California

VEHICLE CODE

2014

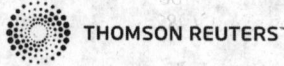
THOMSON REUTERS

Mat #41251369

© 2014 Thomson Reuters

ISBN: 978–0–314–65273–7

SCOPE AND CONTENTS

Legislation

Includes all laws through c. 800 of the 2013 portion of the 2013–2014 Regular Session, the end of the 2013–2014 First Extraordinary Session, and Res. c. 123 (S.C.A.3), subject to approval at the June 3, 2014 election.

Presentation of Legislative Changes

Additions or changes in statutes affected by 2013 legislation are indicated by underlining; deletions are indicated by asterisks.

Effective Dates of Legislation

All California legislative enactments in 2013 are effective January 1, 2014, unless indicated otherwise.

Veto Messages

Codified legislation which is subject to a governor's veto is followed by an italicized note indicating that fact. For the text of the message, please consult the Historical and Statutory Notes for the provision in *West's Annotated California Codes* or the material pertaining to the legislation affecting the provision in *West's California Legislative Service*.

ADDITIONAL INFORMATION OR RESEARCH ASSISTANCE

For additional information or research assistance call the West reference attorneys at 1-800-REF-ATTY (1-800-733-2889). Contact West's editorial department directly with your questions and suggestions by e-mail at west.editor@thomson.com.

*

TABLE OF SECTIONS AFFECTED

This table indicates sections affected by 2013 legislation

Vehicle Code

Sec.	Effect	Chap.	Sec.	Sec.	Effect	Chap.	Sec.
165	Amended	352	516	5205.5	Repealed	414	2
378	Repealed	523	18	9250.1	Amended	401	35
379	Repealed	523	19	9250.2	Amended	401	36
385.2	Added	523	20				37
385.3	Added	523	21	9250.14	Amended	241	1
585	Amended	523	22	9261.1	Amended	401	38
1500	Amended	352	517	9400.1	Amended	35	13
1505	Amended	352	518	9400.4	Amended	35	14
1653.5	Amended	524	3	9706	Amended	352	524
	Added	524	4	9853.6	Amended	401	39
			5	11205	Amended	76	193
1808.51	Amended	352	519	11713.3	Amended	512	18
2100	Amended	352	520	11713.13	Amended	512	19
2109	Amended	352	521	12200	Amended	392	3
2810.2	Amended	472	9	12204	Amended	392	4
2901	Amended	352	522	12505	Amended	649	1
2902	Amended	352	523	12517.1	Amended	523	29
3006	Amended	512	2	12517.2	Amended	160	1
3008	Amended	512	3	12800	Amended	524	6
3012	Amended	512	4		Added	524	7
3050	Amended	512	5				8
3050.7	Amended	512	6	12801	Amended	524	9
3052	Amended	512	7		Added	524	10
3056	Amended	512	8				11
3057	Amended	512	9	12801.5	Amended	524	12
3062	Amended	512	10		Added	524	13
3063	Amended	512	11				14
3064	Amended	512	12	12801.9	Added	524	15
3065	Amended	512	13	12801.10	Added	524	16
3065.1	Amended	512	14	12801.11	Added	524	17
3066	Amended	512	15	12804.9	Amended	649	2
3067	Amended	512	16	12804.11	Amended	76	194
3069.1	Amended	512	17	13001	Added	571	3
4764	Amended	101	1	13353.45	Amended	22	86
4767	Added	101	2	14606	Amended	523	30
4774	Amended	101	3	15210	Amended	649	3
4853	Amended	569	1	15250	Amended	649	4
5022	Amended	523	23	15309.5	Added	649	5
5023	Amended	523	24	16028	Amended	76	195
5066	Amended	28	90	21100	Amended	652	1
5068	Amended	523	25	21107.7	Amended	605	49
5072	Amended	523	26	21650	Amended	426	2
5074	Amended	221	1	21655.9	Amended	405	3
5101.7	Amended	523	27				3.5
5106	Amended	523	28			414	3
5156	Amended	690	1				3.5
5205.5	Amended	405	1	21750	Amended	331	1
			1.5		Added	331	2
	Repealed	405	2	21760	Added	331	3
	Amended	414	1	22352	Amended	240	1
			1.5	22508.5	Amended	71	1

TABLE OF SECTIONS AFFECTED

Sec.	Effect	Chap.	Sec.
22508.5	Added	71	2
22651	Amended	605	50
22651.05	Amended	605	51
22658	Amended	605	52
23112.5	Amended	352	525
23124	Amended	754	1
23538	Amended	22	87
23556	Amended	22	88
23612	Amended	76	196
23646	Amended	22	89
25354	Added	133	1
prec. § 27375 Div. 12 ch. 5 art. 3.4	Added	752	2
27375	Added	752	2
34061	Amended	352	526
34501.12	Amended	500	5
	Added	500	6
34505.5	Amended	500	7
	Added	500	8
34505.6	Amended	500	9
	Added	500	10
34510.5	Amended	76	197
34515	Amended	500	11

Sec.	Effect	Chap.	Sec.
34515	Added	500	12
34601	Amended	392	5
			5.5
		500	13
			13.5
	Added	500	14
34606	Repealed	500	15
34620	Amended	96	1
34622	Amended	500	16
34623	Amended	500	17
	Added	500	18
35400.6	Added	548	1
35400.8	Added	95	1
38603	Amended	179	1
38604	Amended	179	2
40000.20	Amended	76	198
40000.22	Amended	500	19
	Added	500	20
42001.6	Amended	414	4
42007	Amended	523	31
42205	Amended	35	15

TABLE OF CONTENTS

		Page
General Provisions		1

Division

1.	Words and Phrases Defined	7
2.	Administration	49

Chapter

1.	The Department of Motor Vehicles	49
2.	Department of the California Highway Patrol	83
2.5	Licenses Issued by California Highway Patrol	105
3.	The Reciprocity Commission [Repealed]	111
4.	Administration and Enforcement	111
5.	California Traffic Safety Program	120
6.	New Motor Vehicle Board	123
7.	Driver Certification [Repealed]	140

3.	Registration of Vehicles and Certificates of Title	141

Chapter

1.	Original and Renewal of Registration; Issuance of Certificates of Title	141
2.	Transfers of Title or Interest	220
2.5	Miscellaneous Title Provisions	231
3.	Filing Instruments Evidencing Liens or Encumbrances	234
4.	Permits to Nonresident Owners	234
5.	Offenses Against Registration Laws and Suspension, Revocation, and Cancellation of Registration	243
6.	Registration and Weight Fees	244

3.5	Registration and Transfer of Vessels	279

Chapter

1.	General Provisions and Definitions	279
2.	Registration	279
3.	Transfer of Title or Interest in Undocumented Vessel	288

3.6	Vehicle Sales	295

Chapter

1.	Advertising, Brochures, and Manuals	295
2.	Manufacturer's Responsibility for Safety Defects	297
3.	Engine Manufacturers	298
4.	Disclosure of Damage	298

4.	Special Antitheft Laws	301

Chapter

1.	Reports of Stolen Vehicles	301
1.5	Reports of Stolen Vessels	302
2.	Reports of Stored Vehicles	303
3.	Alteration or Removal of Numbers	304

TABLE OF CONTENTS

Page

Chapter

3.5	Motor Vehicle Chop Shops	306
4.	Theft and Injury of Vehicles	307
5.	Motor Vehicle Theft Prevention	309

Division

5. Occupational Licensing and Business Regulations ... 311

Chapter

1.	Driving Schools and Driving Instructors	311
1.5	Traffic Violator Schools	322
2.	Vehicle Verifiers	333
2.5	Registration Services	336
3.	Automobile Dismantlers	340
3.5	Lessor–Retailers	350
4.	Manufacturers, Transporters, Dealers and Salesmen	357
5.	Sale of Housecars	401
6.	Sale of Used Vehicles	402
7.	Sale of Automobile Parts	402
8.	Private Party Vehicle Markets	403
9.	Towing	403
10.	Sales of Vehicles by Private Owners	404
11.	Consumer Recovery Fund	405

6. Drivers' Licenses ... 413

Chapter

1.	Issuance of Licenses, Expiration and Renewal	413
2.	Suspension or Revocation of Licenses	461
3.	Investigation and Hearing	497
4.	Violation of License Provisions	502
5.	License Fees	524
6.	Driver License Compact	527
7.	Commercial Motor Vehicle Safety Program	529

6.5 Motor Vehicle Transactions With Minors ... 541

Chapter

1.	Driver's License Requirements	541

6.7 Unattended Child in Motor Vehicle Safety Act ... 543

Chapter

1.	General Provisions	543
2.	Offenses	543
3.	Educational Provisions	543

7. Financial Responsibility Laws ... 545

Chapter

1.	Compulsory Financial Responsibility	545
2.	Suspension Following Unsatisfied Judgments	558
3.	Proof of Financial Responsibility	562
4.	Commercial Vehicles	566
5.	Transporters of Motor Vehicles [Repealed]	568
6.	Interstate Highway Carriers	568

TABLE OF CONTENTS

Page

Division

9. Civil Liability ----- 569
   Chapter
   1. Civil Liability of Owners and Operators of Vehicles ----- 569
   2. Civil Liability of Persons Signing License Applications of Minors ----- 577
10. Accidents and Accident Reports ----- 581
    Chapter
    1. Accidents and Accident Reports ----- 581
    2. Incident Response Management Program [Repealed] ----- 585
11. Rules of the Road ----- 587
    Chapter
    1. Obedience to and Effect of Traffic Laws ----- 587
    2. Traffic Signs, Signals, and Markings ----- 613
    3. Driving, Overtaking, and Passing ----- 629
    4. Right-of-Way ----- 641
    5. Pedestrians' Rights and Duties ----- 644
    6. Turning and Stopping and Turning Signals ----- 648
    7. Speed Laws ----- 651
    8. Special Stops Required ----- 660
    9. Stopping, Standing, and Parking ----- 664
    10. Removal of Parked and Abandoned Vehicles ----- 684
    11. Parking Lots ----- 716
    12. Public Offenses ----- 717
    13. Vehicular Crossings and Toll Highways ----- 745
    14. Parkways [Repealed] ----- 751
11.5 Sentencing for Driving While Under the Influence ----- 753
    Chapter
    1. Court–Imposed Penalties: Persons Less Than 21 Years of Age ----- 753
    2. Court Penalties ----- 756
    3. Probation ----- 780
    4. Procedures ----- 781
    5. Ignition Interlock Devices ----- 789
12. Equipment of Vehicles ----- 793
    Chapter
    1. General Provisions ----- 793
    2. Lighting Equipment ----- 801
    3. Brakes ----- 834
    4. Windshields and Mirrors ----- 840
    5. Other Equipment ----- 844
    6. Vehicle Equipment Safety Compact [Repealed] ----- 875
    7. Motor Vehicle Pollution Control Device Installation and Inspection Stations [Repealed] ----- 875
13. Towing and Loading Equipment ----- 877
    Chapter
    1. Towing Equipment ----- 877
    2. Logs and Poles [Repealed] ----- 879
    3. Lumber and Lumber Products [Repealed] ----- 879

TABLE OF CONTENTS

Page

Chapter

4. Baled Hay [Repealed] 879
5. Transporting Other Loads 879

Division

14. Transportation of Explosives 887
14.1 Transportation of Hazardous Material 893

Chapter

1. Licensing 893
2. Notification of Routes 895

14.3 Transportation of Inhalation Hazards 897
14.5 Transportation of Radioactive Materials 901
14.7 Flammable and Combustible Liquids 903
14.8 Safety Regulations 907
14.85 Motor Carriers of Property Permit Act 933

Chapter

1. General Provisions and Definitions 933
2. Motor Carrier Permits 935
3. Insurance 939
4. Workers' Compensation 943
5. Identification 943
6. Fines and Penalties 943

14.9 Motor Vehicle Damage Control 945

Chapter

1. Short Title 945
2. General Provisions and Definitions 945
3. Departmental Action 945

15. Size, Weight and Load 947

Chapter

1. General Provisions 947
2. Width 948
3. Height 951
4. Length 951
5. Weight 962
6. Multistate Highway Transportation Agreement [Repealed] 982

16. Implements of Husbandry 983

Chapter

1. Definitions 983
2. Registration of Implements of Husbandry 985
3. Drivers' Licenses 987
4. Speed Laws 987
5. Equipment of Implements of Husbandry 987
6. Size, Weight and Load of Implements of Husbandry 988
7. Other Requirements 989
8. General Provisions 990

16.5 Off–Highway Vehicles 991

Chapter

1. General Provisions 991

TABLE OF CONTENTS

Page

Chapter

2. Registration of Off–Highway Vehicles; Original and Renewal of Identification; Issuance of Certificates of Ownership ----- 992

3. Transfer of Title or Interest [Renumbered] ----- 1006

4. Identification Fees [Renumbered] ----- 1006

5. Off–Highway Vehicle Operating Rules ----- 1006

6. Equipment of Off–Highway Vehicles ----- 1009

7. All–Terrain Vehicles ----- 1013

8. Recreational Off–Highway Vehicles ----- 1014

Division

16.6 Autonomous Vehicles ----- 1017

16.7 Registration and Licensing of Bicycles ----- 1019

16.8 Licensing of Bicycles [Repealed] ----- 1021

17. Offenses and Prosecution ----- 1023

Chapter

1. Offenses ----- 1023

2. Procedure on Arrests ----- 1053

2.5 Administrative Adjudication of Traffic Safety Violations [Repealed] ----- 1075

3. Illegal Evidence ----- 1075

3.5 Evidence ----- 1078

4. Presumptions ----- 1079

5. Defenses ----- 1080

6. Nonprosecution of Violations ----- 1081

7. Arrest Quotas ----- 1082

8. Consolidated Disposition ----- 1082

18. Penalties and Disposition of Fees, Fines, and Forfeitures ----- 1085

Chapter

1. Penalties ----- 1085

2. Disposition of Fees, Fines, and Forfeitures ----- 1102

3. Motor Vehicle Account ----- 1106

VIOLATIONS TABLE
(Page 1109)

INDEX
(Page I–1)

*

VEHICLE CODE

Division		Section
	General Provisions	1
1.	Words and Phrases Defined	95
2.	Administration	1500
3.	Registration of Vehicles and Certificates of Title	4000
3.5.	Registration and Transfer of Vessels	9840
3.6.	Vehicle Sales	9950
4.	Special Antitheft Laws	10500
5.	Occupational Licensing and Business Regulations	11100
6.	Drivers' Licenses	12500
6.5.	Motor Vehicle Transactions with Minors	15500
6.7.	Unattended Child in Motor Vehicle Safety Act	15600
7.	Financial Responsibility Laws	16000
8.	Blank.	
9.	Civil Liability	17000
10.	Accidents and Accident Reports	20000
11.	Rules of the Road	21000
11.5.	Sentencing for Driving While Under the Influence	23500
12.	Equipment of Vehicles	24000
13.	Towing and Loading Equipment	29000
14.	Transportation of Explosives	31600
14.1.	Transportation of Hazardous Material	32000
14.3.	Transportation of Inhalation Hazards	32100
14.5.	Transportation of Radioactive Materials	33000
14.7.	Flammable and Combustible Liquids	34000
14.8.	Safety Regulations	34500
14.85.	Motor Carriers of Property Permit Act	34600
14.9.	Motor Vehicle Damage Control	34700
15.	Size, Weight and Load	35000
16.	Implements of Husbandry	36000
16.5.	Off-Highway Vehicles	38000
16.6.	Autonomous Vehicles	38750
16.7.	Registration and Licensing of Bicycles	39000
16.8.	Licensing of Bicycles [Repealed]	
17.	Offenses and Prosecution	40000
18.	Penalties and Disposition of Fees, Fines, and Forfeitures	42000

GENERAL PROVISIONS

Section
1. Short title.
1.5. Repealed.
2. Continuation of existing law.
3. Tenure of office.
4. Pending proceedings and accrued rights.
5. Constitutionality.
6. Construction of code.
7. Effect of headings.
8. Delegation of powers and duties.
9. Required writings.
10. References to statutes.
11. "Section" and "subdivision".
12. Construction of tenses.
13. Construction of genders.
14. Construction of singular and plural.
15. "Shall" and "may".
16. Oath includes affirmation.
17. Signature by mark.
18. Oaths and acknowledgments.
19. Attested signatures.
20. False statements.
21. Uniformity of code.
22. Method of giving notice.
23. When notice complete.
24. Proof of notice.
24.5. Service of civil process and subpoenas.
25. Unlawful advertising as department; use of department initials or identity.
25.5. False representation to obtain records or information.
26. Repealed.
27. Impersonation of patrol member.
28. Notification of repossession; fine.
29. Method of giving notice.
30. Legislative policy: red lights and sirens.
31. False information to peace officer.
32. Actions local authorities may take by resolution.

§ 1. Short title

This act shall be known as the Vehicle Code. *(Stats. 1959, c. 3, p. 1523, § 1.)*

Cross References

Act to embrace single subject expressed in title, see Const. Art. 4, § 9.

Constitutionality, see Vehicle Code § 5.

Construction of amended statutes, see Government Code § 9605.

Construction of statutes, see Government Code § 9603.

Effective dates, see Const. Art. 4, § 8.

Effective date of statutes, see Government Code § 9600.

Intent of legislature to be pursued in construing statute, see Code of Civil Procedure § 1859.

Maxims of jurisprudence, see Civil Code § 3509 et seq.

Motor clubs, generally, see Insurance Code § 12140 et seq.

Prohibition of legislation granting privileges and immunities, see Const. Art. 1, § 7.

Publication and distribution of Vehicle Code, see Vehicle Code § 1656.

Reference to statutes, see Vehicle Code § 10.

Section and subdivision defined, see Vehicle Code § 11.

Uniform operation of laws of a general nature, see Const. Art. 4, § 16.

§ 1.5. Repealed by Stats.1972, c. 631, p. 1180, § 1, eff. Aug. 9, 1972

1

§ 2. Continuation of existing law

The provisions of this code, insofar as they are substantially the same as existing provisions relating to the same subject matter, shall be construed as restatements and continuations thereof and not as new enactments. *(Stats.1959, c. 3, p. 1523, § 2.)*

Cross References

Construction of statutes, see Government Code § 9603.
Pending actions or proceedings and rights accrued not affected by code, see Vehicle Code § 4.
Restatements and continuations of statutes, see Government Code § 9604.

§ 3. Tenure of office

All persons who, at the time this code goes into effect,[1] hold office under the code repealed by this code, which offices are continued by this code, continue to hold them according to their former tenure. *(Stats.1959, c. 3, p. 1523, § 3.)*

[1] Effective Sept. 18, 1959.

Cross References

Continuance in office until qualification of successor, see Government Code § 1302.
Director of motor vehicles, see Vehicle Code § 1504.
Public officers and employees, terms of office not fixed by law, see Government Code § 1301.
Repeal of statutes, see Government Code § 9606.
Resignations, see Government Code § 1750 et seq.
Vacancies in office, see Government Code § 1770 et seq.

§ 4. Pending proceedings and accrued rights

No action or proceeding commenced before this code takes effect, and no right accrued, is affected by the provisions of this code, but all procedure thereafter taken therein shall conform to the provisions of this code so far as possible. *(Stats.1959, c. 3, p. 1523, § 4.)*

Cross References

Commencement of actions, see Code of Civil Procedure §§ 350 et seq., 411.10.
Definitions,
  Civil actions, see Code of Civil Procedure §§ 22, 30, 363.
  Criminal actions, see Penal Code § 683.
Pending action, definition, see Code of Civil Procedure § 1049.
Vested rights, impairment by repeal of statute, see Government Code § 9606.

§ 5. Constitutionality

If any portion of this code is held unconstitutional, such decision shall not affect the validity of any other portion of this code. *(Stats.1959, c. 3, p. 1523, § 5.)*

Cross References

Constitution of United States, supreme law of the land, see Const. Art. 3, § 1.
Construction of statutes, see Code of Civil Procedure § 1858 et seq.; Government Code § 9600 et seq.

Statute to embrace single subject expressed in title, see Const. Art. 4, § 9.

§ 6. Construction of code

Unless the provision or the context otherwise requires, these general provisions and rules of construction shall govern the construction of this code. *(Stats.1959, c. 3, p. 1523, § 6.)*

Cross References

Common law of England as rule of decision, see Civil Code § 22.2.
Constitutional construction, see Const. Art. 1, §§ 24, 26.
Court's duties, see Code of Civil Procedure § 1858; Evidence Code §§ 310, 400 et seq., 457.
Maxims of jurisprudence, see Civil Code § 3509 et seq.
Pleadings, liberal construction, see Code of Civil Procedure § 452.
Provisions of code or restatements and continuations of existing law, see Vehicle Code § 2.
Questions of law for court, see Evidence Code § 310.
Reference to portion of code, application to all amendments, see Vehicle Code § 10.
Statutory construction,
  Amended statutes, see Government Code § 9605.
  Amendment of repealed statutes, see Government Code § 9609.
  General rules, see Code of Civil Procedure § 1858 et seq.; Government Code § 9603.
  Giving effect to all provisions, see Code of Civil Procedure § 1858.
  Intention of legislature, see Code of Civil Procedure § 1859.
  Natural rights preferred, see Code of Civil Procedure § 1866.
  Particular intent controls general, see Code of Civil Procedure § 1859.
  Repeal of repealing statute, see Government Code § 9607.
  Temporary suspension of law, see Government Code § 9611.
Uniform operation of laws of a general nature, see Const. Art. 4, § 16.
Words and phrases, see Vehicle Code § 100 et seq.; Code of Civil Procedure §§ 16, 17.

§ 7. Effect of headings

Division, chapter, and article headings do not in any manner affect the scope, meaning, or intent of the provisions of this code. *(Stats.1959, c. 3, p. 1523, § 7. Amended by Stats.1959, c. 1996, p. 4614, § 1.)*

§ 8. Delegation of powers and duties

Whenever, by the provisions of this code, a power is granted to a public officer or a duty imposed upon such an officer, the power may be exercised or the duty performed by a deputy of the officer or by a person authorized pursuant to law by the officer. *(Stats.1959, c. 3, p. 1523, § 8.)*

Cross References

Appointment and powers of deputies, see Government Code §§ 7 et seq., 1190, 1191.
Official bonds, protection of deputies, see Government Code § 1504.
Powers and duties of deputies, see Government Code §§ 1194, 18572.

Public officers and employees, see Government Code § 1000 et seq.

§ 9. Required writings

Whenever any notice, report, statement, or record is required by this code, it shall be made in writing in the English language. *(Stats.1959, c. 3, p. 1523, § 9.)*

Cross References

Court proceedings in English, see Code of Civil Procedure § 185.
Judicial notice of English words and phrases, see Evidence Code §§ 450, 451, 459.
Publication of Vehicle Code, see Vehicle Code § 1656.
Writing includes printing and typewriting, see Civil Code § 14; Code of Civil Procedure § 17.
Written words control printed, see Civil Code § 1651; Code of Civil Procedure § 1862.

§ 10. References to statutes

Whenever any reference is made to any portion of this code or of any other law, such reference shall apply to all amendments and additions heretofore or hereafter made. *(Stats.1959, c. 3, p. 1523, § 10.)*

Cross References

Amendment of repealed statutes, see Government Code § 9609.
Amendment of statutes, construction, see Government Code § 9605.
Giving effect to all provisions of statute, see Code of Civil Procedure § 1858.
References to restatements and continuations, see Government Code § 9604.
Requirements relating to amendment of statutes, see Const. Art. 4, § 9.
Rules for construction of statutes contained in code, see Government Code § 9603.

§ 11. "Section" and "subdivision"

"Section" means a section of this code unless some other statute is specifically mentioned and "subdivision" means a subdivision of the section in which that term occurs unless some other section is expressly mentioned. *(Stats.1959, c. 3, p. 1523, § 11.)*

Cross References

Headings of Code, effect, see Vehicle Code § 7.

§ 12. Construction of tenses

The present tense includes the past and future tenses; and the future, the present. *(Stats.1959, c. 3, p. 1524, § 12.)*

Cross References

Construction of statutes, duty of judge, see Code of Civil Procedure § 1858.

§ 13. Construction of genders

The masculine gender includes the feminine and neuter. *(Stats.1959, c. 3, p. 1524, § 13.)*

§ 14. Construction of singular and plural

The singular number includes the plural, and the plural the singular. *(Stats.1959, c. 3, p. 1524, § 14.)*

§ 15. "Shall" and "may"

"Shall" is mandatory and "may" is permissive. *(Stats. 1959, c. 3, p. 1524, § 15.)*

§ 16. Oath includes affirmation

"Oath" includes affirmation. *(Stats.1959, c. 3, p. 1524, § 16.)*

Cross References

Administration of oaths and affirmations, see Vehicle Code § 18; Code of Civil Procedure § 2093 et seq.; Government Code §§ 1225, 1362, 8205, 24057.
Affidavits, see Code of Civil Procedure § 2009 et seq.
Oath of office, see Const. Art. 20, § 3; Government Code § 1360 et seq.
Perjury, see Penal Code § 118 et seq.
Witnesses' oath, option to declare or affirm, see Code of Civil Procedure § 2097.

§ 17. Signature by mark

"Signature" or "subscription" includes mark when the signer or subscriber cannot write, such signer's or subscriber's name being written near the mark by a witness who writes his own name near the signer's or subscriber's name; but a signature or subscription by mark can be acknowledged or can serve as a signature or subscription to a sworn statement only when two witnesses so sign their own names thereto. *(Stats.1959, c. 3, p. 1524, § 17.)*

Cross References

Facsimile signature machines, see Government Code § 11100 et seq.
Signature as including mark, see Civil Code § 14; Code of Civil Procedure § 17; Penal Code § 7; Revenue and Taxation Code § 18.
Signature of persons licensed under this code, see Vehicle Code § 12950.

§ 18. Oaths and acknowledgments

Officers and employees of the Department of Motor Vehicles and the Department of the California Highway Patrol are, for the purposes of this code, authorized to administer oaths and acknowledge signatures, for which no fee shall be charged. *(Stats.1959, c. 3, p. 1524, § 18.)*

Cross References

Irregularity in administration of oath, see Penal Code § 121.
Perjury and subornation of perjury, see Penal Code § 118 et seq.
Persons empowered to administer oaths, see Code of Civil Procedure § 2093; Government Code §§ 1225, 1362, 8205, 24057.
Verification of applications for driver's licenses before persons authorized to administer oaths, see Vehicle Code § 12802.

§ 19. Attested signatures

Whenever the acknowledgment of any document is required by this code or any regulation of either department, the signature of the applicant attested to in his presence by the signature of a subscribing witness is sufficient. *(Stats.1959, c. 3, p. 1524, § 19.)*

Cross References

Signature of persons licensed under this code, see Vehicle Code § 12950.

§ 20. False statements

It is unlawful to use a false or fictitious name, or to knowingly make any false statement or knowingly conceal any material fact in any document filed with the Department of Motor Vehicles or the Department of the California Highway Patrol. *(Stats.1959, c. 3, p. 1524, § 20.)*

Cross References

Automobile dismantler, suspension or revocation of license for use of false or fictitious name, see Vehicle Code § 11509.

Civil liability of persons signing license applications of minors, see Vehicle Code § 17700 et seq.

False evidences of registration as felony, see Vehicle Code § 4463.

False information to peace officer, see Vehicle Code § 31.

False report of theft of vehicle, see Vehicle Code § 10501.

Funds for obtaining evidence on violation of, see Vehicle Code § 42271.

Grounds authorizing refusal to issue or renew a driver's license, see Vehicle Code § 12809.

Procuring or offering false or forged instrument for record, see Penal Code § 115.

Registration, see Vehicle Code § 4000 et seq.

Release from arrest upon promise to appear, use of false or fictitious name, see Vehicle Code § 40504.

Suspension, cancellation or revocation of registration for offense under this section, see Vehicle Code § 8800.

Violation as misdemeanor, punishment, see Vehicle Code §§ 40000.5 et seq., 42002.

§ 21. Uniformity of code

(a) Except as otherwise expressly provided, the provisions of this code are applicable and uniform throughout the state and in all counties and municipalities therein, and a local authority shall not enact or enforce any ordinance or resolution on the matters covered by this code, including ordinances or resolutions that establish regulations or procedures for, or assess a fine, penalty, assessment, or fee for a violation of, matters covered by this code, unless expressly authorized by this code.

(b) To the extent permitted by current state law, this section does not impair the current lawful authority of the Mountains Recreation and Conservation Authority, a joint powers authority, or any member agency constituted therein as of July 1, 2010, to enforce an ordinance or resolution relating to the management of public lands within its jurisdiction. *(Stats.1959, c. 3, p. 1524, § 21. Amended by Stats.1961, c. 2017, p. 4231, § 1; Stats.2010, c. 616 (S.B.949), § 1, operative July 1, 2011.)*

Cross References

Abandoned or inoperative vehicles, local ordinances, see Vehicle Code § 22660.

Curb markings, power of local authorities, see Vehicle Code § 21458.

Distinctive roadway markings for roads under jurisdiction of local authorities, see Vehicle Code § 21459.

Equestrian crossings, local regulation, see Vehicle Code § 21805.

Freeways, local regulation of use, see Vehicle Code § 21960.

Lanes for vehicles required to travel at reduced speeds, designation by local authorities, see Vehicle Code § 21655.

Local authorities defined, see Vehicle Code § 385.

Parking, local regulation, see Vehicle Code § 22506 et seq.

Parking meter zones, powers of local authorities, see Vehicle Code § 22508.

Pedestrians, local regulation, see Vehicle Code § 21961.

Police powers of cities and counties, see Const. Art. 11, § 7.

Speed of vehicles, local regulation, see Vehicle Code §§ 22357 et seq., 22403, 22404, 22407.

Traffic laws, local regulation, see Vehicle Code § 21100 et seq.

Traffic safety program for localities, see Vehicle Code § 2904.

Traffic signs and signals, local regulation, see Vehicle Code § 21351 et seq.

Turning of vehicles, local regulation, see Vehicle Code § 22113.

Unattended vehicles, parking on hills, powers of local authorities, see Vehicle Code § 22509.

Vehicles for hire, regulation by local authorities, see Vehicle Code § 16501.

Weight limits, power of local authorities, see Vehicle Code § 35700 et seq.

§ 22. Method of giving notice

Whenever notice is required to be given under this code by a department or any division, officer, employee, or agent, the notice shall be given either by personal delivery to the person to be notified, by certified mail, return receipt requested, or by mailing the notice, postage prepaid, addressed to the person at his or her address as shown by the records of the department. *(Stats.1959, c. 3, p. 1524, § 22. Amended by Stats.1996, c. 1154 (A.B. 3020), § 54, eff. Sept. 30, 1996.)*

Cross References

Notice by certified mail, see Vehicle Code § 29.

Notice in prosecution of persons owning or controlling vehicles, see Vehicle Code § 40002.

Notice to appear to arrested person, see Vehicle Code § 40500 et seq.

Notices, and filing and service of papers, see Code of Civil Procedure § 1010 et seq.

Notification of repossession, see Vehicle Code § 28.

Service of process, see Vehicle Code § 17450 et seq.

§ 23. When notice complete

The giving of notice by personal delivery is complete upon delivery of a copy of the notice to the person to be notified. The giving of notice by mail is complete upon the expiration of four days after deposit of the notice in the mail, except that in the case of a notice informing any person of an offense against him under Section 40001, the notice is complete 10 days after mailing. *(Stats.1959, c. 3, p. 1524, § 23.)*

Cross References
Notices and filing and service of papers, see Code of Civil Procedure § 1010 et seq.

§ 24. Proof of notice

Proof of the giving of notice may be made by the certificate of any officer, employee, or agent of the Department of Motor Vehicles and the Department of the California Highway Patrol or of any peace officer, or by an affidavit of any person over 18 years of age, naming the person to whom the notice was given and specifying the time, place, and manner of the giving of the notice. *(Stats.1959, c. 3, p. 1524, § 24. Amended by Stats.1996, c. 1154 (A.B.3020), § 55, eff. Sept. 30, 1996.)*

Cross References
Affidavits, see Code of Civil Procedure § 2009 et seq.
Certification or declaration under penalty of perjury, see Code of Civil Procedure § 2015.5.

§ 24.5. Service of civil process and subpoenas

All civil process in actions brought against the director and the Department of Motor Vehicles and all subpoenas for the production of department records shall be served upon the director or his appointed representatives at the department's headquarters. *(Added by Stats.1971, c. 699, p. 1356, § 1, operative May 3, 1972.)*

§ 25. Unlawful advertising as department; use of department initials or identity

(a) It is unlawful for any person to display or cause or permit to be displayed any sign, mark, or advertisement indicating an official connection with either the Department of Motor Vehicles or the Department of the California Highway Patrol unless such person has lawful authority, permission, or right to make such display.

(b) It is unlawful for the holder of any occupational license issued pursuant to Division 5 (commencing with Section 11100) to use the initials "DMV," the Department of Motor Vehicles logogram, or the words "Department of Motor Vehicles" in any business name or telephone number. No occupational licensee may use the initials, logogram, or words in any advertisement in a way that indicates, or could be construed to indicate, any official connection with the Department of Motor Vehicles other than as a licensee. *(Stats.1959, c. 3, p. 1525, § 25. Amended by Stats.1965, c. 595, p. 1931, § 1; Stats.1992, c. 1243 (A.B.3090), § 53, eff. Sept. 30, 1992.)*

Cross References
Penalties for unlawful acts, see Vehicle Code § 40000.1 et seq.
Unlawful advertisements by manufacturers, transporters, dealers and salesmen, see Vehicle Code § 11713.

§ 25.5. False representation to obtain records or information

It is unlawful for any person to falsely represent himself or herself in any manner as an employee of the Department of Motor Vehicles for the purpose of obtaining records or information to which he or she is not entitled. *(Added by Stats.1971, c. 1386, p. 2735, § 1, operative May 3, 1972. Amended by Stats.1982, c. 466, p. 2055, § 105.)*

§ 26. Repealed by Stats.1990, c. 1196 (A.B.4008), § 1, operative July 1, 1991

§ 27. Impersonation of patrol member

Any person who without authority impersonates, or wears the badge of, a member of the California Highway Patrol with intention to deceive anyone is guilty of a misdemeanor. *(Stats.1959, c. 3, p. 1525, § 27.)*

Cross References
Unlawful wearing of badge a misdemeanor, see Penal Code § 538d.
Violations, see Vehicle Code § 40000.1 et seq.

§ 28. Notification of repossession; fine

(a) Whenever possession is taken of any vehicle by or on behalf of any legal owner thereof under the terms of a security agreement or lease agreement, the person taking possession shall notify, within one hour after taking possession of the vehicle, and by the most expeditious means available, the city police department where the taking of possession occurred, if within an incorporated city, or the sheriff's department of the county where the taking of possession occurred, if outside an incorporated city, or the police department of a campus of the University of California or the California State University, if the taking of possession occurred on that campus, and shall within one business day forward a written notice to the city police or sheriff's department.

(b) If possession is taken of more than one vehicle, the possession of each vehicle shall be considered and reported as a separate event.

(c) Any person failing to notify the city police department, sheriff's department, or campus police department as required by this section is guilty of an infraction, and shall be fined a minimum of three hundred dollars ($300), and up to five hundred dollars ($500). The district attorney, city attorney, or city prosecutor shall promptly notify the Bureau of Security and Investigative Services of any conviction resulting from a violation of this section. *(Stats.1959, c. 3, p. 1525, § 28. Amended by Stats.1963, c. 819, p. 2012, § 39, eff. Jan. 1, 1965; Stats.1963, c. 1095, pp. 2556, 2557, §§ 1, 2; Stats.1993, c. 1268 (S.B.984), § 3; Stats.1995, c. 505 (A.B.1541), § 37; Stats.1996, c. 1142 (S.B.1797), § 7, eff. Sept. 30, 1996; Stats.1999, c. 1007 (S.B.532), § 14; Stats.2009, c. 307 (S.B.821), § 106.)*

§ 29. Method of giving notice

Wherever any notice or other communication is required by this code to be mailed by registered mail by or to any person or corporation, the mailing of such notice or other communication by certified mail shall be deemed to be a sufficient compliance with the requirements of law. *(Added by Stats.1959, c. 426, p. 2366, § 10.)*

Giving of notice by personal delivery or by mailing, see Vehicle Code § 22.

Notices, and filing and service of papers, see Code of Civil Procedure § 1010 et seq.

§ 30. Legislative policy: red lights and sirens

It is declared as a matter of legislative policy that red lights and sirens on vehicles should be restricted to authorized emergency vehicles engaged in police, fire and lifesaving services; and that other types of vehicles which are engaged in activities which create special hazards upon the highways should be equipped with flashing amber warning lamps. *(Added by Stats.1961, c. 653, p. 1858, § 1, operative Jan. 1, 1962.)*

Flashing and colored lights,
   Generally, see Vehicle Code § 25250 et seq.,
   Garbage and rubbish vehicles, see Vehicle Code § 21059.
Sirens,
   Armored cars, see Vehicle Code § 27003.

Authorized emergency vehicle, see Vehicle Code §§ 21055, 27002.
Police escort, see Vehicle Code § 21057.
Warning lights and devices, see Vehicle Code § 25300 et seq.

§ 31. False information to peace officer

No person shall give, either orally or in writing, information to a peace officer while in the performance of his duties under the provisions of this code when such person knows that the information is false. *(Added by Stats.1965, c. 1264, p. 3139, § 1.)*

Use of false or fictitious name or false statement in documents, see Vehicle Code § 20.
Violations, see Vehicle Code § 40000.1 et seq.

§ 32. Actions local authorities may take by resolution

Whenever local authorities are given the power to take action by ordinance pursuant to Division 11 (commencing with Section 21000) and Division 15 (commencing with Section 35000), they shall also have the power to take such action by resolution. *(Added by Stats.1972, c. 1095, p. 2056, § 1.)*

Division 1

WORDS AND PHRASES DEFINED

Section	
95.	Renumbered.
100.	Application of definitions.
102.	Ability to respond in damages.
105.	Agricultural water-well boring rig.
108.	Airbrakes.
109.	Alcoholic beverage; intoxicating liquor.
110.	Alley.
111.	All-terrain vehicle.
111.3.	All-terrain vehicle safety instructor.
111.5.	All-terrain vehicle safety training organization.
112.	Amber.
115.	Armored car.
120 to 160.	Repealed.
165.	Authorized emergency vehicle.
165.3, 165.4.	Repealed.
165.5.	Authorized emergency vehicle: rescue team.
166.	Autobroker; auto buying service.
170.	Repealed.
175.	Autoette.
180 to 205.	Repealed.
210.	Automated rail crossing enforcement system.
215.	Repealed.
220.	Automobile dismantler.
221.	Automobile dismantler; exclusions.
223.	Automobile driver training.
225.	Auxiliary dolly.
230.	Axle.
230.5.	B-train assembly.
231.	Bicycle.
231.5.	Bicycle path; bike path.
231.6.	Bicycle path crossing.
232.	Board.
232.5.	Brokering.
233.	Bus.
234.	Business.
235.	Business district.
236.	Business representative.
240.	Business and residence districts: determination.
241.	Buy-here-pay-here dealer; included actions.
241.	Buy-here-pay-here dealer.
241.1.	Buy-here-pay-here dealer; excluded actions.
241.1.	Buy-here-pay-here dealer; exclusions.
242.	Camp trailer.
243.	Camper.
245.	Carry-all.
246.	Certificate of compliance.
250.	Chop Shop.
255.	City.
257.	Clean fuel vehicle.
259.	Collector motor vehicle.
260.	Commercial vehicle.
265.	Commissioner.
266.	Consignment.
267.	Converter.
270.	County.
273.	Crib sheet or cribbing device.
275.	Crosswalk.
280.	Darkness.
285.	Dealer.
286.	Dealer; exclusions.
288.	Declared combined gross weight.
289.	Declared gross vehicle weight.
290.	Department.
291.	Department of transportation.
295.	Director.
295.5.	Disabled person.
295.7.	Disabled veteran.
296.	Distributor.
297.	Distributor branch.
300.	Drawbar.
303.	Driveaway-towaway operation.
305.	Driver.
310.	Driver's license.
310.4.	Driving instructor.
310.6.	Driving school.
310.8.	Driving school operator.
311.	Driving school owner.
311.5.	Renumbered.
312.	Drug.
313.	Electric personal assistive mobility device (EPAMD).
314.	Expressway.
315.	Essential parts.
320.	Established place of business.
320.5.	Extralegal load.
321.	Factory-built housing.
322.	Farm labor vehicle.
323.	Repealed.
324.	Fifth-wheel travel trailer.
324.5.	Former prisoner of war.
325.	Foreign jurisdiction.
330.	Foreign vehicle.
331.	Franchise.
331.1.	Franchisee.
331.2.	Franchisor.
331.3.	Recreational vehicle franchise.
332.	Freeway.
335.	Gantry truck.
336.	General public paratransit vehicle.
340.	Garage.
345.	Golf cart.
350.	Gross vehicle weight rating.
351.	Repealed.
353.	Hazardous material.
355.	Renumbered.
360.	Highway.
362.	House car.
365.	Intersection.
370.	Legal owner.
371.	Lessee.
372.	Lessor.
373.	Lessor-retailer.
375.	Lighting equipment.
377.	Limit line.
378, 379.	Repealed.
380.	Liquefied petroleum gas.
385.	Local authorities.

VEHICLE CODE

Section

385.2.	Logging dolly.
385.3.	Logging vehicle.
385.5.	Low-speed vehicle.
386.	Managerial employee.
387.	Manufactured home.
388.	Repealed.
389.	Manufacturer branch.
390.	Renumbered.
395.	Metal tire.
395.5.	Mobile billboard advertising display.
396.	Mobilehome.
400.	Motorcycle.
405.	Motor-driven cycle.
406.	Motorized bicycle or moped.
407.	Motorized quadricycle and motorized tricycle.
407.5.	Motorized scooter; disclosures.
408.	Motor carrier.
410.	Motor truck.
415.	Motor vehicle.
425.	Muffler.
426.	New motor vehicle dealer.
430.	New vehicle.
431.	Nonrepairable vehicle.
432.	Nonrepairable vehicle certificate.
435.	Nonresident.
435.5.	Nonresident daily commuter.
436.	Off-highway motorcycle.
440.	Official traffic control device.
445.	Official traffic control signal.
450.	Oil well production service unit.
455.	Original driver's license.
460.	Owner.
461.	Owner exemptions.
462.	Paratransit vehicle.
463.	Park or parking.
464.	Passenger transportation vehicle.
465.	Passenger vehicle.
467.	Pedestrian.
467.5.	Pedicab.
468.	Permanent trailer identification plate program.
470.	Person.
471.	Pickup truck.
472.	Pilot car.
473.	Pocket bike.
475.	Pole or pipe dolly.
480.	Power brake.
485.	Pneumatic tire.
490.	Private road or driveway.
492.	Private school.
493.	Repealed.
495.	Repealed.
500.	Recreational off-highway vehicle.
505.	Registered owner.
505.2.	Registration service.
506.	Registration year.
507.	Relevant market area.
507.5.	Remanufactured vehicle.
507.8.	Remanufacturer.
508.	Renter.
510.	Repair shop.
512.	Representative.
515.	Residence district.
516.	Resident.
520.	Retail sale.
521.	Retarder.

Section

521.5.	Revived salvage vehicle.
522.	Ridesharing.
525.	Right-of-way.
527.	Road.
530.	Roadway.
531.	Utility-terrain vehicle.
535.	Safety glazing material.
540.	Safety zone.
543.	Salvage pool.
543.5.	Salvage vehicle rebuilder.
544.	Total loss salvage vehicle; report of total settlement to Department of Motor Vehicles.
545.	Schoolbus.
545.1.	Motor vehicles transporting pupils to or from community colleges.
545.5.	Schoolbus; coach bus exclusion; Trona Unified School District.
546.	School pupil activity bus; driver regulations.
550.	Semitrailer.
553.	Shade trailer.
555.	Sidewalk.
557.	Snowmobile.
558.	Snow-tread tire.
560.	Solid tire.
565.	Special construction equipment.
570.	Special construction equipment: exclusions.
575.	Special mobile equipment.
580.	Specially constructed vehicle.
585.	Station wagon.
587.	Stop or stopping.
590.	Street.
591.	Street or highway.
592.	Highway exceptions.
593.	Supplemental restraint system.
595.	Terminal.
600.	Through highway.
605.	Tire traction devices.
610.	Tire tread.
611.	Toll highway or toll road.
612.	Tour bus.
615.	Tow truck; repossessor's tow vehicle; automobile dismantlers' tow vehicle.
617.	Tow dolly.
620.	Traffic.
625.	Traffic officer.
626.	Traffic violator school.
626.2.	Traffic violator school branch or classroom location.
626.4.	Traffic violator school instructor.
626.6.	Traffic violator school operator.
626.8.	Traffic violator school owner.
627.	Engineering and traffic survey.
630.	Trailer.
635.	Trailer coach.
636.	Trailer bus.
640.	Transferee.
642.	Transit bus.
645.	Transporter.
650.	Trolley coach.
655.	Truck tractor.
657.	Truss.
660.	Unladen weight.
661.	Unladen weight exclusion.
665.	Used vehicle.
665.5.	U–turn.
666.	Repealed.

Section

667. Utility trailer defined.
668. Vanpool vehicle.
670. Vehicle.
670.5. Vehicle frame.
671. Vehicle identification number.
672. Vehicle manufacturer.
675. Vehicle salesperson.
675.5. Vehicle verifier.
675.6. Vehicle verifier; exclusions.
676. Year-round registration.
676.5. Water tender vehicle.
677. Repealed.
680. Youth bus.

Cross References

Approach defined, vehicular crossings, see Vehicle Code § 23255.
Blind person, see Vehicle Code § 21965.
California highway patrol, see Vehicle Code § 2102.
Cause of action defined, financial responsibility, see Vehicle Code § 16251.
Construction of Code, see Vehicle Code § 6.
Department defined, California highway patrol, see Vehicle Code §§ 2101, 24000.
Implement of husbandry defined, see Vehicle Code §§ 36000, 36005, 36015.
Interstate commerce defined, proportionate registration, see Vehicle Code § 8050.
Judgment defined, financial responsibility, see Vehicle Code § 16250.
Motor vehicle liability policy, financial responsibility, see Vehicle Code § 16450.
Motor vehicle pollution control device, defined, see Health and Safety Code § 39040.
Nonresident defined, service of process, see Vehicle Code § 17450.
Private garage, reports of stored vehicles, see Vehicle Code § 10654.
Public entity defined, civil liability, see Vehicle Code § 17000.
Recut or regrooved tires defined, see Vehicle Code §§ 27460.5, 27461.
Refrigerator van defined, see Vehicle Code § 28000.
Revocation defined, driver's licenses, see Vehicle Code § 13101.
Slow moving vehicle, see Vehicle Code § 21656.
Speed trap, see Vehicle Code § 40802.
Station defined as lamp adjusting or brake adjusting station, see Business and Professions Code § 9888.1.
Suspension defined, driver's licenses, see Vehicle Code § 13102.
Total fleet miles defined, proportionate registration, see Vehicle Code § 8057.
Urban and suburban service defined, width of passenger carrying vehicles, see Vehicle Code § 35107.
Vehicular crossing defined, see Vehicle Code § 23254.
Vessels, definitions,
  Registration and transfer, see Vehicle Code § 9840.
  Reports of stolen vessels, see Vehicle Code § 10550.

§ 95. Renumbered § 102 and amended by Stats.1992, c. 974 (S.B.1600), § 2, eff. Sept. 28, 1992

§ 100. Application of definitions

Unless the provision or context otherwise requires, these definitions shall govern the construction of this code. *(Stats.1959, c. 3, p. 1525, § 100.)*

Cross References

Construction of code, see Vehicle Code § 6.
Effect of headings, see Vehicle Code § 7.

§ 102. Ability to respond in damages

"Ability to respond in damages" means financial responsibility. *(Formerly § 95, added by Stats.1989, c. 1157, § 2. Renumbered § 102 and amended by Stats.1992, c. 974 (S.B.1600), § 2, eff. Sept. 28, 1992.)*

§ 105. Agricultural water-well boring rig

An "agricultural water-well boring rig" is a motor vehicle which is used exclusively in the boring of water-wells on agricultural property. *(Stats.1959, c. 3, p. 1525, § 105.)*

§ 108. Airbrakes

"Airbrakes" means a brake system using compressed air either for actuating the service brakes at the wheels of the vehicle or as a source of power for controlling or applying service brakes which are actuated through hydraulic or other intermediate means. *(Added by Stats. 1963, c. 207, p. 945, § 1.)*

Cross References

Airbrakes, see Vehicle Code § 26502 et seq.
Brakes, generally, see Vehicle Code § 26301 et seq.
Operation of brakes, see Vehicle Code § 26450 et seq.
Power brake defined, see Vehicle Code § 480.

§ 109. Alcoholic beverage; intoxicating liquor

"Alcoholic beverage" includes any liquid or solid material intended to be ingested by a person which contains ethanol, also known as ethyl alcohol, drinking alcohol, or alcohol, including, but not limited to, alcoholic beverages as defined in Section 23004 of the Business and Professions Code, intoxicating liquor, malt beverage, beer, wine, spirits, liqueur, whiskey, rum, vodka, cordials, gin, and brandy, and any mixture containing one or more alcoholic beverages. Alcoholic beverage includes a mixture of one or more alcoholic beverages whether found or ingested separately or as a mixture.

For purposes of the Driver License Compact, "intoxicating liquor" as used in Section 15023 has the same meaning as "alcoholic beverage" as used in this code. *(Formerly § 23151, added by Stats.1981, c. 940, p. 3571, § 32. Renumbered § 109 and amended by Stats.1982, c. 53, p. 172, § 25, eff. Feb. 18, 1982.)*

§ 110. Alley

"Alley" is any highway having a roadway not exceeding 25 feet in width which is primarily used for access to the rear or side entrances of abutting property; provided, that the City and County of San Francisco may designate by ordinance or resolution as an "alley" any highway having a roadway not exceeding 25 feet in width. *(Added by Stats.1963, c. 409, p. 1214, § 1. Amended by Stats. 1965, c. 833, p. 2431, § 1.)*

§ 111. All-terrain vehicle

"All-terrain vehicle" means a motor vehicle subject to subdivision (a) of Section 38010 which is all of the following:

(a) Designed for operation off of the highway by an operator with no more than one passenger.

(b) Fifty inches or less in width.

(c) Nine hundred pounds or less unladen weight.

(d) Suspended on three or more low-pressure tires.

(e) Has a single seat designed to be straddled by the operator, or a single seat designed to be straddled by the operator and a seat for no more than one passenger.

(f) Has handlebars for steering control. *(Added by Stats.1987, c. 881, § 1. Amended by Stats.2002, c. 205 (S.B.1302), § 1; Stats.2003, c. 252 (S.B.232), § 1.)*

Cross References

Issuance of licenses and certificates to specified dealers, manufacturers, distributors, or representatives of all-terrain vehicles as defined in this section, payment of license fees and additional fees, see Vehicle Code § 11723.

§ 111.3. All-terrain vehicle safety instructor

An "all-terrain vehicle safety instructor" is a person who is sponsored by an all-terrain vehicle safety training organization, who has completed a course in all-terrain vehicle safety instruction administered by an approved all-terrain vehicle safety training organization, and who has been licensed by the department pursuant to Section 11105.1. *(Added by Stats.1987, c. 881, § 2.)*

§ 111.5. All-terrain vehicle safety training organization

An "all-terrain vehicle safety training organization" is any organization which is approved to offer a program of instruction in all-terrain vehicle safety, including all-terrain vehicle safety instruction training, by the Off-Highway Vehicle Safety Education Committee and which has been issued a license by the department pursuant to Section 11105.6. *(Added by Stats.1987, c. 881, § 3.)*

§ 112. Amber

"Amber" has the same meaning as "yellow," and is within the chromaticity coordinate boundaries for yellow specified in regulations adopted by the Department of the California Highway Patrol. *(Added by Stats.1977, c. 287, p. 1183, § 1.)*

§ 115. Armored car

An "armored car" is a vehicle that is equipped with materials on either the front, sides, or rear for the protection of persons therein from missiles discharged from firearms. *(Stats.1959, c. 3, p. 1525, § 115.)*

Cross References

Armored car not an authorized emergency vehicle, see Vehicle Code § 25262.
License to operate, see Vehicle Code §§ 2510 et seq., 21713.
Red lights, use on armored cars, see Vehicle Code § 25262.

Sirens, use on armored cars, see Vehicle Code § 27003.

§§ 120 to 160. Repealed by Stats.1961, c. 653, p. 1858, §§ 2 to 10, operative Jan. 1, 1962

§ 165. Authorized emergency vehicle

An authorized emergency vehicle is:

(a) Any publicly owned and operated ambulance, lifeguard, or lifesaving equipment or any privately owned or operated ambulance licensed by the Commissioner of the California Highway Patrol to operate in response to emergency calls.

(b) Any publicly owned vehicle operated by the following persons, agencies, or organizations:

(1) Any federal, state, or local agency, department, or district employing peace officers as that term is defined in Chapter 4.5 (commencing with Section 830) of Part 2 of Title 3 of the Penal Code, for use by those officers in the performance of their duties.

(2) Any forestry or fire department of any public agency or fire department organized as provided in the Health and Safety Code.

(c) Any vehicle owned by the state, or any bridge and highway district, and equipped and used either for fighting fires, or towing or servicing other vehicles, caring for injured persons, or repairing damaged lighting or electrical equipment.

(d) Any state-owned vehicle used in responding to emergency fire, rescue, or communications calls and operated either by the * * * Office of Emergency Services or by any public agency or industrial fire department to which the * * * Office of Emergency Services has assigned the vehicle.

(e) Any vehicle owned or operated by any department or agency of the United States government when the vehicle is used in responding to emergency fire, ambulance, or lifesaving calls or is actively engaged in law enforcement work.

(f) Any vehicle for which an authorized emergency vehicle permit has been issued by the Commissioner of the California Highway Patrol. *(Added by Stats.1961, c. 653, p. 1858, § 12, operative Jan. 1, 1962. Amended by Stats.1967, c. 1009, p. 2602, § 2; Stats.1968, c. 1309, p. 2464, § 1, operative Jan. 1, 1969; Stats.1971, c. 438, p. 903, § 178, operative May 3, 1972; Stats.1972, c. 431, p. 796, § 52; Stats.1973, c. 35, p. 55, § 1; Stats.1974, c. 581, p. 1401, § 1; Stats.1977, c. 1017, p. 3051, § 1, eff. Sept. 23, 1977; Stats.1980, c. 1340, p. 4733, § 26.5, eff. Sept. 30, 1980; Stats.1981, c. 973, p. 3712, § 3; Stats.1982, c. 16, p. 29, § 1; Stats.1983, c. 1292, § 8; Stats.2010, c. 618 (A.B.2791), § 291; Stats.2013, c. 352 (A.B.1317), § 516, eff. Sept. 26, 2013, operative July 1, 2013.)*

Cross References

Air horns on authorized emergency vehicles, see Vehicle Code § 27000.
Ambulances, licenses, see Vehicle Code § 2510 et seq.

California highway patrol, generally, see Vehicle Code § 2250 et seq.

California traffic safety program, see Vehicle Code § 2900 et seq.

Civil liability, exemption of operators of authorized emergency vehicles, see Vehicle Code § 17004; Government Code § 830.9.

Colored lights, display on authorized emergency vehicles, see Vehicle Code §§ 30, 25252, 25258.

Coroner vehicles, warning lights, see Vehicle Code § 25264.

County fish and game wardens, powers and duties, see Fish and Game Code § 878.

Equipment of vehicles, see Vehicle Code § 24000 et seq.

Exemption from motor vehicle pollution control devices, see Vehicle Code §§ 27156.2, 27156.3.

Financial responsibility laws, see Vehicle Code § 16000 et seq.

Flashing headlamps on authorized emergency vehicles, see Vehicle Code § 25252.5.

Flashing lights, use on emergency vehicles, see Vehicle Code §§ 25251, 25258.

Following an authorized emergency vehicle, see Vehicle Code § 21706.

Headsets, earplugs or hearing protectors, wearing by operator of emergency vehicle, see Vehicle Code § 27400.

Permit for authorized emergency vehicle, see Vehicle Code § 2416.

Pneumatic tires, see Vehicle Code § 27454.

Right-of-way, authorized emergency vehicles, see Vehicle Code § 21806.

School district security or police patrol vehicles as authorized emergency vehicles, see Education Code §§ 38004, 72332.

Sirens, use by authorized emergency vehicles, see Vehicle Code §§ 30, 27002.

Size, weight and load requirements, exemption of authorized emergency vehicles, see Vehicle Code § 35002.

Special permits for disaster relief work, see Vehicle Code § 4005.

Spotlamps, use on authorized emergency vehicles, see Vehicle Code § 24404.

State vehicle fleet, development and adoption of specifications and standards for passenger cars and light-duty trucks, see Public Resources Code § 25722.5.

Suspension or revocation of permit issued for authorized emergency vehicle, see Vehicle Code § 2417.

Tire energy efficiency program for replacement tires, exemption of certain authorized emergency vehicles from tire efficiency standards, see Public Resources Code § 25773.

Traffic laws, exemption of authorized emergency vehicles, see Vehicle Code § 21055.

Use of areas above or below state highways by authorized emergency vehicles, see Streets and Highways Code § 104.12.

§§ 165.3, 165.4. Repealed by Stats.1980, c. 1340, p. 4733, §§ 27, 28

§ 165.5. Authorized emergency vehicle: rescue team

No act or omission of any rescue team operating in conjunction with an authorized emergency vehicle as defined in Section 165, while attempting to resuscitate any person who is in immediate danger of loss of life, shall impose any liability upon the rescue team or the owners or operators of any authorized emergency vehicle, if good faith is exercised.

For the purposes of this section, "rescue team" means a special group of physicians and surgeons, nurses, volunteers, or employees of the owners or operators of the authorized emergency vehicle who have been trained in cardiopulmonary resuscitation and have been designated by the owners or operators of the emergency vehicle to attempt to resuscitate persons who are in immediate danger of loss of life in cases of emergency.

This section shall not relieve the owners or operators of any other duty imposed upon them by law for the designation and training of members of a rescue team or for any provisions regarding maintenance of equipment to be used by the rescue team.

Members of a rescue team shall receive the training in a program approved by, or conforming to, standards prescribed by an emergency medical care committee established pursuant to Article 3 (commencing with Section 1797.270) of Chapter 4 of Division 2.5 of the Health and Safety Code, or a voluntary area health planning agency established pursuant to Section 127155 of the Health and Safety Code. *(Added by Stats.1970, c. 934, p. 1690, § 1. Amended by Stats.1983, c. 1246, § 44; Stats.1996, c. 1023 (S.B.1497), § 421, eff. Sept. 29, 1996.)*

Cross References

Health facility rescue teams, liability, see Health and Safety Code § 1317.

§ 166. Autobroker; auto buying service

An "autobroker" or "auto buying service" is a dealer, as defined in Section 285, who engages in the business of brokering, as defined in Section 232.5. *(Added by Stats.1994, c. 1253 (A.B.3539), § 3.)*

§ 170. Repealed by Stats.1961, c. 653, p. 1859, § 13

§ 175. Autoette

An "autoette" is a motor vehicle, located on a natural island with an area in excess of 20,000 acres and that is within a county having a population in excess of 4,000,000, that meets all of the following requirements:

(a) Has three or more wheels in contact with the ground.

(b) Has an unladed weight of no greater than 1,800 pounds.

(c) Has an overall length of no more than 120 inches, including the front and rear bumpers.

(d) Has a width of no more than 55 inches, as measured from its widest part. *(Added by Stats.2006, c. 322 (A.B.2401), § 1.)*

Cross References

Autoette registration and license plates, see Vehicle Code § 4000.5.

§§ 180 to 205. Repealed by Stats.1961, c. 653, p. 1859, §§ 15 to 21

§ 210. Automated rail crossing enforcement system

An "automated enforcement system" is any system operated by a governmental agency, in cooperation with a law enforcement agency, that photographically records a driver's responses to a rail or rail transit signal or crossing gate, or both, or to an official traffic control signal described in Section 21450, and is designed to obtain a clear photograph of a vehicle's license plate and the driver of the vehicle.

(Added by Stats.1994, c. 1216 (S.B.1802), § 3. Amended by Stats.1995, c. 922 (S.B.833), § 1; Stats.1998, c. 54 (S.B.1136), § 1.)

§ 215. Repealed by Stats.1961, c. 653, p. 1859, § 23, operative Jan. 1, 1962

§ 220. Automobile dismantler

An "automobile dismantler" is any person not otherwise expressly excluded by Section 221 who:

(a) Is engaged in the business of buying, selling, or dealing in vehicles of a type required to be registered under this code, including nonrepairable vehicles, for the purpose of dismantling the vehicles, who buys or sells the integral parts and component materials thereof, in whole or in part, or deals in used motor vehicle parts. This section does not apply to the occasional and incidental dismantling of vehicles by dealers who have secured dealers plates from the department for the current year whose principal business is buying and selling new and used vehicles, or by owners who desire to dismantle not more than three personal vehicles within any 12–month period.

(b) Notwithstanding the provisions of subdivision (a), keeps or maintains on real property owned by him, or under his possession or control, two or more unregistered motor vehicles no longer intended for, or in condition for, legal use on the highways, whether for the purpose of resale of used parts, for the purpose of reclaiming for use some or all of the materials, whether metal, glass, fabric, or otherwise, or to dispose of them, or for any other purpose. *(Stats.1959, c. 3, p. 1528, § 220. Amended by Stats.1963, c. 1106, p. 2565, § 1; Stats.1967, c. 481, p. 1687, § 1; Stats.1971, c. 1043, p. 1999, § 1, operative May 3, 1972; Stats.1971, c. 1624, p. 3498, § 6, operative May 3, 1972; Stats.1974, c. 613, p. 1458, § 1; Stats.1975, c. 1224, p. 3095, § 1; Stats.1976, c. 937, p. 2145, § 1; Stats.1994, c. 1008 (S.B.1833), § 5, operative July 1, 1995.)*

Cross References

Automobile dismantlers in general, see Vehicle Code § 11500 et seq.

Dealer licenses and certificates, see Vehicle Code § 11700 et seq.

Payment for nonferrous material by junk dealer or recycler, see Business and Professions Code § 21608.5.

Vehicles subject to registration, see Vehicle Code § 4000 et seq.

§ 221. Automobile dismantler; exclusions

(a) The term "automobile dismantler" does not include any of the following:

(1) The owner or operator of any premises on which two or more unregistered and inoperable vehicles are held or stored, if the vehicles are used for restoration or replacement parts or otherwise, in conjunction with any of the following:

(A) Any business of a licensed dealer, manufacturer, or transporter.

(B) The operation and maintenance of any fleet of motor vehicles used for the transportation of persons or property.

(C) Any agricultural, farming, mining, or ranching business that does not sell parts of the vehicles, except for either of the following purposes:

(i) For use in repairs performed by that business.

(ii) For use by a licensed dismantler or an entity described in paragraph (3).

(D) Any motor vehicle repair business registered with the Bureau of Automotive Repair, or those exempt from registration under the Business and Professions Code or applicable regulations, that does not sell parts of the vehicles, except for either of the following purposes:

(i) For use in repairs performed by that business.

(ii) For use by a licensed dismantler or an entity described in paragraph (3).

(2) Any person engaged in the restoration of vehicles of the type described in Section 5004 or in the restoration of other vehicles having historic or classic significance.

(3) The owner of a steel mill, scrap metal processing facility, or similar establishment purchasing vehicles of a type subject to registration, not for the purpose of selling the vehicles, in whole or in part, but exclusively for the purpose of reducing the vehicles to their component materials, if either the facility obtains, on a form approved or provided by the department, a certification by the person from whom the vehicles are obtained that each of the vehicles has been cleared for dismantling pursuant to Section 5500 or 11520, or the facility complies with Section 9564.

(4) Any person who acquires used parts or components for resale from vehicles which have been previously cleared for dismantling pursuant to Section 5500 or 11520.

Nothing in this paragraph permits a dismantler to acquire or sell used parts or components during the time the dismantler license is under suspension.

(b) Any vehicle acquired for the purpose specified in paragraph (3) of subdivision (a) from other than a licensed dismantler, or from other than an independent hauler who obtained the vehicle, or parts thereof from a licensed dismantler, shall be accompanied by either a receipt issued by the department evidencing proof of clearance for dismantling under Section 5500, or a copy of the ordinance or order issued by a local authority for the abatement of the vehicle pursuant to Section 22660. The steel mill, scrap metal processing facility, or similar establishment acquiring the vehicle shall attach the form evidencing clearance or abatement to the certification required pursuant to this section.

All forms specified in paragraph (3) of subdivision (a) and in this subdivision shall be available for inspection by a peace officer during business hours. *(Added by Stats. 1976, c. 937, p. 2145, § 2. Amended by Stats.1979, c. 622, p. 1938, § 1; Stats.1981, c. 271, p. 1365, § 1; Stats.1985, c. 1022, § 1; Stats.1987, c. 709, § 1; Stats.1987, c. 1133, § 2; Stats.1999, c. 316 (A.B.342), § 1.)*

Cross References
Violation as misdemeanor, see Vehicle Code § 40000.5 et seq.

§ 223. Automobile driver training

Any reference in this code to "automobile driver training" shall be deemed to refer to the laboratory phase of driver education described by Section 51852 of the Education Code. *(Added by Stats.1971, c. 1116, p. 2131, § 3, operative May 3, 1972. Amended by Stats.1980, c. 676, p. 2021, § 305.)*

§ 225. Auxiliary dolly

An "auxiliary dolly" is a vehicle, not designed for carrying persons or property on its own structure, which is so constructed and used in conjunction with a semitrailer as to support a portion of the weight of the semitrailer and any load thereon, but not permanently attached to the semitrailer, although a part of the weight of such dolly may rest on another vehicle. *(Stats.1959, c. 3, p. 1529, § 225.)*

Cross References
Brakes, see Vehicle Code § 26305.
Fifth wheel connecting device, affixation, see Vehicle Code § 29001.
Pole or pipe dolly, see Vehicle Code § 475.
Registration,
  Generally, see Vehicle Code § 4000.
  Portable or collapsible dolly used by automobile dismantler, see Vehicle Code § 4014.
Safety regulations, see Vehicle Code § 34500 et seq.
Semitrailer defined, see Vehicle Code § 550.
Turning signals, see Vehicle Code § 24951.
Weight fees, see Vehicle Code § 9400 et seq.

§ 230. Axle

An "axle" is a structure or portion of a structure consisting of one or more shafts, spindles, or bearings in the same vertical transverse plane by means of which, in conjunction with wheels mounted on said shafts, spindles, or bearings, a portion of the weight of a vehicle and its load, if any, is continuously transmitted to the roadway when the vehicle is in motion. *(Stats.1959, c. 3, p. 1529, § 230.)*

Cross References
Number of axles on dollies, see Vehicle Code § 475.
Weight fees, registration, see Vehicle Code § 9400 et seq.
Weight limits, see Vehicle Code § 35550 et seq.

§ 230.5. B-train assembly

A "B-train assembly" is a rigid frame extension attached to the rear frame of a semitrailer which allows for a fifth wheel connection point for a second semitrailer. *(Added by Stats.1991, c. 13 (A.B.37), § 13, eff. Feb. 13, 1991.)*

§ 231. Bicycle

A bicycle is a device upon which any person may ride, propelled exclusively by human power through a belt, chain, or gears, and having one or more wheels. Persons riding bicycles are subject to the provisions of this code specified in Sections 21200 and 21200.5. *(Added by Stats.1978, c. 421, p. 1320, § 1. Amended by Stats.1983, c. 273, § 1; Stats.1985, c. 1013, § 1.)*

§ 231.5. Bicycle path; bike path

A "bicycle path" or "bike path" is a Class I bikeway, as defined in subdivision (a) of Section 890.4 of the Streets and Highways Code. *(Added by Stats.2009, c. 200 (S.B.734), § 5.)*

§ 231.6. Bicycle path crossing

(a) A "bicycle path crossing" is either of the following:

(1) That portion of a roadway included within the prolongation or connection of the boundary lines of a bike path at intersections where the intersecting roadways meet at approximately right angles.

(2) Any portion of a roadway distinctly indicated for bicycle crossing by lines or other markings on the surface.

(b) Notwithstanding subdivision (a), there shall not be a bicycle path crossing where local authorities have placed signs indicating no crossing. *(Added by Stats.2009, c. 200 (S.B.734), § 6.)*

§ 232. Board

The "board" is the New Motor Vehicle Board. *(Added by Stats.1973, c. 996, p. 1964, § 2, operative July 1, 1974.)*

§ 232.5. Brokering

"Brokering" is an arrangement under which a dealer, for a fee or other consideration, regardless of the form or time of payment, provides or offers to provide the service of arranging, negotiating, assisting, or effectuating the purchase of a new or used motor vehicle, not owned by the dealer, for another or others. *(Added by Stats.1994, c. 1253 (A.B.3539), § 4.)*

§ 233. Bus

(a) Except as provided in subdivision (b), a "bus" is any vehicle, including a trailer bus, designed, used, or maintained for carrying more than 15 persons including the driver.

(b) A vehicle designed, used, or maintained for carrying more than 10 persons, including the driver, which is used to transport persons for compensation or profit, or is used by any nonprofit organization or group, is also a bus.

(c) This section does not alter the definition of a schoolbus, school pupil activity bus, general public paratransit vehicle, farm labor vehicle, or youth bus.

(d) A vanpool vehicle is not a bus. *(Added by Stats.1961, c. 263, p. 1292, § 1. Amended by Stats.1969, c. 479, p. 1041, § 1; Stats.1976, c. 844, p. 1923, § 1; Stats.1982, c. 46, p. 139, § 4; Stats.1988, c. 843, § 1; Stats.1992, c. 439 (S.B.1914), § 1; Stats.1994, c. 675 (S.B.1741), § 1.)*

Cross References

Definitions,
Bus, air resources, see Health and Safety Code § 39017.
Charter-party carrier of passengers, see Public Utilities Code § 5360.
Commercial vehicle, see Vehicle Code § 260.
Common carrier, see Public Utilities Code § 211.
Passenger stage, see Public Utilities Code § 225.
Passenger vehicle, see Vehicle Code § 465.
Schoolbus, see Vehicle Code § 545; Education Code § 39830.
Urban and suburban service, see Vehicle Code § 35107.
Length, see Vehicle Code § 35400.
Safety regulations, see Vehicle Code § 34500 et seq.
Size, see Vehicle Code § 35106.
Weight fees, commercial vehicles, see Vehicle Code § 9400 et seq.
Weight limits, see Vehicle Code § 35550 et seq.

§ 234. Business

A "business" includes a proprietorship, partnership, corporation, and any other form of commercial enterprise. *(Added by Stats.1990, c. 1563 (A.B.3243), § 1.)*

§ 235. Business district

A "business district" is that portion of a highway and the property contiguous thereto (a) upon one side of which highway, for a distance of 600 feet, 50 percent or more of the contiguous property fronting thereon is occupied by buildings in use for business, or (b) upon both sides of which highway, collectively, for a distance of 300 feet, 50 percent or more of the contiguous property fronting thereon is so occupied. A business district may be longer than the distances specified in this section if the above ratio of buildings in use for business to the length of the highway exists. *(Stats.1959, c. 3, p. 1529, § 235.)*

Cross References

Lights on parked vehicles in business district, see Vehicle Code § 24802.
Limitations in determining whether highway is within a business district, see Vehicle Code § 240.
Residence district defined, see Vehicle Code § 515.

Speed restriction signs in business districts, see Vehicle Code §§ 21357, 21358, 41100.

§ 236. Business representative

A "business representative" means a proprietor, a limited or general partner, a managerial employee, a stockholder, a director, or an officer who is active in the management, direction, and control of that part of a business which is a licensed activity. *(Added by Stats. 1990, c. 1563 (A.B.3243), § 2.)*

§ 240. Business and residence districts: determination

In determining whether a highway is within a business or residence district, the following limitations shall apply and shall qualify the definitions in Sections 235 and 515:

(a) No building shall be regarded unless its entrance faces the highway and the front of the building is within 75 feet of the roadway.

(b) Where a highway is physically divided into two or more roadways only those buildings facing each roadway separately shall be regarded for the purpose of determining whether the roadway is within a district.

(c) All churches, apartments, hotels, multiple dwelling houses, clubs, and public buildings, other than schools, shall be deemed to be business structures.

(d) A highway or portion of a highway shall not be deemed to be within a district regardless of the number of buildings upon the contiguous property if there is no right of access to the highway by vehicles from the contiguous property. *(Stats.1959, c. 3, p. 1529, § 240.)*

§ 241. Buy-here-pay-here dealer; included actions

Section added by Stats.2012, c. 740 (A.B.1447), § 4. See, also, another section of the same number added by Stats.2012, c. 741 (A.B.1534), § 2.

A "buy-here-pay-here" dealer is a dealer, as defined in Section 285, who is not otherwise expressly excluded by Section 241.1, and who does all of the following:

(a) Enters into conditional sale contracts, within the meaning of subdivision (a) of Section 2981 of the Civil Code, and subject to the provisions of Chapter 2b (commencing with Section 2981) of Title 14 of Part 4 of Division 3 of the Civil Code, or lease contracts, within the meaning of Section 2985.7 of the Civil Code, and subject to the provisions of Chapter 2d (commencing with Section 2985.7) of Title 14 of Part 4 of Division 3 of the Civil Code.

(b) Assigns less than 90 percent of all unrescinded conditional sale contracts and lease contracts to unaffiliated third-party finance or leasing sources within 45 days of the consummation of those contracts.

(c) For purposes of this section, a conditional sale contract does not include a contract for the sale of a motor vehicle if all amounts owed under the contract are paid in full within 30 days.

(d) The department may promulgate regulations as necessary to implement this section. *(Added by Stats. 2012, c. 740 (A.B.1447), § 4.)*

§ 241. Buy-here-pay-here dealer

Section added by Stats.2012, c. 741 (A.B.1534), § 2. See, also, another section of the same number added by Stats.2012, c. 740 (A.B.1447), § 4.

A "buy-here-pay-here" dealer is a dealer, as defined in Section 285, who is not otherwise expressly excluded by Section 241.1, and who does all of the following:

(a) Enters into conditional sale contracts, within the meaning of subdivision (a) of Section 2981 of the Civil Code, and subject to the provisions of Chapter 2b (commencing with Section 2981) of Title 14 of Part 4 of Division 3 of the Civil Code, or lease contracts, within the meaning of Section 2985.7 of the Civil Code, and subject to the provisions of Chapter 2d (commencing with Section 2985.7) of Title 14 of Part 4 of Division 3 of the Civil Code.

(b) Assigns less than 90 percent of all unrescinded conditional sale contracts and lease contracts to unaffiliated third-party finance or leasing sources within 45 days of the consummation of those contracts.

(c) For purposes of this section, a conditional sale contract does not include a contract for the sale of a motor vehicle if all amounts owed under the contract are paid in full within 30 days.

(d) The department may promulgate regulations as necessary to implement this section. *(Added by Stats. 2012, c. 741 (A.B.1534), § 2.)*

§ 241.1. Buy-here-pay-here dealer; excluded actions

Section added by Stats.2012, c. 740 (A.B.1447), § 5. See, also, another section of the same number added by Stats.2012, c. 741 (A.B.1534), § 3.

The term "buy-here-pay-here" dealer does not include any of the following:

(a) A lessor who primarily leases vehicles that are two model years old or newer.

(b) A dealer that does both of the following:

(1) Certifies 100 percent of used vehicle inventory offered for sale at retail price pursuant to Section 11713.18.

(2) Maintains an onsite service and repair facility that is licensed by the Bureau of Automotive Repair and employs a minimum of five master automobile technicians that are certified by the National Institute for Automotive Service Excellence. *(Added by Stats.2012, c. 740 (A.B.1447), § 5.)*

§ 241.1. Buy-here-pay-here dealer; exclusions

Section added by Stats.2012, c. 741 (A.B.1534), § 3. See, also, another section of the same number added by Stats.2012, c. 740 (A.B.1447), § 5.

The term "buy-here-pay-here" dealer does not include any of the following:

(a) A lessor who primarily leases vehicles that are two model years old or newer.

(b) A dealer that does both of the following:

(1) Certifies 100 percent of used vehicle inventory offered for sale at retail price pursuant to Section 11713.18.

(2) Maintains an onsite service and repair facility that is licensed by the Bureau of Automotive Repair and employs a minimum of five master automobile technicians that are certified by the National Institute for Automotive Service Excellence. *(Added by Stats.2012, c. 741 (A.B.1534), § 3.)*

§ 242. Camp trailer

A "camp trailer" is a vehicle designed to be used on a highway, capable of human habitation for camping or recreational purposes, that does not exceed 16 feet in overall length from the foremost point of the trailer hitch to the rear extremity of the trailer body and does not exceed 96 inches in width and includes any tent trailer. Where a trailer telescopes for travel, the size shall apply to the trailer as fully extended. Notwithstanding any other provision of law, a camp trailer shall not be deemed to be a trailer coach. *(Added by Stats.1971, c. 1536, p. 3042, § 1, operative May 3, 1972.)*

§ 243. Camper

A "camper" is a structure designed to be mounted upon a motor vehicle and to provide facilities for human habitation or camping purposes. A camper having one axle shall not be considered a vehicle. *(Added by Stats.1963, c. 688, p. 1694, § 1. Amended by Stats.1968, c. 228, p. 541, § 1, eff. May 29, 1968.)*

§ 245. Carry-all

A "carry-all" is that type of earth-moving equipment which is not self-propelled but which is designed for use behind tractors or other motive power and which is self-loading by means of a cutting blade which is lowered at an angle to dig into the ground. The term includes, but is not limited to, such types of vehicles as carry the trade names of LaPlant-Choate, LeTourneau, and Be Ge. *(Stats.1959, c. 3, p. 1529, § 245.)*

Cross References
Carryalls as included within definition of special highway construction equipment, see Vehicle Code § 565.

§ 246. Certificate of compliance

A "certificate of compliance" for the purposes of this code is an electronic or printed document issued by a state agency, board, or commission, or authorized person, setting forth that the requirements of a particular law, rule or regulation, within its jurisdiction to regulate or administer has been satisfied. *(Added by Stats.1963, c. 666, p. 1654, § 1. Amended by Stats.1967, c. 478, p. 1683, § 1; Stats.1999, c. 1007 (S.B.532), § 15.)*

§ 250. Chop Shop

A "chop shop" is any building, lot, or other premises where any person has been engaged in altering, destroying, disassembling, dismantling, reassembling, or storing any motor vehicle or motor vehicle part known to be illegally obtained by theft, fraud, or conspiracy to defraud, in order to do either of the following:

(a) Alter, counterfeit, deface, destroy, disguise, falsify, forge, obliterate, or remove the identity, including the vehicle identification number, of a motor vehicle or motor vehicle part, in order to misrepresent the identity of the motor vehicle or motor vehicle part, or to prevent the identification of the motor vehicle or motor vehicle part.

(b) Sell or dispose of the motor vehicle or motor vehicle part. *(Added by Stats.1993, c. 386 (S.B.73), § 1, eff. Sept. 8, 1993.)*

§ 255. City

"City" includes every city and city and county within this State. *(Stats.1959, c. 3, p. 1530, § 255.)*

Cross References
County defined, see Vehicle Code § 270.

§ 257. Clean fuel vehicle

A "clean fuel vehicle" means any passenger or commercial vehicle or pickup truck that is fueled by alternative fuels, as defined in Section 301 of the Energy Policy Act of 1992 (P.L. 102-486), and produces emissions which do not exceed whichever of the following standards, as defined by regulations of the State Air Resources Board in effect on January 1, 1994, is applicable to the model year of the vehicle:

(a) For a vehicle of the 1994 to 1996, inclusive, model year, the emission standard applicable to a transitional low-emission vehicle.

(b) For a vehicle of the 1997 model year, the emission standard applicable to a low-emission vehicle.

(c) For a vehicle of the 1998 to 2000, inclusive, model year, the emission standard applicable to an ultra low-emission vehicle. *(Added by Stats.1993, c. 1159 (S.B.314), § 4.)*

§ 259. Collector motor vehicle

"Collector motor vehicle" means a motor vehicle owned by a collector, as defined in subdivision (a) of Section 5051, and the motor vehicle is used primarily in shows, parades, charitable functions, and historical exhibitions for display, maintenance, and preservation, and is not used primarily for transportation. *(Added by Stats. 2004, c. 107 (S.B.1784), § 1.)*

Cross References
Motor vehicle inspection, exemption from testing for collector motor vehicle, see Health and Safety Code § 44011.

§ 260. Commercial vehicle

(a) A "commercial vehicle" is a motor vehicle of a type required to be registered under this code used or maintained for the transportation of persons for hire, compensation, or profit or designed, used, or maintained primarily for the transportation of property.

(b) Passenger vehicles and house cars that are not used for the transportation of persons for hire, compensation, or profit are not commercial vehicles. This subdivision shall not apply to Chapter 4 (commencing with Section 6700) of Division 3.

(c) Any vanpool vehicle is not a commercial vehicle.

(d) The definition of a commercial vehicle in this section does not apply to Chapter 7 (commencing with Section 15200) of Division 6. *(Stats.1959, c. 3, p. 1530, § 260. Amended by Stats.1963, c. 688, p. 1694, § 2; Stats.1982, c. 46, p. 139, § 5; Stats.1988, c. 1509, § 1; Stats.2000, c. 861 (S.B.2084), § 11, eff. Sept. 29, 2000; Stats.2003, c. 222 (A.B.1662), § 1.)*

Cross References
"Bus" defined, see Vehicle Code § 233.
County regulation, see Vehicle Code § 35712 et seq.
Employee meal periods, exception for commercial drivers operating vehicle described in this section and meeting specified conditions, see Labor Code § 512.
Foreign commercial vehicles, see Vehicle Code § 6850 et seq.
"House car" defined, see Vehicle Code § 362.
Identification required, see Vehicle Code § 27900.
Reciprocity with other states, see Vehicle Code §§ 8000 et seq., 8050.
Registration fees, generally, see Vehicle Code § 9250 et seq.
Service stations, services for commercial vehicles, see Business and Professions Code § 13651.
"Vehicle" defined, see Vehicle Code § 670.
Vehicles subject to registration, see Vehicle Code § 4000 et seq.
Weight fees, commercial vehicles, see Vehicle Code § 9400 et seq.

§ 265. Commissioner

The "commissioner" is the Commissioner of the California Highway Patrol. *(Stats.1959, c. 3, p. 1530, § 265.)*

California highway patrol, generally, see Vehicle Code § 2100 et seq.
Powers and duties of commissioner in general, see Vehicle Code §§ 2108, 2400 et seq.

§ 266. Consignment

A "consignment" is an arrangement under which a dealer agrees to accept possession of a vehicle of a type required to be registered under this code from an owner for the purpose of selling the vehicle and to pay the owner or the owner's designee from the proceeds of the sale. *(Added by Stats.1990, c. 735 (A.B.3269), § 1. Amended by Stats.1991, c. 815 (A.B.1063), § 1.)*

§ 267. Converter

A "converter" is a person, other than a vehicle manufacturer, who, prior to the retail sale of a new vehicle, does any of the following to the vehicle:

(a) Assembles, installs, or affixes a body, cab, or special equipment to the vehicle chassis.

(b) Substantially adds to, subtracts from, or modifies the vehicle, if it is a previously assembled or manufactured new vehicle. *(Added by Stats.1995, c. 211 (A.B. 770), § 1.)*

§ 270. County

"County" includes every county and city and county within this State. *(Stats.1959, c. 3, p. 1530, § 270.)*

City as including every city and county within this state, see Vehicle Code § 255.
Counties, see Government Code § 23000 et seq.

§ 273. Crib sheet or cribbing device

A "crib sheet" or "cribbing device" is any paper or device designed for cheating by supplying examination answers without questions to an applicant for the purpose of fraudulently qualifying the applicant for any class of driver's license, permit, or certificate. *(Added by Stats. 1986, c. 960, § 1.)*

§ 275. Crosswalk

"Crosswalk" is either:

(a) That portion of a roadway included within the prolongation or connection of the boundary lines of sidewalks at intersections where the intersecting roadways meet at approximately right angles, except the prolongation of such lines from an alley across a street.

(b) Any portion of a roadway distinctly indicated for pedestrian crossing by lines or other markings on the surface.

Notwithstanding the foregoing provisions of this section, there shall not be a crosswalk where local authorities have placed signs indicating no crossing. *(Stats.1959, c. 3, p. 1530, § 275.)*

"Alley" defined, see Vehicle Code § 110.
Crosswalk near schools, see Vehicle Code § 21368.
Establishment of crosswalks, see Vehicle Code §§ 21106, 21352.
"Intersection" defined, see Vehicle Code § 365.
Pedestrians' crossing at other than crosswalks, right-of-way, see Vehicle Code § 21954.
Pedestrians' right-of-way on crosswalks, see Vehicle Code § 21950.
Prohibition of vehicles on crosswalks, see Vehicle Code § 22500.
"Sidewalk" defined, see Vehicle Code § 555.

§ 280. Darkness

"Darkness" is any time from one-half hour after sunset to one-half hour before sunrise and any other time when visibility is not sufficient to render clearly discernible any person or vehicle on the highway at a distance of 1,000 feet. *(Stats.1959, c. 3, p. 1530, § 280. Amended by Stats.1963, c. 210, p. 951, § 1; Stats.1974, c. 635, p. 1488, § 1.)*

Bicycle operation during darkness, see Vehicle Code § 21201.
Lighting equipment,
    Generally, see Vehicle Code § 24250 et seq.,
    Defined, see Vehicle Code § 375.

§ 285. Dealer

"Dealer" is a person not otherwise expressly excluded by Section 286 who:

(a) For commission, money, or other thing of value, sells, exchanges, buys, or offers for sale, negotiates or attempts to negotiate, a sale or exchange of an interest in, a vehicle subject to registration, a motorcycle, snowmobile, or all-terrain vehicle subject to identification under this code, or a trailer subject to identification pursuant to Section 5014.1, or induces or attempts to induce any person to buy or exchange an interest in a vehicle and, who receives or expects to receive a commission, money, brokerage fees, profit, or any other thing of value, from either the seller or purchaser of the vehicle.

(b) Is engaged wholly or in part in the business of selling vehicles or buying or taking in trade, vehicles for the purpose of resale, selling, or offering for sale, or consigned to be sold, or otherwise dealing in vehicles, whether or not the vehicles are owned by the person. *(Stats.1959, c. 3, p. 1530, § 285. Amended by Stats.1959, c. 173, p. 2068, § 2; Stats.1959, c. 1996, p. 4614, § 1.4; Stats.1961, c. 58, p. 1001, § 2, eff. March 31, 1961; Stats.1979, c. 622, p. 1939, § 2; Stats.2001, c. 539 (S.B. 734), § 1; Stats.2004, c. 836 (A.B.2848), § 1; Stats.2005, c. 270 (S.B.731), § 8.)*

Change of established place of business, see Vehicle Code § 11712.
Fees for special plates, see Vehicle Code § 9262.
Inspection of emission related parts and operations of new vehicle on dealer's premises, see Health and Safety Code § 43012.
Licenses and certificates, see Vehicle Code § 11700 et seq.

New motor vehicle dealer defined, see Vehicle Code § 426.
Vehicle salesman defined, see Vehicle Code § 675.

§ 286. Dealer; exclusions

The term "dealer" does not include any of the following:

(a) Insurance companies, banks, finance companies, public officials, or any other person coming into possession of vehicles in the regular course of business, who sells vehicles under a contractual right or obligation, in performance of an official duty, or in authority of any court of law, if the sale is for the purpose of saving the seller from loss or pursuant to the authority of a court.

(b) Persons who sell or distribute vehicles of a type subject to registration or trailers subject to identification pursuant to Section 5014.1 for a manufacturer to vehicle dealers licensed under this code, or who are employed by manufacturers or distributors to promote the sale of vehicles dealt in by those manufacturers or distributors. However, any of those persons who also sell vehicles at retail are vehicle dealers and are subject to this code.

(c) Persons regularly employed as salespersons by vehicle dealers licensed under this code while acting within the scope of that employment.

(d) Persons engaged exclusively in the bona fide business of exporting vehicles or of soliciting orders for the sale and delivery of vehicles outside the territorial limits of the United States, if no federal excise tax is legally payable or refundable on any of the transactions. Persons not engaged exclusively in the bona fide business of exporting vehicles, but who are engaged in the business of soliciting orders for the sale and delivery of vehicles, outside the territorial limits of the United States are exempt from licensure as dealers only if their sales of vehicles produce less than 10 percent of their total gross revenue from all business transacted.

(e) Persons not engaged in the purchase or sale of vehicles as a business, who dispose of any vehicle acquired and used in good faith, for their own personal use, or for use in their business, and not for the purpose of avoiding the provisions of this code.

(f) Persons who are engaged in the purchase, sale, or exchange of vehicles, other than motorcycles, all-terrain vehicles, or trailers subject to identification under this code, that are not intended for use on the highways.

(g) Persons temporarily retained as auctioneers solely for the purpose of disposing of vehicle stock inventories by means of public auction on behalf of the owners at the owners' place of business, or as otherwise approved by the department, if intermediate physical possession or control of, or an ownership interest in, the inventory is not conveyed to the persons so retained.

(h) Persons who are engaged exclusively in the business of purchasing, selling, servicing, or exchanging racing vehicles, parts for racing vehicles, and trailers designed and intended by the manufacturer to be used exclusively for carrying racing vehicles. For purposes of this subdivision, "racing vehicle" means a motor vehicle of a type used exclusively in a contest of speed or in a competitive trial of speed which is not intended for use on the highways.

(i) A person who is a lessor.

(j) A person who is a renter.

(k) A salvage pool.

(*l*) A yacht broker who is subject to the Yacht and Ship Brokers Act (Article 2 (commencing with Section 700) of Chapter 5 of Division 3 of the Harbors and Navigation Code) and who sells used boat trailers in conjunction with the sale of a vessel.

(m) A licensed automobile dismantler who sells vehicles that have been reported for dismantling as provided in Section 11520.

(n) The Director of Corrections when selling vehicles pursuant to Section 2813.5 of the Penal Code.

(*o*)(1) Any public or private nonprofit charitable, religious, or educational institution or organization that sells vehicles if all of the following conditions are met:

(A) The institution or organization qualifies for state tax-exempt status under Section 23701d of the Revenue and Taxation Code, and tax-exempt status under Section 501(c)(3) of the federal Internal Revenue Code.

(B) The vehicles sold were donated to the nonprofit charitable, religious, or educational institution or organization.

(C) The vehicles subject to retail sale meet all of the applicable equipment requirements of Division 12 (commencing with Section 24000) and are in compliance with emission control requirements as evidenced by the issuance of a certificate pursuant to subdivision (b) of Section 44015 of the Health and Safety Code. Under no circumstances may any institution or organization transfer the responsibility of obtaining a smog inspection certificate to the buyer of the vehicle.

(D) The proceeds of the sale of the vehicles are retained by that institution or organization for its charitable, religious, or educational purposes.

(2) An institution or organization described in paragraph (1) may sell vehicles on behalf of another institution or organization under the following conditions:

(A) The nonselling institution or organization meets the requirements of paragraph (1).

(B) The selling and nonselling institutions or organizations enter into a signed, written agreement pursuant to subparagraph (A) of paragraph (3) of subdivision (a) of Section 1660.

(C) The selling institution or organization transfers the proceeds from the sale of each vehicle to the nonselling institution or organization within 45 days of the sale. All net proceeds transferred to the nonselling institution or organization shall clearly be identifiable to the sale of a specific vehicle. The selling institution or organization may retain a percentage of the proceeds from the sale of a particular vehicle. However, any retained proceeds shall be used by the selling institution or organization for its charitable, religious, or educational purposes.

(D) At the time of transferring the proceeds, the selling institution or organization shall provide to the nonselling institution or organization, an itemized listing of the vehicles sold and the amount for which each vehicle was sold.

(E) In the event the selling institution or organization cannot complete a retail sale of a particular vehicle, or if the vehicle cannot be transferred as a wholesale transaction to a dealer licensed under this code, the vehicle shall be returned to the nonselling institution or organization and the written agreement revised to reflect that return. Under no circumstances may a selling institution or organization transfer or donate the vehicle to a third party that is excluded from the definition of a dealer under this section.

(3) An institution or organization described in this subdivision shall retain all records required to be retained pursuant to Section 1660.

(p) A motor club, as defined in Section 12142 of the Insurance Code, that does not arrange or negotiate individual motor vehicle purchase transactions on behalf of its members but refers members to a new motor vehicle dealer for the purchase of a new motor vehicle and does not receive a fee from the dealer contingent upon the sale of the vehicle. *(Added by Stats.1959, c. 1996, p. 4614, § 1.5. Amended by Stats.1967, c. 394, p. 1617, § 1; Stats.1968, c. 505, p. 1150, § 1; Stats.1970, c. 1290, p. 2384, § 1; Stats.1970, c. 1446, p. 2817, § 1; Stats.1974, c. 687, p. 1551, § 2; Stats.1976, c. 1284, p. 5710, § 3; Stats.1979, c. 622, p. 1939, § 3; Stats.1980, c. 629, p. 1718, § 1; Stats.1984, c. 1407, § 1; Stats.1988, c. 546, § 1; Stats.1989, c. 923, § 2; Stats.1991, c. 13 (A.B.37), § 14, eff. Feb. 13, 1991; Stats.1991, c. 928 (A.B.1886), § 13, eff. Oct. 14, 1991; Stats.1992, c. 127 (A.B.2273), § 1; Stats.1994, c. 1253 (A.B.3539), § 5; Stats.2001, c. 460 (A.B.871), § 1; Stats.2001, c. 539 (S.B.734), § 2.5; Stats.2002, c. 664 (A.B.3034), § 212; Stats.2002, c. 758 (A.B.3024), § 3; Stats.2004, c. 836 (A.B.2848), § 2.)*

Cross References

Inspection of emission related parts and operations of new vehicle on dealer's premises, see Health and Safety Code § 43012.

Nonprofit institution or organization selling vehicles, inspection of records to ascertain meeting of conditions of subd. (*o*) of this section, see Vehicle Code § 1660.

Nonprofit institution or organization selling vehicles, retention of records, see Vehicle Code § 1660.

§ 288. Declared combined gross weight

"Declared combined gross weight" equals the total unladen weight of the combination of vehicles plus the heaviest load that will be transported by that combination of vehicles. *(Added by Stats.2000, c. 861 (S.B.2084), § 12, eff. Sept. 29, 2000.)*

§ 289. Declared gross vehicle weight

"Declared gross vehicle weight" means weight that equals the total unladen weight of the vehicle plus the heaviest load that will be transported on the vehicle. *(Added by Stats.2000, c. 861 (S.B.2084), § 13, eff. Sept. 29, 2000.)*

§ 290. Department

"Department" means the Department of Motor Vehicles except, when used in Chapter 2 (commencing with Section 2100) of Division 2 and in Divisions 11 (commencing with Section 21000), 12 (commencing with Section 24000), 13 (commencing with Section 29000), 14 (commencing with Section 31600), 14.1 (commencing with Section 32000), 14.3 (commencing with Section 32100), 14.5 (commencing with Section 33000), 14.7 (commencing with Section 34000), and 14.8 (commencing with Section 34500), it shall mean the Department of the California Highway Patrol. *(Stats.1959, c. 3, p. 1531, § 290. Amended by Stats.1961, c. 58, p. 1002, § 3, eff. March 31, 1961; Stats.1970, c. 1315, p. 2445, § 1; Stats.1982, c. 1255, p. 4602, § 2.6; Stats.1988, c. 1384, § 1.)*

Cross References

Department of motor vehicles, see Vehicle Code § 1500 et seq.

Department of the California highway patrol, see Vehicle Code § 2100 et seq.

§ 291. Department of transportation

Any reference in this code to the Department of Public Works shall be deemed to refer to the Department of Transportation, which is part of the Business, Transportation and Housing Agency as provided by Section 13975 of the Government Code. *(Added by Stats.1965, c. 1099, p. 2746, § 1. Amended by Stats.1969, c. 138, p. 371, § 276, eff. Sept. 11, 1969; Stats.1974, c. 545, p. 1309, § 153; Stats.1974, c. 773, p. 1696, § 4; Stats.1982, c. 454, p. 1892, § 178.)*

Cross References

"Department" defined, see Streets and Highways Code § 20.

Department of transportation, see Government Code § 14000 et seq.; Streets and Highways Code § 90 et seq.

§ 295. Director

The "director" is the Director of Motor Vehicles. *(Stats.1959, c. 3, p. 1531, § 295.)*

Cross References

Appointment of director, see Vehicle Code § 1504.

Department of Motor Vehicles, powers and duties, see Vehicle Code § 1650 et seq.

Service of process on nonresident, see Vehicle Code § 17451.

§ 295.5. Disabled person

A "disabled person" is any of the following:

(a) Any person who has lost, or has lost the use of, one or more lower extremities or both hands, or who has significant limitation in the use of lower extremities, or who has a diagnosed disease or disorder which substantially impairs or interferes with mobility, or who is so severely disabled as to be unable to move without the aid of an assistant device.

(b) Any person who is blind to the extent that the person's central visual acuity does not exceed $^{20}/_{200}$ in the better eye, with corrective lenses, as measured by the Snellen test, or visual acuity that is greater than $^{20}/_{200}$, but with a limitation in the field of vision such that the widest diameter of the visual field subtends an angle not greater than 20 degrees.

(c) Any person who suffers from lung disease to the extent of any of the following:

(1) The person's forced (respiratory) expiratory volume for one second when measured by spirometry is less than one liter.

(2) The person's arterial oxygen tension (pO_2) is less than 60 mm/Hg on room air while the person is at rest.

(d) Any person who is impaired by cardiovascular disease to the extent that the person's functional limitations are classified in severity as class III or class IV based upon standards accepted by the American Heart Association. *(Added by Stats.1989, c. 554, § 1.)*

§ 295.7. Disabled veteran

A "disabled veteran" is any person who, as a result of injury or disease suffered while on active service with the armed forces of the United States, suffers any of the following:

(a) Has a disability which has been rated at 100 percent by the Department of Veterans Affairs or the military service from which the veteran was discharged, due to a diagnosed disease or disorder which substantially impairs or interferes with mobility.

(b) Is so severely disabled as to be unable to move without the aid of an assistant device.

(c) Has lost, or has lost use of, one or more limbs.

(d) Has suffered permanent blindness, as defined in Section 19153 of the Welfare and Institutions Code. *(Added by Stats.1989, c. 554, § 2.)*

Cross References

Issuance and renewal of disabled parking placard, conditions, certification of disabled veteran status, see Vehicle Code § 22511.55.
Special license plates, certification of disabled veteran status, see Vehicle Code § 5007.

§ 296. Distributor

A "distributor" is any person other than a manufacturer who sells or distributes new vehicles subject to registration under this code, new trailers subject to identification pursuant to Section 5014.1, or new off-highway motorcycles or all-terrain vehicles subject to identification under this code, to dealers in this state and maintains representatives for the purpose of contacting dealers or prospective dealers in this state. *(Added by*

Stats.1973, c. 996, p. 1964, § 3, operative July 1, 1974. Amended by Stats.1975, c. 1224, p. 3096, § 2; Stats.1981, c. 338, p. 1497, § 1; Stats.1982, c. 1584, p. 6260, § 1; Stats.2001, c. 539 (S.B.734), § 3; Stats.2004, c. 836 (A.B.2848), § 3.)

Cross References

Classes of insurance, express warranties, see Insurance Code § 116.6.

§ 297. Distributor branch

A "distributor branch" is an office maintained by a distributor for the sale of new vehicles or new trailers subject to identification pursuant to Section 5014.1 to dealers or for directing or supervising, in whole or in part, the distributor's representatives. *(Added by Stats.1973, c. 996, p. 1964, § 4, operative July 1, 1974. Amended by Stats.1981, c. 338, p. 1497, § 2; Stats.2001, c. 539 (S.B. 734), § 4.)*

§ 300. Drawbar

A "drawbar" is a rigid structure forming a connection between a trailer and a towing vehicle, securely attached to both vehicles by nonrigid means and carrying no part of the load of either vehicle. *(Stats.1959, c. 3, p. 1531, § 300.)*

Cross References

Drawbar, length not included in measuring vehicles, see Vehicle Code § 35402.
Length, see Vehicle Code § 29005.
Towed vehicles, see Vehicle Code § 29004.

§ 303. Driveaway-towaway operation

A "driveaway-towaway operation" is any operation in which any motor vehicle or combination of motor vehicles coupled together constitutes the commodity being transported, when one or more sets of wheels of any such motor vehicle or motor vehicles are on the roadway, and when one or more of such vehicles are being operated under a manufacturer's, dealer's, or transporter's special plates. *(Added by Stats.1961, c. 1989, p. 4185, § 1.)*

Cross References

Clearance and side-marker lamps, see Vehicle Code § 25100.
Exemption from requirement,
For service brakes on all wheels, see Vehicle Code § 26311.
For single control of power brake, see Vehicle Code § 26458.

§ 305. Driver

A "driver" is a person who drives or is in actual physical control of a vehicle. The term "driver" does not include the tillerman or other person who, in an auxiliary capacity, assists the driver in the steering or operation of any articulated firefighting apparatus. *(Stats.1959, c. 3, p. 1531, § 305. Amended by Stats.1971, c. 213, p. 279, § 1, operative May 3, 1972.)*

Cross References

Drivers' licenses, see Vehicle Code § 12500 et seq.

20

Identification cards, see Vehicle Code § 13000 et seq.
Limitation on driving hours, see Vehicle Code § 21702.
Vehicle defined, see Vehicle Code § 670.

§ 310. Driver's license

"Driver's license" is a valid license to drive the type of motor vehicle or combination of vehicles for which a person is licensed under this code or by a foreign jurisdiction. *(Stats.1959, c. 3, p. 1531, § 310. Amended by Stats.1961, c. 1615, p. 3453, § 2; Stats.1963, c. 74, p. 700, § 1; Stats.1971, c. 213, p. 279, § 2, operative May 3, 1972.)*

Cross References

Drivers' licenses, see Vehicle Code § 12500 et seq.

§ 310.4. Driving instructor

A "driving instructor" is, except as provided in Section 11105.5, an employee of a driving school licensed by the department to instruct others in the operation of motor vehicles. *(Added by Stats.1975, c. 703, p. 1664, § 1.)*

§ 310.6. Driving school

A "driving school" is a business which, for compensation, conducts or offers to conduct instruction in the operation of motor vehicles. As used in this section, "instruction" includes classroom driver education, in-vehicle driver training, and correspondence study. *(Added by Stats.1975, c. 703, p. 1664, § 2.)*

§ 310.8. Driving school operator

A "driving school operator" is either a driving school owner who operates his own driving school or an employee of a driving school who is designated by the driving school owner of such school to personally direct and manage the school for the owner. *(Formerly § 311.5, added by Stats.1972, c. 676, p. 1258, § 2. Renumbered § 310.8 and amended by Stats.1975, c. 703, p. 1664, § 3.)*

§ 311. Driving school owner

A "driving school owner" is any person licensed by the department to engage in the business of giving instruction for compensation in the driving of motor vehicles or in the preparation of an applicant for examination for a driver's license issued by the department. *(Added by Stats.1972, c. 676, p. 1257, § 1. Amended by Stats.1975, c. 703, p. 1664, § 4.)*

§ 311.5. Renumbered § 310.8 and amended by Stats. 1975, c. 703, p. 1664, § 3

§ 312. Drug

The term "drug" means any substance or combination of substances, other than alcohol, which could so affect the nervous system, brain, or muscles of a person as to impair, to an appreciable degree, his ability to drive a vehicle in the manner that an ordinarily prudent and cautious man, in full possession of his faculties, using reasonable care, would drive a similar vehicle under like conditions. *(Added by Stats.1971, c. 1530, p. 3022, § 1, operative May 3, 1972.)*

Cross References

Suspension or revocation of license for driving under the influence or engaging in speed contests or exhibitions of speed, reinstatement conditions, see Vehicle Code § 13352.

§ 313. Electric personal assistive mobility device (EP-AMD)

The term "electric personal assistive mobility device" or "EPAMD" means a self-balancing, nontandem two-wheeled device, that is not greater than 20 inches deep and 25 inches wide and can turn in place, designed to transport only one person, with an electric propulsion system averaging less than 750 watts (1 horsepower), the maximum speed of which, when powered solely by a propulsion system on a paved level surface, is no more than 12.5 miles per hour.

(Added by Stats.2002, c. 979 (S.B.1918), § 1, operative March 1, 2003. Amended by Stats.2007, c. 106 (A.B.470), § 1.)

Cross References

Electric personal assistive mobility devices, required safety mechanisms, see Vehicle Code § 21280.5.

§ 314. Expressway

An "expressway" is a portion of highway that is part of either of the following:

(a) An expressway system established by a county under Section 941.4 of the Streets and Highways Code.

(b) An expressway system established by a county before January 1, 1989, as described in subdivision (g) of Section 941.4 of the Streets and Highways Code. *(Added by Stats.2004, c. 615 (S.B.1233), § 17.)*

§ 315. Essential parts

"Essential parts" are all integral and body parts of a vehicle of a type required to be registered under this code, the removal, alteration, or substitution of which would tend to conceal the identity of the vehicle or substantially alter its appearance. *(Stats.1959, c. 3, p. 1531, § 315.)*

Cross References

Alteration or removal of vehicle identification number, motor or serial numbers, etc., see Vehicle Code §§ 4166, 10750, 10751.
Notice of installation of motor in motor vehicle, see Vehicle Code § 4161.

§ 320. Established place of business

"Established place of business" is a place actually occupied either continuously or at regular periods by any of the following:

(a) A dealer, remanufacturer, remanufacturer branch, manufacturer, manufacturer branch, distributor, distributor branch, automobile driving school, or traffic violator school where the books and records pertinent to the type of business being conducted are kept.

(b) An automobile dismantler where the books and records pertinent to the type of business being conducted are kept. A place of business of an automobile dismantler which qualified as an "established place of business" before September 17, 1970, is an "established place of business" as defined in this section.

(c) A registration service where the books and records pertinent to the type of business being conducted are kept. *(Stats.1959, c. 3, p. 1531, § 320. Amended by Stats.1961, c. 1640, p. 3579, § 1, operative Jan. 1, 1962; Stats.1965, c. 1014, p. 2645, § 1; Stats.1970, c. 289, p. 563, § 1; Stats.1970, c. 1381, p. 2563, § 1; Stats.1973, c. 996, p. 1964, § 5, operative July 1, 1974; Stats.1981, c. 665, p. 2447, § 1; Stats.1983, c. 1286, § 8; Stats.1984, c. 193, § 145; Stats.1984, c. 1037, § 1; Stats.1985, c. 106, § 163; Stats.1992, c. 1243 (A.B.3090), § 54, eff. Sept. 30, 1992.)*

Cross References

Automobile dismantler,
  Generally, see Vehicle Code § 11500 et seq.,
  Defined, see Vehicle Code § 220.
Dealers,
  Generally, see Vehicle Code § 11700 et seq.,
  Change of established place of business, see Vehicle Code § 11712.
  Definition, see Vehicle Code §§ 285, 286.
Driving schools and driving instructors, licensing, see Vehicle Code § 11100 et seq.
New motor vehicle dealer defined, see Vehicle Code § 426.
Occupational licensing and business regulations, see Vehicle Code § 11100 et seq.

§ 320.5.   Extralegal load

An "extralegal load" is a single unit or an assembled item which, due to its design, cannot be reasonably reduced or dismantled in size or weight so that it can be legally transported as a load without a permit as required by Section 35780. This section does not apply to loads on passenger cars. *(Added by Stats.1983, c. 145, § 1, urgency, eff. June 28, 1983.)*

Cross References

Special permit to operate or move vehicles transporting trusses or wall panels, see Vehicle Code § 35780.5.

§ 321.   Factory-built housing

"Factory-built housing" is a structure as defined in Section 19971 of the Health and Safety Code. As used in this code, factory-built housing is a trailer coach which is in excess of eight feet in width or in excess of 40 feet in length. *(Added by Stats.1980, c. 1150, p. 3788, § 7.)*

§ 322.   Farm labor vehicle

(a) A "farm labor vehicle" is any motor vehicle designed, used, or maintained for the transportation of nine or more farmworkers, in addition to the driver, to or from a place of employment or employment-related activities.

(b) For the purpose of this section, a farmworker is any person engaged in rendering personal services for hire and compensation in connection with the production or harvesting of any farm products.

(c) "Farm labor vehicle" does not include:

(1) Any vehicle carrying only members of the immediate family of the owner or driver thereof.

(2) Any vehicle while being operated under specific authority granted by the Public Utilities Commission or under specific authority granted to a transit system by an authorized city or county agency. *(Added by Stats.1959, c. 679, p. 2649, § 1. Amended by Stats.1978, c. 488, p. 1616, § 1; Stats.1984, c. 1068, § 1; Stats.2000, c. 308 (A.B.602), § 1.)*

Cross References

Training courses for certification to drive a farm labor vehicle, see Education Code § 40080 et seq.
Vehicles transporting workmen, see Vehicle Code § 31400 et seq.

§ 323.   Repealed by Stats.1978, c. 488, p. 1616, § 2

§ 324.   Fifth-wheel travel trailer

A "fifth-wheel travel trailer" is a vehicle designed for recreational purposes to carry persons or property on its own structure and so constructed as to be drawn by a motor vehicle by means of a kingpin connecting device. *(Added by Stats.1990, c. 1358 (A.B.4261), § 1.)*

§ 324.5.   Former prisoner of war

A "former prisoner of war" is any person who, while serving as a member of the United States Armed Forces, as a member of the Philippine Commonwealth Armed Forces, as a part of a United States Expeditionary Force, or as a United States civilian, was held as a prisoner of war by forces hostile to the United States during any armed conflict and is currently a resident of California. *(Added by Stats.1991, c. 893 (A.B.274), § 1.)*

§ 325.   Foreign jurisdiction

A "foreign jurisdiction" is any other state, the District of Columbia, territories or possessions of the United States, and foreign states, provinces, or countries. *(Stats. 1959, c. 3, p. 1532, § 325.)*

§ 330.   Foreign vehicle

A "foreign vehicle" is a vehicle of a type required to be registered under this code brought into this State from a foreign jurisdiction other than in the ordinary course of business, by or through a manufacturer or dealer and not registered in this State. *(Stats.1959, c. 3, p. 1532, § 330.)*

Cross References

Dealer defined, see Vehicle Code §§ 285, 286.
Foreign jurisdiction defined, see Vehicle Code § 325.
Full faith and credit granted certificates of title issued by other states, see Vehicle Code § 4304.
Permits to nonresident owners, see Vehicle Code § 6700 et seq.
Reciprocity, see Vehicle Code § 8000 et seq.

Registration of foreign commercial vehicles, see Vehicle Code § 6850.

Registration of foreign vehicles, see Vehicle Code § 4300 et seq.

§ 331. Franchise

(a) A "franchise" is a written agreement between two or more persons having all of the following conditions:

(1) A commercial relationship of definite duration or continuing indefinite duration.

(2) The franchisee is granted the right to offer for sale or lease, or to sell or lease at retail new motor vehicles or new trailers subject to identification pursuant to Section 5014.1 manufactured or distributed by the franchisor or the right to perform authorized warranty repairs and service, or the right to perform any combination of these activities.

(3) The franchisee constitutes a component of the franchisor's distribution system.

(4) The operation of the franchisee's business is substantially associated with the franchisor's trademark, trade name, advertising, or other commercial symbol designating the franchisor.

(5) The operation of a portion of the franchisee's business is substantially reliant on the franchisor for a continued supply of new vehicles, parts, or accessories.

(b) The term "franchise" does not include an agreement entered into by a manufacturer or distributor and a person where all the following apply:

(1) The person is authorized to perform warranty repairs and service on vehicles manufactured or distributed by the manufacturer or distributor.

(2) The person is not a new motor vehicle dealer franchisee of the manufacturer or distributor.

(3) The person's repair and service facility is not located within the relevant market area of a new motor vehicle dealer franchisee of the manufacturer or distributor. *(Added by Stats.1973, c. 996, p. 1965, § 6, operative July 1, 1974. Amended by Stats.1998, c. 662 (A.B.2707), § 1; Stats.2001, c. 539 (S.B.734), § 5.)*

Cross References

Recreational vehicle dealer agreements, see Vehicle Code § 11713.22.

§ 331.1. Franchisee

A "franchisee" is any person who, pursuant to a franchise, receives new motor vehicles subject to registration under this code, new off-highway motorcycles, as defined in Section 436, new all-terrain vehicles, as defined in Section 111, or new trailers subject to identification pursuant to Section 5014.1 from the franchisor and who offers for sale or lease, or sells or leases the vehicles at retail or is granted the right to perform authorized warranty repairs and service, or the right to perform any combination of these activities. *(Added by Stats.1973, c. 996, p. 1966, § 7, operative July 1, 1974. Amended by Stats.1982, c. 1584, p. 6260, § 2; Stats.1998, c. 662*

(A.B.2707), § 2; Stats.2001, c. 539 (S.B.734), § 6; Stats. 2004, c. 836 (A.B.2848), § 4.)

§ 331.2. Franchisor

A "franchisor" is any person who manufactures, assembles, or distributes new motor vehicles subject to registration under this code, new off-highway motorcycles, as defined in Section 436, new all-terrain vehicles, as defined in Section 111, or new trailers subject to identification pursuant to Section 5014.1 and who grants a franchise. *(Added by Stats.1973, c. 996, p. 1966, § 8, operative July 1, 1974. Amended by Stats.1982, c. 1584, p. 6260, § 3; Stats.2001, c. 539 (S.B.734), § 7; Stats.2004, c. 836 (A.B.2848), § 5.)*

§ 331.3. Recreational vehicle franchise

A "recreational vehicle franchise" is a written agreement between two or more persons having both of the following conditions:

(a) A commercial relationship of definite duration or continuing indefinite duration.

(b) The franchisee is granted the right to offer for sale or lease, or to sell or lease at retail, new recreational vehicles, as defined in subdivision (a) of Section 18010 of the Health and Safety Code, that are manufactured or distributed by the franchisor, or the right to perform authorized warranty repairs and service, or the right to perform any combination of these activities. *(Added by Stats.2008, c. 743 (A.B.2436), § 1.)*

Cross References

Failure to provide recreational vehicle franchise, see Vehicle Code § 11713.22.

Sale of new recreational vehicles, recreational vehicle franchise required, see Vehicle Code § 11713.23.

§ 332. Freeway

"Freeway" is a highway in respect to which the owners of abutting lands have no right or easement of access to or from their abutting lands or in respect to which such owners have only limited or restricted right or easement of access. *(Stats.1959, c. 3, p. 1532, § 332.)*

Cross References

California freeway and expressway system, see Streets and Highways Code § 250 et seq.

Freeway defined, see Streets and Highways Code § 23.5.

Restriction on use of freeways, see Vehicle Code §§ 21960, 22520.

§ 335. Gantry truck

A "gantry truck" is a motor vehicle so designed and constructed that it straddles the load to be transported and by means of appropriate mechanism picks up the load and supports it during transportation. *(Stats.1959, c. 3, p. 1532, § 335.)*

Cross References

Motor vehicle defined, see Vehicle Code § 415.

§ 336.   General public paratransit vehicle

"General public paratransit vehicle" means any motor vehicle designed for carrying no more than 24 persons and the driver, that provides local transportation to the general public, including transportation of pupils at or below the 12th-grade level to or from a public or private school or school activity, under the exclusive jurisdiction of a publicly owned and operated transit system through one of the following modes: dial-a-ride, subscription service, or route-deviated bus service. Vehicles used in the exclusive transportation of disabled persons as defined in Section 99206.5 of the Public Utilities Code, or of persons 55 years of age or older, including any persons necessary to provide assistance to these passengers, are not general public paratransit vehicles.

However, transportation of attendants, companions, or both traveling together with those individuals with disabilities who are determined to be eligible for complementary paratransit services in accordance with Title II of the Americans with Disabilities Act of 1990 (Public Law 101-336) [1] and federal regulations adopted pursuant thereto, shall not be sufficient to qualify a vehicle as a general public paratransit vehicle.

A vehicle that provides local transportation for the general public through one of the following modes: dial-a-ride, subscription service, or route-deviated bus service, but does not provide transportation of pupils at or below the 12th-grade level to or from a public or private school or school activity, is a transit bus, as defined by Section 642, and is not a general public paratransit vehicle. *(Added by Stats.1987, c. 986, § 2, operative July 1, 1988. Amended by Stats.1988, c. 683, § 3, eff. Aug. 27, 1988; Stats.1992, c. 913 (A.B.1077), § 42; Stats.1993, c. 844 (A.B.402), § 1.)*

[1] 42 U.S.C.A. § 12101 et seq.

§ 340.   Garage

A "garage" is a building or other place wherein the business of storing or safekeeping vehicles of a type required to be registered under this code and which belong to members of the general public is conducted for compensation. *(Stats.1959, c. 3, p. 1532, § 340.)*

Cross References

Private garage defined, see Vehicle Code § 10654.
Records and reports required, see Vehicle Code § 10650.

§ 345.   Golf cart

A "golf cart" is a motor vehicle having not less than three wheels in contact with the ground, having an unladen weight less than 1,300 pounds, which is designed to be and is operated at not more than 15 miles per hour and designed to carry golf equipment and not more than two persons, including the driver. *(Added by Stats.1968, c. 1303, p. 2456, § 1.)*

Cross References

Equipment, see Vehicle Code § 24001.5.
Highway operation, golf carts, see Vehicle Code § 21716.
Local traffic regulation of golf carts, generally, see Vehicle Code §§ 21115, 21115.1.
Registration exemption, see Vehicle Code § 4019.

§ 350.   Gross vehicle weight rating

(a) "Gross vehicle weight rating" (GVWR) means the weight specified by the manufacturer as the loaded weight of a single vehicle.

(b) Gross combination weight rating (GCWR) means the weight specified by the manufacturer as the loaded weight of a combination or articulated vehicle. In the absence of a weight specified by the manufacturer, GCWR shall be determined by adding the GVWR of the power unit and the total unladen weight of the towed units and any load thereon. *(Formerly § 390, enacted by Stats.1959, c. 3, p. 1534, § 390. Renumbered § 350 and amended by Stats.2000, c. 861 (S.B.2084), § 14, eff. Sept. 29, 2000.)*

Cross References

Vehicles without weight rating, see Vehicle Code § 10751.

§ 351.   Repealed by Stats.1963, c. 2149, p. 4486, § 4

§ 353.   Hazardous material

"Hazardous material" is any substance, material, or device posing an unreasonable risk to health, safety, or property during transportation, as defined by regulations adopted pursuant to Section 2402.7. "Hazardous material" includes explosives and hazardous wastes or substances as defined by regulations adopted pursuant to Section 25141 of the Health and Safety Code and medical wastes, as defined in Section 117690 of the Health and Safety Code. *(Added by Stats.1977, c. 825, p. 2495, § 3. Amended by Stats.1981, c. 860, p. 3292, § 1; Stats.1992, c. 878 (A.B.3427), § 22; Stats.1996, c. 1023 (S.B.1497), § 422, eff. Sept. 29, 1996.)*

Cross References

Hazardous waste control, grounds for denial, suspension or revocation of permits, registration or certificates, see Health and Safety Code § 25186.
Operating a motor vehicle in this state without obtaining a driver's license, nonresidents, transporting hazardous material, see Vehicle Code § 12502.

§ 355.   Renumbered § 324 and amended by Stats.1965, c. 1500, p. 3522, § 1

§ 360.   Highway

"Highway" is a way or place of whatever nature, publicly maintained and open to the use of the public for purposes of vehicular travel. Highway includes street. *(Stats.1959, c. 3, p. 1534, § 360.)*

Cross References

County highway defined, see Streets and Highways Code § 25.

Dumping on highways, see Vehicle Code § 23112.
Exclusions from definitions of street or highway, see Vehicle Code §§ 591, 592.
Highway defined, see Streets and Highways Code §§ 23, 660.
Highway segment Safety Awareness Zone designation, see Streets and Highways Code § 97.1.
Liability for damage to streets or highways, see Vehicle Code § 17300 et seq.
Private road or driveway defined, see Vehicle Code § 490.
Removal of material thrown or dropped on highway, see Vehicle Code § 23113.
Right-of-way defined, see Vehicle Code § 525.
Roadway defined, see Vehicle Code § 530.
Speed contest or exhibition on highways, see Vehicle Code § 23109.
Spilling loads on highways, see Vehicle Code § 23114.
State highway defined, see Streets and Highways Code § 24.
Street defined, see Vehicle Code § 590.
Through highway defined, see Vehicle Code § 600.

§ 362. House car

A "house car" is a motor vehicle originally designed, or permanently altered, and equipped for human habitation, or to which a camper has been permanently attached. A motor vehicle to which a camper has been temporarily attached is not a house car except that, for the purposes of Division 11 (commencing with Section 21000) and Division 12 (commencing with Section 24000), a motor vehicle equipped with a camper having an axle that is designed to support a portion of the weight of the camper unit shall be considered a three-axle house car regardless of the method of attachment or manner of registration. A house car shall not be deemed to be a motortruck. *(Added by Stats.1963, c. 688, p. 1694, § 3. Amended by Stats.1967, c. 375, p. 1601, § 1; Stats.1968, c. 228, p. 541, § 2, eff. May 29, 1968; Stats.1968, c. 875, p. 1666, § 1.)*

Cross References

Burglary defined, see Penal Code § 459.
Camper defined, see Vehicle Code § 243.
Clearance and side-marker lamps, see Vehicle Code § 25100.
Exclusion from term "commercial vehicle", see Vehicle Code § 260.
Inclusion in term "passenger vehicle", see Vehicle Code § 465.
Limitation of length on combination of vehicles, see Vehicle Code § 35401.
Motor truck defined, see Vehicle Code § 410.

§ 365. Intersection

An "intersection" is the area embraced within the prolongation of the lateral curb lines, or, if none, then the lateral boundary lines of the roadways, of two highways which join one another at approximately right angles or the area within which vehicles traveling upon different highways joining at any other angle may come in conflict. *(Stats.1959, c. 3, p. 1534, § 365.)*

Cross References

Construction zone, traffic control at intersections, see Vehicle Code § 21370.
Controlled intersections, pedestrians crossing between, see Vehicle Code § 21955.
Crosswalk defined, see Vehicle Code § 275.

Highway defined, see Vehicle Code § 360.
Prohibition on stopping and parking within intersection, see Vehicle Code § 22500.
Right-of-way at intersections, see Vehicle Code § 21800 et seq.
Roadway defined, see Vehicle Code § 530.
Speed limits near intersections, see Vehicle Code § 22352.
Turning upon highways, see Vehicle Code § 22100.

§ 370. Legal owner

A "legal owner" is a person holding a security interest in a vehicle which is subject to the provisions of the Uniform Commercial Code, or the lessor of a vehicle to the State or to any county, city, district, or political subdivision of the State, or to the United States, under a lease, lease-sale, or rental-purchase agreement which grants possession of the vehicle to the lessee for a period of 30 consecutive days or more. *(Stats.1959, c. 3, p. 1534, § 370. Amended by Stats.1963, c. 819, p. 2012, § 40; Stats.1963, c. 1867, p. 3852, § 1.)*

Cross References

Assignment of interest in vehicle by legal owner, see Vehicle Code § 5603.
Legal owner defined,
    Registration and transfer of vessels, see Vehicle Code § 9840.
    Reports of stolen vessels, see Vehicle Code § 10550.
Owner defined, see Vehicle Code §§ 460, 461.
Recording of security interest, see Vehicle Code § 6300 et seq.
Registered owner defined, see Vehicle Code § 505.
Secured party as legal owner, see Vehicle Code § 6302.
Security interest defined, see Commercial Code § 1201.

§ 371. Lessee

Lessee includes "bailee" and is a person who leases, offers to lease, or is offered the lease of a motor vehicle for a term exceeding four months. *(Added by Stats.1976, c. 1284, p. 5711, § 4.)*

§ 372. Lessor

A "lessor" is a person who, for a term exceeding four months, leases or offers for lease, negotiates or attempts to negotiate a lease, or induce any person to lease a motor vehicle; and who receives or expects to receive a commission, money, brokerage fees, profit or any other thing of value from the lessee of said vehicle. "Lessor" includes "bailor" and "lease" includes "bailment." *(Added by Stats.1976, c. 1284, p. 5711, § 5.)*

Cross References

Dealer defined, exclusion for lessors, see Vehicle Code § 286.

§ 373. Lessor-retailer

A "lessor-retailer" is a lessor or renter who, except under the circumstances described in subdivision (a) of Section 286, makes a retail sale or sales of a previously leased or rented vehicle or vehicles to other than any of the following:

(a) The lessee of the vehicle, or the person who, for a period of at least one year, has been designated by the lessee as the driver of the vehicle covered by a written lease agreement.

(b) A buyer for agricultural, business, or commercial purposes.

(c) A government or governmental agency or instrumentality. *(Added by Stats.1976, c. 1284, p. 5711, § 6. Amended by Stats.1979, c. 561, p. 1773, § 1.)*

§ 375. Lighting equipment

"Lighting equipment" is any of the following lamps or devices:

(a) A headlamp, auxiliary driving, passing, or fog lamp, fog taillamp, taillamp, stoplamp, supplemental stoplamp, license plate lamp, clearance lamp, side marker lamp, signal lamp or device, supplemental signal lamp, deceleration signal device, cornering lamp, running lamp, red, blue, amber, or white warning lamp, flashing red schoolbus lamp, side-mounted turn signal lamp, and schoolbus side lamp.

(b) An operating unit or canceling mechanism for turn signal lamps or for the simultaneous flashing of turn signal lamps as vehicular hazard signals, and an advance stoplamp switch.

(c) A flasher mechanism for turn signals, red schoolbus lamps, warning lamps, the simultaneous flashing of turn signal lamps as vehicular hazard signals, and the headlamp flashing systems for emergency vehicles.

(d) Any equipment regulating the light emitted from a lamp or device or the light sources therein.

(e) A reflector, including reflectors for use on bicycles, and reflectors used for required warning devices.

(f) An illuminating device that emits radiation predominantly in the infrared or ultraviolet regions of the spectrum, whether or not these emissions are visible to the unaided eye.

(g) An illuminated sign installed on a bus that utilizes an electronic display to convey the route designation, route number, run number, public service announcement, or any combination of this information, or an illuminated sign utilized pursuant to Section 25353.1. *(Stats.1959, c. 3, p. 1534, § 375. Amended by Stats.1961, c. 58, p. 1002, § 4; Stats.1961, c. 159, p. 1164, § 1; Stats.1961, c. 653, p. 1859, § 24; Stats.1961, c. 1989, p. 4185, § 2; Stats.1963, c. 223, p. 963, § 1; Stats.1965, c. 858, p. 2460, § 1; Stats.1965, c. 1313, p. 3199, § 1.5; Stats.1967, c. 382, p. 1605, § 1; Stats.1970, c. 1477, p. 2922, § 1; Stats.1974, c. 584, p. 1404, § 1; Stats.1977, c. 800, p. 2450, § 1, eff. Sept. 14, 1977; Stats.1979, c. 723, p. 2215, § 1; Stats.1980, c. 399, p. 782, § 1, eff. July 11, 1980; Stats.1991, c. 13 (A.B.37), § 15, eff. Feb. 13, 1991; Stats.2004, c. 198 (S.B.1236), § 1; Stats.2006, c. 881 (S.B.1726), § 1; Stats. 2011, c. 529 (A.B.607), § 2.)*

Cross References

Emergency vehicles, see Vehicle Code § 30.
Illuminated signs on buses, see Vehicle Code § 25353.
Lighting equipment, regulation, see Vehicle Code § 24250 et seq.

Standards and specifications, see Vehicle Code § 26103.

§ 377. Limit line

A "limit line" is a solid white line not less than 12 nor more than 24 inches wide, extending across a roadway or any portion thereof to indicate the point at which traffic is required to stop in compliance with legal requirements. *(Stats.1959, c. 3, p. 1534, § 377.)*

§§ 378, 379. Repealed by Stats.2013, c. 523 (S.B.788), §§ 18, 19

§ 380. Liquefied petroleum gas

"Liquefied petroleum gas" means normal butane, isobutane, propane, or butylene (including isomers) or mixtures composed predominantly thereof in liquid or gaseous state having a vapor pressure in excess of 40 pounds per square inch absolute at a temperature of 100 degrees Fahrenheit. *(Stats.1959, c. 3, p. 1534, § 380. Amended by Stats.1977, c. 825, p. 2495, § 4.)*

Cross References

Exclusion of flammable liquids from vehicle transporting explosives, see Vehicle Code § 31613.
Motor trucks carrying inflammables must stop at railway grade crossings, see Vehicle Code § 22452.
New detector or new automatic high pressure shutoff devices, required approval, see Health and Safety Code § 13117.
Regulations and standards for vehicles propelled by liquified petroleum, see Vehicle Code § 2402.6.
Signs on vehicles carrying inflammable liquid, see Vehicle Code § 27903.

§ 385. Local authorities

"Local authorities" means the legislative body of every county or municipality having authority to adopt local police regulations. *(Stats.1959, c. 3, p. 1534, § 385.)*

Cross References

Limitation on power of local authorities, see Vehicle Code § 21.
Powers of local authorities pertaining to traffic laws,
  Generally, see Vehicle Code § 21100 et seq.
  Parking, stopping, standing, see Vehicle Code § 22501 et seq.
  Speed limits, see Vehicle Code §§ 22357 et seq., 22407.
  Turning at intersections, see Vehicle Code § 22101.
Weight limits, regulation by local authorities, see Vehicle Code § 35700 et seq.

§ 385.2. Logging dolly

A "logging dolly" is a vehicle designed for carrying logs, having one or more axles that, if there are more than one, are not more than 54 inches apart, and used in connection with a motor truck solely for the purpose of transporting logs and securely connected with the towing vehicle both by a reach and by the load. *(Added by Stats.2013, c. 523 (S.B.788), § 20.)*

Cross References

Clearance and side-marker lamps, see Vehicle Code § 25100.
Definitions,
  Auxiliary dolly, see Vehicle Code § 225.
  Axle, see Vehicle Code § 230.

Motor truck, see Vehicle Code § 410.
Tow truck, see Vehicle Code § 615.
Length of vehicles, see Vehicle Code § 35400 et seq.
Registration, see Vehicle Code § 4000.
Safety regulations, see Vehicle Code § 34500 et seq.
Transportation of logging dollies, see Vehicle Code § 31501.
Weight fees, commercial vehicles, see Vehicle Code § 9400 et seq.

§ 385.3. Logging vehicle

A "logging vehicle" is a vehicle used exclusively in the conduct of logging operations and not designed for the transportation of persons or property on a highway. *(Added by Stats.2013, c. 523 (S.B.788), § 21.)*

§ 385.5. Low-speed vehicle

(a) A "low-speed vehicle" is a motor vehicle that meets all of the following requirements:

(1) Has four wheels.

(2) Can attain a speed, in one mile, of more than 20 miles per hour and not more than 25 miles per hour, on a paved level surface.

(3) Has a gross vehicle weight rating of less than 3,000 pounds.

(b)(1) For the purposes of this section, a "low-speed vehicle" is not a golf cart, except when operated pursuant to Section 21115 or 21115.1.

(2) A "low-speed vehicle" is also known as a "neighborhood electric vehicle." *(Added by Stats.1999, c. 140 (S.B.186), § 1. Amended by Stats.2004, c. 422 (A.B.2353), § 2; Stats.2006, c. 66 (S.B.1559), § 1, eff. July 12, 2006.)*

Cross References

Neighborhood electric vehicle transportation plan, plan adoption and implementation, cities of Rocklin and Lincoln, see Streets and Highways Code § 1963.

§ 386. Managerial employee

A "managerial employee" is a person who exercises control over a business licensed under this code, whether compensated by salary or commission, including, but not limited to, any person who is employed as a general manager, business manager, assistant general manager, finance and insurance manager, advertising manager, or sales manager. *(Added by Stats.1982, c. 791, p. 3065, § 1.)*

§ 387. Manufactured home

"Manufactured home" is a manufactured home, as defined in Section 18007 of the Health and Safety Code, a commercial coach, as defined in Section 18001.8 of the Health and Safety Code, a mobilehome, as defined in Section 18008 of the Health and Safety Code, factory-built housing, as defined in Section 18971 [1] of the Health and Safety Code, and a trailer coach which is in excess of 102 inches in width, or in excess of 40 feet in overall length measured from the foremost point of the trailer hitch to the rear extremity of the trailer. Manufactured home does not include a recreational vehicle, as defined in Section 18010 of the Health and Safety Code. *(Added by Stats.1980, c. 1150, p. 3789, § 8. Amended by Stats. 1983, c. 1124, § 50, operative July 1, 1984; Stats.1984, c. 1342, § 25, eff. Sept. 26, 1984, operative Jan. 1, 1985; Stats.1986, c. 248, § 237; Stats.1986, c. 1185, § 1.)*

[1] Probably should read "section 19971".

§ 388. Repealed by Stats.1977, c. 873, p. 2634, § 1.5

§ 389. Manufacturer branch

A "manufacturer branch" is an office maintained by a manufacturer for the sale of new vehicles to dealers or for directing or supervising in whole or in part the manufacturer's representatives. *(Added by Stats.1973, c. 996, p. 1966, § 10, operative July 1, 1974. Amended by Stats.1978, c. 797, p. 2562, § 1.)*

Cross References

Vehicle manufacturer defined, see Vehicle Code § 672.

§ 390. Renumbered § 350 and amended by Stats.2000, c. 861 (S.B.2084), § 14, eff. Sept. 29, 2000

§ 395. Metal tire

A "metal tire" is a tire the surface of which in contact with the highway is wholly or partly of metal or other hard nonresilient material. *(Stats.1959, c. 3, p. 1535, § 395.)*

Cross References

Gross weight per inch, see Vehicle Code § 35601.
Pneumatic tire defined, see Vehicle Code § 485.
Protuberances on tires, see Vehicle Code § 27454.
Restrictions as to tire equipment, see Vehicle Code § 27450 et seq.
Solid tire defined, see Vehicle Code § 560.
Speed law, weight and tire equipment, see Vehicle Code §§ 22409, 22410.
Tire chains, see Vehicle Code § 27459.

§ 395.5. Mobile billboard advertising display

A "mobile billboard advertising display" means an advertising display that is attached to a mobile, nonmotorized vehicle, device, or bicycle, that carries, pulls, or transports a sign or billboard, and is for the primary purpose of advertising. *(Added by Stats.2010, c. 615 (A.B.2756), § 2. Amended by Stats.2011, c. 538 (A.B. 1298), § 1.)*

Cross References

Authority to remove vehicles, mobile advertising displays parked or left standing in violation of local resolution or ordinance, see Vehicle Code § 22651.
Local rules and regulations adopted relating to regulating mobile billboard advertising displays, see Vehicle Code § 21100.

§ 396. Mobilehome

"Mobilehome" is a structure as defined in Section 18008 of the Health and Safety Code. For the purposes of enforcement of highway safety laws and regulations, a mobilehome is a trailer coach which is in excess of 102 inches in width, or in excess of 40 feet in overall length measured from the foremost point of the trailer hitch to the rear extremity of the trailer. *(Added by Stats.1980, c. 1150, p. 3789, § 10. Amended by Stats.1981, c. 975, p. 3796, § 34; Stats.1986, c. 1185, § 2.)*

Cross References

Mobilehome,
   Accessory building or structure, see Health and Safety Code § 18213.
   Defined, see Health and Safety Code §§ 18008, 18211.
   Inclusion in definition of manufactured home, see Vehicle Code § 387.
   Park, see Health and Safety Code § 18214.

§ 400.   Motorcycle

(a) A "motorcycle" is a motor vehicle having a seat or saddle for the use of the rider, designed to travel on not more than three wheels in contact with the ground.

(b) A motor vehicle that has four wheels in contact with the ground, two of which are a functional part of a sidecar, is a motorcycle if the vehicle otherwise comes within the definition of subdivision (a).

(c) A farm tractor is not a motorcycle.

(d) A three-wheeled motor vehicle that otherwise meets the requirements of subdivision (a), has a partially or completely enclosed seating area for the driver and passenger, is used by local public agencies for the enforcement of parking control provisions, and is operated at slow speeds on public streets, is not a motorcycle. However, a motor vehicle described in this subdivision shall comply with the applicable sections of this code imposing equipment installation requirements on motorcycles. *(Added by Stats.1996, c. 453 (A.B.153), § 4. Amended by Stats.2008, c. 672 (A.B.2272), § 1.)*

Cross References

Brakes, see Vehicle Code § 26311.
Consideration for assignment of conditional sale contract, see Civil Code § 2982.10.
Contract cancellation option agreement required, exceptions, purchase price, form, and cancellation procedures, see Vehicle Code § 11731.21.
Equipment limitations, see Vehicle Code § 27801.
Formalities of conditional sale contracts, see Civil Code § 2982.
Law enforcement vehicles, repainting on sale, see Vehicle Code § 27604.
Lighting equipment, see Vehicle Code §§ 25451, 25650 et seq.
Motor vehicle defined, see Vehicle Code § 415.
Motor-driven cycle defined, see Vehicle Code § 405.
Noise limits, see Vehicle Code § 23130.
Passengers on motorcycles, see Vehicle Code § 27800.
Prohibited ownership of vehicle painted as law enforcement vehicle, exceptions, see Vehicle Code § 27605.
Safety helmet regulations, see Vehicle Code § 27802.
Taillamps, see Vehicle Code § 24253.
Windshields, see Vehicle Code §§ 26701, 26705.

§ 405.   Motor-driven cycle

A "motor-driven cycle" is any motorcycle with a motor that displaces less than 150 cubic centimeters. A motor-

driven cycle does not include a motorized bicycle, as defined in Section 406. *(Stats.1959, c. 3, p. 1535, § 405. Amended by Stats.1961, c. 1915, p. 4035, § 1; Stats.1963, c. 422, p. 1239, § 1; Stats.1975, c. 987, p. 2327, § 1; Stats.1990, c. 1359 (A.B.55), § 1; Stats.1991, c. 928 (A.B.1886), § 14, eff. Oct. 14, 1991; Stats.1995, c. 342 (A.B.1604), § 1.)*

Cross References

Bicycle defined, see Vehicle Code § 231.
License plates, see Vehicle Code § 5000.
Motorcycle defined, see Vehicle Code § 400.

§ 406.   Motorized bicycle or moped

(a) A "motorized bicycle" or "moped" is any two-wheeled or three-wheeled device having fully operative pedals for propulsion by human power, or having no pedals if powered solely by electrical energy, and an automatic transmission and a motor which produces less than 2 gross brake horsepower and is capable of propelling the device at a maximum speed of not more than 30 miles per hour on level ground.

(b) A "motorized bicycle" is also a device that has fully operative pedals for propulsion by human power and has an electric motor that meets all of the following requirements:

(1) Has a power output of not more than 1,000 watts.

(2) Is incapable of propelling the device at a speed of more than 20 miles per hour on ground level.

(3) Is incapable of further increasing the speed of the device when human power is used to propel the motorized bicycle faster than 20 miles per hour.

(4) Every manufacturer of motorized bicycles, as defined in this subdivision, shall provide a disclosure to buyers that advises buyers that their existing insurance policies may not provide coverage for these bicycles and that they should contact their insurance company or insurance agent to determine if coverage is provided.

(c) The disclosure required under paragraph (4) of subdivision (b) shall meet both of the following requirements:

(1) The disclosure shall be printed in not less than 14—point boldface type on a single sheet of paper that contains no information other than the disclosure.

(2) The disclosure shall include the following language in capital letters:

"YOUR INSURANCE POLICIES MAY NOT PROVIDE COVERAGE FOR ACCIDENTS INVOLVING THE USE OF THIS BICYCLE. TO DETERMINE IF COVERAGE IS PROVIDED YOU SHOULD CONTACT YOUR INSURANCE COMPANY OR AGENT." *(Added by Stats.1975, c. 987, p. 2327, § 2. Amended by Stats.1985, c. 799, § 1; Stats.1995, c. 342 (A.B.1604), § 2; Stats.1995, c. 804 (A.B.1501), § 1.)*

Cross References

Federal standards, see Vehicle Code § 24015.

Freeways, see Vehicle Code § 21960.
Licensing, see Vehicle Code § 39000 et seq.
Registration, exemption, see Vehicle Code § 4020.
Vehicular crossings, see Vehicle Code § 23330.

§ 407. Motorized quadricycle and motorized tricycle

A "motorized quadricycle" is a four-wheeled device, and a "motorized tricycle" is a three-wheeled device, designed to carry not more than two persons, including the driver, and having either an electric motor or a motor with an automatic transmission developing less than two gross brake horsepower and capable of propelling the device at a maximum speed of not more than 30 miles per hour on level ground. The device shall be utilized only by a person who by reason of physical disability is otherwise unable to move about as a pedestrian or by a senior citizen as defined in Section 13000. *(Added by Stats.1980, c. 756, p. 2261, § 1. Amended by Stats.1993, c. 1292 (S.B.274), § 3.)*

§ 407.5. Motorized scooter; disclosures

(a) A "motorized scooter" is any two-wheeled device that has handlebars, has a floorboard that is designed to be stood upon when riding, and is powered by an electric motor. This device may also have a driver seat that does not interfere with the ability of the rider to stand and ride and may also be designed to be powered by human propulsion. For purposes of this section, a motorcycle, as defined in Section 400, a motor-driven cycle, as defined in Section 405, or a motorized bicycle or moped, as defined in Section 406, is not a motorized scooter.

(b) A device meeting the definition in subdivision (a) that is powered by a source other than electrical power is also a motorized scooter.

(c)(1) A manufacturer of motorized scooters shall provide a disclosure to buyers that advises buyers that the buyers' existing insurance policies may not provide coverage for these scooters and that the buyers should contact their insurance company or insurance agent to determine if coverage is provided.

(2) The disclosure required under paragraph (1) shall meet both of the following requirements:

(A) The disclosure shall be printed in not less than 14–point boldface type on a single sheet of paper that contains no information other than the disclosure.

(B) The disclosure shall include the following language in capital letters:

"YOUR INSURANCE POLICIES MAY NOT PROVIDE COVERAGE FOR ACCIDENTS INVOLVING THE USE OF THIS SCOOTER. TO DETERMINE IF COVERAGE IS PROVIDED, YOU SHOULD CONTACT YOUR INSURANCE COMPANY OR AGENT."

(d)(1) A manufacturer of motorized scooters shall provide a disclosure to a buyer that advises the buyer that the buyer may not modify or alter the exhaust system to cause that system to amplify or create an excessive noise, or to fail to meet applicable emission requirements.

(2) The disclosure required under paragraph (1) shall meet both of the following requirements:

(A) The disclosure shall be printed in not less than 14–point boldface type on a single sheet of paper that contains no information other than the disclosure.

(B) The disclosure shall include the following language in capital letters:

"YOU MAY NOT MODIFY OR ALTER THE EXHAUST SYSTEM OF THIS SCOOTER TO CAUSE IT TO AMPLIFY OR CREATE EXCESSIVE NOISE PER VEHICLE CODE SECTION 21226, OR TO FAIL TO MEET APPLICABLE EMISSION REQUIREMENTS PER VEHICLE CODE 27156."

(e) This section shall become operative on January 1, 2008. *(Added by Stats.2002, c. 979 (S.B.1918), § 3, operative Jan. 1, 2008. Amended by Stats.2004, c. 755 (A.B.1878), § 2, operative Jan. 1, 2008.)*

Cross References

Driver's license, required classification, see Vehicle Code § 12804.9.
Electric personal assistive mobility devices, defined, see Vehicle Code § 313.
Electric personal assistive mobility devices, required safety mechanisms, see Vehicle Code § 21280.5.

§ 408. Motor carrier

"Motor carrier" is the registered owner, lessee, licensee, or bailee of any vehicle set forth in Section 34500, who operates or directs the operation of any such vehicle on either a for-hire or not-for-hire basis. *(Added by Stats.1981, c. 860, p. 3292, § 1.5.)*

§ 410. Motor truck

A "motor truck" or "motortruck" is a motor vehicle designed, used, or maintained primarily for the transportation of property. *(Stats.1959, c. 3, p. 1535, § 410. Amended by Stats.1993, c. 272 (A.B.301), § 11, eff. Aug. 2, 1993.)*

Cross References

Gantry truck defined, see Vehicle Code § 335.
Height limitations, see Vehicle Code § 35250.
Identification required, see Vehicle Code § 27900.
Length, see Vehicle Code § 35400 et seq.
Motor truck as commercial vehicle, see Vehicle Code § 260.
Motor vehicle defined, see Vehicle Code § 415.
Noise limitations, see Vehicle Code § 23130.
Safety regulations, see Vehicle Code § 34500 et seq.
Service brakes, see Vehicle Code § 26304.
Speed limits, see Vehicle Code §§ 22400, 22406.
Truck tractor defined, see Vehicle Code § 655.
Vehicular air pollution control, heavy-duty motor vehicles, emissions standards and inspections, see Health and Safety Code § 43701.

Windshields, see Vehicle Code § 26700.

§ 415. Motor vehicle

(a) A "motor vehicle" is a vehicle that is self-propelled.

(b) "Motor vehicle" does not include a self-propelled wheelchair, motorized tricycle, or motorized quadricycle, if operated by a person who, by reason of physical disability, is otherwise unable to move about as a pedestrian.

(c) For purposes of Chapter 6 (commencing with Section 3000) of Division 2, "motor vehicle" includes a recreational vehicle as that term is defined in subdivision (a) of Section 18010 of the Health and Safety Code, but does not include a truck camper. *(Stats.1959, c. 3, p. 1535, § 415. Amended by Stats.1990, c. 400 (A.B.2953), § 1, eff. July 23, 1990; Stats.1996, c. 124 (A.B.3470), § 112; Stats.2003, c. 703 (S.B.248), § 1; Stats.2004, c. 404 (S.B.1725), § 1.)*

Cross References

Motor vehicle defined,
    Automobile Sales Finance Act, see Civil Code § 2981 et seq.
    Motor vehicle fuel license tax, see Revenue and Taxation Code § 7303.
    Motor vehicle insurance, see Insurance Code § 383.6.
    Use fuel tax, see Revenue and Taxation Code § 8603.
Particular motor vehicles,
    Motor truck, see Vehicle Code § 410.
    Motor-driven cycles, see Vehicle Code § 405.
    Motorcycles, see Vehicle Code § 400.
    Motorized bicycle or moped, see Vehicle Code § 406.
    Motorized quadricycle, see Vehicle Code § 407.
    Tow truck, see Vehicle Code § 615.
    Truck tractor, see Vehicle Code § 655.
Special occupancy parks, eviction, possession and removal of property, and rights of minors, see Civil Code § 1866.
Vehicle defined, see Vehicle Code § 670.
Vehicles required to be registered, see Vehicle Code § 4000.

§ 425. Muffler

A "muffler" is a device consisting of a series of chambers or baffle plates, or other mechanical design, for the purpose of receiving exhaust gas from an internal combustion engine, and effective in reducing noise. *(Stats.1959, c. 3, p. 1535, § 425.)*

Cross References

Exhaust systems, see Vehicle Code § 27150 et seq.
Noise limits, see Vehicle Code § 23130.
Sale, transfer or installation of unlawful equipment, see Vehicle Code § 24005.

§ 426. New motor vehicle dealer

"New motor vehicle dealer" is a dealer, as defined in Section 285, who, in addition to the requirements of that section, either acquires for resale new and unregistered motor vehicles from manufacturers or distributors of those motor vehicles or acquires for resale new off-highway motorcycles, or all-terrain vehicles from manufacturers or distributors of the vehicles. A distinction

shall not be made, nor any different construction be given to the definition of "new motor vehicle dealer" and "dealer" except for the application of the provisions of Chapter 6 (commencing with Section 3000) of Division 2 and Section 11704.5. Sections 3001 and 3003 do not, however, apply to a dealer who deals exclusively in motorcycles, all-terrain vehicles, or recreational vehicles, as defined in subdivision (a) of Section 18010 of the Health and Safety Code. *(Added by Stats.1967, c. 1397, p. 3261, § 1. Amended by Stats.1973, c. 78, p. 137, § 14; Stats.1975, c. 943, p. 2107, § 1; Stats.1982, c. 1584, p. 6260, § 4; Stats.1996, c. 1008 (A.B.2367), § 2; Stats.2000, c. 135 (A.B.2539), § 153; Stats.2003, c. 703 (S.B.248), § 2; Stats.2004, c. 836 (A.B.2848), § 6.)*

Cross References

Dealer defined, see Vehicle Code §§ 285, 286.
"Dealer" defined for purposes of Fair Practices of Equipment Manufacturers, Distributors, Wholesalers, and Dealers Act, see Business and Professions Code § 22901.
Inspection of emission related parts and operations of new vehicle on dealer's premises, see Health and Safety Code § 43012.
Locksmiths, license and registration requirements, exemption for new motor vehicle dealers and employees, see Business and Professions Code § 6980.12.
Motor vehicle defined, see Vehicle Code § 415.
New motor vehicle board, see Vehicle Code § 3000 et seq.

§ 430. New vehicle

A "new vehicle" is a vehicle constructed entirely from new parts that has never been the subject of a retail sale, or registered with the department, or registered with the appropriate agency or authority of any other state, District of Columbia, territory or possession of the United States, or foreign state, province, or country. *(Stats.1959, c. 3, p. 1535, § 430. Amended by Stats.1965, c. 820, p. 2411, § 1; Stats.1983, c. 1286, § 9; Stats.1988, c. 1583, § 1; Stats.1994, c. 1253 (A.B.3539), § 6.)*

Cross References

Motor vehicle defined, see Vehicle Code § 415.
Sale defined, see Vehicle Code § 5901.
Vehicle defined, see Vehicle Code § 670.
Vehicles subject to registration, see Vehicle Code § 4000 et seq.

§ 431. Nonrepairable vehicle

A "nonrepairable vehicle" is a vehicle of a type otherwise subject to registration that meets the criteria specified in subdivision (a), (b), or (c). The vehicle shall be issued a nonrepairable vehicle certificate and the vehicle, the vehicle frame, or unitized frame and body, as applicable, and as defined in Section 670.5, shall not be titled or registered.

(a) A nonrepairable vehicle is a vehicle that has no resale value except as a source of parts or scrap metal, and which the owner irreversibly designates solely as a source of parts or scrap metal.

(b) A nonrepairable vehicle is a completely stripped vehicle (a surgical strip) recovered from theft, missing all of the bolt on sheet metal body panels, all of the doors and hatches, substantially all of the interior components, and substantially all of the grill and light assemblies, or that the owner designates has little or no resale value other than its worth as a source of scrap metal, or as a source of a vehicle identification number that could be used illegally.

(c) A nonrepairable vehicle is a completely burned vehicle (burned hulk) that has been burned to the extent that there are no more usable or repairable body or interior components, tires and wheels, or drive train components, and which the owner irreversibly designates as having little or no resale value other than its worth as scrap metal or as a source of a vehicle identification number that could be used illegally. *(Added by Stats. 1994, c. 1008 (S.B.1833), § 6, operative July 1, 1995. Amended by Stats.2002, c. 670 (S.B.1331), § 1.)*

§ 432. Nonrepairable vehicle certificate

A "nonrepairable vehicle certificate" is a vehicle ownership document issued to the owner of a nonrepairable vehicle. Ownership of the vehicle may only be transferred two times on a nonrepairable vehicle certificate. A vehicle for which a nonrepairable vehicle certificate has been issued may not be titled or registered for use on the roads or highways of California. A nonrepairable vehicle certificate shall be conspicuously labeled with the word "nonrepairable" across the front. *(Added by Stats.1994, c. 1008 (S.B.1833), § 6.5, operative July 1, 1995.)*

§ 435. Nonresident

"Nonresident" is a person who is not a resident of this State. *(Stats.1959, c. 3, p. 1535, § 435.)*

Cross References

Actions against, see Vehicle Code § 16376.
Applicability of cancellation, suspension and revocation of license provisions, see Vehicle Code § 13552.
Exemption from licensing requirements, see Vehicle Code § 12502 et seq.
Exemption from registration, generally, see Vehicle Code § 6700 et seq.
Reciprocity, see Vehicle Code § 8000 et seq.
Resident, defined, see Vehicle Code § 516.
Service of process, see Vehicle Code § 17450 et seq.

§ 435.5. Nonresident daily commuter

"Nonresident daily commuter" means a person who is not a resident of this state, but who enters and leaves this state on a daily basis for the purpose of employment and whose vehicle is principally garaged out of this state. *(Added by Stats.1985, c. 1090, § 1, eff. Sept. 27, 1985.)*

Cross References

Permits, nonresident exemptions, see Vehicle Code § 6700 et seq.

§ 436. Off-highway motorcycle

An "off-highway motorcycle" means a motorcycle or motor-driven cycle which is subject to identification under this code. *(Added by Stats.1982, c. 1584, p. 6260, § 5.)*

§ 440. Official traffic control device

An "official traffic control device" is any sign, signal, marking, or device, consistent with Section 21400, placed or erected by authority of a public body or official having jurisdiction, for the purpose of regulating, warning, or guiding traffic, but does not include islands, curbs, traffic barriers, speed humps, speed bumps, or other roadway design features. *(Stats.1959, c. 3, p. 1535, § 440. Amended by Stats.1980, c. 671, p. 1865, § 1; Stats.1982, c. 749, p. 2966, § 3, eff. Sept. 8, 1982; Stats.1983, c. 291, § 3; Stats.1994, c. 1220 (A.B.3132), § 51, eff. Sept. 30, 1994.)*

Cross References

Official traffic control device, see Vehicle Code §§ 21400, 21401.
Official traffic control signal,
  Generally, see Vehicle Code § 21450 et seq.
  Defined, see Vehicle Code § 445.
Traffic regulation, see Vehicle Code § 21100 et seq.
Traffic signs, signals and markings, generally, see Vehicle Code § 21350 et seq.

§ 445. Official traffic control signal

An "official traffic control signal" is any device, whether manually, electrically or mechanically operated, by which traffic is alternately directed to stop and proceed and which is erected by authority of a public body or official having jurisdiction. *(Stats.1959, c. 3, p. 1535, § 445.)*

Cross References

Official traffic control devices, see Vehicle Code §§ 21400, 21401.
Official traffic control signals, see Vehicle Code § 21450 et seq.
Speed trap defined, see Vehicle Code § 40802.
Traffic-actuated signals, detection of bicycle or motorcycle traffic, see Vehicle Code § 21450.5.
Traffic regulation, see Vehicle Code § 21100 et seq.
Traffic signs, signals and markings, generally, see Vehicle Code § 21350 et seq.

§ 450. Oil well production service unit

An "oil well production service unit" is any vehicle specifically designed for and used exclusively in servicing oil wells which is only incidentally operated or moved on a highway. *(Added by Stats.1969, c. 133, p. 284, § 1.)*

§ 455. Original driver's license

"Original driver's license" means the first driver's license issued a person under this code. *(Stats.1959, c. 3, p. 1535, § 455.)*

Cross References

Drivers' licenses,
  Generally, see Vehicle Code § 12500 et seq.
  Defined, see Vehicle Code § 310.

§ 460. Owner

An "owner" is a person having all the incidents of ownership, including the legal title of a vehicle whether or not such person lends, rents, or creates a security interest in the vehicle; the person entitled to the possession of a vehicle as the purchaser under a security agreement; or the State, or any county, city, district, or political subdivision of the State, or the United States, when entitled to the possession and use of a vehicle under a lease, lease-sale, or rental-purchase agreement for a period of 30 consecutive days or more. *(Stats.1959, c. 3, p. 1530, § 460. Amended by Stats.1963, c. 819, p. 2013, § 41; Stats.1963, c. 1867, p. 3852, § 2.)*

Cross References

Civil liability of private owners, see Vehicle Code § 17150 et seq.
Contract cancellation option agreement required, exceptions, purchase price, form, and cancellation procedures, see Vehicle Code § 11731.21.
Definitions,
  Legal owner, see Vehicle Code § 370.
  Owner, registration and transfer of vessels, see Vehicle Code § 9840.
  Owner, reports of stolen vessels, see Vehicle Code § 10550.
  Registered owner, see Vehicle Code § 505.
  Security agreement, see Commercial Code § 9105.
  Security interest, see Commercial Code § 1201.
Liability of owner of vehicle for damages to or obstruction in highway, or bridge, see Vehicle Code § 17300 et seq.
Nonresident owners, see Vehicle Code § 6700 et seq.
Registration indices and records under name of owner, see Vehicle Code § 1800.
Registration provisions,
  Generally, see Vehicle Code § 4000 et seq.
  Certificate of ownership, contents, see Vehicle Code § 4451.
  Issuance of certificate of ownership and registration card to legal owner and owner, see Vehicle Code § 4450.

§ 461. Owner exemptions

The Senate, Assembly, or any committees thereof, or the Governor's office in possession and using vehicles under a lease, lease-sale, or rental-purchase agreement for a period of 30 consecutive days or more, unless otherwise provided in the lease or rental agreement, shall be exempt from the provisions of Section 460, upon the giving of written notice to the department of the desire to be so exempt. *(Added by Stats.1967, c. 162, p. 1247, § 1, eff. May 16, 1967.)*

§ 462. Paratransit vehicle

A "paratransit vehicle" is a passenger vehicle, other than a bus, schoolbus, school pupil activity bus, youth bus, general public paratransit vehicle, or taxicab that is both of the following:

(a)(1) Operated for hire by a business, nonprofit organization, or the state, or a political subdivision of the state utilizing drivers who receive compensation for their services and who spend a majority of their workweek operating a passenger vehicle.

(2) For the purposes of this subdivision, compensation does not include reimbursement to volunteer drivers of the cost of providing transportation services at a rate not greater than that approved by the United States Internal Revenue Service for volunteers.

(3) For the purposes of this subdivision, "for hire" means that the entity providing transportation services is compensated for the transportation under contract or agreement.

(b) Regularly used to provide transportation services to any of the following:

(1) Disabled persons who meet the definition of handicapped persons, as defined in Section 99206.5 of the Public Utilities Code.

(2) Persons with a developmental disability, as defined in subdivision (a) of Section 4512 of the Welfare and Institutions Code.

(3) Individuals with disabilities who are determined to be eligible for complementary paratransit services under Title II of the Americans with Disabilities Act of 1990 (P.L.101–336).

(4) Persons who are 55 years of age or older. *(Added by Stats.1998, c. 241 (A.B.1634), § 1. Amended by Stats.2004, c. 404 (S.B.1725), § 2.)*

Cross References

Employee meal periods, exception for commercial drivers operating vehicle described in this section and meeting specified conditions, see Labor Code § 512.
Exclusive or preferential use of highway lanes for high-occupancy vehicles, exception for paratransit vehicles, see Vehicle Code § 21655.5.

§ 463. Park or parking

"Park or parking" shall mean the standing of a vehicle, whether occupied or not, otherwise than temporarily for the purpose of and while actually engaged in loading or unloading merchandise or passengers. *(Added by Stats. 1961, c. 1608, p. 3437, § 1.)*

Cross References

Curb markings, see Vehicle Code § 21458.
Parking violations, see Vehicle Code § 40200 et seq.
Removal of parked and abandoned vehicles, see Vehicle Code § 22651 et seq.
Stop or stopping defined, see Vehicle Code § 587.
Stopping, standing and parking, see Vehicle Code § 22500 et seq.

§ 464. Passenger transportation vehicle

A "passenger transportation vehicle" is any vehicle, including a trailer bus, designed, used, or maintained for carrying more than 10 persons including the driver, which requires the person to have in his or her immediate possession a valid driver's license for the appropriate class of vehicle to be driven endorsed for passenger transportation. *(Added by Stats.1990, c. 1360 (S.B.1510), § 1.5.)*

§ 465. Passenger vehicle

A "passenger vehicle" is any motor vehicle, other than a motortruck, truck tractor, or a bus, as defined in Section 233, and used or maintained for the transportation of persons. The term "passenger vehicle" shall include a housecar. *(Stats.1959, c. 3, p. 1536, § 465. Amended by Stats.1961, c. 263, p. 1292, § 2; Stats.1963, c. 688, p. 1694, § 4; Stats.1969, c. 479, p. 1041, § 2; Stats.1976, c. 844, p. 1921, § 2; Stats.1982, c. 46, p. 139, § 6; Stats.1999, c. 1008 (S.B.533), § 1.)*

Cross References
Definitions,
  House car, see Vehicle Code § 362.
  Motor truck, see Vehicle Code § 410.
  Motor vehicle, see Vehicle Code § 415.
  Truck tractor, see Vehicle Code § 655.
Service stations, services for passenger vehicles, see Business and Professions Code § 13651.

§ 467. Pedestrian

(a) A "pedestrian" is a person who is afoot or who is using any of the following:

(1) A means of conveyance propelled by human power other than a bicycle.

(2) An electric personal assistive mobility device.

(b) "Pedestrian" includes a person who is operating a self-propelled wheelchair, motorized tricycle, or motorized quadricycle and, by reason of physical disability, is otherwise unable to move about as a pedestrian, as specified in subdivision (a).

(Added by Stats.1967, c. 586, p. 1931, § 1. Amended by Stats.1990, c. 400 (A.B.2953), § 1.5, eff. July 23, 1990; Stats.2002, c. 979 (S.B.1918), § 4, operative March 1, 2003; Stats.2004, c. 404 (S.B.1725), § 3; Stats.2007, c. 106 (A.B.470), § 2.)

Cross References
Bicycle defined, see Vehicle Code § 231.
Electric personal assistive mobility devices, defined, see Vehicle Code § 313.
Electric personal assistive mobility devices, required safety mechanisms, see Vehicle Code § 21280.5.
Pedestrian traffic control, see Vehicle Code §§ 21456, 21456.1, 21461.5.
Pedestrians' rights and duties, see Vehicle Code § 21950 et seq.

§ 467.5. Pedicab

"Pedicab" means either of the following:

(a) A bicycle that has three or more wheels, that transports, or is capable of transporting, passengers on seats attached to the bicycle, that is operated by a person, and that is being used for transporting passengers for hire.

(b) A bicycle that pulls a trailer, sidecar, or similar device, that transports, or is capable of transporting, passengers on seats attached to the trailer, sidecar, or similar device, that is operated by a person, and that is being used for transporting passengers for hire. *(Added by Stats.2010, c. 614 (A.B.2294), § 1.)*

Cross References
Local rules and regulations adopted relating to licensing and operation of pedicabs for hire, see Vehicle Code § 21100.
Rights and duties of bicycle riders and pedicab operators, see Vehicle Code § 21200.

§ 468. Permanent trailer identification plate program

The department shall commence the "permanent trailer identification plate program," on or after December 31, 2001, and may designate the method, consistent with this code, to be used by trailers, as defined in Section 5014.1, to receive an assigned permanent trailer identification plate for all trailers, except for trailer coaches and park trailers as described in subdivision (b) of Section 18010 of the Health and Safety Code, for identification purposes. An auxiliary dolly or tow dolly may be assigned a permanent trailer identification plate. The plate shall be in a size and design as determined by the department. *(Added by Stats.2000, c. 861 (S.B.2084), § 15, eff. Sept. 29, 2000.)*

§ 470. Person

"Person" includes a natural person, firm, copartnership, association, limited liability company, or corporation. *(Stats.1959, c. 3, p. 1536, § 470. Amended by Stats.1994, c. 1010 (S.B.2053), § 225.)*

Cross References
Corporation included in term, see Corporations Code § 18; Commercial Code § 1201.
Jurisdiction over person, see Government Code § 270.
Protection of person, see Const. Art. 1, § 1; Civil Code § 50; Government Code § 270.
State's rights over person, see Government Code § 200 et seq.

§ 471. Pickup truck

A "pickup truck" is a motor truck with a manufacturer's gross vehicle weight rating of less than 11,500 pounds, an unladen weight of less than 8,001 pounds, and which is equipped with an open box-type bed not exceeding 9 feet in length. "Pickup truck" does not include a motor vehicle otherwise meeting the above definition, that is equipped with a bed-mounted storage compartment unit commonly called a "utility body." *(Added by Stats.1991, c. 13 (A.B.37), § 16, eff. Feb. 13, 1991. Amended by Stats.1991, c. 928 (A.B.1886), § 15, eff. Oct. 14, 1991; Stats.1997, c. 652 (A.B.1518), § 8.)*

§ 472. Pilot car

A "pilot car" is a motor vehicle, except a motorcycle, motorized bicycle, or motorized quadricycle, which is used to escort one or more other vehicles, when required, due to the vehicles' size or character of load, in accordance with conditions set forth in a permit issued by the appropriate state agency or by a local authority. *(Added by Stats.1982, c. 568, p. 2524, § 1.)*

§ 473. Pocket bike

(a) A "pocket bike" is a two-wheeled motorized device that has a seat or saddle for the use of the rider, and that is not designed or manufactured for highway use. "Pocket bike" does not include an off-highway motorcycle, as defined in Section 436.

(b) For purposes of this section, a vehicle is designed for highway use if it meets the applicable Federal Motor Vehicle Safety Standards, as contained in Title 49 of the Code of Federal Regulations, and is equipped in accordance with the requirements of this code. *(Added by Stats.2005, c. 323 (A.B.1051), § 1.)*

Cross References

Operation of pocket bikes, prohibited areas, see Vehicle Code § 21720.
Seizure or removal of pocket bikes, peace officer authority, see Vehicle Code § 21721.

§ 475. Pole or pipe dolly

A "pole or pipe dolly" is a vehicle, other than a motor vehicle, having one or more axles which axles, if there be more than one, are not more than 54 inches apart, and two or more wheels, used in connection with a motor vehicle solely for the purpose of transporting poles, timbers, pipes, or integral structural materials and connected with the towing vehicle both by chain, rope, cable, or drawbar, and by the load, without any part of the weight of the dolly resting upon the towing vehicle. *(Stats.1959, c. 3, p. 1536, § 475.)*

Cross References

Application of chapter on towing and loading equipment to pole or pipe dollies, see Vehicle Code § 29000.
Auxiliary dolly defined, see Vehicle Code § 225.
Axle defined, see Vehicle Code § 230.
Drawbar defined, see Vehicle Code § 300.
Length of loads, see Vehicle Code §§ 35406, 35407, 35411, 35414.
Logging dolly defined, see Vehicle Code § 378.
Registration, see Vehicle Code § 4000.
Regulation of transportation of logs and poles, see Vehicle Code §§ 29200, 29201.
Special series license plates, see Vehicle Code § 5000.
Weight fees, see Vehicle Code § 9400 et seq.

§ 480. Power brake

A "power brake" is any braking gear or mechanism that aids in applying the brakes of a vehicle and which utilizes vacuum, compressed air, electricity, or hydraulic pressure developed by the motive power of that vehicle for that purpose. *(Stats.1959, c. 3, p. 1536, § 480. Amended by Stats.1977, c. 102, p. 523, § 1, eff. June 15, 1977.)*

Cross References

Airbrakes defined, see Vehicle Code § 108.
Brakes, generally, see Vehicle Code § 26301 et seq.

Operation of brakes, see Vehicle Code § 26450 et seq.

§ 485. Pneumatic tire

A "pneumatic tire" is a tire inflated or capable of inflation with compressed air. *(Stats.1959, c. 3, p. 1536, § 485.)*

Cross References

Metal tire defined, see Vehicle Code § 395.
Restrictions as to tire equipment, see Vehicle Code § 27450 et seq.
Snow-tread tire defined, see Vehicle Code § 558.
Solid tire defined, see Vehicle Code § 560.
Tire tread defined, see Vehicle Code § 610.

§ 490. Private road or driveway

"Private road or driveway" is a way or place in private ownership and used for vehicular travel by the owner and those having express or implied permission from the owner but not by other members of the public. *(Stats. 1959, c. 3, p. 1536, § 490.)*

Cross References

Highway defined, see Vehicle Code § 360.
Local regulation of private roads, see Vehicle Code § 21107 et seq.
Ownership of property defined, see Civil Code §§ 654, 679, 680 et seq.
Traffic devices on private road or driveway, see Vehicle Code § 21360.
Yield of right-of-way by driver of vehicle about to enter or cross highway from private property, see Vehicle Code § 21804.

§ 492. Private school

A "private school" is any school, whether conducted for profit or not, giving a course of training similar to that given in a public school at or below the twelfth grade, including but not limited to schools owned or operated by any church. *(Stats.1959, c. 3, p. 1536, § 492. Amended by Stats.1977, c. 406, p. 1414, § 6, eff. Aug. 27, 1977.)*

§ 493. Repealed by Stats.1981, c. 636, p. 2403, § 1

§ 495. Repealed by Stats.2011, c. 315 (A.B.28), § 6

§ 500. Recreational off-highway vehicle

"Recreational off-highway vehicle" means a motor vehicle meeting all of the following criteria:

(a) Designed by the manufacturer for operation primarily off of the highway.

(b) Has a steering wheel for steering control.

(c) Has nonstraddle seating provided by the manufacturer for the operator and all passengers.

(d)(1) Has a maximum speed capability of greater than 30 miles per hour.

(2) A vehicle designed by the manufacturer with a maximum speed capability of 30 miles per hour or less but is modified so that it has a maximum speed capability of greater than 30 miles per hour satisfies the criteria set forth in this subdivision.

(e) Has an engine displacement equal to or less than 1,000cc (61 ci). *(Added by Stats.2012, c. 165 (A.B.1595), § 1.)*

§ 505. Registered owner

A "registered owner" is a person registered by the department as the owner of a vehicle. *(Stats.1959, c. 3, p. 1536, § 505.)*

Cross References

Legal owner defined, see Vehicle Code § 370.

Owner defined, see Vehicle Code § 460.

Registered owner defined, registration and transfer of vessels, see Vehicle Code § 9840.

Registration indices and records under name of owner, see Vehicle Code § 1800.

Responsibility of registered owner to apply for license plates when lost or stolen, see Vehicle Code § 4457.

Vehicles subject to registration, see Vehicle Code § 4000 et seq.

§ 505.2. Registration service

(a) A "registration service" is a person engaged in the business of soliciting or receiving an application for the registration, renewal of registration, or transfer of registration or ownership, of a vehicle of a type subject to registration under this code, or of soliciting or receiving an application for a motor carrier permit under Division 14.85 (commencing with Section 34600), or of transmitting or presenting those documents to the department, when any compensation is solicited or received for the service. "Registration service" includes, but is not limited to, a person who, for compensation, processes registration documents, conducts lien sales, or processes vehicle dismantling documents.

(b) "Registration service" does not include the following:

(1) A person performing registration services on a vehicle acquired by that person for his or her own personal use or for use in the regular course of that person's business.

(2) A person who solicits applications for or sells, for compensation, nonresident permits for the operation of vehicles within this state.

(3) An employee of one or more dealers or dismantlers, or a combination thereof, who performs either of the following:

(A) Registration services for vehicles acquired by, consigned to, or sold by one or more of the employing dealers or dismantlers.

(B) Vehicle transactions on behalf of one or more of the employing dealers or dismantlers, if the transaction is for an employing dealer or dismantler who is a qualified business partner in compliance with the Business Partner Automation Program established by the department pursuant to Section 1685.

(4) A motor club, as defined in Section 12142 of the Insurance Code.

(5) A common carrier acting in the regular course of its business in transmitting applications. *(Added by Stats.1990, c. 1196 (A.B.4008), § 2, operative July 1, 1991. Amended by Stats.1992, c. 1243 (A.B.3090), § 55, eff. Sept. 30, 1992; Stats.1996, c. 1155 (S.B.1587), § 2; Stats.2000, c. 1035 (S.B.1403), § 3; Stats.2005, c. 148 (A.B.785), § 1; Stats.2006, c. 419 (A.B.2557), § 2.)*

§ 506. Registration year

"Registration year" is the period of time beginning with the date the vehicle is first required to be registered in this state and ending on the date designated by the director for expiration of the registration or the period of time designated for subsequent renewal thereof. *(Added by Stats.1973, c. 889, p. 1651, § 21, eff. Sept. 28, 1973.)*

§ 507. Relevant market area

The "relevant market area" is any area within a radius of 10 miles from the site of a potential new dealership. *(Added by Stats.1973, c. 996, p. 1966, § 11, operative July 1, 1974.)*

§ 507.5. Remanufactured vehicle

A "remanufactured vehicle" is a vehicle that has been constructed by a licensed remanufacturer and consists of any used or reconditioned integral parts, including, but not limited to, frame, engine, transmission, axles, brakes, or suspension. Remanufactured vehicles may be sold under a distinctive trade name. An existing vehicle which is incidently repaired, restored, or modified by replacing or adding parts or accessories is not a remanufactured vehicle. *(Added by Stats.1983, c. 1286, § 11.)*

§ 507.8. Remanufacturer

A "remanufacturer" is any person who for commission, money, or other thing of value, produces a vehicle that consists of any used or reconditioned integral parts, including, but not limited to, frame, engine, transmission, axles, brakes, or suspension which is subject to registration under this code. A remanufacturer is not a person who incidently repairs, restores, or modifies an existing vehicle by replacing or adding parts or accessories. *(Added by Stats.1983, c. 1286, § 12.)*

§ 508. Renter

A "renter" is a person who is engaged in the business of renting, leasing or bailing vehicles for a term not exceeding four months and for a fixed rate or price. *(Added by Stats.1976, c. 1284, p. 5711, § 7.)*

Cross References

Dealer defined, exclusion for renters, see Vehicle Code § 286.

§ 510. Repair shop

A "repair shop" is a place where vehicles subject to registration under this code are repaired, rebuilt, reconditioned, repainted, or in any way maintained for the public at a charge. *(Stats.1959, c. 3, p. 1536, § 510.)*

§ 512. Representative

A "representative" is any person regularly employed by a manufacturer or distributor for the purpose of negotiating or promoting the sale of the manufacturer's or distributor's vehicles to their franchisees or for regularly supervising or contacting franchisees or prospective franchisees in this state for any purpose. *(Added by Stats. 1973, c. 996, p. 1966, § 12, operative July 1, 1974.)*

§ 515. Residence district

A "residence district" is that portion of a highway and the property contiguous thereto, other than a business district, (a) upon one side of which highway, within a distance of a quarter of a mile, the contiguous property fronting thereon is occupied by 13 or more separate dwelling houses or business structures, or (b) upon both sides of which highway, collectively, within a distance of a quarter of a mile, the contiguous property fronting thereon is occupied by 16 or more separate dwelling houses or business structures. A residence district may be longer than one-quarter of a mile if the above ratio of separate dwelling houses or business structures to the length of the highway exists. *(Stats. 1959, c. 3, p. 1536, § 515.)*

§ 516. Resident

"Resident" means any person who manifests an intent to live or be located in this state on more than a temporary or transient basis. Presence in the state for six months or more in any 12-month period gives rise to a rebuttable presumption of residency.

The following are evidence of residency for purposes of vehicle registration:

(a) Address where registered to vote.

(b) Location of employment or place of business.

(c) Payment of resident tuition at a public institution of higher education.

(d) Attendance of dependents at a primary or secondary school.

(e) Filing a homeowner's property tax exemption.

(f) Renting or leasing a home for use as a residence.

(g) Declaration of residency to obtain a license or any other privilege or benefit not ordinarily extended to a nonresident.

(h) Possession of a California driver's license.

(i) Other acts, occurrences, or events that indicate presence in the state is more than temporary or transient. *(Added by Stats. 1983, c. 409, § 2. Amended by Stats. 1991, c. 13 (A.B.37), § 17, eff. Feb. 13, 1991.)*

§ 520. Retail sale

A "retail sale" is a sale of goods to a person for the purpose of consumption and use, and not for resale to others, including, but not limited to, an arrangement where a motor vehicle is consigned to a dealer for sale. *(Added by Stats. 1976, c. 1284, p. 5711, § 8.)*

§ 521. Retarder

A "retarder" is a device, other than a brake, which, when activated by the driver, applies a retarding force to the wheels of a vehicle without the use of friction. A retarder may be installed in or on the engine, exhaust system, drive train, or wheels of a motor vehicle, or an axle or wheels of a towed vehicle. A retarder may operate by altering the valve timing of the engine, by controlling the flow of a circulating fluid, by applying an electromagnetic force, by controlling the release of gases from the exhaust system, or by other means. A retarder may or may not be capable of stopping the vehicle upon which it is installed. *(Added by Stats. 1991, c. 648 (S.B.880), § 1.)*

§ 521.5. Revived salvage vehicle

"Revived salvage vehicle" means a total loss salvage vehicle as defined in Section 544, or a vehicle reported for dismantling pursuant to Section 5500 or 11520, that has been rebuilt or restored to legal operating condition with new or used component parts. *(Added by Stats. 2002, c. 670 (S.B.1331), § 2.)*

§ 522. Ridesharing

"Ridesharing" means two or more persons traveling by any mode, including, but not limited to, carpooling, vanpooling, buspooling, taxipooling, jitney, and public transit. *(Added by Stats. 1982, c. 185, p. 566, § 5.)*

§ 525. Right-of-way

"Right-of-way" is the privilege of the immediate use of the highway. *(Stats. 1959, c. 3, p. 1536, § 525.)*

Cross References

Right-of-way in general, see Vehicle Code §§ 21800 et seq., 21950 et seq.

§ 527. Road

(a) "Road" means any existing vehicle route established before January 1, 1979, with significant evidence of prior regular travel by vehicles subject to registration pursuant to Article 1 (commencing with Section 4000) of Chapter 1 of Division 3; provided, that "road" does not mean any route traversed exclusively by bicycles as defined in Section 39001, motorcycles as defined in Section 400, motor-driven cycles as defined in Section 405, or off-highway motor vehicles as defined in Section 38012.

(b) Even though nature may alter or eliminate portions of an existing vehicle route, the route shall still be considered a road where there is evidence of periodic use.

(c) A vehicle route need not necessarily be a publicly or privately maintained surface to be a road, as defined, for purposes of this section. Nothing contained herein shall pertain to any property in an incorporated area or properties held in private ownership.

(d) This section is definitional only and nothing contained herein shall be deemed to affect, alter, create, or destroy any right, title, or interest in real property, including, but not limited to, any permit, license, or easement; nor shall this chapter be deemed to affect the liability, or lack thereof, of any owner of an interest of real property based upon the use, possession, or ownership of such interest in real property or the entry upon such property by any person.

(e) This section shall only apply in a county where the board of supervisors has adopted a resolution or enacted an ordinance providing for such application. (*Added by Stats.1980, c. 361, p. 715, § 1.*)

§ 530. Roadway

A "roadway" is that portion of a highway improved, designed, or ordinarily used for vehicular travel. (*Stats. 1959, c. 3, p. 1537, § 530.*)

Cross References

Definitions,
  Highway, see Vehicle Code § 360.
  Street, see Vehicle Code § 590.
  Street or highway, see Vehicle Code § 591.
  Through highway, see Vehicle Code § 600.
Existing roadway projects, exemption from division requirements, conditions to be met, hearing, notice of exemption, see Public Resources Code § 21080.37.
Markings, see Vehicle Code § 21459.
Pedestrian on roadway, duties, see Vehicle Code § 21956.

§ 531. Utility-terrain vehicle

"Utility-terrain vehicle" means a motor vehicle subject to subdivision (a) of Section 38010 that is all of the following:

(a) Designed for operation off of the highway.

(b) Suspended on four tires.

(c) Has a steering wheel for steering control.

(d) Has one seat to accommodate a driver and one passenger sitting side by side. (*Added by Stats.2012, c. 168 (A.B.2111), § 1.*)

§ 535. Safety glazing material

Safety glazing material is any glazing material so constructed, treated, or combined with other materials as to reduce, in comparison with ordinary sheet, plate, or floatglass, the likelihood of injury to persons by glazing material whether it may be broken or unbroken. (*Added by Stats.1967, c. 1268, p. 3073, § 1. Amended by Stats. 1968, c. 980, p. 1875, § 29; Stats.1979, c. 723, p. 2215, § 2.*)

Cross References

Windshields and mirrors, see Vehicle Code § 26700 et seq.

§ 540. Safety zone

A "safety zone" is the area or space lawfully set apart within a roadway for the exclusive use of pedestrians and which is protected, or which is marked or indicated by vertical signs, raised markers or raised buttons, in order to make such area or space plainly visible at all times while the same is set apart as a safety zone. (*Stats.1959, c. 3, p. 1537, § 540.*)

Cross References

Driving within or through prohibited, see Vehicle Code § 21709.
Parking or stopping between safety zone and curb, see Vehicle Code § 22500.
Passing streetcars at intersection or safety zone, see Vehicle Code § 21756.
Roadway defined, see Vehicle Code § 530.

§ 543. Salvage pool

"Salvage pool" means a person engaged exclusively in the business of disposing of total loss salvage vehicles, nonrepairable vehicles, or recovered stolen vehicles sent to it by, or on behalf of, insurance companies, authorized adjusters, leasing companies, self-insured persons, or financial institutions. (*Added by Stats.1980, c. 629, p. 1720, § 2. Amended by Stats.1986, c. 952, § 1; Stats. 1991, c. 996 (S.B.798), § 1; Stats.1994, c. 1008 (S.B.1833), § 7, operative July 1, 1995.*)

Cross References

Dealer defined, exclusion of salvage pools, see Vehicle Code § 286.

§ 543.5. Salvage vehicle rebuilder

"Salvage vehicle rebuilder" means any person who rebuilds a total loss salvage vehicle, as defined in Section 544, or a vehicle reported for dismantling pursuant to Section 11520, for subsequent resale. A person who, for personal use, rebuilds a total loss salvage vehicle, or a vehicle reported for dismantling, and registers that vehicle in his or her name, is not a salvage vehicle rebuilder. Nothing in this section exempts a salvage vehicle rebuilder from any applicable licensing requirements under this code. *(Added by Stats.2002, c. 670 (S.B.1331), § 3.)*

§ 544. Total loss salvage vehicle; report of total settlement to Department of Motor Vehicles

"Total loss salvage vehicle" means either of the following:

(a) A vehicle, other than a nonrepairable vehicle, of a type subject to registration that has been wrecked, destroyed, or damaged, to the extent that the owner, leasing company, financial institution, or the insurance company that insured or is responsible for repair of the vehicle, considers it uneconomical to repair the vehicle and because of this, the vehicle is not repaired by or for the person who owned the vehicle at the time of the event resulting in damage.

(b) A vehicle that was determined to be uneconomical to repair, for which a total loss payment has been made by an insurer, whether or not the vehicle is subsequently repaired, if prior to or upon making the payment to the claimant, the insurer obtains the agreement of the claimant to the amount of the total loss settlement, and informs the client that, pursuant to subdivision (a) or (b) of Section 11515, the total loss settlement must be reported to the Department of Motor Vehicles, which will issue a salvage certificate for the vehicle. *(Added by Stats.1980, c. 629, p. 1720, § 3. Amended by Stats.1991, c. 996 (S.B.798), § 2; Stats.1994, c. 1008 (S.B.1833), § 8, operative July 1, 1995; Stats.2003, c. 451 (A.B.1718), § 4.)*

§ 545. Schoolbus

A "schoolbus" is a motor vehicle designed, used, or maintained for the transportation of any school pupil at or below the 12th–grade level to or from a public or private school or to or from public or private school activities, except the following:

(a) A motor vehicle of any type carrying only members of the household of the owner of the vehicle.

(b) A motortruck transporting pupils who are seated only in the passenger compartment, or a passenger vehicle designed for and carrying not more than 10 persons, including the driver, unless the vehicle or truck is transporting two or more disabled pupils confined to wheelchairs.

(c) A motor vehicle operated by a common carrier, or by and under the exclusive jurisdiction of a publicly owned or operated transit system, only during the time it is on a scheduled run and is available to the general public, or on a run scheduled in response to a request from a disabled pupil confined to a wheelchair, or from a parent of the disabled pupil, for transportation to or from nonschool activities, and the motor vehicle is designed for and actually carries not more than 16 persons including the driver, is available to eligible persons of the general public, and the school does not provide the requested transportation service.

(d) A school pupil activity bus.

(e) A motor vehicle operated by a carrier licensed by the Interstate Commerce Commission which is transporting pupils on a school activity entering or returning to the state from another state or country.

(f) A youth bus.

(g) Notwithstanding any other provisions of this section, the governing board of a district maintaining a community college may, by resolution, designate any motor vehicle operated by or for the district, a schoolbus within the meaning of this section, if it is primarily used for the transportation of community college students to or from a public community college or to or from public community college activities. The designation shall not be effective until written notification thereof has been filed with the Department of the California Highway Patrol.

(h) A state-owned motor vehicle being operated by a state employee upon the driveways, paths, parking facilities, or grounds specified in Section 21113 that are under the control of a state hospital under the jurisdiction of the State Department of Developmental Services where the posted speed limit is not more than 20 miles per hour. The motor vehicle may also be operated for a distance of not more than one-quarter mile upon a public street or highway that runs through the grounds of a state hospital under the jurisdiction of the State Department of Developmental Services, if the posted speed limit on the public street or highway is not more than 25 miles per hour and if all traffic is regulated by posted stop signs or official traffic control signals at the points of entry and exit by the motor vehicle.

(i) A general public paratransit vehicle, if the general public paratransit vehicle does not duplicate existing schoolbus service, does not transport a public school pupil at or below the 12th grade level to a destination outside of that pupil's school district, and is not used to transport public school pupils in areas where schoolbus services were available during the 1986–87 school year. In areas where expanded school services require expanded transportation of public school pupils, as determined by the governing board of a school district, general public paratransit vehicles shall not be used to transport those pupils for a period of three years from the date that a need for expansion is identified. For purposes of this section, a pupil is defined as a student at or below the 12th grade level who is being transported to a mandated school activity.

(j) A schoolbus with the flashing red light signal system, the amber warning system, and the schoolbus signs covered, while being used for transportation of persons other than pupils, to or from school or school related activities.

(k) A motor vehicle, other than a motor vehicle described in subdivision (b), that is designed to carry not more than 25 persons including the driver, while being used for the transportation of pupils to or from school-related activities if the vehicle is operated by a passenger charter-party carrier certified and licensed by the Public

Utilities Commission pursuant to Chapter 8 (commencing with Section 5351) of Division 2 of the Public Utilities Code that is not under a contractual agreement with a school or school district, and the transportation does not duplicate schoolbus service or any other transportation services for pupils contracted, arranged, or otherwise provided by the school or school district. *(Added by Stats.1987, c. 986, § 3.5, operative July 1, 1988. Amended by Stats.1992, c. 624 (A.B.3144), § 2, eff. Sept. 14, 1992; Stats.2004, c. 404 (S.B.1725), § 5; Stats.2008, c. 649 (A.B.830), § 3.)*

Cross References

Definitions,
  Bus, see Vehicle Code § 233.
  Common carrier, see Public Utilities Code §§ 211, 212.
  Motor vehicle, see Vehicle Code § 415.
  Passenger charter-party carrier, see Public Utilities Code § 5360.
  Passenger vehicle, see Vehicle Code § 465.
  Schoolbus, see Education Code §§ 39830, 82321.
  Station wagon, see Vehicle Code § 585.
Drivers,
  Age limit, see Vehicle Code § 12516.
  First aid examination, see Vehicle Code § 12522.
Flashing red signals,
  Required equipment, see Vehicle Code § 25257.
  Use, see Vehicle Code § 22112.
Inspection and certification, see Vehicle Code §§ 2807, 2807.1.
Instruction in schoolbus emergency procedure and passenger safety, see Education Code § 39831.5.
Railroad grade crossings, full stop required for school bus, see Vehicle Code § 22452.
Registration and weight fees, exemptions, see Vehicle Code § 9101 et seq.
Regulations pertaining to vehicles meeting or passing school bus, see Vehicle Code § 22454.
Safety regulations, see Vehicle Code § 34501.5.
Signs on school buses, see Vehicle Code § 27906.
Speed limitations, see Vehicle Code § 22406.
Training courses for certification to drive a schoolbus, see Education Code § 40080 et seq.
Transporting school pupils, requirements, see Vehicle Code § 12517.45.
Use of school bus in general, see Education Code § 39830 et seq.
Violation as misdemeanor, see Vehicle Code § 40000.11.

§ 545.1. Motor vehicles transporting pupils to or from community colleges

(a) Notwithstanding Section 545, a motor vehicle is not a schoolbus if it is operated for the purpose of transporting any pupil to or from a community college or to or from activities at that college, irrespective of the age of the pupil or the grade level of the pupil, if the pupil is a current enrollee in classes of the college providing the transportation.

(b) A driver of a motor vehicle that meets the criteria established by subdivision (a) shall escort pupils as required by subdivision (d) of Section 22112 and shall meet the requirements of Section 12517.

(c) This section shall apply to a community college district that includes within its boundaries one or more counties, each of which has a population of 250,000 or less. *(Added by Stats.1993, c. 834 (S.B.372), § 3, eff. Oct. 6, 1993. Amended by Stats.1995, c. 542 (S.B.40), § 3, eff. Oct. 4, 1995; Stats.2001, c. 739 (A.B.1707), § 2.)*

§ 545.5. Schoolbus; coach bus exclusion; Trona Unified School District

(a) Notwithstanding Section 545, a bus of the type commonly known as a coach bus is not a schoolbus when it is operated by the Trona Unified School District to transport pupils to route-deviated school activities.

(b) A coach bus operated pursuant to subdivision (a) shall be inspected annually by the Department of the California Highway Patrol, shall meet the equipment safety standards established by the federal government for schoolbuses, and shall be used to transport pupils only if the driver has obtained a certificate to operate a schoolbus pursuant to Section 12517. *(Added by Stats. 1995, c. 400 (A.B.1633), § 1.)*

§ 546. School pupil activity bus; driver regulations

A "school pupil activity bus" is any motor vehicle, other than a schoolbus, operated by a common carrier, or by and under the exclusive jurisdiction of a publicly owned or operated transit system, or by a passenger charter-party carrier, used under a contractual agreement between a school and carrier to transport school pupils at or below the 12th-grade level to or from a public or private school activity, or used to transport pupils to or from residential schools, when the pupils are received and discharged at off-highway locations where a parent or adult designated by the parent is present to accept the pupil or place the pupil on the bus. As used in this section, common carrier, publicly owned or operated transit system, and passenger charter-party carrier refer to carriers in business for the principal purpose of transporting members of the public on a commercial basis. This section shall not apply to a motor vehicle operated by a carrier licensed by the Interstate Commerce Commission that is transporting pupils on a school activity trip entering or returning to the state from another state or country.

The driver of a school pupil activity bus shall be subject to the regulations adopted by the California Highway Patrol governing schoolbus drivers, except that the regulations shall not require drivers to duplicate training or schooling that they have otherwise received which is equivalent to that required pursuant to the regulations, and the regulations shall not require drivers to take training in first aid. However, a valid certificate to drive a school pupil activity bus shall not entitle the bearer to drive a school bus. *(Added by Stats.1981, c. 813, p. 3152, § 6.)*

Cross References

Inspection and certification, see Vehicle Code § 2807.1.
Similar provisions, see Education Code § 39830.1.

Training courses for certification to drive a bus, see Education Code § 40080 et seq.

§ 550.   Semitrailer

A "semitrailer" is a vehicle designed for carrying persons or property, used in conjunction with a motor vehicle, and so constructed that some part of its weight and that of its load rests upon, or is carried by, another vehicle. *(Stats.1959, c. 3, p. 1537, § 550.)*

Cross References

Axle defined, see Vehicle Code § 230.
Brakes, see Vehicle Code §§ 26302, 26304.
License plates, see Vehicle Code § 5000.
Registration, see Vehicle Code § 4000.
Semitrailer as implement of husbandry, see Vehicle Code §§ 36005, 36010, 36015.
Size requirements, see Vehicle Code §§ 35250, 35400 et seq.
Snow tires or tire chain requirement, see Vehicle Code § 27459.
Speed of motor vehicle with semitrailer, see Vehicle Code § 22406.
Trailer coach defined, see Vehicle Code § 635.
Trailer defined, see Vehicle Code § 630.
Truck tractor defined, see Vehicle Code § 655.

§ 553.   Shade trailer

"Shade trailer" means a device designed and utilized to provide shade pursuant to Section 3395 of Title 8 of the California Code of Regulations. *(Added by Stats.2012, c. 168 (A.B.2111), § 2.)*

§ 555.   Sidewalk

"Sidewalk" is that portion of a highway, other than the roadway, set apart by curbs, barriers, markings or other delineation for pedestrian travel. *(Stats.1959, c. 3, p. 1537, § 555. Amended by Stats.1959, c. 979, p. 3007, § 1.)*

Cross References

Crosswalk defined, see Vehicle Code § 275.
Driving on sidewalk, see Vehicle Code § 21663.
Highway defined, see Vehicle Code §§ 360, 591.
Pedestrians' right-of-way on sidewalk, see Vehicle Code § 21952.
Prohibition of vehicles on sidewalk, see Vehicle Code § 22500.
Roadway defined, see Vehicle Code § 530.

§ 557.   Snowmobile

A "snowmobile" is a motor vehicle designed to travel over ice or snow in whole or in part on skis, belts, or cleats, which is commonly referred to as an Over Snow Vehicle (OSV). *(Added by Stats.1969, c. 1075, p. 2062, § 1. Amended by Stats.1989, c. 533, § 2.)*

Cross References

Exemption from requirement of driver's license, see Vehicle Code § 12501.
Identification plate, see Vehicle Code § 5011 et seq.
Off-highway motor vehicle defined, see Vehicle Code § 38012.

Unlawful operation of snowmobiles, see Vehicle Code § 23128.

§ 558.   Snow-tread tire

A "snow-tread tire" is a tire which has a relatively deep and aggressive tread pattern compared with conventional passenger tread pattern. *(Added by Stats.1961, c. 26, p. 932, § 1.)*

Cross References

Pneumatic tire defined, see Vehicle Code § 485.
Protuberances on tires, see Vehicle Code § 27454.
Use of snow-tread tires, see Vehicle Code § 27459.

§ 560.   Solid tire

A "solid tire" is a tire of rubber or other resilient material which does not depend upon compressed air for the support of the load. *(Stats.1959, c. 3, p. 1537, § 560.)*

Cross References

Gross weight per inch, see Vehicle Code § 35600.
Metal tire defined, see Vehicle Code § 395.
Pneumatic tire defined, see Vehicle Code § 485.
Restrictions as to tire equipment, see Vehicle Code § 27450 et seq.
Speed law for vehicle equipped with solid tire, see Vehicle Code § 22409.

§ 565.   Special construction equipment

"Special construction equipment" is:

(a) Any vehicle used primarily off the highways for construction purposes and which moves only occasionally over the highways and which because of the length, height, width, or unladen weight may not move over the public highways unladen without the permit specified in Section 35780.

(b) Any vehicle which is designed and used primarily either for grading of highways, paving of highways, earth moving, and other construction work on highways, or for construction or maintenance work on railroad rights-of-way, and which is not designed or used primarily for the transportation of persons or property and which is only incidentally operated or moved over the highway. It includes, but is not limited to, road and railroad construction and maintenance machinery so designed and used such as portable air compressors, air drills, asphalt spreaders, bituminous mixers, bucket loaders, tracktype tractors, crawler tractors, ditchers, leveling graders, finishing machines, motor graders, paving mixers, road rollers, scarifiers, earth moving scrapers and carryalls, lighting plants, welders, pumps, water wagons, power shovels and draglines, speed swings, skip loaders, weed mowers, self-propelled and tractor-drawn earth moving equipment and machinery, including dump trucks and tractor-dump trailer combinations which either (1) are in excess of 96 inches in width or (2) which, because of their length, height or unladen weight, may not be moved on a public highway without the permit specified in Section 35780 of this code and which are not operated laden except within the boundaries of the job construction site, and other similar types of construction equipment.

(Stats.1959, c. 3, p. 1537, § 565. Amended by Stats.1961, c. 1659, p. 3625, § 1; Stats.1969, c. 90, p. 213, § 1.)

Cross References

Carryall defined, see Vehicle Code § 245.
Exemption of equipment from use fuel tax, see Revenue and Taxation Code § 8652.
Identification plates, see Vehicle Code §§ 5011, 5015 et seq., 9261.
Lighting equipment, exemption of highway construction equipment, see Vehicle Code § 25801.
Off-highway vehicle exemption, see Vehicle Code § 38010.
Registration, exemption, see Vehicle Code § 4010.

§ 570. Special construction equipment: exclusions

"Special construction equipment" does not include any of the following:

(a) A vehicle originally designed for the transportation of persons or property to which machinery has been attached unless specifically designated as such in Section 565.

(b) Dump trucks originally designed to comply with the size and weight provisions of this code notwithstanding any subsequent modification which would require a permit, as specified in Section 35780 of this code, to operate such vehicles on a highway, truck-mounted transit mixers, cranes and shovels. *(Stats.1959, c. 3, p. 1538, § 570. Amended by Stats.1961, c. 1659, p. 3626, § 2.)*

§ 575. Special mobile equipment

"Special mobile equipment" is a vehicle, not self-propelled, not designed or used primarily for the transportation of persons or property, and only incidentally operated or moved over a highway, excepting implements of husbandry. *(Stats.1959, c. 3, p. 1538, § 575).*

Cross References

Exemption from registration, see Vehicle Code § 4010.
Identification plates, see Vehicle Code §§ 5011, 5016, 5017, 9261.
Implement of husbandry defined, see Vehicle Code § 36000.
Lighting equipment, exemption of special mobile equipment, see Vehicle Code § 25800.

§ 580. Specially constructed vehicle

A "specially constructed vehicle" is a vehicle which is built for private use, not for resale, and is not constructed by a licensed manufacturer or remanufacturer. A specially constructed vehicle may be built from (1) a kit; (2) new or used, or a combination of new and used, parts; or (3) a vehicle reported for dismantling, as required by Section 5500 or 11520, which, when reconstructed, does not resemble the original make of the vehicle dismantled. A specially constructed vehicle is not a vehicle which has been repaired or restored to its original design by replacing parts. *(Stats.1959, c. 3, p. 1538, § 580. Amended by Stats.1983, c. 1286, § 13.)*

Cross References

Registration, see Vehicle Code § 4153.

§ 585. Station wagon

A "station wagon" is a dual purpose vehicle designed for the transportation of persons and also designed in such a manner that the seats may be removed or folded out of the way for the purpose of increasing the property carrying space within the vehicle. The term includes, but is not limited to, types of vehicles which carry the trade names of station wagon, estate wagon, town and country wagon, and country sedan. <u>A vehicle used primarily for the transportation of cadavers to or from a funeral home, mortuary, or burial site is not a station wagon.</u> *(Stats. 1959, c. 3, p. 1538, § 585. Amended by Stats.2013, c. 523 (S.B.788), § 22.)*

Cross References

Weight fees, see Vehicle Code § 9404.

§ 587. Stop or stopping

"Stop or stopping" when prohibited shall mean any cessation of movement of a vehicle, whether occupied or not, except when necessary to avoid conflict with other traffic or in compliance with the direction of a police officer or official traffic control device or signal. *(Added by Stats.1961, c. 1917, p. 4036, § 1.)*

Cross References

Park or parking defined, see Vehicle Code § 463.

§ 590. Street

"Street" is a way or place of whatever nature, publicly maintained and open to the use of the public for purposes of vehicular travel. Street includes highway. *(Stats.1959, c. 3, p. 1538, § 590.)*

Cross References

Bicycle lanes, see Vehicle Code § 21207.
Deferred payments by local agency, see Government Code § 8687.
Definitions,
  Alley, see Vehicle Code § 110.
  Highway, see Vehicle Code § 360.
  Roadway, see Vehicle Code § 530.
  Through highway, see Vehicle Code § 600.
Parking on state highways, see Vehicle Code § 22505.

§ 591. Street or highway

A "street" or "highway" shall not include those portions of a way or place in or upon which construction, alteration, or repair work is being performed insofar as the equipment performing such work and its operation are concerned. Where the work consists of a street or highway project, the limits of the project as shown or described in the plans or specifications of the awarding body shall be so excluded with reference to the equipment actually engaged in performing the work. The authority having jurisdiction over such way or place may include any or all of the requirements set forth in

Divisions 11, 12, 13, 14 and 15 in any permit issued for work on such way or place and the awarding body on any such street or highway project may include such requirements in the specifications for such project. It is the intention of the Legislature, in enacting this section, that this section shall not be construed to relieve any person from the duty of exercising due care. *(Added by Stats. 1959, c. 659, p. 2632, § 1.)*

Cross References

Definitions,
   Highway, see Vehicle Code § 360.
   Street, see Vehicle Code § 590.

§ 592. Highway exceptions

"Highway", for the purposes of Division 3 (commencing with Section 4000), Division 12 (commencing with Section 24000), Division 13 (commencing with Section 29000), Division 14.8 (commencing with Section 34500), and Division 15 (commencing with Section 35000), does not include a way or place under the jurisdiction of a federal governmental agency, which lies on national forest or private lands, is open to public use, and for which the cost of maintenance of such way or place is borne or contributed to directly by any users thereof. *(Added by Stats.1967, c. 1682, p. 4215, § 1. Amended by Stats.1969, c. 1213, p. 2353, § 1.)*

Cross References

Deferred payments by local agency, see Government Code
   § 8687.
Highway defined, see Vehicle Code § 360.
Tax exemption, federal road, cost contributed to by users, see
   Revenue and Taxation Code §§ 8101.1, 8653.1.

§ 593. Supplemental restraint system

"Supplemental restraint system" means an automatic passive restraint system consisting of a bag that is designed to inflate upon collision, commonly referred to as an "airbag." *(Added by Stats.2002, c. 670 (S.B.1331), § 4.)*

§ 595. Terminal

"Terminal" is a place where a vehicle of a type listed in Section 34500 is regularly garaged or maintained, or from which the vehicle is operated or dispatched. *(Added by Stats.1994, c. 832 (S.B.2034), § 1.)*

§ 600. Through highway

A "through highway" is a highway or portion thereof at the entrance to which vehicular traffic from intersecting highways is regulated by stop signs or traffic control signals or is controlled when entering on a separated right-turn roadway by a yield-right-of-way sign. *(Stats. 1959, c. 3, p. 1538, § 600. Amended by Stats.1969, c. 168, p. 419, § 1.)*

42

Cross References

Definitions,
   Highway, see Vehicle Code § 360.
   Traffic, see Vehicle Code § 620.
Entering, see Vehicle Code § 21802.
Stop signs, see Vehicle Code §§ 21354, 21355.
Stopping, see Vehicle Code §§ 21802, 22450.

§ 605. Tire traction devices

"Tire traction devices" are devices or mechanisms having a composition and design capable of improving vehicle traction, braking, and cornering ability upon snow or ice-covered surfaces. Tire traction devices shall be constructed and assembled to provide sufficient structural integrity and to prevent accidental detachment from vehicles. Tire traction devices shall, at the time of manufacture or final assembly, bear a permanent impression indicating the name, initials, or trademark of the assembling company or primary manufacturer, and the country in which the devices were manufactured or assembled in final form. *(Added by Stats.1990, c. 71 (A.B.2498), § 1, eff. May 1, 1990.)*

Cross References

Restrictions on use of tire chains, see Vehicle Code § 27454.
Use of tire chains required, see Vehicle Code § 27459.

§ 610. Tire tread

"Tire tread" is that portion of the tire, consisting of the ribs and grooves, which comes in contact with the roadway. *(Added by Stats.1970, c. 216, p. 469, § 1.)*

Cross References

Use of snow-tread tires, see Vehicle Code § 27459.

§ 611. Toll highway or toll road

A "toll highway" or "toll road" is a publicly owned way or place open to the use of the public for purposes of vehicular travel which use requires the payment of a fee. *(Added by Stats.1992, c. 1241 (S.B.1615), § 6.)*

§ 612. Tour bus

"Tour bus" means a bus, which is operated by or for a charter-party carrier of passengers, as defined in Section 5360 of the Public Utilities Code, or a passenger stage corporation, as defined in Section 226 of the Public Utilities Code, or any highway carrier of passengers required to register with the California Public Utilities Commission pursuant to Section 3910 of the Public Utilities Code. *(Added by Stats.1986, c. 1305, § 1; Stats.1986, c. 1306, § 6. Amended by Stats.1987, c. 726, § 2, operative July 1, 1988; Stats.1988, c. 1586, § 2.5; Stats.1989, c. 1216, § 8, eff. Oct. 1, 1989.)*

§ 615. Tow truck; repossessor's tow vehicle; automobile dismantlers' tow vehicle

(a) A "tow truck" is a motor vehicle which has been altered or designed and equipped for, and primarily used in the business of, transporting vehicles by means of a crane, hoist, tow bar, tow line, or dolly or is otherwise primarily used to render assistance to other vehicles. A "roll-back carrier" designed to carry up to two vehicles is also a tow truck. A trailer for hire that is being used to transport a vehicle is a tow truck. "Tow truck" does not include an automobile dismantlers' tow vehicle or a repossessor's tow vehicle.

(b) "Repossessor's tow vehicle" means a tow vehicle which is registered to a repossessor licensed or registered pursuant to Chapter 11 (commencing with Section 7500) of Division 3 of the Business and Professions Code that is used exclusively in the course of the repossession business.

(c) "Automobile dismantlers' tow vehicle" means a tow vehicle which is registered by an automobile dismantler licensed pursuant to Chapter 3 (commencing with Section 11500) of Division 5 and which is used exclusively to tow vehicles owned by that automobile dismantler in the course of the automobile dismantling business. *(Stats.1959, c. 3, p. 1538, § 615. Amended by Stats.1982, c. 1273, p. 4697, § 1; Stats.1985, c. 710, § 1; Stats.1988, c. 924, § 1; Stats.1993, c. 479 (A.B.1113), § 2; Stats.1999, c. 456 (S.B.378), § 14.)*

Cross References

Lighting equipment, requirements, see Vehicle Code §§ 24605, 25253, 25253.1.
Motor vehicle defined, see Vehicle Code § 415.
Repossessors, entry to vehicle or connection of collateral to a tow truck or repossessor's tow vehicle as defined under this section, determination of occurrence of repossession, see Business and Professions Code § 7507.12.
Required equipment, see Vehicle Code § 27700.
Signs required, see Vehicle Code § 27907.

§ 617. Tow dolly

A "tow dolly" is a vehicle towed by a motor vehicle and designed and used exclusively to transport another motor vehicle and upon which the front or rear wheels of the towed motor vehicle are mounted, while the other wheels of the towed motor vehicle remain in contact with the ground. "Tow dolly" does not include a portable or collapsible dolly used as specified in Section 4014. *(Added by Stats.1983, c. 708, § 1.)*

§ 620. Traffic

The term "traffic" includes pedestrians, ridden animals, vehicles, street cars, and other conveyances, either singly or together, while using any highway for purposes of travel. *(Stats.1959, c. 3, p. 1539, § 620.)*

Cross References

Definitions,
Highway, see Vehicle Code § 360.
Vehicle, see Vehicle Code § 670.
Traffic laws, see Vehicle Code § 21000 et seq.

§ 625. Traffic officer

A "traffic officer" is any member of the California Highway Patrol, or any peace officer who is on duty for the exclusive or main purpose of enforcing Division 10

(commencing with Section 20000) or 11 (commencing with Section 21000). *(Stats.1959, c. 3, p. 1539, § 625. Amended by Stats.1961, c. 202, p. 1211, § 1; Stats.1983, c. 142, § 159.)*

Cross References

California highway patrol, generally, see Vehicle Code § 2100 et seq.
Enforcement of regulations for transport of radioactive materials, see Health and Safety Code § 114825.
Minimum standards for public officers or employees having powers of peace officers, see Government Code § 1031.
Obedience to peace officer, see Vehicle Code § 2800.
Peace officer, see Penal Code § 830 et seq.
Waste tire hauler registration, enforcement authority, see Public Resources Code § 42962.5.

§ 626. Traffic violator school

A "traffic violator school" is a business that, for compensation, provides, or offers to provide, instruction in traffic safety, including, but not limited to, classroom traffic violator curricula, for persons referred by a court pursuant to Section 42005 or to other persons who elect to attend. *(Added by Stats.1985, c. 396, § 1, eff. July 30, 1985. Amended by Stats.2001, c. 457 (A.B.509), § 1.)*

§ 626.2. Traffic violator school branch or classroom location

A "traffic violator school branch or classroom location" is any place where a traffic violator school conducts instruction or maintains records. *(Added by Stats.1985, c. 396, § 2, eff. July 30, 1985.)*

§ 626.4. Traffic violator school instructor

A "traffic violator school instructor" is any person who provides instruction to traffic violators on behalf of a traffic violator school. *(Added by Stats.1985, c. 396, § 3, eff. July 30, 1985.)*

§ 626.6. Traffic violator school operator

A "traffic violator school operator" is the person who directs and manages the operations of a traffic violator school.

A "traffic violator school operator" may be either the traffic violator school owner or another person designated by the traffic violator school owner to personally direct and manage the traffic violator school for the traffic violator school owner. *(Added by Stats.1985, c. 396, § 4, eff. July 30, 1985.)*

§ 626.8. Traffic violator school owner

A "traffic violator school owner" is any natural person, association, or corporation that owns a traffic violator school. *(Added by Stats.1985, c. 396, § 5, eff. July 30, 1985.)*

§ 627. Engineering and traffic survey

(a) "Engineering and traffic survey," as used in this code, means a survey of highway and traffic conditions in accordance with methods determined by the Department of Transportation for use by state and local authorities.

(b) An engineering and traffic survey shall include, among other requirements deemed necessary by the department, consideration of all of the following:

(1) Prevailing speeds as determined by traffic engineering measurements.

(2) Accident records.

(3) Highway, traffic, and roadside conditions not readily apparent to the driver.

(c) When conducting an engineering and traffic survey, local authorities, in addition to the factors set forth in paragraphs (1) to (3), inclusive, of subdivision (b) may consider all of the following:

(1) Residential density, if any of the following conditions exist on the particular portion of highway and the property contiguous thereto, other than a business district:

(A) Upon one side of the highway, within a distance of a quarter of a mile, the contiguous property fronting thereon is occupied by 13 or more separate dwelling houses or business structures.

(B) Upon both sides of the highway, collectively, within a distance of a quarter of a mile, the contiguous property fronting thereon is occupied by 16 or more separate dwelling houses or business structures.

(C) The portion of highway is longer than one-quarter of a mile but has the ratio of separate dwelling houses or business structures to the length of the highway described in either subparagraph (A) or (B).

(2) Pedestrian and bicyclist safety. *(Added by Stats. 1959, c. 11, p. 1853, § 10, operative Jan. 1, 1960. Amended by Stats.1974, c. 545, p. 1310, § 154; Stats.1982, c. 466, p. 2055, § 106; Stats.2000, c. 45 (A.B.2767), § 1.)*

Cross References

Rules of the road, speed laws, equestrian safety, see Vehicle Code § 22353.

§ 630. Trailer

A "trailer" is a vehicle designed for carrying persons or property on its own structure and for being drawn by a motor vehicle and so constructed that no part of its weight rests upon any other vehicle. As used in Division 15 (commencing with Section 35000), "trailer" includes a semitrailer when used in conjunction with an auxiliary dolly, if the auxiliary dolly is of a type constructed to replace the function of the drawbar and the front axle or axles of a trailer. *(Stats.1959, c. 3, p. 1539, § 630. Amended by Stats.1983, c. 145, § 1.2, eff. June 28, 1983; Stats.1984, c. 542, § 1.)*

Cross References

Brakes, see Vehicle Code §§ 26302, 26304.
Definitions,
  Drawbar, see Vehicle Code § 300.

Motor vehicle, see Vehicle Code § 415.
  Trailer coach, see Vehicle Code § 635.
License plates, see Vehicle Code § 5000.
Mobilehome, see Health and Safety Code § 18008 et seq.
Registration, see Vehicle Code § 4000.
Speed limit, vehicle with trailer, see Vehicle Code § 22406.
Towing of vehicle, see Vehicle Code § 29000 et seq.

§ 635. Trailer coach

A "trailer coach" is a vehicle, other than a motor vehicle, designed for human habitation or human occupancy for industrial, professional, or commercial purposes, for carrying property on its own structure, and for being drawn by a motor vehicle. A "park trailer," as described in Section 18009.3 of the Health and Safety Code, is a trailer coach. *(Stats.1959, c. 3, p. 1539, § 635. Amended by Stats.1963, c. 1317, p. 2838, § 1; Stats.1971, c. 1536, p. 3042, § 1.5, operative May 3, 1972; Stats.1986, c. 1078, § 5, eff. Sept. 24, 1986, operative Jan. 1, 1987; Stats.1993, c. 272 (A.B.301), § 12, eff. Aug. 2, 1993; Stats.2000, c. 566 (A.B.1912), § 3.)*

Cross References

Brakes, see Vehicle Code § 26303.
Burglary of trailer coach, see Penal Code § 459.
Commercial coach as including trailer coach, see Health and Safety Code § 18218.
Definitions,
  Motor vehicle, see Vehicle Code § 415.
  Trailer, see Vehicle Code § 630.
Recreational vehicle park, see Health and Safety Code § 18215.
Signal devices required, see Vehicle Code § 24950.
Speed limitations, see Vehicle Code § 22406.

§ 636. Trailer bus

A "trailer bus" is a trailer or semitrailer designed, used, or maintained for the transportation of more than 15 persons, including the driver, and includes a connected towing motor vehicle that is a motor truck, truck tractor, or bus. *(Added by Stats.1988, c. 843, § 2. Amended by Stats.1994, c. 58 (A.B.1633), § 1, eff. April 26, 1994.)*

§ 640. Transferee

A "transferee" is a person who has acquired the sole ownership of or an equity in a vehicle of a type required to be registered under this code. *(Stats.1959, c. 3, p. 1539, § 640.)*

Cross References

Transfers of title or interest, see Vehicle Code § 5600 et seq.

§ 642. Transit bus

A "transit bus" is any bus owned or operated by a publicly owned or operated transit system, or operated under contract with a publicly owned or operated transit system, and used to provide to the general public, regularly scheduled transportation for which a fare is charged. A general public paratransit vehicle is not a transit bus. *(Added by Stats.1989, c. 1136, § 2, operative July 1, 1990.)*

Cross References

Training courses for certification to drive a bus, see Education Code § 40080 et seq.

§ 645. Transporter

(a) A "transporter" is a person engaged in the business of moving any owned or lawfully possessed vehicle by lawful methods over the highways for the purpose of delivery of such vehicles to dealers, sales agents of a manufacturer, purchasers, or to a new location as requested by the owner.

(b) The term "transporter" does not include a person engaged in the business of operating a tow car. *(Stats. 1959, c. 3, p. 1539, § 645. Amended by Stats.1963, c. 444, p. 1278, § 1.)*

Cross References

Fees for license plates, see Vehicle Code § 9262.
Issuance of licenses and certificates, see Vehicle Code § 11700 et seq.

§ 650. Trolley coach

A "trolley coach" is a vehicle which is propelled by electric power obtained from overhead trolley wires, but not operated upon rails. *(Stats.1959, c. 3, p. 1539, § 650.)*

§ 655. Truck tractor

(a) A "truck tractor" is a motor vehicle designed and used primarily for drawing other vehicles and not so constructed as to carry a load, other than a part of the weight of the vehicle and the load so drawn. As used in this section, "load" does not include items carried on the truck tractor in conjunction with the operation of the vehicle if the load carrying space for these items does not exceed 34 square feet.

(b) Notwithstanding subdivision (a), a truck tractor, operated by a motor carrier whose owner is licensed by the Department of the California Highway Patrol to transport explosives pursuant to Division 14 (commencing with Section 31600), may be equipped with a cargo container used exclusively for the transportation of explosives or munitions-related security material, as specified by the United States Department of Defense. *(Stats. 1959, c. 3, p. 1539, § 655. Amended by Stats.1991, c. 13 (A.B.37), § 18, eff. Feb. 13, 1991; Stats.1994, c. 88 (S.B.1326), § 1.)*

Cross References

Exemption of tractors used in agricultural operations from use fuel tax, see Revenue and Taxation Code § 8652.
Motor vehicle defined, see Vehicle Code § 415.
Tractor excluded from definition of motorcycle, see Vehicle Code § 400.
Windshields required of truck tractor, see Vehicle Code § 26700.

§ 657. Truss

A "truss" is an assemblage of beams, bars, or rods typically arranged in a triangle or combination of trian-

gles to form a rigid framework and used as a structural support in buildings. *(Added by Stats.1979, c. 299, p. 300, § 1.)*

§ 660. Unladen weight

The "unladen weight" of a vehicle is the weight equipped and ready for operation on the road including the body, fenders, oil in motor, radiator full of water, with five gallons of gasoline or equivalent weight of other motor fuel; also equipment required by law, and unless exempted under Section 661, any special cabinets, boxes or body parts permanently attached to the vehicle, and any machinery, equipment or attachment which is attendant to the efficient operation of the body or vehicle. Unladen weight shall not include any load or any machinery or mechanical apparatus, such as, but not limited to, wood saws, well-drilling machines, spray apparatus, tow truck cranes, and grinding equipment. The unladen weight of a vehicle shall have no application in determining any fee under this code or the Revenue and Taxation Code other than Section 9400. *(Stats.1959, c. 3, p. 1539, § 660. Amended by Stats.1961, c. 58, p. 1002, § 5; Stats.1961, c. 1576, p. 3399, § 1; Stats.1963, c. 2108, p. 4385, § 1; Stats.1988, c. 924, § 2.)*

§ 661. Unladen weight exclusion

Unladen weight shall not include the following machinery, equipment or attachment which is attendant to the efficient operation of the body or vehicle:

(a) Equipment used for loading, compacting, or unloading of refuse.

(b) Transitmix cement equipment.

(c) Temporary equipment used to contain or support the load which does not change the body classification.

(d) Any camper unit that is temporarily attached to a vehicle.

(e) Refrigeration equipment. *(Added by Stats.1963, c. 2108, p. 4386, § 2.)*

§ 665. Used vehicle

A "used vehicle" is a vehicle that has been sold, or has been registered with the department, or has been sold and operated upon the highways, or has been registered with the appropriate agency of authority, of any other state, District of Columbia, territory or possession of the United States or foreign state, province or country, or unregistered vehicles regularly used or operated as demonstrators in the sales work of a dealer or unregistered vehicles regularly used or operated by a manufacturer in the sales or distribution work of such manufacturer. The word "sold" does not include or extend to: (1) any sale made by a manufacturer or a distributor to a dealer, (2) any sale by a new motor vehicle dealer franchised to sell a particular line-make to another new motor vehicle dealer franchised to sell the same line-make, or (3) any sale by a dealer to another dealer licensed under this code involving a mobilehome, as defined in Section 396, a recreational vehicle, as defined in Section 18010.5 of the

Health and Safety Code, a commercial coach, as defined in Section 18012 of the Health and Safety Code, an off-highway motor vehicle subject to identification, as defined in Section 38012, or a commercial vehicle, as defined in Section 260. *(Stats.1959, c. 3, p. 1540, § 665. Amended by Stats.1965, c. 820, p. 2411, § 2; Stats.1967, c. 801, p. 2217, § 1; Stats.1988, c. 1583, § 2.)*

Cross References

Alteration or removal of vehicle numbers, see Vehicle Code §§ 10750, 10751.
Contract cancellation option agreement required, exceptions, purchase price, form, and cancellation procedures, see Vehicle Code § 11731.21.
Engine or motor change, see Vehicle Code § 4161.
Essential parts defined, see Vehicle Code § 315.
Used vehicles, NMVTIS vehicle history report required, requirements for junk or salvage automobile, exceptions, see Vehicle Code § 11713.26.
Vehicles subject to registration, see Vehicle Code § 4000 et seq.

§ 665.5. U–turn

A "U-turn" is the turning of a vehicle upon a highway so as to proceed in the opposite direction whether accomplished by one continuous movement or not. *(Added by Stats.1970, c. 620, p. 1231, § 1.)*

Cross References

Traffic signals, u-turns, see Vehicle Code § 21451.
Turning and stopping, including U-turns, see Vehicle Code § 22100 et seq.

§ 666. Repealed by Stats.2001, c. 826 (A.B.1472), § 7

§ 667. Utility trailer defined

(a) A "utility trailer" is a trailer or semitrailer used solely for the transportation of the user's personal property, not in commerce, which does not exceed a gross weight of 10,000 pounds or a manufacturer's gross vehicle weight rating of 10,000 pounds.

(b) Notwithstanding subdivision (a), a "utility trailer" includes a trailer or semitrailer designed and used for the transportation of livestock, not in commerce, which does not exceed a gross weight of 10,000 pounds or a manufacturer's gross vehicle weight rating of 10,000 pounds. *(Added by Stats.2010, c. 491 (S.B.1318), § 35.)*

§ 668. Vanpool vehicle

A "vanpool vehicle" is any motor vehicle, other than a motortruck or truck tractor, designed for carrying more than 10 but not more than 15 persons including the driver, which is maintained and used primarily for the nonprofit work-related transportation of adults for the purposes of ridesharing. *(Added by Stats.1982, c. 46, p. 139, § 8.)*

Cross References

Ridesharing defined, see Vehicle Code § 522.

Safety regulations, see Vehicle Code § 34509.

§ 670. Vehicle

A "vehicle" is a device by which any person or property may be propelled, moved, or drawn upon a highway, excepting a device moved exclusively by human power or used exclusively upon stationary rails or tracks. *(Stats. 1959, c. 3, p. 1540, § 670. Amended by Stats.1975, c. 987, p. 2327, § 3.)*

Cross References

Definitions,
    Authorized emergency vehicles, see Vehicle Code § 165.
    Commercial vehicle, see Vehicle Code § 260.
    Foreign vehicle, see Vehicle Code § 330.
    Motor vehicle, see Vehicle Code § 415.
    Specially constructed vehicle, see Vehicle Code § 580.
Military Families Financial Relief Act, see Military and Veterans Code § 800 et seq.
Motor vehicle brake friction materials, restrictions, definitions, see Health and Safety Code § 25250.50.
Sales and use tax, vehicle defined, see Revenue and Taxation Code § 6272.
Special mobile equipment as a vehicle, see Vehicle Code § 575.
Trolley coach as a vehicle, see Vehicle Code § 650.
Vehicle License Fee Law, see Revenue and Taxation Code § 10701 et seq.

§ 670.5. Vehicle frame

A "vehicle frame" is defined as the main longitudinal structural members of the chassis of the vehicle, or for vehicles with unitized body construction, the lowest main longitudinal structural members of the body of the vehicle, used as the major support in the construction of the motor vehicle. *(Added by Stats.2002, c. 670 (S.B. 1331), § 5.)*

§ 671. Vehicle identification number

(a) A "vehicle identification number" is the motor number, serial number, or other distinguishing number, letter, mark, character, or datum, or any combination thereof, required or employed by the manufacturer or the department for the purpose of uniquely identifying a motor vehicle or motor vehicle part or for the purpose of registration.

(b) Whenever a vehicle is constructed of component parts identified with one or more different vehicle identification numbers, the vehicle identification number stamped or affixed by the manufacturer or authorized governmental entity on the frame or unitized frame and body, as applicable, and as defined in Section 670.5, shall determine the identity of the vehicle for registration purposes. *(Added by Stats.1993, c. 386 (S.B.73), § 2, eff. Sept. 8, 1993. Amended by Stats.2002, c. 670 (S.B.1331), § 6.)*

§ 672. Vehicle manufacturer

(a) "Vehicle manufacturer" is any person who produces from raw materials or new basic components a vehicle of a type subject to registration under this code, off-highway motorcycles or all-terrain vehicles subject to identification under this code, or trailers subject to identification pursuant to Section 5014.1, or who permanently alters, for purposes of retail sales, new commercial vehicles by converting the vehicles into house cars that display the insignia of approval required by Section 18056 of the Health and Safety Code and any regulations issued pursuant thereto by the Department of Housing and Community Development. As used in this section, "permanently alters" does not include the permanent attachment of a camper to a vehicle.

(b) A vehicle manufacturer that produces a vehicle of a type subject to registration that consists of used or reconditioned parts, for the purposes of the code, is a remanufacturer, as defined in Section 507.8.

(c) Unless a vehicle manufacturer either grants franchises to franchisees in this state, or issues vehicle warranties directly to franchisees in this state or consumers in this state, the manufacturer shall have an established place of business or a representative in this state.

(d) The scope and application of this section are limited to Division 2 (commencing with Section 1500) and Division 5 (commencing with Section 11100). *(Added by Stats.1977, c. 873, p. 2634, § 2. Amended by Stats.1982, c. 1584, p. 6260, § 6; Stats.1983, c. 1286, § 14; Stats.1996, c. 124 (A.B.3470), § 113; Stats.2001, c. 539 (S.B.734), § 8; Stats.2002, c. 664 (A.B.3034), § 213; Stats.2004, c. 836 (A.B.2848), § 7.)*

Cross References

Classes of insurance, express warranties, see Insurance Code § 116.6.

§ 675. Vehicle salesperson

(a) "Vehicle salesperson" is a person not otherwise expressly excluded by this section, who does one or a combination of the following:

(1) Is employed as a salesperson by a dealer, as defined in Section 285, or who, under any form of contract, agreement, or arrangement with a dealer, for commission, money, profit, or other thing of value, sells, exchanges, buys, or offers for sale, negotiates, or attempts to negotiate, a sale, or exchange of an interest in a vehicle required to be registered under this code.

(2) Induces or attempts to induce any person to buy or exchange an interest in a vehicle required to be registered, and who receives or expects to receive a commission, money, brokerage fees, profit, or any other thing of value, from either the seller or purchaser of the vehicle.

(3) Exercises managerial control over the business of a licensed vehicle dealer or who supervises vehicle salespersons employed by a licensed dealer, whether compensated by salary or commission, including, but not limited to, any person who is employed by the dealer as a general manager, assistant general manager, or sales manager, or any employee of a licensed vehicle dealer who negotiates with or induces a customer to enter into a security agreement or purchase agreement or purchase order for the sale of a vehicle on behalf of the licensed vehicle dealer.

(b) The term "vehicle salesperson" does not include any of the following:

(1) Representatives of insurance companies, finance companies, or public officials, who in the regular course of business, are required to dispose of or sell vehicles under a contractual right or obligation of the employer, or in the performance of an official duty, or under the authority of any court of law, if the sale is for the purpose of saving the seller from any loss or pursuant to the authority of a court of competent jurisdiction.

(2) Persons who are licensed as a manufacturer, remanufacturer, transporter, distributor, or representative.

(3) Persons exclusively employed in a bona fide business of exporting vehicles, or of soliciting orders for the sale and delivery of vehicles outside the territorial limits of the United States.

(4) Persons not engaged in the purchase or sale of vehicles as a business, disposing of vehicles acquired for their own use, or for use in their business when the vehicles have been so acquired and used in good faith, and not for the purpose of avoiding the provisions of this code.

(5) Persons regularly employed as salespersons by persons who are engaged in a business involving the purchase, sale, or exchange of boat trailers.

(6) Persons regularly employed as salespersons by persons who are engaged in a business activity which does not involve the purchase, sale, or exchange of vehicles, except incidentally in connection with the purchase, sale, or exchange of vehicles of a type not subject to registration under this code, boat trailers, or midget autos or racers advertised as being built exclusively for use by children.

(7) Persons licensed as a vehicle dealer under this code doing business as a sole ownership or member of a partnership or a stockholder and director of a corporation or a member and manager of a limited liability company licensed as a vehicle dealer under this code. However, those persons shall engage in the activities of a salesperson, as defined in this section, exclusively on behalf of the sole ownership or partnership or corporation or limited liability company in which they own an interest or stock, and those persons owning stock shall be directors of the corporation; otherwise, they are vehicle salespersons and subject to Article 2 (commencing with Section 11800) of Chapter 4 of Division 5.

(8) Persons regularly employed as salespersons by a vehicle dealer authorized to do business in California under Section 11700.1 of the Vehicle Code. *(Stats.1959, c. 3, p. 1540, § 675. Amended by Stats.1959, c. 1668, p. 4051, § 3; Stats.1967, c. 1038, p. 2640, § 1; Stats.1968, c. 1004, p. 1953, § 1; Stats.1976, c. 1286, p. 5949, § 5; Stats.1979, c. 1088, p. 3936, § 1, eff. Sept. 28, 1979; Stats.1983, c. 1286, § 15; Stats.1990, c. 1563 (A.B.3243),*

§ 3.3; Stats.1994, c. 1200 (S.B.469), § 92, eff. Sept. 30, 1994.)

§ 675.5. Vehicle verifier

A "vehicle verifier" is a person not expressly excluded by Section 675.6 who inspects, records, documents, and submits to the department, or its authorized representative, such proof of vehicle identification as may be required by the department for the purpose of registering or transferring the ownership of vehicles. *(Added by Stats.1975, c. 700, p. 1658, § 1.)*

§ 675.6. Vehicle verifier; exclusions

(a) "Vehicle verifier" does not include any of the following:

(1) A peace officer.

(2) An authorized employee of the department.

(3) A special agent of the National Auto Theft Bureau.

(4) An employee of an organization certified under the provisions of Part 5 (commencing with Section 12140) of Division 2 of the Insurance Code whose duties require or authorize the verification of vehicles.

(b) Any person specified in subdivision (a) may perform the duties of a vehicle verifier without obtaining the special permit required in Section 11300. *(Added by Stats.1975, c. 700, p. 1658, § 2.)*

§ 676. Year-round registration

"Year-round registration" is a system whereby the director designates a date for the expiration of registration of a vehicle and renewal thereof in order to equalize the volume of such renewals throughout the year. *(Added by Stats.1973, c. 889, p. 1651, § 22, eff. Sept. 28, 1973.)*

§ 676.5. Water tender vehicle

A "water tender vehicle" is a vehicle designed to carry not less than 1,500 gallons of water and used primarily for transporting and delivering water to be applied by other vehicles or pumping equipment at fire emergency scenes. *(Added by Stats.1994, c. 207 (A.B.2827), § 1, eff. July 18, 1994. Amended by Stats.1995, c. 91 (S.B.975), § 169.)*

§ 677. Repealed by Stats.1998, c. 601 (S.B.1250), § 3

§ 680. Youth bus

(a) A "youth bus" is any bus, other than a schoolbus, designed for and when actually carrying not more than 16 persons and the driver, used to transport children at or below the 12th–grade level directly from a public or private school to an organized nonschool-related youth activity within 25 miles of the school or directly from a location which provides the organized nonschool-related youth activity to a public or private school within 25 miles of that location.

(b) In addition to the destinations specified in subdivision (a), a youth bus may also be used to transport children at or below the 12th–grade level to or from their place of residence if the driver has met the requirements of Section 12523 and received additional instruction and training approved by the Department of the California Highway Patrol. *(Added by Stats.1982, c. 383, p. 1712, § 2, eff. July 4, 1982. Amended by Stats.1987, c. 723, § 2, eff. Sept. 18, 1987; Stats.1996, c. 774 (A.B.2920), § 1.)*

Division 2

ADMINISTRATION

Chapter	Section
1. The Department of Motor Vehicles	1500
2. Department of the California Highway Patrol	2100
2.5. Licenses Issued by California Highway Patrol	2500
3. The Reciprocity Commission [Repealed]	
4. Administration and Enforcement	2800
5. California Traffic Safety Program	2900
6. New Motor Vehicle Board	3000
7. Driver Certification [Repealed]	

CHAPTER 1. THE DEPARTMENT OF MOTOR VEHICLES

Article	Section
1. Organization of Department	1500
2. Powers and Duties	1650
3. Records of Department	1800

ARTICLE 1. ORGANIZATION OF DEPARTMENT

Section
1500. Department of Motor Vehicles; references to Business, Transportation and Housing Agency and Secretary of Business, Transportation and Housing.
1501. Successor to state agencies.
1502. Possession of records and property.
1503. State department provisions.
1504. Director of motor vehicles.
1505. Organization of department.
1506. Repealed.
1507. Appointment of subordinates.
1508. Repealed.

§ 1500. Department of Motor Vehicles; references to Business, Transportation and Housing Agency and Secretary of Business, Transportation and Housing

(a) There is in the Transportation Agency the Department of Motor Vehicles.

(b) Whenever the term "Business, Transportation and Housing Agency" appears within the Vehicle Code, it shall refer to the Transportation Agency, and whenever the term "Secretary of Business, Transportation and Housing" appears within the Vehicle Code, it shall refer to the Secretary of Transportation. *(Stats.1959, c. 3, p. 1541, § 1500. Amended by Stats.1961, c. 2073, p. 4331, § 3; Stats.1965, c. 493, p. 1804, § 9; Stats.1969, c. 138, p. 371, § 277, eff. Sept. 11, 1969; Stats.1984, c. 144, § 201; Gov.Reorg.Plan No. 2 of 2011–2012, § 321, eff. July 3, 2012, operative July 1, 2013; Stats.2013, c. 352 (A.B.1317), § 517, eff. Sept. 26, 2013, operative July 1, 2013.)*

Cross References

Administrative adjudication, applicability of provisions to department, see Government Code § 11501.
Adoption of seal by department, see Government Code § 11151.
Appropriation for support and operation of department, see Vehicle Code § 42271; Revenue and Taxation Code § 11003.
Assistance to other departments, see Government Code § 11253.
Attorney General as legal adviser to department, see Government Code § 11157.
Department defined, see Vehicle Code § 290.
Enforcement of orders by sheriffs, see Government Code § 11158.
Powers and duties, see Vehicle Code § 1650 et seq.
Restriction on use of name of department and false and misleading statements, see Vehicle Code § 25; Business and Professions Code § 17500.
State departments in general, see Government Code § 11150 et seq.

§ 1501. Successor to state agencies

The department is the successor to and is hereby vested with all of the powers, duties, purposes, responsibilities, and jurisdiction now or hereafter vested by law in the Department of Motor Vehicles, the Motor Vehicle Department, the Motor Vehicle Department of California, the Division of Motor Vehicles of the Department of Finance, the Division of Motor Vehicles of the Department of Public Works, and all other state agencies of similar designation, or in the several heads, members, officers, and employees of each thereof. *(Stats.1959, c. 3, p. 1541, § 1501.)*

Cross References

Effect of succession of department, see Government Code § 11159 et seq.

§ 1502. Possession of records and property

The department has possession and control of all records, books, papers, offices, equipment, moneys, funds, appropriations, and all other property, real or personal, now or hereafter held for the benefit or use of any state agency mentioned in Section 1501. *(Stats.1959, c. 3, p. 1541, § 1502.)*

Cross References

Inspection of public records, see Government Code § 6250 et seq.
Registration records and indices, see Vehicle Code § 1800.
Report and deposit of money by department, see Vehicle Code § 42270.
Safekeeping of records during emergency, see Government Code § 1229.
State agencies, reports and records, see Government Code § 11090 et seq.

Withholding, destruction, removal or mutilation of records, money or property, see Government Code § 1855.

§ 1503. State department provisions

Except as in this division otherwise provided, the provisions of Chapter 2 (commencing at Section 11150) of Part 1 of Division 3 of Title 2 of the Government Code shall govern and apply to the conduct of the department in every respect the same as if the provisions were set forth in this code, and wherever in that chapter the term "head of the department" or similar designation occurs, for the purposes of this division, it shall mean the director. *(Stats.1959, c. 3, p. 1541, § 1503. Amended by Stats.1959, c. 1996, p. 4617, § 3.)*

§ 1504. Director of motor vehicles

The department is under the control of a civil executive officer known as the Director of Motor Vehicles. The director shall be appointed by, and hold office at the pleasure of, the Governor. *(Stats.1959, c. 3, p. 1541, § 1504. Amended by Stats.1984, c. 268, § 32.2, eff. June 30, 1984.)*

Cross References

Appointment of subordinates, see Vehicle Code § 1507.
Appointments by governor, see Government Code § 1300 et seq.
Assumption of office without giving bond a misdemeanor, see Government Code § 1303.
Attorney General as legal adviser, see Government Code §§ 11042, 11157.
Attorney General to give opinions in writing, see Government Code § 12519.
Continuance in office until successor has qualified, see Government Code § 1302.
Defense of public employees, see Government Code § 995 et seq.
Director as civil executive officer, see Government Code § 1001.
Disqualification for office or employment, see Government Code § 1020 et seq.
Oath of office, in general, see Government Code § 1360 et seq.
Office and residence of directors, see Government Code §§ 1061, 11151.
Official bonds, generally, see Government Code § 1450 et seq.
Payment of expenses of public officers, see Government Code § 1367.
Powers and duties of directors, see Vehicle Code § 1650 et seq.; Revenue and Taxation Code § 10952.
Resignations, removals and vacancies, see Government Code §§ 1750 et seq., 1770 et seq., 3001 et seq.
Term of office, see Government Code § 1301.
Unlawful exercise of official functions after expiration of term, see Government Code § 1854.

§ 1505. Organization of department

The director, with the approval of the Governor and the Secretary of Transportation, shall organize the department in a manner that he or she may deem necessary to conduct the work of the department. *(Stats.1959, c. 3, p. 1541, § 1505. Amended by Stats.1969, c. 138, p. 371, § 278, eff. Sept. 11, 1969; Stats.1971, c. 509, p. 1003, § 1, operative May 3, 1972; Stats.1982, c. 454, p. 1892, § 179; Gov.Reorg.Plan No. 2 of 2011–2012, § 322, eff. July 3,*

2012, operative July 1, 2013; Stats.2013, c. 352 (A.B.1317), § 518, eff. Sept. 26, 2013, operative July 1, 2013.)

Cross References

Administration of department under Vehicle License Fee Law, see Revenue and Taxation Code §§ 10951, 10952.
Appointment of division chiefs; compensation, see Government Code § 11153.
Appointment of other employees; duties and salaries, see Government Code § 11154.
Classification and arrangement of work by department heads, see Government Code § 11152.
Drivers' licenses, in general, see Vehicle Code § 12500 et seq.
Original and renewal of registration, see Vehicle Code §§ 4150 et seq., 4600 et seq.
Registration and license fees, see Vehicle Code § 9250 et seq.
State departments in general, see Government Code § 11150 et seq.
Vehicles subject to registration, see Vehicle Code § 4000 et seq.

§ 1506. Repealed by Stats.1973, c. 551, p. 1073, § 1

§ 1507. Appointment of subordinates

The director may appoint and in accordance with law, fix the salaries of:

(a) A deputy director.

(b) Such other officers, deputies, technical experts, and employees as may be necessary for the proper discharge of the duties of the department. *(Stats.1959, c. 3, p. 1542, § 1507.)*

Cross References

Additional powers and duties of director, see Vehicle Code §§ 1650 et seq., 4453; Revenue and Taxation Code § 10952.
Chiefs of divisions, appointment of, see Government Code § 11153.
Delegation of powers and duties, see Vehicle Code § 8.
Director may require aides to file bond, see Government Code § 14625.
Director to fix salaries, see Revenue and Taxation Code § 10952.
Oath of office in general, see Government Code § 1360 et seq.
Qualifications and removal from office, see Government Code § 1364 et seq.
Resignations, removals and vacancies, see Government Code §§ 1750 et seq., 1770 et seq., 3001 et seq.
Salaries of state personnel, see Government Code § 18000 et seq.
Terms of office in general, see Government Code § 1301.

§ 1508. Repealed by Stats.1977, c. 516, p. 1656, § 1, operative Dec. 31, 1979

ARTICLE 2. POWERS AND DUTIES

Section
1650.   Administration and enforcement.
1651.   Rules and regulations.
1651.2. Occupational license and permit requirements; offenses; injunctive relief.
1651.3. Commercial driver's licenses; policies to assist armed services personnel.

Section

1651.5. Conversion to year-round registration.

1652. Forms; signature upon applications or documents.

1653. Grant or refusal of applications.

1653.5. Forms; required numbers.

1653.5. Forms; required numbers.

1653.5. Forms; required numbers.

1654. Real property.

1655. Peace officer powers; inspection of vehicles for investigation of title and registration.

1656. Publishing Vehicle Code and related laws; synopsis or summary of laws regulating operation of vehicles and use of highways; distribution.

1656.2. Printed summary of penalties; warning.

1656.3. Material to be included in California Driver's Handbook.

1656.4. Consumer information; internet web site.

1656.5. Message display systems; advertising.

1657. Driver education.

1658. Membership in associations dealing with related subjects.

1659. Driver education and training.

1659.9. Repealed.

1660. Retention and inspection of records by nonprofit institution or organization selling vehicles.

1660.5. Repealed.

1660.6. Repealed.

1660.7. Repealed.

1660.8. Repealed.

1661. Registration renewal fee; due date; notification.

1662. Investigation of dismantler violations.

1663. Shoulder harness; warning regarding lack thereof.

1664. Safe Streets Act of 1994; duty to publicize.

1665. Occupational licenses; time of renewal.

1666. Driver's examination; knowledge of blood alcohol concentration; inclusion of information with license and vehicle registration and renewal.

1666.1. Driver's examination; knowledge of risks and punishments associated with eluding police.

1666.5. Driver's examination; question relating to abandonment or dumping of any animal.

1667. Motor vehicle registration; notice of smog indexing program; form.

1668. Fingerprint service; fee.

1669. Promptness in serving the public; legislative intent; posting hours of operation.

1670. Division between types of business involving vehicles or component parts; inspection of business.

1671. Established place of business; office; display or manufacturing area; dismantling area.

1672. Anatomical gifts; drivers license or identification card designation; signs, notices, pamphlets and brochures.

1672.3. Driver's license and identification card inventory; depletion date; notice.

1672.5. Anatomical gifts; sticker affixed to driver's license or identification card.

1673. Refunding of smog impact fee; "registered owner or lessee".

1673.2. Refunding of smog impact fee; duties of department; interest on claims; filing of claims.

1673.4. Refunding of smog impact fee; time for filing claims; notification of eligibility; disputed claims; parties to law suits.

1673.5. Refunding of smog impact fee; recovering erroneously paid refunds.

Section

1673.6. Refunding of smog impact fee; violations; penalties.

1673.7. Refunding of smog impact fee; notice.

1674. Program of encouragement.

1674.2. Repealed.

1674.4. Sensitivity training for test administrators.

1674.6. Finding and declaration; intent to provide transportation alternatives; task force.

1675. Mature driver improvement courses.

1676. Mature driver improvement courses; fees.

1677. Providers of mature driver improvement courses; fees for approval; responsibilities.

1678. Base fee amounts; adjustment of fees.

1679. Notice to prospective voters; delayed receipt of requested voter registration information.

1680. Repealed.

1685. Vehicle registration and titling transactions; establishment of contracts for electronic programs; transaction fee.

1685.1. Repealed.

§ 1650. Administration and enforcement

The director shall administer and enforce the provisions of this code relating to the department. *(Stats.1959, c. 3, p. 1542, § 1650.)*

Cross References

Additional powers and duties of directors, see Government Code § 11150 et seq.

Approval of contracts, see Government Code § 13325; Public Contract Code § 10295.

Contracts affecting realty, approval by director of general services, see Government Code § 11005.

Office of director, creation, see Vehicle Code § 1504.

Organization of department by director, see Vehicle Code § 1505.

§ 1651. Rules and regulations

(a) The director may adopt and enforce rules and regulations as may be necessary to carry out the provisions of this code relating to the department.

(b) Rules and regulations shall be adopted, amended, or repealed in accordance with the Administrative Procedure Act (Chapter 3.5 (commencing with Section 11340) of Part 1 of Division 3 of Title 2 of the Government Code). *(Stats.1959, c. 3, p. 1542, § 1961. Amended by Stats.1959, c. 1996, p. 4617, § 3.5; Stats.1965, c. 1500, p. 3522, § 2; Stats.2003, c. 594 (S.B.315), § 13.)*

Cross References

Commissioner's powers and duties as department head, see Vehicle Code § 2400 et seq.; Government Code §§ 11153, 11154.

Effect of succession of department, see Government Code § 11159 et seq.

Manufacturers, transporters and dealers, license suspension or revocation for violation of rules adopted pursuant to this section, see Vehicle Code § 11705.

Succession of department to ownership of property and control of records, see Vehicle Code § 2104.

§ 1651.2. Occupational license and permit requirements; offenses; injunctive relief

Whenever in the judgment of the department, any person has engaged, or is about to engage, in any acts or practices that constitute, or will constitute, an offense against Division 5 (commencing with Section 11100) by engaging in any act subject to license requirements without having obtained a license, the department may apply to the appropriate court for an order enjoining the acts or practices, and, upon showing by the department that the person has engaged, or is about to engage, in any of those acts or practices, an injunction, restraining order, or other order that may be appropriate shall be granted by the court, including the costs incurred by the department in obtaining the order. *(Added by Stats.1994, c. 584 (A.B.3312), § 1.)*

§ 1651.3. Commercial driver's licenses; policies to assist armed services personnel

It is the policy of this state to recognize the training and experience that individuals gain while serving in the armed forces of the United States. In furtherance of this policy, the department, in conjunction with the military services of the United States, shall develop policies to assist persons who are leaving active duty to obtain commercial driver's licenses. These policies shall not waive any requisites, fees, or examinations required by law for a commercial driver's license. These policies shall specify how this training and experience may be used to obtain these licenses. The department shall consult with the Department of Veterans Affairs before adopting these policies. The department shall perform the duties required by this section within existing budgetary resources of the agency within which the department operates. *(Added by Stats.1994, c. 987 (S.B.1646), § 3, eff. Sept. 29, 1994.)*

§ 1651.5. Conversion to year-round registration

(a) The director may assign or reassign dates for the expiration of registration for a vehicle registered pursuant to this code. The director may establish a registration year for any vehicle consisting of any period from seven months to 18 months, inclusive, with subsequent renewals being required at yearly intervals thereafter. The director shall assign an expiration date of the last day of the calendar month to all trailers and to all motor vehicles subject to additional fees under the provisions of Section 9400. Any vehicle being registered on a quarterly basis shall be assigned or reassigned an expiration date of December 31 for the registration year. The director shall have the authority to exclude from year-round registration any type of vehicle that the director deems appropriate for exclusion.

(b) In order to implement a year-round registration for vehicles registered pursuant to the International Registration Plan as described in Article 4 (commencing with Section 8050) of Chapter 4 of Division 3, the director, on or before January 1, 2009, shall assign or reassign a date for the expiration of registration of those vehicles described in this subdivision and may utilize the applicable practices and procedures set forth under subdivision (a) in order to implement this subdivision. *(Added by Stats.1973, c. 889, p. 1651, § 24, eff. Sept. 28, 1973.*

Amended by Stats.1974, c. 1330, p. 2892, § 14, eff. Sept. 26, 1974; Stats.2006, c. 169 (A.B.2736), § 1.)

Cross References

Apportioned registration, federal motor vehicle safety program, see Vehicle Code § 8100 et seq.
Registration renewal fee, apportioned increase or decrease, see Vehicle Code § 9559.5.

§ 1652. Forms; signature upon applications or documents

(a) The department shall prescribe and provide suitable forms of applications, certificates of ownership, registration cards, drivers' licenses, and all other forms requisite or deemed necessary for the purposes of this code and shall prepay all transportation charges thereon.

(b) The department may require that any application or document filed with the department be signed and submitted under penalty of perjury. *(Stats.1959, c. 3, p. 1542, § 1652. Amended by Stats.1982, c. 830, p. 3147, § 1.)*

Cross References

Applications,
  Drivers' licenses, see Vehicle Code § 12800.
  Registration of special vehicles, see Vehicle Code § 4153.
  Registration of vehicle previously registered out of state, see Vehicle Code § 4300.
  Registration of vehicles, see Vehicle Code § 4150.
  Special construction and mobile equipment, see Vehicle Code § 5015.
Certificate of ownership and registration card, issuance, see Vehicle Code § 4450 et seq.
Drivers licenses in general,
  Generally, see Vehicle Code § 12500 et seq.
  Contents, see Vehicle Code § 12811.
License plates or stickers, see Vehicle Code §§ 4850, 4853.
One-trip permits, see Vehicle Code § 4003.
Ownership certificate, contents, see Vehicle Code § 4451.
Questions on race or religion in forms a misdemeanor, see Government Code § 8310.
Registration card, contents, see Vehicle Code § 4453.
Restricted licenses, issuance, see Vehicle Code § 12813.
Student licenses, see Vehicle Code § 12650.

§ 1653. Grant or refusal of applications

The department shall examine and determine the genuineness and regularity of every application or document filed with it under this code and may require additional information or reject any such application or document if not satisfied of the genuineness and regularity thereof or the truth of any statement contained therein. *(Stats.1959, c. 3, p. 1542, § 1653. Amended by Stats.1961, c. 58, p. 1003, § 7, eff. March 31, 1961.)*

Cross References

Application for,
  Drivers' license, see Vehicle Code § 12800.
  Registration in general, see Vehicle Code § 4150.
  Registration of vehicle previously registered out of state, see Vehicle Code § 4300.
  Transfer by transferee, see Vehicle Code § 5902.

Driver's licenses in general, see Vehicle Code § 12500 et seq.

False statements, concealment of facts, see Vehicle Code § 20.

Original and renewal of registration of motor vehicles, see Vehicle Code § 4000 et seq.

Refusal of registration, see Vehicle Code §§ 4750, 4751.

Registration and license fees, see Vehicle Code § 9250 et seq.

Registration card and certificate of ownership, contents, see Vehicle Code §§ 4451, 4453.

Transfers of title or interest, see Vehicle Code § 5600 et seq.

§ 1653.5. Forms; required numbers

Section operative until the sooner of Jan. 1, 2015 or the date the director executes a declaration pursuant to § 12801.11. See, also, section operative the sooner of Jan. 1, 2015 or the date the director executes a declaration pursuant to § 12801.11 and operative until the effective date of a judicial determination that any provision of Stats.2013, c. 524 (A.B.60) is enjoined, found unconstitutional or held invalid, and section operative the effective date of a judicial determination that any provision of Stats.2013, c. 524 (A.B.60) is enjoined, found unconstitutional or held invalid.

(a) Every form prescribed by the department for use by an applicant for the issuance or renewal by the department of a driver's license or identification card pursuant to Division 6 (commencing with Section 12500) shall contain a section for the applicant's social security account number.

(b) Every form prescribed by the department for use by an applicant for the issuance, renewal, or transfer of the registration or certificate of title to a vehicle shall contain a section for the applicant's driver's license or identification card number.

(c) A person who submits to the department a form that, pursuant to subdivision (a), contains a section for the applicant's social security account number, or pursuant to subdivision (b), the applicant's driver's license or identification card number, if any, shall furnish the appropriate number in the space provided.

(d) The department shall not complete an application that does not include the applicant's social security account number or driver's license or identification card number as required under subdivision (c).

(e) An applicant's social security account number shall not be included by the department on a driver's license, identification card, registration, certificate of title, or any other document issued by the department.

(f) Notwithstanding any other * * * law, information regarding an applicant's social security account number, obtained by the department pursuant to this section, is not a public record and may not be disclosed by the department except for any of the following purposes:

(1) Responding to a request for information from an agency operating pursuant to, and carrying out the provisions of, Part A (Aid to Families with Dependent Children), or Part D (Child Support and Establishment of Paternity), of Subchapter IV of Chapter 7 of Title 42 of the United States Code.

(2) Implementation of Section 12419.10 of the Government Code.

(3) Responding to information requests from the Franchise Tax Board for the purpose of tax administration.

(g) This section shall become inoperative on January 1, 2015, or on the date that the director executes a declaration pursuant to Section 12801.11, whichever is sooner, and as of January 1, 2015, is repealed, unless a later enacted statute, that is enacted before January 1, 2015, deletes or extends that date. *(Added by Stats.1991, c. 772 (S.B.395), § 1. Amended by Stats.1992, c. 635 (A.B.1823), § 3, eff. Sept. 14, 1992; Stats.1994, c. 1221 (S.B.1758), § 1; Stats.1997, c. 619 (S.B.506), § 6; Stats. 2003, c. 326 (S.B.60), § 1; Stats.2003–2004, 3rd Ex.Sess., c. 1 (S.B.1), § 1, eff. Dec. 4, 2003, operative Jan. 1, 2004; Stats.2013, c. 524 (A.B.60), § 3.)*

Inoperative Date and Repeal

For inoperative date and repeal of this section, see its terms.

Cross References

Marriage, change of name, see Family Code § 306.5.

Offset of amounts overdue and unpaid for fines, penalties, assessments, bail, vehicle parking penalties, or court-ordered reimbursement for court-related services, obtaining of social security number by Franchise Tax Board, see Government Code § 12419.10.

Registered domestic partnership, change of name, see Family Code § 298.6.

§ 1653.5. Forms; required numbers

Section operative the sooner of Jan. 1, 2015 or the date the director executes a declaration pursuant to § 12801.11 and operative until the effective date of a judicial determination that any provision of the act that added this section is enjoined, found unconstitutional or held invalid. See, also, section operative until the sooner of Jan. 1, 2015 or the date the director executes a declaration pursuant to § 12801.11, and section operative the effective date of a judicial determination that any provision of the act that added this section is enjoined, found unconstitutional or held invalid.

(a) Each form prescribed by the department for use by an applicant for the issuance or renewal by the department of a driver's license or identification card pursuant to Division 6 (commencing with Section 12500) shall contain a section for the applicant's social security account number.

(b) Each form prescribed by the department for use by an applicant for the issuance, renewal, or transfer of the registration or certificate of title to a vehicle shall contain a section for the applicant's driver's license or identification card number.

(c) Except as provided in Section 12801, a person who submits to the department a form that, pursuant to subdivision (a), contains a section for the applicant's social security account number, or pursuant to subdivision (b), the applicant's driver's license or identification card number, if any, shall furnish the appropriate number in the space provided.

(d) Except as provided in Section 12801, the department shall not complete an application that does not include the applicant's social security account number or driver's license or identification card number as required under subdivision (c).

(e) An applicant's social security account number shall not be included by the department on a driver's license, identification card, registration, certificate of title, or any other document issued by the department.

(f) Notwithstanding any other law, information regarding an applicant's social security account number, obtained by the department pursuant to this section, is not a public record and shall not be disclosed by the department except for any of the following purposes:

(1) Responding to a request for information from an agency operating pursuant to, and carrying out the provisions of, Part A (Aid to Families with Dependent Children), or Part D (Child Support and Establishment of Paternity), of Subchapter IV of Chapter 7 of Title 42 of the United States Code.

(2) Implementation of Section 12419.10 of the Government Code.

(3) Responding to information requests from the Franchise Tax Board for the purpose of tax administration.

(g) This section shall become operative on January 1, 2015, or on the date that the director executes a declaration pursuant to Section 12801.11, whichever is sooner.

(h) This section shall become inoperative on the effective date of a final judicial determination made by any court of appellate jurisdiction that any provision of the act that added this section, or its application, either in whole or in part, is enjoined, found unconstitutional, or held invalid for any reason. The department shall post this information on its Internet Web site. *(Added by Stats.2013, c. 524 (A.B.60), § 4, operative contingent.)*

Operative Effect

For operative effect of this section, see its terms.

Cross References

Marriage, change of name, see Family Code § 306.5.
Offset of amounts overdue and unpaid for fines, penalties, assessments, bail, vehicle parking penalties, or court-ordered reimbursement for court-related services, obtaining of social security number by Franchise Tax Board, see Government Code § 12419.10.

Registered domestic partnership, change of name, see Family Code § 298.6.

§ 1653.5. Forms; required numbers

Section operative the effective date of a judicial determination that any provision of the act that added this section is enjoined, found unconstitutional or held invalid. See, also, section operative until the sooner of Jan. 1, 2015 or the date the director executes a declaration pursuant to § 12801.11, and section operative the sooner of Jan. 1, 2015 or the date the director executes a declaration pursuant to § 12801.11 and operative until the effective date of a judicial determination that any provision of the act that added this section is enjoined, found unconstitutional or held invalid.

(a) Each form prescribed by the department for use by an applicant for the issuance or renewal by the department of a driver's license or identification card pursuant to Division 6 (commencing with Section 12500) shall contain a section for the applicant's social security account number.

(b) Each form prescribed by the department for use by an applicant for the issuance, renewal, or transfer of the registration or certificate of title to a vehicle shall contain a section for the applicant's driver's license or identification card number.

(c) A person who submits to the department a form that, pursuant to subdivision (a), contains a section for the applicant's social security account number, or pursuant to subdivision (b), the applicant's driver's license or identification card number, if any, shall furnish the appropriate number in the space provided.

(d) The department shall not complete an application that does not include the applicant's social security account number or driver's license or identification card number as required under subdivision (c).

(e) An applicant's social security account number shall not be included by the department on a driver's license, identification card, registration, certificate of title, or any other document issued by the department.

(f) Notwithstanding any other law, information regarding an applicant's social security account number, obtained by the department pursuant to this section, is not a public record and may not be disclosed by the department except for any of the following purposes:

(1) Responding to a request for information from an agency operating pursuant to, and carrying out the provisions of, Part A (Aid to Families with Dependent Children), or Part D (Child Support and Establishment of Paternity), of Subchapter IV of Chapter 7 of Title 42 of the United States Code.

(2) Implementation of Section 12419.10 of the Government Code.

(3) Responding to information requests from the Franchise Tax Board for the purpose of tax administration.

(g) This section shall become operative on the effective date of a final judicial determination made by any court of appellate jurisdiction that any provision of the act that added this section, or its application, either in whole or in part, is enjoined, found unconstitutional, or held invalid for any reason. The department shall post this information on its Internet Web site. *(Added by Stats.2013, c. 524 (A.B.60), § 5, operative contingent.)*

Operative Effect

For operative effect of this section, see its terms.

Cross References

Marriage, change of name, see Family Code § 306.5.

Offset of amounts overdue and unpaid for fines, penalties, assessments, bail, vehicle parking penalties, or court-ordered reimbursement for court-related services, obtaining of social security number by Franchise Tax Board, see Government Code § 12419.10.

Registered domestic partnership, change of name, see Family Code § 298.6.

§ 1654. Real property

The director may purchase or lease such real estate and erect such buildings as the department or any of its divisions require, subject to the approval of the Department of General Services. *(Stats.1959, c. 3, p. 1542, § 1654. Amended by Stats.1965, c. 371, p. 1598, § 285.)*

Cross References

Department of General Services, see Government Code § 14600 et seq.

§ 1655. Peace officer powers; inspection of vehicles for investigation of title and registration

(a) The director and deputy director of the department, the Deputy Director, Investigations Division, the Chief, Field Investigations Branch, and the investigators of the department, including rank-and-file, supervisory, and management personnel, shall have the powers of peace officers for the purpose of enforcing those provisions of law committed to the administration of the department or enforcing the law on premises occupied by the department.

(b) Any person designated in subdivision (a) may inspect any vehicle of a type required to be registered under this code, or any component part thereof, in any garage, repair shop, parking lot, used car lot, automobile dismantler's lot, steel mill, scrap metal processing facility, or other establishment engaged in the business of selling, repairing, or dismantling vehicles, or reducing vehicles or the integral parts thereof to their component materials for the purpose of investigating the title and registration of the vehicle, inspecting wrecked or dismantled vehicles, or locating stolen vehicles. *(Stats.1959, c. 3, p. 1542, § 1655. Amended by Stats.1961, c. 1274, p. 3051, § 1; Stats.1968, c. 1222, p. 2330, § 75; Stats.1974, c. 613, p.*

1459, § 2; Stats.1982, c. 830, p. 3147, § 2; Stats.2000, c. 1035 (S.B.1403), § 4; Stats.2004, c. 615 (S.B.1233), § 18.)

Cross References

False information to peace officer, see Vehicle Code § 31.

Minimum standards for public officers of employees having powers of peace officers, see Government Code § 1031.

Peace officers, generally, see Penal Code § 830 et seq.

§ 1656. Publishing Vehicle Code and related laws; synopsis or summary of laws regulating operation of vehicles and use of highways; distribution

(a) The department shall publish the complete text of the California Vehicle Code together with other laws relating to the use of highways or the operation of motor vehicles once every two years. The department, upon written request of any state or local governmental officer or agency, any federal agency, any public secondary school in this state, or any other person, shall distribute the California Vehicle Code at a charge sufficient to pay the entire cost of publishing and distributing the code. With regard to public secondary schools, the quantities shall be sufficient to provide one copy for each driver training and education instructor and one copy for each public secondary school library. In determining the amount of the charge, a fraction of a dollar shall be disregarded, unless it exceeds fifty cents ($0.50), in which case it shall be treated as one full dollar ($1). The receipts from the sale of such publications shall be deposited in the Motor Vehicle Account, with the intent to reimburse the department for the entire cost to print and distribute the Vehicle Code.

(b) The department shall publish a synopsis or summary of the laws regulating the operation of vehicles and the use of the highways and may deliver a copy thereof without charge with each original vehicle registration and with each original driver's license. The department shall publish such number of copies of the synopsis or summary in the Spanish language as the director determines are needed to meet the demand for such copies. The department shall furnish both English and Spanish copies to its field offices and to law enforcement agencies for general distribution and, when it does so, shall furnish the copies without charge. *(Stats.1959, c. 3, p. 1542, § 1656. Amended by Stats.1961, c. 286, p. 1319, § 1; Stats.1963, c. 686, p. 1692, § 1; Stats.1968, c. 955, p. 1839, § 1; Stats.1978, c. 380, p. 1202, § 142; Stats.1978, c. 818, p. 2606, § 2; Stats.2002, c. 805 (A.B.2996), § 8, eff. Sept. 23, 2002.)*

Cross References

Appropriations for support and operation of department, see Vehicle Code § 42271.

Authority for the appropriation of money in the Motor Vehicle License Fee Fund, see Revenue and Taxation Code § 11002.

Department to tabulate and disseminate traffic accident information, see Vehicle Code § 2408.

Information relating to leaving child unattended in motor vehicle, inclusion in handbook, see Vehicle Code § 15632.

§ 1656.2. Printed summary of penalties; warning

The department shall prepare and publish a printed summary describing the penalties for noncompliance with Sections 16000 and 16028, which shall be included with each motor vehicle registration, registration renewal, and transfer of registration and with each driver's license and license renewal. The printed summary may contain, but is not limited to, the following wording:

"IMPORTANT FACTS ABOUT ENFORCEMENT OF CALIFORNIA'S COMPULSORY FINANCIAL RESPONSIBILITY LAW

California law requires every driver to carry written evidence of valid automobile liability insurance, a thirty-five thousand dollar ($35,000) bond, a thirty-five thousand dollar ($35,000) cash deposit, or a certificate of self-insurance that has been issued by the Department of Motor Vehicles.

You must provide evidence of financial responsibility when you renew the registration of a motor vehicle, and after you are cited by a peace officer for a traffic violation or are involved in any traffic accident. The law requires that you provide the officer with the name and address of your insurer and the policy identification number. Your insurer will provide written evidence of this number. Failure to provide evidence of your financial responsibility can result in fines of up to five hundred dollars ($500) and loss of your driver's license. Falsification of evidence can result in fines of up to seven hundred fifty dollars ($750) or 30 days in jail, or both, in addition to a one-year suspension of driving privileges.

Under existing California law, if you are involved in an accident that results in damages of over seven hundred fifty dollars ($750) to the property of any person or in any injury or fatality, you must file a report of the accident with the Department of Motor Vehicles within 10 days of the accident. If you fail to file a report or fail to provide evidence of financial responsibility on the report, your driving privilege will be suspended for up to four years. Your suspension notice will notify you of the department's action and of your right to a hearing. Your suspension notice will also inform you that if you request a hearing, it must be conducted within 30 days of your written request, and that a decision is to be rendered within 15 days of the conclusion of the hearing." *(Added by Stats.1984, c. 1324, § 1. Amended by Stats.1988, c. 1156, § 1, eff. Sept. 22, 1988, operative Nov. 30, 1988; Stats.1996, c. 124 (A.B.3470), § 114; Stats.2000, c. 375 (A.B.1331), § 15; Stats.2000, c. 787 (S.B.1404), § 16; Stats.2002, c. 766 (S.B.1590), § 1.)*

§ 1656.3. Material to be included in California Driver's Handbook

(a) The department shall include within the California Driver's Handbook, as specified in subdivision (b) of Section 1656, language regarding each of the following:

(1) Rail transit safety.

(2) Abandonment or dumping of any animal on a highway.

(3) The importance of respecting the right-of-way of others, particularly pedestrians, bicycle riders, and motorcycle riders.

(b) In order to minimize costs, the language referred to in paragraphs (2) and (3) of subdivision (a) shall be initially included at the earliest opportunity when the handbook is otherwise revised or reprinted. *(Added by Stats.1993, c. 722 (A.B.1035), § 6. Amended by Stats. 2001, c. 300 (S.B.237), § 1; Stats.2006, c. 898 (S.B.1021), § 1.)*

§ 1656.4. Consumer information; internet web site

(a) The department, in consultation with the Department of Consumer Affairs, shall make available on its Internet web site, on or before July 1, 1997, information to assist consumers who plan to purchase a vehicle or who have purchased a vehicle. The information shall, at a minimum, contain the names, addresses, electronic addresses, and telephone numbers of all of the following:

(1) State and federal government agencies that deal with consumer affairs and vehicles.

(2) Vehicle arbitration services.

(3) Consumer organizations that provide information and direct assistance to consumers with vehicle concerns.

(b) Money deposited in the Consumer Fraud Protection Program Fund shall be available, upon appropriation by the Legislature, for the consumer protection activities of the department, including, but not limited to, expenditures by the department to comply with the requirements specified in subdivision (a). *(Added by Stats.1996, c. 722 (A.B.1383), § 1.)*

§ 1656.5. Message display systems; advertising

(a) The Legislature finds that the department, by virtue of its interaction with millions of California drivers and vehicle owners each year, represents a valuable resource for the disbursement of important public safety and consumer information.

(b) The department may enter into a contract with a private vendor for the purpose of acquiring and utilizing message display systems. These systems may be used on the department's mailings or other property owned, leased, or controlled by the department. The information displayed shall be of appropriate benefit to the motoring public and the state's consumers, as determined by the department.

(c) A vendor under contract with the department may utilize a portion of the available time and space on the display systems that it provides for the purpose of advertising products or services. The advertising on a message display system shall not exceed 15 minutes in a 60–minute period. The extent of the access shall be established under the terms of the contract.

(d) The department shall determine whether a vendor's advertised product or service is consistent with and appropriate to the best interests of the motoring public. The department shall not enter into a contract with a vendor whose advertised product or service the department determines is not consistent with or appropriate to the best interests of the motoring public. *(Added by Stats.2007, c. 407 (A.B.1139), § 1.)*

§ 1657. Driver education

The director may assign qualified employees of the department to advise with the State Board of Education and with the governing boards of districts maintaining secondary schools in the preparation, establishment, and conduct of courses in automobile driver education and automobile driver training in secondary schools under the provisions of the Education Code. *(Stats.1959, c. 3, p. 1543, § 1657. Amended by Stats.1961, c. 58, p. 1003, § 8, eff. March 31, 1961; Stats.1971, c. 438, p. 904, § 179, operative May 3, 1972.)*

Cross References

Automobile driver training costs, see Education Code §§ 41304, 41900 et seq.
Civil liability of public entities in operation of motor vehicles, see Vehicle Code § 17000 et seq.
Compliance with rules and regulations of state board of education on training drivers, see Education Code § 41905.
Driving on school property, restrictions, see Vehicle Code § 21113.
Driving schools and driving instructors, see Vehicle Code § 11100 et seq.
Power of local authorities to close streets during training programs, see Vehicle Code § 21101.

§ 1658. Membership in associations dealing with related subjects

The department may pay membership fees, join, and participate in affairs of associations having for their purpose the interchange of information relating to the registration of vehicles and the issuance of operators' licenses, financial responsibility, and subjects relating to highway safety and to the powers and duties of the department. *(Stats.1959, c. 3, p. 1543, § 1658.)*

§ 1659. Driver education and training

The department may develop criteria, establish standards for, and coordinate a program of motor vehicle driver education and motor vehicle driver training for drivers whose licenses have been suspended or revoked.

The purpose of the program shall be to promote safe driving. To carry out this purpose the department may seek the advice or cooperation of the schools, courts, and other interested persons. *(Added by Stats.1965, c. 447, p. 1758, § 1.)*

§ 1659.9. Repealed by Stats.2006, c. 282 (A.B.2542), § 1, operative Jan. 1, 2012

§ 1660. Retention and inspection of records by nonprofit institution or organization selling vehicles

(a) Any institution or organization described in subdivision (*o*) of Section 286 shall keep the following records for not less than three years:

(1) The name and address of each vehicle donor and the year, make, vehicle identification number, and, if available, the license plate number of the donated vehicle.

(2) An itemized listing by vehicle identification number of the date each vehicle was donated, the date sold, and the amount for which it was sold.

(3) If the donated vehicle is being sold by an institution or organization on behalf of another institution or organization pursuant to paragraph (2) of subdivision (*o*) of Section 286, the following documentation shall be retained in the following manner:

(A) A signed, written agreement shall remain on the premises that identifies the percentage of the proceeds that may be retained by the selling institution or organization, a statement that each vehicle meets, or, unless sold at wholesale, by the time of sale will meet, the equipment requirements of Division 12 (commencing with Section 24000), and a statement that each vehicle is in compliance, or, unless sold at wholesale, at the time of sale will be in compliance, with emission control certification requirements pursuant to subdivision (b) of Section 44015 of the Health and Safety Code.

(B) A separate listing that identifies each vehicle by year, make, and vehicle identification number.

(C) All itemized listings pursuant to subparagraph (D) of paragraph (2) of subdivision (*o*) of Section 286.

(D) The selling institution or organization shall retain all documentation pertaining to the sale of vehicles on behalf of another institution or organization in the same manner as is required for the sale of vehicles donated to the selling institution or organization.

(b) The department may inspect the records of any nonprofit institution or organization that obtains donated vehicles in order to ascertain whether it meets the conditions specified in subdivision (*o*) of Section 286. *(Added by Stats.1992, c. 127 (A.B.2273), § 2. Amended by Stats.2001, c. 460 (A.B.871), § 2.)*

§ 1660.5. Repealed by Stats.1998, c. 877 (A.B.2132), § 33

§ 1660.6. Repealed by Stats.1990, c. 1455 (S.B.2374), § 27

§ 1660.7. Repealed by Stats.1984, c. 904, § 2, operative July 1, 1987

§ 1660.8. Repealed by Stats.1987, c. 1075, § 1, eff. July 1, 1988

§ 1661. Registration renewal fee; due date; notification

(a) Except for vehicles registered pursuant to Article 5 (commencing with Section 9700) of Chapter 6 of Division 3, the department shall notify the registered owner of each vehicle of the date that the registration renewal fees for the vehicle are due, at least 60 days prior to that due date. The department shall indicate the fact that the required notice was mailed by a notation in the department's records.

(b) The department shall include in any final notice of delinquent registration provided to the registered owner of a vehicle whose registration has not been properly renewed as required under this code, information relating to the potential removal and impoundment of that vehicle under subdivision (o) of Section 22651.

(c) Commencing on May 1, 2011, subdivision (a) shall not apply to vehicles with registration expiring on or after July 1, 2011. This subdivision shall become inoperative on January 1, 2012. (Added by Stats.1992, c. 1241 (S.B.1615), § 6.5. Amended by Stats.1999, c. 22 (S.B.24), § 4, operative May 26, 1999; Stats.2002, c. 805 (A.B.2996), § 9, eff. Sept. 23, 2002; Stats.2011, c. 21 (S.B.94), § 2, eff. May 4, 2011.)

§ 1662. Investigation of dismantler violations

Notwithstanding any other provision of law, the department shall have no duty to investigate alleged violations of the provisions of Chapter 3 (commencing with Section 11500) of Division 5 by any person defined as an "automobile dismantler" by subdivision (b) of Section 220 and Section 221, unless notice of such alleged violations has been given the department by the district attorney, county counsel, city attorney, or other duly constituted law enforcement agency. (Added by Stats. 1971, c. 1624, p. 3496, § 1.5, operative May 3, 1972. Amended by Stats.1979, c. 373, p. 1380, § 313.)

§ 1663. Shoulder harness; warning regarding lack thereof

(a) The department shall, in the synopsis or summary of laws regulating the operation of vehicles and the use of the highways published under subdivision (b) of Section 1656, provide a warning which states that, in certain accidents, the lack of a shoulder harness may cause, or aggravate, serious and fatal injuries, especially to the head, spinal column, and abdominal organs.

(b) Nothing in this section limits or impairs the rights or remedies that are otherwise available to any person under existing law. (Added by Stats.1992, c. 562 (A.B. 1751), § 1. Amended by Stats.1998, c. 877 (A.B.2132), § 34.)

§ 1664. Safe Streets Act of 1994; duty to publicize

The department shall publicize the Safe Streets Act of 1994 when mailing vehicle registrations, driver's licenses, and driver's license suspension and revocation notices, and in other educational materials made available by the department. (Added by Stats.1994, c. 1133 (A.B.3148), § 2.)

§ 1665. Occupational licenses; time of renewal

Notwithstanding any other provision of law, the department by rule or regulation may provide for the issuance and renewal on a two-year basis of licenses or other indicia of authority issued pursuant to this code by the department or any agency in the department.

The department may, by rule or regulation, set the fee for such two-year license, certificate of registration, or other indicia, not to exceed twice the annual fee for issuance or renewal set by statute.

This section shall not apply to any driver's license or vehicle or vessel license or certificate of registration issued pursuant to this code. (Added by Stats.1975, c. 57, p. 105, § 3.)

§ 1666. Driver's examination; knowledge of blood alcohol concentration; inclusion of information with license and vehicle registration and renewal

The department shall do all of the following:

(a) Include at least one question in each test of an applicant's knowledge and understanding of the provisions of this code, as administered pursuant to Section 12804 or 12814, to verify that the applicant has read and understands the table of blood alcohol concentration published in the Driver's Handbook made available pursuant to subdivision (b) of Section 1656. In order to minimize costs, the question or questions shall be initially included at the earliest opportunity when the test is otherwise revised or reprinted.

(b) Include with each driver's license or certificate of renewal and each vehicle registration renewal mailed by the department, information that shows with reasonable certainty the amount of alcohol consumption necessary for a person to reach a 0.08 percent blood alcohol concentration by weight.

(c) Include at least one question in each test of an applicant's knowledge and understanding of the provisions of this code as administered pursuant to Section 12804 or 12814, to verify that the applicant has read and understands the rights of pedestrians. In order to minimize costs, the question or questions shall be initially included at the earliest opportunity when the test is otherwise revised or reprinted. (Added by Stats.1984, c. 54, § 1, eff. March 28, 1984, operative Aug. 1, 1984. Amended by Stats.1989, c. 479, § 1; Stats.2000, c. 135 (A.B.2539), § 154; Stats.2000, c. 833 (A.B.2522), § 4.)

§ 1666.1. Driver's examination; knowledge of risks and punishments associated with eluding police

Upon updating the California Driver's Handbook, the department shall include at least one question in any of the noncommercial driver's license examinations, as administered under Section 12804.9, of an applicant's knowledge and understanding of this code, to verify that the applicant has an understanding of the risks and punishments associated with eluding a pursuing officer's motor vehicle. *(Added by Stats.2005, c. 485 (S.B.719), § 5.)*

Cross References

Fleeing a police officer while operating a motor vehicle, penalty, see Vehicle Code § 2800.1.
Vehicle pursuit reports filed by law enforcement agency, contents, see Vehicle Code § 14602.1.

§ 1666.5. Driver's examination; question relating to abandonment or dumping of any animal

The department shall include, on a rotating basis, at least one question in at least 20 percent of the tests of an applicant's knowledge and understanding of the provisions of this code, as administered pursuant to Section 12803 or 12814, to verify that the applicant has read and understands that the abandonment or dumping of any animal is a criminal offense that can create a severe traffic safety hazard. *(Added by Stats.2001, c. 300 (S.B. 237), § 2.)*

§ 1667. Motor vehicle registration; notice of smog indexing program; form

Operation contingent upon fulfillment of conditions specified in Stats.1994, c. 1192 (S.B.2050), § 32.

(a) As part of its motor vehicle registration and registration renewal process, other than upon the initial registration of a new motor vehicle, the department shall inform motor vehicle owners of the vehicle smog indexing program. That notice shall be in the form developed by the State Air Resources Board in consultation with the department pursuant to subdivision (c) of Section 44254 of the Health and Safety Code.

(b) This section shall become inoperative five years from the date determined pursuant to Section 32 of the act adding this section, and on the January 1 following that date is repealed. *(Added by Stats.1994, c. 1192 (S.B.2050), § 31.1.)*

Repeal

By its own terms, this section becomes inoperative 5 years after its operative date and is repealed the following Jan. 1.

§ 1668. Fingerprint service; fee

(a) The department may provide fingerprint service to the general public. When that service is provided, the department shall charge a fee of not less than five dollars ($5) for each person fingerprinted.

(b) Whenever the department submits the fingerprints of an applicant for a license or certificate to the Department of Justice, and is required to pay a fee pursuant to subdivision (e) of Section 11105 of the Penal Code, the department, without the necessity of adopting regulations, shall charge the applicant a fee sufficient to reimburse the department for that fee. *(Added by*

Stats.1978, c. 689, p. 2196, § 1, eff. Sept. 11, 1978. Amended by Stats.1990, c. 1360 (S.B.1510), § 1.5.)

§ 1669. Promptness in serving the public; legislative intent; posting hours of operation

It is the intent of the Legislature that the department implement procedures to ensure, to the fullest extent permitted by the resources made available to it, that any person who is requesting services relating to registration of vessels or vehicles, or who is applying for an original or renewal of a driver's license or identification card, will not be required under normal circumstances to wait in any one line for service longer than one-half hour during the department's published or posted hours of operation. Every office of the department shall have posted, at or near the entrance thereto, its hours of operation. *(Added by Stats.1983, c. 786, § 1.)*

§ 1670. Division between types of business involving vehicles or component parts; inspection of business

A licensee issued an occupational license by the department and conducting more than one type of business from an established place of business shall provide a clear physical division between the types of business involving vehicles or their component parts. The established place of business shall be open to inspection of the premises, pertinent records, and vehicles by any peace officer during business hours. *(Added by Stats.1985, c. 106, § 164.)*

§ 1671. Established place of business; office; display or manufacturing area; dismantling area

(a) The established place of business of a dealer, remanufacturer, remanufacturer branch, manufacturer, manufacturer branch, distributor, distributor branch, automobile driving school, or traffic violator school shall have an office and a dealer, manufacturer, or remanufacturer shall also have a display or manufacturing area situated on the same property where the business peculiar to the type of license issued by the department is or may be transacted. When a room or rooms in a hotel, roominghouse, apartment house building, or a part of any single- or multiple-unit dwelling house is used as an office or offices of an established place of business, the room or rooms shall be devoted exclusively to and occupied for the office or offices of the dealer, manufacturer, manufacturer branch, remanufacturer, remanufacturer branch, distributor, distributor branch, automobile driving school, or traffic violator school, shall be located on the ground floor, and shall be so constructed as to provide a direct entrance into the room or rooms from the exterior of the building. A dealer who does not offer new or used vehicles for sale at retail, a dealer who has been issued an autobroker's endorsement to his or her dealer's license and who does not also sell motor vehicles at retail, or a dealer who is a wholesaler involved for profit only in the sale of vehicles between licensed dealers, shall have an office, but a display area is not required.

(b) The established place of business of an automobile dismantler shall have an office and a dismantling area located in a zone properly zoned for that purpose by the city or county. *(Added by Stats.1985, c. 106, § 165. Amended by Stats.1994, c. 1253 (A.B.3539), § 7; Stats. 1995, c. 211 (A.B.770), § 2; Stats.2006, c. 538 (S.B.1852), § 653.)*

§ 1672. Anatomical gifts; drivers license or identification card designation; signs, notices, pamphlets and brochures

(a) The department shall make available, in the public area of each office of the department where applications for driver's licenses or identification cards are received, space for a sign or notice briefly describing the Uniform Anatomical Gift Act (Chapter 3.5 (commencing with Section 7150) of Part 1 of Division 7 of the Health and Safety Code) and information about the California Organ and Tissue Donor Registry and about how private donations may be made.

(b) The department shall make available to the public in its offices a pamphlet or brochure providing more detailed information on the California Organ and Tissue Donor Registry and information about how private donations may be made.

(c) The signs, notices, pamphlets, and brochures specified in subdivisions (a) and (b) shall be provided without cost to the department by responsible private parties associated with the anatomical gift program. *(Formerly § 1670, added by Stats.1985, c. 526, § 1. Renumbered § 1672 and amended by Stats.1986, c. 248, § 238. Amended by Stats.2001, c. 740 (S.B.108), § 4; Stats.2003, c. 405 (S.B.112), § 5.)*

Cross References

Drivers' licenses, issuance and renewal, information to be provided on organ and tissue donation including a enrollment form for the California Organ and Tissue Donor Registry, see Vehicle Code § 12811.
Organ and Tissue Donor Registry, see Health and Safety Code § 7152.7.

§ 1672.3. Driver's license and identification card inventory; depletion date; notice

(a) The director shall determine the date when the department's inventory of driver's license and identification card forms, as that inventory exists in accordance with the law in effect on December 31, 1998, has been depleted.

(b) The director shall make written notification of the date determined under subdivision (a) to the following persons:

(1) The Secretary of State.

(2) The Chair of the Senate Committee on Transportation.

(3) The Chair of the Assembly Committee on Transportation.

(c) The written notice required under subdivision (b) shall state that it is being submitted in accordance with this section. *(Added by Stats.1998, c. 887 (S.B.1403), § 4.)*

Cross References

Driver's licenses, issuance and contents, operative effect of this section, see Vehicle Code § 12811.
Identification cards, contents and form, operative effect of this section, see Vehicle Code § 13005.

§ 1672.5. Anatomical gifts; sticker affixed to driver's license or identification card

For purposes of providing a means of identifying persons who have elected to make an anatomical gift under the Uniform Anatomical Gift Act (Chapter 3.5 (commencing with Section 7150) of Part 1 of Division 7 of the Health and Safety Code), the department shall design the driver's licenses and identification cards in order that a sticker may be affixed to the licenses and cards. The sticker shall indicate a person's willingness to make an anatomical gift, and shall be affixed with a substance that is resistant to any unintentional removal. *(Added by Stats.1998, c. 887 (S.B.1403), § 5.)*

§ 1673. Refunding of smog impact fee; "registered owner or lessee"

For the purposes of refunding the smog impact fee, as prescribed in Sections 1673.2 and 1673.4, "registered owner or lessee" means the person or persons to whom the registration or title was issued when the transaction that included the imposition of the smog impact fee under Chapter 3.3 (commencing with Section 6261) of Part 1 of Division 2 of the Revenue and Taxation Code was completed. *(Added by Stats.2000, c. 31 (A.B.809), § 3, eff. June 8, 2000.)*

Cross References

Smog Impact Fee Refund Account, see Revenue and Taxation Code § 6909.

§ 1673.2. Refunding of smog impact fee; duties of department; interest on claims; filing of claims

(a) The department, in coordination with the Department of Finance, shall do all of the following:

(1) Search its records to identify the registered owner or lessee. Except as required under Section 1673.4, the department shall mail to the registered owner or lessee a refund notification form notifying the registered owner or lessee that he or she is eligible for a refund of the smog impact fee. This form shall identify the vehicle make and year, and include a refund claim that shall be signed, under penalty of perjury, and returned to the department.

(2) Shall acknowledge by mail claims for refund from registered owners or lessees received prior to the effective date of this section.

(3) Except as provided in Section 1673.4, shall verify whether the information provided in any claim is true and correct and shall refund the three hundred dollar ($300)

smog impact fee, plus the amount of any penalty collected for late payment of the smog impact fee, and any interest earned on those charges, to the person shown to be the registered owner or lessee.

(b) Notwithstanding any other provision of law, interest shall be paid on all claims at a single annual rate, calculated by the Department of Finance, that averages the annualized interest rates earned by the Pooled Money Investment Account for the period beginning October 1990 and ending on the effective date of this section. Interest on each refund shall be calculated from the date the smog impact fee and vehicle registration transaction was completed to the date the refund is issued. Accrual of interest shall terminate one year after the effective date of this section.

(c)(1) Notwithstanding any other provision of law, those who paid the smog impact fee between October 15, 1990, and October 19, 1999, may file a claim for refund.

(2) Claims for refund by a registered owner or lessee shall be filed with the Department of Motor Vehicles within three years of the effective date of this section. *(Added by Stats.2000, c. 31 (A.B.809), § 4, eff. June 8, 2000. Amended by Stats.2010, c. 719 (S.B.856), § 64, eff. Oct. 19, 2010.)*

Cross References

Smog Impact Fee Refund Account, see Revenue and Taxation Code § 6909.

§ 1673.4. Refunding of smog impact fee; time for filing claims; notification of eligibility; disputed claims; parties to law suits

(a) Any claim submitted by a person other than a registered owner or lessee shall be filed within 30 days from the effective date of this section.

(b) If a claimant other than the registered owner or lessee files a claim, or has filed a claim prior to the effective date of this section, for refund in a manner and form verified by the department, the department shall mail a notification to the registered owner or lessee informing that person that he or she is eligible for a refund of the smog impact fee and that a competing claim for that fee has been filed. The registered owner or lessee shall have three years from the effective date of this section to inform the department that the registered owner or lessee opposes payment of the smog impact fee refund to the competing claimant. In that case, the refund shall be made to the registered owner or lessee and notice of that action shall be sent to the competing claimant. If the registered owner or lessee does not notify the department within the three-year period that he or she opposes the payment, the department shall pay the refund to the competing claimant.

(c) If any refund paid by the department under this section is disputed, any party that filed a claim may commence an action in small claims court. The small claims court action may not be filed if three years or more

have elapsed from the date the department mailed the refund to either party.

(d) The State of California, its departments and agencies, and their officers or employees shall not be a party to a lawsuit between competing claimants relating to smog impact fee refunds. *(Added by Stats.2000, c. 31 (A.B.809), § 5, eff. June 8, 2000.)*

Cross References

Smog Impact Fee Refund Account, see Revenue and Taxation Code § 6909.

§ 1673.5. Refunding of smog impact fee; recovering erroneously paid refunds

The department shall attempt to recover any refund of the smog impact fee, or part thereof, that is erroneously made. Collection shall be initiated if the recipient fails to respond to the Department of Motor Vehicles' notice to pay the erroneous refund within 90 days in accordance with existing collection procedures utilized by the department. *(Added by Stats.2000, c. 31 (A.B.809), § 6, eff. June 8, 2000.)*

Cross References

Smog Impact Fee Refund Account, see Revenue and Taxation Code § 6909.

§ 1673.6. Refunding of smog impact fee; violations; penalties

It is unlawful to use a false or fictitious name, to knowingly make any false statement, or conceal any material fact on a refund claim for the smog impact fee that is filed with the department. A violation of this provision is punishable under Section 72 of the Penal Code. Any signed claim form submitted to the department for a refund of the smog impact fee shall be signed under penalty of perjury. *(Added by Stats.2000, c. 31 (A.B.809), § 7, eff. June 8, 2000.)*

Cross References

Smog Impact Fee Refund Account, see Revenue and Taxation Code § 6909.

§ 1673.7. Refunding of smog impact fee; notice

(a) The department shall include the following notice with each check issued as a refund of the smog impact fee:

"The enclosed check is a refund of the $300 Smog Impact Fee you paid to the Department of Motor Vehicles when you initially registered an out-of-state vehicle in California. In the case of Jordan v. Department of Motor Vehicles (1999) 75 Cal.App.4th 449, the court ruled the smog impact fee unconstitutional. The enclosed check includes an interest payment which has been calculated from the date the fee was paid to the date the refund is issued.

"If you have any questions about the enclosed refund, please contact your local office of the Department of Motor Vehicles."

(b) No notice other than the one required under subdivision (a) may be included with a smog impact fee refund check. *(Added by Stats.2000, c. 31 (A.B.809), § 8, eff. June 8, 2000.)*

Cross References

Smog Impact Fee Refund Account, see Revenue and Taxation Code § 6909.

§ 1674. Program of encouragement

The department shall develop a program to foster a positive atmosphere that is conducive to encouraging drivers to succeed in passing any visual tests or written or behind-the-wheel driving tests administered by the department. *(Added by Stats.2000, c. 985 (S.B.335), § 3.)*

§ 1674.2. Repealed by Stats.2000, c. 985 (S.B.335), § 4, operative Jan. 1, 2003

§ 1674.4. Sensitivity training for test administrators

In order to address any conscious or unconscious bias against a driver by persons administering the department's visual tests or written or behind-the-wheel driving tests, the department shall implement a component in its training and development program for test administrators that encourages sensitivity to the issues of youth and aging. *(Added by Stats.2000, c. 985 (S.B.335), § 5.)*

§ 1674.6. Finding and declaration; intent to provide transportation alternatives; task force

(a) The Legislature finds and declares that persons should be provided with transportation alternatives when their privilege to drive is lost because of failure to pass visual tests or written or behind-the-wheel driving tests. While a partial obligation for addressing this issue rests with families, communities, social service agencies, and local governments, the Legislature recognizes an obligation to promote, facilitate, and share in the funding of alternative modes of transportation for persons who have lost their driving privilege.

(b) Accordingly, it is the intent of the Legislature, not later than January 1, 2003, to provide an affordable and equitable mode of transportation to fulfill the reasonable transportation needs of persons who have lost their driver's licenses due to a failure to pass a visual test or a written or behind-the-wheel driving test.

(c) In furtherance of the intent set forth in subdivision (b), the Business, Transportation and Housing Agency shall establish a task force to analyze potential sources of funding and modes of transportation for persons who have lost their driver's licenses due to a failure to pass a visual test or a written or behind-the-wheel driving test. The Business, Transportation and Housing Agency shall prepare and submit a report on the findings of the task force to the Legislature not later than July 1, 2001. *(Added by Stats.2000, c. 985 (S.B.335), § 6.)*

§ 1675. Mature driver improvement courses

(a) The director shall establish standards and develop criteria for the approval of initial and renewal driver improvement courses specifically designed for the safe driving needs of drivers who are 55 years of age or older, which shall be known as mature driver improvement courses.

(b) The curricula for the courses provided for in subdivision (a) shall include, but is not limited to, all of the following components:

(1) How impairment of visual and audio perception affects driving performance and how to compensate for that impairment.

(2) The effects of fatigue, medications, and alcohol on driving performance, when experienced alone or in combination, and precautionary measures to prevent or offset ill effects.

(3) Updates on rules of the road and equipment, including, but not limited to, safety belts and safe and efficient driving techniques under present day road and traffic conditions.

(4) How to plan travel time and select routes for safety and efficiency.

(5) How to make crucial decisions in dangerous, hazardous, and unforeseen situations.

(c) The initial mature driver improvement course shall include not less than 400 minutes of instruction, and shall not exceed 25 students per single day of instruction or 30 students per two days of instruction.

(d) Upon satisfactory completion of an initial mature driver improvement course, participants shall receive and retain a certificate provided by the department, awarded and distributed by the course provider, which shall be suitable evidence of satisfactory course completion, and eligibility for three years, from the date of completion, for the mature driver vehicle liability insurance premium reduction pursuant to Section 11628.3 of the Insurance Code.

(e)(1) The certificate may be renewed by successfully completing a subsequent renewal mature driver improvement course within one year of the expiration of the certificate, or if more than one year has elapsed since the expiration, a mature driver improvement course in accordance with the standards established in subdivision (c).

(2) The renewal mature driver improvement course shall include not less than 240 minutes of instruction.

(f) For the purposes of this section, and Sections 1676 and 1677, "course provider" means any person offering a mature driver improvement course approved by the department pursuant to subdivision (a). *(Added by Stats.1986, c. 1325, § 3, operative July 1, 1987. Amended by Stats.1996, c. 124 (A.B.3470), § 115; Stats.2001, c. 739 (A.B.1707), § 3; Stats.2006, c. 129 (A.B.2407), § 1.)*

§ 1676. Mature driver improvement courses; fees

(a) A course provider conducting a mature driver improvement course pursuant to Section 1675 may charge a tuition not to exceed thirty dollars ($30).

(b) A course provider shall issue a receipt for the tuition it collects from an individual who registers for or attends a mature driver improvement course.

(c) The department shall charge a fee not to exceed three dollars ($3) for each completion certificate issued to a mature driver improvement course provider, pursuant to subdivision (d) of Section 1675. The amount of the fee shall be determined by the department and shall be sufficient to defray the actual costs incurred by the department for administering the mature driver improvement program, for evaluating the program, and for any other activities deemed necessary by the department to assure high quality education for participants of the program. A course provider shall not charge a fee in excess of the fee charged by the department pursuant to this subdivision for furnishing a certificate of completion or duplicate thereof. The department shall transmit all fees it receives for deposit in the Motor Vehicle Account in the State Transportation Fund pursuant to Section 42270. *(Added by Stats.1986, c. 1325, § 4, operative July 1, 1987. Amended by Stats.2006, c. 129 (A.B.2407), § 2.)*

§ 1677. Providers of mature driver improvement courses; fees for approval; responsibilities

(a) The department may collect a fee, to be determined by the department, from each course provider who shall be responsible for the development and operation of a mature driver improvement course, for the approval of the course, but not to exceed the actual cost of approval of the course. The department shall transmit all fees it receives for deposit in the Motor Vehicle Account in the State Transportation Fund pursuant to Section 42270.

(b) Each course provider, who has received course approval from the department, is responsible for the delivery, instruction, and content of his or her mature driver improvement course.

(c) The department shall investigate claims of impropriety on the part of a course provider. The department may withdraw the approval of courses in violation of Section 1675 or 1676, as determined by the department, for just cause, including, but not limited to any of the following:

(1) Furnishing course completion certificates to course enrollees prior to, or in the absence of, completion of the curriculum specified in subdivisions (b) and (c) of Section 1675.

(2) Charging fees in excess of the amounts specified in subdivisions (a) and (c) of Section 1676.

(d) Mature driver improvement courses approved by the department shall continue to be approved until either of the following occurs:

(1) The course provider does not meet the conditions of approval.

(2) The department finds just cause to terminate the approval pursuant to subdivision (c). *(Added by Stats. 1986, c. 1325, § 5, operative July 1, 1987. Amended by Stats.2001, c. 739 (A.B.1707), § 4.)*

§ 1678. Base fee amounts; adjustment of fees

(a) Between January 1, 2004, and December 31, 2004, inclusive, the fee amounts set forth in Section 488.385 of the Code of Civil Procedure, Section 10902 of the Revenue and Taxation Code, and Sections 4604, 5014, 5036, 6700.25, 9102.5, 9250.8, 9250.13, 9252, 9254, 9258, 9261, 9265, 9702, 11515, 11515.2, 14900, 14900.1, 14901, 14902, 15250.6, 15250.7, 15255.1, 15255.2, 38121, 38225.4, 38225.5, 38232, 38255, 38260, and 38265 shall be the base fee amounts charged by the department.

(b) On January 1, 2005, and every January 1 thereafter, the department shall adjust the fees imposed under the sections listed in subdivision (a) by increasing each fee in an amount equal to the increase in the California Consumer Price Index for the prior year, as calculated by the Department of Finance, with amounts equal to or greater than fifty cents ($0.50) rounded to the next highest whole dollar.

(c) Any increases to the fees imposed under the sections listed in subdivision (a) that are enacted by legislation subsequent to January 1, 2005, shall be deemed to be changes to the base fee for purposes of the calculation performed pursuant to subdivision (b). *(Added by Stats.2003, c. 719 (S.B.1055), § 3. Amended by Stats.2008, c. 756 (A.B.268), § 18, eff. Sept. 30, 2008; Stats.2009–2010, 4th Ex.Sess., c. 10 (A.B.10), § 8, eff. July 28, 2009.)*

§ 1679. Notice to prospective voters; delayed receipt of requested voter registration information

On and after July 1, 2006, in any document mailed by the department that offers a person the opportunity to register to vote pursuant to the National Voter Registration Act of 1993 (42 U.S.C. Sec. 1973gg), the department shall include a notice informing prospective voters that if they have not received voter registration information within 30 days of requesting it, they should contact their local elections office or the office of the Secretary of State. *(Added by Stats.2005, c. 660 (S.B.316), § 2.)*

§ 1680. Repealed by Stats.2001, c. 857 (S.B.776), § 2, operative Jan. 1, 2003

§ 1685. Vehicle registration and titling transactions; establishment of contracts for electronic programs; transaction fee

(a) In order to continue improving the quality of products and services it provides to its customers, the department, in conformance with Article 4 (commencing with Section 19130) of Chapter 5 of Part 2 of Division 5 of Title 2 of the Government Code, may establish contracts for electronic programs that allow qualified private industry partners to join the department in providing services that include processing and payment programs for vehicle registration and titling transactions.

(b)(1) The department may enter into contractual agreements with qualified private industry partners. There are the following three types of private industry partnerships authorized under this section:

(A) First-line business partner is an industry partner that receives data directly from the department and uses it to complete registration and titling activities for that partner's own business purposes.

(B) First-line service provider is an industry partner that receives information from the department and then transmits it to another authorized industry partner.

(C) Second-line business partner is a partner that receives information from a first-line service provider.

(2) The private industry partner contractual agreements shall include the following minimum requirements:

(A) Filing of an application and payment of an application fee, as established by the department.

(B) Submission of information, including, but not limited to, fingerprints and personal history statements, focusing on and concerning the applicant's character, honesty, integrity, and reputation as the department may consider necessary.

(C) Posting a bond in an amount consistent with Section 1815.

(3) The department shall, through regulations, establish any additional requirements for the purpose of safeguarding privacy and protecting the information authorized for release under this section.

(c) The director may establish, through the adoption of regulations, the maximum amount that a qualified private industry partner may charge its customers in providing the services authorized under subdivision (a).

(d) The department shall charge a three-dollar ($3) transaction fee for the information and services provided under subdivision (a). The private industry partner may pass the transaction fee to the customer, but the total charge to a customer may not exceed the amount established by the director under subdivision (c).

(e) All fees collected by the department pursuant to subdivision (d) shall be deposited in the Motor Vehicle Account. On January 1 of each year, the department shall adjust the fee in accordance with the California Consumer Price Index. The amount of the fee shall be rounded to the nearest whole dollar, with amounts equal to, or greater than, fifty cents ($0.50) rounded to the next highest whole dollar.

(f) The department shall adopt regulations and procedures that ensure adequate oversight and monitoring of qualified private industry partners to protect vehicle owners from the improper use of vehicle records. These regulations and procedures shall include provisions for qualified private industry partners to periodically submit records to the department, and the department shall

review those records as necessary. The regulations shall also include provisions for the dedication of department resources to program monitoring and oversight; the protection of confidential records in the department's files and databases; and the duration and nature of the contracts with qualified private industry partners.

(g) The department shall, annually, by October 1, provide a report to the Legislature that shall include all of the following information gathered during the fiscal year immediately preceding the report date:

(1) Listing of all qualified private industry partners, including names and business addresses.

(2) Volume of transactions, by type, completed by business partners.

(3) Total amount of funds, by transaction type, collected by business partners.

(4) Total amount of funds received by the department.

(5) Description of any fraudulent activities identified by the department.

(6) Evaluation of the benefits of the program.

(7) Recommendations for any administrative or statutory changes that may be needed to improve the program.

(h) Nothing in this section impairs or limits the authority provided in Section 4610 or Section 12155 of the Insurance Code. *(Added by Stats.2001, c. 127 (S.B.46), § 3, eff. July 30, 2001. Amended by Stats.2003, c. 719 (S.B.1055), § 4; Stats.2004, c. 615 (S.B.1233), § 19.)*

§ 1685.1. Repealed by Stats.2004, c. 615 (S.B.1233), § 20, operative Jan. 1, 2010

ARTICLE 3. RECORDS OF DEPARTMENT

Section
1800.   Registration indices and records.
1801.   Submission of documents; storage of records; electronic media or other approved means; evidentiary use.
1801.1.   Electronic submission of documents; signatures; rules and standards; admissibility.
1802.   Court records.
1803.   Abstract of record of court.
1803.3.   Reversal of conviction; abstract of record of court; notice of dismissal; removal of record of conviction.
1803.4.   Suspension or revocation of driving privileges; notice record; peace officers and courts.
1803.5.   Abstract of record; preparation following designation of conviction as confidential in consideration of attendance at driving instruction school or program.
1803.5.   Abstract of record; preparation following designation of conviction as confidential in consideration of attendance at driving instruction school or program.
1804.   Abstract form; contents; blood alcohol percentages.
1805.   Failure to comply.
1806.   Report of accident or conviction.
1806.1.   Stipulated vehicle release agreement; records.

Section

1806.5. Report of accident or conviction; furnishing information violating federal credit reporting act prohibited.

1807. Destruction of records.

1807.5. Conviction of reckless driving prior to Jan. 1, 1987; not public record; limited disclosure after 5 years.

1808. Records open to public inspection.

1808.1. Prospective employers of drivers of vehicles requiring certain licenses or certificates; pull-notice system and periodic reports.

1808.2. Confidential records; address; inspectors or investigators of district attorney; peace officer employees of board of prison terms.

1808.3. Repealed.

1808.4. Confidential records; home addresses of certain public officials and employees and their spouses and children; penalty.

1808.5. Confidential records: physical, mental condition; controlled substances offenses.

1808.6. Confidential records; home addresses of certain officials.

1808.7. Confidential record; exceptions.

1808.7. Confidential record; exceptions.

1808.8. Schoolbus, pupil activity bus, youth bus, or paratransit vehicle drivers; dismissal for safety-related cause; reinstatement; reporting requirements.

1808.9. Confidential records; demonstration of continued eligibility.

1808.10. Drivers allowed to complete courses at traffic violator schools; conviction records not confidential; disclosures required.

1808.21. Confidential records; residence or mailing address; consent to service of process; grounds for suppression.

1808.22. Application of § 1808.21; violations.

1808.23. Application of confidentiality of records law to specified entities; use of released address information.

1808.24. Confidential information; information regarding motor vehicle liability insurance policy; exceptions.

1808.25. Residence address information to be provided to accredited degree-granting nonprofit independent institutions of higher education; terms of memorandum of understanding and contract.

1808.45. Unauthorized disclosure of information; false representation; misdemeanor.

1808.46. Civil penalties; suspension or revocation of requester code privileges; review of procedure.

1808.47. Procedures to protect confidentiality of records; use of records by agents.

1808.51. Bureau of Real Estate; city attorney and investigators; authority to obtain copies of fullface engraved pictures or photographs of individuals directly from Department of Motor Vehicles.

1809. Traffic accident information.

1810. Inspection or sale of information; identification of requester; notification of subject; photocopies.

1810.2. Commercial requester accounts; issuance of requester code.

1810.3. Use of information in accident reports provided under § 20012.

1810.5. Public records; access by certain officials.

1810.7. Access to electronic database for vehicle registration information for commercial use; special permit;

Section

departmental powers and duties; financial security; fees; report every three years.

1811. Sale of records.

1812. Free to governmental agencies.

1813. Free records.

1814. Automobile registration service.

1815. Bond.

1816. Juvenile traffic offender.

1817. Forwarding information to department of forestry.

1818. Vehicle license notation on abstract.

1819. Records of actual mileage of motor vehicles.

1820. Repealed.

1821. Data and monitoring system; evaluation of intervention programs; recidivism tracking system; report.

1822. Driving under the influence of alcohol or drugs; data system to track violations; legislative intent.

1825. Disabled person placards; annual random audits of applications.

Cross References

Customer records, security procedures, see Civil Code § 1798.81.5.

§ 1800. Registration indices and records

(a) The department shall file each application received for the registration of a vehicle and shall keep a record of each as follows:

(1) Under a distinctive registration number assigned to the vehicle.

(2) Alphabetically, under the name of the owner.

(3) Under the motor or a permanent identifying number of the vehicle as may be determined by the department.

(4) In the discretion of the department, in any other manner it may deem desirable.

(b) The department shall file every application for a license to operate a motor vehicle received by it and maintain all of the following:

(1) A suitable index containing, in alphabetical order, all applications denied. On the applications shall be noted the reasons for the denial.

(2) A suitable index containing, in alphabetical order, all applications granted.

(3) A suitable index containing, in alphabetical order, the name of every licensee whose license has been suspended or revoked by the department or by a court and after each name notes the reasons for the action and the period of revocation or suspension. *(Stats.1959, c. 3, p. 1543, § 1800. Amended by Stats.1965, c. 1715, p. 3848, § 1, eff. Jan. 1, 1966; Stats.1967, c. 476, p. 1682, § 1; Stats.2003, c. 594 (S.B.315), § 14.)*

Cross References

Alteration or change of vehicle numbers, see Vehicle Code § 10750.

Application of this section to trolley coaches, see Vehicle Code § 21051.

Authority to grant or refuse applications, see Vehicle Code § 1653.

Department to prescribe forms of registration, see Vehicle Code § 1652.

Destruction of records, see Vehicle Code § 1807.

Evidences of registration in general, see Vehicle Code § 4450 et seq.

Falsification of registration, see Vehicle Code § 4463.

Lending evidence of registration, see Vehicle Code § 4461.

Notice and submission of records on installation of motor or engine, see Vehicle Code § 4161.

Operation of vehicle pending registration, see Vehicle Code § 4017.

Possession, etc., of motor vehicles with manufacturers' numbers removed, see Vehicle Code § 10751.

Possession of records in department, see Vehicle Code § 1502.

Registered owner as one registered by department, see Vehicle Code § 505.

Restrictions on engaging in registration business, see Vehicle Code § 505.2.

Return of evidences of registration upon cancellation, suspension or revocation, see Vehicle Code § 8802.

§ 1801. Submission of documents; storage of records; electronic media or other approved means; evidentiary use

(a) Whenever any notice, report, statement, court abstract, or record is required to be submitted to the department by this code, the document may be submitted to the department by electronic transmission or other means approved by the department.

(b) All records maintained by the department may be stored in any feasible manner, including, but not limited to, any electronic media or any other form of data compilation.

(c) Notwithstanding any other provision of law, the records shall be deemed original documents and shall be admissible in evidence in all administrative, quasi-judicial, and judicial proceedings. *(Added by Stats.1994, c. 1220 (A.B.3132), § 53, eff. Sept. 30, 1994. Amended by Stats. 1996, c. 10 (A.B.1869), § 9, eff. Feb. 9, 1996.)*

Cross References

Applications for licenses, see Vehicle Code § 12800 et seq.

Cancellation, revocation or suspension of licenses, see Vehicle Code § 13100 et seq.

Duty of court to report conviction to department, see Vehicle Code § 1803.

Duty to stop and report accidents, see Vehicle Code § 20000 et seq.

Issuance and contents of license, see Vehicle Code § 12811.

Maximum period of suspension or revocation in certain cases, see Vehicle Code § 13556.

Possession and control of all records, books, etc., by department, see Vehicle Code § 1502.

Records required to be written in English, see Vehicle Code § 9.

Registration indices and records required, see Vehicle Code § 1800.

Renewal of licenses, see Vehicle Code § 12814.

§ 1801.1. Electronic submission of documents; signatures; rules and standards; admissibility

(a) Notwithstanding any other provision of law, the department may allow a person to submit any document required to be submitted to the department by using electronic media deemed feasible by the department instead of requiring the actual submittal of the original document.

(b) If a signature on a document is required by law in order to complete a transaction, and the document is submitted electronically, that signature requirement may be met by an electronically submitted signature, if the department retains information verifying the identity of the person submitting the electronic signature.

(c) The department may establish minimum transaction volume levels, audit and security standards, and technological requirements, or terms and conditions, including methods of authentication for electronically submitted signatures, it deems necessary for the approval of this process.

(d) An electronically submitted document, once accepted by the department, shall be deemed the same as an original document, and shall be admissible in all administrative, quasi-judicial, and judicial proceedings. *(Added by Stats.1996, c. 440 (S.B.1588), § 1. Amended by Stats.2005, c. 61 (A.B.461), § 1.)*

§ 1802. Court records

Every judge of a court not of record shall keep a full record of every case in which a person is charged with any violation of this code. *(Stats.1959, c. 3, p. 1543, § 1802.)*

Cross References

Departmental file of abstracts of court records of convictions, see Vehicle Code § 1806.

§ 1803. Abstract of record of court

(a)(1) The clerk of a court in which a person was convicted of a violation of this code, was convicted of a violation of subdivision (a), (b), (c), (d), (e), or (f) of Section 655 of the Harbors and Navigation Code pertaining to a mechanically propelled vessel but not to manipulating any water skis, an aquaplane, or similar device, was convicted of a violation of Section 655.2, 655.6, 658, or 658.5 of the Harbors and Navigation Code, a violation of subdivision (a) of Section 192.5 of the Penal Code, or a violation of subdivision (b) of Section 5387 of the Public Utilities Code, was convicted of an offense involving use or possession of controlled substances under Division 10 (commencing with Section 11000) of the Health and Safety Code, was convicted of a felony offense when a commercial motor vehicle, as defined in subdivision (b) of Section 15210, was involved in or incidental to the commission of the offense, or was convicted of a violation of any other statute relating to the safe operation of vehicles, shall prepare within five days after conviction and immediately forward to the department at its office at Sacramento an abstract of the record of the court covering the case in which the person was so convicted. If sentencing is not pronounced in conjunction with the conviction, the abstract shall be forwarded to the department within five days after sentencing and the abstract shall be certified by the person so required to prepare it to be true and correct.

(2) For the purposes of this section, a forfeiture of bail shall be equivalent to a conviction.

(b) The following violations are not required to be reported under subdivision (a):

(1) Division 3.5 (commencing with Section 9840).

(2) Section 21113, with respect to parking violations.

(3) Chapter 9 (commencing with Section 22500) of Division 11, except Section 22526.

(4) Division 12 (commencing with Section 24000), except Sections 24002, 24004, 24250, 24409, 24604, 24800, 25103, 26707, 27151, 27315, 27360, 27800, and 27801 and Chapter 3 (commencing with Section 26301).

(5) Division 15 (commencing with Section 35000), except Chapter 5 (commencing with Section 35550).

(6) Violations for which a person was cited as a pedestrian or while operating a bicycle or a motorized scooter.

(7) Division 16.5 (commencing with Section 38000), except Sections 38301, 38301.3, 38301.5, 38304.1, and 38504.1.

(8) Subdivision (b) of Section 23221, subdivision (b) of Section 23223, subdivision (b) of Section 23225, and subdivision (b) of Section 23226.

(c) If the court impounds a license or orders a person to limit his or her driving pursuant to subdivision (d) of Section 40508, the court shall notify the department concerning the impoundment or limitation on an abstract prepared pursuant to subdivision (a) of this section or on a separate abstract, that shall be prepared within five days after the impoundment or limitation was ordered and immediately forwarded to the department at its office in Sacramento.

(d) If the court determines that a prior judgment of conviction of a violation of Section 23152 or 23153 is valid or is invalid on constitutional grounds pursuant to Section 41403, the clerk of the court in which the determination is made shall prepare an abstract of that determination and forward it to the department in the same manner as an abstract of record pursuant to subdivision (a).

(e) Within five days of an order terminating or revoking probation under Section 23602, the clerk of the court in which the order terminating or revoking probation was entered shall prepare and immediately forward to the department at its office in Sacramento an abstract of the record of the court order terminating or revoking probation and any other order of the court to the department required by law.

(Added by Stats.2007, c. 746 (A.B.421), § 2, operative Oct. 1, 2008. Amended by Stats.2009, c. 248 (A.B.636), § 3; Stats.2009, c. 414 (A.B.134), § 1; Stats.2010, c. 213 (A.B.2768), § 24.)

Cross References

Advisory statement to be given by court to person convicted of violating §§ 23103, 23103.5, 23152 and 23153, inclusion of fact on abstract of conviction, see Vehicle Code § 23593.

Child safety belt and passenger restraint requirements, conviction under Vehicle Code §§ 27360 or 27360.5, reporting pursuant to this section, see Vehicle Code § 27360.6.

Entry of motor vehicle into federal or state wilderness area, public offense and penalties, see Vehicle COde § 38301.3.

Failure to pay fine, driver's license issuance or renewal, see Vehicle Code § 12807.

Influence of alcoholic beverage or drug, suspension or revocation of driving privileges, see Vehicle Code §§ 13352, 13352.5.

Uniform fee for traffic violator school or court-supervised traffic safety instruction, see Vehicle Code § 42007.

§ 1803.3. Reversal of conviction; abstract of record of court; notice of dismissal; removal of record of conviction

(a) The clerk of any court that reverses a conviction for an offense described in subdivision (a) of Section 1803, which is not exempted under subdivision (b) of that section, shall prepare and forward to the department at its office in Sacramento an abstract of the record of the court covering the case in which the conviction was reversed. In addition, if a court dismisses a charge of a violation of Section 40508 for which a notice was given to the department pursuant to Section 40509 or 40509.5, the court shall notify the department of the dismissal.

(b) The abstract shall be forwarded within 30 days of the date the judgment of reversal becomes final. The notice of dismissal shall be given to the department not later than 30 days after the dismissal. Within 30 days of receiving the abstract or notice, the department shall remove any record of that conviction, or notice received pursuant to Section 40509 or 40509.5, from the driver's record.

(c) As used in this section, "reverse" includes any action by which a conviction is nullified or set aside. *(Added by Stats.1989, c. 122, § 1, operative July 1, 1990. Amended by Stats.1991, c. 650 (S.B.131), § 1; Stats.2007, c. 263 (A.B.310), § 31.)*

Law Revision Commission Comments

2007 Amendment

Section 1803.3 is amended to delete unnecessary language authorizing the judge to substitute for the clerk if there is no clerk. See Code Civ. Proc. § 167 (judge may perform any act court clerk may perform); Gov't Code §§ 69840–69848 (duties of clerk of superior court), 71620(b) (executive or administrative officer has authority of clerk of court). [35 Cal.L.Rev.Comm. Reports 219 (2007)].

§ 1803.4. Suspension or revocation of driving privileges; notice record; peace officers and courts

Any record regarding the providing of information pursuant to Section 13106, or record of persons personally given notice by the department or a court, by a peace officer pursuant to Section 13382 or 13388, or otherwise pursuant to this code regarding the suspension or revocation of a person's privilege to operate a motor vehicle shall, upon request, be provided as follows:

(a) Immediately to any peace officer, as defined in Chapter 4.5 (commencing with Section 830) of Title 3 of Part 2 of the Penal Code, acting within the scope of his or her duties.

(b) Clearly stated on the record provided to any court of this state. *(Added by Stats.1998, c. 683 (A.B.2347), § 1. Amended by Stats.1999, c. 22 (S.B.24), § 6, operative May 26, 1999.)*

§ 1803.5. Abstract of record; preparation following designation of conviction as confidential in consideration of attendance at driving instruction school or program

> *Section added by Stats.2010, c. 216 (A.B.2144), § 1.5, operative July 1, 2011. See, also, another section of the same number added by Stats.2010, c. 599 (A.B.2499), § 1.7, operative July 1, 2011.*

(a) In accordance with Section 41501 or 42005, the clerk of a court or hearing officer, when a person who receives a notice to appear at a court or board proceeding for a violation of any statute relating to the safe operation of vehicles is granted a continuance of the proceeding in consideration for completion of a program at a school for traffic violators, that results in a designation of the conviction as confidential in consideration for that completion, shall prepare an abstract of the record of the court or board proceeding that indicates that the person was convicted of the violation and ordered to complete a traffic violator program, certify the abstract to be true and correct, and cause the abstract to be forwarded to the department at its office at Sacramento within five days after receiving proof that the program was completed or the due date to which the proceeding was continued, whichever comes first.

(b) This section shall become operative on July 1, 2011. *(Added by Stats.2010, c. 216 (A.B.2144), § 1.5, operative July 1, 2011.)*

Cross References

Confidential record, see Vehicle Code § 1808.7.
Occupational licensing, traffic violator schools, duties of Judicial Council, see Vehicle Code § 11205.4.

§ 1803.5. Abstract of record; preparation following designation of conviction as confidential in consideration of attendance at driving instruction school or program

> *Section added by Stats.2010, c. 599 (A.B.2499), § 1.7, operative July 1, 2011. See, also, another section of the same number added by Stats.2010, c. 216 (A.B.2144), § 1.5, operative July 1, 2011.*

(a) In accordance with Section 41501 or 42005, the clerk of a court or hearing officer, when a person who receives a notice to appear at a court or board proceeding for a violation of any statute relating to the safe operation of vehicles is granted a continuance of the proceeding in consideration for completion of a program at a school for traffic violators, that results in a designation of the conviction as confidential in consideration for that completion, shall prepare an abstract of the record of the court or board proceeding that indicates that the person was convicted of the violation and ordered to complete a traffic violator program, certify the abstract to be true and correct, and cause the abstract to be forwarded to the department at its office at Sacramento within five days after receiving proof that the program was completed or the due date to which the proceeding was continued, whichever comes first.

(b) This section shall become operative on July 1, 2011. *(Added by Stats.2010, c. 599 (A.B.2499), § 1.7, operative July 1, 2011.)*

Cross References

Confidential record, see Vehicle Code § 1808.7.
Occupational licensing, traffic violator schools, duties of Judicial Council, see Vehicle Code § 11205.4.

§ 1804. Abstract form; contents; blood alcohol percentages

(a) The abstract shall be made upon a form furnished or approved by the department and shall contain all necessary information to identify the defendant, including, but not limited to, the person's driver's license number, name, and date of birth, the date and nature of the offense, the vessel number, if any, of the vessel involved in the offense, the license plate number of the vehicle involved in the offense, the date of hearing, and the judgment, except that in the case of infractions where the court has not directed the department to suspend or restrict the defendant's driver's license, only the conviction and not the judgment need be set forth in the abstract. The abstract shall also indicate whether the vehicle involved in the offense is a commercial motor vehicle, as defined in subdivision (b) of Section 15210, whether the vehicle was of a type requiring the driver to have a certificate issued pursuant to Section 2512, 12517, 12519, 12523, or 12523.5 or any endorsement issued pursuant to paragraph (2) or (5) of subdivision (a) of Section 15278, and whether the vehicle was transporting hazardous material at the time of the offense, or whether the vessel involved in the offense was a recreational vessel, as defined in subdivision (bb) of Section 651 of the Harbors and Navigation Code.

(b) As to any abstract for which the original arrest and final conviction was for a violation of subdivision (b), (c), (d), (e), or (f) of Section 655 of the Harbors and Navigation Code or Section 23152 or 23153 of this code, the abstract shall contain a statement indicating the percentage of alcohol, by weight, in the person's blood whenever that percentage was determined by a chemical test. The information regarding the chemical test shall be compiled if it is available to the clerk of the court. All information required to be compiled pursuant to this subdivision shall be kept confidential in the records of the department pursuant to Section 1808.5. The department may use the information for research and statistical purposes and for determining the eligibility of any person to operate a motor vehicle on the highways of this state. The information shall not be released to any other public or private agency, except for research and statistical summary purposes and, for those purposes, the name and address of the person and any other identifying information shall not be disclosed.

(c) The Legislature finds and declares that blood-alcohol percentages have valuable research potential in providing statistical summary information on impaired drivers but that a specific blood-alcohol percentage is only an item of evidence for purposes of criminal and licensing sanctions imposed by law. The Legislature recognizes that the accuracy of the determination of a specific blood-alcohol percentage is not the critical determination in a conviction for driving under the influence of an alcoholic beverage if the blood-alcohol percentage exceeds the statutory amount. *(Added by Stats.1989, c. 1114, § 17, operative Jan. 1, 1992. Amended by Stats. 1990, c. 1360 (S.B.1510), § 2, operative Jan. 1, 1992; Stats.1991, c. 928 (A.B.1886), § 16, eff. Oct. 14, 1991, operative Jan. 1, 1992; Stats.1993, c. 158 (A.B.392), § 21.5, eff. July 21, 1993; Stats.1995, c. 526 (S.B.1224), § 6; Stats.2007, c. 630 (A.B.1728), § 1.)*

§ 1805. Failure to comply

The failure, refusal, or neglect of any such judicial officer to comply with any of the requirements of Sections 1802, 1803, 1804 and 1816 is misconduct in office and is ground for removal therefrom. *(Stats.1959, c. 3, p. 1544, § 1805. Amended by Stats.1959, c. 1622, p. 3991, § 1.)*

§ 1806. Report of accident or conviction

(a) The department shall file all accident reports and abstracts of court records of convictions received under this code, and in connection therewith, shall maintain convenient records or make suitable notations in order that an individual record of each license showing the convictions of the licensee and all traffic accidents in which the individual was involved, except those where, in the opinion of a reporting officer, another individual was at fault, are readily ascertainable. At its discretion the department may file and maintain these accident reports and abstracts by electronic recording and storage media and after transcribing electronically all available data from the accident reports and abstracts of conviction may destroy the original documents. Notwithstanding any other provisions of law, the recorded facts from any electronic recording and storage device maintained by the department shall constitute evidence of the facts in any administrative actions instituted by the department.

(b) When the department receives notification pursuant to subdivision (c) of Section 1872.45 of the Insurance Code, the department shall remove from the license record of each victim any record of his or her involvement in the accident which is the subject of the criminal complaint. *(Stats.1959, c. 3, p. 1544, § 1806. Amended by Stats.1968, c. 693, p. 1393, § 1; Stats.1968, c. 1062, p. 2062, § 1.5; Stats.1978, c. 974, p. 3037, § 1; Stats.1985, c. 1011, § 1, operative June 30, 1986; Stats.1999, c. 885 (A.B.1050), § 9.)*

Cross References

Duty to report accidents, see Vehicle Code § 20008.
Report of violations to department, see Vehicle Code § 1803.

§ 1806.1. Stipulated vehicle release agreement; records

If a person has entered into a stipulated vehicle release agreement pursuant to paragraph (2) of subdivision (d) of Section 14607.6, the department shall maintain a record of that fact for seven years from the date the person signed the agreement. *(Added by Stats.1994, c. 1133 (A.B.3148), § 3.)*

§ 1806.5. Report of accident or conviction; furnishing information violating federal credit reporting act prohibited

Notwithstanding Section 1808, the department shall not furnish information filed pursuant to Section 1806 to any person if the furnishing of that information would violate the federal Fair Credit Reporting Act (15 U.S.C. Sec. 1681 et seq.). *(Added by Stats.1986, c. 1117, § 1.)*

§ 1807. Destruction of records

(a) The department is not required to maintain records relating to drivers of motor vehicles after the records are, in the opinion of the director, no longer necessary, except as follows:

(1) Records of convictions shall be maintained so long as they may form the basis of license suspensions or revocations as prior convictions or with other records of conviction constitute a person a "negligent driver."

(2) Records of convictions of violating Section 38301.3 shall be maintained for seven years.

(b) Records that are not required to be maintained may be destroyed with the approval of the Department of General Services. *(Stats.1959, c. 3, p. 1544, § 1807. Amended by Stats.1965, c. 371, p. 1598, § 286; Stats.2005, c. 571 (A.B.1086), § 2.)*

Cross References

Department of General Services, see Government Code § 14600 et seq.
Entry of motor vehicle into federal or state wilderness area, public offense and penalties, see Vehicle Code § 38301.3.

§ 1807.5. Conviction of reckless driving prior to Jan. 1, 1987; not public record; limited disclosure after 5 years

(a) Notwithstanding Section 1808, any record of the department of a conviction of Section 23103 as specified in Section 23103.5, or of a conviction of Section 23152 or 23153 which occurred before January 1, 1987, is not a public record on and after a date which is five years after the date of conviction of that offense, and the department shall, thereafter, make any information relating to that conviction available only to persons authorized by law to receive the information.

(b) For the purposes of this section, "persons authorized by law to receive the information" means any of the following:

(1) The courts of the state.

(2) Peace officers, as defined in Section 830.1 of the Penal Code; subdivision (a) of Section 830.2 of the Penal Code; subdivisions (a), (b), and (j) of Section 830.3 of the Penal Code; and subdivisions (a), (b), and (c) of Section 830.5 of the Penal Code.

(3) The Attorney General.

(4) District attorneys of any county within the state.

(5) Prosecuting city attorneys of any city within the state.

(6) Probation officers of any city or county of the state.

(7) Parole officers of any city or county of the state. *(Added by Stats.1988, c. 1273, § 1, operative July 1, 1989. Amended by Stats.1989, c. 1360, § 154; Stats.1998, c. 606 (S.B.1880), § 14; Stats.1998, c. 828 (S.B.1637), § 10.)*

§ 1808. Records open to public inspection

(a) Except where a specific provision of law prohibits the disclosure of records or information or provides for confidentiality, all records of the department relating to the registration of vehicles, other information contained on an application for a driver's license, abstracts of convictions, and abstracts of accident reports required to be sent to the department in Sacramento, except for abstracts of accidents where, in the opinion of a reporting officer, another individual was at fault, shall be open to public inspection during office hours. All abstracts of accident reports shall be available to law enforcement agencies and courts of competent jurisdiction.

(b) The department shall make available or disclose abstracts of convictions and abstracts of accident reports required to be sent to the department in Sacramento, as described in subdivision (a), if the date of the occurrence is not later than the following:

(1) Ten years for a violation pursuant to Section 23140, 23152, or 23153.

(2) Seven years for a violation designated as two points pursuant to Section 12810, except as provided in paragraph (1) of this subdivision.

(3) Three years for accidents and all other violations.

(c) The department shall make available or disclose suspensions and revocations of the driving privilege while the suspension or revocation is in effect and for three years following termination of the action or reinstatement of the privilege, except that driver's license suspension actions taken pursuant to Sections 13202.6 and 13202.7, or Section 256 or 11350.6 of the Welfare and Institutions Code shall be disclosed only during the actual time period in which the suspension is in effect.

(d) The department shall not make available or disclose a suspension or revocation that has been judicially set aside or stayed.

(e) The department shall not make available or disclose personal information about a person unless the disclosure is in compliance with the Driver's Privacy Protection Act of 1994 (18 U.S.C. Sec. 2721 et seq.). However, a disclosure is subject to the prohibition in paragraph (2) of subdivision (a) of Section 12800.5.

(f) The department shall make available or disclose to the courts and law enforcement agencies a conviction of Section 23103, as specified in Section 23103.5, or a conviction of Section 23140, 23152, or 23153, or Section 655 of the Harbors and Navigation Code, or paragraph (1) of subdivision (c) of Section 192 of the Penal Code for a period of 10 years from the date of the offense for the purpose of imposing penalties mandated by this code, or by other applicable provisions of California law.

(g) The department shall make available or disclose to the courts and law enforcement agencies a conviction of Section 191.5, or subdivision (a) of Section 192.5 of the Penal Code, punished as a felony, for the purpose of imposing penalties mandated by Section 23550.5, or by other applicable provisions of California law. *(Added by Stats.1974, c. 1409, p. 3095, § 6. Amended by Stats.1977, c. 504, p. 1633, § 1, operative July 1, 1978; Stats.1980, c. 544, p. 1499, § 1; Stats.1982, c. 1129, p. 4079, § 2; Stats.1985, c. 1011, § 2, operative June 30, 1986; Stats. 1991, c. 946 (S.B.228), § 3.5; Stats.1997, c. 619 (S.B.506), § 7; Stats.1999, c. 489 (A.B.771), § 1; Stats.2001, c. 473 (S.B.485), § 17; Stats.2002, c. 545 (S.B.1852), § 6; Stats. 2004, c. 550 (S.B.1694), § 3; Stats.2006, c. 311 (S.B.1586), § 4; Stats.2007, c. 747 (A.B.678), § 13.)*

Cross References

Accident reports, confidentiality, see Vehicle Code §§ 16005, 20012.

Information concerning taxation of manufactured homes, see Revenue and Taxation Code § 5842.

§ 1808.1. Prospective employers of drivers of vehicles requiring certain licenses or certificates; pull-notice system and periodic reports

(a) The prospective employer of a driver who drives a vehicle specified in subdivision (k) shall obtain a report showing the driver's current public record as recorded by the department. For purposes of this subdivision, a report is current if it was issued less than 30 days prior to the date the employer employs the driver. The report shall be reviewed, signed, and dated by the employer and maintained at the employer's place of business until receipt of the pull-notice system report pursuant to subdivisions (b) and (c). These reports shall be presented upon request to an authorized representative of the Department of the California Highway Patrol during regular business hours.

(b) The employer of a driver who drives a vehicle specified in subdivision (k) shall participate in a pull-notice system, which is a process for the purpose of providing the employer with a report showing the driver's current public record as recorded by the department, and any subsequent convictions, failures to appear, accidents, driver's license suspensions, driver's license revocations, or any other actions taken against the driving privilege or certificate, added to the driver's record while the employer's notification request remains valid and uncanceled. As used in this section, participation in the pull-notice system means obtaining a requester code and enrolling all employed drivers who drive a vehicle specified in subdivision (k) under that requester code.

(c) The employer of a driver of a vehicle specified in subdivision (k) shall, additionally, obtain a periodic report from the department at least every 12 months. The employer shall verify that each employee's driver's license has not been suspended or revoked, the employee's traffic violation point count, and whether the employee has been convicted of a violation of Section 23152 or 23153. The report shall be signed and dated by the employer and maintained at the employer's principal place of business. The report shall be presented upon demand to an authorized representative of the Department of the California Highway Patrol during regular business hours.

(d) Upon the termination of a driver's employment, the employer shall notify the department to discontinue the driver's enrollment in the pull-notice system.

(e) For the purposes of the pull-notice system and periodic report process required by subdivisions (b) and (c), an owner, other than an owner-operator as defined in Section 34624, and an employer who drives a vehicle described in subdivision (k) shall be enrolled as if he or she were an employee. A family member and a volunteer driver who drives a vehicle described in subdivision (k) shall also be enrolled as if he or she were an employee.

(f) An employer who, after receiving a driving record pursuant to this section, employs or continues to employ as a driver a person against whom a disqualifying action has been taken regarding his or her driving privilege or required driver's certificate, is guilty of a public offense, and upon conviction thereof, shall be punished by confinement in a county jail for not more than six months, by a fine of not more than one thousand dollars ($1,000), or by both that confinement and fine.

(g) As part of its inspection of bus maintenance facilities and terminals required at least once every 13 months pursuant to subdivision (c) of Section 34501, the Department of the California Highway Patrol shall determine whether each transit operator, as defined in Section 99210 of the Public Utilities Code, is then in compliance with this section and Section 12804.6, and shall certify each operator found to be in compliance. Funds shall not be allocated pursuant to Chapter 4 (commencing with Section 99200) of Part 11 of Division 10 of the Public Utilities Code to a transit operator that the Department of the California Highway Patrol has not certified pursuant to this section.

(h)(1) A request to participate in the pull-notice system established by this section shall be accompanied by a fee determined by the department to be sufficient to defray the entire actual cost to the department for the notification service. For the receipt of subsequent reports, the employer shall also be charged a fee established by the department pursuant to Section 1811. An employer who qualifies pursuant to Section 1812 shall be exempt from any fee required pursuant to this section. Failure to pay the fee shall result in automatic cancellation of the employer's participation in the notification services.

(2) A regularly organized fire department, having official recognition of the city, county, city and county, or district in which the department is located, shall participate in the pull-notice program and shall not be subject to the fee established pursuant to this subdivision.

(3) The Board of Pilot Commissioners for Monterey Bay and the Bays of San Francisco, San Pablo, and Suisun, and its port agent shall participate in the pull-notice system established by this section, subject to Section 1178.5 of the Harbors and Navigation Code, and shall not be subject to the fees established pursuant to this subdivision.

(i) The department, as soon as feasible, may establish an automatic procedure to provide the periodic reports to an employer by mail or via an electronic delivery method, as required by subdivision (c), on a regular basis without the need for individual requests.

(j)(1) The employer of a driver who is employed as a casual driver is not required to enter that driver's name in the pull-notice system, as otherwise required by subdivision (a). However, the employer of a casual driver shall be in possession of a report of the driver's current public record as recorded by the department, prior to allowing a casual driver to drive a vehicle specified in subdivision (k). A report is current if it was issued less than six months prior to the date the employer employs the driver.

(2) For the purposes of this subdivision, a driver is employed as a casual driver when the employer has employed the driver less than 30 days during the preceding six months. "Casual driver" does not include a driver who operates a vehicle that requires a passenger transportation endorsement.

(k) This section applies to a vehicle for the operation of which the driver is required to have a class A or class B driver's license, a class C license with a hazardous materials endorsement, a class C license issued pursuant to Section 12814.7, or a certificate issued pursuant to Section 12517, 12519, 12520, 12523, 12523.5, or 12527, or a passenger vehicle having a seating capacity of not more than 10 persons, including the driver, operated for compensation by a charter-party carrier of passengers or passenger stage corporation pursuant to a certificate of public convenience and necessity or a permit issued by the Public Utilities Commission.

(*l*) This section shall not be construed to change the definition of "employer," "employee," or "independent contractor" for any purpose.

(m) A motor carrier who contracts with a person to drive a vehicle described in subdivision (k) that is owned by, or leased to, that motor carrier, shall be subject to subdivisions (a), (b), (c), (d), (f), (j), (k), and (*l*) and the employer obligations in those subdivisions.

(n) Reports issued pursuant to this section, but only those for a driver of a taxicab engaged in transportation services as described in subdivision (a) of Section 53075.5 of the Government Code, shall be presented upon request, during regular business hours, to an authorized representative of the administrative agency responsible for issuing permits to taxicab transportation services pursuant to Section 53075.5 of the Government Code. *(Added by Stats.1983, c. 893, § 1, operative July 1, 1984. Amended by Stats.1984, c. 667, § 3, operative July 1, 1985; Stats.1986, c. 1306, § 7; Stats.1987, c. 726, § 3, operative July 1, 1988; Stats.1988, c. 1586, § 3, operative July 1, 1989; Stats.1989, c. 1136, § 3; Stats.1989, c. 1216, § 9, eff. Oct. 1, 1989; Stats.1990, c. 65 (A.B.1790), § 14, eff. May 1, 1990; Stats.1990, c. 104 (S.B.798), § 1, eff. May 23, 1990; Stats.1990, c. 1360 (S.B.1510), § 3; Stats.1991, c. 488 (A.B.123), § 1; Stats.1991, c. 928 (A.B.1886), § 17, eff. Oct. 14, 1991; Stats.1991, c. 1223 (S.B.1073), § 1.3; Stats.1992, c. 690 (S.B.1973), § 1; Stats.1996, c. 1042 (A.B.1683), § 49, eff. Sept. 29, 1996; Stats.1997, c. 652 (A.B.1518), § 9; Stats.2000, c. 1035 (S.B.1403), § 5; Stats.2002, c. 418 (A.B.2273), § 1; Stats.2006, c. 311 (S.B.1586), § 5; Stats.2010, c. 360 (A.B.1648), § 1; Stats. 2010, c. 478 (A.B.2777), § 6.5; Stats.2011, c. 108 (A.B. 807), § 1; Stats.2012, c. 794 (S.B.1408), § 10.)*

Cross References

Provisional restricted class C license for operation of army and national guard vehicles, conditions, see Vehicle Code § 12814.7.
Suspension of permit for motor carriers of property, failure to enroll all drivers in pull notice system, see Vehicle Code § 34623.

§ 1808.2. Confidential records; address; inspectors or investigators of district attorney; peace officer employees of board of prison terms

In addition to those specified in Section 1808.4, the home address of any inspector or investigator regularly employed and paid as such in the office of a district attorney or any peace officer employee of the Board of Prison Terms appearing in any record of the department is confidential. *(Added by Stats.1980, c. 616, p. 1698, § 2, operative July 1, 1981.)*

Cross References

Prohibition against posting on Internet the home address or telephone number of any elected or appointed official, inclusion of active or retired public officer or other persons listed in this section, see Government Code §§ 6254.21 and 6254.24.

§ 1808.3. Repealed by Stats.1996, c. 1042 (A.B.1683), § 50, eff. Sept. 29, 1996

§ 1808.4. Confidential records; home addresses of certain public officials and employees and their spouses and children; penalty

(a) For all of the following persons, his or her home address that appears in a record of the department is confidential if the person requests the confidentiality of that information:

(1) Attorney General.

(2) State Public Defender.

(3) A Member of the Legislature.

(4) A judge or court commissioner.

(5) A district attorney.

(6) A public defender.

(7) An attorney employed by the Department of Justice, the office of the State Public Defender, or a county office of the district attorney or public defender.

(8) A city attorney and an attorney who submits verification from his or her public employer that the attorney represents the city in matters that routinely place the attorney in personal contact with persons under investigation for, charged with, or convicted of, committing criminal acts, if that attorney is employed by a city attorney.

(9) A nonsworn police dispatcher.

(10) A child abuse investigator or social worker, working in child protective services within a social services department.

(11) An active or retired peace officer, as defined in Chapter 4.5 (commencing with Section 830) of Title 3 of Part 2 of the Penal Code.

(12) An employee of the Department of Corrections and Rehabilitation, Division of Juvenile Facilities, or the Prison Industry Authority specified in Sections 20403 and 20405 of the Government Code.

(13) A nonsworn employee of a city police department, a county sheriff's office, the Department of the California Highway Patrol, a federal, state, or local detention facility, or a local juvenile hall, camp, ranch, or home, who submits agency verification that, in the normal course of his or her employment, he or she controls or supervises inmates or is required to have a prisoner in his or her care or custody.

(14) A county counsel assigned to child abuse cases.

(15) An investigator employed by the Department of Justice, a county district attorney, or a county public defender.

(16) A member of a city council.

(17) A member of a board of supervisors.

(18) A federal prosecutor, criminal investigator, or National Park Service Ranger working in this state.

(19) An active or retired city enforcement officer engaged in the enforcement of the Vehicle Code or municipal parking ordinances.

(20) An employee of a trial court.

(21) A psychiatric social worker employed by a county.

(22) A police or sheriff department employee designated by the Chief of Police of the department or the sheriff of the county as being in a sensitive position. A designation pursuant to this paragraph shall, for purposes of this section, remain in effect for three years subject to additional designations that, for purposes of this section, shall remain in effect for additional three-year periods.

(23) A state employee in one of the following classifications:

(A) Licensing Registration Examiner, Department of Motor Vehicles.

(B) Motor Carrier Specialist 1, Department of the California Highway Patrol.

(C) Museum Security Officer and Supervising Museum Security Officer.

(24)(A) The spouse or child of a person listed in paragraphs (1) to (23), inclusive, regardless of the spouse's or child's place of residence.

(B) The surviving spouse or child of a peace officer, as defined in Chapter 4.5 (commencing with Section 830) of Title 3 of Part 2 of the Penal Code, if the peace officer died in the line of duty.

(C)(i) Subparagraphs (A) and (B) shall not apply if the person listed in those subparagraphs was convicted of a crime and is on active parole or probation.

(ii) For requests made on or after January 1, 2011, the person requesting confidentiality for their spouse or child listed in subparagraph (A) or (B) shall declare, at the time of the request for confidentiality, whether the spouse or child has been convicted of a crime and is on active parole or probation.

(iii) Neither the listed person's employer nor the department shall be required to verify, or be responsible for verifying, that a person listed in subparagraph (A) or (B) was convicted of a crime and is on active parole or probation.

(b) The confidential home address of a person listed in subdivision (a) shall not be disclosed, except to any of the following:

(1) A court.

(2) A law enforcement agency.

(3) The State Board of Equalization.

(4) An attorney in a civil or criminal action that demonstrates to a court the need for the home address, if the disclosure is made pursuant to a subpoena.

(5) A governmental agency to which, under any provision of law, information is required to be furnished from records maintained by the department.

(c)(1) A record of the department containing a confidential home address shall be open to public inspection, as provided in Section 1808, if the address is completely obliterated or otherwise removed from the record.

(2) Following termination of office or employment, a confidential home address shall be withheld from public inspection for three years, unless the termination is the result of conviction of a criminal offense. If the termination or separation is the result of the filing of a criminal complaint, a confidential home address shall be withheld from public inspection during the time in which the terminated individual may file an appeal from termination, while an appeal from termination is ongoing, and until the appeal process is exhausted, after which confidentiality shall be at the discretion of the employing agency if the termination or separation is upheld. Upon reinstatement to an office or employment, the protections of this section are available.

(3) With respect to a retired peace officer, his or her home address shall be withheld from public inspection permanently upon request of confidentiality at the time the information would otherwise be opened. The home address of the surviving spouse or child listed in subparagraph (B) of paragraph (24) of subdivision (a) shall be withheld from public inspection for three years following the death of the peace officer.

(4) The department shall inform a person who requests a confidential home address what agency the individual whose address was requested is employed by or the court at which the judge or court commissioner presides.

(d) A violation of subdivision (a) by the disclosure of the confidential home address of a peace officer, as specified in paragraph (11) of subdivision (a), a nonsworn employee of the city police department or county sheriff's office, or the spouses or children of these persons, including, but not limited to, the surviving spouse or child listed in subparagraph (B) of paragraph (24) of subdivision (a), that results in bodily injury to the peace officer, employee of the city police department or county sheriff's office, or the spouses or children of these persons is a felony. *(Added by Stats.1985, c. 745, § 2, operative July 1, 1986. Amended by Stats.1989, c. 335, § 1; Stats.1991, c. 579 (A.B.972), § 2; Stats.1992, c. 427 (A.B.3355), § 164; Stats.1992, c. 1242 (S.B.602), § 2; Stats.1992, c. 1279 (A.B.3442), § 8; Stats.1993, c. 1291 (A.B.2367), § 1; Stats.1993, c. 1292 (S.B.274), § 4.5; Stats.1994, c. 77 (A.B.1931), § 3; Stats.1994, c. 838 (A.B.3161), § 2; Stats.1998, c. 458 (A.B.1389), § 1; Stats.2001, c. 363 (A.B.606), § 7, eff. Sept. 27, 2001; Stats.2001, c. 486 (A.B.1029), § 1; Stats.2001, c. 809 (A.B.84), § 3; Stats. 2002, c. 1 (S.B.65), § 47, eff. Jan. 16, 2002; Stats.2008, c. 91 (A.B.2039), § 1; Stats.2009, c. 140 (A.B.1164), § 178; Stats.2010, c. 280 (S.B.938), § 1.)*

§ 1808.5. Confidential records: physical, mental condition; controlled substances offenses

Except as provided in Section 22511.58, all records of the department relating to the physical or mental condition of any person, and convictions of any offense involving the use or possession of controlled substances under Division 10 (commencing with Section 11000) of the Health and Safety Code not arising from circumstances involving a motor vehicle, are confidential and not open to public inspection. *(Added by Stats.1969, c. 1445, p. 2955, § 1. Amended by Stats.1973, c. 876, p. 1608, § 1; Stats.1984, c. 1635, § 92; Stats.1995, c. 766 (S.B.726), § 4; Stats.1998, c. 828 (S.B.1637), § 11.)*

§ 1808.6.   Confidential records; home addresses of certain officials

(a) In addition to those specified in Section 1808.4, the home address of any of the following persons, that appears in any record of the department, is confidential, if the person requests the confidentiality of that information:

(1) The chairperson, executive officer, commissioners, and deputy commissioners of the Board of Prison Terms.

(2) The chairperson, members, executive director, and hearing representatives of the Youthful Offender Parole Board.

(3) The spouse or children of persons listed in this section, regardless of the spouse's or child's place of residence.

(b) The confidential home address of any of the persons listed in subdivision (a) shall not be disclosed to any person, except a court, a law enforcement agency, the State Board of Equalization, or any governmental agency to which, under any provision of law, information is required to be furnished from records maintained by the department.

(c) Any record of the department containing a confidential home address shall be open to public inspection, as provided in Section 1808, if the address is completely obliterated or otherwise removed from the record. The home address shall be withheld from public inspection for three years following termination of office or employment, except with respect to retired peace officers, whose home addresses shall be withheld from public inspection permanently upon request of confidentiality at the time the information would otherwise be opened. The department shall inform any person who requests a confidential home address of the name of the agency that employs the individual whose address was requested. *(Added by Stats.1993, c. 525 (A.B.807), § 1. Amended by Stats.1995, c. 91 (S.B.975), § 170; Stats.1996, c. 880 (A.B.1941), § 1.)*

§ 1808.7.   Confidential record; exceptions

Section added by Stats.2010, c. 216 (A.B.2144), § 2.5, operative July 1, 2011. See, also, another section of the same number added by Stats.2010, c. 599 (A.B.2499), § 2.5, operative July 1, 2011.

(a) The record of the department relating to the first proceeding and conviction under Section 1803.5 in any 18–month period for completion of a traffic violator school program is confidential, shall not be disclosed to any person, except a court and as provided for in subdivision (b), and shall be used only for statistical purposes by the department. No violation point count shall be assessed pursuant to Section 12810 if the conviction is confidential.

(b) The record of a conviction described in subdivision (a) shall not be confidential if any of the following circumstances applies:

(1) The person convicted holds a commercial driver's license as defined by Section 15210.

(2) The person convicted holds a commercial driver's license in another state, in accordance with Part 383 of Title 49 of the Code of Federal Regulations.

(3) The violation occurred in a commercial motor vehicle, as defined in subdivision (b) of Section 15210.

(4) The conviction would result in a violation point count of more than one point pursuant to Section 12810.

(c) This section shall become operative on July 1, 2011. *(Added by Stats.2010, c. 216 (A.B.2144), § 2.5, operative July 1, 2011.)*

§ 1808.7.   Confidential record; exceptions

Section added by Stats.2010, c. 599 (A.B.2499), § 2.5, operative July 1, 2011. See, also, another section of the same number, added by Stats.2010, c. 216 (A.B.2144), § 2.5, operative July 1, 2011.

(a) The record of the department relating to the first proceeding and conviction under Section 1803.5 in any 18–month period for completion of a traffic violator school program is confidential, shall not be disclosed to any person, except a court and as provided for in subdivision (b), and shall be used only for statistical purposes by the department. No violation point count shall be assessed pursuant to Section 12810 if the conviction is confidential.

(b) The record of a conviction described in subdivision (a) shall not be confidential if any of the following circumstances applies:

(1) The person convicted holds a commercial driver's license as defined by Section 15210.

(2) The person convicted holds a commercial driver's license in another state, in accordance with Part 383 of Title 49 of the Code of Federal Regulations.

(3) The violation occurred in a commercial motor vehicle, as defined in subdivision (b) of Section 15210.

(4) The conviction would result in a violation point count of more than one point pursuant to Section 12810.

(c) This section shall become operative on July 1, 2011. *(Added by Stats.2010, c. 599 (A.B.2499), § 2.5, operative July 1, 2011.)*

Cross References

Occupational licensing, traffic violator schools, duties of Judicial Council, see Vehicle Code § 11205.4.

§ 1808.8. Schoolbus, pupil activity bus, youth bus, or paratransit vehicle drivers; dismissal for safety-related cause; reinstatement; reporting requirements

(a) Dismissal of any driver certified pursuant to Section 12517, 12523, or 12523.5, for a cause relating to pupil transportation safety, shall be reported by the carrier to the department within five days of the dismissal date.

(b) Reinstatement of any driver whose dismissal has been reported under subdivision (a) shall be reported by the carrier to the department within five days of the reinstatement date. *(Added by Stats.1989, c. 359, § 2.)*

§ 1808.9. Confidential records; demonstration of continued eligibility

(a) Except for retired peace officers whose home address is permanently withheld from public inspection under subdivision (c) of Section 1808.4 or subdivision (c) of Section 1808.6, a person whose home address is confidential in any record of the department under Section 1808.2, 1808.4, or 1808.6 may be required by the department to demonstrate his or her continued eligibility for that confidentiality upon renewal of a driver's license or identification card issued by the department. Not later than 90 days prior to the expiration of a driver's license or identification card, the department shall notify the person whose record is confidential of any requirement to demonstrate the continued eligibility.

(b) A person whose driver's license or identification card is renewed within one year of the first request for address confidentiality under this section shall not be required to demonstrate his or her eligibility for that confidentially again until the subsequent renewal. *(Added by Stats.1996, c. 880 (A.B.1941), § 2.)*

§ 1808.10. Drivers allowed to complete courses at traffic violator schools; conviction records not confidential; disclosures required

The record of the department relating to the first proceeding and conviction for a driver licensed with a class A license, class B license, or commercial class C driver's license in any 18–month period who is allowed, for a traffic offense while operating a vehicle requiring only a class C or a class M license, to complete a course of instruction at a traffic violator school, is not confidential and shall be disclosed for purposes of Title 49 of the Code of Federal Regulations and to insurers by the department for insurance underwriting and rating purposes. *(Added by Stats.2012, c. 302 (A.B.1888), § 1.)*

§ 1808.21. Confidential records; residence or mailing address; consent to service of process; grounds for suppression

(a) Any residence address in any record of the department is confidential and shall not be disclosed to any person, except a court, law enforcement agency, or other government agency, or as authorized in Section 1808.22 or 1808.23.

(b) Release of any mailing address or part thereof in any record of the department may be restricted to a release for purposes related to the reasons for which the information was collected, including, but not limited to, the assessment of driver risk, or ownership of vehicles or vessels. This restriction does not apply to a release to a court, a law enforcement agency, or other governmental agency, or a person who has been issued a requester code pursuant to Section 1810.2.

(c) Any person providing the department with a mailing address shall declare, under penalty of perjury, that the mailing address is a valid, existing, and accurate mailing address and shall consent to receive service of process pursuant to subdivision (b) of Section 415.20, subdivision (a) of Section 415.30, and Section 416.90 of the Code of Civil Procedure at the mailing address.

(d)(1) Any registration or driver's license record of a person may be suppressed from any other person, except those persons specified in subdivision (a), if the person requesting the suppression submits either of the following:

(A) A certificate or identification card issued to the person as a program participant by the Secretary of State pursuant to Chapter 3.1 (commencing with Section 6205) of Division 7 of Title 1 of the Government Code.

(B) Verification acceptable to the department that he or she has reasonable cause to believe either of the following:

(i) That he or she is the subject of stalking, as specified in Section 1708.7 of the Civil Code or Section 646.9 of the Penal Code.

(ii) That there exists a threat of death or great bodily injury to his or her person, as defined in Section 12022.7 of the Penal Code.

(2) Upon suppression of a record, each request for information about that record shall be authorized by the subject of the record or verified as legitimate by other investigative means by the department before the information is released.

(e)(1) The suppression of a record pursuant to a verification under subparagraph (B) of paragraph (1) of subdivision (d) shall occur for one year after approval by the department. Not less than 60 days prior to the date the suppression of the record would otherwise expire, the department shall notify the subject of the record of its impending expiration. The suppression may be continued for two additional periods of one year each if a letter is submitted to the department stating that the person continues to have a reasonable cause to believe that he or she is the subject of stalking or that there exists a threat of death or great bodily injury as described in subparagraph (B) of paragraph (1) of subdivision (d). The suppression may be additionally continued at the end of the second one-year period by submitting verification acceptable to the department. The notification described in this subdivision shall instruct the person of the method to reapply for record suppression.

(2) The suppression of a record made in accordance with the submission of a certificate or identification card under subparagraph (A) of paragraph (1) of subdivision (d) shall occur for four years following the submission of the certificate or identification card described in this paragraph. The suppression may be continued for an additional four-year period, and for subsequent four-year periods, upon the submission of a current certificate or identification card described in this paragraph.

(f) For the purposes of subdivisions (d) and (e), "verification acceptable to the department" means recent police reports, court documentation, or other documentation from a law enforcement agency. *(Added by Stats. 1989, c. 1213, § 5. Amended by Stats.1994, c. 395 (A.B.3454), § 1; Stats.1996, c. 440 (S.B.1588), § 1.5; Stats.2000, c. 1008 (S.B.2072), § 1; Stats.2001, c. 854 (S.B.205), § 66; Stats.2003, c. 720 (A.B.184), § 1.)*

Cross References

Address confidentiality for reproductive health care service providers, employees, volunteers and patients, suppression of records by Department of Motor Vehicles, see Government Code § 6215.5.

§ 1808.22. Application of § 1808.21; violations

(a) Section 1808.21 does not apply to a financial institution licensed by the state or federal government to do business in the State of California, if the financial institution states under penalty of perjury that it has obtained a written waiver of Section 1808.21 signed by the individual whose address is requested, or to providing the address of a person who has entered into an agreement held by that institution prior to July 1, 1990, so long as that agreement remains in effect.

(b)(1) Section 1808.21 does not apply to an insurance company licensed to do business in California, or to an authorized contractor acting on behalf of that insurance company, pursuant to a contractual agreement, if the company or contractor, under penalty of perjury, requests the information for the purpose of obtaining the address of another motorist or vehicle owner involved in an accident with the company's insured.

(2) Section 1808.21 does not apply to an insurance company licensed to do business in California if the company, under penalty of perjury, requests the information on an individual who has signed a written waiver of Section 1808.21 or on the individuals insured under a policy if a named insured of that policy has signed a written waiver.

(c)(1) Notwithstanding any other provisions of the Vehicle Code and regulations adopted by the department, all information obtained from the department pursuant to the exemptions in subdivision (b) shall be subject to the existing use or disclosure limitations and data security requirements for the principal under applicable state and federal law.

(2) Use or disclosure limitations and data security requirements imposed on an authorized contractor by this subdivision shall be enforced by the department in compliance with its existing regulations governing the use or disclosure of information obtained from the department pursuant to subdivision (b).

(3) The use or disclosure of information obtained from the department by an authorized contractor of the insurance company pursuant to paragraph (1) of subdivision (b) shall be permitted only for the purpose of obtaining the address of another motorist or vehicle owner involved in an accident with the company's insured. The information shall not be used or disclosed for any other purpose, other than the reason for which the information was requested, or to any other person.

(4) An insurance company shall be responsible for any misuse of the information by the authorized contractor.

(5) An authorized contractor is subject to all of the following requirements:

(A) All information obtained by the contractor from the department pursuant to paragraph (1) of subdivision (b), and any copies made of that information, shall be destroyed by the contractor pursuant to Section 1798.81 of the Civil Code, once the contractor has used the information for the purpose of obtaining the address of a motorist or vehicle owner involved in an accident with individuals insured with the insurer.

(B) The contractor shall not sell the information obtained from the department or store, combine, or link that information with a database for resale or for any purpose other than obtaining the address of a motorist or vehicle owner involved in an accident with individuals insured with the insurer.

(C) The contractor shall maintain a log to track the receipt, use, and dissemination of the information. The log shall be immediately available to the department upon request and maintained for four years from the date of the request.

(D) The contractor shall maintain a surety bond in the amount of fifty thousand dollars ($50,000), consistent with subdivision (c) of Section 1810.2 and Section 350.24 of Title 13 of the California Code of Regulations.

(E) A contractor that violates this section shall be liable to the department for civil penalties up to the amount of one hundred thousand dollars ($100,000), and, if the contractor is a commercial requester pursuant to Section 1810.2, the contractor shall also have his or her requester code suspended for a period of five years, or revoked, pursuant to Section 1808.46.

(d) Section 1808.21 does not apply to an attorney if the attorney states, under penalty of perjury, that the motor vehicle or vessel registered owner or driver residential address information is necessary in order to represent his or her client in a criminal or civil action that directly involves the use of the motor vehicle or vessel that is pending, is to be filed, or is being investigated. Information requested pursuant to this subdivision is subject to all of the following:

(1) The attorney shall state that the criminal or civil action that is pending, is to be filed, or is being investigated relates directly to the use of that motor vehicle or vessel.

(2) The case number, if any, or the names of expected parties to the extent they are known to the attorney requesting the information, shall be listed on the request.

(3) A residence address obtained from the department shall not be used for any purpose other than in furtherance of the case cited or action to be filed or that is being investigated.

(4) If an action is not filed within a reasonable time, the residence address information shall be destroyed.

(5) An attorney shall not request residential address information pursuant to this subdivision in order to sell the information to a person.

(6) Within 10 days of receipt of a request, the department shall notify every individual whose residence address has been requested pursuant to this subdivision.

(e) A knowing violation of paragraph (1), (2), (3), (4), or (5) of subdivision (d) is a misdemeanor. A knowing violation of paragraph (1), (2), (3), (4), or (5) of subdivision (d) in furtherance of another crime is subject to the same penalties as that other crime.

(Added by Stats.2003, c. 649 (A.B.1675), § 2, operative Jan. 1, 2007. Amended by Stats.2010, c. 353 (A.B.953), § 1.)

Cross References

Misdemeanor, definition, penalties, see Penal Code §§ 17, 19 and 19.2.

§ 1808.23. Application of confidentiality of records law to specified entities; use of released address information

(a) Section 1808.21 does not apply to any of the following:

(1) A vehicle manufacturer licensed to do business in this state if the manufacturer, or its agent, under penalty of perjury, requests and uses the information only for the purpose of safety, warranty, including a warranty issued in compliance with Section 1795.92 of the Civil Code, emission, or product recall if the manufacturer offers to make and makes any changes at no cost to the vehicle owner.

(2) A dealer licensed to do business in this state if the dealer, or its agent, under penalty of perjury, requests and uses the information only for the purpose of completing registration transactions and documents.

(3) A person who, under penalty of perjury, requests and uses the information as permitted under subdivision (h) of Section 1798.24 of the Civil Code, if the request specifies that no persons will be contacted by mail or otherwise at the address included with the information released. The information released by the department under this subdivision shall not be in a form that identifies any person.

(4) An electrical corporation as defined in Section 218 of the Public Utilities Code or a local publicly owned electric utility as defined in Section 224.3 of the Public Utilities Code, if the corporation or utility, or its agent, under penalty of perjury, requests and uses the information only for the purposes of identifying where an electric vehicle is registered. All of the following shall apply to this paragraph:

(A) The department may disclose to the electrical corporation or local publicly owned utility only the type of vehicle and address of the electric vehicle owner. The department shall not disclose the name of the electric vehicle owner.

(B) Within 15 days of receiving residence address information from the department pursuant to this section, an electrical corporation or local publicly owned utility shall provide a clear, express disclosure to the electric vehicle owner that his or her residence address information is permitted by law to be shared with the corporation or utility. The disclosure shall not contain marketing information or a solicitation for the purchase of goods or services.

(C) Confidential home address and type of vehicle information of electric vehicle owners disclosed pursuant to this paragraph shall only be used for the purpose of identifying where an electric vehicle is registered and shall not be used or disclosed for any other purpose, including for purposes of identifying the individual or individuals residing at the address, or to any other person.

(D) The electrical corporation or local publicly owned utility and its agents shall not sell, share, or further disclose, including to any subsidiaries, the residence address or type of vehicle information of electric vehicle owners obtained pursuant to this paragraph, or name information determined by matching residence information against the corporation or utility's customer records.

(b) Residential addresses released shall not be used for direct marketing or solicitation for the purchase of any consumer product or service. *(Added by Stats.1990, c. 1635 (A.B.3796), § 1, eff. Sept. 30, 1990. Amended by Stats.1993, c. 814 (S.B.486), § 2; Stats.1995, c. 929 (S.B.501), § 9; Stats.1996, c. 440 (S.B.1588), § 3; Stats. 2011, c. 346 (S.B.859), § 1.)*

§ 1808.24. Confidential information; information regarding motor vehicle liability insurance policy; exceptions

Information regarding any motor vehicle liability insurance policy or surety bond provided to the department pursuant to Section 4000.37 or provided electronically is confidential and shall not be disclosed to any person, except to the following:

(a) A court of competent jurisdiction.

(b) A law enforcement or other governmental agency.

(c) An insurance company or its assigns to verify a record the company or its assigns previously submitted to the department.

(d) A person whose vehicle or property has been involved in an accident reported to the department, or who suffered bodily injury or death in an accident reported to the department, pursuant to Chapter 1 (commencing with Section 16000) of Division 7, or the person's authorized representative, employer, parent, or legal guardian. *(Added by Stats.1999, c. 880 (S.B.652), § 2.)*

§ 1808.25. Residence address information to be provided to accredited degree-granting nonprofit independent institutions of higher education; terms of memorandum of understanding and contract

(a) The department shall implement a program to provide residence address information to an accredited degree-granting nonprofit independent institution of higher education incorporated in the state, that has concluded a memorandum of understanding pursuant to subdivision (b) of Section 830.7 of the Penal Code if, under penalty of perjury, the institution requests and uses the information solely for the purpose of enforcing parking restrictions.

(b) The memorandum of understanding executed by the sheriff or chief of police within whose jurisdiction the independent institution is located shall expressly permit the institution to enforce parking restrictions pursuant to subdivision (b) of Section 830.7 of the Penal Code. For the purposes of this subdivision, a participating institution shall enter into a contractual agreement with the department that, at a minimum, requires the institution to do all of the following:

(1) Establish and maintain procedures, to the satisfaction of the department, for persons to contest parking violation notices issued by the institution.

(2) Remit a fee, as determined by the department, to cover the department's costs of providing each address to the institution.

(3) Agree that access to confidential residence address information from the department's vehicle registration database will be provided only through an approved commercial requester account.

(4) Establish and maintain a system that ensures that confidential address information obtained from the department is used solely for the purpose specified in subdivision (a).

(c) The director may terminate a contract authorized by subdivision (b) at any time the department determines that the independent institution of higher education fails to maintain adequate safeguards to ensure that the operation of the program does not adversely affect those individuals whose records are maintained in the department's files, or that the information is used for any purpose other than that specified in subdivision (a).

(d) Sections 1808.45, 1808.46, and 1808.47 are applicable to persons who obtain department records pursuant to this section and the department may pursue any appropriate civil or criminal action against any individual at an independent institution who violates the provisions of this section.

(e) For purposes of this article only, any confidential information obtained from the department for administration or enforcement of this article shall be held confidential, except to the extent necessary for the enforcement of parking restrictions, and may not be used for any purpose other than the administration or enforcement of parking restrictions.

(Added by Stats.1998, c. 885 (A.B.1730), § 2. Amended by Stats.2001, c. 676 (A.B.370), § 1; Stats.2003, c. 410 (S.B.247), § 1.)

§ 1808.45. Unauthorized disclosure of information; false representation; misdemeanor

The willful, unauthorized disclosure of information from any department record to any person, or the use of any false representation to obtain information from a department record or any use of information obtained from any department record for a purpose other than the one stated in the request or the sale or other distribution of the information to a person or organization for purposes not disclosed in the request is a misdemeanor, punishable by a fine not exceeding five thousand dollars ($5,000) or by imprisonment in the county jail not exceeding one year, or both fine and imprisonment. *(Added by Stats.1989, c. 1213, § 7.)*

Cross References

Use of vehicle report information, see Vehicle Code § 1810.3.

§ 1808.46. Civil penalties; suspension or revocation of requester code privileges; review of procedure

No person or agent shall directly or indirectly obtain information from the department files using false representations or distribute restricted or confidential information to any person or use the information for a reason not authorized or specified in a requester code application. Any person who violates this section, in addition to any other penalty provided in this code, is liable to the department for civil penalties up to one hundred thousand dollars ($100,000) and shall have its requester code privileges suspended for a period of up to five years, or revoked. The regulatory agencies having jurisdiction over any licensed person receiving information pursuant to this chapter shall implement procedures to review the procedures of any licensee which receives information to ensure compliance with the limitations on the use of information as part of the agency's regular oversight of the licensees. The agency shall report noncompliance to the department. *(Added by Stats.1989, c. 1213, § 8. Amended by Stats.1990, c. 431 (S.B.1150), § 1.5, eff. July 26, 1990; Stats.1990, c. 1635 (A.B.3796), § 2, eff. Sept. 30, 1990.)*

Cross References

Use of vehicle report information, see Vehicle Code § 1810.3.

§ 1808.47. Procedures to protect confidentiality of records; use of records by agents

Any person who has access to confidential or restricted information from the department shall establish procedures to protect the confidentiality of those records. If any confidential or restricted information is released to any agent of a person authorized to obtain information, the person shall require the agent to take all steps necessary to ensure confidentiality and prevent the release of any information to a third party. No agent shall obtain or use any confidential or restricted records for any purpose other than the reason the information was requested. *(Added by Stats.1989, c. 1213, § 9. Amended by Stats.1996, c. 440 (S.B.1588), § 4; Stats.1999, c. 880 (S.B.652), § 3.)*

§ 1808.51. Bureau of Real Estate; city attorney and investigators; authority to obtain copies of fullface engraved pictures or photographs of individuals directly from Department of Motor Vehicles

Notwithstanding Sections 1808.5 and 12800.5, both of the following may obtain copies of fullface engraved pictures or photographs of individuals directly from the department:

(a) The Bureau of Real Estate, as a department, individually, or through its staff, for purposes of enforcing the Real Estate Law (Part 1 (commencing with Section 10000) of Division 4 of the Business and Professions Code) or the Subdivided Lands Law (Chapter 1 (commencing with Section 11000) of Part 2 of Division 4 of the Business and Professions Code).

(b) The city attorney of a city and county and his or her investigators for purposes of performing functions related to city and county operations. *(Added by Stats. 2011, c. 717 (S.B.53), § 16. Amended by Stats.2012, c. 304 (A.B.2383), § 1; Stats.2013, c. 352 (A.B.1317), § 519, eff. Sept. 26, 2013, operative July 1, 2013.)*

§ 1809. Traffic accident information

The department may prepare and disseminate information relating to prevention of traffic accidents. *(Stats. 1959, c. 3, p. 1544, § 1809.)*

Cross References

Tabulation and analysis of accident information, see Vehicle Code § 2408.

§ 1810. Inspection or sale of information; identification of requester; notification of subject; photocopies

(a) Except as provided in Sections 1806.5, 1808.2, 1808.4, 1808.5, 1808.6, 1808.7, 1808.8, and paragraph (2) of subdivision (a) of Section 12800.5, the department may permit inspection of, or sell, or both, information from its records concerning the registration of any vehicle or information from the files of drivers' licenses at a charge sufficient to pay at least the actual cost to the department for providing the inspection or sale of the information, including, but not limited to, costs incurred by the department in carrying out subdivision (b), with the charge for the information to be determined by the director. This section does not apply to statistical information of the type previously compiled and distributed by the department.

(b)(1) With respect to the inspection or sale of information concerning the registration of any vehicle or of information from the files of drivers' licenses, the department shall establish, by regulation, administrative procedures under which any person making a request for that information shall be required to identify himself or herself and state the reason for making the request. The procedures shall provide for the verification of the name and address of the person making a request for the information, and the department may require the person to produce that information as it determines is necessary to ensure that the name and address of the person is the true name and address. The procedures may provide for a 10–day delay in the release of the requested information. The procedures shall also provide for notification to the person to whom the information primarily relates, as to what information was provided and to whom it was provided. The department shall establish, by regulation, a reasonable period of time for which a record of all the foregoing shall be maintained.

(2) The procedures required by this subdivision do not apply to any governmental entity, any person who has applied for and has been issued a requester code by the department, or any court of competent jurisdiction.

(c) With respect to the inspection or sale of information from the files of drivers' licenses, the department may require both the full name of the driver and either the driver's license number or date of birth as identifying points of the record, except that the department may disclose a record without two identifying points if the department determines that the public interest in disclosure outweighs the public interest in personal privacy.

(d) With respect to the inspection or sale of information from the files of drivers' licenses, certificates of ownership, and registration cards, the department may not allow, for a fee or otherwise, copying by the public. *(Stats.1959, c. 3, p. 1544, § 1810. Amended by Stats.1961,*

c. 216, p. 1238, § 1; Stats.1977, c. 374, p. 1361, § 1; Stats.1982, c. 1273, p. 4698, § 2; Stats.1987, c. 961, § 2; Stats.1989, c. 1213, § 10; Stats.1996, c. 124 (A.B.3470), § 116; Stats.1997, c. 619 (S.B.506), § 8; Stats.1999, c. 489 (A.B.771), § 2; Stats.2002, c. 805 (A.B.2996), § 10, eff. Sept. 23, 2002; Stats.2003, c. 594 (S.B.315), § 15.)

§ 1810.2. Commercial requester accounts; issuance of requester code

(a) The department may establish commercial requester accounts for individuals or organizations and issue requester codes for the purpose of obtaining information from the department's files, except as prohibited by Section 1808.21.

(b) Commercial requester account applications shall include the requester's name, address, type of business, a specific reason for requesting information, and the name of the person responsible for the business or firm.

(c) The department shall establish a commercial requester account when it determines that the applicant has a legitimate business need for the information requested and when the applicant files a bond in the amount of fifty thousand dollars ($50,000) and pays a two hundred fifty dollar ($250) filing fee. If the applicant does not request and is not issued a requester code permitting the applicant access to residence address information, only a filing fee of fifty dollars ($50) shall be required with the original application and each biennial renewal application.

(d) An individual requester code shall be issued for a period not to exceed five years and may be renewed upon application for additional periods not to exceed five years each.

(e) A requester code may be denied to any person unless the proposed use of the information from department records is related to legitimate business or commercial purposes of that person. A requester code may be canceled immediately if the requested information is used for a purpose other than the purpose for which the requester code was issued. (Added by Stats.1989, c. 1213, § 11. Amended by Stats.1991, c. 579 (A.B.972), § 3.)

§ 1810.3. Use of information in accident reports provided under § 20012

(a) Using the information made available in the accident reports provided to the department by law enforcement agencies under Section 20012, the department may provide information consisting of the following, for each vehicle that is included in those reports:

(1) The license plate number.

(2) The accident report number.

(b) Notwithstanding Section 16005, 20012, or 20014, or any other provision of law, the department may make the information available to a person who has done both of the following:

(1) Established a commercial requester account under Section 1810.2.

(2) Entered into an agreement described under subdivision (c).

(c) The department shall not provide information under this section unless the person requesting the information has entered into an agreement with the department that includes the following stipulations:

(1) The information provided may not be used for the purpose of identifying or contacting any person or for any other purpose, except as specified in paragraph (2).

(2) The information may be used only to identify a vehicle that has been reported to be in a traffic accident.

(3) The law enforcement agency accident report number and license plate number provided under this section shall be used only for the internal verification purposes of the business that receives the information and may not be disclosed to any party other than the department or the Department of the California Highway Patrol.

(4) The requester agrees to investigate and promptly correct any error that is brought to its attention.

(d) Use of the information provided under this section in violation of paragraph (1), (2), or (3) of subdivision (c) is a violation of Sections 1808.45 and 1808.46. (Added by Stats.2004, c. 336 (S.B.871), § 1, eff. Aug. 30, 2004.)

§ 1810.5. Public records; access by certain officials

The Attorney General, district attorneys, law enforcement agencies, city attorneys prosecuting misdemeanor actions under Section 41803. 5 of the Government Code, public defenders, and public defender investigators shall have access, including, but not limited to, telephone access, to the records of the department. For purposes of obtaining a governmental entity requester code from the department, the office of a city attorney engaged in the prosecution of criminal actions shall be deemed a law enforcement entity. (Added by Stats.1986, c. 1056, § 1. Amended by Stats.2003, c. 127 (A.B.365), § 1.)

§ 1810.7. Access to electronic database for vehicle registration information for commercial use; special permit; departmental powers and duties; financial security; fees; report every three years

(a) Except as provided in Sections 1806.5, 1808.2, 1808.4, 1808.5, 1808.6, 1808.7, and 1808.21, the department may authorize, by special permit, any person to access the department's electronic database, as provided for in this section, for the purpose of obtaining information for commercial use.

(b) The department may limit the number of permits issued under this section, and may restrict, or establish priority for, access to its files as the department deems necessary to avoid disruption of its normal operations, or as the department deems is in the best interest of the public.

(c) The department may establish minimum volume levels, audit and security standards, and technological requirements, or any terms and conditions it deems necessary for the permits.

(d) As a condition of issuing a permit under this section, the department shall require each direct-access permittee to file a performance bond or other financial security acceptable to the department, in an amount the department deems appropriate.

(e) The department shall charge fees for direct-access service permits, and shall charge fees pursuant to Section 1810 for any information copied from the files.

(f) The department shall ensure that information provided under this section includes only the public portions of records.

(g) On and after January 1, 1992, the director shall report every three years to the Legislature on the implementation of this section. The report shall include the number and location of direct-access permittees, the volume and nature of direct-access inquiries, procedures the department has taken to ensure the security of its files, and the costs and revenues associated with the project.

(h) The department shall establish procedures to ensure confidentiality of any records of residence addresses and mailing addresses as required by Sections 1808.21, 1808.22, 1808.45, 1808.46, and 1810.2. *(Added by Stats. 1988, c. 1459, § 1, operative July 1, 1989. Amended by Stats.1989, c. 1213, § 12; Stats.2001, c. 745 (S.B.1191), § 224, eff. Oct. 12, 2001; Stats.2002, c. 805 (A.B.2996), § 11, eff. Sept. 23, 2002; Stats.2003, c. 594 (S.B.315), § 16.)*

§ 1811. Sale of records

The department may sell copies of all or any part of its records at a charge sufficient to pay at least the entire actual cost to the department of the copies, the charge for the records and the conditions under which they may be sold to be determined by the director. *(Stats.1959, c. 3, p. 1545, § 1811. Amended by Stats.1961, c. 216, p. 1238, § 2.)*

§ 1812. Free to governmental agencies

The department shall not charge for copies of records or for information from its records given to any county, city, any transit operator as defined in Section 99210 of the Public Utilities Code, state department, or the United States government. *(Stats.1959, c. 3, p. 1545, § 1812. Amended by Stats.1987, c. 726, § 4, operative July 1, 1988.)*

§ 1813. Free records

The director and such officers of the department as he may designate may, upon request, prepare under the seal of the department and deliver without charge a certified copy of any record of the department received or maintained under this code. *(Stats.1959, c. 3, p. 1545, § 1813.)*

§ 1814. Automobile registration service

Any person engaged in the business of examining the records of the department and supplying information relative thereto to the public for compensation shall first obtain a permit from the director. The director shall grant such a permit when he determines that the applicant is qualified and intends in good faith to carry on such business, and when the applicant files with the director a bond in the amount of five thousand dollars ($5,000). *(Stats.1959, c. 3, p. 1545, § 1814.)*

Cross References

Accident reports are confidential, see Vehicle Code §§ 20012, 20014.

Authority for corporations to become sureties, see Code of Civil Procedure § 995.620.

Contents of sureties' affidavits on undertaking or bonds, see Code of Civil Procedure § 995.520.

Department to have possession of records, see Vehicle Code § 1502.

Inspection and copying of public records, see Government Code § 6250 et seq.

§ 1815. Bond

The bond shall be to the satisfaction of the director and shall obligate the principal and sureties to compensate the officers of the department and any other person who may suffer loss or damage by reason of any failure or neglect of the principal, the principal's agents, or employees to preserve carefully and surrender any records examined in the department and by reason of any act of the principal, the principal's agents, or employees in respect to the loss, alteration, substitution, or mutilation of any records of the department. *(Stats.1959, c. 3, p. 1545, § 1815. Amended by Stats.1982, c. 517, p. 2420, § 386.)*

Law Revision Commission Comments

1982 Amendment

Section 1815 is amended to delete a provision duplicated in the Bond and Undertaking Law. See Code Civ.Proc. §§ 995.310 (sureties on bond), 995.140 ("bond" defined). The other changes in Section 1815 are technical. [16 Cal.L.Rev.Comm.Reports 501 (1981)].

Cross References

Bond and Undertaking Law, see Code of Civil Procedure § 995.010 et seq.

Records of Department of Motor Vehicles, vehicle registration and titling, electronic programs, see Vehicle Code § 1685.

§ 1816. Juvenile traffic offender

Every judge of the juvenile court, juvenile hearing officer, duly constituted referee of a juvenile court, or other person responsible for the disposition of cases involving traffic offenses required to be reported under Section 1803 committed by persons under 18 years of age shall keep a full record of every case in which a person is charged with such a violation, and shall report the offense to the department at its office in Sacramento not more than 30 days after the date on which it was committed, and in no case less than 10 days after adjudication. The report required by this section shall be required for any determination that a minor committed the violation, including any determination that because of the act the minor is a person described in Section 601 or 602 of the Welfare and Institutions Code or that a program of supervision should be instituted for the minor. No report shall be made if it is found that the alleged offense was not committed.

The report required by this section shall be made upon a form furnished by the department and shall contain all necessary information as to the identity of the offender, the arresting agency, the date and nature of the offense, and the date the finding was made. *(Added by Stats.1959, c. 1622, p. 3991, § 2. Amended by Stats.1971, c. 1748, p. 3761, § 51.5, operative March 4, 1972; Stats.1972, c. 755, p. 1349, § 1; Stats.1989, c. 1465, § 4; Stats.2003, c. 149 (S.B.79), § 80.)*

Law Revision Commission Comments

2003 Amendment

Section 1816 is amended to reflect the redesignation of traffic hearing officers as juvenile hearing officers. See 1997 Cal. Stat. ch. 679. [33 Cal.L.Rev.Comm. Reports 246 (2003)].

Cross References

Advisory statement to be given by court to person convicted of violating §§ 23103, 23103.5, 23152 and 23153, inclusion of fact on abstract of conviction, see Vehicle Code § 23593.

§ 1817. Forwarding information to department of forestry

Written allegations received by the department from members of the public identifying motor vehicles or other vehicles by license number from which any flaming or glowing substance has been thrown, or discharged, shall be forwarded to the Department of Forestry and Fire Protection together with any information as to the identity of the registered owner of the vehicle as shown by the records of the department. *(Added by Stats.1963, c. 2038, p. 4267, § 29. Amended by Stats.1981, c. 714, p. 2791, § 434; Stats.1992, c. 427 (A.B.3355), § 165.)*

§ 1818. Vehicle license notation on abstract

Any record of, or information from any record concerning, an abstract of conviction kept by the department shall contain an appropriate notation indicating the commercial or noncommercial nature or the license plate number of the vehicle involved in the offense. *(Added by Stats.1967, c. 683, p. 2052, § 2.)*

§ 1819. Records of actual mileage of motor vehicles

All records of the department containing information as to the actual mileage of motor vehicles submitted as required by subdivision (b) of Section 4456 and Sections 5900 and 5901 shall be open to inspection by the public during the office hours of the department. *(Added by Stats.1971, c. 260, p. 417, § 1, operative May 3, 1972. Amended by Stats.1993, c. 852 (A.B.1485), § 1; Stats. 1994, c. 180 (A.B.375), § 4, eff. July 11, 1994.)*

§ 1820. Repealed by Stats.1992, c. 690 (S.B.1973), § 2

§ 1821. Data and monitoring system; evaluation of intervention programs; recidivism tracking system; report

(a) The department shall establish and maintain a data and monitoring system to evaluate the efficacy of intervention programs for persons convicted of violations of Section 23152 or 23153.

(b) The system may include a recidivism tracking system. The recidivism tracking system may include, but not be limited to, jail sentencing, license restriction, license suspension, level I (first offender) and II (multiple offender) alcohol and drug education and treatment program assignment, alcohol and drug education treatment program readmission and dropout rates, adjudicating court, length of jail term, actual jail or alternative sentence served, type of treatment program assigned, actual program compliance status, subsequent accidents related to driving under the influence of alcohol or drugs, and subsequent convictions of violations of Section 23152 or 23153.

(c) The systems described in subdivisions (a) and (b) shall include an evaluation of the efficacy of the increased level of intervention resulting from the act that added this subdivision.

(d) The department shall submit an annual report of its evaluations to the Legislature. The evaluations shall include a ranking of the relative efficacy of criminal penalties, other sanctions, and intervention programs and the various combinations thereof, including, but not limited to, those described in subdivision (c). *(Added by Stats.1989, c. 450, § 2. Amended by Stats.1998, c. 656 (A.B.1916), § 2.)*

Cross References

Public agencies and conditions requiring the preparation or submission of written reports with respect to this section, see Government Code § 7550.5.

§ 1822. Driving under the influence of alcohol or drugs; data system to track violations; legislative intent

The Legislature finds that driving under the influence of alcohol or drugs continues to be a primary safety issue on the state's highways, and the major cause of traffic deaths. It is imperative that violators who drive while under the influence of alcohol or drugs be fully prosecuted under the law. The Legislature also finds that too often violators have not had their driving records at the Department of Motor Vehicles appropriately updated. Therefore, it is the intent of the Legislature that the department, working with the courts, establish and maintain a data and monitoring system to track violations of driving under the influence of alcohol or drugs, including, but not limited to, violations of Article 1.3 (commencing with Section 23136), Article 1.5 (commencing with Section 23140), and Article 2 (commencing with Section 23152), of Chapter 12 of Division 11. The system shall match arrests for driving under the influence of alcohol or drug violations with convictions reported to the department. *(Added by Stats.1996, c. 224 (S.B.1579), § 1.)*

§ 1825. Disabled person placards; annual random audits of applications

(a) The department may conduct an annual, random audit of applications submitted and processed pursuant to Section 22511.55 or subdivision (b) or (c) of Section 22511.59 to verify the authenticity of the certificates and information submitted in support of those applications.

(b) The audit provisions of subdivision (a) only apply to those applications that were initially submitted to the department after January 1, 2001. *(Added by Stats.2000, c. 524 (A.B.1792), § 1.5.)*

CHAPTER 2. DEPARTMENT OF THE CALIFORNIA HIGHWAY PATROL

Article		Section
1.	Administration	2100
2.	The California Highway Patrol	2250
3.	Powers and Duties	2400
3.3.	Tow Truck Drivers	2430
3.5.	Emergency Roadside Assistance	2435
4.	Highway Spill Containment and Abatement of Hazardous Substances	2450
5.	Renderers and Transporters of Inedible Kitchen Grease	2460

ARTICLE 1. ADMINISTRATION

Section
2100. Department of California Highway Patrol.
2101. Reference to department.
2102. Reference to California Highway Patrol.
2103. Successor to California Highway Patrol.
2104. Ownership of property.
2105. State Department provisions.
2106. Office of department.
2107. Commissioner of the California Highway Patrol.
2108. Powers and duties of commissioner.
2109. Organization of department.
2110. Assistant commissioner.
2111. Duties of assistant commissioner.
2112. Administrative officer.
2113. Duties of chief administrative officer.
2114. Membership in associations.

§ 2100. Department of California Highway Patrol

There is in the Transportation Agency the Department of the California Highway Patrol. *(Stats.1959, c. 3, p. 1545, § 2100. Amended by Stats.1961, c. 2073, p. 4331, § 4; Stats.1965, c. 493, p. 1804, § 10; Stats.1969, c. 138, p. 371, § 279, eff. Sept. 11, 1969; Stats.1984, c. 144, § 202; Gov.Reorg.Plan No. 2 of 2011–2012, § 323, eff. July 3, 2012, operative July 1, 2013; Stats.2013, c. 352 (A.B.1317), § 520, eff. Sept. 26, 2013, operative July 1, 2013.)*

Cross References

Accident report forms, supply by department, see Vehicle Code § 2407.

Advertisement as California highway patrol, see Vehicle Code § 25.

Appropriations for support and operation of department, see Vehicle Code § 42271.

Assistance to other departments, see Government Code § 11253.

Cattle protection, cooperation with other peace officers to maintain, see Food and Agricultural Code § 20433.

Commissioner defined, see Vehicle Code § 265.

Department defined, see Vehicle Code §§ 290, 2101, 21000, 24000.

Department personnel, see Vehicle Code § 2250.

Headquarters or substations, establishment, see Vehicle Code § 2404.

Patrol districts and branch offices, establishment, see Vehicle Code § 2403.

Powers and duties of department and commissioner, see Vehicle Code §§ 2108, 2400 et seq.

Services, materials or equipment to other agencies, see Government Code § 11256.

Term of office, see Government Code § 1301.

§ 2101. Reference to department

As used in this chapter, "department" means the Department of the California Highway Patrol. *(Stats. 1959, c. 3, p. 1545, § 2101. Amended by Stats.1959, c. 1996, p. 4617, § 4.)*

§ 2102. Reference to California Highway Patrol

Wherever in any statute "California Highway Patrol" is used, it means the Department of the California Highway Patrol. *(Stats.1959, c. 3, p. 1546, § 2102.)*

Cross References

Traffic officer defined, see Vehicle Code § 625.

§ 2103. Successor to California Highway Patrol

The department is the successor to and is vested with the duties, powers, purposes, responsibilities, and jurisdiction of the former Division of Enforcement of the Department of Motor Vehicles, known as the California Highway Patrol, and of the officers and employees thereof. *(Stats.1959, c. 3, p. 1546, § 2103.)*

§ 2104. Ownership of property

The department has possession and control of all records, books, papers, offices, or equipment, and all other property, real or personal, now or hereafter held for the benefit or use of the former Division of Enforcement of the Department of Motor Vehicles, known as the California Highway Patrol. *(Stats.1959, c. 3, p. 1546, § 2104.)*

§ 2105. State Department provisions

Except as in this chapter otherwise provided, the provisions of Chapter 2 (commencing at Section 11150) of Part 1 of Division 3 of Title 2 of the Government Code shall govern and apply to the conduct of the department in every respect the same as if the provisions were set forth in this code, and wherever in that chapter the term "head of the department" or similar designation occurs, for the purposes of this division, it shall mean the commissioner. *(Stats.1959, c. 3, p. 1546, § 2105. Amended by Stats.1959, c. 1996, p. 4617, § 5.)*

§ 2106. Office of department

The department shall maintain its main office within 20 miles of Sacramento. *(Stats.1959, c. 3, p. 1546, § 2106. Amended by Stats.2007, c. 9 (A.B.443), § 1.)*

Cross References

Creation of patrol districts and branch offices, see Vehicle Code § 2403.
Department to keep office at Sacramento and adopt official seal, see Government Code § 11151.
Establishment of headquarters or substations, see Vehicle Code § 2404.

§ 2107. Commissioner of the California Highway Patrol

The department is under the control of a civil executive officer, known as the Commissioner of the California Highway Patrol. The commissioner shall be appointed by the Governor with the advice and consent of the Senate to serve at the pleasure of the Governor, and shall have resided within the State continuously for at least five years immediately preceding his appointment. *(Stats. 1959, c. 3, p. 1546, § 2107. Amended by Stats.1984, c. 268, § 32.3, eff. June 30, 1984.)*

Cross References

Buying appointment to office prohibited, see Penal Code §§ 73, 74.
Chief administrative officer, of California highway patrol, appointment, see Vehicle Code § 2112.
Civil executive officers enumerated, see Government Code § 1001.
Commissioner defined, see Vehicle Code § 265.
Commissioner's general powers and duties, see Vehicle Code § 2400 et seq.
Disqualification for office or employment, see Government Code § 1020 et seq.
Misdemeanor to exercise offices without furnishing bond, see Government Code § 1303.
Official bonds, generally, see Government Code § 1450 et seq.
Patrol members, compulsory retirement, exception for Commissioner of California Highway Patrol, see Government Code § 21130.
Salary of commissioner, see Government Code § 11550.
Term of office, see Government Code § 1301.

§ 2108. Powers and duties of commissioner

The commissioner shall perform all duties, exercise all powers and jurisdiction, assume and discharge all responsibilities, and carry out and effect all purposes vested by law in the department.

Notwithstanding any other provision of law, the commissioner may administratively determine the geographic area of residence of any member of the department in order to assure the availability of such member for emergency service and the discharge of departmental responsibilities. *(Stats.1959, c. 3, p. 1546, § 2108. Amended by Stats.1963, c. 1231, p. 2758, § 1.)*

Cross References

Commissioner, powers and duties as department head, see Vehicle Code § 2400 et seq.; Government Code §§ 11153, 11154.
Cooperation with department of transportation, see Streets and Highways Code § 127.
Delegation of powers and duties, see Vehicle Code § 8.
Establishment of headquarters or substations, see Vehicle Code § 2404.
Establishment of training school, see Vehicle Code § 2262.
Law enforcement, see Vehicle Code § 2400.
Patrol districts and branch offices, see Vehicle Code § 2403.
Patrol equipment, see Vehicle Code § 2406.
Real property, purchase or lease, see Vehicle Code § 2405.
Rules and regulations, see Vehicle Code § 2402.
School safety patrols, cooperation with local authorities, see Education Code § 49305.

§ 2109. Organization of department

The commissioner shall organize the department with the approval of the Governor and the Secretary of Transportation and may arrange and classify the work of the department and may, with the approval of the Governor and the Secretary of Transportation, create or abolish divisions thereof. *(Stats.1959, c. 3, p. 1546, § 2109. Amended by Stats.1969, c. 138, p. 371, § 280, eff. Sept. 11, 1969; Stats.1984, c. 144, § 203; Gov.Reorg.Plan No. 2 of 2011–2012, § 324, eff. July 3, 2012, operative July 1, 2013; Stats.2013, c. 352 (A.B.1317), § 521, eff. Sept. 26, 2013, operative July 1, 2013.)*

Cross References

Commissioner, powers and duties as department head, see Vehicle Code § 2400 et seq.; Government Code §§ 11153, 11154.
Organization of divisions and making of rules and regulations, see Government Code § 11152.

§ 2110. Assistant commissioner

The Assistant Commissioner of the California Highway Patrol shall be appointed by the commissioner, subject to the approval of the Governor, pursuant to the provisions of Article XXIV [1] of the State Constitution. *(Stats.1959, c. 3, p. 1546, § 2110. Amended by Stats.1984, c. 268, § 32.4, eff. June 30, 1984.)*

[1] Repealed; see, now, Const. Art. 7.

Cross References

Delegation of powers and duties, see Vehicle Code § 8.
Disqualification for office or employment, see Government Code § 1020 et seq.
Misdemeanor to exercise offices without furnishing bond, see Government Code § 1303.

§ 2111. Duties of assistant commissioner

The assistant commissioner shall carry out and execute such duties, with respect to traffic law enforcement, as may be specified by the commissioner. *(Stats.1959, c. 3, p. 1546, § 2111.)*

Cross References

Delegation of powers and duties, see Vehicle Code § 8.

Offenses and prosecution, see Vehicle Code § 40000.1 et seq.

§ 2112. Administrative officer

The chief administrative officer of the department shall be appointed by the commissioner subject to the approval of the Governor, pursuant to the provisions of Article XXIV [1] of the State Constitution. *(Stats.1959, c. 3, p. 1546, § 2112. Amended by Stats.1965, c. 371, p. 1598, § 287; Stats.1984, c. 268, § 32.5, eff. June 30, 1984.)*

[1] Repealed; see, now, Const. Art. 7.

Cross References

Delegation of powers and duties, see Vehicle Code § 8.
Department of General Services, see Government Code § 14600 et seq.
Misdemeanor to exercise offices without furnishing bond, see Government Code § 1303.

§ 2113. Duties of chief administrative officer

The chief administrative officer shall carry out and execute such duties with respect to the administrative affairs of the department as may be specified by the commissioner. *(Stats.1959, c. 3, p. 1547, § 2113.)*

Cross References

Delegation of powers and duties, see Vehicle Code § 8.

§ 2114. Membership in associations

The department may pay membership fees, join, and participate in the affairs of associations having for their purpose the interchange of information relating to law enforcement, accident prevention, and subjects related to the powers and duties of the department. *(Stats.1959, c. 3, p. 1547, § 2114.)*

ARTICLE 2. THE CALIFORNIA HIGHWAY PATROL

Section
2250.   The California Highway Patrol.
2250.1. Special peace officer designation; transfer of responsibilities from state police division; reinstatement to former peace officer positions.
2251.   Promotions.
2252.   Specialized positions.
2253.   Worker's compensation.
2254.   Injury and disability records.
2255.   Service outside county of appointment.
2256.   Entry level peace officers; age limits.
2257.   Badges.
2258.   Issuance of badges.
2259.   Uniforms and equipment.
2259.5. Bulletproof vests.
2260.   Uniforms.
2261.   Wearing of uniforms.
2262.   Training school.
2263.   Firearm training.
2264.   Marksmanship badges.
2265.   Uniform assessment prohibited.
2266.   Communications operators; considerations regarding compensation determinations.
2267.   Citizenship requirements.
2268.   Official duties and other duties necessary for preservation of life and property; permanent limited duty; industrial disability retirement.
2269.   Boots; motorcycle riders; aircraft operations.

§ 2250. The California Highway Patrol

The California Highway Patrol in the Department of the California Highway Patrol consists of the following members: the commissioner, the deputy commissioner, assistant commissioners, chiefs, assistant chiefs, captains, lieutenants, sergeants, and officers. *(Stats.1959, c. 3, p. 1547, § 2250. Amended by Stats.1977, c. 615, p. 2089, § 1; Stats.2005, c. 270 (S.B.731), § 9.)*

Cross References

Exemption of public employees from civil liability for damages, see Vehicle Code § 17004.
Impersonation of patrol member, misdemeanor, see Vehicle Code § 27.
Patrol members, authority of peace officers, see Vehicle Code § 2409; Penal Code § 830.2.
Powers and duties of commissioner, see Vehicle Code § 2400 et seq.

§ 2250.1. Special peace officer designation; transfer of responsibilities from state police division; reinstatement to former peace officer positions

(a) The commissioner shall establish special designations of peace officers within the Department of the California Highway Patrol to assist in the transfer of responsibilities from the California State Police Division to the Department of the California Highway Patrol. The peace officers so designated include all peace officers of the former California State Police Division on July 11, 1995. These specially designated peace officers are peace officers as defined in subdivision (a) of Section 830.2 of the Penal Code.

(b) Peace officers designated in subdivision (a) shall become members of the Department of the California Highway Patrol, as described in Section 2250, by meeting the training requirements and qualifications for those positions as established pursuant to Section 19818.6 of the Government Code or with the approval of the State Personnel Board Executive Officer.

(c) Individuals granted reemployment or reinstatement on or after July 12, 1995, to peace officer positions formerly within the California State Police Division shall be reinstated to the peace officer designations established by the commissioner pursuant to this section. *(Added by Gov.Reorg.Plan No. 1 of 1995, § 64, eff. July 12, 1995; Stats.1996, c. 305 (A.B.3103), § 65.)*

§ 2251. Promotions

All promotions to the classes of deputy chief, assistant chief, captain, lieutenant, and sergeant shall be made from promotional eligible lists resulting from promotional examination of persons in the next lower class. *(Stats.1959, c. 3, p. 1547, § 2251. Amended by Stats.1961,*

c. 425, p. 1490, § 1; Stats.1963, c. 209, p. 948, § 1, eff. April 29, 1963; Stats.1977, c. 615, p. 2088, § 2.)

§ 2252. Specialized positions

Such specialized positions as shall be designated by the commissioner with the approval of the Personnel Board shall be filled pursuant to open competitive examinations held pursuant to law. *(Stats.1959, c. 3, p. 1547, § 2252.)*

§ 2253. Worker's compensation

For the purpose of determining the scope of employment of any member of the California Highway Patrol under the workers' compensation laws, any such member shall be deemed to be on duty and acting within the scope of the person's employment when actually exercising any of the powers or performing any of the duties imposed or authorized by law at any time during the 24 hours of the day. *(Stats.1959, c. 3, p. 1547, § 2253. Amended by Stats.1974, c. 1454, p. 3181, § 20.)*

§ 2254. Injury and disability records

In the event any dispute arises between the department and any of its members in an industrial disability case, such member or his attorney, upon demand, shall be entitled to examine any record of the department or of the State Compensation Insurance Fund which has any bearing on said case. *(Stats.1959, c. 3, p. 1547, § 2254.)*

§ 2255. Service outside county of appointment

No member of the California Highway Patrol, appointed to serve in any county, shall be assigned by the commissioner for service outside the county for a longer period than one week, except:

(a) Pursuant to a request by the employee for a transfer.

(b) As may be necessitated by temporary traffic emergencies requiring an increase in the number of patrol members in one locality or seasonal changes making expedient a decrease in the number of patrol members in one locality, but in such latter events no assignment shall be made for disciplinary purposes.

An assignment under this section shall be made by the commissioner. *(Stats.1959, c. 3, p. 1547, § 2255.)*

§ 2256. Entry level peace officers; age limits

Notwithstanding Section 18932 of the Government Code, the minimum age limit for appointment to the position of entry level peace officer of the Department of the California Highway Patrol, shall be 21 years, and the maximum age limit for examination shall be 35 years. *(Stats.1959, c. 3, p. 1548, § 2256. Amended by Stats.1968, c. 83, p. 240, § 3; Stats.1971, c. 1748, p. 3761, § 52, operative March 4, 1972; Stats.1997, c. 945 (A.B.1561), § 10; Stats.2001, c. 162 (A.B.311), § 1.)*

§ 2257. Badges

The commissioner shall issue to each member of the California Highway Patrol a badge of authority with the seal of the State of California in the center thereof, the words "California Highway Patrol" encircling the seal and below the designation of the position held by each member to whom issued. *(Stats.1959, c. 3, p. 1548, § 2257.)*

§ 2258. Issuance of badges

Neither the commissioner nor any other person shall issue a badge to any person who is not a duly appointed member of the California Highway Patrol. *(Stats.1959, c. 3, p. 1548, § 2258.)*

§ 2259. Uniforms and equipment

The Department of the California Highway Patrol shall pay to the member, or his estate, the cost of repairing the uniforms and equipment of the member of the California

Highway Patrol which are damaged in the line of duty. If the uniforms or equipment are damaged beyond repair, the department shall pay an amount equal to the actual value thereof at the time the damage occurred, which shall be determined by the commissioner.

The term "equipment," as used in this section, shall include equipment required by the department or personal accoutrements necessary for the patrol member to perform his duty. *(Stats.1959, c. 3, p. 1548, § 2259. Amended by Stats.1959, c. 1996, p. 4618, § 6; Stats.1961, c. 1473, p. 3327, § 1.)*

Cross References

Appropriations for support and operation of department, see Vehicle Code § 42271.

Prohibited uniform assessments, see Vehicle Code § 2265.

§ 2259.5. Bulletproof vests

The commissioner shall make certified bulletproof vests available to members of the California Highway Patrol while engaged in enforcement activities. The commissioner may, at his option, make such equipment available to the remainder of the personnel of the California Highway Patrol. Such equipment shall remain the property of the Department of the California Highway Patrol and shall be returned upon request of the commissioner. No provision of this section shall be construed to require that the commissioner provide one certified bulletproof vest for each member of the California Highway Patrol. It is the intent of this section that a sufficient number of such vests be available for the use of members of the California Highway Patrol while engaged in enforcement activities. Such vests may be passed from one shift to another in the interests of economy. *(Added by Stats.1976, c. 951, p. 2176, § 3.)*

Cross References

Acquisition of body armor by commissioner, certification requirement, see Penal Code § 12360 et seq.

§ 2260. Uniforms

The commissioner may advance the cost of, or obtain and furnish, one complete uniform, including such items of clothing and equipment as may be required by the commissioner, to each new member of the California Highway Patrol hereafter employed. The cost to the commissioner shall be deducted from the salary of such member in installments within the first year after he has completed the training school. *(Stats.1959, c. 3, p. 1548, § 2260.)*

§ 2261. Wearing of uniforms

A uniform substantially similar to the official uniform of members of the California Highway Patrol shall not be worn by any other law enforcement officer or by any other person except duly appointed members of the California Highway Patrol and persons authorized by the commissioner to wear such uniform in connection with a program of entertainment. A uniform shall be deemed substantially similar to the uniform of the California Highway Patrol if it so resembles such official uniform as to cause an ordinary reasonable person to believe that the person wearing the uniform is a member of the California Highway Patrol. *(Stats.1959, c. 3, p. 1548, § 2261. Amended by Stats.1968, c. 1192, p. 2256, § 5.2, operative Jan. 1, 1969.)*

Cross References

Unauthorized wearing of uniforms, misdemeanor, see Military and Veterans Code § 422.

Wearing of uniform in traffic law enforcement, see Vehicle Code § 40800.

§ 2262. Training school

The commissioner shall establish a school for the training and education of the members of the California Highway Patrol, and for such other employees of the department deemed necessary, in traffic regulation, in the performance of the duties of such persons, and in the proper enforcement of this code and laws respecting use of the highways. He may contract with any county, city, district, or other subdivision of the State for the use of school facilities in the training of enforcement officers. *(Stats.1959, c. 3, p. 1548, § 2262.)*

Cross References

State miscellaneous or state industrial members of Public Employees' Retirement System, exemptions from credit accrual and employee contribution provisions, see Government Code § 20281.5.

§ 2263. Firearm training

Shooting practice and instruction in the use of firearms shall constitute part of the training to be given to members of the California Highway Patrol. Firearm training may be given in connection with the school or otherwise and may include participation by patrol members in shooting competition. *(Stats.1959, c. 3, p. 1549, § 2263.)*

§ 2264. Marksmanship badges

The commissioner may procure and issue appropriate badges to patrol members for excellence in marksmanship. *(Stats.1959, c. 3, p. 1549, § 2264.)*

§ 2265. Uniform assessment prohibited

The Department of the California Highway Patrol shall not assess against any member of the department the cost of replacing any article of uniform clothing or accessories which employees are required to wear when the replacement is necessary as a result of a change in uniform regulations by the department after the effective date of this section. *(Added by Stats.1959, c. 1704, p. 4107, § 1.)*

§ 2266. Communications operators; considerations regarding compensation determinations

(a) The Legislature finds and declares all of the following:

(1) The communications operators of the Department of the California Highway Patrol are among the lowest

paid when compared to operators employed by other law enforcement agencies in the state. The department's communication centers suffer from significant staff shortages and high turnover rates. Increasing the wages paid to these communications operators will increase their professionalism while reducing their rate of turnover.

(2) The recruitment and retention problem is especially evident in the classifications of Communications Operator I and II.

(3) In order for the state to recruit and retain the highest qualified and capable communications operators, those employees should be compensated in an amount equal to the estimated average total compensation for the classifications corresponding to Communications Operator I and II within the police departments in the Cities of Los Angeles, Oakland, San Diego, and San Jose and the City and County of San Francisco.

(4) According to the Department of the California Highway Patrol, it costs the department thirty-six thousand one hundred ninety-eight dollars ($36,198) to train a Communications Operator I and sixty-five thousand two hundred two dollars ($65,202) to train a Communications Operator II to their respective classifications. After the department has trained an operator, all too often the new, fully trained operator will move to a local agency to a higher wage.

(5) This section is not in violation of the Ralph C. Dills Act (Chapter 10.3 (commencing with Section 3512) of Division 4 of Title 1 of the Government Code), which requires that changes for salaries and benefits be collectively bargained between representatives of the state and the employee's union. This section does not circumvent that process. This section simply authorizes the Department of Human Resources, when determining compensation for communications operators in the Department of the California Highway Patrol, to consider the total compensation for communications operators in other jurisdictions.

(b) When determining compensation for communications operators in the Department of the California Highway Patrol, the Department of Human Resources may consider the total compensation for communications operators in comparable positions in the police departments specified in paragraph (3) of subdivision (a). *(Added by Stats.2001, c. 786 (A.B.1038), § 1. Amended by Gov.Reorg.Plan No. 1 of 2011, § 210, eff. Sept. 9, 2011, operative July 1, 2012; Stats.2012, c. 665 (S.B.1308), § 190.)*

§ 2267. Citizenship requirements

(a) No person shall be appointed as a member of the California Highway Patrol who is not a citizen of the United States.

(b) A member of the patrol appointed prior to the effective date of this act who is not a United States citizen shall become a United States citizen at the earliest possible time. Inability or failure to comply with this subdivision shall result in termination of employment. *(Added by Stats.1982, c. 382, p. 1710, § 1.)*

§ 2268. Official duties and other duties necessary for preservation of life and property; permanent limited duty; industrial disability retirement

(a) Any member of the Department of the California Highway Patrol, as specified in Sections 2250 and 2250.1, shall be capable of fulfilling the complete range of official duties administered by the commissioner pursuant to Section 2400 and other critical duties that may be necessary for the preservation of life and property. Members of the California Highway Patrol shall not be assigned to permanent limited duty positions which do not require the ability to perform these duties.

(b) Subdivision (a) does not apply to any member of the California Highway Patrol who, after sustaining serious job-related physical injuries, returned to duty with the California Highway Patrol and who received a written commitment from the appointing power allowing his or her continued employment as a member of the California Highway Patrol. This subdivision applies only to commitments made prior to January 1, 1984.

(c) Nothing in subdivision (a) entitles a member of the California Highway Patrol to, or precludes a member from receiving, an industrial disability retirement. *(Added by Stats.1983, c. 1004, § 1. Amended by Stats.1996, c. 305 (A.B.3103), § 66.)*

§ 2269. Boots; motorcycle riders; aircraft operations

(a) The commissioner shall provide, as safety equipment, boots to each member of the California Highway Patrol who is assigned to ride motorcycles. This safety equipment shall remain the property of the state. Items lost or damaged because of the negligence of the officer shall be replaced by the officer at his or her expense.

(b) The commissioner shall pay the cost of aviation boots to each member of the California Highway Patrol who is assigned to aircraft operations and shall make aviation boots directly available for purchase by those members.

(Formerly § 2267, added by Stats.1982, c. 23, p. 40, § 1. Renumbered § 2269 and amended by Stats.1987, c. 56, § 168.)

ARTICLE 3. POWERS AND DUTIES

Section
2400. Law enforcement.
2400.5. Repealed.
2400.6. Enforcement of laws regulating use of State Highway Route 1 in City of Malibu.
2400.7. Enforcement of laws regulating the use of expressways in Santa Clara county.
2401. Patrol of highways.
2401.1. Transportation of hazardous waste or medical waste; enforcement of laws.
2402. Rules and regulations.
2402.5. Repealed.

Section
2402.6.   Regulations and standards for fuel containers and systems on vehicles using compressed or liquefied natural or petroleum gas or using compressed or liquefied hydrogen gas or liquid fuels that generate hydrogen gas; motor vehicle compliance; infractions; filling procedure.
2402.7.   Hazardous materials, substances or wastes; definitions.
2403.   Patrol districts and branch offices.
2403.5.   Reciprocal operational agreements with other states.
2404.   Headquarters or substations.
2404.5.   Vehicle for registration and commercial safety inspections at border crossings into Mexico.
2405.   Real property.
2406.   Authorized patrol equipment.
2407.   Accident report forms.
2407.5.   Repealed.
2408.   Accident information.
2408.5.   Repealed.
2409.   Peace officer authority.
2410.   Traffic direction.
2410.5.   Special events; supplemental patrol services; contract provisions; deposit of fees.
2411.   Service of warrants.
2412.   Accident investigation.
2413.   Statewide Vehicle Theft Investigation and Apprehension Coordinator; powers; duties of Department of California Highway Patrol regarding license plate reader (LPR) data.
2414.   Unclaimed property.
2415.   Sale of unclaimed property.
2416.   Issuance of authorized emergency vehicle permit.
2417.   Suspension or revocation of permit.
2418.   Rules and regulations for foreign commercial vehicles.
2418.1.   Vehicle and safety emissions inspections at California–Mexican border.
2418.5.   Resuscitation requirements for ambulances.
2419.   Replacement of flares.
2420.   Motorcycle: gross brake horsepower.
2420.5.   Inspection of specified vehicles; contract.
2421.   Attendance of out-of-state funerals; law enforcement officers.
2421.5.   Service authority for freeway emergencies; contracts to handle calls; service guidelines; reimbursement of costs.
2421.6.   Repealed.
2422.   Emergency medical dispatchers; training.
2423.   Additional training and instruction; approval; considerations.
2424.   Agreements with providers of towing, emergency road, and storage services; enforcement procedures.
2424.5.   Repealed.
2425.   Repealed.
2426.   Designated driver program; information sheets.
2427.   Fingerprints of applicant; submission to department; fee.
2428.   Protective services for state employees and property; payment of cost by state agencies; protective services fund; refusal to pay.
2429.   Public reporting of violations of Article 2; "800" telephone number.
2429.3.   Public awareness and outreach campaign; committee.

Section
2429.5.   Farm labor vehicle certification requirements; education program.

Cross References

Commissioner,
    Definition, see Vehicle Code § 265.
    Powers and duties, see Vehicle Code § 2108.
Department created and defined, see Vehicle Code §§ 1500, 2101.

§ 2400.   Law enforcement

(a) The commissioner shall administer Chapter 4 (commencing with Section 10850) of Division 4, Article 3 (commencing with Section 17300) of Chapter 1 of Division 9, Division 10 (commencing with Section 20000), Division 11 (commencing with Section 21000) except Chapter 11 (commencing with Section 22950), Division 12 (commencing with Section 24000), Division 13 (commencing with Section 29000), Division 14 (commencing with Section 31600), Division 14.1 (commencing with Section 32000), Division 14.5 (commencing with Section 33000), Division 14.7 (commencing with Section 34000), Division 14.8 (commencing with Section 34500), Division 15 (commencing with Section 35000), Division 16 (commencing with Section 36000) except Chapter 2 (commencing with Section 36100) and Chapter 3 (commencing with Section 36300), and Division 16.5 (commencing with Section 38000) except Chapter 2 (commencing with Section 38010).

(b) The commissioner shall enforce all laws regulating the operation of vehicles and the use of the highways except that, on ways or places to which Section 592 makes reference, the commissioner shall not be required to provide patrol or enforce any provisions of this code other than those provisions applicable to private property.

(c) The commissioner shall not be required to provide patrol for or enforce Division 16.5 (commencing with Section 38000).

(d) The commissioner shall have full responsibility and primary jurisdiction for the administration and enforcement of the laws, and for the investigation of traffic accidents, on all toll highways and state highways constructed as freeways, including transit-related facilities located on or along the rights-of-way of those toll highways or freeways, except facilities of the San Francisco Bay Area Rapid Transit District. However, city police officers while engaged primarily in general law enforcement duties may incidentally enforce state and local traffic laws and ordinances on toll highways and state freeways within incorporated areas of the state. In any city having either a population in excess of 2,000,000 or an area of more than 300 square miles, city police officers shall have full responsibility and primary jurisdiction for the administration and enforcement of those laws and ordinances, unless the city council of the city by resolution requests administration and enforcement of those laws by the commissioner.

(e) The commissioner shall have full responsibility and primary jurisdiction for the administration and enforcement of the laws, and for the investigation of traffic accidents, on all highways within a city and county with a population of less than 25,000, if, at the time the city and county government is established, the county contains no municipal corporations.

(f) The commissioner may enter into any interagency agreement with the State Board of Equalization for the purpose of enforcement of statutes requiring commercial vehicles from foreign jurisdictions to have a diesel fuel tax permit and to make payments to the board as required.

(g) The commissioner shall assume those duties and responsibilities of providing protection to state property and employees actually being performed by the California State Police Division on and before July 11, 1995.

(h) The commissioner may provide for the physical security of any current or former constitutional officer of the state and current or former legislator of the state.

(i) Upon request of the Chief Justice of the California Supreme Court, the commissioner may provide appropriate protective services to any current or former member of the State Court of Appeal or the California Supreme Court. *(Stats.1959, c. 3, p. 1549, § 2400. Amended by Stats.1959, c. 1996, p. 4618, § 7; Stats.1961, c. 227, p. 1245, § 1; Stats.1963, c. 2148, p. 4483, § 6; Stats.1963, c. 2149, p. 4486, § 4.6; Stats.1965, c. 1451, p. 3399, § 1; Stats.1969, c. 1213, p. 2354, § 2; Stats.1976, c. 1093, p. 4940, § 2; Stats.1980, c. 875, p. 2746, § 3; Stats.1981, c. 714, p. 2792, § 435; Stats.1981, c. 860, p. 3292, § 2; Stats.1982, c. 794, p. 3073, § 2; Stats.1982, c. 1255, p. 4602, § 3; Stats.1987, c. 958, § 2; Stats.1991, c. 653 (A.B.1850), § 2; Stats.1992, c. 1241 (S.B.1615), § 7; Gov.Reorg.Plan No. 1 of 1995, § 65, eff. July 12, 1995; Stats.1996, c. 305 (A.B.3103), § 67.)*

Cross References

Additional powers and duties, see Vehicle Code § 2108.
Commissioner to cooperate with department of transportation, see Streets and Highways Code § 127.
Freeway defined, see Vehicle Code § 332.
Law governing traffic rules and regulations, see Streets and Highways Code § 27174.1.
Schoolbus regulations, adoption, see Education Code § 39831.
Travel facilities, policing by highway patrol, see Streets and Highways Code § 27177.

§ 2400.5. Repealed by Stats.1997, c. 467 (A.B.379), § 1, eff. Sept. 25, 1997

§ 2400.6. Enforcement of laws regulating use of State Highway Route 1 in City of Malibu

The commissioner shall enforce all laws regulating the operation of vehicles on, and the use of any portion of, State Highway Route 1 in the City of Malibu, if requested by the city, and if a contract is entered into between the state and the city. The contract shall require that an amount be paid to the commissioner that is equal to the costs incurred by the department for services provided

under the contract. *(Added by Stats.1992, c. 394 (S.B. 1327), § 1.)*

§ 2400.7. Enforcement of laws regulating the use of expressways in Santa Clara county

(a) The commissioner may enforce all laws regulating the operation of vehicles and on, and the use of, any portion of any expressway in the County of Santa Clara, if requested by a city or the county with respect to the portion of the highway within that city or county and if a contract is entered into between the state and that city or the county or any combination thereof.

(b) The contract shall require affected cities or the County of Santa Clara, or both, as the case may be, to pay to the commissioner, for deposit in the Motor Vehicle Account in the State Transportation Fund, an amount that is equal to the costs incurred by the department for services provided under the contract. *(Added by Stats. 1997, c. 467 (A.B.379), § 2, eff. Sept. 25, 1997.)*

§ 2401. Patrol of highways

The commissioner shall make adequate provision for patrol of the highways at all times of the day and night. *(Stats.1959, c. 3, p. 1549, § 2401.)*

Cross References

Commissioner to cooperate with department of transportation, see Streets and Highways Code § 127.
Enforcement of travel facilities by highway patrol, see Streets and Highways Code § 27177.
Law governing traffic rules and regulations, see Streets and Highways Code §§ 27174, 27174.1.

§ 2401.1. Transportation of hazardous waste or medical waste; enforcement of laws

The commissioner may enforce those provisions relating to the transportation of hazardous waste found in Article 6 (commencing with Section 25160), Article 6.5 (commencing with Section 25167.1), and Article 8 (commencing with Section 25180), of Chapter 6.5 of Division 20 of the Health and Safety Code, pursuant to subdivision (d) of Section 25180 of the Health and Safety Code and the provisions relating to the transportation of medical waste found in Chapter 6 (commencing with Section 118000) of, and Chapter 10 (commencing with Section 118325) of, Part 14 of Division 104 of the Health and Safety Code. *(Added by Stats.1988, c. 101, § 2. Amended by Stats.1992, c. 54 (A.B.961), § 16, eff. May 14, 1992; Stats.1996, c. 1023 (S.B.1497), § 423, eff. Sept. 29, 1996.)*

§ 2402. Rules and regulations

The commissioner may make and enforce such rules and regulations as may be necessary to carry out the duties of the department. Rules and regulations shall be adopted, amended, or repealed in accordance with the Administrative Procedure Act, commencing with Section 11370 of the Government Code. *(Stats.1959, c. 3, p. 1549, § 2402. Amended by Stats.1965, c. 1500, p. 3522, § 3.)*

§ 2402.5. Repealed by Stats.1979, c. 723, p. 2216, § 4

§ 2402.6. Regulations and standards for fuel containers and systems on vehicles using compressed or liquefied natural or petroleum gas or using compressed or liquefied hydrogen gas or liquid fuels that generate hydrogen gas; motor vehicle compliance; infractions; filling procedure

(a) The commissioner may adopt and enforce regulations and standards with respect to fuel containers and fuel systems on vehicles using compressed or liquefied natural gas and liquefied petroleum gas used in conjunction with a propulsion system certified by the State Air Resources Board as producing as few or fewer emissions as a State Air Resources Board approved system using compressed or liquefied natural gas or liquefied petroleum gas and with respect to the operation of vehicles using any of those fuels to ensure the safety of the equipment and vehicles and of persons and property using the highways.

(b) The commissioner may also adopt and enforce regulations and standards with respect to fuel containers and fuel systems on vehicles using compressed or liquefied hydrogen gas or liquid fuels that generate hydrogen gas.

(c) All motor vehicles with compressed natural gas fuel systems used for propulsion shall comply either with the regulations adopted pursuant to subdivision (a) or with National Fire Protection Administration Standard NFPA 52, "Compressed Natural Gas (CNG) Vehicular Fuel Systems" in effect at the time of manufacture, until standards for those fuel systems have been incorporated into the Federal Motor Vehicle Safety Standards by the United States Department of Transportation. Whenever those Federal Motor Vehicle Safety Standards include requirements for gaseous fuel systems, all motor vehicles with gaseous fuel systems which are manufactured after the effective date of those requirements shall comply with those requirements.

(d) It is an infraction for any person to operate any motor vehicle in violation of any provision of a regulation adopted pursuant to this section.

(e) The operator of every facility for filling portable liquefied natural gas or liquefied petroleum gas containers having a capacity of four pounds or more but not more than 200 pounds of gas shall post in a conspicuous place the regulations applicable to that filling procedure. *(Added by Stats.1970, c. 1507, p. 2993, § 4. Amended by Stats.1971, c. 1257, p. 2470, § 1, operative May 3, 1972; Stats.1991, c. 928 (A.B.1886), § 17.5, eff. Oct. 14, 1991; Stats.1992, c. 1243 (A.B.3090), § 61, eff. Sept. 30, 1992; Stats.2002, c. 610 (S.B.1257), § 2.)*

Cross References

Liquefied petroleum gas defined, see Vehicle Code § 380.

§ 2402.7. Hazardous materials, substances or wastes; definitions

The commissioner shall adopt the definitions designated by the United States Department of Transportation under Title 49 (commencing with Section 1801) of the United States Code and Title 49 (commencing with Section 107) of the Code of Federal Regulations relating to hazardous materials, substances, or wastes, including, but not limited to, definitions relating to any radioactive material, poison, flammable gas, nonflammable gas, flammable liquid, oxidizer, flammable solid, corrosive material (liquid or solid), irritating materials, combustible liquids, explosives, blasting agents, etiologic agents, organic peroxides, hazardous wastes, and other regulated materials of classes A, B, C, D and E. *(Added by Stats.1977, c. 825, p. 2495, § 5. Amended by Stats.1981, c. 860, p. 3293, § 3.)*

Cross References

Hazardous material, defined, see Vehicle Code § 353.
Hazardous substances, highway spill containment and abatement, see Vehicle Code § 2454.

§ 2403. Patrol districts and branch offices

The commissioner may create highway patrol districts for the efficient administration and enforcement of this code and the laws respecting the use of highways. He may establish branch offices wherever he may deem necessary. *(Stats.1959, c. 3, p. 1549, § 2403.)*

§ 2403.5. Reciprocal operational agreements with other states

The commissioner, or a designated representative, may enter into reciprocal operational agreements with authorized representatives of the Oregon State Police, the Nevada Department of Motor Vehicles and Public Safety, and the Arizona Department of Public Safety to promote expeditious and effective law enforcement service to the public, and assistance between the members of the California Highway Patrol and those agencies, in areas adjacent to the borders of this state and each of the adjoining states pursuant to Section 830.32 of the Penal Code. The reciprocal operational agreement shall be in writing and may cover the reciprocal exchange of law enforcement services, resources, facilities and any other necessary and proper matters between the Department of the California Highway Patrol and the respective agency. Any agreement shall specify the involved departments, divisions, or units of the agencies, the duration and purpose of the agreement, the responsibility for damages, the method of financing any joint or cooperative undertaking, and the methods to be employed to terminate an agreement. The commissioner may establish operational procedures in implementation of any reciprocal operational agreement that are necessary to achieve the purposes of the agreement. *(Added by Stats.1989, c. 594, § 8.)*

§ 2404. Headquarters or substations

The commissioner shall establish, in counties having charters, except in counties of the first or second class, headquarters or substations for the efficient performance of the duties of the department, and he may establish, in such other localities as he deems most suitable, such

91

headquarters or substations. *(Stats.1959, c. 3, p. 1549, § 2404.)*

Cross References

Determination of headquarters, see Government Code § 11031.

§ 2404.5. Vehicle for registration and commercial safety inspections at border crossings into Mexico

The department shall obtain a vehicle suitable for registration and commercial safety inspections at border crossings into Mexico. *(Added by Stats.1983, c. 1001, § 1.)*

§ 2405. Real property

The commissioner may purchase or lease such real estate and erect such buildings as the department or any of its divisions require, subject to the approval of the Department of General Services. *(Stats.1959, c. 3, p. 1549, § 2405. Amended by Stats.1965, c. 371, p. 1598, § 288.)*

Cross References

Approval of leases and other contracts by department of general services, see Government Code § 13325; Public Contract Code § 10295.

Department of General Services, see Government Code § 14600 et seq.

Director may hire or lease realty, see Government Code § 14669.

Gifts to state and contracts regarding realty to require finance director's approval, see Government Code § 11005.

§ 2406. Authorized patrol equipment

The commissioner may provide that any highway patrol vehicle shall be equipped with a stretcher and emergency first aid equipment for use in transporting injured persons. *(Stats.1959, c. 3, p. 1549, § 2406.)*

§ 2407. Accident report forms

The department shall prepare and on request supply to police departments, coroners, sheriffs, and other suitable agencies or individuals, forms for accident reports required under this code, which reports shall call for sufficiently detailed information to disclose with reference to a traffic accident the cause, conditions then existing, and the persons and vehicles involved. *(Stats. 1959, c. 3, p. 1550, § 2407.)*

Cross References

Coroners to report vehicular accidental deaths, see Vehicle Code § 20011.

Department to prescribe forms, see Vehicle Code § 1652.

Duty to report accidents, see Vehicle Code § 20008.

Use of accident reports, see Vehicle Code § 20014.

§ 2407.5. Repealed by Stats.2001, c. 710 (A.B.770), § 2, operative Jan. 1, 2003

§ 2408. Accident information

The department shall tabulate and may analyze all accident reports and publish annually or at more frequent intervals statistical information based thereon as to the number and location of traffic accidents, as well as other information relating to traffic accident prevention. Based upon its findings after such analysis, the department may conduct further necessary detailed research to more fully determine the cause and control of highway accidents. It may further conduct experimental field tests within areas of the State to prove the practicability of various ideas advanced in traffic control and accident prevention. *(Stats.1959, c. 3, p. 1550, § 2408.)*

Cross References

Accident reports confidential, see Vehicle Code § 20012.

Accident reports to be kept by department of motor vehicles, see Vehicle Code § 1806.

Duty to report accidents, see Vehicle Code § 20008.

Instruction in public safety and accident prevention, see Education Code § 51202.

Preparation and dissemination of accident prevention information, see Vehicle Code § 1809.

Use of accident reports, see Vehicle Code § 20014.

§ 2408.5. Repealed by Stats.2000, c. 1035 (S.B.1403), § 5.5, operative Jan. 1, 2004

§ 2409. Peace officer authority

All members of the California Highway Patrol have the powers of a peace officer as provided in Section 830.2 of the Penal Code. *(Stats.1959, c. 3, p. 1550, § 2409. Amended by Stats.1971, c. 938, p. 1841, § 1, operative May 3, 1972.)*

Cross References

Arrest by peace officers, see Penal Code § 836.

Department of motor vehicles investigators to have powers of peace officers, see Vehicle Code § 1655.

Inspections by patrol members, see Vehicle Code § 2804 et seq.

Local emergencies, highway patrol officers as peace officers, see Government Code § 8598.

Minimum standards for public officers or employees having powers of peace officers, see Government Code § 1031.

Obedience to peace officer, see Vehicle Code § 2800.

Peace officer defined, see Penal Code § 830 et seq.

Procedure on arrest, see Vehicle Code § 40300 et seq.

Uniform Act on fresh pursuit, see Penal Code § 852 et seq.

§ 2410. Traffic direction

Members of the California Highway Patrol are authorized to direct traffic according to law, and, in the event of a fire or other emergency, or to expedite traffic or insure safety, may direct traffic as conditions may require notwithstanding the provisions of this code. *(Stats.1959, c. 3, p. 1550, § 2410.)*

Cross References

Obedience to peace officer, see Vehicle Code § 2800.

Policing of vehicular crossing by highway patrol, see Vehicle Code §§ 23251, 23253.

Traffic laws, generally, see Vehicle Code § 21000 et seq.

§ 2410.5. Special events; supplemental patrol services; contract provisions; deposit of fees

(a) The department may contract with a person or governmental entity that is conducting a special event which will impose extraordinary traffic control requirements at and near the site of the special event to provide supplemental patrol services to coordinate and direct traffic at and near the special event site. A contract entered into pursuant to this section shall include provisions for reimbursement to the department, and may include a requirement for the posting of a bond, for the cost of providing the supplemental patrol services, as determined by the commissioner.

(b) The patrol services, if any, provided under this section shall be rendered by officers of the department.

(c) Contract patrol services authorized under this section shall not reduce the normal and regular services of the department.

(d) Any contract fees received by the department pursuant to a contract under this section shall be deposited in the Motor Vehicle Account in the State Transportation Fund. *(Added by Stats.1983, c. 54, § 1, eff. May 27, 1983.)*

§ 2411. Service of warrants

Members of the California Highway Patrol are authorized to serve all warrants relating to the enforcement of this code. *(Stats.1959, c. 3, p. 1550, § 2411.)*

Cross References

Officer serving warrants, uniform and color of vehicle, see Vehicle Code § 40800.
Procedure on arrest, see Vehicle Code § 40300 et seq.

§ 2412. Accident investigation

All members of the California Highway Patrol may investigate accidents resulting in personal injuries or death and gather evidence for the purpose of prosecuting the person or persons guilty of any violation of the law contributing to the happening of such accident. *(Stats. 1959, c. 3, p. 1550, § 2412.)*

Cross References

Accident report forms, see Vehicle Code § 2407.
Accident reports confidential, see Vehicle Code § 20012.
Coroners' duty to report accidental death due to motor vehicle, see Vehicle Code § 20011.
Department to tabulate and analyze accident reports, see Vehicle Code § 2408.
Duty of driver to stop and report accident, see Vehicle Code §§ 16000, 20000 et seq.

§ 2413. Statewide Vehicle Theft Investigation and Apprehension Coordinator; powers; duties of Department of California Highway Patrol regarding license plate reader (LPR) data

(a) The Commissioner of the California Highway Patrol is designated as the Statewide Vehicle Theft

Investigation and Apprehension Coordinator. The commissioner may establish vehicle theft prevention, investigation, and apprehension programs. The commissioner may assist local, state, and federal law enforcement agencies by coordinating multijurisdictional vehicle theft investigations and may establish programs to improve the ability of law enforcement to combat vehicle theft.

(b) The Department of the California Highway Patrol may retain license plate data captured by a license plate reader (LPR) for no more than 60 days, except in circumstances when the data is being used as evidence or for all felonies being investigated, including, but not limited to, auto theft, homicides, kidnaping, burglaries, elder and juvenile abductions, Amber Alerts, and Blue Alerts.

(c) The Department of the California Highway Patrol shall not sell LPR data for any purpose and shall not make the data available to an agency that is not a law enforcement agency or an individual who is not a law enforcement officer. The data may be used by a law enforcement agency only for purposes of locating vehicles or persons when either are reasonably suspected of being involved in the commission of a public offense.

(d) The Department of the California Highway Patrol shall monitor internal use of the LPR data to prevent unauthorized use.

(e) The Department of the California Highway Patrol shall, as a part of the annual automobile theft report submitted to the Legislature pursuant to subdivision (b) of Section 10901, report the LPR practices and usage, including the number of LPR data disclosures, a record of the agencies to which data was disclosed and for what purpose, and any changes in policy that affect privacy concerns. *(Added by Stats.1994, c. 1248 (S.B.1743), § 4. Amended by Stats.2011, c. 38 (A.B.115), § 6, eff. June 30, 2011.)*

§ 2414. Unclaimed property

When lost, stolen, abandoned or otherwise unclaimed property, except vehicles subject to registration under this code, comes into possession of the department, the department may hold or store the same with some responsible person until it is claimed and all just and reasonable charges for saving and storage thereof have been paid. *(Stats.1959, c. 3, p. 1550, § 2414.)*

Cross References

Abandoned vehicles, see Vehicle Code §§ 22523, 22524.
Unclaimed property, generally, see Code of Civil Procedure § 1300 et seq.

§ 2415. Sale of unclaimed property

(a) If the owner or other person entitled to the possession thereof fails to claim the property within six months and pay the charges, the department may sell it to the highest bidder at public auction at the place where the same may be held or stored, having first caused notice of sale to be given at least five days before the time fixed therefor, by publication once in a newspaper of general circulation published in the county where the sale is to be held.

(b) Any excess in the proceeds of the sale after paying such charges and expenses of sale including but not limited to the costs of advertising and a fee of not exceeding ten dollars ($10) to be charged by the department for making the sale shall be deposited in the State Treasury in the special deposit fund as money remaining unclaimed in the hands of the department.

(c) On payment of the price bid for the property sold, the delivery of the property with the commissioner's bill of sale vests title in the purchaser.

(d) In any case where there is no bid offered for the property, or if the highest bid offered does not exceed the charges for saving, holding, and storage and the expenses of sale, the same shall become the property of the department as compensation for expenses incurred. *(Stats.1959, c. 3, p. 1551, § 2415.)*

Cross References

Publication, generally, see Government Code § 6000 et seq.
Unclaimed property payable to state treasurer and controller, see Code of Civil Procedure § 1310.

§ 2416. Issuance of authorized emergency vehicle permit

(a) The Commissioner of the California Highway Patrol may issue authorized emergency vehicle permits only for the following vehicles, and then only upon a finding in each case that the vehicle is used in responding to emergency calls for fire or law enforcement or for the immediate preservation of life or property or for the apprehension of law violators:

(1) Any vehicle maintained in whole or in part by the state, a county or a city and privately owned and operated by a marshal, deputy marshal, or person who is a member of, and who receives salary from, and is regularly employed by, a police department or sheriff's department, provided the state, county or city does not furnish to that person a publicly owned authorized emergency vehicle.

(2) Any vehicle owned and operated by a public utility, used primarily to accomplish emergency repairs to utility facilities or used primarily by railroad police officers, who are commissioned by the Governor, in the performance of their duties.

(3) Firefighting or rescue equipment designed and operated exclusively as such.

(4) Any vehicle operated by the chief, assistant chief, or one other uniformed person designated by the chief of a fire department organized as provided in the Health and Safety Code or the Government Code or pursuant to special act of the Legislature.

(5) Any vehicle of an air pollution control district used to enforce provisions of law relating to air pollution from motor vehicles.

(6) Any vehicle operated by the chief of any fire department established on any base of the armed forces of the United States.

(7) Any vehicle owned and operated by any fire company organized pursuant to Part 4 (commencing with Section 14825) of the Health and Safety Code.

(8) Privately owned ambulances licensed pursuant to Chapter 2.5 (commencing with Section 2500).

(9) Vehicles other than privately owned ambulances used by privately owned ambulance operators exclusively to transport medical supplies, lifesaving equipment, or personnel to the scene of an emergency when a request for medical supplies, lifesaving equipment, or personnel has been made by any person or public agency responsible for providing emergency medical transportation. These vehicles shall display a sign or lettering not less than two and one-half inches in height, in a color providing a sharp contrast to its background, on each side showing the name of the ambulance operator.

(10) Any vehicle owned and operated by an office or department of a city, county, or district which is designated by an ordinance adopted by the governing body of that local agency as a hazardous materials response team vehicle for response to hazardous materials emergencies.

(b) The commissioner may adopt and enforce regulations to implement this section.

(c) Violation of any regulation adopted by the commissioner pursuant to this section is a misdemeanor. *(Added by Stats.1961, c. 653, p. 1860, § 25, operative Jan. 1, 1962. Amended by Stats.1967, c. 1216, p. 3486, § 1; Stats.1968, c. 1309, p. 2465, § 2, operative Jan. 1, 1969; Stats.1970, c. 1268, p. 2292, § 1; Stats.1973, c. 35, p. 56, § 2; Stats. 1973, c. 452, p. 917, § 1; Stats.1974, c. 728, p. 1613, § 1; Stats.1975, c. 1190, p. 2948, § 1; Stats.1978, c. 272, p. 557, § 1, eff. June 22, 1978; Stats.1979, c. 517, p. 1696, § 2, eff. Sept. 7, 1979; Stats.1980, c. 1340, p. 4734, § 30, eff. Sept. 30, 1980; Stats.1982, c. 404, p. 1744, § 1; Stats.1983, c. 440, § 2; Stats.1984, c. 1028, § 1; Stats.1985, c. 492, § 1; Stats.1986, c. 102, § 1; Stats.1990, c. 824 (S.B.2858), § 3; Stats.1996, c. 872 (A.B.3472), § 177.)*

Cross References

Authorized emergency vehicle defined, see Vehicle Code § 165.
Violation as misdemeanor, see Vehicle Code § 40000.7.

§ 2417. Suspension or revocation of permit

(a) The commissioner may suspend or revoke any permit issued for an authorized emergency vehicle under the following conditions:

(1) The vehicle is operated in violation of any of the provisions of this code.

(2) The vehicle is operated in violation of the rules and regulations relating to authorized emergency vehicles as promulgated by the commissioner.

(3) The vehicle is not equipped as required by this code.

(b) The permittee of any authorized emergency vehicle whose permit has been suspended or revoked shall be entitled, upon request, to a hearing in accordance with Chapter 5 (commencing with Section 11500) of Part 1 of Division 3 of Title 2 of the Government Code.

(c) When any authorized emergency vehicle permit has been suspended or revoked under provisions of this section, any additional authorized emergency vehicle permit issued in the name of the permittee may be likewise suspended or revoked. *(Formerly § 2416. Stats. 1959, c. 3, p. 1551. Renumbered § 2417 and amended by Stats.1961, c. 653, p. 1860, § 26, operative Jan. 1, 1962. Amended by Stats.1978, c. 272, p. 558, § 2, eff. June 22, 1978.)*

Cross References

Revocation and suspension of licenses, see Vehicle Code § 13100 et seq.

§ 2418. Rules and regulations for foreign commercial vehicles

The department shall adopt reasonable rules and regulations to ensure that all foreign commercial vehicles entering into, and operating within, this state meet those standards already in effect for other commercial vehicles and shall address, but not be limited to, the following concerns:

(a) Vehicle maintenance.

(b) Maximum hours of service for drivers.

(c) Insurance.

(d) Enforcement of criminal, civil, and administrative actions, including, but not limited to, impoundment of vehicles for second or subsequent violations of rules and regulations adopted under this section. *(Added by Stats. 1998, c. 727 (S.B.270), § 3.)*

Contingent Operation

This section is contingent upon funding in the 1998 Budget Act, pursuant to Stats.1998, c. 727 (S.B.270), § 5.

§ 2418.1. Vehicle and safety emissions inspections at California–Mexican border

For purposes of enforcing the provisions of Section 2418, the department and the State Air Resources Board shall, to the maximum extent possible, conduct vehicle safety and emissions inspections at the California–Mexican border crossings. Inspections shall be conducted at the Otay Mesa and Calexico commercial vehicle inspection facilities operated by the department and at other random roadside locations as determined by the department, in consultation with the board. Inspections for safety and emissions shall be consistent with the inspection procedures specified in Title 13 (commencing with Section 2175) of the California Code of Regulations as they pertain to vehicle inspections. *(Added by Stats.1998, c. 727 (S.B.270), § 4.)*

Contingent Operation

This section is contingent upon funding in the 1998 Budget Act, pursuant to Stats.1998, c. 727 (S.B.270), § 5.

§ 2418.5. Resuscitation requirements for ambulances

(a) Notwithstanding any other provision of law, every emergency ambulance that is operated within this state by any public or private agency, including, but not limited to, any emergency ambulance that is operated by the State of California, any charter or general law city or county, or any district, shall be equipped at all times with a resuscitator.

(b) For purposes of this section "emergency ambulance" means a vehicle that is designed or intended to be used in providing emergency transportation of wounded, injured, sick, disabled, or incapacitated human beings.

(c) For the purposes of this section, a " resuscitator" means a device that adequately, effectively and safely restores breathing, including, but not limited to, a portable hand-operated, self-refilling bag-valve mask unit for inflation of the lungs with either air or oxygen. The resuscitator shall not have any straps that could be used to attach the resuscitator to the human head. *(Formerly § 2418.1, added by Stats.1968, c. 1271, p. 2395, § 1. Renumbered § 2418.5 and amended by Stats.1969, c. 680, p. 1350, § 1. Amended by Stats.2004, c. 404 (S.B.1725), § 6.)*

Cross References

Authorized emergency vehicle,
  Defined, see Vehicle Code § 165.
  Rescue team non-liability, see Vehicle Code § 165.5.

§ 2419. Replacement of flares

(a) Any member of the California Highway Patrol may give flares to any person as replacement for flares used by such person to warn traffic of an accident or other hazardous condition on a highway, provided such person was not required by law to give such warning, or was not involved in the accident or the creation of the hazardous condition. The officer shall not replace such flares unless he is reasonably satisfied that such person in fact placed the flares for which replacement is requested.

(b) Notwithstanding any other provision of law, the person requesting replacement of flares shall not be required to file any claim for such flares. *(Added by Stats.1963, c. 939, p. 2192, § 1. Amended by Stats.1969, c. 167, p. 418, § 1.)*

§ 2420. Motorcycle: gross brake horsepower

Upon request of the California Highway Patrol, manufacturers of motorcycles shall furnish a certification of gross brake horsepower to the department. If any manufacturer of motorcycles fails to comply with such request within 30 days from the date such request has been deposited in the mail, then and in that event no dealer shall sell or offer for sale the particular make and model of motorcycle for which the certification was requested. *(Added by Stats.1963, c. 422, p. 1239, § 2.)*

§ 2420.5. Inspection of specified vehicles; contract

(a) The department may enter into a contract to conduct an inspection of vehicles that are subject to Section 500.100 of Title 29 of the Code of Federal Regulations and issue the vehicle inspection sticker authorized under subdivision (b) of that section to qualified vehicles.

(b) Any contract entered into under subdivision (a) shall provide that the amount to be paid to the department shall be equal to the costs incurred by the department for services provided under the contract. *(Added by Stats.1998, c. 877 (A.B.2132), § 36.)*

§ 2421. Attendance of out-of-state funerals; law enforcement officers

Notwithstanding Section 11032 of the Government Code, the commissioner may approve the out-of-state travel within the United States of members of the California Highway Patrol, in numbers the commissioner deems appropriate, to attend out-of-state funerals of law enforcement officers or to attend out-of-state events related to the funerals of law enforcement officers, including the National Peace Officers Memorial. Reimbursement for actual and necessary traveling expenses shall be allowed for members of the California Highway Patrol approved to travel out of state pursuant to this section up to a maximum aggregate amount of forty thousand dollars ($40,000) in any fiscal year. *(Added by Stats.1998, c. 220 (A.B.2236), § 1.)*

§ 2421.5. Service authority for freeway emergencies; contracts to handle calls; service guidelines; reimbursement of costs

(a) When any Service Authority for Freeway Emergencies has imposed additional fees on vehicles pursuant to Section 2555 of the Streets and Highways Code, the authority may contract with the department or a private or public entity to handle calls originating from the authority's motorist aid call box system.

(b)(1) If the contract is with the department, its terms shall comply with the requirements specified in paragraph (2) for the system on the portions of the California Freeway and Expressway System and on county roads in rural, unincorporated areas of the county and on state highway routes that connect segments of these systems, if they are located within the county in which the authority is established and the Department of the California Highway Patrol has law enforcement responsibility over them.

(2) The contract shall contain guidelines, as jointly agreed to between the authority and the department, following consultation with the authority, for services to be provided, including, but not limited to, reporting

requirements, immediate transfer of emergency calls and traffic management information to the department, computer interface capability with the department, performance standards, and coordination with the eligible tow service providers.

(c) If the contract is with a private or public entity, the authority shall ensure that the specifications in the "CHP/Cal Trans Call Box and Motorist Aid Guidelines" are met and coordinate with the department to determine which calls will be transferred to it for response. The authority shall reimburse the department for all costs incurred under this subdivision in accordance with the "CHP/Cal Trans Call Box and Motorist Aid Guidelines." If an authority has a contract with a private or public entity having a commencement date of July 1, 2003, or prior, the performance standards of those contracts shall remain in effect until modifications are made to the applicable sections of the statewide guidelines.

(d) The authority may contract with the Department of the California Highway Patrol to perform duties as mutually agreed by the parties. *(Added by Stats.1985, c. 1350, § 3. Amended by Stats.1986, c. 730, § 2; Stats. 1989, c. 533, § 3; Stats.1996, c. 1154 (A.B.3020), § 56, eff. Sept. 30, 1996; Stats.1997, c. 89 (S.B.396), § 2; Stats. 2003, c. 374 (S.B.795), § 4.)*

§ 2421.6. Repealed by Stats.1997, c. 89 (S.B.396), § 3

§ 2422. Emergency medical dispatchers; training

The department shall determine and implement the basic level of emergency medical dispatcher training for dispatchers employed by the department based on guidelines developed by the California Emergency Medical Services Authority with the concurrence of the department. Implementation shall commence not later than January 1, 1987. Notwithstanding the foregoing, the commissioner may adopt a higher level of training for department dispatchers where appropriate.

The department shall report to the Legislature on progress in the implementation of an emergency medical dispatch training program not later than January 1, 1988. *(Added by Stats.1985, c. 1303, § 1.)*

§ 2423. Additional training and instruction; approval; considerations

In approving the additional instruction and training required under subdivision (b) of Section 680, the department shall consider the requirements of Chapter 3 (commencing with Section 40080) of Part 23.5 of the Education Code, as those provisions relate to instruction and training requirements for schoolbus drivers and school pupil activity bus drivers. *(Added by Stats.1996, c. 774 (A.B.2920), § 2. Amended by Stats.2006, c. 538 (S.B.1852), § 654.)*

§ 2424. Agreements with providers of towing, emergency road, and storage services; enforcement procedures

(a) The Commissioner of the California Highway Patrol may enter into agreements with providers of towing, emergency road, and storage services for the purpose of determining which providers shall be summoned by the department when those services are necessary for public assistance or to carry out the duties and responsibilities of the department. Chapter 3.5 (commencing with Section 11340) of Part 1 of Division 3 of Title 2 of the Government Code shall not apply to the agreements. The department shall confer with the towing industry, as necessary, to reach agreements mutually beneficial to the public, the towing industry, and the department.

(b) This section does not prohibit a member of the public from selecting any vehicle towing, emergency road service, or storage provider, except when towing or storage is ordered by a member of the department under the provisions of law.

(c) These agreements shall be implemented in cooperation with representatives of the towing industry, and shall include, but not be limited to, the following subjects: liability insurance requirements, towing, emergency road service, and storage fees, inspection of business and storage facilities and equipment, recordkeeping, minimum equipment requirements, and the establishment of tow districts.

(d) Failure of a towing, emergency road service, or storage provider to comply with the provisions of the agreement may result in the suspension or termination of the agreement. In the event of suspension or termination of the agreement, and at the request of the towing, emergency road service, or storage provider, the department shall provide a hearing and appeal process to the provider.

(e) Chapter 5 (commencing with Section 11500) of Part 1 of Division 3 of Title 2 of the Government Code does not apply to the hearing and appeal process specified in subdivision (d). *(Added by Stats.1988, c. 554, § 2. Amended by Stats.1991, c. 488 (A.B.123), § 2.)*

§ 2424.5. Repealed by Stats.1995, c. 766 (S.B.726), § 5

§ 2425. Repealed by Stats.2001, c. 127 (S.B.46), § 4, operative Jan. 1, 2003

§ 2426. Designated driver program; information sheets

The department shall prepare a one-page information sheet describing its Designated Driver Program. The sheet shall include information concerning the person or entity an alcoholic beverage licensee may contact for assistance in establishing a Designated Driver Program. *(Added by Stats.1990, c. 1337 (A.B.3620), § 3.)*

§ 2427. Fingerprints of applicant; submission to department; fee

Whenever the department submits the fingerprints of an applicant for a license or certificate to the Department of Justice, and is required to pay a fee pursuant to subdivision (e) of Section 11105 of the Penal Code, the department, without the necessity of adopting regulations, shall charge the applicant a fee sufficient to reimburse the department for that fee. *(Added by Stats.1990, c. 1360 (S.B.1510), § 4.)*

§ 2428. Protective services for state employees and property; payment of cost by state agencies; protective services fund; refusal to pay

(a) The Department of the California Highway Patrol may fix the cost or pro rata share, or, in its discretion, an amount it considers equivalent to the cost or pro rata share, and collect from each state agency in advance or upon any other basis that it may determine the cost of providing protective services for state employees and property.

(b) Payments for services provided shall be made by direct transfer as described in Section 11255 of the Government Code. All money received by the department pursuant to this section shall be deposited in the Protective Services Fund, which is hereby created. When appropriated by the Legislature, funds in the Protective Services Fund shall be used by the department to fulfill those responsibilities set forth in subdivisions (g), (h), and (i) of Section 2400.

(c) If a state agency refuses to pay the charges fixed by the Department of the California Highway Patrol for security services rendered, the department may file a claim for those charges against any appropriations made for the support or maintenance of all or any part of the work and affairs of the state agency. The Controller shall draw his or her warrant in accordance with law upon the claim in favor of the Department of the California Highway Patrol. *(Added by Gov.Reorg.Plan No. 1 of 1995, § 66, eff. July 12, 1995; Stats.1996, c. 305 (A.B. 3103), § 68.)*

§ 2429. Public reporting of violations of Article 2; "800" telephone number

The department shall develop an "800" telephone number system to facilitate public reporting of violations of Article 2 (commencing with Section 31400) of Chapter 5 of Division 13. The department shall include in the department's "El Protector Program" public outreach activities that publicize the "800" telephone number system. *(Added by Stats.1999, c. 557 (A.B.1165), § 1, eff. Sept. 29, 1999.)*

§ 2429.3. Public awareness and outreach campaign; committee

(a) The commissioner shall appoint a committee of 12 members to develop a public awareness and outreach campaign to educate manufacturers, sellers, and owners of house cars, as described in subdivision (b) of Section 12804.10, regarding locations where those vehicles may be legally operated within the state. The committee shall consist of the commissioner, two members representing owners or operators of house cars, and one representative from each of the following:

(1) The Department of Transportation.

(2) The Department of Motor Vehicles.

(3) The Recreational Vehicle Industry Association.

(4) The California Recreational Vehicle Dealers Association.

(5) The National Recreational Vehicle Dealers Association.

(6) The Family Motor Coach Association.

(7) The Good Sam Club.

(8) The recreational vehicle manufacturing industry.

(9) The California Travel Parks Association.

(b) The committee shall develop a driver education safety video for operators of house cars. The video, as well as a map of the approved highways on which those vehicles may operate, shall be made available to dealers of house cars. The committee shall encourage dealers to make copies of the video and map available to purchasers of those vehicles. The video shall be produced at no cost to the state.

(c) Committee members shall serve at the pleasure of the commissioner and without compensation. *(Added by Stats.2001, c. 658 (A.B.67), § 1, eff. Oct. 10, 2001.)*

§ 2429.5. Farm labor vehicle certification requirements; education program

The department, in cooperation with county and local farm bureaus, shall provide a program to educate growers and farmers and farm labor vehicle owners and drivers regarding farm labor vehicle certification requirements, including, but not limited to, certification requirements for farm labor vehicle drivers. *(Added by Stats.1999, c. 556 (A.B.555), § 2, eff. Sept. 29, 1999.)*

ARTICLE 3.3. TOW TRUCK DRIVERS

Section
2430.   Emergency road service organizations; certification and training; pilot project; duration; report to legislature; criminal records of tow truck drivers.
2430.1.   Definitions.
2430.2.   Regional or local entity.
2430.3.   Freeway service patrol tow truck driver and California Highway Patrol rotation tow track operator; notice to employees, prospective employers and Department of California Highway Patrol of arrest or conviction of certain crimes.
2430.5.   Temporary tow truck driver certificates; necessity; files and rosters; inspection; removal of tow truck drivers; violations.
2431.   Criminal history and driver history screening; procedure; application for tow truck driver certificate; fees; fingerprints; confidentiality of information; temporary tow truck driver certificates.
2432.   Providing false information; failure to comply with notification requirements.
2432.1.   Violations by employer; sanctions.
2432.3.   Local government authority; verification of criminal histories; fingerprints; fees; verification of driver's

Section
         licenses; procedure for notification of crimes; confidentiality of information.

§ 2430. Emergency road service organizations; certification and training; pilot project; duration; report to legislature; criminal records of tow truck drivers

(a) The Legislature hereby creates a pilot project to develop recommendations for requiring emergency road service organizations and their specified employees, within the state, to be certified and receive specified training in the interest of public safety. The project shall be limited to freeway service patrol operations for major urban areas. The project includes, but is not limited to, the issuance of tow truck driver certificates to employees and employers involved in freeway service patrol operations, criminal history checks for convictions of specified crimes, and training for enhancement of public safety. The purpose of the project shall be to develop recommendations for requiring all emergency road service organizations and specified employees, within the state, to be certified and receive specified training in the interest of public safety.

(b) This project shall be for a period of two years commencing on July 1, 1992. The department shall submit a report to the Legislature not later than September 1, 1994. The report shall include, but not be limited to, all of the following:

(1) The number of criminal history checks processed by the department.

(2) The number of specified tow truck driver certificates issued.

(3) The number of persons rejected for freeway service patrol operations as a result of the criminal history checks.

(4) The names of participating emergency road service organizations.

(5) An accounting of the number of certified persons who were subsequently disqualified for convictions of specified crimes, including the number of certified persons subsequently disqualified for convictions of specified crimes against those receiving service.

(6) The training received by specified personnel.

(7) Recommendations developed by the Emergency Roadside Assistance Advisory Committee regarding training, as specified in Section 2438, and guidelines for motorist safety, as specified in Section 2439.

(8) Information compiled from reports submitted by highway service organizations pursuant to subdivision (a) of Section 2440.

(9) Recommendations for extending the requirements of this article and Article 3.5 (commencing with Section 2435) to all highway service organizations and their specified employees within the state.

(c) The Legislature declares that it is important to the public safety that tow truck drivers, who perform freeway service patrol operations under agreement with any specified public transportation planning entity, do not have criminal records which include violent crimes against persons. *(Added by Stats.1991, c. 488 (A.B.123), § 3.)*

§ 2430.1. Definitions

As used in this article, each of the following terms has the following meaning:

(a) "Tow truck driver" means a person who operates a tow truck, who renders towing service or emergency road service to motorists while involved in freeway service patrol operations, pursuant to an agreement with a regional or local entity, and who has or will have direct and personal contact with the individuals being transported or assisted. As used in this subdivision, "towing service" has the same meaning as defined in Section 2436.

(b) "Employer" means a person or organization that employs those persons defined in subdivision (a), or who is an owner-operator who performs the activity specified in subdivision (a), and who is involved in freeway service patrol operations pursuant to an agreement or contract with a regional or local entity.

(c) "Regional or local entity" means a public organization established as a public transportation planning entity pursuant to Title 7.1 (commencing with Section 66500) of the Government Code or authorized to impose a transaction and use tax for transportation purposes by the Public Utilities Code or the service authority for freeway emergencies described in Section 2551 of the Streets and Highways Code.

(d) "Emergency road service" has the same meaning as defined in Section 2436.

(e) "Freeway service patrol" has the same meaning as defined in Section 2561 of the Streets and Highways Code. *(Added by Stats.1991, c. 488 (A.B.123), § 3. Amended by Stats.1992, c. 1109 (A.B.3346), § 2; Stats. 2003, c. 374 (S.B.795), § 5; Stats.2008, c. 179 (S.B.1498), § 214.)*

§ 2430.2. Regional or local entity

"Regional or local entity", as defined by subdivision (c) of Section 2430.1, also includes the transportation planning entity established pursuant to Section 130050.1 of the Public Utilities Code or the service authority for freeway emergencies described in Section 2551 of the Streets and Highways Code.

(Added by Stats.1991, c. 1223 (S.B.1073), § 1.5. Amended by Stats.2003, c. 374 (S.B.795), § 6.)

§ 2430.3 Freeway service patrol tow truck driver and California Highway Patrol rotation tow track operator; notice to employees, prospective employers and Department of California Highway Patrol of arrest or conviction of certain crimes

(a) Every freeway service patrol tow truck driver and any California Highway Patrol rotation tow truck operator shall notify each of his or her employers and prospective employers and the Department of the California Highway Patrol of an arrest or conviction of any crime specified in paragraph (1), (2), (3), or (4) of subdivision (a) of Section 13377 prior to beginning the next workshift for that employer.

(b) For the purpose of conducting criminal history and driver history checks of any California Highway Patrol rotation tow truck operator, the commissioner may utilize the California Law Enforcement Telecommunications System (CLETS). *(Added by Stats.1991, c. 488 (A.B.123), § 3. Amended by Stats.2001, c. 127 (S.B.46), § 5, eff. July 30, 2001.)*

§ 2430.5. Temporary tow truck driver certificates; necessity; files and rosters; inspection; removal of tow truck drivers; violations

(a) Every employer intending to hire a tow truck driver on or after July 1, 1992, shall require the applicant for employment to submit a temporary tow truck driver certificate issued by the department or a permanent tow truck driver certificate issued by the Department of Motor Vehicles. The employer shall review the certificate and obtain a copy to be maintained as required by subdivision (c). The employer shall not hire any tow truck driver in any freeway service patrol operations who does not provide a temporary tow truck driver certificate issued by the department or a permanent tow truck driver certificate issued by the Department of Motor Vehicles. The employer shall not allow a tow truck driver who is not certified to participate in any freeway service patrol operations. If the issuance date on the certificate is more than 90 days from the proposed date of hire, the employer shall contact the department to reverify eligibility.

(b) On or after July 1, 1992, every employer, whose currently employed tow truck drivers are required to obtain a tow truck driver certificate pursuant to Section 12520, shall require the employees to submit to the employer a temporary tow truck driver certificate issued by the department or a permanent tow truck driver certificate issued by the Department of Motor Vehicles. The employer shall review the certificate and obtain a copy to be maintained as required by subdivision (c).

(c) Every employer shall maintain a tow truck driver certificate file for all tow truck drivers hired on or after July 1, 1992, or all currently employed tow truck drivers who are required to obtain a tow truck driver certificate pursuant to Section 12520. The employer shall retain employee rosters and copies of tow truck driver certificates for all tow truck drivers. The roster shall be comprised of the following two lists:

(1) Drivers who have valid tow truck driver certificates.

(2) Drivers who would be prohibited, pursuant to subdivision (a) of Section 13377, from involvement in any freeway service patrol operation.

Every employer shall make available for inspection by the department at the employer's primary place of business in this state. In addition, the employer shall maintain a personnel roster, also available for inspection, of all current tow truck drivers and their date of hire by the employer.

(d) Upon notification that a tow truck driver has been arrested for, or convicted of, any crime specified in paragraph (1), (2), (3), or (4) of subdivision (a) of Section 13377, the employer shall remove that tow truck driver from any position involving freeway service patrol operations.

(e) A violation of this section by an employer is a misdemeanor. *(Added by Stats.1991, c. 488 (A.B.123), § 3. Amended by Stats.1992, c. 1241 (S.B.1615), § 8.)*

§ 2431. Criminal history and driver history screening; procedure; application for tow truck driver certificate; fees; fingerprints; confidentiality of information; temporary tow truck driver certificates

(a) For the purposes of conducting criminal history and driver history screening of tow truck drivers and employers, the commissioner shall do all of the following:

(1) Obtain fingerprints from tow truck drivers and employers. The fingerprint cards will be submitted to the Department of Justice for criminal history checks.

(2) Obtain a second set of fingerprints from applicants who have not continuously resided in the state for the previous seven years, and submit that card to the Federal Bureau of Investigation for out-of-state criminal history checks. The department may charge a fee sufficient to cover the additional expense of processing the fingerprint cards through the Federal Bureau of Investigation.

(3) Verify that the tow truck driver or employer, or both, have a valid California driver's license, through the use of the automated records system.

(b) On and after July 1, 1992, all tow truck drivers shall submit an application for the issuance of a tow truck driver certificate with the department and pay an application fee equal to the actual costs of a criminal history check and issuance of the tow truck driver's certificate, but not more than fifty dollars ($50). Applicants for the renewal of an expired tow truck driver certificate or applicants for a duplicate tow truck driver certificate shall submit an application for issuance of a new tow truck driver certificate to the Department of Motor Vehicles and pay an application fee of twelve dollars ($12).

All fees collected pursuant to this section shall be deposited in the Motor Vehicle Account in the State Transportation Fund. An amount equal to the fees paid shall be made available, upon appropriation, to the Department of Motor Vehicles for its administrative costs, for the cost of criminal history checks to be conducted by the Department of Justice, and to the department for its administrative costs. In no case shall the fees collected exceed the costs of administering this section.

(c) Applicants for an original tow truck driver certificate shall be fingerprinted by the department, on a form issued by the department, for submission to the Department of Justice for the purpose of determining whether the applicant has been convicted for a violation of a crime specified in paragraph (1), (2), (3), or (4) of subdivision (a) of Section 13377.

(d) Information released to the department or the Department of Motor Vehicles shall be related to their inquiry and shall remain confidential.

(e) The department shall issue a temporary tow truck driver certificate, provided by the Department of Motor Vehicles, to applicants who have cleared the specified criminal history check pursuant to paragraph (1) of subdivision (a) and the driver history check through the automated records system, and who meet all other applicable provisions of this code. The term of the temporary tow truck driver's certificate shall be for a period of 90 days from the date of issuance. *(Added by Stats.1991, c. 488 (A.B.123), § 3. Amended by Stats.1992, c. 1109 (A.B.3346), § 3; Stats.2010, c. 280 (S.B.938), § 2.)*

§ 2432. Providing false information; failure to comply with notification requirements

(a) It is unlawful for a freeway service patrol tow truck driver to knowingly provide false information on the application prepared and submitted to the department pursuant to subdivision (b) of Section 2431.

(b) It is unlawful for a California Highway Patrol rotation tow truck operator, including, but not limited to, a freeway service patrol tow truck driver, to fail to comply with the notification requirements in Section 2430. 3.

(c) A violation of this section is punishable as a misdemeanor. *(Added by Stats.1991, c. 488 (A.B.123), § 3. Amended by Stats.1992, c. 1241 (S.B.1615), § 9; Stats.2001, c. 127 (S.B.46), § 6, eff. July 30, 2001.)*

§ 2432.1. Violations by employer; sanctions

(a) If the commissioner determines that an employer has failed to comply with the requirements of this article or Article 3.5 (commencing with Section 2435), the commissioner may, after a hearing, suspend the highway safety carrier's identification number issued pursuant to Section 2436.3 for a period not to exceed two years.

(b) If the commissioner determines that an employer has failed to comply with the requirements of this article or Article 3.5 (commencing with Section 2435) twice within a period of 24 consecutive months, the commissioner may, after a hearing, prohibit the employer from participating in any freeway service patrol operation for two years.

(c) Chapter 5 (commencing with Section 11500) of Part 1 of Division 3 of Title 2 of the Government Code does not apply to the hearing specified in subdivision (a) or (b). *(Added by Stats.1991, c. 488 (A.B.123), § 3.)*

§ 2432.3. Local government authority; verification of criminal histories; fingerprints; fees; verification of driver's licenses; procedure for notification of crimes; confidentiality of information

(a) This article does not preempt the authority of any city, city and county, or county to regulate, pursuant to subdivision (g) of Section 21100, any of the matters covered by this article.

(b)(1) For the purposes of verifying the criminal history of individuals involved in the operation of tow truck services, law enforcement agencies of any city, city and county, or county may conduct criminal history checks for all of the following:

(A) Applicants for employment to drive tow trucks.

(B) Those who drive tow trucks.

(C) Tow truck owners-operators.

(2) The law enforcement agency may obtain the fingerprints of the individuals on a form approved by the Department of Justice and provided by the agency. The fingerprint samples shall be submitted to the Department of Justice for the purpose of determining whether the individual has been convicted of any violation, including, but not limited to, Section 220, subdivision (1), (2), (3), or (4) of Section 261, or Section 264.1, 267, 288, or 289 of the Penal Code, or any felony or three misdemeanors as set forth in subparagraph (B) of paragraph (2) of subdivision (a) of Section 5164 of the Public Resources Code.

(3) For purposes of conducting criminal history screening of tow truck driver applicants, employees, and employers who have not resided continuously in the state for the previous seven years, the law enforcement agency of any city, city and county, or county, may obtain a second set of fingerprints, when necessary, and may submit that card to the Federal Bureau of Investigation for out-of-state criminal history checks.

(c) The law enforcement agency of any city, city and county, or county may charge a fee sufficient to cover the cost of obtaining and processing the fingerprint cards through the Department of Justice.

(d) For the purposes of conducting driver history screening of applicants to drive tow trucks, employees, and owners-operators, the law enforcement agency of any city, city and county, or county may verify that the applicant or owner-operator, as the case may be, has a valid California driver's license of the proper class, through the use of the automated records system.

(e) The Department of Justice shall develop a procedure whereby it will notify the requesting law enforcement agency if the person fingerprinted has been convicted of any of the specified crimes or is convicted of a specified crime subsequent to employment or beginning operation of a tow service. The Department of Justice shall release the requested information to the requesting agency.

(f) Information released to the requesting agency may be utilized for licensing and regulating procedures established pursuant to subdivision (g) of Section 21100.

(g) Information released to the requesting agency shall be related to its inquiry, shall remain confidential, and shall not be made public. *(Added by Stats.1991, c. 488*

(A.B.123), § 3. Amended by Stats.2004, c. 184 (S.B.1314), § 5, eff. July 23, 2004.)

Cross References

Counties and cities, persons convicted of Penal Code offenses, supervisory or disciplinary authority over minors, see Public Resources Code § 5164.

ARTICLE 3.5. EMERGENCY ROADSIDE ASSISTANCE

Section
2435.   Legislative findings and declarations.
2436.   Definitions.
2436.3. Carrier identification numbers; effect of suspension; removal of number; penalty for violations.
2436.5. Training for employers and tow truck drivers.
2436.7. Necessity of attending training; certificate of completion; employer files.
2437 to 2440.   Repealed.

§ 2435. Legislative findings and declarations

(a) The Legislature finds and declares that the emergency roadside assistance provided by highway service organizations is a valuable service that benefits millions of California motorists. The Legislature further finds and declares that emergency roadside assistance is provided statewide, in cooperation with, and shares resources with, public safety agencies. The Legislature also finds that the Department of the California Highway Patrol, in cooperation with the Department of Transportation, is responsible for the rapid removal of impediments to traffic on highways within the state and that the Department of the California Highway Patrol may enter into agreements with employers for freeway service patrol operations under an agreement or contract with a regional or local entity. The Legislature declares that it is important to the public safety that drivers who provide emergency roadside service not have criminal records that include violent crimes against persons.

(b) The Legislature also declares that the Department of the California Highway Patrol, in cooperation with the Department of Transportation, shall be responsible for establishing the minimum training standards for highway service organization employees and employers who participate in freeway service patrol operations pursuant to an agreement or contract with a regional or local entity. *(Added by Stats.1991, c. 488 (A.B.123), § 4. Amended by Stats.2003, c. 374 (S.B.795), § 7.)*

§ 2436. Definitions

For the purposes of this article, each of the following terms has the meaning given in this section:

(a) "Emergency road service" is the adjustment, repair, or replacement by a highway service organization of the equipment, tires, or mechanical parts of a motor vehicle so as to permit it to be operated under its own power. "Towing service" is the drafting or moving by a highway service organization of a motor vehicle from one place to another under power other than its own.

(b) "Emergency roadside assistance" means towing service or emergency road service.

(c) "Employer" has the same meaning as defined in Section 2430.1.

(d) "Freeway service patrol" has the same meaning as defined in Section 2561 of the Streets and Highways Code.

(e) "Highway service organization" means a motor club, as defined by Section 12142 of the Insurance Code and, in addition, includes any person or organization that operates or directs the operation of highway service vehicles to provide emergency roadside assistance to motorists, or any person or organization that is reimbursed or reimburses others for the cost of providing emergency roadside assistance, and any employer and includes any person or organization that directly or indirectly, with or without compensation, provides emergency roadside assistance.

(f) "Regional or local entity" has the same meaning as defined in Section 2430.1.

(g) "Tow truck driver" has the same meaning as defined in Section 2430.1. *(Added by Stats.1991, c. 488 (A.B.123), § 4. Amended by Stats.1992, c. 1109 (A.B. 3346), § 4; Stats.2003, c. 374 (S.B.795), § 8.)*

§ 2436.3. Carrier identification numbers; effect of suspension; removal of number; penalty for violations

(a) On and after July 1, 1992, every employer shall obtain from the department a carrier identification number. Application for a carrier identification number shall be on forms furnished by the department. The number shall be displayed on both sides of each tow truck utilized in any freeway service patrol operation, in accordance with Section 27907.

(b) No employer shall operate a tow truck in any freeway service patrol operation if the carrier identification number issued pursuant to subdivision (a) has been suspended by the commissioner pursuant to Section 2432.1.

(c) The carrier identification number shall be removed before sale, transfer, or other disposal of the vehicle, or upon termination of an agreement or contract for freeway service patrol operations.

(d) A violation of this section is a misdemeanor. *(Added by Stats.1991, c. 488 (A.B.123), § 4.)*

§ 2436.5. Training for employers and tow truck drivers

(a) The department, in cooperation with the Department of Transportation, shall provide training, pursuant to a reimbursable agreement or contract with a regional or local entity, for all employers and tow truck drivers who are involved in freeway service patrol operations pursuant to an agreement or contract with the regional or local entity. Dispatchers for freeway service patrol operations shall be employees of the department or the Department of Transportation.

(b) The training shall include, but not be limited to, all of the following:

(1) Tow truck driver and motorist safety.

(2) Patrol responsibility.

(3) Vehicle operation.

(4) Traffic control and scene management.

(5) Communication procedures.

(6) Demeanor and courtesy. *(Added by Stats.1991, c. 488 (A.B.123), § 4.)*

§ 2436.7. Necessity of attending training; certificate of completion; employer files

(a) Every tow truck driver and employer, involved in a freeway service patrol operation under an agreement or contract with a regional or local entity, shall attend the training specified in subdivision (b) of Section 2436.5.

(b) Upon successful completion of the training, each trainee shall be issued a certificate of completion. The certificate shall state the name of the training organization, the name and signature of the trainer, the name of the trainee, and the date of completion of the training.

(c) The trainee shall provide a copy of the certificate of training to the employer. The employer shall maintain this information in the tow truck driver files established pursuant to subdivision (c) of Section 2430.5.

(d) Every employer shall make the file available for inspection by the department at the employer's primary place of business in this state. *(Added by Stats.1991, c. 488 (A.B.123), § 4.)*

§§ 2437 to 2440. Repealed by Stats.2003, c. 374 (S.B. 795), §§ 9 to 12

ARTICLE 4. HIGHWAY SPILL CONTAINMENT AND ABATEMENT OF HAZARDOUS SUBSTANCES

Section
2450. Short title.
2451. Legislative findings and declaration.
2452. Hazardous substance.
2453. Information, assistance, and notification coordinator for hazardous spill incidents on highways.
2454. Authority for incident command at scene of hazardous substance incident; assignment; interagency coordination.

§ 2450. Short title

This article shall be known and may be cited as the Hazardous Substances Highway Spill Containment and Abatement Act. *(Added by Stats.1980, c. 922, p. 2929, § 1.)*

§ 2451. Legislative findings and declaration

The Legislature finds and declares that a statewide program for the management of hazardous substances highway spills, under the jurisdiction of the California

Highway Patrol, is necessary to protect the public health and environment. *(Added by Stats.1980, c. 922, p. 2929, § 1.)*

§ 2452. Hazardous substance

"Hazardous substance" means any hazardous material defined in Section 353 and any toxic substance defined pursuant to Section 108145 of the Health and Safety Code. *(Added by Stats.1980, c. 922, p. 2929, § 1. Amended by Stats.1992, c. 878 (A.B.3427), § 23; Stats. 1996, c. 1023 (S.B.1497), § 424, eff. Sept. 29, 1996.)*

Cross References

Hazardous material, defined, see Vehicle Code § 353.

§ 2453. Information, assistance, and notification coordinator for hazardous spill incidents on highways

The California Highway Patrol shall serve as statewide information, assistance, and notification coordinator for all hazardous substances spill incidents occurring on highways within the State of California. The California Highway Patrol shall establish a single notification mechanism to serve as a central focus point for a hazardous substances spill response system. To assure timely notification of emergency personnel, the notification mechanism established pursuant to this section shall complement and not conflict with the system established pursuant to subdivision (b) of Section 8574.17 of the Government Code. *(Added by Stats.1980, c. 922, p. 2929, § 1. Amended by Stats.1994, c. 1214 (A.B.3404), § 7.)*

§ 2454. Authority for incident command at scene of hazardous substance incident; assignment; interagency coordination

(a) The authority for incident command at the scene of an on-highway hazardous substance incident is vested in the appropriate law enforcement agency having primary traffic investigative authority on the highway where the incident occurs. Responsibility for incident command at the scene of an on-highway hazardous substance incident shall continue until all emergency operations at the scene have been completed and order has been restored.

(b) Notwithstanding subdivision (a), the local governing body of a city, whether general law or chartered, which has jurisdiction over the location where an on-highway hazardous substance incident occurs may assign the authority for incident command at the scene of an on-highway hazardous substance incident on local streets and roads, other than freeways, to either the local law enforcement agency or the local fire protection agency. However, the department is responsible for incident command at the scene of an on-highway hazardous substance incident on all highways where the department has primary traffic investigative authority. Any law enforcement agency having primary traffic investigative authority may enter into written agreements with other public agencies to facilitate incident command at the scene of an on-highway hazardous substance incident on local streets and roads other than freeways.

(c) For purposes of this section, "incident command at the scene of an on-highway hazardous substance incident" means coordination of operations which occur at the location of a hazardous substance incident. This coordinating function does not include how the specialized functions provided by the various other responding agencies are to be performed. The incident commander at the scene of an on-highway hazardous substance incident shall consult with other response agencies at the scene to ensure that all appropriate resources are properly utilized, and shall perform his or her coordinating function in a manner designed to minimize the risk of death or injury to other persons. *(Added by Stats.1980, c. 922, p. 2929, § 1. Amended by Stats.1982, c. 543, p. 2479, § 2; Stats.1983, c. 623, § 1; Stats.1989, c. 265, § 2; Stats.1990, c. 216 (S.B.2510), § 112; Stats.1992, c. 1241 (S.B.1615), § 10.)*

ARTICLE 5. RENDERERS AND TRANSPORTERS OF INEDIBLE KITCHEN GREASE

Section
2460. Definitions.
2462. Required records.
2464. Maintenance of records; access.
2466. Inspections.
2468. Violations of record keeping requirements; punishment.
2470. Transportation without registration certificate unlawful.
2472. Interstate transportation by persons not registered or licensed.
2474. Stealing, contamination, or damage unlawful.
2476. Taking possession of stolen grease or grease from unregistered transporters.
2478. Punishment for violations.

§ 2460. Definitions

(a) The definitions set forth in Article 1 (commencing with Section 19200) of Chapter 5 of Part 3 of Division 9 of the Food and Agricultural Code apply for purposes of this article.

(b) A "licensed renderer" is a renderer licensed under Article 6 (commencing with Section 19300) of Chapter 5 of Part 3 of Division 9 of the Food and Agricultural Code.

(c) A "registered transporter" is a transporter of inedible kitchen grease registered under Article 6.5 (commencing with Section 19310) of Chapter 5 of Part 3 of Division 9 of the Food and Agricultural Code.

(d) A "peace officer" is any peace officer defined in Chapter 4.5 (commencing with Section 830) of Title 3 of Part 2 of the Penal Code. *(Added by Stats.1998, c. 394 (S.B.1738), § 3.)*

§ 2462. Required records

(a) In addition to any other records required to be kept pursuant to Chapter 5 (commencing with Section

19200) of Part 3 of Division 9 of the Food and Agricultural Code, every licensed renderer shall record and keep for two years, in connection with the receipt of kitchen grease that is not intended for human food, all of the following information:

(1) The name, address, and registration number of every transporter of inedible kitchen grease who has delivered that material to the renderer.

(2) The total amount of inedible kitchen grease purchased in each transaction.

(3) The date of each transaction.

(b) Every registered transporter of inedible kitchen grease shall record and maintain for two years all of the following:

(1) The name and address of each location from which the transporter obtained the inedible kitchen grease.

(2) The quantity of material received from each location.

(3) The date on which the inedible kitchen grease was obtained from each location. *(Added by Stats.1998, c. 394 (S.B.1738), § 3. Amended by Stats.2012, c. 303 (A.B. 2378), § 4.)*

§ 2464. Maintenance of records; access

All records required to be retained pursuant to this article shall be maintained at the regular place of business of every licensed renderer and every registered transporter. Those records shall be exhibited on demand to any peace officer. *(Added by Stats.1998, c. 394 (S.B.1738), § 3.)*

§ 2466. Inspections

Any peace officer may, during normal business hours, inspect any premises maintained by a licensed renderer or registered transporter, and any inedible kitchen grease located on the premises, for the purpose of determining whether that renderer or transporter is complying with the record maintenance requirements of this article. *(Added by Stats.1998, c. 394 (S.B.1738), § 3.)*

§ 2468. Violations of record keeping requirements; punishment

(a) Any licensed renderer who fails in any respect to keep the written records required by this article, or to set out in that written record any matter required by this article to be set out in the record, is guilty of a misdemeanor.

(b) Every licensed renderer or registered transporter who refuses, upon demand of any peace officer, to exhibit any written record required by this article, or who destroys that record within two years after making the final entry of any information required by this article, is guilty of a misdemeanor.

(c) Any violation of subdivision (a) or (b) is punishable as follows:

(1) For a first offense, by a fine of not less than five hundred dollars ($500), or by imprisonment in the county jail for not more than 30 days, or by both that fine and imprisonment.

(2) For a second offense within a period of one year, by a fine of not less than one thousand dollars ($1,000), or by imprisonment in the county jail for not more than 30 days, or by both that fine and imprisonment. In addition to any other punishment imposed pursuant to this paragraph, the court may order the defendant to stop engaging in the business as a transporter or renderer for a period not to exceed 30 days.

(3) For a third or any subsequent offense within a period of two years, by a fine of not less than two thousand dollars ($2,000), or by imprisonment in the county jail for not more than six months, or by both that fine and imprisonment. In addition to any other sentence imposed pursuant to this paragraph, the court shall order the defendant to stop engaging in the business as a transporter or renderer for a period of 30 days. *(Added by Stats.1998, c. 394 (S.B.1738), § 3. Amended by Stats.2012, c. 303 (A.B.2378), § 5.)*

§ 2470. Transportation without registration certificate unlawful

It is unlawful for any person to engage in the transportation of inedible kitchen grease without being registered with the Department of Food and Agriculture and without being in possession of a valid registration certificate issued by that department. *(Added by Stats.1998, c. 394 (S.B.1738), § 3.)*

§ 2472. Interstate transportation by persons not registered or licensed

It is unlawful for any person who is not a registered transporter or licensed renderer of inedible kitchen grease to transport that product from any place within this state to any place outside the borders of this state. *(Added by Stats.1998, c. 394 (S.B.1738), § 3.)*

§ 2474. Stealing, contamination, or damage unlawful

It is unlawful for any person to steal, misappropriate, contaminate, or damage inedible kitchen grease, or containers thereof. *(Added by Stats.1998, c. 394 (S.B. 1738), § 3.)*

§ 2476. Taking possession of stolen grease or grease from unregistered transporters

No licensed renderer, registered transporter, or any other person may take possession of inedible kitchen grease from an unregistered transporter or knowingly take possession of stolen inedible kitchen grease. *(Added by Stats.1998, c. 394 (S.B.1738), § 3.)*

§ 2478. Punishment for violations

(a) Any person who is found guilty of violating Section 2470, 2472, 2474, or 2476, or the rules and regulations promulgated under those provisions, is subject to imprisonment in a county jail for not more than one year, or a fine of not more than five thousand dollars ($5,000), or both that imprisonment and fine.

(b) If the conviction is a second or subsequent conviction of a violation described in subdivision (a), or the violation is committed with intent to defraud or mislead, the person is subject to imprisonment pursuant to subdivision (h) of Section 1170 of the Penal Code, or a fine of not more than fifteen thousand dollars ($15,000), or both that imprisonment and fine. *(Added by Stats.1998, c. 394 (S.B.1738), § 3. Amended by Stats.1999, c. 83 (S.B.966), § 186; Stats.2011, c. 15 (A.B.109), § 598, eff. April 4, 2011, operative Oct. 1, 2011; Stats.2012, c. 303 (A.B.2378), § 6.)*

CHAPTER 2.5. LICENSES ISSUED BY CALIFORNIA HIGHWAY PATROL

Article   **Section**
1. General Provisions 2500
2. Privately Owned and Operated Ambulances and Armored Cars 2510
3. Lamp and Brake Adjusting Stations and Motor Vehicle Pollution Control Device Installation and Inspection Stations [Repealed]
3.5 Inspection and Maintenance Stations 2525
4. Transportation of Hazardous Material 2530
5. Denial, Suspension and Revocation 2540
6. Hazardous Waste Inspections [Repealed]
7. Transportation of School Pupils 2570

Cross References

Used oil, refuse removal or curbside collection vehicles, exemption from this chapter, see Health and Safety Code § 25250.15.

ARTICLE 1. GENERAL PROVISIONS

Section
2500. Application of chapter.
2501. Licenses.
2501. Licenses; operative date of section.
2502. Fees; waiver; form and content of application.
2503. Transfer or replacement of license; report of change of address or relocation of licensed service.
2504. Violation of regulations.
2505. Hazardous material transportation; staggering license renewals.

Cross References

Used oil, transportation or collection by refuse removal or curbside collection vehicles, exemption from provisions of this chapter, see Health and Safety Code § 25250.15.

§ 2500. Application of chapter

The provisions of this chapter shall apply to all licenses issued by the Department of the California Highway Patrol unless the particular provisions applicable to each license otherwise provide. *(Added by Stats.1968, c. 1309, p. 2466, § 5, operative Jan. 1, 1969.)*

§ 2501. Licenses

Section as added by Stats.1968, c. 1309, p. 2466, § 5. See, also, another section of the same number, added by Stats.1981, c. 860, p. 3294, § 6, operative Jan. 1, 1988.

The Commissioner of the California Highway Patrol may issue licenses for the operation of privately owned or operated ambulances used to respond to emergency calls, armored cars, fleet owner inspection and maintenance stations, and for the transportation of hazardous material, including the transportation of explosives. Such licenses shall be issued in accordance with the provisions of this chapter and regulations adopted by the commissioner pursuant thereto. All licenses issued by the commissioner shall expire one year from the date of issue. Licenses may be renewed upon application and payment of the renewal fees if the application for renewal is made within the 30-day period prior to the date of expiration. Persons whose licenses have expired shall immediately cease the activity requiring a license, but the commissioner shall accept applications for renewal during the 30-day period following the date of expiration if they are accompanied by the new license fee. In no case shall a license be renewed where the application is received more than 30 days after the date of expiration. *(Added by Stats.1968, c. 1309, p. 2466, § 5, operative Jan. 1, 1969. Amended by Stats.1969, c. 1064, p. 2050, § 1, eff. Aug. 29, 1969; Stats.1970, c. 1067, p. 1902, § 1; Stats.1971, c. 1578, p. 3181, § 2, operative May 3, 1972; Stats.1975, c. 502, p. 1027, § 1; Stats.1981, c. 860, p. 3293, § 4; Stats.1982, c. 16, p. 30, § 2; Stats.1982, c. 294, p. 935, § 2, eff. June 22, 1982.)*

Cross References

Armored car defined, see Vehicle Code § 115.
Hazardous material, defined, see Vehicle Code § 353.

§ 2501. Licenses; operative date of section

Section as added by Stats.1981, c. 860, p. 3294, § 6, operative Jan. 1, 1988. See, also, another section of the same number, added by Stats.1968, c. 1309, p. 2466, § 5.

The Commissioner of the California Highway Patrol may issue licenses for the operation of privately owned and operated ambulances used to respond to emergency calls, armored cars, fleet owner inspection and maintenance stations, and for the transportation of explosives. The licenses shall be issued in accordance with the provisions of this chapter and regulations adopted by the commissioner pursuant thereto. All licenses issued by the commissioner shall expire one year from the date of issue. Licenses may be renewed upon application and payment of the renewal fees if the application for renewal is made within the 30-day period prior to the date of expiration. Persons whose licenses have expired shall immediately cease the activity requiring a license, but the commissioner shall accept applications for renewal during the 30-day period following the date of expiration if they are accompanied by the new license fee. In no case shall a license be renewed where the application is received more than 30 days after the date of expiration.

This section shall become operative January 1, 1988. *(Added by Stats.1981, c. 860, p. 3294, § 6, operative Jan. 1, 1988.)*

§ 2502. Fees; waiver; form and content of application

(a) Except as otherwise provided in this section, each application for a new or renewal license shall be accompanied by a fee of ten dollars ($10) for a new license or five dollars ($5) for a renewal license. This subdivision does not apply to licenses for transportation of hazardous material or operation of ambulances.

(b) Each application for a new or renewal license for the operation of ambulances shall be accompanied by a fee not to exceed two hundred dollars ($200) for a new license or one hundred fifty dollars ($150) for a renewal license.

(c) Each application for a new or renewal license to transport hazardous material shall be accompanied by a fee of not to exceed one hundred dollars ($100) for a new license and not to exceed seventy-five dollars ($75) for a renewal license.

(d) Each application shall be made upon a form furnished by the commissioner. It shall contain information concerning the applicant's background and experience which the commissioner may prescribe, in addition to other information required by law. *(Added by Stats. 1968, c. 1309, p. 2466, § 5, operative Jan. 1, 1969. Amended by Stats.1971, c. 1578, p. 3181, § 3, operative May 3, 1972; Stats.1981, c. 860, p. 3294, § 8; Stats.1983, c. 458, § 1; Stats.1984, c. 955, § 1; Stats.1987, c. 352, § 1; Gov.Reorg.Plan No. 1 of 1991, § 188, eff. July 17, 1991; Stats.1996, c. 539 (A.B.2201), § 26.)*

§ 2503. Transfer or replacement of license; report of change of address or relocation of licensed service

(a) Licenses issued by the commissioner shall not be transferable. A change in ownership or control of the licensed activity shall render the existing license null and void and a new license shall be required. A change in ownership or control includes, but is not limited to, a change in corporate status, or a stock transfer of shares possessing more than 50 percent of the voting power of the corporation. A change in ownership or control does not include the addition or deletion of partners, officers, directors, or board members comprising 50 percent or less ownership or control of the licensed activity if both of the following are complied with:

(1) The new partners, officers, directors, or board members have not committed any acts described in Section 2541.

(2) An amended license application form indicating the changes and any other information required pursuant to subdivision (d) of Section 2502 is submitted to the commissioner within 10 days of the change.

(b) In the event of a change of name, not involving a change of ownership or control, the license shall be returned to the commissioner for cancellation, and a new license application form shall be submitted. The commissioner shall cancel the returned license and issue a new license for the unexpired term without a fee.

(c) In the event of loss, destruction, or mutilation of a license issued by the commissioner, the person to whom it was issued may obtain a duplicate upon paying a fee of five dollars ($5). Any person who loses a license issued by the commissioner and who, after obtaining a duplicate, finds the original license, shall immediately surrender the original license to the commissioner.

(d) Any change of address or relocation of a licensed service shall be reported to the commissioner within 10 days. *(Added by Stats.1968, c. 1309, p. 2466, § 5, operative Jan. 1, 1969. Amended by Stats.1971, c. 1578, p. 3181, § 4, operative May 3, 1972; Stats.1982, c. 16, p. 31, § 3; Stats.1984, c. 955, § 2; Stats.1999, c. 1008 (S.B.533), § 3.)*

§ 2504. Violation of regulations

It is unlawful to violate any regulation adopted by the commissioner pursuant to this chapter. *(Added by Stats. 1968, c. 1309, p. 2466, § 5, operative Jan. 1, 1969. Amended by Stats.1969, c. 9, p. 63, § 3, eff. March 6, 1969; Stats.1970, c. 1067, p. 1903, § 2.)*

§ 2505. Hazardous material transportation; staggering license renewals

Notwithstanding Sections 2501 and 2502, for the purpose of staggering license renewals subject to this chapter, the commissioner may, during any 12-month period, issue licenses that expire 6 to 18 months from the date of issue. Subsequent renewal of these licenses shall be for a period of 12 months. Fees with respect to these licenses for more or less than one year shall be prorated accordingly.

This section applies only to licenses for the transportation of hazardous materials established on or after January 1, 1982. *(Added by Stats.1984, c. 488, § 1; Stats.1984, c. 1230, § 8.)*

Cross References

Hazardous material, defined, see Vehicle Code § 353.

ARTICLE 2. PRIVATELY OWNED AND OPERATED AMBULANCES AND ARMORED CARS

Section
2510. License for ambulance or armored car.
2511. Eligibility for license.
2512. Regulations governing ambulance service; ambulance driver's handbook.

Cross References

Armored car defined, see Vehicle Code § 115.

Authorized emergency vehicle as including privately owned ambulances, see Vehicle Code § 165.

§ 2510. License for ambulance or armored car

(a) A person applying for a license to operate ambulances or armored cars shall provide separate identification data and reports of inspection for each vehicle as prescribed by the commissioner.

(b) No person shall operate a privately owned emergency ambulance or armored car until the California Highway Patrol has determined that the vehicle is in compliance with this code and regulations adopted by the commissioner. Ambulances licensed by the department shall be inspected by the department not less often than once annually. *(Added by Stats.1968, c. 1309, p. 2466, § 5, operative Jan. 1, 1969. Amended by Stats.1982, c. 16, p. 31, § 4; Stats.1984, c. 955, § 3.)*

Cross References

Inspections, see Vehicle Code § 2800 et seq.
Licenses, see Vehicle Code § 2501.

§ 2511. Eligibility for license

Licenses for the operation of ambulances may be issued only to those persons or entities which operate ambulances designed and operated exclusively as such and which are used to respond to emergency calls. *(Added by Stats.1968, c. 1309, p. 2466, § 5, operative Jan. 1, 1969.)*

§ 2512. Regulations governing ambulance service; ambulance driver's handbook

(a) The commissioner, after consultation with, and pursuant to the recommendations of, the Emergency Medical Service Authority and the department, shall adopt and enforce reasonable regulations as the commissioner determines are necessary for the public health and safety regarding the operation, equipment, and certification of drivers of all ambulances used for emergency services. The regulations shall not conflict with standards established by the Emergency Medical Service Authority pursuant to Section 1797.170 of the Health and Safety Code. The commissioner shall exempt, upon request of the county board of supervisors that an exemption is necessary for public health and safety, noncommercial ambulances operated within the county from the regulations adopted under this section as are specified in the board of supervisors' request. The Emergency Medical Service Authority shall be notified by the county boards of supervisors of any exemptions.

(b) The department, in cooperation with the Department of the California Highway Patrol and the Emergency Medical Service Authority, may adopt and administer regulations relating to the issuance, suspension, or revocation of ambulance driver's certificates. In addition to the fee authorized in Section 2427, the department shall charge a fee of twenty-five dollars ($25) for the issuance of an original certificate and twelve dollars ($12) for the renewal of that certificate, and, in the administration

thereof, to exercise the powers granted to the commissioner by this section.

(c) This section shall not preclude the adoption of more restrictive regulations by local authorities, except that inspection of ambulances pursuant to subdivision (b) of Section 2510 shall not be duplicated by local authorities. It is the intent of the Legislature that regulations adopted by the commissioner pursuant to this section shall be the minimum necessary to protect public health and safety, and shall not be so restrictive as to preclude compliance by ambulances operated in sparsely populated areas. This subdivision does not relieve the owner or driver of any ambulance from compliance with Section 21055.

(d) The Department of the California Highway Patrol after consultation with the department and the Emergency Medical Service Authority shall prepare, and make available for purchase, an ambulance driver's handbook. *(Added by Stats.1968, c. 1309, p. 2466, § 5, operative Jan. 1, 1969. Amended by Stats.1970, c. 1469, p. 2900, § 1; Stats.1973, c. 1086, p. 2202, § 4; Stats.1978, c. 429, p. 1434, § 173, eff. July 17, 1978, operative July 1, 1978; Stats.1980, c. 676, p. 2021, § 306; Stats.1982, c. 1273, p. 4698, § 3; Stats.1984, c. 955, § 4; Stats.1985, c. 1303, § 2; Stats.1990, c. 104 (S.B.798), § 2, eff. May 23, 1990; Stats.1990, c. 1360 (S.B.1510), § 4.5; Stats.1996, c. 440 (S.B.1588), § 5.)*

Cross References

Traffic violation point count, number giving rise to presumptions of negligence by certificate or license holder, see Vehicle Code § 12810.5.

ARTICLE 3. LAMP AND BRAKE ADJUSTING STATIONS AND MOTOR VEHICLE POLLUTION CONTROL DEVICE INSTALLATION AND INSPECTION STATIONS [REPEALED]

§§ 2520 to 2523. Repealed by Stats.1971, c. 1578, p. 3182, § 5, operative May 3, 1972

ARTICLE 3.5. INSPECTION AND MAINTENANCE STATIONS

Section
2525. Definitions.
2525.2. Administrative regulations.
2525.4. Installations, adjustments, inspections and maintenance by licensed fleet owners.
2525.6. Stickers certifying compliance.
2525.8. Regulations governing issuance of stickers.
2525.10. Violations.
2525.12. Fee.

§ 2525. Definitions

For purposes of this article:

(a) "Fleet owner" means an owner of a fleet of three or more vehicles that are any one or more of the types specified in Section 34500 who is engaged in the transportation of persons or property and whose vehicles are registered in California.

(b) "Inspection and maintenance station" means a facility operated by a fleet owner to inspect and maintain his own vehicles and licensed by the commissioner pursuant to this chapter.   *(Added by Stats.1970, c. 1067, p. 1903, § 4. Amended by Stats.1975, c. 502, p. 1028, § 3.)*

§ 2525.2. Administrative regulations

The commissioner may adopt such regulations as are necessary to administer the provisions of this article. A fleet owner licensed by the commissioner as an inspection and maintenance station pursuant to this chapter shall comply with such regulations. *(Added by Stats.1970, c. 1067, p. 1904, § 4. Amended by Stats.1975, c. 502, p. 1028, § 4.)*

§ 2525.4. Installations, adjustments, inspections and maintenance by licensed fleet owners

(a) Fleet owners licensed as inspection and maintenance stations shall do all of the following:

(1) Conduct all installations, adjustments, inspections, and maintenance under the supervision of, and subject to the regulations of, the department, and subject to Division 12 (commencing with Section 24000).

(2) If engaged in interstate transportation, also conduct inspections and maintenance in accordance with the requirements of the United States Department of Transportation.

(3) If operating or maintaining vehicles described in subdivisions (a), (b), (d), (e), (f), or (g), of Section 34500, enroll each licensed inspection and maintenance station for inspection by the Department of the California Highway Patrol pursuant to subdivision (d) of Section 34501.12 and pay the fees required by subdivision (e) of that section.

(b) Fleet owners may not certify the adjustment of lamps or brakes or the installation, inspection, repair, or servicing of motor vehicle pollution control devices or systems, except for vehicles in the owner's fleet. *(Added by Stats.1970, c. 1067, p. 1904, § 4. Amended by Stats. 1975, c. 502, p. 1028, § 5; Stats.1992, c. 1243 (A.B.3090), § 62, eff. Sept. 30, 1992.)*

§ 2525.6. Stickers certifying compliance

Each fleet owner licensed as an inspection and maintenance station may place upon a vehicle which it has inspected and maintained, or upon which it has installed or adjusted required equipment, a sticker, in a form approved by the commissioner, certifying the compliance of such vehicle with all pertinent requirements imposed upon such vehicle by this code or regulations adopted thereunder and, if applicable, by the United States Department of Transportation. Such stickers shall remain valid for a period of one year and shall not be placed on any vehicle which is not part of the fleet.

(Added by Stats.1970, c. 1067, p. 1904, § 4. Amended by Stats.1975, c. 502, p. 1028, § 6.)

§ 2525.8. Regulations governing issuance of stickers

The commissioner shall make and enforce regulations with respect to the issuance of stickers to be displayed upon vehicles owned or operated by a fleet owner which has complied with Section 2525.6. *(Added by Stats.1970, c. 1067, p. 1904, § 4.)*

§ 2525.10. Violations

It is unlawful and constitutes a separate offense for any person to knowingly place or knowingly permit to be placed any sticker authorized by this article on any vehicle which does not comply with all the equipment requirements of this code or regulations adopted thereunder. *(Added by Stats.1970, c. 1067, p. 1904, § 4.)*

§ 2525.12. Fee

The commissioner may charge a fee for the stickers furnished to fleet owner inspection and maintenance stations. The fee charged shall be established by regulation and shall not produce a total estimated revenue which, together with license fees charged pursuant to Sections 2502 and 2503, is in excess of the estimated total cost to the department of the administration of the statutes relating to fleet owner inspection and maintenance stations. *(Added by Stats.1970, c. 1067, p. 1904, § 4. Amended by Stats.1975, c. 502, p. 1028, § 7.)*

ARTICLE 4. TRANSPORTATION OF HAZARDOUS MATERIAL

Section
2530. Repealed.
2531. Denial, suspension or revocation of licenses.
2532. Regulations.

Cross References

Hazardous material, defined, see Vehicle Code § 353.
Used oil, transportation or collection by refuse removal or curbside collection vehicles, exemption from provisions of this chapter, see Health and Safety Code § 25250.15.

§ 2530. Repealed by Stats.1989, c. 161, § 1

§ 2531. Denial, suspension or revocation of licenses

In addition to taking action pursuant to Article 5 (commencing with Section 2540), the commissioner may deny, suspend, or revoke a license to transport hazardous material when it is evident that the applicant or licensee or his or her employees have repeatedly violated any provision of law to such an extent as to demonstrate that it would be unsafe and not in the public interest to permit the applicant or licensee to operate or permit the operation of any vehicle owned or controlled by him or her for the transportation of hazardous material upon the public highways. *(Added by Stats.1981, c. 860, p. 3295, § 11. Amended by Stats.1989, c. 161, § 2.)*

§ 2532. Regulations

The commissioner may adopt such regulations as are necessary to administer the provisions of this article. *(Added by Stats.1981, c. 860, p. 3295, § 11.)*

ARTICLE 5. DENIAL, SUSPENSION AND REVOCATION

Section
2540. Denial, suspension or revocation of license.
2541. Grounds for denial of license.
2542. Grounds for disciplinary action.
2543. Convictions.
2544. Disciplinary actions.
2545. Surrender of license.
2546. Continuing jurisdiction.
2547. Period for filing accusations.
2548. Revocation or suspension of additional licenses.
2549. Reinstatement of license.

§ 2540. Denial, suspension or revocation of license

Any license issued may be suspended or revoked by the commissioner. The commissioner may refuse to issue a license to any applicant for the reasons set forth in Section 2531 or 2541. The proceedings under this article shall be conducted in accordance with Chapter 5 (commencing with Section 11500) of Part 1 of Division 3 of Title 2 of the Government Code, and the commissioner shall have all the powers granted therein. *(Added by Stats.1968, c. 1309, p. 2466, § 5, operative Jan. 1, 1969. Amended by Stats.1981, c. 860, p. 3295, § 12.)*

§ 2541. Grounds for denial of license

(a) The commissioner may deny a license if the applicant or any partner, officer, or director thereof:

(1) Fails to meet the qualifications established by the department pursuant to this chapter for the issuance of the license applied for.

(2) Was previously the holder of a license issued under this chapter which license has been revoked and never reissued or which license was suspended and the terms of the suspension have not been fulfilled.

(3) Has committed any act which, if committed by any licensee, would be grounds for the suspension or revocation of a license issued pursuant to this chapter.

(4) Has committed any act involving dishonesty, fraud, or deceit whereby another is injured or whereby the applicant has benefited.

(5) Has acted in the capacity of a licensed person or firm under this chapter without having a license therefor.

(6) Has entered a plea of guilty or nolo contendere to, or been found guilty of, or been convicted of, a felony, or a crime involving moral turpitude, and the time for appeal has elapsed or the judgment of conviction has been affirmed on appeal, irrespective of an order granting probation following such conviction, suspending the imposition of sentence, or of a subsequent order under the provisions of Section 1203.4 of the Penal Code allowing such person to withdraw his plea of guilty and to enter a plea of not guilty, or setting aside the plea or verdict of guilty, or dismissing the accusation or information.

(b) The commissioner may also deny a license if a corporation is the applicant and the policy or activities of the corporation are or will be directed, controlled, or managed by individuals or shareholders who are ineligible for a license, and the licensing of that corporation would likely defeat the purpose of this section. *(Added by Stats.1968, c. 1309, p. 2466, § 5, operative Jan. 1, 1969. Amended by Stats.1982, c. 16, p. 31, § 5.)*

Cross References

Hazardous material transportation licenses, see Vehicle Code §§ 2531, 2532.

§ 2542. Grounds for disciplinary action

The commissioner may suspend, revoke, or take other disciplinary action against a license as provided in this article if the licensee or any partner, officer, director, controlling shareholder, or manager thereof:

(a) Violates any section of this code which relates to his or her licensed activities.

(b) Is convicted of any felony.

(c) Is convicted of any misdemeanor involving moral turpitude.

(d) Violates any of the regulations promulgated by the commissioner pursuant to this chapter.

(e) Commits any act involving dishonesty, fraud, or deceit whereby another is injured or any act involving moral turpitude.

(f) Has misrepresented a material fact in obtaining a license.

(g) Aids or abets an unlicensed person to evade this chapter.

(h) Fails to make and keep records showing his or her transactions as a licensee, or fails to have these records available for inspection by the commissioner or his or her duly authorized representative for a period of not less than three years after completion of any transaction to which the records refer, or refuses to comply with a written request of the commissioner to make such record available for inspection.

(i) Violates or attempts to violate this chapter relating to the particular activity for which he or she is licensed.

(j) Fails to equip or maintain his or her vehicles, as required by this code or by the regulations adopted pursuant to this code. *(Added by Stats.1968, c. 1309, p. 2466, § 5, operative Jan. 1, 1969. Amended by Stats.1982, c. 16, p. 32, § 6; Stats.1989, c. 161, § 3.)*

Cross References

Hazardous material transportation licenses, see Vehicle Code §§ 2531, 2532.

§ 2543. Convictions

A plea or verdict of guilty or a conviction following a plea of nolo contendere is deemed to be a conviction within the meaning of this article. The commissioner may order the license suspended or revoked, or may decline to issue a license, when the time for appeal has elapsed, or the judgment of conviction has been affirmed on appeal, or when an order granting probation is made suspending the imposition of sentence, irrespective of a subsequent order under the provisions of Section 1203.4 of the Penal Code allowing such person to withdraw his plea of guilty and to enter a plea of not guilty, or setting aside the verdict of guilty, or dismissing the accusation, information or indictment. *(Added by Stats.1968, c. 1309, p. 2466, § 5, operative Jan. 1, 1969.)*

Cross References

Hazardous material transportation licenses, see Vehicle Code §§ 2531, 2532.

§ 2544. Disciplinary actions

The commissioner may take disciplinary action against any licensee after a hearing as provided in this chapter by any of the following:

(a) Imposing probation upon terms and conditions to be set forth by the commissioner.

(b) Suspending the license.

(c) Revoking the license. *(Added by Stats.1968, c. 1309, p. 2466, § 5, operative Jan. 1, 1969.)*

Cross References

Hazardous material transportation licenses, see Vehicle Code §§ 2531, 2532.

§ 2545. Surrender of license

Upon the effective date of any order of suspension or revocation of any license governed by this chapter, the licensee shall surrender the license to the commissioner. *(Added by Stats.1968, c. 1309, p. 2466, § 5, operative Jan. 1, 1969.)*

§ 2546. Continuing jurisdiction

The expiration or suspension of a license by operation of law or by order or decision of the commissioner or a court of law, or the voluntary surrender of a license by a licensee shall not deprive the commissioner of jurisdiction to proceed with any investigation of or action or disciplinary proceedings against such licensee, or to render a decision suspending or revoking such license. *(Added by Stats.1968, c. 1309, p. 2466, § 5, operative Jan. 1, 1969.)*

§ 2547. Period for filing accusations

All accusations against licensees shall be filed within three years after the act or omission alleged as the ground for disciplinary action, except that with respect to an accusation alleging a violation of subdivision (f) of Section 2542, the accusation may be filed within two years after the discovery by the California Highway Patrol of the alleged facts constituting the fraud or misrepresentation prohibited by said section. *(Added by Stats.1968, c. 1309, p. 2466, § 5, operative Jan. 1, 1969.)*

§ 2548. Revocation or suspension of additional licenses

When any license has been revoked or suspended following a hearing under the provisions of this chapter, any additional license issued under this chapter in the name of the licensee may be likewise revoked or suspended by the commissioner. *(Added by Stats.1968, c. 1309, p. 2466, § 5, operative Jan. 1, 1969.)*

§ 2549. Reinstatement of license

After suspension of the license upon any of the grounds set forth in this article, the commissioner may reinstate the license upon proof of compliance by the applicant with all provisions of the decision as to reinstatement. After revocation of a license upon any of the grounds set forth in this article, the license shall not be reinstated or reissued within a period of one year after the effective date of revocation. *(Added by Stats.1968, c. 1309, p. 2466, § 5, operative Jan. 1, 1969.)*

ARTICLE 6.   HAZARDOUS WASTE INSPECTIONS [REPEALED]

§ 2560.   Repealed by Stats.1996, c. 539 (A.B.2201), § 27

§ 2561.   Repealed by Stats.1981, c. 912, p. 3452, § 4.5, urgency, eff. Sept. 28, 1981

ARTICLE 7.   TRANSPORTATION OF SCHOOL PUPILS

Section
2570. Legislative intent.
2571. Private schoolbus contractors; licenses; fees.
2572. Regulations; operation by contractor without license; penalty.
2573. Suspension of licenses.
2574. Deposit and use of fees.
2575. Repealed.

§ 2570.   Legislative intent

It is the intent of the Legislature, in enacting this chapter, that the public be provided additional protection through the licensing of private schoolbus contractors transporting school pupils under contracts with school districts, and that the Department of the California Highway Patrol be authorized to inspect and license the contractors described in subdivision (a), giving special attention directed to negligent operators or repeat violators. *(Added by Stats.1990, c. 1563 (A.B.3243), § 3.6.)*

§ 2571.   Private schoolbus contractors; licenses; fees

Every private schoolbus contractor who contracts with a school district for the transportation of school pupils shall be licensed in accordance with regulations adopted by the commissioner. The license fee shall be one hundred dollars ($100) for an initial license and seventy-five dollars ($75) for each annual renewal. *(Added by Stats.1990, c. 1563 (A.B.3243), § 3.6.)*

§ 2572. Regulations; operation by contractor without license; penalty

(a) The commissioner may adopt whatever regulations are necessary to administer this chapter. The regulations shall be consistent with regulations regarding schoolbuses and schoolbus drivers adopted by the commissioner pursuant to other provisions of law.

(b) In addition to any other requirements, it is unlawful for the private schoolbus contractor or the person who directs the driver to operate a vehicle transporting school pupils, when that transportation requires a license, to knowingly cause the operation of the vehicle unless the private schoolbus contractor holds a valid license for the transportation of school pupils. A violation of this subdivision shall be punished by a fine of not more than two thousand dollars ($2,000). *(Added by Stats.1990, c. 1563 (A.B.3243), § 3.6.)*

§ 2573. Suspension of licenses

(a) The commissioner may temporarily suspend a license to transport school pupils under contract with a school district, subject to a hearing conducted pursuant to Chapter 5 (commencing with Section 11500) of Part 1 of Division 3 of Title 2 of the Government Code, when, in the commissioner's opinion, the action is necessary to prevent an imminent and substantial danger to the public health.

(b) The commissioner may, following a hearing, suspend a license to transport school pupils under contract with a school district, for a period of at least 30 days but not more than 90 days, if the holder of the license knowingly permits the transportation of school pupils by a person who does not possess the appropriate driver's license and driver's certificate.

(c) The suspensions authorized pursuant to subdivisions (a) and (b) may, at the discretion of the commissioner, be enforced for all operations of a schoolbus contractor, or for the operations of the contractor in the school district in which the alleged violations occurred, or for the operations of the contractor in the contractor's terminal in which the alleged violations occurred.

(d) The commissioner shall provide notification of a suspension hearing to those school districts whose terminals would be affected by the suspension. *(Added by Stats.1990, c. 1563 (A.B.3243), § 3.6.)*

§ 2574. Deposit and use of fees

(a) All fees collected by the Department of the California Highway Patrol pursuant to the issuance or renewal of a license for the transportation of school pupils under contract with a school district shall be deposited in the Motor Vehicle Account of the State Transportation Fund.

(b) All moneys collected from these fees shall be used for the support of the licensing program of the department upon appropriation therefor by the Legislature. *(Added by Stats.1990, c. 1563 (A.B.3243), § 3.6.)*

§ 2575. Repealed by Stats.2004, c. 193 (S.B.111), § 192

Law Revision Commission Comments

2004 Repeal

Section 2575 is repealed as obsolete. The required report was to be completed by January 1, 1993. [33 Cal.L.Rev.Comm. Reports 494 (2003)].

CHAPTER 3. THE RECIPROCITY COMMISSION [REPEALED]

§§ 2600 to 2603. Repealed by Stats.2011, c. 315 (A.B.28), § 7

§ 2604. Repealed by Stats.1967, c. 1656, p. 4025, § 109

§ 2605. Repealed by Stats.1968, c. 1473, p. 2950, § 71

§§ 2650, 2651. Repealed by Stats.2011, c. 315 (A.B.28), § 7

CHAPTER 4. ADMINISTRATION AND ENFORCEMENT

Article	Section
1. Lawful Orders and Inspections	2800

ARTICLE 1. LAWFUL ORDERS AND INSPECTIONS

Section

2800.　Peace officers, Department of California Highway Patrol or authorized enforcement officers; compliance with lawful orders and lawful out-of-service orders.

2800.1.　Flight from pursuing peace officer.

2800.2.　Driving in willful or wanton disregard for safety of persons or property while fleeing from pursuing police officer; penalties.

2800.3.　Death or serious bodily injury proximately caused by flight from pursuing peace officer; punishment; "serious bodily injury" defined.

2800.4.　Willful driving of vehicle on highway in direction opposite lawful traffic during flight from pursuing peace officer; punishment.

2801.　Obedience to firemen.

2802.　Load inspection; inspection facilities and scales; hours of operation.

2802.5.　Repealed.

2803.　Control of illegal size or weight.

2804.　Inspection by patrol members.

2805.　Inspection of vehicles, vehicle components, title or registration.

2806.　Inspection by police, deputy sheriffs, or reserve police officers.

2807.　School bus inspection.

2807.1.　School pupil activity bus; inspection and certification; display of certificate.

2807.2.　Preventive maintenance inspections.

2807.3.　Inspection and certification of youth bus; display of certificate; fee.

2808.　Private schoolbus requirements.

2809.　California highway patrol scales.

Section
2810.   Inspection to prevent theft.
2810.1. Commercial rental vehicles transporting household goods; stop and inspection; violations; citations.
2810.2. Vehicles transporting agricultural irrigation supplies; inspection of bills of lading, shipping, or delivery papers by peace officer; care of apprehended supplies; expenses incurred; impoundment of vehicle; other violations.
2811.   Damage to fences.
2812.   Closing of highways.
2812.5. Restricting or prohibiting use of highway; visibility limitations.
2813.   Commercial vehicle inspection; violations; misdemeanor.
2813.5. Commercial vehicle inspection stickers; issuance and display; unauthorized or facsimile stickers; misdemeanor.
2814.   Passenger vehicle inspection.
2814.1. Vehicle inspection program; motorcycle only checkpoints prohibited.
2814.2. Conduct of sobriety checkpoint inspection; vehicle impoundment and release.
2815.   Nonstudent school crossing guard.
2816.   Youth bus; loading or discharging children; highways.
2817.   Funeral processions; disregard of traffic signal or direction by peace officer; violation.
2818.   Electronic beacon, flare, or cone patterns or combination; traverse.

§ 2800. Peace officers, Department of California Highway Patrol or authorized enforcement officers; compliance with lawful orders and lawful out-of-service orders

(a) It is unlawful to willfully fail or refuse to comply with a lawful order, signal, or direction of a peace officer, as defined in Chapter 4.5 (commencing with Section 830) of Title 3 of Part 2 of the Penal Code, when that peace officer is in uniform and is performing duties pursuant to any of the provisions of this code, or to refuse to submit to a lawful inspection pursuant to this code.

(b)(1) Except as authorized pursuant to Section 24004, it is unlawful to fail or refuse to comply with a lawful out-of-service order issued by an authorized employee of the Department of the California Highway Patrol or by an authorized enforcement officer as described in subdivision (d).

(2) It is unlawful for a driver transporting hazardous materials in a commercial motor vehicle that is required to display a placard pursuant to Section 27903 to violate paragraph (1).

(3) It is unlawful for a driver of a vehicle designed to transport 16 or more passengers, including the driver, to violate paragraph (1).

(c) It is unlawful to fail or refuse to comply with a lawful out-of-service order issued by the United States Secretary of the Department of Transportation.

(d) "Out-of–Service order" means a declaration by an authorized enforcement officer of a federal, state, Canadian, Mexican, or local jurisdiction that a driver, a commercial motor vehicle, or a motor carrier operation is out-of-service pursuant to Section 386.72, 392.5, 392.9a, 395.13, or 396.9 of Title 49 of the Code of Federal Regulations, state law, or the North American Standard Out-of-Service Criteria. *(Stats.1959, c. 3, p. 1552, § 2800. Amended by Stats.1981, c. 644, p. 2414, § 1; Stats.1999, c. 724 (A.B.1650), § 29.5; Stats.2004, c. 952 (A.B.3049), § 2, operative Sept. 20, 2005; Stats.2006, c. 288 (A.B.3011), § 1; Stats.2010, c. 491 (S.B.1318), § 36; Stats.2012, c. 670 (A.B.2188), § 1.)*

Cross References

Applicability of this section to trolley coaches, see Vehicle Code § 21051.

Authority of highway patrol, see Vehicle Code § 2409.

Commercial motor vehicles, suspension of driving privileges for violations of this section, see Vehicle Code § 15311.

Conditions under which employer prohibited from allowing driver to drive, see Vehicle Code § 15240.

Direction of traffic by members of highway patrol, see Vehicle Code § 2410.

Duration of prohibition against operation of commercial motor vehicle, see Vehicle Code § 15312.

Failure to stop and submit to inspection of equipment or unsafe condition endangering a person, punishment for misdemeanor conviction, see Vehicle Code § 42002.1.

Farm labor vehicles subject to forfeiture as nuisance, and impounding, see Vehicle Code § 34506.5.

Inspections by patrol members, see Vehicle Code § 2804 et seq.

Obedience to traffic control devices and signals, see Vehicle Code §§ 21461, 21462.

Operation of vehicle with unlawful equipment or in unsafe condition, see Vehicle Code § 24002 et seq.

Optional appearance before magistrate, see Vehicle Code § 40303.

Penalty for violations affecting failure to stop and submit to inspection of equipment or for an unsafe condition, see Vehicle Code § 42001.

Possession and display of driver's license, see Vehicle Code § 12951.

Punishment for misdemeanors under this section, see Vehicle Code § 42001 et seq.

Rules of the road, bicycles or animals, see Vehicle Code §§ 21050, 21200.

School safety patrol traffic signals, disregarding, see Education Code § 49307.

Vehicles incidentally operated over highway, applicability of this section, see Vehicle Code § 25802.

Violation a misdemeanor, see Vehicle Code § 40000.7.

§ 2800.1. Flight from pursuing peace officer

(a) Any person who, while operating a motor vehicle and with the intent to evade, willfully flees or otherwise attempts to elude a pursuing peace officer's motor vehicle, is guilty of a misdemeanor punishable by imprisonment in a county jail for not more than one year if all of the following conditions exist:

(1) The peace officer's motor vehicle is exhibiting at least one lighted red lamp visible from the front and the person either sees or reasonably should have seen the lamp.

(2) The peace officer's motor vehicle is sounding a siren as may be reasonably necessary.

(3) The peace officer's motor vehicle is distinctively marked.

(4) The peace officer's motor vehicle is operated by a peace officer, as defined in Chapter 4.5 (commencing with Section 830) of Title 3 of Part 2 of the Penal Code, and that peace officer is wearing a distinctive uniform.

(b) Any person who, while operating a motor vehicle and with the intent to evade, willfully flees or otherwise attempts to elude a pursuing peace officer's bicycle, is guilty of a misdemeanor punishable by imprisonment in a county jail for not more than one year if the following conditions exist:

(1) The peace officer's bicycle is distinctively marked.

(2) The peace officer's bicycle is operated by a peace officer, as defined in paragraph (4) of subdivision (a), and that peace officer is wearing a distinctive uniform.

(3) The peace officer gives a verbal command to stop.

(4) The peace officer sounds a horn that produces a sound of at least 115 decibels.

(5) The peace officer gives a hand signal commanding the person to stop.

(6) The person is aware or reasonably should have been aware of the verbal command, horn, and hand signal, but refuses to comply with the command to stop. *(Added by Stats.1982, c. 947, p. 3433, § 2. Amended by Stats.1988, c. 504, § 1, eff. Aug. 22, 1988; Stats.1995, c. 68 (S.B.170), § 1; Stats.2005, c. 485 (S.B.719), § 6.)*

Cross References

Commercial motor vehicles, suspension of driving privileges for violations of this section, see Vehicle Code §§ 15300, 15302.
Driver's license examinations, knowledge of risks and punishment associated with fleeing a police officer while operating a motor vehicle, see Vehicle Code § 1666.1.
Indemnification of victims of crime, persons injured where police officer is operating a motor vehicle attempting to apprehend a suspect, see Government Code § 13955.
Vehicle pursuit reports filed by law enforcement agency, contents, see Vehicle Code § 14602.1.
Violation as misdemeanor, see Vehicle Code § 40000.7.

§ 2800.2. Driving in willful or wanton disregard for safety of persons or property while fleeing from pursuing police officer; penalties

(a) If a person flees or attempts to elude a pursuing peace officer in violation of Section 2800.1 and the pursued vehicle is driven in a willful or wanton disregard for the safety of persons or property, the person driving the vehicle, upon conviction, shall be punished by imprisonment in the state prison, or by confinement in the county jail for not less than six months nor more than one year. The court may also impose a fine of not less than one thousand dollars ($1,000) nor more than ten thousand dollars ($10,000), or may impose both that imprisonment or confinement and fine.

(b) For purposes of this section, a willful or wanton disregard for the safety of persons or property includes, but is not limited to, driving while fleeing or attempting to elude a pursuing peace officer during which time either three or more violations that are assigned a traffic violation point count under Section 12810 occur, or damage to property occurs. *(Added by Stats.1988, c. 504, § 3, eff. Aug. 22, 1988. Amended by Stats.1996, c. 420 (A.B.1999), § 1; Stats.1998, c. 472 (A.B.2066), § 1.)*

Cross References

Commercial motor vehicles, suspension of driving privileges for violations of this section, see Vehicle Code §§ 15300, 15302.
Traffic violation point count, violation of this section, see Vehicle Code § 12810.

§ 2800.3. Death or serious bodily injury proximately caused by flight from pursuing peace officer; punishment; "serious bodily injury" defined

(a) Whenever willful flight or attempt to elude a pursuing peace officer in violation of Section 2800.1 proximately causes serious bodily injury to any person, the person driving the pursued vehicle, upon conviction, shall be punished by imprisonment in the state prison for three, five, or seven years, by imprisonment in a county jail for not more than one year, or by a fine of not less than two thousand dollars ($2,000) nor more than ten thousand dollars ($10,000), or by both that fine and imprisonment.

(b) Whenever willful flight or attempt to elude a pursuing peace officer in violation of Section 2800.1 proximately causes death to a person, the person driving the pursued vehicle, upon conviction, shall be punished by imprisonment in the state prison for a term of 4, 6, or 10 years.

(c) Nothing in this section shall preclude the imposition of a greater sentence pursuant to Section 190 of the Penal Code or any other provisions of law applicable to punishment for an unlawful death.

(d) For the purposes of this section, "serious bodily injury" has the same meaning as defined in paragraph (4) of subdivision (f) of Section 243 of the Penal Code. *(Formerly § 2800.2, added by Stats.1982, c. 947, p. 3433, § 3. Renumbered § 2800.3, and amended by Stats.1988, c. 504, § 2, eff. Aug. 22, 1988. Amended by Stats.1991, c. 656 (S.B.666), § 1; Stats.1996, c. 420 (A.B.1999), § 2; Stats.1998, c. 256 (A.B.1382), § 1; Stats.2005, c. 485 (S.B.719), § 7.)*

Cross References

Commercial motor vehicles, suspension of driving privileges for violations of this section, see Vehicle Code §§ 15300, 15302.
Driver's license examinations, knowledge of risks and punishment associated with fleeing a police officer while operating a motor vehicle, see Vehicle Code § 1666.1.
Indemnification of victims of crime, persons injured where police officer is operating a motor vehicle attempting to apprehend a suspect, see Government Code § 13955.

§ 2800.4. Willful driving of vehicle on highway in direction opposite lawful traffic during flight from pursuing peace officer; punishment

Whenever a person willfully flees or attempts to elude a pursuing peace officer in violation of Section 2800.1, and the person operating the pursued vehicle willfully drives that vehicle on a highway in a direction opposite to that in which the traffic lawfully moves upon that highway, the person upon conviction is punishable by imprisonment for not less than six months nor more than one year in a county jail or by imprisonment in the state prison, or by a fine of not less than one thousand dollars ($1,000) nor more than ten thousand dollars ($10,000), or by both that fine and imprisonment. *(Added by Stats. 2006, c. 688 (S.B.1735), § 1. Amended by Stats.2011, c. 15 (A.B.109), § 599, eff. April 4, 2011, operative Oct. 1, 2011; Stats.2012, c. 43 (S.B.1023), § 111, eff. June 27, 2012.)*

§ 2801. Obedience to firemen

It is unlawful to wilfully fail or refuse to comply with any lawful order, signal, or direction of any member of any fire department, paid, volunteer, or company operated, when wearing the badge or insignia of a fireman and when in the course of his duties he is protecting the personnel and fire department equipment. *(Stats.1959, c. 3, p. 1552, § 2801.)*

Cross References

Failure to stop and submit to inspection of equipment or unsafe condition endangering a person, punishment for misdemeanor conviction, see Vehicle Code § 42002.1.

Penalty for violations affecting failure to stop and submit to inspection of equipment or for an unsafe condition, see Vehicle Code § 42001.

Punishment for misdemeanors under this section, see Vehicle Code § 42001.

Rules of the road, bicycles or animals, see Vehicle Code §§ 21050, 21200.

Violation a misdemeanor, see Vehicle Code § 40000.7.

§ 2802. Load inspection; inspection facilities and scales; hours of operation

(a) Any traffic officer having reason to believe that a vehicle is not safely loaded or that the height, width, length, or weight of a vehicle and load is unlawful may require the driver to stop and submit to an inspection, measurement, or weighing of the vehicle. The weighing may be done either by means of portable or stationary scales and the officer may require that the vehicle be driven to the nearest scale facility, in the event the scales are within five road miles.

(b) Selected inspection facilities and platform scales operated by the Department of the California Highway Patrol may, at the discretion of the commissioner, be open for extended hours, up to and including 24 hours every day. The primary purpose of the extended hours is to assist in the detection of overweight vehicles. These inspection facilities and platform scales shall be located near primary border route points of entry into the state and key routes within the state.

(c) An amount not to exceed one million dollars ($1,000,000) shall be available annually from the Motor Vehicle Account in the State Transportation Fund, upon appropriation by the Legislature, for the expanded operation of the scale facilities, as specified in subdivision (b). It is the intent of the Legislature that the funds made available pursuant to this subdivision shall be the only funds available for purposes of this section. *(Stats.1959, c. 3, p. 1552, § 2802. Amended by Stats.1981, c. 1170, p. 4700, § 1; Stats.1993, c. 19 (S.B.361), § 1.)*

Cross References

Procedure on arrest for violation of this section, see Vehicle Code § 40303.

Punishment for violations, see Vehicle Code § 42001 et seq.

Size, weight, and load, see Vehicle Code § 35000 et seq.

§ 2802.5. Repealed by Stats.2001, c. 115 (S.B.153), § 37

Law Revision Commission Comments

2001 Repeal

Section 2802.5 is repealed as obsolete. The pilot project established by this section has expired. [30 Cal.L.Rev.Comm. Reports 327 (2000)].

§ 2803. Control of illegal size or weight

(a) If the traffic officer determines that the vehicle is not safely loaded or that the height, width, length, or weight is unlawful, he may require the driver to stop in a suitable place and reload or remove such portion of the load as may be necessary to render the load safe or to reduce it to the limits permitted under this code. A suitable place is an area which allows the least obstruction to the highway and which requires the least travel on the highway by the vehicle. Determination of the suitability of an area shall be made by the traffic officer who requires the adjustment. All material so unloaded shall be cared for by the owner or operator of the vehicle at the risk of the owner or operator.

(b) If a certified weight certificate or bill of lading accompanies a vehicle which has been determined to be overweight due to the load on the vehicle, the driver shall submit the certified weight certificate or bill of lading, whichever is appropriate, to the traffic officer when the overweight load is removed in the presence of the officer. The officer may note on the certified weight certificate or bill of lading submitted by the driver the fact that a portion of the load has been removed to bring the vehicle and load within the allowable weight limit specified in this code, and the officer shall return the certificate or bill of lading to the driver.

(c) If the height, width, or length of the vehicle is unlawful, irrespective of any load thereon, or if an unladen vehicle is overweight, the traffic officer may prohibit further movement of the vehicle until a permit is obtained as provided in Section 35780. *(Stats.1959, c. 3, p. 1552, § 2803. Amended by Stats.1961, c. 1151, p. 2897,*

§ 1; Stats.1965, c. 1196, p. 3017, § 1; Stats.1977, c. 506, p. 1635, § 1.)

§ 2804. Inspection by patrol members

A member of the California Highway Patrol upon reasonable belief that any vehicle is being operated in violation of any provisions of this code or is in such unsafe condition as to endanger any person, may require the driver of the vehicle to stop and submit to an inspection of the vehicle, and its equipment, license plates, and registration card. *(Stats.1959, c. 3, p. 1552, § 2804.)*

§ 2805. Inspection of vehicles, vehicle components, title or registration

(a) For the purpose of locating stolen vehicles, (1) any member of the California Highway Patrol, or (2) a member of a city police department, a member of a county sheriff's office, or a district attorney investigator, whose primary responsibility is to conduct vehicle theft investigations, may inspect any vehicle of a type required to be registered under this code, or any identifiable vehicle component thereof, on a highway or in any public garage, repair shop, terminal, parking lot, new or used car lot, automobile dismantler's lot, vehicle shredding facility, vehicle leasing or rental lot, vehicle equipment rental yard, vehicle salvage pool, or other similar establishment, or any agricultural or construction work location where work is being actively performed, and may inspect the title or registration of vehicles, in order to establish the rightful ownership or possession of the vehicle or identifiable vehicle component.

As used in this subdivision, "identifiable vehicle component" means any component which can be distinguished from other similar components by a serial number or other unique distinguishing number, sign, or symbol.

(b) A member of the California Highway Patrol, a member of a city police department or county sheriff's office, or a district attorney investigator whose primary responsibility is to conduct vehicle theft investigations, may also inspect, for the purposes specified in subdivision (a), implements of husbandry, special construction equipment, forklifts, and special mobile equipment in the places described in subdivision (a) or when that vehicle is incidentally operated or transported upon a highway.

(c) Whenever possible, inspections conducted pursuant to subdivision (a) or (b) shall be conducted at a time and in a manner so as to minimize any interference with, or delay of, business operations. *(Stats.1959, c. 3, p. 1552, § 2805. Amended by Stats.1970, c. 648, p. 1266, § 1; Stats.1977, c. 325, p. 1274, § 1; Stats.1979, c. 252, p. 543, § 1; Stats.1983, c. 1017, § 1; Stats.1988, c. 392, § 1; Stats.2000, c. 688 (A.B.1669), § 21.)*

§ 2806. Inspection by police, deputy sheriffs, or reserve police officers

Any regularly employed and salaried police officer or deputy sheriff, or any reserve police officer or reserve deputy sheriff listed in Section 830.6 of the Penal Code, having reasonable cause to believe that any vehicle or combination of vehicles is not equipped as required by this code or is in any unsafe condition as to endanger any person, may require the driver to stop and submit the vehicle or combination of vehicles to an inspection and those tests as may be appropriate to determine the safety to persons and compliance with the code. *(Stats.1959, c. 3, p. 1553, § 2806. Amended by Stats.1967, c. 1110, p. 2754, § 1; Stats.2003, c. 292 (A.B.1436), § 5.)*

Criminal procedure, deputized or appointed peace officers, see Penal Code § 830.6.

Duty of driver to submit to inspection, see Vehicle Code § 2800.

Equipment of vehicles, see Vehicle Code § 24000 et seq.

Lighting requirements, see Vehicle Code § 24250 et seq.

Operation of vehicle without required equipment or in unsafe condition, see Vehicle Code § 24002 et seq.

Procedure on equipment violations, see Vehicle Code § 40150 et seq.

Punishment for violations, see Vehicle Code § 42001 et seq.

Vehicles incidentally operated over highway, applicability of this section, see Vehicle Code § 25802.

Vehicles transporting explosives, inspection, see Vehicle Code § 31607.

§ 2807. School bus inspection

(a) The California Highway Patrol shall inspect every schoolbus at least once each school year to ascertain whether its construction, design, equipment, and color comply with all provisions of law.

(b) No person shall drive any schoolbus unless there is displayed therein a certificate issued by the California Highway Patrol stating that on a certain date, which shall be within 13 months of the date of operation, an authorized employee of the California Highway Patrol inspected the bus and found that on the date of inspection the bus complied with the applicable provisions of state law relating to construction, design, equipment, and color. The Commissioner of the California Highway Patrol shall provide by rule or regulation for the issuance and display of distinctive inspection certificates. *(Stats. 1959, c. 3, p. 1553, § 2807. Amended by Stats.1963, c. 198, p. 937, § 1; Stats.1969, c. 580, p. 1211, § 1.)*

Cross References

Schoolbus defined, see Vehicle Code § 545.

§ 2807.1. School pupil activity bus; inspection and certification; display of certificate

(a) The Department of the California Highway Patrol shall inspect and certify every school pupil activity bus specified in Section 546 at least once each year to ascertain whether its condition complies with all provisions of the law.

(b) No person shall drive any motor vehicle specified in subdivision (a) unless there is displayed therein a certificate issued by the Department of the California Highway Patrol stating that on a certain date, which shall be within 13 months of the date of operation, an authorized employee of the Department of the California Highway Patrol inspected such motor vehicle and found that on the date of inspection such motor vehicle complied with the applicable provisions of the state law. The Commissioner of the California Highway Patrol shall provide by rule or regulation for the issuance and display of distinctive inspection certificates. *(Added by Stats. 1976, c. 945, p. 2161, § 3, eff. Sept. 15, 1976, operative Jan. 1, 1977. Amended by Stats.1981, c. 813, p. 3153, § 7.)*

§ 2807.2. Preventive maintenance inspections

The Department of the California Highway Patrol shall, by regulation, provide for a preventive maintenance inspection guide for use by operators of tour buses, motor vehicles specified in Sections 2807 and 2807.1, and vehicles described in subdivisions (a), (b), (d), (e), (f), and (g) of Section 34500. The regulations shall provide that the record of inspection shall be signed by the person making the inspection, and the record of the inspections shall be retained on file by the operator for review and inspection by the Department of the California Highway Patrol. *(Added by Stats.1976, c. 945, p. 2161, § 4, eff. Sept. 15, 1976. Amended by Stats.1977, c. 406, p. 1415, § 8, eff. Aug. 27, 1977; Stats.1977, c. 1174, p. 3846, § 2; Stats.1981, c. 813, p. 3153, § 8; Stats.1986, c. 1306, § 8; Stats.1988, c. 1586, § 4, operative July 1, 1989.)*

Cross References

Tour bus defined, see Vehicle Code § 612.

§ 2807.3. Inspection and certification of youth bus; display of certificate; fee

(a) The Department of the California Highway Patrol shall inspect and certify every youth bus at least once each school year to ascertain whether its condition complies with all provisions of law.

(b) No person shall drive any youth bus unless there is displayed therein a certificate issued by the Department of the California Highway Patrol stating that on a certain date, which shall be within 13 months of the date of operation, an authorized employee of the Department of the California Highway Patrol inspected the youth bus and found that on the date of inspection the youth bus complied with the applicable provisions of state law. The Commissioner of the California Highway Patrol shall provide, by rule or regulation, for the issuance and display of distinctive inspection certificates.

(c) The Commissioner of the California Highway Patrol may determine the fee and method of collection for the annual inspection of youth buses. The fee, established by regulation, shall be sufficient to cover the cost to the department for youth bus inspections and testing of drivers pursuant to Section 12523. All fees received shall be deposited in the Motor Vehicle Account in the State Transportation Fund. *(Added by Stats.1982, c. 383, p. 1712, § 3, eff. July 4, 1982. Amended by Stats.1982, c. 1273, p. 4699, § 4.)*

Cross References

Youth bus defined, see Vehicle Code § 680.

§ 2808. Private schoolbus requirements

(a) Except as provided in subdivision (b), all schoolbuses transporting pupils to or from any private school or private school activity shall be subject to the same statutes, rules, and regulations relating to construction, design, operation, equipment, and color as are now or hereafter applicable to schoolbuses transporting pupils to or from any public school or public school activity.

(b) Schoolbuses shall be exempt from such statutes, rules, and regulations relating to construction, design, safe operation, and equipment as the Commissioner of the California Highway Patrol shall determine necessary to permit such schoolbuses to continue in operation or when it appears that the results intended to be attained by such rules and regulations are being accomplished by the use of other methods. Such exemption shall be specified by rule or regulation of the commissioner. No such exemption shall be made which in the opinion of the commissioner would jeopardize the safety of the pupils so transported. *(Stats.1959, c. 3, p. 1553, § 2808. Amended by Stats.1977, c. 406, p. 1415, § 8.5, eff. Aug. 27, 1977.)*

Cross References

Private school, defined, see Vehicle Code § 492.
Schoolbus defined, see Vehicle Code § 545.

§ 2809. California highway patrol scales

All scales and weighing instruments used by any member of the California Highway Patrol to enforce the provisions of this code with respect to weight limitations shall be inspected and certified as to accuracy at least once in each calendar year by the Bureau of Weights and Measures of the Department of Food and Agriculture or by a county sealer of weights and measures. *(Stats.1959, c. 3, p. 1553, § 2809. Amended by Stats.1972, c. 261, p. 510, § 1; Stats.1974, c. 545, p. 1310, § 156.)*

Cross References

Punishment for violations, see Vehicle Code § 42001 et seq.
Size, weight, and load, see Vehicle Code § 35000 et seq.

§ 2810. Inspection to prevent theft

(a) A member of the California Highway Patrol may stop any vehicle transporting any timber products, livestock, poultry, farm produce, crude oil, petroleum products, or inedible kitchen grease, and inspect the bills of lading, shipping or delivery papers, or other evidence to determine whether the driver is in legal possession of the load, and, upon reasonable belief that the driver of the vehicle is not in legal possession, shall take custody of the vehicle and load and turn them over to the custody of the sheriff of the county in which the timber products, livestock, poultry, farm produce, crude oil, petroleum products, or inedible kitchen grease, or any part thereof, is apprehended.

(b) The sheriff shall receive and provide for the care and safekeeping of the apprehended timber products, livestock, poultry, farm produce, crude oil, petroleum products, or inedible kitchen grease, or any part thereof, and immediately, in cooperation with the department, proceed with an investigation and its legal disposition.

(c) Any expense incurred by the sheriff in the performance of his or her duties under this section shall be a legal charge against the county. *(Stats.1959, c. 3, p. 1553, § 2810. Amended by Stats.1981, c. 912, p. 3452, § 4, eff. Sept. 28, 1981; Stats.1998, c. 394 (S.B.1738), § 4; Stats. 1999, c. 83 (S.B.966), § 187.)*

Cross References

Driver defined, see Vehicle Code § 305.

§ 2810.1. Commercial rental vehicles transporting household goods; stop and inspection; violations; citations

(a) Any traffic officer may stop any commercial vehicle, as defined in Section 260, that is a rental vehicle and inspect the bills of lading, shipping, delivery papers, or other evidence to determine whether the driver is transporting household goods in violation of the Household Goods Carriers Act (Chapter 7 (commencing with Sec. 5101) of Division 2 of the Public Utilities Code). The officer may only stop and inspect where the officer has probable cause to believe that the vehicle is being operated in violation of that act.

(b) It is a public offense, for which an officer may issue a citation, for a driver to unlawfully transport household goods in violation of the Household Goods Carriers Act. That public offense is punishable as prescribed in Article 8 (commencing with Section 5311) of Chapter 7 of Division 2 of the Public Utilities Code. It is an infraction to refuse to submit to an inspection as authorized by subdivision (a).

(c) A copy of the citation for any offense described in subdivision (b) shall be sent by the the department that employs the traffic officer to the Director of the Consumer Services Division of the California Public Utilities Commission. A copy of a citation shall be removed from any record of the commission upon a showing that the person was not convicted of the offense or that bail was not forfeited for that offense. A person for whom a copy of a citation has been sent to the commission and is on file with the commission may request the commission for an administrative hearing on that matter. *(Added by Stats.1997, c. 250 (A.B.1261), § 1.)*

§ 2810.2. Vehicles transporting agricultural irrigation supplies; inspection of bills of lading, shipping, or delivery papers by peace officer; care of apprehended supplies; expenses incurred; impoundment of vehicle; other violations

(a)(1) A peace officer, as described in Chapter 4.5 (commencing with Section 830) of Title 3 of Part 2 of the Penal Code, may stop any vehicle transporting agricultural irrigation supplies that are in plain view to inspect the bills of lading, shipping, or delivery papers, or other evidence to determine whether the driver is in legal possession of the load, if the vehicle is on a rock road or unpaved road that is located in a county that has elected to implement this section and the road is located as follows:

(A) Located * * * under the management of the Department of Parks and Recreation, the Department of Fish and Wildlife, the Department of Forestry and Fire Protection, the State Lands Commission, a regional park district, the United States Forest Service, or the Bureau of Land Management.

(B) Located within the respective ownership of a timberland production zone, as defined in Chapter 6.7 (commencing with Section 51100) of Division 1 of Title 5 of the Government Code, either that is larger than 50,000 acres or for which the owner of more than 2,500 acres has given express written permission for a vehicle to be stopped within that zone pursuant to this section.

(2) Upon reasonable belief that the driver of the vehicle is not in legal possession, the law enforcement officer specified in paragraph (1) shall take custody of the vehicle and load and turn them over to the custody of the sheriff of the county that has elected to implement this section where the agricultural irrigation supplies are apprehended.

(b) The sheriff shall receive and provide for the care and safekeeping of the apprehended agricultural irrigation supplies that were in plain view within the boundaries of public lands under the management of the entities listed in subparagraph (A) of paragraph (1) of subdivision (a) or on a timberland production zone as specified in subparagraph (B) of paragraph (1) of subdivision (a), and immediately, in cooperation with the department, proceed with an investigation and its legal disposition.

(c) Any expense incurred by the sheriff in the performance of his or her duties under this section shall be a legal charge against the county.

(d) Except as provided in subdivision (e), a peace officer shall not cause the impoundment of a vehicle at a traffic stop made pursuant to subdivision (a) if the driver's only offense is a violation of Section 12500.

(e) During the conduct of pulling a driver over in accordance with subdivision (a), if the peace officer encounters a driver who is in violation of Section 12500, the peace officer shall make a reasonable attempt to identify the registered owner of the vehicle. If the registered owner is present, or the peace officer is able to identify the registered owner and obtain the registered owner's authorization to release the motor vehicle to a licensed driver during the vehicle stop, the vehicle shall be released to either the registered owner of the vehicle if he or she is a licensed driver or to the licensed driver authorized by the registered owner of the vehicle. If a notice to appear is issued, the name and the driver's license number of the licensed driver to whom the vehicle was released pursuant to this subdivision shall be listed on the officer's copy of the notice to appear issued to the unlicensed driver. When a vehicle cannot be released, the vehicle shall be removed pursuant to subdivision (p) of Section 22651, whether a notice to appear has been issued or not.

(f) For * * * purposes of this section, "agricultural irrigation supplies" include agricultural irrigation water bladder and one-half inch diameter or greater irrigation line.

(g) This section shall be implemented only in a county where the board of supervisors adopts a resolution authorizing the enforcement of this section. *(Added by Stats.2012, c. 390 (A.B.2284), § 3. Amended by Stats. 2013, c. 472 (S.B.814), § 9.)*

§ 2811. Damage to fences

Any traffic officer who observes a fence along any highway, which has been damaged as a result of a traffic accident, shall promptly report same to the owner, lessee, occupant, or person in charge of the property enclosed by the fence, or to the local headquarters of the department. *(Stats.1959, c. 3, p. 1554, § 2811.)*

Cross References

Traffic officer defined, see Vehicle Code § 625.

§ 2812. Closing of highways

Whenever poisonous gas, explosives, dust, smoke, or other similar substances, or fire exist upon or so near a public highway as to create a menace to public health or safety, members of the California Highway Patrol, police departments, or sheriff's office may close any highway to traffic when necessary to protect the public from such dangers. Whenever a highway is closed, the governmental agency having control over the highway shall be immediately notified of the reason of the closing and the location. *(Stats.1959, c. 3, p. 1554, § 2812.)*

Cross References

Punishment for violations, see Vehicle Code § 42001 et seq.

§ 2812.5. Restricting or prohibiting use of highway; visibility limitations

Whenever visibility limitations pose a significant safety hazard, as determined by a member of the California Highway Patrol, that member may restrict or prohibit the use of any highway by any vehicle subject to regulation by the Department of the California Highway Patrol pursuant to Section 34500. *(Added by Stats.1992, c. 119 (A.B.122), § 1.)*

§ 2813. Commercial vehicle inspection; violations; misdemeanor

Every driver of a commercial vehicle shall stop and submit the vehicle to an inspection of the size, weight, equipment, and smoke emissions of the vehicle at any location where members of the California Highway Patrol are conducting tests and inspections of commercial vehicles and when signs are displayed requiring the stop. Every driver who fails or refuses to stop and submit the vehicle to an inspection when signs are displayed requiring that stop is guilty of a misdemeanor. *(Added by Stats.1959, c. 1441, p. 3713, § 1. Amended by Stats.1966, 1st Ex.Sess., c. 91, p. 539, § 1; Stats.1981, c. 675, p. 2469, § 1.)*

Cross References

Commercial vehicle defined, see Vehicle Code § 260.

Violation as misdemeanor, see Vehicle Code § 40000.7.

§ 2813.5. Commercial vehicle inspection stickers; issuance and display; unauthorized or facsimile stickers; misdemeanor

(a) The commissioner shall have exclusive authority in the issuance of stickers as evidence that commercial vehicles have been inspected pursuant to Section 2813 and have been found to be in compliance with minimum safety standards established by the department. The commissioner may make and enforce regulations with respect to the issuance and display of the stickers upon commercial vehicles.

(b) It is unlawful for any unauthorized person, company, corporation, or public or private entity to possess, issue, or display upon a vehicle an unauthorized commercial vehicle safety inspection sticker or a sticker that is either a facsimile of, or is substantially similar to, that issued by the commissioner.

(c) Any violation of subdivision (b) is a misdemeanor. *(Added by Stats.1987, c. 747, § 1. Amended by Stats.2004, c. 183 (A.B.3082), § 345.)*

§ 2814. Passenger vehicle inspection

Every driver of a passenger vehicle shall stop and submit the vehicle to an inspection of the mechanical condition and equipment of the vehicle at any location where members of the California Highway Patrol are conducting tests and inspections of passenger vehicles and when signs are displayed requiring such stop.

The Commissioner of the California Highway Patrol may make and enforce regulations with respect to the issuance of stickers or other devices to be displayed upon passenger vehicles as evidence that the vehicles have been inspected and have been found to be in safe mechanical condition and equipped as required by this code and equipped with certified motor vehicle pollution control devices as required by Part 5 (commencing with Section 43000) of Division 26 of the Health and Safety Code which are correctly installed and in operating condition. Any sticker so issued shall be placed on the windshield within a seven-inch square as provided in Section 26708.

If, upon such inspection of a passenger vehicle, it is found to be in unsafe mechanical condition or not equipped as required by this code and the provisions of Part 5 (commencing with Section 43000) of Division 26 of the Health and Safety Code, the provisions of Article 2 (commencing with Section 40150) of Chapter 1 of Division 17 of this code shall apply.

The provisions of this section relating to motor vehicle pollution control devices apply to vehicles of the United States or its agencies, to the extent authorized by federal law. *(Added by Stats.1965, c. 2031, p. 4611, § 10, eff. July 23, 1965. Amended by Stats.1968, c. 49, p. 194, § 6, eff. April 25, 1968; Stats.1968, c. 178, p. 402, § 1; Stats.1968, c. 764, p. 1480, § 10; Stats.1971, c. 739, p. 1464, § 4, operative May 3, 1972; Stats.1975, c. 957, p. 2230, § 20.)*

Cross References

Passenger vehicle defined, see Vehicle Code § 465.

§ 2814.1. Vehicle inspection program; motorcycle only checkpoints prohibited

(a) A board of supervisors of a county may, by ordinance, establish, on highways under its jurisdiction, a vehicle inspection checkpoint program to check for violations of Sections 27153 and 27153.5. The program shall be conducted by the local agency or department with the primary responsibility for traffic law enforcement.

(b) A driver of a motor vehicle shall stop and submit to an inspection conducted under subdivision (a) when signs and displays are posted requiring that stop.

(c) A county that elects to conduct the program described under subdivision (a) may fund that program through fine proceeds deposited with the county under Section 1463.15 of the Penal Code.

(d) State and local law enforcement agencies shall not conduct motorcycle only checkpoints. *(Added by Stats. 2003, c. 482 (S.B.708), § 3. Amended by Stats.2011, c. 653 (A.B.353), § 1; Stats.2012, c. 89 (A.B.1047), § 2.)*

§ 2814.2. Conduct of sobriety checkpoint inspection; vehicle impoundment and release

(a) A driver of a motor vehicle shall stop and submit to a sobriety checkpoint inspection conducted by a law enforcement agency when signs and displays are posted requiring that stop.

(b) Notwithstanding Section 14602.6 or 14607.6, a peace officer or any other authorized person shall not cause the impoundment of a vehicle at a sobriety checkpoint if the driver's only offense is a violation of Section 12500.

(c) During the conduct of a sobriety checkpoint, if the law enforcement officer encounters a driver who is in violation of Section 12500, the law enforcement officer shall make a reasonable attempt to identify the registered owner of the vehicle. If the registered owner is present, or the officer is able to identify the registered owner and obtain the registered owner's authorization to release the motor vehicle to a licensed driver by the end of the checkpoint, the vehicle shall be released to either the registered owner of the vehicle if he or she is a licensed driver or to the licensed driver authorized by the registered owner of the vehicle. If a notice to appear is issued, the name and driver's license number of the licensed driver to whom the vehicle was released pursuant to this subdivision shall be listed on the officer's copy of the notice to appear issued to the unlicensed driver. When a vehicle cannot be released, the vehicle shall be removed pursuant to subdivision (p) of Section 22651, whether a notice to appear has been issued or not. *(Added by Stats.2011, c. 653 (A.B.353), § 2.)*

Release of vehicle to registered owner or agent, see Vehicle Code § 14602.

§ 2815. Nonstudent school crossing guard

Any person who shall disregard any traffic signal or direction given by a nonstudent school crossing guard, appointed pursuant to Section 21100, or authorized by any city police department, any board of supervisors of a county, or the Department of the California Highway Patrol, when the guard is wearing the official insignia of such a school crossing guard, and when in the course of the guard's duties the guard is protecting any person in crossing a street or highway in the vicinity of a school or while returning thereafter to a place of safety, shall be guilty of an infraction and subject to the penalties provided in Section 42001.1. *(Added by Stats.1969, c. 1131, p. 2197, § 1; Amended by Stats.1976, c. 1018, p. 4598, § 1; Stats.1978, c. 626, p. 2078, § 2; Stats.1984, c. 69, 1, eff. April 5, 1984.)*

Official traffic control signal, defined, see Vehicle Code § 445.

§ 2816. Youth bus; loading or discharging children; highways

It is unlawful to load or discharge children onto or from a youth bus upon a highway at any location where the children must cross the highway upon which the youth bus is stopped, unless traffic is controlled by a traffic officer or an official traffic control signal. *(Added by Stats.1982, c. 383, p. 1712, § 4, eff. July 4, 1982.)*

Official traffic control signal, defined, see Vehicle Code § 445.
Traffic officer defined, see Vehicle Code § 625.
Youth bus defined, see Vehicle Code § 680.

§ 2817. Funeral processions; disregard of traffic signal or direction by peace officer; violation

Any person who disregards any traffic signal or direction given by a peace officer authorized pursuant to subdivision (d) of Section 70 of the Penal Code to escort funeral processions, if the peace officer is in a peace officer's uniform, and is in the process of escorting a funeral procession, shall be guilty of an infraction and subject to the penalties provided in subdivision (a) of Section 42001. *(Added by Stats.1984, c. 1108, § 1.)*

§ 2818. Electronic beacon, flare, or cone patterns or combination; traverse

It is unlawful to traverse an electronic beacon pattern, a flare pattern, cone pattern, or combination of electronic beacon, flare, or cone patterns, provided for the regulation of traffic, or provided in a situation where public safety personnel are engaged in traffic control or emergency scene management. *(Added by Stats.1988, c. 843, § 3. Amended by Stats.2008, c. 120 (S.B.1727), § 1.)*

CHAPTER 5. CALIFORNIA TRAFFIC SAFETY PROGRAM

Article   Section
 1. Traffic Safety 2900
 2. Motorcycle Safety 2930

ARTICLE 1. TRAFFIC SAFETY

Section
2900. Scope of program.
2901. Administration.
2902. Delegation of authority.
2903. Advisory committee.
2904. Local traffic safety program.
2905. Report to legislature.
2906. California traffic safety program fund.
2907. Appropriation of federal funds.
2908. Apportionment of funds.
2909. Local participation.
2910. Local use of funds.
2911. Public awareness campaign associated with risks and penalties resulting from evading a peace officer.

§ 2900. Scope of program

There is in this state, the California Traffic Safety Program, which consists of a comprehensive plan in conformity with the laws of this state to reduce traffic accidents and deaths, injuries, and property damage resulting from accidents. The program shall include, but not be limited to, provisions to improve driver performance, including, but not limited to, driver education, driver testing to determine proficiency to operate motor vehicles, and driver examinations and driver licensing, and provisions to improve bicyclist and pedestrian education and performance. In addition, the program shall include, but not be limited to, provisions for an effective record system of accidents, including injuries and deaths resulting from accidents; accident investigations to determine the probable causes of accidents, injuries, and deaths; vehicle registration, operation, and inspection; highway design and maintenance including lighting, markings, and surface treatment; traffic control; vehicle codes and laws; surveillance of traffic for detection and correction of high or potentially high accident locations; and emergency services. *(Added by Stats.1967, c. 1492, p. 3487, § 2, eff. Aug. 28, 1967. Amended by Stats.1996, c. 674 (S.B.515), § 3; Stats.2000, c. 181 (S.B.2190), § 1.)*

§ 2901. Administration

The Governor may appoint a highway safety representative who shall serve in the Transportation Agency and who shall, in consultation with the Governor and Secretary of Transportation, prepare the California Traffic Safety Program. The Governor is responsible for the administration of the program, and has final approval of all phases of the program, and may take all action necessary to secure the full benefits available to the program under the Federal Highway Safety Act of 1966, and any amendments thereto [1]. The highway safety representative serves at the pleasure of the secretary.

(Added by Stats.1967, c. 1492, p. 3487, § 2, eff. Aug. 28, 1967. Amended by Stats.1969, c. 138, p. 371, § 281, eff. Sept. 11, 1969; Stats.1978, c. 652, p. 2114, § 1; Stats.1984, c. 144, § 204; Gov.Reorg.Plan No. 2 of 2011–2012, § 325, eff. July 3, 2012, operative July 1, 2013; Stats.2013, c. 352 (A.B.1317), § 522, eff. Sept. 26, 2013, operative July 1, 2013.)

[1] 23 U.S.C.A. §§ 105, 303 note, 307, 401 to 404.

§ 2902. Delegation of authority

To the maximum extent permitted by federal law and regulations and the laws of this state, the Governor may delegate to the Secretary of Transportation and the highway safety representative the authority necessary to administer the program, and the secretary and the representative may exercise this authority once delegated. *(Added by Stats.1967, c. 1492, p. 3487, § 2, eff. Aug. 28, 1967. Amended by Stats.1969, c. 138, p. 372, § 282, eff. Sept. 11, 1969; Stats.1978, c. 652, p. 2114, § 2; Gov.Reorg. Plan No. 2 of 2011–2012, § 326, eff. July 3, 2012, operative July 1, 2013; Stats.2013, c. 352 (A.B.1317), § 523, eff. Sept. 26, 2013, operative July 1, 2013.)*

§ 2903. Advisory committee

The Governor may establish an Advisory Committee on the California Traffic Safety Program which shall consist of various officials of state and local government and other persons who are interested in the establishment of a comprehensive program of traffic safety in this state including, but not limited to, representatives of agriculture, railroads, the Institute of Transportation and Traffic Engineering of the University of California, the motor vehicle manufacturing industry, the automobile aftermarket equipment servicing and manufacturing industry, automobile dealers, the trucking industry, labor, motor vehicle user organizations, and traffic safety organizations. *(Added by Stats.1967, c. 1492, p. 3487, § 2, eff. Aug. 28, 1967.)*

§ 2904. Local traffic safety program

The California Traffic Safety Program shall include a local traffic safety program designed to encourage the political subdivisions of this state to establish traffic safety programs consistent with the objectives of the California Traffic Safety Program. *(Added by Stats.1967, c. 1492, p. 3487, § 2, eff. Aug. 28, 1967.)*

§ 2905. Report to legislature

On or before the fifth legislative day of the 1968 legislative session and each year thereafter, the Governor shall submit a report to the Legislature through such interim committee or committees as may be designated by legislative resolution. Such report shall include a detailed presentation of the California Traffic Safety Program, a statement concerning the progress made in implementing the program and recommendations concerning possible legislative action deemed necessary or desirable to implement the program. *(Added by Stats. 1967, c. 1492, p. 3487, § 2, eff. Aug. 28, 1967.)*

§ 2906. California traffic safety program fund

The California Traffic Safety Program Fund is hereby created in the State Treasury to consist of the funds referred to in Section 2907. *(Added by Stats.1967, c. 1492, p. 3487, § 2, eff. Aug. 28, 1967.)*

§ 2907. Appropriation of federal funds

Any funds which are appropriated by Congress for the purposes of carrying out Section 402 of Title 23, United States Code (P.L. 89–564; 80 Stats. 731) and which are apportioned to this state by the Secretary of Commerce pursuant to Section 402 of Title 23, United States Code (P.L. 89–564; 80 Stats. 731) are continuously appropriated for the purposes and uses of the California Traffic Safety Program. *(Added by Stats.1967, c. 1492, p. 3487, § 2, eff. Aug. 28, 1967.)*

§ 2908. Apportionment of funds

The Governor shall apportion any funds contained in the California Traffic Safety Program Fund among the various state agencies and local political subdivisions as shall effectuate the purposes of the program, and, in accordance with any federal formula for apportionment or other federal requirements as contained in federal enactments, regulations, or standards promulgated by the Secretary of Commerce. *(Added by Stats.1967, c. 1492, p. 3487, § 2, eff. Aug. 28, 1967.)*

§ 2909. Local participation

Any local political subdivision of this state, including, but not limited to, a city, a county, a city and county, a district, or a special district, is authorized to participate in a local traffic safety program within its jurisdiction if such local program is approved by the Governor; provided, however, that any local political subdivision may participate in a traffic safety program other than that promulgated pursuant to the federal Highway Safety Act of 1966.[1] *(Added by Stats.1967, c. 1492, p. 3487, § 2, eff. Aug. 28, 1967.)*

[1] 23 U.S.C.A. §§ 105, 303 note, 307, 401 to 404.

§ 2910. Local use of funds

Such local political subdivision may use, in implementing its local traffic safety program, any funds which are apportioned to it from the California Traffic Safety Program Fund by the Governor pursuant to Section 2908. *(Added by Stats.1967, c. 1492, p. 3487, § 2, eff. Aug. 28, 1967.)*

§ 2911. Public awareness campaign associated with risks and penalties resulting from evading a peace officer

All traffic safety programs that receive state funds and that include public awareness campaigns involving emergency vehicle operations shall include in the public awareness campaign, information on the risks to public safety of peace officer motor vehicle pursuits, and the penalties that may result from evading a peace officer. *(Added by Stats.2005, c. 485 (S.B.719), § 8.)*

Cross References

Driver's license examinations, knowledge of risks and punishment associated with fleeing a police officer while operating a motor vehicle, see Vehicle Code § 1666.1.

ARTICLE 2.   MOTORCYCLE SAFETY

Section
2930.   Definitions.
2931.   Establishment of program; administration.
2932.   Commissioner's powers.
2933.   Program services; contracts or grants.
2934.   California Motorcyclist Safety Fund.
2935.   Fees upon registration; deposit in fund.
2936.   Repealed.
2937, 2938.   Repealed.

Cross References

Instruction permits to operate motorcycles, motorized scooters, motorized bicycles, etc., completion of motorcyclist safety program required, see Vehicle Code § 12509.5.

§ 2930.   Definitions

(a) "Commissioner" means the Commissioner of the California Highway Patrol.

(b) "Fund" means the California Motorcyclist Safety Fund.

(c) "Program" means the motorcyclist safety program established in this article. *(Added by Stats.1985, c. 547, § 2.)*

§ 2931.   Establishment of program; administration

A motorcyclist safety program is hereby established in the Department of the California Highway Patrol, to be administered by the commissioner. *(Added by Stats.1985, c. 547, § 2.)*

§ 2932.   Commissioner's powers

The commissioner may, through contracts with other public agencies or with private entities, do all of the following:

(a) Provide financial or other support to projects aimed at enhancing motorcycle operation and safety, including, but not limited to, motorcyclist safety training programs. The motorcyclist safety training programs shall comply with criteria which the commissioner, in consultation with other state agencies and national motorcycle safety organizations, may adopt to provide validated motorcyclist safety training programs in the state.

(b) Sponsor and coordinate efforts aimed at increasing motorists' awareness of motorcyclists.

(c) Sponsor research into effective communication techniques to reach all highway users on matters of motorcyclist safety.

(d) Establish an advisory committee of persons from other state and local agencies with an interest in motorcycle safety; persons from the motorcycle industry; motorcycle safety organizations; motorcycle enthusiast organizations; and others with an interest in motorcycle safety, to assist in the establishment of a comprehensive program of motorcycle safety.

(e) Adopt standards for course content, contact hours, curriculum, instructor training and testing, and instructional quality control, and setting forth a maximum amount for course fees for the novice rider training course specified in subdivisions (g) and (i) of Section 12804.9.

(f)(1) Adopt standards for course content, contact hours, curriculum, instructor training and testing, and instructional quality control, for a premier motorcyclist safety training program. Motorcycle safety training courses offered under a premier motorcyclist safety training program shall meet all of the following requirements:

(A) Provide a core curriculum approved for the novice rider training course specified in subdivision (e).

(B) Additional course requirements established by the commissioner.

(2) On and after January 1, 2008, the commissioner shall not impose a maximum amount for course fees for courses provided under the premier motorcyclist safety training program.

(3) All administrative costs of a premier motorcyclist safety training program shall be paid for by the provider, and none of the costs shall be paid for by the state. *(Added by Stats.1985, c. 547, § 2.   Amended by Stats.1993, c. 789 (A.B.229), § 1; Stats.2006, c. 711 (A.B.1189), § 2.)*

§ 2933.   Program services; contracts or grants

The commissioner shall not directly manage or provide program services. Any program service financed under this article shall be provided under contractual arrangements or grant funding. All public agencies assisting or providing program services under this article shall be fully reimbursed for their costs by the commissioner. The commissioner shall monitor and evaluate any contracts or grants executed pursuant to this article to ensure that the provisions of the contracts or grants are adhered to by the recipients. *(Added by Stats.1985, c. 547, § 2.)*

§ 2934.   California Motorcyclist Safety Fund

(a) The California Motorcyclist Safety Fund is hereby created in the State Treasury. The money in the fund is available, when appropriated by the Legislature, to fund programs established pursuant to this article and to defray related costs incurred. Moneys in the fund are and shall be held as trust funds for the exclusive trust purposes specified in this article.

(b) The commissioner shall not in any way encumber moneys in the fund beyond that amount which is actually available in the fund at the time of encumbrance, and shall not in any manner pledge or encumber future revenues to accrue to the fund from any source. *(Added by Stats.1985, c. 547, § 2.)*

§ 2935. Fees upon registration; deposit in fund

The Department of Motor Vehicles shall, in addition to other fees, collect a fee of two dollars ($2) upon initial registration and renewal of registration of every motorcycle subject to registration fees. These additional fees shall be deposited in the fund. *(Added by Stats.1985, c. 547, § 2.)*

§ 2936. Repealed by Stats.2001, c. 745 (S.B.1191), § 226, eff. Oct. 12, 2001

§§ 2937, 2938. Repealed by Stats.1999, c. 610 (A.B.975), §§ 3, 4

CHAPTER 6. NEW MOTOR VEHICLE BOARD

Article	Section
1. Organization of Board	3000
2. Powers and Duties of Board	3050
3. Appeals from Decisions of the Department	3052
4. Hearings on Franchise Modification, Replacement, Termination, Refusal to Continue, Delivery and Preparation Obligations, and Warranty Reimbursement	3060
5. Hearings on Recreational Vehicle Franchise Modification, Replacement, Termination, Refusal to Continue, Establishment, and Relocation, and Consumer Complaints	3070

ARTICLE 1. ORGANIZATION OF BOARD

Section
3000. Board created.
3001. Qualifications of board members.
3002. Effective date of appointments.
3003. Terms of office; vacancies.
3004. Oath.
3005. Removal from office.
3006. President of board.
3007. Frequency of meetings.
3008. Public meetings.
3009. Repealed.
3010. Quorum.
3011. Effect of vacancy on board.
3012. Per diem.
3013. Seal.
3014. Appointment of executive director; exemption from civil service requirements; personnel, office space, equipment, supplies, and services.
3015. Offices.
3016. Funding of activities; fees; deposits; surplus.

Cross References

Issuance of licenses and certificates to manufacturers, transporters and dealers, unlawful acts, see Vehicle Code § 11713.3.

§ 3000. Board created

There is in the Department of Motor Vehicles a New Motor Vehicle Board, which consists of nine members. *(Added by Stats.1967, c. 1397, p. 3261, § 2. Amended by Stats.1973, c. 996, § 13, operative July 1, 1974.)*

§ 3001. Qualifications of board members

(a) Four of the appointive members of the board shall be new motor vehicle dealers as defined in Section 426 who have engaged for a period of not less than five years preceding their appointment in activities regulated by Article 1 (commencing with Section 11700) of Chapter 4 of Division 5. These members shall be appointed by the Governor.

(b) Each of the five remaining appointive members shall be a public member who is not a licentiate under Article 1 (commencing with Section 11700) or 2 (commencing with Section 11800) of Chapter 4 of Division 5 or an employee of such licentiate at the time of appointment and one of these five appointive members shall have been admitted to practice law in the state for at least 10 years immediately preceding his or her appointment. One public member shall be appointed by the Senate Committee on Rules, one by the Speaker of the Assembly, and three by the Governor.

(c) Each member shall be of good moral character.

(d) This section does not apply to a dealer who deals exclusively in motorcycles or recreational vehicles, as defined in subdivision (a) of Section 18010 of the Health and Safety Code. *(Added by Stats.1967, c. 1397, p. 3261, § 2. Amended by Stats.1975, c. 943, p. 2107, § 2; Stats.1982, c. 1584, p. 6261, § 7; Stats.2003, c. 703 (S.B.248), § 3.)*

Cross References

Motorcycle dealers, inapplicability of section, see Vehicle Code § 426.

§ 3002. Effective date of appointments

The appointments of the appointive members shall be made effective as of the effective date of this article. *(Added by Stats.1967, c. 1397, p. 3261, § 2.)*

§ 3003. Terms of office; vacancies

(a) Each appointive member of the board shall be appointed for a term of four years and shall hold office until the appointment and qualification of his or her successor or until one year has elapsed since the expiration of the time for which he or she was appointed, whichever occurs first.

(b) The terms of the members of the board first appointed shall expire as follows: one public member and one new motor vehicle dealer member, January 15, 1969; two public members and one new motor vehicle dealer member, January 15, 1970; two public members and two new motor vehicle dealer members, January 15, 1971. The terms shall thereupon expire in the same relative order.

(c) Vacancies occurring shall be filled by appointment for the unexpired term.

This section does not apply to a dealer who deals exclusively in motorcycles or recreational vehicles, as defined in subdivision (a) of Section 18010 of the Health and Safety Code. *(Added by Stats.1967, c. 1397, p. 3261, § 2. Amended by Stats.1975, c. 943, p. 2108, § 3; Stats.1982, c. 1584, p. 6261, § 8; Stats.1983, c. 1144, § 1, eff. Sept. 28, 1983; Stats.2003, c. 703 (S.B.248), § 4.)*

Cross References

Motorcycle dealers, inapplicability of section, see Vehicle Code § 426.

§ 3004. Oath

Members of the board shall take an oath of office as provided in the Constitution and the Government Code. *(Added by Stats.1967, c. 1397, p. 3261, § 2.)*

§ 3005. Removal from office

The appointing authority has the power to remove from office at any time, any member of the board appointed by such appointing authority for continued neglect of duties required by law, or for incompetence, or unprofessional or dishonorable conduct. Nothing in this section shall be construed as a limitation or restriction on the power of the appointing authority, conferred by any other provision of law, to remove any member of the board. *(Added by Stats.1967, c. 1397, p. 3261, § 2.)*

§ 3006. President of board

The board shall organize and elect a president from among its members for a term of one year at the first meeting of each year. The newly elected president shall assume his or her duties at the conclusion of the meeting at which he or she was elected. Reelection to office during membership is unrestricted. *(Added by Stats.1967, c. 1397, p. 3261, § 2. Amended by Stats.2013, c. 512 (S.B.155), § 2.)*

§ 3007. Frequency of meetings

The board shall meet at least twice during each calendar year.

Special meetings may be called at any time by the president or by any five members of the board upon notice for such time and in such manner as the board may provide. *(Added by Stats.1967, c. 1397, p. 3261, § 2.)*

§ 3008. Public meetings

(a) All meetings of the board shall be open and public, and all persons shall be permitted to attend any meeting of the board, except that the board may hold executive sessions to deliberate on the decision to be reached upon the evidence introduced in a proceeding conducted in accordance with Chapter 5 (commencing with Section 11500) of Part 1 of Division 3 of Title 2 of the Government Code.

(b) At all meetings of the board, open or executive, involving an appeal from a decision of the Director of Motor Vehicles * * *, the director or his or her authorized representative may attend, present the position of the department, and then shall absent himself or herself from any executive session at the request of any member of the board.

(c) Within the limitations of its powers and authority * * *, and in the event of disagreement between the board and the director regarding the decision to be reached * * *, the decision of the board shall be final. *(Added by Stats.1967, c. 1397, p. 3261, § 2. Amended by Stats.2013, c. 512 (S.B.155), § 3.)*

§ 3009. Repealed by Stats.1968, c. 1473, p. 2950, § 72

§ 3010. Quorum

Five members of the board shall constitute a quorum for the transaction of business, for the performance of any duty or the exercise of any power or authority of the board, except that three members of the board, who are not new motor vehicle dealers, shall constitute a quorum for the purposes of Article 4 (commencing with Section 3060) and the consideration of a petition pursuant to subdivision (c) of Section 3050 that involves a dispute between a franchisee and franchisor. *(Added by Stats. 1967, c. 1397, p. 3261, § 2. Amended by Stats.1977, c. 278, p. 1171, § 1, eff. July 8, 1977; Stats.2000, c. 637 (A.B.2292), § 1.)*

§ 3011. Effect of vacancy on board

A vacancy on the board shall not impair the power of the remaining members to perform all duties and exercise all powers of the board, providing the members remaining constitute a quorum. *(Added by Stats.1967, c. 1397, p. 3261, § 2.)*

§ 3012. Per diem

Each member of the board shall receive a per diem of one hundred dollars ($100) for each day actually spent in the discharge of official duties, and he or she shall be reimbursed for * * * traveling and other expenses necessarily incurred in the performance of his or her duties * * *. The per diem and reimbursement shall be wholly defrayed from funds that shall be provided in the annual budget of the department. *(Added by Stats.1967, c. 1397, p. 3261, § 2. Amended by Stats.1982, c. 1273, p. 4700, § 4.5; Stats.1982, c. 1584, p. 6261, § 9; Stats.1983, c. 1144, § 2, eff. Sept. 28, 1983; Stats.2013, c. 512 (S.B.155), § 4.)*

§ 3013. Seal

The board shall adopt a seal and such other device as the members may desire thereon, by which they shall authenticate all papers and documents under their control.

Copies of all records and papers in the board's office shall be received in evidence in all cases when certified under the hand and seal of the board, equally and with like effect as the originals. *(Added by Stats.1967, c. 1397, p. 3261, § 2.)*

§ 3014. Appointment of executive director; exemption from civil service requirements; personnel, office space, equipment, supplies, and services

The board may appoint an executive director, who shall be exempt from civil service requirements, and who shall devote as much time as may be necessary to discharge the functions of the board as herein provided. The department shall provide the board with the necessary personnel, office space, equipment, supplies, and services that, in the opinion of the board, may be necessary to administer this chapter. However, the board may contract with the department or another state agency for office space, equipment, supplies, and services, as determined by the board to be appropriate, for the administration of this chapter. *(Added by Stats.1967, c. 1397, p. 3261, § 2. Amended by Stats.1983, c. 1144, § 3, eff. Sept. 28, 1983; Stats.1984, c. 247, § 1; Stats.2003, c. 451 (A.B.1718), § 5.)*

§ 3015. Offices

In addition to the office of the executive director in Sacramento, the department shall, as the need therefor occurs, secure adequate rooms for the meetings of the board in Los Angeles, San Francisco, Sacramento, or other locations in the state as may be required in the discretion of the board, to administer this chapter. *(Added by Stats.1967, c. 1397, p. 3261, § 2. Amended by Stats.2003, c. 451 (A.B.1718), § 6.)*

§ 3016. Funding of activities; fees; deposits; surplus

(a) New motor vehicle dealers and other licensees under the jurisdiction of the board shall be charged fees sufficient to fully fund the activities of the board other than those conducted pursuant to Section 472.5 of the Business and Professions Code. The board may recover the direct cost of the activities required by Section 472.5 of the Business and Professions Code by charging the Department of Consumer Affairs a fee which shall be paid by the Department of Consumer Affairs with funds appropriated from the Certification Account in the Consumer Affairs Fund. All fees shall be deposited, and held separate from other moneys, in the Motor Vehicle Account in the State Transportation Fund, and shall not be transferred to the State Highway Account pursuant to Section 42273.

(b) The fees shall be available, when appropriated, exclusively to fund the activities of the board. If, at the conclusion of any fiscal year, the amount of fees collected exceeds the amount of expenditures for this purpose during the fiscal year, the surplus shall be carried over into the succeeding fiscal year. *(Added by Stats.1982, c. 327, p. 1543, § 197, eff. June 30, 1982. Amended by Stats.1983, c. 1144, § 3.2, eff. Sept. 28, 1983; Stats.1985, c. 1201, § 1, eff. Sept. 29, 1985; Stats.1989, c. 193, § 3; Stats.1990, c. 216 (S.B.2510), § 113; Stats.1996, c. 1088 (A.B.2515), § 13, eff. Sept. 30, 1996; Stats.1997, c. 17 (S.B.947), § 143.)*

ARTICLE 2. POWERS AND DUTIES OF BOARD

Section
3050.   Duties.
3050.1.   Oaths, depositions, certification of official acts, subpoenas, discovery.

Section
3050.2.   Enforcement of subpoenas and compliance with discovery procedures.
3050.3.   Witness fees and the mileage allowance.
3050.4.   Mandatory settlement conference.
3050.5.   Fee for initial filing of appeal, protest or petition.
3050.6.   Continuances; costs.
3050.7.   Proposed stipulated decision and order; adoption by board; objections.
3051.   Applicability of provisions.

§ 3050. Duties

The board shall do all of the following:

(a) Adopt rules and regulations in accordance with Chapter 3.5 (commencing with Section 11340) of Part 1 of Division 3 of Title 2 of the Government Code governing those matters that are specifically committed to its jurisdiction.

(b) Hear and determine, within the limitations and in accordance with the procedure provided, an appeal presented by an applicant for, or holder of, a license as a new motor vehicle dealer, manufacturer, manufacturer branch, distributor, distributor branch, or representative when the applicant or licensee submits an appeal provided for in this chapter from a decision arising out of the department.

(c) Consider any matter concerning the activities or practices of any person applying for or holding a license as a new motor vehicle dealer, manufacturer, manufacturer branch, distributor, distributor branch, or representative pursuant to Chapter 4 (commencing with Section 11700) of Division 5 submitted by any person. A member of the board who is a new motor vehicle dealer may not participate in, hear, comment, advise other members upon, or decide any matter considered by the board pursuant to this subdivision that involves a dispute between a franchisee and franchisor. After that consideration, the board may do any one or any combination of the following:

(1) Direct the department to conduct investigation of matters that the board deems reasonable, and make a written report on the results of the investigation to the board within the time specified by the board.

(2) Undertake to mediate, arbitrate, or otherwise resolve any honest difference of opinion or viewpoint existing between any member of the public and any new motor vehicle dealer, manufacturer, manufacturer branch, distributor, distributor branch, or representative.

(3) Order the department to exercise any and all authority or power that the department may have with respect to the issuance, renewal, refusal to renew, suspension, or revocation of the license of any new motor vehicle dealer, manufacturer, manufacturer branch, distributor, distributor branch, or representative as that license is required under Chapter 4 (commencing with Section 11700) of Division 5.

(d) Hear and decide, within the limitations and in accordance with the procedure provided, a protest presented by a franchisee pursuant to Section 3060, 3062, 3064, 3065, * * * 3065.1, 3070, 3072, 3074, 3075, or 3076. A member of the board who is a new motor vehicle dealer may not participate in, hear, comment, advise other members upon, or decide, any matter involving a protest filed pursuant to Article 4 (commencing with Section 3060), unless all parties to the protest stipulate otherwise.

(e) Notwithstanding subdivisions (c) and (d), the courts have jurisdiction over all common law and statutory claims originally cognizable in the courts. For those claims, a party may initiate an action directly in any court of competent jurisdiction. *(Added by Stats.1967, c. 1397, p. 3261, § 2. Amended by Stats.1973, c. 996, p. 1966, § 14, operative July 1, 1974; Stats.1974, c. 384, p. 952, § 1, eff. July 5, 1974, operative July 1, 1974; Stats.1975, c. 943, p. 2108, § 4; Stats.1977, c. 278, p. 1171, § 2, eff. July 8, 1977; Stats.1979, c. 340, p. 1206, § 1, eff. July 27, 1979; Stats.1982, c. 454, p. 1892, § 180; Stats.1985, c. 1201, § 2, urgency, eff. Sept. 29, 1985; Stats.1987, c. 1280, § 7, operative Jan. 1, 1988; Stats.1997, c. 356 (S.B.690), § 1; Stats.2013, c. 512 (S.B.155), § 5.)*

§ 3050.1. Oaths, depositions, certification of official acts, subpoenas, discovery

(a) In a proceeding, hearing, or in the discharge of duties imposed under this chapter, the board, its executive director, or an administrative law judge designated by the board may administer oaths, take depositions, certify to official acts, and issue subpoenas to compel attendance of witnesses and the production of books, records, papers, and other documents in any part of the state.

(b) For purposes of discovery, the board or its executive director may, if deemed appropriate and proper under the circumstances, authorize the parties to engage in the civil action discovery procedures in Title 4 (commencing with Section 2016.010) of Part 4 of the Code of Civil Procedure, excepting the provisions of Chapter 13 (commencing with Section 2030.010) of that title. Discovery shall be completed no later than 15 days prior to the commencement of the proceeding or hearing before the board. This subdivision shall apply only to those proceedings or hearings involving a petition or protest filed pursuant to subdivision (c) or (d) of Section 3050. The board, its executive director, or an administrative law judge designated by the board may issue subpoenas to compel attendance at depositions of persons having knowledge of the acts, omissions, or events that are the basis for the proceedings, as well as the production of books, records, papers, and other documents. *(Added by Stats.1972, c. 1210, p. 2336, § 1. Amended by Stats.1980, c. 964, p. 3058, § 1; Stats.2000, c. 637 (A.B.2292), § 2; Stats.2003, c. 451 (A.B.1718), § 7; Stats.2004, c. 182 (A.B.3081), § 59, operative July 1, 2005.)*

Law Revision Commission Comments
2004 Amendment

Subdivision (b) of Section 3050.1 is amended to reflect nonsubstantive reorganization of the rules governing civil discovery. [33 Cal.L.Rev.Comm. Reports 1070 (2003)].

§ 3050.2. Enforcement of subpoenas and compliance with discovery procedures

(a) Obedience to subpoenas issued to compel attendance of witnesses, or the production of books, records, papers, and other documents at the proceeding or hearing, may be enforced by application to the superior court as set forth in Article 2 (commencing with Section 11180) of Chapter 2 of Part 1 of Division 3 of Title 2 of the Government Code.

(b) Compliance with discovery procedures authorized pursuant to subdivision (b) of Section 3050.1 may be enforced by application to the executive director of the board. The executive director may, at the direction of the board, upon a showing of failure to comply with authorized discovery without substantial justification for that failure, dismiss the protest or petition or suspend the proceedings pending compliance. The executive director may, at the direction of the board, upon a failure to comply with authorized discovery without substantial justification for that failure, require payment of costs incurred by the board, as well as attorney's fees and costs of the party who successfully makes or opposes a motion to compel enforcement of discovery. Nothing in this section precludes the executive director from making application to the superior court to enforce obedience to subpoenas or compliance with other discovery procedures authorized pursuant to subdivision (b) of Section 3050.1. *(Added by Stats.1972, c. 1210, p. 2336, § 2. Amended by Stats.1980, c. 964, p. 3058, § 2; Stats.1983, c. 1144, § 3.5, eff. Sept. 28, 1983; Stats.1990, c. 1325 (A.B.3515), § 1, eff. Sept. 26, 1990; Stats.2003, c. 451 (A.B.1718), § 8.)*

§ 3050.3. Witness fees and the mileage allowance

A witness, other than an officer or employee of the state or of a political subdivision of the state, who appears by order of the board or its executive director, shall receive for his or her attendance the same fees and the same mileage allowed by law to witnesses in civil cases. The amount shall be paid by the party at whose request the witness is subpoenaed. The mileage and fees, if any, of a witness subpoenaed by the board or its executive director, but not at the request of a party, shall be paid from the funds provided for the use of the board in the same manner that other expenses of the board are paid. *(Added by Stats.1972, c. 1210, p. 2336, § 3. Amended by Stats.2003, c. 451 (A.B.1718), § 9.)*

§ 3050.4. Mandatory settlement conference

In a protest or petition before the board, the board, its executive director, or an administrative law judge designated by the board or its executive director, may order a mandatory settlement conference. The failure of a party to appear, to be prepared, or to have authority to settle the matter may result in one or more of the following:

(a) The board, its executive director, or an administrative law judge designated by the board or its executive director, may suspend all proceedings before the board in the matter until compliance.

(b) The board, its executive director, or an administrative law judge designated by the board or its executive director, may dismiss the proceedings or any part thereof before the board with or without prejudice.

(c) The board, its executive director, or an administrative law judge designated by the board or its executive director, may require all the board's costs to be paid by the party at fault.

(d) The board, its executive director, or an administrative law judge designated by the board or its executive director, may deem that the party at fault has abandoned the matter. *(Added by Stats.1983, c. 1144, § 4, eff. Sept. 28, 1983. Amended by Stats.2003, c. 451 (A.B.1718), § 10.)*

§ 3050.5. Fee for initial filing of appeal, protest or petition

Pursuant to Section 3016, the board shall establish a fee for the initial filing by any party in regard to any appeal, protest, or petition filed pursuant to this chapter. *(Added by Stats.1984, c. 268, § 32.55, eff. June 30, 1984. Amended by Stats.1985, c. 1201, § 3, eff. Sept. 29, 1985.)*

§ 3050.6. Continuances; costs

The board or its executive director may, in the event of a granting of a continuance of a scheduled matter, assess costs of the board upon the party receiving the continuance. *(Added by Stats.1983, c. 1144, § 5, eff. Sept. 28, 1983. Amended by Stats.2003, c. 451 (A.B.1718), § 11.)*

§ 3050.7. Proposed stipulated decision and order; adoption by board; objections

(a) The board may adopt stipulated decisions and orders, without a hearing pursuant to Section 3066, to resolve one or more issues raised by a protest or petition filed with the board. Whenever the parties to a protest or petition submit a proposed stipulated decision and * * * order of the board, a copy of the proposed stipulated decision and order shall be transmitted by the executive director of the board to each member of the board. The proposed stipulated decision and order shall be deemed to be adopted by the board unless a member of the board notifies the executive director of the board of an objection thereto within 10 days after that board member has received a copy of the proposed stipulated decision and order.

(b) If the board adopts a stipulated decision and order to resolve a protest filed pursuant to Section 3060 or 3070 in which the parties stipulate that good cause exists for the termination of the franchise of the protestant, and the order provides for a conditional or unconditional termination of the franchise of the protestant, paragraph (2) of subdivision (a) of Section 3060 and paragraph (2) of subdivision (a) of Section 3070, which require a hearing to determine whether good cause exists for termination of the franchise, is inapplicable to the proceedings. If the stipulated decision and order provides for an unconditional termination of the franchise, the franchise may be

terminated without further proceedings by the board. If the stipulated decision and order provides for the termination of the franchise, conditioned upon the failure of a party to comply with specified conditions, the franchise may be terminated upon a determination, according to the terms of the stipulated decision and order, that the conditions have not been met. If the stipulated decision and order provides for the termination of the franchise conditioned upon the occurrence of specified conditions, the franchise may be terminated upon a determination, according to the terms of the stipulated decision and order, that the stipulated conditions have occurred. *(Added by Stats.1985, c. 1201, § 4, eff. Sept. 29, 1985. Amended by Stats.1990, c. 1325 (A.B.3515), § 2, eff. Sept. 26, 1990; Stats.2003, c. 451 (A.B.1718), § 12; Stats.2011, c. 342 (S.B.642), § 2; Stats.2013, c. 512 (S.B.155), § 6.)*

§ 3051. Applicability of provisions

This chapter does not apply to any person licensed as a transporter under Article 1 (commencing with Section 11700) or as a salesperson under Article 2 (commencing with Section 11800) of Chapter 4 of Division 5, or to any licensee who is not a new motor vehicle dealer, motor vehicle manufacturer, manufacturer branch, new motor vehicle distributor, distributor branch, or representative. This chapter does not apply to transactions involving "mobilehomes," as defined in Section 18008 of the Health and Safety Code, "recreational vehicles," as defined in subdivision (b) of Section 18010 of the Health and Safety Code, truck campers, "commercial coaches," as defined in Section 18001.8 of the Health and Safety Code, or off-highway motor vehicles subject to identification, as defined in Section 38012, except off-highway motorcycles, as defined in Section 436, and all-terrain vehicles, as defined in Section 111. Except as otherwise provided in this chapter, this chapter applies to a new motor vehicle dealer, a dealer of new recreational vehicles, as defined in subdivision (a) of Section 18010 of the Health and Safety Code, except a dealer who deals exclusively in truck campers, a vehicle manufacturer as defined in Section 672, a manufacturer branch as defined in Section 389, a distributor as defined in Section 296, a distributor branch as defined in Section 297, a representative as defined in Section 512, or an applicant therefor. *(Added by Stats.1967, c. 1397, p. 3261, § 2. Amended by Stats.1973, c. 996, p. 1967, § 15, operative July 1, 1974; Stats.1975, c. 943, p. 2109, § 5; Stats.1979, c. 622, p. 1941, § 4; Stats.1981, c. 714, p. 2792, § 436; Stats.1982, c. 1584, p. 6262, § 10; Stats.1993, c. 594 (A.B.1821), § 2; Stats.2000, c. 637 (A.B.2292), § 3; Stats.2003, c. 703 (S.B.248), § 5.)*

ARTICLE 3. APPEALS FROM DECISIONS OF THE DEPARTMENT

Section
3052. Filing and content of appeal.
3053. Determination of appeal.
3054. Power to reverse or amend decision.
3055. Power to reverse or amend penalty.

Section
3056.   Reconsideration on reversal of decision.
3057.   Effective date of orders of board; final orders.
3058.   Judicial review.

§ 3052.   Filing and content of appeal

(a) On or before the 10th day after the last day on which reconsideration of a final decision of the department can be ordered, the * * * applicant or licensee may file an appeal with the executive director of the board. The appeal shall be in writing and shall state the grounds therefor. A copy of the appeal shall be mailed by the appellant to the department, and the department shall thereafter be considered as a party to the appeal. The right to appeal is not affected by failure to seek reconsideration before the department.

(b) An appeal is considered to be filed on the date it is received in the office of the executive director of the board, except that an appeal mailed to the executive director by means of registered mail is considered to be filed with the executive director on the postmark date.

(c) The appeal shall be accompanied by evidence that the appellant has requested the administrative record of the department and advanced the cost of preparation of that record. The complete administrative record includes the pleadings, all notices and orders issued by the department, any proposed decision by an administrative law judge, the exhibits admitted or rejected, the written evidence, and any other papers in the case. All parts of the administrative record requested by the appellant may be filed with the appeal together with the appellant's points and authorities. If the board orders the filing of additional parts of the administrative record, the board may order prior payment by the appellant of the cost of providing those additional parts.

(d) Except as provided in subdivisions (e) and (f), a decision of the department may not become effective during the period in which an appeal may be filed, and the filing of an appeal shall stay the decision of the department until a final order is made by the board.

(e) When a decision has ordered revocation of a dealer's license, the department may, on or before the last day upon which an appeal may be filed with the board, petition the board to order the decision of the department into effect.

(f) With respect to the department's petition filed pursuant to subdivision (e), the department shall have the burden of proof. The board shall act upon the petition within 14 days or prior to the effective date of the department's decision, whichever is later. The board may order oral argument on the petition before the board. * * * *(Added by Stats.1967, c. 1397, p. 3261, § 2. Amended by Stats.1990, c. 1563 (A.B.3243), § 4; Stats. 2003, c. 451 (A.B.1718), § 13; Stats.2013, c. 512 (S.B. 155), § 7.)*

128

§ 3053.   Determination of appeal

The board shall determine the appeal upon the administrative record of the department, any evidence adduced at any hearing of the department, and upon any briefs filed by the parties. If any party to the appeal requests the right to appear before the board, the board shall set a time and place for such hearing, the production of any relevant evidence and argument. *(Added by Stats.1967, c. 1397, p. 3261, § 2.)*

§ 3054.   Power to reverse or amend decision

The board shall have the power to reverse or amend the decision of the department if it determines that any of the following exist:

(a) The department has proceeded without or in excess of its jurisdiction.

(b) The department has proceeded in a manner contrary to the law.

(c) The decision is not supported by the findings.

(d) The findings are not supported by the weight of the evidence in the light of the whole record reviewed in its entirety, including any and all relevant evidence adduced at any hearing of the board.

(e) There is relevant evidence, which in the exercise of reasonable diligence, could not have been produced or which was improperly excluded at the hearing.

(f) The determination or penalty, as provided in the decision of the department is not commensurate with the findings. *(Added by Stats.1967, c. 1397, p. 3261, § 2. Amended by Stats.1970, c. 819, p. 1548, § 1.)*

§ 3055.   Power to reverse or amend penalty

The board shall also have the power to amend, modify, or reverse the penalty imposed by the department. *(Added by Stats.1967, c. 1397, p. 3261, § 2.)*

§ 3056.   Reconsideration on reversal of decision

When the order reverses the decision of the department, the board may direct the * * * department to reconsider the matter in the light of its order and may direct the department to take any further action as is specially enjoined upon it by law. In all cases the board shall enter its order within 60 days after the filing of the appeal, except in the case of unavoidable delay in supplying the administrative record, in which event the board shall make its final order within 60 days after receipt * * * of the record. *(Added by Stats.1967, c. 1397, p. 3261, § 2. Amended by Stats.2013, c. 512 (S.B.155), § 8.)*

§ 3057.   Effective date of orders of board; final orders

The board shall fix an effective date for its orders not more than 30 days from the day the order is served upon the parties or remand the case to the department for fixing an effective date. A final order of the board shall be in writing and copies * * * of the order shall be delivered to the parties personally or sent to them by registered mail. The order shall be final upon its delivery or mailing and no reconsideration or rehearing by the board shall be permitted. *(Added by Stats.1967, c. 1397, p. 3261, § 2. Amended by Stats.1970, c. 819, p. 1548, § 2; Stats.2013, c. 512 (S.B.155), § 9.)*

§ 3058. Judicial review

Either party may seek judicial review of final orders of the board. Time for filing an action for such review shall not be more than 30 days from the date on which the final order of the board is delivered to the parties personally or is sent them by registered mail. *(Added by Stats.1967, c. 1397, p. 3261, § 2.)*

Cross References

Judicial review of administrative decisions, see Government Code § 11523.

Review of administrative decisions, see Code of Civil Procedure § 1094.5.

ARTICLE 4. HEARINGS ON FRANCHISE MODIFICATION, REPLACEMENT, TERMINATION, REFUSAL TO CONTINUE, DELIVERY AND PREPARATION OBLIGATIONS, AND WARRANTY REIMBURSEMENT

Section
3060. Termination of franchise.
3061. Good cause.
3062. Establishing or relocating dealerships.
3063. Good cause.
3064. Delivery and preparation obligation.
3065. Warranty reimbursement; disallowance of claim; requirements and process; audits of franchisee warranty records.
3065.1. Franchisor incentive program; claims; audits.
3066. Hearings on protests.
3067. Decision.
3068. Judicial review.
3069. Application of article.
3069.1. Application to franchises authorizing a dealership.

Cross References

Franchise definitions, see Vehicle Code § 331 et seq.

Issuance of licenses and certificates to manufacturers, transporters and dealers, unlawful acts, see Vehicle Code § 11713.3.

§ 3060. Termination of franchise

(a) Notwithstanding Section 20999.1 of the Business and Professions Code or the terms of any franchise, no franchisor shall terminate or refuse to continue any existing franchise unless all of the following conditions are met:

(1) The franchisee and the board have received written notice from the franchisor as follows:

(A) Sixty days before the effective date thereof setting forth the specific grounds for termination or refusal to continue.

(B) Fifteen days before the effective date thereof setting forth the specific grounds with respect to any of the following:

(i) Transfer of any ownership or interest in the franchise without the consent of the franchisor, which consent shall not be unreasonably withheld.

(ii) Misrepresentation by the franchisee in applying for the franchise.

(iii) Insolvency of the franchisee, or filing of any petition by or against the franchisee under any bankruptcy or receivership law.

(iv) Any unfair business practice after written warning thereof.

(v) Failure of the motor vehicle dealer to conduct its customary sales and service operations during its customary hours of business for seven consecutive business days, giving rise to a good faith belief on the part of the franchisor that the motor vehicle dealer is in fact going out of business, except for circumstances beyond the direct control of the motor vehicle dealer or by order of the department.

(C) The written notice shall contain, on the first page thereof in at least 12–point bold type and circumscribed by a line to segregate it from the rest of the text, one of the following statements, whichever is applicable:

[To be inserted when a 60–day notice of termination is given.]

"NOTICE TO DEALER: You have the right to file a protest with the NEW MOTOR VEHICLE BOARD in Sacramento and have a hearing in which you may protest the termination of your franchise under provisions of the California Vehicle Code. You must file your protest with the board within 30 calendar days after receiving this notice or within 30 days after the end of any appeal procedure provided by the franchisor or your protest right will be waived."

[To be inserted when a 15–day notice of termination is given.]

"NOTICE TO DEALER: You have the right to file a protest with the NEW MOTOR VEHICLE BOARD in Sacramento and have a hearing in which you may protest the termination of your franchise under provisions of the California Vehicle Code. You must file your protest with the board within 10 calendar days after receiving this notice or within 10 days after the end of any appeal procedure provided by the franchisor or your protest right will be waived."

(2) Except as provided in Section 3050.7, the board finds that there is good cause for termination or refusal to continue, following a hearing called pursuant to Section 3066. The franchisee may file a protest with the board within 30 days after receiving a 60–day notice, satisfying the requirements of this section, or within 30 days after the end of any appeal procedure provided by the franchisor, or within 10 days after receiving a 15–day notice, satisfying the requirements of this section, or

within 10 days after the end of any appeal procedure provided by the franchisor. When a protest is filed, the board shall advise the franchisor that a timely protest has been filed, that a hearing is required pursuant to Section 3066, and that the franchisor may not terminate or refuse to continue until the board makes its findings.

(3) The franchisor has received the written consent of the franchisee, or the appropriate period for filing a protest has elapsed.

(b)(1) Notwithstanding Section 20999.1 of the Business and Professions Code or the terms of any franchise, no franchisor shall modify or replace a franchise with a succeeding franchise if the modification or replacement would substantially affect the franchisee's sales or service obligations or investment, unless the franchisor has first given the board and each affected franchisee written notice thereof at least 60 days in advance of the modification or replacement. Within 30 days of receipt of the notice, satisfying the requirement of this section, or within 30 days after the end of any appeal procedure provided by the franchisor, a franchisee may file a protest with the board and the modification or replacement does not become effective until there is a finding by the board that there is good cause for the modification or replacement. If, however, a replacement franchise is the successor franchise to an expiring or expired term franchise, the prior franchise shall continue in effect until resolution of the protest by the board. In the event of multiple protests, hearings shall be consolidated to expedite the disposition of the issue.

(2) The written notice shall contain, on the first page thereof in at least 12–point bold type and circumscribed by a line to segregate it from the rest of the text, the following statement:

"NOTICE TO DEALER: Your franchise agreement is being modified or replaced. If the modification or replacement will substantially affect your sales or service obligations or investment, you have the right to file a protest with the NEW MOTOR VEHICLE BOARD in Sacramento and have a hearing in which you may protest the proposed modification or replacement of your franchise under provisions of the California Vehicle Code. You must file your protest with the board within 30 calendar days of your receipt of this notice or within 30 days after the end of any appeal procedure provided by the franchisor or your protest rights will be waived." *(Added by Stats.1973, c. 996, p. 1967, § 16, operative July 1, 1974. Amended by Stats.1974, c. 384, p. 953, § 4, eff. July 5, 1974, operative July 1, 1974; Stats.1983, c. 520, § 1; Stats.1984, c. 247, § 2; Stats.1990, c. 1325 (A.B.3515), § 3, eff. Sept. 26, 1990; Stats.1998, c. 662 (A.B.2707), § 3.)*

§ 3061. Good cause

In determining whether good cause has been established for modifying, replacing, terminating, or refusing to continue a franchise, the board shall take into consid-

eration the existing circumstances, including, but not limited to, all of the following:

(a) Amount of business transacted by the franchisee, as compared to the business available to the franchisee.

(b) Investment necessarily made and obligations incurred by the franchisee to perform its part of the franchise.

(c) Permanency of the investment.

(d) Whether it is injurious or beneficial to the public welfare for the franchise to be modified or replaced or the business of the franchisee disrupted.

(e) Whether the franchisee has adequate motor vehicle sales and service facilities, equipment, vehicle parts and qualified service personnel to reasonably provide for the needs of the consumers for the motor vehicles handled by the franchisee and has been and is rendering adequate services to the public.

(f) Whether the franchisee fails to fulfill the warranty obligations of the franchisor to be performed by the franchisee.

(g) Extent of franchisee's failure to comply with the terms of the franchise. *(Added by Stats.1973, c. 996, p. 1968, § 16, operative July 1, 1974. Amended by Stats.1983, c. 142, § 160.)*

§ 3062. Establishing or relocating dealerships

(a)(1) Except as otherwise provided in subdivision (b), if a franchisor seeks to enter into a franchise establishing an additional motor vehicle dealership * * *, or seeks to relocate an existing motor vehicle dealership, that has a relevant market area * * * within which the same line make is * * * represented, * * * the franchisor shall, in writing, first notify the board and each franchisee in that line-make in the relevant market area of the franchisor's intention to establish an additional dealership or to relocate an existing dealership * * *. Within 20 days of receiving the notice, satisfying the requirements of this section, or within 20 days after the end of an appeal procedure provided by the franchisor, a franchisee required to be given the notice may file with the board a protest to the * * * proposed dealership establishment or relocation described in the franchisor's notice. If within this time, a franchisee files with the board a request for additional time to file a protest, the board or its executive director, upon a showing of good cause, may grant an additional 10 days to file the protest. When a protest is filed, the board shall inform the franchisor that a timely protest has been filed, that a hearing is required pursuant to Section 3066, and that the franchisor may not establish the proposed dealership or relocate the existing dealership until the board has held a hearing as provided in Section 3066, nor thereafter, if the board has determined that there is good cause for not permitting the establishment of the proposed dealership or relocation of the existing dealership. In the event of multiple protests, hearings may be consolidated to expedite the disposition of the issue.

(2) If a franchisor seeks to enter into a franchise that authorizes a satellite warranty facility to be established at, or relocated to, a proposed location that is within two miles of a dealership of the same line-make, the franchisor shall first give notice in writing of the franchisor's intention to establish or relocate a satellite warranty facility at the proposed location to the board and each franchisee operating a dealership of the same line-make within two miles of the proposed location. Within 20 days of receiving the notice satisfying the requirements of this section, or within 20 days after the end of an appeal procedure provided by the franchisor, a franchisee required to be given the notice may file with the board a protest to the establishing or relocating of the satellite warranty facility. If, within this time, a franchisee files with the board a request for additional time to file a protest, the board or its executive director, upon a showing of good cause, may grant an additional 10 days to file the protest. When a protest is filed, the board shall inform the franchisor that a timely protest has been filed, that a hearing is required pursuant to Section 3066, and that the franchisor may not establish or relocate the proposed satellite warranty facility until the board has held a hearing as provided in Section 3066, nor thereafter, if the board has determined that there is good cause for not permitting the satellite warranty facility. In the event of multiple protests, hearings may be consolidated to expedite the disposition of the issue.

(3) The written notice shall contain, on the first page thereof in at least 12–point bold type and circumscribed by a line to segregate it from the rest of the text, the following statement:

"NOTICE TO DEALER: You have the right to file a protest with the NEW MOTOR VEHICLE BOARD in Sacramento and have a hearing on your protest under the terms of the California Vehicle Code if you oppose this action. You must file your protest with the board within 20 days of your receipt of this notice, or within 20 days after the end of any appeal procedure that is provided by us to you. If within this time you file with the board a request for additional time to file a protest, the board or its executive director, upon a showing of good cause, may grant you an additional 10 days to file the protest."

(b) Subdivision (a) does not apply to either of the following:

(1) The relocation of an existing dealership to a location that is both within the same city as, and within one mile from, the existing dealership location.

(2) The establishment at a location that is both within the same city as, and within one-quarter mile from, the location of a dealership of the same line-make that has been out of operation for less than 90 days.

(c) Subdivision (a) does not apply to a display of vehicles at a fair, exposition, or similar exhibit if actual sales are not made at the event and the display does not

exceed 30 days. This subdivision may not be construed to prohibit a new vehicle dealer from establishing a branch office for the purpose of selling vehicles at the fair, exposition, or similar exhibit, even though the event is sponsored by a financial institution, as defined in Section 31041 of the Financial Code or by a financial institution and a licensed dealer. The establishment of these branch offices, however, shall be in accordance with subdivision (a) where applicable.

(d) For the purposes of this section, the reopening of a dealership that has not been in operation for one year or more shall be deemed the establishment of an additional motor vehicle dealership.

(e) As used in this section, the following definitions apply:

(1) "Motor vehicle dealership" or "dealership" means an authorized facility at which a franchisee offers for sale or lease, displays for sale or lease, or sells or leases new motor vehicles.

(2) "Satellite warranty facility" means a facility operated by a franchisee where authorized warranty repairs and service are performed and the offer for sale or lease, the display for sale or lease, or the sale or lease of new motor vehicles is not authorized to take place. *(Added by Stats.1973, c. 996, p. 1969, § 16, operative July 1, 1974. Amended by Stats.1974, c. 384, p. 954, § 5, eff. July 5, 1974, operative July 1, 1974; Stats.1975, c. 653, p. 1413, § 1; Stats.1977, c. 880, p. 2649, § 1; Stats.1978, c. 638, p. 2097, § 1; Stats.1983, c. 709, § 1; Stats.1985, c. 1201, § 5, eff. Sept. 29, 1985; Stats.1985, c. 1566, § 1, eff. Oct. 2, 1985; Stats.1998, c. 662 (A.B.2707), § 4; Stats.2003, c. 451 (A.B.1718), § 14; Stats.2013, c. 512 (S.B.155), § 10.)*

Cross References

Issuance of licenses and certificates to manufacturers, transporters and dealers, unlawful acts, see Vehicle Code § 11713.3.

§ 3063. Good cause

In determining whether good cause has been established for not entering into a franchise or relocating an * * * existing dealership of the same line-make, the board shall take into consideration the existing circumstances, including, but not limited to, all of the following:

(a) Permanency of the investment.

(b) Effect on the retail motor vehicle business and the consuming public in the relevant market area.

(c) Whether it is injurious to the public welfare for an additional franchise to be established or an existing dealership to be relocated.

(d) Whether the franchisees of the same line-make in the relevant market area are providing adequate competition and convenient consumer care for the motor vehicles of the line-make in the market area, which shall include the adequacy of motor vehicle sales and service facilities, equipment, supply of vehicle parts, and qualified service personnel.

(e) Whether the establishment of an additional franchise would increase competition and therefore be in the public interest.

(f) For purposes of this section, the terms "motor vehicle dealership" and "dealership" shall have the same meaning as defined in Section 3062. *(Added by Stats. 1973, c. 996, p. 1969, § 16, operative July 1, 1974. Amended by Stats.1983, c. 142, § 161; Stats.2013, c. 512 (S.B.155), § 11.)*

§ 3064. Delivery and preparation obligation

(a) Every franchisor shall specify to its franchisees the delivery and preparation obligations of the franchisees prior to delivery of new motor vehicles to retail buyers. A copy of the delivery and preparation obligations, which shall constitute the franchisee's only responsibility for product liability between the franchisee and the franchisor but * * * shall not in any way affect the franchisee's responsibility for product liability between the purchaser and either the franchisee or the franchisor, and a schedule of compensation to be paid to franchisees for the work and services they shall be required to perform in connection with those delivery and preparation obligations shall be filed with the board by franchisors, and shall constitute the compensation as set forth on the schedule. The schedule of compensation shall be reasonable, with the reasonableness thereof being subject to the approval of the board, if a franchisee files a notice of protest with the board. In determining the reasonableness of the schedules, the board shall consider all relevant circumstances, including, but not limited to, the time required to perform each function that the dealer is obligated to perform and the appropriate labor rate.

(b) Upon delivery of the vehicle, the franchisee shall give a copy of the delivery and preparation obligations to the purchaser and a written certification that * * * the franchisee has fulfilled these obligations. *(Added by Stats.1973, c. 996, p. 1969, § 16, operative July 1, 1974. Amended by Stats.2013, c. 512 (S.B.155), § 12.)*

Cross References

Manufacturers, transporters and dealers, license suspension or revocation for violation of this section, see Vehicle Code § 11705.

§ 3065. Warranty reimbursement; disallowance of claim; requirements and process; audits of franchisee warranty records

(a) Every franchisor shall properly fulfill every warranty agreement made by it and adequately and fairly compensate each of its franchisees for labor and parts used to fulfill that warranty when the franchisee has fulfilled warranty obligations of diagnostics, repair, and servicing and shall file a copy of its warranty reimbursement schedule or formula with the board. The warranty reimbursement schedule or formula shall be reasonable with respect to the time and compensation allowed to the franchisee for the warranty * * * diagnostics, repair, and servicing, and all other conditions of the obligation. The

reasonableness of the warranty reimbursement schedule or formula shall be determined by the board if a franchisee files a * * * protest with the board. A franchisor shall not replace, modify, or supplement the warranty reimbursement schedule to impose a fixed percentage or other reduction in the time and compensation allowed to the franchisee for warranty repairs not attributable to a specific repair. A franchisor may reduce the allowed time and compensation applicable to a specific warranty repair only upon 15 days' prior written notice to the franchisee. Any protest challenging a reduction in time and compensation applicable to specific parts or labor operations shall be filed within six months following the franchisee's receipt of notice of the reduction, and the franchisor shall have the burden of establishing the reasonableness of the reduction and adequacy and fairness of the resulting compensation.

(b) In determining the adequacy and fairness of the compensation, the franchisee's effective labor rate charged to its various retail customers may be considered together with other relevant criteria. If in a protest permitted by this section filed by any franchisee the board determines that the warranty reimbursement schedule or formula fails to provide adequate and fair compensation or fails to conform with the other requirements of this section, within 30 days after receipt of the board's order, the franchisor shall correct the failure by amending or replacing the warranty reimbursement schedule or formula and implementing the correction as to all franchisees of the franchisor that are located in this state.

(c) If any franchisor disallows a franchisee's claim for a defective part, alleging that the part, in fact, is not defective, the franchisor shall return the part alleged not to be defective to the franchisee at the expense of the franchisor, or the franchisee shall be reimbursed for the franchisee's cost of the part, at the franchisor's option.

(d)(1) All claims made by franchisees pursuant to this section shall be either approved or disapproved within 30 days after their receipt by the franchisor. Any claim not specifically disapproved in writing within 30 days from receipt by the franchisor shall be deemed approved on the 30th day. * * * All claims made by franchisees under this section and Section 3064 for labor and parts shall be paid within 30 days after approval.

(2) A franchisor shall not disapprove a claim unless the claim is false or fraudulent, repairs were not properly made, repairs were inappropriate to correct a nonconformity with the written warranty due to an improper act or omission of the franchisee, or for material noncompliance with reasonable and nondiscriminatory documentation and administrative claims submission requirements.

(3) When any claim is disapproved, the franchisee who submits it shall be notified in writing of its disapproval within the required period, and each notice shall state the specific grounds upon which the disapproval is based. The franchisor shall provide for a reasonable appeal process allowing the franchisee at least 30 days after receipt of the written disapproval notice to provide

132

additional supporting documentation or information rebutting the disapproval. If disapproval is based upon noncompliance with documentation or administrative claims submission requirements, the franchisor shall allow the franchisee at least 30 days from the date of receipt of the notice to cure any material noncompliance. If the disapproval is rebutted, and material noncompliance is cured before the applicable deadline, the franchisor shall approve the claim.

(4) If the franchisee provides additional supporting documentation or information purporting to rebut the disapproval, attempts to cure noncompliance relating to the claim, or otherwise appeals denial of the claim and the franchisor continues to deny the claim, the franchisor shall provide the franchisee with a written notification of the final denial within 30 days of completion of the appeal process, which shall conspicuously state "Final Denial" on the first page.

(5) Failure to approve or pay within the above specified time limits, in individual instances for reasons beyond the reasonable control of the franchisor, shall not constitute a violation of this article.

(6) Within six months after either receipt of the written notice described in paragraph (3) or (4), whichever is later, a franchisee may file a protest with the board for determination of whether the franchisor complied with the requirements of this subdivision. In any protest pursuant to this subdivision, the franchisor shall have the burden of proof.

(e)(1) Audits of franchisee warranty records may be conducted by the franchisor on a reasonable basis * * * for a period of nine months after a claim is paid or credit issued. * * * A franchisor shall not select a franchisee for an audit, or perform an audit, in a punitive, retaliatory, or unfairly discriminatory manner. A franchisor may conduct no more than one random audit of a franchisee in a nine-month period. The franchisor's notification to the franchisee of any additional audit within a nine-month period shall be accompanied by written disclosure of the basis for that additional audit.

(2) Previously approved claims shall not be disapproved or charged back to the franchisee unless the claim is false or fraudulent, repairs were not properly made, repairs were inappropriate to correct a nonconformity with the written warranty due to an improper act or omission of the franchisee, or for material noncompliance with reasonable and nondiscriminatory documentation and administrative claims submission requirements. A franchisor shall not disapprove or chargeback a claim based upon an extrapolation from a sample of claims, unless the sample of claims is selected randomly and the extrapolation is performed in a reasonable and statistically valid manner.

(3) If the franchisor disapproves of a previously approved claim following an audit, the franchisor shall provide to the franchisee, within 30 days after the audit, a written disapproval notice stating the specific grounds upon which the claim is disapproved. The franchisor

shall provide a reasonable appeal process allowing the franchisee a reasonable period of not less than 30 days after receipt of the written disapproval notice to respond to any disapproval with additional supporting documentation or information rebutting the disapproval and to cure noncompliance, with the period to be commensurate with the volume of claims under consideration. If the franchisee rebuts any disapproval and cures any material noncompliance relating to a claim before the applicable deadline, the franchisor shall not chargeback the franchisee for that claim.

(4) If the franchisee provides additional supporting documentation or information purporting to rebut the disapproval, attempts to cure noncompliance relating to the claim, or otherwise appeals denial of the claim and the franchisor continues to deny the claim, the franchisor shall provide the franchisee with a written notification of the final denial within 30 days of completion of the appeal process, which shall conspicuously state "Final Denial" on the first page.

(5) The franchisor shall not chargeback the franchisee until 45 days after receipt of the written notice described in paragraph (3) or paragraph (4), whichever is later. Any chargeback to a franchisee for warranty parts or service compensation shall be made within 90 days of * * * receipt of that written notice. If the franchisee files a protest pursuant to this subdivision prior to the franchisor's chargeback for denied claims, the franchisor shall not offset or otherwise undertake to collect the chargeback until the board issues a final order on the protest. If the board sustains the chargeback or the protest is dismissed, the franchisor shall have 90 days following issuance of the final order or the dismissal to make the chargeback, unless otherwise provided in a settlement agreement.

(6) Within six months after either receipt of the written disapproval notice or completion of the franchisor's appeal process, whichever is later, a franchisee may file a protest with the board for determination of whether the franchisor complied with this subdivision. In any protest pursuant to this subdivision, the franchisor shall have the burden of proof.

(f) If a false claim was submitted by a franchisee with the intent to defraud the franchisor, a longer period for audit and any resulting chargeback may be permitted if the franchisor obtains an order from the board. *(Added by Stats.1973, c. 996, p. 1970, § 16, operative July 1, 1974. Amended by Stats.1993, c. 528 (A.B.1032), § 1; Stats. 2013, c. 512 (S.B.155), § 13.)*

Cross References

Manufacturers, transporters and dealers, license suspension or revocation for violation of this section, see Vehicle Code § 11705.
Warranties, see Civil Code § 1790 et seq.; Commercial Code § 2312 et seq.

§ 3065.1. Franchisor incentive program; claims; audits

(a) All claims made by a franchisee for payment under the terms of a franchisor incentive program shall be either approved or disapproved within 30 days after receipt by the franchisor. When any claim is disapproved, the franchisee who submits it shall be notified in writing of its disapproval within the required period, and each notice shall state the specific grounds upon which the disapproval is based. Any claim not specifically disapproved in writing within 30 days from receipt shall be deemed approved on the 30th day. * * *

(b) Franchisee claims for incentive program compensation shall not be disapproved unless the claim is false or fraudulent, the claim is ineligible under the terms of the incentive program as previously communicated to the franchisee, or for material noncompliance with reasonable and nondiscriminatory documentation and administrative claims submission requirements.

(c) The franchisor shall provide for a reasonable appeal process allowing the franchisee at least 30 days after receipt of the written disapproval notice to respond to any disapproval with additional supporting documentation or information rebutting the disapproval. If disapproval is based upon noncompliance with documentation or administrative claims submission requirements, the franchisor shall allow the franchisee at least 30 days from the date of receipt of the written disapproval notice to cure any material noncompliance. If the disapproval is rebutted, and material noncompliance is cured before the applicable deadline, the franchisor shall approve the claim.

(d) If the franchisee provides additional supporting documentation or information purporting to rebut the disapproval, attempts to cure noncompliance relating to the claim, or otherwise appeals denial of the claim, and the franchisor continues to deny the claim, the franchisor shall provide the franchisee with a written notification of the final denial within 30 days of completion of the appeal process, which shall conspicuously state "Final Denial" on the first page.

(e) Following the disapproval of a claim, a franchisee shall have six months from receipt of the written notice described in either subdivision (a) or (d), whichever is later, to file a protest with the board for determination of whether the franchisor complied with subdivisions (a), (b), (c), and (d). In any hearing pursuant to this subdivision or subdivision (a), (b), (c), or (d), the franchisor shall have the burden of proof.

(f) All claims made by franchisees under this section shall be paid within 30 days following approval. Failure to approve or pay within the above specified time limits, in individual instances for reasons beyond the reasonable control of the franchisor, do not constitute a violation of this article.

* * * (g)(1) Audits of franchisee incentive records may be conducted by the franchisor on a reasonable basis, and for a period of nine months after a claim is paid or credit issued. * * * A franchisor shall not select a franchisee for an audit, or perform an audit, in a punitive, retaliatory, or unfairly discriminatory manner. A franchisor may conduct no more than one random audit of a franchisee in a nine-month period. The franchisor's notification to the franchisee of any additional audit within a nine-month period shall be accompanied by written disclosure of the basis for that additional audit.

(2) Previously approved claims shall not be disapproved and charged back unless the claim is false or fraudulent, the claim is ineligible under the terms of the incentive program as previously communicated to the franchisee, or for material noncompliance with reasonable and nondiscriminatory documentation and administrative claims submission requirements. A franchisor shall not disapprove a claim or chargeback a claim based upon an extrapolation from a sample of claims, unless the sample of claims is selected randomly and the extrapolation is performed in a reasonable and statistically valid manner.

(3) If the franchisor disapproves of a previously approved claim following an audit, the franchisor shall provide to the franchisee, within 30 days after the audit, a written disapproval notice stating the specific grounds upon which the claim is disapproved. The franchisor shall provide a reasonable appeal process allowing the franchisee a reasonable period of not less than 30 days after receipt of the written disapproval notice to respond to any disapproval with additional supporting documentation or information rebutting the disapproval and to cure any material noncompliance, with the period to be commensurate with the volume of claims under consideration. If the franchisee rebuts any disapproval and cures any material noncompliance relating to a claim before the applicable deadline, the franchisor shall not chargeback the franchisee for that claim.

(4) If the franchisee provides additional supporting documentation or information purporting to rebut the disapproval, attempts to cure noncompliance relating to the claim, or otherwise appeals denial of the claim, and the franchisor continues to deny the claim, the franchisor shall provide the franchisee with a written notification of the final denial within 30 days of completion of the appeal process, which shall conspicuously state "Final Denial" on the first page.

(5) The franchisor shall not chargeback the franchisee until 45 days after the franchisee receives the written notice described in paragraph (3) or (4), whichever is later. If the franchisee cures any material noncompliance relating to a claim, the franchisor shall not chargeback the dealer for that claim. Any chargeback to a franchisee for incentive program compensation shall be made within 90 days * * * after the franchisee receives that written notice. If the board sustains the chargeback or the protest is dismissed, the franchisor shall have 90 days following issuance of the final order or the dismissal to make the chargeback, unless otherwise provided in a settlement agreement.

(6) Within six months after either receipt of the written notice described in paragraph (3) or (4), a franchisee may file a protest with the board for determination of whether the franchisor complied with this

subdivision. If the franchisee files a protest pursuant to this subdivision prior to the franchisor's chargeback for denied claims, the franchisor shall not offset or otherwise undertake to collect the chargeback until the board issues a final order on the protest. In any protest pursuant to this subdivision, the franchisor shall have the burden of proof.

(h) If a false claim was submitted by a franchisee with the intent to defraud the franchisor, a longer period for audit and any resulting chargeback may be permitted if the franchisor obtains an order from the board. *(Added by Stats.1993, c. 528 (A.B.1032), § 2. Amended by Stats.2013, c. 512 (S.B.155), § 14.)*

Cross References

Issuance of licenses and certificates to manufacturers, transporters and dealers, unlawful acts, see Vehicle Code § 11713.3.

§ 3066. Hearings on protests

(a) Upon receiving a * * * protest pursuant to Section 3060, 3062, 3064, 3065, 3065.1, 3070, 3072, 3074, 3075, or 3076, the board shall fix a time within 60 days of the order, and place of hearing, and shall send by registered mail a copy of the order to the franchisor, the protesting franchisee, and all individuals and groups that have requested notification by the board of protests and decisions of the board. Except in a case involving a franchisee who deals exclusively in motorcycles, the board or its executive director may, upon a showing of good cause, accelerate or postpone the date initially established for a hearing, but the hearing may not be rescheduled more than 90 days after the board's initial order. For the purpose of accelerating or postponing a hearing date, "good cause" includes, but is not limited to, the effects upon, and any irreparable harm to, the parties or interested persons or groups if the request for a change in hearing date is not granted. The board or an administrative law judge designated by the board shall hear and consider the oral and documented evidence introduced by the parties and other interested individuals and groups, and the board shall make its decision solely on the record so made. Chapter 4.5 (commencing with Section 11400) of Part 1 of Division 3 of Title 2 of the Government Code and Sections 11507.3, 11507.6, 11507.7, 11511, 11511.5, 11513, 11514, 11515, and 11517 of the Government Code apply to these proceedings.

(b) In a hearing on a protest filed pursuant to Section 3060, 3062, 3070, or 3072, the franchisor shall have the burden of proof to establish that there is good cause to modify, replace, terminate, or refuse to continue a franchise. The franchisee shall have the burden of proof to establish that there is good cause not to enter into a franchise establishing or relocating an additional motor vehicle dealership.

(c) Except as otherwise provided in this chapter, in a hearing on a protest alleging a violation of, or filed pursuant to, Section 3064, 3065, 3065.1, 3074, 3075, or 3076, the franchisee shall have the burden of proof, but the franchisor has the burden of proof to establish that a

franchisee acted with intent to defraud the franchisor where that issue is material to a protest filed pursuant to Section 3065, 3065.1, 3075, or 3076.

(d) A member of the board who is a new motor vehicle dealer may not participate in, hear, comment, or advise other members upon, or decide, a matter involving a protest filed pursuant to this article unless all parties to the protest stipulate otherwise. *(Added by Stats.1973, c. 996, p. 1970, § 16, operative July 1, 1974. Amended by Stats.1974, c. 384, p. 955, § 6, eff. July 5, 1974, operative July 1, 1974; Stats.1977, c. 278, p. 1172, § 3, eff. July 8, 1977; Stats.1979, c. 340, p. 1207, § 2, eff. July 27, 1979; Stats.1983, c. 709, § 2; Stats.1985, c. 1566, § 2, eff. Oct. 2, 1985; Stats.1995, c. 938 (S.B.523), § 89, operative July 1, 1997; Stats.1997, c. 356 (S.B.690), § 2; Stats.1998, c. 662 (A.B.2707), § 5; Stats.2003, c. 451 (A.B.1718), § 15; Stats.2003, c. 703 (S.B.248), § 7; Stats.2013, c. 512 (S.B.155), § 15.)*

Law Revision Commission Comments
1995 Amendment

Section 3066 is amended to correct the reference to the Administrative Procedure Act. A number of provisions formerly found in Government Code Sections 11500–11530 are now located in general provisions on administrative adjudication, which apply to all state adjudicative proceedings. See, e.g., Gov't Code §§ 11410.20 (application to state), 11425.10 (administrative adjudication bill of rights), 11430.10–11430.80 (ex parte communications), 11450.10–11450.40 (subpoenas), 11455.10–11455.30 (enforcement of orders and sanctions). See also Gov't Code § 11435.15 (language assistance requirement applicable to Department of Motor Vehicles). [25 Cal.L.Rev.Comm. Reports 55 (1995)].

§ 3067. Decision

(a) The decision of the board shall be in writing and shall contain findings of fact and a determination of the issues presented. The decision shall sustain, conditionally sustain, overrule, or conditionally overrule the protest. Conditions imposed by the board shall be for the purpose of assuring performance of binding contractual agreements between franchisees and franchisors or otherwise serving the purposes of this article or Article 5 (commencing with Section 3070). If the board fails to act within 30 days after the hearing, within 30 days after the board receives a proposed decision where the case is heard before an administrative law judge alone, or within a period necessitated by Section 11517 of the Government Code, or as may be mutually agreed upon by the parties, then the proposed action shall be deemed to be approved. Copies of the board's decision shall be delivered to the parties personally or sent to them by registered mail, as well as to all individuals and groups that have requested notification by the board of protests and decisions by the board. The board's decision shall be final upon its delivery or mailing and a reconsideration or rehearing is not permitted.

(b) Notwithstanding subdivision (c) of Section 11517 of the Government Code, if a protest is heard by an administrative law judge alone, 10 days after receipt by the board of the administrative law judge's proposed decision, a copy of the proposed decision shall be filed by the board as a public record and a copy shall be served by the board on each party and his or her attorney. *(Added by Stats.1973, c. 996, p. 1971, § 16, operative July 1, 1974. Amended by Stats.1974, c. 384, p. 955, § 7, eff. July 5, 1974, operative July 1, 1974; Stats.1983, c. 1144, § 6, eff. Sept. 28, 1983; Stats.1998, c. 662 (A.B.2707), § 6; Stats.2003, c. 451 (A.B.1718), § 16; Stats.2013, c. 512 (S.B.155), § 16.)*

§ 3068. Judicial review

Either party may seek judicial review of final decisions of the board. Time for filing for such review shall not be more than 45 days from the date on which the final order of the board is made public and is delivered to the parties personally or is sent them by registered mail. *(Added by Stats.1973, c. 996, p. 1971, § 16, operative July 1, 1974. Amended by Stats.1974, c. 384, p. 955, § 8, eff. July 5, 1974, operative July 1, 1974.)*

§ 3069. Application of article

The provisions of this article shall be applicable to all franchises existing between dealers and manufacturers, manufacturer branches, distributors and distributor branches at the time of its enactment and to all such future franchises. *(Added by Stats.1973, c. 996, p. 1971, § 16, operative July 1, 1974.)*

§ 3069.1. Application to franchises authorizing a dealership

Sections 3060 to 3065.1, inclusive, do not apply to a franchise authorizing a dealership, as defined in * * * subdivision (d) of Section 3072. *(Added by Stats.2003, c. 703 (S.B.248), § 10. Amended by Stats.2013, c. 512 (S.B.155), § 17.)*

ARTICLE 5. HEARINGS ON RECREATIONAL VEHICLE FRANCHISE MODIFICATION, REPLACEMENT, TERMINATION, REFUSAL TO CONTINUE, ESTABLISHMENT, AND RELOCATION, AND CONSUMER COMPLAINTS

Section
3070. Termination or refusal to continue a franchise; conditions required; modification or replacement of a succeeding franchise; conditions required.
3071. Good cause for modifying, replacing, terminating or refusing to continue; enumerated circumstances.
3072. Additional dealerships or relocation of a dealership; notice within market area; protest hearings; exclusions.
3072.5. "Recreational vehicle line-make" defined.
3073. Good cause; considerations for relocation or new establishment.
3074. Delivery and preparation obligations; written certification.
3075. Warranty agreements.
3076. Incentive payments; claims; audits.
3077. One-time additional fee for issuance or renewal of license; expiration of fee; deposit.
3078. Complaints from the public seeking a refund; remedies under other code provisions.
3079. Application of article; date of franchise agreement or renewal.

Application

For application of Article 5, see Vehicle Code § 3079.

Cross References

New motor vehicle board, hearings on franchise-related protests, decision of the board, see Vehicle Code § 3067.

§ 3070. Termination or refusal to continue a franchise; conditions required; modification or replacement of a succeeding franchise; conditions required

(a) Notwithstanding Section 20999.1 of the Business and Professions Code or the terms of any franchise, a franchisor of a dealer of new recreational vehicles, as defined in subdivision (a) of Section 18010 of the Health and Safety Code, except a dealer who deals exclusively in truck campers, may not terminate or refuse to continue a franchise unless all of the following conditions are met:

(1) The franchisee and the board have received written notice from the franchisor as follows:

(A) Sixty days before the effective date thereof setting forth the specific grounds for termination or refusal to continue.

(B) Fifteen days before the effective date thereof setting forth the specific grounds with respect to any of the following:

(i) Transfer of any ownership or interest in the franchise without the consent of the franchisor, which consent may not be unreasonably withheld.

(ii) Misrepresentation by the franchisee in applying for the franchise.

(iii) Insolvency of the franchisee, or filing of any petition by or against the franchisee under any bankruptcy or receivership law.

(iv) Any unfair business practice after written warning thereof.

(v) Failure of the dealer to conduct its customary sales and service operations during its customary hours of business for seven consecutive business days, giving rise to a good faith belief on the part of the franchisor that the recreational vehicle dealer is in fact going out of business, except for circumstances beyond the direct control of the recreational vehicle dealer or by order of the department.

(C) The written notice shall contain, on the first page thereof in at least 12–point bold type and circumscribed by a line to segregate it from the rest of the text, one of the following statements, whichever is applicable:

(i) To be inserted when a 60–day notice of termination is given:

"NOTICE TO DEALER: You have the right to file a protest with the NEW MOTOR VEHICLE BOARD in Sacramento and have a hearing in which you may protest the termination of your franchise under provisions of the California Vehicle Code. You must file your protest with the board within 30 calendar days after receiving this notice or within 30 days after the end of any appeal procedure provided by the franchisor or your protest right will be waived."

(ii) To be inserted when a 15–day notice of termination is given:

"NOTICE TO DEALER: You have the right to file a protest with the NEW MOTOR VEHICLE BOARD in Sacramento and have a hearing in which you may protest the termination of your franchise under provisions of the California Vehicle Code. You must file your protest with the board within 10 calendar days after receiving this notice or within 10 days after the end of any appeal procedure provided by the franchisor or your protest right will be waived."

(2) Except as provided in Section 3050.7, the board finds that there is good cause for termination or refusal to continue, following a hearing called pursuant to Section 3066. The franchisee may file a protest with the board within 30 days after receiving a 60–day notice, satisfying the requirements of this section, or within 30 days after the end of any appeal procedure provided by the franchisor, or within 10 days after receiving a 15–day notice, satisfying the requirements of this section, or within 10 days after the end of any appeal procedure provided by the franchisor. When a protest is filed, the board shall advise the franchisor that a timely protest has been filed, that a hearing is required pursuant to Section 3066, and that the franchisor may not terminate or refuse to continue until the board makes its findings.

(3) The franchisor has received the written consent of the franchisee, or the appropriate period for filing a protest has elapsed.

(b)(1) Notwithstanding Section 20999.1 of the Business and Professions Code or the terms of any franchise, a franchisor of a dealer of recreational vehicles may not modify or replace a franchise with a succeeding franchise if the modification or replacement would substantially affect the franchisee's sales or service obligations or investment, unless the franchisor has first given the board and each affected franchisee written notice thereof at least 60 days in advance of the modification or replacement. Within 30 days of receipt of a notice satisfying the requirements of this section, or within 30 days after the end of any appeal procedure provided by the franchisor, a franchisee may file a protest with the board and the modification or replacement does not become effective until there is a finding by the board that there is good cause for the modification or replacement. If, however, a replacement franchise is the successor franchise to an expiring or expired term franchise, the prior franchise shall continue in effect until resolution of the protest by the board. In the event of multiple protests, hearings shall be consolidated to expedite the disposition of the issue.

(2) The written notice shall contain, on the first page thereof in at least 12–point bold type and circumscribed by a line to segregate it from the rest of the text, the following statement:

"NOTICE TO DEALER: Your franchise agreement is being modified or replaced. If the modification or replacement will substantially affect your sales or service obligations or investment, you have the right to file a protest with the NEW MOTOR VEHICLE BOARD in Sacramento and have a hearing in which you may protest the proposed modification or replacement of your franchise under provisions of the California Vehicle Code. You must file your protest with the board within 30 calendar days of your receipt of this notice or within 30 days after the end of any appeal procedure provided by the franchiser or your protest rights will be waived." *(Added by Stats.2003, c. 703 (S.B.248), § 11.)*

Cross References

New motor vehicle board, powers and duties, hearing and deciding protests by franchisees, see Vehicle Code § 3050.
New motor vehicle board, protests and petitions, adoption of proposed stipulated decision and order, see Vehicle Code § 3050.7.

§ 3071. Good cause for modifying, replacing, terminating or refusing to continue; enumerated circumstances

In determining whether good cause has been established for modifying, replacing, terminating, or refusing to continue a franchise of a dealer of new recreational vehicles, the board shall take into consideration the existing circumstances, including, but not limited to, all of the following:

(a) The amount of business transacted by the franchisee, as compared to the business available to the franchisee.

(b) The investment necessarily made and obligations incurred by the franchisee to perform its part of the franchise.

(c) The permanency of the investment.

(d) Whether it is injurious or beneficial to the public welfare for the franchise to be modified or replaced or the business of the franchisee disrupted.

(e) Whether the franchisee has adequate new recreational vehicle sales and, if required by the franchise, service facilities, equipment, vehicle parts, and qualified service personnel, to reasonably provide for the needs of the consumers of the recreational vehicles handled by the franchisee and has been and is rendering adequate services to the public.

(f) Whether the franchisee fails to fulfill the warranty obligations agreed to be performed by the franchisee in the franchise.

(g) The extent of franchisee's failure to comply with the terms of the franchise. *(Added by Stats.2003, c. 703 (S.B.248), § 11.)*

§ 3072. Additional dealerships or relocation of a dealership; notice within market area; protest hearings; exclusions

(a)(1) Except as otherwise provided in subdivision (b), if a franchisor seeks to enter into a franchise establishing an additional motor vehicle dealership within a relevant market area where the same recreational vehicle line-make is then represented, or seeks to relocate an existing motor vehicle dealership, the franchisor shall, in writing, first notify the board and each franchisee in that recreational vehicle line-make in the relevant market area of the franchisor's intention to establish an additional dealership or to relocate an existing dealership within or into that market area. Within 20 days of receiving the notice, satisfying the requirements of this section, or within 20 days after the end of any appeal procedure provided by the franchisor, any franchisee required to be given the notice may file with the board a protest to establishing or relocating the dealership. If, within this time, a franchisee files with the board a request for additional time to file a protest, the board or its secretary, upon a showing of good cause, may grant an additional 10 days to file the protest. When a protest is filed, the board shall inform the franchisor that a timely protest has been filed, that a hearing is required pursuant to Section 3066, and that the franchisor shall not establish or relocate the proposed dealership until the board has held a hearing as provided in Section 3066, nor thereafter, if the board has determined that there is good cause for not permitting the dealership. In the event of multiple protests, hearings may be consolidated to expedite the disposition of the issue.

(2) The written notice shall contain, on the first page thereof in at least 12–point bold type and circumscribed by a line to segregate it from the rest of the text, the following statement:

"NOTICE TO DEALER: You have the right to file a protest with the NEW MOTOR VEHICLE BOARD in Sacramento and have a hearing on your protest under the terms of the California Vehicle Code if you oppose this action. You must file your protest with the board within 20 days of your receipt of this notice, or within 20 days after the end of any appeal procedure that is provided by us to you. If, within this time, you file with the board a request for additional time to file a protest, the board or its secretary, upon a showing of good cause, may grant you an additional 10 days to file the protest."

(b) Subdivision (a) does not apply to any of the following:

(1) The relocation of an existing dealership to any location that is both within the same city as, and within one mile of, the existing dealership location.

(2) The establishment at any location that is both within the same city as, and within one-quarter mile of, the location of a dealership of the same recreational vehicle line-make that has been out of operation for less than 90 days.

138

(3) A display of vehicles at a fair, exposition, or similar exhibit if no actual sales are made at the event and the display does not exceed 30 days. This paragraph may not be construed to prohibit a new vehicle dealer from establishing a branch office for the purpose of selling vehicles at the fair, exposition, or similar exhibit, even though that event is sponsored by a financial institution, as defined in Section 31041 of the Financial Code, or by a financial institution and a licensed dealer. The establishment of these branch offices, however, shall be in accordance with subdivision (a) where applicable.

(4) An annual show sponsored by a national trade association of recreational vehicle manufacturers that complies with all of the requirements of subdivision (d) of Section 11713.15.

(5) A motor vehicle dealership protesting the location of another dealership with the same recreational vehicle line-make within its relevant market area, if the dealership location subject to the protest was established on or before January 1, 2004.

(c) For the purposes of this section, the reopening of a dealership that has not been in operation for one year or more shall be deemed the establishment of an additional motor vehicle dealership.

(d) For the purposes of this section and Section 3073, a "motor vehicle dealership" or "dealership" is any authorized facility at which a franchisee offers for sale or lease, displays for sale or lease, or sells or leases new recreational vehicles, as defined in subdivision (a) of Section 18010 of the Health and Safety Code. A " motor vehicle dealership" or "dealership" does not include a dealer who deals exclusively in truck campers. *(Added by Stats.2003, c. 703 (S.B.248), § 11. Amended by Stats. 2004, c. 183 (A.B.3082), § 346.)*

Cross References

New motor vehicle board, powers and duties, hearing and deciding protests by franchisees, see Vehicle Code § 3050.

§ 3072.5. "Recreational vehicle line-make" defined

For the purposes of this article, a "recreational vehicle line-make" is a group or groups of recreational vehicles defined by the terms of a written agreement that complies with Section 331. *(Added by Stats.2003, c. 703 (S.B.248), § 11.)*

§ 3073. Good cause; considerations for relocation or new establishment

In determining whether good cause has been established for not entering into or relocating an additional franchise for the same recreational vehicle line-make, the board shall take into consideration the existing circumstances, including, but not limited to, all of the following:

(a) The permanency of the investment.

(b) The effect on the retail recreational vehicle business and the consuming public in the relevant market area.

(c) Whether it is injurious to the public welfare for an additional franchise to be established.

(d) Whether the franchisees of the same recreational vehicle line-make in that relevant market area are providing adequate competition and convenient consumer care for the motor vehicles of the recreational vehicle line-make in the market area. In making this determination, the board shall consider the adequacy of recreational vehicle sales and, if required by the franchise, service facilities, equipment, supply of vehicle parts, and qualified service personnel.

(e) Whether the establishment of an additional franchise would increase competition and therefore be in the public interest. *(Added by Stats.2003, c. 703 (S.B.248), § 11.)*

§ 3074. Delivery and preparation obligations; written certification

(a) A franchisor shall specify to its franchisees the delivery and preparation obligations of the franchisees prior to delivery of new recreational vehicles to retail buyers. A copy of the delivery and preparation obligations, which shall constitute the franchisee's only responsibility for product liability between the franchisee and the franchisor but which shall not in any way affect the franchisee's responsibility for product liability between the purchaser and either the franchisee or the franchisor, and a schedule of compensation to be paid franchisees for the work and services they shall be required to perform in connection with the delivery and preparation obligations shall be filed with the board by franchisors, and shall constitute the compensation as set forth on the schedule. The schedule of compensation shall be reasonable, with the reasonableness thereof being subject to the approval of the board, providing a franchisee files a notice of protest with the board. In determining the reasonableness of the schedules, the board shall consider all relevant circumstances, including, but not limited to, the time required to perform each function that the dealer is obligated to perform and the appropriate labor rate.

(b) Upon delivery of the vehicle, the franchisee shall give a copy of the delivery and preparation obligations to the purchaser and a written certification that he or she has fulfilled these obligations. *(Added by Stats.2003, c. 703 (S.B.248), § 11.)*

Cross References

New motor vehicle board, powers and duties, hearing and deciding protests by franchisees, see Vehicle Code § 3050.

§ 3075. Warranty agreements

(a) A franchisor shall properly fulfill every warranty agreement made by it and adequately and fairly compensate each of its franchisees for labor and parts used to fulfill that warranty when the franchisee has fulfilled warranty obligations of repair and servicing and shall file a copy of its warranty reimbursement schedule or formula with the board. The warranty reimbursement schedule or formula shall be reasonable with respect to the time and compensation allowed the franchisee for the warranty work and all other conditions of the obligation. The reasonableness of the warranty reimbursement schedule or formula shall be determined by the board if a franchisee files a notice of protest with the board.

(b) In determining the adequacy and fairness of the compensation, the franchisee's effective labor rate charged to its various retail customers may be considered together with other relevant criteria.

(c) If a franchisor disallows a franchisee's claim for a defective part, alleging that the part, in fact, is not defective, the franchisor shall return the part alleged not to be defective to the franchisee at the expense of the franchisor, or the franchisee shall be reimbursed for the franchisee's cost of the part, at the franchisor's option.

(d) All claims made by franchisees pursuant to this section shall be either approved or disapproved within 30 days after their receipt by the franchisor. A claim not specifically disapproved in writing within 30 days from receipt by the franchisor shall be deemed approved on the 30th day. When a claim is disapproved, the franchisee who submits it shall be notified in writing of its disapproval within the required period, and the notice shall state the specific grounds upon which the disapproval is based. All claims made by franchisees under this section and Section 3074 for labor and parts shall be paid within 30 days following approval. Failure to approve or pay within the above specified time limits, in individual instances for reasons beyond the reasonable control of the franchisor, do not constitute a violation of this article.

(e) Audits of franchisee warranty records may be conducted by the franchisor on a reasonable basis, and for a period of 12 months after a claim is paid or credit issued. Franchisee claims for warranty compensation shall not be disapproved except for good cause, including, but not limited to, performance of nonwarranty repairs, lack of material documentation, or fraud. Any chargeback to a franchisee for warranty parts or service compensation shall be made within 90 days of the completion of the audit. If a false claim was submitted by a franchisee with intent to defraud the franchisor, a longer period for audit and any resulting chargeback may be permitted if the franchisor obtains an order from the board. *(Added by Stats.2003, c. 703 (S.B.248), § 11.)*

Cross References

New motor vehicle board, powers and duties, hearing and deciding protests by franchisees, see Vehicle Code § 3050.

§ 3076. Incentive payments; claims; audits

(a) All claims made by a franchisee for payment under the terms of a franchisor incentive program shall be either approved or disapproved within 30 days after receipt by the franchisor. When a claim is disapproved, the franchisee who submits it shall be notified in writing of its disapproval within the required period, and each notice shall state the specific grounds upon which the disapproval is based. A claim not specifically disapproved in writing within 30 days from receipt shall be deemed approved on the 30th day. Following the disapproval of a claim, a franchisee shall have one year from receipt of the notice of disapproval in which to appeal the disapproval to the franchisor and file a protest with the board. All claims made by franchisees under this section shall be paid within 30 days following approval. Failure to approve or pay within the above specified time limits, in individual instances for reasons beyond the reasonable control of the franchisor, do not constitute a violation of this article.

(b) Audits of franchisee incentive records may be conducted by the franchisor on a reasonable basis, and for a period of 18 months after a claim is paid or credit issued. Franchisee claims for incentive program compensation shall not be disapproved except for good cause, such as ineligibility under the terms of the incentive program, lack of material documentation, or fraud. Any chargeback to a franchisee for incentive program compensation shall be made within 90 days of the completion of the audit. If a false claim was submitted by a franchisee with the intent to defraud the franchisor, a longer period for audit and any resulting chargeback may be permitted if the franchisor obtains an order from the board. *(Added by Stats.2003, c. 703 (S.B.248), § 11.)*

Cross References

New motor vehicle board, powers and duties, hearing and deciding protests by franchisees, see Vehicle Code § 3050.

§ 3077. One-time additional fee for issuance or renewal of license; expiration of fee; deposit

(a) In addition to fees imposed under Sections 3016 and 11723, the department shall impose a one-time additional fee on those dealers subject to this article for the issuance or renewal of a license, in an amount determined by the department to be sufficient to cover the costs incurred by the department and the board in the implementation of this article for the first year, or in an amount sufficient to cover costs of not more than three hundred fifty thousand dollars ($350,000), whichever amount is less.

(b) The fee authorized under subdivision (a) may not be imposed on and after January 1, 2005.

(c) All funds derived from the imposition of the fee required under subdivision (a) shall be deposited in the Motor Vehicle Account in the State Transportation Fund and shall be available, upon appropriation, for expenditure to cover the costs incurred by the department and the board in the initial implementation of this article. *(Added by Stats.2003, c. 703 (S.B.248), § 11.)*

§ 3078. Complaints from the public seeking a refund; remedies under other code provisions

(a) If the board receives a complaint from a member of the public seeking a refund involving the sale or lease of, or a replacement of, a recreational vehicle, as defined in subdivision (a) of Section 18010 of the Health and Safety Code, from a motor vehicle dealership, as defined in paragraph (1) of subdivision (e) of Section 3072, the board shall recommend that the complainant consult with the Department of Consumer Affairs.

(b) Nothing in this chapter affects a person's rights regarding a transaction involving a recreational vehicle as defined in subdivision (a), to maintain an action under any other statute, including, but not limited to, applicable provisions of Title 1.7 (commencing with Section 1790) of Part 4 of Division 3 of the Civil Code. *(Added by Stats.2003, c. 703 (S.B.248), § 11.)*

§ 3079. Application of article; date of franchise agreement or renewal

This article applies only to a franchise entered into or renewed on or after January 1, 2004. *(Added by Stats. 2003, c. 703 (S.B.248), § 11.)*

CHAPTER 7. DRIVER CERTIFICATION [REPEALED]

§§ 3100 to 3104. Repealed by Stats.1990, c. 1360 (S.B. 1510), §§ 5 to 9

Division 3

REGISTRATION OF VEHICLES AND CERTIFICATES OF TITLE

Chapter		Section
1.	Original and Renewal of Registration; Issuance of Certificates of Title	4000
2.	Transfers of Title or Interest	5600
2.5.	Miscellaneous Title Provisions	6150
3.	Filing Instruments Evidencing Liens or Encumbrances	6300
4.	Permits to Nonresident Owners	6700
5.	Offenses Against Registration Laws and Suspension, Revocation, and Cancellation of Registration	8800
6.	Registration and Weight Fees	9100

Cross References

Sale of specified vehicles, presumption of sale at retail, rebuttal by taking resale certificate, additional contents of resale certificate, see Revenue and Taxation Code § 6092.5.

CHAPTER 1. ORIGINAL AND RENEWAL OF REGISTRATION; ISSUANCE OF CERTIFICATES OF TITLE

Article		Section
1.	Vehicles Subject to Registration	4000
2.	Original Registration	4150
3.	Registration of Foreign Vehicles	4300
4.	Evidences of Registration	4450
5.	Renewal of Registration	4600
5.5.	Voluntary Common Registration Renewal Dates [Repealed]	
6.	Refusal of Registration	4750
6.5.	Refusal of Registration for Nonpayment of Toll Evasion Penalties	4770
7.	License Plates	4850
8.	Special Plates	5000
8.1.	Motorized Bicycles	5030
8.3.	Historic and Special Interest Vehicles	5050
8.4.	Special Interest License Plates	5060
8.5	Environmental License Plates	5100
8.6.	Specialized License Plates	5115
9.	Display of Plates, Tabs, and Stickers	5200
9.5.	Registration of Fleet Vehicles	5300
10.	Registration of Trailer Coaches	5350
11.	Registration of Mobilehomes Subject to Local Property Taxation [Repealed]	
12.	Surrender of Registration Documents and License Plates	5500

Cross References

Rebuttable presumption for vehicles, vessels, or aircraft bought outside state, see Revenue and Taxation Code § 6248.

ARTICLE 1. VEHICLES SUBJECT TO REGISTRATION

Section
4000. Registration required; offstreet parking facility; compliance with vehicular air pollution control provisions; exceptions; driver's license as rebuttable presumption of ownership.

4000.1. Certificate of compliance or noncompliance; statement in lieu of certificate; exemptions; testing for collector motor vehicle.

4000.11. Repealed.

4000.2. Out-of-state motor vehicles; requirements.

4000.3. Certificate of compliance; periodic issuance.

4000.37. Application for renewal of registration; proof of compliance with financial responsibility laws.

4000.38. Suspension, cancellation, or revocation of registration; false evidence of financial responsibility or cancellation of insurance; notice; reissuance fees; military exemption from fee.

4000.39. Repealed.

4000.4. Vehicle registered to nonresident, and based in or primarily using California highways; registration.

4000.5. Autoette; registration; license plates.

4000.6. Commercial motor vehicles.

4000.7. Repealed.

4001. Registration of exempt vehicles.

4002. Vehicles exempt under permit.

4003. Vehicles exempt under permit.

4003.5. One-trip permit for new trailer, semitrailer, or auxiliary dolly.

4003.6. Repealed.

4004. Foreign commercial motor vehicles; temporary operation and registration.

4004.5. Statement of multiple county use of vehicle.

4004.7. Issuance of unladen operation permit to authorize unladen operation of vehicle or vehicle combination; time period.

4005. Special permit for disaster relief work.

4006. Vehicle crossing highway.

4007. Passenger carriers; temporary operating authority; interagency agreement to establish system.

4008. Repealed.

4008.5. Repealed.

4009. Hauled vehicles.

4010. Special construction and mobile equipment.

4011. Repealed.

4012. Cemetery equipment.

4013. Forklift trucks.

4014. Portable dolly.

4015. Firefighting vehicle.

4016. Loading and unloading by dealer.

4017. Operation of vehicle pending registration.

4018. Logging vehicles.

4019. Golf carts.

4020. Motorized bicycles.

4021. Aircraft refueling vehicles.

4022. Repossessed vehicles.

4023. Low-speed vehicles.

Cross References

Manufacturers, transporters and dealers, license suspension or revocation for violation of this division, see Vehicle Code § 11705.

Notice to correct registration violations, see Vehicle Code § 40303.5.

§ 4000. Registration required; offstreet parking facility; compliance with vehicular air pollution control provisions; exceptions; driver's license as rebuttable presumption of ownership

(a)(1) A person shall not drive, move, or leave standing upon a highway, or in an offstreet public parking facility, any motor vehicle, trailer, semitrailer, pole or pipe dolly, or logging dolly, unless it is registered and the appropriate fees have been paid under this code or registered under the permanent trailer identification program, except that an off-highway motor vehicle which displays an identification plate or device issued by the department pursuant to Section 38010 may be driven, moved, or left standing in an offstreet public parking facility without being registered or paying registration fees.

(2) For purposes of this subdivision, "offstreet public parking facility" means either of the following:

(A) Any publicly owned parking facility.

(B) Any privately owned parking facility for which no fee for the privilege to park is charged and which is held open for the common public use of retail customers.

(3) This subdivision does not apply to any motor vehicle stored in a privately owned offstreet parking facility by, or with the express permission of, the owner of the privately owned offstreet parking facility.

(4) Beginning July 1, 2011, the enforcement of paragraph (1) shall commence on the first day of the second month following the month of expiration of the vehicle's registration. This paragraph shall become inoperative on January 1, 2012.

(b) No person shall drive, move, or leave standing upon a highway any motor vehicle, as defined in Chapter 2 (commencing with Section 39010) of Part 1 of Division 26 of the Health and Safety Code, which has been registered in violation of Part 5 (commencing with Section 43000) of that Division 26.

(c) Subdivisions (a) and (b) do not apply to off-highway motor vehicles operated pursuant to Sections 38025 and 38026.5.

(d) This section does not apply, following payment of fees due for registration, during the time that registration and transfer is being withheld by the department pending the investigation of any use tax due under the Revenue and Taxation Code.

(e) Subdivision (a) does not apply to a vehicle that is towed by a tow truck on the order of a sheriff, marshal, or other official acting pursuant to a court order or on the order of a peace officer acting pursuant to this code.

(f) Subdivision (a) applies to a vehicle that is towed from a highway or offstreet parking facility under the direction of a highway service organization when that organization is providing emergency roadside assistance to that vehicle. However, the operator of a tow truck providing that assistance to that vehicle is not responsible for the violation of subdivision (a) with respect to that vehicle. The owner of an unregistered vehicle that is disabled and located on private property, shall obtain a permit from the department pursuant to Section 4003 prior to having the vehicle towed on the highway.

(g) For purposes of this section, possession of a California driver's license by the registered owner of a vehicle shall give rise to a rebuttable presumption that the owner is a resident of California. *(Stats.1959, c. 3, p. 1554, § 4000. Amended by Stats.1959, c. 1233, p. 3312, § 1; Stats.1960, 1st Ex.Sess., c. 23, p. 351, § 2; Stats.1963, c. 292, p. 1059, § 2; Stats.1963, c. 1858, p. 3835, § 7.5 eff. July 19, 1963, operative Oct. 1, 1963; Stats.1965, 1st Ex.Sess., c. 2, p. 5453, § 36, eff. July 12, 1965, operative Aug. 1, 1965; Stats.1967, c. 551, p. 1900, § 1; Stats.1968 c. 49, p. 194, § 7, eff. April 25, 1968; Stats.1968, c. 764, p. 1480, § 11; Stats.1975, c. 957, p. 2230, § 21; Stats.1976, c. 1206, p. 5492, § 14; Stats.1982, c. 974, p. 3486, § 1; Stats.1984, c. 213, 1, eff. June 20, 1984; Stats.1984, c. 621, § 1; Stats.1987, c. 44, § 1; Stats.1988, c. 1008, § 1; Stats.1993, c. 186 (A.B.1566), § 1; Stats.1996, c. 10 (A.B.1869), § 10, eff. Feb. 9, 1996; Stats.2000, c. 861 (S.B.2084), § 16, eff. Sept. 29, 2000; Stats.2011, c. 21 (S.B.94), § 3, eff. May 4, 2011.)*

Cross References

Certificate of ownership and registration card, see Vehicle Code § 4450 et seq.

Commercial vehicle registration, permits to nonresident owners, applicability of interest on underpaid portion of fees, see Vehicle Code § 8058.

Definitions,
  Auxiliary dolly, see Vehicle Code § 225.
  Highway, see Vehicle Code §§ 360, 591.
  Motor vehicle, see Vehicle Code § 415.
  Person, see Vehicle Code § 470.
  Pole or pipe dolly, see Vehicle Code § 475.
  Semitrailer, see Vehicle Code § 550.
  Trailer, see Vehicle Code § 630.

Entry of motor vehicle into federal or state wilderness area, public offense and penalties, see Vehicle Code § 38301.3.

Environmental license plates, retention fee, see Vehicle Code § 5106.

Foreign commercial vehicles, registration of, see Vehicle Code § 6850.

Identification, identification certificate defined, see Vehicle Code § 38013.

Immobilization of vehicles, see Vehicle Code § 22651.7.

Nonresident vehicles leased for use in state, registration, see Vehicle Code § 6853.

Off-highway vehicles,
  Identification required, see Vehicle Code § 38020.
  Operation on highway, conditions, see Vehicle Code § 38025.

Operation of vehicle displaying special plates, see Vehicle Code § 11715.

Operation of vehicle without registration or plates, when permitted, see Vehicle Code § 11716.

Permits to nonresident owners, see Vehicle Code § 6700 et seq.

Proportionate registration and licensing of vehicles used in interstate commerce, application, see Vehicle Code § 8052.

Refusal of registration, see Vehicle Code §§ 4750, 4751.

Registration and weight fees, generally, see Vehicle Code § 9101 et seq.

Registration indices and records, see Vehicle Code § 1800.

Registration of publicly owned vehicles, see Vehicle Code § 4155.

Suspension, cancellation or revocation of registration, see Vehicle Code § 8800.

Temporary permit pending registration, see Vehicle Code § 4156.

Transportation on highway of motorcycles issued a special identification device, see Vehicle Code § 38022.

Trolley coaches, applicability of this chapter, see Vehicle Code § 21051.

Undertaking on registration, see Vehicle Code §§ 4157, 4158.

Vehicles bought outside of state, rebuttable presumption that purchased for storage or use within state, see Revenue and Taxation Code § 6248.

Vehicles used in interstate commerce, proportionate registration and licensing, see Vehicle Code § 8050 et seq.

Violations, see Vehicle Code § 40000.1 et seq.

§ 4000.1. Certificate of compliance or noncompliance; statement in lieu of certificate; exemptions; testing for collector motor vehicle

(a) Except as otherwise provided in subdivision (b), (c), or (d) of this section, or subdivision (b) of Section 43654 of the Health and Safety Code, the department shall require upon initial registration, and upon transfer of ownership and registration, of any motor vehicle subject to Part 5 (commencing with Section 43000) of Division 26 of the Health and Safety Code, a valid certificate of compliance or a certificate of noncompliance, as appropriate, issued in accordance with Section 44015 of the Health and Safety Code.

(b) With respect to new motor vehicles certified pursuant to Chapter 2 (commencing with Section 43100) of Part 5 of Division 26 of the Health and Safety Code, the department shall accept a statement completed pursuant to subdivision (b) of Section 24007 in lieu of the certificate of compliance.

(c) For purposes of determining the validity of a certificate of compliance or noncompliance submitted in compliance with the requirements of this section, the definitions of new and used motor vehicle contained in Chapter 2 (commencing with Section 39010) of Part 1 of Division 26 of the Health and Safety Code shall control.

(d) Subdivision (a) does not apply to a transfer of ownership and registration under any of the following circumstances:

(1) The initial application for transfer is submitted within the 90–day validity period of a smog certificate as specified in Section 44015 of the Health and Safety Code.

(2) The transferor is the parent, grandparent, sibling, child, grandchild, or spouse of the transferee.

(3) A motor vehicle registered to a sole proprietorship is transferred to the proprietor as owner.

(4) The transfer is between companies the principal business of which is leasing motor vehicles, if there is no change in the lessee or operator of the motor vehicle or between the lessor and the person who has been, for at least one year, the lessee's operator of the motor vehicle.

(5) The transfer is between the lessor and lessee of the motor vehicle, if there is no change in the lessee or operator of the motor vehicle.

(6) The motor vehicle was manufactured prior to the 1976 model-year.

(7) Except for diesel-powered vehicles, the transfer is for a motor vehicle that is four or less model-years old. The department shall impose a fee of eight dollars ($8) on the transferee of a motor vehicle that is four or less model-years old. Revenues generated from the imposition of that fee shall be deposited into the Vehicle Inspection and Repair Fund.

(e) The State Air Resources Board, under Part 5 (commencing with Section 43000) of Division 26 of the Health and Safety Code, may exempt designated classifications of motor vehicles from subdivision (a) as it deems necessary, and shall notify the department of that action.

(f) Subdivision (a) does not apply to a motor vehicle when an additional individual is added as a registered owner of the motor vehicle.

(g) For purposes of subdivision (a), any collector motor vehicle, as defined in Section 259, is exempt from those portions of the test required by subdivision (f) of Section 44012 of the Health and Safety Code, if the collector motor vehicle meets all of the following criteria:

(1) Submission of proof that the motor vehicle is insured as a collector motor vehicle, as shall be required by regulation of the bureau.

(2) The motor vehicle is at least 35 model-years old.

(3) The motor vehicle complies with the exhaust emissions standards for that motor vehicle's class and model year as prescribed by the department, and the motor vehicle passes a functional inspection of the fuel cap and a visual inspection for liquid fuel leaks. *(Added by Stats.1963, c. 2028, p. 4169, § 1. Amended by Stats. 1965, c. 2031, p. 4612, § 10.5, eff. July 23, 1965; Stats. 1968, c. 49, p. 195, § 8, eff. April 25, 1968; Stats.1968, c. 764, p. 1481, § 12.5; Stats.1968, c. 1160, p. 2195, § 2; Stats.1969, c. 622, p. 1260, § 2, eff. July 28, 1969; Stats.1970, c. 766, p. 1450, § 1; Stats.1971, c. 1073, p. 2042, § 4, operative May 3, 1972; Stats.1971, c. 1488, p. 2940, § 3, operative May 3, 1972; Stats.1974, c. 637, p. 1491, § 1; Stats.1975, c. 957, p. 2231, § 22; Stats.1976, c. 231, p. 441, § 4; Stats.1976, c. 1206, p. 5492, § 15; Stats.1977, c. 1038, p. 3137, § 3, eff. Sept. 23, 1977; Stats.1977, c. 1083, p. 3488, § 3, eff. Sept. 27, 1977; Stats.1982, c. 664, p. 2723, § 5; Stats.1982, c. 892, p. 3314, § 3.5; Stats.1984, c. 246, § 4; Stats.1984, c. 631, § 2; Stats.1985, c. 904, § 1; Stats.1988, c. 1544, § 58; Stats. 1989, c. 1154, § 17; Stats.1993, c. 958 (S.B.575), § 1; Stats.1995, c. 292 (A.B.100), § 1; Stats.1996, c. 112 (S.B.1528), § 1; Stats.1997, c. 801 (S.B.42), § 2; Stats. 2002, c. 127 (A.B.2303), § 1; Stats.2004, c. 230 (S.B. 1107), § 18, eff. Aug. 16, 2004; Stats.2004, c. 701 (S.B. 1615), § 3; Stats.2004, c. 702 (A.B.2104), § 12, eff. Sept.*

23, 2004; Stats.2004, c. 704 (A.B.2683), § 3, operative April 1, 2005; Stats.2005, c. 22 (S.B.1108), § 194; Stats. 2009, c. 200 (S.B.734), § 7.)

Cross References

Air pollution control devices, see Vehicle Code § 27156.
Equipment of vehicles, responsibility of dealer or other person selling motor vehicle, see Vehicle Code § 24007.
Vehicle sales by auctioneer or public agency, application to registration requirements pursuant to this section, see Vehicle Code § 24007.5.
Vehicles previously modified to use fuels other than gasoline or diesel, exemption, see Health and Safety Code § 43005.

§ 4000.11. Repealed by Stats.2001, c. 465 (A.B.1258), § 2, operative Jan. 1, 2002

§ 4000.2. Out-of-state motor vehicles; requirements

(a) Except as otherwise provided in subdivision (b) of Section 43654 of the Health and Safety Code, and, commencing on April 1, 2005, except for model-years exempted from biennial inspection pursuant to Section 44011 of the Health and Safety Code, the department shall require upon registration of a motor vehicle subject to Part 5 (commencing with Section 43000) of Division 26 of the Health and Safety Code, previously registered outside this state, a valid certificate of compliance or a certificate of noncompliance, as appropriate, issued in accordance with Section 44015 of the Health and Safety Code.

(b) For the purposes of determining the validity of a certificate of compliance or noncompliance submitted in compliance with the requirements of this section, the definitions of new and used motor vehicle contained in Chapter 2 (commencing with Section 39010) of Part 1 of Division 26 of the Health and Safety Code shall control. *(Added by Stats.1968, c. 1307, p. 2462, § 2. Amended by Stats.1969, c. 11, p. 70, § 2, eff. March 12, 1969; Stats. 1970, c. 766, p. 1450, § 1; Stats.1975, c. 957, p. 2231, § 23; Stats.1976, c. 231, p. 441, § 5; Stats.1976, c. 1206, p. 5493, § 16; Stats.1977, c. 1083, p. 3489, § 4, eff. Sept. 27, 1977; Stats.1982, c. 892, p. 3314, § 4; Stats.1988, c. 1544, § 59; Stats.1989, c. 1154, § 18; Stats.2004, c. 701 (S.B. 1615), § 4.5, operative April 1, 2005; Stats.2004, c. 704 (A.B.2683), § 4, operative April 1, 2005.)*

Cross References

Air pollution control devices, see Vehicle Code § 27156.
Vehicle sales by auctioneer or public agency, application to registration requirements pursuant to this section, see Vehicle Code § 24007.5.

§ 4000.3. Certificate of compliance; periodic issuance

(a) Except as otherwise provided in Section 44011 of the Health and Safety Code, the department shall require biennially, upon renewal of registration of any motor vehicle subject to Part 5 (commencing with Section 43000) of Division 26 of the Health and Safety Code, a valid certificate of compliance issued in accordance with Section 44015 of the Health and Safety Code. The

144

department, in consultation with the Department of Consumer Affairs, shall develop a schedule under which vehicles shall be required biennially to obtain certificates of compliance.

(b) The Department of Consumer Affairs shall provide the department with information on vehicle classes that are subject to the motor vehicle inspection and maintenance program.

(c) The department shall include any information pamphlet provided by the Department of Consumer Affairs with notification of the inspection requirement and with its renewal notices. The information pamphlet in the renewal notice shall also notify the owner of the motor vehicle of the right to have the vehicle pretested pursuant to Section 44011.3 of the Health and Safety Code. *(Added by Stats.1982, c. 892, p. 3315, § 5. Amended by Stats.1988, c. 1544, § 60; Stats.1994, c. 27 (A.B.2018), § 59, eff. March 30, 1994; Stats.1998, c. 938 (S.B.1754), § 2.)*

Cross References

Fees for temporary permits, see Vehicle Code § 9257.5.
Temporary permits, limitations, see Vehicle Code § 4156.
Vehicle sales by auctioneer or public agency, application to registration requirements pursuant to this section, see Vehicle Code § 24007.5.

§ 4000.37. Application for renewal of registration; proof of compliance with financial responsibility laws

(a) Upon application for renewal of registration of a motor vehicle, the department shall require that the applicant submit either a form approved by the department, but issued by the insurer, as specified in paragraph (1), (2), or (3), or any of the items specified in paragraph (4), as evidence that the applicant is in compliance with the financial responsibility laws of this state.

(1) For vehicles covered by private passenger automobile liability policies and having coverage as described in subdivisions (a) and (b) of Section 660 of the Insurance Code, or policies and coverages for private passenger automobile policies as described in subdivisions (a) and (b) of that section and issued by an automobile assigned risk plan, the form shall include all of the following:

(A) The primary name of the insured covered by the policy or the vehicle owner, or both.

(B) The year, make, and vehicle identification number of the vehicle.

(C) The name, the National Association of Insurance Commissioners (NAIC) number, and the address of the insurance company or surety company providing a policy or bond for the vehicle.

(D) The policy or bond number, and the effective date and expiration date of that policy or bond.

(E) A statement from the insurance company or surety company that the policy or bond meets the requirements of Section 16056 or 16500.5. For the purposes of this section, policies described in Section 11629.71 of the Insurance Code are deemed to meet the requirements of Section 16056.

(2) For vehicles covered by commercial or fleet policies, and not private passenger automobile liability policies, as described in paragraph (1), the form shall include all of the following:

(A) The name and address of the vehicle owner or fleet operator.

(B) The name, the NAIC number, and the address of the insurance company or surety company providing a policy or bond for the vehicle.

(C) The policy or bond number, and the effective date and expiration date of the policy or bond.

(D) A statement from the insurance company or surety company that the policy or bond meets the requirements of Section 16056 or 16500.5 and is a commercial or fleet policy. For vehicles registered pursuant to Article 9.5 (commencing with Section 5301) or Article 4 (commencing with Section 8050) of Chapter 4, one form may be submitted per fleet as specified by the department.

(3)(A) The director may authorize an insurer to issue a form that does not conform to paragraph (1) or (2) if the director does all of the following:

(i) Determines that the entity issuing the alternate form is or will begin reporting the insurance information required under paragraph (1) or (2) to the department through electronic transmission.

(ii) Determines that use of the alternate form furthers the interests of the state by enhancing the enforcement of the state's financial responsibility laws.

(iii) Approves the contents of the alternate form as providing an adequate means for persons to prove compliance with the financial responsibility laws.

(B) The director may authorize the use of the alternate form in lieu of the forms otherwise required under paragraph (1) or (2) for a period of four years or less and may renew that authority for additional periods of four years or less.

(4) In lieu of evidence of insurance as described in paragraphs (1), (2), and (3), one of the following documents as evidence of coverage under an alternative form of financial responsibility may be provided by the applicant:

(A) An evidence form, as specified by the department, that indicates either a certificate of self-insurance or an assignment of deposit letter has been issued by the department pursuant to Sections 16053 or 16054.2.

(B) An insurance covering note or binder pursuant to Section 382 or 382.5 of the Insurance Code.

(C) An evidence form that indicates coverage is provided by a charitable risk pool operating under Section 5005.1 of the Corporations Code, if the registered owner of the vehicle is a nonprofit organization that is exempt from taxation under paragraph (3) of subsection (c) of Section 501 of the United States Internal Revenue Code. The evidence form shall include:

(i) The name and address of the vehicle owner or fleet operator.

(ii) The name and address of the charitable risk pool providing the policy for the vehicle.

(iii) The policy number, and the effective date and expiration date of the policy.

(iv) A statement from the charitable risk pool that the policy meets the requirements of subdivision (b) of Section 16054.2.

(b) This section does not apply to any of the following:

(1) A vehicle for which a certification has been filed pursuant to Section 4604, until the vehicle is registered for operation upon the highway.

(2) A vehicle that is owned or leased by, or under the direction of, the United States or any public entity that is included in Section 811.2 of the Government Code.

(3) A vehicle registration renewal application where there is a change of registered owner.

(4) A vehicle for which evidence of liability insurance information has been electronically filed with the department. *(Added by Stats.1999, c. 880 (S.B.652), § 5. Amended by Stats.2000, c. 455 (S.B.1996), § 1; Stats.2000, c. 1035 (S.B.1403), § 6.5; Stats.2001, c. 159 (S.B.662), § 188; Stats.2005, c. 435 (S.B.20), § 18.)*

Application

For application of this section to County of Los Angeles and City and County of San Francisco, see Vehicle Code §§ 16020.1 and 16020.2.

Cross References

County and City of San Francisco Low–Cost Automobile Insurance Pilot Program, policy attributes, see Insurance Code § 11629.91.

County of Los Angeles Low–Cost Automobile Insurance Pilot Program, policy attributes, see Insurance Code § 11629.71.

Evidence of financial responsibility, electronic method for reporting private passenger automobile liability insurance policies and coverages, alternative forms of financial responsibility, see Vehicle Code § 16058.

Financial responsibility, application of this section to vehicle owners with residence address in Los Angeles County, see Vehicle Code § 16020.1.

Financial responsibility, application of this section to vehicle owners with residence address in San Francisco County or City, see Vehicle Code § 16020.2.

§ 4000.38. Suspension, cancellation, or revocation of registration; false evidence of financial responsibility or cancellation of insurance; notice; reissuance fees; military exemption from fee

(a) The department shall suspend, cancel, or revoke the registration of a vehicle when it determines that any of the following circumstances has occurred:

(1) The registration was obtained by providing false evidence of financial responsibility to the department.

(2) Upon notification by an insurance company that the required coverage has been canceled and a sufficient period of time has elapsed since the cancellation notification, as determined by the department, for replacement coverage to be processed and received by the department.

(3) Evidence of financial responsibility has not been submitted to the department within 30 days of the issuance of a registration certificate for the original registration or transfer of registration of a vehicle.

(b)(1) Prior to suspending, canceling, or revoking the registration of a vehicle, the department shall notify the vehicle owner of its intent to suspend, cancel, or revoke the registration, and shall provide the vehicle owner a reasonable time, not less than 45 days in cases under paragraph (2) of subdivision (a), to provide evidence of financial responsibility or to establish that the vehicle is not being operated.

(2) For the low-cost automobile insurance program established under Section 11629.7 of the Insurance Code, the department shall provide residents with information on the notification document, in plain, boldface type not less than 12 point in size, and in both English and Spanish, stating the following:

"California Low–Cost Auto Insurance: A program offering affordable automobile insurance is available. Visit (insert Internet Web site address provided by the Department of Insurance) or call toll free (insert toll-free telephone number for the California Automobile Assigned Risk Plan or its successor as provided by the Department of Insurance). Qualified applicants must be 19 years of age or older, have a driver's license for the past three years, and meet income eligibility requirements (insert income example provided by Department of Insurance)."

(c)(1) Notwithstanding any other provision of this code, before a registration is reinstated after suspension, cancellation, or revocation, there shall be paid to the department, in addition to any other fees required by this code, a fee sufficient to pay the cost of the reissuance as determined by the department.

(2) Commencing on January 1, 2011, the reissuance fee imposed by paragraph (1) shall not apply to a member of the California National Guard or the United States Armed Forces who was on active duty, serving outside of this state in a military conflict during a time of war, as defined in Section 18 of the Military and Veterans Code, at the time of the suspension, cancellation, or revocation of his or her vehicle registration. The person shall submit a copy of his or her official military orders upon requesting the registration reinstatement. *(Added by Stats.2004, c. 920 (S.B.1500), § 3, operative Jan. 1, 2006. Amended by Stats.2005, c. 435 (S.B.20), § 19; Stats.2009, c. 107 (A.B.425), § 1; Stats.2011, c. 401 (A.B.1024), § 4.)*

§ 4000.39. Repealed by Stats.2005, c. 76 (S.B.62), § 9, operative Jan. 1, 2007

§ 4000.4. Vehicle registered to nonresident, and based in or primarily using California highways; registration

(a) Except as provided in Sections 6700, 6702, and 6703, any vehicle which is registered to a nonresident owner, and which is based in California or primarily used on California highways, shall be registered in California.

(b) For purposes of this section, a vehicle is deemed to be primarily or regularly used on the highways of this state if the vehicle is located or operated in this state for a greater amount of time than it is located or operated in any other individual state during the registration period in question. *(Added by Stats.1983, c. 409, § 3. Amended by Stats.1988, c. 1008, § 2.)*

Cross References

Commercial vehicle registration, permits to nonresident owners, applicability of interest on underpaid portion of fees, see Vehicle Code § 8058.
Registration, see Vehicle Code § 6700.

§ 4000.5. Autoette; registration; license plates

(a) The department shall register an autoette, as defined in Section 175, as a motor vehicle.

(b) The owner of an autoette shall remove the license plates from the vehicle and return them to the department when the autoette is removed from a natural island, as described in Section 175. *(Added by Stats.2006, c. 322 (A.B.2401), § 2.)*

§ 4000.6. Commercial motor vehicles

A commercial motor vehicle, singly or in combination, that operates with a declared gross or combined gross vehicle weight that exceeds 10,000 pounds shall be registered pursuant to Section 9400.1.

(a) A person submitting an application for registration of a commercial motor vehicle operated in combination with a semitrailer, trailer, or any combination thereof, shall include the declared combined gross weight of all units when applying for registration with the department, except as exempted under subdivision (a) of Section 9400.1.

(b) This section does not apply to pickups nor to any commercial motor vehicle or combination that does not exceed 10,000 pounds gross vehicle weight.

(c) A peace officer, as defined in Chapter 4.5 (commencing with Section 830) of Title 3 of Part 2 of the Penal Code, having reason to believe that a commercial motor vehicle is being operated, either singly or in combination, in excess of its registered declared gross or combined gross vehicle weight, may require the driver to stop and submit to an inspection or weighing of the vehicle or vehicles and an inspection of registration documents.

(d) A person shall not operate a commercial motor vehicle, either singly or in combination, in excess of its registered declared gross or combined gross vehicle weight.

(e) A violation of this section is an infraction punishable by a fine in an amount equal to the amount specified in Section 42030.1. *(Added by Stats.2000, c. 861 (S.B. 2084), § 17, eff. Sept. 29, 2000. Amended by Stats.2001, c. 825 (S.B.290), § 7.3; Stats.2001, c. 826 (A.B.1472), § 8.5; Stats.2004, c. 615 (S.B.1233), § 21.)*

Cross References

Refusal of registration, renewal, or transfer of registration, see Vehicle Code § 4755.

§ 4000.7. Repealed by Stats.1997, c. 802 (A.B.208), § 12; Stats.1997, c. 803 (A.B.1492), § 14

§ 4001. Registration of exempt vehicles

All vehicles exempt from the payment of registration fees shall be registered as otherwise required by this code by the person having custody thereof, and he shall display upon the vehicle a license plate bearing distinguishing marks or symbols, which shall be furnished by the department free of charge. *(Stats.1959, c. 3, p. 1554, § 4001.)*

Cross References

Exemptions from registration and weight fees, see Vehicle Code § 9101 et seq.
License plates, see Vehicle Code § 4850 et seq.
Trolley coaches, applicability of this section, see Vehicle Code § 21051.

§ 4002. Vehicles exempt under permit

When moved or operated under a permit issued by the department, registration is not required of:

(a) A vehicle not previously registered while being moved or operated from a dealer's, distributor's, or manufacturer's place of business to a place where essential parts of the vehicle are to be altered or supplied.

(b) A vehicle while being moved from a place of storage to another place of storage.

(c) A vehicle while being moved to or from a garage or repair shop for the purpose of repairs or alteration.

(d) A vehicle while being moved or operated for the purpose of dismantling or wrecking the same and permanently removing it from the highways.

(e) A vehicle, while being moved from one place to another for the purpose of inspection by the department, assignment of a vehicle identification number, inspection of pollution control devices, or weighing the vehicle.

(f) A vehicle, the construction of which has not been completed, until such time as the construction thereof is completed and final weights and costs can be determined for registration purposes. *(Stats.1959, c. 3, p. 1554, § 4002. Amended by Stats.1959, c. 517, p. 2482, § 1;*

Stats.1963, c. 1628, p. 3218, § 1; Stats.1977, c. 326, p. 1274, § 1.)

Cross References

Automobile dismantlers, generally, see Vehicle Code § 11500 et seq.
Commercial vehicle registration, permits to nonresident owners, applicability of interest on underpaid portion of fees, see Vehicle Code § 8058.
Exemptions from registration and weight fees, see Vehicle Code § 9101 et seq.
Trolley coaches, applicability of this section, see Vehicle Code § 21051.

§ 4003. Vehicles exempt under permit

A permit, as described in Section 9258, may be issued by the department for operating any of the following vehicles, except a crane:

(a) A vehicle while being moved or operated unladen for one continuous trip from a place within this state to another place either within or without this state or from a place without this state to a place within this state.

(b) A vehicle while being moved or operated for one round trip to be completed within 60 days from one place to another for the purpose of participating as a vehicular float or display in a lawful parade or exhibition, provided that the total round trip does not exceed 100 miles.

The department may issue a quantity of permits under this subsection in booklet form upon payment of the proper fee for each permit contained in such booklet. Each permit shall be valid for only one vehicle and for only one continuous trip. Such permit shall be posted upon the windshield or other prominent place upon a vehicle and shall identify the vehicle to which it is affixed. When so affixed, such permit shall serve in lieu of California registration. *(Stats.1959, c. 3, p. 1555, § 4003. Amended by Stats.1963, c. 1628, p. 3218, § 2; Stats.1974, c. 1430, p. 3133, § 2; Stats.1977, c. 326, p. 1275, § 2.)*

Cross References

Commercial vehicle registration, permits to nonresident owners, applicability of interest on underpaid portion of fees, see Vehicle Code § 8058.
Duty of driver to submit to inspection, see Vehicle Code §§ 2800, 2806.
Exemptions from registration and weight fees, see Vehicle Code § 9101 et seq.
Inspection of vehicles by highway patrol, see Vehicle Code §§ 2804, 2805.
One-trip permits, fees, see Vehicle Code § 9258.
Special plates for dealers, see Vehicle Code § 11714 et seq.
Trailer coaches, exemption under one-trip permit, see Vehicle Code § 5353.
Trolley coaches, applicability of this section, see Vehicle Code § 21051.

§ 4003.5. One-trip permit for new trailer, semitrailer, or auxiliary dolly

(a) Upon payment of the fee specified in Section 9258.5, the department shall issue to a manufacturer or dealer a one-trip permit authorizing a new trailer, semitrailer, or auxiliary dolly which has never been registered in any state, or a used trailer, semitrailer, or auxiliary dolly which is not currently registered to be moved or operated laden within, entering, or leaving this state for not more than five days as part of one continuous trip from the place of manufacture for a new vehicle, or from the place of dispatch or entry into this state for a used vehicle, to a place where the vehicle will be offered for sale.

(b) Any permit issued pursuant to this section authorizes the operation of a single trailer, semitrailer, or auxiliary dolly, and the permit shall identify the trailer, semitrailer, or auxiliary dolly authorized by make, model, and vehicle identification number. The permit shall include the name and license number of the manufacturer from whom the new vehicle is sent, or the name and license number of the dealer from whom the used vehicle is sent, the name and address of the person or business receiving the load, a description of the load being carried, and the name and license number of the dealer who will be offering the trailer, semitrailer, or auxiliary dolly for sale. Each permit shall be completed prior to operation of the trailer or semitrailer or auxiliary dolly on a highway. The permit shall be carried on the trailer, semitrailer, or auxiliary dolly to which it applies in an appropriate receptacle inaccessible from the inside of the cab and shall be readily available for inspection by a peace officer. Each permit is valid at the time of inspection by a peace officer only if it has been completed as required by the department and has been placed in the appropriate receptacle as required by this section. The manufacturer or dealer issued the permit may allow a third party to move or operate the vehicle.

(c) The privilege of securing and displaying a permit authorized pursuant to this section shall not be extended to a manufacturer, carrier, or dealer located in a jurisdiction with which the state does not have vehicle licensing reciprocity.

(d) The privilege of securing and displaying a permit authorized pursuant to this section shall not be granted more than once without the sale and registration of the trailer, semitrailer, or auxiliary dolly. (Added by Stats. 1983, c. 825, § 1. Amended by Stats.1984, c. 933, § 1; Stats.1985, c. 625, § 1; Stats.1986, c. 1071, § 1; Stats. 1987, c. 290, § 1.)

Cross References
Fee, see Vehicle Code § 9258.5.

§ 4003.6. Repealed by Stats.1986, c. 1078, § 6, eff. Sept. 24, 1986, operative Jan. 1, 1987

§ 4004. Foreign commercial motor vehicles; temporary operation and registration

(a)(1) Commercial motor vehicles meeting the registration requirements of a foreign jurisdiction, and subject to registration but not entitled to exemption from registration or licensing under any of the provisions of this code or any agreements, arrangements, or declarations

made under Article 3 (commencing with Section 8000) of Chapter 4, may, as an alternate to registration, secure a temporary registration to operate in this state for a period of not to exceed 90 days, or a trip permit to operate in this state for a period of four consecutive days.

(2) Each trip permit shall authorize the operation of a single commercial motor vehicle for a period of not more than four consecutive days, commencing with the day of first use and three consecutive days thereafter. Every permit shall identify, as the department may require, the commercial motor vehicle for which it is issued. Each trip permit shall be completed prior to operation of the commercial motor vehicle on any highway in this state and shall be carried in the commercial motor vehicle to which it applies and shall be readily available for inspection by a peace officer. Each permit shall be valid at the time of inspection by a peace officer only if it has been completed as required by the department and has been placed in the appropriate receptacle as required by this section. It is unlawful for any person to fail to comply with the provisions of this section.

(b) The privilege of securing and using a trip permit or a temporary registration not to exceed 90 days shall not extend to a vehicle that is based within this state and is operated by a person having an established place of business within this state. For purposes of this paragraph, a commercial motor vehicle shall be considered to be based in this state if it is primarily operated or dispatched from or principally garaged or serviced or maintained at a site with an address within this state.

(c) Any trailer or semitrailer identified in paragraph (1) of subdivision (a) of Section 5014.1 that enters the state without a currently valid license plate issued by California or another jurisdiction shall be immediately subject to full identification fees as specified in subdivision (e) of Section 5014.1. (Stats.1959, c. 3, p. 1555, § 4004. Amended by Stats.1963, c. 1462, p. 3020, § 1; Stats.1977, c. 326, p. 1275, § 3; Stats.1981, c. 245, p. 1297, § 1; Stats.1982, c. 794, p. 3074, § 3; Stats.1983, c. 1000, § 5.5; Stats.2000, c. 861 (S.B.2084), § 18, eff. Sept. 29, 2000; Stats.2001, c. 826 (A.B.1472), § 9; Stats.2011, c. 315 (A.B.28), § 8.)

Cross References
Commercial vehicle registration, permits to nonresident owners, applicability of interest on underpaid portion of fees, see Vehicle Code § 8058.
Display of permit, see Vehicle Code § 4455.
Fee for foreign commercial vehicle permit, see Vehicle Code § 9260.
Registration of foreign commercial vehicles, see Vehicle Code § 6850 et seq.
Trucking reciprocity, issuance of California fuel trip permits, see Revenue and Taxation Code § 8708.

§ 4004.5. Statement of multiple county use of vehicle

The owner of any motor vehicle subject to the registration provisions of this chapter, or exempted therefrom, may file with the department, at the time he registers or renews the registration of such motor vehicle, a signed statement that he resides in more than one county for a period of more than 30 days, or uses such vehicle in a county other than the county of his legal residence for business purposes. Such statement shall specify the address at which the owner resides in any county for more than 30 days, if any, or the length of time during which such owner uses the motor vehicle for business purposes in any county.

The department shall provide forms for the filing of such statements and shall take into consideration the length of time during which owners reside or use motor vehicles in counties, in accordance with the statements filed with the department, to determine the total number of vehicles registered or exempted from registration in any particular county. *(Added by Stats.1967, c. 1485, p. 3480, § 1.)*

Cross References

Commercial vehicle registration, permits to nonresident owners, applicability of interest on underpaid portion of fees, see Vehicle Code § 8058.

§ 4004.7. Issuance of unladen operation permit to authorize unladen operation of vehicle or vehicle combination; time period

(a) If the apportioned registration issued under Article 4 (commencing with Section 8050) of Chapter 4 for a commercial vehicle or vehicle combination that was last registered by a California resident has expired or has been terminated, the department, upon receipt of a completed application, a fee of thirty dollars ($30), and proof of financial responsibility for the vehicle, may issue an unladen operation permit to authorize the unladen operation of that vehicle or vehicle combination for a period of not more than 15 continuous days.

(b) This section does not apply to any vehicle or vehicle combination for which any vehicle registration fees, other than those for the current year, vehicle license fees, or penalties, or any combination of those are due.

(c) Operation of a laden vehicle or vehicle combination under an unladen operation permit issued pursuant to this section is an infraction. *(Added by Stats.2001, c. 539 (S.B.734), § 9.)*

§ 4005. Special permit for disaster relief work

Any vehicle subject to registration may be operated within a disaster area or region for the purpose of assisting in disaster relief work, under a special permit to be issued by the department for such purpose, without the registration of such vehicle.

Said permit shall be issued only if the Department of Transportation or the responsible local authority has determined that the vehicle is necessary for such purpose, and shall be valid only during a period of a state of emergency as proclaimed by the Governor under the provisions of the California Emergency Services Act.[1] *(Stats.1959, c. 3, p. 1555, § 4005. Amended by Stats.1971,*

c. 438, p. 904, § 180, operative May 3, 1972; Stats.1974, c. 545, p. 1310, § 158.)

[1] Gov.C. § 8550 et seq.

§ 4006. Vehicle crossing highway

A vehicle which is driven or moved upon a highway only for the purpose of crossing the highway from one property to another in accordance with a permit issued by the Department of Transportation is exempt from registration. *(Stats.1959, c. 3, p. 1556, § 4006. Amended by Stats.1974, c. 545, p. 1310, § 159.)*

Cross References

Applicability of this section to trolley coaches, see Vehicle Code § 21051.

Off-highway vehicle exemption, see Vehicle Code § 38010.

§ 4007. Passenger carriers; temporary operating authority; interagency agreement to establish system

The department, the Public Utilities Commission, and the State Board of Equalization shall enter into an interagency agreement to establish a coordinated system for the issuance of temporary operating authority to carriers of passengers for compensation by motor vehicles which are operating under the laws of another state or country. The agreement shall designate a lead agency from among the parties to the agreement to which the carrier may make a single application for the temporary operating authority required under the laws of this state. The lead agency shall coordinate and expedite all matters relating to issuance of the temporary operating authority and the collection and distribution of fees therefor with every other state agency having jurisdiction, so as to promptly prepare and issue the required operating authority. *(Added by Stats.1986, c. 510, § 3.)*

§ 4008. Repealed by Stats.1963, c. 2149, p. 4486, § 6

§ 4008.5. Repealed by Stats.1963, c. 2149, p. 4486, § 6

§ 4009. Hauled vehicles

A vehicle transported upon a highway, no part of which is in contact with the highway, is exempt from registration. *(Stats.1959, c. 3, p. 1556, § 4009.)*

Cross References

Applicability of this section to trolley coaches, see Vehicle Code § 21051.

§ 4010. Special construction and mobile equipment

Special construction equipment and special mobile equipment are exempt from registration. *(Stats.1959, c. 3, p. 1556, § 4010. Amended by Stats.1961, c. 1659, p. 3626, § 3.)*

Cross References

Off-highway vehicle exemption, see Vehicle Code § 38010.
Special highway construction equipment, definition, see Vehicle Code § 565.

Special mobile equipment defined, see Vehicle Code § 575.

§ 4011. Repealed by Stats.1990, c. 400 (A.B.2953), § 2, eff. July 23, 1990

§ 4012. Cemetery equipment

Any vehicle, implement, or equipment specifically designed or altered for and used exclusively in the maintenance or operation of cemetery grounds, which is only incidentally operated or moved on a highway is exempt from registration. *(Stats.1959, c. 3, p. 1556, § 4012. Amended by Stats.1968, c. 999, p. 1949, § 1.)*

Cross References

Off-highway vehicle exemption, see Vehicle Code § 38010.

§ 4013. Forklift trucks

Any forklift truck which is designed primarily for loading and unloading and for stacking materials and is operated upon a highway only for the purpose of transporting products or material across a highway in the loading, unloading or stacking process, and is in no event operated along a highway for a greater distance than one-quarter mile is exempt from registration. *(Stats.1959, c. 3, p. 1556, § 4013.)*

Cross References

Off-highway vehicle exemption, see Vehicle Code § 38010.

§ 4014. Portable dolly

Any portable or collapsible dolly carried in a tow truck or in a truck used by an automobile dismantler and used upon a highway exclusively for towing disabled vehicles is exempt from registration. *(Added by Stats.1959, c. 1893, p. 4460, § 1. Amended by Stats.1968, c. 753, p. 1455, § 1; Stats.1988, c. 924, § 3.)*

Cross References

Tow dolly defined, see Vehicle Code § 617.

§ 4015. Firefighting vehicle

Any privately owned vehicle designed or capable of being used for firefighting purposes when operated upon a highway only in responding to, and returning from, emergency fire calls is exempt from registration. *(Added by Stats.1959, c. 577, p. 2538, § 2. Amended by Stats. 1965, c. 1643, p. 3738, § 1.)*

Cross References

Authorized emergency vehicle, firefighting, see Vehicle Code § 165.
Off-highway vehicle exemption, see Vehicle Code § 38010.

§ 4016. Loading and unloading by dealer

Notwithstanding the provisions of Section 4000, unregistered vehicles may be left standing upon a highway adjacent to a vehicle dealer's place of business when done so in connection with the loading and unloading of vehicles to be used in the dealer's business, unless

150

otherwise prohibited by law. *(Added by Stats.1959, c. 1233, p. 3312, § 2.)*

§ 4017. Operation of vehicle pending registration

The provisions of Section 4000 shall not apply to the moving or operating of a vehicle during the period of time in which application may be made for registration of the vehicle without penalty as provided in Section 4152.5. *(Formerly § 4014, added by Stats.1959, c. 1, p. 594, § 5. Renumbered § 4017 and amended by Stats.1961, c. 58, p. 1003, § 10, eff. March 31, 1961. Amended by Stats.1973, c. 889, p. 1652, § 25, eff. Sept. 28, 1973; Stats.1974, c. 1330, p. 2893, § 15, eff. Sept. 26, 1974, operative March 10, 1975.)*

Cross References

Temporary permit pending registration, see Vehicle Code § 4156.

§ 4018. Logging vehicles

Any logging vehicle is exempt from registration. *(Added by Stats.1975, c. 517, p. 1083, § 2.)*

§ 4019. Golf carts

A golf cart operated pursuant to Section 21115 is exempt from registration. *(Added by Stats.1968, c. 1303, p. 2456, § 2.)*

Cross References

Golf cart defined, see Vehicle Code § 345.
Off-highway vehicle exemption, see Vehicle Code § 38010.

§ 4020. Motorized bicycles

A motorized bicycle operated upon a highway is exempt from registration. *(Added by Stats.1975, c. 987, p. 2327, § 4.)*

Cross References

Definition, see Vehicle Code § 406.
Freeways, see Vehicle Code § 21960.
Vehicular crossings, see Vehicle Code § 23330.

§ 4021. Aircraft refueling vehicles

Any vehicle that is designed or altered for, and used exclusively for, the refueling of aircraft at a public airport is exempt from registration, if the vehicle is operated upon a highway under the control of a local authority for a continuous distance not exceeding one-half mile each way to and from a bulk fuel storage facility. *(Added by Stats.1984, c. 270, § 2, eff. July 3, 1984. Amended by Stats.1996, c. 1154 (A.B.3020), § 57, eff. Sept. 30, 1996.)*

§ 4022. Repossessed vehicles

A vehicle repossessed pursuant to the terms of a security agreement is exempt from registration solely for the purpose of transporting the vehicle from the point of repossession to the storage facilities of the repossessor, and from the storage facilities to the legal owner or a licensed motor vehicle auction, provided that the repossessor transports with the vehicle the appropriate documents authorizing the repossession and makes them available to a law enforcement officer on request. *(Added by Stats.1995, c. 505 (A.B.1541), § 38.)*

Cross References
Circumstances permitting removal of parked and abandoned vehicles, see Vehicle Code § 22651.

§ 4023. Low-speed vehicles

A low-speed vehicle operated pursuant to Section 21115 or 21115.1 is exempt from registration. *(Added by Stats.1999, c. 140 (S.B.186), § 2.)*

ARTICLE 2. ORIGINAL REGISTRATION

Section
4150.   Application form; information required.
4150.1.   Commercial motor vehicles; declaration of gross vehicle weight.
4150.2.   Application for motorcycle.
4150.5.   Co-ownership registrations.
4150.7.   Beneficiary form ownership.
4151.   Vehicle in state.
4152.   Vehicle outside state.
4152.5.   Application for registration of vehicles last registered in foreign jurisdiction.
4153.   Special vehicles.
4154.   Farm labor vehicles; registration issuance or renewal; verification of inspection.
4155.   Publicly owned vehicles.
4156.   Temporary permit; limitations.
4157.   Undertaking.
4158.   Return of bond or undertaking; surrender of certificate of ownership.
4159.   Notice of change of address.
4160.   Change of address on card.
4161.   Engine and motor change notification; distinguishing vehicle identification number; replacement engine case for motorcycles.
4162.   Repealed.
4163.   Three or more motor vehicles.
4164, 4165. Repealed.
4166.   Removed, destroyed, or obliterated motor or identifying number; distinguishing vehicle identification number.

§ 4150. Application form; information required

Application for the original or renewal registration of a vehicle of a type required to be registered under this code shall be made by the owner to the department upon the appropriate form furnished by it and shall contain all of the following:

(a) The true, full name, business or residence and mailing address, and driver's license or identification card number, if any, of the owner, and the true, full name and business or residence or mailing address of the legal owner, if any.

(b) The name of the county in which the owner resides.

(c) A description of the vehicle, including the following data insofar as they may exist:

(1) The make, model, and type of body.

(2) The vehicle identification number or any other identifying number as may be required by the department.

(3) The date first sold by a manufacturer, remanufacturer, or dealer to a consumer.

(d) Any other information that is reasonably required by the department to enable it to determine whether the vehicle is lawfully entitled to registration. *(Stats.1959, c. 3, p. 1556, § 4150. Amended by Stats.1959, c. 1996, p. 4618, § 7.5; Stats.1965, c. 1715, p. 3849, § 2, eff. Jan. 1, 1966; Stats.1970, c. 1439, p. 2792, § 1; Stats.1975, c. 389, p. 865, § 1; Stats.1983, c. 1286, § 16; Stats.1989, c. 1213, § 13; Stats.1991, c. 90 (A.B.1297), § 63, eff. June 30, 1991; Stats.1994, c. 1221 (S.B.1758), § 2.)*

Cross References
Ascertaining of type of fuel prior to registration, see Revenue and Taxation Code § 9256.
Change of address after making application, see Vehicle Code § 4159.
Dealers and manufacturers, etc., application for licenses, see Vehicle Code §§ 11701, 11704.
Department of motor vehicles, prescribing and supplying of forms, see Vehicle Code § 1652.
False statements,
  Generally, see Vehicle Code § 20.
  Application as misdemeanor, see Vehicle Code § 40000.5.
Filing of applications for registration, see Vehicle Code § 1800.
Fleet vehicles in interstate commerce, application, see Vehicle Code § 8052.
Foreign vehicles, application for registration, see Vehicle Code § 4300.
Refusal of registration, see Vehicle Code §§ 1653, 4750, 4751.
Renewal of registration, application, see Vehicle Code § 4602.
Soliciting applications, see Vehicle Code § 505.2.
Suspension, cancellation or revocation of registration, see Vehicle Code § 8800 et seq.
Trolley coaches, application of this section, see Vehicle Code § 21051.
Vehicles previously registered outside state, see Vehicle Code § 4300.

§ 4150.1. Commercial motor vehicles; declaration of gross vehicle weight

(a) On a form provided by the department, the registered owner of record, lessee, or the owner's designee shall certify and report the declared gross or combined gross vehicle weight of any commercial motor vehicle, singly or in combination, in excess of 10,000 pounds.

(b) A single form may be used or referenced for multiple vehicles. *(Added by Stats.1984, c. 779, § 1. Amended by Stats.2000, c. 861 (S.B.2084), § 19, eff. Sept. 29, 2000; Stats.2001, c. 826 (A.B.1472), § 10.)*

§ 4150.2. Application for motorcycle

Application for the original registration or renewal of the registration of a motorcycle shall be made by the owner to the department upon the appropriate form furnished by it, and shall contain all of the following:

151

(a) The true, full name, business or residence and mailing address, and driver's license or identification card number, if any, of the owner, and the true, full name and business or residence or mailing address of the legal owner, if any.

(b) The name of the county in which the owner resides.

(c) A description of the motorcycle, including the following data insofar as they may exist:

(1) The make and type of body.

(2) The motor and vehicle identification numbers recorded exactly as they appear on the engine and frame, respectively, by the manufacturer, and any other identifying number of the motorcycle as may be required by the department.

(3) The date first sold by a manufacturer, remanufacturer, or dealer to a consumer.

(d) Any other information that is reasonably required by the department to enable it to determine whether the vehicle is lawfully entitled to registration.

(e) The department shall maintain a cross-index file of motor and vehicle identification numbers registered with it. *(Added by Stats.1970, c. 887, p. 1621, § 1, operative Jan. 1, 1972. Amended by Stats.1971, c. 1353, p. 2671, § 2, operative May 3, 1972; Stats.1972, c. 624, p. 1159, § 1; Stats.1975, c. 389, p. 866, § 2; Stats.1983, c. 1286, § 17; Stats.1984, c. 631, § 3; Stats.1989, c. 1213, § 14; Stats.1991, c. 90 (A.B.1297), § 64, eff. June 30, 1991; Stats.1994, c. 1221 (S.B.1758), § 3.)*

§ 4150.5.　Co-ownership registrations

Ownership of title to a vehicle subject to registration may be held by two (or more) coowners as provided in Section 682 of the Civil Code, except that:

(a) A vehicle may be registered in the names of two (or more) persons as coowners in the alternative by the use of the word "or." A vehicle so registered in the alternative shall be deemed to be held in joint tenancy. Each coowner shall be deemed to have granted to the other coowners the absolute right to dispose of the title and interest in the vehicle. Upon the death of a coowner the interest of the decedent shall pass to the survivor as though title or interest in the vehicle was held in joint tenancy unless a contrary intention is set forth in writing upon the application for registration.

(b) A vehicle may be registered in the names of two (or more) persons as coowners in the alternative by the use of the word "or" and if declared in writing upon the application for registration by the applicants to be community property, or tenancy in common, shall grant to each coowner the absolute power to transfer the title or interest of the other coowners only during the lifetime of such coowners.

(c) A vehicle may be registered in the names of two (or more) persons as coowners in the conjunctive by the use of the word "and" and shall thereafter require the

signature of each coowner or his personal representative to transfer title to the vehicle, except where title to the vehicle is set forth in joint tenancy, the signature of each coowner or his personal representative shall be required only during the lifetime of the coowners, and upon death of a coowner title shall pass to the surviving coowner.

(d) The department may adopt suitable abbreviations to appear upon the certificate of registration and certificate of ownership to designate the manner in which title to the vehicle is held if set forth by the coowners upon the application for registration. *(Added by Stats.1965, c. 891, p. 2495, § 1.)*

§ 4150.7.　Beneficiary form ownership

(a) Ownership of title to a vehicle subject to registration may be held in beneficiary form that includes a direction to transfer ownership of the vehicle to a designated beneficiary on the death of the owner if both of the following requirements are satisfied:

(1) Only one owner is designated.

(2) Only one TOD beneficiary is designated.

(b) A certificate of ownership issued in beneficiary form shall include, after the name of the owner, the words "transfer on death to" or the abbreviation "TOD" followed by the name of the beneficiary.

(c) During the lifetime of the owner, the signature or consent of the beneficiary is not required for any transaction relating to the vehicle for which a certificate of ownership in beneficiary form has been issued.

(d) The fee for registering ownership of a vehicle in a beneficiary form is ten dollars ($10). *(Added by Stats. 1991, c. 1055 (S.B.271), § 58, operative Jan. 1, 1993.)*

Law Revision Commission Comments
1991 Addition

Section 4150.7 is new. Subdivisions (a), (b), and (c) are drawn from Missouri law. See Mo.Ann.Stat. § 301.681 (Vernon Supp. 1991). See also Health & Safety Code §§ 18080.2, 18102.2; Veh.Code §§ 5910.5, 9852.7, 9916.5. [21 Cal.L.Rev.Comm.Reports 71 (1991)].

§ 4151.　Vehicle in state

The department shall not accept an application for the original registration of a vehicle in this State unless the vehicle at the time of application is within this State unless the provisions of Section 4152 are complied with. *(Stats.1959, c. 3, p. 1557, § 4151.)*

Cross References

Application for vehicle previously registered outside state, see Vehicle Code § 4300.

§ 4152.　Vehicle outside state

(a) The department may accept an application for registration of a vehicle which is not within this state, but which is to be registered to a resident of this state, at the time all documents and fees, as determined by the department in accordance with the provisions of this division, are submitted to the department.

(b) Any fees submitted pursuant to subdivision (a) shall not be subject to refund based upon the fact that the vehicle has not been and is not within this state. *(Stats.1959, c. 3, p. 1557, § 4152. Amended by Stats.1965, c. 1715, p. 3849, § 3, eff. Jan. 1, 1966; Stats.1975, c. 1220, p. 3082, § 1.)*

Cross References

Registration fees, generally, see Vehicle Code § 9250 et seq.
Trolley coaches, application of this section, see Vehicle Code § 21051.
Vehicles previously registered outside state, application of this section, see Vehicle Code § 4300.
Weight fees, commercial vehicles, see Vehicle Code § 9400 et seq.

§ 4152.5. Application for registration of vehicles last registered in foreign jurisdiction

Except as provided for in subdivision (c) of Section 9553, when California registration is required of a vehicle last registered in a foreign jurisdiction, an application for registration shall be made to the department within 20 days following the date registration became due. The application shall be deemed an original application. *(Added by Stats.1984, c. 1322, § 5, operative July 1, 1985. Amended by Stats.2000, c. 1035 (S.B.1403), § 7.)*

§ 4153. Special vehicles

If the vehicle to be registered is a specially constructed or remanufactured vehicle, the application shall also state that fact and contain additional information as may reasonably be required by the department to enable it properly to register the vehicle. *(Stats.1959, c. 3, p. 1557, § 4153. Amended by Stats.1983, c. 1286, § 18.)*

Cross References

Applicability of this section to trolley coaches, see Vehicle Code § 21051.
Registration of dismantled vehicle, see Vehicle Code § 11519.
Specially constructed vehicle defined, see Vehicle Code § 580.

§ 4154. Farm labor vehicles; registration issuance or renewal; verification of inspection

The department may not issue or renew the registration of a farm labor vehicle unless the owner of the vehicle provides verification to the department that the inspection required by Section 31401 has been performed. For these purposes, the department shall determine what constitutes appropriate verification. *(Added by Stats.1999, c. 557 (A.B.1165), § 1.5, eff. Sept. 29, 1999.)*

§ 4155. Publicly owned vehicles

Registration under this code shall apply to any vehicle owned by the United States government, the state, or any city, county, or political subdivision of the state, except in the following particulars:

(a) A license plate issued for a vehicle while publicly owned need not display the year number for which it is issued, but shall display a distinguishing symbol or letter.

(b) The registration of the vehicle and the registration card issued therefor shall not be renewed annually but shall remain valid until the certificate of ownership is suspended, revoked, or canceled by the department or upon a transfer of any interest shown in the certificate of ownership. If ownership of the vehicle is transferred to any person, the vehicle shall be reregistered as a privately owned vehicle and the special license plates shall be surrendered to the department.

(c) An identification plate used for special construction, cemetery, or special mobile equipment need not display a distinguishing symbol or letter. *(Stats.1959, c. 3, p. 1557, § 4155. Amended by Stats.1969, c. 1242, p. 2432, § 1.)*

Cross References

Exemptions from registration and weight fees, see Vehicle Code § 9101 et seq.
Issuance of stickers or devices in lieu of license plates, see Vehicle Code § 4853.
Suspension, revocation or cancellation of registration, see Vehicle Code § 8801.
Transfers of title or interest, see Vehicle Code § 5600 et seq.
Trolley coaches, applicability of this section, see Vehicle Code § 21051.

§ 4156. Temporary permit; limitations

(a) Notwithstanding any other provision of this code, and except as provided in subdivision (b), the department in its discretion may issue a temporary permit to operate a vehicle when a payment of fees has been accepted in an amount to be determined by, and paid to the department, by the owner or other person in lawful possession of the vehicle. The permit shall be subject to the terms and conditions, and shall be valid for the period of time, that the department shall deem appropriate under the circumstances.

(b)(1) The department shall not issue a temporary permit pursuant to subdivision (a) to operate a vehicle for which a certificate of compliance is required pursuant to Section 4000.3, and for which that certificate of compliance has not been issued, unless the department is presented with sufficient evidence, as determined by the department, that the vehicle has failed its most recent smog check inspection.

(2) Not more than one temporary permit may be issued pursuant to this subdivision to a vehicle owner in a two-year period.

(3) A temporary permit issued pursuant to paragraph (1) is valid for either 60 days after the expiration of the registration of the vehicle or 60 days after the date that vehicle is removed from nonoperation, whichever is applicable at the time that the temporary permit is issued.

(4) A temporary permit issued pursuant to paragraph (1) is subject to Section 9257.5. *(Stats.1959, c. 3, p. 1557,*

§ 4156. Amended by Stats.1959, c. 1478, p. 3772, § 1; Stats.2008, c. 451 (A.B.2241), § 1; Stats.2009, c. 140 (A.B.1164), § 179.)

Cross References

Applicability of this section to trolley coaches, see Vehicle Code § 21051.

Commercial vehicle registration, permits to nonresident owners, applicability of interest on underpaid portion of fees, see Vehicle Code § 8058.

Permits to nonresident owners, see Vehicle Code § 6700 et seq.

Temporary permits, commercial vehicles of nonresidents, see Vehicle Code § 4004.

Trailer coaches, exemption under temporary permit, see Vehicle Code § 5353.

§ 4157. Undertaking

In the absence of the regularly required supporting evidence of ownership upon application for registration or transfer of a vehicle, the department may accept an undertaking or bond which shall be conditioned to protect the department and all officers and employees thereof and any subsequent purchaser of the vehicle, any person acquiring a lien or security interest thereon, or the successor in interest of such purchaser or person against any loss or damage on account of any defect in or undisclosed claim upon the right, title, and interest of the applicant or other person in and to the vehicle. *(Stats. 1959, c. 3, p. 1558, § 4157. Amended by Stats.1963, c. 819, p. 2013, § 42, eff. Jan. 1, 1965.)*

Cross References

Bond and Undertaking Law, see Code of Civil Procedure § 995.010 et seq.

Registration of foreign vehicles, title in doubt, see Vehicle Code § 4307.

Transfers of title or interest, see Vehicle Code § 5600 et seq.

§ 4158. Return of bond or undertaking; surrender of certificate of ownership

In the event the vehicle is no longer registered in this state and the currently valid certificate of ownership is surrendered to the department, the bond or undertaking shall be returned and surrendered at the end of three years or prior thereto. *(Stats.1959, c. 3, p. 1558, § 4158. Amended by Stats.1982, c. 517, p. 2421, § 387.)*

Law Revision Commission Comments

1982 Amendment

Section 4158 is amended to delete provisions duplicated in the Bond and Undertaking Law. See Code Civ. Proc. §§ 996.430 (action to enforce liability) and 996.470 (limitation on liability of surety). [16 Cal.L.Rev. Comm. Reports 501 (1981)].

Cross References

Applicability of this section to trolley coaches, see Vehicle Code § 21051.

Registration of foreign vehicles, title in doubt, see Vehicle Code § 4307.

§ 4159. Notice of change of address

Whenever any person after making application for the registration of a vehicle required to be registered under this code, or after obtaining registration either as owner or legal owner, moves or acquires a new address different from the address shown in the application or upon the certificate of ownership or registration card, such person shall, within 10 days thereafter, notify the department of his old and new address. *(Stats.1959, c. 3, p. 1558, § 4159. Amended by Stats.1959, c. 964, p. 2995, § 1; Stats.1976, c. 552, p. 1392, § 1.)*

Cross References

Certificate of ownership and registration card, see Vehicle Code § 4450 et seq.

Suspension, cancellation or revocation of registration, see Vehicle Code § 8800.

§ 4160. Change of address on card

Any registered owner of a vehicle who moves or acquires a new address different from the address shown upon the registration card issued for the vehicle shall within 10 days mark out the former address shown on the face of the card and with pen and ink write or type the new address on the face of the card immediately below the former address with the initials of the registered owner. *(Stats.1959, c. 3, p. 1558, § 4160. Amended by Stats.1959, c. 964, p. 2995, § 2.)*

Cross References

Certificate of ownership and registration card, see Vehicle Code § 4450 et seq.

Suspension, cancellation or revocation of registration, see Vehicle Code § 8800.

§ 4161. Engine and motor change notification; distinguishing vehicle identification number; replacement engine case for motorcycles

(a) Whenever a motor vehicle engine or motor is installed, except temporarily, in a motor vehicle which is identified on the ownership and registration certificates by motor or engine number or by both the motor and frame numbers and subject to registration under this code, the owner of the motor vehicle shall, within 10 days thereafter, give notice to the department upon a form furnished by it containing a description of the motor vehicle engine or motor installed, including any identifying number thereon and the date of the installation. The owner of the motor vehicle shall also submit to the department with the notice the certificate of ownership and registration card covering the motor vehicle in which the motor vehicle engine or motor is installed and evidence of ownership covering the new or used motor vehicle engine or motor installed and such other documents as may be required by the department.

(b) Upon receipt of motor vehicle engine or motor change notification and other required documents, the department shall assign a distinguishing vehicle identification number to motor vehicles, other than motorcycles or motor-driven cycles registered under a motor number or motor and frame numbers. When the distinguishing vehicle identification number is placed on the vehicle as authorized, the vehicle shall thereafter be identified by the distinguishing identification number assigned.

(c) Notwithstanding any other provision of this section or any other provision of law, whenever an application is made to the department to register a replacement engine case for any motorcycle, the department shall request the Department of the California Highway Patrol to inspect the motorcycle to determine its proper identity. If the replacement engine case bears the same identifying numbers as the engine case being replaced, the original engine case shall be destroyed. A determination verifying proof of destruction shall be made by the Department of the California Highway Patrol. *(Stats.1959, c. 3, p. 1558, § 4161. Amended by Stats.1970, c. 824, p. 1558, § 1; Stats.1971, c. 1353, p. 2671, § 3, operative May 3, 1972; Stats.1982, c. 755, p. 2984, § 1; Stats.2001, c. 94 (S.B.1173), § 1.)*

Cross References

Certificate of ownership and registration card, see Vehicle Code § 4450 et seq.
Definitions,
  Department, see Vehicle Code § 290.
  Owner, see Vehicle Code § 460.
  Vehicle, see Vehicle Code § 670.
Fee for change of motor or engine, see Vehicle Code § 9257.
Registration indices and records, see Vehicle Code § 1800.
Suspension, cancellation or revocation of registration, see Vehicle Code § 8800.

§ 4162. Repealed by Stats.1970, c. 824, p. 1559, § 2

§ 4163. Three or more motor vehicles

The owner of three or more motor vehicles is not required to notify the department or to pay the fee required under Section 9257 when motor vehicle engines or motors owned by him are installed in or transferred between the motor vehicles owned by him until the motor vehicle is sold, transferred, or otherwise disposed of by him. *(Stats.1959, c. 3, p. 1559, § 4163. Amended by Stats.1961, c. 58, p. 1003, § 11, eff. March 31, 1961.)*

Cross References

Suspension, cancellation or revocation of registration, see Vehicle Code § 8800.

§§ 4164, 4165. Repealed by Stats.1970, c. 824, p. 1559, §§ 3, 4

§ 4166. Removed, destroyed, or obliterated motor or identifying number; distinguishing vehicle identification number

The department may assign a distinguishing vehicle identification number to a motor vehicle whenever the motor or other identifying number thereon is removed, destroyed or obliterated, and any motor vehicle to which a distinguishing vehicle identification number is assigned as authorized herein shall be registered under the number so assigned when registration of the motor vehicle is required under this code. *(Stats.1959, c. 3, p. 1559, § 4166. Amended by Stats.1970, c. 824, p. 1559, § 5.)*

Cross References

Applicability of this section to trolley coaches, see Vehicle Code § 21051.
Registration records of original motor number, see Vehicle Code § 1800.

ARTICLE 3. REGISTRATION OF FOREIGN VEHICLES

Section
4300.   Application.
4300.5.   Payment of sales and use tax required.
4301.   Surrender of plates and documents.
4302.   Disposition of plates.
4303.   Interstate vehicles.
4304.   Effect of foreign certificates of title.
4305.   Validity of foreign certificates.
4306.   Foreign liens and encumbrances.
4307.   Title in doubt.
4308.   Return of documents.
4309.   Notice to other states.

Cross References

Foreign vehicle, definition, see Vehicle Code § 330.
Permits to nonresident owners, see Vehicle Code § 6700 et seq.
Reciprocity, see Vehicle Code § 8000 et seq.

§ 4300. Application

Upon application for registration of a vehicle previously registered outside this State, the application shall be certified by the applicant and shall state that the vehicle previously has been registered outside this State, the time and place of the last registration of such vehicle outside this State, the name and address of the governmental officer, agency, or authority making the registration, and such further information relative to its previous registration as may reasonably be required by the department, including the time and place of original registration, if known, and if different from the last foreign registration. *(Stats.1959, c. 3, p. 1559, § 4300.)*

Cross References

Applicability of this section to trolley coaches, see Vehicle Code § 21051.
Certificates of title issued out of state, full faith and credit, see Vehicle Code § 4304.
Foreign vehicle defined, see Vehicle Code § 330.
Fraudulent applications, see Vehicle Code § 20.
Notice of application for vehicle previously registered out of state, see Vehicle Code § 4309.
Permits to nonresident owners without registration, see Vehicle Code § 6700 et seq.
Registration fees, generally, see Vehicle Code § 9250 et seq.

Registration fees for vehicles registered outside state, see Vehicle Code § 9252.

§ 4300.5. Payment of sales and use tax required

An application for registration under this chapter of a vehicle previously registered outside of this state shall be accompanied by payment of the amount required to be paid under Part 1 (commencing with Section 6001) of Division 2 of the Revenue and Taxation Code with respect to the use of the vehicle by the applicant. *(Added by Stats.1963, c. 1858, p. 3836, § 8, eff. July 19, 1963, operative Oct. 1, 1963. Amended by Stats.1965, 1st Ex.Sess., c. 2, p. 5453, § 37, eff. July 12, 1965, operative Aug. 1, 1965; Stats.1984, c. 144, § 205.)*

§ 4301. Surrender of plates and documents

The applicant shall surrender to the department all unexpired license plates, seals, certificates, or other evidence of foreign registration as may be in his possession or under his control. The department may require a certification from the jurisdiction of last registry when the applicant fails to surrender the last issued unexpired license plates. *(Stats.1959, c. 3, p. 1559, § 4301.)*

Cross References

Applicability of this section to trolley coaches, see Vehicle Code § 21051.
Return of documents when registration refused, see Vehicle Code § 4308.

§ 4302. Disposition of plates

Upon application made at the time of their surrender to the department and upon payment of a fee of one dollar ($1), the department shall return the unexpired license plates to the official in charge of the registration of motor vehicles in the state of issue of the license plates. *(Stats.1959, c. 3, p. 1559, § 4302.)*

Cross References

Applicability of this section to trolley coaches, see Vehicle Code § 21051.

§ 4303. Interstate vehicles

If in the course of interstate operation of a vehicle registered in another state it is desirable to retain registration in such state, the applicant need not surrender the evidence of foreign registration, but shall deliver it to the department for purposes of inspection, and the department upon a proper showing shall register the vehicle in this State, but shall not issue a certificate of ownership for the vehicle. *(Stats.1959, c. 3, p. 1560, § 4303.)*

Cross References

Applicability of this section to trolley coaches, see Vehicle Code § 21051.

§ 4304. Effect of foreign certificates of title

Upon application for registration of a vehicle previously registered outside this State, the department shall grant full faith and credit to the currently valid certificate of title describing the vehicle, the ownership thereof, and any liens thereon, issued by the state in which the vehicle was last registered, except that the laws of the state shall provide for the notation upon the certificate of title of any and all liens and encumbrances other than those dependent upon possession. *(Stats.1959, c. 3, p. 1560, § 4304.)*

Cross References

Applicability of this section to trolley coaches, see Vehicle Code § 21051.
Application for registration of vehicle previously registered outside state, see Vehicle Code § 4300.
Perfection of security interest in multiple state transactions, see Commercial Code § 9103.
Recording security interests, see Vehicle Code § 6300 et seq.

§ 4305. Validity of foreign certificates

In the absence of knowledge by the department that any certificate of title issued by another state is forged, fraudulent, or void, the acceptance thereof by the department shall be a sufficient determination of the genuineness and regularity of the certificate and of the truth of the recitals therein, and no liability shall be incurred by any officer or employee of the department by reason of so accepting a certificate of title. *(Stats.1959, c. 3, p. 1560, § 4305.)*

Cross References

Applicability of this section to trolley coaches, see Vehicle Code § 21051.

§ 4306. Foreign liens and encumbrances

In the event a certificate of title issued by another state shows any lien or encumbrance upon the vehicle therein described, then the department upon registering the vehicle in this State and upon issuing a certificate of ownership shall include therein the name of the lienholder as legal owner unless documents submitted with the foreign certificate of title establish that the lien or encumbrance has been fully satisfied. *(Stats.1959, c. 3, p. 1560, § 4306.)*

Cross References

Applicability of this section to trolley coaches, see Vehicle Code § 21051.
Perfection of security interest in multiple state transactions, see Commercial Code § 9103.
Recording security interests, see Vehicle Code § 6300 et seq.

§ 4307. Title in doubt

In the event application is made in this state for registration of a vehicle and the department is not satisfied as to the ownership of the vehicle or the existence of foreign liens thereon, then the department may register the vehicle and issue a distinctive registration card and appropriate license plates but shall withhold issuance of a California certificate of ownership unless the applicant shall present documents sufficient to reasonably satisfy the department of the applicant's ownership of the vehicle and sufficient to identify any liens thereon or the applicant shall post a bond pursuant to Section 4157. *(Stats.1959, c. 3, p. 1560, § 4307. Amended by Stats.1981, c. 636, p. 2403, § 2.)*

Cross References

Applicability of this section to trolley coaches, see Vehicle Code § 21051.
Return of bond or undertaking, see Vehicle Code § 4158.

§ 4308. Return of documents

In the event the department refuses to grant an application for registration in this State of a vehicle previously registered in another state, the department shall immediately return to the applicant all documents submitted by the applicant with the application. *(Stats. 1959, c. 3, p. 1560, § 4308.)*

Cross References

Applicability of this section to trolley coaches, see Vehicle Code § 21051.
Refusal of registration, generally, see Vehicle Code §§ 4750, 4751.
Surrender of certificates or other evidence of registration in foreign state, see Vehicle Code § 4301.

§ 4309. Notice to other states

The department shall forthwith mail a notice of the filing of any application for registration of a vehicle previously registered outside this state upon written request of the governmental officer, agency, or authority which made the last registration of the vehicle outside this state. The notice shall contain like data as required on the application filed with the department. This section shall not apply to applications to register commercial vehicles operating in interstate transportation nor to vehicles last registered in a foreign province or country. *(Stats.1959, c. 3, p. 1560, § 4309. Amended by Stats.1967, c. 1141, p. 2817, § 1.)*

Cross References

Applicability of this section to trolley coaches, see Vehicle Code § 21051.
Commercial vehicle defined, see Vehicle Code § 260.
Contents of application for registration of out of state vehicles, see Vehicle Code § 4300.

ARTICLE 4. EVIDENCES OF REGISTRATION

Section
4450. Certificate of ownership and registration card.
4450.5. Electronic lien and title program; auto loan business volume minimum threshold for required participation.
4451. Contents of certificate of ownership.
4452. Certificate of ownership without registration.
4452.5. Repealed.
4453. Contents of registration card.
4453.2. Farm labor vehicles; registration card language.
4453.5. Leased vehicles.
4453.6. Leased vehicles; information to law enforcement officer.

Section
4454. Registration card left with vehicle; exceptions.
4455. Display of foreign commercial vehicle permit.
4456. Report of sale forms; conditions; transfer registration; wholesale motor vehicle auctions; required information.
4456.1. Administrative service fee and grounds for suspension or revocation of dealer's license.
4456.3. Fees for vehicles sold; collection and disbursement; reimbursement.
4456.4. Motor vehicle sold or leased by new motor vehicle dealer; electronic registration; exceptions.
4456.5. Allowable dealer charges.
4457. Stolen, lost, or damaged cards and plates.
4458. Both plates lost or stolen.
4458.5. Repealed.
4459. Stolen, lost, or damaged certificate.
4460. Seizure of documents and plates.
4461. Lending evidence of registration or placards; disabled persons; parking; offenses; exception.
4461.3. Authority of city or county to adopt an ordinance or resolution to assess a penalty in addition to those imposed by §§ 4461 and 22507.8; use of proceeds.
4461.5. Additional civil penalties; convictions; disabled person placards; parking.
4462. Presentation and examination of registration card.
4462.5. Display of registration, identification card, etc. not issued for vehicle with intent to avoid compliance with registration requirements.
4463. Forgery, alteration, counterfeit or falsification of registration, license plate, certificate, license, etc., or disabled person placard; penalties.
4463.3. Additional civil penalties; convictions; forgery, alteration, counterfeit or falsification of disabled person placard.
4463.5. Decorative or facsimile license plates; authorization; punishment for violation.
4464. Altered license plates.
4465. Information for legal owner; compliance with federal law and rules; elimination of restrictions on consumer access to titling, branding, and theft information.
4466. Duplicate or substitute certificate of title or license plate; different address; verification.
4467. Victims of domestic violence, stalking, rape, and sexual battery; application for new and different license plates; conditions of issuance.

§ 4450. Certificate of ownership and registration card

The department upon registering a vehicle shall issue a certificate of ownership to the legal owner and a registration card to the owner, or both to the owner if there is no legal owner of the vehicle. *(Stats.1959, c. 3, p. 1561, § 4450.)*

Cross References

Applicability of this section to trolley coaches, see Vehicle Code § 21051.
Application for duplicate certificate, see Vehicle Code §§ 4457, 4459.
Change of address on card, see Vehicle Code § 4160.
Contents of registration card, see Vehicle Code § 4453.
Delivery of certificate and card, see Vehicle Code § 5753.
Department to issue new card on renewal of registration, see Vehicle Code § 4607.

Department to prescribe forms of registration, see Vehicle Code § 1652.

Duplicate certificate of ownership, fee, see Vehicle Code § 9265.

Evidence of registration, improper or false use of, see Vehicle Code §§ 4461 to 4463.

Installation of engine or motor, submission of card and certificate on, see Vehicle Code § 4161.

Legal owner defined, see Vehicle Code § 370.

Notice to state board of equalization of type of fuel used before registration, see Revenue and Taxation Code § 9256.

Owner defined, see Vehicle Code § 460.

Registered owner defined, see Vehicle Code § 505.

Registration card to be kept with vehicle, see Vehicle Code § 4454.

Renewal of registration, issuance of new card, see Vehicle Code § 4607.

Surrender of documents prior to dismantling, see Vehicle Code § 5501.

Suspension, cancellation or revocation of registration, see Vehicle Code § 8800.

Transfers of title or interest, endorsement of certificate, see Vehicle Code § 5750 et seq.

§ 4450.5. Electronic lien and title program; auto loan business volume minimum threshold for required participation

(a) On or before January 1, 2012, the director shall develop an Electronic Lien and Title (ELT) Program, in consultation with lienholders, licensed dealers, and other stakeholders, to require that all lienholders' title information be held in an electronic format, if the department determines that the program is cost effective compared to the current paper title and registration system.

(b) The director may establish an auto loan business volume threshold below which a lienholder is not required to participate in the program developed pursuant to subdivision (a). *(Added by Stats.2009, c. 540 (A.B. 1515), § 1.)*

§ 4451. Contents of certificate of ownership

The certificate of ownership shall contain all of the following:

(a) Not less than the information required upon the face of the registration card.

(b) Provision for notice to the department of a transfer of the title or interest of the owner or legal owner.

(c) Provision for application for transfer of registration by the transferee.

(d) Provision for an odometer disclosure statement pursuant to subsection (a) of Section 32705 of Title 49 of the United States Code. *(Stats.1959, c. 3, p. 1561, § 4451. Amended by Stats.1963, c. 1858, p. 3836, § 8.5, eff. July 19, 1963, operative Oct. 1, 1963; Stats.1965, 1st Ex.Sess., c. 2, p. 5453, § 38, eff. July 12, 1965, operative Aug. 1, 1965; Stats.1981, c. 714, p. 2793, § 437; Stats. 1993, c. 852 (A.B.1485), § 2; Stats.2000, c. 1035 (S.B. 1403), § 8.)*

Cross References

Applicability of this section to trolley coaches, see Vehicle Code § 21051.

Contents of registration card, see Vehicle Code § 4453.

Department to prescribe forms of certificate, see Vehicle Code § 1652.

Evidence of registration, improper or false use of, see Vehicle Code §§ 4461 to 4463.

Legal owner defined, see Vehicle Code § 370.

Owner defined, see Vehicle Code § 460.

Registered owner defined, see Vehicle Code § 505.

Transfers of title or interest, see Vehicle Code § 5600 et seq.

§ 4452. Certificate of ownership without registration

The department may issue a certificate of ownership to the legal owner of a vehicle without requiring registration, and may issue a facsimile copy of the certificate to the owner if there is no legal owner, the application is submitted in proper form, and one of the following conditions exist:

(a) The vehicle is registered pursuant to Section 5014.1.

(b) A certification has been filed with the department, pursuant to subdivision (a) of Section 4604, that the vehicle has not been driven, moved, or left standing upon any highway so as to require payment of fees and that the owner will not thereafter permit that operation or movement of the vehicle or leave the vehicle standing on any highway without surrendering, or arranging to surrender, the certificate of ownership to the department and without first making an application for the regular registration of the vehicle and full payment of all fees required to be paid under this code and Part 5 (commencing with Section 10701) of Division 2 of the Revenue and Taxation Code. *(Stats.1959, c. 3, p. 1561, § 4452. Amended by Stats.1967, c. 551, p. 1901, § 2; Stats.1970, c. 1439, p. 2793, § 2; Stats.1977, c. 456, p. 1494, § 1; Stats.1990, c. 1352 (A.B.2912), § 3, eff. Sept. 27, 1990, operative July 1, 1990; Stats.2001, c. 826 (A.B.1472), § 11.)*

Cross References

Applicability of this section to trolley coaches, see Vehicle Code § 21051.

Application for registration, see Vehicle Code § 4150.

Application for transfer, see Vehicle Code § 5904.

Fees for duplicate certificates of ownership, see Vehicle Code § 9265.

Fees for transfer of registration, see Vehicle Code § 9255.

Issuance of certificate of ownership, see Vehicle Code § 4450.

Legal owner defined, see Vehicle Code § 370.

Owner defined, see Vehicle Code § 460.

Registered owner defined, see Vehicle Code § 505.

Registration of trailer coaches, nonapplicability of this section, see Vehicle Code § 5351.

Service fee, certificate without registration, see Vehicle Code § 9254.

Transfer by department, see Vehicle Code § 6052.

Transfers of title or interest, see Vehicle Code § 5600 et seq.

Vehicle registration amnesty program, development and administration, see Vehicle Code § 9565.

§ 4452.5. Repealed by Stats.1972, c. 973, p. 1757, § 6, urgency, eff. Aug. 16, 1972

§ 4453. Contents of registration card

(a) The registration card shall contain upon its face, the date issued, the name and residence or business address or mailing address of the owner and of the legal owner, if any, the registration number assigned to the vehicle, and a description of the vehicle as complete as that required in the application for registration of the vehicle.

(b) The following motor vehicles shall be identified as such on the face of the registration card whenever the department is able to ascertain that fact at the time application is made for initial registration or transfer of ownership of the vehicle:

(1) A motor vehicle rebuilt and restored to operation that was previously declared to be a total loss salvage vehicle because the cost of repairs exceeds the retail value of the vehicle.

(2) A motor vehicle rebuilt and restored to operation that was previously reported to be dismantled pursuant to Section 11520.

(3) A motor vehicle previously registered to a law enforcement agency and operated in law enforcement work.

(4) A motor vehicle formerly operated as a taxicab.

(5) A motor vehicle manufactured outside of the United States and not intended by the manufacturer for sale in the United States.

(6) A park trailer, as described in Section 18009.3 of the Health and Safety Code, that when moved upon the highway is required to be moved under a permit pursuant to Section 35780.

(7) A motor vehicle that has been reacquired under circumstances described in subdivision (c) of Section 1793.23 of the Civil Code, a vehicle with out-of-state titling documents reflecting a warranty return, or a vehicle that has been identified by an agency of another state as requiring a warranty return title notation, pursuant to the laws of that state. The notation made on the face of the registration and pursuant to this subdivision shall state "Lemon Law Buyback."

(c) The director may modify the form, arrangement, and information appearing on the face of the registration card and may provide for standardization and abbreviation of fictitious or firm names on the registration card whenever the director finds that the efficiency of the department will be promoted by so doing. *(Stats.1959, c. 3, p. 1561, § 4453. Amended by Stats.1965, c. 1715, p. 3849, § 4, eff. Jan. 1, 1966; Stats.1967, c. 474, p. 1679, § 1; Stats.1980, c. 856, p. 2668, § 1, operative Oct. 1, 1981; Stats.1985, c. 1235, § 5; Stats.1986, c. 1078, § 7, eff. Sept. 24, 1986, operative Jan. 1, 1987; Stats.1989, c. 862,*

§ 2; Stats.1993, c. 272 (A.B.301), § 13, eff. Aug. 2, 1993; Stats.1995, c. 503 (A.B.1381), § 5; Stats.2000, c. 566 (A.B.1912), § 4; Stats.2003, c. 451 (A.B.1718), § 17.)

Cross References

Applicability of this section to trolley coaches, see Vehicle Code § 21051.
Application for registration, see Vehicle Code § 4150.
False evidence of registration, see Vehicle Code § 4463.
Legal owner defined, see Vehicle Code § 370.
Owner defined, see Vehicle Code § 460.
Registered owner defined, see Vehicle Code § 505.
Registration card to be kept with vehicle, see Vehicle Code § 4454.

§ 4453.2. Farm labor vehicles; registration card language

In addition to the information required under Section 4453, the registration card of every farm labor vehicle shall contain the words, "Farm Labor Vehicle," in conjunction with the vehicle identification information. *(Added by Stats.1999, c. 557 (A.B.1165), § 2, eff. Sept. 29, 1999.)*

§ 4453.5. Leased vehicles

(a) In the case of leased vehicles, the lessor and the lessee shall be shown on the registration card as the owner and the lessee of a vehicle, and the department shall designate their relationships upon the card and the ownership certificate by the words "lessor" and "lessee" and, at the election of the lessor, the department may designate thereon either the address of the lessor or the lessee.

(b) Transfers of ownership involving vehicles registered as provided in subdivision (a) shall only be effected upon the signature release of the lessor.

(c) The lessor shall provide the address, or the name and address, of the lessee on a form prescribed by the department in all cases where the information is not on the registration card and ownership certificate. Information received under this subdivision shall be used only for law enforcement and shall be available only to law enforcement officials at their request.

(d) A lessor, upon written request of the lessee or, if designated in writing, the lessee's designee, shall disclose any pertinent information regarding the amount of payment and the documents necessary to exercise any option held by the lessee to purchase the leased vehicle. *(Added by Stats.1985, c. 1500, § 2, operative July 1, 1986. Amended by Stats.2003, c. 151 (S.B.237), § 1.)*

Cross References

Purchase or obtaining vehicle subject to prior credit or lease, payment of prior obligation before sale, consignment or transfer, prior good faith notice, see Vehicle Code § 11709.4.
Transfers of title or interest, violation of endorsement and delivery of certificate of ownership and registration card requirements, leased vehicles, see Vehicle Code § 5753.

§ 4453.6. Leased vehicles; information to law enforcement officer

On request of any member of the California Highway Patrol, any regularly employed and salaried police officer or deputy sheriff, or any reserve police officer or reserve deputy sheriff listed in Section 830.6 of the Penal Code, or any employee or officer of the department specified in Section 1655, who is conducting an investigation of a public offense, the lessor of a vehicle shall furnish the name and address of the lessee of a vehicle if that information does not appear on the registration card. *(Added by Stats.1975, c. 358, p. 802, § 1. Amended by Stats.1982, c. 830, p. 3147, § 3; Stats.2003, c. 292 (A.B. 1436), § 6.)*

Cross References

Criminal procedure, deputized or appointed peace officers, see Penal Code § 830.6.

§ 4454. Registration card left with vehicle; exceptions

(a) Every owner, upon receipt of a registration card, shall maintain the same or a facsimile copy thereof with the vehicle for which issued.

(b) This section does not apply when a registration card is necessarily removed from the vehicle for the purpose of application for renewal or transfer of registration, or when the vehicle is left unattended.

(c) Any violation of this section shall be cited in accordance with the provisions of Section 40610. *(Stats. 1959, c. 3, p. 1562, § 4454. Amended by Stats.1961, c. 58, p. 1003, § 12; Stats.1965, c. 442, p. 1750, § 1; Stats.1967, c. 410, p. 1629, § 1; Stats.1982, c. 402, p. 1739, § 1; Stats.1999, c. 106 (A.B.289), § 1.)*

Cross References

Applicability of this section to trolley coaches, see Vehicle Code § 21051.
Auxiliary dolly defined, see Vehicle Code § 225.
Contents of registration card, see Vehicle Code § 4453.
Display of license plates, see Vehicle Code § 5200.
Evidence of registration, improper or false use of, see Vehicle Code §§ 4461 to 4463.
Issuance of card on registration, see Vehicle Code § 4450.
Necessity of registration, see Vehicle Code § 4000.
Operation of vehicle without registration, see Vehicle Code § 4001 et seq.
Owner defined, see Vehicle Code § 460.
Pole or pipe dolly defined, see Vehicle Code § 475.
Registered owner defined, see Vehicle Code § 505.
Registration, license or mechanical violations, conditions for use, see Vehicle Code § 40610.
Renewal of registration, generally, see Vehicle Code § 4600 et seq.
Suspension, cancellation or revocation of registration, see Vehicle Code § 8800 et seq.
Transfers of title or interest, see Vehicle Code § 5600 et seq.
Vehicle defined, see Vehicle Code § 670.

§ 4455. Display of foreign commercial vehicle permit

Any permit issued under Section 4004 shall be carried in the vehicle for which issued at all times while it is being operated in this State. *(Stats.1959, c. 3, p. 1562, § 4455.)*

§ 4456. Report of sale forms; conditions; transfer registration; wholesale motor vehicle auctions; required information

(a) When selling a vehicle, dealers and lessor-retailers shall use numbered report-of-sale forms issued by the department. The forms shall be used in accordance with the following terms and conditions:

(1) The dealer or lessor-retailer shall attach for display a copy of the report of sale on the vehicle before the vehicle is delivered to the purchaser.

(2) The dealer or lessor-retailer shall submit to the department an application accompanied by all fees and penalties due for registration or transfer of registration of the vehicle within 30 days from the date of sale, as provided in subdivision (c) of Section 9553, if the vehicle is a used vehicle, and 20 days if the vehicle is a new vehicle. Penalties due for noncompliance with this paragraph shall be paid by the dealer or lessor-retailer. The dealer or lessor-retailer shall not charge the purchaser for the penalties.

(3) As part of an application to transfer registration of a used vehicle, the dealer or lessor-retailer shall include all of the following information on the certificate of title, application for a duplicate certificate of title, or form prescribed by the department:

(A) Date of sale and report of sale number.

(B) Purchaser's name and address.

(C) Dealer's name, address, number, and signature or signature of authorized agent.

(D) Salesperson number.

(4) If the department returns an application and the application was first received by the department within 30 days of the date of sale of the vehicle if the vehicle is a used vehicle, and 20 days if the vehicle is a new vehicle, the dealer or lessor-retailer shall submit a corrected application to the department within 50 days from the date of sale of the vehicle if the vehicle is a used vehicle, and 40 days if the vehicle is a new vehicle, or within 30 days from the date that the application is first returned by the department if the vehicle is a used vehicle, and 20 days if the vehicle is a new vehicle, whichever is later.

(5) If the department returns an application and the application was first received by the department more than 30 days from the date of sale of the vehicle if the vehicle is a used vehicle, and 20 days if the vehicle is a new vehicle, the dealer or lessor-retailer shall submit a corrected application to the department within 50 days from the date of sale of the vehicle if the vehicle is a used vehicle, and 40 days if the vehicle is a new vehicle.

(6) An application first received by the department more than 50 days from the date of sale of the vehicle if the vehicle is a used vehicle, and 40 days if the vehicle is a new vehicle, is subject to the penalties specified in subdivisions (a) and (b) of Section 4456.1.

(7) The dealer or lessor-retailer shall report the sale pursuant to Section 5901.

(b)(1) A transfer that takes place through a dealer conducting a wholesale vehicle auction shall be reported to the department by that dealer on a single form approved by the department. The completed form shall contain, at a minimum, all of the following information:

(A) The name and address of the seller.

(B) The seller's dealer number, if applicable.

(C) The date of delivery to the dealer conducting the auction.

(D) The actual mileage of the vehicle as indicated by the vehicle's odometer at the time of delivery to the dealer conducting the auction.

(E) The name, address, and occupational license number of the dealer conducting the auction.

(F) The name, address, and occupational license number of the buyer.

(G) The signature of the dealer conducting the auction.

(2) Submission of the completed form specified in paragraph (1) to the department shall fully satisfy the requirements of subdivision (a) and subdivision (a) of Section 5901 with respect to the dealer selling at auction and the dealer conducting the auction.

(3) The single form required by this subdivision does not relieve a dealer of any obligation or responsibility that is required by any other provision of law.

(c) A vehicle displaying a copy of the report of sale may be operated without license plates or registration card until either of the following, whichever occurs first:

(1) The license plates and registration card are received by the purchaser.

(2) A 90–day period, commencing with the date of sale of the vehicle, has expired.

(d) This section shall become operative on July 1, 2012. *(Added by Stats.2011, c. 329 (A.B.1215), § 8, operative July 1, 2012.)*

Cross References

Definitions,
  Dealer, see Vehicle Code § 285.
  Department, see Vehicle Code § 290.
  Vehicle, see Vehicle Code § 670.
Use and display on vehicles of copies of report of sale form and
  identification devices, see Vehicle Code § 38080.

§ 4456.1. Administrative service fee and grounds for suspension or revocation of dealer's license

(a) A dealer or lessor-retailer who violates paragraph (1), (2), or (7) of subdivision (a) of Section 4456 shall pay to the department an administrative service fee of five dollars ($5) for each violation.

(b) A dealer or lessor-retailer who violates paragraph (4), (5), or (6) of subdivision (a) of Section 4456 shall pay to the department an administrative service fee of twenty-five dollars ($25) for each violation.

(c) Subject to subdivision (d), each violation of Section 4456 is, in addition to the obligation to pay an administrative service fee, a separate cause for discipline pursuant to Section 11613 or 11705.

(d) A violation of subdivision (a) of Section 4456 because of a dealer or lessor-retailer's failure to submit to the department an application for registration or transfer of registration is a cause for disciplinary action pursuant to Section 11613 or 11705 only if the initial application is submitted 50 days or more following the date of sale of the vehicle if the vehicle is a used vehicle, and 40 days if the vehicle is a new vehicle. *(Added by Stats.1979, c. 597, p. 1860, § 4. Amended by Stats.1983, c. 1286, § 20; Stats.1984, c. 628, § 2; Stats.1985, c. 1022, § 3; Stats. 1996, c. 813 (A.B.2286), § 2; Stats.1996, c. 1155 (S.B. 1587), § 3.1.)*

Cross References

Use and display on vehicles of copies of report of sale form and
  identification devices, see Vehicle Code § 38080.

§ 4456.3. Fees for vehicles sold; collection and disbursement; reimbursement

(a) The department shall charge a dealer or lessor-retailer a fee, as established by the director pursuant to subdivision (b), for each vehicle sold by a dealer or lessor-retailer and reported on a report-of-sale form issued by the department to a dealer or lessor-retailer, or for every vehicle sold by a dealer or lessor-retailer if that licensee does not use a report-of-sale form issued by the department because the report of the sale is given electronically or otherwise. The department shall collect the fee and the fees shall be paid to the Consumer Motor Vehicle Recovery Corporation as described in Chapter 11 (commencing with Section 12200) of Division 5. The department shall not charge more than a total of two thousand five hundred dollars ($2,500) in fees under this section to a dealer licensee within a calendar year.

(b) The director shall establish the fee at one dollar ($1) and shall collect the fee. The director shall deposit the fees received in the Motor Vehicle Account. Notwithstanding Section 13340 of the Government Code, the revenues from the fees deposited in the Motor Vehicle Account, less an amount that the director determines is equal to the department's costs related to collecting and processing the fees, is hereby continuously appropriated to the department for quarterly payment to the Consumer Motor Vehicle Recovery Corporation until the Consumer Motor Vehicle Recovery Corporation notifies the department that the balance in the recovery fund maintained by the corporation has reached five million dollars ($5,000,000). Within 90 days after being notified by the Consumer Motor Vehicle Recovery Corporation, the director shall cease collecting the fee. Thereafter, if the amount in the recovery fund maintained by the corporation is less than two million dollars ($2,000,000), the Consumer Motor Vehicle Recovery Corporation shall notify the department of the amount necessary to return the recovery fund balance to five million dollars ($5,000,-

000). Within 90 days of being notified, the director shall collect the fee and pay the fee revenue required by this subdivision until the Consumer Motor Vehicle Recovery Corporation notifies the director that the recovery fund has reached five million dollars ($5,000,000). Within 90 days of being notified, the director shall cease collecting the fee.

(c)(1) The Consumer Motor Vehicle Recovery Corporation shall reimburse the department for all reasonable expenses incurred in implementing this section.

(2) The Consumer Motor Vehicle Recovery Corporation shall reimburse the department for all reasonable startup expenses incurred by the department to comply with this section within 90 days after the department begins collecting the fees and transmitting them to the Corporation as provided in this section.

(d) This section shall become operative on July 1, 2008. *(Added by Stats.2007, c. 437 (S.B.729), § 2, operative July 1, 2008.)*

§ 4456.4. Motor vehicle sold or leased by new motor vehicle dealer; electronic registration; exceptions

(a) A motor vehicle sold or leased by a new motor vehicle dealer shall be registered by the dealer using electronic programs provided by a qualified private industry partner pursuant to Section 1685 if the department permits the transaction to be processed electronically.

(b) This section does not apply to the sale or lease of a motorcycle or off-highway motor vehicle subject to identification under Section 38010 or a recreational vehicle as defined in Section 18010 of the Health and Safety Code.

(c) This section shall become operative on July 1, 2012. *(Added by Stats.2011, c. 329 (A.B.1215), § 9, operative July 1, 2012.)*

§ 4456.5. Allowable dealer charges

(a) A dealer may charge the purchaser or lessee of a vehicle the following charges:

(1) A document processing charge for the preparation and processing of documents, disclosures, and titling, registration, and information security obligations imposed by state and federal law. The dealer document processing charge shall not be represented as a governmental fee.

(A) If a dealer has a contractual agreement with the department to be a private industry partner pursuant to Section 1685, the document processing charge shall not exceed eighty dollars ($80).

(B) If a dealer does not have a contractual agreement with the department to be a private industry partner pursuant to Section 1685, the document processing charge shall not exceed sixty-five dollars ($65).

(2) An electronic filing charge, not to exceed the actual amount the dealer is charged by a first-line service provider for providing license plate processing, postage, and the fees and services authorized pursuant to subdivi-

sions (a) and (d) of Section 1685. The director may establish, through the adoption of regulations, the maximum amount that a first-line service provider may charge a dealer. The electronic filing charge shall not be represented as a governmental fee.

(b) As used in this section, the term "first-line service provider" shall have the same meaning as defined in subdivision (b) of Section 1685.

(c) This section shall become operative on July 1, 2012. *(Added by Stats.2011, c. 329 (A.B.1215), § 10, operative July 1, 2012.)*

§ 4457. Stolen, lost, or damaged cards and plates

If any registration card or license plate is stolen, lost, mutilated, or illegible, the owner of the vehicle for which the same was issued, as shown by the records of the department, shall immediately make application for and may, upon the applicant furnishing information satisfactory to the department, obtain a duplicate or a substitute or a new registration under a new registration number, as determined to be most advisable by the department. An application for a duplicate registration card is not required in conjunction with any other application. *(Stats. 1959, c. 3, p. 1562, § 4457. Amended by Stats.1988, c. 1268, § 1.)*

Cross References

Applicability of this section to trolley coaches, see Vehicle Code § 21051.
Dismantling vehicle, application of section, see Vehicle Code § 5501.
Fees for duplicate or substitute cards and plates, see Vehicle Code § 9265.
Inapplicability of provisions to certificate of dismantling, see Vehicle Code § 5501.
Owner defined, see Vehicle Code § 460.
Punishment for false evidences of registration, see Vehicle Code § 4463.
Registration indices and records, see Vehicle Code § 1800.

§ 4458. Both plates lost or stolen

If both license plates or a permanent trailer identification plate are lost or stolen, the registered owner shall immediately notify a law enforcement agency, and shall immediately apply to the department for new plates in lieu of the plates stolen or lost. The department shall in every proper case, except in the case of plates which are exempt from fees, cause to be issued applicable license plates of a different number and assign the registration number to the vehicle for which the plates are issued. *(Stats.1959, c. 3, p. 1563, § 4458. Amended by Stats.2000, c. 861 (S.B.2084), § 20, eff. Sept. 29, 2000; Stats.2001, c. 826 (A.B.1472), § 12.)*

Cross References

Applicability of this section to trolley coaches, see Vehicle Code § 21051.
Dismantling vehicle, application of section, see Vehicle Code § 5501.

Exemptions from registration fees, see Vehicle Code § 4001 et seq.

Fees for duplicate or substitute plates, see Vehicle Code § 9265.

Off-highway vehicles, applicability of registration provisions, see Vehicle Code § 38100.

Registered owner defined, see Vehicle Code § 505.

§ 4458.5. Repealed by Stats.1975, c. 1220, p. 3082, § 2

§ 4459. Stolen, lost, or damaged certificate

If any certificate of ownership is stolen, lost, mutilated or illegible, the legal owner or, if none, then the owner of the vehicle for which the same was issued as shown by the records of the department shall immediately make application for and may, upon the applicant furnishing information satisfactory to the department, obtain a duplicate. *(Stats.1959, c. 3, p. 1563, § 4459.)*

Cross References

Applicability of this section to trolley coaches, see Vehicle Code § 21051.

Dismantling vehicle, application of section, see Vehicle Code § 5501.

Fees for duplicate certificates, see Vehicle Code § 9265.

Legal owner defined, see Vehicle Code § 370.

Owner defined, see Vehicle Code § 460.

Registration indices and records, see Vehicle Code § 1800.

§ 4460. Seizure of documents and plates

(a) The Department of Motor Vehicles, the Traffic Adjudication Board, and the Department of the California Highway Patrol, any regularly employed and salaried police officer or deputy sheriff or any reserve police officer or reserve deputy sheriff listed in Section 830.6 of the Penal Code may take possession of any certificate, card, placard, permit, license, or license plate issued under this code, upon expiration, revocation, cancellation, or suspension thereof or which is fictitious or which has been unlawfully or erroneously issued. Any license plate which is not attached to the vehicle for which issued, when and in the manner required under this code, may be seized, and attachment to the proper vehicle may be made or required.

(b) Any document, placard, or license plate seized shall be delivered to the Department of Motor Vehicles. *(Stats.1959, c. 3, p. 1563, § 4460. Amended by Stats.1967, c. 1110, p. 2754, § 2; Stats.1981, c. 984, p. 3815, § 1; Stats.1982, c. 975, p. 3940, § 1; Stats.1983, c. 142, § 162; Stats.2003, c. 292 (A.B.1436), § 7.)*

Cross References

Applicability of this section to trolley coaches, see Vehicle Code § 21051.

Criminal procedure, deputized or appointed peace officers, see Penal Code § 830.6.

Department to issue certificate of ownership, see Vehicle Code § 4450.

Department to issue reflectorized license plates, see Vehicle Code § 4850.

Driver's license, suspension or revocation by court, see Vehicle Code § 13200 et seq.

Driving motor vehicle when driving privileges suspended or revoked, see Vehicle Code § 14601.

Expiration of driver's license, see Vehicle Code §§ 12816, 12817.

Expiration of registration, see Vehicle Code § 4601.

Grounds permitting refusal of driver's license, see Vehicle Code § 12809.

Off-highway vehicles, applicability of registration provisions, see Vehicle Code § 38100.

Owner to return evidence of registration upon cancellation, suspension or revocation, see Vehicle Code § 8802.

Registration, suspension, revocation and cancellation generally, see Vehicle Code § 8800 et seq.

Suspension or revocation of license by department, see Vehicle Code § 13350 et seq.

Use of false or fictitious name or false statements prohibited, see Vehicle Code § 20.

§ 4461. Lending evidence of registration or placards; disabled persons; parking; offenses; exception

(a) A person shall not lend a certificate of ownership, registration card, license plate, special plate, validation tab, or permit issued to him or her if the person desiring to borrow it would not be entitled to its use, and a person shall not knowingly permit its use by one not entitled to it.

(b) A person to whom a disabled person placard has been issued shall not lend the placard to another person, and a disabled person shall not knowingly permit the use for parking purposes of the placard or identification license plate issued pursuant to Section 5007 by one not entitled to it. A person to whom a disabled person placard has been issued may permit another person to use the placard only while in the presence or reasonable proximity of the disabled person for the purpose of transporting the disabled person. A violation of this subdivision is subject to the issuance of a notice of parking violation imposing a civil penalty of not less than two hundred fifty dollars ($250) and not more than one thousand dollars ($1,000), for which enforcement shall be governed by the procedures set forth in Article 3 (commencing with Section 40200) of Chapter 1 of Division 17 or is a misdemeanor punishable by a fine of not less than two hundred fifty dollars ($250) and not more than one thousand dollars ($1,000), imprisonment in the county jail for not more than six months, or both that fine and imprisonment.

(c) Except for the purpose of transporting a disabled person as specified in subdivision (b), a person shall not display a disabled person placard that was not issued to him or her or that has been canceled or revoked pursuant to Section 22511.6. A violation of this subdivision is subject to the issuance of a notice of parking violation imposing a civil penalty of not less than two hundred fifty dollars ($250) and not more than one thousand dollars ($1,000), for which enforcement shall be governed by the procedures set forth in Article 3 (commencing with Section 40200) of Chapter 1 of Division 17 or is a misdemeanor punishable by a fine of not less than two hundred fifty dollars ($250) and not more than one thousand dollars ($1,000), imprisonment in the county jail for not more than six months, or both that fine and imprisonment.

(d) Notwithstanding subdivisions (a), (b), and (c), a person using a vehicle displaying a special identification license plate issued to another pursuant to Section 5007 shall not park in those parking stalls or spaces designated for disabled persons pursuant to Section 22511.7 or 22511.8, unless transporting a disabled person. A violation of this subdivision is subject to the issuance of a notice of parking violation imposing a civil penalty of not less than two hundred fifty dollars ($250) and not more than one thousand dollars ($1,000), for which enforcement shall be governed by the procedures set forth in Article 3 (commencing with Section 40200) of Chapter 1 of Division 17 or is a misdemeanor punishable by a fine of not less than two hundred fifty dollars ($250) and not more than one thousand dollars ($1,000), imprisonment in the county jail for not more than six months, or both that fine and imprisonment.

(e) For the purposes of subdivisions (b) and (c), "disabled person placard" means a placard issued pursuant to Section 22511.55 or 22511.59. *(Added by Stats. 1986, c. 351, § 2, operative July 1, 1987. Amended by Stats.1991, c. 894 (S.B.234), § 1; Stats.1993, c. 272 (A.B.301), § 14, eff. Aug. 2, 1993; Stats.1994, c. 1149 (A.B.2878), § 2; Stats.1996, c. 116 (S.B.1527), § 1; Stats. 2000, c. 524 (A.B.1792), § 2; Stats.2009, c. 415 (A.B.144), § 2.)*

Cross References

False evidences of registration, see Vehicle Code § 4463.
Fines, disabled parking restrictions, see Penal Code § 1465.6.
Issuance and renewal of disabled parking placards, penalty printing requirements, see Vehicle Code §§ 22511.55 and 22511.59.
Off-highway vehicles, applicability of registration provisions, see Vehicle Code § 38100.
Parking penalties, additional assessments, see Vehicle Code § 40203.6.
Procedure upon registration, see Vehicle Code § 4150 et seq.
Registration indices and records, see Vehicle Code § 1800.
Suspension, revocation or cancellation of registration, see Vehicle Code § 8800 et seq.
Violation as misdemeanor,
  Generally, see Vehicle Code § 40000.7.
  Punishment, see Vehicle Code § 42002.

§ 4461.3. Authority of city or county to adopt an ordinance or resolution to assess a penalty in addition to those imposed by §§ 4461 and 22507.8; use of proceeds

In addition to any fine imposed for conviction of a violation of Section 4461 or 22507.8, a city or county may adopt an ordinance or resolution to assess an additional penalty of one hundred dollars ($100). All revenue generated from imposition of the penalty shall be used specifically for the purpose of improving enforcement of the provisions of this code relating to disabled parking spaces and placards within the city or county. Revenue generated from imposition of the penalty may not be used

164

to supplant funds used for other general parking enforcement purposes, but may be used to offset the cost of establishing a new disabled parking enforcement program. *(Added by Stats.2003, c. 555 (A.B.327), § 4.)*

Cross References

Additional fines imposed for violation of disabled parking restrictions, see Penal Code § 1465.6.
Fines imposed and collected for violation of disabled parking restrictions, see Penal Code § 1465.5.
Issuance and renewal of disabled parking placards, penalty printing requirements, see Vehicle Code §§ 22511.55 and 22511.59.

§ 4461.5. Additional civil penalties; convictions; disabled person placards; parking

In addition to, or instead of, any fine imposed for conviction of a violation of subdivision (c) or (d) of Section 4461, the court may impose a civil penalty of not more than one thousand five hundred dollars ($1,500) for each conviction. *(Added by Stats.2000, c. 215 (A.B.1276), § 1.)*

§ 4462. Presentation and examination of registration card

(a) The driver of a motor vehicle shall present the registration or identification card or other evidence of registration of any or all vehicles under his or her immediate control for examination upon demand of any peace officer.

(b) No person shall display upon a vehicle, nor present to any peace officer, any registration card, identification card, temporary receipt, license plate, device issued pursuant to Section 4853, or permit not issued for that vehicle or not otherwise lawfully used thereon under this code.

(c) This section shall become operative on January 1, 2001. *(Added by Stats.1996, c. 697 (A.B.2852), § 2, operative Jan. 1, 2001.)*

Cross References

Display of license plates, see Vehicle Code § 5200.
Off-highway vehicles, applicability of registration provisions, see Vehicle Code § 38100.
Procedure upon registration, see Vehicle Code § 4150 et seq.
Registration card to be kept with vehicle, see Vehicle Code § 4454.
Violation as misdemeanor, punishment, see Vehicle Code § 42002.

§ 4462.5. Display of registration, identification card, etc. not issued for vehicle with intent to avoid compliance with registration requirements

Every person who commits a violation of subdivision (b) of Section 4462, with intent to avoid compliance with vehicle registration requirements of Article 1 (commencing with Section 4000) of Chapter 1 or Article 1 (commencing with Section 5600) of Chapter 2, is guilty of a misdemeanor. *(Added by Stats.1988, c. 640, § 2.)*

§4463. Forgery, alteration, counterfeit or falsification of registration, license plate, certificate, license, etc., or disabled person placard; penalties

(a) A person who, with intent to prejudice, damage, or defraud, commits any of the following acts is guilty of a felony and upon conviction thereof shall be punished by imprisonment pursuant to subdivision (h) of Section 1170 of the Penal Code for 16 months or two or three years, or by imprisonment in a county jail for not more than one year:

(1) Alters, forges, counterfeits, or falsifies a certificate of ownership, registration card, certificate, license, license plate, device issued pursuant to Section 4853, special plate, or permit provided for by this code or a comparable certificate of ownership, registration card, certificate, license, license plate, device comparable to that issued pursuant to Section 4853, special plate, or permit provided for by a foreign jurisdiction, or alters, forges, counterfeits, or falsifies the document, device, or plate with intent to represent it as issued by the department, or alters, forges, counterfeits, or falsifies with fraudulent intent an endorsement of transfer on a certificate of ownership or other document evidencing ownership, or with fraudulent intent displays or causes or permits to be displayed or have in his or her possession a blank, incomplete, canceled, suspended, revoked, altered, forged, counterfeit, or false certificate of ownership, registration card, certificate, license, license plate, device issued pursuant to Section 4853, special plate, or permit.

(2) Utters, publishes, passes, or attempts to pass, as true and genuine, a false, altered, forged, or counterfeited matter listed in paragraph (1) knowing it to be false, altered, forged, or counterfeited.

(b) A person who, with intent to prejudice, damage, or defraud, commits any of the following acts is guilty of a misdemeanor, and upon conviction thereof shall be punished by imprisonment in a county jail for six months, a fine of not less than five hundred dollars ($500) and not more than one thousand dollars ($1,000), or both that fine and imprisonment, which penalty shall not be suspended:

(1) Forges, counterfeits, or falsifies a disabled person placard or a comparable placard relating to parking privileges for disabled persons provided for by a foreign jurisdiction, or forges, counterfeits, or falsifies a disabled person placard with intent to represent it as issued by the department.

(2) Passes, or attempts to pass, as true and genuine, a false, forged, or counterfeit disabled person placard knowing it to be false, forged, or counterfeited.

(3) Acquires, possesses, sells, or offers for sale a genuine or counterfeit disabled person placard.

(c) A person who, with fraudulent intent, displays or causes or permits to be displayed a forged, counterfeit, or false disabled person placard, is subject to the issuance of a notice of parking violation imposing a civil penalty of not less than two hundred fifty dollars ($250) and not more than one thousand dollars ($1,000), for which enforcement shall be governed by the procedures set forth in Article 3 (commencing with Section 40200) of Chapter 1 of Division 17 or is guilty of a misdemeanor punishable by imprisonment in a county jail for six months, a fine of not less than two hundred fifty dollars ($250) and not more than one thousand dollars ($1,000), or both that fine and imprisonment, which penalty shall not be suspended.

(d) For purposes of subdivision (b) or (c), "disabled person placard" means a placard issued pursuant to Section 22511.55 or 22511.59.

(e) A person who, with intent to prejudice, damage, or defraud, commits any of the following acts is guilty of an infraction, and upon conviction thereof shall be punished by a fine of not less than one hundred dollars ($100) and not more than two hundred fifty dollars ($250) for a first offense, not less than two hundred fifty dollars ($250) and not more than five hundred dollars ($500) for a second offense, and not less than five hundred dollars ($500) and not more than one thousand dollars ($1,000) for a third or subsequent offense, which penalty shall not be suspended:

(1) Forges, counterfeits, or falsifies a Clean Air Sticker or a comparable clean air sticker relating to high occupancy vehicle lane privileges provided for by a foreign jurisdiction, or forges, counterfeits, or falsifies a Clean Air Sticker with intent to represent it as issued by the department.

(2) Passes, or attempts to pass, as true and genuine, a false, forged, or counterfeit Clean Air Sticker knowing it to be false, forged, or counterfeited.

(3) Acquires, possesses, sells, or offers for sale a counterfeit Clean Air Sticker.

(4) Acquires, possesses, sells, or offers for sale a genuine Clean Air Sticker separate from the vehicle for which the department issued that sticker.

(f) As used in this section, "Clean Air Sticker" means a label or decal issued pursuant to Sections 5205.5 and 21655.9. *(Stats.1959, c. 3, p. 1563, § 4463. Amended by Stats.1967, c. 1110, p. 2755, § 3; Stats.1971, c. 605, p. 1209, § 1, operative May 3, 1972; Stats.1976, c. 1139, p. 5171, § 335, operative July 1, 1977; Stats.1980, c. 589, p. 1601, § 1; Stats.1982, c. 975, p. 3490, § 3; Stats.1985, c. 623, § 1; Stats.1988, c. 624, § 2; Stats.1991, c. 630 (A.B.1346), § 1; Stats.1994, c. 1149 (A.B.2878), § 3; Stats.2000, c. 524 (A.B.1792), § 3; Stats.2008, c. 417 (S.B.1720), § 1; Stats.2009, c. 415 (A.B.144), § 3; Stats. 2011, c. 15 (A.B.109), § 600, eff. April 4, 2011, operative Oct. 1, 2011.)*

Cross References

Certificate of ownership and registration card, see Vehicle Code § 4450.

Cigarette tax stamps or meter impressions, counterfeiting, see Revenue and Taxation Code § 30473.

Counterfeiting, see Penal Code § 470 et seq.

Endorsement of certificate of ownership upon transfer, see Vehicle Code § 5750 et seq.

Fines, disabled parking restrictions, see Penal Code § 1465.6.

Off-highway vehicles, applicability of registration provisions, see Vehicle Code § 38100.

Parking penalties, additional assessments, see Vehicle Code § 40203.6.

Procedure upon registration, see Vehicle Code § 4150 et seq.

Surrender of evidences of registration, see Vehicle Code § 8802.

Suspension, revocation or cancellation of registration, see Vehicle Code § 8800 et seq.

Violation as misdemeanor, see Vehicle Code § 40000.7.

§ 4463.3. Additional civil penalties; convictions; forgery, alteration, counterfeit or falsification of disabled person placard

In addition to, or instead of, any fine imposed for conviction of a violation of subdivision (b) or (c) of Section 4463, the court may impose a civil penalty of not more than two thousand five hundred dollars ($2,500) for each conviction. *(Added by Stats.2000, c. 215 (A.B.1276), § 2.)*

§ 4463.5. Decorative or facsimile license plates; authorization; punishment for violation

(a) No person shall manufacture or sell a decorative or facsimile license plate of a size substantially similar to the license plate issued by the department.

(b) Notwithstanding subdivision (a), the director may authorize the manufacture and sale of decorative or facsimile license plates for special events or media productions.

(c) A violation of this section is a misdemeanor punishable by a fine of not less than five hundred dollars ($500). *(Added by Stats.1986, c. 859, § 1.)*

Cross References

Violation as misdemeanor, see Vehicle Code § 40000.7.

§ 4464. Altered license plates

A person shall not display upon a vehicle a license plate that is altered from its original markings. *(Added by Stats.1959, c. 1478, p. 3772, § 2. Amended by Stats. 2012, c. 702 (A.B.2489), § 2.)*

Cross References

Off-highway vehicles, applicability of registration provisions, see Vehicle Code § 38100.

Violation as misdemeanor, punishment, see Vehicle Code § 42002.

§ 4465. Information for legal owner; compliance with federal law and rules; elimination of restrictions on consumer access to titling, branding, and theft information

(a) A legal owner of record of a vehicle may request, and the department shall furnish, information regarding the current registration status of the vehicle, including the license plate number and address of the registered owner

of the vehicle. The department may charge a fee to pay for the cost of furnishing this information.

(b)(1) By January 1, 2010, the department shall be in full compliance with the federal Anti Car Theft Act of 1992 (P.L. 102–519)[1] and the United States Department of Justice (DOJ) rules governing the federal National Motor Vehicle Title Information System (NMVTIS) (49 U.S.C. Sec. 30501 et seq.), to the extent practicable.

(2) Notwithstanding paragraph (1), by January 1, 2010, the department shall eliminate any restrictions to consumer access to titling, branding, and theft information provided by the department to NMVTIS, to ensure that prospective purchasers have instant and reliable access to California's data. *(Added by Stats.1975, c. 1220, p. 3082, § 3. Amended by Stats.2009, c. 461 (A.B.647), § 2; Stats.2010, c. 328 (S.B.1330), § 226.)*

[1] Public law sections classified to U.S.C.A., see U.S.C.A. Tables.

§ 4466. Duplicate or substitute certificate of title or license plate; different address; verification

(a) The department shall not issue a duplicate or substitute certificate of title or license plate if, after a search of the records of the department, the registered owner's address, as submitted on the application, is different from that which appears in the records of the department, unless the registered owner applies in person and presents all of the following:

(1) Proof of ownership of the vehicle that is acceptable to the department. Proof of ownership may be the certificate of title, registration certificate, or registration renewal notice, or a facsimile or photocopy of any of those documents, if the facsimile or photocopy matches the vehicle record of the department.

(2) A driver's license or identification card containing a picture of the licensee or cardholder issued to the registered owner by the department pursuant to Chapter 1 (commencing with Section 12500) of Division 6. The department shall conduct a search of its records to verify the authenticity of any document submitted under this paragraph.

(A) If the registered owner is a resident of another state or country, the registered owner shall present a driver's license or identification card issued by that state or country. In addition, the registered owner shall provide photo documentation in the form of a valid passport, military identification card, identification card issued by a state or United States government agency, student identification card issued by a college or university, or identification card issued by a California-based employer. If a resident of another state is unable to present the required photo identification, the department shall verify the authenticity of the driver's license or identification card by contacting the state that issued the driver's license or identification card.

(B) If the registered owner is not an individual, the person submitting the application shall submit the photo identification required pursuant to this paragraph, as well as documentation acceptable to the department that demonstrates that the person is employed by an officer of the registered owner.

(3) If the application is for the purpose of replacing a license plate that was stolen, a copy of a police report identifying the plate as stolen.

(4) If the application is for the purpose of replacing a certificate of title or license plate that was mutilated or destroyed, the remnants of the mutilated or destroyed document or plate.

(5) If the department has a record of a prior issuance of a duplicate or substitute certificate of title or license plate for the vehicle within the past 90 days, a copy of a report from the Department of the California Highway Patrol verifying the vehicle identification number of the vehicle.

(b) Subdivision (a) does not apply if any of the following applies:

(1) The registered owner's name, address, and driver's license or identification card number submitted on the application match the name, address, and driver's license or identification card number contained in the department's records.

(2) An application for a duplicate or substitute certificate of title or license plate is submitted by or through one of the following:

(A) A legal owner, if the legal owner is not the same person as the registered owner or as the lessee under Section 4453.5.

(B) A dealer or an agent of the dealer.

(C) A dismantler.

(D) An insurer or an agent of the insurer.

(E) A salvage pool.

(c) At the discretion of the department, subdivision (a) does not apply in any of the following circumstances:

(1) An application for a duplicate or substitute certificate of title or license plate is submitted by a licensed registration service representing any of the following:

(A) A person or entity listed in subparagraphs (A) to (E), inclusive, of paragraph (2) of subdivision (b).

(B) A business entity recognized under the laws of this state or the laws of any foreign or domestic jurisdiction whose laws are in parity with the laws of this state.

(C) A court-appointed bankruptcy referee.

(D) A person who is an individual, is not included in subparagraphs (A) to (C), inclusive, and submits to the licensed registration service an application with a signature that is validated by a notary public. The licensed registration service shall maintain full and complete records of its transactions conducted pursuant to this subparagraph and shall make those records available for inspection by an investigator of the Department of Motor Vehicles, investigator of the Department of the California

Highway Patrol, a city police department, a county sheriff's office, or a district attorney's office, if the investigator requests access to the record and the request is for the purpose of a criminal investigation.

(2) The vehicle is registered under the International Registration Plan pursuant to Section 8052 or under the Permanent Fleet Registration program pursuant to Article 9.5 (commencing with Section 5301).

(3) The vehicle is an implement of husbandry, as defined in Section 36000, or a tow dolly, or has been issued an identification plate under Section 5014 or 5014.1.

(d) The department shall issue one or more license plates only to the registered owner or lessee. The department shall issue the certificate of title only to the legal owner, or if none, then to the registered owner, as shown on the department's records. *(Added by Stats. 2004, c. 430 (A.B.2606), § 1.5, operative Jan. 1, 2008. Amended by Stats.2009, c. 481 (A.B.873), § 1; Stats.2010, c. 328 (S.B.1330), § 227.)*

§ 4467. Victims of domestic violence, stalking, rape, and sexual battery; application for new and different license plates; conditions of issuance

(a) Notwithstanding any other provision of law, the department shall issue new and different license plates immediately upon request to the registered owner of a vehicle who appears in person and submits a completed application, if all of the following are provided:

(1) Proof of ownership of the vehicle that is acceptable to the department.

(2) A driver's license or identification card containing a picture of the licensee or cardholder issued to the registered owner by the department pursuant to Chapter 1 (commencing with Section 12500) of Division 6. The department shall conduct a search of its records to verify the authenticity of any document submitted under this paragraph.

(3) The previously issued license plates from the vehicle.

(4) The payment of required fees under subdivision (c) of Section 4850 and subdivision (b) of Section 9265 for the issuance of duplicate license plates.

(5) One of the following:

(A) A copy of a police report, court documentation, or other law enforcement documentation identifying the registered owner of the vehicle as the victim of an incident of domestic violence, as specified in Section 1708. 6 of the Civil Code, the subject of stalking, as specified in Section 1708.7 of the Civil Code or Section 646.9 of the Penal Code, the victim of a rape, as defined in Section 261 or 262 of the Penal Code, or the victim of a sexual battery, as defined in Section 1708.5 of the Civil Code.

(B) A written acknowledgment, dated within 30 days of submission, on the letterhead of a domestic violence agency or a rape crisis center, that the registered owner is actively seeking assistance or has sought assistance from that agency within the past year.

(C) An active protective order as defined in Section 6218 of the Family Code, or issued pursuant to Section 527.6 or 527.8 of the Code of Civil Procedure, which names the registered owner as a protected party.

(b) Subdivision (a) does not apply to special license plates issued under Article 8 (commencing with Section 5000) of Chapter 1 of Division 3, special interest license plates issued under Article 8.4 (commencing with Section 5060) of Chapter 1 of Division 3, or environmental license plates issued under Article 8.5 (commencing with Section 5100) of Chapter 1 of Division 3. *(Added by Stats.2002, c. 80 (A.B.1915), § 1. Amended by Stats.2003, c. 153 (S.B.378), § 1; Stats.2005, c. 60 (A.B.70), § 1.)*

Cross References

Certificate of ownership and registration card, issuance, see Vehicle Code § 4450.
Domestic violence, defined, see Family Code § 6211.
Domestic Violence Centers Act, public social services, generally, see Welfare and Institutions Code § 18920 et seq.
Domestic Violence Prevention Act, generally, see Family Code § 6200 et seq.
Law Enforcement Response to Domestic Violence, generally, see Penal Code § 13700 et seq.
Legal owner defined, see Vehicle Code § 370.
Owner defined, see Vehicle Code § 460.
Registered owner defined, see Vehicle Code § 505.

ARTICLE 5.   RENEWAL OF REGISTRATION

Section
4600.   Certificates of ownership.
4601.   Expiration and renewal of registration.
4601.5.   Exceptions to expiration and renewal of registration requirements.
4601.9.   Repealed.
4602.   Application for renewal.
4602.1.   Repealed.
4602.2.   Repealed.
4602.5.   Repealed.
4603.   Extension of renewal period.
4604.   Nonrenewal; certification required; filing period; fee; exemptions; subsequent registration.
4604.2.   Nonoperation certificate; requirements; payment of fees.
4604.5.   Filing after expiration of vehicle registration; penalty.
4605.   Stolen or embezzled vehicles; accrual of fees or penalties; owner certificate.
4606.   Operation pending renewal.
4607.   New card.
4608.   Repealed.
4609.   Plates, issuance of series.
4610.   Motor clubs.
4611.   Renumbered.

Cross References

Original registration, see Vehicle Code § 4150 et seq.

Refusal of renewal of registration, grounds, see Vehicle Code §§ 4750, 4751.

§ 4600.   Certificates of ownership

Certificates of ownership shall not be renewed annually but shall remain valid until suspended, revoked, or canceled by the department for cause or upon a transfer of any interest shown therein. *(Stats.1959, c. 3, p. 1564, § 4600.)*

Cross References

Applicability of this section to trolley coaches, see Vehicle Code § 21051.
Cancellation, revocation or suspension of license, see Vehicle Code § 13100 et seq.
Certificate of ownership, issuance, see Vehicle Code § 4450.
Transfers of title or interest, see Vehicle Code § 5600 et seq.

§ 4601.   Expiration and renewal of registration

(a) Except as otherwise provided in this code, every vehicle registration and registration card expires at midnight on the expiration date designated by the director pursuant to Section 1651.5, and shall be renewed prior to the expiration of the registration year. The department may, upon payment of the proper fees, renew the registration of vehicles.

(b) Notwithstanding any other provision of law, renewal of registration for any vehicle that is either currently registered or for which a certification pursuant to Section 4604 has been filed may be obtained not more than 75 days prior to the expiration of the current registration or certification.

(c) Notwithstanding subdivision (b) or any other law, commencing upon the effective date of the act[1] that added this subdivision, the renewal of registration for a vehicle that expires on or before June 30, 2011, may be obtained not more than 75 days prior to the expiration of the current registration or certification and the renewal of registration for a vehicle that expires on or after July 1, 2011, or for which a certification, pursuant to Section 4604, has been filed, may not be obtained until the expiration of the current registration or certification or until the department has issued a notice of renewal, whichever occurs first. This subdivision shall become inoperative on January 1, 2012. *(Added by Stats.1974, c. 1330, p. 2893, § 17, eff. Sept. 26, 1974, operative March 8, 1976. Amended by Stats.1983, c. 142, § 163; Stats.1992, c. 1243 (A.B.3090), § 64, eff. Sept. 30, 1992; Stats.2005, c. 270 (S.B.731), § 10; Stats.2011, c. 21 (S.B.94), § 4, eff. May 4, 2011.)*

[1] Stats.2011, c. 21 (S.B.94), eff. May 4, 2011.

Cross References

Applicability of this section to trolley coaches, see Vehicle Code § 21051.
Occupational licenses and special plates, application for renewal, see Vehicle Code § 11717.
Operation of vehicle pending renewal, see Vehicle Code § 4606.
Payment of license fee at time of renewal of registration, see Revenue and Taxation Code § 10851.

Penalty for delinquent renewal of registration, see Vehicle Code § 9553.

Publicly owned vehicles, registration, see Vehicle Code § 4155.

Registration fees, generally, see Vehicle Code § 9250 et seq.

Renewal of registration, issuance of registration cards, see Vehicle Code § 4607.

Renewal of registration subsequent to the expiration of the registration, see Vehicle Code § 4604.

Seizure of plates on expiration of registration, see Vehicle Code § 4460.

§ 4601.5. Exceptions to expiration and renewal of registration requirements

Notwithstanding Section 4601, the registration for vehicles registered pursuant to the Partial Year Registration Program as described in Article 5 (commencing with Section 9700) of Chapter 6 of Division 3, expires at midnight of December 31 of the registration year. However, for the purposes of applying any future reductions or increases in the vehicle license fee, the vehicle registrations subject to this section shall be deemed to have a final expiration date in the succeeding calendar year. *(Added by Stats.2001, c. 868 (A.B.1621), § 1. Amended by Stats.2006, c. 169 (A.B.2736), § 2.)*

Cross References

Apportioned registration, federal motor vehicle safety program, see Vehicle Code § 8100 et seq.

Registration renewal fee, apportioned increase or decrease, see Vehicle Code § 9559.5.

§ 4601.9. Repealed by Stats.1975, c. 393, p. 871, § 1, operative March 8, 1976

§ 4602. Application for renewal

Application for renewal of a vehicle registration shall be made by the owner not later than midnight of the expiration date, and shall be made by presentation of the registration card last issued for the vehicle or by presentation of a potential registration card issued by the department for use at the time of renewal and by payment of the full registration year fee for the vehicle as provided in this code. If the registration card and potential registration card are unavailable, a fee as specified in Section 9265 shall not be paid. *(Stats.1959, c. 3, § 4602. Amended by Stats.1970, c. 943, § 1; Stats.1971, c. 1507, § 6, eff. Nov. 12, 1971, operative May 3, 1972; Stats.1973, c. 889, § 27, eff. Sept. 28, 1973, operative March 10, 1975; Stats.1974, c. 670, § 2; Stats.1974, c. 670, § 3, operative March 10, 1975; Stats.1975, c. 957, § 24; Stats.1975, c. 957, § 25, operative March 8, 1976; Stats.1975, c. 393, § 2; Stats.1983, c. 142, § 164; Stats.1988, c. 1268, § 2.)*

Cross References

Applicability of this section to trolley coaches, see Vehicle Code § 21051.

Application for registration,

Generally, see Vehicle Code § 4150.

Special vehicles, see Vehicle Code § 4153.

Vehicles previously registered outside state, see Vehicle Code § 4300 et seq.

Duplicate and substitute registration card fees, see Vehicle Code § 9265.

Issuance of registration card, see Vehicle Code § 4450.

Registration fees, generally, see Vehicle Code § 9250 et seq.

Renewal of registration for vehicles not operated, see Vehicle Code § 4604.

Use of vehicle pending renewal, see Vehicle Code § 4606.

§ 4602.1. Repealed by Stats.1995, c. 766 (S.B.726), § 6

§ 4602.2. Repealed by Stats.1982, c. 1346, p. 5035, § 9

§ 4602.5. Repealed by Stats.1973, c. 774, p. 1386, § 1

§ 4603. Extension of renewal period

Whenever in his opinion the interests of the State will be promoted thereby, the director with the approval of the Governor may extend for a period not to exceed 10 days the closing of the period during which applications for renewal of registration may be presented without the payment of penalties. *(Stats.1959, c. 3, p. 1564, § 4603.)*

Cross References

Applicability of this section to trolley coaches, see Vehicle Code § 21051.

Penalty for delinquent registration fee, see Vehicle Code § 9553.

§ 4604. Nonrenewal; certification required; filing period; fee; exemptions; subsequent registration

(a) Except as otherwise provided in subdivision (d), prior to the expiration of the registration of a vehicle, if that registration is not to be renewed prior to its expiration, the owner of the vehicle shall file, under penalty of perjury, a certification that the vehicle will not be operated, moved, or left standing upon a highway without first making an application for registration of the vehicle, including full payment of all fees. The certification is valid until the vehicle's registration is renewed pursuant to subdivision (c).

(b) Each certification filed pursuant to subdivision (a) shall be accompanied by a filing fee of fifteen dollars ($15).

(c)(1) An application for renewal of registration, except when accompanied by an application for transfer of title to, or an interest in, the vehicle, shall be submitted to the department with payment of the required fees for the current registration year and without penalty for delinquent payment of fees imposed under this code or under Part 5 (commencing with Section 10701) of Division 2 of the Revenue and Taxation Code if the department receives the application prior to or on the date the vehicle is first operated, moved, or left standing upon a highway during the current registration year and the certification required pursuant to subdivision (a) was timely filed with the department.

(2) If an application for renewal of registration is accompanied by an application for transfer of title, that application may be made without incurring a penalty for delinquent payment of fees not later than 20 days after the date the vehicle is first operated, moved, or left

169

standing on a highway if a certification pursuant to subdivision (a) was timely filed with the department.

(d) A certification is not required to be filed pursuant to subdivision (a) for one or more of the following:

(1) A vehicle on which the registration expires while being held as inventory by a dealer or lessor-retailer or while being held pending a lien sale by the keeper of a garage or operator of a towing service.

(2) A vehicle registered pursuant to Article 4 (commencing with Section 8050) of Chapter 4 of Division 3.

(3) A vehicle described in Section 5004, 5004.5, or 5051, as provided in Section 4604.2. However, the registered owner may file a certificate of nonoperation in lieu of the certification specified in subdivision (a).

(4) A vehicle registered pursuant to Article 5 (commencing with Section 9700) of Chapter 6 if the registered owner has complied with subdivision (c) of Section 9706.

(e) Notwithstanding Section 670, for purposes of this section, a "vehicle" is a device by which a person or property may be propelled, moved, or driven upon a highway having intact and assembled its major component parts including, but not limited to, the frame or chassis, cowl, and floor pan or, in the case of a trailer, the frame and wheels or, in the case of a motorcycle, the frame, front fork, and engine. For purposes of this section, "vehicle" does not include a device moved exclusively by human power, a device used exclusively upon stationary rails or tracks, or a motorized wheelchair. *(Added by Stats.1990, c. 1352 (A.B.2912), § 5, eff. Sept. 27, 1990, operative July 1, 1990. Amended by Stats.1991, c. 362 (A.B.1974), § 1, eff. Aug. 30, 1991; Stats.1993, c. 272 (A.B.301), § 15, eff. Aug. 2, 1993; Stats.1994, c. 1221 (S.B.1758), § 4; Stats.1996, c. 504 (S.B.2162), § 1; Stats. 2003, c. 719 (S.B.1055), § 5; Stats.2006, c. 574 (A.B. 2520), § 4.)*

Cross References

Applicability of this section to trolley coaches, see Vehicle Code § 21051.

Application of this section to fleet vehicle registration, see Vehicle Code § 5302.

Base fee amounts, adjustment of fees, see Vehicle Code § 1678.

Inapplicability of this section to renewal of registration of trailer coach, see Vehicle Code § 5351.

Penalty for delinquent registration fee, see Vehicle Code § 9553.

Registration fees, generally, see Vehicle Code § 9250 et seq.

Registration of fleet vehicles, see Vehicle Code § 5301 et seq.

§ 4604.2. Nonoperation certificate; requirements; payment of fees

(a) When the registration of a vehicle registered on a partial year basis has expired and the vehicle is not thereafter operated, moved, or left standing upon a highway, and the vehicle is in compliance with subdivision (b) of Section 9706 applying to vehicles registered on a partial year basis, an application for renewal made subsequent to that expiration shall be accompanied by a certificate of nonoperation.

170

(b) An application for registration or renewal of registration of a vehicle described in Section 5004 or 5004.5 that has not been operated, moved, or left standing upon a highway shall be accompanied by a certificate of nonoperation for the period during which the vehicle was not registered.

(c) A certificate of nonoperation may be accepted for a vehicle registered pursuant to Article 4 (commencing with Section 8050) of Chapter 4 solely for the purpose of waiver of penalties.

(d) The application for registration or renewal of registration of vehicles specified in subdivisions (a) and (b), whether or not accompanied by an application for transfer of title, shall be accepted by the department upon payment of the proper fees for the current registration year without the payment of delinquent fees imposed under this code or Part 5 (commencing with Section 10701) of Division 2 of the Revenue and Taxation Code if the department receives the application and certificate of nonoperation prior to the date the vehicle is first operated, moved, or left standing upon a highway during the current registration year. *(Added by Stats.1991, c. 362 (A.B.1974), § 2, eff. Aug. 30, 1991. Amended by Stats. 1992, c. 1243 (A.B.3090), § 66, eff. Sept. 30, 1992; Stats.2006, c. 574 (A.B.2520), § 5.)*

§ 4604.5. Filing after expiration of vehicle registration; penalty

(a)(1) If the vehicle has not been operated, moved, or left standing upon any highway subsequent to the expiration of the vehicle's registration, the certification specified in Section 4604 or 4604.2 may be filed after the expiration of the registration of a vehicle, but not later than 90 days after the expiration date, subject to the payment of the filing fee specified in Section 4604 and the penalty specified in paragraph (2).

(2) A penalty shall be collected on any certification specified in Section 4604 or 4604.2 filed later than midnight of the date of expiration of registration. The penalty shall be computed as provided in Sections 9406 and 9559 and after the registration and weight fees have been combined with the license fee specified in Section 10751 of the Revenue and Taxation Code, as follows:

(A) For a delinquency period of 10 days or less, the penalty is 10 percent of the fee.

(B) For a delinquency period of more than 10 days, to and including 30 days, the penalty is 20 percent of the fee.

(C) For a delinquency period of more than 30 days, to and including 90 days, the penalty is 60 percent of the fee.

(3) This subdivision applies to the renewal of registration for vehicles with expiration dates on or before December 31, 2002.

(b) The certification specified in Sections 4604 and 4604.2 may be filed no more than 90 days after the expiration of the registration of a vehicle if the vehicle has not been operated, moved, or left standing upon any highway subsequent to the expiration of the vehicle's registration. A penalty shall be collected on any certification specified in Section 4604 or 4604.2 filed later than midnight of the date of expiration of registration. After 90 days, the vehicle must be registered pursuant to Section 4601. A certification filed pursuant to this subdivision is subject to the payment of the filing fee specified in Section 4604 and the payment of the penalties specified in paragraphs (1), (2), and (3) of this subdivision.

(1) The penalty for late payment of the registration fee provided in Section 9250 is as follows:

(A) For a delinquency period of 10 days or less, the penalty is ten dollars ($10).

(B) For a delinquency period of more than 10 days, to and including 30 days, the penalty is fifteen dollars ($15).

(C) For a delinquency period of more than 30 days, to and including 90 days, the penalty is thirty dollars ($30).

(2) The penalty on the weight fee and the vehicle license fee shall be computed after the weight fee as provided in Section 9400 or 9400.1 plus the vehicle license fee specified in Section 10751 of the Revenue and Taxation Code have been added together as follows:

(A) For a delinquency period of 10 days or less, the penalty is 10 percent of the fee.

(B) For a delinquency period exceeding 10 days, to and including 30 days, the penalty is 20 percent of the fee.

(C) For a delinquency period of more than 30 days, to and including 90 days, the penalty is 60 percent of the fee.

(3) Weight fees not reported and not paid within 20 days, as required by Section 9406, shall be assessed a penalty on the difference in the weight fee, as follows:

(A) For a delinquency period of 10 days or less, the penalty is 10 percent of the fee.

(B) For a delinquency period exceeding 10 days, to and including 30 days, the penalty is 20 percent of the fee.

(C) For a delinquency period of more than 30 days, to and including 90 days, the penalty is 60 percent of the fee.

(c) This section shall apply to registration renewals that expire on or after January 1, 2003. *(Added by Stats.1996, c. 504 (S.B.2162), § 2. Amended by Stats. 1999, c. 724 (A.B.1650), § 30; Stats.2002, c. 805 (A.B. 2996), § 12, eff. Sept. 23, 2002.)*

§ 4605. Stolen or embezzled vehicles; accrual of fees or penalties; owner certificate

Notwithstanding Section 4000 of this code, and notwithstanding Section 38020 of this code, no fees or penalties imposed under this code or under Part 5 (commencing with Section 10701) of Division 2 of the Revenue and Taxation Code shall accrue due to operation of a vehicle in conjunction with the theft or embezzlement of the vehicle if the owner or legal owner submits a certificate in writing setting forth the circumstances of the theft or embezzlement and certifies that the theft or embezzlement of the vehicle has been

reported pursuant to the provisions of this code. *(Added by Stats.1976, c. 935, p. 2142, § 3.)*

Cross References

Applicability of this section to trolley coaches, see Vehicle Code § 21051.
Evidences of registration, see Vehicle Code § 4450 et seq.
Legal owner defined, see Vehicle Code § 370.
Owner defined, see Vehicle Code § 460.
Penalty for late application for renewal of identification for off-highway motor vehicles, exception of this section, see Vehicle Code § 38246.
Registered owner defined, see Vehicle Code § 505.
Reports of stolen vehicles, generally, see Vehicle Code § 10500 et seq.

§ 4606. Operation pending renewal

Notwithstanding any provision of subdivision (a) of Section 5204 to the contrary, when an application for the registration of a vehicle has been made as required in Sections 4152.5 and 4602, the vehicle may be operated on the highways until the new indicia of current registration have been received from the department, upon condition that there be displayed on the vehicle the license plates and validating devices, if any, issued to the vehicle for the previous registration year. *(Stats.1959, c. 3, p. 1565, § 4606. Amended by Stats.1959, c. 1, p. 594, § 6; Stats.1973, c. 889, p. 1653, § 30, eff. Sept. 28, 1973, operative March 10, 1975; Stats.1992, c. 258 (S.B.133), § 1.)*

Cross References

Applicability of this section to trolley coaches, see Vehicle Code § 21051.
Display of license plates, tabs and stickers, see Vehicle Code § 5200 et seq.
Improper display of registration card, license plate or permit, see Vehicle Code § 4462.

§ 4607. New card

The department, upon renewing a registration, shall issue a new registration card to the owner as upon an original registration. *(Stats.1959, c. 3, p. 1565, § 4607.)*

Cross References

Applicability of this section to trolley coaches, see Vehicle Code § 21051.
Issuance of registration card, see Vehicle Code § 4450.

§ 4608. Repealed by Stats.1998, c. 828 (S.B.1637), § 12

§ 4609. Plates, issuance of series

The department may extend the life of the current series of license plates, outstanding during 1957, and may hereafter issue a new series of license plates for an indefinite period of time, but in no event for a period less than five (5) years. During each intervening year of the period for which the plates are issued, the department shall issue a tab, sticker, or other suitable device as herein provided.

Any such series of plates may be canceled by the director with the approval of the Governor at any time after five years from the year of issuance of such series. *(Stats.1959, c. 3, p. 1565, § 4609.)*

Cross References

Applicability of this section to trolley coaches, see Vehicle Code § 21051.

Display of license plates, tabs and stickers, see Vehicle Code § 5200.

Issuance of reflectorized license plates, see Vehicle Code § 4850.

§ 4610. Motor clubs

The department may authorize an endorsement of a receipt or the validation of a registration card or potential registration card as provided in this code by a person or organization holding a certificate of authority issued under the provisions of Part 5 (commencing with Section 12140) of Division 2 of the Insurance Code. *(Stats.1959, c. 3, p. 1565, § 4610. Amended by Stats.1982, c. 454, p. 1893, § 181.)*

Cross References

Applicability of this section to trolley coaches, see Vehicle Code § 21051.

Certificate of authority, in general, see Insurance Code § 12160 et seq.

Delinquent renewal of registration, see Vehicle Code § 9556.

Transmittal of fees by mail, see Vehicle Code § 9557.

§ 4611. Renumbered § 4152.5 and amended by Stats. 1973, c. 889, p. 1644, § 31, urgency, eff. Sept. 28, 1973, operative March 10, 1975

ARTICLE 5.5. VOLUNTARY COMMON REGISTRATION RENEWAL DATES [REPEALED]

§§ 4650 to 4655. Repealed by Stats.1998, c. 828 (S.B. 1637), § 14

ARTICLE 6. REFUSAL OF REGISTRATION

Section
4750.   Grounds requiring refusal.
4750.1. Application for registration of specialty constructed passenger vehicle or pickup truck; assignment of model-year; amnesty program participation fee.
4750.2. Repealed.
4750.4. Information provided by insurers; use by law enforcement agencies.
4750.5. Withholding of registration; nonpayment of use tax.
4751.   Grounds permitting refusal.
4755.   Refusal of registration, renewal, or transfer of registration for commercial motor vehicles subject to Section 4000.6.
4760.   Failure to pay parking penalties and administration fees; receipt for payment; abstract or notice of disposition to renter or lessor of vehicle; citations issued prior to registered owner taking possession of vehicle.

Section
4760.1. Driver's license record check.
4761.   Amount of unpaid parking penalties and administrative fees, and jurisdiction issuing notice on potential registration card.
4762.   Remitting parking penalties and administrative fees collected.
4763.   Fee for recording notice of delinquent parking violation.
4764.   Transfer of vehicle or nonrenewal of registration; department not required to attempt collection of parking penalty; application of section.
4764.1. Repealed.
4764.2. Repealed.
4764.3, 4764.4.   Repealed.
4765.   Obligation to pay parking penalties and administrative fees.
4766.   Notice of noncompliance without certificate of adjudication; notice to department; conditions for renewal of registration.
4767.   Delinquent parking or toll violations; payment or notice of disposition from court or designated processing agency prior to transfer; application of section.

§ 4750. Grounds requiring refusal

The department shall refuse registration, or renewal or transfer of registration, upon any of the following grounds:

(a) The application contains any false or fraudulent statement.

(b) The required fee has not been paid.

(c) The registration, or renewal or transfer of registration, is prohibited by the requirements of Part 5 (commencing with Section 43000) of Division 26 of the Health and Safety Code.

(d) The owner of a heavy vehicle, which is subject to the heavy vehicle use tax imposed pursuant to Section 4481 of Title 26 of the United States Code, has not presented sufficient evidence, as determined by the department, that the tax for the vehicle has been paid pursuant to that section.

(e) Evidence of financial responsibility, that is required for a vehicle registration renewal where there is no change in registered owner, has not been provided to the department pursuant to Section 4000.37 or electronically. This subdivision does not apply to any of the following:

(1) A vehicle for which a certification has been filed pursuant to Section 4604, until the vehicle is registered for operation upon the highway.

(2) A vehicle owned or leased by, or under the direction of, the United States or any public entity that is included in Section 811.2 of the Government Code.

(3) A vehicle registration renewal application where there is a change of registered owner. *(Added by Stats.1985, c. 245, § 2. Amended by Stats.1999, c. 880 (S.B.652), § 7.)*

Cross References

Applicability of this section to trolley coaches, see Vehicle Code § 21051.

Application for apportioned registration, grounds for refusal, see Vehicle Code § 8101.

False statements, see Vehicle Code § 20.

Grounds permitting refusal of registration, see Vehicle Code § 4751.

Registration fees, generally, see Vehicle Code § 9250 et seq.

Registration of dismantled vehicle, see Vehicle Code § 11519.

Suspension, cancellation or revocation of registration, see Vehicle Code § 8800 et seq.

Vehicular air pollution control, see Health and Safety Code § 43000 et seq.

§ 4750.1. Application for registration of specialty constructed passenger vehicle or pickup truck; assignment of model-year; amnesty program participation fee

(a) If the department receives an application for registration of a specially constructed passenger vehicle or pickup truck after it has registered 500 specially constructed vehicles during that calendar year pursuant to Section 44017.4 of the Health and Safety Code, and the vehicle has not been previously registered, the vehicle shall be assigned the same model-year as the calendar year in which the application is submitted, for purposes of determining emissions inspection requirements for the vehicle.

(b)(1) If the department receives an application for registration of a specially constructed passenger vehicle or pickup truck that has been previously registered after it has registered 500 specially constructed vehicles during that calendar year pursuant to Section 44017.4 of the Health and Safety Code, and the application requests a model-year determination different from the model-year assigned in the previous registration, the application for registration shall be denied and the vehicle owner is subject to the emission control and inspection requirements applicable to the model-year assigned in the previous registration.

(2) For a vehicle participating in the amnesty program in effect from July 1, 2011, to June 30, 2012, pursuant to Section 9565, the model-year of the previous registration shall be the calendar year of the year in which the vehicle owner applied for amnesty. However, a denial of an application for registration issued pursuant to this paragraph does not preclude the vehicle owner from applying for a different model-year determination and application for registration under Section 44017.4 of the Health and Safety Code in a subsequent calendar year.

(c)(1) The Bureau of Automotive Repair may charge the vehicle owner who applies to participate in the amnesty program a fee for each referee station inspection conducted pursuant to Section 9565. The fee shall be one hundred sixty dollars ($160) and shall be collected by the referee station performing the inspection.

(2) A contract to perform referee services may authorize direct compensation to the referee contractor from the inspection fees collected pursuant to paragraph (1). The referee contractor shall deposit the inspection fees collected from the vehicle owner into a separate trust account that the referee contractor shall account for and manage in accordance with generally accepted accounting standards and principles. Where the department conducts the inspections pursuant to Section 9565, the inspection fees collected by the department shall be deposited into the Vehicle Inspection and Repair Fund. *(Added by Stats.2002, c. 693 (S.B.1578), § 2. Amended by Stats.2008, c. 420 (A.B.619), § 2; Stats.2009, c. 235 (A.B.318), § 1; Stats.2010, c. 388 (A.B.2461), § 1.)*

§ 4750.2. Repealed by Stats.2004, c. 193 (S.B.111), § 193

Law Revision Commission Comments

2004 Repeal

Section 4750.2 is repealed as obsolete. The required report was to be completed by December 1, 1992. [33 Cal.L.Rev. Comm. Reports 494 (2004)].

§ 4750.4. Information provided by insurers; use by law enforcement agencies

Information provided by an insurer to the department pursuant to Section 11580.10 of the Insurance Code and former Section 4750.2, as added by Chapter 946 of the Statutes of 1991, shall be made available only to law enforcement agencies for law enforcement purposes. *(Added by Stats.1991, c. 946 (S.B.228), § 5. Amended by Stats.2004, c. 193 (S.B.111), § 194.)*

Law Revision Commission Comments

2004 Amendment

Section 4750.4 is amended to reflect the repeal of former Section 4750.2. [33 Cal.L.Rev.Comm. Reports 495 (2004)].

Cross References

Inspection of public records, exemptions from disclosure, Department of Motor Vehicles, information provided by insurer, see Government Code § 6276.14.

§ 4750.5. Withholding of registration; nonpayment of use tax

(a) The department shall withhold the registration or the transfer of registration of any vehicle sold at retail to any applicant by any person other than a vehicle manufacturer or dealer holding a license and certificate issued pursuant to Chapter 4 (commencing with Section 11700) of Division 5, or an automobile dismantler holding a license and certificate issued pursuant to Chapter 3 (commencing with Section 11500) of Division 5, or a lessor-retailer holding a license issued pursuant to Chapter 3.5 (commencing with Section 11600) of Division 5, and subject to the provisions of Section 11615.5, until the applicant pays to the department the use tax measured by the sales price of the vehicle as required by the Sales and Use Tax Law (Part 1 (commencing with Section 6001) of Division 2 of the Revenue and Taxation Code), together with penalty, if any, unless the State Board of Equalization finds that no use tax is due. If the applicant so desires, he may pay the use tax and penalty, if any, to the department so as to secure immediate action upon his application for registration or transfer of registration, and thereafter he may apply through the Department of Motor Vehicles to the State Board of Equalization under the provisions of the Sales and Use Tax Law for a refund of the amount so paid.

(b) The department shall transmit to the State Board of Equalization all collections of use tax and penalty made under this section. This transmittal shall be made at least monthly, accompanied by a schedule in such form as the department and board may prescribe.

(c) The State Board of Equalization shall reimburse the department for its costs incurred in carrying out the provisions of this section. Such reimbursement shall be effected under agreement between the agencies, approved by the Department of Finance.

(d) In computing any use tax or penalty thereon under the provisions of this section, dollar fractions shall be disregarded in the manner specified in Section 9559 of this code. Payment of tax and penalty on this basis shall be deemed full compliance with the requirements of the Sales and Use Tax Law insofar as they are applicable to the use of vehicles to which this section relates. *(Added by Stats.1963, c. 1858, p. 3836, § 9, eff. July 19, 1963, operative Oct. 1, 1963. Amended by Stats.1965, 1st Ex.Sess., c. 2, p. 5454, § 39, eff. July 12, 1965, operative Aug. 1, 1965; Stats.1976, c. 1284, p. 5712, § 8.3.)*

Cross References

Application when retailer not subject to § 11615.5, see Revenue and Taxation Code § 6292.

§ 4751. Grounds permitting refusal

The department may refuse registration or the renewal or transfer of registration of a vehicle in any of the following events:

(a) If the department is not satisfied that the applicant is entitled thereto under this code.

(b) If the applicant has failed to furnish the department with information required in the application or reasonable additional information required by the department.

(c) If the department determines that the applicant has made or permitted unlawful use of any registration certificate, certificate of ownership, or license plates.

(d) If the vehicle is mechanically unfit or unsafe to be operated or moved on the highways.

(e) If the department determines that a manufacturer or dealer has failed during the current or previous year to comply with the provisions of this code relating to the giving of notice to the department of the transfer of a vehicle during the current or previous year.

(f) If the department determines that a lien exists, pursuant to Section 9800, against one or more other vehicles in which the applicant has an ownership interest.

(g) If the applicant has failed to furnish the department with an odometer disclosure statement pursuant to subsection (a) of Section 32705 of Title 49 of the United States Code. *(Stats.1959, c. 3, p. 1566, § 4751. Amended by Stats.1981, c. 636, p. 2403, § 3; Stats.1983, c. 759, § 4; Stats.1993, c. 852 (A.B.1485), § 3; Stats.2000, c. 1035 (S.B.1403), § 9.)*

Cross References

Applicability of this section to trolley coaches, see Vehicle Code § 21051.

Application for apportioned registration, grounds for refusal, see Vehicle Code § 8101.

Application for registration, see Vehicle Code § 4150.

Apportioned registration, reasons for suspension, see Vehicle Code § 8102.

Contents of application for registration of vehicle registered outside state, see Vehicle Code § 4300.

Refusal for false statements and non-payment of fees, see Vehicle Code § 4750.

Suspension,

Revocation and cancellation of registration, see Vehicle Code § 8800 et seq.

Revocation or refusal of renewal of automobile wrecker's certificate, see Vehicle Code § 11509.

§ 4755. Refusal of registration, renewal, or transfer of registration for commercial motor vehicles subject to Section 4000.6

The department shall refuse registration, or renewal or transfer of registration for any commercial motor vehicle subject to Section 4000.6, if the owner or operator of the motor vehicle at the time of the application has been cited for a violation, pertaining to that vehicle, of Division 26 (commencing with Section 39000) of the Health and Safety Code or regulations of the State Air Resources Board adopted pursuant to that division, until the violation has been cleared, as determined by the State Air Resources Board. *(Added by Stats.2007, c. 592 (A.B.233), § 5.)*

§ 4760. Failure to pay parking penalties and administration fees; receipt for payment; abstract or notice of disposition to renter or lessor of vehicle; citations issued prior to registered owner taking possession of vehicle

(a)(1) Except as provided in subdivision (b) or (d), the department shall refuse to renew the registration of a vehicle if the registered owner or lessee has been mailed a notice of delinquent parking violation relating to standing or parking, the processing agency has filed or electronically transmitted to the department an itemization of unpaid parking penalties, including administrative fees pursuant to Section 40220, and the owner or lessee has not paid the parking penalty and administrative fee pursuant to Section 40211, unless he or she pays to the department, at the time of application for renewal, the full amount of all outstanding parking penalties and administrative fees, as shown by records of the department.

(2) When the department receives the full amount of all outstanding parking penalties and administrative fees pursuant to paragraph (1), it shall issue a receipt showing each parking penalty and administrative fee that has been paid, the processing agency for that penalty and fee, and a description of the vehicle involved in the parking violations. The receipt shall also state that, to reduce the possibility of impoundment under Section 22651 or immobilization under Section 22651.7 of the vehicle involved in the parking violation, the registered owner or lessee may transmit to that processing agency a copy or other evidence of the receipt.

(b) The department shall not refuse to renew the registration of a vehicle owned by a renter or lessor if the applicant provides the department with the abstract or notice of disposition of parking violation issued pursuant to subdivision (c) for clearing all outstanding parking penalties and administrative fees as shown by the records of the department.

(c) The court or designated processing agency shall issue an abstract or notice of disposition of parking violation to the renter or lessor of a vehicle issued a notice of delinquent parking violation relating to standing or parking if the renter or lessor provides the court or processing agency with the name, address, and driver's license number of the rentee or lessee at the time of occurrence of the parking violation.

(d) The department shall not refuse to renew the registration of a vehicle if the citation was issued prior to the registered owner taking possession of the vehicle. *(Added by Stats.1975, c. 1179, p. 2908, § 1, operative Jan. 1, 1978. Amended by Stats.1977, c. 804, p. 2453, § 1; Stats.1981, c. 529, p. 1895, § 1; Stats.1986, c. 939, § 8; Stats.1989, c. 750, § 1; Stats.1991, c. 587 (A.B.1126), § 1, operative July 1, 1992; Stats.2008, c. 741 (A.B.2401), § 1.)*

Cross References

Notice of parking or delinquent parking violations, processing agency duties and procedure, application of this section, see Vehicle Code § 40211 et seq.

§ 4760.1. Driver's license record check

(a) The department shall, before renewing the registration of any vehicle, check the driver's license record of all registered owners for conviction of traffic violations and traffic accidents.

(b) The department shall, before renewing the registration of any vehicle, check the driver's license record of all registered owners for notices filed with the department pursuant to subdivision (a) of Section 40509 and notices that the licensee has failed to pay a lawfully imposed fine, penalty, assessment, or bail within the time authorized by the court for any violation which is required to be reported pursuant to Section 1803 and shall refuse to renew the registration of the vehicle if the driver's license record of any registered owner has any such outstanding notices to appear or failures to pay a court ordered fine, unless the department has received a certificate issued by the magistrate or clerk of the court hearing the case in which the promise was given showing that the case has been adjudicated or unless the registered owner's record is cleared as provided in Chapter 6 (commencing with Section 41500) of Division 17. In lieu of the certificate of adjudication, a notice from the court stating that the original records have been lost or destroyed shall permit the department to renew the registration.

(c) Any notice received by the department pursuant to Section 40509 which has been on file five years may be removed from the department records and destroyed, in the discretion of the department.

(d) In lieu of the certificate of adjudication or a notice from the court, the department shall with the consent of all registered owners collect the amounts which it has been notified are due pursuant to Sections 40509 and 40509.5, and authorized to be collected pursuant to Article 2 (commencing with Section 14910) of Chapter 5 of Division 6. *(Added by Stats.1991, c. 90 (A.B.1297), § 65, eff. June 30, 1991. Amended by Stats. 1991, c. 613 (A.B.195), § 10; Stats.1992, c. 635 (A.B. 1823), § 5, eff. Sept. 14, 1992.)*

§ 4761. Amount of unpaid parking penalties and administrative fees, and jurisdiction issuing notice on potential registration card

The department shall include on each potential registration card issued for use at the time of renewal, or on an accompanying document, an itemization of unpaid parking penalties, including administrative fees, showing the amount thereof and the jurisdiction which issued the notice of parking violation relating thereto, which the registered owner or lessee is required to pay pursuant to Section 4760. *(Added by Stats.1975, c. 1179, p. 2908, § 2, operative Jan. 1, 1978. Amended by Stats.1986, c. 939, § 9.)*

§ 4762. Remitting parking penalties and administrative fees collected

The department shall remit all parking penalties and administrative fees collected, after deducting the administrative fee authorized by Section 4763, for each notice of delinquent parking violation for which parking penalties and administrative fees have been collected pursuant to Section 4760, to each jurisdiction in the amounts due to each jurisdiction according to its unadjudicated notices of delinquent parking violation. Within 45 days from the time penalties are recorded by the department, the department shall inform each jurisdiction which of its notices of delinquent parking violation have been discharged. *(Added by Stats.1975, c. 1179, p. 2909, § 3, operative Jan. 1, 1978. Amended by Stats.1977, c. 804, p. 2454, § 2; Stats.1985, c. 1008, § 1; Stats.1985, c. 1289, § 1; Stats.1986, c. 939, § 10.)*

Cross References

Notice of parking or delinquent parking violations, processing agency duties and procedure, application of this section, see Vehicle Code § 40211 et seq.

Tolling of time limitations for delinquent parking violations, see Vehicle Code § 40224.

§ 4763. Fee for recording notice of delinquent parking violation

The department shall assess a fee for the recording of the notice of delinquent parking violation, which is given to the department pursuant to Section 40220, in an amount, as determined by the department, that is sufficient to provide a total amount equal to its actual costs of administering Sections 4760, 4761, 4762, 4764, and 4765. *(Added by Stats.1975, c. 1179, p. 2909, § 4, operative Jan. 1, 1978. Amended by Stats.1977, c. 804, p. 2454, § 3; Stats.1978, c. 497, p. 1632, § 1; Stats.1985, c. 1008, § 2; Stats.1986, c. 939, § 11.)*

§ 4764. Transfer of vehicle or nonrenewal of registration; department not required to attempt collection of parking penalty; application of section

* * * (a) If a vehicle is transferred or the registration is not renewed for two renewal periods and the former registered owner or lessee of the vehicle owes a parking penalty for a notice of delinquent parking violation filed with the department pursuant to Section 40220, the department shall notify each jurisdiction of that fact and is not required thereafter to attempt collection of the undeposited parking penalty and administrative fees.

(b) This section does not apply if the transfer of a vehicle is one described in Section 6285 of the Revenue and Taxation Code. *(Added by Stats.1975, c. 1179, p. 2909, § 5, operative Jan. 1, 1978. Amended by Stats.1986, c. 939, § 12; Stats.2013, c. 101 (A.B.443), § 1.)*

Cross References

Collection of unpaid parking penalty, exception for notice provided pursuant to this section, see Vehicle Code § 40220.
Collection of unpaid toll evasion penalty, exception for notice provided pursuant to this section, see Vehicle Code § 40267.
Notice of parking or delinquent parking violations, processing agency duties and procedure, application of this section, see Vehicle Code § 40211 et seq.
Tolling of time limitations for delinquent parking violations, see Vehicle Code § 40224.

§ 4764.1. Repealed by Stats.2001, c. 115 (S.B.153), § 38

Law Revision Commission Comments

2001 Repeal

Section 4764.1 is repealed as obsolete. The pilot project established by Sections 4764.1–4764.4 has expired. [30 Cal. L.Rev.Comm. Reports 327 (2000)].

§ 4764.2. Repealed by Stats.2000, c. 787 (S.B.1404), § 18

Law Revision Commission Comments

2001 Repeal

Section 4764.2 is repealed as obsolete. The pilot project established by Sections 4764.1–4764.4 has expired. [30 Cal. L.Rev.Comm. Reports 327 (2000)].

§§ 4764.3, 4764.4. Repealed by Stats.2001, c. 115 (S.B. 153), § 40, 41

Law Revision Commission Comments

2001 Amendment

Section 4764.3 is repealed as obsolete. The pilot project established by Sections 4764.1–4764.4 has expired. [30 Cal. L.Rev.Comm. Reports 327 (2000)].

Section 4764.4 is repealed as obsolete. The pilot project established by Sections 4764.1–4764.4 has expired. [30 Cal. L.Rev.Comm. Reports 327 (2000)].

§ 4765. Obligation to pay parking penalties and administrative fees

No exemption from the payment of any fee imposed by this code is an exemption from the obligation of a registered owner or lessee to pay the full amount of parking penalties and administrative fees pursuant to Section 4760. *(Added by Stats.1975, c. 1179, p. 2909, § 6, operative Jan. 1, 1978. Amended by Stats.1986, c. 939, § 13.)*

§ 4766. Notice of noncompliance without certificate of adjudication; notice to department; conditions for renewal of registration

(a) Except as provided in subdivisions (b) and (c), the department shall refuse to renew the registration of a vehicle for which a notice of noncompliance has been transmitted to the department pursuant to subdivision (a) of Section 40002.1 if no certificate of adjudication has been received by the department pursuant to subdivision (b) of that section. The department shall include on each potential registration card issued for use at the time of renewal, or on an accompanying document, an itemization of citations for which notices of noncompliance have been received by the department pursuant to subdivision (a) of Section 40002.1. The itemization shall include the citation number, citation date, and the jurisdiction that issued the underlying notice pursuant to Section 40002 and the administrative service fee for clearing the offense pursuant to subdivision (b) of this section.

(b) Upon application for renewal of vehicle registration for a vehicle subject to subdivision (a), the department shall not refuse registration renewal pursuant to subdivision (a) if the applicant, with respect to each outstanding certificate of noncompliance, has performed both of the following:

(1) Provides the department with a certificate of adjudication for the offense issued pursuant to subdivision (b) of Section 40002.1.

(2) Pays an administrative service fee, which shall be established by the department to, in the aggregate, defray its costs in administering this section.

(c) Whenever registration of a vehicle subject to subdivision (a) is transferred or not renewed for two renewal periods, the department shall notify each court that transmitted a notice of noncompliance affecting the vehicle of the transfer of, or lack of renewal of, the registration and the department shall not thereafter refuse registration renewal pursuant to subdivision (a). *(Added by Stats.1984, c. 881, § 1, operative July 1, 1985; Stats.1984, c. 981, § 1, operative July 1, 1985. Amended by Stats.1985, c. 858, § 1; Stats.2007, c. 452 (A.B.1464), § 1; Stats.2008, c. 179 (S.B.1498), § 215.)*

§ 4767. Delinquent parking or toll violations; payment or notice of disposition from court or designated processing agency prior to transfer; application of section

(a) If delinquent parking or toll violations have been reported to the department for a vehicle for which a transfer of ownership and registration has been requested, the department shall not transfer ownership and registration unless the transferee requesting the transfer pays all of the fines and penalties for those violations to the department, or provides an original abstract or notice of disposition from the court or designated processing agency that the fines and penalties for those violations have been cleared with the parking agency or the court.

(b) This section only applies if the transfer requested is one described in Section 6285 of the Revenue and Taxation Code. *(Added by Stats.2013, c. 101 (A.B.443), § 2.)*

ARTICLE 6.5. REFUSAL OF REGISTRATION FOR NONPAYMENT OF TOLL EVASION PENALTIES

Section
4770. Notice of toll evasion violation; nonrenewal of vehicle registration.
4771. Registration renewal notices; itemization of unpaid toll evasion penalties.
4772. Remittance of toll evasion penalties and fees to each jurisdiction.
4773. Assessment of fee for recording of notice of delinquent toll evasion violation.
4773.5. Cost of implementing article; reimbursement by issuing agencies.
4774. Transfer of vehicle or nonrenewal of registration; department not required to attempt collection of toll evasion penalty; application of section.
4775. Exemptions.

§ 4770. Notice of toll evasion violation; nonrenewal of vehicle registration

(a) Except as provided in subdivision (c) or (d), the department shall refuse to renew the registration of a vehicle if the registered owner or lessee has been mailed a notice of toll evasion violation, the processing agency has transmitted to the department an itemization of unpaid toll evasion penalties, including administrative fees, pursuant to Section 40267, and the toll evasion penalty and administrative fee have not been paid pursuant to Section 40266, unless the full amount of all outstanding toll evasion penalties and administrative fees, as shown by records of the department are paid to the department at the time of application for renewal.

(b) The designated processing agency shall issue a notice of the disposition of the toll evasion violation or violations to a lessor, if the lessor provides the processing agency with the name, address, and driver's license number of the lessee at the time of the occurrence of the toll evasion violation.

(c) The department shall renew the registration of a vehicle if the applicant provides the department with the notice of the disposition of the toll evasion violation or violations issued pursuant to subdivision (b) for clearing all outstanding toll evasion penalties and administrative fees, as shown by the records of the department, and the applicant has met all other requirements for registration.

(d) The department shall not refuse to renew the registration of a vehicle if the toll evasion violation occurred prior to the date that the registered owner or lessee took possession of the vehicle. *(Added by Stats. 1995, c. 739 (A.B.1223), § 5. Amended by Stats.2008, c. 741 (A.B.2401), § 2.)*

§ 4771. Registration renewal notices; itemization of unpaid toll evasion penalties

The department shall include on each vehicle registration renewal notice issued for use at the time of renewal, or on an accompanying document, an itemization of unpaid toll evasion penalties, including administrative fees, showing the amount thereof, the jurisdiction that issued the notice of toll evasion violation, and the date of toll evasion relating thereto, which the registered owner or lessee is required to pay pursuant to Section 4770. *(Added by Stats.1995, c. 739 (A.B.1223), § 5.)*

§ 4772. Remittance of toll evasion penalties and fees to each jurisdiction

(a) Except as provided in subdivision (b), the department shall remit all toll evasion penalties and administrative fees collected, after deducting the administrative fee authorized by Section 4773, for each notice of delinquent toll evasion violation for which toll evasion penalties and administrative fees have been collected pursuant to Section 4770, to each jurisdiction in the amounts due to each jurisdiction according to its unadjudicated notices of delinquent toll violation. Within 45 days from the time penalties are paid to the department, the department shall inform each jurisdiction which of its notices of delinquent toll evasion violation have been collected.

(b) This subdivision applies to facilities developed pursuant to Section 143 of the Streets and Highways Code. For each notice of delinquent toll evasion violation for which toll evasion penalties and administrative fees have been collected by the department pursuant to Section 4770, each issuing agency is due an amount equal to the sum of the unpaid toll, administrative fees, other costs incurred by the issuing agency that are related to toll evasion, process service fees, and fees and collection costs related to civil debt collection. After deducting the department's administrative fee authorized by Section 4773 and the amounts due each issuing agency for unpaid tolls, administrative fees, other costs incurred by the issuing agency that are related to toll evasion, process service fees, and fees and collection costs related to civil debt collection, the department shall deposit the balance of the toll evasion penalties collected pursuant to Section 4770, if any, in the State Highway Account in the State Transportation Fund. *(Added by Stats.1995, c. 739 (A.B. 1223), § 5.)*

§ 4773. Assessment of fee for recording of notice of delinquent toll evasion violation

The department shall assess a fee for the recording of the notice of delinquent toll evasion violation, which is given to the department pursuant to Section 40267, in an amount, as determined by the department, that is sufficient to provide a total amount equal to at least its actual costs of administering Sections 4770, 4771, 4774, and 4775. *(Added by Stats.1995, c. 739 (A.B.1223), § 5.)*

§ 4773.5. Cost of implementing article; reimbursement by issuing agencies

(a) The department shall require the entire cost of initially implementing this article to be reimbursed by the issuing agencies that are private entities and by the local authorities described in Section 40250, on whose behalf toll processing procedures are carried out pursuant to Article 4 (commencing with Section 40250) of Chapter 1 of Division 17. For purposes of this section, the cost to the department of initially implementing this article includes all of the one-time costs that are incurred by the department in order to implement this article, but does not include ongoing administrative costs associated with this article. The issuing agencies and the local authorities shall each be required to reimburse the department for 50 percent of the reimbursable costs.

(b)(1) The amount collected pursuant to subdivision (a) shall be the actual cost.

(2) The amount of the reimbursement required by subdivision (a) for each issuing agency and local authority shall be determined by the department in as equitable a manner as possible. In the event of a dispute of the reimbursement required by subdivision (a), an issuing agency may request an audit of applicable costs by a certified public accountant or public accountant. The cost of the audit shall be borne by the issuing agency requesting the audit. The result of the audit shall determine the actual costs.

(c) The processing agency shall access the department's data base via "on-line" techniques or other methods as the department and the processing agency may agree. *(Added by Stats.1995, c. 739 (A.B.1223), § 5.)*

§ 4774. Transfer of vehicle or nonrenewal of registration; department not required to attempt collection of toll evasion penalty; application of section

* * * (a) If a vehicle is transferred or the registration is not renewed for two renewal periods and the former registered owner or lessee of the vehicle owes a toll

178

evasion penalty for a notice of delinquent toll evasion violation filed with the department pursuant to Section 40267, the department shall notify each jurisdiction of that fact and is not required thereafter to attempt collection of the undeposited toll evasion penalty and administrative fees.

(b) This section does not apply if the transfer of a vehicle is one described in Section 6285 of the Revenue and Taxation Code. *(Added by Stats.1995, c. 739 (A.B. 1223), § 5. Amended by Stats.2013, c. 101 (A.B.443), § 3.)*

§ 4775. Exemptions

No exemption from the payment of any fee imposed by this code is an exemption from the obligation of a registered owner or lessee to pay the full amount of toll evasion penalties and administrative fees pursuant to Section 4770. *(Added by Stats.1995, c. 739 (A.B.1223), § 5.)*

ARTICLE 7. LICENSE PLATES

Section
4850. Issuance of reflectorized plates; fees.
4850.1. Repealed.
4850.5. Truck tractors; one plate on front; contingent operation.
4851. Display on plates.
4852. Size and shape of plates; number and letter requirements.
4853. Devices in lieu of plates; pilot program to evaluate use of alternative products; limitations on exchange of data with electronic devices and receipt and retention of information; report to Legislature.

§ 4850. Issuance of reflectorized plates; fees

(a) The department, upon registering a vehicle, shall issue to the owner two partially or fully reflectorized license plates or devices for a motor vehicle, other than a motorcycle, and one partially or fully reflectorized license plate or device for all other vehicles required to be registered under this code. The plates or devices shall identify the vehicles for which they are issued for the period of their validity.

(b) Notwithstanding any other provision of law, no contract shall be let to any nongovernmental entity for the purchase or securing of reflectorized material for the plates, unless the department has made every reasonable effort to secure qualified bids from as many independent responsible bidders as possible. No contract shall be let to any nongovernmental entity for the manufacturing of reflectorized safety license plates.

(c) In addition to any other fees specified in this code, a fee of one dollar ($1) for reflectorization shall be paid only by those vehicle owners receiving license plates or devices under this section.

(d) This section does not require vehicle owners with nonreflectorized license plates or devices to replace them with reflectorized plates or devices.

(e) This section shall be known as the Schrade-Belotti Act. *(Stats.1959, c. 3, p. 1566, § 4850. Amended by Stats.1972, c. 953, p. 1728, § 1; Stats.1979, c. 696, p. 2170, § 1; Stats.1985, c. 679, § 1, operative Jan. 1, 1987.)*

Cross References

Attachment and display of license plates, see Vehicle Code § 5200 et seq.
Definitions,
   Motor vehicle, see Vehicle Code § 415.
   Motorcycle, see Vehicle Code § 400.
   Owner, see Vehicle Code § 460.
   Vehicle, see Vehicle Code § 670.
Devices in lieu of license plates, see Vehicle Code § 4853.
Domestic violence victims, application for new and different license plates, see Vehicle Code § 4467.
Duplicate or substitute plates, fees, see Vehicle Code § 9265.
Duplicate or substitute registration for lost plates, see Vehicle Code §§ 4457, 4458.
Equipment identification plate on special construction equipment, see Vehicle Code § 5011.
Evidence of registration, improper or false use of, see Vehicle Code § 4461.
Features of license plates of publicly owned vehicles, see Vehicle Code § 4155.
Improper display of license plates, see Vehicle Code § 4462.
Indicia of registration pending renewal, see Vehicle Code § 4606.
Registration of dismantled vehicle, see Vehicle Code § 11519.
Seizure of license plates on expiration, revocation, suspension, or cancellation, see Vehicle Code § 4460.
Series of plates, issuance, see Vehicle Code § 4609.
Special series license plates for exempt vehicles, see Vehicle Code § 5000.
Trolley coaches, applicability of this section, see Vehicle Code § 21051.

§ 4850.1. Repealed by Stats.1992, c. 1243 (A.B.3090), § 67, eff. Sept. 30, 1992

§ 4850.5. Truck tractors; one plate on front; contingent operation

(a) Notwithstanding subdivision (a) of Section 4850 and Section 5200, the department, upon registering a truck tractor, shall issue to the owner one suitable license plate or other device which identifies the vehicle for which it is issued and for the period of its validity. The license plate or other device shall be attached to the front of the vehicle.

(b) This section shall become operative only when and if the Department of the California Highway Patrol implements a program which requires identifying numbers on the right and left sides of truck tractors. *(Added by Stats.1985, c. 183, § 1.)*

Operative Effect

Operative effect of 1985 addition, see subdivision (b).

§ 4851. Display on plates

Every license plate shall have displayed upon it the registration number assigned to the vehicle for which it is issued, together with the word "California" or the abbreviation "Cal." and the year number for which it is issued or a suitable device issued by the department for validation purposes, which device shall contain the year number for which issued. *(Stats.1959, c. 3, p. 1566, § 4851.)*

Cross References

Applicability of this section to trolley coaches, see Vehicle Code § 21051.
Display of plates, tabs and stickers, see Vehicle Code § 5200 et seq.
Exempt vehicles, display of distinguishing marks or symbols on license plates, see Vehicle Code § 4001.
Features of license plates of publicly owned vehicles, see Vehicle Code § 4155.
Improper display of license plates, see Vehicle Code § 4462.

§ 4852. Size and shape of plates; number and letter requirements

(a) License plates issued for motor vehicles, other than motorcycles, shall be rectangular in shape, 12 inches in length and six inches in width. The number and letter characters on the plates shall have a minimum height of two and three-quarter inches, a minimum width of one and one-quarter inches, and a minimum spacing between characters of five-sixteenths of an inch.

(b) Motorcycle license plates shall measure seven inches in length and four inches in width, and the characters on the plates shall have a minimum height of one and one-half inches and a minimum width of nine-sixteenths inches, and shall have a minimum spacing between characters of three-sixteenths of an inch. *(Stats. 1959, c. 3, p. 1566, § 4852. Amended by Stats.2000, c. 163 (S.B.1329), § 1; Stats.2000, c. 859 (A.B.1515), § 1.)*

Cross References

Applicability of this section to trolley coaches, see Vehicle Code § 21051.

§ 4853. Devices in lieu of plates; pilot program to evaluate use of alternative products; limitations on exchange of data with electronic devices and receipt and retention of information; report to Legislature

(a) The department may issue one or more stickers, tabs, or other suitable devices in lieu of the license plates provided for under this code. Except where the physical differences between the stickers, tabs, or devices and license plates by their nature render the provisions of this code inapplicable, all provisions of this code relating to license plates may apply to stickers, tabs, or devices.

(b) The department may establish a pilot program to evaluate the use of alternatives to the stickers, tabs, license plates, and registration cards authorized by this code, subject to all of the following requirements:

179

(1) The alternative products shall be approved by the Department of the California Highway Patrol.

(2) The pilot program shall be limited to no more than 0.5 percent of registered vehicles for the purpose of road testing and evaluation.

(3) The alternative products to be evaluated shall be provided at no cost to the state.

(4) Any pilot program established by the department pursuant to this subdivision shall be completed no later than January 1, 2017.

(5) Any pilot program established by the department pursuant to this subdivision shall be limited to vehicle owners who have voluntarily chosen to participate in the pilot program.

(c) In the conduct of any pilot program pursuant to this section, any data exchanged between the department and any electronic device or the provider of any electronic device shall be limited to that data necessary to display evidence of registration compliance. The department shall not receive or retain any information generated during the pilot program regarding the movement, location, or use of a vehicle participating in the pilot program.

(d) If the department conducts a pilot program authorized in subdivision (b), the department shall, no later than July 1, 2018, submit a report of the results of the pilot program to the Legislature, in compliance with Section 9795 of the Government Code, to include, but not be limited to, the following:

(1) An evaluation of the cost effectiveness of the alternatives used in the pilot program when compared to the department's current use of stickers, tabs, license plates, and registration cards.

(2) A review of all products evaluated in the pilot program and of the features of those products. The report shall note if the devices evaluated in the pilot program are available with the ability to transmit and retain information relating to the movement, location, or use of a vehicle, and if a product contains that feature, the report shall also note if the product includes any security features to protect against unauthorized access to information.

(3) Recommendations for subsequent actions, if any, that should be taken with regard to alternatives evaluated in the pilot program. *(Stats.1959, c. 3, p. 1566, § 4853. Amended by Stats.1973, c. 889, § 32, eff. Sept. 28, 1973; Stats.2013, c. 569 (S.B.806), § 1.)*

Cross References

Applicability of this section to trolley coaches, see Vehicle Code § 21051.

Display of license plates, tabs and stickers, see Vehicle Code § 5200 et seq.

Issuance of reflectorized license plates, see Vehicle Code § 4850.

Special series license plates for certain vehicles, see Vehicle Code § 5000.

Substitute or duplicate license plates for lost or destroyed plates, see Vehicle Code §§ 4457, 4458.

Tabs and stickers, display, see Vehicle Code §§ 5204, 5205.

ARTICLE 8. SPECIAL PLATES

Section

5000. Special series plates.
5000.5. Repealed.
5001. Regular series plates for law enforcement vehicles.
5001.5. Law enforcement license plates; agreements with other states.
5002. Plates for law enforcement vehicles in pools.
5002.5. Regular series plates for legislative vehicles.
5002.6. University chancellor or president; state-owned vehicles; regular series plates.
5002.7. County-owned vehicles; requests for regular series plates; reassignment of vehicle.
5002.8. Legislative or Congressional members; fees; deposit.
5003. Records of law enforcement vehicles.
5004. Vehicles of historic value.
5004.1. License plate corresponding to model year date of licensed historical vehicle.
5004.3. California Legacy License Plate Program.
5004.5. Pre-1943 motorcycles.
5004.6. Repealed.
5005. Amateur radio station licensees.
5006. Honorary consular officer.
5006.5. Foreign organizations; officers and designated employees.
5007. Disabled persons, disabled veterans, or organizations involved in transportation of the disabled; special license plates; application and issuance requirements; return of plates to department upon death of veteran or disabled person, or upon sale of vehicle used for transportation of disabled persons.
5007.5. Physician's certificate substantiating a disability; requests for information; review board or panel.
5008. Press photographers.
5009. Repealed.
5010. School bus lessors; temporary permits.
5011. Identification plates; display.
5011.5. Limousines operated by charter-party carrier; special identification license plates.
5011.6. Memorandum of understanding; special identification license plates for limousines.
5011.9. Charter-party carrier plates; "LIVERY" inscription; issuance as environmental plates.
5012. Repealed.
5013. Repealed.
5014. Identification plate application by person other than manufacturer or dealer; renewal.
5014.1. Permanent trailer identification plate program; implementation; procedure.
5015. Time for application.
5016. Identification plates and certificates.
5016.5. Identification plate; issuance to manufacturer or dealer.
5017. Display of identification plate; carrying of identification certificate; permanent plate and identification certificate.
5018. Transfer of ownership; transferee's duties.
5019. Trailers.
5020. Class D radio station.
5021. Class D radio station.
5022. 1984 Olympic reflectorized license plates.
5023. Commemorative Olympic reflectorized license plates.

Section
5024.   Commemorative collegiate reflectorized license plates.

Cross References
Domestic violence victims, application for new and different license plates, see Vehicle Code § 4467.

§ 5000.   Special series plates

(a) Identification plates issued for trailers, semitrailers, motor-driven cycles, and pole and pipe dollies, and such vehicles as are exempt from the payment of registration fees under this code shall display suitable distinguishing marks or symbols, and the registration numbers assigned to each class of vehicles shall run in a separate numerical series, except that registration numbers assigned to vehicles exempt from the payment of registration fees may run in several separate numerical series.

(b) Vehicles subject to Sections 9400 and 9400.1 shall be issued license plates with suitable distinguishing marks or symbols distinguishing them from other license plates issued.

(c) Vehicles subject to Section 5014.1 shall be issued permanent identification plates with suitable distinguishing marks or symbols that distinguish them from other license plates. *(Stats.1959, c. 3, p. 1566, § 5000. Amended by Stats.1960, 1st Ex.Sess., c. 52, p. 402, § 1; Stats.1978, c. 768, § 1, operative Oct. 1, 1979; Stats.2000, c. 861 (S.B.2084), § 21, eff. Sept. 29, 2000.)*

Cross References
Applicability of this section to trolley coaches, see Vehicle Code § 21051.
Definitions,
    Motor-driven cycles, see Vehicle Code § 405.
    Pole or pipe dolly, see Vehicle Code § 475.
    Semitrailer, see Vehicle Code § 550.
    Trailer, see Vehicle Code § 630.
Evidence of registration, improper or false use of, see Vehicle Code §§ 4461, 4463.
Exemption from registration, generally, see Vehicle Code §§ 4002, 6700 et seq.
Operation of vehicles under special plates by automobile dismantlers, see Vehicle Code § 11516.
Schoolbus lessor temporary permit, display of exempt license plates, see Vehicle Code § 5010.

§ 5000.5.   Repealed by Stats.1996, c. 872 (A.B.3472), § 178

§ 5001.   Regular series plates for law enforcement vehicles

The department may issue license plates for vehicles exempt from registration fees in the same series as plates issued for nonexempt vehicles. The plates may be issued for a one-year period and only upon the certification of the department that the issuance of the plates has been requested by the head of a criminal justice or a law enforcement agency of a city, county, or state or federal department, that the vehicle is assigned to persons responsible for investigating actual or suspected violations of the law or the supervision of persons liberated from a state prison or other institution under the jurisdiction of the Department of Corrections by parole or the supervision of persons liberated from an institution under the jurisdiction of the Department of the Youth Authority by parole, and is intended for use in the line of duty. *(Stats.1959, c. 3, p. 1567, § 5001. Amended by Stats.1961, c. 319, p. 1360, § 1; Stats.1978, c. 617, p. 2068, § 2; Stats.1982, c. 576, p. 2536, § 1.)*

Cross References
Exemptions from registration and weight fees, see Vehicle Code § 9101 et seq.
Registration of exempt vehicles, display of plates, see Vehicle Code § 4001.

§ 5001.5.   Law enforcement license plates; agreements with other states

The director may enter into agreements or arrangements with motor vehicle departments in other states to provide for a reciprocal exchange of regular series license plates for the purposes of and under the conditions provided in Sections 5001 and 5003. *(Added by Stats. 1971, c. 899, p. 1750, § 1, operative May 3, 1972. Amended by Stats.1982, c. 576, p. 2536, § 2.)*

§ 5002.   Plates for law enforcement vehicles in pools

The department may issue regular series plates to the Department of General Services for use on motor vehicles maintained within motor vehicle pools of state-owned vehicles when the vehicles are used for the purposes set forth in Section 5001, except that the Department of General Services shall not assign, dispatch, or otherwise make any of those vehicles available for use by any agency of the state except upon the certification of the department. *(Stats.1959, c. 3, p. 1567, § 5002. Amended by Stats.1965, c. 371, p. 1598, § 289; Stats.1982, c. 576, p. 2536, § 3.)*

Cross References
Department of General Services, see Government Code § 14600 et seq.

§ 5002.5.   Regular series plates for legislative vehicles

The department shall issue regular series license plates for any motor vehicle owned by, or in the possession and use of, the Senate or Assembly, upon the request of the Rules Committee thereof. *(Added by Stats.1967, c. 162, p. 1247, § 2, eff. May 16, 1967.)*

§ 5002.6.   University chancellor or president; state-owned vehicles; regular series plates

(a) The Chancellor or a president of a campus of the California State University, or the president or a chancellor of a campus of the University of California, who is regularly issued a state-owned vehicle may apply to the department for regular series license plates for that vehicle, if a request for that issuance is also made by the Trustees of the California State University or the Regents of the University of California, as applicable. The

181

request by the president or chancellor and by the trustees or regents shall be in the manner specified by the department.

(b) Regular series license plates issued pursuant to subdivision (a) shall be surrendered to the department by the trustees or regents, as applicable, upon the reassignment of a vehicle, for which those plates have been issued, to a person other than the person who requested those plates. *(Added by Stats.1993, c. 1023 (S.B.448), § 1. Amended by Stats.1994, c. 146 (A.B.3601), § 219.)*

§ 5002.7. County-owned vehicles; requests for regular series plates; reassignment of vehicle

(a) For a county of over 20,000 square miles in area, a member of the county board of supervisors, or a county assessor, auditor, controller, treasurer, or tax collector, who is regularly issued a county-owned vehicle may apply to the department for regular series license plates for that vehicle, if a request for that issuance is also made by the county board of supervisors. The application and the request shall be in the manner specified by the department.

(b) Regular series license plates issued pursuant to subdivision (a) shall be surrendered to the department by the board member or administrative officer, as applicable, upon the reassignment of a vehicle, for which those plates have been issued, to a person other than the person who requested those plates. *(Added by Stats.1996, c. 10 (A.B.1869), § 11, eff. Feb. 9, 1996. Amended by Stats. 1999, c. 724 (A.B.1650), § 30.5; Stats.2000, c. 860 (A.B. 2908), § 7; Stats.2007, c. 630 (A.B.1728), § 2.)*

§ 5002.8. Legislative or Congressional members; fees; deposit

(a)(1) Distinctive license plates issued for a motor vehicle owned by a current or retired Member of the California Legislature, which plates denote that the person is, or was, a Member of the Legislature, and distinctive license plates issued for a vehicle owned by a Member of the Congress of the United States, which plates denote that the person is a Member of Congress, shall be subject to the regular fees for an original registration or renewal of registration.

(2) In addition to the regular fees for an original registration or renewal of registration, the applicant shall be charged the following additional fees:

(b) For an original registration, the applicant shall be charged the fee specified in subdivision (a) of Section 5106.

(c) For a renewal of registration, the applicant shall be charged the fee specified in subdivision (b) of Section 5106.

(d) When a Member or former Member of the California Legislature or a Member of the Congress of the United States who has been issued personalized license plates pursuant to this section applies to the department for transfer of the plates to another passenger vehicle, commercial motor vehicle, trailer, or semitrailer, a trans-

fer fee in the amount specified pursuant to Section 5108 shall be charged in addition to all other appropriate fees.

(e) After deducting the costs incurred by the department to administer this section, the department shall deposit in the California Environmental License Plate Fund, all fees received by the department in payment for the issuance, renewal, or transfer of the special license plates authorized under this section.

(f) This section shall become operative on January 1, 2014. *(Added by Stats.1978, c. 444, p. 1524, § 1. Amended by Stats.2012, c. 748 (A.B.2068), § 2, operative Jan. 1, 2014.)*

§ 5003. Records of law enforcement vehicles

The department shall maintain a record of the registration of exempt vehicles with regular series plates, which record shall not be open to public inspection. The record shall be disclosed in the event of any accident involving a vehicle so registered on demand of the Attorney General or upon an order of court. In the event of an inquiry by a county sheriff, city chief of police, or judge of any court relating to such exempt vehicle in connection with an alleged violation of state or local traffic laws, the department shall notify the supervisor of the person to whom the vehicle was assigned of the inquiry and the alleged violation and shall notify the inquiring official that this has been done without disclosing the name of the person involved. *(Stats.1959, c. 3, p. 1567, § 5003. Amended by Stats.1959, c. 536, p. 2504, § 1.)*

§ 5004. Vehicles of historic value

(a) Notwithstanding any other provision of this code, any owner of a vehicle described in paragraph (1), (2), or (3) which is operated or moved over the highway primarily for the purpose of historical exhibition or other similar purpose shall, upon application in the manner and at the time prescribed by the department, be issued special identification plates for the vehicle:

(1) A motor vehicle with an engine of 16 or more cylinders manufactured prior to 1965.

(2) A motor vehicle manufactured in the year 1922 or prior thereto.

(3) A vehicle which was manufactured after 1922, is at least 25 years old, and is of historic interest.

(b) The special identification plates assigned to motor vehicles with an engine of 16 or more cylinders manufactured prior to 1965 and to any motor vehicle manufactured in the year 1922 and prior thereto shall run in a separate numerical series, commencing with "Horseless Carriage No. 1".

The special identification plates assigned to vehicles specified in paragraph (3) of subdivision (a) shall run in a separate numerical series, commencing with "Historical Vehicle No. 1".

Each series of plates shall have different and distinguishing colors.

(c) A fee of twenty-five dollars ($25) shall be charged for the initial issuance of the special identification plates. Such plates shall be permanent and shall not be required to be replaced. If such special identification plates become damaged or unserviceable in any manner, replacement for the plates may be obtained from the department upon proper application and upon payment of such fee as is provided for in Section 9265.

(d) All funds received by the department in payment for such identification plates or the replacement thereof shall be deposited in the California Environmental License Plate Fund.

(e) These vehicles shall not be exempt from the equipment provisions of Sections 26709, 27150, and 27600.

(f) As used in this section, a vehicle is of historic interest if it is collected, restored, maintained, and operated by a collector or hobbyist principally for purposes of exhibition and historic vehicle club activities. (Stats.1959, c. 3, p. 1567, § 5004. Amended by Stats.1961, c. 1285, p. 3065, § 2; Stats.1965, c. 1389, p. 3310, § 1; Stats.1971, c. 1437, p. 2841, § 4, operative May 3, 1972; Stats.1971, c. 1448, p. 2859, § 4, operative Jan. 1, 1972; Stats.1974, c. 1012, p. 2207, § 5; Stats.1981, c. 714, p. 2793, § 438; Stats.1981, c. 415, p. 1613, § 2; Stats.1984, c. 918, § 1.)

Cross References

Annual minimum license fee for vehicle described in this section, see Revenue and Taxation Code § 10753.5.

Automobile dismantler, exclusions, see Vehicle Code § 221.

Environmental license plate fund, see Public Resources Code §§ 21191, 21192.

Exemption from certain pollution control requirements, see Health and Safety Code § 43002.

Historic and special interest vehicles, storage and maintenance, see Vehicle Code § 5050 et seq.

Horseless carriage as any vehicle defined in this section, see Revenue and Taxation Code § 10704.

Motor carrier permits, provisions not applicable to vehicles described in this section, see Vehicle Code § 34622.

Nonoperated vehicles, registration or renewal requirements, Generally, see Vehicle Code § 4604 et seq.

  Certificate of nonoperation exemptions, see Vehicle Code § 4604.

  Certificate of nonoperation requirements, see Vehicle Code § 4604.2.

Registration fees, generally, see Vehicle Code § 9250 et seq.

§ 5004.1. License plate corresponding to model year date of licensed historical vehicle

(a)(1) An owner of a vehicle that is a 1969 or older model-year vehicle or the owner of a commercial vehicle or a pickup truck that is a 1972 or older model-year may, after the requirements for the registration of the vehicle are complied with and with the approval of the department, utilize license plates of this state with the date of year corresponding to the model-year date when the vehicle was manufactured, if the model-year date license plate is legible and serviceable, as determined by the department, in lieu of the license plates otherwise required by this code.

(2) The department may consult with an organization of old car hobbyists in determining whether the date of year of the license plate corresponds to the model-year date when the vehicle was manufactured.

(b) A fee of forty-five dollars ($45) shall be charged for the application for the use of the special plates.

(c) In addition to the regular renewal fee for the vehicle for which the plates are authorized, the applicant for a renewal of the plates shall be charged an additional fee of ten dollars ($10). If payment of a regular vehicle renewal fee is not required by this code, the holder of license plates with a date corresponding to the model-year may retain the plates upon payment of an annual fee of twenty dollars ($20) that shall be due at the expiration of the registration year of the vehicle to which the plates were last assigned under this section.

(d) If a person who is authorized to utilize the special license plates applies to the department for transfer of the plates to another vehicle, a transfer fee of twelve dollars ($12) shall be charged in addition to all other appropriate fees. (Added by Stats.1982, c. 721, p. 2888, § 1. Amended by Stats.1984, c. 918, § 2; Stats.1987, c. 280, § 1; Stats.1988, c. 645, § 1, operative July 1, 1989; Stats.1993, c. 1292 (S.B.274), § 5; Stats.2007, c. 497 (A.B.462), § 1, operative July 1, 2009; Stats.2008, c. 179 (S.B.1498), § 216.)

§ 5004.3. California Legacy License Plate Program

(a) Subject to subdivision (c), the department shall establish the California Legacy License Plate Program and create and issue a series of specialized license plates known as California Legacy License Plates that replicate the look of California license plates from the state's past. The design of the plates shall be identical, to the extent the department determines it to be reasonably feasible under current manufacturing processes, to a regular license plate, except as provided in subdivision (b).

(b) The California Legacy License Plates shall consist of one or more of the following designs:

(1) Yellow background with black lettering per the appearance of California license plates issued by the department from 1956 to 1962, inclusive.

(2) Black background with yellow lettering per the appearance of California license plates issued by the department from 1965 to 1968, inclusive.

(3) Blue background with yellow lettering per the appearance of California license plates issued by the department from 1969 to 1986, inclusive.

(c) In addition to the regular fees for an original registration or renewal of registration, the following additional fees shall be paid for the issuance, renewal, or transfer of the specialized license plates:

(1) Fifty dollars ($50) for the original issuance of the plates.

(2) Forty dollars ($40) for a renewal of registration with the plates.

(3) Fifteen dollars ($15) for transfer of the plates to another vehicle.

(4) Thirty-five dollars ($35) for each substitute replacement plate.

(d) The department shall not issue California Legacy License Plates for a vehicle that is exempt from the payment of registration fees pursuant to Section 9101 or 9103.

(e)(1) The department shall not establish the California Legacy License Plate Program until the department has received not less than 7,500 paid applications for plates. The department shall collect and hold applications for the plates. The department shall not issue a specialized license plate until it has received not less than 7,500 paid applications for any one of the particular plates within the time period prescribed in this section.

(2) The department shall have until January 1, 2015, to receive the required number of applications. If, after that date, 7,500 paid applications have not been received for any one of the three plates described in subdivision (b), the department shall immediately refund to all applicants all fees or deposits that have been collected.

(f)(1) Upon a determination by the department that there are sufficient funds for the program, moneys shall be available, upon appropriation by the Legislature, to the department for the necessary administrative costs of establishing the California Legacy License Plate Program.

(2) After deducting its administrative costs under this subdivision, the department shall deposit any additional revenue derived from the issuance, renewal, transfer, and substitution of the specialized license plates into the California Environmental License Plate Fund, for appropriation by the Legislature pursuant to existing law. *(Added by Stats.2012, c. 720 (A.B.1658), § 1.)*

§ 5004.5. Pre-1943 motorcycles

Notwithstanding any other provision of this code, any owner of a motorcycle manufactured in the year 1942 or prior thereto shall, upon application in the manner and at the time prescribed by the department, be issued special license plates for the motorcycle. The special license plates assigned to such motorcycles shall run in a separate numerical series. An additional fee of fifteen dollars ($15) shall be charged for the initial issuance of the special license plates. Such plates shall be permanent and shall not be required to be replaced. If such special license plates become damaged or unserviceable in any manner, replacement for the plates may be obtained from the department upon proper application and upon payment of such fee as is provided for in Section 9265. Except as otherwise provided in this section, such motorcycles shall be subject to the same annual registration fees and provisions of law as are other motorcycles.

All revenues derived from the fees provided for in this section above actual costs of the production and issuance

184

of the special plates for motorcycles, or the replacement thereof, shall be deposited in the California Environmental License Plate Fund by the department. *(Added by Stats.1972, c. 1198, p. 2320, § 1, operative Jan. 1, 1974. Amended by Stats.1981, c. 714, p. 2794, § 439; Stats.1981, c. 415, p. 1614, § 3.)*

§ 5004.6. Repealed by Stats.2003, c. 594 (S.B.315), § 19

§ 5005. Amateur radio station licensees

(a) Any person holding an unexpired amateur radio station license issued by the Federal Communications Commission may, after the requirements for the registration of the motor vehicle have been complied with, also apply directly to the department for special license plates, and the department may issue special plates in lieu of the regular license plates. The special license plates shall be affixed to the motor vehicle for which registration is sought and, in lieu of the numbers otherwise prescribed by law, shall display the official amateur radio station call letters of the applicant as assigned by the Federal Communications Commission.

The applicant shall, by satisfactory proof, show that he or she is the holder of an unexpired license.

(b) The department shall not issue more than one set of special plates for any licensed amateur radio station.

(c) In addition to the regular fees for an original registration or renewal of registration, the following special fees shall be paid:

(1) Twenty dollars ($20) for the initial issuance of the special plate.

(2) Twelve dollars ($12) for the transfer of the special plate to another motor vehicle. *(Stats.1959, c. 3, p. 1567, § 5005. Amended by Stats.1959, c. 135, p. 2026, § 3; Stats.1970, c. 989, p. 1761, § 1; Stats.1978, c. 444, p. 1524, § 2; Stats.1982, c. 310, p. 978, § 1; Stats.1982, c. 1273, p. 4700, § 5.)*

§ 5006. Honorary consular officer

(a) The department may issue distinctive license plates for motor vehicles owned or leased by an honorary consular officer or a similar official when the department is otherwise satisfied that the issuance of the license plates is in order. An honorary consular officer or similar official is a citizen of the United States, or a permanent resident of this country, who is appointed by a foreign country for the purpose of facilitating and promoting the interest of that country.

(b) The motor vehicles for which the license plates are issued shall be subject to all regular license and registration fees. In addition to the regular fees for an original registration or renewal of registration, the additional fees specified in Sections 5106 and 5108, as applicable, shall be paid, and shall be deposited in the Motor Vehicle Account in the State Transportation Fund. *(Added by Stats.1985, c. 752, § 1.)*

§ 5006.5. Foreign organizations; officers and designated employees

(a) The department may issue, for a fee determined by the department to be sufficient to reimburse the department for actual costs incurred pursuant to this section, distinctive license plates for motor vehicles owned or leased by an officer or a designated employee of a foreign organization recognized by the United States pursuant to the Taiwan Relations Act (22 U.S.C. Sec. 3301 et seq.) when the department is otherwise satisfied that the issuance of the license plates is in order.

(b) The distinctive license plates shall be designed by the department and shall contain the words "Foreign Organization."

(c) The department shall establish procedures for both of the following:

(1) To verify the eligibility of an applicant for plates issued pursuant to this section.

(2) To authorize a recognized foreign organization to apply on behalf of its officers for plates issued pursuant to this section. *(Added by Stats.1994, c. 397 (A.B.2805), § 1.)*

§ 5007. Disabled persons, disabled veterans, or organizations involved in transportation of the disabled; special license plates; application and issuance requirements; return of plates to department upon death of veteran or disabled person, or upon sale of vehicle used for transportation of disabled persons

(a) The department shall, upon application and without additional fees, issue a special license plate or plates pursuant to procedures adopted by the department to all of the following:

(1) A disabled person.

(2) A disabled veteran.

(3) An organization or agency involved in the transportation of disabled persons or disabled veterans if the motor vehicle that will have the special license plate is used solely for the purpose of transporting those persons.

(b) The special license plates issued under subdivision (a) shall run in a regular numerical series that shall include one or more unique two-letter codes reserved for disabled person license plates or disabled veteran license plates. The International Symbol of Access adopted

pursuant to Section 3 of Public Law 100–641, commonly known as the "wheelchair symbol" shall be depicted on each plate.

(c)(1) Except as provided in paragraph (3), prior to issuing a special license plate to a disabled person or disabled veteran, the department shall require the submission of a certificate, in accordance with paragraph (2), signed by the physician and surgeon, or to the extent that it does not cause a reduction in the receipt of federal aid highway funds, by a nurse practitioner, certified nurse midwife, or physician assistant, substantiating the disability, unless the applicant's disability is readily observable and uncontested. The disability of a person who has lost, or has lost the use of, one or more lower extremities or one hand, for a disabled veteran, or both hands for a disabled person, or who has significant limitation in the use of lower extremities, may also be certified by a licensed chiropractor. The blindness of an applicant shall be certified by a licensed physician and surgeon who specializes in diseases of the eye or a licensed optometrist. The physician and surgeon, nurse practitioner, certified nurse midwife, physician assistant, chiropractor, or optometrist certifying the qualifying disability shall provide a full description of the illness or disability on the form submitted to the department.

(2) The physician and surgeon, nurse practitioner, certified nurse midwife, physician assistant, chiropractor, or optometrist who signs a certificate submitted under this subdivision shall retain information sufficient to substantiate that certificate and, upon request of the department, shall make that information available for inspection by the Medical Board of California or the appropriate regulatory board.

(3) For a disabled veteran, the department shall accept, in lieu of the certificate described in paragraph (1), a certificate from the United States Department of Veterans Affairs that certifies that the applicant is a disabled veteran as described in Section 295.7.

(d) A disabled person or disabled veteran who is issued a license plate or plates under this section shall, upon request, present to a peace officer, or person authorized to enforce parking laws, ordinances, or regulations, a certification form that substantiates the eligibility of the disabled person or veteran to possess the plate or plates. The certification shall be on a form prescribed by the department and contain the name of the disabled person or disabled veteran to whom the plate or plates were issued, and the name, address, and telephone number of the medical professional described in subdivision (c) who certified the eligibility of the person or veteran for the plate or plates.

(e) The certification requirements of subdivisions (c) and (d) do not apply to an organization or agency that is issued a special license plate or plates under paragraph (3) of subdivision (a).

(f) The special license plate shall, upon the death of the disabled person or disabled veteran, be returned to

185

the department within 60 days or upon the expiration of the vehicle registration, whichever occurs first.

(g) When a motor vehicle subject to paragraph (3) of subdivision (a) is sold or transferred, the special license plate or plates issued to an organization or agency under paragraph (3) of subdivision (a) for that motor vehicle shall be immediately returned to the department. *(Added by Stats.2004, c. 363 (A.B.1138), § 2, operative July 1, 2005; Stats.2004, c. 404 (S.B.1725), § 8, operative July 1, 2005. Amended by Stats.2006, c. 116 (A.B.2120), § 1; Stats.2006, c. 203 (A.B.1910), § 1.5; Stats.2010, c. 421 (A.B.1944), § 1; Stats.2010, c. 478 (A.B.2777), § 7.5; Stats.2011, c. 296 (A.B.1023), § 301.)*

Cross References

Former prisoners of war, disabled veterans, or Congressional Medal of Honor recipients, exemptions from fees for certain plates, certificates, or cards, see Vehicle Code § 9105.
Public offstreet parking facilities, loading and unloading disabled persons, sufficient space, see Vehicle Code § 22511.85.
Restrictions and prohibitions, disabled person's parking, see Vehicle Code § 22511.57.
Temporary distinguishing placard, see Vehicle Code § 22511.59.
Use of placard in lieu of special identification license plates, see Vehicle Code §§ 22511.5, 22511.55.

§ 5007.5. Physician's certificate substantiating a disability; requests for information; review board or panel

(a) Upon a receipt of request for information by a local law enforcement agency or local or state agency responsible for the administration or enforcement of parking regulations, the department shall make available to the requesting agency any information contained in a physician's certificate submitted to the department to substantiate the disability of a person applying for or who has been issued special license plates pursuant to Section 5007. The department shall not provide the information specified in this subdivision to any private entity or third-party parking citation processing agency.

(b) A local authority may establish a review board or panel, for the purposes of reviewing information contained in applications for special license plates and the certification of qualifying disabilities for persons residing within the jurisdiction of the local authority. The review board shall include a physician or other medical authority. Any findings or determinations by a review board or panel under this section indicating that an application or certification is fraudulent or lacks proper certification shall be transmitted to the department or other appropriate authorities for further review and investigation. *(Added by Stats.2004, c. 404 (S.B.1725), § 9.)*

§ 5008. Press photographers

(a) Any person who is regularly employed or engaged as a bona fide newspaper, newsreel, or television photographer or cameraman, may, after the requirements for the registration of the motor vehicle have been complied with, also apply for special license plates, and the department shall issue special license plates in lieu of the

regular license plates. The special license plates shall be affixed to the vehicle for which registration is sought and shall display the letters "PP" enclosed by a shield.

The applicant shall, by satisfactory proof, show that he or she is a bona fide newspaper, newsreel, or television photographer or cameraman.

(b) The department shall not issue more than one set of the special plates to any person.

(c) In addition to the regular fees for an original registration or renewal of registration, the following special fees shall be paid:

(1) Twenty dollars ($20) for the initial issuance of the special plate.

(2) Twelve dollars ($12) for the transfer of the special plate to another motor vehicle. *(Stats.1959, c. 3, p. 1568, § 5008. Amended by Stats.1959, c. 135, p. 2027, § 4; Stats.1978, c. 444, p. 1525, § 4; Stats.1982, c. 1273, p. 4700, § 5.5.)*

Cross References

Issuance of plates referred to in this section not applicable to trailers, see Vehicle Code § 5019.
Registration fees, generally, see Vehicle Code § 9250 et seq.

§ 5009.   Repealed by Stats.1978, c. 444, p. 1525, § 5

§ 5010.   School bus lessors; temporary permits

Notwithstanding any other provision of this code, when a motor vehicle which is leased to a school district for use as a schoolbus, as defined in Section 545, temporarily reverts to the possession and control of the lessor, and if the motor vehicle thereafter becomes subject to registration, the lessor may, as an alternative to such registration, secure a temporary permit to operate the vehicle in this state for any one or more calendar months. Such permit shall be posted upon the windshield or other prominent place upon the vehicle, and shall identify the vehicle for which it is affixed. When so affixed, such permit shall serve in lieu of registration. If such a lessor operates the motor vehicle under a temporary permit issued pursuant to this section, he shall notwithstanding the provisions of Section 5000 continue to display on the vehicle the exempt license plates issued to the vehicle as a schoolbus. Upon payment of the fees specified in Section 9266, the department may issue a temporary permit under this section. *(Added by Stats.1968, c. 871, p. 1664, § 1.)*

§ 5011.   Identification plates; display

Every piece of special construction equipment, special mobile equipment, cemetery equipment, trailer, semitrailer, and every logging vehicle shall display an identification plate issued pursuant to Section 5014 or 5014.1.

(Stats.1959, c. 3, p. 1568, § 5011. Amended by Stats.1961, c. 1659, p. 3626, § 4; Stats.1967, c. 1069, p. 2700, § 1; Stats.1967, c. 1491, p. 3485, § 1; Stats.1969, c. 1075, p. 2063, § 3; Stats.1972, c. 973, p. 1757, § 7, eff. Aug. 16, 1972; Stats.1975, c. 517, p. 1083, § 3; Stats.1983, c. 708, § 2; Stats.1984, c. 1077, § 1, operative July 1, 1985;

Stats.2000, c. 861 (S.B.2084), § 22, eff. Sept. 29, 2000; Stats.2001, c. 826 (A.B.1472), § 13.)

Exemption from registration, see Vehicle Code § 4010.

Logging vehicle defined, see Vehicle Code § 379.

Motor carrier permits, provisions not applicable to vehicles described in this section, see Vehicle Code § 34622.

Special construction equipment defined, see Vehicle Code §§ 565, 570.

Special mobile equipment defined, see Vehicle Code § 575.

Tow dolly defined, see Vehicle Code § 617.

§ 5011.5. Limousines operated by charter-party carrier; special identification license plates

Every limousine operated by a charter-party carrier, as defined by Section 5371.4 of the Public Utilities Code, shall display a special identification license plate issued pursuant to Section 5385.6 of that code.

This section shall become operative on July 1, 1995. *(Added by Stats.1994, c. 109 (A.B.727), § 7, eff. June 27, 1994, operative July 1, 1995. Amended by Stats.1996, c. 124 (A.B.3470), § 118; Stats.2004, c. 193 (S.B.111), § 195.)*

Law Revision Commission Comments

2004 Amendment

Section 5011.5 is amended to reflect that subdivision (h) of Public Utilities Code Section 5371.4 was redesignated as subdivision (g). [33 Cal.L.Rev.Comm. Reports 495 (2004)].

§ 5011.6. Memorandum of understanding; special identification license plates for limousines

Not later than January 1, 1995, the department and the Public Utilities Commission shall adopt a memorandum of understanding governing the exchange of information regarding vehicle registrations, and reimbursement by the commission of the department's costs in producing and distributing special identification license plates for limousines required by Section 5011.5 and Section 5385.6 of the Public Utilities Code. *(Added by Stats.1994, c. 109 (A.B.727), § 8, eff. June 27, 1994.)*

§ 5011.9. Charter-party carrier plates; "LIVERY" inscription; issuance as environmental plates

(a) The department shall design the license plate specified in Section 5011.5 with the word "LIVERY" inscribed under the license plate number.

(b) The department shall issue the license plate specified in subdivision (a) on and after six months after the operative date of this section.

(c) The license plate specified in subdivision (a) may be issued as an environmental license plate, as defined in Section 5103, subject to the fees specified in Sections 5106 and 5108. *(Added by Stats.1995, c. 358 (A.B.933), § 1, eff. Aug. 4, 1995.)*

§ 5012. Repealed by Stats.1967, c. 1491, p. 3485, § 2

§ 5013. Repealed by Stats.1963, c. 2149, p. 4487, § 8

§ 5014. Identification plate application by person other than manufacturer or dealer; renewal

An application by a person other than a manufacturer or dealer for an identification plate for special construction equipment, cemetery equipment, special mobile equipment, logging vehicle, cotton trailer, or farm trailer as specified in Section 36109, a vehicle that is farmer-owned and used as provided in subdivision (b) of Section 36101, a motor vehicle that is farmer-owned and operated and used as provided in subdivision (a) of Section 36101, an automatic bale wagon operated as specified in subdivision (a) or (b) of Section 36102, or a farm trailer that is owned, rented, or leased by a farmer and is operated and used as provided in subdivision (b) of Section 36010, shall include the following:

(a) The true, full name and the driver's license or identification card number, if any, of the owner.

(b) A statement by the owner of the use or uses which he or she intends to make of the equipment.

(c) A description of the vehicle, including any distinctive marks or features.

(d) A photograph of the vehicle. Only one photograph of one piece of equipment shall be required to be attached to the application when identification plates are to be obtained for more than one piece of equipment, each of which is of the same identical type.

(e) Other information as may reasonably be required by the department to determine whether the applicant is entitled to be issued an identification plate.

(f) A service fee of fifteen dollars ($15) for each vehicle. The plates shall be renewed between January 1 and February 4 every five calendar years, commencing in 1986. Any part of the year of the first application constitutes a calendar year. An application for renewal of an identification plate shall contain a space for the applicant's driver's license or identification card number, and the applicant shall furnish that number, if any, in the space provided. *(Stats.1959, c. 3, p. 1568, § 5014. Amended by Stats.1961, c. 1659, p. 3626, § 5; Stats.1963, c. 2149, p. 4487, § 9; Stats.1967, c. 1069, p. 2700, § 2; Stats.1967, c. 1491, p. 3485, § 3; Stats.1969, c. 1075, p. 2063, § 4; Stats.1970, c. 405, p. 816, § 1; Stats.1972, c. 973, p. 1758, § 8, eff. Aug. 16, 1972; Stats.1977, c. 456, p. 1494, § 2; Stats.1983, c. 708, § 3; Stats.1984, c. 1077, § 2, operative July 1, 1985; Stats.1994, c. 1221 (S.B.1758), § 5; Stats.1996, c. 650 (A.B.2417), § 1; Stats.2000, c. 861 (S.B.2084), § 23, eff. Sept. 29, 2000; Stats.2003, c. 719 (S.B.1055), § 6.)*

Base fee amounts, adjustment of fees, see Vehicle Code § 1678.

Implement of husbandry, identification plates, see Vehicle Code § 36115.

Logging vehicle defined, see Vehicle Code § 379.

Special construction equipment defined, see Vehicle Code §§ 565, 570.

Special mobile equipment defined, see Vehicle Code § 575.

Tow dolly defined, see Vehicle Code § 617.

§ 5014.1. Permanent trailer identification plate program; implementation; procedure

(a) Upon the implementation of the permanent trailer identification plate program, the following applies:

(1) All trailers, except in cases where the registrant has elected to apply for trailer identification plates pursuant to Section 5014 or the trailer is exempt from registration pursuant to Section 36100 or 36109, shall receive an identification certificate upon conversion to the permanent trailer identification program. The following trailers, except as provided in Section 5101, may be assigned a trailer identification plate by the department in accordance with this section or an election may be made to keep the current plate on the expiration date of registration:

(A) Logging dolly.

(B) Pole or pipe dolly.

(C) Semitrailer.

(D) Trailer.

(E) Trailer bus.

(2) An auxiliary dolly or tow dolly may be assigned a permanent trailer identification plate.

(3) Trailer coaches and park trailers, as described in subdivision (b) of Section 18010 of the Health and Safety Code, are exempted from the permanent trailer identification plate program.

(b) The permanent trailer identification plate shall be in a size and design as determined by the department.

(c) The permanent trailer identification plate and the permanent trailer identification certificate shall not expire as long as the appropriate fees have been paid.

(d) Upon sale or transfer of the trailer or semitrailer, the assigned permanent trailer identification plate shall remain with the trailer or semitrailer for the life of the vehicle except as provided in Section 5101. Upon transfer of ownership, a new identification certificate shall be issued and the transferee shall pay a fee of seven dollars ($7).

(e) A service fee, sufficient to pay at least the entire actual costs to the department, not to exceed twenty dollars ($20) shall be assessed by the department upon converting to the permanent trailer identification program.

(f) A fee of seven dollars ($7) for substitute permanent trailer identification plates or certificates shall be charged.

(g) All valid trailer and semitrailer license plates and registration indicia that were issued under this code prior to December 31, 2001, upon which is affixed a permanent trailer identification sticker issued by the department, may be displayed in lieu of a permanent trailer identification plate as described in Sections 5011 and 5014.

(h) Every trailer that is submitted for original registration in this state shall be issued a permanent trailer identification plate and identification certificate.

(i) A service fee of ten dollars ($10) shall be charged for each vehicle renewing identification plates pursuant to this section. These plates shall be renewed on the anniversary date of either the trailer plate expiration date or the date of issuance of the original permanent trailer identification plate, every five calendar years commencing December 31, 2006. *(Added by Stats.2000, c. 861 (S.B. 2084), § 24, eff. Sept. 29, 2000. Amended by Stats.2001, c. 825 (S.B.290), § 8; Stats.2001, c. 826 (A.B.1472), § 14.5.)*

Cross References

Dealers defined, see Vehicle Code §§ 285 and 286.
Distributors defined, see Vehicle Code §§ 296 and 297.
Franchisees defined, see Vehicle Code §§ 331.1 and 331.2.
Issuance of licenses and certificates to specified dealers, manufacturers, distributors, or representatives of trailers subject to identification pursuant to this section, see Vehicle Code § 11723.
Sale of specified vehicles, presumption of sale at retail, rebuttal by taking resale certificate, additional contents of resale certificate, see Revenue and Taxation Code § 6092.5.
Tangible personal property, due dates for use taxes imposed for storage, use or other consumption of property, see Revenue and Taxation Code § 6451.5.
Vehicle manufacturer defined, see Vehicle Code § 672.

§ 5015. Time for application

(a) The application for an identification plate for special construction equipment, special mobile equipment, cemetery equipment, and any logging vehicle shall be made before that piece of equipment is moved over a highway.

(b) The application for an identification plate for a cotton trailer or a farm trailer as specified in Section 36109, a vehicle that is farmer-owned and used as provided in subdivision (b) of Section 36101, a motor vehicle that is farmer-owned and operated and used as provided in subdivision (a) of Section 36101, or an automatic bale wagon operated as specified in subdivision (a) or (b) of Section 36102 shall be made before any such piece of equipment is moved over a highway.

(c) The application for a permanent trailer identification plate, as described in Section 5014.1, shall be made prior to the equipment or vehicle described in subdivision (a) being moved, towed, or left standing on any highway or in any offstreet public parking facility. *(Stats.1959, c. 3, p. 1569, § 5015. Amended by Stats.1961, c. 1659, p. 3627, § 6; Stats.1967, c. 1069, p. 2700, § 3; Stats.1967, c. 1491, p. 3486, § 4; Stats.1969, c. 1075, p. 2063, § 5; Stats.1970, c. 1330, p. 2474, § 1; Stats.1971, c. 438, p. 904, § 181, operative May 3, 1972; Stats.1971, c. 432, p. 838, § 5, operative May 3, 1972; Stats.1972, c. 973, p. 1758, § 9, eff. Aug. 16, 1972; Stats.1977, c. 456, p. 1494, § 3; Stats.1983, c. 708, § 4; Stats.1984, c. 1077, § 3, operative July 1, 1985; Stats.2000, c. 861 (S.B.2084), § 25, eff. Sept. 29, 2000.)*

Authority to prescribe forms for applications, see Vehicle Code § 1652.

§ 5016. Identification plates and certificates

Upon proper application and payment of the fees specified in Section 5014.1 or 9261, the department shall issue an identification plate and an identification certificate for the piece of equipment, vehicle, trailer, semitrailer, or implement of husbandry for which application is made. *(Stats.1959, c. 3, p. 1569, § 5016. Amended by Stats.1969, c. 1075, p. 2063, § 6; Stats.1970, c. 405, p. 816, § 2; Stats.1970, c. 1330, p. 2475, § 2; Stats.1972, c. 973, p. 1758, § 10, eff. Aug. 16, 1972; Stats.1984, c. 1077, § 4, operative July 1, 1985; Stats.2000, c. 861 (S.B.2084), § 26, eff. Sept. 29, 2000.)*

Implement of husbandry, defined, see Vehicle Code § 36000.

§ 5016.5. Identification plate; issuance to manufacturer or dealer

(a) The department may issue a special identification plate or other suitable device to a manufacturer or dealer of special construction equipment, special mobile equipment, cemetery equipment, tow dolly, logging vehicle, or implement of husbandry upon payment of the fee specified in subdivision (b) of Section 9261. The identification plate or other suitable device shall be of a size, color, and configuration determined by the department. The form of the application shall also be determined by the department.

(b) A manufacturer or dealer of special construction equipment, special mobile equipment, cemetery equipment, any tow dolly, any logging vehicle, or any implement of husbandry may operate or move such equipment or vehicle upon the highways during the delivery of or during the demonstration for the sale of such piece of equipment or vehicle upon condition that any such equipment or vehicle display thereon an identification plate or other suitable device issued to such manufacturer or dealer; provided, that special permits have been obtained in accordance with the provisions of Article 6 (commencing with Section 35780) of Chapter 5 of Division 15 for the operation or movement of any such equipment or vehicle of a size, weight, or load exceeding the maximum specified in this code. *(Added by Stats. 1970, c. 405, p. 816, § 3; Stats.1974, c. 545, p. 1310, § 160; Stats.1975, c. 534, p. 1100, § 1; Stats.1977, c. 456, p. 1494, § 4; Stats.1983, c. 708, § 5; Stats.1984, c. 1077, § 5, operative July 1, 1985.)*

Dealer defined, see Vehicle Code §§ 285, 286.
Implement of husbandry,
  Defined, see Vehicle Code § 36000.
  Identification plates, see Vehicle Code § 36115.
Logging vehicle defined, see Vehicle Code § 379.
Special construction equipment defined, see Vehicle Code § 565.

Special mobile equipment defined, see Vehicle Code § 575.
Tow dolly defined, see Vehicle Code § 617.
Vehicle manufacturer defined, see Vehicle Code § 672.

§ 5017. Display of identification plate; carrying of identification certificate; permanent plate and identification certificate

(a) Each identification plate issued under Section 5016 shall bear a distinctive number to identify the equipment, logging vehicle, trailer, semitrailer, or implement of husbandry for which it is issued. The owner, upon being issued a plate, shall attach it to the equipment, logging vehicle, trailer, semitrailer, or implement of husbandry for which it is issued and shall carry the identification certificate issued by the department as provided by Section 4454. It shall be unlawful for any person to attach or use the plate upon any other equipment, logging vehicle, trailer, semitrailer, or implement of husbandry. If the equipment, logging vehicle, trailer, semitrailer, or implement of husbandry is destroyed or the ownership thereof transferred to another person, the person to whom the plate was issued shall, within 10 days, notify the department, on a form approved by the department, that the equipment, logging vehicle, trailer, semitrailer, or implement of husbandry has been destroyed or the ownership thereof transferred to another person.

(b) Upon the implementation of the permanent trailer identification plate program, all trailers except those exempted in paragraphs (1) and (3) of subdivision (a) of Section 5014.1 may be assigned a single permanent plate for identification purposes. Upon issuance of the plate, it shall be attached to the vehicle pursuant to Sections 5200 and 5201.

(c) An identification certificate shall be issued for each trailer or semitrailer assigned an identification plate. The identification certificate shall contain upon its face, the date issued, the name and residence or business address of the registered owner or lessee and of the legal owner, if any, the vehicle identification number assigned to the trailer or semitrailer, and a description of the trailer or semitrailer as complete as that required in the application for registration of the trailer or semitrailer. For those trailers registered under Article 4 (commencing with Section 8050) of Chapter 4 on the effective date of the act adding this sentence that are being converted to the permanent trailer identification program, the identification card may contain only the name of the registrant, and the legal owner's name is not required to be shown. Upon transfer of those trailers, the identification card shall contain the name of the owner and legal owner, if any. When an identification certificate has been issued to a trailer or semitrailer, the owner or operator shall make that certificate available for inspection by a peace officer upon request.

(d) The application for transfer of ownership of a vehicle with a trailer plate or permanent trailer identification plate shall be made within 10 days of sale of the vehicle. The permanent trailer identification certificate is not a certificate of ownership as described in Section

38076. *(Stats.1959, c. 3, p. 1569, § 5017. Amended by Stats.1959, c. 1996, p. 4618, § 8; Stats.1967, c. 410, p. 1630, § 3; Stats.1970, c. 405, p. 817, § 4; Stats.1970, c. 1330, p. 2475, § 3; Stats.1971, c. 235, p. 362, § 1, operative May 3, 1972; Stats.1972, c. 973, p. 1758, § 11, eff. Aug. 16, 1972; Stats.1977, c. 456, p. 1495, § 5; Stats.1984, c. 1077, § 6, operative July 1, 1985; Stats.2000, c. 861 (S.B.2084), § 27, eff. Sept. 29, 2000; Stats.2001, c. 825 (S.B.290), § 8.7; Stats.2001, c. 826 (A.B.1472), § 15.5; Stats.2002, c. 664 (A.B.3034), § 214.)*

§ 5018.   Transfer of ownership; transferee's duties

Whenever the ownership of equipment, a logging vehicle, or an implement of husbandry is transferred, the transferee shall within 10 days thereafter make application to the department for a transfer of ownership and pay the fee specified in subdivision (c) of Section 9261. *(Added by Stats.1984, c. 1077, § 7, operative July 1, 1985.)*

§ 5019.   Trailers

The authorizations for the issuance of special license plates referred to in Sections 5005 and 5008 do not apply to trailers. *(Added by Stats.1959, c. 837, p. 2886, § 1. Amended by Stats.1980, c. 342, p. 689, § 1; Stats.1984, c. 918, § 3.*

Cross References

Trailer defined, see Vehicle Code § 630.

§ 5020.   Class D radio station

Any person holding an unexpired license for a class D radio station in the Citizens Radio Service issued by the Federal Communications Commission may, at the time he or she makes application for an original or a renewal registration for a motor vehicle, also apply directly to the department for special license plates, to be affixed to the motor vehicle for which registration is sought, on which, in lieu of the numbers otherwise prescribed by law, shall be inscribed the official class D radio station call sign of the applicant as assigned by the Federal Communications Commission.

The applicant shall, by satisfactory proof, show that he or she is the holder of an unexpired license and, in addition to the regular registration fee, may be charged a fee of twenty dollars ($20) for each set of special plates when issued and fifteen dollars ($15) each succeeding year the vehicle is registered. Whenever the vehicle or the ownership of the vehicle for which plates are issued is changed, a fee of twenty dollars ($20) may be charged. When the applicant also pays weight fees, the department shall so indicate on the special license plates. *(Added by Stats.1969, c. 1442, p. 2952, § 1. Amended by Stats.1970, c. 989, p. 1762, § 2; Stats.1982, c. 1273, p. 4700, § 6.)*

§ 5021.   Class D radio station

After the requirements for the registration of the vehicle have been complied with, the department shall issue such plates in lieu of the regular license plates. The department shall not issue more than one set of special plates for any licensed class D radio station in the Citizens Radio Service. *(Added by Stats.1969, c. 1442, p. 2952, § 2.)*

§ 5022.   1984 Olympic reflectorized license plates

(a) Until December 31, 1984, a person described in Section 5101 may also apply for a set of commemorative 1984 Olympic reflectorized license plates and the department shall issue those special license plates in lieu of the regular license plates. No commemorative 1984 Olympic reflectorized license plates shall be issued pursuant to an application therefor which is submitted on or after January 1, 1985, but the holder of those plates may thereafter renew or retain them * * *, or transfer them to another vehicle, subject to this section.

(b) The commemorative 1984 Olympic reflectorized license plates shall be of a distinctive design and shall be available in a special series of letters or numbers, or both, as determined by the department after consultation with the Los Angeles Olympic Organizing Committee.

(c) In addition to the regular fees for an original registration or renewal of registration, * * * a special fee of twelve dollars ($12) shall be paid * * * for the transfer of the special plates to another vehicle. * * *

(d) When payment of renewal fees is not required as specified in Section 4000, or when the person determines to retain the plates upon sale, trade, or other release of the vehicle upon which the special plates have been displayed, the person shall notify the department and the person may retain the special plates.

(e) Until December 31, 1989, duplicate, replacement plates shall be identical commemorative 1984 Olympic reflectorized license plates of the same letter, number, and design as originally issued. However, duplicate, replacement plates of the commemorative 1984 Olympic reflectorized license plate series shall not be available on or after January 1, 1990. Thereafter, unless otherwise provided by * * * this code, regular series plates shall be issued for the * * * fee provided in Section 9265 whenever * * * substitute or duplicate plates are requested.

(f) All revenue derived from the additional special fees provided in this section shall be deposited in the California Environmental License Plate Fund pursuant to Section 21191 of the Public Resources Code. *(Added by Stats.1983, c. 1289, § 3, eff. Sept. 30, 1983. Amended by Stats.2013, c. 523 (S.B.788), § 23.)*

Cross References

Commemorative 1984 Olympic reflectorized license plates, see Vehicle Code § 5101.7.

§ 5023.   Commemorative Olympic reflectorized license plates

(a)(1) Until December 31, 2013, a person described in Section 5101 may also apply for a set of commemorative Olympic reflectorized license plates and the department shall issue those special license plates in lieu of regular license plates. The commemorative Olympic reflectorized license plates shall be of a distinctive design and shall be available in a special series of letters or numbers, or both, as determined by the department after consultation with the United States Olympic Committee. The department may issue the commemorative Olympic reflectorized license plates as environmental license plates, as defined in Section 5103, in a combination of numbers or letters, or both, as requested by the owner or lessee of the vehicle.

(2) On or after January 1, 2014, original, substitute, or duplicate Olympic license plates, including those issued as environmental license plates, shall not be available. However, the holder of Olympic license plates may thereafter renew or retain those plates, or transfer them to another vehicle, subject to this section. Unless otherwise provided by this code, regular series plates shall be issued for the fee provided in Section 9265 whenever substitute or duplicate plates are requested.

(3) On or after January 1, 2014, the holder of Olympic license plates issued as environmental license plates, as defined in Section 5103, may apply for other special license plates using the exact combination of numbers or letters, or both, if authorized by this code, whenever the holder requests substitute or duplicate plates.

(b) In addition to the regular fees for an original registration or renewal of registration, the following special fees shall be paid:

* * *

(1) Fifteen dollars ($15) for the transfer of the special plates to another vehicle.

* * *

(2) Thirty dollars ($30) for the annual renewal of the special plates.

(c) When payment of renewal fees is not required as specified in Section 4000, or when the person determines to retain the plates upon sale, trade, or other release of the vehicle upon which the special plates have been displayed, the person shall notify the department and the person may retain the special plates.

(d) All revenue derived from the additional special fees provided in this section, less costs incurred by the department pursuant to this section, shall be deposited in the * * * General Fund * * *. *(Added by Stats.1989, c. 1182, § 3. Amended by Stats.1990, c. 706 (A.B.3911), § 1; Stats.1993, c. 383 (S.B.965), § 1; Stats.1996, c. 270 (S.B.2116), § 1, eff. July 23, 1996; Stats.2001, c. 745 (S.B.1191), § 227, eff. Oct. 12, 2001; Stats.2010, c. 478 (A.B.2777), § 8; Stats.2013, c. 523 (S.B.788), § 24.)*

§ 5024. Commemorative collegiate reflectorized license plates

(a) A person described in Section 5101 may also apply for a set of commemorative collegiate reflectorized license plates, and the department shall issue those special license plates in lieu of the regular license plates. The collegiate reflectorized plates shall be of a distinctive design, and shall be available in a special series of letters or numbers, or both, as determined by the department. The collegiate reflectorized plates shall also contain the name of the participating institution as well as the reflectorized logotype, motto, symbol, or other distinctive design, as approved by the department, representing the participating university or college selected by the applicant. The department may issue the commemorative collegiate reflectorized license plates as environmental license plates, as defined in Section 5103, in a combination of numbers or letters, or both, as requested by the owner or lessee of the vehicle.

(b) Any public or private postsecondary educational institution in the state, which is accredited or has been accepted as a recognized candidate for accreditation by the Western Association of Schools and Colleges, may indicate to the department its decision to be included in the commemorative collegiate license plate program and submit its distinctive design for the logotype, motto, symbol, or other design. However, no public or private postsecondary educational institution may be included in the program until not less than 5,000 applications are received for license plates containing that institution's logotype, motto, symbol, or other design. Each participating institution shall collect and hold applications for collegiate license plates until it has received at least 5,000 applications. Once the institution has received at least 5,000 applications, it shall submit the applications, along with the necessary fees, to the department. Upon receiving the first application, the institution shall have one calendar year to receive the remaining required applications. If, after that one calendar year, 5,000 applications have not been received, the institution shall refund to all applicants any fees or deposits which have been collected.

(c) In addition to the regular fees for an original registration, a renewal of registration, or a transfer of registration, the following commemorative collegiate license plate fees shall be paid:

(1) Fifty dollars ($50) for the initial issuance of the plates. These plates shall be permanent and shall not be required to be replaced.

(2) Forty dollars ($40) for each renewal of registration which includes the continued display of the plates.

(3) Fifteen dollars ($15) for transfer of the plates to another vehicle.

(4) Thirty-five dollars ($35) for replacement plates, if the plates become damaged or unserviceable.

(d) When payment of renewal fees is not required as specified in Section 4000, or when the person determines to retain the commemorative collegiate license plates upon sale, trade, or other release of the vehicle upon which the plates have been displayed, the person shall notify the department and the person may retain the plates.

(e) Of the revenue derived from the additional special fees provided in this section, less costs incurred by the department pursuant to this section, one-half shall be deposited in the California Collegiate License Plate Fund, which is hereby created, and one-half shall be deposited in the Resources License Plate Fund, which is hereby created.

(f) The money in the California Collegiate License Plate Fund is, notwithstanding Section 13340 of the Government Code, continuously appropriated to the Controller for allocation as follows:

(1) To the governing body of participating public institutions in the proportion that funds are collected on behalf of each, to be used for need-based scholarships, distributed according to federal student aid guidelines.

(2) With respect to funds collected on behalf of accredited nonprofit, private, and independent colleges and universities in the state, to the California Student Aid Commission for grants to students at those institutions, in the proportion that funds are collected on behalf of each institution, who demonstrate eligibility and need in accordance with the Cal Grant Program pursuant to Article 3 (commencing with Section 69530) of Chapter 2 of Part 42 of the Education Code, but who did not receive an award based on a listing prepared by the California Student Aid Commission.

(g) The scholarships and grants shall be awarded without regard to race, religion, creed, sex, or age.

(h) The money in the Resources License Plate Fund is available, upon appropriation, for the purposes of natural resources preservation, enhancement, and restoration.

(i) All revenues deposited in, and expenditures from, the California Collegiate License Plate Fund shall be audited by the Auditor General on December 1, 1993, and December 1, 1995. *(Added by Stats.1991, c. 981 (S.B.1092), § 2. Amended by Stats.1992, c. 1282 (A.B. 3632), § 1; Stats.1994, c. 146 (A.B.3601), § 220; Stats. 2010, c. 478 (A.B.2777), § 9.)*

ARTICLE 8.1. MOTORIZED BICYCLES

Section
5030. Special license plates; requirement.
5031. Applications for license plates; contents.
5032. Time for applications for license plates.
5033. Issuance of license plates and identification cards; submission of applications by mail.
5034. Manufacturers or dealers; license plates or other devices; operation or movement of motorized bicycles.
5035. License plates; identification number and distinguishing symbols; attachment; carrying identification card; unlawful use; destruction or transfer of ownership of motorized bicycles.
5036. Service fee.
5037. Movement or operation upon highway; necessity for applications for license plates.
5038. Record system; stolen motorized bicycles.
5039. Dealers, manufacturers, salesmen, or representatives; requirement for other licenses or permits.

§ 5030. Special license plates; requirement

A motorized bicycle, as defined in Section 406, is required to display a special license plate issued by the department. *(Added by Stats.1980, c. 1070, p. 3418, § 1.)*

§ 5031. Applications for license plates; contents

An application by a person other than a manufacturer or dealer for a license plate for a motorized bicycle shall include all the following:

(a) The true, full name and the driver's license or identification card number, if any, of the owner.

(b) A description of the motorized bicycle, including any distinctive marks or features.

(c) Other information as may reasonably be required by the department to determine whether a license plate shall be issued for the motorized bicycle. *(Added by Stats.1980, c. 1070, p. 3418, § 1. Amended by Stats.1994, c. 1221 (S.B.1758), § 6.)*

Cross References

Dealer defined, see Vehicle Code §§ 285, 286.
Vehicle manufacturer defined, see Vehicle Code § 672.

§ 5032. Time for applications for license plates

(a) The application for a special license plate for a motorized bicycle shall be made before the motorized bicycle is operated or moved upon a highway, except that, upon the retail sale of a motorized bicycle when there is no license plate, the operator may operate the motorized bicycle for a period of five days from and including the date of sale, at which time application shall be made to the department for a special license plate. If the fifth day should fall on Saturday, Sunday, or a holiday, the application shall be made on the first business day thereafter.

(b) The five-day operating provision set forth in subdivision (a) shall apply only if the operator has in his immediate possession evidence that the motorized bicycle was purchased within the last five days including the date of sale. *(Added by Stats.1980, c. 1070, p. 3418, § 1.)*

Cross References

Retail sale, defined, see Vehicle Code § 520.

§ 5033. Issuance of license plates and identification cards; submission of applications by mail

Upon proper application and payment of the fees specified in Section 5036, the department shall issue a special license plate and an identification card for the motorized bicycle for which application was made. Applications may be submitted by mail unless the department determines that it is not feasible to complete the identification process by such method. *(Added by Stats. 1980, c. 1070, p. 3418, § 1.)*

§5034. Manufacturers or dealers; license plates or other devices; operation or movement of motorized bicycles

(a) The department may issue a special license plate or other suitable device to a manufacturer or dealer of motorized bicycles upon payment of the fee specified in Section 5036. The license plate shall be of a size, color and configuration determined by the department. The form of the application shall also be determined by the department.

(b) A manufacturer or dealer of motorized bicycles may operate or move a motorized bicycle upon the highways during the delivery of, or during the demonstration for the sale of, the motorized bicycle if the motorized bicycle displays thereon a license plate or other suitable device issued to the manufacturer or dealer. *(Added by Stats.1980, c. 1070, p. 3418, § 1.)*

Cross References

Dealer defined, see Vehicle Code §§ 285, 286.
Vehicle manufacturer defined, see Vehicle Code § 672.

§5035. License plates; identification number and distinguishing symbols; attachment; carrying identification card; unlawful use; destruction or transfer of ownership of motorized bicycles

Each license plate issued under Section 5033 shall bear a distinctive number to identify the motorized bicycle for which it is issued and shall bear a symbol, letter, or word to distinguish license plates issued under this article from license plates issued for motorcycles and motor-driven cycles. The owner, upon being issued a license plate, shall attach it to the motorized bicycle for which it is issued and shall carry the identification card issued by the department as provided in Section 4454. It shall be unlawful for any person to attach or use the license plate upon any other motorized bicycle or vehicle. If the motorized bicycle is destroyed, the owner shall destroy the license plate and shall within 10 days notify the department on a form approved by the department that the motorized bicycle and license plate have been destroyed.

If the ownership of the motorized bicycle is transferred to another person, that person shall submit, within 10 days, proper application as provided in Section 5031. The license plate shall remain with the motorized bicycle. *(Added by Stats.1980, c. 1070, p. 3418, § 1.)*

§5036. Service fee

A service fee of fifteen dollars ($15) shall be paid for the issuance or transfer of a special license plate for motorized bicycles, as defined in Section 406. Publicly-owned motorized bicycles are exempt from the fee. *(Added by Stats.1980, c. 1070, p. 3418, § 1. Amended by Stats.2003, c. 719 (S.B.1055), § 7.)*

Cross References

Base fee amounts, adjustment of fees, see Vehicle Code § 1678.

§5037. Movement or operation upon highway; necessity for applications for license plates

(a) No motorized bicycle first sold on or after July 1, 1981, shall be moved or operated upon a highway unless the owner first makes application for a license plate and, when received, attaches it to the motorized bicycle as provided in this article.

(b) Motorized bicycles first sold prior to July 1, 1981, shall not be moved or operated upon a highway after January 1, 1982, unless the owner makes application for a license plate and, when received, attaches it to the motorized bicycle as provided in this article.

(c) Any motorized bicycle currently licensed pursuant to Division 16.7 (commencing with Section 39000) on July 1, 1981, may be operated upon a highway until July 1, 1982. *(Added by Stats.1980, c. 1070, p. 3418, § 1.)*

§5038. Record system; stolen motorized bicycles

The department shall establish a record system that provides for identification of stolen motorized bicycles. *(Added by Stats.1980, c. 1970, p. 3418, § 1.)*

§5039. Dealers, manufacturers, salesmen, or representatives; requirement for other licenses or permits

Notwithstanding any other provision of law, no dealer, manufacturer, salesman, or representative of motorized bicycles exclusively is required to be licensed or permitted pursuant to Chapter 4 (commencing with Section 11700) of Division 5. *(Added by Stats.1980, c. 1070, p. 3418, § 1.)*

Cross References

Dealer defined, see Vehicle Code §§ 285, 286.
Representative defined, see Vehicle Code § 512.
Vehicle manufacturer defined, see Vehicle Code § 672.
Vehicle salesperson defined, see Vehicle Code § 675.

ARTICLE 8.3. HISTORIC AND SPECIAL INTEREST VEHICLES

Section
5050. Legislative findings.
5051. Definitions.
5052. Storage; manner of maintenance.

Cross References

Special plates for vehicles of historic value, see Vehicle Code §§ 5004, 5004.1.

§5050. Legislative findings

The Legislature finds and declares that constructive leisure pursuits by California citizens is most important. This article is intended to encourage responsible participation in the hobby of collecting, preserving, restoring, and maintaining motor vehicles of historic and special interest, which hobby contributes to the enjoyment of the citizen and the preservation of California's automotive memorabilia. *(Added by Stats.1975, c. 753, p. 1755, § 1.)*

§ 5051. Definitions

As used in this article, unless the context otherwise requires:

(a) "Collector" is the owner of one or more vehicles described in Section 5004 or of one or more special interest vehicles, as defined in this article, who collects, purchases, acquires, trades, or disposes of the vehicle, or parts thereof, for his or her own use, in order to preserve, restore, and maintain the vehicle for hobby or historical purposes.

(b) "Special interest vehicle" is a vehicle of an age that is unaltered from the manufacturer's original specifications and, because of its significance, including, but not limited to, an out-of-production vehicle or a model of less than 2,000 sold in California in a model-year, is collected, preserved, restored, or maintained by a hobbyist as a leisure pursuit.

(c) "Parts car" is a motor vehicle that is owned by a collector to furnish parts for restoration or maintenance of a special interest vehicle or a vehicle described in Section 5004, thus enabling a collector to preserve, restore, and maintain a special interest vehicle or a vehicle described in Section 5004.

(d) "Street rod vehicle" is a motor vehicle, other than a motorcycle, manufactured in, or prior to, 1948 that is individually modified in its body style or design, including through the use of nonoriginal or reproduction components, and may include additional modifications to other components, including, but not limited to, the engine, drivetrain, suspension, and brakes in a manner that does not adversely affect its safe performance as a motor vehicle or render it unlawful for highway use. *(Added by Stats.1975, c. 753, p. 1755, § 1. Amended by Stats.1990, c. 929 (A.B.3449), § 2; Stats.2006, c. 574 (A.B.2520), § 6.)*

Cross References

Words and phrases defined, collector motor vehicle, see Vehicle Code § 259.

§ 5052. Storage; manner of maintenance

Except as otherwise provided by local ordinance, a collector may maintain one or more vehicles described in Section 5051, whether currently licensed or unlicensed, or whether operable or inoperable, in outdoor storage on private property, if every such vehicle and outdoor storage area is maintained in such manner as not to constitute a health hazard and is located away from public view, or screened from ordinary public view, by means of a suitable fence, trees, shrubbery, opaque covering, or other appropriate means. *(Added by Stats.1975, c. 753, p. 1756, § 1.)*

194

Cross References

Exemption from certificate of nonoperation requirements, see Vehicle Code § 4604.

ARTICLE 8.4. SPECIAL INTEREST LICENSE PLATES

Section

5060. Application; issuance; design; participating organizations; developmental and administrative costs; retention and use of plates; use of collected fees.

5060.1. Restrictions on program application participation.

5061. Motorcycle special interest license plates.

5062. Blue sky license plate program; design; application; issuance; fees; deposit of revenues.

5063. Repealed.

5064. Environmental design license plates; design; application; issuance; fees; deposit of revenues.

5065. Repealed.

5066. California memorial license plates; fees; antiterrorism fund established; termination of plate replacement or issuance.

5067. California Coastal Commission design; additional fees; deposit of revenue; creation of California Beach and Coastal Enhancement Account.

5068. Application for special interest plates; fees; Internet Web site link for online orders.

5068.1. Issuance of decal for veteran plates or plates honoring veterans; availability of "support our troops" decal; inventory elimination.

5069. Deposit of revenue in Veterans Service Office Fund.

5070 to 5071.1. Repealed.

5072. Special license plates to fund child health and safety programs; design; fees.

5073. Repealed.

5074. Special interest license plates; arts council participation; fees; use of revenue.

5075. Special environmental design license plates; Lake Tahoe conservancy; fees.

5080. Repealed.

Cross References

Domestic violence victims, application for new and different license plates, see Vehicle Code § 4467.

§ 5060. Application; issuance; design; participating organizations; developmental and administrative costs; retention and use of plates; use of collected fees

(a) An organization may apply to the department for participation in a special interest license plate program and the department shall issue special license plates for that program if the issuance of those plates is required by this article, the sponsoring organization complies with the requirements of this section, and the organization meets all of the following criteria:

(1) Qualifies for tax-exempt status under Section 501(c)(3) of the Internal Revenue Code and Section 23701d of the Revenue and Taxation Code.

(2) Submits a financial plan describing the purposes for which the revenues described in paragraph (2) of subdivision (e) will be used.

(3) Submits a design of the organization's proposed special interest license plate that, among other things, provides for the placement of the number and letter characters in a manner that allows for law enforcement to readily identify those characters.

(b) Any person described in Section 5101 may apply for special interest license plates, in lieu of the regular license plates.

(c) The design criteria for a special interest license plate are as follows:

(1) The license plate for a passenger vehicle, commercial vehicle, or trailer shall provide a space not larger than 2 inches by 3 inches to the left of the numerical series and a space not larger than five-eighths of an inch in height below the numerical series for a distinctive design, decal, or descriptive message as authorized by this article. The plates shall be issued in sequential numerical order or, pursuant to Section 5103, in a combination of numbers or letters.

(2) Special interest license plates authorized under this article may be issued for use on a motorcycle. That license plate shall contain a five digit configuration issued in sequential numerical order or, pursuant to Section 5103, in a combination of numbers or letters. There shall be a space to the left of the numerical series for a distinctive design or decal and the characters shall contrast sharply with the uniform background color. No motorcycle plate containing a full plate graphic design is authorized. Those particular special interest license plates that were issued prior to the discontinuation provided by this paragraph may continue to be used and attached to the vehicle for which they were issued and may be renewed, retained, or transferred pursuant to this code.

(d)(1) No organization may be included in the program until not less than 7,500 applications for the particular special interest license plates are received. Each organization shall collect and hold applications for the plates. Once the organization has received at least 7,500 applications, it shall submit the applications, along with the necessary fees, to the department. The department shall not issue any special interest license plate until an organization has received and submitted to the department not less than 7,500 applications for that particular special interest license plate within the time period prescribed in this section. Advanced payment to the department by an organization representing the department's estimated or actual administrative costs associated with the issuance of a particular special interest license plate shall not constitute compliance with this requirement. The organization shall have 12 months, following the effective date of the enactment of the specific legislation enabling the organization to participate in this program, to receive the required number of applications. If, after that 12 months, 7,500 applications have not been received, the organization shall immediately do either of the following:

(A) Refund to all applicants any fees or deposits that have been collected.

(B) Contact the department to indicate the organization's intent to undertake collection of additional applications and fees or deposits for an additional period, not to exceed 12 months, in order to obtain the minimum 7,500 applications. If an organization elects to exercise the option under this paragraph, it shall contact each applicant who has submitted an application with the appropriate fees or deposits to determine if the applicant wishes a refund of fees or deposits or requests the continuance of the holding of the application and fees or deposits until that time that the organization has received 7,500 applications. The organization shall refund the fees or deposits to any applicant so requesting. In no event shall an organization collect and hold applications for a period exceeding 24 months following the date of authorization as described in paragraph (2) of subdivision (a).

(C) Sequential plate fees shall be paid for the original issuance, renewal, retention, replacement, or transfer of the special interest license plate as determined by the organization and authorized by department's regulations. Those plates containing a personalized message are subject to the fees required pursuant to Sections 5106 and 5108 in addition to any fees required by the special interest license plate program.

(2)(A) If the number of currently outstanding and valid special interest license plates in any particular program provided for in this article is less than 7,500, the department shall notify the sponsoring organization of that fact and shall inform the organization that if that number is less than 7,500 one year from the date of that notification, the department will no longer issue or replace those special interest license plates.

(B) Those particular special interest license plates that were issued prior to the discontinuation provided by subparagraph (A) may continue to be used and attached to the vehicle for which they were issued and may be renewed, retained, or transferred pursuant to this code.

(e)(1) The department shall deduct its costs to develop and administer the special interest license plate program from the revenues collected for the plates.

(2) The department shall deposit the remaining revenues from the original issuance, renewal, retention, replacement, or transfer of the special interest license plate in a fund which shall be established by the Controller.

(f) When payment of renewal fees is not required as specified in Section 4000, or when a person determines to retain the special interest license plate upon a sale, trade, or other release of the vehicle upon which the plate has been displayed, the person shall notify the department and the person may retain and use the plate as authorized by department regulations.

(g) An organization that is eligible to participate in a special interest license plate program pursuant to this article and receives funds from the additional fees collected from the sale of special license plates shall not expend annually more than 25 percent of those funds on administrative costs, marketing, or other promotional activities associated with encouraging application for, or renewal of, the special license plates.

(h)(1) Every organization authorized under this article to offer special interest license plates shall prepare and submit an annual accounting report to the department by June 30. The report shall include an accounting of all revenues and expenditures associated with the special interest license plate program.

(2) If an organization submits a report pursuant to paragraph (1) indicating that the organization violated the expenditure restriction set forth in subdivision (g), the department shall immediately cease depositing fees in the fund created by the Controller for that organization under paragraph (2) of subdivision (e) and, instead, shall deposit those fees that would have otherwise been deposited in that fund in a separate fund created by the Controller, which fund is subject to appropriation by the Legislature. The department shall immediately notify the organization of this course of action. The depositing of funds in the account established pursuant to this paragraph shall continue until the organization demonstrates to the satisfaction of the department that the organization is in compliance or will comply with the requirements of subdivision (g). If one year from the date that the organization receives the notice described in this paragraph, the organization is still unable to satisfactorily demonstrate to the department that it is in compliance or will comply with the requirements of subdivision (g), the department shall no longer issue or replace those special interest license plates associated with that organization. Those particular special interest license plates that were issued prior to the discontinuation provided by this paragraph may continue to be used and attached to the vehicle for which they were issued and may be renewed, retained, or transferred pursuant to this code.

(3) Upon receiving the reports required under paragraph (1), the department shall prepare and transmit an annual consolidated report to the Legislature containing the revenue and expenditure data. *(Added by Stats.1992, c. 1273 (A.B.2700), § 2. Amended by Stats.1993, c. 1303 (S.B.648), § 1, eff. Oct. 11, 1993; Stats.1994, c. 558 (S.B.1411), § 1; Stats.2000, c. 163 (S.B.1329), § 2; Stats. 2003, c. 185 (A.B.1743), § 41.)*

Validity

This section was been held unconstitutional in the case of The Women's Resource Network v. Gourley, E.D.Cal.2004, 305 F.Supp.2d 1145..

§ 5060.1.　Restrictions on program application participation

Notwithstanding Section 5060 or any other provision of law to the contrary, the department shall not accept an application for participation in a special interest license plate program under Section 5060 and shall not issue,

under Section 5060, special interest license plates for a new program. *(Added by Stats.2006, c. 454 (A.B.84), § 2.)*

§ 5061.　Motorcycle special interest license plates

(a) Notwithstanding any other provision of law, if the department permits the issuance of a special interest license plate for display on a motorcycle, the department shall not approve any design for that plate that incorporates either or both of the following:

(1) Full or partial graphic designs appearing behind the license plate number configuration.

(2) Symbols within the license plate number configuration.

(b) Any special interest license plate issued for display on a motorcycle is subject to the same fees that are collected for the issuance and retention of special interest license plates on other vehicles. *(Added by Stats.2000, c. 859 (A.B.1515), § 2.)*

§ 5062.　Blue sky license plate program; design; application; issuance; fees; deposit of revenues

(a) This section shall be known, and may be cited, as the Rosenthal Blue Sky License Plate Program.

(b) The Legislature hereby finds and declares that CALSTART is a California nonprofit consortium dedicated to the development and commercialization of advanced transportation technologies, including clean fuel vehicles, and that CALSTART should be authorized to undertake a special environmental "Blue Sky" license plate program to facilitate the purchase and use of clean fuel vehicles in the state.

(c) CALSTART may, with the approval of the department, participate in this special interest license plate program.

(d) CALSTART may, with the approval of the department, develop a distinctive design, in conformance with Section 5060, for inclusion on a special interest license plate. The license plate shall be known as the Blue Sky license plate and shall signify that the vehicle to which it is assigned is a clean fuel vehicle.

(e) Any person who owns or leases a clean fuel vehicle, as defined in Section 257, and who applies for an original or renewal registration of that vehicle, may apply, through CALSTART, for a set of Blue Sky license plates in lieu of regular license plates.

(f) The Blue Sky license plate is subject to Sections 5106 and 5108. The revenues derived from the sale of the license plates shall be deposited in the California Environmental License Plate Fund, after the department has deducted its costs for developing and administering the program.

(g) Notwithstanding Section 5060, a Blue Sky license plate may, upon application of the holder, be transferred to another clean fuel vehicle. If the vehicle to which transfer is sought is not a clean fuel vehicle, the plates shall be surrendered to the department.

(h) CALSTART, in coordination with the State Air Resources Board, the State Energy Resources Conservation and Development Commission, and the Public Utilities Commission, shall undertake efforts to publicize the availability of Blue Sky license plates.

(i) Notwithstanding Section 5060, CALSTART shall have 12 months, commencing November 1, 1995, to receive the required applications and to notify the department that the requisite number of applications have been received. If, after that 12-month period, 5,000 applications have not been received, CALSTART shall immediately notify the department and refund to all applicants any fees or deposits which have been collected.

(j) If, on November 1, 1996, the department has not received a notice from CALSTART pursuant to subdivision (i) or if, on or before that date CALSTART notifies the department that the requisite number of applications have not been received, the department shall provide that information to the Secretary of State, and this section shall become inoperative upon receipt of that information by the Secretary of State, and shall remain in effect only until January 1, 1997, and as of that date is repealed, unless a later enacted statute, which is enacted before January 1, 1997, deletes or extends that date. *(Added by Stats.1993, c. 1159 (S.B.314), § 5.)*

Inoperative Date and Repeal

By its own terms, this section may become inoperative and may be repealed on Jan. 1, 1997, upon specified conditions.

§ 5063. Repealed by Stats.1998, c. 1002 (S.B.844), § 1

§ 5064. Environmental design license plates; design; application; issuance; fees; deposit of revenues

(a) The department, in consultation with the Yosemite Foundation, shall design and make available for issuance pursuant to this article special environmental design license plates bearing, notwithstanding Section 5060, a full-plate graphic design depicting a significant feature or quality of Yosemite National Park. Any person described in Section 5101, upon payment of the additional fees set forth in subdivision (b), may apply for and be issued a set of special environmental design license plates. Notwithstanding subdivision (a) of Section 5060, the plates may be issued in a combination of numbers or letters, or both, requested by the owner or lessee of the vehicle.

(b) In addition to the regular fees for an original registration or renewal of registration, the following additional fees shall be paid for the issuance, renewal, or transfer of the special environmental design license plates authorized pursuant to this section:

(1) For the original issuance of the plates, fifty dollars ($50).

(2) For a renewal of registration with the plates, forty dollars ($40).

(3) For transfer of the plates to another vehicle, fifteen dollars ($15).

(4) For each substitute replacement plate, thirty-five dollars ($35).

(5) For the conversion of an existing environmental license plate to the special environmental design license plate authorized pursuant to this section, sixty-five dollars ($65).

(c) After deducting its administrative costs under this section, the department shall deposit the additional revenue derived from the issuance, renewal, transfer, and substitution of special environmental design license plates as follows:

(1) One–half in the Yosemite Foundation Account, which is hereby created in the California Environmental License Plate Fund. Upon appropriation by the Legislature, the money in the account shall be allocated by the Controller to the Yosemite Foundation or its successor for expenditure for the exclusive trust purposes of preservation and restoration projects in Yosemite National Park.

(2) One–half in the California Environmental License Plate Fund.

(d) The Yosemite Foundation shall report to the Legislature on or before June 30 of each year on its use and expenditure of the money in the Yosemite Foundation Account, beginning one year after the initial issuance of the special interest license plates authorized by this section. *(Added by Stats.1992, c. 1273 (A.B.2700), § 2. Amended by Stats.1996, c. 1154 (A.B.3020), § 58, eff. Sept. 30, 1996.)*

§ 5065. Repealed by Stats.1998, c. 1002 (S.B.844), § 2

§ 5066. California memorial license plates; fees; anti-terrorism fund established; termination of plate replacement or issuance

(a) The department, in conjunction with the California Highway Patrol, shall design and make available for issuance pursuant to this article the California memorial license plate. Notwithstanding Section 5060, the California memorial license plate may be issued in a combination of numbers or letters, or both, as requested by the applicant for the plates. A person described in Section 5101, upon payment of the additional fees set forth in subdivision (b), may apply for and be issued a set of California memorial license plates.

(b) In addition to the regular fees for an original registration or renewal of registration, the following additional fees shall be paid for the issuance, renewal, retention, or transfer of the California memorial license plates authorized pursuant to this section:

(1) For the original issuance of the plates, fifty dollars ($50).

(2) For a renewal of registration of the plates or retention of the plates, if renewal is not required, forty dollars ($40).

(3) For transfer of the plates to another vehicle, fifteen dollars ($15).

(4) For each substitute replacement plate, thirty-five dollars ($35).

(5) In addition, for the issuance of an environmental license plate, as defined in Section 5103, the additional fees required pursuant to Sections 5106 and 5108 shall be deposited proportionately in the funds described in subdivision (c).

(c) The department shall deposit the additional revenue derived from the issuance, renewal, transfer, and substitution of California memorial license plates as follows:

(1) Eighty-five percent in the Antiterrorism Fund, which is hereby created in the General Fund.

(A) Upon appropriation by the Legislature, one-half of the money in the fund shall be allocated by the Controller to the * * * Office of Emergency Services to be used solely for antiterrorism activities. The office shall not use more than 5 percent of the money appropriated * * * for local antiterrorism efforts for administrative purposes.

(B) Upon appropriation by the Legislature in the annual Budget Act or in another statute, one-half of the money in the fund shall be used solely for antiterrorism activities.

(2) Fifteen percent in the California Memorial Scholarship Fund, which is hereby established in the General Fund. Money deposited in this fund shall be administered by the Scholarshare Investment Board, and shall be available, upon appropriation in the annual Budget Act or in another statute, for distribution or encumbrance by the board pursuant to Article 21. 5 (commencing with Section 70010) of Chapter 2 of Part 42 of the Education Code.

(d) The department shall deduct its costs to administer, but not to develop, the California memorial license plate program. The department may utilize an amount of money, not to exceed fifty thousand dollars ($50,000) annually, derived from the issuance, renewal, transfer, and substitution of California memorial license plates for the continued promotion of the California memorial license plate program of this section.

(e) For the purposes of this section, "antiterrorism activities" means activities related to the prevention, detection, and emergency response to terrorism that are undertaken by state and local law enforcement, fire protection, and public health agencies. The funds provided for these activities, to the extent that funds are available, shall be used exclusively for purposes directly related to fighting terrorism. Eligible activities include, but are not limited to, hiring support staff to perform administrative tasks, hiring and training additional law enforcement, fire protection, and public health personnel, response training for existing and additional law enforcement, fire protection, and public health personnel, and hazardous materials and other equipment expenditures.

(f) Beginning January 1, 2007, and each January 1 thereafter, the department shall determine the number of currently outstanding and valid California memorial license plates. If that number is less than 7,500 in any year, then the department shall no longer issue or replace those plates. *(Added by Stats.2002, c. 38 (A.B.1759), § 2, eff. May 13, 2002. Amended by Stats.2003, c. 719 (S.B. 1055), § 7.5; Stats.2006, c. 69 (A.B.1806), § 34, eff. July 12, 2006; Stats.2010, c. 618 (A.B.2791), § 292; Stats.2013, c. 28 (S.B.71), § 90, eff. June 27, 2013.)*

Cross References

California memorial scholarship program, establishment and administration, see Education Code § 70010.

§ 5067. California Coastal Commission design; additional fees; deposit of revenue; creation of California Beach and Coastal Enhancement Account

(a) The department, in consultation with the California Coastal Commission, shall design and make available for issuance pursuant to this article special environmental design license plates. Notwithstanding subdivision (a) of Section 5060, the special environmental design license plates shall bear a graphic design depicting a California coastal motif and may be issued in a combination of numbers or letters, or both, as requested by the applicant for the plates. Any person described in Section 5101 may, upon payment of the additional fees set forth in subdivision (b), apply for and be issued a set of special environmental design license plates.

(b) In addition to the regular fees for an original registration or renewal of registration, the following additional fees shall be paid for the issuance, renewal, retention, or transfer of the special environmental design license plates authorized pursuant to this section:

(1) For the original issuance of the plates, fifty dollars ($50).

(2) For a renewal of registration of the plates or retention of the plates, if renewal is not required, forty dollars ($40).

(3) For transfer of the plates to another vehicle, fifteen dollars ($15).

(4) For each substitute replacement plate, thirty-five dollars ($35).

(5) In addition, for the issuance of an environmental license plate, as defined in Section 5103, the additional fees prescribed in Section 5106 and 5108. The additional fees prescribed in Sections 5106 and 5108 shall be deposited in the California Environmental License Plate Fund.

(c) After deducting its administrative costs under this section, the department, except as provided in paragraph (5) of subdivision (b), shall deposit the additional revenue derived from the issuance, renewal, transfer, and substitution of special environmental design license plates as follows:

(1) One-half in the California Beach and Coastal Enhancement Account, which is hereby established in the California Environmental License Plate Fund. Upon appropriation by the Legislature, the money in the account shall be allocated by the Controller as follows:

(A) First to the California Coastal Commission for expenditure for the Adopt–A–Beach program, the Beach Cleanup Day program, coastal public education programs, and grants to local governments and nonprofit organizations for the costs of operating and maintaining public beaches related to these programs.

(B) Second, from funds remaining after the allocation required under subparagraph (A), to the State Coastal Conservancy for coastal natural resource restoration and enhancement projects and for other projects consistent with the provisions of Division 21 (commencing with Section 31000) of the Public Resources Code.

(2) One-half in the California Environmental License Plate Fund. *(Added by Stats.1994, c. 558 (S.B.1411), § 3. Amended by Stats.2004, c. 230 (S.B.1107), § 19, eff. Aug. 16, 2004.)*

Cross References

Designation of voluntary contribution on tax return to California Beach and Coastal Enhancement Account, revision of tax return, deduction, see Revenue and Taxation Code § 18745.

§ 5068. Application for special interest plates; fees; Internet Web site link for online orders

(a)(1)(A) A veterans' organization may apply either individually or with other veterans' organizations to meet the application threshold set forth in Section 5060 for special interest plates. An organization that meets the minimum application requirement by applying with other organizations under this subdivision shall be issued a regular license plate bearing a distinctive design or decal approved under subdivision (a) of Section 5060.

(B) The Department of Veterans Affairs may modify the distinctive design or decal described in subparagraph (A), consistent with the design criteria imposed by Section 5060, to honor all veterans, or veterans who served in a particular war or armed conflict as described in subdivision (a) of Section 5068.1. Special interest plates issued under this section and bearing the modified design or decal shall be issued only after all existing plates have been issued.

(2) Any person who is the registered owner or lessee of a passenger vehicle, commercial motor vehicle, motorcycle, trailer, or semitrailer registered or certificated with the department, or any person who applies for an original registration or renewal of registration of that vehicle may apply under this section for a special interest license plate with a decal that honors all veterans or veterans who served in a particular war or armed conflict.

(3) Special interest license plates issued under this section may be issued in a combination of numbers or letters, or both, requested by the owner or lessee of the vehicle, to be displayed in addition to the design or decal authorized under paragraph (1), subject to Section 5105.

(b) In addition to the regular fees for an original registration, a renewal of registration, or a transfer of registration, the following fees shall be paid by individuals applying for a special interest license plate or a decal issued under this section:

(1) Fifty dollars ($50) for the initial issuance of the plates and decals. The plates shall be permanent and shall not be required to be replaced.

(2) Forty dollars ($40) for each renewal of registration that includes the continued display of the plates or decals.

(3) Fifteen dollars ($15) for transfer of the plates to another vehicle.

(4) Thirty-five dollars ($35) for replacement plates, if they become damaged or unserviceable.

(5) Ten dollars ($10) for replacement decals, if they become damaged or unserviceable.

(6) Notwithstanding Section 5106, seventy-eight dollars ($78) for the personalization of the plates, as authorized under paragraph (3) of subdivision (a).

(c) The department shall maintain on its Internet Web site, a link to order online the special interest license plates issued pursuant to this section. *(Added by Stats. 2001, c. 201 (A.B.527), § 2, operative July 1, 2002. Amended by Stats.2002, c. 664 (A.B.3034), § 215; Stats. 2003, c. 62 (S.B.600), § 299; Stats.2003, c. 594 (S.B.315), § 20; Stats.2010, c. 166 (A.B.1908), § 1; Stats.2012, c. 398 (A.B.1550), § 1; Stats.2013, c. 523 (S.B.788), § 25.)*

§ 5068.1. Issuance of decal for veteran plates or plates honoring veterans; availability of "support our troops" decal; inventory elimination

By July 1, 2013, the department shall do all of the following:

(a) Issue a distinctive decal pursuant to subparagraph (B) of paragraph (1) of subdivision (a) of Section 5068 to an applicant for an original or renewal of vehicle registration for veteran plates or plates honoring veterans to allow that applicant the option of recognizing his or her veteran status in, or honoring veterans of, a particular war or armed conflict, including, but not limited to, those who served in the active military, naval, or air service and performed any portion of their service during any of the periods described in Section 980 of the Military and Veterans Code, including active duty in a campaign or expedition for service in which a medal was authorized by the government of the United States.

(b) Make available to an applicant, upon request, a "yellow ribbon/support our troops" decal in lieu of the distinctive decal described in subdivision (a).

(c) Eliminate from inventory any decals for which the department determines that demand is insufficient to maintain that inventory in a cost-effective manner. *(Added by Stats.2012, c. 398 (A.B.1550), § 2.)*

§ 5069. Deposit of revenue in Veterans Service Office Fund

Revenue derived from the additional special fees provided in Section 5068, less costs incurred by the department pursuant to this article, shall be deposited in the Veterans Service Office Fund, created by Section 972.2 of the Military and Veterans Code.

(Added by Stats.1992, c. 1275 (A.B.3033), § 1. Amended by Stats.1994, c. 569 (A.B.1066), § 2, eff. Sept. 16, 1994; Stats.2010, c. 166 (A.B.1908), § 2.)

§§ 5070 to 5071.1. Repealed by Stats.2003, c. 594 (S.B.315), §§ 21 to 23

§ 5072. Special license plates to fund child health and safety programs; design; fees

(a) Any person described in Section 5101 may also apply for a set of "Have a Heart, Be a Star, Help Our Kids" license plates, and the department shall issue those special license plates in lieu of the regular license plates. The "Have a Heart, Be a Star, Help Our Kids" plates shall be distinct from other existing license plates by the inclusion of a well within the portion of the license plate that has the alpha-numeric sequence. The well may be placed in any position within that portion of the license plate. A heart shape, a five-pointed star, a hand shape, a plus-sign shape, shall be imprinted within the well itself. However, for purposes of processing the alpha-numeric sequence, the symbol within the well shall be read as a blank within the alpha-numeric sequence. The Department of Motor Vehicles shall cooperate with representatives of the California Highway Patrol and the Prison Industries Authority to design the final shape and dimension of the symbols for these license plates.

(b) An applicant for a license plate described in subdivision (a) may choose to either accept a license plate character sequence assigned by the department that includes one of the four symbols or request a specialized license plate character sequence determined by the applicant that includes one of the four symbols, in accordance with instructions which shall be provided by the department.

(c) In addition to the regular fees for an original registration, a renewal of registration, or a transfer of registration, the following "Have a Heart, Be a Star, Help Our Kids" license plate fees shall be paid:

(1) Notwithstanding Section 5106, for those specialized license plates whose character sequence is determined by the license owner or applicant:

(A) Fifty dollars ($50) for the initial issuance of the plates. These plates shall be permanent and shall not be required to be replaced.

(B) Forty dollars ($40) for each renewal of registration which includes the continued display of the plates.

(C) Fifteen dollars ($15) for transfer of the plates to another vehicle.

200

(D) Thirty-five dollars ($35) for replacement plates, if the plates become damaged or unserviceable.

(2) For those specialized license plates whose character sequence is assigned by the department:

(A) Twenty dollars ($20) for the initial issuance of the plates. These plates shall be permanent and shall not be required to be replaced.

(B) The legally allowed fee for renewal plus fifteen dollars ($15) for each renewal of registration, which includes the continued display of the plates.

(C) Fifteen dollars ($15) for transfer of the plates to another vehicle.

(D) Twenty dollars ($20) for replacement plates, if the plates become damaged or unserviceable.

(d) When payment of renewal fees is not required as specified in Section 4000, or when the person determines to retain the "Have a Heart, Be a Star, Help Our Kids" license plates upon sale, trade, or other release of the vehicle upon which the plates have been displayed, the person shall notify the department and the person may retain the plates.

(e) The revenue derived from the additional special fees provided in this section, less costs incurred by the department, the Department of the California Highway Patrol, and local law enforcement for developing and administering this license plate program pursuant to this section, shall be deposited in the Child Health and Safety Fund, created pursuant to Chapter 4. 6 (commencing with Section 18285) of Part 6 of Division 9 of the Welfare and Institutions Code, and, when appropriated by the Legislature shall be available for the purposes specified in that chapter.

(f) It is the intent of the Legislature that the additional special fees specified in subdivision (e) are not used to replace existing appropriation levels in the 1991–92 Budget Act.

* * *   *(Added by Stats.1992, c. 1316 (A.B.3087), § 13. Amended by Stats.2013, c. 523 (S.B.788), § 26.)*

Cross References

License plates, child health and safety, funding, see Welfare and Institutions Code § 18285.

§ 5073. Repealed by Stats.2003, c. 594 (S.B.315), § 24

§ 5074. Special interest license plates; arts council participation; fees; use of revenue

(a) This section shall be known and may be cited as the Polanco–Bates License Plates for the Arts Act of 1993. The California Arts Council shall participate in the special interest license plate program.

(b) In addition to the regular fees for an original registration or renewal of registration, the following additional fees shall be paid for the issuance, transfer, or renewal of license plates bearing, notwithstanding Section 5060, a full-plate graphic design * * * that depicts a significant feature or quality of the State of California, approved by the department in consultation with the California Arts Council:

(1) For the original issuance of the plates, fifty dollars ($50).

(2) For a renewal of registration of the plates, forty dollars ($40).

(3) For the transfer of the special plates to another vehicle, fifteen dollars ($15).

(4) In addition, for the issuance of an environmental license plate, as defined in Section 5103, with a full-plate graphic design, the additional fees prescribed in Sections 5106 and 5108. The additional fees prescribed in Sections 5106 and 5108 shall be deposited in the California Environmental License Plate Fund.

(c) Except as provided in paragraph (4) of subdivision (b), all fees collected under this section, after deduction of the department's costs in administering this section, shall be deposited in the Graphic Design License Plate Account, which is hereby established in the General Fund. The funds in the account shall be used by the California Arts Council, upon appropriation by the Legislature, for arts education and local arts programming.

(d) The California Arts Council shall use the revenue derived from the fee increases authorized by amendment of this section during the 2003–04 Regular Session exclusively for arts education and local arts programming.
* * * (Added by Stats.1993, c. 414 (A.B.1895), § 2, operative July 1, 1994. Amended by Stats.1994, c. 569 (A.B.1066), § 4, eff. Sept. 16, 1994; Stats.2004, c. 393 (S.B.1213), § 1; Stats.2013, c. 221 (S.B.789), § 1.)

§ 5075. Special environmental design license plates; Lake Tahoe conservancy; fees

(a) The department, in consultation with the California Tahoe Conservancy, shall design and make available for issuance pursuant to this article special environmental design license plates as described in this section. Notwithstanding subdivision (a) of Section 5060, the special environmental design license plates shall bear a full-plate graphic design depicting a significant feature of Lake Tahoe. Any person described in Section 5101 may, upon payment of the additional fees set forth in subdivision (b), apply for and be issued a set of special environmental design license plates. Notwithstanding subdivision (a) of Section 5060, the special environmental design license plates may be issued as environmental license plates, as defined in Section 5103.

(b) In addition to the regular fees for an original registration or renewal of registration, the following additional fees shall be paid for the issuance, renewal, or transfer of the special environmental design license plates authorized pursuant to this section:

(1) For the original issuance of the plates, fifty dollars ($50).

(2) For a renewal of registration with the plates, forty dollars ($40).

(3) For transfer of the plates to another vehicle, fifteen dollars ($15).

(4) For each substitute replacement plate, thirty-five dollars ($35).

(5) In addition, for the issuance of environmental license plates, as defined in Section 5103, with a full-plate graphic design described in subdivision (a), the additional fees prescribed in Sections 5106 and 5108. The additional fees prescribed in Sections 5106 and 5108 shall be deposited in the Environmental License Plate Fund.

(c) Except as provided in paragraph (5) of subdivision (b), and after deducting its administrative costs under this section, the department shall deposit the additional revenue derived from the issuance, renewal, transfer, and substitution of special environmental design license plates in the Lake Tahoe Conservancy Account, which is hereby created in the California Environmental License Plate Fund. Upon appropriation by the Legislature, the money in the account shall be allocated by the Controller to the California Tahoe Conservancy or its successor for expenditure for the exclusive trust purposes of preservation and restoration projects in the Lake Tahoe area and for the purpose of establishing and improving trails, pathways, and public access for nonmotorized traffic in that area. (Added by Stats.1993, c. 1303 (S.B.648), § 3, eff. Oct. 11, 1993.)

§ 5080. Repealed by Stats.2003, c. 594 (S.B.315), § 25

ARTICLE 8.5. ENVIRONMENTAL LICENSE PLATES

Section
5100. Purpose.
5101. Application.
5101.2. Firefighter license plates; requirements; fees; retention by surviving spouse or family; deposit of revenues.
5101.3. Pearl Harbor Survivor.
5101.4. Legion of Valor license plates; surviving spouse retention; retention as family heirloom.
5101.5. Former prisoners of war.
5101.6. Congressional Medal of Honor license plates; surviving spouse retention.
5101.7. 1984 Olympic reflectorized license plates.
5101.8. Purple Heart license plates; surviving spouse retention; retention as family heirloom.
5101.9. Bill of Rights Bicentennial plates.
5102. Color and design.
5103. Environmental license plates; defined.
5104. Issuance.
5105. Application; cancellation of plates.
5105.5. Repealed.
5106. Additional fees.
5106.5. Repealed.
5107. Disposition of revenue; California environmental license plate fund.
5108. Transfer fee.
5109. Transfer or retention of plates.
5110. Rules and regulations; cost control.

Section
5112.   Link on Web site to order environmental license plates; other informational links; information to be included in replenished supplies or revised forms.

Cross References

Domestic violence victims, application for new and different license plates, see Vehicle Code § 4467.
Environmental license plate fund, see Public Resources Code §§ 21191, 21192.

§ 5100. Purpose

The purpose of this article is to provide revenue for the California Environmental License Plate Fund. *(Added by Stats.1970, c. 779, p. 1470, § 7, eff. Aug. 21, 1970. Amended by Stats.1979, c. 1105, p. 3981, § 4.)*

Cross References

Environmental license plate fund, see Public Resources Code §§ 21191, 21192.

§ 5101. Application

Any person who is the registered owner or lessee of a passenger vehicle, commercial motor vehicle, motorcycle, trailer, or semitrailer registered or certificated with the department, or who makes application for an original registration or renewal registration of that vehicle, may, upon payment of the fee prescribed in Section 5106 and those fees required by Sections 5022 to 5024, inclusive, apply to the department for environmental license plates, in the manner prescribed in Section 5105, which plates shall be affixed to the passenger vehicle, commercial motor vehicle, motorcycle, trailer, or semitrailer for which registration is sought in lieu of the regular license plates. *(Added by Stats.1970, c. 779, p. 1470, § 7, eff. Aug. 21, 1970. Amended by Stats.1971, c. 1273, p. 2492, § 1, eff. Oct. 29, 1971, operative May 3, 1972; Stats.1973, c. 265, p. 661, § 2, eff. July 13, 1973; Stats.2000, c. 163 (S.B.1329), § 3; Stats.2000, c. 859 (A.B.1515), § 3; Stats.2000, c. 861 (S.B.2084), § 28, eff. Sept. 29, 2000; Stats.2000, c; 861 (S.B.2084), § 28.5, eff. Sept. 29, 2000, operative Jan. 1, 2001; Stats.2001, c. 826 (A.B.1472), § 16.)*

Cross References

Commercial vehicle defined, see Vehicle Code § 260.
Lessee defined, see Vehicle Code § 371.
Passenger vehicle defined, see Vehicle Code § 465.
Registered owner defined, see Vehicle Code § 505.
Trailer defined, see Vehicle Code § 630.

§ 5101.2. Firefighter license plates; requirements; fees; retention by surviving spouse or family; deposit of revenues

(a) A person otherwise eligible under this article who is a firefighter or a retired firefighter may apply for special license plates for a vehicle under this article. License plates issued pursuant to this section shall be issued in accordance with Section 5060.

(b) The applicant, by satisfactory proof, shall show all of the following:

(1) The applicant is, or has retired, in good standing as an officer, an employee, or a member of a fire department or a fire service of the state, a county, a city, a district, or any other political subdivision of the state, whether in a volunteer, partly paid, or fully paid status.

(2) The applicant is, or was until retirement, regularly employed as a firefighter or regularly enrolled as a volunteer firefighter.

(3) The applicant's principal duties fall, or fell until retirement, within the scope of active firefighting and any of the following activities:

(A) Fire prevention service.

(B) Fire training.

(C) Hazardous materials abatement.

(D) Arson investigation.

(E) Emergency medical services.

(c) The special license plates issued under this section shall contain the words "California Firefighter" and shall run in a regular numerical series.

(d) In addition to the regular fees for an original registration, a renewal of registration, or a transfer of registration, the following special license plate fees shall be paid:

(1) A fee of fifty dollars ($50) for the initial issuance of the special license plates. These special license plates shall be permanent and shall not be required to be replaced.

(2) A fee of thirty-five dollars ($35) for each renewal of registration that includes the continued display of the special license plates.

(3) If the special license plates become damaged or unserviceable, a fee of thirty-five dollars ($35) for the replacement of the special license plates, obtained from the department upon proper application therefor.

(4) A fee of fifteen dollars ($15) for the transfer of the special license plates to another vehicle qualifying as a vehicle owned by a firefighter who has met the requirements set forth in subdivision (b).

(5) In addition, for the issuance of environmental license plates, as defined in Section 5103, with the special firefighter personal vehicle license plates and distinctive design or decal, the additional fees prescribed in Sections 5106 and 5108. The additional fees collected pursuant to this paragraph shall be deposited in the California Environmental License Plate Fund.

(e)(1) Upon the death of a person issued special license plates pursuant to this section, his or her surviving spouse may retain the special license plates. Except as provided in paragraph (2), upon the death of the surviving spouse, the plates shall be returned to the department or destroyed within 60 days after the death of the surviving spouse or upon the expiration of the vehicle registration, whichever occurs first.

(2) In the absence of a surviving spouse or where the surviving spouse dies while in possession of the special

license plates, a member of the deceased firefighter's family may retain one of the special license plates as a family heirloom, subject to the conditions set forth in subdivision (f).

(f) The special license plates issued under this section are not valid for use for vehicle registration purposes by a person other than the person issued the special license plates under subdivision (a) and the surviving spouse of that person.

(g) For purposes of this section, "family" means grandparents, stepgrandparents, parents, stepparents, siblings, stepsiblings, stepchildren, natural-born children, or adopted children of the person issued the special license plates under subdivision (a).

(h) Except as provided in paragraph (5) of subdivision (d), the revenues derived from the additional special fees provided in this section, less costs incurred by the department pursuant to this section, shall be deposited in the California Firefighters' Memorial Fund established by Section 18802 of the Revenue and Taxation Code. *(Added by Stats.1993, c. 1304 (A.B.941), § 1. Amended by Stats.1994, c. 8 (S.B.568), § 1; Stats.1995, c. 213 (A.B. 613), § 1; Stats.1996, c. 1120 (A.B.3478), § 6, eff. Sept. 30, 1996; Stats.1997, c. 114 (S.B.354), § 1; Stats.1999, c. 988 (S.B.246), § 4; Stats.2003, c. 594 (S.B.315), § 26; Stats.2010, c. 304 (S.B.88), § 2.)*

§ 5101.3. Pearl Harbor Survivor

(a) Any person otherwise eligible under this article who qualifies under subdivision (b) may apply for special license plates that shall run in a separate numerical series and shall contain the words "Pearl Harbor Survivor." The plates may be issued for any vehicle, except a vehicle used for transportation for hire, compensation, or profit, or a motorcycle, which is owned or coowned by the person.

(b) To qualify for issuance of the special plates, the applicant by satisfactory proof shall show all of the following:

(1) The applicant was a member of the United States Armed Forces on December 7, 1941, and received an honorable discharge from military service.

(2) The applicant was on station at Pearl Harbor, the Island of Oahu, or offshore within a distance of three miles, on December 7, 1941, during the hours of 7:55 a.m. to 9:45 a.m., Hawaii time, as certified by a California chapter of the Pearl Harbor Survivors Association.

(c) Upon the death of a person issued special license plates pursuant to this section, his or her surviving spouse may retain the special license plates subject to the conditions set forth in this section. Upon the death of the spouse, the retained special license plates shall be returned to the department either (1) within 60 days following that death or (2) upon the expiration of the vehicle registration, whichever occurs first.

(d) Sections 5106 and 5108 do not apply to this section. *(Added by Stats.1988, c. 1643, § 1. Amended by Stats.*

1990, c. 484 (S.B.2216), § 1, eff. Aug. 9, 1990; Stats.1997, c. 114 (S.B.354), § 2; Stats.1999, c. 612 (A.B.640), § 1.)

Cross References

Veterans displaying special license plates issued under this section, privileges relating to metered parking spaces, see Vehicle Code § 22511.3.

§ 5101.4. Legion of Valor license plates; surviving spouse retention; retention as family heirloom

(a) Any person otherwise eligible under this article who is a recipient of the Army Medal of Honor, Navy Medal of Honor, Air Force Medal of Honor, Army Distinguished Service Cross, Navy Cross, or Air Force Cross may apply for special license plates for the vehicle under this article.

(b) The applicant, by conclusive evidence, shall show that the applicant is a recipient of one of the nation's highest decorations for valor, as specified in subdivision (a).

(c) The special license plates issued under this section shall contain the words "Legion of Valor" and shall run in a regular numerical series. An adhesive sticker denoting which of the nation's highest decorations for valor, as specified in subdivision (a), is held by the applicant shall be affixed in a recess provided for it on the license plates.

(d) Upon the death of a person issued special license plates pursuant to this section, his or her surviving spouse may retain the special license plates subject to the conditions set forth in this section. If there is no surviving spouse, the special license plates shall be returned to the department either (1) within 60 days following that death or (2) upon the expiration of the vehicle registration, whichever occurs first. However, in the absence of a surviving spouse, another surviving member of the deceased medal recipient's family may retain one of the special license plates as a family heirloom, subject to the conditions set forth in subdivision (g).

(e) If a surviving spouse who has elected to retain the special license plates as authorized under subdivision (d) dies while in possession of the special license plates, the special license plates shall be returned to the department either within 60 days following that death, or upon the expiration date of the vehicle registration, whichever date occurs first. However, another surviving member of the deceased medal recipient's family may retain one of the special license plates as a family heirloom, subject to the conditions set forth in subdivision (g).

(f) Sections 5106 and 5108 do not apply to this section.

(g) The special license plates issued under this section are not valid for use for vehicle registration purposes or for the purposes of Section 9105, or Section 10783 or 10783.2 of the Revenue and Taxation Code, by a person other than the person issued the special license plates under subdivision (a) and the surviving spouse of that person.

(h) For purposes of this section, "family" means grandparents, stepgrandparents, parents, stepparents, siblings, stepsiblings, children, and stepchildren of the person issued the special license plates under subdivision (a). *(Added by Stats.1991, c. 358 (A.B.1165), § 1. Amended by Stats.1993, c. 392 (A.B.917), § 1; Stats.1999, c. 612 (A.B.640), § 2; Stats.2010, c. 181 (S.B.1295), § 1.)*

Cross References

Veterans displaying special license plates issued under this section, privileges relating to metered parking spaces, see Vehicle Code § 22511.3.

§ 5101.5. Former prisoners of war

(a) A person otherwise eligible under this article who is a former American prisoner of war may apply for special license plates for the vehicle under this article. The special license plates assigned to the vehicle shall run in a separate numerical series and contain a replica design of the American Prisoner of War Medal followed by the letters "POW" and four numbers. The special license plates issued under this subdivision also shall contain the following words: "Ex–Prisoner of War." The department shall, pursuant to this article, reserve and issue the special license plates provided for by this section only to persons who show by satisfactory proof former prisoner-of-war status. A person otherwise issued license plates within this series pursuant to this article prior to January 1, 1982, may retain them.

(b) Notwithstanding subdivision (a), the department, in consultation with the Department of Veterans Affairs and veterans' service organizations, shall design and make available for issuance pursuant to this article a special environmental design license plate for former American prisoners of war who prefer not to have their former status as a "POW" or "Ex–Prisoner of War" identified by words or other markings or symbols. This section is not intended to prohibit individuals eligible for the special license plate from selecting the existing license plate design specified in subdivision (a). The design criteria for a special interest license plate pursuant to this subdivision are as follows:

(1) The license plate for a passenger vehicle, commercial vehicle, or trailer shall provide a space not larger than two inches by three inches to the left of the numerical series and a space not larger than five-eighths of an inch in height below the numerical series for a distinctive design, decal, or descriptive message as authorized by this subdivision. The license plates shall be issued in sequential numerical order or, pursuant to Section 5103, in a combination of numbers or letters.

(2) The license plate shall not identify "POW" or "Ex–Prisoner of War" by words or other markings or symbols.

(c) Special license plates may be issued pursuant to subdivision (a) only for a vehicle owned or coowned by a former American prisoner of war.

(d) Upon the death of a person issued the special license plates pursuant to this section, his or her surviving spouse may retain the special license plates subject to the conditions set forth in this section. If there is no surviving spouse, the special license plates shall be returned to the department either within 60 days following that death, or upon the expiration date of the vehicle registration, whichever date occurs first. However, in the absence of a surviving spouse, a member of the former prisoner of war's family may retain one of the special license plates as a family heirloom, subject to the conditions set forth in subdivision (i), upon submitting an affidavit to the department agreeing not to attempt to use the special license plates for vehicle registration purposes.

(e) If a surviving spouse who has elected to retain the special license plates as authorized under subdivision (d) dies while in possession of the special license plates, the special license plates shall be returned to the department either within 60 days following that death, or upon the expiration date of the vehicle registration, whichever date occurs first. However, a member of the former prisoner of war's family may retain one of the special license plates as a family heirloom, subject to the conditions set forth in subdivision (i), upon submitting an affidavit to the department agreeing not to attempt to use the special license plates for vehicle registration purposes.

(f) A vehicle exempted from fees by Section 9105 and by Section 10783 of the Revenue and Taxation Code shall lose the exemption upon the death of the former American prisoner of war, except that if a surviving spouse elects to retain the special license plates as authorized under subdivision (d), the exemption pursuant to Section 9105, and Section 10783.2 of the Revenue and Taxation Code, shall extend until the death of that spouse.

(g) Sections 5106 and 5108 do not apply to this section.

(h) The department shall recall all former prisoner-of-war special license plates issued pursuant to this section prior to January 1, 1999, and shall issue to the holder of those special license plates, without charge, the revised special license plates authorized by this section.

(i) The special license plates issued under this section are not valid for use for vehicle registration purposes or for the purposes of Section 9105 or Section 10783 or 10783.2 of the Revenue and Taxation Code by a person other than the person issued the special license plates under subdivision (a) and the surviving spouse of that person.

(j) For purposes of this section, "family" means grandparents, stepgrandparents, parents, stepparents, siblings, stepsiblings, children, and stepchildren of the person issued the special license plates under subdivision (a). *(Added by Stats.1998, c. 563 (S.B.1462), § 4, operative July 1, 1999. Amended by Stats.2007, c. 357 (S.B.386), § 2; Stats.2010, c. 345 (A.B.498), § 2.)*

Cross References

Prisoner of war special license plates, see Public Resources Code § 21191.

Veterans displaying special license plates issued under this section, privileges relating to metered parking spaces, see Vehicle Code § 22511.3.

Veterans' Morale, Welfare and Recreation Fund, see Military and Veterans Code § 1048.

§ 5101.6. Congressional Medal of Honor license plates; surviving spouse retention

(a) A person otherwise eligible under this article who is a Congressional Medal of Honor recipient may apply for special license plates for the vehicle under this article. The special license plates assigned to the vehicle shall run in a separate numerical series and shall have inscribed on the license plate the words "Congressional Medal of Honor" or "Medal of Honor." The department shall reserve and issue the special license plates to all applicants providing the proof required by subdivision (b).

(b) The applicant shall, by satisfactory proof, show that the applicant is a Congressional Medal of Honor recipient.

(c) Special license plates may be issued pursuant to subdivision (a) only for a vehicle owned or coowned by a Congressional Medal of Honor recipient.

(d) Upon the death of a person issued special license plates pursuant to this section, his or her surviving spouse may retain the special license plates subject to the conditions set forth in this section. If there is no surviving spouse, the special license plates shall be returned to the department either within 60 days following that death, or upon the expiration date of the vehicle registration, whichever date occurs first. However, in the absence of a surviving spouse, a member of the Congressional Medal of Honor recipient's family may retain one of the special license plates as a family heirloom, subject to the conditions set forth in subdivision (h), upon submitting an affidavit to the department agreeing not to attempt to use the special license plates for vehicle registration purposes.

(e) If a surviving spouse who has elected to retain the special license plates as authorized under subdivision (d) dies while in possession of the special license plates, the special license plates shall be returned to the department either within 60 days following that death, or upon the expiration date of the vehicle registration, whichever date occurs first. However, a member of the Congressional Medal of Honor recipient's family may retain one of the special license plates as a family heirloom, subject to the conditions set forth in subdivision (h), upon submitting an affidavit to the department agreeing not to attempt to use the special license plates for vehicle registration purposes.

(f) A vehicle exempted from fees by Section 9105 and by Section 10783 of the Revenue and Taxation Code shall lose the exemption upon the death of the Congressional Medal of Honor recipient, except that if a surviving spouse elects to retain the special license plates as authorized under subdivision (d), the exemption pursuant to Section 9105, and Section 10783.2 of the Revenue and Taxation Code, shall extend until the death of that spouse.

(g) Sections 5106 and 5108 do not apply to this section.

(h) The special license plates issued under this section are not valid for use for vehicle registration purposes or for the purposes of Section 9105 or Section 10783 or 10783.2 of the Revenue and Taxation Code by a person other than the person issued the special license plates under subdivision (a) and the surviving spouse of that person.

(i) For the purposes of this section, "family" means grandparents, stepgrandparents, parents, stepparents, siblings, stepsiblings, children, and stepchildren of the person issued the special license plates under subdivision (a). *(Added by Stats.1983, c. 415, § 2. Amended by Stats.1985, c. 1041, § 2; Stats.1993, c. 392 (A.B.917), § 2; Stats.2007, c. 357 (S.B.386), § 3.)*

Cross References

Veterans displaying special license plates issued under this section, privileges relating to metered parking spaces, see Vehicle Code § 22511.3.

§ 5101.7. 1984 Olympic reflectorized license plates

(a) Until December 31, 1984, any person described in Section 5101 may also apply for a set of commemorative 1984 Olympic reflectorized license plates and the department shall issue those special license plates in lieu of the regular license plates. No commemorative 1984 Olympic reflectorized license plates shall be issued pursuant to an application therefor which is submitted on or after January 1, 1985, but the holder of those plates may thereafter renew or retain them, * * * or transfer them to another vehicle, subject to this article.

(b) Except as provided in this section, the issue, renewal, cancellation, retention, and transfer of the commemorative 1984 Olympic reflectorized license plates shall be subject to the provisions of this article as if they were environmental license plates. Until December 31, 1989, duplicate, replacement plates shall be identical commemorative 1984 Olympic reflectorized license plates of the same letter, number, and design as originally issued. On and after January 1, 1990, duplicate or replacement plates shall be provided pursuant to this article.

* * *

(c) Notwithstanding the color, design, and number of digit requirements of Section 5102, the department shall design the commemorative 1984 Olympic reflectorized license plates, which shall be reflectorized license plates issued pursuant to Section 4850. The commemorative 1984 Olympic reflectorized license plates shall be of a distinctive design, as determined by the department after consultation with the Los Angeles Olympic Organizing Committee * * *. *(Added by Stats.1983, c. 1289, § 4, eff. Sept. 30, 1983. Amended by Stats.2013, c. 523 (S.B.788), § 27.)*

Commemorative 1984 Olympic reflectorized license plates, see Vehicle Code § 5022.

§ 5101.8. Purple Heart license plates; surviving spouse retention; retention as family heirloom

(a) Any person otherwise eligible under this article who is a Purple Heart recipient may apply for special license plates for vehicles that are not used for transportation for hire, compensation, or profit, under this article. The special plates assigned to the vehicle shall run in a separate numerical series, shall have inscribed on the plate the Purple Heart insignia, and shall contain the words "Combat Wounded" and "Purple Heart" or at least the letters "PH" as part of the numerical series. The department shall reserve and issue the special plates to all applicants providing the proof required by subdivision (b).

(b) The applicant, by satisfactory proof, shall show that the applicant is a Purple Heart recipient.

(c) Special plates may be issued pursuant to subdivision (a) only for a vehicle owned or coowned by a Purple Heart recipient.

(d) Upon the death of a person issued special license plates pursuant to this section, his or her surviving spouse may retain the special license plates subject to the conditions set forth in this section. If there is no surviving spouse, the special license plates shall be returned to the department either (1) within 60 days following that death or (2) upon the expiration of the vehicle registration, whichever occurs first. However, in the absence of a surviving spouse, another surviving member of the deceased Purple Heart recipient's family may retain one of the special license plates as a family heirloom, subject to the conditions set forth in subdivision (h).

(e) If a surviving spouse who has elected to retain the special license plates as authorized under subdivision (d) dies while in possession of the special license plates, the special license plates shall be returned to the department either within 60 days following that death, or upon the expiration date of the vehicle registration, whichever date occurs first. However, another surviving member of the deceased Purple Heart recipient's family may retain one of the special license plates as a family heirloom, subject to the conditions set forth in subdivision (h).

(f) When an applicant for the Purple Heart license plate qualifies as a disabled veteran, as specified in subdivision (b) of Section 22511.55, the applicant may also apply for a distinguishing placard described in subdivision (a) of Section 22511.55 to be used in conjunction with the Purple Heart license plate for the purpose of allowing special parking privileges pursuant to subdivision (a) of Section 22511.5.

(g) Sections 5106 and 5108 do not apply to this section.

(h) The special license plates issued under this section are not valid for use for vehicle registration purposes or for the purposes of Section 9105, or Section 10783 or 10783.2 of the Revenue and Taxation Code, by a person other than the person issued the special license plates under subdivision (a) and the surviving spouse of that person.

(i) For purposes of this section, "family" means grandparents, stepgrandparents, parents, stepparents, siblings, stepsiblings, children, and stepchildren of the person issued the special license plates under subdivision (a). *(Added by Stats.1988, c. 1644, § 1 operative July 1, 1989. Amended by Stats.1989, c. 176, § 1, eff. July 20, 1989; Stats.1995, c. 91 (S.B.975), § 171; Stats.1999, c. 612 (A.B.640), § 3; Stats.2004, c. 201 (A.B.279), § 1; Stats. 2010, c. 181 (S.B.1295), § 2.)*

Veterans displaying special license plates issued under this section, privileges relating to metered parking spaces, see Vehicle Code § 22511.3.

§ 5101.9. Bill of Rights Bicentennial plates

(a) Until December 31, 1991, any person described in Section 5101 may apply for a set of commemorative Bicentennial of the Bill of Rights reflectorized license plates and the department shall issue those special license plates in lieu of regular license plates. No commemorative Bicentennial of the Bill of Rights reflectorized license plates shall be issued pursuant to an application submitted on or after January 1, 1992, but the holder of those plates may thereafter renew or retain them, obtain substitute replacements for them, or transfer them to another vehicle, subject to this section. However, substitute replacement plates shall not be available on or after January 1, 1997. Thereafter, unless otherwise provided by law, regular series plates shall be issued for the fee provided in Section 9265 whenever substitute plates are required.

(b) The commemorative Bicentennial of the Bill of Rights reflectorized license plates shall be of a distinctive design and shall be available in a special series of letters or numbers, or both, as determined by the department.

(c) In addition to the regular fees for an original or renewal registration, the applicant shall be charged a fee of thirty-five dollars ($35).

(d) Notwithstanding Section 9265, the applicant for substitute commemorative Bicentennial of the Bill of Rights reflectorized license plates shall be charged a fee of thirty-five dollars ($35).

(e) Whenever any person who has been issued commemorative Bicentennial of the Bill of Rights reflectorized license plates applies to the department for transfer of the plates to another vehicle, a transfer fee of fifteen dollars ($15) shall be charged in addition to all other appropriate fees.

(f) Sections 5106 and 5108 do not apply. *(Added by Stats.1989, c. 312, § 1, operative July 1, 1990.)*

§ 5102. Color and design

The environmental license plates shall be the same color and design as regular passenger vehicle, commercial vehicle, motorcycle, or trailer license plates, and shall consist of any combination of numbers or letters, not exceeding seven positions and not less than two positions, if there are no conflicts with existing passenger, commercial, trailer, motorcycle, or special license plates series or with Section 4851. *(Added by Stats.1970, c. 779, p. 1471, § 7, eff. Aug. 21, 1970. Amended by Stats.1971, c. 1273, p. 2492, § 2, eff. Oct. 29, 1971, operative May 3, 1972; Stats.1973, c. 265, p. 662, § 3, eff. July 13, 1973; Stats. 1977, c. 821, p. 2491, § 2, operative July 1, 1978; Stats. 1985, c. 752, § 2.)*

§ 5103. Environmental license plates; defined

"Environmental license plates," as used in this article, means license plates or permanent trailer identification plates that have displayed upon them the registration number assigned to the passenger vehicle, commercial motor vehicle, motorcycle, trailer, or semitrailer for which a registration number was issued in a combination of letters or numbers, or both, requested by the owner or lessee of the vehicle. *(Added by Stats.1970, c. 779, p. 1471, § 7, eff. Aug. 21, 1970. Amended by Stats.1971, c. 1273, p. 2493, § 3, eff. Oct. 29, 1971, operative May 3, 1972; Stats.1973, c. 265, p. 662, § 4, eff. July 13, 1973; Stats.2000, c. 163 (S.B.1329), § 4; Stats.2000, c. 859 (A.B.1515), § 4; Stats.2000, c. 861 (S.B.2084), § 29, eff. Sept. 29, 2000; Stats.2000, c. 861 (S.B.2084), § 29.5, eff. Sept. 29, 2000, operative Jan. 1. 2001.)*

Cross References

Commemorative collegiate reflectorized license plates issued as environmental license plates, see Vehicle Code § 5024.
Commemorative Olympic reflectorized license plates issued as environmental license plates, see Vehicle Code § 5023.

§ 5104. Issuance

Environmental license plates shall be issued only to the registered owner or lessee of the vehicle on which they are to be displayed. *(Added by Stats.1970, c. 779, p. 1471, § 7, eff. Aug. 21, 1970. Amended by Stats.1971, c. 1273, p. 2493, § 4, eff. Oct. 29, 1971, operative May 3, 1972; Stats.1973, c. 265, p. 662, § 5, eff. July 13, 1973.)*

Cross References

Lessee defined, see Vehicle Code § 371.
Registered owner defined, see Vehicle Code § 505.

§ 5105. Application; cancellation of plates

(a) An applicant for issuance of environmental license plates or renewal of such plates in the subsequent year pursuant to this article shall file an application therefor in such form and by such date as the department may require, indicating thereon the combination of letters or numbers, or both, requested as a registration number. There shall be no duplication of registration numbers, and the department may refuse to issue any combination of letters or numbers, or both, that may carry connota-tions offensive to good taste and decency or which would be misleading or a duplication of license plates provided for in Article 8 (commencing with Section 5000) of Chapter 1 of Division 3.

(b) The department may cancel and order the return of any environmental license plate heretofore or hereaf-ter issued, containing any combination of letters, or numbers, or both, which the department determines carries connotations offensive to good taste and decency or which would be misleading. Whenever the depart-ment orders any person to return any such environmental license plate containing any combination of letters or numbers, or both, which the department determines carries connotations offensive to good taste and decency or which would be misleading, the person so ordered may, in writing and within 10 days after receiving the order, demand a hearing, which shall be granted. The provisions of Chapter 5 (commencing with Section 11500), Part 1, Division 3, Title 2 of the Government Code, shall apply to hearings provided for in this subdivision. Any person ordered to return such plates shall either be reimbursed for any additional fees he paid for the plates pursuant to Section 5106 or 5108 for the registration year in which they are recalled, or be given, at no additional cost therefor, replacement environmental license plates, the issuance of which is in compliance with this code.

(c) The department may cancel and order the return of any environmental license plate, without opportunity to be heard, as specified in subdivision (b) of this section, if the license plate issued is a duplication of license plates provided for in Article 8 (commencing with Section 5000) of Chapter 1 of Division 3 or if the fee specified under subdivision (c) of Section 5106 has not been paid. *(Added by Stats.1970, c. 779, p. 1471, § 7, eff. Aug. 21, 1970. Amended by Stats.1973, c. 265, p. 662, § 6, urgency eff. July 13, 1973; Stats.1974, c. 692, p. 1562, § 1.)*

§ 5105.5. Repealed by Stats.1987, c. 1014, § 1, opera-tive Jan. 1, 1992

§ 5106. Additional fees

(a) * * * In addition to the regular registration fee or a permanent trailer identification fee, the applicant shall be charged a fee of forty-eight dollars ($48) for issuance of environmental license plates.

(b) In addition to the regular renewal fee or a perma-nent trailer identification fee for the vehicle to which the plates are assigned, the applicant for a renewal of environmental license plates shall be charged an addition-al fee of thirty-eight dollars ($38). An applicant with a permanent trailer identification plate shall be charged an annual fee of thirty-eight dollars ($38) for renewal of environmental license plates. However, applicants for renewal of prisoner-of-war special license plates issued under Section 5101.5 shall not be charged the additional renewal fee under this subdivision.

(c) When payment of renewal fees is not required as specified in Section 4000, the holder of any environmental license plate may retain the plate upon payment of an annual fee of thirty-eight dollars ($38). The fee shall be due at the expiration of the registration year of the vehicle to which the environmental license plate was last assigned. However, applicants for retention of prisoner-of-war special license plates issued under Section 5101.5 shall not be charged the additional retention fee under this subdivision.

(d) Notwithstanding Section 9265, the applicant for a duplicate environmental license plate * * * shall be charged a fee of thirty-eight dollars ($38). *(Added by Stats.1970, c. 779, p. 1471, § 7, eff. Aug. 21, 1970. Amended by Stats.1974, c. 692, p. 1563, § 2; Stats.1976, c. 935, p. 2142, § 4; Stats.1978, c. 560, p. 1735, § 1; Stats.1982, c. 783, p. 3042, § 1; Stats.1982, c. 1157, p. 4141, § 4; Stats.1983, c. 323, § 93.8, eff. July 21, 1983; Stats.1983, c. 1289, § 6, eff. Sept. 30, 1983; Stats.1991, c. 821 (S.B.514), § 3; Stats.1996, c. 735 (A.B.2788), § 2; Stats.2000, c. 861 (S.B.2084), § 30, eff. Sept. 29, 2000; Stats.2004, c. 540 (A.B.2514), § 4; Stats.2009–2010, 4th Ex.Sess., c. 11 (A.B.11), § 25, eff. July 28, 2009; Stats. 2013, c. 523 (S.B.788), § 28.)*

Cross References

Commemorative 1984 Olympic reflectorized license plates, fee, see Vehicle Code § 5101.7.

Congressional medal of honor recipients, exemption, see Vehicle Code § 5101.6.

Special interest license plates to fund child health and safety programs, fee for specialized plates with character sequence determined by license owner or applicant, see Vehicle Code § 5072.

Special interest license plates, fee for personalization of plates, see Vehicle Code § 5068.

Special plates, legislative or Congressional members, fees, see Vehicle Code § 5002.8.

§ 5106.5.   Repealed by Stats.1987, c. 1014, § 2, operative Jan. 1, 1992

§ 5107.   Disposition of revenue; California environmental license plate fund

(a) All revenue derived from the fees provided for in this article shall be deposited in the California Environmental License Plate Fund.

(b) Not more than fifty cents ($0.50) of the amount collected from each applicant pursuant to Section 5106 on and after January 1, 1999, shall be set aside for use, upon appropriation by the Legislature, by the appropriate agency for the purpose of increasing public awareness of the environmental license plate program. *(Added by Stats.1983, c. 1289, § 7, eff. Sept. 30, 1983. Amended by Stats.1991, c. 821 (S.B.514), § 4; Stats.1998, c. 326 (A.B.2784), § 6, eff. Aug. 21, 1998.)*

§ 5108.   Transfer fee

Whenever any person who has been issued environmental license plates applies to the department for

208

transfer of the plates to another passenger vehicle, commercial motor vehicle, trailer, or semitrailer, a transfer fee of thirty-eight dollars ($38) shall be charged in addition to all other appropriate fees. *(Added by Stats. 1970, c. 779, p. 1471, § 7, eff. Aug. 21, 1970. Amended by Stats.1971, c. 1273, p. 2493, § 5, eff. Oct. 29, 1971, operative May 3, 1972; Stats.1973, c. 265, p. 663, § 7, eff. July 13, 1973; Stats.1982, c. 783, p. 3043, § 2; Stats.2000, c. 861 (S.B.2084), § 31, eff. Sept. 29, 2000; Stats.2004, c. 540 (A.B.2514), § 5; Stats.2009–2010, 4th Ex.Sess., c. 11 (A.B.11), § 26, eff. July 28, 2009.)*

Cross References

Congressional medal of honor recipients, exemption, see Vehicle Code § 5101.6.

Special plates, legislative or Congressional members, fees, deposit, see Vehicle Code § 5002.8.

§ 5109.   Transfer or retention of plates

When any person who has been issued environmental license plates sells, trades, or otherwise releases ownership of the vehicle upon which the environmental license plates have been displayed, such person shall immediately report the transfer of such plates to an acquired passenger vehicle, commercial vehicle, or trailer pursuant to Section 5108, unless such person determines to retain the plates pursuant to subdivision (c) of Section 5106. *(Added by Stats.1970, c. 779, p. 1471, § 7, eff. Aug. 21, 1970. Amended by Stats.1971, c. 1273, p. 2493, § 6, eff. Oct. 29, 1971, operative May 3, 1972; Stats.1973, c. 265, p. 663, § 8, eff. July 13, 1973; Stats.1976, c. 935, p. 2142, § 5.)*

§ 5110.   Rules and regulations; cost control

(a) The director may adopt rules and regulations as necessary to carry out the purposes of this article.

(b) Whenever two or more separate series of special plates are authorized under this article in a period of one year, the director shall coordinate the administrative and technical procedures for preparation and issuance of the plates in order to control costs to the maximum extent. *(Added by Stats.1970, c. 779, p. 1471, § 7, eff. Aug. 21, 1970. Amended by Stats.1991, c. 358 (A.B.1165), § 2.)*

§ 5112.   Link on Web site to order environmental license plates; other informational links; information to be included in replenished supplies or revised forms

(a) The department shall revise its Internet Web site to provide a direct link on the homepage to information on ordering environmental license plates.

(b) The department may provide links on its Internet Web site to other Internet Web sites that have information regarding the protection and management of ocean and coastal resources and other programs that are supported with funds from the Environmental License Plate Fund.

(c) When existing supplies of forms, publications, and signs have been depleted, or if those forms, publications, and signs are required to be revised in the normal course of operations, the department shall include in the replenishing supplies or the revised forms, publications, and signs, information regarding environmental license plates and the procedures for applying for those plates. This subdivision applies only to forms, publications, and signs, that advertise, facilitate the application for, or are an application for environmental license plates. *(Added by Stats.2004, c. 540 (A.B.2514), § 6.)*

ARTICLE 8.6. SPECIALIZED LICENSE PLATES

Section
5115 to 5120. Repealed.
5151. State agency defined; legislative intent.
5152. Qualified applicants.
5154. Display on plate; specialized design or message.
5155. Design criteria.
5156. Program sponsorship; requirements to establish program; discontinuation; Gold Star Family program; veterans program.
5156.1. Repealed.
5157. Fees for issuance, renewal or transfer of specialized plates; donations for Gold Star Family License Plate Account.
5158. Sale, trade or release of vehicle; retention of specialized license plate; notice.
5159. Restrictions on use of collected fees.
5160. Annual accounting report; contents.
5161. State parks environmental design license plates; additional fees; deposit of additional revenue.

Cross References

Competitive grant program to support small capital projects in museums, specialized license plates program, use of funds, see Education Code § 20092.

§§ 5115 to 5120. Repealed by Stats.1979, c. 10078, § 1, operative Jan. 1, 1990

§ 5151. State agency defined; legislative intent

(a) As used in this article, "state agency" means a state office, officer, department, division, bureau, board, or commission, or any other state body or agency.

(b) It is the intent of the Legislature that this article contain the authority for specialized license plates for state agencies. *(Added by Stats.2006, c. 454 (A.B.84), § 3.)*

§ 5152. Qualified applicants

A person described in Section 5101 may apply for a specialized license plate under this article, in lieu of regular license plates. *(Added by Stats.2006, c. 454 (A.B.84), § 3.)*

§ 5154. Display on plate; specialized design or message

Specialized license plates issued under this article shall have a design or contain a message that publicizes or promotes a state agency, or the official policy, mission, or work of a state agency. *(Added by Stats.2006, c. 454 (A.B.84), § 3.)*

§ 5155. Design criteria

The design criteria for a specialized license plate are as follows:

(a) Except as provided in Section 5161, the license plate for a passenger vehicle, commercial vehicle, or trailer shall provide a space not larger than two inches by three inches to the left of the numerical series and a space not larger than five-eighths of an inch in height below the numerical series for a distinctive design, decal, or descriptive message as authorized by this article. The license plates shall be issued in sequential numerical order or, pursuant to Section 5103, in a combination of numbers or letters.

(b) Specialized license plates authorized under this article may be issued for use on a motorcycle. That license plate shall contain a five-digit configuration issued in sequential numerical order or, pursuant to Section 5103, in a combination of numbers or letters. There shall be a space to the left of the numerical series for a distinctive design or decal and the characters shall contrast sharply with the uniform background color. A motorcycle plate containing a full plate graphic design is not authorized.

(c) Specialized license plates may be issued as environmental license plates, as defined in Section 5103. *(Added by Stats.2006, c. 454 (A.B.84), § 3. Amended by Stats. 2012, c. 39 (S.B.1018), § 112, eff. June 27, 2012.)*

§ 5156. Program sponsorship; requirements to establish program; discontinuation; Gold Star Family program; veterans program

(a)(1) A state agency may apply to the department to sponsor a specialized license plate program, and the department shall issue specialized license plates for that program, if the agency complies with all of the requirements of this article.

(2) The department shall not issue specialized license plates to a state agency for a vehicle that is exempt from the payment of registration fees pursuant to Section 9101 or 9103.

(b) Except as provided in subdivision (d), the department shall not establish a specialized license plate program for an agency until the department has received not less than 7,500 applications for that agency's specialized license plates. The agency shall collect and hold applications for the plates. Once the agency has received at least 7,500 applications, it shall submit the applications, along with the necessary fees, to the department. The department shall not issue a specialized license plate until the agency has received and submitted to the department not less than 7,500 applications for that particular specialized license plate within the time period prescribed in this section. Advance payment to the department by the agency representing the department's estimated or actual administrative costs associated with the issuance of a particular specialized license plate shall not constitute compliance with this requirement. The agency shall have 12 months, following the date of approval of the agency's initial application to sponsor a specialized license plate program, to receive the required number of applications. If, after that 12 months, 7,500 applications have not been received, the agency shall immediately do either of the following:

(1) Refund to all applicants all fees or deposits that have been collected.

(2) Contact the department to indicate the agency's intent to undertake collection of additional applications and fees or deposits for an additional period, not to exceed 12 months, in order to obtain the minimum 7,500 applications. If the agency elects to exercise the option under this subparagraph, it shall contact each applicant who has submitted an application with the appropriate fees or deposits to determine if the applicant wishes a refund of fees or deposits or requests the continuance of the holding of the application and fees or deposits until that time that the agency has received 7,500 applications. The agency shall refund the fees or deposits to an applicant so requesting. The agency shall not collect and hold applications for a period exceeding 24 months following the date of approval of the agency's initial application to sponsor a specialized license plate program.

(c)(1) If the number of outstanding and valid specialized license plates in a particular program, except as provided in subdivision (d), provided for in this article is less than 7,500, the department shall notify the sponsoring agency of that fact and shall inform the agency that if that number is less than 7,500 one year from the date of that notification, the department will no longer issue or replace those specialized license plates.

(2) Those particular specialized license plates that were issued prior to the discontinuation provided by paragraph (1) may continue to be used and attached to the vehicle for which they were issued and may be renewed, retained, or transferred pursuant to this code.

(d)(1) The Department of Veterans Affairs may sponsor a Gold Star Family specialized license plate program and the department may establish this specialized license plate program in the absence of 7,500 paid applications as provided in subdivision (d) of Section 5157.

(2) The Department of Veterans Affairs shall, upon receiving proof of eligibility from an applicant, authorize the department to issue Gold Star Family specialized license plates for a vehicle owned by an eligible family member of a member of the Armed Forces of the United States who was killed in the line of duty while on active duty during wartime service, or during an international terrorist attack that has been recognized by the United States Secretary of Defense as an attack against the United States or a foreign nation friendly to the United States, or during military operations while serving outside the United States, including commonwealths, territories, and possessions of the United States, or as part of a peacekeeping force, which includes personnel assigned to a force engaged in a peacekeeping operation authorized

by the United Nations Security Council. An eligible family member is defined as all of the following:

(A) A person who is otherwise eligible under this article to register a motor vehicle.

(B) A person who shows proof from the United States Department of Veterans Affairs or the Department of Defense that the member who was in the Armed Forces of the United States was killed in the line of duty while on active duty in the military.

(C) A person who bears, and shows proof satisfactory to the Department of Veterans Affairs of, one of the following relationships to the member of the Armed Forces killed in the line of duty while serving on active duty:

(i) Widow.

(ii) Widower.

(iii) Biological parent.

(iv) Adoptive parent.

(v) Stepparent.

(vi) Foster parent in loco parentis.

(vii) Biological child.

(viii) Adoptive child.

(ix) Stepchild.

(x) Sibling.

(xi) Half-sibling.

(xii) Grandparent.

(xiii) Grandchild.

(3) Upon the death of a person issued a Gold Star Family specialized license plate, the license plate shall be transferred to the surviving spouse, if he or she requests, or shall be returned to the department within 60 days after the death of the plateholder or upon the expiration of the vehicle registration, whichever occurs first.

(e)(1) The Department of Veterans Affairs shall apply to the department to sponsor a veterans specialized license plate program, and the department shall issue license plates for that program if the Department of Veterans Affairs meets the requirements prescribed by this section.

(2) The design of the veterans specialized license plate shall be identical to the design of the veterans special interest license plate issued pursuant to Section 5068 on or before January 1, 2010, and the decals for the plate shall be identical to those offered pursuant to Section 5068.

(3) Notwithstanding Section 5157, in addition to the regular fees for an original registration, a renewal of registration, or a transfer of registration, the following fees shall be paid by individuals applying for a special interest license plate or a decal issued under this subdivision:

(A) Fifty dollars ($50) for the initial issuance of the plates and decals. The plates shall be permanent and shall not be required to be replaced.

(B) Forty dollars ($40) for each renewal of registration that includes the continued display of the plates or decals.

(C) Fifteen dollars ($15) for transfer of the plates to another vehicle.

(D) Thirty-five dollars ($35) for replacement plates, if they become damaged or unserviceable.

(E) Ten dollars ($10) for replacement decals, if they become damaged or unserviceable.

(F) Seventy-eight dollars ($78) for the personalization of the plates.

(4) After deducting its administrative costs under this subdivision, the department shall deposit the revenue derived from the additional fees provided in paragraph (3) in the Veterans Service Office Fund created by Section 972.2 of the Military and Veterans Code. *(Added by Stats.2006, c. 454 (A.B.84), § 3. Amended by Stats.2008, c. 309 (S.B.1455), § 2; Stats.2013, c. 690 (A.B.244), § 1.)*

Cross References

Competitive grant program to support small capital projects in museums, specialized license plates program, use of funds, see Education Code § 20092.

§ 5156.1. Repealed by Stats.2012, c. 9 (A.B.610), § 1, operative Jan. 1, 2014

§ 5157. Fees for issuance, renewal or transfer of specialized plates; donations for Gold Star Family License Plate Account

(a) In addition to the regular fees for an original registration or renewal of registration, the following additional fees shall be paid for the issuance, renewal, or transfer of the specialized license plates:

(1) For the original issuance of the plates, fifty dollars ($50).

(2) For a renewal of registration with the plates, forty dollars ($40).

(3) For transfer of the plates to another vehicle, fifteen dollars ($15).

(4) For each substitute replacement plate, thirty-five dollars ($35).

(5) In addition, for the issuance of environmental license plates, as defined in Section 5103, with a specialized license plate design, the additional fees prescribed in Sections 5106 and 5108. The additional fees prescribed in Sections 5106 and 5108 shall be deposited in the California Environmental License Plate Fund.

(b) The Gold Star Family specialized license plate program as provided in subdivision (d) of Section 5156 shall not be subject to the fees specified in paragraphs (1), (2), and (5) of subdivision (a) and shall only be issued in a sequential series.

(c) Except as provided in paragraph (5) of subdivision (a), and after deducting its administrative costs under this section, the department shall deposit the additional revenue derived from the issuance, renewal, transfer, and substitution of the specialized license plates in the Specialized License Plate Fund, which is hereby established in the State Treasury. Upon appropriation by the Legislature, the moneys in that fund shall be allocated to each sponsoring agency, in proportion to the amount in the fund that is attributable to the agency's specialized license plate program. Except as authorized under Section 5159, the sponsoring agency shall expend all funds received under this section exclusively for projects and programs that promote the state agency's official policy, mission, or work.

(d)(1) The Department of Veterans Affairs may actively request and receive donations for the Gold Star Family License Plate Account which is hereby created in the Specialized License Plate Fund and which may consist of donations from public and private entities. Earnings generated by the Gold Star Family License Plate Account shall be retained by the account.

(2) Upon the determination of the department that there are sufficient funds in the Gold Star Family License Plate Account for this purpose, moneys in the Gold Star Family License Plate Account shall be available, upon appropriation by the Legislature, to the department for the necessary administrative costs of establishing the Gold Star Family specialized license plate program. *(Added by Stats.2006, c. 454 (A.B.84), § 3. Amended by Stats.2008, c. 309 (S.B.1455), § 3.)*

§ 5158. Sale, trade or release of vehicle; retention of specialized license plate; notice

When payment of renewal fees is not required as specified in Section 4000, or when a person determines to retain the specialized license plate upon a sale, trade, or other release of the vehicle upon which the plate has been displayed, the person shall notify the department and the person may retain and use the plate as authorized by departmental regulations. *(Added by Stats.2006, c. 454 (A.B.84), § 3.)*

§ 5159. Restrictions on use of collected fees

A state agency that is eligible to participate in a specialized license plate program pursuant to this article and receives funds from the additional fees collected from the sale of specialized plates shall not expend annually more than 25 percent of those funds on administrative costs, marketing, or other promotional activities associated with encouraging application for, or renewal of, the specialized plates. *(Added by Stats.2006, c. 454 (A.B.84), § 3.)*

§ 5160. Annual accounting report; contents

(a) A state agency authorized under this article to offer specialized license plates shall prepare and submit an annual accounting report to the department by June 30. The report shall include an accounting of all revenues and expenditures associated with the specialized license plate program.

(b) If a state agency submits a report pursuant to subdivision (a) indicating that the agency violated the expenditure restriction set forth in Section 5159, the department shall immediately cease depositing fees for that agency's specialized license plate program in the Specialized License Plate Fund established under Section 5157 and, instead, shall deposit those fees that would have otherwise been deposited in that fund in a separate fund created by the Controller, which fund is subject to appropriation by the Legislature. The department shall immediately notify the agency of this course of action. The depositing of funds in the account established pursuant to this subdivision shall continue until the agency demonstrates to the satisfaction of the department that the agency is in compliance or will comply with the requirements of Section 5159. If one year from the date that the agency receives the notice described in this subdivision, the agency is still unable to satisfactorily demonstrate to the department that it is in compliance or will comply with Section 5159, the department shall no longer issue or replace those specialized license plates associated with that agency. Those particular specialized license plates that were issued prior to the discontinuation provided by this subdivision may continue to be used and attached to the vehicle for which they were issued and may be renewed, retained, or transferred pursuant to this code.

(c) Upon receiving the reports required under subdivision (a), notwithstanding Section 7550.5 of the Government Code, the department shall prepare and transmit an annual consolidated report to the Legislature containing the revenue and expenditure data. (*Added by Stats.2006, c. 454 (A.B.84), § 3. Amended by Stats.2007, c. 130 (A.B.299), § 233.*)

§ 5161. State parks environmental design license plates; additional fees; deposit of additional revenue

(a) The department, in consultation with the Department of Parks and Recreation, shall design and make available for issuance pursuant to this article special state parks environmental design license plates as described in this section. Notwithstanding Section 5155, the special state parks environmental design license plates shall bear a full-plate graphic design that the department determines, in consultation with the Department of the California Highway Patrol, does not obscure the readability of the license plate depicting a California redwood tree design as an iconic feature of California's state park system, as approved by the Department of Parks and Recreation. The Department of Parks and Recreation may accept and use donated artwork from California artists for purposes of this requirement. Any person described in Section 5101 may, upon payment of the additional fees set forth in subdivision (b), apply for and be issued a set of special state parks environmental design license plates. The special state parks environmental

212

design license plates may be issued as environmental license plates, as defined in Section 5103.

(b) In addition to the regular fees for an original registration or renewal of registration, the following additional fees shall be paid for the issuance, renewal, or transfer of the special state parks environmental design license plates authorized pursuant to this section:

(1) For the original issuance of the plates, fifty dollars ($50).

(2) For a renewal of registration with the plates, forty dollars ($40).

(3) For transfer of the plates to another vehicle, fifteen dollars ($15).

(4) For each substitute replacement plate, thirty-five dollars ($35).

(5) In addition, for the issuance of environmental license plates, as defined in Section 5103, with a full-plate graphic design described in subdivision (a), the additional fees prescribed in Sections 5106 and 5108. The additional fees prescribed in Sections 5106 and 5108 shall be deposited in the Environmental License Plate Fund.

(c) Except as provided in paragraph (5) of subdivision (b), and after deducting its administrative costs under this section, the department shall deposit the additional revenue derived from the issuance, renewal, transfer, and substitution of special environmental design license plates in the California State Parks Account, which is hereby created in the Specialized License Plate Fund. Upon appropriation by the Legislature, the money in the account shall be allocated by the Controller to the Department of Parks and Recreation for expenditure for the exclusive trust purposes of preservation and restoration of California state parks.

(d) The Department of Parks and Recreation shall collect and hold applications for the special state parks environmental license plates described in this section. The department shall not be required to make the special state parks environmental license plates available for issuance pursuant to this section until the Department of Parks and Recreation has submitted not less than 7,500 applications for the plates to the department. (*Added by Stats.2012, c. 39 (S.B.1018), § 113, eff. June 27, 2012.*)

ARTICLE 9. DISPLAY OF PLATES, TABS, AND STICKERS

Section
5200.   Display of license plates.
5201.   Mounting of plates.
5201.1. Product or device that obscures reading of license plates; sale of such device or operation of vehicle with such device prohibited; alteration of license plates prohibited; penalty.
5202.   Period of display.
5203.   Plates surrendered or removed.
5204.   Tabs.
5205.   Stickers.

Section

5205.5. Use of decals, labels and other identifiers to distinguish enumerated hybrid and alternative fuel vehicles from other vehicles; use of high-occupancy lanes; toll-free and reduced-rate passage; accounts.

5206. Partial year certificates or insignia.

§ 5200. Display of license plates

(a) When two license plates are issued by the department for use upon a vehicle, they shall be attached to the vehicle for which they were issued, one in the front and the other in the rear.

(b) When only one license plate is issued for use upon a vehicle, it shall be attached to the rear thereof, unless the license plate is issued for use upon a truck tractor, in which case the license plate shall be displayed in accordance with Section 4850.5. *(Stats.1959, c. 3, p. 1569, § 5200. Amended by Stats.2003, c. 594 (S.B.315), § 27.)*

Cross References

Applicability of this section to trolley coaches, see Vehicle Code § 21051.

Dismantlers, special plates, see Vehicle Code § 11516.

Improper display of plates, see Vehicle Code § 4462.

Issuance and display of special license plates to dealers, see Vehicle Code § 11714 et seq.

Operation of vehicle without license plates, see Vehicle Code § 5202.

Operation of vehicles displaying special plates, see Vehicle Code § 11715.

Reflectorized license plates, issuance, see Vehicle Code § 4850.

Seizure of plates unlawfully or erroneously issued, see Vehicle Code § 4460.

Special series license plates, see Vehicle Code § 5000.

Stickers, tabs or devices in lieu of plates, see Vehicle Code § 4853.

Vehicles exempt from registration, see Vehicle Code § 4002.

§ 5201. Mounting of plates

(a) License plates shall at all times be securely fastened to the vehicle for which they are issued so as to prevent the plates from swinging, shall be mounted in a position so as to be clearly visible, and so that the characters are upright and display from left to right, and shall be maintained in a condition so as to be clearly legible. The rear license plate shall be mounted not less than 12 inches nor more than 60 inches from the ground, and the front license plate shall be mounted not more than 60 inches from the ground, except as follows:

(1) The rear license plate on a tow truck or repossessor's tow vehicle may be mounted on the left-hand side of the mast assembly at the rear of the cab of the vehicle, not less than 12 inches nor more than 90 inches from the ground.

(2) The rear license plate on a tank vehicle hauling hazardous waste, as defined in Section 25117 of the Health and Safety Code, or asphalt material may be mounted not less than 12 inches nor more than 90 inches from the ground.

(3) The rear license plate on a truck tractor may be mounted at the rear of the cab of the vehicle, but not less than 12 inches nor more than 90 inches from the ground.

(4) The rear license plate of a vehicle designed by the manufacturer for the collection and transportation of garbage, rubbish, or refuse that is used regularly for the collection and transportation of that material by a person or governmental entity employed to collect, transport, and dispose of garbage, rubbish, or refuse may be mounted not less than 12 inches nor more than 90 inches from the ground.

(5) The rear license plate on a two-axle livestock trailer may be mounted 12 inches or more, but not more than 90 inches, from the ground.

(6)(A) The rear license plate on a dump bed motortruck equipped with a trailing, load bearing swing axle shall be mounted more than 12 inches, but not more than 107 inches, from the ground.

(B) As used in this section, a trailing, load bearing swing axle is an axle which can be moved from a raised position to a position behind the vehicle that allows for the transfer of a portion of the weight of the vehicle and load to the trailing axle.

(b) A covering shall not be used on license plates except as follows:

(1) The installation of a cover over a lawfully parked vehicle to protect it from the weather and the elements does not constitute a violation of this subdivision. A peace officer or other regularly salaried employee of a public agency designated to enforce laws, including local ordinances, relating to the parking of vehicles may temporarily remove so much of the cover as is necessary to inspect any license plate, tab, or indicia of registration on a vehicle.

(2) The installation of a license plate security cover is not a violation of this subdivision if the device does not obstruct or impair the recognition of the license plate information, including, but not limited to, the issuing state, license plate number, and registration tabs, and the cover is limited to the area directly over the top of the registration tabs. No portion of a license plate security cover shall rest over the license plate number.

(c) A casing, shield, frame, border, product, or other device that obstructs or impairs the reading or recognition of a license plate by an electronic device operated by state or local law enforcement, an electronic device operated in connection with a toll road, high-occupancy toll lane, toll bridge, or other toll facility, or a remote emission sensing device, as specified in Sections 44081 and 44081.6 of the Health and Safety Code, shall not be installed on, or affixed to, a vehicle.

(d)(1) It is the intent of the Legislature that an accommodation be made to persons with disabilities and to those persons who regularly transport persons with disabilities, to allow the removal and relocation of wheelchair lifts and wheelchair carriers without the necessity of removing and reattaching the vehicle's rear

213

license plate. Therefore, it is not a violation of this section if the reading or recognition of a rear license plate is obstructed or impaired by a wheelchair lift or wheelchair carrier and all of the following requirements are met:

(A) The owner of the vehicle has been issued a special identification license plate pursuant to Section 5007, or the person using the wheelchair that is carried on the vehicle has been issued a distinguishing placard under Section 22511.55.

(B)(i) The operator of the vehicle displays a decal, designed and issued by the department, that contains the license plate number assigned to the vehicle transporting the wheelchair.

(ii) The decal is displayed on the rear window of the vehicle, in a location determined by the department, in consultation with the Department of the California Highway Patrol, so as to be clearly visible to law enforcement.

(2) Notwithstanding any other law, if a decal is displayed pursuant to this subdivision, the requirements of this code that require the illumination of the license plate and the license plate number do not apply.

(3) The department shall adopt regulations governing the procedures for accepting and approving applications for decals, and issuing decals, authorized by this subdivision.

(4) This subdivision does not apply to a front license plate. *(Stats.1959, c. 3, p. 1569, § 5201. Amended by Stats.1963, c. 128, p. 804, § 1; Stats.1967, c. 408, p. 1628, § 1; Stats.1976, c. 154, p. 248, § 1; Stats.1979, c. 146, p. 341, § 1; Stats.1980, c. 22, p. 72, § 1; Stats.1980, c. 405, p. 792, § 1; Stats.1984, c. 1281, § 2, eff. Sept. 19, 1984; Stats.1988, c. 924, § 4; Stats.1994, c. 704 (S.B.1699), § 22; Stats.1999, c. 1007 (S.B.532), § 16; Stats.2003, c. 594 (S.B.315), § 28; Stats.2003, c. 626 (A.B.1303), § 2; Stats. 2004, c. 650 (A.B.3047), § 6; Stats.2007, c. 273 (A.B.801), § 1; Stats.2009, c. 307 (S.B.821), § 107; Stats.2010, c. 491 (S.B.1318), § 37; Stats.2012, c. 702 (A.B.2489), § 3; Stats.2012, c. 769 (A.B.2679), § 34.5.)*

Cross References

Applicability of this section to trolley coaches, see Vehicle Code
   § 21051.
Tow truck defined, see Vehicle Code § 615.
Truck tractor defined, see Vehicle Code § 655.

§ 5201.1. Product or device that obscures reading of license plates; sale of such device or operation of vehicle with such device prohibited; alteration of license plates prohibited; penalty

(a) A person shall not sell a product or device that obscures, or is intended to obscure, the reading or recognition of a license plate by visual means, or by an electronic device as prohibited by subdivision (c) of Section 5201.

(b) A person shall not operate a vehicle with a product or device that violates subdivision (a).

214

(c) A person shall not erase the reflective coating of, paint over the reflective coating of, or alter a license plate to avoid visual or electronic capture of the license plate or its characters by state or local law enforcement.

(d) A conviction for a violation of this section is punishable by a fine of two hundred fifty dollars ($250) per item sold or per violation. *(Added by Stats.2007, c. 273 (A.B.801), § 2. Amended by Stats.2012, c. 702 (A.B.2489), § 4.)*

Cross References

Infractions, classification of offenses pursuant to this section, see
   Penal Code § 19.8.

§ 5202. Period of display

(a) A license plate issued by this state or any other jurisdiction within or without the United States shall be attached upon receipt and remain attached during the period of its validity to the vehicle for which it is issued while being operated within this state or during the time the vehicle is being held for sale in this state, or until the time that a vehicle with special or identification plates is no longer entitled to those plates; and a person shall not operate, and an owner shall not knowingly permit to be operated, upon any highway, a vehicle unless the license plate is so attached. A special permit issued in lieu of plates shall be attached and displayed on the vehicle for which the permit was issued during the period of the permit's validity.

(b) This section shall become operative on July 1, 2012. *(Added by Stats.2011, c. 329 (A.B.1215), § 12, operative July 1, 2012.)*

Cross References

Applicability of this section to trolley coaches, see Vehicle Code
   § 21051.
Suspension, cancellation or revocation of registration, see Vehicle Code § 8800 et seq.

§ 5203. Plates surrendered or removed

This chapter does not apply to plates which the department pursuant to law has ordered to be surrendered, transferred to another vehicle, or removed. *(Stats.1959, c. 3, p. 1570, § 5203.)*

Cross References

Applicability of this section to trolley coaches, see Vehicle Code
   § 21051.

§ 5204. Tabs

(a) Except as provided by subdivisions (b) and (c), a tab shall indicate the year of expiration and a tab shall indicate the month of expiration. Current month and year tabs shall be attached to the rear license plate assigned to the vehicle for the last preceding registration year in which license plates were issued, and, when so attached, the license plate with the tabs shall, for the purposes of this code, be deemed to be the license plate, except that truck tractors, and commercial motor vehicles having a declared gross vehicle weight of 10,001 pounds or more, shall display the current month and year tabs upon the front license plate assigned to the truck tractor or commercial motor vehicle. Vehicles that fail to display current month and year tabs or display expired tabs are in violation of this section.

(b) The requirement of subdivision (a) that the tabs indicate the year and the month of expiration does not apply to fleet vehicles subject to Article 9.5 (commencing with Section 5300) or vehicles defined in Section 468.

(c) Subdivision (a) does not apply when proper application for registration has been made pursuant to Section 4602 and the new indicia of current registration have not been received from the department.

(d) This section is enforceable against any motor vehicle that is driven, moved, or left standing upon a highway, or in an offstreet public parking facility, in the same manner as provided in subdivision (a) of Section 4000. *(Stats.1959, c. 3, p. 1570, § 5204. Amended by Stats.1963, c. 150, p. 820, § 1; Stats.1973, c. 889, p. 1654, § 33, eff. Sept. 28, 1973; Stats.1976, c. 908, p. 2082, § 1; Stats.1978, c. 768, p. 2397, § 2, operative Oct. 1, 1979; Stats.1980, c. 784, p. 2377, § 1; Stats.1983, c. 986, § 1; Stats.1987, c. 282, § 1; Stats.1992, c. 258 (S.B.133), § 2; Stats.1994, c. 27 (A.B.2018), § 60, eff. March 30, 1994; Stats.1997, c. 945 (A.B.1561), § 14; Stats.2000, c. 135 (A.B.2539), § 155; Stats.2000, c. 861 (S.B.2084), § 32, eff. Sept. 29, 2000.)*

Cross References

Applicability of this section to trolley coaches, see Vehicle Code § 21051.

§ 5205. Stickers

The department may make appropriate rules and regulations for the use and display of stickers or devices issued in lieu of license plates, and shall publish a summary thereof. *(Stats.1959, c. 3, p. 1570, § 5205.)*

Cross References

Applicability of this section to trolley coaches, see Vehicle Code § 21051.
Issuance of devices in lieu of plates, see Vehicle Code § 4853.

§ 5205.5. Use of decals, labels and other identifiers to distinguish enumerated hybrid and alternative fuel vehicles from other vehicles; use of high-occupancy lanes; toll-free and reduced-rate passage; accounts

(a) For purposes of implementing Section 21655.9, the department shall make available for issuance, for a fee determined by the department to be sufficient to reimburse the department for the actual costs incurred pursuant to this section, distinctive decals, labels, and other identifiers that clearly distinguish the following vehicles from other vehicles:

(1) A vehicle that meets California's super ultra-low emission vehicle (SULEV) standard for exhaust emissions and the federal inherently low-emission vehicle (ILEV) evaporative emission standard, as defined in Part 88 (commencing with Section 88.101–94) of Title 40 of the Code of Federal Regulations.

(2) A vehicle that was produced during the 2004 model-year or earlier and meets California ultra-low emission vehicle (ULEV) standard for exhaust emissions and the federal ILEV standard.

* * *

(3) A vehicle that meets California's enhanced advanced technology partial zero-emission vehicle (enhanced AT PZEV) standard or transitional zero-emission vehicle (TZEV) standard.

* * *

(b) The department shall include a summary of the provisions of this section on each motor vehicle registration renewal notice, or on a separate insert, if space is available and the summary can be included without incurring additional printing or postage costs.

(c) The Department of Transportation shall remove individual HOV lanes, or portions of those lanes, during periods of peak congestion from the access provisions provided in subdivision (a), following a finding by the Department of Transportation as follows:

(1) The lane, or portion thereof, exceeds a level of service C, as discussed in subdivision (b) of Section 65089 of the Government Code.

(2) The operation or projected operation of the vehicles described in subdivision (a) in these lanes, or portions thereof, will significantly increase congestion.

(3) The finding shall also demonstrate the infeasibility of alleviating the congestion by other means, including, but not limited to, reducing the use of the lane by noneligible vehicles or further increasing vehicle occupancy.

(d) The State Air Resources Board shall publish and maintain a listing of all vehicles eligible for participation in the programs described in this section. The board shall provide that listing to the department.

(e)(1) For purposes of subdivision (a), the Department of the California Highway Patrol and the department, in consultation with the Department of Transportation, shall design and specify the placement of the decal, label, or other identifier on the vehicle. Each decal, label, or other identifier issued for a vehicle shall display a unique number, which number shall be printed on, or affixed to, the vehicle registration.

(2) Decals, labels, or other identifiers designed pursuant to this subdivision for a vehicle described in paragraph (3) of subdivision (a) shall be distinguishable from the decals, labels, or other identifiers that are designed for vehicles described in paragraphs (1) and (2) * * * of subdivision (a).

* * *

(f)(1) Except as provided in paragraph (2), for purposes of paragraph (3) of subdivision (a), the department shall issue no more than 40,000 distinctive decals, labels,

215

or other identifiers that clearly distinguish a vehicle specified in paragraph (3) of subdivision (a).

(2) The department may issue a decal, label, or other identifier for a vehicle that satisfies all of the following conditions:

(A) The vehicle is of a type identified in paragraph (3) of subdivision (a).

(B) The owner of the vehicle is the owner of a vehicle for which a decal, label, or other identifier described in paragraph (1) was previously issued and that vehicle for which the decal, label, or other identifier was previously issued is determined by the department, on the basis of satisfactory proof submitted by the owner to the department, to be a nonrepairable vehicle or a total loss salvage vehicle.

(C) The owner of the vehicle applied for a decal, label, or other identifier pursuant to this paragraph within six months of the date on which the vehicle for which a decal, label, or other identifier was previously issued is declared to be a nonrepairable vehicle or a total loss salvage vehicle.

(g) If the Metropolitan Transportation Commission, serving as the Bay Area Toll Authority, grants toll-free and reduced-rate passage on toll bridges under its jurisdiction to a vehicle pursuant to Section 30102.5 of the Streets and Highways Code, it shall also grant the same toll-free and reduced-rate passage to a vehicle displaying an identifier issued by the department pursuant to paragraph (1) or (2) of subdivision (a) * * *.

* * *

(h)(1) Notwithstanding Section 21655.9, and except as provided in paragraph (2), a vehicle described in subdivision (a) that displays a decal, label, or identifier issued pursuant to this section shall be exempt from toll charges imposed on single-occupant vehicles in high-occupancy toll lanes as described in Section 149.7 of the Streets and Highways Code unless prohibited by federal law.

(2)(A) Paragraph (1) does not apply to the imposition of a toll imposed for passage on a toll road or toll highway, that is not a high-occupancy toll lane as described in Section 149.7 of the Streets and Highways Code.

(B) On or before March 1, 2014, paragraph (1) does not apply to the imposition of a toll imposed for passage in lanes designated for tolls pursuant to the federally supported value pricing and transit development demonstration program operated pursuant to Section 149.9 of the Streets and Highways Code for State Highway Route 10 or 110.

(C) Paragraph (1) does not apply to the imposition of a toll charged for crossing a state-owned bridge.

(i) If the Director of Transportation determines that federal law does not authorize the state to allow vehicles that are identified by distinctive decals, labels, or other identifiers on vehicles described in subdivision (a) to use highway lanes or highway access ramps for high-occupan-

cy vehicles regardless of vehicle occupancy, the Director of Transportation shall submit a notice of that determination to the Secretary of State.

* * *

* * * (j) This section shall * * * become inoperative on January 1, 2019, or the date the federal authorization pursuant to Section 166 of Title 23 of the United States Code expires, or the date the Secretary of State receives the notice described in subdivision (i), whichever occurs first, and, as of January 1, 2019, is repealed, unless a later enacted statute, that becomes operative on or before January 1, 2019, deletes or extends the dates on which it becomes inoperative and is repealed.

* * *   *(Added by Stats.1999, c. 330 (A.B.71), § 2. Amended by Stats.2000, c. 686 (S.B.1080), § 1; Stats.2003, c. 715 (S.B.916), § 91; Stats.2004, c. 725 (A.B.2628), § 1; Stats.2005, c. 22 (S.B.1108), § 196; Stats.2006, c. 606 (A.B.1407), § 3; Stats.2006, c. 614 (A.B.2600), § 2; Stats.2008, c. 429 (A.B.1209), § 1; Stats.2010, c. 215 (S.B.535), § 1; Stats.2012, c. 674 (A.B.2405), § 2; Stats. 2013, c. 405 (A.B.266), § 1; Stats.2013, c. 414 (S.B.286), § 1.5.)*

Inoperative Date and Repeal

For inoperative date and repeal of this section, see its terms.

Cross References

Exclusive or preferential use of highway lanes or access ramps for vehicles with distinctive identifiers, see Vehicle Code § 21655.9.

Plan to improve use of alternative fuels, synthetic lubricants, and fuel-efficient vehicles, development, implementation and submittal to Legislature, progress report, and use of alternatively fueled vehicles, see Public Resources Code § 25722.8.

Zero-emission vehicles, parking without displaying decal,
  Penalty amount, see Vehicle Code § 42001.6.
  Prohibition, see Vehicle Code § 22511.1.

§ 5206. Partial year certificates or insignia

Vehicles for which weight fees are paid on a partial year basis shall display a certificate or insignia issued by the department, which shall state the end of the period for which the vehicle is licensed. *(Stats.1959, c. 3, p. 1570, § 5206. Amended by Stats.1981, c. 636, p. 2404, § 4.)*

Cross References

Partial year payment of weight fees, see Vehicle Code § 9700 et seq.

ARTICLE 9.5. REGISTRATION OF FLEET VEHICLES

Section
5300. Repealed.
5301. Application for permanent license plates or decals and registration cards; fleet defined; submission by an association.

Section
5302. Motor vehicles registered outside California; nonoperated vehicles; audits; display.
5303. Form of application; issuance of plate or decal; evidence of registration.
5304. Renewal fees; payment schedule.
5305. Service fees.
5306. Term for which plate or decal and registration card remains valid.
5307. Deletion of vehicles from fleet registration; liens.
5308. Procedures for noncomplying fleet owners or lessees.
5309. Annual registration.
5310. Repealed.

Cross References

Weight decals, see Vehicle Code § 9400.1.

§ 5300. Repealed by Stats.1982, c. 695, p. 2837, § 1

§ 5301. Application for permanent license plates or decals and registration cards; fleet defined; submission by an association

(a) Notwithstanding any other provision of this code and Part 5 (commencing with Section 10701) of Division 2 of the Revenue and Taxation Code, the registered owner or lessee of a fleet of vehicles consisting of commercial motor vehicles base plated in the state, or passenger automobiles may, upon payment of appropriate fees, apply to the department for license plates, permanent decals, and registration cards.

(b)(1) Fleets shall consist of at least 50 motor vehicles to qualify for this program. However, the department may provide for permanent fleet registration through an association providing a combination of fleets of motor vehicles of 250 or more vehicles with no individual fleet of fewer than 25 motor vehicles.

(2) An association submitting an application of participation in the program shall provide within the overall application a listing identifying the registered owner of each fleet and the motor vehicles within each fleet. Identification of the motor vehicles as provided in this article applies to the ownership of the motor vehicles and not the association submitting the application.

(c) With the concurrence of both the department and the participant, the changes made in this section by the enactment of the Commercial Vehicle Registration Act of 2001 shall not affect those participants who were lawfully participating in the permanent fleet registration program on December 31, 2001. Any fleet that qualifies for permanent fleet registration as of December 31, 2001, will continue to count trailers to qualify as a fleet until January 1, 2007. However, five years following the implementation of the permanent trailer identification program, all participants in the permanent fleet registration program shall meet the requirements of this section in order to continue enrollment in the program described in this section. *(Added by Stats.1982, c. 695, p. 2837, § 2. Amended by Stats.1983, c. 986, § 1.5; Stats.1986, c. 687, § 1; Stats.1994, c. 187 (A.B.2666), § 1; Stats.1995, c. 91 (S.B.975), § 172; Stats.2000, c. 861 (S.B.2084), § 33, eff.*

Sept. 29, 2000; Stats.2001, c. 826 (A.B.1472), § 17; Stats.2004, c. 615 (S.B.1233), § 22.)

Cross References

Commercial vehicle defined, see Vehicle Code § 260.
Lessee defined, see Vehicle Code § 371.
Owner defined, see Vehicle Code § 460.
Passenger vehicle defined, see Vehicle Code § 465.
Trailer defined, see Vehicle Code § 630.

§ 5302. Motor vehicles registered outside California; nonoperated vehicles; audits; display

(a) Motor vehicles registered in any state other than California shall not be permitted to participate in this program.

(b) Section 4604 does not apply to vehicles registered under this article.

(c) The department may conduct an audit of the records of each fleet owner or lessee of the vehicle fleets electing to participate in the program. The department shall be fully reimbursed by the fleet owner or lessee for the costs of conducting the audits.

(d) Vehicles registered under this article shall display in a conspicuous place on both the right and the left side of each motor vehicle the name, trademark, or logo of the company. The display of the name, trademark, or logo shall be in letters in sharp contrast to the background and shall be of a size, shape, and color that is readily legible during daylight hours from a distance of 50 feet.

(e) A motor vehicle under 6,000 pounds unladen weight that is owned or leased by a public utility may be registered under this article by displaying the permanent fleet registration number on both the right and left side or on the front and rear of the motor vehicle. The display shall be in sharp contrast to the background and shall be of a size, shape, and color that is readily legible during daylight hours from a distance of 50 feet. *(Added by Stats.1982, c. 695, p. 2837, § 2. Amended by Stats. 1986, c. 687, § 2; Stats.1996, c. 108 (S.B.1491), § 1; Stats.2000, c. 861 (S.B.2084), § 34, eff. Sept. 29, 2000.)*

§ 5303. Form of application; issuance of plate or decal; evidence of registration

(a) The applicant for initial issuance of permanent registration or renewal of registration shall file an application in such form as the department shall require.

(b) Upon initial application, the department shall issue a distinguishing license plate or decal which indicates that the vehicle has been registered under this article.

(c) Display of the distinguishing license plate or decal and registration card shall constitute prima facie evidence that the vehicle is currently registered. *(Added by Stats.1982, c. 695, p. 2837, § 2.)*

§ 5304. Renewal fees; payment schedule

Renewal fees shall be paid pursuant to a schedule established by the department. Submission of renewal fees by an association pursuant to subdivision (b) of

Section 5301 shall be specific as to each fleet and vehicle thereof covered by the renewal application. *(Added by Stats.1982, c. 695, p. 2837, § 2. Amended by Stats.1983, c. 986, p. 2837, § 2.)*

§ 5305. Service fees

In addition to any other fees due for motor vehicles registered pursuant to this article, the department may charge and collect a service fee of one dollar ($1) for each fleet motor vehicle at the time the initial application is submitted to the department and at the time of registration renewal of each fleet vehicle. *(Added by Stats.1982, c. 695, p. 2837, § 2. Amended by Stats.1986, c. 687, § 3; Stats.2000, c. 861 (S.B.2084), § 35, eff. Sept. 29, 2000.)*

§ 5306. Term for which plate or decal and registration card remains valid

Upon payment of appropriate fees, the license plate or decal and registration card issued pursuant to this article for the vehicle shall remain valid until the provisions of Section 5307 have been met. *(Added by Stats.1982, c. 695, p. 2837, § 2.)*

§ 5307. Deletion of vehicles from fleet registration; liens

(a) A fleet vehicle registered under this article may be deleted from the identified fleet when the fleet operator notifies the department of the proposed deletion on a form approved by the department and the distinguishing license plate or decal and registration card issued for the vehicle are surrendered to the department.

(b) Failure to comply with subdivision (a) will require that the payment of fees due for the registration of the vehicle shall be the responsibility of the fleet owner as though the vehicle remained part of the fleet.

(c) The fees determined to be due and owing under this article shall be a lien upon all vehicles of the applicant of a type subject to registration under this code, and the provisions of Article 6 (commencing with Section 9800) of Chapter 6 shall apply. *(Added by Stats.1982, c. 695, p. 2837, § 2.)*

§ 5308. Procedures for noncomplying fleet owners or lessees

The director shall adopt procedures for initial application, payment of fees, fleet additions or deletions, and for the cancellation of the distinguishing plates or decals and registration card issued to a vehicle of a fleet owner or lessee who does not comply with this article. *(Added by Stats.1982, c. 695, p. 2837, § 2.)*

§ 5309. Annual registration

The registration of any identified fleet vehicle is required annually. *(Added by Stats.1982, c. 695, p. 2837, § 2.)*

§ 5310. Repealed by Stats.1982, c. 695, p. 2837, § 1

218

ARTICLE 10. REGISTRATION OF TRAILER COACHES

Section
5350. Provisions applicable.
5350.3, 5350.5. Repealed.
5350.6, 5350.7. Repealed.
5351. Provisions not applicable.
5352. Registration.
5353. Exemption from registration.
5354. Nonresident owner exemption.
5356, 5357. Repealed.

Cross References

Trailer coach defined, see Vehicle Code § 635.

§ 5350. Provisions applicable

The provisions of this division shall apply to trailer coaches except as otherwise provided in this article. *(Stats.1959, c. 3, p. 1570, § 5350. Amended by Stats.1961, c. 58, p. 1004, § 14, eff. March 31, 1961; Stats.1979, c. 194, p. 430, § 8; Stats.1981, c. 975, p. 3796, § 35.)*

§§ 5350.3, 5350.5. Repealed by Stats.1985, c. 426, §§ 1, 2

§§ 5350.6, 5350.7. Repealed by Stats.1981, c. 975, p. 3796, §§ 36, 37

§ 5351. Provisions not applicable

Sections 4452, 4604, 5904, 6052, and 9254, and subdivision (a) of Section 9552 do not apply to the registration or renewal of registration of any trailer coach. *(Stats.1959, c. 3, p. 1570, § 5351.)*

§ 5352. Registration

Subject to the exemptions stated in Section 5353, registration of any trailer coach in this state is required annually. *(Stats.1959, c. 3, p. 1570, § 5352. Amended by Stats.1979, c. 1160, p. 4360, § 14; Stats.1980, c. 285, p. 592, § 14, eff. June 30, 1980, operative July 1, 1980; Stats.1981, c. 975, p. 3796, § 38.)*

§ 5353. Exemption from registration

The registration provisions of this article shall not apply to any of the following:

(a) Any trailer coach which is driven or moved upon a highway in any of the following circumstances:

(1) In conformance with the provisions of this code relating to dealers, manufacturers, transporters, or nonresidents.

(2) Under a temporary permit issued by the department as authorized by Section 4156.

(3) Under a one-trip permit issued by the department as authorized by Section 4003 when such permit is issued to a nonresident.

(b) Any unoccupied trailer coach which is part of an inventory of trailer coaches held for sale by a manufacturer or dealer in the course of his business. *(Stats.1959, c.*

3, p. 1570, § 5353. Amended by Stats.1961, c. 58, p. 1004, § 15, eff. March 31, 1961; Stats.1978, c. 638, p. 2097, § 2; Stats.1981, c. 975, p. 3796, § 39.)

Cross References

Dealers, exemption as to, see Vehicle Code § 4002.
Nonresident exemption from registration, see Vehicle Code § 6700.
Operation of vehicles displaying special plates, see Vehicle Code § 11715.

§ 5354. Nonresident owner exemption

The registration of a foreign trailer coach owned by a nonresident shall be subject to and governed by Section 6700. *(Stats.1959, c. 3, p. 1571, § 5354. Amended by Stats.1959, c. 1021, p. 3043, § 1.)*

Cross References

Exemption of vehicles of nonresidents, see Vehicle Code § 6700.

§§ 5356, 5357. Repealed by Stats.1981, c. 975, p. 3796, §§ 40, 41

ARTICLE 11. REGISTRATION OF MOBILEHOMES SUBJECT TO LOCAL PROPERTY TAXATION [REPEALED]

§§ 5400 to 5405. Repealed by Stats.1981, c. 975, p. 3796, § 42

ARTICLE 12. SURRENDER OF REGISTRATION DOCUMENTS AND LICENSE PLATES

Section
5500. Persons other than licensed dismantlers disassembling vehicle; violations; penalties.
5501. Dismantling of vehicles; inability to furnish certificate of ownership; registration card and license plate or plates; report, application and examination; duplicates; fees.
5505. Total loss salvage vehicles and dismantled vehicles; application to register; inspections; proof of ownership; definitions.
5506. Resale or transfer of vehicle subject to inspection.

§ 5500. Persons other than licensed dismantlers disassembling vehicle; violations; penalties

(a) Any person, other than a licensed dismantler, desiring to disassemble a vehicle of a type required to be registered under this code, either partially or totally, with the intent to use as parts only, to reduce to scrap, or to construct another vehicle shall deliver to the department the certificate of ownership, the registration card, and the license plates last issued to the vehicle before dismantling may begin.

(b) Any person who is convicted of violating subdivision (a) shall be punished upon a first conviction by imprisonment in the county jail for not less than five days or more than six months, or by a fine of not less than fifty dollars ($50) or more than five hundred dollars ($500), or

by both that fine and imprisonment; and, upon a second or any subsequent conviction, by imprisonment in the county jail for not less than 30 days or more than one year, or by a fine of not less than two hundred fifty dollars ($250) or more than one thousand dollars ($1,000), or by both that fine and imprisonment. *(Added by Stats.1983, c. 1286, § 21. Amended by Stats.1985, c. 1022, § 4.)*

Cross References

Automobile dismantler, defined, see Vehicle Code §§ 220, 221.
Violation as misdemeanor, see Vehicle Code § 40000.7.

§ 5501. Dismantling of vehicles; inability to furnish certificate of ownership; registration card and license plate or plates; report, application and examination; duplicates; fees

The provisions of Sections 4457, 4458, and 4459 shall not apply when a vehicle is reported for dismantling. However, any person desiring to dismantle a vehicle shall, in accordance with Section 5500 or 11520, surrender to the department the certificate of ownership, registration card, and license plate or plates last issued for the vehicle. In the event the person so reporting is unable to furnish the certificate of ownership, registration card, and license plate or plates last issued to the vehicle, or any of them, the department may receive the report and application, examine into the circumstances of the case, and may require the filing of suitable affidavits, or other information or documents. No duplicate certificate of ownership, registration card, license plate or plates will be issued when a vehicle is reported for dismantling. No fees shall be required for acceptance of any affidavit provided pursuant to this section or on account of any stolen, lost or damaged certificate, card, plate or plates or duplicates thereof, unless the vehicle is subsequently registered in accordance with Section 11519. *(Added by Stats.1983, c. 1286, § 21.)*

Cross References

Automobile dismantlers, generally, see Vehicle Code § 11500 et seq.
Sale of vehicle by auctioneer or public agency, see Vehicle Code § 24007.5.

§ 5505. Total loss salvage vehicles and dismantled vehicles; application to register; inspections; proof of ownership; definitions

(a) This section applies to any vehicle reported to be a total loss salvage vehicle pursuant to Section 11515 and to any vehicle reported for dismantling pursuant to Section 5500 or 11520.

(b) Whenever an application is made to the Department of Motor Vehicles to register a vehicle described in subdivision (a), that department shall inspect the vehicle to determine its proper identity or request that the inspection be performed by the Department of the California Highway Patrol. An inspection by the Department of Motor Vehicles shall not preclude that department from referring the vehicle to the Department of the

California Highway Patrol for an additional inspection if deemed necessary.

(c) The Department of the California Highway Patrol shall inspect, on a random basis, those vehicles described in subdivision (a) that have been presented to the Department of Motor Vehicles for registration after completion of the reconstruction process to determine the proper identity of those vehicles. The vehicle being presented for inspection shall be a complete vehicle, in legal operating condition. If the vehicle was originally manufactured with a "supplemental restraint system" as defined in Section 593, the reconstructed vehicle shall also be equipped with a supplemental restraint system in good working order that meets applicable federal motor vehicle safety standards and conforms to the manufacturer's specifications for that vehicle. The inspection conducted pursuant to this subdivision shall be a comprehensive, vehicle identification number inspection.

(d) A salvage vehicle rebuilder, as defined in Section 543.5, or other individual in possession of a vehicle described in subdivision (a), who is submitting the vehicle for registration as described in subdivision (b), shall have available, and shall present upon demand of the Department of the California Highway Patrol, bills of sale, invoices, or other acceptable proof of ownership of component parts, and invoices for minor component parts. Additionally, bills of sale and invoices shall include the year, make, model, and the vehicle identification number of the vehicle from which the parts were removed or sold, the name and signature of the person from whom the parts were acquired, and his or her address, and telephone number. To assist in the identification of the seller of new or used parts, the number of the seller's driver's license, identification card, social security card, or Federal Employer Identification Number shall be provided by the seller to the buyer on the bills of sale and invoice. The seller of a salvage vehicle, or the agent of the seller, shall inform the purchaser of the vehicle that ownership documentation for certain replacement parts used in the repair of the vehicle will be required in the inspection required under this section.

(e) As used in this section, the term "component parts for passenger motor vehicles" includes supplemental restraint systems, the cowl or firewall, front-end assembly, rear clip, including the roof panel, the roof panel when installed separately, and the frame or any portion thereof, or in the case of a unitized body, the supporting structure that serves as the frame, each door, the hood, each fender or quarter panel, deck lid or hatchback, each bumper, both T-tops, replacement transmissions or transaxles, and a replacement motor.

(1) As used in this subdivision, "front-end assembly" includes all of the following: hood, fenders, bumper, and radiator supporting members for these items. For vehicles with a unitized body, the front-end assembly also includes the frame support members.

(2) As used in this subdivision, "rear clip" includes the roof, quarter panels, trunk lid, floor pan, and the support members for each item.

(f) As used in this section, "major component parts for trucks, truck-type or bus-type vehicles" includes the cab, the frame or any portion thereof, and, in the case of a unitized body, the supporting structure which serves as a frame, the cargo compartment floor panel or passenger compartment floor pan, roof panel, and replacement transmissions or transaxles, and replacement motors, each door, hood, each fender or quarter panel, each bumper, and the tailgate. All component parts identified in subdivision (e), common to a truck, truck-type or bus-type vehicle, not listed in this section, shall be considered as included in this section if the part is replaced.

(1) "Major component parts for motorcycles" includes the engine or motor, transmission or transaxle, frame, front fork, and crankcase.

(2) "Minor component parts for motorcycles" includes the fairing and any other body molding.

(g) If the vehicle identification number, year, make, or model required under subdivision (d) cannot be determined, the Department of the California Highway Patrol may accept, in lieu of that information, a certification on a form provided by that department, signed by the person submitting the vehicle for inspection, that the part was not obtained by means of theft or fraud.

(Added by Stats.1995, c. 684 (S.B.549), § 2, eff. Oct. 10, 1995, operative Jan. 1, 1997. Amended by Stats.1996, c. 450 (S.B.1713), § 1; Stats.2002, c. 670 (S.B.1331), § 7.)

§ 5506. Resale or transfer of vehicle subject to inspection

No salvage vehicle rebuilder may resell or transfer ownership of any vehicle that is subject to inspection as provided in Section 5505, unless either a certificate of inspection issued by the Department of the California Highway Patrol, or vehicle verification form completed by an authorized employee of the Department of Motor Vehicles is provided to the buyer upon sale or transfer. Responsibility for compliance with this section shall rest with the salvage vehicle rebuilder selling or transferring the vehicle. This section shall not apply to a salvage vehicle rebuilder who has applied for and received a title in accordance with Section 5505. *(Added by Stats.2002, c. 670 (S.B.1331), § 8.)*

Cross References

Misdemeanors, see Vehicle Code § 40000.7.

CHAPTER 2. TRANSFERS OF TITLE OR INTEREST

Article	Section
1. Procedure to Transfer	5600
2. Endorsement and Delivery of Documents	5750
3. Notice and Application	5900
4. Transfer by Department	6050

Article   Section
5.   Transfers Through Wholesale Auctions 6100

ARTICLE 1. PROCEDURE TO TRANSFER

Section
5600.   Transfer requirements.
5600.5.   Co-owners as transferees.
5601.   Involuntary transfer.
5602.   Requirements for releasing liability.
5603.   Transfer by legal owner.
5604.   Notification of insurance coverage.
5604.5.   Insurance policies sold by dealers; notifications re-
          garding policy contents; insurance warning mes-
          sage.

Cross References

Off-highway motor vehicles, applicability of chapter, see Vehicle
    Code § 38195.

§ 5600. Transfer requirements

(a) No transfer of the title or any interest in or to a vehicle registered under this code shall pass, and any attempted transfer shall not be effective, until the parties thereto have fulfilled either of the following requirements:

(1) The transferor has made proper endorsement and delivery of the certificate of ownership to the transferee as provided in this code and the transferee has delivered to the department or has placed the certificate in the United States mail addressed to the department when and as required under this code with the proper transfer fee, together with the amount required to be paid under Part 1 (commencing with Section 6001), Division 2 of the Revenue and Taxation Code with respect to the use by the transferee of the vehicle, and thereby makes application for a transfer of registration except as otherwise provided in Sections 5905, 5906, 5907, and 5908.

(2) The transferor has delivered to the department or has placed in the United States mail addressed to the department the appropriate documents for the registration or transfer of registration of the vehicle pursuant to the sale or transfer except as provided in Section 5602.

(b) Whenever a person transfers ownership of a vehicle and is required to disclose the mileage of the vehicle, the department may prescribe a secured form to be used for purposes of the odometer mileage disclosure requirements pursuant to subsection (a) of Section 32705 of Title 49 of the United States Code. *(Stats.1959, c. 3, p. 1571, § 5600. Amended by Stats.1963, c. 1858, p. 3837, § 10, eff. July 19, 1963, operative Oct. 1, 1963; Stats.1965, 1st Ex.Sess., c. 2, p. 5454, § 40, eff. July 12, 1965, operative Aug. 1, 1965; Stats.1988, c. 1268, § 3; Stats.2000, c. 1035 (S.B.1403), § 10.)*

Cross References

Altering, forging or falsifying endorsement of transfer, see
    Vehicle Code § 4463.
Authority to grant or refuse applications for transfers, see
    Vehicle Code § 1653.

Dealer as transferee, operation of vehicle without application for
    transfer, see Vehicle Code § 5906.
Delivery of certificate of ownership, see Vehicle Code § 5753.
Department to transfer registration, see Vehicle Code § 6050.
Endorsement of certificate of ownership upon transfer, see
    Vehicle Code § 5750 et seq.
Fees on transfer of registration, see Vehicle Code § 9255.
Involuntary transfers, change of registration on, see Vehicle
    Code § 5909.
Legal owner defined, see Vehicle Code § 370.
Notice of sale or transfer, see Vehicle Code §§ 5900, 5901.
Owner defined, see Vehicle Code § 460.
Registered owner defined, see Vehicle Code § 505.
Restriction on engaging in business of transferring registrations,
    see Vehicle Code § 505.2.
Stolen vehicles, notification of transfer, see Vehicle Code
    § 10505.
Transfer when certificate or card unavailable, see Vehicle Code
    § 5911.
Transferee defined, see Vehicle Code § 640.
Transferee to apply for transfer, see Vehicle Code § 5902.

§ 5600.5. Co-owners as transferees

Ownership of title to a vehicle subject to registration may be transferred to two (or more) coowners as transferee to be held provided in Section 682 of the Civil Code, except that:

(a) A vehicle may be registered in the names of two (or more) persons as coowners in the alternative by the use of the word "or." A vehicle so registered in the alternative shall be deemed to be held in joint tenancy. Each coowner shall be deemed to have granted to the other coowners the absolute right to dispose of the title and interest in the vehicle. Upon the death of a coowner the interest of the decedent shall pass to the survivor as though title or interest in the vehicle was held in joint tenancy unless a contrary intention is set forth in writing upon the request for transfer of registration.

(b) A vehicle may be registered in the names of two (or more) persons as coowners in the alternative by the use of the word "or" and if declared in writing upon the application for a transfer of registration by the applicants to be community property, or tenancy in common, shall grant to each coowner the absolute power to transfer the title or interest of the other coowners only during the lifetime of such coowners.

(c) A vehicle may be registered in the names of two (or more) persons as coowners in the conjunctive by the use of the word "and" and shall thereafter require the signature of each coowner or his personal representative to transfer title to the vehicle, except where title to the vehicle is set forth in joint tenancy, the signature of each coowner or his personal representative shall be required only during the lifetime of the coowners, and upon death of a coowner title shall pass to the surviving coowner.

(d) The department may adopt suitable abbreviations to appear upon the certificate of registration and certificate of ownership to designate the manner in which the interest in or title to the vehicle is held if set forth by the coowners upon the application for transfer of registration. *(Added by Stats.1965, c. 891, p. 2496, § 2.)*

§ 5601. Involuntary transfer

Section 5600 does not apply to involuntary transfers, as upon the taking of possession by a secured party under a security agreement, or to transfers involving the creation of security interests subject to Chapter 3, commencing at Section 6300. *(Stats.1959, c. 3, p. 1571, § 5601. Amended by Stats.1963, c. 819, p. 2013, § 43, operative Jan. 1, 1965.)*

Cross References

Transfer of registration upon involuntary transfer, see Vehicle Code § 5909.

§ 5602. Requirements for releasing liability

An owner who has made a bona fide sale or transfer of a vehicle and has delivered possession of the vehicle to a purchaser is not, by reason of any of the provisions of this code, the owner of the vehicle so as to be subject to civil liability or criminal liability for the parking, abandoning, or operation of the vehicle thereafter by another when the selling or transferring owner, in addition to that delivery and that bona fide sale or transfer, has fulfilled either of the following requirements:

(a) He or she has made proper endorsement and delivery of the certificate of ownership as provided in this code.

(b) He or she has delivered to the department or has placed in the United States mail, addressed to the department, either of the following documents:

(1) The notice as provided in subdivision (b) of Section 4456 or Section 5900 or 5901.

(2) The appropriate documents and fees for registration of the vehicle to the new owner pursuant to the sale or transfer. *(Stats.1959, c. 3, p. 1571, § 5602. Amended by Stats.1981, c. 775, p. 3027, § 1; Stats.1987, c. 1097, § 1; Stats.1988, c. 1267, § 1, eff. Sept. 26, 1988; Stats.1988, c. 1268, § 4; Stats.1994, c. 180 (A.B.375), § 6, eff. July 11, 1994.)*

Cross References

Civil liability of private owners, generally, see Vehicle Code § 17000 et seq.
Delivery of certificate and card, see Vehicle Code § 5753.
Endorsement of certificate of ownership, see Vehicle Code § 5750 et seq.
Form for notice to department on certificate of ownership, see Vehicle Code § 4451.
Issuance of certificate of ownership, see Vehicle Code § 4450.
Liability of private owners, see Vehicle Code § 17150.
Owner defined, see Vehicle Code § 460.
Transferor to notify department, see Vehicle Code §§ 5900, 5901.

§ 5603. Transfer by legal owner

A legal owner may assign his title or interest in or to a vehicle registered under this code to a person other than the owner without the consent of and without affecting the interest of the owner. *(Stats.1959, c. 3, p. 1572, § 5603.)*

Cross References

Endorsement of certificate of ownership, see Vehicle Code § 5750 et seq.
Issuance of original registration card and certificate of ownership, see Vehicle Code § 4450.
Legal owner defined, see Vehicle Code § 370.
Owner defined, see Vehicle Code § 460.
Registration card to be kept with vehicle, see Vehicle Code § 4454.
Transfer of registration by department, see Vehicle Code § 6050.

§ 5604. Notification of insurance coverage

Every dealer who, upon transferring by sale, lease, or otherwise, any new or used vehicle of a type subject to registration, requires the transferee to insure the vehicle, and every lending agency which, as the holder of any security interest in the vehicle, requires its obligor to insure the vehicle, shall, if the required insurance policy is obtained by the dealer or lending agency and the policy does not insure the transferee or obligor against damages resulting from ownership or operation of the vehicle arising by reason of personal injury or death of any person, or from injury to property, notify the transferee or obligor of that fact in writing on a document other than the insurance policy. The document shall be in duplicate and signed by the transferee or obligor.

If the required insurance policy is obtained by the dealer or lending agency because of the failure or refusal of the transferee or obligor to furnish or renew insurance in accordance with the terms of the contract of sale or the security agreement, and the policy does not insure the transferee or obligor against damages resulting from ownership or operation of the vehicle arising by reason of personal injury or death of any person, or from injury to property, the dealer or lending agency shall notify the transferee or obligor that the policy obtained does not insure the transferee or obligor for liability from any claims. The notice shall be made in writing on a document other than the insurance policy, or the declaration page attached to the policy, and shall be mailed, with postage paid and properly addressed, to the transferee or obligor within 30 days of obtaining the policy. *(Stats. 1959, c. 3, p. 1572, § 5604. Amended by Stats.1963, c. 819, p. 2013, § 44; Stats.1965, c. 666, p. 2043, § 2; Stats.1988, c. 1407, § 1.)*

Cross References

Automobile,
　Dealers, acceptance of insurance assignment by, see Business and Professions Code §§ 18450, 18451.
　Insurance, generally, see Insurance Code § 11620 et seq.
　Sales finance contracts, see Civil Code § 2984.1.
Civil liability and financial responsibility of vehicle owners and operators, generally, see Vehicle Code § 17000 et seq.
Dealer defined, see Vehicle Code §§ 285, 286.
Exemption from registration, see Vehicle Code §§ 4002, 4003.
Proof of financial responsibility, see Vehicle Code § 16430.

Transferee defined, see Vehicle Code § 640.

Vehicles subject to registration, see Vehicle Code § 4000 et seq.

§ 5604.5. Insurance policies sold by dealers; notifications regarding policy contents; insurance warning message

(a) Every dealer who, upon transferring by sale, lease, or otherwise, any new or used vehicle of a type subject to registration, requires the transferee to insure the motor vehicle shall, if the required insurance policy is sold by that dealer at the time of the transfer and the policy does not insure the transferee against damages resulting from ownership or operation of the vehicle arising by reason of personal injury or death of any person, or from damage to property, notify the transferee of that fact in writing on a document other than the insurance policy. The document shall be signed by the transferee and an exact copy shall be furnished to the transferee by the dealer at the time of signature.

(b) The document required under subdivision (a) shall contain a notice in English and Spanish in at least 10–point type that reads as follows:

"INSURANCE WARNING

The motor vehicle physical damage insurance policy you are buying does not allow you to legally drive on the streets of California. Generally, in order to legally drive on the streets of California, you must either purchase a type of insurance called "liability insurance" or deposit a bond with the Department of Motor Vehicles. If you drive this or any other motor vehicle without liability insurance or a bond, a police officer may request evidence of liability insurance or a bond at the time of a traffic stop. If you do not have evidence of liability insurance or a bond during a traffic stop, the fines can be from several hundreds of dollars to an amount that exceeds $1,000. If you get into an accident and do not have liability insurance or a bond, you will lose your driver's license for one year. If you cause the accident and do not have liability insurance or a bond, you may have to pay the injured person yourself and these costs may be substantial.

Liability insurance as well as the insurance needed to obtain a loan for your motor vehicle may be purchased through a licensed insurance agent or broker. The price for both types of insurance may be more or less than the price for the insurance you are being offered by the dealer. The State of California advises you to shop for insurance because prices may vary substantially.

I have read this notice and understand that I am about to buy a type of insurance that is available elsewhere and that does not allow me to drive the motor vehicle legally on the streets of California.

I also understand that if I drive on the streets of California without liability insurance or a bond, then I may be subject to severe financial penalties, including fines and personal payment for any damage to others that I may cause while driving.

(Spanish translation of the above text to be developed by the Department of Motor Vehicles and to be inserted below the above English version text)

Dated: _____   Signed: _____"

(c) The department shall also make available a translation of the Insurance Warning notice set forth in subdivision (b) in any of the languages used in the most recent statewide voter pamphlet. *(Added by Stats.2000, c. 455 (S.B.1996), § 2.)*

ARTICLE 2. ENDORSEMENT AND DELIVERY OF DOCUMENTS

Section

5750.   Transfer by legal owner.

5751.   Transfer by registered owner.

5751.5.   Transfer; statement; modification of emissions system; form.

5752.   Endorsement when certificate unavailable.

5753.   Delivery of certificate of ownership and registration card.

Cross References

Operation of vehicle without transfer, see Vehicle Code § 5906.

§ 5750. Transfer by legal owner

Upon transfer of the title or any interest of the legal owner or owners in a vehicle registered under this code, the transferor shall write his signature, and the transferee shall write his signature and address, in the appropriate spaces provided on the certificate of ownership issued for the vehicle. *(Stats.1959, c. 3, p. 1572, § 5750. Amended by Stats.1959, c. 1996, p. 4618, § 9; Stats.1967, c. 723, p. 2094, § 1.)*

Cross References

Certificate of ownership,
    Contents, see Vehicle Code § 4451.
    Issuance, see Vehicle Code § 4450.
Dealer defined, see Vehicle Code §§ 285, 286.
Delivery of certificate and card, see Vehicle Code § 5753.
Endorsement and delivery of certificate to complete transfer, see Vehicle Code § 5600.
Falsification or forgery of endorsement as a felony, see Vehicle Code § 4463.
Fees for transfer of registration, see Vehicle Code § 9255.
Legal owner defined, see Vehicle Code § 370.
Limitations on transfers of registration as a business, see Vehicle Code § 505.2.
Notice by dealer, see Vehicle Code § 5901.
Owner defined, see Vehicle Code § 460.
Report of possession required of automobile dismantler, see Vehicle Code § 11520.
Special plates to dealers, issuance, see Vehicle Code § 11714 et seq.
Transfer of title to stolen vehicle, see Vehicle Code § 10505.

Transferee defined, see Vehicle Code § 640.

§ 5751. Transfer by registered owner

Upon transfer of the title or interest of the registered owner only in a vehicle registered under this code, the registered owner shall write his signature and address and the transferee shall write his signature and address in the appropriate spaces provided on the certificate of ownership for the vehicle, and the legal owner shall write his signature in the space provided for the new legal owner indicating that he is to retain his legal title and interest. *(Stats.1959, c. 3, p. 1572, § 5751. Amended by Stats.1967, c. 723, p. 2094, § 2.)*

Cross References

Fees for transfer of registration, see Vehicle Code § 9255.
Registered owner defined, see Vehicle Code § 505.

§ 5751.5. Transfer; statement; modification of emissions system; form

(a) Upon transfer of the title or interest of the registered owner of a motor vehicle that is subject to Part 5 (commencing with Section 43000) of Division 26 of the Health and Safety Code, if no certificate of compliance or certificate of noncompliance is submitted to the department pursuant to the exemptions described in paragraph (1) of subdivision (d) of Section 4000.1, the transferor of that vehicle shall sign and deliver to the transferee, upon completion of the transaction, the original copy of a statement, under penalty of perjury, that he or she has not modified the emissions system of the vehicle and does not have any personal knowledge of anyone else modifying the system in a manner that causes the emission system to fail to qualify for the issuance of a certificate of compliance pursuant to Section 44015 of the Health and Safety Code. The transferor shall keep a duplicate copy of the statement delivered to the transferee pursuant to this section. The department shall prescribe and make available to transferors the necessary forms to comply with this subdivision.

(b) Any form prescribed by the department pursuant to subdivision (a) shall contain the following statement and a space for the signatures of the transferor and transferee at the end of the statement:

"WARNING TO THE BUYER

"A valid certificate of compliance was submitted to the Department of Motor Vehicles with an application for the renewal of registration of this vehicle. If an application for transfer is submitted to the department within the 90–day validity period of the smog certification, no new smog certification will be required. However, at present, you may be purchasing a vehicle that may not be in compliance with specified emission standards.

"By signing this statement, you acknowledge that the seller is not required to provide you with an additional certificate of compliance prior to the completion of this transaction.

"You may have this vehicle tested at a licensed smog check station prior to completion of this transaction to verify compliance. If the vehicle passes the test, you shall be responsible for the costs of the test. If the vehicle fails the test, the seller is obligated to reimburse you the cost of having the vehicle tested and, without expense to you, must have the vehicle repaired to comply with specified emission standards prior to completion of this transaction.

———————————————   ———————————————
      (Transferor)   (Date)

———————————————   ———————————————
      (Transferee)   (Date)"

(Added by Stats.1993, c. 958 (S.B.575), § 2. Amended by Stats.2002, c. 127 (A.B.2303), § 2; Stats.2004, c. 650 (A.B.3047), § 7.)

§ 5752. Endorsement when certificate unavailable

(a) When the required certificate of ownership is lost, stolen, damaged, or mutilated, the application for transfer may be made upon a form provided by the department for a duplicate certificate of ownership. The transferor shall write his or her signature and address in the appropriate spaces provided upon the application and file the same together with the proper fees for duplicate certificate of ownership and transfer. The application shall also include, if applicable, the notarized [1] signature of the lienholder.

(b) An insurance company or its agent is exempt from the notarized signature requirement of subdivision (a) and may apply, upon a form provided by the department, for a duplicate certificate of ownership and transfer of ownership to the insurance company, if all of the following occur:

(1) The insurance company or its agent obtains from the lienholder a document to verify satisfaction of the lien.

(2) The insurance company has paid a total loss claim for the vehicle.

(3) A lienholder is indicated on the department's records.

(4) The certificate of ownership is lost, stolen, damaged, or mutilated. *(Stats.1959, c. 3, p. 1572, § 5752. Amended by Stats.1967, c. 723, p. 2094, § 3; Stats.1996, c. 451 (S.B.2144), § 1.)*

[1] So in original.

Cross References

Fees for duplicate or substitute certificates of ownership, see
   Vehicle Code § 9265.

§ 5753. Delivery of certificate of ownership and registration card

(a) It is unlawful for any person to fail or neglect properly to endorse, date, and deliver the certificate of ownership and, when having possession, to deliver the registration card to a transferee who is lawfully entitled to a transfer of registration.

(b) Except when the certificate of ownership is demanded in writing by a purchaser, a vehicle dealer licensed under this code shall satisfy the delivery requirement of this section by submitting appropriate documents and fees to the department for transfer of registration in accordance with Sections 5906 and 4456 of this code and rules and regulations promulgated thereunder.

(c)(1) Within 15 business days after receiving payment in full for the satisfaction of a security interest and a written instrument signed by the grantor of the security interest designating the transferee and authorizing release of the legal owner's interest, the legal owner shall release its security interest and mail, transmit, or deliver the vehicle's certificate of ownership to the transferee who, due to satisfaction of the security interest, is lawfully entitled to the transfer of legal ownership.

(2) If a lease provides a lessee with the option to purchase the leased vehicle, within 15 business days after receiving payment in full for the purchase, and all documents necessary to effect the transfer, the lessor shall mail, transmit, or deliver the vehicle's certificate of ownership to the transferee, who, due to purchase of the vehicle, is lawfully entitled to the transfer of legal ownership.

(d) The certificate of ownership delivered pursuant to subdivision (c) shall be signed by the legal owner or lessor to reflect release of the legal owner's interest or transfer of the lessor's interest in the vehicle or accompanied by a form provided by the department to accomplish the same result and signed by the legal owner or lessor. If the legal owner or lessor is not in possession or control of the certificate of ownership, the legal owner or lessor shall, within the time provided in subdivision (c) for the mailing, transmittal, or delivery of the certificate of ownership, take any action required by the department to release the legal owner's security interest or transfer the lessor's interest in the vehicle and within that time shall mail, transmit, or deliver written notice of its taking that action to the transferee.

(e) A legal owner or lessor that fails to satisfy the requirements of subdivisions (c) and (d), shall, without offset or reduction, pay the transferee twenty-five dollars ($25) per day for each day that the requirements of subdivisions (c) and (d) remain unsatisfied, not to exceed a maximum payment of two thousand five hundred dollars ($2,500). If the legal owner or lessor fails to pay this amount within 60 days following written demand by the transferee, the amount shall be trebled, not to exceed a maximum payment of seven thousand five hundred dollars ($7,500), and the transferee shall be entitled to costs and reasonable attorneys fees incurred in any court action brought to collect the payment. The right to recover these payments is cumulative with and is not in substitution or derogation of any remedy otherwise available at law or equity.

(f) A legal owner, upon written request of the transferee, shall disclose any pertinent information regarding the amount of payment and the documents necessary to release the obligation secured by the legal owner's interest. *(Stats.1959, c. 3, p. 1572, § 5753. Amended by Stats.1968, c. 147, p. 369, § 1; Stats.2003, c. 151 (S.B.237), § 2.)*

Cross References

Certificate of ownership,
  Generally, see Vehicle Code § 4451.
  Issuance on original registration, see Vehicle Code § 4450.
Endorsement of certificate of ownership, see Vehicle Code § 5750 et seq.
Leased vehicles, evidences of registration, see Vehicle Code § 4453.5
Necessity of delivery for completion of title, see Vehicle Code § 5600.
Transfer of certificate by legal owner only, see Vehicle Code § 5603.
Violation as misdemeanor, see Vehicle Code § 40000.7.

ARTICLE 3. NOTICE AND APPLICATION

Section
5900.   Notice by owners; sale or transfer; mileage of vehicle.
5901.   Dealer or lessor-retailer; written notice of transfer; mileage.
5901.1. Repealed.
5902.   Application for transfer of registration.
5902.5. Applications filed during 30 days preceding expiration of vehicle registration; inclusion of full renewal fee for ensuing year; exception.
5903.   Receipt by department of judgment of abandonment and evidence of sale as specified in Civil Code § 798.61; transfer of registration or reregistration; issuance of new certificate of ownership and registration card.
5904.   Application for vehicles not registered.
5905.   Continuation of security interest.
5906.   Operation without transfer.
5906.5. Transfer of vehicle; recordation of mileage of vehicle.
5907.   Security interest in dealer's inventory.
5908.   Security interests.
5909.   Involuntary transfers.
5910.   Transfer upon death of owner; persons eligible; requirements; form.
5910.5. Beneficiary form ownership.
5910.7. Beneficiary form ownership; transfer; department liability.
5911.   Transfer when certificate unavailable.
5912.   Card held by department.

§ 5900. Notice by owners; sale or transfer; mileage of vehicle

(a) Whenever the owner of a vehicle registered under this code sells or transfers his or her title or interest in, and delivers the possession of, the vehicle to another, the owner shall, within five calendar days, notify the department of the sale or transfer giving the date thereof, the name and address of the owner and of the transferee, and the description of the vehicle that is required in the appropriate form provided for that purpose by the department.

(b) Except as otherwise provided in subdivision (c), pursuant to subsection (a) of Section 32705 of Title 49 of the United States Code, the owner shall also notify the department of the actual mileage of the vehicle as indicated by the vehicle's odometer at the time of sale or transfer. However, if the vehicle owner has knowledge that the mileage displayed on the odometer is incorrect, the owner shall indicate on the appropriate form the true mileage, if known, of the vehicle at the time of sale or transfer.

Providing false or inaccurate mileage is not a violation of this subdivision unless it is done with the intent to defraud.

(c) If the registered owner is not in possession of the vehicle that is sold or transferred, the person in physical possession of that vehicle shall give the notice required by subdivisions (a) and (b). If the registered owner sells or transfers the vehicle through a dealer conducting a wholesale motor vehicle auction, the owner shall furnish the information required by subdivisions (a) and (b) to that dealer.

(Added by Stats.1992, c. 745 (A.B.2414), § 3, operative July 1, 1993. Amended by Stats.1993, c. 852 (A.B.1485), § 4; Stats.2000, c. 1035 (S.B.1403), § 11.)

Cross References

Civil liability of private owners, see Vehicle Code § 17150 et seq.
Mileage records, inspection, see Vehicle Code § 1819.
Mobilehome licensees, unlawful acts, see Health and Safety Code § 18060.5.
Notice of transfer by dealers, off-highway motor vehicles, see Vehicle Code § 38200.
Presumption of abandonment, see Vehicle Code § 22524.
Release from liability upon transfer, notice for, see Vehicle Code § 5602.
Suspension or revocation of dealers' certificates and plates, see Vehicle Code § 11705.

§ 5901. Dealer or lessor-retailer; written notice of transfer; mileage

(a) Every dealer or lessor-retailer, upon transferring by sale, lease, or otherwise any vehicle, whether new or used, of a type subject to registration under this code, shall, not later than the end of the fifth calendar day thereafter not counting the day of sale, give written notice of the transfer to the department at its headquarters upon an appropriate form provided by it.

(b) Except as otherwise provided in this subdivision or in subdivision (c), the dealer or lessor-retailer shall enter on the form and pursuant to Section 32705(a) of Title 49 of the United States Code, on the ownership certificate, the actual mileage of the vehicle as indicated by the vehicle's odometer at the time of the transfer. However, if the vehicle dealer or lessor-retailer has knowledge that the mileage displayed on the odometer is incorrect, the licensee shall indicate on the form on which the mileage

is entered that the mileage registered by the odometer is incorrect. A vehicle dealer or lessor-retailer need not give the notice when selling or transferring a new unregistered vehicle to a dealer or lessor-retailer.

(c) When the dealer or lessor-retailer is not in possession of the vehicle that is sold or transferred, the person in physical possession of the vehicle shall give the information required by subdivision (b).

(d) A sale is deemed completed and consummated when the purchaser of the vehicle has paid the purchase price, or, in lieu thereof, has signed a purchase contract or security agreement, and has taken physical possession or delivery of the vehicle. *(Added by Stats.1992, c. 745 (A.B.2414), § 5, operative July 1, 1993. Amended by Stats.1993, c. 852 (A.B.1485), § 5; Stats.1994, c. 180 (A.B.375), § 7, eff. July 11, 1994; Stats.1998, c. 828 (S.B.1637), § 13.)*

Cross References

Civil liability of private owners, see Vehicle Code § 17150 et seq.
Dealer defined, see Vehicle Code §§ 285, 286.
Mileage records, inspection, see Vehicle Code § 1819.
Off-highway motor vehicles, applicability of section, see Vehicle Code § 38195.
Release of liability upon transfer of title, requisites, see Vehicle Code § 5602.
Violation a misdemeanor, see Vehicle Code § 40000.7.

§ 5901.1. Repealed by Stats.1980, c. 743, p. 2219, § 1

§ 5902. Application for transfer of registration

Whenever any person has received as transferee a properly endorsed certificate of ownership, that person shall, within 10 days thereafter, forward the certificate with the proper transfer fee to the department and thereby make application for a transfer of registration. The certificate of ownership shall contain a space for the applicant's driver's license or identification card number, and the applicant shall furnish that number, if any, in the space provided.

(Stats.1959, c. 3, p. 1573, § 5902. Amended by Stats.1967, c. 723, p. 2095, § 5; Stats.1970, c. 1252, p. 2264, § 1; Stats.1972, c. 296, p. 568, § 1; Stats.1984, c. 779, § 2; Stats.1988, c. 1268, § 5; Stats.1994, c. 1221 (S.B.1758), § 7; Stats.2000, c. 861 (S.B.2084), § 36, eff. Sept. 29, 2000; Stats.2001, c. 826 (A.B.1472), § 18.)

Cross References

Civil liability of private owners, see Vehicle Code § 17150 et seq.
Contents of registration card, see Vehicle Code § 4453.
Fees for transfer of registration, see Vehicle Code § 9255.
Issuance of original certificate of ownership, see Vehicle Code § 4450.
Off-highway motor vehicles, applicability of section, see Vehicle Code § 38195.
Registration fees, generally, see Vehicle Code § 9250 et seq.

Undertaking or bond in absence of evidence of ownership, see Vehicle Code § 4157.

§ 5902.5. Applications filed during 30 days preceding expiration of vehicle registration; inclusion of full renewal fee for ensuing year; exception

(a) If an application for a registration transaction is filed with the department during the 30 days immediately preceding the date of expiration of registration of the vehicle, the application shall be accompanied by the full renewal fees for the ensuing registration year in addition to any other fees that are due and payable.

(b) The requirements of subdivision (a) shall not apply if the expiration of registration occurs on or after July 1, 2011. This subdivision shall become inoperative on January 1, 2012. *(Added by Stats.1993, c. 1292 (S.B.274), § 6. Amended by Stats.2011, c. 21 (S.B.94), § 5, eff. May 4, 2011.)*

§ 5903. Receipt by department of judgment of abandonment and evidence of sale as specified in Civil Code § 798.61; transfer of registration or reregistration; issuance of new certificate of ownership and registration card

When the department receives a copy of the judgment of abandonment and evidence of sale as specified in Section 798.61 of the Civil Code, the department shall transfer the registration of the trailer coach or recreational vehicle which has been deemed abandoned pursuant to that section, or reregister the trailer coach or vehicle under a new registration number, and issue a new certificate of ownership and registration card to the person or persons presenting the copy of the judgment of abandonment and evidence of sale to the department. *(Added by Stats.1991, c. 564 (A.B.743), § 2.)*

Cross References

Off-highway motor vehicles, applicability of section, see Vehicle Code § 38195.

§ 5904. Application for vehicles not registered

Whenever the ownership of any vehicle for which a certificate of ownership has been issued without registration under Section 4452 is transferred, an application for transfer shall be made as provided in this chapter. *(Stats.1959, c. 3, p. 1573, § 5904. Amended by Stats.1961, c. 58, p. 1004, § 16, eff. March 31, 1961.)*

Cross References

Applicability of this section to trolley coaches, see Vehicle Code § 21051.
Off-highway motor vehicles, applicability of section, see Vehicle Code § 38195.
Registration of trailer coaches, nonapplicability of this section, see Vehicle Code § 5351.

§ 5905. Continuation of security interest

When a security interest upon a registered vehicle is satisfied, canceled, or released by the parties thereto duly registered as owner and legal owner respectively and thereafter within a period of 10 days a new security agreement covering the vehicle is executed between the same parties, no application for transfer of registration by reason thereof shall be made and no new certificate of ownership or registration card shall be issued, and all provisions of this code relating to transfers of any title or interest in a vehicle and the registration of the transfers shall be deemed to have been fully complied with, and the new security agreement shall be deemed perfected at the time the new security agreement is executed. *(Stats.1959, c. 3, p. 1573, § 5905. Amended by Stats.1963, c. 819, p. 2014, § 45, eff. Jan. 1, 1965.)*

Cross References

Legal owner defined, see Vehicle Code § 370.
Owner defined, see Vehicle Code § 460.
Security interests, generally, see Vehicle Code § 6300 et seq.
Transfer requirements, see Vehicle Code § 5600.

§ 5906. Operation without transfer

When the transferee of a vehicle is a dealer who holds the same for resale and operates or moves the same upon the highways under special plates, the dealer is not required to make application for transfer, but upon transferring his title or interest to another person he shall comply with this division. *(Stats.1959, c. 3, p. 1573, § 5906.)*

Cross References

Dealer defined, see Vehicle Code §§ 285, 286.
Off-highway motor vehicles, applicability of section, see Vehicle Code § 38195.
Procedure relating to transfer, see Vehicle Code § 5750 et seq.
Transfer requirements, see Vehicle Code § 5600.

§ 5906.5. Transfer of vehicle; recordation of mileage of vehicle

(a) Except as otherwise provided in subdivision (b), in the case of any transfer, including, but not limited to, a transfer resulting from a sale, lease, gift, or auction, of a vehicle under 6,001 pounds, manufacturer's maximum gross weight rating, where no application for transfer is required, the person making such transfer, or his authorized representative, shall sign and shall record on the document evidencing the transfer of the vehicle the actual mileage of the vehicle as indicated by the vehicle's odometer at the time of the transfer. However, if the person making the transfer, or his authorized representative, has knowledge that the mileage displayed on the odometer is incorrect, such person shall record on the document the true mileage, if known, of the vehicle at the time of transfer.

(b) Whenever the person making such transfer is not in possession of the vehicle that is transferred, the person in physical possession of such vehicle shall provide the information required by subdivision (a). *(Added by Stats.1971, c. 260, p. 419, § 5, operative May 3, 1972. Amended by Stats.1978, c. 797, p. 2563, § 4.)*

§ 5907.　Security interest in dealer's inventory

A secured party who holds a security interest in a registered vehicle that constitutes inventory as defined in the Uniform Commercial Code, who has possession of the certificate of ownership issued for that vehicle, if the certificate of ownership has been issued, need not make application for a transfer of registration and the Uniform Commercial Code shall exclusively control the validity and perfection of that security interest. This section does not apply to the extent that subdivisions (a) to (c), inclusive, of Section 9311 of the Uniform Commercial Code apply to a security interest, because the transaction is not described in subdivision (d) of Section 9311 of that code. *(Stats.1959, c. 3, p. 1574, § 5907. Amended by Stats.1963, c. 819, p. 2014, § 46, eff. Jan. 1, 1965; Stats.2003, c. 235 (S.B.283), § 9.)*

Cross References

Enforceability of security interest, see Commercial Code § 9203.
Legal owner defined, see Vehicle Code § 370.
Motor vehicles, security interest in dealer's inventory, application of this section to security interest, see Vehicle Code § 5907.
Security interest, generally, see Vehicle Code § 6300 et seq.
Transfer requirements, see Vehicle Code § 5600.
Transferee defined, see Vehicle Code § 640.

§ 5908.　Security interests

The transferee of a security interest in a registered vehicle need not make application for a transfer of registration when the interest of such transferee arises from a transfer of a security agreement or a lease agreement by the legal owner to the transferee to secure payment or performance of an obligation, and the Uniform Commercial Code shall exclusively control the validity and perfection of such a security interest. *(Stats. 1959, c. 3, p. 1574, § 5908. Amended by Stats.1963, c. 819, p. 2014, § 47, eff. Jan. 1, 1965.)*

Cross References

Legal owner defined, see Vehicle Code § 370.
Secured transactions, see Commercial Code § 9101 et seq.
Security interests, generally, see Vehicle Code § 6300 et seq.
Transfer requirements, see Vehicle Code § 5600.
Transferee defined, see Vehicle Code § 640.

§ 5909.　Involuntary transfers

(a) Whenever the title or interest of any owner or legal owner in or to a vehicle registered under this code passes to another otherwise than by voluntary transfer the new owner or legal owner may obtain a transfer of registration upon application therefor and upon presentation of the last certificate of ownership and registration card issued for the vehicle, if available, and any instruments or documents of authority or certified copies thereof as may be required by the department, or required by law, to evidence or effect a transfer of title or interest in or to chattels in such case.

(b) The department when satisfied of the genuineness and regularity of the transfer shall give notice by mail to the owner and legal owner of the vehicle as shown by the records of the department and five days after the giving of the notice, if still satisfied of the genuineness and regularity of such transfer, shall transfer the registration of the vehicle accordingly. Such notice shall not be required for a transfer described in Section 5601. *(Stats. 1959, c. 3, p. 1574, § 5909. Amended by Stats.1969, c. 384, p. 917, § 1.)*

Cross References

Delivery of card and certificate to transferee, exceptions as to involuntary transfers, see Vehicle Code § 5601.
Issuance of original certificate of ownership and registration card, see Vehicle Code § 4450.
Legal owner defined, see Vehicle Code § 370.
Owner defined, see Vehicle Code § 460.
Registration records, see Vehicle Code § 1800 et seq.
Use fuel tax sale, sale for delinquency in payment of, see Revenue and Taxation Code § 9011.

§ 5910.　Transfer upon death of owner; persons eligible; requirements; form

(a) Upon the death of an owner or legal owner of a vehicle registered under this code, without the decedent leaving other property necessitating probate, and irrespective of the value of the vehicle, the following person or persons may secure transfer of registration of the title or interest of the decedent:

(1) The sole person or all of the persons who succeeded to the property of the decedent under Sections 6401 and 6402 of the Probate Code unless the vehicle is, by will, otherwise bequeathed.

(2) The sole beneficiary or all of the beneficiaries who succeeded to the vehicle under the will of the decedent where the vehicle is, by will, so bequeathed.

(b) The person authorized by subdivision (a) may secure a transfer of registration of the title or interest of the decedent upon presenting to the department all of the following:

(1) The appropriate certificate of ownership and registration card, if available.

(2) A certificate of the heir or beneficiary under penalty of perjury containing the following statements:

(A) The date and place of the decedent's death.

(B) The decedent left no other property necessitating probate and no probate proceeding is now being or has been conducted in this state for the decedent's estate.

(C) The declarant is entitled to the vehicle either (i) as the sole person or all of the persons who succeeded to the property of the decedent under Sections 6401 and 6402 of the Probate Code if the decedent left no will or (ii) as the beneficiary or beneficiaries under the decedent's last will if the decedent left a will, and no one has a right to the decedent's vehicle that is superior to that of the declarant.

(D) There are no unsecured creditors of the decedent or, if there are, the unsecured creditors of the decedent have been paid in full or their claims have been otherwise discharged.

(3) If required by the department, a certificate of the death of the decedent.

(4) If required by the department, the names and addresses of any other heirs or beneficiaries.

(c) If the department is presented with the documents specified in paragraphs (1) and (2) of subdivision (b), no liability shall be incurred by the department or any officer or employee of the department by reason of the transfer of registration of the vehicle pursuant to this section. The department or officer or employee of the department may rely in good faith on the statements in the certificate specified in paragraph (2) of subdivision (b) and has no duty to inquire into the truth of any statement in the certificate. The person who secures the transfer of the vehicle pursuant to this section is subject to the provisions of Sections 13109 to 13113, inclusive, of the Probate Code to the same extent as a person to whom transfer of property is made under Chapter 3 (commencing with Section 13100) of Part 1 of Division 8 of the Probate Code.

(d) The department may prescribe a combined form for use under this section and Section 9916. *(Added by Stats.1985, c. 982, § 24. Amended by Stats.1986, c. 783, § 26, operative July 1, 1987.)*

Cross References

Issuance of original certificate of ownership and registration card, see Vehicle Code § 4450.

Legal owner defined, see Vehicle Code § 370.

Owner defined, see Vehicle Code § 460.

§ 5910.5. Beneficiary form ownership

(a) On death of the owner of a vehicle owned in beneficiary form, the vehicle belongs to the surviving beneficiary, if any. If there is no surviving beneficiary, the vehicle belongs to the estate of the deceased owner or of the last coowner to die.

(b) A certificate of ownership in beneficiary form may be revoked or the beneficiary changed at any time before the death of the owner by either of the following methods:

(1) By sale of the vehicle with proper assignment and delivery of the certificate of ownership to another person.

(2) By application for a new certificate of ownership without designation of a beneficiary or with the designation of a different beneficiary.

(c) Except as provided in subdivision (b), designation of a beneficiary in a certificate of ownership issued in beneficiary form may not be changed or revoked by will, by any other instrument, by a change of circumstances, or otherwise.

(d) The beneficiary's interest in the vehicle at death of the owner is subject to any contract of sale, assignment, or security interest to which the owner was subject during his or her lifetime.

(e) The surviving beneficiary may secure a transfer of ownership for the vehicle upon presenting to the department all of the following:

(1) The appropriate certificate of ownership.

(2) A certificate under penalty of perjury stating the date and place of the owner's death and that the declarant is entitled to the vehicle as the designated beneficiary.

(3) If required by the department, a certificate of the death of the owner.

(f) After the death of the owner, the surviving beneficiary may transfer his or her interest in the vehicle to another person without securing transfer of ownership into his or her own name by appropriately signing the certificate of ownership for the vehicle and delivering the document to the transferee for forwarding to the department with appropriate fees. The transferee may secure a transfer of ownership upon presenting to the department (1) the certificate of ownership signed by the beneficiary, (2) the certificate described in paragraph (2) of subdivision (e) executed by the beneficiary under penalty of perjury; and (3) if required by the department, a certificate of death of the owner.

(g) A transfer at death pursuant to this section is effective by reason of this section, and shall not be deemed to be a testamentary disposition of property. The right of the designated beneficiary to the vehicle shall not be denied, abridged, or affected on the grounds that the right has not been created by a writing executed in accordance with the laws of this state prescribing the requirements to effect a valid testamentary disposition of property.

(h) A transfer at death pursuant to this section is subject to Section 9653 of the Probate Code.

(i) If there is no surviving beneficiary, the person or persons described in Section 5910 may secure transfer of the vehicle as provided in that section.

(j) The department may prescribe forms for use pursuant to this section. *(Added by Stats.1991, c. 1055 (S.B.271), § 59, operative Jan. 1, 1993.)*

Law Revision Commission Comments

1991 Addition

Section 5910.5 is new. Subdivisions (a) through (d) are drawn from Missouri law. See Mo.Ann.Stat. § 301.681 (Vernon Supp. 1991). Subdivision (e) is drawn from Health and Safety Code Section 18102(b) and Vehicle Code Sections 5910(b) and 9916(b). Subdivision (g) is drawn from Probate Code Section 5304. Subdivision (h) is comparable to Health and Safety Code Section 18102.2(h), Probate Code Section 5705 (gift in view of impending death), and Vehicle Code Section 9916.5(h). Subdivision (j) is drawn from Vehicle Code Section 5910(c). See also Health & Safety Code §§ 18080.2, 18102.2; Veh.Code §§ 4150.7, 9852.7, 9916.5. [21 Cal.L.Rev.Comm.Reports 71 (1991)].

§ 5910.7. Beneficiary form ownership; transfer; department liability

(a) If the department makes a transfer pursuant to Section 5910.5, the department is discharged from all liability, whether or not the transfer is consistent with the beneficial ownership of the vehicle transferred.

(b) The protection provided by subdivision (a) does not extend to a transfer made after the department has been served with a court order restraining the transfer. No other notice or information shown to have been available to the department shall affect its right to the protection afforded by subdivision (a).

(c) The protection provided by this section has no bearing on the rights of parties in disputes between themselves or their successors concerning the beneficial ownership of the vehicle.

(d) The protection provided by this section is in addition to, and not exclusive of, any other protection provided to the department by any other provision of law. *(Added by Stats.1991, c. 1055 (S.B.271), § 60, operative Jan. 1, 1993.)*

Law Revision Commission Comments

1991 Addition

Section 5910.7 is drawn from Probate Code Section 5405 (Multiple-Party Accounts Law). See also Health and Safety Code § 18102.3; Veh.Code 9916.7. [20 Cal.L.Rev.Comm.Reports 2883 (1990)].

§ 5911. Transfer when certificate unavailable

Whenever application is made to the department for a transfer of registration of a vehicle to a new owner or legal owner and the applicant is unable to present the certificate of ownership issued for the vehicle by reason of the same being lost or otherwise not available, the department may receive the application and examine into the circumstances of the case and may require the filing of certifications or other information, and when the department is satisfied that the applicant is entitled to a transfer of registration the department may transfer the registration of the vehicle, or reregister the vehicle under a new registration number, and issue a new certificate of ownership and registration card to the person or persons found to be entitled thereto. The department, however, shall not issue a new certificate of ownership and registration card to the applicant if the department has received notice by registered or certified mail in which it is indicated that the existing ownership certificate is being held for nonpayment of the vehicle. The notice may be forwarded by the registered owner, recorded lienholder, or by a person exempted from recording ownership by Section 5906. *(Stats.1959, c. 3, p. 1574, § 5911. Amended by Stats.1973, c. 943, p. 1774, § 1; Stats.1977, c. 456, p. 1495, § 6; Stats.1988, c. 1268, § 6.)*

230

Cross References

Application for new or substitute registration where registration certificates or cards stolen, lost, or damaged, see Vehicle Code §§ 4457, 4459.
Issuance of original registration card and certificate of ownership, see Vehicle Code § 4450.
Renewal of registration of stolen or embezzled vehicles, see Vehicle Code § 4605.

§ 5912. Card held by department

Whenever application is made to the department for a transfer of registration of a vehicle to a new owner or legal owner and the applicant is unable to present the registration card issued for the vehicle by reason of the same being in the possession of the department upon an application for renewal of registration, the department may transfer the registration of such vehicle upon production of the properly endorsed certificate of ownership to the vehicle and a temporary receipt upon a form prescribed by the department and containing such information as the department shall deem necessary, including, but not limited to, the license number assigned to the vehicle for the ensuing registration year, the amount of the fees payable upon renewal of registration, and the vehicle identification number of the vehicle. *(Stats.1959, c. 3, p. 1575, § 5912. Amended by Stats.1973, c. 889, p. 1654, § 35, eff. Sept. 28, 1973.)*

Cross References

Application by transferee for transfer of registration, see Vehicle Code § 5902.
Application for new registration card where original lost, see Vehicle Code § 4457.
Endorsement of certificate of ownership upon transfer, see Vehicle Code § 5750 et seq.
Issuance of original registration card, see Vehicle Code § 4450.
Legal owner defined, see Vehicle Code § 370.
Registration fees, generally, see Vehicle Code § 9250 et seq.

ARTICLE 4. TRANSFER BY DEPARTMENT

Section
6050. Transfer of registration; nonrepairable vehicle certificate.
6051. Transfer under regular application.
6052. Transfer of vehicle not registered.

§ 6050. Transfer of registration; nonrepairable vehicle certificate

(a) The department upon receipt of a properly endorsed certificate of ownership and the required fee shall reregister the vehicle under its registration number in the name of the new owner and new legal owner, if any, and shall issue a new registration card and certificate of ownership as provided upon an original registration.

(b) The department shall not issue a new registration card and certificate of ownership pursuant to subdivision (a) on a vehicle that has been issued a nonrepairable vehicle certificate pursuant to Section 11515.2. *(Stats. 1959, c. 3, p. 1575, § 6050. Amended by Stats.1988, c.*

1268, § 7; Stats.1994, c. 1008 (S.B.1833), § 10, operative July 1, 1995.)

Cross References

Certificate or registration card lost, procedure on transfer, see Vehicle Code § 5911.
Endorsement of certificate of ownership, see Vehicle Code § 5750 et seq.
Fees on transfer of registration, see Vehicle Code § 9255.
Issuance of registration card and certificate of ownership, see Vehicle Code § 4450.
Legal owner defined, see Vehicle Code § 370.
Owner defined, see Vehicle Code § 460.
Refusal of transfer, grounds, see Vehicle Code §§ 4750, 4751.
Registration fees, generally, see Vehicle Code § 9250 et seq.
Transfer of registration where transfers involuntary, see Vehicle Code § 5909.
Transfer where registration card not available, see Vehicle Code § 5912.
Transfer without probate, see Vehicle Code § 5910.

§ 6051. Transfer under regular application

If the application for a transfer is made in the manner provided in this code the department shall not be required to withhold the transfer of any right, title, or interest in or to a vehicle if the application on its face appears to be genuine and regular and the department has received neither a request from any law enforcement agency that action on the application be deferred nor an order of a court of the United States or of the State of California restraining the transfer within two years prior thereto. *(Stats.1959, c. 3, p. 1575, § 6051.)*

Cross References

Transfers of title or interest, see Vehicle Code § 5600 et seq.

§ 6052. Transfer of vehicle not registered

When application is made for transfer of the ownership of a vehicle for which a certificate of ownership has been issued without registration, upon payment of registration, transfer, and other fees required by law, the department shall issue the usual certificate of ownership and registration card unless the vehicle is not to be operated on the highways and the new owner submits an affidavit satisfactory to the department as to those facts required by subdivision (b) of Section 4452, in which case the new certificate of title and facsimile thereof may be issued as provided for in that section. *(Stats.1959, c. 3, p. 1575, § 6052.)*

Cross References

Applicability of this section to trolley coaches, see Vehicle Code § 21051.
Off-highway motor vehicles, applicability of section, see Vehicle Code § 38195.
Registration of trailer coaches, nonapplicability of this section, see Vehicle Code § 5351.

ARTICLE 5. TRANSFERS THROUGH WHOLESALE AUCTIONS

Section
6100. Certificate of title; dealer name; auction date.
6102. Documents to be retained by dealer.
6104. Sales between dealers; purchasers rights and remedies.
6105. Operative date.

§ 6100. Certificate of title; dealer name; auction date

A dealer who conducts a wholesale motor vehicle auction and who uses the form prescribed in subdivision (b) of Section 4456 shall include the phrase "SOLD THROUGH [name of dealer conducting the auction]" and the date of the auction on the certificate of title of every vehicle sold, in a manner prescribed by the department. *(Added by Stats.1992, c. 745 (A.B.2414), § 6, operative July 1, 1993. Amended by Stats.1994, c. 180 (A.B.375), § 8, eff. July 11, 1994.)*

§ 6102. Documents to be retained by dealer

For each vehicle sold pursuant to this article, the dealer who conducts the auction shall maintain a copy of the following documents for a period of not less than five years:

(a) The form required by subdivision (b) of Section 4456.

(b) A copy of the auction sales agreement.

(c) A copy of the odometer statement required by Section 5900. *(Added by Stats.1992, c. 745 (A.B.2414), § 6, operative July 1, 1993. Amended by Stats.1994, c. 180 (A.B.375), § 9, eff. July 11, 1994.)*

§ 6104. Sales between dealers; purchasers rights and remedies

Notwithstanding any other provision of law, a dealer who purchases a vehicle pursuant to this article has the same rights and remedies against the dealer who conducts the auction sale as if that dealer were an owner and seller of the auctioned vehicle. The purchaser dealer's rights and remedies are in addition to any right or remedy he or she may have against the seller of a vehicle sold at a wholesale motor vehicle auction. The provisions of this section may not be waived or modified by agreement, or by recharacterization of the transaction. *(Added by Stats.1992, c. 745 (A.B.2414), § 6, operative July 1, 1993.)*

§ 6105. Operative date

This article shall become operative on July 1, 1993. *(Added by Stats.1992, c. 745 (A.B.2414), § 6, operative July 1, 1993.)*

CHAPTER 2.5. MISCELLANEOUS TITLE PROVISIONS

Article	Section
1. Certificate of Title as Evidence	6150
2. Inspection and Cancellation of Titles for Exported Vehicles	6160
3. Return of Stolen Motor Vehicle Retained as Evidence	6171

ARTICLE 1. CERTIFICATE OF TITLE AS EVIDENCE

Section
6150. Certified copy of record of title of motor vehicle; evidence of ownership.
6151. Showing of need; notice; testimony of owner or person in control of motor vehicle.
6152. Showing of need; continuance; preservation of witness' testimony.
6153. Preservation of testimony; examination in open court subject to cross-examination.
6154. Severability.

§ 6150. Certified copy of record of title of motor vehicle; evidence of ownership

In any criminal proceeding in which ownership, possession, or use of a motor vehicle is an issue, a copy certified by the department as its record of title on file, or with the official custodian of those documents of another state, shall be admissible as evidence of ownership of the motor vehicle. Upon the introduction of evidence that the legal owner of a motor vehicle is not named in the certificate of title or that use or possession was with the consent or authority of the owner, a reasonable continuance shall be granted any party to enable the owner of the vehicle to be brought into court to testify. *(Added by Stats.1994, c. 1247 (A.B.1926), § 6.)*

§ 6151. Showing of need; notice; testimony of owner or person in control of motor vehicle

A party to a proceeding described in Section 6150 may provide notice to the opposing party that a showing of need will be made at the arraignment or at any other pretrial hearing, and upon the proof of that notice and the showing of need, the court shall take testimony from the owner or person in control of the motor vehicle which shall be admissible at trial. *(Added by Stats.1994, c. 1247 (A.B.1926), § 6.)*

§ 6152. Showing of need; continuance; preservation of witness' testimony

At any hearing, including, but not limited to, a scheduled trial date, involving a proceeding described in Section 6150, upon a showing of need, the court shall order as a condition of granting a continuance that the testimony of a witness then present in court be taken and preserved for subsequent use at a trial or any other stage of the proceeding. *(Added by Stats.1994, c. 1247 (A.B. 1926), § 6.)*

§ 6153. Preservation of testimony; examination in open court subject to cross-examination

Where testimony is taken and preserved for use at trial or other stage of the proceeding pursuant to Sections 6151 and 6152, the witness shall be examined in open court by the party on whose behalf he or she is present, and the adverse party shall have the right of cross-examination. *(Added by Stats.1994, c. 1247 (A.B.1926), § 6.)*

232

§ 6154. Severability

If any provision of this act or the application thereof to any person or circumstances is held invalid, that invalidity shall not affect other provisions or applications of the act which can be given effect without the invalid provision or application, and to this end the provisions of this act are severable. *(Added by Stats.1994, c. 1247 (A.B.1926), § 6.)*

ARTICLE 2. INSPECTION AND CANCELLATION OF TITLES FOR EXPORTED VEHICLES

Section
6160. Legislative findings and declarations; vehicle exportation.
6161. Definitions.
6161. Definitions.
6162. Vehicle exportation; procedure.

§ 6160. Legislative findings and declarations; vehicle exportation

The Legislature finds and declares that when vehicles are exported and their title records are not amended to reflect exportation, it is conducive to vehicle theft and insurance fraud. The certificates of title issued by this state are used in insurance frauds in which a claimant falsely states that a vehicle has been stolen or uses that certificate to fraudulently procure insurance when in fact the vehicle has previously been exported from the United States. In the interest of the general welfare of the people of this state, and in order to combat vehicle theft and insurance fraud, it is necessary that the department's record of title reflect the fact that a vehicle is being exported either temporarily or permanently, based upon the true owner's declaration prior to exportation. *(Added by Stats.1994, c. 1247 (A.B.1926), § 6.)*

§ 6161. Definitions

Section added by Stats.1994, c. 1008 (S.B. 1833), § 11. See, also, another section of the same number, added by Stats.1994, c. 1247 (A.B. 1926), § 6.

For the purposes of this chapter, the following provisions and definitions apply to the following terms:

(a) "Certified record of permanent exportation" shall include all of the following:

(1) The titled owner's name and address.

(2) A description of the vehicle, including year, make, body type, vehicle identification number, license registration number, and state registration.

(3) The destination of vehicle.

(4) The purpose of export, whether sale, lease, or personal use.

(b) "Declaration that the vehicle will not be permanently located outside the United States" shall include the items specified in paragraphs (1) to (3), inclusive, of subdivision (a), and shall also state the period of time for which it is anticipated that the vehicle will be outside the United States.

(c) "Export" means the shipping or transporting of a vehicle out of the United States by means other than its own power or that of a vehicle drawing or towing it.

(d) "Owner" means the owner of record indicated in a certificate of title issued by this state and includes an agent of that owner acting under a valid power of attorney executed by an owner.

(e) "Title" means the certificate of ownership issued by the department pursuant to Section 4450, but excludes a salvage certificate, as described in Section 11515, a nonrepairable vehicle certificate, as defined in Section 432, and an acquisition bill of sale, as described in Section 11519.

(f) "Vehicle" means every device designed for transportation of persons or property upon land, for which a certificate of title is required. *(Added by Stats.1994, c. 1008 (S.B.1833), § 11.)*

§ 6161. Definitions

Section added by Stats.1994, c. 1247 (A.B. 1926), § 6. See, also, another section of the same number, added by Stats.1994, c. 1008 (S.B.1833), § 11.

For the purposes of this act, the term:

(a) "Certified record of permanent exportation" shall include the following:

(1) Titled owner's name and address.

(2) Description of the vehicle, including year, make, body type, vehicle identification number, license registration number, and state registration.

(3) Destination of vehicle.

(4) Purpose of export, whether sale, lease, or personal use.

(b) "Declaration that the vehicle will not be permanently located outside the United States" shall include the items specified in paragraphs (1) to (3), inclusive, of subdivision (a), and shall also state the period of time for which it is anticipated that the vehicle will be outside the United States.

(c) "Export" means the shipping or transporting of a vehicle out of the United States by means other than its own power or that of a vehicle drawing or towing it.

(d) "Owner" means the owner of record indicated in a certificate of title issued by this state and includes an agent of that owner acting under a valid power of attorney executed by an owner.

(e) "Title" means the certificate of ownership issued by the department pursuant to Section 4450, but excludes a salvage certificate as described in Section 11515 and an acquisition bill of sale as described in Section 11519.

(f) "Vehicle" means every device designed for transportation of persons or property upon land, for which a certificate of title is required. *(Added by Stats.1994, c. 1247 (A.B.1926), § 6.)*

§ 6162. Vehicle exportation; procedure

An owner of a vehicle who seeks to export a vehicle titled in this state shall appear at the department with the certificate of title to ascertain whether there are any liens of record outstanding and whether the person exporting the vehicle is the lawful owner. If the certificate of title is found to be in proper order and no unsatisfied lien appears, the department shall enter into its record of title that the vehicle is intended for permanent exportation from the United States. If the owner certifies by filing a declaration with the department that the vehicle will not be permanently located outside the United States, and that he or she intends to return the vehicle to the United States, the department shall enter into its record of title a declaration that the vehicle will not be permanently located outside the United States until notification by the owner that the vehicle has been returned. *(Added by Stats.1994, c. 1247 (A.B.1926), § 6. Amended by Stats. 1995, c. 91 (S.B.975), § 173.)*

ARTICLE 3. RETURN OF STOLEN MOTOR VEHICLE RETAINED AS EVIDENCE

Section

6171. Return of allegedly stolen vehicle; opportunity for examination by prosecution and defense.
6172. Release of vehicle; time; order for additional time for examination or retention.

§ 6171. Return of allegedly stolen vehicle; opportunity for examination by prosecution and defense

When criminal charges have been filed involving a motor vehicle alleged to have been stolen and the vehicle is in the custody of a peace officer for evidentiary purposes, it shall be held in custody or, if a request for its release from custody is made, until the prosecutor has notified the defendant or his or her attorney of that request and both the prosecution and defense have been afforded a reasonable opportunity for an examination of the motor vehicle to determine its true value and to produce or reproduce, by photographs or other identifying techniques, legally sufficient evidence for introduction at trial or other criminal proceedings. *(Added by Stats. 1994, c. 1247 (A.B.1926), § 6.)*

§ 6172. Release of vehicle; time; order for additional time for examination or retention

Upon expiration of a reasonable time for the completion of the examination, which in no event shall exceed 30 days from the date of service of the notice of request or return of the motor vehicle as provided in Section 6171, the property shall be released to the person making that request after satisfactory proof of the person's entitlement to the possession. Notwithstanding the foregoing, upon ex parte application by either party with notice to the other, the court may grant additional time for the examination or order retention of the motor vehicle if it determines that either is necessary to further the interests of justice; however, this provision shall not be construed to require a noticed hearing. *(Added by Stats.1994, c. 1247 (A.B.1926), § 6.)*

CHAPTER 3. FILING INSTRUMENTS EVIDENCING LIENS OR ENCUMBRANCES

Section
6300. Recording of security interest.
6301. Perfection of security interest.
6302. Secured party as legal owner.
6303. Method is exclusive.

§ 6300. Recording of security interest

Except as provided in Sections 5905, 5907, and 5908, no security interest in any vehicle registered under this code, irrespective of whether the registration was effected prior or subsequent to the creation of the security interest, is perfected until the secured party or his or her successor or assignee has deposited, either physically or by electronic transmission pursuant to Section 1801.1, with the department, at its office in Sacramento, or at any other office as may be designated by the director, a properly endorsed certificate of ownership to the vehicle subject to the security interest showing the secured party as legal owner if the vehicle is then registered under this code, or, if the vehicle is not so registered, an application in usual form for an original registration, together with an application for registration of the secured party as legal owner, and upon payment of the fees as provided in this code. *(Stats.1959, c. 3, p. 1576, § 6300. Amended by Stats.1963, c. 819, p. 2014, § 48, eff. Jan. 1, 1965; Stats.1996, c. 440 (S.B.1588), § 6.)*

Cross References

Application for original registration of vehicle, see Vehicle Code § 4150.
Definitions,
  Legal owner, see Vehicle Code § 370.
  Owner, see Vehicle Code § 460.
  Registered owner, see Vehicle Code § 505.
  Vehicle, see Vehicle Code § 670.
Fee for filing chattel mortgage, see Vehicle Code § 9256.
Involuntary transfers, see Vehicle Code § 5601.
Secured party, defined, see Commercial Code § 9105.
Security interest, defined, see Commercial Code § 1201.

§ 6301. Perfection of security interest

When the secured party, his or her successor, or his or her assignee, has deposited, either physically or by electronic transmission pursuant to Section 1801.1, with the department a properly endorsed certificate of ownership showing the secured party as legal owner or an application in usual form for an original registration, together with an application for registration of the secured party as legal owner, the deposit constitutes perfection of the security interest and the rights of all persons in the vehicle shall be subject to the provisions of the Uniform Commercial Code, but the vehicle subject to

the security interest shall be subject to a lien for services and materials as provided in Chapter 6.5 (commencing with Section 3068) of Title 14 of Part 4 of Division 3 of the Civil Code. *(Stats.1959, c. 3, p. 1576, § 6301. Amended by Stats.1963, c. 819, p. 2014, § 49, eff. Jan. 1, 1965; Stats.1982, c. 454, p. 1893, § 182; Stats.1996, c. 440 (S.B.1588), § 7.)*

Cross References

Legal owner defined, see Vehicle Code § 370.
Secured party, defined, see Commercial Code § 9105.
Security interest, defined, see Commercial Code § 1201.

§ 6302. Secured party as legal owner

Upon the deposit of an application for registration of a secured party as legal owner and upon the payment of the fees as provided in this code, the department shall register the secured party, his successor or assignee as legal owner in the manner provided for the registration of motor vehicles under the provisions of this chapter. *(Stats.1959, c. 3, p. 1576, § 6302. Amended by Stats.1961, c. 58, p. 1005, § 17; Stats.1963, c. 819, p. 2015, § 50, eff. Jan. 1, 1965.)*

Cross References

Fee for filing chattel mortgage, see Vehicle Code § 9256.
Legal owner defined, see Vehicle Code § 370.
Procedure upon registration, see Vehicle Code § 4450 et seq.
Secured party, defined, see Commercial Code § 9105.

§ 6303. Method is exclusive

Except as provided in Sections 5905, 5907 and 5908, the method provided in this chapter for perfecting a security interest on a vehicle registered under this code is exclusive, but the effect of such perfection, and the creation, attachment, priority and validity of such security interest shall be governed by the Uniform Commercial Code. *(Stats.1959, c. 3, p. 1576, § 6303. Amended by Stats.1961, c. 58, p. 1005, § 18; Stats.1963, c. 819, p. 2015, § 51, eff. Jan. 1, 1965.)*

CHAPTER 4. PERMITS TO NONRESIDENT OWNERS

Article	Section
1. Exemption of Nonresidents	6700
2. Foreign Commercial Vehicles	6850
3. Reciprocity Agreements	8000
4. Apportioned Registration	8050
5. Federal Motor Vehicle Safety Program	8100
6. Enforcement of Liens on Apportioned Fleet Vehicles	8200
7. International Registration Plan and Reciprocal Agreements [Repealed]	

ARTICLE 1. EXEMPTION OF NONRESIDENTS

Section
6700. Nonresidents and vehicles owned by nonresidents: registration.

Section

6700.1.   Foreign residents purchasing vehicles made in United States; in-transit permits; duration of permit; reimbursement of sales tax and registration charges; penalties.

6700.2.   Nonresident daily commuters; motor vehicle operation conditions; foreign country residents.

6700.25.   Nonresident daily commuters; identification indicia and card; service fees.

6700.3.   Nonresident daily commuters; applications for identification indicia and card.

6700.4.   Nonresident daily commuters; display of identification indicia and card.

6700.5.   Repealed.

6701.   Nonresident owners who are members or spouses of members of United States armed forces on active duty in state.

6702.   Nonresidents having established place of business.

6703.   Persons discharged from armed forces.

6704 to 6706.   Repealed.

§ 6700. Nonresidents and vehicles owned by nonresidents: registration

(a) Except as provided in Section 6700.2, the owner of any vehicle of a type otherwise subject to registration under this code, other than a commercial vehicle registered in a foreign jurisdiction, may operate the vehicle in this state until gainful employment is accepted in this state or until residency is established in this state, whichever occurs first, if the vehicle displays valid license plates and has a valid registration issued to the owner, and the owner was a resident of that state at the time of issuance. Application to register the vehicle shall be made within 20 days after gainful employment is accepted in this state or residency is established in this state.

(b) A nonresident owner of a vehicle, otherwise exempt from registration pursuant to this section or Section 6700.2, may operate or permit operation of the vehicle in this state without registering the vehicle in this state if the vehicle is registered in the place of residence of the owner and displays upon it valid license plates issued by that place. This exemption does not apply if the nonresident owner rents, leases, lends, or otherwise furnishes the vehicle to a California resident for regular use on the highways of this state, as defined in subdivision (b) of Section 4000.4.

(c) Any resident who operates upon a highway of this state a vehicle owned by a nonresident who furnished the vehicle to the resident operator for his or her regular use within this state, as defined in subdivision (b) of Section 4000.4, shall cause the vehicle to be registered in California within 20 days after its first operation within this state by the resident.

(Added by Stats.1984, c. 1322, § 7, operative July 1, 1985. Amended by Stats.1985, c. 1090, § 2, eff. Sept. 27, 1985; Stats.2003, c. 594 (S.B.315), § 30.)

Cross References

Definitions,
   Legal owner, see Vehicle Code § 370.
   Nonresident, see Vehicle Code § 435.

   Owner, see Vehicle Code § 460.
   Vehicle, see Vehicle Code § 670.
Exemption of vehicles from registration, see Vehicle Code § 4002 et seq.
Foreign commercial vehicles, see Vehicle Code § 6850 et seq.
Registration fees for vehicles registered outside state, see Vehicle Code § 9252.
Registration of nonresident vehicles leased for use in this state, see Vehicle Code § 6853.
Registration of trailer coaches, nonresident exemptions, see Vehicle Code § 5354.
Suspension or revocation of license provisions applicable to nonresidents, see Vehicle Code § 13205.

§ 6700.1. Foreign residents purchasing vehicles made in United States; in-transit permits; duration of permit; reimbursement of sales tax and registration charges; penalties

(a) Notwithstanding any other provision of law, the department may issue an in-transit permit to a resident of a foreign country not more than 30 days before or after the foreign resident purchases a new motor vehicle in California which was manufactured in the United States. The permit authorizes the operation of the vehicle for which it is purchased for up to 30 consecutive days after the first date of operation, and is in lieu of any other registration requirements, including, but not limited to, fees or taxes required by this code or the Revenue and Taxation Code. The seller shall ship or drive the vehicle out of this country before or at the end of 30 consecutive days from the first date of operation, or thereafter shall be subject to, and shall be required to pay, all charges and registration requirements for vehicles subject to registration in this state. In addition, if the vehicle is not so removed from this country, the department shall assess, and the seller shall be required to pay, a penalty of 20 percent of the vehicle registration and license fees and sales tax due upon the vehicle becoming subject to registration.

(b) Subdivision (a) does not apply to commercial vehicles.

(c) Proof of residency in a foreign country for purposes of this section shall be established through the presentation of a valid visa, passport, or other suitable documentation, as determined by the department.

(d) A fee of sixty dollars ($60) shall be paid to the department for each in-transit permit issued.

(e) A permit issued under this section shall be displayed in the manner permitted by paragraph (3) of subdivision (b) of Section 26708.

(f) The permit issued by the department shall clearly and prominently indicate the date of expiration of the authorized in-transit driving privilege.

(g) No California certificate of ownership shall be issued.

(h) A manufacturer's certificate of origin shall prominently indicate that the certificate is valid for transfer of ownership to the purchaser only outside of the United

States, the District of Columbia, or the Commonwealth of Puerto Rico.

(i) Notwithstanding Part 1 (commencing with Section 6001) of Division 2 of the Revenue and Taxation Code, the manufacturer of a new motor vehicle sold to a foreign purchaser under the conditions specified in Section 6366.2 of the Revenue and Taxation Code shall reimburse the retailer for an amount equal to the sales tax and all registration charges and fees, and a penalty of 20 percent of those taxes, charges, and fees if the conditions of the in-transit permit are not met, as specified in this section. *(Added by Stats.1989, c. 762, § 3, eff. Sept. 25, 1989.)*

§ 6700.2. Nonresident daily commuters; motor vehicle operation conditions; foreign country residents

(a) Notwithstanding Section 4000.4, subdivision (a) of Section 6700, or Section 6702, a nonresident daily commuter may operate a motor vehicle on the highways of this state only if all of the following conditions are met:

(1) The motor vehicle is a passenger vehicle or a commercial vehicle of less than 8,001 pounds unladen weight with not more than two axles of the type commonly referred to as a pickup truck.

(2) The motor vehicle is used regularly to transport passengers on the highways of this state principally between, and to and from, the place of residence in a contiguous state and the place of employment in this state by the owner of the motor vehicle and for no other business purpose.

(3) The motor vehicle is not used in the course of a business within this state, including the transportation of property other than incidental personal property between, and to or from, the place of residence in a contiguous state and the place of employment of the motor vehicle owner in this state.

(4) Nothing in paragraphs (2) and (3) prohibits a nonresident daily commuter operating a motor vehicle that displays currently valid external vehicle identification indicia and who possess a corresponding identification card issued pursuant to Section 6700.25 from using that vehicle for other lawful purposes.

(b) The exception to registration of a motor vehicle under the conditions specified in this section does not supersede any other exception to registration under other conditions provided by law.

(c) This section does not apply to a resident of a foreign country. *(Added by Stats.1985, c. 1090, § 3, eff. Sept. 27, 1985. Amended by Stats.1993, c. 633 (A.B.2008), § 2; Stats.1995, c. 91 (S.B.975), § 174; Stats.2000, c. 30 (A.B.1763), § 1; Stats.2001, c. 825 (S.B.290), § 9.)*

Cross References

Nonresident daily commuter, defined, see Vehicle Code § 435.5.

§ 6700.25. Nonresident daily commuters; identification indicia and card; service fees

(a) The department shall provide a nonresident daily commuter with external vehicle identification indicia and

a corresponding identification card, upon application therefor and completion of the form required by Section 6700.3, which indicia and card shall be valid for a period of two years. A vehicle shall be exempt from Sections 4000.4 and 6700 when operated with the requisite indicia and otherwise in accordance with this chapter.

(b) Subdivision (a) applies only to residents and vehicles of residents of a contiguous state which has enacted laws that provide reciprocal privileges to California residents who are employed in the contiguous state. Subdivision (a) does not apply to residents of foreign countries.

(c) Subdivision (a) applies only to the vehicles specified in paragraph (1) of subdivision (a) of Section 6700.2.

(d) Subdivision (a) applies only to vehicles which are licensed in a foreign jurisdiction that are used to commute into California to a destination within a corridor in this state that parallels the border between California and the contiguous state and extends not more than 35 air miles into California from the border at any point. The privilege accorded by subdivision (a) shall be revoked by operation of the vehicle for commuter purposes beyond that 35-mile corridor.

(e) The department shall charge a service fee of fifteen dollars ($15) for each vehicle. *(Added by Stats.1985, c. 1090, § 4, eff. Sept. 27, 1985. Amended by Stats.2003, c. 719 (S.B.1055), § 8.)*

Cross References

Base fee amounts, adjustment of fees, see Vehicle Code § 1678.
Nonresident daily commuter, defined, see Vehicle Code § 435.5.

§ 6700.3. Nonresident daily commuters; applications for identification indicia and card

(a) An application by a nonresident daily commuter for indicia and an identification card pursuant to Section 6700.25 shall be filed with the department.

(b) The department shall prescribe a form to be completed by the applicant which shall include all of the following information:

(1) The vehicle license number and the vehicle identification number (VIN) of the vehicle that will display the nonresident daily commuter indicia.

(2) The name of the registered owner of the vehicle that will display the indicia.

(3) A statement that the applicant is a nonresident daily commuter as defined in Section 435.5.

(4) A statement that the indicia will be displayed upon a qualified vehicle as specified in Section 6700.4.

(5) A statement that the place of employment of the nonresident daily commuter is within the 35-mile corridor specified in subdivision (d) of Section 6700.25. *(Added by Stats.1985, c. 1090, § 5, eff. Sept. 27, 1985.)*

§ 6700.4. Nonresident daily commuters; display of identification indicia and card

A nonresident daily commuter indicia shall be displayed in a location on the vehicle which is clearly visible and adjacent to the rear license plate. The corresponding nonresident daily commuter identification card shall be carried at all times in the assigned vehicle and shall be presented to any California peace officer upon demand. *(Added by Stats.1985, c. 1090, § 6, eff. Sept. 27, 1985.)*

Cross References

Nonresident daily commuter, defined, see Vehicle Code § 435.5.

§ 6700.5. Repealed by Stats.1986, c. 248, § 240

§ 6701. Nonresident owners who are members or spouses of members of United States armed forces on active duty in state

(a) Any nonresident owner of a vehicle registered in a foreign state who is a member or spouse of a member of the armed forces of the United States on active duty within this state, and any resident owner of a vehicle registered in a foreign state who is a member or spouse of a member of the armed forces of the United States returning from active duty in a foreign state, may operate the vehicle in this state without securing California registration after satisfying all of the following requirements:

(1) The license plates displayed on the vehicle are valid plates issued by a foreign jurisdiction.

(2) The vehicle registration and license plates are issued to the military person or spouse of the military person.

(3) The vehicle registration and license plates were issued by the foreign jurisdiction where the military person was last regularly assigned and stationed for duty by military orders or a jurisdiction claimed by the nonresident military person as the permanent state of residence.

(4) If the vehicle is a motor vehicle, the owner or driver has in force one of the forms of financial responsibility specified in Section 16021.

(b) For purposes of paragraph (3) of subdivision (a), military orders do not include military orders for leave, for temporary duty, or for any other assignment of any nature requiring the military person's presence outside the foreign jurisdiction where the owner was regularly assigned and stationed for duty.

(c) This section applies to all vehicles owned by the military person or spouse except any commercial vehicle used in any business manner wherein the military person or spouse receives compensation. *(Added by Stats.1984, c. 1322, § 7, operative July 1, 1985. Amended by Stats. 1986, c. 1212, § 1; Stats.1999, c. 100 (S.B.594), § 1.)*

§ 6702. Nonresidents having established place of business

Every nonresident, including any foreign corporation, having an established place of business within this state, and regularly using a vehicle of a type subject to registration under this code, shall immediately register the vehicle upon entry into this state. *(Added by Stats.1984, c. 1322, § 7, operative July 1, 1985.)*

§ 6703. Persons discharged from armed forces

Any person entering California following discharge from the armed forces of the United States is exempted from registration of passenger vehicles, trailer coaches, and utility trailers only, as provided for and under the conditions prescribed in Section 6700. *(Added by Stats. 1984, c. 1322, § 7, operative July 1, 1985.)*

§§ 6704 to 6706. Repealed by Stats.1984, c. 1322, § 6, operative July 1, 1985

ARTICLE 2. FOREIGN COMMERCIAL VEHICLES

Section
6850. Registration.
6851. Repealed.
6851.5. Repealed.
6852. Reciprocity.
6853. Vehicles leased for use in this state.
6854. Lack of reciprocal privileges; proof of financial responsibility; vehicles affected.
6855. Renumbered.

Cross References

Foreign jurisdiction defined, see Vehicle Code § 325.

§ 6850. Registration

A nonresident owner of any foreign commercial vehicle shall register the vehicle in this state and pay the fees applicable thereto under this code, except as provided in this article and Article 3 (commencing with Section 8000), and except in the event the vehicle is lawfully registered as a private passenger vehicle in the foreign jurisdiction in which the owner has residence, in which case Section 6700 shall apply. *(Stats.1959, c. 3, p. 1577, § 6850. Amended by Stats.1959, c. 1996, p. 4619, § 10; Stats.1984, c. 1322, § 8, operative July 1, 1985.)*

Cross References

Definitions,
  Commercial vehicle, see Vehicle Code § 260.
  Nonresident, see Vehicle Code § 435.
  Owner, see Vehicle Code § 460.
Registration in general, see Vehicle Code § 4000 et seq.

§ 6851. Repealed by Stats.2000, c. 861 (S.B.2084), § 37, eff. Sept. 29, 2000

§ 6851.5. Repealed by Stats.2000, c. 861 (S.B.2084), § 38, eff. Sept. 29, 2000

§ 6852. Reciprocity

The nonresident owner of a foreign vehicle shall be granted such privileges and freedom from registration and payment of fees imposed by this code, or Part 5 of Division 2 of the Revenue and Taxation Code, commencing at Section 10701, as the foreign jurisdiction in which the foreign commercial vehicle is registered or licensed grants to like vehicles registered under this code or as provided in agreements, arrangements, or declarations made under Article 3, commencing at Section 8000. *(Stats.1959, c. 3, p. 1578, § 6852.)*

Cross References

Definitions,
   Commercial vehicle, see Vehicle Code § 260.
   Foreign vehicle, see Vehicle Code § 330.
   Nonresident, see Vehicle Code § 435.
   Owner, see Vehicle Code § 460.
   Reciprocity commission, see Vehicle Code § 495.
Reciprocity, see Vehicle Code § 8000 et seq.
Reciprocity commission, see Vehicle Code § 2600 et seq.
Registration in general, see Vehicle Code § 4000 et seq.

§ 6853. Vehicles leased for use in this state

Any vehicle owned by a nonresident owner not registered under this code, which vehicle is leased or rented to a user having an established place of business or residence in this State, for use on the highways of this State shall be subject to registration either by the owner or lessee of the vehicle, unless the vehicle is exempted from registration by the provisions of this division or under any agreement, arrangement, or declaration made pursuant to Article 3, commencing at Section 8000. *(Stats.1959, c. 3, p. 1578, § 6853.)*

Cross References

Definitions,
   Nonresident, see Vehicle Code § 435.
   Owner, see Vehicle Code § 460.
   Vehicle, see Vehicle Code § 670.
Reciprocity, see Vehicle Code §§ 6852, 8000 et seq.
Registration, see Vehicle Code § 4000 et seq.

§ 6854. Lack of reciprocal privileges; proof of financial responsibility; vehicles affected

(a) Any owner or lessor of a commercial vehicle with primary registration and plates issued in a foreign jurisdiction which does not grant reciprocal privileges to California owners of commercial vehicles shall submit to the department proof of financial responsibility issued by an insurance company authorized to do business in California. This section shall apply only to commercial vehicles having an unladen weight of over 7,000 pounds that are used in the transportation of property in the conduct of a business.

(b) As an alternative to the requirements of subdivision (a), proof of financial responsibility may be met by submitting to the department either of the following:

(1) A certificate of registration as a foreign motor carrier or foreign motor private carrier issued by the

Interstate Commerce Commission under Part 1171 of Title 49 of the Code of Federal Regulations.

(2) Contractual documents showing to the satisfaction of the department that a trailer or semitrailer subject to registration under Part 1171 of Title 49 of the Code of Federal Regulations will be towed by a truck or truck tractor operated by a motor carrier having highway carrier operating authority issued by the Public Utilities Commission. *(Added by Stats.1983, c. 1000, § 6. Amended by Stats.1985, c. 1162, § 1; Stats.1992, c. 974 (S.B.1600), § 3, eff. Sept. 28, 1992.)*

Cross References

Commercial vehicle defined, see Vehicle Code § 260.
Reciprocity, see Vehicle Code §§ 6852, 8000 et seq.

§ 6855. Renumbered § 34518 and amended by Stats. 2006, c. 288 (A.B.3011), § 2

ARTICLE 3. RECIPROCITY AGREEMENTS

Section
8000. Agreements authorized; fee exemptions.
8001. Declarations of reciprocity.
8002. Repealed.
8003 to 8006. Repealed.
8007. Repealed.
8008 to 8010. Repealed.

Cross References

Collection of administrative service fee for each registration, renewal of registration or supplement apportioned registration, see Vehicle Code § 9250.15.
Reciprocity commission,
   Generally, see Vehicle Code § 2600 et seq.
   Definition, see Vehicle Code § 495.

§ 8000. Agreements authorized; fee exemptions

The director, or his or her designee, may enter into agreements with foreign jurisdictions that provide for the exemption of fees for commercial vehicles if the foreign jurisdictions provide equivalent exemptions to vehicles registered in this state. The agreements shall be applicable to vehicles that are properly licensed and registered in the foreign jurisdictions. The director, or his or her designee, may also enter into agreements that provide for the exemption of regulatory fees which are, or may be, imposed, by the Public Utilities Code or the department. *(Added by Stats.1989, c. 533, § 6. Amended by Stats.2000, c. 861 (S.B.2084), § 39, eff. Sept. 29, 2000; Stats.2011, c. 315 (A.B.28), § 9.)*

Cross References

Foreign commercial vehicle, temporary operation, see Vehicle Code § 4004.
Nonresident vehicles leased for use in this state, see Vehicle Code § 6853.
Reciprocity commission, powers, see Vehicle Code § 2650.
Registration in general, see Vehicle Code § 4000 et seq.

Registration of foreign commercial vehicles, see Vehicle Code § 6850.

§ 8001. Declarations of reciprocity

The director, or his or her designee, is authorized to examine the legal requirements of commercial vehicle registration fee statutes of foreign jurisdictions which grant reciprocal privileges to out-of-state vehicles, but which do not authorize negotiations or execution of agreements. After examination of the statutes, the director, or his or her designee, may declare the exemptions, benefits, and privileges that commercial vehicles registered in foreign jurisdictions shall be entitled to in this state. *(Added by Stats.1989, c. 533, § 6. Amended by Stats.2011, c. 315 (A.B.28), § 10.)*

§ 8002. Repealed by Stats.2011, c. 315 (A.B.28), § 11

§§ 8003 to 8006. Repealed by Stats.1989, c. 533, § 5

§ 8007. Repealed by Stats.1980, c. 622, p. 1705, § 1

§§ 8008 to 8010. Repealed by Stats.1989, c. 533, § 5

ARTICLE 4. APPORTIONED REGISTRATION

Section

8050. Legislative declaration.
8051. Repealed.
8052. International Registration Plan Agreement membership; collection of fees due other jurisdictions.
8053. Other code provisions to apply.
8054. Transfer of ownership of fleets apportionately registered.
8055. Commercial vehicles from non-reciprocal jurisdictions; application of article.
8056. Diesel-powered vehicles; application information.
8057. Fleet records; record retention date; audits.
8058. Interest on underpaid fees due under this article; penalty.

Cross References

Apportioned registration, operation of a vehicle or a fleet for which apportioned registration has been suspended, see Vehicle Code § 8104.

Collection of administrative service fee for each registration, renewal of registration or supplement apportioned registration, see Vehicle Code § 9250.15.

Department of motor vehicles, conversion to year-round registration, see Vehicle Code § 1651.5.

Deposits to cover the inclusion of additional operating area or registration issued under this article, see Vehicle Code § 9259.3.

Expiration of registration for vehicles registered pursuant to this article, see Vehicle Code § 4601.5

Fee to cover immediate telephone service for registration issued under this article, see Vehicle Code § 9259.5.

Issuance of unladen operation permit to authorize unladen operation of vehicle or vehicle combination, see Vehicle Code § 4004.7.

Nonoperated vehicles, registration or renewal requirements, Generally, see Vehicle Code § 4604 et seq.
  Certificate of nonoperation exemptions, see Vehicle Code § 4604.

Certificate of nonoperation requirements, see Vehicle Code § 4604.2.

Reciprocity commission,
  Generally, see Vehicle Code § 2600 et seq.
  Definition, see Vehicle Code § 495.

§ 8050. Legislative declaration

The Legislature declares that in enacting this article, it adheres to the principle that each state should have the freedom to develop the kind of highway user tax structure that it determines to be most appropriate to itself, that the method of taxation of interstate vehicles should not be a determining factor in developing its user tax structure and that annual taxes or other taxes of the fixed fee type which are not imposed on a basis that reflects the amount of highway use should be apportioned among the states on the basis of vehicle miles traveled within each of the states. If the department determines that apportionment of the taxes on the basis of vehicle miles for a particular fleet of vehicles is impractical, the department may require the taxes on the fleet to be apportioned on an equivalent basis other than miles, as determined by the department. *(Added by Stats.1989, c. 533, § 8.)*

Cross References

Delinquent payment of licensing fees, notice to registrant, time to pay, see Vehicle Code § 9553.5.

§ 8051. Repealed by Stats.2011, c. 315 (A.B.28), § 12

§ 8052. International Registration Plan Agreement membership; collection of fees due other jurisdictions

(a) The director, or his or her designee, may, on behalf of the state, enter into, and become, a member of the International Registration Plan Agreement developed by the American Association of Motor Vehicle Administrators. The director, or his or her designee, may adopt rules and regulations necessary to carry out the provisions of the International Registration Plan or other apportioned registration agreements entered into under the authority of this article.

(b) In administering the International Registration Plan, the state may collect all appropriate registration and license fees due other jurisdictions. Foreign jurisdictions that are members of the agreement shall be authorized to collect all appropriate registration and license fees due to the State of California, and remit the fees to this state pursuant to the terms of the agreement. *(Added by Stats.1989, c. 533, § 8. Amended by Stats.2011, c. 315 (A.B.28), § 13.)*

§ 8053. Other code provisions to apply

Provisions of this code which specify and govern application filing, fee assignment, penalty assessment, and issuance of license plates and registration certificates, shall be applicable to vehicles registered pursuant to this article. *(Added by Stats.1989, c. 533, § 8.)*

§ 8054. Transfer of ownership of fleets apportionately registered

(a) Upon the application for transfer of ownership of a fleet of vehicles apportionately registered pursuant to this article, the department shall permit registration in the new owners name without reassessing the registration and vehicle license fees, if the application of the new ownership is for the same fleet interstate operation as the previous owner.

(b) The new owner, lessee, or their designee, shall certify the declared gross vehicle weight of the vehicle or vehicles on a single form for all commercial motor vehicles registered in the fleet owner's or lessee's name. The department shall reassess the weight fees if the declared gross vehicle weight is increased. The weight fees will be assessed at a prorated rate. *(Added by Stats.1989, c. 533, § 8. Amended by Stats.2000, c. 861 (S.B.2084), § 40, eff. Sept. 29, 2000.)*

§ 8055. Commercial vehicles from non-reciprocal jurisdictions; application of article

This article does not apply to any owner or lessee of a commercial vehicle with primary registration and license plates issued in a foreign jurisdiction which does not grant reciprocity or apportioned registration to residents of this state owning commercial vehicles while operating within that foreign jurisdiction. *(Added by Stats.1989, c. 533, § 8.)*

§ 8056. Diesel-powered vehicles; application information

Any application filed pursuant to this article which contains vehicles powered by diesel fuel shall include information concerning any diesel fuel tax permit issued by the Board of Equalization. *(Added by Stats.1989, c. 533, § 8.)*

§ 8057. Fleet records; record retention date; audits

Any person issued fleet registration pursuant to Article 9.5 (commencing with Section 5301) of Chapter 1 or this article shall:

(a) Maintain fleet records that support the reported mileage, cost, and declared gross or combined gross vehicle weight of all vehicles. Any registrant whose application for apportioned registration has been accepted shall preserve the mileage records on which the application is based, including copies of all permits, for a period of three years after the close of the registration year. Vehicle cost and declared gross or combined gross weight records shall be retained for four years after the close of the registration year in which the vehicle was deleted.

(b) Make fleet records available to the department at its request for audit to verify the accuracy of the records. In the event the records are not made available within 30 days of the request, the department may assess full California fees and penalties and may suspend or cancel apportioned registration privileges. The registrant may

240

be required to reimburse the department auditor per diem and travel expenses under certain conditions as determined by the director. *(Added by Stats.1989, c. 533, § 8. Amended by Stats.2002, c. 758 (A.B.3024), § 4.)*

§ 8058. Interest on underpaid fees due under this article; penalty

(a) The department shall charge interest on any underpaid fees due under this article, at the rate of 1 percent per month of the underpaid portion of the fees, commencing on the date the underpaid portion of the fees were originally due and accruing monthly until paid.

(b) Interest charged under subdivision (a) shall continue to accumulate during any disputation of the underpaid fees or any hearing regarding the underpaid fees. During any disputation or hearing, the registrant may pay the underpaid fees and other charges to avoid additional interest charges and may request a refund of any overpaid fees after final review.

(c) For any underpaid fees, the department may impose a penalty of fifty dollars ($50) or 10 percent of the underpaid fees, whichever is greater, commencing on the date the underpaid fees were determined to be due.

(d) For the purposes of this section, "underpaid fees" include additional vehicle registration, weight, and license fees found to be due to this state.

(e) The director shall have discretion to apply subdivision (b) of Section 9562 instead of subdivision (c) of this section.

(f) The penalty structure set forth in Sections 9554 and 9554.5 shall apply in place of the provisions of this section in those cases where there is a violation of Section 4000, 4000.4, 4002, 4003, 4004, 4004.5, or 4156 for commercial registration that is not apportioned pursuant to Section 8050. *(Added by Stats.2001, c. 539 (S.B.734), § 10. Amended by Stats.2002, c. 758 (A.B.3024), § 5.)*

ARTICLE 5. FEDERAL MOTOR VEHICLE SAFETY PROGRAM

Section
8100. Application for apportioned registration.
8101. Grounds for refusal of application.
8102. Suspension of apportioned registration.
8103. Suspension hearing.
8104. Operation of a vehicle or a fleet for which apportioned registration has been suspended.
8150 to 8164. Repealed.

Cross References

Exceptions to expiration and renewal of registration requirements, see Vehicle Code § 4601.5.
Registration renewal fee, apportioned increase or decrease, see Vehicle Code § 9559.5.

Year-round registration of motor vehicles, see Vehicle Code § 1651.5.

§ 8100. Application for apportioned registration

An application for apportioned registration received on and after January 1, 2008, and filed pursuant to Article 4 (commencing with Section 8050) shall contain the following information:

(a) The United States Department of Transportation Number issued to the person responsible for the safe operation of each vehicle being registered.

(b) The taxpayer identification number corresponding to the United States Department of Transportation number provided in the apportioned registration application. The taxpayer identification number may consist of the federal employer identification number or the social security number, as applicable.

(c) Notwithstanding any other provision of law, the taxpayer identification number provided pursuant to this section is confidential and shall not be disclosed by the department except to law enforcement or a federal agency, or as required by law. *(Added by Stats.2006, c. 169 (A.B.2736), § 3.)*

§ 8101. Grounds for refusal of application

In addition to the reasons specified in Section 4750 or 4751, the department shall refuse an application for apportioned registration for the following grounds:

(a) The applicant has failed to furnish the department with information required in the application under Section 8100.

(b) The person responsible for the safety of the vehicle or fleet is prohibited from operating in interstate commerce by a federal agency. *(Added by Stats.2006, c. 169 (A.B.2736), § 3.)*

§ 8102. Suspension of apportioned registration

(a) In addition to the reasons specified in Section 8800, the department may suspend the apportioned registration of a vehicle or a fleet, when the person responsible for the safety of the vehicle or a fleet of vehicles is prohibited from operating in interstate commerce by a federal agency.

(b) Whenever the department suspends the apportioned registration of a vehicle or a fleet pursuant to subdivision (a), the department may refuse the issuance of vehicle registration as authorized pursuant to Section 4751.

(c) Whenever the department suspends the apportioned registration under subdivision (a), the department shall furnish the person responsible for the vehicle or fleet with written notice of the suspension.

(d) When an apportioned registration is suspended pursuant to this section, and that suspension is based wholly or in part on the failure of the person to maintain a vehicle or a fleet in safe operating condition, the person to whom the registration was issued shall not lease, or otherwise allow, another person to operate a vehicle that is subject to the suspension during the period of the suspension.

(e) A person shall not knowingly lease, operate, dispatch, or otherwise utilize a vehicle from another person whose apportioned registration is suspended, when that suspension is based wholly or in part on the failure of the person to maintain a vehicle or a fleet in safe operating condition.

(f) The apportioned registration of a vehicle or a fleet, that was suspended because the vehicle or fleet is prohibited from operating in interstate commerce by a federal agency may be reinstated upon notification from the federal agency that the prohibition has been lifted.

(g) Notwithstanding any other provision of this code, before an apportioned registration may be reissued after a suspension is terminated, there shall, in addition to other fees required by this code, be paid to the department a fee of one hundred fifty dollars ($150). This fee shall be deposited in the Motor Vehicle Account to cover the department's cost of administering this program. *(Added by Stats.2006, c. 169 (A.B.2736), § 3.)*

§ 8103. Suspension hearing

Notwithstanding any other provision of this code, a hearing shall not be provided when the suspension is based solely on notification by a federal agency that interstate operation is prohibited. *(Added by Stats.2006, c. 169 (A.B.2736), § 3.)*

§ 8104. Operation of a vehicle or a fleet for which apportioned registration has been suspended

Except as provided in subdivision (e), a vehicle or a fleet for which the apportioned registration has been suspended pursuant to this article shall not be operated in interstate or intrastate commerce unless evidence is provided to the department that the vehicle or the fleet is to be operated by a person whose apportioned registration is not subject to a suspension pursuant to this article and who has a valid apportioned registration pursuant to Article 4 (commencing with Section 8050) or Division 14.85. *(Added by Stats.2006, c. 169 (A.B.2736), § 3.)*

§§ 8150 to 8164. Repealed by Stats.1989, c. 533, § 9

ARTICLE 6. ENFORCEMENT OF LIENS ON APPORTIONED FLEET VEHICLES

Section
8200. Registrant.
8201. Lien; fees; expiration; perfected; notice; waiver.
8202. Documentation; suspension or cancellation of operating privileges; hearing; review.
8203. Perfected lien; time for submission of documentation or hearing passed; suspension on cancellation of fleet operations; seizure of vehicles; agents; notice; sale.
8204. Transfer or purchase of fleet vehicle; outstanding lien; fees; waiver; liability.
8205 to 8210. Repealed.

§ 8200. Registrant

"Registrant," for purposes of this article, means any person issued apportioned fleet registration pursuant to Article 4 (commencing with Section 8050). *(Added by Stats.1989, c. 187, § 2. Amended by Stats.1996, c. 124 (A.B.3470), § 120.)*

§ 8201. Lien; fees; expiration; perfected; notice; waiver

(a) Fees determined to be due, including penalties and service fees, for the operation of a fleet apportionately registered vehicle shall be a lien upon all vehicles operated as part of the fleet and on any other fleet vehicles operated by the registrant. The department may collect the amount of the lien, plus costs, not to exceed two hundred fifty dollars ($250), in an appropriate civil action and by seizure and sale of the vehicle.

(b) Liens arising as the result of an audit expire four years from the date the registration fees first become due unless the lien is perfected pursuant to subdivision (d).

(c) Any lien arising under this section that is not subject to subdivision (b) expires three years from the date the fee or penalty first became due unless the lien is perfected pursuant to subdivision (d).

(d) A lien shall be perfected when a notice is mailed to the registrant at the address shown on the department's records and the lien is recorded on the electronic vehicle registration records of the department. A perfected lien shall expire five years from the date of perfection.

(e) Prior to the expiration of the statute of limitations, the registrant may consent to a waiver which would allow the assessment of fees and penalties past the statute of limitations. *(Added by Stats.1989, c. 187, § 2. Amended by Stats.2002, c. 758 (A.B.3024), § 6.)*

§ 8202. Documentation; suspension or cancellation of operating privileges; hearing; review

(a) Within 30 days of the date the notice is mailed pursuant to Section 8201, the registrant may submit documentation not previously available or may request a hearing to contest the existence or the amount of the lien. If no additional documentation is submitted, or if no hearing is requested, the operating privileges of the fleet may be suspended or canceled and a sufficient number of vehicles may be seized and sold to satisfy the lien.

(b) If additional documentation is submitted, the department shall review the documentation and issue its findings to the registrant. Within 30 days of the date the findings are mailed, the registrant may request a hearing.

(c) If a hearing is requested, 10 days' notice shall be given of the time and place of the hearing, which shall be held within the county of residence of the person requesting the hearing or within the county of the established place of business of the registrant. The hearing shall be conducted by a referee who shall submit findings and recommendations to the director or his or her authorized representative, who shall decide the

242

matter. The decision shall be effective on notice thereof to the interested parties. However, the director, or his or her authorized representative, may rescind the decision and reconsider the matter for good cause shown at any time within three years after the date the disputed fee or penalty first became due, or one year from the hearing whichever is later.

(d) Upon final completion of all administrative appeals, the department shall give written notice to the registrant of the right to a review of the decision by a court of competent jurisdiction. Any action brought in court shall be commenced within 90 days from the date notice of the decision is mailed. *(Added by Stats.1989, c. 187, § 2. Amended by Stats.2010, c. 478 (A.B.2777), § 10.)*

§ 8203. Perfected lien; time for submission of documentation or hearing passed; suspension on cancellation of fleet operations; seizure of vehicles; agents; notice; sale

(a) When a lien is perfected pursuant to Section 8200 and the opportunity to submit additional documentation or to request a hearing has passed, the department may suspend or cancel the operating privileges of the fleet. When the suspension takes effect, the department may seize a sufficient number of vehicles to satisfy the lien without further notice, upon obtaining authorization for the seizure and sale from the director or his or her authorized representative.

(b) Members of the California Highway Patrol, and peace officers employed by local authorities, are agents of the department for the purposes of this section.

(c) In all cases, prior to the sale, a notice of the lien and intent to sell the vehicle shall be given by the department to the registrant, the known legal and registered owners, and to any other person known to be claiming an interest in the vehicle. The department shall also give public notice of the lien by placing an advertisement in a newspaper of general circulation published in the county in which the registrant's place of business is located.

(d) At any time before seizure and sale, any person claiming an interest in the vehicle may pay the department the amount of the lien, plus costs. In that event, the seizure and sale shall not be held, and the vehicle, shall be returned by the department to the person entitled to its possession.

(e) Any property found by the department in any vehicle seized under the provisions of this article shall be handled by the department in the manner provided in Sections 2414 and 2415.

(f) The sale shall be conducted and proceeds distributed pursuant to Section 9802. *(Added by Stats.1989, c. 187, § 2.)*

§ 8204. Transfer or purchase of fleet vehicle; outstanding lien; fees; waiver; liability

(a) When a transferee or purchaser of an apportionately registered fleet vehicle applies to the department for transfer of ownership and it is determined by the department that there is an outstanding lien against the fleet in which the vehicle was operated, that fees became due prior to the transfer or purchase of the vehicle, and that the transferee or purchaser was not cognizant of the fact that a lien existed, the department may waive apportioned registration fees and any penalties that are due.

(b) When fees and penalties are waived pursuant to subdivision (a), the apportioned registration fees and penalties shall become the liability of the registrant who failed to pay the fees and penalties when they became due. The fees and penalties may be collected by the department in an appropriate civil action. *(Added by Stats.1989, c. 187, § 2.)*

§§ 8205 to 8210. Repealed by Stats.1986, c. 687, § 4

ARTICLE 7. INTERNATIONAL REGISTRATION PLAN AND RECIPROCAL AGREEMENTS [REPEALED]

§§ 8300 to 8302. Repealed by Stats.1989, c. 533, § 10

CHAPTER 5. OFFENSES AGAINST REGISTRATION LAWS AND SUSPENSION, REVOCATION, AND CANCELLATION OF REGISTRATION

Section
8800. General powers.
8801. Publicly owned vehicles.
8802. Owner to return evidence of registration.
8803. Licensee to return evidence of license.
8804. Registration or renewal of registration of vehicle in foreign jurisdiction; failure to pay fees and taxes in this state.

§ 8800. General powers

(a) The department may suspend, cancel, or revoke the registration of a vehicle or a certificate of ownership, registration card, license plate, or permit under any of the following circumstances:

(1) When the department is satisfied that the registration or the certificate, card, plate, or permit was fraudulently obtained or erroneously issued.

(2) When the department determines that a registered vehicle is mechanically unfit or unsafe to be operated or moved upon the highways.

(3) When a registered vehicle has been dismantled or wrecked.

(4) When the department determines that the required fee has not been paid and the same is not paid upon reasonable notice and demand.

(5) When a registration card, license plate, or permit is knowingly displayed upon a vehicle other than the one for which issued.

(6) When the registration could have been refused when last issued or renewed.

(7) When the department determines that the owner or legal owner has committed an offense under Sections 20 (with respect to an application for the registration of a vehicle), 4000, 4159 to 4163, inclusive, 4454, 4456, 4461, 4463, 5202, 10750, and 10751, involving the registration or the certificate, card, plate, or permit to be suspended, canceled, or revoked.

(8) When the department is so authorized pursuant to any other provision of law.

(b) The department may suspend the registration of all vehicles registered in the name of a person, under any of the following circumstances:

(1) When the United States Secretary of the Department of Transportation or his or her designee issues a lawful out-of-service order pursuant to Title 49 of the Code of Federal Regulations.

(2) When the department suspends or revokes a motor carrier of property permit.

(3) When the Public Utilities Commission suspends or revokes operating authority or private registration.

(c) A suspension imposed pursuant to subdivision (b) shall remain in effect and a vehicle for which registration has been suspended shall not be registered in the name of the person until the department verifies that person's federal registration, federal operating authority, California operating authority, California private registration, or motor carrier of property permit is reissued. *(Stats.1959, c. 3, p. 1583, § 8800. Amended by Stats.1972, c. 618, p. 1147, § 137; Stats.2006, c. 288 (A.B.3011), § 3.)*

Cross References

Apportioned registration, reasons for suspension, see Vehicle Code § 8102.
Automobile dismantler, possession of stolen vehicle, presumption, see Vehicle Code § 11511.
Judgment unsatisfied, suspension of driving privilege, see Vehicle Code § 16370.
Refusal of registration, see Vehicle Code §§ 4750, 4751.
Registration fees, generally, see Vehicle Code § 9250 et seq.
Suspension or revocation of license,
  Court, see Vehicle Code § 13200 et seq.
  Department, see Vehicle Code § 13350 et seq.

§ 8801. Publicly owned vehicles

The department may suspend, cancel, revoke, or renew any permanent registration made under Section 4155 when the department determines that it is advisable to reissue the registration. *(Stats.1959, c. 3, p. 1583, § 8801.)*

Applicability of this section to trolley coaches, see Vehicle Code § 21051.

§ 8802. Owner to return evidence of registration

Whenever the department cancels, suspends, or revokes the registration of a vehicle or a certificate of ownership, registration card, or license plates, or any nonresident or other permit, the owner or person in possession shall immediately return the documents, plates, certificates, or other evidence of registration to the department. *(Stats.1959, c. 3, p. 1583, § 8802. Amended by Stats.1967, c. 482, p. 1687, § 1.)*

False evidences of registration, see Vehicle Code § 4463.
Registration indices and records, see Vehicle Code § 1800.
Seizure of documents and plates, see Vehicle Code § 4460.
Violation as misdemeanor, see Vehicle Code § 40000.7.

§ 8803. Licensee to return evidence of license

Whenever the department cancels, suspends, or revokes any license issued pursuant to Division 5 (commencing with Section 11100), the licensee or person in possession shall immediately return the license, documents, plates, certificates, and other evidence of the license to the department. *(Added by Stats.1967, c. 482, p. 1687, § 2. Amended by Stats.1983, c. 1286, § 21.5; Stats.1990, c. 1563 (A.B.3243), § 5.)*

Violation as misdemeanor, see Vehicle Code § 40000.7.

§ 8804. Registration or renewal of registration of vehicle in foreign jurisdiction; failure to pay fees and taxes in this state

Every person who, while a resident, as defined in Section 516, of this state, with respect to any vehicle owned by him and operated in this state, registers or renews the registration for the vehicle in a foreign jurisdiction, without the payment of appropriate fees and taxes to this state, is guilty of a misdemeanor. *(Added by Stats.1983, c. 409, § 4.)*

CHAPTER 6. REGISTRATION AND WEIGHT FEES

Article	Section
1. **Exemptions**	9100
2. **Registration Fees**	9250
3. **Weight Fees**	9400
4. **Payment of Fees**	9550
5. **Partial Year Payment of Weight Fees**	9700
6. **Enforcement of Liens**	9800

ARTICLE 1. EXEMPTIONS

Section
9100.   Repealed.
9101.   Publicly operated vehicles.
9102.   Educational institution vehicles.

Section
9102.5. Privately owned schoolbus; inapplicability of section; temporary permit.
9103.   Publicly owned vehicles.
9104.   Fire department vehicles.
9104.2. Payment of fees; federally recognized Indian tribes; vehicles used for firefighting or rescue purposes only.
9104.5. Payment of fees; federally recognized Indian tribes.
9105.   Former prisoners of war, disabled veterans, or Congressional Medal of Honor recipients; surviving spouse of former prisoner of war or Congressional Medal of Honor recipient.
9106.   Civil air patrol vehicles.
9107.   Common carrier passenger stage, intra-city and van-pool vehicles; specialized transportation vehicles for senior citizens and handicapped persons.

Registration of exempt vehicles, see Vehicle Code § 4001.

§ 9100. Repealed by Stats.1985, c. 752, § 3

§ 9101. Publicly operated vehicles

No fees specified in this code, except fees not exempted under Section 9103, need be paid for any vehicle operated by the state, or by any county, city, district, or political subdivision of the state, or the United States, as lessee under a lease, lease-sale, or rental-purchase agreement that grants possession of the vehicle to the lessee for a period of 30 consecutive days or more. *(Stats.1959, c. 3, p. 1584, § 9101. Amended by Stats.1963, c. 1867, p. 3852, § 3; Stats.2003, c. 594 (S.B.315), § 31.)*

California Legacy License Plate Program, registration fees, exemptions, see Vehicle Code § 5004.3.
Refund of fees and penalties, see Vehicle Code § 42230 et seq.
Registration of exempt vehicles, see Vehicle Code § 4001.
Special plates, see Vehicle Code § 5000 et seq.

§ 9102. Educational institution vehicles

The fees specified in this code except fees for duplicate plates, certificates, or cards need not be paid for any vehicle owned by an educational institution of collegiate grade not conducted for profit and having an enrollment of 5,000 students or more and having an acreage of 5,000 acres or more, if such vehicle is used for fire-fighting purposes within the limits of the acreage of such institution and is operated principally on roads owned by such institution. *(Stats.1959, c. 3, p. 1584, § 9102.)*

Duplicate or substitute plates, certificates and cards, see Vehicle Code §§ 4457 et seq., 9265.
Fire fighting equipment of certain colleges, exemption, see Revenue and Taxation Code § 10786.
Refund of fees and penalties, see Vehicle Code § 42230 et seq.
Registration of exempt vehicles, see Vehicle Code § 4001.

Special plates, see Vehicle Code § 5000 et seq.

§ 9102.5. Privately owned schoolbus; inapplicability of section; temporary permit

(a) In lieu of all other fees which are specified in this code, except fees for duplicate plates, certificates, or cards, a fee of fifteen dollars ($15) shall be paid for the registration and licensing of any privately owned schoolbus, as defined in Section 545, which is either of the following:

(1) Owned by a private nonprofit educational organization and operated in accordance with the rules and regulations of the Department of Education and the Department of the California Highway Patrol exclusively in transporting school pupils, or school pupils and employees, of the private nonprofit educational organization.

(2) Operated in accordance with the rules and regulations of the Department of Education and the Department of the California Highway Patrol exclusively in transporting school pupils, or school pupils and employees, of any public school or private nonprofit educational organization pursuant to a contract between a public school district or nonprofit educational organization and the owner or operator of the schoolbus.

This section does not apply to any schoolbus which is operated pursuant to any contract which requires the public school district or nonprofit educational organization to pay any amount representing the costs of registration and weight fees unless and until the contract is amended to require only the payment of an amount representing the fee required by this section.

(b) When a schoolbus under contract and registered pursuant to subdivision (a) is to be temporarily operated in such a manner that it becomes subject to full registration fees specified in this code, the owner may, prior to that operation, as an alternative to the full registration, secure a temporary permit to operate the vehicle in this state for any one or more calendar months. The permit shall be posted upon the windshield or other prominent place upon the vehicle, and shall identify the vehicle to which it is affixed. When so affixed, the permit shall serve as indicia of full registration for the period designated on the permit. Upon payment of the fees specified in Section 9266.5, the department may issue a temporary permit under this section.

(c) Notwithstanding any other provision, any schoolbus used exclusively to transport students at or below the 12th–grade level to or from any school, for an education-related purpose, or for an activity sponsored by a nonprofit organization shall be deemed to be a schoolbus for the purposes of this section and shall pay a fee of fifteen dollars ($15) in lieu of all other fees which are specified in this code, except fees for duplicate plates, certificates, or cards.

(d) This section does not apply to a schoolbus, operated to transport persons who are developmentally disabled, as defined by the Lanterman Developmental Disabilities Services Act (Division 4.5 (commencing with Section 4500) of the Welfare and Institutions Code), to or from vocational, prevocational, or work training centers sponsored by the State Department of Developmental Services. *(Added by Stats.1969, c. 1444, p. 2954, § 1. Amended by Stats.1971, c. 1489, p. 2942, § 1, operative May 3, 1972; Stats.1973, c. 411, p. 875, § 2, eff. Sept. 10, 1973; Stats.1977, c. 406, p. 1416, § 9, eff. Aug. 27, 1977; Stats.1978, c. 497, p. 1633, § 2; Stats.1980, c. 147, p. 344, § 2; Stats.1981, c. 813, p. 3153, § 8.5; Stats.1983, c. 142, § 165; Stats.1986, c. 678, § 1; Stats.2003, c. 719 (S.B. 1055), § 9.)*

Cross References
Base fee amounts, adjustment of fees, see Vehicle Code § 1678.

§ 9103. Publicly owned vehicles

(a) Fees specified in this code, except fees for duplicate plates, certificates, or cards, are not required to be paid for any vehicle of a type subject to registration under this code owned by the United States or by any state or political subdivision of a state or by any municipality duly organized under the California Constitution or laws of this state.

(b) The registration fees specified in this code, except fees for duplicate plates, certificates, or cards, are not required to be paid for any vehicle owned by a public entity described in subdivision (f) of Section 15975 of the Government Code. *(Stats.1959, c. 3, p. 1584, § 9103. Amended by Stats.1975, c. 575, p. 1155, § 5, eff. Sept. 6, 1975, operative Jan. 1, 1976; Stats.2009, c. 200 (S.B.734), § 8.)*

Cross References
California Legacy License Plate Program, registration fees, exemptions, see Vehicle Code § 5004.3.
Duplicate plates, certificates and cards, see Vehicle Code §§ 4457 et seq., 9265.
Refund of fees and penalties, see Vehicle Code § 42230 et seq.
Registration of exempt vehicles, see Vehicle Code § 4001.
Special plates, see Vehicle Code § 5000 et seq.

§ 9104. Fire department vehicles

The fees specified in this code except fees for duplicate plates, certificates, or cards need not be paid for any vehicle of a type subject to registration under this code owned by a public fire department organized as a nonprofit corporation and used exclusively for firefighting or rescue purposes or exclusively as an ambulance, nor for any vehicle owned by a voluntary fire department organized under the laws of this state and used exclusively for firefighting or rescue purposes or exclusively as an ambulance. *(Stats.1959, c. 3, p. 1584, § 9104. Amended by Stats.1967, c. 1445, p. 3366, § 1; Stats.1979, c. 517, p. 1697, § 3, eff. Sept. 7, 1979.)*

Cross References
Duplicate or substitute plates, certificates and cards, see Vehicle Code §§ 4457 et seq., 9265.

§ 9104.2. Payment of fees; federally recognized Indian tribes; vehicles used for firefighting or rescue purposes only

The fees specified in this code, except fees for duplicate plates, certificates, or cards need not be paid for a vehicle of a type subject to registration under this code owned by a federally recognized Indian tribe that has entered into a mutual aid agreement with a state, county, city, or other governmental municipality for fire protection and emergency response, and the equipment is used exclusively for firefighting or rescue purposes or exclusively as an ambulance. *(Added by Stats.2008, c. 92 (A.B.2060), § 1.)*

§ 9104.5. Payment of fees; federally recognized Indian tribes

The fees specified in this code, except fees for registration under Section 9250, need not be paid for any vehicle of a type subject to registration under this code if the vehicle is owned by a federally recognized Indian tribe and the vehicle is used exclusively within the boundaries of lands under the jurisdiction of that Indian tribe, including the incidental use of that vehicle on highways within those boundaries. *(Added by Stats.1999, c. 911 (A.B.1474), § 2.)*

§ 9105. Former prisoners of war, disabled veterans, or Congressional Medal of Honor recipients; surviving spouse of former prisoner of war or Congressional Medal of Honor recipient

(a) Except for fees for duplicate license plates, duplicate certificates, or duplicate cards, the fees specified in this code need not be paid for a vehicle that is of a type subject to registration under this code, and that is not used for transportation for hire, compensation, or profit, when owned by any of the following:

(1) A disabled veteran.

(2) A former American prisoner of war.

(3) The surviving spouse of a former American prisoner of war who has elected to retain the special license plates issued under Section 5101.5.

(4) A Congressional Medal of Honor recipient.

(5) The surviving spouse of a Congressional Medal of Honor recipient who has elected to retain the special license plates issued under Section 5101.6.

(b) The exemption granted by subdivision (a) shall not extend to more than one vehicle owned by a former American prisoner of war, a disabled veteran, or a Congressional Medal of Honor recipient, or a surviving spouse, and is applicable to the same vehicle as described in subdivision (b) of Section 10783, or subdivision (b) of Section 10783.2, of the Revenue and Taxation Code.

(c)(1) The department may require a disabled veteran applying for an exemption under this section to submit a certificate signed by a physician and surgeon, or to the extent that it does not cause a reduction in the receipt of federal aid highway funds, by a nurse practitioner, certified nurse midwife, physician assistant, chiropractor, or optometrist, substantiating the disability.

(2) The department may require a person applying for an exemption under this section for either of the following reasons to do any of the following:

(A) By reason of the person's status as a former prisoner of war, to show, by satisfactory proof, his or her former prisoner-of-war status.

(B) By reason of the person's status of receiving the Congressional Medal of Honor, to show, by satisfactory proof, that he or she is a Congressional Medal of Honor recipient.

(d) For the purposes of this section, the term "vehicle" means any of the following:

(1) A passenger motor vehicle.

(2) A motorcycle.

(3) A commercial motor vehicle of less than 8,001 pounds unladen weight. *(Added by Stats.1998, c. 563 (S.B.1462), § 6, operative July 1, 1999. Amended by Stats.2006, c. 116 (A.B.2120), § 2; Stats.2007, c. 357 (S.B.386), § 4.)*

Cross References

Commercial vehicle defined, see Vehicle Code § 260.
Congressional medal of honor recipients, special license plates, loss of exemption upon death, see Vehicle Code § 5101.6.
Duplicate or substitute plates, certificates and cards, see Vehicle Code §§ 4457 et seq., 9265.
Issuance and renewal of disabled parking placard, conditions, fee exemptions, see Vehicle Code § 22511.55.
Legion of Valor, license plates, retention as family heirloom, see Vehicle Code § 5101.4.
Parking facilities, state agencies, see Government Code § 14679.
Purple Heart, license plates, retention as family heirloom, see Vehicle Code § 5101.8.

§ 9106. Civil air patrol vehicles

The fees specified in this code, except fees for duplicate plates, certificates or cards, need not be paid for any vehicle of a type subject to registration under this code which is operated by the Civil Air Patrol, when the vehicle has been transferred to the Civil Air Patrol by the United States Government, or any agency thereof, if by federal regulation or directive the use of such vehicle is restricted to defined activities of the Civil Air Patrol, and if by federal regulation or directive the vehicle must be returned to the United States Government when no longer required or suited for use by the Civil Air Patrol. Such vehicles shall be registered as otherwise required under this code by the Civil Air Patrol and the Civil Air Patrol shall display a license plate or plates bearing distinguishing marks or symbols as specified in this code, which plate or plates shall be furnished by the department free of charge. *(Stats.1959, c. 3, p. 1585, § 9106.)*

Cross References

Duplicate or substitute plates, certificates and cards, see Vehicle Code §§ 4457 et seq., 9265.

§ 9107. Common carrier passenger stage, intra-city and vanpool vehicles; specialized transportation vehicles for senior citizens and handicapped persons

The weight fees for commercial vehicles specified in Sections 9400 and 9400.1 do not apply to any of the following:

(a) A vehicle operated by a passenger stage corporation, as defined in Section 226 of the Public Utilities Code, that is subject to the jurisdiction of the Public Utilities Commission, if all of the following conditions are met:

(1) The vehicle is operated exclusively on any line or lines having a one-way route mileage not exceeding 15 miles, and each of those lines is operated in either of the following areas:

(A) In urban or suburban areas or between cities in close proximity.

(B) Between nonadjacent urban or suburban areas or cities, the area between which is substantially residential, commercial, or industrial as distinguished from rural.

(2) The principal business of the passenger stage corporation is the operation of vehicles on a route or routes as defined in paragraph (1).

(b) A vehicle operated exclusively on any line or lines within the limits of a single city by a person engaged as a common carrier of passengers between fixed termini or over a regular route, 98 percent of whose operations, as measured by total route mileage operated, are exclusively within the limits of a single city, and who by reason thereof is not a passenger stage corporation subject to the jurisdiction of the Public Utilities Commission.

(c) Vanpool vehicles.

(d) A vehicle purchased with federal funds under the authority of paragraph (2) of subsection (a) of Section 5310 of Title 49 of the United States Code or Chapter 35 (commencing with Section 3001) of Title 42 of the United States Code for the purpose of providing specialized transportation services to senior citizens and handicapped persons by public and private nonprofit operators of specialized transportation service agencies.

(e) A vehicle operated solely for the purpose of providing specialized transportation services to senior citizens and persons with disabilities, by a nonprofit, public benefit consolidated transportation service agency designated under Section 15975 of the Government Code. *(Added by Stats.1964, 2nd Ex.Sess., c. 1, p. 711, § 1. Amended by Stats.1982, c. 46, p. 139, § 9; Stats. 1987, c. 673, § 8; Stats.1997, c. 667 (S.B.812), § 2; Stats.2003, c. 594 (S.B.315), § 32.)*

ARTICLE 2. REGISTRATION FEES

Section
9250.   Amount; application of section.
9250.1.   Fee increase.
9250.2.   Surcharge collected for Sacramento Metropolitan Air Quality Management District.
9250.2.   Surcharge collected for Sacramento Metropolitan Air Quality Management District.
9250.4.   Collection of motor vehicle registration fee increase for congestion or pollution reduction program; costs; distribution.
9250.5.   San Mateo County; local registration fee; program costs; distribution of revenue.

Section
9250.7.   Fee; service authority for abatement of abandoned vehicles.
9250.8.   Additional fees.
9250.9.   Additional fees; deposit; use.
9250.10. Service authority for freeway emergencies; additional fees; distribution after deduction of administrative costs.
9250.11. Registration renewal fee; approval and adoption; memorandum of understanding; accounting procedures.
9250.12. City and county of San Francisco; local registration fee.
9250.13. Fee to offset costs of increasing uniformed field strength of highway patrol.
9250.14. Additional fee; vehicle theft programs; prosecution of crimes involving driving under the influence of alcohol or drugs or vehicular manslaughter; reports.
9250.15. Collection of administrative service fee for each registration, renewal of registration or supplement apportioned registration; amount; use of money collected.
9250.16. Surcharge imposed by San Joaquin Valley Unified Air Pollution Control District; allocation of funds.
9250.17. Collection of fees to be used to reduce air pollution; distribution of revenues after deduction of costs; limitation on costs.
9250.18. Administrative fees; collection; disposition.
9250.19. Fingerprint identification program.
9251.   Repealed.
9252.   Vehicles purchased new or registered outside state.
9253.   Repealed.
9254.   Certificate without registration.
9255.   Transfer of registration.
9255.1.   Service fee; initial issuance of registration card.
9255.2.   Initial registration or transfer of ownership; inspection fee; deposit.
9255.3.   Title transfer fees; vehicles transferred pursuant to § 14607.6.
9255.5.   Transfer of registration; unavailable certificate; additional fee.
9256.   Filing chattel mortgage.
9257.   Installation of engine or motor.
9257.5.   Fee for temporary permit.
9258.   One-trip payment.
9258.5.   New trailer or semitrailer, one-trip permit.
9259.   Fleet vehicles; sticker or device; fee.
9259.3.   Deposits to cover the inclusion of additional operating area or registration issued under Article 4 for each application.
9259.5.   Fee to cover immediate telephone service for registration issued under Article 4 for each application.
9260.   Temporary registration; trip permit; fees.
9261.   Service fees; transfer fee; renewal fee.
9261.1.   Fee increase.
9262.   Fees; license; special plates.
9262.5.   Disposition of increase in fee by 2009 amendment of § 9262.
9263.   Investigation service fee.
9264.   Repealed.
9265.   Duplicates.
9266.   School bus lessors; temporary permit fee.
9266.5.   Privately owned schoolbuses; fee for temporary permit.

Section
9267.   Repealed.
9268.   Motorcycles; original registration.
9269.   Automobile dismantlers; exemption from fees or penalties.
9270.   Expedited service fees for initial registration, transfer, or issuance of duplicate certificate of ownership.
9271.   Inspection fees; total loss salvage vehicles; dismantled vehicles.

§ 9250.   Amount; application of section

(a) A registration fee of thirty-one dollars ($31) shall be paid to the department for the registration of every vehicle or trailer coach of a type subject to registration under this code, except those vehicles that are expressly exempted under this code from the payment of registration fees. This subdivision applies to all of the following:

(1) The initial or original registration, on or after January 1, 2004, but before July 1, 2011, of any vehicle not previously registered in this state.

(2) The renewal of registration of any vehicle for which the registration period expires on or after January 1, 2004, but before July 1, 2011, regardless of whether a renewal application was mailed to the registered owner prior to January 1, 2004.

(b) A registration fee of forty-three dollars ($43) shall be paid to the department for the registration of each vehicle or trailer coach of a type subject to registration under this code, except those vehicles that are expressly exempted under this code from the payment of registration fees. This subdivision applies to all of the following:

(1) The initial or original registration, on or after July 1, 2011, of any vehicle not previously registered in this state.

(2) The renewal of registration of any vehicle for which the registration period expires on or after July 1, 2011, regardless of whether a renewal application was mailed to the registered owner prior to July 1, 2011.

(c) The registration fee imposed under this section applies to all vehicles described in Section 5004, whether or not special identification plates are issued to that vehicle.

(d) Trailer coaches are subject to the registration fee provided in subdivision (a) or (b) for each unit of the trailer coach.

(e) The amounts collected pursuant to the increase in the registration fee as specified in subdivision (b) shall be used only for costs incurred in connection with the regulation of vehicles, including administrative costs for vehicle registration. *(Added by Stats.1998, c. 877 (A.B. 2132), § 39. Amended by Stats.2003, c. 719 (S.B.1055), § 10; Stats.2011, c. 35 (S.B.89), § 10, eff. June 30, 2011.)*

Cross References

Applicability of this section to trolley coaches, see Vehicle Code § 21051.

248

Authorization to refrain from collecting sums of two hundred and fifty dollars or less, see Government Code § 13943.2.

Certificate of ownership without registration on payment of service fee, see Vehicle Code §§ 4452, 9254.

Collection of and receipt for license fee, see Revenue and Taxation Code § 10852.

Delinquent fees and penalties, see Vehicle Code § 9552 et seq.

Department, definition, see Vehicle Code §§ 290, 2101, 21000.

Disposition of overpayments of fees less than ten dollars, see Government Code § 16302.1.

Drivers' licenses, generally, see Vehicle Code § 12500 et seq.

Exemptions, generally, see Vehicle Code § 9101 et seq.

Fees for duplicate or substitute plates, certificates and cards, see Vehicle Code § 9265.

Filing after expiration of vehicle registration, penalty, see Vehicle Code § 4604.5.

Foreign vehicles, exemption from fees on reciprocity basis, see Vehicle Code § 6852.

License fee, generally, see Revenue and Taxation Code § 10701 et seq.

Payment of registration fees, payment on application, see Vehicle Code § 9550.

Penalties for delinquency of fees, see Vehicle Code § 9554.

Penalty on application for original registration after date of expiration or date penalties due, see Vehicle Code § 9554.5.

Registration, generally, see Vehicle Code § 4000 et seq.

Special highway construction equipment, see Vehicle Code § 9261.

Special permits for oversized vehicles, see Vehicle Code § 35780.

Special plates, see Vehicle Code § 5000 et seq.

Suspension, revocation or cancellation of registration when fee not paid, see Vehicle Code § 8800.

Temporary permit pending registration, see Vehicle Code § 4156.

Time for payment of fees, see Vehicle Code § 9550.

Unclaimed refunds, disposition, see Government Code § 16302.1.

Vehicle defined, see Vehicle Code § 670.

§ 9250.1.   Fee increase

(a) Beginning July 1, 2008, the fee described in Section 9250 shall be increased by three dollars ($3).

(b) Two dollars ($2) of the increase shall be deposited into the Alternative and Renewable Fuel and Vehicle Technology Fund created by Section 44273 of the Health and Safety Code, and one dollar ($1) shall be deposited into the Enhanced Fleet Modernization Subaccount created by Section 44126 of the Health and Safety Code.

(c) This section shall remain in effect only until January 1, 2024, and as of that date is repealed, unless a later enacted statute, that is enacted before January 1, 2024, deletes or extends that date. *(Added by Stats.2007, c. 750 (A.B.118), § 6. Amended by Stats.2013, c. 401 (A.B.8), § 35, eff. Sept. 28, 2013.)*

Repeal

For repeal of this section, see its terms.

§ 9250.2.   Surcharge collected for Sacramento Metropolitan Air Quality Management District

Section operative until Jan. 1, 2024. See, also, section operative Jan. 1, 2024.

(a) The department, if requested by the Sacramento Metropolitan Air Quality Management District pursuant to Section 41081 of the Health and Safety Code, shall impose and collect a surcharge on the registration fees for every motor vehicle registered in that district, not to exceed the amount of six dollars ($6), as specified by the governing body of that district.

(b) This section shall remain in effect only until January 1, 2024, and as of that date is repealed, unless a later enacted statute, that is enacted before January 1, 2024, deletes or extends that date. *(Added by Stats.1988, c. 1541, § 5. Amended by Stats.2004, c. 707 (A.B.923), § 15; Stats.2013, c. 401 (A.B.8), § 36, eff. Sept. 28, 2013.)*

Repeal

For repeal of this section, see its terms.

§ 9250.2. Surcharge collected for Sacramento Metropolitan Air Quality Management District

Section operative Jan. 1, 2024. See, also, section operative until Jan. 1, 2024.

(a) The department, if requested by the Sacramento Metropolitan Air Quality Management District pursuant to Section 41081 of the Health and Safety Code, shall impose and collect a surcharge on the registration fees for every motor vehicle registered in that district, not to exceed * * * four dollars ($4).

* * *

(b) This section shall become operative on January 1, 2024. *(Added by Stats.2004, c. 707 (A.B.923), § 15.5, operative Jan. 1, 2015. Amended by Stats.2013, c. 401 (A.B.8), § 37, eff. Sept. 28, 2013, operative Jan. 1, 2024.)*

§ 9250.4. Collection of motor vehicle registration fee increase for congestion or pollution reduction program; costs; distribution

(a) The department shall, if requested by a countywide transportation planning agency, collect the fee imposed pursuant to Section 65089.20 of the Government Code upon the registration or renewal of registration of a motor vehicle registered in the county, except those vehicles that are expressly exempted under this code from the payment of registration fees.

(b) The countywide transportation planning agency shall pay for the initial setup and programming costs identified by the department through a direct contract with the department. Any direct contract payment by the board shall be repaid, with no restriction on the funds, to the countywide transportation planning agency as part of the initial revenues available for distribution.

(c)(1) After deducting all costs incurred pursuant to this section, the department shall distribute the net revenues pursuant to subdivision (a) of Section 65089.20 of the Government Code.

(2) The costs deducted under paragraph (1) shall not be counted against the 5–percent administrative cost limit specified in subdivision (d) of Section 65089.20 of the

Government Code. *(Added by Stats.2009, c. 554 (S.B.83), § 3.)*

§ 9250.5. San Mateo County; local registration fee; program costs; distribution of revenue

(a) The department shall, if requested by the City/County Association of Governments of San Mateo County, collect the fee imposed pursuant to Section 65089.11 of the Government Code upon the registration or renewal of registration of any motor vehicle registered in the county, except those vehicles that are expressly exempted under this code from the payment of registration fees.

(b) The City/County Association of Governments of San Mateo County shall pay for the initial setup and programming costs identified by the Department of Motor Vehicles through a direct contract with the department. Any direct contract payment by the City/County Association of Governments of San Mateo County shall be repaid, with no restriction on the funds, to the City/County Association of Governments of San Mateo County as part of the initial revenues distributed. Regular Department of Motor Vehicles collection costs shall be in accordance with subdivision (c). These costs shall not be counted against the 5–percent administration cost limit specified in subdivision (e) of Section 65089.12.

(c) After deducting all costs incurred pursuant to this section, the department shall distribute the revenues to the City/County Association of Governments of San Mateo County. *(Added by Stats.2004, c. 931 (A.B.1546), § 2.)*

§ 9250.7. Fee; service authority for abatement of abandoned vehicles

(a)(1) A service authority established under Section 22710 may impose a service fee of one dollar ($1) on all vehicles, except vehicles described in subdivision (a) of Section 5014.1, registered to an owner with an address in the county that established the service authority. The fee shall be paid to the department at the time of registration, or renewal of registration, or when renewal becomes delinquent, except on vehicles that are expressly exempted under this code from the payment of registration fees.

(2) In addition to the one-dollar ($1) service fee, and upon the implementation of the permanent trailer identification plate program, and as part of the Commercial Vehicle Registration Act of 2001, all commercial motor vehicles subject to Section 9400.1 registered to an owner with an address in the county that established a service authority under this section shall pay an additional service fee of two dollars ($2).

(b) The department, after deducting its administrative costs, shall transmit, at least quarterly, the net amount collected pursuant to subdivision (a) to the Treasurer for deposit in the Abandoned Vehicle Trust Fund, which is hereby created. All money in the fund is continuously appropriated to the Controller for allocation to a service authority that has an approved abandoned vehicle abatement program pursuant to Section 22710, and for payment of the administrative costs of the Controller. After deduction of its administrative costs, the Controller shall allocate the money in the Abandoned Vehicle Trust Fund to each service authority in proportion to the revenues received from the fee imposed by that authority pursuant to subdivision (a). If any funds received by a service authority pursuant to this section are not expended to abate abandoned vehicles pursuant to an approved abandoned vehicle abatement program that has been in existence for at least two full fiscal years within 90 days of the close of the fiscal year in which the funds were received and the amount of those funds exceeds the amount expended by the service authority for the abatement of abandoned vehicles in the previous fiscal year, the fee imposed pursuant to subdivision (a) shall be suspended for one year, commencing on July 1 following the Controller's determination pursuant to subdivision (e).

(c) Every service authority that imposes a fee authorized by subdivision (a) shall issue a fiscal yearend report to the Controller on or before October 31 of each year summarizing all of the following:

(1) The total revenues received by the service authority during the previous fiscal year.

(2) The total expenditures by the service authority during the previous fiscal year.

(3) The total number of vehicles abated during the previous fiscal year.

(4) The average cost per abatement during the previous fiscal year.

(5) Any additional, unexpended fee revenues for the service authority during the previous fiscal year.

(6) The number of notices to abate issued to vehicles during the previous fiscal year.

(7) The number of vehicles disposed of pursuant to an ordinance adopted pursuant to Section 22710 during the previous fiscal year.

(8) The total expenditures by the service authority for towing and storage of abandoned vehicles during the previous fiscal year.

(d) Each service authority that fails to submit the report required pursuant to subdivision (c) by October 31 of each year shall have its fee pursuant to subdivision (a) suspended for one year commencing on July 1 following the Controller's determination pursuant to subdivision (e).

(e) On or before January 1 annually, the Controller shall review the fiscal yearend reports, submitted by each service authority pursuant to subdivision (c) and due no later than October 31, to determine if fee revenues are being utilized in a manner consistent with the service authority's approved program. If the Controller determines that the use of the fee revenues is not consistent with the service authority's program as approved by the Department of the California Highway Patrol, or that an

250

excess of fee revenues exists, as specified in subdivision (b), the authority to collect the fee shall be suspended for one year pursuant to subdivision (b). If the Controller determines that a service authority has not submitted a fiscal yearend report as required in subdivision (c), the authorization to collect the service fee shall be suspended for one year pursuant to subdivisions (b) and (d). The Controller shall inform the Department of Motor Vehicles on or before January 1 annually, that the authority to collect the fee is suspended. A suspension shall only occur if the service authority has been in existence for at least two full fiscal years and the revenue fee surpluses are in excess of those allowed under this section, the use of the fee revenue is not consistent with the service authority's approved program, or the required fiscal yearend report has not been submitted by October 31.

(f) On or before January 1, 2010, and biennially thereafter, the service authority shall have a financial audit of the service authority conducted by a qualified independent third party.

(g) The fee imposed by a service authority shall remain in effect only for a period of 10 years from the date that the actual collection of the fee commenced unless the fee is extended pursuant to this subdivision. The fee may be extended in increments of up to 10 years each if the board of supervisors of the county, by a two-thirds vote, and a majority of the cities having a majority of the incorporated population within the county adopt resolutions providing for the extension of the fee. *(Added by Stats.1990, c. 1684 (A.B.4114), § 3. Amended by Stats.1992, c. 1241 (S.B.1615), § 11; Stats.1995, c. 819 (A.B.135), § 1; Stats. 1997, c. 272 (S.B.112), § 1, eff. Aug. 15, 1997; Stats.2000, c. 861 (S.B.2084), § 41, eff. Sept. 29, 2000; Stats.2001, c. 175 (S.B.106), § 1; Stats.2001, c. 826 (A.B.1472), § 19.5; Stats.2002, c. 664 (A.B.3034), § 216; Stats.2004, c. 650 (A.B.3047), § 8; Stats.2007, c. 389 (A.B.468), § 1; Stats. 2012, c. 728 (S.B.71), § 176.)*

Cross References

Reimbursement of governmental or private agency for removal of abandoned vehicles, see Vehicle Code § 22710.

§ 9250.8. Additional fees

(a) In addition to any other fees specified in this code and the Revenue and Taxation Code, a fee of three dollars ($3) shall be paid at the time of registration or renewal of registration of every vehicle, except vehicles described in subdivision (a) of Section 5014.1, subject to registration under this code, except those vehicles that are expressly exempted under this code from the payment of registration fees.

(b) In addition to the fee required under subdivision (a), upon the implementation of the permanent trailer identification plate program, and as part of the Commercial Vehicle Registration Act of 2001, all commercial motor vehicles subject to Section 9400.1 shall pay a fee of six dollars ($6). *(Added by Stats.1985, c. 797, § 2. Amended by Stats.1990, c. 954 (A.B.2545), § 1; Stats. 1992, c. 1109 (A.B.3346), § 5; Stats.1994, c. 1197 (A.B.*

3080), § 1; Stats.2000, c. 861 (S.B.2084), § 42, eff. Sept. 29, 2000; Stats.2001, c. 826 (A.B.1472), § 20; Stats.2003, c. 719 (S.B.1055), § 11.)

Base fee amounts, adjustment of fees, see Vehicle Code § 1678.

§ 9250.9. Additional fees; deposit; use

All fees received by the department pursuant to Section 9250.8 shall be deposited in the Motor Vehicle Account in the State Transportation Fund. The money deposited in the account pursuant to this section shall be available, upon appropriation by the Legislature, for expenditure to accomplish the following:

(a) To ensure sufficient support for those peace officer members employed on December 31, 1994, and to support an additional 130 peace officer members of the California Highway Patrol.

(b) To offset the costs of maintaining the uniformed field strength of the Department of the California Highway Patrol.

(Added by Stats.1981, c. 933, p. 3521, § 3, eff. Sept. 29, 1981. Amended by Stats.1985, c. 797, § 3; Stats.1990, c. 954 (A.B.2545), § 2; Stats.1992, c. 1109 (A.B.3346), § 6; Stats.1994, c. 1197 (A.B.3080), § 2.)

§ 9250.10. Service authority for freeway emergencies; additional fees; distribution after deduction of administrative costs

(a)(1) In addition to any other fees specified in this code and the Revenue and Taxation Code, any additional fees imposed by a service authority for freeway emergencies pursuant to Section 2555 of the Streets and Highways Code shall be paid to the department at the time of registration or renewal of registration of every vehicle, except vehicles described in subdivision (a) of Section 5014.1, subject to registration under this code in the subject counties, except those vehicles that are expressly exempted under this code from the payment of registration fees.

(2) In addition to the additional fees imposed for freeway emergencies, and upon the implementation of the permanent trailer identification plate program, and as part of the Commercial Vehicle Registration Act of 2001, all commercial motor vehicles subject to Section 9400.1 registered to an owner with an address in the county that established a service authority under this section, shall pay an additional service fee of two dollars ($2).

(b) After deducting its administrative costs, the department shall distribute the additional fees collected pursuant to subdivision (a) to the authority in the county in which they were collected. *(Added by Stats.1985, c. 1350, § 4. Amended by Stats.1988, c. 1132, § 13, eff. Sept. 22, 1988; Stats.2000, c. 861 (S.B.2084), § 43, eff. Sept. 29, 2000; Stats.2001, c. 826 (A.B.1472), § 21.)*

San Diego County service authority, dissolution, succession by SANDAG, see Streets and Highways Code § 2555.1.

§ 9250.11. Registration renewal fee; approval and adoption; memorandum of understanding; accounting procedures

(a) In addition to any other fees specified in this code and the Revenue and Taxation Code, a fee of one dollar ($1) may be imposed by the South Coast Air Quality Management District and shall be paid to the department, upon renewal of registration of any motor vehicle subject to Part 5 (commencing with Section 43000) of Division 26 of the Health and Safety Code and registered in the south coast district, except any vehicle that is expressly exempted under this code from the payment of registration fees.

(b) Prior to imposing fees pursuant to this section, the south coast district board shall approve the imposition of the fees through the adoption of a resolution by both a majority of the district board and a majority of the district board who are elected officials. After deducting all costs incurred pursuant to this section, the department shall distribute the additional fees collected pursuant to subdivision (a) to the south coast district, which shall use the fees to reduce air pollution from motor vehicles through implementation of Sections 40448.5 and 40448.5.1 of the Health and Safety Code.

(c) Any memorandum of understanding reached between the district and a county prior to the imposition of a one dollar ($1) fee by a county shall remain in effect and govern the allocation of the funds generated in that county by that fee.

(d) The South Coast Air Quality Management District shall adopt accounting procedures to ensure that revenues from motor vehicle registration fees are not commingled with other program revenues.

(Added by Stats.1999, c. 36 (S.B.98), § 4, eff. June 8, 1999. Amended by Stats.2003, c. 476 (S.B.288), § 2; Stats.2008, c. 724 (S.B.1646), § 2.)

§ 9250.12. City and county of San Francisco; local registration fee

(a) For purposes of this section, "county" means the City and County of San Francisco.

(b) In addition to any other fees specified in this code and the Revenue and Taxation Code, a fee of four dollars ($4) shall be paid at the time of registration or renewal of registration of every vehicle registered to an address within a county, except those vehicles expressly exempted from payment of registration fees and commercial vehicles weighing more than 4,000 pounds, unladen, if all of the following occur:

(1) The county board of supervisors finds both of the following:

(A) That there is traffic congestion within the county that can be alleviated by the operation of public transit

251

and that the cost of funding public transit exceeds the revenues to be collected from a service fee imposed on vehicles.

(B) That the imposition of the additional registration fee will reduce the need for any public transit fare increases during the period that the fee is in effect.

(2) The county board of supervisors adopts an ordinance or resolution imposing the additional registration fee.

(3) The ordinance or resolution adopted pursuant to paragraph (2) is approved by two-thirds of the voters in the county who voted on the measure.

(c) The fee imposed pursuant to this section shall apply to any original registration occurring on or after the January 1 following the adoption of the ordinance pursuant to paragraph (3) of subdivision (b) and to any renewal of registration with an expiration date on or after that January 1.

(d) After deducting all costs incurred pursuant to this section, the department shall distribute the revenues to the county. The amount of revenues distributed by the department to the county shall be equal to the net amount of revenues received from that county that were derived from the imposition of the additional fees.

(e) Money allocated to the county pursuant to this section shall be expended only to fund programs for the provision of public transit, including capital outlay, security, and maintenance costs, and including, but not limited to, removal of graffiti from public transit vehicles and facilities, and to pay the costs of compliance with paragraph (3) of subdivision (b).

(f) If public transit fees are increased at any time the additional registration fee authorized by the section is in effect, the fee may not continue to be imposed. This section shall become inoperative on the date those fares are increased and shall be repealed on January 1 next following that date. The board of supervisors shall notify the department of any increase in public transit fares occurring while the additional registration fee is in effect. *(Added by Stats.1993, c. 966 (A.B.925), § 2.)*

Inoperative Date and Repeal

For inoperative date and repeal of this section, see subd. (f).

§ 9250.13. Fee to offset costs of increasing uniformed field strength of highway patrol

(a)(1) In addition to any other fees specified in this code and the Revenue and Taxation Code, a fee of eighteen dollars ($18) shall be paid at the time of registration or renewal of registration of every vehicle, except vehicles described in subdivision (a) of Section 5014.1, subject to registration under this code, except those vehicles that are expressly exempted under this code from the payment of registration fees.

(2) In addition to the fee required under paragraph (1), upon the implementation of the permanent trailer

252

identification plate program, and as part of the Commercial Vehicle Registration Act of 2001 (Chapter 861 of the Statutes of 2000), all commercial motor vehicles subject to Section 9400.1 shall pay a fee of six dollars ($6).

(b) The money realized pursuant to this section shall be available, upon appropriation by the Legislature, for expenditure to offset the costs of increasing the uniformed field strength of the Department of the California Highway Patrol beyond its 1994 staffing level and those costs associated with maintaining this new level of uniformed field strength and carrying out those duties specified in subdivision (a) of Section 830.2 of the Penal Code. *(Added by Stats.1994, c. 1196 (A.B.2949), § 1. Amended by Stats.2000, c. 861 (S.B.2084), § 44, eff. Sept. 29, 2000; Stats.2001, c. 826 (A.B.1472), § 22; Stats.2003, c. 719 (S.B.1055), § 12; Stats.2004, c. 183 (A.B.3082), § 347; Stats.2008, c. 756 (A.B.268), § 19, eff. Sept. 30, 2008.)*

Cross References

Base fee amounts, adjustment of fees, see Vehicle Code § 1678.

§ 9250.14. Additional fee; vehicle theft programs; prosecution of crimes involving driving under the influence of alcohol or drugs or vehicular manslaughter; reports

(a)(1) In addition to any other fees specified in this code and the Revenue and Taxation Code, upon the adoption of a resolution by any county board of supervisors, a fee of one dollar ($1) shall be paid at the time of registration or renewal of registration of every vehicle, except vehicles described in subdivision (a) of Section 5014.1, registered to an address within that county except those expressly exempted from payment of registration fees. The fees, after deduction of the administrative costs incurred by the department in carrying out this section, shall be paid quarterly to the Controller.

(2)(A) If * * * a county * * * has adopted a resolution to impose a one-dollar ($1) fee pursuant to paragraph (1), the county may increase the fee specified in paragraph (1) to two dollars ($2) in the same manner as the imposition of the initial fee pursuant to paragraph (1). The two dollars ($2) shall be paid at the time of registration or renewal of registration of a vehicle, and quarterly to the Controller, as provided in paragraph (1).

(B) If a county has not adopted a resolution to impose a one-dollar ($1) fee pursuant to paragraph (1), the county may instead adopt a fee of two dollars ($2) in the manner prescribed in paragraph (1).

(C) A resolution to * * * impose a fee of two dollars ($2) pursuant to subparagraph (A) or (B) shall be submitted to the department at least six months prior to the operative date of the fee increase.

(3) In addition to the service fee imposed pursuant to paragraph (1), and upon the implementation of the permanent trailer identification plate program, and as part of the Commercial Vehicle Registration Act of 2001 (Chapter 861 of the Statutes of 2000), all commercial

motor vehicles subject to Section 9400.1 registered to an owner with an address in the county that established a service authority under this section, shall pay an additional service fee of two dollars ($2).

(4)(A) If a county imposes a service fee of two dollars ($2) by adopting a resolution pursuant to subparagraph (A) or (B) of paragraph (2), the fee specified in paragraph (3) shall be increased to four dollars ($4). The four dollars ($4) shall be paid at the time of registration or renewal of registration of a vehicle, and quarterly to the Controller as provided in paragraph (1).

(B) A resolution to increase the additional service fee from two dollars ($2) to four dollars ($4) pursuant to subparagraph (A) or (B) of paragraph (2) shall be submitted to the department at least six months prior to the operative date of the fee increase.

(b) Notwithstanding Section 13340 of the Government Code, the moneys paid to the Controller are continuously appropriated, without regard to fiscal years, for the administrative costs of the Controller, and for disbursement by the Controller to each county that has adopted a resolution pursuant to subdivision (a), based upon the number of vehicles registered, or whose registration is renewed, to an address within that county.

(c) Except as otherwise provided in this subdivision, moneys allocated to a county pursuant to subdivision (b) shall be expended exclusively to fund programs that enhance the capacity of local police and prosecutors to deter, investigate, and prosecute vehicle theft crimes. In any county with a population of 250,000 or less, the moneys shall be expended exclusively for those vehicle theft crime programs and for the prosecution of crimes involving driving while under the influence of alcohol or drugs, or both, in violation of Section 23152 or 23153, or vehicular manslaughter in violation of Section 191.5 of the Penal Code or subdivision (c) of Section 192 of the Penal Code, or any combination of those crimes.

(d) The moneys collected pursuant to this section shall not be expended to offset a reduction in any other source of funds, nor for any purpose not authorized under this section.

(e) Any funds received by a county prior to January 1, 2000, pursuant to this section, that are not expended to deter, investigate, or prosecute crimes pursuant to subdivision (c) shall be returned to the Controller, for deposit in the Motor Vehicle Account in the State Transportation Fund. Those funds received by a county shall be expended in accordance with this section.

(f) Each county that adopts a resolution under subdivision (a) shall submit, on or before the 13th day following the end of each quarter, a quarterly expenditure and activity report to the designated statewide Vehicle Theft Investigation and Apprehension Coordinator in the Department of the California Highway Patrol.

(g) A county that imposes a fee under subdivision (a) shall issue a fiscal yearend report to the Controller on or before August 31 of each year. The report shall include a detailed accounting of the funds received and expended in the immediately preceding fiscal year, including, at a minimum, all of the following:

(1) The amount of funds received and expended by the county under subdivision (b) for the immediately preceding fiscal year.

(2) The total expenditures by the county under subdivision (c) for the immediately preceding fiscal year.

(3) Details of expenditures made by the county under subdivision (c), including salaries and expenses, purchase of equipment and supplies, and any other expenditures made listed by type with an explanatory comment.

(4) A summary of vehicle theft abatement activities and other vehicle theft programs funded by the fees collected * * * pursuant to this section.

(5) The total number of stolen vehicles recovered and the value of those vehicles during the immediately preceding fiscal year.

(6) The total number of vehicles stolen during the immediately preceding fiscal year as compared to the fiscal year prior to the immediately preceding fiscal year.

(7) Any additional, unexpended fee revenues received under subdivision (b) for the county for the immediately preceding fiscal year.

(h) Each county that fails to submit the report required pursuant to subdivision (g) by November 30 of each year shall have the fee suspended by the Controller for one year, commencing on July 1 following the Controller's determination that a county has failed to submit the report.

(i)(1) On or before January 1, 2013, and on or before January 1 of each year, the Controller shall provide to the Department of the California Highway Patrol copies of the yearend reports submitted by the counties under subdivision (g) * * * and, in consultation with the Department of the California Highway Patrol, shall review the fiscal yearend reports submitted by each county pursuant to subdivision (g) to determine if fee revenues are being utilized in a manner consistent with this section. If the Controller determines that the use of the fee revenues is not consistent with this section, the Controller shall consult with the participating counties' designated regional coordinators. If the Controller determines that use of the fee revenues is still not consistent with this section, the authority to collect the fee by that county shall be suspended for one year.

(2) If the Controller determines that a county has not submitted a fiscal yearend report as required in subdivision (g), the authorization to collect the service fee shall be suspended for one year pursuant to subdivision (h).

(3) When the Controller determines that a fee shall be suspended for a county, the Controller shall inform the Department of Motor Vehicles on or before January 1 of each year that the authority to collect a fee for that county is suspended.

(j) On or before January 1 of each year, the Controller shall prepare and submit to the Legislature a revenue and expenditure summary for each participating county that includes all of the following:

(1) The total revenues received by each county.

(2) The total expenditures by each county.

(3) The unexpended revenues for each county.

(k) For the purposes of this section, a county-designated regional coordinator is that agency designated by the participating county's board of supervisors as the agency in control of its countywide vehicle theft apprehension program.

* * *   *(Added by Stats.1990, c. 1670 (S.B.2139), § 1. Amended by Stats.1992, c. 820 (S.B.2014), § 1; Stats.1995, c. 819 (A.B.135), § 2; Stats.1999, c. 232 (A.B.183), § 1; Stats.2000, c. 861 (S.B.2084), § 45, eff. Sept. 29, 2000; Stats.2000, c. 1064 (A.B.2227), § 5, eff. Sept. 30, 2000; Stats.2000, c; 1064 (A.B.2227), § 5.5, eff. Sept. 30, 2000; Stats.2001, c. 826 (A.B.1472), § 23; Stats.2004, c. 514 (A.B.1663), § 1; Stats.2009, c. 230 (A.B.286), § 1; Stats. 2012, c. 728 (S.B.71), § 177; Stats.2012, c. 775 (A.B. 1404), § 1; Stats.2013, c. 241 (A.B.767), § 1.)*

§ 9250.15. Collection of administrative service fee for each registration, renewal of registration or supplement apportioned registration; amount; use of money collected

(a) In addition to any other fees specified in this code, the department shall collect an administrative service fee in the amount authorized under subdivision (b) for each application for registration, renewal of registration, or supplement apportioned registration pursuant to Article 4 (commencing with Section 8050) of Chapter 4.

(b) The administrative service fee required to be collected under subdivision (a) shall be at least the amount determined by the department to be sufficient to pay membership dues to the association acting as the repository for the International Registration Plan under Article 3 (commencing with Section 8000) of Chapter 4, but may not be more than two dollars ($2) for each application.

(c) The money collected by the department under this section, less the department's administrative costs in collecting and transmitting the money, shall be available, upon appropriation, to the department for payment to the association described in subdivision (b).

(d) Funds provided to the association under this section shall be used exclusively for the administration and support of reciprocity activities under the International Registration Plan. *(Added by Stats.1990, c. 880 (S.B.2546), § 1. Amended by Stats.2001, c. 539 (S.B.734), § 11.)*

§ 9250.16. Surcharge imposed by San Joaquin Valley Unified Air Pollution Control District; allocation of funds

(a) In addition to any other fees specified in this code, the Health and Safety Code, and the Revenue and Taxation Code, a surcharge of one dollar ($1) may be imposed by the San Joaquin Valley Unified Air Pollution Control District and shall be paid to the department as follows:

(1) Upon initial registration of any motor vehicle not previously registered in this state that is registered on or after the date the department begins collecting the fee.

(2) Upon renewal of registration of any motor vehicle for which the registration period expires after the date the department begins collecting the fee.

(3) This subdivision applies to any motor vehicle subject to Part 5 (commencing with Section 43000) of Division 26 of the Health and Safety Code, except any vehicle that is expressly exempted under this code from the payment of registration fees. The department shall begin collecting the fee on January 1 of the fiscal year immediately following the date the department receives the request to do so from the San Joaquin Valley Unified Air Pollution Control District Board.

(b) Prior to the adoption of any surcharge pursuant to this subdivision, the San Joaquin Valley Unified Air Pollution Control District board shall approve the imposition of the surcharge through the adoption of a resolution, as specified in Section 44225 of the Health and Safety Code.

(c) The San Joaquin Valley Unified Air Pollution Control District shall pay for the costs identified by the department to establish the fee collection procedure. After deducting the on-going costs incurred by the department in collecting the fees, the department shall deposit the revenue collected pursuant to this section into the Motor Vehicle Account in the State Transportation Fund for allocation to the district. Subdivision (c) of Section 40605 of the Health and Safety Code does not apply to the costs described in this subdivision. *(Added by Stats.2003, c. 483 (S.B.709), § 3.)*

§ 9250.17. Collection of fees to be used to reduce air pollution; distribution of revenues after deduction of costs; limitation on costs

(a) The department shall, if requested by a county air pollution control district, air quality management district, or unified or regional air pollution control district, collect fees established pursuant to Sections 44223 and 44225 of the Health and Safety Code upon the registration or renewal of registration of any motor vehicle registered in the district, except those vehicles which are expressly exempted under this code from the payment of registration fees.

(b) After deducting all costs incurred pursuant to this section, the department shall distribute the revenues to the districts based upon the amount of fees collected from motor vehicles registered within each district.

(c) The department may annually expend for its costs not more than the following percentages of the fees collected pursuant to subdivision (a):

(1) Five percent during the first year after the operative date the fee is imposed or increased.

(2) Three percent during the second year after the operative date the fee is imposed or increased.

(3) One percent during any subsequent year. *(Added by Stats.1990, c. 1705 (A.B.2766), § 2.)*

§ 9250.18. Administrative fees; collection; disposition

(a) The department shall collect the administrative fee established pursuant to Sections 44081 and 44081.6 of the Health and Safety Code upon the renewal of registration or transfer of ownership of any motor vehicle registered in the state.

(b) On a monthly basis, after deducting its reasonable costs, the department shall transmit all revenues, including accrued interest, received pursuant to this section, for deposit in the Vehicle Inspection and Repair Fund, for use by the Department of Consumer Affairs pursuant to Chapter 5 (commencing with Section 44000) of Part 5 of Division 26 of the Health and Safety Code. Alternatively, the department and the Department of Consumer Affairs may, by interagency agreement, establish a procedure for the Department of Consumer Affairs to reimburse the department for its reasonable costs incurred in collecting the administrative fees. *(Added by Stats.1994, c. 27 (A.B.2018), § 61, eff. March 30, 1994. Amended by Stats.1994, c. 1220 (A.B.3132), § 54.2, eff. Sept. 30, 1994.)*

§ 9250.19. Fingerprint identification program

(a)(1) In addition to any other fees specified in this code and the Revenue and Taxation Code, upon the adoption of a resolution pursuant to this subdivision by any county board of supervisors, a fee of one dollar ($1) shall be paid at the time of registration, renewal, or supplemental application for apportioned registration pursuant to Article 4 (commencing with Section 8050) of Chapter 4 of every vehicle, except vehicles described in subdivision (a) of Section 5014.1, registered to an address within that county except those expressly exempted from payment of registration fees. The fees, after deduction of the administrative costs incurred by the department in carrying out this section, shall be paid quarterly to the Controller.

(2) In addition to the one-dollar ($1) service fee, and upon the implementation of the permanent trailer identification plate program, and as part of the Commercial Vehicle Registration Act of 2001, all commercial motor vehicles subject to Section 9400.1 registered to an owner with an address in the county that established a service authority under this section, shall pay an additional service fee of two dollars ($2).

(3) A resolution adopted pursuant to paragraph (1) shall include findings as to the purpose of, and the need for, imposing the additional registration fee.

(b) Notwithstanding Section 13340 of the Government Code, the money paid to the Controller pursuant to subdivision (a) is continuously appropriated, without regard to fiscal years, for disbursement by the Controller to each county that has adopted a resolution pursuant to subdivision (a), based upon the number of vehicles registered, or whose registration is renewed, to an address within that county, or supplemental application for apportioned registration, and for the administrative costs of the Controller incurred under this section.

(c) Money allocated to a county pursuant to subdivision (b) shall be expended exclusively to fund programs that enhance the capacity of local law enforcement to provide automated mobile and fixed location fingerprint identification of individuals who may be involved in driving under the influence of alcohol or drugs in violation of Section 23152 or 23153, or vehicular manslaughter in violation of Section 191.5 of the Penal Code or subdivision (c) of Section 192 of the Penal Code, or any combination of those and other vehicle-related crimes, and other crimes committed while operating a motor vehicle.

(d) The data from a program funded pursuant to subdivision (c) shall be made available by the local law enforcement agency to a local public agency that is required by law to obtain a criminal history background of persons as a condition of employment with that local public agency. A local law enforcement agency that provides the data may charge a fee to cover its actual costs in providing that data.

(e)(1) Money collected pursuant to this section shall not be used to offset a reduction in any other source of funds for the purposes authorized under this section.

(2) Funds collected pursuant to this section, upon recommendation of local or regional Remote Access Network Boards to the board of supervisors, shall be used exclusively for the purchase, by competitive bidding procedures, and the operation of equipment that is compatible with the Department of Justice's Cal–ID master plan, as described in Section 11112.2 of the Penal Code, and the equipment shall interface in a manner that is in compliance with the requirement described in the Criminal Justice Information Services, Electronic Fingerprint Transmission Specification, prepared by the Federal Bureau of Investigation and dated August 24, 1995.

(f) Every county that has authorized the collection of the fee pursuant to subdivision (a) shall issue a fiscal yearend report to the Controller on or before November 1 of each year, summarizing all of the following with respect to those fees:

(1) The total revenues received by the county for the fiscal year.

(2) The total expenditures and encumbered funds by the county for the fiscal year. For purposes of this

subdivision, "encumbered funds" means funding that is scheduled to be spent pursuant to a determined schedule and for an identified purchase consistent with this section.

(3) Any unexpended or unencumbered fee revenues for the county for the fiscal year.

(4) The estimated annual cost of the purchase, operation, and maintenance of automated mobile and fixed location fingerprint equipment, related infrastructure, law enforcement enhancement programs, and personnel created or utilized in accordance with this section for the fiscal year. The listing shall detail the make and model number of the equipment, and include a succinct description of the related infrastructure items, law enforcement enhancement programs, and the classification or title of any personnel.

(5) How the use of the funds benefits the motoring public.

(g) For each county that fails to submit the report required pursuant to subdivision (f) by November 1 of each year, the Controller shall notify the Department of Motor Vehicles to suspend the fee for that county imposed pursuant to subdivision (a) for one year.

(h) If any funds received by a county pursuant to subdivision (a) are not expended or encumbered in accordance with this section by the close of the fiscal year in which the funds were received, the Controller shall notify the Department of Motor Vehicles to suspend the fee for that county imposed pursuant to subdivision (a) for one year. For purposes of this subdivision, "encumbered funds" means funding that is scheduled to be spent pursuant to a determined schedule and for an identified purchase consistent with this section.

(Added by Stats.1997, c. 587 (S.B.720), § 1. Amended by Stats.1998, c. 921 (A.B.2790), § 1; Stats.2000, c. 861 (S.B.2084), § 46, eff. Sept. 29, 2000; Stats.2001, c. 826 (A.B.1472), § 24; Stats.2002, c. 986 (A.B.879), § 1; Stats.2003, c. 62 (S.B.600), § 300; Stats.2005, c. 470 (A.B.857), § 1; Stats.2011, c. 205 (A.B.674), § 1; Stats. 2012, c. 728 (S.B.71), § 178.)

§ 9251. Repealed by Stats.1970, c. 1007, p. 1814, § 1

§ 9252. Vehicles purchased new or registered outside state

(a) In addition to the registration fee specified in Section 9250 and any weight fee, there shall be paid a service fee of fifteen dollars ($15) for the registration within this state of every vehicle purchased new outside this state or previously registered outside this state. If the vehicle has been registered and operated in this state during the same registration year in which application for registration is made, a fee of fifteen dollars ($15) shall be paid.

(b) This section does not apply to vehicles registered as fleet vehicles under Article 4 (commencing with Section 8050) of Chapter 4, except upon application for a

256

certificate of ownership. *(Stats.1959, c. 3, p. 1585, § 9252. Amended by Stats.1967, c. 1717, p. 4279, § 1; Stats.1970, c. 1439, p. 2793, § 4; Stats.1973, c. 889, p. 1654, § 37, eff. Sept. 28, 1973; Stats.1976, c. 1079, p. 4888, § 87; Stats.1981, c. 541, p. 2181, § 26, eff. Sept. 17, 1981, operative, eff. Jan. 1, 1982; Stats.1988, c. 907, § 1; Stats.1996, c. 124 (A.B.3470), § 121; Stats.2003, c. 719 (S.B.1055), § 13.)*

Cross References

Application for registration of vehicle previously registered outside state, see Vehicle Code § 4300.

Base fee amounts, adjustment of fees, see Vehicle Code § 1678.

Exemption of foreign vehicles from fees on reciprocity basis, see Vehicle Code § 6852.

Nonresident owners, permits, see Vehicle Code § 6700 et seq.

Weight fees, commercial vehicles, see Vehicle Code § 9400 et seq.

§ 9253. Repealed by Stats.1973, c. 1010, p. 2006, § 2

§ 9254. Certificate without registration

A service fee of fifteen dollars ($15) shall be paid to the department for a certificate of ownership issued without registration of the vehicle. *(Stats.1959, c. 3, p. 1586, § 9254. Amended by Stats.1970, c. 1439, p. 2794, § 5; Stats.1988, c. 1268, § 8; Stats.2003, c. 719 (S.B.1055), § 14.)*

Cross References

Applicability of this section to trolley coaches, see Vehicle Code § 21051.

Base fee amounts, adjustment of fees, see Vehicle Code § 1678.

Issuance of certificate without registration, see Vehicle Code § 4452.

Registration of trailer coaches, nonapplicability of this section, see Vehicle Code § 5351.

§ 9255. Transfer of registration

Upon application for the transfer of the title or any interest of an owner or legal owner in or to a vehicle registered under this code, or for which a certificate of ownership has been issued without registration under Section 4452, other than upon a transfer to a chattel mortgagee and other than upon a transfer to a transferee not required under this code to obtain the issuance to the owner of a new certificate of ownership and registration card, there shall be paid the following fees:

(1) For a transfer by the owner of an automobile or
motorcycle .... $ 15

(2) For a transfer by the owner of a trailer coach or commercial
vehicle $15

(3) For a transfer by the legal owner $15

(4) When an application is presented showing a transfer by both
the owner and legal owner of an automobile or
motorcycle $15

(5) When an application is presented showing a transfer by both the

owner and legal owner of a trailer coach or commercial vehicle $15

(Added by Stats.1997, c. 291 (A.B.1591), § 5, eff. Aug. 18, 1997, operative July 1, 1999. Amended by Stats.1999, c. 1007 (S.B.532), § 17; Stats.2002, c. 758 (A.B.3024), § 7.)

Cross References

Delinquent fees and penalties, see Vehicle Code § 9552 et seq.
"Legal owner" defined, see Vehicle Code § 370.
Secured party to appear as legal owner, see Vehicle Code § 6300.
Transfer of registration, see Vehicle Code § 6050.
Transfers of title or interest, see Vehicle Code § 5600 et seq.

§ 9255.1. Service fee; initial issuance of registration card

A service fee of two dollars ($2), in addition to other required fees, shall be paid to the department upon the initial issuance of a registration card identifying a motor vehicle of a type included in subdivision (b) of Section 4453. Subsequent transfers of title are exempted from the two-dollar ($2) service fee. *(Added by Stats.1980, c. 856, p. 2669, § 2, operative Oct. 1, 1981.)*

§ 9255.2. Initial registration or transfer of ownership; inspection fee; deposit

(a) In addition to any other fees specified in this code and the Revenue and Taxation Code, a fee of not more than fifty dollars ($50), as determined by the Department of the California Highway Patrol to cover the costs of implementing and conducting the inspection program required under Section 5505, shall be paid to the Department of Motor Vehicles at the time inspection is made for initial registration or transfer of ownership of a vehicle included in paragraphs (1) and (2) of subdivision (b) of Section 4453.

(b) The fees collected pursuant to subdivision (a) shall be deposited in the Motor Vehicle Account in the State Transportation Fund. The money deposited in the account shall be available, upon appropriation by the Legislature, for distribution as follows:

(1) Not more than three dollars ($3) of each fee collected under subdivision (a) to the Department of Motor Vehicles.

(2) The remainder to the Department of the California Highway Patrol.

(Added by Stats.1994, c. 1008 (S.B.1833), § 12, operative July 1, 1995. Amended by Stats.1996, c. 450 (S.B.1713), § 2; Stats.2002, c. 670 (S.B.1331), § 9.)

§ 9255.3. Title transfer fees; vehicles transferred pursuant to § 14607.6

Notwithstanding Section 9255, any vehicle transferred pursuant to Section 14607.6 shall be subject to a title transfer fee equal to the department's actual cost of

processing that transfer. *(Added by Stats.1994, c. 1133 (A.B.3148), § 4.)*

§ 9255.5. Transfer of registration; unavailable certificate; additional fee

Upon application for transfer of registration pursuant to Section 5911, a fee as specified in Section 9265 shall be paid to the department in addition to the regular transfer fee. *(Added by Stats.1978, c. 497, p. 1634, § 3.)*

§ 9256. Filing chattel mortgage

Upon filing with the department an application for transfer of registration to the chattel mortgagee as provided herein there shall be paid to the department a fee of three dollars ($3) for each vehicle registered under this code described in and subject to the chattel mortgage. *(Stats.1959, c. 3, p. 1586, § 9256. Amended by Stats.1967, c. 1717, p. 4279, § 3.)*

Cross References

Department, definition, see Vehicle Code §§ 290, 2101, 21000.
Recording of security interest, see Vehicle Code § 6300.

§ 9257. Installation of engine or motor

Every notice of the installation in a vehicle of a motor vehicle engine or motor required to be filed under Section 4161 shall be accompanied by a filing fee of two dollars ($2). *(Stats.1959, c. 3, p. 1586, § 9257.)*

Cross References

Alteration or change of vehicle numbers, see Vehicle Code § 10750.
Delinquent fee penalty, see Vehicle Code § 9553.
Owners of three or more vehicles, time of payment, see Vehicle Code § 4163.
Registration, engine or motor change, see Vehicle Code § 4161.

§ 9257.5. Fee for temporary permit

(a) Except as provided in subdivision (c), a fee of fifty dollars ($50) shall be paid for each temporary permit issued pursuant to Section 4156 when a certificate of compliance is required pursuant to Section 4000.3.

(b) After deducting its administrative costs, the department shall deposit fees collected pursuant to subdivision (a) in the High Polluter Repair or Removal Account in the Vehicle Inspection and Repair Fund.

(c) The department shall not charge a fee pursuant to subdivision (a) if the department is presented at the time the temporary permit is issued with sufficient evidence, as determined by the department, that the owner of the vehicle is an income eligible applicant who had his or her vehicle accepted into the Bureau of Automotive Repair Consumer Assistance Program as established pursuant to Chapter 5 (commencing with Section 44000) of Part 5 of Division 26 of the Health and Safety Code. *(Added by Stats.2008, c. 451 (A.B.2241), § 2.)*

§ 9258. One-trip payment

A fee of fifteen dollars ($15) shall be paid to the department for each one-trip permit issued pursuant to

Section 4003. *(Stats.1959, c. 3, p. 1586, § 9258. Amended by Stats.1961, c. 58, p. 1005, § 21; Stats.1963, c. 1628, p. 3219, § 3; Stats.1981, c. 541, p. 2181, § 28, eff. Sept. 17, 1981, operative Jan. 1, 1982; Stats.2003, c. 719 (S.B.1055), § 15.)*

Cross References

Base fee amounts, adjustment of fees, see Vehicle Code § 1678.
Department, definition, see Vehicle Code §§ 290, 2101, 21000.

§ 9258.5. New trailer or semitrailer, one-trip permit

A fee of thirty-five dollars ($35) shall be paid to the department for each one-trip permit issued pursuant to Section 4003.5. *(Added by Stats.1983, c. 825, § 2. Amended by Stats.1985, c. 625, § 2.)*

Cross References

One-trip permits, issuance, see Vehicle Code § 4003.5.

§ 9259. Fleet vehicles; sticker or device; fee

A fee of two dollars ($2) shall be paid for each sticker or device issued under Article 4 (commencing with Section ·8050) of Chapter 4 of Division 3 or for each vehicle in a fleet upon transfer of ownership as provided in Section 8054. *(Stats.1959, c. 3, p. 1586, § 9259. Amended by Stats.1961, c. 58, p. 1005, § 22, eff. March 31, 1961; Stats.1983, c. 986, § 4; Stats.1992, c. 1241 (S.B. 1615), § 12.)*

§ 9259.3. Deposits to cover the inclusion of additional operating area or registration issued under Article 4 for each application

For each application to include an additional operating area or a registration issued under Article 4 (commencing with Section 8050) of Chapter 4 of Division 3, the department shall require a deposit in an amount determined by the department to be sufficient to ensure compliance with that article. *(Added by Stats.2001, c. 539 (S.B.734), § 12.)*

§ 9259.5. Fee to cover immediate telephone service for registration issued under Article 4 for each application

For each application for immediate telephone service for a registration issued under Article 4 (commencing with Section 8050) of Chapter 4 of Division 3, the department shall impose a fee in an amount determined by the department to be sufficient to cover its administrative costs under this section. *(Added by Stats.2001, c. 539 (S.B.734), § 13.)*

§ 9260. Temporary registration; trip permit; fees

(a) The fee for a temporary registration issued under Section 4004 is one-quarter of the annual fees in Division 3 (commencing with Section 4000) of this code and Part 5 (commencing with Section 10701) of Division 2 of the Revenue and Taxation Code, for the period that the vehicle is to be operated in this state.

258

(b) The fee for a trip permit issued under Section 4004 is forty-five dollars ($45) for each commercial motor vehicle. *(Stats.1959, c. 3, p. 1586, § 9260. Amended by Stats.1963, c. 1433, p. 2980, § 4; Stats.1963, c. 1462, p. 3021, § 3; Stats.1967, c. 1333, p. 3166, § 1; Stats.1981, c. 245, p. 1298, § 2; Stats.1992, c. 1241 (S.B.1615), § 13; Stats.2000, c. 861 (S.B.2084), § 47, eff. Sept. 29, 2000.)*

§ 9261. Service fees; transfer fee; renewal fee

(a) A service fee of fifteen dollars ($15) shall be paid for an identification plate issued pursuant to Section 5014. Publicly owned special construction equipment, cemetery equipment, special mobile equipment, logging vehicles, and implements of husbandry are exempt from the service charge.

(b) A service fee of fifteen dollars ($15) shall be paid for an identification plate issued pursuant to Section 5016.5.

(c) Upon application for the transfer of interest of an owner in a piece of equipment, vehicle, or implement of husbandry identified pursuant to Section 5014, the transferee shall pay a fee of fifteen dollars ($15).

(d) A fee of fifteen dollars ($15) shall be paid upon the renewal of an identification plate issued pursuant to Section 5014 or 5016.5. *(Stats.1959, c. 3, p. 1586, § 9261. Amended by Stats.1961, c. 1659, p. 3627, § 7; Stats.1963, c. 209, p. 948, § 4, eff. April 29, 1963; Stats.1963, c. 2149, p. 4487, § 11; Stats.1967, c. 1069, p. 2701, § 4; Stats. 1967, c. 1491, p. 3486, § 5; Stats.1969, c. 1075, p. 2063, § 7.5; Stats.1969, c. 1242, p. 2063, § 3; Stats.1970, c. 1330, p. 2475, § 4; Stats.1972, c. 973, p. 1758, § 12, eff. Aug. 16, 1972; Stats.1975, c. 517, p. 1083, § 4; Stats.1983, c. 708, § 6; Stats.1984, c. 1077, § 8, operative July 1, 1985; Stats.2000, c. 861 (S.B.2084), § 48, eff. Sept. 29, 2000; Stats.2003, c. 719 (S.B.1055), § 16.)*

Cross References

Base fee amounts, adjustment of fees, see Vehicle Code § 1678.
Implements of husbandry, exemption from registration, see Vehicle Code § 36100.
Special construction and mobile equipment, exemption from registration, see Vehicle Code § 4010.

§ 9261.1. Fee increase

(a) Beginning July 1, 2008, the fee described in Section 9261, as adjusted pursuant to Section 1678, shall be increased by five dollars ($5).

(b) Two dollars and <u>fifty</u> cents ($2.50) of the increase shall be deposited into the Alternative and Renewable Fuel and Vehicle Technology Fund created by Section 44273 of the Health and Safety Code, and two dollars and fifty cents ($2.50) shall be deposited into the Air Quality Improvement Fund created by Section 44274.5 of the Health and Safety Code.

(c) This section shall remain in effect only until January 1, <u>2024,</u> and as of that date is repealed, unless a later enacted statute, that is enacted before January 1, <u>2024,</u> deletes or extends that date. *(Added by Stats.2007, c. 750 (A.B.118), § 7. Amended by Stats.2013, c. 401 (A.B.8), § 38, eff. Sept. 28, 2013.)*

Repeal

For repeal of this section, see its terms.

§ 9262. Fees; license; special plates

(a) The fee for a license issued to dealers and lessor-retailers is as follows:

(1) For the original license, or an ownership change which requires a new application, except as provided by Section 42231, a nonrefundable fee of one hundred seventy-five dollars ($175).

(2) For the annual renewal of a license, a fee of one hundred twenty-five dollars ($125).

(3) If an alteration of an existing license is caused by a firm name change, address change, change in the corporate officer structure, or the addition of a branch location, a fee of seventy dollars ($70).

(b) The fee for a license issued to dismantlers, manufacturers, manufacturer branches, remanufacturers, remanufacturer branches, transporters, distributors, and distributor branches is as follows:

(1) For the original license, or an ownership change which requires a new application, except as provided by Section 42231, a nonrefundable fee of one hundred dollars ($100).

(2) For the annual renewal of a license, a fee of eighty-five dollars ($85).

(3) If an alteration of an existing license is caused by a firm name change, address change, or the addition of a branch location, a fee of fifty dollars ($50).

(4) If an alteration of an existing license is caused by a change in the corporate officer structure, a fee of seventy dollars ($70).

(c) The fee for a license issued to representatives is as follows:

(1) For the original license, or an ownership change which requires a new application, except as provided by Section 42231, a nonrefundable fee of fifty dollars ($50).

(2) For the annual renewal of a license, a fee of eighty-five dollars ($85).

(d) The fee for an autobroker's endorsement to a dealer's license is as follows:

(1) For the original endorsement, a nonrefundable fee of one hundred dollars ($100).

(2) For the annual renewal of the endorsement, a fee of seventy-five dollars ($75).

(e) When the holder of a license for which a fee is provided in this section applies for special plates as provided in subdivision (b) of Section 11505 or subdivision (b) of Section 11714, the fee for the plates and the annual renewal of the plates is the prevailing vehicle registration fee as set forth in Section 9250 for the period for which the special plates are issued or renewed.

(Added by Stats.1975, c. 182, p. 529, § 2, eff. July 5, 1975. Amended by Stats.1980, c. 608, p. 1676, § 1; Stats.1982, c. 1273, p. 4701, § 7; Stats.1983, c. 1286, § 22; Stats.1984, c. 499, § 1; Stats.1985, c. 1022, § 5; Stats.1990, c. 90 (A.B.2445), § 1, eff. May 9, 1990, operative July 1, 1990; Stats.1994, c. 1253 (A.B.3539), § 8; Stats.1995, c. 211 (A.B.770), § 3; Stats.2009, c. 556 (S.B.95), § 3.)

Cross References

Return of fees after rejection of application, see Vehicle Code § 42230.

§ 9262.5. Disposition of increase in fee by 2009 amendment of § 9262

It is the intent of the Legislature, in amending Section 9262 in 2009 to increase the fee for the annual renewal of the license of a dealer and of a lessor-retailer to one hundred twenty-five dollars ($125), that forty dollars ($40) of that fee shall, when appropriated, be utilized by the department for the investigation of those dealers and lessor-retailers who demonstrate the greatest potential for causing losses to consumers as shown by repeated consumer complaints, habitual violations of the requirements of their licenses, the issuance of a probationary license by the department, or a violation of other standards and criteria established by the department for these purposes. *(Added by Stats.1990, c. 90 (A.B.2445), § 2, eff. May 9, 1990. Amended by Stats.2009, c. 556 (S.B.95), § 4.)*

§ 9263. Investigation service fee

Any automobile dismantler who fails to comply with Section 11520, or any other person who fails to comply with Section 5500 or 11520, shall pay an investigation service fee of fifteen dollars ($15). *(Stats.1959, c. 3, p. 1587, § 9263. Amended by Stats.1961, c. 1640, p. 3579, § 2, operative Jan. 1, 1962; Stats.1963, c. 1106, p. 2565, § 2; Stats.1972, c. 791, p. 1405, § 1; Stats.1974, c. 613, p. 1460, § 3; Stats.1985, c. 1022, § 6.)*

§ 9264. Repealed by Stats.1982, c. 1273, p. 4702, § 9

§ 9265. Duplicates

Upon application for duplicates or substitutes as permitted under this code, the following fees shall be paid:

(a) For a duplicate certificate of ownership or registration card or equipment identification card $15

(b) For any duplicate license plates, except environmental license plates, or substitute plates, or equipment identification plate for the same vehicle 15

(Stats.1959, c. 3, p. 1587, § 9265. Amended by Stats.1967, c. 1717, p. 4280, § 4; Stats.1981, c. 541, p. 2181, § 30, eff. Sept. 17, 1981, operative Jan. 1, 1982; Stats.1982, c. 783, p. 3403, § 3; Stats.1984, c. 1077, § 9, operative July 1, 1985; Stats.2003, c. 719 (S.B.1055), § 17.)

Cross References

Applicability of this section to trolley coaches, see Vehicle Code § 21051.

Base fee amounts, adjustment of fees, see Vehicle Code § 1678.
Certificate of ownership, see Vehicle Code § 4450 et seq.
Domestic violence victims, application for new and different license plates, see Vehicle Code § 4467.
Duplicate driver's license, see Vehicle Code §§ 12815, 14901.
Duplicate environmental license plate fee, see Vehicle Code § 5106.
Duplicate plates, cards or certificates, issuance, see Vehicle Code § 4457 et seq.
Reflectorized license plates, issuance, see Vehicle Code § 4850.
Registration card, see Vehicle Code § 4450 et seq.
Registration card unavailable, waiver of fee, see Vehicle Code § 9706.1.

§ 9266. School bus lessors; temporary permit fee

The fee for a temporary permit issued under Section 5010 is one-tenth of the annual fees in Division 3 (commencing with Section 4000) of this code and Part 5 (commencing with Section 10701) of Division 2 of the Revenue and Taxation Code, for each calendar month that the vehicle is to be operated in this state. There shall be no proration of fees for any fraction of a calendar month. *(Added by Stats.1968, c. 871, p. 1664, § 2.)*

§ 9266.5. Privately owned schoolbuses; fee for temporary permit

The fee for a temporary permit issued under subdivision (b) of Section 9102.5 is one-tenth of the annual fees in Division 3 (commencing with Section 4000) of this code and Part 5 (commencing with Section 10701) of Division 2 of the Revenue and Taxation Code, for each calendar month that the vehicle is to be operated in this state. There shall be no proration of fees for any fraction of a calendar month. *(Added by Stats.1971, c. 1489, p. 2942, § 2, operative May 3, 1972. Amended by Stats.1980, c. 147, p. 345, § 3.)*

§ 9267. Repealed by Stats.1973, c. 889, p. 1655, § 39, urgency, eff. Sept. 28, 1973, operative March 8, 1976

§ 9268. Motorcycles; original registration

In addition to any other registration fee and notwithstanding Section 9559, an additional fee of one dollar ($1) shall be collected upon the original registration of a motorcycle pursuant to Section 4150.2. *(Added by Stats. 1970, c. 887, p. 1622, § 2, operative Jan. 1, 1972.)*

§ 9269. Automobile dismantlers; exemption from fees or penalties

A licensed automobile dismantler who acquires, for the purpose of dismantling, a vehicle of a type subject to registration under this code, and who complies with Section 11520, is not required to pay fees or penalties that would otherwise be required if that vehicle were to be currently registered. *(Added by Stats.1974, c. 613, p. 1460, § 4. Amended by Stats.1990, c. 1352 (A.B.2912), § 7, eff. Sept. 27, 1990, operative July 1, 1990.)*

260

§ 9270. Expedited service fees for initial registration, transfer, or issuance of duplicate certificate of ownership

(a) The department may charge a service fee of not more than fifteen dollars ($15), in addition to other fees payable under this code, for the expedited completion of any of the following services within 72 hours after receipt of a complete and proper application for the service:

(1) Initial registration of a vehicle.

(2) Transfer of registration of a vehicle.

(3) Issuance of a duplicate certificate of ownership.

(b) The services in subdivision (a) shall be available only at the department's headquarters office in Sacramento. *(Added by Stats.1983, c. 825, § 3, operative July 1, 1984. Amended by Stats.1984, c. 628, § 3, operative July 1, 1985; Stats.2004, c. 430 (A.B.2606), § 2.)*

§ 9271. Inspection fees; total loss salvage vehicles; dismantled vehicles

In addition to any other fees specified in this code, a fee sufficient to cover the department's costs for the inspections performed pursuant to Section 5505 shall be charged to register a vehicle which has been declared a total loss salvage vehicle pursuant to Section 11515 or which has been reported to have been dismantled pursuant to Section 5500 or 11520. *(Added by Stats.1988, c. 529, § 2. Amended by Stats.1989, c. 1360, § 155.)*

ARTICLE 3.   WEIGHT FEES

Section
9400.   Weight fees for commercial motor vehicles.
9400.1.   Additional fees for commercial motor vehicles with declared gross vehicle weight of 10,001 pounds or more; weight decals.
9400.3.   Cargo Theft Interdiction Program fees.
9400.4.   Weight fee revenue deposited in State Highway Account or Transportation Debt Service Fund; use.
9400.7.   Restricting by local agencies of hours of operation of trucks paying increased weight fees.
9400.8.   Local agency imposition of use fee or charge for use of streets or highways; effect of constitutional amendment; fees existing prior to June 1, 1989.
9401.   Vehicles manufactured in or prior to 1936.
9402.   Repealed.
9403.   Repealed.
9404.   Station wagons; exemption; option to pay by person engaged in a business.
9405.   Agricultural water-well boring rigs.
9406.   Alterations or additions to vehicles.
9406.1.   Vehicles operated at weight greater than declared gross vehicle weight; application and fees.
9407.   Reduction of fees; partial year registrations.
9408.   Credit for fees paid.
9409.   Forklift trucks.
9410.   Disabled person's exemption.

Display by contractor of business name and license number on motor vehicles used in construction business, see Business and Professions Code § 7029.6.

Plumbing contractor, required signs on commercial vehicles, see Business and Professions Code § 7029.5.

§ 9400.   Weight fees for commercial motor vehicles

Except as provided in Section 9400.1, and in addition to any other registration fee, there shall be paid the fees set forth in this section for the registration of any commercial motor vehicle that operates with unladen weight.   Weight fees for pickup trucks are calculated under this section.   Whenever a camper is temporarily attached to a motor vehicle designed to transport property, the motor vehicle shall be subject to the fees imposed by this section.   The camper shall be deemed to be a load, and fees imposed by this section upon the motor vehicle shall be based upon the unladen weight of the motor vehicle, exclusive of the camper.

(a) For any electric vehicle designed, used, or maintained as described in this section, fees shall be paid according to the following schedule:

Unladen Weight	Fee
Less than 6,000 lbs.	$ 87
6,000 lbs. or more but less than 10,000 lbs.	266
10,000 lbs. or more	358

(b) For any motor vehicle having not more than two axles and designed, used, or maintained as described in this section, other than an electric vehicle, fees shall be paid according to the following schedule:

Unladen Weight	Fee
Less than 3,000 lbs.	$ 8
3,000 lbs. to and including 4,000 lbs.	24
4,001 lbs. to and including 5,000 lbs.	80
5,001 lbs. to and including 6,000 lbs.	154
6,001 lbs. to and including 7,000 lbs.	204
7,001 lbs. to and including 8,000 lbs.	257
8,001 lbs. to and including 9,000 lbs.	308
9,001 lbs. to and including 10,000 lbs.	360

(c) For any motor vehicle having three or more axles designed, used, or maintained as described in this section, other than an electric vehicle, fees shall be paid according to the following schedule:

Unladen Weight	Fee
2,000 lbs. to and including 3,000 lbs.	$ 43
3,001 lbs. to and including 4,000 lbs.	77
4,001 lbs. to and including 5,000 lbs.	154
5,001 lbs. to and including 6,000 lbs.	231
6,001 lbs. to and including 7,000 lbs.	308
7,001 lbs. to and including 8,000 lbs.	385
8,001 lbs. to and including 9,000 lbs.	462
9,001 lbs. to and including 10,000 lbs.	539

(d) This section is not applicable to any vehicle that is operated or moved over the highway exclusively for the purpose of historical exhibition or other similar noncommercial purpose.

(e) The fee changes effected by this section apply to (1) initial or original registration on or after January 1, 1995, and prior to December 31, 2001, of any commercial vehicle never before registered in this state and (2) to renewal of registration of any commercial vehicle whose registration expires on or after January 1, 1995, and prior to December 31, 2001.

(f) Commercial vehicles, other than those specified in Section 9400.1, with an initial registration or renewal of registration that is due on or after December 31, 2001, are subject to the payment of fees specified in this section. *(Added by Stats.1989, c. 106, § 23, eff. July 10, 1989, operative July 1, 1994. Amended by Stats.2000, c. 861 (S.B.2084), § 49, eff. Sept. 29, 2000; Stats.2000, c. 973 (A.B.2749), § 3.5; Stats.2001, c. 826 (A.B.1472), § 25.)*

Additional fees for extra weight, see Vehicle Code § 9406.

Applicability of this section to trolley coaches, see Vehicle Code § 21051.

Credit for fees paid, see Vehicle Code § 9408.

Definitions,
   Axle, see Vehicle Code § 230.
   Commercial vehicle, see Vehicle Code § 260.
   Motor vehicle, see Vehicle Code § 415.
   Pole or pipe dolly, see Vehicle Code § 475.
   Semitrailer, see Vehicle Code § 550.
   Trailer, see Vehicle Code § 630.
   Unladen weight, see Vehicle Code § 660.

Disposition of fees collected under this section, see Vehicle Code § 42205.

Exemptions, weight fees for commercial vehicles, see Vehicle Code § 9107.

Filing after expiration of vehicle registration, penalty, see Vehicle Code § 4604.5.

License plates with distinguishing marks, see Vehicle Code § 5000.

Partial year payment of weight fees, see Vehicle Code § 9700 et seq.

Penalties for delinquency of fees, see Vehicle Code § 9554.

Penalty on application for original registration after date of expiration or date penalties due, see Vehicle Code § 9554.5.

Reduced fees for portion of year, see Vehicle Code § 9407.

Transportation Debt Service Fund, creation, use of moneys, Transportation Bond Direct Payment Account, state covenant regarding alteration, amendment, or restriction of specified provisions relating to transfer of weight fees, transfers to General Fund, see Government Code § 16965.

§ 9400.1.   Additional fees for commercial motor vehicles with declared gross vehicle weight of 10,001 pounds or more; weight decals

(a)(1) In addition to any other required fee, there shall be paid the fees set forth in this section for the registration of commercial motor vehicles operated either singly or in combination with a declared gross vehicle weight of 10,001 pounds or more. Pickup truck and electric vehicle weight fees are not calculated under this section.

(2) The weight of a vehicle issued an identification plate pursuant to an application under Section 5014, and the weight of an implement of husbandry as defined in

Section 36000, shall not be considered when calculating, pursuant to this section, the declared gross vehicle weight of a towing commercial motor vehicle that is owned and operated exclusively by a farmer or an employee of a farmer in the conduct of agricultural operations.

(3) Tow trucks that are utilized to render assistance to the motoring public or to tow or carry impounded vehicles shall pay fees in accordance with this section, except that the fee calculation shall be based only on the gross vehicle weight rating of the towing or carrying vehicle. Upon each initial or transfer application for registration of a tow truck described in this paragraph, the registered owner or lessee or that owner's or lessee's designee, shall certify to the department the gross vehicle weight rating of the tow truck:

Gross Vehicle Weight Range	Fee
10,001–15,000	$ 257
15,001–20,000	353
20,001–26,000	435
26,001–30,000	552
30,001–35,000	648
35,001–40,000	761
40,001–45,000	837
45,001–50,000	948
50,001–54,999	1,039
55,000–60,000	1,173
60,001–65,000	1,282
65,001–70,000	1,398
70,001–75,000	1,650
75,001–80,000	1,700

(b) The fees specified in subdivision (a) apply to both of the following:

(1) An initial or original registration occurring on or after December 31, 2001, to December 30, 2003, inclusive, of a commercial motor vehicle operated either singly or in combination with a declared gross vehicle weight of 10,001 pounds or more.

(2) The renewal of registration of a commercial motor vehicle operated either singly or in combination, with a declared gross vehicle weight of 10,001 pounds or more for which registration expires on or after December 31, 2001, to December 30, 2003, inclusive.

(c)(1) For both an initial or original registration occurring on or after December 31, 2003, of a commercial motor vehicle operated either singly or in combination with a declared gross vehicle weight of 10,001 pounds or more, and the renewal of registration of a commercial motor vehicle operated either singly or in combination, with a declared gross vehicle weight of 10,001 pounds or more for which registration expires on or after December 31, 2003, there shall be paid fees as follows:

Gross Vehicle Weight Range	Weight Code	Fee
10,001–15,000	A	$ 332
15,001–20,000	B	447
20,001–26,000	C	546
26,001–30,000	D	586
30,001–35,000	E	801
35,001–40,000	F	937

Gross Vehicle Weight Range	Weight Code	Fee
40,001–45,000	G	1,028
45,001–50,000	H	1,161
50,001–54,999	I	1,270
55,000–60,000	J	1,431
60,001–65,000	K	1,562
65,001–70,000	L	1,701
70,001–75,000	M	2,004
75,001–80,000	N	2,064

(2) For the purpose of obtaining "revenue neutrality" as described in Sections 1 and 59 of Senate Bill 2084 of the 1999–2000 Regular Session (Chapter 861 of the Statutes of 2000), the Director of Finance shall review the final 2003–04 Statement of Transactions of the State Highway Account. If that review indicates that the actual truck weight fee revenues deposited in the State Highway Account do not total at least seven hundred eighty-nine million dollars ($789,000,000), the Director of Finance shall instruct the department to adjust the schedule set forth in paragraph (1), but not to exceed the following fee amounts:

Gross Vehicle Weight Range	Weight Code	Fee
10,001–15,000	A	$ 354
15,001–20,000	B	482
20,001–26,000	C	591
26,001–30,000	D	746
30,001–35,000	E	874
35,001–40,000	F	1,024
40,001–45,000	G	1,125
45,001–50,000	H	1,272
50,001–54,999	I	1,393
55,000–60,000	J	1,571
60,001–65,000	K	1,716
65,001–70,000	L	1,870
70,001–75,000	M	2,204
75,001–80,000	N	2,271

(d)(1) In addition to the fees set forth in subdivision (a), a Cargo Theft Interdiction Program fee of three dollars ($3) shall be paid at the time of initial or original registration or renewal of registration of each motor vehicle subject to weight fees under this section.

(2) This subdivision does not apply to vehicles used or maintained for the transportation of persons for hire, compensation or profit, and tow trucks.

(3) For vehicles registered under Article 4 (commencing with Section 8050) of Chapter 4, the fee imposed under this subdivision shall be apportioned as required for registration fees under that article.

(4) Funds collected pursuant to the Cargo Theft Interdiction Program shall not be proportionately reduced for each month and shall be transferred to the Motor Carriers Safety Improvement Fund.

(e) Notwithstanding Section 42270 or any other provision of law, of the moneys collected by the department under this section, one hundred twenty-two dollars ($122) for each initial, original, and renewal registration shall be reported monthly to the Controller, and at the same time, deposited in the State Treasury to the credit of the Motor Vehicle Account in the State Transportation Fund. All other moneys collected by the department under this section shall be deposited to the credit of the State Highway Account in the State Transportation Fund, or directly to the credit of the Transportation Debt Service Fund as provided in paragraph (2) of subdivision (c) of Section 9400.4, as applicable. One hundred twenty-two dollars ($122) of the fee imposed under this section shall not be proportionately reduced for each month. For vehicles registered under Article 4 (commencing with Section 8050) of Chapter 4, the fee shall be apportioned as required for registration under that article.

(f)(1) The department, in consultation with the Department of the California Highway Patrol, shall design and make available a set of distinctive weight decals that reflect the declared gross combined weight or gross operating weight reported to the department at the time of initial registration, registration renewal, or when a weight change is reported to the department pursuant to Section 9406.1. A new decal shall be issued on each renewal or when the weight is changed pursuant to Section 9406.1. The decal for a tow truck that is subject to this section shall reflect the gross vehicle weight rating or weight code.

(2) The department may charge a fee, not to exceed ten dollars ($10), for the department's actual cost of producing and issuing each set of decals issued under paragraph (1).

(3) The weight decal shall be in sharp contrast to the background and shall be of a size, shape, and color that is readily legible during daylight hours from a distance of 50 feet.

(4) Each vehicle subject to this section shall display the weight decal on both the right and left sides of the vehicle.

(5) A person may not display upon a vehicle a decal issued pursuant to this subdivision that does not reflect the declared weight reported to the department.

(6) Notwithstanding subdivision (e) or any other provision of law, the moneys collected by the department under this subdivision shall be deposited in the State Treasury to the credit of the Motor Vehicle Account in the State Transportation Fund.

(7) This subdivision shall apply to vehicles subject to this section at the time of an initial registration, registration renewal, or reported weight change that occurs on or after July 1, 2004.

(8) The following shall apply to vehicles registered under the permanent fleet registration program pursuant to Article 9.5 (commencing with Section 5301) of Chapter 1:

(A) The department, in consultation with the Department of the California Highway Patrol, shall distinguish the weight decals issued to permanent fleet registration vehicles from those issued to other vehicles.

(B) The department shall issue the distinguishable weight decals only to the following:

(i) A permanent fleet registration vehicle that is registered with the department on January 1, 2005.

(ii) On and after January 1, 2005, a vehicle for which the department has an application for initial registration as a permanent fleet registration vehicle.

(iii) On and after January 1, 2005, a permanent fleet registration vehicle that has a weight change pursuant to Section 9406.1.

(C) The weight decal issued under this paragraph shall comply with the applicable provisions of paragraphs (1) to (6), inclusive. *(Added by Stats.2000, c. 861 (S.B.2084), § 50, eff. Sept. 29, 2000. Amended by Stats.2001, c. 825 (S.B.290), § 10; Stats.2001, c. 826 (A.B.1472), § 26.5; Stats.2003, c. 719 (S.B.1055), § 17.5; Stats.2004, c. 183 (A.B.3082), § 348; Stats.2004, c. 615 (S.B.1233), § 23; Stats.2005, c. 22 (S.B.1108), § 197; Stats.2013, c. 35 (S.B.85), § 13, eff. June 27, 2013.)*

Cross References

Filing after expiration of vehicle registration, penalty, see Vehicle Code § 4604.5.
Penalties for delinquency of fees, see Vehicle Code § 9554.
Penalty on application for original registration after date of expiration or date penalties due, see Vehicle Code § 9554.5.
State Highway Account revenues derived from weight fees, use of revenues to make remaining authorized bond debt service reimbursement and loans to the General Fund, see Streets and Highways Code § 2103.
Transportation Debt Service Fund, creation, use of moneys, Transportation Bond Direct Payment Account, state covenant regarding alteration, amendment, or restriction of specified provisions relating to transfer of weight fees, transfers to General Fund, see Government Code § 16965.

§ 9400.3. Cargo Theft Interdiction Program fees

(a) In order to ensure that Chapter 973 of the Statutes of 2000 is implemented as originally intended by the Legislature, the department may not assess the Cargo Theft Interdiction Program fee upon any commercial motor vehicle that has a declared gross vehicle weight of less than 10,001 pounds.

(b) The department shall issue refunds of, or credits for, any Cargo Theft Interdiction Program fee that is assessed upon a vehicle that does not meet the minimum weights described in Section 9400.1 or is a pickup truck or an electric vehicle. *(Added by Stats.2001, c. 826 (A.B. 1472), § 27. Amended by Stats.2004, c. 183 (A.B.3082), § 349.)*

§ 9400.4. Weight fee revenue deposited in State Highway Account or Transportation Debt Service Fund; use

Weight fee revenue deposited into the State Highway Account pursuant to subdivision (e) of Section 9400.1 and subdivision (a) of Section 42205 net of amounts appropriated for other purposes pursuant to subdivision (b) of Section 42205, and weight fee revenues deposited directly into the Transportation Debt Service Fund pursuant to subdivision (e) of Section 9400.1 and subdivision (a) of Section 42205, as applicable, shall be used as follows:

(a) For the 2010–11 fiscal year, seven hundred fifty-six million three hundred ninety-six thousand dollars ($756,-396,000) is hereby appropriated from weight fee revenues in the State Highway Account for transfer to the General Fund as transportation bond debt service reimbursement and loans as follows:

(1) The Controller shall transfer all weight fee revenues deposited into the State Highway Account in any month to the Transportation Debt Service Fund for transfer to the General Fund as reimbursement for debt service costs until all of the debt service paid on transportation bonds for projects that the Director of Finance indicates qualify for reimbursement as provided for in Section 16965 of the Government Code have been reimbursed.

(2) After the Director of Finance has notified the Controller that all debt service costs for the 2010–11 fiscal year have been reimbursed, the Controller shall transfer any remaining monthly weight fee revenues in the State Highway Account to the General Fund as a loan until the full amount appropriated in this subdivision has been transferred to the General Fund. The Director of Finance may repay any remaining portion of the outstanding balance of this loan in any year in which the Director of Finance determines the funds are needed to reimburse the General Fund for current year transportation bond debt service or to redeem or retire those bonds, pursuant to Section 16774 of the Government Code, maturing in a subsequent fiscal year, provided that the loans shall be repaid no later than June 30, 2021. All funds loaned pursuant to this section, upon repayment to the State Highway Account, shall be immediately transferred by the Controller to the Transportation Debt Service Fund for use pursuant to Section 16965 of the Government Code.

(3) By June 15, 2011, the Director of Finance in consultation with the Treasurer shall notify the Controller regarding the final amount of debt service paid from the General Fund during the 2010–11 fiscal year pursuant to Section 16965 of the Government Code and shall direct the Controller to reverse and adjust any transfers made as debt service reimbursements or loans so that a maximum amount of transfers are made for debt service reimbursements and with any loan amounts limited to the difference between this amount and the total amount appropriated in this subdivision. The total amount of weight fee revenues transferred from the State Highway Account for the 2010–11 fiscal year shall not be greater than the total amount of weight fee revenues deposited into the State Highway Account for that year.

(4) With respect to transfers or portions of transfers that cannot be made in any given month if weight fee revenues are insufficient, the first weight fee revenues available in the following month or months shall be used to complete the transfers for the previous month or

months prior to making additional transfers for later months.

(b) For the 2011–12 fiscal year, all revenue generated from weight fees in the State Highway Account, as determined by Sections 9400.1 and 42205, excluding an amount equal to the loan of forty-three million seven hundred thousand dollars ($43,700,000) authorized pursuant to Item 2660–013–0042 of Section 2.00 of the Budget Act of 2011, is hereby appropriated for transfer to the General Fund as debt service reimbursement and loans as follows:

(1) The Controller shall transfer all weight fee revenues deposited into the State Highway Account in any month to the Transportation Debt Service Fund for transfer to the General Fund as reimbursement for debt service costs until all of the debt service paid on transportation bonds for projects that the Director of Finance indicates qualify for reimbursement as provided for in Section 16965 of the Government Code have been reimbursed.

(2) After the Director of Finance has notified the Controller that all debt service costs for the 2011–12 fiscal year have been reimbursed, the Controller shall transfer any remaining weight fee revenues for that fiscal year in the State Highway Account to the General Fund as a loan until all weight fee revenues for that fiscal year appropriated in this subdivision have been transferred to the General Fund, excluding forty-two million dollars ($42,-000,000), which shall be transferred to the General Fund as a loan on July 1, 2012. The Director of Finance may repay any portion of the balance of this loan in any year in which the Director of Finance determines the funds are needed to reimburse the General Fund for current year transportation bond debt service or to redeem or retire those bonds, pursuant to Section 16774 of the Government Code, maturing in a subsequent year, provided that the loans shall be repaid no later than June 30, 2021. All funds loaned pursuant to this section, upon repayment to the State Highway Account, shall be immediately transferred by the Controller to the Transportation Debt Service Fund for use pursuant to Section 16965 of the Government Code.

(3) By June 15, 2012, the Director of Finance in consultation with the Treasurer shall notify the Controller regarding the final amount of debt service paid from the General Fund during the 2011–12 fiscal year pursuant to Section 16965 of the Government Code and shall direct the Controller to reverse and adjust any transfers made as debt service reimbursements or loans so that a maximum amount of transfers are made for debt service reimbursements and with any loan amounts limited to the difference between this amount and the total amount appropriated in this subdivision. The total amount of weight fee revenues transferred from the State Highway Account for the 2011–12 fiscal year shall not be greater than the total amount of weight fee revenues deposited into the State Highway Account in that year.

(4) With respect to transfers or portions of transfers that cannot be made in any given month if weight fee revenues are insufficient, the first weight fee revenues available in the following month or months shall be used to complete the transfers for the previous month or months prior to making additional transfers for later months.

(c)(1)(A) Until the month of first issuance of designated bonds as defined in subdivision (c) of Section 16773 of the Government Code, and at any time thereafter that a Treasurer's certification pursuant to subparagraph (B) of paragraph (3) of subdivision (a) of Section 16965 of the Government Code applies, all weight fee revenues subject to this section in any month shall be transferred from the State Highway Account to the Transportation Debt Service Fund.

(B) Except as provided in paragraph (3), or when subparagraph (A) applies pursuant to a Treasurer's certification, upon the first issuance of designated bonds, as defined in subdivision (c) of Section 16773 of the Government Code, starting in the month following that first issuance, all weight fee revenues received by the Controller from the first day through the 14th day of every month shall be transferred from the State Highway Account to the Transportation Debt Service Fund.

* * * (C) All funds transferred pursuant to subparagraphs (A) and (B) are hereby appropriated for transfer to the General Fund by the Controller as reimbursement for debt service costs paid with respect to eligible bonds described in subparagraph (A) of paragraph (2) of subdivision (a) of Section 16965 of the Government Code, until all * * * debt service * * * that the Director of Finance indicates qualifies for reimbursement as provided for in subdivision (d), (e), or (f) of Section 16965 of the Government Code has been reimbursed, or to redeem or retire bonds, pursuant to Section 16774 of the Government Code, as referenced in subdivision * * * (d), (e), or (f) of Section 16965 of the Government Code, that are maturing in a subsequent year. After the Director of Finance has notified the Controller that all debt service costs for the fiscal year have been reimbursed, the Controller shall transfer any remaining revenue generated from weight fees subject to this section for that fiscal year in the State Highway Account to the General Fund as a loan. The Director of Finance may repay any portion of the balance of this loan in any year in which the Director of Finance determines that the funds are needed to reimburse the General Fund for current year transportation bond debt service or to redeem or retire those bonds pursuant to Section 16774 of the Government Code, maturing in a future fiscal year, provided that the loans shall be repaid no later than June 30, 2021. All funds loaned pursuant to this section, upon repayment to the State Highway Account, shall be immediately transferred by the Controller to the Transportation Debt Service Fund for use pursuant to Section 16965 of the Government Code. By June 15 of each year, the Director of Finance, in consultation with the Treasurer, shall notify the Controller regarding the final amount of debt service paid from the General Fund during that fiscal year pursuant to subdivision (d), (e), or (f) of Section 16965 of the Government Code and shall direct the Controller to reverse or adjust any transfers made as debt service reimbursements or loans so that a maximum amount of transfers are made for debt service reimbursements and with any loan amounts limited to the difference between this amount and the total amount of revenue for that fiscal year generated from weight fees, as determined by Sections 9400.1 and 42205. The total amount of weight fee revenues transferred from the State Highway Account in any fiscal year shall not be greater than the total amount of weight fee revenues deposited into the State Highway Account in that year.

(2) Starting in the month following the first issuance of any designated bonds, unless a Treasurer's certification pursuant to subparagraph (B) of paragraph (3) of subdivision (a) of Section 16965 of the Government Code applies, all weight fee revenues subject to this section that are received by the Controller from the 15th day of every month, or the first business day thereafter if not a business day, through the last day of the month shall be deposited directly in the Transportation Debt Service Fund and are hereby appropriated for transfer as follows:

(A) First, to the Transportation Bond Direct Payment Account as set forth in subdivision (b) of Section 16965 of the Government Code, to provide for payment of debt service with respect to designated bonds.

(B) Thereafter, as provided in subparagraph (C) of paragraph (1).

(3) Notwithstanding paragraphs (1) and (2), if by the last day of a month the transfer for that month relating to designated bonds required by the Treasurer's certificate described in subdivision (b) of Section 16965 of the Government Code has not been made due to insufficient weight fee revenue, weight fee revenue shall continue to be transferred pursuant to paragraph (2) beginning with the first day of the subsequent month and continuing every day until such time as sufficient revenue for full compliance with the certificate has been transferred.

* * * (4) Except as otherwise provided in paragraph (1), (2), or (3), with respect to any transfers or portions of transfers that cannot be made in any given month if weight fee revenues are insufficient, the first weight fee revenues available in the following month or months shall be used to complete the transfers for the previous month or months prior to making additional transfers for later months. *(Added by Stats.2011, c. 6 (A.B.105), § 35, eff. March 24, 2011. Amended by Stats.2011, c. 38 (A.B.115), § 7, eff. June 30, 2011; Stats.2012, c. 22 (A.B.1465), § 7, eff. June 27, 2012; Stats.2013, c. 35 (S.B.85), § 14, eff. June 27, 2013.)*

Cross References

Disposition of weight fees for commercial vehicles, see Vehicle Code § 42205.

State Highway Account revenues derived from weight fees, use of revenues to make remaining authorized bond debt service reimbursement and loans to the General Fund, see Streets and Highways Code § 2103.

§ 9400.7. Restricting by local agencies of hours of operation of trucks paying increased weight fees

(a) Notwithstanding any other provision of law, except for restrictions in existence on June 1, 1989, and except as provided in subdivision (d), so long as any increases in the weight fees required by Section 9400, as enacted by Assembly Bill 471 of the 1989–90 Regular Session, remain in effect, no local agency located within an urbanized area within a county which is required to prepare a congestion management plan pursuant to Section 65089 of the Government Code may restrict the hours of operation on any street or highway which is otherwise open to truck use unless the local agency determines that the restriction is consistent with the adopted congestion management plan and is coordinated with adjacent local agencies so as to not unreasonably interfere with truck operations.

(b) If an inconsistency in access occurs between cities and counties, the inconsistent access provisions of the congestion management plan may be appealed to the California Transportation Commission. The commission shall review the inconsistent access plan and make a finding within 90 days of the appeal being filed. If the commission fails to make a finding within 90 days, the Director of Transportation shall review the issue and make a finding within 30 days.

(c) The access provisions of the congestion management plan shall not go into effect while an appeal is being made. If the commission makes a finding of inconsistency, the access provisions of the congestion management plan shall not become operative.

(d) (1) This section does not apply to Los Angeles County if the City of Los Angeles establishes restrictions on the hours of operation on any street or highway which is otherwise open to truck use.

(2) If the City of Los Angeles establishes restrictions under paragraph (1) and any other city in the County of Los Angeles establishes restrictions on the hours of operation on any street or highway which is otherwise open to truck use, the restrictions in that other city shall conform to the restrictions imposed by the City of Los Angeles, except that the other city may appeal noncomforming restrictions to the commission pursuant to subdivision (b) for a determination as to whether a variance from this paragraph should be granted.

(3) The Legislature finds and declares that, because of unique and special traffic congestion problems in the County of Los Angeles and in the City of Los Angeles, the general provisions of this section cannot be made applicable to that county. (Added by Stats.1989, c. 1337, § 1.)

266

§ 9400.8. Local agency imposition of use fee or charge for use of streets or highways; effect of constitutional amendment; fees existing prior to June 1, 1989

Notwithstanding any other provision of law, if the voters approve Senate Constitutional Amendment 1 of the 1989–90 Regular Session, no local agency may impose a tax, permit fee, or other charge for the privilege of using its streets or highways, other than a permit fee for extra legal loads, after December 31, 1990, unless the local agency had imposed the fee prior to June 1, 1989. (Added by Stats.1989, c. 1337, § 2.)

§ 9401. Vehicles manufactured in or prior to 1936

(a) Motor vehicles manufactured in or prior to 1936, are exempted from the payment of the weight fees provided for in Section 9400.

(b) Notwithstanding subdivision (a), any person who owns and operates a commercial vehicle manufactured in or prior to 1936 which is registered to such person, may pay the appropriate weight fees, and the department shall issue license plates of the same type as are issued to vehicles which are required to pay weight fees for such vehicles. (Added by Stats.1980, c. 622, p. 1706, § 3.)

Cross References

Exemptions, weight fees for commercial vehicles, see Vehicle Code § 9107.

§ 9402. Repealed by Stats.1981, c. 636, p. 2404, § 5

§ 9403. Repealed by Stats.1963, c. 2149, p. 4487, § 12

§ 9404. Station wagons; exemption; option to pay by person engaged in a business

(a) Station wagons, except those used in the transportation of passengers for hire, are exempted from the payment of weight fees provided for in Section 9400.

Any provision of this code notwithstanding, any person (1) who is bona fide engaged in a business and who owns and operates a station wagon which is registered in the name of such business, or (2) who is bona fide engaged in a business as an employee and who is required by such employment to own and operate a station wagon, which is registered to such person, may pay the appropriate weight fees, and the department shall issue license plates of the same type as are issued to vehicles which are required to pay weight fees.

(b) For purposes of this section, "engaged in a business" means engaged in a bona fide trade, business,,[1] commerce, or in a profession in which the measurement of land, construction quantities, or the dimension of structures, is a function authorized to be performed by the license issued for such profession, but does not include being engaged in any other type of profession. (Stats.1959, c. 3, p. 1590, § 9404. Amended by Stats.1959, c. 6, p. 1838, § 8; Stats.1961, c. 1909, p. 4027, § 1;

Stats.1970, c. 1226, p. 2146, § 1; Stats.1975, c. 531, p. 1097, § 1.)

[1] So in enrolled bill.

§ 9405. Agricultural water-well boring rigs

Agricultural water-well boring rigs are exempt from the fees provided in Section 9400. *(Stats.1959, c. 3, p. 1590, § 9405.)*

§ 9406. Alterations or additions to vehicles

Alterations or additions to registered vehicles for which fees have been paid under Section 9400 or 9400.1 placing the vehicles in weight fee classifications under Section 9400 or 9400.1 greater than the weight fees previously paid shall be reported to the department and at the same time the difference between the weight fee previously paid, reduced as provided in Section 9407, and the greater weight fee, reduced as provided in Section 9407, shall be paid to the department upon the operation of the vehicles in the greater weight fee classification under Section 9400 or 9400.1. *(Stats.1959, c. 3, p. 1590, § 9406. Amended by Stats.2000, c. 861 (S.B.2084), § 51, eff. Sept. 29, 2000.)*

§ 9406.1. Vehicles operated at weight greater than declared gross vehicle weight; application and fees

Prior to operation of a vehicle at a declared gross vehicle weight greater than reported to, and registered by, the department, the owner shall make application to the department and pay all appropriate fees. *(Added by Stats.2000, c. 861 (S.B.2084), § 52, eff. Sept. 29, 2000.)*

§ 9407. Reduction of fees; partial year registrations

The fee required under Section 9400 and 9400.1 shall be reduced proportionately for each month which has elapsed since the expiration of the last issued registration certificate if either of the following applies:

(a) Application for registration is made after the first month of any registration year and a certification was filed pursuant to subdivision (a) of Section 4604.

(b) Application for registration of a vehicle registered on a partial year basis is made after the first month

following expiration and a certification was filed pursuant to subdivision (b) of Section 9706. *(Added by Stats.1991, c. 362 (A.B.1974), § 4, eff. Aug. 30, 1991. Amended by Stats.1992, c. 1243 (A.B.3090), § 69, eff. Sept. 30, 1992; Stats.2001, c. 826 (A.B.1472), § 28.)*

§ 9408. Credit for fees paid

(a) Whenever any registered commercial vehicle, including, but not limited to, any commercial vehicle operating in California with apportioned registration, for which fees have been paid under Section 9400 or 9400.1 is withdrawn from service in this state before the expiration of the registration, the owner may surrender the registration card and license plates previously issued for the vehicle to the department and, within 90 days of the time of withdrawal, make application for the registration of another commercial vehicle which is subject to the fees specified in Section 9400 or 9400.1. If the vehicle that is withdrawn from service is operating in this state under Article 4 (commencing with Section 8050 of Chapter 4, credit for any unused fees paid under Section 9400 or 9400.1 may be applied only to a commercial vehicle concurrently added to the same apportioned fleet.

(b) Under the circumstances described in subdivision (a), and upon a proper showing of the facts, the department upon determining the fees payable under this division shall allow as credit thereon the unexpired portion, as of the month of the application, of the fee paid under Section 9400 or 9400.1 for the previous registration, but, in addition to fees otherwise payable under this division less any credit, shall charge and collect an additional fee of two dollars ($2) for issuance of the new registration. *(Stats.1959, c. 3, p. 1590, § 9408. Amended by Stats.2000, c. 861 (S.B.2084), § 53, eff. Sept. 29, 2000; Stats.2001, c. 826 (A.B.1472), § 29.)*

§ 9409. Forklift trucks

Any forklift truck which is designed primarily for loading and unloading and for stacking materials and is operated or drawn along a highway unladen is exempt from the provisions of Section 9400. *(Added by Stats. 1963, c. 1395, p. 2935, § 1.)*

§ 9410. Disabled person's exemption

(a) One commercial vehicle weighing less than 8,001 pounds unladen, which displays the distinguishing license plate designated in, and is registered to a person who qualifies for the exemption provided by, Section 22511.5, is exempt from the weight fees provided for in Section 9400.

(b) A commercial vehicle displaying a distinguishing placard pursuant to Section 22511.5 is not exempt from weight fees. *(Added by Stats.1969, c. 812, p. 1634, § 1. Amended by Stats.1970, c. 923, p. 1676, § 1; Stats.1974, c. 234, p. 440, § 1; Stats.1978, c. 560, p. 1735, § 2; Stats.1992, c. 1243 (A.B.3090), § 70, eff. Sept. 30, 1992; Stats.2001, c. 825 (S.B.290), § 11; Stats.2004, c. 404 (S.B.1725), § 10.)*

ARTICLE 4.　PAYMENT OF FEES

Section
9550.　Fees for license or special plates.
9551.　Automobile dismantlers.
9551.1.　Repealed.
9551.2.　Offset amounts.
9552.　Delinquent fees.
9553.　Penalties for delinquency.
9553.5.　Delinquency fees for vehicles subject to apportioned registration; time to comply; penalty.
9553.7.　Delinquent transfer penalty.
9554.　Computation of penalty.
9554.1.　Reduction of penalty.
9554.2.　Commercial vehicles operated at greater gross vehicle weight than reported; new registration application.
9554.5.　Penalty on application for original registration after date of expiration or date penalties due.
9555.　Delinquent trailer coach fees.
9556.　Application through motor club; date of delinquency.
9557.　Transmittal of fees by mail.
9558.　Bad check in payment of fee or penalty; redeposit.
9558.5.　Repealed.
9559.　Computation of fees.
9559.5.　Apportionment of Renewal fee.
9560.　Waiver of penalties for late payment of registration renewal fees; definitions; application of section.
9561.　Waiver of renewal penalties on repossessed vehicle or sale at auction of repossessed vehicle.
9561.5.　Waiver of renewal penalties on auction sale of leased vehicle.
9562.　Waiver of penalties and registration fees; transferred vehicles' registration fees and penalties.
9563.　Rebuilt and restored passenger vehicle; registration application and fees.
9564.　Scrap metal processor; compliance with code; certificate of nonoperation or fees not required; reconstruction.
9565.　Repealed.

§ 9550.　Fees for license or special plates

All fees required to be paid by a vehicle dealer, manufacturer, manufacturer branch, remanufacturer, remanufacturer branch, distributor, distributor branch, representative, or transporter, in accordance with this code, for any license or special plates shall be paid at the time application is made to the department. *(Stats.1959, c. 3, p. 1590, § 9550. Amended by Stats.1971, c. 1214, p. 2341, § 3, operative May 3, 1972; Stats.1973, c. 996, p. 1972, § 18, operative July 1, 1974; Stats.1974, c. 384, p. 956, § 9, eff. July 5, 1974, operative July 1, 1974; Stats.1983, c. 1286, § 23.)*

268

Cross References

Applicability of this section to trolley coaches, see Vehicle Code § 21051.
Dealer defined, see Vehicle Code §§ 285, 286.
Distributor branch defined, see Vehicle Code § 297.
Distributor defined, see Vehicle Code § 296.
Lien for fees and penalties, see Vehicle Code § 9800.
Manufacturer branch defined, see Vehicle Code § 389.
Penalties, see Vehicle Code §§ 9553, 9554.
Remanufacturer defined, see Vehicle Code § 507.8.
Representative defined, see Vehicle Code § 512.
Time for payment of vehicle license fee, see Revenue and Taxation Code § 10851.
Transporter defined, see Vehicle Code § 645.
Vehicle manufacturer defined, see Vehicle Code § 672.

§ 9551.　Automobile dismantlers

All fees required to be paid by an automobile dismantler, in accordance with this code, for any license, or special plates, shall be paid at the time application is made to the department. *(Stats.1959, c. 3, p. 1591, § 9551. Amended by Stats.1961, c. 1640, p. 3580, § 4, operative Jan. 1, 1962; Stats.1963, c. 1106, p. 2566, § 4; Stats.1971, c. 1214, p. 2341, § 4, operative May 3, 1972.)*

Cross References

Definitions,
　Automobile dismantler, see Vehicle Code § 220.
　Department, see Vehicle Code §§ 290, 2101, 21000.
Fee, lien upon vehicle, see Vehicle Code § 9800.
Penalties for delinquent fees, see Vehicle Code §§ 9553, 9554.

§ 9551.1.　Repealed by Stats.1998, c. 322 (A.B.2797), § 103, eff. Aug. 20, 1998, operative July 1, 1999

§ 9551.2.　Offset amounts

(a) When an application is made for a renewal or initial registration of a vehicle, the department shall apply the amount of any operative offset established by subdivision (a) of Section 10754 of the Revenue and Taxation Code. The department shall alter its billing notice for vehicle license fees to indicate the amount of the vehicle license fee for each vehicle as calculated under Section 10752 or 10752.1 of the Revenue and Taxation Code, or under Section 18115 of the Health and Safety Code, and the amount of the applicable offset as required by subdivision (a) of Section 10754 of the Revenue and Taxation Code. The amount of the offset shall be identified on the billing notice as the "VLF Offset." The Department of Motor Vehicles shall, as required by Section 11000 of the Revenue and Taxation Code, provide information to the Controller with respect to the amount of offsets subject to this subdivision.

(b) This section shall become operative on July 1, 1999, or on that earlier date that is determined by both the director of the department, and the Director of the Department of Housing and Community Development, to be feasible for the implementation of this section. *(Added by Stats.1998, c. 322 (A.B.2797), § 104, eff. Aug. 20, 1998.)*

§ 9552. Delinquent fees

(a) Whenever any vehicle is operated upon any highway of this state without the fees first having been paid as required by this code, and those fees have not been paid within 20 days of its first operation, those fees are delinquent, except as provided in subdivision (b).

(b) Fees are delinquent whenever application for renewal of registration, or any application for renewal of special license plates, is made after midnight of the expiration date of the registration or special plates, or 60 days after the date the registered owner is notified by the department pursuant to Section 1661, whichever is later.

(c) Whenever any person has received as transferee a properly endorsed certificate of ownership and the transfer fee has not been paid as required by this code within 10 days, the fee is delinquent.

(d) Whenever any person becomes an automobile dismantler, dealer, manufacturer, manufacturer branch, distributor, distributor branch, or transporter without first having paid the license and special plate fees as required by this code, the fees are delinquent. *(Stats.1959, c. 3, p. 1591, § 9552. Amended by Stats.1963, c. 1106, p. 2566, § 5; Stats.1967, c. 1064, p. 2693, § 3; Stats.1973, c. 996, p. 1972, § 19, operative July 1, 1974; Stats.1988, c. 1268, § 10; Stats.1992, c. 1241 (S.B.1615), § 13.5; Stats.2002, c. 805 (A.B.2996), § 13, eff. Sept. 23, 2002.)*

Cross References

Applicability of section to trolley coaches, see Vehicle Code § 21051.

Automobile dismantler, payment of fees, see Vehicle Code § 9551.

Delinquent license fee, see Revenue and Taxation Code § 10853 et seq.

Fees for transfer of registration, see Vehicle Code § 9255.

Licenses or temporary permits, automobile dismantlers, see Vehicle Code §§ 9262, 11500, 11502.

Registration of trailer coaches, nonapplicability of this section, see Vehicle Code § 5351.

§ 9553. Penalties for delinquency

(a) A penalty shall be added upon any delinquent application as provided in Section 9552, except as provided in Section 4604 or 9706, or in subdivision (b).

(b) When renewal fee penalties have not accrued with respect to a vehicle and the vehicle is transferred, the transferee has 20 days from the date of the transfer to pay the registration fees which become due without payment of penalties or to file a certification pursuant to subdivision (a) of Section 4604 if the vehicle will not be operated, moved, or left standing upon any highway during the subsequent registration year, except as provided in subdivision (c).

(c)(1) A dealer or lessor-retailer submitting an application for registration or transfer of a used vehicle shall have 30 days from the date of sale to submit the fees, without the penalty that otherwise would be required under subdivision (a).

(2) This subdivision does not apply to penalties due or accrued prior to the date of sale by the dealer or lessor-retailer.

(d) A penalty shall be added if the fees specified in Section 9255 are not paid within 20 days after they become delinquent.

(e) In addition to the imposition of monetary fines or fees as specified in this section, delinquent registration may result in impoundment of the vehicle pursuant to Section 22651. *(Added by Stats.1974, c. 1330, p. 2895, § 22, eff. Sept. 26, 1974, operative March 8, 1976. Amended by Stats.1982, c. 1273, p. 4702, § 10; Stats.1990, c. 1352 (A.B.2912), § 9, eff. Sept. 27, 1990, operative July 1, 1990; Stats.1991, c. 362 (A.B.1974), § 5, eff. Aug. 30, 1991; Stats.1992, c. 1243 (A.B.3090), § 71, eff. Sept. 30, 1992; Stats.1998, c. 600 (S.B.619), § 3; Stats.1999, c. 22 (S.B.24), § 6.2, eff. May 26, 1999, operative July 1, 1999; Stats.2002, c. 805 (A.B.2996), § 14, eff. Sept. 23, 2002.)*

Cross References

Applicability of this section to trolley coaches, see Vehicle Code § 21051.

Lien for penalties, see Vehicle Code § 9800.

Penalties accrued before purchase, waiver, see Vehicle Code § 9562.

Proportionate registration and licensing, see Vehicle Code § 8050 et seq.

Renewal of registration, see Vehicle Code § 4600 et seq.

Report and deposit of money received by Departments of Motor Vehicles and California Highway Patrol, see Vehicle Code § 42270.

Special license plates, see Vehicle Code § 5000 et seq.

Waiver of penalties on repossessed vehicle, see Vehicle Code § 9561.

§ 9553.5. Delinquency fees for vehicles subject to apportioned registration; time to comply; penalty

(a) Whenever fees have not been paid in full for an application for registration of vehicles registered pursuant to Article 4 (commencing with Section 8050) of Chapter 4, the registrant shall have 20 days from the date of notice by the department to pay the balance of the fees due.

(b) Failure to pay the balance of the fees due within 20 days shall subject the application to penalties, as defined in Sections 9554 and 9554.5, on the unpaid portion of the California fees due. *(Added by Stats.2002, c. 758 (A.B. 3024), § 8. Amended by Stats.2008, c. 756 (A.B.268), § 20, eff. Sept. 30, 2008.)*

§ 9553.7. Delinquent transfer penalty

The penalty for delinquency with respect to any transfer is fifteen dollars ($15) and applies only to the last transfer. *(Added by Stats.2008, c. 756 (A.B.268), § 21, eff. Sept. 30, 2008.)*

§ 9554. Computation of penalty

(a)(1) A penalty shall be added on any application for renewal of registration made later than midnight of the date of expiration or on or after the date penalties

269

become due. Penalties shall be computed as provided in Section 9559 and shall be collected with the fee.

(2) Notwithstanding paragraph (1), commencing on July 1, 2011, a penalty shall not be added if an application for renewal of registration, or an application for renewal of special license plates, is made within 30 days after midnight of the expiration date of the registration or special plates. This paragraph shall become inoperative on January 1, 2012.

(b) The penalty assessment for the delinquent payment of the registration fee specified in Section 9250 shall be as follows:

(1) Ten dollars ($10) for a delinquency period of 10 days or less.

(2) Fifteen dollars ($15) for a delinquency period of more than 10 days, to and including 30 days.

(3) Thirty dollars ($30) for a delinquency period of more than 30 days, to and including one year.

(4) Fifty dollars ($50) for a delinquency period of more than one year, to and including two years.

(5) One hundred dollars ($100) for a delinquency period of more than two years.

(c) The penalty assessment for the delinquent payment of the weight fee specified in Section 9400 or 9400.1 and the vehicle license fee as specified in Section 10751 of the Revenue and Taxation Code shall be as follows:

(1) Ten percent of the vehicle license fee, or the combined amount of the vehicle license fee and the weight fee if the vehicle is subject to both fees, for a delinquency period of 10 days or less.

(2) Twenty percent of the vehicle license fee, or the combined amount of the vehicle license fee and the weight fee if the vehicle is subject to both fees, for a delinquency period of more than 10 days, to and including 30 days.

(3) Sixty percent of the vehicle license fee, or the combined amount of the vehicle license fee and the weight fee if the vehicle is subject to both fees, for a delinquency period of more than 30 days, to and including one year.

(4) Eighty percent of the vehicle license fee, or the combined amount of the vehicle license fee and the weight fee if the vehicle is subject to both fees, for a delinquency period of more than one year, to and including two years.

(5) One hundred sixty percent of the vehicle license fee, or the combined amount of the vehicle license fee and the weight fee if the vehicle is subject to both fees, for a delinquency period of more than two years.

(d) On or after January 1, 2003, a penalty assessment for weight fees not reported and not paid within 20 days as required by Section 9406 shall be applied to the difference in the weight fee as follows:

(1) Ten percent of the fee for a delinquency period of 10 days or less.

(2) Twenty percent of the fee for a delinquency period more than 10 days, to and including 30 days.

(3) Sixty percent of the fee for a delinquency period more than 30 days, to and including one year.

(4) Eighty percent of the fee for a delinquency period more than one year, to and including two years.

(5) One hundred sixty percent for a delinquency period more than two years.

(e) A single penalty assessment for the delinquent payment of the fees specified in Sections 9250.8 and 9250.13 shall be as follows:

(1) Ten dollars ($10) for a delinquency period of 10 days or less.

(2) Fifteen dollars ($15) for a delinquency period of more than 10 days, to and including 30 days.

(3) Thirty dollars ($30) for a delinquency period of more than 30 days, to and including one year.

(4) Fifty dollars ($50) for a delinquency period of more than one year, to and including two years.

(5) One hundred dollars ($100) for a delinquency period of more than two years.

(6) This subdivision applies to the renewal of registration for vehicles with expiration dates on or after December 1, 2008. *(Added by Stats.2008, c. 756 (A.B. 268), § 23, eff. Sept. 30, 2008, operative Jan. 1, 2009. Amended by Stats.2011, c. 21 (S.B.94), § 6, eff. May 4, 2011.)*

§ 9554.1. Reduction of penalty

The amount of any penalty calculated pursuant to Section 9554 or subdivision (b) of Section 18116 of the Health and Safety Code shall be reduced by the amount of any offset implemented pursuant to Section 10754 of the Revenue and Taxation Code, or any portion of the amount of that offset. *(Added by Stats.1998, c. 322 (A.B.2797), § 105, eff. Aug. 20, 1998.)*

§ 9554.2. Commercial vehicles operated at greater gross vehicle weight than reported; new registration application

Upon the operation of a commercial motor vehicle at a greater gross vehicle weight than had been reported to and registered by the department, a new registration application shall be made to the department. The greater declared gross vehicle weight fee as required in Section 9400.1 and any penalties defined in this code shall be paid to the department. *(Added by Stats.2000, c. 861 (S.B.2084), § 54, eff. Sept. 29, 2000.)*

§ 9554.5. Penalty on application for original registration after date of expiration or date penalties due

(a) On and after January 1, 2003, a penalty shall be added on any application for original registration made later than midnight of the date of expiration or on or after the date penalties become due. Penalties shall be computed as provided in Section 9559 and shall be collected with the fee.

(b) The penalty assessment for the delinquent payment of the registration fee specified in Section 9250 shall be as follows:

(1) Thirty dollars ($30) for a delinquency period of one year or less.

(2) Fifty dollars ($50) for a delinquency period of more than one year, to and including two years.

(3) One hundred dollars ($100) for a delinquency period of more than two years.

(c) The penalty assessment for the delinquent payment of the weight fee specified in Section 9400 or 9400.1 and the vehicle license fee as specified in Section 10751 of the Revenue and Taxation Code shall be as follows:

(1) Forty percent of the vehicle license fee, or the combined amount of the vehicle license fee and the weight fee if the vehicle is subject to both fees, for a delinquency period of one year or less.

(2) Eighty percent of the vehicle license fee, or the combined amount of the vehicle license fee and the weight fee if the vehicle is subject to both fees, for a delinquency period of more than one year, to and including two years.

(3) One hundred sixty percent of the vehicle license fee, or the combined amount of the vehicle license fee and the weight fee if the vehicle is subject to both fees, for a delinquency period of more than two years.

(d) A single penalty assessment for the delinquent payment of the fees specified in Sections 9250.8 and 9250.13 shall be as follows:

(1) Thirty dollars ($30) for a delinquency period of one year or less.

(2) Fifty dollars ($50) for a delinquency period of more than one year, to and including two years.

(3) One hundred dollars ($100) for a delinquency period of more than two years.

(4) This subdivision shall apply to applications for an original registration where the date the fee is due is on or after December 1, 2008.

(e) This section shall become operative January 1, 2009. *(Added by Stats.2008, c. 756 (A.B.268), § 25, eff. Sept. 30, 2008, operative Jan. 1, 2009.)*

§ 9555. Delinquent trailer coach fees

Whenever any trailer coach is in this State without the registration fee having first been paid as required by this code, the fee is delinquent. *(Stats.1959, c. 3, p. 1591, § 2.)*

Cross References

Delinquent fees and penalties, see Vehicle Code § 9552 et seq.
Proportionate registration and licensing, see Vehicle Code § 8050 et seq.
Similar provision, see Revenue and Taxation Code § 10769.

Trailer coach defined, see Vehicle Code § 635.

§ 9556. Application through motor club; date of delinquency

Whenever any person or organization authorized by the department under Section 4610 receives an application for renewal of registration accompanied by the proper fee and endorses a receipt or validates a registration card or potential registration card in respect to the application for renewal of registration prior to midnight on the date registration expires in any year, the application and payment of fees shall not be deemed delinquent or subject to penalty, except that the person or organization so receiving the application and fees shall transmit the application and fees to the department as promptly as practicable in the immediate course of business.

This section shall become operative on March 8, 1976, unless a later enacted statute, which is chaptered before March 8, 1976, deletes or extends such date. *(Added by Stats.1974, c. 1330, p. 2896, § 26, eff. Sept. 26, 1974, operative March 8, 1976.)*

§ 9557. Transmittal of fees by mail

(a) No penalty shall be imposed for delinquent payment of any fee required to be paid under this code in the event any instrument for effective payment of such fee is placed in the United States mail or in any postal box maintained by the United States Postal Service with sufficient identification in an envelope with postage thereon prepaid and addressed to the Department of Motor Vehicles at Sacramento, or to one of the regularly established branch offices of the department or to any person or organization authorized by the department under Section 4610, prior to the date or time the fee becomes delinquent.

(b) Any person so mailing an instrument for payment of any fee may file with the department a certificate in writing showing compliance with the provisions of this section. The certificate shall be accepted by the department as prima facie evidence of such mailing. *(Stats. 1959, c. 3, p. 1591, § 9557. Amended by Stats.1975, c. 389, p. 866, § 4.)*

Cross References

Statute making one fact prima facie evidence of another fact, see Evidence Code § 602.

§ 9558. Bad check in payment of fee or penalty; redeposit

If a check in payment of a fee or penalty is not paid by the bank on which it is drawn on its first presentation, the person tendering the check remains liable for the payment of the fee, or fee and penalty, as if he had not tendered the check. The department in its discretion may redeposit a check in payment of the fee, or the fee and penalty, not more than once without assessing additional penalties. *(Stats.1959, c. 3, p. 1592, § 9558. Amended by Stats.1969, c. 214, p. 544, § 2.)*

Department, definition, see Vehicle Code §§ 290, 2101, 21000.
Similar provision, see Revenue and Taxation Code § 10854.1.

§ 9558.5. Repealed by Stats.1988, c. 1268, § 11.5, operative Jan. 1, 1992

§ 9559. Computation of fees

In computing any registration or weight fee or penalty imposed by this code, whether on a proration or otherwise, a fraction of a dollar is disregarded, unless it equals or exceeds fifty cents ($0.50), in which case it is treated as one full dollar ($1). Computation of any penalty shall be made from the fee after the same has been computed as provided in this section.

Any fee or penalty in an amount of forty-nine cents ($0.49) or less shall be deemed to be one dollar ($1). *(Stats.1959, c. 3, p. 1592, § 9559. Amended by Stats.1992, c. 1241 (S.B.1615), § 14.)*

Delinquent fees and penalties, see Vehicle Code § 9552 et seq.
Payment of use tax for transfer of title or interest in off-highway
    motor vehicle, see Vehicle Code § 38211.

§ 9559.5. Apportionment of Renewal fee

When, by reason of the assignment or reassignment of a renewal registration date by the director, the registration year is less than, or more than, 12 months, the fee due for that renewal shall be decreased or increased by one-twelfth of the annual fee for each month of the period less than, or in excess of, 12 months. *(Added by Stats.2006, c. 169 (A.B.2736), § 4.)*

Apportioned registration, federal motor vehicle safety program,
    see Vehicle Code § 8100 et seq.
Exceptions to expiration and renewal of registration require-
    ments, see Vehicle Code § 4601.5.
Year-round registration of motor vehicles, see Vehicle Code
    § 1651.5.

§ 9560. Waiver of penalties for late payment of registration renewal fees; definitions; application of section

(a) The department shall waive all penalties that may be due for late payment of registration renewal fees on a vehicle for any period during which the registered owner is deployed to a location outside of the state.

(b)(1) For the purposes of this section, "deployed" means being ordered to temporary military duty during a period when a Presidential Executive order specifies that the United States is engaged in combat or homeland defense and the registered owner is one of the following:

(A) A member of the armed forces.

(B) A member of the armed forces reserve or the National Guard who has been called to active duty or active service.

(2) "Deployed" does not include either of the following:

(A) Temporary duty for the sole purpose of training or processing.

(B) A permanent change of station.

(c) This section does not apply to a registered owner who applies for registration renewal more than 60 days after termination of his or her deployment. *(Added by Stats.2004, c. 188 (A.B.1787), § 1.)*

§ 9561. Waiver of renewal penalties on repossessed vehicle or sale at auction of repossessed vehicle

(a) When a legal owner or his or her agent repossesses a vehicle on which renewal fees are due, the department shall waive any renewal penalties that are due for late payment if the fees are paid within 60 days of taking possession.

(b) Notwithstanding any other provisions of this code, when a repossessed vehicle is sold through a dealer conducting a wholesale motor vehicle auction as provided in subdivision (b) of Section 4456 and Article 5 (commencing with Section 6100) of Chapter 2 of Division 3, any penalties that may be due are waived, if all renewal fees that are due are paid not later than 60 days after the date of sale at the auction. *(Added by Stats.1959, c. 791, p. 2804, § 1. Amended by Stats.1965, c. 355, p. 1460, § 1; Stats.1965, c. 1014, p. 2646, § 4; Stats.1968, c. 712, p. 1414, § 1; Stats.1970, c. 1439, p. 2794, § 6; Stats.1971, c. 433, p. 841, § 1, operative May 3, 1972; Stats.1973, c. 889, p. 1657, § 48, eff. Sept. 28, 1973, operative March 10, 1975; Stats.1974, c. 1330, p. 2897, § 29, eff. Sept. 26, 1974, operative March 10, 1975; Stats.1978, c. 841, p. 2646, § 1; Stats.1993, c. 200 (A.B.82), § 1; Stats.1994, c. 180 (A.B. 375), § 10, eff. July 11, 1994.)*

§ 9561.5. Waiver of renewal penalties on auction sale of leased vehicle

The department shall waive any penalties that may be due for late payment of registration renewal fees on a vehicle if all of the following criteria are met:

(a) The vehicle is sold through a dealer conducting a wholesale motor vehicle auction as provided in subdivision (b) of Section 4456 and Article 5 (commencing with Section 6100) of Chapter 2 of Division 3.

(b) Immediately prior to the sale the vehicle was registered as a leased vehicle.

(c) Delivery of the vehicle to the dealer conducting the wholesale motor vehicle auction was not later than 25 days after the termination of the lease.

(d) The date of termination of the lease and the date of delivery to the auction is reported on the application for registration, or application for transfer and registration, in a format that is acceptable to the department. *(Added by Stats.1997, c. 311 (S.B.192), § 1.)*

§ 9562. Waiver of penalties and registration fees; transferred vehicles' registration fees and penalties

(a) When a transferee or purchaser of a vehicle applies for transfer of registration, as provided in Section 5902, and it is determined by the department that registration penalties accrued prior to the purchase of the vehicle, and that the transferee or purchaser was not cognizant of the nonpayment of the fees for registration for the current or prior registration years, the department may waive the registration penalties upon payment of the fees for registration due.

(b) Other provisions of this code notwithstanding, the director may, at his or her discretion, investigate into the circumstances of any application for registration to ascertain if penalties had accrued through no fault or intent of the owner. If the director determines that the circumstances justify it, he or she may waive any penalties upon payment of the fees for registration then due.

(c) When a transferee or purchaser of a vehicle applies for transfer of registration of a vehicle, and it is determined by the department that fees for registration of the vehicle for any year are unpaid and due, that the fees became due prior to the transfer or purchase of the vehicle by the transferee or purchaser and that the transferee or purchaser was not cognizant of the fact that the fees were unpaid and due, the department may waive the fees and any penalty thereon if the license plate assigned to the vehicle displays a validating device issued by the department and the validating device contains the year number of the registration year for which the transferee or purchaser is requesting a waiver of fees and penalties.

(d) Upon the transfer of a vehicle for which fees for registration and any penalties thereon are unpaid and due, the fees and penalties are, notwithstanding the provisions of Article 6 (commencing with Section 9800) of this chapter, the personal debt of the transferor of the vehicle who did not pay the fees and penalties when they became due or accrued. The fees and penalties may be collected by the department in an appropriate civil action if the department has waived the fees and penalties pursuant to subdivision (c). *(Added by Stats.1959, c. 791, p. 2805, § 2. Amended by Stats.1973, c. 889, p. 1657, § 49, eff. Sept. 28, 1973; Stats.1976, c. 935, p. 2142, § 6; Stats.1983, c. 759, § 5; Stats.1993, c. 223 (A.B.822), § 1.)*

§ 9563. Rebuilt and restored passenger vehicle; registration application and fees

Notwithstanding any other provisions of this code, when a vehicle is rebuilt and restored to operation after it has been reported to be dismantled pursuant to Section 11520, the application shall be deemed to be an application for original registration of a new vehicle for determination of fees. *(Added by Stats.1971, c. 1353, p. 2672, § 4, operative May 3, 1972. Amended by Stats.1973, c. 889, p. 1657, § 50, eff. Sept. 28, 1973.)*

§ 9564. Scrap metal processor; compliance with code; certificate of nonoperation or fees not required; reconstruction

(a) A scrap metal processor, as described in paragraph (3) of subdivision (a) of Section 221, who acquires a vehicle of a type subject to registration under this code, and who complies with all the provisions of this section, is not required to submit a certificate of nonoperation in lieu of fees or to pay fees that would otherwise be required if the vehicle were to be currently registered.

(b) A scrap metal processor who acquires a vehicle as provided in subdivision (a) shall submit either of the following to the department before reducing the vehicle to its component materials:

(1) Documentation that the vehicle was acquired pursuant to Section 22669 and disposed of in compliance with Article 2 (commencing with Section 22850) of Chapter 10 of Division 11.

(2) The properly endorsed certificate of title transferring title to the scrap iron processor and any available license plates or registration documents.

(c) A vehicle delivered to a scrap metal processor under subdivision (a) shall not be reconstructed or made operable, unless it is a vehicle which qualifies for either horseless carriage license plates or historical vehicle license plates pursuant to Section 5004, in which case the vehicle may be reconstructed or made operable. *(Added by Stats.1987, c. 1133, § 3. Amended by Stats.1999, c. 316 (A.B.342), § 2.)*

§ 9565. Repealed by Stats.2010, c. 388 (A.B.2461), § 2, operative Jan. 1, 2013

ARTICLE 5. PARTIAL YEAR PAYMENT OF WEIGHT FEES

Section
9700. Amount of proportional payment.
9701. Repealed.
9702. Additional fee for partial year registration or renewal.
9703. Repealed.
9704. Expiration and renewal of registrations and certificates or insignia.
9705. Repealed.
9706. Application for partial year registration or renewal; application for certificate of nonoperation; support to firefighting operations.
9706.1. Registration card unavailable; waiver of fee.
9708. Repealed.
9710. Operation of vehicle prior to receipt of certificate or insignia of registration.
9711. Commercial vehicles based in foreign jurisdictions not granting reciprocity or proportionate registration; nonapplicability of article.

Cross References

Expiration of registration for vehicles registered pursuant to this article, see Vehicle Code § 4601.5

Registration renewal, notification, exception for vehicles registered pursuant to this article, see Vehicle Code § 1661.

Weight fees, see Vehicle Code § 9400 et seq.

§ 9700. Amount of proportional payment

With respect to vehicles subject to additional registration fees under Section 9400 or 9400.1, a proportionate share of the additional fees may be paid for any partial period of one month or more, but less than 12 months, in an amount determined to be one-twelfth of the annual registration times the consecutive months, or fraction thereof, of the period of registration. *(Added by Stats. 1981, c. 636, p. 2404, § 8. Amended by Stats.2001, c. 826 (A.B.1472), § 30.)*

Cross References

Display of certificates or insignia, fees paid on a partial year basis, see Vehicle Code § 5206.

§ 9701. Repealed by Stats.1973, c. 889, p. 1657, § 52, urgency, eff. Sept. 28, 1973, operative Dec. 1, 1974

§ 9702. Additional fee for partial year registration or renewal

An additional fee of fifteen dollars ($15) shall be charged for each application for partial year registration, or renewal thereof, whenever a person pays the fee under Section 9400 or 9400.1, as provided in Section 9700. *(Added by Stats.1981, c. 636, p. 2404, § 8. Amended by Stats.2003, c. 719 (S.B.1055), § 19.)*

Cross References

Base fee amounts, adjustment of fees, see Vehicle Code § 1678.

§ 9703. Repealed by Stats.1981, c. 636, p. 2404, § 7

§ 9704. Expiration and renewal of registrations and certificates or insignia

Every partial year vehicle registration and every certificate or insignia issued under this article shall expire at midnight on the last day of the period for which issued. The department may, upon payment of the proper fees, renew the registration of the vehicle for a period of months less than the remainder of the registration year or for the remainder of the registration year. *(Added by Stats.1981, c. 636, p. 2404, § 8.)*

§ 9705. Repealed by Stats.1981, c. 636, p. 2404, § 7

§ 9706. Application for partial year registration or renewal; application for certificate of nonoperation; support to firefighting operations

(a) Application for partial year registration in conjunction with an application for original California registration shall be made by the owner within 20 days of the date the vehicle first becomes subject to California registration. Any application for partial year registration submitted after that 20–day period shall be denied registration for a partial year, and the vehicle shall be subject to payment of the fees for the entire registration year. In addition to the fee for the registration year, a penalty, as specified in Section 9554, shall be added to the fee for registration.

(b) Any application to renew registration for a part of the remainder of the registration year or for the entire remainder of the registration year shall be made prior to midnight of the expiration date of the last issued registration certificate. Application shall be made upon presentation of the last issued registration card or of a potential registration issued by the department for use at the time of renewal and by payment of the required partial year fees, or, if renewal is for the remainder of the registration year, by payment of the annual fee required by Section 9400 or 9400.1, as reduced pursuant to Section 9407.

(c) Notwithstanding any other provision of law, an owner who registers a vehicle pursuant to this article during a calendar year shall, if the vehicle was not operated, moved, or left standing upon a highway, file a certificate of nonoperation prior to the date of the first operation of the vehicle on the highways in a manner which requires that registration and shall, by December 31 of each calendar year thereafter, file a certification pursuant to subdivisions (a) and (b) of Section 4604 when the vehicle is not registered for operation on the highways for the succeeding calendar year.

(d) Notwithstanding subdivision (c), the owner of any vehicle being moved or operated for the purpose of providing support to firefighting operations while the vehicle or owner is under contract to the United States Forestry Service, the United States Department of the Interior, the Bureau of Land Management, the Department of Forestry and Fire Protection, or the * * * Office of Emergency Services may obtain partial year registration if application is made within 20 days of the date the vehicle is first operated, moved, or left standing on the highway and the owner has obtained a letter of authorization from the department prior to the date that the vehicle is first operated, moved, or left standing on the highway. *(Added by Stats.1981, c. 636, p. 2405, § 8. Amended by Stats.1983, c. 142, § 166; Stats.1983, c. 185, § 1, eff. July 11, 1983; Stats.1990, c. 1352 (A.B.2912), § 11, eff. Sept. 27, 1990, operative July 1, 1990; Stats.1991, c. 362 (A.B.1974), § 6, eff. Aug. 30, 1991; Stats.1992, c. 1243 (A.B.3090), § 72, eff. Sept. 30, 1992; Stats.2001, c. 826 (A.B.1472), § 31; Stats.2010, c. 618 (A.B.2791), § 293; Stats.2013, c. 352 (A.B.1317), § 524, eff. Sept. 26, 2013, operative July 1, 2013.)*

Cross References

Nonoperated vehicles, certificate of nonoperation requirements, see Vehicle Code § 4604.2.

§ 9706.1. Registration card unavailable; waiver of fee

If the registration card or potential registration card is unavailable, payment of the fee prescribed by Section 9265 for the issuance of a duplicate registration shall not be required in addition to the other fees prescribed by subdivision (b) of Section 9706. *(Added by Stats.1991, c. 13 (A.B.37), § 22, eff. Feb. 13, 1991.)*

§ 9708. Repealed by Stats.1990, c. 1352 (A.B.2912), § 12, eff. Sept. 27, 1990, operative July 1, 1990

§ 9710. Operation of vehicle prior to receipt of certificate or insignia of registration

When an application for renewal of registration of a vehicle has been made as required by Section 9706, the vehicle may be operated on the highways until the new certificate or insignia of current registration has been received from the department if there is displayed on the vehicle, in addition to the license plates or validating devices issued to the vehicle for the previous year, the certificate or insignia issued to the vehicle for the previous partial year. *(Added by Stats.1981, c. 636, p. 2405, § 8. Amended by Stats.1990, c. 1352 (A.B.2912), § 13, eff. Sept. 27, 1990, operative July 1, 1990.)*

§ 9711. Commercial vehicles based in foreign jurisdictions not granting reciprocity or proportionate registration; nonapplicability of article

This article does not apply to any owner or lessor of a commercial vehicle based in a foreign jurisdiction which does not grant reciprocity or proportionate registration to residents of this state while operating within that jurisdiction. *(Added by Stats.1988, c. 907, § 2.)*

ARTICLE 6. ENFORCEMENT OF LIENS

Section
9800. Lien for fees and penalties; perfected lien; expiration; agents of department.
9801. Delinquent registration; filing certificate requesting judgment, or civil action and seizure and sale; application to leased vehicles; notice; hearing; payment and return; highway patrol assistance; unclaimed property.
9801.2. Inoperative.
9802. Conduct of sale; bids; disposition of proceeds.
9803. Review.
9804. Action to review; time; notice of right.
9805. Filing certificate; specifications; notice; hearing.
9806. Entry of judgment; filing.
9807. Repealed.
9808. Execution of judgment.
9809, 9810. Repealed.

Cross References

Application of this Article to nonpayment of fees for permanent fleet registration of proportionately registered commercial trailers, see Vehicle Code § 5307.
Transferred vehicles, registration fees and penalties as transferor debt notwithstanding this article, see Vehicle Code § 9562.
Waiver of penalties and registration fees for off-highway motor vehicles, see Vehicle Code § 38247.

§ 9800. Lien for fees and penalties; perfected lien; expiration; agents of department

(a) Payments for any of the following, and any interest, penalties, or service fees added thereto, required to register or transfer the registration of a vehicle, constitute a lien on the vehicle on which they are due or which was involved in the offense, and on any other vehicle owned by the owner of that vehicle:

(1) Registration fees.

(2) Transfer fees.

(3) License fees.

(4) Use taxes.

(5) Penalties for offenses relating to the standing or parking of a vehicle for which a notice of parking violation has been served on the owner, and any administrative service fee added to the penalty.

(6) Any court-imposed fine or penalty assessment, and any administrative service fee added thereto, which is subject to collection by the department.

(b) Notwithstanding subdivision (a), if a person is cited for a foreign registered auxiliary dolly, semitrailer, or trailer having been operated without current year registration or valid California permits or registration, an amount equal to the minimum registration fees or transfer fees, and any penalty added thereto, from the date they became due, shall, by election of the power unit operator, constitute a lien upon the California registered power unit which was pulling the dolly, semitrailer, or trailer. However, this subdivision is not applicable if the citation is issued at a scale operated by the Department of the California Highway Patrol and registration for the vehicle can be issued there immediately upon payment of the fees due.

(c) Every lien arising under this section expires three years from the date the fee, tax, or parking penalty first became due unless the lien is perfected pursuant to subdivision (d).

(d) A lien is perfected when a notice is mailed to the registered and legal owners at the addresses shown in the department's records and the lien is recorded on the electronic vehicle registration records of the department. A perfected lien shall expire five years from the date of perfection.

(e) Employees and members of the Department of the California Highway Patrol assigned to commercial vehicle scale facilities may possess and sell trip permits approved by the Department of Motor Vehicles. *(Added by Stats.1982, c. 664, p. 2725, § 8. Amended by Stats.1983, c. 759, § 6; Stats.1983, c. 986, § 6; Stats.1986, c. 939, § 14; Stats.1989, c. 187, § 3; Stats.1992, c. 1199 (A.B.2409), § 10, eff. Sept. 30, 1992.)*

Cross References

Applicability of this section to trolley coaches, see Vehicle Code § 21051.
Fleet vehicles, fees due as liens, see Vehicle Code § 5307.
Lien on vehicles, notice of failure to appear or failure to pay fine, see Vehicle Code § 14911.

§ 9801. Delinquent registration; filing certificate requesting judgment, or civil action and seizure and sale; application to leased vehicles; notice; hearing; payment and return; highway patrol assistance; unclaimed property

(a)(1) When the payment required for the registration or transfer of a vehicle is delinquent pursuant to subdivision (a) of Section 9800, the department may collect the amount of the lien on the vehicle plus costs, not to exceed two hundred fifty dollars ($250), by the filing of a certificate requesting judgment pursuant to Section 9805, or by appropriate civil action and by the seizure and sale of the vehicle or any other vehicle owned by the owner of the unregistered vehicle.

(2) In the case of a leased vehicle, the authority provided in paragraph (1) to seize and sell the vehicle or any other vehicle owned by the owner of that vehicle shall not apply to a lien for any delinquency for which only the lessee is liable pursuant to paragraph (1) of subdivision (a) of Section 10879 of the Revenue and Taxation Code.

(b) At least 10 days before the seizure, notice of the lien and of the intent to seize and sell the vehicle shall be given by the department to the registered and legal owners, and to any other person known to be claiming an interest in the vehicle, by registered mail addressed to those persons at the last known addresses appearing on the records of the department.

(c) Any person receiving the notice of the lien and the intent to seize and sell the vehicle may request a hearing to contest the existence or amount of the lien. If no hearing is requested, the vehicle shall be seized and sold.

(d) If a hearing is requested, 10 days' notice shall be given of the time and place of the hearing, which shall be held within the county of residence of the person requesting the hearing or of the registered owner. The hearing shall be conducted by a referee who shall submit findings and recommendations to the director or his or her authorized representative, who shall decide the matter. The decision shall be effective on notice thereof to the interested parties. However, the director or his or her authorized representative may rescind the decision and reconsider the matter for good cause shown at any time within three years after the date the disputed fee or tax first became due, or within one year from the hearing, whichever is later.

(e) At any time before seizure or sale, any registered owner, legal owner, or person claiming an interest in the vehicle may pay the department the amount of the lien, plus costs. In that event, the seizure or sale shall not be held and the vehicle, if seized, shall be returned by the department to the person entitled to its possession. This payment shall not constitute a waiver of the right to a hearing.

(f) When the department or an authorized agent has reasonable cause to believe that the lien may be jeopardized within the 10-day notice-of-intent period, the vehicle may be seized without prior notice to the registered or legal owner, upon obtaining authorization for the seizure from the Registrar of Vehicles or authorized representative. In all those cases, a notice of the lien and the intent to sell the vehicle shall be given by the department to the legal and registered owner, and to any other person known to be claiming an interest in the vehicle, within 48 hours after seizure excluding Saturdays, Sundays, and holidays specified in Section 6700 of the Government Code. Any hearing to contest the lien and the seizure shall be requested within 10 days following transmittal of that notice.

(g) When a lien exists against one or more vehicles owned by the same person or persons, the department may seize and sell a sufficient number of the vehicles to pay the lien, plus costs, on one or more of the vehicles in accordance with subdivision (a).

(h) The Department of the California Highway Patrol shall assist with the seizure and impounding of the vehicle. Any municipality or county law enforcement agency may assist with the seizure and impounding of the vehicle.

(i) Any property found by the department in any vehicle seized under the provisions of this article shall be handled by the department in the same manner as is provided in Sections 2414 and 2415. *(Added by Stats. 1982, c. 664, p. 2725, § 8. Amended by Stats.1983, c. 759, § 7; Stats.1989, c. 187, § 4; Stats.1990, c. 676 (A.B.1822), § 1; Stats.1992, c. 1199 (A.B.2409), § 11, eff. Sept. 30, 1992; Stats.1994, c. 1211 (A.B.3032), § 3, eff. Sept. 30, 1994.)*

Cross References

Applicability of this section to trolley coaches, see Vehicle Code § 21051.

§ 9801.2. Inoperative

§ 9802. Conduct of sale; bids; disposition of proceeds

(a) The Registrar of Vehicles or authorized representative shall conduct the sale in the same manner as provided by law for the seizure and sale of personal property by the assessor for the collection of taxes due on personal property.

(b) The department may bid for the vehicle an amount equal to the lien held by the department for registration, transfer, and license fees, use taxes, parking penalties, and any interest, penalties, and costs added thereto. In all cases where the vehicle becomes the property of the department, it shall be reduced to junk and sold.

(c) The proceeds of any sale shall be allocated by the department for the following purposes and in the following order:

(1) Costs incurred by the department.

(2) Registration and transfer fees and any penalty added thereto.

(3) License fees and any penalty added thereto.

(4) Use taxes and any interest or penalty added thereto.

(5) Perfected mechanics' liens.

(6) Perfected security interests.

(7) Penalties for offenses relating to the standing or parking of a vehicle and any administrative service fee added thereto. Any other court-induced liability, and

any administrative service fee added thereto, which is subject to collection by the department.

(8) All other fees due the department.

(9) Any remainder to the person whose claim of interest in the vehicle is approved by the department.

(d) Notwithstanding Section 42270, the proceeds of a sale allocated pursuant to paragraphs (4) to (9), inclusive, of subdivision (c) shall not be transmitted to the Treasurer for deposit in the Motor Vehicle Account in the State Transportation Fund.

(e) The department shall transmit to the State Board of Equalization all use taxes, interest, and penalties collected under this article within 60 days after receipt thereof in the form which may be prescribed and approved jointly by the department and the board. *(Added by Stats.1982, c. 664, p. 1275, § 8. Amended by Stats.1983, c. 759, § 8; Stats.1988, c. 1268, § 12; Stats. 1989, c. 187, § 5; Stats.1992, c. 1199 (A.B.2409), § 11.5, eff. Sept. 30, 1992.)*

Cross References

Mechanics' liens, generally, see Civil Code § 3109 et seq.
Taxes due on unsecured property, seizure and sale, see Revenue and Taxation Code § 2951 et seq.

§ 9803. Review

Nothing in this code prevents a review or other action as may be permitted by the Constitution and laws of this state by a court of competent jurisdiction of any order of the department to seize and sell a vehicle. *(Added by Stats.1986, c. 1212, § 2.)*

§ 9804. Action to review; time; notice of right

(a) Any action brought in a court of competent jurisdiction to review any order of the department to seize and sell a vehicle shall be commenced within 90 days from the date notice is given of the order.

(b) Upon final completion of all administrative appeals, the department shall give written notice to the owner of a vehicle ordered for seizure and sale of his or her right to a review of the order by a court pursuant to subdivision (a). *(Added by Stats.1986, c. 1212, § 3.)*

§ 9805. Filing certificate; specifications; notice; hearing

(a) The department may file in the office of the Clerk of the Superior Court of Sacramento County, or any other county, a certificate specifying the amount of any fee, tax, penalty, and collection cost due, the name and last known address of the individual, company, or corporation liable for the amount due, and the fact that the department has complied with all the provisions of this division in the computation of the amount due, and a request that judgment be entered against the individual, company, or corporation in the amount of the fee, tax, penalty, and collection cost set forth in the certificate if the fee, tax, penalty, or collection cost constitutes either of the following:

(1) A lien under this division on the vehicle on which it is due is not paid when due, and there is evidence that the vehicle has been operated in violation of this code or any regulations adopted pursuant to this code.

(2) A lessee liability as provided in Section 10879 of the Revenue and Taxation Code.

(b) Prior to the filing of the certificate, the department shall, by mail, notify the individual, company, or corporation of the amount which is due and of the opportunity for a hearing as provided in this subdivision. At the request of the individual, company, or corporation, the department shall conduct a hearing pursuant to Section 9801, at which it shall be determined whether the claimed fee, tax, penalty, or collection cost in the amount claimed by the department is due and constitutes a lien on the vehicle, and whether the individual, company, or corporation is liable therefor.

(c) If no hearing is requested within 15 days after mailing the notice required by subdivision (b), the certificate required by subdivision (b) may be filed. *(Added by Stats.1990, c. 676 (A.B.1822), § 2. Amended by Stats.1994, c. 1211 (A.B.3032), § 4, eff. Sept. 30, 1994; Stats.2002, c. 784 (S.B.1316), § 593.)*

Law Revision Commission Comments
2002 Amendment

Subdivision (a) of Section 9805 is amended to reflect elimination of the county clerk's role as ex officio clerk of the superior court. See former Gov't Code § 26800 (county clerk acting as clerk of superior court). The powers, duties, and responsibilities formerly exercised by the county clerk as ex officio clerk of the court are delegated to the court administrative or executive officer, and the county clerk is relieved of those powers, duties, and responsibilities. See Gov't Code §§ 69840 (powers, duties, and responsibilities of clerk of court and deputy clerk of court), 71620 (trial court personnel). [32 Cal.L.Rev.Comm. Reports 533 (2002)].

§ 9806. Entry of judgment; filing

The clerk of the court, immediately upon the filing of the certificate specified in Section 9805, shall enter a judgment for the people of the State of California against the individual, company, or corporation in the amount of any fee, tax, penalty, and collection cost set forth in the certificate. The clerk may file the judgment in a looseleaf book entitled "Department of Motor Vehicles Registration Judgments." *(Added by Stats.1990, c. 676 (A.B.1822), § 3. Amended by Stats.2002, c. 784 (S.B. 1316), § 594.)*

Law Revision Commission Comments
2002 Amendment

Section 9806 is amended to reflect elimination of the county clerk's role as ex officio clerk of the superior court. See former Gov't Code § 26800 (county clerk acting as clerk of superior court). The powers, duties, and responsibilities formerly exercised by the county clerk as ex officio clerk of the court are delegated to the court administrative or executive officer, and the county clerk is relieved of those powers, duties, and responsibilities. See Gov't Code §§ 69840 (powers, duties, and responsibilities of clerk of court and deputy clerk of court),

71620 (trial court personnel). [32 Cal.L.Rev.Comm. Reports 534 (2002)].

§ 9807. Repealed by Stats.1982, c. 664, § 7

§ 9808. Execution of judgment

Execution shall issue upon the judgment specified in Section 9806 upon request of the department in the same manner as execution may issue upon other judgments, and sales shall be held under the execution as prescribed in the Code of Civil Procedure, except that attachment may not issue against any real property. *(Added by Stats.1990, c. 676 (A.B.1822), § 4.)*

§§ 9809, 9810. Repealed by Stats.1982, c. 664, § 7

Division 3.5

REGISTRATION AND TRANSFER OF VESSELS

Chapter   Section
1. General Provisions and Definitions 9840
2. Registration 9850
3. Transfer of Title or Interest in Undocu-
    mented Vessel 9900

CHAPTER 1. GENERAL PROVISIONS AND DEFINITIONS

Section
9840. Definitions.
9845. Inspection for ownership and registration of vessels at
      specified places; authority.

§ 9840. Definitions

As used in this division, unless the context clearly requires a different meaning:

(a) "Vessel" includes every description of watercraft used or capable of being used as a means of transportation on water, except the following:

(1) A seaplane on the water.

(2) A watercraft specifically designed to operate on a permanently fixed course, the movement of which is restricted to or guided on such permanently fixed course by means of a mechanical device on a fixed track or arm to which the watercraft is attached or by which the watercraft is controlled, or by means of a mechanical device attached to the watercraft itself.

(3) A floating structure which is designed and built to be used as a stationary waterborne residential dwelling, which (A) does not have and is not designed to have a mode of power of its own, (B) is dependent for utilities upon a continuous utility linkage to a source originating on shore, and (C) has a permanent, continuous hookup to a shoreside sewage system.

(b) "Owner" is a person having all the incidents of ownership, including the legal title, of a vessel whether or not such person lends, rents, or pledges such vessel; the person entitled to the possession of a vessel as the purchaser under a conditional sale contract; or the mortgagor of a vessel. "Owner" does not include a person holding legal title to a vessel under a conditional sales contract, the mortgagee of a vessel, or the renter or lessor of a vessel to the state or to any county, city, district, or political subdivision of the state under a lease, lease-sale, or rental-purchase agreement which grants possession of the vessel to the lessee for a period of 30 consecutive days or more.

(c) "Legal owner" is a person holding the legal title to a vessel under a conditional sale contract, the mortgagee of a vessel, or the renter or lessor of a vessel to the state, or to any county, city, district or political subdivision of the state, under a lease, lease-sale, or rental-purchase agreement which grants possession of the vessel to the lessee for a period of 30 consecutive days or more.

(d) "Registered owner" is the person registered by the department as the owner of the vessel.

(e) "Waters of this state" means any waters within the territorial limits of this state.

(f) "State of principal use" means the state on which waters a vessel is used or intended to be used most during a calendar year.

(g) "Undocumented vessel" means any vessel which is not required to have and does not have a valid marine document issued by the Bureau of Customs of the United States or any federal agency successor thereto.

(h) "Use" means operate, navigate, or employ. *(Added by Stats.1970, c. 1428, p. 2737, § 61. Amended by Stats.1973, c. 759, p. 1368, § 1; Stats.1984, c. 411, § 1.)*

§ 9845. Inspection for ownership and registration of vessels at specified places; authority

The director, deputy director, registrar, deputy registrar, investigators of the department, and peace officers, as defined in Chapter 4.5 (commencing with Section 830) of the Penal Code, may inspect the hull identification number, certificate of number, and certificate of ownership of any vessel, as defined in Section 9840, when transported on a highway, or in any public garage, repair shop, public or private marina, dry storage facility, new or used vessel sales lot or boat yard, or other similar establishment for the purpose of investigating the ownership and registration of vessels, locating stolen vessels, and for inspection of wrecked, dismantled, or abandoned vessels. The authority to inspect pursuant to this section does not extend to any enclosed living area aboard a vessel. *(Added by Stats.1987, c. 298, § 1.)*

CHAPTER 2. REGISTRATION

Section
9850. Numbering of undocumented vessels.
9851. Registration of public undocumented vehicles; exemption.
9852. Proof of ownership.
9852.5. Ownership of two or more undocumented vessels by two or more coowners.
9852.7. Beneficiary form ownership.
9852.9. Initial application for a number; form contents.
9853. Application for number; fees; documentation of administrative costs.
9853.1. Issuance of certificate of ownership and certificate of number.
9853.2. Display of number.

Section

9853.3. Retention of certificate of number for leased or rented vessels.

9853.4. Stickers, tabs, or other devices.

9853.5. Vessels of historical interest; special plaques; fees.

9853.6. Fee increases.

9853.7. Retail sellers of specified vessels containing spark-ignition marine engines; obligations.

9853.8. Application.

9854. Federal or out-of-state registration.

9855. Change of ownership.

9856. Transfer to dealer.

9857. Conformity with federal system.

9858. Issuance of certificates: department or agent.

9858.1. Maximum documentary preparation charge.

9858.5. Licensed yacht and ship brokers; use tax collection.

9859. Funds received by agent.

9860. Renewal of certificates of number; fee for renewal; quagga and zebra mussel infestation prevention fee; documentation of administrative costs.

9861. Expiration date of certificates of number.

9862. Penalties for delinquency.

9862.2. Repealed.

9862.5. Computation of penalties.

9863. Harbors and Watercraft Revolving Fund; distribution of funds.

9864. Wrecked, dismantled, destroyed or abandoned undocumented vessels.

9865. Change of address.

9866. Display of other numbers on bow.

9867. Fee; duplicate certificates or stickers.

9867.5. Transfer of registration; unavailable certificate; additional fee.

9868. Refunds.

9869. Information to be transmitted to county assessor.

9870. Nonprofit public benefit corporation.

9871. Assignment and marking of hull identification number.

9871.5. Renewal of registration; hull identification number.

9872. Defacing, destroying, or altering hull identification number.

9872.1. Vessel or component part with hull identification number removed, defaced, altered or destroyed; prohibition of purchase, sale, offer for sale, receipt or possession; impoundment; hearing on disposition; notice and receipt; contents; return to owner; conditions.

9872.5. Amphibious vehicles.

9873. Undocumented vessels not required to be numbered.

9874. Suspension, cancellation, or revocation.

9875. Penalties.

9880. Withholding of renewal of certificate of vessel number or transfer of title or interest; receipt of notice of tax delinquency; record of notice; satisfaction; notification of vessel transfer or nonrenewal.

Cross References

Violation of chapter a misdemeanor, see Vehicle Code § 40000.8.

§ 9850. Numbering of undocumented vessels

Every undocumented vessel using the waters or on the waters of this state shall be currently numbered. No person shall operate nor shall any county, city, or political subdivision give permission for the operation of any undocumented vessel on those waters unless the undocumented vessel is numbered in accordance with this chapter, or in accordance with applicable federal law, or in accordance with a federally approved numbering system of another state, and unless (1) the certificate of number issued to such undocumented vessel is in full force and effect, and (2) the identifying number set forth in the certificate of number is displayed on each side of the bow of the undocumented vessel for which the identifying number was issued. *(Added by Stats.1970, c. 1428, p. 2758, § 61. Amended by Stats.1975, c. 988, p. 2333, § 1; Stats.1987, c. 298, § 2.)*

Cross References

Exemptions from numbering requirement, see Vehicle Code § 9873.

Federal or out-of-state registration, see Vehicle Code § 9854.

Motorized recreational vessels numbered pursuant to this section, restrictions pertaining to noise levels, see Harbors and Navigation Code § 654.05.

§ 9851. Registration of public undocumented vehicles; exemption

The department may adopt rules and regulations for the registration of undocumented vessels belonging to the state, local public agencies, or to the United States without payment of fees specified in this code, except fees for duplicate certificates of ownership, duplicate certificates of number, or substitute current year registration stickers. Any vessel owned by the Department of Boating and Waterways is exempt from any fees specified in this division. *(Added by Stats.1970, c. 1428, p. 2758, § 61. Amended by Stats.1970, c. 1544, p. 3137, § 17; Stats.1973, c. 759, p. 1368, § 2; Stats.1984, c. 411, § 2; Stats.1990, c. 951 (S.B.2708), § 1, operative July 1, 1991.)*

§ 9852. Proof of ownership

The department shall promulgate rules and regulations setting forth requirements relative to establishing proof of ownership to be submitted by the owner at the time of filing initial application for a certificate of number and a certificate of ownership. The issuance of a certificate of ownership or certificate of number under this chapter shall not in any way be construed that the department is warranting or guaranteeing the title of the vessel as it appears on such certificates. *(Added by Stats.1970, c. 1428, p. 2758, § 61. Amended by Stats.1970, c. 1544, p. 3157, § 18; Stats.1973, c. 759, p. 1368, § 3.)*

§ 9852.5. Ownership of two or more undocumented vessels by two or more coowners

Ownership of an undocumented vessel subject to registration may be held by two or more coowners as follows:

(a) A vessel may be registered in the names of two or more persons as coowners in the alternative by the use of the word "or". A vessel so registered in the alternative shall be deemed to be held in joint tenancy. Each coowner shall be deemed to have granted to the other coowners the absolute right to dispose of the title and interest in the vessel. Upon the death of a coowner the interest of the decedent shall pass to the survivor as though title or interest in the vessel was held in joint tenancy unless a contrary intention is set forth in writing upon the application for registration.

(b) A vessel may be registered in the names of two or more persons as coowners in the alternative by the use of the word "or" and if declared in writing upon the application for registration by the applicants to be community property, or tenancy in common, shall grant to each coowner the absolute power to transfer the title or interest of the other coowners only during the lifetime of such coowners.

(c) A vessel may be registered in the names of two or more persons as coowners in the conjunctive by the use of the word "and" and shall thereafter require the signature of each coowner or his personal representative to transfer title to the vessel, except where title to the vessel is set forth in joint tenancy, the signature of each coowner or his or her personal representative shall be required only during the lifetime of the coowners, and upon death of a coowner title shall pass to the surviving coowner.

(d) The department may adopt suitable abbreviations to appear upon the certificate of ownership and certificate of number to designate the manner in which title to the vessel is held if set forth by the coowners upon the application for registration. *(Added by Stats.1985, c. 982, § 25.)*

Law Revision Commission Comments

1985 Addition

Section 9852.5 is drawn from Section 4150.5 (vehicles). [18 Cal.L.Rev.Comm. Reports 129 (1984)].

§ 9852.7. Beneficiary form ownership

(a) Ownership of an undocumented vessel subject to registration may be held in beneficiary form that includes a direction to transfer ownership of the vessel to a designated beneficiary on death of the owner if both of the following requirements are satisfied:

(1) Only one owner is designated.

(2) Only one TOD beneficiary is designated.

(b) Ownership registration and title issued in beneficiary form shall include, after the name of the owner, the words "transfer on death to" or the abbreviation "TOD" followed by the name of the beneficiary.

(c) During the lifetime of the owner, the signature or consent of the beneficiary is not required for any transaction relating to the vessel for which a certificate of ownership in beneficiary form has been issued.

(d) The fee for registering ownership of a vessel in a beneficiary form is ten dollars ($10). *(Added by Stats. 1991, c. 1055 (S.B.271), § 61, operative Jan. 1, 1993.)*

Law Revision Commission Comments

1991 Addition

Section 9852.7 is new. Subdivisions (a), (b), and (c) are drawn from Missouri law. See Mo.Ann.Stat. § 301.681 (Vernon Supp. 1991). See also Health & Safety Code §§ 18080.2, 18102.2; Veh.Code §§ 4150.7, 5910.5, 9916.5. [21 Cal.L.Rev.Comm.Reports 71 (1991)].

§ 9852.9. Initial application for a number; form contents

(a) On and after July 1, 2008, the form for an initial application for a number prepared by the department pursuant to Section 9853 shall include both of the following:

(1) Checkoff boxes or line alternatives for the retail seller of an undocumented vessel to certify that a sterndrive or inboard vessel that contains a spark-ignition marine engine below 373 kW (500 hp) rated power output that was manufactured on or after January 1, 2008, and a sterndrive or inboard vessel that contains a spark-ignition marine engine with any rated power output that was manufactured on or after January 1, 2009, has a permanently affixed label indicating that the engine meets or exceeds the 2008 California emissions standards required by Section 2442 of Title 13 of the California Code of Regulations.

(2) A line requiring that an initial application for a vessel described in paragraph (1) be accompanied by the hang tag required by Section 2443.3 of Title 13 of the California Code of Regulations for the engine described in paragraph (1).

(b) As used in this section, "spark-ignition marine engine" has the same meaning as that term is defined in Section 9853.7. *(Added by Stats.2007, c. 609 (A.B.695), § 1, operative July 1, 2008.)*

§ 9853. Application for number; fees; documentation of administrative costs

(a) The owner of each vessel requiring numbering by this state shall file an initial application for a number with the department or with an agent authorized by the department on forms approved by the department. The forms shall be prepared in cooperation with the Department of Boating and Waterways. The application shall contain the true name and address of the owner and of the legal owner, if any, and the hull identification number of the vessel as may be required by the department. The application shall be signed by the owner of the vessel and shall be accompanied by a fee of nine dollars ($9), in addition to the fees required under subdivision (b), except that an owner of a vessel registered outside this state who is submitting an application for registration in this state shall pay a fee of thirty-seven dollars ($37), in addition to the fees required under subdivision (b).

(b)(1) Whenever the fee for original registration of a vessel becomes due between January 1 and December 31 of any even-numbered year, the application shall be accompanied by a fee of ten dollars ($10), in addition to any other fees that are then due and payable.

(2) Whenever the fee for original registration of a vessel becomes due, or is filed with the department, between January 1 and December 31 of any odd-numbered year, the application shall be accompanied by a fee of twenty dollars ($20) in addition to any other fees that are then due and payable.

(c) The department shall additionally collect a quagga and zebra mussel infestation prevention fee in an amount established by the Department of Boating and Waterways pursuant to Section 675 of the Harbors and Navigation Code.

(d) The department shall provide documentation of its administrative costs pursuant to this section to the Department of Boating and Waterways. *(Added by Stats.1973, c. 759, p. 1369, § 5. Amended by Stats.1975, c. 389, p. 867, § 5; Stats.1980, c. 617, p. 1699, § 1; Stats.1980, c. 881, p. 2762, § 1; Stats.1982, c. 582, p. 2542, § 1; Stats.1990, c. 951 (S.B.2708), § 2, operative July 1, 1991; Stats.1997, c. 257 (A.B.299), § 3, eff. Aug. 11, 1997; Stats.2005, c. 473 (S.B.255), § 1; Stats.2012, c. 485 (A.B.2443), § 3.)*

Cross References

Distribution of funds derived from registration fee, see Vehicle Code § 9863.
Nonprofit public benefit corporations, fee exemption, see Vehicle Code § 9870.

§ 9853.1. Issuance of certificate of ownership and certificate of number

Upon receipt of the application in approved form, the department shall issue a certificate of ownership to the legal owner and a certificate of number to the owner, or both to the owner if there is no legal owner, stating the number issued to the vessel and the name and address of the owner. *(Added by Stats.1973, c. 759, p. 1369, § 6.)*

§ 9853.2. Display of number

The owner shall paint on or attach to each side of the forward half of the vessel the identification number in such manner as may be prescribed by rules and regulations of the department in order that it may be clearly visible. Any such rules and regulations shall be developed in cooperation with the Department of Boating and Waterways. The number shall be maintained in a legible condition. The certificate of number shall be pocket size and shall be available at all times for inspection on the vessel for which issued, whenever the vessel is in use, except as to those vessels subject to Section 9853.3. *(Added by Stats.1973, c. 759, p. 1369, § 7. Amended by Stats.1984, c. 144, § 206.)*

§ 9853.3. Retention of certificate of number for leased or rented vessels

The certificate of number for vessels less than 26 feet in length and leased or rented to another for the latter's noncommercial use of less than 24 hours may be retained

on shore by the vessel's owner or his representative at the place from which the vessel departs or returns to the possession of the owner or his representative. A copy of the lease or rental agreement signed by the owner or his authorized representative and by the person leasing or renting the vessel shall be carried aboard the vessel at all times during use. *(Added by Stats.1973, c. 759, p. 1369, § 8.)*

§ 9853.4. Stickers, tabs, or other devices

(a) The department may issue one or more stickers, tabs, or other suitable devices to identify vessels as being currently registered. The size, shape, and color of the sticker, tab, or other device and the positioning of the sticker, tab, or other device on the vessel shall be as determined by the department after consultation with the Department of Boating and Waterways, such consultation to consider the responsibilities and duties of the Department of Boating and Waterways as prescribed in the Harbors and Navigation Code.

(b) Whenever the department issues a sticker, tab, or other device pursuant to subdivision (a), the sticker, tab, or device shall only be displayed on the vessel for which it was issued. *(Added by Stats.1973, c. 759, p. 1369, § 9. Amended by Stats.1983, c. 142, § 167; Stats.1987, c. 298, § 3.)*

§ 9853.5. Vessels of historical interest; special plaques; fees

Upon request, the department shall issue for any power-driven pleasure craft which is constructed of wood and which was constructed prior to December 31, 1942, a special plaque which identifies the craft as a vessel of historical interest. The provisions of this section shall apply to documented as well as undocumented vessels. The size, shape, and content of such plaque and its positioning on the vessel shall be determined by the department after consultation with the Department of Boating and Waterways; provided, that such plaque shall be of a durable material and shall be no smaller than six inches in height and six inches in width. A reasonable fee, as determined by the department, sufficient to support the administration of such program, shall be charged for issuance of the plaque. The plaque shall be valid for the life of the vessel. *(Added by Stats.1980, c. 577, p. 1577, § 1.)*

§ 9853.6. Fee increases

(a)(1) Beginning July 1, 2008, the fee described in paragraph (1) of subdivision (b) of Section 9853 shall be increased by ten dollars ($10).

(2) Five dollars ($5) of the increase shall be deposited into the Alternative and Renewable Fuel and Vehicle Technology Fund created by Section 44273 of the Health and Safety Code and five dollars ($5) shall be deposited into the Air Quality Improvement Fund created by Section 44274.5 of the Health and Safety Code.

(b)(1) Beginning July 1, 2008, the fee described in paragraph (2) of subdivision (b) of Section 9853 shall be increased by twenty dollars ($20).

(2) Ten dollars ($10) of the increase shall be deposited into the Alternative and Renewable Fuel and Vehicle Technology Fund created by Section 44273 of the Health and Safety Code and ten dollars ($10) shall be deposited into the Air Quality Improvement Fund created by Section 44274.5 of the Health and Safety Code.

(c) This section shall remain in effect only until January 1, 2024, and as of that date is repealed, unless a later enacted statute, that is enacted before January 1, 2024, deletes or extends that date. *(Added by Stats.2007, c. 750 (A.B.118), § 8. Amended by Stats.2008, c. 179 (S.B.1498), § 217; Stats.2013, c. 401 (A.B.8), § 39, eff. Sept. 28, 2013.)*

Repeal

For repeal of this section, see its terms.

§ 9853.7. Retail sellers of specified vessels containing spark-ignition marine engines; obligations

(a)(1) When the retail seller of an undocumented sterndrive or inboard vessel, that contains a spark-ignition marine engine below 373 kW (500 hp) rated power output that was manufactured on or after January 1, 2008, or contains a spark-ignition marine engine with any rated power output that was manufactured on or after January 1, 2009, files for the purchaser of the vessel the initial application for a number for the vessel, the retail seller shall do both of the following:

(A) Certify on that application, by marking in indelible ink the affirmative checkoff boxes or line alternatives described in subdivision (a) of Section 9852.9, that the spark-ignition marine engine has a permanently affixed label indicating that the engine meets or exceeds the 2008 California emissions standards required by Section 2442 of Title 13 of the California Code of Regulations. The retail seller shall make that certification only after examining the permanently affixed label for the engine and only if the label indicates compliance with Section 2442 of Title 13 of the California Code of Regulations.

(B) Submit with the application, the hang tag required by Section 2443.3 of Title 13 of the California Code of Regulations for the engine, after including on the reserved white space of the hang tag, the engine family name, from the permanently affixed engine label, and the serial number of the engine.

(2) If the retail seller does not file for the purchaser of a vessel described in paragraph (1) the initial application for a number for the vessel, the applicant, upon filing an initial application for a number, shall submit the hang tag required by Section 2443.3 of Title 13 of the California Code of Regulations for the engine. The hang tag shall contain the engine family name, from the permanently affixed engine label, and the serial number of the engine, as inserted by the retail seller of the vessel.

(b) Subdivision (a) does not apply to a vessel originally purchased in another state by a resident of that state who subsequently establishes residence in this state and who provides satisfactory evidence to the department, or the department's agent authorized pursuant to Section 9858, of the previous residence.

(c) The department, and the department's agent authorized pursuant to Section 9858, shall not number a vessel subject to subdivision (a), unless the retail seller certifies on the initial application for a number filed for the purchaser of the vessel that the spark-ignition marine engine has the label described in paragraph (1) of subdivision (a) permanently affixed to the engine, or the applicant submits an application that is accompanied by the hang tag required by subdivision (a).

(d) For the purposes of this section, "spark-ignition marine engine" has the same meaning as that term is defined in paragraph (48) of subdivision (a) of Section 2441 of Title 13 of the California Code of Regulations. *(Added by Stats.2007, c. 609 (A.B.695), § 2, operative July 1, 2008.)*

§ 9853.8. Application

(a) This section applies only to a sterndrive or inboard vessel that contains a spark-ignition marine engine below 373 kW (500 hp) rated power output that was manufactured on or after January 1, 2008, or contains a spark-ignition marine engine with any rated power output that was manufactured on or after January 1, 2009.

(b) It is an infraction, punishable by a fine of two hundred fifty dollars ($250), for a person to operate an undocumented vessel, requiring numbering by the state, that is not currently numbered by the state, and that does not comply with the emissions standards required by Section 2442 of Title 13 of the California Code of Regulations.

(c) As used in this section, "spark-ignition marine engine" has the same meaning as that term is defined in Section 9853.7. *(Added by Stats.2007, c. 609 (A.B.695), § 3, operative July 1, 2008.)*

§ 9854. Federal or out-of-state registration

The owner of any vessel already covered by a number in full force and effect which has been issued to it pursuant to then operative federal law or a federally approved numbering system of another state shall make application within 30 days after the 90-day reciprocity period provided for in Section 9873. Such application shall be in a manner and pursuant to the procedure required for the issuance of a number under Section 9853. *(Added by Stats.1970, c. 1428, p. 2759, § 61. Amended by Stats.1972, c. 618, p. 1148, § 139.)*

§ 9855. Change of ownership

If the ownership of an undocumented vessel changes, the existing certificate of ownership and a new application form accompanied by a fee of fifteen dollars ($15) shall be filed with the department and a new certificate of

283

ownership and a new certificate of number shall be issued in the same manner as provided for in the initial issuance of number and the number shall be reassigned to the new owner. *(Added by Stats.1970, c. 1428, p. 2759, § 61. Amended by Stats.1980, c. 881, p. 2762, § 2; Stats.1982, c. 582, p. 2542, § 3; Stats.1990, c. 951 (S.B.2708), § 3, operative July 1, 1991.)*

Cross References

Nonprofit public benefit corporations, fee exemption, see Vehicle Code § 9870.

§ 9856.   Transfer to dealer

(a) It is not required that the department issue, or that an application be made for a new certificate of ownership or a new certificate of number, or that the fee prescribed in Section 9855 be paid on transfer of an undocumented vessel to a dealer in the course of his business as is otherwise provided in this division, if both of the following conditions are satisfied:

(1) The vessel is held and operated by the dealer only for the purpose of resale in the course of his business.

(2) The dealer has been issued a sales permit by the Board of Equalization covering sale of such property.

(b) The certificate of ownership bearing the endorsement of the transferor to the dealer of a vessel registered pursuant to this section and the certificate of number thereof shall be retained by the dealer until a transfer of the vessel by him. During that time the certificates shall be subject to inspection by the department or other authorized agency. Upon transfer of the vessel by the dealer the certificate of ownership shall be endorsed by the dealer and transfer further accomplished as otherwise provided in this division. *(Added by Stats.1970, c. 1428, p. 2759, § 61. Amended by Stats.1984, c. 411, § 3.)*

§ 9857.   Conformity with federal system

If an agency of the United States government shall have in force an overall system of identification numbering for undocumented vessels within the United States, the numbering system employed pursuant to this chapter shall be in conformity therewith. *(Added by Stats.1970, c. 1428, p. 2760, § 61.)*

§ 9858.   Issuance of certificates: department or agent

The department may issue any certificate of ownership and certificate of number or temporary certificate of number directly or the department may authorize any person to act as agent for the issuance of a certificate of number or temporary certificate of number. If a person accepts such authorization, he may be assigned a block of numbers which upon issuance, in conformity with this chapter and with any rules and regulations of the department, shall be valid as if issued directly by the department. Registration of vessels pursuant to the provisions of this code shall be conducted by the department or by any agent authorized by the department to conduct such registration. *(Added by Stats.1970, c. 1428, p. 2760, § 61.)*

§ 9858.1.   Maximum documentary preparation charge

Any documentary preparation charge by an authorized agent of the department shall not exceed twenty dollars ($20). *(Added by Stats.1984, c. 1407, § 2.)*

§ 9858.5.   Licensed yacht and ship brokers; use tax collection

Any licensed yacht and ship broker acting as an authorized agent of the department may collect use tax on a vessel transfer when applicable, and transmit the use tax and the registration application and applicable fees to the department, or may submit the registration application and applicable fees to the department for collection of any use tax due. *(Added by Stats.1982, c. 665, p. 2728, § 2.)*

Cross References

Undocumented vessels, retail sellers lacking seller's permit and not regularly engaged in the business, see Revenue and Taxation Code § 6294.

§ 9859.   Funds received by agent

All money received by an agent from the sale of certificates of number or temporary certificates of number and use tax shall be kept separate and apart from any other funds of the agent, and shall at all times belong to the state.

In case of an assignment for the benefit of creditors, receivership, or bankruptcy, the state shall have a preferred claim against the assignee, receiver, or trustee for all moneys owing the state for the sale of certificates as provided in this code and any use tax, and shall not be estopped from asserting such claim by reason of the commingling of funds or otherwise. *(Added by Stats. 1970, c. 1428, p. 2760, § 61. Amended by Stats.1982, c. 665, p. 2728, § 3; Stats.2009, c. 500 (A.B.1059), § 61.)*

§ 9860.   Renewal of certificates of number; fee for renewal; quagga and zebra mussel infestation prevention fee; documentation of administrative costs

(a) Certificates of number shall be renewed before midnight of the expiration date by presentation of the certificate of number last issued for the vessel or by presentation of a potential registration card issued by the department.

(b) The fee for renewal shall be twenty dollars ($20) for each two-year period, and shall accompany the request for renewal.

(c) If the certificate of number and potential registration card are unavailable, the fee specified in Section 9867 shall not be paid.

(d) The department shall additionally collect a quagga and zebra mussel infestation prevention fee in an amount established by the Department of Boating and Waterways pursuant to Section 675 of the Harbors and Navigation Code.

(e) The department shall provide documentation of its administrative costs pursuant to this section to the

Department of Boating and Waterways. *(Added by Stats.1996, c. 971 (A.B.122), § 4, operative Jan. 1, 1998. Amended by Stats.1997, c. 257 (A.B.299), § 5, eff. Aug. 11, 1997, operative Sept. 1, 1997; Stats.2005, c. 473 (S.B.255), § 2; Stats.2012, c. 485 (A.B.2443), § 4.)*

Cross References

Distribution of funds derived from registration fee, see Vehicle Code § 9863.
Nonprofit public benefit corporations, fee exemption, see Vehicle Code § 9870.

§ 9861. Expiration date of certificates of number

All certificates of number expire on December 31 of every odd-numbered year.

(Added by Stats.1970, c. 1428, p. 2761, § 61. Amended by Stats.1970, c. 1439, p. 2794, § 7; Stats.1996, c. 971 (A.B.122), § 5; Stats.1997, c. 257 (A.B.299), § 6, eff. Aug. 11, 1997; Stats.2005, c. 473 (S.B.255), § 3.)

§ 9862. Penalties for delinquency

(a) If the initial application for a number is not received by the department on or before the date set by the department, a penalty of one-half of the fee shall be assessed. If a certificate of number is not renewed on or before midnight of the expiration date, a penalty of one-half of the fee shall be assessed.

(b) If any person has received as the transferee of a vessel a properly endorsed certificate of ownership and certificate of number describing that vessel and the transfer fee has not been paid as required by this code within 30 days, a penalty of one-half of the transfer fee specified in Section 9855 shall be assessed. *(Added by Stats.1970, c. 1428, p. 2761, § 61. Amended by Stats.1973, c. 759, p. 1370, § 10; Stats.1982, c. 665, p. 2729, § 4; Stats.1984, c. 411, § 5; Stats.1990, c. 1352 (A.B.2912), § 14, eff. Sept. 27, 1990, operative July 1, 1990.)*

§ 9862.2. Repealed by Stats.1990, c. 1352 (A.B.2912), § 15, operative Jan. 1, 1995

§ 9862.5. Computation of penalties

In computing any penalty imposed under this chapter, a fraction of a dollar shall be disregarded unless it equals or exceeds fifty cents ($0. 50), in which case it shall be treated as one dollar ($1). *(Added by Stats.1970, c. 1439, p. 2761, § 8. Amended by Stats.2001, c. 825 (S.B.290), § 12.)*

§ 9863. Harbors and Watercraft Revolving Fund; distribution of funds

(a) Except as required under subdivisions (b) and (c), and except moneys collected under Section 9875, fees received pursuant to this chapter shall be deposited in the Harbors and Watercraft Revolving Fund and, notwithstanding Section 13340 of the Government Code, are continuously appropriated, without regard to fiscal years, for the administration of this chapter by the department. Funds in the Harbors and Watercraft Revolving Fund

derived pursuant to this chapter in excess of the amount determined by the Director of Finance, from time to time, to be necessary for expenditure for the administration of this chapter, notwithstanding Section 13340 of the Government Code, are continuously appropriated to the Department of Boating and Waterways, without regard to fiscal years, for expenditure in accordance with Section 663.7 of the Harbors and Navigation Code.

(b) Funds derived from imposition of the biennial registration fee under paragraph (2) of subdivision (b) of Section 9853, or under subdivision (b) of Section 9860, shall be distributed as follows:

(1) One-half shall be continuously appropriated pursuant to subdivision (a).

(2) One-half shall be allocated, upon appropriation, to the Department of Boating and Waterways for expenditure in support of programs under the department's jurisdiction.

(c) Funds derived from the imposition of the quagga and zebra mussel prevention fee under subdivision (c) of Section 9853, or under subdivision (d) of Section 9860, shall be distributed as specified in Section 676 of the Harbors and Navigation Code. *(Added by Stats.1970, c. 1428, p. 2761, § 61. Amended by Stats.1980, c. 881, p. 2763, § 4; Stats.1996, c. 971 (A.B.122), § 6; Stats.1998, c. 475 (A.B.2268), § 7; Stats.2005, c. 473 (S.B.255), § 4; Stats.2012, c. 485 (A.B.2443), § 5.)*

§ 9864. Wrecked, dismantled, destroyed or abandoned undocumented vessels.

The owner shall furnish the department notice of the wrecking or dismantling, or the destruction or abandonment of an undocumented vessel within 15 days thereof. The wrecking, dismantling, destruction or abandonment shall terminate the certificate of ownership and certificate of number of such undocumented vessel which if in existence shall be surrendered to the department.

The department, upon receiving notice of the abandonment of an undocumented vessel, or upon an official determination that an undocumented vessel has been abandoned, may order the destruction of such vessel at the expiration of 30 days if an investigation by the department has disclosed that no owner, legal owner, or lienholder claims an interest in the vessel, or if those persons have waived their interest. Nothing in this section shall be construed to deny the legal rights, otherwise provided for by law, of any person claiming an interest in an abandoned vessel if that person notifies the department within the time specified therefor. *(Added by Stats.1970, c. 1428, p. 2761, § 61. Amended by Stats.1987, c. 298, § 4.)*

§ 9865. Change of address

Any holder of a certificate of number shall notify the department within 15 days, if his address no longer conforms to the address appearing on the certificate and shall, as part of such notification, furnish the department with his new address. The department may provide for

285

the surrender of the certificate bearing the former address and its replacement with a certificate bearing the new address or for the alteration of an outstanding certificate to show the new address of the holder. *(Added by Stats.1970, c. 1428, p. 2762, § 61. Amended by Stats.1973, c. 759, p. 1370, § 11.)*

§ 9866. Display of other numbers on bow

No number other than the number issued to an undocumented vessel or granted reciprocity pursuant to this chapter shall be painted, attached, or otherwise displayed on either side of the bow of such undocumented vessel. *(Added by Stats.1970, c. 1428, p. 2762, § 61.)*

§ 9867. Fee; duplicate certificates or stickers

A fee of fifteen dollars ($15) shall be charged for a duplicate of certificate of number, certificate of ownership, or current year registration stickers. *(Added by Stats.1970, c. 1428, p. 2762, § 61. Amended by Stats.1973, c. 759, p. 1370, § 12; Stats.1980, c. 881, p. 2763, § 5; Stats.1982, c. 582, p. 2543, § 7; Stats.1990, c. 951 (S.B. 2708), § 4, operative July 1, 1991.)*

§ 9867.5. Transfer of registration; unavailable certificate; additional fee

Upon application for transfer of registration pursuant to Section 9917, a fee as specified in Section 9867 shall be paid to the department in addition to the regular transfer fee. *(Added by Stats.1978, c. 497, p. 1634, § 4.)*

§ 9868. Refunds

Fees received pursuant to this chapter are appropriated for payment of refunds of money received or collected in the payment of fees, permits, or services whenever the fee, permit or service cannot lawfully be issued or rendered to the applicant, and in cases where the payment in whole or in part represents overpayment or payment in duplicate. *(Added by Stats.1970, c. 1428, p. 2762, § 61.)*

§ 9869. Information to be transmitted to county assessor

The department shall transmit information from each initial application and each transfer application or renewal application to the county assessor in the county of residence of the owner of the vessel and to the county assessor in the county in which the vessel is principally kept if other than the county of residence of the owner, if such other county is known to the department. If an application shows that the owner of the vessel has changed his residence from one county to another county or shows that there has been a change in the county in which the vessel is principally kept, the department shall transmit information of the change to the assessor of the county in which the owner of the vessel formerly resided or to the assessor of the county in which the vessel formerly was principally kept. After the department receives a notice pursuant to Section 9864, the department shall transmit information of the destruction or abandonment to the assessor of the county in which the owner of the vessel resides and to the assessor of the county in which the vessel is or was principally kept, if other than the county of residence of the owner, if such other county was known to the department. *(Added by Stats.1970, c. 1428, p. 2762, § 61.)*

§ 9870. Nonprofit public benefit corporation

A nonprofit public benefit corporation governed by the Nonprofit Public Benefit Corporation Law (Part 2 (commencing with Section 5110) of Division 2 of Title 1 of the Corporations Code), which purposes relate to promoting the ability of boys and girls to do things for themselves, to train them in scoutcraft and camping, and to teach them patriotism, courage, self-reliance and kindred virtues, shall not be required to pay the fees provided for in Sections 9853, 9855, and 9860. *(Added by Stats.1970, c. 1428, p. 2762, § 61. Amended by Stats.1978, c. 1305, p. 4292, § 43, operative Jan. 1, 1980; Stats.1984, c. 411, § 6.)*

§ 9871. Assignment and marking of hull identification number

Upon application for original registration or transfer of registration of an undocumented vessel, the department may assign an appropriate hull identification number to such vessel whenever there is no hull identification number thereon, or when a hull identification number thereon has been destroyed or obliterated; and such hull identification number shall be permanently marked in an integral part of the hull which is accessible for inspection. *(Added by Stats.1970, c. 1428, p. 2763, § 61. Amended by Stats.1980, c. 617, p. 1699, § 2.)*

§ 9871.5. Renewal of registration; hull identification number

Upon application for renewal of registration of an undocumented vessel, the applicant is required to furnish the hull identification number if the records of the department do not contain such number. If the vessel does not have a hull number, the department may assign an appropriate hull identification number. *(Added by Stats.1980, c. 617, p. 1699, § 3.)*

§ 9872. Defacing, destroying, or altering hull identification number

No person shall intentionally deface, destroy, or alter the hull identification number of a vessel required to be numbered under this chapter without written authorization from the department; nor shall any person place or stamp any serial or other number or mark upon an undocumented vessel which might interfere with identification of the hull identification number. This does not prohibit the restoration by an owner of an original number or mark when the restoration is authorized by the department, nor prevent any manufacturer from placing, in the ordinary course of business, numbers or marks upon new vessels or new parts thereof. *(Added by*

Stats.1970, c. 1428, p. 2763, § 61. Amended by Stats.1980, c. 617, p. 1699, § 4.)

§ 9872.1. Vessel or component part with hull identification number removed, defaced, altered or destroyed; prohibition of purchase, sale, offer for sale, receipt or possession; impoundment; hearing on disposition; notice and receipt; contents; return to owner; conditions.

(a) No person shall knowingly buy, sell, offer for sale, receive, or have in his or her possession any vessel, or component part thereof, from which the hull identification number has been removed, defaced, altered, or destroyed, unless the vessel or component part has attached thereto a hull identification number assigned or approved by the department in lieu of the manufacturer's number.

(b) Whenever a vessel, or component part thereof, from which the hull identification number has been removed, defaced, altered, or destroyed, and which does not have attached thereto an assigned or approved number as described in subdivision (a), comes into the custody of a peace officer, the seized vessel or component part is subject, in accordance with the procedures specified in this section, to impoundment and to such disposition as may be provided by order of a court having jurisdiction. This subdivision does not apply with respect to a seized vessel or component part used as evidence in any criminal action or proceeding.

(c) Whenever a vessel or component part described in subdivision (a) comes into the custody of a peace officer, any person from whom the property was seized, and all claimants to the property whose interest or title is on registration records in the department, shall be notified within five days, excluding Saturdays, Sundays, and holidays, after the seizure, of the date, time, and place of the hearing required in subdivision (e). The notice shall contain the information specified in subdivision (d).

(d) Whenever a peace officer seizes a vessel or component part as provided in subdivision (b), any person from whom the property was seized shall be provided a notice of impoundment of the vessel or component part which shall serve as a receipt and contain the following information:

(1) Name and address of person from whom the property was seized.

(2) A statement that the vessel or component part seized has been impounded for investigation of a violation of this section and that the property will be released upon a determination that the hull identification number has not been removed, defaced, altered, or destroyed, or upon the presentation of satisfactory evidence of ownership of the vessel or component part, provided that no other person claims an interest in the property; otherwise, a hearing regarding the disposition of the vessel or component part shall take place in the proper court.

(3) A statement that any person from whom the property was seized, and all claimants to the property whose interest or title is on registration records in the department, will receive written notification of the date, time, and place of the hearing within five days, excluding Saturdays, Sundays, and holidays, after the seizure.

(4) Name and address of the law enforcement agency where evidence of ownership of the vessel or component part may be presented.

(5) A statement of the contents of this section.

(e) A hearing on the disposition of the property shall be held by the superior court within 60 days after the seizure. The hearing shall be before the court without a jury. A proceeding under this section is a limited civil case.

(1) If the evidence reveals either that the hull identification number has not been removed, altered, or destroyed or that the hull identification number has been removed, altered, or destroyed but satisfactory evidence of ownership has been presented to the seizing agency or court, the property shall be released to the person entitled thereto.

(2) If the evidence reveals that the hull identification number has been removed, altered, or destroyed, and satisfactory evidence of ownership has not been presented, the property shall be destroyed, sold, or otherwise disposed of as provided by court order.

(3) At the hearing, the seizing agency shall have the burden of establishing that the hull identification number has been removed, defaced, altered, or destroyed and that no satisfactory evidence of ownership has been presented.

(f) Nothing in this section precludes the return of a seized vessel or component part to the owner by the seizing agency following presentation of satisfactory evidence of ownership and, if determined necessary, upon the assignment of an identification number to the vessel or component part by the department. *(Added by Stats.1987, c. 302, § 1. Amended by Stats.1998, c. 931 (S.B.2139), § 454, eff. Sept. 28, 1998; Stats.2002, c. 784 (S.B.1316), § 595.)*

Law Revision Commission Comments

1998 Amendment

Section 9872.1 is amended to accommodate unification of the municipal and superior courts in a county. Cal. Const. art. VI, § 5(e). The section is also amended to reflect elimination of the justice court. Cal. Const. art. VI, §§ 1, 5(b).

A limited civil case is within the original jurisdiction of the municipal court or of the superior court in a county in which there is no municipal court. Cal. Const. art. VI, 10 (superior court jurisdiction); Code Civ. Proc. §§ 85, 85.1 (limited civil cases). See also Code Civ. Proc. §§ 91, 904.2, 1085 (trial procedures and writ and appellate jurisdiction for limited civil cases). [28 Cal.L.Rev.Comm. Reports 51 (1998)].

2002 Amendment

Subdivision (e) of Section 9872.1 is amended to reflect unification of the municipal and superior courts pursuant to

Article VI, Section 5(e), of the California Constitution. [32 Cal.L.Rev.Comm. Reports 534 (2002)].

§ 9872.5. Amphibious vehicles

No certificate of ownership shall be issued under this chapter for any "amphibious vehicle" for which a certificate of ownership may be issued by the department under other provisions of this code.

For the purposes of this section, an "amphibious vehicle" is a device by which any person or property may be propelled, moved, or drawn, both upon water and upon a highway on land. *(Added by Stats.1970, c. 1439, p. 2794, § 9.)*

§ 9873. Undocumented vessels not required to be numbered

An undocumented vessel shall not be required to be numbered under this chapter if it is:

(a) Already covered by a number in full force and effect which has been issued to it pursuant to federal law or a federally approved numbering system of another state; provided, that such undocumented vessel shall be subject to the numbering requirements of this chapter if it has changed its state of principal use and has been within this state for a period in excess of 90 consecutive days.

(b) A vessel from a country other than the United States temporarily using the waters of this state.

(c) A public vessel of the United States, another state or subdivision thereof or municipality of such other state.

(d) A ship's lifeboat.

(e) Any vessel belonging to a class of boats which has been exempted from numbering by the department after the department has found that the numbering of vessels of such class will not materially aid in their identification; and, if any agency of the federal government has a numbering system applicable to the class of vessels to which the vessel in question belongs, after the department has further found that the vessel would also be exempt from numbering if it were subject to the federal law. An undocumented vessel propelled solely by oars or paddles and an undocumented vessel eight feet or less propelled solely by sail are exempt from the provisions of this chapter. *(Added by Stats.1970, c. 1428, p. 2763, § 61. Amended by Stats.1973, c. 759, p. 1370, § 13.)*

Cross References

Federal or out of state registration, see Vehicle Code § 9854.

§ 9874. Suspension, cancellation, or revocation

The department may suspend, cancel, or revoke the registration of a vessel, a certificate of number, sticker, certificate of ownership, or temporary certificate of number in any of the following cases:

(a) When the department is satisfied that the registration or the certificate of number, sticker, certificate of ownership, or temporary certificate of number was fraudulently obtained or erroneously issued.

(b) When the department determines that the required fee has not been paid and the same is not paid upon reasonable notice and demand. *(Added by Stats. 1970, c. 1428, p. 2764, § 61.)*

§ 9875. Penalties

Except as provided in Section 40000.8, any person who violates any provision of this chapter or any rule or regulation of the department adopted pursuant to this chapter is guilty of an infraction, punishable under Section 42001. *(Added by Stats.1970, c. 1428, p. 2764, § 61. Amended by Stats.1983, c. 1092, § 379, eff. Sept. 27, 1983, operative Jan. 1, 1984; Stats.1991, c. 922 (A.B.1201), § 6.)*

§ 9880. Withholding of renewal of certificate of vessel number or transfer of title or interest; receipt of notice of tax delinquency; record of notice; satisfaction; notification of vessel transfer or nonrenewal

(a) The department shall not renew the certificate of number of, or allow a transfer of any title to or interest in, a vessel if the county tax collector has notified the department pursuant to Section 3205 of the Revenue and Taxation Code, that taxes are delinquent upon the vessel, and the department shall not subsequently issue a certificate of number for, or a new certificate of ownership reflecting a transfer of title to or interest in, that vessel until the department receives a certificate of clearance from the county tax collector that the delinquent taxes have been paid on that vessel or until the county tax collector has provided notice to the department that the delinquency has been satisfied.

(b) The department shall record the notice of delinquent taxes on the vessel. If the department is notified by the county tax collector that the delinquency has been satisfied, the department shall, if all other requirements are satisfied, issue a certificate of number for, or a new certificate of ownership reflecting a transfer of title to or interest in, the vessel. The department shall assess a fee upon each county tax collector in an amount that is sufficient to reimburse the department for its actual costs of administering this section.

(c) Whenever a vessel subject to this section is transferred, or not renewed for 26 months, the department shall notify the county tax collector of that fact. *(Added by Stats.1989, c. 183, § 2. Amended by Stats.1994, c. 940 (S.B.1626), § 4, operative July 1, 1995; Stats.1997, c. 546 (S.B.1107), § 13.)*

CHAPTER 3. TRANSFER OF TITLE OR INTEREST IN UNDOCUMENTED VESSEL

Section
9900.   Requirements for transfer.
9901.   Application by transferee for certificates of ownership and number; fee.
9902.   Issuance of new certificates of ownership and number.

Section
9903.   Statement by transferee or transferor: information to be transmitted to state board of equalization.
9904.   Repealed.
9905.   Requirements for releasing liability.
9906.   Transfer by legal owner.
9907.   Endorsement of certificate of ownership upon transfer by legal owner.
9908.   Transfer by registered owner.
9909.   Endorsement when certificate of ownership unavailable.
9910.   Delivery of certificates.
9911.   Notice by owners.
9912.   Notice by dealers.
9913.   New security interest executed by parties to prior security agreement.
9914.   Pledge of security interest by legal owner.
9915.   Involuntary transfers.
9916.   Transfer of ownership upon death of owner; persons eligible; requirements.
9916.5.   Beneficiary form ownership.
9916.7.   Beneficiary form ownership; transfer; department liability.
9917.   Transfer when certificates unavailable.
9918.   Transfer under regular application.
9919.   Recording of security interest.
9920.   Perfection of security interest.
9921.   Secured party as legal owner.
9922.   Method as exclusive.
9923.   Undertaking on bond.
9924.   Return and surrender of bond or undertaking.
9928.   Withholding number certificates or transfer registration pending payment of use tax or penalties; transmittal of collections; computation of tax; collection agreements.

Cross References

Definitions, see Vehicle Code § 9840.

§ 9900.   Requirements for transfer

No transfer of the title or any interest in or to an undocumented vessel numbered under this code shall pass, and any attempted transfer shall not be effective, until the parties thereto have paid any delinquent property taxes with respect to that vessel and fulfilled either of the following requirements:

(a) The transferor has made proper endorsement and delivery of the certificate of ownership to the transferee as provided in this code and the transferee has delivered to the department or has placed the certificates in the United States mail addressed to the department when and as required under this code with the proper transfer fee and thereby makes application for a new certificate of ownership and a new certificate of number.

(b) The transferor has delivered to the department or has placed in the United States mail addressed to the department the appropriate documents for the transfer of ownership of the vessel pursuant to the sale or transfer except as otherwise provided. *(Added by Stats.1970, c. 1428, p. 2764, § 61.   Amended by Stats.1988, c. 1268, § 14; Stats.1994, c. 940 (S.B.1626), § 5, operative July 1, 1995.)*

§ 9901.   Application by transferee for certificates of ownership and number; fee

Whenever any person has received as transferee a properly endorsed certificate of ownership, he or she shall, within 10 days thereafter, forward the certificates with the transfer fee specified in Section 9855 to the department, and thereby make application for a certificate of ownership and certificate of number. *(Added by Stats.1970, c. 1428, p. 2764, § 61.   Amended by Stats.1970, c. 1439, p. 2794, § 10; Stats.1980, c. 881, p. 2764, § 6; Stats.1982, c. 582, p. 2543, § 9; Stats.1988, c. 1268, § 15; Stats.1995, c. 766 (S.B.726), § 7.)*

§ 9902.   Issuance of new certificates of ownership and number

The department, upon receipt of a properly endorsed certificate of ownership and a new application form and the required fee, shall issue a new certificate of ownership and a new certificate of number in the same manner as provided for in the initial issuance of number and the number may be reassigned to the new owner, provided, however, in the case of a transfer of a part interest which does not affect the owner's right to operate such undocumented vessel the transfer shall not terminate the certificate of number. *(Added by Stats.1970, c. 1428, p. 2764, § 61.   Amended by Stats.1988, c. 1268, § 16.)*

§ 9903.   Statement by transferee or transferor: information to be transmitted to state board of equalization

(a) Prior to the issuance of any certificate of ownership the department shall obtain a statement in writing, signed by the transferee or transferor, showing:

(1) The date of the sale or other transfer of ownership of the vessel.

(2) The name and address of the seller or transferor.

(3) The name and address of the buyer or transferee.

(4) The total consideration (valued in money) given for the sale or other transfer of the vessel, including any motor or other component part of the vessel included in the sale or other transfer.

(b) Upon the transfer of ownership of a vessel the department shall forward to the State Board of Equalization information from its records identifying the vessel together with the data required by subdivision (a). The information shall be transmitted as promptly as feasible and in such form and manner as shall be agreed between the department and the board. *(Added by Stats.1970, c. 1428, p. 2765, § 61.)*

§ 9904.   Repealed by Stats.1975, c. 918, p. 2025, § 1

§ 9905.   Requirements for releasing liability

An owner who has made a bona fide sale or transfer of an undocumented vessel and has delivered possession of the vessel to a purchaser shall not by reason of any of the provisions of this code or the Harbors and Navigation Code be deemed the owner of the vessel so as to be subject to civil liability for the operation of the vessel thereafter by another when the owner, in addition to the foregoing, has fulfilled either of the following requirements:

(a) Made proper endorsement and delivery of the certificate of ownership as provided in this code.

(b) Delivered to the department or placed in the United States mail, addressed to the department, either the notice as provided in Sections 9911 and 9912 or appropriate documents for transfer of the vessel pursuant to the sale or transfer. *(Added by Stats.1970, c. 1428, p. 2765, § 61. Amended by Stats.1988, c. 1268, § 17; Stats.1991, c. 13 (A.B.37), § 23, eff. Feb. 13, 1991.)*

Cross References

Certificate of ownership, procedures upon change of ownership, see Vehicle Code § 9855.
Transfers to dealers, see Vehicle Code § 9856.
Undocumented vessel, defined, see Vehicle Code § 9840.

§ 9906. Transfer by legal owner

A legal owner may assign his title or interest in or to an undocumented vessel numbered under this code to a person other than the owner without the consent of and without affecting the interest of the owner. *(Added by Stats.1970, c. 1428, p. 2765, § 61.)*

§ 9907. Endorsement of certificate of ownership upon transfer by legal owner

Upon transfer of the title or any interest of the legal owner or legal owners in an undocumented vessel numbered under this code, the transferor shall write his signature, and the transferee shall write his signature and address, in the appropriate spaces provided upon the reverse side of the certificate of ownership issued for the vessel. *(Added by Stats.1970, c. 1428, p. 2765, § 61.)*

§ 9908. Transfer by registered owner

Upon transfer of the title or interest or any part thereof of the registered owner only in an undocumented vessel numbered under this code, the registered owner shall write his signature and address and the transferee shall write his signature and address in the appropriate spaces provided on the reverse side of the certificate of ownership for the vessel, and the legal owner shall write his signature in the space provided for the new legal owner indicating that he is to retain his legal title and interest. *(Added by Stats.1970, c. 1428, p. 2765, § 61.)*

§ 9909. Endorsement when certificate of ownership unavailable

When the required certificate of ownership is lost, stolen, damaged, or mutilated, application for transfer may be made upon a form provided by the department for a duplicate certificate of ownership. The transferor shall write his signature and address in the appropriate spaces provided upon the application and file the same together with the proper fees for duplicate certificate of

ownership and transfer. *(Added by Stats.1970, c. 1428, p. 2766, § 61.)*

§ 9910. Delivery of certificates

It is unlawful for any person to fail or neglect to deliver the certificate of number and, when having possession, to properly endorse, date, and deliver the certificate of ownership to a transferee who is lawfully entitled to a transfer of ownership. *(Added by Stats.1970, c. 1428, p. 2766, § 61.)*

§ 9911. Notice by owners

Whenever the owner of an undocumented vessel numbered under this code sells or transfers his or her title or interest in, or any part thereof, and delivers the possession of, the vessel to another, the owner shall, within five calendar days, notify the department of the sale or transfer by giving the date thereof, the name and address of the owner and of the transferee and a description of the vessel as may be required in the appropriate form provided for the purpose by the department. *(Added by Stats.1970, c. 1428, p. 2766, § 61. Amended by Stats.1986, c. 1212, § 4; Stats.1991, c. 13 (A.B.37), § 24, eff. Feb. 13, 1991; Stats.1992, c. 427 (A.B.3355), § 166.)*

Cross References

Undocumented vessels,
   Defined, see Vehicle Code § 9840.
   Numbering, see Vehicle Code § 9850.

§ 9912. Notice by dealers

Every dealer upon transferring by sale, lease or otherwise any undocumented vessel, whether new or used, required to be numbered under this code, shall, not later than the end of the next business day of the dealer, give written notice of the transfer to the department upon an appropriate form provided by it, but a dealer need not give the notice when selling or transferring a new unnumbered vessel to another dealer. *(Added by Stats. 1970, c. 1428, p. 2766, § 61.)*

§ 9913. New security interest executed by parties to prior security agreement

When a security interest upon a numbered vessel is satisfied, canceled, or released by the parties thereto who are the registered owner and legal owner respectively of said vessel and thereafter within a period of 10 days a new security interest covering the vessel is executed between the same parties, no application for transfer of ownership by reason thereof shall be made, no new certificate of ownership or certificate of number shall be issued, and all provisions of this code relating to transfers of any title or interest in a vessel shall be deemed to have been fully complied with. *(Added by Stats.1970, c. 1428, p. 2766, § 61.)*

§ 9914. Pledge of security interest by legal owner

The transferee of a security interest in the interest of a legal owner of a numbered vessel need not make application for a transfer of ownership when the security interest arises from a pledge of security agreement by the legal owner to the pledgee. *(Added by Stats.1970, c. 1428, p. 2766, § 61.)*

§ 9915. Involuntary transfers

(a) Whenever the title or interest of any owner or legal owner in or to a vessel numbered under this code passes to another otherwise than by a voluntary transfer, the new owner or legal owner may obtain a transfer of ownership upon application therefor and upon presentation of the last certificate of ownership and certificate of number issued for the vessel, if available, and any instruments or documents of authority or certified copies thereof as may be required by the department, or required by law, to evidence or effect a transfer of title or interest in or to chattels in such case.

(b) The department when satisfied of the genuineness and regularity of the transfer shall give notice by mail to the owner and legal owner of the vessel as shown by the records of the department, and five days after the giving of the notice, if still satisfied of the genuineness and regularity of such transfer, shall transfer the ownership of the vessel accordingly and issue a new certificate of ownership and certificate of number to the person or persons entitled thereto. Such notice shall not be required for an involuntary transfer when repossession involves a secured party. *(Added by Stats.1970, c. 1428, p. 2765, § 61. Amended by Stats.1975, c. 918, p. 2025, § 2.)*

§ 9916. Transfer of ownership upon death of owner; persons eligible; requirements

(a) If 40 days have elapsed since the death of an owner or legal owner of any vessel numbered under this division without the decedent leaving other property necessitating probate, and irrespective of the value of the vessel, the following person may secure a transfer of ownership of the title or interest of the decedent:

(1) The sole person or all of the persons who succeeded to the property of the decedent under Sections 6401 and 6402 of the Probate Code unless the vessel is, by will, otherwise bequeathed.

(2) The sole beneficiary or all of the beneficiaries who succeeded to the vessel under the will of the decedent where the vessel is, by will, so bequeathed.

(b) The person authorized by subdivision (a) may secure a transfer of ownership of the title or interest of the decedent upon presenting to the department all of the following:

(1) The appropriate certificate of ownership and certificate of number, if available.

(2) A certificate of the heir or beneficiary under penalty of perjury containing the following statements:

(A) The date and place of the decedent's death.

(B) The decedent left no other property necessitating probate and no probate proceeding is now being or has been conducted in this state for the decedent's estate.

(C) The declarant is entitled to the vessel either (i) as the sole person or all of the persons who succeeded to the property of the decedent under Sections 6401 and 6402 of the Probate Code if the decedent left no will or (ii) as the beneficiary or beneficiaries under the decedent's last will if the decedent left a will, and no one has a right to the decedent's vessel that is superior to that of the declarant.

(D) There are no unsecured creditors of the decedent or, if there are, the unsecured creditors of the decedent have been paid in full or their claims have been otherwise discharged.

(3) If required by the department, a certificate of the death of the decedent.

(4) If required by the department, the names and addresses of any other heirs or beneficiaries.

(c) If the department is presented with the documents specified in paragraphs (1) and (2) of subdivision (b), no liability shall be incurred by the department or any officer or employee of the department by reason of the transfer of registration of the vessel pursuant to this section. The department or officer or employee of the department may rely in good faith on the statements in the certificate specified in paragraph (2) of subdivision (b) and has no duty to inquire into the truth of any statement in the certificate. The person who secures the transfer of the vessel pursuant to this section is subject to the provisions of Section 13109 to 13113, inclusive, of the Probate Code to the same extent as a person to whom transfer of property is made under Chapter 3 (commencing with Section 13100) of Part 1 of Division 8 of the Probate Code. *(Added by Stats.1985, c. 982, § 27. Amended by Stats.1986, c. 783, § 27, operative July 1, 1987.)*

§ 9916.5. Beneficiary form ownership

(a) On death of the owner of a vessel numbered under this division and owned in beneficiary form, the vessel belongs to the surviving beneficiary, if any. If there is no surviving beneficiary, the vessel belongs to the estate of the deceased owner.

(b) A certificate of ownership in beneficiary form may be revoked or the beneficiary changed at any time before the death of the owner by either of the following methods:

(1) By sale of the vessel with property assignment and delivery of the certificate of ownership to another person.

(2) By application for a new certificate of ownership without designation of a beneficiary or with the designation of a different beneficiary.

(c) Except as provided in subdivision (b), designation of a beneficiary in a certificate of ownership issued in beneficiary form may not be changed or revoked by will, by any other instrument, by a change of circumstances, or otherwise.

(d) The beneficiary's interest in the vessel at death of the owner is subject to any contract of sale, assignment, or security interest to which the owner was subject during his or her lifetime.

(e) The surviving beneficiary may secure a transfer of ownership for the vessel upon presenting to the department all of the following:

(1) The appropriate certificate of ownership.

(2) A certificate under penalty of perjury stating the date and place of the owner's death and that the declarant is entitled to the vessel as the designated beneficiary.

(3) If required by the department, a certificate of the death of the owner.

(f) After the death of the owner, the surviving beneficiary may transfer his or her interest in the vessel to another person without securing transfer of ownership into his or her own name by appropriately signing the certificate of ownership for the vessel and delivering the document to the transferee for forwarding to the department with appropriate fees. The transferee may secure a transfer of ownership upon presenting to the department (1) the certificate of title signed by the beneficiary, (2) the certificate described in paragraph (2) of subdivision (e) executed by the beneficiary under penalty of perjury, and (3) if required by the department, a certificate of death of the owner.

(g) A transfer at death pursuant to this section is effective by reason of this section, and shall not be deemed to be a testamentary disposition of property. The right of the designated beneficiary to the vessel shall not be denied, abridged, or affected on the grounds that the right has not been created by a writing executed in accordance with the laws of this state prescribing the requirements to effect a valid testamentary disposition of property.

(h) A transfer at death pursuant to this section is subject to Section 9653 of the Probate Code.

(i) If there is no surviving beneficiary, the person or persons described in Section 9916 may secure transfer of the vessel as provided in that section.

(j) The department may prescribe forms for use pursuant to this section. *(Added by Stats.1991, c. 1055 (S.B.271), § 62, operative Jan. 1, 1993.)*

Law Revision Commission Comments

1991 Addition

Section 9916.5 is new. Subdivisions (a) through (d) are drawn from Missouri law. See Mo.Ann.Stat. § 301.681 (Vernon Supp. 1991). Subdivision (e) is drawn from Health and Safety Code Section 18102(b) and Vehicle Code Sections 5910(b) and 9916(b). Subdivision (g) is drawn from Probate Code Section 5304. Subdivision (h) is comparable to Health and Safety Code Section 18102.2(h), Probate Code Section 5705 (gift in view of impending death), and Vehicle Code Section 5910.5(h). Subdivision (j) is drawn from Vehicle Code Section 5910(c). See also Health & Safety Code §§ 18080.2, 18102.2; Veh. Code §§ 4150.7, 5910.5, 9852.7, 9916.5. [21 Cal.L.Rev.Comm.Reports 71 (1991)].

292

§ 9916.7. Beneficiary form ownership; transfer; department liability

(a) If the department makes a transfer pursuant to Section 9916.5, the department is discharged from all liability, whether or not the transfer is consistent with the beneficial ownership of the vessel transferred.

(b) The protection provided by subdivision (a) does not extend to a transfer made after the department has been served with a court order restraining the transfer. No other notice or information shown to have been available to the department shall affect its right to the protection afforded by subdivision (a).

(c) The protection provided by this section has no bearing on the rights of parties in disputes between themselves or their successors concerning the beneficial ownership of the vessel.

(d) The protection provided by this section is in addition to, and not exclusive of, any other protection provided to the department by any other provision of law. *(Added by Stats.1991, c. 1055 (S.B.271), § 63, operative Jan. 1, 1993.)*

Law Revision Commission Comments

1991 Addition

Section 9916.7 is drawn from Probate Code Section 5405 (Multiple-Party Accounts Law). See also Health & Safety Code § 18102.3; Veh. Code § 5910.7. [20 Cal.L.Rev.Comm.Reports 2883 (1990)].

§ 9917.   Transfer when certificates unavailable

Whenever application is made to the department for a transfer of ownership of a vessel to a new owner or legal owner and the applicant is unable to present the certificate of ownership issued for the vessel by reason of the same being lost or otherwise not available, the department may receive the application and examine into the circumstances of the case and may require the filing of affidavits or other information, and when the department is satisfied that the applicant is entitled to a transfer of ownership, the department may transfer the ownership of the vessel, and issue a new certificate of ownership, and certificate of number to the person or persons found to be entitled thereto. *(Added by Stats.1970, c. 1428, p. 2767, § 61. Amended by Stats.1988, c. 1268, § 18.)*

Cross References

Fees, see Vehicle Code § 9867.5.

§ 9918.   Transfer under regular application

If the application for a transfer is made in the manner provided in this code, the department shall not be required to withhold the transfer of any right, title or interest in or to a vessel if the application on its face appears to be genuine and regular and the department has received neither a request from any law enforcement agency that action on the application be deferred nor an order of a court of the United States or of the State of

California restraining the transfer within two years prior thereto. *(Added by Stats.1970, c. 1428, p. 2767, § 61.)*

§ 9919. Recording of security interest

No security interest in any vessel numbered under this code, irrespective of whether such number was effected prior or subsequent to the creation of such security interest, is perfected, until the secured party, or his successor or assignee, has deposited with the department a properly endorsed certificate of ownership to the vessel, subject to the security interest, showing the secured party as legal owner if the vessel is then numbered under this code; or if the vessel is not so numbered, the owner shall file an initial application for number as provided for in this code, and the certificate of ownership issued under said application shall contain the name and address of the legal owner. *(Added by Stats.1970, c. 1428, p. 2768, § 61.)*

§ 9920. Perfection of security interest

When the secured party, his successor or assignee, has deposited with the department a properly endorsed certificate of ownership showing the secured party as legal owner, or if the vessel is not numbered when the owner shall file an initial application for number as provided for in this code, and the certificate of ownership issued under said application shows said secured party as the legal owner, and said certificate of ownership is deposited with the department, the deposit constitutes perfection of the security interest. *(Added by Stats.1970, c. 1428, p. 2768, § 61.)*

§ 9921. Secured party as legal owner

Upon the deposit with the department of the certificate of ownership showing the secured party as legal owner as provided in Section 9919 hereof, the department shall on its records show the secured party, his successor or assignee, as legal owner with respect to such vessel. *(Added by Stats.1970, c. 1428, p. 2768, § 61.)*

§ 9922. Method as exclusive

The method provided in this chapter for perfecting a security interest in a vessel numbered under this code is exclusive. *(Added by Stats.1970, c. 1428, p. 2768, § 61.)*

§ 9923. Undertaking on bond

In the absence of the regularly required supporting evidence of ownership upon application for registration or transfer of a vessel, the department may accept an undertaking or bond in the amount of the fair market value of the vessel at the time of the application, as determined by the department, which shall be conditioned to protect the department and all officers and employees thereof and any subsequent purchaser of the vessel, any person acquiring a lien or security interest thereon, or the successor in interest of such purchaser or person, against any loss or damage on account of any defect in or undisclosed claim upon the right, title, and interest of the applicant or other person in and to the vessel. *(Added by Stats.1970, c. 1428, p. 2768, § 61.)*

§ 9924. Return and surrender of bond or undertaking

In the event the vessel is no longer registered in this state and the currently valid certificate of ownership is surrendered to the department or the vessel has been destroyed or lost, the bond or undertaking shall be returned and surrendered after three years. *(Added by Stats.1970, c. 1428, p. 2768, § 61. Amended by Stats.1982, c. 517, p. 2421, § 389.)*

Law Revision Commission Comments

1982 Amendment

Section 9924 is amended to delete provisions duplicated in the Bond and Undertaking Law. See Code Civ. Proc. §§ 996.430 (action to enforce liability) and 996.470 (limitation on liability of surety). [16 Cal.L.Rev. Comm. Reports 501 (1981)].

Cross References

Bond and Undertaking Law, see Code of Civil Procedure § 995.010 et seq.

§ 9928. Withholding number certificates or transfer registration pending payment of use tax or penalties; transmittal of collections; computation of tax; collection agreements

The department shall withhold the certificate of number or the transfer of registration of any vessel sold at retail to any applicant by any person other than a person holding a seller's permit pursuant to Section 6066 of the Revenue and Taxation Code, and regularly engaged in the business of selling vessels, until the applicant pays to the department the use tax measured by the sales price of the vessel as required by the Sales and Use Tax Law, together with penalty, if any, unless the State Board of Equalization finds that no use tax is due. If the applicant so desires, he may pay the use tax and penalty, if any, to the department so as to secure immediate action upon his application for registration or transfer of registration and thereafter he may apply through the Department of Motor Vehicles to the State Board of Equalization under the provisions of the Sales and Use Tax Law for a refund of the amount so paid.

(b) The department shall transmit to the State Board of Equalization all collections of the use tax and penalty made under this section. This transmittal shall be made at least monthly, accompanied by a schedule in such form as the department and board may prescribe.

(c) The State Board of Equalization shall reimburse the department for its costs incurred in carrying out the provisions of this section.

(d) In computing any use tax or penalty thereon under the provisions of the section, dollar fractions shall be disregarded in the manner specified in Section 9559. Payment of tax and penalty on this basis shall be deemed full compliance with the requirements of the Sales and Use Tax Law insofar as they are applicable to the use of vessels to which this section relates.

293

(e) The department and the State Board of Equalization shall enter into an agreement for the collection of the use tax pursuant to this section and Section 6294 of the Revenue and Taxation Code. The agreement shall specify the procedures agreed upon by the department and the board for collection of the tax and the reimbursement provided for in subdivision (c). The agreement shall be approved by the Department of Finance. *(Added by Stats.1982, c. 665, p. 2729, § 5.)*

Division 3.6

VEHICLE SALES

Chapter	Section
1. Advertising, Brochures, and Manuals	9950
2. Manufacturer's Responsibility for Safety Defects	9975
3. Engine Manufacturers	9980
4. Disclosure of Damage	9990

CHAPTER 1. ADVERTISING, BROCHURES, AND MANUALS

Section
9950. Statement of horsepower rating of engine.
9951. Disclosure in owner's vehicle manual of event data recorders or sensing and diagnostic modules; use or release of recorded data; subscription service agreements.
9952. Violations.
9953. Tire chains; vehicles which may not be operated with chains; notice.
9954. Replacement motor vehicle keys or other functionally similar devices; 24 hour availability; exemptions; severability.
9955. Pocket bikes; manufacturer's sticker information and disclosure statement.

§ 9950. Statement of horsepower rating of engine

Any advertisement, brochure, owner's manual, or sales manual relating to any gasoline-powered motor vehicle of a type subject to registration with a manufacturer's gross vehicle weight rating of under 6,000 pounds of 1972 or later year model which contains any reference to the horsepower of the engine of the vehicle shall state only the Society of Automotive Engineers horsepower rating of such engine, as installed (net), as determined by S.A.E. Standard J1349. *(Added by Stats.1970, c. 1246, p. 2236, § 1. Amended by Stats.1971, c. 181, p. 248, § 1, eff. June 25, 1971, operative May 3, 1972; Stats.1973, c. 73, p. 121, § 1, eff. May 31, 1973; Stats.1986, c. 1212, § 5.)*

Cross References

Motor vehicle defined, see Vehicle Code § 415.

§ 9951. Disclosure in owner's vehicle manual of event data recorders or sensing and diagnostic modules; use or release of recorded data; subscription service agreements

(a) A manufacturer of a new motor vehicle sold or leased in this state that is equipped with one or more recording devices commonly referred to as "event data recorders (EDR)" or "sensing and diagnostic modules (SDM)," shall disclose that fact in the owner's manual for the vehicle.

(b) As used in this section, "recording device" means a device that is installed by the manufacturer of the vehicle and does one or more of the following, for the purpose of retrieving data after an accident:

(1) Records how fast and in which direction the motor vehicle is traveling.

(2) Records a history of where the motor vehicle travels.

(3) Records steering performance.

(4) Records brake performance, including, but not limited to, whether brakes were applied before an accident.

(5) Records the driver's seatbelt status.

(6) Has the ability to transmit information concerning an accident in which the motor vehicle has been involved to a central communications system when an accident occurs.

(c) Data described in subdivision (b) that is recorded on a recording device may not be downloaded or otherwise retrieved by a person other than the registered owner of the motor vehicle, except under one of the following circumstances:

(1) The registered owner of the motor vehicle consents to the retrieval of the information.

(2) In response to an order of a court having jurisdiction to issue the order.

(3) For the purpose of improving motor vehicle safety, including for medical research of the human body's reaction to motor vehicle accidents, and the identity of the registered owner or driver is not disclosed in connection with that retrieved data. The disclosure of the vehicle identification number (VIN) for the purpose of improving vehicle safety, including for medical research of the human body's reaction to motor vehicle accidents, does not constitute the disclosure of the identity of the registered owner or driver.

(4) The data is retrieved by a licensed new motor vehicle dealer, or by an automotive technician as defined in Section 9880.1 of the Business and Professions Code, for the purpose of diagnosing, servicing, or repairing the motor vehicle.

(d) A person authorized to download or otherwise retrieve data from a recording device pursuant to paragraph (3) of subdivision (c), may not release that data, except to share the data among the motor vehicle safety and medical research communities to advance motor vehicle safety, and only if the identity of the registered owner or driver is not disclosed.

(e)(1) If a motor vehicle is equipped with a recording device that is capable of recording or transmitting information as described in paragraph (2) or (6) of subdivision (b) and that capability is part of a subscription service, the fact that the information may be recorded or transmitted shall be disclosed in the subscription service agreement.

(2) Subdivision (c) does not apply to subscription services meeting the requirements of paragraph (1).

(f) This section applies to all motor vehicles manufactured on or after July 1, 2004. *(Added by Stats.2003, c. 427 (A.B.213), § 1. Amended by Stats.2004, c. 183 (A.B.3082), § 350.)*

§ 9952. Violations

Any person who publishes, or causes to be published, or offers for sale or sells, or gives to another person, any advertisement, brochure, owner's manual, or sales manual which violates Section 9950 is guilty of an infraction. *(Added by Stats.1970, c. 1246, p. 2237, § 1. Amended by Stats.1973, c. 73, p. 121, § 3, eff. May 31, 1973.)*

Cross References

Infractions, see Penal Code §§ 17, 19.6, 19.7.

§ 9953. Tire chains; vehicles which may not be operated with chains; notice

Every manufacturer of a new motor vehicle sold in this state which, as equipped, may not be operated with tire chains shall do both of the following:

(a) Indicate that fact in the owner's manual for the vehicle or other written material provided by the manufacturer regarding the vehicle.

(b) Provide each of its franchised new motor vehicle dealers in this state with a list of the affected vehicle models on an annual basis and prior to the manufacturer's introduction of its new model year vehicles. The list shall include sufficient information, including information regarding tire sizes where necessary, to allow the selling dealer to determine when disclosure is required pursuant to Section 11713.6. *(Added by Stats.1991, c. 6 (A.B.39), § 1, eff. Dec. 13, 1990, operative Jan. 1, 1991. Amended by Stats.1995, c. 452 (A.B.28), § 1.)*

§ 9954. Replacement motor vehicle keys or other functionally similar devices; 24 hour availability; exemptions; severability

(a) This section applies only to new vehicles sold or leased in this state on or after January 1, 2008, except as provided in subdivision (d) or (e).

(b) A motor vehicle manufacturer of a motor vehicle sold or leased in this state shall provide the means whereby the registered owner of that motor vehicle, through a registered locksmith, can access the information, and only that information, that is necessary to permit the production of a replacement key or other functionally similar device by the registered locksmith that will allow the registered vehicle's owner to enter, start, and operate his or her vehicle. The means to access this information shall be available by telephone or electronically 24 hours a day and seven days a week, as follows:

(1) When a registered locksmith is requested by the motor vehicle's registered owner or the registered owner's family member, to produce a replacement key or other functionally similar device that will allow the vehicle to be entered, started, and operated, and the information is needed from the vehicle manufacturer in order to produce the requested key or other functionally similar device, in addition to the requirement in Section 466.6 of the Penal Code, the registered locksmith shall visually verify the identity of the requesting party through that party's driver's license; shall visually verify that the registration of the vehicle matches the requesting party's identity and address (or last name and address if the requesting party is a family member of the registered owner); and shall visually verify that the vehicle identification number of the vehicle matches with the vehicle identification number on the registration. Upon satisfactory verification of all three requirements, the registered locksmith shall sign an affidavit that he or she has visually verified the information and file the affidavit along with, and for the same time period as, the work order required by Section 466.6 of the Penal Code, and proceed to access the needed information from the vehicle manufacturer.

(2) Upon completing the services, the registered locksmith shall give any key code information obtained from the vehicle manufacturer to the registered owner, or if applicable, the owner's family member, and shall destroy all information accessed from the vehicle manufacturer in his or her possession.

(3) Except in cases of fraud or misappropriation, a registered locksmith who follows these procedures shall incur no liability for theft of the vehicle related to the locksmith's production of a replacement key or functionally similar device that will allow the vehicle to be entered, started, and operated.

(4) When a vehicle manufacturer receives a request from a registered locksmith for information to enable the locksmith to produce a replacement key or other functionally similar device that will allow the vehicle to be entered, started, and operated, and that request is made at the behest of the vehicle's registered owner or the registered owner's family member, the vehicle manufacturer shall require the registered locksmith to confirm the locksmith's registration with the manufacturer's registry; provide the security password issued by the manufacturer; and comply with any other reasonable authentication procedure. The manufacturer shall also require the registered locksmith to confirm the locksmith's visual identity and vehicle verifications, pursuant to paragraph (1). Upon satisfactory verification of these requirements, and upon presentation of the vehicle identification number and model number, the vehicle manufacturer shall provide to the registered locksmith, for the vehicle identified by the vehicle identification number and model number, the information necessary to enable production of a replacement key or other functionally similar device that allows the vehicle to be entered, started, and operated.

(5) A motor vehicle manufacturer subject to this section shall retain and make the information available in

accordance with this section for at least 25 years from the date of manufacture.

(6) A vehicle manufacturer that follows these procedures shall incur no liability for theft of the vehicle related to furnishing the information to a registered locksmith for the production of a replacement key or functionally similar device that will allow the vehicle to be entered, started, and operated.

(c) For purposes of this section the following definitions apply:

(1) "Information" includes, but is not limited to, the vehicle's key code and, if applicable, immobilizer or access code, and its successor technology and terminology.

(2) "Motor vehicle" is a passenger vehicle as defined in Section 465 and pickup truck as defined in Section 471, and does not include a housecar, a motorcycle, or other two-wheeled motor vehicle.

(3) A "registered locksmith" means a locksmith licensed and bonded in California that has registered with a motor vehicle manufacturer, and has been issued a registry number and security password by the manufacturer.

(4) A registered owner, as defined in Section 505, also includes a lessee of the vehicle when the lessee's name appears on the vehicle registration.

(d)(1) This section does not apply to a vehicle line of a motor vehicle manufacturer that on January 1, 2006, does not provide for the production of a replacement key or other functionally similar device that allows the vehicle to be entered, started, and operated, by anyone other than the vehicle manufacturer itself and only itself, provided that the vehicle manufacturer operates a telephone or electronic request line 24 hours a day and seven days a week, and upon a request of the registered owner or family member of the registered owner of the vehicle, a replacement key or other functionally similar device that will allow the vehicle to be entered, started, and operated, is furnished to the registered owner at a reasonable cost within one day of the request or via the next overnight delivery.

(2) If subsequent to January 1, 2008, a vehicle line of the manufacturer exempted by this subdivision provides for the production of a replacement by anyone, other than the vehicle manufacturer itself, of a key or other functionally similar device that will allow the vehicle to be entered, started, and operated, this section shall apply to that vehicle line.

(3) This subdivision shall remain operative until January 1, 2013, and as of that date shall become inoperative, unless a later enacted statute, that is enacted before January 1, 2013, deletes or extends that date.

(e)(1) This section does not apply to a vehicle line of a motor vehicle manufacturer that sold between 2,500 and 5,000 vehicles of that line in the prior calendar year in the state.

(2) This subdivision shall remain operative until January 1, 2013, and as of that date shall become inoperative, unless a later enacted statute, that is enacted before January 1, 2013, deletes or extends that date.

(f) This section shall not apply to a make that sold fewer than 2,500 vehicles in the prior calendar year in the state.

(g) The duties imposed on a manufacturer pursuant to this section may be performed either by the manufacturer or by an agent through a contract.

(h) The provisions of this section are severable. If any provision of this section or its application is held invalid, that invalidity shall not affect other provisions or applications that can be given effect without the invalid provision or application. *(Added by Stats.2006, c. 433 (S.B.1542), § 2.)*

§ 9955. Pocket bikes; manufacturer's sticker information and disclosure statement

(a) A manufacturer of a pocket bike shall affix on the pocket bike a sticker with a disclosure stating that the device is prohibited from being operated on a sidewalk, roadway, or any part of a highway, or on a bikeway, bicycle path or trail, equestrian trail, hiking or recreational trail, or on public lands open to off-highway motor vehicle use.

(b) The disclosure required under subdivision (a) shall meet both of the following requirements:

(1) Be printed in not less than 14–point boldface type on a sticker that contains only the disclosure.

(2) Include the following statement:

"THE POCKET BIKE YOU HAVE PURCHASED OR OBTAINED IS STRICTLY PROHIBITED FROM BEING OPERATED ON A SIDEWALK, ROADWAY, OR ANY OTHER PART OF A HIGHWAY, OR ON A BIKEWAY, BICYCLE PATH OR TRAIL, EQUESTRIAN TRAIL, HIKING OR RECREATIONAL TRAIL, OR ON PUBLIC LANDS OPEN TO OFF–HIGHWAY VEHICLE USE. A VIOLATION OF THIS REGULATION MAY RESULT IN PROSECUTION AND SEIZURE OF THE DEVICE." *(Added by Stats. 2005, c. 323 (A.B.1051), § 2.)*

Cross References

"Pocket bike", defined, see Vehicle Code § 473.

CHAPTER 2. MANUFACTURER'S RESPONSIBILITY FOR SAFETY DEFECTS

Section
9975. Correction of safety defects.

§ 9975. Correction of safety defects

Every manufacturer of a motor vehicle who furnishes notification to the registered owner of the motor vehicle of any defect in the motor vehicle or motor vehicle equipment which relates to motor vehicle safety, shall, notwithstanding any limitation in any warranty relating to the motor vehicle, correct such defect without charge to the registered owner of the vehicle or, at the manufacturer's election, reimburse the registered owner for the cost of making such correction.

The manufacturer of such motor vehicle shall not be liable for the cost of such correction if the registered owner of the motor vehicle does not seek to have the correction made within 45 days after receipt of the notification or within the warranty period of the motor vehicle, whichever is longer. *(Added by Stats.1972, c. 954, p. 1729, § 1.)*

Cross References

Motor vehicle defined, see Vehicle Code § 415.
Registered owner defined, see Vehicle Code § 505.

CHAPTER 3.   ENGINE MANUFACTURERS

Section
9980. Labeling of engine; different manufacturer of engine and vehicle.
9981. Labeling; location; exception.
9982. Application of chapter.

§ 9980.   Labeling of engine; different manufacturer of engine and vehicle

If the manufacturer of the engine of a new motor vehicle is different from the manufacturer of the vehicle, the vehicle shall be labeled as required by Section 9981.

For purposes of this chapter, the manufacturer of a motor vehicle engine is different from the vehicle manufacturer if a majority of parts, or most of the work of assembly, of the engine is provided by a person other than the vehicle manufacturer or a subsidiary or affiliate of the vehicle manufacturer. For purposes of this chapter, an "affiliate" is an entity that directly, or indirectly through one or more intermediaries, controls or is controlled by, or is under common control with, the manufacturer of the vehicle. *(Added by Stats.1984, c. 1264, § 1. Amended by Stats.2000, c. 135 (A.B.2539), § 156.)*

§ 9981.   Labeling; location; exception

The manufacturer of any vehicle subject to Section 9980 shall affix a prominent label to the vehicle stating that the engine in the vehicle may have been manufactured by another manufacturer. The label shall be located on or adjacent to the window sticker identifying the manufacturer's suggested retail price for the vehicle or, if none, it shall be located on or adjacent to the window sticker identifying the equipment provided with the vehicle. This label, however, is not required if the manufacturer of the engine contained in the vehicle is disclosed in sales literature or is noted in the sales contract. *(Added by Stats.1984, c. 1264, § 1.)*

298

§ 9982.   Application of chapter

This chapter applies only to new passenger vehicles and to new motortrucks with an unladen weight under 6,000 pounds, except housecars. *(Added by Stats.1984, c. 1264, § 1.)*

Cross References

Motor truck defined, see Vehicle Code § 410.
Passenger vehicle defined, see Vehicle Code § 465.

CHAPTER 4.   DISCLOSURE OF DAMAGE

Section
9990. Material damage sustained by motor vehicle defined.
9991. Disclosure in writing to purchaser of material damage to new or previously unregistered vehicle known by dealer to be subsequently repaired.
9992. Disclosure in writing of damage to new or previously unregistered vehicle known by dealer and not repaired.
9993. Prohibition of response to inquiry by purchaser in untrue or misleading manner.

§ 9990.   Material damage sustained by motor vehicle defined

For purposes of this chapter, damage sustained by a motor vehicle is material under any of the following circumstances:

(a) The damage required repairs having a value, including parts and labor calculated at the repairer's cost, exceeding 3 percent of the manufacturer's suggested retail price of the vehicle or five hundred dollars ($500), whichever is greater. The replacement of damaged or stolen components, excluding the cost of repainting or refinishing those components, if replaced by the installation of new original manufacturer's equipment, parts, or accessories that are bolted or otherwise attached as a unit to the vehicle, including, but not limited to, the hood, bumpers, fenders, mechanical parts, instrument panels, moldings, glass, tires, wheels, and electronic instruments, shall be excluded from the damage calculation, except that any damage having a cumulative repair or replacement value which exceeds 10 percent of the manufacturer's suggested retail price of the vehicle shall be deemed material.

(b) The damage was to the frame or drive train of the motor vehicle.

(c) The damage occurred in connection with a theft of the entire vehicle.

(d) The damage was to the suspension of the vehicle requiring repairs other than wheel balancing or alignment. *(Added by Stats.1990, c. 1373 (S.B.2434), § 1.)*

§ 9991.   Disclosure in writing to purchaser of material damage to new or previously unregistered vehicle known by dealer to be subsequently repaired

Every dealer shall disclose in writing to the purchaser of a new or previously unregistered motor vehicle, prior to entering into a contract for the vehicle or, if unknown at that time, prior to delivery of the vehicle, any material damage known by the dealer to have been sustained by the vehicle and subsequently repaired. *(Added by Stats. 1990, c. 1373 (S.B.2434), § 1.)*

§ 9992. Disclosure in writing of damage to new or previously unregistered vehicle known by dealer and not repaired

Every dealer shall disclose in writing to the purchaser of a new or previously unregistered motor vehicle, prior to entering into a contract for the vehicle or, if unknown at that time, prior to delivery of the vehicle, any damage, including, but not limited to, material damage, known by the dealer to have been sustained by the vehicle and not repaired. *(Added by Stats.1990, c. 1373 (S.B.2434), § 1.)*

§ 9993. Prohibition of response to inquiry by purchaser in untrue or misleading manner

Nothing in this chapter permits any dealer to respond to the inquiry of a purchaser in any untrue or misleading manner. *(Added by Stats.1990, c. 1373 (S.B.2434), § 1.)*

Division 4

SPECIAL ANTITHEFT LAWS

Chapter		Section
1.	Reports of Stolen Vehicles	10500
1.5.	Reports of Stolen Vessels	10550
2.	Reports of Stored Vehicles	10650
3.	Alteration or Removal of Numbers	10750
3.5.	Motor Vehicle Chop Shops	10801
4.	Theft and Injury of Vehicles	10850
5.	Motor Vehicle Theft Prevention	10900

Cross References

Manufacturers, transporters and dealers, license suspension or revocation for violation of this division, see Vehicle Code § 11705.

CHAPTER 1. REPORTS OF STOLEN VEHICLES

Section
10500. Stolen, or unlawfully driven or taken vehicles; lost or stolen license plates; notification to reporting party.
10501. False report of theft; prior conviction; penalty.
10502. Reports by owners.
10503. Notice to Department of Motor Vehicles.
10504. Action by department.
10505. Notification of transfer.

§ 10500. Stolen, or unlawfully driven or taken vehicles; lost or stolen license plates; notification to reporting party

(a) Every peace officer, upon receiving a report based on reliable information that any vehicle registered under this code has been stolen, taken, or driven in violation of Section 10851, or that a leased or rented vehicle has not been returned within five days after its owner has made written demand for its return, by certified or registered mail, following the expiration of the lease or rental agreement, or that license plates for any vehicle have been lost or stolen, shall, immediately after receiving that information, report the information to the Department of Justice Stolen Vehicle System. An officer, upon receiving information of the recovery of any vehicle described in this subdivision, or of the recovery of plates which have been previously reported as lost or stolen, shall immediately report the fact of the recovery to the Department of Justice Stolen Vehicle System. At the same time, the recovering officer shall advise the Department of Justice Stolen Vehicle System and the original reporting police agency of the location and condition of the vehicle or license plates recovered. The original reporting police agency, upon receipt of the information from the recovering officer, shall, immediately attempt to notify the reporting party by telephone, if the telephone number of the reporting party is available or readily accessible, of the location and condition of the recovered vehicle. If the reporting party's telephone number is unknown, or notification attempts were unsuccessful, the original re-porting police agency shall notify the reporting party by placing, in the mail, a notice providing the location and condition of the recovered vehicle. This written notice shall be mailed within 24 hours of the original reporting police agency's receipt of the information of the recovery of the vehicle, excluding holidays and weekends.

(b) If the recovered vehicle is subject to parking or storage charges, Section 10652.5 applies. *(Added by Stats.1982, c. 581, p. 2541, § 2, operative Jan. 1, 1989. Amended by Stats.1990, c. 337 (A.B.2717), § 1; Stats. 1992, c. 290 (A.B.1583), § 1; Stats.1994, c. 675 (S.B. 1741), § 3.)*

Cross References

Departmental action on report of stolen, taken or driven vehicle, see Vehicle Code § 10504.
Owners' reports of stolen and recovered vehicles, see Vehicle Code § 10502.

§ 10501. False report of theft; prior conviction; penalty

(a) It is unlawful for any person to make or file a false or fraudulent report of theft of a vehicle required to be registered under this code with any law enforcement agency with intent to deceive.

(b) If a person has been previously convicted of a violation of subdivision (a), he or she is punishable by imprisonment pursuant to subdivision (h) of Section 1170 of the Penal Code for 16 months, or two or three years, or in a county jail for not to exceed one year. *(Stats.1959, c. 3, p. 1594, § 10501. Amended by Stats.1982, c. 958, p. 3458, § 1; Stats.2011, c. 15 (A.B.109), § 601, eff. April 4, 2011, operative Oct. 1, 2011.)*

Cross References

Registration, see Vehicle Code § 4000 et seq.
Violations, see Vehicle Code §§ 40000.9, 42002.

§ 10502. Reports by owners

(a) The owner or legal owner of a vehicle registered under this code which has been stolen or embezzled may notify the Department of the California Highway Patrol of the theft or embezzlement, but in the event of an embezzlement other than an embezzlement as specified in Section 10855, may make the report only after having procured the issuance of a warrant for the arrest of the person charged with the embezzlement.

(b) Every owner or legal owner who has given any notice under subdivision (a) shall notify the Department of the California Highway Patrol of a recovery of the vehicle. *(Stats.1959, c. 3, p. 1595, § 10502. Amended by Stats.1992, c. 290 (A.B.1583), § 2.)*

Cross References

Definitions,
  Legal owner, see Vehicle Code § 370.
  Owner, see Vehicle Code § 460.
  Vehicle, see Vehicle Code § 670.
Effective period of report, see Vehicle Code § 10504.
Embezzlement, see Penal Code § 503 et seq.
Registration, see Vehicle Code § 4000 et seq.

§ 10503.   Notice to Department of Motor Vehicles

The Department of Justice upon receiving notice under this chapter that a vehicle has been stolen, or taken or driven in violation of Section 10851, or that a vehicle reported stolen, or taken or driven in violation of Section 10851 has been recovered, shall notify the Department of Motor Vehicles of the reported theft, taking or driving, or recovery. *(Stats.1959, c. 3, p. 1595, § 10503. Amended by Stats.1972, c. 98, p. 133, § 2, eff. May 30, 1972, operative Oct. 1, 1972.)*

§ 10504.   Action by department

The department upon receiving a report of a stolen vehicle, or of a vehicle taken or driven in violation of Section 10851, shall place an appropriate notice in the electronic file system which will identify such vehicles during the processing of new certificates of registration, ownership, or registration and ownership. When such vehicles are thus identified, processing shall be discontinued and the Department of Justice shall be notified. New certificates shall not be issued until cleared by the Department of Justice. Notices shall remain in the Department of Motor Vehicles system until a Department of Justice deletion is received.

A report of a stolen vehicle, or of a vehicle taken or driven in violation of Section 10851, is effective for a period of not less than one year from the date first reported or longer as the department may determine. *(Stats.1959, c. 3, p. 1595, § 10504. Amended by Stats. 1970, c. 1439, p. 2794, § 11; Stats.1972, c. 98, p. 133, § 3, eff. May 30, 1972, operative Oct. 1, 1972.)*

Cross References

Definitions,
  Department, see Vehicle Code § 290.
  Vehicle, see Vehicle Code § 670.
Registration indices and records, see Vehicle Code § 1800 et seq.

§ 10505.   Notification of transfer

Upon the transfer of registration of a vehicle reported as stolen or embezzled, the department shall immediately notify the reporting agency of such fact. *(Stats.1959, c. 3, p. 1595, § 10505.)*

CHAPTER 1.5.   REPORTS OF STOLEN VESSELS

Section
10550.   Definitions.
10551.   Peace officers duty to report to department.
10551.5.   Notice of reported theft or recovery by department of justice.
10552.   False or fraudulent reports.
10553.   Report by owner or legal owner.
10554.   Notice in electronic file system; processing of new certificates; duration of effectiveness of reports.

§ 10550.   Definitions

In this chapter, unless the context clearly requires a different meaning, the terms and definitions set forth in Section 9840 shall apply. *(Added by Stats.1970, c. 1428, p. 2769, § 62.   Amended by Stats.1973, c. 759, p. 1371, § 14.)*

§ 10551.   Peace officers duty to report to department

Every peace officer upon receiving a report based on reliable information that any undocumented vessel numbered under this code has been stolen shall immediately after receiving such information report the theft to the Department of Justice, Automated Boat System, and such peace officer upon receiving information of the recovery of any such vessel which he has previously reported as stolen, shall immediately report the fact of the recovery to the Department of Justice, Automated Boat System. *(Added by Stats.1970, c. 1428, p. 2769, § 62.   Amended by Stats.1980, c. 617, p. 1700, § 5.)*

Cross References

Peace officers, see Penal Code § 830 et seq.

§ 10551.5.   Notice of reported theft or recovery by department of justice

The Department of Justice upon receiving notice under this chapter that a vessel has been stolen or that a vessel reported stolen has been recovered shall notify the Department of Motor Vehicles of the reported theft or recovery. *(Added by Stats.1980, c. 617, p. 1700, § 6.)*

§ 10552.   False or fraudulent reports

It is unlawful for any person to make or file a false or fraudulent report of the theft of an undocumented vessel required to be numbered under this code with any law enforcement agents with intent to deceive. *(Added by Stats.1970, c. 1428, p. 2769, § 62.)*

Cross References

False reporting of criminal offense, misdemeanor, see Penal Code § 148.5.

§ 10553.   Report by owner or legal owner

The owner or legal owner of a vessel numbered under this code which has been stolen or embezzled may notify a law enforcement agency of the theft or embezzlement, but in the event of an embezzlement may make the report only after having procured the issuance of a warrant for the arrest of the person charged with such embezzlement. Every owner or legal owner who has given any such notice shall notify the law enforcement agency of a recovery of the vessel. *(Added by Stats.1970, c. 1428, p. 2770, § 62. Amended by Stats.1980, c. 617, p. 1700, § 7.)*

Cross References
Embezzlement, see Penal Code § 503 et seq.
Theft or larceny, see Penal Code § 484 et seq.

§ 10554. Notice in electronic file system; processing of new certificates; duration of effectiveness of reports

The department upon receiving a report of a stolen or embezzled vessel shall place an appropriate notice in the electronic file system which will identify such vessel during the processing of new certificates of number, ownership, or number and ownership. When such vessels are thus identified, processing shall be discontinued and the agency holding the theft report and the Department of Justice shall be notified. New certificates shall not be issued until cleared by the Department of Justice. Notices shall remain in the Department of Motor Vehicles system until a Department of Justice deletion is received.

A report of a stolen or embezzled vessel is effective for a period of not less than one year from the date first reported, or for such longer period as the department may determine. *(Added by Stats.1970, c. 1428, p. 2770, § 62. Amended by Stats.1980, c. 617, p. 1700, § 8.)*

CHAPTER 2. REPORTS OF STORED VEHICLES

Section
10650. Required written record of storage.
10651. Repealed.
10652. Report of vehicles.
10652.5. Motor vehicle storage fees.
10653. Report of vehicles showing bullet marks.
10654. Renting of private building.
10655. Failure to make reports or keep records.
10656. Inspection of vehicles.
10658. Recreational vehicle stored in mobilehome park; exemption.

§ 10650. Required written record of storage

(a) Every operator of a towing service and every keeper of a garage or trailer park shall keep a written record of every vehicle of a type subject to registration under this code stored for a period longer than 12 hours.

(b) The record shall contain the name and address of the person storing the vehicle or requesting the towing, the names of the owner and driver of the vehicle, if ascertainable, and a brief description of the vehicle including the name or make, the motor or other number of the vehicle, the nature of any damage to the vehicle, and the license number and registration number shown by the license plates or registration card, if either of the latter is attached to the vehicle in a clearly discernible place.

(c) All records shall be kept for one year from the commencement of storage and shall be open to inspection by any peace officer.

(d) Upon termination of the storage, a statement shall be added to the record as to the disposition of the vehicle, including the name and address of the person to whom the vehicle was released and the date of such release. *(Stats.1959, c. 3, p. 1595, § 10650. Amended by Stats. 1974, c. 271, p. 497, § 1.)*

Cross References
Definitions,
 Garage, see Vehicle Code § 340.
 Vehicle, see Vehicle Code § 670.
Failure to keep records or make reports, misdemeanor, see Vehicle Code § 10655.
Improperly causing vehicle to be towed or removed to create or acquire lien, forfeiture of claims and liability to owner or lessee, see Civil Code § 3070.
Lien for vehicle care, storage, etc., necessity of compliance with this section, see Civil Code § 3068.
Unauthorized use or tampering with vehicle by bailee, misdemeanor, see Vehicle Code § 10854.
Vehicles subject to registration, see Vehicle Code § 4000 et seq.

§ 10651. Repealed by Stats.1965, c. 1135, p. 2787, § 3

§ 10652. Report of vehicles

Whenever any vehicle of a type subject to registration under this code has been stored in a garage, repair shop, parking lot, or trailer park for 30 days, the keeper shall report such fact to the Department of Justice by receipted mail, which shall at once notify the legal owner as of record. This section shall not apply to any vehicle stored by a peace officer or employee designated in Section 22651 pursuant to Article 3 (commencing with Section 22850) of Chapter 10 of Division 11. *(Stats.1959, c. 3, p. 1596, § 10652. Amended by Stats.1965, c. 1135, p. 2787, § 4; Stats.1968, c. 1070, p. 2076, § 1; Stats.1972, c. 98, p. 133, § 4, eff. May 30, 1972, operative Oct. 1, 1972; Stats.1979, c. 373, p. 1380, § 314; Stats.2008, c. 699 (S.B.1241), § 24.)*

Cross References
Definitions,
 Garage, see Vehicle Code § 340.
 Legal owner, see Vehicle Code § 370.
 Registered owner, see Vehicle Code § 505.
 Vehicle, see Vehicle Code § 670.
Failure to keep records or make reports, see Vehicle Code § 10655.
Lien for vehicle care, storage, etc., necessity of compliance with this section, see Civil Code § 3068.
Vehicles subject to registration, see Vehicle Code § 4000 et seq.

§ 10652.5. Motor vehicle storage fees

(a) Whenever the name and address of the legal owner of a motor vehicle is known, or may be ascertained from the registration records in the vehicle or from the records of the Department of Motor Vehicles, no fee or service charge may be imposed upon the legal owner for the parking and storage of the motor vehicle except as follows: (1) The first 15 days of possession and (2) following that 15–day period, the period commencing three days after written notice is sent by the person in

303

possession to the legal owner by certified mail, return receipt requested, and continuing for a period not to exceed any applicable time limit set forth in Section 3068 or 3068.1 of the Civil Code.

(b) The costs of notifying the legal owner may be charged as part of the storage fee when the motor vehicle has been stored for an indefinite period of time and notice is given no sooner than the third day of possession. This subdivision also applies if the legal owner refuses to claim possession of the motor vehicle.

(c) In any action brought by, or on behalf of, a legal owner of a motor vehicle to which subdivision (a) applies, to recover a motor vehicle alleged to be withheld by the person in possession of the motor vehicle by demanding storage fees or charges for any number of days in excess of that permitted pursuant to subdivision (a), the prevailing party shall be entitled to reasonable attorney's fees, not to exceed one thousand seven hundred fifty dollars ($1,750). The recovery of those fees is in addition to any other right, remedy, or cause of action of that party.

(d) This section is not applicable to any motor vehicle stored by a levying officer acting under the authority of judicial process. *(Added by Stats.1973, c. 911, p. 1693, § 1. Amended by Stats.1983, c. 913, § 1; Stats.1988, c. 1092, § 5; Stats.1991, c. 727 (A.B.1882), § 3; Stats.1995, c. 289 (A.B.323), § 1.)*

Cross References

Improperly causing vehicle to be towed or removed to create or acquire lien, forfeiture of claims and liability to owner or lessee, see Civil Code § 3070.
Service lien, see Civil Code § 3068.

§ 10653. Report of vehicles showing bullet marks

Whenever any vehicle of a type subject to registration under this code which shows evidence of having been struck by a bullet is stored in a garage or repair shop, the keeper thereof shall within 24 hours after receiving the vehicle report such fact to the sheriff's office of the county or police department of the city wherein the garage or repair shop is located, giving the motor or other number of the vehicle, the license number if ascertainable, and the name and address of the person storing the same or the name and address of the owner shown by the registration card, if the same is attached to the vehicle in a clearly discernible place. *(Stats.1959, c. 3, p. 1596, § 10653.)*

Cross References

Failure to make reports or keep records, see Vehicle Code § 10655.

§ 10654. Renting of private building

Every person other than the keeper of a garage renting any private building used as a private garage or space therein for the storage of a vehicle of a type subject to registration under this code, when the agreement to rent includes only the building or space therein, shall within 24 hours after the vehicle is stored therein report such fact

together with the name of the tenant, and a description of the vehicle, including the name or make, the motor or other number of the vehicle, and the license number to the sheriff's office of the county or the police department of the city wherein the building is located. "Private garage" as used in this section does not include a public warehouse or public garage. *(Stats.1959, c. 3, p. 1596, § 10654.)*

§ 10655. Failure to make reports or keep records

No person required to keep a record or make a report under this chapter shall wilfully fail, refuse, or neglect to comply with this chapter. *(Stats.1959, c. 3, p. 1596, § 10655.)*

Cross References

Improperly causing vehicle to be towed or removed to create or acquire lien, forfeiture of claims and liability to owner or lessee, see Civil Code § 3070.
Violations, see Vehicle Code §§ 40000.1 et seq., 42002.

§ 10656. Inspection of vehicles

The director, deputy director, registrar, deputy registrar, investigators of the department, and members of a city police department or county sheriff's office whose primary responsibility is to conduct vehicle theft investigations, may inspect any vehicle of a type required to be registered under this code in any garage, repair shop, parking lot, used car lot, automobile dismantlers lot, or other similar establishment for the purpose of investigating the title and registration of vehicles and inspection of vehicles wrecked or dismantled. *(Stats.1959, c. 3, p. 1596, § 10656. Amended by Stats.1963, c. 1106, p. 2566, § 6; Stats.1979, c. 252, p. 544, § 2.)*

Cross References

Definitions,
   Automobile dismantler, see Vehicle Code § 220.
   Garage, see Vehicle Code § 340.
   Repair shop, see Vehicle Code § 510.
Vehicles subject to registration, see Vehicle Code § 4000 et seq.

§ 10658. Recreational vehicle stored in mobilehome park; exemption

(a) The provisions of this chapter shall not apply to the storage of any recreational vehicle owned by a mobilehome park resident and stored in a mobilehome park.

(b) As used in this section, "recreational vehicle" shall have the same meaning as defined in Section 18215.5 of the Health and Safety Code, and "mobilehome park" shall have the same meaning as defined in Section 18214 of the Health and Safety Code. *(Added by Stats.1974, c. 646, p. 1509, § 3.)*

CHAPTER 3. ALTERATION OR REMOVAL OF NUMBERS

Section
10750. Altering or changing vehicle numbers.

Section

10751. Manufacturer's serial or identification numbers; disposition; hearing; notice; application of section.

10752. Manufacturer's or governmental serial or identification numbers; possession or sale; penalties.

§ 10750. Altering or changing vehicle numbers

(a) No person shall intentionally deface, destroy, or alter the motor number, other distinguishing number, or identification mark of a vehicle required or employed for registration purposes without written authorization from the department, nor shall any person place or stamp any serial, motor, or other number or mark upon a vehicle, except one assigned thereto by the department.

(b) This section does not prohibit the restoration by an owner of the original vehicle identification number when the restoration is authorized by the department, nor prevent any manufacturer from placing in the ordinary course of business numbers or marks upon new motor vehicles or new parts thereof. *(Stats.1959, c. 3, p. 1596, § 10750. Amended by Stats.1970, c. 824, p. 1559, § 6.)*

Cross References

Definitions,

Department, see Vehicle Code § 290.

Owner, see Vehicle Code § 460.

Person, see Vehicle Code § 470.

Vehicle, see Vehicle Code § 670.

Registration indices and records, see Vehicle Code § 1800.

Suspension, cancellation or revocation of registration, see Vehicle Code § 8800.

Violation a misdemeanor, see Vehicle Code § 40000.9.

§ 10751. Manufacturer's serial or identification numbers; disposition; hearing; notice; application of section

(a) No person shall knowingly buy, sell, offer for sale, receive, or have in his or her possession, any vehicle, or component part thereof, from which any serial or identification number, including, but not limited to, any number used for registration purposes, that is affixed by the manufacturer to the vehicle or component part, in whatever manner deemed proper by the manufacturer, has been removed, defaced, altered, or destroyed, unless the vehicle or component part has attached thereto an identification number assigned or approved by the department in lieu of the manufacturer's number.

(b) Whenever a vehicle described in subdivision (a), including a vehicle assembled with any component part which is in violation of subdivision (a), comes into the custody of a peace officer, it shall be destroyed, sold, or otherwise disposed of under the conditions as provided in an order by the court having jurisdiction. No court order providing for disposition shall be issued unless the person from whom the property was seized, and all claimants to the property whose interest or title is on registration records in the Department of Motor Vehicles, are provided a postseizure hearing by the court having jurisdiction within 90 days after the seizure. This subdivision shall not apply with respect to a seized vehicle or

component part used as evidence in any criminal action or proceeding. Nothing in this section shall, however, preclude the return of a seized vehicle or a component part to the owner by the seizing agency following presentation of satisfactory evidence of ownership and, if determined necessary, upon the assignment of an identification number to the vehicle or component part by the department.

(c) Whenever a vehicle described in subdivision (a) comes into the custody of a peace officer, the person from whom the property was seized, and all claimants to the property whose interest or title is on registration records in the Department of Motor Vehicles, shall be notified within five days, excluding Saturdays, Sundays, and holidays, after the seizure, of the date, time, and place of the hearing required in subdivision (b). The notice shall contain the information specified in subdivision (d).

(d) Whenever a peace officer seizes a vehicle described in subdivision (a), the person from whom the property was seized shall be provided a notice of impoundment of the vehicle which shall serve as a receipt and contain the following information:

(1) Name and address of person from whom the property was seized.

(2) A statement that the vehicle seized has been impounded for investigation of a violation of Section 10751 of the California Vehicle Code and that the property will be released upon a determination that the serial or identification number has not been removed, defaced, altered, or destroyed, or upon the presentation of satisfactory evidence of ownership of the vehicle or a component part, if no other person claims an interest in the property; otherwise, a hearing regarding the disposition of the vehicle shall take place in the proper court.

(3) A statement that the person from whom the property was seized, and all claimants to the property whose interest or title is on registration records in the Department of Motor Vehicles, will receive written notification of the date, time, and place of the hearing within five days, excluding Saturdays, Sundays, and holidays, after the seizure.

(4) Name and address of the law enforcement agency where evidence of ownership of the vehicle or component part may be presented.

(5) A statement of the contents of Section 10751 of the Vehicle Code.

(e) A hearing on the disposition of the property shall be held by the superior court within 90 days after the seizure. The hearing shall be before the court without a jury. A proceeding under this section is a limited civil case.

(1) If the evidence reveals either that the serial or identification number has not been removed, defaced, altered, or destroyed or that the number has been removed, defaced, altered, or destroyed but satisfactory evidence of ownership has been presented to the seizing

agency or court, the property shall be released to the person entitled thereto. Nothing in this section precludes the return of the vehicle or a component part to a good faith purchaser following presentation of satisfactory evidence of ownership thereof upon the assignment of an identification number to the vehicle or component part by the department.

(2) If the evidence reveals that the identification number has been removed, defaced, altered, or destroyed, and satisfactory evidence of ownership has not been presented, the vehicle shall be destroyed, sold, or otherwise disposed of as provided by court order.

(3) At the hearing, the seizing agency has the burden of establishing that the serial or identification number has been removed, defaced, altered, or destroyed and that no satisfactory evidence of ownership has been presented.

(f) This section does not apply to a scrap metal processor engaged primarily in the acquisition, processing, and shipment of ferrous and nonferrous scrap, and who receives dismantled vehicles from licensed dismantlers, licensed junk collectors, or licensed junk dealers as scrap metal for the purpose of recycling the dismantled vehicles for their metallic content, the end product of which is the production of material for recycling and remelting purposes for steel mills, foundries, smelters, and refiners. *(Added by Stats.1981, c. 599, p. 2314, § 2, operative Jan. 1, 1988. Amended by Stats.1990, c. 481 (S.B.2809), § 1; Stats.1991, c. 13 (A.B.37), § 25, eff. Feb. 13, 1991; Stats.1998, c. 931 (S.B.2139), § 455, eff. Sept. 28, 1998; Stats.2002, c. 784 (S.B.1316), § 596.)*

Law Revision Commission Comments

1998 Amendment

Section 10751 is amended to accommodate unification of the municipal and superior courts in a county. Cal. Const. art. VI, § 5(e). The section is also amended to reflect elimination of the justice court. Cal. Const. art. VI, §§ 1, 5(b).

A limited civil case is within the original jurisdiction of the municipal court or of the superior court in a county in which there is no municipal court. Cal. Const. art. VI, 10 (superior court jurisdiction); Code Civ. Proc. §§ 85, 85.1 (limited civil cases). See also Code Civ. Proc. §§ 91, 904.2, 1085 (trial procedures and writ and appellate jurisdiction for limited civil cases). [28 Cal.L.Rev.Comm. Reports 51 (1998)].

2002 Amendment

Subdivision (e) of Section 10751 is amended to reflect unification of the municipal and superior courts pursuant to Article VI, Section 5(e), of the California Constitution. [32 Cal.L.Rev.Comm. Reports 537 (2002)].

Cross References

Alteration or change of vehicle numbers, see Vehicle Code § 10750.
Definitions,
  Department, see Vehicle Code § 290.
  Manufacturer's gross vehicle weight rating, see Vehicle Code § 390.
  Motor vehicle, see Vehicle Code § 415.

Person, see Vehicle Code § 470.
Vehicle, see Vehicle Code § 670.
Punishment for violation of section, see Vehicle Code § 42002.4.
Registration indices and records, see Vehicle Code § 1800.
Suspension, revocation or cancellation of registration, see Vehicle Code § 8800 et seq.
Violation as misdemeanor, see Vehicle Code § 40000.9.

§ 10752. Manufacturer's or governmental serial or identification numbers; possession or sale; penalties

(a) No person shall, with intent to prejudice, damage, injure, or defraud, acquire, possess, sell, or offer for sale any genuine or counterfeit manufacturer's serial or identification number from or for, or purporting to be from or for, a vehicle or component part thereof.

(b) No person shall, with intent to prejudice, damage, injure, or defraud, acquire, possess, sell, or offer for sale any genuine or counterfeit serial or identification number issued by the department, the Department of the California Highway Patrol, or the vehicle registration and titling agency of any foreign jurisdiction which is from or for, or purports to be from or for, a vehicle or component part thereof.

(c) Every person convicted of a violation of subdivision (a) or (b) shall be punished by imprisonment pursuant to subdivision (h) of Section 1170 of the Penal Code, or in the county jail for not less than 90 days nor more than one year, and by a fine of not less than two hundred fifty dollars ($250) nor more than five thousand dollars ($5,000). *(Added by Stats.1980, c. 608, p. 1677, § 4. Amended by Stats.1985, c. 623, § 2; Stats.2011, c. 15 (A.B.109), § 602, eff. April 4, 2011, operative Oct. 1, 2011.)*

CHAPTER 3.5. MOTOR VEHICLE CHOP SHOPS

Section
10801. Ownership or operation; punishment.
10802. Vehicle identification numbers; alteration, destruction, forgery or removal; punishment.
10803. Possession, purchase, sale or transfer of more than one motor vehicle or parts; knowledge of altered, destroyed, forged or removed vehicle identification numbers; punishment.
10804. Exemption; motor vehicle scrap processor; owner or authorized possessor of recovered stolen vehicle.

§ 10801. Ownership or operation; punishment

Any person who knowingly and intentionally owns or operates a chop shop is guilty of a public offense and, upon conviction, shall be punished by imprisonment pursuant to subdivision (h) of Section 1170 of the Penal Code for two, three, or four years, or by a fine of not more than fifty thousand dollars ($50,000), or by both the fine and imprisonment, or by up to one year in the county jail, or by a fine of not more than one thousand dollars ($1,000), or by both the fine and imprisonment. *(Added by Stats.1993, c. 386 (S.B.73), § 3, eff. Sept. 8, 1993. Amended by Stats.2011, c. 15 (A.B.109), § 603, eff. April 4, 2011, operative Oct. 1, 2011.)*

§ 10802. Vehicle identification numbers; alteration, destruction, forgery or removal; punishment

Any person who knowingly alters, counterfeits, defaces, destroys, disguises, falsifies, forges, obliterates, or removes vehicle identification numbers, with the intent to misrepresent the identity or prevent the identification of motor vehicles or motor vehicle parts, for the purpose of sale, transfer, import, or export, is guilty of a public offense and, upon conviction, shall be punished by imprisonment pursuant to subdivision (h) of Section 1170 of the Penal Code for 16 months, or two or three years, or by a fine of not more than twenty-five thousand dollars ($25,000), or by both the fine and imprisonment, or by up to one year in the county jail, or by a fine of not more than one thousand dollars ($1,000), or by both the fine and imprisonment. *(Added by Stats.1993, c. 386 (S.B.73), § 3, eff. Sept. 8, 1993. Amended by Stats.2011, c. 15 (A.B.109), § 604, eff. April 4, 2011, operative Oct. 1, 2011.)*

§ 10803. Possession, purchase, sale or transfer of more than one motor vehicle or parts; knowledge of altered, destroyed, forged or removed vehicle identification numbers; punishment

(a) Any person who buys with the intent to resell, disposes of, sells, or transfers, more than one motor vehicle or parts from more than one motor vehicle, with the knowledge that the vehicle identification numbers of the motor vehicles or motor vehicle parts have been altered, counterfeited, defaced, destroyed, disguised, falsified, forged, obliterated, or removed for the purpose of misrepresenting the identity or preventing the identification of the motor vehicles or motor vehicle parts, is guilty of a public offense and, upon conviction, shall be punished by imprisonment pursuant to subdivision (h) of Section 1170 of the Penal Code for two, four, or six years, or by a fine of not more than sixty thousand dollars ($60,000), or by both the fine and imprisonment, or by up to one year in the county jail, or by a fine of not more than one thousand dollars ($1,000), or by both the fine and imprisonment.

(b) Any person who possesses, for the purpose of sale, transfer, import, or export, more than one motor vehicle or parts from more than one motor vehicle, with the knowledge that the vehicle identification numbers of the motor vehicles or motor vehicle parts have been altered, counterfeited, defaced, destroyed, disguised, falsified, forged, obliterated, or removed for the purpose of misrepresenting the identity or preventing the identification of the motor vehicles or motor vehicle parts, is guilty of a public offense and, upon conviction, shall be punished by imprisonment pursuant to subdivision (h) of Section 1170 of the Penal Code for 16 months, or two or three years, or by a fine of not more than thirty thousand dollars ($30,000), or by both the fine and imprisonment, or by imprisonment in the county jail not exceeding one year or by a fine of not more than one thousand dollars ($1,000) or by both the fine and imprisonment. *(Added by Stats.1993, c. 386 (S.B.73), § 3, eff. Sept. 8, 1993.*

Amended by Stats.2011, c. 15 (A.B.109), § 605, eff. April 4, 2011, operative Oct. 1, 2011.)

§ 10804. Exemption; motor vehicle scrap processor; owner or authorized possessor of recovered stolen vehicle

(a) Section 10803 does not apply to a motor vehicle scrap processor who, in the normal legal course of business and in good faith, processes a motor vehicle or motor vehicle part by crushing, compacting, or other similar methods, if any vehicle identification number is not removed from the motor vehicle or motor vehicle part prior to or during the processing.

(b) Section 10803 does not apply to any owner or authorized possessor of a motor vehicle or motor vehicle part which has been recovered by law enforcement authorities after having been stolen or if the condition of the vehicle identification number of the motor vehicle or motor vehicle part is known to, or has been reported to, law enforcement authorities. Law enforcement authorities are presumed to have knowledge of all vehicle identification numbers on a motor vehicle or motor vehicle part which are altered, counterfeited, defaced, disguised, falsified, forged, obliterated, or removed, when law enforcement authorities deliver or return the motor vehicle or motor vehicle part to its owner or an authorized possessor after it has been recovered by law enforcement authorities after having been reported stolen. *(Added by Stats.1993, c. 386 (S.B.73), § 3, eff. Sept. 8, 1993.)*

CHAPTER 4. THEFT AND INJURY OF VEHICLES

Section
10850. Application of chapter.
10851. Theft and unlawful driving or taking of a vehicle.
10851.5. Theft of binder chains.
10852. Breaking or removing vehicle parts.
10853. Malicious mischief to vehicle.
10854. Unlawful use or tampering by bailee.
10855. Leased and rented vehicles.

§ 10850. Application of chapter

The provisions of this chapter apply to vehicles upon the highways and elsewhere throughout the State. *(Stats. 1959, c. 3, p. 1597, § 10850.)*

Cross References

Highway defined, see Vehicle Code §§ 360, 590.
Law enforcement, California highway patrol, see Vehicle Code § 2400.
Vehicle defined, see Vehicle Code § 670.

§ 10851. Theft and unlawful driving or taking of a vehicle

(a) Any person who drives or takes a vehicle not his or her own, without the consent of the owner thereof, and with intent either to permanently or temporarily deprive the owner thereof of his or her title to or possession of the vehicle, whether with or without intent to steal the vehicle, or any person who is a party or an accessory to or an accomplice in the driving or unauthorized taking or stealing, is guilty of a public offense and, upon conviction thereof, shall be punished by imprisonment in a county jail for not more than one year or pursuant to subdivision (h) of Section 1170 of the Penal Code or by a fine of not more than five thousand dollars ($5,000), or by both the fine and imprisonment.

(b) If the vehicle is (1) an ambulance, as defined in subdivision (a) of Section 165, (2) a distinctively marked vehicle of a law enforcement agency or fire department, taken while the ambulance or vehicle is on an emergency call and this fact is known to the person driving or taking, or any person who is party or an accessory to or an accomplice in the driving or unauthorized taking or stealing, or (3) a vehicle which has been modified for the use of a disabled veteran or any other disabled person and which displays a distinguishing license plate or placard issued pursuant to Section 22511.5 or 22511.9 and this fact is known or should reasonably have been known to the person driving or taking, or any person who is party or an accessory in the driving or unauthorized taking or stealing, the offense is a felony punishable by imprisonment pursuant to subdivision (h) of Section 1170 of the Penal Code for two, three, or four years or by a fine of not more than ten thousand dollars ($10,000), or by both the fine and imprisonment.

(c) In any prosecution for a violation of subdivision (a) or (b), the consent of the owner of a vehicle to its taking or driving shall not in any case be presumed or implied because of the owner's consent on a previous occasion to the taking or driving of the vehicle by the same or a different person.

(d) The existence of any fact which makes subdivision (b) applicable shall be alleged in the accusatory pleading, and either admitted by the defendant in open court, or found to be true by the jury trying the issue of guilt or by the court where guilt is established by plea of guilty or nolo contendere or by trial by the court sitting without a jury.

(e) Any person who has been convicted of one or more previous felony violations of this section, or felony grand theft of a vehicle in violation of subdivision (d) of Section 487 of the former Penal Code subdivision (3) of Section 487 of the Penal Code, as that section read prior to being amended by Section 4 of Chapter 1125 of the Statutes of 1993, or Section 487h of the Penal Code, is punishable as set forth in Section 666.5 of the Penal Code. The existence of any fact that would bring a person under Section 666.5 of the Penal Code shall be alleged in the information or indictment and either admitted by the defendant in open court, or found to be true by the jury trying the issue of guilt or by the court where guilt is established by plea of guilty or nolo contendere, or by trial by the court sitting without a jury.

(f) This section shall become operative on January 1, 1997. *(Added by Stats.1993, c. 1125 (A.B.1630), § 14, eff. Oct. 11, 1993, operative Jan. 1, 1997. Amended by*

Stats.1995, c. 101 (S.B.317), § 4, operative Jan. 1, 1997; Stats.2011, c. 15 (A.B.109), § 606, eff. April 4, 2011, operative Oct. 1, 2011.)

Cross References

Applicability of this section to trolley coaches, see Vehicle Code § 21051.

Department of justice reports of theft, taking, driving or recovery, see Vehicle Code § 10503.

Electronic file record of stolen vehicles, withholding registration, see Vehicle Code § 10504.

Grand theft as including taking of automobile, see Penal Code § 487.

Juvenile court rules related to this section, see California Rules of Court, Rule 5.514.

Owner defined, see Vehicle Code § 460.

Police reports, see Vehicle Code § 10500.

Revocation of driver's license by department, see Vehicle Code § 13350.

Subsequent conviction of petit theft following conviction of auto theft under this section, punishment, see Penal Code § 666.

Suspension or revocation of driver's license, recommendation of court, see Vehicle Code § 13357.

Taking vehicle for temporary use, see Penal Code § 499b.

§ 10851.5.　Theft of binder chains

Any person who takes binder chains, required under regulations adopted pursuant to Section 31510, having a value of nine hundred fifty dollars ($950) or less which chains are not his own, without the consent of the owner thereof, and with intent either permanently or temporarily to deprive the owner thereof of his title to or possession of the binder chains whether with or without intent to steal the same, or any person who is a party or accessory to or an accomplice in the unauthorized taking or stealing is guilty of a misdemeanor, and upon conviction thereof shall be punished by imprisonment in the county jail for not less than six months or by a fine of not less than one thousand dollars ($1,000) or by both such fine and imprisonment. The consent of the owner of the binder chain to its taking shall not in any case be presumed or implied because of such owner's consent on a previous occasion to the taking of the binder chain by the same or a different person. *(Added by Stats.1963, c. 1780, p. 3560, § 1. Amended by Stats.1983, c. 1092, § 380, eff. Sept. 27, 1983, operative Jan. 1, 1984; Stats. 2009–2010, 3rd Ex.Sess., c. 28 (S.B.18), § 54, eff. Jan. 25, 2010.)*

Cross References

Misdemeanor, see Penal Code §§ 17, 19, 19.2.
Violation a misdemeanor, see Vehicle Code § 40000.9.

§ 10852.　Breaking or removing vehicle parts

No person shall either individually or in association with one or more other persons, wilfully injure or tamper with any vehicle or the contents thereof or break or remove any part of a vehicle without the consent of the owner. *(Stats.1959, c. 3, p. 1597, § 10852.)*

Cross References

Applicability of this section to trolley coaches, see Vehicle Code § 21051.

Procedure on arrest for violation of this section, see Vehicle Code § 40303.

Violation a misdemeanor, see Vehicle Code § 40000.9.

Violation of this section involving vehicle modified for use of disabled person, penalty, see Vehicle Code § 42002.5.

§ 10853. Malicious mischief to vehicle

No person shall with intent to commit any malicious mischief, injury, or other crime, climb into or upon a vehicle whether it is in motion or at rest, nor shall any person attempt to manipulate any of the levers, starting mechanism, brakes, or other mechanism or device of a vehicle while the same is at rest and unattended, nor shall any person set in motion any vehicle while the same is at rest and unattended. *(Stats.1959, c. 3, p. 1597, § 10853.)*

Cross References

Applicability of this section to trolley coaches, see Vehicle Code § 21051.

Procedure on arrest for violation of this section, see Vehicle Code § 40303.

Violation a misdemeanor, see Vehicle Code § 40000.9.

Violation of this section involving vehicle modified for use of disabled person, penalty, see Vehicle Code § 42002.5.

§ 10854. Unlawful use or tampering by bailee

Every person having the storage, care, safe-keeping, custody, or possession of any vehicle of a type subject to registration under this code who, without the consent of the owner, takes, hires, runs, drives, or uses the vehicle or who takes or removes any part thereof is guilty of a misdemeanor and upon conviction shall be punished by a fine of not exceeding one thousand dollars ($1,000) or by imprisonment in the county jail for not exceeding one year or by both. *(Stats.1959, c. 3, p. 1598, § 10854.)*

Cross References

Misdemeanor, see Penal Code §§ 17, 19, 19.2.

Owner defined, see Vehicle Code § 460.

Vehicles subject to registration, see Vehicle Code § 4000 et seq.

Violation a misdemeanor, see Vehicle Code § 40000.9.

§ 10855. Leased and rented vehicles

Whenever any person who has leased or rented a vehicle wilfully and intentionally fails to return the vehicle to its owner within five days after the lease or rental agreement has expired, that person shall be presumed to have embezzled the vehicle. *(Stats.1959, c. 3, p. 1598, § 10855.)*

Cross References

Embezzlement, see Penal Code §§ 487, 490a, 503 et seq.

CHAPTER 5. MOTOR VEHICLE THEFT PREVENTION

Section
10900.   Short title.

Section
10901.   Disposition of funds; use; periodic report.
10902.   CAL H.E.A.T. program.
10903.   Repealed.
10904.   Public education campaign against auto insurance fraud.
10905.   Repealed.

Operative Effect

Legislative intent relating to prevailing provisions of Stats.1994, c. 1248, § 5, see § 7 of that Act. Section affected by two or more acts at the same session of the legislature, see Government Code § 9605.

§ 10900. Short title

This chapter shall be known and may be cited as the "Motor Vehicle Theft Prevention Act." *(Added by Stats.1994, c. 1247 (A.B.1926), § 7; Stats.1994, c. 1248 (S.B.1743), § 5.)*

§ 10901. Disposition of funds; use; periodic report

(a) Pursuant to Section 1872.8 of the Insurance Code, proceeds from the assessment imposed thereunder shall be used to fund prevention and increased investigation of economic automobile theft.

Funds received pursuant to Section 1872.8 of the Insurance Code shall be deposited in the Motor Vehicle Account and appropriated to the Department of the California Highway Patrol for prevention and enhanced investigative efforts to deter economic automobile theft.

(b) Moneys received by the commissioner pursuant to this section shall be used to fund (1) enhanced programs to prevent and investigate economic automobile theft; (2) a program directed at investigating and interdicting the export of stolen motor vehicles and stolen motor vehicle components across an international border; and (3) to operate the CAL H.E.A.T (Californians Help Eliminate Auto Theft) program. Moneys received by a local law enforcement agency pursuant to this section shall be used to fund enhanced programs to prevent and investigate economic automobile theft and shall not be used to supplant or replace funding of existing personnel or equipment.

The commissioner shall submit an annual report to the Legislature, no later than 90 days following the completion of the fiscal year, accounting for all funds received and disbursed pursuant to this section. The report shall detail (A) the uses to which those funds were put, including payment of salaries and expenses, purchase of equipment and supplies, and other expenditures by type; and (B) results achieved as a consequence of expenditures made, including the number of investigations, arrests, complaints filed, convictions, and the number of vehicles recovered and amounts of property losses saved.

(c) As used in this section, "economic automobile theft" means automobile theft perpetrated for financial gain, including, but not limited to, the following:

(1) Theft of a motor vehicle for financial gain.

(2) Reporting that a motor vehicle has been stolen for the purpose of filing a false insurance claim.

(3) Engaging in any act prohibited by Chapter 3.5 (commencing with Section 10801) of Division 4.

(4) Switching of vehicle identification numbers to obtain title to a stolen motor vehicle. *(Added by Stats.1994, c. 1247 (A.B.1926), § 7; Stats.1994, c. 1248 (S.B.1743), § 5.)*

Cross References

License plate reader (LPR) data, inclusion of LPR practices and usage in annual automobile theft report submitted pursuant to this section, see Vehicle Code § 2413.

§ 10902. CAL H.E.A.T. program

The Department of the California Highway Patrol shall establish a program entitled "CAL H.E.A.T." (Californians Help Eliminate Auto Theft) for the purpose of reducing the incidence of economic auto theft in California. The program shall be an anti-auto theft program with a toll-free telephone hotline operator funded by the department using funds distributed to it pursuant to Section 10901. The hotline operator shall channel reports from the public regarding auto thefts to state and local law enforcement agencies. In the annual report, the commissioner shall report on the results of this program, including the number of calls from the public reporting a suspected motor vehicle theft, the number of arrests, complaints filed, convictions, and vehicles recovered, and the amount of property losses saved as a result of the program.

If funded by admitted insurers in this state, the program may offer rewards for reports that lead to the arrest and conviction of a person engaged in economic automobile theft. If so funded, the Department of the California Highway Patrol shall establish a claims board, which shall include appointments from state and local law enforcement agencies and the insurance industry, to determine the amount of individual awards. *(Added by Stats.1994, c. 1247 (A.B.1926), § 7; Stats.1994, c. 1248 (S.B.1743), § 5.)*

§ 10903. Repealed by Stats.1989, c. 1119, § 7

§ 10904. Public education campaign against auto insurance fraud

The commissioner may develop a public education campaign to deter participation in auto insurance fraud and to encourage reporting of fraudulent claims. *(Added by Stats.2000, c. 867 (S.B.1988), § 22.)*

§ 10905. Repealed by Stats.1989, c. 1119, § 7

Division 5

OCCUPATIONAL LICENSING AND BUSINESS REGULATIONS

Chapter		Section
1.	Driving Schools and Driving Instructors	11100
1.5.	Traffic Violator Schools	11200
2.	Vehicle Verifiers	11300
2.5.	Registration Services	11400
3.	Automobile Dismantlers	11500
3.5.	Lessor-Retailers	11600
4.	Manufacturers, Transporters, Dealers, and Salesmen	11700
5.	Sale of Housecars	11930
6.	Sale of Used Vehicles	11950
7.	Sale of Automobile Parts	12000
8.	Private Party Vehicle Markets	12101
9.	Towing	12110
10.	Sales of Vehicles by Private Owners	12120
11.	Consumer Recovery Fund	12200

CHAPTER 1. DRIVING SCHOOLS AND DRIVING INSTRUCTORS

Section

11100. License requirement; truck driving school exemption.

11100.1. All-terrain vehicle instruction; operative date of section.

11100.5. Certification by department of education.

11101. Schools and persons exempted.

11102. Driving school owners or principals in all-terrain vehicle safety training organizations; requirements.

11102.1. Deposit; return; actions for recovery; costs.

11102.5. Requirements for driving school operators.

11103. Insurance requirements.

11103.1. Insurance requirements; all-terrain vehicle safety training organizations; operative date of section.

11103.2. Workers' compensation requirements; owner compliance.

11104. Requirements for driving instructor.

11104.3. Instructors for all-terrain vehicle safety; requirements.

11104.5. License application; owner, operator, or instructor; evidence of character and reputation.

11104.6. License applications; form; contents; operative date of section.

11105. Issuance and renewal of license to owners and operators.

11105.1. Instructors' licenses; issuance and renewal; operative date of section.

11105.2. Fees; operative date of section.

11105.3. Failure to renew license; operative date of section.

11105.5. Independent driving instructor.

11105.6. All-terrain vehicle safety training organization license.

11106. Temporary permit; operative date of section.

11107. Refusal to issue license.

11108. Records of licensees; operative date of section.

11108.5. Notice or reports of changes to department; operative date of section.

11109. Vehicles of licensee.

11110. Suspension or revocation of license.

11110.1. Causes for suspension and revocation of licenses.

11110.2. Cancellation of license; grounds.

11110.5. Cancellation of license when issued in error or surrendered; reapplication; operative date of section.

11110.7. Conviction of crime involving moral turpitude; refusal to issue or suspension of license.

11111. Notice and hearing prior to cancellation, suspension or revocation of license; review; temporary suspension; effect of suspension, expiration or cancellation.

11111.2. Owners of closed businesses or operators or instructors not residing at address last filed; service of process.

11111.5. Compromise settlement agreements; terms and conditions; operative date of section.

11112. Hearings: refusal to issue.

11113. Conduct of courses; rules and regulations.

11113.3. Curriculum includes rights and duties of motorist; rules and regulations.

11113.5. Standards for licensing and control; rules and regulations.

11114. Reexamination.

11115. Repealed.

11116. Repealed.

Cross References

Attendance at licensed traffic violator school, see Vehicle Code § 42005.

Brady–Jared Teen Driver Safety Act of 1997, see Vehicle Code § 12814.6.

Driver training vehicles, safety belt requirement, see Vehicle Code § 27304.

Instruction permits, motor vehicles, see Vehicle Code § 12509.

Instruction permits to operate motorcycles, motorized scooters, motorized bicycles, etc., carrying of passengers prohibited, exception for licensed instructors under this chapter, see Vehicle Code § 12509.5.

Provisions of this division not to preclude application of any other statutory provision which applies to an act violating these provisions, see Vehicle Code § 40007.

Violation as misdemeanor, see Vehicle Code § 40000.11.

§ 11100. License requirement; truck driving school exemption

(a) No person shall own or operate a driving school or give driving instruction for compensation, unless a license therefor has been secured from the department.

(b) This section does not apply to the ownership or operation of any school, or the giving of instruction, for the driving of motortrucks of three or more axles which are more than 6,000 pounds unladen weight. *(Stats.1959, c. 3, p. 1598, § 11100. Amended by Stats.1975, c. 703, p. 1664, § 5; Stats.1988, c. 1399, § 2.)*

Cross References

Brady–Jared Teen Driver Safety Act of 1997, see Vehicle Code § 12814.6.

Definitions,
Department, see Vehicle Code § 290.
Motor vehicle, see Vehicle Code § 415.
Person, see Vehicle Code § 470.

Truck driving school or instruction, certification, see Education Code § 94925.

Violation as misdemeanor, punishment, see Vehicle Code §§ 40000.11, 42002.

§ 11100.1. All-terrain vehicle instruction; operative date of section

No person who instructs others in the operation of all-terrain vehicles shall represent that the instruction given satisfies the requirements of Sections 38503 and 38504, and no certificate shall be issued or awarded for participation in all-terrain vehicle safety instruction unless the instruction is conducted by a licensed all-terrain vehicle safety instructor who is sponsored by an all-terrain vehicle safety training organization.

This section shall become operative on July 1, 1988. *(Added by Stats.1987, c. 881, § 4, operative July 1, 1988.)*

§ 11100.5. Certification by department of education

Whenever it is necessary for a driving school or independent driving instructor to be certified by the Department of Education, or any agency thereof, in order to participate in any state or federal program directed at training or retraining persons in occupational skills, licensing or certification by the Department of Motor Vehicles pursuant to this chapter may operate to fully qualify such school or instructor to participate in the program.

Costs incurred by the department in exercising its functions pursuant to this section shall be borne by the applicant for licensing or certification, and the department may charge the applicant a reasonable fee therefor. *(Added by Stats.1965, c. 1957, p. 4485, § 1.)*

§ 11101. Schools and persons exempted

(a) This chapter does not apply to any of the following:

(1) Public schools or educational institutions in which driving instruction is part of the curriculum.

(2) Nonprofit public service organizations offering instruction without a tuition fee.

(3) Nonprofit organizations engaged exclusively in giving off-the-highway instruction in the operation of motorcycles, if the course of instruction is approved by the National Highway Traffic Safety Administration and is not designed to prepare students for examination by the department for an M1 or M2 drivers license or endorsement.

(4) Commercial schools giving only off-the-highway instruction in the operation of special construction equipment, as defined in this code.

(5) Vehicle dealers or their salesmen giving instruction without charge to purchasers of motor vehicles.

(6) Employers giving instruction to their employees.

(7) Commercial schools engaged exclusively in giving off-the-highway instruction in the operation of racing vehicles or in advanced driving skills to persons holding valid drivers' licenses, except whenever that instruction is given to persons who are being prepared for examination by the department for any class of driver's license.

(b) For purposes of this section, "racing vehicle" means a motor vehicle of a type that is used exclusively in a contest of speed and that is not intended for use on the highways.

(c)(1) Nothing in this chapter shall be construed to direct or restrict courses of instruction in driver education offered by private secondary schools or to require the use of credentialed or certified instructors in driver education courses offered by private secondary schools.

(2) For the purposes of this section, private secondary schools are those subject to Sections 33190 and 48222 of the Education Code. *(Added by Stats.1975, c. 703, p. 1664, § 7. Amended by Stats.1984, c. 499, § 2; Stats. 2002, c. 774 (S.B.2079), § 2, eff. Sept. 21, 2002; Stats. 2004, c. 587 (S.B.524), § 2; Stats.2006, c. 311 (S.B.1586), § 6.)*

§ 11102. Driving school owners or principals in all-terrain vehicle safety training organizations; requirements

(a) A driving school owner, or the principal in an all-terrain vehicle safety training organization, shall meet all of the following requirements:

(1) Maintain an established place of business open to the public. No office or place of business shall be situated within 500 feet of any building used by the department as an office, unless the owner was established at that location on or before January 1, 1976.

(2) Have the proper equipment necessary to give instruction in the operation of the class of vehicles for which the course is designed, which shall include, but not be limited to, training vehicles equipped with all of the following:

(A) An additional functional foot brake affixed to the right side of the front floor.

(B) A rearview mirror placed on the inside of the windshield on the right side, which is additional to the factory-installed mirror in the center of the windshield.

(3) Procure and file with the department a bond of ten thousand dollars ($10,000) executed by an admitted surety insurer and conditioned that the applicant shall not practice any fraud or make any fraudulent representation that will cause a monetary loss to a person taking instruction from the applicant.

(4) Meet the requirements of Section 11105.2 and, if the person is the owner of a driving school, meet the requirements of Section 11102.5. If the owner is not the

operator of the driving school, the owner shall designate an operator who shall meet the requirements of Section 11102.5.

(5)(A) File with the department an instrument, in writing, appointing the director as the agent of the applicant upon whom a process may be served in any action commenced against the applicant arising out of any claim for damages suffered by any person by the applicant's violation of any provision of this code or any condition of the bond.

(B) The applicant shall stipulate in the instrument that any process directed to the applicant, when personal service cannot be made in this state after due diligence, may be served upon the director or, if the director is absent from the office, upon any employee in charge of the office of the director, in which case the service is of the same effect as if served upon the applicant personally. The applicant shall further stipulate, in writing, that the agency created by the instrument shall continue during the period covered by the license and so long thereafter as the applicant may be made to answer in damages for a violation of this code or any condition of the bond.

(C) The instrument appointing the director as agent for the applicant for service of process shall be acknowledged by the applicant before a notary public.

(D) If the licensee is served with process by service upon the director, one copy of the summons and complaint shall be left with the director or in the director's office in Sacramento or mailed to the office of the director in Sacramento. A fee of five dollars ($5) shall also be paid to the director at the time of service of the copy of the summons and complaint.

(E) The service on the director is a sufficient service on the licensee if the plaintiff or the plaintiff's attorney also, on the same day, sends notice of the service and a copy of the summons and complaint by registered mail to the licensee. A copy of the summons and complaint shall also be mailed by the plaintiff or his or her attorney to the surety of the applicant's bond at the address of the surety given in the bond, postpaid and registered with request for return receipt.

(F) The director shall keep a record of all process served upon the director under this paragraph showing the day and hour of service, and the director shall retain the summons and complaint served on file.

(G) If the licensee is served with process by service thereof upon the director, the licensee has 30 days after that service within which to answer any complaint or other pleading filed in the cause. For purposes of venue, if the licensee is served with process by service upon the director, the service is deemed to have been made upon the licensee in the county in which the licensee has or last had the licensee's established place of business.

(b) The qualifying requirements referred to in this section shall be met within one year from the date of application for a license, or a new application, examination, and a fee shall be required. *(Added by Stats.1987, c.*

881, § 6, operative July 1, 1988. Amended by Stats.1990, c. 1563 (A.B.3243), § 6; Stats.2000, c. 243 (S.B.1112), § 1.)

Law Revision Commission Comments

1982 Amendment

Section 11102 is amended to delete provisions duplicated in the Bond and Undertaking Law. See Code Civ. Proc. §§ 996.470 (limitation on liability of surety), 995.710 (deposit in lieu of bond); see also Code Civ. Proc. § 995.120 ("admitted surety insurer" defined). The other changes in Section 11102 are technical. [16 Cal.L.Rev. Comm. Reports 501 (1981)].

Cross References

Bond and Undertaking Law, see Code of Civil Procedure § 995.010 et seq.

§ 11102.1. Deposit; return; actions for recovery; costs

If a deposit is given instead of the bond required by Section 11102:

(a) The director may order the deposit returned at the expiration of three years from the date a driving school licensee has ceased to do business, or three years from the date a licensee has ceased to be licensed, if the director is satisfied that there are no outstanding claims against the deposit. A judge of a superior court may order the return of the deposit prior to the expiration of three years upon evidence satisfactory to the judge that there are no outstanding claims against the deposit.

(b) If either the director, department, or state is a defendant in any action instituted to recover all or any part of the deposit, or any action is instituted by the director, department, or state to determine those entitled to any part of the deposit, the director, department, or state shall be paid reasonable attorney fees and costs from the deposit. Costs shall include those administrative costs incurred in processing claims against the deposit. *(Added by Stats.1974, c. 918, p. 1931, § 1. Amended by Stats.1982, c. 517, p. 2423, § 391; Stats.2002, c. 784 (S.B.1316), § 597.)*

Law Revision Commission Comments

1982 Amendment

Section 11102.1 is amended for consistency with Section 11102. The other changes in Section 11102.1 are technical. [16 Cal.L.Rev. Comm. Reports 501 (1981)].

2002 Amendment

Subdivision (a) of Section 11102.1 is amended to reflect unification of the municipal and superior courts pursuant to Article VI, Section 5(e), of the California Constitution. [32 Cal.L.Rev.Comm. Reports 539 (2002)].

§ 11102.5. Requirements for driving school operators

(a) A driving school operator shall meet all of the following requirements:

(1) Within three attempts, pass an examination that the department requires on traffic laws, safe driving practices, operation of motor vehicles, teaching methods

and techniques, driving school statutes and regulations, and office procedures and recordkeeping.

(2) Pay the department a fee of one hundred dollars ($100), which shall entitle the applicant to three examinations.

(3) Be 21 years of age or older.

(4) Have worked for an established licensed California driving school as a driving instructor for a period of not less than 2,000 hours of actual behind-the-wheel teaching and, on and after July 1, 1973, have satisfactorily completed a course in the teaching of driver education and driver training acceptable to the department, except that the operator, including an owner who is also the operator, of a driving school that exclusively teaches motorcycle driving may, in lieu of the behind-the-wheel teaching requirement, have worked for an established licensed California driving school as a motorcycle driving instructor for not less than 300 hours of actual motorcycle range and street teaching, have taught 300 hours of actual motorcycle range and street instruction under the guidance of the Motorcycle Safety Foundation, or have given comparable training instruction that is acceptable to the department. This paragraph does not apply to any person who is certified by the State Department of Education as fully qualified to teach driver education and driver training and has taught those subjects in the public school system for not less than 1,000 hours.

(b) The qualifying requirements referred to in this section shall be met within one year from the date of application for a license, or a new application, examination, and a fee shall be required. *(Added by Stats.1972, c. 676, p. 1258, § 4. Amended by Stats.1975, c. 703, p. 1666, § 10; Stats.1981, c. 842, p. 3245, § 2; Stats.1982, c. 1273, p. 4702, § 12; Stats.1984, c. 499, § 3; Stats.1990, c. 1563 (A.B.3243), § 7; Stats.2000, c. 243 (S.B.1112), § 2.)*

§ 11103. Insurance requirements

A driving school owner and an independent instructor licensed under Section 11105.5 shall maintain bodily injury and property damage liability insurance on motor vehicles while being used in driving instruction, insuring the liability of the driving school, the driving instructor, and any person taking instruction in at least the following amounts: one hundred fifty thousand dollars ($150,000) for bodily injury to or death of one person in any one accident and, subject to the limit for one person, three hundred thousand dollars ($300,000) for bodily injury to or death of two or more persons in any one accident, and the amount of fifty thousand dollars ($50,000) for damage to property of others in any one accident.

The owner or instructor shall file evidence of that insurance coverage in the form of a certificate from the insurance carrier with the department, and the certificate shall stipulate that the insurance shall not be canceled except upon 30 days' prior written notice to the department. *(Stats.1959, c. 3, p. 1599, § 11103. Amended by Stats.1961, c. 430, p. 1498, § 2; Stats.1972, c. 676, p. 1259,*

§ 5; Stats.1975, c. 703, p. 1666, § 11; Stats.1982, c. 571, p. 2526, § 1; Stats.1986, c. 403, § 1.)*

Cross References

Driving school owner, maintenance of liability insurance, see Vehicle Code § 12660.

§ 11103.1. Insurance requirements; all-terrain vehicle safety training organizations; operative date of section

An all-terrain vehicle safety training organization shall maintain bodily injury and property damage liability insurance on motor vehicles while being used in all-terrain vehicle safety instruction, insuring the liability of the organization, the instructors, and any person taking instruction in at least the following amounts:

(a) One hundred fifty thousand dollars ($150,000) for bodily injury to or death of one person in any one accident.

(b) Subject to the limit specified in paragraph (1) for one person, three hundred thousand dollars ($300,000) for bodily injury to or death of two or more persons in any one accident.

(c) Fifty thousand dollars ($50,000) for damage to property of others in any one accident.

This section shall become operative on July 1, 1988. *(Added by Stats.1987, c. 881, § 7, operative July 1, 1988.)*

§ 11103.2. Workers' compensation requirements; owner compliance

A driving school owner who employs one or more driving instructors or other employees shall sign, under penalty of perjury, a statement in a form determined and retained by the department stating that the owner is in compliance with worker's compensation requirements set forth in Section 3700 of the Labor Code. *(Added by Stats.1996, c. 47 (S.B.636), § 1.)*

§ 11104. Requirements for driving instructor

(a) Every person, in order to qualify as a driving instructor, as defined in Section 310.4, shall meet all of the following requirements:

(1) On and after July 1, 1973, have a high school education or its equivalent and have satisfactorily completed a course in the teaching of driver education and driver training acceptable to the department.

(2) Within three attempts, pass an examination that the department requires on traffic laws, safe driving practices, operation of motor vehicles, and teaching methods and techniques.

(3) Be physically able to safely operate a motor vehicle and to train others in the operation of motor vehicles.

(4) Hold a valid California driver's license in a class appropriate for the type of vehicle in which instruction will be given.

(5) Not be on probation to the department as a negligent operator.

(6) Have a driving record that does not have an outstanding notice for violating a written promise to appear in court or for willfully failing to pay a lawfully imposed fine, as provided in Section 40509.

(7) Be 21 years of age or older.

(b) If an applicant cannot meet the requirements of paragraphs (3) and (4) of subdivision (a) because of a physical disability, the department may, at its discretion, issue the applicant a driving school instructor's license restricted to classroom driver education instruction only.

(c) The qualifying requirements referred to in this section shall be met within one year from the date of application for a license, or a new application, examination, and a fee shall be required. *(Stats.1959, c. 3, p. 1599, § 11104. Amended by Stats.1959, c. 1312, p. 3583, § 2; Stats.1961, c. 430, p. 1499, § 3; Stats.1965, c. 1957, p. 4485, § 2; Stats.1971, c. 851, p. 1686, § 2, operative May 3, 1972; Stats.1971, c. 1748, p. 3763, § 54, operative March 4, 1972; Stats.1972, c. 590, p. 1052, § 33; Stats.1972, c. 231, p. 474, § 1; Stats.1975, c. 703, p. 1667, § 12; Stats.1981, c. 842, p. 3245, § 3; Stats.1984, c. 499, § 4; Stats.1990, c. 1563 (A.B.3243), § 8; Stats.2000, c. 243 (S.B.1112), § 3; Stats.2003, c. 768 (A.B.1343), § 1.)*

§ 11104.3. Instructors for all-terrain vehicle safety; requirements

(a) An all-terrain vehicle safety instructor shall meet all of the following requirements:

(1) Be a person who has not been convicted of a crime involving an act of dishonesty, fraud, or deceit with the intent to benefit himself or herself or another substantially, or to injure another substantially; or has not committed any act which, if done as an all-terrain vehicle safety instructor, would be grounds for the suspension or revocation of the all-terrain vehicle safety instructor's license. A conviction after a plea of nolo contendere shall be deemed to be a conviction within the meaning of this section.

(2) Have a high school education or its equivalent and have satisfactorily completed a course of instruction training in all-terrain vehicle safety as approved by the Off-Highway Vehicle Safety Education Committee.

(3) Within three attempts, pass the examination that the department requires on off-highway vehicle laws, safe driving practices, operation of all-terrain vehicles, and teaching methods and techniques.

(4) Be physically able to safely operate a motor vehicle and to train others in the operation of all-terrain vehicles.

(5) Hold a valid driver's license issued by this state or any contiguous state.

(6) Not be on probation to the department as a negligent operator or the equivalent of that in the state that issued the driver's license.

(7) Have a driver record which does not have an outstanding notice for violating a written promise to appear in court or for willfully failing to pay a lawfully imposed fine, as provided in Section 40509 or 40509.5 or as provided in equivalent statutes in the state that issued the driver's license.

(8) Be 18 years of age or older.

(9) Be sponsored by an all-terrain vehicle safety training organization.

(b) The qualifying requirements in this section shall be met within one year from the date of application for a license, or a new application, examination, and a fee shall be required.

(Added by Stats.1987, c. 881, § 8, operative July 1, 1988. Amended by Stats.1990, c. 1460 (A.B.2735), § 4; Stats.1990, c. 1563 (A.B.3243), § 9.)

§ 11104.5. License application; owner, operator, or instructor; evidence of character and reputation

Each applicant for a license as a driving school owner, driving school operator, or driving instructor shall submit an application to the department on the forms prescribed by the department. The applicant shall provide the department with any information concerning the applicant's character, honesty, integrity, and reputation which the department may consider necessary. *(Added by Stats.1987, c. 75, § 1.)*

§ 11104.6. License applications; form; contents; operative date of section

Each applicant for a license or for renewal of a license under this chapter shall submit an application to the department on the forms prescribed by the department. The applicant shall provide the department any information concerning the applicant's character, honesty, integrity, and reputation which the department considers to be necessary.

This section shall become operative on July 1, 1988. *(Added by Stats.1987, c. 881, § 9, operative July 1, 1988.)*

§ 11105. Issuance and renewal of license to owners and operators

(a) The department shall issue a license certificate to each driving school owner and to each driving school operator when it is satisfied that the owner has met the qualifications required under this chapter. The license shall be for a period of one year from midnight of the last day of the month of issuance unless canceled, suspended, or revoked by the department.

(b) The license shall be renewed annually. The department shall require all of the following for the renewal of the license:

(1) Compliance with the provisions of Sections 11102 and 11105.2 for renewal of a driving school owner's license or Section 11102.5, except paragraph (2) of subdivision (a) of Section 11102.5, for renewal of a driving school operator's license.

(2) Satisfactory completion of an examination as provided in Section 11102.5 at least once during each

succeeding three-year period after the initial issuance of a license certificate.

In lieu of any examination for renewal of the license, the department may accept submission by the licensee of evidence of continuing professional education. Professional education, as used in this subdivision, means satisfactory completion of courses related to traffic safety, teaching techniques, or the teaching of driver instruction acceptable to the department or participation in professional seminars approved by the department.

(c) The department may issue a probationary license and certificate subject to conditions to be observed by the licensee in the exercise of the privilege granted. The conditions to be attached to the exercise of the privilege shall not appear on the face of the license or certificate but shall be such as may, in the judgment of the department, be in the public interest and suitable to the qualifications of the applicant as disclosed by the application and investigation by the department of the information contained therein.

(d) Upon notification of death of a driving school licensee the department may issue a certificate of convenience to the executor, executrix, administrator or administratrix of the estate of a deceased holder of a validly outstanding certificate to conduct a driving school, or if no executor, executrix, administrator or administratrix has been appointed, and until a certified copy of an order making such appointment is filed with the department, to the surviving spouse or other heir otherwise entitled to conduct the business of the deceased, permitting such person to conduct the driving school for a period of one year from and after the date of death, and necessary one-year renewals thereafter pending, but not later than, disposal of the business and qualification of the vendee of the business or such surviving spouse or heir for a license certificate to conduct a driving school under the provisions of this division. The department may restrict or condition the certificate and attach to the exercise of the privilege thereunder such terms and conditions as in its judgment the protection of the public requires.

(e) The department shall not issue or renew a license certificate unless it determines that the driving school owner has complied with Section 11103.2. *(Stats.1959, c. 3, p. 1599, § 11105. Amended by Stats.1959, c. 1312, p. 3583, § 3; Stats.1967, c. 1140, p. 2816, § 3; Stats.1971, c. 851, p. 1686, § 3, operative May 3, 1972; Stats.1972, c. 676, p. 1259, § 6; Stats.1974, c. 918, p. 1931, § 2; Stats.1976, c. 1171, p. 5260, § 30; Stats.1981, c. 842, p. 3246, § 4; Stats.1984, c. 499, § 5; Stats.1996, c. 47 (S.B.636), § 2.)*

§ 11105.1. Instructors' licenses; issuance and renewal; operative date of section

(a) The department shall issue a license certificate to each driving school instructor and to each all-terrain vehicle safety instructor when it is satisfied that the person has met the qualifications required under this chapter. The original instructor's license and any in-

316

structor's license renewed pursuant to subdivisions (b) and (c) is valid for three years from the date issued unless canceled, suspended, or revoked by the department.

(b) A licensee may apply for the renewal of an instructor's license prior to the expiration date of the license. In no event shall an instructor renew the license after the date of expiration.

(c) The department shall require all of the following for the renewal of the instructor's license:

(1) Compliance with Section 11104, except subdivision (c) thereof, for a driving school instructor, or compliance with Section 11104.3, except paragraph (3) of subdivision (a) thereof, for an all-terrain vehicle safety instructor, and, for either, compliance with Section 11105.2.

(2) Satisfactory completion of an examination as provided in Section 11104 or 11104.3, as applicable, at least once during each succeeding three-year period after the initial issuance of an instructor license certificate.

In lieu of any examination for renewal of the license, the department may accept submission by the licensee of evidence of continuing professional education as defined in paragraph (2) of subdivision (b) of Section 11105.

(d) The department may issue a probationary instructor's license and certificate subject to conditions to be observed by the licensee in the exercise of the privilege granted. The conditions to be attached to the exercise of the privilege shall not appear on the face of the license or certificate, but shall be such as may, in the judgment of the department, be in the public interest and suitable to the qualifications of the applicant as disclosed by the application and investigation by the department of the information contained therein.

(e) This section shall become operative on July 1, 1988. *(Added by Stats.1987, c. 881, § 11, operative July 1, 1988.)*

§ 11105.2. Fees; operative date of section

(a) The fee for a license issued to a driving school owner or to an all-terrain vehicle safety training organization shall be as follows:

(1) For the original license, or an ownership change which requires a new application, except as provided by Section 42231, a nonrefundable fee of one hundred fifty dollars ($150).

(2) For the annual renewal of a license, a fee of fifty dollars ($50).

(3) If an alteration of an existing license is caused by a firm name change, a change in corporate officer structure, address change, or the addition of a branch location, a fee of seventy dollars ($70).

(4) For replacement of the license when the original license is lost, stolen, or mutilated, a fee of fifteen dollars ($15).

(b) The fee for a license issued to a driving school operator shall be as follows:

(1) For the original license a nonrefundable fee of one hundred dollars ($100).

(2) For the annual renewal of a license, a fee of one hundred dollars ($100).

(3) If an alteration of an existing license is caused by a change in school name or location, or the addition of a branch location, a fee of fifteen dollars ($15).

(4) For replacement of the license when the original license is lost, stolen, or mutilated, a fee of fifteen dollars ($15).

(c) The fee for a license issued to a driving school instructor or to an all-terrain vehicle safety instructor shall be as follows:

(1) For the original license, except as provided by Section 42231, a nonrefundable fee of thirty dollars ($30).

(2) For the triennial renewal of a license, a fee of thirty dollars ($30).

(3) If an alteration of an existing license is caused by a change in the instructor's employing school's name or location, or transfer of the instructor's license to another employing school, a fee of fifteen dollars ($15).

(4) For the replacement of the instructor's license when the original license is lost, stolen, or mutilated, a fee of fifteen dollars ($15).

(d) This section shall become operative on July 1, 1988. *(Added by Stats.1987, c. 881, § 13, operative July 1, 1988.)*

§ 11105.3. Failure to renew license; operative date of section

Any school owner, operator, or instructor required to be licensed under this chapter who fails to renew the license prior to the expiration of the license in accordance with Sections 11105 and 11105.1 and whose license was not canceled, suspended, or revoked by the department at the time of expiration, may reapply for an original license pursuant to Section 11102, 11102.5, 11104, or 11104.3.

This section shall become operative on July 1, 1988. *(Added by Stats.1987, c. 881, § 15, operative July 1, 1988.)*

§ 11105.5. Independent driving instructor

The department shall issue an independent driving instructor's license to permit instruction in any city with a population of less than 50,000, which does not have within it an established licensed driving school, to any person who meets the requirements of this chapter relating to instructor's and independent instructor's licenses, even though such person is not an employee of, or otherwise associated with or instructing through, a driving school, except that no independent driving instructor's license shall be issued to a person to instruct in counties with a population in excess of 400,000. In addition, an independent instructor must at all times be employed as an accredited teacher of automobile driver education or automobile driver training under the provisions of the Education Code. *(Added by Stats.1961, c. 430, p. 1499,*

§ 4. Amended by Stats.1971, c. 438, p. 905, § 183, operative May 3, 1972.)

Cross References
Driving school owner, maintenance of liability insurance, see Vehicle Code § 12660.
Insurance requirement, independent instructor, see Vehicle Code § 11103.

§ 11105.6. All-terrain vehicle safety training organization license

(a) The department shall issue a license to an all-terrain vehicle safety training organization when the department is satisfied that the organization has met the qualifications required under this chapter and has been approved and certified by the Off-Highway Vehicle Safety Education Committee. The license shall be valid for a period of one year from midnight of the last day of the month of issuance unless canceled, suspended, or revoked by the department.

(b) The license shall be renewed annually. The department shall require compliance with Sections 11102 and 11105.2 for the renewal of the license.

(c) This section shall become operative on July 1, 1988. *(Added by Stats.1987, c. 881, § 16, operative July 1, 1988.)*

§ 11106. Temporary permit; operative date of section

(a) Until the department is satisfied that the applicant has met the requirements under this chapter, it may issue a temporary permit to any person applying for a license issued pursuant to this chapter. The temporary permit authorizes the operation of a school or the giving of instruction for a period not to exceed 120 days while the department is completing its investigation and determination of all facts relative to the qualifications of the applicant for the license.

(b) A temporary permit valid for 30 days may be issued to any applicant for an original instructor's license pending satisfactory completion of the course required by subdivision (b) of Section 11104 or paragraph 2 of subdivision (a) of Section 11104.3, as applicable. This subdivision does not extend the period of validity of any temporary permit issued pursuant to subdivision (a).

(c) The department may cancel a temporary permit when it has determined, or has reasonable cause to believe, that the application is incorrect or incomplete or the temporary permit was issued in error. A temporary permit is invalid when canceled or when the applicant's license has been issued or refused.

(d) This section shall become operative on July 1, 1988. *(Added by Stats.1987, c. 881, § 18.)*

§ 11107. Refusal to issue license

(a) The department may refuse to issue a license certificate under this chapter to any applicant to own or operate a school or to any instructor when it finds and determines any of the following to exist:

(1) The applicant has not met the qualifications required under this chapter.

(2) The applicant was previously the holder of a license under this chapter which was revoked or suspended, which was never reissued by the department after revocation, or which was never reinstated after suspension.

(3) The applicant was previously the holder of an occupational license issued by another state, authorizing the same or similar activities of a license issued under this division; and that license was revoked or suspended for cause and was never reissued, or was suspended for cause, and the terms of suspension have not been fulfilled.

(4) The applicant has done any act or series of acts which would be a cause for suspension or revocation under Section 11110.

(5) If the applicant is a business, a business representative was the holder of a revoked or suspended license previously issued under this chapter which was never reissued after revocation or which was never reinstated after suspension, or a business representative, though not previously the holder of a license, has done any act or series of acts which would be a cause for revocation or suspension under Section 11110.

(6) By reason of the facts and circumstances relating to the organization, control, and management of the business, it is likely that the policy or operation of the business will be directed, controlled, or managed by a business representative who, by reason of any act, series of acts, or conduct described in paragraph (4) or (5), would be ineligible for a license and that, by licensing the business, the purposes of this division would be defeated.

(7) The applicant has knowingly made a false statement or knowingly concealed a material fact in applying for a license.

(8) The applicant, or one of the business representatives if the applicant is a business, has been convicted of a crime, or has committed any act or engaged in conduct involving moral turpitude, which is substantially related to the qualifications, functions, or duties of the licensed activity. A conviction after a plea of nolo contendere is a conviction within the meaning of this section.

(b) Upon refusal of the department to issue a license, the applicant may demand, in writing, a hearing before the director or the director's representative within 60 days after notice of refusal.

The hearing shall be conducted pursuant to Chapter 5 (commencing with Section 11500) of Part 1 of Division 3 of Title 2 of the Government Code.

(c) A person whose license has been revoked, or whose application for a license has been refused, may reapply for the license after a period of not less than one year has elapsed from the effective date of the decision revoking the license or refusing the application. *(Added by Stats.1987, c. 881, § 20, operative July 1, 1988. Amended*

318

by Stats.1990, c. 1563 (A.B.3243), § 10; Stats.1998, c. 877 (A.B.2132), § 42.)

Cross References

Refusal to issue license, right to a hearing, see Vehicle Code § 11112.

§ 11108. Records of licensees; operative date of section

(a) Every person licensed under this chapter shall keep a record showing all of the following:

(1) The name and address and license number of the school.

(2) The name and address of each person given instruction.

(3) Excepting all-terrain vehicle safety training organizations, the instruction permit number or driver's license number of every person given instruction in the driving of a motor vehicle.

(4) Excepting all-terrain vehicle safety training organizations, the date any instruction permit was issued.

(5) The name and instructor's license number of each instructor.

(6) The particular type of instruction given and the date of the instruction.

(7) The amount of time devoted to each type of instruction.

(8) The total number of hours of instruction.

(9) The total cost to the student of the instruction.

(b) The records shall be retained for at least three years and shall be open to the inspection of the department at all reasonable times, but shall be only for the confidential use of the department.

(c) Whenever the licensee suspends or terminates the licensed activity, the licensee shall surrender the records to the department for examination not later than the end of the third day, excluding Saturdays, Sundays, and legal holidays, after the date of suspension or termination. The department may duplicate or make a record of any information contained in the licensee's records. All of the licensee's records shall be returned to the licensee not later than 30 days after the date of surrender.

(d) Every all-terrain vehicle safety training organization shall maintain records for all-terrain vehicle safety instructors who are authorized to offer that organization's courses of instruction.

(e) Each all-terrain vehicle safety instructor shall report the information required under this section to the all-terrain vehicle safety training organization no later than the 15th day of the month following the date instruction was provided. Instructors shall notify the organization, which shall, in turn, notify the department at least 30 days in advance of providing a course of instruction, of the time, date, location, and type of instruction to be given.

(f) This section shall become operative on July 1, 1988. *(Added by Stats.1987, c. 881, § 22, operative July 1, 1988.)*

§ 11108.5. Notice or reports of changes to department; operative date of section

(a) Every school owner licensed pursuant to this chapter shall notify the department within 10 days of any change in the ownership or corporate structure of the licensee.

(b) Every school owner licensed pursuant to this chapter shall immediately notify the department upon changing the site or location of the school's established place of business.

(c) Every school operator and every instructor licensed pursuant to this chapter shall report to the department every change of residence address within five days of the change.

(d) This section shall become operative on July 1, 1988. *(Added by Stats.1987, c. 881, § 24, operative July 1, 1988.)*

§ 11109. Vehicles of licensee

Every licensee under this chapter shall maintain all vehicles used in driver training in safe mechanical condition at all times. *(Stats.1959, c. 3, p. 1600, § 11109.)*

§ 11110. Suspension or revocation of license

(a) The department, after notice and hearing, may suspend or revoke a license issued under this chapter if any of the following occurs:

(1) The department finds and determines that the licensee fails to meet the requirements to receive or hold a license under this chapter.

(2) The licensee fails to keep the records required by this chapter.

(3) The licensee (A) permits fraud or engages in fraudulent practices either with reference to an applicant for a driver's license or an all-terrain vehicle safety certificate from the department, or (B) induces or countenances fraud or fraudulent practices on the part of an applicant.

(4) The licensee fails to comply with this chapter or regulation or requirement of the department adopted pursuant thereto.

(5) The licensee represents himself or herself as an agent or employee of the department or uses advertising designed to create the impression, or that would reasonably have the effect of leading persons to believe, that the licensee is in fact an employee or representative of the department; or the licensee makes an advertisement, in any manner or by any means, that is untrue or misleading and that is known, or that by the exercise of reasonable care should be known, to be untrue or misleading.

(6) The licensee, or an employee or agent of the licensee, solicits driver training or instruction or all-terrain vehicle safety instruction in, or within 200 feet of, an office of the department.

(7) The licensee is convicted of violating Section 14606, 20001, 20002, 20003, 20004, 20006, 20008, 23103, 23104, 23105, 23152, or 23153 of this code or subdivision (b) of Section 191.5 or subdivision (c) of Section 192 of the Penal Code. A conviction, after a plea of nolo contendere, is a conviction within the meaning of this paragraph.

(8) The licensee teaches, or permits a student to be taught, the specific tests administered by the department through use of the department's forms or testing facilities.

(9) The licensee conducts training, or permits training by an employee, in an unsafe manner or contrary to safe driving practices.

(10) The licensed school owner or licensed driving school operator teaches, or permits an employee to teach, driving instruction or all-terrain vehicle safety instruction without a valid instructor's license.

(11) The licensed school owner does not have in effect a bond as required by Section 11102.

(12) The licensee permits the use of the license by any other person for the purpose of permitting that person to engage in the ownership or operation of a school or in the giving of driving instruction or all-terrain vehicle safety instruction for compensation.

(13) The licensee holds a secondary teaching credential and explicitly or implicitly recruits or attempts to recruit a pupil who is enrolled in a junior or senior high school to be a customer for a business licensed pursuant to this article that is owned by the licensee or for which the licensee is an employee.

(b) In the interest of the public's safety, as determined by the department, the department may immediately suspend the license of a licensee for an alleged violation under this chapter and shall conduct a hearing of the alleged violation within 30 days of the suspension. *(Added by Stats.1994, c. 699 (S.B.1390), § 2, operative Jan. 1, 1998. Amended by Stats.1996, c. 47 (S.B.636), § 4, operative Jan. 1, 1998; Stats.1996, c. 922 (A.B.3003), § 2, operative Jan. 1, 1999; Stats.2000, c. 243 (S.B.1112), § 4; Stats.2007, c. 682 (A.B.430), § 8; Stats.2007, c. 747 (A.B.678), § 14.5.)*

Law Revision Commission Comments

1982 Amendment

Section 11110 is amended for consistency with Section 11102. The other changes in Section 11110 are technical. [16 Cal. L.Rev. Comm. Reports 501 (1981)].

§ 11110.1. Causes for suspension and revocation of licenses

Any of the causes specified in this chapter as a cause for refusal to issue a license under this chapter is cause to suspend or revoke a license under this chapter. *(Added by Stats.1990, c. 1563 (A.B.3243), § 12.)*

§ 11110.2. Cancellation of license; grounds

The license issued to a school owner shall be automatically canceled upon the happening of any of the following:

(a) The abandonment of the established place of business or the change thereof without notice to the department pursuant to Section 11108.5.

(b) The failure to maintain an adequate bond or to procure and file another bond, as required by Section 11102, prior to the effective date of the termination by the surety of any existing bond.

(c) The voluntary or involuntary surrender of the license, except that a surrender or cessation of business by the licensee, or the suspension or revocation of the corporate status of the licensee, does not preclude the department from filing an accusation for revocation or suspension of the surrendered license, as provided in Section 11110, or affect the department's decision to suspend or revoke the license.

(d) Notification to the department that the person designated as licensee has changed.

(e) Suspension or revocation of the corporate status of the licensee. *(Added by Stats.1987, c. 881, § 28, operative July 1, 1988. Amended by Stats.1990, c. 1563 (A.B.3243), § 13.)*

§ 11110.5. Cancellation of license when issued in error or surrendered; reapplication; operative date of section

The department may cancel any license issued under this chapter when that license has been issued in error or voluntarily surrendered to the department for cancellation. Whenever a driving school operator's license or an instructor's license is canceled, it shall be without prejudice and shall be surrendered to the department. Any person whose license has been canceled may immediately apply for a license, and the application may be accepted without additional fee or examination under rules and regulations adopted by the department.

This section shall become operative on July 1, 1988. *(Added by Stats.1987, c. 881, § 30, operative July 1, 1988.)*

§ 11110.7. Conviction of crime involving moral turpitude; refusal to issue or suspension of license

(a) The department, after notice and hearing, on an interim basis, may refuse to issue or may suspend a license issued under this chapter when the applicant or licensee, or a business representative if the applicant or licensee is a business, has been convicted of a crime involving moral turpitude which is substantially related to the qualifications, functions, or duties of the licensed activity, if an appeal of the conviction is pending or the conviction has otherwise not become final. A conviction after a plea of nolo contendere is a conviction within the meaning of this section.

(b) If a conviction, upon which an interim refusal to issue or suspension under subdivision (a) is based, is affirmed on appeal or otherwise becomes final, the refusal to issue or the suspension shall automatically become effective as a denial or revocation, as the case may be, of the license. If the interim refusal to issue or the suspension was stayed under probationary terms and conditions, the subsequent automatic denial or revocation shall also be stayed under the same terms and conditions for a term not to exceed the original term of probation for the interim refusal to issue or suspension.

(c) If a conviction, upon which an interim refusal to issue or suspension under subdivision (a) is based, is reversed on appeal, the department shall set aside immediately that refusal or suspension. *(Added by Stats.1990, c. 1563 (A.B.3243), § 14.)*

§ 11111. Notice and hearing prior to cancellation, suspension or revocation of license; review; temporary suspension; effect of suspension, expiration or cancellation

(a) Every licensee under this chapter is entitled to notice and hearing prior to cancellation, suspension, or revocation of the license by the department, except that the department shall immediately cancel the license without a hearing for failure of the licensee to meet and maintain the requirements of paragraph (1), (3), or (4) of subdivision (a) of Section 11102, or Section 11103 or 11103.1, or paragraph (4), (5), or (6) of subdivision (a) of Section 11104, or paragraph (4), (5), or (6) of subdivision (a) of Section 11104.3, or Section 11110.2.

(b) The notice and hearings provided for in this chapter shall be pursuant to Chapter 5 (commencing with Section 11500) of Part 1 of Division 3 of Title 2 of the Government Code.

(c) Any action of the department in suspending, canceling, or revoking, or failing to renew a license may be reviewed by any court of competent jurisdiction.

(d) The department may, pending a hearing, temporarily suspend the license or permit of any person licensed under this chapter for not more than 30 days if the director finds that the action is required in the public interest. In that case, a hearing shall be held and a decision issued within 30 days after notice of the temporary suspension.

(e) The suspension, expiration, or cancellation of a license issued under this chapter does not preclude the filing of an accusation for the revocation or suspension of the suspended, expired, or canceled license as provided in Section 11110, and does not invalidate or otherwise preclude a decision by the department to suspend or revoke the license. That determination may be considered in granting or refusing to grant any subsequent license authorized by this chapter to the same licensee, or to any partner, officer, director, or stockholder of the same licensee.

(Added by Stats.1987, c. 881, § 32, operative July 1, 1988. Amended by Stats.1990, c. 1563 (A.B.3243), § 15.)

Cross References

Departmental action, court review, see Vehicle Code § 14400.

Investigation prior to suspension, etc., see Vehicle Code § 13800 et seq.

Notice, see Vehicle Code § 13950 et seq.

Suspension or revocation of licenses, see Vehicle Code § 13100 et seq.

§ 11111.2. Owners of closed businesses or operators or instructors not residing at address last filed; service of process

Any owner licensed under this chapter who has closed his or her established place of business or any operator or instructor currently or previously licensed under this chapter who no longer resides at the address last filed with the department, may be served with process issued pursuant to Chapter 5 (commencing with Section 11500) of Part 1 of Division 3 of Title 2 of the Government Code by registered mail at that place of business, in the case of an owner, or at that residence, in the case of an operator or instructor, unless the person has notified the department in writing of another address where service may be made. *(Added by Stats.1988, c. 751, § 1.)*

§ 11111.5. Compromise settlement agreements; terms and conditions; operative date of section

(a) After the filing of an accusation under this chapter, the director may enter into a stipulated compromise settlement agreement with the consent of the licensee on terms and conditions mutually agreeable to the director, the respondent licensee, and the accuser without further hearing or appeal. The agreement may include, but is not limited to, a period of probation or monetary penalties, or both. The monetary penalty shall not exceed one thousand dollars ($1,000) for driving school owners or for a principal in an all-terrain vehicle safety training organization or five hundred dollars ($500) for driving school operators or for driving instructors or all-terrain vehicle safety instructors for each violation, and the monetary penalty shall be based on the nature of the violation and the effect of the violation on the purposes of this chapter.

(b) A compromise settlement agreement may be entered before, during, or after the hearing, but is valid only if executed and filed pursuant to subdivision (d) before the proposed decision of the hearing officer, if any, is adopted or the case is decided.

(c) The department shall adopt, by regulation, a schedule of maximum and minimum amounts of monetary penalties, the payment of which may be included as a term or condition of a compromise settlement agreement entered under subdivision (a). Any monetary penalty included in a compromise settlement agreement shall be within the range of monetary penalties in that schedule.

(d) Any compromise settlement agreement entered under this section shall be signed by the director, the respondent licensee, and the accuser, or by their authorized representatives. The director shall file, or cause to be filed, the agreement with the Office of Administrative Hearings, together with the department's notice of withdrawal of the accusation or statement of issues upon which the action was initiated.

(e) If the respondent licensee fails to perform all of the terms and conditions of the compromise settlement agreement, the agreement is void and the department may take any action authorized by law notwithstanding the agreement, including, but not limited to, refiling the accusation or imposing license sanctions.

(f) This section shall become operative on July 1, 1988. *(Added by Stats.1987, c. 881, § 34, operative July 1, 1988.)*

§ 11112. Hearings: refusal to issue

Upon refusal of the department to issue a license, the applicant shall be entitled to demand in writing a hearing before the director or his representative within 60 days after notice of refusal.

The hearing shall be conducted pursuant to Chapter 5 (commencing at Section 11500), Part 1, Division 3, Title 2 of the Government Code. *(Added by Stats.1959, c. 1996, p. 4622, § 15.6.)*

§ 11113. Conduct of courses; rules and regulations

(a) The director may prescribe rules and regulations for driving schools regarding the conduct of courses of driver education and driver training, including curriculum, facilities, and equipment. The rules and regulations regarding curriculum shall require both of the following:

(1) A component relating to the dangers involved in consuming alcohol or drugs in connection with the operation of a motor vehicle.

(2) A component examining driver attitude and motivation that focuses on the reduction of future driving violations, with particular emphasis on aggressive driving behavior and behavior commonly known as "road rage."

(b) The director may also prescribe rules and regulations for the conduct of driving instructor training courses required by Sections 11102.5 and 11104, including curriculum, facilities, and equipment. The department shall monitor instruction given by driving schools. *(Added by Stats.1975, c. 703, p. 1671, § 21. Amended by Stats.1985, c. 1455, § 6; Stats.2000, c. 642 (A.B.2733), § 2.)*

§ 11113.3. Curriculum includes rights and duties of motorist; rules and regulations

The rules and regulations adopted pursuant to Section 11113 regarding the curriculum shall include, but are not limited to, the rights and duties of a motorist as they relate to traffic laws and traffic safety. *(Added by Stats.2000, c. 833 (A.B.2522), § 5.)*

§ 11113.5. Standards for licensing and control; rules and regulations

The department shall establish rules and regulations prescribing standards for the licensing and control, as provided in this chapter, of owners, operators, and instructors and the courses of driver education and driver training for driving schools providing training courses for class 1 and class 2 licensed drivers. The standards shall provide for requirements of licensing, training, and control to assure that the owners, operators, and instructors are qualified to provide the type of training needed by drivers for safe operation of large commercial vehicles on the highway. *(Added by Stats.1985, c. 387, § 1.)*

§ 11114.　Reexamination

The department may require any person licensed under this chapter to submit to a reexamination of his qualifications when there is reasonable cause to believe that the licensee does not have the ability to give driving instruction. If the licensee refuses or fails to submit to such reexamination, the department may peremptorily suspend his license until such time as the licensee shall have submitted to reexamination. The suspension shall be effective upon notice. *(Added by Stats.1975, c. 703, p. 1671, § 23.)*

§ 11115.　Repealed by Stats.1975, c. 703, p. 1672, § 24

§ 11116.　Repealed by Stats.1990, c. 1563 (A.B.3243), § 16

CHAPTER 1.5.　TRAFFIC VIOLATOR SCHOOLS

Section
11200.　License; consumer disclosure statement; notification of court; receipt.
11201.　Repealed.
11202.　Criteria for issuance of license.
11202.5.　Licensing of operators; necessity of valid license; criteria for qualifying; time for license qualification.
11203.　Deposit in lieu of bond.
11203.5.　Actions upon bond.
11204.　Issuance of license certificates to owners and operators; term; renewal; probationary and temporary licenses.
11205.　List of licensed schools; use.
11205.　List of licensed schools on Internet Web site; hard copy lists; database to monitor, report, and track participation and course completion.
11205.1.　Application of fee authorized in § 11205.2.
11205.2.　Traffic assistance program (TAP); processing of traffic violators.
11205.4.　Use of traffic assistance program (TAP) or court assistance program (CAP) for monitoring of licensed traffic violator schools.
11206.　Instructor's licenses; qualifying requirements; exemptions.
11206.5.　License application; owner, operator, or instructor; evidence of character and reputation.
11207.　Issuance of instructors' licenses; term; renewal requirements; probationary licenses.
11208.　Fees for traffic violator school program activities; administrative fee assessed against drivers.
11208.5.　Report on status and progress of implementation.
11209.　Failure to renew license; reapplication; cancellation, suspension or revocation; reinstatement or reissuance.
11210.　Temporary permits.

Section
11211.　Refusal to issue license; grounds; hearing; reapplication.
11212.　Student records.
11213.　Notice; change in ownership, corporate structure, or address; addition or deletion of branch or classroom location; reports.
11214.　Audit, inspection and monitoring; department authority.
11215.　Suspension or revocation of license; grounds.
11215.5.　Suspension or revocation of license; further grounds.
11215.7.　Causes for suspension and revocation of licenses.
11216.　Cancellation of licenses; grounds.
11216.2.　Suspension of licenses; discrimination against individuals with disabilities.
11216.5.　Conviction of crime involving moral turpitude; refusal to issue or suspension of license.
11217.　Suspension or revocation of license; notice and hearing; reinstatement fee; review; temporary suspension.
11217.5.　Owners of closed businesses or operators or instructors not residing at address last filed; service of process.
11218.　Filing of accusation; compromise settlement agreement; terms and conditions; monetary penalties.
11219.　Rules and regulations; curriculum.
11219.3.　Content to be included in curriculum pursuant to § 11219.
11219.5.　Receipt for fees collected; cancellation of scheduled class.
11220.　Reexamination.
11221.　Repealed.
11222.　Contracts for administrative services.

§ 11200.　License; consumer disclosure statement; notification of court; receipt

(a) The department shall license schools for traffic violators for purposes of Section 41501 or 42005 and to provide traffic safety instruction to other persons who elect to attend. A person may not own or operate a traffic violator school or, except as provided in Section 11206, give instruction for compensation in a traffic violator school without a currently valid license issued by the department.

(b)(1) Any person who elects to attend a traffic violator school shall receive from the traffic violator school and shall sign a copy of the following consumer disclosure statement prior to the payment of the school fee and attending the school:

"Course content is limited to traffic violator curricula approved by the Department of Motor Vehicles. Students in the classroom include traffic offenders, repeat traffic offenders, adults, and teenagers, and those who have and those who have not been referred by a court. Instructor training, business regulatory standards, and Vehicle Code requirements of traffic violator schools are not equal to the training, standards, and Vehicle Code requirements of licensed driving schools (California Vehicle Code Section 11200(b)(1))."

(2) In the case of a minor who elects to attend a traffic violator school, the minor's parent or guardian shall sign the consumer disclosure statement.

(3) A copy of each signed disclosure statement shall be retained by the traffic violator school for a minimum of 36 months.

(c) New and modified departmental regulations necessitated by this section shall be adopted and effective no later than September 1, 2011.

(d) A licensed traffic violator school shall notify the court by posting on the department's Web-based database established pursuant to subdivision (b) of Section 11205 information regarding successful course completions.

(e) A licensed traffic violator school shall give every person who attends the school for purposes of Sections 41501 or 42005, upon successful completion of the lesson plan and passage of the postlesson knowledge test, a receipt indicating successful completion. The receipt shall include contact information, including the name of the traffic violator school, address of the school's business location, name of the course instructor if classroom-based, telephone number, e-mail address if appropriate, hours of operation, and any other information that may be used to confirm course completion.

(f) This section shall become operative on September 1, 2011. *(Added by Stats.2010, c. 599 (A.B.2499), § 3.5, operative Sept. 1, 2011.)*

Cross References

Traffic violator school, defined, see Vehicle Code § 626.

§ 11201. Repealed by Stats.1979, c. 373, § 315

§ 11202. Criteria for issuance of license

(a) Except as provided in subdivision (c), a traffic violator school owner shall meet all of the following criteria before a license may be issued for the traffic violator school:

(1) Maintain an established place of business in this state that is open to the public. An office or place of business of a traffic violator school, including any traffic violator school branch or classroom location, shall not be situated within 500 feet of any court of law.

(2) Conform to standards established by regulation of the department. In adopting the standards, the department shall consider those practices and instructional programs that may reasonably foster the knowledge, skills, and judgment necessary for compliance with traffic laws. The department shall establish standards for each instructional modality, which may include requirements specific to each modality. The standards may include, but are not limited to, classroom facilities, school personnel, equipment, curriculum, procedures for the testing and evaluation of students, recordkeeping, and business practices.

(3) Procure and file with the department a bond of fifteen thousand dollars ($15,000) for home study schools and two thousand dollars ($2,000) for classroom-based schools executed by an admitted surety and conditioned upon the applicant not practicing fraud or making a fraudulent representation that will cause a monetary loss to a person taking instruction from the applicant or to the state or any local authority.

(4) Have the proper equipment necessary for giving instruction to traffic violators.

(5) Have a lesson plan approved by the department, except as provided for in paragraph (2) of subdivision (c), and provide not less than the minimum instructional time specified in the approved plan. The approved plan shall include a postlesson knowledge test. The lesson plan for each instructional modality shall require separate approval by the department.

(6)(A) Execute and file with the department an instrument designating the director as agent of the applicant for service of process, as provided in this paragraph, in any action commenced against the applicant arising out of a claim for damages suffered by a person by the applicant's violation of a provision of this code committed in relation to the specifications of the applicant's traffic violator school or a condition of the bond required by paragraph (3).

(B) The applicant shall stipulate in the instrument that a process directed to the applicant, when personal service cannot be made in this state after due diligence, may be served instead upon the director or, in the director's absence from the department's principal offices, upon an employee in charge of the office of the director, and this substituted service is of the same effect as personal service on the applicant. The instrument shall further stipulate that the agency created by the designation shall continue during the period covered by the license issued pursuant to this section and so long thereafter as the applicant may be made to answer in damages for a violation of this code for which the surety may be made liable or a condition of the bond.

(C) The instrument designating the director as agent for service of process shall be acknowledged by the applicant before a notary public.

(D) If the director or an employee of the department, in lieu of the director, is served with a summons and complaint on behalf of the licensee, one copy of the summons and complaint shall be left with the director or in the director's office in Sacramento or mailed to the office of the director in Sacramento. A fee of five dollars ($5) shall also be paid to the director or employee at the time of service of the copy of the summons and complaint, or shall be included with a summons and complaint served by mail.

(E) The service on the director or department employee pursuant to this paragraph is sufficient service on the licensee if a notice of the service and a copy of the summons and complaint are, on the same day as the service or mailing of the summons and complaint, sent by registered mail by the plaintiff or his or her attorney to the licensee. A copy of the summons and complaint shall also be mailed by the plaintiff or plaintiff's attorney to the surety on the licensee's bond at the address of the surety given in the bond, postpaid and registered with request for return receipt.

(F) The director shall keep a record of all processes served pursuant to this paragraph showing the day and hour of service, and shall retain the documents served in the department's files.

(G) If the licensee is served with process by service upon the director or a department employee in lieu of the director, the licensee has 30 days after that service within which to answer any complaint or other pleading filed in the cause. For purposes of venue, if the licensee is served with process by service upon the director or a department employee in lieu of the director, the service is considered to have been made upon the licensee in the county in which the licensee has or last had his or her established place of business.

(7)(A) Meet the requirements of Section 11202.5, relating to traffic violator school operators, if the owner is also the operator of the traffic violator school. If the owner is not the operator of the traffic violator school, the owner shall designate an employee as operator who shall meet the requirements of Section 11202.5.

(B) A person may be an operator for more than one traffic school if (i) the schools have a common owner or owners and (ii) the schools share a single established business address.

(C) A traffic violator school with multiple branch locations may designate a separate operator for each location, but shall designate one of the operators as the primary contact for the department.

(8) Have an instructor who meets the requirements of Section 11206. An owner who is designated as the operator for the school is authorized to act as an instructor without meeting the requirements of Section 11206. The owner license may also include authorization to act as an instructor if the owner is not designated as the operator but meets the requirements of Section 11206. The owner license shall specify if the owner is authorized to offer instruction. If the owner is not approved to act as an instructor, the school must employ an instructor licensed pursuant to Section 11206.

(9) Provide the department with a written assurance that the school will comply with the applicable provisions of Subchapter II or III of the Americans with Disabilities Act of 1990 (42 U.S.C. Sec. 12101 et seq.), and any other federal and state laws prohibiting discrimination against individuals with disabilities. Compliance may include providing sign language interpreters or other accommodations for students with disabilities.

(b) The qualifying requirements specified in subdivision (a) shall be met within one year from the date of

application for a license, or a new application and fee are required.

(c) A court-approved program that was in operation prior to July 1, 2011, shall file an application for licensure as a traffic violator school by March 1, 2012. A court shall not approve a traffic violator school program after July 1, 2011.

(1) A court-approved program may continue to operate as approved by a court until the department makes a licensing decision.

(2) The department shall approve or deny all completed applications filed pursuant to this subdivision no later than December 31, 2012.

(3) A court-approved program shall be exempt from paragraph (5) of subdivision (a). The licensed program may continue to use the curriculum approved by the court until the department establishes curriculum standards in regulation. The court-approved program must comply with the new curriculum standards by the effective date established in regulation.

(d) Paragraphs (3) and (6) of subdivision (a) do not apply to public schools or other public agencies, which shall also not be required to post a cash deposit pursuant to Section 11203.

(e) Paragraph (7) of subdivision (a) does not apply to public schools or other public educational institutions.

(f) A notice approved by the department shall be posted in every traffic violator school, branch, and classroom location, and prominently displayed on a home study or Internet program, stating that any person involved in the offering of, or soliciting for, a completion certificate for attendance at a traffic violator school program in which the person does not attend or does not complete the minimum amount of instruction time may be guilty of violating Section 134 of the Penal Code.

(g) This section shall become operative on September 1, 2011. *(Added by Stats.2010, c. 599 (A.B.2499), § 4.5, operative Sept. 1, 2011.)*

Cross References

Bonds and undertakings, see Code of Civil Procedure § 995.010 et seq.

§ 11202.5. Licensing of operators; necessity of valid license; criteria for qualifying; time for license qualification

(a) The department shall license traffic violator school operators. A person shall not act as a traffic violator school operator without a currently valid license issued by the department, unless the person is an owner/operator and is so designated on the owner's license. Every person, in order to qualify as a traffic violator school operator, shall meet all of the following criteria in order to be issued a traffic violator school operator's license:

(1) Have not committed any act which, if the applicant were licensed as a traffic violator school operator, would be grounds for suspension or revocation of the license.

(2) Within three attempts, pass an examination that the department requires on traffic laws, safe driving practices, operation of motor vehicles, teaching methods and techniques, traffic violator school statutes and regulations, and office procedures and recordkeeping.

(3) Be 21 years of age or older.

(4) Have successfully completed an educational program of not less than four hours. The program shall include, but is not limited to, operator responsibilities, current laws, and the regulations in Article 4 of Title 13 of the California Code of Regulations. The instruction may be provided by generally accredited educational institutions, private vocational schools, and education programs and seminars offered by professional societies, organizations, trade associations, and other educational and technical programs that meet the requirements of this section.

(5) Provide a certification from the owner that the applicant has the knowledge necessary to perform the duties of the operator.

(b) All the qualifying requirements specified in this section shall be met within one year from the date of application for the license or the application shall lapse. However, the applicant may thereafter submit a new application upon payment of the required fee. *(Added by Stats.1985, c. 396, § 8, eff. July 30, 1985. Amended by Stats.1986, c. 1067, § 2; Stats.1990, c. 1563 (A.B.3243), § 18; Stats.1999, c. 282 (A.B.467), § 1; Stats.2000, c. 243 (S.B.1112), § 5; Stats.2010, c. 599 (A.B.2499), § 7.)*

§ 11203. Deposit in lieu of bond

In lieu of the bond otherwise required by paragraph (3) of subdivision (a) of Section 11202, the applicant may make a deposit pursuant to Article 7 (commencing with Section 995.710) of Chapter 2 of Title 14 of Part 2 of the Code of Civil Procedure. The director may order the deposit returned at the expiration of three years from the date a traffic violator school licensee has ceased to do business, or three years from the date a licensee has ceased to be licensed, if the director is satisfied that there are no outstanding claims against the deposit. A superior court may, upon petition, order the return of the deposit prior to the expiration of three years upon evidence satisfactory to the court that there are no outstanding claims against the deposit. If either the director, department, or state is a defendant in any civil action instituted to recover all or any part of the deposit, or any civil action is instituted by the director, department, or state to determine those entitled to any part of the deposit, the director, department, or state shall be paid reasonable attorney fees and costs from the deposit. Costs shall include those administrative costs incurred in processing claims against the licensee recoverable from the deposit. *(Added by Stats.1984, c. 1037, § 4. Amended by Stats.1988, c. 1221, § 2; Stats.1992, c. 1241 (S.B. 1615), § 15; Stats.2002, c. 784 (S.B.1316), § 598.)*

Law Revision Commission Comments

2002 Amendment

Section 11203 is amended to reflect unification of the municipal and superior courts pursuant to Article VI, Section 5(e), of the California Constitution. [32 Cal.L.Rev.Comm. Reports 540 (2002)].

Cross References

Bonds and undertakings, see Code of Civil Procedure § 995.010 et seq.

§ 11203.5. Actions upon bond

If the state or any of its political subdivisions suffers any loss or damage by reason of any fraudulent practice or representation or by reason of any violation of this division by a traffic violator school owner, the department may bring a cause of action against the traffic violator school owner and the surety upon the owner's bond. *(Added by Stats.1988, c. 1221, § 3.)*

§ 11204. Issuance of license certificates to owners and operators; term; renewal; probationary and temporary licenses

(a) The department shall issue a license certificate to each traffic violator school owner and each traffic violator school operator licensed pursuant to this chapter. The term of the license shall be for a period of one year from the date of issue unless canceled, suspended, or revoked by the department. The license shall be renewed annually. The department shall require compliance with Section 11202 for renewal of the license of a traffic violator school owner. The department shall require compliance with Section 11202.5 for renewal of the license of a traffic violator school operator.

(b)(1) In lieu of the examination required by Section 11202.5 for renewal of the license of a traffic violator school operator, the department may accept submission of evidence by the licensee of continuing professional education.

(2) "Professional education," as used in paragraph (1), means the satisfactory completion of courses acceptable to the department related to traffic safety, teaching techniques, or the teaching of driver instruction, or the participation in professional seminars approved by the department.

(c) Whenever in its judgment the public interest so requires, the department may issue a probationary license subject to special conditions to be observed by the licensee in the conduct of the traffic violator school. The conditions to be attached to the license shall be any that may, in the judgment of the department, be in the public interest and suitable to the qualifications of the applicant as disclosed by the application and investigation by the department of the information contained therein. The conditions may not appear on the license certificate.

(d) Upon notification of the death of a traffic violator school licensee, the department may issue a temporary license to the executor or administrator of the estate of a deceased holder of a validly outstanding license to conduct a traffic violator school, or if no executor or administrator has been appointed and until a certified copy of an order making an appointment is filed with the department, a temporary license may be issued to the surviving spouse or other heir entitled to conduct the business of the deceased. The temporary license shall permit the holder to conduct the traffic violator school for a period of one year from and after the date of the original licensee's death, and necessary one-year extensions may be granted to permit disposal of the business and qualification for a license of a purchaser of the business or the surviving spouse or heir. The department may restrict or condition a temporary license and attach to the exercise of the privilege thereunder any terms and conditions that in the department's judgment are required for the protection of the public. *(Added by Stats.1984, c. 1037, § 4. Amended by Stats.1985, c. 396, § 9, eff. July 30, 1985; Stats.2003, c. 594 (S.B.315), § 33.)*

§ 11205. List of licensed schools; use

Section operative if subd. (d) or (e), as added to former § 11205 by Stats.1991, c. 411 (A.B.185), § 4, or application thereof, is held unconstitutional, under the terms of subd. (f). See, also, section operative Sept. 1, 2011.

(a) The department shall publish semiannually, or more often as necessary to serve the purposes of this act, a list of all traffic violator schools which are licensed pursuant to this section. The list shall identify classroom facilities within a judicial district that are at a different location from a licensed school's principal facility. The department shall transmit the list to each municipal court and to each superior court in a county in which there is no municipal court, with a sufficient number of copies to allow the courts to provide one copy to each person referred to a licensed traffic violator school. The department shall, at least semiannually, revise the list to ensure that each court has a current list of all licensed traffic violator schools.

(b) Each licensed traffic violator school owner shall be permitted one school name per judicial district.

(c) The referral list shall be organized alphabetically, in sections for each county, and contain subsections for each judicial district within the county. The order of the names within each judicial district shall be random pursuant to a drawing or lottery conducted by the department.

(d) Except as otherwise provided in subdivision (d) of Section 42005, the court shall use either the current referral list of traffic violator schools published by the department when it orders a person to complete a traffic violator school pursuant to subdivision (a) or (b) of Section 42005 or, when a court utilizing a nonprofit agency for traffic violator school administration and monitoring services in which all traffic violator schools licensed by the department are allowed the opportunity to participate, a statewide referral list may be published

by the nonprofit agency and distributed by the court. The agency shall monitor each classroom location situated within the judicial districts in which that agency provides services to the courts and is represented on its referral list. The monitoring shall occur at least once every 90 days with reports forwarded to the department and the respective courts on a monthly basis.

(e) The court may charge a traffic violator a fee to defray the costs incurred by the agency for the monitoring reports and services provided to the court. The court may delegate collection of the fee to the agency. Fees shall be approved and regulated by the court. Until December 31, 1996, the fee shall not exceed the actual cost incurred by the agency or five dollars ($5), whichever is less.

* * *   *(Added by Stats.1991, c. 411 (A.B.185), § 5. Amended by Stats.1994, c. 308 (A.B.2544), § 33, eff. July 21, 1994; Stats.1995, c. 58 (S.B.1263), § 2, eff. July 6, 1995; Stats.1997, c. 571 (A.B.1088), § 48.5; Stats.1998, c. 931 (S.B.2139), § 456, eff. Sept. 28, 1998; Stats.2013, c. 76 (A.B.383), § 193.)*

Law Revision Commission Comments

1998 Amendment

Section 11205 is amended to accommodate unification of the municipal and superior courts in a county. Cal. Const. art. VI, § 5(e). *Cf.* Code Civ. Proc. § 38 & Comment ("judicial district" defined). The section is also amended to reflect elimination of the justice court. Cal. Const. art. VI, 1, 5(b). [28 Cal.L.Rev. Comm. Reports 51 (1998)].

§ 11205. List of licensed schools on Internet Web site; hard copy lists; database to monitor, report, and track participation and course completion

Section operative Sept. 1, 2011. See, also, section operative upon a decision that subd. (d) or (e), as added to former § 11205 by Stats.1991, c. 411 (A.B.185), § 4, or application thereof, is unconstitutional.

(a) The department shall provide a list of licensed traffic violator schools on its Internet Web site. For each licensed school, the list shall indicate the modalities of instruction offered and specify the cities where classroom instruction is offered. The sequential listing of licensed schools shall be randomized daily.

(b) When a court or traffic assistance program (TAP) provides a hard copy list of licensed traffic violator schools to a traffic violator, the court or TAP shall provide only a current date-stamped list downloaded from the department's Internet Web site. The hard copy list shall be as current as practicable, but in no event shall a list be distributed with a date stamp that is more than 60 days old.

(c) The department shall, by April 1, 2012, develop a Web-based database that will enable the department, the courts, and traffic violator schools to monitor, report, and track participation and course completion. Traffic violator schools shall update course information within three business days of class completion and provide to the courts class completion information on a daily basis.

(d) This section shall become operative on September 1, 2011. *(Added by Stats.2010, c. 599 (A.B.2499), § 5.5, operative Sept. 1, 2011.)*

§ 11205.1. Application of fee authorized in § 11205.2

Until January 1, 2013, the fee authorized in subdivision (d) of Section 11205.2, and after January 1, 2013, the fee authorized in subdivision (c) of Section 11205.2, shall be applicable only in those instances where a traffic violator has agreed to attend or has been ordered to attend a traffic violator school pursuant to Section 41501 or 42005. *(Added by Stats.1997, c. 850 (A.B.233), § 58. Amended by Stats.2010, c. 599 (A.B.2499), § 6.)*

Cross References

Occupational licensing, traffic violator schools, duties of Judicial Council, see Vehicle Code § 11205.4.

§ 11205.2. Traffic assistance program (TAP); processing of traffic violators

(a) As used in this chapter, a traffic assistance program (TAP) is a public or private nonprofit agency that provides services, under contract with a court to process traffic violators or under contract with the department to assist in oversight activities.

(b) A court may use a TAP to assist the court in performing services related to the processing of traffic violators. As used in this section, "services" means those services relating to the processing of traffic infraction cases at, and for, the court, including printing and providing to the court and traffic violators hard copy county-specific lists printed from the department's Internet Web site, administratively assisting traffic violators, and any other lawful activity relating to the administration of the court's traffic infraction caseload.

(c) The court may charge a traffic violator a fee to defray the costs incurred by a TAP for traffic case administration services provided to the court pursuant to subdivision (b). The court may delegate collection of the fee to the TAP. Fees shall be approved and regulated by the court. The fee shall not exceed the actual costs incurred by the TAP for the activities authorized under subdivision (b).

(d) This section shall become operative on January 1, 2013. *(Added by Stats.2010, c. 599 (A.B.2499), § 7.5, operative Jan. 1, 2013.)*

Cross References

Carry over of unexpended funds by trial courts, funds excluded from calculation of amount authorized to be carried over commencing June 30, 2014, see Government Code § 77203.

§ 11205.4. Use of traffic assistance program (TAP) or court assistance program (CAP) for monitoring of licensed traffic violator schools

(a) The department may use a traffic assistance program (TAP), or until January 1, 2013, a CAP established pursuant to Section 11205.2, for monitoring of licensed traffic violator schools, including, but not limited to, audits, inspections, review and examination of business records, class records, business practices, the content of the program of instruction set forth in the lesson plan, or curriculum of a licensee. Inspection includes, but is not limited to, the review of the business office, branch office, and applicable classroom facilities of a licensee. Monitoring includes onsite review of actual presentation of the traffic safety instruction provided in a classroom and any other activity deemed necessary to ensure high-quality education of traffic violators.

(b) This section shall become operative on September 1, 2011. *(Added by Stats.2010, c. 599 (A.B.2499), § 8.5, operative Sept. 1, 2011. Amended by Stats.2011, c. 296 (A.B.1023), § 302.)*

§ 11206. Instructor's licenses; qualifying requirements; exemptions

(a) The department shall license traffic violator school instructors. Except as exempted by this section, no person shall act as a traffic violator school instructor without a currently valid instructor's license issued by the department. Every person, in order to qualify as a traffic violator school instructor, shall meet all of the following requirements before an instructor's license may be issued:

(1) Have a high school education.

(2) Within three attempts, pass an examination, as required by the department, on traffic laws, safe driving practices, operation of motor vehicles, and teaching methods and techniques.

(3) Hold a currently valid California driver's license, which is not subject to probation pursuant to Section 14250 due to the applicant being a negligent operator within the meaning of Section 12810 or 12810.5. The applicant's driving record shall not have any outstanding notice for violating a written promise to appear in court or for willfully failing to pay a lawfully imposed fine, as provided in Section 40509.

(4) Be 18 years of age or older.

(b) All the qualifying requirements specified by this section shall be met within one year from the date of application for a license or the application shall lapse. However, the applicant may thereafter submit a new application upon payment of the requisite fee.

(c) A license issued pursuant to this section is not required to provide instruction to traffic violators in a public school or other public educational institution by a person holding a valid teaching credential with satisfactory training or experience in the subject area, as determined by the department. Persons exempt from licensure under this section are not required to obtain a license certificate pursuant to Section 11207. *(Added by Stats.1984, c. 1037, § 4. Amended by Stats.1985, c. 396, § 11, eff. July 30, 1985; Stats.1990, c. 1563 (A.B.3243), § 19.)*

§ 11206.5. License application; owner, operator, or instructor; evidence of character and reputation

Each applicant for a license as a traffic violator school owner, traffic violator school operator, or traffic violator school instructor shall submit an application to the department on the forms prescribed by the department. The applicant shall provide the department with any information concerning the applicant's character, honesty, integrity, and reputation which the department may consider necessary. *(Added by Stats.1987, c. 75, § 2.)*

§ 11207. Issuance of instructors' licenses; term; renewal requirements; probationary licenses

(a) The department shall issue a license certificate to each traffic violator school instructor when it is satisfied that he or she has met the qualifications required under this chapter. The original instructor license and any license renewed pursuant to subdivisions (b) and (c) shall be valid for a period of three years from the date of issuance unless canceled, suspended, or revoked by the department.

(b) Every application for the renewal of a traffic violator school instructor license may be made by the licensee prior to the expiration date of the license by presenting to the department a completed application on a form provided by the department. In no event shall a traffic violator school instructor renew the license after the date of expiration.

(c) The department shall require all of the following for the renewal of an instructor's license:

(1) Compliance with Section 11206, except subdivision (c) thereof.

(2) Satisfactory completion of an examination as provided in Section 11206 at least once during each succeeding three-year period after the initial issuance of the license. However, in lieu of examination for renewal of the license, the department may accept submission by the licensee of evidence of continuing professional education.

(d) When, in its judgment, the public interest so requires, the department may issue a probationary license subject to special conditions to be observed by the licensee in the exercise of the privilege granted. The conditions to be attached to the license shall be such as may, in the judgment of the department, be in the public interest and suitable to the qualifications of the applicant, as disclosed by the application and investigation by the department of the information contained therein. *(Added by Stats.1984, c. 1037, § 4. Amended by Stats.1987, c. 111, § 2.)*

§ 11208. Fees for traffic violator school program activities; administrative fee assessed against drivers

(a) The department shall charge a fee, to be determined by the department, for the following traffic violator school program activities:

(1) Original issuance of a traffic violator school owner, operator, instructor, and branch or classroom location license.

(2) Renewal of a traffic violator school owner, operator, instructor, and branch or classroom location license.

(3) Issuance of a duplicate or corrected traffic violator school owner, operator, instructor, and branch or classroom location license.

(4) Transfer of an operator or instructor license from one traffic violator school to another.

(5) Approval of curriculum, based on the instructional modality of the curriculum.

(6) Fees for administering the examinations pursuant to Sections 11206 and 11207.

(b) The fees authorized under subdivision (a) shall be sufficient to defray the actual cost to the department to administer the traffic violator school program, except for routine monitoring of instruction.

(c) A single administrative fee shall be assessed against, and collected by the court pursuant to Section 42007.1 from, each driver who is allowed or ordered to attend traffic violator school. Included in this fee shall be an amount determined by the department to be sufficient to defray the cost of routine monitoring of traffic violator school instruction.

(d) This section shall become operative on September 1, 2011. *(Added by Stats.2010, c. 599 (A.B.2499), § 10, operative Sept. 1, 2011.)*

Cross References

Traffic violator school defined, see Vehicle Code § 626.

§ 11208.5. Report on status and progress of implementation

(a) By December 31, 2011, and by December 31 of each year thereafter, the department shall report to the Legislature on the status and progress of its efforts to implement the act that adds this section. This annual report shall include information on all of the following:

(1) The number and type of programs licensed.

(2) The average number of days required to process each application for licensure.

(3) The performance measures established for its monitoring activities, including those contracted out to third parties.

(4) Details with respect to costs to show how fees authorized by the act that adds this section were expended.

(5) A breakdown of all complaints received and their disposition or resolution.

(b) A report to be submitted pursuant to subdivision (a) shall be submitted in compliance with Section 9795 of the Government Code.

(c) Pursuant to Section 10231.5 of the Government Code, this section is repealed on January 1, 2016. *(Added by Stats.2010, c. 599 (A.B.2499), § 10.5.)*

Repeal

For repeal of this section, see its terms.

§ 11209. Failure to renew license; reapplication; cancellation, suspension or revocation; reinstatement or reissuance

Any traffic violator school owner, traffic violator school operator, or traffic violator school instructor required to be licensed under this chapter who fails to renew the license before the expiration of the license may not renew that license, but may reapply for an original license pursuant to this chapter. For purposes of this section, a license that has been canceled may not be renewed and a license that is suspended or revoked may not be renewed, until reinstatement or reissuance by the department. If the period of suspension or revocation extends beyond the expiration of a license, it may not be renewed, but the person may apply for a new license thereafter. *(Added by Stats.1984, c. 1037, § 4. Amended by Stats.1985, c. 396, § 13, eff. July 30, 1985; Stats.1987, c. 111, § 3.)*

§ 11210. Temporary permits

Pending determination by the department that an applicant for a license fully satisfies the requirements of this chapter, the department may issue a temporary permit to the applicant. A temporary permit may authorize the operation of a traffic violator school or acting as a traffic violator school operator or traffic violator school instructor for a period not to exceed 120 days while the department is completing its investigation and determination of all facts relative to the qualifications of the applicant for the license.

The department may cancel a temporary permit when it has determined or has reasonable cause to believe that the application is incorrect or incomplete or the temporary permit was issued in error. A temporary permit is invalid upon cancellation or once the applicant has been issued or denied the license applied for. *(Added by Stats.1984, c. 1037, § 4. Amended by Stats.1985, c. 396, § 14, eff. July 30, 1985.)*

§ 11211. Refusal to issue license; grounds; hearing; reapplication

(a) The department may refuse to issue a license to any applicant under this chapter when it finds and determines that any of the following exist:

(1) The applicant was previously the holder of a license under this chapter which was revoked or suspended.

(2) The applicant was previously the holder of an occupational license issued by another state, authorizing the same or similar activities of a license issued under this division; and that license was revoked or suspended for cause and was never reissued, or was suspended for cause, and the terms of suspension have not been fulfilled.

(3) The applicant has done any act or series of acts which would be a cause for suspension or revocation of licensure under Section 11215, regardless of whether the applicant was licensed under this chapter at the time of the act or acts.

(4) If the applicant is a business, a business representative was the holder of a previously issued license under this chapter that was suspended or revoked or has done any act or series of acts which would be a cause for suspension or revocation of a license under Section 11215, regardless of whether the business representative was licensed under this chapter at the time of the act or acts.

(5) By reason of the facts and circumstances relating to the organization, control, and management of the business, it is likely that both of the following will occur:

(A) The policy or operation of the business will be directed, controlled, or managed by an individual who, by reason of an act, series of acts, or conduct described in paragraph (3) or (4), would be ineligible for a license.

(B) By licensing the business, the purposes of this division would be defeated.

(6) The applicant has knowingly made a false statement or knowingly concealed a material fact in applying for a license under this chapter.

(7) The applicant, or a business representative if the applicant is a business, has been convicted of a crime, or committed any act or engaged in conduct involving moral turpitude which is substantially related to the qualifications, functions, or duties of the licensed activity. A conviction after a plea of nolo contendere is a conviction within the meaning of this section.

(b) Upon refusal of the department to issue a license under this chapter, the applicant is entitled to a hearing upon demand in writing submitted to the department within 60 days after notice of refusal. The hearing shall be conducted pursuant to Chapter 5 (commencing with Section 11500) of Part 1 of Division 3 of Title 2 of the Government Code.

(c) A person whose license has been revoked or application for a license has been refused may reapply for the license after a period of not less than one year has elapsed from the effective date of the decision revoking the license or refusing the application. *(Added by Stats.1984, c. 1037, § 4. Amended by Stats.1985, c. 396, § 15, eff. July 30, 1985; Stats.1990, c. 1563 (A.B.3243), § 20; Stats.1998, c. 877 (A.B.2132), § 43.)*

§ 11212. Student records

(a) Every owner licensed under this chapter shall keep a record at the traffic violator school's primary business location showing all of the following for each student:

(1) The name and address and license number of the traffic violator school providing instruction.

329

(2) The name and address of each person given instruction.

(3) The instruction permit number or driver's license number of every person given instruction.

(4) The name and number of the license issued pursuant to Section 11207 of the traffic violator school instructor.

(5) The particular type of instruction given and the date or dates of the instruction.

(6) A statement as to whether the approved lesson plan was followed.

(7) The total number of hours of instruction.

(8) The total cost to the student of the instruction, which shall not exceed the amount of the fee represented or advertised by the traffic violator school at the time of the student's enrollment.

(9) The court docket number under which the student was referred to a traffic violator school.

(10) The number of the completion certificate issued to the student pursuant to subdivision (e) of Section 11208 and, if different, the number of any copy thereof issued to the student.

(b) The records shall be retained for a minimum of three years and shall be open to the inspection during business hours and at all other reasonable times by the department, the court, a private entity providing monitoring pursuant to Section 11222, the Legislative Analyst, and the State Auditor or authorized employees thereof, but shall be only for confidential use.

(c) Whenever a licensee suspends or terminates the licensed activity, the licensee shall surrender the records specified in subdivision (a) to the department for examination not later than the end of the third day, excluding Saturdays, Sundays, and legal holidays, after the date of suspension or termination. The department may duplicate or make a record of any information contained therein. All these records shall be returned to the licensee not later than 30 days after the date of surrender.

(d) The address of any person kept pursuant to paragraph (2) of subdivision (a) shall only be used by the school for school administrative purposes. (Added by Stats.1984, c. 1037, § 4. Amended by Stats.1985, c. 396, § 16, eff. July 30, 1985; Stats.2001, c. 739 (A.B.1707), § 5.)

§ 11213. Notice; change in ownership, corporate structure, or address; addition or deletion of branch or classroom location; reports.

(a) Every traffic violator school owner licensed pursuant to this chapter shall notify the department within 10 days of any change in the ownership or corporate structure of the licensee.

(b) Every traffic violator school owner shall immediately notify the department of the following activities:

(1) Change of the site or location of the school's established principal place of business.

(2) Addition or deletion of a traffic violator school branch or classroom location.

(c) Every traffic violator school operator and traffic violator school instructor licensed pursuant to this chapter shall report to the department every change of residence address within five days of the change.

(d) The department may require persons licensed pursuant to this chapter to submit additional reports as determined necessary by the department to serve the purposes of this chapter. (Added by Stats.1984, c. 1037, § 4. Amended by Stats.1985, c. 396, § 17, eff. July 30, 1985.)

§ 11214. Audit, inspection and monitoring; department authority

(a) Except as provided in this chapter, the department may audit, inspect, and monitor, all licensed traffic violator schools.

(b) The department may annually audit the records of a licensee. Auditing includes, but is not limited to, the review and examination of business records, class records when applicable, business practices, and the content of the program of instruction set forth in the lesson plan or curriculum of a licensee.

(c) Inspecting includes, but is not limited to, the review of the business office, branch office, and applicable classroom facilities of a licensee.

(d) Monitoring includes the onsite review of the actual presentation of the program of traffic safety instruction provided in a classroom mode of instruction. (Added by Stats.2003, c. 518 (A.B.1479), § 4.)

§ 11215. Suspension or revocation of license; grounds

The department, after notice and hearing, may suspend or revoke a license issued under this chapter if any of the following circumstances exist:

(a) The department finds and determines that the licensee ceases to meet any requirement to obtain a license under this chapter.

(b) The holder fails to comply with, or otherwise violates, a provision of this chapter or a regulation or requirement of the department adopted pursuant to this chapter.

(c) The licensee engages in fraudulent practices with respect to its activities licensed under this chapter or induces or fails to promptly report to the department any known fraud or fraudulent practices on the part of an employee of the traffic violator school.

(d) The licensee represents himself or herself as an agent or employee of the department or uses advertising designed to create the impression, or that would reasonably have the effect of leading persons to believe that the licensee was in fact an employee or representative of the department, or whenever the licensee advertises, in any manner or means, a statement that is untrue or misleading and that is known, or that by the exercise of reasonable care should be known, to be untrue or misleading.

(e) The licensee or an employee or agent of the licensee collects fees for or preregisters a person in traffic violator school or solicits traffic violator school instruction in an office of the department or in a court or within 500 feet of a court.

(f) The licensee is convicted of violating Section 20001, 20002, 20003, 20004, 20006, 20008, 23103, 23104, 23105, 23152, or 23153 of this code or subdivision (b) of Section 191.5 or Section 192 of the Penal Code. A conviction after a plea of nolo contendere is a conviction within the meaning of this section.

(g) The traffic violator school owner teaches, or permits an employee to teach, traffic safety instruction without a valid instructor's license.

(h) The traffic violator school owner does not have in effect a bond as provided in paragraph (3) of subdivision (a) of Section 11202 or a deposit in lieu of the bond, as specified in Section 11203. *(Added by Stats.1984, c. 1037, § 4. Amended by Stats.1985, c. 396, § 19, eff. July 30, 1985; Stats.1990, c. 1563 (A.B.3243), § 21; Stats.1992, c. 969 (S.B.895), § 2; Stats.2007, c. 682 (A.B.430), § 9; Stats.2007, c. 747 (A.B.678), § 15.5.)*

§ 11215.5. Suspension or revocation of license; further grounds

The department, after notice and hearing, may also suspend or revoke any license issued under this chapter when any of the following circumstances exist:

(a) If the main business office of the traffic violator school is located in any county with a population of 400,000 or more in which the traffic violator school conducts its instructional program, and the main business office does not maintain office hours during the time that the day courts in that county are open for business. This subdivision shall not apply to public schools.

(b) If the licensee is found by the department to be selling, or knowingly permitting the sale of, completion certificates.

(c) If the licensee is found by the department to be intentionally cutting instructional time short.

(d) If the licensee is found by the department to be intentionally diverting any student to a traffic school other than the school initially contacted by that student, without disclosure to that student, through the use of the department's list of licensed traffic violator schools. *(Added by Stats.1986, c. 1067, § 4. Amended by Stats. 1988, c. 1196, § 3.)*

§ 11215.7. Causes for suspension and revocation of licenses

Any of the causes specified in this chapter as a cause for refusal to issue a license under this chapter is cause to suspend or revoke a license under this chapter. *(Added by Stats.1990, c. 1563 (A.B.3243), § 22.)*

§ 11216. Cancellation of licenses; grounds

Any license issued to a traffic violator school owner under this chapter shall be automatically canceled upon the happening of any of the following:

(a) The abandonment of the established place of business or the change thereof without notice to the department pursuant to Section 11213.

(b) The failure to maintain an adequate bond or to procure and file another bond, as required by Section 11202, prior to the effective date of the termination by the surety of any existing bond.

(c) The voluntary or involuntary surrender of the license, except that a surrender or cessation of business by the licensee, or the suspension or revocation of the corporate status of the licensee, does not preclude the department from filing an accusation for revocation or suspension of the surrendered license, as provided in Section 11215 or 11215.5, or affect the department's decision to suspend or revoke the license.

(d) Notification to the department that the person designated as the licensee has changed.

(e) Suspension or cancellation of the corporate status of the licensee. *(Added by Stats.1984, c. 1037, § 4. Amended by Stats.1990, c. 1563 (A.B.3243), § 23.)*

§ 11216.2. Suspension of licenses; discrimination against individuals with disabilities

(a) Any license issued to the owner or operator of a traffic violator school under this chapter shall be automatically suspended for 30 days by the department if the department has been notified that more than one final determination has been made that the traffic violator school has violated a student's rights under the federal Americans with Disabilities Act of 1990 (42 U.S.C. Sec. 12101, et seq.) or any other federal or state law prohibiting discrimination against individuals with disabilities. The final determination shall be made by a federal or state court of competent jurisdiction or an appropriate federal or state administrative agency, including, but not limited to, the Department of Fair Employment and Housing, or any combination thereof.

For the purpose of this subdivision, "final determination" means that no further appeal of a determination can be taken to any court because the time period for the appeal has expired.

(b) If a traffic violator school subject to suspension under this section is operated by a traffic school operator licensed pursuant to Section 11202.5 who is operating other traffic schools, the licenses of the owners of those traffic schools operated by that traffic school operator also shall be suspended for the 30–day period. *(Added by Stats.1994, c. 1053 (A.B.3162), § 3. Amended by Stats. 1996, c. 124 (A.B.3470), § 122.)*

§ 11216.5. Conviction of crime involving moral turpitude; refusal to issue or suspension of license

(a) The department, after notice and hearing, on an interim basis, may refuse to issue or may suspend a license issued under this chapter when the applicant or licensee, or a business representative if the applicant or licensee is a business, has been convicted of a crime involving moral turpitude which is substantially related to the qualifications, functions, or duties of the licensed activity, if an appeal of the conviction is pending or the conviction has otherwise not become final. A conviction after a plea of nolo contendere is a conviction within the meaning of this section.

(b) If a conviction, on which an interim refusal to issue or suspension under subdivision (a) is based, is affirmed on appeal or otherwise becomes final, the refusal to issue or the suspension shall automatically take effect as a denial or revocation, as the case may be, of the license. If the interim refusal to issue or suspension was stayed under probationary terms and conditions, the subsequent automatic denial or revocation shall also be stayed under the same terms and conditions for a term not to exceed the original term of probation for the interim refusal to issue or suspension.

(c) If a conviction, upon which an interim refusal to issue or suspension under subdivision (a) is based, is reversed on appeal, the refusal or suspension shall be set aside immediately by the department. *(Added by Stats. 1990, c. 1563 (A.B.3243), § 24.)*

§ 11217. Suspension or revocation of license; notice and hearing; reinstatement fee; review; temporary suspension

(a) Every licensee under this chapter is entitled to notice and hearing prior to suspension or revocation of the license by the department, except that the department shall immediately suspend the license pursuant to subdivision (e) for any act of fraud specified in subdivision (c) or (d) of Section 11215.

(b) Before reinstatement of any license suspended pursuant to subdivision (a) of Section 11215, the licensee shall pay the department a reinstatement fee of five dollars ($5).

(c) The notice and hearings provided for in this division shall be pursuant to Chapter 5 (commencing with Section 11500) of Part 1 of Division 3 of Title 2 of the Government Code.

(d) Any action of the department, in suspending, canceling, revoking, or failing to renew a license issued pursuant to this chapter, may be reviewed by any court of competent jurisdiction.

(e) The department may, pending a hearing, temporarily suspend the license or permit of any traffic violator school owner, operator, or instructor for a period of not more than 30 days if the director finds that the public interest so requires. In that case, a hearing shall be held

and a decision issued within 30 days after issuance of the notice of temporary suspension.

(f) The suspension, expiration, or cancellation of a license issued pursuant to this chapter does not preclude the filing of an accusation for the revocation or suspension of the suspended, expired, or canceled license, and does not invalidate or otherwise preclude a decision by the department to suspend or revoke the license, and this determination may be considered by the department in granting or refusing to grant any subsequent license under this chapter to the same licensee or to any business representative of the same licensee. *(Added by Stats. 1984, c. 1037, § 4. Amended by Stats.1990, c. 1563 (A.B.3243), § 25.)*

§ 11217.5. Owners of closed businesses or operators or instructors not residing at address last filed; service of process

Any owner licensed under this chapter who has closed his or her established place of business or any operator or instructor currently or previously licensed under this chapter who no longer resides at the address last filed with the department, may be served with process issued pursuant to Chapter 5 (commencing with Section 11500) of Part 1 of Division 3 of Title 2 of the Government Code by registered mail at that place of business, in the case of an owner, or at that residence, in the case of an operator or instructor, unless the person has notified the department in writing of another address where service may be made. *(Added by Stats.1988, c. 751, § 2.)*

§ 11218. Filing of accusation; compromise settlement agreement; terms and conditions; monetary penalties

(a) After the filing of an accusation under this chapter, the director may enter into a stipulated compromise settlement agreement with the consent of the licensee on terms and conditions mutually agreeable to the director, the respondent licensee, and the accuser without further hearing or appeal. The agreement may include, but is not limited to, a period of probation or monetary penalties, or both. The monetary penalty shall not exceed one thousand dollars ($1,000) per violation for a traffic violator school owner or five hundred dollars ($500) per violation for traffic violator school operators or instructors, and shall be based on the nature of the violation and the effect of the violation on the purposes of this chapter.

(b) A compromise settlement agreement may be entered before, during, or after the hearing, but is valid only if executed and filed pursuant to subdivision (d) before the proposed decision of the hearing officer, if any, is adopted or the case is decided.

(c) The department shall adopt, by regulation, a schedule of maximum and minimum amounts of monetary penalties, the payment of which may be included as a term or condition of a compromise settlement agreement entered under subdivision (a). Any monetary penalty included in a compromise settlement agreement shall be within the range of monetary penalties in that schedule.

(d) Any compromise settlement agreement entered under this section shall be signed by the director, the respondent licensee, and the accuser, or by their authorized representatives. The director shall file, or cause to be filed, the agreement with the Office of Administrative Hearings, together with the department's notice of withdrawal of the accusation or statement of issues upon which the action was initiated, unless that accusation or statement has not yet been forwarded to the Office of Administrative Hearings.

(e) If the respondent licensee fails to perform all of the terms and conditions of the compromise settlement agreement, the agreement is void and the department may take any action authorized by law notwithstanding the agreement, including, but not limited to, refiling the accusation or imposing license sanctions. *(Added by Stats.1985, c. 1022, § 13. Amended by Stats.1992, c. 1243 (A.B.3090), § 73, eff. Sept. 30, 1992.)*

§ 11219. Rules and regulations; curriculum

The director may prescribe rules and regulations for traffic violator schools regarding the conduct of courses of education including curriculum, facilities, and equipment. The curriculum shall include, but is not limited to, the rights and duties of a motorist as they pertain to pedestrians and the rights and duties of a pedestrian as they relate to traffic laws and traffic safety. The director may also prescribe rules and regulations for the conduct of instructor training courses. *(Added by Stats.1984, c. 1037, § 4. Amended by Stats.2000, c. 642 (A.B.2733), § 3; Stats.2000, c. 833 (A.B.2522), § 5.5.)*

§ 11219.3. Content to be included in curriculum pursuant to § 11219

The curriculum prescribed pursuant to Section 11219 shall include, but is not limited to, the following:

(a) The rights and duties of a motorist as they pertain to pedestrians.

(b) The rights and duties of a pedestrian as they relate to traffic laws and traffic safety.

(c) Information that emphasizes respecting the right-of-way of others, particularly with respect to pedestrians, bicycle riders, and motorcycle riders. *(Added by Stats. 2000, c. 833 (A.B.2522), § 5.. Amended by Stats.2006, c. 898 (S.B.1021), § 2.)*

§ 11219.5. Receipt for fees collected; cancellation of scheduled class

(a) A traffic violator school shall issue a receipt for a fee collected by the traffic violator school from a person who registers for, attends, or completes a program of instruction in traffic safety at the licensed traffic violator school.

(b) In the event of a cancellation of a scheduled class, a licensee under this chapter shall not be required by the department to provide a program of instruction in traffic

safety to a person for a fee that is less than the standard fee normally charged by the licensee for its program, if a notice of cancellation of a class is given to a student at least 72 hours prior to the start of the class, or if the class was canceled based upon exigent circumstances beyond the control of the licensee. *(Added by Stats.1985, c. 396, § 19.5, eff. July 30, 1985. Amended by Stats.2007, c. 396 (A.B.758), § 3.)*

§ 11220. Reexamination

The department may require any person licensed under this chapter to submit to a reexamination of his or her qualifications when there is reasonable cause to believe that the licensee does not have the ability to give instruction. If the licensee refuses or fails to submit to the reexamination, the department may, without a hearing, temporarily suspend his or her license until such time as the licensee submits to the reexamination. The suspension shall be effective upon receipt of notice by the licensee. *(Added by Stats.1984, c. 1037, § 4.)*

§ 11221. Repealed by Stats.1990, c. 1563 (A.B.3243), § 26

§ 11222. Contracts for administrative services

The department may contract with a nongovernmental entity to administer any part of this chapter, subject to limitations in other laws regarding contracting out for services. No contract shall exceed three years' duration. The contracting entity, and any affiliate or subsidiary thereof monitoring traffic violator schools, shall conform to all of the following requirements:

(a) Engage in no other business activity with traffic violator schools or any of the principals of the traffic violator schools, including the provision of services or supplies.

(b) Provide reports in statistical form to the department and to the Legislature as instructed by the department. These reports shall be issued not less frequently than annually.

(c) Make its records available for inspection by authorized representatives of the department, the Legislative Analyst, and the State Auditor. *(Added by Stats.1984, c. 1037, § 4. Amended by Stats.1985, c. 396, § 21, eff. July 30, 1985; Stats.2001, c. 739 (A.B.1707), § 6.)*

CHAPTER 2. VEHICLE VERIFIERS

Section
11300.	Permit required.
11301.	Requirements for application.
11301.3.	Repealed.
11301.5.	Refund of deposits; grounds for orders; attorney fees and costs of actions.
11302.	Issuance, refusal to issue, suspension, revocation.
11302.2.	Change of address; report; service of process.
11302.5.	Filing of accusation; compromise settlement agreement; terms and conditions.
11305.	Unlawful acts; causes for disciplinary action.
11306.	Hearing, probationary permit, reapplication.

Section
11307. Record required.
11308. Rules and regulations.
11309. Fees.
11310. Time for compliance.
11312. Accusation for revocation or suspension of suspended, expired, or cancelled permit.

Cross References

Vehicle verifier defined, see Vehicle Code § 675.5.

§ 11300. Permit required

It shall be unlawful for any person to act as a vehicle verifier without first having procured a vehicle verifier's permit issued by the department, or when such permit has been canceled, suspended, revoked or invalidated. *(Added by Stats.1975, c. 700, p. 1659, § 3.)*

§ 11301. Requirements for application

Every vehicle verifier shall make application to the department upon the appropriate form, accompanied by a good and sufficient bond, approved as to form by the Attorney General, in the amount of five thousand dollars ($5,000) with corporate surety thereon, duly licensed to do business within the State of California.

(a) The department shall prescribe and provide forms to be used for application for permits to be issued under the terms and provisions of this chapter and require of applicants information including, but not limited to, residence address, fingerprints, and personal history statements touching on and concerning the applicant's character, honesty, integrity, and reputation as it may consider necessary.

(b) Upon receipt of an application in proper form accompanied by the appropriate fee, the department shall within 120 days, make a thorough investigation of the information contained in the application. *(Added by Stats.1975, c. 700, p. 1659, § 3. Amended by Stats.1988, c. 751, § 3.)*

Cross References

Bonds and undertakings, see Code of Civil Procedure § 995.010 et seq.

§ 11301.3. Repealed by Stats.1982, c. 517, p. 2424, § 393

Law Revision Commission Comments

1982 Repeal

The substance of former Section 11301.3 is continued in Code of Civil Procedure Section 995.710 (deposit in lieu of bond). [16 Cal.L.Rev. Comm. Reports 501 (1981)].

§ 11301.5. Refund of deposits; grounds for orders; attorney fees and costs of actions

If a deposit is given instead of the bond required by Section 11301:

(a) The Director of Motor Vehicles may order the refund of the deposit three years from the date a vehicle verifier has ceased to be licensed, if the director is satisfied that there are no outstanding claims against the deposit. A judge of a superior court may order the return of the deposit prior to the expiration of three years from the date a vehicle verifier has ceased to be licensed if there is evidence satisfactory to the court that there are no outstanding claims against the deposit.

(b) If the director, department, or state is a defendant in any action instituted to recover all or any part of the deposit, or any action is instituted by the director, department, or state to determine those entitled to any part of the deposit, the director, department, or state shall be paid reasonable attorney fees and costs from the deposit. Costs shall include those administrative costs incurred in processing claims against the deposit. *(Added by Stats.1978, c. 347, p. 728, § 2. Amended by Stats.1982, c. 517, p. 2424, § 394; Stats.1982, c. 466, p. 2055, § 108; Stats.1983, c. 18, § 37, eff. April 21, 1983. Amended by Stats.2002, c. 784 (S.B.1316), § 599.)*

Law Revision Commission Comments

1983 Amendment

Section 11301.5 is amended to reflect the repeal of Section 11301.3. [16 Cal.L.Rev.Comm.Reports 501 (1981), 2239 (1982)].

2002 Amendment

Subdivision (a) of Section 11301.5 is amended to reflect unification of the municipal and superior courts pursuant to Article VI, Section 5(e), of the California Constitution. [32 Cal.L.Rev.Comm. Reports 540 (2002)].

§ 11302. Issuance, refusal to issue, suspension, revocation

(a) The department may issue, or for reasonable cause shown, refuse to issue, a vehicle verifier's permit to any applicant, or may, after notice and hearing, suspend or revoke the permit when satisfied that the applicant or permittee:

(1) Has violated any of the provisions of this division or has committed any acts which are grounds for the refusal to issue, or the suspension or revocation of a permit or license issued under this division.

(2) Was previously the holder of an occupational license issued by another state, authorizing the same or similar activities of a license issued under this division; and that license was revoked or suspended for cause and was never reissued, or was suspended for cause, and the terms of suspension have not been fulfilled.

(3) Has purchased, sold, or otherwise acquired or disposed of, a vehicle which was stolen or embezzled or has performed or submitted to the department, or its authorized representative, documents purporting verification of a vehicle which was stolen or embezzled.

(4) Has, in the course of performing a vehicle verification, acted with negligence or incompetence in the reporting of erroneous information to the department, or its authorized representative, and has thereby caused the department to issue inaccurate certificates of ownership

or registration, or any other documents or indices which it would not otherwise have issued.

(b) Every hearing as provided for in this chapter shall be pursuant to the provisions of Chapter 5 (commencing with Section 11500) of Part 1 of Division 3 of Title 2 of the Government Code. *(Added by Stats.1975, c. 700, p. 1659, § 3. Amended by Stats.1998, c. 877 (A.B.2132), § 44.)*

§ 11302.2. Change of address; report; service of process

(a) Every person licensed under this chapter shall report to the department every change of residence address within 10 days of the change.

(b) Any person currently or previously licensed under this chapter who no longer resides at the address last filed with the department may be served with process issued pursuant to Chapter 5 (commencing with Section 11500) of Part 1 of Division 3 of Title 2 of the Government Code by registered mail at that residence, unless the person has notified the department in writing of another address where service may be made. *(Added by Stats.1988, c. 751, § 4.)*

§ 11302.5. Filing of accusation; compromise settlement agreement; terms and conditions

(a) After the filing of an accusation under this chapter, the director may enter into a stipulated compromise settlement agreement with the consent of the licensee on terms and conditions mutually agreeable to the director, the respondent licensee, and the accuser without further hearing or appeal. The agreement may include, but is not limited to, a period of probation or monetary penalties, or both. The monetary penalty shall not exceed five hundred dollars ($500) for each violation, and it shall be based on the nature of the violation and the effect of the violation on the purposes of this chapter.

(b) A compromise settlement agreement may be entered before, during, or after the hearing, but is valid only if executed and filed pursuant to subdivision (d) before the proposed decision of the hearing officer, if any, is adopted or the case is decided.

(c) The department shall adopt, by regulation, a schedule of maximum and minimum amounts of monetary penalties, the payment of which may be included as a term or condition of a compromise settlement agreement entered under subdivision (a). Any monetary penalty included in a compromise settlement agreement shall be within the range of monetary penalties in that schedule.

(d) Any compromise settlement agreement entered under this section shall be signed by the director, the respondent licensee, and the accuser, or by their authorized representatives. The director shall file, or cause to be filed, the agreement with the Office of Administrative Hearings, together with the department's notice of withdrawal of the accusation or statement of issues upon which the action was initiated.

(e) If the respondent licensee fails to perform all of the terms and conditions of the compromise settlement agreement, the agreement is void and the department may take any action authorized by law notwithstanding the agreement, including, but not limited to, refiling the accusation or imposing license sanctions. *(Added by Stats.1985, c. 1022, § 14.)*

§ 11305. Unlawful acts; causes for disciplinary action

It shall be unlawful and cause of disciplinary action for the holder of a vehicle verifier's permit:

(a) To submit to the department, or its authorized representative, any document which purports to evidence the verification of any vehicle, without having actually physically inspected such vehicle to determine the existence of proper vehicle identification.

(b) To fail to report to the department, in a manner prescribed by the department, the absence, alteration, or obvious attempt to alter or obliterate any identifying number or number plate, or remove or attempt to remove such plate on any vehicle for which verification is performed.

(c) To fail to physically compare identifying numbers on a vehicle inspected to the information contained in any document of title, registration, or any other form describing such vehicle.

(d) To cause any person to suffer any loss or damage by reason of any fraud or deceit practiced upon such person in the course of the conducting of business under the vehicle verifier's permit.

(e) To violate one or more terms and provisions of Section 20, or of Division 3 (commencing with Section 4000), or of this division of this code, or any rules or regulations adopted pursuant thereto, or of Part 5 (commencing with Section 10701) of Division 2 of the Revenue and Taxation Code. *(Added by Stats.1975, c. 700, p. 1660, § 3.)*

§ 11306. Hearing, probationary permit, reapplication

(a) If the department issues or renews a vehicle verifier's permit requiring conditions of probation, or if the department refuses to issue a vehicle verifier's permit, the applicant shall be entitled to demand, in writing, a hearing as provided in this chapter, before the director, or his representative, within 60 days after notice of refusal or issuance of the probationary permit.

(b) Except where the provisions of this code require the refusal to issue a permit, the department may issue a probationary permit subject to conditions to be observed by the permittee in the exercise of the privilege granted. The conditions to be attached to the exercise of the privilege shall be such as may, in the judgment of the department, be in the public interest and suitable to the qualifications of the applicant as disclosed by the application and investigation by the department of the information contained therein.

(c) The department may, pending a hearing, temporarily suspend the permit issued to a vehicle verifier for a period not to exceed 30 days if the director finds that such action is required in the public interest. In any such case, a hearing shall be held and a decision thereon issued within 30 days after notice of the temporary suspension.

(d) A person whose application for a permit has been denied may reapply for such permit after a period of not less than one year has elapsed from the date of filing of such denial. *(Added by Stats.1975, c. 700, p. 1660, § 3.)*

§ 11307. Record required

(a) A vehicle verifier shall maintain a record of each verification made. The record shall contain all of the following:

(1) The name and address of the person requesting the verification and the fee charged for such verification.

(2) The year model, vehicle identification number, license plate number of the vehicle verified and the state in which the vehicle was last registered.

(b) All records maintained by a vehicle verifier shall be open to inspection by any peace officer. *(Added by Stats.1975, c. 700, p. 1660, § 3.)*

§ 11308. Rules and regulations

The department may adopt rules and regulations concerning the issuance, use, and renewal of a vehicle verifier's permit, and for determining the competence of an applicant therefor. *(Added by Stats.1975, c. 700, p. 1661, § 3.)*

§ 11309. Fees

(a) The following fees for a vehicle verifier's permit shall be paid to the department:

(1) For the application and original permit, except as provided by Section 42231, a nonrefundable fee of fifty dollars ($50).

(2) For an application for renewal, fifteen dollars ($15).

(b) All permits shall be renewed on a biennial basis. All original permits shall be issued for a period of not less than two years, except in the case of a probationary license which, in the discretion of the department, may be issued for a shorter term. *(Added by Stats.1975, c. 700, p. 1661, § 3. Amended by Stats.1980, c. 608, p. 1677, § 5; Stats.1982, c. 1273, p. 4703, § 13.)*

Cross References

Return of fees after rejection of application, see Vehicle Code § 42230.

§ 11310. Time for compliance

Any person who holds a vehicle verifier's permit issued before the operative date of this chapter shall comply with the provisions of this chapter within three months after its operative date. *(Added by Stats.1975, c. 700, p. 1661, § 3.)*

336

§ 11312. Accusation for revocation or suspension of suspended, expired, or cancelled permit

The suspension, expiration, or cancellation of a vehicle verifier's permit provided for in this chapter shall not prevent the filing of an accusation for the revocation or suspension of the suspended, expired, or canceled permit as provided in Section 11302 or 11305 or any rules or regulations adopted pursuant to Section 11308, and the department's decision that the permit should be suspended or revoked. That determination may be considered in granting or refusing to grant any subsequent license or permit authorized by this division to that vehicle verifier or to a business representative of that prior vehicle verifier's permit. *(Added by Stats.1998, c. 877 (A.B.2132), § 45.)*

CHAPTER 2.5. REGISTRATION SERVICES

Section
11400. License to act as registration service.
11401. Application for license.
11402. Bond requirement.
11403. Agent for service of process; service on director.
11404. Temporary permits.
11405. Refusal, suspension, revocation or cancellation of license; grounds.
11406. Business records; required information; copy to customer.
11406.5. Incomplete application submitted to registration service; return to customer.
11407. Retention and inspection of business records.
11408. Orders relating to license; service of accusation; hearing; compromise settlements.
11409. License fees.
11410. Duration of license; renewal of license.
11411. Termination of registration service; notice to department.
11413. Accusation for revocation or suspension of suspended, expired, or cancelled license.

§ 11400. License to act as registration service

No person shall act as a registration service, engage in the business of soliciting or receiving any application for the registration, renewal of registration, or transfer of registration or ownership of any vehicle of a type subject to registration under this code, or of soliciting or receiving an application for a motor carrier permit under Division 14.85 (commencing with Section 34600), or transmit or present any of those documents to the department, if any compensation is solicited or received for the service, without a license or temporary permit issued by the department pursuant to this chapter, or if that license or temporary permit has expired or been canceled, suspended, or revoked, or the terms and conditions of an agreement entered into pursuant to Section 11408 have not been fulfilled. *(Added by Stats. 1990, c. 1196 (A.B.4008), § 3, operative July 1, 1991. Amended by Stats.1996, c. 1155 (S.B.1587), § 4; Stats. 2005, c. 148 (A.B.785), § 2.)*

Cross References

Registration service defined, see Vehicle Code § 505.2.

§ 11401. Application for license

An applicant for a license to be a registration service shall submit an application to the department upon the appropriate form for a license and a distinguishing number. The applicant shall also include with the application any information as to the applicant's character, honesty, integrity, and reputation which the department requires. The application shall include, but not be limited to, all of the following:

(a) The type of ownership, whether an individual, a partnership, or a corporation. If the applicant is a partnership, the names and titles of all partners, except limited partners, shall be furnished. If the applicant is a corporation, the names and titles of all controlling stockholders, directors, and officers who, by reason of the facts and circumstances, could direct, control, or manage the business of the registration service shall be furnished.

(b) The name and address of the business, including street, city, and postal zip code of the principal place of business and any branch location.

(c) A personal history statement and fingerprints from any person required to be identified in subdivision (a), containing the information the department requires.

(d) The name, address, driver's license number, and a brief physical description of all persons employed or otherwise engaged by the registration service to perform registration work.

(e) A bond executed by an admitted surety insurer, approved as to form by the Attorney General, to cover any loss to the public or the State of California arising out of the operation of the registration service.

(f) A nonrefundable application fee, as specified in Section 11409. *(Added by Stats.1990, c. 1196 (A.B.4008), § 3, operative July 1, 1991.)*

§ 11402. Bond requirement

(a) The amount of the bond required by subdivision (e) of Section 11401 for the issuance of a registration service license, or for the renewal of such a license is twenty-five thousand dollars ($25,000). Liability under the bond shall remain at that amount.

(b) If the amount of the liability under the bond is decreased, or there is outstanding a final court judgment arising out of a violation of any provision of this code for which the registration service is liable, the license of the registration service shall be automatically suspended. In order to reinstate the license, the registration service shall either file an additional bond or restore the bond on file to the original amount, or shall satisfy the outstanding judgment for which the registration service and surety are liable.

(c) The bond shall remain in effect for three years after cessation of business of the registration service. *(Added by Stats.1990, c. 1196 (A.B.4008), § 3, operative*

July 1, 1991. Amended by Stats.2004, c. 430 (A.B.2606), § 3.)

§ 11403. Agent for service of process; service on director

(a) A license to conduct a registration service, or a renewal of that license, shall not be issued to any applicant unless the applicant files with the department an instrument, in writing, in which the applicant appoints the director as the agent of the applicant upon whom all process may be served in any action which may be commenced against the applicant arising out of any claim for damages by any person by reason of the violation by the applicant of any provision of this code in connection with the registration service or any condition of the registration service's bond.

(b) The applicant shall agree in the instrument that any process directed to the applicant, when personal service of process upon the applicant cannot be made in this state after due diligence and, in that case, is served upon the director or, in the event of the director's absence from the office, upon any employee in charge of the office of the director, is of the same force and effect as if served upon the applicant personally.

(c) The applicant shall further agree, in writing, that the agency created by the instrument shall continue during the period covered by any license that may be issued and so long thereafter as the applicant may be required to answer in damages for a violation of this code in connection with the registration service or any condition of the bond.

(d) The instrument appointing the director as the agent for the applicant for service of process shall be acknowledged by the applicant before a notary public.

(e) If the registration service is served with process by service upon the director, one copy of the summons and complaint shall be left with the director or in the director's office in Sacramento or mailed to the office of the director in Sacramento. A fee of five dollars ($5) shall also be paid to the director at the time of service of the copy of the summons and complaint.

(f) Service on the director is a sufficient service on the registration service if a notice of service and a copy of the summons and complaint are immediately sent by registered mail by the plaintiff or the plaintiff's attorney to the registration service. A copy of the summons and complaint shall also be mailed by the plaintiff or the plaintiff's attorney to the surety on the registration service's bond at the address of the surety given in the bond, postpaid and registered with request for return receipt.

(g) The director shall keep a record of all process served on the director pursuant to this section, which shall show the day and hour of service, and shall retain the summons and complaint so served on file.

(h) If the registration service is served with process by service upon the director, the registration service has 30 days from the date of that service within which to answer

337

any complaint or other pleading which may be filed in the cause.

(i) For purposes of venue, if the registration service is served with process by service upon the director, the service is deemed to have been made upon the registration service in the county in which the registration service has, or last had, its principal place of business. *(Added by Stats.1990, c. 1196 (A.B.4008), § 3, operative July 1, 1991.)*

§ 11404. Temporary permits

(a) Until the department determines that the applicant meets all of the requirements of this chapter, it may issue a temporary permit to the person applying for a license as a registration service.

(b) The temporary permit shall permit the operation by the registration service or registration agent for not more than 120 days while the department is completing its investigation and determination of all facts relative to the qualifications of the applicant for the license. The department may cancel the temporary permit when it has determined that the application is incorrect or incomplete or that the temporary permit was issued in error.

(c) The temporary permit is invalid when canceled or when the license has been issued or refused. *(Added by Stats.1990, c. 1196 (A.B.4008), § 3, operative July 1, 1991.)*

§ 11405. Refusal, suspension, revocation or cancellation of license; grounds

The department may refuse to issue a license to, or may suspend, revoke, or cancel the license of, a person to act as a registration service for any of the following reasons:

(a) The person has been convicted of a felony or a crime involving moral turpitude which is substantially related to the qualifications, functions, or duties of the licensed activity.

(b) The person is, or has been, the holder, or a managerial employee of the holder, of any occupational license issued by the department which has been suspended or revoked.

(c) The applicant was previously the holder of an occupational license issued by another state, authorizing the same or similar activities of a license issued under this division; and that license was revoked or suspended for cause and was never reissued, or was suspended for cause, and the terms of suspension have not been fulfilled.

(d) The person has used a false or fictitious name, knowingly made any false statement, or knowingly concealed any material fact, in the application for the license.

(e) The person has knowingly made, or acted with negligence or incompetence, or knowingly or negligently accepted or failed to inquire about any false, erroneous, or incorrect statement or information submitted to the registration service or the department in the course of the licensed activity.

(f) The person has knowingly or negligently permitted fraud, or willfully engaged in fraudulent practices, with reference to clients, vehicle registrants, applicants for motor carrier permits under Division 14.85 (commencing with Section 34600), or members of the public, or the department in the course of the licensed activity.

(g) The person has knowingly or negligently committed or was responsible for any violation, cause for license refusal, or cause for discipline under Section 20 or Division 3 (commencing with Section 4000), Division 3.5 (commencing with Section 9840), Division 4 (commencing with Section 10500), or Division 5 (commencing with Section 11100), or Division 14.85 (commencing with Section 34600), or any rules or regulations adopted under those provisions.

(h) The person has failed to obtain and maintain an established place of business in California.

(i) The person has failed to keep the business records required by Section 11406.

(j) The person has violated any term or condition of a restricted license to act as a registration service.

(k) The person has committed or was responsible for any other act, occurrence, or event in California or any foreign jurisdiction which would be cause to refuse to issue a license to, or to suspend, revoke, or cancel the license of, a person to act as a registration service. *(Added by Stats.1990, c. 1196 (A.B.4008), § 3, operative July 1, 1991. Amended by Stats.1992, c. 1243 (A.B.3090), § 74, eff. Sept. 30, 1992; Stats.1996, c. 1155 (S.B.1587), § 5; Stats.1998, c. 877 (A.B.2132), § 46; Stats.2005, c. 148 (A.B.785), § 3.)*

§ 11406. Business records; required information; copy to customer

(a) Every registration service shall keep accurate business records containing all of the following information:

(1) The name, address, and license number of the registration service and the name and address of every employee who performs registration work.

(2) The name and address of each client for whom registration work was performed.

(3) The identity of every vehicle by year, make, type, license number, and vehicle identification number on which registration work was performed.

(4) The amount of registration fees or payments collected for each vehicle on which registration work was performed, including the method of payment to the registration service.

(5) The amount of registration fees or payments submitted to the department for each vehicle on which registration work was performed, including the date and method of payment to the department.

(6) The amount of any refunds or additional charges on registration fees or payments collected for each vehicle on which registration work was performed, including the date and method of payment of the refund or

additional charge by or to the client, the registration service, or the department.

(7) The name, signature, or initials of each employee performing work on each transaction and the date the work was done.

(8) The cost to each client for the registration work performed on each of the client's vehicles or to obtain a motor carrier permit.

(9) For each motor carrier for which motor carrier permit work was performed, the carrier identification number, business type, business address, carrier type, activities, and number of vehicles.

(10) For each motor carrier for which motor carrier permit work was performed, the amount of fees or payment collected and the method of payment.

(11) For each motor carrier for which motor carrier permit work was performed, the amount of fees or payment submitted to the department, including the date submitted and the method of payment to the department.

(b) As an alternative to maintaining the records required by paragraphs (1) to (11), inclusive, of subdivision (a), a registration service may retain a copy of the listing sheet approved by the department for transmitting registration or motor carrier permit documents to the department.

(c) Every registration service shall provide each customer with a document containing all of the information required by subdivision (a) relative to that customer's transaction, excluding paragraph (7) and excluding the addresses of employees and other customers' names and addresses. This requirement does not apply to transactions for customers of a dealer or dismantler.

(d) Every registration service shall display prominently at its place of business a sign indicating that the service is not a branch of the department and shall inform each customer of that fact. *(Added by Stats.1990, c. 1196 (A.B.4008), § 3, operative July 1, 1991. Amended by Stats.1992, c. 1243 (A.B.3090), § 75, eff. Sept. 30, 1992; Stats.1995, c. 766 (S.B.726), § 8; Stats.2004, c. 430 (A.B.2606), § 4; Stats.2005, c. 148 (A.B.785), § 4.)*

§ 11406.5. Incomplete application submitted to registration service; return to customer

Whenever a customer fails to submit to a registration service any documents, compensation, or fees requested in writing by the registration service, the registration service shall return all documents pertaining to the incomplete transaction, including the department receipt evidencing any fees paid, within 60 days after the request was sent to the customer, to the last known address of the customer, by registered mail. *(Added by Stats.1992, c. 1243 (A.B.3090), § 76, eff. Sept. 30, 1992.)*

§ 11407. Retention and inspection of business records

The business records required by Section 11406 shall be maintained for at least four years and shall be open to inspection by the department during normal business hours.

The department may duplicate or make a record of any information contained in any of those records, which shall be for the official use of the department.

All records shall be returned to the licensee not later than 30 days after receipt of the records by the department. *(Added by Stats.1990, c. 1196 (A.B.4008), § 3, operative July 1, 1991.)*

§ 11408. Orders relating to license; service of accusation; hearing; compromise settlements

(a) The director may issue an order to grant an unrestricted or a restricted license to act as a registration service, or an order to deny, suspend, revoke, or cancel a license to act as a registration service.

(b) The order shall become final 30 days from issuance, unless the denied or restricted applicant or licensee files with the department a request for a hearing. Hearings shall be held pursuant to Chapter 5 (commencing with Section 11500) of Part 1 of Division 3 of Title 2 of the Government Code.

(c) Any registration service may be served with an accusation issued pursuant to Chapter 5 (commencing with Section 11500) of Part 1 of Division 3 of Title 2 of the Government Code by registered mail to the address of the principal place of business on file with the department, whether or not the business has been closed or terminated, unless the registration service has notified the department in writing of another address where service shall be made.

(d) The department may, pending a hearing, temporarily suspend the license issued to a registration service for not more than 30 days if the director finds that action is required in the public interest. In that case, a hearing shall be held and a decision issued within 30 days after notice of the temporary suspension or cancellation.

(e) The director may, following the filing of a statement of issues or an accusation against an applicant or a registration service, with the consent of the applicant or licensee, enter into a compromise settlement agreement with a stipulated restriction or penalty whereby the applicant or licensee accepts the terms and conditions of the agreement without hearing or appeal by any party thereto.

(1) The compromise settlement agreement may provide for a restricted license, special operating terms and conditions, a higher bond, a monetary penalty, or any other term or condition agreeable to the parties.

(2) The compromise settlement agreement shall be signed by the respondent applicant or licensee, the director, and the accuser, or their authorized representatives, and filed with the Office of Administrative Hearings, together with the department's notice of withdrawal of the statement of issues or the accusation upon which the action was initiated.

(3) A failure of the respondent applicant or licensee to carry out a compromise settlement agreement entered into under this section is a separate cause to refuse to issue, or to suspend, revoke, or cancel, any license authorizing the respondent to act as a registration service.

(f) Any person whose license to act as a registration service was suspended for cause and the terms of the suspension are unfulfilled, or whose license was revoked for cause, may reapply for a license to act as a registration service after not less than one year from the effective date of the suspension or revocation action.

(g) The issuance of a new license to that person is within the sole discretion of the department, and a hearing regarding that issuance shall be held only upon the consent of the director. *(Added by Stats.1990, c. 1196 (A.B.4008), § 3, operative July 1, 1991.)*

§ 11409. License fees

The fee for a license issued to a registration service is as follows:

(a) For the original license, or an ownership change which requires a new application, one hundred fifty dollars ($150), which is nonrefundable.

(b) For the annual renewal of a license, fifteen dollars ($15).

(c) For the alteration of an existing license required by a name change, address change, change in corporate officer structure, or the addition of a branch location, seventy dollars ($70). *(Added by Stats.1990, c. 1196 (A.B.4008), § 3, operative July 1, 1991.)*

§ 11410. Duration of license; renewal of license

(a) Every license issued under this chapter is valid for a period of one year from the last day of the month of issuance. Except as provided in subdivision (c), renewal of the license for the ensuing year may be obtained by the person to whom the license was issued upon application to the department and payment of the fee required by Section 11409.

(b) An application for the renewal of a license shall be made by the licensee not more than 90 days prior to the expiration date and shall be made by presenting the completed application form provided by the department and by payment of the renewal fee.

(c) If the application for renewal of the license is not made by midnight of the expiration date, the application may be made within 30 days following expiration of the license by paying the annual renewal fee and a penalty fee equal to the amount of the original application fee for each license held.

(d) A licensee shall not renew the license after the expiration of the 30-day period specified in subdivision (c). *(Added by Stats.1990, c. 1196 (A.B.4008), § 3, operative July 1, 1991. Amended by Stats.2008, c. 179 (S.B.1498), § 218.)*

§ 11411. Termination of registration service; notice to department

If a registration service ceases operation for any reason, the owner of the service immediately shall notify the department and, upon demand by the department, shall deliver to the department the registration service license, all records kept pursuant to Section 11406, and all customer transactions then in his or her possession, including any fees or receipts for fees due to the department or to the customer. *(Added by Stats.1992, c. 1243 (A.B.3090), § 77, eff. Sept. 30, 1992.)*

§ 11413. Accusation for revocation or suspension of suspended, expired, or cancelled license

The suspension, expiration, or cancellation of a registration service license provided for in this chapter shall not prevent the filing of an accusation for the revocation or suspension of the suspended, expired, or canceled license as provided in Section 11405 or 11408 or any related rules or regulations, and the department's decision that the license should be suspended or revoked. That determination may be considered in granting or refusing to grant any subsequent license authorized by this division to that licensee or to a business representative of that prior licensee. *(Added by Stats.1998, c. 877 (A.B.2132), § 47.)*

CHAPTER 3. AUTOMOBILE DISMANTLERS

Section
11500.   Unlawful acts.
11501.   Application for license.
11502.   Refusal to issue.
11503.   Grounds for refusal.
11503.1. Additional grounds for refusal.
11503.5. Conviction of crime involving moral turpitude; refusal to issue or suspension of license.
11504.   License applications; contents; perjury; investigation of information; notification of corporate changes.
11505.   Issuance of license and special plates.
11506.   Restricted license.
11507.   Temporary permit.
11508.   Expiration and renewal.
11508.1. Repealed.
11509.   Suspension or revocation.
11509.1. Filing of accusation; compromise settlement agreement; terms and conditions.
11509.5. Reapplication for license.
11510.   Temporary suspension.
11511.   Possession of stolen vehicle or part thereof; presumption.
11512.   Hearing upon refusal.
11513.   Established place of business required; service of process when business closed.
11514.   Dismantling site requirements.
11515.   Total loss salvage vehicle; evidence of ownership; salvage certificate; reporting requirements; violations.
11515.1. Salvage pool; sale of vehicle.
11515.2. Total loss settlement on nonrepairable vehicle; properly endorsed certificate of ownership; vehi-

Section

11516.   cle retained by owner; vehicles not subject of insurance settlement; certificate; violations.

11516.   Operation of vehicle under special plates.

11517.   Certificate of convenience.

11518.   Automatic cancellation of special plates and license.

11519.   Registration of total loss salvage and dismantled vehicles.

11520.   Notice of acquisition; transmittal of documents and license plates; records.

11521.   Advertisements; license or permit numbers required.

11522.   Local regulation.

11540.   Salvage pools; records; notice of disposition of vehicle; license plates; submission to department.

11541.   Duties of department; operative date.

11568.   Inoperative.

Cross References

Dismantling of off-highway motor vehicles, applicability of chapter, see Vehicle Code § 38180.

§ 11500. Unlawful acts

It shall be unlawful for any person to act as an automobile dismantler without first having an established place of business which meets the requirements set forth in Section 11514 and without first having procured a license or temporary permit issued by the department, or when such license or temporary permit has been canceled, suspended, revoked, invalidated, expired, or the terms and conditions of an agreement effected pursuant to Section 11509.1 have not been fulfilled. *(Added by Stats.1961, c. 1640, p. 3580, § 6, operative Jan. 1, 1962. Amended by Stats.1963, c. 1106, p. 2566, § 8; Stats.1967, c. 557, p. 1906, § 1; Stats.1971, c. 1043, p. 1999, § 2, operative May 3, 1972; Stats.1976, c. 619, p. 1468, § 1.)*

Cross References

Definitions,
   Automobile dismantler, see Vehicle Code § 220.
   Vehicle, see Vehicle Code § 670.

§ 11501. Application for license

Every automobile dismantler shall make application to the department upon the appropriate form for a license containing a general distinguishing number. The applicant shall submit proof of his status as a bona fide automobile dismantler as may reasonably be required by the department. *(Added by Stats.1961, c. 1640, p. 3580, § 6, operative Jan. 1, 1962. Amended by Stats.1963, c. 1106, p. 2567, § 9; Stats.1971, c. 1214, p. 2341, § 5, operative May 3, 1972; Stats.1975, c. 182, p. 530, § 5, eff. July 5, 1975.)*

Cross References

Fees, see Vehicle Code §§ 9262, 9263, 9551.

Issuance of special plates to manufacturers, dealers, etc., see Vehicle Code § 11714.

Operation of vehicles displaying special plates, see Vehicle Code § 11715.

Vehicles subject to registration, see Vehicle Code § 4000 et seq.

§ 11502. Refusal to issue

The department shall have the power and duty to issue and for reasonable cause shown to refuse to issue a license. The department may refuse to any applicant therefor a license provided for herein, if such applicant does not meet the requirements of the terms and provisions of this code relating to the conduct of an automobile dismantling business. *(Added by Stats.1961, c. 1640, p. 3580, § 6, operative Jan. 1, 1962. Amended by Stats.1963, c. 1106, p. 2567, § 10; Stats.1971, c. 1214, p. 2341, § 6, operative May 3, 1972; Stats.1975, c. 182, p. 530, § 6, eff. July 5, 1975.)*

Cross References

Hearing upon refusal, see Vehicle Code § 11512.

Suspension or revocation as a ground of refusal, see Vehicle Code § 11509.

§ 11503. Grounds for refusal

The department may refuse to issue a license to an applicant when it determines any of the following:

(a) The applicant was previously the holder, or a managerial employee of the holder, of a license issued under this chapter which was revoked for cause and never reissued by the department, or which was suspended for cause and the terms of suspension have not been fulfilled.

(b) The applicant was previously a business representative whose license issued under this chapter was revoked for cause and never reissued or was suspended for cause and the terms of suspension have not been fulfilled.

(c) If the applicant is a business, a business representative was previously the holder of a license, or was a business representative of a business whose license, issued under this chapter was revoked for cause and never reissued or was suspended for cause and the terms of suspension have not been fulfilled; or, by reason of the facts and circumstances related to the organization, control, and management of the business, the operation of that business will be directed, controlled, or managed by individuals who, by reason of their conviction of violations of this code, would be ineligible for a license and, by licensing that business, the purposes of this chapter would be defeated.

(d) The applicant, or a business representative if the applicant is a business, has been convicted of a crime or has committed any act or engaged in conduct involving moral turpitude which is substantially related to the qualifications, functions, or duties of the licensed activity. A conviction after a plea of nolo contendere is a conviction within the meaning of this section.

(e) The applicant was previously the holder of an occupational license issued by another state, authorizing the same or similar activities of a license issued under this division; and that license was revoked or suspended for cause and was never reissued, or was suspended for

341

cause, and the terms of suspension have not been fulfilled.

(f) The information contained in an application is incorrect.

(g) A decision of the department to cancel, suspend, or revoke a license has been made, and the applicant was a business representative of the business regulated under that license. *(Added by Stats.1961, c. 1640, p. 3580, § 6, operative Jan. 1, 1962. Amended by Stats.1965, c. 652, p. 2007, § 1; Stats.1968, c. 667, p. 1355, § 1; Stats.1969, c. 240, p. 585, § 1; Stats.1971, c. 1214, p. 2341, § 7, operative May 3, 1972; Stats.1971, c. 1293, p. 2532, § 3, operative May 3, 1972; Stats.1975, c. 182, p. 530, § 7, eff. July 5, 1975; Stats.1990, c. 1563 (A.B.3243), § 27; Stats. 1994, c. 428 (A.B.3085), § 1; Stats.1998, c. 877 (A.B. 2132), § 48.)*

Cross References

Hearing upon refusal, see Vehicle Code § 11512.

§ 11503.1.   Additional grounds for refusal

Any of the causes specified in this chapter as a cause to suspend or revoke the license issued to an automobile dismantler is cause to refuse to issue a license to an automobile dismantler. *(Added by Stats.1968, c. 667, p. 1356, § 1.5. Amended by Stats.1971, c. 1214, p. 2342, § 8, operative May 3, 1972; Stats.1975, c. 182, p. 531, § 8, eff. July 5, 1975; Stats.1990, c. 1563 (A.B.3243), § 28.)*

§ 11503.5.   Conviction of crime involving moral turpitude; refusal to issue or suspension of license

(a) The department, after notice and hearing, on an interim basis, may refuse to issue or may suspend a license issued under this chapter when the applicant or licensee, or a business representative if the applicant or licensee is a business, has been convicted of a crime involving moral turpitude which is substantially related to the qualifications, functions, or duties of the licensed activity, if an appeal of the conviction is pending or the conviction has otherwise not become final. A conviction after a plea of nolo contendere is a conviction within the meaning of this section.

(b) When a conviction, upon which an interim refusal to issue or suspension under subdivision (a) is based, is affirmed on appeal or otherwise becomes final, the refusal to issue or suspension shall automatically take effect as a denial or revocation, as the case may be, of the license. If the interim refusal to issue or suspension was stayed under probationary terms and conditions, the subsequent automatic denial or revocation shall also be stayed under the same terms and conditions for a term not to exceed the original term of probation for the interim refusal or suspension.

(c) If a conviction, upon which an interim refusal to issue or suspension under subdivision (a) is based, is reversed on appeal, the refusal or suspension shall be set aside immediately by the department. *(Added by Stats. 1990, c. 1563 (A.B.3243), § 29.)*

§ 11504.   License applications; contents; perjury; investigation of information; notification of corporate changes

(a) An applicant who applies for a license pursuant to Section 11501 shall submit an application to the department on the forms prescribed by the department. The applicant shall provide the department with information as to the applicant's character, honesty, integrity, and reputation, as the department may consider necessary. The department, by regulation, shall prescribe what information is required of the applicant for the purposes of this subdivision, and the applicant shall provide that information under penalty of perjury. In addition to any other information required by the department, the department shall require the applicant to furnish all of the following information on any application for a new license or the renewal of a license, if the applicant is required by other provisions of law to have the following permits, numbers, or plan:

(1) Board of Equalization resale permit number.

(2) Identification number issued by the California Environmental Protection Agency.

(3) A statement indicating that the applicant has either filed an application for a stormwater permit or is not required to obtain a stormwater permit.

(4) A statement indicating that the applicant has either filed a hazardous materials business plan or is not required to file that plan.

(5) The tax identification number assigned by the Franchise Tax Board.

(b) Upon receipt of an application for a new license that is accompanied by the appropriate fee, the department shall, not later than 120 days from the receipt of that application, make a thorough investigation of all of the information contained in the application.

(c)(1) Upon receipt of an application for renewal of a license that is accompanied by the appropriate fee, the department shall, not later than 120 days from the receipt of that application, make a thorough investigation of the information contained in the application, except the information specified in paragraphs (1) to (5), inclusive, of subdivision (a).

(2) As of January 1, 2011, upon receipt of an application for the renewal of a license that is accompanied by the appropriate fee, the department shall, not later than 120 days from the receipt of that application, make a thorough investigation of all of the information contained in the application.

(d) A person holding a license issued pursuant to Section 11501 shall notify the department, within 10 days, of any change in the ownership or corporate structure of the licensee. *(Added by Stats.1977, c. 452, p. 1488, § 2. Amended by Stats.1994, c. 428 (A.B.3085), § 2; Stats. 2009, c. 475 (A.B.805), § 1.)*

§ 11505. Issuance of license and special plates

(a) The department, upon granting a license shall issue to the applicant a license containing the applicant's name and address and the general distinguishing number assigned to the applicant.

(b) When the department has issued a license pursuant to subdivision (a), the licensee may apply for and the department shall issue special plates which shall have displayed thereon the general distinguishing number assigned to the applicant. Each plate so issued shall also contain a number or symbol identifying the plate from every other plate bearing a like general distinguishing number.

(c) The department shall also furnish books and forms as it may determine necessary, which books and forms are and shall remain the property of the department and may be taken up at any time for inspection. (*Added by Stats.1961, c. 1640, p. 3582, § 6, operative Jan. 1, 1962. Amended by Stats.1971, c. 1214, p. 2343, § 10, operative May 3, 1972; Stats.1975, c. 182, p. 531, § 9, eff. July 5, 1975.*)

§ 11506. Restricted license

Except where the provisions of this code require the refusal to issue a license, the department may issue a license restricted by conditions to be observed in the exercise of the privilege granted. The terms and conditions to be attached to the exercise of the privilege under such restricted license shall be such as may, in the judgment of the department, be in the public interest and suitable to the qualifications of the applicant as disclosed by the application and investigation by the department. (*Added by Stats.1961, c. 1640, p. 3582, § 6, operative Jan. 1, 1962. Amended by Stats.1971, c. 1214, p. 2343, § 11, operative May 3, 1972; Stats.1975, c. 182, p. 531, § 10, eff. July 5, 1975.*)

§ 11507. Temporary permit

Pending the satisfaction of the department that the applicant has met the requirements under this code, it may issue a temporary permit to any person applying for an automobile dismantler license. The temporary permit shall permit the operation by the automobile dismantler for a period not to exceed 120 days while the department is completing its investigation and determination of all facts relative to the qualification of the applicant to such license. The department may cancel such temporary permit when it has determined or has reasonable cause to believe that the application is incorrect or incomplete or the temporary permit was issued in error. Such temporary permit shall be invalid when canceled or when the applicant's license has been issued or refused. (*Added by Stats.1961, c. 1640, p. 3582, § 6, operative Jan. 1, 1962. Amended by Stats.1963, c. 1106, p. 2567, § 12; Stats.1971, c. 1214, p. 2344, § 12, operative May 3, 1972; Stats.1972, c. 215, p. 447, § 2; Stats.1975, c. 182, p. 531, § 11, eff. July 5, 1975.*)

§ 11508. Expiration and renewal

(a) Every occupational license and special plate issued under this chapter shall be valid for a period of one year from midnight of the last day of the month of issuance. Renewal of the occupational license and special plates for the ensuing year may be obtained by the person to whom any plates and license were issued upon application to the department and payment of the fee provided in this code.

(b) Except as provided in subdivision (c), every application for the renewal of an occupational license and special plates which expire pursuant to this section shall be made by the person to whom issued not more than 90 days prior to the expiration date, and shall be made by presenting the completed application form provided by the department and by payment of the full annual renewal fee for the occupational license and special plates.

(c) If the application for renewal of the occupational license and special plates is not made by midnight of the expiration date, the application may be made within 30 days following expiration of the license by paying the annual renewal fee and a penalty fee equal to the amount of the original application fee for each occupational license held. A penalty as specified in Sections 9553 and 9554 shall also be added to each special plate renewed during the 30-day period following expiration of the special plates.

(d) In no event may the licensee renew the occupational license or special plates after the expiration of the 30-day period authorized in subdivision (c). (*Added by Stats.1961, c. 1640, p. 3582, § 6, operative Jan. 1, 1962. Amended by Stats.1971, c. 1214, p. 2344, § 13, operative May 3, 1972; Stats.1982, c. 571, p. 2527, § 2; Stats.1984, c. 499, § 10.*)

§ 11508.1. Repealed by Stats.1992, c. 1241 (S.B.1615), § 16

§ 11509. Suspension or revocation

(a) The department, after notice and hearing, may suspend or revoke the license issued to an automobile dismantler upon the determination that the person to whom the license was issued is not lawfully entitled thereto or has done any of the following:

(1) Made or knowingly or negligently permitted any illegal use of the special plates issued to him or her.

(2) Used a false or fictitious name or knowingly made any false statement or concealed any material fact in any application or other document filed with the department.

(3) Failed to provide and maintain a clear physical division between the type of business licensed pursuant to this chapter and any other type of business conducted at the established place of business.

(4) Violated any provision of Division 3 (commencing with Section 4000) or any rule or regulation adopted pursuant thereto.

(5) Violated any provision of Division 4 (commencing with Section 10500) or any rule or regulation adopted pursuant thereto.

(6) Violated any provision of this chapter, except Section 11520, or any rule or regulation adopted pursuant thereto.

(7) Knowingly, repeatedly, or flagrantly violated Section 11520.

(8) Violated any provision of Part 5 (commencing with Section 10701) of Division 2 of the Revenue and Taxation Code or any rule or regulation adopted pursuant thereto.

(9) Purchased, concealed, possessed, or otherwise acquired or disposed of a vehicle, or a part thereof, knowing it to be stolen.

(10) Failed to meet and maintain the requirements for the issuance of an automobile dismantler's license as provided in this code.

(11) Failed to pay, within 30 days after written demand from the department, any fees or penalties due on vehicles acquired for dismantling which are not the subject of dispute. If the dismantler disputes the validity of the fees or penalties, the 30-day period shall not commence until the department, after review, has determined the fee or penalty to be due.

(12) Submitted a check, draft, or money order to the department for any obligation or fees due the state, and it is thereafter dishonored or refused payment upon presentation.

(13) Failed to meet the terms and conditions of a previous agreement entered into pursuant to Section 11509.1.

(b) Any of the causes specified in this chapter as a cause for refusal to issue a license to an automobile dismantler applicant is cause, after notice and hearing, to suspend or revoke a license and special plates issued to an automobile dismantler.

(c) Except as provided in Section 11509.1, every hearing provided for in this chapter shall be held pursuant to Chapter 5 (commencing with Section 11500) of Part 1 of Division 3 of Title 2 of the Government Code. *(Added by Stats.1975, c. 1224, p. 3096, § 4. Amended by Stats.1976, c. 619, p. 1468, § 2; Stats.1977, c. 99, p. 520, § 1; Stats.1980, c. 608, p. 1677, § 6; Stats.1985, c. 1022, § 14.5; Stats.1990, c. 1563 (A.B.3243), § 30.)*

Cross References

Definitions,
  Department, see Vehicle Code § 290.
  Vehicle, see Vehicle Code § 670.

§ 11509.1. Filing of accusation; compromise settlement agreement; terms and conditions

(a) After the filing of an accusation under this chapter, the director may enter into a stipulated compromise settlement agreement with the consent of the licensee on terms and conditions mutually agreeable to the director, the respondent licensee, and the accuser without further

hearing or appeal. The agreement may include, but is not limited to, a period of probation or monetary penalties, or both. The monetary penalty shall not exceed one thousand dollars ($1,000) for each violation, and it shall be based on the nature of the violation and the effect of the violation on the purposes of this chapter.

(b) A compromise settlement agreement may be entered before, during, or after the hearing, but is valid only if executed and filed pursuant to subdivision (d) before the proposed decision of the hearing officer, if any, is adopted or the case is decided.

(c) The department shall adopt, by regulation, a schedule of maximum and minimum amounts of monetary penalties, the payment of which may be included as a term or condition of a compromise settlement agreement entered under subdivision (a). Any monetary penalty included in a compromise settlement agreement shall be within the range of monetary penalties in that schedule.

(d) Any compromise settlement agreement entered under this section shall be signed by the director, the respondent licensee, and the accuser, or by their authorized representatives. The director shall file, or cause to be filed, the agreement with the Office of Administrative Hearings, together with the department's notice of withdrawal of the accusation or statement of issues upon which the action was initiated.

(e) If the respondent licensee fails to perform all of the terms and conditions of the compromise settlement agreement, the agreement is void and the department may take any action authorized by law notwithstanding the agreement, including, but not limited to, refiling the accusation or imposing license sanctions. *(Added by Stats.1985, c. 1022, § 16.)*

§ 11509.5.   Reapplication for license

A person whose automobile dismantler's license has been revoked or whose application for a license has been denied may reapply for such license after a period of not less than one year has elapsed from the effective date of the decision revoking the license or denying the application; provided, however, that if such decision was based upon paragraph (3), (9), or (10) of subdivision (a) of Section 11509, or Section 11513, an earlier reapplication may be made accompanied by evidence satisfactory to the department that such grounds no longer exist. *(Added by Stats.1976, c. 934, p. 2138, § 1. Amended by Stats.1979, c. 373, p. 1380, § 316.)*

§ 11510.   Temporary suspension

The department may, pending a hearing, temporarily suspend the license and special plates issued to an automobile dismantler for a period not to exceed 30 days if the director finds that such action is required in the public interest. In any such case a hearing shall be held and a decision thereon issued within 30 days after notice of temporary suspension.

Every hearing as provided for in this section shall be pursuant to the provisions of Chapter 5 (commencing with Section 11500) of Part 1 of Division 3 of Title 2 of the Government Code. *(Added by Stats.1961, c. 1640, p. 3583, § 6, operative Jan. 1, 1962. Amended by Stats.1963, c. 1106, § 14; Stats.1968, c. 667, p. 1357, § 3; Stats.1971, c. 1214, p. 2345, § 15, operative May 3, 1972.)*

§ 11511. Possession of stolen vehicle or part thereof; presumption

In any administrative action to revoke or suspend an automobile dismantler's license:

(a) Proof that a stolen vehicle of a type subject to registration under this code, or a part thereof, was found in the possession of, or upon the premises of, the dismantler shall constitute in evidence a prima facie presumption that the dismantler had knowledge that the vehicle was stolen. This presumption may be rebutted by satisfactory evidence that the dismantler has complied with paragraphs (1), (2), (3), and (5) of subdivision (a) of Section 11520.

(b) Proof that a vehicle of a type subject to registration under this code is found in a partially dismantled condition in the possession of, or upon the premises of, the dismantler shall constitute in evidence a prima facie presumption that the vehicle was partially dismantled by the dismantler. The presumption may be rebutted by a business record of the dismantler reflecting the partially dismantled condition of the vehicle on the date of acquisition. *(Added by Stats.1963, c. 1106, p. 2568, § 16. Amended by Stats.1968, c. 667, p. 1357, § 4; Stats.1974, c. 613, p. 1460, § 5; Stats.1980, c. 608, p. 1679, § 7; Stats.1981, c. 714, p. 2795, § 441; Stats.1982, c. 466, p. 2056, § 109.)*

Cross References

Prima facie evidence, see Evidence Code § 602.

§ 11512. Hearing upon refusal

(a) Upon refusal of the department to issue a license to an automobile dismantler the applicant shall be entitled to demand in writing a hearing before the director or his representative within 60 days after notice of refusal.

(b) The hearing shall be conducted pursuant to the provisions of Chapter 5 (commencing with Section 11500) of Part 1 of Division 3 of Title 2 of the Government Code. *(Added by Stats.1961, c. 1640, p. 3584, § 6, operative Jan. 1, 1962. Amended by Stats.1963, c. 1106, p. 2569, § 17; Stats.1971, c. 1214, p. 2345, § 16, operative May 3, 1972; Stats.1975, c. 182, p. 532, § 13, eff. July 5, 1975.)*

Cross References

Application for license, see Vehicle Code § 11501.
Department, definition, see Vehicle Code § 290.

§ 11513. Established place of business required; service of process when business closed

(a) The department shall not issue an automobile dismantler's license to any applicant for that license who has not an established place of business as defined in this code. If the automobile dismantler changes the site or location of his or her established place of business, he or she shall immediately upon making the change notify the department. If the automobile dismantler, for any reason ceases to be in possession of an established place of business from and on which he or she conducts the business for which he or she is licensed, he or she shall immediately notify the department and, upon demand by the department, shall deliver to the department the automobile dismantler's license, and all books and forms provided by the department in his or her possession.

(b) Any person licensed under this chapter who has closed his or her established place of business may be served with process issued pursuant to Chapter 5 (commencing with Section 11500) of Part 1 of Division 3 of Title 2 of the Government Code by registered mail at that place of business, unless the person has notified the department in writing of another address where service may be made. *(Added by Stats.1961, c. 1640, p. 3584, § 6, operative Jan. 1, 1962. Amended by Stats.1963, c. 1106, p. 2569, § 18; Stats.1971, c. 1214, p. 2346, § 17, operative May 3, 1972; Stats.1975, c. 182, p. 532, § 14, eff. July 5, 1975; Stats.1988, c. 751, § 5.)*

§ 11514. Dismantling site requirements

(a) An automobile dismantler's established place of business and such other sites or locations as may be operated and maintained by such automobile dismantler in conjunction with his principal established place of business shall have posted, in a place conspicuous to the public in each and every site or location, the license issued by the department and shall have erected or posted thereon such signs or devices providing information relating to the automobile dismantler's name and the location and address of his established place of business so as to enable any person doing business with such automobile dismantler to identify him properly. Every such sign erected or posted on an established place of business shall have an area of not less than 32 square feet per side displayed and shall contain lettering not less than six inches in height. The sign shall indicate the nature of the dismantler's business by inclusion of "Automobile Dismantler", "Automobile Wrecker", "Motorcycle Dismantler", "Trailer Dismantler", "Vehicle Dismantler", or a combination of such designations on such sign.

(b) Any local authority may provide for a sign and lettering smaller than that specified in subdivision (a); however, no local authority shall require a sign to have an area of less than four square feet per side displayed. *(Added by Stats.1961, c. 1640, p. 3584, § 6, operative Jan. 1, 1962. Amended by Stats.1963, c. 1106, p. 2569, § 19; Stats.1971, c. 212, p. 277, § 1, operative May 3, 1972; Stats.1971, c. 285, p. 591, § 1, operative May 3, 1972; Stats.1971, c. 1214, p. 2346, § 18, operative May 3, 1972; Stats.1976, c. 55, p. 84, § 1; Stats.1977, c. 579, p. 1911, § 180.)*

§ 11515. Total loss salvage vehicle; evidence of ownership; salvage certificate; reporting requirements; violations

(a)(1) Whenever an insurance company makes a total loss settlement on a total loss salvage vehicle, the insurance company, an occupational licensee of the department authorized by the insurance company, or a salvage pool authorized by the insurance company, within 10 days from the settlement of the loss, shall forward the properly endorsed certificate of ownership or other evidence of ownership acceptable to the department, the license plates, and a fee in the amount of fifteen dollars ($15), to the department. An occupational licensee of the department may submit a certificate of license plate destruction in lieu of the actual license plate.

(2) If an insurance company, an occupational licensee of the department authorized by the insurance company, or a salvage pool authorized by the insurance company is unable to obtain the properly endorsed certificate of ownership or other evidence of ownership acceptable to the department within 30 days following oral or written acceptance by the owner of an offer of an amount in settlement of a total loss, that insurance company, licensee, or salvage pool, on a form provided by the department and signed under penalty of perjury, may request the department to issue a salvage certificate for the vehicle. The request shall include and document that the requester has made at least two written attempts to obtain the certificate of ownership or other acceptable evidence of title, and shall include the license plates and fee described in paragraph (1).

(3) The department, upon receipt of the certificate of ownership, other evidence of title, or properly executed request described in paragraph (2), the license plates, and the fee, shall issue a salvage certificate for the vehicle.

(b) Whenever the owner of a total loss salvage vehicle retains possession of the vehicle, the insurance company shall notify the department of the retention on a form prescribed by the department. The insurance company shall also notify the insured or owner of the insured's or owner's responsibility to comply with this subdivision. The owner shall, within 10 days from the settlement of the loss, forward the properly endorsed certificate of ownership or other evidence of ownership acceptable to the department, the license plates, and a fee in the amount of fifteen dollars ($15) to the department. The department, upon receipt of the certificate of ownership or other evidence of title, the license plates, and the fee, shall issue a salvage certificate for the vehicle.

(c) Whenever a total loss salvage vehicle is not the subject of an insurance settlement, the owner shall, within 10 days from the loss, forward the properly endorsed certificate of ownership or other evidence of ownership acceptable to the department, the license plates, and a fee in the amount of fifteen dollars ($15) to the department.

(d) Whenever a total loss salvage vehicle is not the subject of an insurance settlement, a self-insurer, as defined in Section 16052, shall, within 10 days from the loss, forward the properly endorsed certificate of ownership or other evidence of ownership acceptable to the department, the license plates, and a fee in the amount of fifteen dollars ($15) to the department.

(e) Prior to the sale or disposal of a total loss salvage vehicle, the owner, owner's agent, or salvage pool, shall obtain a properly endorsed salvage certificate and deliver it to the purchaser within 10 days after payment in full for the salvage vehicle and shall also comply with Section 5900. The department shall accept the endorsed salvage certificate in lieu of the certificate of ownership or other evidence of ownership when accompanied by an application and other documents and fees, including, but not limited to, the fees required by Section 9265, as may be required by the department.

(f) This section does not apply to a vehicle that has been driven or taken without the consent of the owner thereof, until the vehicle has been recovered by the owner and only if the vehicle is a total loss salvage vehicle.

(g) A violation of subdivision (a), (b), (d), or (e) is a misdemeanor, pursuant to Section 40000.11. Notwithstanding Section 40000.11, a violation of subdivision (c) is an infraction, except that, if committed with the intent to defraud, a violation of subdivision (c) is a misdemeanor.

(h)(1) A salvage certificate issued pursuant to this section shall include a statement that the seller and subsequent sellers that transfer ownership of a total loss vehicle pursuant to a properly endorsed salvage certificate are required to disclose to the purchaser at, or prior to, the time of sale that the vehicle has been declared a total loss salvage vehicle.

(2) Effective on and after the department includes in the salvage certificate form the statement described in paragraph (1), a seller who fails to make the disclosure described in paragraph (1) shall be subject to a civil penalty of not more than five hundred dollars ($500).

(3) Nothing in this subdivision affects any other civil remedy provided by law, including, but not limited to, punitive damages. *(Added by Stats.1980, c. 629, p. 1720, § 5. Amended by Stats.1981, c. 714, p. 2796, § 442; Stats.1984, c. 1026, § 1; Stats.1986, c. 952, § 3; Stats. 1991, c. 470 (A.B.779), § 1, operative July 1, 1992; Stats.1998, c. 453 (A.B.218), § 1; Stats.2002, c. 826 (S.B.2076), § 1; Stats.2003, c. 719 (S.B.1055), § 20; Stats.2006, c. 412 (A.B.1122), § 1.)*

Cross References

Base fee amounts, adjustment of fees, see Vehicle Code § 1678.
Misdemeanors, definition and penalties, see Penal Code §§ 17, 19 and 19.2.
Sale of specified vehicles, presumption of sale at retail, rebuttal by taking resale certificate, additional contents of resale certificate, see Revenue and Taxation Code § 6092.5.
Total loss salvage vehicle, report to Department of Motor Vehicles, see Vehicle Code § 544.

§ 11515.1. Salvage pool; sale of vehicle

A salvage pool shall sell a vehicle only with either of the following:

(a) A salvage certificate, except those vehicles described in subdivision (f) of Section 11515, which may be sold with a certificate of title.

(b) A nonrepairable vehicle certificate, except those vehicles described in subdivision (f) of Section 11515.2, which may be sold with a certificate of title. *(Added by Stats.1991, c. 996 (S.B.798), § 3. Amended by Stats.1994, c. 1008 (S.B.1833), § 13, operative July 1, 1995.)*

§ 11515.2. Total loss settlement on nonrepairable vehicle; properly endorsed certificate of ownership; vehicle retained by owner; vehicles not subject of insurance settlement; certificate; violations

(a)(1) If an insurance company makes a total loss settlement on a nonrepairable vehicle and takes possession of that vehicle, either itself or through an agent, the insurance company, an occupational licensee of the department authorized by the insurance company, or a salvage pool authorized by the insurance company, shall, within 10 days after receipt of title by the insurer, free and clear of all liens, forward the properly endorsed certificate of ownership or other evidence of ownership acceptable to the department, the license plates, and a fee in the amount of fifteen dollars ($15) to the department. An occupational licensee of the department may submit a certificate of license plate destruction in lieu of the actual license plate. The department, upon receipt of the certificate of ownership or other evidence of title, the license plates, and the fee, shall issue a nonrepairable vehicle certificate for the vehicle.

(2) If an insurance company, an occupational licensee of the department authorized by the insurance company, or a salvage pool authorized by the insurance company is unable to obtain the properly endorsed certificate of ownership or other evidence of ownership acceptable to the department within 30 days following oral or written acceptance by the owner of an offer of an amount in settlement of a total loss, that insurance company, licensee, or salvage pool, on a form provided by the department and signed under penalty of perjury, may request the department to issue a nonrepairable vehicle certificate for the vehicle. The request shall include and document that the requester has made at least two written attempts to obtain the certificate of ownership or other acceptable evidence of title, and shall include the license plates and fee described in paragraph (1).

(3) The department, upon receipt of the certificate of ownership, other evidence of title, or properly executed request described in paragraph (2), the license plates, and the fee, shall issue a nonrepairable vehicle certificate for the vehicle.

(b) If the owner of a nonrepairable vehicle retains possession of the vehicle, the insurance company shall notify the department of the retention on a form prescribed by the department. The insurance company shall also notify the insured or owner of the insured's or owner's responsibility to comply with this subdivision. The owner shall, within 10 days from the settlement of the loss, forward the properly endorsed certificate of ownership or other evidence of ownership acceptable to the department, the license plates, and a fee in the amount of fifteen dollars ($15) to the department. The department, upon receipt of the certificate of ownership or other evidence of title, the license plates, and the fee, shall issue a nonrepairable vehicle certificate for the vehicle.

(c) If a nonrepairable vehicle is not the subject of an insurance settlement, the owner shall, within 10 days from the loss, forward the properly endorsed certificate of ownership or other evidence of ownership acceptable to the department, the license plates, and a fee in the amount of fifteen dollars ($15) to the department.

(d) If a nonrepairable vehicle is not the subject of an insurance settlement, a self-insurer, as defined in Section 16052, shall, within 10 days of the loss, forward the properly endorsed certificate of ownership or other evidence of ownership acceptable to the department, the license plates, and a fee in the amount of fifteen dollars ($15) to the department.

(e) Prior to sale or disposal of a nonrepairable vehicle, the owner, owner's agent, or salvage pool shall obtain a properly endorsed nonrepairable vehicle certificate and deliver it to the purchaser within 10 days after payment in full for the nonrepairable vehicle and shall also comply with Section 5900. The department shall accept the endorsed nonrepairable vehicle certificate in lieu of the certificate of ownership or other evidence of ownership when accompanied by an application and other documents and fees, including, but not limited to, the fees required by Section 9265, as may be required by the department.

(f) This section does not apply to a vehicle that has been driven or taken without the consent of the owner thereof, until the vehicle has been recovered by the owner and only if the vehicle is a nonrepairable vehicle.

(g) A nonrepairable vehicle certificate shall be conspicuously labeled with the words "NONREPAIRABLE VEHICLE" across the front of the certificate.

(h) A violation of subdivision (a), (b), (d), or (e) is a misdemeanor, pursuant to Section 40000.11. Notwithstanding Section 40000.11, a violation of subdivision (c) is an infraction, except that, if committed with intent to defraud, a violation of subdivision (c) is a misdemeanor. *(Added by Stats.1994, c. 1008 (S.B.1833), § 14, operative July 1, 1995. Amended by Stats.2003, c. 719 (S.B.1055), § 21; Stats.2004, c. 183 (A.B.3082), § 351; Stats.2008, c. 97 (A.B.2273), § 1.)*

Cross References

Base fee amounts, adjustment of fees, see Vehicle Code § 1678.
Misdemeanors, definition and penalties, see Penal Code §§ 17, 19 and 19.2.

§ 11516. Operation of vehicle under special plates

(a) Any automobile dismantler owning or controlling any vehicle of a type otherwise required to be registered under this code, may operate or move the vehicle upon the highways without subjecting the vehicle to registration or transfer, or both, solely for the purpose of moving the vehicle from its location to the established place of business of the automobile dismantler or to a scrap processor, if there are displayed on the vehicle special plates issued to the automobile dismantler as provided in this chapter, in addition to other license plates or permits already assigned and attached to the vehicle in the manner prescribed in Article 9 (commencing with Section 5200) of Chapter 1 of Division 3.

(b) The provisions of this section do not apply to work or service vehicles owned by an automobile dismantler.

(c) Every owner, upon receipt of a registration card issued for special plates, shall maintain the registration card or a facsimile copy of it with the vehicle bearing the special plates. *(Added by Stats.1961, c. 1640, p. 3585, § 6, operative Jan. 1, 1962. Amended by Stats.1963, c. 1106, p. 2570, § 20; Stats.1971, c. 929, p. 1826, § 1, operative May 3, 1972; Stats.1994, c. 1220 (A.B.3132), § 55, eff. Sept. 30, 1994.)*

Cross References

Display of license plates, see Vehicle Code §§ 5200, 5201.

§ 11517. Certificate of convenience

The department may issue a certificate of convenience to the executor, executrix, administrator or administratrix of the estate of a deceased holder of validly outstanding special plates and license issued under this chapter, or if no executor, executrix, administrator or administratrix had been appointed, and until a certified copy of an order making such appointment is filed with the department, to the widow or other heir otherwise entitled to conduct the business of the deceased, permitting such person to exercise the privileges granted by such special plates and license for a period of one year from and after the date of death, pending, but not later than, disposal of the business and qualifications of the vendor of the business or such surviving widow or heir for such special plates and license under the provisions of this chapter. The department may restrict or condition the license and special plates and attach to the exercise of the privileges thereunder such terms and conditions as in its judgment the protection of the public requires. *(Added by Stats.1961, c. 1640, p. 3585, § 6, operative Jan. 1, 1962. Amended by Stats.1971, c. 1214, p. 2346, § 19, operative May 3, 1972.)*

§ 11518. Automatic cancellation of special plates and license

The special plates and license provided for in this chapter shall be automatically canceled if any of the following occurs:

(a) The abandonment of the established place of business of the automobile dismantler or the change thereof without notice to the department pursuant to Section 11513.

(b) The voluntary or involuntary surrender for any cause by the licensee of the special plates and license, except that a surrender of the special plates and license, the cessation of business by the licensee, or the suspension or revocation of the corporate status of the licensee, does not preclude the filing of an accusation for revocation or suspension of the surrendered license as provided in Section 11509, and does not affect the department's decision to suspend or revoke the license. The department's decision to suspend or revoke the license may be considered in issuing or refusing to issue any subsequent license authorized by this division to that licensee or any business representative of that licensee.

(c) When the person designated as the licensee has changed, except that the special plates issued to the original licensee may be transferred upon application as provided in Section 11501 and the newly designated licensee, as transferee, shall succeed to the privileges evidenced by the plates until their expiration.

(d) The suspension or revocation of the corporate status of the licensee.

(e) The suspension or revocation of the seller's permit of the licensee by the State Board of Equalization. *(Added by Stats.1961, c. 1640, p. 3585, § 6, operative Jan. 1, 1962. Amended by Stats.1963, c. 1106, p. 2570, § 21; Stats.1965, c. 652, p. 2009, § 3; Stats.1971, c. 1214, p. 2347, § 20, operative May 3, 1972; Stats.1977, c. 452, p. 1488, § 3; Stats.1990, c. 1563 (A.B.3243), § 31.)*

§ 11519. Registration of total loss salvage and dismantled vehicles

(a) A vehicle that has been reported as a total loss salvage vehicle or dismantled vehicle may not be subsequently registered until there is submitted to the department all of the following:

(1) The prescribed bill of sale.

(2) An appropriate application.

(3) Official lamp and brake adjustment certificates issued by an official lamp and brake adjusting station licensed by the Director of Consumer Affairs, except that a fleet owner of motor trucks of three or more axles that are more than 6,000 pounds unladen weight, and a fleet owner of truck tractors, may instead submit an official lamp and brake certification for his or her rebuilt vehicle if the fleet owner operates an inspection and maintenance station licensed by the commissioner under subdivision (b) of Section 2525.

(4) With respect to a motor vehicle subject to Part 5 (commencing with Section 43000) of Division 26 of the Health and Safety Code, a valid certificate of compliance from a licensed motor vehicle pollution control device installation and inspection station indicating that the vehicle is properly equipped with a motor vehicle pollution control device that is in proper operating condition and is in compliance with Part 5 (commencing with Section 43000) of Division 26 of the Health and Safety Code.

(5) Any other documents or fees required under law.

(b) The department may not register a vehicle that has been referred to the Department of the California Highway Patrol under subdivision (b) of Section 5505 or that has been selected for inspection by that department under subdivision (c) of that section, until the applicant for registration submits to the department a certification of inspection issued by the Department of the California Highway Patrol and all of the documents required under subdivision (a). *(Added by Stats.2003, c. 594 (S.B.315), § 34.)*

§ 11520. Notice of acquisition; transmittal of documents and license plates; records

(a) A licensed automobile dismantler who acquired, for the purpose of dismantling, actual possession, as a transferee, of a vehicle of a type subject to registration under this code shall do all of the following:

(1) Within five calendar days, not including the day of acquisition, mail a notice of acquisition to the department at its headquarters.

(2) Within five calendar days, not including the day of acquisition, mail a copy of the notice of acquisition to the Department of Justice at its headquarters.

(3) Not begin dismantling until 10 calendar days have elapsed after mailing the notice of acquisition. In the alternative, dismantling may begin any time after the dismantler complies with paragraph (4).

(4) Deliver to the department, within 90 calendar days of the date of acquisition, the documents evidencing ownership and the license plates last issued for the vehicle. Proof that a registered or certified letter of demand for the documents was sent within 90 days of the date of acquisition to the person from whom the vehicle was acquired may be substituted for documents that cannot otherwise be obtained. A certificate of license plate destruction, when authorized by the director, may be delivered in lieu of the license plates.

(5) Maintain a business record of all vehicles acquired for dismantling. The record shall contain the name and address of the person from whom the vehicle was acquired; the date the vehicle was acquired; the license plate number last assigned to the vehicle; and a brief description of the vehicle, including its make, type, and the vehicle identification number used for registration purposes. The record required by this paragraph shall be a business record of the dismantler separate and distinct from the records maintained in those books and forms furnished by the department.

(b) Paragraphs (1) and (2) of subdivision (a) do not apply to vehicles acquired pursuant to Section 11515, 11515.2, 22851.2, or 22851.3 of this code or Section 3071, 3072, or 3073 of the Civil Code.

(c) Paragraphs (1), (2), (3), and (4) of subdivision (a) do not apply to a vehicle acquired from another person if the other person has already notified and cleared the vehicle for dismantling with the department pursuant to

this code and a bill of sale has been executed to the dismantler that properly identifies the vehicle and contains evidence of clearance by the department, including, but not limited to, a dismantling report number, temporary receipt number, or other proof of compliance with this section. *(Added by Stats.1974, c. 613, p. 1460, § 7. Amended by Stats.1983, c. 142, § 168; Stats.1983, c. 1092, § 384, eff. Sept. 27, 1983, operative Jan. 1, 1984; Stats. 1983, c. 1286, § 23.2; Stats.1984, c. 216, § 6; Stats.1985, c. 1022, § 17; Stats.1987, c. 1091, § 4; Stats.1994, c. 1008 (S.B.1833), § 16, operative July 1, 1995; Stats.1997, c. 945 (A.B.1561), § 15.)*

Cross References

Automobile dismantler, exclusions, see Vehicle Code § 221.
Dismantler's investigation service fee, see Vehicle Code § 9263.
Registration fees for rebuilt vehicles reported to be dismantled, see Vehicle Code § 9563.
Surrender of documents upon reporting dismantling of vehicle, see Vehicle Code §§ 5500, 5501.
Waiver of reporting requirements and fees, see Vehicle Code § 22664.

§ 11521. Advertisements; license or permit numbers required

No person required to be licensed as an automobile dismantler under this code shall advertise the services of an automobile dismantler without indicating in the advertisement the occupational license or permit number of the automobile dismantler as issued by the department. *(Added by Stats.1996, c. 265 (A.B.2047), § 1.)*

§ 11522. Local regulation

The provisions of this chapter shall not prevent the local authorities of any city, city and county or county by ordinance, within the exercise of the police power of such city, city and county or county, from imposing local regulations with respect to traffic in loose vehicle parts and vehicle accessories. *(Added by Stats.1961, c. 1640, p. 3588, § 6, operative Jan. 1, 1962.)*

§ 11540. Salvage pools; records; notice of disposition of vehicle; license plates; submission to department

(a) A salvage pool shall maintain an accurate record of every vehicle it acquires and every vehicle it disposes of, and shall notify the department of the disposition of any vehicle pursuant to Section 5900.

(b) Whenever a salvage pool acquires a total loss salvage vehicle, a nonrepairable vehicle, or a recovered stolen vehicle and the license plates on the vehicle have not been removed pursuant to subdivision (a) of Section 11515, subdivision (a) of Section 11515.2, or any other provision of law, the salvage pool shall, prior to disposing of that vehicle, remove and submit the license plates to the department. The salvage pool shall maintain an accurate record of every license plate it acquires and disposes of, which records shall be maintained for two years and be open for inspection by any peace officer during the regular business hours of that salvage pool. *(Added by Stats.1986, c. 952, § 4. Amended by Stats.1991, c. 470 (A.B.779), § 2, operative July 1, 1992; Stats.1994, c. 1008 (S.B.1833), § 17, operative July 1, 1995.)*

§ 11541. Duties of department; operative date

The department shall administer and enforce all provisions of this code pertaining to salvage pools.

This section shall become operative on July 1, 1987. *(Added by Stats.1986, c. 952, § 5, operative July 1, 1987.)*

§ 11568. Inoperative

CHAPTER 3.5.   LESSOR–RETAILERS

Section
11600.   License or temporary permit required.
11601.   Application for license.
11602.   Contents of application.
11603.   Issuance or refusal of license.
11604.   Refusal to issue; grounds.
11604.1. Causes for suspension or revocation of license.
11604.5. Conviction of crime involving moral turpitude; refusal to issue or suspension of license.
11605.   Hearing upon refusal.
11606.   Probationary license.
11607.   Temporary permit.
11608.   Certificate of convenience.
11609.   Posting of license; other sign requirements.
11609.5. Notice; right of inspection.
11610.   Change of principal place of business or branch office; notice; service of process.
11612.   Bond.
11613.   Suspension or revocation.
11613.5. Filing of accusation; compromise settlement agreement; terms and conditions.
11614.   Prohibited acts.
11614.1. Prohibited acts in advertising.
11615.   Additional unlawful acts.
11615.5. Sales tax payment.
11616.   Refund of excess fees.
11617.   Automatic cancellation.
11618.   Temporary suspension.
11620.   Expiration of licenses; renewal; fees.
11620.1. Repealed.

Cross References

Advisory safety equipment maintenance check, exclusion, see Health and Safety Code § 44018.
"Lessor-retailer" defined, see Vehicle Code § 373.

§ 11600.   License or temporary permit required

It shall be unlawful for any lessor-retailer to make a retail sale of a vehicle of a type subject to registration without having first procured either a vehicle dealer license or a lessor-retailer license or temporary permit issued by the department or when such license or temporary permit issued by the department has been canceled, suspended, revoked, or invalidated or has expired. *(Added by Stats.1976, c. 1284, p. 5714, § 11.)*

Cross References

Unlicensed lessor-retailers, enforceability of security interest and other legal actions, see Vehicle Code § 11711.3.

§ 11601.   Application for license

(a) Every lessor-retailer who sells at retail a vehicle of a type subject to registration shall make application to the department for a license. The applicant shall submit proof of his status as a bona fide lessor-retailer as may reasonably be required by the department.

(b) An application shall be made for the principal place of business, and a separate branch office application shall be made for each branch office location of the licensee as shall be operated and maintained by the applicant in conjunction with the retail sale or sales of vehicles.

(c) "Principal place of business," for the purposes of this chapter, means the place designated by the lessor-retailer as the main business or office location in California whether or not retail sales are made from such location. *(Added by Stats.1976, c. 1284, p. 5714, § 11.)*

§ 11602.   Contents of application

(a) The department shall prescribe and provide forms to be used for application for licenses to be issued under the terms and provisions of this chapter and require of such applicants, where appropriate as a condition precedent to issuance of such license, such information, including but not limited to, fingerprints and personal history statements, touching on and concerning the applicant's character, honesty, integrity and reputation as it may consider necessary; provided, however, that every application for a lessor-retailer license shall contain, in addition to such information that the department may require, a statement of the following facts:

(1) The name and residence address of the applicant and the trade name, if any, under which he intends to conduct his business; and if the applicant be a partnership, the name and residence address of each member thereof, whether a limited or general partner, and the name under which the partnership business is to be conducted; and if the applicant be a corporation, the name of the corporation and the name and address of each of its principal officers and directors.

(2) A complete description, including the city, town or village with the street and number, if any, of its principal place of business in California and such other and additional branch location or locations.

(b) Upon receipt of an application accompanied with the appropriate fee, the department shall make a thorough investigation of the information contained in the application. *(Added by Stats.1976, c. 1284, p. 5714, § 11.)*

§ 11603.   Issuance or refusal of license

(a) The department may issue, or for reasonable cause shown, refuse to issue, a license to any applicant applying for a lessor-retailer license or branch office location.

(b) The license shall contain the applicant's name, location address and the general distinguishing number assigned to the applicant. *(Added by Stats.1976, c. 1284, p. 5714, § 11.)*

§ 11604. Refusal to issue; grounds

The department may refuse to issue a lessor-retailer license when it makes any of the following determinations:

(a) The applicant has outstanding an unsatisfied final court judgment rendered in connection with an activity licensed under the authority of this division.

(b) The applicant was previously the holder, or a managerial employee of the holder, of a license issued under this division which was revoked for cause and never reissued by the department, or which was suspended for cause and the terms of suspension have not been fulfilled.

(c) The applicant was previously a business representative whose license issued under this division was revoked for cause and never reissued or was suspended for cause and the terms of suspension have not been fulfilled.

(d) If the applicant is a business, a business representative was previously the holder of a license, or was a business representative of a business whose license, issued under this division, was revoked for cause and never reissued or was suspended for cause and the terms of suspension have not been fulfilled; or, by reason of the facts and circumstances related to the organization, control, and management of the business, the operation of that business will be directed, controlled, or managed by individuals who, by reason of their conviction of violations of this code, would be ineligible for a license and, by licensing that business, the purposes of this chapter would be defeated.

(e) The applicant, or a business representative if the applicant is a business, has been convicted of a crime or committed any act or engaged in conduct involving moral turpitude which is substantially related to the qualifications, functions, or duties of the licensed activity. A conviction after a plea of nolo contendere is a conviction within the meaning of this section.

(f) The applicant was previously the holder of an occupational license issued by another state, authorizing the same or similar activities of a license issued under this division; and that license was revoked or suspended for cause and was never reissued, or was suspended for cause, and the terms of suspension have not been fulfilled.

(g) The information contained in the application is incorrect.

(h) A decision of the department to cancel, suspend, or revoke a license has been made, and the applicant was a business representative of the business regulated under that license.

(i) The applicant does not have a principal place of business in California.

(j) The applicant has failed to pay the full amount of a claim paid by the Consumer Motor Vehicle Recovery Corporation, plus interest at the rate of 10 percent per annum, as described in subdivision (i) of Section 11703. *(Added by Stats.1976, c. 1284, p. 5714, § 11. Amended by Stats.1990, c. 1563 (A.B.3243), § 32; Stats.1998, c. 877 (A.B.2132), § 49; Stats.2007, c. 437 (S.B.729), § 3.)*

§ 11604.1. Causes for suspension or revocation of license

Any cause specified in this chapter as a cause to suspend or revoke the license issued to a lessor-retailer is a cause to refuse to issue a license to a lessor-retailer. *(Added by Stats.1990, c. 1563 (A.B.3243), § 33.)*

§ 11604.5. Conviction of crime involving moral turpitude; refusal to issue or suspension of license

(a) The department, after notice and hearing, on an interim basis, may refuse to issue or may suspend a license issued under this chapter when the applicant or licensee, or a business representative if the applicant or licensee is a business, has been convicted of a crime involving moral turpitude which is substantially related to the qualifications, functions, or duties of the licensed activity, if an appeal of the conviction is pending or the conviction has otherwise not become final. A conviction after a plea of nolo contendere is a conviction within the meaning of this section.

(b) When a conviction, upon which an interim refusal to issue or suspension under subdivision (a) is based, is affirmed on appeal or otherwise becomes final, the refusal to issue or suspension shall automatically take effect as a denial or revocation, as the case may be, of the license. If the interim refusal to issue or suspension was stayed under probationary terms and conditions, the subsequent automatic denial or revocation shall also be stayed under the same terms and conditions for a term not to exceed the original term of probation for the interim refusal to issue or suspension.

(c) If a conviction, upon which an interim refusal to issue or suspension under subdivision (a) is based, is reversed on appeal, the refusal or suspension shall be set aside immediately by the department. *(Added by Stats. 1990, c. 1563 (A.B.3243), § 34.)*

§ 11605. Hearing upon refusal

(a) Upon refusal of the department to issue a license to a lessor-retailer, the applicant shall be entitled to demand in writing a hearing before the director or his representative within 60 days after notice of refusal.

(b) The hearing shall be conducted pursuant to the provisions of Chapter 5 (commencing with Section 11500) of Part 1 of Division 3 of Title 2 of the Government Code. *(Added by Stats.1976, c. 1284, p. 5714, § 11.)*

§ 11606. Probationary license

Except where the provisions of this code require the refusal to issue a license, the department may issue a

351

probationary license subject to conditions to be observed by the licensee in the exercise of the privilege granted. The conditions to be attached to the exercise of the privilege shall not appear on the face of the license but shall be such as may, in the judgment of the department, be in the public interest and suitable to the qualifications of the applicant as disclosed by the application and investigation by the department of the information contained therein. *(Added by Stats.1976, c. 1284, p. 5714, § 11.)*

§ 11607.   Temporary permit

Pending the satisfaction of the department that the applicant has met the requirements under this chapter, it may issue a temporary permit to any person applying for a lessor-retailer license or branch office location. The temporary permit shall permit the operation by the lessor-retailer while the department is completing its investigation and determination of all facts relative to the qualifications of the applicant to such license. The department may cancel such temporary permit when it has determined or has reasonable cause to believe that the application is incorrect or incomplete or the temporary permit was issued in error. Such temporary permit shall be invalid when canceled or when the applicant's license has been issued or refused. *(Added by Stats.1976, c. 1284, p. 5714, § 11.)*

§ 11608.   Certificate of convenience

The department may issue a certificate of convenience to the executor, executrix, administrator or administratrix of the estate of a deceased holder of a valid license issued under this chapter, or if no executor, executrix, administrator or administratrix has been appointed, and until a certified copy of an order making such appointment is filed with the department, to the widow or other heir otherwise entitled to conduct the business of the deceased, permitting such person to exercise the privileges granted by such license for a period of one year from and after the date of death and necessary one-year renewals thereafter, pending, but not later than, disposal of the business and qualification of the vendee of the business or such surviving widow, heir or other persons for such license under the provisions of this chapter. The department may restrict or condition the license and attach to the exercise of the privileges thereunder such terms and conditions as in its judgment the protection of the public requires. *(Added by Stats.1976, c. 1284, p. 5714, § 11.)*

§ 11609.   Posting of license; other sign requirements

Each office location operated and maintained by a lessor-retailer in conjunction with its retail sale of a vehicle or vehicles shall have posted in a place conspicuous to the public the license issued by the department to the lessor, and shall have erected or posted thereon such signs or devices providing information relating to the lessor-retailer's name, the office location and the office address, to enable any person doing business with such

352

lessor to identify him properly. *(Added by Stats.1976, c. 1284, p. 5714, § 11.)*

§ 11609.5.   Notice; right of inspection

Every lessor-retailer who displays or offers one or more used vehicles for sale at retail shall post a notice not less than 8 inches high and 10 inches wide, in a place conspicuous to the public, which states the following:

"The prospective purchaser of a vehicle may, at his or her own expense and with the approval of the lessor-retailer, have the vehicle inspected by an independent third party either on or off these premises." *(Added by Stats.1990, c. 1563 (A.B.3243), § 35.)*

§ 11610.   Change of principal place of business or branch office; notice; service of process

(a) If the lessor-retailer changes the location of its principal place of business or any branch office location in California, the lessor-retailer shall immediately upon making the change notify the department.

(b) If a lessor-retailer, for any reason, ceases to be in possession of its principal place of business or any branch office location, the lessor-retailer shall immediately notify the department, and shall deliver to the department the lessor-retailer license issued for the location, and, upon demand, all report of sale books in his or her possession.

(c) Any person licensed under this chapter who has closed his or her principal place of business may be served with process issued pursuant to Chapter 5 (commencing with Section 11500) of Part 1 of Division 3 of Title 2 of the Government Code by registered mail at that place of business, unless the person has notified the department in writing of another address where service may be made. *(Added by Stats.1976, c. 1284, p. 5714, § 11. Amended by Stats.1988, c. 751, § 6; Stats.1990, c. 216 (S.B.2510), § 114.)*

§ 11612.   Bond

(a) Before any lessor-retailer license shall be issued or renewed by the department to any applicant therefor, the applicant shall procure and file with the department a bond meeting the same requirements as specified for a vehicle dealer's license in Sections 11710 and 11710.2.

(b) Any cause of action or claim specified in Section 11711 against a vehicle dealer's bond shall also be a cause of action or claim against a lessor-retailer's bond. *(Added by Stats.1976, c. 1284, p. 5714, § 11. Amended by Stats.1982, c. 517, p. 2425, § 395.)*

Law Revision Commission Comments

1982 Amendment

Section 11612 is amended to reflect the repeal of Section 11710.1. See also Code Civ. Proc. § 995.310 (sureties on bond). [16 Cal.L.Rev. Comm. Reports 501 (1981)].

Cross References

Bond and Undertaking Law, see Code of Civil Procedure § 995.010 et seq.

§ 11613. Suspension or revocation

(a) The department, after notice and hearing, may suspend or revoke the license issued to a lessor-retailer upon determining that the person to whom the license was issued is not lawfully entitled thereto, or has done any of the following:

(1) Filed an application for the license using a false or fictitious name not registered with the proper authorities, or knowingly made any false statement or knowingly concealed any material fact, in the application for the license.

(2) Used a false or fictitious name, knowingly made any false statement or knowingly concealed any material fact in any application for the registration of a vehicle, or otherwise committed a fraud in the application.

(3) Knowingly purchased, sold, or otherwise acquired or disposed of a stolen motor vehicle.

(4) Violated any provision of Division 3 (commencing with Section 4000) or rule or regulation adopted pursuant thereto.

(5) Violated any provision of Division 4 (commencing with Section 10500) or rule or regulation adopted pursuant thereto.

(6) Violated any provision of this chapter or rule or regulation adopted pursuant thereto.

(7) Violated any provision of Chapter 2b (commencing with Section 2981) of Title 14 of Part 4 of Division 3 of the Civil Code or rule or regulation adopted pursuant thereto under the authority of Section 1651.

(8) Submitted a check, draft, or money order to the department for any obligation or fee due the state which was thereafter dishonored or refused payment upon presentation.

(9) Caused any person to suffer any loss or damage by reason of any fraud or deceit practiced on, or fraudulent representations made to, that person in the sale of a vehicle or parts or accessories thereof.

For purposes of this subdivision, "fraud" includes any act or omission which is included within the definition of either "actual fraud" or "constructive fraud" as defined in Sections 1572 and 1573 of the Civil Code, and "deceit" has the same meaning as defined in Section 1710 of the Civil Code. In addition, "fraud" and "deceit" include, but are not limited to, a misrepresentation in any manner, whether intentionally false or due to gross negligence, of a material fact; a promise or representation not made honestly and in good faith; an intentional failure to disclose a material fact; and any act within Section 484 of the Penal Code.

For purposes of this subdivision, "person" also includes a governmental entity.

(b) Any of the causes specified in this chapter as a cause for refusal to issue a license to a lessor-retailer applicant is cause to suspend or revoke a license issued to a lessor-retailer.

(c) Every hearing provided for in this section shall be conducted pursuant to Chapter 5 (commencing with Section 11500) of Part 1 of Division 3 of Title 2 of the Government Code. *(Added by Stats.1976, c. 1284, p. 5714, § 11. Amended by Stats.1980, c. 676, p. 2023, § 308; Stats.1990, c. 1563 (A.B.3243), § 36.)*

§ 11613.5. Filing of accusation; compromise settlement agreement; terms and conditions

(a) After the filing of an accusation under this chapter, the director may enter into a stipulated compromise settlement agreement with the consent of the licensee on terms and conditions mutually agreeable to the director, the respondent licensee, and the accuser without further hearing or appeal. The agreement may include, but is not limited to, a period of probation or monetary penalties, or both. The monetary penalty shall not exceed one thousand dollars ($1,000) for each violation, and it shall be based on the nature of the violation and the effect of the violation on the purposes of this chapter.

(b) A compromise settlement agreement may be entered before, during, or after the hearing, but is valid only if executed and filed pursuant to subdivision (d) before the proposed decision of the hearing officer, if any, is adopted or the case is decided.

(c) The department shall adopt, by regulation, a schedule of maximum and minimum amounts of monetary penalties, the payment of which may be included as a term or condition of a compromise settlement agreement entered under subdivision (a). Any monetary penalty included in a compromise settlement agreement shall be within the range of monetary penalties in that schedule.

(d) Any compromise settlement agreement entered under this section shall be signed by the director, the respondent licensee, and the accuser, or by their authorized representatives. The director shall file, or cause to be filed, the agreement with the Office of Administrative Hearings, together with the department's notice of withdrawal of the accusation or statement of issues upon which the action was initiated.

(e) If the respondent licensee fails to perform all of the terms and conditions of the compromise settlement agreement, the agreement is void and the department may take any action authorized by law notwithstanding the agreement, including, but not limited to, refiling the accusation or imposing license sanctions. *(Added by Stats.1985, c. 1022, § 18.)*

§ 11614. Prohibited acts

No lessor-retailer licensed under this chapter may do any of the following in connection with any activity for which this license is required:

(a) Make or disseminate, or cause to be made or disseminated, before the public in this state, in any

353

newspaper or other publication, or any advertising device, or by oral representation, or in any other manner or means whatever, any statement that is untrue or misleading and that is known, or which by the exercise of reasonable care should be known, to be untrue or misleading; or make or disseminate, or cause to be made or disseminated, any statement as part of a plan or scheme with the intent not to sell any vehicle, or service so advertised, at the price stated therein, or as so advertised.

(b) Advertise, or offer for sale in any manner, any vehicle not actually for sale at the premises of the lessor-retailer or available within a reasonable time to the lessor-retailer at the time of the advertisement or offer.

(c) Fail within 48 hours to give, in writing, notification to withdraw any advertisement of a vehicle that has been sold or withdrawn from sale.

(d) Advertise any specific vehicle for sale without identifying the vehicle by its model, model year, and either its license number or that portion of the vehicle identification number that distinguishes the vehicle from all other vehicles of the same make, model, and model-year. Model-year is not required to be advertised for current model-year vehicles. Year models are no longer current when ensuing year models are available for purchase at retail in California.

(e) Advertise the total price of a vehicle without including all costs to the purchaser at the time of delivery at the lessor-retailer's premises, except sales tax, vehicle registration fees, finance charges, certificate of compliance or noncompliance fees not exceeding thirty-five dollars ($35) pursuant to any statute, and any dealer documentary preparation charge. The dealer documentary charge shall not exceed thirty-five dollars ($35).

(f)(1) Fail to disclose, in an advertisement of a vehicle for sale, that there will be added to the advertised total price, at the time of sale, charges for sales tax, vehicle registration fees, the fee charged by the state for the issuance of any certificate of compliance or noncompliance pursuant to any statute, finance charges, or any dealer documentary preparation charge.

(2) For purposes of paragraph (1), "advertisement" means any advertisement in a newspaper, magazine, direct mail publication, or handbill that is two or more columns in width or one column in width and more than seven inches in length, or on any Web page of a lessor-retailer's Web site that displays the price of a vehicle offered for sale on the Internet, as that term is defined in paragraph (6) of subdivision (e) of Section 17538 of the Business and Professions Code.

(g) Advertise or otherwise represent, or knowingly allow to be advertised or represented on the lessor-retailer's behalf or at the lessor-retailer's place of business, that no downpayment is required in connection with the sale of a vehicle when a downpayment is in fact required and the buyer is advised or induced to finance the downpayment by a loan in addition to any other loan

financing the remainder of the purchase price of the vehicle. The terms "no downpayment," "zero down delivers," or similar terms shall not be advertised unless the vehicle will be sold to any qualified purchaser without a prior payment of any kind or trade-in.

(h) Refuse to sell a vehicle to any person at the advertised total price, exclusive of sales tax, vehicle registration fees, finance charges, certificate of compliance or noncompliance pursuant to any statute, and any dealer documentary preparation charge, which charges shall not exceed thirty-five dollars ($35) for the documentary preparation charge and thirty-five dollars ($35) for the certificate of compliance or noncompliance pursuant to any statute, while the vehicle remains unsold or unleased, unless the advertisement states the advertised total price is good only for a specified time and the time has elapsed.

(i) Engage in the business for which the licensee is licensed without having in force and effect a bond required by Section 11612.

(j) Engage in the business for which the lessor-retailer is licensed without at all times maintaining a principal place of business and any branch office location required by this chapter.

(k) Permit the use of the lessor-retailer license, supplies, or books by any other person for the purpose of permitting that person to engage in the sale of vehicles required to be registered under this code, or to permit the use of the lessor-retailer license, supplies, or books to operate a branch office location to be used by any other person, if, in either situation, the licensee has no financial or equitable interest or investment in the vehicles sold by, or the business of, or branch office location used by, the person, or has no interest or investment other than commissions, compensations, fees, or any other thing of value received for the use of the lessor-retailer license, supplies, or books to engage in the sale of vehicles.

(l) Violate any provision of Article 10 (commencing with Section 28050) of Chapter 5 of Division 12.

(m) Represent the dealer documentary preparation charge, or certificate of compliance or noncompliance fee, as a governmental fee.

(n) Advertise free merchandise, gifts, or services provided by a lessor-retailer contingent on the purchase of a vehicle. "Free" includes merchandise or services offered for sale at a price less than the lessor-retailer's cost of the merchandise or services.

(o) Advertise vehicles and related goods or services with the intent not to supply reasonably expectable demand, unless the advertisement discloses a limitation of quantity.

(p) Use the term "rebate" or similar words such as "cash back" in advertising the sale of a vehicle.

(q) Require a person to pay a higher price for a vehicle and related goods or services for receiving advertised credit terms than the cash price the same person would have to pay to purchase the same vehicle and related goods or services. For the purpose of this subdivision, "cash price" has the meaning as defined in subdivision (e) of Section 2981 of the Civil Code.

(r) Misrepresent the authority of a representative or agent to negotiate the final terms of a transaction.

(s) Violate any law prohibiting bait and switch advertising, including, but not limited to, the guides against bait advertising set forth in Part 238 of Title 16 of the Code of Federal Regulations, as those regulations read on January 1, 1988.

(t) Make any untrue or misleading statement indicating that a vehicle is equipped with all the factory installed optional equipment the manufacturer offers, including, but not limited to, a false statement that a vehicle is "fully factory equipped."

(u) Advertise any underselling claim, such as "we have the lowest prices" or "we will beat any dealer's price," unless the lessor-retailer has conducted a recent survey showing that the lessor-retailer sells its vehicles at lower prices than any other licensee in its trade area and maintains records to adequately substantiate the claim. The substantiating records shall be made available to the department upon request.

(v) To display or offer for sale any used vehicle unless there is affixed to the vehicle the Federal Trade Commission's Buyer's Guide as required by Part 455 of Title 16 of the Code of Federal Regulations.

(w) This section shall become operative on July 1, 2001. *(Added by Stats.2000, c. 773 (S.B.2060), § 2, operative July 1, 2001. Amended by Stats.2002, c. 947 (A.B.2397), § 1.)*

§ 11614.1. Prohibited acts in advertising

No lessor-retailer licensed under this chapter may do any of the following in connection with any activity for which this license is required:

(a) Use a picture in connection with any advertisement of the price of a specific vehicle or class of vehicles, unless the picture is of the year, make, and model being offered for sale. The picture may not depict a vehicle with optional equipment or a design not actually offered at the advertised price.

(b) Advertise a vehicle for sale that was used by the selling lessor-retailer in its business as a demonstrator, executive vehicle, service vehicle, rental, loaner, or lease vehicle, unless the advertisement clearly and conspicuously discloses the previous use made by that licensee of the vehicle. An advertisement may not describe any of those vehicles as "new."

(c) Advertise any used vehicle of the current or prior model-year without expressly disclosing the vehicle as "used," "previously owned," or a similar term that indicates that the vehicle is used, as defined in this code.

(d) Use the terms "on approved credit" or "on credit approval" in an advertisement for the sale of a vehicle

unless those terms are clearly and conspicuously disclosed and unabbreviated.

(e) Advertise an amount described by terms such as "unpaid balance" or "balance can be financed" unless the total sale price is clearly and conspicuously disclosed and is in close proximity to the advertised balance.

(f) Advertise credit terms that fail to comply with the disclosure requirements of Section 226.24 of Title 12 of the Code of Federal Regulations. Advertisements of terms that include escalated payments, balloon payments, or deferred downpayments shall clearly and conspicuously identify those payments as to amounts and time due.

(g) Advertise claims such as "everyone financed," "no credit rejected," or similar claims unless the dealer is willing to extend credit to any person under any and all circumstances.

(h) Advertise the amount of any downpayment unless it represents the total payment required of a purchaser prior to delivery of the vehicle, including any payment for sales tax or license. A statement such as "$_____ delivers," is an example of an advertised downpayment.

(i) Fail to clearly and conspicuously disclose in an advertisement for the sale of a vehicle any disclosure required by this code or any qualifying term used in conjunction with advertised credit terms. Unless otherwise provided by statute, the specific size of disclosures or qualifying terms is not prescribed. *(Added by Stats.2002, c. 947 (A.B.2397), § 2. Amended by Stats.2003, c. 62 (S.B.600), § 302.)*

Cross References

False advertising, see Business and Professions Code § 17500 et seq.
Unfair Practices Act, see Business and Professions Code § 17000 et seq.

§ 11615. Additional unlawful acts

It shall be unlawful and a violation of this code for a lessor-retailer licensed under this chapter when selling at retail a vehicle in a transaction for which this license is required:

(a) To deliver, following sale, a vehicle for operation on California highways, if such vehicle does not meet all of the equipment requirements of Division 12 (commencing with Section 24000) of this code.

(b) To fail to deliver to a transferee lawfully entitled thereto a properly endorsed certificate of ownership.

(c) To violate any of the terms or provisions of Part 5 (commencing with Section 10701) of Division 2 of the Revenue and Taxation Code or rules and regulations adopted pursuant thereto or adopted pursuant to Section 1651 of this code.

(d) To take a vehicle in trade in part or total payment for a vehicle sold by the lessor-retailer.

(e) To sell a vehicle which has not been previously leased, bailed or rented or acquired or contracted for lease or rental by the lessor-retailer.

(f) To display a vehicle for sale at a location other than the principal place of business or branch office authorized by the department for that lessor-retailer. *(Added by Stats.1976, c. 1284, p. 5714, § 11. Amended by Stats.1990, c. 1563 (A.B.3243), § 36.7.)*

§ 11615.5. Sales tax payment

It is unlawful and a violation of this code for a person holding a license under this chapter to make a retail sale of a motor vehicle, except to the lessee of such vehicle, required to be registered pursuant to Division 3 (commencing with Section 4000) or subject to identification pursuant to Division 16.5 (commencing with Section 38000) if such person files with the department a report of sale as provided in Section 4456 with respect to such retail sale, without making the return and payment of any sales tax due and required by Section 6451 of the Revenue and Taxation Code. *(Added by Stats.1976, c. 1284, p. 5714, § 11. Amended by Stats.1979, c. 373, p. 1381, § 317.)*

Cross References

Sale by person not subject to this section, see Revenue and Taxation Code §§ 6292, 6293.

§ 11616. Refund of excess fees

If a purchaser of a vehicle pays to the lessor-retailer an amount for the licensing or transfer of title of the vehicle, which amount is in excess of the actual fees due for such licensing or transfer, or which amount is in excess of the amount which has been paid, prior to the sale, by the lessor-retailer to the state in order to avoid penalties that would have accrued because of late payment of such fees, the lessor-retailer shall return such excess amount to the purchaser, whether or not such purchaser requests the return of the excess amount. *(Added by Stats.1976, c. 1284, p. 5714, § 11.)*

§ 11617. Automatic cancellation

(a) The license provided for in this chapter shall be automatically canceled upon the happening of any of the following:

(1) The abandonment of the principal place of business of the lessor-retailer or the change thereof without notice to the department as provided in Section 11610.

(2) The failure of the licensee to maintain an adequate bond or to procure and file another bond as required by Section 11612 prior to the effective date of the termination by the surety of any existing bond.

(3) The voluntary or involuntary surrender for any cause by the licensee of the license, except that a surrender of the license, or cessation of business by the licensee, or the suspension or revocation of the corporate status of the licensee, does not preclude the filing of an accusation for revocation or suspension of the surrendered license as provided in Section 11613, and does not affect the department's decision to suspend or revoke the license. The department's determination to suspend or revoke the license may be considered in issuing or

356

refusing to issue any subsequent license authorized by this division to that licensee or any business representative of that licensee.

(4) Notification to the department that the person designated as licensee has changed.

(5) The suspension or cancellation of the corporate status of the licensee .

(6) The suspension or revocation of the seller's permit of the licensee by the State Board of Equalization.

(b) The branch office location license provided for in this chapter shall be automatically canceled upon the abandonment of the branch office location of the lessor-retailer or the change of that branch office without notice to the department as provided in Section 11610. *(Added by Stats.1976, c. 1284, p. 5714, § 11. Amended by Stats.1990, c. 1563 (A.B.3243), § 37.)*

§ 11618. Temporary suspension

The department may, pending a hearing, temporarily suspend the license issued to a lessor-retailer for a period not to exceed 30 days, if the director finds that such action is required in the public interest. In any such case a hearing shall be held and a decision thereon issued within 30 days after notice of the temporary suspension.

Every hearing as provided for in this section shall be pursuant to the provisions of Chapter 5 (commencing with Section 11500) of Part 1 of Division 3 of Title 2 of the Government Code. *(Added by Stats.1976, c. 1284, p. 5714, § 11.)*

§ 11620. Expiration of licenses; renewal; fees

(a) Every occupational license issued under this chapter shall be valid for a period of one year from midnight of the last day of the month of issuance. Except as provided in subdivision (c), renewal of an occupational license for the ensuing year may be obtained by the person to whom the occupational license was issued upon application to the department and payment of the fee provided in this code.

(b) Every application for the renewal of an occupational license which expires pursuant to this section shall be made by the person to whom issued not more than 90 days prior to the expiration date, and shall be made by presenting the completed application form provided by the department and by payment of the full annual renewal fee for the occupational license.

(c) If the application for renewal of the occupational license is not made by midnight of the expiration date, the application may be made within 30 days following expiration of the license by paying the annual renewal fee and a penalty fee equal to the amount of the original application fee for each occupational license held.

(d) In no event may the licensee renew the occupational license after the expiration of the 30-day period authorized in subdivision (c). *(Added by Stats.1981, c. 338, p. 1497, § 3. Amended by Stats.1982, c. 571, p. 2527, § 4; Stats.1984, c. 499, § 11.)*

§ 11620.1. Repealed by Stats.1992, c. 1241 (S.B.1615)
§ 17

CHAPTER 4. MANUFACTURERS, TRANSPORTERS, DEALERS, AND SALESMEN

Article   Section
1. Issuance of Licenses and Certificates to Manufacturers, Transporters, and Dealers 11700
2. Vehicle Salespersons 11800
3. Representatives 11900

ARTICLE 1. ISSUANCE OF LICENSES AND CERTIFICATES TO MANUFACTURERS, TRANSPORTERS, AND DEALERS

Section
11700.   License or temporary permit.
11700.1.   Out of state dealer exemption; limitation on scope
            of business in state.
11700.2.   Autobroker's endorsement; dealer licensing, ad-
            vertising, and other statutory and regulatory
            requirements and prohibitions.
11700.3.   Aiding and abetting.
11701.   Application for license.
11702.   Issuance or refusal of license.
11703.   Refusal to issue; grounds.
11703.1.   Additional grounds for refusal.
11703.2.   Refusal to issue license; unsatisfied final judgment
            or restitution order.
11703.3.   Reapplication after revocation or denial; time.
11703.4.   Additional grounds for refusal.
11704.   Application for license; information; investigation
            of applicant; notice of ownership or corporate
            structure change.
11704.5.   License examination requirement; contents; pre-
            liminary educational program; application of
            section.
11704.6.   Repealed.
11704.7.   Examination fee.
11705.   Suspension or revocation.
11705.2.   Repealed.
11705.4.   Suspension or revocation; violation of warranty
            responsibilities.
11705.5.   Repealed.
11706.   Temporary suspension.
11707.   Filing of accusation; compromise settlement
            agreement; terms and conditions.
11708.   Refusal to issue license and special plates; hear-
            ings.
11709.   Display of license by dealers; requirements.
11709.1.   Notice; right of inspection.
11709.2.   Vehicle lease or purchase contract; notice; cool-
            ing–off period.
11709.3.   Automobile dealers; clear and conspicuous display
            of vehicle for sale; requirements.
11709.4.   Purchase or obtaining of vehicle subject to prior
            credit or lease balance; payment of prior obli-
            gation; sale, consignment or other transfer;
            prior good faith notice of rescission of contract.
11709.5.   Repealed.
11710.   Bond; service of process.
11710.1.   Amount of bond; certain wholesale dealers.
11710.2.   Refund of deposits; grounds for orders; attorney
            fees and costs for actions.
11710.5.   Repealed.
11711.   Fraud and other violations of law; failure to pay
            for vehicles; priority of claims.
11711.3.   Unlicensed dealers and lessor-retailers; enforce-
            ability of security interest and other actions.
11712.   Change of established place of business; service of
            administrative process.
11712.5.   Motorcycle and light duty truck sales; required
            price information.
11713.   Unlawful acts.
11713.05.   Inoperative.
11713.1.   Additional violations.
11713.2.   Additional unlawful acts; coercion or attempted
            coercion of dealer.
11713.3.   Additional unlawful acts; direct actions and indi-
            rect actions through affiliate.
11713.4.   Refund of excess fees by dealer.
11713.5.   Unlawful representation of vehicle model year;
            housecars; applicability of section.
11713.6.   Tire chains; vehicles which may not be operated
            with chains; disclosures to buyers and lessees.
11713.7.   Remanufactured vehicles; disclosure methods.
11713.8.   Remanufacturers; illegalities and code violations.
11713.9.   Unlabeled engine where manufacturer of engine
            and vehicle differ; offer of vehicle for sale.
11713.10.   Low-speed vehicles; sale; disclosure of risks.
11713.11.   Auctions; advertisements; identification of vehi-
            cles; costs included in price; buyer's fee.
11713.12.   Affixation of "Lemon Law Buyback" decal.
11713.13.   Additional unlawful acts.
11713.14.   Auctions; rights and remedies of purchasers.
11713.15.   Temporary branch license to sell new recreational
            vehicles; manufacturer's written authorization.
11713.16.   Additional violations; advertising.
11713.17.   Conditions allowing dealer to deliver motor vehicle
            following retail sale or lease of motor vehicle for
            which department issues two license plates.
11713.18.   Advertisement of used vehicle as certified.
11713.19.   Disclosure of additional charges for goods or
            services.
11713.20.   Consumer credit score obtained by a dealer; infor-
            mation to be provided to the consumer.
11713.21.   Contract cancellation option agreement required;
            exceptions; purchase price; form; cancellation
            procedures.
11713.22.   Recreational vehicle franchises.
11713.23.   Sale or shipment of new recreational vehicles;
            recreational vehicle franchise required; invento-
            ry; application.
11713.25.   Computer vendors; consent required from dealer
            to access, modify, or extract information from
            confidential dealer computer records or person-
            ally identifiable consumer data; dealer right to
            revoke consent.
11713.26.   Used vehicles; NMVTIS vehicle history report
            required; requirements for junk or salvage auto-
            mobiles; exceptions.
11714.   Issuance of license; posting at sales location;
            wholesale dealers; special plates.
11715.   Operation of vehicles displaying special plates.
11716.   When a vehicle may be operated without plates.
11717.   Expiration of occupational licenses and special
            plates.

Section
11717.1. Repealed.
11718. Issuance of probationary license.
11719. Temporary permit.
11720. Certificate of convenience.
11721. Automatic cancellation.
11722. Claims against surety on dealer's bond of a financing agency.
11723. License fees; additional fees.
11724. Repossession of vehicle connected with incident of violence notice; notice to subsequent assignee.
11725. Transfer of motor vehicles to foreign jurisdictions for registration or sale; removal and delivery of license plates to state; misdemeanor.
11726. Recovery of damages; injunctive relief.
11727. Revocation or suspension of license.
11728. Penalties.
11729. Consignment agreements.
11730. Contents of consignment agreement.
11735. Dealer; autobroker's endorsement; log; required information; fiduciary duty.
11736. Retail sale brokering; unlawful acts.
11737. Dealer-brokered motor vehicle sale; purchase money deposit into trust account; management.
11738. Brokering agreement; contents.
11739. Brokered retail new motor vehicle sale; title registration, warranties, rebates, and incentives; dealer's duties.
11740. Remedies and penalties; cumulative effect.

Cross References

Administrative decisions rendered against licensees under this Article, restitution, see Government Code § 11519.1.

Advisory safety equipment maintenance check, exclusion, see Health and Safety Code § 44018.

Mobilehomes, listing or showing by ownership or management, see Civil Code §§ 798.71, 799.2.

Motorized bicycle dealer, manufacturer, salesperson, or representative, application of chapter, see Vehicle Code § 5039.

Off-highway vehicles, special plates or permit, see Vehicle Code § 38021.

Use and display on vehicles of copies of report of sale form and identification devices, see Vehicle Code § 38080.

§ 11700. License or temporary permit

No person shall act as a dealer, remanufacturer, manufacturer, or transporter, or as a manufacturer branch, remanufacturer branch, distributor, or distributor branch, without having first been issued a license as required in Section 11701 or temporary permit issued by the department, except that, when the license or temporary permit has been canceled, suspended, or revoked or has expired, any vehicle in the dealer's inventory and owned by the dealer when the dealer ceased to be licensed may be sold at wholesale to a licensed dealer. The former licensee shall give the purchasing dealer a statement of facts stating that the seller is not a licensed dealer. Any vehicle on consignment with the dealer when the dealer ceased to be licensed shall be returned to the consignor. Any vehicle in the dealer's possession, but not owned by the dealer and not on consignment when the dealer ceased to be licensed, shall be returned to the owner of the vehicle. (Stats.1959, c. 3, p. 1605, § 11700.

358

Amended by Stats.1967, c. 557, p. 1906, § 2; Stats.1971, c. 1214, p. 2347, § 21, operative May 3, 1972; Stats.1973, c. 996, p. 1972, § 20, operative July 1, 1974; Stats.1975, c. 182, p. 533, § 15, eff. July 5, 1975; Stats.1976, c. 619, p. 1470, § 4; Stats.1977, c. 105, p. 536, § 2; Stats.1983, c. 1286, § 24; Stats.1990, c. 1563 (A.B.3243), § 38.)

Cross References

Definitions,
  Dealer, see Vehicle Code §§ 285, 286.
  Department, see Vehicle Code § 290.
  Person, see Vehicle Code § 470.
Violation as misdemeanor, punishment, see Vehicle Code §§ 40000.11, 42002.

§ 11700.1. Out of state dealer exemption; limitation on scope of business in state

A dealer who does not have an established place of business in this state but who is currently authorized to do business as, and who has an established place of business as, a vehicle dealer in another state is not subject to licensure under this article if the business transacted in California is limited to the importation of vehicles for sale to, or the export of vehicles purchased from, persons licensed in California under this chapter. (Added by Stats.1979, c. 1088, p. 3937, § 3, eff. Sept. 28, 1979.)

§ 11700.2. Autobroker's endorsement; dealer licensing, advertising, and other statutory and regulatory requirements and prohibitions

A dealer who obtains an autobroker's endorsement to his or her dealer's license is subject to all of the licensing, advertising, and other statutory and regulatory requirements and prohibitions applicable to a dealer, regardless of whether that dealer acts as the buyer of a vehicle, the seller of a vehicle, or provides brokering services on behalf of another or others for the purpose of arranging, negotiating, assisting, or effectuating the sale of a vehicle not owned by that dealer. (Added by Stats.1995, c. 211 (A.B.770), § 4.)

§ 11700.3. Aiding and abetting

No person may aid and abet a person in the performance of any act in violation of this chapter. (Added by Stats.2002, c. 407 (S.B.91), § 1.)

§ 11701. Application for license

Every manufacturer, manufacturer branch, remanufacturer, remanufacturer branch, distributor, distributor branch, transporter, or dealer of vehicles of a type subject to registration, or snowmobiles, motorcycles, all-terrain vehicles, or trailers of a type subject to identification, shall make application to the department for a license containing a general distinguishing number. The applicant shall submit proof of his or her status as a bona fide manufacturer, manufacturer branch, remanufacturer, remanufacturer branch, distributor, distributor branch, transporter, or dealer as may reasonably be required by the department. (Stats.1959, c. 3, p. 1605, § 11701. Amended by Stats.1970, c. 1290, p. 2385, § 2; Stats.1971, *c. 1214, p. 2348, § 22, operative May 3, 1972; Stats.1973, c. 996, p. 1972, § 21, operative July 1, 1974; Stats.1975, c. 182, p. 533, § 16, eff. July 5, 1975; Stats.1979, c. 622, p. 1941, § 5; Stats.1983, c. 1286, § 25; Stats.2002, c. 758 (A.B.3024), § 9; Stats.2003, c. 62 (S.B.600), § 303; Stats. 2004, c. 836 (A.B.2848), § 8.)*

Cross References

Definitions,
  Dealer, see Vehicle Code §§ 285, 286.
  Snowmobile, see Vehicle Code § 557.
  Transporter, see Vehicle Code § 645.
  Vehicle, see Vehicle Code § 670.
Vehicles subject to registration, see Vehicle Code § 4000 et seq.

§ 11702. Issuance or refusal of license

The department may issue, or for reasonable cause shown, refuse to issue a license to any applicant applying for a manufacturer's, manufacturer's branch, remanufacturer's, remanufacturer's branch, distributor's, distributor's branch, transporter's, or dealer's license. *(Stats. 1959, c.-3, p. 1605, § 11702. Amended by Stats.1971, c. 1214, p. 2348, § 23, operative May 3, 1972; Stats.1973, c. 996, p. 1972, § 22, operative July 1, 1974; Stats.1974, c. 384, p. 956, § 10, eff. July 5, 1974, operative July 1, 1974; Stats.1975, c. 182, p. 533, § 17, eff. July 5, 1975; Stats. 1983, c. 1286, § 26.)*

§ 11703. Refusal to issue; grounds

The department may refuse to issue a license to a manufacturer, manufacturer branch, remanufacturer, re-manufacturer branch, distributor, distributor branch, transporter, or dealer, if it determines any of the following:

(a) The applicant was previously the holder, or a managerial employee of the holder, of a license issued under this chapter which was revoked for cause and never reissued by the department, or which was suspended for cause and the terms of suspension have not been fulfilled.

(b) The applicant was previously a business representative of a business whose license issued under this chapter was revoked for cause and never reissued or was suspended for cause and the terms of suspension have not been fulfilled.

(c) If the applicant is a business, a business representative of the business was previously the holder of a license, or was a business representative of a business whose license, issued under this chapter was revoked for cause and never reissued or was suspended for cause and the terms of suspension have not been fulfilled; or, by reason of the facts and circumstances related to the organization, control, and management of the business, the operation of that business will be directed, controlled, or managed by individuals who, by reason of their conviction of violations of the provisions of this code, would be ineligible for a license and, by licensing the business, the purposes of this chapter would be defeated.

(d) The applicant, or a business representative if the applicant is a business, has been convicted of a crime or

committed an act or engaged in conduct involving moral turpitude which is substantially related to the qualifications, functions, or duties of the licensed activity. A conviction after a plea of nolo contendere is a conviction within the meaning of this section.

(e) The applicant was previously the holder of an occupational license issued by another state, authorizing the same or similar activities of a license issued under this division; and that license was revoked or suspended for cause and was never reissued, or was suspended for cause, and the terms of suspension have not been fulfilled.

(f) The information contained in the application is incorrect.

(g) Upon investigation, the business history required by Section 11704 contains incomplete or incorrect information, or reflects substantial business irregularities.

(h) A decision of the department to cancel, suspend, or revoke a license has been made and the applicant was a business representative of the business regulated under that license.

(i) The applicant has failed to repay the full amount of a claim paid by the Consumer Motor Vehicle Recovery Corporation, plus interest at the rate of 10 percent per annum. The dealer or lessor-retailer's discharge in bankruptcy shall not relieve the dealer or lessor-retailer from the provisions of this subdivision, except to the extent, if any, mandated by bankruptcy law. *(Stats.1959, c. 3, p. 1605, § 11703. Amended by Stats.1959, c. 1996, p. 4623, § 15.8; Stats.1965, c. 1014, p. 2647, § 8; Stats.1968, c. 667, p. 1357, § 5; Stats.1969, c. 240, p. 586, § 2; Stats.1971, c. 1214, p. 2348, § 24, operative May 3, 1972; Stats.1971, c. 1293, p. 2533, § 4, operative May 3, 1972; Stats.1973, c. 996, p. 1973, § 23, operative July 1, 1974; Stats.1974, c. 1034, p. 2233, § 1; Stats.1975, c. 182, p. 533, § 18, eff. July 5, 1975; Stats.1975, c. 1248, p. 3214, § 4.2; Stats.1982, c. 791, p. 2555, § 2; Stats.1983, c. 1286, § 27; Stats.1990, c. 1563 (A.B.3243), § 39; Stats.1998, c. 877 (A.B.2132), § 50; Stats.2007, c. 437 (S.B.729), § 4.)*

Cross References

Grounds for refusal to issue lessor-retailer license, see Vehicle Code § 11604.

§ 11703.1. Additional grounds for refusal

Any of the causes specified in this chapter as a cause to suspend or revoke the license issued to a dealer, manufacturer, manufacturer branch, remanufacturer, remanufacturer branch, distributor, distributor branch, or transporter, is cause to refuse to issue a license to a dealer, manufacturer, manufacturer branch, remanufacturer, re-manufacturer branch, distributor, distributor branch, or transporter. *(Added by Stats.1968, c. 667, p. 1358, § 5.5. Amended by Stats.1971, c. 1214, p. 2349, § 25, operative May 3, 1972; Stats.1973, c. 996, p. 1973, § 24, operative July 1, 1974; Stats.1975, c. 182, p. 534, § 19, eff. July 5, 1975; Stats.1983, c. 1286, § 28; Stats.1990, c. 1563 (A.B.3243), § 40.)*

§ 11703.2. Refusal to issue license; unsatisfied final judgment or restitution order

The department may refuse to issue a license to a manufacturer, manufacturer branch, remanufacturer, remanufacturer branch, distributor, distributor branch, transporter, or dealer, when the department determines that either of the following apply to the applicant:

(a) An outstanding and unsatisfied final judgment rendered against the applicant exists in connection with the purchase, sale, or lease of any vehicle.

(b) An outstanding and unsatisfied restitution order issued against the applicant under subdivision (a) of Section 11519.1 of the Government Code exists. *(Added by Stats.1975, c. 891, p. 1971, § 1, operative July 1, 1976. Amended by Stats.1983, c. 1286, § 29; Stats.2007, c. 93 (S.B.525), § 2.)*

§ 11703.3. Reapplication after revocation or denial; time

A person whose license has been revoked or whose application for a license has been denied may reapply for a license after a period of not less than one year has elapsed from the effective date of the decision revoking the license or denying the application; except that if the decision was entered under the authority of subdivision (a), (b), (c), or (g) of Section 11703, or 11703.2, or paragraph (6) of subdivision (a) of Section 11705, a reapplication accompanied by evidence satisfactory to the department that such grounds no longer exist may be made earlier than such one-year period. *(Added by Stats.1975, c. 891, p. 1972, § 2, operative July 1, 1976. Amended by Stats.1976, c. 934, p. 2138, § 2.)*

§ 11703.4. Additional grounds for refusal

The department may refuse to issue a license to a dealer when it determines that an applicant for a dealer's license has failed to effectively endorse an authorization for disclosure of an account or accounts relating to the operation of the dealership as provided for in Section 7473 of the Government Code. *(Added by Stats.1976, c. 1320, p. 2138, § 10.)*

Cross References

California Right to Financial Privacy Act, see Government Code § 7460 et seq.

§ 11704. Application for license; information; investigation of applicant; notice of ownership or corporate structure change

(a) Every applicant who applies for a license pursuant to Section 11701 shall submit an application to the department on the forms prescribed by the department. Such applicant shall provide the department with information as to the applicant's character, honesty, integrity, and reputation, as the department may consider necessary. The department, by regulation, shall prescribe what information is required of such an applicant for the purposes of this subdivision.

(b) Upon receipt of an application for a license which is accompanied by the appropriate fee, the department shall, within 120 days, make a thorough investigation of the information contained in the application.

(c) Every person holding a license issued pursuant to Section 11701 shall notify the department, within 10 days, of any change in the ownership or corporate structure of the licensee. *(Added by Stats.1977, c. 452, p. 1488, § 5.)*

§ 11704.5. License examination requirement; contents; preliminary educational program; application of section

(a) Except as provided in subdivision (e), every person who applies for a dealer's license pursuant to Section 11701 for the purpose of transacting sales of used vehicles on a retail or wholesale basis only shall be required to take and successfully complete a written examination prepared and administered by the department before a license may be issued. The examination shall include, but need not be limited to, all of the following laws and subjects:

(1) Division 12 (commencing with Section 24000), relating to equipment of vehicles.

(2) Advertising.

(3) Odometers.

(4) Vehicle licensing and registration.

(5) Branch locations.

(6) Offsite sales.

(7) Unlawful dealer activities.

(8) Handling, completion, and disposition of departmental forms.

(b) Prior to the first taking of an examination under subdivision (a), every applicant shall successfully complete a preliminary educational program of not less than four hours. The program shall address, but not be limited to, all of the following topics:

(1) Chapter 2B (commencing with Section 2981) of Title 14 of Part 4 of Division 3 of the Civil Code, relating to motor vehicle sales finance.

(2) Motor vehicle financing.

(3) Truth in lending.

(4) Sales and use taxes.

(5) Division 12 (commencing with Section 24000), relating to equipment of vehicles.

(6) Advertising.

(7) Odometers.

(8) Vehicle licensing and registration.

(9) Branch locations.

(10) Offsite sales.

(11) Unlawful dealer activities.

(12) Air pollution control requirements.

(13) Regulations of the Bureau of Automotive Repair.

(14) Handling, completion, and disposition of departmental forms.

(c)(1) Except as provided in paragraph (2) or (3), every dealer who is required to complete a written examination and an educational program pursuant to subdivisions (a) and (b) and who is thereafter issued a dealer's license shall successfully complete, every two years after issuance of that license, an educational program of not less than four hours that offers instruction in the subjects listed under subdivision (a) and the topics listed under subdivision (b), in order to maintain or renew that license.

(2) A dealer is not required to complete the educational program set forth in paragraph (1) if the educational program is completed by a managerial employee employed by the dealer.

(3) Paragraph (1) does not apply to dealers who sell vehicles on a wholesale basis only and who, in a one-year period, deal with less than 50 vehicles that are subject to registration.

(d) Instruction described in subdivisions (b) and (c) may be provided by generally accredited educational institutions, private vocational schools, and educational programs and seminars offered by professional societies, organizations, trade associations, and other educational and technical programs that meet the requirements of this section or by the department.

(e) This section does not apply to any of the following:

(1) An applicant for a new vehicle dealer's license or any employee of that dealer.

(2) A person who holds a valid license as an automobile dismantler, an employee of that dismantler, or an applicant for an automobile dismantler's license.

(3) An applicant for a motorcycle only dealer's license or any employee of that dealer.

(4) An applicant for a trailer only dealer's license or any employee of that dealer.

(5) An applicant for an all-terrain only dealer's license or any employee of that dealer. *(Added by Stats.1996, c. 1008 (A.B.2367), § 3. Amended by Stats.1997, c. 619 (S.B.506), § 10; Stats.1999, c. 230 (A.B.159), § 1; Stats. 2000, c. 221 (A.B.2807), § 1; Stats.2001, c. 93 (S.B.1100), § 1; Stats.2004, c. 836 (A.B.2848), § 9.)*

§ 11704.6. Repealed by Stats.1984, c. 1342, § 27, eff. Sept. 26, 1984, operative Jan. 1, 1985

§ 11704.7. Examination fee

Every person who applies to the department to take or retake the examination required under Section 11704.5 shall pay to the department a fee of sixteen dollars ($16). *(Added by Stats.1996, c. 1008 (A.B.2367), § 4.)*

§ 11705. Suspension or revocation

(a) The department, after notice and hearing, may suspend or revoke the license issued to a dealer, transporter, manufacturer, manufacturer branch, remanufacturer, remanufacturer branch, distributor, or distributor branch upon determining that the person to whom the license was issued is not lawfully entitled thereto, or has done any of the following:

(1) Filed an application for the license using a false or fictitious name not registered with the proper authorities, or knowingly made a false statement or knowingly concealed a material fact, in the application for the license.

(2) Made, or knowingly or negligently permitted, an illegal use of the special plates issued to the licensee.

(3) Used a false or fictitious name, knowingly made a false statement, or knowingly concealed a material fact, in an application for the registration of a vehicle, or otherwise committed a fraud in the application.

(4) Failed to deliver to a transferee lawfully entitled thereto a properly endorsed certificate of ownership.

(5) Knowingly purchased, sold, or otherwise acquired or disposed of a stolen motor vehicle.

(6) Failed to provide and maintain a clear physical division between the type of business licensed pursuant to this chapter and any other type of business conducted at the established place of business.

(7) Willfully violated Section 3064 or 3065 or any rule or regulation adopted pursuant thereto.

(8) Violated any provision of Division 3 (commencing with Section 4000) or any rule or regulation adopted pursuant thereto, or subdivision (a) of Section 38200.

(9) Violated any provision of Division 4 (commencing with Section 10500) or any rule or regulation adopted pursuant thereto.

(10) Violated any provision of Article 1 (commencing with Section 11700) of Chapter 4 of Division 5 or any rule or regulation adopted pursuant thereto.

(11) Violated any provision of Part 5 (commencing with Section 10701) of Division 2 of the Revenue and Taxation Code or any rule or regulation adopted pursuant thereto.

(12) Violated any provision of Chapter 2b (commencing with Section 2981) of Title 14 of Part 4 of Division 3 of the Civil Code or any rule or regulation adopted pursuant thereto.

(13) Submitted a check, draft, or money order to the department for any obligation or fee due the state which was dishonored or refused payment upon presentation.

(14) Has caused any person to suffer any loss or damage by reason of any fraud or deceit practiced on that person or fraudulent representations made to that person in the course of the licensed activity.

For purposes of this paragraph, "fraud" includes any act or omission which is included within the definition of either "actual fraud" or "constructive fraud" as defined in Sections 1572 and 1573 of the Civil Code, and "deceit" has the same meaning as defined in Section 1710 of the

Civil Code. In addition, "fraud" and " deceit" include, but are not limited to, a misrepresentation in any manner, whether intentionally false or due to gross negligence, of a material fact; a promise or representation not made honestly and in good faith; an intentional failure to disclose a material fact; and any act within Section 484 of the Penal Code.

For purposes of this paragraph, "person" also includes a governmental entity.

(15) Failed to meet the terms and conditions of an agreement entered into pursuant to Section 11707.

(16) Violated Section 43151, 43152, or 43153 of, or subdivision (b) of Section 44072.10 of, the Health and Safety Code.

(17) Failed to repay a claim paid by the Consumer Motor Vehicle Recovery Corporation as provided in subdivision (i) of Section 11703.

(b) Any of the causes specified in this chapter as a cause for refusal to issue a license to a transporter, manufacturer, manufacturer branch, remanufacturer, re-manufacturer branch, distributor, distributor branch, or dealer applicant is cause to suspend or revoke a license issued to a transporter, manufacturer, manufacturer branch, remanufacturer, remanufacturer branch, distributor, distributor branch, or dealer.

(c) Except as provided in Section 11707, every hearing provided for in this section shall be conducted pursuant to Chapter 5 (commencing with Section 11500) of Part 1 of Division 3 of Title 2 of the Government Code. *(Stats.1959, c. 3, p. 1607, § 11705. Amended by Stats. 1960, 1st Ex.Sess., c. 35, p. 380, § 3; Stats.1963, c. 1863, p. 3846, § 3; Stats.1965, c. 1014, p. 2648, § 9; Stats.1967, c. 475, p. 1681, § 2; Stats.1968, c. 1021, p. 1972, § 1; Stats.1969, c. 240, p. 587, § 3; Stats.1970, c. 1106, p. 1970, § 3; Stats.1971, c. 708, p. 1372, § 1, operative May 3, 1972; Stats.1973, c. 66, p. 108, § 1; Stats.1973, c. 996, p. 1975, § 26, operative July 1, 1974; Stats.1974, c. 384, p. 957, § 12, eff. July 5, 1974, operative July 1, 1974; Stats.1974, c. 1025, p. 2224, § 1; Stats.1974, c. 1034, p. 2234, § 2; Stats.1974, c. 1286, p. 2792, § 2, operative July 1, 1975; Stats.1975, c. 182, p. 534, § 20, eff. July 5, 1975, operative July 1, 1975; Stats.1976, c. 619, p. 1470, § 5; Stats.1982, c. 791, p. 3066, § 3; Stats.1983, c. 1286, § 30; Stats.1984, c. 1342, § 28, eff. Sept. 26, 1984, operative Jan. 1, 1985; Stats.1985, c. 1235, § 6; Stats.1990, c. 1563 (A.B.3243), § 41; Stats.1994, c. 1220 (A.B.3132), § 56, eff. Sept. 30, 1994; Stats.2007, c. 437 (S.B.729), § 5.)*

§ 11705.2. Repealed by Stats.1984, c. 1342, § 29, eff. Sept. 26, 1984, operative Jan. 1, 1985

§ 11705.4. Suspension or revocation; violation of warranty responsibilities

(a) The department, after notice and hearing, may suspend or revoke the license issued to a dealer, transporter, manufacturer, manufacturer branch, distributor, or distributor branch upon determining that the person to whom the license was issued is not lawfully entitled

362

thereto or has willfully violated the terms and conditions of any warranty responsibilities as set forth in Title 1.7 (commencing with Section 1790) of Part 4 of Division 3 of the Civil Code.

(b) Every hearing as provided for in this section shall be pursuant to the provisions of Chapter 5 (commencing with Section 11500) of Part 1 of Division 3 of Title 2 of the Government Code. *(Added by Stats.1975, c. 891, p. 1972, § 3, operative July 1, 1976. Amended by Stats.1977, c. 873, p. 2634, § 3.)*

§ 11705.5. Repealed by Stats.2004, c. 615 (S.B.1233), § 25

§ 11706. Temporary suspension

The department may, pending a hearing, temporarily suspend the license and special plates issued to a manufacturer, manufacturer branch, remanufacturer, re-manufacturer branch, distributor, distributor branch, transporter, or dealer, for a period not to exceed 30 days, if the director finds that such action is required in the public interest. In any such case, a hearing shall be held and a decision thereon issued within 30 days after notice of the temporary suspension.

Every hearing, as provided for in this section, shall be conducted pursuant to Chapter 5 (commencing with Section 11500) of Part 1 of Division 3 of Title 2 of the Government Code. *(Stats.1959, c. 3, p. 1607, § 11706. Amended by Stats.1968, c. 667, p. 1358, § 6; Stats.1971, c. 1214, p. 2350, § 28, operative May 3, 1972; Stats.1973, c. 996, p. 1976, § 27, operative July 1, 1974; Stats.1983, c. 1286, § 32.)*

§ 11707. Filing of accusation; compromise settlement agreement; terms and conditions

(a) After the filing of an accusation under this article, the director may enter into a stipulated compromise settlement agreement with the consent of the licensee on terms and conditions mutually agreeable to the director, the respondent licensee, and the accuser without further hearing or appeal. The agreement may include, but is not limited to, a period of probation or monetary penalties, or both. Except as provided in Section 11728, the monetary penalty shall not exceed one thousand dollars ($1,000) for each violation, and it shall be based on the nature of the violation and the effect of the violation on the purposes of this article.

(b) A compromise settlement agreement may be entered before, during, or after the hearing, but is valid only if executed and filed pursuant to subdivision (d) before the proposed decision of the hearing officer, if any, is adopted or the case is decided.

(c) The department shall adopt, by regulation, a schedule of maximum and minimum amounts of monetary penalties, the payment of which may be included as a term or condition of a compromise settlement agreement entered under subdivision (a). Any monetary penalty included in a compromise settlement agreement shall be within the range of monetary penalties in that schedule.

(d) Any compromise settlement agreement entered under this section shall be signed by the director, the respondent licensee, and the accuser, or by their authorized representatives. The director shall file, or cause to be filed, the agreement with the Office of Administrative Hearings, together with the department's notice of withdrawal of the accusation or statement of issues upon which the action was initiated.

(e) If the respondent licensee fails to perform all of the terms and conditions of the compromise settlement agreement, the agreement is void and the department may take any action authorized by law, notwithstanding the agreement, including, but not limited to, refiling the accusation or imposing license sanctions. *(Added by Stats.1985, c. 1022, § 20. Amended by Stats.1990, c. 90 (A.B.2445), § 3, eff. May 9, 1990.)*

§ 11708. Refusal to issue license and special plates; hearings

(a) Upon refusal of the department to issue a license and special plates to a manufacturer, manufacturer branch, remanufacturer, remanufacturer branch, distributor, distributor branch, transporter, or dealer, the applicant shall be entitled to demand, in writing, a hearing before the director or his or her representative within 60 days after notice of refusal.

(b) The hearing shall be conducted pursuant to Chapter 5 (commencing with Section 11500) of Part 1 of Division 3 of Title 2 of the Government Code. *(Stats. 1959, c. 3, p. 1607, § 11708. Amended by Stats.1971, c. 1214, p. 2350, § 29, operative May 3, 1972; Stats.1973, c. 996, p. 1976, § 28, operative July 1, 1974; Stats.1983, c. 1286, § 33.)*

§ 11709. Display of license by dealers; requirements

(a) A dealer's established place of business, and other sites or locations as may be operated and maintained by the dealer in conjunction with his or her established place of business, shall have posted, in a place conspicuous to the public in each and every location, the license, or a true and exact copy of the license, issued by the department to the dealer and to each salesperson employed by the dealer and shall have erected or posted thereon signs or devices providing information relating to the dealer's name and the location and address of the dealer's established place of business to enable any person doing business with the dealer to identify him or her properly. A sign erected or posted pursuant to this subdivision, on an established place of business, shall have an area of not less than two square feet per side displayed and shall contain lettering of sufficient size to enable the sign to be read from a distance of at least 50 feet. This section shall not apply to a dealer who is a wholesaler involved for profit only in the sale of vehicles between licensed dealers.

(b) Notwithstanding Section 11704 and this section, a dealer may display vehicles at a fair, exposition, or similar exhibit without securing a branch license, if no actual sales are made at those events and the display does not exceed 30 days.

(c) A vehicle displayed pursuant to subdivision (b) or (e) shall be identified by a sign or device providing information relating to the dealer's name and the location and address of the dealer's established place of business.

(d) This section shall not be applicable to a dealer who deals only in off-highway vehicles subject to identification, as defined in Section 38012.

(e) Notwithstanding Section 11704 and this section, a vessel dealer may display a trailer and may sell a trailer in conjunction with the sale of a vessel at a fair, exposition, or similar exhibit without securing a branch license if the display does not exceed 30 days. *(Stats.1959, c. 3, p. 1607, § 11709. Amended by Stats.1965, c. 319, p. 1419, § 1; Stats.1970, c. 1290, p. 2385, § 3; Stats.1971, c. 212, p. 2350, § 2, operative May 3, 1972; Stats.1971, c. 1214, p. 2350, § 30, operative May 3, 1972; Stats.1973, c. 331, p. 751, § 1; Stats.1977, c. 94, p. 515, § 1; Stats.1978, c. 638, p. 2098, § 3; Stats.1979, c. 622, p. 1942, § 7; Stats.1981, c. 665, p. 2448, § 2; Stats.1984, c. 1342, § 31, eff. Sept. 26, 1984, operative Jan. 1, 1985; Stats.1989, c. 147, § 1; Stats.2010, c. 483 (S.B.1004), § 1.)*

§ 11709.1. Notice; right of inspection

Every dealer who displays or offers one or more used vehicles for sale at retail shall post a notice not less than 8 inches high and 10 inches wide, in a place conspicuous to the public, which states the following:

"The prospective purchaser of a vehicle may, at his or her own expense and with the approval of the dealer, have the vehicle inspected by an independent third party either on or off these premises." *(Added by Stats.1990, c. 1563 (A.B.3243), § 42.)*

§ 11709.2. Vehicle lease or purchase contract; notice; cooling–off period

Every dealer shall conspicuously display a notice, not less than eight inches high and 10 inches wide, in each sales office and sales cubicle of a dealer's established place of business where written terms of specific sale or lease transactions are discussed with prospective purchasers or lessees, and in each room of a dealer's established place of business where sale and lease contracts are regularly executed, which states the following:

"THERE IS NO COOLING–OFF PERIOD
UNLESS YOU OBTAIN A CONTRACT
CANCELLATION OPTION

California law does not provide for a "cooling-off" or other cancellation period for vehicle lease or purchase contracts. Therefore, you cannot later cancel such a contract simply because you change your mind, decide the vehicle costs too much, or wish you had acquired a different vehicle. After you sign a motor vehicle pur-

363

chase or lease contract, it may only be canceled with the agreement of the seller or lessor or for legal cause, such as fraud.

However, California law does require a seller to offer a 2–day contract cancellation option on used vehicles with a purchase price of less than $40,000, subject to certain statutory conditions. This contract cancellation option requirement does not apply to the sale of a recreational vehicle, a motorcycle, or an off-highway motor vehicle subject to identification under California law. See the vehicle contract cancellation option agreement for details." *(Added by Stats.1993, c. 1092 (A.B.431), § 5, operative July 1, 1994. Amended by Stats.1994, c. 146 (A.B.3601), § 221; Stats.2005, c. 128 (A.B.68), § 7, operative July 1, 2006; Stats.2006, c. 567 (A.B.2303), § 24.)*

§ 11709.3. Automobile dealers; clear and conspicuous display of vehicle for sale; requirements

(a) Every dealer shall clearly and conspicuously display in its showroom at its established place of business, in a place that is easily accessible to prospective purchasers, a clear and conspicuous listing of each vehicle that the dealer has advertised for sale if the vehicle meets all of the following requirements:

(1) The vehicle is advertised for sale in a newspaper or other publication of general circulation, or in any other advertising medium that is disseminated to the public generally, including, but not limited to, radio, television, or the Internet.

(2) The vehicle is advertised at a specific price and is required pursuant to subdivision (a) of Section 11713.1 to be identified in the advertisement by its vehicle identification number or license number.

(3) The vehicle has not been sold or leased during the time that the advertised price is valid.

(4) The vehicle does not clearly and conspicuously have displayed on or in it the advertised price.

(b) The listing required by subdivision (a) may be satisfied by clearly and conspicuously posting in the showroom a complete copy of any print advertisement that includes vehicles currently advertised for sale or by clearly and conspicuously displaying in the showroom a list of currently advertised vehicles described by make, model, model-year, vehicle identification number, or license number, and the advertised price. *(Added by Stats.2001, c. 441 (S.B.481), § 1.)*

§ 11709.4. Purchase or obtaining of vehicle subject to prior credit or lease balance; payment of prior obligation; sale, consignment or other transfer; prior good faith notice of rescission of contract

(a) When a dealer purchases or obtains a vehicle in trade in a retail sale or lease transaction and the vehicle is subject to a prior credit or lease balance, all of the following apply:

(1) If the dealer agreed to pay a specified amount on the prior credit or lease balance owing on the vehicle purchased or obtained in trade, and the agreement to pay the specified amount is contained in a written agreement documenting the transaction, the dealer shall tender the agreed upon amount as provided in the written agreement to the lessor registered in accordance with Section 4453.5, or to the legal owner reflected on the ownership certificate, or to the designee of that lessor or legal owner of the vehicle purchased or obtained in trade within 21 calendar days of purchasing or obtaining the vehicle in trade.

(2) If the dealer did not set forth an agreement regarding payment of a prior credit or lease balance owed on the vehicle purchased or obtained in trade, in a written agreement documenting the transaction, the dealer shall tender to the lessor registered in accordance with Section 4453.5, or to the legal owner reflected on the ownership certificate, or to the designee of that lessor or legal owner of the vehicle purchased or obtained in trade, an amount necessary to discharge the prior credit or lease balance owing on the vehicle purchased or obtained in trade within 21 calendar days of purchasing or obtaining the vehicle in trade.

(3) The time period specified in paragraph (1) or (2) may be shortened if the dealer and consumer agree, in writing, to a shorter time period.

(4) A dealer shall not sell, consign for sale, or transfer any ownership interest in the vehicle purchased or obtained in trade until an amount necessary to discharge the prior credit or lease balance owing on the vehicle has been tendered to the lessor registered in accordance with Section 4453.5, or to the legal owner reflected on the ownership certificate, or to the designee of that lessor or legal owner of the vehicle purchased or obtained in trade.

(b) A dealer does not violate this section if the dealer reasonably and in good faith gives notice of rescission of the contract promptly, but no later than 21 days after the date on which the vehicle was purchased or obtained in trade, and the contract is thereafter rescinded on any of the grounds in Section 1689 of the Civil Code. *(Added by Stats.2009, c. 556 (S.B.95), § 5. Amended by Stats.2010, c. 328 (S.B.1330), § 228.)*

§ 11709.5. Repealed by Stats.1984, c. 1342, § 32, eff. Sept. 26, 1984, operative Jan. 1, 1985

§ 11710. Bond; service of process

(a) Before any dealer's or remanufacturer's license is issued or renewed by the department to any applicant therefor, the applicant shall procure and file with the department a bond executed by an admitted surety insurer, approved as to form by the Attorney General, and conditioned that the applicant shall not practice any fraud or make any fraudulent representation which will cause a monetary loss to a purchaser, seller, financing agency, or governmental agency.

(b) A dealer's bond shall be in the amount of fifty thousand dollars ($50,000), except the bond of a dealer who deals exclusively in motorcycles or all-terrain vehicles shall be in the amount of ten thousand dollars ($10,000). Before the license is renewed by the department, the dealer, other than a dealer who deals exclusively in motorcycles or all-terrain vehicles, shall procure and file a bond in the amount of fifty thousand dollars ($50,000). A remanufacturer bond shall be in the amount of fifty thousand dollars ($50,000).

(c) Liability under the bond is to remain at full value. If the amount of liability under the bond is decreased or there is outstanding a final court judgment for which the dealer or remanufacturer and sureties are liable, the dealer's or remanufacturer's license shall be automatically suspended. In order to reinstate the license and special plates, the licensee shall either file an additional bond or restore the bond on file to the original amount, or shall terminate the outstanding judgment for which the dealer or remanufacturer and sureties are liable.

(d) A dealer's or remanufacturer's license, or renewal of the license, shall not be issued to any applicant therefor, unless and until the applicant files with the department a good and sufficient instrument, in writing, in which the applicant appoints the director as the true and lawful agent of the applicant upon whom all process may be served in any action, or actions, which may thereafter be commenced against the applicant, arising out of any claim for damages suffered by any firm, person, association, or corporation, by reason of the violation of the applicant of any of the terms and provisions of this code or any condition of the dealer's or remanufacturer's bond. The applicant shall stipulate and agree in the appointment that any process directed to the applicant, when personal service of process upon the applicant cannot be made in this state after due diligence and, in that case, is served upon the director or, in the event of the director's absence from the office, upon any employee in charge of the office of the director, shall be of the same legal force and effect as if served upon the applicant personally. The applicant shall further stipulate and agree, in writing, that the agency created by the appointment shall continue for and during the period covered by any license that may be issued and so long thereafter as the applicant may be made to answer in damages for a violation of this code or any condition of the bond. The instrument appointing the director as the agent for the applicant for service of process shall be acknowledged by the applicant before a notary public. In any case where the licensee is served with process by service upon the director, one copy of the summons and complaint shall be left with the director or in the director's office in Sacramento or mailed to the office of the director in Sacramento. A fee of five dollars ($5) shall also be paid to the director at the time of service of the copy of the summons and complaint. Service on the director shall be a sufficient service on the licensee if a notice of service and a copy of the summons and complaint are immediately sent by registered mail by the plaintiff or the plaintiff's attorney to the licensee. A copy of the summons and complaint shall also be mailed by the plaintiff or the plaintiff's attorney to the surety on the applicant's bond at the address of the surety given in the bond, postpaid and registered with request for return receipt. The director shall keep a record of all process so served upon the director, which record shall show the day and hour of service and shall retain the summons and complaint so served on file. Where the licensee is served with process by service upon the director, the licensee shall have and be allowed 30 days from and after the service within which to answer any complaint or other pleading which may be filed in the cause. However, for purposes of venue, where the licensee is served with process by service upon the director, the service is deemed to have been made upon the licensee in the county in which the licensee has or last had an established place of business. *(Stats.1959, c. 3, p. 1608, § 11710. Amended by Stats.1959, c. 1827, p. 4342, § 6; Stats.1963, c. 660, p. 1649, § 1; Stats.1971, c. 1214, p. 2351, § 31, operative May 3, 1972; Stats.1982, c. 517, p. 2426, § 397; Stats.1983, c. 1286, § 34; Stats.1989, c. 622, § 2; Stats. 2002, c. 303 (S.B.1458), § 1; Stats.2004, c. 836 (A.B. 2848), § 10.)*

Law Revision Commission Comments

1982 Amendment

Section 11710 is amended for consistency with the Bond and Undertaking Law. See Code Civ. Proc. §§ 995.310 (sureties on bond), 995.120 ("admitted surety insurer" defined), 995.710 (deposit in lieu of bond). The other changes in Section 11710 are technical. [16 Cal.L.Rev. Comm. Reports 501(1981)].

Cross References

Attorney General, generally, see Government Code § 12500 et seq.

Automatic cancellation of plates, license and certificate upon failure to procure and file bond upon termination of existing bond, see Vehicle Code § 11721.

Bond and Undertaking Law, see Code of Civil Procedure § 995.010 et seq.

Bond not to protect interest of financing agency loaning money to licensee or assignee, see Vehicle Code § 11722.

§ 11710.1. Amount of bond; certain wholesale dealers

Notwithstanding subdivision (b) of Section 11710, the bond amount of a dealer who sells vehicles on a wholesale basis only, and who sells fewer than 25 vehicles per year, shall be ten thousand dollars ($10,000). *(Added by Stats.2002, c. 1110 (S.B.2073), § 1.)*

§ 11710.2. Refund of deposits; grounds for orders; attorney fees and costs for actions

If a deposit is given instead of the bond required by Section 11710 both of the following apply:

(a)(1) The director may order the deposit returned at the expiration of any of the following dates:

(A) Three years from the date an applicant for a dealer's license who has operated a business of selling vehicles under a temporary permit has ceased to do business.

(B) Three years from the date a licensee has ceased to be licensed, if the director is satisfied that there are no outstanding claims against the deposit.

(C) Five years from the date a licensee secured and maintained a dealer bond, pursuant to Section 11710, after posting a deposit, if the director is satisfied that there are no outstanding claims against the deposit.

(2) A judge of a superior court may order the return of the deposit prior to the expiration of the dates provided in paragraph (1) upon evidence satisfactory to the judge that there are no outstanding claims against the deposit.

(b) If either the director, department, or state is a defendant in any action instituted to recover all or any part of the deposit, or any action is instituted by the director, department, or state to determine those entitled to any part of the deposit, the director, department, or state shall be paid reasonable attorney fees and costs from the deposit. Costs shall include those administrative costs incurred in processing claims against the deposit. *(Added by Stats.1971, c. 846, p. 1679, § 1, operative May 3, 1972. Amended by Stats.1982, c. 517, p. 2427, § 399; Stats.1990, c. 216 (S.B.2510), § 115; Stats. 2002, c. 784 (S.B.1316), § 600; Stats.2010, c. 483 (S.B. 1004), § 2.)*

Law Revision Commission Comments

1982 Amendment

Section 11710.2 is amended to reflect the repeal of Section 11710.1. The other changes in Section 11710.2 are technical. [16 Cal.L.Rev. Comm. Reports 501 (1981)].

2002 Amendment

Subdivision (a) of Section 11710.2 is amended to reflect unification of the municipal and superior courts pursuant to Article VI, Section 5(e), of the California Constitution. [32 Cal.L.Rev.Comm. Reports 541 (2002)].

§ 11710.5. Repealed by Stats.1979, c. 622, p. 1943, § 8

§ 11711. Fraud and other violations of law; failure to pay for vehicles; priority of claims

(a) If any person (1) shall suffer any loss or damage by reason of any fraud practiced on him or fraudulent representation made to him by a licensed dealer or one of such dealer's salesmen acting for the dealer, in his behalf, or within the scope of the employment of such salesman and such person has possession of a written instrument furnished by the licensee, containing stipulated provisions and guarantees which the person believes have been violated by the licensee, or (2) if any person shall suffer any loss or damage by reason of the violation by such dealer or salesman of any of the provisions of Division 3 (commencing with Section 4000) of this code, or (3) if any person is not paid for a vehicle sold to and purchased by a licensee, then any such person shall have a right of action against such dealer, his salesman, and the surety upon the

dealer's bond, in an amount not to exceed the value of the vehicle purchased from or sold to the dealer.

(b) If the state or any political subdivision thereof shall suffer any loss or damage by reason of any fraud practiced on the state or fraudulent representation made to the state by a licensed dealer, or one of such dealer's representatives acting for the dealer, in his behalf, or within the scope of employment of such representatives, or shall suffer any loss or damage by reason of the violation of such dealer or representative of any of the provisions of Division 3 (commencing with Section 4000) of this code, or Part 5 (commencing with Section 10701), Division 2 of the Revenue and Taxation Code, the state or any political subdivision thereof, through the department, shall have a right of action against such dealer, his representative, and the surety upon the dealer's bond in an amount not to exceed the value of the vehicles involved.

(c) The failure of a dealer upon demand to pay the fees and penalties determined to be due as provided in Section 4456 hereof is declared to be a violation of Division 3 (commencing with Section 4000) of this code, and Part 5 (commencing with Section 10701), Division 2 of the Revenue and Taxation Code and to constitute loss or damage to the state in the amounts of such fees and penalties determined to be due and not paid.

(d) The claims of the state under subdivision (b) shall be satisfied first and entitled to preference over all claims under subdivision (a).

(e) The claims of any person under subdivision (a) who is not a licensee shall be satisfied first and entitled to preference over all other claims under subdivision (a). *(Stats.1959, c. 3, p. 1609, § 11711. Amended by Stats. 1959, c. 1827, p. 4344, § 7; Stats.1960, 1st Ex.Sess., c. 35, p. 379, § 1; Stats.1963, c. 1863, p. 3846, § 5; Stats.1972, c. 1106, p. 2114, § 1.)*

Cross References

Damages for fraud,
  Generally, see Civil Code § 1709.
  Exemplary damages, see Civil Code § 3294.
  Interest, see Civil Code § 3288.
  Sale, purchase or exchange of property, see Civil Code § 3343.
"Dealer" defined, see Vehicle Code §§ 285, 286.
False statements, use in documents filed with department, see Vehicle Code § 20.
Fraud, actual and constructive, see Civil Code § 1571 et seq.

§ 11711.3. Unlicensed dealers and lessor-retailers; enforceability of security interest and other actions

A person acting as a dealer, who was not licensed as a dealer as required by this article, or a person acting as a lessor-retailer, who was not licensed as a lessor-retailer as required by Chapter 3.5 (commencing with Section 11600), may not enforce any security interest or bring or maintain any action in law or equity to recover any money or property or obtain other relief from the purchaser or lessee of a vehicle in connection with a transaction in which the person was, at the time of the transaction, required to be licensed as a dealer or a lessor-retailer. *(Added by Stats.2002, c. 407 (S.B.91), § 2. Amended by Stats.2003, c. 62 (S.B.600), § 304.)*

§ 11712. Change of established place of business; service of administrative process

(a) The department shall not issue a dealer's license to any applicant therefor who has not an established place of business as defined in this code. Should the dealer change the site or location of his established place of business, he or she shall, immediately upon making that change, so notify the department. Should a dealer for any reason whatsoever, cease to be in possession of an established place of business from and on which he or she conducts the business for which he or she is licensed, he or she shall immediately notify the department and, upon demand by the department, shall deliver to the department the dealer's license, dealer's special plate or plates, and all report of sale books in his or her possession.

(b) Should the dealer change to, or add another franchise for the sale of new vehicles, or cancel or, for any cause whatever, otherwise lose a franchise for the sale of new vehicles, he or she shall immediately so notify the department.

(c) Any person licensed under this article who has closed his or her established place of business may be served with process issued pursuant to Chapter 5 (commencing with Section 11500) of Part 1 of Division 3 of Title 2 of the Government Code by registered mail at that place of business or at the mailing address of record if different from the established place of business, unless the person has notified the department in writing of another address where service may be made. *(Stats.1959, c. 3, p. 1609, § 11712. Amended by Stats.1971, c. 1214, p. 2352, § 33, operative May 3, 1972; Stats.1982, c. 535, p. 2466, § 2; Stats.1988, c. 751, § 7.)*

Cross References

"Dealer" defined, see Vehicle Code §§ 285, 286.
"Established place of business" defined, see Vehicle Code § 320.
Operation of vehicles displaying special plates, see Vehicle Code § 11715.

§ 11712.5. Motorcycle and light duty truck sales; required price information

It is unlawful and a violation of this code for a dealer issued a license pursuant to this article to sell, offer for sale, or display any new vehicle, as follows:

(a) A new motorcycle unless there is securely attached thereto a statement as required by Section 24014.

(b) A new light duty truck with a manufacturer's gross vehicle weight rating of 8,500 pounds or less unless there is affixed to the light duty truck the label required by Section 24013.5. *(Added by Stats.1974, c. 1089, p. 2315, § 1. Amended by Stats.1987, c. 418, § 1.)*

§ 11713. Unlawful acts

No holder of any license issued under this article shall do any of the following:

(a) Make or disseminate, or cause to be made or disseminated, before the public in this state, in any newspaper or other publication, or any advertising device, or by public outcry or proclamation, or in any other manner or means whatever, any statement which is untrue or misleading and which is known, or which by the exercise of reasonable care should be known, to be untrue or misleading; or to so make or disseminate, or cause to be so disseminated, any statement as part of a plan or scheme with the intent not to sell any vehicle or service so advertised at the price stated therein, or as so advertised.

(b)(1)(A) Advertise or offer for sale or exchange in any manner, any vehicle not actually for sale at the premises of the dealer or available to the dealer directly from the manufacturer or distributor of the vehicle at the time of the advertisement or offer. However, a dealer who has been issued an autobroker's endorsement to his or her dealer's license may advertise his or her service of arranging or negotiating the purchase of a new motor vehicle from a franchised new motor vehicle dealer and may specify the line-makes and models of those new vehicles. Autobrokering service advertisements may not advertise the price or payment terms of any vehicle and shall disclose that the advertiser is an autobroker or auto buying service, and shall clearly and conspicuously state the following: "All new cars arranged for sale are subject to price and availability from the selling franchised new car dealer."

(B) As to printed advertisements, the disclosure statement required by subparagraph (A) shall be printed in not less than 10-point bold type size and shall be textually segregated from the other portions of the printed advertisement.

(2) Notwithstanding subparagraph (A), classified advertisements for autobrokering services that measure two column inches or less are exempt from the disclosure statement in subparagraph (A) pertaining to price and availability.

(3) Radio advertisements of a duration of less than 11 seconds that do not reference specific line-makes or models of motor vehicles are exempt from the disclosure statement required in subparagraph (A).

(c) Fail, within 48 hours, in writing to withdraw any advertisement of a vehicle that has been sold or withdrawn from sale.

(d) Advertise or represent a vehicle as a new vehicle if the vehicle is a used vehicle.

(e) Engage in the business for which the licensee is licensed without having in force and effect a bond as required by this article.

(f) Engage in the business for which the dealer is licensed without at all times maintaining an established place of business as required by this code.

(g) Include, as an added cost to the selling price of a vehicle, an amount for licensing or transfer of title of the vehicle, which is not due to the state unless, prior to the sale, that amount has been paid by a dealer to the state in order to avoid penalties that would have accrued because of late payment of the fees. However, a dealer may collect from the second purchaser of a vehicle a prorated fee based upon the number of months remaining in the registration year for that vehicle, if the vehicle had been previously sold by the dealer and the sale was subsequently rescinded and all the fees that were paid, as required by this code and Chapter 2 (commencing with Section 10751) of Division 2 of the Revenue and Taxation Code, were returned to the first purchaser of the vehicle.

(h) Employ any person as a salesperson who has not been licensed pursuant to Article 2 (commencing with Section 11800), and whose license is not displayed on the premises of the dealer as required by Section 11812, or willfully fail to notify the department by mail within 10 days of the employment or termination of employment of a salesperson.

(i) Deliver, following the sale, a vehicle for operation on California highways, if the vehicle does not meet all of the equipment requirements of Division 12 (commencing with Section 24000). This subdivision does not apply to the sale of a leased vehicle to the lessee if the lessee is in possession of the vehicle immediately prior to the time of the sale and the vehicle is registered in this state.

(j) Use, or permit the use of, the special plates assigned to him or her for any purpose other than as permitted by Section 11715.

(k) Advertise or otherwise represent, or knowingly allow to be advertised or represented on behalf of, or at the place of business of, the licenseholder that no downpayment is required in connection with the sale of a vehicle when a downpayment is in fact required and the buyer is advised or induced to finance the downpayment by a loan in addition to any other loan financing the remainder of the purchase price of the vehicle. The terms "no downpayment," "zero down delivers," or similar terms shall not be advertised unless the vehicle will be sold to any qualified purchaser without a prior payment of any kind or trade-in.

(l) Participate in the sale of a vehicle required to be reported to the Department of Motor Vehicles under Section 5900 or 5901 without making the return and payment of the full sales tax due and required by Section 6451 of the Revenue and Taxation Code.

(m) Permit the use of the dealer's license, supplies, or books by any other person for the purpose of permitting that person to engage in the purchase or sale of vehicles required to be registered under this code, or permit the use of the dealer's license, supplies, or books to operate a branch location to be used by any other person, whether or not the licensee has any financial or equitable interest or investment in the vehicles purchased or sold by, or the business of, or branch location used by, the other person.

368

(n) Violate any provision of Article 10 (commencing with Section 28050) of Chapter 5 of Division 12.

(o) Sell a previously unregistered vehicle without disclosing in writing to the purchaser the date on which any manufacturer's or distributor's warranty commenced.

(p) Accept a purchase deposit relative to the sale of a vehicle, unless the vehicle is present at the premises of the dealer or available to the dealer directly from the manufacturer or distributor of the vehicle at the time the dealer accepts the deposit. Purchase deposits accepted by an autobroker when brokering a retail sale shall be governed by Sections 11736 and 11737.

(q) Consign for sale to another dealer a new vehicle.

(r) Display a vehicle for sale at a location other than an established place of business authorized by the department for that dealer or display a new motor vehicle at the business premises of another dealer registered as an autobroker. This subdivision does not apply to the display of a vehicle pursuant to subdivision (b) of Section 11709 or the demonstration of the qualities of a motor vehicle by way of a test drive.

(s) Use a picture in connection with any advertisement of the price of a specific vehicle or class of vehicles, unless the picture is of the year, make and model being offered for sale. The picture shall not depict a vehicle with optional equipment or a design not actually offered at the advertised price.

(t) Advertise a vehicle for sale that was used by the selling licensee in its business as a demonstrator, executive vehicle, service vehicle, rental, loaner, or lease vehicle, unless the advertisement clearly and conspicuously discloses the previous use made by that licensee of the vehicle. An advertisement shall not describe any of those vehicles as "new." *(Stats.1959, c. 3, p. 1610, § 11713. Amended by Stats.1959, c. 1827, p. 4340, § 1; Stats.1961, c. 58, p. 1007, § 28; Stats.1961, c. 346, p. 1386, § 1; Stats.1961, c. 1626, p. 3541, § 5; Stats.1963, c. 1858, p. 3838, § 11.5, eff. July 19, 1963, operative Oct. 1, 1963; Stats.1967, c. 482, p. 1687, § 3; Stats.1968, c. 1021, p. 1973, § 2; Stats.1970, c. 395, p. 808, § 1; Stats.1970, c. 522, p. 1016, § 2; Stats.1971, c. 1214, p. 2353, § 34, operative May 3, 1972; Stats.1972, c. 475, p. 845, § 1; Stats.1972, c. 799, p. 1422, § 1; Stats.1973, c. 774, p. 1386, § 2, eff. Sept. 25, 1973; Stats.1974, c. 1286, p. 2794, § 3, operative July 1, 1975; Stats.1975, c. 842, p. 1904, § 1; Stats.1975, c. 1248, p. 3217, § 7; Stats.1976, c. 843, p. 1921, § 2; Stats.1977, c. 579, p. 1911, § 181; Stats.1978, c. 797, p. 2563, § 5; Stats.1982, c. 517, p. 2428, § 400; Stats.1982, c. 535, p. 2467, § 3; Stats.1983, c. 18, § 38, eff. April 21, 1983; Stats.1983, c. 1286, § 35; Stats.1984, c. 1342, § 33, eff. Sept. 26, 1984, operative Jan. 1, 1985; Stats.1985, c. 1136, § 1; Stats.1988, c. 1583, § 3; Stats. 1990, c. 89 (A.B.1314), § 1; Stats.1990, c. 1484 (S.B. 2735), § 4; Stats.1990, c. 1563 (A.B.3243), § 43; Stats. 1994, c. 1253 (A.B.3539), § 9; Stats.1995, c. 211 (A.B. 770), § 5; Stats.1995, c. 766 (S.B.726), § 9.5; Stats.1998, c. 517 (S.B.559), § 1; Stats.2002, c. 947 (A.B.2397), § 3.)*

Law Revision Commission Comments

1983 Amendment

Section 11713 is amended for consistency with Section 11710. The other changes in Section 11713 are technical. [16 Cal. L.Rev.Comm. Reports 501 (1981), 2239 (1982)].

Cross References

Advertisement of used vehicle as certified, see Vehicle Code § 11713.18.
"Established place of business" defined, see Vehicle Code § 320.
Violation as misdemeanor, punishment, see Vehicle Code §§ 40000.11, 42002.

§ 11713.05. Inoperative

§ 11713.1. Additional violations

It is a violation of this code for the holder of a dealer's license issued under this article to do any of the following:

(a) Advertise a specific vehicle for sale without identifying the vehicle by its model, model-year, and either its license number or that portion of the vehicle identification number that distinguishes the vehicle from all other vehicles of the same make, model, and model-year. Model-year is not required to be advertised for current model-year vehicles. Year models are no longer current when ensuing year models are available for purchase at retail in California. An advertisement that offers for sale a class of new vehicles in a dealer's inventory, consisting of five or more vehicles, that are all of the same make, model, and model-year is not required to include in the advertisement the vehicle identification numbers or license numbers of those vehicles.

(b) Advertise the total price of a vehicle without including all costs to the purchaser at time of sale, except taxes, vehicle registration fees, the California tire fee, as defined in Section 42885 of the Public Resources Code, emission testing charges not exceeding fifty dollars ($50), actual fees charged for certificates pursuant to Section 44060 of the Health and Safety Code, finance charges, and any dealer document processing charge or charge to electronically register or transfer the vehicle.

(c)(1) Exclude from an advertisement of a vehicle for sale that there will be added to the advertised total price at the time of sale, charges for sales tax, vehicle registration fees, the California tire fee, the fee charged by the state for the issuance of a certificate of compliance or noncompliance pursuant to a statute, finance charges, a charge to electronically register or transfer the vehicle, and a dealer document processing charge.

(2) The obligations imposed by paragraph (1) are satisfied by adding to the advertisement a statement containing no abbreviations and that is worded in substantially the following form: "Plus government fees and taxes, any finance charges, any dealer document processing charge, any electronic filing charge, and any emission testing charge."

(3) For purposes of paragraph (1), "advertisement" means an advertisement in a newspaper, magazine, or direct mail publication that is two or more columns in width or one column in width and more than seven inches in length, or on a Web page of a dealer's Internet Web site that displays the price of a vehicle offered for sale on the Internet, as that term is defined in paragraph (6) of subdivision (f) of Section 17538 of the Business and Professions Code.

(d) Represent the dealer document processing charge, electronic registration or transfer charge, or emission testing charge, as a governmental fee.

(e) Fail to sell a vehicle to a person at the advertised total price, exclusive of taxes, vehicle registration fees, the California tire fee, the fee charged by the state for the issuance of a certificate of compliance or noncompliance pursuant to a statute, finance charges, mobilehome escrow fees, the amount of a city, county, or city and county imposed fee or tax for a mobilehome, a dealer document processing charge, an electronic registration or transfer charge, and a charge for emission testing not to exceed fifty dollars ($50) plus the actual fees charged for certificates pursuant to Section 44060 of the Health and Safety Code, while the vehicle remains unsold, unless the advertisement states the advertised total price is good only for a specified time and the time has elapsed. Advertised vehicles shall be sold at or below the advertised total price, with statutorily permitted exclusions, regardless of whether the purchaser has knowledge of the advertised total price.

(f)(1) Advertise for sale, sell, or purchase for resale a new vehicle of a line-make for which the dealer does not hold a franchise.

(2) This subdivision does not apply to a transaction involving the following:

(A) A mobilehome.

(B) A recreational vehicle as defined in Section 18010 of the Health and Safety Code.

(C) A commercial coach, as defined in Section 18001.8 of the Health and Safety Code.

(D) An off-highway motor vehicle subject to identification as defined in Section 38012.

(E) A manufactured home.

(F) A new vehicle that will be substantially altered or modified by a converter prior to resale.

(G) A commercial vehicle with a gross vehicle weight rating of more than 10,000 pounds.

(H) A vehicle purchased for export and exported outside the territorial limits of the United States without being registered with the department.

(I) A vehicle acquired in the ordinary course of business as a new vehicle by a dealer franchised to sell that vehicle, if all of the following apply:

(i) The manufacturer or distributor of the vehicle files a bankruptcy petition.

(ii) The franchise agreement of the dealer is terminated, canceled, or rejected by the manufacturer or distributor as part of the bankruptcy proceedings and the termination, cancellation, or rejection is not a result of the revocation by the department of the dealer's license or the dealer's conviction of a crime.

(iii) The vehicle is held in the inventory of the dealer on the date the bankruptcy petition is filed.

(iv) The vehicle is sold by the dealer within six months of the date the bankruptcy petition is filed.

(3) Subparagraph (I) of paragraph (2) does not entitle a dealer whose franchise agreement has been terminated, canceled, or rejected to continue to perform warranty service repairs or continue to be eligible to offer or receive consumer or dealer incentives offered by the manufacturer or distributor.

(g) Sell a park trailer, as specified in Section 18009.3 of the Health and Safety Code, without disclosing in writing to the purchaser that a park trailer is required to be moved by a transporter or a licensed manufacturer or dealer under a permit issued by the Department of Transportation or a local authority with respect to highways under their respective jurisdictions.

(h) Advertise free merchandise, gifts, or services provided by a dealer contingent on the purchase of a vehicle. "Free" includes merchandise or services offered for sale at a price less than the seller's cost of the merchandise or services.

(i)(1) Advertise vehicles, and related goods or services, at a specified dealer price, with the intent not to supply reasonably expectable demand, unless the advertisement discloses the number of vehicles in stock at the advertised price. In addition, whether or not there are sufficient vehicles in stock to supply a reasonably expectable demand, when phrases such as "starting at," "from," "beginning as low as," or words of similar import are used in reference to an advertised price, the advertisement shall disclose the number of vehicles available at that advertised price.

(2) For purposes of this subdivision, in a newspaper advertisement for a vehicle that is two model-years old or newer, the actual phrase that states the number of vehicles in stock at the advertised price shall be printed in a type size that is at least equal to one-quarter of the type size, and in the same style and color of type, used for the advertised price. However, in no case shall the phrase be printed in less than 8–point type size, and the phrase shall be disclosed immediately above, below, or beside the advertised price without intervening words, pictures, marks, or symbols.

(3) The disclosure required by this subdivision is in addition to any other disclosure required by this code or any regulation regarding identifying vehicles advertised for sale.

(j) Use "rebate" or similar words, including, but not limited to, "cash back," in advertising the sale of a vehicle unless the rebate is expressed in a specific dollar amount

and is in fact a rebate offered by the vehicle manufacturer or distributor directly to the retail purchaser of the vehicle or to the assignee of the retail purchaser.

(k) Require a person to pay a higher price for a vehicle and related goods or services for receiving advertised credit terms than the cash price the same person would have to pay to purchase the same vehicle and related goods or services. For the purpose of this subdivision, "cash price" has the meaning as defined in subdivision (e) of Section 2981 of the Civil Code.

(l) Advertise a guaranteed trade-in allowance.

(m) Misrepresent the authority of a salesperson, representative, or agent to negotiate the final terms of a transaction.

(n)(1) Use "invoice," "dealer's invoice," "wholesale price," or similar terms that refer to a dealer's cost for a vehicle in an advertisement for the sale of a vehicle or advertise that the selling price of a vehicle is above, below, or at either of the following:

(A) The manufacturer's or distributor's invoice price to a dealer.

(B) A dealer's cost.

(2) This subdivision does not apply to either of the following:

(A) A communication occurring during face-to-face negotiations for the purchase of a specific vehicle if the prospective purchaser initiates a discussion of the vehicle's invoice price or the dealer's cost for that vehicle.

(B) A communication between a dealer and a prospective commercial purchaser that is not disseminated to the general public. For purposes of this subparagraph, a "commercial purchaser" means a dealer, lessor, lessor-retailer, manufacturer, remanufacturer, distributor, financial institution, governmental entity, or person who purchases 10 or more vehicles during a year.

(o) Violate a law prohibiting bait and switch advertising, including, but not limited to, the guides against bait advertising set forth in Part 238 (commencing with Section 238) of Title 16 of the Code of Federal Regulations, as those regulations read on January 1, 1988.

(p) Make an untrue or misleading statement indicating that a vehicle is equipped with all the factory-installed optional equipment the manufacturer offers, including, but not limited to, a false statement that a vehicle is "fully factory equipped."

(q) Affix on a new vehicle a supplemental price sticker containing a price that represents the dealer's asking price that exceeds the manufacturer's suggested retail price unless all of the following occur:

(1) The supplemental sticker clearly and conspicuously discloses in the largest print appearing on the sticker, other than the print size used for the dealer's name, that the supplemental sticker price is the dealer's asking price, or words of similar import, and that it is not the manufacturer's suggested retail price.

(2) The supplemental sticker clearly and conspicuously discloses the manufacturer's suggested retail price.

(3) The supplemental sticker lists each item that is not included in the manufacturer's suggested retail price, and discloses the additional price of each item. If the supplemental sticker price is greater than the sum of the manufacturer's suggested retail price and the price of the items added by the dealer, the supplemental sticker price shall set forth that difference and describe it as "added mark-up."

(r) Advertise an underselling claim, including, but not limited to, "we have the lowest prices" or "we will beat any dealer's price," unless the dealer has conducted a recent survey showing that the dealer sells its vehicles at lower prices than another licensee in its trade area and maintains records to adequately substantiate the claims. The substantiating records shall be made available to the department upon request.

(s)(1) Advertise an incentive offered by the manufacturer or distributor if the dealer is required to contribute to the cost of the incentive as a condition of participating in the incentive program, unless the dealer discloses in a clear and conspicuous manner that dealer participation may affect consumer cost.

(2) For purposes of this subdivision, "incentive" means anything of value offered to induce people to purchase a vehicle, including, but not limited to, discounts, savings claims, rebates, below-market finance rates, and free merchandise or services.

(t) Display or offer for sale a used vehicle unless there is affixed to the vehicle the Federal Trade Commission's Buyer's Guide as required by Part 455 of Title 16 of the Code of Federal Regulations.

(u) Fail to disclose in writing to the franchisor of a new motor vehicle dealer the name of the purchaser, date of sale, and the vehicle identification number of each new motor vehicle sold of the line-make of that franchisor, or intentionally submit to that franchisor a false name for the purchaser or false date for the date of sale.

(v) Enter into a contract for the retail sale of a motor vehicle unless the contract clearly and conspicuously discloses whether the vehicle is being sold as a new vehicle or a used vehicle, as defined in this code.

(w) Use a simulated check, as defined in subdivision (a) of Section 22433 of the Business and Professions Code, in an advertisement for the sale or lease of a vehicle.

(x) Fail to disclose, in a clear and conspicuous manner in at least 10–point boldface type on the face of a contract for the retail sale of a new motor vehicle that this transaction is, or is not, subject to a fee received by an autobroker from the selling new motor vehicle dealer, and the name of the autobroker, if applicable.

(y) Sell or lease a new motor vehicle after October 1, 2012, unless the dealer has a contractual agreement with the department to be a private industry partner pursuant to Section 1685. This subdivision does not apply to the sale or lease of a motorcycle or off-highway motor vehicle subject to identification under Section 38010 or a recreational vehicle as defined in Section 18010 of the Health and Safety Code.

(z) As used in this section, "make" and "model" have the same meaning as is provided in Section 565.3 of Title 49 of the Code of Federal Regulations.

(aa) This section shall become operative on July 1, 2012. *(Added by Stats.2011, c. 329 (A.B.1215), § 14, operative July 1, 2012.)*

Cross References

Occupational licensing, automobiles, vehicles for sale, see Vehicle Code § 11709.3.

§ 11713.2. Additional unlawful acts; coercion or attempted coercion of dealer

It shall be unlawful and a violation of this code for any manufacturer, manufacturer branch, distributor, or distributor branch licensed under this code to coerce or attempt to coerce any dealer in this state:

(a) To order or accept delivery of any motor vehicle, part or accessory thereof, appliance, equipment or any other commodity not required by law which shall not have been voluntarily ordered by the dealer.

(b) To order or accept delivery of any motor vehicle with special features, appliances, accessories or equipment not included in the list price of such motor vehicles as publicly advertised by the manufacturer or distributor.

(c) To order for any person any parts, accessories, equipment, machinery, tools, appliances, or any commodity whatsoever.

(d) To participate in an advertising campaign or contest, any promotional campaign, promotional materials, training materials, showroom or other display decorations or materials at the expense of the dealer.

(e) To enter into any agreement with the manufacturer, manufacturer branch, distributor, or distributor branch, or to do any other act prejudicial to the dealer by threatening to cancel a franchise or any contractual agreement existing between the dealer and manufacturer, manufacturer branch, distributor, or distributor branch. Notice in good faith to any dealer of the dealer's violation of any terms or provisions of such franchise or contractual agreement shall not constitute a violation of this article. *(Formerly § 11713.1, added by Stats.1973, c. 996, p. 1976, § 29, operative July 1, 1974. Renumbered § 11713.2 and amended by Stats.1979, c. 943, p. 3247, § 1.)*

§ 11713.3. Additional unlawful acts; direct actions and indirect actions through affiliate

It is unlawful and a violation of this code for a manufacturer, manufacturer branch, distributor, or distributor branch licensed pursuant to this code to do, directly or indirectly through an affiliate, any of the following:

(a) To refuse or fail to deliver in reasonable quantities and within a reasonable time after receipt of an order from a dealer having a franchise for the retail sale of a new vehicle sold or distributed by the manufacturer or distributor, a new vehicle or parts or accessories to new vehicles as are covered by the franchise, if the vehicle, parts, or accessories are publicly advertised as being available for delivery or actually being delivered. This subdivision is not violated, however, if the failure is caused by acts or causes beyond the control of the manufacturer, manufacturer branch, distributor, or distributor branch.

(b) To prevent or require, or attempt to prevent or require, by contract or otherwise, a change in the capital structure of a dealership or the means by or through which the dealer finances the operation of the dealership, if the dealer at all times meets reasonable capital standards agreed to by the dealer and the manufacturer or distributor, and if a change in capital structure does not cause a change in the principal management or have the effect of a sale of the franchise without the consent of the manufacturer or distributor.

(c) To prevent or require, or attempt to prevent or require, a dealer to change the executive management of a dealership, other than the principal dealership operator or operators, if the franchise was granted to the dealer in reliance upon the personal qualifications of that person.

(d)(1) Except as provided in subdivision (t), to prevent or require, or attempt to prevent or require, by contract or otherwise, a dealer, or an officer, partner, or stockholder of a dealership, the sale or transfer of a part of the interest of any of them to another person. A dealer, officer, partner, or stockholder shall not, however, have the right to sell, transfer, or assign the franchise, or a right thereunder, without the consent of the manufacturer or distributor except that the consent shall not be unreasonably withheld.

(2)(A) For the transferring franchisee to fail, prior to the sale, transfer, or assignment of a franchisee or the sale, assignment, or transfer of all, or substantially all, of the assets of the franchised business or a controlling interest in the franchised business to another person, to notify the manufacturer or distributor of the franchisee's decision to sell, transfer, or assign the franchise. The notice shall be in writing and shall include all of the following:

(i) The proposed transferee's name and address.

(ii) A copy of all of the agreements relating to the sale, assignment, or transfer of the franchised business or its assets.

(iii) The proposed transferee's application for approval to become the successor franchisee. The application shall include forms and related information generally utilized by the manufacturer or distributor in reviewing prospective franchisees, if those forms are readily made available to existing franchisees. As soon as practicable after receipt of the proposed transferee's application, the manufacturer or distributor shall notify the franchisee and the proposed transferee of information needed to make the application complete.

(B) For the manufacturer or distributor, to fail, on or before 60 days after the receipt of all of the information required pursuant to subparagraph (A), or as extended by a written agreement between the manufacturer or distributor and the franchisee, to notify the franchisee of the approval or the disapproval of the sale, transfer, or assignment of the franchise. The notice shall be in writing and shall be personally served or sent by certified mail, return receipt requested, or by guaranteed overnight delivery service that provides verification of delivery and shall be directed to the franchisee. A proposed sale, assignment, or transfer shall be deemed approved, unless disapproved by the franchisor in the manner provided by this subdivision. If the proposed sale, assignment, or transfer is disapproved, the franchisor shall include in the notice of disapproval a statement setting forth the reasons for the disapproval.

(3) In an action in which the manufacturer's or distributor's withholding of consent under this subdivision or subdivision (e) is an issue, whether the withholding of consent was unreasonable is a question of fact requiring consideration of all the existing circumstances.

(e) To prevent, or attempt to prevent, a dealer from receiving fair and reasonable compensation for the value of the franchised business. There shall not be a transfer or assignment of the dealer's franchise without the consent of the manufacturer or distributor, which consent shall not be unreasonably withheld or conditioned upon the release, assignment, novation, waiver, estoppel, or modification of a claim or defense by the dealer.

(f) To obtain money, goods, services, or another benefit from a person with whom the dealer does business, on account of, or in relation to, the transaction between the dealer and that other person, other than for compensation for services rendered, unless the benefit is promptly accounted for, and transmitted to, the dealer.

(g)(1) Except as provided in paragraph (3), to obtain from a dealer or enforce against a dealer an agreement, provision, release, assignment, novation, waiver, or estoppel that does any of the following:

(A) Modifies or disclaims a duty or obligation of a manufacturer, manufacturer branch, distributor, distributor branch, or representative, or a right or privilege of a dealer, pursuant to Chapter 4 (commencing with Section 11700) of Division 5 or Chapter 6 (commencing with Section 3000) of Division 2.

(B) Limits or constrains the right of a dealer to file, pursue, or submit evidence in connection with a protest before the board.

(C) Requires a dealer to terminate a franchise.

(D) Requires a controversy between a manufacturer, manufacturer branch, distributor, distributor branch, or representative and a dealer to be referred to a person for a binding determination. However, this subparagraph does not prohibit arbitration before an independent arbitrator, provided that whenever a motor vehicle franchise contract provides for the use of arbitration to resolve a controversy arising out of, or relating to, that contract, arbitration may be used to settle the controversy only if, after the controversy arises, all parties to the controversy consent in writing to use arbitration to settle the controversy. For the purpose of this subparagraph, the terms "motor vehicle" and "motor vehicle franchise contract" shall have the same meaning as defined in Section 1226 of Title 15 of the United States Code. If arbitration is elected to settle a dispute under a motor vehicle franchise contract, the arbitrator shall provide the parties to the arbitration with a written explanation of the factual and legal basis for the award.

(2) An agreement, provision, release, assignment, novation, waiver, or estoppel prohibited by this subdivision shall be unenforceable and void.

(3) This subdivision does not do any of the following:

(A) Limit or restrict the terms upon which parties to a protest before the board, civil action, or other proceeding can settle or resolve, or stipulate to evidentiary or procedural matters during the course of, a protest, civil action, or other proceeding.

(B) Affect the enforceability of any stipulated order or other order entered by the board.

(C) Affect the enforceability of any provision in a contract if the provision is not prohibited under this subdivision or any other law.

(D) Affect the enforceability of a provision in any contract entered into on or before December 31, 2011.

(E) Prohibit a dealer from waiving its right to file a protest pursuant to Section 3065.1 if the waiver agreement is entered into after a franchisor incentive program claim has been disapproved by the franchisor and the waiver is voluntarily given as part of an agreement to settle that claim.

(F) Prohibit a voluntary agreement supported by valuable consideration, other than granting or renewing a franchise, that does both of the following:

(i) Provides that a dealer establish or maintain exclusive facilities, personnel, or display space or provides that a dealer make a material alteration, expansion, or addition to a dealership facility.

(ii) Contains no waiver or other provision prohibited by subparagraph (A), (B), (C), or (D) of paragraph (1).

(G) Prohibit an agreement separate from the franchise agreement that implements a dealer's election to terminate the franchise if the agreement is conditioned only on a specified time for termination or payment of consideration to the dealer.

(H)(i) Prohibit a voluntary waiver agreement, supported by valuable consideration, other than the consideration of renewing a franchise, to waive the right of a

dealer to file a protest under Section 3062 for the proposed establishment or relocation of a specific proposed dealership, if the waiver agreement provides all of the following:

(I) The approximate address at which the proposed dealership will be located.

(II) The planning potential used to establish the proposed dealership's facility, personnel, and capital requirements.

(III) An approximation of projected vehicle and parts sales, and number of vehicles to be serviced at the proposed dealership.

(IV) Whether the franchisor or affiliate will hold an ownership interest in the proposed dealership or real property of the proposed dealership, and the approximate percentage of any franchisor or affiliate ownership interest in the proposed dealership.

(V) The line-makes to be operated at the proposed dealership.

(VI) If known at the time the waiver agreement is executed, the identity of the dealer who will operate the proposed dealership.

(VII) The date the waiver agreement is to expire, which may not be more than 30 months after the date of execution of the waiver agreement.

(ii) Notwithstanding the provisions of a waiver agreement entered into pursuant to the provisions of this subparagraph, a dealer may file a protest under Section 3062 if any of the information provided pursuant to clause (i) has become materially inaccurate since the waiver agreement was executed. Any determination of the enforceability of a waiver agreement shall be determined by the board and the franchisor shall have the burden of proof.

(h) To increase prices of motor vehicles that the dealer had ordered for private retail consumers prior to the dealer's receipt of the written official price increase notification. A sales contract signed by a private retail consumer is evidence of the order. In the event of manufacturer price reductions, the amount of the reduction received by a dealer shall be passed on to the private retail consumer by the dealer if the retail price was negotiated on the basis of the previous higher price to the dealer. Price reductions apply to all vehicles in the dealer's inventory that were subject to the price reduction. Price differences applicable to new model or series motor vehicles at the time of the introduction of new models or series shall not be considered a price increase or price decrease. This subdivision does not apply to price changes caused by either of the following:

(1) The addition to a motor vehicle of required or optional equipment pursuant to state or federal law.

(2) Revaluation of the United States dollar in the case of a foreign-make vehicle.

(i) To fail to pay to a dealer, within a reasonable time following receipt of a valid claim by a dealer thereof, a payment agreed to be made by the manufacturer or distributor to the dealer by reason of the fact that a new vehicle of a prior year model is in the dealer's inventory at the time of introduction of new model vehicles.

(j) To deny the widow, widower, or heirs designated by a deceased owner of a dealership the opportunity to participate in the ownership of the dealership or successor dealership under a valid franchise for a reasonable time after the death of the owner.

(k) To offer refunds or other types of inducements to a person for the purchase of new motor vehicles of a certain line-make to be sold to the state or a political subdivision of the state without making the same offer to all other dealers in the same line-make within the relevant market area.

(*l*) To modify, replace, enter into, relocate, terminate, or refuse to renew a franchise in violation of Article 4 (commencing with Section 3060) of Chapter 6 of Division 2.

(m) To employ a person as a representative who has not been licensed pursuant to Article 3 (commencing with Section 11900) of Chapter 4 of Division 5.

(n) To deny a dealer the right of free association with another dealer for a lawful purpose.

(*o*)(1) To compete with a dealer in the same line-make operating under an agreement or franchise from a manufacturer or distributor in the relevant market area.

(2) A manufacturer, branch, or distributor or an entity that controls or is controlled by, a manufacturer, branch, or distributor, shall not, however, be deemed to be competing in the following limited circumstances:

(A) Owning or operating a dealership for a temporary period, not to exceed one year at the location of a former dealership of the same line-make that has been out of operation for less than six months. However, after a showing of good cause by a manufacturer, branch, or distributor that it needs additional time to operate a dealership in preparation for sale to a successor independent franchisee, the board may extend the time period.

(B) Owning an interest in a dealer as part of a bona fide dealer development program that satisfies all of the following requirements:

(i) The sole purpose of the program is to make franchises available to persons lacking capital, training, business experience, or other qualities ordinarily required of prospective franchisees and the dealer development candidate is an individual who is unable to acquire the franchise without assistance of the program.

(ii) The dealer development candidate has made a significant investment subject to loss in the franchised business of the dealer.

(iii) The program requires the dealer development candidate to manage the day-to-day operations and business affairs of the dealer and to acquire, within a reasonable time and on reasonable terms and conditions, beneficial ownership and control of a majority interest in

the dealer and disassociation of any direct or indirect ownership or control by the manufacturer, branch, or distributor.

(C) Owning a wholly owned subsidiary corporation of a distributor that sells motor vehicles at retail, if, for at least three years prior to January 1, 1973, the subsidiary corporation has been a wholly owned subsidiary of the distributor and engaged in the sale of vehicles at retail.

(3)(A) A manufacturer, branch, and distributor that owns or operates a dealership in the manner described in subparagraph (A) of paragraph (2) shall give written notice to the board, within 10 days, each time it commences or terminates operation of a dealership and each time it acquires, changes, or divests itself of an ownership interest.

(B) A manufacturer, branch, and distributor that owns an interest in a dealer in the manner described in subparagraph (B) of paragraph (2) shall give written notice to the board, annually, of the name and location of each dealer in which it has an ownership interest, the name of the bona fide dealer development owner or owners, and the ownership interests of each owner expressed as a percentage.

(p) To unfairly discriminate among its franchisees with respect to warranty reimbursement or authority granted to its franchisees to make warranty adjustments with retail customers.

(q) To sell vehicles to a person not licensed pursuant to this chapter for resale.

(r) To fail to affix an identification number to a park trailer, as described in Section 18009.3 of the Health and Safety Code, that is manufactured on or after January 1, 1987, and that does not clearly identify the unit as a park trailer to the department. The configuration of the identification number shall be approved by the department.

(s) To dishonor a warranty, rebate, or other incentive offered to the public or a dealer in connection with the retail sale of a new motor vehicle, based solely upon the fact that an autobroker arranged or negotiated the sale. This subdivision shall not prohibit the disallowance of that rebate or incentive if the purchaser or dealer is ineligible to receive the rebate or incentive pursuant to any other term or condition of a rebate or incentive program.

(t) To exercise a right of first refusal or other right requiring a franchisee or an owner of the franchise to sell, transfer, or assign to the franchisor, or to a nominee of the franchisor, all or a material part of the franchised business or of the assets of the franchised business unless all of the following requirements are met:

(1) The franchise authorizes the franchisor to exercise a right of first refusal to acquire the franchised business or assets of the franchised business in the event of a proposed sale, transfer, or assignment.

(2) The franchisor gives written notice of its exercise of the right of first refusal no later than 45 days after the franchisor receives all of the information required pursuant to subparagraph (A) of paragraph (2) of subdivision (d).

(3) The sale, transfer, or assignment being proposed relates to not less than all or substantially all of the assets of the franchised business or to a controlling interest in the franchised business.

(4) The proposed transferee is neither a family member of an owner of the franchised business, nor a managerial employee of the franchisee owning 15 percent or more of the franchised business, nor a corporation, partnership, or other legal entity owned by the existing owners of the franchised business. For purposes of this paragraph, a "family member" means the spouse of an owner of the franchised business, the child, grandchild, brother, sister, or parent of an owner, or a spouse of one of those family members. This paragraph does not limit the rights of the franchisor to disapprove a proposed transferee as provided in subdivision (d).

(5) Upon the franchisor's exercise of the right of first refusal, the consideration paid by the franchisor to the franchisee and owners of the franchised business shall equal or exceed all consideration that each of them were to have received under the terms of, or in connection with, the proposed sale, assignment, or transfer, and the franchisor shall comply with all the terms and conditions of the agreement or agreements to sell, transfer, or assign the franchised business.

(6) The franchisor shall reimburse the proposed transferee for expenses paid or incurred by the proposed transferee in evaluating, investigating, and negotiating the proposed transfer to the extent those expenses do not exceed the usual, customary, and reasonable fees charged for similar work done in the area in which the franchised business is located. These expenses include, but are not limited to, legal and accounting expenses, and expenses incurred for title reports and environmental or other investigations of real property on which the franchisee's operations are conducted. The proposed transferee shall provide the franchisor a written itemization of those expenses, and a copy of all nonprivileged reports and studies for which expenses were incurred, if any, within 30 days of the proposed transferee's receipt of a written request from the franchisor for that accounting. The franchisor shall make payment within 30 days of exercising the right of first refusal.

(u)(1) To unfairly discriminate in favor of a dealership owned or controlled, in whole or in part, by a manufacturer or distributor or an entity that controls or is controlled by the manufacturer or distributor. Unfair discrimination includes, but is not limited to, the following:

(A) The furnishing to a franchisee or dealer that is owned or controlled, in whole or in part, by a manufacturer, branch, or distributor of any of the following:

(i) A vehicle that is not made available to each franchisee pursuant to a reasonable allocation formula that is applied uniformly, and a part or accessory that is not made available to all franchisees on an equal basis when there is no reasonable allocation formula that is applied uniformly.

(ii) A vehicle, part, or accessory that is not made available to each franchisee on comparable delivery terms, including the time of delivery after the placement of an order. Differences in delivery terms due to geographic distances or other factors beyond the control of the manufacturer, branch, or distributor shall not constitute unfair competition.

(iii) Information obtained from a franchisee by the manufacturer, branch, or distributor concerning the business affairs or operations of a franchisee in which the manufacturer, branch, or distributor does not have an ownership interest. The information includes, but is not limited to, information contained in financial statements and operating reports, the name, address, or other personal information or buying, leasing, or service behavior of a dealer customer, and other information that, if provided to a franchisee or dealer owned or controlled by a manufacturer or distributor, would give that franchisee or dealer a competitive advantage. This clause does not apply if the information is provided pursuant to a subpoena or court order, or to aggregated information made available to all franchisees.

(iv) Sales or service incentives, discounts, or promotional programs that are not made available to all California franchises of the same line-make on an equal basis.

(B) Referring a prospective purchaser or lessee to a dealer in which a manufacturer, branch, or distributor has an ownership interest, unless the prospective purchaser or lessee resides in the area of responsibility assigned to that dealer or the prospective purchaser or lessee requests to be referred to that dealer.

(2) This subdivision does not prohibit a franchisor from granting a franchise to prospective franchisees or assisting those franchisees during the course of the franchise relationship as part of a program or programs to make franchises available to persons lacking capital, training, business experience, or other qualifications ordinarily required of prospective franchisees.

(v)(1) To access, modify, or extract information from a confidential dealer computer record, as defined in Section 11713.25, without obtaining the prior written consent of the dealer and without maintaining administrative, technical, and physical safeguards to protect the security, confidentiality, and integrity of the information.

(2) Paragraph (1) does not limit a duty that a dealer may have to safeguard the security and privacy of records maintained by the dealer.

(w)(1) To use electronic, contractual, or other means to prevent or interfere with any of the following:

(A) The lawful efforts of a dealer to comply with federal and state data security and privacy laws.

(B) The ability of a dealer to do either of the following:

(i) Ensure that specific data accessed from the dealer's computer system is within the scope of consent specified in subdivision (v).

(ii) Monitor specific data accessed from or written to the dealer's computer system.

(2) Paragraph (1) does not limit a duty that a dealer may have to safeguard the security and privacy of records maintained by the dealer.

(x)(1) To unfairly discriminate against a franchisee selling a service contract, debt cancellation agreement, maintenance agreement, or similar product not approved, endorsed, sponsored, or offered by the manufacturer, manufacturer branch, distributor, or distributor branch or affiliate. For purposes of this subdivision, unfair discrimination includes, but is not limited to, any of the following:

(A) Express or implied statements that the dealer is under an obligation to exclusively sell or offer to sell service contracts, debt cancellation agreements, or similar products approved, endorsed, sponsored, or offered by the manufacturer, manufacturer branch, distributor, or distributor branch or affiliate.

(B) Express or implied statements that selling or offering to sell service contracts, debt cancellation agreements, maintenance agreements, or similar products not approved, endorsed, sponsored, or offered by the manufacturer, manufacturer branch, distributor, or distributor branch or affiliate, or the failure to sell or offer to sell service contracts, debt cancellation agreements, maintenance agreements, or similar products approved, endorsed, sponsored, or offered by the manufacturer, manufacturer branch, distributor, or distributor branch or affiliate will have any negative consequences for the dealer.

(C) Measuring a dealer's performance under a franchise agreement based upon the sale of service contracts, debt cancellation agreements, or similar products approved, endorsed, sponsored, or offered by the manufacturer, manufacturer branch, distributor, or distributor branch or affiliate.

(D) Requiring a dealer to actively promote the sale of service contracts, debt cancellation agreements, or similar products approved, endorsed, sponsored, or offered by the manufacturer, manufacturer branch, distributor, or distributor branch or affiliate.

(E) Conditioning access to vehicles or parts, or vehicle sales or service incentives upon the sale of service contracts, debt cancellation agreements, or similar products approved, endorsed, sponsored, or offered by the manufacturer, manufacturer branch, distributor, or distributor branch or affiliate.

(2) Unfair discrimination does not include, and nothing shall prohibit a manufacturer from, offering an incentive program to vehicle dealers who voluntarily sell or offer to sell service contracts, debt cancellation agreements, or similar products approved, endorsed, sponsored, or offered by the manufacturer, manufacturer branch, distributor, or distributor branch or affiliate, if the program does not provide vehicle sales or service incentives.

(3) This subdivision does not prohibit a manufacturer, manufacturer branch, distributor, or distributor branch from requiring a franchisee that sells a used vehicle as "certified" under a certified used vehicle program established by the manufacturer, manufacturer branch, distributor, or distributor branch to provide a service contract approved, endorsed, sponsored, or offered by the manufacturer, manufacturer branch, distributor, or distributor branch.

(4) Unfair discrimination does not include, and nothing shall prohibit a franchisor from requiring a franchisee to provide, the following notice prior to the sale of the service contract if the service contract is not provided or backed by the franchisor and the vehicle is of the franchised line-make:

"Service Contract Disclosure
The service contract you are purchasing is not provided or backed by the manufacturer of the vehicle you are purchasing. The manufacturer of the vehicle is not responsible for claims or repairs under this service contract.

_____

Signature of Purchaser"

(y) To take or threaten to take any adverse action against a dealer pursuant to an export or sale-for-resale prohibition because the dealer sold or leased a vehicle to a customer who either exported the vehicle to a foreign country or resold the vehicle in violation of the prohibition, unless the export or sale-for-resale prohibition policy was provided to the dealer in writing prior to the sale or lease, and the dealer knew or reasonably should have known of the customer's intent to export or resell the vehicle in violation of the prohibition at the time of sale or lease. If the dealer causes the vehicle to be registered in this or any other state, and collects or causes to be collected any applicable sales or use tax due to this state, a rebuttable presumption is established that the dealer did not have reason to know of the customer's intent to export or resell the vehicle.

(z) As used in this section, "area of responsibility" is a geographic area specified in a franchise that is used by the franchisor for the purpose of evaluating the franchisee's performance of its sales and service obligations. *(Formerly § 11713.2, added by Stats.1973, c. 996, p. 1977, § 30, operative July 1, 1974. Amended by Stats.1974, c. 384, p. 958, § 13, eff. July 5, 1974, operative July 1, 1974.)*

Renumbered § 11713.3 and amended by Stats.1979, c. 943, p. 3249, § 3. Amended by Stats.1986, c. 1078, § 9, eff. Sept. 24, 1986, operative Jan. 1, 1987; Stats.1993, c. 272 (A.B.301), § 16, eff. Aug. 2, 1993; Stats.1994, c. 1253 (A.B.3539), § 11; Stats.1998, c. 662 (A.B.2707), § 7; Stats.2000, c. 566 (A.B.1912), § 6; Stats.2000, c. 789 (S.B.1819), § 2.5; Stats.2006, c. 353 (A.B.2291), § 1; Stats.2011, c. 342 (S.B.642), § 3; Stats.2012, c. 162 (S.B.1171), § 180; Stats.2013, c. 512 (S.B.155), § 18.)

§ 11713.4. Refund of excess fees by dealer

If a purchaser of a vehicle pays to the dealer an amount for the licensing or transfer of title of the vehicle, which amount is in excess of the actual fees due for such licensing or transfer, or which amount is in excess of the amount which has been paid, prior to the sale, by the dealer to the state in order to avoid penalties that would have accrued because of late payment of such fees, the dealer shall return such excess amount to the purchaser, whether or not such purchaser requests the return of the excess amount. *(Formerly § 11713.3, added by Stats.1974, c. 222, p. 420, § 1. Renumbered § 11713.4 and amended by Stats.1979, c. 943, p. 3251, § 4.)*

§ 11713.5. Unlawful representation of vehicle model year; housecars; applicability of section

(a) It is unlawful and a violation of this code for the holder of any license issued under this article to display for sale, offer for sale, or sell, a motor vehicle, representing the motor vehicle to be of a year model different from the year model designated at the time of manufacture or first assembly as a completed vehicle.

(b) It is unlawful and a violation of this code for the holder of any license issued under this article to directly or indirectly authorize or advise another holder of a license issued under this article to change the year model of a motor vehicle in the inventory of the other holder.

(c) It is unlawful and a violation of this code for the holder of any license issued under this article to display for sale, offer for sale, or sell, a housecar which has been manufactured in two or more stages, unless the licensee informs the buyer that the housecar has been so manufactured and the licensee provides the buyer with a form, approved by the department, which sets forth the date of chassis and engine manufacture and the date and model year of the other stages of the vehicle. The licensee shall retain a copy of the form, which shall be signed by the purchaser prior to entering into any sales contract, indicating that the purchaser has received a copy of the form.

(d) This section does not apply to the displaying or offering for sale, or selling, of any new motortruck or truck tractor weighing over 10,000 pounds.

(e) This section does not apply to a vehicle which has been remanufactured by a licensed remanufacturer. The year model of a remanufactured vehicle will be the year the vehicle was remanufactured. *(Added by Stats.1974, c.*

1025, p. 2226, § 2. Amended by Stats.1977, c. 873, p. 2634, § 4; Stats.1983, c. 1286, § 36.)*

§ 11713.6. Tire chains; vehicles which may not be operated with chains; disclosures to buyers and lessees

(a) It is unlawful and a violation of this code for the holder of any dealer's license issued under this article to fail to disclose in writing to the buyer or lessee of a new motor vehicle, that the vehicle, as equipped, may not be operated on a highway signed for the requirement of tire chains if the owner's manual or other material provided by the manufacturer states that the vehicle, as equipped, may not be operated with tire chains.

(b) The disclosure required under subdivision (a) shall meet both of the following requirements:

(1) The disclosure shall be printed in not less than 14–point boldface type on a single sheet of paper that contains no information other than the disclosure.

(2) The disclosure shall include the following language in capital letters: "AS EQUIPPED, THIS VEHICLE MAY NOT BE OPERATED WITH TIRE CHAINS BUT MAY ACCOMMODATE SOME OTHER TYPE OF TIRE TRACTION DEVICE. SEE THE OWNER'S MANUAL FOR DETAILS."

(c) Prior to the sale or lease, the dealer shall present the disclosure statement for the buyer's or lessee's signature and then shall provide the buyer or lessee with a copy of the signed disclosure. *(Added by Stats.1991, c. 6 (A.B.39), § 2, eff. Dec. 13, 1990, operative Jan. 1, 1991. Amended by Stats.1995, c. 452 (A.B.28), § 2.)*

§ 11713.7. Remanufactured vehicles; disclosure methods

Disclosure to a buyer that a vehicle has been remanufactured is required. Disclosure shall be accomplished by all of the following:

(a) Oral notification to the buyer.

(b) The statement "THIS VEHICLE HAS BEEN REMANUFACTURED AND CONTAINS USED OR RECONDITIONED PARTS" shall appear in a type size at least the same as the bulk of the text on the purchase order or conditional sales contract signed by the buyer.

(c) The statement that the vehicle is remanufactured and contains used or reconditioned parts shall appear in any advertisement pertaining to remanufactured vehicles.

(d) Remanufactured vehicles displayed for retail purposes shall be clearly designated as remanufactured. The disclosure statement required in subdivision (b) shall appear on the vehicle or at the location where the vehicles are displayed. *(Added by Stats.1983, c. 1286, § 37.)*

§ 11713.8. Remanufacturers; illegalities and code violations

It is unlawful and a violation of this code for a remanufacturer licensed under this code to fail to do any of the following:

(a) Report to the department an existing vehicle identification number when a used frame is utilized.

(b) Die stamp the vehicle identification number to the frame of the vehicle when a new vehicle identification number is assigned.

(c) Disclose that a vehicle is remanufactured and contains used or reconditioned parts as required by Section 11713.7.

(d) Remove the trade name of the original manufacturer from the vehicle, unless the remanufacturer and the original manufacturer are same.

(e) Maintain for three years bills of sale or invoices for used parts utilized in a remanufactured vehicle.

(f) Maintain for three years proof that the vehicle was reported dismantled, as required by Section 5500 or 11520, when a used frame is utilized in a remanufactured vehicle.

(g) Disclose, on the vehicle identification number plate or label, that the vehicle is remanufactured and includes used parts.

(h) Disclose to the dealer on a document signed by the dealer that the vehicle is remanufactured and contains used parts. *(Added by Stats.1983, c. 1286, § 38.)*

§ 11713.9. Unlabeled engine where manufacturer of engine and vehicle differ; offer of vehicle for sale

(a) It is unlawful and a violation of this code for the holder of a dealer's license to knowingly display for sale or offer for sale any new motor vehicle specified in subdivision (b) with an engine manufactured by a manufacturer that is not the same as the vehicle manufacturer, as defined in Section 9980, unless the vehicle is prominently labeled as specified in Section 9981.

(b) This section applies only to new passenger vehicles and to new motortrucks with an unladen weight under 6,000 pounds, except housecars. *(Added by Stats.1984, c. 1264, § 2.)*

§ 11713.10. Low-speed vehicles; sale; disclosure of risks

It is unlawful and a violation of this code to sell a low-speed vehicle, as defined in Section 385.5, without disclosing to the buyer the vehicle's maximum speed and the potential risks of driving a low-speed vehicle. *(Added by Stats.1999, c. 140 (S.B.186), § 3.)*

§ 11713.11. Auctions; advertisements; identification of vehicles; costs included in price; buyer's fee

No holder of a dealer's license shall do any of the following when conducting an auction of vehicles to the public:

(a) Advertise that a vehicle will be auctioned to the public unless all of the following information is clearly and conspicuously disclosed in the advertisement:

(1) The date or the day of the week of the public auction, or if subdivision (b) applies to the auction, the date of the public auction.

(2) The location of the public auction.

(3) Whether a fee will be charged to attend the auction and the amount of that fee.

(4) The name and dealer number of the auctioning dealer.

(5) Whether a buyer's fee will be charged to a purchaser, in addition to the accepted auction bid price, and, if the fee is a set amount, the dollar amount of that fee. If the buyer's fee is not a set amount, the advertisement shall state the formula or percentage used to calculate the fee.

(b) If vehicles seized by a federal, state, or local public agency or authority are being advertised, advertise that a vehicle will be auctioned to the public unless, in addition to the information required by subdivision (a), the following information is clearly and conspicuously disclosed in the advertisement:

(1) A good faith estimate of the number of vehicles to be auctioned at that date.

(2) A good faith estimate of the number of vehicles seized by a federal, state, or local public agency or authority to be auctioned at that date.

(c) Fail, on the day of auction, to identify each vehicle seized by a federal, state, or local public agency or authority, either in a printed catalog or orally, before bidding begins on the vehicle.

(d) Include in the total price of an auctioned vehicle any costs to the purchaser at the completion of the sale, except the accepted auction bid price, taxes, vehicle registration fees, any charge for emission testing, not to exceed fifty dollars ($50), plus the actual fees charged to a consumer for a certificate pursuant to Section 44060 of the Health and Safety Code, any dealer document preparation charge not exceeding forty-five dollars ($45), and any buyer's fee.

(e) Charge a buyer's fee, unless the dealer conducting the auction delivers to any person permitted to submit bids, and at a time prior to accepting any bids from that person, a disclosure statement required by this subdivision and signed by that person. The disclosure statement, if the buyer's fee is a set amount, shall disclose the amount of the fee, or if the buyer's fee is not a set amount, disclose the formula or percentage used to calculate the fee. The disclosure statement shall be on a separate 8½ x 11 inch sheet of paper. Except for the information set forth in this subdivision, the disclosure statement shall not contain any other text, except as necessary to identify the dealer conducting the auction sale and to disclose the amount, percentage, or formula used to calculate the buyer's fee, and to provide for the date and the person's acknowledgment of receipt. The heading shall be printed in no smaller than 24–point bold type and the text of the statement shall be printed in no smaller than 12–point type and shall read substantially as follows:

BUYER'S FEE REQUIRED

A buyer's fee is an amount charged by the auctioning dealer for conducting the auction sale. If your bid price is accepted as the winning bid on any vehicle, you will be charged a buyer's fee in addition to the accepted bid price.

The buyer's fee that will be added to your accepted bid price is $_____.

OR

The buyer's fee that will be added to your accepted bid price will be calculated as follows (insert percentage or other formula for calculating the buyer's fee):

The buyer's fee is part of the purchase price and is subject to sales tax.

Date: _____ Signature of Bidder _____

(f) Fail to comply with or violate this chapter, Title 2.95 (commencing with Section 1812.600) of Part 4 of Division 3 of the Civil Code, Section 2328 of the Commercial Code, or Section 535 of the Penal Code, or any law administered by the State Board of Equalization, relating to the auctioneering business, including, but not limited to, sales and the transfer of title of goods.

(g) For purposes of this section, a "buyer's fee" is any amount that is in addition to the accepted auction bid price, taxes, vehicle registration fees, certificate of compliance or noncompliance fee, or any dealer document preparation charge, which is charged to a purchaser by an auctioning dealer. *(Added by Stats.1995, c. 585 (A.B. 192), § 3. Amended by Stats.1999, c. 672 (S.B.974), § 2.)*

§ 11713.12. Affixation of "Lemon Law Buyback" decal

(a) The decal required by subdivision (c) of Section 1793.23 of the Civil Code to be affixed by a manufacturer to a motor vehicle, shall be affixed to the left front doorframe of the vehicle, or, if the vehicle does not have a left front doorframe, it shall be affixed in a location designated by the department. The decal shall specify that title to the motor vehicle has been inscribed with the notation "Lemon Law Buyback" and shall be affixed to the vehicle in a manner prescribed by the department.

(b) No person shall knowingly remove or alter any decal affixed to a vehicle pursuant to subdivision (a), whether or not licensed under this code. *(Added by Stats.1995, c. 503 (A.B.1381), § 6.)*

§ 11713.13. Additional unlawful acts

It is unlawful and a violation of this code for any manufacturer, manufacturer branch, distributor, or distributor branch licensed under this code to do, directly or indirectly through an affiliate, any of the following:

(a) Prevent, or attempt to prevent, by contract or otherwise, a dealer from acquiring, adding, or maintaining a sales or service operation for another line-make of motor vehicles at the same or expanded facility at which the dealer currently operates a dealership if the dealer complies with any reasonable facilities and capital requirements of the manufacturer or distributor.

(b) Require a dealer to establish or maintain exclusive facilities, personnel, or display space if the imposition of the requirement would be unreasonable in light of all existing circumstances, including economic conditions. In any proceeding * * * in which the reasonableness of a facility or capital requirement is an issue, the manufacturer or distributor shall have the burden of proof.

(c) Require, by contract or otherwise, a dealer to make a material alteration, expansion, or addition to any dealership facility, unless the required alteration, expansion, or addition is reasonable in light of all existing circumstances, including economic conditions and advancements in vehicular technology. This subdivision does not limit the obligation of a dealer to comply with any applicable health or safety laws.

(1) A required facility alteration, expansion, or addition shall not be deemed reasonable if it requires that the dealer purchase goods or services from a specific vendor when goods or services of substantially similar kind, quality, and general design concept are available from another vendor. Notwithstanding the prohibitions in this paragraph, a manufacturer, manufacturer branch, distributor, or distributor branch may require the dealer to request approval for the use of alternative goods or services in writing. Approval for these requests shall not be unreasonably withheld, and the request shall be deemed approved if not specifically denied in writing within 20 business days of receipt of the dealer's written request. This paragraph does not authorize a dealer to impair or eliminate the intellectual property or trademark rights of the manufacturer, manufacturer branch, distributor, or distributor branch, or to permit a dealer to erect or maintain signs that do not conform to the intellectual property usage guidelines of the manufacturer, manufacturer branch, distributor, or distributor branch. This paragraph shall not apply to a specific good or service if the manufacturer, manufacturer branch, distributor, or distributor branch provides the dealer with a lump-sum payment or series of payments of a substantial portion of the cost of that good or service, if the payment is intended solely to reimburse the dealer for the purchase of the specified good or service.

(2) In any proceeding in which a required facility alteration, expansion, or addition is an issue, the manufacturer* * * , manufacturer branch, distributor, distributor branch, or affiliate shall have the burden of proof.

(d)(1) Fail to pay to a dealer, within 90 days of termination, cancellation, or nonrenewal of a franchise, all of the following:

(A) The dealer cost, plus any charges made by the manufacturer or distributor for vehicle distribution or

379

delivery and the cost of any dealer-installed original equipment accessories, less any amount invoiced to the vehicle and paid by the manufacturer or distributor to the dealer, for all new and undamaged vehicles with less than 500 miles in the dealer's inventory that were acquired by the dealer from the manufacturer, distributor, or another new motor vehicle dealer franchised to sell vehicles of the same line-make, in the ordinary course of business, within 18 months of termination, cancellation, or nonrenewal of the franchise.

(B) The dealer cost for all unused and undamaged supplies, parts, and accessories listed in the manufacturer's current parts catalog and in their original packaging, except that sheet metal may be packaged in a comparable substitute for the original package.

(C) The fair market value of each undamaged sign owned by the motor vehicle dealer and bearing a common name, trade name, or trademark of the manufacturer or distributor if acquisition of the sign was required or made a condition of participation in an incentive program by the manufacturer or distributor.

(D) The fair market value of all special tools, computer systems, and equipment that were required or made a condition of participation in an incentive program by the manufacturer or distributor that are in usable condition, excluding normal wear and tear.

(E) The dealer costs of handling, packing, loading, and transporting any items or inventory for repurchase by the manufacturer or distributor.

(2) This subdivision does not apply to a franchisor of a dealer of new recreational vehicles, as defined in subdivision (a) of Section 18010 of the Health and Safety Code.

(3) This subdivision does not apply to a termination that is implemented as a result of the sale of substantially all of the inventory and fixed assets or stock of a franchised dealership if the dealership continues to operate as a franchisee of the same line-make.

(e)(1)(A) Fail to pay to a dealer of new recreational vehicles, as defined in subdivision (a) of Section 18010 of the Health and Safety Code, within 90 days of termination, cancellation, or nonrenewal of a franchise for a recreational vehicle line-make, as defined in Section 3072.5, the dealer cost, plus any charges made by the manufacturer or distributor for vehicle distribution or delivery and the cost of any dealer-installed original equipment accessories, less any amount invoiced to the vehicle and paid by the manufacturer or distributor to the dealer, for a new recreational vehicle when the termination, cancellation, or nonrenewal is initiated by a recreational vehicle manufacturer. This paragraph only applies to new and unused recreational vehicles that do not currently have or have had in the past, material damage, as defined in Section 9990, and that the dealer acquired from the manufacturer, distributor, or another new motor vehicle dealer franchised to sell recreational vehicles of the same line-make in the ordinary course of

business within 12 months of the termination, cancellation, or nonrenewal of the franchise.

(B) For those recreational vehicles with odometers, paragraph (1) shall apply to only those vehicles that have no more than 1,500 miles on the odometer, in addition to the number of miles incurred while delivering the vehicle from the manufacturer's facility that produced the vehicle for delivery to the dealer's retail location.

(C) Damaged recreational vehicles shall be repurchased by the manufacturer provided there is an offset in value for damages, except recreational vehicles that have or had material damage, as defined in Section 9990, may be repurchased at the manufacturer's option provided there is an offset in value for damages.

(2) Fail to pay to a dealer of new recreational vehicles, as defined in subdivision (a) of Section 18010 of the Health and Safety Code, within 90 days of termination, cancellation, or nonrenewal of a franchise, all of the following:

(A) The dealer cost for all unused and undamaged supplies, parts, and accessories listed in the manufacturer's current parts catalog and in their original packaging, except that sheet metal may be packaged in a comparable substitute for the original package.

(B) The fair market value of each undamaged sign owned by the motor vehicle dealer and bearing a common name, trade name, or trademark of the manufacturer or distributor if acquisition of the sign was required or made a condition of participation in an incentive program by the manufacturer or distributor.

(C) The fair market value of all special tools, computer systems, and equipment that were required or made a condition of participation in an incentive program by the manufacturer or distributor that are in usable condition, excluding normal wear and tear.

(D) The dealer costs of handling, packing, loading, and transporting any items or inventory for repurchase by the manufacturer or distributor.

(f)(1) Fail, upon demand, to indemnify any existing or former franchisee and the franchisee's successors and assigns from any and all damages sustained and attorney's fees and other expenses reasonably incurred by the franchisee that result from or relate to any claim made or asserted by a third party against the franchisee to the extent the claim results from any of the following:

(A) The condition, characteristics, manufacture, assembly, or design of any vehicle, parts, accessories, tools, or equipment, or the selection or combination of parts or components manufactured or distributed by the manufacturer or distributor.

(B) Service systems, procedures, or methods the franchisor required or recommended the franchisee to use if the franchisee properly uses the system, procedure, or method.

(C) Improper use or disclosure by a manufacturer or distributor of nonpublic personal information obtained from a franchisee concerning any consumer, customer, or employee of the franchisee.

(D) Any act or omission of the manufacturer or distributor for which the franchisee would have a claim for contribution or indemnity under applicable law or under the franchise, irrespective of and without regard to any prior termination or expiration of the franchise.

(2) This subdivision does not limit, in any way, the existing rights, remedies, or recourses available to any person who purchases or leases vehicles at retail.

(g)(1) Establish or maintain a performance standard, sales objective, or program for measuring a dealer's sales, service, or customer service performance that may materially affect the dealer, including, but not limited to, the dealer's right to payment under any incentive or reimbursement program or establishment of working capital requirements, unless both of the following requirements are satisfied:

(A) The performance standard, sales objective, or program for measuring dealership sales, service, or customer service performance is reasonable in light of all existing circumstances, including, but not limited to, the following:

(i) Demographics in the dealer's area of responsibility.

(ii) Geographical and market characteristics in the dealer's area of responsibility.

(iii) The availability and allocation of vehicles and parts inventory.

(iv) Local and statewide economic circumstances.

(v) Historical sales, service, and customer service performance of the line-make within the dealer's area of responsibility, including vehicle brand preferences of consumers in the dealer's area of responsibility.

(B) Within 30 days after a request by the dealer, the manufacturer, manufacturer branch, distributor, distributor branch, or affiliate provides a written summary of the methodology and data used in establishing the performance standard, sales objective, or program for measuring dealership sales or service performance. The summary shall be in detail sufficient to permit the dealer to determine how the standard was established and applied to the dealer.

(2) In any proceeding in which the reasonableness of a performance standard, sales objective, or program for measuring dealership sales, service, or customer service performance is an issue, the manufacturer, manufacturer branch, distributor, distributor branch, or affiliate shall have the burden of proof.

(3) As used in this subdivision, "area of responsibility" shall have the same meaning as defined in subdivision (z) of Section 11713.3. *(Added by Stats.2009, c. 12 (S.B.424), § 3, eff. July 2, 2009. Amended by Stats.2013, c. 512 (S.B.155), § 19.)*

Cross References

Burden of proof, generally, see Evidence Code § 500 et seq.

§ 11713.14. Auctions; rights and remedies of purchasers

(a) Notwithstanding any other provision of law, a person who purchases a vehicle that is sold through a dealer at an auction of vehicles open to the general public shall have the same rights and remedies against the dealer who conducts the auction sale as if that dealer were the owner and seller of the auctioned vehicle. The purchaser's rights and remedies are in addition to any right or remedy he or she may have against an owner of a vehicle sold at a public auto auction.

(b) If any claim or action is filed against a dealer pursuant to subdivision (a) and the vehicle that is the subject of the claim or action was owned by a person other than the dealer at the time of sale by auction, the owner of the vehicle that consigned it to the dealer shall indemnify the dealer for any liability resulting from misrepresentations or other misconduct by the consignor.

(c) A purchaser's rights and remedies under this section may not be waived or modified by an agreement or by a recharacterization of the sales transaction. *(Added by Stats.1999, c. 672 (S.B.974), § 3.)*

§ 11713.15. Temporary branch license to sell new recreational vehicles; manufacturer's written authorization

(a)(1) Prior to being issued a temporary branch license for selling new recreational vehicles, as defined in Section 18010 of the Health and Safety Code, at a show, a dealer shall submit to the department a manufacturer's written authorization for the sale specifying the dates of the show, the location of the show, and the makes of those new recreational vehicles being offered for sale.

(2) If nine or fewer dealers are participating in the show, a temporary branch license may only be issued to a dealer under this subdivision if the location of the show is 50 miles or less from that dealer's established place of business or permanent branch location.

Each dealer described in this paragraph shall certify in his or her application for a temporary branch license that the show location is 50 miles or less from his or her established place of business or permanent branch location.

(3) A temporary branch license may be issued to a dealer for purposes of participating in a show if all of the following conditions exist:

(A) The location of the show is 50 miles or more from the dealer's place of business or that dealer's branch locations, or both.

(B) Ten or more dealers apply for temporary branch licenses for purposes of participating in that show.

(C) Not less than 10 days prior to the conduct of the show, the department receives at least 10 applications for temporary branch licenses together at one of the department's field offices.

(b)(1) Any advertising and promotional materials designed to attract the public to attend a show of recreational vehicles where there are nine or fewer dealers participating shall include the business name of each participating dealer and that dealer's established place of business in a type size that is equivalent to the second largest type used in the advertisement or promotional materials. This information shall be placed at the top of any advertisement or promotional materials.

(2) If the recreational vehicles being offered for sale are used, the word "used" shall immediately precede the identification of the make of the vehicle or be immediately adjacent to the depiction of any used vehicles.

(3) In addition, the promoters of the show shall cause a sign to be conspicuously displayed at the major, public entrance leading directly to the show, printed in 50–point type, containing the information required in paragraph (1).

(c) A recreational vehicle dealer participating in a show for which a temporary branch license is required shall provide each buyer, prior to the sale of any vehicle at the show, a written statement disclosing the identity and the established business location of the dealer that has agreed to render service or warranty work with respect to the vehicle being purchased by the buyer, and if there is no agreement with any dealer to render the service or warranty, to state that fact.

(d) Paragraphs (2) and (3) of subdivision (a) and subdivision (b) do not apply to a dealer participating in an annual show sponsored by a national trade association of recreational vehicle manufacturers, the show is located in a county with a population of 6,000,000 or more persons, and at least 25 manufacturers are participating in the show, and, if the dealer is otherwise eligible to participate in the show, the department shall issue a temporary branch license if all the following occur:

(1) A national trade association of recreational vehicle manufacturers submits a letter to the department that certifies its status as a national trade association of recreational vehicle manufacturers and specifies the dates and location of the show.

(2) Upon receipt of the letter from a national trade association described in paragraph (1) notifying the department of the dates and location of the show, the department provides written acknowledgement to the national trade association submitting the letter.

(3) Each dealer participating in the show attaches a copy of the department letter described in paragraph (2) to the application for a temporary branch license submitted to the department. *(Added by Stats.1995, c. 923 (S.B.325), § 1. Amended by Stats.1997, c. 339 (S.B.1057), § 1, eff. Aug. 21, 1997.)*

382

§ 11713.16. Additional violations; advertising

It is a violation of this code for the holder of any dealer's license issued under this article to do any of the following:

(a) Advertise any used vehicle of the current or prior model-year without expressly disclosing the vehicle as "used," "previously owned," or a similar term that indicates that the vehicle is used, as defined in this code.

(b) Use the terms "on approved credit" or "on credit approval" in an advertisement for the sale of a vehicle unless those terms are clearly and conspicuously disclosed and unabbreviated.

(c) Advertise an amount described by terms such as "unpaid balance" or "balance can be financed" unless the total sale price is clearly and conspicuously disclosed and in close proximity to the advertised balance.

(d) Advertise credit terms that fail to comply with the disclosure requirements of Section 226.24 of Title 12 of the Code of Federal Regulations. Advertisements of terms that include escalated payments, balloon payments, or deferred downpayments shall clearly and conspicuously identify those payments as to amounts and time due.

(e) Advertise as the total sales price of a vehicle an amount that includes a deduction for a rebate. However, a dealer may advertise a separate amount that includes a deduction for a rebate provided that the advertisement clearly and conspicuously discloses, in close proximity to the amount advertised, the price of the vehicle before the rebate deduction and the amount of the rebate, each so identified.

(f) Advertise claims such as "everyone financed," "no credit rejected," or similar claims unless the dealer is willing to extend credit to any person under any and all circumstances.

(g) Advertise the amount of any downpayment unless it represents the total payment required of a purchaser prior to delivery of the vehicle, including any payment for sales tax or license. Statements such as "$____ delivers," "$____ puts you in a new car" are examples of advertised downpayments.

(h) Advertise the price of a new vehicle or class of new vehicles unless the vehicle or vehicles have all of the equipment listed as standard by the manufacturer or distributor or the dealer has replaced the standard equipment with equipment of higher value.

(i) Fail to clearly and conspicuously disclose in an advertisement for the sale of a vehicle any disclosure required by this code or any qualifying term used in conjunction with advertised credit terms. Unless otherwise provided by statute, the specific size of disclosures or qualifying terms is not prescribed. *(Added by Stats.2002, c. 947 (A.B.2397), § 5.)*

Cross References

False advertising, see Business and Professions Code § 17500 et seq.

Unfair Practices Act, see Business and Professions Code § 17000 et seq.

§ 11713.17. Conditions allowing dealer to deliver motor vehicle following retail sale or lease of motor vehicle for which department issues two license plates

(a) Following the retail sale or lease of a motor vehicle for which the department issues two license plates, a dealer may not deliver the motor vehicle unless either of the following occurs:

(1) The motor vehicle is equipped with a bracket or other means of securing a front license plate.

(2) The dealer obtains a signed written acknowledgment from the person taking delivery of the motor vehicle acknowledging both of the following:

(A) The person expressly refused installation of a bracket or other means of securing the front license plate.

(B) The person understands that California law requires a license plate to be displayed from and securely fastened to the front of the motor vehicle and that the hardware necessary to securely fasten the front plate is available from the dealer.

(b) A manufacturer or distributor may not sell or distribute in this state a new motor vehicle for which the department issues two license plates, unless that motor vehicle is equipped or provided with a bracket or other means of securing the license plates. *(Added by Stats. 2004, c. 365 (A.B.1272), § 1.)*

§ 11713.18. Advertisement of used vehicle as certified

(a) It is a violation of this code for the holder of any dealer's license issued under this article to advertise for sale or sell a used vehicle as "certified" or use any similar descriptive term in the advertisement or the sale of a used vehicle that implies the vehicle has been certified to meet the terms of a used vehicle certification program if any of the following apply:

(1) The dealer knows or should have known that the odometer on the vehicle does not indicate actual mileage, has been rolled back or otherwise altered to show fewer miles, or replaced with an odometer showing fewer miles than actually driven.

(2) The dealer knows or should have known that the vehicle was reacquired by the vehicle's manufacturer or a dealer pursuant to state or federal warranty laws.

(3) The title to the vehicle has been inscribed with the notation "Lemon Law Buyback," "manufacturer repurchase," "salvage," "junk," "nonrepairable," "flood," or similar title designation required by this state or another state.

(4) The vehicle has sustained damage in an impact, fire, or flood, that after repair prior to sale substantially impairs the use or safety of the vehicle.

(5) The dealer knows or should have known that the vehicle has sustained frame damage.

(6) Prior to sale, the dealer fails to provide the buyer with a completed inspection report indicating all the components inspected.

(7) The dealer disclaims any warranties of merchantability on the vehicle.

(8) The vehicle is sold "AS IS."

(9) The term "certified" or any similar descriptive term is used in any manner that is untrue or misleading or that would cause any advertisement to be in violation of subdivision (a) of Section 11713 of this code or Section 17200 or 17500 of the Business and Professions Code.

(b) A violation of this section is actionable under the Consumers Legal Remedies Act (Title 1.5 (commencing with Section 1750) of Part 4 of Division 3 of the Civil Code), the Unfair Competition Law (Chapter 5 (commencing with Section 17200) of Part 2 of Division 7 of the Business and Professions Code), Section 17500 of the Business and Professions Code, or any other applicable state or federal law. The rights and remedies provided by this section are cumulative and shall not be construed as restricting any right or remedy that is otherwise available.

(c) This section does not abrogate or limit any disclosure obligation imposed by any other law.

(d) This section does not apply to the advertisement or sale of a used motorcycle or a used off-highway motor vehicle subject to identification under Section 38010. *(Added by Stats.2005, c. 128 (A.B.68), § 8, operative July 1, 2006.)*

Cross References
Buy-here-pay-here dealer, exclusions from definition, see Vehicle Code § 241.1.

§ 11713.19. Disclosure of additional charges for goods or services

(a) It is unlawful and a violation of this code for the holder of any dealer's license issued under this article to do any of the following:

(1) Negotiate the terms of a vehicle sale or lease contract and then add charges to the contract for any goods or services without previously disclosing to the consumer the goods and services to be added and obtaining the consumer's consent.

(2)(A) Inflate the amount of an installment payment or down payment or extend the maturity of a sale or lease contract for the purpose of disguising the actual charges for goods or services to be added by the dealer to the contract.

(B) For purposes of subparagraph (A), "goods or services" means any type of good or service, including, but not limited to, insurance and service contracts.

(b) Subdivision (a) does not apply to the sale or lease of a motorcycle or an off-highway motor vehicle subject to identification under Section 38010. *(Added by Stats. 2005, c. 128 (A.B.68), § 9, operative July 1, 2006.)*

§ 11713.20. Consumer credit score obtained by a dealer; information to be provided to the consumer

(a) A dealer that obtains a consumer credit score, as defined in subdivision (b) of Section 1785.15.1 of the Civil Code, from a consumer credit reporting agency, as defined in subdivision (d) of Section 1785.3 of the Civil Code, for use in connection with an application for credit initiated by a consumer for the purchase or lease of a motor vehicle for personal, family, or household use, shall provide, prior to the sale or lease of the vehicle, the following information to the consumer in at least 10–point type on a document separate from the sale or lease contract:

(1) Each credit score obtained and used by the dealer.

(2) A statement that a consumer report, or a credit report, is a record of the consumer's credit history and includes information about whether the consumer pays his or her obligations on time and how much the consumer owes to creditors.

(3) A statement that a credit score is a number that takes into account information in a consumer report and that a credit score can change over time to reflect changes in the consumer's credit history.

(4) A statement that the consumer's credit score can affect whether the consumer can obtain credit and what the cost of that credit will be.

(5) The range of possible credit scores under the model used to generate that credit score.

(6) The distribution of credit scores among consumers who are scored under the same scoring model that is used to generate the consumer's credit score using the same scale as that of the credit score that is provided to the consumer, presented in the form of a bar graph containing a minimum of six bars that illustrates the percentage of consumers with credit scores within the range of scores reflected in each bar, or by other clear and readily understandable graphical means, or a clear and readily understandable statement informing the consumer how his or her credit score compares to the scores of other consumers. Use of a graph or statement obtained from the person providing the credit score that meets the requirements of this paragraph is deemed to comply with this requirement.

(7) The date the credit score was created.

(8) The name of the consumer reporting agency or other person that provided each credit score obtained and used by the dealer.

(9) A statement that the consumer is encouraged to verify the accuracy of the information contained in the consumer report and has the right to dispute any inaccurate information in the report.

(10) A statement that federal law gives the consumer the right to obtain copies of his or her consumer reports directly from the consumer reporting agencies, including a free report from each of the nationwide consumer reporting agencies once during any 12–month period.

(11) Contact information for the centralized source from which consumers may obtain their free annual consumer reports.

(12) A statement directing consumers to the Internet Web sites of the Federal Reserve Board and Federal Trade Commission to obtain more information about consumer reports.

(b) Appropriate use by a dealer of the model form described in Section 640.5(e)(5) of Title 16 of the Code of Federal Regulations and contained in Title 16 of the Code of Federal Regulations Part B, Appendix B, Model Form B–4, as promulgated on January 15, 2010, is deemed to comply with the requirements of this section. Use of the model form is optional.

(c) This section does not apply to the purchase or lease of a motorcycle or an off-highway motor vehicle subject to identification under Section 38010.

(d) This section does not limit or restrict any rights or remedies otherwise available under existing law. *(Added by Stats.2005, c. 128 (A.B.68), § 10, operative July 1, 2006. Amended by Stats.2010, c. 483 (S.B.1004), § 3.)*

§ 11713.21. Contract cancellation option agreement required; exceptions; purchase price; form; cancellation procedures

(a)(1) A dealer shall not sell a used vehicle, as defined in Section 665 and subject to registration under this code, at retail to an individual for personal, family, or household use without offering the buyer a contract cancellation option agreement that allows the buyer to return the vehicle without cause. This section does not apply to a used vehicle having a purchase price of forty thousand dollars ($40,000) or more, a motorcycle, as defined in Section 400, or a recreational vehicle, as defined in Section 18010 of the Health and Safety Code.

(2) The purchase price for the contract cancellation option shall not exceed the following:

(A) Seventy-five dollars ($75) for a vehicle with a cash price of five thousand dollars ($5,000) or less.

(B) One hundred fifty dollars ($150) for a vehicle with a cash price of more than five thousand dollars ($5,000), but not more than ten thousand dollars ($10,000).

(C) Two hundred fifty dollars ($250) for a vehicle with a cash price of more than ten thousand dollars ($10,000), but not more than thirty thousand dollars ($30,000).

(D) One percent of the purchase price for a vehicle with a cash price of more than thirty thousand dollars ($30,000), but less than forty thousand dollars ($40,000).

The term "cash price" as used in this paragraph has the same meaning as described in subparagraph (A) of paragraph (1) of subdivision (a) of Section 2982 of the Civil Code. "Cash price" also excludes registration, transfer, titling, and license fees, the California tire fee, and any charge to electronically register or transfer the vehicle.

(b) To comply with subdivision (a), and notwithstanding Section 2981.9 of the Civil Code, a contract cancellation option agreement shall be contained in a document separate from the conditional sales contract or other vehicle purchase agreement and shall contain, at a minimum, the following:

(1) The name of the seller and the buyer.

(2) A description and the Vehicle Identification Number of the vehicle purchased.

(3) A statement specifying the time within which the buyer must exercise the right to cancel the purchase under the contract cancellation option and return the vehicle to the dealer. The dealer shall not specify a time that is earlier than the dealer's close of business on the second day following the day on which the vehicle was originally delivered to the buyer by the dealer.

(4) A statement that clearly and conspicuously specifies the dollar amount of any restocking fee the buyer must pay to the dealer to exercise the right to cancel the purchase under the contract cancellation option. The restocking fee shall not exceed one hundred seventy-five dollars ($175) if the vehicle's cash price is five thousand dollars ($5,000) or less, three hundred fifty dollars ($350) if the vehicle's cash price is less than ten thousand dollars ($10,000), and five hundred dollars ($500) if the vehicle cash price is ten thousand dollars ($10,000) or more. The dealer shall apply toward the restocking fee the price paid by the buyer for the contract cancellation option. The price for the purchase of the contract cancellation option is not otherwise subject to setoff or refund.

(5) Notwithstanding paragraph (4), when a buyer, who leased the purchased vehicle immediately preceding the dealer's sale of the vehicle to the buyer, exercises the contract cancellation option, the limit on the amount of a restocking fee required to be paid by the buyer shall be increased. That increased amount shall be the amount the buyer would have been obligated to pay the lessor, at the time of the termination of the lease, for the following charges, as specified in the lease, and as if the buyer had not purchased the contract cancellation option:

(A) Excess mileage.

(B) Unrepaired damage.

(C) Excess wear and tear.

(6) A statement specifying the maximum number of miles that the vehicle may be driven after its original delivery by the dealer to the buyer to remain eligible for cancellation under the contract cancellation option. A dealer shall not specify fewer than 250 miles in the contract cancellation option agreement.

(7) A statement that the contract cancellation option gives the buyer the right to cancel the purchase and obtain a full refund, minus the purchase price for the contract cancellation option agreement; and that the right to cancel will apply only if, within the time specified in the contract cancellation option agreement, the following are personally delivered to the selling dealer by the buyer: a written notice exercising the right to cancel the purchase signed by the buyer; any restocking fee specified in the contract cancellation option agreement minus the purchase price for the contract cancellation option agreement; the original contract cancellation option agreement and vehicle purchase contract and related documents, if the seller gave those original documents to the buyer; all original vehicle titling and registration documents, if the seller gave those original documents to the buyer; and the vehicle, free of all liens and encumbrances, other than any lien or encumbrance created by or incidental to the conditional sales contract, any loan arranged by the dealer, or any purchase money loan obtained by the buyer from a third party, and in the same condition as when it was delivered by the dealer to the buyer, reasonable wear and tear and any defect or mechanical problem that manifests or becomes evident after delivery that was not caused by the buyer excepted, and which must not have been driven beyond the mileage limit specified in the contract cancellation option agreement. The agreement may also provide that the buyer will execute documents reasonably necessary to effectuate the cancellation and refund and as reasonably required to comply with applicable law.

(8) At the bottom of the contract cancellation option agreement, a statement that may be signed by the buyer to indicate the buyer's election to exercise the right to cancel the purchase under the terms of the contract cancellation option agreement, and the last date and time by which the option to cancel may be exercised, followed by a line for the buyer's signature. A particular form of statement is not required, but the following statement is sufficient: "By signing below, I elect to exercise my right to cancel the purchase of the vehicle described in this agreement." The buyer's delivery of the purchase cancellation agreement to the dealer with the buyer's signature following this statement shall constitute sufficient written notice exercising the right to cancel the purchase pursuant to paragraph (6). The dealer shall provide the buyer with the statement required by this paragraph in duplicate to enable the buyer to return the signed cancellation notice and retain a copy of the cancellation agreement.

(9) If, pursuant to paragraph (5), the limit on the restocking fee is increased by the amount the buyer, who exercises a contract cancellation option would have been obligated to pay the lessor, upon termination of the lease, for charges for excess mileage, unrepaired damage, or excess wear and tear, as specified in the lease, the dealer shall provide the buyer with a notice of the contents of paragraph (5), including a statement regarding the increased restocking fee.

(c)(1) No later than the second day following the day on which the buyer exercises the right to cancel the purchase in compliance with the contract cancellation option agreement, the dealer shall cancel the contract and provide the buyer with a full refund, including that portion of the sales tax attributable to amounts excluded pursuant to Section 6012.3 of the Revenue and Taxation Code.

(2) If the buyer was not charged for the contract cancellation option agreement, the dealer shall return to the buyer, no later than the day following the day on which the buyer exercises the right to cancel the purchase, any motor vehicle the buyer left with the seller as a downpayment or trade-in. If the dealer has sold or otherwise transferred title to the motor vehicle that was left as a downpayment or trade-in, the full refund described in paragraph (1) shall include the fair market value of the motor vehicle left as a downpayment or trade-in, or its value as stated in the contract or purchase order, whichever is greater.

(3) If the buyer was charged for the contract cancellation option agreement, the dealer shall retain any motor vehicle the buyer left with the dealer as a downpayment or trade-in until the buyer exercises the right to cancel or the right to cancel expires. If the buyer exercises the right to cancel the purchase, the dealer shall return to the buyer, no later than the day following the day on which the buyer exercises the right to cancel the purchase, any motor vehicle the buyer left with the seller as a downpayment or trade-in. If the dealer has inadvertently sold or otherwise transferred title to the motor vehicle as the result of a bona fide error, notwithstanding reasonable procedures designed to avoid that error, the inadvertent sale or transfer of title shall not be deemed a violation of this paragraph, and the full refund described in paragraph (1) shall include the retail market value of the motor vehicle left as a downpayment or trade-in, or its value as stated in the contract or purchase order, whichever is greater.

(d) If the dealer received a portion of the purchase price by credit card, or other third-party payer on the buyer's account, the dealer may refund that portion of the purchase price to the credit card issuer or third-party payer for credit to the buyer's account.

(e) Notwithstanding subdivision (a), a dealer is not required to offer a contract cancellation option agreement to an individual who exercised his or her right to cancel the purchase of a vehicle from the dealer pursuant to a contract cancellation option agreement during the immediately preceding 30 days. A dealer is not required to give notice to a subsequent buyer of the return of a vehicle pursuant to this section. This subdivision does not abrogate or limit any disclosure obligation imposed by any other law.

(f) This section does not affect or alter the legal rights, duties, obligations, or liabilities of the buyer, the dealer, or the dealer's agents or assigns, that would exist in the absence of a contract cancellation option agreement. The buyer is the owner of a vehicle when he or she takes delivery of a vehicle until the vehicle is returned to the dealer pursuant to a contract cancellation option agreement, and the existence of a contract cancellation option agreement shall not impose permissive user liability on

the dealer, or the dealer's agents or assigns, under Section 460 or 17150 or otherwise.

(g) This section does not affect the ability of a buyer to rescind the contract or revoke acceptance under any other law.

(h) This section shall become operative on July 1, 2012. *(Added by Stats.2011, c. 329 (A.B.1215), § 16, operative July 1, 2012.)*

Cross References

Gross receipts and sales price, contract cancellation option, see Revenue and Taxation Code § 6012.3.

§ 11713.22. Recreational vehicle franchises

(a) Upon mutual agreement of the parties to enter into a recreational vehicle franchise, it is unlawful and a violation of this code for a manufacturer, manufacturer branch, distributor, or distributor branch licensed under this code to fail or refuse to provide a recreational vehicle dealer with a written recreational vehicle franchise that complies with the requirements of Section 331.3.

(b) Notwithstanding Section 331.3, a recreational vehicle franchise described in this section shall include, but not be limited to, provisions regarding dealership transfer, dealership termination, sales territory, and reimbursement for costs incurred by the dealer for work related to the manufacturer's warranty for each line-make of recreational vehicle covered by the agreement.

(c) This section applies only to a dealer and manufacturer agreement involving recreational vehicles, as defined in subdivision (a) of Section 18010 of the Health and Safety Code, but does not include an agreement with a dealer who deals exclusively in truck campers. *(Added by Stats.2007, c. 406 (A.B.1092), § 1. Amended by Stats.2008, c. 743 (A.B.2436), § 2.)*

§ 11713.23. Sale or shipment of new recreational vehicles; recreational vehicle franchise required; inventory; application

(a) A recreational vehicle manufacturer, manufacturer branch, distributor, or distributor branch licensed under this code shall not sell a new recreational vehicle in this state to or through a recreational vehicle dealer without having first entered into a written recreational vehicle franchise with that recreational vehicle dealer, that complies with the requirements of Section 331.3 and that has been signed by both parties.

(b) A recreational vehicle dealer shall not sell a new recreational vehicle in this state without having first entered into a written recreational vehicle franchise, that complies with the requirements of Section 331.3, with a recreational vehicle manufacturer, manufacturer branch, distributor, or distributor branch licensed under this code, that has been signed by both parties.

(c)(1) A recreational vehicle manufacturer, manufacturer branch, distributor, or distributor branch shall not ship a new recreational vehicle to a recreational dealer on or after January 1, 2009, without a recreational vehicle franchise that has been signed by both parties.

(2) A recreational vehicle dealer shall not receive a new recreational vehicle from a recreational vehicle manufacturer, manufacturer branch, distributor, or distributor branch on or after January 1, 2009, without a recreational vehicle franchise that has been signed by both parties.

(d) Any new recreational vehicle inventory that has been purchased by a recreational vehicle dealer, or shipped by a manufacturer, manufacturer branch, distributor, or distributor branch, before January 1, 2009, may be sold at any time without a recreational vehicle franchise.

(e) This section applies only to a dealer and manufacturer agreement involving recreational vehicles, as defined in subdivision (a) of Section 18010 of the Health and Safety Code, but does not include an agreement with a dealer who deals exclusively in truck campers. *(Added by Stats.2008, c. 743 (A.B.2436), § 3.)*

§ 11713.25. Computer vendors; consent required from dealer to access, modify, or extract information from confidential dealer computer records or personally identifiable consumer data; dealer right to revoke consent

(a) A computer vendor shall not do any of the following:

(1) Access, modify, or extract information from a confidential dealer computer record or personally identifiable consumer data from a dealer without first obtaining express written consent from the dealer and without maintaining administrative, technical, and physical safeguards to protect the security, confidentiality, and integrity of the information.

(2)(A) Except as provided in subparagraph (B), require a dealer as a condition of doing or continuing to do business, to give express consent to perform the activities specified in paragraph (1).

(B) Express consent may be required as a condition of doing or continuing to do business if the consent is limited to permitting access to personally identifiable consumer data to the extent necessary to do any of the following:

(i) To protect against, or prevent actual or potential fraud, unauthorized transactions, claims, or other liability, or to protect against breaches of confidentiality or security of consumer records.

(ii) To comply with institutional risk control or to resolve consumer disputes or inquiries.

(iii) To comply with federal, state, or local laws, rules, and other applicable legal requirements, including lawful requirements of a law enforcement or governmental agency.

(iv) To comply with lawful requirements of a self-regulatory organization or as necessary to perform an investigation on a matter related to public safety.

(v) To comply with a properly authorized civil, criminal, or regulatory investigation, or subpoena or summons by federal, state, or local authorities.

(vi) To make other use of personally identifiable consumer data with the express written consent of the consumer that has not been revoked by the consumer.

(3) Use electronic, contractual, or other means to prevent or interfere with the lawful efforts of a dealer to comply with federal and state data security and privacy laws and to maintain the security, integrity, and confidentiality of confidential dealer computer records, including, but not limited to, the ability of a dealer to monitor specific data accessed from or written to the dealer computer system. Waiver of this subdivision or purported consents authorizing the activities proscribed by the subdivision is void.

(b) A dealer shall have the right to prospectively revoke an express consent by providing a 10–day written notice to the computer vendor to whom the consent was provided or on any shorter period of notice agreed to by the computer vendor and the dealer. An agreement that requires a dealer to waive its right to prospectively revoke an express consent is void.

(c) For the purposes of this section, the following terms mean as follows:

(1) "Confidential dealer computer record" means a computer record residing on the dealer's computer system that contains, in whole or in part, any personally identifiable consumer data, or the dealer's financial or other proprietary data.

(2) "Computer vendor" means a person, other than a manufacturer, manufacturer branch, distributor, or distributor branch, who in the ordinary course of that person's business configured, sold, leased, licensed, maintained, or otherwise made available to a dealer, a dealer computer system.

(3) "Dealer computer system" means a computer system or computerized application primarily designed for use by and sold to a motor vehicle dealer that, by ownership, lease, license, or otherwise, is used by and in the ordinary course of business of a dealer.

(4) "Express consent" means the unrevoked written consent signed by a dealer that specifically describes the data that may be accessed, the means by which it may be accessed, the purpose for which it may be used, and the person or class of persons to whom it may be disclosed.

(5) "Personally identifiable consumer data" means information that is any of the following:

(A) Information of the type specified in subparagraph (A) of paragraph (6) of subdivision (e) of Section 1798.83 of the Civil Code.

(B) Information that is nonpublic personal information as defined in Section 313.3(n)(1) of Title 16 of the Code of Federal Regulations.

(C) Information that is nonpublic personal information as defined in subdivision (a) of Section 4052 of the Financial Code.

(d) This section does not limit a duty that a dealer may have to safeguard the security and privacy of records maintained by the dealer. *(Added by Stats.2006, c. 353 (A.B.2291), § 2.)*

§ 11713.26. Used vehicles; NMVTIS vehicle history report required; requirements for junk or salvage automobiles; exceptions

(a) A dealer shall not display or offer for sale at retail a used vehicle, as defined in Section 665 and subject to registration under this code, unless the dealer first obtains a NMVTIS vehicle history report from a NMVTIS data provider for the vehicle identification number of the vehicle.

(b) If a NMVTIS vehicle history report for a used vehicle indicates that the vehicle is or has been a junk automobile or a salvage automobile or the vehicle has been reported as a junk automobile or a salvage automobile by a junk yard, salvage yard, or insurance carrier pursuant to Section 30504 of Title 49 of the United States Code, or the certificate of title contains a brand, a dealer shall do both of the following:

(1) Post the following disclosure on the vehicle while it is displayed for sale at retail in at least 14–point bold black type, except for the title "Warning" which shall be in at least 18–point bold black type, on at least a 4 x 5.5 inch red background in close proximity to the Federal Trade Commission's Buyer's Guide:

"WARNING

According to a vehicle history report issued by the National Motor Vehicle Title Information System (NMVTIS), this vehicle has been reported as a total-loss vehicle by an insurance company, has been reported into NMVTIS by a junk or salvage reporting entity, or has a title brand which may materially affect the value, safety, and/or condition of the vehicle. Because of its history as a junk, salvage, or title-branded vehicle, the manufacturer's warranty or service contract on this vehicle may be affected. Ask the dealer to see a copy of the NMVTIS vehicle history report. You may independently obtain the report by checking NMVTIS online at www. vehiclehistory.gov."

(2) Provide the retail purchaser with a copy of the NMVTIS vehicle history report upon request prior to sale.

(c) Subdivisions (a) and (b) do not apply to a used vehicle for which NMVTIS does not have a record if the dealer attempts to obtain a NMVTIS vehicle history report for the vehicle.

(d) As used in this section the following terms have the following meanings:

(1) "NMVTIS" means the National Motor Vehicle Title Information System established pursuant to Section 30501 et seq. of Title 49 of the United States Code.

(2) "NMVTIS vehicle history report" means a report obtained by an NMVTIS data provider that contains:

(A) The date of the report.

(B) Any disclaimer required by the operator of NMVTIS.

(C) If available from NMVTIS, information establishing the following:

(i) Whether the vehicle is titled in a particular state.

(ii) Whether the title to the vehicle was branded by a state.

(iii) The validity and status of a document purporting to be a certificate of title for the vehicle.

(iv) Whether the vehicle is or has been a junk automobile or a salvage automobile.

(v) The odometer mileage disclosure required pursuant to Section 32705 of Title 49 of the United States Code for that vehicle on the date the certificate of title for that vehicle was issued and any later mileage information.

(vi) Whether the vehicle has been reported as a junk automobile or a salvage automobile pursuant to Section 30504 of Title 49 of the United States Code.

(3) "Junk automobile," "operator," and "salvage automobile" shall have the same meanings as defined in Section 25.52 of Title 28 of the Code of Federal Regulations.

(4) "NMVTIS data provider" means a person authorized by the NMVTIS operator as an access portal provider for NMVTIS. .

(5) "NMVTIS operator" means the individual or entity authorized or designated as the operator of NMVTIS pursuant to subdivision (b) of Section 30502 of Title 49 of the United States Code, or the office designated by the United States Attorney General, if there is no authorized or designated individual or entity.

(e) Nothing in this section shall prohibit a NMVTIS data provider from including, in a NMVTIS vehicle history report containing the information required by paragraph (2) of subdivision (d), additional vehicle history information obtained from resources other than NMVTIS.

(f) This section shall not create any legal duty upon the dealer related to the accuracy, errors, or omissions contained in a NMVTIS vehicle history report that is obtained from a NMVTIS data provider or any legal duty to provide information added to NMVTIS after the dealer obtained the NMVTIS vehicle history report pursuant to subdivision (a).

(g)(1) In the event that all NMVTIS data providers cease to make NMVTIS vehicle history reports available to the public, this section shall become inoperative.

(2) In the event that all NMVTIS data providers cease to make NMVTIS vehicle history reports available to the public, it is the intent of the Legislature that the United States Department of Justice notify the Legislature and the department.

(h) This section does not apply to the sale of a recreational vehicle, a motorcycle, or an off-highway motor vehicle subject to identification under Section 38010.

(i) This section shall become operative on July 1, 2012. *(Added by Stats.2011, c. 329 (A.B.1215), § 17, operative July 1, 2012.)*

§ 11714. Issuance of license; posting at sales location; wholesale dealers; special plates

(a) The department, upon granting a license, shall issue to the applicant a license containing the applicant's name and address and the general distinguishing number assigned to the applicant.

(b) A dealer shall not sell any vehicle at retail at a location that is not posted pursuant to Section 11709.

(c) A dealer who is authorized by the department to sell motor vehicles only at wholesale shall not sell any vehicle at retail and shall report every sale to the department on the wholesale report of sale form prescribed by the department.

(d) When the department has issued a license pursuant to subdivision (a), the licensee may apply for and the department shall issue special plates which shall have displayed thereon the general distinguishing number assigned to the applicant. Each plate so issued shall also contain a number or symbol identifying the plate from every other plate bearing a like general distinguishing number.

(e) The department shall also furnish books and forms as it may determine necessary. Such books and forms are and shall remain the property of the department and may be taken up at any time for inspection. *(Stats.1959, c. 3, p. 1610, § 11714. Amended by Stats.1971, c. 929, p. 1827, § 2, operative May 3, 1972; Stats.1975, c. 182, p. 536, § 21, eff. July 5, 1975; Stats.1987, c. 444, § 1.)*

Cross References

Expiration and renewal of occupational licenses and special plates, see Vehicle Code § 11717.
Operation of vehicles by dealers without evidences of registration, see Vehicle Code § 4456.

§ 11715. Operation of vehicles displaying special plates

(a) A manufacturer, remanufacturer, distributor, or dealer owning or lawfully possessing any vehicle of a type otherwise required to be registered under this code may operate or move the vehicle upon the highways without registering the vehicle upon condition that the vehicle displays special plates issued to the owner as provided in this chapter, in addition to other license plates or permits already assigned and attached to the vehicle in the manner prescribed in Sections 5200 to 5203, inclusive. A vehicle for sale or lease by a dealer may also be operated or moved upon the highways without registration for a period not to exceed seven days by a prospective buyer or lessee who is test- driving the vehicle for possible purchase or lease, if the vehicle is in compliance with this condition. The vehicle may also be moved or operated for the purpose of towing or transporting by any lawful method other vehicles.

(b) A transporter may operate or move any owned or lawfully possessed vehicle of like type by any lawful method upon the highways solely for the purpose of delivery, upon condition that there be displayed upon each vehicle in contact with the highway special license plates issued to the transporter as provided in this chapter, in addition to any license plates or permits already assigned and attached to the vehicle in the manner prescribed in Sections 5200 to 5203, inclusive. The vehicles may be used for the purpose of towing or transporting by any lawful method other vehicles when the towing or transporting vehicle is being delivered for sale or to the owner thereof.

(c) This section does not apply to any manufacturer, remanufacturer, transporter, distributor, or dealer operating or moving a vehicle as provided in Section 11716.

(d) This section does not apply to work or service vehicles owned by a manufacturer, remanufacturer, transporter, distributor, or dealer. This section does not apply to vehicles owned and leased by dealers, except those vehicles rented or leased to vehicle salespersons in the course of their employment for purposes of display or demonstration, nor to any unregistered vehicles used to transport more than one load of other vehicles for the purpose of sale.

(e) This section does not apply to vehicles currently registered in this state that are owned and operated by a licensed dealer when the notice of transfer has been forwarded to the department by the former owner of record pursuant to Section 5900 and when a copy of the notice is displayed as follows:

(1) For a motorcycle or motor-driven cycle, the notice is displayed in a conspicuous manner upon the vehicle.

(2) For a vehicle other than a motorcycle or motor-driven cycle, the notice is displayed in the lower right-hand corner of the windshield of the vehicle, as specified in paragraph (3) of subdivision (b) of Section 26708.

(f) Every owner, upon receipt of a registration card issued for special plates, shall maintain the same or a facsimile copy thereof with the vehicle bearing the special plates. *(Stats.1959, c. 3, p. 1611, § 11715. Amended by Stats.1959, c. 421, p. 2360, § 1; Stats.1959, c. 1391, p. 3669, § 1; Stats.1961, c. 346, p. 1387, § 2; Stats.1967, c.*

801, p. 2218, § 2; Stats.1971, c. 929, p. 1827, § 3, operative May 3, 1972; Stats.1975, c. 182, p. 536, § 22, eff. July 5, 1975; Stats.1977, c. 105, p. 536, § 3; Stats.1983, c. 1286, § 39; Stats.2001, c. 739 (A.B.1707), § 6.5.)

Cross References

Definitions,
    Dealer, see Vehicle Code §§ 285, 286.
    Transporter, see Vehicle Code § 645.
    Vehicle, see Vehicle Code § 670.
Exemption from registration of vehicles, see Vehicle Code § 4002.
Reflectorized license plates to be furnished by department, see Vehicle Code § 4850.

§ 11716. When a vehicle may be operated without plates

A manufacturer, remanufacturer, transporter, distributor, or dealer, in the course of business, may operate or move any vehicle of a type otherwise required to be registered under this code without registering the vehicle, and without license or special plates attached thereto, from a vessel, railroad depot, or warehouse over the highways to a warehouse or salesroom upon first having obtained a written permit from the department authorizing that operation. *(Stats.1959, c. 3, p. 1611, § 11716. Amended by Stats.1983, c. 1286, § 40; Stats.1990, c. 1563 (A.B.3243), § 45.)*

Cross References

Definitions,
    Dealer, see Vehicle Code §§ 285, 286.
    Transporter, see Vehicle Code § 645.
    Vehicle, see Vehicle Code § 670.
Exception from operation of vehicles displaying special plate, see Vehicle Code § 11715.
Operation of vehicles by dealers without evidences of registration, see Vehicle Code § 4456.

§ 11717. Expiration of occupational licenses and special plates

(a) Every occupational license and special plate issued under this article shall be valid for a period of one year from midnight of the last day of the month of issuance. Except as provided in subdivision (c), renewal of the occupational license and special plates for the ensuing year may be obtained by the person to whom the occupational license and special plates were issued upon application to the department and payment of the fee provided in this code.

(b) Every application for the renewal of an occupational license and special plates which expire pursuant to this section shall be made by the person to whom issued not more than 90 days prior to the expiration date, and shall be made by presenting the completed application form provided by the department and by payment of the full annual renewal fee for the occupational license and special plates.

(c) If the application for renewal of the occupational license and special plates is not made by midnight of the expiration date, the application may be made within 30 days following expiration of the license by paying the annual renewal fee and a penalty fee equal to the amount of the original application fee for each occupational license held. A penalty as specified in Sections 9553 and 9554 shall also be added to each special plate renewed during the 30-day period following expiration of the special plates.

(d) In no event may the licensee renew the occupational license or special plates after the expiration of the 30-day period authorized in subdivision (c). *(Stats.1959, c. 3, p. 1611, § 11717. Amended by Stats.1971, c. 1214, p. 2355, § 35, operative May 3, 1972; Stats.1982, c. 571, p. 2527, § 6; Stats.1984, c. 499, § 12.)*

Cross References

Fees for special plates, see Vehicle Code § 9262.

§ 11717.1. Repealed by Stats.1992, c. 1241 (S.B.1615), § 18

§ 11718. Issuance of probationary license

Except where the provisions of this code require the refusal to issue a license, the department may issue a probationary license subject to conditions to be observed by the licensee in the exercise of the privilege granted. The conditions to be attached to the exercise of the privilege shall not appear on the face of the license but shall be such as may, in the judgment of the department, be in the public interest and suitable to the qualifications of the applicant as disclosed by the application and investigation by the department of the information contained therein. *(Added by Stats.1959, c. 1827, p. 4341, § 2. Amended by Stats.1971, c. 1214, p. 2355, § 36, operative May 3, 1972.)*

§ 11719. Temporary permit

Pending the satisfaction of the department that the applicant has met the requirements under this article, it may issue a temporary permit to any person applying for a manufacturer's, manufacturer's branch, remanufacturer's, remanufacturer's branch, distributor's, distributor's branch, transporter's, or dealer's license and special plates. The temporary permit shall permit the operation by the manufacturer, manufacturer branch, remanufacturer, remanufacturer branch, distributor, distributor branch, transporter, or dealer for a period not to exceed 120 days while the department is completing its investigation and determination of all facts relative to the qualifications of the applicant to the license and special plates. The department may cancel the temporary permit when it has determined, or has reasonable cause to believe, that the application is incorrect or incomplete or the temporary permit was issued in error. The temporary permit is invalid when canceled or when the applicant's license has been issued or refused. *(Added by Stats.1959, c. 1827, p. 4341, § 3. Amended by Stats.1971, c. 1214, p. 2355, § 37, operative May 3, 1972; Stats.1972, c. 215, p. 447, § 3;*

Stats.1973, c. 996, p. 1979, § 31, operative July 1, 1974; Stats.1983, c. 1286, § 41.)

§ 11720. Certificate of convenience

The department may issue a certificate of convenience to the executor, executrix, administrator or administratrix of the estate of a deceased holder of validly outstanding special plates and license issued under this article, or if no executor, executrix, administrator or administratrix has been appointed, and until a certified copy of an order making such appointment is filed with the department, to the surviving spouse or other heir otherwise entitled to conduct the business of the deceased, permitting such person to exercise the privileges granted by such special plates and license for a period of one year from and after the date of death and necessary one-year renewals thereafter, pending, but not later than, disposal of the business and qualification of the vendee of the business or such surviving spouse, heir or other persons for such special plates and license under the provisions of this article. The department may restrict or condition the license and attach to the exercise of the privileges thereunder such terms and conditions as in its judgment the protection of the public requires. *(Added by Stats. 1959, c. 1827, p. 4341, § 4. Amended by Stats.1971, c. 1214, p. 2355, § 38, operative May 3, 1972; Stats.1976, c. 1171, p. 5261, § 31.)*

§ 11721. Automatic cancellation

The special plates and licenses provided for in this article shall be automatically canceled upon the happening of any of the following:

(a) The abandonment of the established place of business of the dealer or the change thereof without notice to the department as provided in Section 11712.

(b) The failure of the licensee to maintain an adequate bond or to procure and file another bond as provided in Section 11710 prior to the effective date of the termination by the surety of any existing bond.

(c) The voluntary or involuntary surrender for any cause by the licensee of the special plates and license, except that the surrender of the special plates and license, the cessation of business by the licensee, or the suspension or revocation of the corporate status of the licensee, does not preclude the filing of an accusation for revocation or suspension of the surrendered license as provided in Section 11705, does not affect the department's decision to suspend or revoke the license. The department's determination to suspend or revoke the license may be considered in issuing or refusing to issue any subsequent license authorized by this division to that licensee or to a business representative of that prior licensee.

(d) Notification to the department that the person designated as licensee has changed, except that the special plates issued to the original licensee may be transferred and the newly designated licensee as transfer-ee shall succeed to the privileges evidenced by the plates until their expiration.

(e) The suspension or revocation of the corporate status of the licensee.

(f) The suspension or revocation of the seller's permit of the licensee by the State Board of Equalization. *(Added by Stats.1959, c. 1827, p. 4342, § 5. Amended by Stats.1965, c. 1014, p. 2648, § 10; Stats.1971, c. 1214, p. 2356, § 39, operative May 3, 1972; Stats.1974, c. 274, p. 499, § 1; Stats.1982, c. 791, p. 3068, § 4; Stats.1990, c. 1563 (A.B.3243), § 46.)*

§ 11722. Claims against surety on dealer's bond of a financing agency

Claims, against the surety upon a dealer's bond, of a financing agency that has loaned money to a licensee or assignee thereof shall be allowed only to the extent that the claims of any other person or entity with respect to the bond under Section 11711 shall be satisfied first and entitled to preference over the claims of the financing agency with respect to the bond; provided, however, that as to any conditional sales contract as defined in Section 2981 of the Civil Code, acquired by way of purchase or pledge, a financing agency shall be entitled to protection under the bond with the same preference set forth under Section 11711 if the financing agency is defrauded by a licensee. *(Added by Stats.1960, 1st Ex.Sess., c. 35, p. 379, § 2. Amended by Stats.2002, c. 303 (S.B.1458), § 2.)*

§ 11723. License fees; additional fees

The board may require that fees shall be paid to the department for the issuance or renewal of a license to do business as a new motor vehicle dealer, dealer branch, manufacturer, manufacturer branch, distributor, distributor branch, or representative. The fees shall be to reimburse the department for costs incurred in licensing those dealers, manufacturers, distributors, branches, and representatives and for related administrative costs incurred on behalf of the board. The board may also require that an additional fee be paid to the department when the licensee has failed to pay the fee authorized by Section 3016 prior to the expiration of its occupational license and special plates and the licensee utilizes the 30–day late renewal period authorized by subdivision (c) of Section 11717.

This section shall not apply to dealers, manufacturers, distributors, or representatives of vehicles not subject to registration under this code, except dealers, manufacturers, manufacturer branches, distributors, distributor branches, or representatives of, off-highway motorcycles, as defined in Section 436, all-terrain vehicles, as defined in Section 111, and trailers subject to identification pursuant to Section 5014.1. *(Added by Stats.1967, c. 1397, p. 3266, § 3. Amended by Stats.1973, c. 996, p. 1980, § 32, operative July 1, 1974; Stats.1975, c. 943, p. 2109, § 6; Stats.1982, c. 1584, p. 6262, § 11; Stats.1983, c. 1144, § 7, eff. Sept. 28, 1983; Stats.1985, c. 1201, § 6, eff. Sept. 29, 1985; Stats.2004, c. 836 (A.B.2848), § 11.)*

§ 11724. Repossession of vehicle connected with incident of violence notice; notice to subsequent assignee

A dealer, or the agent of a dealer, who has received a notice pursuant to Section 7507.6 of the Business and Professions Code, shall not make a subsequent assignment to skip trace, locate, or repossess a vehicle without simultaneously, and in the same manner by which the assignment is given, advising the assignee of the assignment of the information contained in the notice. As used in this section, "assignment" has the same meaning set forth in Section 7500.1 of the Business and Professions Code. *(Added by Stats.2007, c. 192 (S.B.659), § 9, eff. Sept. 7, 2007.)*

§ 11725. Transfer of motor vehicles to foreign jurisdictions for registration or sale; removal and delivery of license plates to state; misdemeanor

(a) No person shall transport or drive any motor vehicle from this state outside of the United States with the intent to register or sell such vehicle in a foreign jurisdiction, without first removing the license plates and delivering them to the department. Such person may obtain a permit from the department authorizing the operation of the unlicensed motor vehicle on the public highways of this state in order to reach such foreign jurisdiction. Failure to deliver the license plates as required by this subdivision shall be a misdemeanor.

(b) No holder of any license, or any temporary permit for such license issued under this division, shall deliver any vehicle following sale without first removing all license plates from such vehicle when it is known by the licensee that the vehicle is to be exported to a foreign jurisdiction outside of the United States. *(Added by Stats.1970, c. 1147, p. 2028, § 1. Amended by Stats.1976, c. 934, p. 2139, § 3.)*

Cross References

Misdemeanors, definition and penalties, see Penal Code §§ 17, 19 and 19.2.
Offenses and prosecutions, see Vehicle Code § 40000.1 et seq.

§ 11726. Recovery of damages; injunctive relief

Any licensee suffering pecuniary loss because of any willful failure by any other licensee to comply with any provision of Article 1 (commencing with Section 11700) or 3 (commencing with Section 11900) of Chapter 4 of Division 5 or Article 3 (commencing with Section 3052) of Chapter 6 of Division 2 or with any regulation adopted by the department or any rule adopted or decision rendered by the board under authority vested in them may recover damages and reasonable attorney fees therefor in any court of competent jurisdiction. Any such licensee may also have appropriate injunctive relief in any such court. *(Added by Stats.1973, c. 996, p. 1980, § 34, operative July 1, 1974.)*

§ 11727. Revocation or suspension of license

The revocation or suspension of a license of a manufacturer, manufacturer branch, distributor, distributor branch, or representative may be limited to one or more municipalities or counties or any other defined area, or may be revoked or suspended in a defined area only as to certain aspects of its business, or as to a specified dealer or dealers. *(Added by Stats.1973, c. 996, p. 1980, § 35, operative July 1, 1974.)*

§ 11728. Penalties

As part of a compromise settlement agreement entered into pursuant to Section 11707 or 11808.5, the department may assess a monetary penalty of not more than two thousand five hundred dollars ($2,500) per violation and impose a license suspension of not more than 30 days for any dealer who violates subdivision (r) of Section 11713. The extent of the penalties shall be based on the nature of the violation and effect of the violation on the purposes of this article. Except for the penalty limits provided for in Sections 11707 and 11808.5, all the provisions governing compromise settlement agreements for dealers, salespersons, and wholesalers apply to this section, and Section 11415.60 of the Government Code does not apply. *(Added by Stats.1990, c. 90 (A.B.2445), § 4, eff. May 9, 1990. Amended by Stats.1990, c. 1563 (A.B.3243), § 47; Stats.1991, c. 928 (A.B.1886), § 18, eff. Oct. 14, 1991; Stats.1995, c. 938 (S.B.523), § 90, operative July 1, 1997.)*

Law Revision Commission Comments
1995 Amendment

Section 11728 is amended to make the settlement provisions of the Administrative Procedure Act inapplicable to this section. [25 Cal.L.Rev.Comm. Reports 55 (1995)].

§ 11729. Consignment agreements

(a) Except as provided in subdivision (b), any dealer engaging in a consignment with an owner not licensed as a dealer, manufacturer, manufacturer branch, distributor, or a distributor branch licensed under this code, and the consignment is not otherwise prohibited by this code, shall execute a consignment agreement as prescribed by Section 11730. The failure of a dealer, when required under this section, to complete and comply with the terms of the prescribed consignment agreement for any vehicle which the dealer agrees to accept on consignment, or to pay the agreed amount to the consignor or his or her designee within 20 days after the date of sale of the vehicle, is cause for suspending or revoking the license of the dealer under paragraph (10) of subdivision (a) of Section 11705.

(b)(1) A dealer conducting retail auction sales on behalf of a fleet owner shall execute a consignment agreement applicable to all vehicles consigned for sale during the term of the agreement which contains, at a minimum, substantially all of the terms, phrases, conditions, and disclosures required by Section 11730, except the following are not required:

(A) The description of a specific vehicle by year, make, identification number, license, state, or mileage.

(B) The information contained in paragraph (4) of subdivision (b) of Section 11730.

(2) If mutually agreeable, in lieu of the requirements of paragraph (7) of subdivision (b) of Section 11730, the consignor may provide the documents necessary to transfer the ownership of the vehicle to the consignee prior to the auction being held.

(3) For purposes of this subdivision, "fleet owner" is either of the following:

(A) A person who is the registered or legal owner of 25 or more vehicles registered in this state and is the owner, as recorded in the department's records, of the vehicles consigned for sale to the dealer.

(B) A bankruptcy trustee who owns or has legal control of the vehicles consigned for sale to the dealer, government agency, or financial institution. *(Added by Stats.1990, c. 735 (A.B.3269), § 2. Amended by Stats. 1991, c. 815 (A.B.1063), § 2; Stats.1999, c. 672 (S.B.974), § 4.)*

§ 11730. Contents of consignment agreement

The consignment agreement required by Section 11729 shall contain all the following terms, phrases, conditions, and disclosures:

(a) The date the agreement is executed.

(b) All of the following statements:

(1) "I (We), the undersigned consigner(s), hereby consign and deliver possession of my(our) vehicle, which is a (Year) ____ (Make) ____ (ID#) ____ (License) ____ (State) ____ (Mileage) ____, to (Consignee) ____ (Dealer #) ____ for the sole purpose of selling the vehicle and paying, to the consignor or his or her designee from the proceeds of the sale of the vehicle, the amount agreed upon under terms of this agreement. This agreement is effective and valid only for a period of ____ days from this date."

(2) "At the termination of this agreement, the consignee shall return the vehicle to the consignor, or, at the option of both the consignor and consignee, enter into a new agreement."

(3) "If the vehicle is sold by the consignee during the term of this agreement, the money due the consignor shall be disbursed within 20 days after the date of sale in accordance with the terms of this agreement. As used in this agreement, a "sale" occurs when the consignee either (A) receives the purchase price or its equivalent or executes a conditional sales contract for the vehicle, or (B) when the purchaser takes delivery of the vehicle, whichever occurs first."

(4) "The following information shall be completed prior to the signing of this agreement:

Current market value: $____ Source: ____.

Outstanding liens: $____ Lienholder: ____.

(Any difference between the outstanding amount shown and the actual payoff to the lienholder will be credited to the consignor.)

Repairs to be made: $____ Work Order #____.

Moneys to the consignor: ____ percent of sale price, flat fee of $____ or the following specific formula: ____."

(5) "Within 20 days after sale, the consignee shall make an accounting to the consignor of all of the following: date of sale, repairs authorized by consignor (supported by work records), exact amount of any liens payable to lienholders, evidence of payment of any liens, and the total sales price."

(6) "The consigned vehicle is delivered to the consignee in trust for the exact terms set forth in this agreement. The consignee agrees to receive this vehicle in trust and not to permit its use for any other purpose other than contained in this agreement without the express written consent of the consignor."

(7) "Upon payment of the moneys due the consignor, the consignor agrees to furnish the consignee those documents necessary to transfer the ownership of the vehicle to the purchaser.

Signatures:

Consignor	Date
Address	
Consignee	Date
Address	"

(8) "NOTICE TO CONSIGNOR: Failure of the consignee to comply with the terms of this agreement may be a violation of statute which could result in criminal or administrative sanctions, or both. If you feel the consignee has not complied with the terms of this agreement, please contact an investigator of the Department of Motor Vehicles." *(Added by Stats.1990, c. 735 (A.B.3269), § 3. Amended by Stats.1991, c. 815 (A.B. 1063), § 3; Stats.2000, c. 1035 (S.B.1403), § 12.)*

§ 11735. Dealer; autobroker's endorsement; log; required information; fiduciary duty

(a) No dealer shall engage in brokering a retail sales transaction without first paying the fee required by subdivision (d) of Section 9262 and obtaining from the department an autobroker's endorsement to the dealer's license. An autobroker's endorsement shall be automatically cancelled upon the cancellation, suspension, revocation, surrender, or expiration of a dealer's license.

(b) Upon the issuance of an autobroker's endorsement to a dealer's license, the department shall furnish the dealer with an autobroker's log. The autobroker's log shall remain the property of the department and may be taken up at any time for inspection.

(c) The autobroker's log shall contain spaces sufficient for the dealer to record the following information with respect to each retail sale brokered by that dealer:

(1) Vehicle identification number of brokered vehicle.

(2) Date of brokering agreement.

(3) Selling dealer's name, address, and dealer number.

(4) Name of consumer.

(5) Brokering dealer's name and dealer number.

(d) Nothing in this code prohibits a dealer who has been issued an autobroker's endorsement to his or her dealer's license from delivering, with the selling dealer's written approval, motor vehicles that have been sold pursuant to a duly executed motor vehicle purchase agreement or obtaining a consumer's signature on a selling dealer's motor vehicle purchase agreement that has already been executed by the selling dealer.

(e) When brokering a retail sale as an agent of the consumer, selling dealer, or both, the brokering dealer owes a fiduciary duty of utmost care, integrity, honesty, and loyalty in dealings with its principal or principals.

(f) For purposes of this section and Sections 11736, 11737, and 11738, "consumer" means any person who retains a dealer to perform brokering services in connection with a retail sale. *(Added by Stats.1994, c. 1253 (A.B.3539), § 12.   Amended by Stats.1995, c. 211 (A.B. 770), § 7.)*

§ 11736. Retail sale brokering; unlawful acts

It is unlawful for any dealer licensed under this article to do any of the following when brokering a retail sale:

(a) Fail to execute a written brokering agreement, as described in Section 11738, and provide a completed copy to both of the following:

(1) Any consumer entering into the brokering agreement. The completed copy shall be provided prior to the consumer's signing of an agreement for the purchase of the vehicle described in the brokering agreement or, prior to accepting one hundred dollars ($100) or more from that consumer, whichever occurs first.

(2) The selling dealer. The completed copy shall be provided prior to the selling dealer's entering into a purchase agreement with the consumer.

(b) Accept a purchase deposit from any consumer that exceeds 2.5 percent of the selling price of the vehicle described in the brokering agreement.

(c) Fail to refund any purchase money, including purchase deposits, upon demand by a consumer at any time prior to the consumer's signing of a vehicle purchase agreement with a selling dealer and taking delivery of the vehicle described in the brokering agreement.

(d) Fail to cancel a brokering agreement and refund, upon demand, any money paid by a consumer, including any brokerage fee, under any of the following circumstances:

(1) When the final price of the brokered vehicle exceeds the purchase price listed in the brokering agreement.

(2) When the vehicle delivered is not as described in the brokering agreement.

(3) When the brokering agreement expires prior to the customer being presented with a purchase agreement from a selling dealer arranged through the brokering dealer that contains a purchase price at or below the price listed in the brokering agreement.

(e) Act as a seller and provide brokering services, both in the same transaction.

(f) Fail to disclose to the consumer and selling dealer, as soon as practicable, whether the autobroker receives or does not receive a fee or other compensation, regardless of the form or time of payment, from the selling dealer and the dollar amount of any fee that the consumer is obligated to pay to the autobroker. This arrangement shall be confirmed in a brokering agreement.

(g) Fail to record in the dealer's autobroker log, for each brokered sale, all of the information specified in subdivision (c) of Section 11735.

(h) Fail to maintain for a minimum of three years a copy of the executed brokering agreement and other notices and documents related to each brokered transaction.

(i) Fail to advise the consumer, prior to accepting any money, that a full refund will be given if the motor vehicle ordered through the autobroker is not obtained for the consumer or if the service orally contracted for is not provided. *(Added by Stats.1994, c. 1253 (A.B.3539), § 13. Amended by Stats.1995, c. 211 (A.B.770), § 8.)*

§ 11737. Dealer-brokered motor vehicle sale; purchase money deposit into trust account; management

(a) A dealer who brokers a motor vehicle sale shall deposit directly into a trust account any purchase money, including purchase deposits, it receives from a consumer or a consumer's lender. This subdivision does not require a separate trust account for each brokered transaction.

(b) The brokering dealer shall not in any manner encumber the corpus of the trust account except as follows:

(1) In partial or full payment to a selling dealer for a vehicle purchased by the brokering dealer's consumer.

(2) To make refunds.

(c) Subdivision (b) shall not prevent payment of the interest earned on the trust account to the brokering dealer.

(d) The brokering dealer shall serve as trustee of the trust account required by this section. If the brokering dealer is a partnership or a corporation, the managing partner of the partnership or the chief executive officer of the corporation shall be the trustee. The trustee may designate in writing that an officer or employee may manage the trust account if that officer or employee is under the trustee's supervision and control, and the original of that writing is on file with the department.

(e) All trust accounts required by this section shall be maintained at a branch of a bank, savings and loan association, or credit union regulated by the state or the government of the United States.

(f) The brokering dealer has a fiduciary responsibility with respect to all purchase money received from a consumer or consumer's lender relative to a brokered sale transaction.

(g) The following are deemed to be held in trust for consumers who have paid purchase money to a brokering dealer:

(1) All sums received by the brokering dealer whether or not required to be deposited in an actual trust account and regardless of whether any of these sums were required to be deposited or actually were deposited in a trust account.

(2) All property with which any of the sums described in paragraph (1) has been commingled if any of these sums cannot be identified because of the commingling.

(h) Upon any judicially ordered distribution of any money or property required to be held in trust and after all expenses of distribution approved by the court have been paid, every consumer of a brokering dealer has a claim on the trust for purchase money payments made to the brokering dealer. Unless a consumer can identify his or her funds in the trust within the time established by the court, each consumer shall receive a proportional share based on the amount paid. *(Added by Stats.1994, c. 1253 (A.B.3539), § 14.)*

§ 11738. Brokering agreement; contents

The brokering agreement required by Section 11736 shall be printed in no smaller than 10–point type and shall contain not less than the following terms, conditions, requirements, and disclosures:

(a) The name, address, license number, and telephone number of the autobroker.

(b) A complete description, including line-make, model, year model, and color, of the vehicle and the desired options.

(c) The following statement:

"The following information shall be completed prior to the signing of this brokering agreement:

Dollar Purchase Price of Vehicle: _____.

Date this agreement will expire if a purchase agreement from a selling dealer is not presented for your signature: _____.

Fee that you will be obligated to pay us, if any: _____."

(d) One of the following notices, as appropriate, printed in at least 10–point bold type and placed immediately below the statement required by subdivision (c):

(1) "We do not receive a fee from the selling dealer."

(2) "We receive a fee from the selling dealer."

(e) The following notice on the face of the brokering agreement with a heading in at least 14–point bold type and the text in at least 10–point bold type, circumscribed by a line, that reads as follows:

NOTICE

This is an agreement to provide services; it is not an agreement for the purchase of a vehicle. California law gives you the following rights and protection.

Once you have signed this agreement, you have the right to cancel it and receive a full refund of any money paid, including any brokerage fee you may have paid, under any of the following circumstances:

(1) The final price of the vehicle exceeds the purchase price listed above.

(2) The vehicle is not as described above upon delivery.

(3) This agreement expires prior to your being presented with a selling dealer's purchase agreement.

If you have paid a purchase deposit, you have the right to receive a refund of that deposit at any time prior to your signing a vehicle purchase agreement with a selling dealer. Purchase deposits are limited by law to no more than 2.5 percent of the purchase price of a vehicle and must be deposited by an autobroker or auto buying service in a federally insured trust account. If you are unable to resolve a dispute with your autobroker or auto buying service, please contact an investigator of the Department of Motor Vehicles.

(f) The date the agreement is executed.

(g) The signature of the autobroker and consumer. *(Added by Stats.1994, c. 1253 (A.B.3539), § 15. Amended by Stats.2000, c. 1035 (S.B.1403), § 13.)*

§ 11739. Brokered retail new motor vehicle sale; title registration, warranties, rebates, and incentives; dealer's duties

For purposes of title registration, warranties, rebates, and incentives, in a brokered retail new motor vehicle sale, the selling, franchised new car dealer, and not the autobroker, is responsible to apply for title in the name of the purchaser, to secure vehicle registration and the license plates for the purchaser, to secure the manufacturer's warranty in the name of the purchaser, and to make all applications for any manufacturer's rebates and incentives due the purchaser. If there is a manufacturer's recall, the consumer shall be notified directly by the manufacturer. *(Added by Stats.1994, c. 1253 (A.B.3539), § 16.)*

§ 11740. Remedies and penalties; cumulative effect

The remedies and penalties provided in this code for a violation of this article are cumulative to the remedies and penalties provided by other laws. *(Added by Stats. 2002, c. 407 (S.B.91), § 3.)*

ARTICLE 2. VEHICLE SALESPERSONS

Section
11800. Acting as salesperson without license.
11801. Repealed.
11801.5. Repealed.
11802. Contents of application; format of license.
11803. Temporary permit.
11804. Authority to issue or refuse license.
11805. Repealed.
11806. Refusal to issue and suspension or revocation of license: grounds.
11807. Repealed.
11808. Conduct of hearing.
11808.5. Filing of accusation; compromise settlement agreement; terms and conditions.
11809. Repealed.
11810. Temporary suspension, probation, and reapplication.
11811. Repealed.
11812. Display of licenses; termination; report of change of residence; service of process.
11814. Term of license; renewal; duplicate.
11816. Repealed.
11818. Repealed.
11819. Unlawful actions; licenses.
11820. Fees.
11822. Automatic cancellation.
11824. Department's authority after suspension, expiration, or cancellation of license.

§ 11800. Acting as salesperson without license

It shall be unlawful for any person to act as a vehicle salesperson without having first procured a license or temporary permit issued by the department or when that license or temporary permit issued by the department has been canceled, suspended, revoked, or invalidated or has expired. *(Added by Stats.1975, c. 505, p. 1030, § 2. Amended by Stats.1990, c. 1563 (A.B.3243), § 48.)*

Cross References

Violation as misdemeanor, punishment, see Vehicle Code §§ 40000.11, 42002.

§ 11801. Repealed by Stats.1975, c. 505, p. 1030, § 1

§ 11801.5. Repealed by Stats.1967, c. 1038, p. 2641, § 2

§ 11802. Contents of application; format of license

(a) The department shall prescribe and provide forms to be used for application for licenses to be issued under this article and require of applicants, as a condition of the issuance of a license, that information concerning the applicant's character, honesty, integrity, and reputation as it considers necessary. Every application for a vehicle salesperson's license shall contain, in addition to that information which the department requires, a statement of all of the following facts:

(1) The name and address of the applicant.

(2) Whether the applicant has ever had a court judgment rendered for which he or she has been liable as a result of his or her activities in conjunction with an occupational license issued under this division, and whether that judgment remains unpaid or unsatisfied.

(3) Whether the applicant ever had a license, issued under this division, revoked, suspended, or subjected to other disciplinary action and whether the applicant was ever a partner in a partnership or an officer, director, or stockholder in a corporation licensed under this division, the license of which was revoked, suspended, or subjected to other disciplinary action.

(b) The department shall issue a license bearing a fullface photograph of the licensee and the following information:

(1) Name and address.

(2) Physical description.

(3) The licensee's usual signature.

(4) Distinguishing vehicle salesperson's license number. *(Added by Stats.1975, c. 505, p. 1030, § 2. Amended by Stats.1990, c. 1563 (A.B.3243), § 49.)*

§ 11803. Temporary permit

Pending the satisfaction of the department that the applicant has met the requirements of this chapter, it may issue a temporary permit to any person applying for a vehicle salesperson's license. The temporary permit shall permit the operation by the salesperson for a period of not more than 120 days while the department is completing its investigation of the applicant for the license. If the department determines to its satisfaction that the temporary permit was issued upon a fraudulent application or determines or has reasonable cause to believe that the application is incorrect or incomplete or the temporary permit was issued in error, the department may cancel the temporary permit, effective immediately. The temporary permit shall become invalid when canceled or when the applicant's license has been issued or refused. *(Added by Stats.1977, c. 645, p. 2144, § 1. Amended by Stats.1990, c. 1563 (A.B.3243), § 50; Stats.2002, c. 758 (A.B.3024), § 10.)*

§ 11804. Authority to issue or refuse license

The department may issue or, for reasonable cause shown, refuse to issue, a license to any applicant applying for a vehicle salesperson's license. *(Added by Stats.1975, c. 505, p. 1031, § 2. Amended by Stats.1990, c. 1563 (A.B.3243), § 51.)*

§ 11805. Repealed by Stats.1975, c. 505, p. 1031, § 1

§ 11806. Refusal to issue and suspension or revocation of license: grounds

The department, after notice and hearing, may refuse to issue, or may suspend or revoke, a vehicle salesperson's license when it makes any of the following findings and determinations:

(a) The applicant or licensee has outstanding an unsatisfied final court judgment rendered in connection with an activity licensed under this division.

(b) The applicant or licensee has failed to pay funds or property received in the course of employment to a dealer entitled thereto.

(c) The applicant or licensee has failed to surrender possession of, or failed to return, a vehicle to a dealer lawfully entitled thereto upon termination of employment.

(d) A cause for refusal, suspension, or revocation exists under any provision of Sections 11302 to 11909, inclusive.

(e) The applicant was previously the holder of an occupational license issued by another state authorizing the same or similar activities of a license issued under this division and that license was revoked or suspended for cause and was never reissued, or was suspended for cause, and the terms of suspension have not been fulfilled.

(f) The applicant or licensee has acted as a dealer by purchasing or selling vehicles while employed by a licensed dealer without reporting that fact to the dealer or without utilizing the report of sale documents issued to the dealer.

(g) The applicant or licensee has concurrently acted as a vehicle salesperson and engaged in that activity for, or on behalf of, more than one licensed dealer unless all of the licensed dealers for whom that salesperson works have common controlling ownership. Nothing in this section restricts the number of dealerships of which a person may be an owner, officer, or director, or precludes a vehicle salesperson from working for more than one dealer, provided that all of the licensed dealers for whom that salesperson works have common controlling ownership. For purposes of this subdivision, dealers have common controlling ownership when more than 50 percent of the ownership interests in each dealer are held by the same person or persons, either directly or through one or more wholly owned subsidiary entities.

(h) The applicant or licensee has acted as a vehicle salesperson without having first complied with Section 11812.

(i) The applicant or licensee was a managerial employee of a dealer during the time a person under the direction or control of the managerial employee committed wrongful acts which resulted in the suspension or revocation of the dealer's license.

(j) The applicant or licensee has acted as a dealer by purchasing or selling any vehicle and using the license, report of sale books, purchase drafts, financial institution accounts, or other supplies of a dealer to facilitate that purchase or sale, when the applicant or licensee is not acting on behalf of that dealer. *(Added by Stats.1975, c. 505, p. 1031, § 2. Amended by Stats.1976, c. 934, p. 2139, § 4; Stats.1977, c. 645, p. 2144, § 2; Stats.1982, c. 791, p. 3069, § 5; Stats.1990, c. 1563 (A.B.3243), § 52; Stats. 1998, c. 877 (A.B.2132), § 51; Stats.2010, c. 483 (S.B. 1004), § 4.)*

§ 11807. Repealed by Stats.1975, c. 505, p. 1030, § 1

§ 11808. Conduct of hearing

Every hearing provided for in this article shall be conducted pursuant to Chapter 5 (commencing with Section 11500) of Part 1 of Division 3 of Title 2 of the Government Code. *(Added by Stats.1975, c. 505, p. 1031, § 2. Amended by Stats.1977, c. 645, p. 2145, § 3; Stats.1990, c. 1563 (A.B.3243), § 53.)*

§ 11808.5. Filing of accusation; compromise settlement agreement; terms and conditions

(a) After the filing of an accusation under this article, the director may enter into a stipulated compromise settlement agreement with the consent of the licensee on terms and conditions mutually agreeable to the director, the respondent licensee, and the accuser without further hearing or appeal. The agreement may include, but is not limited to, a period of probation or monetary penalties, or both. Except as provided in Section 11728, the monetary penalty shall not exceed five hundred dollars ($500) for each violation, and it shall be based on the nature of the violation and the effect of the violation on the purposes of this article.

(b) A compromise settlement agreement may be entered before, during, or after the hearing, but is valid only if executed and filed pursuant to subdivision (d) before the proposed decision of the hearing officer, if any, is adopted or the case is decided.

(c) The department shall adopt, by regulation, a schedule of maximum and minimum amounts of monetary penalties, the payment of which may be included as a term or condition of a compromise settlement agreement entered under subdivision (a). Any monetary penalty included in a compromise settlement agreement shall be within the range of monetary penalties in that schedule.

(d) Any compromise settlement agreement entered under this section shall be signed by the director, the respondent licensee, and the accuser, or by their authorized representatives. The director shall file, or cause to be filed, the agreement with the Office of Administrative Hearings, together with the department's notice of withdrawal of the accusation or statement of issues upon which the action was initiated.

(e) If the respondent licensee fails to perform all of the terms and conditions of the compromise settlement agreement, the agreement is void and the department may take any action authorized by law, notwithstanding the agreement, including, but not limited to, refiling the accusation or imposing license sanctions. *(Added by Stats.1985, c. 1022, § 21. Amended by Stats.1990, c. 90 (A.B.2445), § 5, eff. May 9, 1990.)*

§ 11809. Repealed by Stats.1975, c. 505, p. 1030, § 1

§ 11810. Temporary suspension, probation, and reapplication

(a) The department may, pending a hearing, temporarily suspend the license issued to a vehicle salesperson for a period of not more than 30 days if the director finds that action to be required in the public interest. In that case, a hearing shall be held and a decision thereon issued within 30 days after notice of the temporary suspension.

(b) Except where the provisions of this code require the refusal to issue a license, the department may issue a probationary license subject to conditions to be observed by the licensee in the exercise of the privilege granted. The conditions to be attached to the exercise of the privilege shall be those which may, in the judgment of the department, be in the public interest and suitable to the qualifications of the applicant, as disclosed by the application and investigation by the department of the information contained in the application.

(c) If the department issues or renews a vehicle salesperson's license requiring conditions of probation or if the department refuses to issue a vehicle salesperson's license, the applicant may demand in writing a hearing before the director or the director's representative within 60 days after notice of refusal to issue or issuance of the probationary license.

(d) A person whose license has been revoked or whose application for a license has been denied may reapply for a license after not less than one year has elapsed from the effective date of the decision revoking the license or denying the application, except that if the decision was based upon subdivision (a) of Section 11806, an earlier reapplication may be made accompanied by evidence satisfactory to the department that those grounds for revocation or denial of the license no longer exist. *(Added by Stats.1975, c. 505, p. 1031, § 2. Amended by Stats.1976, c. 934, p. 2139, § 5; Stats.1979, c. 373, p. 1381, § 319; Stats.1990, c. 1563 (A.B.3243), § 54.)*

Cross References

Hearing on demand of holder of temporary permit, see Vehicle Code § 11803.

§ 11811.   Repealed by Stats.1975, c. 505, p. 1030, § 1

§ 11812.   Display of licenses; termination; report of change of residence; service of process

(a) A vehicle salesperson licensed under this article shall, at the time of employment, deliver his or her salesperson's license to his or her employing dealer for the posting of the salesperson's license or a true and exact copy of the salesperson's license in a place conspicuous to the public at each location where he or she is actually engaged in the selling of vehicles for the employing dealer.

(b) The license, or a true and exact copy of the license, shall be displayed continuously at each location where he or she is actually engaged in the selling of vehicles during the employment. If a vehicle salesperson's employment

398

is terminated, the license shall be returned to the salesperson and all copies of the license used by the dealer for posting or display shall be destroyed by the dealer.

(c) A vehicle salesperson licensed pursuant to this article shall report in writing to the department every change of residence address within five days of the change.

(d) A person currently or previously licensed under this article who no longer resides at the address last filed with the department may be served with process issued pursuant to Chapter 5 (commencing with Section 11500) of Part 1 of Division 3 of Title 2 of the Government Code by registered mail at that residence, unless the person has notified the department in writing of another address where service may be made. *(Added by Stats.1975, c. 505, p. 1032, § 2. Amended by Stats.1976, c. 388, p. 1038, § 1; Stats.1978, c. 422, p. 1322, § 1; Stats.1982, c. 571, p. 2528, § 8; Stats.1988, c. 751, § 8; Stats.1990, c. 1563 (A.B. 3243), § 55; Stats.2010, c. 483 (S.B.1004), § 5.)*

Cross References

Noncompliance as ground for suspension, revocation or refusal to issue license, see Vehicle Code § 11806.

§ 11814.   Term of license; renewal; duplicate

(a) Every original vehicle salesperson's license issued, and every vehicle salesperson's license renewed pursuant to subdivision (b), shall be valid for a period of three years from the date of issuance unless canceled, suspended, or revoked by the department.

(b) Renewal of a vehicle salesperson's license may be made prior to the expiration date. In no event may a vehicle salesperson renew his or her license after the date of expiration.

(c) A salesperson's license may be renewed by mail if that license was not renewed by mail for the immediately preceding period.

(d) A salesperson shall obtain a duplicate license when the original is either lost or mutilated. *(Added by Stats.1975, c. 505, p. 1032, § 2. Amended by Stats.1987, c. 111, § 4; Stats.1992, c. 1243 (A.B.3090), § 78, eff. Sept. 30, 1992.)*

§ 11816.   Repealed by Stats.1980, c. 676, p. 2024, § 309

§ 11818.   Repealed by Stats.1977, c. 645, p. 2145, § 4

§ 11819.   Unlawful actions; licenses

It is unlawful for a person:

(a) To lend a salesperson's license to any other person or knowingly permit its use by another.

(b) To display or represent a salesperson's license not issued to the person as being his or her license.

(c) To fail or refuse to surrender to the department, upon its lawful demand, a salesperson's license that has been suspended, revoked, or canceled.

(d) To permit any unlawful use of a salesperson's license issued to him or her.

(e) To photograph, photostat, duplicate, or in any way reproduce a salesperson's license or facsimile thereof in a manner that it could be mistaken for a valid license, or to display or have in possession a photograph, photostat, duplicate, reproduction, or facsimile unless for display by a dealer, or as authorized by this code. *(Added by Stats.1978, c. 422, p. 1322, § 2. Amended by Stats.1990, c. 1563 (A.B.3243), § 56; Stats.2010, c. 483 (S.B.1004), § 6.)*

§ 11820. Fees

The following fees shall be paid to the department:

(a) Except as provided by Section 42231, a nonrefundable fee for the original issuance of a license, fifty dollars ($50).

(b) Fee for license renewal, fifty dollars ($50).

(c) Fee for a duplicate license, fifteen dollars ($15). *(Added by Stats.1975, c. 505, p. 1033, § 2. Amended by Stats.1980, c. 608, p. 1679, § 8; Stats.1982, c. 1273, p. 4703, § 15; Stats.1987, c. 111, § 5; Stats.1990, c. 90 (A.B.2445), § 6, eff. May 9, 1990, operative July 1, 1990.)*

Cross References

Return of fees after rejection of application, see Vehicle Code § 42230.

§ 11822. Automatic cancellation

The vehicle salesperson's license or any permit provided in this article shall be automatically canceled upon the failure of a licensee to pay the required fees or to file an application for renewal of the license or permit before the date of expiration of the current license or permit. *(Added by Stats.1975, c. 505, p. 1033, § 2. Amended by Stats.1984, c. 499, § 13.)*

§ 11824. Department's authority after suspension, expiration, or cancellation of license

The suspension, expiration, or cancellation of a vehicle salesperson's license issued under this article does not prevent the filing of an accusation for the revocation or suspension of the suspended, expired, or canceled license as provided in Section 11806, and the department's decision that the license should be suspended or revoked. That determination may be considered in granting or refusing to grant any subsequent license authorized by this division to that licensee. *(Added by Stats.1975, c. 505, p. 1033, § 2. Amended by Stats.1980, c. 676, p. 2024, § 310; Stats.1990, c. 1563 (A.B.3243), § 57.)*

ARTICLE 3. REPRESENTATIVES

Section
11900.   License or temporary permit required.
11901.   Application forms.
11902.   Authority to issue, refuse, suspend, or revoke license or temporary permit.
11902.5.   Conviction of crime involving moral turpitude; refusal to issue or suspension of license.
11903.   Suspension or revocation; probationary licenses; hearings; reapplication after denial or revocation.
11903.5.   Filing of accusation; compromise settlement agreement; terms and conditions.
11904.   Expiration of representative license.
11905.   Renewal of representative license.
11906.   Repealed.
11907.   Automatic cancellation.
11908.   Department's authority after suspension, expiration or cancellation of license.
11909.   Posting of license.

Cross References

"Representative" defined, see Vehicle Code § 512.

§ 11900. License or temporary permit required

It shall be unlawful for any person to act as a representative on or after July 1, 1974, without having first procured a license or temporary permit issued by the department or when such license or temporary permit has been canceled, suspended, revoked, or invalidated or has expired. *(Added by Stats.1973, c. 996, p. 1981, § 36, operative July 1, 1974. Amended by Stats.1974, c. 384, p. 961, § 14, eff. July 5, 1974, operative July 1, 1974.)*

§ 11901. Application forms

The department shall prescribe and provide forms to be used for application for licenses to be issued under the terms and provisions of this chapter and require of such applicants, as a condition precedent to issuance of such license, such information touching on and concerning the applicant's character, honesty, integrity and reputation as it may consider necessary. Every application for a representative's license shall contain, in addition to such information as the department may require, a statement of the following facts:

(a) Name and address of the applicant.

(b) Whether the applicant has ever had a court judgment rendered for which he has been liable as a result of his activity in connection with an occupation licensed under this chapter and whether such judgment remains unpaid or unsatisfied.

(c) Whether the applicant ever had a license, issued under the authority of this chapter, revoked, suspended, or subjected to other disciplinary action and whether the applicant was ever a partner in a partnership or an officer, director, or stockholder in a corporation licensed under the authority of this chapter, the license of which was revoked, suspended, or subjected to other disciplinary action.

(d) Name, address, and license number of the manufacturer, manufacturer branch, distributor, or distributor branch employing the applicant. *(Added by Stats.1973, c. 996, p. 1981, § 36, operative July 1, 1974.)*

§ 11902. Authority to issue, refuse, suspend, or revoke license or temporary permit

(a) The department shall issue a representative's license when it finds and determines that the applicant has furnished the required information, and that the applicant intends in good faith to act as a representative and has paid the fees required by Sections 9262 and 11723.

(b) The department may refuse to issue, or may suspend or revoke, a license for any of the following reasons:

(1) The information in the application is incorrect.

(2) The applicant or licensee has been convicted of a crime or committed any act or engaged in any conduct involving moral turpitude which is substantially related to the qualifications, functions, or duties of the licensed activity. A conviction after a plea of nolo contendere is a conviction within the meaning of this section.

(3) The applicant or licensee has outstanding an unpaid final court judgment rendered in connection with an activity licensed under this chapter.

(4) The applicant or licensee was previously the holder of, or was a business representative of a business which was the holder of, a license and certificate issued under this chapter which were revoked for cause and not reissued by the department or which were suspended for cause and the terms of suspension have not been fulfilled.

(5) The applicant was previously the holder of an occupational license issued by another state, authorizing the same or similar activities of a license issued under this division; and that license was revoked or suspended for cause and was never reissued, or was suspended for cause, and the terms of suspension have not been fulfilled.

(6) The applicant or licensee has committed any act prohibited by Section 11713.2 or 11713.3.

(c) Pending the determination of the department that the applicant has met the requirements of this chapter, it may issue a temporary permit to any person applying for a representative's license. The temporary permit shall permit the operation by the representative for a period not to exceed 120 days while the department is completing its investigation and determination of all facts relative to the qualifications of the applicant for a license. The temporary permit is invalid after the applicant's license has been issued or refused.

(d) The department may issue a probationary representative's license based upon the existence of any circumstance set forth in subdivision (b), subject to conditions to be observed in the exercise of the privilege granted, either upon application for the issuance of a license or upon application for the renewal of a license. The conditions to be attached to the exercise of the privilege shall not appear on the face of the license but shall be those which, in the judgment of the department, are in the public interest and suitable to the qualifications of the applicant as disclosed by the application and investigation by the department of the information contained therein. *(Added by Stats.1973, c. 996, p. 1981, § 36, operative July 1, 1974. Amended by Stats.1977, c. 579, p. 1913, § 182; Stats.1981, c. 714, p. 2798, § 444; Stats.1990, c. 1563 (A.B.3243), § 58; Stats.1998, c. 877 (A.B.2132), § 52.)*

§ 11902.5. Conviction of crime involving moral turpitude; refusal to issue or suspension of license

(a) The department, after notice and hearing, on an interim basis, may refuse to issue or may suspend a license issued under this chapter when the applicant or licensee has been convicted of a crime involving moral turpitude which is substantially related to the qualifications, functions, or duties of the licensed activity, if an appeal of the conviction is pending or the conviction has otherwise not become final. A conviction after a plea of nolo contendere is a conviction within the meaning of this section.

(b) If a conviction, upon which an interim refusal to issue or suspension under subdivision (a) is based, is affirmed on appeal or otherwise becomes final, the refusal to issue or suspension shall automatically take effect as a denial or revocation, as the case may be, of the license. If the interim refusal to issue or suspension was stayed under probationary terms and conditions, the subsequent automatic denial or revocation shall also be stayed under the same terms and conditions for a term not to exceed the original term of probation for the interim refusal or suspension.

(c) If a conviction, upon which an interim refusal to issue or suspension under subdivision (a) is based, is reversed on appeal, the refusal or suspension shall be set aside immediately by the department. *(Added by Stats. 1990, c. 1563 (A.B.3243), § 59.)*

§ 11903. Suspension or revocation; probationary licenses; hearings; reapplication after denial or revocation

(a) If the department suspends or revokes a representative's license, the licensee shall be entitled to an appropriate hearing. Such hearing shall be conducted pursuant to Chapter 5 (commencing with Section 11500) of Part 1 of Division 3 of Title 2 of the Government Code.

(b) If the department issues or renews a representative's license requiring conditions of probation or if the department refuses to issue such license, the applicant shall be entitled to demand in writing a hearing as hereinabove provided before the director or his representative within 60 days after notice of refusal or issuance of the probationary license.

(c) A person whose representative's license has been revoked or whose application for a license has been denied may reapply for such license after a period of not less than one year has elapsed from the effective date of the decision revoking the license or denying the application; provided, however, that if such decision was based upon paragraph (3) or (4) of subdivision (b) of Section 11902, an earlier reapplication may be made accompanied by evidence satisfactory to the department that such grounds no longer exist. *(Added by Stats.1973, c. 996, p. 1982, § 36, operative July 1, 1974. Amended by Stats.1976, c. 934, p. 2140, § 6.)*

§ 11903.5. Filing of accusation; compromise settlement agreement; terms and conditions

(a) After the filing of an accusation under this article, the director may enter into a stipulated compromise settlement agreement with the consent of the licensee on terms and conditions mutually agreeable to the director, the respondent licensee, and the accuser without further hearing or appeal. The agreement may include, but is not limited to, a period of probation or monetary penalties, or both. The monetary penalty shall not exceed five hundred dollars ($500) for each violation, and it shall be based on the nature of the violation and the effect of the violation on the purposes of this article.

(b) A compromise settlement agreement may be entered before, during, or after the hearing, but is valid only if executed and filed pursuant to subdivision (d) before the proposed decision of the hearing officer, if any, is adopted or the case is decided.

(c) The department shall adopt, by regulation, a schedule of maximum and minimum amounts of monetary penalties, the payment of which may be included as a term or condition of a compromise settlement agreement entered under subdivision (a). Any monetary penalty included in a compromise settlement agreement shall be within the range of monetary penalties in that schedule.

(d) Any compromise settlement agreement entered under this section shall be signed by the director, the respondent licensee, and the accuser, or by their authorized representatives. The director shall file, or cause to be filed, the agreement with the Office of Administrative Hearings, together with the department's notice of withdrawal of the accusation or statement of issues upon which the action was initiated.

(e) If the respondent licensee fails to perform all of the terms and conditions of the compromise settlement agreement, the agreement is void and the department may take any action authorized by law notwithstanding the agreement, including, but not limited to, refiling the accusation or imposing license sanctions. *(Added by Stats.1985, c. 1022, § 22.)*

§ 11904. Expiration of representative license

Every representative's license issued hereunder shall expire at midnight on the 30th day of June of each year. *(Added by Stats.1973, c. 996, p. 1982, § 36, operative July 1, 1974.)*

§ 11905. Renewal of representative license

Every application for the renewal of a representative's license which expires on the 30th day of June shall be made by the person to whom issued between June 1st and midnight of June 30th preceding such expiration date and shall be made by presenting the application form provided by the department and by payment of the full annual renewal fee for such license. *(Added by Stats.1973, c. 996, p. 1982, § 36, operative July 1, 1974.)*

§ 11906. Repealed by Stats.1975, c. 182, p. 537, § 23, eff. July 5, 1975

§ 11907. Automatic cancellation

The representative's license, or any permit provided for in this chapter, shall be automatically canceled upon the failure of the licensee to file an application for renewal of the license or permit before July 1st following the expiration date of the current license or permit. *(Added by Stats.1973, c. 996, p. 1983, § 36, operative July 1, 1974.)*

§ 11908. Department's authority after suspension, expiration or cancellation of license

The suspension, expiration, or cancellation of the representative's license provided for in this chapter shall not prevent the filing of an accusation for revocation or suspension of the suspended, expired, or canceled license as provided in Section 11903, and the department's decision that such license should be suspended or revoked. Such determination may be considered in granting or refusing to grant any subsequent license authorized by Division 5 (commencing with Section 11100) to such licensee. *(Added by Stats.1973, c. 996, p. 1983, § 36, operative July 1, 1974.)*

§ 11909. Posting of license

Upon issuance by the department to the licensee, the license provided in this article shall be immediately delivered to and posted in a place conspicuous to the public at the place of business of the manufacturer, manufacturer's branch, distributor, distributor's branch from which the representative is directly supervised and shall be continuously exhibited in such place while the representative is employed by such employer.

In the event a representative's employment is terminated, the license shall be forwarded to the department by the manufacturer, manufacturer's branch, distributor, distributor's branch not later than the end of the third business day after termination. *(Added by Stats.1974, c. 384, p. 961, § 16, eff. July 5, 1974, operative July 1, 1974.)*

CHAPTER 5. SALE OF HOUSECARS

Section
11930. Definitions.
11931. Express warranty list; signature of purchaser and dealer; violation.

Cross References

"House car" defined, see Vehicle Code § 362.

§ 11930. Definitions

As used in this chapter:

(a) "First-stage manufacturer" with reference to a housecar means the manufacturer of the engine, chassis, and drive train of the vehicle.

(b) "Second-stage manufacturer" means the installer of the structure and equipment permanently upon the engine, chassis, and drive train of the vehicle rendering the vehicle complete and suitable for human habitation and ready for delivery to the dealer or the buyer. *(Added by Stats.1980, c. 853, p. 2661, § 1.)*

§ 11931. Express warranty list; signature of purchaser and dealer; violation

(a) The dealer shall give the purchaser of a new housecar a list of every express warranty, of which he has notice, that has been issued on the housecar, or a part thereof, by the first-stage manufacturer, the second-stage manufacturer, the dealer, or any other party. The dealer shall also give the purchaser a copy of each warranty.

(b) The purchaser shall sign the list as an acknowledgment that he has received each warranty listed. The dealer shall sign to signify that all express warranties applicable to the housecar appear on the list. Both the purchaser and the dealer shall retain a copy of the list.

(c) Violation of this section is an infraction. *(Added by Stats.1980, c. 853, p. 2661, § 1.)*

CHAPTER 6. SALE OF USED VEHICLES

Section
11950. Buy-here-pay-here dealer; label on used vehicle for retail sale; requirements; reasonable market value.
11951. Repealed.

§ 11950. Buy-here-pay-here dealer; label on used vehicle for retail sale; requirements; reasonable market value

(a) A buy-here-pay-here dealer shall affix a label on any used vehicle being offered for retail sale that states the reasonable market value of that vehicle. The label shall meet all of the following conditions:

(1) Be in writing.

(2) Be printed with a heading that reads "REASONABLE MARKET VALUE OF THIS VEHICLE" in at least 16–point bold type and text in at least 12–point type.

(3) Be located adjacent to the window sticker identifying the equipment provided with the vehicle or, if none, it shall be located prominently and conspicuously on the vehicle so that it is readily readable.

(4) Contain the information used to determine the reasonable market value of the vehicle, including, but not limited to, the use of a nationally recognized pricing guide for used vehicles.

(5) Contain the date the reasonable market value was determined.

(6) Indicate that the reasonable market value is being provided only for comparison shopping and is not the retail sale price or the advertised price of the vehicle.

(b) A buy-here-pay-here dealer shall provide to a prospective buyer of the used vehicle a copy of any information obtained from a nationally recognized pricing guide that the buy-here-pay-here dealer used to determine the reasonable market value of the vehicle.

(c) As used in this section:

(1) "Reasonable market value" means the average retail value of a used vehicle based on the condition, mileage, year, make, and model of the vehicle, as determined within the last 60 days by a nationally recognized pricing guide that provides used vehicle retail values or pricing reports to vehicle dealers or the public.

(2) "Nationally recognized pricing guide" includes, but is not limited to, the Kelley Blue Book (KBB), Edmunds, the Black Book, or the National Automobile Dealers' Association (NADA) Guide. *(Added by Stats.2012, c. 741 (A.B.1534), § 1.)*

Cross References

Buy-here-pay-here dealer defined, see Vehicle Code §§ 241, 241.1.

§ 11951. Repealed by Stats.1980, c. 1149, p. 3783, § 53

CHAPTER 7. SALE OF AUTOMOBILE PARTS

Section
12000. Investigation and enforcement.
12001. Invoice; required information.
12002. Defective vehicle parts.
12003. Violation.

§ 12000. Investigation and enforcement

The Bureau of Automotive Repair in the Department of Consumer Affairs shall enforce the provisions of this chapter. The Bureau of Automotive Repair shall investigate and inspect retail outlets to insure compliance with this chapter. *(Added by Stats.1975, c. 678, p. 1500, § 70.)*

§ 12001. Invoice; required information

(a) Any person who sells and installs new parts in passenger cars, in the ordinary course of his business, shall provide the customer with an invoice which identifies by brand name, or other comparable designation, the part or parts installed.

(b) Any person who sells and installs used or factory rebuilt parts in passenger cars, in the ordinary course of his business, shall provide the customer with an invoice which specifically designates the used part or parts installed.

(c) This section shall not apply to any fitting or other device necessary to the installation of any new, used or factory rebuilt part subject to the provisions of this section. *(Added by Stats.1975, c. 678, p. 1500, § 70.)*

§ 12002. Defective vehicle parts

No person shall knowingly manufacture, sell, or install in any vehicle, any vehicle part which, under the provisions of the National Traffic and Motor Vehicle Safety

Act of 1966 (15 U.S.C., Sec. 1381 et seq.), is, or has been, determined to be defective and subject to customer notification or recall. *(Added by Stats.1975, c. 678, p. 1500, § 70.)*

§ 12003. Violation

Any violation of this chapter shall be a misdemeanor. *(Added by Stats.1975, c. 678, p. 1500, § 70.)*

Cross References

Misdemeanors, definition and penalties, see Penal Code §§ 17, 19 and 19.2.

CHAPTER 8. PRIVATE PARTY VEHICLE MARKETS

Section
12101. Secondhand tangible personal property law; application.
12102. Definitions.
12103. Market operators; records.
12104. Market operators; obligation to supply forms and information.

§ 12101. Secondhand tangible personal property law; application

Any transaction which is regulated by this chapter shall not be subject to the provisions of Article 4 (commencing with Section 21625) of Chapter 9 of Division 8 of the Business and Professions Code, regulating transactions in identifiable secondhand tangible personal property. No person shall be considered a "secondhand dealer" within the meaning of Section 21661 [1] of the Business and Professions Code because of activities regulated by this chapter. *(Added by Stats.1978, c. 525, p. 1684, § 1.)*

[1] "Secondhand dealer" is defined in Business and Professions Code § 21626.

§ 12102. Definitions

The following definitions apply with respect to this chapter:

(a) "Private party vehicle market" means any event conducted under any of the following circumstances:

(1) An event at which two or more vehicles are offered or displayed for sale or exchange and a fee is charged for the privilege of offering or displaying the vehicles for sale or exchange.

(2) An event at which a fee is charged to prospective buyers for admission to the area where vehicles are offered or displayed for sale or exchange.

(3) An event, other than one conducted by a person listed in subdivision (a) of Section 286, at which used vehicles are offered or displayed for sale or exchange if such event is held at the same place more than six times in any 12-month period, regardless of the number of persons offering or displaying vehicles or the absence of fees.

(b) "Private party vehicle market operator" means any person who controls, manages, conducts, or otherwise administers a private party vehicle market.

(c) "Vendor" means any person who exchanges, sells, or offers for sale or exchange any vehicle at a private party vehicle market.

(d) Any event arranged or sponsored, or both, by a dealer licensed pursuant to Division 5 (commencing with Section 11100) shall not be considered a private party vehicle market. *(Added by Stats.1978, c. 525, p. 1684, § 1.)*

Cross References

"Dealer" defined, see Vehicle Code § 285.

§ 12103. Market operators; records

(a) Every private party vehicle market operator shall maintain a record, for not less than one year, of all of the following information:

(1) The name of each vendor selling, exchanging, or offering for sale or exchange, any vehicle at a private party vehicle market.

(2) The vendor's driver's license number.

(3) The registration number assigned to the vehicle and the vehicle identification number.

(4) The number of the vehicle's current and valid certificate of compliance.

(5) The make, model, and color of the vehicle.

(b) That information shall be made available, upon request, to any peace officer and to any employee of the department designated by the director. *(Added by Stats. 1978, c. 525, p. 1684, § 1. Amended by Stats.1991, c. 1054 (S.B.245), § 4.)*

§ 12104. Market operators; obligation to supply forms and information

(a) Every private party vehicle market operator shall supply, to vendors, sufficient forms which are necessary to comply with Section 5900.

(b) Every private party vehicle market operator shall supply, to vendors, all information made available by the department to the general public regarding all existing provisions of law pertaining to requirements for the transfer of vehicle ownership and registration between parties who are not dealers. *(Added by Stats.1978, c. 525, p. 1684, § 1.)*

CHAPTER 9. TOWING

Section
12110. Compensation for arranging or requesting towing services; restrictions; exceptions; towing franchise awards; offense; penalties.
12111. Business license taxes; imposition on tow truck operations.

§ 12110. Compensation for arranging or requesting towing services; restrictions; exceptions; towing franchise awards; offense; penalties

(a) Except as provided in subdivision (b), no towing service shall provide and no person or public entity shall accept any direct or indirect commission, gift, or any compensation whatever from a towing service in consideration of arranging or requesting the services of a tow truck. As used in this section, "arranging" does not include the activities of employees or principals of a provider of towing services in responding to a request for towing services.

(b) Subdivision (a) does not preclude a public entity otherwise authorized by law from requiring a fee in connection with the award of a franchise for towing vehicles on behalf of that public entity. However, the fee in those cases may not exceed the amount necessary to reimburse the public entity for its actual and reasonable costs incurred in connection with the towing program.

(c) Any towing service or any employee of a towing service that accepts or agrees to accept any money or anything of value from a repair shop and any repair shop or any employee of a repair shop that pays or agrees to pay any money or anything of value as a commission, referral fee, inducement, or in any manner a consideration, for the delivery or the arranging of a delivery of a vehicle, not owned by the repair shop or towing service, for the purpose of storage or repair, is guilty of a misdemeanor, punishable as set forth in subdivision (d). Nothing in this subdivision prevents a towing service from towing a vehicle to a repair shop owned by the same company that owns the towing service.

(d) Any person convicted of a violation of subdivision (a) or (c) shall be punished as follows:

(1) Upon first conviction, by a fine of not more than five thousand dollars ($5,000) or imprisonment in the county jail for not more than six months, or by both that fine and imprisonment. If the violation of subdivision (a) or (c) is committed by a tow truck driver, the person's privilege to operate a motor vehicle shall be suspended by the department under Section 13351.85. The clerk of the court shall send a certified abstract of the conviction to the department. If the violation of either subdivision (a) or (c) is committed by a tow truck driver, the court may order the impoundment of the tow truck involved for not more than 15 days.

(2) Upon a conviction of a violation of subdivision (a) or (c) that occurred within seven years of one or more separate convictions of violations of subdivision (a) or (c), by a fine of not more than ten thousand dollars ($10,000) or imprisonment in the county jail for not more than one year, or by both that fine and imprisonment. If the violation of subdivision (a) or (c) is committed by a tow truck driver, the person's privilege to operate a motor vehicle shall be suspended by the department under Section 13351.85. The clerk of the court shall send a certified abstract of the conviction to the department. If the violation of either subdivision (a) or (c) is committed

by a tow truck owner, the court may order the impoundment of the tow truck involved for not less than 15 days but not more than 30 days. *(Added by Stats.1983, c. 746, § 1. Amended by Stats.1988, c. 924, § 5; Stats.1994, c. 268 (A.B.3017), § 1; Stats.1994, c. 675 (S.B.1741), § 4; Stats.2000, c. 641 (A.B.2729), § 1.)*

Cross References

Misdemeanors, definition and penalties, see Penal Code §§ 17, 19 and 19.2.
"Tow truck" defined, see Vehicle Code § 615.

§ 12111. Business license taxes; imposition on tow truck operations

(a) Except as provided in subdivision (b), no city or city and county may impose a business license tax for revenue-raising purposes on the operation of a tow truck in its jurisdiction if the vehicle tower maintains no fixed place of business within the boundaries of the city or city and county.

(b) A city or city and county may impose a business license tax upon a vehicle tower doing business within its jurisdiction who has no fixed place of business therein, if the license tax is graduated according to gross receipts attributable to work done within the city or city and county. *(Added by Stats.1984, c. 1334, § 1. Amended by Stats.1988, c. 924, § 6.)*

Cross References

"Tow truck" defined, see Vehicle Code § 615.

CHAPTER 10. SALES OF VEHICLES BY PRIVATE OWNERS

Section
12120. Vehicles required to be registered or identified; persons authorized to sell or offer for sale.
12121. Exemptions.
12122. Repealed.

§ 12120. Vehicles required to be registered or identified; persons authorized to sell or offer for sale

Only a dealer, a person described in Section 286, or the registered owner of record shall sell or offer for sale a vehicle of a type required to be registered pursuant to Division 3 (commencing with Section 4000) or identified pursuant to Division 16.5 (commencing with Section 38000), except as provided in Section 12121. *(Added by Stats.1986, c. 668, § 1.)*

Cross References

"Registered owner" defined, see Vehicle Code § 505.

§ 12121. Exemptions

(a) Section 12120 does not apply to a dealer licensed pursuant to Chapter 4 (commencing with Section 11700) when acting under authority of the license, or to his or her authorized agent.

(b) Section 12120 does not prohibit the sale of a vehicle by any of the following persons not engaged in the business of selling vehicles:

(1) Anyone related by blood, adoption, or marriage to the registered owner.

(2) The receiver, administrator, executor, guardian, or other person appointed by, or acting under, a judgment or order of any court.

(3) The trustee of a trust in which the vehicle is registered as an asset.

(4) Any public officer in the performance of his or her official duties.

(5) An attorney on behalf of a client who is the registered owner.

(6) The owner, officer, or designated representative of a business in whose name the vehicle, is registered.

(7) The legal owner as shown on the certificate of ownership.

(8) A person who has prior written authorization from the registered owner of the vehicle, and that person does not receive or expect to receive a commission, money, brokerage fees, profit, or any other thing of value from either the seller or purchaser of the vehicle.

(9) An insurer selling the salvage of one of its insured's vehicle or the stolen vehicle of one of its insured which has been recovered. *(Added by Stats.1986, c. 668, § 1.)*

Cross References

"Legal owner" defined, see Vehicle Code § 370.

§ 12122. Repealed by Stats.1988, c. 1029, § 33

CHAPTER 11. CONSUMER RECOVERY FUND

Section
12200. Definitions.
12201. Consumer Motor Vehicle Recovery Corporation.
12202. Board of directors.
12203. Consumer recovery fund; operations account; investment of funds; funds held in trust; accounting; bylaws, rules, and procedures.
12204. Applications for eligible consumer claims; evidentiary requirements; time for filing.
12205. Notice of consumer rights.
12206. Receipt of application; notice; payment or denial of claim; conflict of interest.
12207. Notice to alleged nonpaying dealer or lessor-retailer.
12208. Payments; maximum allowed.
12209. Denied claims; notice; final decisions; review.
12210. Subrogation of paid amounts; recovery actions; payment report; disposition of claim notice; effect of payment.
12211. Insufficient funds available; priority of claims.
12212. Year-end statement; information to be made public; disseminating information.
12213. Attorney General examination and review.
12214. Failure or cessation of recovery corporation operations; findings.
12215. Settling of outstanding debts or obligations.
12216. Administrative costs and expenses.
12217. Construction of chapter.
12300 to 12304. Repealed.

Cross References

Fees for vehicles sold, see Vehicle Code § 4456.3.

§ 12200. Definitions

The following definitions apply to this chapter:

(a) "Application" means an application to the recovery corporation for the payment of an eligible claim from the recovery fund that is filed with the recovery corporation after January 1, 2009.

(b) "Consumer" means a person who either (1) purchased or leased, or became obligated to purchase or lease, a motor vehicle to be used primarily for personal, family, or household purposes from a dealer or lessor-retailer licensed under this code, or (2) consigned for sale a motor vehicle that was used primarily for personal, family, or household purposes to a dealer licensed under this code.

(c) "Eligible claim" means an unsatisfied claim for economic loss, not barred by the statutes of limitation, that accrues after July 1, 2008, as a result of the failure of a dealer licensed under this code, or, if applicable, a lessor-retailer licensed under this code, to do any of the following:

(1) Remit license or registration fees received or contractually obligated to be paid from a consumer to the department.

(2) Pay to the legal owner of a vehicle transferred as a trade-in by a consumer to the dealer or lessor-retailer the amount necessary to discharge the prior credit balance owed to the legal owner.

(3) Pay to the lessor registered in accordance with Section 4453.5 of a vehicle transferred as a trade-in by a consumer to the dealer or lessor-retailer the amount the dealer or lessor-retailer agreed to pay to the lessor.

(4) Pay the amount specified in a consignment agreement to a consumer after the sale of a consigned vehicle.

(5) Provide a consumer who purchased a vehicle from the dealer or lessor-retailer with good title to the vehicle, free from any security interest or other lien, encumbrance, or claim, unless otherwise clearly and conspicuously provided for by the written sale agreement.

(6) Pay to a third party any amount received from, or contractually obligated to be paid by, a consumer for insurance, service contracts, or goods or services purchased through the dealer or lessor-retailer and to be provided by the third party.

(d) "Participant" means a dealer licensed under this code or a lessor-retailer licensed under this code.

(e) "Recovery corporation" means the Consumer Motor Vehicle Recovery Corporation.

(f) "Recovery fund" means the consumer recovery fund established by the recovery corporation pursuant to Section 12203 for the payment of eligible claims. *(Added by Stats.2007, c. 437 (S.B.729), § 6. Amended by Stats. 2013, c. 392 (A.B.501), § 3.)*

§ 12201. Consumer Motor Vehicle Recovery Corporation

(a) Participants shall maintain a corporation under the Nonprofit Mutual Benefit Corporation Law (Part 3 (commencing with Section 7110) of Division 2 of Title 1 of the Corporations Code) that shall operate under the name "Consumer Motor Vehicle Recovery Corporation."

(b) The purpose of the Consumer Motor Vehicle Recovery Corporation is to provide payments to consumers on eligible claims subject to the requirements and limitations set forth in this chapter.

(c) A participant may not charge or collect from a consumer a separate fee or charge to recoup the fee paid by the participant pursuant to Section 4456.3.

(d) The State of California and its officers, agents, or employees shall not be liable for any act or omission of the recovery corporation or its directors, officers, agents, or employees. *(Added by Stats.2007, c. 437 (S.B.729), § 6.)*

Cross References

"Consumer" defined for purposes of this Chapter, see Vehicle Code § 12200.
"Eligible claim" defined for purposes of this Chapter, see Vehicle Code § 12200.
"Participant" defined for purposes of this Chapter, see Vehicle Code § 12200.
"Recovery corporation" defined for purposes of this Chapter, see Vehicle Code § 12200.

§ 12202. Board of directors

(a) The recovery corporation shall have a board of directors composed of six directors, as follows:

(1) One public consumer representative member appointed by the Director of Consumer Affairs who shall serve until the appointment is revoked, another appointment is made, or until the appointed director resigns. The consumer representative shall be either of the following:

(A) A current or former prosecutor with at least two years of direct experience in the civil or criminal enforcement of consumer protection laws, including laws prohibiting deceptive advertising and unlawful and fraudulent practices.

(B) A current or former employee of a government agency who has at least two years of direct experience in one of the following:

(i) The investigation, mediation, and resolution of consumer complaints.

(ii) Providing counseling, information, education, or referral services to consumers.

(iii) Administering a consumer protection program that provides any of the services described in clause (i) or (ii).

(2) A representative of the Attorney General, who shall serve as an ex officio, nonvoting member.

(3) One member of the general public appointed by the Senate Committee on Rules to a two-year term.

(4) One member of the general public appointed by the Speaker of the Assembly to a two-year term, except that the initial appointment to the board of directors shall be for a one-year term.

(5) Two participants, who shall be appointed by the Governor for two-year terms, except that the initial term of the position of one of the participant directors shall be for a one-year term.

(b) A person is eligible to be nominated and to serve as a participant director if the person satisfies all of the following conditions:

(1) The person's primary occupation, at the time of nomination and continuously during the previous three years, has been as an owner or general manager of a licensed dealer or lessor-retailer.

(2) The person has not been convicted of a crime, including a plea or verdict of guilty or a conviction following a plea of nolo contendere.

(3) The person is not subject to a judgment or administrative order, whether entered after adjudication or stipulation, predicated on that person's commission of an act of dishonesty, fraud, deceit, or violation of this chapter or Chapter 5 (commencing with Section 17200) of Part 2 of Division 7 of the Business and Professions Code.

(4) The person is not a defendant in a pending criminal or civil law enforcement action brought by a public prosecutor.

(5) The person has not served as a participant director of the recovery corporation at any time during the previous 18 months.

(c) A director who does not qualify to be a participant director, whose term has lapsed, or who otherwise becomes unable to serve shall not continue to serve as a director. *(Added by Stats.2007, c. 437 (S.B.729), § 6.)*

Cross References

Attorney General, generally, see Government Code § 12500 et seq.
"Consumer" defined for purposes of this Chapter, see Vehicle Code § 12200.
"Participant" defined for purposes of this Chapter, see Vehicle Code § 12200.
"Recovery corporation" defined for purposes of this Chapter, see Vehicle Code § 12200.

§ 12203. Consumer recovery fund; operations account; investment of funds; funds held in trust; accounting; bylaws, rules, and procedures

(a) The recovery corporation shall establish a consumer recovery fund for the payment of claims as provided in this chapter.   The recovery corporation shall receive funds from the department as provided in Section 4456.3 and shall promptly notify the department when the recovery fund balance reaches the amounts specified in subdivision (b) of Section 4456.3.

(b) The recovery corporation shall establish and maintain an operations account within the recovery fund for the payment of costs of operations and administration. The recovery corporation shall prepare, prior to its fiscal year end, an estimated annual operational budget projecting the costs of operations and administration for the succeeding fiscal year, excluding the amount paid for claims.   The recovery corporation shall not expend more than two hundred fifty thousand dollars ($250,000) each fiscal year from the operations account for the administration of this chapter.

(c) The recovery corporation shall invest all funds received from the department pursuant to Section 4456.3, and interest earned on those funds, deposited in the recovery fund, in a federally insured account or in federally insured certificates of deposit at a California state or federally chartered bank or savings bank.

(d) The recovery corporation holds all money in the recovery fund in trust for the purposes provided in this chapter and shall disburse funds only as provided in this chapter.

(e) The recovery corporation shall separately account for disbursements and collections.   The accounting shall include a record of each claim paid that indicates the name, address, and phone number of each claimant receiving payment, the amount of the payment, and the name of the participant for which a claim was paid. Quarterly reports shall be provided to the office of the Attorney General, Consumer Law Section, commencing on or before October 31, 2008, and within 30 days after the end of each quarter thereafter.

(f) The recovery corporation may adopt reasonable written bylaws, rules, and procedures to carry out the purposes of this chapter.   The representative of the Attorney General may vote on the adoption of bylaws, rules, and procedures notwithstanding paragraph (2) of subdivision (a) of Section 12202.   *(Added by Stats.2007, c. 437 (S.B.729), § 6.)*

Cross References

Attorney General, generally, see Government Code § 12500 et seq.
"Consumer" defined for purposes of this Chapter, see Vehicle Code § 12200.
"Participant" defined for purposes of this Chapter, see Vehicle Code § 12200.
"Recovery corporation" defined for purposes of this Chapter, see Vehicle Code § 12200.

§ 12204. Applications for eligible consumer claims; evidentiary requirements; time for filing

(a) A consumer may file an application with the recovery corporation for the payment of the consumer's eligible claim if a dealer or lessor-retailer against whom the claim is asserted has ceased selling and leasing motor vehicles to the general public or has become subject to a petition in bankruptcy.

(b)(1) The application shall be verified and shall set forth all of the following information:

(A) The consumer's name, address, and telephone number.

(B) The amount of the eligible claim.

(C) A description of the circumstances demonstrating an eligible claim.

(D) A statement indicating the consumer's belief that the dealer or lessor-retailer has ceased selling and leasing motor vehicles to the general public or has become subject to a petition in bankruptcy and the reasons for this belief.

(E) A statement indicating what action, if any, the applicant has taken to recover the amount of the eligible claim.

(F) A statement indicating that the consumer's application for payment does not include any amount for which the consumer has obtained recovery under the dealer's bond required by Section 11710.

(2) Nothing in this chapter shall be construed to require a consumer to bring a civil action to obtain recovery, file a bankruptcy claim, or file a crime report with a law enforcement agency in order to obtain payment of an eligible claim submitted to the recovery corporation.

(c) The application shall be accompanied by a copy of the agreement between the consumer and the dealer or lessor-retailer, unless the agreement is unnecessary to the recovery corporation's determination of the validity of the claim.

(d) If the eligible claim is based on the failure to remit license or registration fees, the application shall be accompanied by evidence demonstrating that the consumer paid money or other consideration for the fees, or became obligated to pay the fees, and that the fees had not been remitted.   The eligible claim shall be limited to the dollar amount of the license or registration fees not remitted and a late charge or penalty.

(e) If the eligible claim is based on the failure to pay the proceeds of a consignment sale, the application shall be accompanied by the consignment agreement, evidence that the consigned vehicle was sold, and by the consumer's verified statement that the consumer did not receive the portion of the proceeds of the sale to which the consumer was entitled.   The eligible claim is limited to the dollar amount specified in a written consignment agreement to be paid to the consignor.

(f) If the eligible claim is based on the failure to pay the legal owner of the consumer's trade-in vehicle, the application shall be accompanied by a statement from the legal owner of the amount, if any, that he or she received from the dealer or lessor-retailer.   The eligible claim is limited to the dollar amount necessary to discharge the credit balance owing on the trade-in vehicle.

(g) If the eligible claim is based on the failure to pay the lessor of the consumer's trade-in vehicle, the application shall be accompanied by a statement from the lessor of the amount, if any, that the lessor received from the dealer or lessor-retailer. The eligible claim is limited to the dollar amount necessary to pay the lessor the total amount that the dealer or lessor-retailer agreed with the consumer to pay the lessor.

(h) If the eligible claim is based on the failure to provide good title, the application shall be accompanied by a statement from the legal owner or other claimant of the amount, if any, that he or she received from the dealer or lessor-retailer. The eligible claim is limited to the remaining dollar amount necessary to discharge the valid security interest, lien, encumbrance, or other claim clouding title to the vehicle.

(i) If the eligible claim is based on the failure to pay third parties for insurance, service contracts, or goods or services, the application shall be accompanied by a statement from the third party of the amount, if any, that he or she received from the dealer or lessor-retailer. The eligible claim is limited to the difference between the dollar amount the consumer paid or was contractually obligated to pay to the dealer or lessor-retailer for the insurance, service contracts, or goods or services purchased through the dealer or lessor-retailer and to be provided by the third party and the dollar amount actually received by the third party from the dealer or lessor-retailer for the insurance, service contracts, or goods or services.

(j) The recovery corporation may require reasonable additional information designed to facilitate payment of eligible claims.

(k)(1) For claims that have accrued on or after July 1, 2008, and before January 1, 2009, the application shall be filed within 18 months of the date upon which the dealer or lessor-retailer ceased selling or leasing motor vehicles to the general public or became subject to a petition in bankruptcy.

(2) For claims that have accrued on or after January 1, 2009, the application shall be filed within one year of the date upon which the dealer or lessor-retailer ceased selling or leasing motor vehicles to the general public or became subject to a petition in bankruptcy. *(Added by Stats.2007, c. 437 (S.B.729), § 6. Amended by Stats.2013, c. 392 (A.B.501), § 4.)*

Cross References

"Application" defined for purposes of this Chapter, see Vehicle Code § 12200.
"Consumer" defined for purposes of this Chapter, see Vehicle Code § 12200.
"Eligible claim" defined for purposes of this Chapter, see Vehicle Code § 12200.

"Recovery corporation" defined for purposes of this Chapter, see Vehicle Code § 12200.

§ 12205. Notice of consumer rights

The recovery corporation shall develop a notice fully explaining a consumer's right to make a claim from the fund, an application form, and an explanation of how to complete the application. The notice, application, and explanation shall be in English and Spanish and shall be provided to a person upon request. *(Added by Stats.2007, c. 437 (S.B.729), § 6.)*

Cross References

"Application" defined for purposes of this Chapter, see Vehicle Code § 12200.
"Consumer" defined for purposes of this Chapter, see Vehicle Code § 12200.
"Recovery corporation" defined for purposes of this Chapter, see Vehicle Code § 12200.

§ 12206. Receipt of application; notice; payment or denial of claim; conflict of interest

(a) Within 30 days of receiving an application, the recovery corporation shall notify the applicant, in writing, that the application is complete or, if the application is incomplete, what additional information is required.

(b)(1) Within 60 days of the recovery corporation providing notice to the applicant of a complete application, the recovery corporation shall either pay the eligible claim from the fund as prescribed in this chapter or deny the claim. A claim shall be deemed granted unless the directors affirmatively vote to deny the claim.

(2) The recovery corporation, for good cause, may extend the 60–day period not more than an additional 90 days to investigate the accuracy of the application or evidence submitted by a dealer or lessor-retailer.

(c) A director shall not be involved in the decision of a claim if the director has a financial interest in the outcome of the decision; has a financial interest in or is employed by the participant that is the subject of the claim; or has a familial or close personal relationship with the claimant or an owner, officer, director, or manager of the participant. *(Added by Stats.2007, c. 437 (S.B.729), § 6.)*

Cross References

"Application" defined for purposes of this Chapter, see Vehicle Code § 12200.
"Eligible claim" defined for purposes of this Chapter, see Vehicle Code § 12200.
"Participant" defined for purposes of this Chapter, see Vehicle Code § 12200.
"Recovery corporation" defined for purposes of this Chapter, see Vehicle Code § 12200.

§ 12207. Notice to alleged nonpaying dealer or lessor-retailer

(a) Within 15 days of receiving a complete application, the recovery corporation shall serve a copy of the complete application and the following notice on the dealer or lessor-retailer that is the subject of the claim:

"NOTICE"

"The attached application has been made to the Consumer Motor Vehicle Recovery Corporation for payment of a claim allegedly arising out of your conduct or omission. If you wish to contest payment, you must file a written response to the application that describes any evidence that you have showing that the application is inaccurate or that payment from the fund is not authorized under Section 12200 and following of the Vehicle Code, a copy of which is provided.

"The allegations stated in the attached application may constitute grounds on which disciplinary action may be taken to suspend or revoke your license. In addition, the Department of Motor Vehicles may suspend your license until you have repaid in full the amount paid by the Consumer Motor Vehicle Recovery Corporation on the attached application, plus interest at the rate of 10 percent per annum."

(b) The notice prescribed by subdivision (a), a copy of the application for payment, and a copy of this chapter shall be served on the dealer or lessor-retailer by personal service or certified mail, return receipt requested, at the department's mailing address of record for that licensee. *(Added by Stats.2007, c. 437 (S.B.729), § 6.)*

Cross References

"Application" defined for purposes of this Chapter, see Vehicle Code § 12200.
"Consumer" defined for purposes of this Chapter, see Vehicle Code § 12200.
"Recovery corporation" defined for purposes of this Chapter, see Vehicle Code § 12200.

§ 12208. Payments; maximum allowed

If the recovery corporation pays the claim, the amount of the payment shall be the total of the amount of the eligible claim, but in no event may the payment exceed thirty-five thousand dollars ($35,000) for a transaction. *(Added by Stats.2007, c. 437 (S.B.729), § 6.)*

Cross References

"Eligible claim" defined for purposes of this Chapter, see Vehicle Code § 12200.
"Recovery corporation" defined for purposes of this Chapter, see Vehicle Code § 12200.

§ 12209. Denied claims; notice; final decisions; review

If the recovery corporation denies the claim, the recovery corporation shall notify the applicant in writing of the denial, the legal and factual bases for the denial, and the applicant's right to contest the denial in writing within 60 days or any longer period permitted by the recovery corporation. If the applicant does not contest the denial within 60 days or an additional period reasonably requested by the consumer, the decision shall be final. The recovery corporation shall act on the applicant's objection within 30 days. If the claim is denied in whole or in part, the applicant may seek review in the superior court of any of the following counties in which the office of the Attorney General maintains an office: Sacramento, San Francisco, Los Angeles, or San Diego. Review shall be limited to the written record before the recovery corporation and any relevant evidence that could not have been previously presented to the recovery corporation despite the applicant's reasonable diligence. The superior court shall affirm the decision of the recovery corporation if it is supported by substantial evidence. *(Added by Stats.2007, c. 437 (S.B.729), § 6.)*

Cross References

Attorney General, generally, see Government Code § 12500 et seq.
"Consumer" defined for purposes of this Chapter, see Vehicle Code § 12200.
"Recovery corporation" defined for purposes of this Chapter, see Vehicle Code § 12200.

§ 12210. Subrogation of paid amounts; recovery actions; payment report; disposition of claim notice; effect of payment

After the recovery corporation pays or rejects a claim, all of the following apply:

(a) Immediately upon payment, the recovery corporation shall be subrogated to all of the consumer's rights against the dealer or lessor-retailer to the extent of the amount of the payment.

(b) The recovery corporation may bring an action to recover the amount of the payment plus interest at the rate of 10 percent per annum and shall be entitled to recover costs and reasonable attorney's fees.

(c) Within 10 days of paying the claim, the recovery corporation shall inform the department of the payment of the claim, the amount of the payment, and the name and address of the dealer or lessor-retailer that is the subject of the claim. Upon the department's request, the recovery corporation shall provide the department with a copy of the claim application and other documents received by the recovery corporation in connection with the claim.

(d) Within 15 days of paying or rejecting the claim, the recovery corporation shall serve the dealer or lessor-retailer that is the subject of the claim with notice of the recovery corporation's disposition of the claim in the manner provided for service in subdivision (b) of Section 12207.

(e) After the consumer receives payment of the eligible claim from the recovery corporation, the consumer shall not seek to recover the amount received from the recovery corporation for the eligible claim from the dealer's bond required by Section 11710. Nothing in this subdivision affects any other rights the consumer may have as provided in Section 12217. *(Added by Stats.2007, c. 437 (S.B.729), § 6.)*

§ 12211. Insufficient funds available; priority of claims

If the recovery corporation has insufficient funds to pay all eligible claims, the recovery corporation shall pay eligible claims in the order that the claim applications were received and shall hold the remaining claims until funds are available to pay those claims. *(Added by Stats.2007, c. 437 (S.B.729), § 6.)*

§ 12212. Year-end statement; information to be made public; disseminating information

(a) Within 30 days after the close of the fiscal year or other reasonable period established by the board of directors, the recovery corporation shall make publicly available a statement of the following information concerning the most recently concluded fiscal year:

(1) The number of claims and approximate dollar amount of the claims received.

(2) The total number of claims and total dollar amount of claims paid.

(3) The approximate number and dollar amount of claims denied or abandoned.

(4) The dollar balance in the recovery fund.

(5) The dollar amount of fees received pursuant to Section 4456.3.

(6) The administrative costs and expenses of the recovery corporation.

(b) The recovery corporation shall make publicly available within 15 days of approval by the board of directors or other reasonable period established by the board of directors, the following information:

(1) The approved minutes of meetings of the board of directors.

(2) The approved estimated annual operational budget projecting the costs of operations and administration for the succeeding fiscal year, excluding the amount to be paid for claims.

(3) The approved bylaws, as amended, of the recovery corporation.

(c) Information may be made publicly available as required by this section by disseminating the information on an Internet Web site or providing the information by electronic mail to a person who has requested the information and provided a valid electronic mail address. *(Added by Stats.2007, c. 437 (S.B.729), § 6.)*

§ 12213. Attorney General examination and review

The operation of the recovery corporation shall at all times be subject to the examination and review of the Attorney General and the Attorney General's representatives. The Attorney General and his or her representatives may at any time investigate the affairs and examine the books, accounts, records, and files used by the recovery corporation. The Attorney General and his or her representatives shall have free access to the offices, books, accounts, papers, records, files, safes, and vaults of the recovery corporation and may copy any documents of, or in the possession of, the recovery corporation. *(Added by Stats.2007, c. 437 (S.B.729), § 6.)*

§ 12214. Failure or cessation of recovery corporation operations; findings

The Attorney General or his or her representative may determine that the recovery corporation has failed or ceased to operate upon a finding that any one of the following has occurred with respect to the recovery corporation:

(a) The recovery corporation was not created.

(b) The recovery corporation is dissolved.

(c) The recovery corporation ceased to operate.

(d) The recovery corporation is insolvent or bankrupt.

(e) The recovery corporation failed to pay its operating costs.

(f) The recovery corporation failed to pay any claim or judgment in a timely manner.

(g) The recovery corporation violated its articles of incorporation or any law of this state.

(h) The recovery corporation invested its funds in violation of this chapter.

(i) The recovery corporation has not diligently made a decision upon a claim made by a person aggrieved.

(j) The recovery corporation violated any section of this chapter.

(k) The recovery corporation neglected or refused to submit its books, papers, and affairs to the inspection of the Attorney General or his or her representatives. *(Added by Stats.2007, c. 437 (S.B.729), § 6.)*

§ 12215. Settling of outstanding debts or obligations

If the recovery corporation is dissolved or ceases to exist, or if the Attorney General or his or her representative makes a determination, pursuant to Section 12214, that the recovery corporation has failed or ceased to operate, all outstanding debts, obligations of the recovery corporation, and amounts due for services rendered shall first be paid from the remaining assets, including the recovery fund. The assets remaining, after settling those liabilities, shall be distributed to the participants, less the costs of that distribution. *(Added by Stats.2007, c. 437 (S.B.729), § 6.)*

§ 12216. Administrative costs and expenses

All costs and expenses incurred by the Department of Justice in the administration of this chapter shall be paid to the Department of Justice by the recovery corporation. The Department of Justice may institute an action for the recovery of costs and expenses incurred in the administration of this article in any court of competent jurisdiction. *(Added by Stats.2007, c. 437 (S.B.729), § 6.)*

§ 12217. Construction of chapter

Nothing in this chapter is intended to limit or restrict actions, remedies, penalties, or procedures otherwise available pursuant to any other provision of law. *(Added by Stats.2007, c. 437 (S.B.729), § 6.)*

§§ 12300 to 12304. Repealed by Stats.1971, c. 1578, p. 3182, § 7, operative May 3, 1972

Division 6

DRIVERS' LICENSES

Chapter	Section
1. Issuance of Licenses, Expiration, and Renewal	12500
2. Suspension or Revocation of Licenses	13100
3. Investigation and Hearing	13800
4. Violation of License Provisions	14600
5. License Fees	14900
6. Driver License Compact	15000
7. Commercial Motor Vehicle Safety Program	15200

Cross References

Application for driver's license or identification card, required numbers or identifiers, see Vehicle Code § 1653.5.

Confidentiality of driver's license information, authorization for businesses to swipe driver's license or identification card in electronic device for certain purposes, violation, see Civil Code § 1798.90.1.

Requirements for drivers of fifteen-passenger vans for students, Community colleges and state university, see Public Contract Code § 10326.1.

School districts and private schools, see Education Code § 39800.5.

CHAPTER 1. ISSUANCE OF LICENSES, EXPIRATION, AND RENEWAL

Article	Section
1. Persons Required to be Licensed, Exemptions, and Age Limits	12500
2. Student Licenses	12650
3. Issuance and Renewal of Licenses	12800
4. Signature and Display of Licenses	12950
5. Identification Cards	13000

Cross References

Confidentiality of driver's license information, authorization for businesses to swipe driver's license or identification card in electronic device for certain purposes, violation, see Civil Code § 1798.90.1.

ARTICLE 1. PERSONS REQUIRED TO BE LICENSED, EXEMPTIONS, AND AGE LIMITS

Section
12500. License requirements; motorized scooter engine requirements.
12501. Persons exempt.
12502. Persons who may operate a motor vehicle without obtaining a driver's license; exemption requiring a medical certificate; compliance with medical certificate restrictions.
12502. Persons who may operate a motor vehicle without obtaining a driver's license; exemption requiring a medical certificate; compliance with medical certificate restrictions.
12503. Unlicensed nonresident.
12504. Nonresident minors.
12505. Residency.
12506. Temporary licenses.
12507. Repealed.
12507.1. Repealed.
12508. Limited term license.
12509. Instruction permits for certain motor vehicles; duration of permit.
12509.5. Instruction permits; motorcycles, motorized scooters, motorized bicycles, etc.
12510. Repealed.
12511. Licensee entitled to one license.
12512. Issuance of licenses to persons under the age of 18 years.
12512.5. Repealed.
12513. Junior permits; issuance.
12514. Junior permits; duration; revocation.
12515. Driving for hire; age limit.
12516. Age for driving school bus.
12517. Schoolbus and pupil activity bus drivers; qualifications; certificates; fees.
12517.1. Schoolbus accident.
12517.2. Bus drivers and farm labor vehicle operators; applications for certificates; medical examination.
12517.3. Fingerprints; bus and ambulance drivers.
12517.4. Regulations for issuance of certificate to drive a schoolbus, school pupil activity bus, youth bus, paratransit vehicle, or farm labor vehicle.
12517.45. Transporting school pupils; requirements.
12517.5. Driver of paratransit vehicles; qualifications.
12518. Nonresident minor member of armed forces.
12519. Farm labor vehicle license.
12519.5. Repealed.
12520. Tow truck drivers; necessity of valid driver's license; permanent tow truck driver certificate.
12520.5, 12520.7. Repealed.
12521. Tour bus operators; use of safety belts; report of accidents.
12522. First aid examination for schoolbus or youth bus operator.
12523. Youth bus operators; licensing requirements; renewals; applicability of regulations for schoolbus drivers; operating rules.
12523.5. Paratransit vehicle operator; driver's license and certificate; fee; qualifications; renewals; operating rules.
12523.6. Driver of persons with developmental disabilities; special driver certificate.
12524. Vehicles hauling fissile class III shipments or large quantity radioactive materials; driver's license and certificate.
12525. Mechanics or other maintenance personnel; operation of certain vehicles requiring endorsement or certificates; exemption.
12526. Repealed.
12527. Ambulance drivers; application for certificate; requirements.

§ 12500. License requirements; motorized scooter engine requirements

(a) A person may not drive a motor vehicle upon a highway, unless the person then holds a valid driver's license issued under this code, except those persons who are expressly exempted under this code.

(b) A person may not drive a motorcycle, motor-driven cycle, or motorized bicycle upon a highway, unless the person then holds a valid driver's license or endorsement issued under this code for that class, except those persons who are expressly exempted under this code, or those persons specifically authorized to operate motorized bicycles or motorized scooters with a valid driver's license of any class, as specified in subdivision (h) of Section 12804.9.

(c) A person may not drive a motor vehicle in or upon any offstreet parking facility, unless the person then holds a valid driver's license of the appropriate class or certification to operate the vehicle. As used in this subdivision, "offstreet parking facility" means any offstreet facility held open for use by the public for parking vehicles and includes any publicly owned facilities for offstreet parking, and privately owned facilities for offstreet parking where no fee is charged for the privilege to park and which are held open for the common public use of retail customers.

(d) A person may not drive a motor vehicle or combination of vehicles that is not of a type for which the person is licensed.

(e) A motorized scooter operated on public streets shall at all times be equipped with an engine that complies with the applicable State Air Resources Board emission requirements. *(Stats.1959, c. 3, p. 1613, § 12500. Amended by Stats.1961, c. 1615, p. 3453, § 5; Stats.1963, c. 74, p. 700, § 2; Stats.1984, c. 621, § 2; Stats.1990, c. 1359 (A.B.55), § 3; Stats.1993, c. 272 (A.B.301), § 17, eff. Aug. 2, 1993; Stats.1993, c. 1292 (S.B.274), § 7; Stats.1996, c. 10 (A.B.1869), § 12, eff. Feb. 9, 1996; Stats.2004, c. 755 (A.B.1878), § 3; Stats.2007, c. 630 (A.B.1728), § 3.)*

Cross References

Certain violations constituting misdemeanors, see Vehicle Code § 40000.11.
Conduct of sobriety checkpoint inspection, vehicle impoundment and release, see Vehicle Code § 2814.2.
Driver license compact, see Vehicle Code § 15000 et seq.
Driver's license defined, see Vehicle Code § 310.
Driving when privileges suspended or revoked, see Vehicle Code § 14601.
Employment of unlicensed motor vehicle attendant, see Vehicle Code § 14605.
Highway defined, see Vehicle Code § 360.
Offense under this section as infraction, see Penal Code § 19.8.
Permitting unlicensed person to drive as offense, see Vehicle Code § 14606.
Removal of vehicle, circumstances permitting, see Vehicle Code § 22651.
Renting vehicle to unlicensed person, see Vehicle Code § 14608.

Transportation of agricultural irrigation supplies, inspection of bills of lading, shipping, or delivery papers, care of apprehended supplies, see Vehicle Code § 2810.2.

§ 12501. Persons exempt

The following persons are not required to obtain a driver's license:

(a) An officer or employee of the United States, while operating a motor vehicle owned or controlled by the United States on the business of the United States, except when the motor vehicle being operated is a commercial motor vehicle, as defined in Section 15210.

(b) Any person while driving or operating implements of husbandry incidentally operated or moved over a highway, except as provided in Section 36300 or 36305.

(c) Any person driving or operating an off-highway motor vehicle subject to identification, as defined in Section 38012, while driving or operating such motor vehicle as provided in Section 38025. Nothing in this subdivision authorizes operation of a motor vehicle by a person without a valid driver's license upon any offstreet parking facility, as defined in subdivision (c) of Section 12500. *(Stats.1959, c. 3, p. 1614, § 12501. Amended by Stats.1959, c. 1685, p. 4084, § 1; Stats.1963, c. 268, p. 1025, § 2; Stats.1963, c. 2149, p. 4487, § 13; Stats.1969, c. 1075, p. 2064, § 8; Stats.1972, c. 973, p. 1758, § 16, eff. Aug. 16, 1972; Stats.1984, c. 621, § 3; Stats.1986, c. 973, § 2; Stats.1990, c. 1360 (S.B.1510), § 10.)*

Cross References

Definitions,
  Implement of husbandry, see Vehicle Code § 36000.
  Motor vehicle, see Vehicle Code § 415.
Nonresidents exempt, see Vehicle Code § 12502 et seq.
Vehicles exempt from registration, see Vehicle Code §§ 4002, 4006 et seq., 6700 et seq.

§ 12502. Persons who may operate a motor vehicle without obtaining a driver's license; exemption requiring a medical certificate; compliance with medical certificate restrictions

Section operative until Jan. 30, 2014. See, also, section operative Jan. 31, 2014.

(a) The following persons may operate a motor vehicle in this state without obtaining a driver's license under this code:

(1) A nonresident over the age of 18 years having in his or her immediate possession a valid driver's license issued by a foreign jurisdiction of which he or she is a resident, except as provided in Section 12505.

(2) A nonresident, 21 years of age or older, if transporting hazardous material, as defined in Section 353, in a commercial vehicle, having in his or her immediate possession a valid license with the appropriate endorsement issued by another state or other jurisdiction that is recognized by the department, or a Canadian driver's license and a copy of his or her current training certificate to transport hazardous material that complies with all

federal laws and regulations with respect to hazardous materials, both of which shall be in his or her immediate possession.

(3) A nonresident having in his or her immediate possession a valid driver's license, issued by the Diplomatic Motor Vehicle Office of the Office of Foreign Missions of the United States Department of State, for the type of motor vehicle or combination of vehicles that the person is operating.

(b) Any person entitled to the exemption contained in subdivision (a), while operating, within this state, a commercial motor vehicle, as defined in subdivision (b) of Section 15210, shall have in his or her possession a current medical certificate of a type described in subdivision (c) of Section 12804.9, that has been issued within two years of the date of operation of the vehicle.

(c) A nonresident possessing a medical certificate in accordance with subdivision (b) shall comply with any restriction of the medical certificate issued to that nonresident.

(d) This section shall remain in effect only until January 30, 2014, and as of that date is repealed, unless a later enacted statute, that is enacted before January 30, 2014, deletes or extends that date. *(Stats.1959, c. 3, p. 1614, § 12502. Amended by Stats.1961, c. 1615, p. 3453, § 6; Stats.1963, c. 237, p. 978, § 2; Stats.1963, c. 666, p. 1654, § 2; Stats.1971, c. 1748, p. 3763, § 54.5, operative March 4, 1972; Stats.1981, c. 245, p. 1298, § 3; Stats.1988, c. 436, § 1; Stats.1988, c. 1509, § 3.5; Stats.1989, c. 23, § 1, eff. May 25, 1989; Stats.1990, c. 1360 (S.B.1510), § 10.5; Stats.1992, c. 711 (A.B.2874), § 118, eff. Sept. 15, 1992; Stats.1993, c. 272 (A.B.301), § 18, eff. Aug. 2, 1993; Stats.2002, c. 103 (A.B.2112), § 1, eff. July 2, 2002; Stats.2012, c. 670 (A.B.2188), § 2.)*

Repeal

For repeal of this section, see its terms.

Cross References

Nonresident defined, see Vehicle Code § 435.
Renting vehicle to nonresident licensed in his own state, see Vehicle Code § 14608.

§ 12502. Persons who may operate a motor vehicle without obtaining a driver's license; exemption requiring a medical certificate; compliance with medical certificate restrictions

Section operative Jan. 31, 2014. See, also, section operative until Jan. 30, 2014.

(a) The following persons may operate a motor vehicle in this state without obtaining a driver's license under this code:

(1) A nonresident over the age of 18 years having in his or her immediate possession a valid driver's license issued by a foreign jurisdiction of which he or she is a resident, except as provided in Section 12505.

(2) A nonresident, 21 years of age or older, if transporting hazardous material, as defined in Section 353, in a commercial vehicle, having in his or her immediate possession, a valid license with the appropriate endorsement issued by another state or other jurisdiction that is recognized by the department, or a Canadian driver's license and a copy of his or her current training certificate to transport hazardous material that complies with all federal laws and regulations with respect to hazardous materials, both of which shall be in his or her immediate possession.

(3) A nonresident having in his or her immediate possession a valid driver's license, issued by the Diplomatic Motor Vehicle Office of the Office of Foreign Missions of the United States Department of State, for the type of motor vehicle or combination of vehicles that the person is operating.

(b)(1) A driver required to have a commercial driver's license under Part 383 of Title 49 of the Code of Federal Regulations who submits a current medical examiner's certificate to the licensing state in accordance with Section 383.71(h) of Subpart E of Part 383 of Title 49 of the Code of Federal Regulations, documenting that he or she meets the physical qualification requirements of Section 391.41 of Subpart E of Part 391 of Title 49 of the Code of Federal Regulations, is not required to carry on his or her person the medical examiner's certificate or a copy of that certificate.

(2) A driver may use the date-stamped receipt, given to the driver by the licensing state agency, for up to 15 days after the date stamped on the receipt, as proof of medical certification.

(c) A nonresident possessing a medical certificate in accordance with subdivision (b) shall comply with any restriction of the medical certificate issued to that nonresident.

(d) This section shall become operative on January 31, 2014. *(Added by Stats.2012, c. 670 (A.B.2188), § 2.5, operative Jan. 31, 2014.)*

Cross References

Nonresident defined, see Vehicle Code § 435.
Renting vehicle to nonresident licensed in his own state, see Vehicle Code § 14608.

§ 12503. Unlicensed nonresident

A nonresident over the age of 18 years whose home state or country does not require the licensing of drivers may operate a foreign vehicle owned by him for not to exceed 30 days without obtaining a license under this code. *(Stats.1959, c. 3, p. 1614, § 12503. Amended by Stats.1961, c. 1615, p. 3453, § 7; Stats.1971, c. 1748, p. 3763, § 55, operative March 4, 1972.)*

§ 12504. Nonresident minors

(a) Sections 12502 and 12503 apply to any nonresident over the age of 16 years but under the age of 18 years. The maximum period during which that nonresident may operate a motor vehicle in this state without obtaining a driver's license is limited to a period of 10 days immediately following the entry of the nonresident into this state except as provided in subdivision (b) of this section.

(b) Any nonresident over the age of 16 years but under the age of 18 years who is a resident of a foreign jurisdiction which requires the licensing of drivers may continue to operate a motor vehicle in this state after 10 days from his or her date of entry into this state if he or she meets both the following:

(1) He or she has a valid driver's license, issued by the foreign jurisdiction, in his or her immediate possession.

(2) He or she has been issued and has in his or her immediate possession a nonresident minor's certificate, which the department issues to a nonresident minor who holds a valid driver's license issued to him or her by his or her home state or country, and who files proof of financial responsibility.

(c) Whenever any of the conditions for the issuance of a nonresident minor's certificate cease to exist, the department shall cancel the certificate and require the minor to surrender it to the department. *(Stats.1959, c. 3, p. 1614, § 12504. Amended by Stats.1963, c. 237, p. 978, § 3; Stats.1963, c. 666, p. 1654, § 3; Stats.1967, c. 478, p. 1683, § 2; Stats.1971, c. 1748, p. 3763, § 56, operative March 4, 1972; Stats.1992, c. 974 (S.B.1600), § 4, eff. Sept. 28, 1992.)*

Cross References

Application of this section to nonresident members of the armed forces under the age of 18, see Vehicle Code § 12518.

Failure to surrender nonresident minor's certificate as ground for refusal to issue or renew a driver's license, see Vehicle Code § 12809.

Permitting unlicensed minor to drive, see Vehicle Code § 14607.

Student licenses if parent or guardian is nonresident, see Vehicle Code § 12650.

§ 12505. Residency

(a)(1) For purposes of this division only and notwithstanding Section 516, residency shall be determined as a person's state of domicile. "State of domicile" means the state where a person has his or her true, fixed, and permanent home and principal residence and to which he or she has manifested the intention of returning whenever he or she is absent.

Prima facie evidence of residency for driver's licensing purposes includes, but is not limited to, the following:

(A) Address where registered to vote.

(B) Payment of resident tuition at a public institution of higher education.

(C) Filing a homeowner's property tax exemption.

(D) Other acts, occurrences, or events that indicate presence in the state is more than temporary or transient.

(2) California residency is required of a person in order to be issued a commercial driver's license under this code.

(b) The presumption of residency in this state may be rebutted by satisfactory evidence that the licensee's primary residence is in another state.

(c) Any person entitled to an exemption under Section 12502, 12503, or 12504 may operate a motor vehicle in this state for not to exceed 10 days from the date he or she establishes residence in this state, except that * * * a person shall not operate a motor vehicle for employment in this state after establishing residency without first obtaining a license from the department * * *.

(d) If the State of California is decertified by the federal government and prohibited from issuing an initial, renewal, or upgraded commercial driver's license pursuant to Section 384.405 of Title 49 of the Code of Federal Regulations, the following applies:

(1) An existing commercial driver's license issued pursuant to this code prior to the date that the state is notified of its decertification shall remain valid until its expiration date.

(2) A person who is a resident of this state may obtain a * * * nondomiciled commercial learner's permit or commercial driver's license from any state that elects to issue a * * * nondomiciled commercial learner's permit or commercial driver's license and that complies with the testing and licensing standards contained in subparts F, G, and H of Part 383 of Title 49 of the Code of Federal Regulations.

(3) For the purposes of this subdivision, a * * * nondomiciled commercial learner's permit or commercial driver's license is a commercial learner's permit or commercial driver's license issued by a state to an individual domiciled in a foreign country or in another state.

(e) The department may issue a nondomiciled commercial learner's permit or nondomiciled commercial driver's license to a person who is domiciled in a state or jurisdiction that has been decertified by the federal government or not determined to be in compliance with the testing and licensing standards contained in subparts F, G, and H of Part 383 of Title 49 of the Code of Federal Regulations.

(f) Subject to Section 12504, a person over the age of 16 years who is a resident of a foreign jurisdiction other than a state, territory, or possession of the United States, the District of Columbia, the Commonwealth of Puerto Rico, or Canada, having a valid driver's license issued to him or her by any other foreign jurisdiction * * * may operate a motor vehicle in this state without obtaining a license from the department, * * * unless the department determines that the foreign jurisdiction does not meet the licensing standards imposed by this code.

(g) A person who is 18 years of age or older and in possession of a valid commercial learner's permit or commercial driver's license issued by any state, territory, or possession of the United States, the District of Columbia, the Commonwealth of Puerto Rico, or a foreign jurisdiction that meets the licensing standards contained in subparts F, G, and H of Part 383 of Title 49 of the Code of Federal Regulations shall be granted reciprocity to operate vehicles of the appropriate class on the highways of this state.

(h) Any person from a foreign * * * jurisdiction that does not meet the licensing standards contained in subparts F, G, and H of Part 383 of Title 49 of the Code of Federal Regulations shall obtain a commercial learner's permit or commercial driver's license from the department before operating on the highways a motor vehicle for which a * * * commercial driver's license is required, as described in Section 12804.9. The medical examination form required for issuance of a * * * commercial driver's license shall be completed by a health care professional, as defined in paragraph (2) of subdivision (a) of Section 12804.9, who is licensed, certified, or registered to perform physical examinations in the United States of America. This subdivision does not apply to (1) drivers of schoolbuses operated in California on a trip for educational purposes or (2) drivers of vehicles used to provide the services of a local public agency.

(i) This section does not authorize the employment of a person in violation of Section 12515.

* * *   (Stats.1959, c. 3, p. 1614, § 12505. Amended by Stats.1961, c. 1614, p. 3451, § 1; Stats.1963, c. 209, p. 949, § 5, eff. April 29, 1963; Stats.1963, c. 237, p. 978, § 4; Stats.1963, c. 666, p. 1655, § 4; Stats.1970, c. 166, p. 408, § 1; Stats.1983, c. 1000, § 8; Stats.1991, c. 13 (A.B.37), § 27, eff. Feb. 13, 1991; Stats.1993, c. 272 (A.B.301), § 19, eff. Aug. 2, 1993; Stats.1995, c. 766 (S.B.726), § 10; Stats.2004, c. 952 (A.B.3049), § 3, operative Sept. 20, 2005; Stats.2013, c. 649 (A.B.1047), § 1.)

§ 12506. Temporary licenses

The department may issue a temporary driver's license to any person applying for a driver's license, to any person applying for renewal of a driver's license, or to any licensee whose license is required to be changed, added to, or modified. Notwithstanding subdivision (b) of Section 12805, the department may issue a temporary driver's license to an applicant who has previously been licensed in this state or in any other state, territory, or possession of the United States, the District of Columbia, the Commonwealth of Puerto Rico, or the Dominion of Canada, notwithstanding that the applicant has failed the written examination on the person's first attempt.

A temporary license permits the operation of a motor vehicle upon the highways for a period of 60 days, if the licensee has the temporary license in his or her immediate possession, and while the department is completing its investigation and determination of all facts relative to the applicant's right to receive a license. The temporary license is invalid when the applicant's license has been issued or refused. (Stats.1959, c. 3, p. 1614, § 12506. Amended by Stats.1961, c. 1615, p. 3453, § 9; Stats.1971, c. 1214, p. 2343, § 11, operative May 3, 1972; Stats.1973, c. 891, p. 1661, § 1, eff. Sept. 28, 1973, operative Oct. 1, 1973; Stats.1985, c. 743, § 1; Stats.1987, c. 321, § 2.)

Cross References

Application for license, contents, see Vehicle Code § 12800.

§ 12507. Repealed by Stats.1997, c. 760 (S.B.1329), § 2

§ 12507.1. Repealed by Stats.1997, c. 760 (S.B.1329), § 3, operative Jan. 1, 1999

§ 12508. Limited term license

When in the opinion of the department it would be in the interest of safety, the department may issue, in individual cases, to any applicant for a driver's license, a license limited in duration to less than the regular term. Upon the expiration of a limited term license the department may extend its duration for an additional period without fee but the duration of the license and extensions shall not exceed the term of a regular license. (Stats.1959, c. 3, p. 1615, § 12508.)

Cross References

Expiration of driver's license, see Vehicle Code § 12816.

§ 12509. Instruction permits for certain motor vehicles; duration of permit

(a) Except as otherwise provided in subdivision (f) of Section 12514, the department, for good cause, may issue an instruction permit to a physically and mentally qualified person who meets one of the following requirements and who applies to the department for an instruction permit:

(1) Is 15 years and 6 months of age or older, and has successfully completed approved courses in automobile driver education and driver training as provided in paragraph (3) of subdivision (a) of Section 12814.6.

(2) Is 15 years and 6 months of age or older, and has successfully completed an approved course in automobile driver education and is taking driver training as provided in paragraph (3) of subdivision (a) of Section 12814.6.

(3) Is 15 years and 6 months of age and enrolled and participating in an integrated automobile driver education and training program as provided in subparagraph (B) of paragraph (3) of subdivision (a) of Section 12814.6.

(4) Is over 16 years of age and is applying for a restricted driver's license pursuant to Section 12814.7.

(5) Is over 17 years and 6 months of age.

(b) The applicant shall qualify for, and be issued, an instruction permit within 12 months from the date of the application.

(c) An instruction permit issued pursuant to subdivision (a) shall entitle the applicant to operate a vehicle, subject to the limitations imposed by this section and any other provisions of law, upon the highways for a period not exceeding 24 months from the date of the application.

(d) Except as provided in Section 12814.6, a person, while having in his or her immediate possession a valid permit issued pursuant to paragraphs (1) to (3), inclusive, of subdivision (a), may operate a motor vehicle, other than a motorcycle, motorized scooter, or a motorized bicycle, when accompanied by, and under the immediate supervision of, a California-licensed driver with a valid license of the appropriate class who is 18 years of age or over and whose driving privilege is not subject to probation. An accompanying licensed driver at all times shall occupy a position within the driver's compartment that would enable the accompanying licensed driver to assist the person in controlling the vehicle as may be necessary to avoid a collision and to provide immediate guidance in the safe operation of the vehicle.

(e) A person, while having in his or her immediate possession a valid permit issued pursuant to paragraph (4) of subdivision (a), may only operate a government-owned motor vehicle, other than a motorcycle, motorized scooter, or a motorized bicycle, when taking driver training instruction administered by the California National Guard.

(f) The department may also issue an instruction permit to a person who has been issued a valid driver's license to authorize the person to obtain driver training instruction and to practice that instruction in order to obtain another class of driver's license or an endorsement.

(g) The department may further restrict permits issued under subdivision (a) as it may determine to be appropriate to ensure the safe operation of a motor vehicle by the permittee. *(Added by Stats.1974, c. 644, p. 1507, § 2. Amended by Stats.1976, c. 645, p. 1594, § 1; Stats.1977, c. 579, p. 1914, § 183; Stats.1995, c. 766 (S.B.726), § 11; Stats.1997, c. 760 (S.B.1329), § 4; Stats.2000, c. 1035 (S.B.1403), § 14; Stats.2001, c. 825 (S.B.290), § 13; Stats.2002, c. 418 (A.B.2273), § 2; Stats.2002, c. 758 (A.B.3024), § 11.5; Stats.2003, c. 62 (S.B.600), § 305; Stats.2003, c. 768 (A.B.1343), § 2; Stats.2004, c. 183 (A.B.3082), § 352; Stats.2004, c. 755 (A.B.1878), § 4; Stats.2005, c. 22 (S.B.1108), § 198; Stats.2006, c. 538 (S.B.1852), § 656; Stats.2010, c. 586 (A.B.1952), § 2; Stats.2011, c. 296 (A.B.1023), § 303.)*

Cross References

Provisional driver's licenses, demonstration program, see Vehicle Code § 12814.6.
Provisional restricted class C license for operation of army and national guard vehicles, conditions, see Vehicle Code § 12814.7.
Student licenses, see Vehicle Code § 12650 et seq.

§ 12509.5. Instruction permits; motorcycles, motorized scooters, motorized bicycles, etc.

(a) A person shall obtain an instruction permit issued pursuant to this section prior to operating, or being issued a class M1 or M2 driver's license to operate, a two-wheel motorcycle, motor-driven cycle, motorized scooter, motorized bicycle, moped, or bicycle with an attached motor. The person shall meet the following requirements to obtain an instruction permit for purposes of this section:

(1) If age 15 years and 6 months or older, but under the age of 18 years, the applicant shall meet all of the following requirements:

(A) Have a valid class C license or complete driver education and training pursuant to paragraph (3) of subdivision (a) of Section 12814.6.

(B) Successfully complete a motorcyclist safety program that is operated pursuant to Article 2 (commencing with Section 2930) of Chapter 5 of Division 2.

(C) Pass the motorcycle driver's written exam.

(2) If 18 years of age or older, but under 21 years of age, the applicant shall meet both of the following requirements:

(A) Successfully complete a motorcyclist safety program that is operated pursuant to Article 2 (commencing with Section 2930) of Chapter 5 of Division 2.

(B) Pass the motorcycle driver's written exam.

(3) If 21 years of age or older, pass the motorcycle driver's written exam.

(b) A person described in paragraph (1) or (2) of subdivision (a) shall hold an instruction permit issued pursuant to this section for a minimum of six months prior to being issued a class M1 or M2 license.

(c) A person issued an instruction permit pursuant to this section shall not operate a two-wheel motorcycle, motor-driven cycle, motorized scooter, motorized bicycle, moped, or bicycle with an attached motor during the hours of darkness, shall stay off any freeways that have full control of access and have no crossings at grade, and shall not carry any passenger except an instructor licensed under Chapter 1 (commencing with Section 11100) of Division 5 or a qualified instructor as defined in Section 41907 of the Education Code.

(d) An instruction permit issued pursuant to this section shall be valid for a period not exceeding 24 months from the date of application.

(e) The department may perform, during regularly scheduled computer system maintenance and upgrades, any necessary software updates related to the changes made by the addition, during the 2009–2010 Regular Session, of this section. *(Added by Stats.2010, c. 586 (A.B.1952), § 3.)*

§ 12510. Repealed by Stats.1967, c. 253, p. 1401, § 2

§ 12511. Licensee entitled to one license

No person shall have in his or her possession or otherwise under his or her control more than one driver's license. *(Added by Stats.1959, c. 298, p. 2207, § 2. Amended by Stats.1961, c. 1615, p. 3453, § 11; Stats.1988, c. 1509, § 4.)*

§ 12512. Issuance of licenses to persons under the age of 18 years

Except as provided in Sections 12513, 12514, and 12814.6, no license to drive shall be issued to a person under the age of 18 years. *(Added by Stats.2000, c. 596 (A.B.2909), § 6.)*

Cross References

Prospective employers of drivers of vehicles requiring certain licenses or certificates, class C license issued pursuant to this section, see Vehicle Code § 1808.1.

§ 12512.5. Repealed by Stats.1992, c. 1243 (A.B.3090), § 79, eff. Sept. 30, 1992

§ 12513. Junior permits; issuance

(a) Upon application, successful completion of tests and compliance with Sections 17700 to 17705, inclusive, the department may issue a junior permit to any person 14 years of age, but less than 18, who establishes eligibility as required by this section. A person is eligible when, in the opinion of the department, any one or more of the following circumstances exist:

School or other transportation facilities are inadequate for regular attendance at school and at activities authorized by the school. The application for a junior permit shall be accompanied by a signed statement from the school principal verifying such facts. A junior permit issued under this subsection shall be restricted to operating a vehicle from residence to the school and return.

Reasonable transportation facilities are inadequate and operation of a vehicle by a minor is necessary due to illness of a family member. The application shall be accompanied by a signed statement from a physician familiar with the condition, containing a diagnosis and probable date when sufficient recovery will have been made to terminate the emergency.

Transportation facilities are inadequate, and use of a motor vehicle is necessary in the transportation to and from the employment of the applicant and the applicant's income from such employment is essential in the support of the family, or where the applicant's operation of a motor vehicle is essential to an enterprise from which an appreciable portion of the income of the family will be derived. The application shall be accompanied by a signed statement from the parents or the guardian, setting forth the reasons a permit is necessary under this subsection.

(b) The existence of public transportation at reasonable intervals within one mile of the residence of the applicant may be considered adequate grounds for refusal of a junior permit.

(c) The department shall impose restrictions upon junior permits appropriate to the conditions and area under which they are intended to be used. *(Stats.1959, c. 3, p. 1615, § 12513. Amended by Stats.1959, c. 1996, p. 4624, § 16.5; Stats.1969, c. 947, p. 1891, § 1.)*

§ 12514. Junior permits; duration; revocation

(a) Junior permits issued pursuant to Section 12513 shall not be valid for a period exceeding that established on the original request as the approximate date the minor's operation of a vehicle will no longer be necessary. In any event, no permit shall be valid on or after the 18th birthday of the applicant.

(b) The department may revoke any permit when to do so is necessary for the welfare of the minor or in the interests of safety.

(c) If conditions or location of residence, which required the minor's operation of a vehicle, change prior to expiration of the permit, the department may cancel the permit.

(d) Upon a determination that the permittee has operated a vehicle in violation of restrictions, the department shall revoke the permit.

(e) A junior permit is a form of driver's license that shall include all information required by subdivision (a) of Section 12811 except for an engraved picture or photograph of the permittee, and is subject to all provisions of this code applying to driver's licenses, except as otherwise provided in this section and Section 12513.

(f) An instruction permit valid for a period of not more than six months may be issued after eligibility has been established under Section 12513.

(g) The department shall cancel any permit six months from the date of issuance unless the permittee has complied with one of the conditions prescribed by paragraph (3) of subdivision (a) of Section 12814.6. *(Stats.1959, c. 3, p. 1616, § 12514. Amended by Stats. 1959, c. 1996, p. 4624, § 17; Stats.1961, c. 1615, p. 3454, § 13; Stats.1969, c. 947, p. 1893, § 2; Stats.1992, c. 1243 (A.B.3090), § 80, eff. Sept. 30, 1992; Stats.1997, c. 760 (S.B.1329), § 6; Stats.1998, c. 485 (A.B.2803), § 158; Stats.2000, c. 1035 (S.B.1403), § 15.)*

Cross References

Instruction permits, see Vehicle Code § 12509.

§ 12515. Driving for hire; age limit

(a) No person under the age of 18 years shall be employed for compensation by another for the purpose of driving a motor vehicle on the highways.

(b) No person under the age of 21 years shall be employed for compensation by another to drive, and no person under the age of 21 years may drive a motor vehicle, as defined in Section 34500 or subdivision (b) of Section 15210, that is engaged in interstate commerce, or any motor vehicle that is engaged in the interstate or intrastate transportation of hazardous material, as defined in Section 353. *(Stats.1959, c. 3, p. 1617, § 12515. Amended by Stats.1961, c. 1615, p. 3454, § 14; Stats.1984, c. 779, § 3; Stats.1986, c. 434, § 2; Stats.1988, c. 1509, § 5.)*

Cross References

Parents' or guardian's signature to minor's application for license, see Vehicle Code § 17701.

Permitting unlicensed minor to drive as offense, see Vehicle Code § 14607.

Persons not of legal age, denial of license, see Vehicle Code
   § 12805.

Prima facie evidence, see Evidence Code § 602.

Violation as misdemeanor, see Vehicle Code § 40000.11.

§ 12516.   Age for driving school bus

It is unlawful for any person under the age of 18 years
to drive a school bus transporting pupils to or from
school. *(Stats.1959, c. 3, p. 1617, § 12516.)*

Cross References

Minimum age, driving for hire license, see Vehicle Code
   § 12515.

Schoolbus defined, see Vehicle Code § 545.

§ 12517.   Schoolbus and pupil activity bus drivers; qualifications; certificates; fees

(a)(1) A person may not operate a schoolbus while
transporting pupils unless that person has in his or her
immediate possession a valid driver's license for the
appropriate class of vehicle to be driven endorsed for
schoolbus and passenger transportation.

(2) When transporting one or more pupils at or below
the 12th–grade level to or from a public or private school
or to or from public or private school activities, the
person described in paragraph (1) shall have in his or her
immediate possession a certificate issued by the department to permit the operation of a schoolbus.

(b) A person may not operate a school pupil activity
bus unless that person has in his or her immediate
possession a valid driver's license for the appropriate
class of vehicle to be driven endorsed for passenger
transportation. When transporting one or more pupils at
or below the 12th–grade level to or from public or private
school activities, the person shall also have in his or her
immediate possession a certificate issued by the department to permit the operation of school pupil activity
buses.

(c) The applicant for a certificate to operate a schoolbus or school pupil activity bus shall meet the eligibility
and training requirements specified for schoolbus and
school pupil activity busdrivers in this code, the Education Code, and regulations adopted by the Department
of the California Highway Patrol, and, in addition to the
fee authorized in Section 2427, shall pay a fee of twenty-
five dollars ($25) with the application for issuance of an
original certificate, and a fee of twelve dollars ($12) for
the renewal of that certificate.

*(Stats.1959, c. 3, p. 1617, § 12517. Amended by
Stats.1961, c. 1615, p. 3454, § 15; Stats.1982, c. 1233, p.
4544, § 1; Stats.1982, c. 1273, p. 4703, § 16; Stats.1990, c.
104 (S.B.798), § 3, eff. May 23, 1990; Stats.1990, c. 1360
(S.B.1510), § 11; Stats.1996, c. 440 (S.B.1588), § 8;
Stats.2004, c. 952 (A.B.3049), § 4, operative Sept. 20, 2005;
Stats.2005, c. 199 (A.B.1748), § 2; Stats.2006, c. 574
(A.B.2520), § 7.)*

420

Cross References

School pupil activity bus, definition and driver regulations, see
   Vehicle Code § 546.

Schoolbus and school pupil activity bus driver training course,
   see Education Code § 40070.

Schoolbus defined, see Vehicle Code § 545.

Traffic violation point count, number giving rise to presumptions
   of negligence by certificate or license holder, see Vehicle
   Code § 12810.5.

Training courses for certification under this section, see Education Code § 40080 et seq.

Violation as misdemeanor, see Vehicle Code § 40000.11.

§ 12517.1.   Schoolbus accident

(a) A "schoolbus accident" means any of the following:

(1) A motor vehicle accident resulting in property
damage in excess of seven hundred fifty dollars ($750) or
personal injury, on public or private property, and
involving a schoolbus, youth bus, school pupil activity bus,
or general public paratransit vehicle transporting a pupil.

(2) A collision between a vehicle and a pupil or a
schoolbus driver while the pupil or driver is crossing the
highway when the schoolbus flashing red signal lamps are
required to be operated pursuant to Section 22112 or
when the schoolbus is stopped for the purpose of loading
or unloading pupils.

(3) Injury of a pupil inside a vehicle described in
paragraph (1) as a result of acceleration, deceleration, or
other movement of the vehicle.

(b) The Department of the California Highway Patrol
shall investigate all schoolbus accidents, except that
accidents involving only property damage and occurring
entirely on private property shall be investigated only if
they involve a violation of this code. *(Added by Stats.
1990, c. 1360 (S.B.1510), § 12. Amended by Stats.2002, c.
766 (S.B.1590), § 2; Stats.2013, c. 523 (S.B.788), § 29.)*

§ 12517.2.   Bus drivers and farm labor vehicle opera-
tors; applications for certificates; medical examination

(a) Applicants for an original or renewal certificate to
drive a schoolbus, school pupil activity bus, youth bus,
general public paratransit vehicle, or farm labor vehicle
shall submit a report of a medical examination of the
applicant given not more than two years prior to the date
of the application by a physician licensed to practice
medicine, a licensed advanced practice registered nurse
qualified to perform a medical examination, * * * a
licensed physician assistant, or a licensed doctor of
chiropractic listed on the most current National Registry
of Certified Medical Examiners, as adopted by the United
States Department of Transportation, as published by the
notice in the Federal Register, Volume 77, Number 77,
Friday, April 20, 2012, on pages 24104 to 24135, inclusive,
and pursuant to Section 391.42 of Title 49 of the Code of
Federal Regulations. The report shall be on a form
approved by the department.

(b) Schoolbus drivers, within the same month of reaching 65 years of age and each 12th month thereafter, shall undergo a medical examination, pursuant to Section 12804.9, and shall submit a report of that medical examination on a form as specified in subdivision (a). *(Added by Stats.1990, c. 1360 (S.B.1510), § 13. Amended by Stats.1993, c. 272 (A.B.301), § 20, eff. Aug. 2, 1993; Stats.2007, c. 158 (A.B.139), § 1; Stats.2012, c. 670 (A.B.2188), § 3; Stats.2013, c. 160 (A.B.722), § 1.)*

§ 12517.3. Fingerprints; bus and ambulance drivers

(a)(1) An applicant for an original certificate to drive a schoolbus, school pupil activity bus, youth bus, or general public paratransit vehicle shall be fingerprinted by the Department of the California Highway Patrol, on a form provided or approved by the Department of the California Highway Patrol for submission to the Department of Justice, utilizing the Applicant Expedite Service or an electronic fingerprinting system.

(2) An applicant fingerprint form shall be processed and returned to the office of the Department of the California Highway Patrol from which it originated not later than 15 working days from the date on which the fingerprint form was received by the Department of Justice, unless circumstances, other than the administrative duties of the Department of Justice, warrant further investigation.

(3) Applicant fingerprints that are submitted by utilizing an electronic fingerprinting system shall be processed and returned to the appropriate office of the Department of the California Highway Patrol within three working days.

(4) The commissioner may utilize the California Law Enforcement Telecommunications System to conduct a preliminary criminal and driver history check to determine an applicant's eligibility to hold an original or renewal certificate to drive a schoolbus, school pupil activity bus, youth bus, or general public paratransit vehicle.

(b)(1) Notwithstanding subdivision (a), an applicant for an original certificate to drive a schoolbus, school pupil activity bus, youth bus, or general public paratransit vehicle may be fingerprinted by a public law enforcement agency, a school district, or a county office of education utilizing an electronic fingerprinting system with terminals managed by the Department of Justice.

(2) The Department of Justice shall provide the fingerprint information processed pursuant to this subdivision to the appropriate office of the Department of the California Highway Patrol within three working days of receipt of the information.

(3) An applicant for an original certificate to drive an ambulance shall submit a completed fingerprint card to the department. *(Added by Stats.1990, c. 1360 (S.B. 1510), § 14. Amended by Stats.1997, c. 738 (A.B.1238), § 1; Stats.1999, c. 229 (A.B.128), § 1, eff. Aug. 25, 1999; Stats.2006, c. 311 (S.B.1586), § 7.)*

Cross References

Fingerprint rollers, qualification and certification of persons, necessity of certificate, see Penal Code § 11102.1.

§ 12517.4. Regulations for issuance of certificate to drive a schoolbus, school pupil activity bus, youth bus, paratransit vehicle, or farm labor vehicle

This section governs the issuance of a certificate to drive a schoolbus, school pupil activity bus, youth bus, general public paratransit vehicle, or farm labor vehicle.

(a) The driver certificate shall be issued only to applicants meeting all applicable provisions of this code and passing the examinations prescribed by the department and the Department of the California Highway Patrol. The examinations shall be conducted by the Department of the California Highway Patrol, pursuant to Sections 12517, 12519, 12522, 12523, and 12523.5.

(b) A temporary driver certificate shall be issued by the Department of the California Highway Patrol after an applicant has cleared a criminal history background check by the Department of Justice and, if applicable, the Federal Bureau of Investigation, and has passed the examinations and meets all other applicable provisions of this code.

(c) A permanent driver's certificate shall be issued by the department after an applicant has passed all tests and met all applicable provisions of this code. Certificates are valid for a maximum of five years and shall expire on the fifth birthday following the issuance of an original certificate or the expiration of the certificate renewed.

(d) A holder of a certificate may not violate any restriction placed on the certificate. Depending upon the type of vehicle used in the driving test and the abilities and physical condition of the applicant, the Department of the California Highway Patrol and the department may place restrictions on a certificate to assure the safe operation of a motor vehicle and safe transportation of passengers. These restrictions may include, but are not limited to, all of the following:

(1) Automatic transmission only.

(2) Hydraulic brakes only.

(3) Type 2 bus only.

(4) Conventional or type 2 bus only.

(5) Two-axle motor truck or passenger vehicle only.

(e) A holder of a certificate may not drive a motor vehicle equipped with a two-speed rear axle unless the certificate is endorsed: "May drive vehicle with two-speed rear axle."

(f) This section shall become operative on September 20, 2005. *(Added by Stats.1990, c. 1360 (S.B.1510), § 15. Amended by Stats.1996, c. 1043 (A.B.2352), § 1; Stats. 2004, c. 952 (A.B.3049), § 5, operative Sept. 20, 2005.)*

§ 12517.45. Transporting school pupils; requirements

(a) A person shall not operate a motor vehicle described in subdivision (k) of Section 545 while transporting school pupils at or below the 12th–grade level to or from a public or private school or to or from public or private school activities, unless all of the following requirements are met:

(1) The person has in his or her immediate possession all of the following:

(A) A valid driver's license of a class appropriate to the vehicle driven and that is endorsed for passenger transportation.

(B) Either a certificate to drive a schoolbus as described in Section 40082 of the Education Code, or a certificate to drive a school pupil activity bus as described in Section 40083 of the Education Code, issued by the department in accordance with eligibility and training requirements specified by the department, the State Department of Education, and the Department of the California Highway Patrol.

(C) A parental authorization form for each pupil signed by a parent or a legal guardian of the pupil that gives permission for that pupil to be transported to or from the school or school-related activity.

(2)(A) The motor vehicle has passed an annual inspection conducted by the Department of the California Highway Patrol and is in compliance with the charter-party carrier's responsibilities under Section 5374 of the Public Utilities Code.

(B) The Department of the California Highway Patrol may charge a charter-party carrier a reasonable fee sufficient to cover the costs incurred by the Department of the California Highway Patrol in conducting the annual inspection of a motor vehicle.

(b) A driver of a motor vehicle described in subdivision (k) of Section 545 shall comply with the duties specified in subdivision (a) of Section 5384.1 of the Public Utilities Code. *(Added by Stats.2008, c. 649 (A.B.830), § 4.)*

Cross References
Violation as misdemeanor, see Vehicle Code § 40000.11.

§ 12517.5. Driver of paratransit vehicles; qualifications

A person who is employed as a driver of a paratransit vehicle shall not operate that vehicle unless the person meets both of the following requirements:

(a) Has in his or her immediate possession a valid driver's license of a class appropriate to the vehicle driven.

(b) Successfully completes, during each calendar year, four hours of training administered by, or at the direction of, his or her employer or the employer's agent on the safe operation of paratransit vehicles and four hours of training on the special transportation needs of the persons he or she is employed to transport.

This subdivision may be satisfied if the driver receives transportation training or a certificate, or both, pursuant

to Section 40082, 40083, 40085, 40085.5, or 40088 of the Education Code.

The employer shall maintain a record of the current training received by each driver in his or her employ and shall present that record on demand to any authorized representative of the Department of the California Highway Patrol. *(Added by Stats.1998, c. 241 (A.B.1634), § 2. Amended by Stats.1999, c. 1007 (S.B.532), § 18; Stats. 2002, c. 664 (A.B.3034), § 217.)*

§ 12518. Nonresident minor member of armed forces

The provisions of Section 12504 shall apply to any nonresident who is under the age of 18 years and who is a member of the armed forces of the United States on active duty within this state, except that the maximum period during which such nonresident may operate a motor vehicle in this state without obtaining a driver's license or a nonresident minor's certificate shall be limited to a period of 60 days immediately following the entry of such nonresident into this state. *(Added by Stats.1959, c. 17, p. 1865, § 2. Amended by Stats.1961, c. 1615, p. 3454, § 16; Stats.1963, c. 237, p. 979, § 5; Stats.1963, c. 666, p. 1655, § 5; Stats.1967, c. 478, p. 1684, § 3; Stats.1971, c. 1748, p. 3764, § 57, operative March 4, 1972.)*

§ 12519. Farm labor vehicle license

(a) No person shall operate a farm labor vehicle unless the person has in his or her possession a driver's license for the appropriate class of vehicle to be driven, endorsed for passenger transportation, and, when transporting one or more farmworker passengers, a certificate issued by the department to permit the operation of farm labor vehicles.

(b) The applicants shall present evidence that they have successfully completed the driver training course developed by the Department of Education pursuant to Section 40081 of the Education Code, and approved by the Department of Motor Vehicles and the Department of the California Highway Patrol before a permanent certificate will be issued.

(c) The certificate shall be issued only to applicants qualified by examinations prescribed by the Department of Motor Vehicles and the Department of the California Highway Patrol and upon payment of a fee of twelve dollars ($12) to the Department of the California Highway Patrol. The examinations shall be conducted by the Department of the California Highway Patrol.

(d) A person holding a valid certificate to permit the operation of a farm labor vehicle, issued prior to January 1, 1991, shall not be required to reapply for a certificate to satisfy any additional requirements imposed by the act adding this subdivision until the certificate he or she holds expires or is canceled or revoked. *(Added by Stats.1959, c. 679, p. 2650, § 3. Amended by Stats.1961, c. 1615, p. 3454, § 17; Stats.1965, c. 1555, p. 3647, § 1; Stats.1974, c. 1447, p. 3160, § 3, eff. Sept. 26, 1974; Stats.1975, c. 791, p. 1815, § 2, eff. Sept. 16, 1975;*

Stats.1978, c. 488, p. 1616, § 3; Stats.1981, c. 813, p. 3154, § 9; Stats.1982, c. 1273, p. 4703, § 17; Stats.1990, c. 1360 (S.B.1510), § 17.)

Cross References

Farm labor contractor or employee operating bus or truck transporting individuals, licenses, see Labor Code § 1696.3.

Farm labor vehicle defined, see Vehicle Code § 322.

Persons driving or operating implements of husbandry, exemption, see Vehicle Code § 36300.

Traffic violation point count, number giving rise to presumptions of negligence by certificate or license holder, see Vehicle Code § 12810.5.

Training courses for certification under this section, see Education Code § 40080 et seq.

Violation as misdemeanor, see Vehicle Code § 40000.11.

§ 12519.5. Repealed by Stats.1990, c. 1360 (S.B.1510), § 18, operative Jan. 1, 1993

§ 12520. Tow truck drivers; necessity of valid driver's license; permanent tow truck driver certificate

(a) No person employed as a tow truck driver, as defined in Section 2430.1, shall operate a tow truck unless that person has, in his or her immediate possession, a valid California driver's license of an appropriate class for the vehicle to be driven, and a tow truck driver certificate issued by the department or a temporary tow truck driver certificate issued by the Department of the California Highway Patrol, to permit the operation of the tow truck.

(b) When notified that the applicant has been cleared through the Department of Justice or the Federal Bureau of Investigation, or both, and if the applicant meets all other applicable provisions of this code, the department shall issue a permanent tow truck driver certificate. The permanent tow truck driver certificate shall be valid for a maximum of five years and shall expire on the same date as that of the applicant's driver's license. *(Added by Stats.1991, c. 488 (A.B.123), § 5. Amended by Stats.1996, c. 1043 (A.B.2352), § 2.)*

§§ 12520.5, 12520.7. Repealed by Stats.1990, c. 1360 (S.B.1510), §§ 20, 21

§ 12521. Tour bus operators; use of safety belts; report of accidents

An operator of a tour bus shall, at all times when operating the tour bus, do all the following:

(a) Use a safety belt.

(b) Report any accidents involving the tour bus to the Department of the California Highway Patrol. *(Added by Stats.1990, c. 1360 (S.B.1510), § 22.5.)*

§ 12522. First aid examination for schoolbus or youth bus operator

(a) Every person who operates a schoolbus or youth bus in the transportation of school pupils shall, in addition to any other requirement for a schoolbus or youth bus driver's certificate, qualify by an examination on first aid practices deemed necessary for schoolbus operators or youth bus operators. Standards for examination shall be determined by the Emergency Medical Services Authority after consultation with the State Department of Education, the Department of Motor Vehicles, and the Department of the California Highway Patrol. The local school authority employing the applicant shall provide a course of instruction concerning necessary first aid practices.

(b) The Department of the California Highway Patrol shall conduct the first aid examination as part of the examination of applicants for a schoolbus or youth bus driver's certificate and shall certify to the Department of Motor Vehicles that the applicant has satisfactorily demonstrated his or her qualifications in first aid practices, knowledge of schoolbus or youth bus laws and regulations, and ability to operate a schoolbus or youth bus. The first aid certifications shall be valid for the term of the schoolbus or youth bus driver's certificate.

(c) The first aid examination may be waived if the applicant possesses either of the following minimum qualifications:

(1) A current first aid certificate issued by the American Red Cross or by an organization whose first aid training program is at least equivalent to the American Red Cross first aid training program, as determined by the Emergency Medical Services Authority. The Emergency Medical Services Authority may charge a fee, sufficient to cover its administrative costs of approval, to an organization that applies to have its first aid training program approved for purposes of this paragraph.

(2) A current license as a physician and surgeon, osteopathic physician and surgeon, or registered nurse, or a current certificate as a physician's assistant or emergency medical technician. The first aid certificate or license shall be maintained throughout the term of the schoolbus or youth bus driver's certificate and shall be presented upon demand of any traffic officer. The schoolbus or youth bus driver's certificate shall not be valid during any time that the driver fails to maintain and possess that license or certificate after the first aid examination has been waived. *(Added by Stats.1965, c. 1315, p. 3204, § 1. Amended by Stats.1967, c. 565, p. 1912, § 1; Stats.1969, c. 26, p. 127, § 6; Stats.1974, c. 545, p. 1311, § 162; Stats.1978, c. 429, p. 1436, § 174, eff. July 17, 1978, operative July 1, 1978; Stats.1983, c. 1246, § 45, operative July 1, 1984; Stats.1987, c. 723, § 3, eff. Sept. 18, 1987; Stats.1992, c. 624 (A.B.3144), § 3, eff. Sept. 14, 1992; Stats.1993, c. 226 (A.B.1987), § 15.)*

Cross References

Youth bus defined, see Vehicle Code § 680.

§ 12523. Youth bus operators; licensing requirements; renewals; applicability of regulations for schoolbus drivers; operating rules

(a) No person shall operate a youth bus without having in possession a valid driver's license of the appropriate class, endorsed for passenger transportation and a certificate issued by the department to permit the operation of a youth bus.

(b) Applicants for a certificate to drive a youth bus shall present evidence that they have successfully completed a driver training course administered by or at the direction of their employer consisting of a minimum of 10 hours of classroom instruction covering applicable laws and regulations and defensive driving practices and a minimum of 10 hours of behind-the-wheel training in a vehicle to be used as a youth bus. Applicants seeking to renew a certificate to drive a youth bus shall present evidence that they have received two hours of refresher training during each 12 months of driver certificate validity.

(c) The driver certificate shall be issued only to applicants qualified by examinations prescribed by the Department of Motor Vehicles and the Department of the California Highway Patrol, and upon payment of a fee of twenty-five dollars ($25) for an original certificate and twelve dollars ($12) for the renewal of that certificate to the Department of the California Highway Patrol. The examinations shall be conducted by the Department of the California Highway Patrol. The Department of Motor Vehicles may deny, suspend, or revoke a certificate valid for driving a youth bus for the causes specified in this code or in regulations adopted pursuant to this code.

(d) An operator of a youth bus shall, at all times when operating a youth bus, do all of the following:

(1) Use seat belts.

(2) Refrain from smoking.

(3) Report any accidents reportable under Section 16000 to the Department of the California Highway Patrol.

(e) A person holding a valid certificate to permit the operation of a youth bus, issued prior to January 1, 1991, shall not be required to reapply for a certificate to satisfy any additional requirements imposed by the act adding this subdivision until the certificate he or she holds expires or is canceled or revoked. *(Added by Stats.1982, c. 383, p. 1712, § 5, eff. July 4, 1982. Amended by Stats.1990, c. 104 (S.B.798), § 4, eff. May 23, 1990; Stats.1990, c. 1360 (S.B.1510), § 23.)*

Cross References

Traffic violation point count, number giving rise to presumptions of negligence by certificate or license holder, see Vehicle Code § 12810.5.

Youth bus defined, see Vehicle Code § 680.

§ 12523.5. Paratransit vehicle operator; driver's license and certificate; fee; qualifications; renewals; operating rules

(a) No person shall operate a general public paratransit vehicle unless he or she has in his or her possession a valid driver's license of the appropriate class endorsed for passenger transportation when operating a vehicle designed, used, or maintained for carrying more than 10 persons including the driver and either (1) a certificate issued by the department to permit the operation of a general public paratransit vehicle, or (2) a certificate issued by the department to drive a schoolbus or school pupil activity bus pursuant to Section 12517.

(b) Applicants for a certificate to drive a general public paratransit vehicle shall pay a fee to the Department of the California Highway Patrol of twenty-five dollars ($25) for an original certificate and twelve dollars ($12) for a renewal certificate. Applicants for an original certificate shall present evidence that they have successfully completed a driver training course consisting of a minimum of 40 hours of instruction within the previous two years. The instruction shall have covered applicable laws and regulations and defensive driving practices, a minimum of eight hours of certified defensive driving, and a minimum of 20 hours of behind-the-wheel training in a vehicle to be used as a general public paratransit vehicle. Applicants seeking to renew a certificate valid for driving a general public paratransit vehicle shall present evidence that they have received two hours of refresher training during each 12 months of driver certificate validity.

(c) The driver certificate shall be issued only to applicants qualified by examinations prescribed by the Department of Motor Vehicles and the Department of the California Highway Patrol. The examinations shall be conducted by the Department of the California Highway Patrol. The Department of Motor Vehicles may deny, suspend, or revoke a certificate valid for driving a general public paratransit vehicle for the causes specified in this code or the Education Code or in regulations adopted pursuant to this code or the Education Code.

(d) An operator of a general public paratransit vehicle shall do all of the following:

(1) Use seatbelts.

(2) Refrain from smoking.

(3) Report any accident reportable under Section 16000 to the Department of the California Highway Patrol.

(e) A person holding a valid certificate to permit the operation of a general public paratransit vehicle, issued prior to January 1, 1991, shall not be required to reapply for a certificate to satisfy any additional requirements imposed by the act adding this subdivision until the certificate he or she holds expires or is canceled or revoked. *(Added by Stats.1987, c. 986, § 4, operative July 1, 1988. Amended by Stats.1988, c. 683, § 4, eff. Aug. 27, 1988, operative Jan. 1, 1989; Stats.1989, c. 1136, § 5, operative July 1, 1990; Stats.1990, c. 104 (S.B.798), § 5, eff. May 23, 1990; Stats.1990, c. 1360 (S.B.1510), § 24.)*

§ 12523.6. Driver of persons with developmental disabilities; special driver certificate

(a)(1) On and after March 1, 1998, no person who is employed primarily as a driver of a motor vehicle that is used for the transportation of persons with developmental disabilities, as defined in subdivision (a) of Section 4512 of the Welfare and Institutions Code, shall operate that motor vehicle unless that person has in his or her possession a valid driver's license of the appropriate class and a valid special driver certificate issued by the department.

(2) This subdivision only applies to a person who is employed by a business, a nonprofit organization, or a state or local public agency.

(b) The special driver certificate shall be issued only to an applicant who has cleared a criminal history background check by the Department of Justice and, if applicable, by the Federal Bureau of Investigation.

(1) In order to determine the applicant's suitability as the driver of a vehicle used for the transportation of persons with developmental disabilities, the Department of the California Highway Patrol shall require the applicant to furnish to that department, on a form provided or approved by that department for submission to the Department of Justice, a full set of fingerprints sufficient to enable a criminal background investigation.

(2) Except as provided in paragraph (3), an applicant shall furnish to the Department of the California Highway Patrol evidence of having resided in this state for seven consecutive years immediately prior to the date of application for the certificate.

(3) If an applicant is unable to furnish the evidence required under paragraph (2), the Department of the California Highway Patrol shall require the applicant to furnish an additional full set of fingerprints. That department shall submit those fingerprint cards to the Department of Justice. The Department of Justice shall, in turn, submit the additional full set of fingerprints required under this paragraph to the Federal Bureau of Investigation for a national criminal history record check.

(4) Applicant fingerprint forms shall be processed and returned to the area office of the Department of the California Highway Patrol from which they originated not later than 15 working days from the date on which the fingerprint forms were received by the Department of Justice, unless circumstances, other than the administrative duties of the Department of Justice, warrant further investigation. Upon implementation of an electronic fingerprinting system with terminals located statewide and managed by the Department of Justice, the Department of Justice shall ascertain the information required pursuant to this subdivision within three working days.

(5) The applicant shall pay, in addition to the fees authorized in Section 2427, a fee of twenty-five dollars ($25) for an original certificate and twelve dollars ($12) for the renewal of that certificate to the Department of the California Highway Patrol.

(c) A certificate issued under this section shall not be deemed a certification to operate a particular vehicle that otherwise requires a driver's license or endorsement for a particular class under this code.

(d) On or after March 1, 1998, no person who operates a business or a nonprofit organization or agency shall employ a person who is employed primarily as a driver of a motor vehicle for hire that is used for the transportation of persons with developmental disabilities unless the employed person operates the motor vehicle in compliance with subdivision (a).

(e) Nothing in this section precludes an employer of persons who are occasionally used as drivers of motor vehicles for the transportation of persons with developmental disabilities from requiring those persons, as a condition of employment, to obtain a special driver certificate pursuant to this section or precludes any volunteer driver from applying for a special driver certificate.

(f) As used in this section, a person is employed primarily as driver if that person performs at least 50 percent of his or her time worked including, but not limited to, time spent assisting persons onto and out of the vehicle, or at least 20 hours a week, whichever is less, as a compensated driver of a motor vehicle for hire for the transportation of persons with developmental disabilities.

(g) This section does not apply to any person who has successfully completed a background investigation prescribed by law, including, but not limited to, health care transport vehicle operators, or to the operator of a taxicab regulated pursuant to Section 21100. This section does not apply to a person who holds a valid certificate, other than a farm labor vehicle driver certificate, issued under Section 12517.4 or 12527. This section does not apply to a driver who provides transportation on a noncommercial basis to persons with developmental disabilities. *(Added by Stats.1997, c. 595 (A.B.1611), § 1, eff. Sept. 30, 1997. Amended by Stats.1998, c. 485 (A.B.2803), § 159; Stats.1998, c. 877 (A.B.2132), § 53.)*

§ 12524. Vehicles hauling fissile class III shipments or large quantity radioactive materials; driver's license and certificate

(a) No class A, class B, or class C driver's licenseholder shall operate a vehicle hauling fissile class III shipments or large quantity radioactive materials, as defined in Section 173.403 of Title 49 of the Code of Federal Regulations, unless the driver possesses a valid license of the appropriate class and a radioactive materials driver's certificate, issued by the Department of Motor Vehicles, which permits the driver to operate those vehicles.

(b) Applicants for the certificates shall present evidence to the Department of Motor Vehicles that they have successfully completed the radioactive materials hauler driving training course developed by the Department of Motor Vehicles and the Department of the California Highway Patrol before a certificate may be issued. Either the employer of the driver or a driving school licensed pursuant to Chapter 1 (commencing with Section 11100) of Division 5 may administer the training course.

(c) The certificate shall be issued only to applicants qualified by examinations prescribed by the Department of Motor Vehicles and the Department of the California Highway Patrol. These examinations shall be conducted by the Department of Motor Vehicles, and an examination fee of twelve dollars ($12) shall be paid by the applicant to the Department of Motor Vehicles.

(d) Any application for an original radioactive materials driver's certificate or renewal of the certificate and any radioactive materials driver's certificate issued pursuant to this section shall be subject to the provisions of Section 13369. *(Added by Stats.1990, c. 1360 (S.B.1510), § 25.1. Amended by Stats.1992, c. 1241 (S.B.1615), § 19; Stats.1993, c. 272 (A.B.301), § 21, eff. Aug. 2, 1993.)*

Cross References

Directing operation of vehicle transporting fissile class III shipments or large quantity radioactive materials by unauthorized driver, see Vehicle Code § 14611.

Medical certificate of person employed to drive class 1 or class 2 vehicle, employer responsibilities, see Vehicle Code § 14606.

§ 12525. Mechanics or other maintenance personnel; operation of certain vehicles requiring endorsement or certificates; exemption

Mechanics or other maintenance personnel may operate vehicles requiring a schoolbus endorsement or certificates issued pursuant to Section 2512, 12517, 12519, 12523, or 12523.5 without obtaining a schoolbus endorsement or those certificates if that operation is within the course of their employment and they do not transport pupils or members of the public. *(Added by Stats.1990, c. 1360 (S.B.1510), § 27. Amended by Stats.2006, c. 574 (A.B.2520), § 8.)*

§ 12526. Repealed by Stats.1990, c. 1360 (S.B.1510), § 27.5

§ 12527. Ambulance drivers; application for certificate; requirements

In addition to satisfying all requirements specified in this code and regulations adopted pursuant to this code, an applicant for an ambulance driver certificate shall satisfy all of the following requirements:

(a) Except as otherwise provided, every ambulance driver responding to an emergency call or transporting patients shall be at least 18 years of age, hold a driver's license valid in California, possess a valid ambulance driver certificate, and be trained and competent in ambulance operation and the use of safety and emergency care equipment required by the California Code of Regulations governing ambulances.

(b) Except as provided in subdivision (f), no person shall operate an ambulance unless the person has in his or her immediate possession a driver's license for the appropriate class of vehicle to be driven, and a certificate issued by the department to permit the operation of an ambulance.

(c) An ambulance driver certificate may be issued by the department only upon the successful completion of an examination conducted by the department and subject to all of the following conditions:

(1) An applicant for an original or renewal driver certificate shall submit a report of medical examination on a form approved by the department, the Federal Highway Administration, or the Federal Aviation Administration. The report shall be dated within the two years preceding the application date.

(2) An applicant for an original driver certificate shall submit an acceptable fingerprint card.

(3) The certificate to drive an ambulance shall be valid for a period not exceeding five years and six months and shall expire on the same date as the driver's license. The ambulance driver certificate shall be valid only when both of the following conditions exist:

(A) The certificate is accompanied by a medical examination certificate that was issued within the preceding two years and approved by the department, Federal Highway Administration, or Federal Aviation Administration.

(B) A copy of the medical examination report from which the certificate was issued is on file with the department.

(4) The ambulance driver certificate is renewable under conditions prescribed by the department. Except as permitted under paragraphs (2) and (3) of subdivision (d), applicants renewing an ambulance driver certificate shall possess certificates or licenses evidencing compliance with the emergency medical training and educational standards for ambulance attendants established by the Emergency Medical Service Authority.

(d)(1) Every ambulance driver shall have been trained to assist the ambulance attendant in the care and handling of the ill and injured.

Except as provided in paragraph (2), the driver of a California-based ambulance shall, within one year of initial issuance of the driver's ambulance driver certificate, possess a certificate or license evidencing compliance with the emergency medical training and educational standards for ambulance attendants by the Emergency Medical Service Authority. In those emergencies requiring both the regularly assigned driver and attendant to be utilized in providing patient care, the specialized emergency medical training requirement shall not apply to persons temporarily detailed to drive the ambulance.

(2) Paragraph (1) does not apply to an ambulance driver who is a volunteer driver for a volunteer ambulance service under the circumstances specified in this paragraph, if the service is provided in the unincorporated areas of a county with a population of less than 125,000 persons, as determined by the most recent federal decennial census. The operation of an ambulance under this paragraph shall only apply if the name of the driver and the volunteer ambulance service and facts

substantiating the public health necessity for an exemption are submitted to the department by the county board of supervisors and by at least one of the following entities in the county where the driver operates the ambulance:

(A) The county health officer.

(B) The county medical care committee.

(C) The local emergency medical services agency coordinator.

(3) The information required by paragraph (2) shall be submitted to the department at the time of application for an ambulance driver certificate. Upon receipt of that information, the department shall restrict the certificate holder to driving an ambulance for the volunteer ambulance service.

(4) The director may terminate any certificate issued pursuant to paragraph (2) at any time the department determines that the qualifying conditions specified therein no longer exist.

(5) The exemption granted pursuant to paragraph (2) shall expire on the expiration date of the ambulance driver certificate.

(e) A person holding a valid certificate to permit the operation of an ambulance, issued prior to January 1, 1991, shall not be required to reapply for a certificate to satisfy the requirements of this section until the certificate he or she holds expires or is canceled or revoked.

(f) An ambulance certificate is not required for persons operating ambulances in the line of duty as salaried, regular, full-time police officers, deputy sheriffs, or members of a fire department of a public agency. This exemption does not include volunteers and part-time employees or members of a department whose duties are primarily clerical or administrative. *(Added by Stats. 1990, c. 1360 (S.B.1510), § 28. Amended by Stats.1994, c. 954 (A.B.2635), § 1; Stats.1995, c. 766 (S.B.726), § 12; Stats.1996, c. 1043 (A.B.2352), § 3.)*

Cross References

Drivers' licenses, issuance and expiration, traffic violation point count, see Vehicle Code § 12810.5.

Prospective employers of drivers of vehicles requiring certain licenses or certificates, pull-notice system and periodic reports, application to vehicles for which certificate under this section is required, see Vehicle Code § 1808.1.

ARTICLE 2. STUDENT LICENSES

Section
12650. Application.
12651. Issuance.
12652. Limitations.
12653. Cancellation.
12654. Repealed.
12660. Program authorizing driving schools to issue student licenses.
12661. Regulations for issuance of student licenses by driving schools.

§ 12650. Application

(a) Any student over 15 years of age taking a course in automobile driver training, maintained pursuant to Article 12 (commencing with Section 41900) of Chapter 5 of Part 24 of Division 3 of Title 2 of the Education Code, in a secondary school or enrolled in a driver training course offered by a private or parochial school of secondary level may apply to the principal of the school for a student license.

(b) The application shall be signed by the applicant before the principal of the school, or a staff member assigned to such duty. The application shall be accompanied by a statement signed by the parents or guardian or person having custody of the minor, consenting to the issuance of a student license to the student and accepting liability for civil damages arising out of the student driving a motor vehicle upon a highway as provided for in Division 9 (commencing with Section 17000) of this code.

(c) Notwithstanding any other provision of this code, if the person or persons required to sign a statement consenting to the issuance of a student license and accepting liability as provided in subdivision (b) are not residents of this state and the student resides at the school, or the student is a foster child with no parents or guardian available to sign this statement, the application may be accepted if the principal of the school or staff member assigned such duties certifies that the school has filed with the department a certificate of insurance carrier or surety company that there is in effect a policy or bond meeting the requirements of Section 16056, and that such policy or bond will cover the liability for civil damages arising out of the student driving a motor vehicle upon a highway. *(Stats.1959, c. 3, p. 1617, § 12650. Amended by Stats.1961, c. 58, p. 1008, § 31, eff. March 31, 1961; Stats.1969, c. 382, p. 916, § 1; Stats.1971, c. 357, p. 715, § 1, operative May 3, 1972; Stats.1976, c. 1079, p. 4888, § 88; Stats.1977, c. 579, p. 1916, § 184.)*

Cross References

Application forms, see Vehicle Code § 1652.
Instruction permits, see Vehicle Code § 12509.

§ 12651. Issuance

The principal or staff member assigned such duty may issue or reissue a student license without cost whenever in his opinion the applicant is qualified to take the course of instruction and has filed a proper application therefor. *(Stats.1959, c. 3, p. 1617, § 12651. Amended by Stats. 1978, c. 162, p. 393, § 1.)*

§ 12652. Limitations

A student license shall limit the operation of a motor vehicle to such times as the licensee is taking driver training in connection with the driver education program and then only at the direction and under the supervision of the instructor and shall be valid only for the period covered by the course and for not more than one year from the date of issuance. *(Stats.1959, c. 3, p. 1617, § 12652.)*

§ 12653. Cancellation

A student license may be canceled by the principal of the school or by the department whenever, in the opinion of either, the safety of the licensee or other persons requires the action and shall be canceled upon the written request of the parent or other person who signed the consent to issue the license. *(Stats.1959, c. 3, p. 1617, § 12653. Amended by Stats.1978, c. 162, p. 393, § 2.)*

§ 12654. Repealed by Stats.1968, c. 1469, p. 2936, § 2

§ 12660. Program authorizing driving schools to issue student licenses

(a) The department may establish a program authorizing a driving school licensed under Chapter 1 (commencing with Section 11100) of Division 5 to issue a student license to operate a class 3 vehicle to any applicant 15 years of age or older, subject to the conditions specified in subdivision (d).

(b) The department may charge any driving school participating in the program a fee not to exceed two dollars ($2) per applicant to recover the department's cost in establishing and monitoring the program. The fee that a participating school may charge an applicant for a student license may not exceed the fee that the department charges the school for the license.

(c) The department may remove a driving school from the program if the department determines that the school has issued a student license fraudulently, or has otherwise not followed the requirements of the program. This fraudulent conduct may result in cause for suspension or revocation of the driving school license.

(d)(1) Applicants shall meet the qualification standards specified in regulations adopted by the department pursuant to Section 12661. The student license application shall be accompanied by a statement signed by the parents or guardian, or person having custody of the minor, consenting to the issuance of a student license to the applicant.

(2) No licensed driving school may issue a student license to any applicant under the age of 17 years and 6 months unless that applicant shows proof of satisfactory completion of an approved course in driver education, pursuant to standards specified in paragraph (4) of subdivision (a) of Section 12814.6.

(e) A driving school owner or an independent instructor licensed under Section 11105.5 shall maintain liability insurance for bodily injury or property damage caused by the use of a motor vehicle in driving instruction, and for the liability of the driving school, the instructor, and the student, in accordance with Section 11103.

(f) The department shall submit a report to the Legislature on the progress of the program established under subdivision (a) within two years after the program is implemented. The report shall include, but not be limited to, an analysis of the costs and benefits of the program and shall include recommendations by the department.

(g) The director may terminate the program at any time the department determines that continued operation of the program would have an adverse effect on traffic safety. The finding upon which the termination is based shall be reported to the Legislature within 30 days following termination of the program. *(Added by Stats.1987, c. 1029, § 1. Amended by Stats.1992, c. 399 (S.B.1476), § 1; Stats.1997, c. 760 (S.B.1329), § 7; Stats.2003, c. 768 (A.B.1343), § 3.)*

§ 12661. Regulations for issuance of student licenses by driving schools

The department, in consultation with the State Department of Education, shall adopt regulations for the issuance of student licenses pursuant to Section 12660. The department and the State Department of Education shall seek advice and input on those regulations from the public, law enforcement, and the driving school industry. The regulations shall include all of the following:

(a) Standards and procedures for the issuance of student licenses pursuant to Section 12660, including the determination of an applicant's qualifications under Section 12805.

(b) Standards and procedures to ensure that all records of a driving school relating to the physical or mental condition of any student are confidential, except to the department.

(c) Standards and procedures for monitoring the issuance of student licenses.

(d) A requirement that each student license issued pursuant to Section 12660 be accompanied by a verbal and written description of the limitations of that license in terms of duration and use.

(e) Any other requirements necessary to carry out Section 12660. *(Added by Stats.1987, c. 1029, § 2.)*

ARTICLE 3. ISSUANCE AND RENEWAL OF LICENSES

Section
12800.	Applications.
12800.	Applications.
12800.	Applications.
12800.5.	Engraved picture or photo; disclaimer; proof of age.
12800.7.	Verification of name and address.
12801.	Applications; driver's license; social security numbers; display not allowed.
12801.	Applications; driver's license; social security numbers; display not allowed.
12801.	Applications; driver's license; social security numbers; display not allowed.
12801.2.	Repealed.
12801.5.	Proof of authorized presence in United States under federal law; verification; appeal; supplemental budget report; detention or arrest on belief that person is unlicensed driver; duty to

Section

obey motor vehicle laws regardless of licensed status.

12801.5. Proof of authorized presence in United States under federal law; verification; appeal; supplemental budget report; detention or arrest on belief that person is unlicensed driver; duty to obey motor vehicle laws regardless of licensed status.

12801.5. Proof of authorized presence in United States under federal law; verification; appeal; supplemental budget report; detention or arrest on belief that person is unlicensed driver; duty to obey motor vehicle laws regardless of licensed status.

12801.6. Deferred action for childhood arrivals; driver's license.

12801.7. Deported aliens; cancellation of license; review.

12801.8. Legal, nonimmigrant applicants; temporary licenses; expiration; extensions.

12801.9. Persons unable to submit satisfactory proof of authorized presence in United States under federal law; issuance of driver's license; emergency regulations; documents acceptable to prove identity and residency.

12801.10. Commercial driver's license; submission of social security account number required.

12801.11. Determination that department is prepared to issue licenses pursuant to § 12801.09; issuance of declaration.

12802. Signature and verification.

12802.5. Applicant under age 21; notice regarding driving with blood-alcohol concentration of .01 percent or greater.

12803. Examinations for license.

12804. Repealed.

12804.1. Repealed.

12804.2. Agricultural operations; exemption from certain endorsement requirements.

12804.3. Repealed.

12804.4. Repealed.

12804.5. Changes in classification of vehicles minors licensed to operate; consent of parents.

12804.6. Transit busdrivers; required certification; qualifications; employee records.

12804.7. Two-axle motortruck or implement of husbandry; towing implement of husbandry; class C; speed and distance.

12804.8. Competency test; safe operation of motor vehicle; development and use; liability.

12804.9. Examination and driving test.

12804.10. Driving of house cars; noncommercial class B driver's license with endorsement.

12804.11. Requirements to operate firefighting equipment; qualifications for firefighter endorsement; fees; conditions; license requirements of employees or volunteers.

12804.12. Restricted class A driver's license for certain 2-axle vehicles; medical information.

12804.13. Repealed.

12804.14. Restricted class A driver's licenses for certain two-axle vehicles towing livestock trailers.

12804.15. Driving of house cars; license requirements.

12805. Refusal to issue or renew driver's license; mandatory grounds.

Section

12806. Refusal to issue or renew driver's license; discretionary grounds.

12806.5. Schoolbus, school pupil activity, youth busdriver, farm labor vehicle, or general public paratransit vehicle certificate; suspension or revocation; regulations.

12807. Additional grounds for refusal.

12808. Record of applicant.

12808.1. Delinquent parking violations; refusal to issue or renew license.

12809. Grounds permitting refusal; operative date.

12810. Traffic violation point counts; allocation of points.

12810.2. Convictions of § 27315, use of seatbelts; no point count.

12810.3. Violation points.

12810.4. Conviction of Anti-Gridlock Act of 1987; no violation point counts.

12810.5. Traffic violation point count; number for presumption of negligent operation; proof of financial responsibility.

12811. Issuance and contents of license.

12811.1. Medical information card; issuance; contents; design.

12812. Driver with class C or M license not required to have certificate; negligent operator; restricted license for employment.

12813. Restricted licenses.

12814. Renewal of licenses; applications; examinations; extensions; terms and conditions; selective testing.

12814.1. Repealed.

12814.5. Renewal by mail.

12814.6. Brady–Jared Teen Driver Safety Act of 1997; provisional licenses; persons under age 18.

12814.7. Provisional restricted class C license for operation of army and national guard vehicles; conditions.

12814.8. Repealed.

12815. Licenses lost, destroyed, or mutilated.

12816. Term of license; period for renewal; exception.

12817. Persons in the armed forces; spouses.

12818. Reexamination upon request; actions relating to driving privilege; notice of results to law enforcement agency.

12819. Failure to request reexamination pursuant to notice; suspension of driving privilege.

Cross References

Confidentiality of driver's license information, authorization for businesses to swipe driver's license or identification card in electronic device for certain purposes, violation, see Civil Code § 1798.90.1.

§ 12800. Applications

Section operative until the sooner of Jan. 1, 2015 or the date the director executes a declaration pursuant to § 12801.11. See, also, section operative the sooner of Jan. 1, 2015 or the date the director executes a declaration pursuant to § 12801.11 and operative until the effective date of a judicial determination that any provision of Stats.2013, c. 524 (A.B.60) is enjoined, found unconstitutional or held invalid, and section operative the effective date of a judicial determination that any provision of Stats.2013, c. 524 (A.B.60) is enjoined, found unconstitutional or held invalid.

Every application for an original or a renewal of a driver's license shall contain all of the following information:

(a) The applicant's true full name, age, sex, mailing address, residence address, and social security account number.

(b) A brief description of the applicant for the purpose of identification.

(c) A legible print of the thumb or finger of the applicant.

(d) The type of motor vehicle or combination of vehicles the applicant desires to operate.

(e) Whether the applicant has ever previously been licensed as a driver and, if so, when and in what state or country and whether or not the license has been suspended or revoked and, if so, the date of and reason for the suspension or revocation.

(f) Whether the applicant has ever previously been refused a driver's license in this state and, if so, the date of and the reason for the refusal.

(g) Whether the applicant, within the last three years, has experienced, on one or more occasions, either a lapse of consciousness or an episode of marked confusion caused by a condition that may bring about recurrent lapses, or whether the applicant has a disease, disorder, or disability that affects his or her ability to exercise reasonable and ordinary control in operating a motor vehicle upon a highway.

(h) Whether the applicant understands traffic signs and signals.

(i) Whether the applicant has ever previously been issued an identification card by the department.

(j) Any other information that is necessary to enable the department to determine whether the applicant is entitled to a license under this code.

(k) This section shall become inoperative on January 1, 2015, or on the date that the director executes a declaration pursuant to Section 12801.11, whichever is sooner, and as of January 1, 2015, is repealed, unless a later enacted statute, that is enacted before January 1, 2015, deletes or extends that date. *(Stats.1959, c. 3, p. 1618, § 12800. Amended by Stats.1961, c. 53, p. 991, § 1; Stats.1961, c. 1615, p. 3455, § 18; Stats.1968, c. 494, p. 1136, § 1; Stats.1975, c. 659, p. 1424, § 1, operative July 1, 1976; Stats.1981, c. 772, p. 3017, § 1; Stats.1981, c. 1102, p. 4310, § 1.5; Stats.1982, c. 1042, p. 3799, § 2; Stats. 1984, c. 737, § 2, operative July 1, 1985; Stats.1991, c. 90 (A.B.1297), § 66, eff. June 30, 1991; Stats.1991, c. 928 (A.B.1886), § 18.5, eff. Oct. 14, 1991; Stats.2003, c. 326 (S.B.60), § 2; Stats.2003–2004, 3rd Ex.Sess., c. 1 (S.B.1), § 2, eff. Dec. 4, 2003, operative Jan. 1, 2004; Stats.2013, c. 524 (A.B.60), § 6.)*

430

Inoperative Date and Repeal

For inoperative date and repeal of this section, see its terms.

Cross References

Application forms, see Vehicle Code § 1652.
Authority to grant or refuse applications, see Vehicle Code § 1653.
Department retention and indexing of applications, see Vehicle Code § 1800.
False or fictitious name, false statement, concealment of facts, or fraud in application as offense, see Vehicle Code § 20.
Fees,
　Driver's license, see Vehicle Code § 14900.
　Duplicate licenses or change of name, see Vehicle Code § 14901.
Grounds,
　Permitting denial of license, see Vehicle Code § 12809.
　Requiring denial of license, see Vehicle Code § 12805 et seq.
Notice of suspension or revocation of driving privilege, address of driver, see Vehicle Code § 13106.
Renewal of licenses, see Vehicle Code § 12814.
Signature, verification, see Vehicle Code § 12802.

§ 12800. Applications

Section operative the sooner of Jan. 1, 2015 or the date the director executes a declaration pursuant to § 12801.11 and operative until the effective date of a judicial determination that any provision of the act that added this section is enjoined, found unconstitutional or held invalid. See, also, section operative until the sooner of Jan. 1, 2015 or the date the director executes a declaration pursuant to § 12801.11, and section operative the effective date of a judicial determination that any provision of the act that added this section is enjoined, found unconstitutional or held invalid.

Each application for an original or a renewal of a driver's license shall contain all of the following information:

(a) The applicant's true full name, age, sex, mailing address, residence address, and, except as provided in Section 12801, social security account number.

(b) A brief description of the applicant for the purpose of identification.

(c) A legible print of the thumb or finger of the applicant.

(d) The type of motor vehicle or combination of vehicles the applicant desires to operate.

(e) Whether the applicant has ever previously been licensed as a driver and, if so, when and in what state or country and whether or not the license has been suspended or revoked and, if so, the date of and reason for the suspension or revocation.

(f) Whether the applicant has ever previously been refused a driver's license in this state and, if so, the date of and the reason for the refusal.

(g) Whether the applicant, within the last three years, has experienced, on one or more occasions, either a lapse of consciousness or an episode of marked confusion caused by a condition that may bring about recurrent lapses, or whether the applicant has a disease, disorder, or disability that affects his or her ability to exercise reasonable and ordinary control in operating a motor vehicle upon a highway.

(h) Whether the applicant understands traffic signs and signals.

(i) Whether the applicant has ever previously been issued an identification card by the department.

(j) Any other information that is necessary to enable the department to determine whether the applicant is entitled to a license under this code.

(k) This section shall become operative on January 1, 2015, or on the date that the director executes a declaration pursuant to Section 12801.11, whichever is sooner.

(*l*) This section shall become inoperative on the effective date of a final judicial determination made by any court of appellate jurisdiction that any provision of the act that added this section, or its application, either in whole or in part, is enjoined, found unconstitutional, or held invalid for any reason. The department shall post this information on its Internet Web site. *(Added by Stats.2013, c. 524 (A.B.60), § 7, operative contingent.)*

Operative Effect

For operative effect of this section, see its terms.

Cross References

Application forms, see Vehicle Code § 1652.
Authority to grant or refuse applications, see Vehicle Code § 1653.
Department retention and indexing of applications, see Vehicle Code § 1800.
False or fictitious name, false statement, concealment of facts, or fraud in application as offense, see Vehicle Code § 20.
Fees,
    Driver's license, see Vehicle Code § 14900.
    Duplicate licenses or change of name, see Vehicle Code § 14901.
Grounds,
    Permitting denial of license, see Vehicle Code § 12809.
    Requiring denial of license, see Vehicle Code § 12805 et seq.
Notice of suspension or revocation of driving privilege, address of driver, see Vehicle Code § 13106.
Renewal of licenses, see Vehicle Code § 12814.
Signature, verification, see Vehicle Code § 12802.

§ 12800. Applications

Section operative the effective date of a judicial determination that any provision of the act that added this section is enjoined, found unconstitutional or held invalid. See, also, section operative until the sooner of Jan. 1, 2015 or the date the director executes a declaration pursuant to § 12801.11, and section operative the sooner of Jan. 1, 2015 or the date the director executes a declaration pursuant to § 12801.11 and operative until the effective date of a judicial determination that any provision of the act that added this section is enjoined, found unconstitutional or held invalid.

Each application for an original or a renewal of a driver's license shall contain all of the following information:

(a) The applicant's true full name, age, sex, mailing address, residence address, and social security account number.

(b) A brief description of the applicant for the purpose of identification.

(c) A legible print of the thumb or finger of the applicant.

(d) The type of motor vehicle or combination of vehicles the applicant desires to operate.

(e) Whether the applicant has ever previously been licensed as a driver and, if so, when and in what state or country and whether or not the license has been suspended or revoked and, if so, the date of and reason for the suspension or revocation.

(f) Whether the applicant has ever previously been refused a driver's license in this state and, if so, the date of and the reason for the refusal.

(g) Whether the applicant, within the last three years, has experienced, on one or more occasions, either a lapse of consciousness or an episode of marked confusion caused by a condition that may bring about recurrent lapses, or whether the applicant has a disease, disorder, or disability that affects his or her ability to exercise reasonable and ordinary control in operating a motor vehicle upon a highway.

(h) Whether the applicant understands traffic signs and signals.

(i) Whether the applicant has ever previously been issued an identification card by the department.

(j) Any other information that is necessary to enable the department to determine whether the applicant is entitled to a license under this code.

(k) This section shall become operative on the effective date of a final judicial determination made by any court of appellate jurisdiction that any provision of the act that added this section, or its application, either in whole or in part, is enjoined, found unconstitutional, or held invalid for any reason. The department shall post this information on its Internet Web site. *(Added by Stats.2013, c. 524 (A.B.60), § 8, operative contingent.)*

Operative Effect

For operative effect of this section, see its terms.

Cross References

Application forms, see Vehicle Code § 1652.

Authority to grant or refuse applications, see Vehicle Code § 1653.

Department retention and indexing of applications, see Vehicle Code § 1800.

False or fictitious name, false statement, concealment of facts, or fraud in application as offense, see Vehicle Code § 20.

Fees,
  Driver's license, see Vehicle Code § 14900.
  Duplicate licenses or change of name, see Vehicle Code § 14901.

Grounds,
  Permitting denial of license, see Vehicle Code § 12809.
  Requiring denial of license, see Vehicle Code § 12805 et seq.

Notice of suspension or revocation of driving privilege, address of driver, see Vehicle Code § 13106.

Renewal of licenses, see Vehicle Code § 12814.

Signature, verification, see Vehicle Code § 12802.

§ 12800.5. Engraved picture or photo; disclaimer; proof of age

(a)(1) A license shall bear a fullface engraved picture or photograph of the licensee.

(2) Notwithstanding any other provision of law, the department shall not, unless requested by the licensee, distribute or sell the licensee's picture or photograph or any information pertaining to the licensee's physical characteristics to any private individual, other than the licensee, or to any firm, copartnership, association, or corporation. This paragraph does not apply to any private business entity that contracts with the department for the production of driver's licenses and identification cards, if the contract prohibits the unauthorized use and disclosure of the information.

(b) A license, including a temporary license issued pursuant to Section 12506, shall bear the following notice: "This license is issued as a license to drive a motor vehicle; it does not establish eligibility for employment, voter registration, or public benefits."

(c) The department may demand proof of age prior to the issuance of a license. *(Added by Stats.1965, c. 1817, p. 4191, § 1. Amended by Stats.1971, c. 1748, p. 3764, § 58, operative March 4, 1972; Stats.1973, c. 463, p. 932, § 1; Stats.1981, c. 1006, p. 3895, § 1; Stats.1993, c. 820 (S.B.976), § 1; Stats.1996, c. 10 (A.B.1869), § 13, eff. Feb. 9, 1996; Stats.1999, c. 489 (A.B.771), § 3.)*

Cross References

Department of Real Estate, city attorney and investigators, authority to obtain copies of fullface engraved pictures or photographs of individuals directly from Department of Motor Vehicles, see Vehicle Code § 1808.51.

§ 12800.7. Verification of name and address

Upon application for an original or duplicate license the department may require the applicant to produce any identification that it determines is necessary in order to ensure that the name of the applicant stated in the application is his or her true, full name and that his or her residence address as set forth in the application is his or her true residence address. *(Added by Stats.1965, c. 1832,*

432

p. 4228, § 1. Amended by Stats.1999, c. 1008 (S.B.533), § 4.)

Cross References

Marriage, change of name, see Family Code § 306.5.
Registered domestic partnership, change of name, see Family Code § 298.6.

§ 12801. Applications; driver's license; social security numbers; display not allowed

Section operative until the sooner of Jan. 1, 2015 or the date the director executes a declaration pursuant to § 12801.11. See, also, section operative the sooner of Jan. 1, 2015 or the date the director executes a declaration pursuant to § 12801.11 and operative until the effective date of a judicial determination that any provision of Stats.2013, c. 524 (A.B.60) is enjoined, found unconstitutional or held invalid, and section operative the effective date of a judicial determination that any provision of Stats.2013, c. 524 (A.B.60) is enjoined, found unconstitutional or held invalid.

(a) Notwithstanding any other law, the department shall require an application for a driver's license to contain the applicant's social security account number and any other number or identifier determined to be appropriate by the department.

(b) Notwithstanding subdivision (a), an applicant who provides satisfactory proof that his or her presence in the United States is authorized under federal law, but who is not eligible for a social security account number, is eligible to receive an original driver's license if he or she meets all other qualifications for licensure.

(c) Notwithstanding any other law, the social security account number collected on a driver's license application shall not be displayed on the driver's license including, but not limited to, inclusion on a magnetic tape or strip used to store data on the license.

(d) This section shall become inoperative on January 1, 2015, or on the date that the director executes a declaration pursuant to Section 12801.11, whichever is sooner, and as of January 1, 2015, is repealed, unless a later enacted statute, that is enacted before January 1, 2015, deletes or extends that date. *(Added by Stats.1988, c. 1509, § 6. Amended by Stats.1992, c. 635 (A.B.1823), § 4, eff. Sept. 14, 1992; Stats.2003, c. 326 (S.B.60), § 3; Stats.2003–2004, 3rd Ex.Sess., c. 1 (S.B.1), § 3, eff. Dec. 4, 2003, operative Jan. 1, 2004; Stats.2012, c. 862 (A.B.2189), § 2; Stats.2013, c. 524 (A.B.60), § 9.)*

Inoperative Date and Repeal

For inoperative date and repeal of this section, see its terms.

Cross References

Application for driver's license or identification card, required numbers or identifiers, see Vehicle Code § 1653.5.

Marriage, change of name, see Family Code § 306.5.
Registered domestic partnership, change of name, see Family Code § 298.6.

§ 12801. Applications; driver's license; social security numbers; display not allowed

Section operative the sooner of Jan. 1, 2015 or the date the director executes a declaration pursuant to § 12801.11 and operative until the effective date of a judicial determination that any provision of the act that added this section is enjoined, found unconstitutional or held invalid. See, also, section operative until the sooner of Jan. 1, 2015 or the date the director executes a declaration pursuant to § 12801.11, and section operative the effective date of a judicial determination that any provision of the act that added this section is enjoined, found unconstitutional or held invalid.

(a) Except as provided in subdivisions (b) and (c) and Section 12801.9, the department shall require an application for a driver's license to contain the applicant's social security account number and any other number or identifier determined to be appropriate by the department.

(b) An applicant who provides satisfactory proof that his or her presence in the United States is authorized under federal law, but who is not eligible for a social security account number, is eligible to receive an original driver's license if he or she meets all other qualifications for licensure.

(c)(1) An applicant who is unable to provide satisfactory proof that his or her presence in the United States is authorized under federal law may sign an affidavit attesting that he or she is both ineligible for a social security account number and unable to submit satisfactory proof that his or her presence in the United States is authorized under federal law. This affidavit is not a public record.

(2) The submission of this affidavit shall be accepted by the department in lieu of a social security account number.

(3) This subdivision shall not apply to applications for a commercial driver's license. The department shall require all applications for a commercial driver's license to include the applicant's social security account number.

(4) Nothing in this section shall be used to consider an individual's citizenship or immigration status as a basis for a criminal investigation, arrest, or detention.

(d) The department shall not complete an application for a driver's license unless the applicant is in compliance with the requirements of subdivision (a), (b) or (c).

(e) Notwithstanding any other law, the social security account number collected on a driver's license application shall not be displayed on the driver's license including, but not limited to, inclusion on a magnetic tape or strip used to store data on the license.

(f) This section shall become operative on January 1, 2015, or on the date that the director executes a declaration pursuant to Section 12801.11, whichever is sooner.

(g) This section shall become inoperative on the effective date of a final judicial determination made by any court of appellate jurisdiction that any provision of the act that added this section, or its application, either in whole or in part, is enjoined, found unconstitutional, or held invalid for any reason. The department shall post this information on its Internet Web site. *(Added by Stats.2013, c. 524 (A.B.60), § 10, operative contingent.)*

Operative Effect

For operative effect of this section, see its terms.

Cross References

Application for driver's license or identification card, required numbers or identifiers, see Vehicle Code § 1653.5.
Marriage, change of name, see Family Code § 306.5.
Registered domestic partnership, change of name, see Family Code § 298.6.

§ 12801. Applications; driver's license; social security numbers; display not allowed

Section operative the effective date of a judicial determination that any provision of the act that added this section is enjoined, found unconstitutional or held invalid. See, also, section operative until the sooner of Jan. 1, 2015 or the date the director executes a declaration pursuant to § 12801.11, and section operative the sooner of Jan. 1, 2015 or the date the director executes a declaration pursuant to § 12801.11 and operative until the effective date of a judicial determination that any provision of the act that added this section is enjoined, found unconstitutional or held invalid.

(a) Notwithstanding any other law, the department shall require an application for a driver's license to contain the applicant's social security account number and any other number or identifier determined to be appropriate by the department.

(b) Notwithstanding subdivision (a), an applicant who provides satisfactory proof that his or her presence in the United States is authorized under federal law, but who is not eligible for a social security account number, is eligible to receive an original driver's license if he or she meets all other qualifications for licensure.

(c) Notwithstanding any other law, the social security account number collected on a driver's license application shall not be displayed on the driver's license including, but not limited to, inclusion on a magnetic tape or strip used to store data on the license.

(d) This section shall become operative on the effective date of a final judicial determination made by any court of appellate jurisdiction that any provision of the act that added this section, or its application, either in whole or in part, is enjoined, found unconstitutional, or held invalid for any reason. The department shall post this information on its Internet Web site. *(Added by Stats.2013, c. 524 (A.B.60), § 11, operative contingent.)*

§ 12801.2. Repealed by Stats.2003–2004, 3rd Ex.Sess., c. 1 (S.B.1), § 4, eff. Dec. 4, 2003, operative Jan. 1, 2004

§ 12801.5. Proof of authorized presence in United States under federal law; verification; appeal; supplemental budget report; detention or arrest on belief that person is unlicensed driver; duty to obey motor vehicle laws regardless of licensed status

Section operative until the sooner of Jan. 1, 2015 or the date the director executes a declaration pursuant to § 12801.11. See, also, section operative the sooner of Jan. 1, 2015 or the date the director executes a declaration pursuant to § 12801.11 and operative until the effective date of a judicial determination that any provision of Stats.2013, c. 524 (A.B.60) is enjoined, found unconstitutional or held invalid, and section operative the effective date of a judicial determination that any provision of Stats.2013, c. 524 (A.B.60) is enjoined, found unconstitutional or held invalid.

(a) Notwithstanding any other * * * law, the department shall require an applicant for an original driver's license or identification card to submit satisfactory proof that the applicant's presence in the United States is authorized under federal law.

(b) The department shall not issue an original driver's license or identification card to a person who does not submit satisfactory proof that the applicant's presence in the United States is authorized under federal law.

(c) The department shall adopt regulations to carry out the purposes of this section, including procedures for, but not limited to, (1) verifying that the applicant's presence in the United States is authorized under federal law, (2) issuance of a temporary license pending verification of the applicant's status, and (3) appeal hearings from a denial of a license, temporary license, or identification card.

(d) On January 10 of each year, the department shall submit a supplemental budget report to the Governor and the Legislature detailing the costs of verifying the citizenship or legal residency of applicants for driver's

licenses and identification cards, in order for the state to request reimbursement from the federal government.

(e) Notwithstanding Section 40300 or any other * * * law, a peace officer may not detain or arrest a person solely on the belief that the person is an unlicensed driver, unless the officer has reasonable cause to believe the person driving is under * * * 16 years of age.

(f) The inability to obtain a driver's license pursuant to this section does not abrogate or diminish in any respect the legal requirement of every driver in this state to obey the motor vehicle laws of this state, including laws with respect to licensing, motor vehicle registration, and financial responsibility.

(g) This section shall become inoperative on January 1, 2015, or on the date that the director executes a declaration pursuant to Section 12801.11, whichever is sooner, and as of January 1, 2015, is repealed, unless a later enacted statute, that is enacted before January 1, 2015, deletes or extends that date. *(Added by Stats.1993, c. 820 (S.B.976), § 2, operative March 1, 1994. Amended by Stats.1994, c. 675 (S.B.1741), § 5; Stats.2003, c. 326 (S.B.60), § 5; Stats.2003–2004, 3rd Ex.Sess., c. 1 (S.B.1), § 5, eff. Dec. 4, 2003, operative Jan. 1, 2004; Stats.2013, c. 524 (A.B.60), § 12.)*

§ 12801.5. Proof of authorized presence in United States under federal law; verification; appeal; supplemental budget report; detention or arrest on belief that person is unlicensed driver; duty to obey motor vehicle laws regardless of licensed status

Section operative the sooner of Jan. 1, 2015 or the date the director executes a declaration pursuant to § 12801.11 and operative until the effective date of a judicial determination that any provision of the act that added this section is enjoined, found unconstitutional or held invalid. See, also, section operative until the sooner of Jan. 1, 2015 or the date the director executes a declaration pursuant to § 12801.11, and section operative the effective date of a judicial determination that any provision of the act that added this section is enjoined, found unconstitutional or held invalid.

(a) Except as provided in Section 12801.9, the department shall require an applicant for an original driver's license or identification card to submit satisfactory proof that the applicant's presence in the United States is authorized under federal law.

(b) Except as provided in Section 12801.9, the department shall not issue an original driver's license or identification card to a person who does not submit satisfactory proof that the applicant's presence in the United States is authorized under federal law.

(c) The department shall adopt regulations to carry out the purposes of this section, including, but not limited to, procedures for (1) verifying that the applicant's presence in the United States is authorized under federal law, (2) issuance of a temporary license pending verification of the applicant's status, and (3) hearings to appeal a denial of a license, temporary license, or identification card.

(d) On January 10 of each year, the department shall submit a supplemental budget report to the Governor and the Legislature detailing the costs of verifying the citizenship or legal residency of applicants for driver's licenses and identification cards, in order for the state to request reimbursement from the federal government.

(e) Notwithstanding Section 40300 or any other law, a peace officer shall not detain or arrest a person solely on the belief that the person is an unlicensed driver, unless the officer has reasonable cause to believe the person driving is under 16 years of age.

(f) The inability of an individual to obtain a driver's license pursuant to this section does not abrogate or diminish in any respect the legal requirement of every driver in this state to obey the motor vehicle laws of this state, including laws with respect to licensing, motor vehicle registration, and financial responsibility.

(g) This section shall become operative on January 1, 2015, or on the date that the director executes a declaration pursuant to Section 12801.11, whichever is sooner.

(h) This section shall become inoperative on the effective date of a final judicial determination made by any court of appellate jurisdiction that any provision of the act that added this section, or its application, either in whole or in part, is enjoined, found unconstitutional, or held invalid for any reason. The department shall post this information on its Internet Web site. *(Added by Stats.2013, c. 524 (A.B.60), § 13.)*

Operative Effect

For operative effect of this section, see its terms.

Cross References

Application for driver's license or identification card, required numbers or identifiers, see Vehicle Code § 1653.5.
Knowingly assisting person present in United States in violation of federal law to procure license or identification, violation, see Vehicle Code § 14610.7.

§ 12801.5. Proof of authorized presence in United States under federal law; verification; appeal; supplemental budget report; detention or arrest on belief that person is unlicensed driver; duty to obey motor vehicle laws regardless of licensed status

Section operative the effective date of a judicial determination that any provision of the act that

added this section is enjoined, found unconstitutional or held invalid. See, also, section operative until the sooner of Jan. 1, 2015 or the date the director executes a declaration pursuant to § 12801.11, and section operative the sooner of Jan. 1, 2015 or the date the director executes a declaration pursuant to § 12801.11 and operative until the effective date of a judicial determination that any provision of the act that added this section is enjoined, found unconstitutional or held invalid.

(a) Notwithstanding any other law, the department shall require an applicant for an original driver's license or identification card to submit satisfactory proof that the applicant's presence in the United States is authorized under federal law.

(b) The department shall not issue an original driver's license or identification card to a person who does not submit satisfactory proof that the applicant's presence in the United States is authorized under federal law.

(c) The department shall adopt regulations to carry out the purposes of this section, including, but not limited to, procedures for (1) verifying that the applicant's presence in the United States is authorized under federal law, (2) issuance of a temporary license pending verification of the applicant's status, and (3) hearings to appeal a denial of a license, temporary license, or identification card.

(d) On January 10 of each year, the department shall submit a supplemental budget report to the Governor and the Legislature detailing the costs of verifying the citizenship or legal residency of applicants for driver's licenses and identification cards, in order for the state to request reimbursement from the federal government.

(e) Notwithstanding Section 40300 or any other law, a peace officer shall not detain or arrest a person solely on the belief that the person is an unlicensed driver, unless the officer has reasonable cause to believe the person driving is under 16 years of age.

(f) The inability of an individual to obtain a driver's license pursuant to this section does not abrogate or diminish in any respect the legal requirement of every driver in this state to obey the motor vehicle laws of this state, including laws with respect to licensing, motor vehicle registration, and financial responsibility.

(g) This section shall become operative on the effective date of a final judicial determination made by any court of appellate jurisdiction that any provision of the act that added this section, or its application, either in whole or in part, is enjoined, found unconstitutional, or held invalid for any reason. The department shall post this information on its Internet Web site. *(Added by Stats.2013, c. 524 (A.B.60), § 14.)*

Operative Effect

For operative effect of this section, see its terms.

Application for driver's license or identification card, required numbers or identifiers, see Vehicle Code § 1653.5.

Knowingly assisting person present in United States in violation of federal law to procure license or identification, violation, see Vehicle Code § 14610.7.

§ 12801.6. Deferred action for childhood arrivals; driver's license

(a) Any federal document demonstrating favorable action by the federal government for acceptance of a person into the deferred action for childhood arrivals program shall satisfy the requirements of Section 12801.5.

(b) The department may issue an original driver's license to the person who submits proof of presence in the United States as authorized under federal law pursuant to subdivision (a) and either a social security account number or ineligibility for a social security account number. *(Added by Stats.2012, c. 862 (A.B.2189), § 3.)*

§ 12801.7. Deported aliens; cancellation of license; review

(a) The department shall not issue an original driver's license or identification card, or a renewal, duplicate, or replacement driver's license or identification card to any person for whom the department has received notice from the United States Immigration and Naturalization Service that the person has been determined and found by the United States Immigration and Naturalization Service to be a deported alien under Section 1252 of Title 8 of the United States Code.

(b)(1) The department shall cancel any driver's license or identification card issued to any person identified as specified in subdivision (a).

(2) The cancellation shall become effective on the 30th day after the date the cancellation notice is mailed to the person, except as authorized under paragraph (3).

(3) The person may request a review of the intended cancellation during the 30–day period specified in paragraph (2) and, if proof is provided to show the person is legally present in the United States as authorized under federal law, the department shall rescind the cancellation.

(4) The cancellation notice shall be mailed to the person's last known address.

(c) The department shall require an applicant for a driver's license whose license was canceled under this section to submit satisfactory proof that the applicant's presence in the United States is authorized under federal law.

(d) This section shall become operative on, and apply only to persons determined and found to be a deported alien after, July 1, 1997. *(Added by Stats.1996, c. 1168 (A.B.33), § 1, operative July 1, 1997.)*

This section applies only to persons determined and found to be a deported alien after July 1, 1997.

§ 12801.8. Legal, nonimmigrant applicants; temporary licenses; expiration; extensions

(a) In the case of a legal, nonimmigrant driver's license applicant, the department shall issue a temporary driver's license, valid for 90 days, if the applicant has successfully completed the application and the related requirements for the issuance of a driver's license under this code, including subdivision (a) of Section 12805. If the United States Immigration and Naturalization Service is unable to verify the applicant's presence before the temporary driver's license expires, the department shall, at least 15 days before the temporary driver's license expires, extend the temporary driver's license for an additional 120 days and notify the applicant by mail that the temporary driver's license is being extended.

(b) If the department adjusts the expiration date of any driver's license issued pursuant to this code so that the date does not exceed the expiration date of a federal document submitted pursuant to subdivision (a) of Section 12801.5, the applicant may, upon receipt of a notice of renewal of the driver's license by the department sent prior to the expiration of the license, request an extension of the term of the driver's license by submitting to the department satisfactory proof that the applicant's presence in the United States has been reauthorized or extended under federal law. After verifying that the applicant's presence in the United States has been reauthorized or extended by federal law, the department shall adjust the expiration date of the driver's license so that it does not exceed the expiration date of the revised federal document submitted pursuant to subdivision (a) of Section 12801.5 and complies with the related requirements of this code.

(c) On or before July 1, 1997, the department shall establish a procedure for receiving mailed requests for the extension of driver's licenses as described in this section. *(Added by Stats.1996, c. 531 (S.B.1717), § 1.)*

§ 12801.9. Persons unable to submit satisfactory proof of authorized presence in United States under federal law; issuance of driver's license; emergency regulations; documents acceptable to prove identity and residency

Section operative the sooner of Jan. 1, 2015 or the date the director executes a declaration pursuant to § 12801.11 and operative until the effective date of a judicial determination that any provision of the act that added this section is enjoined, found unconstitutional or held invalid.

(a) Notwithstanding Section 12801.5, the department shall issue an original driver's license to a person who is unable to submit satisfactory proof that the applicant's presence in the United States is authorized under federal law if he or she meets all other qualifications for licensure and provides satisfactory proof to the department of his or her identity and California residency.

(b) The department shall adopt emergency regulations to carry out the purposes of this section, including, but not limited to, procedures for (1) identifying documents acceptable for the purposes of proving identity and California residency, (2) procedures for verifying the authenticity of the documents, (3) issuance of a temporary license pending verification of any document's authenticity, and (4) hearings to appeal a denial of a license or temporary license.

(c) Emergency regulations adopted for purposes of establishing the documents acceptable to prove identity and residency pursuant to subdivision (b) shall be promulgated by the department in consultation with appropriate interested parties, in accordance with the Administrative Procedure Act (Chapter 3.5 (commencing with Section 11340) of Part 1 of Division 3 of Title 2 of the Government Code), including law enforcement representatives, immigrant rights representatives, labor representatives, and other stakeholders, which may include, but are not limited to, the California Highway Patrol, the California State Sheriffs' Association, and the California Police Chiefs Association. The department shall accept various types of documentation for this purpose, including, but not limited to, the following documents:

(1) A valid, unexpired consular identification document issued by a consulate from the applicant's country of citizenship, or a valid, unexpired passport from the applicant's country of citizenship.

(2) An original birth certificate, or other proof of age, as designated by the department.

(3) A home utility bill, lease or rental agreement, or other proof of California residence, as designated by the department.

(4) The following documents, which, if in a language other than English, shall be accompanied by a certified translation or an affidavit of translation into English:

(A) A marriage license or divorce certificate.

(B) A foreign federal electoral photo card issued on or after January 1, 1991.

(C) A foreign driver's license.

(5) A United States Department of Homeland Security Form I–589, Application for Asylum and for Withholding of Removal.

(6) An official school or college transcript that includes the applicant's date of birth, or a foreign school record that is sealed and includes a photograph of the applicant at the age the record was issued.

(7) A United States Department of Homeland Security Form I–20 or Form DS–2019.

(8) A deed or title to real property.

(9) A property tax bill or statement issued within the previous 12 months.

(10) An income tax return.

(d)(1) A license issued pursuant to this section, including a temporary license issued pursuant to Section 12506, shall include a recognizable feature on the front of the card, such as the letters "DP" instead of, and in the same font size as, the letters "DL," with no other distinguishable feature.

(2) The license shall bear the following notice: "This card is not acceptable for official federal purposes. This license is issued only as a license to drive a motor vehicle. It does not establish eligibility for employment, voter registration, or public benefits."

(3) The notice described in paragraph (2) shall be in lieu of the notice provided in Section 12800.5.

(e) If the United States Department of Homeland Security determines a license issued pursuant to this section does not satisfy the requirements of Section 37.71 of Title 6 of the Code of Federal Regulations, adopted pursuant to paragraph (11) of subdivision (d) of Section 202 of the Real ID Act of 2005 (Public Law 109–13), the department shall modify the license only to the extent necessary to satisfy the requirements of that section.

(f) Notwithstanding Section 40300 or any other law, a peace officer shall not detain or arrest a person solely on the belief that the person is an unlicensed driver, unless the officer has reasonable cause to believe the person driving is under 16 years of age.

(g) The inability to obtain a driver's license pursuant to this section does not abrogate or diminish in any respect the legal requirement of every driver in this state to obey the motor vehicle laws of this state, including laws with respect to licensing, motor vehicle registration, and financial responsibility.

(h) It shall be a violation of law, including, but not limited to, a violation of the Unruh Civil Rights Act (Section 51 of the Civil Code), to discriminate against an individual because he or she holds or presents a license issued under this section.

(i) Information collected pursuant to this section is not a public record and shall not be disclosed by the department, except as required by law.

(j) A license issued pursuant to this section shall not be used to consider an individual's citizenship or immigration status as a basis for a criminal investigation, arrest, or detention.

(k) On or before January 1, 2018, the California Research Bureau shall compile and submit to the Legislature and the Governor a report of any violations of subdivisions (h) and (j). Information pertaining to any specific individual shall not be provided in the report.

(*l*) In addition to the fees required by Section 14900, a person applying for an original license pursuant to this section may be required to pay an additional fee determined by the department that is sufficient to offset the reasonable administrative costs of implementing the provisions of the act that added this section. If this additional fee is assessed, it shall only apply until June 30, 2017.

(m) This section shall become operative on January 1, 2015, or on the date that the director executes a declaration pursuant to Section 12801.11, whichever is sooner.

(n) This section shall become inoperative on the effective date of a final judicial determination made by any court of appellate jurisdiction that any provision of the act that added this section, or its application, either in whole or in part, is enjoined, found unconstitutional, or held invalid for any reason. The department shall post this information on its Internet Web site. *(Added by Stats.2013, c. 524 (A.B.60), § 15, operative contingent.)*

§ 12801.10. Commercial driver's license; submission of social security account number required

Section operative the sooner of Jan. 1, 2015 or the date the director executes a declaration pursuant to § 12801.11 and operative until the effective date of a judicial determination that any provision of the act that added this section is enjoined, found unconstitutional or held invalid.

(a) Nothing in Section 1653.5, 12800, 12801, 12801.5, or 12801.9 authorizes an individual to apply for, or be issued, a commercial driver's license without the submission of his or her social security account number upon application.

(b) This section shall become operative on January 1, 2015, or on the date that the director executes a declaration pursuant to Section 12801.11, whichever is sooner.

(c) This section shall become inoperative on the effective date of a final judicial determination made by any court of appellate jurisdiction that any provision of the act that added this section, or its application, either in whole or in part, is enjoined, found unconstitutional, or held invalid for any reason. The department shall post this information on its Internet Web site. *(Added by Stats.2013, c. 524 (A.B.60), § 16, operative contingent.)*

§ 12801.11. Determination that department is prepared to issue licenses pursuant to § 12801.09; issuance of declaration

Section operative until the effective date of a judicial determination that any provision of the act that added this section is enjoined, found unconstitutional or held invalid.

(a) If the director determines that the department is prepared to begin issuing driver's licenses pursuant to Section 12801.9 on a date sooner than January 1, 2015,

the director shall execute a declaration stating that determination and date and, within five business days, provide a copy of that declaration to the appropriate fiscal and policy committees of the Legislature and to the Governor, and shall post this information on its Internet Web site.

(b) This section shall become inoperative on the effective date of a final judicial determination made by any court of appellate jurisdiction that any provision of the act that added this section, or its application, either in whole or in part, is enjoined, found unconstitutional, or held invalid for any reason. The department shall post this information on its Internet Web site. *(Added by Stats.2013, c. 524 (A.B.60), § 17.)*

§ 12802. Signature and verification

Every original application shall be signed and verified by the applicant before a person authorized to administer oaths and the applicant shall submit such evidence of age as the department may require, and, if the applicant is a minor, the application shall also be signed and verified as provided in Chapter 2 (commencing with Section 17700) of Division 9. *(Stats.1959, c. 3, p. 1618, § 12802. Amended by Stats.1965, c. 622, p. 1959, § 1; Stats.1993, c. 272 (A.B.301), § 22, eff. Aug. 2, 1993.)*

§ 12802.5. Applicant under age 21; notice regarding driving with blood-alcohol concentration of .01 percent or greater

Before issuing a driver's license or permit to any person under 21 years of age, both of the following shall occur:

(a) The department shall inform the applicant of the following:

(1) It is unlawful to drive with a blood-alcohol concentration of 0.01 percent or greater, as measured by a preliminary alcohol screening test or other chemical test.

(2) The penalty for so driving is a one-year suspension of the driving privilege.

(3) A refusal to take, or a failure to complete, a preliminary alcohol screening test or other chemical test for the purpose of determining the level of alcohol pursuant to Section 13388 shall result in a one-year suspension of the driving privilege.

(4) The fee for reissuance of a driver's license after suspension for a violation of Section 23136 is one hundred dollars ($100). This fee is in addition to any

other fees that may be imposed by the department in connection with reissuance of a driver's license.

(b) The applicant shall sign a statement that acknowledges that he or she has been notified of the information specified in subdivision (a). *(Added by Stats.1993, c. 899 (S.B.689), § 2. Amended by Stats.1998, c. 118 (S.B.1186), § 1.27, operative July 1, 1999; Stats.1999, c. 22 (S.B.24), § 7, eff. May 26, 1999, operative July 1, 1999.)*

§ 12803. Examinations for license

Upon application for an original license, except student licenses, the department shall require an examination of the applicant and shall make provision therefor before an officer or employee or authorized representative of the department in the county wherein the applicant resides. *(Stats.1959, c. 3, p. 1619, § 12803.)*

Cross References

Abandonment or dumping of animals,
    Driver's examination questions, see Vehicle Code § 1666.5.
    Driver's handbook, information relating to abandonment or dumping, see Vehicle Code § 1656.3.
    Highway signs, warnings relating to abandonment or dumping of any animal, see Vehicle Code § 21376.
Grounds,
    Permitting denial of license, see Vehicle Code § 12809.
    Requiring denial of license, see Vehicle Code § 12805 et seq.
Renewal of licenses, see Vehicle Code § 12814.
Scope of examination, see Vehicle Code § 12804.9.
Student licenses, see Vehicle Code § 12650 et seq.

§ 12804. Repealed by Stats.1993, c. 272 (A.B.301), § 23, eff. Aug. 2, 1993

§ 12804.1. Repealed by Stats.1990, c. 1360 (S.B.1510), § 30

§ 12804.2. Agricultural operations; exemption from certain endorsement requirements

(a) Notwithstanding Section 15275, a person with at least a class C driver's license is exempt from the endorsement requirements of Section 15275 if all of the following conditions are met:

(1) The person is employed in an agricultural operation and is driving a vehicle, other than a vehicle used in common or contract motor carriage, controlled by a farmer and transporting agricultural products or farm machinery or supplies to or from a farm.

(2)(A) The person has completed an agricultural hazardous materials transportation program offered or approved by the Department of the California Highway Patrol. The Department of the California Highway Patrol shall make the program available at no cost, and the program shall contain information specifically applicable to the safe transportation of agricultural chemicals and shall not be less than two hours in length. If the commissioner determines that the program cannot be offered in a particular area of the state because of personnel constraints, a person in that area may instead comply with this requirement by receiving agricultural

hazardous materials training, in a program and manner approved by the Department of the California Highway Patrol, from an organization or a person in a supervisory position that has been certified by the Department of the California Highway Patrol.

(B) Upon successful completion of the program specified in subparagraph (A), a verification of training, valid for four years, shall be issued by the instructor and shall be carried by the person when operating an implement of husbandry or a motor vehicle required to display placards or markings pursuant to Section 27903 or which is hauling hazardous waste, as defined in Sections 25115 and 25117 of the Health and Safety Code. Within 10 days of issuance by the instructor, a copy of the verification shall be forwarded by the person completing the training to the department for inclusion on the permanent driving record of the person, together with a fee of twelve dollars ($12).

(C) The department, in consultation with the Department of the California Highway Patrol, shall develop a suitable form for verification of training.

(3) The person has, within the vehicle, informational material approved by the Department of the California Highway Patrol, in both English and Spanish, outlining basic safety procedures to be followed in the event of an accident. The Department of the California Highway Patrol shall provide the information required by this subdivision and make it available at no cost to the person.

(4) The person is operating a vehicle which is an implement of husbandry or a motor vehicle requiring a class C driver's license and the distance which the vehicle is being operated between the final point of distribution and the ultimate point of application or from part of a farm to another part thereof, or from one farm to another, is not more than 50 miles.

(5) In lieu of a report of a medical examination required by Section 12804.9, an applicant for a certificate pursuant to paragraph (3) shall, upon application and every two years thereafter, submit medical information on a form approved by the department. A person who obtains a verification of training pursuant to this section, but does not meet the medical requirements for a hazardous materials endorsement established by the department under Section 12804.9, is not qualified to transport hazardous materials.

(6) For purposes of the penalties and sanctions prescribed by Article 7 (commencing with Section 15300) of Chapter 7, the operation of a vehicle pursuant to this subdivision is deemed to be the operation of a commercial motor vehicle.

(b) Implementation dates for this section may be established by the Department of Motor Vehicles by regulation in order to accomplish an orderly certification program. *(Added by Stats.1986, c. 741, § 3. Amended by Stats.1990, c. 115 (S.B.1581), § 1, eff. May 25, 1990; Stats.1990, c. 1360 (S.B.1510), § 30.5; Stats.1993, c. 272 (A.B.301), § 24, eff. Aug. 2, 1993.)*

§ 12804.3.   Repealed by Stats.1990, c. 1360 (S.B.1510), § 31

§ 12804.4.   Repealed by Stats.1988, c. 913, § 2, operative Jan. 1, 1993

§ 12804.5.   Changes in classification of vehicles minors licensed to operate; consent of parents

The class of vehicles permitted to be operated as shown on a driver's license held by a minor shall not be changed, unless the parents, guardians, or person having custody of such minor gives written consent to the department for such a change. *(Added by Stats.1972, c. 97, p. 132, § 1.)*

§ 12804.6.   Transit busdrivers; required certification; qualifications; employee records

(a) A person shall not operate a transit bus transporting passengers unless that person has received from the department a certificate to operate a transit bus or is certified to drive a schoolbus or school pupil activity bus pursuant to Section 12517.

(b) All transit busdrivers shall comply with standards established in Section 40083 of the Education Code. The Department of Motor Vehicles shall establish an implementation program for transit busdrivers to meet these requirements. A transit busdriver who was employed as a busdriver on or before July 1, 1990, shall comply with Section 40085.5 of the Education Code instead of Section 40083 of that code in order to receive his or her original certificate.

(c) Implementation procedures for the issuance of transit busdrivers' certificates may be established by the Department of Motor Vehicles as necessary to implement an orderly transit busdriver training program.

(d) The department shall issue a transit busdriver certificate to a person who provides either of the following:

(1) Proof that he or she has complied with Section 40083 of the Education Code.

(2) Proof that he or she has complied with Section 40085.5 of the Education Code.

(e) The department may charge a fee of ten dollars ($10) to an applicant for an original or a duplicate or renewal certificate under this section.

(f) The department shall issue a certificate to the applicant. The status of the certificate shall also become part of the pull notice and periodic reports issued pursuant to Section 1808.1. The certificate or the pull notice or periodic reports shall become part of, the person's employee records for the purpose of inspection pursuant to Sections 1808.1 and 34501. It shall be unlawful for the employer to permit a person to drive a transit bus who does not have a valid certificate.

(g) The term of a certificate shall be a period not to exceed five years, and shall expire with the driver's license. *(Added by Stats.1989, c. 1136, § 4, operative July 1, 1990. Amended by Stats.1990, c. 65 (A.B.1790), § 15,*

440

eff. May 1, 1990; Stats.1996, c. 1043 (A.B.2352), § 4; Stats.2006, c. 574 (A.B.2520), § 9.)

Cross References

Training courses for certification under this section, see Education Code § 40080 et seq.

§ 12804.7.   Two-axle motortruck or implement of husbandry; towing implement of husbandry; class C; speed and distance

Notwithstanding subdivision (b) of Section 12804.9, class C also includes any two-axle motortruck or implement of husbandry weighing 4,000 pounds or more unladen when towing an implement of husbandry as specified in subdivision (n) of Section 36005, except that those vehicles shall not be operated in excess of 25 miles per hour on the highways and for not more than 25 miles on the highway from their point of origin. *(Added by Stats.1987, c. 645, § 1. Amended by Stats.1993, c. 272 (A.B.301), § 25, eff. Aug. 2, 1993.)*

§ 12804.8.   Competency test; safe operation of motor vehicle; development and use; liability

(a) Notwithstanding any other provision of law, the department may conduct studies to develop and identify examinations and tests, to more accurately identify persons who, due to physical or mental factors, or both, are not competent or qualified to safely operate a motor vehicle.

(b) In addition to any other tests or examinations required under this code, the department may require any person applying for an original driver's license or renewal of a driver's license, or any person subject to reexamination under Section 13801, to submit to one or more tests or examinations which are part of a study.

(c) The results and information obtained during the study, through the tests and examinations specified in subdivision (a), shall be used only to assess and evaluate the effectiveness of the tests and examinations and to select tests and examinations for use by the department, and for no other purpose. The results of the tests are confidential and shall not be disclosed to any person.

(d) No public entity or employee shall be liable for any loss, detriment, or injury resulting directly or indirectly from the department's acts or failure to act on information received through the studies. *(Added by Stats.1993, c. 546 (A.B.2284), § 2.)*

§ 12804.9.   Examination and driving test

(a)(1) The examination shall include all of the following:

(A) A test of the applicant's knowledge and understanding of the provisions of this code governing the operation of vehicles upon the highways.

(B) A test of the applicant's ability to read and understand simple English used in highway traffic and directional signs.

(C) A test of the applicant's understanding of traffic signs and signals, including the bikeway signs, markers, and traffic control devices established by the Department of Transportation.

(D) An actual demonstration of the applicant's ability to exercise ordinary and reasonable control in operating a motor vehicle by driving it under the supervision of an examining officer. The applicant shall submit to an examination appropriate to the type of motor vehicle or combination of vehicles he or she desires a license to drive, except that the department may waive the driving test part of the examination for any applicant who submits a license issued by another state, territory, or possession of the United States, the District of Columbia, or the Commonwealth of Puerto Rico if the department verifies through any acknowledged national driver record data source that there are no stops, holds, or other impediments to its issuance. The examining officer may request to see evidence of financial responsibility for the vehicle prior to supervising the demonstration of the applicant's ability to operate the vehicle. The examining officer may refuse to examine an applicant who is unable to provide proof of financial responsibility for the vehicle, unless proof of financial responsibility is not required by this code.

(E) A test of the hearing and eyesight of the applicant, and of other matters that may be necessary to determine the applicant's mental and physical fitness to operate a motor vehicle upon the highways, and whether any grounds exist for refusal of a license under this code.

(2)(A) Before a class A or class B driver's license, or class C driver's license with a commercial endorsement, may be issued or renewed, the applicant shall have in his or her driver record a valid report of a medical examination of the applicant given not more than two years prior to the date of the application by a health care professional. As used in this paragraph, "health care professional" means a person who is licensed, certified, or registered in accordance with applicable state laws and regulations to practice medicine and perform physical examinations in the United States. Health care professionals are doctors of medicine, doctors of osteopathy, physician assistants, and registered advanced practice nurses, or doctors of chiropractic who are clinically competent to perform the medical examination presently required of motor carrier drivers by the United States Department of Transportation. The report shall be on a form approved by the department. In establishing the requirements, consideration may be given to the standards presently required of motor carrier drivers by the Federal Motor Carrier Safety Administration.

(B) The department may accept a federal waiver of one or more physical qualification standards if the waiver is accompanied by a report of a nonqualifying medical examination for a class A or class B driver's license, or class C driver's license with a commercial endorsement, pursuant to Section 391.41(a)(3)(ii) of Subpart E of Part 391 of Title 49 of the Code of Federal Regulations.

(3) A physical defect of the applicant that, in the opinion of the department, is compensated for to ensure safe driving ability, shall not prevent the issuance of a license to the applicant.

(b) In accordance with the following classifications, an applicant for a driver's license shall be required to submit to an examination appropriate to the type of motor vehicle or combination of vehicles the applicant desires a license to drive:

(1) Class A includes the following:

(A) Except as provided in subparagraph (H) of paragraph (3), a combination of vehicles, if a vehicle being towed has a gross vehicle weight rating or gross vehicle weight of more than 10,000 pounds.

(B) A vehicle towing more than one vehicle.

(C) A trailer bus.

(D) The operation of all vehicles under class B and class C.

(2) Class B includes the following:

(A) Except as provided in subparagraph (H) of paragraph (3), a single vehicle with a gross vehicle weight rating or gross vehicle weight of more than 26,000 pounds.

(B) A single vehicle with three or more axles, except any three-axle vehicle weighing less than 6,000 pounds.

(C) A bus with a gross vehicle weight rating or gross vehicle weight of more than 26,000 pounds, except a trailer bus.

(D) A farm labor vehicle.

(E) A single vehicle with three or more axles or a gross vehicle weight rating or gross vehicle weight of more than 26,000 pounds towing another vehicle with a gross vehicle weight rating or gross vehicle weight of 10, 000 pounds or less.

(F) A house car over 40 feet in length, excluding safety devices and safety bumpers.

(G) The operation of all vehicles covered under class C.

(3) Class C includes the following:

(A) A two-axle vehicle with a gross vehicle weight rating or gross vehicle weight of 26,000 pounds or less, including when the vehicle is towing a trailer or semitrailer with a gross vehicle weight rating or gross vehicle weight of 10,000 pounds or less.

(B) Notwithstanding subparagraph (A), a two-axle vehicle weighing 4,000 pounds or more unladen when towing a trailer coach not exceeding 9,000 pounds gross.

(C) A house car of 40 feet in length or less.

(D) A three-axle vehicle weighing 6,000 pounds gross or less.

(E) A house car of 40 feet in length or less or a vehicle towing another vehicle with a gross vehicle weight rating of 10,000 pounds or less, including when a tow dolly is used. A person driving a vehicle may not tow another vehicle in violation of Section 21715.

(F)(i) A two-axle vehicle weighing 4,000 pounds or more unladen when towing either a trailer coach or a fifth-wheel travel trailer not exceeding 10,000 pounds gross vehicle weight rating, when the towing of the trailer is not for compensation.

(ii) A two-axle vehicle weighing 4,000 pounds or more unladen when towing a fifth-wheel travel trailer exceeding 10,000 pounds, but not exceeding 15,000 pounds, gross vehicle weight rating, when the towing of the trailer is not for compensation, and if the person has passed a specialized written examination provided by the department relating to the knowledge of this code and other safety aspects governing the towing of recreational vehicles upon the highway.

The authority to operate combinations of vehicles under this subparagraph may be granted by endorsement on a class C license upon completion of that written examination.

(G) A vehicle or combination of vehicles with a gross combination weight rating or a gross vehicle weight rating, as those terms are defined in subdivisions (j) and (k), respectively, of Section 15210, of 26,000 pounds or less, if all of the following conditions are met:

(i) Is operated by a farmer, an employee of a farmer, or an instructor credentialed in agriculture as part of an instructional program in agriculture at the high school, community college, or university level.

(ii) Is used exclusively in the conduct of agricultural operations.

(iii) Is not used in the capacity of a for-hire carrier or for compensation.

(H) Firefighting equipment, provided that the equipment is operated by a person who holds a firefighter endorsement pursuant to Section 12804.11.

(I) A motorized scooter.

(J) A bus with a gross vehicle weight rating or gross vehicle weight of 26,000 pounds or less, except a trailer bus.

(K) Class C does not include a two-wheel motorcycle or a two-wheel motor-driven cycle.

(4) Class M1. A two-wheel motorcycle or a motor-driven cycle. Authority to operate a vehicle included in a class M1 license may be granted by endorsement on a class A, B, or C license upon completion of an appropriate examination.

(5)(A) Class M2 includes the following:

(i) A motorized bicycle or moped, or a bicycle with an attached motor, except a motorized bicycle described in subdivision (b) of Section 406.

(ii) A motorized scooter.

(B) Authority to operate vehicles included in class M2 may be granted by endorsement on a class A, B, or C license upon completion of an appropriate examination,

except that no endorsement is required for a motorized scooter. Persons holding a class M1 license or endorsement may operate vehicles included in class M2 without further examination.

(c) A driver's license or driver certificate is not valid for operating a commercial motor vehicle, as defined in subdivision (b) of Section 15210, any other motor vehicle defined in paragraph (1) or (2) of subdivision (b), or any other vehicle requiring a driver to hold any driver certificate or any driver's license endorsement under Section 15275, unless a medical certificate approved by the department that has been issued within two years of the date of the operation of that vehicle and a copy of the medical examination report from which the certificate was issued is on file with the department. Otherwise, the license is valid only for operating class C vehicles that are not commercial vehicles, as defined in subdivision (b) of Section 15210, and for operating class M1 or M2 vehicles, if so endorsed, that are not commercial vehicles, as defined in subdivision (b) of Section 15210.

(d) A license or driver certificate issued prior to the enactment of Chapter 7 (commencing with Section 15200) is valid to operate the class or type of vehicles specified under the law in existence prior to that enactment until the license or certificate expires or is otherwise suspended, revoked, or canceled. Upon application for renewal or replacement of a driver's license, endorsement, or certificate required to operate a commercial motor vehicle, a valid medical certificate on a form approved by the department shall be submitted to the department.

(e) The department may accept a certificate of driving skill that is issued by an employer, authorized by the department to issue a certificate under Section 15250, of the applicant, in lieu of a driving test, on class A or B applications, if the applicant has first qualified for a class C license and has met the other examination requirements for the license for which he or she is applying. The certificate may be submitted as evidence of the applicant's skill in the operation of the types of equipment covered by the license for which he or she is applying.

(f) The department may accept a certificate of competence in lieu of a driving test on class M1 or M2 applications, when the certificate is issued by a law enforcement agency for its officers who operate class M1 or M2 vehicles in their duties, if the applicant has met the other examination requirements for the license for which he or she is applying.

(g) The department may accept a certificate of satisfactory completion of a novice motorcyclist training program approved by the commissioner pursuant to Section 2932 in lieu of a driving test on class M1 or M2 applications, if the applicant has met the other examination requirements for the license for which he or she is applying. The department shall review and approve the written and driving test used by a program to determine whether the program may issue a certificate of completion.

(h) Notwithstanding subdivision (b), a person holding a valid California driver's license of any class may operate a short-term rental motorized bicycle without taking any special examination for the operation of a motorized bicycle, and without having a class M2 endorsement on that license. As used in this subdivision, "short-term" means 48 hours or less.

(i) A person under the age of 21 years shall not be issued a class M1 or M2 license or endorsement unless he or she provides evidence satisfactory to the department of completion of a motorcycle safety training program that is operated pursuant to Article 2 (commencing with Section 2930) of Chapter 5 of Division 2.

(j) A driver of a vanpool vehicle may operate with a class C license but shall possess evidence of a medical examination required for a class B license when operating vanpool vehicles. In order to be eligible to drive the vanpool vehicle, the driver shall keep in the vanpool vehicle a statement, signed under penalty of perjury, that he or she has not been convicted of reckless driving, drunk driving, or a hit-and-run offense in the last five years. *(Added by Stats.2004, c. 952 (A.B.3049), § 6.5, operative Sept. 20, 2005. Amended by Stats.2005, c. 199 (A.B.1748), § 3; Stats.2006, c. 574 (A.B.2520), § 10; Stats.2007, c. 130 (A.B.299), § 235; Stats.2010, c. 360 (A.B.1648), § 2; Stats.2011, c. 296 (A.B.1023), § 304; Stats.2011, c. 92 (A.B.82), § 1, eff. July 25, 2011; Stats. 2012, c. 670 (A.B.2188), § 4; Stats.2013, c. 649 (A.B. 1047), § 2.)*

Cross References

Driver's examination, question on punishment for eluding police, see Vehicle Code § 1666.1.

Medical report, physical examination, bus drivers and farm labor vehicle operators, see Vehicle Code § 12517.2.

§ 12804.10. Driving of house cars; noncommercial class B driver's license with endorsement

(a) Notwithstanding any other provision of law, a person issued a class C license under paragraph (3) of subdivision (b) of Section 12804.9 may drive any house car of 40 feet in length or less without obtaining a noncommercial class B driver's license with house car endorsement as described in subdivision (b).

(b) Any person seeking to drive any house car over 40 feet in length, excluding safety devices and safety bumpers, shall obtain a noncommercial class B driver's license with house car endorsement as described in this subdivision. The applicant for that endorsement shall pass a specialized written examination and demonstrate the ability to exercise ordinary and reasonable control in operating that vehicle by driving it under the supervision of an examining officer. Upon satisfactory completion of the examination and demonstration, the applicant shall be issued a noncommercial class B driver's license with house car endorsement by the department. Upon application for an endorsement to operate this vehicle, and

every two years thereafter, the applicant shall submit medical information on a form approved by the department. *(Added by Stats.2001, c. 658 (A.B.67), § 3, eff. Oct. 10, 2001.)*

§ 12804.11. Requirements to operate firefighting equipment; qualifications for firefighter endorsement; fees; conditions; license requirements of employees or volunteers

(a) To operate firefighting equipment, a driver, including a tiller operator, is required to do either of the following:

(1) Obtain and maintain a firefighter endorsement issued by the department and obtain and maintain a class C license as described in Section 12804.9, a restricted class A license as described in Section 12804.12, or a noncommercial class B license as described in Section 12804.10.

(2) Obtain and maintain a class A or B license as described in Section 12804.9 * * * and, as appropriate, for the size and configuration of the firefighting equipment operated.

(b) To qualify for a firefighter endorsement the driver shall do all of the following:

(1)(A) Provide to the department proof of current employment as a firefighter or registration as a volunteer firefighter with a fire department and evidence of fire equipment operation training by providing a letter * * * or other indication * * * from the chief of the fire department * * * or his or her designee.

(B) For purposes of this section, evidence of fire equipment operation training means the applicant has successfully completed Fire Apparatus Driver/Operator 1A taught by an instructor registered with the Office of the State Fire Marshal or fire department driver training that meets all of the following requirements:

(i) Meets or exceeds the standards outlined in NFPA 1002, Chapter 4 (2008 version) or the Fire Apparatus Driver/Operator 1A course adopted by the Office of the State Fire Marshal.

(ii) Prepares the applicant to safely operate the department's fire equipment that the applicant will be authorized to operate.

(iii) Includes a classroom (cognitive) portion of at least 16 hours.

(iv) Includes a manipulative portion of at least 14 hours, which includes directly supervised behind-the-wheel driver training.

(C) Driver training shall be conducted by a person who is registered with the Office of the State Fire Marshal to instruct a Fire Apparatus Driver/Operator 1A course or a person who meets all of the following criteria:

(i) Possesses a minimum of five years of fire service experience as an emergency vehicle operator, three of which must be at the rank of engineer or higher.

443

(ii) Possesses a valid California class A or B license or a class A or B license restricted to the operation of firefighting equipment.

(iii) Is certified as a qualified training instructor or training officer by the State of California, the federal government, or a county training officers' association.

(2) Pass the written firefighter examination developed by the department with the cooperation of the Office of the State Fire * * * Marshal.

(3) Upon application and every two years thereafter, submit medical information on a form approved by the department.

(c) There shall be no additional charge for adding a firefighter endorsement to an original license or when renewing a license. To add a firefighter endorsement to an existing license when not renewing the license, the applicant shall pay the fee for a duplicate license pursuant to Section 14901.

(d)(1) A driver of firefighting equipment is subject to the requirements of subdivision (a) if both of the following conditions exist:

(A) The equipment is operated by a person employed as a firefighter by a federal or state agency, by a regularly organized fire department of a city, county, city and county, or district, or by a tribal fire department or registered as a volunteer member of a regularly organized fire department having official recognition of the city, county, city and county, or district in which the department is located, or of a tribal fire department.

(B) The motor vehicle is used to travel to and from the scene of an emergency situation, or to transport equipment used in the control of an emergency situation, and which is owned, leased, or rented by, or under the exclusive control of, a federal or state agency, a regularly organized fire department of a city, county, city and county, or district, a volunteer fire department having official recognition of the city, county, city and county, or district in which the department is located, or a tribal fire department.

(2) A driver of firefighting equipment is not required to obtain and maintain a firefighter endorsement pursuant to paragraph (1) of subdivision (a) if the driver is operating the firefighting equipment for training purposes, during a nonemergency, while under the direct supervision of a fire department employee who is properly licensed to operate the equipment and is authorized by the fire department to provide training.

(e) For purposes of this section, a tiller operator is the driver of the rear free-axle portion of a ladder truck.

(f) For purposes of this section, "firefighting equipment" means a motor vehicle, that meets the definition of a class A or class B vehicle described in subdivision (b) of Section 12804.9, that is used to travel to and from the scene of an emergency situation, or to transport equipment used in the control of an emergency situation, and that is owned, leased, or rented by, or under the exclusive

control of, a federal or state agency, a regularly organized fire department of a city, county, city and county, or district, or a volunteer fire department having official recognition of the city, county, city and county, or district in which the department is located.

(g) Notwithstanding paragraph (1) of subdivision (a), a regularly organized fire department, having official recognition of the city, county, city and county, or district in which the department is located, may require an employee or a volunteer of the fire department who is a driver or operator of firefighting equipment to hold a class A or B license.

(h) This section applies to a person hired by a fire department, or to a person renewing a driver's license, on or after January 1, 2011. *(Added by Stats.2010, c. 360 (A.B.1648), § 3. Amended by Stats.2011, c. 296 (A.B. 1023), § 305; Stats.2011, c. 92 (A.B.82), § 2, eff. July 25, 2011; Stats.2012, c. 162 (S.B.1171), § 181; Stats.2012, c. 111 (A.B.1567), § 1; Stats.2013, c. 76 (A.B.383), § 194.)*

§ 12804.12. Restricted class A driver's license for certain 2-axle vehicles; medical information

(a) The department may issue a restricted class A driver's license for the operation of any two-axle vehicle weighing 4,000 pounds or more unladen when towing a trailer coach exceeding 10,000 pounds gross vehicle weight rating, or a fifth-wheel travel trailer exceeding 15,000 pounds gross vehicle weight rating, when the towing of the trailer is not for compensation.

(b) In lieu of a report of a medical examination required by Section 12804.9, an applicant for a restricted license issued pursuant to subdivision (a) shall, upon application and every two years thereafter, submit medical information on a form approved by the department.

(Added by Stats.1990, c. 1358 (A.B.4261), § 5. Amended by Stats.1993, c. 272 (A.B.301), § 28, eff. Aug. 2, 1993.)

§ 12804.13. Repealed by Stats.1995, c. 766 (S.B.726), § 14, operative Jan. 1, 1997

§ 12804.14. Restricted class A driver's licenses for certain two-axle vehicles towing livestock trailers

(a) The department may issue a restricted class A driver's license for the operation of any two-axle vehicle weighing 4,000 pounds or more unladen when towing a livestock trailer exceeding 10,000 pounds, but not exceeding 15,000 pounds gross vehicle weight rating or gross vehicle weight, if all of the following conditions are met:

(1) The vehicle is controlled and operated by a farmer.

(2) The vehicle is used to transport livestock to or from a farm.

(3) The vehicle is not used in the operations of a common or contract carrier.

(4) The vehicle is used within 150 miles of the person's farm.

(b) The requirements of subdivision (a) incorporate the guidelines published by the Federal Highway Administration in the Federal Register on September 26, 1988 (53 FR 37313). The department shall follow those guidelines in acting pursuant to this section as those guidelines now exist and as they are hereafter amended.

(c) In lieu of a report of a medical examination required by Sections 12804 and 12804.9, a licensed California driver applying for a restricted license issued pursuant to subdivision (a) shall, upon application and every two years thereafter, submit medical information on a form approved by the department. *(Added by Stats. 1993, c. 1012 (A.B.1597), § 1. Amended by Stats.1994, c. 515 (A.B.2818), § 2; Stats.1995, c. 766 (S.B.726), § 15; Stats.1996, c. 10 (A.B.1869), § 14, eff. Feb. 9, 1996.)*

§ 12804.15. Driving of house cars; license requirements

(a) Notwithstanding Section 362, for purposes of this section "house car" means a vehicle described in subdivision (b) of Section 12804.10.

(b)(1) Except as provided under paragraph (2), no person may operate a house car unless that person has in his or her possession a valid driver's license of the appropriate class and an endorsement thereto issued by the department to permit operation of the house car.

(2) A nonresident may not operate a house car in this state unless that person is in possession of an out-of-state driver's license authorizing the operation of that vehicle.

(c) An endorsement to drive a house car may be issued only if the applicant meets all of the following conditions:

(1) The applicant successfully completes an examination prescribed by the department to determine qualification for the endorsement.

(2) Upon initial application and every two years thereafter, the applicant submits medical information on a form approved by the department to verify that the person meets the minimum medical requirements established by the department for operation of a house car.

(3) Upon application for issuance of an original driver's license or renewal driver's license pursuant to subdivision (b) of Section 12804.10, there shall be paid to the department a fee of thirty-four dollars ($34) for a license that will expire on the applicant's fifth birthday following the date of the application.

(d) The department may deny, suspend, or revoke an endorsement to drive a house car when the applicant does not meet any requirement for the issuance or retention of the endorsement. *(Added by Stats.2001, c. 658 (A.B.67), § 4, eff. Oct. 10, 2001.)*

§ 12805. Refusal to issue or renew driver's license; mandatory grounds

The department shall not issue a driver's license to, or renew a driver's license of, any person:

(a) Who is not of legal age to receive a driver's license.

(b) Whose best corrected visual acuity is $20/200$ or worse in that person's better eye, as verified by an optometrist or ophthalmologist. No person may use a bioptic telescopic or similar lens to meet the $20/200$ visual acuity standards.

(c) Who is unable, as shown by examination, to understand traffic signs or signals or who does not have a reasonable knowledge of the provisions of this code governing the operations of vehicles upon the highways.

(d) When it is determined, by examination or other evidence, that the person is unable to safely operate a motor vehicle upon a highway.

(e) Who is unable to read and understand simple English used in highway traffic and directional signs. This subdivision does not apply to any person holding an operator's or chauffeur's license issued by this state and valid on September 11, 1957.

(f) Who holds a valid driver's license issued by a foreign jurisdiction unless the license has been surrendered to the department, or is lost or destroyed.

(g) Who has ever held, or is the holder of, a license to drive issued by another state, territory, or possession of the United States, the District of Columbia, or the Commonwealth of Puerto Rico, and that license has been suspended by reason, in whole or in part, of a conviction of a traffic violation until the suspension period has terminated, except that the department may issue a license to the applicant if, in the opinion of the department, it will be safe to issue a license to a person whose license to drive was suspended by a state that is not a party to the Driver License Compact provided for in Chapter 6 (commencing with Section 15000) of Division 6.

(h) Who has ever held, or is the holder of, a license to drive issued by another state, territory, or possession of the United States, the District of Columbia or the Commonwealth of Puerto Rico, and that license has been revoked by reason, in whole or in part, of a conviction of a traffic violation, until the revocation has been terminated or after the expiration of one year from the date the license was revoked, whichever occurs first, except that the department may issue a license to the applicant if, in the opinion of the department, it will be safe to issue a license to a person whose license to drive was revoked by a state that is not a party to the Driver License Compact provided for in Chapter 6 (commencing with Section 15000) of Division 6. *(Added by Stats.1987, c. 321, § 4. Amended by Stats.2000, c. 985 (S.B.335), § 7.)*

Cross References

Court determination that grounds exist, investigation, see Vehicle Code § 13208.
Driving when license suspended or revoked as offense, see Vehicle Code § 14601.
Grounds,
  Permitting denial of license, see Vehicle Code § 12809.
  Permitting revocation or suspension of license, see Vehicle Code §§ 13352, 13359.

Requiring denial of license, see Vehicle Code §§ 12807, 15024.

Requiring revocation of license, see Vehicle Code § 13350.

Minimum age for issuance of license,

Driving for hire, see Vehicle Code § 12515.

School bus driver, see Vehicle Code § 12516.

Temporary license issuance notwithstanding failure of written examination on first attempt, see Vehicle Code § 12506.

Traffic laws, see Vehicle Code § 21000 et seq.

§ 12806. Refusal to issue or renew driver's license; discretionary grounds

The department may refuse to issue to, or renew a driver's license of, any person:

(a) Who is rendered incapable of safely operating a motor vehicle because of alcoholism, excessive and chronic use of alcoholic beverages, or addiction to, or habitual use of, any drug.

(b) Who is addicted to the use of narcotic drugs unless the person is participating in a narcotic treatment program approved pursuant to Article 3 (commencing with Section 11875) of Chapter 1 of Part 3 of Division 10.5 of the Health and Safety Code, in which case the person may be issued a probationary license, subject to reasonable terms and conditions, if that drug usage does not affect the person's ability to exercise reasonable and ordinary control in operating a motor vehicle on the highway.

(c) Who has a disorder characterized by lapses of consciousness or who has experienced, within the last three years, either a lapse of consciousness or an episode of marked confusion caused by any condition which may bring about recurrent lapses, or who has any physical or mental disability, disease, or disorder which could affect the safe operation of a motor vehicle unless the department has medical information which indicates the person may safely operate a motor vehicle. In making its determination, the department may rely on any relevant information available to the department. *(Added by Stats.1987, c. 321, § 6. Amended by Stats.1991, c. 13 (A.B.37), § 28, eff. Feb. 13, 1991; Stats.1995, c. 455 (A.B.1113), § 30, eff. Sept. 5, 1995.)*

Cross References

Personal service, notice of suspension or revocation of driving license for violation of this section, see Vehicle Code § 13106.

§ 12806.5. Schoolbus, school pupil activity, youth bus-driver, farm labor vehicle, or general public paratransit vehicle certificate; suspension or revocation; regulations

The department may adopt regulations specifying, in addition to any cause provided by statute, the circumstances which are grounds for the suspension or revocation of a schoolbus, school pupil activity, youth busdriver, farm labor vehicle, or general public paratransit vehicle certificate. *(Added by Stats.1985, c. 535, § 1. Amended by Stats.1990, c. 1360 (S.B.1510), § 32.)*

446

§ 12807. Additional grounds for refusal

The department shall not issue or renew a driver's license to any person:

(a) When a license previously issued to the person under this code has been suspended until the expiration of the period of the suspension, unless cause for suspension has been removed.

(b) When a license previously issued to the person under this code has been revoked until the expiration of one year after the date of the revocation, except where a different period of revocation is prescribed by this code, or unless the cause for revocation has been removed.

(c) When the department has received a notice pursuant to Section 40509 or 40509.5, unless the department has received a certificate as provided in those sections.

(Stats.1959, c. 3, p. 1620, § 12807. Amended by Stats.1961, c. 1653, p. 3608, § 1; Stats.1971, c. 1532, p. 3036, § 1, operative May 3, 1972; Stats.1996, c. 224 (S.B.1579), § 2.)

Cross References

Grounds,

Permitting denial of license, see Vehicle Code § 12809.

Requiring denial of license, see Vehicle Code §§ 12805 et seq., 15024.

Suspension or revocation of license, see Vehicle Code §§ 13352, 13355, 13357, 13359, 13361.

Renewal of licenses, see Vehicle Code § 12814.

§ 12808. Record of applicant

(a) The department shall, before issuing or renewing any license, check the record of the applicant for conviction of traffic violations and traffic accidents.

(b) The department shall, before issuing or renewing any license, check the record of the applicant for notices of failure to appear in court filed with it and shall withhold or shall not issue a license to any applicant who has violated his or her written promise to appear in court unless the department has received a certificate issued by the magistrate or clerk of the court hearing the case in which the promise was given showing that the case has been adjudicated or unless the applicant's record is cleared as provided in Chapter 6 (commencing with Section 41500) of Division 17. In lieu of the certificate of adjudication, a notice from the court stating that the original records have been lost or destroyed shall permit the department to issue a license.

(c)(1) Any notice received by the department pursuant to Section 40509, 40509.1, or 40509.5, except subdivision (c) of Section 40509.5, that has been on file five years may be removed from the department records and destroyed at the discretion of the department.

(2) Any notice received by the department under subdivision (c) of Section 40509.5 that has been on file 10 years may be removed from the department records and destroyed at the discretion of the department.

(d) This section shall become operative on January 1, 2011. *(Added by Stats.2000, c. 985 (S.B.335), § 9, operative Jan. 1, 2011.)*

Cross References

Release from arrest on promise to appear, see Vehicle Code § 40500 et seq.

§ 12808.1. Delinquent parking violations; refusal to issue or renew license

The department shall refuse to issue or renew any license if the applicant has been mailed a notice of delinquent parking violation relating to standing or parking, the processing agency has filed or electronically transmitted to the department an itemization of unpaid parking penalties, including administrative fees pursuant to Section 40220, and the applicant has not paid the parking penalty and administrative fee pursuant to Section 40211, unless he or she pays to the department, at the time of application, the full amount of all outstanding parking penalties and administrative fees, as shown by records of the department. *(Added by Stats.1991, c. 90 (A.B.1297), § 67, eff. June 30, 1991.)*

§ 12809. Grounds permitting refusal; operative date

The department may refuse to issue or renew a driver's license to any person:

(a) If the department is satisfied that the applicant is not entitled to the license under this code.

(b) If the applicant has failed to furnish the department the information required in the application or reasonable additional information requested by the department.

(c) If the department determines that the applicant has made or permitted unlawful use of any driver's license.

(d) If the department determines that the person has knowingly used a false or fictitious name in any application for a license or has impersonated another in making application or in taking any test, or has knowingly made a false statement or knowingly concealed a material fact, or otherwise committed any fraud in any application.

(e) If the department determines that the applicant is a negligent or incompetent operator of a motor vehicle.

(f) If the applicant is convicted of any offense involving the transportation for purpose of sale, or the transportation for compensation, of a controlled substance under Division 10 (commencing with Section 11000) of the Health and Safety Code, and the commission of the offense involved the use or operation of a motor vehicle.

If, however, the driving privilege of the applicant is on probation for a cause related to the use or possession of a narcotic controlled substance, the department may refuse to issue or renew a driver's license to the applicant if the applicant is subsequently convicted of any offense involving the use or possession of a narcotic controlled

substance, whether or not the commission of the offense involved the use or operation of a motor vehicle.

The maximum period of time for which the department may refuse to issue or renew a driver's license to any person pursuant to this subdivision shall be three years from the date of conviction.

(g) If the applicant fails or refuses to surrender to the department, upon its lawful demand, a nonresident minor's certificate which has been canceled.

(h) If the applicant has failed to appear regarding a citation issued for vehicle abandonment as specified in Section 22523.

(i) This section shall become operative on July 1, 1989. *(Added by Stats.1988, c. 1267, § 3, operative July 1, 1989.)*

Cross References

Driving when license suspended or revoked, see Vehicle Code § 14601.
Grounds,
  Permitting revocation or suspension of license, see Vehicle Code §§ 13352, 13359.
  Requiring denial of license, see Vehicle Code § 12805 et seq.
Information required in application, see Vehicle Code § 12800.
Suspension or revocation of driving privilege for a violation of this section, notice by personal service, see Vehicle Code § 13106.

§ 12810. Traffic violation point counts; allocation of points

In determining the violation point count, the following shall apply:

(a) A conviction of failure to stop in the event of an accident in violation of Section 20001 or 20002 shall be given a value of two points.

(b) A conviction of a violation of Section 23152 or 23153 shall be given a value of two points.

(c) A conviction of reckless driving shall be given a value of two points.

(d)(1) A conviction of a violation of subdivision (b) of Section 191.5 or subdivision (c) of Section 192 of the Penal Code, or of Section 2800.2 or 2800.3, subdivision (b) of Section 21651, subdivision (b) of Section 22348, subdivision (a) or (c) of Section 23109, Section 23109.1, or Section 31602 of this code, shall be given a value of two points.

(2) A conviction of a violation of subdivision (a) or (b) of Section 23140 shall be given a value of two points.

(e) A conviction of a violation of Section 14601, 14601.1, 14601.2, 14601.3, or 14601.5 shall be given a value of two points.

(f) Except as provided in subdivision (i), any other traffic conviction involving the safe operation of a motor vehicle upon the highway shall be given a value of one point.

(g) A traffic accident in which the operator is deemed by the department to be responsible shall be given a value of one point.

(h) A conviction of a violation of Section 27360 or 27360.5 shall be given a value of one point.

(i)(1) A violation of paragraph (1), (2), (3), or (5) of subdivision (b) of Section 40001 shall not result in a violation point count being given to the driver if the driver is not the owner of the vehicle.

(2) A conviction of a violation of paragraph (1) or (2) of subdivision (b) of Section 12814.6, subdivision (a) of Section 21116, Section 21207.5, 21708, 21710, 21716, 23120, 24800, or 26707 shall not be given a violation point count.

(3) A violation of subdivision (d) of Section 21712 shall not result in a violation point count.

(4) A violation of Section 23136 shall not result in a violation point count.

(5) A violation of Section 38301, 38301.3, 38301.5, 38304.1, or 38504.1 shall not result in a violation point count.

(j) A conviction for only one violation arising from one occasion of arrest or citation shall be counted in determining the violation point count for the purposes of this section. *(Added by Stats.1984, c. 667, § 9, operative July 1, 1985. Amended by Stats.1985, c. 720, § 1; Stats.1991, c. 13 (A.B.37), § 29, eff. Feb. 13, 1991; Stats.1991, c. 1223 (S.B.1073), § 2; Stats.1992, c. 291 (A.B.1600), § 1; Stats. 1993, c. 899 (S.B.689), § 3; Stats.1994, c. 1220 (A.B. 3132), § 58, eff. Sept. 30, 1994; Stats.1996, c. 1154 (A.B.3020), § 59, eff. Sept. 30, 1996; Stats.2000, c. 675 (S.B.567), § 1; Stats.2000, c. 1035 (S.B.1403), § 18.1; Stats.2002, c. 758 (A.B.3024), § 12; Stats.2004, c. 650 (A.B.3047), § 9; Stats.2005, c. 571 (A.B.1086), § 3; Stats.2006, c. 900 (A.B.1850), § 1; Stats.2007, c. 682 (A.B.430), § 10; Stats.2007, c. 747 (A.B.678), § 16.5; Stats.2009, c. 414 (A.B.134), § 2.)*

Cross References

Accident reports, see Vehicle Code § 20000 et seq.
Driving when license refused, suspended, or revoked as offense, see Vehicle Code § 14601.
Entry of motor vehicle into federal or state wilderness area, public offense and penalties, see Vehicle Code § 38301.3.
Habitual traffic offender defined based on point count pursuant to this section, see Vehicle Code § 14601.3.
Obedience to traffic laws required, see Vehicle Code § 2800 et seq.
Offenses and prosecutions, see Vehicle Code § 40000.1 et seq.
Prohibition on teak surfing, platform dragging, bodysurfing, see Harbors and Navigation Code § 681.
Reckless driving, see Vehicle Code §§ 23103, 23104.
Suspension or revocation of driving privilege for a violation of this section, notice by personal service, see Vehicle Code § 13106.
Traffic violator schools, instructors' licenses, qualifying requirements, see Vehicle Code § 11206.

§ 12810.2. Convictions of § 27315, use of seatbelts; no point count

Notwithstanding subdivision (e) of Section 12810, no violation point count shall be given for a conviction of a

violation of Section 27315. *(Added by Stats.1985, c. 1361, § 1. Amended by Stats.1992, c. 1243 (A.B.3090), § 82, eff. Sept. 30, 1992.)*

§ 12810.3. Violation points

Notwithstanding subdivision (f) of Section 12810, a violation point shall not be given for a conviction of a violation of subdivision (a) of Section 23123, subdivision (a) of Section 23123.5, or subdivision (b) of Section 23124.

(Added by Stats.2006, c. 290 (S.B.1613), § 3, operative July 1, 2008. Amended by Stats.2007, c. 214 (S.B.33), § 1, operative July 1, 2008; Stats.2008, c. 270 (S.B.28), § 1; Stats.2009, c. 200 (S.B.734), § 9.)

§ 12810.4. Conviction of Anti-Gridlock Act of 1987; no violation point counts

Notwithstanding any other provision of law, no violation point shall be given for a conviction of a violation of Section 22526. *(Added by Stats.1993, c. 647 (S.B.952), § 1.)*

§ 12810.5. Traffic violation point count; number for presumption of negligent operation; proof of financial responsibility

(a) Except as otherwise provided in subdivision (b), a person whose driving record shows a violation point count of four or more points in 12 months, six or more points in 24 months, or eight or more points in 36 months shall be prima facie presumed to be a negligent operator of a motor vehicle. In applying this subdivision to a driver, if the person requests and appears at a hearing conducted by the department, the department shall give due consideration to the amount of use or mileage traveled in the operation of a motor vehicle.

(b)(1) A class A or class B licensed driver, except persons holding certificates pursuant to Section 12517, 12519, 12523, 12523.5, or 12527, or an endorsement issued pursuant to paragraph (2) or (5) of subdivision (a) of Section 15278, who is presumed to be a negligent operator pursuant to subdivision (a), and who requests and appears at a hearing and is found to have a driving record violation point count of six or more points in 12 months, eight or more points in 24 months, or 10 or more points in 36 months is presumed to be a prima facie negligent operator. However, the higher point count does not apply if the department reasonably determines that four or more points in 12 months, six or more points in 24 months, or eight or more points in 36 months are attributable to the driver's operation of a vehicle requiring only a class C license, and not requiring a certificate or endorsement, or a class M license.

(2) For purposes of this subdivision, each point assigned pursuant to Section 12810 shall be valued at one and one-half times the value otherwise required by that section for each violation reasonably determined by the department to be attributable to the driver's operation of a vehicle requiring a class A or class B license, or

requiring a certificate or endorsement described in this section.

(c) The department may require a negligent operator whose driving privilege is suspended or revoked pursuant to this section to submit proof of financial responsibility, as defined in Section 16430, on or before the date of reinstatement following the suspension or revocation. The proof of financial responsibility shall be maintained with the department for three years following that date of reinstatement. *(Added by Stats.1991, c. 928 (A.B.1886), § 21, eff. Oct. 14, 1991, operative Jan. 1, 1993. Amended by Stats.1993, c. 272 (A.B.301), § 30, eff. Aug. 2, 1993, operative Jan. 1, 1993; Stats.2003, c. 451 (A.B.1718), § 18; Stats.2007, c. 630 (A.B.1728), § 4.)*

Cross References

Statute making one fact prima facie evidence of another fact, see Evidence Code § 602.

Traffic violator schools, convictions not added to violation point counts for purposes of this section, see Vehicle Code § 42005.

Traffic violator schools, instructors' licenses, qualifying requirements, see Vehicle Code § 11206.

§ 12811. Issuance and contents of license

(a)(1)(A) When the department determines that the applicant is lawfully entitled to a license, it shall issue to the person a driver's license as applied for. The license shall state the class of license for which the licensee has qualified and shall contain the distinguishing number assigned to the applicant, the date of expiration, the true full name, age, and mailing address of the licensee, a brief description and engraved picture or photograph of the licensee for the purpose of identification, and space for the signature of the licensee.

(B) Each license shall also contain a space for the endorsement of a record of each suspension or revocation thereof.

(C) The department shall use whatever process or processes, in the issuance of engraved or colored licenses, that prohibit, as near as possible, the ability to alter or reproduce the license, or prohibit the ability to superimpose a picture or photograph on the license without ready detection.

(2) In addition to the requirements of paragraph (1), a license issued to a person under 18 years of age shall display the words "provisional until age 18."

(b)(1) On and after July 1, 2011, an application for an original or renewal driver's license or identification card shall contain a space for the applicant to enroll in the Donate Life California Organ and Tissue Donor Registry. The application shall include check boxes for an applicant to mark either (A) Yes, add my name to the donor registry or (B) I do not wish to register at this time.

(2) The department shall inquire verbally of an applicant applying in person for an original or renewal driver's license or identification card at a department office as to whether the applicant wishes to enroll in the Donate Life

California Organ and Tissue Donor Registry. Failure or refusal to answer this question or check a box on the application form shall not be a basis for the department to deny an applicant a driver's license or identification card.

(3) The following language shall be included with the question required by paragraph (1):

"Marking 'Yes' adds your name to the Donate Life California Organ and Tissue Donor Registry and a pink 'donor' dot will appear on your license. If you wish to remove your name from the registry you must contact Donate Life California (see back); DMV can remove the pink dot from your licenses but cannot remove you from the registry."

(4) The back of the application shall contain the following statement:

"If, on the front of this form, you marked 'Yes' to register as an organ and tissue donor you are legally authorizing the recovery of organs and tissues in the event of your death. Registering as a donor will not affect your medical treatment in any way. As outlined in the California Anatomical Gift Act, your authorization is legally binding and, unless the donor is under 18 years of age, your decision does not require the consent of any other person. For registered donors under 18 years of age, the legal guardian shall make the final donation decision. You may limit your donation to specific organs or tissues, place usage restrictions, for example transplantation or research, obtain more information about donation, or remove your name from the registry on the Internet Web site of Donate Life California: www.donate LIFEcalifornia.org."

(5) Notwithstanding any other provision of law, a person under 18 years of age may register as a donor. However, the legal guardian of that person shall make the final decision regarding the donation.

(6) The department shall collect donor designation information on all applications for an original or renewal driver's license or identification card.

(7) The department shall print the word "DONOR" or another appropriate designation on the face of a driver's license or identification card to a person who has indicated on the application his or her intent to enroll in the organ donation program pursuant to this section.

(8) On a weekly basis, the department shall electronically transmit to Donate Life California, a nonprofit organization established and designated as the California Organ and Tissue Donor Registrar pursuant to Section 7150.90 of the Health and Safety Code, all of the following information from every application that indicates the applicant's decision to enroll in the organ donation program:

(A) His or her true full name.

(B) His or her residence or mailing address.

(C) His or her year of birth.

(D) His or her California driver's license number or identification card number.

(9)(A) A person who applies for an original or renewal driver's license or identification card may designate a voluntary contribution of two dollars ($2) for the purpose of promoting and supporting organ and tissue donation. This contribution shall be collected by the department, and treated as a voluntary contribution to Donate Life California and not as a fee for the issuance of a driver's license or identification card.

(B) The department may use the donations collected pursuant to this paragraph to cover its actual administrative costs incurred pursuant to paragraphs (6) to (8), inclusive. The department shall deposit all revenue derived pursuant to this paragraph and remaining after the department's deduction for administrative costs in the Donate Life California Trust Subaccount, that is hereby created in the Motor Vehicle Account in the State Transportation Fund. Notwithstanding Section 13340 of the Government Code, all revenue in this subaccount is continuously appropriated, without regard to fiscal years, to the Controller for allocation to Donate Life California and shall be expended for the purpose of increasing participation in organ donation programs.

(C) The department shall transmit to the Donate Life California Organ and Tissue Donor Registry and the appropriate policy and fiscal committees of the Legislature an annual report, and shall make available quarterly updates, detailing funds collected through voluntary contributions as well as a summary of applicants, including all of the following nonidentifiable information:

(i) Date of application.

(ii) Method of application (field office, online, or mail).

(iii) Donor registration status.

(iv) ZIP code.

(v) Gender.

(vi) Year of birth.

(D)(i) The annual report to be submitted to the appropriate policy and fiscal committees of the Legislature pursuant to subparagraph (C) shall be submitted in compliance with Section 9795 of the Government Code.

(ii) Pursuant to Section 10231.5 of the Government Code, the requirement for submitting the annual report to the appropriate policy and fiscal committees of the Legislature imposed under subparagraph (C) is inoperative four years after the date the first annual report is due.

(10) The enrollment form shall be posted on the Internet Web sites for the department and the California Health and Human Services Agency.

(11) The enrollment shall constitute a legal document pursuant to the Uniform Anatomical Gift Act (Chapter

450

3.5 (commencing with Section 7150) of Part 1 of Division 7 of the Health and Safety Code) and shall remain binding after the donor's death despite any express desires of next of kin opposed to the donation. Except as provided in paragraph (5) of subdivision (b), the donation does not require the consent of any other person.

(12) Donate Life California shall ensure that all additions and deletions to the California Organ and Tissue Donor Registry, established pursuant to Section 7150.90 of the Health and Safety Code, shall occur within 30 days of receipt.

(13) Information obtained by Donate Life California for the purposes of this subdivision shall be used for these purposes only and shall not be disseminated further by Donate Life California.

(c)(1) All applications for a driver's license or identification card shall contain a space for an applicant to indicate whether he or she has served in the Armed Forces of the United States and to give his or her consent to be contacted regarding eligibility to receive state or federal veterans benefits. The application shall contain the following statement:

"By marking the veteran box on this application, I certify that I am a veteran of the United States Armed Forces and that I want to receive veterans benefits information from the California Department of Veterans Affairs. By marking the veteran box on this application, I also consent to DMV transmitting my name and mailing address to the California Department of Veterans Affairs for this purpose only, and I certify that I have been notified that this transmittal will occur."

(2) The department shall collect the information obtained pursuant to paragraph (1).

(3) As mutually agreed between the department and the Department of Veterans Affairs, the department shall electronically transmit to the Department of Veterans Affairs the following information on each applicant who has identified that he or she has served in the Armed Forces of the United States since the last data transfer and has consented to be contacted about veterans benefits:

(A) His or her true full name.

(B) His or her mailing address.

(4) Information obtained by the Department of Veterans Affairs for the purposes of this subdivision shall be used for the purpose of assisting individuals to access veterans benefits and shall not be disseminated except as needed for this purpose.

(d) A public entity or employee shall not be liable for loss, detriment, or injury resulting directly or indirectly from false or inaccurate information contained in the form provided pursuant to subdivision (b).

(e) A contract shall not be awarded to a nongovernmental entity for the processing of driver's licenses, unless the contract conforms to all applicable state contracting laws and all applicable procedures set forth in the State Contracting Manual.

(Added by Stats.1998, c. 887 (S.B.1403), § 7. Amended by Stats.1999, c. 1008 (S.B.533), § 5; Stats.2001, c. 740 (S.B.108), § 5; Stats.2001, c. 740 (S.B.108), § 5.5; Stats. 2003, c. 405 (S.B.112), § 6; Stats.2004, c. 615 (S.B.1233), § 26; Stats.2005, c. 665 (S.B.689), § 1, operative July 1, 2006; Stats.2006, c. 538 (S.B.1852), § 657; Stats.2006, c. 311 (S.B.1586), § 8; Stats.2007, c. 629 (A.B.1689), § 3; Stats.2007, c. 630 (A.B.1728), § 5.5; Stats.2010, c. 217 (S.B.1395), § 2; Stats.2011, c. 6 (A.B.105), § 36, eff. March 24, 2011.)

Cross References

Altruistic Living Donor Registry Act of 2010, see Health and Safety Code § 7152 et seq.

Change of address, see Vehicle Code § 14600.

Confidentiality of driver's license information, authorization for businesses to swipe driver's license or identification card in electronic device for certain purposes, violation, see Civil Code § 1798.90.1 et seq.

Department of Motor Vehicles, duty to make available on licenses and identification cards space for sign or notice describing this Act, duty to make available information about registry and how donations may be made, see Vehicle Code § 1672.

Department to prescribe forms, see Vehicle Code § 1652.

Identification cards, contents and form, see Vehicle Code § 13005.

Restricted licenses, see Vehicle Code § 12813.

Signature, possession, and display of license, see Vehicle Code § 12950 et seq.

State Controller, generally, see Government Code § 12402 et seq.

Surrender of license upon suspension, see Vehicle Code § 13206.

Suspension or revocation of license by,
  Court, see Vehicle Code § 13200 et seq.
  Department, see Vehicle Code § 13350 et seq.

Unlawful use of license, see Vehicle Code § 14610.

§ 12811.1. Medical information card; issuance; contents; design

(a) Upon the applicant's request, the department shall issue an adhesive backed medical information card which contains a format permitting the licensee to specify blood type, allergies, past or present medical problems, any medication being taken, the name of the licensee's doctor, the person to notify in case of an emergency, and whether the licensee is under a doctor's care.

(b) The medical information card, which shall be a different color than the anatomical gift card authorized by Section 12811, shall be the same size as a driver's license.

(Added by Stats.1979, c. 884, p. 3070, § 1, operative Jan. 1, 1981. Amended by Stats.1991, c. 928 (A.B.1886), § 23, eff. Oct. 14, 1991.)

§ 12812. Driver with class C or M license not required to have certificate; negligent operator; restricted license for employment

If a driver with a class C or M license, who is not required to have a certificate under any provision of this code, is presumed to be a negligent operator pursuant to Section 12810.5, the department may, as a condition of probation, issue a restricted driver's license to permit driving of a vehicle while in the course of the driver's employment during specified hours of employment or any other restrictions as determined by the department. The restrictions shall be noted on the driver's license. *(Added by Stats.1965, c. 1819, p. 4196, § 1. Amended by Stats. 1984, c. 667, § 12, operative July 1, 1985; Stats.1987, c. 726, § 5, operative July 1, 1988; Stats.1993, c. 272 (A.B.301), § 31, eff. Aug. 2, 1993.)*

§ 12813. Restricted licenses

(a) The department may, upon issuing a driver's license or after issuance whenever good cause appears, impose restrictions suitable to the licensee's driving ability with respect to the type of, or special mechanical control devices required on, a motor vehicle which the licensee may operate or impose other restrictions applicable to the licensee that the department may determine to be appropriate to assure the safe operation of a motor vehicle by the licensee.

(b) The department may issue either a special restricted license or may set forth the restrictions upon the usual license form.

(c) The authority of the department to issue restricted licenses under this section is subject to Sections 12812, 13352, 13353.3, and 13352.5. *(Stats.1959, c. 3, p. 1621, § 12813. Amended by Stats.1961, c. 1615, p. 3456, § 23; Stats.1976, c. 552, p. 1392, § 2; Stats.1987, c. 726, § 6, operative July 1, 1988; Stats.1998, c. 756 (A.B.762), § 5, operative July 1, 1999; Stats.2011, c. 657 (A.B.520), § 1.)*

Cross References

Operation in violation of license restrictions, see Vehicle Code § 14603.

Revocation for violation of license restrictions, see Vehicle Code § 13360.

Signature, possession, and display of license, see Vehicle Code § 12950 et seq.

Vehicles covered by certificate of proof of financial responsibility, restrictions, see Vehicle Code § 16457.

§ 12814. Renewal of licenses; applications; examinations; extensions; terms and conditions; selective testing

(a) Application for renewal of a license shall be made at an office of the department by the person to whom the license was issued. The department may in its discretion require an examination of the applicant as upon an original application, or an examination deemed by the department to be appropriate considering the licensee's record of convictions and accidents, or an examination deemed by the department to be appropriate in relation

451

to evidence of a condition which may affect the ability of the applicant to safely operate a motor vehicle. The age of a licensee, by itself, may not constitute evidence of a condition requiring an examination of the driving ability. If the department finds any evidence, the department shall disclose the evidence to the applicant or licensee. If the person is absent from the state at the time the license expires, the director may extend the license for a period of one year from the expiration date of the license.

(b) Renewal of a driver's license shall be under terms and conditions prescribed by the department.

(c) The department may adopt and administer those regulations as shall be deemed necessary for the public safety in the implementation of a program of selective testing of applicants, and, with reference to this section, the department may waive tests for purposes of evaluation of selective testing procedures.

(d) This section shall become operative on January 1, 2011. *(Added by Stats.2000, c. 985 (S.B.335), § 11, operative Jan. 1, 2011. Amended by Stats.2003, c. 594 (S.B.315), § 36, operative Jan. 1, 2011.)*

Cross References

Application for license, contents, see Vehicle Code § 12800.

Blood alcohol concentration table, inclusion of question on examination administered pursuant to this section, see Vehicle Code § 1666.

Confidentiality of driver's license information, authorization for businesses to swipe driver's license or identification card in electronic device for certain purposes, violation, see Civil Code § 1798.90.1.

Disorders characterized by lapses of consciousness, medical reports regarding persons with disorders, see Health and Safety Code § 103900.

Driver's examination, questions relating to abandonment or dumping of any animal, see Vehicle Code § 1666.5.

Driver's handbook, information relating to abandonment or dumping of any animal, see Vehicle Code § 1656.3.

Examination on original application for license, see Vehicle Code § 12803.

Fee for renewal of license, see Vehicle Code § 14900.

Highway signs, warnings relating to abandonment or dumping of any animal, see Vehicle Code § 21376.

Notice to appear in court after arrest, see Vehicle Code § 40500 et seq.

§ 12814.1. Repealed by Stats.2000, c. 985 (S.B.335), § 12, operative Jan. 1, 2002

§ 12814.5. Renewal by mail

(a) The director may establish a program to evaluate the traffic safety and other effects of renewing driver's licenses by mail. Pursuant to that program, the department may renew by mail driver's licenses for licensees not holding a probationary license, and whose records, for the two years immediately preceding the determination of eligibility for the renewal, show no notification of a violation of subdivision (a) of Section 40509, a total violation point count not greater than one as determined in accordance with Section 12810, no suspension of the driving privilege pursuant to Section 13353.2, and no

refusal to submit to or complete chemical testing pursuant to Section 13353 or 13353.1.

(b) The director may terminate the renewal by mail program authorized by this section at any time the department determines that the program has an adverse impact on traffic safety.

(c) No renewal by mail shall be granted to any person who is 70 years of age or older.

(d) The department shall notify each licensee granted a renewal by mail pursuant to this section of major changes to the Vehicle Code affecting traffic laws occurring during the prior five-year period.

(e) The department shall not renew a driver's license by mail if the license has been previously renewed by mail two consecutive times for five-year periods. *(Added by Stats.1978, c. 658, p. 2120, § 1. Amended by Stats.1979, c. 625, p. 1945, § 2; Stats.1981, c. 541, p. 2184, § 34, eff. Sept. 17, 1981, operative Jan. 1, 1982; Stats.1982, c. 776, p. 3027, § 1; Stats.1984, c. 985, § 1; Stats.1986, c. 57, § 1; Stats.1987, c. 429, § 1; Stats.1992, c. 1241 (S.B.1615), § 20; Stats.1993, c. 546 (A.B.2284), § 3; Stats.1994, c. 675 (S.B.1741), § 6; Stats.1995, c. 766 (S.B.726), § 16; Stats.1996, c. 1043 (A.B.2352), § 5; Stats.2003, c. 326 (S.B.60), § 7; Stats.2003, c. 719 (S.B.1055), § 22; Stats. 2009–2010, 4th Ex.Sess., c. 10 (A.B.10), § 9, eff. July 28, 2009.)*

Cross References

Base fee amounts, adjustment of fees, see Vehicle Code § 1678.

§ 12814.6. Brady–Jared Teen Driver Safety Act of 1997; provisional licenses; persons under age 18

(a) Except as provided in Section 12814.7, a driver's license issued to a person at least 16 years of age but under 18 years of age shall be issued pursuant to the provisional licensing program contained in this section. The program shall consist of all of the following components:

(1) Upon application for an original license, the applicant shall be issued an instruction permit pursuant to Section 12509. A person who has in his or her immediate possession a valid permit issued pursuant to Section 12509 may operate a motor vehicle, other than a motorcycle or motorized bicycle, only when the person is either taking the driver training instruction referred to in paragraph (3) or practicing that instruction, provided the person is accompanied by, and is under the immediate supervision of, a California licensed driver 25 years of age or older whose driving privilege is not on probation. The age requirement of this paragraph does not apply if the licensed driver is the parent, spouse, or guardian of the permitholder or is a licensed or certified driving instructor.

(2) The person shall hold an instruction permit for not less than six months prior to applying for a provisional driver's license.

(3) The person shall have complied with one of the following:

(A) Satisfactory completion of approved courses in automobile driver education and driver training maintained pursuant to provisions of the Education Code in any secondary school of California, or equivalent instruction in a secondary school of another state.

(B) Satisfactory completion of an integrated driver education and training program that is approved by the department and conducted by a driving instructor licensed under Chapter 1 (commencing with Section 11100) of Division 5. The program shall utilize segmented modules, whereby a portion of the educational instruction is provided by, and then reinforced through, specific behind-the-wheel training before moving to the next phase of driver education and training. The program shall contain a minimum of 30 hours of classroom instruction and six hours of behind-the-wheel training.

(C) Satisfactory completion of six hours or more of behind-the-wheel instruction by a driving school or an independent driving instructor licensed under Chapter 1 (commencing with Section 11100) of Division 5 and either an accredited course in automobile driver education in any secondary school of California pursuant to provisions of the Education Code or satisfactory completion of equivalent professional instruction acceptable to the department. To be acceptable to the department, the professional instruction shall meet minimum standards to be prescribed by the department, and the standards shall be at least equal to the requirements for driver education and driver training contained in the rules and regulations adopted by the State Board of Education pursuant to the Education Code. A person who has complied with this subdivision shall not be required by the governing board of a school district to comply with subparagraph (A) in order to graduate from high school.

(D) Except as provided under subparagraph (B), a student may not take driver training instruction, unless he or she has successfully completed driver education.

(4) The person shall complete 50 hours of supervised driving practice prior to the issuance of a provisional license, which is in addition to any other driver training instruction required by law. Not less than 10 of the required practice hours shall include driving during darkness, as defined in Section 280. Upon application for a provisional license, the person shall submit to the department the certification of a parent, spouse, guardian, or licensed or certified driving instructor that the applicant has completed the required amount of driving practice and is prepared to take the department's driving test. A person without a parent, spouse, guardian, or who is an emancipated minor, may have a licensed driver 25 years of age or older or a licensed or certified driving instructor complete the certification. This requirement does not apply to motorcycle practice.

(5) The person shall successfully complete an examination required by the department. Before retaking a test, the person shall wait for not less than one week after failure of the written test and for not less than two weeks after failure of the driving test.

(b) Except as provided in Section 12814.7, the provisional driver's license shall be subject to all of the following restrictions:

(1) Except as specified in paragraph (2), during the first 12 months after issuance of a provisional license the licensee may not do any of the following unless accompanied and supervised by a licensed driver who is the licensee's parent or guardian, a licensed driver who is 25 years of age or older, or a licensed or certified driving instructor:

(A) Drive between the hours of 11 p.m. and 5 a.m.

(B) Transport passengers who are under 20 years of age.

(2) A licensee may drive between the hours of 11 p.m. and 5 a.m. or transport an immediate family member without being accompanied and supervised by a licensed driver who is the licensee's parent or guardian, a licensed driver who is 25 years of age or older, or a licensed or certified driving instructor, in the following circumstances:

(A) Medical necessity of the licensee when reasonable transportation facilities are inadequate and operation of a vehicle by a minor is necessary. The licensee shall keep in his or her possession a signed statement from a physician familiar with the condition, containing a diagnosis and probable date when sufficient recovery will have been made to terminate the necessity.

(B) Schooling or school-authorized activities of the licensee when reasonable transportation facilities are inadequate and operation of a vehicle by a minor is necessary. The licensee shall keep in his or her possession a signed statement from the school principal, dean, or school staff member designated by the principal or dean, containing a probable date that the schooling or school-authorized activity will have been completed.

(C) Employment necessity of the licensee when reasonable transportation facilities are inadequate and operation of a vehicle by a minor is necessary. The licensee shall keep in his or her possession a signed statement from the employer, verifying employment and containing a probable date that the employment will have been completed.

(D) Necessity of the licensee or the licensee's immediate family member when reasonable transportation facilities are inadequate and operation of a vehicle by a minor is necessary to transport the licensee or the licensee's immediate family member. The licensee shall keep in his or her possession a signed statement from a parent or legal guardian verifying the reason and containing a probable date that the necessity will have ceased.

(E) The licensee is an emancipated minor.

(c) A law enforcement officer shall not stop a vehicle for the sole purpose of determining whether the driver is in violation of the restrictions imposed under subdivision (b).

(d) A law enforcement officer shall not stop a vehicle for the sole purpose of determining whether a driver who is subject to the license restrictions in subdivision (b) is in violation of Article 2.5 (commencing with Section 118947) of Chapter 4 of Part 15 of Division 104 of the Health and Safety Code.

(e)(1) Upon a finding that any licensee has violated paragraph (1) of subdivision (b), the court shall impose one of the following:

(A) Not less than eight hours nor more than 16 hours of community service for a first offense and not less than 16 hours nor more than 24 hours of community service for a second or subsequent offense.

(B) A fine of not more than thirty-five dollars ($35) for a first offense and a fine of not more than fifty dollars ($50) for a second or subsequent offense.

(2) If the court orders community service, the court shall retain jurisdiction until the hours of community service have been completed.

(3) If the hours of community service have not been completed within 90 days, the court shall impose a fine of not more than thirty-five dollars ($35) for a first offense and not more than fifty dollars ($50) for a second or subsequent offense.

(f) A conviction of paragraph (1) of subdivision (b), when reported to the department, may not be disclosed as otherwise specified in Section 1808 or constitute a violation point count value pursuant to Section 12810.

(g) Any term of restriction or suspension of the driving privilege imposed on a person pursuant to this subdivision shall remain in effect until the end of the term even though the person becomes 18 years of age before the term ends.

(1) The driving privilege shall be suspended when the record of the person shows one or more notifications issued pursuant to Section 40509 or 40509.5. The suspension shall continue until any notification issued pursuant to Section 40509 or 40509.5 has been cleared.

(2) A 30–day restriction shall be imposed when a driver's record shows a violation point count of two or more points in 12 months, as determined in accordance with Section 12810. The restriction shall require the licensee to be accompanied by a licensed parent, spouse, guardian, or other licensed driver 25 years of age or older, except when operating a class M vehicle, or so licensed, with no passengers aboard.

(3) A six-month suspension of the driving privilege and a one-year term of probation shall be imposed whenever a licensee's record shows a violation point count of three or more points in 12 months, as determined in accordance with Section 12810. The terms and conditions of probation shall include, but not be limited to, both of the following:

(A) The person shall violate no law which, if resulting in conviction, is reportable to the department under Section 1803.

(B) The person shall remain free from accident responsibility.

(h) Whenever action by the department under subdivision (g) arises as a result of a motor vehicle accident, the person may, in writing and within 10 days, demand a hearing to present evidence that he or she was not responsible for the accident upon which the action is based. Whenever action by the department is based upon a conviction reportable to the department under Section 1803, the person has no right to a hearing pursuant to Article 3 (commencing with Section 14100) of Chapter 3.

(i) The department shall require a person whose driving privilege is suspended or revoked pursuant to subdivision (g) to submit proof of financial responsibility as defined in Section 16430. The proof of financial responsibility shall be filed on or before the date of reinstatement following the suspension or revocation. The proof of financial responsibility shall be maintained with the department for three years following the date of reinstatement.

(j)(1) Notwithstanding any other provision of this code, the department may issue a distinctive driver's license, that displays a distinctive color or a distinctively colored stripe or other distinguishing characteristic, to persons at least 16 years of age and older but under 18 years of age, and to persons 18 years of age and older but under 21 years of age, so that the distinctive license feature is immediately recognizable. The features shall clearly differentiate between driver's licenses issued to persons at least 16 years of age or older but under 18 years of age and to persons 18 years of age or older but under 21 years of age.

(2) If changes in the format or appearance of driver's licenses are adopted pursuant to this subdivision, those changes may be implemented under any new contract for the production of driver's licenses entered into after the adoption of those changes.

(k) The department shall include, on the face of the provisional driver's license, the original issuance date of the provisional driver's license in addition to any other issuance date.

(l) This section shall be known and may be cited as the Brady–Jared Teen Driver Safety Act of 1997. *(Added by Stats.1992, c. 1243 (A.B.3090), § 85.1, eff. Sept. 30, 1992, operative Jan. 1, 1993. Amended by Stats.1997, c. 760 (S.B.1329), § 8, operative Jan. 1, 1998; Stats.2000, c. 1035 (S.B.1403), § 19; Stats.2002, c. 418 (A.B.2273), § 2.5; Stats.2002, c. 758 (A.B.3024), § 13.5; Stats.2003, c. 768 (A.B.1343), § 4; Stats.2005, c. 337 (A.B.1474), § 1; Stats.2007, c. 425 (S.B.7), § 2.)*

Driver education, satisfaction of requirements by Internet-based, correspondence, or distance-learning courses offered by private secondary schools, conditions, see Education Code § 51220.6.

Instruction permits to operate motorcycles, motorized scooters, motorized bicycles, etc., license or driver education and training requirements, see Vehicle Code § 12509.5.

§ 12814.7. Provisional restricted class C license for operation of army and national guard vehicles; conditions

(a) Notwithstanding the provisional licensing requirements of subdivisions (a) to (e), inclusive, of Section 12814.6, the department shall issue to a person who is at least 16 years of age, but under 18 years of age, a restricted class C driver's license valid for the operation of United States Army and California National Guard vehicles during the course and scope of their duties with the California National Guard if the following conditions are met:

(1) Upon application, the person provides the department with the executed enlistment contract for the applicant.

(2) The person qualifies for and is issued an instruction permit pursuant to Section 12509.

(3) Prior to the issuance of the class C license, the applicant provides proof satisfactory to the department of successful completion of a driver education and training course administered by the California National Guard.

(b) A driver's license issued pursuant to this section shall be subject to both of the following:

(1) Subdivisions (f) to (k), inclusive, of Section 12814.6.

(2) Pull-notice and periodic reports issued pursuant to Section 1808.1.

(c) The licensee shall comply with all other licensing requirements of this code, including, but not limited to, the requirements of Section 12804.9. *(Added by Stats. 2002, c. 418 (A.B.2273), § 3.)*

Cross References

Instruction permits, application for restricted driver's license pursuant to this section, see Vehicle Code § 12509.

§ 12814.8. Repealed by Stats.1999, c. 206 (S.B.946), § 1, operative Jan. 1, 2004

§ 12815. Licenses lost, destroyed, or mutilated

(a) If a driver's license issued under this code is lost, destroyed or mutilated, or a new true, full name is acquired, the person to whom it was issued shall obtain a duplicate upon furnishing to the department (1) satisfactory proof of that loss, destruction, or mutilation and (2) if the licensee is a minor, evidence of permission to obtain a duplicate secured from the parents, guardian, or person having custody of the minor. Any person who loses a driver's license and who, after obtaining a duplicate, finds the original license shall immediately destroy the original license.

(b) A person in possession of a valid driver's license who has been informed either by the department or by a law enforcement agency that the document is mutilated shall surrender the license to the department not later than 10 days after that notification.

(c) For purposes of this section, a mutilated license is one that has been damaged sufficiently to render any or all of the elements of identity set forth in Sections 12800.5 and 12811 unreadable or unidentifiable through visual, mechanical, or electronic means. *(Stats.1959, c. 3, p. 1622, § 12815. Amended by Stats.1959, c. 298, p. 2207, § 3; Stats.1970, c. 166, p. 409, § 2; Stats.1996, c. 1154 (A.B.3020), § 60, eff. Sept. 30, 1996; Stats.1999, c. 1008 (S.B.533), § 6; Stats.2000, c. 135 (A.B.2539), § 158.)*

Cross References

Fees for duplicates or change of name, see Vehicle Code § 14901.

Unlawful use of license, see Vehicle Code § 14610.

§ 12816. Term of license; period for renewal; exception

(a) Every original driver's license expires on the fifth birthday of the applicant following the date of the application for the license.

(b) Renewal of a driver's license shall be made for a term which expires on the fifth birthday of the applicant following the expiration of the license renewed, if application for renewal is made within six months prior to the expiration of the license to be renewed, or within 90 days after expiration of the license. If renewal is not applied for within 90 days after expiration of the license, the application and fee is considered the same as an application for an original license.

(c) The department may accept application for a renewal of a driver's license made more than six months prior to the date of expiration. The renewal shall be made for a term which expires on the fifth birthday of the applicant following the date of the application for the renewal license.

(d) The department may accept an application for a license of a different class made more than six months before the expiration of the license previously issued, if the previously issued license is surrendered for cancellation in accordance with Section 13100. The driver's license issued from that application expires on the fifth birthday of the applicant following the date of the application.

(e) Notwithstanding subdivisions (a), (b), (c), and (d), the department may adjust the expiration date for any driver's license issued pursuant to this code. *(Stats.1959, c. 3, p. 1622, § 12816. Amended by Stats.1959, c. 1996, p. 4625, § 17.5; Stats.1963, c. 49, p. 675, § 1; Stats.1965, c. 1445, p. 3389, § 2; Stats.1973, c. 891, p. 1662, § 4, eff. Sept. 28, 1973, operative Jan. 1, 1975; Stats.1974, c. 428, p. 1040, § 2; Stats.1984, c. 34, § 1, operative July 1, 1985;*

Stats.1992, c. 1240 (A.B.862), § 3; Stats.1996, c. 1043 (A.B.2352), § 6.)

Cross References

Renewal of license, see Vehicle Code §§ 12808, 12814.

§ 12817.   Persons in the armed forces; spouses

(a) A California driver's license held by a person who enters or is in the United States Armed Forces shall continue in full force and effect, so long as the service continues and the person remains absent from this state, and for a period not to exceed 30 days following the date the holder of the license is honorably separated from that service or returns to this state, whichever is earlier, unless the license was suspended, canceled, or revoked for cause as provided by law. The license is valid only if it is in the immediate possession of the licensee and the licensee has in his or her immediate possession discharge or separation papers if the licensee has been discharged or separated from the service.

(b) A California driver's license held by a spouse of a person described in subdivision (a) shall continue in full force and effect, so long as the person described in subdivision (a) continues in the service and remains absent from this state and the spouse remains absent from this state, and for a period not to exceed 30 days following the date the person described in subdivision (a) is honorably separated from that service or the date that the person or the spouse returns to this state, whichever is earlier, unless the spouse's license was suspended, canceled, or revoked for cause as provided by law. The license is valid only if it is in the immediate possession of the licensee and the licensee has in his or her immediate possession discharge or separation papers of the person described in subdivision (a). *(Stats.1959, c. 3, p. 1622, § 12817. Amended by Stats.1963, c. 73, p. 700, § 1; Stats.2011, c. 154 (S.B.720), § 1.)*

Cross References

Possession and display of license, see Vehicle Code §§ 12951, 12952.

Renewal of license, see Vehicle Code §§ 12808, 12814.

§ 12818.   Reexamination upon request; actions relating to driving privilege; notice of results to law enforcement agency

(a) Upon receipt of a request for reexamination and presentation of a legible copy of a notice of reexamination by a person issued the notice pursuant to Section 21061, the department shall reexamine the person's qualifications to operate a motor vehicle pursuant to Section 13801, notwithstanding the notice requirement of Section 13801.

(b) Based on the department's reexamination of the person's qualifications pursuant to subdivision (a), the department shall determine if either of the following actions should be taken:

(1) Suspend or revoke the driving privilege of that person if the department finds that any of the grounds exist which authorize the refusal to issue a license.

(2) Restrict, make subject to terms and conditions of probation, suspend, or revoke the driving privilege of that person based upon the records of the department as provided in Chapter 3 (commencing with Section 13800).

(c) As an alternative to subdivision (a), the department may suspend or revoke the person's driving privilege as provided under Article 2 (commencing with Section 13950) of Chapter 3.

(d) Upon request, the department shall notify the law enforcement agency which employs the traffic officer who issued the notice of reexamination of the results of the reexamination.

(e) This section shall become operative on January 1, 2011. *(Added by Stats.2000, c. 985 (S.B.335), § 14, operative Jan. 1, 2011.)*

§ 12819.   Failure to request reexamination pursuant to notice; suspension of driving privilege

Unless the person issued the notice of reexamination requests the reexamination pursuant to Section 12818 within five working days after the department receives the notice of reexamination transmitted pursuant to Section 21062, the department shall peremptorily suspend the driving privilege of the person until the person has completed the reexamination and the department has taken the action prescribed in subdivision (b) of Section 12818. *(Added by Stats.1986, c. 304, § 2, operative July 1, 1987.)*

ARTICLE 4.   SIGNATURE AND DISPLAY OF LICENSES

Section
12950.   Signature of licensee.
12950.5.   Digitized signatures on driver's license; digitized signatures of persons who register to vote on voter registration cards and change of address information to be provided to Secretary of State.
12951.   Possession of valid driver's license.
12952.   Display of license to court.
12953.   Accidents or violations causing detention of crewmember of train by police; furnishing of license; issuance of citation.
12954.   Repealed.

Cross References

Confidentiality of driver's license information, authorization for businesses to swipe driver's license or identification card in electronic device for certain purposes, violation, see Civil Code § 1798.90.1.

§ 12950.   Signature of licensee

(a) Every person licensed under this code shall write his or her usual signature with pen and ink in the space provided for that purpose on the license issued to him or her, immediately on receipt thereof, and the license is not valid until so signed, except that if the department issues a form of license which bears the facsimile signature of the applicant as shown upon the application, the license is valid even though not so signed.

(b) For purposes of subdivision (a), signature includes a digitized signature. *(Stats.1959, c. 3, p. 1623, § 12950. Amended by Stats.2003, c. 819 (A.B.593), § 3.)*

Cross References

Space for signature of licensee, see Vehicle Code § 12811.
Unlawful use of license, see Vehicle Code § 14610.

§ 12950.5. Digitized signatures on driver's license; digitized signatures of persons who register to vote on voter registration cards and change of address information to be provided to Secretary of State

(a) The department shall require digitized signatures on each driver's license. A digitized signature is an electronic representation of a handwritten signature.

(b) The department shall provide to the Secretary of State the digitized signature of every person who registers to vote on the voter registration card provided by the department.

(c) The department shall provide the Secretary of State with change-of-address information for every voter who indicates that he or she desires to have his or her address changed for voter registration purposes. *(Added by Stats.2003, c. 819 (A.B.593), § 4.)*

§ 12951. Possession of valid driver's license

(a) The licensee shall have the valid driver's license issued to him or her in his or her immediate possession at all times when driving a motor vehicle upon a highway.

Any charge under this subdivision shall be dismissed when the person charged produces in court a driver's license duly issued to that person and valid at the time of his or her arrest, except that upon a third or subsequent charge the court in its discretion may dismiss the charge. When a temporary, interim, or duplicate driver's license is produced in court, the charge shall not be dismissed unless the court has been furnished proof by the Department of Motor Vehicles that the temporary, interim, or duplicate license was issued prior to the arrest, that the driving privilege and license had not been suspended or revoked, and that the person was eligible for the temporary, interim, or duplicate license.

(b) The driver of a motor vehicle shall present his or her license for examination upon demand of a peace officer enforcing the provisions of this code. *(Stats.1959, c. 3, p. 1623, § 12951. Amended by Stats.1965, c. 175, p. 1141, § 1; Stats.1965, c. 495, p. 1804, § 1; Stats.1965, c. 1177, p. 2977, § 1; Stats.1968, c. 1192, p. 2257, § 6, operative Jan. 1, 1969; Stats.1993, c. 1292 (S.B.274), § 8.)*

Cross References

Certain violations constituting misdemeanors, see Vehicle Code § 40000.11.
Notice to correct driver's license infraction, see Vehicle Code § 40303.5.

Unlawful use of license, see Vehicle Code § 14610.

§ 12952. Display of license to court

A licensee shall display his driver's license upon request of a magistrate or judge before whom he may be brought for violation of any traffic law. *(Stats.1959, c. 3, p. 1623, § 12952.)*

§ 12953. Accidents or violations causing detention of crewmember of train by police; furnishing of license; issuance of citation

In any circumstances involving accidents or violations in which the engineer or any other crewmember of any train is detained by state or local police, the engineer or any other crew member shall not be required to furnish a motor vehicle operator's license, nor shall any citation involving the operation of a train be issued against the motor vehicle operator's license of the engineer or any other crew member of the train. *(Added by Stats.1980, c. 1134, p. 3660, § 11.)*

§ 12954. Repealed by Stats.2010, c. 360 (A.B.1648), § 4

ARTICLE 5. IDENTIFICATION CARDS

Section
13000. Issuance; contents; senior citizen notation; application.
13000.1. Grounds to refuse to issue or renew identification cards.
13000.5. Repealed.
13001. Documentation of acceptance into federal Deferred Action for Childhood Arrivals program; proof of authorized presence in the United States; identification card issuance.
13002. Expiration of identification cards.
13002.1. Renewal of identification cards; mail or Internet Web site; duration of renewal.
13003. Loss, destruction, mutilation or acquisition of new name; application for original identification card; fee.
13004. Unlawful acts.
13004.1. Manufacture or sale of similar identification document prohibited; penalties; other prosecution not precluded.
13005. Contents and form of identification card.
13005.3. Senior citizen identification cards.
13005.5. Engraved picture or photograph.
13006. Public entities or employees; no liability.
13007. Change of address.
13007.5. Identity verification.
13008. Cancellation.

Cross References

Confidentiality of driver's license information, authorization for businesses to swipe driver's license or identification card in electronic device for certain purposes, violation, see Civil Code § 1798.90.1.

§ 13000. Issuance; contents; senior citizen notation; application

(a) The department may issue an identification card to any person attesting to the true full name, correct age, and other identifying data as certified by the applicant for the identification card.

(b) Any person 62 years of age or older may apply for, and the department upon receipt of a proper application therefor shall issue, an identification card bearing the notation "Senior Citizen".

(c) Every application for an identification card shall be signed and verified by the applicant before a person authorized to administer oaths and shall be supported by bona fide documentary evidence of the age and identity of the applicant as the department may require, and shall include a legible print of the thumb or finger of the applicant.

(d) Any person 62 years of age or older, and any other qualified person, may apply for, or possess, an identification card under the provisions of either subdivision (a) or (b), but not under both of those provisions. *(Added by Stats.1968, c. 494, p. 1138, § 3. Amended by Stats.1969, c. 1340, p. 2687, § 1; Stats.1973, c. 965, p. 1856, § 2; Stats.1975, c. 1198, p. 2964, § 1; Stats.1979, c. 373, p. 1382, § 320; Stats.1981, c. 1102, p. 4311, § 2; Stats.1999, c. 1008 (S.B.533), § 7; Stats.2003, c. 326 (S.B.60), § 8.)*

Cross References

Confidentiality of driver's license information, authorization for businesses to swipe driver's license or identification card in electronic device for certain purposes, violation, see Civil Code § 1798.90.1.

Fees, see Vehicle Code § 14902.

Oath as including affirmation, see Vehicle Code § 16.

Persons authorized to administer oaths, see Vehicle Code § 18.

§ 13000.1. Grounds to refuse to issue or renew identification cards

(a) The department may refuse to issue or renew an identification card to any person for any of the following reasons:

(1) The department determines that the person has knowingly used a false or fictitious name in any application.

(2) The department determines that the person has impersonated another in making an application.

(3) The department determines that the person has knowingly made a false statement, knowingly concealed a material fact, or otherwise committed any fraud on any application.

(b) The department may declare an identification card invalid upon any of the grounds specified in subdivision (a) as reason to refuse to reissue or renew an identification card. The holder of an identification card that has been declared invalid shall surrender the identification card to the department. *(Added by Stats.2000, c. 787 (S.B.1404), § 19.)*

§ 13000.5. Repealed by Stats.1991, c. 928 (A.B.1886), § 24, eff. Oct. 14, 1991

§ 13001. Documentation of acceptance into federal Deferred Action for Childhood Arrivals program; proof of authorized presence in the United States; identification card issuance

(a) Any federal document demonstrating favorable action by the federal government for acceptance of a person into the federal Deferred Action for Childhood Arrivals program shall satisfy the requirement that the applicant submit satisfactory proof that the applicant's presence in the United States is authorized under federal law.

(b) The department may issue an original identification card to the person who submits proof of presence in the United States as authorized under federal law pursuant to subdivision (a) and either a social security account number or ineligibility for a social security account number. *(Added by Stats.2013, c. 571 (A.B.35), § 3.)*

§ 13002. Expiration of identification cards

(a) Except as otherwise provided in subdivision (b), every identification card shall expire, unless canceled earlier, on the sixth birthday of the applicant following the date of application for the identification card. Renewal of any identification card, other than a senior citizen identification card, shall be made for a term which shall expire on the sixth birthday of the applicant following expiration of the identification card renewed, unless surrendered earlier. Any application for renewal received after 90 days after expiration of the identification card, including a senior citizen identification card, shall be considered the same as an application for an original identification card. The department shall, at the end of six years and six months after the issuance or renewal of an identification card, other than a senior citizen identification card, destroy any record of the card if it has expired and has not been renewed.

(b) Every senior citizen identification card issued pursuant to subdivision (b) of Section 13000 shall expire, unless canceled earlier, on the 10th birthday of the applicant following the date of application for the identification card. Renewal of any senior citizen identification card shall be made for a term which shall expire on the 10th birthday of the applicant following expiration of the senior citizen identification card renewed, unless surrendered earlier. The department shall, at the end of 10 years and six months after the issuance or renewal of a senior citizen identification card, destroy any record of the card if it has expired and has not been renewed.

(c) An identification card may be issued to a person in exchange for the person's driver's license which is surrendered to the department for either of the following reasons:

(1) The person has a physical or mental condition and requests cancellation of the driver's license.

(2) The department has revoked the person's driving privilege based on the person's physical or mental condition.

That card shall be issued without the payment of any additional fee.

(d) Notwithstanding subdivisions (a) and (b), the department may adjust the expiration date of any identification card issued pursuant to this code so that the date does not exceed the expiration date of a document submitted pursuant to subdivision (a) of Section 12801.5. *(Added by Stats.1968, c. 494, p. 1138, § 3. Amended by Stats.1969, c. 1143, p. 2213, § 2; Stats.1969, c. 1340, p. 2689, § 8; Stats.1975, c. 1198, p. 2964, § 2; Stats.1978, c. 821, p. 2610, § 1; Stats.1990, c. 607 (S.B.2311), § 1; Stats.1991, c. 928 (A.B.1886), § 25, eff. Oct. 14, 1991; Stats.1994, c. 675 (S.B.1741), § 7.)*

§ 13002.1. Renewal of identification cards; mail or Internet Web site; duration of renewal

(a) The director shall establish by January 1, 2011, a program that permits the renewal of identification cards by mail or through the department's Internet Web site.

(b) The initial application for the identification card shall be pursuant to Section 13000. The first renewal for a person 62 years of age or older shall be for a 10–year period with a maximum of one renewal by mail or through the department's Internet Web site. All other renewals shall be for a six-year period with a maximum of two renewals by mail or through the department's Internet Web site. *(Added by Stats.2008, c. 674 (A.B.2319), § 1.)*

§ 13003. Loss, destruction, mutilation or acquisition of new name; application for original identification card; fee

(a) If an identification card issued under this code is lost, destroyed, mutilated, or a new true full name is acquired, the person to whom it was issued shall make application for an original identification card as specified in Section 13000. The fee provided in Section 14902 shall be paid to the department upon application for the card. Every identification card issued pursuant to this section shall expire as provided in Section 13002 and shall be deemed an original identification card for that purpose.

(b) A person in possession of a valid identification card who has been informed either by the department or by a law enforcement agency that the document is mutilated shall surrender the identification card to the department not later than 10 days after that notification.

(c) For purposes of this section a mutilated identification card is one that has been damaged sufficiently to render any or all of the elements of identity set forth in Sections 13005 and 13005.5 unreadable or unidentifiable through visual, mechanical, or electronic means. *(Added by Stats.1968, c. 494, p. 1138, § 3. Amended by Stats. 1978, c. 821, p. 2610, § 2; Stats.1996, c. 1154 (A.B.3020), § 61, eff. Sept. 30, 1996; Stats.1999, c. 1008 (S.B.533), § 8.)*

§ 13004. Unlawful acts

It is unlawful for any person:

(a) To display or cause or permit to be displayed or have in his possession any canceled, fictitious, fraudulently altered, or fraudulently obtained identification card.

(b) To lend his identification card to any other person or knowingly permit the use thereof by another.

(c) To display or represent any identification card not issued to him as being his card.

(d) To permit any unlawful use of an identification card issued to him.

(e) To do any act forbidden or fail to perform any act required by this article.

(f) To photograph, photostat, duplicate, or in any way reproduce any identification card or facsimile thereof in such a manner that it could be mistaken for a valid identification card, or to display or have in his possession any such photograph, photostat, duplicate, reproduction, or facsimile unless authorized by the provisions of this code.

(g) To alter any identification card in any manner not authorized by this code. *(Added by Stats.1968, c. 494, p. 1138, § 3. Amended by Stats.1969, c. 1340, p. 2688, § 4; Stats.1971, c. 1174, p. 2239, § 3, operative May 3, 1972.)*

Cross References

Violation a misdemeanor, see Vehicle Code § 40000.11.

§ 13004.1. Manufacture or sale of similar identification document prohibited; penalties; other prosecution not precluded

(a) A person shall not manufacture or sell an identification document of a size and form substantially similar to, or that purports to confer the same privileges as, the identification cards issued by the department.

(b) A violation of this section is a misdemeanor punishable as follows:

(1) The court shall impose a fine of not less than two hundred fifty dollars ($250) and not more than one thousand dollars ($1,000), and 24 hours of community service, to be served when the person is not employed or is not attending school. No part of the fine or community service shall be suspended or waived.

(2) In lieu of the penalties imposed under paragraph (1), the court, in its discretion, may impose a jail term of up to one year and a fine of up to one thousand dollars ($1,000). In exercising its discretion the court shall consider the extent of the defendant's commercial motivation for the offense.

(c) Prosecution under this section shall not preclude prosecution under any other applicable provision of law. *(Added by Stats.1990, c. 170 (S.B.1873), § 1. Amended by Stats.2007, c. 743 (A.B.1658), § 5; Stats.2010, c. 684 (A.B.2471), § 1.)*

Misdemeanors, definition and penalties, see Penal Code §§ 17, 19 and 19.2.

Violation of license provisions, manufacture or sale of similar identification document prohibited, see Vehicle Code § 14610.1.

§ 13005. Contents and form of identification card

(a) The identification card shall resemble in appearance, so far as is practicable, a driver's license issued pursuant to this code. It shall adequately describe the applicant, bear his or her picture, and be produced in color or engraved by a process or processes that prohibit, as near as possible, the ability to alter or reproduce the identification card, or prohibit the ability to superimpose a picture or photograph on the identification card without ready detection.

(b)(1) Upon issuance of a new identification card, or renewal of an identification card, the department shall provide information on organ and tissue donation, including a standardized form to be filled out by an individual who desires to enroll in the California Organ and Tissue Donor Registry with instructions for mailing the completed form to the California Organ and Tissue Donor Registrar established pursuant to subdivision (a) of Section 7150.90 of the Health and Safety Code.

(2) The enrollment form shall be simple in design and shall be produced by the department, in cooperation with the California Organ and Tissue Donor Registrar, and shall require all of the following information to be supplied by the enrollee:

(A) Date of birth, sex, full name, address, and home telephone number.

(B) Consent for organs or tissues to be donated for transplant after death.

(C) Any limitation of the donation to specific organs, tissues, or research.

(3) The form shall also include a description of the process for having a name removed from the registry, and the process for donating money for the benefit of the registry.

(4) The registry enrollment form shall be posted on the Internet Web sites for the department and the California Health and Human Services Agency.

(5) The form shall constitute a legal document under the Uniform Anatomical Gift Act (Chapter 3.5 (commencing with Section 7150) of Part 1 of Division 7 of the Health and Safety Code).

(6) The registrar shall ensure that all additions and deletions to the registry shall occur within 30 days of receipt.

(7) Information obtained by the registrar for the purposes of this subdivision shall be used for these purposes only and shall not further be disseminated by the registrar.

(c) A contract shall not be awarded to a nongovernmental entity for the processing of identification cards unless the contract conforms to all applicable state contracting laws and all applicable procedures set forth in the State Contracting Manual. *(Added by Stats.1998, c. 887 (S.B.1403), § 9. Amended by Stats.2001, c. 740 (S.B.108), § 6.5; Stats.2003, c. 405 (S.B.112), § 8; Stats. 2007, c. 629 (A.B.1689), § 4; Stats.2007, c. 630 (A.B. 1728), § 6.5; Stats.2009, c. 229 (A.B.282), § 4.)*

Department of Motor Vehicles, duty to make available on licenses and identification cards space for sign or notice describing this Act, duty to make available information about registry and how donations may be made, see Vehicle Code § 1672.

Organ and tissue donation, information to be provided upon issuance and renewal of drivers' licenses on organ and tissue donation including a enrollment form for the California Organ and Tissue Donor Registry, see Vehicle Code § 12811.

§ 13005.3. Senior citizen identification cards

In addition to the requirements of Section 13005, any identification card issued pursuant to subdivision (b) of Section 13000 shall contain the words "Senior Citizen". *(Added by Stats.1975, c. 1198, p. 2964, § 3. Amended by Stats.1981, c. 1006, p. 3897, § 4; Stats.1982, c. 1042, p. 3800, § 4.)*

§ 13005.5. Engraved picture or photograph

(a) An identification card issued to any person shall bear a fullface engraved picture or photograph of the person.

(b) Notwithstanding any other provision of law, the department shall not, unless requested by the applicant, distribute or sell the applicant's picture or photograph or any information pertaining to the applicant's physical characteristics to any private individual, other than the applicant, or to any firm, copartnership, association, or corporation. This subdivision does not apply to any private business entity that contracts with the department for the production of driver's licenses and identification cards, if the contract prohibits the unauthorized use and disclosure of the information. *(Added by Stats.1969, c. 1340, p. 2688, § 6. Amended by Stats.1971, c. 1748, p. 3764, § 58.5, operative March 4, 1972; Stats.1981, c. 1006, p. 3897, § 5; Stats.1999, c. 489 (A.B.771), § 4.)*

§ 13006. Public entities or employees; no liability

No public entity or employee shall be liable for any loss or injury resulting directly or indirectly from false or inaccurate information contained in identification cards provided for in this article.

No public entity or employee shall be liable for any loss, detriment, or injury resulting directly or indirectly from false or inaccurate information contained in the sticker provided pursuant to subdivision (b) of Section 13005. *(Added by Stats.1968, c. 494, p. 1138, § 3.*

Amended by Stats.1973, c. 965, p. 1857, § 5; Stats.1975, c. 325, p. 773, § 3.)

§ 13007. Change of address

Whenever any person after applying for or receiving an identification card acquires an address different from the address shown on the identification card issued to him, he shall within 10 days thereafter notify the department of his old and new address. The department may thereupon take such action as necessary to insure that the identification card reflects the proper address of the identification card holder. *(Added by Stats.1968, c. 494, p. 1138, § 3. Amended by Stats.1976, c. 552, p. 1392, § 3.)*

§ 13007.5. Identity verification

Notwithstanding anything to the contrary in this code or in the regulations adopted thereunder, including specifically the Driver's License Manual of Procedure, the department may verify the identity of any person born prior to 1916 who applies for an identification card, through United States Census records even though the date and month of birth are not included.

It is unlawful for an applicant to knowingly declare to the department, in writing, that no birth certificate exists for the applicant when, in fact, a birth certificate does exist. *(Added by Stats.1982, c. 199, p. 674, § 1. Amended by Stats.1992, c. 1243 (A.B.3090), § 86, eff. Sept. 30, 1992.)*

Cross References

Confidentiality of driver's license information, authorization for businesses to swipe driver's license or identification card in electronic device for certain purposes, violation, see Civil Code § 1798.90.1.

§ 13008. Cancellation

When used in reference to an identification card, "cancellation" means that an identification card is terminated without prejudice and must be surrendered. Cancellation of card may be made when a card has been issued through error or when voluntarily surrendered to the department. *(Added by Stats.1969, c. 1340, p. 2689, § 7.)*

CHAPTER 2. SUSPENSION OR REVOCATION OF LICENSES

Article	Section
1. General Provisions	13100
2. Suspension or Revocation by Court	13200
3. Suspension and Revocation by Department	13350
4. Procedure	13550

ARTICLE 1. GENERAL PROVISIONS

Section
13100. Cancellation.
13101. Revocation.
13102. Suspension; examination.
13103. Equivalents of conviction.
13105. Conviction of a juvenile.
13106. Notice of suspension or revocation of driving privilege; presumptions; alternative methods for determining whereabouts of drivers.

Cross References

Driver license compact, see Vehicle Code § 15000 et seq.
Surrender of license, see Vehicle Code §§ 13207, 13551.
Suspension or revocation of license, driving schools, see Vehicle Code § 11110.

§ 13100. Cancellation

When used in reference to a driver's license, "cancellation" means that a driver's license certificate is terminated without prejudice and must be surrendered. Any person whose license has been canceled may immediately apply for a license. Cancellation of license may be made only when specifically authorized in this code, when application is made for a license to operate vehicles of a higher class, or when a license has been issued through error or voluntarily surrendered to the department. *(Stats.1959, c. 3, p. 1623, § 13100. Amended by Stats. 1961, c. 1615, p. 3457, § 25; Stats.1974, c. 428, p. 1040, § 3.)*

Cross References

Application for license, see Vehicle Code § 12800.
Cancellation of minor's license, see Vehicle Code §§ 17711, 17712.
Records of licenses suspended, revoked and cancelled, see Vehicle Code §§ 1801, 1807.
Renewal of license, see Vehicle Code §§ 12808, 12814.
Seizure of documents and plates, see Vehicle Code § 4460.

§ 13101. Revocation

When used in reference to a driver's license, "revocation" means that the person's privilege to drive a motor vehicle is terminated and a new driver's license may be obtained after the period of revocation. *(Stats.1959, c. 3, p. 1623, § 13101.)*

Cross References

Suspension or revocation of,
  Emergency vehicle permit, grounds, see Vehicle Code § 2417.
  License by court, see Vehicle Code § 13200 et seq.

§ 13102. Suspension; examination

When used in reference to a driver's license, "suspension" means that the person's privilege to drive a motor vehicle is temporarily withdrawn. The department may, before terminating any suspension based upon a physical or mental condition of the licensee, require such examination of the licensee as deemed appropriate in relation to evidence of any condition which may affect the ability of the licensee to safely operate a motor vehicle. *(Stats. 1959, c. 3, p. 1623, § 13102. Amended by Stats.1976, c. 498, p. 1238, § 1; Stats.1999, c. 724 (A.B.1650), § 31.)*

Definitions,
  Highway, see Vehicle Code §§ 360, 590.
  Motor vehicle, see Vehicle Code § 415.

§ 13103. Equivalents of conviction

For purposes of this division, a plea of nolo contendere or a plea of guilty or judgment of guilty, whether probation is granted or not, a forfeiture of bail, or a finding reported under Section 1816, constitutes a conviction of any offense prescribed by this code, other than offenses relating to the unlawful parking of vehicles. *(Added by Stats.1959, c. 1622, p. 3991, § 3. Amended by Stats.1972, c. 1207, p. 2333, § 3.)*

Cross References

Forfeiture of bail, see Penal Code § 1305 et seq.
Judgments in criminal cases, see Penal Code § 1191 et seq.
Plea of guilty, see Penal Code § 1016 et seq.

§ 13105. Conviction of a juvenile

For the purposes of this chapter, "convicted" or "conviction" includes a finding by a judge of a juvenile court, a juvenile hearing officer, or referee of a juvenile court that a person has committed an offense, and "court" includes a juvenile court except as otherwise specifically provided. *(Added by Stats.1972, c. 755, p. 1349, § 2. Amended by Stats.2003, c. 149 (S.B.79), § 81.)*

Law Revision Commission Comments

2003 Amendment

Section 13105 is amended to reflect the redesignation of traffic hearing officers as juvenile hearing officers. See 1997 Cal. Stat. ch. 679. [33 Cal.L.Rev.Comm. Reports 246 (2003)].

§ 13106. Notice of suspension or revocation of driving privilege; presumptions; alternative methods for determining whereabouts of drivers

(a) When the privilege of a person to operate a motor vehicle is suspended or revoked, the department shall notify the person by first-class mail, of the action taken and of the effective date thereof, except for those persons personally given notice by the department or a court, by a peace officer pursuant to Section 13388 or 13382, or otherwise pursuant to this code. It shall be a rebuttable presumption, affecting the burden of proof, that a person has knowledge of the suspension or revocation if notice has been sent by first-class mail by the department pursuant to this section to the most recent address reported to the department pursuant to Section 12800 or 14600, or any more recent address on file if reported by the person, a court, or a law enforcement agency, and the notice has not been returned to the department as undeliverable or unclaimed. It is the responsibility of every holder of a driver's license to report changes of address to the department pursuant to Section 14600.

(b) The department may utilize alternative methods for determining the whereabouts of a driver, whose driving privilege has been suspended or revoked under

this code, for the purpose of providing the driver with notice of suspension or revocation. Alternative methods may include, but are not limited to, cooperating with other state agencies that maintain more current address information than the department's driver's license files.

(Added by Stats.1994, c. 1133 (A.B.3148), § 5, operative June 30, 1995. Amended by Stats.1998, c. 683 (A.B.2347), § 2; Stats.1999, c. 22 (S.B.24), § 8, eff. May 26, 1999, operative July 1, 1999; Stats.2002, c. 805 (A.B.2996), § 17, eff. Sept. 23, 2002.)

Cross References

Burden of proof, generally, see Evidence Code § 500 et seq.
Driving after revocation or suspension of driving privilege, mailed notice as presumption affecting burden of proof, see Vehicle Code § 14601 et seq.

ARTICLE 2. SUSPENSION OR REVOCATION BY COURT

Section
13200.   Speeding or reckless driving.
13200.5. Driving at speeds over 100 m.p.h.; suspension of privilege to operate a motor vehicle.
13201.   Certain misdemeanors.
13201.5. Violations of Penal Code § 647; suspension or restriction of driving privileges.
13202.   Controlled substance offenses.
13202.3. Repealed.
13202.4. Public offense by minor involving concealable firearm; suspension, restriction or delay of driving privileges; community service.
13202.5. Drug and alcohol related offenses by person under age of 21, but aged 13 or over; suspension, delay, or restriction of driving privileges.
13202.6. Vandalism by defacing or destroying property; convictions of persons age 13 or older; suspension or delay of driving privilege; reduction of period for community service.
13202.7. Minor 13 to 18 years old; habitual truant or ward of juvenile court; suspension, delay, or restriction of driving privileges.
13202.8. Ignition interlock device; installation and maintenance; restrictions under § 13202.5.
13203.   Limitation on suspension.
13204.   Repealed.
13205.   Nonresidents.
13206.   Surrender of license.
13207.   Licenses affected by suspension.
13208.   Recommendation of court to department.
13209.   Record of prior conviction.
13210.   Suspensions of driving privileges; commission of assault; road rage.

Cross References

Driver license compact, see Vehicle Code § 15000 et seq.

§ 13200. Speeding or reckless driving

Whenever any person licensed under this code is convicted of a violation of any provision of this code relating to the speed of vehicles or a violation of Section 23103 the court may, unless this code makes mandatory a revocation by the department, suspend the privilege of the person to operate a motor vehicle for a period of not to exceed 30 days upon a first conviction, for a period of not to exceed 60 days upon a second conviction, and for a period of not to exceed six months upon a third or any subsequent conviction. *(Stats.1959, c. 3, p. 1623, § 13200.)*

Cross References

Conviction, equivalents, see Vehicle Code § 13103.
Maximum period of suspension, see Vehicle Code § 13203.
Offenses,
    Driving while intoxicated, see Vehicle Code §§ 23152, 23153.
    Failure to stop after accident, see Vehicle Code § 20001 et seq.
    Reckless driving, see Vehicle Code §§ 23103, 23104.
Seizure of documents and plates, see Vehicle Code § 4460.
Speed laws, see Vehicle Code § 22348 et seq.
Surrender of suspended or revoked licenses, see Vehicle Code § 13550.
Suspension or revocation,
    Emergency vehicle permit, see Vehicle Code § 2417.
    Failure to satisfy judgment, see Vehicle Code § 16370 et seq.
    Failure to stop after accident, see Vehicle Code § 13201.
    Registration of vehicles, see Vehicle Code § 8800 et seq.
    Violating provisions of restricted license, see Vehicle Code §§ 13360, 14603.

§ 13200.5. Driving at speeds over 100 m.p.h.; suspension of privilege to operate a motor vehicle

Whenever any person licensed under this code is convicted of a violation of subdivision (b) of Section 22348, the court may, unless this code makes mandatory a revocation by the department, suspend the privilege of the person to operate a motor vehicle for a period of not to exceed 30 days. *(Added by Stats.1983, c. 980, § 1. Amended by Stats.1984, c. 276, § 2.)*

Cross References

Driving at speed greater than 100 miles per hour, see Vehicle Code § 22348.

§ 13201. Certain misdemeanors

A court may suspend, for not more than six months, the privilege of a person to operate a motor vehicle upon conviction of any of the following offenses:

(a) Failure of the driver of a vehicle involved in an accident to stop or otherwise comply with Section 20002.

(b) Reckless driving proximately causing bodily injury to a person under Section 23104 or 23105.

(c) Failure of the driver of a vehicle to stop at a railway grade crossing as required by Section 22452.

(d) Evading a peace officer in violation of Section 2800.1 or 2800.2, or in violation of Section 2800.3 if the person's license is not revoked for that violation pursuant to paragraph (3) of subdivision (a) of Section 13351.

(e)(1) Knowingly causing or participating in a vehicular collision, or any other vehicular accident, for the purpose of presenting or causing to be presented any false or fraudulent insurance claim.

(2) In lieu of suspending a person's driving privilege pursuant to paragraph (1), the court may order the privilege to operate a motor vehicle restricted to necessary travel to and from that person's place of employment for not more than six months. If driving a motor vehicle is necessary to perform the duties of the person's employment, the court may restrict the driving privilege to allow driving in that person's scope of employment. Whenever a person's driving privilege is restricted pursuant to this paragraph, the person shall be required to maintain proof of financial responsibility. *(Stats.1959, c. 3, p. 1624, § 13201. Amended by Stats.1971, c. 1530, p. 3024, § 5, operative May 3, 1972; Stats.1972, c. 92, p. 118, § 3; Stats.1975, c. 1133, p. 2804, § 1; Stats.1981, c. 939, p. 3548, § 3; Stats.1981, c. 940, p. 3563, § 2; Stats.1988, c. 504, § 4, eff. Aug. 22, 1988; Stats.1991, c. 656 (S.B.666), § 2; Stats.1992, c. 490 (A.B.2699), § 1; Stats.2007, c. 682 (A.B.430), § 11.)*

Cross References

Grounds for suspension, see Vehicle Code § 13361.

§ 13201.5. Violations of Penal Code § 647; suspension or restriction of driving privileges

(a) A court may suspend, for not more than 30 days, the privilege of any person to operate a motor vehicle upon conviction of subdivision (b) of Section 647 of the Penal Code where the violation was committed within 1,000 feet of a private residence and with the use of a vehicle.

(b) A court may suspend, for not more than 30 days, the privilege of any person to operate a motor vehicle upon conviction of subdivision (a) of Section 647 of the Penal Code, where a peace officer witnesses the violator pick up a person who is engaging in loitering with the intent to commit prostitution, as described in Section 653.22 of the Penal Code, and the violator subsequently engages with that person in a lewd act within 1,000 feet of a private residence and with the use of a vehicle.

(c) Instead of ordering the suspension under subdivision (a) or (b), a court may order a person's privilege to operate a motor vehicle restricted for not more than six months to necessary travel to and from the person's place of employment or education. If driving a motor vehicle is necessary to perform the duties of the person's employment, the court may also allow the person to drive in that person's scope of employment. *(Added by Stats. 1996, c. 1019 (A.B.2949), § 3. Amended by Stats.1998, c. 758 (A.B.1788), § 2.)*

§ 13202. Controlled substance offenses

(a) A court may suspend or order that the department revoke in which case the department shall revoke the privilege of any person to operate a motor vehicle upon conviction of any offense related to controlled substances as defined in Division 10 (commencing with Section 11000) of the Health and Safety Code when the use of a motor vehicle was involved in, or incidental to, the commission of the offense.

(b) A court shall order that the department revoke and the department shall revoke the privilege of any person to operate a motor vehicle upon conviction of a violation of Section 11350, 11351, 11352, 11353, 11357, 11359, 11360, or 11361 of the Health and Safety Code when a motor vehicle was involved in, or incidental to, the commission of such offense.

(c) The period of time for suspension or the period after revocation during which the person may not apply for a license shall be determined by the court, but in no event shall such period exceed three years from the date of conviction. *(Stats.1959, c. 3, p. 1624, § 13202. Amended by Stats.1961, c. 274, p. 1308, § 15; Stats.1967, c. 549, p. 1897, § 1; Stats.1972, c. 1407, p. 3044, § 11; Stats.1974, c. 1194, p. 2570, § 2; Stats.1984, c. 1635, § 93.)*

§ 13202.3. Repealed by Stats.1997 c. 5 (A.B.74), § 1, operative Jan. 1, 2000

§ 13202.4. Public offense by minor involving concealable firearm; suspension, restriction or delay of driving privileges; community service

(a)(1) For each conviction of a minor who commits a public offense involving a pistol, revolver, or other firearm capable of being concealed upon the person, the court may suspend the minor's driving privilege for five years. If the minor convicted does not yet have the privilege to drive, the court may order the department to delay issuing the privilege to drive for five years subsequent to the time the person becomes legally eligible to drive. For each successive offense, the court may suspend the minor's driving privilege for those possessing a license or delay the eligibility for those not in possession of a license at the time of their conviction for one additional year.

(2)(A) Any minor whose driving privilege is suspended pursuant to this section may elect to reduce the period of suspension or delay imposed by the court by performing community service under the supervision of the probation department if both of the following conditions are met:

(i) At least 50 percent of the suspension or delay period has expired.

(ii) The person has not been the subject of any other criminal conviction during the suspension or delay period.

(B) If the conditions specified in subparagraph (A) are met, the period of suspension or delay ordered under paragraph (1) shall be reduced at the rate of one day for each hour of community service performed.

(3) As used in this section, the term "conviction" includes the findings in juvenile proceedings specified in Section 13105.

(b)(1) Whenever the court suspends driving privileges pursuant to subdivision (a), the court in which the conviction is had shall require all driver's licenses held by the person to be surrendered to the court. The court shall, within 10 days following the conviction, transmit a certified abstract of the conviction, together with any driver's licenses surrendered, to the department.

(2) Violations of restrictions imposed pursuant to this section are subject to Section 14603.

(c) When the court is considering suspending or delaying driving privileges pursuant to subdivision (a), the court shall consider if a personal or family hardship exists that requires the person to have a driver's license for his or her own, or a member of his or her family's, employment or medically related purposes.

(d) The suspension, restriction, or delay of driving privileges pursuant to this section shall be in addition to any penalty imposed upon conviction for the offense. *(Added by Stats.1993–94, 1st Ex.Sess., c. 33 (S.B.36), § 11, eff. Nov. 30, 1994. Amended by Stats.2001, c. 854 (S.B.205), § 67.)*

§ 13202.5. Drug and alcohol related offenses by person under age of 21, but aged 13 or over; suspension, delay, or restriction of driving privileges

(a) For each conviction of a person for an offense specified in subdivision (d), committed while the person was under the age of 21 years, but 13 years of age or older, the court shall suspend the person's driving privilege for one year. If the person convicted does not yet have the privilege to drive, the court shall order the department to delay issuing the privilege to drive for one year subsequent to the time the person becomes legally eligible to drive. However, if there is no further conviction for an offense specified in subdivision (d) in a 12–month period after the conviction, the court, upon petition of the person affected, may modify the order imposing the delay of the privilege. For each successive offense, the court shall suspend the person's driving privilege for those possessing a license or delay the eligibility for those not in possession of a license at the time of their conviction for one additional year.

As used in this section, the term "conviction" includes the findings in juvenile proceedings specified in Section 13105.

(b) Whenever the court suspends driving privileges pursuant to subdivision (a), the court in which the conviction is had shall require all driver's licenses held by the person to be surrendered to the court. The court shall within 10 days following the conviction transmit a certified abstract of the conviction, together with any driver's licenses surrendered, to the department.

(c)(1) After a court has issued an order suspending or delaying driving privileges pursuant to subdivision (a), the court, upon petition of the person affected, may review the order and may impose restrictions on the person's privilege to drive based upon a showing of a critical need to drive.

(2) As used in this section, "critical need to drive" means the circumstances that are required to be shown for the issuance of a junior permit pursuant to Section 12513.

(3) The restriction shall remain in effect for the balance of the period of suspension or restriction in this section. The court shall notify the department of any modification within 10 days of the order of modification.

(d) This section applies to violations involving controlled substances or alcohol contained in the following provisions:

(1) Article 7 (commencing with Section 4110) of Chapter 9 of Division 2 of, and Sections 25658, 25658.5, 25661, and 25662 of, the Business and Professions Code.

(2) Division 10 (commencing with Section 11000) of the Health and Safety Code.

(3) Section 191.5, subdivision (a) or (b) of Section 192.5, and subdivision (f) of Section 647 of the Penal Code.

(4) Section 23103 when subject to Section 23103.5, Section 23140, and Article 2 (commencing with Section 23152) of Chapter 12 of Division 11 of this code.

(e) Suspension, restriction, or delay of driving privileges pursuant to this section shall be in addition to any penalty imposed upon conviction of a violation specified in subdivision (d). *(Added by Stats.1984, c. 658, § 1. Amended by Stats.1988, c. 1254, § 3; Stats.1990, c. 1696 (S.B.1756), § 3; Stats.1990, c. 1697 (S.B.2635), § 4; Stats.2007, c. 747 (A.B.678), § 17.)*

§ 13202.6. Vandalism by defacing or destroying property; convictions of persons age 13 or older; suspension or delay of driving privilege; reduction of period for community service

(a)(1) For every conviction of a person for a violation of Section 594, 594.3, or 594.4 of the Penal Code, committed while the person was 13 years of age or older, the court shall suspend the person's driving privilege for not more than two years, except when the court finds that a personal or family hardship exists that requires the person to have a driver's license for his or her own, or a member of his or her family's, employment, school, or medically related purposes. If the person convicted does not yet have the privilege to drive, the court shall order the department to delay issuing the privilege to drive for not less than one year nor more than three years subsequent to the time the person becomes legally eligible to drive. However, if there is no further conviction for violating Section 594, 594.3, or 594.4 of the Penal Code in a 12–month period after the conviction, the court, upon petition of the person affected, may modify the order imposing the delay of the privilege. For each successive offense, the court shall suspend the person's driving privilege for those possessing a license or delay the eligibility for those not in possession of a license at the time of their conviction for one additional year.

(2) A person whose driving privilege is suspended or delayed for an act involving vandalism in violation of Section 594, 594.3, or 594.4 of the Penal Code, may elect to reduce the period of suspension or delay imposed by the court by performing community service under the supervision of the probation department. The period of suspension or delay ordered under paragraph (1) shall be reduced at the rate of one day for each hour of community service performed. If the jurisdiction has adopted a graffiti abatement program as defined in subdivision (f) of Section 594 of the Penal Code, the period of suspension or delay ordered under paragraph (1) shall be reduced at the rate of one day for each day of community service performed in the graffiti abatement program when the defendant and his or her parents or legal guardians are responsible for keeping a specified property in the community free of graffiti for a specified period of time. The suspension shall be reduced only when the specified period of participation has been completed. Participation of a parent or legal guardian is not required under this paragraph if the court deems this participation to be detrimental to the defendant, or if the parent or legal guardian is a single parent who must care for young children. For purposes of this paragraph, "community service" means cleaning up graffiti from any public property, including public transit vehicles.

(3) As used in this section, the term "conviction" includes the findings in juvenile proceedings specified in Section 13105.

(b)(1) Whenever the court suspends driving privileges pursuant to subdivision (a), the court in which the conviction is had shall require all drivers' licenses held by the person to be surrendered to the court. The court shall, within 10 days following the conviction, transmit a certified abstract of the conviction, together with any drivers' licenses surrendered, to the department.

(2) Violations of restrictions imposed pursuant to this section are subject to Section 14603.

(c) The suspension, restriction, or delay of driving privileges pursuant to this section shall be in addition to any penalty imposed upon conviction of a violation of Section 594, 594.3, or 594.4 of the Penal Code. *(Added by Stats.1990, c. 712 (S.B.1977), § 1. Amended by Stats.1993, c. 605 (A.B.1179), § 14; Stats.1994, c. 909 (S.B.1779), § 9; Stats.1996, c. 600 (A.B.2295), § 9; Stats. 1996, c. 918 (A.B.2331), § 2; Stats.2006, c. 434 (A.B. 2923), § 1.)*

§ 13202.7. Minor 13 to 18 years old; habitual truant or ward of juvenile court; suspension, delay, or restriction of driving privileges

(a) Any minor under the age of 18 years, but 13 years of age or older, who is an habitual truant within the meaning of Section 48262 of the Education Code, or who is adjudged by the juvenile court to be a ward of the court under subdivision (b) of Section 601 of the Welfare and Institutions Code, may have his or her driving privilege suspended for one year by the court. If the minor does not yet have the privilege to drive, the court may order the department to delay issuing the privilege to drive for one year subsequent to the time the person becomes legally eligible to drive. However, if there is no further truancy in the 12-month period, the court, upon petition

465

of the person affected, may modify the order imposing the delay of the driving privilege. For each successive time the minor is found to be an habitual truant, the court may suspend the minor's driving privilege for a minor possessing a driver's license, or delay the eligibility for the driving privilege for those not in possession of a driver's license, for one additional year.

(b) Whenever the juvenile court suspends a minor's driving privilege pursuant to subdivision (a), the court may require all driver's licenses held by the minor to be surrendered to the court. The court shall, within 10 days following the surrender of the license, transmit a certified abstract of the findings, together with any driver's licenses surrendered, to the department.

(c) When the juvenile court is considering suspending or delaying a minor's driving privilege pursuant to subdivision (a), the court shall consider whether a personal or family hardship exists that requires the minor to have a driver's license for his or her own, or a member of his or her family's, employment or for medically related purposes.

(d) The suspension, restriction, or delay of a minor's driving privilege pursuant to this section shall be in addition to any other penalty imposed by law on the minor. *(Added by Stats.1991, c. 425 (S.B.558), § 2. Amended by Stats.1994, c. 1023 (S.B.1728), § 5.)*

§ 13202.8. Ignition interlock device; installation and maintenance; restrictions under § 13202.5

The restrictions specified in Section 13202.5 for the violations specified in that section may include, but are not limited to, the installation and maintenance of a certified ignition interlock device pursuant to Section 13386. Any restriction is subject to the provisions of Section 13202.5 relating to restrictions. *(Formerly § 13202.7, added by Stats.1990, c. 1403 (A.B.2040), § 5, eff. Sept. 28, 1990. Renumbered § 13202.8 and amended by Stats.1991, c. 425 (S.B.558), § 1. Amended by Stats. 1998, c. 118 (S.B.1186), § 1.33, operative July 1, 1999.)*

§ 13203. Limitation on suspension

In no event shall a court suspend the privilege of any person to operate a motor vehicle or as a condition of probation prohibit the operation of a motor vehicle for a period of time longer than that specified in this code. Any such prohibited order of a court, whether imposed as a condition of probation or otherwise, shall be null and void, and the department shall restore or reissue a license to any person entitled thereto irrespective of any such invalid order of a court. *(Stats.1959, c. 3, p. 1624, § 13203. Amended by Stats.1963, c. 917, p. 2169, § 13; Stats.1967, c. 549, p. 1897, § 2; Stats.1972, c. 755, p. 1349, § 2.5; Stats.1973, c. 903, p. 1683, § 1; Stats.1974, c. 1283, p. 2776, § 1, eff. Sept. 23, 1974.)*

§ 13204. Repealed by Stats.1959, c. 1622, p. 3992, § 4

466

§ 13205. Nonresidents

The privileges of a nonresident to operate vehicles in this State may be suspended or revoked under the provisions of this chapter in the same manner and to the same extent as the privileges of a resident driver. *(Stats.1959, c. 3, p. 1624, § 13205.)*

§ 13206. Surrender of license

Whenever a court suspends the privilege of a person to operate a motor vehicle, the court shall require the person's license to be surrendered to it. Unless required by the provisions of Section 13550 to send the license to the department, the court shall retain the license during the period of suspension and return it to the licensee at the end of the period after indorsing thereon a record of the suspension. *(Stats.1959, c. 3, p. 1624, § 13206.)*

§ 13207. Licenses affected by suspension

Whenever a court suspends the privilege of any person to operate a motor vehicle, the suspension shall apply to all driver's licenses held by him, and all licenses shall be surrendered to the court. *(Stats.1959, c. 3, p. 1625, § 13207.)*

§ 13208. Recommendation of court to department

In any criminal proceeding, without regard to its disposition, wherein the defendant is charged with a violation of Division 11 (commencing with Section 21000), the court may, if it has reason to believe that any of the conditions specified in Section 12805 or 12806 exist, recommend to the department that an investigation be conducted to determine whether the driving privilege of that person should be suspended or revoked. In making the recommendation, the court shall state the basis for the belief that the condition exists and whether the defendant relied upon the condition as a part of his or her defense. The department may provide a form for the court's convenience. *(Added by Stats.1959, c. 1477, p. 3772, § 1. Amended by Stats.1987, c. 321, § 7.)*

§ 13209. Record of prior conviction

Before sentencing a person upon a conviction of a violation of Section 23152 or 23153, the court shall obtain from the department a record of any prior convictions of that person for traffic violations. The department shall furnish that record upon the written request of the court.

Notwithstanding the provisions of Section 1449 of the Penal Code, in any such criminal action the time for pronouncement of judgment shall not commence to run until the time that the court receives the record of prior convictions from the department. *(Added by Stats.1961, c. 1936, p. 4087, § 1. Amended by Stats.1971, c. 1530, p. 3025, § 6, operative May 3, 1972; Stats.1981, c. 939, p. 3548, § 4.5.)*

§ 13210. Suspensions of driving privileges; commission of assault; road rage

In addition to the penalties set forth in subdivision (a) of Section 245 of the Penal Code, the court may order the suspension of the driving privilege of any operator of a motor vehicle who commits an assault as described in subdivision (a) of Section 245 of the Penal Code on an operator or passenger of another motor vehicle, an operator of a bicycle, or a pedestrian and the offense occurs on a highway. The suspension period authorized under this section for an assault commonly known as "road rage," shall be six months for a first offense and one year for a second or subsequent offense to commence, at the discretion of the court, either on the date of the person's conviction, or upon the person's release from confinement or imprisonment. The court may, in lieu of or in addition to the suspension of the driving privilege, order a person convicted under this section to complete a court-approved anger management or "road rage" course, subsequent to the date of the current violation. *(Added by Stats.2000, c. 642 (A.B.2733), § 4.)*

ARTICLE 3. SUSPENSION AND REVOCATION BY DEPARTMENT

Section
13350.   Required revocation; affidavit of understanding; reinstatement.
13350.5.   Conviction of vehicular manslaughter for driving under influence or influence of alcohol and drugs causing bodily injury as conviction of § 23153.
13351.   Required revocation; conviction of manslaughter, three or more violations of §§ 20001, 20002, 23103, 23104 or 23105, or Penal Code §§ 191.5, 192.5, or 2800.3; reinstatement.
13351.5.   Vehicle used to commit assault with a deadly weapon or force likely to produce great bodily injury; revocation of driving privilege.
13351.8.   Suspension of driving privilege; receipt of certified abstract of record.
13351.85.   Conviction under § 12110; suspension of driving privileges.
13352.   Conviction for driving under the influence or engaging in speed contests or exhibitions of speed; terms of suspension or revocation of

Section
            license; eligibility for restricted license; reinstatement conditions.
13352.1.   Conviction or finding of violation of § 23152; ten month suspension of privilege for certain offenders; conditions for reinstatement.
13352.2.   Driving-under-the-influence programs; filing of proof of enrollment and proof of completion by program provider.
13352.3.   Persons under eighteen years of age convicted of violations of §§ 23152 or 23153; term of revocation; reinstatement of privilege.
13352.4.   Restricted driver's licenses.
13352.5.   Restricted driver's licenses.
13352.6.   Conviction of person under 21 drinking and driving; reinstatement; driving-under-the-influence program.
13353.   Chemical blood, breath, or urine tests.
13353.1.   Preliminary alcohol screening test; refusal or failure to complete; notice; review.
13353.2.   Immediate suspension; grounds; notice of order of suspension; determination of facts.
13353.3.   Order of suspension under Vehicle Code § 13353.2; effective date, period, and termination of suspension.
13353.4.   Restoration of driving privilege and issuance of restricted or hardship permit to operate motor vehicle during suspension or revocation period.
13353.45.   Certificate of completion; fees.
13353.5.   Expiration of suspension or revocation period; out of state residence; reinstatement; conditions.
13353.6.   Repealed.
13353.7.   Restricted driver's licenses.
13353.8.   Order suspending or delaying driving privileges; showing of critical need to drive; review of order; imposition of restrictions on driving privilege.
13354.   Repealed.
13355.   Driving upon a highway at a speed greater than one hundred miles per hour; suspension of privilege to operate motor vehicle.
13355.5.   Repealed.
13356.   Repealed.
13357.   Revocation or suspension for theft or unlawful taking of a vehicle.
13358.   Repealed.
13359.   Grounds for suspension or revocation.
13360.   Violation of license restrictions.
13361.   Grounds for suspension.
13362.   Surrender of license erroneously issued.
13363.   Conviction in another state.
13364.   Driver's license; suspension; dishonored check; notice; reinstatement.
13365.   Section 40508 (promise to appear) violations.
13365.2.   Persons charged with driving under the influence of drugs or alcohol; failure to make appearance; effective date of suspension.
13365.5.   Notification of willful failure to comply with court order; suspension; effective date of suspension.
13366.   Effective date of suspension or revocation.
13366.5.   Commencement of suspension or revocation.
13367.   Determining minor's suspension.
13368.   Driver training requirement.
13369.   Certificate or endorsement for specified vehicles.
13370.   Schoolbus, school pupil activity bus, general public paratransit vehicle, youth bus, or vehicle for

Section

         transportation of developmentally disabled persons; grounds to refuse or revoke driver certificate.

13371.   Schoolbus, activity bus, youth bus, paratransit vehicle, and developmentally disabled person vehicle certificate; hearing.

13372.   Ambulance driver certificate; refusal to issue or renew; suspension or revocation; grounds; conditions for reapplication.

13373.   Dismissal of ambulance drivers or attendants; causes.

13374.   Denial, suspension, or revocation of ambulance drivers license; hearing; request; waiver; findings and recommendations; review committee; final decision.

13375.   Plea or verdict of guilty or plea of nolo contendere; conviction.

13376.   Bus or public paratransit driver certificates; revocation or suspension; positive test result or refusal to submit to test for a controlled substance; sex offense prosecution.

13377.   Tow truck driver certificates; grounds for revocation or refusal to issue or renew; reapplication for certificate.

13378.   Request for hearing; stay; appointment of hearing officer.

13380.   Peace officer's report; service of notice of suspension; arrest.

13382.   Blood alcohol of specified level; suspension or revocation of driving privilege; notice; confiscation of license; temporary license.

13384.   Consent to chemical test of blood, breath or urine.

13385.   Driving under the influence; declaration required in application forms or renewal notices as condition of licensure.

13386.   Certification and list of ignition interlock devices; prohibitions.

13388.   Preliminary alcohol screening test or other chemical testing; procedure upon failure to take or complete test.

13389.   Persons previously convicted of driving under the influence; lawful detention during probation; preliminary alcohol screening test; suspension of driving privileges.

13390.   Repealed.

13392.   Fee for reissuance, return or issuance of license.

Cross References

Driver license compact, see Vehicle Code § 15000 et seq.

Probation in lieu of suspension or revocation, see Vehicle Code § 14250.

Recommendations of court to department, see Vehicle Code § 13208.

§ 13350.   Required revocation; affidavit of understanding; reinstatement

(a) The department immediately shall revoke the privilege of a person to drive a motor vehicle upon receipt of a duly certified abstract of the record of a court showing that the person has been convicted of any of the following crimes or offenses:

(1) Failure of the driver of a vehicle involved in an accident resulting in injury or death to a person to stop or otherwise comply with Section 20001.

(2) A felony in the commission of which a motor vehicle is used, except as provided in Section 13351, 13352, or 13357.

(3) Reckless driving causing bodily injury.

(b) If a person is convicted of a violation of Section 23152 punishable under Section 23546, 23550, or 23550.5, or a violation of Section 23153 punishable under Section 23550.5 or 23566, including a violation of subdivision (b) of Section 191.5 of the Penal Code as provided in Section 193.7 of that code, the court shall, at the time of surrender of the driver's license or temporary permit, require the defendant to sign an affidavit in a form provided by the department acknowledging his or her understanding of the revocation required by paragraph (5), (6), or (7) of subdivision (a) of Section 13352, and an acknowledgment of his or her designation as a habitual traffic offender. A copy of this affidavit shall be transmitted, with the license or temporary permit, to the department within the prescribed 10 days.

(c) The department shall not reinstate the privilege revoked under subdivision (a) until the expiration of one year after the date of revocation and until the person whose privilege was revoked gives proof of financial responsibility as defined in Section 16430. *(Stats.1959, c. 3, p. 1625, § 13350. Amended by Stats.1959, c. 1048, p. 3089, § 1; Stats.1961, c. 58, p. 1009, § 33; Stats.1965, c. 1060, p. 2706, § 1; Stats.1967, c. 1110, p. 2756, § 7; Stats.1971, c. 1530, p. 3025, § 8, operative May 3, 1972; Stats.1982, c. 655, p. 2671, § 1; Stats.1988, c. 1415, § 1; Stats.1990, c. 44 (A.B.1648), § 2; Stats.1991, c. 656 (S.B.666), § 3; Stats.1992, c. 974 (S.B.1600), § 5, eff. Sept. 28, 1992; Stats.1997, c. 901 (A.B.130), § 1; Stats. 1998, c. 118 (S.B.1186), § 1.35, operative July 1, 1999; Stats.1999, c. 22 (S.B.24), § 9, eff. May 26, 1999, operative July 1, 1999; Stats.2002, c. 545 (S.B.1852), § 7; Stats. 2007, c. 747 (A.B.678), § 18.)*

Cross References

Commercial motor vehicles, multiple violations, see Vehicle Code § 15302.

Definitions,

   Felony, see Penal Code § 17.

   Manslaughter in driving of vehicle, see Penal Code § 192.

Driver license compact party states, reported conduct as ground for suspension or revocation, see Vehicle Code § 15023.

Grand theft of motor vehicle, see Penal Code § 487.

Proof of financial responsibility, see Vehicle Code § 16430.

Theft and unlawful driving or taking of a vehicle, see Vehicle Code § 10851.

§ 13350.5.   Conviction of vehicular manslaughter for driving under influence or influence of alcohol and drugs causing bodily injury as conviction of § 23153

Notwithstanding Section 13350, for the purposes of this article, conviction of a violation of subdivision (b) of Section 191.5 of the Penal Code is a conviction of a violation of Section 23153. *(Added by Stats.1983, c. 937, § 3. Amended by Stats.1987, c. 309, § 1; Stats.1991, c. 656 (S.B.666), § 4; Stats.1998, c. 118 (S.B.1186), § 1.37, operative July 1, 1999; Stats.1999, c. 22 (S.B.24), § 10, eff. May 26, 1999, operative July 1, 1999; Stats.2007, c. 747 (A.B.678), § 19.)*

§ 13351. Required revocation; conviction of manslaughter, three or more violations of §§ 20001, 20002, 23103, 23104 or 23105, or Penal Code §§ 191.5, 192.5, or 2800.3; reinstatement

(a) The department immediately shall revoke the privilege of a person to drive a motor vehicle upon receipt of a duly certified abstract of the record of a court showing that the person has been convicted of any of the following crimes or offenses:

(1) Manslaughter resulting from the operation of a motor vehicle, except when convicted under paragraph (2) of subdivision (c) of Section 192 of the Penal Code.

(2) Conviction of three or more violations of Section 20001, 20002, 23103, 23104, or 23105 within a period of 12 months from the time of the first offense to the third or subsequent offense, or a combination of three or more convictions of violations within the same period.

(3) Violation of subdivision (a) of Section 191.5 or subdivision (a) of Section 192.5 of the Penal Code or of Section 2800.3 causing serious bodily injury resulting in a serious impairment of physical condition, including, but not limited to, loss of consciousness, concussion, serious bone fracture, protracted loss or impairment of function of any bodily member or organ, and serious disfigurement.

(b) The department shall not reinstate the privilege revoked under subdivision (a) until the expiration of three years after the date of revocation and until the person whose privilege was revoked gives proof of financial responsibility, as defined in Section 16430. *(Added by Stats.1982, c. 655, p. 2671, § 3. Amended by Stats.1985, c. 6, § 2, eff. Feb. 21, 1985; Stats.1991, c. 656 (S.B.666), § 5; Stats.1992, c. 974 (S.B.1600), § 6, eff. Sept. 28, 1992; Stats.2007, c. 682 (A.B.430), § 12; Stats. 2007, c. 747 (A.B.678), § 20.5.)*

Cross References

Renewal of licenses, see Vehicle Code §§ 12808, 12814.

§ 13351.5. Vehicle used to commit assault with a deadly weapon or force likely to produce great bodily injury; revocation of driving privilege

(a) Upon receipt of a duly certified abstract of the record of any court showing that a person has been convicted of a felony for a violation of Section 245 of the Penal Code and that a vehicle was found by the court to constitute the deadly weapon or instrument used to commit that offense, the department immediately shall revoke the privilege of that person to drive a motor vehicle.

(b) The department shall not reinstate a privilege revoked under subdivision (a) under any circumstances.

(c) Notwithstanding subdivision (b), the department shall terminate any revocation order issued under this section on or after January 1, 1995, for a misdemeanor conviction of violating Section 245 of the Penal Code. *(Added by Stats.1994, c. 1221 (S.B.1758), § 9. Amended by Stats.1998, c. 606 (S.B.1880), § 15.)*

Cross References

Felonies, definition and penalties, see Penal Code §§ 17 and 18.
Misdemeanors, definition and penalties, see Penal Code §§ 17, 19 and 19.2.

§ 13351.8. Suspension of driving privilege; receipt of certified abstract of record

Upon receipt of a duly certified abstract of the record of any court showing that the court has ordered the suspension of a driver's license pursuant to Section 13210, on or after January 1, 2001, the department shall suspend the person's driving privilege in accordance with that suspension order commencing either on the date of the person's conviction or upon the person's release from confinement or imprisonment. *(Added by Stats.2000, c. 642 (A.B.2733), § 5.)*

§ 13351.85. Conviction under § 12110; suspension of driving privileges

Upon receipt of a duly certified abstract of any court showing that a person has been convicted of a violation of Section 12110, the department shall suspend that person's driving privilege for four months if the conviction was a first conviction, and for one year, if the conviction was a second or subsequent conviction of a violation of that section that occurred within seven years of the current conviction. *(Added by Stats.2000, c. 641 (A.B.2729), § 2.)*

§ 13352. Conviction for driving under the influence or engaging in speed contests or exhibitions of speed; terms of suspension or revocation of license; eligibility for restricted license; reinstatement conditions

(a) The department shall immediately suspend or revoke the privilege of a person to operate a motor vehicle upon the receipt of an abstract of the record of a court showing that the person has been convicted of a violation of Section 23152 or 23153, subdivision (a) of Section 23109, or Section 23109.1, or upon the receipt of a report of a judge of the juvenile court, a juvenile traffic hearing officer, or a referee of a juvenile court showing that the person has been found to have committed a violation of Section 23152 or 23153 or subdivision (a) of Section 23109 or Section 23109.1. If an offense specified in this section occurs in a vehicle defined in Section 15210, the suspension or revocation specified below shall apply to the noncommercial driving privilege. The commercial driving privilege shall be disqualified as specified in Sections 15300 to 15302, inclusive. For the purposes of this section, suspension or revocation shall be as follows:

(1) Except as required under Section 13352.1 or 13352.4, upon a conviction or finding of a violation of Section 23152 punishable under Section 23536, the privilege shall be suspended for a period of six months. The privilege shall not be reinstated until the person gives proof of financial responsibility and gives proof satisfactory to the department of successful completion of a driving-under-the-influence program licensed pursuant to Section 11836 of the Health and Safety Code described in subdivision (b) of Section 23538. If the court, as authorized under paragraph (3) of subdivision (b) of Section 23646, elects to order a person to enroll in, participate in, and complete either program described in subdivision (b) of Section 23542, the department shall require that program in lieu of the program described in subdivision (b) of Section 23538. For the purposes of this paragraph, enrollment in, participation in, and completion of an approved program shall be subsequent to the date of the current violation. Credit shall not be given to any program activities completed prior to the date of the current violation.

(2) Upon a conviction or finding of a violation of Section 23153 punishable under Section 23554, the privilege shall be suspended for a period of one year. The privilege shall not be reinstated until the person gives proof of financial responsibility and gives proof satisfactory to the department of successful completion of a driving-under-the-influence program licensed pursuant to Section 11836 of the Health and Safety Code as described in subdivision (b) of Section 23556. If the court, as authorized under paragraph (3) of subdivision (b) of Section 23646, elects to order a person to enroll in, participate in, and complete either program described in subdivision (b) of Section 23542, the department shall require that program in lieu of the program described in Section 23556. For the purposes of this paragraph, enrollment, participation, and completion of an approved program shall be subsequent to the date of the current violation. Credit shall not be given to any program activities completed prior to the date of the current violation.

(3) Except as provided in Section 13352.5, upon a conviction or finding of a violation of Section 23152 punishable under Section 23540, the privilege shall be suspended for two years. The privilege shall not be reinstated until the person gives proof of financial responsibility and gives proof satisfactory to the department of successful completion of a driving-under-the-influence program licensed pursuant to Section 11836 of the Health and Safety Code as described in subdivision (b) of Section 23542. For the purposes of this paragraph, enrollment in, participation in, and completion of an approved program shall be subsequent to the date of the current violation. Credit shall not be given to any program activities completed prior to the date of the current violation. The department shall advise the

person that he or she may apply to the department for a restriction of the driving privilege, which may include credit for a suspension period served under subdivision (c) of Section 13353.3, subject to the following conditions:

(A) Completion of 12 months of the suspension period, or completion of 90 days of the suspension period if the underlying conviction did not include the use of drugs as defined in Section 312 and the person was found to be only under the influence of an alcoholic beverage at the time of the violation.

(B) The person satisfactorily provides, subsequent to the violation date of the current underlying conviction, either of the following:

(i) Proof of enrollment in an 18–month driving-under-the-influence program licensed pursuant to Section 11836 of the Health and Safety Code.

(ii) Proof of enrollment in a 30–month driving-under-the-influence program licensed pursuant to Section 11836 of the Health and Safety Code, if available in the county of the person's residence or employment.

(C) The person agrees, as a condition of the restriction, to continue satisfactory participation in the program described in subparagraph (B).

(D) The person submits the "Verification of Installation" form described in paragraph (2) of subdivision (g) of Section 13386.

(E) The person agrees to maintain the ignition interlock device as required under subdivision (g) of Section 23575.

(F) The person provides proof of financial responsibility, as defined in Section 16430.

(G) The person pays all reissue fees and any restriction fee required by the department.

(H) The person pays to the department a fee sufficient to cover the costs of administration of this paragraph, as determined by the department.

(I) The restriction shall remain in effect for the period required in subdivision (f) of Section 23575.

(4) Except as provided in this paragraph, upon a conviction or finding of a violation of Section 23153 punishable under Section 23560, the privilege shall be revoked for a period of three years. The privilege may not be reinstated until the person gives proof of financial responsibility, and the person gives proof satisfactory to the department of successful completion of a driving-under-the-influence program licensed pursuant to Section 11836 of the Health and Safety Code, as described in paragraph (4) of subdivision (b) of Section 23562 of this code. For the purposes of this paragraph, enrollment in, participation in, and completion of an approved program shall be subsequent to the date of the current violation. Credit shall not be given to any program activities completed prior to the date of the current violation. The department shall advise the person that after the completion of 12 months of the revocation period, which may include credit for a suspension period served under

subdivision (c) of Section 13353.3, the person may apply to the department for a restricted driver's license, subject to the following conditions:

(A) The person has satisfactorily completed, subsequent to the violation date of the current underlying conviction, either of the following:

(i) The initial 12 months of an 18–month driving-under-the-influence program licensed pursuant to Section 11836 of the Health and Safety Code.

(ii) The initial 12 months of a 30–month driving-under-the-influence program licensed pursuant to Section 11836 of the Health and Safety Code, if available in the county of the person's residence or employment, and the person agrees, as a condition of the restriction, to continue satisfactory participation in that 30–month program.

(B) The person submits the "Verification of Installation" form described in paragraph (2) of subdivision (g) of Section 13386.

(C) The person agrees to maintain the ignition interlock device as required under subdivision (g) of Section 23575.

(D) The person provides proof of financial responsibility, as defined in Section 16430.

(E) The person pays all applicable reinstatement or reissue fees and any restriction fee required by the department.

(F) The restriction shall remain in effect for the period required in subdivision (f) of Section 23575.

(5) Except as provided in this paragraph, upon a conviction or finding of a violation of Section 23152 punishable under Section 23546, the privilege shall be revoked for a period of three years. The privilege shall not be reinstated until the person files proof of financial responsibility and gives proof satisfactory to the department of successful completion of one of the following programs: an 18–month driving-under-the-influence program licensed pursuant to Section 11836 of the Health and Safety Code, as described in subdivision (b) or (c) of Section 23548 of this code, or, if available in the county of the person's residence or employment, a 30–month driving-under-the-influence program licensed pursuant to Section 11836 of the Health and Safety Code, or a program specified in Section 8001 of the Penal Code. For the purposes of this paragraph, enrollment in, participation in, and completion of an approved program shall be subsequent to the date of the current violation. Credit shall not be given to any program activities completed prior to the date of the current violation. The department shall advise the person that he or she may apply to the department for a restriction of the driving privilege, which may include credit for a suspension period served under subdivision (c) of Section 13353. 3, subject to the following conditions:

(A) Completion of 12 months of the suspension period, or completion of six months of the suspension period

if the underlying conviction did not include the use of drugs as defined in Section 312 and the person was found to be only under the influence of an alcoholic beverage at the time of the violation.

(B) The person satisfactorily provides, subsequent to the violation date of the current underlying conviction, either of the following:

(i) Proof of enrollment in an 18–month driving-under-the-influence program licensed pursuant to Section 11836 of the Health and Safety Code.

(ii) Proof of enrollment in a 30–month driving-under-the-influence program licensed pursuant to Section 11836 of the Health and Safety Code, if available in the county of the person's residence or employment, and the person agrees, as a condition of the restriction, to continue satisfactory participation in the 30–month driving-under-the-influence program.

(C) The person submits the "Verification of Installation" form described in paragraph (2) of subdivision (g) of Section 13386.

(D) The person agrees to maintain the ignition interlock device as required under subdivision (g) of Section 23575.

(E) The person provides proof of financial responsibility, as defined in Section 16430.

(F) An individual convicted of a violation of Section 23152 punishable under Section 23546 may also, at any time after sentencing, petition the court for referral to an 18–month driving-under-the-influence program licensed pursuant to Section 11836 of the Health and Safety Code, or, if available in the county of the person's residence or employment, a 30–month driving-under-the-influence program licensed pursuant to Section 11836 of the Health and Safety Code. Unless good cause is shown, the court shall order the referral.

(G) The person pays all applicable reinstatement or reissue fees and any restriction fee required by the department.

(H) The person pays to the department a fee sufficient to cover the costs of administration of this paragraph, as determined by the department.

(I) The restriction shall remain in effect for the period required in subdivision (f) of Section 23575.

(6) Except as provided in this paragraph, upon a conviction or finding of a violation of Section 23153 punishable under Section 23550.5 or 23566, the privilege shall be revoked for a period of five years. The privilege may not be reinstated until the person gives proof of financial responsibility and gives proof satisfactory to the department of successful completion of a driving-under-the-influence program licensed pursuant to Section 11836 of the Health and Safety Code as described in subdivision (b) of Section 23568, or if available in the county of the person's residence or employment, a 30–month driving-under-the-influence program licensed pursuant to Section 11836 of the Health and Safety Code, or a program

specified in Section 8001 of the Penal Code. For the purposes of this paragraph, enrollment in, participation in, and completion of an approved program shall be subsequent to the date of the current violation. Credit shall not be given to any program activities completed prior to the date of the current violation. The department shall advise the person that after completion of 12 months of the revocation period, which may include credit for a suspension period served under subdivision (c) of Section 13353.3, the person may apply to the department for a restricted driver's license, subject to the following conditions:

(A) The person has satisfactorily provided, subsequent to the violation date of the current underlying conviction, either of the following:

(i) Completion of the initial 12 months of a 30–month driving-under-the-influence program licensed pursuant to Section 11836 of the Health and Safety Code, if available in the county of the person's residence or employment, and the person agrees, as a condition of the restriction, to continue satisfactory participation in the 30–month driving-under-the-influence program.

(ii) Completion of the initial 12 months of an 18–month driving-under-the-influence program licensed pursuant to Section 11836 of the Health and Safety Code, if a 30–month program is unavailable in the person's county of residence or employment.

(B) The person submits the "Verification of Installation" form described in paragraph (2) of subdivision (g) of Section 13386.

(C) The person agrees to maintain the ignition interlock device as required under subdivision (g) of Section 23575.

(D) The person provides proof of financial responsibility, as defined in Section 16430.

(E) An individual convicted of a violation of Section 23153 punishable under Section 23566 may also, at any time after sentencing, petition the court for referral to an 18–month driving-under-the-influence program licensed pursuant to Section 11836 of the Health and Safety Code, or, if available in the county of the person's residence or employment, a 30–month driving-under-the-influence program licensed pursuant to Section 11836 of the Health and Safety Code. Unless good cause is shown, the court shall order the referral.

(F) The person pays all applicable reinstatement or reissue fees and any restriction fee required by the department.

(G) The restriction shall remain in effect for the period required in subdivision (f) of Section 23575.

(7) Except as provided in this paragraph, upon a conviction or finding of a violation of Section 23152 punishable under Section 23550 or 23550.5, or of a violation of Section 23153 punishable under Section 23550.5, the privilege shall be revoked for a period of four years. The privilege shall not be reinstated until the

person files proof of financial responsibility and gives proof satisfactory to the department of successful completion of an 18–month driving-under-the-influence program licensed pursuant to Section 11836 of the Health and Safety Code, or, if available in the county of the person's residence or employment, a 30–month driving-under-the-influence program licensed pursuant to Section 11836 of the Health and Safety Code, or a program specified in Section 8001 of the Penal Code. For the purposes of this paragraph, enrollment in, participation in, and completion of an approved program shall be subsequent to the date of the current violation. Credit shall not be given to any program activities completed prior to the date of the current violation. The department shall advise the person that after completion of 12 months of the revocation period, which may include credit for a suspension period served under subdivision (c) of Section 13353.3, the person may apply to the department for a restricted driver's license, subject to the following conditions:

(A) The person has satisfactorily completed, subsequent to the violation date of the current underlying conviction, either of the following:

(i) The initial 12 months of an 18–month driving-under-the-influence program licensed pursuant to Section 11836 of the Health and Safety Code.

(ii) The initial 12 months of a 30–month driving-under-the-influence program licensed pursuant to Section 11836 of the Health and Safety Code, if available in the county of the person's residence or employment, and the person agrees, as a condition of the restriction, to continue satisfactory participation in the 30–month driving-under-the-influence program.

(B) The person submits the "Verification of Installation" form described in paragraph (2) of subdivision (g) of Section 13386.

(C) The person agrees to maintain the ignition interlock device as required under subdivision (g) of Section 23575.

(D) The person provides proof of financial responsibility, as defined in Section 16430.

(E) An individual convicted of a violation of Section 23152 punishable under Section 23550 may also, at any time after sentencing, petition the court for referral to an 18–month driving-under-the-influence program licensed pursuant to Section 11836 of the Health and Safety Code, or, if available in the county of the person's residence or employment, a 30–month driving-under-the-influence program licensed pursuant to Section 11836 of the Health and Safety Code. Unless good cause is shown, the court shall order the referral.

(F) The person pays all applicable reinstatement or reissue fees and any restriction fee required by the department.

(G) The restriction shall remain in effect for the period required in subdivision (f) of Section 23575.

(8) Upon a conviction or finding of a violation of subdivision (a) of Section 23109 that is punishable under subdivision (e) of that section or Section 23109.1, the privilege shall be suspended for a period of 90 days to six months, if ordered by the court. The privilege shall not be reinstated until the person gives proof of financial responsibility, as defined in Section 16430.

(9) Upon a conviction or finding of a violation of subdivision (a) of Section 23109 that is punishable under subdivision (f) of that section, the privilege shall be suspended for a period of six months, if ordered by the court. The privilege shall not be reinstated until the person gives proof of financial responsibility, as defined in Section 16430.

(b) For the purpose of paragraphs (2) to (9), inclusive, of subdivision (a), the finding of the juvenile court judge, the juvenile hearing officer, or the referee of a juvenile court of a commission of a violation of Section 23152 or 23153 or subdivision (a) of Section 23109 or Section 23109.1, as specified in subdivision (a) of this section, is a conviction.

(c) A judge of a juvenile court, juvenile hearing officer, or referee of a juvenile court shall immediately report the findings specified in subdivision (a) to the department.

(d) A conviction of an offense in a state, territory, or possession of the United States, the District of Columbia, the Commonwealth of Puerto Rico, or Canada that, if committed in this state, would be a violation of Section 23152, is a conviction of Section 23152 for the purposes of this section, and a conviction of an offense that, if committed in this state, would be a violation of Section 23153, is a conviction of Section 23153 for the purposes of this section. The department shall suspend or revoke the privilege to operate a motor vehicle pursuant to this section upon receiving notice of that conviction.

(e) For the purposes of the restriction conditions specified in paragraphs (3) to (7), inclusive, of subdivision (a), the department shall terminate the restriction imposed pursuant to this section and shall suspend or revoke the person's driving privilege upon receipt of notification from the driving-under-the-influence program that the person has failed to comply with the program requirements. The person's driving privilege shall remain suspended or revoked for the remaining period of the original suspension or revocation imposed under this section and until all reinstatement requirements described in this section are met.

(f) For the purposes of this section, completion of a program is the following:

(1) Satisfactory completion of all program requirements approved pursuant to program licensure, as evidenced by a certificate of completion issued, under penalty of perjury, by the licensed program.

(2) Certification, under penalty of perjury, by the director of a program specified in Section 8001 of the Penal Code, that the person has completed a program specified in Section 8001 of the Penal Code.

(g) The holder of a commercial driver's license who was operating a commercial motor vehicle, as defined in Section 15210, at the time of a violation that resulted in a suspension or revocation of the person's noncommercial driving privilege under this section is not eligible for the restricted driver's license authorized under paragraphs (3) to (7), inclusive, of subdivision (a). *(Added by Stats.2004, c. 595 (S.B.1541), § 1.5, operative Sept. 20, 2005. Amended by Stats.2005, c. 22 (S.B.1108), § 199; Stats.2005, c. 646 (A.B.979), § 1; Stats.2006, c. 692 (S.B.1756), § 2; Stats.2007, c. 130 (A.B.299), § 236; Stats.2007, c. 682 (A.B.430), § 13; Stats.2008, c. 699 (S.B.1241), § 25; Stats.2009, c. 193 (S.B.598), § 1, operative July 1, 2010; Stats.2010, c. 301 (A.B.1601), § 1; Stats.2011, c. 296 (A.B.1023), § 306.)*

Cross References

Commercial motor vehicles, multiple violations, see Vehicle Code § 15302.

Consecutive imposition of restriction, suspension, or revocation imposed under this section and suspension or revocation for refusing chemical testing, see Vehicle Code § 13353.1.

Conviction and punishment for violation of driving while under the influence of an alcoholic beverage, see Vehicle Code §§ 23612, 23620.

Driving under influence of alcohol or drugs, juvenile court finding in another jurisdiction deemed conviction for purpose of this section, see Vehicle Code § 23521.

Maximum period of suspension in certain cases, see Vehicle Code § 13556.

Participation of convicted person in alcohol services program, see Health and Safety Code § 11837.

Proof of financial responsibility, see Vehicle Code § 16430.

Separate offense involving alcohol or drugs and operation of vessel, etc., as separate offense under this section, see Vehicle Code § 23620.

Surrender of revoked licenses, see Vehicle Code §§ 13207, 13550.

§ 13352.1. Conviction or finding of violation of § 23152; ten month suspension of privilege for certain offenders; conditions for reinstatement

(a) Pursuant to subdivision (a) of Section 13352 and except as required under Section 13352.4, upon a conviction or finding of a violation of Section 23152 punishable under Section 23536, if the court refers the person to a program pursuant to paragraph (2) of subdivision (b) of Section 23538, the privilege shall be suspended for 10 months.

(b) The privilege may not be reinstated until the person gives proof of financial responsibility and gives proof satisfactory to the department of successful completion of a driving-under-the-influence program licensed pursuant to Section 11836 of the Health and Safety Code described in subdivision (b) of Section 23538 of this code. For the purposes of this subdivision, enrollment, participation, and completion of an approved program shall be subsequent to the date of the current violation. Credit may not be given to any program activities completed prior to the date of the current violation. *(Added by*

473

Stats.2006, c. 692 (S.B.1756), § 3. Amended by Stats. 2007, c. 130 (A.B.299), § 237.)

§ 13352.2. Driving-under-the-influence programs; filing of proof of enrollment and proof of completion by program provider

(a) If a person is required under Section 13352 to provide the department with proof of enrollment in a driving-under-the-influence program licensed pursuant to Section 11836 of the Health and Safety Code, or a program specified in Section 8001 of the Penal Code, the department shall deem that requirement satisfied upon receiving at its headquarters proof of enrollment that is satisfactory to the department and has been forwarded to the department by the program provider.

(b) If a person is required under Section 13352 to provide the department with proof of completion of a driving-under-the-influence program licensed pursuant to Section 11836 of the Health and Safety Code, or a program specified in Section 8001 of the Penal Code, the department shall deem that requirement satisfied upon receiving at its headquarters proof of completion that is satisfactory to the department and has been forwarded to the department by the program provider. *(Added by Stats.2004, c. 403 (S.B.1696), § 1.)*

§ 13352.3. Persons under eighteen years of age convicted of violations of §§ 23152 or 23153; term of revocation; reinstatement of privilege

(a) Notwithstanding any other provision of law, except subdivisions (b), (c), and (d) of Section 13352 and Sections 13367 and 23521, the department immediately shall revoke the privilege of any person to operate a motor vehicle upon receipt of a duly certified abstract of the record of any court showing that the person was convicted of a violation of Section 23152 or 23153 while under 18 years of age, or upon receipt of a report of a judge of the juvenile court, a juvenile hearing officer, or a referee of a juvenile court showing that the person has been found to have committed a violation of Section 23152 or 23153.

(b) The term of the revocation shall be until the person reaches 18 years of age, for one year, or for the period prescribed for restriction, suspension, or revocation specified in subdivision (a) of Section 13352, whichever is longer. The privilege may not be reinstated until the person gives proof of financial responsibility as defined in Section 16430. *(Added by Stats.1983, c. 934, § 2. Amended by Stats.1992, c. 974 (S.B.1600), § 7, eff. Sept. 28, 1992; Stats.1998, c. 118 (S.B.1186), § 3.2, operative July 1, 1999; Stats.2003, c. 149 (S.B.79), § 83.)*

Law Revision Commission Comments

2003 Amendment

Subdivision (a) of Section 13352.3 is amended to reflect the redesignation of traffic hearing officers as juvenile hearing officers. See 1997 Cal. Stat. ch. 679. [33 Cal.L.Rev.Comm. Reports 257 (2003)].

474

Cross References

Driving under influence of alcohol or drugs, juvenile court finding in another jurisdiction deemed conviction for purpose of this section, see Vehicle Code § 23521.

§ 13352.4. Restricted driver's licenses

(a) Except as provided in subdivision (h), the department shall issue a restricted driver's license to a person whose driver's license was suspended under paragraph (1) of subdivision (a) of Section 13352 or Section 13352.1, if the person meets all of the following requirements:

(1) Submits proof satisfactory to the department of enrollment in, or completion of, a driving-under-the-influence program licensed pursuant to Section 11836 of the Health and Safety Code, as described in subdivision (b) of Section 23538.

(2) Submits proof of financial responsibility, as defined in Section 16430.

(3) Pays all applicable reinstatement or reissue fees and any restriction fee required by the department.

(b) The restriction of the driving privilege shall become effective when the department receives all of the documents and fees required under subdivision (a) and shall remain in effect until the final day of the original suspension imposed under paragraph (1) of subdivision (a) of Section 13352 or Section 13352.1, or until the date all reinstatement requirements described in Section 13352 or Section 13352.1 have been met, whichever date is later, and may include credit for any suspension period served under subdivision (c) of Section 13353.3.

(c) The restriction of the driving privilege shall be limited to the hours necessary for driving to and from the person's place of employment, driving during the course of employment, and driving to and from activities required in the driving-under-the-influence program.

(d) Whenever the driving privilege is restricted under this section, proof of financial responsibility, as defined in Section 16430, shall be maintained for three years. If the person does not maintain that proof of financial responsibility at any time during the restriction, the driving privilege shall be suspended until the proof required under Section 16484 is received by the department.

(e) For the purposes of this section, enrollment, participation, and completion of an approved program shall be subsequent to the date of the current violation. Credit may not be given to a program activity completed prior to the date of the current violation.

(f) The department shall terminate the restriction issued under this section and shall suspend the privilege to operate a motor vehicle pursuant to paragraph (1) of subdivision (a) of Section 13352 or Section 13352.1 immediately upon receipt of notification from the driving-under-the-influence program that the person has failed to comply with the program requirements. The privilege shall remain suspended until the final day of the original suspension imposed under paragraph (1) of subdivision (a) of Section 13352 or Section 13352.1, or until the date all reinstatement requirements described in Section 13352 or Section 13352.1 have been met, whichever date is later.

(g) The holder of a commercial driver's license who was operating a commercial motor vehicle, as defined in Section 15210, at the time of a violation that resulted in a suspension or revocation of the person's noncommercial driving privilege under paragraph (1) of subdivision (a) of Section 13352 or Section 13352.1 is not eligible for the restricted driver's license authorized under this section.

(h) If, upon conviction, the court has made the determination, as authorized under subdivision (d) of Section 23536 or paragraph (3) of subdivision (a) of Section 23538, to disallow the issuance of a restricted driver's license, the department may not issue a restricted driver's license under this section.

(Added by Stats.2004, c. 551 (S.B.1697), § 5, operative Sept. 20, 2005. Amended by Stats.2006, c. 692 (S.B.1756), § 4.)

§ 13352.5. Restricted driver's licenses

(a) The department shall issue a restricted driver's license to a person whose driver's license was suspended under paragraph (3) of subdivision (a) of Section 13352, if all of the following requirements have been met:

(1) Proof satisfactory to the department of enrollment in, or completion of, a driving-under-the-influence program licensed pursuant to Section 11836 of the Health and Safety Code, as described in subdivision (b) of Section 23542 has been received in the department's headquarters.

(2) The person submits proof of financial responsibility, as described in Section 16430.

(3) The person completes not less than 12 months of the suspension period imposed under paragraph (3) of subdivision (a) of Section 13352. The 12 months may include credit for any suspension period served under subdivision (c) of Section 13353.3.

(4) The person pays all applicable reinstatement or reissue fees and any restriction fee required by the department.

(b) The restriction of the driving privilege shall become effective when the department receives all of the documents and fees required under subdivision (a) and shall remain in effect until the final day of the original suspension imposed under paragraph (3) of subdivision (a) of Section 13352, or until the date all reinstatement requirements described in Section 13352 have been met, whichever date is later.

(c) The restriction of the driving privilege shall be limited to the hours necessary for driving to and from the person's place of employment, driving during the course of employment, and driving to and from activities required in the driving-under-the-influence program.

(d) Whenever the driving privilege is restricted under this section, proof of financial responsibility, as defined in Section 16430, shall be maintained for three years. If the person does not maintain that proof of financial responsibility at any time during the restriction, the driving privilege shall be suspended until the proof required under Section 16484 is received by the department.

(e) For the purposes of this section, enrollment in, participation in, and completion of an approved program shall be subsequent to the date of the current violation. Credit shall not be given to any program activities completed prior to the date of the current violation.

(f) The department shall terminate the restriction imposed pursuant to this section and shall suspend the privilege to drive under paragraph (3) of subdivision (a) of Section 13352 upon receipt of notification from the driving-under-the-influence program that the person has failed to comply with the program requirements.

(g) If, upon conviction, the court has made the determination, as authorized under subdivision (b) of Section 23540 or subdivision (d) of Section 23542, to disallow the issuance of a restricted driver's license, the department shall not issue a restricted driver's license under this section.

(h) A person restricted pursuant to this section may apply to the department for a restricted driver's license, subject to the conditions specified in paragraph (3) of subdivision (a) of Section 13352. Whenever proof of financial responsibility has already been provided and a restriction fee has been paid in compliance with restrictions described in this section, and the offender subsequently receives an ignition interlock device restriction described in paragraph (3) of subdivision (a) of Section 13352, the proof of financial responsibility period shall not be extended beyond the previously established term and no additional restriction fee shall be required.

(i) This section applies to a person who meets all of the following conditions:

(1) Has been convicted of a violation of Section 23152 that occurred on or before July 1, 1999, and is punishable under Section 23540, or former Section 23165.

(2) Was granted probation for the conviction subject to conditions imposed under subdivision (b) of Section 23542, or under subdivision (b) of former Section 23166.

(3) Is no longer subject to the probation described in paragraph (2).

(4) Has not completed the licensed driving-under-the-influence program under paragraph (3) of subdivision (a) of Section 13352 for reinstatement of the driving privilege.

(5) Has no violations in his or her driving record that would preclude issuance of a restricted driver's license. *(Added by Stats.2004, c. 551 (S.B.1697), § 6.5, operative Sept. 20, 2005. Amended by Stats.2009, c. 193 (S.B.598), § 2, operative July 1, 2010; Stats.2010, c. 30 (S.B.895), § 1, eff. June 22, 2010, operative July 1, 2010.)*

Cross References

Consecutive imposition of restriction, suspension, or revocation under this section and suspension or revocation for refusing chemical testing, see Vehicle Code § 13353.1.

Driving under influence of alcohol or drugs, juvenile court finding in another jurisdiction deemed conviction for purpose of this section, see Vehicle Code § 23521.

Probation conditions, see Vehicle Code §§ 23542, 23562.

§ 13352.6. Conviction of person under 21 drinking and driving; reinstatement; driving-under-the-influence program

(a) The department shall immediately suspend the driving privilege of a person who is 18 years of age or older and is convicted of a violation of Section 23140, upon the receipt of a duly certified abstract of the record of a court showing that conviction. The privilege may not be reinstated until the person provides the department with proof of financial responsibility and until proof satisfactory to the department, of successful completion of a driving-under-the-influence program licensed under Section 11836 of the Health and Safety Code has been received in the department's headquarters. That attendance shall be as follows:

(1) If, within 10 years of the current violation of Section 23140, the person has not been convicted of a separate violation of Section 23140, 23152, or 23153, or of Section 23103, with a plea of guilty under Section 23103.5, or of Section 655 of the Harbors and Navigation Code, or of Section 191.5 of, or subdivision (a) of Section 192.5 of, the Penal Code, the person shall complete, at a minimum, the education component of that licensed driving-under-the-influence program.

(2) If the person does not meet the requirements of paragraph (1), the person shall complete, at a minimum, the program described in paragraph (1) of subdivision (c) of Section 11837 of the Health and Safety Code.

(b) For the purposes of this section, enrollment, participation, and completion of the program shall be subsequent to the date of the current violation. Credit for enrollment, participation, or completion may not be given for any program activities completed prior to the date of the current violation. *(Added by Stats.2000, c. 1063 (A.B.803), § 2. Amended by Stats.2004, c. 403 (S.B.1696), § 3; Stats.2004, c. 550 (S.B.1694), § 5.5; Stats.2007, c. 747 (A.B.678), § 21.)*

§ 13353. Chemical blood, breath, or urine tests

(a) If a person refuses the officer's request to submit to, or fails to complete, a chemical test or tests pursuant to Section 23612, upon receipt of the officer's sworn statement that the officer had reasonable cause to believe the person had been driving a motor vehicle in violation of Section 23140, 23152, or 23153, and that the person had refused to submit to, or did not complete, the test or tests after being requested by the officer, the department shall do one of the following:

(1) Suspend the person's privilege to operate a motor vehicle for a period of one year.

(2) Revoke the person's privilege to operate a motor vehicle for a period of two years if the refusal occurred within 10 years of either (A) a separate violation of Section 23103 as specified in Section 23103.5, or of Section 23140, 23152, or 23153, or of Section 191.5 or subdivision (a) of Section 192.5 of the Penal Code, that resulted in a conviction, or (B) a suspension or revocation of the person's privilege to operate a motor vehicle pursuant to this section or Section 13353.2 for an offense that occurred on a separate occasion.

(3) Revoke the person's privilege to operate a motor vehicle for a period of three years if the refusal occurred within 10 years of any of the following:

(A) Two or more separate violations of Section 23103 as specified in Section 23103.5, or of Section 23140, 23152, or 23153, or of Section 191.5 or subdivision (a) of Section 192.5 of the Penal Code, or any combination thereof, that resulted in convictions.

(B) Two or more suspensions or revocations of the person's privilege to operate a motor vehicle pursuant to this section or Section 13353.2 for offenses that occurred on separate occasions.

(C) Any combination of two or more of those convictions or administrative suspensions or revocations.

The officer's sworn statement shall be submitted pursuant to Section 13380 on a form furnished or approved by the department. The suspension or revocation shall not become effective until 30 days after the giving of written notice thereof, or until the end of a stay of the suspension or revocation, as provided for in Section 13558.

(D) For the purposes of this section, a conviction of an offense in any state, territory, or possession of the United States, the District of Columbia, the Commonwealth of Puerto Rico, or the Dominion of Canada that, if committed in this state, would be a violation of Section 23103, as specified in Section 23103.5, or Section 23140, 23152, or 23153, or Section 191.5 or subdivision (a) of Section 192.5 of the Penal Code, is a conviction of that particular section of the Vehicle Code or Penal Code.

(b) If a person on more than one occasion in separate incidents refuses the officer's request to submit to, or fails to complete, a chemical test or tests pursuant to Section 23612 while driving a motor vehicle, upon the receipt of the officer's sworn statement that the officer had reasonable cause to believe the person had been driving a motor vehicle in violation of Section 23140, 23152, or 23153, the department shall disqualify the person from operating a commercial motor vehicle for the rest of his or her lifetime.

(c) The notice of the order of suspension or revocation under this section shall be served on the person by a peace officer pursuant to Section 23612. The notice of the order of suspension or revocation shall be on a form provided by the department. If the notice of the order of suspension or revocation has not been served by the peace officer pursuant to Section 23612, the department immediately shall notify the person in writing of the action taken. The peace officer who serves the notice, or the department, if applicable, also shall provide, if the officer or department, as the case may be, determines that it is necessary to do so, the person with the appropriate non-English notice developed pursuant to subdivision (d) of Section 14100.

(d) Upon the receipt of the officer's sworn statement, the department shall review the record. For purposes of this section, the scope of the administrative review shall cover all of the following issues:

(1) Whether the peace officer had reasonable cause to believe the person had been driving a motor vehicle in violation of Section 23140, 23152, or 23153.

(2) Whether the person was placed under arrest.

(3) Whether the person refused to submit to, or did not complete, the test or tests after being requested by a peace officer.

(4) Whether, except for a person described in subdivision (a) of Section 23612 who is incapable of refusing, the person had been told that his or her driving privilege would be suspended or revoked if he or she refused to submit to, or did not complete, the test or tests.

(e) The person may request an administrative hearing pursuant to Section 13558. Except as provided in subdivision (e) of Section 13558, the request for an administrative hearing does not stay the order of suspension or revocation.

(f) The suspension or revocation imposed under this section shall run concurrently with any restriction, suspension, or revocation imposed under Section 13352, 13352.4, or 13352.5 that resulted from the same arrest.

(Added by Stats.2004, c. 952 (A.B.3049), § 7.5, operative Sept. 20, 2005. Amended by Stats.2005, c. 279 (S.B.1107), § 21; Stats.2007, c. 747 (A.B.678), § 22.)

§ 13353.1. Preliminary alcohol screening test; refusal or failure to complete; notice; review

(a) If a person refuses an officer's request to submit to, or fails to complete, a preliminary alcohol screening test pursuant to Section 13388 or 13389, upon the receipt of the officer's sworn statement, submitted pursuant to Section 13380, that the officer had reasonable cause to believe the person had been driving a motor vehicle in violation of Section 23136 or 23154, and that the person had refused to submit to, or did not complete, the test after being requested by the officer, the department shall do one of the following:

(1) Suspend the person's privilege to operate a motor vehicle for a period of one year.

(2) Revoke the person's privilege to operate a motor vehicle for a period of two years if the refusal occurred within 10 years of either of the following:

(A) A separate violation of subdivision (a) of Section 23136, that resulted in a finding of a violation, or a separate violation, that resulted in a conviction, of Section 23103, as specified in Section 23103.5, of Section

23140, 23152, or 23153, or of Section 191.5 or subdivision (a) of Section 192.5 of the Penal Code.

(B) A suspension or revocation of the person's privilege to operate a motor vehicle if that action was taken pursuant to this section or Section 13353 or 13353.2 for an offense that occurred on a separate occasion.

(3) Revoke the person's privilege to operate a motor vehicle for a period of three years if the refusal occurred within 10 years of any of the following:

(A) Two or more separate violations of subdivision (a) of Section 23136, that resulted in findings of violations, or two or more separate violations, that resulted in convictions, of Section 23103, as specified in Section 23103.5, of Section 23140, 23152, or 23153, or of Section 191.5 or subdivision (a) of Section 192.5 of the Penal Code, or any combination thereof.

(B) Two or more suspensions or revocations of the person's privilege to operate a motor vehicle if those actions were taken pursuant to this section, or Section 13353 or 13353.2, for offenses that occurred on separate occasions.

(C) Any combination of two or more of the convictions or administrative suspensions or revocations described in subparagraph (A) or (B).

(b) For the purposes of this section, a conviction of an offense in any state, territory, or possession of the United States, the District of Columbia, the Commonwealth of Puerto Rico, or Canada that, if committed in this state, would be a violation of Section 23103, as specified in Section 23103.5, or Section 23140, 23152, or 23153, or Section 191.5 or subdivision (a) of Section 192.5 of the Penal Code, is a conviction of that particular section of the Vehicle or Penal Code.

(c) The notice of the order of suspension or revocation under this section shall be served on the person by the peace officer pursuant to Section 13388 and shall not become effective until 30 days after the person is served with that notice. The notice of the order of suspension or revocation shall be on a form provided by the department. If the notice of the order of suspension or revocation has not been served by the peace officer pursuant to Section 13388, the department immediately shall notify the person in writing of the action taken. The peace officer who serves the notice, or the department, if applicable, also shall provide, if the officer or department, as the case may be, determines that it is necessary to do so, the person with the appropriate non-English notice developed pursuant to subdivision (d) of Section 14100.

(d) Upon the receipt of the officer's sworn statement, the department shall review the record. For the purposes of this section, the scope of the administrative review shall cover all of the following issues:

(1) Whether the peace officer had reasonable cause to believe the person had been driving a motor vehicle in violation of Section 23136.

(2) Whether the person was lawfully detained.

(3) Whether the person refused to submit to, or did not complete, the test after being requested to do so by a peace officer.

(e) The person may request an administrative hearing pursuant to Section 13558. Except as provided in subdivision (e) of Section 13558, the request for an administrative hearing does not stay the order of suspension or revocation. *(Added by Stats.1993, c. 899 (S.B. 689), § 4. Amended by Stats.1994, c. 938 (S.B.1295), § 2, eff. Sept. 28, 1994; Stats.1998, c. 118 (S.B.1186), § 3.10, operative July 1, 1999; Stats.2001, c. 473 (S.B.485), § 19; Stats.2004, c. 550 (S.B.1694), § 7; Stats.2007, c. 747 (A.B.678), § 23; Stats.2007, c. 749 (A.B.1165), § 1.5, operative Jan. 1, 2009.)*

Cross References

Driving motor vehicle following suspension or revocation of license pursuant to this section, punishment, see Vehicle Code § 14601.5.

§ 13353.2. Immediate suspension; grounds; notice of order of suspension; determination of facts

(a) The department shall immediately suspend the privilege of a person to operate a motor vehicle for any one of the following reasons:

(1) The person was driving a motor vehicle when the person had 0.08 percent or more, by weight, of alcohol in his or her blood.

(2) The person was under 21 years of age and had a blood-alcohol concentration of 0.01 percent or greater, as measured by a preliminary alcohol screening test, or other chemical test.

(3) The person was driving a vehicle that requires a commercial driver's license when the person had 0.04 percent or more, by weight, of alcohol in his or her blood.

(4) The person was driving a motor vehicle when both of the following applied:

(A) The person was on probation for a violation of Section 23152 or 23153.

(B) The person had 0.01 percent or more, by weight, of alcohol in his or her blood, as measured by a preliminary alcohol screening test or other chemical test.

(b) The notice of the order of suspension under this section shall be served on the person by a peace officer pursuant to Section 13382 or 13388. The notice of the order of suspension shall be on a form provided by the department. If the notice of the order of suspension has not been served upon the person by the peace officer pursuant to Section 13382 or 13388, upon the receipt of the report of a peace officer submitted pursuant to Section 13380, the department shall mail written notice of the order of the suspension to the person at the last known address shown on the department's records and, if the address of the person provided by the peace officer's report differs from the address of record, to that address.

(c) The notice of the order of suspension shall specify clearly the reason and statutory grounds for the suspension, the effective date of the suspension, the right of the person to request an administrative hearing, the procedure for requesting an administrative hearing, and the date by which a request for an administrative hearing shall be made in order to receive a determination prior to the effective date of the suspension.

(d) The department shall make a determination of the facts in subdivision (a) on the basis of the report of a peace officer submitted pursuant to Section 13380. The determination of the facts, after administrative review pursuant to Section 13557, by the department is final, unless an administrative hearing is held pursuant to Section 13558 and any judicial review of the administrative determination after the hearing pursuant to Section 13559 is final.

(e) The determination of the facts in subdivision (a) is a civil matter that is independent of the determination of the person's guilt or innocence, shall have no collateral estoppel effect on a subsequent criminal prosecution, and shall not preclude the litigation of the same or similar facts in the criminal proceeding. If a person is acquitted of criminal charges relating to a determination of facts under subdivision (a), or if the person's driver's license was suspended pursuant to Section 13388 and the department finds no basis for a suspension pursuant to that section, the department shall immediately reinstate the person's privilege to operate a motor vehicle if the department has suspended it administratively pursuant to subdivision (a), and the department shall return or reissue for the remaining term any driver's license that has been taken from the person pursuant to Section 13382 or otherwise. Notwithstanding subdivision (b) of Section 13558, if criminal charges under Section 23140, 23152, or 23153 are not filed by the district attorney because of a lack of evidence, or if those charges are filed but are subsequently dismissed by the court because of an insufficiency of evidence, the person has a renewed right to request an administrative hearing before the department. The request for a hearing shall be made within one year from the date of arrest.

(f) The department shall furnish a form that requires a detailed explanation specifying which evidence was defective or lacking and detailing why that evidence was defective or lacking. The form shall be made available to the person to provide to the district attorney. The department shall hold an administrative hearing, and the hearing officer shall consider the reasons for the failure to prosecute given by the district attorney on the form provided by the department. If applicable, the hearing officer shall consider the reasons stated on the record by a judge who dismisses the charges. A fee shall not be imposed pursuant to Section 14905 for the return or reissuing of a driver's license pursuant to this subdivision. The disposition of a suspension action under this section does not affect an action to suspend or revoke the person's privilege to operate a motor vehicle under another provision of this code, including, but not limited to, Section 13352 or 13353, or Chapter 3 (commencing with Section 13800). *(Added by Stats.1989, c. 1460, § 7, operative July 1, 1990. Amended by Stats.1990, c. 431 (S.B.1150), § 4, eff. July 26, 1990; Stats.1992, c. 1281 (A.B.3580), § 4; Stats.1993, c. 899 (S.B.689), § 5; Stats. 1993, c. 1244 (S.B.126), § 12.1; Stats.1994, c. 938 (S.B. 1295), § 3, eff. Sept. 28, 1994; Stats.1998, c. 118 (S.B. 1186), § 3.12, operative July 1, 1999; Stats.1999, c. 22 (S.B.24), § 14, eff. May 26, 1999, operative July 1, 1999; Stats.2006, c. 574 (A.B.2520), § 11; Stats.2007, c. 130 (A.B.299), § 238; Stats.2007, c. 749 (A.B.1165), § 2, operative Jan. 1, 2009; Stats.2008, c. 179 (S.B.1498), § 219.)*

Cross References

Driving with knowledge of suspension, revocation, or restriction of driving privilege, punishment, see Vehicle Code § 14601.5.

Fee for license issued following suspension under this section, see Vehicle Code § 14905.

§ 13353.3. Order of suspension under Vehicle Code § 13353.2; effective date, period, and termination of suspension

(a) An order of suspension of a person's privilege to operate a motor vehicle pursuant to Section 13353.2 shall become effective 30 days after the person is served with the notice pursuant to Section 13382 or 13388, or subdivision (b) of Section 13353.2.

(b) The period of suspension of a person's privilege to operate a motor vehicle under Section 13353.2 is as follows:

(1) If the person has not been convicted of a separate violation of Section 23103, as specified in Section 23103.5, or Section 23140, 23152, or 23153, or Section 191.5 or subdivision (a) of Section 192.5 of the Penal Code, the person has not been administratively determined to have refused chemical testing pursuant to Section 13353 or 13353.1, or the person has not been administratively determined to have been driving with an excessive concentration of alcohol pursuant to Section 13353.2 on a separate occasion, which offense or occurrence occurred within 10 years of the occasion in question, the person's privilege to operate a motor vehicle shall be suspended for four months.

(2)(A) If the person has been convicted of one or more separate violations of Section 23103, as specified in Section 23103.5, or Section 23140, 23152, or 23153, or Section 191.5 or subdivision (a) of Section 192.5 of the Penal Code, the person has been administratively determined to have refused chemical testing pursuant to Section 13353 or 13353.1, or the person has been administratively determined to have been driving with an excessive concentration of alcohol pursuant to Section 13353.2 on a separate occasion, which offense or occasion occurred within 10 years of the occasion in question, the person's privilege to operate a motor vehicle shall be suspended for one year, except as provided in subparagraphs (B) and (C).

(B) The one-year suspension pursuant to subparagraph (A) shall terminate if the person has been convicted of a violation arising out of the same occurrence and all of the following conditions are met:

(i) The person is eligible for a restricted driver's license pursuant to Section 13352.

(ii) The person installs an ignition interlock device as required in Section 13352 for that restricted driver's license.

(iii) The person complies with all other applicable conditions of Section 13352 for a restricted driver's license.

(C) The one-year suspension pursuant to subparagraph (A) shall terminate after completion of a 90–day suspension period, and the person shall be eligible for a restricted license if the person has been convicted of a violation of Section 23103, as specified in Section 23103.5, arising out of the same occurrence, has no more than two prior alcohol-related convictions within 10 years, as specified pursuant to subparagraph (A), and all of the following conditions are met:

(i) The person satisfactorily provides, subsequent to the underlying violation date, proof satisfactory to the department of enrollment in a nine-month driving-under-the-influence program licensed pursuant to Chapter 9 (commencing with Section 11836) of Part 2 of Division 10.5 of the Health and Safety Code that consists of at least 60 hours of program activities, including education, group counseling, and individual interview sessions.

(ii) The person agrees, as a condition of the restriction, to continue satisfactory participation in the program described in clause (i).

(iii) The person installs an ignition interlock device and submits the "Verification of Installation" form described in paragraph (2) of subdivision (h) of Section 13386.

(iv) The person agrees to maintain the ignition interlock device as required pursuant to subdivision (g) of Section 23575.

(v) The person provides proof of financial responsibility, as defined in Section 16430.

(vi) The person pays all license fees and any restriction fee required by the department.

(vii) The person pays to the department a fee sufficient to cover the costs of administration of this paragraph, as determined by the department.

(D) The department shall advise those persons that are eligible under subparagraph (C) that after completion of 90 days of the suspension period, the person may apply to the department for a restricted driver's license, subject to the conditions set forth in subparagraph (C).

(E) The restricted driving privilege shall become effective when the department receives all of the documents and fees required under subparagraph (C) and remain in effect for at least the remaining period of the original suspension and until the person provides satisfactory proof to the department of successful completion of a driving-under-the-influence program licensed pursuant to Section 11836 of the Health and Safety Code. The restricted driving privilege shall be subject to the following conditions:

(i) If the driving privilege is restricted under this section, proof of financial responsibility, as described in Section 16430, shall be maintained for three years. If the person does not maintain that proof of financial responsibility at any time during the restriction, the driving privilege shall be suspended until the proof required pursuant to Section 16484 is received by the department.

(ii) For the purposes of this section, enrollment, participation, and completion of an approved program shall be subsequent to the date of the current violation. Credit may not be given to a program activity completed prior to the date of the current violation.

(iii) The department shall terminate the restriction issued pursuant to this section and shall suspend the privilege to operate a motor vehicle pursuant to subparagraph (A) immediately upon receipt of notification from the driving-under-the-influence program that the person has failed to comply with the program requirements. The privilege shall remain suspended until the final day of the original suspension imposed pursuant to subparagraph (A).

(iv) The department shall terminate the restriction issued pursuant to this section and shall immediately suspend the privilege to operate a motor vehicle pursuant to subparagraph (A) immediately upon receipt of notification from the installer that a person has attempted to remove, bypass, or tamper with the ignition interlock device, has removed the device prior to the termination date of the restriction, or fails three or more times to comply with any requirement for the maintenance or calibration of the ignition interlock device ordered pursuant to this section. The privilege shall remain suspended for the remaining period of the original suspension imposed pursuant to subparagraph (A).

(3) Notwithstanding any other law, if a person has been administratively determined to have been driving in violation of Section 23136 or to have refused chemical testing pursuant to Section 13353.1, the period of suspension shall not be for less than one year.

(c) If a person's privilege to operate a motor vehicle is suspended pursuant to Section 13353.2 and the person is convicted of a violation of Section 23152 or 23153, including, but not limited to, a violation described in Section 23620, arising out of the same occurrence, both the suspension under Section 13353.2 and the suspension or revocation under Section 13352 shall be imposed, except that the periods of suspension or revocation shall run concurrently, and the total period of suspension or revocation shall not exceed the longer of the two suspension or revocation periods.

480

(d) For the purposes of this section, a conviction of an offense in any state, territory, or possession of the United States, the District of Columbia, the Commonwealth of Puerto Rico, or the Dominion of Canada that, if committed in this state, would be a violation of Section 23103, as specified in Section 23103.5, or Section 23140, 23152, or 23153, or Section 191.5 or subdivision (a) of Section 192.5 of the Penal Code, is a conviction of that particular section of the Vehicle Code or Penal Code.

(e) The holder of a commercial driver's license who was operating a commercial motor vehicle, as defined in Section 15210, at the time of a violation that resulted in a suspension or revocation of the person's noncommercial driving privilege is not eligible for the restricted driver's license authorized pursuant to this section. *(Added by Stats.2004, c. 551 (S.B.1697), § 8.5, operative Sept. 20, 2005. Amended by Stats.2007, c. 747 (A.B.678), § 24; Stats.2010, c. 30 (S.B.895), § 2, eff. June 22, 2010; Stats.2011, c. 657 (A.B.520), § 2.)*

§ 13353.4.   Restoration of driving privilege and issuance of restricted or hardship permit to operate motor vehicle during suspension or revocation period

(a) Except as provided in Section 13353.3, 13353.7, or 13353.8, the driving privilege shall not be restored, and a restricted or hardship permit to operate a motor vehicle shall not be issued, to a person during the suspension or revocation period specified in Section 13353, 13353.1, or 13353.3.

(b) The privilege to operate a motor vehicle shall not be restored after a suspension or revocation pursuant to Section 13352, 13353, 13353.1, or 13353.2 until all applicable fees, including the fees prescribed in Section 14905, have been paid and the person gives proof of financial responsibility, as defined in Section 16430, to the department.

(Added by Stats.1992, c. 1181 (S.B.1650), § 4, eff. Sept. 30, 1992, operative July 1, 1993. Amended by Stats.1993, c. 1244 (S.B.126), § 13, operative July 1, 1993; Stats.1994, c. 938 (S.B.1295), § 5, eff. Sept. 28, 1994; Stats.2002, c. 545 (S.B.1852), § 12; Stats.2004, c. 952 (A.B.3049), § 8, operative Sept. 20, 2005; Stats.2011, c. 657 (A.B.520), § 3.)

§ 13353.45.   Certificate of completion; fees

The department shall, in consultation with the State Department of * * * Health Care Services, with representatives of the county alcohol program administrators, and with representatives of licensed drinking driver program providers, develop a certificate of completion for the purposes of Sections 13352, 13352.4, and 13352.5 and shall develop, implement, and maintain a system for safeguarding the certificates against misuse. The department may charge a reasonable fee for each blank completion certificate distributed to a drinking driver program. The fee shall be sufficient to cover, but shall not exceed, the costs incurred in administering this section, Sections 13352, 13352.4, and 13352.5 or twelve dollars ($12) per person, whichever is less. *(Added by Stats.1992, c. 1181 (S.B.1650), § 5, eff. Sept. 30, 1992, operative July 1, 1993. Amended by Stats.1994, c. 938 (S.B.1295), § 6, eff. Sept. 28, 1994; Stats.2002, c. 545 (S.B.1852), § 13; Stats.2013, c. 22 (A.B.75), § 86, eff. June 27, 2013, operative July 1, 2013.)*

§ 13353.5. Expiration of suspension or revocation period; out of state residence; reinstatement; conditions

(a) If a person whose driving privilege is suspended or revoked under Section 13352, former Section 13352.4, Section 13352.4, 13352.6, paragraph (1) of subdivision (g) of Section 23247, or paragraph (2) of subdivision (f) of Section 23575 is a resident of another state at the time the mandatory period of suspension or revocation expires, the department may terminate the suspension or revocation, upon written application of the person, for the purpose of allowing the person to apply for a license in his or her state of residence. The application shall include, but need not be limited to, evidence satisfactory to the department that the applicant now resides in another state.

(b) If the person submits an application for a California driver's license within three years after the date of the action to terminate suspension or revocation pursuant to subdivision (a), a license shall not be issued until evidence satisfactory to the department establishes that the person is qualified for reinstatement and no grounds exist including, but not limited to, one or more subsequent convictions for driving under the influence of alcohol or other drugs that would support a refusal to issue a license. The department may waive the three-year requirement if the person provides the department with proof of financial responsibility, as defined in Section 16430, and proof satisfactory to the department of successful completion of a driving-under-the-influence program described in Section 13352, and the driving-under-the-influence program is of the length required under paragraphs (1) to (7), inclusive, of subdivision (a) of Section 13352.

(c) For the purposes of this section, "state" includes a foreign province or country.

(d) This section shall become operative on September 20, 2005. *(Added by Stats.1992, c. 1181 (S.B.1650), § 6, eff. Sept. 30, 1992. Amended by Stats.1994, c. 938 (S.B.1295), § 7, eff. Sept. 28, 1994; Stats.2002, c. 545 (S.B.1852), § 14; Stats.2004, c. 551 (S.B.1697), § 9, operative Sept. 20, 2005.)*

§ 13353.6. Repealed by Stats.2004, c. 952 (A.B.3049), § 9, operative Jan. 1, 2006

§ 13353.7. Restricted driver's licenses

(a) Subject to subdivision (c), if the person whose driving privilege has been suspended under Section 13353.2 has not been convicted of, or found to have committed, a separate violation of Section 23103, as specified in Section 23103.5, or Section 23140, 23152, or 23153 of this code, or Section 191.5 or subdivision (a) of Section 192.5 of the Penal Code, and if the person's privilege to operate a motor vehicle has not been suspended or revoked pursuant to Section 13353 or 13353.2 for an offense that occurred on a separate occasion within 10 years of the occasion in question and, if the person subsequently enrolls in a driving-under-the-influence program licensed under Section 11836 of the Health and Safety Code, as described in subdivision (b) of Section 23538, that person, if 21 years of age or older at the time the offense occurred, may apply to the department for a restricted driver's license limited to travel to and from the activities required by the program and to and from and in the course of the person's employment. After receiving proof of enrollment in the program, and if the person has not been arrested ,subsequent to the offense for which the person's driving privilege has been suspended under Section 13353.2 for a violation of Section 23103, as specified in Section 23103.5, or Section 23140, 23152, or 23153 of this code, or Section 191.5 or subdivision (a) of Section 192.5 of the Penal Code, and if the person's privilege to operate a motor vehicle has not been suspended or revoked pursuant to Section 13353 or 13353.2 for an offense that occurred on a separate occasion, notwithstanding Section 13551, the department shall, after review pursuant to Section 13557, suspend the person's privilege to operate a motor vehicle for 30 days and then issue the person a restricted driver's license under the following conditions:

(1) The program shall report any failure to participate in the program to the department and shall certify successful completion of the program to the department.

(2) The person was 21 years of age or older at the time the offense occurred and gives proof of financial responsibility as defined in Section 16430.

(3) The restriction shall be imposed for a period of five months.

(4) If a person who has been issued a restricted license under this section fails at any time to participate in the program, the department shall suspend the restricted license immediately. The department shall give notice of the suspension under this paragraph in the same manner as prescribed in subdivision (b) of Section 13353.2 for the period specified in Section 13353.3, that is effective upon receipt by the person.

(b) Notwithstanding subdivision (a), and upon a conviction of Section 23152 or 23153, the department shall suspend or revoke the person's privilege to operate a motor vehicle under Section 13352.

(c) If the driver was operating a commercial vehicle, as defined in Section 15210, at the time of the violation that resulted in the suspension of that person's driving privilege under Section 13353.2, the department shall, pursuant to this section, if the person is otherwise eligible, issue the person a class C or class M driver's license restricted in the same manner and subject to the same conditions as specified in subdivision (a), except that the license may

481

not allow travel to and from or in the course of the person's employment.

(d) If the holder of a commercial driver's license was operating a motor vehicle, other than a commercial vehicle as defined in Section 15210, at the time of the violation that resulted in the suspension of that person's driving privilege pursuant to Section 13353.2, the department shall, pursuant to this section, if the person is otherwise eligible, issue the person a class C or class M driver's license restricted in the same manner and subject to the same conditions as specified in subdivision (a).

(e) This section does not apply to a person whose driving privilege has been suspended or revoked pursuant to Section 13353 or 13353.2 for an offense that occurred on a separate occasion, or as a result of a conviction of a separate violation of Section 23103, as specified in Section 23103.5, or Section 23140, 23152, or 23153, when that violation occurred within 10 years of the offense in question. This subdivision shall be operative only so long as a one-year suspension of the driving privilege for a second or subsequent occurrence or offense, with no restricted or hardship licenses permitted, is required by Section 408 or 410 of Title 23 of the United States Code. *(Added by Stats.2004, c. 952 (A.B.3049), § 10.5, operative Sept. 20, 2005. Amended by Stats.2007, c. 747 (A.B.678), § 25; Stats.2012, c. 670 (A.B.2188), § 5.)*

§ 13353.8. Order suspending or delaying driving privileges; showing of critical need to drive; review of order; imposition of restrictions on driving privilege

(a) After the department has issued an order suspending or delaying driving privileges as a result of a violation of subdivision (a) of Section 23136, the department, upon the petition of the person affected, may review the order and may impose restrictions on the person's privilege to drive based upon a showing of a critical need to drive, if the department determines that, within 10 years of the current violation of Section 23136, the person has not violated Section 23136 or been convicted of a separate violation of Section 23140, 23152, or 23153, or of Section 23103, with a plea of guilty under Section 23103.5, or of Section 191.5 or subdivision (a) of Section 192.5 of, the Penal Code, and that the person's driving privilege has not been suspended or revoked under Section 13353, 13353.1, or 13353.2 within that 10–year period.

(b) For purposes of this section, a conviction of an offense in a state, territory, or possession of the United States, the District of Columbia, the Commonwealth of Puerto Rico, or the Dominion of Canada that, if committed in this state, would be a violation of Section 23103, as specified in Section 23103.5, or Section 23140, 23152, 23153, or Section 191.5 or subdivision (a) of Section 192.5 of the Penal Code, is a conviction of that particular section of the Vehicle Code or Penal Code.

(c) As used in this section, "critical need to drive" means the circumstances that are required to be shown for the issuance of a junior permit pursuant to Section 12513.

(d) The restriction shall be imposed not earlier than the 31st day after the date the order of suspension became effective and shall remain in effect for the balance of the period of suspension or restriction in this section. *(Added by Stats.1993, c. 899 (S.B.689), § 7. Amended by Stats.1994, c. 938 (S.B.1295), § 8, eff. Sept. 28, 1994; Stats.1995, c. 766 (S.B.726), § 17; Stats.2003, c. 254 (S.B.408), § 1; Stats.2004, c. 550 (S.B.1694), § 10; Stats.2007, c. 747 (A.B.678), § 26.)*

Cross References

Driving motor vehicle following restriction of driving privilege pursuant to this section, punishment, see Vehicle Code § 14601.5.

§ 13354. Repealed by Stats.2005, c. 551 (S.B.1697), § 11, operative Jan. 1, 2006

§ 13355. Driving upon a highway at a speed greater than one hundred miles per hour; suspension of privilege to operate motor vehicle

The department shall immediately suspend the privilege of any person to operate a motor vehicle upon receipt of a duly certified abstract of the record of any court showing that the person has been convicted of a violation of subdivision (b) of Section 22348, or upon a receipt of a report of a judge of a juvenile court, a juvenile hearing officer, or a referee of a juvenile court showing that the person has been found to have committed a violation of subdivision (b) of Section 22348 under the following conditions and for the periods, as follows:

(a) Upon a conviction or finding of an offense under subdivision (b) of Section 22348 that occurred within three years of a prior offense resulting in a conviction of an offense under subdivision (b) of Section 22348, the privilege shall be suspended for a period of six months, or the privilege shall be restricted for six months to necessary travel to and from the person's place of employment and, if driving a motor vehicle is necessary to perform the duties of the person's employment, restricted to driving within the person's scope of employment.

(b) Upon a conviction or finding of an offense under subdivision (b) of Section 22348 that occurred within five years of two or more prior offenses resulting in convictions of offenses under subdivision (b) of Section 22348, the privilege shall be suspended for a period of one year, or the privilege shall be restricted for one year to necessary travel to and from the person's place of employment and, if driving a motor vehicle is necessary to perform the duties of the person's employment, restricted to driving within the person's scope of employment. *(Added by Stats.1983, c. 980, § 2. Amended by Stats.2003, c. 149 (S.B.79), § 84.)*

Law Revision Commission Comments

2003 Amendment

Section 13355 is amended to reflect the redesignation of traffic hearing officers as juvenile hearing officers. See 1997 Cal. Stat. ch. 679. [33 Cal.L.Rev.Comm. Reports 258 (2003)].

Cross References

Driving at speed greater than 100 miles per hour, see Vehicle Code § 22348.

§ 13355.5. Repealed by Stats.1973, c. 257, p. 651, § 1, eff. July 12, 1973

§ 13356. Repealed by Stats.1972, c. 755, p. 1349, § 5

§ 13357. Revocation or suspension for theft or unlawful taking of a vehicle

Upon the recommendation of the court the department shall suspend or revoke the privilege to operate a motor vehicle of any person who has been found guilty of a violation of Section 10851. *(Added by Stats.1967, c. 1110, p. 2757, § 9.)*

Cross References

Commercial motor vehicles, multiple violations, see Vehicle Code § 15302.

§ 13358. Repealed by Stats.1972, c. 755, p. 1349, § 6

§ 13359. Grounds for suspension or revocation

The department may suspend or revoke the privilege of any person to operate a motor vehicle upon any of the grounds which authorize the refusal to issue a license. *(Stats.1959, c. 3, p. 1627, § 13359. Amended by Stats. 1976, c. 498, p. 1238, § 2.)*

Cross References

Grounds authorizing refusal to issue a license, see Vehicle Code § 12805 et seq.

§ 13360. Violation of license restrictions

Upon receiving satisfactory evidence of any violation of the restrictions of a driver's license, the department may suspend or revoke the same. *(Stats.1959, c. 3, p. 1627, § 13360.)*

Cross References

Restricted licenses, issuance, see Vehicle Code § 12813.

§ 13361. Grounds for suspension

The department may suspend the privilege of any person to operate a motor vehicle upon receipt of a duly certified abstract of the record of any court showing that the person has been convicted of any of the following crimes or offenses:

(a) Failure to stop in the event of an accident resulting in damage to property only, or otherwise failing to comply with the requirements of Section 20002.

(b) A second or subsequent conviction of reckless driving.

(c) Manslaughter resulting from the operation of a motor vehicle as provided in paragraph (2) of subdivision (c) of Section 192 of the Penal Code.

In any case under this section the department is authorized to require proof of ability to respond in damages as defined in Section 16430. *(Stats.1959, c. 3, p. 1627, § 13361. Amended by Stats.1959, c. 1048, p. 3089, § 2; Stats.1963, c. 87, p. 715, § 1; Stats.1965, c. 1060, p. 2706, § 2; Stats.1967, c. 236, p. 1371, § 5; Stats.1967, c. 253, p. 1401, § 3; Stats.1982, c. 655, p. 2672, § 4; Stats.1982, c. 1339, p. 4983, § 10, eff. Sept. 24, 1982; Stats.1985, c. 6, § 3, eff. Feb. 21, 1985.)*

Cross References

Proof of financial responsibility, see Vehicle Code § 16430.
Reckless driving, see Vehicle Code §§ 23103, 23104.
Stopping at scene of accident, see Vehicle Code § 20000 et seq.

§ 13362. Surrender of license erroneously issued

The department may require the surrender to it of any driver's license which has been issued erroneously or which contains any erroneous or false statement, or which does not contain any notation required by law or by the department. In the event a licensee does not surrender the license upon proper demand, the department may suspend the licensee's privilege to operate a motor vehicle. The suspension shall continue until the correction of the license by the department or until issuance of another license or temporary license in lieu thereof. *(Stats.1959, c. 3, p. 1627, § 13362.)*

Cross References

Surrender of license during suspension, see Vehicle Code § 13206.

§ 13363. Conviction in another state

(a) The department may, in its discretion, except as provided in Chapter 6 (commencing with Section 15000) of Division 6, of this code, suspend or revoke the privilege of any resident or nonresident to drive a motor vehicle in this State upon receiving notice of the conviction of the person in a state, territory, or possession of the United States, the District of Columbia, the Commonwealth of Puerto Rico, or the Dominion of Canada of an offense therein which, if committed in this State, would be grounds for the suspension or revocation of the privilege to operate a motor vehicle.

(b) Whenever any state, territory, or possession of the United States, the District of Columbia, the Commonwealth of Puerto Rico, or the Dominion of Canada reports the conviction of a violation in such place by a person licensed in this State, the department shall not give effect to such report pursuant to subdivision (a) of this section or Section 15023 unless the department is satisfied that the law of such other place pertaining to the conviction is substantially the same as the law of this State pertaining to such conviction and that the description of the violation from which the conviction arose, is sufficient and that the interpretation and enforcement of such law are substantially the same in such other place as they are in this State. *(Stats.1959, c. 3, p. 1627, § 13363. Amended by Stats.1963, c. 237, p. 980, § 9.)*

Cross References

Definitions,
  Conviction, see Vehicle Code § 13103.
  Nonresident, see Vehicle Code § 435.

§ 13364. Driver's license; suspension; dishonored check; notice; reinstatement

(a) Notwithstanding any other provision of this code, a person's privilege to operate a motor vehicle shall be suspended upon notification by a bank or financial institution that a check has been dishonored when that check was presented to the department for either of the following reasons:

(1) In payment of a fine that resulted from an outstanding violation pursuant to Section 40508 or a suspension pursuant to Section 13365.

(2) In payment of a fee or penalty owed by the person, if the fee or penalty is required by this code for the issuance, reissuance, or return of the person's driver's license after suspension, revocation, or restriction of the driving privilege.

(b) The suspension shall remain in effect until payment of all fines, fees, and penalties is made to the department or to the court, as appropriate, and the person's driving record does not contain any notification of a court order issued pursuant to subdivision (a) of Section 42003 or of a violation of subdivision (a) or (b) of Section 40508.

(c) No suspension imposed pursuant to this section shall become effective until 30 days after the mailing of a written notice of the intent to suspend.

(d) The written notice of a suspension imposed pursuant to this section shall be delivered by certified mail.

(e) If any personal check is offered in payment of fines described in paragraph (1) of subdivision (a) and is returned for any reason, the related notice issued pursuant to Section 40509 or 40509.5 shall be restored to the person's record.

(f) Notwithstanding any other provision of law, any license that has been suspended pursuant to this section shall immediately be reinstated, and the fees and penalties waived, upon the submission of proof acceptable to the department that the check has been erroneously dishonored by the bank or financial institution. *(Added by Stats.1993, c. 845 (A.B.484), § 1. Amended by Stats. 1998, c. 877 (A.B.2132), § 56.)*

§ 13365. Section 40508 (promise to appear) violations

(a) Upon receipt of notification of a violation of subdivision (a) or (b) of Section 40508, the department shall take the following action:

(1) If the notice is given pursuant to subdivision (a) or (b) of Section 40509, if the driving record of the person who is the subject of the notice contains one or more prior notifications of a violation issued pursuant to Section 40509 or 40509.5, and if the person's driving privilege is not currently suspended under this section,

the department shall suspend the driving privilege of the person.

(2) If the notice is given pursuant to subdivision (a) or (b) of Section 40509.5, and if the driving privilege of the person who is the subject of the notice is not currently suspended under this section, the department shall suspend the driving privilege of the person.

(b) A suspension under this section shall not be effective before a date 60 days after the date of receipt, by the department, of the notice given specified in subdivision (a), and the notice of suspension shall not be mailed by the department before a date 30 days after receipt of the notice given specified in subdivision (a).

The suspension shall continue until the suspended person's driving record does not contain any notification of a violation of subdivision (a) or (b) of Section 40508. *(Added by Stats.1963, c. 354, p. 1145, § 1. Amended by Stats.1971, c. 1532, p. 3037, § 2, operative May 3, 1972; Stats.1981, c. 584, p. 2250, § 1, operative July 1, 1982; Stats.1983, c. 983, § 5, eff. Sept. 21, 1983; Stats.1984, c. 858, § 1, operative July 1, 1985; Stats.1990, c. 472 (S.B.1826), § 1; Stats.1998, c. 877 (A.B.2132), § 57.)*

§ 13365.2. Persons charged with driving under the influence of drugs or alcohol; failure to make appearance; effective date of suspension

(a) Upon receipt of the notice required under subdivision (c) of Section 40509.5, the department shall suspend the driving privilege of the person upon whom notice was received and shall continue that suspension until receipt of the certificate required under that subdivision.

(b) The suspension required under subdivision (a) shall become effective on the 45th day after the mailing of written notice by the department. *(Added by Stats.1996, c. 224 (S.B.1579), § 4.)*

§ 13365.5. Notification of willful failure to comply with court order; suspension; effective date of suspension

(a) Upon receipt of a notification issued pursuant to Section 40509.1, the department shall suspend the person's privilege to operate a motor vehicle until compliance with the court order is shown or as prescribed in subdivision (c) of Section 12808. The suspension under this section shall not be effective until 45 days after the giving of written notice by the department.

(b) This section does not apply to a notification of failure to comply with a court order issued for a violation enumerated in paragraph (1), (2), (3), (6), or (7) of subdivision (b) of Section 1803. *(Added by Stats.1993, c. 158 (A.B.392), § 21.7, eff. July 21, 1993.)*

§ 13366. Effective date of suspension or revocation

Whenever in this code the department is required to suspend or revoke the privilege of a person to operate a motor vehicle upon the conviction of such person of violating this code, such suspension or revocation shall begin upon a plea, finding or verdict of guilty. *(Stats. 1959, c. 3, p. 1628, § 13366.)*

Cross References

Consecutive imposition of restriction, suspension or revocation for driving under influence or refusing chemical testing, see Vehicle Code § 13353.1.

§ 13366.5.   Commencement of suspension or revocation

(a) Notwithstanding Section 13366, whenever in this code the department is required to disqualify the commercial driving privilege of a person to operate a commercial motor vehicle upon the conviction of that person of a violation of this code, the suspension or revocation shall begin upon receipt by the department of a duly certified abstract of any court record showing that the person has been so convicted.

(b) This section shall become operative on September 20, 2005. *(Added by Stats.2004, c. 952 (A.B.3049), § 11, operative Sept. 20, 2005.)*

Cross References

Commercial vehicles, sanctions, serious traffic violations occurring within three years of two or more separate offenses, see Vehicle Code § 15308.

§ 13367.   Determining minor's suspension

For purposes of the suspension or revocation of any driver's license issued to a minor, the department shall not provide any lighter penalty than would be given to an adult under similar circumstances. *(Added by Stats.1959, c. 562, p. 2524, § 4.)*

§ 13368.   Driver training requirement

The department, as a condition to the reinstatement of a suspended license or the issuance of a new license to an individual whose prior license has been revoked, may require the individual to attend the program authorized by the provisions of Section 1659. *(Added by Stats.1965, c. 447, p. 1758, § 2.)*

§ 13369.   Certificate or endorsement for specified vehicles

(a) This section applies to the following endorsements and certificates:

(1) Passenger transportation vehicle.

(2) Hazardous materials.

(3) Schoolbus.

(4) School pupil activity bus.

(5) Youth bus.

(6) General public paratransit vehicle.

(7) Farm labor vehicle.

(8) Vehicle used for the transportation of developmentally disabled persons.

(b) The department shall refuse to issue or renew, or shall revoke, the certificate or endorsement of any person who meets the following conditions:

(1) Within three years, has committed any violation that results in a conviction assigned a violation point count of two or more, as defined in Sections 12810 and 12810.5. The department may not refuse to issue or renew, nor may it revoke, a person's hazardous materials or passenger transportation vehicle endorsement if the violation leading to the conviction occurred in the person's private vehicle and not in a commercial motor vehicle, as defined in Section 15210.

(2) Within three years, has had his or her driving privilege suspended, revoked, or on probation for any reason involving unsafe operation of a motor vehicle. The department may not refuse to issue or renew, nor may it revoke, a person's passenger transportation vehicle endorsement if the person's driving privilege has, within three years, been placed on probation only for any reason involving unsafe operation of a motor vehicle.

(3) Notwithstanding paragraphs (1) and (2), does not meet the qualifications for issuance of a hazardous materials endorsement set forth in Parts 383, 384, and 1572 of Title 49 of the Code of Federal Regulations.

(c) The department may refuse to issue or renew, or may suspend or revoke, the certificate or endorsement of any person who meets any of the following conditions:

(1) Within 12 months, has been involved as a driver in three accidents in which the driver caused or contributed to the causes of the accidents.

(2) Within 24 months, as a driver, caused or contributed to the cause of an accident resulting in a fatality or serious injury or serious property damage in excess of seven hundred fifty dollars ($750).

(3) Has violated any provision of this code, or any rule or regulation pertaining to the safe operation of a vehicle for which the certificate or endorsement was issued.

(4) Has violated any restriction of the certificate, endorsement, or commercial driver's license.

(5) Has knowingly made a false statement or failed to disclose a material fact on an application for a certificate or endorsement.

(6) Has been determined by the department to be a negligent or incompetent operator.

(7) Has demonstrated irrational behavior to the extent that a reasonable and prudent person would have reasonable cause to believe that the applicant's ability to perform the duties of a driver may be impaired.

(8) Excessively or habitually uses, or is addicted to, alcoholic beverages, narcotics, or dangerous drugs.

(9) Does not meet the minimum medical standards established or approved by the department.

(d) The department may cancel the certificate or endorsement of any driver who meets any of the following conditions:

(1) Does not have a valid driver's license of the appropriate class.

(2) Has requested cancellation of the certificate or endorsement.

(3) Has failed to meet any of the requirements for issuance or retention of the certificate or endorsement, including, but not limited to, payment of the proper fee, submission of an acceptable medical report and fingerprint cards, and compliance with prescribed training requirements.

(4) Has had his or her driving privilege suspended or revoked for a cause involving other than the safe operation of a motor vehicle.

(e)(1) The department shall refuse to issue or renew, or shall suspend or revoke, the passenger vehicle endorsement of a person who violates subdivision (b) of Section 5387 of the Public Utilities Code.

(2) A person found to be in violation of subdivision (b) of Section 5387 of the Public Utilities Code shall be ineligible for a passenger vehicle endorsement that would permit him or her to drive a bus of any kind, including, but not limited to, a bus, schoolbus, youth bus, school pupil activity bus, trailer bus, or a transit bus, with passengers, for a period of five years.

(f)(1) Reapplication following refusal or revocation under subdivision (b) or (c) may be made after a period of not less than one year from the effective date of denial or revocation, except in cases where a longer period of suspension or revocation is required by law.

(2) Reapplication following cancellation under subdivision (d) may be made at any time without prejudice. *(Added by Stats.2004, c. 952 (A.B.3049), § 12.5, operative Sept. 20, 2005. Amended by Stats.2005, c. 66 (A.B.637), § 1; Stats.2009, c. 248 (A.B.636), § 4.)*

§ 13370. Schoolbus, school pupil activity bus, general public paratransit vehicle, youth bus, or vehicle for transportation of developmentally disabled persons; grounds to refuse or revoke driver certificate

(a) The department shall refuse to issue or shall revoke a schoolbus, school pupil activity bus, general public paratransit vehicle, or youth bus driver certificate, or a certificate for a vehicle used for the transportation of developmentally disabled persons, if any of the following causes apply to the applicant or certificate holder:

(1) Has been convicted of a sex offense as defined in Section 44010 of the Education Code.

(2) Has been convicted, within two years, of an offense specified in Section 11361.5 of the Health and Safety Code.

(3) Has failed to meet prescribed training requirements for certificate issuance.

(4) Has failed to meet prescribed testing requirements for certificate issuance.

(5) Has been convicted of a violent felony listed in subdivision (c) of Section 667.5 of the Penal Code, or a serious felony listed in subdivision (c) of Section 1192.7 of the Penal Code. This paragraph shall not be applied to

486

revoke a license that was valid on January 1, 2005, unless the certificate holder is convicted for an offense that is committed on or after that date.

(b) The department may refuse to issue or renew, or may suspend or revoke a schoolbus, school pupil activity bus, general public paratransit vehicle, or youth bus driver certificate, or a certificate for a vehicle used for the transportation of developmentally disabled persons if any of the following causes apply to the applicant or certificate holder:

(1) Has been convicted of a crime specified in Section 44424 of the Education Code within seven years. This paragraph does not apply if denial is mandatory.

(2) Has committed an act involving moral turpitude.

(3) Has been convicted of an offense, not specified in this section and other than a sex offense, that is punishable as a felony, within seven years.

(4) Has been dismissed as a driver for a cause relating to pupil transportation safety.

(5) Has been convicted, within seven years, of an offense relating to the use, sale, possession, or transportation of narcotics, habit-forming drugs, or dangerous drugs, except as provided in paragraph (3) of subdivision (a).

(c)(1) Reapplication following refusal or revocation under paragraph (1), (2), or (3) of subdivision (a) or (b) may be made after a period of not less than one year after the effective date of refusal or revocation.

(2) Reapplication following refusal or revocation under paragraph (4) of subdivision (a) may be made after a period of not less than 45 days after the date of the applicant's third testing failure.

(3) An applicant or holder of a certificate may reapply for a certificate whenever a felony or misdemeanor conviction is reversed or dismissed. A termination of probation and dismissal of charges pursuant to Section 1203.4 of the Penal Code or a dismissal of charges pursuant to Section 1203.4a of the Penal Code is not a dismissal for purposes of this section. *(Added by Stats. 1990, c. 1360 (S.B.1510), § 36. Amended by Stats.1998, c. 877 (A.B.2132), § 59; Stats.2003, c. 594 (S.B.315), § 37; Stats.2004, c. 615 (S.B.1233), § 27; Stats.2005, c. 66 (A.B.637), § 2.)*

Cross References

Felonies, definition and penalties, see Penal Code §§ 17 and 18.
Misdemeanors, definition and penalties, see Penal Code §§ 17, 19 and 19.2.

§ 13371. Schoolbus, activity bus, youth bus, paratransit vehicle, and developmentally disabled person vehicle certificate; hearing

This section applies to schoolbus, school pupil activity bus, youth bus, general public paratransit vehicle certificates, and a certificate for a vehicle used for the transportation of developmentally disabled persons.

(a) Any driver or applicant who has received a notice of refusal, suspension, or revocation, may, within 15 days after the mailing date, submit to the department a written request for a hearing. Failure to demand a hearing within 15 days is a waiver of the right to a hearing.

(1) Upon receipt by the department of the hearing request, the department may stay the action until a hearing is conducted and the final decision has been rendered by the Certificate Action Review Board pursuant to paragraph (2) of subdivision (d). The department shall not stay an action when there is reasonable cause to believe the stay would pose a significant risk to the safety of pupils being transported in a schoolbus, school pupil activity bus, youth bus, or persons being transported in a general public paratransit vehicle.

(2) An applicant or driver is not entitled to a hearing whenever the action by the department is made mandatory by this article or any other applicable law or regulation except where the cause for refusal is based on failure to meet medical standards or excessive and habitual use of or addiction to alcoholic beverages, narcotics, or dangerous drugs.

(b) The department shall appoint a hearing officer to conduct the hearing in accordance with Section 14112. After the hearing, the hearing officer shall prepare and submit findings and recommendations to the department.

(c) The department shall mail, as specified in Section 22, a copy of the hearing officer's findings and recommendations to the driver or applicant and to the driver or applicant's hearing representative, either of whom may file a statement of exception to the findings and recommendations within 24 days after the mailing date.

(d)(1) The Certificate Action Review Board consists of the following three members: a chairperson appointed by the director of the department, a member appointed by the Commissioner of the California Highway Patrol, and a member appointed by the Superintendent of Public Instruction.

(2) After a hearing, the board shall review the findings and recommendations of the hearing officer, and any statement of exception, and make a decision concerning disposition of the action taken by the department, which decision shall be final. At this stage, no evidence shall be heard that was not presented at the hearing, unless the person wishing to present the new evidence establishes, to the satisfaction of the board, that it could not have been obtained with due diligence prior to the hearing. *(Added by Stats.1990, c. 1360 (S.B.1510), § 37. Amended by Stats.1992, c. 731 (S.B.1606), § 1; Stats.1998, c. 877 (A.B.2132), § 60; Stats.2005, c. 66 (A.B.637), § 3.)*

§ 13372. Ambulance driver certificate; refusal to issue or renew; suspension or revocation; grounds; conditions for reapplication

(a) The department shall refuse to issue or renew, or shall suspend or revoke an ambulance driver certificate if any of the following apply to the applicant or certificate holder:

(1) Is required to register as a sex offender under Section 290 of the Penal Code for any offense involving force, violence, threat, or intimidation.

(2) Habitually or excessively uses or is addicted to narcotics or dangerous drugs.

(3) Is on parole or probation for any felony, theft, or any crime involving force, violence, threat, or intimidation.

(b) The department may refuse to issue or renew, or may suspend or revoke an ambulance driver certificate if any of the following apply to the applicant or certificate holder:

(1) Has been convicted within seven years of any offense punishable as a felony or has been convicted during that period of any theft.

(2) Has committed any act involving moral turpitude, including fraud or intentional dishonesty for personal gain, within seven years.

(3) Habitually and excessively uses intoxicating beverages.

(4) Has been convicted within seven years of any offense relating to the use, sale, possession, or transportation of narcotics or addictive or dangerous drugs, or of any misdemeanor involving force, violence, threat, or intimidation.

(5) Is on probation to the department for a cause involving the unsafe operation of a motor vehicle.

(6) Within three years has had his or her driver's license suspended or revoked by the department for a cause involving the unsafe operation of a motor vehicle, or, within the same period, has been convicted of any of the following:

(A) Failing to stop and render aid in an accident involving injury or death.

(B) Driving-under-the-influence of intoxicating liquor, any drug, or under the combined influence of intoxicating liquor and any drug.

(C) Reckless driving, or reckless driving involving bodily injury.

(7) Has knowingly made a false statement or failed to disclose a material fact in his or her application.

(8) Has been involved as a driver in any motor vehicle accident causing death or bodily injury or in three or more motor vehicle accidents within one year.

(9) Does not meet minimum medical standards specified in this code or in regulations adopted pursuant to this code.

(10) Has demonstrated irrational behavior or incurred a physical disability to the extent that a reasonable and prudent person would have reasonable cause to believe that the ability to perform the duties normally expected of an ambulance driver may be impaired.

(11) Has violated any provision of this code or any rule or regulation adopted by the Commissioner of the

California Highway Patrol relating to the operation of emergency ambulances within one year.

(12) Has committed any act that warrants dismissal, as provided in Section 13373.

(c)(1) Reapplication following refusal or revocation under subdivision (a) or (b) may be made after a period of not less than one year after the effective date of the refusal or revocation, except in cases where a longer period of refusal, suspension, or revocation is required by law.

(2) Reapplication following refusal or revocation under subdivision (a) or (b) may be made if a felony or misdemeanor conviction supporting the refusal or revocation is reversed or dismissed. A termination of probation and dismissal of charges under Section 1203.4 of the Penal Code or a dismissal of charges under Section 1203.4a of the Penal Code is not a dismissal for purposes of this section. *(Added by Stats.1990, c. 1360 (S.B.1510), § 38. Amended by Stats.2005, c. 66 (A.B.637), § 4.)*

Cross References

Felonies, definition and penalties, see Penal Code §§ 17 and 18.
Misdemeanors, definition and penalties, see Penal Code §§ 17, 19 and 19.2.

§ 13373. Dismissal of ambulance drivers or attendants; causes

The receipt of satisfactory evidence of any violation of Article 1 (commencing with Section 1100) of Subchapter 5 of Chapter 2 of Title 13 of the California Code of Regulations, the Vehicle Code, or any other applicable law that would provide grounds for refusal, suspension, or revocation of an ambulance driver's certificate or evidence of an act committed involving intentional dishonesty for personal gain or conduct contrary to justice, honesty, modesty, or good morals, may be sufficient cause for the dismissal of any ambulance driver or attendant. Dismissal of a driver or attendant under this section shall be reported by the employer to the Department of Motor Vehicles at Sacramento within 10 days. *(Added by Stats.1990, c. 1360 (S.B.1510), § 39. Amended by Stats. 2005, c. 66 (A.B.637), § 5.)*

§ 13374. Denial, suspension, or revocation of ambulance drivers license; hearing; request; waiver; findings and recommendations; review committee; final decision

(a) An applicant for, or the holder of, an ambulance driver certificate who has received a notice of refusal, suspension, or revocation may submit, within 15 days after the notice has been mailed by the department, a written request for a hearing. Upon receipt of the request, the department shall appoint a referee who shall conduct an informal hearing in accordance with Section 14104. Failure to request a hearing within 15 days after the notice has been mailed by the department is a waiver of the right to a hearing. A request for a hearing shall not operate to stay the action for which notice is given.

(b) Upon conclusion of an informal hearing, the referee shall prepare and submit findings and recommendations through the department to a committee of three members one each appointed by the Director of the Emergency Medical Service Authority, the director, and the Commissioner of the California Highway Patrol with the appointee of the Commissioner of the California Highway Patrol serving as chairperson. After a review of the findings and recommendations, the committee shall render a final decision on the action taken, and the department shall notify the person involved of the decision. *(Added by Stats.1990, c. 1360 (S.B.1510), § 40. Amended by Stats.2005, c. 66 (A.B.637), § 6.)*

§ 13375. Plea or verdict of guilty or plea of nolo contendere; conviction

For the purposes of this article, any plea or verdict of guilty, plea of nolo contendere, or court finding of guilt in a trial without a jury, or forfeiture of bail, is deemed a conviction, notwithstanding subsequent action under Section 1203.4 or 1203.4a of the Penal Code allowing withdrawal of the plea of guilty and entering a plea of not guilty, setting aside the verdict of guilty, or dismissing the accusation or information. *(Added by Stats.1990, c. 1360 (S.B.1510), § 41.)*

§ 13376. Bus or public paratransit driver certificates; revocation or suspension; positive test result or refusal to submit to test for a controlled substance; sex offense prosecution

(a) This section applies to the following certificates:

(1) Schoolbus.

(2) School pupil activity bus.

(3) Youth bus.

(4) General public paratransit vehicle.

(5) Vehicle used for the transportation of developmentally disabled persons.

(b)(1) The department shall revoke a certificate listed in subdivision (a) for three years if the certificate holder refuses to submit to a test for, fails to comply with the testing requirements for, or receives a positive test for a controlled substance, as specified in Part 382 (commencing with Section 382.101) of Title 49 of the Code of Federal Regulations and Section 34520. However, the department shall not revoke a certificate under this paragraph if the certificate holder is in compliance with any rehabilitation or return to duty program that is imposed by the employer that meets the controlled substances and alcohol use and testing requirements set forth in Part 382 (commencing with Section 382.101) of Title 49 of the Code of Federal Regulations. The driver shall be allowed to participate in a rehabilitation or return to duty program only once within a three-year period. The employer or program shall report any subsequent positive test result or drop from the program to the department on a form approved by the department.

(2) If an applicant refuses to submit to a test for, fails to comply with the testing requirements for, or receives a positive test for a controlled substance, the department shall refuse the application for a certificate listed in subdivision (a) for three years from the date of the confirmed positive test result.

(3) The carrier that requested the test shall report the refusal, failure to comply, or positive test result to the department not later than five days after receiving notification of the test result on a form approved by the department.

(4) The department shall maintain a record of any action taken for a refusal, failure to comply, or positive test result in the driving record of the applicant or certificate holder for three years from the date of the refusal, failure to comply, or positive test result.

(c)(1) The department may temporarily suspend a schoolbus, school pupil activity bus, youth bus, or general public paratransit driver certificate, or temporarily withhold issuance of a certificate to an applicant, if the holder or applicant is arrested for or charged with any sex offense, as defined in Section 44010 of the Education Code.

(2) Upon receipt of a notice of temporary suspension, or of the department's intent to withhold issuance, of a certificate, the certificate holder or applicant may request a hearing within 10 days of the effective date of the department's action.

(3) The department shall, upon request of the holder of, or applicant for, a certificate, within 10 working days of the receipt of the request, conduct a hearing on whether the public interest requires suspension or withholding of the certificate pursuant to paragraph (1).

(4) If the charge is dismissed or results in a finding of not guilty, the department shall immediately terminate the suspension or resume the application process, and shall expunge the suspension action taken pursuant to this subdivision from the record of the applicant or certificate holder.

(d) An applicant or holder of a certificate may reapply for a certificate whenever a felony or misdemeanor conviction is reversed or dismissed. A termination of probation and dismissal of charges pursuant to Section 1203.4 of the Penal Code or a dismissal of charges pursuant to Section 1203.4a of the Penal Code is not a dismissal for purposes of this section.

(e) The determination of the facts pursuant to this section is a civil matter which is independent of the determination of the person's guilt or innocence, has no collateral estoppel effect on a subsequent criminal prosecution, and does not preclude the litigation of the same or similar facts in a criminal proceeding. *(Added by Stats. 1990, c. 741 (A.B.3636), § 1. Amended by Stats.1997, c. 738 (A.B.1238), § 2; Stats.2005, c. 66 (A.B.637), § 7.)*

Cross References

Felonies, definition and penalties, see Penal Code §§ 17 and 18.

Misdemeanors, definition and penalties, see Penal Code §§ 17, 19 and 19.2.

§ 13377. Tow truck driver certificates; grounds for revocation or refusal to issue or renew; reapplication for certificate

(a) The department shall not issue or renew, or shall revoke, the tow truck driver certificate of an applicant or holder for any of the following causes:

(1) The tow truck driver certificate applicant or holder has been convicted of a violation of Section 220 of the Penal Code.

(2) The tow truck driver certificate applicant or holder has been convicted of a violation of paragraph (1), (2), (3), or (4) of subdivision (a) of Section 261 of the Penal Code.

(3) The tow truck driver certificate applicant or holder has been convicted of a violation of Section 264.1, 267, 288, or 289 of the Penal Code.

(4) The tow truck driver certificate applicant or holder has been convicted of any felony or three misdemeanors as set forth in subparagraph (B) of paragraph (2) of subdivision (a) of Section 5164 of the Public Resources Code.

(5) The tow truck driver certificate applicant's or holder's driving privilege has been suspended or revoked in accordance with any provisions of this code.

(b) For purposes of this section, a conviction means a plea or verdict of guilty or a conviction following a plea of nolo contendere. For purposes of this section, the record of a conviction, or a copy thereof certified by the clerk of the court or by a judge of the court in which the conviction occurred, is conclusive evidence of the conviction.

(c) Whenever the department receives information from the Department of Justice, or the Federal Bureau of Investigation, that a tow truck driver has been convicted of an offense specified in paragraph (1), (2), (3), or (4) of subdivision (a), the department shall immediately notify the employer and the Department of the California Highway Patrol.

(d) An applicant or holder of a tow truck driver certificate, whose certificate was denied or revoked, may reapply for a certificate whenever the applicable felony or misdemeanor conviction is reversed or dismissed. If the cause for the denial or revocation was based on the suspension or revocation of the applicant's or holder's driving privilege, he or she may reapply for a certificate upon restoration of his or her driving privilege. A termination of probation and dismissal of charges pursuant to Section 1203.4 of the Penal Code or a dismissal of charges pursuant to Section 1203.4a of the Penal Code is not a dismissal for purposes of this section. *(Added by Stats.1991, c. 488 (A.B.123), § 6. Amended by Stats.1992, c. 1243 (A.B.3090), § 86.2, eff. Sept. 30, 1992; Stats.2000, c. 135 (A.B.2539), § 159; Stats.2002, c. 787 (S.B.1798), § 34; Stats.2004, c. 184 (S.B.1314), § 6, eff. July 23, 2004.)*

489

Cross References

Counties and cities, persons convicted of Penal Code offenses, supervisory or disciplinary authority over minors, see Public Resources Code § 5164.
Felonies, definition and penalties, see Penal Code §§ 17 and 18.
Misdemeanors, definition and penalties, see Penal Code §§ 17, 19 and 19.2.

§ 13378.　Request for hearing; stay; appointment of hearing officer

(a) Any applicant for, or holder of, a tow truck driver certificate who has received a notice of refusal or revocation, may submit to the department, within 15 days after the mailing of the notice, a written request for a hearing. Failure to request a hearing, in writing, within 15 days is a waiver of the right to a hearing.

(b) Upon receipt by the department of the hearing request, the department may stay the action until a hearing is conducted and the final decision is made by the hearing officer. The department shall not stay the action when there is reasonable cause to believe that the stay would pose a threat to a member of the motoring public who may require the services of the tow truck driver in question.

(c) An applicant for, or a holder of, a tow truck driver certificate, whose certificate has been refused or revoked, is not entitled to a hearing whenever the action by the department is made mandatory by this article or any other applicable law or regulation.

(d) Upon receipt of a request for a hearing, and when the requesting party is entitled to a hearing under this article, the department shall appoint a hearing officer to conduct a hearing in accordance with Section 14112. *(Added by Stats.1991, c. 488 (A.B.123), § 7. Amended by Stats.1996, c. 124 (A.B.3470), § 123; Stats.2005, c. 66 (A.B.637), § 8.)*

§ 13380.　Peace officer's report; service of notice of suspension; arrest

(a) If a peace officer serves a notice of an order of suspension pursuant to Section 13388, or arrests any person for a violation of Section 23140, 23152, or 23153, the peace officer shall immediately forward to the department a sworn report of all information relevant to the enforcement action, including information that adequately identifies the person, a statement of the officer's grounds for belief that the person violated Section 23136, 23140, 23152, or 23153, a report of the results of any chemical tests that were conducted on the person or the circumstances constituting a refusal to submit to or complete the chemical testing pursuant to Section 13388 or 23612, a copy of any notice to appear under which the person was released from custody, and, if immediately available, a copy of the complaint filed with the court. For the purposes of this section and subdivision (g) of Section 23612, "immediately" means on or before the end of the fifth ordinary business day following the arrest, except that with respect to Section 13388 only, "immedi-

490

ately" has the same meaning as that term is defined in paragraph (3) of subdivision (b) of Section 13388.

(b) The peace officer's sworn report shall be made on forms furnished or approved by the department.

(c) For the purposes of this section, a report prepared pursuant to subdivision (a) and received pursuant to subdivision (a) of Section 1801, is a sworn report when it bears an entry identifying the maker of the document or a signature that has been affixed by means of an electronic device approved by the department. *(Added by Stats. 1998, c. 118 (S.B.1186), § 3.24, operative July 1, 1999.)*

§ 13382.　Blood alcohol of specified level; suspension or revocation of driving privilege; notice; confiscation of license; temporary license

(a) If the chemical test results for a person who has been arrested for a violation of Section 23152 or 23153 show that the person has 0.08 percent or more, by weight, of alcohol in the person's blood, or if the chemical test results for a person who has been arrested for a violation of Section 23140 show that the person has 0.05 percent or more, by weight, of alcohol in the person's blood, the peace officer, acting on behalf of the department, shall serve a notice of order of suspension or revocation of the person's privilege to operate a motor vehicle personally on the arrested person.

(b) If the peace officer serves the notice of order of suspension or revocation, the peace officer shall take possession of any driver's license issued by this state which is held by the person. When the officer takes possession of a valid driver's license, the officer shall issue, on behalf of the department, a temporary driver's license. The temporary driver's license shall be an endorsement on the notice of the order of suspension or revocation and shall be valid for 30 days from the date of arrest.

(c) The peace officer shall immediately forward a copy of the completed notice of order of suspension form, and any driver's license taken into possession under subdivision (b), with the report required by Section 13380, to the department. For the purposes of this section, "immediately" means on or before the end of the fifth ordinary business day following the arrest. *(Added by Stats.1998, c. 118 (S.B.1186), § 4, operative July 1, 1999.)*

§ 13384.　Consent to chemical test of blood, breath or urine

(a) The department shall not issue or renew a driver's license to any person unless the person consents in writing to submit to a chemical test or tests of that person's blood, breath, or urine pursuant to Section 23612, or a preliminary alcohol screening test pursuant to Section 23136, when requested to do so by a peace officer.

(b) All application forms for driver's licenses or driver's license renewal notices shall include a requirement that the applicant sign the following declaration as a condition of licensure:

"I agree to submit to a chemical test of my blood, breath, or urine for the purpose of determining the alcohol or drug content of my blood when testing is requested by a peace officer acting in accordance with Section 13388 or 23612 of the Vehicle Code."

(c) The department is not, incident to this section, required to maintain, copy, or store any information other than that to be incorporated into the standard application form. *(Added by Stats.1998, c. 118 (S.B. 1186), § 5, operative July 1, 1999.)*

§ 13385. Driving under the influence; declaration required in application forms or renewal notices as condition of licensure

(a) On or after July 1, 2008, all application forms for driver's licenses or driver's license renewal notices shall include a requirement that the applicant sign the following declaration as a condition of licensure:

"I am hereby advised that being under the influence of alcohol or drugs, or both, impairs the ability to safely operate a motor vehicle. Therefore, it is extremely dangerous to human life to drive while under the influence of alcohol or drugs, or both. If I drive while under the influence of alcohol or drugs, or both, and as a result, a person is killed, I can be charged with murder."

(b) On all application forms for driver's licenses or driver's license renewal notices printed by the department, in English or a language other than English, the department shall include the declaration in the same language as the application or renewal notice.

(c) The department is not, incident to this section, required to maintain, copy, or store any information other than that to be incorporated into the standard application form. *(Added by Stats.2007, c. 748 (A.B.808), § 2.)*

§ 13386. Certification and list of ignition interlock devices; prohibitions

(a)(1) The Department of Motor Vehicles shall certify or cause to be certified ignition interlock devices required by Article 5 (commencing with Section 23575) of Chapter 2 of Division 11.5 and publish a list of approved devices.

(2)(A) The Department of Motor Vehicles shall ensure that ignition interlock devices that have been certified according to the requirements of this section continue to meet certification requirements. The department may periodically require manufacturers to indicate in writing whether the devices continue to meet certification requirements.

(B) The department may use denial of certification, suspension or revocation of certification, or decertification of an ignition interlock device in another state as an indication that the certification requirements are not met, if either of the following apply:

(i) The denial of certification, suspension or revocation of certification, or decertification in another state constitutes a violation by the manufacturer of Article 2.55

(commencing with Section 125.00) of Chapter 1 of Division 1 of Title 13 of the California Code of Regulations.

(ii) The denial of certification for an ignition interlock device in another state was due to a failure of an ignition interlock device to meet the standards adopted by the regulation set forth in clause (i), specifically Sections 1 and 2 of the model specification for breath alcohol ignition interlock devices, as published by notice in the Federal Register, Vol. 57, No. 67, Tuesday, April 7, 1992, on pages 11774 to 11787, inclusive.

(C) Failure to continue to meet certification requirements shall result in suspension or revocation of certification of ignition interlock devices.

(b)(1) A manufacturer shall not furnish an installer, service center, technician, or consumer with technology or information that allows a device to be used in a manner that is contrary to the purpose for which it is certified.

(2) Upon a violation of paragraph (1), the department shall suspend or revoke the certification of the ignition interlock device that is the subject of that violation.

(c) An installer, service center, or technician shall not tamper with, change, or alter the functionality of the device from its certified criteria.

(d) The department shall utilize information from an independent laboratory to certify ignition interlock devices on or off the premises of the manufacturer or manufacturer's agent, in accordance with the guidelines. The cost of certification shall be borne by the manufacturers of ignition interlock devices. If the certification of a device is suspended or revoked, the manufacturer of the device shall be responsible for, and shall bear the cost of, the removal of the device and the replacement of a certified device of the manufacturer or another manufacturer.

(e) No model of ignition interlock device shall be certified unless it meets the accuracy requirements and specifications provided in the guidelines adopted by the National Highway Traffic Safety Administration.

(f) All manufacturers of ignition interlock devices that meet the requirements of subdivision (e) and are certified in a manner approved by the Department of Motor Vehicles, who intend to market the devices in this state, first shall apply to the Department of Motor Vehicles on forms provided by that department. The application shall be accompanied by a fee in an amount not to exceed the amount necessary to cover the costs incurred by the department in carrying out this section.

(g) A manufacturer and a manufacturer's agent certified by the department to provide ignition interlock devices shall provide each year to the department information on the number of false positives and the time to reset the device. The department shall use this information in evaluating the continued certification of an ignition interlock device.

491

(h) The department shall ensure that standard forms and procedures are developed for documenting decisions and compliance and communicating results to relevant agencies. These forms shall include all of the following:

(1) An "Option to Install," to be sent by the Department of Motor Vehicles to repeat offenders along with the mandatory order of suspension or revocation. This shall include the alternatives available for early license reinstatement with the installation of an ignition interlock device and shall be accompanied by a toll-free telephone number for each manufacturer of a certified ignition interlock device. Information regarding approved installation locations shall be provided to drivers by manufacturers with ignition interlock devices that have been certified in accordance with this section.

(2) A "Verification of Installation" to be returned to the department by the reinstating offender upon application for reinstatement. Copies shall be provided for the manufacturer or the manufacturer's agent.

(3) A "Notice of Noncompliance" and procedures to ensure continued use of the ignition interlock device during the restriction period and to ensure compliance with maintenance requirements. The maintenance period shall be standardized at 60 days to maximize monitoring checks for equipment tampering.

(i) Every manufacturer and manufacturer's agent certified by the department to provide ignition interlock devices shall adopt fee schedules that provide for the payment of the costs of the device by applicants in amounts commensurate with the applicant's ability to pay. *(Formerly § 23235, added by Stats.1994, c. 1237 (A.B.2639), § 3, eff. Sept. 30, 1994. Amended by Stats. 1998, c. 756 (A.B.762), § 19, operative July 1, 1999. Renumbered § 13386 and amended by Stats.1999, c. 22 (S.B.24), § 25, eff. May 26, 1999, operative July 1, 1999. Amended by Stats.2000, c. 1064 (A.B.2227), § 6, eff. Sept. 30, 2000; Stats.2001, c. 473 (S.B.485), § 21; Stats.2002, c. 545 (S.B.1852), § 15; Stats.2006, c. 835 (A.B.3045), § 2; Stats.2009, c. 217 (A.B.91), § 1; Stats.2010, c. 328 (S.B. 1330), § 229.)*

Cross References

Causing bodily injury to another while driving with license suspended or revoked, reinstatement of driving privileges, application of this section, see Vehicle Code § 14601.4.

Driving with knowledge of suspension, revocation, or restriction of driving privilege, punishment, reinstatement of driving privileges, see Vehicle Code § 14601.5.

Pilot program to reduce driving under the influence offenses, establishment in Alameda, Los Angeles, Sacramento, and Tulare Counties, see Vehicle Code § 23700.

Suspension or revocation of driving privilege for driving under the influence of alcoholic beverages or drugs, compliance with this section, see Vehicle Code § 14601.2.

§ 13388. Preliminary alcohol screening test or other chemical testing; procedure upon failure to take or complete test

(a) If a peace officer lawfully detains a person under 21 years of age who is driving a motor vehicle, and the officer has reasonable cause to believe that the person is in violation of Section 23136, the officer shall request that the person take a preliminary alcohol screening test to determine the presence of alcohol in the person, if a preliminary alcohol screening test device is immediately available. If a preliminary alcohol screening test device is not immediately available, the officer may request the person to submit to chemical testing of his or her blood, breath, or urine, conducted pursuant to Section 23612.

(b) If the person refuses to take, or fails to complete, the preliminary alcohol screening test or refuses to take or fails to complete a chemical test if a preliminary alcohol device is not immediately available, or if the person takes the preliminary alcohol screening test and that test reveals a blood-alcohol concentration of 0.01 percent or greater, or if the results of a chemical test reveal a blood-alcohol concentration of 0.01 percent or greater, the officer shall proceed as follows:

(1) The officer, acting on behalf of the department, shall serve the person with a notice of an order of suspension of the person's driving privilege.

(2) The officer shall take possession of any driver's license issued by this state which is held by the person. When the officer takes possession of a valid driver's license, the officer shall issue, on behalf of the department, a temporary driver's license. The temporary driver's license shall be an endorsement on the notice of the order of suspension and shall be valid for 30 days from the date of issuance, or until receipt of the order of suspension from the department, whichever occurs first.

(3) The officer immediately shall forward a copy of the completed notice of order of suspension form, and any driver's license taken into possession under paragraph (2), with the report required by Section 13380, to the department. For the purposes of this paragraph, "immediately" means on or before the end of the fifth ordinary business day after the notice of order of suspension was served.

(c) For the purposes of this section, a preliminary alcohol screening test device is an instrument designed and used to measure the presence of alcohol in a person based on a breath sample. *(Added by Stats.1998, c. 118 (S.B.1186), § 7, operative July 1, 1999.)*

§ 13389. Persons previously convicted of driving under the influence; lawful detention during probation; preliminary alcohol screening test; suspension of driving privileges

(a) If a peace officer lawfully detains a person previously convicted of Section 23152 or 23153 who is driving a motor vehicle, while the person is on probation for a violation of Section 23152 or 23153, and the officer has reasonable cause to believe that the person is in violation of Section 23154, the officer shall request that the person take a preliminary alcohol screening test to determine the presence of alcohol in the person, if a preliminary alcohol screening test device is immediately available. If a preliminary alcohol screening test device is not immediately available, the officer may request the person to submit to chemical testing of his or her blood, breath, or urine, conducted pursuant to Section 23612.

(b) If the person refuses to take, or fails to complete, the preliminary alcohol screening test or refuses to take or fails to complete a chemical test if a preliminary alcohol device is not immediately available, or if the person takes the preliminary alcohol screening test and that test reveals a blood-alcohol concentration of 0.01 percent or greater, the officer shall proceed as follows:

(1) The officer, acting on behalf of the department, shall serve the person with a notice of an order of suspension of the person's driving privilege.

(2)(A) The officer shall take possession of any driver's license issued by this state that is held by the person. When the officer takes possession of a valid driver's license, the officer shall issue, on behalf of the department, a temporary driver's license.

(B) The temporary driver's license shall be an endorsement on the notice of the order of suspension and shall be valid for 30 days from the date of issuance, or until receipt of the order of suspension from the department, whichever occurs first.

(3)(A) The officer shall immediately forward a copy of the completed notice of order of suspension form, and any driver's license taken into possession under paragraph (2), with the report required by Section 13380, to the department.

(B) For the purposes of subparagraph (A), "immediately" means on or before the end of the fifth ordinary business day after the notice of order of suspension was served.

(c) For the purposes of this section, a preliminary alcohol screening test device is an instrument designed and used to measure the presence of alcohol in a person based on a breath sample. *(Added by Stats.2007, c. 749 (A.B.1165), § 3, operative Jan. 1, 2009.)*

Cross References

Drivers' licenses, review of suspension or revocation order, see Vehicle Code § 13557.

§ 13390. Repealed by Stats.2006, c. 899 (A.B.2752), § 1

§ 13392. Fee for reissuance, return or issuance of license

Any person whose license is suspended or delayed issuance pursuant to Section 13388 shall pay to the department, in addition to any other fees required for the reissuance, return, or issuance of a driver's license, one hundred dollars ($100) for the reissuance, return, or issuance of his or her driver's license. *(Added by Stats.1998, c. 118 (S.B.1186), § 9, operative July 1, 1999.)*

ARTICLE 4. PROCEDURE

Section
13550. Surrender of license or temporary permit to court.

Section
13551. Surrender of licenses to department.
13551.1. Repealed.
13552. Nonresidents.
13553. Unlicensed persons.
13554. Repealed.
13555. Termination of probation and dismissal of charges.
13556. Duration of suspension.
13557. Review of suspension or revocation order.
13558. Hearing on suspension or revocation.
13559. Blood alcohol content of .08 percent or more, or refusal of chemical test; judicial review of suspension; stay; effect on criminal prosecution.

Cross References

Driver license compact, see Vehicle Code § 15000 et seq.

§ 13550. Surrender of license or temporary permit to court

Whenever any person is convicted of any offense for which this code makes mandatory the revocation or suspension by the department of the privilege of the person to operate a motor vehicle, the privilege of the person to operate a motor vehicle is suspended or revoked until the department takes the action required by this code, and the court in which the conviction is had shall require the surrender to it of the driver's license or temporary permit issued to the person convicted and the court shall within 10 days after the conviction forward the same with the required report of the conviction to the department. *(Stats.1959, c. 3, p. 1628, § 13550. Amended by Stats.1961, c. 1615, p. 3457, § 26; Stats.1971, c. 1530, p. 3027, § 11, operative May 3, 1972; Stats.1972, c. 1129, p. 2170, § 3; Stats.1990, c. 44 (A.B.1648), § 3.)*

Cross References

Conviction of driving under the influence, first time offense, surrender of license, see Vehicle Code § 23536.
Driving under the influence and causing bodily injury to another, punishment and conditions of probation, surrender of license, see Vehicle Code §§ 23554 to 23568.
Driving while under the influence of alcoholic beverages or drugs, surrender of license for conviction, see Vehicle Code § 23660.
Licenses affected by suspension or revocation, see Vehicle Code § 13207.
Multiple offenses with respect to driving under the influence, punishment and conditions of probation, surrender of license, see Vehicle Code §§ 23550 and 23552.
Retention of license by court during suspension, see Vehicle Code § 13206.
Second offense with respect to driving under the influence, punishment and conditions of probation, surrender of license, see Vehicle Code §§ 23540 and 23542.

§ 13551. Surrender of licenses to department

(a) Whenever the department revokes or suspends the privilege of any person to operate a motor vehicle, the revocation or suspension shall apply to all driver's licenses held by that person, and, unless previously surrendered to the court, all of those licenses shall be surrendered to the department, or, pursuant to Section 13388, 23612, or 13382, to a peace officer on behalf of the department.

Whenever the department cancels a driver's license, the license shall be surrendered to the department. All suspended licenses shall be retained by the department. The department shall return the license to the licensee, or may issue the person a new license upon the expiration of the period of suspension or revocation, if the person is otherwise eligible for a driver's license.

(b) The department shall return the license to the licensee, or may issue the person a new license, whenever the department determines that the grounds for suspension, revocation, or cancellation did not exist at the time the action was taken, if the person is otherwise eligible for a driver's license. *(Stats.1959, c. 3, p. 1628, § 13551. Amended by Stats.1961, c. 1615, p. 3457, § 27; Stats.1963, c. 154, p. 822, § 1; Stats.1967, c. 769, p. 2157, § 1; Stats.1989, c. 1460, § 12, operative July 1, 1990; Stats. 1990, c. 431 (S.B.1150), § 9, eff. July 26, 1990; Stats.1993, c. 899 (S.B.689), § 8; Stats.1998, c. 118 (S.B.1186), § 3.18, operative July 1, 1999.)*

Cross References

Cancellation, revocation and suspension of license, defined, see Vehicle Code § 13100 et seq.

Driver's license,

     Surrender on suspension by court, see Vehicle Code § 13206.

     Suspension for failure to report accident, see Vehicle Code § 16004.

Motor vehicle defined, see Vehicle Code § 415.

Seizure of documents and plates upon expiration, revocation, cancellation or suspension, see Vehicle Code § 4460.

Suspension or revocation of driver's license by,

     Court, see Vehicle Code § 13200 et seq.

     Department, see Vehicle Code § 13350 et seq.

§ 13551.1. Repealed by Stats.1999, c. 1008 (S.B.533), § 9

§ 13552. Nonresidents

(a) The privileges of a nonresident to operate vehicles in this state may be suspended or revoked under the provisions of this chapter in the same manner and to the same extent as the privileges of a resident driver.

(b) Any nonresident, whether or not licensed to drive in a foreign jurisdiction, who operates a motor vehicle upon a highway after his privilege of operating a motor vehicle in this state has been suspended or revoked is in violation of Section 14601 or 14601.1.

(c) Whenever the department revokes or suspends the privileges of a nonresident to operate vehicles in this state, it shall send a certified copy of the order to the proper authorities in the state wherein the person is a resident. *(Stats.1959, c. 3, p. 1628, § 13552. Amended by Stats.1971, c. 438, p. 908, § 189, operative May 3, 1972.)*

Cross References

Nonresident defined, see Vehicle Code § 435.

Suspension or revocation,

     Of license by court, provisions applicable to nonresidents, see Vehicle Code § 13205.

     Of privilege of nonresident to drive in this state, see Vehicle Code § 13363.

§ 13553. Unlicensed persons

Whenever a court or the department suspends or revokes the privilege of any person to operate a motor vehicle and the person does not hold a valid driver's license, or has never applied for or received a driver's license in this State, the person shall be subject to any and all penalties and disabilities provided in this code for a violation of the terms and conditions of a suspension or revocation of the privilege to operate a motor vehicle. *(Stats.1959, c. 3, p. 1629, § 13553.)*

Cross References

Driving when license, suspended or revoked, see Vehicle Code § 14601.

Penalties, generally, see Vehicle Code § 42000 et seq.

Suspension or revocation of license by,

     Court, see Vehicle Code § 13200 et seq.

     Department, see Vehicle Code § 13350 et seq.

Violation of code as misdemeanor, see Vehicle Code § 40000.5 et seq.

§ 13554. Repealed by Stats.1959, c. 1622, p. 3992, § 5

§ 13555. Termination of probation and dismissal of charges

A termination of probation and dismissal of charges pursuant to Section 1203.4 or a dismissal of charges pursuant to Section 1203.4a of the Penal Code does not affect any revocation or suspension of the privilege of the person convicted to drive a motor vehicle under this chapter. Such person's prior conviction shall be considered a conviction for the purpose of revoking or suspending or otherwise limiting such privilege on the ground of two or more convictions. *(Stats.1959, c. 3, p. 1629, § 13555. Amended by Stats.1959, c. 1996, p. 4626, § 18.6; Stats.1963, c. 1994, p. 4075, § 1.)*

§ 13556. Duration of suspension

(a) Unless otherwise specifically provided in this chapter, no suspension of a license by the department shall be for a longer period than six months, except that the department may suspend a license for a maximum period of 12 months in those cases when a discretionary revocation would otherwise be authorized pursuant to this chapter.

(b) Any discretionary suspension, the ending of which is dependent upon an action by the person suspended and which has been in effect for eight years, may be ended at the election of the department.

(c) Notwithstanding any other provisions of this code, a suspension based upon a physical or mental condition shall continue until evidence satisfactory to the department establishes that the cause for which the action was taken has been removed or no longer renders the person incapable of operating a motor vehicle safely. *(Stats. 1959, c. 3, p. 1629, § 13556. Amended by Stats.1976, c. 498, p. 1298, § 3; Stats.1982, c. 612, p. 2596, § 1.)*

Cross References

Grounds for suspension, see Vehicle Code § 13361.

§ 13557. Review of suspension or revocation order

(a) The department shall review the determination made pursuant to Section 13353, 13353.1, or 13353.2 relating to a person who has received a notice of an order of suspension or revocation of the person's privilege to operate a motor vehicle pursuant to Section 13353, 13353.1, 13353.2, 13382, or 23612, [1]. The department shall consider the sworn report submitted by the peace officer pursuant to Section 23612 or 13380 and any other evidence accompanying the report.

(b)(1) If the department determines in the review of a determination made under Section 13353 or 13353.1, by a preponderance of the evidence, all of the following facts, the department shall sustain the order of suspension or revocation:

(A) The peace officer had reasonable cause to believe that the person had been driving a motor vehicle in violation of Section 23136, 23140, 23152, 23153, or 23154.

(B) The person was placed under arrest or, if the alleged violation was of Section 23136, that the person was lawfully detained.

(C) The person refused or failed to complete the chemical test or tests after being requested by a peace officer.

(D) Except for the persons described in Section 23612 who are incapable of refusing, the person had been told that his or her privilege to operate a motor vehicle would be suspended or revoked if he or she refused to submit to, and complete, the required testing.

(2) If the department determines, by a preponderance of the evidence, that any of the facts required under paragraph (1) were not proven, the department shall rescind the order of suspension or revocation and, if the person is otherwise eligible, return or reissue the person's driver's license pursuant to Section 13551. The determination of the department upon administrative review is final unless a hearing is requested pursuant to Section 13558.

(3) If the department determines in the review of a determination made under Section 13353.2, by the preponderance of the evidence, all of the following facts, the department shall sustain the order of suspension or revocation, or if the person is under 21 years of age and does not yet have a driver's license, the department shall delay issuance of that license for one year:

(A) The peace officer had reasonable cause to believe that the person had been driving a motor vehicle in violation of Section 23136, 23140, 23152, 23153, or 23154.

(B) The person was placed under arrest or, if the alleged violation was of Section 23136, the person was lawfully detained.

(C) The person was driving a motor vehicle under any of the following circumstances:

(i) When the person had 0.08 percent or more, by weight, of alcohol in his or her blood.

(ii) When the person was under 21 years of age and had 0.05 percent or more, by weight, of alcohol in his or her blood.

(iii) When the person was under 21 years of age and had a blood-alcohol concentration of 0.01 percent or greater, as measured by a preliminary alcohol screening test, or other chemical test.

(iv) When the person was driving a vehicle that requires a commercial driver's license and the person had 0.04 percent or more, by weight, of alcohol in his or her blood.

(v) When the person was on probation for a violation of Section 23152 or 23153 and had a blood-alcohol concentration of 0.01 percent or greater, as measured by a preliminary alcohol screening test or other chemical test.

(4) If the department determines that any of those facts required under paragraph (3) were not proven by the preponderance of the evidence, the department shall rescind the order of suspension or revocation and, if the person is otherwise eligible, return or reissue the person's driver's license pursuant to Section 13551. For persons under 21 years of age, the determination of the department pursuant to paragraph (3) is final unless a hearing is requested within 10 days of the determination, which hearing shall be conducted according to Section 13558. For persons over 21 years of age, the determination of the department upon administrative review is final unless a hearing is requested pursuant to Section 13558.

(c) The department shall make the determination upon administrative review before the effective date of the order of suspension or revocation.

(d) The administrative review does not stay the suspension or revocation of a person's privilege to operate a motor vehicle. If the department is unable to make a determination on administrative review within the time limit in subdivision (c), the department shall stay the effective date of the order of suspension or revocation pending the determination and, if the person's driver's license has been taken by the peace officer pursuant to Section 13382, 13388, 13389, or 23612, the department shall notify the person before the expiration date of the temporary permit issued pursuant to Section 13382, 13388, 13389, or 23612, or the expiration date of any previous extension issued pursuant to this subdivision, in a form that permits the person to establish to any peace officer that his or her privilege to operate a motor vehicle is not suspended or revoked.

(e) A person may request and be granted a hearing pursuant to Section 13558 without first receiving the results of an administrative review pursuant to this section. After receiving a request for a hearing, the department is not required to conduct an administrative review of the same matter pursuant to this section.

(f) A determination of facts by the department under this section has no collateral estoppel effect on a subsequent criminal prosecution and does not preclude litigation of those same facts in the criminal proceeding. *(Added by Stats.1989, c. 1460, § 13, operative July 1, 1990. Amended by Stats.1990, c. 431 (S.B.1150), § 10, eff. July 26, 1990; Stats.1992, c. 974 (S.B.1600), § 9, eff. Sept. 28, 1992; Stats.1993, c. 899 (S.B.689), § 9; Stats.1993, c. 1244 (S.B.126), § 15.5; Stats.1994, c. 938 (S.B.1295), § 9, eff. Sept. 28, 1994; Stats.1998, c. 118 (S.B.1186), § 3.20, operative July 1, 1999; Stats.2010, c. 244 (A.B.1928), § 1; Stats.2011, c. 296 (A.B.1023), § 307.)*

¹ So in enrolled bill.

§ 13558. Hearing on suspension or revocation

(a) Any person, who has received a notice of an order of suspension or revocation of the person's privilege to operate a motor vehicle pursuant to Section 13353, 13353.1, 13353.2, 13388, 23612, or 13382 or a notice pursuant to Section 13557, may request a hearing on the matter pursuant to Article 3 (commencing with Section 14100) of Chapter 3, except as otherwise provided in this section.

(b) If the person wishes to have a hearing before the effective date of the order of suspension or revocation, the request for a hearing shall be made within 10 days of the receipt of the notice of the order of suspension or revocation. The hearing shall be held at a place designated by the department as close as practicable to the place where the arrest occurred, unless the parties agree to a different location. Any evidence at the hearing shall not be limited to the evidence presented at an administrative review pursuant to Section 13557.

(c)(1) The only issues at the hearing on an order of suspension or revocation pursuant to Section 13353 or 13353.1 shall be those facts listed in paragraph (1) of subdivision (b) of Section 13557. Notwithstanding Section 14106, the period of suspension or revocation specified in Section 13353 or 13353.1 shall not be reduced and, notwithstanding Section 14105.5, the effective date of the order of suspension or revocation shall not be stayed pending review at a hearing pursuant to this section.

(2) The only issues at the hearing on an order of suspension pursuant to Section 13353.2 shall be those facts listed in paragraph (2) of subdivision (b) of Section 13557. Notwithstanding Section 14106, the period of suspension specified in Section 13353.3 shall not be reduced.

(d) The department shall hold the administrative hearing before the effective date of the order of suspension or revocation if the request for the hearing is postmarked or received by the department on or before 10 days after the person's receipt of the service of the notice of the order of suspension or revocation pursuant to Section 13353.2, 13388, 23612, or 13382.

(e) A request for an administrative hearing does not stay the suspension or revocation of a person's privilege

to operate a motor vehicle. If the department does not conduct an administrative hearing and make a determination after an administrative hearing within the time limit in subdivision (d), the department shall stay the effective date of the order of suspension or revocation pending the determination and, if the person's driver's license has been taken by the peace officer pursuant to Section 13388, 23612, or 13382, the department shall notify the person before the expiration date of the temporary permit issued pursuant to Section 13388, 23612, or 13382, or the expiration date of any previous extension issued pursuant to this subdivision, provided the person is otherwise eligible, in a form that permits the person to establish to any peace officer that his or her privilege to operate a motor vehicle is not suspended or revoked.

(f) The department shall give written notice of its determination pursuant to Section 14105. If the department determines, upon a hearing of the matter, to suspend or revoke the person's privilege to operate a motor vehicle, notwithstanding the term of any temporary permit issued pursuant to Section 13388, 23612, or 13382, the temporary permit shall be revoked and the suspension or revocation of the person's privilege to operate a motor vehicle shall become effective five days after notice is given. If the department sustains the order of suspension or revocation, the department shall include notice that the person has a right to review by the court pursuant to Section 13559.

(g) A determination of facts by the department upon a hearing pursuant to this section has no collateral estoppel effect on a subsequent criminal prosecution and does not preclude litigation of those same facts in the criminal proceeding. *(Added by Stats.1989, c. 1460, § 14, operative July 1, 1990. Amended by Stats.1990, c. 216 (S.B.2510), § 117; Stats.1990, c. 431 (S.B.1150), § 11, eff. July 26, 1990; Stats.1992, c. 974 (S.B.1600), § 10, eff. Sept. 28, 1992; Stats.1993, c. 899 (S.B.689), § 10; Stats.1994, c. 938 (S.B.1295), § 10, eff. Sept. 28, 1994; Stats.1998, c. 118 (S.B.1186), § 3.22, operative July 1, 1999.)*

§ 13559. Blood alcohol content of .08 percent or more, or refusal of chemical test; judicial review of suspension; stay; effect on criminal prosecution

(a) Notwithstanding Section 14400 or 14401, within 30 days of the issuance of the notice of determination of the department sustaining an order of suspension or revocation of the person's privilege to operate a motor vehicle after the hearing pursuant to Section 13558, the person may file a petition for review of the order in the court of competent jurisdiction in the person's county of residence. The filing of a petition for judicial review shall not stay the order of suspension or revocation. The review shall be on the record of the hearing and the court shall not consider other evidence. If the court finds that the department exceeded its constitutional or statutory authority, made an erroneous interpretation of the law, acted in an arbitrary and capricious manner, or made a determination which is not supported by the evidence in the record, the court may order the department to rescind the order of suspension or revocation and return, or reissue a new license to, the person.

(b) A finding by the court after a review pursuant to this section shall have no collateral estoppel effect on a subsequent criminal prosecution and does not preclude litigation of those same facts in the criminal proceeding. *(Added by Stats.1989, c. 1460, § 15, operative July 1, 1990. Amended by Stats.1990, c. 431 (S.B.1150), § 12, eff. July 26, 1990.)*

CHAPTER 3. INVESTIGATION AND HEARING

Article	Section
1. Investigation and Re-examination	13800
2. Notice	13950
3. Hearing	14100
4. Probation	14250
5. Review of Orders	14400

ARTICLE 1. INVESTIGATION AND RE–EXAMINATION

Section
13800. Investigations by the department.
13801. Re-examination by department.
13802. Special consideration for amount of use.
13803. Repealed.

§ 13800. Investigations by the department

The department may conduct an investigation to determine whether the privilege of any person to operate a motor vehicle should be suspended or revoked or whether terms or conditions of probation should be imposed upon receiving information or upon a showing by its records:

(a) That the licensee has been involved as a driver in any accident causing death or personal injury or serious damage to property.

(b) That the licensee has been involved in three or more accidents within a period of 12 consecutive months.

(c) That the person in three consecutive years has committed three or more offenses which have resulted in convictions involving the consumption of an alcoholic beverage or drug, or both, while operating a motor vehicle, including, but not limited to, offenses under Section 23103.5, 23152, 23153, 23222, or 23224; has been involved in three or more accidents in which the accident reports show that the person was driving and had consumed alcoholic beverages or drugs, or both; or had any combination of three or more of those offenses and accidents.

(d) That the licensee is a reckless, negligent, or incompetent driver of a motor vehicle.

(e) That the licensee has permitted an unlawful or fraudulent use of his driver's license.

(f) That any ground exists for which a license might be refused. The receipt by the department of an abstract of the record of conviction of any offense involving the use or possession of narcotic controlled substances under Division 10 (commencing with Section 11000) of the Health and Safety Code shall be a sufficient basis for an investigation by the department to determine whether grounds exist for which a license might be refused. *(Stats.1959, c. 3, p. 1629, § 13800. Amended by Stats. 1961, c. 1845, p. 3928, § 2; Stats.1972, c. 1407, p. 3045, § 13; Stats.1982, c. 1339, p. 4984, § 11, eff. Sept. 24, 1982.)*

Cross References

Grounds permitting refusal of license, see Vehicle Code § 12809.

§ 13801. Re-examination by department

In addition to the investigation, the department may require the re-examination of the licensee, and shall give 10 days' written notice of the time and place thereof. If the licensee refuses or fails to submit to the re-examination, the department may peremptorily suspend the driving privilege of the person until such time as the licensee shall have submitted to re-examination. The suspension shall be effective upon notice. *(Stats.1959, c. 3, p. 1629, § 13801.)*

Cross References

License examination and driving test, see Vehicle Code § 12804.9.
Method of giving notice, see Vehicle Code § 22 et seq.

§ 13802. Special consideration for amount of use

In applying the provisions of Section 13800 the department shall give due consideration to the amount of use or mileage traveled in the operation of a motor vehicle. *(Stats.1959, c. 3, p. 1630, § 13802. Amended by Stats. 1961, c. 1615, p. 3457, § 28.)*

§ 13803. Repealed by Stats.2000, c. 985 (S.B.335), § 15, operative Jan. 1, 2011

ARTICLE 2. NOTICE

Section
13950. Notice required.
13951. Notice upon refusal of license.
13952. Contents of notice.
13953. Alternative action.
13954. Suspension or revocation of license upon accident occurring under specified circumstances; application of section.

§ 13950. Notice required

Whenever the department determines upon investigation or re-examination that any of the grounds for re-examination are true, or that the safety of the person investigated or re-examined or other persons upon the highways requires such action, and it proposes to revoke or suspend the driving privilege of the person or proposes to impose terms of probation on his driving privilege, notice and an opportunity to be heard shall be given before taking the action. *(Stats.1959, c. 3, p. 1630, § 13950.)*

Cross References

Hearings by department, see Vehicle Code § 14100 et seq.
Issuance of license, see Vehicle Code § 12800 et seq.
Method of giving notice, see Vehicle Code § 22 et seq.
Renewal of licenses, see Vehicle Code §§ 12808, 12814.

§ 13951. Notice upon refusal of license

Whenever the department proposes to refuse to issue or renew a driver's license, it shall notify the applicant of such fact and give him an opportunity to be heard. *(Stats.1959, c. 3, p. 1630, § 13951.)*

Cross References

Hearings, see Vehicle Code § 14100 et seq.

§ 13952. Contents of notice

The notice shall contain a statement setting forth the proposed action and the grounds therefor, and notify the person of his right to a hearing as provided in this chapter, or the department, at the time it gives notice of its intention to act may set the date of hearing, giving 10 days' notice thereof. *(Stats.1959, c. 3, p. 1630, § 13952. Amended by Stats.1961, c. 58, p. 1009, § 34, eff. March 31, 1961.)*

Cross References

Hearings, see Vehicle Code § 14100 et seq.

§ 13953. Alternative action

In the alternative to the procedure under Sections 13950, 13951, and 13952 and in the event the department determines upon investigation or reexamination that the safety of the person subject to investigation or reexamination or other persons upon the highways require such action, the department shall forthwith and without hearing suspend or revoke the privilege of the person to operate a motor vehicle or impose reasonable terms and conditions of probation which shall be relative to the safe operation of a motor vehicle. No order of suspension or revocation or the imposition of terms or conditions of probation shall become effective until 30 days after the giving of written notice thereof to the person affected, except that the department shall have authority to make any such order effective immediately upon the giving of notice when in its opinion because of the mental or physical condition of the person such immediate action is required for the safety of the driver or other persons upon the highways. *(Stats.1959, c. 3, p. 1630, § 13953. Amended by Stats.1959, c. 1996, p. 4626, § 19; Stats.1969, c. 1045, p. 2029, § 1.)*

§ 13954. Suspension or revocation of license upon accident occurring under specified circumstances; application of section

(a) Notwithstanding any other provision of this code, the department immediately shall suspend or revoke the driving privilege of a person who the department has

reasonable cause to believe was in some manner involved in an accident while operating a motor vehicle under the following circumstances at the time of the accident:

(1) The person had 0.08 percent or more, by weight, of alcohol in his or her blood.

(2) He or she proximately caused the accident as a result of an act prohibited, or the neglect of any duty imposed, by law.

(3) The accident occurred within five years of the date of a violation of subdivision (b) of Section 191.5 of the Penal Code that resulted in a conviction.

(b) If an accident described in subdivision (a) does not result in a conviction or finding of a violation of Section 23152 or 23153, the department shall suspend the driving privilege under this section for one year from the date of commencement of the original suspension. After the one-year suspension period, the driving privilege may be reinstated if evidence establishes to the satisfaction of the department that no grounds exist that would authorize the refusal to issue a license and that reinstatement of the driving privilege would not jeopardize the safety of the person or other persons upon the highways, and if the person gives proof of financial responsibility, as defined in Section 16430.

(c) If an accident described in subdivision (a) does result in a conviction or finding of a violation of Section 23152 or 23153, the department shall revoke the driving privilege under this section for three years from the date of commencement of the original revocation. After the three-year revocation period, the driving privilege may be reinstated if evidence establishes to the satisfaction of the department that no grounds exist that would authorize the refusal to issue a license and that reinstatement of the driving privilege would not jeopardize the safety of the person or other persons upon the highways, and if the person gives proof of financial responsibility.

(d) Any revocation action under subdivision (c) shall be imposed as follows:

(1) If the accident results in a first conviction of a violation of Section 23152 or 23153, or if the person was convicted of a separate violation of Section 23152 or 23153 that occurred within five years of the accident, the period of revocation under subdivision (c) shall be concurrent with any period of restriction, suspension, or revocation imposed under Section 13352, 13352.4, or 13352.5.

(2) If the person was convicted of two or more separate violations of Section 23152 or 23153, or both, that occurred within five years of the accident, the period of revocation under subdivision (c) shall be cumulative and shall be imposed consecutively with any period of restriction, suspension, or revocation imposed under Section 13352 or 13352.5.

(e) The department immediately shall notify the person in writing of the action taken and, upon the person's request in writing and within 15 days from the date of receipt of that request, shall grant the person an opportunity for a hearing in the same manner and under the same conditions as provided in Article 3 (commencing with Section 14100) of Chapter 3, except as otherwise provided in this section. For purposes of this section, the scope of the hearing shall cover the following issues:

(1) Whether the peace officer had reasonable cause to believe the person had been driving a motor vehicle in violation of Section 23152 or 23153.

(2) Whether the person had been placed under lawful arrest.

(3) Whether a chemical test of the person's blood, breath, or urine indicated that the blood-alcohol level was 0.08 percent or more, by weight, at the time of testing.

If the department determines, upon a hearing of the matter, that the person had not been placed under lawful arrest, or that a chemical test of the person's blood, breath, or urine did not indicate a blood-alcohol level of 0.08 percent or more, by weight, at the time of testing, the suspension or revocation shall be terminated immediately.

(f) This section applies if the accident occurred on or after January 1, 1990, without regard for the dates of the violations referred to in subdivisions (a) and (d).

(g) Notwithstanding subdivision (f), if a person's privilege to operate a motor vehicle is required to be suspended or revoked pursuant to this section as it read before January 1, 1990, as a result of an accident that occurred before January 1, 1990, the privilege shall be suspended or revoked pursuant to this section as it read before January 1, 1990.

(Added by Stats.1985, c. 1071, § 1. Amended by Stats.1989, c. 479, § 2; Stats.1992, c. 974 (S.B.1600), § 11, eff. Sept. 28, 1992; Stats.2004, c. 551 (S.B.1697), § 12, operative Sept. 20, 2005; Stats.2007, c. 747 (A.B.678), § 27.)

Cross References

Chemical testing for blood-alcohol level, see Vehicle Code § 23612.

Grounds permitting refusal to issue license, see Vehicle Code § 12809.

ARTICLE 3. HEARING

Section
14100.   Demand for hearing; application; notice; contents.
14100.1.   Denial, suspension, or revocation of passenger transportation vehicle, hazardous materials endorsement, or farm labor vehicle certificate; conduct of hearings.
14101.   Entitlement to hearing.
14102.   Repealed.
14103.   Waiver of hearing.
14104.   Time and place; notice.
14104.2.   Conduct of hearing; recordings.
14104.5.   Subpoenas; issuance.
14104.7.   Evidence.
14105.   Finding and decision; notice; review; correction of errors.

Section
14105.5.   Review of decision; stay; scope; notice; correction of errors.
14106.   Reopening case.
14107 to 14111.   Repealed.
14112.   Procedures; law governing.

§ 14100. Demand for hearing; application; notice; contents

(a) Whenever the department has given notice, or has taken or proposes to take action under Section 12804.15, 13353, 13353.2, 13950, 13951, 13952, or 13953, the person receiving the notice or subject to the action may, within 10 days, demand a hearing which shall be granted, except as provided in Section 14101.

(b) An application for a hearing does not stay the action by the department for which the notice is given.

(c) The fact that a person has the right to request an administrative hearing within 10 days after receipt of the notice of the order of suspension under this section and Section 16070, and that the request is required to be made within 10 days in order to receive a determination prior to the effective date of the suspension shall be made prominent on the notice.

(d) The department shall make available notices, to accompany the notice provided pursuant to this section, that provide the information required pursuant to subdivision (c) in all non-English languages spoken by a substantial number of the public served by the department, and shall distribute the notices as it determines is appropriate.

(e) The department shall implement the provisions of subdivisions (c) and (d) as soon as practicable, but not later than January 1, 1994. *(Stats.1959, c. 3, p. 1630, § 14100. Amended by Stats.1959, c. 1996, p. 4626, § 20; Stats.1989, c. 1460, § 16, operative July 1, 1990; Stats. 1990, c. 431 (S.B.1150), § 13, eff. July 26, 1990; Stats. 1991, c. 13 (A.B.37), § 31, eff. Feb. 13, 1991; Stats.1992, c. 1281 (A.B.3580), § 7; Stats.2001, c. 658 (A.B.67), § 5, eff. Oct. 10, 2001.)*

§ 14100.1. Denial, suspension, or revocation of passenger transportation vehicle, hazardous materials endorsement, or farm labor vehicle certificate; conduct of hearings

Hearings granted on refusal, suspension, or revocation of a passenger transportation vehicle or hazardous materials endorsement, or farm labor vehicle certificate shall be conducted according to Chapter 3 (commencing with Section 13800) of Division 6. *(Added by Stats.1990, c. 1360 (S.B.1510), § 42.)*

§ 14101. Entitlement to hearing

A person is not entitled to a hearing in either of the following cases:

(a) If the action by the department is made mandatory by this code.

(b) If the person has previously been given an opportunity with appropriate notice for a hearing and failed to request a hearing within the time specified by law. *(Stats.1959, c. 3, p. 1631, § 14101. Amended by Stats. 1991, c. 13 (A.B.37), § 32, eff. Feb. 13, 1991.)*

§ 14102. Repealed by Stats.1991, c. 13 (A.B.37), § 33, eff. Feb. 13, 1991

§ 14103. Waiver of hearing

Failure to respond to a notice given under this chapter within 10 days is a waiver of the right to a hearing, and the department may take action without a hearing or may, upon request of the person whose privilege of driving is in question, or at its own option, reopen the question, take evidence, change, or set aside any order previously made, or grant a hearing. *(Stats.1959, c. 3, p. 1631, § 14103. Amended by Stats.1991, c. 13 (A.B.37), § 34, eff. Feb. 13, 1991.)*

§ 14104. Time and place; notice

If the department grants a hearing as provided in this chapter, it shall fix a time and place for the hearing and shall give 10 days' notice of the hearing to the applicant or licensee. The notice of hearing shall also include a statement of the discovery rights of the applicant or licensee to review the department's records prior to the hearing.

(Stats.1959, c. 3, p. 1631, § 14104. Amended by Stats.1961, c. 58, p. 1009, § 35, eff. March 31, 1961; Stats.1991, c. 13 (A.B.37), § 35, eff. Feb. 13, 1991.)

§ 14104.2. Conduct of hearing; recordings

(a) Any hearing shall be conducted by the director or by a hearing officer or hearing board appointed by him or her from officers or employees of the department.

(b) The entire proceedings at any hearing may be recorded by a phonographic recorder or by mechanical, electronic, or other means capable of reproduction or transcription. *(Added by Stats.1991, c. 13 (A.B.37), § 36, eff. Feb. 13, 1991.)*

§ 14104.5. Subpoenas; issuance

(a) Before a hearing has commenced, the department, or the hearing officer or hearing board, shall issue subpoenas or subpoenas duces tecum, or both, at the request of any party, for attendance or production of documents at the hearing. After the hearing has commenced, the department, if it is hearing the case, or the hearing officer sitting alone, or the hearing board, may issue subpoenas or subpoenas duces tecum, or both.

(b) Notwithstanding Section 11450.20 of the Government Code, subpoenas and subpoenas duces tecum issued in conjunction with the hearings may be served by first-class mail. *(Added by Stats.1976, c. 891, p. 2048, § 1. Amended by Stats.1991, c. 13 (A.B.37), § 37, eff. Feb. 13, 1991; Stats.1999, c. 724 (A.B.1650), § 32.)*

500

§ 14104.7. Evidence

At any hearing, the department shall consider its official records and may receive sworn testimony. At the hearing, or subsequent to the hearing with the consent of the applicant or licensee, any or all of the following may be submitted as evidence concerning any fact relating to the ability of the applicant or licensee to safely operate a motor vehicle:

(a) Reports of attending or examining physicians and surgeons.

(b) Reports of special investigators appointed by the department to investigate and report upon any facts relating to the ability of the person to operate a vehicle safely.

(c) Properly authenticated reports of hospital records, excerpts from expert testimony received by the department or a hearing board upon similar issues of scientific fact in other cases, and the prior decision of the director upon those issues. *(Added by Stats.1991, c. 13 (A.B.37), § 38, eff. Feb. 13, 1991.)*

§ 14105. Finding and decision; notice; review; correction of errors

(a) Upon the conclusion of a hearing, the hearing officer or hearing board shall make findings and render a decision on behalf of the department and shall notify the person involved. Notice of the decision shall include a statement of the person's right to a review. The decision shall take effect as stated in the notice, but not less than four nor more than 15 days after the notice is mailed.

(b) The decision may be modified at any time after issuance to correct mistakes or clerical errors. *(Stats. 1959, c. 3, p. 1631, § 14105. Amended by Stats.1976, c. 891, p. 2048, § 2; Stats.1980, c. 92, p. 230, § 1; Stats. 1991, c. 13 (A.B.37), § 39, eff. Feb. 13, 1991; Stats.1999, c. 724 (A.B.1650), § 33.)*

§ 14105.5. Review of decision; stay; scope; notice; correction of errors

(a) The person subject to a hearing may request a review of the decision taken under Section 14105 within 15 days of the effective date of the decision.

(b) On receipt of a request for review, the department shall stay the action pending a decision on review, unless the hearing followed an action pursuant to Section 13353, 13353.2, or 13953. The review shall include an examination of the hearing report, documentary evidence, and findings. The hearing officer or hearing board conducting the original hearing may not participate in the review process.

(c) Following the review, a written notice of the department's decision shall be mailed to the person involved. If the action has been stayed pending review, the department's decision shall take effect as stated in the notice, but not less than four nor more than 15 days after the notice is mailed.

(d) The decision may be modified at any time after issuance to correct mistakes or clerical errors. *(Added by Stats.1980, c. 92, p. 231, § 2. Amended by Stats.1991, c. 13 (A.B.37), § 40, eff. Feb. 13, 1991; Stats.1999, c. 724 (A.B.1650), § 34.)*

§ 14106. Reopening case

Following the mailing of the notice of the department's decision pursuant to Section 14105.5, the department, at its own option or upon the request of the person whose privilege of driving is in question, may reopen the question, take further evidence, or change or set aside any order previously made. *(Stats.1959, c. 3, p. 1631, § 14106. Amended by Stats.1991, c. 13 (A.B.37), § 41, eff. Feb. 13, 1991.)*

§§ 14107 to 14111. Repealed by Stats.1991, c. 13 (A.B.37), §§ 42 to 46, eff. Feb. 13, 1991

§ 14112. Procedures; law governing

(a) All matters in a hearing not covered by this chapter shall be governed, as far as applicable, by Chapter 5 (commencing with Section 11500) of Part 1 of Division 3 of Title 2 of the Government Code.

(b) Subdivision (a) of Section 11425.30 of the Government Code does not apply to a proceeding for issuance, denial, revocation, or suspension of a driver's license pursuant to this division. *(Stats.1959, c. 3, p. 1632, § 14112. Amended by Stats.1961, c. 58, p. 1010, § 37, eff. March 31, 1961; Stats.1991, c. 13 (A.B.37), § 47, eff. Feb. 13, 1991; Stats.1995, c. 938 (S.B.523), § 91, operative July 1, 1997; Stats.2004, c. 193 (S.B.111), § 196.)*

Law Revision Commission Comments

1995 Amendment

Subdivision (b) is added to Section 14112 in recognition of the personnel problem faced by the Department of Motor Vehicles due to the large volume of drivers' licensing cases. Subdivision (b) makes separation of functions requirements inapplicable in drivers' licensing cases, including license classifications and endorsements. However, the separation of functions requirements remain applicable in other Department of Motor Vehicle hearings, including schoolbus and ambulance operation certificate hearings, on which the department is required to report. [25 Cal.L.Rev.Comm. Reports 55 (1995)].

2004 Amendment

Section 14112 is amended to delete reference to an obsolete reporting requirement. The required report was to be completed by December 31, 1999. [33 Cal.L.Rev.Comm. Reports 495 (2003)].

ARTICLE 4. PROBATION

Section
14250. Probation.
14250.5. Driver training requirement.
14251. Termination or modification of probation.
14252. Withdrawal of probationary license.
14253. Termination of probation.

§ 14250. Probation

Whenever by any provision of this code the department has discretionary authority to suspend or revoke the privilege of a person to operate a motor vehicle, the department may in lieu of suspension or revocation place the person on probation, the terms of which may include a suspension as a condition of probation, issuing a probationary license with such reasonable terms and conditions as shall be deemed by the department to be appropriate. *(Stats.1959, c. 3, p. 1632, § 14250. Amended by Stats.1963, c. 154, p. 822, § 2.)*

Cross References

Traffic violator schools, instructors' licenses, qualifying requirements, see Vehicle Code § 11206.

§ 14250.5. Driver training requirement

The department, as a condition of probation, may require a person whose privilege to operate a motor vehicle is subject to suspension or revocation to attend, for not to exceed 24 hours, the program authorized by the provisions of Section 1659. *(Added by Stats.1965, c. 447, p. 1758, § 3.)*

§ 14251. Termination or modification of probation

The department shall have authority to terminate or to modify the terms or conditions of any order of probation whenever good cause appears therefor. *(Stats.1959, c. 3, p. 1633, § 14251.)*

§ 14252. Withdrawal of probationary license

The department upon receiving satisfactory evidence of a violation of any of the terms or conditions of probation imposed under this code, may withdraw the probationary license and order the suspension or revocation of the privilege to operate a motor vehicle. *(Stats.1959, c. 3, p. 1633, § 14252.)*

§ 14253. Termination of probation

Unless probation was imposed for a cause which is continuing, the probationer, after not less than one year, may request in writing the termination of the probation and the return of his regular license. Upon a showing that there has been no violation of the terms or conditions of the probation for a period of one year immediately preceding the request, the department shall terminate the probation and either restore to the person his driver's license or require an application for a new license. *(Stats.1959, c. 3, p. 1633, § 14253.)*

ARTICLE 5. REVIEW OF ORDERS

Section
14400. Court review.
14401. Requirements regarding court review.

§ 14400. Court review

Nothing in this code shall be deemed to prevent a review or other action as may be permitted by the

Constitution and laws of this State by a court of competent jurisdiction of any order of the department refusing, canceling, suspending, or revoking the privilege of a person to operate a motor vehicle. *(Stats.1959, c. 3, p. 1633, § 14400.)*

Cross References

Blood alcohol content of .08 percent or more, or refusal of chemical test, judicial review of suspension, see Vehicle Code § 13559.

§ 14401. Requirements regarding court review

(a) Any action brought in a court of competent jurisdiction to review any order of the department refusing, canceling, placing on probation, suspending, or revoking the privilege of a person to operate a motor vehicle shall be commenced within 90 days from the date the order is noticed.

(b) Upon final completion of all administrative appeals, the person whose driving privilege was refused, canceled, placed on probation, suspended, or revoked shall be given written notice by the department of his or her right to a review by a court pursuant to subdivision (a). *(Added by Stats.1973, c. 628, p. 1156, § 1. Amended by Stats.1985, c. 1008, § 3.)*

Cross References

Blood alcohol content of .08 percent or more, or refusal of chemical test, judicial review of suspension, see Vehicle Code § 13559.

CHAPTER 4. VIOLATION OF LICENSE PROVISIONS

Section
14600.   Change of address.
14601.   Driving when privileges suspended or revoked for certain offenses; knowledge; punishment; driving on private property; requiring installation of ignition interlock device.
14601.1.   Driving when privilege revoked or suspended for other reasons.
14601.2.   Driving when privilege suspended or revoked for driving under the influence of alcoholic beverage or drug; compliance with restriction; punishment.
14601.3.   Habitual traffic offender; accumulation of driving record history while driving privilege suspended or revoked; penalty.
14601.4.   Causing bodily injury to another while driving with license suspended or revoked; penalty; reinstatement of driving privileges.
14601.5.   Driving with knowledge of suspension, revocation, or restriction of driving privilege; punishment; reinstatement of driving privileges.
14601.8.   Service of sentence.
14601.9.   Repealed.
14601.10.   Repealed.
14602.   Release of vehicle to registered owner or agent.
14602.1.   Vehicle pursuit reports.

Section
14602.5.   Driving class M1 or M2 motor vehicle while driving privilege suspended or revoked; impounding vehicle.
14602.6.   Driving without a license, while privilege suspended or revoked, or while privilege is restricted and vehicle is not equipped with interlock device; arrest; seizure and impoundment of vehicle; notice to owner; storage hearing; release of vehicle; liability of law enforcement agency and impounding agency.
14602.7.   Fleeing or evading a peace officer; reckless driving; removal and impoundment.
14602.8.   Immediate removal and seizure of vehicle driven by repeat offender; storage and impoundment; vehicle owner's rights and responsibilities.
14602.9.   Charter-party carrier buses; impoundment; notice; storage hearing; release of vehicle; towing and storage charges.
14603.   Violation of license restrictions.
14604.   Non-owner driver of vehicle; owner to determine that driver has valid license; standard of inquiry; rental companies.
14605.   Operation of motor vehicles in offstreet parking facilities.
14606.   Employment of person to drive motor vehicle; license and medical certificate.
14606.   Employment of person to drive motor vehicle; license and medical certificate; operation of commercial motor vehicles.
14607.   Permitting unlicensed minor to drive.
14607.4.   Legislative findings and declarations.
14607.6.   Motor vehicles subject to forfeiture; driving without a license; impoundment; officer's discretion; hearings; release of vehicle; community property interests; surrender; redemption and sale; stolen vehicles; distribution of filing fee.
14607.8.   Motor vehicles subject to forfeiture as a nuisance; first misdemeanor convictions.
14608.   Rental of vehicles; requirements; rental to blind or disabled persons who are nondrivers.
14609.   Records of rental.
14610.   Unlawful use of license; license defined.
14610.1.   Manufacture or sale of similar identification document prohibited; penalties; other prosecution not precluded.
14610.5.   Unlawful sale, offer to sell, distribution or use of crib sheet or cribbing device; unlawful impersonation; punishment.
14610.7.   Assisting in obtaining a license or identification card for persons present in United States in violation of federal law.
14611.   Vehicles transporting highway route controlled quantity of Class 7 radioactive materials; directing operation of vehicle with driver not possessing training certificate and proper license; penalty.

Cross References

Confidentiality of driver's license information, authorization for businesses to swipe driver's license or identification card in electronic device for certain purposes, violation, see Civil Code § 1798.90.1.

Driver license compact, see Vehicle Code § 15000 et seq.

§ 14600. Change of address

(a) Whenever any person after applying for or receiving a driver's license moves to a new residence, or acquires a new mailing address different from the address shown in the application or in the license as issued, he or she shall within 10 days thereafter notify the department of both the old and new address. The department may issue a document to accompany the driver's license reflecting the new address of the holder of the license.

(b) When, pursuant to subdivision (b) of Section 12951, a driver presents his or her driver's license to a peace officer, he or she shall, if applicable, also present the document issued pursuant to subdivision (a) if the driver's license does not reflect the driver's current residence or mailing address. *(Stats.1959, c. 3, p. 1633, § 14600. Amended by Stats.1959, c. 964, p. 2995, § 3; Stats.1976, c. 552, p. 1392, § 4; Stats.1992, c. 1243 (A.B.3090), § 86.4, eff. Sept. 30, 1992.)*

Cross References

Contents of license, see Vehicle Code §§ 12811, 12813.
Notice of change of address by registered owner, see Vehicle Code § 4159.

§ 14601. Driving when privileges suspended or revoked for certain offenses; knowledge; punishment; driving on private property; requiring installation of ignition interlock device

(a) No person shall drive a motor vehicle at any time when that person's driving privilege is suspended or revoked for reckless driving in violation of Section 23103, 23104, or 23105, any reason listed in subdivision (a) or (c) of Section 12806 authorizing the department to refuse to issue a license, negligent or incompetent operation of a motor vehicle as prescribed in subdivision (e) of Section 12809, or negligent operation as prescribed in Section 12810.5, if the person so driving has knowledge of the suspension or revocation. Knowledge shall be conclusively presumed if mailed notice has been given by the department to the person pursuant to Section 13106. The presumption established by this subdivision is a presumption affecting the burden of proof.

(b) A person convicted under this section shall be punished as follows:

(1) Upon a first conviction, by imprisonment in a county jail for not less than five days or more than six months and by a fine of not less than three hundred dollars ($300) or more than one thousand dollars ($1,000).

(2) If the offense occurred within five years of a prior offense that resulted in a conviction of a violation of this section or Section 14601.1, 14601.2, or 14601.5, by imprisonment in a county jail for not less than 10 days or more than one year and by a fine of not less than five hundred dollars ($500) or more than two thousand dollars ($2,000).

(c) If the offense occurred within five years of a prior offense that resulted in a conviction of a violation of this section or Section 14601.1, 14601.2, or 14601.5, and is granted probation, the court shall impose as a condition of probation that the person be confined in a county jail for at least 10 days.

(d) Nothing in this section prohibits a person from driving a motor vehicle, that is owned or utilized by the person's employer, during the course of employment on private property that is owned or utilized by the employer, except an offstreet parking facility as defined in subdivision (c) of Section 12500.

(e) When the prosecution agrees to a plea of guilty or nolo contendere to a charge of a violation of this section in satisfaction of, or as a substitute for, an original charge of a violation of Section 14601.2, and the court accepts that plea, except, in the interest of justice, when the court finds it would be inappropriate, the court shall, pursuant to Section 23575, require the person convicted, in addition to any other requirements, to install a certified ignition interlock device on any vehicle that the person owns or operates for a period not to exceed three years.

(f) This section also applies to the operation of an off-highway motor vehicle on those lands to which the Chappie-Z'berg Off-Highway Motor Vehicle Law of 1971 (Division 16.5 (commencing with Section 38000)) applies as to off-highway motor vehicles, as described in Section 38001. *(Added by Stats.1968, c. 963, p. 1849, § 3; Stats.1968, c. 1195, p. 2270, § 7. Amended by Stats.1971, c. 1530, p. 3027, § 12, operative May 3, 1972; Stats.1972, c. 618, p. 1148, § 140; Stats.1981, c. 939, p. 3559, § 9; Stats.1981, c. 940, p. 3565, § 7; Stats.1982, c. 53, p. 169, § 19, eff. Feb. 18, 1982; Stats.1982, c. 1339, p. 4984, § 12, eff. Sept. 24, 1982; Stats.1983, c. 1092, § 385, eff. Sept. 27, 1983, operative Jan. 1, 1984; Stats.1985, c. 1522, § 1; Stats.1986, c. 1306, § 9; Stats.1987, c. 321, § 8; Stats. 1994, c. 253 (A.B.2416), § 1; Stats.1994, c. 1133 (A.B. 3148), § 7, operative June 30, 1995; Stats.1995, c. 91 (S.B.975), § 176; Stats.1995, c. 766 (S.B.726), § 18; Stats.2000, c. 1064 (A.B.2227), § 7, eff. Sept. 30, 2000; Stats.2003, c. 468 (S.B.851), § 26; Stats.2004, c. 908 (A.B.2666), § 14; Stats.2007, c. 682 (A.B.430), § 14.)*

Cross References

Burden of proof, generally, see Evidence Code § 500 et seq.
Cancellation, suspension and revocation of license by department, see Vehicle Code § 13350 et seq.
Challenging constitutional validity of separate conviction, see Vehicle Code § 41403.
Constitutional challenge to validity of conviction, see Vehicle Code § 23624.
Grounds requiring refusal of license, see Vehicle Code § 12805 et seq.
Guilty plea, see Vehicle Code § 41610.
Interest of justice exceptions to the statutory requirements for installation of an ignition interlock device under Vehicle Code § 23575, findings, statement of reasons, see California Rules of Court, Rule 4.325.
Nonresidents, effect of operation while driver's license is suspended or revoked, see Vehicle Code § 13552.

Optional appearance before magistrate, see Vehicle Code § 40303.

Presumption affecting burden of proof, see Evidence Code §§ 605, 606.

Removal of vehicle, circumstances permitting, see Vehicle Code § 22651.

Suspension or revocation of license by court, see Vehicle Code § 13200 et seq.

Traffic violation point counts, allocation of points, see Vehicle Code § 12810.

Unlicensed persons, penalties, see Vehicle Code § 13553.

Violation a misdemeanor, see Vehicle Code § 40000.11.

§ 14601.1. Driving when privilege revoked or suspended for other reasons

(a) No person shall drive a motor vehicle when his or her driving privilege is suspended or revoked for any reason other than those listed in Section 14601, 14601.2, or 14601.5, if the person so driving has knowledge of the suspension or revocation. Knowledge shall be conclusively presumed if mailed notice has been given by the department to the person pursuant to Section 13106. The presumption established by this subdivision is a presumption affecting the burden of proof.

(b) Any person convicted under this section shall be punished as follows:

(1) Upon a first conviction, by imprisonment in the county jail for not more than six months or by a fine of not less than three hundred dollars ($300) or more than one thousand dollars ($1,000), or by both that fine and imprisonment.

(2) If the offense occurred within five years of a prior offense which resulted in a conviction of a violation of this section or Section 14601, 14601.2, or 14601.5, by imprisonment in the county jail for not less than five days or more than one year and by a fine of not less than five hundred dollars ($500) or more than two thousand dollars ($2,000).

(c) Nothing in this section prohibits a person from driving a motor vehicle, which is owned or utilized by the person's employer, during the course of employment on private property which is owned or utilized by the employer, except an offstreet parking facility as defined in subdivision (d) of Section 12500.

(d) When the prosecution agrees to a plea of guilty or nolo contendere to a charge of a violation of this section in satisfaction of, or as a substitute for, an original charge of a violation of Section 14601.2, and the court accepts that plea, except, in the interest of justice, when the court finds it would be inappropriate, the court shall, pursuant to Section 23575, require the person convicted, in addition to any other requirements, to install a certified ignition interlock device on any vehicle that the person owns or operates for a period not to exceed three years.

(e) This section also applies to the operation of an off-highway motor vehicle on those lands to which the Chappie–Z'berg Off–Highway Motor Vehicle Law of 1971 (Division 16.5 (commencing with Section 38000)) applies as to off-highway motor vehicles, as described in

504

Section 38001. *(Added by Stats.1968, c. 1195, p. 2271, § 8. Amended by Stats.1972, c. 618, p. 1149, § 142; Stats.1981, c. 940, p. 3565, § 8; Stats.1982, c. 53, p. 170, § 20, eff. Feb. 18, 1982; Stats.1982, c. 1339, c. p. 4985, § 13, eff. Sept. 24, 1982; Stats.1983, c. 1092, § 386, eff. Sept. 27, 1983, operative Jan. 1, 1984; Stats.1984, c. 216, § 9; Stats.1985, c. 1522, § 2; Stats.1986, c. 1306, § 10; Stats. 1994, c. 253 (A.B.2416), § 2; Stats.1994, c. 1133 (A.B. 3148), § 8, operative June 30, 1995; Stats.1995, c. 91 (S.B.975), § 178; Stats.1995, c. 766 (S.B.726), § 19; Stats.2000, c. 1064 (A.B.2227), § 8, eff. Sept. 30, 2000; Stats.2004, c. 908 (A.B.2666), § 15.)*

Cross References

Burden of proof, generally, see Evidence Code § 500 et seq.

Cancellation, suspension and revocation of license by department, see Vehicle Code § 13350 et seq.

Challenging constitutional validity of separate conviction, see Vehicle Code § 41403.

Guilty plea, see Vehicle Code § 41610.

Interest of justice exceptions to the statutory requirements for installation of an ignition interlock device under Vehicle Code § 23575, findings, statement of reasons, see California Rules of Court, Rule 4.325.

Nonresident operating vehicle after license suspension or revocation, see Vehicle Code § 13552.

Offense under this section as infraction, see Penal Code § 19.8.

Optional appearance before magistrate, see Vehicle Code § 40303.

Presumption affecting burden of proof, see Evidence Code §§ 605, 606.

Removal of vehicle, circumstances permitting, see Vehicle Code § 22651.

Suspension or revocation of license by court, see Vehicle Code § 13200 et seq.

Traffic violation point counts, allocation of points, see Vehicle Code § 12810.

Violation a misdemeanor, see Vehicle Code § 40000.11.

§ 14601.2. Driving when privilege suspended or revoked for driving under the influence of alcoholic beverage or drug; compliance with restriction; punishment

(a) A person shall not drive a motor vehicle at any time when that person's driving privilege is suspended or revoked for a conviction of a violation of Section 23152 or 23153 if the person so driving has knowledge of the suspension or revocation.

(b) Except in full compliance with the restriction, a person shall not drive a motor vehicle at any time when that person's driving privilege is restricted if the person so driving has knowledge of the restriction.

(c) Knowledge of the suspension or revocation of the driving privilege shall be conclusively presumed if mailed notice has been given by the department to the person pursuant to Section 13106. Knowledge of the restriction of the driving privilege shall be presumed if notice has been given by the court to the person. The presumption established by this subdivision is a presumption affecting the burden of proof.

(d) A person convicted of a violation of this section shall be punished as follows:

(1) Upon a first conviction, by imprisonment in the county jail for not less than 10 days or more than six months and by a fine of not less than three hundred dollars ($300) or more than one thousand dollars ($1,000), unless the person has been designated a habitual traffic offender under subdivision (b) of Section 23546, subdivision (b) of Section 23550, or subdivision (d) of Section 23550.5, in which case the person, in addition, shall be sentenced as provided in paragraph (3) of subdivision (e) of Section 14601.3.

(2) If the offense occurred within five years of a prior offense that resulted in a conviction of a violation of this section or Section 14601, 14601.1, or 14601.5, by imprisonment in the county jail for not less than 30 days or more than one year and by a fine of not less than five hundred dollars ($500) or more than two thousand dollars ($2,000), unless the person has been designated a habitual traffic offender under subdivision (b) of Section 23546, subdivision (b) of Section 23550, or subdivision (d) of Section 23550.5, in which case the person, in addition, shall be sentenced as provided in paragraph (3) of subdivision (e) of Section 14601.3.

(e) If a person is convicted of a first offense under this section and is granted probation, the court shall impose as a condition of probation that the person be confined in the county jail for at least 10 days.

(f) If the offense occurred within five years of a prior offense that resulted in a conviction of a violation of this section or Section 14601, 14601.1, or 14601.5 and is granted probation, the court shall impose as a condition of probation that the person be confined in the county jail for at least 30 days.

(g) If a person is convicted of a second or subsequent offense that results in a conviction of this section within seven years, but over five years, of a prior offense that resulted in a conviction of a violation of this section or Section 14601, 14601.1, or 14601.5 and is granted probation, the court shall impose as a condition of probation that the person be confined in the county jail for at least 10 days.

(h) Pursuant to Section 23575, the court shall require a person convicted of a violation of this section to install a certified ignition interlock device on a vehicle the person owns or operates. Upon receipt of the abstract of a conviction under this section, the department shall not reinstate the privilege to operate a motor vehicle until the department receives proof of either the "Verification of Installation" form as described in paragraph (2) of subdivision (g) of Section 13386 or the Judicial Council Form I.D. 100.

(i) This section does not prohibit a person who is participating in, or has completed, an alcohol or drug rehabilitation program from driving a motor vehicle that is owned or utilized by the person's employer, during the course of employment on private property that is owned or utilized by the employer, except an offstreet parking facility as defined in subdivision (c) of Section 12500.

(j) This section also applies to the operation of an off-highway motor vehicle on those lands that the Chappie–Z'berg Off–Highway Motor Vehicle Law of 1971 (Division 16.5 (commencing with Section 38000)) applies as to off-highway motor vehicles, as described in Section 38001.

(k) If Section 23573 is applicable, then subdivision (h) is not applicable. *(Added by Stats.2004, c. 908 (A.B. 2666), § 16.5, operative Sept. 20, 2005. Amended by Stats.2005, c. 279 (S.B.1107), § 22; Stats.2006, c. 835 (A.B.3045), § 3; Stats.2008, c. 404 (S.B.1388), § 1.)*

Cross References

Burden of proof, generally, see Evidence Code § 500 et seq.
Challenging constitutional validity of separate conviction, see Vehicle Code § 41403.
Constitutional challenge to validity of conviction, see Vehicle Code § 23624.
Guilty plea, see Vehicle Code § 41610.
Presumption affecting burden of proof, see Evidence Code §§ 605, 606.
Removal of vehicle, circumstances permitting, see Vehicle Code § 22651.
Traffic violation point counts, allocation of points, see Vehicle Code § 12810.
Violation as misdemeanor, see Vehicle Code § 40000.11.

§ 14601.3. Habitual traffic offender; accumulation of driving record history while driving privilege suspended or revoked; penalty

(a) It is unlawful for a person whose driving privilege has been suspended or revoked to accumulate a driving record history which results from driving during the period of suspension or revocation. A person who violates this subdivision is designated an habitual traffic offender.

For purposes of this section, a driving record history means any of the following, if the driving occurred during any period of suspension or revocation:

(1) Two or more convictions within a 12–month period of an offense given a violation point count of two pursuant to Section 12810.

(2) Three or more convictions within a 12–month period of an offense given a violation point count of one pursuant to Section 12810.

(3) Three or more accidents within a 12–month period that are subject to the reporting requirements of Section 16000.

(4) Any combination of convictions or accidents, as specified in paragraphs (1) to (3), inclusive, which results during any 12–month period in a violation point count of three or more pursuant to Section 12810.

(b) Knowledge of suspension or revocation of the driving privilege shall be conclusively presumed if mailed notice has been given by the department to the person pursuant to Section 13106. The presumption established

505

by this subdivision is a presumption affecting the burden of proof.

(c) The department, within 30 days of receipt of a duly certified abstract of the record of any court or accident report which results in a person being designated an habitual traffic offender, may execute and transmit by mail a notice of that designation to the office of the district attorney having jurisdiction over the location of the person's last known address as contained in the department's records.

(d)(1) The district attorney, within 30 days of receiving the notice required in subdivision (c), shall inform the department of whether or not the person will be prosecuted for being an habitual traffic offender.

(2) Notwithstanding any other provision of this section, any habitual traffic offender designated under subdivision (b) of Section 23546, subdivision (b) of Section 23550, or subdivision (b) of Section 23550.5, who is convicted of violating Section 14601.2 shall be sentenced as provided in paragraph (3) of subdivision (e).

(e) Any person convicted under this section of being an habitual traffic offender shall be punished as follows:

(1) Upon a first conviction, by imprisonment in the county jail for 30 days and by a fine of one thousand dollars ($1,000).

(2) Upon a second or any subsequent offense within seven years of a prior conviction under this section, by imprisonment in the county jail for 180 days and by a fine of two thousand dollars ($2,000).

(3) Any habitual traffic offender designated under Section 193.7 of the Penal Code or under subdivision (b) of Section 23546, subdivision (b) of Section 23550, subdivision (b) of Section 23550.5, or subdivision (d) of Section 23566 who is convicted of a violation of Section 14601.2 shall be punished by imprisonment in the county jail for 180 days and by a fine of two thousand dollars ($2,000). The penalty in this paragraph shall be consecutive to that imposed for the violation of any other law.

(f) This section also applies to the operation of an off-highway motor vehicle on those lands to which the Chappie–Z'berg Off–Highway Motor Vehicle Law of 1971 (Division 16.5 (commencing with Section 38000)) applies as to off-highway motor vehicles, as described in Section 38001. *(Added by Stats.1982, c. 655, p. 2672, § 5. Amended by Stats.1984, c. 239, § 1; Stats.1986, c. 1306, § 12; Stats.1988, c. 1415, § 7; Stats.1990, c. 44 (A.B. 1648), § 4; Stats.1994, c. 1133 (A.B.3148), § 10, operative June 30, 1995; Stats.1995, c. 91 (S.B.975), § 179; Stats. 1997, c. 901 (A.B.130), § 4; Stats.1998, c. 118 (S.B.1186), § 10.2, operative July 1, 1999; Stats.1999, c. 22 (S.B.24), § 16, eff. May 26, 1999, operative July 1, 1999; Stats.2004, c. 908 (A.B.2666), § 17.)*

Cross References

Burden of proof, generally, see Evidence Code § 500 et seq.
Guilty plea, see Vehicle Code § 41610.

Presumption affecting burden of proof, see Evidence Code §§ 605, 606.
Removal of vehicle, circumstances permitting, see Vehicle Code § 22651.
Traffic violation point counts, allocation of points, see Vehicle Code § 12810.

§ 14601.4. Causing bodily injury to another while driving with license suspended or revoked; penalty; reinstatement of driving privileges

(a) It is unlawful for a person, while driving a vehicle with a license suspended or revoked pursuant to Section 14601.2 to do an act forbidden by law or neglect a duty imposed by law in the driving of the vehicle, which act or neglect proximately causes bodily injury to a person other than the driver. In proving the person neglected a duty imposed by law in the driving of the vehicle, it is not necessary to prove that a specific section of this code was violated.

(b) A person convicted under this section shall be imprisoned in the county jail and shall not be released upon work release, community service, or other release program before the minimum period of imprisonment, prescribed in Section 14601.2, is served. If a person is convicted of that offense and is granted probation, the court shall require that the person convicted serve at least the minimum time of imprisonment, as specified in those sections, as a term or condition of probation.

(c) When the prosecution agrees to a plea of guilty or nolo contendere to a charge of a violation of this section in satisfaction of, or as a substitute for, an original charge of a violation of Section 14601.2, and the court accepts that plea, except, in the interest of justice, when the court finds it should be inappropriate, the court shall, pursuant to Section 23575, require the person convicted, in addition to other requirements, to install a certified ignition interlock device on a vehicle that the person owns or operates for a period not to exceed three years.

(d) This section also applies to the operation of an off-highway motor vehicle on those lands that the Chappie–Z'berg Off–Highway Motor Vehicle Law of 1971 (Division 16.5 (commencing with Section 38000)) applies as to off-highway motor vehicles, as described in Section 38001.

(e) Upon receipt of the abstract of a conviction under this section, the department shall not reinstate the privilege to operate a motor vehicle until the department receives proof of either the "Verification of Installation" form as described in paragraph (2) of subdivision (g) of Section 13386 or the Judicial Council Form I.D. 100.

(f) If Section 23573 is applicable, then subdivisions (c) and (e) are not applicable. *(Added by Stats.1988, c. 1254, § 4. Amended by Stats.2000, c. 1064 (A.B.2227), § 9, eff. Sept. 30, 2000; Stats.2004, c. 908 (A.B.2666), § 18; Stats.2006, c. 835 (A.B.3045), § 4; Stats.2008, c. 404 (S.B.1388), § 2.)*

Cross References

Interest of justice exceptions to the statutory requirements for installation of an ignition interlock device under Vehicle Code § 23575, findings, statement of reasons, see California Rules of Court, Rule 4.325.

Removal of vehicle, circumstances permitting, see Vehicle Code § 22651.

§ 14601.5. Driving with knowledge of suspension, revocation, or restriction of driving privilege; punishment; reinstatement of driving privileges

(a) A person shall not drive a motor vehicle at any time when that person's driving privilege is suspended or revoked pursuant to Section 13353, 13353.1, or 13353.2 and that person has knowledge of the suspension or revocation.

(b) Except in full compliance with the restriction, a person shall not drive a motor vehicle at any time when that person's driving privilege is restricted pursuant to Section 13353.7 or 13353.8 and that person has knowledge of the restriction.

(c) Knowledge of suspension, revocation, or restriction of the driving privilege shall be conclusively presumed if notice has been given by the department to the person pursuant to Section 13106. The presumption established by this subdivision is a presumption affecting the burden of proof.

(d) A person convicted of a violation of this section is punishable, as follows:

(1) Upon a first conviction, by imprisonment in the county jail for not more than six months or by a fine of not less than three hundred dollars ($300) or more than one thousand dollars ($1,000), or by both that fine and imprisonment.

(2) If the offense occurred within five years of a prior offense that resulted in a conviction for a violation of this section or Section 14601, 14601.1, 14601.2, or 14601.3, by imprisonment in the county jail for not less than 10 days or more than one year, and by a fine of not less than five hundred dollars ($500) or more than two thousand dollars ($2,000).

(e) In imposing the minimum fine required by subdivision (d), the court shall take into consideration the defendant's ability to pay the fine and may, in the interest of justice, and for reasons stated in the record, reduce the amount of that minimum fine to less than the amount otherwise imposed.

(f) This section does not prohibit a person who is participating in, or has completed, an alcohol or drug rehabilitation program from driving a motor vehicle, that is owned or utilized by the person's employer, during the course of employment on private property that is owned or utilized by the employer, except an offstreet parking facility as defined in subdivision (c) of Section 12500.

(g) When the prosecution agrees to a plea of guilty or nolo contendere to a charge of a violation of this section in satisfaction of, or as a substitute for, an original charge of a violation of Section 14601.2, and the court accepts that plea, except, in the interest of justice, when the court finds it would be inappropriate, the court shall, pursuant to Section 23575, require the person convicted, in addition to other requirements, to install a certified ignition interlock device on a vehicle that the person owns or operates for a period not to exceed three years.

(h) This section also applies to the operation of an off-highway motor vehicle on those lands that the Chappie–Z'berg Off–Highway Motor Vehicle Law of 1971 (Division 16.5 (commencing with Section 38000)) applies as to off-highway motor vehicles, as described in Section 38001.

(i) Upon receipt of the abstract of a conviction under this section, the department shall not reinstate the privilege to operate a motor vehicle until the department receives proof of either the "Verification of Installation" form as described in paragraph (2) of subdivision (g) of Section 13386 or the Judicial Council Form I.D. 100.

(j) If Section 23573 [1] is applicable, then subdivisions (g) and (i) are not applicable. *(Added by Stats.2004, c. 952 (A.B.3049), § 13.5, operative Sept. 20, 2005. Amended by Stats.2006, c. 835 (A.B.3045), § 5; Stats.2008, c. 404 (S.B.1388), § 3.)*

[1] Added by Stats.2008, c. 404 (S.B.1388), § 4, operative July 1, 2009.

Cross References

Burden of proof, generally, see Evidence Code § 500 et seq.

§ 14601.8. Service of sentence

The judge may, in his or her discretion, allow any person convicted of a violation of Section 14601 or 14601.1 to serve his or her sentence on a sufficient number of consecutive weekend days to complete the sentence. *(Formerly § 14601.5, added by Stats.1961, c. 278, § 2. Amended by Stats.1968, c. 1195, § 5. Renumbered § 14601.8 and amended by Stats.1992, c. 982 (S.B.2022), § 1.)*

§ 14601.9. Repealed by Stats.2004, c. 594 (S.B.1848), § 1, operative Jan. 1, 2008

§ 14601.10. Repealed by Stats.1999, c. 877 (A.B.402), § 1, operative Jan. 1, 2004

§ 14602. Release of vehicle to registered owner or agent

In accordance with subdivision (p) of Section 22651, a vehicle removed pursuant to subdivision (c) of Section 2814.2 shall be released to the registered owner or his or her agent at any time the facility to which the vehicle has been removed is open upon presentation of the registered owner's or his or her agent's currently valid driver's license to operate the vehicle and proof of current vehicle registration. *(Added by Stats.2011, c. 653 (A.B.353), § 3.)*

§ 14602.1. Vehicle pursuit reports

(a) Every state and local law enforcement agency, including, but not limited to, city police departments and county sheriffs' offices, shall report to the Department of the California Highway Patrol, on a paper or electronic form developed and approved by the Department of the California Highway Patrol, all motor vehicle pursuit data.

(b) Effective January 1, 2006, the form shall require the reporting of all motor vehicle pursuit data, which shall include, but not be limited to, all of the following:

(1) Whether any person involved in a pursuit or a subsequent arrest was injured, specifying the nature of that injury. For all purposes of this section, the form shall differentiate between the suspect driver, a suspect passenger, and the peace officers involved.

(2) The violations that caused the pursuit to be initiated.

(3) The identity of the peace officers involved in the pursuit.

(4) The means or methods used to stop the suspect being pursued.

(5) All charges filed with the court by the district attorney.

(6) The conditions of the pursuit, including, but not limited to, all of the following:

(A) Duration.

(B) Mileage.

(C) Number of peace officers involved.

(D) Maximum number of law enforcement vehicles involved.

(E) Time of day.

(F) Weather conditions.

(G) Maximum speeds.

(7) Whether a pursuit resulted in a collision, and a resulting injury or fatality to an uninvolved third party, and the corresponding number of persons involved.

(8) Whether the pursuit involved multiple law enforcement agencies.

(9) How the pursuit was terminated.

(c) In order to minimize costs, the department, upon updating the form, shall update the corresponding database to include all of the reporting requirements specified in subdivision (b).

(d) All motor vehicle pursuit data obtained pursuant to subdivision (b) shall be submitted to the Department of the California Highway Patrol no later than 30 days following a motor vehicle pursuit.

(e) The Department of the California Highway Patrol shall submit annually to the Legislature a report that includes, but is not limited to, the following information:

(1) The number of motor vehicle pursuits reported to the Department of the California Highway Patrol during that year.

(2) The number of those motor vehicle pursuits that reportedly resulted in a collision in which an injury or fatality to an uninvolved third party occurred.

508

(3) The total number of uninvolved third parties who were injured or killed as a result of those collisions during that year. *(Added by Stats.1991, c. 1048 (S.B.185), § 2. Amended by Stats.2001, c. 745 (S.B.1191), § 228, eff. Oct. 12, 2001; Stats.2005, c. 485 (S.B.719), § 9.)*

§ 14602.5. Driving class M1 or M2 motor vehicle while driving privilege suspended or revoked; impounding vehicle

(a) Whenever a person is convicted for driving any class M1 or M2 motor vehicle, while his or her driving privilege has been suspended or revoked, of which vehicle he or she is the owner, or of which the owner permitted the operation, knowing the person's driving privilege was suspended or revoked, the court may, at the time sentence is imposed on the person, order the motor vehicle impounded in any manner as the court may determine, for a period not to exceed six months for a first conviction, and not to exceed 12 months for a second or subsequent conviction. For the purposes of this section, a "second or subsequent conviction" includes a conviction for any offense described in this section. The cost of keeping the vehicle shall be a lien on the vehicle, pursuant to Chapter 6.5 (commencing with Section 3067) of Title 14 of Part 4 of Division 3 of the Civil Code.

(b) Notwithstanding subdivision (a), any motor vehicle impounded pursuant to this section which is subject to a chattel mortgage, conditional sale contract, or lease contract shall, upon the filing of an affidavit by the legal owner that the chattel mortgage, conditional sale contract, or lease contract is in default, be released by the court to the legal owner, and shall be delivered to him or her upon payment of the accrued cost of keeping the motor vehicle. *(Added by Stats.1990, c. 1359 (A.B.55), § 5.)*

§ 14602.6. Driving without a license, while privilege suspended or revoked, or while privilege is restricted and vehicle is not equipped with interlock device; arrest; seizure and impoundment of vehicle; notice to owner; storage hearing; release of vehicle; liability of law enforcement agency and impounding agency

(a)(1) Whenever a peace officer determines that a person was driving a vehicle while his or her driving privilege was suspended or revoked, driving a vehicle while his or her driving privilege is restricted pursuant to Section 13352 or 23575 and the vehicle is not equipped with a functioning, certified interlock device, or driving a vehicle without ever having been issued a driver's license, the peace officer may either immediately arrest that person and cause the removal and seizure of that vehicle or, if the vehicle is involved in a traffic collision, cause the removal and seizure of the vehicle without the necessity of arresting the person in accordance with Chapter 10 (commencing with Section 22650) of Division 11. A vehicle so impounded shall be impounded for 30 days.

(2) The impounding agency, within two working days of impoundment, shall send a notice by certified mail,

return receipt requested, to the legal owner of the vehicle, at the address obtained from the department, informing the owner that the vehicle has been impounded. Failure to notify the legal owner within two working days shall prohibit the impounding agency from charging for more than 15 days' impoundment when the legal owner redeems the impounded vehicle. The impounding agency shall maintain a published telephone number that provides information 24 hours a day regarding the impoundment of vehicles and the rights of a registered owner to request a hearing. The law enforcement agency shall be open to issue a release to the registered owner or legal owner, or the agent of either, whenever the agency is open to serve the public for regular, nonemergency business.

(b) The registered and legal owner of a vehicle that is removed and seized under subdivision (a) or their agents shall be provided the opportunity for a storage hearing to determine the validity of, or consider any mitigating circumstances attendant to, the storage, in accordance with Section 22852.

(c) Any period in which a vehicle is subjected to storage under this section shall be included as part of the period of impoundment ordered by the court under subdivision (a) of Section 14602.5.

(d)(1) An impounding agency shall release a vehicle to the registered owner or his or her agent prior to the end of 30 days' impoundment under any of the following circumstances:

(A) When the vehicle is a stolen vehicle.

(B) When the vehicle is subject to bailment and is driven by an unlicensed employee of a business establishment, including a parking service or repair garage.

(C) When the license of the driver was suspended or revoked for an offense other than those included in Article 2 (commencing with Section 13200) of Chapter 2 of Division 6 or Article 3 (commencing with Section 13350) of Chapter 2 of Division 6.

(D) When the vehicle was seized under this section for an offense that does not authorize the seizure of the vehicle.

(E) When the driver reinstates his or her driver's license or acquires a driver's license and proper insurance.

(2) No vehicle shall be released pursuant to this subdivision without presentation of the registered owner's or agent's currently valid driver's license to operate the vehicle and proof of current vehicle registration, or upon order of a court.

(e) The registered owner or his or her agent is responsible for all towing and storage charges related to the impoundment, and any administrative charges authorized under Section 22850.5.

(f) A vehicle removed and seized under subdivision (a) shall be released to the legal owner of the vehicle or the legal owner's agent prior to the end of 30 days' impoundment if all of the following conditions are met:

(1) The legal owner is a motor vehicle dealer, bank, credit union, acceptance corporation, or other licensed financial institution legally operating in this state or is another person, not the registered owner, holding a security interest in the vehicle.

(2)(A) The legal owner or the legal owner's agent pays all towing and storage fees related to the seizure of the vehicle. No lien sale processing fees shall be charged to the legal owner who redeems the vehicle prior to the 15th day of impoundment. Neither the impounding authority nor any person having possession of the vehicle shall collect from the legal owner of the type specified in paragraph (1), or the legal owner's agent any administrative charges imposed pursuant to Section 22850.5 unless the legal owner voluntarily requested a poststorage hearing.

(B) A person operating or in charge of a storage facility where vehicles are stored pursuant to this section shall accept a valid bank credit card or cash for payment of towing, storage, and related fees by a legal or registered owner or the owner's agent claiming the vehicle. A credit card shall be in the name of the person presenting the card. "Credit card" means "credit card" as defined in subdivision (a) of Section 1747.02 of the Civil Code, except, for the purposes of this section, credit card does not include a credit card issued by a retail seller.

(C) A person operating or in charge of a storage facility described in subparagraph (B) who violates subparagraph (B) shall be civilly liable to the owner of the vehicle or to the person who tendered the fees for four times the amount of the towing, storage, and related fees, but not to exceed five hundred dollars ($500).

(D) A person operating or in charge of a storage facility described in subparagraph (B) shall have sufficient funds on the premises of the primary storage facility during normal business hours to accommodate, and make change in, a reasonable monetary transaction.

(E) Credit charges for towing and storage services shall comply with Section 1748.1 of the Civil Code. Law enforcement agencies may include the costs of providing for payment by credit when making agreements with towing companies on rates.

(3) The legal owner or the legal owner's agent presents a copy of the assignment, as defined in subdivision (b) of Section 7500.1 of the Business and Professions Code; a release from the one responsible governmental agency, only if required by the agency; a government-issued photographic identification card; and any one of the following, as determined by the legal owner or the legal owner's agent: a certificate of repossession for the vehicle, a security agreement for the vehicle, or title, whether paper or electronic, showing proof of legal ownership for the vehicle. Any documents presented may be originals, photocopies, or facsimile copies, or may be transmitted electronically. The law enforcement

agency, impounding agency, or any other governmental agency, or any person acting on behalf of those agencies, shall not require any documents to be notarized. The law enforcement agency, impounding agency, or any person acting on behalf of those agencies may require the agent of the legal owner to produce a photocopy or facsimile copy of its repossession agency license or registration issued pursuant to Chapter 11 (commencing with Section 7500) of Division 3 of the Business and Professions Code, or to demonstrate, to the satisfaction of the law enforcement agency, impounding agency, or any person acting on behalf of those agencies, that the agent is exempt from licensure pursuant to Section 7500.2 or 7500.3 of the Business and Professions Code.

No administrative costs authorized under subdivision (a) of Section 22850.5 shall be charged to the legal owner of the type specified in paragraph (1), who redeems the vehicle unless the legal owner voluntarily requests a poststorage hearing. No city, county, city and county, or state agency shall require a legal owner or a legal owner's agent to request a poststorage hearing as a requirement for release of the vehicle to the legal owner or the legal owner's agent. The law enforcement agency, impounding agency, or other governmental agency, or any person acting on behalf of those agencies, shall not require any documents other than those specified in this paragraph. The law enforcement agency, impounding agency, or other governmental agency, or any person acting on behalf of those agencies, shall not require any documents to be notarized. The legal owner or the legal owner's agent shall be given a copy of any documents he or she is required to sign, except for a vehicle evidentiary hold logbook. The law enforcement agency, impounding agency, or any person acting on behalf of those agencies, or any person in possession of the vehicle, may photocopy and retain the copies of any documents presented by the legal owner or legal owner's agent.

(4) A failure by a storage facility to comply with any applicable conditions set forth in this subdivision shall not affect the right of the legal owner or the legal owner's agent to retrieve the vehicle, provided all conditions required of the legal owner or legal owner's agent under this subdivision are satisfied.

(g)(1) A legal owner or the legal owner's agent that obtains release of the vehicle pursuant to subdivision (f) shall not release the vehicle to the registered owner of the vehicle, or the person who was listed as the registered owner when the vehicle was impounded, or any agents of the registered owner, unless the registered owner is a rental car agency, until after the termination of the 30–day impoundment period.

(2) The legal owner or the legal owner's agent shall not relinquish the vehicle to the registered owner or the person who was listed as the registered owner when the vehicle was impounded until the registered owner or that owner's agent presents his or her valid driver's license or valid temporary driver's license to the legal owner or the legal owner's agent. The legal owner or the legal owner's

510

agent or the person in possession of the vehicle shall make every reasonable effort to ensure that the license presented is valid and possession of the vehicle will not be given to the driver who was involved in the original impoundment proceeding until the expiration of the impoundment period.

(3) Prior to relinquishing the vehicle, the legal owner may require the registered owner to pay all towing and storage charges related to the impoundment and any administrative charges authorized under Section 22850.5 that were incurred by the legal owner in connection with obtaining custody of the vehicle.

(4) Any legal owner who knowingly releases or causes the release of a vehicle to a registered owner or the person in possession of the vehicle at the time of the impoundment or any agent of the registered owner in violation of this subdivision shall be guilty of a misdemeanor and subject to a fine in the amount of two thousand dollars ($2,000) in addition to any other penalties established by law.

(5) The legal owner, registered owner, or person in possession of the vehicle shall not change or attempt to change the name of the legal owner or the registered owner on the records of the department until the vehicle is released from the impoundment.

(h)(1) A vehicle removed and seized under subdivision (a) shall be released to a rental car agency prior to the end of 30 days' impoundment if the agency is either the legal owner or registered owner of the vehicle and the agency pays all towing and storage fees related to the seizure of the vehicle.

(2) The owner of a rental vehicle that was seized under this section may continue to rent the vehicle upon recovery of the vehicle. However, the rental car agency may not rent another vehicle to the driver of the vehicle that was seized until 30 days after the date that the vehicle was seized.

(3) The rental car agency may require the person to whom the vehicle was rented to pay all towing and storage charges related to the impoundment and any administrative charges authorized under Section 22850.5 that were incurred by the rental car agency in connection with obtaining custody of the vehicle.

(i) Notwithstanding any other provision of this section, the registered owner and not the legal owner shall remain responsible for any towing and storage charges related to the impoundment, any administrative charges authorized under Section 22850.5, and any parking fines, penalties, and administrative fees incurred by the registered owner.

(j) The law enforcement agency and the impounding agency, including any storage facility acting on behalf of the law enforcement agency or impounding agency, shall comply with this section and shall not be liable to the registered owner for the improper release of the vehicle to the legal owner or the legal owner's agent provided the release complies with the provisions of this section. The legal owner shall indemnify and hold harmless a storage facility from any claims arising out of the release of the vehicle to the legal owner or the legal owner's agent and from any damage to the vehicle after its release, including the reasonable costs associated with defending any such claims. A law enforcement agency shall not refuse to issue a release to a legal owner or the agent of a legal owner on the grounds that it previously issued a release. *(Added by Stats.1994, c. 1221 (S.B.1758), § 13. Amended by Stats.1995, c. 922 (S.B.833), § 3; Stats.1998, c. 582 (S.B.117), § 5; Stats.2001, c. 480 (A.B.360), § 1; Stats. 2001, c. 554 (A.B.783), § 2.5; Stats.2002, c. 664 (A.B. 3034), § 219; Stats.2002, c; 402 (A.B.1883), § 7; Stats. 2005, c. 646 (A.B.979), § 2; Stats.2006, c. 538 (S.B.1852), § 658; Stats.2006, c. 418 (A.B.2318), § 7; Stats.2007, c. 192 (S.B.659), § 10, eff. Sept. 7, 2007; Stats.2009, c. 322 (A.B.515), § 5.)*

Cross References

Misdemeanors, definition and penalties, see Penal Code §§ 17, 19 and 19.2.

§ 14602.7. Fleeing or evading a peace officer; reckless driving; removal and impoundment

(a) A magistrate presented with the affidavit of a peace officer establishing reasonable cause to believe that a vehicle, described by vehicle type and license number, was an instrumentality used in the peace officer's presence in violation of Section 2800.1, 2800.2, 2800.3, or 23103, shall issue a warrant or order authorizing any peace officer to immediately seize and cause the removal of the vehicle. The warrant or court order may be entered into a computerized database. A vehicle so impounded may be impounded for a period not to exceed 30 days.

The impounding agency, within two working days of impoundment, shall send a notice by certified mail, return receipt requested, to the legal owner of the vehicle, at the address obtained from the department, informing the owner that the vehicle has been impounded and providing the owner with a copy of the warrant or court order. Failure to notify the legal owner within two working days shall prohibit the impounding agency from charging for more than 15 days impoundment when a legal owner redeems the impounded vehicle. The law enforcement agency shall be open to issue a release to the registered owner or legal owner, or the agent of either, whenever the agency is open to serve the public for regular, nonemergency business.

(b)(1) An impounding agency shall release a vehicle to the registered owner or his or her agent prior to the end of the impoundment period and without the permission of the magistrate authorizing the vehicle's seizure under any of the following circumstances:

(A) When the vehicle is a stolen vehicle.

(B) When the vehicle is subject to bailment and is driven by an unlicensed employee of the business establishment, including a parking service or repair garage.

(C) When the registered owner of the vehicle causes a peace officer to reasonably believe, based on the totality of the circumstances, that the registered owner was not the driver who violated Section 2800.1, 2800.2, or 2800.3, the agency shall immediately release the vehicle to the registered owner or his or her agent.

(2) No vehicle shall be released pursuant to this subdivision, except upon presentation of the registered owner's or agent's currently valid driver's license to operate the vehicle and proof of current vehicle registration, or upon order of the court.

(c)(1) Whenever a vehicle is impounded under this section, the magistrate ordering the storage shall provide the vehicle's registered and legal owners of record, or their agents, with the opportunity for a poststorage hearing to determine the validity of the storage.

(2) A notice of the storage shall be mailed or personally delivered to the registered and legal owners within 48 hours after issuance of the warrant or court order, excluding weekends and holidays, by the person or agency executing the warrant or court order, and shall include all of the following information:

(A) The name, address, and telephone number of the agency providing the notice.

(B) The location of the place of storage and a description of the vehicle, which shall include, if available, the name or make, the manufacturer, the license plate number, and the mileage of the vehicle.

(C) A copy of the warrant or court order and the peace officer's affidavit, as described in subdivision (a).

(D) A statement that, in order to receive their poststorage hearing, the owners, or their agents, are required to request the hearing from the magistrate issuing the warrant or court order in person, in writing, or by telephone, within 10 days of the date of the notice.

(3) The poststorage hearing shall be conducted within two court days after receipt of the request for the hearing.

(4) At the hearing, the magistrate may order the vehicle released if he or she finds any of the circumstances described in subdivision (b) or (e) that allow release of a vehicle by the impounding agency. The magistrate may also consider releasing the vehicle when the continued impoundment will cause undue hardship to persons dependent upon the vehicle for employment or to a person with a community property interest in the vehicle.

(5) Failure of either the registered or legal owner, or his or her agent, to request, or to attend, a scheduled hearing satisfies the poststorage hearing requirement.

(6) The agency employing the peace officer who caused the magistrate to issue the warrant or court order shall be responsible for the costs incurred for towing and storage if it is determined in the poststorage hearing that reasonable grounds for the storage are not established.

(d) The registered owner or his or her agent is responsible for all towing and storage charges related to

511

the impoundment, and any administrative charges authorized under Section 22850.5.

(e) A vehicle removed and seized under subdivision (a) shall be released to the legal owner of the vehicle or the legal owner's agent prior to the end of the impoundment period and without the permission of the magistrate authorizing the seizure of the vehicle if all of the following conditions are met:

(1) The legal owner is a motor vehicle dealer, bank, credit union, acceptance corporation, or other licensed financial institution legally operating in this state or is another person, not the registered owner, holding a financial interest in the vehicle.

(2)(A) The legal owner or the legal owner's agent pays all towing and storage fees related to the seizure of the vehicle. No lien sale processing fees shall be charged to the legal owner who redeems the vehicle prior to the 15th day of impoundment. Neither the impounding authority nor any person having possession of the vehicle shall collect from the legal owner of the type specified in paragraph (1), or the legal owner's agent any administrative charges imposed pursuant to Section 22850.5 unless the legal owner voluntarily requested a poststorage hearing.

(B) A person operating or in charge of a storage facility where vehicles are stored pursuant to this section shall accept a valid bank credit card or cash for payment of towing, storage, and related fees by a legal or registered owner or the owner's agent claiming the vehicle. A credit card shall be in the name of the person presenting the card. "Credit card" means "credit card" as defined in subdivision (a) of Section 1747.02 of the Civil Code, except, for the purposes of this section, credit card does not include a credit card issued by a retail seller.

(C) A person operating or in charge of a storage facility described in subparagraph (B) who violates subparagraph (B) shall be civilly liable to the owner of the vehicle or to the person who tendered the fees for four times the amount of the towing, storage and related fees, but not to exceed five hundred dollars ($500).

(D) A person operating or in charge of a storage facility described in subparagraph (B) shall have sufficient funds on the premises of the primary storage facility during normal business hours to accommodate, and make change in, a reasonable monetary transaction.

(E) Credit charges for towing and storage services shall comply with Section 1748.1 of the Civil Code. Law enforcement agencies may include the costs of providing for payment by credit when making agreements with towing companies on rates.

(3) The legal owner or the legal owner's agent presents, to the law enforcement agency, impounding agency, person in possession of the vehicle, or any person acting on behalf of those agencies, a copy of the assignment, as defined in subdivision (b) of Section 7500.1 of the Business and Professions Code; a release from the one responsible governmental agency, only if required by the

agency; a government-issued photographic identification card; and any one of the following, as determined by the legal owner or the legal owner's agent: a certificate of repossession for the vehicle, a security agreement for the vehicle, or title, whether paper or electronic, showing proof of legal ownership for the vehicle. Any documents presented may be originals, photocopies, or facsimile copies, or may be transmitted electronically. The law enforcement agency, impounding agency, or any other governmental agency, or any person acting on behalf of those agencies, shall not require any documents to be notarized. The law enforcement agency, impounding agency, or any person acting on behalf of those agencies, may require the agent of the legal owner to produce a photocopy or facsimile copy of its repossession agency license or registration issued pursuant to Chapter 11 (commencing with Section 7500) of Division 3 of the Business and Professions Code, or to demonstrate, to the satisfaction of the law enforcement agency, impounding agency, or any person acting on behalf of those agencies that the agent is exempt from licensure pursuant to Section 7500.2 or 7500.3 of the Business and Professions Code.

No administrative costs authorized under subdivision (a) of Section 22850.5 shall be charged to the legal owner of the type specified in paragraph (1), who redeems the vehicle unless the legal owner voluntarily requests a poststorage hearing. No city, county, city and county, or state agency shall require a legal owner or a legal owner's agent to request a poststorage hearing as a requirement for release of the vehicle to the legal owner or the legal owner's agent. The law enforcement agency, impounding agency, or other governmental agency, or any person acting on behalf of those agencies, shall not require any documents other than those specified in this paragraph. The law enforcement agency, impounding agency, or other governmental agency, or any person acting on behalf of those agencies, shall not require any documents to be notarized. The legal owner or the legal owner's agent shall be given a copy of any documents he or she is required to sign, except for a vehicle evidentiary hold logbook. The law enforcement agency, impounding agency, or any person acting on behalf of those agencies, or any person in possession of the vehicle, may photocopy and retain the copies of any documents presented by the legal owner or legal owner's agent.

(4) A failure by a storage facility to comply with any applicable conditions set forth in this subdivision shall not affect the right of the legal owner or the legal owner's agent to retrieve the vehicle, provided all conditions required of the legal owner or legal owner's agent under this subdivision are satisfied.

(f)(1) A legal owner or the legal owner's agent that obtains release of the vehicle pursuant to subdivision (e) shall not release the vehicle to the registered owner or the person who was listed as the registered owner when the vehicle was impounded of the vehicle or any agents of the registered owner, unless a registered owner is a rental car agency, until the termination of the impound period.

(2) The legal owner or the legal owner's agent shall not relinquish the vehicle to the registered owner or the person who was listed as the registered owner when the vehicle was impounded until the registered owner or that owner's agent presents his or her valid driver's license or valid temporary driver's license to the legal owner or the legal owner's agent. The legal owner or the legal owner's agent shall make every reasonable effort to ensure that the license presented is valid and possession of the vehicle will not be given to the driver who was involved in the original impoundment proceeding until the expiration of the impound period.

(3) Prior to relinquishing the vehicle, the legal owner may require the registered owner to pay all towing and storage charges related to the impoundment and the administrative charges authorized under Section 22850.5 that were incurred by the legal owner in connection with obtaining the custody of the vehicle.

(4) Any legal owner who knowingly releases or causes the release of a vehicle to a registered owner or the person in possession of the vehicle at the time of the impoundment or any agent of the registered owner in violation of this subdivision shall be guilty of a misdemeanor and subject to a fine in the amount of two thousand dollars ($2,000) in addition to any other penalties established by law.

(5) The legal owner, registered owner, or person in possession of the vehicle shall not change or attempt to change the name of the legal owner or the registered owner on the records of the department until the vehicle is released from the impoundment.

(g)(1) A vehicle impounded and seized under subdivision (a) shall be released to a rental car agency prior to the end of the impoundment period if the agency is either the legal owner or registered owner of the vehicle and the agency pays all towing and storage fees related to the seizure of the vehicle.

(2) The owner of a rental vehicle that was seized under this section may continue to rent the vehicle upon recovery of the vehicle. However, the rental car agency shall not rent another vehicle to the driver who used the vehicle that was seized to evade a police officer until 30 days after the date that the vehicle was seized.

(3) The rental car agency may require the person to whom the vehicle was rented and who evaded the peace officer to pay all towing and storage charges related to the impoundment and any administrative charges authorized under Section 22850.5 that were incurred by the rental car agency in connection with obtaining custody of the vehicle.

(h) Notwithstanding any other provision of this section, the registered owner and not the legal owner shall remain responsible for any towing and storage charges related to the impoundment and the administrative charges authorized under Section 22850.5 and any parking fines, penalties, and administrative fees incurred by the registered owner.

(i)(1) This section does not apply to vehicles abated under the Abandoned Vehicle Abatement Program pursuant to Sections 22660 to 22668, inclusive, and Section 22710, or to vehicles impounded for investigation pursuant to Section 22655, or to vehicles removed from private property pursuant to Section 22658.

(2) This section does not apply to abandoned vehicles removed pursuant to Section 22669 that are determined by the public agency to have an estimated value of three hundred dollars ($300) or less.

(j) The law enforcement agency and the impounding agency, including any storage facility acting on behalf of the law enforcement agency or impounding agency, shall comply with this section and shall not be liable to the registered owner for the improper release of the vehicle to the legal owner or the legal owner's agent provided the release complies with the provisions of this section. The legal owner shall indemnify and hold harmless a storage facility from any claims arising out of the release of the vehicle to the legal owner or the legal owner's agent and from any damage to the vehicle after its release, including the reasonable costs associated with defending any such claims. A law enforcement agency shall not refuse to issue a release to a legal owner or the agent of a legal owner on the grounds that it previously issued a release. *(Added by Stats.1997, c. 743 (A.B.662), § 1. Amended by Stats.1998, c. 485 (A.B.2803), § 160; Stats.2001, c. 554 (A.B.783), § 3; Stats.2002, c. 664 (A.B.3034), § 220; Stats.2002, c. 402 (A.B.1883), § 8; Stats.2006, c. 418 (A.B.2318), § 8; Stats.2007, c. 192 (S.B.659), § 11, eff. Sept. 7, 2007; Stats.2009, c. 322 (A.B.515), § 6.)*

Cross References

Misdemeanors, definition and penalties, see Penal Code §§ 17, 19 and 19.2.

§ 14602.8. Immediate removal and seizure of vehicle driven by repeat offender; storage and impoundment; vehicle owner's rights and responsibilities

(a)(1) If a peace officer determines that a person has been convicted of a violation of Section 23140, 23152, or 23153, that the violation occurred within the preceding 10 years, and that one or more of the following circumstances applies to that person, the officer may immediately cause the removal and seizure of the vehicle that the person was driving, under either of the following circumstances:

(A) The person was driving a vehicle when the person had 0.10 percent or more, by weight, of alcohol in his or her blood.

(B) The person driving the vehicle refused to submit to or complete a chemical test requested by the peace officer.

(2) A vehicle impounded pursuant to paragraph (1) shall be impounded for the following period of time:

(A) Five days, if the person has been convicted once of violating Section 23140, 23152, or 23153, and the violation occurred within the preceding 10 years.

(B) Fifteen days, if the person has been convicted two or more times of violating Section 23140, 23152, or 23153, or any combination thereof, and the violations occurred within the preceding 10 years.

(3) Within two working days after impoundment, the impounding agency shall send a notice by certified mail, return receipt requested, to the legal owner of the vehicle, at the address obtained from the department, informing the owner that the vehicle has been impounded. Failure to notify the legal owner within two working days shall prohibit the impounding agency from charging for more than five days' impoundment when the legal owner redeems the impounded vehicle. The impounding agency shall maintain a published telephone number that provides information 24 hours a day regarding the impoundment of vehicles and the rights of a registered owner to request a hearing. The law enforcement agency shall be open to issue a release to the registered owner or legal owner, or the agent of either, whenever the agency is open to serve the public for regular, nonemergency business.

(b) The registered and legal owner of a vehicle that is removed and seized under subdivision (a) or his or her agent shall be provided the opportunity for a storage hearing to determine the validity of, or consider any mitigating circumstances attendant to, the storage, in accordance with Section 22852.

(c) Any period during which a vehicle is subjected to storage under this section shall be included as part of the period of impoundment ordered by the court under Section 23594.

(d)(1) The impounding agency shall release the vehicle to the registered owner or his or her agent prior to the end of the impoundment period under any of the following circumstances:

(A) When the vehicle is a stolen vehicle.

(B) When the vehicle is subject to bailment and is driven by an unlicensed employee of a business establishment, including a parking service or repair garage.

(C) When the driver of the vehicle is not the sole registered owner of the vehicle and the vehicle is being released to another registered owner of the vehicle who agrees not to allow the driver to use the vehicle until after the end of the impoundment period.

(2) A vehicle shall not be released pursuant to this subdivision without presentation of the registered owner's or agent's currently valid driver's license to operate the vehicle and proof of current vehicle registration, or upon order of a court.

(e) The registered owner or his or her agent is responsible for all towing and storage charges related to the impoundment, and any administrative charges authorized under Section 22850.5.

(f) A vehicle removed and seized under subdivision (a) shall be released to the legal owner of the vehicle or the legal owner's agent prior to the end of the impoundment period if all of the following conditions are met:

(1) The legal owner is a motor vehicle dealer, bank, credit union, acceptance corporation, or other licensed financial institution legally operating in this state, or is another person who is not the registered owner and holds a security interest in the vehicle.

(2)(A) The legal owner or the legal owner's agent pays all towing and storage fees related to the seizure of the vehicle. A lien sale processing fee shall not be charged to the legal owner who redeems the vehicle prior to the 10th day of impoundment. The impounding authority or any person having possession of the vehicle shall not collect from the legal owner of the type specified in paragraph (1) or the legal owner's agent any administrative charges imposed pursuant to Section 22850.5 unless the legal owner voluntarily requested a poststorage hearing.

(B) A person operating or in charge of a storage facility where vehicles are stored pursuant to this section shall accept a valid bank credit card or cash for payment of towing, storage, and related fees by a legal or registered owner or the owner's agent claiming the vehicle. A credit card shall be in the name of the person presenting the card. "Credit card" means "credit card" as defined in subdivision (a) of Section 1747.02 of the Civil Code, except, for the purposes of this section, credit card does not include a credit card issued by a retail seller.

(C) A person operating or in charge of a storage facility described in subparagraph (B) who violates subparagraph (B) shall be civilly liable to the owner of the vehicle or to the person who tendered the fees for four times the amount of the towing, storage, and other related fees, but not to exceed five hundred dollars ($500).

(D) A person operating or in charge of a storage facility described in subparagraph (B) shall have sufficient funds on the premises of the primary storage facility during normal business hours to accommodate, and make change in, a reasonable monetary transaction.

(E) Credit charges for towing and storage services shall comply with Section 1748.1 of the Civil Code. Law enforcement agencies may include the costs of providing for payment by credit when making agreements with towing companies on rates.

(3)(A) The legal owner or the legal owner's agent presents to the law enforcement agency or impounding agency, or any person acting on behalf of those agencies, a copy of the assignment, as defined in subdivision (b) of Section 7500.1 of the Business and Professions Code; a release from the one responsible governmental agency, only if required by the agency; a government-issued photographic identification card; and any one of the following as determined by the legal owner or the legal owner's agent: a certificate of repossession for the vehicle, a security agreement for the vehicle, or title, whether paper or electronic, showing proof of legal ownership for the vehicle. The law enforcement agency, impounding agency, or any other governmental agency, or any person acting on behalf of those agencies, shall not require the presentation of any other documents.

(B) The legal owner or the legal owner's agent presents to the person in possession of the vehicle, or any person acting on behalf of the person in possession, a copy of the assignment, as defined in subdivision (b) of Section 7500.1 of the Business and Professions Code; a release from the one responsible governmental agency, only if required by the agency; a government-issued photographic identification card; and any one of the following as determined by the legal owner or the legal owner's agent: a certificate of repossession for the vehicle, a security agreement for the vehicle, or title, whether paper or electronic, showing proof of legal ownership for the vehicle. The person in possession of the vehicle, or any person acting on behalf of the person in possession, shall not require the presentation of any other documents.

(C) All presented documents may be originals, photocopies, or facsimile copies, or may be transmitted electronically. The law enforcement agency, impounding agency, or any person acting on behalf of them, shall not require a document to be notarized. The law enforcement agency, impounding agency, or any person in possession of the vehicle, or anyone acting on behalf of those agencies may require the agent of the legal owner to produce a photocopy or facsimile copy of its repossession agency license or registration issued pursuant to Chapter 11 (commencing with Section 7500) of Division 3 of the Business and Professions Code, or to demonstrate, to the satisfaction of the law enforcement agency, the impounding agency, any other governmental agency, or any person in possession of the vehicle, or anyone acting on behalf of them, that the agent is exempt from licensure pursuant to Section 7500.2 or 7500.3 of the Business and Professions Code.

(D) Administrative costs authorized under subdivision (a) of Section 22850.5 shall not be charged to the legal owner of the type specified in paragraph (1) who redeems the vehicle unless the legal owner voluntarily requests a poststorage hearing. A city, county, city and county, or state agency shall not require a legal owner or a legal owner's agent to request a poststorage hearing as a requirement for release of the vehicle to the legal owner or the legal owner's agent. The law enforcement agency, the impounding agency, any governmental agency, or any person acting on behalf of those agencies shall not require any documents other than those specified in this paragraph. The law enforcement agency, impounding agency, or other governmental agency, or any person acting on behalf of those agencies, shall not require any documents to be notarized. The legal owner or the legal owner's agent shall be given a copy of any documents he or she is required to sign, except for a vehicle evidentiary

hold logbook. The law enforcement agency, impounding agency, or any person acting on behalf of those agencies, or any person in possession of the vehicle, may photocopy and retain the copies of any documents presented by the legal owner or legal owner's agent.

(4) A failure by a storage facility to comply with any applicable conditions set forth in this subdivision shall not affect the right of the legal owner or the legal owner's agent to retrieve the vehicle, provided all conditions required of the legal owner or legal owner's agent under this subdivision are satisfied.

(g)(1) A legal owner or the legal owner's agent who obtains release of the vehicle pursuant to subdivision (f) shall not release the vehicle to the registered owner of the vehicle or the person who was listed as the registered owner when the vehicle was impounded or any agents of the registered owner unless the registered owner is a rental car agency, until after the termination of the impoundment period.

(2) The legal owner or the legal owner's agent shall not relinquish the vehicle to the registered owner or the person who was listed as the registered owner when the vehicle was impounded until the registered owner or that owner's agent presents his or her valid driver's license or valid temporary driver's license to the legal owner or the legal owner's agent. The legal owner or the legal owner's agent or the person in possession of the vehicle shall make every reasonable effort to ensure that the license presented is valid and possession of the vehicle will not be given to the driver who was involved in the original impoundment proceeding until the expiration of the impoundment period.

(3) Prior to relinquishing the vehicle, the legal owner may require the registered owner to pay all towing and storage charges related to the impoundment and any administrative charges authorized under Section 22850.5 that were incurred by the legal owner in connection with obtaining custody of the vehicle.

(4) A legal owner who knowingly releases or causes the release of a vehicle to a registered owner or the person in possession of the vehicle at the time of the impoundment or an agent of the registered owner in violation of this subdivision is guilty of a misdemeanor and subject to a fine in the amount of two thousand dollars ($2,000) in addition to any other penalties established by law.

(5) The legal owner, registered owner, or person in possession of the vehicle shall not change or attempt to change the name of the legal owner or the registered owner on the records of the department until the vehicle is released from the impoundment.

(h)(1) A vehicle removed and seized under subdivision (a) shall be released to a rental car agency prior to the end of the impoundment period if the agency is either the legal owner or registered owner of the vehicle and the agency pays all towing and storage fees related to the seizure of the vehicle.

(2) The owner of a rental vehicle that was seized under this section may continue to rent the vehicle upon recovery of the vehicle. However, the rental car agency shall not rent another vehicle to the driver of the vehicle that was seized until the impoundment period has expired.

(3) The rental car agency may require the person to whom the vehicle was rented to pay all towing and storage charges related to the impoundment and any administrative charges authorized under Section 22850.5 that were incurred by the rental car agency in connection with obtaining custody of the vehicle.

(i) Notwithstanding any other provision of this section, the registered owner, and not the legal owner, shall remain responsible for any towing and storage charges related to the impoundment, any administrative charges authorized under Section 22850.5, and any parking fines, penalties, and administrative fees incurred by the registered owner.

(j) The law enforcement agency and the impounding agency, including any storage facility acting on behalf of the law enforcement agency or impounding agency, shall comply with this section and shall not be liable to the registered owner for the improper release of the vehicle to the legal owner or the legal owner's agent provided the release complies with the provisions of this section. The legal owner shall indemnify and hold harmless a storage facility from any claims arising out of the release of the vehicle to the legal owner or the legal owner's agent and from any damage to the vehicle after its release, including the reasonable costs associated with defending any such claims. A law enforcement agency shall not refuse to issue a release to a legal owner or the agent of a legal owner on the grounds that it previously issued a release. *(Added by Stats.2005, c. 656 (S.B.207), § 1. Amended by Stats.2009, c. 322 (A.B.515), § 7; Stats.2011, c. 341 (S.B.565), § 2.)*

Cross References

Misdemeanors, definition and penalties, see Penal Code §§ 17, 19 and 19.2.

§ 14602.9. Charter-party carrier buses; impoundment; notice; storage hearing; release of vehicle; towing and storage charges

(a) An officer of the Department of the California Highway Patrol may impound a bus of a charter-party carrier for 30 days if the officer determines that any of the following violations occurred while the bus driver was operating the bus of a charter-party carrier:

(1) The driver was operating the bus of a charter-party carrier when the charter-party carrier did not have a permit or certificate issued by the Public Utilities Commission, pursuant to Section 5375 of the Public Utilities Code.

(2) The driver was operating the bus of a charter-party carrier when the charter-party carrier was operating the

bus with a suspended permit or certificate from the Public Utilities Commission.

(3) The driver was operating the bus of a charter-party carrier without having a current and valid driver's license of the proper class, a passenger vehicle endorsement, or the required certificate.

(b) Within two working days after impoundment, the impounding agency shall send a notice by certified mail, return receipt requested, to the legal owner of the vehicle, at the address obtained from the department, informing the owner that the vehicle has been impounded. Failure to notify the legal owner within two working days shall prohibit the impounding agency from charging for more than 15 day's impoundment when the legal owner redeems the impounded vehicle. The impounding agency shall maintain a published telephone number that provides information 24 hours a day regarding the impoundment of vehicles and the rights of a registered owner to request a hearing.

(c) The registered and legal owner of a vehicle that is removed and seized under subdivision (a) or his or her agent shall be provided the opportunity for a storage hearing to determine the validity of, or consider any mitigating circumstances attendant to, the storage, in accordance with Section 22852.

(d)(1) The impounding agency shall release the vehicle to the registered owner or his or her agent prior to the end of the impoundment period under any of the following circumstances:

(A) When the vehicle is a stolen vehicle.

(B) When the vehicle is subject to bailment and is driven by an unlicensed employee of a business establishment, including a parking service or repair garage.

(C) When the driver of the vehicle is not the sole registered owner of the vehicle and the vehicle is being released to another registered owner of the vehicle who agrees not to allow the driver to use the vehicle until after the end of the impoundment period and the charter-party carrier has been issued a valid permit from the Public Utilities Commission, pursuant to Section 5375 of the Public Utilities Code.

(2) A vehicle shall not be released pursuant to this subdivision without presentation of the registered owner's or agent's currently valid driver's license to operate the vehicle and proof of current vehicle registration, or upon order of a court.

(e) The registered owner or his or her agent is responsible for all towing and storage charges related to the impoundment, and any administrative charges authorized under Section 22850.5.

(f) A vehicle removed and seized under subdivision (a) shall be released to the legal owner of the vehicle or the legal owner's agent prior to the end of the impoundment period if all of the following conditions are met:

(1) The legal owner is a motor vehicle dealer, bank, credit union, acceptance corporation, or other licensed

financial institution legally operating in this state, or is another person who is not the registered owner and holds a security interest in the vehicle.

(2) The legal owner or the legal owner's agent pays all towing and storage fees related to the seizure of the vehicle. A lien sale processing fee shall not be charged to the legal owner who redeems the vehicle prior to the 10th day of impoundment. The impounding authority or any person having possession of the vehicle shall not collect from the legal owner of the type specified in paragraph (1), or the legal owner's agent, any administrative charges imposed pursuant to Section 22850.5 unless the legal owner voluntarily requested a poststorage hearing.

(3)(A) The legal owner or the legal owner's agent presents either lawful foreclosure documents or an affidavit of repossession for the vehicle, and a security agreement or title showing proof of legal ownership for the vehicle. All presented documents may be originals, photocopies, or facsimile copies, or may be transmitted electronically. The impounding agency shall not require a document to be notarized. The impounding agency may require the agent of the legal owner to produce a photocopy or facsimile copy of its repossession agency license or registration issued pursuant to Chapter 11 (commencing with Section 7500) of Division 3 of the Business and Professions Code, or to demonstrate, to the satisfaction of the impounding agency, that the agent is exempt from licensure pursuant to Section 7500.2 or 7500.3 of the Business and Professions Code.

(B) Administrative costs authorized under subdivision (a) of Section 22850.5 shall not be charged to the legal owner of the type specified in paragraph (1), who redeems the vehicle unless the legal owner voluntarily requests a poststorage hearing. A city, county, or state agency shall not require a legal owner or a legal owner's agent to request a poststorage hearing as a requirement for release of the vehicle to the legal owner or the legal owner's agent. The impounding agency shall not require any documents other than those specified in this paragraph. The impounding agency shall not require any documents to be notarized.

(C) As used in this paragraph, "foreclosure documents" means an "assignment" as that term is defined in subdivision (o) of Section 7500.1 of the Business and Professions Code.

(g)(1) A legal owner or the legal owner's agent who obtains release of the vehicle pursuant to subdivision (f) may not release the vehicle to the registered owner of the vehicle or any agents of the registered owner, unless the registered owner is a rental car agency, until after the termination of the impoundment period.

(2) The legal owner or the legal owner's agent shall not relinquish the vehicle to the registered owner until the registered owner or that owner's agent presents his or her valid driver's license or valid temporary driver's license to the legal owner or the legal owner's agent. The legal owner or the legal owner's agent shall make every reasonable effort to ensure that the license presented is valid.

(3) Prior to relinquishing the vehicle, the legal owner may require the registered owner to pay all towing and storage charges related to the impoundment and any administrative charges authorized under Section 22850.5 that were incurred by the legal owner in connection with obtaining custody of the vehicle.

(h)(1) A vehicle removed and seized under subdivision (a) shall be released to a rental agency prior to the end of the impoundment period if the agency is either the legal owner or registered owner of the vehicle and the agency pays all towing and storage fees related to the seizure of the vehicle.

(2) The owner of a rental vehicle that was seized under this section may continue to rent the vehicle upon recovery of the vehicle. However, the rental agency shall not rent another vehicle to the driver of the vehicle that was seized until the impoundment period has expired.

(3) The rental agency may require the person to whom the vehicle was rented to pay all towing and storage charges related to the impoundment and any administrative charges authorized under Section 22850.5 that were incurred by the rental agency in connection with obtaining custody of the vehicle.

(i) Notwithstanding any other provision of this section, the registered owner, and not the legal owner, shall remain responsible for any towing and storage charges related to the impoundment, any administrative charges authorized under Section 22850.5, and any parking fines, penalties, and administrative fees incurred by the registered owner.

(j) The impounding agency is not liable to the registered owner for the improper release of the vehicle to the legal owner or the legal owner's agent provided the release complies with this section.

(k) For the purposes of this section, a "bus" means a bus as defined by Section 233 or a tour bus as defined by Section 612.

(l) For the purposes of this section, a "charter-party carrier" means a charter-party carrier as defined by Section 5360 of the Public Utilities Code. (*Added by Stats.2009, c. 248 (A.B.636), § 5.*)

Cross References

Charter-party carriers, grounds for impounding of bus, see Public Utilities Code § 5387.

§ 14603. Violation of license restrictions

No person shall operate a vehicle in violation of the provisions of a restricted license issued to him. (*Stats. 1959, c. 3, p. 1634, § 14603.*)

Restricted license, issuance, see Vehicle Code § 12813.

§ 14604. Non-owner driver of vehicle; owner to determine that driver has valid license; standard of inquiry; rental companies

(a) No owner of a motor vehicle may knowingly allow another person to drive the vehicle upon a highway unless the owner determines that the person possesses a valid driver's license that authorizes the person to operate the vehicle. For the purposes of this section, an owner is required only to make a reasonable effort or inquiry to determine whether the prospective driver possesses a valid driver's license before allowing him or her to operate the owner's vehicle. An owner is not required to inquire of the department whether the prospective driver possesses a valid driver's license.

(b) A rental company is deemed to be in compliance with subdivision (a) if the company rents the vehicle in accordance with Sections 14608 and 14609. *(Added by Stats.1994, c. 1221 (S.B.1758), § 14. Amended by Stats. 1995, c. 922 (S.B.833), § 3.5.)*

§ 14605. Operation of motor vehicles in offstreet parking facilities

(a) No person who owns or is in control of a motor vehicle shall cause or permit another person to operate the vehicle within or upon an offstreet parking facility if the person has knowledge that the driver does not have a driver's license of the appropriate class or certification to operate the vehicle.

(b) No operator of an offstreet parking facility shall hire or retain in his employment an attendant whose duties involve the operating of motor vehicles unless such attendant, at all times during such employment, is licensed as a driver under the provisions of this code.

(c) As used in this section, "offstreet parking facility" means any offstreet facility held open for use by the public for parking vehicles and includes all publicly owned facilities for offstreet parking, and privately owned facilities for offstreet parking where no fee is charged for the privilege to park and which are held open for the common public use of retail customers. *(Stats.1959, c. 3, p. 1634, § 14605. Amended by Stats.1961, c. 1615, p. 3457, § 30; Stats.1984, c. 621, § 4.)*

Regulation in cities over 2,000,000 population, see Vehicle Code § 22950.
Use of street or alley by parking facility operator prohibited, see Vehicle Code § 22951.

§ 14606. Employment of person to drive motor vehicle; license and medical certificate

Section operative until Jan. 30, 2014. See, also, section operative Jan. 30, 2014.

(a) A person shall not employ or hire any person to drive a motor vehicle or knowingly permit or authorize

518

the driving of a motor vehicle, owned by him or her or under his or her control, upon the highways by any person unless that person is licensed for the appropriate class of vehicle to be driven.

(b)(1) Whenever a person fails to qualify, on reexamination, to operate a commercial motor vehicle, an employer shall report that failure to the department within 10 days.

(2) Until January 30, 2014, if a driver has no medical certification status information in the Commercial Driver License Information System motor vehicle record obtained from the driver's state licensing agency, the employing motor carrier may accept as proof of medical certification a medical examiner's certificate issued to that driver prior to January 30, 2012, and shall retain a copy as part of a driver qualification file.

(c) This section shall remain in effect only until January 30, 2014, and as of that date is repealed, unless a later enacted statute, that is enacted before January 30, 2014, deletes or extends that date. *(Stats.1959, c. 3, p. 1634, § 14606. Amended by Stats.1961, c. 1615, p. 3458, § 31; Stats.1963, c. 140, p. 813, § 3; Stats.1971, c. 1279, p. 2509, § 3, operative May 3, 1972; Stats.1993, c. 272 (A.B.301), § 33, eff. Aug. 2, 1993; Stats.2012, c. 670 (A.B.2188), § 6.)*

For repeal of this section, see its terms.

Civil liability of owners and operators, see Vehicle Code § 17000 et seq.
Driving school or driving instructor, cancellation revocation or suspension of license for violation of this section, see Vehicle Code § 11110.
Driving without a license, see Vehicle Code § 12500.
Owner, definitions of, see Vehicle Code §§ 370, 460, 505.
Person defined, see Vehicle Code § 470.

§ 14606. Employment of person to drive motor vehicle; license and medical certificate; operation of commercial motor vehicles

Section operative Jan. 30, 2014. See, also, section operative until Jan. 30, 2014.

(a) A person shall not employ, hire, knowingly permit, or authorize any person to drive a motor vehicle owned by him or her or under his or her control upon the highways unless that person is licensed for the appropriate class of vehicle to be driven.

(b) Whenever a person fails to qualify, on reexamination, to operate a commercial motor vehicle, an employer shall report that failure to the department within 10 days.

(c) An employer shall obtain from a driver required to have a commercial driver's license or commercial endorsement a copy of the driver's medical certification before allowing the driver to operate a commercial motor vehicle. The employer shall retain the certification as part of a driver qualification file.

(d) This section shall become operative on January 30, 2014. *(Added by Stats.2012, c. 670 (A.B.2188), § 7, operative Jan. 1, 2014. Amended by Stats.2013, c. 523 (S.B.788), § 30, operative Jan. 30, 2014.)*

Cross References

Civil liability of owners and operators, see Vehicle Code § 17000 et seq.

Driving school or driving instructor, cancellation revocation or suspension of license for violation of this section, see Vehicle Code § 11110.

Driving without a license, see Vehicle Code § 12500.

Owner, definitions of, see Vehicle Code §§ 370, 460, 505.

Person defined, see Vehicle Code § 470.

§ 14607. Permitting unlicensed minor to drive

No person shall cause or knowingly permit his child, ward, or employee under the age of 18 years to drive a motor vehicle upon the highways unless such child, ward, or employee is then licensed under this code. *(Stats. 1959, c. 3, p. 1634, § 14607. Amended by Stats.1961, c. 1615, p. 3458, § 32; Stats.1971, c. 1748, p. 3764, § 59, operative March 4, 1972.)*

Cross References

Age limit for issuance of license,
  Junior permits, see Vehicle Code §§ 12513, 12514.

Civil liability of persons signing license applications of minors, see Vehicle Code § 17700 et seq.

Definitions,
  Highway, see Vehicle Code §§ 360, 590.
  Motor vehicle, see Vehicle Code § 415.

Licensing of nonresident minors, see Vehicle Code § 12504.

§ 14607.4. Legislative findings and declarations

The Legislature finds and declares all of the following:

(a) Driving a motor vehicle on the public streets and highways is a privilege, not a right.

(b) Of all drivers involved in fatal accidents, more than 20 percent are not licensed to drive. A driver with a suspended license is four times as likely to be involved in a fatal accident as a properly licensed driver.

(c) At any given time, it is estimated by the Department of Motor Vehicles that of some 20 million driver's licenses issued to Californians, 720,000 are suspended or revoked. Furthermore, 1,000,000 persons are estimated to be driving without ever having been licensed at all.

(d) Over 4,000 persons are killed in traffic accidents in California annually, and another 330,000 persons suffer injuries.

(e) Californians who comply with the law are frequently victims of traffic accidents caused by unlicensed drivers. These innocent victims suffer considerable pain and property loss at the hands of people who flaunt the law. The Department of Motor Vehicles estimates that 75 percent of all drivers whose driving privilege has been withdrawn continue to drive regardless of the law.

(f) It is necessary and appropriate to take additional steps to prevent unlicensed drivers from driving, including

the civil forfeiture of vehicles used by unlicensed drivers. The state has a critical interest in enforcing its traffic laws and in keeping unlicensed drivers from illegally driving. Seizing the vehicles used by unlicensed drivers serves a significant governmental and public interest, namely the protection of the health, safety, and welfare of Californians from the harm of unlicensed drivers, who are involved in a disproportionate number of traffic incidents, and the avoidance of the associated destruction and damage to lives and property.

(g) The Safe Streets Act of 1994 is consistent with the due process requirements of the United States Constitution and the holding of the Supreme Court of the United States in Calero-Toledo v. Pearson Yacht Leasing Co., 40 L.Ed.2d 452. *(Added by Stats.1994, c. 1133 (A.B.3148), § 11.)*

§ 14607.6. Motor vehicles subject to forfeiture; driving without a license; impoundment; officer's discretion; hearings; release of vehicle; community property interests; surrender; redemption and sale; stolen vehicles; distribution of filing fee

(a) Notwithstanding any other provision of law, and except as provided in this section, a motor vehicle is subject to forfeiture as a nuisance if it is driven on a highway in this state by a driver with a suspended or revoked license, or by an unlicensed driver, who is a registered owner of the vehicle at the time of impoundment and has a previous misdemeanor conviction for a violation of subdivision (a) of Section 12500 or Section 14601, 14601.1, 14601.2, 14601.3, 14601.4, or 14601.5.

(b) A peace officer shall not stop a vehicle for the sole reason of determining whether the driver is properly licensed.

(c)(1) If a driver is unable to produce a valid driver's license on the demand of a peace officer enforcing the provisions of this code, as required by subdivision (b) of Section 12951, the vehicle shall be impounded regardless of ownership, unless the peace officer is reasonably able, by other means, to verify that the driver is properly licensed. Prior to impounding a vehicle, a peace officer shall attempt to verify the license status of a driver who claims to be properly licensed but is unable to produce the license on demand of the peace officer.

(2) A peace officer shall not impound a vehicle pursuant to this subdivision if the license of the driver expired within the preceding 30 days and the driver would otherwise have been properly licensed.

(3) A peace officer may exercise discretion in a situation where the driver without a valid license is an employee driving a vehicle registered to the employer in the course of employment. A peace officer may also exercise discretion in a situation where the driver without a valid license is the employee of a bona fide business establishment or is a person otherwise controlled by such an establishment and it reasonably appears that an owner of the vehicle, or an agent of the owner, relinquished possession of the vehicle to the business establishment

519

solely for servicing or parking of the vehicle or other reasonably similar situations, and where the vehicle was not to be driven except as directly necessary to accomplish that business purpose. In this event, if the vehicle can be returned to or be retrieved by the business establishment or registered owner, the peace officer may release and not impound the vehicle.

(4) A registered or legal owner of record at the time of impoundment may request a hearing to determine the validity of the impoundment pursuant to subdivision (n).

(5) If the driver of a vehicle impounded pursuant to this subdivision was not a registered owner of the vehicle at the time of impoundment, or if the driver of the vehicle was a registered owner of the vehicle at the time of impoundment but the driver does not have a previous conviction for a violation of subdivision (a) of Section 12500 or Section 14601, 14601.1, 14601.2, 14601.3, 14601.4, or 14601.5, the vehicle shall be released pursuant to this code and is not subject to forfeiture.

(d)(1) This subdivision applies only if the driver of the vehicle is a registered owner of the vehicle at the time of impoundment. Except as provided in paragraph (5) of subdivision (c), if the driver of a vehicle impounded pursuant to subdivision (c) was a registered owner of the vehicle at the time of impoundment, the impounding agency shall authorize release of the vehicle if, within three days of impoundment, the driver of the vehicle at the time of impoundment presents his or her valid driver's license, including a valid temporary California driver's license or permit, to the impounding agency. The vehicle shall then be released to a registered owner of record at the time of impoundment, or an agent of that owner authorized in writing, upon payment of towing and storage charges related to the impoundment, and any administrative charges authorized by Section 22850.5, providing that the person claiming the vehicle is properly licensed and the vehicle is properly registered. A vehicle impounded pursuant to the circumstances described in paragraph (3) of subdivision (c) shall be released to a registered owner whether or not the driver of the vehicle at the time of impoundment presents a valid driver's license.

(2) If there is a community property interest in the vehicle impounded pursuant to subdivision (c), owned at the time of impoundment by a person other than the driver, and the vehicle is the only vehicle available to the driver's immediate family that may be operated with a class C driver's license, the vehicle shall be released to a registered owner or to the community property interest owner upon compliance with all of the following requirements:

(A) The registered owner or the community property interest owner requests release of the vehicle and the owner of the community property interest submits proof of that interest.

(B) The registered owner or the community property interest owner submits proof that he or she, or an authorized driver, is properly licensed and that the

impounded vehicle is properly registered pursuant to this code.

(C) All towing and storage charges related to the impoundment and any administrative charges authorized pursuant to Section 22850.5 are paid.

(D) The registered owner or the community property interest owner signs a stipulated vehicle release agreement, as described in paragraph (3), in consideration for the nonforfeiture of the vehicle. This requirement applies only if the driver requests release of the vehicle.

(3) A stipulated vehicle release agreement shall provide for the consent of the signator to the automatic future forfeiture and transfer of title to the state of any vehicle registered to that person, if the vehicle is driven by a driver with a suspended or revoked license, or by an unlicensed driver. The agreement shall be in effect for only as long as it is noted on a driving record maintained by the department pursuant to Section 1806.1.

(4) The stipulated vehicle release agreement described in paragraph (3) shall be reported by the impounding agency to the department not later than 10 days after the day the agreement is signed.

(5) No vehicle shall be released pursuant to paragraph (2) if the driving record of a registered owner indicates that a prior stipulated vehicle release agreement was signed by that person.

(e)(1) The impounding agency, in the case of a vehicle that has not been redeemed pursuant to subdivision (d), or that has not been otherwise released, shall promptly ascertain from the department the names and addresses of all legal and registered owners of the vehicle.

(2) The impounding agency, within two days of impoundment, shall send a notice by certified mail, return receipt requested, to all legal and registered owners of the vehicle, at the addresses obtained from the department, informing them that the vehicle is subject to forfeiture and will be sold or otherwise disposed of pursuant to this section. The notice shall also include instructions for filing a claim with the district attorney, and the time limits for filing a claim. The notice shall also inform any legal owner of its right to conduct the sale pursuant to subdivision (g). If a registered owner was personally served at the time of impoundment with a notice containing all the information required to be provided by this paragraph, no further notice is required to be sent to a registered owner. However, a notice shall still be sent to the legal owners of the vehicle, if any. If notice was not sent to the legal owner within two working days, the impounding agency shall not charge the legal owner for more than 15-days' impoundment when the legal owner redeems the impounded vehicle.

(3) No processing charges shall be imposed on a legal owner who redeems an impounded vehicle within 15 days of the impoundment of that vehicle. If no claims are filed and served within 15 days after the mailing of the notice in paragraph (2), or if no claims are filed and served within five days of personal service of the notice

specified in paragraph (2), when no other mailed notice is required pursuant to paragraph (2), the district attorney shall prepare a written declaration of forfeiture of the vehicle to the state. A written declaration of forfeiture signed by the district attorney under this subdivision shall be deemed to provide good and sufficient title to the forfeited vehicle. A copy of the declaration shall be provided on request to any person informed of the pending forfeiture pursuant to paragraph (2). A claim that is filed and is later withdrawn by the claimant shall be deemed not to have been filed.

(4) If a claim is timely filed and served, then the district attorney shall file a petition of forfeiture with the appropriate juvenile or superior court within 10 days of the receipt of the claim. The district attorney shall establish an expedited hearing date in accordance with instructions from the court, and the court shall hear the matter without delay. The court filing fee of one hundred dollars ($100) shall be paid by the claimant, but shall be reimbursed by the impounding agency if the claimant prevails. To the extent practicable, the civil and criminal cases shall be heard at the same time in an expedited, consolidated proceeding. A proceeding in the civil case is a limited civil case.

(5) The burden of proof in the civil case shall be on the prosecuting agency, by a preponderance of the evidence. All questions that may arise shall be decided and all other proceedings shall be conducted as in an ordinary civil action. A judgment of forfeiture does not require as a condition precedent the conviction of a defendant of an offense which made the vehicle subject to forfeiture. The filing of a claim within the time limits specified in paragraph (3) is considered a jurisdictional prerequisite for the availing of the action authorized by that paragraph.

(6) All right, title, and interest in the vehicle shall vest in the state upon commission of the act giving rise to the forfeiture.

(7) The filing fee in paragraph (4) shall be distributed as follows:

(A) To the county law library fund as provided in Section 6320 of the Business and Professions Code, the amount specified in Sections 6321 and 6322.1 of the Business and Professions Code.

(B) To the Trial Court Trust Fund, the remainder of the fee.

(f) Any vehicle impounded that is not redeemed pursuant to subdivision (d) and is subsequently forfeited pursuant to this section shall be sold once an order of forfeiture is issued by the district attorney of the county of the impounding agency or a court, as the case may be, pursuant to subdivision (e).

(g) Any legal owner who is a motor vehicle dealer, bank, credit union, acceptance corporation, or other licensed financial institution legally operating in this state, or the agent of that legal owner, may take possession and conduct the sale of the forfeited vehicle if the legal owner or agent notifies the agency impounding the vehicle of its intent to conduct the sale within 15 days of the mailing of the notice pursuant to subdivision (e). Sale of the vehicle after forfeiture pursuant to this subdivision may be conducted at the time, in the manner, and on the notice usually given for the sale of repossessed or surrendered vehicles. The proceeds of any sale conducted by or on behalf of the legal owner shall be disposed of as provided in subdivision (i). A notice pursuant to this subdivision may be presented in person, by certified mail, by facsimile transmission, or by electronic mail.

(h) If the legal owner or agent of the owner does not notify the agency impounding the vehicle of its intent to conduct the sale as provided in subdivision (g), the agency shall offer the forfeited vehicle for sale at public auction within 60 days of receiving title to the vehicle. Low value vehicles shall be disposed of pursuant to subdivision (k).

(i) The proceeds of a sale of a forfeited vehicle shall be disposed of in the following priority:

(1) To satisfy the towing and storage costs following impoundment, the costs of providing notice pursuant to subdivision (e), the costs of sale, and the unfunded costs of judicial proceedings, if any.

(2) To the legal owner in an amount to satisfy the indebtedness owed to the legal owner remaining as of the date of sale, including accrued interest or finance charges and delinquency charges, providing that the principal indebtedness was incurred prior to the date of impoundment.

(3) To the holder of any subordinate lien or encumbrance on the vehicle, other than a registered or legal owner, to satisfy any indebtedness so secured if written notification of demand is received before distribution of the proceeds is completed. The holder of a subordinate lien or encumbrance, if requested, shall furnish reasonable proof of its interest and, unless it does so upon request, is not entitled to distribution pursuant to this paragraph.

(4) To any other person, other than a registered or legal owner, who can reasonably establish an interest in the vehicle, including a community property interest, to the extent of his or her provable interest, if written notification is received before distribution of the proceeds is completed.

(5) Of the remaining proceeds, funds shall be made available to pay any local agency and court costs, that are reasonably related to the implementation of this section, that remain unsatisfied.

(6) Of the remaining proceeds, half shall be transferred to the Controller for deposit in the Vehicle Inspection and Repair Fund for the high-polluter repair assistance and removal program created by Article 9 (commencing with Section 44090) of Chapter 5 of Part 5 of Division 26 of the Health and Safety Code, and half shall be transferred to the general fund of the city or county of the impounding agency, or the city or county

where the impoundment occurred. A portion of the local funds may be used to establish a reward fund for persons coming forward with information leading to the arrest and conviction of hit-and-run drivers and to publicize the availability of the reward fund.

(j) The person conducting the sale shall disburse the proceeds of the sale as provided in subdivision (i) and shall provide a written accounting regarding the disposition to the impounding agency and, on request, to any person entitled to or claiming a share of the proceeds, within 15 days after the sale is conducted.

(k) If the vehicle to be sold pursuant to this section is not of the type that can readily be sold to the public generally, the vehicle shall be conveyed to a licensed dismantler or donated to an eleemosynary institution. License plates shall be removed from any vehicle conveyed to a dismantler pursuant to this subdivision.

(l) No vehicle shall be sold pursuant to this section if the impounding agency determines the vehicle to have been stolen. In this event, the vehicle may be claimed by the registered owner at any time after impound, providing the vehicle registration is current and the registered owner has no outstanding traffic violations or parking penalties on his or her driving record or on the registration record of any vehicle registered to the person. If the identity of the legal and registered owners of the vehicle cannot be reasonably ascertained, the vehicle may be sold.

(m) Any owner of a vehicle who suffers any loss due to the impound or forfeiture of any vehicle pursuant to this section may recover the amount of the loss from the unlicensed, suspended, or revoked driver. If possession of a vehicle has been tendered to a business establishment in good faith, and an unlicensed driver employed or otherwise directed by the business establishment is the cause of the impoundment of the vehicle, a registered owner of the impounded vehicle may recover damages for the loss of use of the vehicle from the business establishment.

(n)(1) The impounding agency, if requested to do so not later than 10 days after the date the vehicle was impounded, shall provide the opportunity for a poststorage hearing to determine the validity of the storage to the persons who were the registered and legal owners of the vehicle at the time of impoundment, except that the hearing shall be requested within three days after the date the vehicle was impounded if personal service was provided to a registered owner pursuant to paragraph (2) of subdivision (e) and no mailed notice is required.

(2) The poststorage hearing shall be conducted not later than two days after the date it was requested. The impounding agency may authorize its own officer or employee to conduct the hearing if the hearing officer is not the same person who directed the storage of the vehicle. Failure of either the registered or legal owner to request a hearing as provided in paragraph (1) or to attend a scheduled hearing shall satisfy the poststorage hearing requirement.

(3) The agency employing the person who directed the storage is responsible for the costs incurred for towing and storage if it is determined that the driver at the time of impoundment had a valid driver's license.

(o) As used in this section, "days" means workdays not including weekends and holidays.

(p) Charges for towing and storage for any vehicle impounded pursuant to this section shall not exceed the normal towing and storage rates for other vehicle towing and storage conducted by the impounding agency in the normal course of business.

(q) The Judicial Council and the Department of Justice may prescribe standard forms and procedures for implementation of this section to be used by all jurisdictions throughout the state.

(r) The impounding agency may act as the agent of the state in carrying out this section.

(s) No vehicle shall be impounded pursuant to this section if the driver has a valid license but the license is for a class of vehicle other than the vehicle operated by the driver.

(t) This section does not apply to vehicles subject to Sections 14608 and 14609, if there has been compliance with the procedures in those sections.

(u) As used in this section, "district attorney" includes a city attorney charged with the duty of prosecuting misdemeanor offenses.

(v) The agent of a legal owner acting pursuant to subdivision (g) shall be licensed, or exempt from licensure, pursuant to Chapter 11 (commencing with Section 7500) of Division 3 of the Business and Professions Code. *(Added by Stats.1994, c. 1133 (A.B.3148), § 12. Amended by Stats.1995, c. 404 (S.B.240), § 4; Stats.1998, c. 582 (S.B.117), § 6; Stats.1998, c. 931 (S.B.2139), § 457, eff. Sept. 28, 1998; Stats.1998, c. 931 (S.B.2139), § 457.5, eff. Sept. 28, 1998, operative Jan. 1, 1999; Stats.2005, c. 75 (A.B.145), § 151, eff. July 19, 2005, operative Jan. 1, 2006.)*

Cross References

Burden of proof, generally, see Evidence Code § 500 et seq.

Deposit of fees or fines collected pursuant to this section in the Trial Court Trust Fund, effect of prior agreements or practices, long-term revenue allocation schedule proposal, see Government Code § 68085.5.

Maintenance of records, stipulated vehicle release agreements entered into pursuant to this section, see Vehicle Code § 1806.1

Misdemeanors, definition and penalties, see Penal Code §§ 17, 19 and 19.2.

Organization and government of courts, collection of fees and fines pursuant to this section, distributions, see Government Code § 68085.1.

State Controller, generally, see Government Code § 12402 et seq.

Title transfer fees for vehicles transferred pursuant to this section, see Vehicle Code § 9255.3.

§ 14607.8. Motor vehicles subject to forfeiture as a nuisance; first misdemeanor convictions

Upon a first misdemeanor conviction of a violation of subdivision (a) of Section 12500 or Section 14601, 14601.1, 14601.2, 14601.3, 14601.4, or 14601.5, the court shall inform the defendant that, pursuant to Section 14607.6, a motor vehicle is subject to forfeiture as a nuisance if it is driven on a highway in this state by a driver with a suspended or revoked license, or by an unlicensed driver, who is a registered owner of the vehicle and has a previous misdemeanor conviction for a violation of subdivision (a) of Section 12500 or Section 14601, 14601.1, 14601.2, 14601.3, 14601.4, or 14601.5. *(Added by Stats.1994, c. 1133 (A.B.3148), § 13.)*

Cross References

Misdemeanors, definition and penalties, see Penal Code §§ 17, 19 and 19.2.

§ 14608. Rental of vehicles; requirements; rental to blind or disabled persons who are nondrivers

(a) A person shall not rent a motor vehicle to another person unless both of the following requirements have been met:

(1) The person to whom the vehicle is rented is licensed under this code or is a nonresident who is licensed under the laws of the state or country of his or her residence.

(2) The person renting to another person has inspected the driver's license of the person to whom the vehicle is to be rented and compared either the signature thereon with that of the person to whom the vehicle is to be rented or the photograph thereon with the person to whom the vehicle is to be rented.

(b) This section does not prohibit a blind or disabled person who is a nondriver from renting a motor vehicle if both of the following conditions exist at the time of rental:

(1) The blind or disabled person either holds an identification card issued pursuant to this code or is a resident of this state.

(2) The blind or disabled person has a driver present who is either licensed to drive a vehicle pursuant to this code or is a nonresident licensed to drive a vehicle pursuant to the laws of the state or country of the driver's residence. *(Stats.1959, c. 3, p. 1634, § 14608. Amended by Stats.1993, c. 1292 (S.B.274), § 11; Stats.2012, c. 406 (A.B.2659), § 2; Stats.2012, c. 862 (A.B.2189), § 4.)*

Cross References

Duties of persons renting automobiles to keep records, see Vehicle Code § 14609.
Issuance and contents of license, see Vehicle Code § 12811.
Nonresident defined, see Vehicle Code § 435.
Persons who must be licensed, see Vehicle Code § 12500 et seq.
Rental company, hiring, see Civil Code § 1936.5.

Vehicle rental agreements, rental company not subject to requirements of this section, conditions, see Civil Code § 1936.5.

§ 14609. Records of rental

(a) Every person renting a motor vehicle to another person shall keep a record of the registration number of the motor vehicle rented, the name and address of the person to whom the vehicle is rented, his or her driver's license number, the jurisdiction that issued the driver's license, and the expiration date of the driver's license.

(b) If the person renting the vehicle is a nondriver pursuant to subdivision (c) of Section 14608, the record maintained pursuant to this section shall include the name and address of the person renting the vehicle and, if applicable, his or her identification card number, the jurisdiction that issued the identification card, and the expiration date of the identification card. The record shall also include the name and address of the licensed driver, his or her driver's license number, and the expiration date of his or her driver's license. *(Stats.1959, c. 3, p. 1634, § 14609. Amended by Stats.1975, c. 389, p. 867, § 6; Stats.1993, c. 1292 (S.B.274), § 12.)*

§ 14610. Unlawful use of license; license defined

(a) It is unlawful for any person:

(1) To display or cause or permit to be displayed or have in his possession any canceled, revoked, suspended, fictitious, fraudulently altered, or fraudulently obtained driver's license.

(2) To lend his driver's license to any other person or knowingly permit the use thereof by another.

(3) To display or represent any driver's license not issued to him as being his license.

(4) To fail or refuse to surrender to the department upon its lawful demand any driver's license which has been suspended, revoked or canceled.

(5) To permit any unlawful use of a driver's license issued to him.

(6) To do any act forbidden or fail to perform any act required by this division.

(7) To photograph, photostat, duplicate, or in any way reproduce any driver's license or facsimile thereof in such a manner that it could be mistaken for a valid license, or to display or have in his possession any such photograph, photostat, duplicate, reproduction, or facsimile unless authorized by the provisions of this code.

(8) To alter any driver's license in any manner not authorized by this code.

(b) For purposes of this section, "driver's license" includes a temporary permit to operate a motor vehicle. *(Stats.1959, c. 3. p. 1634, § 14610. Amended by Stats. 1967, c. 545, p. 1894, § 1; Stats.1971, c. 1174, p. 2240, § 4, operative May 3, 1972; Stats.1990, c. 44 (A.B.1648), § 5.)*

Cancellation, suspension and revocation of license by department, see Vehicle Code § 13350 et seq.

Contents,
  Application for license, see Vehicle Code § 12800.
  License, see Vehicle Code § 12811.

Minor's use of fraudulent license for purpose of purchasing or leasing a vehicle, see Vehicle Code § 15501.

Permitting unlicensed person to drive, see Vehicle Code § 14606.

Person defined, see Vehicle Code § 470.

Procedure upon revocation, suspension or cancellation, see Vehicle Code § 13351.

Suspension or revocation of license by court, see Vehicle Code § 13200 et seq.

Violation a misdemeanor, see Vehicle Code § 40000.11.

§ 14610.1. Manufacture or sale of similar identification document prohibited; penalties; other prosecution not precluded

(a) A person shall not manufacture or sell an identification document of a size and form substantially similar to, or that purports to confer the same privileges as, the drivers' licenses issued by the department.

(b) A violation of this section is a misdemeanor punishable as follows:

(1) The court shall impose a fine of not less than two hundred fifty dollars ($250) and not more than one thousand dollars ($1,000), and 24 hours of community service, to be served when the person is not employed or is not attending school. No part of the fine or community service shall be suspended or waived.

(2) In lieu of the penalties imposed under paragraph (1), the court, in its discretion, may impose a jail term of up to one year and a fine of up to one thousand dollars ($1,000). In exercising its discretion the court shall consider the extent of the defendant's commercial motivation for the offense.

(c) Prosecution under this section shall not preclude prosecution under any other applicable provision of law. *(Added by Stats.1990, c. 170 (S.B.1873), § 2. Amended by Stats.2007, c. 743 (A.B.1658), § 6; Stats.2010, c. 684 (A.B.2471), § 2.)*

Identification cards, manufacture or sale of similar identification document prohibited, see Vehicle Code § 13004.1.

Misdemeanors, definition and penalties, see Penal Code §§ 17, 19 and 19.2.

§ 14610.5. Unlawful sale, offer to sell, distribution or use of crib sheet or cribbing device; unlawful impersonation; punishment

(a) It is unlawful for any person to do any of the following:

(1) Sell, offer for sale, distribute, or use any crib sheet or cribbing device that contains the answers to any examination administered by the department for any class of driver's license, permit, or certificate.

(2) Impersonate or allow the impersonation of an applicant for any class of driver's license, permit, or certificate for the purpose of fraudulently qualifying the applicant for any class of driver's license, permit, or certificate.

(b) A first conviction under this section is punishable as either an infraction or a misdemeanor; a second or subsequent conviction is punishable as a misdemeanor. *(Added by Stats.1986, c. 960, § 2. Amended by Stats.1995, c. 243 (S.B.307), § 1.)*

Crib sheet or cribbing device defined, see Vehicle Code § 273.

License examination and driving test, see Vehicle Code §§ 12803, 12804.9.

Misdemeanors, definition and penalties, see Penal Code §§ 17, 19 and 19.2.

§ 14610.7. Assisting in obtaining a license or identification card for persons present in United States in violation of federal law

It is a misdemeanor for any person to knowingly assist in obtaining a driver's license or identification card for any person whose presence in the United States is not authorized under federal law. *(Added by Stats.1993, c. 820 (S.B.976), § 3.)*

License requirements, authorized presence in United States under federal law, see Vehicle Code § 12801.5.

Misdemeanors, definition and penalties, see Penal Code §§ 17, 19 and 19.2.

§ 14611. Vehicles transporting highway route controlled quantity of Class 7 radioactive materials; directing operation of vehicle with driver not possessing training certificate and proper license; penalty

(a) A person shall not knowingly direct the operation of a vehicle transporting a highway route controlled quantity of Class 7 radioactive materials, as defined in Section 173.403 of Title 49 of the Code of Federal Regulations, by a person who does not possess a training certificate pursuant to subdivision (b) of Section 12524 and a valid driver's license of the appropriate class.

(b) A person convicted under this section shall be punished by a fine of not less than five thousand dollars ($5,000) nor more than ten thousand dollars ($10,000). *(Added by Stats.1983, c. 893, § 5, operative July 1, 1984. Amended by Stats.2010, c. 491 (S.B.1318), § 38.)*

Driver's license and certification for hauling fissile class III shipments or large quantity radioactive materials, see Vehicle Code § 12524.

CHAPTER 5. LICENSE FEES

Article	Section
1. Imposition of Fees	14900

Article   Section
  2. Collection of Fees 14910

ARTICLE 1. IMPOSITION OF FEES

Section

14900.   Class C or M license; fees.
14900.1.   Driver's license fees.
14900.5.   Fee for identification card in lieu of driver's license; expiration of card.
14901.   Duplicate license or name change; fees.
14901.1.   Repealed.
14902.   Fee for identification cards.
14903.   Repealed.
14904.   Fee for issuance, reissuance, or return of license after termination of suspension or revocation; exceptions.
14905.   Suspension pursuant to § 13353 or § 13353.2; additional fee.
14906.   Fee covering cost of giving notice; suspension or revocation.
14907.   Fee in addition to one required by § 14904.
14908.   Repealed.

§ 14900. Class C or M license; fees

(a) Upon application for an original class C or M driver's license, a fee of twenty-four dollars ($24), and on and after January 1, 2010, a fee of thirty dollars ($30), shall be paid to the department for a license that will expire on the fifth birthday of the applicant following the date of the application. The payment of the fee entitles the person paying the fee to apply for a driver's license and to take three examinations within a period of 12 months from the date of the application or during the period that an instruction permit is valid, as provided in Section 12509.

(b) In addition to the application fee specified in subdivision (a), a person who fails to successfully complete the driving skill test on the first attempt shall be required to pay an additional fee of five dollars ($5) for each additional driving skill test administered under that application.

(Stats.1959, c. 3, p. 1635, § 14900. Amended by Stats.1961, c. 1615, p. 3458, § 33; Stats.1968, c. 1469, p. 2937, § 4; Stats.1971, c. 1324, p. 2625, § 2, operative July 1, 1972; Stats.1973, c. 891, p. 1663, § 5, eff. Sept. 28, 1973, operative Oct. 1, 1973; Stats.1974, c. 428, p. 1040, § 4; Stats.1976, c. 552, p. 1393, § 5; Stats.1981, c. 541, p. 2185, § 35, eff. Sept. 17, 1981, operative Jan. 1, 1982; Stats.1984, c. 34, § 2, operative July 1, 1985; Stats.1988, c. 1509, § 8; Stats.1990, c. 104 (S.B.798), § 6, eff. May 23, 1990; Stats.1990, c. 400 (A.B.2953), § 3; Stats.1991, c. 217 (S.B.184), § 3; Stats.1996, c. 1043 (A.B.2352), § 7; Stats. 2000, c. 787 (S.B.1404), § 20; Stats.2002, c. 805 (A.B. 2996), § 18, eff. Sept. 23, 2002; Stats.2003, c. 719 (S.B. 1055), § 23; Stats.2009–2010, 4th Ex.Sess., c. 10 (A.B.10), § 10, eff. July 28, 2009.)

Cross References

Base fee amounts, adjustment of fees, see Vehicle Code § 1678.
Driver's license defined, see Vehicle Code § 310.

Duplicate license or change of name fee, see Vehicle Code § 14901.
Issuance of licenses, see Vehicle Code § 12800 et seq.
Licenses, generally, see Vehicle Code § 12500 et seq.
Renewal of license, see Vehicle Code § 12807 et seq.
Vehicle license fee, see Revenue and Taxation Code § 10751 et seq.

§ 14900.1. Driver's license fees

(a) Except as provided in Sections 15250.6 and 15255.1, upon application for the renewal of a driver's license or for a license to operate a different class of vehicle, a fee of twenty-four dollars ($24), and on and after January 1, 2010, a fee of thirty dollars ($30), shall be paid to the department for a license that will expire on the fifth birthday of the applicant following the date of the application. The payment of the fee entitles the person paying the fee to apply for a driver's license and to take three examinations within a period of 12 months from the date of the application or during the period that an instruction permit is valid, as provided in Section 12509.

(b) In addition to the application fee specified in subdivision (a), a person who fails to successfully complete the driving skill test on the first attempt shall be required to pay an additional fee of five dollars ($5) for each additional driving skill test administered under that application.

(Added by Stats.1991, c. 217 (S.B.184), § 4. Amended by Stats.1996, c. 1043 (A.B.2352), § 8; Stats.2000, c. 787 (S.B.1404), § 21; Stats.2001, c. 739 (A.B.1707), § 7; Stats.2002, c. 805 (A.B.2996), § 19, eff. Sept. 23, 2002; Stats.2003, c. 719 (S.B.1055), § 24; Stats.2009–2010, 4th Ex.Sess., c. 10 (A.B.10), § 11, eff. July 28, 2009.)

Cross References

Base fee amounts, adjustment of fees, see Vehicle Code § 1678.

§ 14900.5. Fee for identification card in lieu of driver's license; expiration of card

Upon application and payment of the fees for a driver's license pursuant to Section 14900, an identification card may be issued to the applicant if it is determined that a driver's license cannot be issued due to the applicant's physical or mental condition. The identification card, unless canceled earlier, shall expire on the applicant's sixth birthday following the date of application. *(Added by Stats.1990, c. 607 (S.B.2311), § 2.)*

§ 14901. Duplicate license or name change; fees

Upon an application for a duplicate driver's license or for a change of name on a driver's license, a fee of nineteen dollars ($19), and on and after January 1, 2010, a fee of twenty-four dollars ($24), shall be paid to the department. *(Stats.1959, c. 3, p. 1635, § 14901. Amended by Stats.1971, c. 1324, p. 2625, § 3, operative July 1, 1972; Stats.1981, c. 541, p. 2185, § 36, eff. Sept. 17, 1981, operative Jan. 1, 1982; Stats.1982, c. 1273, p. 4705, § 20; Stats.1991, c. 217 (S.B.184), § 5; Stats.1996, c. 1043 (A.B.2352), § 9; Stats.2003, c. 719 (S.B.1055), § 25;*

Stats.2009–2010, 4th Ex.Sess., c. 10 (A.B.10), § 12, eff. July 28, 2009.)

Cross References

Applicability of this section to trolley coaches, see Vehicle Code § 21051.

Base fee amounts, adjustment of fees, see Vehicle Code § 1678.

Duplicate license, see Vehicle Code § 12815.

Firefighter endorsement required to operate firefighting equipment, qualifications, fees for adding endorsement to existing license, see Vehicle Code § 12804.11.

§ 14901.1. Repealed by Stats.1996, c. 1043 (A.B.2352), § 10

§ 14902. Fee for identification cards

(a) Except as otherwise provided in subdivisions (b) and (c) of this section, subdivision (c) of Section 13002, and subdivision (c) of Section 14900, upon an application for an identification card a fee of twenty dollars ($20), and on and after January 1, 2010, a fee of twenty-six dollars ($26), shall be paid to the department.

(b) An original or replacement senior citizen identification card issued pursuant to subdivision (b) of Section 13000 shall be issued free of charge.

(c) The fee for an original or replacement identification card issued to a person who has been determined to have a current income level that meets the eligibility requirements for assistance programs under Chapter 2 (commencing with Section 11200) or Chapter 3 (commencing with Section 12000) of Part 3 of, or Part 5 (commencing with Section 17000) of, or Article 9 (commencing with Section 18900) of Chapter 10 of Part 6 of, or Chapter 10.1 (commencing with Section 18930) or Chapter 10.3 (commencing with Section 18937) of Part 6 of, Division 9 of the Welfare and Institutions Code shall be six dollars ($6). The determination of eligibility under this subdivision shall be made by a governmental or nonprofit entity, which shall be subject to regulations adopted by the department.

(d) All fees received pursuant to this section shall be deposited in the Motor Vehicle Account. *(Added by Stats.1968, c. 494, p. 1139, § 4. Amended by Stats.1971, c. 1324, p. 2626, § 4, operative July 1, 1972; Stats.1975, c. 1198, p. 2965, § 4; Stats.1978, c. 821, p. 2610, § 3; Stats.1981, c. 541, p. 2185, § 37, eff. Sept. 17, 1981, operative Jan. 1, 1982; Stats.1990, c. 607, (S.B.2311), § 3; Stats.2003, c. 719 (S.B.1055), § 26; Stats.2004, c. 212 (S.B.1098), § 7, eff. Aug. 11, 2004; Stats.2009–2010, 4th Ex.Sess., c. 10 (A.B.10), § 13, eff. July 28, 2009.)*

Cross References

Base fee amounts, adjustment of fees, see Vehicle Code § 1678.

Identification cards, see Vehicle Code § 13000 et seq.

§ 14903. Repealed by Stats.1978, c. 821, p. 2611, § 4

§ 14904. Fee for issuance, reissuance, or return of license after termination of suspension or revocation; exceptions

(a) Notwithstanding any other provision of this code, before a driver's license may be issued, reissued, or returned to the licensee after a suspension or a revocation of a person's driving privilege ordered by the department has been terminated, there shall, in addition to any other fees required by this code, be paid to the department a fee sufficient to pay the actual costs of the issuance, reissuance, or return as determined by the department.

(b) This section shall not apply to any suspension or revocation that is set aside by the department or a court.

(c) This section shall not apply to any suspension or revocation based upon a physical or mental condition. *(Added by Stats.1970, c. 1012, p. 1819, § 1. Amended by Stats.1974, c. 333, p. 664, § 2; Stats.1974, c. 1409, p. 3095, § 6.5, operative July 1, 1975; Stats.1981, c. 584, p. 2250, § 2; Stats.1982, c. 612, p. 2596, § 2; Stats.1991, c. 1177 (S.B.35), § 2, eff. Oct. 14, 1991.)*

Cross References

Suspension or revocation of licenses, see Vehicle Code § 13100 et seq.

§ 14905. Suspension pursuant to § 13353 or § 13353.2; additional fee

(a) Notwithstanding any other provision of this code, in lieu of the fees in Section 14904, before a driver's license may be issued, reissued, or returned to a person after suspension or revocation of the person's privilege to operate a motor vehicle pursuant to Section 13353 or 13353.2, there shall be paid to the department a fee in an amount of one hundred twenty-five dollars ($125) to pay the costs of the administration of the administrative suspension and revocation programs for persons who refuse or fail to complete chemical testing, as provided in Section 13353, or who drive with an excessive amount of alcohol in their blood, as provided in Section 13353.2, any costs of the Department of the California Highway Patrol related to the payment of compensation for overtime for attending any administrative hearings pursuant to Article 3 (commencing with Section 14100) of Chapter 3 and Section 13382, and any reimbursement for costs mandated by the state pursuant to subdivisions (f) and (g) of Section 23612.

(b) This section does not apply to a suspension or revocation that is set aside by the department or a court. *(Added by Stats.1989, c. 1460, § 18, operative July 1, 1990. Amended by Stats.1990, c. 431 (S.B.1150), § 14, eff. July 26, 1990; Stats.1998, c. 118 (S.B.1186), § 11, operative July 1, 1999; Stats.2002, c. 805 (A.B.2996), § 20, eff. Sept. 23, 2002.)*

§ 14906. Fee covering cost of giving notice; suspension or revocation

(a) In addition to the fees required by Section 14904, the department may require payment of a fee sufficient to pay the actual costs, as determined by the department, for giving any notices in connection with suspensions or revocations in accordance with Sections 22, 29, and 13106.

(b) This section does not apply to any suspension or revocation that is set aside by the department or a court. *(Added by Stats.1993, c. 546 (A.B.2284), § 4. Amended by Stats.1994, c. 1221 (S.B.1758), § 15.)*

Cross References

Recovery of costs of notice of suspension or revocation of license, fees authorized pursuant to this section, see Vehicle Code § 13106.

§ 14907. Fee in addition to one required by § 14904

In addition to the fees required pursuant to Section 14904, there shall be paid to the department a fee of one hundred twenty dollars ($120) to pay the costs of a departmental review when requested pursuant to Section 14105.5, following a hearing conducted pursuant to Section 13353 or 13353.2. The fee authorized under this section shall be collected in conjunction with any request for a departmental review received on or after January 1, 2003. *(Added by Stats.2002, c. 805 (A.B.2996), § 21, eff. Sept. 23, 2002.)*

§ 14908. Repealed by Stats.1999, c. 1008 (S.B.533), § 10

ARTICLE 2. COLLECTION OF FEES

Section
14910. Collection; remittance; bail posting fees.
14911. Notice of failure to appear or failure to pay fine; lien on vehicles; collection.

§ 14910. Collection; remittance; bail posting fees

(a) The department shall, with the consent of the applicant, collect the amounts which it has been notified are due pursuant to Sections 40509 and 40509.5, and any service fees added to those amounts, at the time it collects from the applicant any fees and penalties required to issue or renew a driver's license or identification card.

(b) Except as provided in subdivision (c), the department shall remit all amounts collected pursuant to subdivision (a), after deducting the administrative fee authorized in subdivision (c), to each jurisdiction in the amounts due to each jurisdiction according to its notices filed with the department. Within 45 days from the time payment is received by the department, the department shall inform each jurisdiction which of its notices of failure to appear or failure to pay have been discharged.

(c) The department shall assess a fee for posting the bail on each notice of failure to appear or failure to pay

which is given to the department pursuant to Section 40509 or 40509.5, in an amount, as determined by the department, that is sufficient to provide a sum equal to its actual costs of administering this section, not to exceed one dollar ($1) per notice. The fees shall be assessed to each jurisdiction on a regular basis by deducting the amount due to the department pursuant to this subdivision from the bails and fines collected pursuant to subdivision (a), prior to remitting the balance to each jurisdiction pursuant to subdivision (b).

(d) Except as provided in subdivision (e) of Section 13364, if bail is collected under this section for the violation of any provisions of this code, the person shall be deemed to be convicted of those sections violated.

(e) Any amounts collected by the department under this section are nonrefundable by the department.

(f) Notwithstanding Section 42003, payment of bail to the department in accordance with this section shall be paid in full and not in installments. *(Added by Stats.1991, c. 13 (A.B.37), § 49, eff. Feb. 13, 1991, operative July 1, 1992. Amended by Stats.1998, c. 877 (A.B.2132), § 61.)*

§ 14911. Notice of failure to appear or failure to pay fine; lien on vehicles; collection

(a) When a notice of failure to appear or failure to pay a fine is recorded on the department records pursuant to Sections 40509 and 40509.5, the fine and any penalty assessments shall be a lien upon all vehicles of the defendant of a type subject to registration under this code.

(b) For every lien arising pursuant to subdivision (a) which is due and not paid, the department may collect the amount of the lien plus costs, and Article 6 (commencing with Section 9800) of Chapter 6 of Division 3.5 shall apply. *(Added by Stats.1992, c. 1199 (A.B.2409), § 12, eff. Sept. 30, 1992.)*

CHAPTER 6. DRIVER LICENSE COMPACT

Article	Section
1. Generally	15000
2. Compact Terms	15020

Cross References

Conviction outside state, suspension or revocation of driver's license, see Vehicle Code § 13363.

ARTICLE 1. GENERALLY

Section
15000. Compact enacted.
15001. Licensing authority.
15002. Expenses of administrator.
15003. Executive head.

§ 15000. Compact enacted

The Driver License Compact is hereby enacted into law and entered into with all other jurisdictions legally joining therein in the form substantially contained in Article 2 (commencing with Section 15020), of Chapter 6, Division 6 of this code. *(Added by Stats.1963, c. 237, p. 981, § 10.)*

§ 15001.   Licensing authority

As used in the compact, the term "licensing authority" with reference to this State shall mean the Department of Motor Vehicles. That department shall furnish to the appropriate authorities of any other party state any information or documents reasonably necessary to facilitate the administration of Sections 15022, 15023, and 15024 of the compact. *(Added by Stats.1963, c. 237, p. 981, § 10.)*

§ 15002.   Expenses of administrator

The compact administrator provided for in Section 15026 of this compact shall not be entitled to any additional compensation on account of his service as such administrator, but shall be entitled to expenses incurred in connection with his duties and responsibilities as such administrator, in the same manner as for expenses incurred in connection with any other duties or responsibilities of his office or employment. *(Added by Stats. 1963, c. 237, p. 981, § 10. Amended by Stats.1972, c. 618, p. 1149, § 143.)*

§ 15003.   Executive head

As used in the compact, with reference to this State, the term "executive head" shall mean the Governor. *(Added by Stats.1963, c. 237, p. 981, § 10.)*

ARTICLE 2.   COMPACT TERMS

Section
15020.   Findings and policy statement.
15021.   Compact definitions.
15022.   Reports of convictions.
15023.   Effect of conviction in party state.
15024.   Grounds requiring refusal to issue license.
15025.   Application of other state laws.
15026.   Administrator of compact.
15027.   Compact as law; withdrawal procedure.
15028.   Construction and validity; severability.

§ 15020.   Findings and policy statement

(a) The party states find that:

(1) The safety of their streets and highways is materially affected by the degree of compliance with state laws and local ordinances relating to the operation of motor vehicles.

(2) Violation of such a law or ordinance is evidence that the violator engages in conduct which is likely to endanger the safety of persons and property.

(3) The continuance in force of a license to drive is predicated upon compliance with laws and ordinances relating to the operation of motor vehicles, in whichever jurisdiction the vehicle is operated.

(b) It is the policy of the party states to:

528

(1) Promote compliance with the laws, ordinances and administrative rules and regulations relating to the operation of motor vehicles by their drivers in each of the jurisdictions where such drivers operate motor vehicles.

(2) Make the reciprocal recognition of licenses to drive and eligibility therefor more just and equitable by considering the overall compliance with motor vehicle laws, ordinances and administrative rules and regulations as a condition precedent to the continuance or issuance of any license by reason of which the licensee is authorized or permitted to operate a motor vehicle in any of the party states. *(Added by Stats.1963, c. 237, p. 981, § 10.)*

§ 15021.   Compact definitions

As used in the compact:

(a) "State" means a state, territory or possession of the United States, the District of Columbia, or the Commonwealth of Puerto Rico.

(b) "Home state" means the state which has issued and has the power to suspend or revoke the use of the license or permit to operate a motor vehicle.

(c) "Conviction" means a conviction of any offense related to the use or operation of a motor vehicle which is prohibited by state law, municipal ordinance or administrative rule or regulation, or a forfeiture of bail, bond or other security deposited to secure appearance by a person charged with having committed any such offense, and which conviction or forfeiture is required to be reported to the licensing authority. *(Added by Stats.1963, c. 237, p. 982, § 10.)*

§ 15022.   Reports of convictions

The licensing authority of a party state shall report each conviction of a person from another party state occurring within its jurisdiction to the licensing authority of the home state of the licensee. Such report shall clearly identify the person convicted; describe the violation specifying the section of the statute, code, or ordinance violated; identify the court in which action was taken; indicate whether a plea of guilty or not guilty was entered, or the conviction was a result of the forfeiture of bail, bond or other security; and shall include any special findings made in connection therewith. *(Added by Stats. 1963, c. 237, p. 982, § 10.)*

§ 15023.   Effect of conviction in party state

(a) The licensing authority in the home state, for the purposes of suspending, revoking, or limiting the license to operate a motor vehicle, shall give the same effect to the conduct reported, pursuant to Section 15022 of this compact, as it would if such conduct had occurred in the home state, in the case of a conviction for:

(1) Manslaughter or negligent homicide resulting from the operation of a motor vehicle;

(2) Driving a motor vehicle while under the influence of intoxicating liquor or a narcotic drug, or under the influence of any other drug to a degree which renders the driver incapable of safely driving a motor vehicle;

(3) Any felony in the commission of which a motor vehicle is used;

(4) Failure to stop and render aid in the event of a motor vehicle accident resulting in the death or personal injury of another.

(b) As to any other conviction, reported pursuant to Section 15022, the licensing authority in the home state shall give such effect to the conduct as is provided by the laws of the home state.

(c) If the laws of a party state do not provide for offenses or violations denominated or described in precisely the words employed in subdivision (a) of this section, such party state shall construe the denominations and descriptions appearing in subdivision (a) hereof as being applicable to and identifying those offenses or violations of a substantially similar nature, and the laws of such party state shall contain such provisions as may be necessary to ensure that full force and effect is given to this section. *(Added by Stats.1963, c. 237, p. 982, § 10.)*

Cross References

Intoxicating liquor, defined, see Vehicle Code § 109.
Revocation or suspension of driver's license,
  Generally, see Vehicle Code § 13100 et seq.
  Conviction in foreign jurisdiction, see Vehicle Code § 13363.

§ 15024. Grounds requiring refusal to issue license

Upon application for a license to drive, the licensing authority in a party state shall ascertain whether the applicant has ever held, or is the holder of a license to drive issued by any other party state. The licensing authority in the state where application is made shall not issue a license to drive to the applicant if:

(1) The applicant has held such a license, but the license has been suspended by reason, in whole or in part, of a violation, and if such suspension period has not terminated.

(2) The applicant has held such a license, but the license has been revoked by reason, in whole or in part, of a violation, and if such revocation has not terminated; except that after the expiration of one year from the date the license was revoked, such person may make application for a new license if permitted by law. The licensing authority may refuse to issue a license to any such applicant if, after investigation, the licensing authority determines that it will not be safe to grant to such person the privilege of driving a motor vehicle on the public highways.

(3) The applicant is the holder of a license to drive issued by another party state and currently in force, unless the applicant surrenders such license. *(Added by Stats.1963, c. 237, p. 983, § 10.)*

Cross References

Grounds requiring denial of license, see Vehicle Code § 12805 et seq.

§ 15025. Application of other state laws

Except as expressly required by provisions of this compact, nothing contained herein shall be construed to affect the right of any party state to apply any of its other laws relating to licenses to drive to any person or circumstance, nor to invalidate or prevent any driver license agreement or other co-operative arrangement between a party state and a nonparty state. *(Added by Stats.1963, c. 237, p. 983, § 10.)*

§ 15026. Administrator of compact

(a) The head of the licensing authority of each party state shall be the administrator of this compact for his state. The administrators of all party states, acting jointly, shall have the power to formulate all necessary and proper procedures for the exchange of information under this compact.

(b) The administrator of each party state shall furnish to the administrator of each other party state any information or documents reasonably necessary to facilitate the administration of this compact. *(Added by Stats.1963, c. 237, p. 983, § 10.)*

§ 15027. Compact as law; withdrawal procedure

(a) This compact shall become effective as to any state in which this compact becomes effective as the law of that state.

(b) Any party state may withdraw from this compact by enacting a statute repealing this compact as the law of that state, but no such withdrawal shall take effect until six months after the executive head of the withdrawing state has given notice of the withdrawal to the executive heads of all other party states. No withdrawal shall affect the validity or applicability by the licensing authorities of states remaining party to the compact of any report of conviction occurring prior to the withdrawal. *(Added by Stats.1963, c. 237, p. 984, § 10.)*

§ 15028. Construction and validity; severability

The compact shall be liberally construed so as to effectuate the purposes thereof. The provisions of the compact shall be severable and if any phrase, clause, sentence, or provisions of the compact is declared to be contrary to the constitution of any party state or of the United States or the applicability thereof to any government, agency, person or circumstance is held invalid, the validity of the remainder of the compact and the applicability thereof to any government, agency, person or circumstance shall not be affected thereby. If the compact shall be held contrary to the constitution of any state party thereto, the compact shall remain in full force and effect as to the remaining states and in full force and effect as to the state affected as to all severable matters. *(Added by Stats.1963, c. 237, p. 984, § 10.)*

CHAPTER 7. COMMERCIAL MOTOR VEHICLE SAFETY PROGRAM

Article	Section
1. Intent	15200
2. Definitions	15210
3. Driver Notification Requirements	15215

Article	Section
4. Employer Responsibilities	15240
5. Commercial Driver's License	15250
6. Endorsements	15275
7. Sanctions	15300

ARTICLE 1. INTENT

Section
15200. Legislative intent; liberal construction; conflict with general provisions; fee support.

§ 15200. Legislative intent; liberal construction; conflict with general provisions; fee support

It is the intent of the Legislature, in enacting this chapter, to adopt those standards required of drivers by the Federal Motor Carrier Safety Administration of the United States Department of Transportation, as set forth in the federal Motor Carrier Safety Improvement Act of 1999 (Public Law 106–159)[1] and to reduce or prevent commercial motor vehicle accidents, fatalities, and injuries by permitting drivers to hold only one license, disqualifying drivers for certain criminal offenses and serious traffic violations, and strengthening licensing and testing standards. This act is a remedial law and shall be liberally construed to promote the public health, safety and welfare. To the extent that this chapter conflicts with general driver licensing provisions, this chapter shall prevail. Where this chapter is silent, the general driver licensing provisions shall apply. It is the further intent of the Legislature that this program be fee supported, and that the department fully recoup its costs within four years of the program's enactment. *(Added by Stats.1988, c. 1509, § 9. Amended by Stats.2010, c. 216 (A.B.2144), § 3.)*

[1] Public law sections classified to U.S.C.A., see U.S.C.A. Tables.

ARTICLE 2. DEFINITIONS

Section
15210. Definitions applicable to chapter.

§ 15210. Definitions applicable to chapter

Notwithstanding any other provision of this code, as used in this chapter, the following terms have the following meanings:

(a) "Commercial driver's license" means a driver's license issued by a state or other jurisdiction, in accordance with the standards contained in Part 383 of Title 49 of the Code of Federal Regulations, which authorizes the licenseholder to operate a class or type of commercial motor vehicle.

(b)(1) "Commercial motor vehicle" means any vehicle or combination of vehicles that requires a class A or class B license, or a class C license with an endorsement issued pursuant to paragraph (2), (3), (4), or (5) of subdivision (a) of Section 15278.

(2) "Commercial motor vehicle" does not include any of the following:

(A) A recreational vehicle, as defined in Section 18010 of the Health and Safety Code.

(B) An implement of husbandry operated by a person who is not required to obtain a driver's license under this code.

(C) Vehicles operated by persons exempted pursuant to Section 25163 of the Health and Safety Code or a vehicle operated in an emergency situation at the direction of a peace officer pursuant to Section 2800.

(c) "Controlled substance" has the same meaning as defined by the federal Controlled Substances Act (21 U.S.C. Sec. 802).

(d) "Conviction" means an unvacated adjudication of guilt, or a determination that a person has violated or failed to comply with the law in a court of original jurisdiction or by an authorized administrative tribunal, an unvacated forfeiture of bail or collateral deposited to secure the person's appearance in court, a plea of guilty or nolo contendere accepted by the court, the payment of a fine or court costs, or violation of a condition of release without bail, regardless of whether or not the penalty is rebated, suspended, or probated.

(e) "Disqualification" means a prohibition against driving a commercial motor vehicle.

(f) "Driving a commercial vehicle under the influence" means committing any one or more of the following unlawful acts in a commercial motor vehicle:

(1) Driving a commercial motor vehicle while the operator's blood-alcohol concentration level is 0.04 percent or more, by weight in violation of subdivision (d) of Section 23152.

(2) Driving under the influence of alcohol, as prescribed in subdivision (a) or (b) of Section 23152.

(3) Refusal to undergo testing as required under this code in the enforcement of Subpart D of Part 383 or Subpart A of Part 392 of Title 49 of the Code of Federal Regulations.

(g) "Employer" means any person, including the United States, a state, or political subdivision of a state, who owns or leases a commercial motor vehicle or assigns drivers to operate that vehicle. A person who employs himself or herself as a commercial vehicle driver is considered to be both an employer and a driver for purposes of this chapter.

(h) "Fatality" means the death of a person as a result of a motor vehicle accident.

(i) "Felony" means an offense under state or federal law that is punishable by death or imprisonment for a term exceeding one year.

(j) "Gross combination weight rating" means the value specified by the manufacturer as the maximum loaded weight of a combination or articulated vehicle. In the absence of a value specified by the manufacturer, gross vehicle weight rating will be determined by adding the gross vehicle weight rating of the power unit and the total weight of the towed units and any load thereon.

(k) "Gross vehicle weight rating" means the value specified by the manufacturer as the maximum loaded weight of a single vehicle, as defined in Section 390.

(*l*) "Imminent hazard" means the existence of a condition that presents a substantial likelihood that death, serious illness, severe personal injury, or substantial endangerment to health, property, or the environment may occur before the reasonable foreseeable completion date of a formal proceeding begun to lessen the risk of death, illness, injury, or endangerment.

(m) "Noncommercial motor vehicle" means a motor vehicle or combination of motor vehicles that is not included within the definition in subdivision (b).

(n) "Nonresident commercial driver's license" means a commercial driver's license issued to an individual by a state under one of the following provisions:

(1) The individual is domiciled in a foreign country.

(2) The individual is domiciled in another state.

(*o*) "Schoolbus" is a commercial motor vehicle, as defined in Section 545.

(p) "Serious traffic violation" includes any of the following:

(1) Excessive speeding, as defined pursuant to the federal Commercial Motor Vehicle Safety Act (P.L. 99–570) involving any single offense for any speed of 15 miles an hour or more above the posted speed limit.

(2) Reckless driving, as defined pursuant to the federal Commercial Motor Vehicle Safety Act (P.L. 99–570), and driving in the manner described under Section 2800.1, 2800.2, or 2800.3, including, but not limited to, the offense of driving a commercial motor vehicle in willful or wanton disregard for the safety of persons or property.

(3) A violation of a state or local law involving the safe operation of a motor vehicle, arising in connection with a fatal traffic accident.

(4) A similar violation of a state or local law involving the safe operation of a motor vehicle, as defined pursuant to the Commercial Motor Vehicle Safety Act (Title XII of P.L. 99–570).

(5) Driving a commercial motor vehicle without a commercial driver's license.

(6) Driving a commercial motor vehicle without the driver having in his or her possession a commercial driver's license, unless the driver provides proof at the subsequent court appearance that he or she held a valid commercial driver's license on the date of the violation.

(7) Driving a commercial motor vehicle when the driver has not met the minimum testing standards for that vehicle as to the class or type of cargo the vehicle is carrying.

(8) Driving a commercial motor vehicle while using an electronic wireless communication device to write, send, or read a text-based communication, as defined in Section 23123.5.

In the absence of a federal definition, existing definitions under this code shall apply.

(q) "State" means a state of the United States or the District of Columbia.

(r) "Tank vehicle" means a commercial motor vehicle that is designed to transport any liquid or gaseous material within a tank or tanks having an individual rated capacity of more than 119 gallons and an aggregate rated capacity of at least 1,000 gallons that is permanently or temporarily attached to the vehicle or the chassis, including, but not limited to, cargo tanks and portable tanks, as defined in Part 171 of Title 49 of the Code of Federal Regulations. * * * A commercial motor vehicle transporting an empty storage container tank not designed for transportation, with a rated capacity of at least 1,000 gallons that is temporarily attached to a flatbed trailer, is not a tank vehicle. *(Added by Stats.1988, c. 1509, § 9. Amended by Stats.1990, c. 1360 (S.B.1510), § 43; Stats. 2001, c. 504 (A.B.1280), § 1; Stats.2003, c. 222 (A.B. 1662), § 2; Stats.2003, c. 594 (S.B.315), § 38; Stats.2004, c. 952 (A.B.3049), § 14, operative Sept. 20, 2005; Stats. 2006, c. 574 (A.B.2520), § 12; Stats.2007, c. 630 (A.B. 1728), § 7; Stats.2012, c. 670 (A.B.2188), § 8; Stats.2013, c. 649 (A.B.1047), § 3.)*

Cross References

Employee meal periods, exception for commercial drivers operating vehicle described in this section and meeting specified conditions, see Labor Code § 512.

ARTICLE 3. DRIVER NOTIFICATION REQUIREMENTS

Section
15215. Conviction in this state of persons holding commercial licenses from other states; report to other state.
15220. Convictions in other states; notice to department.
15222. Convictions; notice to employer.
15224. Suspension, revocation, cancellation of license; disqualification from driving; notice to employer.
15226. Out-of-service orders; notice to employer.
15228. Out-of-service orders; report to employers.
15230. Applications for employment; information.

§ 15215. Conviction in this state of persons holding commercial licenses from other states; report to other state

(a) The department shall report each conviction of a person who holds a commercial driver's licence [1] from another state occurring within this state to the licensing authority of the home state of the licencee.[1] This report shall clearly identify the person convicted; violation date; describe the violation specifying the section of the statute, code, or ordinance violated; identify the court in which action was taken; indicate whether a plea of guilty or not guilty was entered, or the conviction was a result of the forfeiture of bail, bond, or other security; and include special findings made in connection with the conviction.

(b) For the purposes of subdivision (a), "conviction" has the same meaning as defined in subdivision (d) of Section 15210. *(Added by Stats.2006, c. 574 (A.B.2520), § 13.)*

¹ So in enrolled bill.

§ 15220. Convictions in other states; notice to department

Any driver of a commercial motor vehicle who has a driver's license issued by the department, and who is convicted of any offense involving the safe operation of a motor vehicle in any other state, shall notify the department, in the manner provided by the department, of the conviction within 30 days of the date of conviction. *(Added by Stats.1988, c. 1509, § 9.)*

§ 15222. Convictions; notice to employer

Any driver of a commercial motor vehicle, who has a driver's license issued by the department, and who is convicted of any offense involving the safe operation of a motor vehicle, shall notify his or her employer of the conviction, within 30 days of the date of conviction. *(Added by Stats.1988, c. 1509, § 9.)*

§ 15224. Suspension, revocation, cancellation of license; disqualification from driving; notice to employer

Any driver who has a driver's license or privilege suspended, revoked, or canceled by any state for any period, or who is disqualified from driving a commercial motor vehicle for any period, shall notify his or her employer of the suspension, revocation, cancellation, or disqualification, before the end of the business day following the action. *(Added by Stats.1988, c. 1509, § 9.)*

§ 15226. Out-of-service orders; notice to employer

Any driver who is issued an out-of-service order under the federal Motor Carrier Safety Regulations of the United States Department of Transportation (49 C.F.R. 392.5) shall report the issuance to his or her employer within 24 hours. *(Added by Stats.1988, c. 1509, § 9.)*

§ 15228. Out-of-service orders; report to employers

The driver shall also report the issuance of an out-of-service order described in Section 15226 to the department in the manner provided by the department within 30 days unless the driver requests a review of the order by the United States Department of Transportation. If so, the driver shall report the order to the department within 30 days of an affirmation of the order. *(Added by Stats.1988, c. 1509, § 9.)*

§ 15230. Applications for employment; information

Each person who applies for employment as a driver of a commercial motor vehicle shall provide the employer, at the time of the application, with the following information for the 10 years preceding the date of application:

(a) A list of the names and addresses of the applicant's previous employers for which the applicant was a driver of a commercial motor vehicle.

(b) The dates the applicant was employed by each employer.

(c) The reason for leaving that employment.

The applicant shall certify that all information furnished is true and complete. An employer may require an applicant to provide additional information. *(Added by Stats.1988, c. 1509, § 9.)*

ARTICLE 4. EMPLOYER RESPONSIBILITIES

Section
15240. Conditions under which employer prohibited from allowing driver to drive.
15242. Self employment as drivers; requirements; certain other persons engaged by motor carrier; direction and control of motor carrier; definitions.

§ 15240. Conditions under which employer prohibited from allowing driver to drive

No employer shall knowingly allow, permit, require, or authorize a driver to drive a commercial motor vehicle under any of the following conditions:

(a) The driver has a driver's license or privilege suspended, revoked, or canceled by any state or has been disqualified from operating a commercial motor vehicle.

(b) The driver has more than one driver's license.

(c) The driver or the commercial motor vehicle or motor carrier operation is subject to an out-of-service order as described in subdivision (b) of Section 2800.

(d) In violation of any law or regulation pertaining to a railroad-highway grade crossing. *(Added by Stats.1988, c. 1509, § 9. Amended by Stats.2001, c. 504 (A.B.1280), § 2.)*

§ 15242. Self employment as drivers; requirements; certain other persons engaged by motor carrier; direction and control of motor carrier; definitions

(a) A person who is self-employed as a commercial motor vehicle driver shall comply with both the requirements of this chapter pertaining to employers and those pertaining to employees.

(b) Notwithstanding subdivision (a), a motor carrier that engages a person who owns, leases, or otherwise operates not more than one motor vehicle listed in Section 34500 to provide transportation services under the direction and control of that motor carrier is responsible for the compliance of that person with this chapter and for purposes of the regulations adopted by the department pursuant to Section 34501 during the period of that direction and control.

(c) For the purposes of subdivision (b), "direction and control" means either of the following:

(1) The person is operating under the motor carrier's interstate operating authority issued by the United States Department of Transportation.

(2) The person is operating under a subcontract with the motor carrier that requires the person to operate in intrastate commerce and the person has performed transportation services for a minimum of 60 calendar days within the past 90 calendar days for the motor carrier and has been on duty for that carrier for no less than 36 hours within any week in which transportation services were provided.

(d) Subdivision (b) shall not be construed to change the definition of "employer," "employee," or "independent contractor" for any purpose. *(Added by Stats.1988, c. 1509, § 9. Amended by Stats.1990, c. 1360 (S.B.1510), § 44; Stats.2001, c. 298 (S.B.871), § 2; Stats.2002, c. 774 (S.B.2079), § 3, eff. Sept. 21, 2002; Stats.2005, c. 226 (A.B.1048), § 1; Stats.2006, c. 538 (S.B.1852), § 659.)*

Cross References

Compliance with federal drug and alcohol regulations, notification by owner-operators of fulfillment of requirements under terms of this section, punishment for violation, see Vehicle Code § 34520.

Suspension of motor carrier permit of motor carrier of property, grounds, see Vehicle Code § 34623.

ARTICLE 5. COMMERCIAL DRIVER'S LICENSE

Section
15250.   License necessary for operation of vehicle; written and driving tests; employer administration; active duty personnel operating motor vehicles for military purposes exempt from commercial driver's license requirements and sanctions.
15250.3.   Organized camp employees; license requirements.
15250.5.   Repealed.
15250.6.   Repealed.
15250.7.   Repealed.
15255.   Repealed.
15255.1.   Commercial driver's license; alternate fees.
15255.2.   Duplicate commercial driver's license.
15260.   Restricted licenses; vehicles with air brakes.
15263.   Restricted licenses; vehicles with manual transmissions.
15265.   Repealed.

§ 15250. License necessary for operation of vehicle; written and driving tests; employer administration; active duty personnel operating motor vehicles for military purposes exempt from commercial driver's license requirements and sanctions

(a)(1) A person shall not operate a commercial motor vehicle unless that person has in his or her immediate possession a valid commercial driver's license of the appropriate class.

(2) A person shall not operate a commercial motor vehicle while transporting hazardous materials unless that person has in his or her possession a valid commercial driver's license with a hazardous materials endorsement.

An instruction permit does not authorize the operation of a vehicle transporting hazardous materials.

(b)(1) Before an application for an original or renewal of a commercial driver's license with a hazardous materials endorsement is submitted to the United States Transportation Security Administration for the processing of a security threat assessment, as required under Part 1572 of Title 49 of the Code of Federal Regulations, the department shall complete a check of the applicant's driving record to ensure that the person is not subject to a disqualification under Part 383.51 of Title 49 of the Code of Federal Regulations.

(2)(A) A person shall not be issued a commercial driver's license until he or she has passed a written and driving test for the operation of a commercial motor vehicle that complies with the minimum federal standards established by the federal Commercial Motor Vehicle Safety Act of 1986 (Public Law 99–570) and Part 383 of Title 49 of the Code of Federal Regulations, and has satisfied all other requirements of that act as well as any other requirements imposed by this code.

(B) The driving skills test as specified in Section 383.113 of Title 49 of the Code of Federal Regulations may be waived for a commercial motor vehicle driver with military commercial motor vehicle experience who is currently licensed with the United States Armed Forces at the time of his or her application for a commercial driver's license, and whose driving record in combination with his or her driving experience meets, at a minimum, the conditions required by Section 383.77(a) and (b) of Title 49 of the Code of Federal Regulations.

(c) The tests shall be prescribed and conducted by or under the direction of the department. The department may allow a third-party tester to administer the driving test part of the examination required under this section and Section 15275 if all of the following conditions are met:

(1) The tests given by the third party are the same as those that would otherwise be given by the department.

(2) The third party has an agreement with the department that includes, but is not limited to, the following provisions:

(A) Authorization for the United States Secretary of Transportation, or his or her representative, and the department, or its representative, to conduct random examinations, inspections, and audits without prior notice.

(B) Permission for the department, or its representative, to conduct onsite inspections at least annually.

(C) A requirement that all third-party testers meet the same qualification and training standards as the department's examiners, to the extent necessary to conduct the driving skill tests in compliance with the requirements of Part 383 of Title 49 of the Code of Federal Regulations.

(D) The department may cancel, suspend, or revoke the agreement with a third-party tester if the third-party tester fails to comply with the standards for the commercial driver's license testing program, or with any other term of the third-party agreement, upon 15 days' prior written notice of the action to cancel, suspend, or revoke the agreement by the department to the third party. Any action to appeal or review any order of the department canceling, suspending, or revoking a third-party testing agreement shall be brought in a court of competent jurisdiction under Section 1085 of the Code of Civil Procedure, or as otherwise permitted by the laws of this state. The action shall be commenced within 90 days from the effective date of the order.

(E) Any third-party tester whose agreement has been canceled pursuant to subparagraph (D) may immediately apply for a third-party testing agreement.

(F) A suspension of a third-party testing agreement pursuant to subparagraph (D) shall be for a term of less than 12 months as determined by the department. After the period of suspension, the agreement shall be reinstated upon request of the third-party tester.

(G) A revocation of a third-party testing agreement pursuant to subparagraph (D) shall be for a term of not less than one year. A third-party tester may apply for a new third-party testing agreement after the period of revocation and upon submission of proof of correction of the circumstances causing the revocation.

(H) Authorization for the department to charge the third-party tester a fee, as determined by the department, that is sufficient to defray the actual costs incurred by the department for administering and evaluating the third-party testing program, and for carrying out any other activities deemed necessary by the department to ensure sufficient training for the drivers participating in the program.

(3) Except as provided in Section 15250.3, the tests given by the third party shall not be accepted in lieu of tests prescribed and conducted by the department for applicants for a passenger vehicle endorsement specified in paragraph (2) of subdivision (a) of Section 15278, if the applicant operates or will operate a tour bus.

(d) Commercial driver's license applicants who take and pass driving tests administered by a third party shall provide the department with certificates of driving skill satisfactory to the department that the applicant has successfully passed the driving tests administered by the third party.

(e) If a driving test is administered to a commercial driver's license applicant who is to be licensed in another state pursuant to Section 383.79 of Subpart E of Part 383 of Title 49 of the Code of Federal Regulations, the department may impose a fee on the applicant that does not exceed the reasonable cost of conducting the tests and reporting the results to the driver's state of record.

(f) Implementation dates for the issuance of a commercial driver's license pursuant to this chapter may be established by the department as it determines is necessary to accomplish an orderly commercial driver's license program.

(g) Active duty members of the United States Armed Forces, members of the military reserves, members of the National Guard who are on active duty, including personnel on full-time National Guard duty, personnel on part-time National Guard training, and National Guard military technicians (civilians who are required to wear military uniforms), and active duty personnel of the United States Coast Guard are exempt from all commercial driver's license requirements and sanctions, as provided in Section 383.3(c) of Subpart A of Part 383 of Title 49 of the Code of Federal Regulations when operating motor vehicles for military purposes. This exception shall not apply to United States Armed Forces reserve technicians. *(Added by Stats.1988, c. 1509, § 9. Amended by Stats.1990, c. 1360 (S.B.1510), § 45; Stats.1992, c. 208 (A.B.2332), § 1; Stats.1998, c. 828 (S.B.1637), § 16; Stats.2004, c. 801 (A.B.2040), § 2; Stats.2005, c. 22 (S.B.1108), § 200; Stats.2012, c. 406 (A.B.2659), § 3; Stats.2012, c. 670 (A.B.2188), § 9.5; Stats.2013, c. 649 (A.B.1047), § 4.)*

§ 15250.3. Organized camp employees; license requirements

The department may allow any employee of an organized camp, as defined in Section 18897 of the Health and Safety Code, regulated by the Public Utilities Commission pursuant to Chapter 8 (commencing with Section 5351) of Division 2 of the Public Utilities Code to operate a tour bus pursuant to employment by the operator of that organized camp, if that employee satisfies the requirements for a class B license and a passenger vehicle endorsement by passing a test administered by a third party in accordance with subdivisions (c), (d), and (e) of Section 15250. *(Added by Stats.1992, c. 208 (A.B.2332), § 2.)*

§ 15250.5. Repealed by Stats.2001, c. 739 (A.B.1707), § 8

§ 15250.6. Repealed by Stats.2010, c. 360 (A.B.1648), § 5

§ 15250.7. Repealed by Stats.2010, c. 360 (A.B.1648), § 6

§ 15255. Repealed by Stats.2001, c. 739 (A.B.1707), § 9

§ 15255.1. Commercial driver's license; alternate fees

(a) Except as otherwise specified in subdivisions (b) and (c), upon an application for an original commercial driver's license, a fee of sixty-four dollars ($64), and on and after January 1, 2010, a fee of sixty-six dollars ($66), shall be paid to the department for a license that will expire on the fifth birthday of the applicant following the date of the application. A fee of sixty-four dollars ($64), and on and after January 1, 2010, a fee of sixty-six dollars ($66), shall also be paid to the department upon an application to change a license classification or to remove a restriction if the change or removal requires a driving-skill test and the license will expire on the fifth birthday of the applicant following the date of the application.

(b) Upon application for an original commercial driver's license or for the renewal of commercial driver's license by a currently licensed class A or class B, or class A or class B, driver who meets the driver record requirements and all other requirements established by Section 383.77 of Title 49 of the Code of Federal Regulations, a fee of thirty-four dollars ($34), and on and after January 1, 2010, a fee of thirty-nine dollars ($39), shall be paid to the department for a license that will expire on the fifth birthday of the applicant following the date of the application.

(c) Upon application for an original class C commercial driver's license or for the renewal of a class C commercial driver's license which requires an endorsement as provided in Section 15278, a fee of thirty-four dollars ($34), and on and after January 1, 2010, a fee of thirty-nine dollars ($39), shall be paid to the department for a license that will expire on the fifth birthday of the applicant following the date of the application.

(d) Following failure in taking a driving-skill test, a fee of thirty dollars ($30) shall be paid to the department for each subsequent administration of the driving-skill test required by the application. *(Added by Stats.1991, c. 217 (S.B.184), § 10. Amended by Stats.1993, c. 272 (A.B.301), § 37, eff. Aug. 2, 1993; Stats.1996, c. 1043 (A.B.2352), § 15; Stats.2009–2010, 4th Ex.Sess., c. 10 (A.B.10), § 16, eff. July 28, 2009.)*

§ 15255.2. Duplicate commercial driver's license

Upon application for a duplicate commercial driver's license by a currently licensed class A or class B driver, or a class C commercial driver's license which requires an endorsement as provided in Section 15278, from an applicant who meets the driver record requirements and all other requirements established by Section 383.77 of Title 49 of the Code of Federal Regulations, a fee of twenty-seven dollars ($27), on and after January 1, 2010, a fee of twenty-nine dollars ($29), shall be paid to the department. *(Added by Stats.1996, c. 1043 (A.B.2352), § 16. Amended by Stats.2009–2010, 4th Ex.Sess., c. 10 (A.B.10), § 17, eff. July 28, 2009.)*

§ 15260. Restricted licenses; vehicles with air brakes

(a) Any applicant for a commercial driver's license who does not successfully complete the air-brake component of the knowledge test, or who does not successfully complete the driving-skill test in a vehicle or combination of vehicles equipped with air brakes, shall, if otherwise qualified, receive a commercial driver's license that restricts the licenseholder from operating a commercial motor vehicle equipped with air brakes.

(b) To remove the restriction described in subdivision (a) from a commercial driver's license, the driver is required to make a new application for a commercial driver's license, and, in addition to any other require-

ments specified in this code, to successfully complete the air-brake component of the knowledge test prescribed by the department, and to pass the driver-skill test in a vehicle or combination of vehicles equipped with air brakes.

(c) For the purposes of the driving-skill test and the restriction described in this section, air brakes shall include any braking system operating fully or partially on the air-brake principle. *(Added by Stats.1988, c. 1509, § 9.)*

§ 15263. Restricted licenses; vehicles with manual transmissions

(a) Any applicant for a commercial driver's license who successfully completes the driving-skill test in a vehicle or combination of vehicles equipped with an automatic transmission, shall, if otherwise qualified, receive a commercial driver's license that restricts the licenseholder from operating a commercial motor vehicle or combination of vehicles equipped with a manual transmission.

(b) To remove the restriction described in subdivision (a) from a commercial driver's license, the driver is required to make a new application for a commercial driver's license, and, in addition to any other requirements specified in this code, successfully complete the driving-skill test in a vehicle or combination of vehicles equipped with a manual transmission. *(Added by Stats. 1988, c. 1509, § 9.)*

§ 15265. Repealed by Stats.1990, c. 62 (A.B.264), § 2, eff. May 1, 1990, operative July 1, 1990

ARTICLE 6.   ENDORSEMENTS

Section
15275.   Endorsement necessary for operation of vehicles; examinations; denial, suspension, or revocation of endorsements; application of article.
15275.1.   Schoolbus endorsement.
15278.   Vehicles for which endorsement required.

Cross References

Requirements for drivers of 15–passenger vans for students,
  Community colleges and state university, see Public Contract Code § 10326.1.
  School districts and private schools, see Education Code § 39800.5.

§ 15275. Endorsement necessary for operation of vehicles; examinations; denial, suspension, or revocation of endorsements; application of article

(a) A person may not operate a commercial motor vehicle described in this chapter unless that person has in his or her possession a valid commercial driver's license for the appropriate class, and an endorsement issued by the department to permit the operation of the vehicle unless exempt from the requirement to obtain an endorsement pursuant to subdivision (b) of Section 15278.

(b)(1) An endorsement to drive vehicles specified in this article shall be issued only to applicants who are qualified by examinations prescribed by the department and who meet the minimum standards established in Part 383 of Title 49 of the Code of Federal Regulations.

(2) A hazardous materials endorsement shall be issued only to applicants who comply with paragraph (1) and the requirements set forth in Part 1572 of Title 49 of the Code of Federal Regulations.

(c) The department may deny, suspend, revoke, or cancel an endorsement to drive vehicles specified in this article when the applicant does not meet the qualifications for the issuance or retention of the endorsement.

(d) If the department denies, suspends, revokes, or cancels a hazardous materials endorsement because the department received notification that the applicant poses a security threat pursuant to Part 1572 of Title 49 of the Code of Federal Regulations, and, upon appeal by the United States Transportation Security Administration, that endorsement is ordered reinstated, the department shall issue or restore the hazardous materials endorsement to the applicant within the period specified under those federal regulations. *(Added by Stats.1988, c. 1509, § 9. Amended by Stats.1990, c. 1360 (S.B.1510), § 46.5; Stats.1993, c. 272 (A.B.301), § 38, eff. Aug. 2, 1993; Stats.1999, c. 224 (A.B.787), § 1; Stats.2004, c. 801 (A.B.2040), § 3; Stats.2005, c. 22 (S.B.1108), § 201.)*

§ 15275.1. Schoolbus endorsement

(a) Except as provided in subdivision (b), a schoolbus endorsement is valid only when the operator possesses or qualifies for a valid commercial driver's license with a passenger endorsement and possesses a schoolbus driver's certificate issued pursuant to Section 12517.

(b) A schoolbus endorsement is valid without a schoolbus driver's certificate for an operator who is employed as a mechanic or a schoolbus driver-trainee if the schoolbus endorsement is restricted to operating a schoolbus when there is no pupil being transported. *(Added by Stats. 2004, c. 952 (A.B.3049), § 15, operative Sept. 20, 2005. Amended by Stats.2005, c. 199 (A.B.1748), § 4.)*

§ 15278. Vehicles for which endorsement required

(a) A driver is required to obtain an endorsement issued by the department to operate any commercial motor vehicle that is any of the following:

(1) A double trailer.

(2) A passenger transportation vehicle, which includes, but is not limited to, a bus, farm labor vehicle, or general public paratransit vehicle when designed, used, or maintained to carry more than 10 persons including the driver.

(3) A schoolbus.

(4) A tank vehicle.

(5) A vehicle carrying hazardous materials, as defined in Section 353, that is required to display placards pursuant to Section 27903, unless the driver is exempt from the endorsement requirement as provided in subdi-

vision (b). This paragraph does not apply to any person operating an implement of husbandry who is not required to obtain a driver's license under this code.

(b) This section does not apply to any person operating a vehicle in an emergency situation at the direction of a peace officer pursuant to Section 2800.

(Added by Stats.1988, c. 1509, § 9. Amended by Stats.1990, c. 1360 (S.B.1510), § 47; Stats.1996, c. 183 (S.B.1595), § 1; Stats.1999, c. 224 (A.B.787), § 2; Stats. 2002, c. 758 (A.B.3024), § 14; Stats.2004, c. 952 (A.B. 3049), § 16, operative Sept. 20, 2005; Stats.2010, c. 360 (A.B.1648), § 7.)

ARTICLE 7. SANCTIONS

Section
15300.   First time violations; hazardous material violations.
15301.   Suspension of commercial motor vehicle licenses for unlawful transportation of certain dangerous fireworks.
15302.   More than one violation.
15304.   Felonies involving controlled substances.
15306.   Serious traffic violations occurring within three years of separate offense.
15308.   Serious traffic violations occurring within three years of two or more separate offenses.
15309.   Falsified driver's license applications.
15309.5.   Selling or using crib sheet or device containing answers to commercial driver's license or permit examination; impersonating applicant; unauthorized assistance during examination; punishment.
15310.   Repealed.
15311.   Out-of-service order violations.
15311.1.   Allowing or requiring employee to violate out-of-service order.
15312.   Drivers; duration of prohibition against operation of commercial motor vehicle.
15312.1.   Allowing or requiring employee to violate railroad crossing laws.
15315.   Issuance of license during period of prohibition or suspension of license; surrender of out-of-state licenses.
15319.   Agreements to carry out chapter.
15320.   Record of conviction.
15325.   Imminent hazards; disqualification.
15326.   Suspension, revocation, or disqualification based upon specified violations.

§ 15300. First time violations; hazardous material violations

(a) A driver shall not operate a commercial motor vehicle for a period of one year if the driver is convicted of a first violation of any of the following:

(1) Subdivision (a), (b), or (c) of Section 23152 while operating a motor vehicle.

(2) Subdivision (d) of Section 23152.

(3) Subdivision (a) or (b) of Section 23153 while operating a motor vehicle.

(4) Subdivision (d) of Section 23153.

(5) Leaving the scene of an accident involving a motor vehicle operated by the driver.

(6) Using a motor vehicle to commit a felony, other than a felony described in Section 15304.

(7) Driving a commercial motor vehicle when the driver's commercial driver's license is revoked, suspended, or canceled based on the driver's operation of a commercial motor vehicle or when the driver is disqualified from operating a commercial motor vehicle based on the driver's operation of a commercial motor vehicle.

(8) Causing a fatality involving conduct defined pursuant to Section 191.5 of the Penal Code or subdivision (c) of Section 192 of the Penal Code.

(9) While operating a motor vehicle, refuses to submit to, or fails to complete, a chemical test or tests in violation of Section 23612.

(10) A violation of Section 2800.1, 2800.2, or 2800.3 that involves a commercial motor vehicle.

(b) If a violation listed in subdivision (a), or a violation listed in paragraph (2) of subdivision (a) of Section 13350 or Section 13352 or 13357, occurred while transporting a hazardous material, the period specified in subdivision (a) shall be three years. *(Added by Stats.1988, c. 1509, § 9. Amended by Stats.1991, c. 13 (A.B.37), § 50, eff. Feb. 13, 1991; Stats.1999, c. 724 (A.B.1650), § 35; Stats. 2001, c. 504 (A.B.1280), § 3; Stats.2004, c. 952 (A.B. 3049), § 17, operative Sept. 20, 2005; Stats.2006, c. 574 (A.B.2520), § 14; Stats.2007, c. 747 (A.B.678), § 28; Stats.2010, c. 216 (A.B.2144), § 4.)*

Cross References

Hazardous material, defined, see Vehicle Code § 353.
Offenses involving alcohol or drugs, see Vehicle Code § 23152 et seq.

§ 15301. Suspension of commercial motor vehicle licenses for unlawful transportation of certain dangerous fireworks

The Department of Motor Vehicles, in conjunction with the State Fire Marshal, shall develop regulations and procedures to temporarily suspend the commercial motor vehicle license of a person who is operating a commercial motor vehicle while transporting dangerous fireworks having a gross weight of 10,000 pounds or more. A driver of a commercial motor vehicle shall not operate a commercial motor vehicle for three years if the driver is convicted of transporting dangerous fireworks having a gross weight of 10,000 pounds or more. *(Added by Stats.2007, c. 563 (S.B.839), § 13.)*

Cross References

State Fire Marshal, development of regulations for suspension of commercial motor vehicle license for transportation of certain dangerous fireworks, see Health and Safety Code § 12703.

§ 15302. More than one violation

A driver shall not operate a commercial motor vehicle for the rest of his or her life if convicted of more than one violation of any of the following:

(a) Subdivision (a), (b), or (c) of Section 23152 while operating a motor vehicle.

(b) Subdivision (d) of Section 23152.

(c) Subdivision (a) or (b) of Section 23153 while operating a motor vehicle.

(d) Subdivision (d) of Section 23153.

(e) Leaving the scene of an accident involving a motor vehicle operated by the driver.

(f) Using a motor vehicle to commit a felony, other than a felony described in Section 15304.

(g) Driving a commercial motor vehicle when the driver's commercial driver's license is revoked, suspended, or canceled based on the driver's operation of a commercial motor vehicle or when the driver is disqualified from operating a commercial motor vehicle based on the driver's operation of a commercial motor vehicle.

(h) Causing a fatality involving conduct defined pursuant to Section 191.5 of the Penal Code or in subdivision (c) of Section 192 of the Penal Code.

(i) While operating a motor vehicle, refuses to submit to, or fails to complete, a chemical test or tests in violation of Section 23612.

(j) A violation of Section 2800.1, 2800.2, or 2800.3 that involves a commercial motor vehicle.

(k) Any combination of the above violations or a violation listed in paragraph (2) of subdivision (a) of Section 13350 or Section 13352 or 13357 that occurred while transporting a hazardous material. *(Added by Stats.1988, c. 1509, § 9. Amended by Stats.1999, c. 724 (A.B.1650), § 35.2; Stats.2001, c. 504 (A.B.1280), § 4; Stats.2002, c. 787 (S.B.1798), § 35; Stats.2002, c. 664 (A.B.3034), § 221; Stats.2004, c. 952 (A.B.3049), § 18, operative Sept. 20, 2005; Stats.2006, c. 574 (A.B.2520), § 15; Stats.2007, c. 747 (A.B.678), § 29; Stats.2010, c. 216 (A.B.2144), § 5.)*

§ 15304. Felonies involving controlled substances

(a) A driver may not operate a commercial motor vehicle for the rest of his or her life who uses a motor vehicle in the commission of a felony involving manufacturing, distributing, or dispensing a controlled substance, or possession with intent to manufacture, distribute, or dispense a controlled substance.

(b) This section shall become operative on September 20, 2005. *(Added by Stats.1988, c. 1509, § 9. Amended by Stats.2004, c. 952 (A.B.3049), § 19, operative Sept. 20, 2005.)*

§ 15306. Serious traffic violations occurring within three years of separate offense

A driver shall not operate a commercial motor vehicle for a period of 60 days if the person is convicted of a serious traffic violation involving a commercial or a noncommercial motor vehicle and the offense occurred within three years of a separate offense of a serious traffic violation that resulted in a conviction.

(Added by Stats.1988, c. 1509, § 9. Amended by Stats.2004, c. 952 (A.B.3049), § 20, operative Sept. 20, 2005; Stats.2010, c. 216 (A.B.2144), § 6.)

Cross References

Speeding constituting serious traffic violation, see Vehicle Code § 22406.

§ 15308. Serious traffic violations occurring within three years of two or more separate offenses

(a) A driver shall not operate a commercial motor vehicle for a period of 120 days if the person is convicted of a serious traffic violation involving a commercial or noncommercial motor vehicle and the offense occurred within three years of two or more separate offenses of serious traffic violations that resulted in convictions.

(b) Notwithstanding Section 13366.5, the time period under subdivision (a) shall not commence until all existing suspensions or revocations of the commercial driving privilege have ended.

(Added by Stats.1988, c. 1509, § 9. Amended by Stats.2004, c. 952 (A.B.3049), § 21, operative Sept. 20, 2005; Stats.2010, c. 216 (A.B.2144), § 7.)

§ 15309. Falsified driver's license applications

In addition to any other action taken under this code, no driver may operate a commercial motor vehicle for a period of 60 days if the department determines, after a hearing, that the person falsified information on his or her application for a driver's license in violation of the standards set forth in subpart J of part 383 or Section 383.71(a) of Title 49 of the Code of Federal Regulations. *(Added by Stats.1999, c. 724 (A.B.1650), § 35.4.)*

§ 15309.5. Selling or using crib sheet or device containing answers to commercial driver's license or permit examination; impersonating applicant; unauthorized assistance during examination; punishment

(a) It is unlawful for any person to do any of the following:

(1) Sell, offer for sale, distribute, or use a crib sheet or cribbing device, as defined in Section 273, that contains answers to any examination administered by the department for a commercial driver's license or permit.

(2) Impersonate or allow the impersonation of an applicant for a commercial driver's license or permit for the purpose of fraudulently qualifying the applicant for a commercial driver's license or permit.

(3) Provide, or use, any unauthorized assistance during any examination administered by the department for a commercial driver's license or permit.

(b) A first conviction under this section is punishable as either an infraction or a misdemeanor, and the driver shall not operate a commercial motor vehicle for a period of one year. A second or subsequent conviction is punishable as a misdemeanor, and the driver shall not operate a commercial motor vehicle for a period of one year. *(Added by Stats.2013, c. 649 (A.B.1047), § 5.)*

§ 15310. Repealed by Stats.1999, c. 1008 (S.B.533), § 11

§ 15311. Out-of-service order violations

(a) A driver shall not operate a commercial motor vehicle for a period of 180 days if the person is convicted of a first violation of an out-of-service order under subdivision (b), (c), or (d) of Section 2800.

(b) A driver shall not operate a commercial motor vehicle for a period of two years if the person is convicted of violating an out-of-service order under subdivision (b), (c), or (d) of Section 2800 while transporting hazardous materials required to be placarded or while operating a vehicle designed to transport 16 or more passengers, including the driver.

(c) A driver shall not operate a commercial motor vehicle for a period of two years if the person is convicted of a second violation of an out-of-service order under subdivision (b), (c), or (d) of Section 2800 during any 10-year period, arising from separate incidents.

(d) A driver shall not operate a commercial motor vehicle for a period of three years if the person is convicted of a second violation of an out-of-service order under subdivision (b), (c), or (d) of Section 2800 while transporting hazardous materials that are required to be placarded or while operating a vehicle designed to transport 16 or more passengers, including the driver.

(e) In addition to the disqualification period required in subdivision (a), (b), (c), or (d), a driver who is convicted of violating an out-of-service order under subdivision (b) of Section 2800 is subject to a civil penalty of not less than two thousand five hundred dollars ($2,500) for a first conviction, and a civil penalty of five thousand dollars ($5,000) for a second or subsequent conviction.

(f) A driver shall not operate a commercial motor vehicle for a period of three years if the person is convicted of a third or subsequent violation of an out-of-service order under subdivision (b), (c), or (d) of Section 2800 during any 10-year period, arising from separate incidents.

(Added by Stats.1999, c. 724 (A.B.1650), § 36. Amended by Stats.2004, c. 952 (A.B.3049), § 22, operative Sept. 20, 2005; Stats.2010, c. 216 (A.B.2144), § 8.)

§ 15311.1. Allowing or requiring employee to violate out-of-service order

An employer that knowingly allows or requires an employee to operate a commercial motor vehicle in violation of an out-of- service order is, upon conviction, subject to a civil penalty of not less than two thousand seven hundred fifty dollars ($2,750) nor more than twenty- five thousand dollars ($25,000).

(Added by Stats.2004, c. 952 (A.B.3049), § 23, operative Sept. 20, 2005. Amended by Stats.2010, c. 216 (A.B.2144), § 9.)

§ 15312. Drivers; duration of prohibition against operation of commercial motor vehicle

A driver may not operate a commercial motor vehicle for the following periods:

(a) Not less than 60 days if that person is convicted of a violation of subdivision (a) of Section 2800, or Section 21462, 22451, or 22452, or subdivision (c) or (d) of Section 22526, involving a commercial motor vehicle and the violation occurred at a railroad-highway crossing.

(b) Not less than 120 days if that person is convicted of a violation of subdivision (a) of Section 2800, or Section 21462, 22451, or 22452, or subdivision (c) or (d) of Section 22526, involving a commercial motor vehicle, and that violation occurred at a railroad-highway crossing, during any three-year period of a separate, prior offense of a railroad-highway grade crossing violation, that resulted in a conviction.

(c) Not less than one year if that person is convicted of a violation of subdivision (a) of Section 2800, or Section 21462, 22451, or 22452, or subdivision (c) or (d) of Section 22526, involving a commercial motor vehicle, and that violation occurred at a railroad-highway crossing, at a railroad-highway grade crossing, during any three-year period of two or more prior offenses of a railroad-highway grade crossing violation, that resulted in convictions. *(Added by Stats.2001, c. 504 (A.B.1280), § 5. Amended by Stats.2004, c. 952 (A.B.3049), § 24, operative Sept. 20, 2005; Stats.2010, c. 216 (A.B.2144), § 10.)*

§ 15312.1. Allowing or requiring employee to violate railroad crossing laws

(a) An employer that knowingly allows or requires an employee to operate a commercial motor vehicle in violation of a federal, state, or local law or regulation pertaining to railroad crossings is, upon conviction, subject to a civil penalty of not more than ten thousand dollars ($10,000).

(b) This section shall become operative on September 20, 2005. *(Added by Stats.2004, c. 952 (A.B.3049), § 25, operative Sept. 20, 2005.)*

§ 15315. Issuance of license during period of prohibition or suspension of license; surrender of out-of-state licenses

(a) The department shall not issue a commercial driver's license to a person during a period in which the person is prohibited from operating a commercial motor vehicle, or the person's driving privilege is suspended, revoked, or canceled.

(b) No commercial driver's license may be issued to a person who has a commercial driver's license issued by any other state unless the person first surrenders the commercial driver's license issued by the other state, which license shall be returned to the issuing state. *(Added by Stats.1988, c. 1509, § 9.)*

§ 15319. Agreements to carry out chapter

The department may execute or make agreements, arrangements, or declarations to carry out this chapter. *(Added by Stats.1988, c. 1509, § 9.)*

§ 15320. Record of conviction

The department shall suspend, revoke, or cancel, the privilege of any person to operate a commercial motor vehicle for the periods specified in this article upon receipt of a duly certified abstract of the record of any court that the person has been convicted of any of the offenses set forth in this article. *(Added by Stats.1999, c. 724 (A.B.1650), § 37.)*

§ 15325. Imminent hazards; disqualification

(a) Pursuant to subpart D of Part 383 of Title 49 of the Code of Federal Regulations, a driver whose driving is determined to constitute an imminent hazard is disqualified from operating a commercial motor vehicle for the period specified by the Federal Motor Carrier Safety Administration.

(b) The disqualification action shall be made part of the driver's record.

(c) A driver who is simultaneously disqualified under this section and any other state law or regulation, shall serve those disqualification periods concurrently.

(d) This section shall become operative on September 20, 2005. *(Added by Stats.2004, c. 952 (A.B.3049), § 26, operative Sept. 20, 2005.)*

§ 15326. Suspension, revocation, or disqualification based upon specified violations

Upon receiving notification of an administrative action or conviction of a commercial licenseholder in a state, territory, or possession of the United States, the District of Columbia, the Commonwealth of Puerto Rico, or the Dominion of Canada, the department shall impose a suspension, revocation, or disqualification action on that person's commercial driving privilege based upon violations that would result in an administrative action or a conviction pursuant to Section 383.51 of Subpart D of Part 383 and Sections 384.206(b)(3), 384.213, and 384.231 of Subpart B of Part 384 of Title 49 of the Federal Code of Regulations. Those violations include, but are not limited to, all of the following:

(a) Violations of Sections 15300, 15302, and 15304.

(b) Serious traffic violations, as defined in subdivision (p) of Section 15210 and subject to the penalties under Section 15306 or 15308.

(c) Providing false information under Section 15309.

(d) Out-of-service order violations under Section 15311.

(e) Railroad-highway crossing violations under Section 15312. *(Added by Stats.2012, c. 670 (A.B.2188), § 10.)*

Division 6.5

MOTOR VEHICLE TRANSACTIONS WITH MINORS

Chapter   Section
1. Driver's License Requirements 15500

CHAPTER 1. DRIVER'S LICENSE REQUIREMENTS

Section
15500. Acquisition of vehicle by minor; drivers' license required.
15501. Unlawful for minor to present false driver's license.

§ 15500. Acquisition of vehicle by minor; drivers' license required

It is unlawful for any minor who does not possess a valid driver's license issued under this code to order, purchase or lease, attempt to purchase or lease, contract to purchase or lease, accept, or otherwise obtain, any vehicle of a type subject to registration. *(Added by Stats.1968, c. 1020, p. 1972, § 1.)*

§ 15501. Unlawful for minor to present false driver's license

It is unlawful for any minor to present or offer to any person offering for sale or lease or to give or otherwise furnish thereto any motor vehicle of a type subject to registration, a driver's license which is false, fraudulent, or not actually his own for the purpose of ordering, purchasing or leasing, attempting to purchase or lease, contracting to purchase or lease, accepting, or otherwise obtaining such a vehicle. *(Added by Stats.1968, c. 1020, p. 1972, § 1.)*

Cross References

Unlawful use of driver's license, see Vehicle Code § 14610.
Violation a misdemeanor, see Vehicle Code § 40000.11.

Division 6.7

UNATTENDED CHILD IN MOTOR VEHICLE SAFETY ACT

Chapter   Section
1. General Provisions 15600
2. Offenses 15620
3. Educational Provisions 15630

CHAPTER 1.   GENERAL PROVISIONS

Section
15600.   Division title.
15602.   Application of division to motor vehicles upon high-
         ways and elsewhere throughout state.
15603.   Purpose of division.

§ 15600.   Division title

This division shall be known and may be cited as "Kaitlyn's Law." *(Added by Stats.2001, c. 855 (S.B.255), § 2.)*

§ 15602.   Application of division to motor vehicles upon highways and elsewhere throughout state

This division applies to motor vehicles upon the highways and elsewhere throughout the state unless expressly provided otherwise. *(Added by Stats.2001, c. 855 (S.B.255), § 2.)*

§ 15603.   Purpose of division

The purpose of this division is to help prevent injuries to, and the death of, young children from the effects of being left alone in a motor vehicle, to help educate parents and caretakers about the dangers of leaving children alone in a motor vehicle, and to authorize a monetary fine to be imposed on a person for leaving a young child alone in a motor vehicle in circumstances that pose a life safety risk. *(Added by Stats.2001, c. 855 (S.B.255), § 2.)*

CHAPTER 2.   OFFENSES

Section
15620.   Leaving a child unsupervised inside a motor vehicle;
         violations and punishment.

§ 15620.   Leaving a child unsupervised inside a motor vehicle; violations and punishment

(a) A parent, legal guardian, or other person responsible for a child who is 6 years of age or younger may not leave that child inside a motor vehicle without being subject to the supervision of a person who is 12 years of age or older, under either of the following circumstances:

(1) Where there are conditions that present a significant risk to the child's health or safety.

(2) When the vehicle's engine is running or the vehicle's keys are in the ignition, or both.

(b) A violation of subdivision (a) is an infraction punishable by a fine of one hundred dollars ($100), except that the court may reduce or waive the fine if the defendant establishes to the satisfaction of the court that he or she is economically disadvantaged and the court, instead, refers the defendant to a community education program that includes education on the dangers of leaving young children unattended in motor vehicles, and provides certification of completion of that program. Upon completion of that program, the defendant shall provide that certification to the court. The court may, at its discretion, require any defendant described in this section to attend an education program on the dangers of leaving young children unattended in motor vehicles.

(c) Nothing in this section shall preclude prosecution under both this section and Section 192 of the Penal Code, or Section 273a of that code, or any other provision of law.

(d)(1) Subdivision (b) and Section 40000.1 do not apply if an unattended child is injured or medical services are rendered on that child because of a violation described in subdivision (a).

(2) Nothing in this subdivision precludes prosecution under any other provision of law. *(Added by Stats.2001, c. 855 (S.B.255), § 2. Amended by Stats.2002, c. 664 (A.B.3034), § 222.)*

CHAPTER 3.   EDUCATIONAL PROVISIONS

Section
15630.   Allocation of fines collected for violation of this
         division.
15632.   Educational materials; included publications.

§ 15630.   Allocation of fines collected for violation of this division

Notwithstanding any other provision of law, the fines collected for a violation of this division shall be allocated by the county treasurer, as follows:

(a)(1) Seventy percent to the county or city health department where the violation occurred, to be used for the development and implementation of community education programs on the dangers of leaving young children unattended in motor vehicles.

(2) A county or city health department may develop and implement the community education program described in paragraph (1) or may contract for the development and implementation of that program.

(3) As the proceeds from fines collected under this division become available, each county or city health department shall prepare and annually update a listing of community education programs that provide information

543

on the dangers of leaving young children unattended in motor vehicles and ways to avoid that danger. The county or city health department shall forward the listing to the courts and shall make the listing available to the public, and may distribute it to other agencies or organizations.

(b) Fifteen percent to the county or city for the administration of the program, from which will be paid the cost of the county to account for and disburse fine revenues.

(c) Fifteen percent to the city, to be deposited in its general fund except that, if the violation occurred in an unincorporated area, this amount shall be deposited in the county's general fund. *(Added by Stats.2001, c. 855 (S.B.255), § 2.)*

§ 15632. Educational materials; included publications

(a) The department shall include information concerning the dangers of leaving children unattended in motor vehicles, including, but not limited to, the effect of solar heat on the temperature of vehicle interiors and the penalties for noncompliance with Chapter 2 (commencing with Section 15620), in the following materials distributed by the department:

(1) The California Driver's Handbook published under subdivision (b) of Section 1656.

(2) The driver's license examination administered under Section 12804.9, by including, on a rotating basis, at least one question in one version of the driver's license examination that is periodically administered to applicants.

(3) Any driver's education materials certified by the department.

(4) Courses and examinations for traffic violator schools.

(5) Materials provided to secondary and post-secondary schools and educational institutions.

(6) Any materials provided to community education campaigns undertaken by the department and other state agencies, including, but not limited to, the Department of the California Highway Patrol and the Department of Transportation.

(b) The department shall not republish materials before existing supplies are exhausted, but shall arrange for compliance with this section in the next edition or publication of those materials in the normal course of business. *(Added by Stats.2001, c. 855 (S.B.255), § 2.)*

Division 7

FINANCIAL RESPONSIBILITY LAWS

Chapter	Section
1. Compulsory Financial Responsibility	16000
2. Suspension Following Unsatisfied Judgments	16250
3. Proof of Financial Responsibility	16430
4. Commercial Vehicles	16500
5. Transporters of Motor Vehicles [Repealed]	
6. Interstate Highway Carriers	16560

CHAPTER 1. COMPULSORY FINANCIAL RESPONSIBILITY

Article	Section
1. Accident Reports	16000
2. Financial Responsibility	16020
3. Evidence of Financial Responsibility	16050
4. Suspensions	16070
5. Suspension of Registration of Motor Vehicles Involved in Accidents [Repealed]	

Cross References

Neighborhood electric vehicle transportation plan, operator compliance with this Chapter, see Streets and Highways Code § 1965.5.

ARTICLE 1. ACCIDENT REPORTS

Section
16000. Report required.
16000.1. Reportable off-highway accident.
16000.7. Uninsured motor vehicle.
16000.8. Failure of driver to prove financial responsibility due to fraudulent acts by insurance agent or broker; termination of suspension actions; conditions.
16001. Driverless runaway vehicle.
16002. Vehicle of employer; vehicle owned or operated by publicly owned or operated transit system.
16003. Driver incapacity.
16004. Mandatory suspension of license; exemption.
16005. Use of reports.

§ 16000. Report required

(a) The driver of a motor vehicle who is in any manner involved in an accident originating from the operation of the motor vehicle on a street or highway, or is involved in a reportable off-highway accident, as defined in Section 16000.1, that has resulted in damage to the property of any one person in excess of seven hundred fifty dollars ($750), or in bodily injury, or in the death of any person shall report the accident, within 10 days after the accident, either personally or through an insurance agent, broker, or legal representative, on a form approved by the department, to the office of the department at Sacramento, subject to this chapter. The driver shall identify on the form, by name and current residence address, if available, any person involved in the accident complaining of bodily injury.

(b) A report is not required under subdivision (a) if the motor vehicle involved in the accident was owned or leased by, or under the direction of, the United States, this state, another state, or a local agency.

(c) If none of the parties involved in an accident has reported the accident to the department under this section within one year following the date of the accident, the department is not required to file a report on the accident and the driver's license suspension requirements of Section 16004 or 16070 do not apply. *(Added by Stats.1974, c. 1409, p. 3096, § 8. Amended by Stats.1978, c. 997, p. 3070, § 1; Stats.1979, c. 549, p. 1753, § 1; Stats.1984, c. 1324, § 2, operative July 1, 1985; Stats.1989, c. 808, § 2, operative July 1, 1990; Stats.1991, c. 1177 (S.B.35), § 3, eff. Oct. 14, 1991; Stats.1994, c. 1247 (A.B.1926), § 8; Stats.1996, c. 1154 (A.B.3020), § 63, eff. Sept. 30, 1996; Stats.1998, c. 601 (S.B.1250), § 4; Stats. 2001, c. 739 (A.B.1707), § 10; Stats.2001, c. 84 (S.B.42), § 1, eff. July 19, 2001; Stats.2002, c. 766 (S.B.1590), § 4; Stats.2003, c. 594 (S.B.315), § 40.)*

Cross References

Accidents and accident reports, in general, see Vehicle Code § 20000 et seq.

Definitions,

Commercial vehicle, see Vehicle Code § 260.

Department, see Vehicle Code § 290.

Driver, see Vehicle Code § 305.

Owner, see Vehicle Code § 460.

Registered owner, see Vehicle Code § 505.

Street and highway, see Vehicle Code §§ 360, 590, 591.

Department to prescribe forms, see Vehicle Code § 1652.

Duty to report accident to police, etc., see Vehicle Code §§ 20008, 20009.

Evidence of financial responsibility, see Vehicle Code § 16020 et seq.

Habitual traffic offender as person whose license is suspended or revoked and is involved in three or more accidents under this section in one year, see Vehicle Code § 14601.3.

Report or action of department as evidence, see Vehicle Code § 40833.

§ 16000.1. Reportable off-highway accident

(a) For purposes of this division, a "reportable off-highway accident" means an accident which includes all of the following:

(1) Occurs off the street or highway.

(2) Involves a vehicle that is subject to registration under this code.

(3) Results in damages to the property of any one person in excess of seven hundred fifty dollars ($750) or in bodily injury or in the death of any person.

(b) A "reportable off-highway accident" does not include any accident which occurs off-highway in which

545

damage occurs only to the property of the driver or owner of the motor vehicle and no bodily injury or death of a person occurs. *(Added by Stats.1989, c. 808, § 3, operative July 1, 1990. Amended by Stats.2002, c. 766 (S.B. 1590), § 5.)*

§ 16000.7.   Uninsured motor vehicle

As used in this division an "uninsured motor vehicle" is a motor vehicle for which financial responsibility as provided in Section 16021 was not in effect at the time of the accident. *(Added by Stats.1979, c. 549, p. 1753, § 3.)*

§ 16000.8.   Failure of driver to prove financial responsibility due to fraudulent acts by insurance agent or broker; termination of suspension actions; conditions

(a) Notwithstanding any other provision of this chapter, if the failure of the driver of a motor vehicle involved in an accident to prove the existence of financial responsibility, as required by Section 16020, was due to the fraudulent acts of an insurance agent or broker, the department shall terminate any suspension action taken pursuant to Section 16070, when both of the following conditions are met:

(1) The driver provides documentation from the Department of Insurance that the insurance agent or broker has been found to have committed fraud in the transaction of automobile liability insurance, or provides documentation that criminal charges have been filed against the agent or broker due to fraud or theft related to the sale of automobile liability insurances.

(2) The driver furnishes proof to the department that financial responsibility meeting the requirements of Section 16021 is currently in effect.

(b) It is the intent of the Legislature in enacting this section that individuals who are the victims of insurance fraud not be penalized for violating the financial responsibility laws when that violation was due to the fraudulent acts of others. Persons with documented evidence of fraud involving their insurance coverage, such as where an insurance agent accepted the premium payment for coverage but willfully failed to obtain the coverage and led the customer to believe insurance was in effect, should retain their driving privileges provided they give evidence that valid liability insurance is currently in effect. *(Added by Stats.1996, c. 1155 (S.B.1587), § 6.)*

§ 16001.   Driverless runaway vehicle

If the vehicle involved was a driverless runaway vehicle and was parked with the express or implied permission of the registered owner, the registered owner of the vehicle shall be construed to have been the driver of the vehicle for the purposes of this chapter. *(Added by Stats.1974, c. 1409, p. 3096, § 8.)*

Cross References

Definitions,
  Driver, see Vehicle Code § 305.

546

Registered owner, see Vehicle Code § 505.
Vehicle, see Vehicle Code § 670.
Report or action of department as evidence, see Vehicle Code § 40833.

§ 16002.   Vehicle of employer; vehicle owned or operated by publicly owned or operated transit system

(a) If the driver at the time of the accident was driving a motor vehicle owned, operated, or leased by the employer of the driver and with the permission of the employer, then the driver shall within five days after the accident report the accident to his employer on a form approved by the employer. Within 10 days after receipt of the report the employer shall transmit a report on a form approved by the department to the office of the department at Sacramento, except that an employer need not transmit such report when the vehicle involved in the accident is owned or operated as described in Section 16051 or 16052, or is owned or operated by any person or corporation who has filed with the department a certificate of an insurance carrier or surety company that there is in effect a policy or bond meeting the requirements of Section 16056 and when such policy or bond is in force with respect to the vehicle at the time of the accident.

(b) The driver of a vehicle that is owned or operated by a publicly owned or operated transit system, or that is operated under contract with a publicly owned or operated transit system, and that is used to provide regularly scheduled transportation to the general public or for other official business of the system shall, within 10 days of the occurrence of the accident, report to the transit system any accident of a type otherwise required to be reported pursuant to subdivision (a) of Section 16000. The transit system shall maintain records of any report filed pursuant to this paragraph. Within 10 days after receipt of the report, the transit system shall transmit a report on a form approved by the department to the office of the department in Sacramento, except that a transit system is not required to submit a report when the vehicle involved in the accident is owned or operated as described in subdivision (b) of Section 16000. *(Added by Stats.1974, c. 1409, p. 3096, § 8. Amended by Stats.2001, c. 84 (S.B.42), § 2, eff. July 19, 2001.)*

Cross References

Accident reports, see Vehicle Code § 20000 et seq.
Definitions,
  Department, see Vehicle Code § 290.
  Driver, see Vehicle Code § 305.
  Motor vehicle, see Vehicle Code § 415.
  Owner, see Vehicle Code § 460.
Duty of department to prescribe and provide forms, see Vehicle Code § 1652.
Evidence of financial responsibility, see Vehicle Code § 16020 et seq.
Report or action of department as evidence, see Vehicle Code § 40833.

§ 16003.   Driver incapacity

If any driver is physically incapable of making the report, and is not the owner of the motor vehicle involved in the accident, the owner shall, as soon as he learns of the accident, report the matter in writing to the department. *(Added by Stats.1974, c. 1409, p. 3096, § 8.)*

§ 16004. Mandatory suspension of license; exemption

(a) The department shall suspend the driving privilege of any person who fails, refuses, or neglects to make a report of an accident as required in this chapter.

(b) A suspension taken under this section shall remain in effect until terminated by receipt of the report of the accident or upon receipt of evidence that financial responsibility as provided in Section 16021 is in effect.

(c) The driving privilege shall not be suspended under this section, and, if a suspension has been imposed and is in effect under this section, that suspension shall be terminated, if the driving privilege is suspended under Section 16370 or 16381 as the result of a judgment arising out of the same accident for which the report of the accident is required by this section. The department may suspend or reimpose the suspension of the driving privilege of a person under this section if the suspension under Section 16370 or 16381 is later set aside for a reason other than that the person has satisfied the judgment in full or to the extent provided in Chapter 2 (commencing with Section 16250) and has given proof of financial responsibility, as provided in Chapter 3 (commencing with Section 16430). *(Added by Stats.1974, c. 1409, p. 3096, § 8. Amended by Stats.1976, c. 891, p. 2049, § 4; Stats.1982, c. 746, p. 2961, § 1; Stats.1984, c. 1324, § 3, operative July 1, 1985; Stats.1989, c. 1157, § 3; Stats.1990, c. 314 (S.B.2673), § 3, eff. July 17, 1990.)*

§ 16005. Use of reports

(a) All reports and supplemental reports required by this chapter including insurance information forms shall be without prejudice to the individual so reporting and shall be for the confidential use of the department and any other state department requiring such information, except that the department shall upon request disclose from the reports:

(1) The names and addresses of persons involved in the accident.

(2) The registration numbers and descriptions of vehicles involved in the accident.

(3) The date, time, and location of the accident.

(4) Any suspension action taken by the department.

(5) The names and addresses of insurers.

(b) The information specified in subdivision (a) may be given to any person having a proper interest therein, including:

(1) The driver or drivers involved, or the employer, parent, or legal guardian thereof.

(2) The authorized representative of any person involved in the accident.

(3) Any person injured in the accident.

(4) The owners of vehicles or property damaged in the accident.

(5) Any law enforcement agency.

(6) Any court of competent jurisdiction. *(Added by Stats.1974, c. 1409, p. 3096, § 8.)*

ARTICLE 2. FINANCIAL RESPONSIBILITY

Section
16020. Evidence of financial responsibility.
16020.1. Applicability of Sections 4000.37 and 16028.
16020.2. Applicability of certain provisions to City and County of San Francisco.
16020.3. Employer–owned vanpool vehicles; evidence of financial responsibility.
16021. Establishing financial responsibility.
16022. Repealed.
16023. Repealed.
16024. Repealed.
16025. Accidents; exchange of information; fines and penalties.
16026. Repealed.
16027. Refund of cash deposit.
16028. Proof of financial responsibility to be provided upon demand of peace officer or traffic collision investigator; notice to appear for violation of code; employer vehicle; method of appearance; viewing content on mobile electronic device; liability for mobile electronic device damage.
16028.1. Inoperative.
16028.2. Repealed.
16028.4. Repealed.
16029. Violations; offense; punishment; conditions for impoundment of vehicles.
16030. False evidence of financial responsibility; offense; punishment.
16031. Repealed.

Section
16032.   Repealed.
16033.   Liability of public entities, employees and specified
          persons or organizations.
16034.   Repealed.
16035.   Repealed.

§ 16020.   Evidence of financial responsibility

(a) All drivers and all owners of a motor vehicle shall at all times be able to establish financial responsibility pursuant to Section 16021, and shall at all times carry in the vehicle evidence of the form of financial responsibility in effect for the vehicle.

(b) "Evidence of financial responsibility" means any of the following:

(1) A form issued by an insurance company or charitable risk pool, as specified by the department pursuant to Section 4000.37.

(2) If the owner is a self-insurer, as provided in Section 16052 or a depositor, as provided in Section 16054.2, the certificate of self-insurance or the assignment of deposit letter issued by the department.

(3) An insurance covering note or binder pursuant to Section 382 or 382.5 of the Insurance Code.

(4) A showing that the vehicle is owned or leased by, or under the direction of, the United States or a public entity, as defined in Section 811.2 of the Government Code.

(c) For purposes of this section, "evidence of financial responsibility" also may be obtained by a law enforcement officer and court personnel from an electronic reporting system when that system becomes available for use by law enforcement officers.

(d) For purposes of this section, "evidence of financial responsibility" also includes any of the following:

(1) The name of the insurance company and the number of an insurance policy or surety bond that was in effect at the time of the accident or at the time that evidence of financial responsibility is required to be provided pursuant to Section 16028, if that information is contained in the vehicle registration records of the department.

(2) The identifying motor carrier of property permit number issued by the Department of the California Highway Patrol to the motor carrier of property as defined in Section 34601, and displayed on the motor vehicle in the manner specified by the Department of the California Highway Patrol.

(3) The identifying number issued to the household goods carrier, passenger stage carrier, or transportation charter party carrier by the Public Utilities Commission and displayed on the motor vehicle in the manner specified by the commission.

(e) Evidence of financial responsibility does not include an identification number in paragraph (1), (2), or (3) of subdivision (d) if the carrier is currently suspended by the issuing agency for lack or lapse of insurance or

548

other form of financial responsibility. *(Added by Stats. 1974, c. 1409, p. 3095, § 8. Amended by Stats.1988, c. 1156, § 2, eff. Sept. 22, 1988; Stats.1992, c. 621 (A.B. 2517), § 1; Stats.1996, c. 1126 (A.B.650), § 4, operative Jan. 1, 1997; Stats.1997, c. 652 (A.B.1518), § 10; Stats. 1999, c. 880 (S.B.652), § 8; Stats.2000, c. 1035 (S.B.1403), § 20; Stats.2001, c. 825 (S.B.290), § 14; Stats.2005, c. 706 (A.B.1742), § 37; Stats.2006, c. 288 (A.B.3011), § 4.)*

Cross References

Custody and disposition of security, see Vehicle Code § 16025. Exemptions from security requirement, see Vehicle Code § 16050 et seq.

§ 16020.1.   Applicability of Sections 4000.37 and 16028

(a) On and after January 1, 2016, Section 4000.37 does not apply to vehicle owners with a residence address in the County of Los Angeles at the time of registration renewal.

(b) On and after January 1, 2016, subdivisions (a) and (b) of Section 16028 do not apply to a person who drives a motor vehicle upon a highway in the County of Los Angeles. *(Added by Stats.1999, c. 794 (S.B.171), § 3. Amended by Stats.2000, c. 135 (A.B.2539), § 160; Stats. 2000, c. 1035 (S.B.1403), § 21; Stats.2002, c. 666 (S.B. 180), § 1; Stats.2005, c. 435 (S.B.20), § 20; Stats.2010, c. 234 (A.B.1597), § 6.)*

§ 16020.2.   Applicability of certain provisions to City and County of San Francisco

(a) On and after January 1, 2016, Section 4000.37 does not apply to vehicle owners with a residence address in the City and County of San Francisco at the time of registration renewal.

(b) On and after January 1, 2016, subdivisions (a) and (b) of Section 16028 do not apply to a person who drives a motor vehicle upon a highway in the City and County of San Francisco. *(Added by Stats.1999, c. 807 (S.B.527), § 3. Amended by Stats.2000, c. 1035 (S.B.1403), § 22; Stats.2002, c. 666 (S.B.180), § 2; Stats.2005, c. 435 (S.B.20), § 21; Stats.2010, c. 234 (A.B.1597), § 7.)*

Cross References

Low-cost automobile policies, satisfaction of requirements of this section, see Insurance Code § 11629.991.

§ 16020.3.   Employer–owned vanpool vehicles; evidence of financial responsibility

Notwithstanding any other provision of law, any employer that owns a vanpool vehicle, as described in paragraph (1) of subdivision (c) of Section 17149 of the Revenue and Taxation Code, shall maintain evidence of financial responsibility with respect to that vehicle in the same form and amount as described in Section 5391.2 of the Public Utilities Code. *(Added by Stats.1994, c. 622 (S.B.1360), § 4.)*

§ 16021. Establishing financial responsibility

Financial responsibility of the driver or owner is established if the driver or owner of the vehicle involved in an accident described in Section 16000 is:

(a) A self-insurer under the provisions of this division.

(b) An insured or obligee under a form of insurance or bond that complies with the requirements of this division and that covers the driver for the vehicle involved in the accident.

(c) The United States of America, this state, any municipality or subdivision thereof, or the lawful agent thereof.

(d) A depositor in compliance with subdivision (a) of Section 16054.2.

(e) An obligee under a policy issued by a charitable risk pool that complies with subdivision (b) of Section 16054.2.

(f) In compliance with the requirements authorized by the department by any other manner which effectuates the purposes of this chapter. *(Added by Stats.1974, c. 1409, p. 3097, § 8. Amended by Stats.1975, c. 1082, p. 2643, § 1; Stats.1978, c. 997, p. 3070, § 1.5; Stats.2000, c. 1035 (S.B.1403), § 23; Stats.2003, c. 594 (S.B.315), § 41.)*

Cross References

Assigned Risk Plans required coverage, see Insurance Code § 11622.
County and City of San Francisco Low–Cost Automobile Insurance Pilot Program, policy attributes, see Insurance Code § 11629.91.
County of Los Angeles Low–Cost Automobile Insurance Pilot Program, policy attributes, see Insurance Code § 11629.71.
Evidence of financial responsibility, electronic method for reporting private passenger automobile liability insurance policies and coverages, alternative forms of financial responsibility, see Vehicle Code § 16058.

§ 16022. Repealed by Stats.1984, c. 1324, § 4

§ 16023. Repealed by Stats.1984, c. 1324, § 5

§ 16024. Repealed by Stats.1974, c. 1409, p. 3095, § 7

§ 16025. Accidents; exchange of information; fines and penalties

(a) Every driver involved in the accident shall, unless rendered incapable, exchange with any other driver or property owner involved in the accident and present at the scene, all of the following information:

(1) Driver's name and current residence address, driver's license number, vehicle identification number, and current residence address of registered owner.

(2) Evidence of financial responsibility, as specified in Section 16020. If the financial responsibility of a person is a form of insurance, then that person shall supply the name and address of the insurance company and the number of the insurance policy.

(b) Any person failing to comply with all of the requirements of this section is guilty of an infraction punishable by a fine not to exceed two hundred fifty dollars ($250). *(Added by Stats.1992, c. 621 (A.B.2517), § 2. Amended by Stats.1999, c. 880 (S.B.652), § 10.)*

§ 16026. Repealed by Stats.1974, c. 1409, p. 3095, § 7

§ 16027. Refund of cash deposit

(a) Whenever proof of financial responsibility has been established under subdivision (a) of Section 16054.2 and a period of four years has elapsed following the effective date of the suspension, the cash deposit, or any balance thereof remaining, shall be refunded to the person entitled thereto, if the director is satisfied that there are no outstanding or pending claims against the deposit.

(b) If the deposit, or any balance thereof, is refundable under this section but remains unclaimed by the depositor or any other person entitled thereto for a period of six years from the effective date of the suspension, the unclaimed deposit shall be transferred to the Motor Vehicle Account in the State Transportation Fund. *(Added by Stats.1977, c. 723, p. 2307, § 1. Amended by Stats.1985, c. 619, § 1.)*

§ 16028. Proof of financial responsibility to be provided upon demand of peace officer or traffic collision investigator; notice to appear for violation of code; employer vehicle; method of appearance; viewing content on mobile electronic device; liability for mobile electronic device damage

(a) Upon the demand of a peace officer pursuant to subdivision (b) or upon the demand of a peace officer or traffic collision investigator pursuant to subdivision (c), every person who drives a motor vehicle upon a highway shall provide evidence of financial responsibility for the vehicle that is in effect at the time the demand is made. The evidence of financial responsibility may be provided using a mobile electronic device. However, a peace officer shall not stop a vehicle for the sole purpose of determining whether the vehicle is being driven in violation of this subdivision.

(b) If a notice to appear is issued for any alleged violation of this code, except a violation specified in Chapter 9 (commencing with Section 22500) of Division 11 or any local ordinance adopted pursuant to that chapter, the cited driver shall furnish written evidence of financial responsibility or may provide electronic verification of evidence of financial responsibility using a mobile electronic device upon request of the peace officer issuing the citation. The peace officer shall request and write the driver's evidence of financial responsibility on the notice to appear, except when the peace officer is unable to write the driver's evidence of financial responsibility on the notice to appear due to an emergency that requires his or her presence elsewhere. If the cited driver fails to provide evidence of financial responsibility at the time the notice to appear is issued, the peace officer may issue the

549

driver a notice to appear for violation of subdivision (a). The notice to appear for violation of subdivision (a) shall be written on the same citation form as the original violation.

(c) If a peace officer, or a regularly employed and salaried employee of a city or county who has been trained as a traffic collision investigator, is summoned to the scene of an accident described in Section 16000, the driver of a motor vehicle that is in any manner involved in the accident shall furnish written evidence of financial responsibility or may provide electronic verification of evidence of financial responsibility using a mobile electronic device upon the request of the peace officer or traffic collision investigator. If the driver fails to provide evidence of financial responsibility when requested, the peace officer may issue the driver a notice to appear for violation of this subdivision. A traffic collision investigator may cause a notice to appear to be issued for a violation of this subdivision, upon review of that citation by a peace officer.

(d)(1) If, at the time a notice to appear for a violation of subdivision (a) is issued, the person is driving a motor vehicle owned or leased by the driver's employer, and the vehicle is being driven with the permission of the employer, this section shall apply to the employer rather than the driver. In that case, a notice to appear shall be issued to the employer rather than the driver, and the driver may sign the notice on behalf of the employer.

(2) The driver shall notify the employer of the receipt of the notice issued pursuant to paragraph (1) not later than five days after receipt.

(e) A person issued a notice to appear for a violation of subdivision (a) may personally appear before the clerk of the court, as designated in the notice to appear, and provide written evidence of financial responsibility in a form consistent with Section 16020, showing that the driver was in compliance with that section at the time the notice to appear for violating subdivision (a) was issued. In lieu of the personal appearance, the person may submit by mail to the court written evidence of having had financial responsibility at the time the notice to appear was issued. Upon receipt by the clerk of that written evidence of financial responsibility in a form consistent with Section 16020, further proceedings on the notice to appear for the violation of subdivision (a) shall be dismissed.

(f) For the purposes of this section, "mobile electronic device" means a portable computing and communication device that has a display screen with touch input or a miniature keyboard.

(g) For the purposes of this section, when a person provides evidence of financial responsibility using a mobile electronic device to a peace officer, the peace officer shall only view the evidence of financial responsibility and is prohibited from viewing any other content on the mobile electronic device.

(h) If a person presents a mobile electronic device pursuant to this section, that person assumes all liability for any damage to the mobile electronic device. (*Added by Stats.1996, c. 1126 (A.B.650), § 6, operative Jan. 1, 1997. Amended by Stats.1997, c. 945 (A.B.1561), § 16; Stats.1999, c. 880 (S.B.652), § 11; Stats.2001, c. 825 (S.B.290), § 15; Stats.2012, c. 236 (A.B.1708), § 2; Stats. 2013, c. 76 (A.B.383), § 195.*)

Application

For application of subds. (a) and (b) to drivers in County of Los Angeles and City and County of San Francisco, see Vehicle Code §§ 16020.1 and 16020.2.

§ 16028.1. Inoperative

§ 16028.2. Repealed by Stats.1990, c. 1595 (S.B.2137), § 1, operative Jan. 1, 1992

§ 16028.4. Repealed by Stats.1989, c. 1465, § 10, operative Jan. 1, 1991

§ 16029. Violations; offense; punishment; conditions for impoundment of vehicles

Notwithstanding any other provision of law, a violation of subdivision (a) of Section 16028 is an infraction and shall be punished as follows:

(a) Upon a first conviction, by a fine of not less than one hundred dollars ($100) and not more than two hundred dollars ($200), plus penalty assessments.

(b) Upon a subsequent conviction, occurring within three years of a prior conviction, by a fine of not less than two hundred dollars ($200) and not more than five hundred dollars ($500), plus penalty assessments.

(c)(1) At the discretion of the court, for good cause, and in addition to the penalties specified in subdivisions (a) and (b), the court may order the impoundment of the vehicle for which the owner could not produce evidence of financial responsibility in violation of subdivision (a) of Section 16028.

(2) A vehicle impounded pursuant to paragraph (1) shall be released to the legal owner of the vehicle or the legal owner's agent if all of the following conditions are met:

(A) The legal owner is a motor vehicle dealer, bank, credit union, acceptance corporation, or other licensed financial institution legally operating in this state.

(B) The legal owner or the legal owner's agent pays all towing and storage fees related to the seizure of the vehicle.

(C) The legal owner or the legal owner's agent presents foreclosure documents or an affidavit of repossession for the vehicle.

(3)(A) A legal owner or the legal owner's agent that obtains release of the vehicle pursuant to paragraph (2) shall not release the vehicle to the registered owner of the vehicle or any agents of the registered owner, unless the registered owner is a rental car agency, except upon presentation of evidence of financial responsibility, as defined in Section 16020, for the vehicle. The legal owner or the legal owner's agent shall make every reasonable effort to ensure that the evidence of financial responsibility that is presented is valid.

(B) Prior to relinquishing the vehicle, the legal owner may require the registered owner to pay all towing and storage charges related to impoundment and any administrative charges authorized under Section 22850.5 that were incurred by the legal owner in connection with obtaining custody of the vehicle.

(4) A vehicle impounded under paragraph (1) shall be released to a rental car agency if the agency is either the legal owner or the registered owner of the vehicle and the agency pays all towing and storage fees related to the seizure of the vehicle.

(5) A vehicle impounded under paragraph (1) shall be released to the registered owner of the vehicle only upon presentation of evidence of financial responsibility, as defined in Section 16020, for that vehicle, and evidence that all towing and storage fees related to the seizure of the vehicle are paid.

This paragraph does not apply to a person, entity, or agency who is entitled to release of a vehicle under paragraph (2) or (4) and is either:

(A) The registered and the legal owner and is described in subparagraph (A) of paragraph (2).

(B) The registered owner or legal owner and is described in paragraph (4).

(d) It is the intent of the Legislature that fines collected pursuant to this section be used to reduce the number of uninsured drivers and not be used to generate revenue for general purposes.

(e)(1) Except as provided in this subdivision, the court shall impose a fine that is greater than the minimum fine specified in subdivision (a) or (b), and may not reduce that fine to the minimum specified fine authorized under those provisions, unless the defendant has presented the court with evidence of financial responsibility, as defined in Section 16020, for the vehicle. In no event may the court impose a fine that is less than the minimum specified in subdivision (a) or (b), or impose a fine that exceeds the maximum specified fine authorized under those subdivisions. In addition to the fine authorized under subdivision (a) or (b), the court may issue an order directing the defendant to maintain insurance coverage satisfying the financial responsibility laws for at least one year from the date of the order.

(2) Notwithstanding any other provision of law, the imposition of the fine required under subdivision (a) or (b) is mandatory upon conviction of a violation of subdivision (a) of Section 16028 and may not be waived, suspended, or reduced below the minimum fines, unless the court in its discretion reduces or waives the fine based on the defendant's ability to pay. The court may direct that the fine and penalty assessments be paid within a limited time or in installments on specified dates. The Legislature hereby declares that it is in the interest of justice that the minimum fines set forth in subdivisions (a) and (b) for these offenses be enforced by the court, as provided in this subdivision. *(Added by Stats.1996, c. 1126 (A.B.650), § 7, operative Jan. 1, 1997. Amended by Stats.1999, c. 880 (S.B.652), § 12.)*

§ 16030. False evidence of financial responsibility; offense; punishment

(a) Except as provided in subdivision (c), any person who knowingly provides false evidence of financial responsibility (1) when requested by a peace officer pursuant to Section 16028 or (2) to the clerk of the court as permitted by subdivision (e) of Section 16028, including an expired or canceled insurance policy, bond, certificate of self-insurance, or assignment of deposit letter, is guilty of a misdemeanor punishable by a fine not exceeding seven hundred fifty dollars ($750) or imprisonment in the county jail not exceeding 30 days, or by both that fine and imprisonment. Upon receipt of the court's abstract of conviction, the department shall suspend the driving privilege, effective upon the date of conviction, for a period of one year. The court shall impose an interim suspension of the person's driving privileges pursuant to Section 13550, and shall notify the driver of the suspension pursuant to Section 13106, and all driver's licenses in the possession of the driver shall be surrendered to the court pursuant to Section 13550. Any driver's license surrendered to the court pursuant to this section shall be transmitted by the court, together with the required report of the conviction, to the department within 10 days of the conviction. The suspension may not be terminated until one year has elapsed from the date of the suspension and until the person files proof of financial responsibility, as provided in Chapter 3 (commencing with Section 16430) except that the suspension shall be reinstated if the person fails to maintain proof of financial responsibility for three years.

(b) However, in lieu of suspending a person's driving privileges pursuant to subdivision (a), the court shall restrict the person's driving privileges to driving that is required in the person's course of employment, if driving of a motor vehicle is necessary in order to perform the duties of the person's primary employment. The restriction shall remain in effect for the period of suspension otherwise required by subdivision (a). The court shall provide for endorsement of the restriction on the person's driver's license, and violation of the restriction constitutes a violation of Section 14603 and grounds for suspension or revocation of the license under Section 13360.

(c) This section does not apply to a driver who is driving a motor vehicle owned or leased by the employer of the driver and driven in the course of the driver's employment with the permission of the employer.

(Added by Stats.1996, c. 1126 (A.B.650), § 8, operative Jan. 1, 1997. Amended by Stats.1999, c. 880 (S.B.652), § 13.)

§ 16031. Repealed by Stats.1989, c. 1465, § 13, operative Jan. 1, 1991

§ 16032. Repealed by Stats.1989, c. 1465, § 14, operative Jan. 1, 1991

§ 16033. Liability of public entities, employees and specified persons or organizations

No public entity or employee, agent, or any person or organization authorized under Section 4610 to endorse receipts or validate registration cards or potential registration cards, is liable for any loss, detriment, or injury resulting, directly or indirectly, from any of the following:

(a) Failure to request evidence of financial responsibility.

(b) Failure to notify a vehicle owner that an insurance policy has been terminated.

(c) The discretionary failure to cancel, suspend, or revoke a vehicle registration when an insurance policy has been terminated.

(d) Inaccurately recording that evidence under Section 16028 or as a result of the driver producing false or inaccurate financial responsibility information.

(Added by Stats.1996, c. 1126 (A.B.650), § 9, operative Jan. 1, 1997. Amended by Stats.1999, c. 880 (S.B.652), § 14.)

§ 16034. Repealed by Stats.1990, c. 314 (S.B.2673), § 4, eff. July 17, 1990, operative Jan. 1, 1991

§ 16035. Repealed by Stats.1989, c. 1465, § 17, operative Jan. 1, 1991

ARTICLE 3. EVIDENCE OF FINANCIAL RESPONSIBILITY

Section
16050.   Establishing evidence of financial responsibility.
16050.5. Permitted driver.
16051.   Publicly owned or controlled vehicles.
16052.   Self-insurer.
16053.   Certificate of self-insurance.
16054.   Liability policy or bond.
16054.2. Other forms of financial responsibility.
16055.   Evidence of insurance or bond coverage.
16056.   Requirements of policy or bond.
16056.1. Automobile insurance policies described in Insurance Code provisions; effectiveness.
16057.   Notice by insurer to the department.
16058.   Electronic method for reporting private passenger automobile liability insurance policies and coverages; reporting issuance and termination of policies; alternative forms of financial responsibility; regulations.
16058.1. Electronic verification of insurance by law enforcement officers.
16059, 16060. Repealed.

§ 16050. Establishing evidence of financial responsibility

In order to establish evidence of financial responsibility, every driver or employer involved in an accident and required to report the accident under Section 16000 shall establish to the satisfaction of the department that the provisions of this article are applicable to his or her responsibilities arising out of the accident. *(Added by Stats.1974, c. 1409, p. 3098, § 8. Amended by Stats.2001, c. 739 (A.B.1707), § 12.)*

Cross References

Evidence of financial responsibility, see Vehicle Code § 16020.
Reports of accidents, disclosure, see Vehicle Code § 16005.

§ 16050.5. Permitted driver

The owner of a vehicle, who has a liability insurance policy with respect to the vehicle, shall, upon request, furnish insurance information to a person who, while operating the vehicle with the owner's permission, is involved in a reportable accident with the insured vehicle, or to the department whenever the department is required to establish whether the permitted driver meets the financial responsibility requirements of Section 16020. *(Added by Stats.1990, c. 602 (S.B.2215), § 1. Amended by Stats.1991, c. 1177 (S.B.35), § 4, eff. Oct. 14, 1991.)*

§ 16051. Publicly owned or controlled vehicles

(a) Evidence may be established by filing a report indicating that the motor vehicle involved in the accident was owned, rented, or leased by or under the direction of the United States, this state, or any political subdivision of this state or municipality thereof.

(b) Evidence may be established by filing a report indicating that the motor vehicle involved in the accident was owned and operated by a peace officer, member of the Department of the California Highway Patrol, or firefighter in the performance of his or her duty, and at the request of or under the direction of the United States, this state, or any political subdivision or municipality of this state. *(Added by Stats.1974, c. 1409, p. 3098, § 8. Amended by Stats.2001, c. 739 (A.B.1707), § 13; Stats. 2008, c. 85 (A.B.1115), § 2; Stats.2012, c. 823 (A.B.2298), § 4.)*

Cross References

Registration of public owned vehicles, see Vehicle Code § 4155.
Report of accident, vehicle of employer, see Vehicle Code § 16002.

§ 16052. Self-insurer

Evidence may be established if the owner of the motor vehicle involved in the accident was a self-insurer. Any person in whose name more than 25 motor vehicles are registered may qualify as a self-insurer by obtaining a certificate of self-insurance issued by the department as provided in this article. *(Added by Stats.1974, c. 1409, p.*

3098, § 8. Amended by Stats.2001, c. 739 (A.B.1707), § 14.)

Cross References

Evidence of financial responsibility, see Vehicle Code § 16020.

§ 16053. Certificate of self-insurance

(a) The department may in its discretion, upon application, issue a certificate of self-insurance when it is satisfied that the applicant in whose name more than 25 motor vehicles are registered is possessed and will continue to be possessed of ability to pay judgments obtained against him or her in amounts at least equal to the amounts provided in Section 16056. The certificate may be issued authorizing the applicant to act as a self-insurer for either property damage or bodily injury or both. Any person duly qualified under the laws or ordinances of any city or county to act as self-insurer and then acting as such, may upon filing with the department satisfactory evidence thereof, along with the application as may be required by the department, be entitled to receive a certificate of self-insurance.

(b) Upon not less than five days' notice and a hearing pursuant to the notice, the department may upon reasonable grounds cancel a certificate of self-insurance. Failure to pay any judgment within 30 days after the judgment has become final and has not been stayed or satisfied shall constitute a reasonable ground for the cancellation of a certificate of self-insurance. *(Added by Stats.1974, c. 1409, p. 3098, § 8. Amended by Stats.1991, c. 1177 (S.B.35), § 5, eff. Oct. 14, 1991.)*

Cross References

Vehicles designed to carry 16 or more passengers or over 7,000 pounds, self-insurance under this section permitted, see Vehicle Code § 16500.5.

§ 16054. Liability policy or bond

(a) Evidence may be established by filing with the department satisfactory documentation:

(1) That the owner had an automobile liability policy, a motor vehicle liability policy, or bond in effect at the time of the accident with respect to the driver or the motor vehicle involved in the accident, unless it is established that at the time of the accident the motor vehicle was being operated without the owner's permission, express or implied, or was parked by a driver who had been operating the vehicle without permission.

(2) That the driver of the motor vehicle involved in the accident, if he or she was not the owner of the motor vehicle, had in effect at the time of the accident an automobile liability policy or bond with respect to his or her operation of the motor vehicle not owned by him or her.

(3) That the liability as may arise from the driver's operation of the motor vehicle involved in the accident is, in the judgment of the department, covered by some form of liability insurance or bond.

(4) That the owner or driver, if he or she is involved in an accident while operating a vehicle of less than four wheels, had in effect at the time of the accident with respect to the driver or vehicle a liability policy or bond that meets the requirements of Section 16056.

(b) Any automobile liability policy or bond referred to in this section shall comply with the requirements of Section 16056 and Sections 11580, 11580.011, 11580.1, and 11580.2 of the Insurance Code, but need not contain provisions other than those required by those sections, and shall not be governed by Chapter 3 (commencing with Section 16430). *(Added by Stats.1974, c. 1409, p. 3098, § 8. Amended by Stats.1975, c. 1082, p. 2644, § 4; Stats.1982, c. 466, p. 2056, § 110; Stats.1990, c. 314 (S.B.2673), § 5, eff. July 17, 1990; Stats.1999, c. 183 (S.B.363), § 2; Stats.2001, c. 739 (A.B.1707), § 15.)*

§ 16054.2. Other forms of financial responsibility

Evidence may also be established by any of the following:

(a) By depositing with the department cash in the amount specified in Section 16056.

(b) By providing documentation of a liability policy covering the operation of the vehicle that (A) is issued by a charitable risk pool operating under Section 5005.1 of the Corporations Code, if the registered owner of the vehicle is a nonprofit organization that is exempt from taxation under paragraph (3) of subsection (c) of Section 501 of the United States Internal Revenue Code and (B) the policy is subject, if the accident has resulted in bodily injury or death, to a limit, exclusive of interest and costs, of not less than fifteen thousand dollars ($15,000) because of bodily injury to or death of one person in any one accident and, subject to that limit for one person, to a limit of not less than thirty thousand dollars ($30,000) because of bodily injury to or death of two or more persons in any one accident, and, if the accident has resulted in injury to, or destruction of property, to a limit of not less than five thousand dollars ($5,000) because of injury to or destruction of property of others in any one accident.

(c) By any other manner authorized by the department which effectuates the purposes of this chapter. *(Added by Stats.1974, c. 1409, p. 3099, § 8. Amended by Stats. 2000, c. 1035 (S.B.1403), § 24; Stats.2001, c. 739 (A.B. 1707), § 16.)*

Cross References

Evidence of financial responsibility, see Vehicle Code § 16020.

§ 16055. Evidence of insurance or bond coverage

Evidence of insurance or bond shall be submitted by the insurer or surety in conformance with the requirements of Section 16057. In the event of notice to the department by the company that issued one of the above stated policies or bonds that coverage was not in effect, then the policy or bond shall not operate to establish evidence as provided for by Section 16054. *(Added by*

Stats.1974, c. 1409, p. 3099, § 8. Amended by Stats.1975, c. 1082, p. 2645, § 5; Stats.2001, c. 739 (A.B.1707), § 17.)

Report of accident, vehicle of employer, see Vehicle Code § 16002.

§ 16056. Requirements of policy or bond

(a) No policy or bond shall be effective under Section 16054 unless issued by an insurance company or surety company admitted to do business in this state by the Insurance Commissioner, except as provided in subdivision (b) of this section, nor unless the policy or bond is subject, if the accident has resulted in bodily injury or death, to a limit, exclusive of interest and costs, of not less than fifteen thousand dollars ($15,000) because of bodily injury to or death of one person in any one accident and, subject to that limit for one person, to a limit of not less than thirty thousand dollars ($30,000) because of bodily injury to or death of two or more persons in any one accident, and, if the accident has resulted in injury to, or destruction of property, to a limit of not less than five thousand dollars ($5,000) because of injury to or destruction of property of others in any one accident.

(b) No policy or bond shall be effective under Section 16054 with respect to any vehicle which was not registered in this state or was a vehicle which was registered elsewhere than in this state at the effective date of the policy or bond or the most recent renewal thereof, unless the insurance company or surety company issuing the policy or bond is admitted to do business in this state, or if the company is not admitted to do business in this state, unless it executes a power of attorney authorizing the department to accept service on its behalf of notice or process in any action upon the policy or bond arising out of an accident mentioned in subdivision (a).

(c) Any nonresident driver whose driving privilege has been suspended or revoked based upon an action that requires proof of financial responsibility may, in lieu of providing a certificate of insurance from a company admitted to do business in California, provide a written certificate of proof of financial responsibility that is satisfactory to the department, covers the operation of a vehicle in this state, meets the liability requirements of this section, and is from a company that is admitted to do business in that person's state of residence. *(Added by Stats.1974, c. 1409, p. 3099, § 8. Amended by Stats.1996, c. 1154 (A.B.3020), § 64, eff. Sept. 30, 1996; Stats.2000, c. 1035 (S.B.1403), § 25.)*

Commercial passenger vehicles, proof of financial responsibility, see Vehicle Code § 16500 et seq.
County and City of San Francisco Low–Cost Automobile Insurance Pilot Program, policy attributes, see Insurance Code § 11629.91.
County of Los Angeles Low–Cost Automobile Insurance Pilot Program, policy attributes, see Insurance Code § 11629.71.

Evidence of financial responsibility, see Vehicle Code § 16020.

§ 16056.1. Automobile insurance policies described in Insurance Code provisions; effectiveness

Notwithstanding the coverage limits specified in Section 16056, an automobile insurance policy described in Section 11629.71 of the Insurance Code shall be effective under Section 16054 when issued by an insurance company admitted to do business in this state by the Insurance Commissioner and the policy is subject, if the accident has resulted in bodily injury or death, to a limit, exclusive of interest and costs, of not less than ten thousand dollars ($10,000) because of bodily injury to or death of one person in any one accident and, subject to that limit for one person, to a limit of not less than twenty thousand dollars ($20,000) because of bodily injury to or death of two or more persons in any one accident, and if the accident has resulted in injury to, or destruction of property, to a limit of not less than three thousand dollars ($3,000) because of injury to or destruction of property of others in any one accident.

(Added by Stats.2000, c. 1035 (S.B.1403), § 26. Amended by Stats.2002, c. 742 (S.B.1427), § 15; Stats. 2005, c. 435 (S.B.20), § 22.)

§ 16057. Notice by insurer to the department

Upon receipt of notice of an accident from the department, the insurance company or surety company named in the notice shall notify the department within such time and in such manner as the department may require whenever the policy or bond was not in effect at the time of the accident. *(Added by Stats.1974, c. 1409, p. 3100, § 8.)*

§ 16058. Electronic method for reporting private passenger automobile liability insurance policies and coverages; reporting issuance and termination of policies; alternative forms of financial responsibility; regulations

(a) On or before July 1, 2005, each insurer that issues private passenger automobile liability insurance policies and coverages, or private passenger automobile policies and coverages issued by an automobile assigned risk plan, as those policies, coverages, and plans are described in paragraph (1) of subdivision (a) of Section 4000.37 shall advise the department of the electronic method to be used for reporting liability insurance information under subdivisions (b), (c), and (d). The department shall establish an electronic conversion schedule.

(b) On or before January 1, 2006, each insurer shall report all existing motor vehicle liability insurance policies or coverages described in subdivision (a) issued for vehicles registered in this state or to policyholders with a California address, to the department in a manner that preserves existing reporting relationships and that allows for smaller insurers and those with unusual circumstances to be accommodated, consistent with the intent of this section. Consistent with the intent of this section, a small insurer or those with unusual circumstances may be accommodated by, among other methods, an extension of the mandatory electronic reporting deadline set forth in this section to no later than July 1, 2006.

(c) On and after January 1, 2006, each insurer shall electronically report to the department all issued motor vehicle liability policies or coverages, as described in subdivision (a), within 30 days of the effective date of the coverage.

(d) On and after January 1, 2006, an insurer shall electronically report to the department the termination of a reported policy or any change of information previously reported under subdivision (b) or (c), as specified by the department, within 45 days of the date of termination or change. This report shall include the effective date of the termination, amendment, or cancellation and any other information that does not exceed that required under subdivision (c).

(e)(1) Those persons with alternative forms of financial responsibility pursuant to subdivision (a), (c), (d), or (e) of Section 16021 shall provide satisfactory evidence of that responsibility as determined by the department.

(2) In addition, the department shall establish an alternative procedure for establishment of satisfactory evidence of financial responsibility to permit the timely renewal of vehicle registration when the electronic data has not been updated due to circumstances beyond the vehicle owner's immediate control. Those circumstances may include, but are not limited to, a vehicle identification error in either the department's or the insurer's records or insurance purchased too recently to have been electronically transmitted to the department. Whenever this alternative procedure is used, the department shall, subsequent to the issuance of the registration certificate and indicia, contact the insurer to obtain electronic data pursuant to subdivision (c).

(f) The department shall adopt regulations for reporting insurance information, including, but not limited to, establishing acceptable timeframes and approved methods for reporting information. *(Added by Stats.2004, c. 920 (S.B.1500), § 4.)*

§ 16058.1. Electronic verification of insurance by law enforcement officers

The department shall develop a method by which law enforcement officers and court personnel, on and after July 1, 2006, may electronically verify that an insurance policy or bond for a motor vehicle has been issued. *(Added by Stats.2004, c. 948 (A.B.2709), § 1. Amended by Stats.2005, c. 706 (A.B.1742), § 38.)*

Application

For application of 2005 amendment, see Stats.2005, c. 706 (A.B.1742), § 41.

§§ 16059, 16060. Repealed by Stats.1974, c. 1409, p. 3095, § 7

ARTICLE 4. SUSPENSIONS

Section
16070. Suspension of driving privilege; notice of intent; requisites; proof of financial responsibility.
16071. Suspension by another state.
16072. Period of suspension; restriction in lieu of suspension; suspension under other sections; deposit of revenues from penalty fees.
16073. Course of employment; exemption.
16074. Correction of errors.
16075. Hearing; decision.
16076. Notification of restricted driving privilege; printed summary.
16077. Restricted license to permit driving to prolonged, repetitive medical or mental health treatments; fee; application contents and review; penalty fee.
16078. Application and fee for restricted license under § 16072 or § 16077 after payment of fee under the other section.
16080 to 16084. Repealed.

§ 16070. Suspension of driving privilege; notice of intent; requisites; proof of financial responsibility

(a) Whenever a driver involved in an accident described in Section 16000 fails to provide evidence of financial responsibility, as required by Section 16020, at the time of the accident, the department shall, pursuant to subdivision (b), suspend the privilege of the driver or owner to drive a motor vehicle, including the driving privilege of a nonresident in this state.

(b) Whenever the department receives an accident report pursuant to this article that alleges that any of the drivers involved in the accident was not in compliance with Section 16020 at the time of the accident, the department shall immediately mail to that driver a notice of intent to suspend the driving privilege of that driver. The department shall suspend the driving privilege 30 days after mailing the notice, unless the driver has, prior to that date, established evidence of financial responsibility at the time of the accident, as specified in Section 16021, with the department. The suspension notice shall notify the driver of the action taken and the right to a hearing under Section 16075. *(Added by Stats.1974, c. 1409, p. 3100, § 8. Amended by Stats.1978, c. 997, p. 3070, § 2; Stats.1979, c. 549, p. 1753, § 4; Stats.1983, c. 1252, § 6; Stats.1984, c. 1324, § 7, operative July 1, 1985; Stats.1992, c. 668 (A.B.3481), § 1; Stats.1996, c. 1126 (A.B.650), § 10, operative Jan. 1, 1997; Stats.1999, c. 880 (S.B.652), § 15; Stats.2001, c. 739 (A.B.1707), § 18.)*

Cross References

Stay of suspension upon request for hearing, see Vehicle Code § 16075.

§ 16071. Suspension by another state

The department shall suspend the driving privilege of any person upon receiving notice from another state that the person's driving privilege in that state has been suspended for failure to meet the financial responsibility provisions of the law in that state, if the suspension in that state was taken on grounds that would have resulted in a suspension in this state.

(Added by Stats.1974, c. 1409, p. 3100, § 8. Amended by Stats.1982, c. 466, p. 2057, § 111; Stats.1996, c. 1126 (A.B.650), § 12, operative Jan. 1, 1997; Stats.1999, c. 880 (S.B.652), § 17.)

§ 16072. Period of suspension; restriction in lieu of suspension; suspension under other sections; deposit of revenues from penalty fees

(a) The suspension of the driving privilege of a person as provided in Section 16070 shall not be terminated until one year has elapsed from the date of actual commencement of the suspension and until the person files proof of financial responsibility as provided in Chapter 3 (commencing with Section 16430), except that the suspension shall be reinstated if the person fails to maintain proof of financial responsibility for three years. However, in lieu of suspending a person's driving privilege pursuant to this section, the department, upon application, if the person files and thereafter maintains proof of financial responsibility as provided in this section and pays a penalty fee to the department of two hundred fifty dollars ($250), may restrict the person's driving privilege to any of the following situations:

(1) Necessary travel to and from that person's place of employment.

(2) Driving that is required in the person's course of employment, when driving a motor vehicle is necessary in order to perform the duties of the person's primary employment.

(3) Necessary travel to transport a minor dependent in that person's immediate family to and from an institute of primary or secondary instruction, if the chief administrative officer or principal of the educational institution certifies in writing to the department that the minor dependent is enrolled in the educational institution and no form of public transportation or schoolbus is available between the applicant's place of residence and the educational institution.

The restriction shall remain in effect for the period of suspension required by this section, so long as proof of financial responsibility is maintained.

(b) If a suspension has been imposed under Section 16070 and one year has elapsed from the date the suspension actually commenced, that suspension shall be terminated if the driving privilege is suspended under Section 16370 or 16381 as the result of a judgment arising out of the accident for which proof of financial responsibility was required to be established. The department may reimpose the suspension of the driving privilege of a person under Section 16070 if the suspension under Section 16370 or 16381 is later set aside for a reason other than that the person has satisfied the judgment in full or to the extent provided in Chapter 2 (commencing with Section 16250) and has given proof of ability to respond in damages as provided in Chapter 3 (commencing with Section 16430).

556

(c) Notwithstanding Chapter 2 (commencing with Section 42200) of Division 18, all revenues derived from the penalty fees provided in subdivision (a) shall, after deduction by the department of the costs incurred by the department in administering this section, be deposited in the Financial Responsibility Penalty Account in the General Fund. The balance in this fund on each July 1, which is not subject to appropriation as provided in Section 12980 of the Insurance Code, shall revert to the General Fund.

(d)(1) Subdivision (a) does not apply to a commercial driver's license holder.

(2) A commercial driver's license holder whose driving privilege is otherwise suspended under this chapter is not entitled to a restricted license, unless that person surrenders his or her commercial driver's license and is issued a noncommercial class C or M driver's license. *(Added by Stats.1974, c. 1409, p. 3100, § 8. Amended by Stats.1978, c. 974, p. 3037, § 2; Stats.1982, c. 746, p. 2961, § 2; Stats.1983, c. 1252, p. 2961, § 8; Stats.1984, c. 1324, § 9, operative July 1, 1985; Stats.1985, c. 1494, § 2, eff. Oct. 2, 1985; Stats.1987, c. 903, § 1; Stats.1989, c. 1157, § 5; Stats.1990, c. 1407 (A.B.2817), § 1; Stats.2006, c. 574 (A.B.2520), § 16.)*

§ 16073. Course of employment; exemption

(a) The privilege of a person employed for the purpose of driving a motor vehicle for compensation whose occupation requires the use of a motor vehicle in the course of his or her employment to drive a motor vehicle not registered in his or her name and in the course of that person's employment may not be suspended under this chapter even though his or her privilege to drive is otherwise suspended under this chapter.

(b) Subdivision (a) does not apply to a commercial driver's licenseholder. A commercial driver's licenseholder whose driving privilege is otherwise suspended under this chapter may not operate a commercial motor vehicle.

(c) This section shall become operative on September 20, 2005. *(Added by Stats.1974, c. 1409, p. 3100, § 8. Amended by Stats.2004, c. 952 (A.B.3049), § 27, operative Sept. 20, 2005.)*

§ 16074. Correction of errors

Whenever the department has taken any action or has failed to take any action under this chapter by reason of having received erroneous information, or by reason of having received no information, it shall take appropriate action to carry out the purposes and effect of this chapter upon receiving correct information. *(Added by Stats. 1974, c. 1409, p. 3100, § 8.)*

§ 16075. Hearing; decision

(a) The suspension provisions of this article shall not apply to a driver or owner until 30 days after the department sends to the driver or owner notice of its intent to suspend his or her driving privilege, pursuant to subdivision (b) of Section 16070, and advises the driver or owner of his or her right to a hearing as hereinafter provided.

(b) If the driver or owner receiving the notice of intent to suspend wishes to have a hearing, the request for a hearing shall be made in writing to the department within 10 days of the receipt of the notice. Failure to respond to a notice of intent within 10 days of receipt of the notice is a waiver of the person's right to a hearing.

(c) If the driver or owner makes a timely request for a hearing, the department shall hold the hearing before the effective date of the suspension to determine the applicability of this chapter to the driver or owner, including a determination of whether:

(1) The accident has resulted in property damage in excess of seven hundred fifty dollars ($750), or bodily injury, or death.

(2) The driver or owner has established financial responsibility, as provided in Article 3 (commencing with Section 16050), was in effect at the time of the accident.

(d) A request for a hearing does not stay the suspension of a person's driving privilege. However, if the department does not conduct a hearing and make a determination pursuant thereto within the time limit provided in subdivision (b) of Section 16070, the department shall stay the effective date of the order of suspension pending a determination.

(e) The hearing provided for by this section shall be held in the county of residence of the person requesting the hearing. The hearing shall be conducted pursuant to Article 3 (commencing with Section 14100) of Chapter 3 of Division 6.

(f) The department shall render its decision within 15 days after conclusion of the hearing. *(Added by Stats. 1974, c. 1409, p. 3101, § 8. Amended by Stats.1978, c. 974, p. 3037, § 3; Stats.1978, c. 997, p. 3071, § 3.5; Stats.1979, c. 549, p. 1754, § 5; Stats.1984, c. 1324, § 11, operative July 1, 1985; Stats.1992, c. 668 (A.B.3481), § 2; Stats.2002, c. 766 (S.B.1590), § 6.)*

§ 16076. Notification of restricted driving privilege; printed summary

(a) The department shall notify every person whose driving privilege is suspended, pursuant to Section 16070, of that person's right to apply for a restricted driving privilege authorized under Section 16072.

(b) For purposes of subdivision (a), the department shall prepare and publish a printed summary. The printed summary may contain, but is not limited to, the following wording:

"If your driving privilege is suspended due to involvement in an accident while you were uninsured, you may apply for a restricted license at any office of the Department of Motor Vehicles, accompanied with proof of financial responsibility, payment of a penalty fee of two hundred fifty dollars ($250), and, unless already paid, payment of a reissuance fee.

The Mello–McAlister Restricted Employment Driving Privilege Act allows you to apply for a driver's license limiting you to driving to and from work, and during the course of your primary employment, during the one-year mandatory term of suspension. The restricted license will not be issued if any other suspension or revocation action has been taken against your driving privilege."

(c) This section shall be known and may be cited as the Mello–McAlister Restricted Employment Driving Privilege Act. *(Added by Stats.1985, c. 1494, § 3, eff. Oct. 2, 1985. Amended by Stats.1988, c. 1156, § 3, eff. Sept. 22, 1988, operative Nov. 30, 1988; Stats.2003, c. 451 (A.B. 1718), § 19.)*

§ 16077. Restricted license to permit driving to prolonged, repetitive medical or mental health treatments; fee; application contents and review; penalty fee

(a) The department, upon application and payment of a fifty dollar ($50) fee and a penalty fee of two hundred dollars ($200), may issue a restricted license to an applicant with serious health problems, or to an applicant with an immediate family member with serious health problems, when the applicant's privilege to drive is otherwise suspended under this chapter. The restricted license may be issued to enable the applicant to drive a motor vehicle for the purpose of receiving medical or mental health treatments of a prolonged and repetitive nature for the applicant or the member of the applicant's immediate family with serious health problems, if the applicant files and maintains proof of financial responsibility on file with the department pursuant to Section 16021 and there is no other suitable means of transportation available.

(b) The application shall set forth the nature of the health problem, the nature of the treatments, the duration and location of the treatments, and the schedule for visits. The applicant shall submit documentation signed by the treating physician and surgeon or licensed psychotherapist, as defined in subdivisions (a), (b), (c), and (e) of Section 1010 of the Evidence Code, as necessary to assist the department in its decision to grant or deny the restricted license. Upon reviewing the application, the department may determine that an investigation as to the person's fitness to operate a motor vehicle is warranted. If the department makes this determination, the department may conduct an investigation in a manner provided for in Chapter 3 (commencing with Section 13800) of Division 6.

(c) In reviewing the application, the department shall give due consideration to the circumstances set forth in the application and shall be guided by principles of fairness and humanity.

(d) Notwithstanding Chapter 2 (commencing with Section 42200) of Division 18, all revenues derived from the penalty fees provided in subdivision (a) shall, after deduction by the department of the costs incurred by the

557

department in administering this section, be deposited in the Financial Responsibility Penalty Account in the General Fund.

(e)(1) Subdivision (a) does not apply to a commercial driver's license holder.

(2) A commercial driver's license holder whose driving privilege is otherwise suspended under this chapter is not entitled to a restricted license unless that person surrenders his or her commercial driver's license and is issued a noncommercial class C or M driver's license. *(Added by Stats.1988, c. 846, § 1, operative July 1, 1989. Amended by Stats.1990, c. 1407 (A.B.2817), § 2; Stats.1990, c. 1410 (A.B.3470), § 2; Stats.2006, c. 574 (A.B.2520), § 17.)*

§ 16078. Application and fee for restricted license under § 16072 or § 16077 after payment of fee under the other section

Any person who has paid the penalty fee prescribed in subdivision (a) of Section 16072, whether or not the person has received the license restriction authorized by that section, may also apply for and receive a restricted license under Section 16077 without paying the fees prescribed in Section 16077. Any person who has paid the fees prescribed in subdivision (a) of Section 16077, whether or not the person has received the restricted license authorized by that section, may also apply for and receive the license restriction prescribed in Section 16072. *(Added by Stats.1990, c. 1407 (A.B.2817), § 4.)*

§§ 16080 to 16084. Repealed by Stats.1974, c. 1409, p. 3095, § 7

ARTICLE 5. SUSPENSION OF REGISTRATION OF MOTOR VEHICLES INVOLVED IN ACCIDENTS [REPEALED]

§§ 16100 to 16108. Repealed by Stats.1974, c. 1409, p. 3095, § 7

§ 16109. Repealed by Stats.1969, c. 9, p. 63, § 4

§ 16110. Repealed by Stats.1974, c. 1409, § 7

CHAPTER 2. SUSPENSION FOLLOWING UNSATISFIED JUDGMENTS

Article		Section
1.	Definitions	16250
2.	Suspension of Driving Privilege	16370

ARTICLE 1. DEFINITIONS

Section
16250. Judgment defined.
16251. Cause of action defined.

§ 16250. Judgment defined

As used in this chapter and Chapter 3 (commencing with Section 16430), "judgment" means a final judgment
558

of any court of competent jurisdiction in this or any other state or of the United States against a person as defendant upon a cause of action. *(Stats.1959, c. 3, p. 1645, § 16250. Amended by Stats.1984, c. 144, § 207.)*

Cross References

Entry of judgment, see Code of Civil Procedure § 664.
Judgment, defined, see Code of Civil Procedure § 577.

§ 16251. Cause of action defined

As used in this chapter and Chapter 3 (commencing with Section 16430), "cause of action" means any cause of action for damage to property in excess of seven hundred fifty dollars ($ 750) or for damage in any amount on account of bodily injury to or death of any person resulting from the operation by the defendant or any other person of any motor vehicle upon a highway in this state, except a cause of action based upon statutory liability by reason of signing the application of a minor for a driver's license. *(Stats.1959, c. 3, p. 1645, § 16251. Amended by Stats.1969, c. 486, p. 1094, § 4; Stats.1974, c. 1409, p. 3101, § 9; Stats.1978, c. 997, p. 3071, § 4; Stats.1979, c. 549, p. 1754, § 6; Stats.1984, c. 144, § 208; Stats.1984, c. 126, § 1; Stats.2002, c. 766 (S.B.1590), § 7.)*

Cross References

Civil liability of persons signing license applications of minors, see Vehicle Code § 17700 et seq.
Definition,
  Highway, see Vehicle Code § 360.
  Motor vehicle, see Vehicle Code § 415.

ARTICLE 2. SUSPENSION OF DRIVING PRIVILEGE

Section
16370.   Judgment unsatisfied.
16370.5. Small claims judgments unsatisfied; license suspension procedure.
16370.7. Filing fees.
16371.   Period of suspension.
16372.   Repealed.
16373.   Certified copy of judgment or certified copy of register of actions and certificate of facts relative to the judgment; rights of judgment creditor.
16374.   Judgments not covered by proof.
16375.   Affidavit of insurance.
16376.   Action against nonresident.
16377.   When judgment deemed satisfied.
16378.   Disposition of money deposited.
16379.   Installment payments of judgments.
16380.   Conditions for installment payment.
16381.   Default in payments.

§ 16370. Judgment unsatisfied

The department shall suspend the privilege of any person to operate a motor vehicle upon receiving a certified copy of a judgment, or a certified copy of the register of actions (or a comparable court record of another jurisdiction) in an action resulting in a judgment for damages, and a certificate of facts relative to the judgment, on a form provided by the department, indicating that the person has failed for a period of 30 days to satisfy a judgment rendered against him or her. *(Stats. 1959, c. 3, p. 1645, § 16370. Amended by Stats.1963, c. 713, p. 1719, § 3; Stats.1969, c. 486, p. 1094, § 5; Stats.1974, c. 714, p. 1596, § 1; Stats.1974, c. 1409, p. 3101, § 10; Stats.1975, c. 354, p. 799, § 2, eff. Aug. 25, 1975; Stats.1985, c. 619, § 2; Stats.2001, c. 44 (S.B.562), § 10.)*

Law Revision Commission Comments
2001 Amendment

Section 16370 is amended to delete the reference to "docket entries," and substitute a reference to the register of actions, because courts no longer maintain a record denominated a "docket" in civil cases. Formerly, justice courts maintained a docket in civil cases, which was a record of actions taken in open court, as well as documents filed and other proceedings in the case. See former Gov't Code 71614 (1953 Cal. Stat. ch. 206, 1, repealed by 1977 Cal. Stat. ch. 1257, 71) (judge of justice court shall keep a book denominated a "docket"), 71614.5 (1959 Cal. Stat. ch. 671, 2, repealed by 1977 Cal. Stat. ch. 1257, 72) (clerk or judge of justice court shall keep the "docket" and other records of the court). Now actions taken in open court are recorded in the minutes of a superior court. Gov't Code 69844; see also Copley Press v. Superior Court, 6 Cal.App.4th 106, 110, 7 Cal.Rptr.2d 841 (1992). Documents filed or lodged and other proceedings in a civil case are recorded in the register of actions. See Gov't Code 69845 (clerk of superior court may keep a register of actions), 69845.5 (alternative to maintaining register of actions in superior court). Section 16370 is amended to refer not only to the register of actions but also to a comparable court record of another jurisdiction, because the provision applies to judgments rendered by courts in other states, not just judgments rendered by the California courts. See Section 16250 ("judgment" defined); see also Section 16251 ("cause of action" defined). [30 Cal.L.Rev.Comm. Reports 479 (2000)].

Cross References

Civil liability of persons signing license applications of minors, see Vehicle Code § 17700 et seq.
Duty of court to report judgment, see Vehicle Code § 16373.
Installment payment of civil judgment, see Vehicle Code §§ 16379, 16380.
Judgment defined, see Vehicle Code § 16250.
Motor vehicle defined, see Vehicle Code § 415.
Nonresidents, failure to satisfy judgment, see Vehicle Code § 16376.
Proof of financial responsibility, see Vehicle Code § 16430.
Restoration of privileges, see Vehicle Code § 16482.
Satisfaction of judgment, amount required, see Vehicle Code § 16377.
Suspension,
  Defined, see Vehicle Code § 13102.
  Licenses, generally, see Vehicle Code §§ 13102, 13200 et seq., 16004.
  Registrations, generally, see Vehicle Code §§ 8800, 8801, 16503.

§ 16370.5. Small claims judgments unsatisfied; license suspension procedure

The department shall suspend the privilege of any person to operate a motor vehicle as specified in Section 116.880 of the Code of Civil Procedure. Except as provided in this section, an action brought under Section 116.880 of the Code of Civil Procedure is not governed by Chapter 2 (commencing with Section 16250) of Division 7. *(Added by Stats.1988, c. 395, § 3, eff. Aug. 11, 1988. Amended by Stats.1990, c. 1305 (S.B.2627), § 12; Stats. 2003, c. 594 (S.B.315), § 42.)*

§ 16370.7. Filing fees

Documents filed with the department pursuant to Section 16370 shall be accompanied by a fee of not to exceed twenty dollars ($20) to pay for processing the documents and issuing the suspension order. *(Added by Stats.1988, c. 395, § 4, eff. Aug. 11, 1988.)*

§ 16371. Period of suspension

The suspension shall remain in effect, and no license shall be issued to the judgment debtor until the judgment debtor gives proof of financial responsibility as provided in Chapter 3 (commencing with Section 16430), and until either the judgment is satisfied in full or to the extent provided in this chapter, subject to the exemption provided in Section 16375. *(Stats.1959, c. 3, p. 1645, § 16371. Amended by Stats.1974, c. 714, p. 1596, § 2; Stats.1982, c. 746, p. 2962, § 3; Stats.1989, c. 1157, § 6.)*

Cross References

Proof of financial responsibility, see Vehicle Code § 16430.
Release of proof, see Vehicle Code § 16480 et seq.
Restoration of privileges despite failure to satisfy judgment, grounds, see Vehicle Code § 16482.
Suspension following unsatisfied judgments, see Vehicle Code § 16250 et seq.

§ 16372. Repealed by Stats.1973, c. 436, p. 904, § 1

§ 16373. Certified copy of judgment or certified copy of register of actions and certificate of facts relative to the judgment; rights of judgment creditor

(a) The clerk of a court shall, subject to subdivision (b), issue upon the request of a judgment creditor a certified copy of any judgment or a certified copy of the register of actions in an action resulting in a judgment for damages, and a certificate of facts relative to the judgment on a form provided by the department.

(b) The judgment creditor may pay the required fees and request the documents specified in subdivision (a) upon the expiration of 30 days after the judgment has become final, if the judgment has not been stayed or satisfied within the amounts specified in this chapter as shown by the records of the court. The court shall determine the required fees, which shall be commensurate with the cost incurred by the court in carrying out this section. *(Stats.1959, c. 3, p. 1646, § 16373. Amended by Stats.1974, c. 714, p. 1596, § 3; Stats.1981, c. 362, p. 1538, § 1; Stats.1985, c. 619, § 4; Stats.2001, c. 44 (S.B.562), § 11.)*

Law Revision Commission Comments
2001 Amendment

Section 16373 is amended to delete the reference to "docket entries," and substitute a reference to the register of actions, because courts no longer maintain a record denominated a "docket" in civil cases. Formerly, justice courts maintained a docket in civil cases, which was a record of actions taken in open court, as well as documents filed and other proceedings in the case. See former Gov't Code 71614 (1953 Cal. Stat. ch. 206, 1, repealed by 1977 Cal. Stat. ch. 1257, 71) (judge of justice court shall keep a book denominated a "docket"), 71614.5 (1959 Cal. Stat. ch. 671, 2, repealed by 1977 Cal. Stat. ch. 1257, 72) (clerk or judge of justice court shall keep the "docket" and other records of the court). Now actions taken in open court are recorded in the minutes of a superior court. Gov't Code 69844; see also Copley Press v. Superior Court, 6 Cal.App.4th 106, 110, 7 Cal.Rptr.2d 841 (1992). Documents filed or lodged and other proceedings in a civil case are recorded in the register of actions. See Gov't Code 69845 (clerk of superior court may keep a register of actions), 69845.5 (alternative to maintaining register of actions in superior court).

The amendment also deletes the clause authorizing the judge to substitute for the clerk if there is no clerk. That provision is obsolete because every superior court has a clerk. See Gov't Code 24000(c) (county clerk), 26800 (county clerk as clerk of superior court). Additionally, a judge has authority to perform any act that a court clerk is allowed to perform. Code Civ. Proc. 167. [31 Cal.L.Rev.Comm. Reports 69 (2001)].

Cross References

Organization and government of courts, collection of fees and fines pursuant to this section, deposits, see Government Code § 68085.1.

§ 16374. Judgments not covered by proof

Whenever after a judgment is satisfied and proof of financial responsibility is given, another judgment is rendered against the same person for any accident occurring prior to the date of the giving of the proof and the person fails to satisfy the latter judgment within the amounts specified in this chapter within 15 days after the latter judgment became final, then the department shall again suspend the driver's license of the judgment debtor and shall not issue to him or her any driver's license while the latter judgment remains unsatisfied and subsisting within the amounts specified in this chapter. *(Stats.1959, c. 3, p. 1646, § 16374. Amended by Stats.1974, c. 714, p. 1596, § 4; Stats.1989, c. 1157, § 7.)*

Cross References

Proof of financial responsibility, see Vehicle Code § 16430.
Satisfaction of judgment, amount required, see Vehicle Code § 16377.

§ 16375. Affidavit of insurance

Any person whose driver's license has been suspended, or is about to be suspended or shall become subject to suspension under this chapter, may relieve himself from the effect of the judgment by filing with the department an affidavit stating that at the time of the accident upon which the judgment has been rendered he was insured, that the insurer is liable to pay such judgment, and the

reason, if known, why the insurance company has not paid the judgment. He shall also file the original policy of insurance or a certified copy thereof, if available, and such other documents as the department may require to show that the loss, injury, or damage for which the judgment was rendered, was covered by the policy of insurance.

If the department is satisfied from such papers that the insurer was authorized to issue the policy of insurance in this state at the time of issuing the policy and that such insurer is liable to pay such judgment, at least to the extent and for the amounts provided in this chapter, the department shall not suspend the license, or if already suspended, shall reinstate it. *(Stats.1959, c. 3, p. 1646, § 16375. Amended by Stats.1974, c. 714, p. 1596, § 5.)*

Cross References

Proof of financial responsibility, see Vehicle Code § 16430.
Satisfaction of judgment, amount required, see Vehicle Code § 16377.

§ 16376. Action against nonresident

(a) If the person against whom judgment is rendered is a nonresident and the person fails within the prescribed time to satisfy the judgment in full or to the extent specified in this chapter, all privileges of operating a motor vehicle in this state given to the person under this code shall be suspended while the judgment remains in effect and unsatisfied and until the nonresident gives proof of his or her financial responsibility in the manner and to the extent provided in Chapter 3 (commencing with Section 16430) for accidents occurring after the date of the giving of proof.

(b) The department shall forward a certified copy of the judgment of a court of record to the appropriate officer in charge of the licensing of drivers in the state of which the person is a resident. *(Stats.1959, c. 3, p. 1646, § 16376. Amended by Stats.1963, c. 209, p. 949, § 6, eff. April 29, 1963; Stats.1974, c. 714, p. 1597, § 6; Stats.1989, c. 1157, § 8; Stats.2001, c. 44 (S.B.562), § 12.)*

Law Revision Commission Comments
2001 Amendment

Section 16376 is amended to insert subdivisions and eliminate the reference to "the docket of a court not of record," which is obsolete because all courts are "courts of record." Cal. Const. art. VI, 1. [31 Cal.L.Rev.Comm. Reports 69 (2001)].

Cross References

Nonresident defined, see Vehicle Code §§ 435, 17450.
Permit for registration of foreign vehicles, see Vehicle Code § 6700 et seq.
Privilege of operating motor vehicle, see Vehicle Code §§ 13205, 13552.
Proof of financial responsibility, see Vehicle Code § 16430.

Service of process on nonresident, see Vehicle Code § 17450 et seq.

§ 16377. When judgment deemed satisfied

Every judgment shall for the purposes of this chapter be deemed satisfied:

(a) When fifteen thousand dollars ($15,000) has been credited, upon any judgment in excess of that amount, or upon all judgments, collectively, which together total in excess of that amount, for personal injury to or death of one person as a result of any one accident.

(b) When, subject to the limit of fifteen thousand dollars ($15,000) as to one person, the sum of thirty thousand dollars ($30,000) has been credited, upon any judgment in excess of that amount, or upon all judgments, collectively, which together total in excess of that amount, for personal injury to or death of more than one person as a result of any one accident.

(c) When five thousand dollars ($5,000) has been credited, upon any judgment in excess of that amount, or upon all judgments, collectively, each of which is in excess of seven hundred fifty dollars ($750), and which together total in excess of five thousand dollars ($5,000), for damage to property of others as a result of any one accident.

(d) When the judgment debtor or a person designated by him or her has deposited with the department a sum equal to the amount of the unsatisfied judgment for which the suspension action was taken and presents proof, satisfactory to the department, of inability to locate the judgment creditor. *(Stats.1959, c. 3, p. 1647, § 16377. Amended by Stats.1965, c. 1525, p. 3617, § 1; Stats.1967, c. 862, p. 2304, § 4, operative July 1, 1968; Stats.1969, c. 486, p. 1094, § 6; Stats.1974, c. 1409, p. 3101, § 11; Stats.1978, c. 997, p. 3072, § 5; Stats.1979, c. 549, p. 1754, § 7; Stats.2002, c. 766 (S.B.1590), § 8.)*

§ 16378. Disposition of money deposited

Money deposited pursuant to subdivision (d) of Section 16377 shall be:

(a) Deposited by the department in the special deposit fund with the State Treasurer.

(b) Payable to the judgment creditor upon presentation of a valid claim establishing that he is the judgment creditor for which the deposit was made and that the judgment remains unsatisfied.

(c) Refunded to the person making the deposit or to a person designated by him if the deposit remains unclaimed by the judgment creditor for a period of two years following the date of the deposit.

(d) The State Controller shall draw his warrant on the State Treasurer for any payment ordered pursuant to this section as ordered by the department. *(Added by Stats. 1965, c. 1525, p. 3617, § 2.)*

§ 16379. Installment payments of judgments

(a) The department shall not suspend a license and shall restore any suspended license following nonpayment of a final judgment when the judgment debtor gives proof of financial responsibility for future damages and when the trial court in which the judgment was rendered orders the payment of the judgment in installments and while the payment of any installment payment is not in default.

(b) Whenever the trial court orders the payment of a judgment in installments as provided in this section, upon payment of the required fees by the judgment creditor, it shall forward a certified copy of the order to the department, together with a certified copy of the judgment or a certified copy of the register of actions in an action resulting in a judgment for damages and a certificate of facts relative to the judgment on a form provided by the department.

(c) The court shall determine the required fees, which shall be commensurate with the cost incurred by the court in carrying out the provisions of this section. *(Formerly § 16485, Stats.1959, c. 3, p. 1651, § 16485. Renumbered § 16379 and amended by Stats.1967, c. 211, p. 1337, § 1. Amended by Stats.1974, c. 714, p. 1597, § 7; Stats.1981, c. 362, p. 1538, § 2; Stats.2001, c. 44 (S.B.562), § 13.)*

Law Revision Commission Comments

2001 Amendment

Section 16379 is amended to delete the reference to "docket entries," and substitute a reference to the register of actions, because courts no longer maintain a record denominated a "docket" in civil cases. Formerly, justice courts maintained a docket in civil cases, which was a record of actions taken in open court, as well as documents filed and other proceedings in the case. See former Gov't Code 71614 (1953 Cal. Stat. ch. 206, 1, repealed by 1977 Cal. Stat. ch. 1257, 71) (judge of justice court shall keep a book denominated a "docket"), 71614.5 (1959 Cal. Stat. ch. 671, 2, repealed by 1977 Cal. Stat. ch. 1257, 72) (clerk or judge of justice court shall keep the "docket" and other records of the court). Now actions taken in open court are recorded in the minutes of a superior court. Gov't Code 69844; see also Copley Press v. Superior Court, 6 Cal.App.4th 106, 110, 7 Cal.Rptr.2d 841 (1992). Documents filed or lodged and other proceedings in a civil case are recorded in the register of actions. See Gov't Code 69845 (clerk of superior court may keep a register of actions), 69845.5 (alternative to maintaining register of actions in superior court). [31 Cal.L.Rev.Comm. Reports 69 (2001)].

Cross References

Satisfaction of judgment, amount required, see Vehicle Code § 16377.

§ 16380. Conditions for installment payment

The trial court may order the payment of a judgment in installments only when the defendant is not insured or the insurance policy covering the automobile involved in the accident, for the ownership or operation of which the defendant is held liable, is not sufficient to pay the amount of the judgment, and then only as to such portion of the judgment not covered by the insurance policy.

The order shall fix the amounts and times of payment of the installments and shall be without prejudice to any other legal remedies available to the judgment creditor. *(Formerly § 16486, Stats.1959, c. 3, p. 1651, § 16486. Renumbered § 16380 and amended by Stats.1967, c. 211, p. 1338, § 2.)*

Cross References

Creation and duration of lien, see Code of Civil Procedure § 697.310.

Satisfaction of judgment, amount required, see Vehicle Code § 16377.

§ 16381. Default in payments

In the event that it is made to appear to the court that the judgment debtor has failed to pay any installment as permitted by the order of the court, upon the payment of required fees by the judgment creditor, the court shall give notice of the default to the department and the department shall forthwith suspend the driving privilege of the judgment debtor until the judgment is satisfied as provided in this chapter. The court shall determine the required fees, which shall be commensurate with the cost incurred by the court in carrying out the provisions of this section. *(Formerly § 16487, Stats.1959, c. 3, p. 1652, § 16487. Renumbered § 16381 and amended by Stats. 1967, c. 211, p. 1338, § 3. Amended by Stats.1974, c. 714, p. 1597, § 8; Stats.1981, c. 362, p. 1539, § 3.)*

CHAPTER 3. PROOF OF FINANCIAL RESPONSIBILITY

Article	Section
1. **Proof Requirements**	**16430**
2. **Insurance Policy**	**16450**
3. **Release of Proof**	**16480**

ARTICLE 1. PROOF REQUIREMENTS

Section
16430.   Proof required.
16431.   Proof of financial responsibility; written certificate by insurer; sufficiency; exceptions.
16432.   Repealed.
16432.5. Repealed.
16433.   Cancellation of policy; notice to department; coverage not extended.
16434.   Proof by bond.
16435.   Proof by deposit of money.
16436.   Proof by self-insurer.

§ 16430. Proof required

Proof of financial responsibility when required by this code means proof of financial responsibility resulting from the ownership or operation of a motor vehicle and arising by reason of personal injury to, or death of, any one person, of at least fifteen thousand dollars ($15,000), and, subject to the limit of fifteen thousand dollars ($15,000) for each person injured or killed, of at least thirty thousand dollars ($30,000) for the injury to, or the death of, two or more persons in any one accident, and

for damages to property (in excess of seven hundred fifty dollars ($750)), of at least five thousand dollars ($5,000) resulting from any one accident. Proof of financial responsibility may be given in any manner authorized in this chapter. *(Stats.1959, c. 3, p. 1647, § 16430. Amended by Stats.1967, c. 862, p. 2305, § 5, operative July 1, 1968; Stats.1969, c. 486, p. 1095, § 7; Stats.1974, c. 1409, p. 3102, § 12; Stats.1978, c. 997, p. 3072, § 6; Stats.1979, c. 549, p. 1755, § 8; Stats.1989, c. 1157, § 9; Stats.2002, c. 766 (S.B.1590), § 9.)*

Cross References

Commercial passenger vehicles, proof of financial responsibility, see Vehicle Code § 16500 et seq.

Influence of alcoholic beverage or drug, suspension or revocation of driving privileges, see Vehicle Code § 13352.

Minor's application for license, proof of financial responsibility, see Vehicle Code § 17702.

Motor vehicle liability policy, see Vehicle Code § 16450 et seq.

Nonresident minor, necessity of filing proof of financial responsibility to secure certificate of compliance, see Vehicle Code §§ 246, 12504.

Nonresident minor operating within state without obtaining driver's license, proof of financial responsibility, see Vehicle Code § 12504.

Persons certified or granted probation on conviction of driving under the influence of alcohol or drugs or combined influence on certain conditions, restriction, revocation or suspension of driving privilege, consent to participation in treatment program, see Vehicle Code § 13352.5.

Removal of restriction on privilege to operate a motor vehicle, see Vehicle Code § 23168.

Renewal of driving privilege, see Vehicle Code §§ 13351, 13352.

Revoked licenses, reinstatement, proof of financial responsibility as defined in this section, see Vehicle Code § 13350.

Signature on behalf of minors, see Vehicle Code §§ 17702, 17703.

Substitution of proof of financial responsibility, suspension upon failure of proof, see Vehicle Code §§ 16483, 16484.

Suspension of driver's license, grounds, see Vehicle Code § 13361.

Suspension of driving privileges following accident, duration, see Vehicle Code § 19082.

§ 16431. Proof of financial responsibility; written certificate by insurer; sufficiency; exceptions

(a) Proof of financial responsibility may be given by the written certificate or certificates of any insurance carrier duly authorized to do business within the state, that it has issued to or for the benefit of the person named therein a motor vehicle liability policy as defined in Section 16450, an automobile liability policy as defined in Section 16054, or any other liability policy issued for vehicles with less than four wheels that meets the requirements of Section 16056, which, at the date of the certificate or certificates, is in full force and effect. Except as provided in subdivision (b), the certificate or certificates issued under any liability policy set forth in this section shall be accepted by the department and satisfy the requirements of proof of financial responsibility of this chapter. Nothing in this chapter requires that an insurance carrier certify that there is coverage broader than that provided by the actual policy issued by the carrier.

(b) The department shall require that a person whose driver's license has been revoked, suspended, or restricted under Section 13350, 13351, 13352, 13353, 13353.2, 13353.3, 13353.7, or 16370, provide, as proof of financial responsibility, a certificate or certificates that covers all motor vehicles registered to the person before reinstatement of his or her driver's license.

(c) Subdivision (b) does not apply to vehicles in storage if the current license plates and registration cards are surrendered to the department in Sacramento.

(d)(1) A resident of another state may provide proof of financial responsibility when required to do so under this code from a company authorized to do business in that person's state of residence, if that proof is satisfactory to the department, covers the operation of a vehicle in this state, and meets the minimum coverage limit requirements specified in Section 16056.

(2) If the person specified in paragraph (1) becomes a resident of this state during the period that the person is required to maintain proof of financial responsibility with the department, the department may not issue or return a driver's license to that person until the person files a written certificate or certificates, as authorized under subdivision (a), that meets the minimum coverage limit requirements specified in Section 16056 and covers the period during which the person is required to maintain proof of financial responsibility.

(e) This section shall become operative on September 20, 2005. *(Stats.1959, c. 3, p. 1647, § 16431. Amended by Stats.1965, c. 2003, p. 4531, § 1, operative Jan. 1, 1966; Stats.1989, c. 1157, § 10; Stats.1990, c. 314 (S.B.2673), § 6, eff. July 17, 1990; Stats.1991, c. 1177 (S.B.35), § 6, eff. Oct. 14, 1991; Stats.1996, c. 1154 (A.B.3020), § 66, eff. Sept. 30, 1996; Stats.2003, c. 594 (S.B.315), § 43; Stats. 2004, c. 952 (A.B.3049), § 28, operative Sept. 20, 2005.)*

Cross References

Commercial passenger vehicles, proof of financial responsibility, see Vehicle Code § 16500 et seq.
Completion and filing of certificate by insurer, see Insurance Code § 655.
County and City of San Francisco Low–Cost Automobile Insurance Pilot Program, policy attributes, see Insurance Code § 11629.91.
County of Los Angeles Low–Cost Automobile Insurance Pilot Program, policy attributes, see Insurance Code § 11629.71.
Minor's application for license, proof of financial responsibility, see Vehicle Code § 17702.
Motor vehicle liability policy, see Vehicle Code § 16450 et seq.
Release of proof, see Vehicle Code § 16480 et seq.
Restriction on drivers licenses, see Vehicle Code § 16457.

§ 16432. Repealed by Stats.1991, c. 1177 (S.B.35), § 7, eff. Oct. 14, 1991

§ 16432.5. Repealed by Stats.1989, c. 1157, § 11

§ 16433. Cancellation of policy; notice to department; coverage not extended

A certificate or certificates shall certify, if the liability policy therein cited has been canceled, that the department shall be notified in writing within 10 days after the cancellation of insurance becomes final.

Nothing in this section extends coverage beyond the date stated in the notice of cancellation. *(Stats.1959, c. 3, p. 1648, § 16433. Amended by Stats.1982, c. 466, p. 2057, § 112; Stats.1989, c. 1269, § 1; Stats.1990, c. 314 (S.B. 2673), § 8, eff. July 17, 1990.)*

Cross References

Department defined, see Vehicle Code § 290.
Motor vehicle liability policy, see Vehicle Code § 16450 et seq.

§ 16434. Proof by bond

Proof of financial responsibility may be given by a bond. The bond shall be conditioned for the payment of the amount specified in Section 16430, and shall provide for the entry of judgment on motion of the state in favor of any holder of any final judgment on account of damages to property over seven hundred fifty dollars ($750) in amount, or injury to any person caused by the operation of the person's motor vehicle. *(Stats.1959, c. 3, p. 1648, § 16434. Amended by Stats.1969, c. 486, p. 1095, § 8; Stats.1971, c. 438, p. 908, § 190, operative May 3, 1972; Stats.1974, c. 1409, p. 3102, § 13; Stats.1978, c. 997, p. 3072, § 7; Stats.1979, c. 549, p. 1755, § 9; Stats.1982, c. 517, p. 2430, § 401; Stats.1983, c. 18, § 38.5, eff. April 21, 1983; Stats.1989, c. 1157, § 12; Stats.2002, c. 766 (S.B. 1590), § 10.)*

Law Revision Commission Comments

1982 Amendment

Section 16434 is amended to delete provisions duplicated in the Bond and Undertaking Law. See Code Civ. Proc. §§ 995.310 (sureties on bond), 996.440 (motion to enforce liability). (16 Cal.L.Rev. Comm. Reports 501).

1983 Amendment

Section 16434 is amended to delete the unnecessary court approval procedure. A bond given under Section 16434 is subject to disapproval by the Department of Motor Vehicles pursuant to Code of Civil Procedure Section 996.020. [16 Cal.L.Rev.Comm.Reports 2239 (1982); 83 S.J. 1127].

Cross References

Bond and Undertaking Law, see Code of Civil Procedure § 995.010 et seq.
Commercial passenger vehicles, proof of financial responsibility, see Vehicle Code § 16500.
Minor's application for license, proof of financial responsibility, see Vehicle Code § 17702.
Motor vehicle liability policy, see Vehicle Code § 16450 et seq.
Release of proof, see Vehicle Code § 16480 et seq.
Substitution of proof, see Vehicle Code § 16483.
Vehicles designed to carry 16 or more passengers or over 7,000 pounds, bond under this section permitted, see Vehicle Code § 16500.5.

§ 16435. Proof by deposit of money

Proof of financial responsibility may be given by the deposit of thirty-five thousand dollars ($35,000), as provided in Section 16054.2. The department shall not accept a deposit where any judgment theretofore obtained against that person as a result of damages arising from the operation of any motor vehicle shall not have been paid in full. *(Stats.1959, c. 3, p. 1648, § 16435. Amended by Stats.1989, c. 1157, § 13.)*

Cross References

Commercial passenger vehicles, proof of financial responsibility, see Vehicle Code § 16500 et seq.
Department defined, see Vehicle Code § 290.
Minor's application for license, proof of financial responsibility, see Vehicle Code § 17702.
Release of proof, see Vehicle Code § 16480 et seq.
Substitution of proof, see Vehicle Code § 16483.

§ 16436. Proof by self-insurer

Proof of financial responsibility may be given by the written certificate of a self-insurer holding a certificate of self-insurance for bodily injury and property damage issued by the department.

The certification shall name the employee in whose behalf it is filed and shall bind the self-insurer in a like manner and to the same amounts as provided for in Section 16430 for damages arising from the operation of a motor vehicle by the employee within the scope of his or her employment by the self-insurer. In that case, the department shall restrict any driver's license issued to the employee to the operation of motor vehicles owned by the self-insurer within the scope of his or her employment by the self-insurer.

The certificate shall be canceled upon 10 days' prior written notice to the department by the self-insurer. *(Stats.1959, c. 3, p. 1648, § 16436. Amended by Stats. 1971, c. 438, p. 908, § 191, operative May 3, 1972; Stats.1982, c. 466, p. 2057, § 113; Stats.1989, c. 1157, § 14.)*

Cross References

Commercial passenger vehicles, financial responsibility, see Vehicle Code § 16500 et seq.
Commercial vehicle defined, see Vehicle Code § 260.
Department defined, see Vehicle Code § 290.
Minor's application for license, proof of financial responsibility, see Vehicle Code § 17702.
Operation of vehicle not covered by certificate of proof of financial responsibility, see Vehicle Code § 16457.
Release of proof, see Vehicle Code § 16480 et seq.
Restrictions on drivers licenses, see Vehicle Code § 16457.
Substitution of proof, see Vehicle Code § 16483.

ARTICLE 2. INSURANCE POLICY

Section
16450. Motor vehicle liability policy.
16451. Owner's policy.
16452. Operator's policy.
16453. Permitted provisions.

564

Section
16454. Worker's compensation.
16455. Stored vehicles.
16456. Repealed.
16457. Operation of vehicle not covered by certificate; disclosure of ownership.

§ 16450. Motor vehicle liability policy

A "motor vehicle liability policy," as used in Chapters 1 (commencing with Section 16000), 2 (commencing with Section 16250), and 4 (commencing with Section 16500), and this chapter, means an owner's policy or an operator's policy, or both, of liability insurance, certified as provided in Section 16431 as proof of financial responsibility, issued by an insurance carrier authorized to transact that business in this state to or for the benefit of the person named therein as assured. Any requirements set forth in Chapters 1 (commencing with Section 16000), 2 (commencing with Section 16250), and 4 (commencing with Section 16500), and this chapter relating to a motor vehicle liability policy shall apply only to those policies which have been certified as proof of financial responsibility as provided in Section 16431. *(Stats.1959, c. 3, p. 1649, § 16450. Amended by Stats.1963, c. 1259, p. 2781, § 3; Stats.1989, c. 1157, § 15.)*

Cross References

General regulations of insurance business, see Insurance Code § 680 et seq.
Proof of financial responsibility, see Vehicle Code § 16430.
Rosenthal Auto Insurance Nondiscrimination Law, see Insurance Code § 11628.
Workers' compensation, generally, see Labor Code § 3201 et seq.

§ 16451. Owner's policy

An owner's policy of motor vehicle liability insurance shall insure the named insured and any other person using any motor vehicle registered to the named insured with the express or implied permission of the named insured, against loss from the liability imposed by law for damages arising out of ownership, maintenance, or use of the motor vehicle within the continental limits of the United States to the extent and aggregate amount, exclusive of interest and costs, with respect to each motor vehicle, of fifteen thousand dollars ($15,000) for bodily injury to or death of each person as a result of any one accident and, subject to the limit as to one person, the amount of thirty thousand dollars ($30,000) for bodily injury to or death of all persons as a result of any one accident and the amount of five thousand dollars ($5,000) for damage to property of others as a result of any one accident. *(Stats.1959, c. 3, p. 1649, § 16451. Amended by Stats.1965, c. 2003, p. 4531, § 2; Stats.1967, c. 862, p. 2305, § 6, operative July 1, 1968; Stats.1968, c. 1314, p. 2484, § 4; Stats.1983, c. 1244, § 4; Stats.1989, c. 1157, § 16.)*

Cross References

General regulations of insurance business, see Insurance Code § 680 et seq.

Owner defined, see Vehicle Code § 460.

Vehicles designed to carry 16 or more passengers or over 7,000 pounds, minimum coverage under this section required even though agent is misinformed by owner, see Vehicle Code § 16500.5.

§ 16452. Operator's policy

An operator's policy of motor vehicle liability insurance shall insure the person named as insured therein against loss from the liability imposed on that person by law for damages arising out of use by that person of any motor vehicle not owned by that person, and for any subsequently acquired motor vehicle for a period not to exceed 10 days from date of purchase, within the same territorial limits and subject to the same limits of liability as are provided for in an owner's policy of liability insurance. *(Stats.1959, c. 3, p. 1649, § 16452. Amended by Stats. 1965, c. 2003, p. 4532; § 3; Stats.1968, c. 1314, p. 2484, § 5; Stats.1989, c. 1157, § 17.)*

Cross References

Liability of operator, see Vehicle Code § 17152.
Owner defined, see Vehicle Code § 460.

§ 16453. Permitted provisions

Any motor vehicle liability policy may grant any lawful coverage in excess of or in addition to the coverage herein specified or contain any agreements, provisions or stipulations not in conflict with the provisions of this code and not otherwise contrary to law. *(Stats.1959, c. 3, p. 1649, § 16453.)*

§ 16454. Worker's compensation

Any motor vehicle liability policy need not cover any liability for injury to the assured or any liability of the assured assumed by or imposed upon the assured under any workers' compensation law nor any liability for damage to property in charge of the assured or the assured's employees or agents. *(Stats.1959, c. 3, p. 1649, § 16454. Amended by Stats.1974, c. 1454, p. 3181, § 21.)*

§ 16455. Stored vehicles

The provisions of Section 16451 shall not apply to vehicles in storage if the current license plates and registration cards are surrendered to the department in Sacramento. *(Stats.1959, c. 3, p. 1649, § 16455.)*

§ 16456. Repealed by Stats.1979, c. 549, p. 1755, § 10

§ 16457. Operation of vehicle not covered by certificate; disclosure of ownership

Whenever proof of financial responsibility is required to be filed pursuant to this chapter, no person of whom that proof is required shall drive any motor vehicle not covered by the certificate of proof of financial responsibility filed by him or her with the department, nor shall any applicant for that proof knowingly fail to disclose ownership of a motor vehicle in the application for proof of financial responsibility or to disclose any subsequently acquired motor vehicle.

(Stats.1959, c. 3, p. 1650, § 16457. Amended by Stats.1959, c. 1742, p. 4201, § 3; Stats.1967, c. 473, p. 1679, § 1; Stats.1982, c. 746, p. 2962, § 5; Stats.1989, c. 1157, § 18; Stats.1990, c. 314 (S.B.2673), § 9, eff. July 17, 1990; Stats.1995, c. 91 (S.B.975), § 180; Stats.1996, c. 1126 (A.B.650), § 14, operative Jan. 1, 1997; Stats.1999, c. 880 (S.B.652), § 19.)

Cross References

Certificate of proof of financial responsibility, see Vehicle Code § 16431.
Penalty for misdemeanor, see Vehicle Code § 42002.

ARTICLE 3. RELEASE OF PROOF

Section
16480. Release of proof.
16481. Repealed.
16482. Restoration of privileges when judgment unsatisfied.
16483. Substitution of proof.
16484. Failure of proof.
16485. Renumbered.
16486. Renumbered.
16487. Renumbered.

§ 16480. Release of proof

(a) The department shall upon request, or may at its own discretion, cancel any bond or any certificate of insurance, or the department shall direct the return to the person entitled thereto of any money or securities deposited pursuant to this code as proof of financial responsibility, or the department shall waive the requirement of filing proof of financial responsibility in any of the following events:

(1) When the person is no longer required to maintain the proof under the provisions of this code.

(2) At any time after three years from the date the proof was required.

(3) Upon the death of the person on whose behalf the proof was filed.

(4) The permanent incapacity of the person to operate a motor vehicle if the person surrenders for cancellation his or her driver's license to the department.

(b) The department shall not release proof filed by the bond of individual sureties as set forth in Section 16434, or if given in the manner prescribed by Section 16435, if any action for damages upon a liability referred to in this code is then pending or if any judgment upon any the liability is outstanding and unsatisfied. An affidavit of the applicant of the nonexistence of those facts shall be prima facie evidence thereof. *(Stats.1959, c. 3, p. 1650, § 16480. Amended by Stats.1963, c. 865, p. 2101, § 1; Stats.1965, c. 316, p. 1415, § 1; Stats.1971, c. 1023, p. 1969, § 1, operative May 3, 1972; Stats.1974, c. 714, p. 1598, § 9; Stats.1989, c. 1157, § 19.)*

Cross References

Bond as proof of financial responsibility, see Vehicle Code § 16434.

Certificate of proof of financial responsibility, see Vehicle Code § 16431.

Commercial passenger vehicles, return of deposit, see Vehicle Code § 16500.

Department defined, see Vehicle Code § 290.

Deposit of money or proof of financial responsibility, see Vehicle Code § 16435.

Proof of financial responsibility, see Vehicle Code § 16430.

§ 16481. Repealed by Stats.1965, c. 316, p. 1416, § 2

§ 16482. Restoration of privileges when judgment unsatisfied

(a) Any person whose privilege to operate a motor vehicle has been suspended because of failure to satisfy a judgment and the judgment has been outstanding for a period of three years or more, may be relieved of the penalties therein provided and the privilege of the person to operate a motor vehicle may be restored in the event the person files with the department and thereafter maintains proof of financial responsibility notwithstanding that the judgment which gave rise to the order of suspension has not been paid or fully satisfied.

(b) Any person who has filed proof of financial responsibility as required for three years, or who has been eligible to file that proof for three years, may be relieved of the requirement of filing proof as provided in paragraph (2) of subdivision (a) of Section 16480. *(Stats. 1959, c. 3, p. 1651, § 16482. Amended by Stats.1959, c. 1996, p. 4629, § 20.9; Stats.1967, c. 1014, p. 2609, § 2; Stats.1969, c. 26, p. 128, § 7; Stats.1974, c. 714, p. 1598, § 10; Stats.1989, c. 1157, § 20.)*

Cross References

Suspensions following unsatisfied judgments, see Vehicle Code § 16250 et seq.

§ 16483. Substitution of proof

The department shall cancel any bond or any certificate of insurance or direct the return of any money or securities to the person entitled thereto, upon the substitution and acceptance of other adequate proof of financial responsibility pursuant to this code. *(Stats.1959, c. 3, p. 1651, § 16483. Amended by Stats.1989, c. 1157, § 21.)*

Cross References

Certificate of proof of financial responsibility, see Vehicle Code § 16431.

Commercial passenger vehicles, return of deposit, see Vehicle Code § 16500.

Department defined, see Vehicle Code § 290.

Proof of financial responsibility,
  Generally, see Vehicle Code § 16430.
  Bond, see Vehicle Code § 16434.
  Deposit of money, see Vehicle Code § 16435.
  Self-insurer, see Vehicle Code § 16436.

§ 16484. Failure of proof

Except when a nonresident minor's certificate or minor's license is canceled as required by Sections 12504 and 17704, respectively, whenever any evidence of proof of financial responsibility filed by any person under the provisions of this code no longer fulfills the purpose for which required, the department shall require other evidence of financial responsibility as required by Article 1 (commencing with Section 16430) and shall suspend the privilege of the person to operate a motor vehicle upon a highway. The suspension shall remain in effect until adequate proof of financial responsibility is filed with the department by the person. *(Stats.1959, c. 3, p. 1651, § 16484. Amended by Stats.1970, c. 923, p. 1676, § 3; Stats.1974, c. 714, p. 1598, § 11; Stats.1989, c. 1157, § 22.)*

Cross References

Department defined, see Vehicle Code § 290.

Proof of financial responsibility, see Vehicle Code § 16430.

§ 16485. Renumbered § 16379 and amended by Stats. 1967, c. 211, p. 1337, § 1

§ 16486. Renumbered § 16380 and amended by Stats. 1967, c. 211, p. 1338, § 2

§ 16487. Renumbered § 16381 and amended by Stats. 1967, c. 211, p. 1338, § 3

CHAPTER 4. COMMERCIAL VEHICLES

Section
16500.   Proof of financial responsibility required.
16500.5. Proof of financial responsibility; vehicle used to carry passengers for hire, except taxicabs; vehicles over 7000 pounds; exceptions; coverage of policy based on incorrect information.
16501.   Power of local authorities.
16502.   Violations; denial of entry into the state.
16503.   Suspension of registration.

§ 16500. Proof of financial responsibility required

Every owner of a vehicle used in the transportation of passengers for hire, including taxicabs, when the operation of the vehicle is not subject to regulation by the Public Utilities Commission, shall maintain, whenever he or she may be engaged in conducting those operations, proof of financial responsibility resulting from the ownership or operation of the vehicle and arising by reason of personal injury to, or death of, any one person, of at least fifteen thousand dollars ($15,000), and, subject to the limit of fifteen thousand dollars ($15,000) for each person injured or killed, of at least thirty thousand dollars ($30,000) for the injury to, or the death of, two or more persons in any one accident, and for damages to property of at least five thousand dollars ($5,000) resulting from any one accident. Proof of financial responsibility may be maintained by either:

(a) Being insured under a motor vehicle liability policy against that liability.

(b) Obtaining a bond of the same kind, and containing the same provisions, as those bonds specified in Section 16434.

(c) By depositing with the department thirty-five thousand dollars ($35,000), which amount shall be deposited in a special deposit account with the Controller for the purpose of this section.

(d) Qualifying as a self-insurer under Section 16053.

The department shall return the deposit to the person entitled thereto when he or she is no longer required to maintain proof of financial responsibility as required by this section or upon his or her death. *(Stats.1959, c. 3, p. 1652, § 16500. Amended by Stats.1967, c. 862, p. 2306, § 7, operative July 1, 1968; Stats.1976, c. 1079, p. 4889, § 89; Stats.1989, c. 1157, § 23.)*

Cross References

Definitions,
  Commercial vehicle, see Vehicle Code § 260.
  Department, see Vehicle Code § 290.
  Owner, see Vehicle Code § 460.
  Passenger vehicle, see Vehicle Code § 465.
  Vehicle, see Vehicle Code § 670.
Motor vehicle liability policy, see Vehicle Code § 16450 et seq.
Release of proof of financial responsibility, see Vehicle Code § 16480 et seq.

§ 16500.5. Proof of financial responsibility; vehicle used to carry passengers for hire, except taxicabs; vehicles over 7000 pounds; exceptions; coverage of policy based on incorrect information

(a) Except as specified in subdivision (b), the owner of the following commercial vehicles shall maintain proof of financial responsibility in the amount required by the director:

(1) A vehicle used to carry passengers for hire, except taxicabs as defined in subdivision (c) of Section 27908.

(2) A vehicle having an unladen weight of over 7,000 pounds which is used in the transportation of property in the conduct of a business.

(b) Subdivision (a) does not apply to the following vehicles:

(1) A schoolbus.

(2) A motor vehicle used by a farmer exclusively in the transportation of his or her livestock, implements of husbandry, and agricultural commodities or in the transportation of supplies to his or her farm.

(3) A motor vehicle used by a resident farmer of this state to occasionally transport from the place of production to a warehouse, regular market, place of storage, or place of shipment the farm products of neighboring farmers in exchange for like services, farm products, or other compensation.

(4) A vehicle used in for-hire transportation which is subject to regulation by the Public Utilities Commission.

(5) A rented vehicle used for noncommercial transportation of property.

(c) The director shall establish the amounts which are determined adequate to cover damages resulting from the ownership or operation of a commercial vehicle or vehicles subject to this section arising by reason of personal injury to, or death of, any person or damage to property, or both. The director shall establish the amounts at levels equal to those prescribed by the Public Utilities Commission for owners and operators of for-hire vehicles subject to its jurisdiction and control.

(d) Proof of financial responsibility may be maintained by any of the following:

(1) Being insured under one or more motor vehicle liability policies against that liability.

(2) Obtaining a bond of the same kind, and containing the same provisions, as those bonds specified in Section 16434.

(3) By depositing with the department five hundred thousand dollars ($500,000), which amount shall be deposited in a special deposit account with the Controller for the purpose of this section.

(4) Qualifying as a self-insurer under Section 16053.

(e) The department shall return the deposit made pursuant to paragraph (3) of subdivision (d) to the person entitled thereto when the owner is no longer required to maintain proof of financial responsibility as required by this section or upon the owner's death.

(f) An insurer, agent, or broker who has been incorrectly informed by an owner of a vehicle or his or her representative that the vehicle is 7,000 pounds or less unladen weight, or is incorrectly informed by the owner or his or her representative that the vehicle is exempt from the requirements of subdivisions (a) and (c) pursuant to the exemptions set forth in subdivision (b), may issue a policy of motor vehicle liability insurance in any amount less than that required by the director but not less than the amounts required under Section 16451. The policy of motor vehicle liability insurance when issued shall not be deemed to provide liability coverage amounts greater than that specifically set forth in the policy notwithstanding that the vehicle weighs in excess of 7,000 pounds unladen weight or is subsequently used in a manner which would have required the vehicle to be insured in the amounts established by the director pursuant to subdivision (c). *(Added by Stats.1980, c. 983, p. 3116, § 2. Amended by Stats.1981, c. 924, p. 3479, § 1; Stats.1982, c. 245, p. 788, § 1; Stats.1984, c. 1715, § 5; Stats.1989, c. 1157, § 24.)*

§ 16501. Power of local authorities

The provisions of this chapter shall not prevent local authorities, within the reasonable exercise of the police power, from adopting rules and regulations, by ordinance or resolution, licensing and regulating the operation of any vehicle for hire and the drivers of passenger vehicles for hire. *(Stats.1959, c. 3, p. 1652, § 16501. Amended by Stats.1965, c. 1554, p. 3647, § 1.)*

Cross References

Local authorities defined, see Vehicle Code § 385.

§ 16502. Violations; denial of entry into the state

(a) An owner shall not use, or with his or her consent permit the use of, a vehicle used in the transportation of persons or property in the conduct of a business, without maintaining proof of financial responsibility as required by this chapter.

(b) A motor vehicle from another country in which there is no evidence of financial responsibility required pursuant to this chapter or Part 387 (commencing with Section 387.1) of Title 49 of the Code of Federal Regulations shall be denied entry into the state. *(Stats. 1959, c. 3, p. 1652, § 16502. Amended by Stats.1980, c. 983, p. 3117, § 3; Stats.1989, c. 1157, § 25; Stats.2006, c. 288 (A.B.3011), § 5.)*

Cross References

Owner defined, see Vehicle Code § 460.

§ 16503. Suspension of registration

The department shall suspend the registration of all vehicles used in the transportation of persons or property in the conduct of a business, except vehicles subject to regulation by the Public Utilities Commission, which are registered in the name of any person convicted of violating Section 16502 immediately upon receipt of a duly certified abstract of the record of the court in which the person was convicted.

The suspension shall remain in effect and no such vehicle shall be registered in the name of the person until he or she gives the department proof of his or her financial responsibility as required by Section 16500. *(Stats.1959, c. 3, p. 1652, § 16503. Amended by Stats. 1980, c. 983, p. 3117, § 4; Stats.1989, c. 1157, § 26.)*

Cross References

Department defined, see Vehicle Code § 290.
Proof of financial responsibility, see Vehicle Code § 16430.

Violation of license restrictions, see Vehicle Code §§ 13360, 14603.

CHAPTER 5. TRANSPORTERS OF MOTOR VEHICLES [REPEALED]

§§ 16550 to 16553. Repealed by Stats.1980, c. 983, p. 3117, § 5

CHAPTER 6. INTERSTATE HIGHWAY CARRIERS

Section
16560. Interstate or foreign transportation of property or passengers; failure to comply with requirements; penalty.

§ 16560. Interstate or foreign transportation of property or passengers; failure to comply with requirements; penalty

(a) Any person or corporation who operates or causes to be operated on the highways of this state any motor vehicle in the interstate or foreign transportation of property, other than household goods, for compensation without having first complied with the requirements of paragraph (1) of subdivision (g) of Section 7232 of the Revenue and Taxation Code is guilty of a misdemeanor, and is punishable by a fine of not more than one thousand dollars ($1,000), or by imprisonment in the county jail for not more than three months, or by both that fine and imprisonment.

(b) Any person or corporation who operates or causes to be operated on the highways of this state any motor vehicle in the interstate or foreign transportation of household goods or passengers for compensation without having first complied with the requirements of Chapter 1 (commencing with Section 3901) of Division 2 of the Public Utilities Code is guilty of a misdemeanor, and is punishable by a fine of not more than one thousand dollars ($1,000), or by imprisonment in the county jail for not more than three months, or both that fine and imprisonment. *(Added by Stats.1969, c. 1279, p. 2503, § 5. Amended by Stats.1983, c. 1092, § 388, eff. Sept. 27, 1983, operative Jan. 1, 1984; Stats.1984, c. 1715, § 6; Stats.1999, c. 1007 (S.B.532), § 19.)*

Cross References

Violation a misdemeanor, see Vehicle Code § 40000.13.

Division 9

CIVIL LIABILITY

Chapter	Section
1. Civil Liability of Owners and Operators of Vehicles	17000
2. Civil Liability of Persons Signing License Applications of Minors	17700

CHAPTER 1. CIVIL LIABILITY OF OWNERS AND OPERATORS OF VEHICLES

Article	Section
1. Public Agencies	17000
2. Private Owners	17150
2.5. Uninsured Owners	17200
3. Liability for Damage to Highway	17300
4. Service of Process	17450

ARTICLE 1. PUBLIC AGENCIES

Section
17000. Definitions.
17001. Liability of a public entity.
17002. Extent of liability.
17003. Repealed.
17004. Authorized emergency vehicles.
17004.5. Liability of private fire department.
17004.7. Liability of public agency employing peace officers conducting vehicular pursuits.

§ 17000. Definitions

As used in this chapter:

(a) "Employee" includes an officer, employee, or servant, whether or not compensated, but does not include an independent contractor.

(b) "Employment" includes office or employment.

(c) "Public entity" includes the state, the Regents of the University of California, a county, city, district, public authority, public agency, and any other political subdivision or public corporation in the state. *(Stats.1959, c. 3, p. 1653, § 17000. Amended by Stats.1965, c. 1527, p. 3620, § 1.)*

Law Revision Commission Comments

This amendment makes applicable to motor vehicle cases the same definitions that apply to other tort actions against public entities. See Govt.Code §§ 810.2, 810.4 and 811.2.

§ 17001. Liability of a public entity

A public entity is liable for death or injury to person or property proximately caused by a negligent or wrongful act or omission in the operation of any motor vehicle by an employee of the public entity acting within the scope of his employment. *(Stats.1959, c. 3, p. 1653, § 17001. Amended by Stats.1965, c. 1527, p. 3620, § 2.)*

Law Revision Commission Comments

The Governmental Liability Act specifically imposes liability on public entities for the intentional as well as the negligent torts committed by public employees in the scope of their employment. This amendment removes any doubt which may exist concerning the applicability of this principle to torts involving the operation of motor vehicles. See Van Alstyne, California Government Tort Liability § 7.67 (Cal.Cont.Ed.Bar 1964).

To the extent that the term "servant" can be considered to describe a narrower classification of persons than the term "agent," the amendment restricts the liability of public entities to cases involving the former class of persons in conformity with the Governmental Liability Act. See Govt.Code § 810.2; Vehicle Code § 17000 (amended).

Cross References

Actions on claims, see Government Code § 940 et seq.

Allowance and payment of claims, see Government Code § 965 et seq.

Claims against county, see Government Code § 29700 et seq.

Exemption of authorized emergency vehicles, see Vehicle Code §§ 21055, 21056.

Liability of public entities generally, see Government Code § 814 et seq.

Nonliability for operation of authorized emergency vehicles, see Vehicle Code § 17004.

Public entity, defined, see Government Code § 811.2.

Suits against state, see Const. Art. 3, § 5.

Tort Claims Act, see Government Code § 810 et seq.

Tort liability of public entities, see Government Code § 810 et seq.

Violations of Code as not constituting negligence as matter of law, see Vehicle Code § 40830.

§ 17002. Extent of liability

Subject to Article 4 (commencing with Section 825) of Chapter 1 of Part 2 of Division 3.6 of Title 1 of the Government Code, a public entity is liable for death or injury to person or property to the same extent as a private person under the provisions of Article 2 (commencing with Section 17150) of this chapter. *(Added by Stats.1965, c. 1527, p. 3620, § 4.)*

Law Revision Commission Comments

Comment on repeal of former section:

Vehicle Code Section 17002, which grants a right of subrogation against the public employee to a public entity vicariously liable for his negligent operation of a motor vehicle, probably was impliedly repealed by the 1963 legislation which makes a public entity ultimately liable for the torts of public personnel within the scope of their public service unless the officer, servant, or employee was guilty of actual fraud, corruption, or actual malice. See Govt.Code § 825.2. It should, therefore, be explicitly repealed.

Comment on 1965 addition:

Prior to the decision of the California Supreme Court in Muskopf v. Corning Hospital District, 55 Cal.2d 211, 11 Cal. Rptr. 89, 359 P.2d 457 (1961), the liability of public entities as vehicle owners had been limited by judicial decision to vehicles maintained for use in "proprietary" activities; no vehicle ownership liability existed where the publicly owned vehicle was maintained solely for use in "governmental" activities. This "governmental-proprietary" distinction, however, was abolished by the Muskopf decision and by the 1963 legislation enacting the Governmental Liability Act. Hence, it is probable that ownership liability exists today for public entities. See Van Alstyne, California Government Tort Liability § 7.65 (Cal.Cont.Ed.Bar 1964). The addition of Section 17002 to the Vehicle Code states this liability explicitly. Of course, liability based solely on vehicle ownership and not arising out of a master-servant relationship is only a secondary liability that is expressly limited in dollar amount. See Vehicle Code §§ 17151, 17152.

The reference at the beginning of this section to the indemnification provisions of the Governmental Liability Act makes it clear that these provisions, rather than Vehicle Code Section 17153, control subrogation rights of the public entity where liability is based upon the acts or omissions of public personnel acting within the scope of their public employment. This does not, of course, affect the application of the subrogation rights expressed in Section 17153 where the liability of the public entity is based solely upon vehicle ownership and does not arise by reason of the entity's vicarious responsibility for the acts or omissions of public personnel acting within the scope of public employment.

§ 17003. Repealed by Stats.1963, c. 1682, p. 3292, § 8

§ 17004. Authorized emergency vehicles

A public employee is not liable for civil damages on account of personal injury to or death of any person or damage to property resulting from the operation, in the line of duty, of an authorized emergency vehicle while responding to an emergency call or when in the immediate pursuit of an actual or suspected violator of the law, or when responding to but not upon returning from a fire alarm or other emergency call. *(Stats.1959, c. 3, p. 1653, § 17004. Amended by Stats.1965, c. 1527, p. 3620, § 5.)*

Law Revision Commission Comments

This amendment extends to all public employees the immunity granted by this section. This extension of immunity is appropriate in light of the broad definition of "authorized emergency vehicle" contained in Vehicle Code Section 165 (added by Cal.Stats.1961, Ch. 653, § 12, p. 1858).

Cross References

California highway patrol, see Vehicle Code § 2250 et seq.
Definition of authorized emergency vehicle, see Vehicle Code §§ 165, 165.5.
Exemptions of authorized emergency vehicles, see Vehicle Code §§ 21055, 21056.
Suspension or revocation of authorized emergency vehicle permit, see Vehicle Code § 2417.

§ 17004.5. Liability of private fire department

Any private firm or corporation, or employee thereof, which maintains a fire department and has entered into a mutual aid agreement pursuant to Section 13855, 14095, or 14455.5 of the Health and Safety Code shall have the

same immunity from liability for civil damages on account of personal injury to or death of any person or damage to property resulting from the operation of an authorized emergency vehicle while responding to, but not upon returning from, a fire alarm or other emergency call as is provided by law for the district and its employees with which the firm or corporation has entered into a mutual aid agreement, except when the act or omission causing the personal injury to or death of any person or damage to property occurs on property under the control of such firm or corporation. *(Added by Stats.1961, c. 1880, p. 3980, § 5.)*

§ 17004.7. Liability of public agency employing peace officers conducting vehicular pursuits

(a) The immunity provided by this section is in addition to any other immunity provided by law. The adoption of a vehicle pursuit policy by a public agency pursuant to this section is discretionary.

(b)(1) A public agency employing peace officers that adopts and promulgates a written policy on, and provides regular and periodic training on an annual basis for, vehicular pursuits complying with subdivisions (c) and (d) is immune from liability for civil damages for personal injury to or death of any person or damage to property resulting from the collision of a vehicle being operated by an actual or suspected violator of the law who is being, has been, or believes he or she is being or has been, pursued in a motor vehicle by a peace officer employed by the public entity.

(2) Promulgation of the written policy under paragraph (1) shall include, but is not limited to, a requirement that all peace officers of the public agency certify in writing that they have received, read, and understand the policy. The failure of an individual officer to sign a certification shall not be used to impose liability on an individual officer or a public entity.

(c) A policy for the safe conduct of motor vehicle pursuits by peace officers shall meet all of the following minimum standards:

(1) Determine under what circumstances to initiate a pursuit. The policy shall define a "pursuit," articulate the reasons for which a pursuit is authorized, and identify the issues that should be considered in reaching the decision to pursue. It should also address the importance of protecting the public and balancing the known or reasonably suspected offense, and the apparent need for immediate capture against the risks to peace officers, innocent motorists, and others to protect the public.

(2) Determine the total number of law enforcement vehicles authorized to participate in a pursuit. Establish the authorized number of law enforcement units and supervisors who may be involved in a pursuit, describe the responsibility of each authorized unit and the role of each peace officer and supervisor, and specify if and when additional units are authorized.

(3) Determine the communication procedures to be followed during a pursuit. Specify pursuit coordination

and control procedures and determine assignment of communications responsibility by unit and organizational entity.

(4) Determine the role of the supervisor in managing and controlling a pursuit. Supervisory responsibility shall include management and control of a pursuit, assessment of risk factors associated with a pursuit, and when to terminate a pursuit.

(5) Determine driving tactics and the circumstances under which the tactics may be appropriate.

(6) Determine authorized pursuit intervention tactics. Pursuit intervention tactics include, but are not limited to, blocking, ramming, boxing, and roadblock procedures. The policy shall specify under what circumstances and conditions each approved tactic is authorized to be used.

(7) Determine the factors to be considered by a peace officer and supervisor in determining speeds throughout a pursuit. Evaluation shall take into consideration public safety, peace officer safety, and safety of the occupants in a fleeing vehicle.

(8) Determine the role of air support, where available. Air support shall include coordinating the activities of resources on the ground, reporting on the progress of a pursuit, and providing peace officers and supervisors with information to evaluate whether or not to continue the pursuit.

(9) Determine when to terminate or discontinue a pursuit. Factors to be considered include, but are not limited to, all of the following:

(A) Ongoing evaluation of risk to the public or pursuing peace officer.

(B) The protection of the public, given the known or reasonably suspected offense and apparent need for immediate capture against the risks to the public and peace officers.

(C) Vehicular or pedestrian traffic safety and volume.

(D) Weather conditions.

(E) Traffic conditions.

(F) Speeds.

(G) Availability of air support.

(H) Procedures when an offender is identified and may be apprehended at a later time or when the location of the pursuit vehicle is no longer known.

(10) Determine procedures for apprehending an offender following a pursuit. Safety of the public and peace officers during the law enforcement effort to capture an offender shall be an important factor.

(11) Determine effective coordination, management, and control of interjurisdictional pursuits. The policy shall include, but shall not be limited to, all of the following:

(A) Supervisory control and management of a pursuit that enters another jurisdiction.

(B) Communications and notifications among the agencies involved.

(C) Involvement in another jurisdiction's pursuit.

(D) Roles and responsibilities of units and coordination, management, and control at the termination of an interjurisdictional pursuit.

(12) Reporting and postpursuit analysis as required by Section 14602.1. Establish the level and procedures of postpursuit analysis, review, and feedback. Establish procedures for written postpursuit review and followup.

(d) "Regular and periodic training" under this section means annual training that shall include, at a minimum, coverage of each of the subjects and elements set forth in subdivision (c) and that shall comply, at a minimum, with the training guidelines established pursuant to Section 13519.8 of the Penal Code.

(e) The requirements of subdivision (c) represent minimum policy standards and do not limit an agency from adopting additional policy requirements. The requirements in subdivision (c) are consistent with the 1995 California Law Enforcement Vehicle Pursuit Guidelines developed by the Commission on Peace Officer Standards and Training pursuant to Section 13519. 8 of the Penal Code that will assist agencies in the development of their pursuit policies. Nothing in this section precludes the adoption of a policy that limits or restricts pursuits.

(f) A determination of whether a public agency has complied with subdivisions (c) and (d) is a question of law for the court.

(g) This section shall become operative on July 1, 2007. *(Added by Stats.2005, c. 485 (S.B.719), § 11, operative July 1, 2007.)*

ARTICLE 2. PRIVATE OWNERS

Section
17150.   Liability of private owners.
17150.5.   Limitation on Family Code presumptions.
17151.   Limitation of liability.
17152.   Liability of operator.
17153.   Subrogation of owner.
17154.   Bailee as operator.
17155.   Settlement of claims.
17156.   Vendee as owner.
17157.   School district bailee as owner.
17158.   Owner as passenger; liability.
17159.   Liability of personal representative.

§ 17150. Liability of private owners

Every owner of a motor vehicle is liable and responsible for death or injury to person or property resulting from a negligent or wrongful act or omission in the operation of the motor vehicle, in the business of the owner or otherwise, by any person using or operating the same with the permission, express or implied, of the owner. *(Stats.1959, c. 3, p. 1654, § 17150. Amended by Stats.1967, c. 702, p. 2072, § 1.)*

Cross References

Civil liability of owners and operators, see Vehicle Code § 17000 et seq.
Contract cancellation option agreement required, exceptions, purchase price, form, and cancellation procedures, see Vehicle Code § 11731.21.
Definitions,
  Legal owner, see Vehicle Code § 370.
  Motor vehicle, see Vehicle Code § 415.
  Owner, see Vehicle Code § 460.
  Person, see Vehicle Code § 470.
Liability for minors' negligence, see Vehicle Code § 17707 et seq.
Liability for wilful or negligent damage to highway, see Vehicle Code § 17300.
Negligence of minors imputed to third persons and parents, see Vehicle Code § 17706 et seq.
Owner released from liability for negligence upon transfer, see Vehicle Code § 5602.
Persons signing license applications of minors, limitation on liability, see Vehicle Code § 17714.
Report or action of department as evidence in civil action, see Vehicle Code § 40833.
Responsibility for willful acts and negligence, see Civil Code § 1714.
State liability for injury or damage during operation during emission inspection, see Health and Safety Code § 43012.
Suspension or revocation of driving, privilege as evidence in civil action, see Vehicle Code § 40832.
Theft and unlawful driving or taking of a vehicle, see Vehicle Code § 10851.
Violations of code as evidence of negligence, see Vehicle Code § 40830 et seq.

§ 17150.5.   Limitation on Family Code presumptions

The presumptions created by Section 803 of the Family Code as to the acquisition of property by a married woman by an instrument in writing shall not apply in an action based on Section 17150 with respect to the acquisition of a motor vehicle by a married woman and her husband. *(Added by Stats.1965, c. 1598, p. 3692, § 1. Amended by Stats.1971, c. 438, p. 909, § 192, operative May 3, 1972; Stats.1992, c. 163 (A.B.2641), § 134, operative Jan. 1, 1994.)*

Cross References

Presumptions, see Evidence Code § 600 et seq.

§ 17151.   Limitation of liability

(a) The liability of an owner, bailee of an owner, or personal representative of a decedent imposed by this chapter and not arising through the relationship of principal and agent or master and servant is limited to the amount of fifteen thousand dollars ($15,000) for the death of or injury to one person in any one accident and, subject to the limit as to one person, is limited to the amount of thirty thousand dollars ($30,000) for the death of or injury to more than one person in any one accident and is limited to the amount of five thousand dollars ($5,000) for damage to property of others in any one accident.

(b) An owner, bailee of an owner, or personal representative of a decedent is not liable under this chapter for damages imposed for the sake of example and by way of punishing the operator of the vehicle. Nothing in this subdivision makes an owner, bailee, or personal representative immune from liability for damages imposed for the sake of example and by way of punishing him for his own wrongful conduct. *(Stats.1959, c. 3, p. 1654, § 17151. Amended by Stats.1961, c. 1734, p. 3742, § 1; Stats.1963, c. 403, p. 1211, § 1; Stats.1967, c. 702 p. 2073, § 2.5; Stats.1967, c. 862, p. 2307, § 8.5, operative July 1, 1968.)*

Cross References

Definitions,
  Agent, see Civil Code § 2295.
  Owner, see Vehicle Code § 460.
  Person, see Vehicle Code § 470.
Maximum liability when negligence of minor is imputed, see Vehicle Code § 17709.

§ 17152.   Liability of operator

In any action against an owner, bailee of an owner, or personal representative of a decedent on account of liability imposed by Sections 17150, 17154, or 17159 for the negligent or wrongful act or omission of the operator of a vehicle, the operator shall be made a party defendant if service of process can be made in a manner sufficient to secure personal jurisdiction over the operator. Upon recovery of judgment, recourse shall first be had against the property of the operator so served. *(Stats.1959, c. 3, p. 1654, § 17152. Amended by Stats.1961, c. 1734, p. 3742, § 2; Stats.1967, c. 702, p. 2073, § 3.)*

Law Revision Commission Comments

This amendment conforms the section to section 17150 as amended. It also requires that the operator be made a party if personal jurisdiction over him can be obtained in any manner. Code of Civil Procedure section 417 [now repealed] and Vehicle Code sections 17450–17463 prescribe various ways in which personal jurisdiction can be secured other than by personal service within the state.

Cross References

Definitions,
  Owner, see Vehicle Code § 460.
  Vehicle, see Vehicle Code § 670.
Joinder of parties, generally, see Code of Civil Procedure § 378 et seq.
Personal service of process, see Code of Civil Procedure § 1011.

§ 17153.   Subrogation of owner

If there is recovery under this chapter against an owner, bailee of an owner, or personal representative of a decedent, the owner, bailee of an owner, or personal representative of a decedent is subrogated to all the rights of the person injured or whose property has been injured and may recover from the operator the total amount of any judgment and costs recovered against the owner, bailee of an owner, or personal representative of a decedent. *(Stats.1959, c. 3, p. 1654, § 17153. Amended* by *Stats.1961, c. 1734, p. 3742, § 3; Stats.1967, c. 702, p. 2073, § 4.)*

Law Revision Commission Comments

This amendment merely conforms the section to section 17150 as amended.

Cross References

Definitions,
  Owner, see Vehicle Code § 460.
  Person, see Vehicle Code § 470.

§ 17154. Bailee as operator

If the bailee of an owner with the permission, express or implied, of the owner permits another to operate the motor vehicle of the owner, then the bailee and the driver shall both be deemed operators of the vehicle of the owner within the meaning of Sections 17152 and 17153.

Every bailee of a motor vehicle is liable and responsible for death or injury to person or property resulting from a negligent or wrongful act or omission in the operation of the motor vehicle, in the business of the bailee or otherwise, by any person using or operating the same with the permission, express or implied, of the bailee. *(Stats. 1959, c. 3, p. 1654, § 17154. Amended by Stats.1961, c. 1734, p. 3743, § 4; Stats.1967, c. 702, p. 2073, § 5.)*

Law Revision Commission Comments

This amendment to section 17154 is in substance the same as the amendment to section 17150. See the Comment to section 17150.

Cross References

Definitions,
  Owner, see Vehicle Code § 460.
  Vehicle, see Vehicle Code § 670.

§ 17155. Settlement of claims

If two or more persons are injured or killed in one accident, the owner, bailee of an owner, or personal representative of a decedent may settle and pay any bona fide claims for damages arising out of personal injuries or death, whether reduced by judgment or not, and the payments shall diminish, to the extent of those payments, the person's total liability on account of the accident. Payments aggregating the full sum of thirty thousand dollars ($30,000) shall extinguish all liability of the owner, bailee of an owner, or personal representative of a decedent for death or personal injury arising out of the accident that exists pursuant to this chapter, and did not arise through the negligent or wrongful act or omission of the owner, bailee of an owner, or personal representative of a decedent nor through the relationship of principal and agent or master and servant. *(Stats.1959, c. 3, p. 1654, § 17155. Amended by Stats.1961, c. 1734, p. 3743, § 5; Stats.1963, c. 403, p. 1211, § 2; Stats.1967, c. 702, p. 2074, § 6.5; Stats.1967, c. 862, p. 2307, § 9.5, operative July 1, 1968; Stats.2006, c. 538 (S.B.1852), § 660.)*

Law Revision Commission Comments

This amendment merely conforms the section to section 17150 as amended.

§ 17156. Vendee as owner

If a motor vehicle is sold under a contract of conditional sale whereby the title to such motor vehicle remains in the vendor, such vendor or his assignee shall not be deemed an owner within the provisions of this chapter, but the vendee or his assignee shall be deemed the owner notwithstanding the terms of such contract, until the vendor or his assignee retake possession of the motor vehicle. A chattel mortgagee of a motor vehicle out of possession is not an owner within the provisions of this chapter. *(Stats.1959, c. 3, p. 1654, § 17156. Amended by Stats.1967, c. 702, p. 2074, § 7.)*

Law Revision Commission Comments

This amendment merely conforms the section to section 17150 as amended.

Cross References

Automobile Sales Finance Act, see Civil Code § 2981 et seq.
Definitions,
  Legal owner, see Vehicle Code § 370.
  Motor vehicle, see Vehicle Code § 415.
  Owner, see Vehicle Code § 460.
Requirements for releasing liability of owner, see Vehicle Code § 5602.
Secured party as legal owner, see Vehicle Code § 6300 et seq.

§ 17157. School district bailee as owner

If a motor vehicle is gratuitously loaned to a school district, the bailee and not the bailor shall be deemed to be the owner within the provisions of this chapter notwithstanding the terms of any contract, until the bailor retakes possession of the motor vehicle. *(Added by Stats.1969, c. 289, p. 641, § 2.)*

Cross References

Elementary school district defined, see Education Code § 41606.

§ 17158. Owner as passenger; liability

No person riding in or occupying a vehicle owned by him and driven by another person with his permission has any right of action for civil damages against the driver of the vehicle or against any other person legally liable for the conduct of the driver on account of personal injury to or the death of the owner during the ride, unless the plaintiff in any such action establishes that the injury or death proximately resulted from the intoxication or willful misconduct of the driver. *(Stats.1959, c. 3, p. 1655, § 17158. Amended by Stats.1961, c. 1600, p. 3429, § 1; Stats.1973, c. 803, p. 1426, § 4.)*

Validity

This section was held unconstitutional in the case of Brown v. Merlo (1973) 106 Cal.Rptr. 388.

Cross References

Civil liability of owners and operators, see Vehicle Code § 17000 et seq.
Damages, generally, see Civil Code § 3281 et seq.
Definitions,
  Driver, see Vehicle Code § 305.
  Highway, see Vehicle Code §§ 360, 590, 591.
  Vehicle, see Vehicle Code § 670.
Degree of care required of carrier of persons without reward, see Civil Code § 2096.
Driving while intoxicated,
  Generally, see Vehicle Code §§ 13201, 13352, 23100 et seq., 23220 et seq.
  Chemical blood, breath or urine tests, see Vehicle Code §§ 13353, 13354.
Financial responsibility law, see Vehicle Code § 16000 et seq.
Imputation of liability of minor to parents, see Vehicle Code § 17707.
Imputation of liability to private owners, see Vehicle Code § 17150.
Reckless driving,
  Generally, see Vehicle Code §§ 23103, 23104.
  Investigations by department, see Vehicle Code § 13800 et seq.
Responsibility for willful acts and negligence, see Civil Code § 1714.
Speed laws, see Vehicle Code § 22349 et seq.

§ 17159.   Liability of personal representative

Every person who is a personal representative of a decedent who has control or possession of a motor vehicle subject to administration for the purpose of administration of an estate is, during the period of such administration, or until the vehicle has been distributed under order of the court or he has complied with the requirements of subdivision (a) or (b) of Section 5602, liable and responsible for death or injury to person or property resulting from a negligent or wrongful act or omission in the operation of the motor vehicle by any person using or operating the same with the permission, express or implied, of the personal representative. *(Added by Stats.1961, c. 1734, p. 3743, § 6. Amended by Stats.1963, c. 145, p. 817, § 1; Stats.1967, c. 702, p. 2075, § 8.)*

Law Revision Commission Comments

This amendment to section 17159 is in substance the same as the amendment to Section 17150. See the Comment to section 17150.

ARTICLE 2.5.   UNINSURED OWNERS

Section
17200.   Judgment or settlement obtained by uninsured owner or operator; reduction by amount from uninsured motorist coverage.
17201.   Payment of settlement or judgment; prerequisites.
17202.   Subrogation rights; effect of article.
17203.   Repealed.

574

§ 17200.   Judgment or settlement obtained by uninsured owner or operator; reduction by amount from uninsured motorist coverage

Where an uninsured owner or operator has obtained a judgment against or agreed to a settlement with the owner or operator of an insured motor vehicle based on the negligence of the insured owner or operator, the amount of the judgment or settlement payable by the insured or his or her insurer shall be reduced by the amount paid or payable to the insured owner or operator or occupants of the insured motor vehicles or their heirs or legal representatives from coverage provided by an uninsured motorist endorsement where the claim of the insured, the owner, or occupants of the insured motor vehicle and the uninsured motorist arise out of the same accident. If the insured or his or her insurer becomes entitled to a reduction, the reduction shall not exceed the amount of the settlement or judgment awarded the uninsured owner or operator. *(Added by Stats.1983, c. 1252, § 10.)*

§ 17201.   Payment of settlement or judgment; prerequisites

The payment of any settlement with an uninsured owner or operator or the payment of any final judgment for damages obtained by an uninsured owner or operator in a civil action against an insured owner or operator shall not be made until the claims of the owner, the operator, or the occupants of the insured motor vehicle, if any, or their heirs or legal representatives for benefits under the uninsured motorist endorsement are settled by the insurer and the claimants under the uninsured motorist endorsement or are determined by the arbitrator in arbitration proceedings conducted pursuant to Section 11580.2 of the Insurance Code. *(Added by Stats.1983, c. 1252, § 10.)*

§ 17202.   Subrogation rights; effect of article

This article is not intended to affect the rights granted pursuant to subdivision (g) of Section 11580.2 of the Insurance Code. *(Added by Stats.1983, c. 1252, § 10.)*

§ 17203.   Repealed by Stats.1988, c. 1471, § 4

ARTICLE 3.   LIABILITY FOR DAMAGE TO HIGHWAY

Section
17300.   Willful or negligent damage; claims for liability.
17301.   Damage by illegal operation of vehicle.
17302.   Damage from weight or size.
17303.   Recovery of damages.

Cross References

Damage to highway as misdemeanor, see Penal Code § 588.
Injuries to county highways, see Streets and Highways Code § 1480 et seq.

Law enforcement, california Highway Patrol, see Vehicle Code § 2400.

§ 17300. Willful or negligent damage; claims for liability

(a) A person who willfully or negligently damages a street or highway, or its appurtenances, including, but not limited to, guardrails, signs, traffic signals, snow poles, and similar facilities, is liable for the reasonable cost of repair or replacement thereof.

(b) A person who willfully damages or destroys a memorial sign placed by the Department of Transportation, including, but not limited to, a sign memorializing a victim under Section 101.10 of the Streets and Highways Code, is liable for that damage or destruction for the highest of the following amounts:

(1) One thousand five hundred dollars ($1,500).

(2) The actual repair cost or replacement cost, whichever is applicable.

(c) A person who willfully or negligently causes or permits the contents of a vehicle to be deposited upon a street or highway, or its appurtenances, is liable for the reasonable costs of removing those contents from the street or highway or its appurtenances.

(d) The liability stated in this section also applies to an owner of a vehicle operated with the owner's permission, as provided in Article 2 (commencing with Section 17150), and includes liability for the reasonable cost of necessary safety precautions, including, but not limited to, warning traffic, the removal of debris resulting from accidents, the removal of any materials, or providing detours.

(e) The Department of Transportation and local authorities, with respect to highways under their respective jurisdictions, may present claims for liability under this section, bring actions for recovery thereon, and settle and compromise, in their discretion, claims arising under this section.

(f) If the Department of Transportation or a local authority provides services on a highway outside its jurisdiction, at the request of the department or the local authority that has jurisdiction over that highway, the department or the local authority may present a claim for liability for rendering this service under this section, bring actions for recovery thereon, and, in its discretion, settle and compromise the claim. *(Stats.1959, c. 3, p. 1655, § 17300. Amended by Stats.1974, c. 545, p. 1313, § 165; Stats.1985, c. 691, § 1; Stats.1990, c. 692 (A.B.3398), § 1; Stats.2006, c. 419 (A.B.2557), § 3.)*

Cross References

Stock damage to highways, liability, see Streets and Highways Code § 105.

§ 17301. Damage by illegal operation of vehicle

(a) Any person driving any vehicle, object, or contrivance over a highway or bridge is liable for all damages which the highway or bridge may sustain as a result of any illegal operation, driving or moving of the vehicle, object, or contrivance, or as a result of operating, driving, or moving any vehicle, object, or contrivance weighing in excess of the maximum weight specified in this code which is operated under a special permit issued by the Department of Transportation.

(b) Whenever the driver is not the owner of the vehicle, object, or contrivance but is operating, driving, or moving the same with the express or implied permission of the owner, the owner and driver are jointly and severally liable for the damage. *(Stats.1959, c. 3, p. 1655, § 17301. Amended by Stats.1974, c. 545, p. 1313, § 166.)*

Cross References

Applicability of this section to trolley coaches, see Vehicle Code § 21051.

§ 17302. Damage from weight or size

The driver, or the owner and driver, jointly, as the case may be, are also liable for all damages that any highway or bridge sustains as the result of any operation, driving, or moving of any vehicle that exceeds any of the limitations imposed by Division 15 (commencing with Section 35000), Chapter 1 (commencing with Section 29000) of Division 13, Section 21461 with respect to a sign erected under Section 35655, and Sections 21712 and 23114 even though the vehicle is exempted from the limitations by Section 35001, 35104, 35105, 35106, 35108, 35250, 35400, 35414, or 36615. *(Stats.1959, c. 3, p. 1656, § 17302. Amended by Stats.1979, c. 373, p. 1382, § 321; Stats.1996, c. 124 (A.B.3470), § 124.)*

Cross References

Applicability of this section to trolley coaches, see Vehicle Code § 21051.

§ 17303. Recovery of damages

Damages under Sections 17301 and 17302 may be recovered in a civil action brought by the authorities in control of the highway or bridge. *(Stats.1959, c. 3, p. 1656, § 17303).*

Cross References

Applicability of this section to trolley coaches, see Vehicle Code § 21051.

ARTICLE 4. SERVICE OF PROCESS

Section
17450. Nonresident defined.
17451. Service of process on nonresident.
17452. Service on personal representative.
17453. Agreement on validity of process.
17454. Service of process.
17455. Notice by registered mail.
17456. Proof of service.
17457. Continuance.
17458. Records of process served.
17459. Resident accepting certificate of ownership or registration.
17460. Resident accepting or retaining driver's license.

Section
17461. Manner of serving process.
17462. Time to appear.
17463. Effect on statutes of limitation.

§ 17450. Nonresident defined

As used in this chapter, "nonresident" means a person who is not a resident of this State at the time the accident or collision occurs. *(Stats.1959, c. 3, p. 1656, § 17450.)*

Cross References

Nonresident defined, see Vehicle Code § 435.

§ 17451. Service of process on nonresident

The acceptance by a nonresident of the rights and privileges conferred upon him by this code or any operation by himself or agent of a motor vehicle anywhere within this state, or in the event the nonresident is the owner of a motor vehicle then by the operation of the vehicle anywhere within this state by any person with his express or implied permission, is equivalent to an appointment by the nonresident of the director or his successor in office to be his true and lawful attorney upon whom may be served all lawful processes in any action or proceeding against the nonresident operator or nonresident owner growing out of any accident or collision resulting from the operation of any motor vehicle anywhere within this state by himself or agent, which appointment shall also be irrevocable and binding upon his executor or administrator. *(Stats.1959, c. 3, p. 1656, § 17451. Amended by Stats.1967, c. 720, p. 2092, § 1.)*

Cross References

Definitions,
  Director, see Vehicle Code § 295.
  Highway, see Vehicle Code § 360.
  Motor vehicle, see Vehicle Code § 415.
  Nonresident, see Vehicle Code § 435.
  Owner, see Vehicle Code § 460.

§ 17452. Service on personal representative

Where the nonresident has died prior to the commencement of an action brought pursuant to this article, service of process shall be made on the executor or administrator of the nonresident in the same manner and on the same notice as is provided in the case of the nonresident. Where an action has been duly commenced under the provisions of this article by service upon a defendant who dies thereafter, the court shall allow the action to be continued against his executor or administrator upon motion with such notice as the court deems proper. *(Stats.1959, c. 3, p. 1656, § 17452.)*

Cross References

Nonresident defined, see Vehicle Code §§ 435, 17450.

§ 17453. Agreement on validity of process

The acceptance of rights and privileges under this code or any operation of a motor vehicle anywhere within this state as specified in Section 17451 shall be a signification

576

of the irrevocable agreement of the nonresident, binding as well upon his executor or administrator, that process against him which is served in the manner provided in this article shall be of the same legal force and validity as if served on him personally in this state. *(Stats.1959, c. 3, p. 1656, § 17453. Amended by Stats.1967, c. 720, p. 2092, § 2.)*

Cross References

Highway defined, see Vehicle Code § 360.
Nonresident defined, see Vehicle Code §§ 435, 17450.

§ 17454. Service of process

Service of process shall be made by leaving one copy of the summons and complaint in the hands of the director or in his office at Sacramento or by mailing either by certified or registered mail, addressee only, return receipt requested, the copy of the summons and complaint to the office of the director in Sacramento. Service shall be effective as of the day the return receipt is received from the director's office. A fee of two dollars ($2) for each nonresident to be served shall be paid to the director at the time of service of the copy of the summons and complaint and such service shall be a sufficient service on the nonresident subject to compliance with Section 17455. *(Stats.1959, c. 3, p. 1657, § 17454. Amended by Stats. 1959, c. 1313, p. 3586, § 1.)*

Cross References

Definitions,
  Director, see Vehicle Code § 295.
  Nonresident, see Vehicle Code §§ 435, 17450.

§ 17455. Notice by registered mail

A notice of service and a copy of the summons and complaint shall be forthwith sent by registered mail by the plaintiff or his attorney to the defendant. Personal service of the notice and a copy of the summons and complaint upon the defendant wherever found outside this State shall be the equivalent of service by mail. *(Stats.1959, c. 3, p. 1657, § 17455.)*

§ 17456. Proof of service

Proof of compliance with Section 17455 shall be made in the event of service by mail by affidavit of the plaintiff or his attorney showing said mailing, together with the return receipt of the United States post office bearing the signature of the defendant. The affidavit and receipt shall be appended to the original summons which shall be filed with the court from out of which the summons issued within such time as the court may allow for the return of the summons.

In the event of personal service outside this State, compliance with Section 17455 may be proved by the return of any duly constituted public officer, qualified to serve like process of and in the state or jurisdiction where the defendant is found, showing such service to have been made. The return shall be appended to the original summons which shall be filed as aforesaid. *(Stats.1959, c. 3, p. 1657, § 17456.)*

§ 17457. Continuance

The court in which the action is pending may order such continuances as may be necessary to afford the defendant reasonable opportunity to defend the action. *(Stats.1959, c. 3, p. 1657, § 17457.)*

§ 17458. Records of process served

The director shall keep a record of all process served upon him under this article which record shall show the day and hour of service. *(Stats.1959, c. 3, p. 1657, § 17458.)*

Cross References

Director defined, see Vehicle Code § 295.

§ 17459. Resident accepting certificate of ownership or registration

The acceptance by a resident of this state of a certificate of ownership or a certificate of registration of any motor vehicle or any renewal thereof, issued under the provisions of this code, shall constitute the consent by the person that service of summons may be made upon him within or without this state, whether or not he is then a resident of this state, in any action brought in the courts of this state upon a cause of action arising in this state out of the ownership or operation of the vehicle. *(Stats.1959, c. 3, p. 1657, § 17459. Amended by Stats.1971, c. 622, p. 1223, § 1, operative May 3, 1972.)*

Cross References

Issuance of certificate of ownership or registration, see Vehicle Code § 4450 et seq.
Service of summons, see Code of Civil Procedure § 413.10 et seq.

§ 17460. Resident accepting or retaining driver's license

The acceptance or retention by a resident of this state of a driver's license issued pursuant to the provisions of this code, shall constitute the consent of the person that service of summons may be made upon him within or without this state, whether or not he is then a resident of this state, in any action brought in the courts of this state upon a cause of action arising in this state out of his operation of a motor vehicle anywhere within this state. *(Stats.1959, c. 3, p. 1657, § 17460. Amended by Stats. 1967, c. 720, p. 2093, § 3; Stats.1971, c. 622, p. 1223, § 2, operative May 3, 1972; Stats.1972, c. 618, p. 1150, § 145.)*

Cross References

Driver's license defined, see Vehicle Code § 310.
Issuance of driver's licenses, generally, see Vehicle Code § 12500 et seq.

§ 17461. Manner of serving process

In the event summons is served outside of this state, pursuant to Sections 17459 and 17460, it may be served and proof of service shall be made, in the manner provided by Sections 17454, 17455, and 17456 for service of summons upon a nonresident, or it may be served pursuant to Chapter 4 (commencing with Section 413.10) of Title 5 of Part 2 of the Code of Civil Procedure. *(Stats.1959, c. 3, p. 1658, § 17461. Amended by Stats. 1971, c. 622, p. 1223, § 3, operative May 3, 1972.)*

Cross References

Appearance defined, see Code of Civil Procedure § 1014.
Elisor, execution of process of orders, see Code of Civil Procedure § 262.8.

§ 17462. Time to appear

In the event of service outside the State, the person so served shall have 60 days in which to appear in the action in which the summons is issued. *(Stats.1959, c. 3, p. 1658, § 17462.)*

§ 17463. Effect on statutes of limitation

Notwithstanding any provisions of Section 351 of the Code of Civil Procedure to the contrary, when summons may be personally served upon a person as provided in Sections 17459 and 17460, the time of his absence from this State is part of the time limited for the commencement of the action described in those sections, except when he is out of this State and cannot be located through the exercise of reasonable diligence, except this section in no event shall be applicable in any action or proceeding commenced on or before September 7, 1956. *(Stats.1959, c. 3, p. 1658, § 17463.)*

CHAPTER 2. CIVIL LIABILITY OF PERSONS SIGNING LICENSE APPLICATIONS OF MINORS

Section
17700. Minor defined.
17701. Signature by parents, guardian, or person having custody; child as dependent or ward of the court.
17702. Signature by adult spouse.
17703. Nonresident signers.
17704. Failure of proof.
17705. Application verified by minor only.
17706. Minor's negligence imputed to employer.
17707. Minor's negligence; exceptions.
17708. Liability of parent or guardian.
17709. Limit of liability.
17710. Minor agent or servant.
17711. Release from liability.
17712. Cancellation of license; transfer of liability.
17713. Repealed.
17714. Limitation of double liability.

§ 17700. Minor defined

For the purposes of this chapter, all persons under 18 years of age are minors. *(Stats.1959, c. 3, p. 1658, § 17700. Amended by Stats.1959, c. 1996, p. 4629, § 21; Stats.1971, c. 1748, p. 3765, § 60, operative March 4, 1972.)*

Cross References

Minor defined, see Family Code § 6500.

§ 17701. Signature by parents, guardian, or person having custody; child as dependent or ward of the court

No application for a driver's license shall be granted by the department to any minor unless it is signed and verified by the father and mother of such minor, if both father and mother are living and have custody of the minor.

If only one parent is living or has custody, the application shall be signed and verified by that parent.

If neither parent is living or has custody, the application shall be signed and verified by the guardian, or if there is no guardian, by a person having custody of the minor.

If the minor is a dependent or ward of the court, the application may be signed by a grandparent, sibling over the age of 18 years, aunt, uncle, or foster parent with whom the minor resides. The probation officer or child protective services worker acting as an officer of the court, on behalf of a child, may also sign and verify the application of a minor who is a dependent or ward of the court, if the minor files proof of financial responsibility as provided in Article 1 (commencing with Section 16430) of Chapter 3 of Division 7 at the time of application. Prior to signing the application, the probation officer or child protective services worker shall notify the foster parents or other responsible party of his or her intent to sign and verify the application. *(Stats.1959, c. 3, p. 1658, § 17701. Amended by Stats.1967, c. 485, p. 1692, § 1; Stats.1970, c. 166, p. 409, § 3; Stats.1992, c. 865 (A.B.2691), § 2.)*

Cross References

Application for driver's license, signature and verification, see Vehicle Code § 12802.
Appointment of guardians for minors, see Probate Code § 1510 et seq.
Custody of minors, see Family Code § 3020 et seq.
Employed minors, see Vehicle Code § 17706.
Grounds for cancellation of minor's license, see Vehicle Code § 17712.
Issuance and renewal of licenses, generally, see Vehicle Code § 12800 et seq.
Issuance of junior permits, see Vehicle Code § 12513.
Issuance of licenses, generally, see Vehicle Code § 12500 et seq.
Release from liability, cancellation of minor's license, see Vehicle Code § 17711.
Signature includes mark, see Vehicle Code § 17.
Temporary licenses for minors, see Vehicle Code § 12506.

§ 17702. Signature by adult spouse

If a minor under the age of 18 years is married, the application may be signed and verified by the adult spouse of the minor or by the parents of either spouse or in lieu of the signature, the minor may file proof of financial responsibility, as defined in Section 16430. *(Stats.1959, c. 3, p. 1658, § 17702. Amended by Stats.*

1984, c. 144, § 209; Stats.1992, c. 974 (S.B.1600), § 12, eff. Sept. 28, 1992.)

§ 17703. Nonresident signers

If the person or persons required to sign and verify the application of a minor are not residents of this state, the application shall be signed and verified by a person residing within this state who has custody of the minor, or the department may accept an application signed and verified by the minor and accompanied by proof of financial responsibility, as defined in Section 16430. *(Stats.1959, c. 3, p. 1658, § 17703. Amended by Stats. 1959, c. 1048, p. 3090, § 5; Stats.1984, c. 144, § 210; Stats.1992, c. 974 (S.B.1600), § 13, eff. Sept. 28, 1992.)*

§ 17704. Failure of proof

If, at any time during the minority of the person who has given proof of financial responsibility, as defined in Section 16430, the proof fails, the department shall immediately cancel the license until proof of the licensee's continued financial responsibility has been given or until the minor has otherwise complied with the requirements of this code relative to the issuance of a driver's license. *(Stats.1959, c. 3, p. 1659, § 17704. Amended by Stats.1959, c. 1048, p. 3090, § 6; Stats.1992, c. 974 (S.B.1600), § 14, eff. Sept. 28, 1992.)*

Cross References

Proof of financial responsibility, see Vehicle Code § 16430.

§ 17705. Application verified by minor only

If the person who is required to sign and verify the application of a minor gives his or her written consent, or the minor is emancipated other than by marriage, the department may accept an application signed and verified only by the minor and accompanied by proof of financial responsibility, as defined in Section 16430. The person giving the consent to but not signing or verifying the application shall not be subject to the civil liability specified in Sections 17707 and 17708 merely by reason of having given consent. *(Stats.1959, c. 3, p. 1659, § 17705. Amended by Stats.1959, c. 1048, p. 3090, § 7; Stats.1992, c. 974 (S.B.1600), § 15, eff. Sept. 28, 1992.)*

Cross References

Proof of financial responsibility, see Vehicle Code § 16430.

§ 17706. Minor's negligence imputed to employer

(a) If the person who is required by the provisions of this code to sign and verify the application of a minor gives his written consent, the department may accept an application signed and verified by the minor and his employer, but in such case the department shall issue to the minor only a driver's license restricted to the operation of vehicles by the minor within the scope of his employment by the employer, unless the employer in writing authorizes the issuance of an unrestricted driver's license.

(b) The person giving his consent to, but not signing or verifying, the application as provided in this section shall not be subject to the civil liability specified in Sections 17707 and 17708 merely by reason of having given such consent. *(Stats.1959, c. 3, p. 1659, § 17706.)*

Cross References

Grounds for cancellation of minor's license, see Vehicle Code § 17712.

Restricted licenses, issuance of, see Vehicle Code § 12813.

§ 17707. Minor's negligence; exceptions

Any civil liability of a minor arising out of his driving a motor vehicle upon a highway during his minority is hereby imposed upon the person who signed and verified the application of the minor for a license and the person shall be jointly and severally liable with the minor for any damages proximately resulting from the negligent or wrongful act or omission of the minor in driving a motor vehicle, except that an employer signing the application shall be subject to the provisions of this section only if an unrestricted driver's license has been issued to the minor pursuant to the employer's written authorization.

No liability may be imposed under this section or under Section 17708 on the state or county, or on a probation officer or child protective services worker acting as an officer of the court for damages caused solely by the negligence or willful misconduct of a minor driver whose application for a driver's license was signed by the child protective services worker or probation officer while the minor was a dependent or ward of the court. *(Stats.1959, c. 3, p. 1659, § 17707. Amended by Stats.1967, c. 702, p. 2075, § 9; Stats.1992, c. 865 (A.B.2691), § 3.)*

Law Revision Commission Comments
1967 Amendment

This amendment to section 17707 merely substitutes the term that has been used in Vehicle Code Section 17001 and in sections 17150–17159 for that which appeared in section 17707. The substitution has been made in order to make it clear that the same meaning is intended. No substantive change is made by the revision.

Cross References

Civil liability of owners and operators, generally, see Vehicle Code § 17000 et seq.

Death of person signing minor's application, see Vehicle Code § 17712.

Liability of private owner of motor vehicle, see Vehicle Code § 17150.

Limitation of double liability, see Vehicle Code § 17714.

Release from liability, cancellation of minor's license, see Vehicle Code § 17711.

§ 17708. Liability of parent or guardian

Any civil liability of a minor, whether licensed or not under this code, arising out of his driving a motor vehicle upon a highway with the express or implied permission of the parents or the person or guardian having custody of the minor is hereby imposed upon the parents, person, or guardian and the parents, person, or guardian shall be jointly and severally liable with the minor for any damages proximately resulting from the negligent or wrongful act or omission of the minor in driving a motor vehicle. *(Stats.1959, c. 3, p. 1659, § 17708. Amended by Stats.1967, c. 702, p. 2075, § 10.)*

Law Revision Commission Comments
1967 Amendment

The same reasons which justify the deletion of the provisions for imputed contributory negligence from section 17150 justify the removal of the similar provisions from section 17708. The language of the section has been revised to conform to that use in section 17707.

Cross References

Effect on civil liability of person who consents to, but does not sign nor verify, minor's application, see Vehicle Code §§ 17705, 17706.

§ 17709. Limit of liability

(a) No person, or group of persons collectively, shall incur liability for a minor's negligent or wrongful act or omission under Sections 17707 and 17708 in any amount exceeding fifteen thousand dollars ($15,000) for injury to or death of one person as a result of any one accident or, subject to the limit as to one person, exceeding thirty thousand dollars ($30,000) for injury to or death of all persons as a result of any one accident or exceeding five thousand dollars ($5,000) for damage to property of others as a result of any one accident.

(b) No person is liable under Section 17707 or 17708 for damages imposed for the sake of example and by way of punishing the minor. Nothing in this subdivision makes any person immune from liability for damages imposed for the sake of example and by way of punishing him for his own wrongful conduct. *(Stats.1959, c. 3, p. 1660, § 17709. Amended by Stats.1963, c. 403, p. 1211, § 3; Stats.1967, c. 702, p. 2076, § 11.5; Stats.1967, c. 862, p. 2308, § 11, operative July 1, 1968.)*

Cross References

Effect on civil liability of person who consents to, but does not sign nor verify, minor's application, see Vehicle Code §§ 17705, 17706.

Limitation of double liability, see Vehicle Code § 17714.

§ 17710. Minor agent or servant

The person signing a minor's application for a license is not liable under this chapter for a negligent or wrongful act or omission of the minor committed when the minor is acting as the agent or servant of any person. *(Stats. 1959, c. 3, p. 1660, § 17710. Amended by Stats.1967, c. 702, p. 2076, § 12.)*

Law Revision Commission Comments
1967 Amendment

This amendment merely conforms the section to section 17707 as amended.

§ 17711. Release from liability

Any person who has signed and verified the application of a minor for a driver's license or any employer who has authorized the issuance of a license to a minor and who desires to be relieved from the joint and several liability imposed by reason of having signed and verified such application, may file a verified application with the department requesting that the license of the minor be canceled. The department shall cancel the license, except as provided in subdivision (e) of Section 17712. Thereafter, the person shall be relieved from the liability imposed under this chapter by reason of having signed and verified the original application on account of any subsequent willful misconduct or negligent operation of a motor vehicle by the minor. *(Stats.1959, c. 3, p. 1660, § 17711. Amended by Stats.1976, c. 645, p. 1595, § 2.)*

Cross References

Cancellation,
  Defined, see Vehicle Code § 13100.
  Procedure on, see Vehicle Code § 13551.
Suspension or revocation of license by,
  Court, see Vehicle Code § 13200 et seq.
  Department, see Vehicle Code § 13350 et seq.

§ 17712. Cancellation of license; transfer of liability

(a) The department, upon receipt of satisfactory evidence of the death of the father and mother or the person or guardian who signed and verified the application of any minor under Section 17701 or any employer who signed and verified the application of any minor under subdivision (a) of Section 17706, shall cancel the license, except as provided in subdivision (e).

(b) The department, upon receipt of the verified application of a person who has given written consent to the issuance of a license to a minor as prescribed in Sections 17705 and 17706, for the cancellation of such minor's license, shall cancel the license, except as provided in subdivision (e).

(c) The department, upon receipt of satisfactory evidence that there has been a change of custody of a minor licensed under Chapter 1 (commencing with Section 12500) of Division 6, and upon written request by the person to whom custody has been transferred, shall cancel the license.

(d) The department, upon receipt of satisfactory evidence showing that any minor to whom was issued a license pursuant to Section 17706, has left the employ of the employer who signed and verified the application for the license, shall cancel the license, except as provided in subdivision (e).

(e) The department, upon written request by the person to whom custody of a minor has been transferred, shall transfer the liability imposed under this chapter to such person upon receipt of such person's written verified application for acceptance of liability. Upon receipt, by the department, of such application for acceptance of liability, the person who had signed and verified the application of the minor for the driver's license presently held by the minor shall be relieved from the liability imposed under this chapter. If such application for acceptance of liability is on file with the department prior to the receipt of a request for cancellation by the person who had signed the application of the minor for a driver's license, the license issued under such application shall not be canceled so long as the license is otherwise valid. If, however, such application for acceptance of liability is not on file with the department prior to the receipt of a request for cancellation by the person who had signed the application of the minor for a driver's license, the license issued under such application shall be canceled. *(Stats. 1959, c. 3, p. 1660, § 17712. Amended by Stats.1965, c. 466, p. 1772, § 1; Stats.1976, c. 645, p. 1595, § 3.)*

Cross References

Cancellation,
  Defined, see Vehicle Code § 13100.
  Procedure on, see Vehicle Code § 13551.

§ 17713. Repealed by Stats.1965, c. 466, p. 1772, § 2

§ 17714. Limitation of double liability

In the event, in one or more actions, judgment is rendered against a defendant under this chapter based upon the negligent or wrongful act or omission of a minor in the operation of a vehicle, and also by reason of such act or omission rendered against such defendant under Article 2 (commencing with Section 17150) of Chapter 1 of Division 9, then such judgment or judgments shall not be cumulative but recovery shall be limited to the amount specified in Section 17709. *(Stats.1959, c. 3, p. 1660, § 17714. Amended by Stats.1961, c. 58, p. 1010, § 39, eff. March 31, 1961; Stats.1967, c. 702, p. 2076, § 13.)*

Law Revision Commission Comments

1967 Amendment

This amendment merely conforms the section to sections 17707 and 17708 as amended.

Cross References

Liability of parent or guardian, see Vehicle Code § 17708.
Private owners, liability, see Vehicle Code § 17150 et seq.

Division 10

ACCIDENTS AND ACCIDENT REPORTS

Chapter   **Section**
1. Accidents and Accident Reports **20000**
2. Incident Response Management Program [Repealed]

CHAPTER 1. ACCIDENTS AND ACCIDENT REPORTS

Section
20000. Application of division.
20001. Duty to stop at scene of injury accident; penalties.
20002. Duty where property damaged.
20003. Duty upon injury or death.
20004. Duty upon death.
20005. Repealed.
20006. Driver without license.
20007. Renumbered.
20008. Duty to report accidents.
20009. Supplemental reports.
20010. Driver unable to report.
20011. Coroner's report.
20012. Reports confidential; exceptions; copies; fee.
20013. Reports as evidence.
20014. Use of reports.
20015. Counter report of a property-damage accident; exclusion of determination of fault; exceptions; definition.
20016. Persons injured on highways.
20017. Spill or accidental release of pesticide.
20018. Written policy for law enforcement officers providing assistance to disabled motorists.
20019, 20020. Repealed.

Cross References

Law enforcement vehicles, repainting on sale, see Vehicle Code § 27604.
Prohibited ownership of vehicle painted as law enforcement vehicle, see Vehicle Code § 27605.

§ 20000. Application of division

The provisions of this division apply upon highways and elsewhere throughout the State, unless expressly provided otherwise. *(Stats.1959, c. 3, p. 1661, § 20000.)*

Cross References

Administration and enforcement, see Vehicle Code § 2800 et seq.
Highway defined, see Vehicle Code § 360.
Rules of the road, applicability to animals, see Vehicle Code § 21050.
Uniformity of code, see Vehicle Code § 21.

§ 20001. Duty to stop at scene of injury accident; penalties

(a) The driver of a vehicle involved in an accident resulting in injury to a person, other than himself or herself, or in the death of a person shall immediately stop the vehicle at the scene of the accident and shall fulfill the requirements of Sections 20003 and 20004.

(b)(1) Except as provided in paragraph (2), a person who violates subdivision (a) shall be punished by imprisonment in the state prison, or in a county jail for not more than one year, or by a fine of not less than one thousand dollars ($1,000) nor more than ten thousand dollars ($10,000), or by both that imprisonment and fine.

(2) If the accident described in subdivision (a) results in death or permanent, serious injury, a person who violates subdivision (a) shall be punished by imprisonment in the state prison for two, three, or four years, or in a county jail for not less than 90 days nor more than one year, or by a fine of not less than one thousand dollars ($1,000) nor more than ten thousand dollars ($10,000), or by both that imprisonment and fine. However, the court, in the interests of justice and for reasons stated in the record, may reduce or eliminate the minimum imprisonment required by this paragraph.

(3) In imposing the minimum fine required by this subdivision, the court shall take into consideration the defendant's ability to pay the fine and, in the interests of justice and for reasons stated in the record, may reduce the amount of that minimum fine to less than the amount otherwise required by this subdivision.

(c) A person who flees the scene of the crime after committing a violation of Section 191.5 of, or paragraph (1) of subdivision (c) of Section 192 of the Penal Code, upon conviction of any of those sections, in addition and consecutive to the punishment prescribed, shall be punished by an additional term of imprisonment of five years in the state prison. This additional term shall not be imposed unless the allegation is charged in the accusatory pleading and admitted by the defendant or found to be true by the trier of fact. The court shall not strike a finding that brings a person within the provisions of this subdivision or an allegation made pursuant to this subdivision.

(d) As used in this section, "permanent, serious injury" means the loss or permanent impairment of function of a bodily member or organ. *(Stats.1959, c. 3, p. 1661, § 20001. Amended by Stats.1967, c. 652, p. 2009, § 1; Stats.1976, c. 1139, p. 5171, § 337, operative July 1, 1977; Stats.1983, c. 1092, § 389, eff. Sept. 29, 1983, operative Jan. 1, 1984; Stats.1988, c. 1207, § 1; Stats.1992, c. 501 (S.B.143), § 1; Stats.1996, c. 645 (A.B.1985), § 4; Stats. 1999, c. 854 (S.B.1282), § 1, eff. Oct. 10, 1999; Stats.2007, c. 747 (A.B.678), § 30.)*

Cross References

Accident report forms, see Vehicle Code § 2407.

Applicability of this section to trolley coaches, see Vehicle Code § 21051.

Conviction of a violation of this section as a ground for cancelling, suspending or revoking license to teach driving, see Vehicle Code § 11110.

Crime of violence, within act for indemnification of victims of crime, see Government Code § 13960.

Definitions,
  Driver, see Vehicle Code § 305.
  Negligent operator, see Vehicle Code § 12810.
  Vehicle, see Vehicle Code § 670.

Department of the California highway patrol,
  Accident report forms, see Vehicle Code § 2407.
  Dissemination of traffic accident information, see Vehicle Code § 2408.
  Investigation of accidents, see Vehicle Code § 2412.
  Tabulation and analyzation of accident reports, see Vehicle Code § 2408.

Non-compliance with this section as a ground for revoking license, see Vehicle Code § 13350.

Number of convictions for prima facie presumption as negligent operator, see Vehicle Code § 12810.

Public offense defined, see Penal Code § 15.

Records to be kept by department of motor vehicles, see Vehicle Code § 1800.

Report of accident or conviction, see Vehicle Code § 1806.

Revocation of driver's license, juvenile offenders, see Vehicle Code § 13355.

Revocation or suspension of occupational licenses, see Vehicle Code § 11110.

Time of commencing criminal actions, tolling or extension of time periods, see Penal Code § 803.

Traffic violation point count, violation of this section, see Vehicle Code § 12810.

Traffic violator schools, suspension or revocation of license for violation of this section, see Vehicle Code § 11215.

§ 20002. Duty where property damaged

(a) The driver of any vehicle involved in an accident resulting only in damage to any property, including vehicles, shall immediately stop the vehicle at the nearest location that will not impede traffic or otherwise jeopardize the safety of other motorists. Moving the vehicle in accordance with this subdivision does not affect the question of fault. The driver shall also immediately do either of the following:

(1) Locate and notify the owner or person in charge of that property of the name and address of the driver and owner of the vehicle involved and, upon locating the driver of any other vehicle involved or the owner or person in charge of any damaged property, upon being requested, present his or her driver's license, and vehicle registration, to the other driver, property owner, or person in charge of that property. The information presented shall include the current residence address of the driver and of the registered owner. If the registered owner of an involved vehicle is present at the scene, he or she shall also, upon request, present his or her driver's license information, if available, or other valid identification to the other involved parties.

(2) Leave in a conspicuous place on the vehicle or other property damaged a written notice giving the name

582

and address of the driver and of the owner of the vehicle involved and a statement of the circumstances thereof and shall without unnecessary delay notify the police department of the city wherein the collision occurred or, if the collision occurred in unincorporated territory, the local headquarters of the Department of the California Highway Patrol.

(b) Any person who parks a vehicle which, prior to the vehicle again being driven, becomes a runaway vehicle and is involved in an accident resulting in damage to any property, attended or unattended, shall comply with the requirements of this section relating to notification and reporting and shall, upon conviction thereof, be liable to the penalties of this section for failure to comply with the requirements.

(c) Any person failing to comply with all the requirements of this section is guilty of a misdemeanor and, upon conviction thereof, shall be punished by imprisonment in the county jail not exceeding six months, or by a fine not exceeding one thousand dollars ($1,000), or by both that imprisonment and fine. *(Formerly § 20007, enacted by Stats.1959, c. 3, p. 1662, § 20007. Amended by Stats.1963, c. 406, p. 1213, § 1. Renumbered § 20002 and amended by Stats.1965, c. 872, p. 2474, § 3. Amended by Stats. 1967, c. 652, p. 2009, § 2; Stats.1980, c. 680, p. 2063, § 1; Stats.1983, c. 1092, § 390, eff. Sept. 27, 1983, operative Jan. 1, 1984; Stats.1991, c. 1103 (S.B.148), § 2; Stats.1992, c. 621 (A.B.2517), § 3; Stats.1999, c. 421 (S.B.681), § 1; Stats.2001, c. 825 (S.B.290), § 16.)*

Cross References

Applicability of this section to trolley coaches, see Vehicle Code § 21051.

Conviction of violation of this section as ground for cancelling, suspending or revoking license to teach driving, see Vehicle Code § 11110.

Conviction under this section counted as two convictions for prima facie presumption as negligent operator, see Vehicle Code § 12810.

Driver's license, suspension or revocation by department, see Vehicle Code § 13350.

Guilty plea, see Vehicle Code § 41610.

Impounding vehicles for investigations, see Vehicle Code § 22655.

Procedure on arrest for violation of this section, see Vehicle Code § 40303.

Revocation of driver's license, juvenile offenders, see Vehicle Code § 13355.

Suspension of driver's license, grounds, see Vehicle Code § 13361.

Suspension of license by court upon conviction for violating this section, see Vehicle Code § 13201.

Traffic violation point count, violation of this section, see Vehicle Code § 12810.

Traffic violator schools, suspension or revocation of license for violation of this section, see Vehicle Code § 11215.

Violation as misdemeanor, see Vehicle Code § 40000.13.

§ 20003. Duty upon injury or death

(a) The driver of any vehicle involved in an accident resulting in injury to or death of any person shall also give his or her name, current residence address, the names and current residence addresses of any occupant of the driver's vehicle injured in the accident, the registration number of the vehicle he or she is driving, and the name and current residence address of the owner to the person struck or the driver or occupants of any vehicle collided with, and shall give the information to any traffic or police officer at the scene of the accident. The driver also shall render to any person injured in the accident reasonable assistance, including transporting, or making arrangements for transporting, any injured person to a physician, surgeon, or hospital for medical or surgical treatment if it is apparent that treatment is necessary or if that transportation is requested by any injured person.

(b) Any driver or injured occupant of a driver's vehicle subject to the provisions of subdivision (a) shall also, upon being requested, exhibit his or her driver's license, if available, or, in the case of an injured occupant, any other available identification, to the person struck or to the driver or occupants of any vehicle collided with, and to any traffic or police officer at the scene of the accident. *(Stats.1959, c. 3, p. 1661, § 20003. Amended by Stats. 1980, c. 680, p. 2064, § 2; Stats.1991, c. 1103 (S.B.148), § 3; Stats.1992, c. 621 (A.B.2517), § 4; Stats.1994, c. 1247 (A.B.1926), § 9.)*

Cross References

Applicability of this section to trolley coaches, see Vehicle Code § 21051.
Conviction of a violation of this section as a ground for cancelling, suspending or revoking license to teach driving, see Vehicle Code § 11110.
Impounding vehicle for investigation on reasonable belief of failure of compliance with this section, see Vehicle Code § 22655.
Traffic violator schools, suspension or revocation of license for violation of this section, see Vehicle Code § 11215.
Violation as misdemeanor, see Vehicle Code § 40000.13.

§ 20004. Duty upon death

In the event of death of any person resulting from an accident, the driver of any vehicle involved after fulfilling the requirements of this division, and if there be no traffic or police officer at the scene of the accident to whom to give the information required by Section 20003, shall, without delay, report the accident to the nearest office of the Department of the California Highway Patrol or office of a duly authorized police authority and submit with the report the information required by Section 20003. *(Stats.1959, c. 3, p. 1661, § 20004.)*

Cross References

Applicability of this section to trolley coaches, see Vehicle Code § 21051.
Impounding vehicles for investigations, see Vehicle Code § 22655.
Revocation or suspension of occupational licenses, see Vehicle Code § 11110.

Traffic violator schools, suspension or revocation of license for violation of this section, see Vehicle Code § 11215.

§ 20005. Repealed by Stats.1965, c. 872, p. 2474, § 2

§ 20006. Driver without license

If the driver does not have his driver's license in his possession, he shall exhibit other valid evidences of identification to the occupants of a vehicle with which he collided. *(Stats.1959, c. 3, p. 1662, § 20006.)*

Cross References

Applicability of this section to trolley coaches, see Vehicle Code § 21051.
Impounding vehicles for investigations, see Vehicle Code § 22655.
Revocation or suspension of occupational licenses, see Vehicle Code § 11110.
Traffic violator schools, suspension or revocation of license for violation of this section, see Vehicle Code § 11215.

§ 20007. Renumbered § 20002 and amended by Stats. 1965, c. 872, p. 2474, § 3

§ 20008. Duty to report accidents

(a) The driver of a vehicle, other than a common carrier vehicle, involved in any accident resulting in injuries to or death of any person shall within 24 hours after the accident make or cause to be made a written report of the accident to the Department of the California Highway Patrol or, if the accident occurred within a city, to either the Department of the California Highway Patrol or the police department of the city in which the accident occurred. If the agency which receives the report is not responsible for investigating the accident, it shall immediately forward the report to the law enforcement agency which is responsible for investigating the accident.

On or before the fifth day of each month, every police department which received a report during the previous calendar month of an accident which it is responsible for investigating shall forward the report or a copy thereof to the main office of the Department of the California Highway Patrol at Sacramento.

(b) The owner or driver of a common carrier vehicle involved in any such accident shall make a like report to the Department of California Highway Patrol on or before the 10th day of the month following the accident. *(Stats.1959, c. 3, § 20008. Amended by Stats.1970, c. 224, p. 474, § 1.)*

Cross References

Accident reports as evidence, see Vehicle Code § 20013.
Applicability of this section to trolley coaches, see Vehicle Code § 21051.
Confidential nature of report, see Vehicle Code § 20012.
Department of motor vehicles to prescribe forms, see Vehicle Code § 1652.
Department of the California Highway Patrol,
    Accident report forms, duty to supply, see Vehicle Code § 2407.

Dissemination of traffic accident information, see Vehicle
    Code § 2408.
Investigation of accidents, see Vehicle Code § 2412.
Tabulation and analyzation of accident reports, see Vehicle
    Code § 2408.
Driving schools and driving instructors, revocation or suspension
    of license for violation of this section, see Vehicle Code
    § 11110.
Physical inability to report, see Vehicle Code § 20010.
Traffic violator schools, suspension or revocation of license for
    violation of this section, see Vehicle Code § 11215.

§ 20009. Supplemental reports

The Department of the California Highway Patrol may
require any driver, or the owner of a common carrier
vehicle, involved in any accident of which a report must
be made as provided in Section 20008 to file supplemental reports and may require witnesses of accidents to
render reports to it whenever the original report is
insufficient in the opinion of such department. *(Stats.
1959, c. 3, p. 1663, § 20009.)*

Cross References

Accident reports as evidence, see Vehicle Code § 20013.
Applicability of this section to trolley coaches, see Vehicle Code
    § 21051.
Confidential nature of report, see Vehicle Code § 20012.
Department of California highway patrol,
    Accident report forms, duty to supply, see Vehicle Code
        § 2407.
    Dissemination of traffic accident information, see Vehicle
        Code § 2408.
    Investigation of accidents, see Vehicle Code § 2412.
    Tabulation and analyzation of accident reports, see Vehicle
        Code § 2408.
Department of motor vehicles to prescribe forms, see Vehicle
    Code § 1652.

§ 20010. Driver unable to report

Whenever the driver of a vehicle is physically incapable
of making a required accident report, any occupant in the
vehicle at the time of the accident shall make the report
or cause it to be made. *(Stats.1959, c. 3, p. 1663,
§ 20010.)*

§ 20011. Coroner's report

Every coroner shall on or before the tenth day of each
month report in writing to the Department of the
California Highway Patrol the death of any person during
the preceding calendar month as the result of an accident
involving a motor vehicle and the circumstances of the
accident. *(Stats.1959, c. 3, p. 1663, § 20011.)*

§ 20012. Reports confidential; exceptions; copies; fee

All required accident reports, and supplemental reports, shall be without prejudice to the individual so
reporting and shall be for the confidential use of the
Department of Motor Vehicles and the Department of
the California Highway Patrol, except that the Department of the California Highway Patrol or the law
enforcement agency to whom the accident was reported
shall disclose the entire contents of the reports, including,

but not limited to, the names and addresses of persons
involved or injured in, or witnesses to, an accident, the
registration numbers and descriptions of vehicles involved, the date, time and location of an accident, all
diagrams, statements of the drivers involved or occupants
injured in the accident and the statements of all witnesses, to any person who may have a proper interest
therein, including, but not limited to, the driver or drivers
involved, or the guardian or conservator thereof, the
parent of a minor driver, the authorized representative of
a driver, or to any named person injured therein, the
owners of vehicles or property damaged thereby, persons
who may incur civil liability, including liability based upon
a breach of warranty arising out of the accident, and any
attorney who declares under penalty of perjury that he or
she represents any of the above persons.

A request for a copy of an accident report shall be
accompanied by payment of a fee, provided such fee shall
not exceed the actual cost of providing the copy. *(Stats.
1959, c. 3, p. 1663, § 20012. Amended by Stats.1965, c.
1285, p. 3168, § 1; Stats.1969, c. 19, p. 80, § 1; Stats.
1979, c. 730, p. 2521, § 115, operative Jan. 1, 1981;
Stats.1979, c. 932, p. 3227, § 1; Stats.1979, c. 932, p. 3227,
§ 2, operative Jan. 1, 1981; Stats.1994, c. 1247 (A.B.1926),
§ 10.)*

Law Revision Commission Comments
1979 Amendment

Section 20012 is amended to add the reference to a conservator.

Cross References

Department of highway patrol to tabulate and analyze accident
    reports, see Vehicle Code § 2408.
Insurance Information and Privacy Protection Act, disclosure of
    personal or privileged information, see Insurance Code
    § 791.13.
Use of vehicle report information, see Vehicle Code § 1810.3.

§ 20013. Reports as evidence

No such accident report shall be used as evidence in
any trial, civil or criminal, arising out of an accident,
except that the department shall furnish upon demand of
any person who has, or claims to have, made such a
report or upon demand of any court, a certificate showing
that a specified accident report has or has not been made
to the department solely to prove a compliance or failure
to comply with the requirement that such a report be
made to the department. *(Stats.1959, c. 3, p. 1663,
§ 20013. Amended by Stats.1959, c. 1996, p. 4629, § 22.)*

§ 20014. Use of reports

All required accident reports and supplemental reports
and all reports made to the Department of the California
Highway Patrol by any peace officer, member of the
Department of the California Highway Patrol, or other
employee of the Department of Motor Vehicles and the
Department of the California Highway Patrol, shall be
immediately available for the confidential use of any
division in the department needing the same, for confi-

dential use of the Department of Transportation, and, with respect to accidents occurring on highways other than state highways, for the confidential use of the local authority having jurisdiction over the highway. *(Stats. 1959, c. 3, p. 1663, § 20014. Amended by Stats.1959, c. 1627, p. 3999, § 2; Stats.1974, c. 545, p. 1314, § 167.)*

Cross References

Department of the highway patrol to tabulate and analyze accident reports, see Vehicle Code § 2408.

Use of vehicle report information, see Vehicle Code § 1810.3.

§ 20015. Counter report of a property-damage accident; exclusion of determination of fault; exceptions; definition

(a) No traffic or police officer shall include in any counter report of a property-damage accident, as defined in this section, any determination by the peace officer of fault of the reporting person, including, but not limited to, inattentiveness. This section does not apply to a determination which is the result of an examination of the physical evidence of the accident at the site of the accident by the traffic or police officer or the result of an express, knowing admission of the reporting person if the basis for the determination is also included in the report.

(b) As used in this section, "counter report of a property-damage accident" means any report of an accident involving one or more vehicles which meets the following criteria:

(1) The accident reported caused damage to property, but did not cause personal injury to or the death of any person.

(2) The report is prepared at an office of the California Highway Patrol or local law enforcement agency.

(3) The report is written or recorded by, or with the assistance of, a peace officer. *(Added by Stats.1984, c. 861, § 1.)*

§ 20016. Persons injured on highways

Any peace officer, any member of an organized fire department or fire protection district, any employee of the Department of Transportation assigned to maintenance operations, or any member of the California Highway Patrol may transport or arrange for the transportation of any person injured in an accident upon any highway to a physician and surgeon or hospital, if the injured person does not object to such transportation. Any officer, member, or employee exercising ordinary care and precaution shall not be liable for any damages due to any further injury or for any medical, ambulance, or hospital bills incurred in behalf of the injured party. *(Stats.1959, c. 3, p. 1664, § 20016. Amended by Stats. 1967, c. 1000, p. 2592, § 1; Stats.1974, c. 545, p. 1314, § 168.)*

§ 20017. Spill or accidental release of pesticide

Any peace officer who knows, or has reasonable cause to believe, that a pesticide has been spilled or otherwise accidentally released, shall report the spill as required in Section 105215 of the Health and Safety Code. *(Added by Stats.1979, c. 935, p. 3235, § 5. Amended by Stats. 1996, c. 1023 (S.B.1497), § 425, eff. Sept. 29, 1996.)*

§ 20018. Written policy for law enforcement officers providing assistance to disabled motorists

Every law enforcement agency having traffic law enforcement responsibility as specified in subdivision (a) of Section 830.1 and in subdivision (a) of Section 830.2 of the Penal Code may develop, adopt, and implement a written policy for its officers to provide assistance to disabled motorists on highways within its primary jurisdiction. A copy of the policy, if adopted, shall be available to the public upon request. *(Added by Stats.1985, c. 1203, § 1. Amended by Stats.1993, c. 59 (S.B.443), § 18, eff. June 30, 1993.)*

§§ 20019, 20020. Repealed by Stats.1991, c. 13 (A.B.37), §§ 51, 52, eff. Feb. 13, 1991

CHAPTER 2. INCIDENT RESPONSE MANAGEMENT PROGRAM [REPEALED]

§§ 20050 to 20052. Repealed by Stats.1989, c. 281, § 3, operative Jan. 1, 1991

Division 11

RULES OF THE ROAD

Chapter		Section
1.	Obedience to and Effect of Traffic Laws	21000
2.	Traffic Signs, Signals, and Markings	21350
3.	Driving, Overtaking, and Passing	21650
4.	Right-of-way	21800
5.	Pedestrians' Rights and Duties	21949
6.	Turning and Stopping and Turning Signals	22100
7.	Speed Laws	22348
8.	Special Stops Required	22450
9.	Stopping, Standing, and Parking	22500
10.	Removal of Parked and Abandoned Vehicles	22650
11.	Parking Lots	22950
12.	Public Offenses	23100
13.	Vehicular Crossings and Toll Highways	23250
14.	Parkways [Repealed]	

CHAPTER 1. OBEDIENCE TO AND EFFECT OF TRAFFIC LAWS

Article		Section
1.	Definitions	21000
2.	Effect of Traffic Laws	21050
3.	Local Regulations	21100
4.	Operation of Bicycles	21200
5.	Operation of Motorized Scooters	21220
5.	Operation of Low–Speed Vehicles	21250
6.	Electric Personal Assistive Mobility Devices	21280

ARTICLE 1. DEFINITIONS

Section
21000. Department.
21001. Scope of division.

Cross References

Law enforcement vehicles, repainting on sale, see Vehicle Code § 27604.

Power to act by ordinance as power to act by resolution, see Vehicle Code § 32.

Prohibited ownership of vehicle painted as law enforcement vehicle, see Vehicle Code § 27605.

§ 21000. Department

Wherever in this division "department" occurs, it means the Department of the California Highway Patrol. *(Stats.1959, c. 3, p. 1664, § 21000.)*

Cross References

Department defined, see Vehicle Code §§ 290, 2101, 24000.

Department of the California highway patrol, generally, see Vehicle Code § 2100 et seq.

Powers and duties of commissioner, see Vehicle Code § 2400 et seq.

§ 21001. Scope of division

The provisions of this division refer exclusively to the operation of vehicles upon the highways, unless a differ-ent place is specifically referred to. *(Stats.1959, c. 3, p. 1664, § 21001.)*

Cross References

Highway defined, see Vehicle Code § 360.
Vehicle defined, see Vehicle Code § 670.

ARTICLE 2. EFFECT OF TRAFFIC LAWS

Section
21050. Animals.
21051. Trolley coaches.
21052. Public officers and employees.
21053. Public employees working on highway.
21054. Representative of public agency.
21055. Exemption of authorized emergency vehicles.
21056. Effect of exemption.
21057. Sirens and illegal speed of escorts.
21058. Vehicles owned by physicians.
21059. Rubbish and garbage vehicles.
21060. Streetsweeping and watering vehicles.
21061. Notice of reexamination; evidence of incapacity to operate vehicle.
21062. Copy of notice of reexamination to department; record of notice in driver's license record.
21070. Offense of unsafe operation of motor vehicle with bodily injury or great bodily injury; punishment.

§ 21050. Animals

Every person riding or driving an animal upon a highway has all of the rights and is subject to all of the duties applicable to the driver of a vehicle by this division and Division 10 (commencing with Section 20000), except those provisions which by their very nature can have no application. *(Stats.1959, c. 3, p. 1664, § 21050. Amended by Stats.1963, c. 479, p. 1337, § 1; Stats.1967, c. 586, p. 1931, § 2.)*

Cross References

Animals on highway, generally, see Food and Agricultural Code § 16902 et seq.

Animals prohibited on vehicular crossing, see Vehicle Code § 23330.

Caution required in passing animals, see Vehicle Code § 21759.

§ 21051. Trolley coaches

The following sections apply to trolley coaches:

(a) Sections 1800, 4000, 4001, 4002, 4003, 4006, 4009, 4150, 4151, 4152, 4153, 4155, 4156, 4158, 4166, 4300 to 4309, inclusive, 4450 to 4454, inclusive, 4457, 4458, 4459, 4460, 4600 to 4610, inclusive, 4750, 4751, 4850, 4851, 4852, 4853, 5000, 5200 to 5205, inclusive, 5904, 6052, 8801, 9254, and 40001 with respect to 4000, relating to original and renewal of registration.

(b) Sections 9250, 9265, 9400, 9406, 9407, 9408, 9550, 9552, 9553, 9554, 9800 to 9808, inclusive, 14901, 42230 to 42233, inclusive, relating to registration and other fees.

(c) Sections 2800, 10851, 10852, 10853, 20001 to 20009, inclusive, 21052, 21053, 21054, 21450 to 21457, inclusive, 21461, 21650, 21651, 21658, 21659, 21700, 21701, 21702, 21703, 21709, 21712, 21750, 21753, 21754, 21755, 21800, 21801, 21802, 21806, 21950, 21951, 22106, 22107, 22108, 22109, 22350, 22351, 22352, 22400, 22450 to 22453, inclusive, 23103, 23104, 23105, 23110, 23152, 23153, 40831, 42002 with respect to 10852 and 10853, and 42004, relating to traffic laws.

(d) Sections 26706, 26707, and 26708, relating to equipment.

(e) Sections 17301, 17302, 17303, 21461, 35000, 35100, 35101, 35105, 35106, 35111, 35550, 35551, 35750, 35751, 35753, 40000.1 to 40000.25, inclusive, 40001, 40003, and 42031, relating to the size, weight, and loading of vehicles. *(Stats.1959, c. 3, p. 1664, § 21051. Amended by Stats. 1977, c. 579, p. 1917, § 186; Stats.1981, c. 714, p. 2799, § 445; Stats.1982, c. 53, p. 171, § 22, eff. Feb. 18, 1982; Stats.2000, c. 135 (A.B.2539), § 161; Stats.2007, c. 682 (A.B.430), § 15.)*

Cross References

Trolley coach defined, see Vehicle Code § 650.

§ 21052. Public officers and employees

The provisions of this code applicable to the drivers of vehicles upon the highways apply to the drivers of all vehicles while engaged in the course of employment by this State, any political subdivision thereof, any municipal corporation, or any district, including authorized emergency vehicles subject to those exemptions granted such authorized emergency vehicles in this code. *(Stats.1959, c. 3, p. 1665, § 21052.)*

Cross References

Applicability of this section to trolley coaches, see Vehicle Code § 21051.
Definitions,
   Driver, see Vehicle Code § 305.
   Emergency vehicle, see Vehicle Code §§ 165, 165.5.
   Highway, see Vehicle Code §§ 360, 590.
Exemptions granted to drivers of authorized emergency vehicles, see Vehicle Code § 21055.

§ 21053. Public employees working on highway

This code, except Chapter 1 (commencing with Section 20000) of Division 10, Article 2 (commencing with Section 23152) of Chapter 12 of Division 11, and Sections 25268 and 25269, does not apply to public employees and publicly owned teams, motor vehicles, and other equipment while actually engaged in work upon the surface of a highway, or work of installation, removal, repairing, or maintaining official traffic control devices. This code does apply to those persons and vehicles when traveling to or from their work. *(Stats.1959, c. 3, p. 1665, § 21053. Amended by Stats.1961, c. 653, p. 1860, § 27, operative*

588

Jan. 1, 1962; Stats.1995, c. 766 (S.B.726), § 21; Stats. 1998, c. 877 (A.B.2132), § 62.)

Cross References

Applicability of this section to trolley coaches, see Vehicle Code § 21051.
Definitions,
   Highway, see Vehicle Code §§ 360, 590.
   Motor vehicle, see Vehicle Code § 415.
   Official traffic control device, see Vehicle Code § 440.

§ 21054. Representative of public agency

The provisions of this division do not apply to the duly authorized representatives of any public agency while actually engaged in performing any of the work described in Section 21053 but apply to such persons when traveling to and from such work. *(Stats.1959, c. 3, p. 1665, § 21054.)*

Cross References

Applicability of this section to trolley coaches, see Vehicle Code § 21051.

§ 21055. Exemption of authorized emergency vehicles

The driver of an authorized emergency vehicle is exempt from Chapter 2 (commencing with Section 21350), Chapter 3 (commencing with Section 21650), Chapter 4 (commencing with Section 21800), Chapter 5 (commencing with Section 21950), Chapter 6 (commencing with 22100), Chapter 7 (commencing with Section 22348), Chapter 8 (commencing with Section 22450), Chapter 9 (commencing with Section 22500), and Chapter 10 (commencing with Section 22650) of this division, and Article 3 (commencing with Section 38305) and Article 4 (commencing with Section 38312) of Chapter 5 of Division 16.5, under all of the following conditions:

(a) If the vehicle is being driven in response to an emergency call or while engaged in rescue operations or is being used in the immediate pursuit of an actual or suspected violator of the law or is responding to, but not returning from, a fire alarm, except that fire department vehicles are exempt whether directly responding to an emergency call or operated from one place to another as rendered desirable or necessary by reason of an emergency call and operated to the scene of the emergency or operated from one fire station to another or to some other location by reason of the emergency call.

(b) If the driver of the vehicle sounds a siren as may be reasonably necessary and the vehicle displays a lighted red lamp visible from the front as a warning to other drivers and pedestrians.

A siren shall not be sounded by an authorized emergency vehicle except when required under this section. *(Stats.1959, c. 3, p. 1665, § 21055. Amended by Stats. 1961, c. 524, p. 1627, § 1; Stats.1976, c. 1079, p. 4889, § 90; Stats.1977, c. 1017, p. 3050, § 2, eff. Sept. 23, 1977.)*

Cross References

Additional lights, see Vehicle Code § 25258.

Additional lights on emergency vehicles, see Vehicle Code §§ 25252, 25252.5.

Civil liability of owners and operators, see Vehicle Code § 17000 et seq.

Definitions,
Authorized emergency vehicle, see Vehicle Code §§ 165, 165.5.
Driver, see Vehicle Code § 305.
Highway, see Vehicle Code §§ 360, 590.

Exemption for physicians on emergency calls, see Vehicle Code § 21058.

Flashing headlamps, see Vehicle Code § 25252.5.

Following emergency vehicle, see Vehicle Code § 21706.

Highway patrol regulations, effect on compliance with this section, see Vehicle Code § 2512.

Obedience to traffic control signals, see Vehicle Code § 21462.

Police and traffic officer's use of siren and illegal speed in escorting vehicles, see Vehicle Code § 21057.

Right-of-way of authorized emergency vehicles, see Vehicle Code § 21806.

Traffic control signal changing devices, priority of emergency vehicle over bus, see Vehicle Code § 25352.

§ 21056. Effect of exemption

Section 21055 does not relieve the driver of a vehicle from the duty to drive with due regard for the safety of all persons using the highway, nor protect him from the consequences of an arbitrary exercise of the privileges granted in that section. *(Stats.1959, c. 3, p. 1666, § 21056.)*

Cross References

Liability of operator of authorized emergency vehicles, see Vehicle Code § 17004.

§ 21057. Sirens and illegal speed of escorts

Every police and traffic officer is hereby expressly prohibited from using a siren or driving at an illegal speed when serving as an escort of any vehicle, except when the escort or conveyance is furnished for the preservation of life or when expediting movements of supplies and personnel for any federal, state, or local governmental agency during a national emergency, or state of war emergency, or state of emergency, or local emergency as defined in Section 8558 of the Government code. *(Stats. 1959, c. 3, p. 1666, § 21057. Amended by Stats.1971, c. 131, p. 178, § 1, operative May 3, 1972.)*

Cross References

Speed laws, see Vehicle Code § 22349 et seq.

§ 21058. Vehicles owned by physicians

A physician traveling in response to an emergency call shall be exempt from the provisions of Sections 22351 and 22352 if the vehicle so used by him displays an insigne approved by the department indicating that the vehicle is owned by a licensed physician. The provisions of this section do not relieve the driver of the vehicle from the duty to drive with due regard for the safety of all persons using the highway, nor protect the driver from the consequences of an arbitrary exercise of the privileges of this section. *(Stats.1959, c. 3, p. 1666, § 21058. Amended by Stats.1959, c. 1996, p. 4629, § 23.)*

§ 21059. Rubbish and garbage vehicles

Sections 21211, 21650, 21660, 22502, 22504, and subdivision (h) of Section 22500 do not apply to the operation of a rubbish or garbage truck while actually engaged in the collection of rubbish or garbage within a business or residence district, if the front turn signal lamps at each side of the vehicle are being flashed simultaneously and the rear turn signal lamps at each side of the vehicle are being flashed simultaneously.

This provision does not apply when the vehicle is being driven to and from work, and it does not relieve the driver of the vehicle from the duty to drive with due regard for the safety of all persons using the highway or protect him or her from the consequences of an arbitrary exercise of the privilege granted. *(Added by Stats.1965, c. 490, p. 1800, § 1. Amended by Stats.1999, c. 1007 (S.B.532), § 20.)*

§ 21060. Streetsweeping and watering vehicles

Between the hours of 1 a.m. and 5 a.m., Sections 21650, 21660, 22502, 22504, and subdivision (h) of Section 22500 do not apply to the operation of a streetsweeper vehicle or watering vehicle, operated by a local authority, while the vehicle is actually sweeping streets or watering landscaping or vegetation within a business or residence district. The exemption is not applicable unless the turn signal lamps at each side of the front and rear of the streetsweeper vehicle or watering vehicle are being flashed simultaneously.

This provision shall not apply when the vehicle is being driven to and from such work, nor does it relieve the driver of such a vehicle from the duty to drive with due regard for the safety of all persons using the highway or protect the driver from the consequences of an arbitrary exercise of the privilege granted. *(Added by Stats.1979, c. 469, p. 1626, § 1.)*

§ 21061. Notice of reexamination; evidence of incapacity to operate vehicle

(a) In addition to any action prescribed in Division 17 (commencing with Section 40000.1), a traffic officer may issue a notice of reexamination to any person who violates any provision of this division and who, at the time of the violation, exhibits evidence of incapacity to the traffic officer which leads the traffic officer to reasonably believe that the person is incapable of operating a motor vehicle in a manner so as not to present a clear or potential danger of risk of injury to that person or others if that person is permitted to resume operation of a motor vehicle.

(b) For purposes of this section, "evidence of incapacity" means evidence, other than violations of this division, of serious physical injury or illness or mental impairment or disorientation which is apparent to the traffic officer and which presents a clear or potential danger or risk of

589

injury to the person or others if that person is permitted to resume operation of a motor vehicle. *(Added by Stats.1986, c. 304, § 3, operative July 1, 1987.)*

Cross References

Reexamination pursuant to notice, see Vehicle Code § 12818.
Three-tier assessment system, pilot study, see Vehicle Code § 1659.9.

§ 21062. Copy of notice of reexamination to department; record of notice in driver's license record

The arresting officer shall, before the end of the next working day, transmit, or cause to be transmitted, a legible copy of the notice of reexamination to the Department of Motor Vehicles, and the department shall enter the record of the notice in the driver's license record maintained by electronic recording and storage media by the department within five working days of its receipt. *(Added by Stats.1986, c. 304, § 4, operative July 1, 1987.)*

§ 21070. Offense of unsafe operation of motor vehicle with bodily injury or great bodily injury; punishment

Notwithstanding any other provision of law, a driver who violates any provision of this division, that is punishable as an infraction, and as a result of that violation proximately causes bodily injury or great bodily injury, as defined in Section 12022.7 of the Penal Code, to another person is guilty of the public offense of unsafe operation of a motor vehicle with bodily injury or great bodily injury. That violation is punishable as an infraction pursuant to Section 42001.19. *(Added by Stats.2006, c. 898 (S.B.1021), § 3.)*

Cross References

Conviction under Vehicle Code § 21070, fines, see Vehicle Code § 42001.19.
Infractions, see Penal Code § 16.

ARTICLE 3. LOCAL REGULATIONS

Section
21100.   Rules and regulations; adoption by ordinance or resolution; subject matter.
21100.1.   Traffic control devices; uniform standards and specifications.
21100.3.   Obedience to persons regulating traffic.
21100.4.   Issuance of warrant or order authorizing peace officer or designated local transportation officer to seize vehicle illegally being operated as a taxi; notice and period of impoundment; release of impounded vehicles; towing and storage charges; registered owners.
21100.5.   Island city vehicle regulation.
21100.7.   Repealed.
21101.   Regulation of highways.
21101.2.   Local traffic regulation; reasonable flow impaired; diversion.
21101.4.   Temporary closure of highway by local authorities; extension of closure period; conditions; notice.

Section
21101.6.   Placement of gates or other selective devices on streets denying or restricting access to certain members of public; prohibition; codification of existing law.
21102.   Local authority to close streets.
21102.1.   Local authorities; regulations relating to alleys.
21103.   Signs required.
21104.   Approval of local regulations.
21105.   Boundary line streets.
21106.   Establishment of crosswalks.
21107.   Private roads.
21107.5.   Private roads open for public use.
21107.6.   Private roads to commercial establishments.
21107.7.   Private roads not open to public use.
21107.8.   Private parking facilities.
21107.9.   Private roads within mobilehome parks.
21108.   Private roads leading to airports.
21109.   Tunnels, bridges, or viaducts, cargo tank vehicles displaying flammable liquids placards.
21109.5.   Notice and hearing; cargo tank vehicle restrictions or prohibitions.
21110.   Railroad crossings.
21111.   Housing projects.
21112.   Taxicab and bus stands.
21113.   Public grounds.
21114.   Aircraft on local roads.
21114.5.   Electric carts on sidewalks; disabled persons; persons over 50; governmental and utility employees; permits; exemption.
21114.6.   Repealed.
21115.   Golf carts on local highways; crossing zones; low-speed vehicles.
21115.1.   Golf carts and low-speed vehicles on streets.
21115.5.   Repealed.
21116.   Levees, banks of waterways, and pipeline rights-of-way.
21117.   Public access to highways in environmentally sensitive areas; local agreements.

§ 21100. Rules and regulations; adoption by ordinance or resolution; subject matter

Local authorities may adopt rules and regulations by ordinance or resolution regarding all of the following matters:

(a) Regulating or prohibiting processions or assemblages on the highways.

(b) Licensing and regulating the operation of vehicles for hire and drivers of passenger vehicles for hire.

(c) Regulating traffic by means of traffic officers.

(d) Regulating traffic by means of official traffic control devices meeting the requirements of Section 21400.

(e)(1) Regulating traffic by means of a person given temporary or permanent appointment for that duty by the local authority when official traffic control devices are disabled or otherwise inoperable, at the scenes of accidents or disasters, or at locations as may require traffic direction for orderly traffic flow.

(2) A person shall not be appointed pursuant to this subdivision unless and until the local authority has

submitted to the commissioner or to the chief law enforcement officer exercising jurisdiction in the enforcement of traffic laws within the area in which the person is to perform the duty, for review, a proposed program of instruction for the training of a person for that duty, and unless and until the commissioner or other chief law enforcement officer approves the proposed program. The commissioner or other chief law enforcement officer shall approve a proposed program if he or she reasonably determines that the program will provide sufficient training for persons assigned to perform the duty described in this subdivision.

(f) Regulating traffic at the site of road or street construction or maintenance by persons authorized for that duty by the local authority.

(g)(1) Licensing and regulating the operation of tow truck service or tow truck drivers whose principal place of business or employment is within the jurisdiction of the local authority, excepting the operation and operators of any auto dismantlers' tow vehicle licensed under Section 11505 or any tow truck operated by a repossessing agency licensed under Chapter 11 (commencing with Section 7500) of Division 3 of the Business and Professions Code and its registered employees.

(2) The Legislature finds that the safety and welfare of the general public is promoted by permitting local authorities to regulate tow truck service companies and operators by requiring licensure, insurance, and proper training in the safe operation of towing equipment, thereby ensuring against towing mistakes that may lead to violent confrontation, stranding motorists in dangerous situations, impeding the expedited vehicle recovery, and wasting state and local law enforcement's limited resources.

(3) This subdivision does not limit the authority of a city or city and county pursuant to Section 12111.

(h) Operation of bicycles, and, as specified in Section 21114.5, electric carts by physically disabled persons, or persons 50 years of age or older, on * * * public sidewalks.

(i) Providing for the appointment of nonstudent school crossing guards for the protection of persons who are crossing a street or highway in the vicinity of a school or while returning thereafter to a place of safety.

(j) Regulating the methods of deposit of garbage and refuse in streets and highways for collection by the local authority or by any person authorized by the local authority.

(k)(1) Regulating cruising.

(2) The ordinance or resolution adopted pursuant to this subdivision shall regulate cruising, which is the repetitive driving of a motor vehicle past a traffic control point in traffic that is congested at or near the traffic control point, as determined by the ranking peace officer on duty within the affected area, within a specified time period and after the vehicle operator has been given an adequate written notice that further driving past the

control point will be a violation of the ordinance or resolution.

(3) A person is not in violation of an ordinance or resolution adopted pursuant to this subdivision unless both of the following apply:

(A) That person has been given the written notice on a previous driving trip past the control point and then again passes the control point in that same time interval.

(B) The beginning and end of the portion of the street subject to cruising controls are clearly identified by signs that briefly and clearly state the appropriate provisions of this subdivision and the local ordinance or resolution on cruising.

(l) Regulating or authorizing the removal by peace officers of vehicles unlawfully parked in a fire lane, as described in Section 22500.1, on private property. A removal pursuant to this subdivision shall be consistent, to the extent possible, with the procedures for removal and storage set forth in Chapter 10 (commencing with Section 22650).

(m) Regulating mobile billboard advertising displays, as defined in Section 395.5, including the establishment of penalties, which may include, but are not limited to, removal of the mobile billboard advertising display, civil penalties, and misdemeanor criminal penalties, for a violation of the ordinance or resolution. The ordinance or resolution may establish a minimum distance that a mobile billboard advertising display shall be moved after a specified time period.

(n) Licensing and regulating the operation of pedicabs for hire, as defined in Section 467.5, and operators of pedicabs for hire, including requiring one or more of the following documents:

(1) A valid California driver's license.

(2) Proof of successful completion of a bicycle safety training course certified by the League of American Bicyclists or an equivalent organization as determined by the local authority.

(3) A valid California identification card and proof of successful completion of the written portion of the California driver's license examination administered by the department. The department shall administer, without charging a fee, the original driver's license written examination on traffic laws and signs to a person who states that he or she is, or intends to become, a pedicab operator, and who holds a valid California identification card or has successfully completed an application for a California identification card. If the person achieves a passing score on the examination, the department shall issue a certificate of successful completion of the examination, bearing the person's name and identification card number. The certificate shall not serve in lieu of successful completion of the required examination administered as part of any subsequent application for a driver's license. The department is not required to enter the results of the examination into the computerized

record of the person's identification card or otherwise retain a record of the examination or results.

(*o*)(1) This section does not authorize a local authority to enact or enforce an ordinance or resolution that establishes a violation if a violation for the same or similar conduct is provided in this code, nor does it authorize a local authority to enact or enforce an ordinance or resolution that assesses a fine, penalty, assessment, or fee for a violation if a fine, penalty, assessment, or fee for a violation involving the same or similar conduct is provided in this code.

(2) This section does not preclude a local authority from enacting parking ordinances pursuant to existing authority in Chapter 9 (commencing with Section 22500) of Division 11.

(p)(1) Regulating advertising signs on motor vehicles parked or left standing upon a public street. The ordinance or resolution may establish a minimum distance that the advertising sign shall be moved after a specified time period.

(2) Paragraph (1) does not apply to any of the following:

(A) Advertising signs that are permanently affixed to the body of, an integral part of, or a fixture of a motor vehicle for permanent decoration, identification, or display and that do not extend beyond the overall length, width, or height of the vehicle.

(B) If the license plate frame is installed in compliance with Section 5201, paper advertisements issued by a dealer contained within that license plate frame or any advertisements on that license plate frame.

(3) As used in paragraph (2), "permanently affixed" means any of the following:

(A) Painted directly on the body of a motor vehicle.

(B) Applied as a decal on the body of a motor vehicle.

(C) Placed in a location on the body of a motor vehicle that was specifically designed by a vehicle manufacturer as defined in Section 672 and licensed pursuant to Section 11701, in compliance with both state and federal law or guidelines, for the express purpose of containing an advertising sign. *(Stats.1959, c. 3, p. 1666, § 21100. Amended by Stats.1965, c. 1554, p. 3647, § 2; Stats.1968, c. 1071, p. 2078, § 1; Stats.1972, c. 490, p. 862, § 1; Stats.1974, c. 821, p. 1780, § 1, eff. Sept. 18, 1974; Stats.1976, c. 15, p. 13, § 1; Stats.1976, c. 213, p. 398, § 1; Stats.1976, c. 1018, p. 4599, § 3; Stats.1978, c. 183, p. 413, § 1; Stats.1980, c. 671, p. 1865, § 2; Stats.1982, c. 710, p. 2869, § 2, eff. Sept. 8, 1982; Stats.1984, c. 1426, § 1; Stats.1985, c. 710, § 2; Stats.1988, c. 924, § 7; Stats.2006, c. 609 (A.B.2210), § 1; Stats.2010, c. 614 (A.B.2294), § 2; Stats.2010, c. 615 (A.B.2756), § 3.5; Stats.2010, c. 616 (S.B.949), § 2.7, operative July 1, 2011; Stats.2011, c. 538 (A.B.1298), § 3; Stats.2012, c. 373 (A.B.2291), § 1; Stats.2013, c. 652 (A.B.1253), § 1.)*

Cross References

Authority to remove vehicles, mobile advertising displays parked or left standing in violation of local resolution or ordinance adopted pursuant to this section, see Vehicle Code § 22651.
Bicycle lanes, see Vehicle Code § 21207.
Definitions,
    Local authorities, see Vehicle Code § 385.
    Official traffic control devices and signals, see Vehicle Code §§ 440, 445.
    Traffic, see Vehicle Code § 620.
    Traffic officer, see Vehicle Code § 625.
    Vehicle, see Vehicle Code § 670.
Local establishment of crosswalks, see Vehicle Code § 21106.
Local regulation of state highways, stopping, standing and parking, see Vehicle Code § 22501.
Operation of vehicles on sidewalks, see Vehicle Code § 21663.
Penalties for failure to obey person or control devices at site of construction, maintenance or repair, see Vehicle Code § 40000.14.
Powers of local authorities to regulate,
    Boundary line streets and highways, see Vehicle Code § 21105.
    Parking, see Vehicle Code § 22507.
    Pedestrians and vehicle turning movements, see Vehicle Code §§ 21961, 22113.
    Speed limits, see Vehicle Code §§ 22357, 22358.
    Stop signs on local highways, see Vehicle Code § 21354.
    Taxicab and bus stands, see Vehicle Code § 21112.
    Traffic at highway railroad grade crossings, see Vehicle Code § 21110.
    Traffic on private roads in housing projects, see Vehicle Code § 21111.
    Traffic on private roads in private airports, see Vehicle Code § 21108.
    Traffic on subways, tubes, tunnels, bridges and viaducts, see Vehicle Code § 21109.
Scope of Division, see Vehicle Code § 21101.
Stopping electric cart on sidewalk, see Vehicle Code § 22500.
Traffic signs, signals and markings, powers of local authority to erect, see Vehicle Code §§ 21351, 21353 et seq., 22113.
Uniformity of Code, see Vehicle Code § 21.

§ 21100.1. Traffic control devices; uniform standards and specifications

Whenever any city or county, by ordinance or resolution, permits, restricts, or prohibits the use of public or private highways pursuant to this article, any traffic control device erected by it on or after January 1, 1981, shall conform to the uniform standards and specifications adopted by the Department of Transportation pursuant to Section 21400. *(Added by Stats.1980, c. 671, p. 1866, § 3.)*

§ 21100.3. Obedience to persons regulating traffic

It is unlawful for any person to disobey the traffic directions of a person appointed or authorized by a local authority to regulate traffic pursuant to subdivision (e) of Section 21100 when such appointee is wearing an official insignia issued by the local authority and is acting in the course of his appointed duties. *(Added by Stats.1974, c. 821, p. 1780, § 2, eff. Sept. 18, 1974. Amended by Stats.1976, c. 15, p. 13, § 2.)*

§ **21100.4. Issuance of warrant or order authorizing peace officer or designated local transportation officer to seize vehicle illegally being operated as a taxi; notice and period of impoundment; release of impounded vehicles; towing and storage charges; registered owners**

(a)(1) A magistrate presented with the affidavit of a peace officer or a designated local transportation officer establishing reasonable cause to believe that a vehicle, described by vehicle type and license number, is being operated as a taxicab or other passenger vehicle for hire in violation of licensing requirements adopted by a local authority under subdivision (b) of Section 21100 shall issue a warrant or order authorizing the peace officer or designated local transportation officer to immediately seize and cause the removal of the vehicle. As used in this section, "designated local transportation officer" means any local public officer employed by a local authority to investigate and enforce local taxicab and vehicle for hire laws and regulations.

(2) The warrant or court order may be entered into a computerized database.

(3) A vehicle so impounded may be impounded for a period not to exceed 30 days.

(4) The impounding agency, within two working days of impoundment, shall send a notice by certified mail, return receipt requested, to the legal owner of the vehicle, at an address obtained from the department, informing the owner that the vehicle has been impounded and providing the owner with a copy of the warrant or court order. Failure to notify the legal owner within two working days shall prohibit the impounding agency from charging for more than 15 days' impoundment when a legal owner redeems the impounded vehicle. The law enforcement agency shall be open to issue a release to the registered owner or legal owner, or the agent of either, whenever the agency is open to serve the public for regular, nonemergency business.

(b)(1) An impounding agency shall release a vehicle to the registered owner or his or her agent prior to the end of the impoundment period and without the permission of the magistrate authorizing the vehicle's seizure under any of the following circumstances:

(A) When the vehicle is a stolen vehicle.

(B) When the vehicle was seized under this section for an offense that does not authorize the seizure of the vehicle.

(C) When the vehicle is a rental car.

(2) A vehicle may not be released under this subdivision, except upon presentation of the registered owner's or agent's currently valid license to operate the vehicle under the licensing requirements adopted by the local authority under subdivision (b) of Section 21100, and proof of current vehicle registration, or upon order of the court.

(c)(1) Whenever a vehicle is impounded under this section, the magistrate ordering the storage shall provide the vehicle's registered and legal owners of record, or their agents, with the opportunity for a poststorage hearing to determine the validity of the storage.

(2) A notice of the storage shall be mailed or personally delivered to the registered and legal owners within 48 hours after issuance of the warrant or court order, excluding weekends and holidays, by the person or agency executing the warrant or court order, and shall include all of the following information:

(A) The name, address, and telephone number of the agency providing the notice.

(B) The location of the place of storage and a description of the vehicle, which shall include, if available, the name or make, the manufacturer, the license plate number, and the mileage of the vehicle.

(C) A copy of the warrant or court order and the peace officer's affidavit, as described in subdivision (a).

(D) A statement that, in order to receive their poststorage hearing, the owners, or their agents, are required to request the hearing from the magistrate issuing the warrant or court order in person, in writing, or by telephone, within 10 days of the date of the notice.

(3) The poststorage hearing shall be conducted within two court days after receipt of the request for the hearing.

(4) At the hearing, the magistrate may order the vehicle released if he or she finds any of the circumstances described in subdivision (b) or (e) that allow release of a vehicle by the impounding agency.

(5) Failure of either the registered or legal owner, or his or her agent, to request, or to attend, a scheduled hearing satisfies the poststorage hearing requirement.

(6) The agency employing the peace officer or designated local transportation officer who caused the magistrate to issue the warrant or court order shall be responsible for the costs incurred for towing and storage if it is determined in the poststorage hearing that reasonable grounds for the storage are not established.

(d) The registered owner or his or her agent is responsible for all towing and storage charges related to the impoundment, and any administrative charges authorized under Section 22850.5.

(e) A vehicle removed and seized under subdivision (a) shall be released to the legal owner of the vehicle or the legal owner's agent prior to the end of the impoundment period and without the permission of the magistrate authorizing the seizure of the vehicle if all of the following conditions are met:

(1) The legal owner is a motor vehicle dealer, bank, credit union, acceptance corporation, or other licensed financial institution legally operating in this state or is another person, not the registered owner, holding a security interest in the vehicle.

(2)(A) The legal owner or the legal owner's agent pays all towing and storage fees related to the seizure of the vehicle. A lien sale processing fee shall not be charged to the legal owner who redeems the vehicle prior to the 15th day of impoundment. Neither the impounding authority nor any person having possession of the vehicle shall collect from the legal owner of the type specified in paragraph (1), or the legal owner's agent, any administrative charges imposed pursuant to Section 22850.5 unless the legal owner voluntarily requested a poststorage hearing.

(B) A person operating or in charge of a storage facility where vehicles are stored pursuant to this section shall accept a valid bank credit card or cash for payment of towing, storage, and related fees by a legal or registered owner or the owner's agent claiming the vehicle. A credit card shall be in the name of the person presenting the card. "Credit card" means "credit card" as defined in subdivision (a) of Section 1747.02 of the Civil Code, except, for the purposes of this section, credit card does not include a credit card issued by a retail seller.

(C) A person operating or in charge of a storage facility described in subparagraph (B) who violates subparagraph (B) shall be civilly liable to the owner of the vehicle or to the person who tendered the fees for four times the amount of the towing, storage, and related fees, but not to exceed five hundred dollars ($500).

(D) A person operating or in charge of a storage facility described in subparagraph (B) shall have sufficient funds on the premises of the primary storage facility during normal business hours to accommodate, and make change in, a reasonable monetary transaction.

(E) Credit charges for towing and storage services shall comply with Section 1748.1 of the Civil Code. Law enforcement agencies may include the costs of providing for payment by credit when making agreements with towing companies on rates.

(3)(A) The legal owner or the legal owner's agent presents to the law enforcement agency or impounding agency, or any person acting on behalf of those agencies, a copy of the assignment, as defined in subdivision (b) of Section 7500.1 of the Business and Professions Code; a release from the one responsible governmental agency, only if required by the agency; a government-issued photographic identification card; and any one of the following as determined by the legal owner or the legal owner's agent: a certificate of repossession for the vehicle, a security agreement for the vehicle, or title, whether paper or electronic, showing proof of legal ownership for the vehicle. The law enforcement agency, impounding agency, or any other governmental agency, or any person acting on behalf of those agencies, shall not require the presentation of any other documents.

(B) The legal owner or the legal owner's agent presents to the person in possession of the vehicle, or any person acting on behalf of the person in possession, a copy of the assignment, as defined in subdivision (b) of

Section 7500.1 of the Business and Professions Code; a release from the one responsible governmental agency, only if required by the agency; a government-issued photographic identification card; and any one of the following as determined by the legal owner or the legal owner's agent: a certificate of repossession for the vehicle, a security agreement for the vehicle, or title, whether paper or electronic, showing proof of legal ownership for the vehicle. The person in possession of the vehicle, or any person acting on behalf of the person in possession, shall not require the presentation of any other documents.

(C) All presented documents may be originals, photocopies, or facsimile copies, or may be transmitted electronically. The law enforcement agency, impounding agency, or any person in possession of the vehicle, or anyone acting on behalf of them, shall not require any documents to be notarized. The law enforcement agency, impounding agency, or any person acting on behalf of those agencies, may require the agent of the legal owner to produce a photocopy or facsimile copy of its repossession agency license or registration issued pursuant to Chapter 11 (commencing with Section 7500) of Division 3 of the Business and Professions Code, or to demonstrate, to the satisfaction of the law enforcement agency, impounding agency, or any person in possession of the vehicle, or anyone acting on behalf of them, that the agent is exempt from licensure pursuant to Section 7500.2 or 7500.3 of the Business and Professions Code.

(D) An administrative cost authorized under subdivision (a) of Section 22850.5 shall not be charged to the legal owner of the type specified in paragraph (1) who redeems the vehicle unless the legal owner voluntarily requests a poststorage hearing. A city, county, city and county, or state agency shall not require a legal owner or a legal owner's agent to request a poststorage hearing as a requirement for release of the vehicle to the legal owner or the legal owner's agent. The law enforcement agency, impounding agency, or any other governmental agency, or any person acting on behalf of those agencies, shall not require any documents other than those specified in this paragraph. The law enforcement agency, impounding agency, or other governmental agency, or any person acting on behalf of those agencies, may not require any documents to be notarized. The legal owner or the legal owner's agent shall be given a copy of any documents he or she is required to sign, except for a vehicle evidentiary hold logbook. The law enforcement agency, impounding agency, or any person acting on behalf of those agencies, or any person in possession of the vehicle, may photocopy and retain the copies of any documents presented by the legal owner or legal owner's agent.

(4) A failure by a storage facility to comply with any applicable conditions set forth in this subdivision shall not affect the right of the legal owner or the legal owner's agent to retrieve the vehicle, provided all conditions required of the legal owner or legal owner's agent under this subdivision are satisfied.

(f)(1) A legal owner or the legal owner's agent that obtains release of the vehicle pursuant to subdivision (e) shall not release the vehicle to the registered owner of the vehicle or the person who was listed as the registered owner when the vehicle was impounded or any agents of the registered owner until the termination of the impoundment period.

(2) The legal owner or the legal owner's agent shall not relinquish the vehicle to the registered owner or the person who was listed as the registered owner when the vehicle was impounded until the registered owner or that owner's agent presents his or her valid driver's license or valid temporary driver's license, and an operator's license that is in compliance with the licensing requirements adopted by the local authority under subdivision (b) of Section 21100, to the legal owner or the legal owner's agent. The legal owner or the legal owner's agent or the person in possession of the vehicle shall make every reasonable effort to ensure that the licenses presented are valid and possession of the vehicle will not be given to the driver who was involved in the original impoundment proceeding until the expiration of the impoundment period.

(3) Prior to relinquishing the vehicle, the legal owner may require the registered owner to pay all towing and storage charges related to the impoundment and the administrative charges authorized under Section 22850.5 that were incurred by the legal owner in connection with obtaining the custody of the vehicle.

(4) Any legal owner who knowingly releases or causes the release of a vehicle to a registered owner or the person in possession of the vehicle at the time of the impoundment or any agent of the registered owner in violation of this subdivision shall be guilty of a misdemeanor and subject to a civil penalty in the amount of two thousand dollars ($2,000).

(5) The legal owner, registered owner, or person in possession of the vehicle shall not change or attempt to change the name of the legal owner or the registered owner on the records of the department until the vehicle is released from the impoundment.

(g) Notwithstanding any other provision of this section, the registered owner and not the legal owner shall remain responsible for any towing and storage charges related to the impoundment and the administrative charges authorized under Section 22850.5 and any parking fines, penalties, and administrative fees incurred by the registered owner.

(h) The law enforcement agency and the impounding agency, including any storage facility acting on behalf of the law enforcement agency or impounding agency, shall comply with this section and shall not be liable to the registered owner for the improper release of the vehicle to the legal owner or the legal owner's agent if the release complies with this section. The legal owner shall indemnify and hold harmless a storage facility from any claims arising out of the release of the vehicle to the legal owner or the legal owner's agent and from any damage to the

vehicle after its release, including the reasonable costs associated with defending any such claims. A law enforcement agency shall not refuse to issue a release to a legal owner or the agent of a legal owner on the grounds that it previously issued a release. *(Added by Stats.2003, c. 658 (A.B.299), § 2. Amended by Stats.2008, c. 26 (A.B.2693), § 1; Stats.2009, c. 229 (A.B.282), § 5; Stats. 2009, c. 322 (A.B.515), § 8; Stats.2011, c. 536 (A.B.957), § 14.)*

Cross References

Archaeological, paleontological, and historic sites, unlawful excavation or removal, conviction and release of vehicles subject to forfeiture, see Public Resources Code § 5097.7.

§ 21100.5. Island city vehicle regulation

Notwithstanding any other provisions of law, local authorities of any city which is on a natural island with an area in excess of 20,000 acres and which is within a county having a population in excess of 4,000,000, may, if they determine such rules and regulations to be necessary in view of the special problem existing thereon with respect to the size and nature of the streets of the city and with respect to the characteristics and nature of the city itself, adopt rules and regulations by ordinance or resolution on the following matters:

(a) Regulating the size of vehicles used on streets under their jurisdiction.

(b) Regulating the number of vehicles permitted on streets under their jurisdiction.

(c) Prohibiting the operation, on streets under their jurisdiction, of designated classes of vehicles.

(d) Establishing noise limits, which are different from those prescribed by this code, for vehicles operated on streets under their jurisdiction and prohibiting the operation of vehicles which exceed such limits.

(e) Establishing a maximum speed limit lower than that which the local authority otherwise permitted by this code to establish.

This section shall not apply to vehicles of utilities which are under the jurisdiction of the Public Utilities Commission while engaged in maintenance and construction type service work. *(Added by Stats.1972, c. 168, p. 388, § 1. Amended by Stats.1974, c. 286, p. 551, § 1.)*

§ 21100.7. Repealed by Stats.1998, c. 480 (A.B.2509), § 1, operative Jan. 1, 2002

§ 21101. Regulation of highways

Local authorities, for those highways under their jurisdiction, may adopt rules and regulations by ordinance or resolution on the following matters:

(a) Closing any highway to vehicular traffic when, in the opinion of the legislative body having jurisdiction, the highway is either of the following:

(1) No longer needed for vehicular traffic.

595

(2) The closure is in the interests of public safety and all of the following conditions and requirements are met:

(A) The street proposed for closure is located in a county with a population of 6,000,000 or more.

(B) The street has an unsafe volume of traffic and a significant incidence of crime.

(C) The affected local authority conducts a public hearing on the proposed street closure.

(D) Notice of the hearing is provided to residents and owners of property adjacent to the street proposed for closure.

(E) The local authority makes a finding that closure of the street likely would result in a reduced rate of crime.

(b) Designating any highway as a through highway and requiring that all vehicles observe official traffic control devices before entering or crossing the highway or designating any intersection as a stop intersection and requiring all vehicles to stop at one or more entrances to the intersection.

(c) Prohibiting the use of particular highways by certain vehicles, except as otherwise provided by the Public Utilities Commission pursuant to Article 2 (commencing with Section 1031) of Chapter 5 of Part 1 of Division 1 of the Public Utilities Code.

(d) Closing particular streets during regular school hours for the purpose of conducting automobile driver training programs in the secondary schools and colleges of this state.

(e) Temporarily closing a portion of any street for celebrations, parades, local special events, and other purposes when, in the opinion of local authorities having jurisdiction or a public officer or employee that the local authority designates by resolution, the closing is necessary for the safety and protection of persons who are to use that portion of the street during the temporary closing.

(f) Prohibiting entry to, or exit from, or both, from any street by means of islands, curbs, traffic barriers, or other roadway design features to implement the circulation element of a general plan adopted pursuant to Article 6 (commencing with Section 65350) of Chapter 3 of Division 1 of Title 7 of the Government Code. The rules and regulations authorized by this subdivision shall be consistent with the responsibility of local government to provide for the health and safety of its citizens. *(Stats.1959, c. 3, p. 1667, § 21101. Amended by Stats.1965, c. 764, p. 2345, § 1, eff. June 30, 1965; Stats.1969, c. 136, p. 288, § 1.5; Stats.1969, c. 168, p. 419, § 3; Stats.1969, c. 1365, p. 2790, § 1; Stats.1982, c. 681, p. 2811, § 83; Stats.1982, c. 749, p. 2966, § 5, eff. Sept. 8, 1982; Stats.1983, c. 291, § 5; Stats.1998, c. 876 (S.B.1649), § 24; Stats.1998, c. 877 (A.B.2132), § 63.5.)*

Validity

This section was held to be preempted, to the extent it extends authority to enact a regulation related to a price, route, or service of any motor carrier that is not based on a safety concern or size or weight restriction, by the Federal Aviation Administration Authorization Act, 49 U.S.C.A. § 14501, in the decision of California Dump Truck Owners Ass'n v. Davis, E.D.Cal.2002, 302 F.Supp.2d 1139.

Cross References

Definitions,
  Highway, see Vehicle Code §§ 360, 590.
  Local authorities, see Vehicle Code § 385.
  Through highway, see Vehicle Code § 600.
  Vehicle, see Vehicle Code § 670.
Failure to obey local traffic ordinance or resolution, see Vehicle Code § 21461.
Official traffic control device defined, see Vehicle Code § 440.
Pedestrian Mall Law of 1960, see Streets and Highways Code § 11000 et seq.
Stop signs, see Vehicle Code §§ 21351, 21354, 21355.

§ 21101.2. Local traffic regulation; reasonable flow impaired; diversion

Local authorities may adopt rules and regulations by ordinance or resolution to provide that if a peace officer, as defined in Chapter 4.5 (commencing with Section 830) of Title 3 of Part 2 of the Penal Code, determines that the traffic load on a particular street or highway, or a portion thereof, is such that little or no vehicular flow is occurring and, additionally, if the peace officer finds that a significant number of vehicles are not promptly moving when an opportunity arises to do so, then the peace officer may divert vehicles, excepting public safety or emergency vehicles, from that street or highway, or portion thereof, subject to traffic congestion until such time as reasonably flowing traffic is restored. *(Added by Stats.1982, c. 710, p. 2871, § 3, eff. Sept. 8, 1982.)*

§ 21101.4. Temporary closure of highway by local authorities; extension of closure period; conditions; notice

(a) A local authority may, by ordinance or resolution, adopt rules and regulations for temporarily closing to through traffic a highway under its jurisdiction when all of the following conditions are, after a public hearing, found to exist:

(1) The local authority finds and determines that there is serious and continual criminal activity in the portion of the highway recommended for temporary closure. This finding and determination shall be based upon the recommendation of the police department or, in the case of a highway in an unincorporated area, on the joint recommendation of the sheriff's department and the Department of the California Highway Patrol.

(2) The highway is not designated as a through highway or arterial street.

(3) Vehicular or pedestrian traffic on the highway contributes to the criminal activity.

(4) The closure will not substantially adversely affect traffic flow, safety on the adjacent streets or in the surrounding neighborhoods, the operation of emergency

vehicles, the performance of municipal or public utility services, or the delivery of freight by commercial vehicles in the area of the highway proposed to be temporarily closed.

(b) A highway may be temporarily closed pursuant to subdivision (a) for not more than 18 months, except that this period may be extended for not more than eight additional consecutive periods of not more than 18 months each if, prior to each of those extensions, the local authority holds a public hearing and finds, by ordinance or resolution, that all of the following conditions exist:

(1) Continuation of the temporary closure will assist in preventing the occurrence or reoccurrence of the serious and continual criminal activity found to exist when the immediately preceding temporary closure was authorized. This finding and determination shall be based upon the recommendation of the police department or, in the case of a highway in an unincorporated area, on the joint recommendation of the sheriff's department and the Department of the California Highway Patrol.

(2) The highway is not designated as a through highway or arterial street.

(3) Vehicular or pedestrian traffic on the highway contributes to the criminal activity.

(4) The immediately preceding closure has not substantially adversely affected traffic flow, safety on the adjacent streets or in the surrounding neighborhoods, the operation of emergency vehicles, the performance of municipal or public utility services, or the delivery of freight by commercial vehicles in the area of the highway that was temporarily closed.

(c) The local authority shall mail written notice of the public hearing required under subdivision (a) or (b) to all residents and owners, as shown on the last equalized assessment roll, of property adjacent to the portion of highway where a temporary closure or extension of temporary closure is proposed. *(Added by Stats.1992, c. 80 (S.B.1334), § 1. Amended by Stats.1996, c. 231 (A.B.964), § 1; Stats.2007, c. 173 (S.B.79), § 9, eff. Aug. 24, 2007.)*

§ 21101.6. Placement of gates or other selective devices on streets denying or restricting access to certain members of public; prohibition; codification of existing law

Notwithstanding Section 21101, local authorities may not place gates or other selective devices on any street which deny or restrict the access of certain members of the public to the street, while permitting others unrestricted access to the street.

This section is not intended to make a change in the existing law, but is intended to codify the decision of the Court of Appeal in City of Lafayette v. County of Contra Costa (91 Cal.App.3d 749).

This section shall become operative on January 1, 1990. *(Added by Stats.1987, c. 689, § 3, operative Jan. 1, 1990.)*

§ 21102. Local authority to close streets

Local authorities may adopt rules and regulations by ordinance or resolution closing to vehicular traffic that portion of any street or highway crossing or dividing any school ground or grounds when in the opinion of the legislative body having jurisdiction such closing is necessary for the protection of persons attending such school or school grounds. The closing to vehicular traffic may be limited to such hours and days as the legislative body may specify. No such ordinance or resolution shall be effective until appropriate signs giving notice thereof are posted along the street or highway affected, nor in the case of state highways, until such ordinance or resolution is approved by the Department of Transportation. *(Stats.1959, c. 3, p. 1667, § 21102. Amended by Stats. 1974, c. 545, p. 1314, § 169.)*

Cross References

Failure to obey local traffic ordinance or resolution, see Vehicle Code § 21461.

§ 21102.1. Local authorities; regulations relating to alleys

Notwithstanding any other provision of law, local authorities may, by ordinance or resolution, adopt rules and regulations restricting vehicular or pedestrian traffic through any alley by means of gates, barriers, or other control devices, when, in the opinion of the local authority having jurisdiction over the alley, the restriction is necessary for the protection or preservation of the public peace, safety, health, or welfare, subject to the following conditions:

(a) No ordinance or resolution adopted pursuant to this section shall be enforceable until appropriate signs giving notice of the restriction are posted at every entrance to the alley.

(b) In the coastal zone, as defined in subdivision (a) of Section 30103 of the Public Resources Code, where the alley provides direct access to any public beach or state waters, the local authority shall comply with Division 20 (commencing with Section 30000) of the Public Resources Code.

(c) In the area administered by the San Francisco Bay Conservation and Development Commission, where the alley provides direct access to any public beach, state waters, or wetlands, the local authority shall first obtain the concurrence by, or on behalf of, the San Francisco Bay Conservation and Development Commission. The concurrence or objection shall be based on the permits issued by the San Francisco Bay Conservation and Development Commission and in conformance with the policies contained in Title 7.2 (commencing with Section 66600) of the Government Code and Division 19 (commencing with Section 29000) of the Public Resources Code.

(d) The local authority shall provide access to utility vehicular or pedestrian traffic in order that the utility may maintain, operate, replace, remove, or renew existing and functioning utility facilities.

(e) No ordinance or resolution adopted pursuant to this section shall prohibit the delivery of freight by commercial vehicles.

(f) No ordinance or resolution adopted pursuant to this section shall be implemented in a manner that adversely affects the operation of emergency vehicles or the performance of municipal services.

(g) No ordinance or resolution adopted pursuant to this section shall restrict the access of certain members of the public to the alley, while permitting others unrestricted access to the alley. *(Added by Stats.1995, c. 215 (A.B.356), § 1.)*

§ 21103. Signs required

No ordinance or resolution enacted under Section 21101 shall be effective until signs giving notice of the local traffic laws are posted at all entrances to the highway or part thereof affected. *(Stats.1959, c. 3, p. 1667, § 21103. Amended by Stats.1965, c. 987, p. 2609, § 1; Stats.1973, c. 78, p. 137, § 16; Stats.1980, c. 671, p. 1866, § 4.)*

Cross References

Power of local authorities to place and maintain traffic control devices, see Vehicle Code § 21351.
Stop signs on local highways, see Vehicle Code § 21354.
Traffic control devices on state highways, powers of local authorities, see Vehicle Code § 21353.

§ 21104. Approval of local regulations

No ordinance or resolution proposed to be enacted under Section 21101 or subdivision (d) of Section 21100 is effective as to any highway not under the exclusive jurisdiction of the local authority enacting the same, except that an ordinance or resolution which is submitted to the Department of Transportation by a local legislative body in complete draft form for approval prior to the enactment thereof is effective as to any state highway or part thereof specified in the written approval of the department.

This section does not preclude the application of an ordinance or resolution adopted under Section 21101 or subdivision (d) of Section 21100 to streets maintained by a community services district organized pursuant to Division 3 (commencing with Section 61000) of Title 6 of the Government Code. An ordinance or resolution enacted by a local authority pursuant to subdivision (c) of Section 21101 may impose a fine or penalty of up to one hundred dollars ($100) for a violation of this code. *(Stats.1959, c. 3, p. 1667, § 21104. Amended by Stats. 1969, c. 1365, p. 2791, § 2; Stats.1974, c. 545, p. 1314, § 170; Stats.1979, c. 373, p. 1382, § 322; Stats.1984, c. 598, § 1; Stats.1998, c. 877 (A.B.2132), § 64; Stats.2002, c. 177 (S.B.1729), § 1.)*

§ 21105. Boundary line streets

No rule or regulation adopted under Sections 21100 or 21101 shall be effective as to boundary line streets where portions thereof are within different jurisdictions unless all authorities having jurisdiction of such portions of the street concerned have approved the same. *(Stats.1959, c. 3, p. 1667, § 21105.)*

§ 21106. Establishment of crosswalks

(a) Local authorities, by ordinance or resolution, may establish crosswalks between intersections.

(b) Local authorities may install signs at or adjacent to an intersection directing that pedestrians shall not cross in a crosswalk indicated at the intersection. It is unlawful for any pedestrian to cross at the crosswalk prohibited by a sign. *(Stats.1959, c. 3, p. 1668, § 21106. Amended by Stats.1959, c. 417, p. 2358, § 2.)*

Cross References

Definitions,
   Crosswalk, see Vehicle Code § 275.
   Intersection, see Vehicle Code § 365.
   Local authorities, see Vehicle Code § 385.
Failure to obey local traffic ordinance or resolution, see Vehicle Code § 21461.
Ordinances, regulation of crosswalks, see Vehicle Code § 21961.
Power of local authorities to erect signs, see Vehicle Code §§ 21351, 21353.
Right-of-way of pedestrian at crosswalk, see Vehicle Code §§ 21950, 21951.

§ 21107. Private roads

The provisions of this code shall not prevent any city from adopting rules and regulations by ordinance or resolution, regulating vehicular traffic on privately owned and maintained roads located within the boundary of such city, except that no such ordinance or resolution shall be effective until signs giving notice thereof are posted on the roads affected. The provisions of this section shall not apply to any city in which there are publicly maintained city streets. *(Stats.1959, c. 3, p. 1668, § 21107.)*

Cross References

Private road or driveway defined, see Vehicle Code § 490.

§ 21107.5. Private roads open for public use

(a) Any city or county may, by ordinance or resolution, find and declare that there are privately owned and maintained roads as described in the ordinance or resolution within the city or county that are generally held open for use by the public for vehicular travel and which so connect with highways that the public cannot determine that the roads are not highways. Upon enactment by a city or county of the ordinance or resolution, this code shall apply to the privately owned and maintained road, except as provided in subdivision (b).

(b) No ordinance or resolution enacted under subdivision (a) shall apply to any road on which the owner has erected a notice of a size, shape, and color as to be readily legible during daylight hours from a distance of 100 feet to the effect that the road is privately owned and maintained and that it is not subject to public traffic regulations or control.

(c) No ordinance or resolution shall be enacted under subdivision (a) without a public hearing after 10 days' written notice to the owner of the privately owned and maintained road involved.

(d) The department is not required to provide patrol or enforce any provision of this code on any privately owned and maintained road, except those provisions applicable to private property, other than pursuant to this section. *(Added by Stats.1963, c. 1873, p. 3859, § 2. Amended by Stats.1989, c. 160, § 1.)*

§ 21107.6. Private roads to commercial establishments

(a) Any city or county may, by ordinance, find and declare that there are privately owned and maintained roads as described in such ordinance within the city or county which are generally held open to the public for purposes of vehicular travel to serve commercial establishments. Upon enactment by a city or county of such an ordinance, the provisions of this code shall apply to any such privately owned and maintained road. No ordinance shall be enacted under this section without a public hearing thereon and 10 days' prior notice to the owner of the privately owned and maintained road involved.

(b) Notwithstanding the provisions of subdivision (a) no ordinance enacted thereunder shall apply to any road described therein on which the owner has caused to be erected a notice of such size, shape and color as to be readily legible during daylight hours from a distance of 100 feet, to the effect that the road is privately owned and maintained and that it is not subject to public traffic regulations or control.

(c) The department shall not be required to provide patrol or enforce any provisions of this code on any privately owned and maintained road subjected to the provisions of this code under this section, except those provisions applicable to private property other than by action under this section. *(Added by Stats.1968, c. 514, p. 1157, § 1.)*

§ 21107.7. Private roads not open to public use

(a) Any city or county may, by ordinance or resolution, find and declare that there are privately owned and maintained roads as described in the ordinance or resolution within the city or county that are not generally held open for use of the public for purposes of vehicular travel but, by reason of their proximity to or connection with highways, the interests of any residents residing along the roads and the motoring public will best be served by application of the provisions of this code to those roads. No ordinance or resolution shall be enacted unless there is first filed with the city or county a petition requesting it by a majority of the owners of any privately owned and maintained road, or by at least a majority of

the board of directors of a common interest development, as defined by Section 4100 or 6534 of the Civil Code, that is responsible for maintaining the road, and without a public hearing thereon and 10 days' prior written notice to all owners of the road or all of the owners in the development. Upon enactment of the ordinance or resolution, the provisions of this code shall apply to the privately owned and maintained road if appropriate signs are erected at the entrance to the road of the size, shape, and color as to be readily legible during daylight hours from a distance of 100 feet, to the effect that the road is subject to the provisions of this code. The city or county may impose reasonable conditions and may authorize the owners, or board of directors of the common interest development, to erect traffic signs, signals, markings, and devices which conform to the uniform standards and specifications adopted by the Department of Transportation.

(b) The department shall not be required to provide patrol or enforce any provisions of this code on any privately owned and maintained road subjected to the provisions of this code under this section, except those provisions applicable to private property other than by action under this section.

(c) As used in this section, "privately owned and maintained roads" includes roads owned and maintained by a city, county, or district that are not dedicated to use by the public or are not generally held open for use of the public for purposes of vehicular travel. *(Added by Stats.1963, c. 1914, p. 3916, § 1. Amended by Stats.1965, c. 1500, p. 3523, § 5; Stats.1965, c. 1840, p. 4266, § 1; Stats.1968, c. 1043, p. 2013, § 1; Stats.1988, c. 605, § 1; Stats.2012, c. 181 (A.B.806), § 80, operative Jan. 1, 2014; Stats.2013, c. 605 (S.B.752), § 49.)*

Law Revision Commission Comments
2012 Amendment

Section 21107.7 is amended to correct a cross-reference to former Civil Code Section 1351(c). [40 Cal.L.Rev.Comm. Reports 235 (2010)].

2013 Amendment

Section 21107.7 is amended to add a cross-reference to Civil Code Section 6534, reflecting the enactment of the Commercial and Industrial Common Interest Development Act (Civ. Code §§ 6500–6876). [42 Cal.L.Rev.Comm. Reports 1 (2012)].

§ 21107.8. Private parking facilities

(a) Any city or county may, by ordinance or resolution, find and declare that there are privately owned and maintained offstreet parking facilities as described in the ordinance or resolution within the city or county that are generally held open for use of the public for purposes of vehicular parking. Upon enactment by a city or county of the ordinance or resolution, Sections 22350, 23103, and 23109 and the provisions of Division 16.5 (commencing with Section 38000) shall apply to privately owned and maintained offstreet parking facilities, except as provided in subdivision (b).

(b) Notwithstanding the provisions of subdivision (a), no ordinance or resolution enacted thereunder shall apply to any offstreet parking facility described therein unless the owner or operator has caused to be posted in a conspicuous place at each entrance to that offstreet parking facility a notice not less than 17 by 22 inches in size with lettering not less than one inch in height, to the effect that the offstreet parking facility is subject to public traffic regulations and control.

(c) No ordinance or resolution shall be enacted under subdivision (a) without a public hearing thereon and 10 days prior written notice to the owner and operator of the privately owned and maintained offstreet parking facility involved.

(d) Section 22507.8 may be enforced without enactment of an ordinance or resolution as required under subdivision (a) or the posting of a notice at each entrance to the offstreet parking facility as required under subdivision (b).

(e) The department shall not be required to provide patrol or enforce any provisions of this code on any privately owned and maintained offstreet parking facility subject to the provisions of this code under this section except those provisions applicable to private property other than by action under this section. *(Added by Stats.1971, c. 1013, p. 1952, § 1, operative May 3, 1972. Amended by Stats.1974, c. 927, p. 1942, § 1; Stats.1976, c. 1093, p. 4937, § 4; Stats.1976, c. 1096, p. 4960, § 1.6; Stats.1979, c. 18, p. 57, § 1, eff. April 3, 1979; Stats.1981, c. 522, p. 1882, § 1; Stats.1982, c. 975, p. 3492, § 5.)*

Cross References

Off-highway vehicles, applicability of provisions, see Vehicle Code § 38001.

§ 21107.9. Private roads within mobilehome parks

(a) Any city or county, or city and county, may, by ordinance or resolution, find and declare that there are privately owned and maintained roads within a mobilehome park, as defined in Section 18214 of the Health and Safety Code, or within a manufactured housing community, as defined in Section 18801 of the Health and Safety Code, within the city or county, or city and county, that are generally not held open for use by the public for vehicular travel. Upon enactment of the ordinance or resolution, the provisions of this code shall apply to the privately owned and maintained roads within a mobilehome park or manufactured housing community if appropriate signs are erected at the entrance or entrances to the mobilehome park or manufactured housing community of the size, shape, and color as to be readily legible during daylight hours from a distance of 100 feet, to the effect that the roads within the park or community are subject to the provisions of this code. The city or county, or city and county, may impose reasonable conditions and may authorize the owners of the mobilehome park or manufactured housing community to erect traffic signs, markings, or devices which conform to the uniform standards and specifications adopted by the Department of Transportation.

(b) No ordinance or resolution shall be enacted unless there is first filed with the city or county a petition requested by the owner or owners of any privately owned and maintained roads within a mobilehome park or manufactured housing community, who are responsible for maintaining the roads.

(c) No ordinance or resolution shall be enacted without a public hearing thereon and 10 days' prior written notice to all owners of the roads within a mobilehome park or manufactured housing community proposed to be subject to the ordinance or resolution. At least seven days prior to the public hearing, the owner or manager of the mobilehome park or manufactured housing community shall post a written notice about the hearing in a conspicuous area in the park or community clubhouse, or if no clubhouse exists, in a conspicuous public place in the park or community.

(d) For purposes of this section, the prima facie speed limit on any road within a mobilehome park or manufactured housing community shall be 15 miles per hour. This section does not preclude a mobilehome park or manufactured housing community from requesting a higher or lower speed limit if an engineering and traffic survey has been conducted within the community supporting that request.

(e) The department is not required to provide patrol or enforce any provision of this code on any privately owned and maintained road within a mobilehome park or manufactured housing community, except those provisions applicable to private property other than by action under this section. *(Added by Stats.2002, c. 284 (S.B. 1556), § 1.)*

§ 21108. Private roads leading to airports

Local authorities may adopt rules and regulations by ordinance or resolution regulating vehicular traffic on privately owned and maintained roads or ways within the boundaries of a privately owned airport, when the roads or ways are expressly open to the general public for purposes of vehicular traffic.

The rules or regulations shall not be effective until appropriate signs giving notice thereof are posted along the roads or ways affected. *(Stats.1959, c. 3, p. 1668, § 21108.)*

Cross References

Highway signs, markers or warning notices, failure to observe, see Vehicle Code §§ 21367, 40000.14.
Local authorities defined, see Vehicle Code § 385.
Power of local authority to erect traffic signs, signals and markings, see Vehicle Code §§ 21351, 21353.
Private road or driveway defined, see Vehicle Code § 490.

§ 21109. Tunnels, bridges, or viaducts, cargo tank vehicles displaying flammable liquids placards

(a) Local authorities may adopt rules and regulations by ordinance or resolution regulating vehicular and pedestrian traffic in subways, tubes, and tunnels or upon bridges or viaducts.

(b) The proposed ordinance or resolution shall not be effective as to any state highway until approved in writing by the Department of Transportation. The Department of Transportation, in considering any proposed ordinance or resolution to prohibit or restrict the use by cargo tank vehicles displaying flammable liquids placards in tunnels of a length of 300 feet or greater, shall consult with the Department of the California Highway Patrol and hold a public hearing as provided in Section 21109.5 of the Vehicle Code. In evaluating the feasibility of prohibiting or restricting the use of the structure by cargo tank vehicles displaying flammable liquids placards, the Department of Transportation shall conduct a traffic and engineering survey which includes an analysis of the relative risks to public safety in determining the feasibility of reasonable alternative routes.

(c) The rules or regulations shall not be effective until appropriate signs have been posted giving notice thereof to drivers and pedestrians approaching the highway structures. *(Stats.1959, c. 3, p. 1668, § 21109. Amended by Stats.1974, c. 545, p. 1315, § 171; Stats.1982, c. 1255, p. 4603, § 4.)*

Cross References

Local authorities defined, see Vehicle Code § 385.
Power of local authorities to erect traffic signs, signals and markings, see Vehicle Code §§ 21351, 21353.

§ 21109.5. Notice and hearing; cargo tank vehicle restrictions or prohibitions

(a) No restriction or prohibition shall be effective pursuant to subdivision (b) of Section 21109 or Section 34020.5 except upon notice and hearing in the manner prescribed in this section.

(b) Notice of hearing shall be published pursuant to Section 6064 of the Government Code. The notice shall advise all interested parties that they may submit written or oral objections to the proposed action and shall designate a time and place for presentation of the objections. The time for submission of objections shall not expire, and the hearings shall not be held, less than 60 days after the first publication of notice. The hearing shall be conducted by the Department of Transportation and interested parties shall be accorded an adequate opportunity to be heard with respect to their objections. *(Added by Stats.1982, c. 1255, p. 4603, § 5.)*

§ 21110. Railroad crossings

Local authorities may adopt rules and regulations by ordinance or resolution to require that all vehicles stop before entering or crossing the tracks at any highway railroad grade crossing when signs are in place giving notice thereof, but no such ordinance shall be effective unless approved by an order of the Public Utilities Commission. *(Stats.1959, c. 3, p. 1668, § 21110.)*

Cross References

Highway signs, markers or warning notices, failure to observe, see Vehicle Code §§ 21367, 40000.14.
Local authorities defined, see Vehicle Code § 385.
Railway grade crossings,
   Signs, see Vehicle Code § 21362.
   Speed at, see Vehicle Code § 22352.
   Vehicles required to stop at, see Vehicle Code § 22452.

§ 21111. Housing projects

Local authorities may adopt rules and regulations by ordinance or resolution regulating vehicular traffic on privately owned and maintained roads or ways within the boundaries of any housing project or within the site of any housing owned or operated by a housing authority created under and by virtue of the Housing Authorities Law, commencing at Section 34200 of the Health and Safety Code, on privately owned and maintained roads or ways within areas which would be a residence district if the road or way were a public highway, or, with the consent of the owner, on publicly owned and maintained roads and ways within areas which are not owned by such local authorities. The rules or regulations shall not be effective until appropriate signs giving notice thereof are posted along the roads or ways affected. *(Stats.1959, c. 3, p. 1668, § 21111.)*

Cross References

Definitions,
   Local authorities, see Vehicle Code § 385.
   Private road or driveway, see Vehicle Code § 490.
   Residence district, see Vehicle Code § 515.
Highway signs, markers or warning notices, failure to observe, see Vehicle Code §§ 21367, 40000.14.
Power of local authority to create traffic signs, markings and signals, see Vehicle Code §§ 21351, 21353.

§ 21112. Taxicab and bus stands

Local authorities may by ordinance license and regulate the location of stands on streets and highways for use by taxicabs and other public carriers for hire in their respective jurisdictions. No such ordinance shall be effective as to any state highway until approved in writing by the Department of Transportation. Where maintenance of any state highway is delegated by such department to a city, such approval is not required. *(Stats.1959, c. 3, p. 1669, § 21112. Amended by Stats.1974, c. 545, p. 1315, § 172.)*

Cross References

Delegation of powers to city by department of transportation, see Streets and Highways Code § 116.
Local authorities defined, see Vehicle Code § 385.
Parking of utility vehicles, see Vehicle Code § 22512.
Powers of local authorities on traffic, see Vehicle Code § 21101.
Rules of the road, exemption of authorized emergency vehicles, see Vehicle Code § 21054.

§ 21113. Public grounds

(a) A person shall not drive any vehicle or animal, or stop, park, or leave standing any vehicle or animal, whether attended or unattended, upon the driveways, paths, parking facilities, or the grounds of any public school, state university, state college, unit of the state park system, county park, municipal airport, rapid transit district, transit development board, transit district, joint powers agency operating or managing a commuter rail system, or any property under the direct control of the legislative body of a municipality, or any state, county, or hospital district institution or building, or any educational institution exempted, in whole or in part, from taxation, or any harbor improvement district or harbor district formed pursuant to Part 2 (commencing with Section 5800) or Part 3 (commencing with Section 6000) of Division 8 of the Harbors and Navigation Code, a district organized pursuant to Part 3 (commencing with Section 27000) of Division 16 of the Streets and Highways Code, or state grounds served by the Department of the California Highway Patrol, or any property under the possession or control of a housing authority formed pursuant to Article 2 (commencing with Section 34240) of Part 2 of Division 24 of the Health and Safety Code, except with the permission of, and upon and subject to any condition or regulation that may be imposed by the legislative body of the municipality, or the governing board or officer of the public school, state university, state college, county park, municipal airport, rapid transit district, transit development board, transit district, joint powers agency operating or managing a commuter rail system, or state, county, or hospital district institution or building, or educational institution, or harbor district, or a district organized pursuant to Part 3 (commencing with Section 27000) of Division 16 of the Streets and Highways Code, or housing authority, or the Director of Parks and Recreation regarding units of the state park system or the state agency with jurisdiction over the grounds served by the Department of the California Highway Patrol.

(b) A governing board, legislative body, or officer shall erect or place appropriate signs giving notice of any special conditions or regulations that are imposed under this section and the governing board, legislative body, or officer shall also prepare and keep available at the principal administrative office of the governing board, legislative body, or officer, for examination by all interested persons, a written statement of all those special conditions and regulations adopted pursuant to this section.

(c) When a governing board, legislative body, or officer permits public traffic upon the driveways, paths, parking facilities, or grounds under their control then, except for those conditions imposed or regulations enacted by the governing board, legislative body, or officer applicable to the traffic, all the provisions of this code relating to traffic upon the highways shall be applicable to the traffic upon the driveways, paths, parking facilities, or grounds.

(d) A public transportation agency that imposes any condition or regulation upon a person who parks or leaves standing any vehicle, pursuant to subdivision (a), is authorized to do either of the following:

(1) Enforce that condition or regulation in the manner provided in Article 3 (commencing with Section 40200) of Chapter 1 of Division 17 of this code. The public transportation agency shall be considered the issuing agency for that purpose.

(2) Designate regularly employed and salaried employees, who are engaged in directing traffic or enforcing parking laws and regulations, for the purpose of removing any vehicle in the same manner as a city, county, or jurisdiction of a state agency pursuant to Chapter 10 (commencing with Section 22650) of Division 11 of this code.

(e) With respect to the permitted use of vehicles or animals on property under the direct control of the legislative body of a municipality, no change in the use of vehicles or animals on the property, that had been permitted on January 1, 1976, shall be effective unless and until the legislative body, at a meeting open to the general public, determines that the use of vehicles or animals on the property should be prohibited or regulated.

(f) A transit development board may adopt ordinances, rules, or regulations to restrict, or specify the conditions for, the use of bicycles, motorized bicycles, skateboards, and roller skates on property under the control of, or any portion of property used by, the board.

(g) A public agency, including, but not limited to, the Regents of the University of California and the Trustees of the California State University, may adopt rules or regulations to restrict, or specify the conditions for, the use of bicycles, motorized bicycles, skateboards, and roller skates on public property under the jurisdiction of that agency.

(h) "Housing authority," for the purposes of this section, means a housing authority located within a county with a population of over six million people, and any other housing authority that complies with the requirements of this section.

(i) "Public transportation agency," for purposes of this section, means a public agency that provides public transportation as defined in paragraph (1) of subdivision (f) of Section 1 of Article XIX A of the California Constitution. *(Stats.1959, c. 3, p. 1669, § 21113. Amended by Stats.1965, c. 1149, p. 2893, § 1; Stats.1969, c. 26, p. 128, § 8; Stats.1969, c. 77, p. 196, § 1; Stats.1970, c. 596, p. 1175, § 1; Stats.1971, c. 508, p. 1002, § 1, eff. Aug. 10, 1971, operative May 3, 1972; Stats.1972, c. 208, p. 437, § 1; Stats.1972, c. 235, p. 477, § 2; Stats.1975, c. 501, p. 1026, § 1; Stats.1981, c. 775, p. 3028, § 1.5; Stats.1981, c. 813, p. 3154, § 10; Stats.1981, c. 1055, p. 4078, § 11; Stats.1982, c. 993, p. 3609, § 1; Stats.1983, c. 258, § 1; Stats.1984, c. 193, § 148; Stats.1984, c. 50, § 10, eff. March 22, 1984; Stats.1990, c. 1037 (A.B.4186), § 2; Stats.1993, c. 274 (A.B.425), § 1, eff. Aug. 2, 1993; Gov.Reorg.Plan No. 1 of 1995, § 67, eff. July 12, 1995;*

Stats.1996, c. 305 (A.B.3103), § 69; Stats.2012, c. 724 (A.B.2104), § 1.)

§ 21114. Aircraft on local roads

If a local authority finds that a city street or county road under its jurisdiction adjacent to an airport has been specifically designed and constructed, with the prior approval of the local authority, so as to safely permit the use thereof by regular vehicular traffic and also the taxiing of aircraft thereon between the airport and the place where such aircraft are hangared or tied down, the local authority may by resolution or ordinance designate such street or road or portion thereof for such combined use and prescribe rules and regulations therefor which shall have the force of law. No such street or road shall be so designated for a distance of more than one-half mile from the airport, provided, the finding of the local authority in this respect shall be conclusive. Upon such designation becoming effective, it shall be the sole responsibility of the local authority to enforce the provisions of the Vehicle Code and all rules and regulations adopted by it upon such street or road. Upon such designation becoming effective it shall be lawful to taxi aircraft upon such street or road in accordance with the rules and regulations prescribed as aforesaid and said aircraft need not be licensed under this code or comply with other provisions thereof. *(Added by Stats.1963, c. 537, p. 1417, § 1.)*

§ 21114.5. Electric carts on sidewalks; disabled persons; persons over 50; governmental and utility employees; permits; exemption

Notwithstanding Section 21663 or any other provision of this code, local authorities may, by ordinance, authorize the operation of electric carts by physically disabled persons, by persons 50 years of age or older, or, while in the course of their employment, by employees of the United States Postal Service, state and local governmental agencies, or utility companies, on public sidewalks. Any ordinance shall, however, contain provisions requiring any disabled person or person 50 years of age or older who owns or leases an electric cart to apply to the local authority for a permit and an identification sticker to so operate the cart, and requiring the person to affix the sticker to the cart in order to operate it on the sidewalk. The permit and sticker shall become invalid if the person ceases to operate, own, or lease the cart.

This section does not apply to devices described in subdivision (b) of Section 415. *(Added by Stats.1972, c. 490, p. 862, § 2. Amended by Stats.1975, c. 503, p. 1029, § 2; Stats.1987, c. 600, § 1; Stats.1988, c. 17, § 1; Stats.1996, c. 124 (A.B.3470), § 125.)*

Stopping electric cart on sidewalk, see Vehicle Code § 22500.

§ 21114.6. Repealed by Stats.1990, c. 400 (A.B.2953), § 4, eff. July 23, 1990

§ 21115. Golf carts on local highways; crossing zones; low-speed vehicles

(a) If a local authority finds that a highway under its jurisdiction is located adjacent to, or provides access to, a golf course and between the golf course and the place where golf carts are parked or stored or is within or bounded by a real estate development offering golf facilities and is designed and constructed, so as to safely permit the use of regular vehicular traffic and also the driving of golf carts on the highway, the local authority may, by resolution or ordinance, designate the highway or portion of the highway for combined use and prescribe rules and regulations that shall have the force of law. No highway shall be so designated for a distance of more than one mile from the golf course if the highway is not located within a development or beyond the area of a development, provided, the finding of the local authority in this respect shall be conclusive. Upon the designation becoming effective it shall be lawful to drive golf carts upon the highway in accordance with the prescribed rules and regulations. The rules and regulations may establish crossing zones and speed limits and other operating standards but shall not require that the golf carts conform to any requirements of this code with respect to registration, licensing, or equipment, except that if operated during darkness the golf cart shall be subject to the provisions of Section 24001.5 regarding equipment.

The rules and regulations shall not be effective until appropriate signs giving notice thereof are posted along the highway affected.

A "real estate development offering golf facilities," for purposes of this section, means an area of single-family or multiple-family residences, the owners or occupants of which are eligible for membership in, or the use of, one or more golf courses within the development by virtue of their ownership or occupancy of a residential dwelling unit in the development.

(b) For purposes of this section, a "golf cart" includes a low-speed vehicle. *(Added by Stats.1968, c. 1303, p. 2456, § 3. Amended by Stats.1970, c. 792, p. 1507, § 1; Stats.1977, c. 124, p. 560, § 1; Stats.1989, c. 389, § 1; Stats.1999, c. 140 (S.B.186), § 4.)*

§ 21115.1. Golf carts and low-speed vehicles on streets

(a) Notwithstanding Section 21115, a local authority may, by ordinance or resolution, establish crossing zones, for use by golf carts at any time other than during

603

darkness, on any street, other than a state highway, that has a posted speed limit of 45 miles per hour or less and that is immediately adjacent to a golf course. The crossing zones shall be at an angle of approximately 90 degrees to the direction of the roadway. The ordinance or resolution shall not become effective until submitted to the law enforcement agency having primary jurisdiction over the street, the law enforcement agency finds and determines that the conditions pertaining to that street, with the addition of proper signs, markers, or lighting, or any combination of those, will permit the establishment of a golf cart crossing with reasonable safety, and the signs, markers, or lighting specified by the law enforcement agency are in place.

(b) Subdivision (a) does not constitute precedent for the operation of golf carts on any street or highway other than in a crossing zone established pursuant to subdivision (a).

(c) For purposes of this section, a "golf cart" includes a low-speed vehicle. *(Added by Stats.1991, c. 192 (A.B. 789), § 1. Amended by Stats.1992, c. 1243 (A.B.3090), § 87, eff. Sept. 30, 1992; Stats.1999, c. 140 (S.B.186), § 5.)*

Cross References

Golf cart defined, see Vehicle Code § 345.
Operation of low-speed vehicles generally, see Vehicle Code § 21250 et seq.

§ 21115.5.   Repealed by Stats.2005, c. 26 (A.B.188), § 1, operative Jan. 1, 2007

§ 21116.   Levees, banks of waterways, and pipeline rights-of-way

(a) No person shall drive any motor vehicle upon a roadway located on a levee, canal bank, natural watercourse bank, or pipeline right-of-way if the responsibility for maintenance of the levee, canal bank, natural watercourse bank, or pipeline right-of-way is vested in the state or in a reclamation, levee, drainage, water or irrigation district, or other local agency, unless such person has received permission to drive upon such roadway from the agency responsible for such maintenance, or unless such roadway has been dedicated as a public right-of-way.

(b) For this section to be applicable to a particular levee, canal bank, natural watercourse bank, or pipeline right-of-way, the state or other agency having responsibility for maintenance of the levee, canal bank, natural watercourse bank, or pipeline right-of-way shall erect or place appropriate signs giving notice that permission is required to be obtained to drive a motor vehicle thereon and giving notice of any special conditions or regulations that are imposed pursuant to this section and shall prepare and keep available at the principal office of the state agency or other agency affected or of the board of such agency, for examination by all interested persons, a written statement, in conformity with the existing rights of such agency to control access to the roadway, describing the nature of the vehicles, if any, to which such permission might be granted and the conditions, regulations,

and procedure for the acquisition of such permission adopted pursuant to this section.

(c) Nothing in this section prohibits the establishment of bicycle paths or routes (as prescribed by Article 6.5 (commencing with Section 5078) of Chapter 1 of Division 5 of the Public Resources Code) on levees, canal banks, natural watercourse banks, or pipeline rights-of-way. *(Added by Stats.1970, c. 926, p. 1684, § 1. Amended by Stats.1971, c. 1361, p. 2682, § 2, operative May 3, 1972.)*

§ 21117.   Public access to highways in environmentally sensitive areas; local agreements

(a) Local authorities may, notwithstanding Section 21101 or 21101.6, by written agreement approved by their legislative bodies, transfer among themselves the responsibility for maintaining, operating, or controlling public access to any highway under their respective jurisdictions located in or adjacent to an ecological reserve or an environmentally sensitive area within their respective jurisdictions.

(b) An agreement entered into pursuant to subdivision (a) may authorize the local authority having responsibility for the highway under the agreement to do all of the following:

(1) Limit access by motor vehicles to the highway during certain hours of the day or certain days of the week.

(2) Prohibit access by motor vehicles during certain hours of the day or certain days of the week.

(3) Provide for the construction or erection of barricades or other devices designed or intended to separate pedestrians from vehicles or motor vehicles.

(4) Establish and operate a program by which vehicular access is permitted only in conjunction with specified educational programs or for disabled persons, or both.

(5) Issue temporary permits for special events valid for less than one day.

(c) As used in this section, the term "ecological reserve" has the same meaning as defined in Section 1584 of the Fish and Game Code, and "environmentally sensitive area" has the same meaning as defined in Section 30107.5 of the Public Resources Code. *(Added by Stats.1991, c. 541 (S.B.1153), § 1.)*

ARTICLE 4.   OPERATION OF BICYCLES

Section
21200.   Rights and duties of bicycle riders and pedicab operators; exemption for peace officers operating bicycles.
21200.5.   Riding under influence of alcohol and drugs; chemical tests; punishment.
21201.   Equipment requirements.
21201.3.   Peace officer; blue light.
21201.5.   Reflectorized equipment.
21202.   Operation on roadway.
21203.   Hitching rides on vehicles.
21204.   Seating of persons riding bicycle.

Section
21205. Carrying articles.
21206. Local regulations.
21207. Bicycle lanes; establishment by local authorities.
21207.5. Motorized bicycles; prohibited operation.
21208. Permitted movements from bicycle lanes.
21209. Motor vehicles and motorized bicycles in bicycle lanes.
21210. Bicycle parking.
21211. Blocking bikeways or paths; exemptions.
21212. Bicycle helmets required for persons under 18 to operate a bicycle, nonmotorized scooter, skateboard, or in-line or roller skates; passenger requirements; helmet conformity to safety standards; sales of helmet; violations; allocation of fines collected.

Cross References

Local regulations, see Vehicle Code § 21100.

§ 21200. Rights and duties of bicycle riders and pedicab operators; exemption for peace officers operating bicycles

(a) A person riding a bicycle or operating a pedicab upon a highway has all the rights and is subject to all the provisions applicable to the driver of a vehicle by this division, including, but not limited to, provisions concerning driving under the influence of alcoholic beverages or drugs, and by Division 10 (commencing with Section 20000), Section 27400, Division 16.7 (commencing with Section 39000), Division 17 (commencing with Section 40000.1), and Division 18 (commencing with Section 42000), except those provisions which by their very nature can have no application.

(b)(1) A peace officer, as defined in Chapter 4.5 (commencing with Section 830) of Title 3 of Part 2 of the Penal Code, operating a bicycle during the course of his or her duties is exempt from the requirements of subdivision (a), except as those requirements relate to driving under the influence of alcoholic beverages or drugs, if the bicycle is being operated under any of the following circumstances:

(A) In response to an emergency call.

(B) While engaged in rescue operations.

(C) In the immediate pursuit of an actual or suspected violator of the law.

(2) This subdivision does not relieve a peace officer from the duty to operate a bicycle with due regard for the safety of all persons using the highway. *(Added by Stats.1963, c. 479, p. 1337, § 2. Amended by Stats.1965, c. 1500, p. 3523, § 6; Stats.1967, c. 586, p. 1931, § 3; Stats.1975, c. 987, p. 2331, § 6; Stats.1978, c. 421, p. 1320, § 2; Stats.1982, c. 6, p. 5, § 1; Stats.1983, c. 273, § 2; Stats.1985, c. 1013, § 2.5; Stats.1994, c. 357 (A.B.2499), § 1; Stats.2010, c. 614 (A.B.2294), § 3.)*

§ 21200.5. Riding under influence of alcohol and drugs; chemical tests; punishment

Notwithstanding Section 21200, it is unlawful for any person to ride a bicycle upon a highway while under the influence of an alcoholic beverage or any drug, or under the combined influence of an alcoholic beverage and any drug. Any person arrested for a violation of this section may request to have a chemical test made of the person's blood, breath, or urine for the purpose of determining the alcoholic or drug content of that person's blood pursuant to Section 23612, and, if so requested, the arresting officer shall have the test performed. A conviction of a violation of this section shall be punished by a fine of not more than two hundred fifty dollars ($250). Violations of this section are subject to Section 13202.5. *(Added by Stats.1985, c. 1013, § 3. Amended by Stats.1990, c. 1697 (S.B.2635), § 5; Stats.1998, c. 740 (S.B.1890), § 3; Stats. 1999, c. 22 (S.B.24), § 17, eff. May 26, 1999.)*

§ 21201. Equipment requirements

(a) No person shall operate a bicycle on a roadway unless it is equipped with a brake which will enable the operator to make one braked wheel skid on dry, level, clean pavement.

(b) No person shall operate on the highway a bicycle equipped with handlebars so raised that the operator must elevate his hands above the level of his shoulders in order to grasp the normal steering grip area.

(c) No person shall operate upon a highway a bicycle that is of a size that prevents the operator from safely stopping the bicycle, supporting it in an upright position with at least one foot on the ground, and restarting it in a safe manner.

(d) A bicycle operated during darkness upon a highway, a sidewalk where bicycle operation is not prohibited by the local jurisdiction, or a bikeway, as defined in Section 890.4 of the Streets and Highways Code, shall be equipped with all of the following:

(1) A lamp emitting a white light that, while the bicycle is in motion, illuminates the highway, sidewalk, or bikeway in front of the bicyclist and is visible from a distance of 300 feet in front and from the sides of the bicycle.

(2) A red reflector on the rear that shall be visible from a distance of 500 feet to the rear when directly in front of lawful upper beams of headlamps on a motor vehicle.

(3) A white or yellow reflector on each pedal, shoe, or ankle visible from the front and rear of the bicycle from a distance of 200 feet.

(4) A white or yellow reflector on each side forward of the center of the bicycle, and a white or red reflector on each side to the rear of the center of the bicycle, except that bicycles that are equipped with reflectorized tires on the front and the rear need not be equipped with these side reflectors.

The reflectors and reflectorized tires shall be of a type meeting requirements established by the department.

(e) A lamp or lamp combination, emitting a white light, attached to the operator and visible from a distance of 300 feet in front and from the sides of the bicycle, may be used in lieu of the lamp required by paragraph (1) of subdivision (d). *(Added by Stats.1963, c. 479, p. 1337, § 2. Amended by Stats.1967, c. 586, p. 1931, § 4; Stats.1970, c. 1477, p. 2922, § 2; Stats.1972, c. 726, p. 1316, § 1; Stats.1974, c. 971, p. 2018, § 2, eff. Sept. 20, 1974, operative Jan. 1, 1975; Stats.1975, c. 1157, p. 2847, § 1; Stats.1979, c. 723, p. 2216, § 5; Stats.2007, c. 232 (A.B.478), § 1.)*

Cross References

Approval of modifying devices, see Vehicle Code § 26101.
Color of lights and reflectors, see Vehicle Code § 25950.
Darkness defined, see Vehicle Code § 280.
Notice to correct violations, see Vehicle Code § 40303.5.
Test and approval of lamps, lamp equipment and other devices, see Vehicle Code § 26100 et seq.

§ 21201.3. Peace officer; blue light

(a) A bicycle or motorized bicycle used by a peace officer, as defined in Section 830.1 of, subdivision (a), (b), (c), (d), (e), (f), (g), or (i) of Section 830.2 of, subdivision (b) or (d) of Section 830.31 of, subdivision (a) or (b) of Section 830.32 of, Section 830.33 of, subdivision (a) of Section 830.36 of, subdivision (a) of Section 830.4 of, or Section 830.6 of, the Penal Code, in the performance of the peace officer's duties, may display a steady or flashing blue warning light that is visible from the front, sides, or rear of the bicycle or motorized bicycle.

(b) No person shall display a steady or flashing blue warning light on a bicycle or motorized bicycle except as authorized under subdivision (a). *(Added by Stats.1998, c. 877 (A.B.2132), § 65.)*

§ 21201.5. Reflectorized equipment

(a) No person shall sell, or offer for sale, a reflex reflector or reflectorized tire of a type required on a bicycle unless it meets requirements established by the department. If there exists a federal Consumer Product Safety Commission regulation applicable to bicycle reflectors, the provisions of that regulation shall prevail over provisions of this code or requirements established by the department pursuant to this code relative to bicycle reflectors.

(b) No person shall sell, or offer for sale, a new bicycle that is not equipped with a red reflector on the rear, a white or yellow reflector on each pedal visible from the front and rear of the bicycle, a white or yellow reflector on each side forward of the center of the bicycle, and a white or red reflector on each side to the rear of the center of the bicycle, except that bicycles which are equipped with reflectorized tires on the front and rear need not be equipped with these side reflectors.

(c) Area reflectorizing material meeting the requirements of Section 25500 may be used on a bicycle. *(Added by Stats.1974, c. 971, p. 2018, § 3, eff. Sept. 20, 1974, operative Jan. 1, 1975. Amended by Stats.1975, c. 1157, p. 2848, § 2; Stats.1978, c. 252, p. 532, § 1, eff. June 16, 1978; Stats.1979, c. 723, p. 2216, § 6; Stats.1980, c. 399, p. 782, § 2, eff. July 11, 1980.)*

§ 21202. Operation on roadway

(a) Any person operating a bicycle upon a roadway at a speed less than the normal speed of traffic moving in the same direction at that time shall ride as close as practicable to the right-hand curb or edge of the roadway except under any of the following situations:

(1) When overtaking and passing another bicycle or vehicle proceeding in the same direction.

(2) When preparing for a left turn at an intersection or into a private road or driveway.

(3) When reasonably necessary to avoid conditions (including, but not limited to, fixed or moving objects, vehicles, bicycles, pedestrians, animals, surface hazards, or substandard width lanes) that make it unsafe to continue along the right-hand curb or edge, subject to the provisions of Section 21656. For purposes of this section, a "substandard width lane" is a lane that is too narrow for a bicycle and a vehicle to travel safely side by side within the lane.

(4) When approaching a place where a right turn is authorized.

(b) Any person operating a bicycle upon a roadway of a highway, which highway carries traffic in one direction only and has two or more marked traffic lanes, may ride as near the left-hand curb or edge of that roadway as practicable. *(Added by Stats.1963, c. 479, p. 1337, § 2. Amended by Stats.1972, c. 928, p. 1655, § 1; Stats.1976, c. 751, p. 1783, § 1; Stats.1996, c. 674 (S.B.515), § 4.)*

§ 21203. Hitching rides on vehicles

No person riding upon any motorcycle, motorized bicycle, bicycle, coaster, roller skates, sled, or toy vehicle shall attach the same or himself to any streetcar or vehicle on the roadway. *(Added by Stats.1963, c. 479, p. 1338, § 2. Amended by Stats.1981, c. 813, p. 3155, § 11.)*

§ 21204. Seating of persons riding bicycle

(a) A person operating a bicycle upon a highway shall not ride other than upon or astride a permanent and regular seat attached thereto, unless the bicycle was designed by the manufacturer to be ridden without a seat.

(b) An operator shall not allow a person riding as a passenger, and a person shall not ride as a passenger, on a bicycle upon a highway other than upon or astride a separate seat attached thereto. If the passenger is four years of age or younger, or weighs 40 pounds or less, the seat shall have adequate provision for retaining the passenger in place and for protecting the passenger from the moving parts of the bicycle. *(Added by Stats.1976, c. 751, p. 1783, § 5. Amended by Stats.1986, c. 58, § 1; Stats.1993, c. 1000 (A.B.2268), § 1; Stats.2009, c. 594 (S.B.527), § 1.)*

§ 21205. Carrying articles

No person operating a bicycle shall carry any package, bundle or article which prevents the operator from keeping at least one hand upon the handlebars. *(Added by Stats.1963, c. 479, p. 1338, § 2.)*

§ 21206. Local regulations

This chapter does not prevent local authorities, by ordinance, from regulating the registration of bicycles and the parking and operation of bicycles on pedestrian or bicycle facilities, provided such regulation is not in conflict with the provisions of this code. *(Added by Stats.1963, c. 479, p. 1338, § 2. Amended by Stats.1976, c. 751, p. 1783, § 6.)*

§ 21207. Bicycle lanes; establishment by local authorities

(a) This chapter does not prohibit local authorities from establishing, by ordinance or resolution, bicycle lanes separated from any vehicular lanes upon highways, other than state highways as defined in Section 24 of the Streets and Highways Code and county highways established pursuant to Article 5 (commencing with Section 1720) of Chapter 9 of Division 2 of the Streets and Highways Code.

(b) Bicycle lanes established pursuant to this section shall be constructed in compliance with Section 891 of the Streets and Highways Code. *(Added by Stats.1967, c. 1048, p. 2655, § 1. Amended by Stats.1972, c. 1095, p. 2056, § 2; Stats.1975, c. 1235, p. 3136, § 8; Stats.1976, c. 751, p. 1783, § 7; Stats.1993, c. 517 (S.B.1095), § 4.)*

Cross References
Local regulation of bicycle operation, see Vehicle Code § 21100.

§ 21207.5. Motorized bicycles; prohibited operation

Notwithstanding Sections 21207 and 23127 of this code, or any other provision of law, no motorized bicycle may be operated on a bicycle path or trail, bikeway, bicycle lane established pursuant to Section 21207, equestrian trail, or hiking or recreational trail, unless it is within or adjacent to a roadway or unless the local authority or the governing body of a public agency having jurisdiction over such path or trail permits, by ordinance, such operation. *(Added by Stats.1975, c. 987, p. 2331, § 7. Amended by Stats.1977, c. 664, p. 2180, § 1; Stats.1979, c. 373, p. 1383, § 323.)*

§ 21208. Permitted movements from bicycle lanes

(a) Whenever a bicycle lane has been established on a roadway pursuant to Section 21207, any person operating a bicycle upon the roadway at a speed less than the normal speed of traffic moving in the same direction at that time shall ride within the bicycle lane, except that the person may move out of the lane under any of the following situations:

(1) When overtaking and passing another bicycle, vehicle, or pedestrian within the lane or about to enter the lane if the overtaking and passing cannot be done safely within the lane.

(2) When preparing for a left turn at an intersection or into a private road or driveway.

(3) When reasonably necessary to leave the bicycle lane to avoid debris or other hazardous conditions.

(4) When approaching a place where a right turn is authorized.

(b) No person operating a bicycle shall leave a bicycle lane until the movement can be made with reasonable safety and then only after giving an appropriate signal in the manner provided in Chapter 6 (commencing with Section 22100) in the event that any vehicle may be affected by the movement. *(Added by Stats.1976, c. 751, p. 1783, § 8. Amended by Stats.1996, c. 674 (S.B.515), § 5.)*

§ 21209. Motor vehicles and motorized bicycles in bicycle lanes

(a) No person shall drive a motor vehicle in a bicycle lane established on a roadway pursuant to Section 21207 except as follows:

(1) To park where parking is permitted.

(2) To enter or leave the roadway.

(3) To prepare for a turn within a distance of 200 feet from the intersection.

(b) This section does not prohibit the use of a motorized bicycle in a bicycle lane, pursuant to Section 21207.5, at a speed no greater than is reasonable or prudent, having due regard for visibility, traffic conditions, and the condition of the roadway surface of the bicycle lane, and in a manner which does not endanger the safety of bicyclists. *(Added by Stats.1976, c. 751, p. 1783, § 9. Amended by Stats.1977, c. 664, p. 2181, § 2; Stats.1988, c. 262, § 1.)*

§ 21210. Bicycle parking

No person shall leave a bicycle lying on its side on any sidewalk, or shall park a bicycle on a sidewalk in any other position, so that there is not an adequate path for pedestrian traffic. Local authorities may, by ordinance or resolution, prohibit bicycle parking in designated areas of the public highway, provided that appropriate signs are erected. *(Added by Stats.1976, c. 751, p. 1783, § 10.)*

§ 21211. Blocking bikeways or paths; exemptions

(a) No person may stop, stand, sit, or loiter upon any class I bikeway, as defined in subdivision (a) of Section 890.4 of the Streets and Highways Code, or any other public or private bicycle path or trail, if the stopping, standing, sitting, or loitering impedes or blocks the normal and reasonable movement of any bicyclist.

(b) No person may place or park any bicycle, vehicle, or any other object upon any bikeway or bicycle path or trail, as specified in subdivision (a), which impedes or blocks the normal and reasonable movement of any bicyclist unless the placement or parking is necessary for safe operation or is otherwise in compliance with the law.

(c) This section does not apply to drivers or owners of utility or public utility vehicles, as provided in Section 22512.

(d) This section does not apply to owners or drivers of vehicles who make brief stops while engaged in the delivery of newspapers to customers along the person's route.

(e) This section does not apply to the driver or owner of a rubbish or garbage truck while actually engaged in the collection of rubbish or garbage within a business or residence district if the front turn signal lamps at each side of the vehicle are being flashed simultaneously and the rear turn signal lamps at each side of the vehicle are being flashed simultaneously.

(f) This section does not apply to the driver or owner of a tow vehicle while actually engaged in the towing of a vehicle if the front turn signal lamps at each side of the vehicle are being flashed simultaneously and the rear turn signal lamps at each side of the vehicle are being flashed simultaneously. *(Added by Stats.1987, c. 499, § 1. Amended by Stats.1988, c. 1452, § 2; Stats.1993, c. 517 (S.B.1095), § 5; Stats.1999, c. 1007 (S.B.532), § 21; Stats.2001, c. 127 (S.B.46), § 7, eff. July 30, 2001.)*

Cross References

Utility vehicle exemptions from traffic statutes, see Vehicle Code § 22512.

§ 21212. Bicycle helmets required for persons under 18 to operate a bicycle, nonmotorized scooter, skateboard, or in-line or roller skates; passenger requirements; helmet conformity to safety standards; sales of helmet; violations; allocation of fines collected

(a) A person under 18 years of age shall not operate a bicycle, a nonmotorized scooter, or a skateboard, nor shall they wear in-line or roller skates, nor ride upon a bicycle, a nonmotorized scooter, or a skateboard as a passenger, upon a street, bikeway, as defined in Section 890.4 of the Streets and Highways Code, or any other public bicycle path or trail unless that person is wearing a properly fitted and fastened bicycle helmet that meets the standards of either the American Society for Testing and Materials (ASTM) or the United States Consumer Product Safety Commission (CPSC), or standards subsequently established by those entities. This requirement also applies to a person who rides upon a bicycle while in a restraining seat that is attached to the bicycle or in a trailer towed by the bicycle.

(b) Any helmet sold or offered for sale for use by operators and passengers of bicycles, nonmotorized scooters, skateboards, or in-line or roller skates shall be conspicuously labeled in accordance with the standard described in subdivision (a) which shall constitute the manufacturer's certification that the helmet conforms to the applicable safety standards.

(c) No person shall sell, or offer for sale, for use by an operator or passenger of a bicycle, nonmotorized scooter, skateboard, or in-line or roller skates any safety helmet which is not of a type meeting requirements established by this section.

(d) Any charge under this subdivision shall be dismissed when the person charged alleges in court, under oath, that the charge against the person is the first charge against that person under this subdivision, unless it is otherwise established in court that the charge is not the first charge against the person.

(e) Except as provided in subdivision (d), a violation of this section is an infraction punishable by a fine of not more than twenty-five dollars ($25).

The parent or legal guardian having control or custody of an unemancipated minor whose conduct violates this section shall be jointly and severally liable with the minor for the amount of the fine imposed pursuant to this subdivision.

(f) Notwithstanding Section 1463 of the Penal Code or any other provision of law, the fines collected for a violation of this section shall be allocated as follows:

(1) Seventy-two and one-half percent of the amount collected shall be deposited in a special account of the county health department, to be used for bicycle, nonmotorized scooter, skateboard, and in-line and roller skate safety education and for assisting low-income families in obtaining approved bicycle helmets for children under the age of 18 years, either on a loan or purchase basis. The county may contract for the implementation of this program, which, to the extent practicable, shall be operated in conjunction with the child passenger restraint program pursuant to Section 27360.

(2) Two and one-half percent of the amount collected shall be deposited in the county treasury to be used by the county to administer the program described in paragraph (1).

(3) If the violation occurred within a city, 25 percent of the amount collected shall be transferred to and deposited in the treasury of that city. If the violation occurred in an unincorporated area, this 25 percent shall be deposited and used pursuant to paragraph (1). *(Added by Stats. 1993, c. 1000 (A.B.2268), § 2. Amended by Stats.1996, c. 10 (A.B.1869), § 15, eff. Feb. 9, 1996; Stats.1996, c. 674 (S.B.515), § 6; Stats.2002, c. 475 (S.B.1924), § 1.)*

ARTICLE 5. OPERATION OF
MOTORIZED SCOOTERS

Section
21220.   Legislative findings and declaration.
21220.5.   Motorized scooter defined.
21221.   Applicability of provisions.
21221.5.   Driving under the influence.
21223.   Visibility.
21224.   Exemption from certain vehicle provisions.
21225.   Local regulation.
21226.   Excessive noise.
21227.   Motor function.
21228.   Rules of the road.
21229.   Bicycle lanes.
21230.   Bicycle paths, trails or bikeways.
21235.   Operation restrictions.

For another Article 5, "Operation of Low–Speed Vehicles", see Vehicle Code § 21250 et seq.

§ 21220. Legislative findings and declaration

(a) The Legislature finds and declares both of the following:

(1) This state has severe traffic congestion and air pollution problems, particularly in its cities, and finding ways to reduce these problems is of paramount importance.

(2) Motorized scooters that meet the definition of Section 407.5 produce no emissions and, therefore, do not contribute to increased air pollution or increase traffic congestion.

(b) It is the intent of the Legislature in adding this article to promote the use of alternative low-emission or no-emission transportation. *(Added by Stats.1999, c. 722 (S.B.441), § 5.)*

§ 21220.5. Motorized scooter defined

For the purposes of this article, a motorized scooter is defined in Section 407.5. *(Added by Stats.1999, c. 722 (S.B.441), § 5.)*

§ 21221. Applicability of provisions

Every person operating a motorized scooter upon a highway has all the rights and is subject to all the provisions applicable to the driver of a vehicle by this division, including, but not limited to, provisions concerning driving under the influence of alcoholic beverages or drugs, and by Division 10 (commencing with Section 20000), Division 17 (commencing with Section 40000.1), and Division 18 (commencing with Section 42000), except those provisions which, by their very nature, can have no application. *(Added by Stats.1999, c. 722 (S.B.441), § 5.)*

§ 21221.5. Driving under the influence

Notwithstanding Section 21221, it is unlawful for any person to operate a motorized scooter upon a highway while under the influence of an alcoholic beverage or any drug, or under the combined influence of an alcoholic beverage and any drug. Any person arrested for a violation of this section may request to have a chemical test made of the person's blood or breath for the purpose of determining the alcoholic or drug content of that person's blood pursuant to subdivision (d) of Section 23612, and, if so requested, the arresting officer shall have the test performed. A conviction of a violation of this section shall be punished by a fine of not more than two hundred fifty dollars ($250). *(Added by Stats.1999, c. 722 (S.B.441), § 5. Amended by Stats.2000, c. 287 (S.B.1955), § 25.)*

§ 21223. Visibility

(a) Every motorized scooter operated upon any highway during darkness shall be equipped with the following:

(1) Except as provided in subdivision (b), a lamp emitting a white light which, while the motorized scooter is in motion, illuminates the highway in front of the operator and is visible from a distance of 300 feet in front and from the sides of the motorized scooter.

(2) Except as provided in subdivision (c), a red reflector on the rear that is visible from a distance of 500 feet to the rear when directly in front of lawful upper beams of headlamps on a motor vehicle.

(3) A white or yellow reflector on each side visible from the front and rear of the motorized scooter from a distance of 200 feet.

(b) A lamp or lamp combination, emitting a white light, attached to the operator and visible from a distance of 300 feet in front and from the sides of the motorized scooter, may be used in lieu of the lamp required by paragraph (1) of subdivision (a).

(c) A red reflector, or reflectorized material meeting the requirements of Section 25500, attached to the operator and visible from a distance of 500 feet to the rear when directly in front of lawful upper beams of headlamps on a motor vehicle, may be used in lieu of the reflector required by paragraph (2) of subdivision (a). *(Added by Stats.1999, c. 722 (S.B.441), § 5.)*

§ 21224. Exemption from certain vehicle provisions

(a) A person operating a motorized scooter is not subject to the provisions of this code relating to financial responsibility, registration, and license plate requirements, and, for those purposes, a motorized scooter is not a motor vehicle.

(b) A motorized scooter is exempt from the equipment requirements in Division 12 (commencing with Section 24000), except for Sections 24003 and 27400, Article 4 (commencing with Section 27450) of Chapter 5 of Division 12, and Section 27602.

(c) Notwithstanding subdivision (b), any motorized scooter may be equipped with equipment authorized by Division 12 (commencing with Section 24000).

(d) Any motorized scooter equipped with lighting equipment that is authorized by Division 12 (commencing with Section 24000) shall meet the lighting requirements in Article 1 (commencing with Section 24250) of Chapter 2 of Division 12 for that equipment. *(Added by Stats. 1999, c. 722 (S.B.441), § 5.)*

§ 21225. Local regulation

This article does not prevent a local authority, by ordinance, from regulating the registration of motorized scooters and the parking and operation of motorized scooters on pedestrian or bicycle facilities and local streets and highways, if that regulation is not in conflict with this code. *(Added by Stats.1999, c. 722 (S.B.441), § 5. Amended by Stats.2004, c. 755 (A.B.1878), § 6.)*

§ 21226. Excessive noise

(a) A person shall not sell or offer for sale a motorized scooter that produces a maximum noise level exceeding 80 dbA at a distance of 50 feet from the centerline of travel when tested in accordance with Society of Automotive Engineers (SAE) Recommended Practice J331 JAN00.

(b) A motorized scooter, as defined in subdivision (b) of Section 407.5, shall at all times be equipped with a muffler meeting the requirements of this section, in constant operation and properly maintained to prevent any excessive or unusual noise, and a muffler or exhaust system shall not be equipped with a cutout, bypass, or similar device.

(c) A motorized scooter, as defined in subdivision (b) of Section 407.5, operated off the highways shall at all times be equipped with a muffler meeting the requirements of this section, in constant operation and properly maintained to prevent any excessive or unusual noise, and a muffler or exhaust system shall not be equipped with a cutout, bypass, or similar device.

(d) A person shall not modify the exhaust system of a motorized scooter in a manner that will amplify or increase the noise level emitted by the motor of the scooter so that it is not in compliance with this section or exceeds the noise level limit established by subdivision (a). A person shall not operate a motorized scooter with an exhaust system so modified. *(Added by Stats.2004, c. 755 (A.B.1878), § 7.)*

§ 21227. Motor function

(a) A motorized scooter shall comply with one of the following:

(1) Operate in a manner so that the electric motor is disengaged or ceases to function when the brakes are applied.

(2) Operate in a manner so that the motor is engaged through a switch or mechanism that, when released, will cause the electric motor to disengage or cease to function.

(b) It is unlawful for a person to operate a motorized scooter that does not meet one of the requirements of subdivision (a). *(Added by Stats.1999, c. 722 (S.B.441), § 5.)*

§ 21228. Rules of the road

Any person operating a motorized scooter upon a highway at a speed less than the normal speed of traffic moving in the same direction at that time shall ride as close as practicable to the right-hand curb or right edge of the roadway, except under the following situations:

(a) When overtaking and passing another vehicle proceeding in the same direction.

(b) When preparing for a left turn, the operator shall stop and dismount as close as practicable to the right-hand curb or right edge of the roadway and complete the turn by crossing the roadway on foot, subject to the restrictions placed on pedestrians in Chapter 5 (commencing with Section 21950).

(c)(1) When reasonably necessary to avoid conditions, including, but not limited to, fixed or moving objects, vehicles, bicycles, pedestrians, animals, surface hazards, or substandard width lanes, which make it unsafe to continue along the right-hand curb or right edge of the roadway, subject to Section 21656.

(2) For the purposes of paragraph (1), a " substandard width lane" is a lane that is too narrow for a motorized scooter and another vehicle to travel safely side by side within the lane.

(d) Any person operating a motorized scooter upon a highway that carries traffic in one direction only and has two or more marked traffic lanes may operate the motorized scooter as near the left-hand curb or left edge of that roadway as practicable.

However, when preparing for a right turn, the operator shall stop and dismount as close as practicable to the left-hand curb or left edge of the highway and complete the turn by crossing the roadway on foot, subject to the restrictions placed on pedestrians in Chapter 5 (commencing with Section 21950). *(Added by Stats.1999, c. 722 (S.B.441), § 5. Amended by Stats.2003, c. 62 (S.B. 600), § 306.)*

§ 21229. Bicycle lanes

(a) Whenever a class II bicycle lane has been established on a roadway, any person operating a motorized scooter upon the roadway shall ride within the bicycle lane, except that the person may move out of the lane under any of the following situations:

(1) When overtaking and passing another vehicle or pedestrian within the lane or when about to enter the lane if the overtaking and passing cannot be done safely within the lane.

(2) When preparing for a left turn, the operator shall stop and dismount as close as practicable to the right-hand curb or right edge of the roadway and complete the turn by crossing the roadway on foot, subject to the restrictions placed on pedestrians in Chapter 5 (commencing with Section 21950).

(3) When reasonably necessary to leave the bicycle lane to avoid debris or other hazardous conditions.

(4) When approaching a place where a right turn is authorized.

(b) No person operating a motorized scooter shall leave a bicycle lane until the movement can be made with reasonable safety and then only after giving an appropriate signal in the manner provided in Chapter 6 (commencing with Section 22100) in the event that any vehicle may be affected by the movement. *(Added by Stats.1999, c. 722 (S.B.441), § 5.)*

§ 21230. Bicycle paths, trails or bikeways

Notwithstanding any other provision of law, a motorized scooter may be operated on a bicycle path or trail or bikeway, unless the local authority or the governing body of a local agency having jurisdiction over that path, trail, or bikeway prohibits that operation by ordinance. *(Added by Stats.1999, c. 722 (S.B.441), § 5.)*

§ 21235. Operation restrictions

The operator of a motorized scooter shall not do any of the following:

(a) Operate a motorized scooter unless it is equipped with a brake that will enable the operator to make a braked wheel skid on dry, level, clean pavement.

(b) Operate a motorized scooter on a highway with a speed limit in excess of 25 miles per hour unless the motorized scooter is operated within a class II bicycle lane.

(c) Operate a motorized scooter without wearing a properly fitted and fastened bicycle helmet that meets the standards described in Section 21212.

(d) Operate a motorized scooter without a valid driver's license or instruction permit.

(e) Operate a motorized scooter with any passengers in addition to the operator.

(f) Operate a motorized scooter carrying any package, bundle, or article that prevents the operator from keeping at least one hand upon the handlebars.

(g) Operate a motorized scooter upon a sidewalk, except as may be necessary to enter or leave adjacent property.

(h) Operate a motorized scooter on the highway with the handlebars raised so that the operator must elevate his or her hands above the level of his or her shoulders in order to grasp the normal steering grip area.

(i) Leave a motorized scooter lying on its side on any sidewalk, or park a motorized scooter on a sidewalk in any other position, so that there is not an adequate path for pedestrian traffic.

(j) Attach the motorized scooter or himself or herself while on the roadway, by any means, to any other vehicle on the roadway. *(Added by Stats.1999, c. 722 (S.B.441), § 5. Amended by Stats.2004, c. 755 (A.B.1878), § 8.)*

ARTICLE 5. OPERATION OF LOW–SPEED VEHICLES

Section
21250. Low-speed vehicle.
21251. Application of provisions applicable to motor vehicles; exceptions.
21252. Disclosure to buyer.
21253. Application of federal standards.
21254. Low-speed vehicles modified to exceed 25 miles per hour.
21260. Maximum speed; crossing of intersections.
21266. Restrictions imposed by local authorities.

Explanatory Note

For another Article 5, "Operation of Motorized Scooters", see Vehicle Code § 21220 et seq.

§ 21250. Low-speed vehicle

For the purposes of this article, a low-speed vehicle means a vehicle as defined in Section 385.5. A "low-speed vehicle" is also known as a "neighborhood electric vehicle." *(Added by Stats.1999, c. 140 (S.B.186), § 6. Amended by Stats.2004, c. 422 (A.B.2353), § 3.)*

Cross References

Neighborhood electric vehicle transportation plan, plan adoption and implementation, cities of Rocklin and Lincoln, see Streets and Highways Code § 1963.

§ 21251. Application of provisions applicable to motor vehicles; exceptions

Except as provided in Chapter 6.2 (commencing with Section 1962), Chapter 7 (commencing with Section 1963), Chapter 7.1 (commencing with Section 1964), Chapter 8 (commencing with Section 1965), and Chapter 8.1 (commencing with Section 1966) of Division 2.5 of the Streets and Highways Code, and Sections 4023, 21115, and 21115.1, a low-speed vehicle is subject to all the provisions applicable to a motor vehicle, and the driver of a low-speed vehicle is subject to all the provisions applicable to the driver of a motor vehicle or other vehicle, when applicable, by this code or another code, with the exception of those provisions that, by their very nature, can have no application. *(Added by Stats.1999, c. 140 (S.B.186), § 6. Amended by Stats.2004, c. 422 (A.B.2353), § 4; Stats.2007, c. 442 (S.B.956), § 2; Stats. 2008, c. 179 (S.B.1498), § 220; Stats.2010, c. 437 (A.B. 584), § 2; Stats.2010, c. 452 (A.B.1781), § 2.5; Stats. 2011, c. 170 (A.B.61), § 2.)*

Cross References

Neighborhood electric vehicle transportation plan, plan adoption and implementation, cities of Rocklin and Lincoln, see Streets and Highways Code § 1963.

§ 21252. Disclosure to buyer

A vehicle dealer, selling a low-speed vehicle, shall provide to the buyer a disclosure statement regarding the operation of the vehicle that is in compliance with existing provisions of the California Code of Regulations. *(Added by Stats.1999, c. 140 (S.B.186), § 6.)*

§ 21253. Application of federal standards

A low-speed vehicle operated or parked on the roadway shall at all times meet federal Motor Vehicle Safety Standards established for low-speed vehicles in Section 571.500 of Title 49 of the Code of Federal Regulations. *(Added by Stats.1999, c. 140 (S.B.186), § 6.)*

§ 21254. Low-speed vehicles modified to exceed 25 miles per hour

A motor vehicle that was originally designated as a low-speed vehicle and that has been modified or altered to exceed 25 miles per hour shall not qualify for the relaxed federal Motor Vehicle Safety Standards established for low-speed vehicles and instead shall meet all federal Motor Vehicle Safety Standards for a passenger vehicle. *(Added by Stats.1999, c. 140 (S.B.186), § 6.)*

§ 21260. Maximum speed; crossing of intersections

(a) Except as provided in paragraph (1) of subdivision (b), or in an area where a neighborhood electric vehicle transportation plan has been adopted pursuant to Chapter 6.2 (commencing with Section 1962), Chapter 7 (commencing with Section 1963), Chapter 7.1 (commencing with Section 1964), Chapter 8 (commencing with Section 1965), or Chapter 8.1 (commencing with Section 1966) of Division 2.5 of the Streets and Highways Code, the operator of a low-speed vehicle shall not operate the vehicle on any roadway with a speed limit in excess of 35 miles per hour.

(b)(1) The operator of a low-speed vehicle may cross a roadway with a speed limit in excess of 35 miles per hour if the crossing begins and ends on a roadway with a speed limit of 35 miles per hour or less and occurs at an intersection of approximately 90 degrees.

(2) Notwithstanding paragraph (1), the operator of a low-speed vehicle shall not traverse an uncontrolled intersection with any state highway unless that intersection has been approved and authorized by the agency having primary traffic enforcement responsibilities for that crossing by a low-speed vehicle. *(Added by Stats. 1999, c. 140 (S.B.186), § 6. Amended by Stats.2004, c. 422 (A.B.2353), § 5; Stats.2007, c. 442 (S.B.956), § 3; Stats.2010, c. 437 (A.B.584), § 3; Stats.2010, c. 452 (A.B.1781), § 3.5; Stats.2011, c. 170 (A.B.61), § 3.)*

§ 21266. Restrictions imposed by local authorities

(a) Notwithstanding Section 21260, local authorities, by ordinance or resolution, may restrict or prohibit the use of low-speed vehicles.

(b) Notwithstanding Section 21260, a local law enforcement agency with primary traffic enforcement responsibilities or the Department of the California Highway Patrol may prohibit the operation of a low-speed vehicle on any roadway under that agency's or department's jurisdiction when the agency or the department deems the prohibition to be in the best interest of public safety. Any such prohibition shall become effective when appropriate signs giving notice thereof are erected upon the roadway. *(Added by Stats.1999, c. 140 (S.B.186), § 6.)*

ARTICLE 6. ELECTRIC PERSONAL ASSISTIVE MOBILITY DEVICES

Section
21280.   Legislative findings, declarations and intent.

Section
21280.5.   "Electric personal assistive mobility device" defined.
21281.   Safety mechanisms required.
21281.5.   Speeding; operation with willful or wanton disregard for safety; right-of-way.
21282.   Time, place and manner ordinances.
21283.   Repealed.

§ 21280. Legislative findings, declarations and intent

(a) The Legislature finds and declares all of the following:

(1) This state has severe traffic congestion and air pollution problems, particularly in its cities, and finding ways to reduce these problems is of paramount importance.

(2) Reducing the millions of single passenger automobile trips of five miles or less that Californians take each year will significantly reduce the pollution caused by fuel emissions and aggravated by automobile congestion.

(3) Electric personal assistive mobility devices that meet the definition in Section 313 operate solely on electricity and employ advances in technology to safely integrate the user in pedestrian transportation.

(4) Electric personal assistive mobility devices enable California businesses, public officials, and individuals to travel farther and carry more without the use of traditional vehicles, thereby promoting gains in productivity, minimizing environmental impacts, and facilitating better use of public ways.

(b) The Legislature is adding this article as part of its program to promote the use of no-emission transportation. *(Added by Stats.2002, c. 979 (S.B.1918), § 6, operative March 1, 2003. Amended by Stats.2007, c. 106 (A.B.470), § 4.)*

§ 21280.5. "Electric personal assistive mobility device" defined

For purposes of this article, an electric personal assistive mobility device is defined in Section 313. *(Added by Stats.2002, c. 979 (S.B.1918), § 6, operative March 1, 2003.)*

§ 21281. Safety mechanisms required

Every electric personal assistive mobility device, or EPAMD, shall be equipped with the following safety mechanisms:

(a) Front, rear, and side reflectors.

(b) A system that enables the operator to bring the device to a controlled stop.

(c) If the EPAMD is operated between one-half hour after sunset and one-half hour before sunrise, a lamp emitting a white light that, while the EPAMD is in motion, illuminates the area in front of the operator and is visible from a distance of 300 feet in front of the EPAMD.

(d) A sound emitting device that can be activated from time to time by the operator, as appropriate, to alert nearby persons. *(Added by Stats.2002, c. 979 (S.B.1918), § 6, operative March 1, 2003.)*

§ 21281.5. Speeding; operation with willful or wanton disregard for safety; right-of-way

(a) A person shall not operate an EPAMD on a sidewalk, bike path, pathway, trail, bike lane, street, road, or highway at a speed greater than is reasonable and prudent having due regard for weather, visibility, pedestrians, and other conveyance traffic on, and the surface, width, and condition of, the sidewalk, bike path, pathway, trail, bike lane, street, road, or highway.

(b) A person shall not operate an EPAMD at a speed that endangers the safety of persons or property.

(c) A person shall not operate an EPAMD on a sidewalk, bike path, pathway, trail, bike lane, street, road, or highway with willful or wanton disregard for the safety of persons or property.

(d) A person operating an EPAMD on a sidewalk, bike path, pathway, trail, bike lane, street, road, or highway shall yield the right-of-way to all pedestrians on foot, including persons with disabilities using assistive devices and service animals that are close enough to constitute a hazard. *(Added by Stats.2007, c. 106 (A.B. 470), § 5.)*

§ 21282. Time, place and manner ordinances

Notwithstanding Section 21966, for the purpose of assuring the safety of pedestrians, including seniors, persons with disabilities, and others using sidewalks, bike paths, pathways, trails, bike lanes, streets, roads, and highways, a city, county, or city and county may, by ordinance, regulate the time, place, and manner of the operation of electric personal assistive mobility devices as defined in Section 313, and their use as a pedestrian pursuant to paragraph (2) of subdivision (a) of Section 467, including limiting, prohibiting entirely in the local jurisdiction, or prohibiting use in specified areas as determined to be appropriate by local entities. State agencies may limit or prohibit the time, place, and manner of use on state property. *(Added by Stats.2002, c. 979 (S.B.1918), § 6, operative March 1, 2003.)*

§ 21283. Repealed by Stats.2007, c. 106 (A.B.470), § 6

CHAPTER 2. TRAFFIC SIGNS, SIGNALS, AND MARKINGS

Article	Section
1. Erection and Maintenance	21350
2. Official Traffic Control Devices	21400
3. Offenses Relating to Traffic Devices	21450

ARTICLE 1. ERECTION AND MAINTENANCE

Section
21350. State authority.
21351. Local authority.
21351.3. Use of metric system designations.

Section
21351.5. Stop signs at railroad crossings.
21351.7. Signs indicating deaf child is near; local authority.
21352. Traffic and pedestrian regulation on state highways.
21353. Local regulation affecting state highway traffic.
21354. Stop signs on local highways.
21355. Stop signs.
21356. Yield right-of-way signs.
21356.5. Exits from alleys; placement of signs, mirrors, or other visual or audible devices.
21357. Speed signs for business or residence districts.
21358. Speed signs at district boundaries.
21359. Speed signs for special areas.
21360. Traffic devices on private road or driveway.
21361. Closely adjoining intersections.
21362. Railroad warning approach signs.
21362.5. Automated rail crossing enforcement system.
21363. Detour signs.
21364. Stock crossings.
21365. Open range warning signs.
21366. Street name signs.
21367. Construction, maintenance or repair of highway; restriction of use by and regulation of traffic; violations.
21368. Crosswalk near schools.
21369. Speed signs ratified.
21370. Regulation of traffic; construction zone.
21370.1. Repealed.
21372. Guidelines for traffic control devices near schools.
21373. School board request for traffic control devices.
21374. Directional markings for tourists.
21375. Postsecondary education institutions; directional freeway signs; costs.
21376. Erection and maintenance of sign on major state highway entering state relating to abandonment or dumping of any animal.

§ 21350. State authority

The Department of Transportation shall place and maintain, or cause to be placed and maintained, with respect to highways under its jurisdiction, appropriate signs, signals, and other traffic control devices as required hereunder, and may place and maintain, or cause to be placed and maintained, such appropriate signs, signals, or other traffic control devices as may be authorized hereunder, or as may be necessary properly to indicate and to carry out the provisions of this code, or to warn or guide traffic upon the highways. The Department of Transportation may, with the consent of the local authorities, also place and maintain, or cause to be placed and maintained, in or along city streets and county roads, appropriate signs, signals, and other traffic control devices, or may perform, or cause to be performed, such other work on city streets and county roads, as may be necessary or desirable to control, or direct traffic, or to facilitate traffic flow, to or from or on state highways. *(Stats.1959, c. 3, p. 1669, § 21350. Amended by Stats.1965, c. 483, p. 1795, § 1; Stats.1968, c. 754, p. 1455, § 1; Stats.1970, c. 968, p. 1736, § 1, eff. Sept. 14, 1970; Stats.1974, c. 545, p. 1315, § 173; Stats.1974, c. 648, p. 1511, § 1.)*

Cross References

Bypass of city or business district, erection of directional signs, see Streets and Highways Code § 100.9.

Display of unauthorized signs and signals, see Vehicle Code § 21465 et seq.

Flashing red or yellow signal, see Vehicle Code § 21457.

Flashing signals at school approaches, see Vehicle Code § 21367.

Highway defined, see Vehicle Code §§ 360, 590.

Interference with official signs and signals, see Vehicle Code § 21464.

Obedience to traffic signals, see Vehicle Code § 21462.

Offenses relating to traffic devices, see Vehicle Code § 21450 et seq.

Official traffic control device defined, see Vehicle Code § 440.

Official traffic control signal defined, see Vehicle Code § 445.

Official traffic signals, see Vehicle Code § 21450.

Rules of the road, exemption of authorized emergency vehicles, see Vehicle Code § 21055.

Signs,
   Livestock crossings, see Vehicle Code § 21364.
   Open livestock range, see Vehicle Code § 21365.

Speed restriction signs, erection, see Vehicle Code § 21357 et seq.

Stop requirements, see Vehicle Code § 22450.

Traffic control signal changing devices, see Vehicle Code § 25352.

§ 21351. Local authority

Local authorities in their respective jurisdictions shall place and maintain or cause to be placed and maintained such traffic signs, signals and other traffic control devices upon streets and highways as required hereunder, and may place and maintain or cause to be placed and maintained, such appropriate signs, signals or other traffic control devices as may be authorized hereunder or as may be necessary properly to indicate and to carry out the provisions of this code or local traffic ordinances or to warn or guide traffic. *(Stats.1959, c. 3, p. 1669, § 21351.)*

Cross References

Definitions,
   Highway, see Vehicle Code §§ 360, 590.
   Local authorities, see Vehicle Code § 385.
   Official traffic control device, see Vehicle Code § 440.
   Street, see Vehicle Code § 590.

Interference with traffic devices, see Vehicle Code § 21464.

Obedience to traffic control signals, see Vehicle Code § 21462.

Offenses relating to traffic devices, see Vehicle Code § 21450 et seq.

Traffic control signal changing devices, see Vehicle Code § 25352.

Uniform standards and specifications for traffic control devices, see Vehicle Code § 21400 et seq.

§ 21351.3. Use of metric system designations

Local authorities in their respective jurisdictions may place and maintain, or cause to be placed and maintained, speed limit, speed advisory, and mileage signs, or suitable plates affixed to or near existing signs, which indicate speeds and distances both in common standards of measures, as specified in Section 12302 of the Business and Professions Code, and in measures of the metric

614

system authorized by Congress. *(Added by Stats.1974, c. 462, p. 1085, § 1.)*

§ 21351.5. Stop signs at railroad crossings

The Department of Transportation or local authorities, with respect to highways under their respective jurisdictions, may erect stop signs to require the traffic on a highway to stop before crossing any railroad grade crossing designated by the agency having jurisdiction of the highway as a major crossing with a demonstrated need for stop signs, except a railroad grade crossing which is controlled by automatic signals, gates, or other train-actuated control devices. *(Added by Stats.1974, c. 58, p. 127, § 1, eff. March 8, 1974.)*

§ 21351.7. Signs indicating deaf child is near; local authority

Local authorities in their respective jurisdictions may place and maintain, or cause to be placed and maintained, appropriate signs along city streets or county roads which indicate that a deaf child is near. *(Added by Stats.1983, c. 719, § 1.)*

§ 21352. Traffic and pedestrian regulation on state highways

The Department of Transportation may erect stop signs at any entrance to any state highway and whenever the department determines that it is necessary for the public safety and the orderly and efficient use of the highways by the public, the department may erect and maintain, or cause to be erected and maintained, on any state highway any traffic control signal or any official traffic control device regulating or prohibiting the turning of vehicles upon the highway, allocating or restricting the use of specified lanes or portions of the highway by moving vehicular traffic, establishing crosswalks at or between intersections, or restricting use of the right-of-way by the public for other than highway purposes. *(Stats.1959, c. 3, p. 1670, § 21352. Amended by Stats. 1974, c. 545, p. 1316, § 174; Stats.1981, c. 413, p. 1609, § 1.)*

Cross References

Definitions,
   Crosswalk, see Vehicle Code § 275.
   Highway, see Vehicle Code §§ 360, 590.
   Intersection, see Vehicle Code § 365.
   Official traffic control device, see Vehicle Code § 440.
   Official traffic control signal, see Vehicle Code § 445.
   Right-of-way, see Vehicle Code § 525.
   Through highway, see Vehicle Code § 600.

Highway signs, markers or warning notices, failure to observe, see Vehicle Code §§ 21367, 40000.14.

Obedience to official traffic control devices, see Vehicle Code § 21461.

Uniform standards and specifications for traffic control devices, see Vehicle Code § 21400.

§ 21353. Local regulation affecting state highway traffic

No local authority, except by permission of the Department of Transportation, shall erect or maintain any stop sign or traffic control signal in such manner as to require the traffic on any state highway to stop before entering or crossing any intersecting highway or any railroad grade crossing. *(Stats.1959, c. 3, p. 1670, § 21353. Amended by Stats.1974, c. 545, p. 1316, § 175; Stats.1981, c. 413, p. 1609, § 2.)*

Cross References

Authority to erect stop signs, see Vehicle Code §§ 21350, 21351.
Definitions,
  Highway, see Vehicle Code § 360.
  Local authorities, see Vehicle Code § 385.
  Official traffic control device, see Vehicle Code § 440.
  Official traffic control signal, see Vehicle Code § 445.
Failure to obey local traffic ordinance or resolution, see Vehicle Code § 21461.
Highway signs, markers or warning notices, failure to observe, see Vehicle Code §§ 21367, 40000.14.

§ 21354. Stop signs on local highways

Subject to the provisions of Section 21353, a local authority may designate any highway under its jurisdiction as a through highway and may erect stop signs at entrances thereto or may designate any intersection under its exclusive jurisdiction as a stop intersection and erect stop signs at one or more entrances thereto. *(Stats.1959, c. 3, p. 1670, § 21354.)*

Cross References

Definitions,
  Highway, see Vehicle Code § 360.
  Intersection, see Vehicle Code § 365.
  Local authorities, see Vehicle Code § 385.
  Through highway, see Vehicle Code § 600.
Highway signs, markers or warning notices, failure to observe, see Vehicle Code §§ 21367, 40000.14.
Obedience to official traffic control devices, see Vehicle Code § 21461.
Right-of-way, see Vehicle Code § 21800 et seq.
Stop requirements, see Vehicle Code § 22450.
Uniform standards and specifications for traffic control devices, see Vehicle Code § 21400.

§ 21355. Stop signs

(a) Stop signs erected under Section 21350, 21351, 21352, or 21354 may be erected either at or near the entrance to an intersection.

The Department of Transportation and local authorities in their respective jurisdictions may erect stop signs at any location so as to control traffic within an intersection.

When a required stop is to apply at the entrance to an intersection from a one-way street with a roadway of 30 feet or more in width, stop signs shall be erected both on the left and the right sides of the one-way street at or near the entrance to the intersection.

Notwithstanding any other provision of this code, stop signs shall not be erected at any entrance to an intersection controlled by official traffic control signals, nor at any railroad grade crossing which is controlled by automatic signals, gates, or other train-actuated control devices except where a stop sign may be necessary to control traffic on intersecting highways adjacent to the grade crossing or when a local authority determines, with the approval of the Public Utilities Commission pursuant to Section 21110, that a railroad grade crossing under its jurisdiction presents a danger warranting a stop sign in addition to a train-activated control device.

(b) Notwithstanding subdivision (a), local authorities, with respect to streets under their jurisdiction, are not required to conform lawfully established intersection configurations existing on January 1, 1985, to meet the requirements of subdivision (a) until January 1, 1990. *(Stats.1959, c. 3, p. 1670, § 21355. Amended by Stats. 1963, c. 2042, p. 4275, § 1; Stats.1969, c. 840, p. 1671, § 1; Stats.1973, c. 606, p. 1128, § 1; Stats.1984, c. 700, § 1.)*

Cross References

Definitions,
  Intersection, see Vehicle Code § 365.
  Local authorities, see Vehicle Code § 385.
  Roadway, see Vehicle Code § 530.
  Street, see Vehicle Code § 590.
  Through highway, see Vehicle Code § 600.
Highway signs, markers or warning notices, failure to observe, see Vehicle Code §§ 21367, 40000.14.
Obedience to official traffic control devices, see Vehicle Code § 21461.
Right-of-way, see Vehicle Code § 21800 et seq.
Stop requirements, see Vehicle Code § 22450.
Uniform standards and specifications for traffic control devices, see Vehicle Code § 21400.

§ 21356. Yield right-of-way signs

The Department of Transportation or local authorities, with respect to highways under their respective jurisdictions, may erect yield right-of-way signs at the entrances to intersections or highways. Such yield right-of-way signs shall not be erected upon the approaches to more than one of the intersecting streets.

Yield right-of-way signs shall be located at or near the entrance to the intersection or highway where motorists are required to yield the right-of-way. *(Stats.1959, c. 3, p. 1670, § 21356. Amended by Stats.1967, c. 370, p. 1597, § 1; Stats.1969, c. 834, p. 1667, § 1; Stats.1969, c. 1101, p. 2101, § 3, operative July 1, 1969; Stats.1974, c. 545, p. 1316, § 176; Stats.1978, c. 287, p. 578, § 3.)*

Cross References

Definitions,
  Highway, see Vehicle Code § 360.
  Intersection, see Vehicle Code § 365.
  Local authorities, see Vehicle Code § 385.
  Street, see Vehicle Code § 590.
  Through highway, see Vehicle Code § 600.
Right-of-way, generally, see Vehicle Code § 21800 et seq.

§ 21356.5. Exits from alleys; placement of signs, mirrors, or other visual or audible devices

Local authorities may place signs, mirrors, or other visual or audible devices at exits from alleys that are under their jurisdiction to warn drivers to watch for pedestrians and bicyclists on the sidewalk prior to exiting the alley. *(Added by Stats.1997, c. 150 (A.B.296), § 2.)*

§ 21357. Speed signs for business or residence districts

Speed restriction signs may, but need not, be erected upon any highway other than a state highway at the entrance thereof into a business or residence district unless required in this chapter. *(Stats.1959, c. 3, p. 1671, § 21357. Amended by Stats.1959, c. 11, p. 1853, § 11, operative Jan. 1, 1960.)*

Cross References

Business and residence districts, determination, see Vehicle Code § 240.
Definitions,
  Business district, see Vehicle Code § 235.
  Highway, see Vehicle Code §§ 360, 590.
  Residence district, see Vehicle Code § 515.
Highway signs, markers or warning notices, failure to observe, see Vehicle Code §§ 21367, 40000.14.
Prima facie speed limit, see Vehicle Code § 22352.
Speed laws, see Vehicle Code § 22349 et seq.

§ 21358. Speed signs at district boundaries

Where one or more business and residence districts are contiguous, or where, as authorized by this code, speed is to be restricted between two districts, either business or residence, or at the end of either thereof, speed restriction signs affecting traffic on other than state highways as required by Sections 21357 and 21359 need be erected and maintained only at the boundaries of the outside limits of the area in which speed is to be restricted. *(Stats.1959, c. 3, p. 1671, § 21358. Amended by Stats. 1959, c. 11, p. 1853, § 12, operative Jan. 1, 1960.)*

Cross References

Business and residence districts, determination, see Vehicle Code § 240.
Definitions,
  Business district, see Vehicle Code § 235.
  Residence district, see Vehicle Code § 515.
Highway signs, markers or warning notices, failure to observe, see Vehicle Code §§ 21367, 40000.14.

§ 21359. Speed signs for special areas

Whenever the Department of Transportation or a local authority as authorized by this code determines and declares a speed limit different from the limit otherwise applicable under Sections 22349 and 22352, appropriate speed restriction signs shall be erected and maintained at the outside entrance of the highway or portion thereof upon which the special speed limit is applicable. The special speed limit is not effective until appropriate signs have been erected. *(Stats.1959, c. 3, p. 1671, § 21359. Amended by Stats.1959, c. 11, p. 1853, § 13, operative Jan. 1, 1960; Stats.1963, c. 209, p. 949, § 7, eff. April 29, 1963; Stats.1974, c. 545, p. 1316, § 177.)*

Cross References

Decreasing truck speed limit, see Vehicle Code § 22407.
Highway defined, see Vehicle Code § 360.

616

Multiple-lane highways, speed limits, see Vehicle Code § 22361.
Snow or ice conditions, speed restrictions, see Vehicle Code § 22363.
Speed limits, see Vehicle Code § 22350.

§ 21360. Traffic devices on private road or driveway

Local authorities in their respective jurisdictions may, within the reasonable exercise of their police power and subject to Section 21353, place and maintain official traffic control devices to regulate traffic at the intersection of a highway and a private road or driveway. Official traffic control devices may be erected at or near such intersection, except no such device shall be erected upon a private road or driveway without consent of the owner thereof. When official traffic control devices are installed and in operation, the private road or driveway shall be deemed a highway only for the purpose of determining the existence and location of an intersection. *(Stats.1959, c. 3, p. 1671, § 21360.)*

Cross References

Definitions,
  Highway, see Vehicle Code §§ 360, 590.
  Intersection, see Vehicle Code § 365.
  Local authorities, see Vehicle Code § 385.
  Official traffic control device, see Vehicle Code § 440.
  Private road or driveway, see Vehicle Code § 490.

§ 21361. Closely adjoining intersections

(a) When the outermost boundaries of two or more intersections are confined within a distance of 200 feet, the Department of Transportation in respect to state highways, and a local authority with respect to highways under its jurisdiction, shall have the power to designate a single intersection by the installation and operation of traffic signals which may be supplemented by signs or markings. When so designated, the single intersection shall be the legal intersection for the purposes of traffic movement and regulation.

(b) Whenever a single intersection has been designated by the Department of Transportation or by local authorities as set forth in subdivision (a), the department or such authorities may designate marked crosswalks at certain locations within the intersection or contiguous thereto, and when the marked crosswalks are established, they shall constitute the only crosswalks at the intersection. The department or the local authorities shall erect signs prohibiting pedestrian crossing at locations which, except for the provisions of this section, would constitute unmarked crosswalks. *(Stats.1959, c. 3, p. 1671, § 21361. Amended by Stats.1961, c. 1948, p. 4119, § 1; Stats.1974, c. 545, p. 1316, § 178.)*

Cross References

Definitions,
  Crosswalk, see Vehicle Code § 275.
  Highway, see Vehicle Code §§ 360, 590.
  Intersection, see Vehicle Code § 365.
  Local authorities, see Vehicle Code § 385.
  Official traffic control signal, see Vehicle Code § 445.

Right-of-way, see Vehicle Code § 21800 et seq.

§ 21362. Railroad warning approach signs

Railroad warning approach signs shall be erected by local authorities upon the right-hand side of each approach of every highway under their jurisdiction to a grade crossing of a railroad or electric interurban railway at a reasonable distance from the crossing. *(Stats.1959, c. 3, p. 1671, § 21362. Amended by Stats.1959, c. 450, p. 2389, § 1.)*

Cross References

Definitions,
Highway, see Vehicle Code § 360.
Local authorities, see Vehicle Code § 385.

§ 21362.5. Automated rail crossing enforcement system

(a) Railroad and rail transit grade crossings may be equipped with an automated rail crossing enforcement system if the system is identified by signs clearly indicating the system's presence and visible to traffic approaching from each direction.

Only a governmental agency, in cooperation with a law enforcement agency, may operate an automated rail crossing enforcement system.

(b) Notwithstanding Section 6253 of the Government Code, or any other provision of law, photographic records made by an automated rail crossing enforcement system shall be confidential, and shall be made available only to governmental agencies and law enforcement agencies for the purposes of this section. *(Added by Stats.1994, c. 1216 (S.B.1802), § 4.)*

§ 21363. Detour signs

Detour signs shall be erected at the nearest points of detour from that portion of a highway, or from any bridge, which is closed to traffic while under construction or repair. *(Stats.1959, c. 3, p. 1672, § 21363.)*

Cross References

Highway defined, see Vehicle Code §§ 360, 590.
Highway signs, markers or warning notices, failure to observe, see Vehicle Code §§ 21367, 40000.14.

§ 21364. Stock crossings

The Department of Transportation may authorize an owner of land adjacent to a state highway to erect and maintain signs to indicate the existence of those places where livestock regularly and frequently cross a state highway, and any sign so erected and maintained shall be an official sign. The department shall prescribe the size, shape and character of the signs, which shall be uniform. *(Stats.1959, c. 3, p. 1672, § 21364. Amended by Stats. 1974, c. 545, p. 1317, § 179.)*

Cross References

Caution in passing animals, see Vehicle Code § 21759.
Livestock on highway, restrictions, see Food and Agricultural Code § 16902 et seq.

Rights and duties of those riding animals on highway, see Vehicle Code § 21050.
Signs indicating open livestock range, see Vehicle Code § 21365.

§ 21365. Open range warning signs

The Department of Transportation, with respect to state highways in open range country, and the board of supervisors of each county, with respect to county highways under its jurisdiction, may place and maintain appropriate signs indicating that the territory traversed is open livestock range and warning against the danger of livestock on the highway. *(Stats.1959, c. 3, p. 1672, § 21365. Amended by Stats.1974, c. 545, p. 1317, § 180.)*

Cross References

Animals at large, see Food and Agricultural Code § 16901 et seq.
Grazing areas, see Food and Agricultural Code § 17123.

§ 21366. Street name signs

At each signal-controlled intersection on streets and highways, there shall be a street name sign clearly visible to traffic approaching from all directions. The cost of erecting and maintaining the street name signs may be paid out of funds derived from the Highway Users Tax Fund or the Motor Vehicle License Fee Fund. *(Stats. 1959, c. 3, p. 1672, § 21366. Amended by Stats.1963, c. 1574, p. 3260, § 1.)*

Cross References

Definitions,
Highway, see Vehicle Code §§ 360, 590.
Intersection, see Vehicle Code § 365.
Street, see Vehicle Code § 590.

§ 21367. Construction, maintenance or repair of highway; restriction of use by and regulation of traffic; violations

(a) As provided in Section 125 of the Streets and Highways Code and in Section 21100 of this code, respectively, the duly authorized representative of the Department of Transportation or local authorities, with respect to highways under their respective jurisdictions, including, but not limited to, persons contracting to perform construction, maintenance, or repair of a highway, may, with the approval of the department or local authority, as the case may be, and while engaged in the performance of that work, restrict the use of, and regulate the movement of traffic through or around, the affected area whenever the traffic would endanger the safety of workers or the work would interfere with or endanger the movement of traffic through the area. Traffic may be regulated by warning signs, lights, appropriate control devices, or by a person or persons controlling and directing the flow of traffic.

(b) It is unlawful to disobey the instructions of a person controlling and directing traffic pursuant to subdivision (a).

(c) It is unlawful to fail to comply with the directions of warning signs, lights, or other control devices provided

617

for the regulation of traffic pursuant to subdivision (a). *(Added by Stats.1986, c. 748, § 2.)*

§ 21368. Crosswalk near schools

Whenever a marked pedestrian crosswalk has been established in a roadway contiguous to a school building or the grounds thereof, it shall be painted or marked in yellow as shall be all the marked pedestrian crosswalks at an intersection in case any one of the crosswalks is required to be marked in yellow. Other established marked pedestrian crosswalks may be painted or marked in yellow if either (a) the nearest point of the crosswalk is not more than 600 feet from a school building or the grounds thereof, or (b) the nearest point of the crosswalk is not more than 2,800 feet from a school building or the grounds thereof, there are no intervening crosswalks other than those contiguous to the school grounds, and it appears that the facts and circumstances require special painting or marking of the crosswalks for the protection and safety of persons attending the school. There shall be painted or marked in yellow on each side of the street in the lane or lanes leading to all yellow marked crosswalks the following words, "SLOW—SCHOOL XING," except that such words shall not be painted or marked in any lane leading to a crosswalk at an intersection controlled by stop signs, traffic signals, or yield right-of-way signs. A crosswalk shall not be painted or marked yellow at any location other than as required or permitted in this section. *(Stats.1959, c. 3, p. 1672, § 21368. Amended by Stats.1961, c. 1289, p. 3068, § 1; Stats.1976, c. 232, p. 443, § 1.)*

§ 21369. Speed signs ratified

All speed restriction signs in place on January 1, 1960, are hereby ratified and confirmed and shall establish the applicable prima facie speed limit unless and until changed pursuant to engineering and traffic surveys provided for by this code. *(Added by Stats.1959, c. 1317, p. 3592, § 1.)*

§ 21370. Regulation of traffic; construction zone

The Department of Transportation, or its duly authorized representatives with the approval of the department, while engaged in the construction of a state highway upon new alignment may restrict the use of and regulate the movement of traffic upon any highway intersecting the project at or near the place of intersection whenever such work interferes with or endangers the safe movement of

traffic through the work. *(Added by Stats.1961, c. 1415, p. 3218, § 1. Amended by Stats.1974, c. 545, p. 1317, § 181.)*

§ 21370.1. Repealed by Stats.2004, c. 193 (S.B.111), § 197

§ 21372. Guidelines for traffic control devices near schools

The Department of Transportation and local authorities shall, with respect to highways under their respective jurisdictions, establish and promulgate warrants to be used as guidelines for the placement of traffic control devices near schools for the purpose of protecting students going to and from school. Such devices may include flashing signals. Such warrants shall be based upon, but need not be limited to, the following items: pedestrian volumes, vehicle volumes, width of the roadway, physical terrain, speed of vehicle traffic, horizontal and vertical alignment of the roadway, the distance to existing traffic control devices, proximity to the school, and the degree of urban or rural environment of the area. *(Added by Stats.1968, c. 1443, p. 2854, § 2. Amended by Stats.1971, c. 253, p. 401, § 2, operative May 3, 1972; Stats.1974, c. 545, p. 1317, § 182.)*

§ 21373. School board request for traffic control devices

The governing board of any school district may request the appropriate city, county, city and county or state agency to install traffic control devices in accordance with the warrants established pursuant to Section 21372. Within 90 days thereafter, the city, county, city and county or state agency involved shall undertake an engineering and traffic survey to determine whether the requested crossing protection meets the warrants established pursuant to Section 21372. The city, county, city and county, or state agency involved may require the requesting school district to pay an amount not to exceed 50 percent of the cost of the survey. If it is determined that such requested protection is warranted, it shall be installed by the city, county, city and county or state agency involved. *(Added by Stats.1968, c. 1443, p. 2854, § 2. Amended by Stats.1969, c. 1061, p. 2049, § 1.)*

§ 21374. Directional markings for tourists

A local authority may mark or paint the surface of any street or highway under its jurisdiction, or of any state highway, with the approval of the Department of Transportation, with lines, arrows, or other suitable symbols for the purpose of directing visitors and tourists to local points of interest. No such marking shall be of a color or configuration which, as determined by the Department of Transportation, would cause it to be confused with an official traffic control device. *(Added by Stats.1976, c. 472, p. 1218, § 1.)*

§ 21375. Postsecondary education institutions; directional freeway signs; costs

(a) The Department of Transportation shall place and maintain, or cause to be placed and maintained, directional signs on freeways indicating the location of the freeway off ramp which may be used to reach a public or private postsecondary education institution having an enrollment of either 1,000 or more full-time students or the equivalent in part-time students, at the request of the institution. No signs shall be erected pursuant to this subdivision until the department has received donations from private sources covering the costs of erecting the signs.

(b) The Department of Transportation shall place and maintain, or cause to be placed and maintained, freeway directional signs for any institution described in subdivision (a) for which freeway directional signs had previously been erected and which has, on or after January 1, 1980, moved to another location, if that move was done to contribute to the improvement of the institution, as determined by the department. Freeway directional signs erected pursuant to this subdivision shall be at no cost to the institution.

(c) Subdivision (a) applies to a public or private postsecondary institution which is located within two miles of the freeway in a major metropolitan area, within four miles of the freeway in an urban area, or within five miles of the freeway in a rural area. Subdivision (b) applies to a public or private postsecondary education institution which has moved to a location which is within the distances specified in this subdivision. *(Added by Stats.1990, c. 635 (A.B.2670), § 1.)*

§ 21376. Erection and maintenance of sign on major state highway entering state relating to abandonment or dumping of any animal

The Department of Transportation shall place and maintain on each major state highway entering the state within 500 feet after the state line, a sign that states that the abandonment or dumping of any animal is a crime punishable by a fine of up to one thousand dollars ($1,000) or confinement in a county jail of up to six months, or both. *(Added by Stats.2001, c. 300 (S.B.237), § 3.)*

ARTICLE 2. OFFICIAL TRAFFIC CONTROL DEVICES

Section
21400. Uniform standards and specifications prescribed by Department of Transportation; revision of California Manual on Uniform Traffic Control Devices.
21401. Conformity to uniform standards; two-way communication; optional training for local agencies.
21402 to 21406. Repealed.

§ 21400. Uniform standards and specifications prescribed by Department of Transportation; revision of California Manual on Uniform Traffic Control Devices

(a)(1) The Department of Transportation shall, after consultation with local agencies and public hearings, adopt rules and regulations prescribing uniform standards and specifications for all official traffic control devices placed pursuant to this code, including, but not limited to, stop signs, yield right-of-way signs, speed restriction signs, railroad warning approach signs, street name signs, lines and markings on the roadway, and stock crossing signs placed pursuant to Section 21364.

(2) The Department of Transportation shall, after notice and public hearing, determine and publicize the specifications for uniform types of warning signs, lights, and devices to be placed upon a highway by a person engaged in performing work that interferes with or endangers the safe movement of traffic upon that highway.

(3) Only those signs, lights, and devices as are provided for in this section shall be placed upon a highway to warn traffic of work that is being performed on the highway.

(4) Control devices or markings installed upon traffic barriers on or after January 1, 1984, shall conform to the uniform standards and specifications required by this section.

(b) The Department of Transportation shall revise the California Manual on Uniform Traffic Control Devices, as it read on January 1, 2012, to require the Department of Transportation or a local authority to round speed limits to the nearest five miles per hour of the 85th percentile of the free-flowing traffic. However, in cases in which the speed limit needs to be rounded up to the nearest five miles per hour increment of the 85th-percentile speed, the Department of Transportation or a local authority may decide to instead round down the speed limit to the lower five miles per hour increment, but then the Department of Transportation or a local authority shall not reduce the speed limit any further for any reason. *(Added by Stats.1969, c. 1033, p. 2011, § 2. Amended by Stats.1971, c. 988, p. 1903, § 1, operative May 3, 1972; Stats.1974, c. 545, p. 1317, § 183; Stats.1980, c. 487, p. 1023, § 1; Stats.1983, c. 291, § 7; Stats.2011, c. 528 (A.B.529), § 2.)*

Cross References

Authority to place railroad crossing stop exempt signs, see Vehicle Code § 22452.5.
Maximum weight signs over bridges or other structures, see Vehicle Code § 35752.
Railroad crossing stop exempt sign, effect, see Vehicle Code § 22452.
Traffic control devices, uniform standards and specifications, see Vehicle Code § 21100.1.

§ 21401. Conformity to uniform standards; two-way communication; optional training for local agencies

(a) Except as provided in Section 21374, only those official traffic control devices that conform to the uniform standards and specifications promulgated by the Department of Transportation shall be placed upon a street or highway.

(b) Any traffic signal controller that is newly installed or upgraded by the Department of Transportation shall be of a standard traffic signal communication protocol capable of two-way communications. A local authority may follow this requirement.

(c) In recognition of the state and local interests served by the action made optional for a local authority in subdivision (b), the Legislature encourages local agencies to continue taking the action formerly mandated by this section. However nothing in this subdivision may be construed to impose any liability on a local agency that does not continue to take the formerly mandated action. *(Added by Stats.1969, c. 1033, p. 2011, § 2. Amended by Stats.1974, c. 545, p. 1318, § 184; Stats.1976, c. 472, p. 1218, § 2; Stats.1994, c. 1297 (A.B.3418), § 2; Stats.2004, c. 227 (S.B.1102), § 101, eff. Aug. 16, 2004; Stats.2004, c. 889 (A.B.2853), § 6, eff. Sept. 29, 2004.)*

§§ 21402 to 21406.   Repealed by Stats.1969, c. 1033, p. 2011, § 1

ARTICLE 3.   OFFENSES RELATING TO TRAFFIC DEVICES

Section
21450.   Official traffic control signals.
21450.5.   Traffic-actuated signal; detection of bicycle or motorcycle traffic.
21451.   Circular green signal; green arrow signal.
21452.   Steady circular yellow or yellow arrow signal.
21453.   Steady circular red signal; steady red arrow signal.
21454.   Lane use control signals placed over individual lanes.
21455.   Official traffic control signal at place other than intersection.
21455.5.   Automated traffic enforcement system; requirements; use of printed representation as evidence; confidentiality and retention of records; review of alleged violation by registered owner; manufacturers and suppliers; duties and contract limitations.
21455.6.   Automated enforcement system; public hearing; activities that can be contracted out; photo radar.
21455.7.   Intersections with automated enforcement system; minimum yellow light change intervals.
21456.   Walk, wait, or don't walk.
21456.1.   Pedestrian traffic control.
21456.2.   Bicycle operators; obeying provisions of this article; bicycle signals.
21456.3.   Bicycle signals.
21457.   Illuminated flashing red or yellow lights used in traffic signal or with traffic sign.
21458.   Curb markings.
21459.   Distinctive roadway markings.
21460.   Double lines.
21460.5.   Two-way left-turn lanes.
21461.   Obedience by driver to official traffic control devices.

Section
21461.5.   Obedience by pedestrian to official traffic control devices.
21462.   Obedience to traffic control signals.
21463.   Illegal operation of signals.
21464.   Interference with traffic devices; limitations on use and purchase, possession, manufacture, sale, etc. of mobile infrared transmitters and related devices; penalties.
21465.   Unauthorized traffic devices.
21466.   Light preventing recognition of official traffic control device.
21466.5.   Light impairing driver's vision.
21467.   Prohibited signs and devices.
21468.   Public utilities.

Cross References

Penalties, public offenses, fines in misdemeanor cases for violation pertaining to passing a school building or grounds, see Vehicle Code § 42011.

§ 21450.   Official traffic control signals

Text of section as amended by Stats.2005, c. 126 (A.B.56), § 1, eff. July 25, 2005.

Section 21450 was added by Stats.1959, c. 3, § 21450, amended by Stats.1981, c. 413, § 3; Stats.1999, c. 277 (A.B.134), § 1, and repealed by its own terms, operative Jan. 1, 2005. Therefore, this section was not in effect from Jan. 1, 2005 until July 25, 2005.

Stats.2005, c. 126 (A.B.56), § 1, might be given effect as a new addition of this section; but see Government Code § 9609.

Whenever traffic is controlled by official traffic control signals showing different colored lights, color-lighted arrows, or color-lighted bicycle symbols, successively, one at a time, or in combination, only the colors green, yellow, and red shall be used, except for pedestrian control signals, and those lights shall indicate and apply to drivers of vehicles, operators of bicycles, and pedestrians as provided in this chapter.

(Amended by Stats.2005, c. 126 (A.B.56), § 1, eff. July 25, 2005.)

Cross References

Applicability of this section to trolley coaches, see Vehicle Code § 21051.
Disobedience to traffic laws as misdemeanor, see Vehicle Code §§ 40000.1 et seq., 42001.
Flashing signals, see Vehicle Code § 21457.
Illegal signs, signals and lights, see Vehicle Code §§ 21465 to 21467.
Obedience to official traffic signals, see Vehicle Code § 21462.
Obedience to peace officers, see Vehicle Code § 2800.
Official traffic control signal defined, see Vehicle Code § 445.
Pedestrian control signals, see Vehicle Code § 21456.
Right of way, see Vehicle Code § 21800 et seq.

Traffic defined, see Vehicle Code § 620.

§ 21450.5. Traffic-actuated signal; detection of bicycle or motorcycle traffic

(a) A traffic-actuated signal is an official traffic control signal, as specified in Section 445, that displays one or more of its indications in response to the presence of traffic detected by mechanical, visual, electrical, or other means.

(b) Upon the first placement of a traffic-actuated signal or replacement of the loop detector of a traffic-actuated signal, the traffic-actuated signal shall, to the extent feasible and in conformance with professional traffic engineering practice, be installed and maintained so as to detect lawful bicycle or motorcycle traffic on the roadway.

(c) Cities, counties, and cities and counties shall not be required to comply with the provisions contained in subdivision (b) until the Department of Transportation, in consultation with these entities, has established uniform standards, specifications, and guidelines for the detection of bicycles and motorcycles by traffic-actuated signals and related signal timing.

(d) This section shall remain in effect only until January 1, 2018, and as of that date is repealed, unless a later enacted statute, that is enacted before January 1, 2018, deletes or extends that date. *(Added by Stats.2007, c. 337 (A.B.1581), § 2.)*

Repeal

For repeal of this section, see its terms.

§ 21451. Circular green signal; green arrow signal

(a) A driver facing a circular green signal shall proceed straight through or turn right or left or make a U–turn unless a sign prohibits a U–turn. Any driver, including one turning, shall yield the right-of-way to other traffic and to pedestrians lawfully within the intersection or an adjacent crosswalk.

(b) A driver facing a green arrow signal, shown alone or in combination with another indication, shall enter the intersection only to make the movement indicated by that green arrow or any other movement that is permitted by other indications shown at the same time. A driver facing a left green arrow may also make a U-turn unless prohibited by a sign. A driver shall yield the right-of-way to other traffic and to pedestrians lawfully within the intersection or an adjacent crosswalk.

(c) A pedestrian facing a circular green signal, unless prohibited by sign or otherwise directed by a pedestrian control signal as provided in Section 21456, may proceed across the roadway within any marked or unmarked crosswalk, but shall yield the right-of-way to vehicles lawfully within the intersection at the time that signal is first shown.

(d) A pedestrian facing a green arrow turn signal, unless otherwise directed by a pedestrian control signal as

provided in Section 21456, shall not enter the roadway. *(Stats.1959, c. 3, p. 1674, § 21451. Amended by Stats. 1959, c. 971, p. 3002, § 1; Stats.1973, c. 228, p. 612, § 1, operative July 1, 1974; Stats.1976, c. 394, p. 1043, § 1; Stats.1977, c. 1017, p. 3052, § 3, eff. Sept. 23, 1977; Stats.1981, c. 413, p. 1609, § 4.)*

Cross References

Applicability of this section to trolley coaches, see Vehicle Code § 21051.
Crossing between controlled intersections, see Vehicle Code § 21955.
Definitions,
  Crosswalk, see Vehicle Code § 275.
  Intersection, see Vehicle Code § 365.
  Official traffic control signal, see Vehicle Code § 445.
  Right-of-way, see Vehicle Code § 525.
  Traffic, see Vehicle Code § 620.
  Vehicle, see Vehicle Code § 670.
Violation as misdemeanor, punishment, see Vehicle Code §§ 40000.5 et seq., 42001.

§ 21452. Steady circular yellow or yellow arrow signal

(a) A driver facing a steady circular yellow or yellow arrow signal is, by that signal, warned that the related green movement is ending or that a red indication will be shown immediately thereafter.

(b) A pedestrian facing a steady circular yellow or a yellow arrow signal, unless otherwise directed by a pedestrian control signal as provided in Section 21456, is, by that signal, warned that there is insufficient time to cross the roadway and shall not enter the roadway. *(Stats.1959, c. 3, p. 1675, § 21452. Amended by Stats. 1981, c. 413, p. 1610, § 5; Stats.1986, c. 256, § 1.)*

Cross References

Applicability of this section to trolley coaches, see Vehicle Code § 21051.
Definitions,
  Official traffic control signal, see Vehicle Code § 445.
  Roadway, see Vehicle Code § 530.
  Traffic, see Vehicle Code § 620.
Violation as misdemeanor, punishment, see Vehicle Code §§ 40000.5 et seq., 42002.

§ 21453. Steady circular red signal; steady red arrow signal

(a) A driver facing a steady circular red signal alone shall stop at a marked limit line, but if none, before entering the crosswalk on the near side of the intersection or, if none, then before entering the intersection, and shall remain stopped until an indication to proceed is shown, except as provided in subdivision (b).

(b) Except when a sign is in place prohibiting a turn, a driver, after stopping as required by subdivision (a), facing a steady circular red signal, may turn right, or turn left from a one-way street onto a one-way street. A driver making that turn shall yield the right-of-way to pedestrians lawfully within an adjacent crosswalk and to any vehicle that has approached or is approaching so closely as to constitute an immediate hazard to the driver,

621

and shall continue to yield the right-of-way to that vehicle until the driver can proceed with reasonable safety.

(c) A driver facing a steady red arrow signal shall not enter the intersection to make the movement indicated by the arrow and, unless entering the intersection to make a movement permitted by another signal, shall stop at a clearly marked limit line, but if none, before entering the crosswalk on the near side of the intersection, or if none, then before entering the intersection, and shall remain stopped until an indication permitting movement is shown.

(d) Unless otherwise directed by a pedestrian control signal as provided in Section 21456, a pedestrian facing a steady circular red or red arrow signal shall not enter the roadway. (Stats.1959, c. 3, p. 1675, § 21453. Amended by Stats.1969, c. 246, p. 595, § 1; Stats.1981, c. 413, p. 1610, § 6; Stats.1982, c. 741, p. 2944, § 1; Stats.2001, c. 14 (A.B.563), § 1.)

Cross References

Applicability of this section to trolley coaches, see Vehicle Code § 21051.
Definitions,
  Crosswalk, see Vehicle Code § 275.
  Driver, see Vehicle Code § 305.
  Intersection, see Vehicle Code § 365.
  Local authorities, see Vehicle Code § 385.
  Official traffic control signal, see Vehicle Code § 445.
  Traffic, see Vehicle Code § 620.
  Vehicle, see Vehicle Code § 670.
Local authorities, maintenance of traffic signs, signals and devices, see Vehicle Code § 21351.
Notice to appear, violation recorded by automated enforcement system, see Vehicle Code § 40518.
Violation as misdemeanor, punishment, see Vehicle Code §§ 40000.5 et seq., 42002.

§ 21454. Lane use control signals placed over individual lanes

When lane use control signals are placed over individual lanes, those signals shall indicate and apply to drivers of vehicles as follows:

(a) Green indication: A driver may travel in any lane over which a green signal is shown.

(b) Steady yellow indication: A driver is thereby warned that a lane control change is being made.

(c) Steady red indication: A driver shall not enter or travel in any lane over which a red signal is shown.

(d) Flashing yellow indication: A driver may use the lane only for the purpose of making a left turn to or from the highway. (Stats.1959, c. 3, p. 1675, § 21454. Amended by Stats.1959, c. 1342, p. 3615, § 1; Stats.1961, c. 1727, p. 3737, § 1; Stats.1965, c. 183, p. 1150, § 1; Stats.1973, c. 228, p. 612, § 2, operative July 1, 1974; Stats.1975, c. 529, p. 1095, § 1; Stats.1977, c. 1017, p. 3053, § 4, eff. Sept. 23, 1977; Stats.1981, c. 413, p. 1610, § 7.)

Cross References

Applicability of this section to trolley coaches, see Vehicle Code § 21051.
Definitions,
  Crosswalk, see Vehicle Code § 275.
  Intersection, see Vehicle Code § 365.
  Official traffic control signal, see Vehicle Code § 445.
  Right-of-way, see Vehicle Code § 525.
  Traffic, see Vehicle Code § 620.
  Vehicle, see Vehicle Code § 670.
Violation as misdemeanor, punishment, see Vehicle Code §§ 40000.5 et seq., 42002.

§ 21455. Official traffic control signal at place other than intersection

When an official traffic control signal is erected and maintained at a place other than an intersection, the provisions of this article shall be applicable except those provisions which by their nature can have no application. Any stop required shall be made at a sign or crosswalk or limit line indicating where the stop shall be made, but in the absence of any such sign or marking the stop shall be made at the signal. (Stats.1959, c. 3, p. 1676, § 21455. Amended by Stats.1981, c. 413, p. 1611, § 8.)

Cross References

Applicability of this section to trolley coaches, see Vehicle Code § 21051.
Violation as misdemeanor, punishment, see Vehicle Code §§ 40000.5 et seq., 42002.

§ 21455.5. Automated traffic enforcement system; requirements; use of printed representation as evidence; confidentiality and retention of records; review of alleged violation by registered owner; manufacturers and suppliers; duties and contract limitations

(a) The limit line, the intersection, or a place designated in Section 21455, where a driver is required to stop, may be equipped with an automated traffic enforcement system if the governmental agency utilizing the system meets all of the following requirements:

(1) Identifies the system by signs posted within 200 feet of an intersection where a system is operating that clearly indicate the system's presence and are visible to traffic approaching from all directions in which the automated traffic enforcement system is being utilized to issue citations. A governmental agency utilizing such a system does not need to post signs visible to traffic approaching the intersection from directions not subject to the automated traffic enforcement system. Automated traffic enforcement systems installed as of January 1, 2013, shall be identified no later than January 1, 2014.

(2) Locates the system at an intersection and ensures that the system meets the criteria specified in Section 21455.7.

(b) Prior to issuing citations under this section, a local jurisdiction utilizing an automated traffic enforcement system shall commence a program to issue only warning notices for 30 days. The local jurisdiction shall also make a public announcement of the automated traffic enforcement system at least 30 days prior to the commencement of the enforcement program.

(c) Only a governmental agency, in cooperation with a law enforcement agency, may operate an automated traffic enforcement system. A governmental agency that operates an automated traffic enforcement system shall do all of the following:

(1) Develop uniform guidelines for screening and issuing violations and for the processing and storage of confidential information, and establish procedures to ensure compliance with those guidelines. For systems installed as of January 1, 2013, a governmental agency that operates an automated traffic enforcement system shall establish those guidelines by January 1, 2014.

(2) Perform administrative functions and day-to-day functions, including, but not limited to, all of the following:

(A) Establishing guidelines for the selection of a location. Prior to installing an automated traffic enforcement system after January 1, 2013, the governmental agency shall make and adopt a finding of fact establishing that the system is needed at a specific location for reasons related to safety.

(B) Ensuring that the equipment is regularly inspected.

(C) Certifying that the equipment is properly installed and calibrated, and is operating properly.

(D) Regularly inspecting and maintaining warning signs placed under paragraph (1) of subdivision (a).

(E) Overseeing the establishment or change of signal phases and the timing thereof.

(F) Maintaining controls necessary to ensure that only those citations that have been reviewed and approved by law enforcement are delivered to violators.

(d) The activities listed in subdivision (c) that relate to the operation of the system may be contracted out by the governmental agency, if it maintains overall control and supervision of the system. However, the activities listed in paragraph (1) of, and subparagraphs (A), (D), (E), and (F) of paragraph (2) of, subdivision (c) shall not be contracted out to the manufacturer or supplier of the automated traffic enforcement system.

(e) The printed representation of computer-generated information, video, or photographic images stored by an automated traffic enforcement system does not constitute an out-of-court hearsay statement by a declarant under Division 10 (commencing with Section 1200) of the Evidence Code.

(f)(1) Notwithstanding Section 6253 of the Government Code, or any other law, photographic records made by an automated traffic enforcement system shall be confidential, and shall be made available only to governmental agencies and law enforcement agencies and only for the purposes of this article.

(2) Confidential information obtained from the Department of Motor Vehicles for the administration or enforcement of this article shall be held confidential, and shall not be used for any other purpose.

(3) Except for court records described in Section 68152 of the Government Code, the confidential records and information described in paragraphs (1) and (2) may be retained for up to six months from the date the information was first obtained, or until final disposition of the citation, whichever date is later, after which time the information shall be destroyed in a manner that will preserve the confidentiality of any person included in the record or information.

(g) Notwithstanding subdivision (f), the registered owner or any individual identified by the registered owner as the driver of the vehicle at the time of the alleged violation shall be permitted to review the photographic evidence of the alleged violation.

(h)(1) A contract between a governmental agency and a manufacturer or supplier of automated traffic enforcement equipment shall not include provision for the payment or compensation to the manufacturer or supplier based on the number of citations generated, or as a percentage of the revenue generated, as a result of the use of the equipment authorized under this section.

(2) Paragraph (1) does not apply to a contract that was entered into by a governmental agency and a manufacturer or supplier of automated traffic enforcement equipment before January 1, 2004, unless that contract is renewed, extended, or amended on or after January 1, 2004.

(3) A governmental agency that proposes to install or operate an automated traffic enforcement system shall not consider revenue generation, beyond recovering its actual costs of operating the system, as a factor when considering whether or not to install or operate a system within its local jurisdiction.

(i) A manufacturer or supplier that operates an automated traffic enforcement system pursuant to this section shall, in cooperation with the governmental agency, submit an annual report to the Judicial Council that includes, but is not limited to, all of the following information if this information is in the possession of, or readily available to, the manufacturer or supplier:

(1) The number of alleged violations captured by the systems they operate.

(2) The number of citations issued by a law enforcement agency based on information collected from the automated traffic enforcement system.

(3) For citations identified in paragraph (2), the number of violations that involved traveling straight through the intersection, turning right, and turning left.

(4) The number and percentage of citations that are dismissed by the court.

623

(5) The number of traffic collisions at each intersection that occurred prior to, and after the installation of, the automated traffic enforcement system.

(j) If a governmental agency utilizing an automated traffic enforcement system has posted signs on or before January 1, 2013, that met the requirements of paragraph (1) of subdivision (a) of this section, as it read on January 1, 2012, the governmental agency shall not remove those signs until signs are posted that meet the requirements specified in this section, as it reads on January 1, 2013. *(Added by Stats.1995, c. 922 (S.B.833), § 4. Amended by Stats.1998, c. 54 (S.B.1136), § 3; Stats.2001, c. 496 (S.B.667), § 1; Stats.2003, c. 511 (A.B.1022), § 1; Stats. 2010, c. 328 (S.B.1330), § 230; Stats.2012, c. 735 (S.B. 1303), § 3.)*

Cross References

Inspection of public records, exemptions from disclosure, automated traffic enforcement system, photographic records, see Government Code § 6276.04.

Printed representation of computer-generated information, see Evidence Code § 1552.

Printed representation of video or digital images, see Evidence Code § 1553.

Procedure, certain violations recorded by automated traffic enforcement system, notice to appear, contents, notice of nonliability, form, dismissal, see Vehicle Code § 40518.

§ 21455.6. Automated enforcement system; public hearing; activities that can be contracted out; photo radar

(a) A city council or county board of supervisors shall conduct a public hearing on the proposed use of an automated enforcement system authorized under Section 21455.5 prior to authorizing the city or county to enter into a contract for the use of the system.

(b)(1) The activities listed in subdivision (c) of Section 21455.5 that relate to the operation of an automated enforcement system may be contracted out by the city or county, except that the activities listed in paragraph (1) of, and subparagraphs (A), (D), (E), or (F) of paragraph (2) of, subdivision (c) of Section 21455.5 may not be contracted out to the manufacturer or supplier of the automated enforcement system.

(2) Paragraph (1) does not apply to a contract that was entered into by a city or county and a manufacturer or supplier of automated enforcement equipment before January 1, 2004, unless that contract is renewed, extended, or amended on or after January 1, 2004.

(c) The authorization in Section 21455.5 to use automated enforcement systems does not authorize the use of photo radar for speed enforcement purposes by any jurisdiction. *(Added by Stats.1998, c. 828 (S.B.1637), § 17. Amended by Stats.2000, c. 833 (A.B.2522), § 7; Stats.2000, c. 860 (A.B.2908), § 8; Stats.2003, c. 511 (A.B.1022), § 2.)*

§ 21455.7. Intersections with automated enforcement system; minimum yellow light change intervals

(a) At an intersection at which there is an automated enforcement system in operation, the minimum yellow light change interval shall be established in accordance with the Traffic Manual of the Department of Transportation.

(b) For purposes of subdivision (a), the minimum yellow light change intervals relating to designated approach speeds provided in the Traffic Manual of the Department of Transportation are mandatory minimum yellow light intervals.

(c) A yellow light change interval may exceed the minimum interval established pursuant to subdivision (a). *(Added by Stats.2001, c. 496 (S.B.667), § 2. Amended by Stats.2003, c. 511 (A.B.1022), § 3.)*

§ 21456. Walk, wait, or don't walk

Whenever a pedestrian control signal showing the words "WALK" or "WAIT" or "DONT WALK" or other approved symbol is in place, the signal shall indicate as follows:

(a) "WALK" or approved "Walking Person" symbol. A pedestrian facing the signal may proceed across the roadway in the direction of the signal, but shall yield the right-of-way to vehicles lawfully within the intersection at the time that signal is first shown.

(b) Flashing or steady "DONT WALK" or "WAIT" or approved "Upraised Hand" symbol. No pedestrian shall start to cross the roadway in the direction of the signal, but any pedestrian who has partially completed crossing shall proceed to a sidewalk or safety zone or otherwise leave the roadway while the "WAIT" or "DONT WALK" or approved "Upraised Hand" symbol is showing. *(Stats.1959, c. 3, p. 1676, § 21456. Amended by Stats.1981, c. 413, p. 1611, § 9.)*

Cross References

Applicability of this section to trolley coaches, see Vehicle Code § 21051.

Definitions,
Intersection, see Vehicle Code § 365.
Official traffic control signal, see Vehicle Code § 445.
Roadway, see Vehicle Code § 530.

Duty of driver to yield right-of-way to pedestrian at crosswalk, see Vehicle Code § 21950.

Violation as misdemeanor, punishment, see Vehicle Code §§ 40000.5 et seq., 42002.

§ 21456.1. Pedestrian traffic control

Whenever an official traffic control signal exhibiting an approved "Walking Person" symbol, an approved "Upraised Hand" symbol, or the words "WALK" or "WAIT" or "DON'T WALK" is shown concurrently with official traffic control signals exhibiting the words "GO" or "CAUTION" or "STOP" or exhibiting different colored lights successively, one at a time or with arrows, a pedestrian facing those traffic control signals shall obey the "Walking Person," "Upraised Hand," "WALK" or

"WAIT" or "DON'T WALK" control signal as provided in Section 21456. *(Added by Stats.1961, c. 810, p. 2089, § 1. Amended by Stats.1993, c. 272 (A.B.301), § 39, eff. Aug. 2, 1993.)*

§ 21456.2. Bicycle operators; obeying provisions of this article; bicycle signals

Text of section as amended by Stats.2005, c. 126 (A.B.56), § 3, eff. July 25, 2005.

Section 21456.2 was added by Stats.1999, c. 277 (A.B.134), § 2, and repealed by its own terms, operative Jan. 1, 2005. Therefore, this section was not in effect from Jan. 1, 2005 until July 25, 2005.

Stats.2005, c. 126 (A.B.56), § 3, might be given effect as a new addition of this section; but see Government Code § 9609.

(a) Unless otherwise directed by a bicycle signal as provided in Section 21456.3, an operator of a bicycle shall obey the provisions of this article applicable to the driver of a vehicle.

(b) Whenever an official traffic control signal exhibiting different colored bicycle symbols is shown concurrently with official traffic control signals exhibiting different colored lights or arrows, an operator of a bicycle facing those traffic control signals shall obey the bicycle signals as provided in Section 21456.3.

(Amended by Stats.2005, c. 126 (A.B.56), § 3, eff. July 25, 2005.)

§ 21456.3. Bicycle signals

Text of section as amended by Stats.2005, c. 126 (A.B.56), § 4, eff. July 25, 2005.

Section 21456.3 was added by Stats.1999, c. 277 (A.B.134), § 3, and repealed by its own terms, operative Jan. 1, 2005. Therefore, this section was not in effect from Jan. 1, 2005 until July 25, 2005.

Stats.2005, c. 126 (A.B.56), § 4, might be given effect as a new addition of this section; but see Government Code § 9609.

(a) An operator of a bicycle facing a green bicycle signal shall proceed straight through or turn right or left or make a U-turn unless a sign prohibits a U-turn. An operator of a bicycle, including one turning, shall yield the right-of-way to other traffic and to pedestrians lawfully within the intersection or an adjacent crosswalk.

(b) An operator of a bicycle facing a steady yellow bicycle signal is, by that signal, warned that the related green movement is ending or that a red indication will be shown immediately thereafter.

(c) Except as provided in subdivision (d), an operator of a bicycle facing a steady red bicycle signal shall stop at a marked limit line, but if none, before entering the crosswalk on the near side of the intersection, or, if none, then before entering the intersection, and shall remain stopped until an indication to proceed is shown.

(d) Except when a sign is in place prohibiting a turn, an operator of a bicycle, after stopping as required by subdivision (c), facing a steady red bicycle signal, may turn right, or turn left from a one-way street onto a one-way street. An operator of a bicycle making a turn shall yield the right-of-way to pedestrians lawfully within an adjacent crosswalk and to traffic lawfully using the intersection.

(e) A bicycle signal may be used only at those locations that meet geometric standards or traffic volume standards, or both, as adopted by the Department of Transportation.

(Amended by Stats.2005, c. 126 (A.B.56), § 4, eff. July 25, 2005.)

§ 21457. Illuminated flashing red or yellow lights used in traffic signal or with traffic sign

Whenever an illuminated flashing red or yellow light is used in a traffic signal or with a traffic sign, it shall require obedience by drivers as follows:

(a) Flashing red (stop signal): When a red lens is illuminated with rapid intermittent flashes, a driver shall stop at a clearly marked limit line, but if none, before entering the crosswalk on the near side of the intersection, or if none, then at the point nearest the intersecting roadway where the driver has a view of approaching traffic on the intersecting roadway before entering it, and the driver may proceed subject to the rules applicable after making a stop at a stop sign.

(b) Flashing yellow (caution signal): When a yellow lens is illuminated with rapid intermittent flashes, a driver may proceed through the intersection or past the signal only with caution. *(Stats.1959, c. 3, p. 1676, § 21457. Amended by Stats.1959, c. 975, p. 3004, § 1; Stats.1972, c. 46, p. 64, § 1; Stats.1981, c. 413, p. 1611, § 10.)*

Cross References

Applicability of this section to trolley coaches, see Vehicle Code § 21051.
Definitions,
  Crosswalk, see Vehicle Code § 275.
  Intersection, see Vehicle Code § 365.
  Official traffic control device, see Vehicle Code § 440.
  Traffic, see Vehicle Code § 620.
Right of way, see Vehicle Code § 21802.
Violation as misdemeanor, punishment, see Vehicle Code §§ 40000.5 et seq., 42002.

§ 21458. Curb markings

(a) Whenever local authorities enact local parking regulations and indicate them by the use of paint upon curbs, the following colors only shall be used, and the colors indicate as follows:

(1) Red indicates no stopping, standing, or parking, whether the vehicle is attended or unattended, except that a bus may stop in a red zone marked or signposted as a bus loading zone.

(2) Yellow indicates stopping only for the purpose of loading or unloading passengers or freight for the time as may be specified by local ordinance.

(3) White indicates stopping for either of the following purposes:

(A) Loading or unloading of passengers for the time as may be specified by local ordinance.

(B) Depositing mail in an adjacent mailbox.

(4) Green indicates time limit parking specified by local ordinance.

(5) Blue indicates parking limited exclusively to the vehicles of disabled persons and disabled veterans.

(b) Regulations adopted pursuant to subdivision (a) shall be effective on days and during hours or times as prescribed by local ordinances. *(Stats.1959, c. 3, p. 1676, § 21458. Amended by Stats.1975, c. 688, p. 1636, § 1; Stats.1985, c. 1041, § 4; Stats.1992, c. 1243 (A.B.3090), § 88, eff. Sept. 30, 1992.)*

Cross References

Local authorities defined, see Vehicle Code § 385.
Stopping, standing or parking, see Vehicle Code § 22500 et seq.
Violation as misdemeanor, punishment, see Vehicle Code §§ 40000.5 et seq., 42002.

§ 21459. Distinctive roadway markings

(a) The Department of Transportation in respect to state highways and a local authority with respect to highways under its jurisdiction, is authorized to place and maintain upon highways distinctive roadway markings as described and with the effect set forth in Section 21460.

(b) The distinctive roadway markings shall be employed to designate any portion of a highway where the volume of traffic or the vertical or other curvature of the roadway renders it hazardous to drive on the left side of the marking or to indicate no driving to the left as provided in Section 21460, and shall not be employed for any other purpose.

(c) Any pavement marking other than as described in this section placed by the Department of Transportation or any local authority shall not be effective to indicate no driving over or to the left of the marking. *(Stats.1959, c. 3, p. 1677, § 21459. Amended by Stats.1974, c. 545, p. 1318, § 185.)*

Cross References

Definitions,
  Highway, see Vehicle Code § 360.
  Local authorities, see Vehicle Code § 385.
  Roadway, see Vehicle Code § 530.
Powers of local authorities, generally, see Vehicle Code § 21100 et seq.
Traffic signs, signals, and markings, maintenance and placing by State Department of Transportation and local authorities, see Vehicle Code §§ 21350, 21351.

§ 21460. Double lines

(a) If double parallel solid yellow lines are in place, a person driving a vehicle shall not drive to the left of the lines, except as permitted in this section.

(b) If double parallel solid white lines are in place, a person driving a vehicle shall not cross any part of those double solid white lines, except as permitted in this section or Section 21655.8.

(c) If the double parallel lines, one of which is broken, are in place, a person driving a vehicle shall not drive to the left of the lines, except as follows:

(1) If the driver is on the side of the roadway in which the broken line is in place, the driver may cross over the double lines or drive to the left of the double lines when overtaking or passing other vehicles.

(2) As provided in Section 21460.5.

(d) The markings as specified in subdivision (a), (b), or (c) do not prohibit a driver from crossing the marking if (1) turning to the left at an intersection or into or out of a driveway or private road, or (2) making a U–turn under the rules governing that turn, and the markings shall be disregarded when authorized signs have been erected designating offcenter traffic lanes as permitted pursuant to Section 21657.

(e) Raised pavement markers may be used to simulate painted lines described in this section if the markers are placed in accordance with standards established by the Department of Transportation. *(Stats.1959, c. 3, p. 1677, § 21460. Amended by Stats.1959, c. 255, p. 2157, § 1; Stats.1959, c. 1996, p. 4630, § 25; Stats.1961, c. 446, p. 1519, § 1; Stats.1968, c. 508, p. 1152, § 1; Stats.1971, c. 988, p. 1903, § 2, operative May 3, 1972; Stats.1974, c. 545, p. 1318, § 186; Stats.1976, c. 482, p. 1226, § 1; Stats.1984, c. 462, § 1; Stats.2011, c. 114 (A.B.1105), § 2.)*

Cross References

Definitions,
  Driver, see Vehicle Code § 305.
  Intersection, see Vehicle Code § 365.
  Roadway, see Vehicle Code § 530.
  Vehicle, see Vehicle Code § 670.
Violation as misdemeanor, punishment, see Vehicle Code §§ 40000.5 et seq., 42002.

§ 21460.5. Two-way left-turn lanes

(a) The Department of Transportation and local authorities in their respective jurisdictions may designate a two-way left-turn lane on a highway. A two-way left-turn lane is a lane near the center of the highway set aside for use by vehicles making left turns in both directions from or into the highway.

(b) Two-way left-turn lanes shall be designated by distinctive roadway markings consisting of parallel double yellow lines, interior line dashed and exterior line solid, on each side of the lane. The Department of Transportation may determine and prescribe standards and specifications governing length, width, and positioning of the distinctive pavement markings. All pavement markings designating a two-way left-turn lane shall conform to the Department of Transportation's standards and specifications.

(c) A vehicle shall not be driven in a designated two-way left-turn lane except when preparing for or making a left turn from or into a highway or when preparing for or making a U-turn when otherwise permitted by law, and shall not be driven in that lane for more than 200 feet while preparing for and making the turn or while preparing to merge into the adjacent lanes of travel. A left turn or U-turn shall not be made from any other lane where a two-way left-turn lane has been designated.

(d) This section does not prohibit driving across a two-way left-turn lane.

(e) Raised pavement markers may be used to simulate the painted lines described in this section when those markers are placed in accordance with standards established by the Department of Transportation.

(Added by Stats.1976, c. 482, p. 1227, § 3, operative Jan. 1, 1980. Amended by Stats.1979, c. 364, p. 1229, § 1; Stats.1990, c. 232 (A.B.2769), § 1.)

§ 21461. Obedience by driver to official traffic control devices

(a) It is unlawful for a driver of a vehicle to fail to obey a sign or signal defined as regulatory in the federal Manual on Uniform Traffic Control Devices, or a Department of Transportation approved supplement to that manual of a regulatory nature erected or maintained to enhance traffic safety and operations or to indicate and carry out the provisions of this code or a local traffic ordinance or resolution adopted pursuant to a local traffic ordinance, or to fail to obey a device erected or maintained by lawful authority of a public body or official.

(b) Subdivision (a) does not apply to acts constituting violations under Chapter 9 (commencing with Section 22500) of this division or to acts constituting violations of a local traffic ordinance adopted pursuant to Chapter 9 (commencing with Section 22500). *(Stats.1959, c. 3, p. 1677, § 21461. Amended by Stats.1970, c. 827, p. 1561, § 1; Stats.1981, c. 775, p. 3029, § 2; Stats.2004, c. 203 (A.B.1951), § 1.)*

Cross References

Applicability of this section to trolley coaches, see Vehicle Code § 21051.
Damage to highway, weight or size of vehicle, see Vehicle Code § 17302.
Highway signs, markers or warning notices, failure to observe, see Vehicle Code §§ 21367, 40000.14.
Official traffic control device defined, see Vehicle Code § 440.
Weight violations, penalty, see Vehicle Code § 42030 et seq.

§ 21461.5. Obedience by pedestrian to official traffic control devices

It shall be unlawful for any pedestrian to fail to obey any sign or signal erected or maintained to indicate or carry out the provisions of this code or any local traffic ordinance or resolution adopted pursuant to a local traffic ordinance, or to fail to obey any device erected or maintained pursuant to Section 21352. *(Added by Stats. 1970, c. 827, p. 1561, § 2.)*

§ 21462. Obedience to traffic control signals

The driver of any vehicle, the person in charge of any animal, any pedestrian, and the motorman of any streetcar shall obey the instructions of any official traffic signal applicable to him and placed as provided by law, unless otherwise directed by a police or traffic officer or when it is necessary for the purpose of avoiding a collision or in case of other emergency, subject to the exemptions granted by Section 21055. *(Stats.1959, c. 3, p. 1677, § 21462.)*

Cross References

Crossing between controlled intersections, see Vehicle Code § 21955.
Duration of prohibition against operation of commercial motor vehicle, see Vehicle Code § 15312.
Emergency vehicles, right-of-way, see Vehicle Code § 21806.
Exemption of authorized emergency vehicles, see Vehicle Code § 21055.
Obedience to peace officers, see Vehicle Code § 2800.
Official traffic control signal defined, see Vehicle Code § 445.
Violations, see Vehicle Code § 40000.1 et seq.

§ 21463. Illegal operation of signals

No person shall operate a manually or traffic actuated signal other than for the purpose of permitting a pedestrian or vehicle to cross a roadway. *(Stats.1959, c. 3, p. 1678, § 21463.)*

Cross References

Violations, see Vehicle Code § 40000.1 et seq.

§ 21464. Interference with traffic devices; limitations on use and purchase, possession, manufacture, sale, etc. of mobile infrared transmitters and related devices; penalties

(a) A person, without lawful authority, may not deface, injure, attach any material or substance to, knock down, or remove, nor may a person shoot at, any official traffic control device, traffic guidepost, traffic signpost, motorist callbox, or historical marker placed or erected as authorized or required by law, nor may a person without lawful authority deface, injure, attach any material or substance to, or remove, nor may a person shoot at, any inscription, shield, or insignia on any device, guide, or marker.

(b) A person may not use, and a vehicle, other than an authorized emergency vehicle or a public transit passenger vehicle, may not be equipped with, any device, including, but not limited to, a mobile infrared transmitter, that is capable of sending a signal that interrupts or changes the sequence patterns of an official traffic control signal unless that device or use is authorized by the Department of Transportation pursuant to Section 21350 or by local authorities pursuant to Section 21351.

(c) A person may not buy, possess, manufacture, install, sell, offer for sale, or otherwise distribute a device described in subdivision (b), including, but not limited to, a mobile infrared transmitter (MIRT), unless the purchase, possession, manufacture, installation, sale, offer for sale, or distribution is for the use of the device by a peace officer or other person authorized to operate an authorized emergency vehicle or a public transit passenger vehicle, in the scope of his or her duties.

(d) Any willful violation of subdivision (a), (b), or (c) that results in injury to, or the death of, a person is punishable by imprisonment pursuant to subdivision (h) of Section 1170 of the Penal Code, or by imprisonment in a county jail for a period of not more than six months, and by a fine of not less than five thousand dollars ($5,000) nor more than ten thousand dollars ($10,000).

(e) Any willful violation of subdivision (a), (b), or (c) that does not result in injury to, or the death of, a person is punishable by a fine of not more than five thousand dollars ($5,000).

(f) The court shall allow the offender to perform community service designated by the court in lieu of all or part of any fine imposed under this section. *(Stats.1959, c. 3, p. 1678, § 21464. Amended by Stats.1959, c. 1996, p. 4630, § 26; Stats.1963, c. 659, p. 1648, § 1; Stats.1970, c. 810, p. 1532, § 1; Stats.1976, c. 1139, p. 5172, § 338, operative July 1, 1977; Stats.1977, c. 805, p. 2457, § 1; Stats.1990, c. 447 (A.B.2723), § 1; Stats.1992, c. 1243 (A.B.3090), § 89, eff. Sept. 30, 1992; Stats.2004, c. 338 (A.B.340), § 1; Stats.2004, c. 391 (S.B.1085), § 1; Stats. 2011, c. 15 (A.B.109), § 607, eff. April 4, 2011, operative Oct. 1, 2011.)*

Cross References

Highway signs, markers or warning notices, failure to observe, see Vehicle Code §§ 21367, 40000.14.
Illegal operation of signals, see Vehicle Code § 21463.
Official traffic control device, see Vehicle Code § 440.
Public offenses, infractions and special misdemeanors, see Vehicle Code § 42001.
Violations, see Vehicle Code § 40000.1 et seq.

§ 21465. Unauthorized traffic devices

No person shall place, maintain, or display upon, or in view of, any highway any unofficial sign, signal, device, or marking, or any sign, signal, device, or marking which purports to be or is an imitation of, or resembles, an official traffic control device or which attempts to direct the movement of traffic or which hides from view any official traffic control device. *(Stats.1959, c. 3, p. 1678, § 21465. Amended by Stats.1967, c. 486, p. 1693, § 1.)*

Cross References

Definitions,
  Highway, see Vehicle Code § 360.
  Official traffic control device, see Vehicle Code § 440.
  Traffic, see Vehicle Code § 620.
Highway signs, markers or warning notices, failure to observe, see Vehicle Code §§ 21367, 40000.14.

Violations, see Vehicle Code § 40000.1 et seq.

§ 21466. Light preventing recognition of official traffic control device

No person shall place or maintain or display upon or in view of any highway any light in such position as to prevent the driver of a vehicle from readily recognizing any official traffic control device. *(Stats.1959, c. 3, p. 1678, § 21466. Amended by Stats.1970, c. 968, p. 1736, § 2, eff. Sept. 14, 1970.)*

Cross References

Definitions,
  Driver, see Vehicle Code § 305.
  Highway, see Vehicle Code § 360.
  Official traffic control device, see Vehicle Code § 440.
  Vehicle, see Vehicle Code § 670.
Violations, see Vehicle Code § 40000.1 et seq.

§ 21466.5. Light impairing driver's vision

No person shall place or maintain or display, upon or in view of any highway, any light of any color of such brilliance as to impair the vision of drivers upon the highway. A light source shall be considered vision impairing when its brilliance exceeds the values listed below.

The brightness reading of an objectionable light source shall be measured with a 1½-degree photoelectric brightness meter placed at the driver's point of view. The maximum measured brightness of the light source within 10 degrees from the driver's normal line of sight shall not be more than 1,000 times the minimum measured brightness in the driver's field of view, except that when the minimum measured brightness in the field of view is 10 foot-lamberts or less, the measured brightness of the light source in foot-lambert shall not exceed 500 plus 100 times the angle, in degrees, between the driver's line of sight and the light source.

The provisions of this section shall not apply to railroads as defined in Section 229 of the Public Utilities Code. *(Added by Stats.1970, c. 968, p. 1736, § 3, eff. Sept. 14, 1970.)*

§ 21467. Prohibited signs and devices

Every prohibited sign, signal, device, or light is a public nuisance, and the Department of Transportation, members of the California Highway Patrol, and local authorities are hereby authorized and empowered without notice to remove the same, or cause the same to be removed, or the Director of Transportation, the commissioner, or local authorities may bring an action as provided by law to abate such nuisance. *(Stats.1959, c. 3, p. 1678, § 21467. Amended by Stats.1974, c. 545, p. 1319, § 188.)*

Cross References

Abatement of public nuisance, see Civil Code § 3494; Code of Civil Procedure § 731.
Definition,
  Commissioner, see Vehicle Code § 265.
  Local authorities, see Vehicle Code § 385.

§ 21468. Public utilities

This division does not modify or limit the authority of the Public Utilities Commission to erect or maintain, or cause to be erected and maintained, signs, signals or other traffic control devices as authorized by law. *(Stats. 1959, c. 3, p. 1678, § 21468.)*

Cross References

Official traffic control device defined, see Vehicle Code § 440.

CHAPTER 3. DRIVING, OVERTAKING, AND PASSING

Article	Section
1. Driving on Right Side	21650
2. Additional Driving Rules	21700
3. Overtaking and Passing	21750

Cross References

Penalties, public offenses, fines in misdemeanor cases for violation pertaining to passing a school building or grounds, see Vehicle Code § 42011.

ARTICLE 1. DRIVING ON RIGHT SIDE

Section
21650. Highways; vehicles required to drive on right side of roadway; exceptions.
21650.1. Bicycles; operation on roadway or shoulder; direction.
21651. Divided highways.
21652. Entering or leaving public highway via service road.
21653. Repealed.
21654. Slow-moving vehicles.
21655. Designated lanes for certain vehicles.
21655.3. Repealed.
21655.5. Exclusive or preferential use of highway lanes for high-occupancy vehicles; exceptions for motorcycles, mass transit vehicles and paratransit vehicles.
21655.6. Highway lanes for high-occupancy vehicles; approval required.
21655.7. Public mass transit guideway; highway use; local permit.
21655.8. Exclusive or preferential use lanes for high-occupancy vehicles; entrance or exit.
21655.9. Exclusive or preferential use of highway lanes or access ramps for vehicles with distinctive identifiers.
21655.12. Repealed.
21655.16. Repealed.
21656. Turning out of slow-moving vehicles.
21657. Designated traffic direction.
21658. Laned roadways.
21659. Three-laned highways.
21660. Approaching vehicles.
21661. Narrow roadways.
21662. Mountain driving.
21663. Driving on sidewalk.
21664. On-ramp exit.

§ 21650. Highways; vehicles required to drive on right side of roadway; exceptions

Upon all highways, a vehicle shall be driven upon the right half of the roadway, except as follows:

(a) When overtaking and passing another vehicle proceeding in the same direction under the rules governing that movement.

(b) When placing a vehicle in a lawful position for, and when the vehicle is lawfully making, a left turn.

(c) When the right half of a roadway is closed to traffic under construction or repair.

(d) Upon a roadway restricted to one-way traffic.

(e) When the roadway is not of sufficient width.

(f) When the vehicle is necessarily traveling so slowly as to impede the normal movement of traffic, that portion of the highway adjacent to the right edge of the roadway may be utilized temporarily when in a condition permitting safe operation.

(g) This section does not prohibit the operation of bicycles on any shoulder of a highway, on any sidewalk, on any bicycle path within a highway, or along any crosswalk or bicycle path crossing, where the operation is not otherwise prohibited by this code or local ordinance.

(h) This section does not prohibit the operation of a transit bus on the shoulder of a state highway in conjunction with the implementation of a program authorized pursuant to Section 148.1 of the Streets and Highways Code on state highways within the areas served by the transit services of the Monterey–Salinas Transit District or the Santa Cruz Metropolitan Transit District. *(Stats.1959, c. 3, p. 1678, § 21650. Amended by Stats. 1961, c. 1185, p. 2919, § 1; Stats.1969, c. 136, p. 288, § 2; Stats.1988, c. 58, § 1; Stats.2009, c. 200 (S.B.734), § 10; Stats.2013, c. 426 (A.B.946), § 2.)*

Cross References

Applicability of this section to trolley coaches, see Vehicle Code § 21051.

Limitations on overtaking on left, see Vehicle Code §§ 21751, 21752.

Overtaking and passing of vehicles on right, see Vehicle Code §§ 21754, 21755.

Overtaking and passing on grades prohibited, see Vehicle Code § 21758.

Overtaking animals, caution required in, see Vehicle Code § 21759.

Passing of vehicles going in opposite directions, see Vehicle Code §§ 21660, 21661.

Roadways laned for traffic, regulations as to driving on, see Vehicle Code §§ 21658, 21659.

Rubbish or garbage trucks, exemption, see Vehicle Code § 21059.

Rules governing overtaking of vehicle on left, see Vehicle Code § 21750 et seq.

Rules of the road, exemption of authorized emergency vehicles, see Vehicle Code § 21054.

School bus, overtaking of, see Vehicle Code § 22454.

§ 21650.1.   Bicycles; operation on roadway or shoulder; direction

A bicycle operated on a roadway, or the shoulder of a highway, shall be operated in the same direction as vehicles are required to be driven upon the roadway. *(Added by Stats.1988, c. 58, § 2.)*

§ 21651.   Divided highways

(a) Whenever a highway has been divided into two or more roadways by means of intermittent barriers or by means of a dividing section of not less than two feet in width, either unpaved or delineated by curbs, double-parallel lines, or other markings on the roadway, it is unlawful to do either of the following:

(1) To drive any vehicle over, upon, or across the dividing section.

(2) To make any left, semicircular, or U-turn with the vehicle on the divided highway, except through an opening in the barrier designated and intended by public authorities for the use of vehicles or through a plainly marked opening in the dividing section.

(b) It is unlawful to drive any vehicle upon a highway, except to the right of an intermittent barrier or a dividing section which separates two or more opposing lanes of traffic. Except as otherwise provided in subdivision (c), a violation of this subdivision is a misdemeanor.

(c) Any willful violation of subdivision (b) which results in injury to, or death of, a person shall be punished by imprisonment pursuant to subdivision (h) of Section 1170 of the Penal Code, or imprisonment in a county jail for a period of not more than six months. *(Added by Stats.1982, c. 569, p. 2525, § 2. Amended by Stats.1986, c. 362, § 2; Stats.1988, c. 765, § 1; Stats.2011, c. 15 (A.B.109), § 608, eff. April 4, 2011, operative Oct. 1, 2011.)*

Cross References

Animals, caution in passing, see Vehicle Code § 21759.
Applicability of this section to trolley coaches, see Vehicle Code § 21051.
Overtaking and passing, see Vehicle Code § 21750 et seq.
Overtaking school bus, see Vehicle Code § 22454.
Passing on grades, see Vehicle Code § 21758.
Passing on the right, see Vehicle Code §§ 21754, 21755.
Traffic violation point count, violation of this section, see Vehicle Code § 12810.
Violation as misdemeanor, see Vehicle Code § 40000.13.

§ 21652.   Entering or leaving public highway via service road

When any service road has been constructed on or along any public highway and the main thoroughfare of the highway has been separated from the service road, it is unlawful for any person to drive any vehicle into the main thoroughfare from the service road or from the main thoroughfare into the service road except through an opening in the dividing curb, section, separation, or line. *(Stats.1959, c. 3, p. 1679, § 21652. Amended by*

630

Stats.1959, c. 507, p. 2468, § 2; Stats.1963, c. 335, p. 1124, § 1.)

Cross References

Highway defined, see Vehicle Code §§ 360, 590.

§ 21653.   Repealed by Stats.1969, c. 136, p. 288, § 3

§ 21654.   Slow-moving vehicles

(a) Notwithstanding the prima facie speed limits, any vehicle proceeding upon a highway at a speed less than the normal speed of traffic moving in the same direction at such time shall be driven in the right-hand lane for traffic or as close as practicable to the right-hand edge or curb, except when overtaking and passing another vehicle proceeding in the same direction or when preparing for a left turn at an intersection or into a private road or driveway.

(b) If a vehicle is being driven at a speed less than the normal speed of traffic moving in the same direction at such time, and is not being driven in the right-hand lane for traffic or as close as practicable to the right-hand edge or curb, it shall constitute prima facie evidence that the driver is operating the vehicle in violation of subdivision (a) of this section.

(c) The Department of Transportation, with respect to state highways, and local authorities, with respect to highways under their jurisdiction, may place and maintain upon highways official signs directing slow-moving traffic to use the right-hand traffic lane except when overtaking and passing another vehicle or preparing for a left turn. *(Stats.1959, c. 3, p. 1679, § 21654. Amended by Stats. 1959, c. 1747, p. 4205, § 2, eff. July 13, 1959; Stats.1965, c. 448, p. 1758, § 1; Stats.1974, c. 545, p. 1319, § 189.)*

Cross References

Conditions for overtaking and passing vehicle on right, see Vehicle Code §§ 21754, 21755.
Highway defined, see Vehicle Code § 590.
Intersection defined, see Vehicle Code § 365.
Prima facie speed limits, see Vehicle Code § 22352.
Private road or driveway defined, see Vehicle Code § 490.
Speed laws generally, see Vehicle Code § 22349 et seq.

§ 21655.   Designated lanes for certain vehicles

(a) Whenever the Department of Transportation or local authorities with respect to highways under their respective jurisdictions determines upon the basis of an engineering and traffic investigation that the designation of a specific lane or lanes for the travel of vehicles required to travel at reduced speeds would facilitate the safe and orderly movement of traffic, the department or local authority may designate a specific lane or lanes for the travel of vehicles which are subject to the provisions of Section 22406 and shall erect signs at reasonable intervals giving notice thereof.

(b) Any trailer bus, except as provided in Section 21655.5, and any vehicle subject to the provisions of Section 22406 shall be driven in the lane or lanes designated pursuant to subdivision (a) whenever signs have been erected giving notice of that designation. Except as otherwise provided in this subdivision, when a specific lane or lanes have not been so designated, any of those vehicles shall be driven in the right-hand lane for traffic or as close as practicable to the right edge or curb. If, however, a specific lane or lanes have not been designated on a divided highway having four or more clearly marked lanes for traffic in one direction, any of those vehicles may also be driven in the lane to the immediate left of that right-hand lane, unless otherwise prohibited under this code. When overtaking and passing another vehicle proceeding in the same direction, the driver shall use either the designated lane, the lane to the immediate left of the right-hand lane, or the right-hand lane for traffic as permitted under this code.

This subdivision does not apply to a driver who is preparing for a left- or right-hand turn or who is entering into or exiting from a highway or to a driver who must necessarily drive in a lane other than the right-hand lane to continue on his or her intended route. *(Stats.1959, c. 3, p. 1679, § 21655. Amended by Stats.1963, c. 323, p. 1110, § 1; Stats.1963, c. 1585, p. 3165, § 1; Stats.1965, c. 69, p. 949, § 1; Stats.1967, c. 78, p. 975, § 1; Stats.1970, c. 219, p. 471, § 1; Stats.1974, c. 545, p. 1320, § 190; Stats.1975, c. 542, p. 1109, § 1; Stats.1988, c. 843, § 4.)*

Cross References

Highway defined, see Vehicle Code §§ 360, 590.
Intersection defined, see Vehicle Code § 365.
Overtaking on right, when permitted, see Vehicle Code §§ 21754, 21755.
Private road or driveway defined, see Vehicle Code § 490.

§ 21655.3. Repealed by Stats.2008, c. 27 (A.B.2906), § 1, eff. June 6, 2008

§ 21655.5. Exclusive or preferential use of highway lanes for high-occupancy vehicles; exceptions for motorcycles, mass transit vehicles and paratransit vehicles

(a) The Department of Transportation and local authorities, with respect to highways under their respective jurisdictions, may authorize or permit exclusive or preferential use of highway lanes for high-occupancy vehicles. Prior to establishing the lanes, competent engineering estimates shall be made of the effect of the lanes on safety, congestion, and highway capacity.

(b) The Department of Transportation and local authorities, with respect to highways under their respective jurisdictions, shall place and maintain, or cause to be placed and maintained, signs and other official traffic control devices to designate the exclusive or preferential lanes, to advise motorists of the applicable vehicle occupancy levels, and, except where ramp metering and bypass lanes are regulated with the activation of traffic signals, to advise motorists of the hours of high-occupancy vehicle usage. No person shall drive a vehicle upon those lanes except in conformity with the instructions imparted by the official traffic control devices. A motorcycle, a mass transit vehicle, or a paratransit vehicle that is clearly and identifiably marked on all sides of the vehicle with the name of the paratransit provider may be operated upon those exclusive or preferential use lanes unless specifically prohibited by a traffic control device.

(c) When responding to an existing emergency or breakdown in which a mass transit vehicle is blocking an exclusive or preferential use lane, a clearly marked mass transit vehicle, mass transit supervisor's vehicle, or mass transit maintenance vehicle that is responding to the emergency or breakdown may be operated in the segment of the exclusive or preferential use lane being blocked by the mass transit vehicle, regardless of the number of persons in the vehicle responding to the emergency or breakdown, if both vehicles are owned or operated by the same agency, and that agency provides public mass transit services.

(d) For purposes of this section, a "paratransit vehicle" is defined in Section 462.

(e) For purposes of this section, a "mass transit vehicle" means a transit bus regularly used to transport paying passengers in mass transit service.

(f) It is the intent of the Legislature, in amending this section, to stimulate and encourage the development of ways and means of relieving traffic congestion on California highways and, at the same time, to encourage individual citizens to pool their vehicular resources and thereby conserve fuel and lessen emission of air pollutants.

(g) The provisions of this section regarding mass transit vehicles and paratransit vehicles shall only apply if the Director of Transportation determines that the application will not subject the state to a reduction in the amount of federal aid for highways. *(Added by Stats. 1970, c. 1295, p. 2399, § 12. Amended by Stats.1974, c. 545, p. 1320, § 191; Stats.1974, c. 773, p. 1697, § 5; Stats.1982, c. 466, p. 2057, § 114; Stats.1984, c. 826, § 1, eff. Aug. 31, 1984; Stats.1991, c. 143 (A.B.340), § 1; Stats.1993, c. 133 (S.B.948), § 1; Stats.1997, c. 579 (S.B.236), § 1; Stats.2002, c. 277 (A.B.2582), § 1.)*

Cross References

Administration of state highways, San Diego Association of Governments (SANDAG), value pricing and transit development demonstration program, see Streets and Highways Code § 149.4.
State highway administration, Santa Clara Valley Transportation Authority, value pricing program on high-occupancy vehicle lane systems, see Streets and Highways Code § 149.6.
State highway administration, Sunol Smart Carpool Lane Joint Powers Authority, value pricing high-occupancy vehicle program, see Streets and Highways Code § 149.5.
Value pricing and transit development program on State Highway Route 5 in managed lanes serving as high-occupancy vehicle expressway, single-occupant vehicles meeting specified requirements exempt from this section, see Streets and Highways Code § 149.10.

§ 21655.6. Highway lanes for high-occupancy vehicles; approval required

(a) Whenever the Department of Transportation authorizes or permits exclusive or preferential use of highway lanes for high-occupancy vehicles on any highway located within the territory of a transportation planning agency, as defined in Section 99214 of the Public Utilities Code, or a county transportation commission, the department shall obtain the approval of the transportation planning agency or county transportation commission prior to establishing the exclusive or preferential use of the highway lanes.

(b) If the department authorizes or permits additional exclusive or preferential use of highway lanes for high-occupancy vehicles on that portion of State Highway Route 101 located within the boundaries of the City of Los Angeles, the department shall obtain the approval of the Los Angeles County Transportation Commission by at least a two-thirds majority vote of the entire membership eligible to vote prior to establishing the additional exclusion or preferential use of the highway lanes.

(c) If the department restricts or requires the restriction of the use of any lane on any federal-aid highway in the unincorporated areas of Alameda County to high-occupancy vehicles, the Metropolitan Transportation Commission shall review the use patterns of those lanes and shall determine if congestion relief is being efficiently achieved by the creation of the high-occupancy vehicle lanes. The commission shall report its findings and recommendations in its HOV Master Plan Update for the San Francisco Bay area no later than two years after those high-occupancy vehicle lanes become operational. *(Added by Stats.1982, c. 588, p. 2548, § 1, eff. Aug. 25, 1982. Amended by Stats.1984, c. 25, § 1; Stats.1998, c. 653 (A.B.1624), § 1.)*

Cross References

State highway administration, Santa Clara Valley Transportation Authority, value pricing program on high-occupancy vehicle lane systems, see Streets and Highways Code § 149.6.
State highway administration, Sunol Smart Carpool Lane Joint Powers Authority, value pricing high-occupancy vehicle program, see Streets and Highways Code § 149.5.

§ 21655.7. Public mass transit guideway; highway use; local permit

A local authority, with respect to any highway under its jurisdiction, may authorize or permit a portion of the highway to be used exclusively for a public mass transit guideway. *(Added by Stats.1981, c. 1055, p. 4079, § 12.)*

§ 21655.8. Exclusive or preferential use lanes for high-occupancy vehicles; entrance or exit

(a) Except as required under subdivision (b), when exclusive or preferential use lanes for high-occupancy vehicles are established pursuant to Section 21655.5 and double parallel solid lines are in place to the right thereof, no person driving a vehicle may cross over these double lines to enter into or exit from the exclusive or preferential use lanes, and entrance or exit may be made only in areas designated for these purposes or where a single broken line is in place to the right of the exclusive or preferential use lanes.

(b) Upon the approach of an authorized emergency vehicle displaying a red light or siren, as specified in Section 21806, a person driving a vehicle in an exclusive or preferential use lane shall exit that lane immediately upon determining that the exit can be accomplished with reasonable safety.

(c) Raised pavement markers may be used to simulate painted lines described in this section. *(Added by Stats. 1988, c. 1054, § 2. Amended by Stats.1996, c. 1154 (A.B.3020), § 67, eff. Sept. 30, 1996.)*

§ 21655.9. Exclusive or preferential use of highway lanes or access ramps for vehicles with distinctive identifiers

(a)(1) Whenever the Department of Transportation or a local authority authorizes or permits exclusive or preferential use of highway lanes or highway access ramps for high-occupancy vehicles pursuant to Section 21655.5, the use of those lanes or ramps shall also be extended to vehicles that are issued distinctive decals, labels, or other identifiers pursuant to Section 5205.5 regardless of vehicle occupancy or ownership.

(2) A local authority during periods of peak congestion shall suspend for a lane the access privileges extended pursuant to paragraph (1) for those vehicles issued distinctive decals, labels, or other identifiers pursuant to Section 5205.5, if a periodic review of lane performance by that local authority discloses both of the following factors regarding the lane:

(A) The lane, or a portion of the lane, exceeds a level of service C, as described in subdivision (b) of Section 65089 of the Government Code.

(B) The operation or projected operation of vehicles in the lane, or a portion of the lane, will significantly increase congestion.

(b) A person shall not drive a vehicle described in subdivision (a) of Section 5205.5 with a single occupant upon a high-occupancy vehicle lane pursuant to this section unless the decal, label, or other identifier issued pursuant to Section 5205.5 is properly displayed on the vehicle, and the vehicle registration described in Section 5205.5 is with the vehicle.

(c) A person shall not operate or own a vehicle displaying a decal, label, or other identifier, as described in Section 5205.5, if that decal, label, or identifier was not issued for that vehicle pursuant to Section 5205.5. A violation of this subdivision is a misdemeanor.

(d) If the provisions in Section 5205.5 authorizing the department to issue decals, labels, or other identifiers to hybrid and alternative fuel vehicles are repealed, vehicles displaying those decals, labels, or other identifiers shall not access high-occupancy vehicle lanes without meeting the occupancy requirements otherwise applicable to those lanes.

* * *

* * * (e) This section shall * * * become inoperative on January 1, 2019, or the date the federal authorization pursuant to Section 166 of Title 23 of the United States Code expires, or the date the Secretary of State receives the notice described in subdivision (i) of Section 5205.5, whichever occurs first, and, as of January 1, 2019, is repealed, unless a later enacted statute, that becomes operative on or before January 1, 2019, deletes or extends the dates on which it becomes inoperative and is repealed.

* * * *(Added by Stats.1999, c. 330 (A.B.71), § 3. Amended by Stats.2004, c. 725 (A.B.2628), § 2; Stats. 2006, c. 606 (A.B.1407), § 4; Stats.2006, c. 614 (A.B. 2600), § 4; Stats.2010, c. 37 (A.B.1500), § 2; Stats.2010, c. 215 (S.B.535), § 2; Stats.2013, c. 405 (A.B.266), § 3; Stats.2013, c. 414 (S.B.286), § 3.5.)*

Inoperative Date and Repeal

For inoperative date and repeal of this section, see its terms.

Cross References

Violation of subd.(c) of this section considered as misdemeanor, see Vehicle Code § 40000.13.

§ 21655.12. Repealed by Stats.2000, c. 63 (A.B.769), § 1, operative Jan. 1, 2002

§ 21655.16. Repealed by Stats.2000, c. 337 (A.B.1871), § 1, operative Jan. 1, 2003

§ 21656. Turning out of slow-moving vehicles

On a two-lane highway where passing is unsafe because of traffic in the opposite direction or other conditions, a slow-moving vehicle, including a passenger vehicle, behind which five or more vehicles are formed in line, shall turn off the roadway at the nearest place designated as a turnout by signs erected by the authority having jurisdiction over the highway, or wherever sufficient area for a safe turnout exists, in order to permit the vehicles following it to proceed. As used in this section a slow-moving vehicle is one which is proceeding at a rate of speed less than the normal flow of traffic at the particular time and place. *(Stats.1959, c. 3, p. 1680, § 21656. Amended by Stats.1961, c. 528, p. 1631, § 1; Stats.1965, c. 448, p. 1759, § 2.)*

§ 21657. Designated traffic direction

The authorities in charge of any highway may designate any highway, roadway, part of a roadway, or specific lanes upon which vehicular traffic shall proceed in one direction at all or such times as shall be indicated by official traffic control devices. When a roadway has been so designated, a vehicle shall be driven only in the direction designated at all or such times as shall be indicated by

traffic control devices. *(Stats.1959, c. 3, p. 1680, § 21657. Amended by Stats.1969, c. 136, p. 288, § 4.)*

Cross References

Department of California highway patrol, generally, see Vehicle Code § 2100 et seq.

Driving on one-way street, see Vehicle Code § 21650.

Obedience to traffic signals, etc., see Vehicle Code §§ 21461, 21462.

Powers and duties of California highway patrol, see Vehicle Code § 2400 et seq.

Powers of local authorities with respect to regulating use of highways, see Vehicle Code §§ 21100, 21101.

Traffic signs, signals, and markings, generally, see Vehicle Code § 21350 et seq.

Violations, see Vehicle Code § 40000.1 et seq.

§ 21658. Laned roadways

Whenever any roadway has been divided into two or more clearly marked lanes for traffic in one direction, the following rules apply:

(a) A vehicle shall be driven as nearly as practical entirely within a single lane and shall not be moved from the lane until such movement can be made with reasonable safety.

(b) Official signs may be erected directing slow-moving traffic to use a designated lane or allocating specified lanes to traffic moving in the same direction, and drivers of vehicles shall obey the directions of the traffic device. *(Stats.1959, c. 3, p. 1680, § 21658. Amended by Stats. 1961, c. 528, p. 1632, § 2; Stats.1970, c. 405, p. 817, § 5; Stats.1973, c. 670, p. 1226, § 1; Stats.1975, c. 450, p. 948, § 1.)*

Cross References

Application of this section to trolley coaches, see Vehicle Code § 21051.

Driving on right side of roadway, exceptions to, see Vehicle Code § 21650.

Roadway defined, see Vehicle Code § 530.

Traffic signs and markings, generally, see Vehicle Code § 21350 et seq.

Violations, see Vehicle Code § 40000.1 et seq.

§ 21659. Three-laned highways

Upon a roadway which is divided into three lanes a vehicle shall not be driven in the extreme left lane at any time, nor in the center lane except when overtaking and passing another vehicle where the roadway ahead is clearly visible and the center lane is clear of traffic within a safe distance, or in preparation for a left turn, or where the center lane is at the time allocated exclusively to traffic moving in the direction the vehicle is proceeding and is signposted to give notice of such allocation. This section does not apply upon a one-way roadway. *(Stats. 1959, c. 3, p. 1680, § 21659.)*

Cross References

Application of this section to trolley coaches, see Vehicle Code § 21051.

Roadway defined, see Vehicle Code § 530.

Violations, see Vehicle Code § 40000.1 et seq.

§ 21660.   Approaching vehicles

Drivers of vehicles proceeding in opposite directions shall pass each other to the right, and, except when a roadway has been divided into traffic lanes, each driver shall give to the other at least one-half of the main traveled portion of the roadway whenever possible. *(Stats.1959, c. 3, p. 1680, § 21660.)*

Cross References

Roadway defined, see Vehicle Code § 530.
Rubbish or garbage trucks, exemption, see Vehicle Code § 21059.
Violations, see Vehicle Code § 40000.1 et seq.

§ 21661.   Narrow roadways

Whenever upon any grade the width of the roadway is insufficient to permit the passing of vehicles approaching from opposite directions at the point of meeting, the driver of the vehicle descending the grade shall yield the right-of-way to the vehicle ascending the grade and shall, if necessary, back his vehicle to a place in the highway where it is possible for the vehicles to pass. *(Stats.1959, c. 3, p. 1680, § 21661.)*

Cross References

Roadway defined, see Vehicle Code § 530.

§ 21662.   Mountain driving

The driver of a motor vehicle traveling through defiles or canyons or upon mountain highways shall hold the motor vehicle under control at all times and shall do the following when applicable:

(a) If the roadway has no marked centerline, the driver shall drive as near the right-hand edge of the roadway as is reasonably possible.

(b) If the roadway has insufficient width to permit a motor vehicle to be driven entirely to the right of the center of the roadway, the driver shall give audible warning with the horn of the motor vehicle upon approaching any curve where the view is obstructed within a distance of 200 feet along the highway. *(Stats.1959, c. 3, p. 1681, § 21662. Amended by Stats.1959, c. 973, p. 3004, § 1; Stats.1984, c. 462, § 2.)*

Cross References

Driving on right side of highway, generally, see Vehicle Code § 21650.
Exemption of emergency vehicles from rules of the road, exceptions, see Vehicle Code § 21054.
Overtaking vehicles when approaching crest of grade or where view obstructed, see Vehicle Code § 21752.
Passing without sufficient clearance, see Vehicle Code § 21751.

§ 21663.   Driving on sidewalk

Except as expressly permitted pursuant to this code, including Sections 21100.4 and 21114.5, no person shall operate or move a motor vehicle upon a sidewalk except as may be necessary to enter or leave adjacent property.

634

(Added by Stats.1965, c. 1343, p. 3230, § 1. Amended by Stats.1987, c. 600, § 2; Stats.1996, c. 124 (A.B.3470), § 126.)

Cross References

Electric carts on sidewalks, local regulations, see Vehicle Code §§ 21100, 21114.5.

§ 21664.   On-ramp exit

It is unlawful for the driver of any vehicle to enter or exit any freeway which has full control of access and no crossings at grade, except upon a designated on ramp with respect to entering the freeway or a designated off ramp with respect to exiting the freeway. *(Added by Stats.1965, c. 1100, p. 2747, § 1. Amended by Stats.1988, c. 765, § 2.)*

ARTICLE 2.   ADDITIONAL DRIVING RULES

Section
21700.   Obstruction to driving.
21700.5.   Buses transporting school pupils in City of San Diego.
21701.   Interference with driver or mechanism.
21702.   Limitation on driving hours.
21703.   Following too closely.
21704.   Distance between vehicles subject to special speed restrictions.
21705.   Caravans.
21706.   Following emergency vehicle.
21706.5.   Operation of vehicle in unsafe manner within emergency incident zone.
21707.   Fire areas.
21708.   Fire hoses.
21709.   Safety zones.
21710.   Coasting prohibited.
21711.   Towed vehicles swerving.
21712.   Unlawful riding and towing.
21713.   Privately-owned armored cars.
21714.   Fully enclosed 3-wheeled motor vehicles of specified dimensions; operation of vehicles; prohibited areas.
21715.   Passenger vehicle combinations; number and weight limits.
21716.   Golf carts; operation.
21717.   Turning across bicycle lanes.
21718.   Freeways; stopping, parking or leaving vehicles standing; exceptions to prohibition; violation; conviction.
21720.   Pocket bikes; operation of vehicles; prohibited areas.
21721.   Pocket bikes; removal or seizure; costs associated with removal, seizure or storage; return of bike.

§ 21700.   Obstruction to driving

No person shall drive a vehicle when it is so loaded, or when there are in the front seat such number of persons as to obstruct the view of the driver to the front or sides of the vehicle or as to interfere with the driver's control over the driving mechanism of the vehicle. *(Stats.1959, c. 3, p. 1681, § 21700. Amended by Stats.1965, c. 1500, p. 3523, § 7.)*

Application of this section to trolley coaches, see Vehicle Code § 21051.

§ 21700.5. Buses transporting school pupils in City of San Diego

No person shall knowingly drive a bus within the City of San Diego which is transporting any public or private school pupil who is enrolled in kindergarten or any of grades 1 to 12, inclusive, to or from a public or private school, unless every such pupil is seated in a seat. *(Added by Stats.1972, c. 1124, p. 2161, § 1.)*

§ 21701. Interference with driver or mechanism

No person shall wilfully interfere with the driver of a vehicle or with the mechanism thereof in such manner as to affect the driver's control of the vehicle. The provisions of this section shall not apply to a drivers' license examiner or other employee of the Department of Motor Vehicles when conducting the road or driving test of an applicant for a driver's license nor to a person giving instruction as a part of a course in driver training conducted by a public school, educational institution or a driver training school licensed by the Department of Motor Vehicles. *(Stats.1959, c. 3, p. 1681, § 21701.)*

Application of this section to trolley coaches, see Vehicle Code § 21051.
License examination and driving test, see Vehicle Code §§ 12803, 12804.9.
Violation of this section with intent to capture image, recording or impression for a commercial purpose, see Vehicle Code § 40008.

§ 21702. Limitation on driving hours

(a) No person shall drive upon any highway any vehicle designed or used for transporting persons for compensation for more than 10 consecutive hours nor for more than 10 hours spread over a total of 15 consecutive hours. Thereafter, such person shall not drive any such vehicle until eight consecutive hours have elapsed.

Regardless of aggregate driving time, no driver shall drive for more than 10 hours in any 24-hour period unless eight consecutive hours off duty have elapsed.

(b) No person shall drive upon any highway any vehicle designed or used for transporting merchandise, freight, materials or other property for more than 12 consecutive hours nor for more than 12 hours spread over a total of 15 consecutive hours. Thereafter, such person shall not drive any such vehicle until eight consecutive hours have elapsed.

Regardless of aggregate driving time, no driver shall drive for more than 12 hours in any 24-hour period unless eight consecutive hours off duty have elapsed.

(c) This section does not apply in any case of casualty or unavoidable accident or an act of God.

(d) In computing the number of hours under this section, any time spent by a person in driving such a vehicle outside this state shall, upon the vehicle entering this state, be included.

(e) Any person who violates any provision of this section is guilty of a misdemeanor and is punishable by a fine of not less than one hundred dollars ($100) nor more than one thousand dollars ($1,000) for each offense.

(f) This section shall not apply to the driver of a vehicle which is subject to the provisions of Section 34500. *(Stats.1959, c. 3, p. 1681, § 21702. Amended by Stats.1963, c. 2148, p. 4483, § 7; Stats.1967, c. 564, p. 1911, § 1; Stats.1983, c. 1092, § 391, eff. Sept. 27, 1983, operative Jan. 1, 1984.)*

Application of this section to trolley coaches, see Vehicle Code § 21051.
Misdemeanor defined, see Penal Code § 17.
Uncertified highway carriers of persons, see Penal Code § 654.1 et seq.

§ 21703. Following too closely

The driver of a motor vehicle shall not follow another vehicle more closely than is reasonable and prudent, having due regard for the speed of such vehicle and the traffic upon, and the condition of, the roadway. *(Stats. 1959, c. 3, p. 1682, § 21703.)*

Application of this section to trolley coaches, see Vehicle Code § 21051.
Following emergency vehicle, see Vehicle Code § 21706.
Rules of the road, exemption of authorized emergency vehicles, see Vehicle Code § 21054.
Violation of this section with intent to capture image, recording or impression for a commercial purpose, see Vehicle Code § 40008.

§ 21704. Distance between vehicles subject to special speed restrictions

(a) The driver of any motor vehicle subject to the speed restriction of Section 22406 that is operated outside of a business or residence district, shall keep the vehicle he is driving at a distance of not less than 300 feet to the rear of any other motor vehicle subject to such speed restriction which is preceding it.

(b) The provisions of this section shall not prevent overtaking and passing nor shall they apply upon a highway with two or more lanes for traffic in the direction of travel. *(Stats.1959, c. 3, p. 1682, § 21704. Amended by Stats.1967, c. 371, p. 1598, § 1; Stats.1969, c. 226, p. 558, § 1.)*

Definitions,
  Business district, see Vehicle Code § 235.
  Driver, see Vehicle Code § 305.
  Motor vehicle, see Vehicle Code § 415.
  Residence district, see Vehicle Code § 515.
Rules of the road, exemption of authorized emergency vehicles, see Vehicle Code § 21054.

Speed laws generally, see Vehicle Code § 22349 et seq.

§ 21705. Caravans

Motor vehicles being driven outside of a business or residence district in a caravan or motorcade, whether or not towing other vehicles, shall be so operated as to allow sufficient space and in no event less than 100 feet between each vehicle or combination of vehicles so as to enable any other vehicle to overtake or pass. *(Stats.1959, c. 3, p. 1682, § 21705.)*

Cross References

Rules of the road, exemption of authorized emergency vehicles, see Vehicle Code § 21054.

§ 21706. Following emergency vehicle

No motor vehicle, except an authorized emergency vehicle, shall follow within 300 feet of any authorized emergency vehicle being operated under the provisions of Section 21055.

This section shall not apply to a police or traffic officer when serving as an escort within the purview of Section 21057. *(Stats.1959, c. 3, p. 1682, § 21706. Amended by Stats.1963, c. 564, p. 1444, § 1; Stats.1972, c. 46, p. 64, § 2.)*

Cross References

Authorized emergency vehicle defined, see Vehicle Code § 165.
Rules of the road, exemption of authorized emergency vehicles, see Vehicle Code § 21054.

§ 21706.5. Operation of vehicle in unsafe manner within emergency incident zone

(a) For purposes of this section, the following terms have the following meanings:

(1) "Emergency incident zone" means an area on a freeway that is within 500 feet of, and in the direction of travel of, a stationary authorized emergency vehicle that has its emergency lights activated. Traffic in the opposite lanes of the freeway is not in an "emergency incident zone."

(2) "Operate a vehicle in an unsafe manner" means operating a motor vehicle in violation of an act made unlawful under this division, except a violation of Section 21809.

(b) A person shall not operate a vehicle in an unsafe manner within an emergency incident zone. *(Added by Stats.2006, c. 375 (S.B.1610), § 1.)*

§ 21707. Fire areas

No motor vehicle, except an authorized emergency vehicle or a vehicle of a duly authorized member of a fire or police department, shall be operated within the block wherein an emergency situation responded to by any fire department vehicle exists, except that in the event the nearest intersection to the emergency is more than 300 feet therefrom, this section shall prohibit operation of vehicles only within 300 feet of the emergency, unless directed to do so by a member of the fire department or police department, sheriff, deputy sheriff, or member of the California Highway Patrol. The emergency shall be deemed to have ceased to exist when the official of the fire department in charge at the scene of the emergency shall so indicate. Officials of the fire department or police department or the Department of the California Highway Patrol who are present shall make every effort to prevent the closing off entirely of congested highway traffic passing the scene of any such emergency. *(Stats. 1959, c. 3, p. 1682, § 21707.)*

Cross References

Authorized emergency vehicle defined, see Vehicle Code § 165.
California highway patrol, see Vehicle Code § 2100 et seq.
Emergency vehicles, suspension or revocation of permits, see Vehicle Code § 2417.
Exemptions of authorized emergency vehicles, see Vehicle Code §§ 21055, 21056.
Operation of fire department vehicles, see Vehicle Code § 21055.
Parking of utility vehicles, see Vehicle Code § 22512.
Rules of the road, exemption of authorized emergency vehicles, see Vehicle Code § 21054.

§ 21708. Fire hoses

No person shall drive or propel any vehicle or conveyance upon, over, or across, or in any manner damage any fire hose or chemical hose used by or under the supervision and control of any organized fire department. However, any vehicle may cross a hose provided suitable jumpers or other appliances are installed to protect the hose. *(Stats.1959, c. 3, p. 1683, § 21708.)*

Cross References

Parking of utility vehicles, see Vehicle Code § 22512.
Rules of the road, exemption of authorized emergency vehicles, see Vehicle Code § 21054.

§ 21709. Safety zones

No vehicle shall at any time be driven through or within a safety zone. *(Stats.1959, c. 3, p. 1683, § 21709.)*

Cross References

Application of this section to trolley coaches, see Vehicle Code § 21051.
Rules of the road, exemption of authorized emergency vehicles, see Vehicle Code § 21054.
Safety zone defined, see Vehicle Code § 540.
Stopping, standing or parking in safety zone prohibited, see Vehicle Code § 22500.
Vehicle defined, see Vehicle Code § 670.

§ 21710. Coasting prohibited

The driver of a motor vehicle when traveling on down grade upon any highway shall not coast with the gears of such vehicle in neutral. *(Stats.1959, c. 3, p. 1683, § 21710.)*

§ 21711. Towed vehicles swerving

No person shall operate a train of vehicles when any vehicle being towed whips or swerves from side to side or fails to follow substantially in the path of the towing vehicle. *(Stats.1959, c. 3, p. 1683, § 21711. Amended by Stats.1959, c. 44, p. 1902, § 3.)*

Cross References
Safety chains, see Vehicle Code § 29004.
Size of drawbar, see Vehicle Code § 29005.

§ 21712. Unlawful riding and towing

(a) A person driving a motor vehicle shall not knowingly permit a person to ride on a vehicle or upon a portion of a vehicle that is not designed or intended for the use of passengers.

(b) A person shall not ride on a vehicle or upon a portion of a vehicle that is not designed or intended for the use of passengers.

(c) A person driving a motor vehicle shall not knowingly permit a person to ride in the trunk of that motor vehicle.

(d) A person shall not ride in the trunk of a motor vehicle.

(e) A person violating subdivision (c) or (d) shall be punished as follows:

(1) By a fine of one hundred dollars ($100).

(2) For a second violation occurring within one year of a prior violation that resulted in a conviction, a fine of two hundred dollars ($200).

(3) For a third or a subsequent violation occurring within one year of two or more prior violations that resulted in convictions, a fine of two hundred fifty dollars ($250).

(f) Subdivisions (a) and (b) do not apply to an employee engaged in the necessary discharge of his or her duty or in the case of persons riding completely within or upon vehicle bodies in the space intended for a load on the vehicle.

(g) A person shall not drive a motor vehicle that is towing a trailer coach, camp trailer, or trailer carrying a vessel, containing a passenger, except when a trailer carrying or designed to carry a vessel is engaged in the launching or recovery of the vessel.

(h) A person shall not knowingly drive a motor vehicle that is towing a person riding upon a motorcycle, motorized bicycle, bicycle, coaster, roller skates, sled, skis, or toy vehicle.

(i) Subdivision (g) does not apply to a trailer coach that is towed with a fifth-wheel device if the trailer coach is equipped with safety glazing materials wherever glazing materials are used in windows or doors, with an audible or visual signaling device that a passenger inside the trailer coach can use to gain the attention of the motor vehicle driver, and with at least one unobstructed exit capable of being opened from both the interior and exterior of the trailer coach. *(Stats.1959, c. 3, p. 1683, § 21712. Amended by Stats.1961, c. 117, p. 1128, § 1; Stats.1965, c. 333, p. 1440, § 1; Stats.1971, c. 1536, p. 3043, § 2; Stats.1972, c. 262, p. 511, § 1; Stats.1972, c.*

881, p. 1559, § 3; Stats.1974, c. 578, p. 1397, § 1; Stats.1981, c. 813, p. 3155, § 12; Stats.1992, c. 1243 (A.B.3090), § 90, eff. Sept. 30, 1992; Stats.2006, c. 900 (A.B.1850), § 2.)

Cross References
Application of this section to trolley coaches, see Vehicle Code § 21051.
Traffic violation point counts, allocation of points, see Vehicle Code § 12810.

§ 21713. Privately-owned armored cars

No person shall operate on any highway any privately owned armored car unless a license to operate such car has first been obtained from the commissioner in accordance with Chapter 2.5 (commencing with Section 2500) of Division 2.

Violation of this section is a misdemeanor and upon conviction is punishable by a fine not exceeding one thousand dollars ($1,000) or by imprisonment in the county jail for not to exceed six months or by both such fine and imprisonment. *(Stats.1959, c. 3, p. 1683, § 21713. Amended by Stats.1968, c. 1309, p. 2473, § 9, operative Jan. 1, 1969; Stats.1973, c. 89, p. 149, § 1; Stats.1983, c. 1092, § 392, eff. Sept. 27, 1983, operative Jan. 1, 1984.)*

Cross References
Armored car defined, see Vehicle Code § 115.
Misdemeanor defined, see Penal Code § 17.

§ 21714. Fully enclosed 3-wheeled motor vehicles of specified dimensions; operation of vehicles; prohibited areas

The driver of a vehicle described in subdivision (f) of Section 27803 shall not operate the vehicle in either of the following areas:

(a) On, or immediately adjacent to, the striping or other markers designating adjacent traffic lanes.

(b) Between two or more vehicles that are traveling in adjacent traffic lanes. *(Added by Stats.1997, c. 710 (A.B.1029), § 1. Amended by Stats.2008, c. 672 (A.B. 2272), § 2.)*

§ 21715. Passenger vehicle combinations; number and weight limits

(a) No passenger vehicle regardless of weight, or any other motor vehicle under 4,000 pounds unladen, shall draw or tow more than one vehicle in combination, except that an auxiliary dolly or tow dolly may be used with the towed vehicle.

(b) No motor vehicle under 4,000 pounds unladen shall tow any vehicle weighing 6,000 pounds or more gross. *(Added by Stats.1961, c. 643, p. 1849, § 1. Amended by Stats.1963, c. 134, p. 807, § 1; Stats.1963, c. 850, p. 2074, § 1; Stats.1963, c. 2149, p. 4487, § 13.5; Stats.1977, c. 770, p. 2399, § 3; Stats.1983, c. 708, § 8.)*

Cross References

Almond trailers, see Vehicle Code § 36627.
Cotton trailers, see Vehicle Code § 36626.
Vehicle drawing or towing unladen implements of husbandry,
   see Vehicle Code § 36625.

§ 21716.   Golf carts; operation

Except as provided in Section 21115.1 and Chapter 6 (commencing with Section 1950) of Division 2.5 of the Streets and Highways Code, no person shall operate a golf cart on any highway except in a speed zone of 25 miles per hour or less. *(Added by Stats.1968, c. 1303, p. 2457, § 4. Amended by Stats.1991, c. 192 (A.B.789), § 2; Stats.1992, c. 44 (A.B.1229), § 2; Stats.1994, c. 598 (S.B.2016), § 2; Stats.1995, c. 334 (A.B.110), § 12; Stats. 1997, c. 536 (S.B.525), § 3; Stats.2000, c. 155 (A.B.2221), § 2.)*

Cross References

Golf cart defined, see Vehicle Code § 345.
Highway defined, see Vehicle Code § 360.

§ 21717.   Turning across bicycle lanes

Whenever it is necessary for the driver of a motor vehicle to cross a bicycle lane that is adjacent to his lane of travel to make a turn, the driver shall drive the motor vehicle into the bicycle lane prior to making the turn and shall make the turn pursuant to Section 22100. *(Added by Stats.1976, c. 751, p. 1785, § 12.)*

§ 21718.   Freeways; stopping, parking or leaving vehicles standing; exceptions to prohibition; violation; conviction

(a) No person shall stop, park, or leave standing any vehicle upon a freeway which has full control of access and no crossings at grade except:

(1) When necessary to avoid injury or damage to persons or property.

(2) When required by law or in obedience to a peace officer or official traffic control device.

(3) When any person is actually engaged in maintenance or construction on freeway property or any employee of a public agency is actually engaged in the performance of official duties.

(4) When any vehicle is so disabled that it is impossible to avoid temporarily stopping and another vehicle has been summoned to render assistance to the disabled vehicle or driver of the disabled vehicle. This paragraph applies when the vehicle summoned to render assistance is a vehicle owned by the donor of free emergency assistance that has been summoned by display upon or within a disabled vehicle of a placard or sign given to the driver of the disabled vehicle by the donor for the specific purpose of summoning assistance, other than towing service, from the donor.

(5) Where stopping, standing, or parking is specifically permitted. However, buses may not stop on freeways unless sidewalks are provided with shoulders of sufficient width to permit stopping without interfering with the normal movement of traffic and without the possibility of crossing over fast lanes to reach the bus stop.

(6) Where necessary for any person to report a traffic accident or other situation or incident to a peace officer or any person specified in paragraph (3), either directly or by means of an emergency telephone or similar device.

(7) When necessary for the purpose of rapid removal of impediments to traffic by the owner or operator of a tow truck operating under an agreement with the Department of the California Highway Patrol.

(b) A conviction of a violation of this section is a conviction involving the safe operation of a motor vehicle upon the highway if a notice to appear for the violation was issued by a peace officer described in Section 830.1 or 830.2 of the Penal Code. *(Added by Stats.1997, c. 945 (A.B.1561), § 17.)*

§ 21720.   Pocket bikes; operation of vehicles; prohibited areas

A pocket bike shall not be operated on a sidewalk, roadway, or any other part of a highway, or on a bikeway, bicycle path or trail, equestrian trail, hiking or recreational trail, or on public lands open to off-highway motor vehicle use. *(Added by Stats.2005, c. 323 (A.B.1051), § 3.)*

Cross References

Pocket bike defined, see Vehicle Code § 473.

§ 21721.   Pocket bikes; removal or seizure; costs associated with removal, seizure or storage; return of bike

(a) A peace officer, as defined in Chapter 4.5 (commencing with Section 830) of Title 3 of Part 2 of the Penal Code, may cause the removal and seizure of a pocket bike, upon the notice to appear for a violation of Section 21720. A pocket bike so seized shall be held for a minimum of 48 hours.

(b) A violator of this section shall be responsible for all costs associated with the removal, seizure, and storage of the pocket bike.

(c) A city, county, or city and county may adopt a regulation, ordinance, or resolution imposing charges equal to its administrative costs relating to the removal, seizure, and storage costs of a pocket bike. The charges shall not exceed the actual costs incurred for the expenses directly related to removing, seizing, and storing a pocket bike.

(d) An agency shall release a seized pocket bike to the owner, violator, or the violator's agent after 48 hours, if all of the following conditions are met:

(1) The violator or authorized agent's request is made during normal business hours.

(2) The applicable removal, seizure, and storage costs have been paid by the owner, or any other responsible party. *(Added by Stats.2005, c. 323 (A.B.1051), § 4.)*

Pocket bike defined, see Vehicle Code § 473.

ARTICLE 3. OVERTAKING AND PASSING

Section
21750. Overtake and pass to left.
21750. Overtake and pass to left.
21751. Passing without sufficient clearance.
21752. When driving on left prohibited.
21753. Yielding for passing.
21754. Passing on the right.
21755. Passing on the right safely; use of bicycle in bicycle lane or on shoulder not prohibited.
21756. Passing standing streetcar, trolley coach, or bus.
21757. Passing streetcar on left.
21758. Passing on grades.
21759. Caution in passing animals.
21760. Three Feet for Safety Act; overtaking and passing bicycles; violations and penalties.

§ 21750. Overtake and pass to left

*Section operative until Sept. 16, 2014. See,
also, section operative Sept. 16, 2014.*

(a) The driver of a vehicle overtaking another vehicle or a bicycle proceeding in the same direction shall pass to the left at a safe distance without interfering with the safe operation of the overtaken vehicle or bicycle, subject to the limitations and exceptions * * * set forth in this article.

(b) This section shall become inoperative on September 16, 2014, and, as of January 1, 2015, is repealed, unless a later enacted statute, that becomes operative on or before January 1, 2015, deletes or extends the dates on which it becomes inoperative and is repealed. *(Stats. 1959, c. 3, p. 1683, § 21750. Amended by Stats.1961, c. 577, p. 1718, § 1; Stats.1996, c. 674 (S.B.515), § 7; Stats.2013, c. 331 (A.B.1371), § 1.)*

Inoperative Date and Repeal

*For inoperative date and repeal of
this section, see its terms.*

Cross References

Application of this section to trolley coaches, see Vehicle Code § 21051.
Rules of the road, exemption of authorized emergency vehicles, see Vehicle Code § 21055.

§ 21750. Overtake and pass to left

*Section operative Sept. 16, 2014. See, also,
section operative until Sept. 16, 2014.*

(a) The driver of a vehicle overtaking another vehicle proceeding in the same direction shall pass to the left at a safe distance without interfering with the safe operation of the overtaken vehicle, subject to the limitations and exceptions set forth in this article.

(b) This section shall become operative on September 16, 2014. *(Added by Stats.2013, c. 331 (A.B.1371), § 2, operative Sept. 16, 2014.)*

Cross References

Application of this section to trolley coaches, see Vehicle Code § 21051.
Rules of the road, exemption of authorized emergency vehicles, see Vehicle Code § 21055.

§ 21751. Passing without sufficient clearance

On a two-lane highway, no vehicle shall be driven to the left side of the center of the roadway in overtaking and passing another vehicle proceeding in the same direction unless the left side is clearly visible and free of oncoming traffic for a sufficient distance ahead to permit such overtaking and passing to be completely made without interfering with the safe operation of any vehicle approaching from the opposite direction. *(Stats.1959, c. 3, p. 1684, § 21751. Amended by Stats.1961, c. 577, p. 1718, § 2; Stats.1973, c. 50, p. 83, § 1.)*

Cross References

Overtaking and passing vehicles on left, see Vehicle Code § 21750.

§ 21752. When driving on left prohibited

No vehicle shall be driven to the left side of the roadway under the following conditions:

(a) When approaching or upon the crest of a grade or a curve in the highway where the driver's view is obstructed within such distance as to create a hazard in the event another vehicle might approach from the opposite direction.

(b) When the view is obstructed upon approaching within 100 feet of any bridge, viaduct, or tunnel.

(c) When approaching within 100 feet of or when traversing any railroad grade crossing.

(d) When approaching within 100 feet of or when traversing any intersection.

This section shall not apply upon a one-way roadway. *(Stats.1959, c. 3, p. 1684, § 21752. Amended by Stats. 1969, c. 417, p. 948, § 1; Stats.2000, c. 596 (A.B.2909), § 7.)*

Cross References

Traffic school, rail transit safety film or fine, see Penal Code § 369b.

§ 21753. Yielding for passing

Except when passing on the right is permitted, the driver of an overtaken vehicle shall safely move to the right-hand side of the highway in favor of the overtaking vehicle after an audible signal or a momentary flash of headlights by the overtaking vehicle, and shall not increase the speed of his or her vehicle until completely passed by the overtaking vehicle. This section does not require the driver of an overtaken vehicle to drive on the shoulder of the highway in order to allow the overtaking vehicle to pass. *(Stats.1959, c. 3, p. 1684, § 21753. Amended by Stats.1996, c. 440 (S.B.1588), § 9; Stats.1999, c. 724 (A.B.1650), § 40.)*

Cross References

Application of this section to trolley coaches, see Vehicle Code § 21051.
Overtaking and passing vehicles on right, see Vehicle Code § 21755.

§ 21754.   Passing on the right

The driver of a vehicle may overtake and pass to the right of another vehicle only under the following conditions:

(a) When the vehicle overtaken is making or about to make a left turn.

(b) Upon a highway within a business or residence district with unobstructed pavement of sufficient width for two or more lines of moving vehicles in the direction of travel.

(c) Upon any highway outside of a business or residence district with unobstructed pavement of sufficient width and clearly marked for two or more lines of moving traffic in the direction of travel.

(d) Upon a one-way street.

(e) Upon a highway divided into two roadways where traffic is restricted to one direction upon each of such roadways.

The provisions of this section shall not relieve the driver of a slow moving vehicle from the duty to drive as closely as practicable to the right hand edge of the roadway. *(Stats.1959, c. 3, p. 1684, § 21754. Amended by Stats.2010, c. 491 (S.B.1318), § 39.)*

Cross References

Application of this section to trolley coaches, see Vehicle Code § 21051.
Driving in right hand lane, slow-moving vehicles, see Vehicle Code § 21654.

§ 21755.   Passing on the right safely; use of bicycle in bicycle lane or on shoulder not prohibited

(a) The driver of a vehicle may overtake and pass another vehicle upon the right only under conditions permitting that movement in safety. In no event shall that movement be made by driving off the paved or main-traveled portion of the roadway.

(b) This section does not prohibit the use of a bicycle in a bicycle lane or on a shoulder. *(Stats.1959, c. 3, p. 1684, § 21755. Amended by Stats.2010, c. 491 (S.B.1318), § 40.)*

Cross References

Application of this section to trolley coaches, see Vehicle Code § 21051.

Driving, overtaking or passing slow-moving vehicles, see Vehicle Code § 21654.

§ 21756.   Passing standing streetcar, trolley coach, or bus

(a) The driver of a vehicle overtaking any interurban electric or streetcar stopped or about to stop for the purpose of receiving or discharging any passenger shall stop the vehicle to the rear of the nearest running board or door of such car and thereupon remain standing until all passengers have boarded the car or upon alighting have reached a place of safety, except as provided in subdivision (b) hereof.

(b) Where a safety zone has been established or at an intersection where traffic is controlled by an officer or a traffic control signal device, a vehicle need not be brought to a stop before passing any interurban electric or streetcar but may proceed past such car at a speed not greater than 10 miles per hour and with due caution for the safety of pedestrians.

(c) Whenever any trolley coach or bus has stopped at a safety zone to receive or discharge passengers, a vehicle may proceed past such trolley coach or bus at a speed not greater than 10 miles per hour. *(Stats.1959, c. 3, p. 1685, § 21756. Amended by Stats.1959, c. 969, p. 3001, § 1.)*

Cross References

Driving through safety zone prohibited, see Vehicle Code § 21709.
Intersection defined, see Vehicle Code § 365.
Pedestrians' rights and duties, see Vehicle Code § 21950 et seq.
Prima facie speed limits at intersections, see Vehicle Code § 22352.
Safety zone defined, see Vehicle Code § 540.
Stopping, standing or parking prohibited between safety zone and adjacent curb, see Vehicle Code § 22500.

§ 21757.   Passing streetcar on left

The driver of a vehicle shall not overtake and pass upon the left, nor shall any driver of a vehicle drive upon the left side of, any interurban electric or streetcar proceeding in the same direction whether the streetcar is actually in motion or temporarily at rest, except:

(a) When so directed by a police or traffic officer.

(b) When upon a one-way street.

(c) When upon a street where the tracks are so located as to prevent compliance with this section. *(Stats.1959, c. 3, p. 1685, § 21757.)*

Cross References

Limitations on overtaking on left, see Vehicle Code §§ 21751, 21752.
Obedience to peace officers, see Vehicle Code § 2800.
Overtaking vehicles on left or right, generally, see Vehicle Code § 21750 et seq.
Passing school bus, see Vehicle Code § 22454.

§ 21758.   Passing on grades

In the event any vehicle is being operated on any grade outside of a business or residence district at a speed of less than 20 miles per hour, no person operating any other motor vehicle shall attempt to overtake and pass such slow moving vehicle unless the overtaking vehicle is operated at a speed of at least 10 miles per hour in excess of the speed of the overtaken vehicle, nor unless the passing movement is completed within a total distance not greater than one-quarter of a mile. *(Stats.1959, c. 3, p. 1685, § 21758.)*

§ 21759. Caution in passing animals

The driver of any vehicle approaching any horse drawn vehicle, any ridden animal, or any livestock shall exercise proper control of his vehicle and shall reduce speed or stop as may appear necessary or as may be signalled or otherwise requested by any person driving, riding or in charge of the animal or livestock in order to avoid frightening and to safeguard the animal or livestock and to insure the safety of any person driving or riding the animal or in charge of the livestock. *(Stats.1959, c. 3, p. 1685, § 21759.)*

Cross References

Livestock on highways, duties of owners, see Food and Agricultural Code § 16902.
Open range country, warning against livestock on highway, see Vehicle Code § 21365.
Riding or driving animal on highway, effect of traffic laws, see Vehicle Code § 21050.
Signs at livestock crossing, erection, see Vehicle Code § 21364.

§ 21760. Three Feet for Safety Act; overtaking and passing bicycles; violations and penalties

Section operative Sept. 16, 2014.

(a) This section shall be known and may be cited as the Three Feet for Safety Act.

(b) The driver of a motor vehicle overtaking and passing a bicycle that is proceeding in the same direction on a highway shall pass in compliance with the requirements of this article applicable to overtaking and passing a vehicle, and shall do so at a safe distance that does not interfere with the safe operation of the overtaken bicycle, having due regard for the size and speed of the motor vehicle and the bicycle, traffic conditions, weather, visibility, and the surface and width of the highway.

(c) A driver of a motor vehicle shall not overtake or pass a bicycle proceeding in the same direction on a highway at a distance of less than three feet between any part of the motor vehicle and any part of the bicycle or its operator.

(d) If the driver of a motor vehicle is unable to comply with subdivision (c), due to traffic or roadway conditions, the driver shall slow to a speed that is reasonable and prudent, and may pass only when doing so would not endanger the safety of the operator of the bicycle, taking into account the size and speed of the motor vehicle and bicycle, traffic conditions, weather, visibility, and surface and width of the highway.

(e)(1) A violation of subdivision (b), (c), or (d) is an infraction punishable by a fine of thirty-five dollars ($35).

(2) If a collision occurs between a motor vehicle and a bicycle causing bodily injury to the operator of the bicycle, and the driver of the motor vehicle is found to be in violation of subdivision (b), (c), or (d), a two-hundred-twenty-dollar ($220) fine shall be imposed on that driver.

(f) This section shall become operative on September 16, 2014. *(Added by Stats.2013, c. 331 (A.B.1371), § 3, operative Sept. 16, 2014.)*

CHAPTER 4. RIGHT–OF–WAY

Section
21800. Intersections without functioning traffic control signals or yield sign, or with all-direction stop signs, except left-turning vehicle with vehicle approaching from opposite direction.
21801. Left turn or U–turn right of way.
21802. Approaching intersection entrance.
21803. Yield right-of-way.
21804. Entry onto highway; yield to approaching traffic constituting immediate hazard; yield by approaching traffic.
21805. Equestrian crossings.
21806. Authorized emergency vehicles.
21807. Effect of exemption.
21809. Driving vehicle in lane immediately adjacent to stationary emergency vehicle, tow truck, or Department of Transportation vehicle; penalty; exceptions.
21810. Repealed.

Cross References

Penalties, public offenses, fines in misdemeanor cases for violation pertaining to passing a school building or grounds, see Vehicle Code § 42011.

§ 21800. Intersections without functioning traffic control signals or yield sign, or with all-direction stop signs, except left-turning vehicle with vehicle approaching from opposite direction

(a) The driver of a vehicle approaching an intersection shall yield the right-of-way to any vehicle which has entered the intersection from a different highway.

(b)(1) When two vehicles enter an intersection from different highways at the same time, the driver of the vehicle on the left shall yield the right-of-way to the vehicle on his or her immediate right, except that the driver of any vehicle on a terminating highway shall yield the right-of-way to any vehicle on the intersecting continuing highway.

(2) For the purposes of this section, "terminating highway" means a highway which intersects, but does not continue beyond the intersection, with another highway which does continue beyond the intersection.

(c) When two vehicles enter an intersection from different highways at the same time and the intersection is controlled from all directions by stop signs, the driver of the vehicle on the left shall yield the right-of-way to the vehicle on his or her immediate right.

(d)(1) The driver of any vehicle approaching an intersection which has official traffic control signals that are inoperative shall stop at the intersection, and may proceed with caution when it is safe to do so.

(2) When two vehicles enter an intersection from different highways at the same time, and the official traffic control signals for the intersection are inoperative, the driver of the vehicle on the left shall yield the right-of-way to the vehicle on his or her immediate right, except that the driver of any vehicle on a terminating highway shall yield the right-of-way to any vehicle on the intersecting continuing highway.

(e) This section does not apply to any of the following:

(1) Any intersection controlled by an official traffic control signal or yield right-of-way sign.

(2) Any intersection controlled by stop signs from less than all directions.

(3) When vehicles are approaching each other from opposite directions and the driver of one of the vehicles intends to make, or is making, a left turn. *(Stats.1959, c. 3, p. 1685, § 21800. Amended by Stats.1980, c. 195, p. 418, § 1; Stats.1982, c. 349, § 1; Stats.1987, c. 455, § 1; Stats.1988, c. 623, § 1; Stats.2001–2002, 2nd Ex.Sess., c. 6 (S.B.84), § 2, eff. Oct. 1, 2001; Stats.2009, c. 200 (S.B. 734), § 11.)*

Cross References

Applicability of this section to trolley coaches, see Vehicle Code § 21051.
Intersection defined, see Vehicle Code § 365.
Local regulation of turning movements at intersection, see Vehicle Code § 22113.
Markings or signs for turning, see Vehicle Code § 22101.
Method of turning at intersections, see Vehicle Code § 22100.
Pedestrians, see Vehicle Code § 21950.
Program to provide battery backup power for official traffic control signals determined to be high priority, see Public Resources Code § 25403.8.
Right-of-way defined, see Vehicle Code § 525.
Rights and duties of pedestrians, see Vehicle Code § 21950 et seq.
Rules of the road, exemption of authorized emergency vehicles, see Vehicle Code § 21055.
Speed of vehicles at intersections, see Vehicle Code § 22352.
Turning signals, see Vehicle Code § 22110.
Vehicle entering through highway, stopping and yielding of right of way, see Vehicle Code § 21802.

§ 21801.   Left turn or U–turn right of way

(a) The driver of a vehicle intending to turn to the left or to complete a U-turn upon a highway, or to turn left into public or private property, or an alley, shall yield the right-of-way to all vehicles approaching from the opposite direction which are close enough to constitute a hazard at any time during the turning movement, and shall continue to yield the right-of-way to the approaching vehicles until the left turn or U-turn can be made with reasonable safety.

(b) A driver having yielded as prescribed in subdivision (a), and having given a signal when and as required by this code, may turn left or complete a U-turn, and the drivers of vehicles approaching the intersection or the entrance to the property or alley from the opposite direction shall yield the right-of-way to the turning vehicle. *(Stats.1959, c. 3, p. 1686, § 21801. Amended by Stats.1963, c. 1844, p. 3793, § 1; Stats.1969, c. 312, p. 679, § 1; Stats.1988, c. 623, § 2; Stats.1993, c. 272 (A.B.301), § 40, eff. Aug. 2, 1993.)*

Cross References

Applicability of this section to trolley coaches, see Vehicle Code § 21051.
Intersection defined, see Vehicle Code § 365.
Markings or signs for turning, see Vehicle Code § 22101.
Signals on turning and stopping, see Vehicle Code § 22107 et seq.
Speed limit at intersection, see Vehicle Code § 22352.
Turning at intersections, required position and method of, see Vehicle Code § 22100.

§ 21802.   Approaching intersection entrance

(a) The driver of any vehicle approaching a stop sign at the entrance to, or within, an intersection shall stop as required by Section 22450. The driver shall then yield the right-of-way to any vehicles which have approached from another highway, or which are approaching so closely as to constitute an immediate hazard, and shall continue to yield the right-of-way to those vehicles until he or she can proceed with reasonable safety.

(b) A driver having yielded as prescribed in subdivision (a) may proceed to enter the intersection, and the drivers of all other approaching vehicles shall yield the right-of-way to the vehicle entering or crossing the intersection.

(c) This section does not apply where stop signs are erected upon all approaches to an intersection. *(Stats. 1959, c. 3. p. 1686, § 21802. Amended by Stats.1959, c. 975, p. 3005, § 2; Stats.1963, c. 1844, p. 3793, § 2; Stats.1969, c. 1101, p. 2100, § 2; Stats.1988, c. 623, § 3.)*

Cross References

Applicability of this section to trolley coaches, see Vehicle Code § 21051.
Definitions,
  Intersection, see Vehicle Code § 365.
  Right-of-way, see Vehicle Code § 525.
  Through highway, see Vehicle Code § 600.
Flashing signals at intersections, see Vehicle Code § 21457.
Markings or signs for turning at intersections, see Vehicle Code § 22101.
Speed limit at intersection, see Vehicle Code § 22352.
Stop signs at through highway, see Vehicle Code § 21352 et seq.
Turning at intersections, required position and method, see Vehicle Code § 22100.

§ 21803.   Yield right-of-way

(a) The driver of any vehicle approaching any intersection which is controlled by a yield right-of-way sign shall, upon arriving at the sign, yield the right-of-way to any vehicles which have entered the intersection, or which are approaching on the intersecting highway close enough to constitute an immediate hazard, and shall continue to yield the right-of-way to those vehicles until he or she can proceed with reasonable safety.

(b) A driver having yielded as prescribed in subdivision (a) may proceed to enter the intersection, and the drivers of all other approaching vehicles shall yield the right-of-way to the vehicle entering or crossing the intersection. *(Stats.1959, c. 3, p. 1686, § 21803. Amended by Stats. 1959, c. 255, p. 2158, § 2; Stats.1963, c. 1844, p. 3793, § 3; Stats.1967, c. 370, p. 1597, § 2; Stats.1969, c. 834, p. 1668, § 2, operative July 1, 1970; Stats.1988, c. 623, § 4.)*

Cross References

Definitions,
 Intersection, see Vehicle Code § 365.
 Right-of-way, see Vehicle Code § 525.
Official traffic control devices, see Vehicle Code §§ 21400, 21401.
Signs, see Vehicle Code § 21356.
Speed limits, yield right-of-way signs, see Vehicle Code § 22352.
Traffic signs, signals and markings, see Vehicle Code § 21350 et seq.

§ 21804. Entry onto highway; yield to approaching traffic constituting immediate hazard; yield by approaching traffic

(a) The driver of any vehicle about to enter or cross a highway from any public or private property, or from an alley, shall yield the right-of-way to all traffic, as defined in Section 620, approaching on the highway close enough to constitute an immediate hazard, and shall continue to yield the right-of-way to that traffic until he or she can proceed with reasonable safety.

(b) A driver having yielded as prescribed in subdivision (a) may proceed to enter or cross the highway, and the drivers of all other vehicles approaching on the highway shall yield the right-of-way to the vehicle entering or crossing the intersection. *(Stats.1959, c. 3, p. 1686, § 21804. Amended by Stats.1959, c. 970, p. 3002, § 1; Stats.1963, c. 409, p. 1214, § 2; Stats.1963, c. 1844, p. 3794, § 4; Stats.1969, c. 312, p. 680, § 2; Stats.1976, c. 751, p. 1785, § 13; Stats.1978, c. 122, p. 291, § 1; Stats.1987, c. 284, § 1; Stats.1988, c. 623, § 5.)*

Cross References

Airports, see Vehicle Code § 21108.
Definitions,
 Highway, see Vehicle Code §§ 360, 590, 591.
 Private road or driveway, see Vehicle Code § 490.
 Right-of-way, see Vehicle Code § 525.
Housing projects, see Vehicle Code § 21111.
Traffic control, see Vehicle Code § 21360.
Traffic control by local authorities, see Vehicle Code § 21107.

§ 21805. Equestrian crossings

(a) The Department of Transportation, and local authorities with respect to highways under their jurisdiction, may designate any intersection of a highway as a bridle path or equestrian crossing by erecting appropriate signs.

The signs shall be erected on the highway at or near the approach to the intersection, and shall be of a type approved by the Department of Transportation. The signs shall indicate the crossing and any crossmarks, safety devices, or signals the authorities deem necessary to safeguard vehicular and equestrian traffic at the intersection.

(b) The driver of any vehicle shall yield the right-of-way to any horseback rider who is crossing the highway at any designated equestrian crossing which is marked by signs as prescribed in subdivision (a).

(c) Subdivision (b) does not relieve any horseback rider from the duty of using due care for his or her own safety. No horseback rider shall leave a curb or other place of safety and proceed suddenly into the path of a vehicle which is close enough to constitute an immediate hazard. *(Stats.1959, c. 3, p. 1686, § 21805. Amended by Stats.1973, c. 495, p. 970, § 1; Stats.1988, c. 623, § 6.)*

Cross References

Highway signs, markers or warning notices, failure to observe, see Vehicle Code §§ 21367, 40000.14.
Intersection defined, see Vehicle Code § 365.
Livestock crossings, signs, see Vehicle Code § 21364.
Livestock on highways, see Food and Agricultural Code § 16902.
Rights and duties of persons riding or driving animals, see Vehicle Code § 21050.
Traffic signs, signals and markings, generally, see Vehicle Code § 21350 et seq.

§ 21806. Authorized emergency vehicles

Upon the immediate approach of an authorized emergency vehicle which is sounding a siren and which has at least one lighted lamp exhibiting red light that is visible, under normal atmospheric conditions, from a distance of 1,000 feet to the front of the vehicle, the surrounding traffic shall, except as otherwise directed by a traffic officer, do the following:

(a)(1) Except as required under paragraph (2), the driver of every other vehicle shall yield the right-of-way and shall immediately drive to the right-hand edge or curb of the highway, clear of any intersection, and thereupon shall stop and remain stopped until the authorized emergency vehicle has passed.

(2) A person driving a vehicle in an exclusive or preferential use lane shall exit that lane immediately upon determining that the exit can be accomplished with reasonable safety.

(b) The operator of every street car shall immediately stop the street car, clear of any intersection, and remain stopped until the authorized emergency vehicle has passed.

(c) All pedestrians upon the highway shall proceed to the nearest curb or place of safety and remain there until the authorized emergency vehicle has passed. *(Stats. 1959, c. 3, p. 1687, § 21806. Amended by Stats.1978, c. 252, p. 533, § 2, eff. June 16, 1978; Stats.1988, c. 623, § 7; Stats.1996, c. 1154 (A.B.3020), § 68, eff. Sept. 30, 1996.)*

643

Cross References

Applicability of this section to trolley coaches, see Vehicle Code § 21051.

Authorized emergency vehicles, see Vehicle Code § 165.

Coroner vehicles, see Vehicle Code § 25264.

Exemptions of authorized emergency vehicles, see Vehicle Code §§ 21055, 21056.

Punishment for violation of section, see Vehicle Code § 42001.12.

Right-of-way, definition, see Vehicle Code § 525.

Sirens, use of on authorized emergency vehicles, see Vehicle Code § 27002.

Utility vehicles, see Vehicle Code §§ 25260, 25260.1.

§ 21807. Effect of exemption

The provisions of Section 21806 shall not operate to relieve the driver of an authorized emergency vehicle from the duty to drive with due regard for the safety of all persons and property. *(Added by Stats.1961, c. 653, p. 1861, § 28, operative Jan. 1, 1962.)*

§ 21809. Driving vehicle in lane immediately adjacent to stationary emergency vehicle, tow truck, or Department of Transportation vehicle; penalty; exceptions

(a) A person driving a vehicle on a freeway approaching a stationary authorized emergency vehicle that is displaying emergency lights, a stationary tow truck that is displaying flashing amber warning lights, or a stationary marked Department of Transportation vehicle that is displaying flashing amber warning lights, shall approach with due caution and, before passing in a lane immediately adjacent to the authorized emergency vehicle, tow truck, or Department of Transportation vehicle, absent other direction by a peace officer, proceed to do one of the following:

(1) Make a lane change into an available lane not immediately adjacent to the authorized emergency vehicle, tow truck, or Department of Transportation vehicle, with due regard for safety and traffic conditions, if practicable and not prohibited by law.

(2) If the maneuver described in paragraph (1) would be unsafe or impracticable, slow to a reasonable and prudent speed that is safe for existing weather, road, and vehicular or pedestrian traffic conditions.

(b) A violation of subdivision (a) is an infraction, punishable by a fine of not more than fifty dollars ($50).

(c) The requirements of subdivision (a) do not apply if the stationary authorized emergency vehicle that is displaying emergency lights, the stationary tow truck that is displaying flashing amber warning lights, or the stationary marked Department of Transportation vehicle that is displaying flashing amber warning lights is not adjacent to the freeway or is separated from the freeway by a protective physical barrier. *(Added by Stats.2006, c. 375 (S.B.1610), § 2. Amended by Stats.2009, c. 33 (S.B.159), § 1; Stats.2009, c. 175 (S.B.240), § 1.)*

Cross References

Infractions, see Penal Code § 16.

Operation of vehicle in unsafe manner within emergency incident zone, see Vehicle Code § 21706.5.

§ 21810. Repealed by Stats.2002, c. 937 (A.B.629), § 2, operative Jan. 1, 2004

CHAPTER 5. PEDESTRIANS' RIGHTS AND DUTIES

Section
21949.   Legislative findings and declarations; pedestrian travel and access.
21950.   Right-of-way at crosswalks.
21950.5. Removal of crosswalk; notice.
21951.   Vehicles stopped for pedestrians.
21952.   Right-of-way on sidewalk.
21953.   Tunnel or overhead crossing.
21954.   Pedestrians outside crosswalks.
21955.   Crossing between controlled intersections.
21956.   Pedestrian on roadway.
21957.   Hitchhiking.
21958.   Repealed.
21959.   Skiing or tobogganing.
21960.   Freeways and expressways.
21961.   Local regulation of pedestrians.
21962.   Pedestrian on bridge.
21963.   Visually handicapped pedestrian.
21964.   White canes.
21965.   Definitions.
21966.   Pedestrian in bicycle lane.
21967.   Skateboards on highways, sidewalks or roadways.
21968.   Motorized skateboards; propulsion restrictions on sidewalks, roadways, bikeways, etc.
21969.   Roller skating on highways, sidewalks or roadways; adoption of rules and regulations by ordinance.
21970.   Vehicle blocking crosswalk or sidewalk; one-way streets.
21971.   Specified violations of sections 21451, 21453, 21950 or 21952 causing bodily injury; punishment.

§ 21949. Legislative findings and declarations; pedestrian travel and access

(a) The Legislature hereby finds and declares that it is the policy of the State of California that safe and convenient pedestrian travel and access, whether by foot, wheelchair, walker, or stroller, be provided to the residents of the state.

(b) In accordance with the policy declared under subdivision (a), it is the intent of the Legislature that all levels of government in the state, particularly the Department of Transportation, work to provide convenient and safe passage for pedestrians on and across all streets and highways, increase levels of walking and pedestrian travel, and reduce pedestrian fatalities and injuries. *(Added by Stats.2000, c. 833 (A.B.2522), § 6.)*

§ 21950. Right-of-way at crosswalks

(a) The driver of a vehicle shall yield the right-of-way to a pedestrian crossing the roadway within any marked crosswalk or within any unmarked crosswalk at an intersection, except as otherwise provided in this chapter.

(b) This section does not relieve a pedestrian from the duty of using due care for his or her safety. No pedestrian may suddenly leave a curb or other place of safety and walk or run into the path of a vehicle that is so close as to constitute an immediate hazard. No pedestrian may unnecessarily stop or delay traffic while in a marked or unmarked crosswalk.

(c) The driver of a vehicle approaching a pedestrian within any marked or unmarked crosswalk shall exercise all due care and shall reduce the speed of the vehicle or take any other action relating to the operation of the vehicle as necessary to safeguard the safety of the pedestrian.

(d) Subdivision (b) does not relieve a driver of a vehicle from the duty of exercising due care for the safety of any pedestrian within any marked crosswalk or within any unmarked crosswalk at an intersection. *(Stats.1959, c. 3, p. 1687, § 21950. Amended by Stats.1965, c. 1265, p. 3140, § 1; Stats.1970, c. 1001, p. 1799, § 1; Stats.1982, c. 741, p. 2944, § 2; Stats.2000, c. 833 (A.B.2522), § 8.)*

Cross References

Applicability of this section to trolley coaches, see Vehicle Code § 21051.
Blind persons, right-of-way, see Vehicle Code § 21963 et seq.
Crossing at other than crosswalks, see Vehicle Code § 21954.
Crosswalks, establishment of, see Vehicle Code § 21106.
Definitions,
    Crosswalk, see Vehicle Code § 275.
    Driver, see Vehicle Code § 305.
    Intersection, see Vehicle Code § 365.
    Right-of-way, see Vehicle Code § 525.
    Roadway, see Vehicle Code § 530.
    Vehicle, see Vehicle Code § 670.
Emergency vehicles, right-of-way, see Vehicle Code § 21806.
Pedestrian at controlled intersections, see Vehicle Code § 21955.
Pedestrian right-of-way on sidewalk, see Vehicle Code § 21952.
Pedestrian traffic control, see Vehicle Code § 21456.1.
Pedestrian tunnel or overhead crossing, right-of-way, see Vehicle Code § 21953.
Rules of the road, exemption of authorized emergency vehicles, see Vehicle Code § 21055.
Violations, see Vehicle Code § 40000.1 et seq.

§ 21950.5. Removal of crosswalk; notice

(a) An existing marked crosswalk may not be removed unless notice and opportunity to be heard is provided to the public not less than 30 days prior to the scheduled date of removal. In addition to any other public notice requirements, the notice of proposed removal shall be posted at the crosswalk identified for removal.

(b) The notice required by subdivision (a) shall include, but is not limited to, notification to the public of both of the following:

(1) That the public may provide input relating to the scheduled removal.

(2) The form and method of providing the input authorized by paragraph (1). *(Added by Stats.2000, c. 833 (A.B.2522), § 9.)*

§ 21951. Vehicles stopped for pedestrians

Whenever any vehicle has stopped at a marked crosswalk or at any unmarked crosswalk at an intersection to permit a pedestrian to cross the roadway the driver of any other vehicle approaching from the rear shall not overtake and pass the stopped vehicle. *(Stats.1959, c. 3, p. 1687, § 21951.)*

Cross References

Applicability of this section to trolley coaches, see Vehicle Code § 21051.
Definitions,
    Crosswalk, see Vehicle Code § 275.
    Driver, see Vehicle Code § 305.
    Intersection, see Vehicle Code § 365.
    Right-of-way, see Vehicle Code § 525.
    Roadway, see Vehicle Code § 530.
    Vehicle, see Vehicle Code § 670.
Establishment of crosswalks, see Vehicle Code § 21106.
Violations, see Vehicle Code § 40000.1 et seq.

§ 21952. Right-of-way on sidewalk

The driver of any motor vehicle, prior to driving over or upon any sidewalk, shall yield the right-of-way to any pedestrian approaching thereon. *(Stats.1959, c. 3, p. 1687, § 21952.)*

Cross References

Sidewalk defined, see Vehicle Code § 555.

§ 21953. Tunnel or overhead crossing

Whenever any pedestrian crosses a roadway other than by means of a pedestrian tunnel or overhead pedestrian crossing, if a pedestrian tunnel or overhead crossing serves the place where the pedestrian is crossing the roadway, such pedestrian shall yield the right-of-way to all vehicles on the highway so near as to constitute an immediate hazard.

This section shall not be construed to mean that a marked crosswalk, with or without a signal device, cannot be installed where a pedestrian tunnel or overhead crossing exists. *(Stats.1959, c. 3, p. 1687, § 21953. Amended by Stats.1971, c. 1017, p. 1956, § 1, operative May 3, 1972; Stats.1972, c. 680, p. 1264, § 1.)*

§ 21954. Pedestrians outside crosswalks

(a) Every pedestrian upon a roadway at any point other than within a marked crosswalk or within an unmarked crosswalk at an intersection shall yield the right-of-way to all vehicles upon the roadway so near as to constitute an immediate hazard.

(b) The provisions of this section shall not relieve the driver of a vehicle from the duty to exercise due care for the safety of any pedestrian upon a roadway. *(Stats.1959, c. 3, p. 1687, § 21954. Amended by Stats.1961, c. 1308, p.*

3088, § 1; Stats.1971, c. 1015, p. 1955, § 1, operative May 3, 1972.)

Cross References

Definitions,
Crosswalk, see Vehicle Code § 275.
Intersection, see Vehicle Code § 365.
Roadway, see Vehicle Code § 530.
Local regulations prohibiting pedestrians from crossing at other than crosswalks, see Vehicle Code § 21961.
Right-of-way of pedestrians at crosswalk, see Vehicle Code § 21950.

§ 21955. Crossing between controlled intersections

Between adjacent intersections controlled by traffic control signal devices or by police officers, pedestrians shall not cross the roadway at any place except in a crosswalk. *(Stats.1959, c. 3, p. 1688, § 21955.)*

Cross References

Crosswalks defined, see Vehicle Code § 275.
Intersection defined, see Vehicle Code § 365.
Local regulation of pedestrians, see Vehicle Code § 21961.
Official traffic control devices, see Vehicle Code § 21350 et seq.
Official traffic signals, see Vehicle Code § 21450 et seq.
Pedestrians' right-of-way at crosswalks, see Vehicle Code § 21951.
Powers of local authorities on traffic regulations, see Vehicle Code § 21100 et seq.
Roadway defined, see Vehicle Code § 530.

§ 21956. Pedestrian on roadway

(a) No pedestrian may walk upon any roadway outside of a business or residence district otherwise than close to his or her left-hand edge of the roadway.

(b) A pedestrian may walk close to his or her right-hand edge of the roadway if a crosswalk or other means of safely crossing the roadway is not available or if existing traffic or other conditions would compromise the safety of a pedestrian attempting to cross the road. *(Stats.1959, c. 3, p. 1688, § 21956. Amended by Stats. 2000, c. 833 (A.B.2522), § 10.)*

Cross References

Business district defined, see Vehicle Code § 235.
Limitations in determining business and residence districts, see Vehicle Code § 240.
Residence district defined, see Vehicle Code § 515.

§ 21957. Hitchhiking

No person shall stand in a roadway for the purpose of soliciting a ride from the driver of any vehicle. *(Stats. 1959, c. 3, p. 1688, § 21957.)*

Cross References

Roadway defined, see Vehicle Code § 530.

§ 21958. Repealed by Stats.1969, c. 207, p. 490, § 1

§ 21959. Skiing or tobogganing

It is unlawful for any person to ski or toboggan on or across any roadway in such a manner as to interfere with the movement of vehicles thereon. A person on skis proceeding on or across a highway at a pace no greater than a walk is not within the prohibition of this section and shall be considered to be a pedestrian with all the rights and duties thereof as prescribed in this code. *(Stats.1959, c. 3, p. 1688, § 21959. Amended by Stats. 1972, c. 46, p. 64, § 3.)*

§ 21960. Freeways and expressways

(a) The Department of Transportation and local authorities, by order, ordinance, or resolution, with respect to freeways, expressways, or designated portions thereof under their respective jurisdictions, to which vehicle access is completely or partially controlled, may prohibit or restrict the use of the freeways, expressways, or any portion thereof by pedestrians, bicycles or other nonmotorized traffic or by any person operating a motor-driven cycle, motorized bicycle, or motorized scooter. A prohibition or restriction pertaining to bicycles, motor-driven cycles, or motorized scooters shall be deemed to include motorized bicycles; and no person may operate a motorized bicycle wherever that prohibition or restriction is in force. Notwithstanding any provisions of any order, ordinance, or resolution to the contrary, the driver or passengers of a disabled vehicle stopped on a freeway or expressway may walk to the nearest exit, in either direction, on that side of the freeway or expressway upon which the vehicle is disabled, from which telephone or motor vehicle repair services are available.

(b) The prohibitory regulation authorized by subdivision (a) shall be effective when appropriate signs giving notice thereof are erected upon any freeway or expressway and the approaches thereto. If any portion of a county freeway or expressway is contained within the limits of a city within the county, the county may erect signs on that portion as required under this subdivision if the ordinance has been approved by the city pursuant to subdivision (b) of Section 1730 of the Streets and Highways Code.

(c) No ordinance or resolution of local authorities shall apply to any state highway until the proposed ordinance or resolution has been presented to, and approved in writing by, the Department of Transportation.

(d) An ordinance or resolution adopted under this section on or after January 1, 2005, to prohibit pedestrian access to a county freeway or expressway shall not be effective unless it is supported by a finding by the local authority that the freeway or expressway does not have pedestrian facilities and pedestrian use would pose a safety risk to the pedestrian. *(Stats.1959, c. 3, p. 1688, § 21960. Amended by Stats.1972, c. 498, p. 869, § 1; Stats.1974, c. 545, p. 1321, § 192; Stats.1975, c. 987, p. 2331, § 7.5; Stats.1999, c. 722 (S.B.441), § 6; Stats.2004, c. 615 (S.B.1233), § 28.)*

Cross References

Definition, see Vehicle Code § 332.

Exemption of emergency vehicles from rules of the road, exceptions, see Vehicle Code § 21055.
Local authorities defined, see Vehicle Code § 385.
Motor-driven cycle defined, see Vehicle Code § 405.
Motorized bicycle, see Vehicle Code § 406.
Powers of local authorities, see Vehicle Code § 21100 et seq.
Traffic signs, generally, see Vehicle Code § 21350 et seq.

§ 21961. Local regulation of pedestrians

This chapter does not prevent local authorities from adopting ordinances prohibiting pedestrians from crossing roadways at other than crosswalks. *(Stats.1959, c. 3, p. 1688, § 21961.)*

Cross References

Definitions,
  Crosswalk, see Vehicle Code § 275.
  Intersection, see Vehicle Code § 365.
  Local authorities, see Vehicle Code § 385.
  Roadway, see Vehicle Code § 530.
Establishment of crosswalks by local authorities, see Vehicle Code § 21106.
Exemption of emergency vehicles from rules of the road, exemptions, see Vehicle Code § 21055.
Local regulation of traffic, see Vehicle Code § 21100 et seq.
Pedestrian Mall Law of 1960, see Streets and Highways Code § 11000 et seq.
Pedestrians' right-of-way in crosswalks, see Vehicle Code § 21950.

§ 21962. Pedestrian on bridge

Any peace officer having reasonable cause to believe that any pedestrian is stopped or standing on any bridge or overpass for the purpose of violating Section 23110, may lawfully order such person from the bridge or overpass. *(Added by Stats.1965, c. 1673, p. 3794, § 1.)*

§ 21963. Visually handicapped pedestrian

A totally or partially blind pedestrian who is carrying a predominantly white cane (with or without a red tip), or using a guide dog, shall have the right-of-way, and the driver of any vehicle approaching this pedestrian, who fails to yield the right-of-way, or to take all reasonably necessary precautions to avoid injury to this blind pedestrian, is guilty of a misdemeanor, punishable by imprisonment in the county jail not exceeding six months, or by a fine of not less than five hundred dollars ($500) nor more than one thousand dollars ($1,000), or both. This section shall not preclude prosecution under any other applicable provision of law. *(Added by Stats.1968, c. 461, p. 1094, § 7. Amended by Stats.1993, c. 1149 (A.B.1419), § 7.)*

§ 21964. White canes

No person, other than those totally or partially blind, shall carry or use on any highway or in any public building, public facility, or other public place, a predominantly white cane (with or without a red tip). *(Added by Stats.1968, c. 461, p. 1094, § 8.)*

§ 21965. Definitions

As used in Sections 21963 and 21964, "blind," "totally blind," and "partially blind," mean having central visual acuity not to exceed $^{20}/_{200}$ in the better eye, with corrected lenses, as measured by the Snellen test, or visual acuity greater than $^{20}/_{200}$, but with a limitation in the field of vision such that the widest diameter of the visual field subtends an angle not greater than 20 degrees. *(Added by Stats.1968, c. 461, p. 1094, § 9.)*

§ 21966. Pedestrian in bicycle lane

No pedestrian shall proceed along a bicycle path or lane where there is an adjacent adequate pedestrian facility. *(Added by Stats.1976, c. 751, p. 1785, § 14.)*

Cross References

Electric personal assistive mobility devices, use by a pedestrian, authority to impose time, place or manner ordinances, see Vehicle Code § 21282.

§ 21967. Skateboards on highways, sidewalks or roadways

Except as provided in Section 21968, a local authority may adopt rules and regulations by ordinance or resolution prohibiting or restricting persons from riding or propelling skateboards on highways, sidewalks, or roadways. *(Formerly § 21114.6, added by Stats.1976, c. 1359, p. 6202, § 1. Renumbered § 21967 and amended by Stats.1977, c. 275, p. 1169, § 1, eff. July 8, 1977. Amended by Stats.1978, c. 380, p. 1203, § 144; Stats.1987, c. 1184, § 35.)*

§ 21968. Motorized skateboards; propulsion restrictions on sidewalks, roadways, bikeways, etc.

No motorized skateboard may be propelled on any sidewalk, roadway, or any other part of a highway or on any bikeway, bicycle path or trail, equestrian trail, or hiking or recreational trail. *(Added by Stats.1977, c. 275, p. 1169, § 2, eff. July 8, 1977.)*

§ 21969. Roller skating on highways, sidewalks or roadways; adoption of rules and regulations by ordinance

A local authority may adopt rules and regulations by ordinance regulating persons engaged in roller skating on a highway, sidewalk, or roadway. *(Added by Stats.1981, c. 145, p. 944, § 1.)*

§ 21970. Vehicle blocking crosswalk or sidewalk; one-way streets

(a) No person may stop a vehicle unnecessarily in a manner that causes the vehicle to block a marked or unmarked crosswalk or sidewalk.

(b) Subdivision (a) does not preclude the driver of a vehicle facing a steady circular red light from turning right or turning left from a one-way street onto a one-way street pursuant to subdivision (b) of Section 21453. *(Added by Stats.2000, c. 833 (A.B.2522), § 11.)*

§ 21971. Specified violations of sections 21451, 21453, 21950 or 21952 causing bodily injury; punishment

Notwithstanding any other provision of law, any person who violates subdivision (a) or (b) of Section 21451, subdivision (b) of Section 21453, subdivision (a) of Section 21950, or Section 21952, and causes the bodily injury of anyone other than the driver is guilty of an infraction punishable under Section 42001.18. *(Added by Stats.2000, c. 833 (A.B.2522), § 12.)*

CHAPTER 6. TURNING AND STOPPING AND TURNING SIGNALS

Section
22100.   Turning upon a highway.
22100.5.   U-turn at intersection controlled by traffic signals or devices.
22101.   Regulation of turns at intersection.
22102.   U-turn in business district.
22103.   U-turn in residence district.
22104.   U-turns near fire stations.
22105.   Unobstructed view necessary for U-turn.
22106.   Starting parked vehicles or backing.
22107.   Turning movements and required signals.
22108.   Duration of signal.
22109.   Signal when stopping.
22110.   Method of signaling.
22111.   Hand signals.
22112.   Operation of amber warning light system, flashing red signal lights and stop signal arm system; stopping to load or unload pupils.
22113.   Local authorities.

Cross References

Penalties, public offenses, fines in misdemeanor cases for violation pertaining to passing a school building or grounds, see Vehicle Code § 42011.

§ 22100. Turning upon a highway

Except as provided in Section 22100.5 or 22101, the driver of any vehicle intending to turn upon a highway shall do so as follows:

(a) Right Turns. Both the approach for a right-hand turn and a right-hand turn shall be made as close as practicable to the right-hand curb or edge of the roadway except:

(1) Upon a highway having three marked lanes for traffic moving in one direction that terminates at an intersecting highway accommodating traffic in both directions, the driver of a vehicle in the middle lane may turn right into any lane lawfully available to traffic moving in that direction upon the roadway being entered.

(2) If a right-hand turn is made from a one-way highway at an intersection, a driver shall approach the turn as provided in this subdivision and shall complete the turn in any lane lawfully available to traffic moving in that direction upon the roadway being entered.

(3) Upon a highway having an additional lane or lanes marked for a right turn by appropriate signs or markings,

the driver of a vehicle may turn right from any lane designated and marked for that turning movement.

(b) Left Turns. The approach for a left turn shall be made as close as practicable to the left-hand edge of the extreme left-hand lane or portion of the roadway lawfully available to traffic moving in the direction of travel of the vehicle and, when turning at an intersection, the left turn shall not be made before entering the intersection. After entering the intersection, the left turn shall be made so as to leave the intersection in a lane lawfully available to traffic moving in that direction upon the roadway being entered, except that upon a highway having three marked lanes for traffic moving in one direction that terminates at an intersecting highway accommodating traffic in both directions, the driver of a vehicle in the middle lane may turn left into any lane lawfully available to traffic moving in that direction upon the roadway being entered. *(Added by Stats.1971, c. 286, p. 592, § 2, operative May 3, 1972. Amended by Stats.1972, c. 1060, p. 1970, § 1; Stats.1982, c. 741, p. 2944, § 3; Stats.2004, c. 183 (A.B.3082), § 353.)*

Cross References

Division of highways of state department of public works, see Streets and Highways Code §§ 50, 70 et seq.
Duration of signal, see Vehicle Code § 22108.
Highway signs, markers or warning notices, failure to observe, see Vehicle Code §§ 21367, 40000.14.
Intersection defined, see Vehicle Code § 365.
Means and method of giving signal, see Vehicle Code §§ 22110, 22111.
Regulations, state highways, see Vehicle Code § 21352.
Right-of-way, see Vehicle Code § 21800 et seq.
Rules of the road, exemption of authorized emergency vehicles, see Vehicle Code § 21055.
Signs reducing speed limits in exercise of authority to link districts, see Vehicle Code § 22360.
Streetcars, see Vehicle Code § 21455.
Traffic signs, signals and markings, see Vehicle Code § 21350 et seq.

§ 22100.5. U-turn at intersection controlled by traffic signals or devices

No driver shall make a U-turn at an intersection controlled by official traffic signals except as provided in Section 21451, and then only from the far lefthand lane that is lawfully available to traffic moving in the direction of travel from which the turn is commenced. No driver shall make a U-turn at an intersection controlled by official traffic control devices except from the far lefthand lane that is lawfully available to traffic moving in the direction of travel from which the turn is commenced. *(Added by Stats.1981, c. 413, p. 1611, § 11. Amended by Stats.1984, c. 700, § 2.)*

§ 22101. Regulation of turns at intersection

(a) The Department of Transportation or local authorities in respect to highways under their respective jurisdictions, may cause official traffic control devices to be placed or erected within or adjacent to intersections to regulate or prohibit turning movements at such intersections.

(b) When turning movements are required at an intersection notice of such requirement shall be given by erection of a sign, unless an additional clearly marked traffic lane is provided for the approach to the turning movement, in which event notice as applicable to such additional traffic lane shall be given by any official traffic control device.

(c) When right- or left-hand turns are prohibited at an intersection notice of such prohibition shall be given by erection of a sign.

(d) When official traffic control devices are placed as required in subdivisions (b) or (c), it shall be unlawful for any driver of a vehicle to disobey the directions of such official traffic control devices. *(Stats.1959, c. 3, p. 1689, § 22101. Amended by Stats.1963, c. 481, p. 1339, § 1; Stats.1974, c. 545, p. 1321, § 193.)*

Cross References

Intersection defined, see Vehicle Code § 365.
Local authorities, regulation,
    Determination of speed limit in linking districts on local highways, see Vehicle Code § 22360.
    Pedestrians crossing roadways, see Vehicle Code § 21961.
    Traffic control devices, see Vehicle Code § 21100 et seq.
    Turning movements at intersections, see Vehicle Code § 22113.
Notice to appear, violation recorded by automated enforcement system, see Vehicle Code § 40518.
Street name signs, see Vehicle Code § 21366.
Traffic signs, signals and markings, see Vehicle Code § 21350 et seq.

§ 22102. U-turn in business district

No person in a business district shall make a U-turn, except at an intersection, or on a divided highway where an opening has been provided in accordance with Section 21651. This turning movement shall be made as close as practicable to the extreme left-hand edge of the lanes moving in the driver's direction of travel immediately prior to the initiation of the turning movement, when more than one lane in the direction of travel is present. *(Stats.1959, c. 3, p. 1689, § 22102. Amended by Stats. 1961, c. 1312, p. 3091, § 1; Stats.1970, c. 620, p. 1231, § 2; Stats.1985, c. 47, § 1.)*

Cross References

Definitions,
    Business district, see Vehicle Code § 235.
    Intersection, see Vehicle Code § 365.
    Residence district, see Vehicle Code § 515.
Turning near fire stations or on curve or crest of grade prohibited, see Vehicle Code §§ 22104, 22105.

§ 22103. U-turn in residence district

No person in a residence district shall make a U-turn when any other vehicle is approaching from either direction within 200 feet, except at an intersection when the approaching vehicle is controlled by an official traffic control device. *(Stats.1959, c. 3, p. 1689, § 22103. Amended by Stats.1963, c. 255, p. 1016, § 1; Stats.1970, c. 620, p. 1231, § 3.)*

Cross References

Intersection defined, see Vehicle Code § 365.
Residence district defined, see Vehicle Code § 515.

§ 22104. U-turns near fire stations

No person shall make a U-turn in front of the driveway entrance or approaches to a fire station. No person shall use the driveway entrance or approaches to a fire station for the purpose of turning a vehicle so as to proceed in the opposite direction. *(Stats.1959, c. 3, p. 1689, § 22104. Amended by Stats.1970, c. 620, p. 1231, § 4.)*

§ 22105. Unobstructed view necessary for U-turn

No person shall make a U-turn upon any highway where the driver of such vehicle does not have an unobstructed view for 200 feet in both directions along the highway and of any traffic thereon. *(Stats.1959, c. 3, p. 1689, § 22105. Amended by Stats.1970, c. 620, p. 1231, § 5; Stats.1972, c. 64, p. 84, § 1.)*

§ 22106. Starting parked vehicles or backing

No person shall start a vehicle stopped, standing, or parked on a highway, nor shall any person back a vehicle on a highway until such movement can be made with reasonable safety. *(Stats.1959, c. 3, p. 1689, § 22106.)*

Cross References

Applicability of this section to trolley coaches, see Vehicle Code § 21051.
Parking regulations, see Vehicle Code § 22500 et seq.

§ 22107. Turning movements and required signals

No person shall turn a vehicle from a direct course or move right or left upon a roadway until such movement can be made with reasonable safety and then only after the giving of an appropriate signal in the manner provided in this chapter in the event any other vehicle may be affected by the movement. *(Stats.1959, c. 3, p. 1689, § 22107. Amended by Stats.1959, c. 1996, p. 4630, § 27.)*

Cross References

Applicability of this section to trolley coaches, see Vehicle Code § 21051.
Manner and method of giving signal, see Vehicle Code §§ 22110, 22111.
Position and method of turning at intersection, see Vehicle Code §§ 22100, 22101.
Restrictions on turning of vehicles, see Vehicle Code § 22102 et seq.

§ 22108. Duration of signal

Any signal of intention to turn right or left shall be given continuously during the last 100 feet traveled by the vehicle before turning. *(Stats.1959, c. 3, p. 1689, § 22108.)*

Applicability of this section to trolley coaches, see Vehicle Code § 21051.

§ 22109. Signal when stopping

No person shall stop or suddenly decrease the speed of a vehicle on a highway without first giving an appropriate signal in the manner provided in this chapter to the driver of any vehicle immediately to the rear when there is opportunity to give the signal. *(Stats.1959, c. 3, p. 1689, § 22109.)*

Cross References

Applicability of this section to trolley coaches, see Vehicle Code § 21051.

§ 22110. Method of signaling

(a) The signals required by this chapter shall be given by signal lamp, unless a vehicle is not required to be and is not equipped with turn signals. Drivers of vehicles not required to be and not equipped with turn signals shall give a hand and arm signal when required by this chapter.

(b) In the event the signal lamps become inoperable while driving, hand and arm signals shall be used in the manner required in this chapter. *(Stats.1959, c. 3, p. 1690, § 22110. Amended by Stats.1961, c. 118, p. 1128, § 1; Stats.1965, c. 1012, p. 2643, § 1; Stats.1967, c. 859, p. 2300, § 1; Stats.1999, c. 1008 (S.B.533), § 12.)*

Cross References

Approval of signal device, see Vehicle Code § 26100 et seq.
Unauthorized signals, see Vehicle Code § 21465.

§ 22111. Hand signals

All required signals given by hand and arm shall be given from the left side of a vehicle in the following manner:

(a) Left turn—hand and arm extended horizontally beyond the side of the vehicle.

(b) Right turn—hand and arm extended upward beyond the side of the vehicle, except that a bicyclist may extend the right hand and arm horizontally to the right side of the bicycle.

(c) Stop or sudden decrease of speed signal—hand and arm extended downward beyond the side of the vehicle. *(Stats.1959, c. 3, p. 1690, § 22111. Amended by Stats. 1963, c. 153, p. 821, § 1; Stats.1976, c. 751, p. 1785, § 15.)*

Cross References

Means of giving signal, see Vehicle Code § 22110.

§ 22112. Operation of amber warning light system, flashing red signal lights and stop signal arm system; stopping to load or unload pupils

(a) On approach to a schoolbus stop where pupils are loading or unloading from a schoolbus, the schoolbus driver shall activate an approved amber warning light system, if the schoolbus is so equipped, beginning 200 feet before the schoolbus stop. The schoolbus driver shall

650

deactivate the amber warning light system after reaching the schoolbus stop. The schoolbus driver shall operate the flashing red light signal system and stop signal arm, as required on the schoolbus, at all times when the schoolbus is stopped for the purpose of loading or unloading pupils. The flashing red light signal system, amber warning lights system, and stop signal arm shall not be operated at any place where traffic is controlled by a traffic officer or at any location identified in subdivision (e) of this section. The schoolbus flashing red light signal system, amber warning lights system, and stop signal arm shall not be operated at any other time.

(b) The schoolbus driver shall stop to load or unload pupils only at a schoolbus stop designated for pupils by the school district superintendent or the head or principal of a private school, or authorized by any of those individuals for school activity trips.

(c) When a schoolbus is stopped on a highway or private road for the purpose of loading or unloading pupils, at a location where traffic is not controlled by a traffic officer, the driver shall, before opening the door, ensure that the flashing red light signal system and stop signal arm are activated, and that it is safe to enter or exit the schoolbus.

(d) When a schoolbus is stopped on a highway or private road for the purpose of loading or unloading pupils, at a location where traffic is not controlled by a traffic officer or official traffic control signal, the schoolbus driver shall do all of the following:

(1) Escort all pupils in prekindergarten, kindergarten, or any of grades 1 to 8, inclusive, who need to cross the highway or private road upon which the schoolbus is stopped. The driver shall use an approved hand-held "STOP" sign while escorting all pupils.

(2) Require all pupils who need to cross the highway or private road upon which the schoolbus is stopped to walk in front of the bus as they cross.

(3) Ensure that all pupils who need to cross the highway or private road upon which the schoolbus is stopped have crossed safely, and that all other pupils and pedestrians are a safe distance from the schoolbus before setting the schoolbus in motion.

(e) Except at a location where pupils are loading or unloading from a schoolbus and must cross a highway or private road upon which the schoolbus is stopped, the schoolbus driver may not activate the amber warning light system, the flashing red light signal system and stop signal arm at any of the following locations:

(1) Schoolbus loading zones on or adjacent to school grounds or during an activity trip, if the schoolbus is lawfully stopped or parked.

(2) Where the schoolbus is disabled due to mechanical breakdown. The driver of a relief bus that arrives at the scene to transport pupils from the disabled schoolbus shall not activate the amber warning light system, the flashing red light system, and stop signal arm.

(3) Where a pupil requires physical assistance from the driver or authorized attendant to board or leave the schoolbus and providing the assistance extends the length of time the schoolbus is stopped beyond the time required to load or unload a pupil that does not require physical assistance.

(4) Where the roadway surface on which the bus is stopped is partially or completely covered by snow or ice and requiring traffic to stop would pose a safety hazard as determined by the schoolbus motor carrier.

(5) On a state highway with a posted speed limit of 55 miles per hour or higher where the schoolbus is completely off the main traveled portion of the highway.

(6) Any location determined by a school district or a private school, with the approval of the Department of the California Highway Patrol, to present a traffic or safety hazard.

(f) Notwithstanding subdivisions (a) to (d), inclusive, the Department of the California Highway Patrol may require the activation of an approved flashing amber warning light system, if the schoolbus is so equipped, or the flashing red light signal system and stop signal arm, as required on the schoolbus, at any location where the department determines that the activation is necessary for the safety of school pupils loading or unloading from a schoolbus. *(Stats.1959, c. 3, p. 1690, § 22112. Amended by Stats.1977, c. 553, p. 1778, § 1; Stats.1981, c. 813, p. 3156, § 13; Stats.1992, c. 624 (A.B.3144), § 4, eff. Sept. 14, 1992; Stats.1994, c. 831 (S.B.2019), § 2, eff. Sept. 27, 1994; Stats.1997, c. 739 (A.B.1297), § 3; Stats.1999, c. 647 (A.B.1573), § 2, eff. Oct. 10, 1999; Stats.2002, c. 397 (S.B.1685), § 1; Stats.2012, c. 769 (A.B.2679), § 35.)*

Cross References

Crossing control arm, use of control arm by operator of a schoolbus, responsibility for safety of students, see Vehicle Code § 35400.
Display of signs, see Vehicle Code § 27906.
Duties of drivers, see Vehicle Code § 22454.
Schoolbus defined, see Vehicle Code § 545.
Signal equipment, see Vehicle Code § 25257.

§ 22113. Local authorities

This chapter does not prevent local authorities, by ordinance, from prohibiting the making of any turning movement by any vehicle at any intersection or between any designated intersections. *(Stats.1959, c. 3, p. 1690, § 22113.)*

Cross References

Adoption of rules and regulations, see Vehicle Code § 21100 et seq.
Definitions,
  Intersection, see Vehicle Code § 365.
  Local authorities, see Vehicle Code § 385.
  Vehicle, see Vehicle Code § 670.
Exemption of emergency vehicles from rules of the road, exceptions, see Vehicle Code § 21055.

Traffic regulation, see Vehicle Code § 21100 et seq.

CHAPTER 7. SPEED LAWS

Article	Section
1. Generally	22348
2. Other Speed Laws	22400

Cross References

Penalties, public offenses, fines in misdemeanor cases for violation pertaining to passing a school building or grounds, see Vehicle Code § 42011.

ARTICLE 1. GENERALLY

Section
22348. Exceeding the speed limit on highways; punishment for driving at a speed greater than 100 miles per hour; driving in designated lanes.
22349. Maximum speed limit.
22349.5. Repealed.
22350. Basic speed law.
22351. Speed law violations.
22352. Prima facie speed limits.
22352.1. Repealed.
22353. Equestrian safety; factors in engineering and traffic surveys.
22354. Decrease of state highway limits.
22354.5. Increase or decrease of state highway limits.
22355. Variable speed limits.
22356. Increase of highway speed limit.
22357. Increase of local limits.
22357.1. Park playground; adjacent streets; 25 m.p.h. prima facie limit.
22358. Decrease of local limits.
22358.3. Decrease on narrow street.
22358.4. Decrease of local limits near schools.
22358.5. Downward speed zoning.
22359. Boundary line streets.
22360. Decrease of limit; portion of highway between districts.
22361. Multiple-lane highways.
22362. Speed limit where persons at work.
22363. Restrictions because of snow or ice conditions.
22364. Lane speed limits.
22365. South Coast Air Quality Management District; unpaved roads; ordinances to establish speed limits lower than limits otherwise permitted by code.
22366. Highway speed limit of 65 miles per hour; date when state not subject to reduction in federal aid; notice.

Cross References

Highway defined, see Vehicle Code §§ 360, 590, 591.
Number of convictions for prima facie presumption as negligent operator, see Vehicle Code § 12810.
Penalties, see Vehicle Code §§ 40000.1, 42001.
Presumptions as to correctness of official signs and traffic control devices, see Vehicle Code §§ 41100, 41101.
Speed trap defined and prohibited, see Vehicle Code § 40801 et seq.

Suspension of license for speeding, see Vehicle Code § 13200.

§ 22348. Exceeding the speed limit on highways; punishment for driving at a speed greater than 100 miles per hour; driving in designated lanes

(a) Notwithstanding subdivision (b) of Section 22351, a person shall not drive a vehicle upon a highway with a speed limit established pursuant to Section 22349 or 22356 at a speed greater than that speed limit.

(b) A person who drives a vehicle upon a highway at a speed greater than 100 miles per hour is guilty of an infraction punishable, as follows:

(1) Upon a first conviction of a violation of this subdivision, by a fine of not to exceed five hundred dollars ($500). The court may also suspend the privilege of the person to operate a motor vehicle for a period not to exceed 30 days pursuant to Section 13200.5.

(2) Upon a conviction under this subdivision of an offense that occurred within three years of a prior offense resulting in a conviction of an offense under this subdivision, by a fine of not to exceed seven hundred fifty dollars ($750). The person's privilege to operate a motor vehicle shall be suspended by the Department of Motor Vehicles pursuant to subdivision (a) of Section 13355.

(3) Upon a conviction under this subdivision of an offense that occurred within five years of two or more prior offenses resulting in convictions of offenses under this subdivision, by a fine of not to exceed one thousand dollars ($1,000). The person's privilege to operate a motor vehicle shall be suspended by the Department of Motor Vehicles pursuant to subdivision (b) of Section 13355.

(c) A vehicle subject to Section 22406 shall be driven in a lane designated pursuant to Section 21655, or if a lane has not been so designated, in the right-hand lane for traffic or as close as practicable to the right-hand edge or curb. When overtaking and passing another vehicle proceeding in the same direction, the driver shall use either the designated lane, the lane to the immediate left of the right-hand lane, or the right-hand lane for traffic as permitted under this code. If, however, specific lane or lanes have not been designated on a divided highway having four or more clearly marked lanes for traffic in one direction, a vehicle may also be driven in the lane to the immediate left of the right- hand lane, unless otherwise prohibited under this code. This subdivision does not apply to a driver who is preparing for a left- or right-hand turn or who is in the process of entering into or exiting from a highway or to a driver who is required necessarily to drive in a lane other than the right- hand lane to continue on his or her intended route. *(Added by Stats.1973, c. 1218, p. 2935, § 1, eff. Dec. 12, 1973, operative Jan. 1, 1974. Amended by Stats.1975, c. 153, p. 285, § 1, eff. June 28, 1975; Stats.1978, c. 217, p. 466, § 1, eff. June 8, 1978; Stats.1983, c. 980, § 3; Stats.1984, c. 276, § 3; Stats.1987, c. 25, § 1, eff. May 28, 1987; Stats.1987, c. 72, § 2, eff. June 30, 1987; Stats.2004, c. 300 (A.B.2237), § 1.)*

652

Cross References
Fine for violation of this section, see Vehicle Code § 42000.1.
Suspension of privilege to operate motor vehicle, violation of this section, see Vehicle Code §§ 13200.5, 13355.
Traffic violation point count, violation of this section, see Vehicle Code § 12810.

§ 22349.   Maximum speed limit

(a) Except as provided in Section 22356, no person may drive a vehicle upon a highway at a speed greater than 65 miles per hour.

(b) Notwithstanding any other provision of law, no person may drive a vehicle upon a two-lane, undivided highway at a speed greater than 55 miles per hour unless that highway, or portion thereof, has been posted for a higher speed by the Department of Transportation or appropriate local agency upon the basis of an engineering and traffic survey. For purposes of this subdivision, the following apply:

(1) A two-lane, undivided highway is a highway with not more than one through lane of travel in each direction.

(2) Passing lanes may not be considered when determining the number of through lanes.

(c) It is the intent of the Legislature that there be reasonable signing on affected two-lane, undivided highways described in subdivision (b) in continuing the 55 miles-per-hour speed limit, including placing signs at county boundaries to the extent possible, and at other appropriate locations. *(Added by Stats.1995, c. 766 (S.B.726), § 23. Amended by Stats.1996, c. 20 (S.B.848), § 1, eff. March 29, 1996; Stats.1999, c. 724 (A.B.1650), § 41.)*

§ 22349.5.   Repealed by Stats.1996, c. 20 (S.B.848), § 2, eff. March 29, 1996, operative Jan. 1, 1997

§ 22350.   Basic speed law

No person shall drive a vehicle upon a highway at a speed greater than is reasonable or prudent having due regard for weather, visibility, the traffic on, and the surface and width of, the highway, and in no event at a speed which endangers the safety of persons or property. *(Stats.1959, c. 3, p. 1690, § 22350. Amended by Stats. 1963, c. 252, p. 1014, § 1.)*

Validity

This statute was held preempted by the Commercial Motor Vehicle Safety Act with respect to speed limits for commercial vehicles, in the decision of Weaver v. Chavez (App. 2 Dist. 2005) 35 Cal.Rptr.3d 514, 133 Cal.App.4th 1350, rehearing denied, review denied.

Cross References
Applicability of this section to trolley coaches, see Vehicle Code § 21051.
Buses, motor trucks or truck tractors, fine for violation of this section, see Vehicle Code § 42000.5.

Highway defined, see Vehicle Code § 590.
Other speed laws, see Vehicle Code § 22400 et seq.
Passing animals, see Vehicle Code § 21759.
Passing on grades, see Vehicle Code § 21758.
Passing streetcar or bus, see Vehicle Code § 21756.
Physicians and surgeons, vehicles, see Vehicle Code § 21058.
Police escorts, see Vehicle Code § 21057.
Reckless driving defined, see Vehicle Code §§ 23103, 23104.
Rules of the road, exemption of authorized emergency vehicles, see Vehicle Code § 21055.
Signs restricting speed, see Vehicle Code §§ 21357, 21359.
Speed contests, see Vehicle Code § 23109.
Speeding, suspension or revocation of license by court, see Vehicle Code § 13200.

§ 22351. Speed law violations

(a) The speed of any vehicle upon a highway not in excess of the limits specified in Section 22352 or established as authorized in this code is lawful unless clearly proved to be in violation of the basic speed law.

(b) The speed of any vehicle upon a highway in excess of the prima facie speed limits in Section 22352 or established as authorized in this code is prima facie unlawful unless the defendant establishes by competent evidence that the speed in excess of said limits did not constitute a violation of the basic speed law at the time, place and under the conditions then existing. *(Stats.1959, c. 3, p. 1690, § 22351.)*

Cross References

Applicability of this section to trolley coaches, see Vehicle Code § 21051.
Definitions,
  Business district, see Vehicle Code § 235.
  Residence district, see Vehicle Code § 515.
Emergency call of physician, exemption from this section, see Vehicle Code § 21058.
Other speed laws, see Vehicle Code § 22400 et seq.
Presumption as to correctness of speed restriction signs, see Vehicle Code § 41100.
Prima facie speed limit,
  Authority to alter, see Vehicle Code § 22354 et seq.
  Necessity of alleging in notice, complaint, or information charging violation of speed laws, see Vehicle Code § 40503.
Proof of speed in excess of prima facie limit as not constituting negligence as matter of law, see Vehicle Code § 40831.

§ 22352. Prima facie speed limits

* * * The prima facie limits are as follows and shall be applicable unless changed as authorized in this code and, if so changed, only when signs have been erected giving notice thereof:

(a) Fifteen miles per hour:

(1) When traversing a railway grade crossing, if during the last 100 feet of the approach to the crossing the driver does not have a clear and unobstructed view of the crossing and of any traffic on the railway for a distance of 400 feet in both directions along the railway. This subdivision does not apply in the case of any railway grade crossing where a human flagman is on duty or a clearly visible electrical or mechanical railway crossing signal device is installed but does not then indicate the immediate approach of a railway train or car.

(2) When traversing any intersection of highways if during the last 100 feet of the driver's approach to the intersection the driver does not have a clear and unobstructed view of the intersection and of any traffic upon all of the highways entering the intersection for a distance of 100 feet along all those highways, except at an intersection protected by stop signs or yield right-of-way signs or controlled by official traffic control signals.

(3) On any alley.

(b) Twenty-five miles per hour:

(1) On any highway other than a state highway, in any business or residence district unless a different speed is determined by local authority under procedures set forth in this code.

(2) When approaching or passing a school building or the grounds thereof, contiguous to a highway and posted with a standard "SCHOOL" warning sign, while children are going to or leaving the school either during school hours or during the noon recess period. The prima facie limit shall also apply when approaching or passing any school grounds which are not separated from the highway by a fence, gate, or other physical barrier while the grounds are in use by children and the highway is posted with a standard "SCHOOL" warning sign. For purposes of this subparagraph, standard "SCHOOL" warning signs may be placed at any distance up to 500 feet away from school grounds.

(3) When passing a senior center or other facility primarily used by senior citizens, contiguous to a street other than a state highway and posted with a standard "SENIOR" warning sign. A local authority * * * may erect a sign pursuant to this paragraph * * * when the local agency makes a determination that the proposed signing should be implemented. A local authority may * * * request grant funding from the Pedestrian Safety Account pursuant to Section 894.7 of the Streets and Highways Code, or any other grant funding available to it, and use that grant funding to pay for the erection of those signs, or may utilize any other funds available to it to pay for the erection of those signs, including, but not limited to, donations from private sources.

* * * *(Added by Stats.1997, c. 421 (A.B.1209), § 2, operative March 1, 2001. Amended by Stats.2000, c. 521 (A.B.280), § 2, operative March 1, 2001; Stats.2013, c. 240 (A.B.707), § 1.)*

Cross References

Applicability of this section to trolley coaches, see Vehicle Code § 21051.
Definitions,
  Business district, see Vehicle Code § 235.
  Residence district, see Vehicle Code § 515.
Emergency call of physician, exemption from this section, see Vehicle Code § 21058.
Multiple highways, prima facie speed limit, see Vehicle Code § 22361.

Speed in excess of prima facie limit not negligence as a matter of
    law, see Vehicle Code § 40831.
Speed signs for business or residence districts, see Vehicle Code
    § 21357.
Speed trap defined, see Vehicle Code § 40802.

§ 22352.1. Repealed by Stats.1997, c. 421 (A.B.1209), § 3, operative March 1, 2001

§ 22353. Equestrian safety; factors in engineering and traffic surveys

When conducting an engineering and traffic survey, the City of Norco, in addition to the factors set forth in Section 627, may also consider equestrian safety. *(Added by Stats.2002, c. 186 (A.B.2402), § 1.)*

§ 22354. Decrease of state highway limits

(a) Whenever the Department of Transportation determines upon the basis of an engineering and traffic survey that the limit of 65 miles per hour is more than is reasonable or safe upon any portion of a state highway where the limit of 65 miles is applicable, the department may determine and declare a prima facie speed limit of 60, 55, 50, 45, 40, 35, 30 or 25 miles per hour, whichever is found most appropriate to facilitate the orderly movement of traffic and is reasonable and safe, which declared prima facie speed limit shall be effective when appropriate signs giving notice thereof are erected upon the highway.

(b) This section shall become operative on the date specified in subdivision (c) of Section 22366. *(Added by Stats.1995, c. 766 (S.B.726), § 25.)*

Cross References
Department of Transportation,
    Authority to install and maintain traffic control devices, see
        Vehicle Code §§ 21350 et seq., 21654, 21655, 23300,
        23334.
    Closing or restricting use of highways, see Streets and
        Highways Code §§ 124, 125.
    Delegation of powers and jurisdiction to city, see Streets and
        Highways Code §§ 116, 676.
    Determination of speed on bridges and structures, see Vehicle
        Code § 22402 et seq.
    Publishing and distribution of copies of traffic rules, see
        Vehicle Code § 23335.
Multiple lane highways, see Vehicle Code § 22361.
Speed trap defined, see Vehicle Code § 40802.

§ 22354.5. Increase or decrease of state highway limits

(a) Whenever the Department of Transportation determines, upon the basis of an engineering and traffic survey, to increase or decrease the existing speed limit on a particular portion of a state highway pursuant to Section 22354, it shall, prior to increasing or decreasing that speed limit, consult with, and take into consideration the recommendations of, the Department of the California Highway Patrol.

(b) The city council or board of supervisors of a city or county through which any portion of a state highway subject to subdivision (a) extends may conduct a public

hearing on the proposed increase or decrease at a convenient location as near as possible to that portion of state highway. The Department of Transportation shall take into consideration the results of the public hearing in determining whether to increase or decrease the speed limit. *(Added by Stats.1991, c. 219 (A.B.289), § 1.)*

§ 22355. Variable speed limits

Whenever the Department of Transportation determines upon the basis of an engineering and traffic survey that the safe and orderly movement of traffic upon any state highway which is a freeway will be facilitated by the establishment of variable speed limits, the department may erect, regulate, and control signs upon the state highway which is a freeway, or any portion thereof, which signs shall be so designed as to permit display of different speed limits at various times of the day or night. Such signs need not conform to the standards and specifications established by regulations of the Department of Transportation pursuant to Section 21400, but shall be of sufficient size and clarity to give adequate notice of the applicable speed limit. The speed limit upon the freeway at a particular time and place shall be that which is then and there displayed upon such sign. *(Stats.1959, c. 3, p. 1692, § 22355. Amended by Stats.1959, c. 11, p. 1855, § 19, operative Jan. 1, 1960; Stats.1973, c. 78, p. 137, § 17.)*

Cross References
Department of Transportation,
    Authority to install and maintain traffic control devices, see
        Vehicle Code §§ 21350 et seq., 21654, 21655, 23300,
        23334.
    Closing or restricting use of highways, see Streets and
        Highways Code §§ 124, 125.
    Delegation of powers and jurisdiction to city, see Streets and
        Highways Code §§ 116, 676.
    Determination of speed on bridges and structures, see Vehicle
        Code § 22402 et seq.
    Publishing and distribution of copies of traffic rules, see
        Vehicle Code § 23335.
Multiple lane highways, see Vehicle Code § 22361.

§ 22356. Increase of highway speed limit

(a) Whenever the Department of Transportation, after consultation with the Department of the California Highway Patrol, determines upon the basis of an engineering and traffic survey on existing highway segments, or upon the basis of appropriate design standards and projected traffic volumes in the case of newly constructed highway segments, that a speed greater than 65 miles per hour would facilitate the orderly movement of vehicular traffic and would be reasonable and safe upon any state highway, or portion thereof, that is otherwise subject to a maximum speed limit of 65 miles per hour, the Department of Transportation, with the approval of the Department of the California Highway Patrol, may declare a higher maximum speed of 70 miles per hour for vehicles not subject to Section 22406, and shall cause appropriate signs to be erected giving notice thereof. The Department of Transportation shall only make a determination under this section that is fully consistent with, and in full compliance with, federal law.

(b) No person shall drive a vehicle upon that highway at a speed greater than 70 miles per hour, as posted.

(c) This section shall become operative on the date specified in subdivision (c) of Section 22366. *(Added by Stats.1995, c. 766 (S.B.726), § 27.)*

§ 22357. Increase of local limits

(a) Whenever a local authority determines upon the basis of an engineering and traffic survey that a speed greater than 25 miles per hour would facilitate the orderly movement of vehicular traffic and would be reasonable and safe upon any street other than a state highway otherwise subject to a prima facie limit of 25 miles per hour, the local authority may by ordinance determine and declare a prima facie speed limit of 30, 35, 40, 45, 50, 55, or 60 miles per hour or a maximum speed limit of 65 miles per hour, whichever is found most appropriate to facilitate the orderly movement of traffic and is reasonable and safe. The declared prima facie or maximum speed limit shall be effective when appropriate signs giving notice thereof are erected upon the street and shall not thereafter be revised except upon the basis of an engineering and traffic survey. This section does not apply to any 25–mile–per–hour prima facie limit which is applicable when passing a school building or the grounds thereof or when passing a senior center or other facility primarily used by senior citizens.

(b) This section shall become operative on the date specified in subdivision (c) of Section 22366. *(Added by Stats.1995, c. 766 (S.B.726), § 29.)*

Cross References

Delegation of powers to local authorities by department of transportation, see Streets and Highways Code §§ 116, 676.
Local authorities defined, see Vehicle Code § 385.
Powers of local authorities, see Vehicle Code § 21100 et seq.
Speed trap defined, see Vehicle Code § 40802.
Speed zoning on multiple lane highways, see Vehicle Code § 22361.

§ 22357.1. Park playground; adjacent streets; 25 m.p.h. prima facie limit

Notwithstanding Section 22357, a local authority may, by ordinance or resolution, set a prima facie speed limit of 25 miles per hour on any street, other than a state highway, adjacent to any children's playground in a public park but only during particular hours or days when children are expected to use the facilities. The 25 mile per hour speed limit shall be effective when signs giving notice of the speed limit are posted. *(Added by Stats. 1989, c. 508, § 1.)*

§ 22358. Decrease of local limits

(a) Whenever a local authority determines upon the basis of an engineering and traffic survey that the limit of 65 miles per hour is more than is reasonable or safe upon any portion of any street other than a state highway

where the limit of 65 miles per hour is applicable, the local authority may by ordinance determine and declare a prima facie speed limit of 60, 55, 50, 45, 40, 35, 30, or 25 miles per hour, whichever is found most appropriate to facilitate the orderly movement of traffic and is reasonable and safe, which declared prima facie limit shall be effective when appropriate signs giving notice thereof are erected upon the street.

(b) This section shall become operative on the date specified in subdivision (c) of Section 22366. *(Added by Stats.1995, c. 766 (S.B.726), § 31.)*

Cross References

Delegation of powers to local authorities by department of transportation, see Streets and Highways Code §§ 116, 676.
Local authorities,
    Definition, see Vehicle Code § 385.
    Powers, see Vehicle Code § 21100 et seq.
Speed trap defined, see Vehicle Code § 40802.
Speed zoning on multiple lane highways, see Vehicle Code § 22361.

§ 22358.3. Decrease on narrow street

Whenever a local authority determines upon the basis of an engineering and traffic survey that the prima facie speed limit of 25 miles per hour in a business or residence district or in a public park on any street having a roadway not exceeding 25 feet in width, other than a state highway, is more than is reasonable or safe, the local authority may, by ordinance or resolution, determine and declare a prima facie speed limit of 20 or 15 miles per hour, whichever is found most appropriate and is reasonable and safe. The declared prima facie limit shall be effective when appropriate signs giving notice thereof are erected upon the street. *(Added by Stats.1965, c. 1614, p. 3702, § 1. Amended by Stats.1972, c. 372, p. 692, § 1; Stats.1972, c. 1095, p. 2056, § 3.)*

Cross References

Speed trap defined, see Vehicle Code § 40802.

§ 22358.4. Decrease of local limits near schools

(a)(1) Whenever a local authority determines upon the basis of an engineering and traffic survey that the prima facie speed limit of 25 miles per hour established by paragraph (2) of subdivision (a) of Section 22352 is more than is reasonable or safe, the local authority may, by ordinance or resolution, determine and declare a prima facie speed limit of 20 or 15 miles per hour, whichever is justified as the appropriate speed limit by that survey.

(2) An ordinance or resolution adopted under paragraph (1) shall not be effective until appropriate signs giving notice of the speed limit are erected upon the highway and, in the case of a state highway, until the ordinance is approved by the Department of Transportation and the appropriate signs are erected upon the highway.

(b)(1) Notwithstanding subdivision (a) or any other provision of law, a local authority may, by ordinance or resolution, determine and declare prima facie speed limits as follows:

(A) A 15 miles per hour prima facie limit in a residence district, on a highway with a posted speed limit of 30 miles per hour or slower, when approaching, at a distance of less than 500 feet from, or passing, a school building or the grounds of a school building, contiguous to a highway and posted with a school warning sign that indicates a speed limit of 15 miles per hour, while children are going to or leaving the school, either during school hours or during the noon recess period. The prima facie limit shall also apply when approaching, at a distance of less than 500 feet from, or passing, school grounds that are not separated from the highway by a fence, gate, or other physical barrier while the grounds are in use by children and the highway is posted with a school warning sign that indicates a speed limit of 15 miles per hour.

(B) A 25 miles per hour prima facie limit in a residence district, on a highway with a posted speed limit of 30 miles per hour or slower, when approaching, at a distance of 500 to 1,000 feet from, a school building or the grounds thereof, contiguous to a highway and posted with a school warning sign that indicates a speed limit of 25 miles per hour, while children are going to or leaving the school, either during school hours or during the noon recess period. The prima facie limit shall also apply when approaching, at a distance of 500 to 1,000 feet from, school grounds that are not separated from the highway by a fence, gate, or other physical barrier while the grounds are in use by children and the highway is posted with a school warning sign that indicates a speed limit of 25 miles per hour.

(2) The prima facie limits established under paragraph (1) apply only to highways that meet all of the following conditions:

(A) A maximum of two traffic lanes.

(B) A maximum posted 30 miles per hour prima facie speed limit immediately prior to and after the school zone.

(3) The prima facie limits established under paragraph (1) apply to all lanes of an affected highway, in both directions of travel.

(4) When determining the need to lower the prima facie speed limit, the local authority shall take the provisions of Section 627 into consideration.

(5)(A) An ordinance or resolution adopted under paragraph (1) shall not be effective until appropriate signs giving notice of the speed limit are erected upon the highway and, in the case of a state highway, until the ordinance is approved by the Department of Transportation and the appropriate signs are erected upon the highway.

(B) For purposes of subparagraph (A) of paragraph (1), school warning signs indicating a speed limit of 15 miles per hour may be placed at a distance up to 500 feet away from school grounds.

(C) For purposes of subparagraph (B) of paragraph (1), school warning signs indicating a speed limit of 25 miles per hour may be placed at any distance between 500 and 1,000 feet away from the school grounds.

(D) A local authority shall reimburse the Department of Transportation for all costs incurred by the department under this subdivision. *(Added by Stats.1974, c. 102, p. 217, § 1. Amended by Stats.1990, c. 441 (A.B.2883), § 3; Stats.1990, c. 542 (S.B.1860), § 3; Stats.2005, c. 279 (S.B.1107), § 23; Stats.2007, c. 384 (A.B.321), § 1.)*

§ 22358.5.   Downward speed zoning

It is the intent of the Legislature that physical conditions such as width, curvature, grade and surface conditions, or any other condition readily apparent to a driver, in the absence of other factors, would not require special downward speed zoning, as the basic rule of section 22350 is sufficient regulation as to such conditions. *(Added by Stats.1959, c. 11, p. 1856, § 23, operative Jan. 1, 1960.)*

§ 22359.   Boundary line streets

With respect to boundary line streets and highways where portions thereof are within different jurisdictions, no ordinance adopted under Sections 22357 and 22358 shall be effective as to any such portion until all authorities having jurisdiction of the portions of the street concerned have approved the same. This section shall not apply in the case of boundary line streets consisting of separate roadways within different jurisdictions. *(Stats. 1959, c. 3, p. 1693, § 22359. Amended by Stats.1963, c. 209, p. 949, § 8, eff. April 29, 1963.)*

Cross References

Boundary line streets and highways, traffic laws with respect to, see Vehicle Code § 21105.

Delegation of powers to local authorities by department of transportation, see Streets and Highways Code §§ 116, 676.

Local authorities,
 Definition, see Vehicle Code § 385.
 Powers, see Vehicle Code § 21100 et seq.

Speed zoning on multiple lane highways, see Vehicle Code § 22361.

§ 22360.   Decrease of limit; portion of highway between districts

(a) Whenever a local authority determines upon the basis of an engineering and traffic survey that the limit of 65 miles per hour is more than is reasonable or safe upon any portion of a highway other than a state highway for a distance of not exceeding 2,000 feet in length between districts, either business or residence, the local authority may determine and declare a reasonable and safe prima facie limit thereon lower than 65 miles per hour, but not less than 25 miles per hour, which declared prima facie speed limit shall be effective when appropriate signs giving notice thereof are erected upon the street or highway.

(b) This section shall become operative on the date specified in subdivision (c) of Section 22366. *(Added by Stats.1995, c. 766 (S.B.726), § 33.)*

§ 22361. Multiple-lane highways

On multiple-lane highways with two or more separate roadways different prima facie speed limits may be established for different roadways under any of the procedures specified in Sections 22354 to 22359, inclusive. *(Stats.1959, c. 3, p. 1693, § 22361. Amended by Stats.1963, c. 209, p. 949, § 9, eff. April 29, 1963.)*

§ 22362. Speed limit where persons at work

It is prima facie a violation of the basic speed law for any person to operate a vehicle in excess of the posted speed limit upon any portion of a highway where officers or employees of the agency having jurisdiction of the same, or any contractor of the agency or his employees, are at work on the roadway or within the right-of-way so close thereto as to be endangered by passing traffic. This section applies only when appropriate signs, indicating the limits of the restricted zone, and the speed limit applicable therein, are placed by such agency within 400 feet of each end of such zone. The signs shall display the figures indicating the applicable limit, which shall not be less than 25 miles per hour, and shall indicate the purpose of the speed restriction. Nothing in this section shall be deemed to relieve any operator of a vehicle from complying with the basic speed law. *(Stats.1959, c. 3, p. 1693, § 22362. Amended by Stats.1970, c. 515, p. 1001, § 1.)*

§ 22363. Restrictions because of snow or ice conditions

Notwithstanding any speed limit that may be in effect upon the highway, the Department of Transportation in respect to state highways, or a local authority with respect to highways under its jurisdiction, may determine and declare a prima facie speed limit of 40, 35, 30, or 25 miles per hour, whichever is found most appropriate and is reasonable and safe based on the prevailing snow or ice conditions upon such highway or any portion thereof.

Signs may be placed and removed as snow or ice conditions vary. *(Stats.1959, c. 3, p. 1694, § 22363. Amended by Stats.1970, c. 515, p. 1001, § 2; Stats.1974, c. 545, p. 1322, § 196.)*

§ 22364. Lane speed limits

Whenever the Department of Transportation determines, upon the basis of an engineering and traffic survey, that the safe and orderly movement of traffic upon any state highway will be facilitated by the establishment of different speed limits for the various lanes of traffic, the department may place signs upon the state highway, or any portion thereof. The signs shall designate the speed limits for each of the lanes of traffic. *(Added by Stats.1965, c. 1542, p. 3636, § 1. Amended by Stats.1974, c. 545, p. 1322, § 197; Stats.1982, c. 681, p. 2812, § 84.)*

§ 22365. South Coast Air Quality Management District; unpaved roads; ordinances to establish speed limits lower than limits otherwise permitted by code

Notwithstanding any other provision of law, any county or city, which is contained, in whole or in part, within the South Coast Air Quality Management District, may, if the county or city determines that it is necessary to achieve or maintain state or federal ambient air quality standards for particulate matter, determine and declare by ordinance a prima facie speed limit that is lower than that which the county or city is otherwise permitted by this code to establish, for any unpaved road under the jurisdiction of the county or city and within the district. That declared prima facie speed limit shall be effective when appropriate signs giving notice thereof are erected along the road. *(Added by Stats.1997, c. 16 (S.B.191), § 1, eff. May 30, 1997.)*

§ 22366. Highway speed limit of 65 miles per hour; date when state not subject to reduction in federal aid; notice

(a) Whenever the Director of Transportation determines the date upon which the state may establish a maximum speed limit of 65 miles per hour on highways without subjecting the state to a reduction in the amount of federal aid for highways, the director shall notify the Secretary of State of that determination.

(b) The notice required under subdivision (a) shall state that it is being made pursuant to this section.

(c) The notice shall specify a date which is either the date determined pursuant to subdivision (a), or a later date designated by the director. [1] *(Added by Stats.1995, c. 766 (S.B.726), § 34.)*

[1] The Secretary of State notified that the date was Jan. 3, 1996.

ARTICLE 2.   OTHER SPEED LAWS

Section
22400.   Minimum speed law.
22401.   Traffic signals.
22402.   Bridges and structures.
22403.   Local bridges and structures.
22404.   Revision of speed limit on bridges and structures.
22405.   Violations on bridges and structures.
22406.   Maximum speed limit for certain vehicles.
22406.1. Commercial motor vehicles; violations.
22406.5. Tank vehicles transporting flammable liquids.
22407.   Decreasing maximum speed law for certain vehicles.
22408.   Repealed.
22409.   Solid tire.
22410.   Metal tires.
22411.   Speed limit for motorized scooters.
22412.   Repealed.
22413.   Decreasing speed limit on grades.
22414.   Repealed.

§ 22400.   Minimum speed law

(a) No person shall drive upon a highway at such a slow speed as to impede or block the normal and reasonable movement of traffic unless the reduced speed is necessary for safe operation, because of a grade, or in compliance with law.

No person shall bring a vehicle to a complete stop upon a highway so as to impede or block the normal and reasonable movement of traffic unless the stop is necessary for safe operation or in compliance with law.

(b) Whenever the Department of Transportation determines on the basis of an engineering and traffic survey that slow speeds on any part of a state highway consistently impede the normal and reasonable movement of traffic, the department may determine and declare a minimum speed limit below which no person shall drive a vehicle, except when necessary for safe operation or in compliance with law, when appropriate signs giving notice thereof are erected along the part of the highway for which a minimum speed limit is established.

Subdivision (b) of this section shall apply only to vehicles subject to registration. *(Stats.1959, c. 3, p. 1694, § 22400. Amended by Stats.1959, c. 1304, p. 3577, § 1; Stats.1974, c. 545, p. 1322, § 198; Stats.1979, c. 364, p. 1230, § 2.)*

Cross References

Application of this section to trolley coaches, see Vehicle Code § 21051.
Driving at reduced rate of speed, see Vehicle Code § 22350.
Motor truck defined, see Vehicle Code § 410.

658

Rules of the road, exemption of authorized emergency vehicles, see Vehicle Code § 21054.

§ 22401.   Traffic signals

Local authorities in timing traffic signals may so regulate the timing thereof as to permit the movement of traffic in an orderly and safe manner at speeds slightly at variance from the speed otherwise applicable under this code. *(Stats.1959, c. 3, p. 1694, § 22401.)*

Cross References

Department of Transportation to maintain and install official traffic control devices, see Vehicle Code § 21350 et seq.
Local authorities defined, see Vehicle Code § 385.
Local regulation,
  Parking, see Vehicle Code § 22507.
  Pedestrians, see Vehicle Code § 21961.
  Turning movement, intersections, see Vehicle Code § 22113.
Power of local authorities to regulate traffic, see Vehicle Code § 21100 et seq.
Subways, tubes, tunnels, bridges or viaducts, local regulation of vehicular and pedestrian traffic, see Vehicle Code § 21109.
Traffic signs, signals and markings, generally, see Vehicle Code § 21350 et seq.

§ 22402.   Bridges and structures

The Department of Transportation may, in the manner provided in Section 22404 determine the maximum speed, not less than five miles per hour, which can be maintained with safety to any bridge, elevated structure, tube, or tunnel on a state highway. Said department may also make a determination with reference to any other highway upon receiving a request therefor from the board of supervisors or road commissioner of the county, the governing body of the local authority having jurisdiction over the bridge, elevated structure, tube, or tunnel. *(Stats.1959, c. 3, p. 1694, § 22402. Amended by Stats. 1974, c. 545, p. 1323, § 199.)*

Cross References

Department of transportation to maintain and install official traffic control devices, see Vehicle Code § 21350 et seq.
Powers and duties of director of department of transportation, see Government Code § 14005.

§ 22403.   Local bridges and structures

Any local authority may, in the manner provided in Section 22404, determine the maximum speed, not less than five miles per hour, which can be maintained with safety to any bridge, elevated structure, tube, or tunnel under its jurisdiction, or may request the Department of Transportation to make such determination. *(Stats.1959, c. 3, p. 1694, § 22403. Amended by Stats.1974, c. 545, p. 1323, § 200.)*

Cross References

Powers of local authorities, see Vehicle Code § 21109.

§ 22404.   Revision of speed limit on bridges and structures

The Department of Transportation or local authority making a determination of the maximum safe speed upon a bridge, elevated structure, tube, or tunnel shall first make an engineering investigation and shall hold a public hearing.

Notice of the time and place of the public hearing shall be posted upon the bridge, elevated structure, tube, or tunnel at least five days before the date fixed for the hearing. Upon the basis of the investigation and all evidence presented at the hearing, the department or local authority shall determine by order in writing the maximum speed which can be maintained with safety to the bridge, elevated structure, tube or tunnel. Thereupon, the authority having jurisdiction over the bridge, elevated structure, tube, or tunnel shall erect and maintain suitable signs specifying the maximum speed so determined at a distance of not more than 500 feet from each end of the bridge, elevated structure, tube, tunnel, or any approach thereto. *(Stats.1959, c. 3, p. 1694, § 22404. Amended by Stats.1974, c. 545, p. 1323, § 201.)*

Cross References

Department of transportation, see Government Code § 14000 et seq.

Powers of local authorities, see Vehicle Code § 21109.

Traffic signs, signals and markings, see Vehicle Code § 21350 et seq.

§ 22405. Violations on bridges and structures

(a) No person shall drive a vehicle on any bridge, elevated structure, tube, or tunnel constituting a part of a highway, at a speed which is greater than the maximum speed which can be maintained with safety to such structure.

(b) Upon the trial of any person charged with a violation of this section with respect to a sign erected under Section 22404, proof of the determination of the maximum speed by the Department of Transportation or local authority and the erection and maintenance of the speed signs shall constitute prima facie evidence of the maximum speed which can be maintained with safety to the bridge, elevated structure, tube, or tunnel. *(Stats. 1959, c. 3, p. 1695, § 22405. Amended by Stats.1974, c. 545, p. 1323, § 202.)*

§ 22406. Maximum speed limit for certain vehicles

No person may drive any of the following vehicles on a highway at a speed in excess of 55 miles per hour:

(a) A motortruck or truck tractor having three or more axles or any motortruck or truck tractor drawing any other vehicle.

(b) A passenger vehicle or bus drawing any other vehicle.

(c) A schoolbus transporting any school pupil.

(d) A farm labor vehicle when transporting passengers.

(e) A vehicle transporting explosives.

(f) A trailer bus, as defined in Section 636.

(Added by Stats.1967, c. 78, p. 976, § 4. Amended by Stats.1980, c. 676, p. 2025, § 312; Stats.1988, c. 843, § 5;

Stats.1999, c. 724 (A.B.1650), § 42; Stats.2000, c. 787 (S.B.1404), § 22.)

Cross References

Buses, motor trucks or truck tractors, fine for violation of this section, see Vehicle Code § 42000.5.

Definitions,
  Motor truck, see Vehicle Code § 410.
  Passenger vehicle, see Vehicle Code § 465.
  Schoolbus, see Vehicle Code § 545; Education Code §§ 39830, 82321.
  Trailer, see Vehicle Code § 630.
  Truck tractor, see Vehicle Code § 655.

Distance between vehicles subject to speed limits of this section, see Vehicle Code § 21704.

Driving lanes, see Vehicle Code § 22348.

Lanes for vehicles described in this section, see Vehicle Code § 22348.

Liability for damage to highway or bridge as result of maximum weight, see Vehicle Code § 17301.

Maximum weights on bridges and other structures, see Vehicle Code § 35750 et seq.

Penalties for violating weight restrictions, see Vehicle Code § 42030 et seq.

Power of department of transportation to issue permits for increased size and weight, see Vehicle Code § 35780 et seq.

Power of local authorities to increase or decrease weight limits, see Vehicle Code § 35700 et seq.

Reduction of weights on secondary highways, see Vehicle Code § 35651 et seq.

§ 22406.1. Commercial motor vehicles; violations

(a) A person who operates a commercial motor vehicle, as defined in subdivision (b) of Section 15210, upon a highway at a speed exceeding a posted speed limit established under this code by 15 miles per hour or more, is guilty of a misdemeanor.

(b) A person who holds a commercial driver's license, as defined in subdivision (a) of Section 15210, and operates a noncommerical motor vehicle upon a highway at a speed exceeding a posted speed limit established under this code by 15 miles per hour or more, is guilty of an infraction.

(c) A violation of either subdivision (a) or (b) is a "serious traffic violation," as defined in subdivision (p) of Section 15210, and is subject to the sanctions provided under Section 15306 or 15308, in addition to any other penalty provided by law.

(d) This section shall become operative on September 20, 2005. *(Added by Stats.2000, c. 787 (S.B.1404), § 23. Amended by Stats.2004, c. 952 (A.B.3049), § 29, operative Sept. 20, 2005.)*

§ 22406.5. Tank vehicles transporting flammable liquids

Any person who drives a tank vehicle subject to Division 14.7 (commencing with Section 34000) while transporting more than 500 gallons of flammable liquid at a speed greater than the applicable speed limit or in willful or wanton disregard for the safety of persons or property is, in addition to any other applicable penalty, subject to a fine of not less than five hundred dollars ($500) for a first offense and, for a second or subsequent offense within two years of a prior offense, to a fine of not less than two thousand dollars ($2,000) and a suspension of up to six months of a hazardous materials or cargo tank endorsement, or both. *(Added by Stats.1991, c. 1043 (S.B.123), § 1.)*

§ 22407. Decreasing maximum speed law for certain vehicles

Whenever the Department of Transportation or local authority determines upon the basis of engineering studies and a traffic survey that the speed of 55 miles per hour is more than is reasonable or safe for vehicles mentioned in subdivision (a) of Section 22406, which have a manufacturer's gross vehicle weight rating of 10,000 pounds or more, in descending a grade upon any portion of a highway, the department or local authority, with respect to highways under their respective jurisdiction, may determine and declare a speed limit of 50, 45, 40, 35, 30, 25, or 20 miles per hour, whichever is found most appropriate to facilitate the orderly movement of traffic and is reasonable and safe, which declared speed limit shall be effective for such vehicles when appropriate signs giving notice thereof are erected upon the highway. *(Stats.1959, c. 3, p. 1695, § 22407. Amended by Stats. 1965, c. 184, p. 1150, § 1; Stats.1965, c. 1210, p. 3031, § 1; Stats.1967, c. 78, p. 977, § 5; Stats.1973, c. 82, p. 143, § 1.)*

Cross References

Buses, motor trucks or truck tractors, fine for violation of this section, see Vehicle Code § 42000.5.

§ 22408. Repealed by Stats.1967, c. 78, p. 977, § 6

§ 22409. Solid tire

No person shall operate any vehicle equipped with any solid tire when such vehicle has a gross weight as set forth in the following table at any speed in excess of the speed set forth opposite such gross weight:

When gross weight of vehicle and load is:	Maximum speed in miles per hour:
10,000 lbs. or more but less than 16,000 lbs.	25
16,000 lbs. or more but less than 22,000 lbs.	15
22,000 lbs. or more	12

(Stats.1959, c. 3, p. 1695, § 22409.)

Cross References

Restriction as to tire equipment, see Vehicle Code § 27450 et seq.
Solid tire defined, see Vehicle Code § 560.

Weight permitted per inch on certain tires, see Vehicle Code §§ 35600, 35601.

§ 22410. Metal tires

No person shall operate any vehicle equipped with any metal tire in contact with the surface of the highway at a speed in excess of six miles per hour. *(Stats.1959, c. 3, p. 1695, § 22410.)*

Cross References

Metal tire defined, see Vehicle Code § 395.
Restriction as to tire equipment, see Vehicle Code § 27450 et seq.
Weight permitted per inch on certain tires, see Vehicle Code §§ 35600, 35601.

§ 22411. Speed limit for motorized scooters

No person shall operate a motorized scooter at a speed in excess of 15 miles per hour. *(Added by Stats.1999, c. 722 (S.B.441), § 7.)*

§ 22412. Repealed by Stats.1967, c. 78, p. 977, § 7

§ 22413. Decreasing speed limit on grades

Whenever a local authority determines upon the basis of an engineering and traffic survey that the prima facie limit of 25 miles per hour is more than is reasonable and safe on any portion of a street having a grade in excess of 10 percent, the local authority may by ordinance determine and declare a maximum limit of 20 or 15 miles per hour, whichever is found most appropriate and is reasonable and safe. The declared maximum speed shall be effective when appropriate signs giving notice thereof are erected upon the street. *(Added by Stats.1959, c. 318, p. 2245, § 2, eff. May 8, 1959.)*

§ 22414. Repealed by Stats.1967, c. 78, p. 977, § 8

CHAPTER 8. SPECIAL STOPS REQUIRED

Section
22450. Stop requirements.
22451. Train signals.
22452. Railroad crossings.
22452.5. Railroad crossings; signs authorizing certain vehicles to traverse crossings without stopping.
22453. Effect of negligence on passengers.
22454. Meeting or overtaking schoolbus stopped to load or unload pupils; stop requirement; violation; warning letter; form.
22454.5. Violations of § 22454; penalties.
22455. Street vendors; parking in residential districts; ordinances or resolutions.
22456. Destiny Nicole Stout Memorial Act; trucks vending ice cream and similar foods.

Cross References

Penalties, public offenses, fines in misdemeanor cases for violation pertaining to passing a school building or grounds, see Vehicle Code § 42011.
Punishment for violations of provisions of this chapter, see Vehicle Code § 42001.

Violation of chapter a misdemeanor, see Vehicle Code § 40000.15.

§ 22450. Stop requirements

(a) The driver of any vehicle approaching a stop sign at the entrance to, or within, an intersection shall stop at a limit line, if marked, otherwise before entering the crosswalk on the near side of the intersection.

If there is no limit line or crosswalk, the driver shall stop at the entrance to the intersecting roadway.

(b) The driver of a vehicle approaching a stop sign at a railroad grade crossing shall stop at a limit line, if marked, otherwise before crossing the first track or entrance to the railroad grade crossing.

(c) Notwithstanding any other provision of law, a local authority may adopt rules and regulations by ordinance or resolution providing for the placement of a stop sign at any location on a highway under its jurisdiction where the stop sign would enhance traffic safety. *(Stats.1959, c. 3, p. 1696, § 22450. Amended by Stats.1969, c. 364, p. 890, § 1; Stats.1993, c. 272 (A.B.301), § 41, eff. Aug. 2, 1993; Stats.2007, c. 630 (A.B.1728), § 8.)*

Cross References

Application of this section to trolley coaches, see Vehicle Code § 21051.
Contributory negligence, see Civil Code § 1714.
Definitions,
 Crosswalk, see Vehicle Code § 275.
 Highway, see Vehicle Code §§ 360, 590, 592.
 Intersection, see Vehicle Code § 365.
 Roadway, see Vehicle Code § 530.
 Stop or stopping, see Vehicle Code §§ 587, 21453.
 Through highway, see Vehicle Code § 600.
Farm or private grade crossing of a railroad, see Public Utilities Code § 7538.
Obstructing railroad track, punishment, see Penal Code § 218.1.
Prohibition of stopping, see Vehicle Code § 22500.
Rail transit related traffic violations, county populations greater than 500,000, punishment, see Penal Code § 369b.
Railroad grade crossing violations, see Vehicle Code § 42001.16.
Regulations for intersections,
 Required position and method of turning, see Vehicle Code §§ 22100, 22101.
 Right-of-way, see Vehicle Code § 21800 et seq.
 Signals, see Vehicle Code § 22107 et seq.
Rules of the road, exemption of authorized emergency vehicles, see Vehicle Code § 21054.
Signs indicating railroad crossings, see Vehicle Code § 21362.
Stop signs indicating through highway, see Vehicle Code § 21352 et seq.
Traffic devices on private road or driveway, see Vehicle Code § 21360.
Vehicle entering through highway, see Vehicle Code § 21802.

§ 22451. Train signals

(a) The driver of any vehicle or pedestrian approaching a railroad or rail transit grade crossing shall stop not less than 15 feet from the nearest rail and shall not proceed until he or she can do so safely, whenever the following conditions exist:

(1) A clearly visible electric or mechanical signal device or a flagman gives warning of the approach or passage of a train or car.

(2) An approaching train or car is plainly visible or is emitting an audible signal and, by reason of its speed or nearness, is an immediate hazard.

(b) No driver or pedestrian shall proceed through, around, or under any railroad or rail transit crossing gate while the gate is closed.

(c) Whenever a railroad or rail transit crossing is equipped with an automated enforcement system, a notice of a violation of this section is subject to the procedures provided in Section 40518. *(Added by Stats. 1967, c. 406, p. 1627, § 3. Amended by Stats.1970, c. 608, p. 1189, § 1; Stats.1994, c. 1216 (S.B.1802), § 5; Stats. 1995, c. 922 (S.B.833), § 5; Stats.1998, c. 54 (S.B.1136), § 4; Stats.2000, c. 1035 (S.B.1403), § 27.)*

Cross References

Application of this section to trolley coaches, see Vehicle Code § 21051.
Contributory negligence, see Civil Code § 1714.
Duration of prohibition against operation of commercial motor vehicle, see Vehicle Code § 15312.
Locomotive bell to be rung at intersections, see Public Utilities Code § 7604.
Rail transit related traffic violations, county populations greater than 500,000, punishment, see Penal Code § 369b.
Railroad warning approach signs, see Vehicle Code § 21362.
Regulation of railroad grade crossing, see Vehicle Code § 21110.
Requirement that certain vehicles stop at all railway crossings, see Vehicle Code §§ 22452, 22453.
Safety devices, authority of public utility commission to direct use, see Public Utilities Code § 768.
Speed limits and violations, see Vehicle Code §§ 22351, 22352.
Traffic school, rail transit safety film or fine, see Penal Code § 369b.

§ 22452. Railroad crossings

(a) Subdivisions (b) and (d) apply to the operation of the following vehicles:

(1) A bus or farm labor vehicle carrying passengers.

(2) A motortruck transporting employees in addition to those riding in the cab.

(3) A schoolbus and a school pupil activity bus transporting school pupils, except as otherwise provided in paragraph (4) of subdivision (d).

(4) A commercial motor vehicle transporting any quantity of a Division 2.3 chlorine, as classified by Title 49 of the Code of Federal Regulations.

(5) A commercial motor vehicle that is required to be marked or placarded in accordance with the regulations of Title 49 of the Code of Federal Regulations with one of the following federal classifications:

(A) Division 1.1.

(B) Division 1.2, or Division 1.3.

(C) Division 2.3 Poison gas.

(D) Division 4.3.

(E) Class 7.

(F) Class 3 Flammable.

(G) Division 5.1.

(H) Division 2.2.

(I) Division 2.3 Chlorine.

(J) Division 6.1 Poison.

(K) Division 2.2 Oxygen.

(L) Division 2.1.

(M) Class 3 Combustible liquid.

(N) Division 4.1.

(O) Division 5.1.

(P) Division 5.2.

(Q) Class 8.

(R) Class Division 1.4.

(S) A cargo tank motor vehicle, whether loaded or empty, used for the transportation of a hazardous material, as defined in Parts 107 to 180, inclusive, of Title 49 of the Code of Federal Regulations.

(6) A cargo tank motor vehicle transporting a commodity that at the time of loading has a temperature above its flashpoint, as determined under Section 173.120 of Title 49 of the Code of Federal Regulations.

(7) A cargo tank motor vehicle, whether loaded or empty, transporting a commodity under exemption in accordance with Subpart B of Part 107 of Title 49 of the Code of Federal Regulations.

(b) Before traversing a railroad grade crossing, the driver of a vehicle described in subdivision (a) shall stop that vehicle not less than 15 nor more than 50 feet from the nearest rail of the track and while so stopped shall listen, and look in both directions along the track, for an approaching train and for signals indicating the approach of a train, and shall not proceed until he or she can do so safely. Upon proceeding, the gears shall not be shifted manually while crossing the tracks.

(c) The driver of a commercial motor vehicle, other than those listed in subdivision (a), upon approaching a railroad grade crossing, shall be driven at a rate of speed that allows the commercial vehicle to stop before reaching the nearest rail of that crossing, and shall not be driven upon, or over, the crossing until due caution is taken to ascertain that the course is clear.

(d) A stop need not be made at a crossing in the following circumstances:

(1) Of railroad tracks running along and upon the roadway within a business or residence district.

(2) Where a traffic officer or an official traffic control signal directs traffic to proceed.

(3) Where an exempt sign was authorized by the Public Utilities Commission prior to January 1, 1978.

(4) Where an official railroad crossing stop exempt sign in compliance with Section 21400 has been placed by the Department of Transportation or a local authority pursuant to Section 22452.5. This paragraph does not apply with respect to a schoolbus or to a school pupil activity bus transporting school pupils. *(Stats.1959, c. 3, p. 1696, § 22452. Amended by Stats.1959, c. 1881, p. 4442, § 1; Stats.1963, c. 828, p. 2023, § 1; Stats.1967, c. 406, p. 1627, § 1; Stats.1969, c. 26, p. 129, § 9; Stats. 1970, c. 608, p. 1189, § 2; Stats.1977, c. 1053, p. 3187, § 1; Stats.1981, c. 813, p. 3157, § 15; Stats.2001, c. 504 (A.B.1280), § 6; Stats.2006, c. 574 (A.B.2520), § 18; Stats.2007, c. 630 (A.B.1728), § 9; Stats.2010, c. 491 (S.B.1318), § 41.)*

Cross References

Application of this section to trolley coaches, see Vehicle Code § 21051.

Definitions,
  Bus, see Vehicle Code § 233.
  Business district, see Vehicle Code § 235.
  Liquefied petroleum gas, see Vehicle Code § 380.
  Motor truck, see Vehicle Code § 410.
  Residence district, see Vehicle Code § 515.
  Schoolbus, see Vehicle Code § 545.

Degree of care and skill required of carriers of persons for reward, see Civil Code § 2100.

Duration of prohibition against operation of commercial motor vehicle, see Vehicle Code § 15312.

Public utilities commission's power over state highways, see Streets and Highways Code § 661.

Rail transit related traffic violations, county populations greater than 500,000, punishment, see Penal Code § 369b.

Stopping at intersections signposted with stop sign, see Vehicle Code § 22450.

Suspension of license by court upon conviction for violating this section, see Vehicle Code § 13201.

§ 22452.5. Railroad crossings; signs authorizing certain vehicles to traverse crossings without stopping

The Department of Transportation and local authorities, with respect to highways under their respective jurisdictions, may place signs at railroad grade crossings permitting any vehicle described in subdivision (a) of Section 22452 to traverse such crossings without stopping. Such signs shall be placed in accordance with criteria adopted by the Public Utilities Commission. Prior to placing such signs, the Department of Transportation or local authority shall consult with the Department of the California Highway Patrol, railroad corporations involved, and the operators involved and shall secure the permission of the Public Utilities Commission if a railroad corporation under the jurisdiction of the Public Utilities Commission is affected. Prior to permitting the placement of such signs, the Public Utilities Commission shall seek the concurrence of the Department of the California Highway Patrol. *(Added by Stats.1977, c. 1053, p. 3188, § 2. Amended by Stats.1979, c. 373, p. 1383, § 324.)*

§ 22453. Effect of negligence on passengers

Failure of the driver of a motor vehicle carrying any passenger for hire to stop as required in Section 22452 shall not be imputed to any bona fide passenger for hire in such vehicle. *(Stats.1959, c. 3, p. 1697, § 22453.)*

§ 22454. Meeting or overtaking schoolbus stopped to load or unload pupils; stop requirement; violation; warning letter; form

(a) The driver of any vehicle, upon meeting or overtaking, from either direction, any schoolbus equipped with signs as required in this code, that is stopped for the purpose of loading or unloading any schoolchildren and displays a flashing red light signal and stop signal arm, as defined in paragraph (4) of subdivision (b) of Section 25257, if equipped with a stop signal arm, visible from front or rear, shall bring the vehicle to a stop immediately before passing the schoolbus and shall not proceed past the schoolbus until the flashing red light signal and stop signal arm, if equipped with a stop signal arm, cease operation.

(b)(1) The driver of a vehicle upon a divided highway or multiple-lane highway need not stop upon meeting or passing a schoolbus that is upon the other roadway.

(2) For the purposes of this subdivision, a multiple-lane highway is any highway that has two or more lanes of travel in each direction.

(c)(1) If a vehicle was observed overtaking a schoolbus in violation of subdivision (a), and the driver of the schoolbus witnessed the violation, the driver may, within 24 hours, report the violation and furnish the vehicle license plate number and description and the time and place of the violation to the local law enforcement agency having jurisdiction of the offense. That law enforcement agency shall issue a letter of warning prepared in accordance with paragraph (2) with respect to the alleged violation to the registered owner of the vehicle. The issuance of a warning letter under this paragraph shall not be entered on the driving record of the person to whom it is issued, but does not preclude the imposition of any other applicable penalty.

(2) The Attorney General shall prepare and furnish to every law enforcement agency in the state a form letter for purposes of paragraph (1), and the law enforcement agency may issue those letters in the exact form prepared by the Attorney General. The Attorney General may charge a fee to any law enforcement agency that requests a copy of the form letter to recover the costs of preparing and providing that copy.

(d) This section also applies to a roadway upon private property. *(Stats.1959, c. 3, p. 1697, § 22454. Amended by Stats.1971, c. 877, p. 1722, § 2, operative May 3, 1972; Stats.1981, c. 813, p. 3157, § 16; Stats.1990, c. 1296 (S.B.2061), § 1; Stats.1992, c. 624 (A.B.3144), § 5, eff. Sept. 14, 1992; Stats.1993, c. 589 (A.B.2211), § 18; Stats.1999, c. 647 (A.B.1573), § 3, eff. Oct. 10, 1999.)*

§ 22454.5. Violations of § 22454; penalties

Notwithstanding Section 42001, a person convicted of a first violation of Section 22454 shall be punished by a fine of not less than one hundred fifty dollars ($150) or more than two hundred fifty dollars ($250). A person convicted of a second separate violation of Section 22454 shall be punished by a fine of not less than five hundred dollars ($500) or more than one thousand dollars ($1,000). If a person is convicted of a third or subsequent violation of Section 22454 and the offense occurred within three years of two or more separate violations of Section 22454, the Department of Motor Vehicles shall suspend the person's privilege to operate a motor vehicle for one year. *(Added by Stats.1986, c. 699, § 1. Amended by Stats.1990, c. 1296 (S.B.2061), § 2.)*

§ 22455. Street vendors; parking in residential districts; ordinances or resolutions

(a) The driver of any commercial vehicle engaged in vending upon a street may vend products on a street in a residence district only after bringing the vehicle to a complete stop and lawfully parking adjacent to the curb, consistent with the requirements of Chapter 9 (commencing with Section 22500) and local ordinances adopted pursuant thereto.

(b) Notwithstanding subdivision (a) of Section 114315 of the Health and Safety Code or any other provision of law, a local authority may, by ordinance or resolution, adopt additional requirements for the public safety regulating the type of vending and the time, place, and manner of vending from vehicles upon any street. *(Added by Stats.1984, c. 362, § 1. Amended by Stats.1985, c. 495, § 1; Stats.2008, c. 139 (A.B.2588), § 3.)*

§ 22456. Destiny Nicole Stout Memorial Act; trucks vending ice cream and similar foods

(a) This section shall be known and may be cited as the Destiny Nicole Stout Memorial Act.

(b) The Legislature finds and declares that motor vehicles engaged in vending ice cream and similar food items in residential neighborhoods can increase the danger to children, and it is necessary that these vehicles are clearly seen and noticed by motorists and pedestrians to protect public safety.

(c) As used in this section, the term "ice cream truck" means a motor vehicle engaged in the curbside vending or sale of frozen or refrigerated desserts, confections, or novelties commonly known as ice cream, or prepackaged candies, prepackaged snack foods, or soft drinks, primarily intended for the sale to children under 12 years of age.

(d) Any ice cream truck shall be equipped at all times, while engaged in vending in a residential area, with signs mounted on both the front and the rear and clearly legible from a distance of 100 feet under daylight conditions, incorporating the words "WARNING" and "CHILDREN CROSSING." Each sign shall be at least 12 inches high by 48 inches wide, with letters of a dark color and at least four inches in height, a one-inch wide solid border, and a sharply contrasting background.

(e) A person may not vend from an ice cream truck that is stopped, parked, or standing on any public street, alley, or highway under any of the following conditions:

(1) On a street, alley, or highway with a posted speed limit greater than 25 miles per hour.

(2) If the street, alley, or highway is within 100 feet of an intersection with an opposing highway that has a posted speed limit greater than 25 miles per hour.

(3) If the vendor does not have an unobstructed view for 200 feet in both directions along the highway and of any traffic on the highway. *(Added by Stats.2000, c. 344 (S.B.2185), § 1.)*

CHAPTER 9. STOPPING, STANDING, AND PARKING

Section
22500. Prohibited stopping, standing, or parking.
22500.1. Fire lanes; parking violations; signs.
22500.5. Schoolbus stopping; local ordinance.
22501. Local regulation of state highways.
22502. Curb parking; local ordinances; exception.
22503. Local ordinance; angle parking.
22503.5. Two or three-wheeled motor vehicle parking regulations.
22504. Unincorporated area parking; exception; school bus stops.
22505. Stopping, standing, or parking in certain areas.
22506. Local regulation of state highways.
22507. Local regulation; preferential parking.
22507.1. Designation of streets or portions thereof for exclusive parking privilege for participants in car share or ridesharing program.
22507.2. Parking in front of private driveways; ordinance; permits.
22507.5. Local regulation; overnight parking; commercial vehicles or trailer component thereof; vehicles transporting hazardous waste.
22507.6. Local regulation; street sweeping; commercial vehicles; signs.
22507.8. Disabled persons' and veterans' parking spaces; unauthorized parking or obstructing; offstreet parking facilities.
22507.9. Special enforcement units; handicapped parking enforcement; compensation and benefits; application of section.

Section
22508. Parking meter zones; fee rates; fee payment.
22508.5. Inoperable parking meter or payment center; prohibitions or restrictions.
22508.5. Inoperable parking meter or payment center; prohibitions or restrictions.
22509. Parking on hills.
22510. Snow removal areas; parking restrictions; signs.
22511. Electric vehicle parking stalls or spaces; removal of vehicles not connected for electric charging purposes; off-street parking facility posting and signage requirements; local ordinances.
22511.1. Electric vehicle parking stalls or spaces; unauthorized parking or obstructing.
22511.3. Veterans displaying special license plates; metered parking spaces; privileges.
22511.5. Disabled persons or disabled veterans; parking privileges.
22511.55. Issuance and renewal of disabled parking placard; conditions; printing requirements.
22511.56. Placard or specialty license plate; presentation of identification and evidence of issuance; failure to present; penalties for misuse; confiscation; cancellation.
22511.57. Disabled person placards lost or stolen; owner of placard deceased; vehicle parking restrictions and prohibitions.
22511.58. Physician's certificate information; release to specified local agencies; local review board.
22511.59. Temporary distinguishing placard; renewal.
22511.6. Cancellation or revocation of distinguishing placards.
22511.7. Designation of parking for disabled persons and veterans.
22511.8. Offstreet parking; designation of parking for disabled persons and veterans; removal of unauthorized vehicles.
22511.85. Public offstreet parking facilities; loading and unloading disabled persons; sufficient space.
22511.9. Replacement signs relating to parking privileges for disabled persons; contents.
22511.95. New or replacement signs installed after July 1, 2008; content; parking privileges for disabled persons.
22511.10. Disabled persons; Legislative findings.
22511.11. Office of State Architect; regulations; location of disabled person parking stalls or spaces.
22512. Driver or owner of utility service vehicle; exemption from provisions.
22513. Tow trucks; stopping or parking; solicitation of engagement for services; removal of vehicle without authorization; misdemeanor; exceptions.
22514. Fire hydrants.
22515. Unattended vehicles.
22516. Locked vehicle.
22517. Opening and closing doors.
22518. Fringe and transportation corridor parking facilities; authorized vehicles.
22519. Regulation of offstreet parking.
22520. Repealed.
22520.5. Vending merchandise or services near freeways; exceptions; violations; penalties.
22520.6. Roadside rest areas or vista points; violations; penalties.
22521. Parking upon or near railroad track.

Section
22522. Parking near sidewalk access ramps.
22523. Abandonment; fine; liability for cost of removal and disposition; offense; liability for deficiency.
22524. Presumption; overcoming presumption.
22524.5. Automobile insurance; ordinary and reasonable towing and storage charges; accident or stolen recovery; discharge of obligation.
22525. Vanpool vehicles; use of state highway bus stops; local ordinance or resolution.
22526. Anti–Gridlock Act of 1987; parking or stopping violation.

Cross References

Exemption of driver of authorized emergency vehicle from this chapter, see Vehicle Code § 21055.

Park or parking, defined, see Vehicle Code § 463.

Report of convictions to department, exceptions, see Vehicle Code § 1803 et seq.

Rules and regulations adopted, subject matter, local authority not precluded from enacting parking ordinances pursuant to this Chapter, see Vehicle Code § 21100.

Stop or stopping, defined, see Vehicle Code § 587.

Violations of chapter as infractions, see Vehicle Code §§ 40000.1, 40000.15.

§ 22500. Prohibited stopping, standing, or parking

No person shall stop, park, or leave standing any vehicle whether attended or unattended, except when necessary to avoid conflict with other traffic or in compliance with the directions of a peace officer or official traffic control device, in any of the following places:

(a) Within an intersection, except adjacent to curbs as may be permitted by local ordinance.

(b) On a crosswalk, except that a bus engaged as a common carrier or a taxicab may stop in an unmarked crosswalk to load or unload passengers when authorized by the legislative body of any city pursuant to an ordinance.

(c) Between a safety zone and the adjacent right-hand curb or within the area between the zone and the curb as may be indicated by a sign or red paint on the curb, which sign or paint was erected or placed by local authorities pursuant to an ordinance.

(d) Within 15 feet of the driveway entrance to any fire station. This subdivision does not apply to any vehicle owned or operated by a fire department and clearly marked as a fire department vehicle.

(e) In front of a public or private driveway, except that a bus engaged as a common carrier, schoolbus, or a taxicab may stop to load or unload passengers when authorized by local authorities pursuant to an ordinance.

In unincorporated territory, where the entrance of a private road or driveway is not delineated by an opening in a curb or by other curb construction, so much of the surface of the ground as is paved, surfaced, or otherwise plainly marked by vehicle use as a private road or driveway entrance, shall constitute a driveway.

(f) On any portion of a sidewalk, or with the body of the vehicle extending over any portion of a sidewalk, except electric carts when authorized by local ordinance, as specified in Section 21114.5. Lights, mirrors, or devices that are required to be mounted upon a vehicle under this code may extend from the body of the vehicle over the sidewalk to a distance of not more than 10 inches.

(g) Alongside or opposite any street or highway excavation or obstruction when stopping, standing, or parking would obstruct traffic.

(h) On the roadway side of any vehicle stopped, parked, or standing at the curb or edge of a highway, except for a schoolbus when stopped to load or unload pupils in a business or residence district where the speed limit is 25 miles per hour or less.

(i) Except as provided under Section 22500.5, alongside curb space authorized for the loading and unloading of passengers of a bus engaged as a common carrier in local transportation when indicated by a sign or red paint on the curb erected or painted by local authorities pursuant to an ordinance.

(j) In a tube or tunnel, except vehicles of the authorities in charge, being used in the repair, maintenance, or inspection of the facility.

(k) Upon a bridge, except vehicles of the authorities in charge, being used in the repair, maintenance, or inspection of the facility, and except that buses engaged as a common carrier in local transportation may stop to load or unload passengers upon a bridge where sidewalks are provided, when authorized by local authorities pursuant to an ordinance, and except that local authorities pursuant to an ordinance or the Department of Transportation pursuant to an order, within their respective jurisdictions, may permit parking on bridges having sidewalks and shoulders of sufficient width to permit parking without interfering with the normal movement of traffic on the roadway. Local authorities, by ordinance or resolution, may permit parking on these bridges on state highways in their respective jurisdictions if the ordinance or resolution is first approved in writing by the Department of Transportation. Parking shall not be permitted unless there are signs in place, as may be necessary, to indicate the provisions of local ordinances or the order of the Department of Transportation.

(*l*) In front of or upon that portion of a curb that has been cut down, lowered, or constructed to provide wheelchair accessibility to the sidewalk. (*Stats.1959, c. 3, p. 1698, § 22500. Amended by Stats.1963, c. 1661, p. 3252, § 1; Stats.1965, c. 85, p. 1026, § 1; Stats.1965, c. 295, p. 1293, § 1; Stats.1965, c. 1092, p. 2736, § 1; Stats.1972, c. 490, p. 862, § 3; Stats.1974, c. 545, p. 1324, § 203; Stats.1982, c. 822, p. 3125, § 1; Stats.1984, c. 852, § 1; Stats.1992, c. 624 (A.B.3144), § 6, eff. Sept. 14, 1992; Stats.1998, c. 877 (A.B.2132), § 66; Stats.2002, c. 640 (A.B.1314), § 1.)*

Cross References

Definitions,
Bus, see Vehicle Code § 233.
Crosswalk, see Vehicle Code § 275.
Driving through safety zone prohibited, see Vehicle Code § 21709.
Intersection, see Vehicle Code § 365.
Local authorities, see Vehicle Code § 385.
Park or parking, see Vehicle Code § 463.
Private road or driveway, see Vehicle Code § 490.
Roadway, see Vehicle Code § 530.
Safety zone, see Vehicle Code § 540.
Schoolbus, see Vehicle Code § 545.
Sidewalk, see Vehicle Code § 555.
Stop or stopping, see Vehicle Code § 587.
Street or highway, see Vehicle Code §§ 360, 590, 592.
Local regulation of electric carts on sidewalks, see Vehicle Code § 21100.
Markings to indicate parking regulations, see Vehicle Code § 21458.
Moving vehicle from one place to another, see Vehicle Code § 22654.
Official traffic control devices, see Vehicle Code § 21350 et seq.
Parking on educational institution grounds, restrictions, see Vehicle Code § 21113.
Parking violations, see Vehicle Code § 40200 et seq.
Removal of parked vehicles, authorization, see Vehicle Code § 22654.
Report of convictions to department, exceptions, see Vehicle Code § 1803 et seq.
Rubbish or garbage trucks, exemption, see Vehicle Code § 21059.
Rules of the road, exemption of authorized emergency vehicles, see Vehicle Code § 21054.
Stopping,
Standing or parking in unincorporated areas, see Vehicle Code § 22504.
Standing or parking on vehicular crossing prohibited, see Vehicle Code § 23333.
Streetsweeping and watering vehicles, application of section, see Vehicle Code § 21060.
Warning devices on disabled or parked vehicles, see Vehicle Code §§ 25300, 25301, 25305.

§ 22500.1. Fire lanes; parking violations; signs

In addition to Section 22500, no person shall stop, park, or leave standing any vehicle, whether attended or unattended, except when necessary to avoid conflict with other traffic or in compliance with the directions of a peace officer or official traffic control device along the edge of any highway, at any curb, or in any location in a publicly or privately owned or operated off-street parking facility, designated as a fire lane by the fire department or fire district with jurisdiction over the area in which the place is located.

The designation shall be indicated (1) by a sign posted immediately adjacent to, and visible from, the designated place clearly stating in letters not less than one inch in height that the place is a fire lane, (2) by outlining or painting the place in red and, in contrasting color, marking the place with the words "FIRE LANE", which are clearly visible from a vehicle, or (3) by a red curb or red paint on the edge of the roadway upon which is clearly marked the words "FIRE LANE". *(Added by Stats.1983, c. 328, § 1. Amended by Stats.1984, c. 129, § 1, eff. May 21, 1984.)*

§ 22500.5. Schoolbus stopping; local ordinance

Upon agreement between a transit system operating buses engaged as common carriers in local transportation and a public school district or private school, local authorities may, by ordinance, permit schoolbuses owned by, or operated under contract for, that public school district or private school to stop for the loading or unloading of passengers alongside any or all curb spaces designated for the loading or unloading of passengers of the transit system buses. *(Added by Stats.1982, c. 822, p. 3126, § 2. Amended by Stats.2012, c. 769 (A.B.2679), § 36.)*

§ 22501. Local regulation of state highways

No ordinance enacted by local authorities pursuant to subdivisions (e) and (k) of Section 22500 or Section 22507.2 shall become effective as to any state highway without prior submission to and approval by the Department of Transportation in the same manner as required by Section 21104. Nothing contained in this section and Section 22500 shall be construed as authorizing local authorities to enact legislation which is contrary to the provisions of Sections 22512 and 25301. *(Stats.1959, c. 3, p. 1698, § 22501. Amended by Stats.1965, c. 1500, p. 3524, § 8; Stats.1974, c. 545, p. 1325, § 204; Stats.1980, c. 158, p. 356, § 1, eff. June 11, 1980.)*

Cross References

Department of transportation, see Streets and Highways Code § 90 et seq.
Local authorities defined, see Vehicle Code § 385.
Local regulation, see Vehicle Code § 21100 et seq.

§ 22502. Curb parking; local ordinances; exception

(a) Except as otherwise provided in this chapter, a vehicle stopped or parked upon a roadway where there are adjacent curbs shall be stopped or parked with the right-hand wheels of the vehicle parallel with and within 18 inches of the right-hand curb, except that a motorcycle shall be parked with at least one wheel or fender touching the right-hand curb. Where no curbs or barriers bound a two-way roadway, right-hand parallel parking is required unless otherwise indicated.

(b)(1) The provisions of subdivision (a) or (e) do not apply to a commercial vehicle if a variation from the requirements of subdivision (a) or (e) is reasonably necessary to accomplish the loading or unloading of merchandise or passengers on, or from, a vehicle and while anything connected with the loading, or unloading, is being executed.

(2) This subdivision does not permit a vehicle to stop or park upon a roadway in a direction opposite to that in which traffic normally moves upon that half of the roadway on which the vehicle is stopped or parked.

(c) Notwithstanding subdivision (b), a local authority may, by ordinance, prohibit a commercial vehicle from stopping, parking, or standing on one side of a roadway in a business district with the wheels of the vehicle more than 18 inches from the curb. The ordinance shall be effective only if signs are placed in the areas to which it is applicable clearly indicating the prohibition.

(d) This section does not apply to vehicles of a public utility when the vehicles are being used in connection with the operation, maintenance, or repair of facilities of the public utility or are being used in connection with providing public utility service.

(e)(1) Upon a one-way roadway, a vehicle may be stopped or parked as provided in subdivision (a) or with the left-hand wheels parallel to and within 18 inches of the left-hand curb, except that a motorcycle, if parked on the left-hand side, shall have either one wheel or one fender touching the curb. Where no curb or barriers bound a one-way roadway, parallel parking on either side is required unless otherwise indicated.

(2) This subdivision does not apply upon a roadway of a divided highway.

(f)(1) The City of Long Beach may, by ordinance or resolution, implement a pilot program to authorize vehicles to park on the left-hand side of the roadway parallel to and within 18 inches of the left-hand curb on two-way local residential streets that dead-end with no cul-de-sac or other designated area in which to turn around, if the City of Long Beach has first made a finding, supported by a professional engineering study, that the ordinance or resolution is justified by the need to facilitate the safe and orderly movement of vehicles on the roadways affected by the resolution or ordinance. The area covered by the ordinance or resolution shall be limited to the streets perpendicular to Ocean Boulevard beginning at Balboa Place and ending at 72nd Place, but shall not cover 62nd Place. The ordinance or resolution permitting that parking shall not apply until signs or markings giving adequate notice have been placed near the designated roadways. The city shall submit to the Legislature, two years from the date of the enactment of the ordinance or resolution that establishes the pilot program, a report that outlines the advantages and disadvantages of the pilot program. The report submitted pursuant to this subdivision shall be submitted in compliance with Section 9795 of the Government Code.

(2) The pilot program authorized under this subdivision shall terminate, and this subdivision shall become inoperative, three years from the date of enactment of the ordinance or resolution that establishes the pilot program. *(Stats.1959, c. 3, p. 1699, § 22502. Amended by Stats.1959, c. 978, p. 3006, § 1; Stats.1965, c. 308, p. 1404, § 1; Stats.1967, c. 767, p. 2155, § 1; Stats.1969, c. 777, p. 1555, § 1; Stats.1971, c. 448, p. 933, § 1, operative May 3, 1972; Stats.2010, c. 135 (A.B.2067), § 1.)*

Cross References

Commercial vehicles defined, see Vehicle Code § 260.

Curb markings to indicate parking regulations, see Vehicle Code § 21458.
Local authorities defined, see Vehicle Code § 385.
Park or parking defined, see Vehicle Code § 463.
Report of convictions to department, exceptions, see Vehicle Code § 1803 et seq.
Rubbish or garbage trucks, exemptions, see Vehicle Code § 21059.
Stop or stopping defined, see Vehicle Code § 587.
Streetsweeping and watering vehicles, application of section, see Vehicle Code § 21060.

§ 22503. Local ordinance; angle parking

Local authorities may by ordinance permit angle parking on any roadway, or left-hand parking upon one-way roadways of divided highways, except that no ordinance is effective with respect to any state highway until the proposed ordinance has been submitted to and approved in writing by the Department of Transportation. *(Stats. 1959, c. 3, p. 1699, § 22503. Amended by Stats.1971, c. 448, p. 933, § 2, operative May 3, 1972; Stats.1974, c. 545, p. 1325, § 205.)*

Cross References

Authority of Department of Transportation over local authorities in traffic rules, see Vehicle Code §§ 21104, 21350, 21353.
Highway defined, see Vehicle Code § 360.
Local authorities defined, see Vehicle Code § 385.
Report of convictions to department, exceptions, see Vehicle Code § 1803 et seq.
Roadway defined, see Vehicle Code § 530.

§ 22503.5. Two or three-wheeled motor vehicle parking regulations

Notwithstanding any other provision of this code, any local authority may, by ordinance or resolution, establish special parking regulations for two-wheeled or three-wheeled motor vehicles. *(Added by Stats.1965, c. 1131, p. 2777, § 1. Amended by Stats.1972, c. 1095, p. 2056, § 4.)*

Cross References

Motor vehicle defined, see Vehicle Code § 415.

§ 22504. Unincorporated area parking; exception; school bus stops

(a) Upon any highway in unincorporated areas, a person shall not stop, park, or leave standing any vehicle, whether attended or unattended, upon the roadway when it is practicable to stop, park, or leave the vehicle off such portion of the highway, but in every event an unobstructed width of the highway opposite a standing vehicle shall be left for the free passage of other vehicles and a clear view of the stopped vehicle shall be available from a distance of 200 feet in each direction upon the highway. This section shall not apply upon a highway where the roadway is bounded by adjacent curbs.

(b) This section does not apply to the driver of any vehicle which is disabled in such a manner and to such extent that it is impossible to avoid stopping and temporarily leaving the disabled vehicle on the roadway.

(c) (1) A schoolbus stop shall not be designated where there is not a clear view of a proposed or existing schoolbus stop from a distance of 200 feet in each direction along a highway, or upon the main traveled portion of a highway where there is not a clear view of the stop from 500 feet in each direction along the highway and the speed limit is more than 25 miles per hour, unless approved by the Department of the California Highway Patrol upon the request of the school district superintendent or the head or principal of a private school. If the schoolbus stop is approved by the Department of the California Highway Patrol, the Department of Transportation, in respect to state highways, and local authorities, in respect to highways under their jurisdiction, shall place sufficient signs along the highway to give adequate notice to motorists that they are approaching such bus stops.

(2) A school bus stop shall not be designated on any divided or multiple-lane highway where pupils must cross the highway to board or after exiting the bus, unless traffic is controlled by a traffic officer or official traffic control signal. For purposes of this section, a multiple-lane highway is defined as any highway having two or more lanes of travel in each direction. *(Stats.1959, c. 3, p. 1699, § 22504. Amended by Stats.1961, c. 1429, p. 3230, § 1; Stats.1974, c. 545, p. 1325, § 206; Stats.2012, c. 769 (A.B.2679), § 37.)*

Cross References

Curb markings indicating parking regulations, see Vehicle Code § 21458.
Definitions,
  Roadway, see Vehicle Code § 530.
  Street or highway, see Vehicle Code §§ 360, 590, 592.
  Vehicle, see Vehicle Code § 670.
Display of warning devices when commercial vehicle disabled, see Vehicle Code § 25300.
Illegal parking, see Vehicle Code § 40200 et seq.
Impounding of vehicle by officer for inspection, see Vehicle Code § 22655.
Local parking regulations, see Vehicle Code § 22507.
Parking facility, use of street by, see Vehicle Code § 22951.
Removal of parked vehicles, authorization, see Vehicle Code § 22654.
Roadway with adjacent curbs, parking of vehicles upon, see Vehicle Code §§ 22502, 22508.
Rubbish or garbage trucks, exemption, see Vehicle Code § 21059.
Selling or vending from vehicle parked on highway, see Streets and Highways Code § 731.
Snow areas, parking in, see Vehicle Code § 22510.
Stopping, standing or parking prohibited in specified places, see Vehicle Code § 22500.
Stopping for school buses, see Vehicle Code § 22454.
Streetsweeping and watering vehicles, application of section, see Vehicle Code § 21060.
Tow cars, right to park to assist disabled vehicles, see Vehicle Code § 22513.
Utility vehicles, stopping, standing or parking of, see Vehicle Code §§ 22512, 25301.

§ 22505. Stopping, standing, or parking in certain areas

(a) The Department of Transportation with respect to highways under its jurisdiction may place signs or mark-ings prohibiting or restricting the stopping, standing, or parking of vehicles, including, but not limited to, vehicles which are six feet or more in height (including any load thereon), in any of the following areas and under the following conditions:

(1) In areas where, in its opinion, stopping, standing, or parking is dangerous to those using the highway or where the stopping, standing, or parking of vehicles would unduly interfere with the free movement of traffic thereon.

(2) In areas within one-half mile of the boundary of any unit of the state park system which the Director of Conservation has determined are unusually high fire hazard areas, upon notification of the Department of Transportation of such determination by the Director of Conservation.

(3) In areas within one-half mile of the boundary of any unit of the state park system which the county health officer has determined are areas where a substantial public health hazard would result if camping were allowed, upon notification of the Department of Transportation of such determination by the county health officer.

(b) No person shall stop, park, or leave standing any vehicle in violation of the restrictions stated on the signs or markings.

(c) This section does not apply to any of the following:

(1) Public utility vehicles while performing a work operation.

(2) The driver of any vehicle which is disabled in such a manner and to such an extent that it is impossible to avoid stopping, parking, or leaving the disabled vehicle standing on the roadway. *(Stats.1959, c. 3, p. 1699, § 22505. Amended by Stats.1963, c. 888, p. 2132, § 1; Stats.1970, c. 515, p. 1002, § 3; Stats.1974, c. 52, p. 115, § 1; Stats.1985, c. 912, § 1; Stats.1987, c. 455, § 2.)*

Cross References

Department of transportation may close or restrict use of highway, see Streets and Highways Code § 124.
Official traffic control devices by Department of Transportation and by local authorities, see Vehicle Code §§ 21350, 21351.
Parking defined, see Vehicle Code § 463.
Stopping defined, see Vehicle Code § 587.

§ 22506. Local regulation of state highways

Local authorities may by ordinance or resolution prohibit or restrict the stopping, standing, or parking of vehicles on a state highway, in their respective jurisdictions, if the ordinance or resolution is first submitted to and approved in writing by the Department of Transportation, except that where maintenance of any state highway is delegated by the Department of Transportation to a city, the department may also delegate to the city the powers conferred on the department. *(Stats.1959, c. 3, p. 1699, § 22506. Amended by Stats.1974, c. 545, p. 1325, § 207; Stats.1987, c. 455, § 3.)*

Cross References

Delegation of powers to city by department of transportation, see Streets and Highways Code § 116.

Local authorities defined, see Vehicle Code § 385.

Parking defined, see Vehicle Code § 463.

§ 22507. Local regulation; preferential parking

(a) Local authorities may, by ordinance or resolution, prohibit or restrict the stopping, parking, or standing of vehicles, including, but not limited to, vehicles that are six feet or more in height (including any load thereon) within 100 feet of any intersection, on certain streets or highways, or portions thereof, during all or certain hours of the day. The ordinance or resolution may include a designation of certain streets upon which preferential parking privileges are given to residents and merchants adjacent to the streets for their use and the use of their guests, under which the residents and merchants may be issued a permit or permits that exempt them from the prohibition or restriction of the ordinance or resolution. With the exception of alleys, the ordinance or resolution shall not apply until signs or markings giving adequate notice thereof have been placed. A local ordinance or resolution adopted pursuant to this section may contain provisions that are reasonable and necessary to ensure the effectiveness of a preferential parking program.

(b) An ordinance or resolution adopted under this section may also authorize preferential parking permits for members of organizations, professions, or other designated groups, including, but not limited to, school personnel, to park on specified streets if the local authority determines that the use of the permits will not adversely affect parking conditions for residents and merchants in the area. *(Stats.1959, c. 3, p. 1700, § 22507. Amended by Stats.1963, c. 1070, p. 2530, § 1; Stats.1969, c. 541, p. 1168, § 1; Stats.1976, c. 1102, p. 4982, § 1; Stats.1980, c. 140, p. 334, § 1; Stats.1984, c. 181, § 2; Stats.1985, c. 912, § 2; Stats.1987, c. 455, § 4; Stats.1997, c. 343 (S.B.626), § 2; Stats.2001, c. 223 (S.B.779), § 1.)*

Cross References

Authority to remove vehicles, mobile advertising displays parked or left standing in violation of local resolution or ordinance, warning citations issued in lieu of posting signs giving notice of ordinance, see Vehicle Code § 22651.

Definitions,

Alley, see Vehicle Code § 110.

Highway, see Vehicle Code §§ 360, 592.

Local authorities, see Vehicle Code § 385.

Park or parking, see Vehicle Code § 463.

Street, see Vehicle Code § 590.

Vehicle, see Vehicle Code § 670.

Exemption of emergency vehicles from rules of the road, exceptions, see Vehicle Code § 21055.

Stopping, standing or parking, generally, see Vehicle Code § 22500 et seq.

Traffic regulation by local authorities, see Vehicle Code § 21100 et seq.

Utility vehicles, application of this section, see Vehicle Code § 22512.

§ 22507.1. Designation of streets or portions thereof for exclusive parking privilege for participants in car share or ridesharing program

(a) A local authority may, by ordinance or resolution, designate certain streets or portions of streets for the exclusive parking privilege of motor vehicles participating in a car share vehicle program or ridesharing program. The ordinance or resolution shall establish the criteria for a public or private company or organization to participate in the program, and may limit the types of motor vehicles that may be included in the program. Under the car share vehicle program a car share vehicle or ridesharing vehicle shall be assigned a permit by the local authority that allows that vehicle to park in the exclusive designated parking areas.

(b) The ordinance or resolution described in subdivision (a) does not apply until signs or markings giving adequate notice thereof have been placed.

(c) A local ordinance or resolution adopted pursuant to subdivision (a) may contain provisions that are reasonable and necessary to ensure the effectiveness of a car share vehicle program or ridesharing program.

(d) For purposes of this section, a "car share vehicle" is a motor vehicle that is operated as part of a regional fleet by a public or private car sharing company or organization and provides hourly or daily service. *(Added by Stats.2006, c. 189 (A.B.2154), § 1.)*

§ 22507.2. Parking in front of private driveways; ordinance; permits

Notwithstanding subdivision (e) of Section 22500, a local authority may, by ordinance, authorize the owner or lessee of property to park a vehicle in front of the owner's or lessee's private driveway when the vehicle displays a permit issued pursuant to the ordinance authorizing such parking.

The local authority may charge a nonrefundable fee to defray the costs of issuing and administering the permits.

A local ordinance adopted pursuant to this section may not authorize parking on a sidewalk in violation of subdivision (f) of Section 22500. *(Added by Stats.1980, c. 158, p. 356, § 2, eff. June 11, 1980. Amended by Stats.1984, c. 219, § 1, eff. June 20, 1984; Stats.1985, c. 45, § 1.)*

§ 22507.5. Local regulation; overnight parking; commercial vehicles or trailer component thereof; vehicles transporting hazardous waste

(a) Notwithstanding Section 22507, local authorities may, by ordinance or resolution, prohibit or restrict the parking or standing of vehicles on certain streets or highways, or portions thereof, between the hours of 2 a.m. and 6 a.m., and may, by ordinance or resolution, prohibit or restrict the parking or standing, on any street, or portion thereof, in a residential district, of commercial vehicles having a manufacturer's gross vehicle weight rating of 10,000 pounds or more. The ordinance or resolution relating to parking between the hours of 2 a.m. and 6 a.m. may provide for a system of permits for the purpose of exempting from the prohibition or restriction of the ordinance or resolution, disabled persons, residents, and guests of residents of residential areas, including, but not limited to, high-density and multiple-family dwelling areas, lacking adequate offstreet parking facilities. The ordinance or resolution relating to the parking or standing of commercial vehicles in a residential district, however, shall not be effective with respect to any commercial vehicle, or trailer component thereof, making pickups or deliveries of goods, wares, and merchandise from or to any building or structure located on the restricted streets or highways or for the purpose of delivering materials to be used in the actual and bona fide repair, alteration, remodeling, or construction of any building or structure upon the restricted streets or highways for which a building permit has previously been obtained.

(b) Subdivision (a) of this section is applicable to vehicles specified in subdivision (a) of Section 31303, except that an ordinance or resolution adopted pursuant to subdivision (a) of this section shall not permit the parking of those vehicles which is otherwise prohibited under this code.

(c) For the purpose of implementing this section, each local authority may, by ordinance, define the term "residential district" in accordance with its zoning ordinance. The ordinance is not effective unless the legislative body of the local authority holds a public hearing on the proposed ordinance prior to its adoption, with notice of the public hearing given in accordance with Section 65090 of the Government Code. *(Added by Stats.1969, c. 541, p. 1168, § 2. Amended by Stats.1975, c. 1213, p. 3069, § 1; Stats.1976, c. 37, p. 64, § 1, eff. March 9, 1976; Stats.1987, c. 349, § 1; Stats.1989, c. 533, § 11; Stats. 1996, c. 1156 (A.B.3157), § 1; Stats.2004, c. 404 (S.B. 1725), § 11; Stats.2004, c. 518 (A.B.2201), § 3.)*

Cross References

Definitions,
  Highway, see Vehicle Code §§ 360, 592.
  Local authorities, see Vehicle Code § 385.
  Parking, see Vehicle Code § 463.
  Street, see Vehicle Code § 590.
  Vehicle, see Vehicle Code § 670.

§ 22507.6. Local regulation; street sweeping; commercial vehicles; signs

Local authorities may, by ordinance or resolution, prohibit or restrict the parking or standing of vehicles on designated streets or highways, or portions thereof, for the purpose of street sweeping. No ordinance or resolution relating to the parking or standing of commercial vehicles in a residential district shall be effective with respect to any commercial vehicle making pickups or deliveries of goods, wares, or merchandise from or to any

building or structure located on the restricted street or highway, or for the purpose of delivering materials to be used in the repair, alteration, remodeling, or reconstruction of any building or structure for which a building permit has previously been obtained. No such ordinance or resolution shall be effective until the street or highway, or portion thereof, has been sign-posted in accordance with the uniform standards and specifications of the Department of Transportation, or local authorities have caused to be posted in a conspicuous place at each entrance to the street a notice not less than 17 inches by 22 inches in size, with lettering not less than one inch in height, setting forth the day or days and hours parking is prohibited. As used in this section, "entrance" means the intersection of any street or streets comprising an area of restricted parking for street-sweeping purposes on the same day or days and hours with another street or highway not subject to such a parking restriction, or subject to parking restrictions on different days and hours. *(Added by Stats.1980, c. 391, p. 772, § 1. Amended by Stats.1981, c. 80, p. 196, § 1; Stats.1982, c. 466, p. 2058, § 115.)*

Cross References

Parking of utility vehicles, see Vehicle Code § 22512.

§ 22507.8. Disabled persons' and veterans' parking spaces; unauthorized parking or obstructing; offstreet parking facilities

(a) It is unlawful for any person to park or leave standing any vehicle in a stall or space designated for disabled persons and disabled veterans pursuant to Section 22511.7 or 22511.8 of this code or Section 14679 of the Government Code, unless the vehicle displays either a special identification license plate issued pursuant to Section 5007 or a distinguishing placard issued pursuant to Section 22511.55 or 22511.59.

(b) It is unlawful for any person to obstruct, block, or otherwise bar access to those parking stalls or spaces except as provided in subdivision (a).

(c) It is unlawful for any person to park or leave standing any vehicle, including a vehicle displaying a special identification license plate issued pursuant to Section 5007 or a distinguishing placard issued pursuant to Section 22511.55 or 22511.59, in either of the following places:

(1) On the lines marking the boundaries of a parking stall or space designated for disabled persons or disabled veterans.

(2) In any area of the pavement adjacent to a parking stall or space designated for disabled persons or disabled veterans that is marked by crosshatched lines and is thereby designated, pursuant to any local ordinance, for the loading and unloading of vehicles parked in the stall or space.

(d) Subdivisions (a), (b), and (c) apply to all offstreet parking facilities owned or operated by the state, and to all offstreet parking facilities owned or operated by a local authority. Subdivisions (a), (b), and (c) also apply to any privately owned and maintained offstreet parking facility. *(Added by Stats.1989, c. 338, § 2, eff. Sept. 11, 1989, operative Jan. 1, 1991. Amended by Stats.1990, c. 303 (A.B.3849), § 1; Stats.1994, c. 1149 (A.B.2878), § 4; Stats.1997, c. 945 (A.B.1561), § 18; Stats.2009, c. 200 (S.B.734), § 12.)*

Cross References

Authority of city or county to adopt an ordinance or resolution to assess an additional penalty relating to disabled parking violations, see Vehicle Code § 4461.3.

Fines and penalties, limits, see Vehicle Code § 40203.5.

Issuance and renewal of disabled parking placards, penalty printing requirements, see Vehicle Code §§ 22511.55 and 22511.59.

Parking penalties, additional assessments, see Vehicle Code § 40203.6.

Penalty for person convicted of infraction for violation of this section, see Vehicle Code § 42001.13.

Private parking facilities, see Vehicle Code § 21107.8.

Removal of unauthorized vehicle from physically handicapped parking space, see Vehicle Code § 22652.

Violation, punishment, see Vehicle Code § 42001.5.

§ 22507.9. Special enforcement units; handicapped parking enforcement; compensation and benefits; application of section

Local authorities may establish a special enforcement unit for the sole purpose of providing adequate enforcement of Section 22507.8 and local ordinances and resolutions adopted pursuant to Section 22511.7.

Local authorities may establish recruitment and employment guidelines that encourage and enable employment of qualified disabled persons in these special enforcement units.

Members of the special enforcement unit may issue notices of parking violation for violations of Section 22507.8 and local ordinances adopted pursuant to Section 22511.7. Members of the special enforcement unit shall not be peace officers and shall not make arrests in the course of their official duties, but shall wear distinctive uniforms and badges while on duty. A two-way radio unit, which may utilize police frequencies or citizens' band, may be issued by the local authority to each member of the special enforcement unit for use while on duty.

The local authority may pay the cost of uniforms and badges for the special enforcement unit, and may provide daily cleaning of the uniforms. Additionally, the local authority may provide motorized wheelchairs for use by members of the special unit while on duty, including batteries and necessary recharging thereof. Any motorized wheelchair used by a member of the special enforcement unit while on duty shall be equipped with a single headlamp in the front and a single stoplamp in the rear.

Members of the special enforcement unit may be paid an hourly wage without the compensatory benefits provided other permanent and temporary employees, but shall be entitled to applicable workers' compensation

benefits as provided by law. Insurance provided by the local authority for disability or liability of a member of the special enforcement unit shall be the same as for other employees performing similar duties.

Nothing in this section precludes a local authority from using regular full-time employees to enforce this chapter and ordinances adopted pursuant thereto.

This section applies to all counties and cities, including every charter city and city and county. *(Added by Stats.1984, c. 1095, § 1. Amended by Stats.1996, c. 124 (A.B.3470), § 127.)*

§ 22508. Parking meter zones; fee rates; fee payment

(a) A local authority shall not establish parking meter zones or fix the rate of fees for those zones except by ordinance. The rate of fees may be variable, based upon criteria identified by the local authority in the ordinance. An ordinance establishing a parking meter zone shall describe the area that would be included within the zone.

(b) A local authority may by ordinance cause streets and highways to be marked with white lines designating parking spaces and require vehicles to park within the parking spaces.

(c) An ordinance adopted by a local authority pursuant to this section with respect to any state highway shall not become effective until the proposed ordinance has been submitted to and approved in writing by the Department of Transportation. The proposed ordinance shall be submitted to the department only by action of the local legislative body and the proposed ordinance shall be submitted in complete draft form.

(d) An ordinance adopted pursuant to this section establishing a parking meter zone or fixing rates of fees for that zone shall be subject to local referendum processes in the same manner as if the ordinance dealt with a matter of purely local concern.

(e) A local authority may accept but shall not require payment of parking meter fees by a mobile device. *(Stats.1959, c. 3, p. 1700, § 22508. Amended by Stats. 1961, c. 2017, p. 4231, § 2; Stats.1974, c. 545, p. 1326, § 208; Stats.2012, c. 70 (S.B.1388), § 1.)*

Cross References

Colors used in curb markings, see Vehicle Code § 21458.

Definitions,
    Highway, see Vehicle Code §§ 360, 591, 592.
    Local authorities, see Vehicle Code § 385.
    Park or parking, see Vehicle Code § 463.
    Street, see Vehicle Code §§ 590, 591.

Local regulation of traffic matters, see Vehicle Code § 21100 et seq.

Referendum in municipalities, see Elections Code § 9235 et seq.

Report of previous convictions, see Vehicle Code § 1803.

§ 22508.5. Inoperable parking meter or payment center; prohibitions or restrictions

Section inoperative from Jan. 1, 2014 until Jan. 1, 2017. See, also, section operative from Jan. 1, 2014 until Jan. 1, 2017.

(a) Except as provided in subdivision (b), a vehicle may park, for up to the posted time limit, in any parking space that is * * * regulated by an inoperable parking meter or an inoperable parking payment center.

(b) * * * A local authority may, by ordinance or resolution, prohibit or restrict the parking of vehicles * * * in a parking space regulated by an inoperable parking meter or inoperable parking payment * * * center. An ordinance or resolution adopted by a local authority pursuant to this section shall not become effective until signs or markings giving adequate notice of the restriction or prohibition on parking have been placed at parking locations, parking meters, or parking payment centers.

(c) For purposes of this section:

(1) "Inoperable parking meter" means a meter located next to and designated for an individual parking space, which has become inoperable and cannot accept payment in any form or cannot register that a payment in any form has been made.

(2) "Inoperable parking payment center" means an electronic parking meter or pay station serving one or more parking spaces that is closest to the space where a person has parked and that cannot accept payment in any form, cannot register that a payment in any form has been made, or cannot issue a receipt that is required to be displayed in a conspicuous location on or in the vehicle.

(d) This section shall become inoperative on January 1, 2014, and shall remain inoperative until January 1, 2017. *(Added by Stats.2012, c. 70 (S.B.1388), § 2. Amended by Stats.2013, c. 71 (A.B.61), § 1.)*

Operative Effect

For operative effect of this section, see its terms.

§ 22508.5. Inoperable parking meter or payment center; prohibitions or restrictions

Section operative from Jan. 1, 2014 to Jan. 1, 2017. See, also, section inoperative from Jan. 1, 2014 to Jan. 1, 2017.

(a) A vehicle may park, for up to the posted time limit, in any parking space that is regulated by an inoperable parking meter or an inoperable parking payment center.

(b) A local authority shall not, by ordinance or resolution, prohibit or restrict the parking of vehicles in a space that is regulated by an inoperable parking meter or inoperable parking payment center.

(c) For purposes of this section:

(1) "Inoperable parking meter" means a meter located next to and designated for an individual parking space, which has become inoperable and cannot accept payment in any form or cannot register that a payment in any form has been made.

(2) "Inoperable parking payment center" means an electronic parking meter or pay station serving one or more parking spaces that is closest to the space where a

person has parked and that cannot accept payment in any form, cannot register that a payment in any form has been made, or cannot issue a receipt that is required to be displayed in a conspicuous location on or in the vehicle.

(d) This section shall remain in effect only until January 1, 2017, and as of that date is repealed, unless a later enacted statute, that is enacted before January 1, 2017, deletes or extends that date. *(Added by Stats.2013, c. 71 (A.B.61), § 2.)*

Repeal

For repeal of this section, see its terms.

§ 22509. Parking on hills

Local authorities within the reasonable exercise of their police powers may adopt rules and regulations by ordinance or resolution providing that no person driving, or in control of, or in charge of, a motor vehicle shall permit it to stand on any highway unattended when upon any grade exceeding 3 percent within any business or residence district without blocking the wheels of the vehicle by turning them against the curb or by other means. *(Stats.1959, c. 3, p. 1700, § 22509.)*

Cross References

Business and residence districts defined, see Vehicle Code §§ 235, 515.

Exemption of emergency vehicles from rules of the road, exceptions, see Vehicle Code § 21055.

Local authorities defined, see Vehicle Code § 385.

Motor vehicle defined, see Vehicle Code § 415.

Utility vehicles, application of this section, see Vehicle Code § 22512.

§ 22510. Snow removal areas; parking restrictions; signs

(a) Local authorities may, by ordinance or resolution, prohibit or restrict the parking or standing of vehicles on designated streets or highways within their jurisdiction, or portions thereof, for the purpose of snow removal. The ordinance or resolution shall not be effective until the street or highway, or portion thereof, has been sign-posted in accordance with the uniform standards and specifications of the Department of Transportation, or until the local authorities have caused to be posted in a conspicuous place at each entrance to the street or highway, a notice not less than 17 inches by 22 inches in size, with lettering not less than one inch in height, setting forth the days parking is prohibited. The signs shall, at a minimum, be placed on each affected street or highway, at the boundary of the local authority, and at the beginning and end of each highway or highway segment included in that area. No person shall stop, park, or leave standing any vehicle, whether attended or unattended, within the area marked by signs, except when necessary to avoid conflict with other traffic or in compliance with the directions of a traffic or peace officer.

(b) No ordinance or resolution authorized by subdivision (a) which affects a state highway shall be effective until it is submitted to, and approved by, the Department of Transportation.

(c) The Department of Transportation, with respect to state highways, may restrict the parking or standing of vehicles for purposes of snow removal. The restrictions shall not be effective until the highway, or portion thereof, has been posted with signs in accordance with the uniform standards and specifications of the department. No person shall stop, park, or leave standing any vehicle, whether attended or unattended, within the area marked by parking restriction signs, except when necessary to avoid conflict with other traffic or in compliance with the directions of a traffic or peace officer. *(Added by Stats.1990, c. 692 (A.B.3398), § 3.)*

Cross References

Department of transportation may close or restrict use of highway, see Streets and Highways Code § 124.
Local authorities defined, see Vehicle Code § 385.
Official traffic control device defined, see Vehicle Code § 440.
Traffic signs, signals and markings, generally, see Vehicle Code § 21350 et seq.

§ 22511. Electric vehicle parking stalls or spaces; removal of vehicles not connected for electric charging purposes; off-street parking facility posting and signage requirements; local ordinances

(a) A local authority, by ordinance or resolution, and a person in lawful possession of an offstreet parking facility may designate stalls or spaces in an offstreet parking facility owned or operated by that local authority or person for the exclusive purpose of charging and parking a vehicle that is connected for electric charging purposes.

(b) If posted in accordance with subdivision (d) or (e), the owner or person in lawful possession of a privately owned or operated offstreet parking facility, after notifying the police or sheriff's department, may cause the removal of a vehicle from a stall or space designated pursuant to subdivision (a) in the facility to the nearest public garage if the vehicle is not connected for electric charging purposes.

(c) If posted in accordance with subdivision (d), the local authority owning or operating an offstreet parking facility, after notifying the police or sheriff's department, may cause the removal of a vehicle from a stall or space designated pursuant to subdivision (a) in the facility to the nearest garage, as defined in Section 340, that is owned, leased, or approved for use by a public agency if the vehicle is not connected for electric charging purposes.

(d) The posting required for an offstreet parking facility owned or operated either privately or by a local authority shall consist of a sign not less than 17 by 22 inches in size with lettering not less than one inch in height that clearly and conspicuously states the following:
" Unauthorized vehicles not connected for electric charging purposes will be towed away at owner's expense. Towed vehicles may be reclaimed at

_____ or by telephoning
(Address)
                                                  ,"
_____
                                                  ,"
(Telephone number of local law enforcement agency)

The sign shall be posted in either of the following locations:

(1) Immediately adjacent to, and visible from, the stall or space.

(2) In a conspicuous place at each entrance to the offstreet parking facility.

(e) If the parking facility is privately owned and public parking is prohibited by the posting of a sign meeting the requirements of paragraph (1) of subdivision (a) of Section 22658, the requirements of subdivision (b) may be met by the posting of a sign immediately adjacent to, and visible from, each stall or space indicating that a vehicle not meeting the requirements of subdivision (a) will be removed at the owner's expense and containing the telephone number of the local traffic law enforcement agency.

(f) This section does not interfere with existing law governing the ability of local authorities to adopt ordinances related to parking programs within their jurisdiction, such as programs that provide free parking in metered areas or municipal garages for electric vehicles. *(Added by Stats.2002, c. 640 (A.B.1314), § 2. Amended by Stats.2011, c. 274 (A.B.475), § 1.)*

§ 22511.1. Electric vehicle parking stalls or spaces; unauthorized parking or obstructing

(a) A person shall not park or leave standing a vehicle in a stall or space designated pursuant to Section 22511 unless the vehicle is connected for electric charging purposes.

(b) A person shall not obstruct, block, or otherwise bar access to parking stalls or spaces described in subdivision (a) except as provided in subdivision (a).

(Added by Stats.2002, c. 640 (A.B.1314), § 3. Amended by Stats.2011, c. 274 (A.B.475), § 2.)

Cross References

Punishment upon conviction, penalty amount, see Vehicle Code § 42001.6.

§ 22511.3. Veterans displaying special license plates; metered parking spaces; privileges

(a) A veteran displaying special license plates issued under Section 5101.3, 5101.4, 5101.5, 5101.6, or 5101.8 may park his or her motor vehicle, weighing not more than 6,000 pounds gross weight, without charge, in a metered parking space.

(b) Nothing in this section restricts the rights of a person displaying either a special identification license plate issued pursuant to Section 5007 or a distinguishing placard issued pursuant to Section 22511.55 or 22511.59.

(c)(1) This section does not exempt a vehicle displaying special license plates issued under Section 5101.3, 5101.4, 5101.5, 5101.6, or 5101.8 from compliance with any other state law or ordinance, including, but not limited to, vehicle height restrictions, zones that prohibit stopping, parking, or standing of all vehicles, parking time limitations, street sweeping, restrictions of the parking space to a particular type of vehicle, or the parking of a vehicle that is involved in the operation of a street vending business.

(2) This section does not authorize a vehicle displaying special license plates issued under Section 5101.3, 5101.4, 5101.5, 5101.6, or 5101.8 to park in a state parking facility that is designated only for state employees.

(3) This section does not authorize a vehicle displaying special license plates issued under Section 5101.3, 5101.4, 5101.5, 5101.6, or 5101.8 to park during time periods other than the normal business hours of, or the maximum time allotted by, a state or local authority parking facility.

(4) This section does not require the state or a local authority to designate specific parking spaces for vehicles displaying special license plates issued under Section 5101.3, 5101.4, 5101.5, 5101.6, or 5101.8.

(d) A local authority's compliance with subdivision (a) is solely contingent upon the approval of its governing body. *(Added by Stats.2008, c. 588 (A.B.190), § 1.)*

§ 22511.5. Disabled persons or disabled veterans; parking privileges

(a)(1) A disabled person or disabled veteran displaying special license plates issued under Section 5007 or a distinguishing placard issued under Section 22511.55 or 22511.59 is allowed to park for unlimited periods in any of the following zones:

(A) In any restricted zone described in paragraph (5) of subdivision (a) of Section 21458 or on streets upon which preferential parking privileges and height limits have been given pursuant to Section 22507.

(B) In any parking zone that is restricted as to the length of time parking is permitted as indicated by a sign erected pursuant to a local ordinance.

(2) A disabled person or disabled veteran is allowed to park in any metered parking space without being required to pay parking meter fees.

(3) This subdivision does not apply to a zone for which state law or ordinance absolutely prohibits stopping, parking, or standing of all vehicles, or which the law or ordinance reserves for special types of vehicles, or to the parking of a vehicle that is involved in the operation of a street vending business.

(b) A disabled person or disabled veteran is allowed to park a motor vehicle displaying a special disabled person license plate or placard issued by a foreign jurisdiction with the same parking privileges authorized in this code

674

for any motor vehicle displaying a special license plate or a distinguishing placard issued by the Department of Motor Vehicles. *(Added by Stats.1978, c. 457, p. 1550, § 2. Amended by Stats.1980, c. 261, p. 533, § 1; Stats. 1982, c. 974, p. 3487, § 2; Stats.1982, c. 975, p. 3494, § 6.5; Stats.1984, c. 510, § 1; Stats.1984, c. 1118, § 1; Stats.1985, c. 1041, § 7; Stats.1986, c. 351, § 3; Stats. 1988, c. 115, § 1; Stats.1989, c. 554, § 3; Stats.1991, c. 893 (A.B.274), § 4; Stats.1992, c. 785 (A.B.2289), § 3; Stats.1992, c. 1241 (S.B.1615), § 21; Stats.1994, c. 1149 (A.B.2878), § 5; Stats.2004, c. 404 (S.B.1725), § 12; Stats.2010, c. 478 (A.B.2777), § 11.)*

Cross References

Exemption of disabled person from weight fees, see Vehicle Code § 9410.
Parking facilities, state agencies, see Government Code § 14679.

§ 22511.55. Issuance and renewal of disabled parking placard; conditions; printing requirements

(a)(1) A disabled person or disabled veteran may apply to the department for the issuance of a distinguishing placard. The placard may be used in lieu of the special license plate or plates issued under Section 5007 for parking purposes described in Section 22511.5 when (A) suspended from the rearview mirror, (B) if there is no rearview mirror, when displayed on the dashboard of a vehicle, or (C) inserted in a clip designated for a distinguishing placard and installed by the manufacturer on the driver's side of the front window. It is the intent of the Legislature to encourage the use of distinguishing placards because they provide law enforcement officers with a more readily recognizable symbol for distinguishing vehicles qualified for the parking privilege. The placard shall be the size, shape, and color determined by the department and shall bear the International Symbol of Access adopted pursuant to Section 3 of Public Law 100–641, commonly known as the "wheelchair symbol." The department shall incorporate instructions for the lawful use of a placard, and a summary of the penalties for the unlawful use of a placard, into the identification card issued to the placard owner.

(2)(A) The department may establish procedures for the issuance and renewal of the placards. The procedures shall include, but are not limited to, advising an applicant in writing on the application for a placard of the procedure to apply for a special license plate or plates, as described in Section 5007, and the fee exemptions established pursuant to Section 9105 and in subdivision (a) of Section 10783 of the Revenue and Taxation Code. The placards shall have a fixed expiration date of June 30 every two years. A portion of the placard shall be printed in a contrasting color that shall be changed every two years. The size and color of this contrasting portion of the placard shall be large and distinctive enough to be readily identifiable by a law enforcement officer in a passing vehicle.

(B) As used in this section, "year" means the period between the inclusive dates of July 1 through June 30.

(C) Prior to the end of each year, the department shall, for the most current three years available, compare its record of disability placards issued against the records of the Office of Vital Records of the State Department of Public Health, or its successor, and withhold any renewal notices that otherwise would have been sent for a placardholder identified as deceased.

(3) Except as provided in paragraph (4), a person shall not be eligible for more than one placard at a time.

(4) Organizations and agencies involved in the transportation of disabled persons or disabled veterans may apply for a placard for each vehicle used for the purpose of transporting disabled persons or disabled veterans.

(b)(1) Except as provided in paragraph (4), prior to issuing an original distinguishing placard to a disabled person or disabled veteran, the department shall require the submission of a certificate, in accordance with paragraph (2), signed by the physician and surgeon, or to the extent that it does not cause a reduction in the receipt of federal aid highway funds, by a nurse practitioner, certified nurse midwife, or physician assistant, substantiating the disability, unless the applicant's disability is readily observable and uncontested. The disability of a person who has lost, or has lost use of, one or more lower extremities or one hand, for a disabled veteran, or both hands, for a disabled person, or who has significant limitation in the use of lower extremities, may also be certified by a licensed chiropractor. The blindness of an applicant shall be certified by a licensed physician and surgeon who specializes in diseases of the eye or a licensed optometrist. The physician and surgeon, nurse practitioner, certified nurse midwife, physician assistant, chiropractor, or optometrist certifying the qualifying disability shall provide a full description of the illness or disability on the form submitted to the department.

(2) The physician and surgeon, nurse practitioner, certified nurse midwife, physician assistant, chiropractor, or optometrist who signs a certificate submitted under this subdivision shall retain information sufficient to substantiate that certificate and, upon request of the department, shall make that information available for inspection by the Medical Board of California or the appropriate regulatory board.

(3) The department shall maintain in its records all information on an applicant's certification of permanent disability and shall make that information available to eligible law enforcement or parking control agencies upon a request pursuant to Section 22511.58.

(4) For a disabled veteran, the department shall accept, in lieu of the certificate described in paragraph (1), a certificate from the United States Department of Veterans Affairs that certifies that the applicant is a disabled veteran as described in Section 295.7.

(c) A person who is issued a distinguishing placard pursuant to subdivision (a) may apply to the department for a substitute placard without recertification of eligibility, if that placard is lost or stolen.

(d) The distinguishing placard shall be returned to the department not later than 60 days after the death of the disabled person or disabled veteran to whom the placard was issued.

(e) The department shall print on any distinguishing placard issued on or after January 1, 2005, the maximum penalty that may be imposed for a violation of Section 4461. For purposes of this subdivision, the "maximum penalty" is the amount derived from adding all of the following:

(1) The maximum fine that may be imposed under Section 4461.

(2) The penalty required to be imposed under Section 70372 of the Government Code.

(3) The penalty required to be levied under Section 76000 of the Government Code.

(4) The penalty required to be levied under Section 1464 of the Penal Code.

(5) The surcharge required to be levied under Section 1465.7 of the Penal Code.

(6) The penalty authorized to be imposed under Section 4461.3. *(Added by Stats.1991, c. 893 (A.B.274), § 5. Amended by Stats.1991, c. 894 (S.B.234), § 3; Stats.1993, c. 1292 (S.B.274), § 13; Stats.1994, c. 1149 (A.B.2878), § 6; Stats.1996, c. 1033 (S.B.1498), § 1; Stats.2000, c. 524 (A.B.1792), § 5; Stats.2001, c. 708 (A.B.677), § 3; Stats.2003, c. 555 (A.B.327), § 5; Stats. 2004, c. 404 (S.B.1725), § 13; Stats.2006, c. 116 (A.B. 2120), § 3; Stats.2010, c. 196 (A.B.1855), § 1; Stats.2010, c. 421 (A.B.1944), § 2; Stats.2010, c. 491 (S.B.1318), § 42.3.)*

Cross References

Additional fines imposed for violation of disabled parking restrictions, see Penal Code § 1465.6.

Authority of city or county to adopt an ordinance or resolution to assess an additional penalty relating to disabled parking violations, see Vehicle Code § 4461.3.

Fines and penalties, suspension, see Vehicle Code § 40203.5.

Fines imposed and collected for violation of disabled parking restrictions, see Penal Code § 1465.5.

Former prisoners of war, disabled veterans, or Congressional Medal of Honor recipients, exemptions from fees for certain plates, certificates, or cards, see Vehicle Code § 9105.

Parking facilities for physically handicapped persons and disabled veterans, display of distinguishing placard, see Government Code § 14679.

Revenue allocations under § 30914, performance measures, operating agreement, report, regional transit connectivity plan, TransLink Consortium integrated fare program, Bay Area Regional Rail Plan, see Vehicle Code § 5201.

§ 22511.56. Placard or specialty license plate; presentation of identification and evidence of issuance; failure to present; penalties for misuse; confiscation; cancellation

(a) A person using a distinguishing placard issued under Section 22511.55 or 22511.59, or a special license plate issued under Section 5007, for parking as permitted by Section 22511.5 shall, upon request of a peace officer or person authorized to enforce parking laws, ordinances, or regulations, present identification and evidence of the issuance of that placard or plate to that person, or that vehicle if the plate was issued pursuant to paragraph (3) of subdivision (a) of Section 5007.

(b) Failure to present the requested identification and evidence of the issuance of that placard or plate shall be a rebuttable presumption that the placard or plate is being misused and that the associated vehicle has been parked in violation of Section 22507.8, or has exercised a disabled person's parking privilege pursuant to Section 22511.5.

(c) In addition to any other applicable penalty for the misuse of a placard, the officer or parking enforcement person may confiscate a placard being used for parking purposes that benefit a person other than the person to whom the placard was issued by the Department of Motor Vehicles. A placard lawfully used by a person transporting a disabled person pursuant to subdivision (b) of Section 4461 may not be confiscated.

(d) In addition to any other applicable penalty for the misuse of a special license plate issued under Section 5007, a peace officer may confiscate the plate being used for parking purposes that benefit a person other than the person to whom the plate was issued by the Department of Motor Vehicles.

(e) After verification with the Department of Motor Vehicles that the user of the placard or plate is not the registered owner of the placard or plate, the appropriate agency that confiscated the placard or plate shall notify the department of the placard or plate number and the department shall cancel the placard or plate. A placard or plate canceled by the department pursuant to this subdivision may be destroyed by the agency that confiscated the placard or plate. *(Added by Stats.1991, c. 894 (S.B.234), § 4. Amended by Stats.1994, c. 1149 (A.B. 2878), § 7; Stats.2000, c. 135 (A.B.2539), § 162; Stats. 2004, c. 363 (A.B.1138), § 3; Stats.2006, c. 203 (A.B. 1910), § 2.)*

§ 22511.57. Disabled person placards lost or stolen; owner of placard deceased; vehicle parking restrictions and prohibitions

A local authority may, by ordinance or resolution, prohibit or restrict the parking or standing of a vehicle on streets or highways or in a parking stall or space in a privately or publicly owned or operated offstreet parking facility within its jurisdiction when the vehicle displays, in order to obtain special parking privileges, a distinguishing placard or special license plate, issued pursuant to Section 5007, 22511.55, or 22511.59, and any of the following conditions are met:

(a) The records of the Department of Motor Vehicles for the identification number assigned to the placard or license plate indicate that the placard or license plate has been reported as lost, stolen, surrendered, canceled, revoked, or expired, or was issued to a person who has been reported as deceased for a period exceeding 60 days.

(b) The placard or license plate is displayed on a vehicle that is not being used to transport, and is not in the reasonable proximity of, the person to whom the license plate or placard was issued or a person who is authorized to be transported in the vehicle displaying that placard or license plate.

(c) The placard or license plate is counterfeit, forged, altered, or mutilated. *(Added by Stats.1994, c. 221 (S.B.1378), § 1, operative July 1, 1995. Amended by Stats.2004, c. 363 (A.B.1138), § 4; Stats.2004, c. 404 (S.B.1725), § 14; Stats.2009, c. 415 (A.B.144), § 4; Stats. 2011, c. 341 (S.B.565), § 3.)*

Cross References

Fines and penalties, limits, see Vehicle Code § 40203.5.
Parking penalties, additional assessments, see Vehicle Code § 40203.6.

§ 22511.58. Physician's certificate information; release to specified local agencies; local review board

(a) Upon a request to the department by a local public law enforcement agency or local agency responsible for the administration or enforcement of parking regulations, the department shall make available to the requesting agency any information contained in a physician's certificate submitted to the department as part of the application for a disabled person's parking privileges, substantiating the disability of a person applying for or who has been issued a parking placard pursuant to Section 22511.55. The department shall not provide the information specified in this subdivision to any private or other third-party parking citation processing agency.

(b) Local authorities may establish a review board or panel, which shall include a qualified physician or medical authority, for purposes of reviewing information contained in the applications for special parking privileges and the certification of qualifying disabilities for persons residing within the jurisdiction of the local authority. Any findings or determinations by a review board or panel under this section indicating that an application or certification is fraudulent or lacks proper certification may be transmitted to the department or other appropriate authorities for further review and investigation. *(Added by Stats.1996, c. 1033 (S.B.1498), § 2.)*

§ 22511.59. Temporary distinguishing placard; renewal

(a) Upon the receipt of the applications and documents required by subdivision (b), (c), or (d), the department shall issue a temporary distinguishing placard bearing the International Symbol of Access adopted pursuant to Section 3 of Public Law 100–641 commonly known as the "wheelchair symbol." During the period for which it is valid, the temporary distinguishing placard may be used for the parking purposes described in Section 22511.5 in the same manner as a distinguishing placard issued pursuant to Section 22511.55.

(b)(1) A person who is temporarily disabled for a period of not more than six months may apply to the department for the issuance of the temporary distinguishing placard described in subdivision (a).

(2) Prior to issuing a placard pursuant to this subdivision, the department shall require the submission of a certificate signed by a physician and surgeon, or to the extent that it does not cause a reduction in the receipt of federal aid highway funds, by a nurse practitioner, certified nurse midwife, physician assistant, chiropractor, or optometrist, as described in subdivision (b) of Section 22511.55, substantiating the temporary disability and stating the date upon which the disability is expected to terminate.

(3) The physician and surgeon, nurse practitioner, certified nurse midwife, physician assistant, chiropractor, or optometrist who signs a certificate submitted under this subdivision shall maintain information sufficient to substantiate that certificate and, upon request of the department, shall make that information available for inspection by the Medical Board of California or the appropriate regulatory board.

(4) A placard issued pursuant to this subdivision shall expire not later than 180 days from the date of issuance or upon the expected termination date of the disability, as stated on the certificate required by paragraph (2), whichever is less.

(5) The fee for a temporary placard issued pursuant to this subdivision shall be six dollars ($6).

(6) A placard issued pursuant to this subdivision shall be renewed a maximum of six times consecutively.

(c)(1) A permanently disabled person or disabled veteran who is not a resident of this state and plans to travel within the state may apply to the department for the issuance of the temporary distinguishing placard described in subdivision (a).

(2) Prior to issuing a placard pursuant to this subdivision, the department shall require certification of the disability, as described in subdivision (b) of Section 22511.55.

(3) The physician and surgeon, nurse practitioner, certified nurse midwife, physician assistant, chiropractor, or optometrist who signs a certificate submitted under this subdivision shall maintain information sufficient to substantiate that certificate and, upon request of the department, shall make that information available for inspection by the Medical Board of California or the appropriate regulatory board.

(4) A placard issued pursuant to this subdivision shall expire not later than 90 days from the date of issuance.

(5) The department shall not charge a fee for issuance of a placard under this subdivision.

(6) A placard issued pursuant to this subdivision shall be renewed a maximum of six times consecutively.

(d)(1) A permanently disabled person or disabled veteran who has been issued either a distinguishing placard pursuant to Section 22511.55 or special license plates pursuant to Section 5007, but not both, may apply

to the department for the issuance of the temporary distinguishing placard described in subdivision (a) for the purpose of travel.

(2) Prior to issuing a placard pursuant to this subdivision, the department shall require the applicant to submit either the number identifying the distinguishing placard issued pursuant to Section 22511.55 or the number on the special license plates.

(3) A placard issued pursuant to this subdivision shall expire not later than 30 days from the date of issuance.

(4) The department shall not charge a fee for issuance of a placard under this subdivision.

(5) A placard issued pursuant to this subdivision shall be renewed a maximum of six times consecutively.

(e) The department shall print on a temporary distinguishing placard, the maximum penalty that may be imposed for a violation of Section 4461. For the purposes of this subdivision, the "maximum penalty" is the amount derived from adding all of the following:

(1) The maximum fine that may be imposed under Section 4461.

(2) The penalty required to be imposed under Section 70372 of the Government Code.

(3) The penalty required to be levied under Section 76000 of the Government Code.

(4) The penalty required to be levied under Section 1464 of the Penal Code.

(5) The surcharge required to be levied under Section 1465.7 of the Penal Code.

(6) The penalty authorized to be imposed under Section 4461.3. *(Added by Stats.1994, c. 1149 (A.B.2878), § 8. Amended by Stats.2000, c. 524 (A.B.1792), § 6; Stats.2001, c. 708 (A.B.677), § 4; Stats.2003, c. 555 (A.B.327), § 6; Stats.2004, c. 404 (S.B.1725), § 15; Stats. 2006, c. 116 (A.B.2120), § 4; Stats.2007, c. 413 (A.B. 1531), § 2.)*

Cross References

Fines and penalties, suspension, see Vehicle Code § 40203.5.
Parking facilities for physically handicapped persons and disabled veterans, display of distinguishing placard, see Government Code § 14679.

§ 22511.6. Cancellation or revocation of distinguishing placards

(a) The Department of Motor Vehicles may cancel or revoke a distinguishing placard issued pursuant to Section 22511.55 or 22511.59 in any of the following events:

(1) When the department is satisfied that the placard was fraudulently obtained or erroneously issued.

(2) When the department determines that the required fee has not been paid and the fee is not paid upon reasonable notice and demand.

(3) When the placard could have been refused when last issued or renewed.

(4) When the department determines that the owner of the placard has committed any offense described in Section 4461 or 4463, involving the placard to be canceled or revoked.

(5) When the department determines that the owner of the placard is deceased.

(b) Whenever the Department of Motor Vehicles cancels or revokes a distinguishing placard, the owner or person in possession of the placard shall immediately return the placard to the department. *(Added by Stats. 1984, c. 510, § 2; Stats.1984, c. 1118, § 2. Amended by Stats.1993, c. 1292 (S.B.274), § 14; Stats.1994, c. 1149 (A.B.2878), § 9.)*

§ 22511.7. Designation of parking for disabled persons and veterans

(a) In addition to Section 22511.8 for offstreet parking, a local authority may, by ordinance or resolution, designate onstreet parking spaces for the exclusive use of a vehicle that displays either a special identification license plate issued pursuant to Section 5007 or a distinguishing placard issued pursuant to Section 22511.55 or 22511.59.

(b)(1) Whenever a local authority so designates a parking space, it shall be indicated by blue paint on the curb or edge of the paved portion of the street adjacent to the space. In addition, the local authority shall post immediately adjacent to and visible from the space a sign consisting of a profile view of a wheelchair with occupant in white on a blue background.

(2) The sign required pursuant to paragraph (1) shall clearly and conspicuously state the following: "Minimum Fine $250." This paragraph applies only to signs for parking spaces constructed on or after July 1, 2008, and signs that are replaced on or after July 1, 2008.

(3) If the loading and unloading area of the pavement adjacent to a parking stall or space designated for disabled persons or disabled veterans is to be marked by a border and hatched lines, the border shall be painted blue and the hatched lines shall be painted a suitable contrasting color to the parking space. Blue or white paint is preferred. In addition, within the border the words "No Parking" shall be painted in white letters no less than 12 inches high. This paragraph applies only to parking spaces constructed on or after July 1, 2008, and painting that is done on or after July 1, 2008.

(c) This section does not restrict the privilege granted to disabled persons and disabled veterans by Section 22511.5. *(Added by Stats.1975, c. 688, p. 1636, § 2. Amended by Stats.1976, c. 1096, p. 4961, § 4; Stats.1983, c. 270, § 2, eff. July 15, 1983; Stats.1985, c. 1041, § 8; Stats.1987, c. 314, § 2; Stats.1989, c. 554, § 4; Stats.1990, c. 692 (A.B.3398), § 4; Stats.1994, c. 1149 (A.B.2878), § 10; Stats.2007, c. 413 (A.B.1531), § 3; Stats.2009, c. 200 (S.B.734), § 13.)*

Cross References
Removal of unauthorized vehicle from physically handicapped parking space, see Vehicle Code § 22652.

678

Request by state agency for local agency to provide handicapped parking, see Government Code § 14679.

§ 22511.8. Offstreet parking; designation of parking for disabled persons and veterans; removal of unauthorized vehicles

(a) A local authority, by ordinance or resolution, and a person in lawful possession of an offstreet parking facility may designate stalls or spaces in an offstreet parking facility owned or operated by the local authority or person for the exclusive use of a vehicle that displays either a special license plate issued pursuant to Section 5007 or a distinguishing placard issued pursuant to Section 22511.55 or 22511.59. The designation shall be made by posting a sign as described in paragraph (1), and by either of the markings described in paragraph (2) or (3):

(1)(A) By posting immediately adjacent to, and visible from, each stall or space, a sign consisting of a profile view of a wheelchair with occupant in white on a blue background.

(B) The sign shall also clearly and conspicuously state the following: "Minimum Fine $250." This subparagraph applies only to signs for parking spaces constructed on or after July 1, 2008, and signs that are replaced on or after July 1, 2008, or as the State Architect deems necessary when renovations, structural repair, alterations, and additions occur to existing buildings and facilities on or after July 1, 2008.

(2)(A) By outlining or painting the stall or space in blue and outlining on the ground in the stall or space in white or suitable contrasting color a profile view depicting a wheelchair with occupant.

(B) The loading and unloading area of the pavement adjacent to a parking stall or space designated for disabled persons or disabled veterans shall be marked by a border and hatched lines. The border shall be painted blue and the hatched lines shall be painted a suitable contrasting color to the parking space. Blue or white paint is preferred. In addition, within the border the words "No Parking" shall be painted in white letters no less than 12 inches high. This subparagraph applies only to parking spaces constructed on or after July 1, 2008, and painting that is done on or after July 1, 2008, or as the State Architect deems necessary when renovations, structural repair, alterations, and additions occur to existing buildings and facilities on or after July 1, 2008.

(3) By outlining a profile view of a wheelchair with occupant in white on a blue background, of the same dimensions as in paragraph (2). The profile view shall be located so that it is visible to a traffic enforcement officer when a vehicle is properly parked in the space.

(b) The Department of General Services under the Division of the State Architect shall develop pursuant to Section 4450 of the Government Code, as appropriate, conforming regulations to ensure compliance with subparagraph (B) of paragraph (1) of subdivision (a) and subparagraph (B) of paragraph (2) of subdivision (a).

Initial regulations to implement these provisions shall be adopted as emergency regulations. The adoption of these regulations shall be considered by the Department of General Services to be an emergency necessary for the immediate preservation of the public peace, health and safety, or general welfare.

(c) If posted in accordance with subdivision (e) or (f), the owner or person in lawful possession of a privately owned or operated offstreet parking facility, after notifying the police or sheriff's department, may cause the removal of a vehicle from a stall or space designated pursuant to subdivision (a) in the facility to the nearest public garage unless a special license plate issued pursuant to Section 5007 or distinguishing placard issued pursuant to Section 22511.55 or 22511.59 is displayed on the vehicle.

(d) If posted in accordance with subdivision (e), the local authority owning or operating an offstreet parking facility, after notifying the police or sheriff's department, may cause the removal of a vehicle from a stall or space designated pursuant to subdivision (a) in the facility to the nearest public garage unless a special license plate issued pursuant to Section 5007 or a distinguishing placard issued pursuant to Section 22511.55 or 22511.59 is displayed on the vehicle.

(e) Except as provided in Section 22511.9, the posting required for an offstreet parking facility owned or operated either privately or by a local authority shall consist of a sign not less than 17 by 22 inches in size with lettering not less than one inch in height which clearly and conspicuously states the following: "Unauthorized vehicles parked in designated accessible spaces not displaying distinguishing placards or special license plates issued for persons with disabilities will be towed away at the owner's expense. Towed vehicles may be reclaimed at:

_____or by telephoning
(Address)
_____."
(Telephone number of local law enforcement agency)

The sign shall be posted in either of the following locations:

(1) Immediately adjacent to, and visible from, the stall or space.

(2) In a conspicuous place at each entrance to the offstreet parking facility.

(f) If the parking facility is privately owned and public parking is prohibited by the posting of a sign meeting the requirements of paragraph (1) of subdivision (a) of Section 22658, the requirements of subdivision (c) may be met by the posting of a sign immediately adjacent to, and visible from, each stall or space indicating that a vehicle not meeting the requirements of subdivision (a) will be removed at the owner's expense and containing the telephone number of the local traffic law enforcement agency.

(g) This section does not restrict the privilege granted to disabled persons and disabled veterans by Section 22511.5. *(Added by Stats.1975, c. 688, p. 1636, § 3. Amended by Stats.1976, c. 1096, p. 4962, § 5; Stats.1982, c. 975, p. 3495, § 7; Stats.1983, c. 270, § 3, eff. July 15, 1983; Stats.1985, c. 312, § 1; Stats.1985, c. 1041, § 9; Stats.1987, c. 314, § 3; Stats.1989, c. 554, § 5; Stats.1990, c. 216 (S.B.2510), § 118; Stats.1991, c. 928 (A.B.1886), § 27, eff. Oct. 14, 1991; Stats.1994, c. 1149 (A.B.2878), § 11; Stats.2004, c. 404 (S.B.1725), § 16; Stats.2007, c. 413 (A.B.1531), § 4; Stats.2009, c. 200 (S.B.734), § 14.)*

Cross References

Immunity from liability removal of vehicle from handicapped parking, see Vehicle Code § 22652.5.
Private parking facilities, see Vehicle Code § 21107.8.
Removal of unauthorized vehicle from physically handicapped parking space, see Vehicle Code § 22652.

§ 22511.85. Public offstreet parking facilities; loading and unloading disabled persons; sufficient space

A vehicle, identified with a special license plate issued pursuant to Section 5007 or a distinguishing placard issued pursuant to Section 22511.55 or 22511.59, which is equipped with a lift, ramp, or assistive equipment that is used for the loading and unloading of a person with a disability may park in not more than two adjacent stalls or spaces on a street or highway or in a public or private off-street parking facility if the equipment has been or will be used for loading or unloading a person with a disability, and if there is no single parking space immediately available on the street or highway or within the facility that is suitable for that purpose, including, but not limited to, when there is not sufficient space to operate a vehicle lift, ramp, or assistive equipment, or there is not sufficient room for a person with a disability to exit the vehicle or maneuver once outside the vehicle. *(Added by Stats. 2000, c. 215 (A.B.1276), § 3. Amended by Stats.2007, c. 387 (A.B.463), § 1; Stats.2008, c. 179 (S.B.1498), § 221.)*

§ 22511.9. Replacement signs relating to parking privileges for disabled persons; contents

Every new or replacement sign installed on or after January 1, 1992, relating to parking privileges for disabled persons shall refer to "disabled persons" rather than "physically handicapped persons" or any other similar term, whenever such a reference is required on a sign. *(Added by Stats.1991, c. 928 (A.B.1886), § 28, eff. Oct. 14, 1991.)*

§ 22511.95. New or replacement signs installed after July 1, 2008; content; parking privileges for disabled persons

All new or replacement signs installed on or after July 1, 2008, relating to parking privileges for disabled persons shall refer to "persons with disabilities" rather than "disabled persons" or any other similar term, whenever the reference is required on the sign. *(Added by Stats. 2007, c. 413 (A.B.1531), § 5.)*

§ 22511.10. Disabled persons; Legislative findings

The Legislature hereby finds and declares all of the following:

(a) Two and one-half million Californians suffer from some form of chronic obstructive pulmonary disease. Those persons who are not in wheelchairs have difficulty walking long distances.

(b) Encouraging those with physical disabilities to engage in activities outside of the home promotes better health and self-esteem, thereby lowering health costs.

(c) Placing disabled person parking spaces closest to the main entrances of buildings does not cost taxpayers, but provides accessibility to the physically disabled.

(d) It is the intent of the Legislature, in enacting Section 22511.11, to direct the Office of the State Architect to propose regulations that require disabled person parking spaces to be located on the shortest accessible route of travel to an accessible entrance or exit of a building or parking facility. *(Added by Stats.1992, c. 1187 (S.B.2043), § 1.)*

§ 22511.11. Office of State Architect; regulations; location of disabled person parking stalls or spaces

(a) The Office of the State Architect shall propose regulations specifying the location of disabled person parking stalls or spaces designated pursuant to Section 22511.8, for parking facilities constructed or reconstructed pursuant to a building permit issued on or after October 1, 1993. In specifying the placement of those stalls or spaces near buildings or facilities and within parking structures, consideration shall be given to the special access needs of disabled persons.

(b) The Office of the State Architect shall submit the regulations proposed pursuant to subdivision (a) to the State Building Standards Commission on or before July 1, 1993, for approval, adoption, and publication in Title 24 of the California Code of Regulations. *(Added by Stats.1992, c. 1187 (S.B.2043), § 2.)*

§ 22512. Driver or owner of utility service vehicle; exemption from provisions

Except as otherwise indicated in subdivision (b), none of the following provisions shall apply to the driver or owner of any service vehicle owned or operated by or for or operated under contract with a utility or public utility, whether privately, municipally, or publicly owned, used in the construction, operation, removal, or repair of utility or public utility property or facilities, if warning devices are displayed and when the vehicle is stopped, standing, or parked at the site of work involving the construction, operation, removal, or repair of the utility or public utility property or facilities upon, in, over, under, or adjacent to a highway, bicycle lane, bikeway, or bicycle path or trail, or of a vehicle, whether privately, municipally, or publicly owned, if warning devices are displayed and when the vehicle is engaged in authorized work on the highway, bicycle lane, bikeway, or bicycle path or trail:

(a) Sections 21112, 21211, 21707, 21708, 22507.6, 24605, 25253, 25300, 27700, and 27907.

(b) This chapter, except Sections 22507, 22509, 22515, and 22517.

(c) Chapter 10 (commencing with Section 22650). *(Stats.1959, c. 3, p. 1700, § 22512. Amended by Stats. 1972, c. 618, p. 1150, § 146; Stats.1974, c. 545, p. 1327, § 210; Stats.1980, c. 391, p. 773, § 2; Stats.1987, c. 499, § 2; Stats.1996, c. 124 (A.B.3470), § 128.)*

Cross References

Off-highway vehicle exemption, see Vehicle Code § 38010.
Public utility defined, see Const. Art. 12, § 3; Public Utilities Code § 216.
Regulations governing color of lights on public utility repair vehicles, see Vehicle Code §§ 25260, 25260.1.
Speed limit on highways where persons are at work, see Vehicle Code § 22362.
Warning lights and devices on utility vehicles, see Vehicle Code § 25301.

§ 22513. Tow trucks; stopping or parking; solicitation of engagement for services; removal of vehicle without authorization; misdemeanor; exceptions

(a) Except as provided in subdivision (b) or (c), the owner or operator of a tow truck who complies with the requirements of this code relating to tow trucks may stop or park the tow truck upon a highway for the purpose of rendering assistance to a disabled vehicle.

(b) It is a misdemeanor for the owner or operator of a tow truck to stop at the scene of an accident or near a disabled vehicle for the purpose of soliciting an engagement for towing services, either directly or indirectly, or to furnish any towing services, unless summoned to the scene, requested to stop, or flagged down by the owner or operator of a disabled vehicle or requested to perform the service by a law enforcement officer or public agency pursuant to that agency's procedures.

(c) It is a misdemeanor for the owner or operator of a tow truck to move any vehicle from a highway, street, or public property without the express authorization of the owner or operator of the vehicle or a law enforcement officer or public agency pursuant to that agency's procedures, when the vehicle has been left unattended or when there is an injury as the result of an accident.

(d) This section shall not apply to the following:

(1) A vehicle owned or operated by, or under contract to, a motor club, as defined by Section 12142 of the Insurance Code, which stops to provide services for which compensation is neither requested nor received, provided that those services may not include towing other than that which may be necessary to remove the vehicle to the nearest safe shoulder. The owner or operator of such a vehicle may contact a law enforcement agency or other public agency on behalf of a motorist, but may not refer a motorist to a tow truck owner or operator, unless the motorist is a member of the motor club, the motorist is referred to a tow truck owner or operator under contract

680

to the motor club, and, if there is a dispatch facility which services the area and is owned or operated by the motor club, the referral is made through that dispatch facility.

(2) A tow truck operator employed by a law enforcement agency or other public agency.

(3) A tow truck owner or operator acting under contract with a law enforcement or other public agency to abate abandoned vehicles, or to provide towing service or emergency road service to motorists while involved in freeway service patrol operations, to the extent authorized by law. *(Stats.1959, c. 3, p. 1701, § 22513. Amended by Stats.1967, c. 441, p. 1654, § 1; Stats.1988, c. 924, § 8; Stats.1991, c. 755 (S.B.600), § 1; Stats.1991, c. 1004 (S.B.887), § 3.)*

Cross References
Freeway defined, see Vehicle Code § 332.
Rear lighting equipment for tow trucks and towed vehicles, see Vehicle Code § 24605.
Tow truck defined, see Vehicle Code § 615.
Towing and loading equipment, see Vehicle Code § 29000 et seq.
Warning lights on tow trucks, see Vehicle Code § 25253.

§ 22514. Fire hydrants

No person shall stop, park, or leave standing any vehicle within 15 feet of a fire hydrant except as follows:

(a) If the vehicle is attended by a licensed driver who is seated in the front seat and who can immediately move such vehicle in case of necessity.

(b) If the local authority adopts an ordinance or resolution reducing that distance. If the distance is less than 10 feet total length when measured along the curb or edge of the street, the distance shall be indicated by signs or markings.

(c) If the vehicle is owned or operated by a fire department and is clearly marked as a fire department vehicle. *(Stats.1959, c. 3, p. 1701, § 22514. Amended by Stats.1961, c. 1615, p. 3458, § 35; Stats.1987, c. 488, § 1.)*

Cross References
Local authorities defined, see Vehicle Code § 385.
Park defined, see Vehicle Code § 463.
Report of convictions to department, exceptions, see Vehicle Code § 1803 et seq.
Stop or stopping defined, see Vehicle Code § 587.

§ 22515. Unattended vehicles

(a) No person driving, or in control of, or in charge of, a motor vehicle shall permit it to stand on any highway unattended without first effectively setting the brakes thereon and stopping the motor thereof.

(b) No person in control of, or in charge of, any vehicle, other than a motor vehicle, shall permit it to stand on any highway without first effectively setting the brakes thereon, or blocking the wheels thereof, to effectively prevent the movement of the vehicle. *(Stats.1959, c. 3, p. 1701, § 22515. Amended by Stats.1986, c. 362, § 3.)*

Cross References
Exemption of emergency vehicles from rules of the road, exceptions, see Vehicle Code § 21055.
Utility vehicles, application of this section, see Vehicle Code § 22512.

§ 22516. Locked vehicle

No person shall leave standing a locked vehicle in which there is any person who cannot readily escape therefrom. *(Stats.1959, c. 3, p. 1701, § 22516.)*

§ 22517. Opening and closing doors

No person shall open the door of a vehicle on the side available to moving traffic unless it is reasonably safe to do so and can be done without interfering with the movement of such traffic, nor shall any person leave a door open on the side of a vehicle available to moving traffic for a period of time longer than necessary to load or unload passengers. *(Stats.1959, c. 3, p. 1701, § 22517. Amended by Stats.1963, c. 162, p. 895, § 1.)*

Cross References
Exemption of emergency vehicles from rules of the road, exceptions, see Vehicle Code § 21055.
Utility vehicles, application of this section, see Vehicle Code § 22512.
Vehicle defined, see Vehicle Code § 670.

§ 22518. Fringe and transportation corridor parking facilities; authorized vehicles

(a) Fringe and transportation corridor parking facilities constructed, maintained, or operated by the Department of Transportation pursuant to Section 146.5 of the Streets and Highways Code shall be used only by persons using a bicycle or public transit, or engaged in ridesharing, including, but not limited to, carpools or vanpools. A person shall not park a vehicle 30 feet or more in length, engage in loitering or camping, or engage in vending or any other commercial activity on any fringe or transportation corridor parking facility.

(b) This section does not apply to alternatively fueled infrastructure programs in park-and-ride lots owned and operated by the Department of Transportation. *(Added by Stats.1992, c. 1243 (A.B.3090), § 91, eff. Sept. 30, 1992. Amended by Stats.2012, c. 676 (A.B.2583), § 3.)*

§ 22519. Regulation of offstreet parking

Local authorities may by ordinance or resolution prohibit, restrict or regulate the parking, stopping or standing of vehicles on any offstreet parking facility which it owns or operates. No such ordinance or resolution shall apply until signs giving notice thereof have been erected. *(Added by Stats.1959, c. 1486, p. 3778, § 1.)*

Cross References
Local authorities defined, see Vehicle Code § 385.

§ 22520. Repealed by Stats.1997, c. 945 (A.B.1561), § 19

§ **22520.5. Vending merchandise or services near freeways; exceptions; violations; penalties**

(a) No person shall solicit, display, sell, offer for sale, or otherwise vend or attempt to vend any merchandise or service while being wholly or partly within any of the following:

(1) The right-of-way of any freeway, including any on ramp, off ramp, or roadway shoulder which lies within the right-of-way of the freeway.

(2) Any roadway or adjacent shoulder within 500 feet of a freeway off ramp or on ramp.

(3) Any sidewalk within 500 feet of a freeway off ramp or on ramp, when vending or attempting to vend to vehicular traffic.

(b) Subdivision (a) does not apply to a roadside rest area or vista point located within a freeway right-of-way which is subject to Section 22520.6, to a tow truck or service vehicle rendering assistance to a disabled vehicle, or to a person issued a permit to vend upon the freeway pursuant to Section 670 of the Streets and Highways Code.

(c) A violation of this section is an infraction. A second or subsequent conviction of a violation of this section is a misdemeanor. *(Added by Stats.1981, c. 936, p. 3540, § 1. Amended by Stats.1983, c. 275, § 2, eff. July 15, 1983; Stats.1984, c. 487, § 1; Stats.1988, c. 924, § 10.)*

Cross References

Displaying, selling, or vending merchandise, foodstuffs, or services within vista points or safety roadside rest areas prohibited, exception, see Streets and Highways Code § 225.5.
Violation as misdemeanor, see Vehicle Code § 40000.13.

§ **22520.6. Roadside rest areas or vista points; violations; penalties**

(a) No person shall engage in any activity within a highway roadside rest area or vista point prohibited by rules and regulations adopted pursuant to Section 225 of the Streets and Highways Code.

(b) A violation of this section is an infraction. A second or subsequent conviction of a violation of this section is a misdemeanor. *(Added by Stats.1983, c. 275, § 3, eff. July 15, 1983.)*

Cross References

Displaying, selling, or vending merchandise, foodstuffs, or services within vista points or safety roadside rest areas prohibited, exception, see Streets and Highways Code § 225.5.
Violation as misdemeanor, see Vehicle Code § 40000.13.

§ **22521. Parking upon or near railroad track**

No person shall park a vehicle upon any railroad track or within 7½ feet of the nearest rail. *(Added by Stats. 1968, c. 625, p. 1309, § 1.)*

§ **22522. Parking near sidewalk access ramps**

No person shall park a vehicle within three feet of any sidewalk access ramp constructed at, or adjacent to, a crosswalk or at any other location on a sidewalk so as to be accessible to and usable by the physically disabled, if the area adjoining the ramp is designated by either a sign or red paint. *(Added by Stats.1974, c. 760, p. 1675, § 1. Amended by Stats.1994, c. 221 (S.B.1378), § 2, operative July 1, 1995; Stats.1999, c. 1007 (S.B.532), § 22.)*

Cross References

Parking penalties, additional assessments, see Vehicle Code § 40203.6.

§ **22523. Abandonment; fine; liability for cost of removal and disposition; offense; liability for deficiency**

(a) No person shall abandon a vehicle upon any highway.

(b) No person shall abandon a vehicle upon public or private property without the express or implied consent of the owner or person in lawful possession or control of the property.

(c) Any person convicted of a violation of this section shall be punished by a fine of not less than one hundred dollars ($100) and shall provide proof that the costs of removal and disposition of the vehicle have been paid. No part of any fine imposed shall be suspended. The fine may be paid in installments if the court determines that the defendant is unable to pay the entire amount in one payment.

(d) Proof that the costs of removal and disposition of the vehicle have been paid shall not be required if proof is provided to the court that the vehicle was stolen prior to abandonment. That proof may consist of a police report or other evidence acceptable to the court.

(e) The costs required to be paid for the removal and disposition of any vehicle determined to be abandoned pursuant to Section 22669 shall not exceed those for towing and seven days of storage. This subdivision does not apply if the registered owner or legal owner has completed and returned to the lienholder a "Declaration of Opposition" form within the time specified in Section 22851.8.

(f)(1) If a vehicle is abandoned in violation of subdivision (b) and is not redeemed after impound, the last registered owner is guilty of an infraction. In addition to any other penalty, the registered owner shall be liable for any deficiency remaining after disposal of the vehicle under Section 3071 or 3072 of the Civil Code or Section 22851.10 of this code.

(2) The filing of a report of sale or transfer of the vehicle pursuant to Section 5602, the filing of a vehicle theft report with a law enforcement agency, or the filing of a form or notice with the department pursuant to subdivision (b) of Section 4456 or Section 5900 or 5901 relieves the registered owner of liability under this

subdivision. *(Added by Stats.1988, c. 1267, § 5, eff. Sept. 26, 1988, operative July 1, 1989. Amended by Stats.1990, c. 111 (S.B.2006), § 1; Stats.1996, c. 676 (S.B.1111), § 2.)*

Cross References

Highway defined, see Vehicle Code §§ 360, 591, 592.
Movement of abandoned vehicle standing on highway, authority of peace officer, see Vehicle Code § 22654.
Removal of abandoned vehicles, see Vehicle Code § 22669.
Report of vehicles stored in a garage, repair shop, parking lot or trailer park or public parking area for 30 days, see Vehicle Code § 10652.
Violation, punishment, see Vehicle Code § 42001.5.

§ 22524. Presumption; overcoming presumption

(a) The abandonment of any vehicle in a manner as provided in Section 22523 shall constitute a prima facie presumption that the last registered owner of record is responsible for the abandonment and is thereby liable for the cost of removal and disposition of the vehicle.

(b) An owner who has made a bona fide sale or transfer of a vehicle and has delivered possession of the vehicle to a purchaser may overcome the presumption prescribed in subdivision (a) by demonstrating that he or she has complied with Section 5900 or providing other proof satisfactory to the court.

(c) This section shall become operative on July 1, 1989. *(Added by Stats.1988, c. 1267, § 7, eff. Sept. 26, 1988, operative July 1, 1989.)*

Cross References

Presumptions, see Evidence Code § 600 et seq.

§ 22524.5. Automobile insurance; ordinary and reasonable towing and storage charges; accident or stolen recovery; discharge of obligation

(a) Any insurer that is responsible for coverage for ordinary and reasonable towing and storage charges under an automobile insurance policy to an insured or on behalf of an insured to a valid claimant, is liable for those charges to the person performing those services when a vehicle is towed and stored as a result of an accident or stolen recovery. The insurer may discharge the obligation by making payment to the person performing the towing and storage services or to the insured or on behalf of the insured to the claimant.

(b) Any insured or claimant who has received payment, which includes towing and storage charges, from an insurer for a loss relating to a vehicle is liable for those charges to the person performing those services. *(Added by Stats.1986, c. 1380, § 1.)*

§ 22525. Vanpool vehicles; use of state highway bus stops; local ordinance or resolution

Local authorities may by ordinance or resolution authorize vanpool vehicles to utilize designated state highway bus stops.

The ordinance or resolution shall be submitted to the Department of Transportation for approval. No ordinance or resolution shall become effective until approved by the department. The department shall review the ordinance or resolution within 45 days after receipt. *(Added by Stats.1987, c. 262, § 1.)*

§ 22526. Anti–Gridlock Act of 1987; parking or stopping violation

(a) Notwithstanding any official traffic control signal indication to proceed, a driver of a vehicle shall not enter an intersection or marked crosswalk unless there is sufficient space on the other side of the intersection or marked crosswalk to accommodate the vehicle driven without obstructing the through passage of vehicles from either side.

(b) A driver of a vehicle which is making a turn at an intersection who is facing a steady circular yellow or yellow arrow signal shall not enter the intersection or marked crosswalk unless there is sufficient space on the other side of the intersection or marked crosswalk to accommodate the vehicle driven without obstructing the through passage of vehicles from either side.

(c) A driver of a vehicle shall not enter a railroad or rail transit crossing, notwithstanding any official traffic control device or signal indication to proceed, unless there is sufficient undercarriage clearance to cross the intersection without obstructing the through passage of a railway vehicle, including, but not limited to, a train, trolley, or city transit vehicle.

(d) A driver of a vehicle shall not enter a railroad or rail transit crossing, notwithstanding any official traffic control device or signal indication to proceed, unless there is sufficient space on the other side of the railroad or rail transit crossing to accommodate the vehicle driven and any railway vehicle, including, but not limited to, a train, trolley, or city transit vehicle.

(e) A local authority may post appropriate signs at the entrance to intersections indicating the prohibition in subdivisions (a), (b), and (c).

(f) A violation of this section is not a violation of a law relating to the safe operation of vehicles and is the following:

(1) A stopping violation when a notice to appear has been issued by a peace officer described in Section 830.1, 830.2, or 830.33 of the Penal Code.

(2) A parking violation when a notice of parking violation is issued by a person, other than a peace officer described in paragraph (1), who is authorized to enforce parking statutes and regulations.

(g) This section shall be known and may be cited as the Anti–Gridlock Act of 1987. *(Added by Stats.1987, c. 739, § 1. Amended by Stats.1993, c. 647 (S.B.952), § 2; Stats.1996, c. 116 (S.B.1527), § 2; Stats.2001, c. 504 (A.B.1280), § 7; Stats.2005, c. 716 (A.B.1067), § 6; Stats.2010, c. 216 (A.B.2144), § 11.)*

Cross References

Conviction of infraction for violation of section, see Vehicle Code § 42001.1.

Duration of prohibition against operation of commercial motor vehicle, see Vehicle Code § 15312.

Obstructing railroad track, punishment, see Penal Code § 218.1.

Rail transit related traffic violations, county populations greater than 500,000, punishment, see Penal Code § 369b.

Railroad grade crossing violations, see Vehicle Code § 42001.16.

Suspension or revocation of driver's license, conviction of a violation pursuant to this section, no violation point count, see Vehicle Code § 12810.4.

CHAPTER 10. REMOVAL OF PARKED AND ABANDONED VEHICLES

Article	Section
1. **Authority to Remove Vehicles**	22650
2. **Vehicle Disposition**	22850

Cross References

Arrest of persons engaged in speed contests or reckless driving, removal and seizure of vehicles, see Vehicle Code § 23109.2.

Local regulations, public grounds, enforcement of conditions or regulations regarding employees designated to remove vehicles, see Vehicle Code § 21113.

ARTICLE 1. AUTHORITY TO REMOVE VEHICLES

Section

22650. Prohibition of removal; hearings concerning storage; court actions.

22651. Circumstances permitting removal.

22651.05. Trained volunteers of state or local law enforcement agencies; requirements; circumstances permitting removal.

22651.07. Charges for towing or storage; Towing Fees and Access Notice; rights of vehicle owner; payment by bank draft; penalties; exceptions.

22651.1. Towing and service charges; credit card or cash payment.

22651.2. Removal of vehicles from highways or public lands; conditions.

22651.3. Offstreet parking facility; removal of vehicles without current registration or known to have been issued multiple notices of parking violations.

22651.4. Impounding or storing vehicle from another country.

22651.5. Removal of vehicles with activated alarm devices or horns; report.

22651.6. Removal of vehicles used in motor vehicle speed contests.

22651.7. Immobilization of certain vehicles on highway or public lands; five or more delinquent notices of parking violation.

22651.8. Satisfactory evidence for payment of notices of parking violations defined.

22651.9. Vehicle removal; location; private sale advertisement.

22651.10. Repealed.

22652. Removal of unauthorized vehicle from physically handicapped person's parking space.

Section

22652.5. Handicapped parking; vehicle removal; immunity from liability.

22652.6. Disabled person placard; unlawful use; vehicle removal.

22653. Removal from private property.

22654. Authorization for moving a vehicle.

22655. Vehicles involved in hit-and-run accidents; removal for inspection; release of vehicle; transfer of cargo.

22655.3. Impounding vehicle used to flee or evade peace officer.

22655.5. Impoundment of motor vehicle by peace officer with probable cause to believe vehicle used as means to commit public offense or is evidence or contains evidence of crime.

22656. Removal from railroad, railway or light rail right of way.

22657. Repealed.

22657.5. Repealed.

22658. Removal of vehicle from private property by property owner; towing companies and charges.

22658.1. Damaging of fence while removing vehicle; location and notification of property owner by towing company.

22658.2. Repealed.

22659. State or district agricultural association property.

22659.5. Vehicle used in commission of specified offenses; public nuisance; notice of impounding; poststorage hearing; release of vehicle; towing and storage charges.

22660. Local ordinances.

22661. Contents of ordinance.

22662. Disposition of vehicle or parts.

22663. Administration of ordinance.

22664. Waiver: reporting requirements and fees.

22665. Administration of abandoned vehicle abatement and removal program.

22666. Regulations of highway patrol.

22667. Abatement and removal: priorities.

22668. Abandoned Vehicle Trust Fund: prohibited disbursements.

22669. Removal of abandoned vehicles.

22670. Determination of estimated value of vehicle.

22671. Local franchise or contract for removal.

22700. Renumbered.

22701. Renumbered.

22702. Renumbered.

22703. Repealed.

22704. Repealed.

22705. Renumbered.

22705.1. Repealed.

22706. Renumbered.

22707. Repealed.

22710. Service authority for abatement of abandoned vehicles.

22711. Transportation to and disposition of abandoned vehicle at institution under jurisdiction of director of corrections for restoration and rebuilding.

Cross References

Exemption of driver of authorized emergency vehicle from this chapter, see Vehicle Code § 21055.

Highway defined, see Vehicle Code §§ 360, 591, 592.

Procedure to remove and store vehicles, see Vehicle Code §22850 et seq.

Stopping, standing or parking of utility vehicles, see Vehicle Code §22512.

Street defined, see Vehicle Code §§590, 591.

Violations of chapter as infractions, see Vehicle Code §40000.1.

§22650. Prohibition of removal; hearings concerning storage; court actions

It is unlawful for any peace officer or any unauthorized person to remove any unattended vehicle from a highway to a garage or to any other place, except as provided in this code.

(a) Those law enforcement and other agencies identified in this chapter as having the authority to remove vehicles shall also have the authority to provide hearings in compliance with the provisions of Section 22852. During these hearings the storing agency shall have the burden of establishing the authority for, and the validity of, the removal.

(b) Nothing in this section shall be deemed to prevent a review or other action as may be permitted by the laws of this state by a court of competent jurisdiction. *(Stats. 1959, c. 3, p. 1701, §22650. Amended by Stats.1979, c. 1022, p. 3490, §1.)*

Cross References

Abandoned vehicle, removal, see Vehicle Code §22669.

Movement of vehicle standing on highway, authority of peace officer, see Vehicle Code §22654.

Parking of utility vehicles, see Vehicle Code §22512.

Peace officer defined, see Penal Code §§7, 830 et seq., 852.1.

Private property, removal of vehicles, see Vehicle Code §22653.

Rules of the road, exemption of authorized emergency vehicles, see Vehicle Code §21055.

§22651. Circumstances permitting removal

A peace officer, as defined in Chapter 4.5 (commencing with Section 830) of Title 3 of Part 2 of the Penal Code, or a regularly employed and salaried employee, who is engaged in directing traffic or enforcing parking laws and regulations, of a city, county, or jurisdiction of a state agency in which a vehicle is located, may remove a vehicle located within the territorial limits in which the officer or employee may act, under the following circumstances:

(a) When a vehicle is left unattended upon a bridge, viaduct, or causeway or in a tube or tunnel where the vehicle constitutes an obstruction to traffic.

(b) When a vehicle is parked or left standing upon a highway in a position so as to obstruct the normal movement of traffic or in a condition so as to create a hazard to other traffic upon the highway.

(c) When a vehicle is found upon a highway or public land and a report has previously been made that the vehicle is stolen or a complaint has been filed and a warrant thereon is issued charging that the vehicle was embezzled.

(d) When a vehicle is illegally parked so as to block the entrance to a private driveway and it is impractical to move the vehicle from in front of the driveway to another point on the highway.

(e) When a vehicle is illegally parked so as to prevent access by firefighting equipment to a fire hydrant and it is impracticable to move the vehicle from in front of the fire hydrant to another point on the highway.

(f) When a vehicle, except highway maintenance or construction equipment, is stopped, parked, or left standing for more than four hours upon the right-of-way of a freeway that has full control of access and no crossings at grade and the driver, if present, cannot move the vehicle under its own power.

(g) When the person in charge of a vehicle upon a highway or public land is, by reason of physical injuries or illness, incapacitated to an extent so as to be unable to provide for its custody or removal.

(h)(1) When an officer arrests a person driving or in control of a vehicle for an alleged offense and the officer is, by this code or other law, required or permitted to take, and does take, the person into custody.

(2) When an officer serves a notice of an order of suspension or revocation pursuant to Section 13388 or 13389.

(i)(1) When a vehicle, other than a rented vehicle, is found upon a highway or public land, or is removed pursuant to this code, and it is known that the vehicle has been issued five or more notices of parking violations to which the owner or person in control of the vehicle has not responded within 21 calendar days of notice of citation issuance or citation issuance or 14 calendar days of the mailing of a notice of delinquent parking violation to the agency responsible for processing notices of parking violations, or the registered owner of the vehicle is known to have been issued five or more notices for failure to pay or failure to appear in court for traffic violations for which a certificate has not been issued by the magistrate or clerk of the court hearing the case showing that the case has been adjudicated or concerning which the registered owner's record has not been cleared pursuant to Chapter 6 (commencing with Section 41500) of Division 17, the vehicle may be impounded until that person furnishes to the impounding law enforcement agency all of the following:

(A) Evidence of his or her identity.

(B) An address within this state at which he or she can be located.

(C) Satisfactory evidence that all parking penalties due for the vehicle and all other vehicles registered to the registered owner of the impounded vehicle, and all traffic violations of the registered owner, have been cleared.

(2) The requirements in subparagraph (C) of paragraph (1) shall be fully enforced by the impounding law enforcement agency on and after the time that the

685

Department of Motor Vehicles is able to provide access to the necessary records.

(3) A notice of parking violation issued for an unlawfully parked vehicle shall be accompanied by a warning that repeated violations may result in the impounding of the vehicle. In lieu of furnishing satisfactory evidence that the full amount of parking penalties or bail has been deposited, that person may demand to be taken without unnecessary delay before a magistrate, for traffic offenses, or a hearing examiner, for parking offenses, within the county in which the offenses charged are alleged to have been committed and who has jurisdiction of the offenses and is nearest or most accessible with reference to the place where the vehicle is impounded. Evidence of current registration shall be produced after a vehicle has been impounded, or, at the discretion of the impounding law enforcement agency, a notice to appear for violation of subdivision (a) of Section 4000 shall be issued to that person.

(4) A vehicle shall be released to the legal owner, as defined in Section 370, if the legal owner does all of the following:

(A) Pays the cost of towing and storing the vehicle.

(B) Submits evidence of payment of fees as provided in Section 9561.

(C) Completes an affidavit in a form acceptable to the impounding law enforcement agency stating that the vehicle was not in possession of the legal owner at the time of occurrence of the offenses relating to standing or parking. A vehicle released to a legal owner under this subdivision is a repossessed vehicle for purposes of disposition or sale. The impounding agency shall have a lien on any surplus that remains upon sale of the vehicle to which the registered owner is or may be entitled, as security for the full amount of the parking penalties for all notices of parking violations issued for the vehicle and for all local administrative charges imposed pursuant to Section 22850.5. The legal owner shall promptly remit to, and deposit with, the agency responsible for processing notices of parking violations from that surplus, on receipt of that surplus, the full amount of the parking penalties for all notices of parking violations issued for the vehicle and for all local administrative charges imposed pursuant to Section 22850.5.

(5) The impounding agency that has a lien on the surplus that remains upon the sale of a vehicle to which a registered owner is entitled pursuant to paragraph (4) has a deficiency claim against the registered owner for the full amount of the parking penalties for all notices of parking violations issued for the vehicle and for all local administrative charges imposed pursuant to Section 22850.5, less the amount received from the sale of the vehicle.

(j) When a vehicle is found illegally parked and there are no license plates or other evidence of registration displayed, the vehicle may be impounded until the owner or person in control of the vehicle furnishes the impounding law enforcement agency evidence of his or her

identity and an address within this state at which he or she can be located.

(k) When a vehicle is parked or left standing upon a highway for 72 or more consecutive hours in violation of a local ordinance authorizing removal.

(*l*) When a vehicle is illegally parked on a highway in violation of a local ordinance forbidding standing or parking and the use of a highway, or a portion thereof, is necessary for the cleaning, repair, or construction of the highway, or for the installation of underground utilities, and signs giving notice that the vehicle may be removed are erected or placed at least 24 hours prior to the removal by a local authority pursuant to the ordinance.

(m) When the use of the highway, or a portion of the highway, is authorized by a local authority for a purpose other than the normal flow of traffic or for the movement of equipment, articles, or structures of unusual size, and the parking of a vehicle would prohibit or interfere with that use or movement, and signs giving notice that the vehicle may be removed are erected or placed at least 24 hours prior to the removal by a local authority pursuant to the ordinance.

(n) Whenever a vehicle is parked or left standing where local authorities, by resolution or ordinance, have prohibited parking and have authorized the removal of vehicles. Except as provided in subdivisions (v) and (w), a vehicle shall not be removed unless signs are posted giving notice of the removal.

(*o*)(1) When a vehicle is found or operated upon a highway, public land, or an offstreet parking facility under the following circumstances:

(A) With a registration expiration date in excess of six months before the date it is found or operated on the highway, public lands, or the offstreet parking facility.

(B) Displaying in, or upon, the vehicle, a registration card, identification card, temporary receipt, license plate, special plate, registration sticker, device issued pursuant to Section 4853, or permit that was not issued for that vehicle, or is not otherwise lawfully used on that vehicle under this code.

(C) Displaying in, or upon, the vehicle, an altered, forged, counterfeit, or falsified registration card, identification card, temporary receipt, license plate, special plate, registration sticker, device issued pursuant to Section 4853, or permit.

(2) When a vehicle described in paragraph (1) is occupied, only a peace officer, as defined in Chapter 4.5 (commencing with Section 830) of Title 3 of Part 2 of the Penal Code, may remove the vehicle.

(3) For the purposes of this subdivision, the vehicle shall be released under either of the following circumstances:

(A) To the registered owner or person in control of the vehicle only after the owner or person furnishes the storing law enforcement agency with proof of current registration and a currently valid driver's license to operate the vehicle.

(B) To the legal owner or the legal owner's agency, without payment of any fees, fines, or penalties for parking tickets or registration and without proof of current registration, if the vehicle will only be transported pursuant to the exemption specified in Section 4022 and if the legal owner does all of the following:

(i) Pays the cost of towing and storing the vehicle.

(ii) Completes an affidavit in a form acceptable to the impounding law enforcement agency stating that the vehicle was not in possession of the legal owner at the time of occurrence of an offense relating to standing or parking. A vehicle released to a legal owner under this subdivision is a repossessed vehicle for purposes of disposition or sale. The impounding agency has a lien on any surplus that remains upon sale of the vehicle to which the registered owner is or may be entitled, as security for the full amount of parking penalties for any notices of parking violations issued for the vehicle and for all local administrative charges imposed pursuant to Section 22850.5. Upon receipt of any surplus, the legal owner shall promptly remit to, and deposit with, the agency responsible for processing notices of parking violations from that surplus, the full amount of the parking penalties for all notices of parking violations issued for the vehicle and for all local administrative charges imposed pursuant to Section 22850.5.

(4) The impounding agency that has a lien on the surplus that remains upon the sale of a vehicle to which a registered owner is entitled has a deficiency claim against the registered owner for the full amount of parking penalties for any notices of parking violations issued for the vehicle and for all local administrative charges imposed pursuant to Section 22850.5, less the amount received from the sale of the vehicle.

(5) As used in this subdivision, "offstreet parking facility" means an offstreet facility held open for use by the public for parking vehicles and includes a publicly owned facility for offstreet parking, and a privately owned facility for offstreet parking if a fee is not charged for the privilege to park and it is held open for the common public use of retail customers.

(p) When the peace officer issues the driver of a vehicle a notice to appear for a violation of Section 12500, 14601, 14601.1, 14601.2, 14601.3, 14601.4, 14601.5, or 14604 and the vehicle is not impounded pursuant to Section 22655.5. A vehicle so removed from the highway or public land, or from private property after having been on a highway or public land, shall not be released to the registered owner or his or her agent, except upon presentation of the registered owner's or his or her agent's currently valid driver's license to operate the vehicle and proof of current vehicle registration, to the impounding law enforcement agency, or upon order of a court.

(q) When a vehicle is parked for more than 24 hours on a portion of highway that is located within the boundaries of a common interest development, as defined in Section 4100 or 6534 of the Civil Code, and signs, as required by paragraph (1) of subdivision (a) of Section 22658 of this code, have been posted on that portion of highway providing notice to drivers that vehicles parked thereon for more than 24 hours will be removed at the owner's expense, pursuant to a resolution or ordinance adopted by the local authority.

(r) When a vehicle is illegally parked and blocks the movement of a legally parked vehicle.

(s)(1) When a vehicle, except highway maintenance or construction equipment, an authorized emergency vehicle, or a vehicle that is properly permitted or otherwise authorized by the Department of Transportation, is stopped, parked, or left standing for more than eight hours within a roadside rest area or viewpoint.

(2) Notwithstanding paragraph (1), when a commercial motor vehicle, as defined in paragraph (1) of subdivision (b) of Section 15210, is stopped, parked, or left standing for more than 10 hours within a roadside rest area or viewpoint.

(3) For purposes of this subdivision, a roadside rest area or viewpoint is a publicly maintained vehicle parking area, adjacent to a highway, utilized for the convenient, safe stopping of a vehicle to enable motorists to rest or to view the scenery. If two or more roadside rest areas are located on opposite sides of the highway, or upon the center divider, within seven miles of each other, then that combination of rest areas is considered to be the same rest area.

(t) When a peace officer issues a notice to appear for a violation of Section 25279.

(u) When a peace officer issues a citation for a violation of Section 11700 and the vehicle is being offered for sale.

(v)(1) When a vehicle is a mobile billboard advertising display, as defined in Section 395.5, and is parked or left standing in violation of a local resolution or ordinance adopted pursuant to subdivision (m) of Section 21100, if the registered owner of the vehicle was previously issued a warning citation for the same offense, pursuant to paragraph (2).

(2) Notwithstanding subdivision (a) of Section 22507, a city or county, in lieu of posting signs noticing a local ordinance prohibiting mobile billboard advertising displays adopted pursuant to subdivision (m) of Section 21100, may provide notice by issuing a warning citation advising the registered owner of the vehicle that he or she may be subject to penalties upon a subsequent violation of the ordinance, that may include the removal of the vehicle as provided in paragraph (1). A city or county is not required to provide further notice for a subsequent violation prior to the enforcement of penalties for a violation of the ordinance.

(w)(1) When a vehicle is parked or left standing in violation of a local ordinance or resolution adopted pursuant to subdivision (p) of Section 21100, if the registered owner of the vehicle was previously issued a warning citation for the same offense, pursuant to paragraph (2).

(2) Notwithstanding subdivision (a) of Section 22507, a city or county, in lieu of posting signs noticing a local ordinance regulating advertising signs adopted pursuant to subdivision (p) of Section 21100, may provide notice by issuing a warning citation advising the registered owner of the vehicle that he or she may be subject to penalties upon a subsequent violation of the ordinance that may include the removal of the vehicle as provided in paragraph (1). A city or county is not required to provide further notice for a subsequent violation prior to the enforcement of penalties for a violation of the ordinance. (Stats.1959, c. 3, p. 1701, § 22651. Amended by Stats. 1959, c. 972, p. 3003, § 1; Stats.1960, 1st Ex.Sess., c. 59, p. 408, § 3; Stats.1963, c. 1004, p. 2271, § 2; Stats.1967, c. 543, p. 1891, § 1; Stats.1968, c. 749, p. 1452, § 1; Stats.1969, c. 1116, p. 2177, § 1; Stats.1970, c. 886, p. 1620, § 1; Stats.1971, c. 130, p. 172, § 1, operative May 3, 1972; Stats.1974, c. 545, p. 1327, § 211; Stats.1977, c. 73, p. 477, § 1; Stats.1977, c. 486, p. 1605, § 2; Stats.1977, c. 1129, p. 3624, § 2; Stats.1979, c. 831, p. 2874, § 1; Stats.1979, c. 909, p. 3123, § 2.3; Stats.1980, c. 1340, p. 4735, § 31, eff. Sept. 30, 1980; Stats.1981, c. 343, p. 1501, § 1; Stats.1982, c. 344, p. 1647, § 1; Stats.1983, c. 816, § 1; Stats.1983, c. 1017, § 3; Stats.1985, c. 1007, § 1; Stats.1985, c. 1126, § 5, eff. Sept. 28, 1985; Stats.1985, c. 1126, § 6, eff. Sept. 28, 1985, operative April 1, 1986; Stats.1986, c. 328, § 2; Stats.1986, c. 1236, § 2; Stats. 1986, c. 1262, § 1; Stats.1987, c. 521, § 1, eff. Sept. 11, 1987; Stats.1988, c. 619, § 1; Stats.1988, c. 1008, § 3; Stats.1989, c. 331, § 1; Stats.1991, c. 90 (A.B.1297), § 68, eff. June 30, 1991; Stats.1991, c. 189 (A.B.544), § 40, eff. July 29, 1991; Stats.1992, c. 633 (A.B.1067), § 3; Stats. 1992, c. 1242 (S.B.602), § 3; Stats.1992, c. 1244 (A.B. 408), § 5, operative July 1, 1993; Stats.1993, c. 272 (A.B.301), § 42, eff. Aug. 2, 1993; Stats.1993, c. 614 (A.B.481), § 1; Stats.1993, c. 1093 (A.B.780), § 1.5; Stats.1994, c. 268 (A.B.3017), § 2; Stats.1994, c. 938 (S.B.1295), § 12, eff. Sept. 28, 1994; Stats.1994, c. 1220 (A.B.3132), § 60, eff. Sept. 30, 1994; Stats.1994, c. 1221 (S.B.1758), § 17; Stats.1995, c. 734 (A.B.1228), § 1; Stats.1996, c. 10 (A.B.1869), § 16, eff. Feb. 9, 1996; Stats.1996, c. 1142 (S.B.1797), § 8, eff. Sept. 30, 1996; Stats.1996, c. 1154 (A.B.3020), § 69, eff. Sept. 30, 1996; Stats.1996, c. 1156 (A.B.3157), § 3.7; Stats.1998, c. 118 (S.B.1186), § 11.5, operative July 1, 1999; Stats.1999, c. 22 (S.B.24), § 17.5, eff. May 26, 1999, operative July 1, 1999; Stats.2007, c. 453 (A.B.1589), § 1; Stats.2007, c. 749 (A.B.1165), § 4.5, operative Jan. 1, 2009; Stats.2008, c. 460 (A.B.2402), § 1; Stats.2008, c. 736 (A.B.2042), § 2; Stats.2009, c. 140 (A.B.1164), § 180; Stats.2010, c. 615 (A.B.2756), § 4; Stats.2011, c. 341 (S.B.565), § 4; Stats. 2011, c. 538 (A.B.1298), § 4.5; Stats.2012, c. 181 (A.B. 688

806), § 81, operative Jan. 1, 2014; Stats.2012, c. 769 (A.B.2679), § 38; Stats.2013, c. 605 (S.B.752), § 50.)

Law Revision Commission Comments

2012 Amendment

Subdivision (q) of Section 22651 is amended to correct a cross-reference to former Civil Code Section 1351(c). [40 Cal.L.Rev. Comm. Reports 235 (2010)].

2013 Amendment

Subdivision (q) of Section 22651 is amended to add a cross-reference to Civil Code Section 6534, reflecting the enactment of the Commercial and Industrial Common Interest Development Act (Civ. Code §§ 6500–6876). [42 Cal.L.Rev.Comm. Reports 1 (2012)].

Cross References

Abandoned vehicle, removal, see Vehicle Code § 22669.
Arrested person, taking before magistrate, see Vehicle Code §§ 40302, 40303.
Department of the California highway patrol, generally, see Vehicle Code § 2100 et seq.
Freeway defined, see Vehicle Code § 332.
Lien sales, impounded vehicles, see Vehicle Code § 22851.1.
Local regulations, see Vehicle Code § 21100 et seq.
Private property, removal of vehicles, see Vehicle Code § 22653.
Private road or driveway defined, see Vehicle Code § 490.
Registered owner, responsibility for unattended vehicle, see Vehicle Code § 40200 et seq.
Release of vehicle to registered owner or agent, see Vehicle Code § 14602.
Removal of unauthorized vehicle from physically handicapped parking space, see Vehicle Code § 22652.
Removing standing vehicle from highway by authorized peace officer, see Vehicle Code § 22654.
Snow areas, parking in, see Vehicle Code § 22510.
Stolen vehicles, reports, see Vehicle Code § 10500 et seq.
Storage of vehicles, see Vehicle Code § 22850 et seq.
Transportation of agricultural irrigation supplies, inspection of bills of lading, shipping, or delivery papers, care of apprehended supplies, see Vehicle Code § 2810.2.
Utility vehicles, stopping, standing or parking, see Vehicle Code §§ 22512, 25301.
Vehicle parked or placed on highway for purpose of selling articles, removal, see Streets and Highways Code § 731.

§ 22651.05. Trained volunteers of state or local law enforcement agencies; requirements; circumstances permitting removal

(a) A trained volunteer of a state or local law enforcement agency, who is engaged in directing traffic or enforcing parking laws and regulations, of a city, county, or jurisdiction of a state agency in which a vehicle is located, may remove or authorize the removal of a vehicle located within the territorial limits in which an officer or employee of that agency may act, under any of the following circumstances:

(1) When a vehicle is parked or left standing upon a highway for 72 or more consecutive hours in violation of a local ordinance authorizing the removal.

(2) When a vehicle is illegally parked or left standing on a highway in violation of a local ordinance forbidding

standing or parking and the use of a highway, or a portion thereof, is necessary for the cleaning, repair, or construction of the highway, or for the installation of underground utilities, and signs giving notice that the vehicle may be removed are erected or placed at least 24 hours prior to the removal by local authorities pursuant to the ordinance.

(3) Wherever the use of the highway, or a portion thereof, is authorized by local authorities for a purpose other than the normal flow of traffic or for the movement of equipment, articles, or structures of unusual size, and the parking of a vehicle would prohibit or interfere with that use or movement, and signs giving notice that the vehicle may be removed are erected or placed at least 24 hours prior to the removal by local authorities pursuant to the ordinance.

(4) Whenever a vehicle is parked or left standing where local authorities, by resolution or ordinance, have prohibited parking and have authorized the removal of vehicles. A vehicle may not be removed unless signs are posted giving notice of the removal.

(5) Whenever a vehicle is parked for more than 24 hours on a portion of highway that is located within the boundaries of a common interest development, as defined in Section 4100 or 6534 of the Civil Code, and signs, as required by Section 22658.2, have been posted on that portion of highway providing notice to drivers that vehicles parked thereon for more than 24 hours will be removed at the owner's expense, pursuant to a resolution or ordinance adopted by the local authority.

(b) The provisions of this chapter that apply to a vehicle removed pursuant to Section 22651 apply to a vehicle removed pursuant to subdivision (a).

(c) For purposes of subdivision (a), a "trained volunteer" is a person who, of his or her own free will, provides services, without any financial gain, to a local or state law enforcement agency, and who is duly trained and certified to remove a vehicle by a local or state law enforcement agency. *(Added by Stats.2004, c. 371 (A.B.1847), § 1. Amended by Stats.2012, c. 181 (A.B.806), § 82, operative Jan. 1, 2014; Stats.2013, c. 605 (S.B.752), § 51.)*

Law Revision Commission Comments

2012 Amendment

Section 22651.05 is amended to correct a cross-reference to former Civil Code Section 1351(c). [40 Cal.L.Rev.Comm. Reports 235 (2010)].

2013 Amendment

Section 22651.05 is amended to add a cross-reference to Civil Code Section 6534, reflecting the enactment of the Commercial and Industrial Common Interest Development Act (Civ. Code §§ 6500–6876). [42 Cal.L.Rev.Comm. Reports 1 (2012)].

Cross References

Local regulations, see Vehicle Code § 21100 et seq.
Registered owner, responsibility for unattended vehicle, see Vehicle Code § 40200 et seq.
Snow areas, parking in, see Vehicle Code § 22510.

Utility vehicles, stopping, standing or parking, see Vehicle Code §§ 22512, 25301.
Vehicle parked or placed on highway for purpose of selling articles, removal, see Streets and Highways Code § 731.

§ 22651.07. Charges for towing or storage; Towing Fees and Access Notice; rights of vehicle owner; payment by bank draft; penalties; exceptions

(a) A person that charges for towing or storage, or both, except for storage unrelated to a tow, shall do all of the following:

(1)(A) Except as provided in subparagraph (B), post in the office area of the storage facility, in plain view of the public, the Towing Fees and Access Notice and have copies readily available to the public.

(B) An automotive repair dealer, registered pursuant to Article 3 (commencing with Section 9884) of Chapter 20.3 of Division 3 of the Business and Professions Code, that does not provide towing services is exempt from the requirement to post the Towing Fees and Access Notice in the office area.

(2) Provide, upon request, a copy of the Towing Fees and Access Notice to any owner or operator of a towed or stored vehicle.

(3) Provide a distinct notice on an itemized invoice for any towing or storage, or both, charges stating: "Upon request, you are entitled to receive a copy of the Towing Fees and Access Notice." This notice shall be contained within a bordered text box, printed in no less than 10–point type.

(b) Prior to receiving payment for any towing, recovery, or storage-related fees, a person that charges for towing or storage, or both, shall provide an itemized invoice of actual charges to the vehicle owner or his or her agent. If an automotive repair dealer, registered pursuant to Article 3 (commencing with Section 9884) of Chapter 20.3 of Division 3 of the Business and Professions Code, did not provide the tow, and passes along, from the tower to the consumer, any of the information required on the itemized invoice, pursuant to subdivision (e), the automotive repair dealer shall not be responsible for the accuracy of those items of information that remain unaltered.

(c) Prior to paying any towing, recovery, or storage-related fees, a vehicle owner or his or her agent shall have the right to all of the following:

(1) Receive his or her personal property, at no charge, during normal business hours. Normal business hours are Monday through Friday from 8:00 a.m. to 5:00 p.m., inclusive, except state holidays.

(2) Retrieve his or her vehicle during the first 72 hours of storage and not pay a lien fee.

(3) Request a copy of the Towing Fees and Access Notice.

(4) Be permitted to pay by cash or a valid bank credit card. Credit charges for towing and storage services shall comply with Section 1748.1 of the Civil Code. Law

enforcement agencies may include the costs of providing for payment by credit when agreeing with a towing or storage provider on rates.

(d) The Towing Fees and Access Notice shall be a standardized document plainly printed in no less that 10–point type. A person may distribute the form using its own letterhead, but the language of the Towing Fees and Access Notice shall read as follows:

Towing Fees and Access Notice

Note: The following information is intended to serve as a general summary of some of the laws that provide vehicle owners certain rights when their vehicle is towed. It is not intended to summarize all of the laws that may be applicable nor is it intended to fully and completely state the entire law in any area listed. Please review the applicable California code for a definitive statement of the law in your particular situation.

How much can a towing company charge?

Rates for public tows and storage are generally established by an agreement between the law enforcement agency requesting the tow and the towing company (to confirm the approved rates, you may contact the law enforcement agency that initiated the tow; additionally, these rates are required to be posted at the storage facility).
Rates for private property tows and storage cannot exceed the approved rates for the law enforcement agency that has primary jurisdiction for the property from which the vehicle was removed or the towing company's approved CHP rate. Rates for owner's request tows and storage are generally established by mutual agreement between the requestor and the towing company, but may be dictated by agreements established between the requestor's motor club and motor club service provider.

Where can you complain about a towing company?
For public tows: Contact the law enforcement agency initiating the tow.

Your rights if your vehicle is towed:

Generally, prior to paying any towing and storage-related fees you have the right to:
● Receive an itemized invoice of actual charges.
● Receive your personal property, at no charge, during normal business hours.
● Retrieve your vehicle during the first 72 hours of storage and not pay a lien fee.
● Request a copy of the Towing Fees and Access Notice.
● Pay by cash or valid bank credit card.
● Inspect your vehicle or have your insurance carrier inspect your vehicle at the storage facility, at no charge, during normal business hours.

You have the right to have the vehicle released to you upon (1) payment of all towing and storage-related fees, (2) presentation of a valid photo identification, (3) presentation of reliable documentation showing that you are the owner of the vehicle or that the owner has authorized you to take possession of the vehicle, and (4), if applicable, presentation of any required police or law enforcement release documents.

Prior to your vehicle being repaired:
● You have the right to choose the repair facility and to have no repairs made to your vehicle unless you authorize them in writing.

● Any authorization you sign for towing and any authorization you sign for repair must be on separate forms.

What if I do not pay the towing and storage-related fees or abandon my vehicle at the towing company?
Pursuant to Sections 3068.1 to 3074, inclusive, of the Civil Code, a towing company may sell your vehicle and any moneys received will be applied to towing and storage-related fees that have accumulated against your vehicle.
You are responsible for paying the towing company any outstanding balance due on any of these fees once the sale is complete.

Who is liable if my vehicle was damaged during towing or storage?
Generally the owner of a vehicle may recover for any damage to the vehicle resulting from any intentional or negligent act of a person causing the removal of, or removing, the vehicle.

What happens if a towing company violates the law?
If a tow company does not satisfactorily meet certain requirements detailed in this notice, you may bring a lawsuit in court, generally in small claims court. The tower may be civilly liable for damages up to two times the amount charged, not to exceed $500, and possibly more for certain violations.

(e) "Itemized invoice," as used in this section, means a written document that contains the following information. Any document that substantially complies with this subdivision shall be deemed an "itemized invoice" for purposes of this section:

(1) The name, address, telephone number, and carrier identification number as required by subdivision (a) of Section 34507.5 of the person that is charging for towing and storage.

(2) If ascertainable, the registered owner or operator's name, address, and telephone number.

(3) The date service was initiated.

(4) The location of the vehicle at the time service was initiated, including either the address or nearest intersecting roadways.

(5) A vehicle description that includes, if ascertainable, the vehicle year, make, model, odometer reading, license plate number, or if a license plate number is unavailable, the vehicle identification number (VIN).

(6) The service dispatch time, the service arrival time of the tow truck, and the service completion time.

(7) A clear, itemized, and detailed explanation of any additional services that caused the total towing-related service time to exceed one hour between service dispatch time and service completion time.

(8) The hourly rate or per item rate used to calculate the total towing and recovery-related fees. These fees shall be listed as separate line items.

(9) If subject to storage fees, the daily storage rate and the total number of days stored. The storage fees shall be listed as a separate line item.

(10) If subject to a gate fee, the date and time the vehicle was either accessed, for the purposes of returning personal property, or was released after normal business hours. Normal business hours are Monday through

Friday from 8:00 a.m. to 5:00 p.m., inclusive, except state holidays. A gate fee shall be listed as a separate line item.

(11) A description of the method of towing.

(12) If the tow was not requested by the vehicle's owner or driver, the identity of the person or governmental agency that directed the tow. This paragraph shall not apply to information otherwise required to be redacted under Section 22658.

(13) A clear, itemized, and detailed explanation of any additional services or fees.

(f) "Person," as used in this section, has the same meaning as described in Section 470.

(g) An insurer or insurer's agent shall be permitted to pay for towing and storage charges by bank draft.

(h) A person who violates this section is civilly liable to a registered or legal owner of the vehicle, or a registered owner's insurer, for up to two times the amount charged. For any action brought under this section, liability shall not exceed five hundred dollars ($500) per vehicle.

(i) This section shall not apply to the towing or storage of a repossessed vehicle by any person subject to, or exempt from, the Collateral Recovery Act (Chapter 11 (commencing with Section 7500) of Division 3 of the Business and Professions Code).

(j) This section does not relieve a person from the obligation to comply with the provision of any other law. *(Added by Stats.2010, c. 566 (A.B.519), § 2.)*

§ 22651.1. Towing and service charges; credit card or cash payment

Persons operating or in charge of any storage facility where vehicles are stored pursuant to Section 22651 shall accept a valid bank credit card or cash for payment of towing and storage by the registered owner, legal owner, or the owner's agent claiming the vehicle. A credit card shall be in the name of the person presenting the card. "Credit card" means "credit card" as defined in subdivision (a) of Section 1747.02 of the Civil Code, except, for the purposes of this section, credit card does not include a credit card issued by a retail seller. A person operating or in charge of any storage facility who refuses to accept a valid bank credit card shall be liable to the owner of the vehicle or to the person who tendered the fees for four times the amount of the towing and storage charges, but not to exceed five hundred dollars ($500). In addition, persons operating or in charge of the storage facility shall have sufficient funds on the premises to accommodate and make change in a reasonable monetary transaction.

Credit charges for towing and storage services shall comply with Section 1748.1 of the Civil Code. Law enforcement agencies may include the costs of providing for payment by credit when agreeing with a towing or storage provider on rates. *(Added by Stats.1989, c. 502, § 1. Amended by Stats.1990, c. 309 (S.B.1763), § 2; Stats.1992, c. 246 (A.B.2895), § 1; Stats.2009, c. 322 (A.B.515), § 9.)*

§ 22651.2. Removal of vehicles from highways or public lands; conditions

(a) Any peace officer, as defined in Chapter 4.5 (commencing with Section 830) of Title 3 of Part 2 of the Penal Code, or any regularly employed and salaried employee, who is engaged in directing traffic or enforcing parking laws and regulations of a city, county, or jurisdiction of a state agency in which a vehicle is located, may remove a vehicle located within the territorial limits in which the officer or employee may act when the vehicle is found upon a highway or any public lands, and if all of the following requirements are satisfied:

(1) Because of the size and placement of signs or placards on the vehicle, it appears that the primary purpose of parking the vehicle at that location is to advertise to the public an event or function on private property or on public property hired for a private event or function to which the public is invited.

(2) The vehicle is known to have been previously issued a notice of parking violation that was accompanied by a notice warning that an additional parking violation may result in the impoundment of the vehicle.

(3) The registered owner of the vehicle has been mailed a notice advising of the existence of the parking violation and that an additional violation may result in the impoundment of the vehicle.

(b) Subdivision (a) does not apply to a vehicle bearing any sign or placard advertising any business or enterprise carried on by or through the use of that vehicle.

(c) Section 22852 applies to the removal of any vehicle pursuant to this section. *(Added by Stats.1990, c. 73 (S.B.819), § 1. Amended by Stats.1996, c. 1142 (S.B. 1797), § 9, eff. Sept. 30, 1996; Stats.1997, c. 17 (S.B.947), § 144.)*

§ 22651.3. Offstreet parking facility; removal of vehicles without current registration or known to have been issued multiple notices of parking violations

(a) Any peace officer, as that term is defined in Chapter 4.5 (commencing with Section 830) of Title 3 of Part 2 of the Penal Code, or any regularly employed and salaried employee, who is engaged in directing traffic or enforcing parking laws and regulations, of a city, county, or jurisdiction of a state agency in which any vehicle, other than a rented vehicle, is located may remove the vehicle from an offstreet public parking facility located within the territorial limits in which the officer or employee may act when the vehicle is known to have been issued five or more notices of parking violation over a period of five or more days, to which the owner or person in control of the vehicle has not responded or when any vehicle is illegally parked so as to prevent the movement of a legally parked vehicle.

A notice of parking violation issued to a vehicle which is registered in a foreign jurisdiction or is without current California registration and is known to have been issued five or more notices of parking violation over a period of

691

five or more days shall be accompanied by a warning that repeated violations may result in the impounding of the vehicle.

(b) The vehicle may be impounded until the owner or person in control of the vehicle furnishes to the impounding law enforcement agency evidence of his or her identity and an address within this state at which he or she can be located and furnishes satisfactory evidence that bail has been deposited for all notices of parking violation issued for the vehicle. In lieu of requiring satisfactory evidence that the bail has been deposited, the impounding law enforcement agency may, in its discretion, issue a notice to appear for the offenses charged, as provided in Article 2 (commencing with Section 40500) of Chapter 2 of Division 17. In lieu of either furnishing satisfactory evidence that the bail has been deposited or accepting the notice to appear, the owner or person in control of the vehicle may demand to be taken without unnecessary delay before a magistrate within the county in which the offenses charged are alleged to have been committed and who has jurisdiction of the offenses and is nearest or most accessible with reference to the place where the vehicle is impounded.

(c) Evidence of current registration shall be produced after a vehicle has been impounded. At the discretion of the impounding law enforcement agency, a notice to appear for violation of subdivision (a) of Section 4000 may be issued to the owner or person in control of the vehicle, if the two days immediately following the day of impoundment are weekend days or holidays. *(Added by Stats.1985, c. 858, § 2. Amended by Stats.1988, c. 619, § 2; Stats.1994, c. 1220 (A.B.3132), § 61, eff. Sept. 30, 1994; Stats.1996, c. 1142 (S.B.1797), § 10, eff. Sept. 30, 1996.)*

§ 22651.4. Impounding or storing vehicle from another country

(a) A peace officer, as defined in Chapter 4.5 (commencing with Section 830) of Title 3 of Part 2 of the Penal Code, may impound a vehicle and its cargo pursuant to Section 34517.

(b) A member of the department may impound a vehicle and its cargo pursuant to Section 34518.

(c) A member of the department may store or impound a vehicle upon determination that the registrant of the vehicle or the driver of the vehicle has failed to pay registration, regulatory, fuel permit, or other fees, or has an outstanding warrant in a county in the state. The impound charges are the responsibility of the owner of the vehicle. The stored or impounded vehicle shall be released upon payment of those fees or fines or the posting of bail. The driver or owner of the vehicle may request a hearing to determine the validity of the seizure. *(Added by Stats.1991, c. 707 (A.B.1355), § 1. Amended by Stats.2006, c. 288 (A.B.3011), § 6.)*

692

§ 22651.5. Removal of vehicles with activated alarm devices or horns; report

(a) Any peace officer, as defined in Chapter 4.5 (commencing with Section 830) of Title 3 of Part 2 of the Penal Code, or any regularly employed and salaried employee who is engaged in directing traffic or enforcing parking laws or regulations, may, upon the complaint of any person, remove a vehicle parked within 500 feet of any occupied building of a school, community college, or university during normal hours of operation, or a vehicle parked within a residence or business district, from a highway or from public or private property, if an alarm device or horn has been activated within the vehicle, whether continuously activated or intermittently and repeatedly activated, the peace officer or designated employee is unable to locate the owner of the vehicle within 20 minutes from the time of arrival at the vehicle's location, and the alarm device or horn has not been completely silenced prior to removal.

(b) Upon removal of a vehicle from a highway or from public or private property pursuant to this section, the peace officer or designated employee ordering the removal shall immediately report the removal and the location to which the vehicle is removed to the Stolen Vehicle System of the Department of Justice. *(Added by Stats.1983, c. 1267, § 1. Amended by Stats.1991, c. 928 (A.B.1886), § 29, eff. Oct. 14, 1991; Stats.1993, c. 540 (A.B.1849), § 1; Stats.1997, c. 945 (A.B.1561), § 20.)*

§ 22651.6. Removal of vehicles used in motor vehicle speed contests

A peace officer or employee specified in Section 22651 may remove a vehicle located within the territorial limits in which the officer or employee may act when the vehicle was used by a person who was engaged in a motor vehicle speed contest, as described in subdivision (a) of Section 23109, and the person was arrested and taken into custody for that offense by a peace officer. *(Added by Stats.1996, c. 884 (A.B.2288), § 1.)*

Cross References

Release of vehicles removed and seized pursuant to this section, liability for towing and storage fees, see Vehicle Code § 23109.2.

§ 22651.7. Immobilization of certain vehicles on highway or public lands; five or more delinquent notices of parking violation

(a) In addition to, or as an alternative to, removal, a peace officer, as defined in Chapter 4.5 (commencing with Section 830) of Title 3 of Part 2 of the Penal Code, or a regularly employed and salaried employee who is engaged in directing traffic or enforcing parking laws and regulations, of a jurisdiction in which a vehicle is located may immobilize the vehicle with a device designed and manufactured for the immobilization of vehicles, on a highway or any public lands located within the territorial limits in which the officer or employee may act if the vehicle is found upon a highway or public lands and it is known to have been issued five or more notices of parking violations that are delinquent because the owner or person in control of the vehicle has not responded to the agency responsible for processing notices of parking violation within 21 calendar days of notice of citation issuance or citation issuance or 14 calendar days of the mailing of a notice of delinquent parking violation, or the registered owner of the vehicle is known to have been issued five or more notices for failure to pay or failure to appear in court for traffic violations for which no certificate has been issued by the magistrate or clerk of the court hearing the case showing that the case has been adjudicated or concerning which the registered owner's record has not been cleared pursuant to Chapter 6 (commencing with Section 41500) of Division 17. The vehicle may be immobilized until that person furnishes to the immobilizing law enforcement agency all of the following:

(1) Evidence of his or her identity.

(2) An address within this state at which he or she can be located.

(3) Satisfactory evidence that the full amount of parking penalties has been deposited for all notices of parking violation issued for the vehicle and any other vehicle registered to the registered owner of the immobilized vehicle and that bail has been deposited for all traffic violations of the registered owner that have not been cleared. The requirements in this paragraph shall be fully enforced by the immobilizing law enforcement agency on and after the time that the Department of Motor Vehicles is able to provide access to the necessary records. A notice of parking violation issued to the vehicle shall be accompanied by a warning that repeated violations may result in the impounding or immobilization of the vehicle. In lieu of furnishing satisfactory evidence that the full amount of parking penalties or bail, or both, have been deposited that person may demand to be taken without unnecessary delay before a magistrate, for traffic offenses, or a hearing examiner, for parking offenses, within the county in which the offenses charged are alleged to have been committed and who has jurisdiction of the offenses and is nearest or most accessible with reference to the place where the vehicle is immobilized. Evidence of current registration shall be produced after a vehicle has been immobilized or, at the discretion of the immobilizing law enforcement agency, a notice to appear for violation of subdivision (a) of Section 4000 shall be issued to that person.

(b) A person, other than a person authorized under subdivision (a), shall not immobilize a vehicle. *(Added by Stats.1986, c. 181, § 1, eff. June 23, 1986. Amended by Stats.1991, c. 90 (A.B.1297), § 69, eff. June 30, 1991; Stats.1991, c. 189 (A.B.544), § 41, eff. July 29, 1991; Stats.1992, c. 1244 (A.B.408), § 6, operative July 1, 1993; Stats.1993, c. 1093 (A.B.780), § 2; Stats.1994, c. 1220 (A.B.3132), § 62, eff. Sept. 30, 1994; Stats.1995, c. 734 (A.B.1228), § 2; Stats.1996, c. 1156 (A.B.3157), § 4; Stats.2006, c. 609 (A.B.2210), § 2.)*

§ 22651.8. Satisfactory evidence for payment of notices of parking violations defined

For purposes of paragraph (1) of subdivision (i) of Section 22651 and Section 22651.7, "satisfactory evidence" includes, but is not limited to, a copy of a receipt issued by the department pursuant to subdivision (a) of Section 4760 for the payment of notices of parking violations appearing on the department's records at the time of payment. The processing agency shall, within 72 hours of receiving that satisfactory evidence, update its records to reflect the payments made to the department. If the processing agency does not receive the amount of the parking penalties and administrative fees from the department within four months of the date of issuance of that satisfactory evidence, the processing agency may revise its records to reflect that no payments were received for the notices of parking violation. *(Added by Stats.1991, c. 587 (A.B.1126), § 2, operative July 1, 1992.)*

§ 22651.9. Vehicle removal; location; private sale advertisement

(a) Any peace officer, as defined in Chapter 4.5 (commencing with Section 830) of Title 3 of Part 2 of the Penal Code, or any regularly employed and salaried employee, who is engaged in directing traffic or enforcing parking laws and regulations, of a city, county, or city and county in which a vehicle is located, may remove a vehicle located within the territorial limits in which the officer or employee may act when the vehicle is found upon a street or any public lands, if all of the following requirements are satisfied:

(1) Because of a sign or placard on the vehicle, it appears that the primary purpose of parking the vehicle at that location is to advertise to the public the private sale of that vehicle.

(2) Within the past 30 days, the vehicle is known to have been previously issued a notice of parking violation, under local ordinance, which was accompanied by a notice containing all of the following:

(A) A warning that an additional parking violation may result in the impoundment of the vehicle.

(B) A warning that the vehicle may be impounded pursuant to this section, even if moved to another street, so long as the signs or placards offering the vehicle for sale remain on the vehicle.

(C) A listing of the streets or public lands subject to the resolution or ordinance adopted pursuant to paragraph (4), or if all streets are covered, a statement to that effect.

(3) The notice of parking violation was issued at least 24 hours prior to the removal of the vehicle.

(4) The local authority of the city, county, or city and county has, by resolution or ordinance, authorized the removal of vehicles pursuant to this section from the street or public lands on which the vehicle is located.

(b) Section 22852 applies to the removal of any vehicle pursuant to this section. *(Added by Stats.1993, c. 481 (A.B.1169), § 1, eff. Sept. 27, 1993.)*

§ 22651.10. Repealed by Stats.2007, c. 747 (A.B.678), § 31, operative Jan. 1, 2010

§ 22652. Removal of unauthorized vehicle from physically handicapped person's parking space

(a) A peace officer, as defined in Chapter 4.5 (commencing with Section 830) of Title 3 of Part 2 of the Penal Code, or any regularly employed and salaried employee engaged in directing traffic or enforcing parking laws and regulations of a city, county, or jurisdiction of a state agency may remove any vehicle from a stall or space designated for physically disabled persons pursuant to Section 22511.7 or 22511.8, located within the jurisdictional limits in which the officer or employee is authorized to act, if the vehicle is parked in violation of Section 22507.8 and if the police or sheriff's department or the Department of the California Highway Patrol is notified.

(b) In a privately or publicly owned or operated offstreet parking facility, this section applies only to those stalls and spaces if the posting requirements under subdivisions (a) and (d) of Section 22511.8 have been complied with and if the stalls or spaces are clearly signed or marked. *(Added by Stats.1982, c. 975, p. 3497, § 9. Amended by Stats.1983, c. 270, § 4, eff. July 15, 1983; Stats.1985, c. 312, § 2; Stats.1985, c. 1041, § 11; Stats. 1996, c. 1142 (S.B.1797), § 11, eff. Sept. 30, 1996; Stats.2004, c. 404 (S.B.1725), § 17.)*

§ 22652.5. Handicapped parking; vehicle removal; immunity from liability

The owner or person in lawful possession of an offstreet parking facility, or any local authority owning or operating an offstreet parking facility, who causes a vehicle to be removed from the parking facility pursuant to Section 22511.8, or any state, city, or county employee, is not civilly liable for the removal if the police or sheriff's department in whose jurisdiction the offstreet parking facility or the stall or space is located or the Department of the California Highway Patrol has been notified prior to the removal. *(Added by Stats.1983, c. 232, § 1, eff. July 14, 1983.)*

§ 22652.6. Disabled person placard; unlawful use; vehicle removal

Any peace officer, as defined in Chapter 4.5 (commencing with Section 830) of Title 3 of Part 2 of the Penal Code, or any regularly employed and salaried employee engaged in directing traffic or enforcing parking laws and regulations of a city or county, may remove any vehicle parked or standing on the streets or highways or from a stall or space of a privately or publicly owned or operated offstreet parking facility within the jurisdiction of the city or county when the vehicle is in violation of a local ordinance or resolution adopted pursuant to Section

694

22511.57. *(Added by Stats.1994, c. 221 (S.B.1378), § 3, operative July 1, 1995.)*

§ 22653. Removal from private property

(a) Any peace officer, as that term is defined in Chapter 4.5 (commencing with Section 830) of Title 3 of Part 2 of the Penal Code, other than an employee directing traffic or enforcing parking laws and regulations, may remove a vehicle from private property located within the territorial limits in which the officer is empowered to act, when a report has previously been made that the vehicle has been stolen or a complaint has been filed and a warrant thereon issued charging that the vehicle has been embezzled.

(b) Any peace officer, as that term is defined in Chapter 4.5 (commencing with Section 830) of Title 3 of Part 2 of the Penal Code, may, after a reasonable period of time, remove a vehicle from private property located within the territorial limits in which the officer is empowered to act, if the vehicle has been involved in, and left at the scene of, a traffic accident and no owner is available to grant permission to remove the vehicle. This subdivision does not authorize the removal of a vehicle where the owner has been contacted and has refused to grant permission to remove the vehicle.

(c) Any peace officer, as that term is defined in Chapter 4.5 (commencing with Section 830) of Title 3 of Part 2 of the Penal Code, may, at the request of the property owner or person in lawful possession of any private property, remove a vehicle from private property located within the territorial limits in which the officer is empowered to act when an officer arrests any person driving or in control of a vehicle for an alleged offense and the officer is, by this code or other law, required or authorized to take, and does take the person arrested before a magistrate without unnecessary delay. *(Stats. 1959, c. 3, p. 1702, § 22653. Amended by Stats.1977, c. 73, p. 479, § 3; Stats.1978, c. 427, p. 1327, § 1; Stats. 1980, c. 1340, p. 4737, § 32, eff. Sept. 30, 1980; Stats.1985, c. 912, § 3.)*

Cross References

Department of the California highway patrol, generally, see Vehicle Code § 2100 et seq.

Local authorities, powers, see Vehicle Code § 21100 et seq.

Obstructing traffic, removal of vehicle, see Vehicle Code § 22651.

Peace officer, definition, see Penal Code §§ 7, 830 et seq., 852.1.

Procedure to remove and store vehicles, see Vehicle Code § 22850 et seq.

Removal from private property, see Vehicle Code § 22658.

Removal of abandoned vehicles, see Vehicle Code § 22523 et seq.

Stolen vehicles, reports, see Vehicle Code § 10500 et seq.

§ 22654. Authorization for moving a vehicle

(a) Whenever any peace officer, as that term is defined in Chapter 4.5 (commencing with Section 830) of Title 3 of Part 2 of the Penal Code, or other employee directing traffic or enforcing parking laws and regulations, finds a vehicle standing upon a highway, located within the territorial limits in which the officer or employee is empowered to act, in violation of Sections 22500 and 22504, the officer or employee may move the vehicle or require the driver or other person in charge of the vehicle to move it to the nearest available position off the roadway or to the nearest parking location, or may remove and store the vehicle if moving it off the roadway to a parking location is impracticable.

(b) Whenever the officer or employee finds a vehicle standing upon a street, located within the territorial limits in which the officer or employee is empowered to act, in violation of a traffic ordinance enacted by local authorities to prevent flooding of adjacent property, he or she may move the vehicle or require the driver or person in charge of the vehicle to move it to the nearest available location in the vicinity where parking is permitted.

(c) Any state, county, or city authority charged with the maintenance of any highway may move any vehicle which is disabled or abandoned or which constitutes an obstruction to traffic from the place where it is located on a highway to the nearest available position on the same highway as may be necessary to keep the highway open or safe for public travel. In addition, employees of the Department of Transportation may remove any disabled vehicle which constitutes an obstruction to traffic on a freeway from the place where it is located to the nearest available location where parking is permitted; and, if the vehicle is unoccupied, the department shall comply with the notice requirements of subdivision (d).

(d) Any state, county, or city authority charged with the maintenance or operation of any highway, highway facility, or public works facility, in cases necessitating the prompt performance of any work on or service to the highway, highway facility, or public works facility, may move to the nearest available location where parking is permitted, any unattended vehicle which obstructs or interferes with the performance of the work or service or may remove and store the vehicle if moving it off the roadway to a location where parking is permitted would be impracticable. If the vehicle is moved to another location where it is not readily visible from its former parked location or it is stored, the person causing the movement or storage of the vehicle shall immediately, by the most expeditious means, notify the owner of the vehicle of its location. If for any reason the vehicle owner cannot be so notified, the person causing the vehicle to be moved or stored shall immediately, by the most expeditious means, notify the police department of the city in which the vehicle was parked, or, if the vehicle had been parked in an unincorporated area of a county, notify the sheriff's department and nearest office of the California Highway Patrol in that county. No vehicle may be removed and stored pursuant to this subdivision unless signs indicating that no person shall stop, park, or leave standing any vehicle within the areas marked by the signs because the work or service would be done, were placed at least 24 hours prior to the movement or removal and storage.

(e) Whenever any peace officer finds a vehicle parked or standing upon a highway in a manner so as to obstruct necessary emergency services, or the routing of traffic at the scene of a disaster, the officer may move the vehicle or require the driver or other person in charge of the vehicle to move it to the nearest available parking location. If the vehicle is unoccupied, and moving the vehicle to a parking location is impractical, the officer may store the vehicle pursuant to Sections 22850 and 22852 and subdivision (a) or (b) of Section 22853. If the vehicle so moved or stored was otherwise lawfully parked, no moving or storage charges shall be assessed against or collected from the driver or owner. *(Stats.1959, c. 3, p. 1702, § 22654. Amended by Stats.1969, c. 1229, p. 2382, § 1; Stats.1971, c. 874, p. 1719, § 1, operative May 3, 1972; Stats.1974, c. 545, p. 1328, § 212; Stats.1977, c. 73, p. 479, § 4; Stats.1980, c. 1340, p. 4737, § 33, eff. Sept. 30, 1980; Stats.1981, c. 281, p. 4737, § 1; Stats.1983, c. 913, § 2.)*

Cross References

Local impounding ordinances, see Vehicle Code § 22850 et seq.
Obstructing traffic, removal of vehicle, see Vehicle Code § 22651.
Peace officer, definition, see Penal Code §§ 7, 830 et seq., 852.1.
Private property, removal of vehicles, see Vehicle Code §§ 22653, 22658, 22852.
Procedure to remove and store vehicles, see Vehicle Code § 22850 et seq.
Removal of abandoned vehicles, see Vehicle Code § 22669.
Removal of vehicle parked or placed on highway for purpose of selling articles, see Streets and Highways Code § 731.

§ 22655. Vehicles involved in hit-and-run accidents; removal for inspection; release of vehicle; transfer of cargo

(a) When any peace officer, as that term is defined in Chapter 4.5 (commencing with Section 830) of Title 3 of Part 2 of the Penal Code or any regularly employed and salaried employee who is engaged in directing traffic or enforcing parking statutes and regulations, has reasonable cause to believe that a motor vehicle on a highway or on private property open to the general public onto which the public is explicitly or implicitly invited, located within the territorial limits in which the officer is empowered to act, has been involved in a hit-and-run accident, and the operator of the vehicle has failed to stop and comply with Sections 20002 to 20006, inclusive, the officer may remove the vehicle from the highway or from public or private property for the purpose of inspection.

(b) Unless sooner released, the vehicle shall be released upon the expiration of 48 hours after the removal from the highway or private property upon demand of the owner. When determining the 48-hour period, weekends, and holidays shall not be included.

(c) Notwithstanding subdivision (b), when a motor vehicle to be inspected pursuant to subdivision (a) is a

695

commercial vehicle, any cargo within the vehicle may be removed or transferred to another vehicle.

This section shall not be construed to authorize the removal of any vehicle from an enclosed structure on private property that is not open to the general public. *(Stats.1959, c. 3, p. 1703, § 22655. Amended by Stats. 1961, c. 1198, p. 2932, § 1; Stats.1963, c. 804, p. 1834, § 1; Stats.1967, c. 236, p. 1371, § 6; Stats.1967, c. 253, p. 1403, § 7; Stats.1969, c. 1116, p. 2178, § 2; Stats.1971, c. 130, p. 173, § 2, operative May 3, 1972; Stats.1974, c. 545, p. 1329, § 213; Stats.1975, c. 109, p. 181, § 1; Stats.1977, c. 486, p. 1606, § 3; Stats.1978, c. 505, p. 1650, § 1; Stats.1979, c. 791, p. 2693, § 1; Stats.1979, c. 831, p. 2878, § 2; Stats.1979, c. 909, p. 3126, § 3.2; Stats.1980, c. 1340, p. 4738, § 34, eff. Sept. 30, 1980; Stats.1997, c. 945 (A.B.1561), § 21.)*

Cross References

Department of the California highway patrol, generally, see Vehicle Code § 2100 et seq.
Peace officer, definition, see Penal Code §§ 7, 830 et seq., 852.1.

§ 22655.3. Impounding vehicle used to flee or evade peace officer

Any peace officer, as defined in Chapter 4.5 (commencing with Section 830) of Title 3 of Part 2 of the Penal Code, pursuing a fleeing or evading person in a motor vehicle may remove and store, or cause to be removed and stored, any vehicle used in violation of Section 2800.1 or 2800.2 from property other than that of the registered owner of the vehicle for the purposes of investigation, identification, or apprehension of the driver if the driver of the vehicle abandons the vehicle and leaves it unattended. All towing and storage fees for a vehicle removed under this section shall be paid by the owner, unless the vehicle was stolen or taken without permission.

No vehicle shall be impounded under this section if the driver is arrested before arrival of the towing equipment or if the registered owner is in the vehicle.

As used in this section, "remove and store a vehicle" means that the peace officer may cause the removal of a vehicle to, and storage of a vehicle in, a private lot where the vehicle may be secured by the owner of the facility or by the owner's representative.

This section is not intended to change current statute and case law governing searches and seizures. *(Formerly § 22651.7, added by Stats.1987, c. 279, § 1. Renumbered § 22655.3 and amended by Stats.1988, c. 160, § 181.)*

§ 22655.5. Impoundment of motor vehicle by peace officer with probable cause to believe vehicle used as means to commit public offense or is evidence or contains evidence of crime

A peace officer, as defined in Chapter 4.5 (commencing with Section 830) of Title 3 of Part 2 of the Penal Code, may remove a motor vehicle from the highway or from public or private property within the territorial

limits in which the officer may act under the following circumstances:

(a) When any vehicle is found upon a highway or public or private property and a peace officer has probable cause to believe that the vehicle was used as the means of committing a public offense.

(b) When any vehicle is found upon a highway or public or private property and a peace officer has probable cause to believe that the vehicle is itself evidence which tends to show that a crime has been committed or that the vehicle contains evidence, which cannot readily be removed, which tends to show that a crime has been committed.

(c) Notwithstanding Section 3068 of the Civil Code or Section 22851 of this code, no lien shall attach to a vehicle removed under this section unless the vehicle was used by the alleged perpetrator of the crime with the express or implied permission of the owner of the vehicle.

(d) In any prosecution of the crime for which a vehicle was impounded pursuant to this section, the prosecutor may request, and the court may order, the perpetrator of the crime, if convicted, to pay the costs of towing and storage of the vehicle, and any administrative charges imposed pursuant to Section 22850.5.

(e) This section shall become operative on January 1, 1993. *(Added by Stats.1990, c. 1515 (A.B.3410), § 2, operative Jan. 1, 1993. Amended by Stats.1993, c. 614 (A.B.481), § 2; Stats.1996, c. 1142 (S.B.1797), § 12, eff. Sept. 30, 1996.)*

§ 22656. Removal from railroad, railway or light rail right of way

Any peace officer, as that term is defined in Chapter 4.5 (commencing with Section 830) of Title 3 of Part 2 of the Penal Code, may remove a vehicle from the right-of-way of a railroad, street railway, or light rail line located within the territorial limits in which the officer is empowered to act if the vehicle is parked or abandoned upon any track or within 7½ feet of the nearest rail. The officer may also remove a vehicle that is parked beyond 7½ feet of the nearest rail but within the right-of-way of a railroad, street railway, or light rail if signs are posted giving notice that vehicles may be removed. *(Added by Stats.1968, c. 625, p. 1310, § 2. Amended by Stats.1969, c. 1116, p. 2178, § 3; Stats.1971, c. 130, p. 174, § 3, operative May 3, 1972; Stats.1974, c. 545, p. 1330, § 214; Stats.1974, c. 797, p. 1745, § 1; Stats.1975, c. 110, p. 181, § 1; Stats.1977, c. 486, p. 1607, § 4; Stats.1978, c. 182, p. 412, § 1; Stats.1979, c. 831, p. 2881, § 3; Stats.1979, c. 909, p. 3129, § 4.5; Stats.1980, c. 1340, p. 4739, § 35, eff. Sept. 30, 1980; Stats.1988, c. 18, § 1; Stats.2002, c. 438 (A.B.3026), § 29.)*

Cross References

Department of the California highway patrol, generally, see Vehicle Code § 2100 et seq.

Unauthorized driving of vehicle on railroad track or right-of-way, see Penal Code § 369g.

§ 22657. Repealed by Stats.1977, c. 73, p. 480, § 5

§ 22657.5. Repealed by Stats.1980, c. 1340, p. 4739, § 36

§ 22658. Removal of vehicle from private property by property owner; towing companies and charges

(a) The owner or person in lawful possession of private property, including an association of a common interest development as defined in Sections 4080 and 4100 or Sections 6528 and 6534 of the Civil Code, may cause the removal of a vehicle parked on the property to a storage facility that meets the requirements of subdivision (n) under any of the following circumstances:

(1) There is displayed, in plain view at all entrances to the property, a sign not less than 17 inches by 22 inches in size, with lettering not less than one inch in height, prohibiting public parking and indicating that vehicles will be removed at the owner's expense, and containing the telephone number of the local traffic law enforcement agency and the name and telephone number of each towing company that is a party to a written general towing authorization agreement with the owner or person in lawful possession of the property. The sign may also indicate that a citation may also be issued for the violation.

(2) The vehicle has been issued a notice of parking violation, and 96 hours have elapsed since the issuance of that notice.

(3) The vehicle is on private property and lacks an engine, transmission, wheels, tires, doors, windshield, or any other major part or equipment necessary to operate safely on the highways, the owner or person in lawful possession of the private property has notified the local traffic law enforcement agency, and 24 hours have elapsed since that notification.

(4) The lot or parcel upon which the vehicle is parked is improved with a single-family dwelling.

(b) The tow truck operator removing the vehicle, if the operator knows or is able to ascertain from the property owner, person in lawful possession of the property, or the registration records of the Department of Motor Vehicles the name and address of the registered and legal owner of the vehicle, shall immediately give, or cause to be given, notice in writing to the registered and legal owner of the fact of the removal, the grounds for the removal, and indicate the place to which the vehicle has been removed. If the vehicle is stored in a storage facility, a copy of the notice shall be given to the proprietor of the storage facility. The notice provided for in this section shall include the amount of mileage on the vehicle at the time of removal and the time of the removal from the property. If the tow truck operator does not know and is not able to ascertain the name of the owner or for any other reason is unable to give the notice to the owner as provided in this section, the tow truck operator shall comply with the requirements of subdivision (c) of Section 22853 relating to notice in the same manner as applicable to an officer removing a vehicle from private property.

(c) This section does not limit or affect any right or remedy that the owner or person in lawful possession of private property may have by virtue of other provisions of law authorizing the removal of a vehicle parked upon private property.

(d) The owner of a vehicle removed from private property pursuant to subdivision (a) may recover for any damage to the vehicle resulting from any intentional or negligent act of a person causing the removal of, or removing, the vehicle.

(e)(1) An owner or person in lawful possession of private property, or an association of a common interest development, causing the removal of a vehicle parked on that property is liable for double the storage or towing charges whenever there has been a failure to comply with paragraph (1), (2), or (3) of subdivision (a) or to state the grounds for the removal of the vehicle if requested by the legal or registered owner of the vehicle as required by subdivision (f).

(2) A property owner or owner's agent or lessee who causes the removal of a vehicle parked on that property pursuant to the exemption set forth in subparagraph (A) of paragraph (1) of subdivision (l) and fails to comply with that subdivision is guilty of an infraction, punishable by a fine of one thousand dollars ($1,000).

(f) An owner or person in lawful possession of private property, or an association of a common interest development, causing the removal of a vehicle parked on that property shall notify by telephone or, if impractical, by the most expeditious means available, the local traffic law enforcement agency within one hour after authorizing the tow. An owner or person in lawful possession of private property, an association of a common interest development, causing the removal of a vehicle parked on that property, or the tow truck operator who removes the vehicle, shall state the grounds for the removal of the vehicle if requested by the legal or registered owner of that vehicle. A towing company that removes a vehicle from private property in compliance with subdivision (l) is not responsible in a situation relating to the validity of the removal. A towing company that removes the vehicle under this section shall be responsible for the following:

(1) Damage to the vehicle in the transit and subsequent storage of the vehicle.

(2) The removal of a vehicle other than the vehicle specified by the owner or other person in lawful possession of the private property.

(g)(1)(A) Possession of a vehicle under this section shall be deemed to arise when a vehicle is removed from private property and is in transit.

(B) Upon the request of the owner of the vehicle or that owner's agent, the towing company or its driver shall

697

immediately and unconditionally release a vehicle that is not yet removed from the private property and in transit.

(C) A person failing to comply with subparagraph (B) is guilty of a misdemeanor.

(2) If a vehicle is released to a person in compliance with subparagraph (B) of paragraph (1), the vehicle owner or authorized agent shall immediately move that vehicle to a lawful location.

(h) A towing company may impose a charge of not more than one-half of the regular towing charge for the towing of a vehicle at the request of the owner, the owner's agent, or the person in lawful possession of the private property pursuant to this section if the owner of the vehicle or the vehicle owner's agent returns to the vehicle after the vehicle is coupled to the tow truck by means of a regular hitch, coupling device, drawbar, portable dolly, or is lifted off the ground by means of a conventional trailer, and before it is removed from the private property. The regular towing charge may only be imposed after the vehicle has been removed from the property and is in transit.

(i)(1)(A) A charge for towing or storage, or both, of a vehicle under this section is excessive if the charge exceeds the greater of the following:

(i) That which would have been charged for that towing or storage, or both, made at the request of a law enforcement agency under an agreement between a towing company and the law enforcement agency that exercises primary jurisdiction in the city in which is located the private property from which the vehicle was, or was attempted to be, removed, or if the private property is not located within a city, then the law enforcement agency that exercises primary jurisdiction in the county in which the private property is located.

(ii) That which would have been charged for that towing or storage, or both, under the rate approved for that towing operator by the Department of the California Highway Patrol for the jurisdiction in which the private property is located and from which the vehicle was, or was attempted to be, removed.

(B) A towing operator shall make available for inspection and copying his or her rate approved by the Department of the California Highway Patrol, if any, within 24 hours of a request without a warrant to law enforcement, the Attorney General, district attorney, or city attorney.

(2) If a vehicle is released within 24 hours from the time the vehicle is brought into the storage facility, regardless of the calendar date, the storage charge shall be for only one day. Not more than one day's storage charge may be required for a vehicle released the same day that it is stored.

(3) If a request to release a vehicle is made and the appropriate fees are tendered and documentation establishing that the person requesting release is entitled to possession of the vehicle, or is the owner's insurance representative, is presented within the initial 24 hours of

698

storage, and the storage facility fails to comply with the request to release the vehicle or is not open for business during normal business hours, then only one day's storage charge may be required to be paid until after the first business day. A business day is any day in which the lienholder is open for business to the public for at least eight hours. If a request is made more than 24 hours after the vehicle is placed in storage, charges may be imposed on a full calendar day basis for each day, or part thereof, that the vehicle is in storage.

(j)(1) A person who charges a vehicle owner a towing, service, or storage charge at an excessive rate, as described in subdivision (h) or (i), is civilly liable to the vehicle owner for four times the amount charged.

(2) A person who knowingly charges a vehicle owner a towing, service, or storage charge at an excessive rate, as described in subdivision (h) or (i), or who fails to make available his or her rate as required in subparagraph (B) of paragraph (1) of subdivision (i), is guilty of a misdemeanor, punishable by a fine of not more than two thousand five hundred dollars ($2,500), or by imprisonment in a county jail for not more than three months, or by both that fine and imprisonment.

(k)(1) A person operating or in charge of a storage facility where vehicles are stored pursuant to this section shall accept a valid bank credit card or cash for payment of towing and storage by a registered owner, the legal owner, or the owner's agent claiming the vehicle. A credit card shall be in the name of the person presenting the card. "Credit card" means "credit card" as defined in subdivision (a) of Section 1747.02 of the Civil Code, except, for the purposes of this section, credit card does not include a credit card issued by a retail seller.

(2) A person described in paragraph (1) shall conspicuously display, in that portion of the storage facility office where business is conducted with the public, a notice advising that all valid credit cards and cash are acceptable means of payment.

(3) A person operating or in charge of a storage facility who refuses to accept a valid credit card or who fails to post the required notice under paragraph (2) is guilty of a misdemeanor, punishable by a fine of not more than two thousand five hundred dollars ($2,500), or by imprisonment in a county jail for not more than three months, or by both that fine and imprisonment.

(4) A person described in paragraph (1) who violates paragraph (1) or (2) is civilly liable to the registered owner of the vehicle or the person who tendered the fees for four times the amount of the towing and storage charges.

(5) A person operating or in charge of the storage facility shall have sufficient moneys on the premises of the primary storage facility during normal business hours to accommodate, and make change in, a reasonable monetary transaction.

(6) Credit charges for towing and storage services shall comply with Section 1748.1 of the Civil Code. Law

enforcement agencies may include the costs of providing for payment by credit when making agreements with towing companies as described in subdivision (i).

(*l*)(1)(A) A towing company shall not remove or commence the removal of a vehicle from private property without first obtaining the written authorization from the property owner or lessee, including an association of a common interest development, or an employee or agent thereof, who shall be present at the time of removal and verify the alleged violation, except that presence and verification is not required if the person authorizing the tow is the property owner, or the owner's agent who is not a tow operator, of a residential rental property of 15 or fewer units that does not have an onsite owner, owner's agent or employee, and the tenant has verified the violation, requested the tow from that tenant's assigned parking space, and provided a signed request or electronic mail, or has called and provides a signed request or electronic mail within 24 hours, to the property owner or owner's agent, which the owner or agent shall provide to the towing company within 48 hours of authorizing the tow. The signed request or electronic mail shall contain the name and address of the tenant, and the date and time the tenant requested the tow. A towing company shall obtain, within 48 hours of receiving the written authorization to tow, a copy of a tenant request required pursuant to this subparagraph. For the purpose of this subparagraph, a person providing the written authorization who is required to be present on the private property at the time of the tow does not have to be physically present at the specified location of where the vehicle to be removed is located on the private property.

(B) The written authorization under subparagraph (A) shall include all of the following:

(i) The make, model, vehicle identification number, and license plate number of the removed vehicle.

(ii) The name, signature, job title, residential or business address, and working telephone number of the person, described in subparagraph (A), authorizing the removal of the vehicle.

(iii) The grounds for the removal of the vehicle.

(iv) The time when the vehicle was first observed parked at the private property.

(v) The time that authorization to tow the vehicle was given.

(C)(i) When the vehicle owner or his or her agent claims the vehicle, the towing company prior to payment of a towing or storage charge shall provide a photocopy of the written authorization to the vehicle owner or the agent.

(ii) If the vehicle was towed from a residential property, the towing company shall redact the information specified in clause (ii) of subparagraph (B) in the photocopy of the written authorization provided to the vehicle owner or the agent pursuant to clause (i).

(iii) The towing company shall also provide to the vehicle owner or the agent a separate notice that provides the telephone number of the appropriate local law enforcement or prosecuting agency by stating "If you believe that you have been wrongfully towed, please contact the local law enforcement or prosecuting agency at [insert appropriate telephone number]." The notice shall be in English and in the most populous language, other than English, that is spoken in the jurisdiction.

(D) A towing company shall not remove or commence the removal of a vehicle from private property described in subdivision (a) of Section 22953 unless the towing company has made a good faith inquiry to determine that the owner or the property owner's agent complied with Section 22953.

(E)(i) General authorization to remove or commence removal of a vehicle at the towing company's discretion shall not be delegated to a towing company or its affiliates except in the case of a vehicle unlawfully parked within 15 feet of a fire hydrant or in a fire lane, or in a manner which interferes with an entrance to, or exit from, the private property.

(ii) In those cases in which general authorization is granted to a towing company or its affiliate to undertake the removal or commence the removal of a vehicle that is unlawfully parked within 15 feet of a fire hydrant or in a fire lane, or that interferes with an entrance to, or exit from, private property, the towing company and the property owner, or owner's agent, or person in lawful possession of the private property shall have a written agreement granting that general authorization.

(2) If a towing company removes a vehicle under a general authorization described in subparagraph (E) of paragraph (1) and that vehicle is unlawfully parked within 15 feet of a fire hydrant or in a fire lane, or in a manner that interferes with an entrance to, or exit from, the private property, the towing company shall take, prior to the removal of that vehicle, a photograph of the vehicle that clearly indicates that parking violation. Prior to accepting payment, the towing company shall keep one copy of the photograph taken pursuant to this paragraph, and shall present that photograph and provide, without charge, a photocopy to the owner or an agent of the owner, when that person claims the vehicle.

(3) A towing company shall maintain the original written authorization, or the general authorization described in subparagraph (E) of paragraph (1) and the photograph of the violation, required pursuant to this section, and any written requests from a tenant to the property owner or owner's agent required by subparagraph (A) of paragraph (1), for a period of three years and shall make them available for inspection and copying within 24 hours of a request without a warrant to law enforcement, the Attorney General, district attorney, or city attorney.

(4) A person who violates this subdivision is guilty of a misdemeanor, punishable by a fine of not more than two thousand five hundred dollars ($2,500), or by imprison-

ment in a county jail for not more than three months, or by both that fine and imprisonment.

(5) A person who violates this subdivision is civilly liable to the owner of the vehicle or his or her agent for four times the amount of the towing and storage charges.

(m)(1) A towing company that removes a vehicle from private property under this section shall notify the local law enforcement agency of that tow after the vehicle is removed from the private property and is in transit.

(2) A towing company is guilty of a misdemeanor if the towing company fails to provide the notification required under paragraph (1) within 60 minutes after the vehicle is removed from the private property and is in transit or 15 minutes after arriving at the storage facility, whichever time is less.

(3) A towing company that does not provide the notification under paragraph (1) within 30 minutes after the vehicle is removed from the private property and is in transit is civilly liable to the registered owner of the vehicle, or the person who tenders the fees, for three times the amount of the towing and storage charges.

(4) If notification is impracticable, the times for notification, as required pursuant to paragraphs (2) and (3), shall be tolled for the time period that notification is impracticable. This paragraph is an affirmative defense.

(n) A vehicle removed from private property pursuant to this section shall be stored in a facility that meets all of the following requirements:

(1)(A) Is located within a 10–mile radius of the property from where the vehicle was removed.

(B) The 10–mile radius requirement of subparagraph (A) does not apply if a towing company has prior general written approval from the law enforcement agency that exercises primary jurisdiction in the city in which is located the private property from which the vehicle was removed, or if the private property is not located within a city, then the law enforcement agency that exercises primary jurisdiction in the county in which is located the private property.

(2)(A) Remains open during normal business hours and releases vehicles after normal business hours.

(B) A gate fee may be charged for releasing a vehicle after normal business hours, weekends, and state holidays. However, the maximum hourly charge for releasing a vehicle after normal business hours shall be one-half of the hourly tow rate charged for initially towing the vehicle, or less.

(C) Notwithstanding any other provision of law and for purposes of this paragraph, "normal business hours" are Monday to Friday, inclusive, from 8 a.m. to 5 p.m., inclusive, except state holidays.

(3) Has a public pay telephone in the office area that is open and accessible to the public.

(o)(1) It is the intent of the Legislature in the adoption of subdivision (k) to assist vehicle owners or their agents

700

by, among other things, allowing payment by credit cards for towing and storage services, thereby expediting the recovery of towed vehicles and concurrently promoting the safety and welfare of the public.

(2) It is the intent of the Legislature in the adoption of subdivision (l) to further the safety of the general public by ensuring that a private property owner or lessee has provided his or her authorization for the removal of a vehicle from his or her property, thereby promoting the safety of those persons involved in ordering the removal of the vehicle as well as those persons removing, towing, and storing the vehicle.

(3) It is the intent of the Legislature in the adoption of subdivision (g) to promote the safety of the general public by requiring towing companies to unconditionally release a vehicle that is not lawfully in their possession, thereby avoiding the likelihood of dangerous and violent confrontation and physical injury to vehicle owners and towing operators, the stranding of vehicle owners and their passengers at a dangerous time and location, and impeding expedited vehicle recovery, without wasting law enforcement's limited resources.

(p) The remedies, sanctions, restrictions, and procedures provided in this section are not exclusive and are in addition to other remedies, sanctions, restrictions, or procedures that may be provided in other provisions of law, including, but not limited to, those that are provided in Sections 12110 and 34660.

(q) A vehicle removed and stored pursuant to this section shall be released by the law enforcement agency, impounding agency, or person in possession of the vehicle, or any person acting on behalf of them, to the legal owner or the legal owner's agent upon presentation of the assignment, as defined in subdivision (b) of Section 7500.1 of the Business and Professions Code; a release from the one responsible governmental agency, only if required by the agency; a government-issued photographic identification card; and any one of the following as determined by the legal owner or the legal owner's agent: a certificate of repossession for the vehicle, a security agreement for the vehicle, or title, whether paper or electronic, showing proof of legal ownership for the vehicle. Any documents presented may be originals, photocopies, or facsimile copies, or may be transmitted electronically. The storage facility shall not require any documents to be notarized. The storage facility may require the agent of the legal owner to produce a photocopy or facsimile copy of its repossession agency license or registration issued pursuant to Chapter 11 (commencing with Section 7500) of Division 3 of the Business and Professions Code, or to demonstrate, to the satisfaction of the storage facility, that the agent is exempt from licensure pursuant to Section 7500.2 or 7500.3 of the Business and Professions Code. *(Added by Stats.1959, c. 963, p. 2994, § 1. Amended by Stats.1963, c. 639, p. 1632, § 1; Stats.1971, c. 1698, p. 3639, § 1, operative May 3, 1972; Stats.1979, c. 1022, p. 3491, § 2; Stats.1980, c. 308, p. 634, § 1; Stats.1982, c. 738, p. 2935,*

§ 1; Stats.1983, c. 913, § 3; Stats.1984, c. 255, § 1; Stats.1984, c. 325, § 1; Stats.1984, c. 1334, § 2; Stats. 1985, c. 312, § 3; Stats.1985, c. 1335, § 1; Stats.1986, c. 1262, § 2; Stats.1987, c. 572, § 1; Stats.1990, c. 309 (S.B.1763), § 3; Stats.1990, c. 998 (A.B.2789), § 2; Stats. 1991, c. 711 (A.B.1390), § 3; Stats.1991, c. 1004 (S.B. 887), § 4; Stats.1992, c. 246 (A.B.2895), § 2; Stats.1992, c. 1220 (A.B.3424), § 7; Stats.1993, c. 272 (A.B.301), § 43, eff. Aug. 2, 1993; Stats.1994, c. 1220 (A.B.3132), § 63, eff. Sept. 30, 1994; Stats.1995, c. 404 (S.B.240), § 5; Stats.1999, c. 1007 (S.B.532), § 23; Stats.2003, c. 212 (A.B.792), § 1; Stats.2006, c. 609 (A.B.2210), § 3; Stats. 2009, c. 322 (A.B.515), § 10; Stats.2012, c. 181 (A.B.806), § 83, operative Jan. 1, 2014; Stats.2013, c. 605 (S.B.752), § 52.)

Law Revision Commission Comments

2012 Amendment

Subdivision (a) of Section 22658 is amended to correct a cross-reference to former Civil Code Section 1351(a), (c). [40 Cal.L.Rev.Comm. Reports 235 (2010)].

2013 Amendment

Subdivision (a) of Section 22658 is amended to add cross-references to Civil Code Section 6528 and 6534, reflecting the enactment of the Commercial and Industrial Common Interest Development Act (Civ. Code §§ 6500–6876). [42 Cal.L.Rev. Comm. Reports 1 (2012)].

Cross References

Disabled persons and veterans, designation of parking, removal of unauthorized vehicles from private parking facilities, see Vehicle Code § 22511.8.

Improperly causing vehicle to be towed or removed to create or acquire lien, forfeiture of claims and liability to owner or lessee, see Civil Code § 3070.

Mobilehome parks, removal of vehicles pursuant to this section, see Civil Code § 798.285.

Removal from private property, see Vehicle Code § 22653.

§ 22658.1. Damaging of fence while removing vehicle; location and notification of property owner by towing company

(a) Any towing company that, in removing a vehicle, cuts, removes, otherwise damages, or leaves open a fence without the prior approval of the property owner or the person in charge of the property shall then and there do either of the following:

(1) Locate and notify the owner or person in charge of the property of the damage or open condition of the fence, the name and address of the towing company, and the license, registration, or identification number of the vehicle being removed.

(2) Leave in a conspicuous place on the property the name and address of the towing company, and the license, registration, or identification number of the vehicle being removed, and shall without unnecessary delay, notify the police department of the city in which the property is located, or if the property is located in unincorporated territory, either the sheriff or the local

headquarters of the Department of the California Highway Patrol, of that information and the location of the damaged or opened fence.

(b) Any person failing to comply with all the requirements of this section is guilty of an infraction. *(Added by Stats.1985, c. 608, § 1. Amended by Stats.2001, c. 854 (S.B.205), § 68.)*

§ 22658.2. Repealed by Stats.2006, c. 609 (A.B.2210), § 4

§ 22659. State or district agricultural association property

Any peace officer of the Department of the California Highway Patrol or any person duly authorized by the state agency in possession of property owned by the state, or rented or leased from others by the state and any peace officer of the Department of the California Highway Patrol providing policing services to property of a district agricultural association may, subsequent to giving notice to the city police or county sheriff, whichever is appropriate, cause the removal of a vehicle from the property to the nearest public garage, under any of the following circumstances:

(a) When the vehicle is illegally parked in locations where signs are posted giving notice of violation and removal.

(b) When an officer arrests any person driving or in control of a vehicle for an alleged offense and the officer is by this code or other law required to take the person arrested before a magistrate without unnecessary delay.

(c) When any vehicle is found upon the property and report has previously been made that the vehicle has been stolen or complaint has been filed and a warrant thereon issued charging that the vehicle has been embezzled.

(d) When the person or persons in charge of a vehicle upon the property are by reason of physical injuries or illness incapacitated to that extent as to be unable to provide for its custody or removal.

The person causing removal of the vehicle shall comply with the requirements of Sections 22852 and 22853 relating to notice. *(Added by Stats.1981, c. 32, p. 76, § 4, eff. May 14, 1981. Amended by Gov.Reorg.Plan No. 1 of 1995, § 68, eff. July 12, 1995; Stats.1996, c. 305 (A.B. 3103), § 70.)*

§ 22659.5. Vehicle used in commission of specified offenses; public nuisance; notice of impounding; poststorage hearing; release of vehicle; towing and storage charges

Notwithstanding any other provision of law, a city or a county may adopt an ordinance declaring a motor vehicle to be a public nuisance subject to seizure and an impound period of up to 30 days when the motor vehicle is used in the commission or attempted commission of an act that violates Section 266h or 266i of, subdivision (h) of Section 374.3 of, or subdivision (b) of Section 647 of, the Penal Code, if the owner or operator of the vehicle has had a prior conviction for the same offense within the past three years. An ordinance adopted pursuant to this section may incorporate any combination or all of these offenses. The vehicle may only be impounded pursuant to a valid arrest of the driver for a violation of one of these provisions. An ordinance adopted pursuant to this section shall, at a minimum, contain all of the following provisions:

(a) Within two working days after impound, the impounding agency shall send a notice by certified mail, return receipt requested, to the legal owner of the vehicle, at the address obtained from the department, informing the owner that the vehicle has been impounded. The notice shall also include notice of the opportunity for a poststorage hearing to determine the validity of the storage or to determine mitigating circumstances establishing that the vehicle should be released. The impounding agency shall be prohibited from charging for more than five days' storage if it fails to notify the legal owner within two working days after the impoundment when the legal owner redeems the impounded vehicle. The impounding agency shall maintain a published telephone number that provides information 24 hours a day regarding the impoundment of vehicles and the rights of a legal owner and a registered owner to request a hearing. The notice shall include all of the following information:

(1) The name, address, and telephone number of the agency providing the notice.

(2) The location of the place of storage and description of the vehicle, that shall include, if available, the model or make, the manufacturer, the license plate number, and the mileage.

(3) The authority and purpose for the removal of the vehicle.

(4) A statement that, in order to receive a poststorage hearing, the owners, or their agents, shall request the hearing in person, writing, or by telephone within 10 days of the date appearing on the notice.

(b) The poststorage hearing shall be conducted within 48 hours of the request, excluding weekends and holidays. The public agency may authorize one of its own officers or employees to conduct the hearing if that hearing officer is not the same person who directed the seizure of the vehicle.

(c) Failure of the legal and the registered owners, or their agents, to request or to attend a scheduled hearing shall satisfy the poststorage hearing requirement.

(d) The agency employing the person who directed the storage shall be responsible for the costs incurred for towing and storage if it is determined in the poststorage hearing that reasonable grounds for the storage are not established.

(e) Any period during which a vehicle is subjected to storage under an ordinance adopted pursuant to this section shall be included as part of the period of impoundment.

702

(f) The impounding agency shall release the vehicle to the registered owner or his or her agent prior to the end of the impoundment period under any of the following circumstances:

(1) The driver of the impounded vehicle was arrested without probable cause.

(2) The vehicle is a stolen vehicle.

(3) The vehicle is subject to bailment and was driven by an unlicensed employee of a business establishment, including a parking service or repair garage.

(4) The driver of the vehicle is not the sole registered owner of the vehicle and the vehicle is being released to another registered owner of the vehicle who agrees not to allow the driver to use the vehicle until after the end of the impoundment period.

(5) The registered owner of the vehicle was neither the driver nor a passenger of the vehicle at the time of the alleged violation, or was unaware that the driver was using the vehicle to engage in activities subject to Section 266h or 266i of, or subdivision (b) of Section 647 of, the Penal Code.

(6) A spouse, registered domestic partner, or other affected third party objects to the impoundment of the vehicle on the grounds that it would create a hardship if the subject vehicle is the sole vehicle in a household. The hearing officer shall release the vehicle where the hardship to a spouse, registered domestic partner, or other affected third party created by the impoundment of the subject vehicle, or the length of the impoundment, outweigh the seriousness and the severity of the act in which the vehicle was used.

(g) Notwithstanding any provision of law, if a motor vehicle is released prior to the conclusion of the impoundment period because the driver was arrested without probable cause, neither the arrested person nor the registered owner of the motor vehicle shall be responsible for the towing and storage charges.

(h) Except as provided in subdivision (g), the registered owner or his or her agent shall be responsible for all towing and storage charges related to the impoundment.

(i) A vehicle removed and seized under an ordinance adopted pursuant to this section shall be released to the legal owner of the vehicle or the legal owner's agent prior to the end of the impoundment period if both of the following conditions are met:

(1) The legal owner is a motor vehicle dealer, bank, credit union, acceptance corporation, or other licensed financial institution legally operating in this state, or is another person who is not the registered owner and holds a security interest in the vehicle.

(2) The legal owner or the legal owner's agent pays all towing and storage fees related to the seizure and impoundment of the vehicle.

(j)(1) No lien sale processing fees shall be charged to the legal owner who redeems the vehicle prior to the 15th day of the impoundment period. Neither the impounding authority nor any person having possession of the vehicle shall collect from the legal owner as described in paragraph (1) of subdivision (i), or the legal owner's agent, any administrative charges imposed pursuant to Section 22850.5, unless the legal owner voluntarily requested a poststorage hearing.

(2) A person operating or in charge of a storage facility where vehicles are stored pursuant to this section shall accept a valid bank credit card or cash for payment of towing, storage, and related fees by a legal or registered owner or the owner's agent claiming the vehicle. A credit card or debit card shall be in the name of the person presenting the card. For purposes of this section, "credit card" is as defined in subdivision (a) of Section 1747.02 of the Civil Code. Credit card does not include a credit card issued by a retail seller.

(3) A person operating or in charge of a storage facility described in paragraph (2) who violates paragraph (2) shall be civilly liable to the owner of the vehicle or the person who tendered the fees for four times the amount of the towing, storage, and related fees not to exceed five hundred dollars ($500).

(4) A person operating or in charge of the storage facility described in paragraph (2) shall have sufficient funds on the premises of the primary storage facility during normal business hours to accommodate, and make change for, a reasonable monetary transaction.

(5) Credit charges for towing and storage services shall comply with Section 1748.1 of the Civil Code. Law enforcement agencies may include the costs of providing for payment by credit when making agreements with towing companies on rates.

(6) A failure by a storage facility to comply with any applicable conditions set forth in this subdivision shall not affect the right of the legal owner or the legal owner's agent to retrieve the vehicle if all conditions required of the legal owner or legal owner's agent under this subdivision are satisfied.

(k)(1) The legal owner or the legal owner's agent shall present to the law enforcement agency, impounding agency, person in possession of the vehicle, or any person acting on behalf of those agencies, a copy of the assignment, as defined in subdivision (b) of Section 7500.1 of the Business and Professions Code, a release from the one responsible governmental agency, only if required by the agency, a government-issued photographic identification card, and any one of the following as determined by the legal owner or the legal owner's agent: a certificate of repossession for the vehicle, a security agreement for the vehicle, or title, whether or not paperless or electronic, showing proof of legal ownership for the vehicle. Any documents presented may be originals, photocopies, or facsimile copies, or may be transmitted electronically. The law enforcement agency, impounding agency, or other governmental agency, or any person acting on behalf of those agencies, shall not require any documents to be notarized. The law enforcement agency, impounding agency, or any person acting on

behalf of those agencies may require the agent of the legal owner to produce a photocopy or facsimile copy of its repossession agency license or registration issued pursuant to Chapter 11 (commencing with Section 7500) of Division 3 of the Business and Professions Code, or to demonstrate, to the satisfaction of the law enforcement agency, impounding agency, or any person acting on behalf of those agencies that the agent is exempt from licensure pursuant to Section 7500.2 or 7500.3 of the Business and Professions Code.

(2) Administrative costs authorized under subdivision (a) of Section 22850.5 shall not be charged to the legal owner of the type specified in paragraph (1) of subdivision (i) who redeems the vehicle unless the legal owner voluntarily requests a poststorage hearing. A city, county, city and county, or state agency shall not require a legal owner or a legal owner's agent to request a poststorage hearing as a requirement for release of the vehicle to the legal owner or the legal owner's agent. The law enforcement agency, impounding agency, or other governmental agency, or any person acting on behalf of those agencies, shall not require any documents other than those specified in this paragraph. The legal owner or the legal owner's agent shall be given a copy of any documents he or she is required to sign, except for a vehicle evidentiary hold log book. The law enforcement agency, impounding agency, or any person acting on behalf of those agencies, or any person in possession of the vehicle, may photocopy and retain the copies of any documents presented by the legal owner or legal owner's agent. The legal owner shall indemnify and hold harmless a storage facility from any claims arising out of the release of the vehicle to the legal owner or the legal owner's agent and from any damage to the vehicle after its release, including the reasonable costs associated with defending any such claims.

(l) A legal owner, who meets the requirements for release of a vehicle pursuant to subdivision (i), or the legal owner's agent, shall not be required to request a poststorage hearing as a requirement for release of the vehicle to the legal owner or the legal owner's agent.

(m)(1) A legal owner, who meets the requirements for release of a vehicle pursuant to subdivision (i), or the legal owner's agent, shall not release the vehicle to the registered owner of the vehicle or an agent of the registered owner, unless the registered owner is a rental car agency, until after the termination of the impoundment period.

(2) Prior to relinquishing the vehicle, the legal owner may require the registered owner to pay all towing and storage charges related to the seizure and impoundment.

(n)(1) A vehicle removed and seized pursuant to an ordinance adopted pursuant to this section shall be released to a rental car agency prior to the end of the impoundment period if the agency is either the legal owner or registered owner of the vehicle and the agency pays all towing and storage fees related to the seizure and impoundment of the vehicle.

(2) The owner of a rental vehicle that was seized under an ordinance adopted pursuant to this section may continue to rent the vehicle upon recovery of the vehicle. However, the rental car agency shall not rent another vehicle to the driver of the vehicle that was seized until the impoundment period has expired.

(3) The rental car agency may require the person to whom the vehicle was rented to pay all towing and storage charges related to the seizure and impoundment. *(Added by Stats.2009, c. 210 (A.B.14), § 2.)*

§ 22660. Local ordinances

Notwithstanding any other provision of law, a city, county, or city and county may adopt an ordinance establishing procedures for the abatement and removal, as public nuisances, of abandoned, wrecked, dismantled, or inoperative vehicles or parts thereof from private or public property, and for the recovery, pursuant to Section 25845 or 38773.5 of the Government Code, or assumption by the local authority, of costs of administration and the removal. *(Added by Stats.1967, c. 1055, p. 2660, § 1. Amended by Stats.1970, c. 427, p. 855, § 1; Stats.1971, c. 130, p. 174, § 3.5, operative May 3, 1972; Stats.1975, c. 627, p. 1358, § 1; Stats.1976, c. 29, p. 45, § 1; Stats.1988, c. 126, § 1.)*

Cross References

Automobile dismantler,
  Generally, see Vehicle Code § 11500 et seq.
  Defined, see Vehicle Code § 220.
Dealer,
  Generally, see Vehicle Code § 11700 et seq.
  Defined, see Vehicle Code § 285.
Equalized county assessment roll, see Revenue and Taxation
    Code § 2050 et seq.
Evidences of registration, see Vehicle Code § 4450 et seq.
Junkyards, see Business and Professions Code § 21600 et seq.
Public nuisances,
  Generally, see Penal Code § 370 et seq.
  Defined, see Civil Code § 3480.
  Remedies, see Civil Code § 3490 et seq.
Reimbursement of governmental or private agency for removal
    of abandoned vehicles, see Vehicle Code § 22710.
Service authority for abatement of abandoned vehicles, see
    Vehicle Code § 22710.

§ 22661. Contents of ordinance

Any ordinance establishing procedures for the removal of abandoned vehicles shall contain all of the following provisions:

(a) The requirement that notice be given to the Department of Motor Vehicles within five days after the date of removal, identifying the vehicle or part thereof and any evidence of registration available, including, but not limited to, the registration card, certificates of ownership, or license plates.

(b) Making the ordinance inapplicable to (1) a vehicle or part thereof that is completely enclosed within a building in a lawful manner where it is not visible from the street or other public or private property or (2) a vehicle or part thereof that is stored or parked in a lawful manner on private property in connection with the business of a licensed dismantler, licensed vehicle dealer, or a junkyard. This exception shall not, however, authorize the maintenance of a public or private nuisance as defined under provisions of law other than this chapter.

(c) The requirement that not less than a 10-day notice of intention to abate and remove the vehicle or part thereof as a public nuisance be issued, unless the property owner and the owner of the vehicle have signed releases authorizing removal and waiving further interest in the vehicle or part thereof. However, the notice of intention is not required for removal of a vehicle or part thereof that is inoperable due to the absence of a motor, transmission, or wheels and incapable of being towed, is valued at less than two hundred dollars ($200) by a person specified in Section 22855, and is determined by the local agency to be a public nuisance presenting an immediate threat to public health or safety, provided that the property owner has signed a release authorizing removal and waiving further interest in the vehicle or part thereof. Prior to final disposition under Section 22662 of such a low-valued vehicle or part for which evidence of registration was recovered pursuant to subdivision (a), the local agency shall provide notice to the registered and legal owners of intent to dispose of the vehicle or part, and if the vehicle or part is not claimed and removed within 12 days after the notice is mailed, from a location specified in Section 22662, final disposition may proceed. No local agency or contractor thereof shall be liable for damage caused to a vehicle or part thereof by removal pursuant to this section.

This subdivision applies only to inoperable vehicles located upon a parcel that is (1) zoned for agricultural use or (2) not improved with a residential structure containing one or more dwelling units.

(d) The 10-day notice of intention to abate and remove a vehicle or part thereof, when required by this section, shall contain a statement of the hearing rights of the owner of the property on which the vehicle is located and of the owner of the vehicle. The statement shall include notice to the property owner that he or she may appear in person at a hearing or may submit a sworn written statement denying responsibility for the presence of the vehicle on the land, with his or her reasons for such denial, in lieu of appearing. The notice of intention to abate shall be mailed, by registered or certified mail, to the owner of the land as shown on the last equalized assessment roll and to the last registered and legal owners of record unless the vehicle is in such condition that identification numbers are not available to determine ownership.

(e) The requirement that a public hearing be held before the governing body of the city, county, or city and county, or any other board, commissioner, or official of the city, county, or city and county as designated by the governing body, upon request for such a hearing by the owner of the vehicle or the owner of the land on which the vehicle is located. This request shall be made to the appropriate public body, agency, or officer within 10 days after the mailing of notice of intention to abate and remove the vehicle or at the time of signing a release pursuant to subdivision (c). If the owner of the land on which the vehicle is located submits a sworn written statement denying responsibility for the presence of the vehicle on his or her land within that time period, this statement shall be construed as a request for hearing that does not require the presence of the owner submitting the request. If the request is not received within that period, the appropriate public body, agency, or officer shall have the authority to remove the vehicle.

(f) The requirement that after a vehicle has been removed, it shall not be reconstructed or made operable, unless it is a vehicle that qualifies for either horseless carriage license plates or historical vehicle license plates, pursuant to Section 5004, in which case the vehicle may be reconstructed or made operable.

(g) A provision authorizing the owner of the land on which the vehicle is located to appear in person at the hearing or present a sworn written statement denying responsibility for the presence of the vehicle on the land, with his or her reasons for the denial. If it is determined at the hearing that the vehicle was placed on the land without the consent of the landowner and that he or she has not subsequently acquiesced to its presence, then the local authority shall not assess costs of administration or removal of the vehicle against the property upon which the vehicle is located or otherwise attempt to collect those costs from the owner. *(Added by Stats.1976, c. 29, p. 45, § 2. Amended by Stats.1983, c. 372, § 1; Stats. 1993, c. 589 (A.B.2211), § 187.)*

§ 22662. Disposition of vehicle or parts

Vehicles or parts thereof may be disposed of by removal to a scrapyard, automobile dismantler's yard, or any suitable site operated by a local authority for processing as scrap, or other final disposition consistent with subdivision (e) of Section 22661. A local authority may operate such a disposal site when its governing body determines that commercial channels of disposition are not available or are inadequate, and it may make final disposition of such vehicles or parts, or the local agency may transfer such vehicle or parts to another, provided such disposal shall be only as scrap. *(Added by Stats. 1976, c. 29, p. 46, § 3.)*

Cross References

Local authorities defined, see Vehicle Code § 385.

§ 22663. Administration of ordinance

Any ordinance adopted pursuant to Section 22660 shall provide for administration of the ordinance by regularly salaried full-time employees of the city, county, or city and county, except that the removal of vehicles or parts thereof from property may be by any other duly authorized person. Any such authorized person may enter upon private property for the purposes specified in the

ordinance to examine a vehicle or parts thereof, obtain information as to the identity of a vehicle, and remove or cause the removal of a vehicle or part thereof declared to be a nuisance pursuant to the ordinance. *(Added by Stats.1976, c. 29, p. 46, § 4.)*

§ 22664. Waiver: reporting requirements and fees

Any licensed dismantler or commercial enterprise acquiring vehicles removed pursuant to such ordinance shall be excused from the reporting requirements of Section 11520; and any fees and penalties which would otherwise be due the Department of Motor Vehicles are hereby waived, provided that a copy of the resolution or order authorizing disposition of the vehicle is retained in the dismantler's or commercial enterprise's business records. *(Added by Stats.1976, c. 29, p. 46, § 5.)*

§ 22665. Administration of abandoned vehicle abatement and removal program

Notwithstanding Section 22710 or any other provision of law, the department may, at the request of a local authority, other than a service authority, administer on behalf of the authority its abandoned vehicle abatement and removal program established pursuant to Section 22660. *(Added by Stats.1976, c. 29, p. 47, § 6. Amended by Stats.1990, c. 1684 (A.B.4114), § 4.)*

Cross References

Local authorities defined, see Vehicle Code § 385.

§ 22666. Regulations of highway patrol

Whenever the department is administering a program pursuant to Section 22665, it shall by regulation establish procedures for the abatement and removal of vehicles that are identical to the requirements specified in Section 22661, except that the department shall provide by agreement with the requesting local authority for the conduct of a public hearing pursuant to subdivision (d) of Section 22661 by the local authority and for the reimbursement of the department for its costs of administration and removal which the local authority is authorized to recover from the property owner pursuant to Section 22660. Such regulations shall also provide for the administration of the regulations by regularly salaried, full-time personnel of the department, except that the removal of vehicles or parts thereof from property may be done by any other duly authorized person. Any such person may enter upon private property for the purposes specified in the regulations to examine a vehicle or parts thereof, obtain information as to the identity of a vehicle, and remove or cause the removal of a vehicle or part thereof declared to be a nuisance pursuant to the regulations.

The provisions of Sections 22662 and 22664 shall also apply to any vehicle removed by the department. *(Added by Stats.1976, c. 29, p. 47, § 7.)*

Local authorities defined, see Vehicle Code § 385.

§ 22667. Abatement and removal: priorities

In establishing procedures for the abatement and removal of abandoned vehicles, the department shall give priority to the removal of abandoned vehicles from corridors of the state highway system, from public lands and parks, and from river and wildlife areas. *(Added by Stats.1976, c. 29, p. 47, § 8.)*

§ 22668. Abandoned Vehicle Trust Fund: prohibited disbursements

No local authority whose abandoned vehicle abatement and removal program is administered pursuant to Section 22665 shall be eligible for any disbursement from the Abandoned Vehicle Trust Fund pursuant to Section 22710. *(Added by Stats.1976, c. 29, p. 47, § 9.)*

Local authorities defined, see Vehicle Code § 385.

§ 22669. Removal of abandoned vehicles

(a) Any peace officer, as that term is defined in Chapter 4.5 (commencing with Section 830) of Title 3 of Part 2 of the Penal Code, or any other employee of the state, county, or city designated by an agency or department of the state or the board of supervisors or city council to perform this function, in the territorial limits in which the officer or employee is authorized to act, who has reasonable grounds to believe that the vehicle has been abandoned, as determined pursuant to Section 22523, may remove the vehicle from a highway or from public or private property.

(b) Any person performing a franchise or contract awarded pursuant to subdivision (a) of Section 22710, may remove a vehicle from a highway or place to which it has been removed pursuant to subdivision (c) of Section 22654 or from public or private property, after a determination by a peace officer, as that term is defined in Chapter 4.5 (commencing with Section 830) of Title 3 of Part 2 of the Penal Code, or other designated employee of the state, county, or city in which the vehicle is located that the vehicle is abandoned, as determined pursuant to Section 22523.

(c) A state, county, or city employee, other than a peace officer or employee of a sheriff's department or a city police department, designated to remove vehicles pursuant to this section may do so only after he or she has mailed or personally delivered a written report identifying the vehicle and its location to the office of the Department of the California Highway Patrol located nearest to the vehicle.

(d) Motor vehicles which are parked, resting, or otherwise immobilized on any highway or public right-of-way and which lack an engine, transmission, wheels, tires, doors, windshield, or any other part or equipment necessary to operate safely on the highways of this state, are hereby declared a hazard to public health, safety, and welfare and may be removed immediately upon discovery by a peace officer or other designated employee of the state, county, or city. *(Formerly § 22702, added by Stats.1959, c. 3, p. 1703, § 22702. Amended by Stats.1960, 1st Ex.Sess., c. 57, p. 406, § 6; Stats.1965, c. 1135, p. 2789, § 9; Stats.1967, c. 1055, p. 2662, § 2; Stats.1969, c. 547, p. 1174, § 2; Stats.1969, c. 1116, p. 2180, § 7; Stats.1970, c. 1431, p. 2775, § 2; Stats.1971, c. 130, p. 176, § 4, operative May 3, 1972; Stats.1971, c. 1624, p. 3499, § 7, operative May 3, 1972; Stats.1973, c. 78, p. 138, § 18; Stats.1973, c. 49, p. 81, § 2, eff. May 15, 1973; Stats.1974, c. 797, p. 1746, § 3; Stats.1979, c. 831, p. 2883, § 4; Stats.1979, c. 909, p. 3131, § 5.5; Stats.1980, c. 1340, p. 4739, § 38, eff. Sept. 30, 1980. Renumbered § 22669 and amended by Stats.1980, c. 1111, p. 3569, § 22; Stats.1980, c. 1340, p. 4739, § 38.2, eff. Sept. 30, 1980, operative Jan. 1, 1981. Amended by Stats.1987, c. 1133, § 4.)*

Department of the California highway patrol, generally, see Vehicle Code § 2100 et seq.
Peace officer, definition, see Penal Code §§ 7, 830 et seq., 852.1.
Private property, removal of vehicles, see Vehicle Code §§ 22653, 22658, 22852.
Report of abandoned or unlawfully stored vehicle, see Vehicle Code § 10652.
Storage of vehicles, see Vehicle Code § 22850.

§ 22670. Determination of estimated value of vehicle

(a) For lien sale purposes, the public agency causing the removal of the vehicle shall determine if the estimated value of the vehicle that has been ordered removed, towed, or stored is five hundred dollars ($ 500) or less, over five hundred dollars ($500) but four thousand dollars ($4,000) or less, or over four thousand dollars ($4,000).

(b) If the public agency fails or refuses to put a value on, or to estimate the value of, the vehicle within three days after the date of removal of the vehicle, the garage keeper specified in Section 22851 or the garage keeper's agent shall determine, under penalty of perjury, if the estimated value of the vehicle that has been ordered removed, towed, or stored, is five hundred dollars ($500) or less, over five hundred dollars ($500) but four thousand dollars ($4,000) or less, or over four thousand dollars ($4,000). *(Added by Stats.1980, c. 1111, p. 3568, § 18. Amended by Stats.1984, c. 73, § 4; Stats.1984, c. 1381, § 1; Stats.1987, c. 1091, § 5; Stats.1992, c. 1220 (A.B.3424), § 8; Stats.1998, c. 203 (S.B.1650), § 6; Stats. 2004, c. 650 (A.B.3047), § 10.)*

Disposal of low-valued vehicle, see Vehicle Code § 22851.10.
Lien sales, impounded vehicles, see Vehicle Code §§ 22851.4, 22851.6.

Satisfaction of lien, see Vehicle Code § 22851.4.

§ 22671. Local franchise or contract for removal

A local authority may either issue a franchise or execute a contract for the removal of abandoned vehicles in accordance with the provisions of this chapter. *(Formerly § 22706, added by Stats.1967, c. 1055, p. 2663, § 4. Renumbered § 22671 and amended by Stats.1980, c. 1111, p. 3570, § 26.)*

Cross References

Local authorities defined, see Vehicle Code § 385.

§ 22700. Renumbered § 22523 and amended by Stats. 1980, c. 1111, p. 3568, § 20

§ 22701. Renumbered § 22524 and amended by Stats. 1980, c. 1111, p. 3568, § 21

§ 22702. Renumbered § 22669 and amended by Stats. 1980, c. 1111, p. 3569, § 22; Stats.1980, c. 1340, p. 4739, § 38.2

§ 22703. Repealed by Stats.1965, c. 1135, p. 2789, § 10

§ 22704. Repealed by Stats.1980, c. 1111, p. 3570, § 23

§ 22705. Renumbered § 22851.2 and amended by Stats.1980, c. 1111, p. 3570, § 24

§ 22705.1. Repealed by Stats.1980, c. 1111, p. 3570, § 25

§ 22706. Renumbered § 22671 and amended by Stats. 1980, c. 1111, p. 3570, § 26

§ 22707. Repealed by Stats.1980, c. 1111, p. 3571, § 27

§ 22710. Service authority for abatement of abandoned vehicles

(a) A service authority for the abatement of abandoned vehicles may be established, and a one dollar ($1) vehicle registration fee imposed, in a county if the board of supervisors of the county, by a two-thirds vote, and a majority of the cities having a majority of the incorporated population within the county have adopted resolutions providing for the establishment of the authority and imposition of the fee. The membership of the authority shall be determined by concurrence of the board of supervisors and a majority vote of the majority of the cities within the county having a majority of the incorporated population.

(b) The authority may contract and may undertake any act convenient or necessary to carry out a law relating to the authority. The authority shall be staffed by existing personnel of the city, county, or county transportation commission.

(c)(1) Notwithstanding any other provision of law, a service authority may adopt an ordinance establishing procedures for the abatement, removal, and disposal, as a public nuisance, of an abandoned, wrecked, dismantled, or inoperative vehicle or part of the vehicle from private or public property; and for the recovery, pursuant to Section 25845 or 38773.5 of the Government Code, or assumption by the service authority, of costs associated with the enforcement of the ordinance. Cost recovery shall only be undertaken by an entity that may be a county or city or the department, pursuant to contract with the service authority as provided in this section.

(2)(A) The money received by an authority pursuant to Section 9250.7 and this section shall be used only for the abatement, removal, or the disposal as a public nuisance of any abandoned, wrecked, dismantled, or inoperative vehicle or part of the vehicle from private or public property. The money received shall not be used to offset the costs of vehicles towed under authorities other than an ordinance adopted pursuant to paragraph (1) or when costs are recovered under Section 22850.5.

(B) The money received by a service authority pursuant to Section 9250.7 and this section that are unexpended in a fiscal year may be carried forward by the service authority for the abandoned vehicle abatement program in the following fiscal year as agreed upon by the service authority and its member agencies.

(d)(1) An abandoned vehicle abatement program and plan of a service authority shall be implemented only with the approval of the county and a majority of the cities having a majority of the incorporated population.

(2)(A) The department shall provide guidelines for an abandoned vehicle abatement program. An authority's abandoned vehicle abatement plan and program shall be consistent with those guidelines, and shall provide for, but not be limited to, an estimate of the number of abandoned vehicles, a disposal and enforcement strategy including contractual agreements, and appropriate fiscal controls.

(B) The department's guidelines provided pursuant to this paragraph shall include, but not be limited to, requiring each service authority receiving funds from the Abandoned Vehicle Trust Fund to report to the Controller on an annual basis pursuant to subdivision (c) of Section 9250.7, in a manner prescribed by the department, and pursuant to an approved abandoned vehicle abatement program.

(C) A service authority may carry out an abandoned vehicle abatement from a public property after providing a notice as specified by the local ordinance adopted pursuant to Section 22660 of the jurisdiction in which the abandoned vehicle is located and that notice has expired.

(3) After a plan has been approved pursuant to paragraph (1), the service authority shall, not later than August 1 of the year in which the plan was approved, submit it to the department for review, and the department shall, not later than October 1 of that same year, either approve the plan as submitted or make recommendations for revision. After the plan has received the department's approval as being consistent with the de-

partment's guidelines, the service authority shall submit it to the Controller.

(4) Except as provided in subdivision (e), the Controller shall not make an allocation for a fiscal year, commencing on July 1 following the Controller's determination to suspend a service authority when a service authority has failed to comply with the provisions set forth in Section 9250.7.

(5) A governmental agency shall not receive funds from a service authority for the abatement of abandoned vehicles pursuant to an approved abandoned vehicle abatement program unless the governmental agency has submitted an annual report to the service authority stating the manner in which the funds were expended, and the number of vehicles abated. The governmental agency shall receive that percentage of the total funds collected by the service authority that is equal to its share of the formula calculated pursuant to paragraph (6).

(6) Each service authority shall calculate a formula for apportioning funds to each governmental agency that receives funds from the service authority and submit that formula to the Controller with the annual report required pursuant to paragraph (2). The formula shall apportion 50 percent of the funds received by the service authority to a governmental agency based on the percentage of vehicles abated by that governmental agency of the total number of abandoned vehicles abated by all member agencies, and 50 percent based on population and geographic area, as determined by the service authority. When the formula is first submitted to the Controller, and each time the formula is revised thereafter, the service authority shall include a detailed explanation of how the service authority determined the apportionment between per capita abatements and service area.

(7) Notwithstanding any other provision of this subdivision, the Controller may allocate to the service authority in the County of Humboldt the net amount of the abandoned vehicle abatement funds received from the fee imposed by that authority, as described in subdivision (b) of Section 9250.7, for calendar years 2000 and 2001.

(e) A plan that has been submitted to the Controller pursuant to subdivision (d) may be revised pursuant to the procedure prescribed in that subdivision, including compliance with any dates described therein for submission to the department and the Controller, respectively, in the year in which the revisions are proposed by the service authority. Compliance with that procedure shall only be required if the revisions are substantial.

(f) For purposes of this section, "abandoned vehicle abatement" means the removal of a vehicle from public or private property by towing or any other means after the vehicle has been marked as abandoned by an official of a governmental agency that is a member of the service authority.

(g) A service authority shall cease to exist on the date that all revenues received by the authority pursuant to this section and Section 9250.7 have been expended.

(h) In the event of a conflict with other provisions of law, this section shall govern the disbursement of money collected pursuant to this section and from the Abandoned Vehicle Trust Fund for the implementation of the abandoned vehicle abatement program. *(Added by Stats. 1990, c. 1684 (A.B.4114), § 6. Amended by Stats.1991, c. 928 (A.B.1886), § 30, eff. Oct. 14, 1991; Stats.1995, c. 819 (A.B.135), § 3; Stats.1997, c. 272 (S.B.112), § 2, eff. Aug. 15, 1997; Stats.2001, c. 175 (S.B.106), § 2; Stats.2002, c. 500 (S.B.1329), § 3; Stats.2004, c. 650 (A.B.3047), § 11; Stats.2007, c. 389 (A.B.468), § 2.)*

Cross References

Registration fee, service authority for abatement of abandoned vehicles, see Vehicle Code § 9250.7.

§ 22711. Transportation to and disposition of abandoned vehicle at institution under jurisdiction of director of corrections for restoration and rebuilding

Notwithstanding any other provision of law, the California Highway Patrol, any city, county, or city and county which has an abandoned vehicle abatement program, and any service authority established under Section 22710, upon satisfying all applicable reporting requirements provided in this chapter, may, with the consent of the Director of Corrections, transport any abandoned vehicle to, and dispose of any abandoned vehicle at, any institution under the jurisdiction of the director which has a program established pursuant to Section 2813.5 of the Penal Code. *(Added by Stats.1991, c. 1157 (A.B.2157), § 2.)*

ARTICLE 2.   VEHICLE DISPOSITION

Section
22850.   Storage of vehicle; mileage.
22850.3.   Release to owner or person in control on proof of current registration or on issuance of notice to appear for registration violation; posting of notice.
22850.5.   Impounded vehicles; release procedures; charges for administrative costs.
22851.   Lien on stored vehicle.
22851.1.   Impounded vehicles; lien sales; priorities; defenses; bail.
22851.2.   Disposition of low-valued vehicle.
22851.3.   Disposal of low-value vehicle by public agency after removal of abandoned vehicle; procedure.
22851.4.   Satisfaction of lien.
22851.6.   Satisfaction of lien; low-valued vehicles; forms.
22851.8.   Disposal of low-valued vehicle.
22851.10.   Disposal of low-valued vehicle; dismantler or scrap iron processor; forms and information; reconstruction of vehicle.
22851.12.   Lien–sale preparations; fees.
22852.   Storage; notice; hearing; application of section.
22852.5.   Loss of lien through trick, fraud, or device; revival of lien; misdemeanor.
22853.   Notice to department of justice and proprietor of storage garage; reports; notice to owner.
22854.   Notice to owner.

Section
22854.5. Notifying National Law Enforcement Telecommunication System whenever officer or employee of public agency directs storage of vehicle under this chapter; means of notification.
22855. Appraisers.
22856. Despoliation of evidence; actions against towing companies.

Cross References

Authorization for moving a vehicle, see Vehicle Code § 22654.
Violation of provisions of code or infraction, see Vehicle Code § 40000.1.

§ 22850. Storage of vehicle; mileage

Whenever an officer or employee removes a vehicle from a highway, or from public or private property, unless otherwise provided, he shall take the vehicle to the nearest garage or other place of safety or to a garage designated or maintained by the governmental agency of which the officer or employee is a member, where the vehicle shall be placed in storage.

At the time of such removal, the officer or employee shall determine the amount of mileage on the vehicle. *(Stats.1959, c. 3, p. 1705, § 22850. Amended by Stats. 1960, 1st Ex.Sess., c. 57, p. 405, § 2; Stats.1968, c. 1070, p. 2077, § 3; Stats.1975, c. 239, p. 629, § 1.)*

Cross References

Individual violations of code governing repossessors, penalties, investigations and actions, see Business and Professions Code § 7502.1.
Liens on vehicles, see Civil Code § 3068 et seq.
Removal of abandoned vehicles, see Vehicle Code § 22669.
Removal of vehicles, see Vehicle Code § 22651.
Storage of unclaimed property, see Vehicle Code § 2414.
Unlawful use or tampering with vehicle by bailee, see Vehicle Code § 10854.

§ 22850.3. Release to owner or person in control on proof of current registration or on issuance of notice to appear for registration violation; posting of notice

(a) A vehicle placed in storage pursuant to Section 22850 shall be released to the owner or person in control of the vehicle only if the owner or person furnishes, to the law enforcement agency or employee who placed the vehicle in storage, satisfactory proof of current vehicle registration. The agency which caused the vehicle to be stored may, in its discretion, issue a notice to appear for the registration violation, if the two days immediately following the day of impoundment are weekend days or holidays.

(b) At every storage facility there shall be posted in a conspicuous place a notice to the effect that a vehicle placed in storage pursuant to Section 22850 may be released only on proof of current registration or, at the discretion of the impounding agency, upon the issuance of a notice to appear for the registration violation by the local agency which caused the vehicle to be stored, specifying the name and telephone number of that local agency. *(Added by Stats.1990, c. 1199 (A.B.4191), § 1. Amended by Stats.1994, c. 1220 (A.B.3132), § 64, eff. Sept. 30, 1994.)*

§ 22850.5. Impounded vehicles; release procedures; charges for administrative costs

(a) A city, county, or city and county, or a state agency may adopt a regulation, ordinance, or resolution establishing procedures for the release of properly impounded vehicles and for the imposition of a charge equal to its administrative costs relating to the removal, impound, storage, or release of the vehicles. Those administrative costs may be waived by the local or state authority upon verifiable proof that the vehicle was reported stolen at the time the vehicle was removed.

(b) The following apply to any charges imposed for administrative costs pursuant to subdivision (a):

(1) The charges shall only be imposed on the registered owner or the agents of that owner and shall not include any vehicle towed under an abatement program or sold at a lien sale pursuant to Sections 3068.1 to 3074, inclusive, of, and Section 22851 of, the Civil Code unless the sale is sufficient in amount to pay the lienholder's total charges and proper administrative costs.

(2) Any charges shall be collected by the local or state authority only from the registered owner or an agent of the registered owner.

(3) The charges shall be in addition to any other charges authorized or imposed pursuant to this code.

(4) No charge may be imposed for any hearing or appeal relating to the removal, impound, storage, or release of a vehicle unless that hearing or appeal was requested in writing by the registered or legal owner of the vehicle or an agent of that registered or legal owner. In addition, the charge may be imposed only upon the person requesting that hearing or appeal.

No administrative costs authorized under subdivision (a) shall be charged to the legal owner who redeems the vehicle unless the legal owner voluntarily requests a poststorage hearing. No city, county, city and county, or state agency shall require a legal owner or a legal owner's agent to request a poststorage hearing as a requirement for release of the vehicle to the legal owner or the legal owner's agent. The impounding agency, or any person acting on behalf of the agency, shall not require the legal owner or the legal owner's agent to produce any documents other than those specified in paragraph (3) of subdivision (f) of Section 14602.6 or paragraph (3) of subdivision (e) of Section 14602.7. The impounding agency, or any person acting on behalf of the agency, shall not require any documents to be notarized. *(Added by Stats.1993, c. 614 (A.B.481), § 3. Amended by Stats.1996, c. 1142 (S.B.1797), § 13, eff. Sept. 30, 1996; Stats.1996, c. 1156 (A.B.3157), § 5.5; Stats.1998, c. 169 (A.B.1329), § 1; Stats.1999, c. 456 (S.B.378), § 15; Stats.2001, c. 554 (A.B.783), § 4; Stats.2002, c. 402 (A.B.1883), § 9; Stats. 2007, c. 192 (S.B.659), § 12, eff. Sept. 7, 2007.)*

Cross References

Arrest of persons engaged in speed contests or reckless driving, removal and seizure of vehicles, see Vehicle Code § 23109.2.

Charter-party carrier buses, impoundment and storage, hearing, release of vehicle, see Vehicle Code § 14602.9.

Driving under the influence, arrest of person with prior DUI conviction, impoundment of vehicle, see Vehicle Code § 22651.10.

Driving without a license, impounding vehicle, see Vehicle Code § 14602.6.

Fleeing or evading a peace officer, impounding vehicle, see Vehicle Code § 14602.7.

Immediate removal and seizure of vehicle driven by repeat offender, storage and impoundment, vehicle owner's rights and responsibilities, see Vehicle Code § 14602.8.

Service authority for abatement of abandoned vehicles, see Vehicle Code § 22710.

Traffic laws, seizure and impoundment of vehicles, see Vehicle Code § 21100.4.

Vehicle used in commission of specified offenses, public nuisance, see Vehicle Code § 22659.5.

Vehicle used in violation of code governing repossessors, seizure, release and liability, including fees, see Vehicle Code § 23118.

§ 22851. Lien on stored vehicle

(a)(1) Whenever a vehicle has been removed to a garage under this chapter and the keeper of the garage has received the notice or notices as provided herein, the keeper shall have a lien dependent upon possession for his or her compensation for towage and for caring for and keeping safe the vehicle for a period not exceeding 60 days or, if an application for an authorization to conduct a lien sale has been filed pursuant to Section 3068. 1 of the Civil Code within 30 days after the removal of the vehicle to the garage, 120 days and, if the vehicle is not recovered by the owner within that period or the owner is unknown, the keeper of the garage may satisfy his or her lien in the manner prescribed in this article. The lien shall not be assigned. Possession of the vehicle is deemed to arise when a vehicle is removed and is in transit, or when vehicle recovery operations or load salvage operations that have been requested by a law enforcement agency have begun at the scene.

(2) Whenever a vehicle owner returns to a vehicle that is in possession of a towing company prior to the removal of the vehicle, the owner may regain possession of the vehicle from the towing company if the owner pays the towing company the towing charges.

(b) No lien shall attach to any personal property in or on the vehicle. The personal property in or on the vehicle shall be given to the current registered owner or the owner's authorized agent upon demand and without charge during normal business hours. Notwithstanding any other provision of law, normal business hours are Monday to Friday, inclusive, from 8 a.m. to 5 p.m., inclusive, except state holidays. A gate fee may be charged for returning property after normal business hours, weekends, and state holidays. The maximum hourly charge for nonbusiness hours releases shall be

one-half the hourly tow rate charged for initially towing the vehicle, or less. The lienholder is not responsible for property after any vehicle has been disposed of pursuant to this chapter. *(Stats.1959, c. 3, p. 1705, § 22851. Amended by Stats.1959, c. 963, p. 2994, § 2; Stats.1965, c. 1135, p. 2790, § 15; Stats.1967, c. 993, p. 2587, § 1; Stats.1971, c. 510, p. 1005, § 3, operative May 3, 1972; Stats.1974, c. 1262, p. 2741, § 7, eff. Sept. 23, 1974, operative Nov. 1, 1974 to Dec. 31, 1976; Stats.1980, c. 1111, p. 3571, § 29; Stats.1989, c. 457, § 2; Stats.1995, c. 404 (S.B.240), § 6; Stats.2001, c. 127 (S.B.46), § 8, eff. July 30, 2001.)*

Cross References

Determination of estimated value of vehicle, duration of amendment, see Vehicle Code § 22670.

Garage defined, see Vehicle Code § 340.

Liens on vehicles, see Civil Code § 3068 et seq.

Method of giving notice, see Vehicle Code §§ 22 et seq., 29.

§ 22851.1. Impounded vehicles; lien sales; priorities; defenses; bail

(a) If the vehicle is impounded pursuant to subdivision (i) of Section 22651 and not released as provided in that subdivision, the vehicle may be sold pursuant to this chapter to satisfy the liens specified in Section 22851 and in subdivision (b) of this section.

(b) A local authority impounding a vehicle pursuant to subdivision (i) of Section 22651 shall have a lien dependent upon possession by the keeper of the garage for satisfaction of bail for all outstanding notices of parking violation issued by the local authority for the vehicle, when the conditions specified in subdivision (c) have been met. This lien shall be subordinate in priority to the lien established by Section 22851, and the proceeds of any sale shall be applied accordingly. Consistent with this order of priority, the term "lien," as used in this article and in Chapter 6.5 (commencing with Section 3067) of Title 14 of Part 4 of Division 3 of the Civil Code, includes a lien imposed by this subdivision. In any action brought to perfect the lien, where required by subdivision (d) of Section 22851.8 of this code, or by subdivision (d) of Section 3071 or subdivision (d) of Section 3072 of the Civil Code, it shall be a defense to the recovery of bail that the owner of the vehicle at the time of impoundment was not the owner of the vehicle at the time of the parking offense.

(c) A lien shall exist for bail with respect to parking violations for which no person has answered the charge in the notice of parking violation given, or filed an affidavit of nonownership pursuant to and within the time specified in subdivision (b) of Section 41103. *(Added by Stats.1984, c. 138, § 1. Amended by Stats.1996, c. 124 (A.B.3470), § 129.)*

§ 22851.2. Disposition of low-valued vehicle

(a) Excepting a vehicle removed pursuant to Section 22669, if the vehicle is determined to have a value not exceeding five hundred dollars ($500) pursuant to Section

22670, the public agency that removed the vehicle shall do all of the following:

(1) Within 48 hours after removal of the vehicle, notify the Stolen Vehicle System of the Department of Justice in Sacramento of the removal.

(2) Prepare and give to the lienholder a report that includes all of the following:

(A) The value of the vehicle estimated pursuant to Section 22670.

(B) The identification of the estimator.

(C) The location of the vehicle.

(D) A description of the vehicle, including the make, year model, identification number, license number, state of registration, and, if a motorcycle, an engine number.

(E) The statutory authority for storage.

(b) If the vehicle is in a condition that there is no means of determining ownership, the public agency that removed the vehicle may give authorization to dispose of the vehicle. If authorization for disposal is not issued, a vehicle identification number shall be assigned prior to commencing the lien sale proceedings. *(Formerly § 22705, added by Stats.1965, c. 1135, p. 2789, § 13. Amended by Stats.1967, c. 1055, p. 2662, § 3; Stats.1970, c. 1431, p. 2776, § 3; Stats.1971, c. 510, p. 1004, § 2, operative May 3, 1972; Stats.1972, c. 98, p. 135, § 6, eff. May 30, 1972, operative Oct. 1, 1972; Stats.1972, c. 791, p. 1407, § 4; Stats.1974, c. 1262, p. 2741, § 6, eff. Sept. 23, 1974, operative Nov. 1, 1974; Stats.1975, c. 1036, p. 2450, § 4, eff. Sept. 24, 1975; Stats.1977, c. 821, p. 2492, § 4; Stats.1978, c. 1005, p. 3091, § 12. Renumbered § 22851.2 and amended by Stats.1980, c. 1111, p. 3570, § 24. Amended by Stats.1983, c. 913, § 4; Stats.1986, c. 1059, § 1, eff. Sept. 24, 1986; Stats.1987, c. 530, § 1; Stats.1987, c. 1091, § 6; Stats.2004, c. 650 (A.B.3047), § 12.)*

Cross References

Automobile dismantler,
  Generally, see Vehicle Code § 11500 et seq.
  Defined, see Vehicle Code § 220.
Evidences of registration, see Vehicle Code § 4450 et seq.

§ 22851.3. Disposal of low-value vehicle by public agency after removal of abandoned vehicle; procedure

Whenever a peace officer, as defined in Chapter 4.5 (commencing with Section 830) of Title 3 of Part 2 of the Penal Code, or any other employee of a public agency authorized pursuant to Section 22669, removes, or causes the removal of, a vehicle pursuant to Section 22669 and the public agency or, at the request of the public agency, the lienholder determines the estimated value of the vehicle is five hundred dollars ($500) or less, the public agency that removed, or caused the removal of, the vehicle shall cause the disposal of the vehicle under this section, subject to all of the following requirements:

(a) Not less than 72 hours before the vehicle is removed, the peace officer or the authorized public employee has securely attached to the vehicle a distinc-

tive notice which states that the vehicle will be removed by the public agency. This subdivision does not apply to abandoned vehicles removed pursuant to subdivision (d) of Section 22669 which are determined by the public agency to have an estimated value of three hundred dollars ($300) or less.

(b) Immediately after removal of the vehicle, the public agency which removed, or caused the removal of, the vehicle shall notify the Stolen Vehicle System of the Department of Justice in Sacramento of the removal.

(c) The public agency that removed, or caused the removal of, the vehicle or, at the request of the public agency, the lienholder shall obtain a copy of the names and addresses of all persons having an interest in the vehicle, if any, from the Department of Motor Vehicles either directly or by use of the California Law Enforcement Telecommunications System. This subdivision does not require the public agency or lienholder to obtain a copy of the actual record on file at the Department of Motor Vehicles.

(d) Within 48 hours of the removal, excluding weekends and holidays, the public agency that removed, or caused the removal of, the vehicle or, at the request of the public agency, the lienholder shall send a notice to the registered and legal owners at their addresses of record with the Department of Motor Vehicles, and to any other person known to have an interest in the vehicle. A notice sent by the public agency shall be sent by certified or first-class mail, and a notice sent by the lienholder shall be sent by certified mail. The notice shall include all of the following information:

(1) The name, address, and telephone number of the public agency providing the notice.

(2) The location of the place of storage and description of the vehicle which shall include, if available, the vehicle make, license plate number, vehicle identification number, and mileage.

(3) The authority and purpose for the removal of the vehicle.

(4) A statement that the vehicle may be disposed of 15 days from the date of the notice.

(5) A statement that the owners and interested persons, or their agents, have the opportunity for a poststorage hearing before the public agency that removed, or caused the removal of, the vehicle to determine the validity of the storage if a request for a hearing is made in person, in writing, or by telephone within 10 days from the date of notice; that, if the owner or interested person, or his or her agent, disagrees with the decision of the public agency, the decision may be reviewed pursuant to Section 11523 of the Government Code; and that during the time of the initial hearing, or during the time the decision is being reviewed pursuant to Section 11523 of the Government Code, the vehicle in question may not be disposed of.

(e)(1) A requested hearing shall be conducted within 48 hours of the request, excluding weekends and holidays.

711

The public agency that removed the vehicle may author-ize its own officers to conduct the hearing if the hearing officer is not the same person who directed the storage of the vehicle.

(2) Failure of either the registered or legal owner or interested person, or his or her agent, to request or to attend a scheduled hearing shall satisfy the poststorage validity hearing requirement of this section.

(f) The public agency employing the person, or utiliz-ing the services of a contractor or franchiser pursuant to subdivision (b) of Section 22669, that removed, or caused the removal of, the vehicle and that directed any towing or storage, is responsible for the costs incurred for towing and storage if it is determined in the hearing that reasonable grounds to believe that the vehicle was abandoned are not established.

(g) An authorization for disposal may not be issued by the public agency that removed, or caused the removal of, the vehicle to a lienholder who is storing the vehicle prior to the conclusion of a requested poststorage hearing or any judicial review of that hearing.

(h) If, after 15 days from the notification date, the vehicle remains unclaimed and the towing and storage fees have not been paid, and if no request for a poststorage hearing was requested or a poststorage hearing was not attended, the public agency that re-moved, or caused the removal of, the vehicle shall provide to the lienholder who is storing the vehicle, on a form approved by the Department of Motor Vehicles, authorization to dispose of the vehicle. The lienholder may request the public agency to provide the authoriza-tion to dispose of the vehicle.

(i) If the vehicle is claimed by the owner or his or her agent within 15 days of the notice date, the lienholder who is storing the vehicle may collect reasonable fees for services rendered, but may not collect lien sale fees as provided in Section 22851.12.

(j) Disposal of the vehicle by the lienholder who is storing the vehicle may only be to a licensed dismantler or scrap iron processor. A copy of the public agency's authorization for disposal shall be forwarded to the licensed dismantler within five days of disposal to a licensed dismantler. A copy of the public agency's authorization for disposal shall be retained by the lien-holder who stored the vehicle for a period of 90 days if the vehicle is disposed of to a scrap iron processor.

(k) If the names and addresses of the registered and legal owners of the vehicle are not available from the records of the Department of Motor Vehicles, either directly or by use of the California Law Enforcement Telecommunications System, the public agency may issue to the lienholder who stored the vehicle an authorization for disposal at any time after the removal.

The lienholder may request the public agency to issue an authorization for disposal after the lienholder ascer-tains that the names and addresses of the registered and legal owners of the vehicle are not available from the

records of the Department of Motor Vehicles either directly or by use of the California Law Enforcement Telecommunications System.

(*l*) A vehicle disposed of pursuant to this section may not be reconstructed or made operable, unless it is a vehicle that qualifies for either horseless carriage license plates or historical vehicle license plates, pursuant to Section 5004, in which case the vehicle may be recon-structed or made operable. *(Added by Stats.1986, c. 1059, § 2, eff. Sept. 24, 1986. Amended by Stats.1987, c. 530, § 2; Stats.1987, c. 1091, § 7; Stats.1987, c. 1133, § 5; Stats.2003, c. 67 (A.B.478), § 1.)*

Cross References

Failure of registered owner of mobilehome, manufactured home, or recreational vehicle to pay costs of remediation, ware-houseman's lien, see Health and Safety Code § 25400.47.

§ 22851.4.   Satisfaction of lien

If the vehicle is determined to have a value exceeding five hundred dollars ($500) pursuant to Section 22670, the lien shall be satisfied pursuant to Sections 3067 to 3074, inclusive, of the Civil Code. *(Added by Stats.1980, c. 1111, p. 3571, § 31. Amended by Stats.1984, c. 1381, § 2; Stats.1987, c. 1091, § 9; Stats.2004, c. 650 (A.B. 3047), § 13.)*

§ 22851.6.   Satisfaction of lien; low-valued vehicles; forms

(a) Lienholders who acquire a vehicle subject to Sec-tion 22851.2 shall satisfy their lien pursuant to Sections 22851.8 and 22851.10 if the vehicle has a value not exceeding five hundred dollars ($500), as determined pursuant to Section 22670.

(b) All forms required by Sections 22851.8 and 22851.10 shall be prescribed by the Department of Motor Vehicles. The language used in the notices and declara-tions shall be simple and nontechnical. *(Added by Stats.1980, c. 1111, p. 3571, § 32. Amended by Stats.1984, c. 1381, § 3; Stats.1986, c. 1059, § 3, eff. Sept. 24, 1986; Stats.1987, c. 530, § 3; Stats.1987, c. 1091, § 10; Stats. 2004, c. 650 (A.B.3047), § 14.)*

§ 22851.8.   Disposal of low-valued vehicle

(a) The lienholder shall, within 15 working days fol-lowing the date of possession of the vehicle, make a request to the Department of Motor Vehicles for the names and addresses of all persons having an interest in the vehicle. A storage charge may not accrue beyond the 15–day period unless the lienholder has made a request to the Department of Motor Vehicles as provided for in this section.

(b) By certified mail with return receipt requested or by United States Postal Service Certificate of Mailing, the lienholder shall immediately, upon receipt of this infor-mation, send the following prescribed forms and enclo-sures to the registered owner and legal owner at their addresses of record with the Department of Motor

Vehicles, and to any other person known to have an interest in the vehicle:

(1) A completed form entitled "Notice of Intent to Dispose of a Vehicle Valued at $500 or Less."

(2) A blank form entitled "Declaration of Opposition."

(3) A return envelope preaddressed to the lienholder.

(c) All notices to persons having an interest in the vehicle shall be signed under penalty of perjury and shall include all of the following:

(1) A description of the vehicle, including make, year, model, identification number, license number, and state of registration. For motorcycles, the engine number shall also be included.

(2) The names and addresses of the registered and legal owners of the vehicle and any other person known to have an interest in the vehicle.

(3) The following statements and information:

(A) The amount of the lien.

(B) The facts concerning the claim that gives rise to the lien.

(C) The person has a right to a hearing in court.

(D) If a hearing in court is desired, a Declaration of Opposition form shall be signed under penalty of perjury and returned to the lienholder within 10 days of the date the notice form specified in paragraph (1) of subdivision (b) was mailed.

(E) If the Declaration of Opposition form is signed and mailed, the lienholder shall be allowed to dispose of the vehicle only if the lienholder obtains a court judgment or a subsequent release from the declarant or if the declarant cannot be served as described in subdivision (e).

(F) If a court action is filed, the declarant shall be notified of the lawsuit at the address shown on the Declaration of Opposition form, and the declarant may appear to contest the claim.

(G) The declarant may be liable for court costs if a judgment is entered in favor of the lienholder.

(4) A statement that the lienholder may dispose of the vehicle to a licensed dismantler or scrap iron processor if it is not redeemed or if a Declaration of Opposition form is not signed and mailed to the lienholder within 10 days of the date the notice form specified in paragraph (1) of subdivision (b) was mailed.

(d) If the lienholder receives a completed Declaration of Opposition form within the time prescribed, the vehicle shall not be disposed of unless the lienholder files an action in court within 20 days of the date the notice form specified in paragraph (1) of subdivision (b) was mailed and a judgment is subsequently entered in favor of the lienholder or unless the declarant subsequently releases his or her interest in the vehicle. If a money judgment is entered in favor of the lienholder and the judgment is not paid within five days after becoming final,

then the lienholder may dispose of the vehicle through a dismantler or scrap iron processor.

(e)(1) Service on the declarant in person or by certified mail, return receipt requested, signed by the addressee at the address shown on the Declaration of Opposition form, shall be effective for the serving of process.

(2) If the lienholder has served the declarant by certified mail, return receipt requested, at the address shown on the Declaration of Opposition form and the mail has been returned unclaimed, or if the lienholder has attempted to effect service on the declarant in person with a marshal, sheriff, or licensed process server and the marshal, sheriff, or licensed process server has been unable to effect service on the declarant, the lienholder may proceed with the judicial proceeding or proceed with the lien sale without a judicial proceeding. The lienholder shall notify the Department of Motor Vehicles of the inability to effect service on the declarant and shall provide the Department of Motor Vehicles with a copy of the documents with which service on the declarant was attempted. Upon receipt of the notification of unsuccessful service, the Department of Motor Vehicles shall send authorization of the sale to the lienholder and send notification of the authorization to the declarant. If service is effected on the declarant, the proof of service shall be submitted to the Department of Motor Vehicles with the documents specified in Section 22851.10. *(Added by Stats.1980, c. 1111, p. 3571, § 33. Amended by Stats.1987, c. 1091, § 11; Stats.1990, c. 1284 (A.B.3049), § 5; Stats.1992, c. 1220 (A.B.3424), § 9; Stats.1996, c. 676 (S.B.1111), § 3; Stats.2004, c. 650 (A.B.3047), § 15.)*

Cross References

Failure of registered owner of mobilehome, manufactured home, or recreational vehicle to pay costs of remediation, warehouseman's lien, see Health and Safety Code § 25400.47.

§ 22851.10. Disposal of low-valued vehicle; dismantler or scrap iron processor; forms and information; reconstruction of vehicle

(a) A vehicle determined to have a value not exceeding five hundred dollars ($500) pursuant to Section 22670 that was stored pursuant to this chapter, and that remains unclaimed, or for which reasonable towing and storage charges remain unpaid, shall be disposed of only to a licensed dismantler or scrap iron processor not earlier than 15 days after the date the Notice of Intent to Dispose of a Vehicle Valued at $ 500 or Less form required pursuant to subdivision (b) of Section 22851.8 was mailed, unless a Declaration of Opposition form has been signed and returned to the lienholder.

(b) If the vehicle has been disposed of to a licensed dismantler or scrap iron processor, the lienholder shall forward the following forms and information to the licensed dismantler or scrap iron processor within five days:

(1) A statement, signed under penalty of perjury, that a properly executed Declaration of Opposition form was not received.

(2) A copy of the notice sent to all interested parties.

(3) A certification from the public agency that made the determination of value pursuant to Section 22670.

(4) The proof of service pursuant to subdivision (e) of Section 22851.8 or a copy of the court judgment, if any in favor of the lienholder entered pursuant to subdivision (d) of Section 22851.8.

(5) The name, address, and telephone number of the licensed dismantler or scrap iron processor who received the vehicle.

(6) The amount the lienholder received for the vehicle.

(c) A vehicle disposed of pursuant to this section shall not be reconstructed or made operable, unless it is a vehicle that qualifies for either horseless carriage license plates or historical vehicle license plates, pursuant to Section 5004, in which case the vehicle may be reconstructed or made operable. *(Added by Stats.1980, c. 1111, p. 3573, § 34. Amended by Stats.1982, c. 664, p. 2725, § 8; Stats.1987, c. 1091, § 12; Stats.1990, c. 1284 (A.B. 3049), § 6; Stats.2004, c. 650 (A.B.3047), § 16.)*

§ 22851.12.   Lien–sale preparations; fees

The lienholder may charge a fee for lien-sale preparations not to exceed seventy dollars ($70) in the case of a vehicle having a value determined to be four thousand dollars ($4,000) or less and not to exceed one hundred dollars ($100) in the case of a vehicle having a value determined to be greater than four thousand dollars ($4,000), from any person who redeems the vehicle prior to disposal or is sold through a lien sale pursuant to this chapter. These charges may commence and become part of the possessory lien when the lienholder requests the names and addresses of all persons having an interest in the vehicle from the department. Not more than 50 percent of the allowable fee may be charged until the lien sale notifications are mailed to all interested parties and the lienholder or the registration service agent has possession of the required lien processing documents. This charge shall not be made in the case of any vehicle redeemed prior to 72 hours from the initial storage. *(Added by Stats.1995, c. 404 (S.B.240), § 8. Amended by Stats.1996, c. 676 (S.B.1111), § 4; Stats.1998, c. 203 (S.B.1650), § 7.)*

§ 22852.   Storage; notice; hearing; application of section

(a) Whenever an authorized member of a public agency directs the storage of a vehicle, as permitted by this chapter, or upon the storage of a vehicle as permitted under this section (except as provided in subdivision (f) or (g)), the agency or person directing the storage shall provide the vehicle's registered and legal owners of record, or their agents, with the opportunity for a poststorage hearing to determine the validity of the storage.

(b) A notice of the storage shall be mailed or personally delivered to the registered and legal owners within 48 hours, excluding weekends and holidays, and shall include all of the following information:

(1) The name, address, and telephone number of the agency providing the notice.

(2) The location of the place of storage and description of the vehicle, which shall include, if available, the name or make, the manufacturer, the license plate number, and the mileage.

(3) The authority and purpose for the removal of the vehicle.

(4) A statement that, in order to receive their poststorage hearing, the owners, or their agents, shall request the hearing in person, writing, or by telephone within 10 days of the date appearing on the notice.

(c) The poststorage hearing shall be conducted within 48 hours of the request, excluding weekends and holidays. The public agency may authorize its own officer or employee to conduct the hearing if the hearing officer is not the same person who directed the storage of the vehicle.

(d) Failure of either the registered or legal owner, or his or her agent, to request or to attend a scheduled hearing shall satisfy the poststorage hearing requirement.

(e) The agency employing the person who directed the storage shall be responsible for the costs incurred for towing and storage if it is determined in the poststorage hearing that reasonable grounds for the storage are not established.

(f) This section does not apply to vehicles abated under the Abandoned Vehicle Abatement Program pursuant to Sections 22660 to 22668, inclusive, and Section 22710, or to vehicles impounded for investigation pursuant to Section 22655, or to vehicles removed from private property pursuant to Section 22658.

(g) This section does not apply to abandoned vehicles removed pursuant to Section 22669 that are determined by the public agency to have an estimated value of five hundred dollars ($500) or less. *(Added by Stats.1979, c. 1022, p. 3491, § 4. Amended by Stats.1986, c. 1059, § 4, eff. Sept. 24, 1986; Stats.1987, c. 530, § 4; Stats.1987, c. 1091, § 14; Stats.2004, c. 650 (A.B.3047), § 17.)*

Cross References

Arrest of persons engaged in speed contests or reckless driving, removal and seizure of vehicles, see Vehicle Code § 23109.2.

Charter-party carrier buses, impoundment and storage, hearing, release of vehicle, see Vehicle Code § 14602.9.

Driving under the influence, arrest of person with prior DUI conviction, impoundment of vehicle, see Vehicle Code § 22651.10.

Garage defined, see Vehicle Code § 340.

Legal owner defined, see Vehicle Code § 370.

Notice,

   Illegal parking, see Vehicle Code § 40202 et seq.

   Method of giving, see Vehicle Code §§ 22 et seq., 29.

Notifying National Law Enforcement Telecommunication System whenever officer or employee of public agency directs storage of vehicle, see Vehicle Code § 22854.5.
Registered owner defined, see Vehicle Code § 505.
Registration of vehicles, generally, see Vehicle Code § 4000 et seq.

§ 22852.5. Loss of lien through trick, fraud, or device; revival of lien; misdemeanor

(a) Whenever the possessory lien upon any vehicle is lost through trick, fraud, or device, the repossession of the vehicle by the lienholder revives the possessory lien, but any lien so revived is subordinate to any right, title, or interest of any person under any sale, transfer, encumbrance, lien, or other interest acquired or secured in good faith and for value between the time of the loss of possession and the time of repossession.

(b) It is a misdemeanor for any person to obtain possession of any vehicle or any part thereof subject to a lien pursuant to the provisions of this chapter by trick, fraud, or device.

(c) It is a misdemeanor for any person claiming a lien on a vehicle to knowingly violate any provision of this chapter. *(Added by Stats.1980, c. 1111, p. 3573, § 36.)*

§ 22853. Notice to department of justice and proprietor of storage garage; reports; notice to owner

(a) Whenever an officer or an employee removing a California registered vehicle from a highway or from public property for storage under this chapter does not know and is not able to ascertain the name of the owner or for any other reason is unable to give notice to the owner as required by Section 22852, the officer or employee shall immediately notify, or cause to be notified, the Department of Justice, Stolen Vehicle System, of its removal. The officer or employee shall file a notice with the proprietor of any public garage in which the vehicle may be stored. The notice shall include a complete description of the vehicle, the date, time, and place from which removed, the amount of mileage on the vehicle at the time of removal, and the name of the garage or place where the vehicle is stored.

(b) Whenever an officer or an employee removing a vehicle not registered in California from a highway or from public property for storage under this chapter does not know and is not able to ascertain the owner or for any other reason is unable to give the notice to the owner as required by Section 22852, the officer or employee shall immediately notify, or cause to be notified, the Department of Justice, Stolen Vehicle System. If the vehicle is not returned to the owner within 120 hours, the officer or employee shall immediately send, or cause to be sent, a written report of the removal by mail to the Department of Justice at Sacramento and shall file a copy of the notice with the proprietor of any public garage in which the vehicle may be stored. The report shall be made on a form furnished by that department and shall include a complete description of the vehicle, the date, time, and place from which the vehicle was removed, the amount of

mileage on the vehicle at the time of removal, the grounds for removal, and the name of the garage or place where the vehicle is stored.

(c) Whenever an officer or employee or private party removing a vehicle from private property for storage under this chapter does not know and is not able to ascertain the name of the owner or for any other reason is unable to give the notice to the owner as required by Section 22852 and if the vehicle is not returned to the owner within a period of 120 hours, the officer or employee or private party shall immediately send, or cause to be sent, a written report of the removal by mail to the Department of Justice at Sacramento and shall file a copy of the notice with the proprietor of any public garage in which the vehicle may be stored. The report shall be made on a form furnished by that department and shall include a complete description of the vehicle, the date, time, and place from which the vehicle was removed, the amount of mileage on the vehicle at the time of removal, the grounds for removal, and the name of the garage or place where the vehicle is stored. *(Added by Stats.1983, c. 913, § 6.)*

Cross References

Notifying National Law Enforcement Telecommunication System whenever officer or employee of public agency directs storage of vehicle, see Vehicle Code § 22854.5.
Removal of vehicle from private property, see Vehicle Code § 22658.

§ 22854. Notice to owner

The Department of Justice upon receiving notice under Section 22853 of the removal of a vehicle from a highway, or from public or private property, shall notify the registered and legal owner in writing at the addresses of such persons as shown by the records of the Department of Motor Vehicles, if the vehicle is registered in this state, of the removal of such vehicle, and give the name of the officer reporting such removal, the grounds upon which the removal was authorized and the location of the vehicle. If the vehicle is not registered in this state, the department shall make reasonable effort to notify the legal or registered owner of the removal and location of the vehicle. The notice to the registered or legal owner shall list the amount of mileage on the vehicle at the time of removal. *(Stats.1959, c. 3, p. 1706, § 22854. Amended by Stats.1960, 1st Ex.Sess., c. 57, p. 406, § 5; Stats.1972, c. 98, p. 137, § 8, eff. May 30, 1972, operative Oct. 1, 1972; Stats.1975, c. 239, p. 630, § 4.)*

Cross References

Legal owner defined, see Vehicle Code § 370.
Registered owner defined, see Vehicle Code § 505.

§ 22854.5. Notifying National Law Enforcement Telecommunication System whenever officer or employee of public agency directs storage of vehicle under this chapter; means of notification

Whenever an officer or employee of a public agency directs the storage of a vehicle under this chapter, the

715

officer, employee, or agency directing that storage may notify the National Law Enforcement Telecommunication System by transmitting by any means available, including, but not limited to, electronic means, the vehicle identification number, the information listed in paragraphs (1), (2), and (3) of subdivision (b) of Section 22852, and the information described under Section 22853. *(Added by Stats.2003, c. 622 (A.B.616), § 1.)*

§ 22855. Appraisers

The following persons shall have the authority to make appraisals of the value of vehicles for purposes of this chapter, subject to the conditions stated in this chapter:

(a) Any peace officer of the Department of the California Highway Patrol designated by the commissioner.

(b) Any regularly employed and salaried deputy sheriff, any reserve deputy sheriff listed under Section 830.6 of the Penal Code, or any other employee designated by the sheriff of any county.

(c) Any regularly employed and salaried police officer, any reserve police officer listed under Section 830.6 of the Penal Code, or any other employee designated by the chief of police of any city.

(d) Any officer or employee of the Department of Motor Vehicles designated by the director of that department.

(e) Any regularly employed and salaried police officer, or reserve police officer, or other employee of the University of California Police Department designated by the chief of the department.

(f) Any regularly salaried employee of a city, county, or city and county designated by a board of supervisors or a city council pursuant to subdivision (a) of Section 22669.

(g) Any regularly employed and salaried police officer, or reserve police officer, or other employee of the police department of a California State University designated by the chief thereof.

(h) Any regularly employed and salaried security officer or other employee of a transit district security force designated by the chief thereof.

(i) Any regularly employed and salaried peace officer, or reserve peace officer, or other employee of the Department of Parks and Recreation designated by the director of that department. *(Stats.1959, c. 3, p. 1706, § 22855. Amended by Stats.1965, c. 1135, p. 2790, § 16; Stats.1967, c. 1055, p. 2663, § 6; Stats.1969, c. 1116, p. 2179, § 5; Stats.1970, c. 1431, p. 2777, § 5; Stats.1971, c. 130, p. 177, § 5, operative May 3, 1972; Stats.1974, c. 545, p. 1330, § 215; Stats.1974, c. 798, p. 1748, § 1; Stats. 1979, c. 909, p. 3132, § 6; Stats.1983, c. 143, § 218; Stats.1986, c. 1019, § 68; Gov.Reorg.Plan No. 1 of 1995, § 69, eff. July 12, 1995; Stats.1996, c. 305 (A.B.3103), § 71; Stats.2003, c. 292 (A.B.1436), § 8.)*

716

Cross References

Criminal procedure, deputized or appointed peace officers, see Penal Code § 830.6.
Disposition of low-valued vehicles, see Vehicle Code §§ 22851.2, 22851.6 et seq.
Ordinance for removal of abandoned vehicles, contents, see Vehicle Code § 22661.

§ 22856. Despoliation of evidence; actions against towing companies

Notwithstanding any other provision of law, no cause of action for despoliation of evidence shall arise against any towing company that sells any vehicle at, or disposes of any vehicle after, a lien sale, unless the company knew, or should have known, that the vehicle will be needed as evidence in a legal action. *(Added by Stats.1989, c. 457, § 3.)*

CHAPTER 11. PARKING LOTS

Section
22950. Offstreet parking facilities: regulation by city of Los Angeles.
22951. Street and alley parking.
22952. Towing or removal; violations.
22953. Towing or removal; parking of vehicles at no fee; exceptions; liability.

Cross References

Law enforcement, California highway patrol, see Vehicle Code § 2400.

§ 22950. Offstreet parking facilities: regulation by city of Los Angeles

Any city having a population of over 2,000,000 inhabitants shall regulate offstreet parking facilities within its jurisdiction in a manner not inconsistent with any provisions of this chapter. *(Added by Stats.1976, c. 802, p. 1851, § 2.)*

§ 22951. Street and alley parking

No operator of any offstreet parking facility shall park the vehicle of a patron of the facility in any street or alley. *(Formerly § 22518, Stats.1959, c. 3, p. 1701, § 22518. Renumbered § 22951 and amended by Stats.1965, c. 1041, p. 2680, § 2.)*

Cross References

Alley defined, see Vehicle Code § 110.
Street defined, see Vehicle Code §§ 590, 591.

§ 22952. Towing or removal; violations

Every person engaged in the operation of off-street parking facilities is guilty of a violation, who:

(a) Tows or removes or authorizes the towing and removal of any vehicle within 24 hours of the expiration of the period for which a particular fee is charged. This subdivision shall not affect or limit any parking lot operator from charging parking fees in accordance with his posted schedule for the additional time such vehicle is parked.

(b) Tows or removes or authorizes the towing and removal of any vehicle when such parking facilities are held open for public use and there was no attendant on duty or other facilities permitting the patron to pay or remit the parking charges at the time such vehicle was first parked. This subdivision shall not affect or limit any parking lot operator from charging parking fees in accordance with his posted schedule for the time such vehicle is parked. *(Added by Stats.1963, c. 1346, p. 2874, § 3. Amended by Stats.1965, c. 1055, p. 2704, § 1; Stats.1968, c. 1192, p. 2258, § 8, operative Jan. 1, 1969.)*

§ 22953. Towing or removal; parking of vehicles at no fee; exceptions; liability

(a) An owner or person in lawful possession of private property that is held open to the public, or a discernible portion thereof, for parking of vehicles at no fee, or an employee or agent thereof, shall not tow or remove, or cause the towing or removal, of a vehicle within one hour of the vehicle being parked.

(b) Notwithstanding subdivision (a), a vehicle may be removed immediately after being illegally parked within 15 feet of a fire hydrant, in a fire lane, in a manner that interferes with an entrance to, or an exit from, the private property, or in a parking space or stall legally designated for disabled persons.

(c) Subdivision (a) does not apply to property designated for parking at residential property, or to property designated for parking at a hotel or motel where the parking stalls or spaces are clearly marked for a specific room.

(d) It is the intent of the Legislature in the adoption of subdivision (a) to avoid causing the unnecessary stranding of motorists and placing them in dangerous situations, when traffic citations and other civil remedies are available, thereby promoting the safety of the general public.

(e) A person who violates subdivision (a) is civilly liable to the owner of the vehicle or his or her agent for two times the amount of the towing and storage charges. *(Added by Stats.1985, c. 1335, § 2. Amended by Stats. 2006, c. 609 (A.B.2210), § 5.)*

CHAPTER 12. PUBLIC OFFENSES

Article		Section
1.	Driving Offenses	23100
1.3.	Offenses by Persons Under 21 Years of Age Involving Alcohol	23136
1.5.	Juvenile Offenses Involving Alcohol	23140
1.7.	Youthful Drunk Driver Visitation Program [Repealed]	
2.	Offenses Involving Alcohol and Drugs	23151
3.	Alcohol Rehabilitation Facilities [Repealed]	
4.	Ignition Interlock Device	23235
4.5.	Installation of Ignition Interlock Devices [Repealed]	
5.	Alcohol and Drug Problem Assessment Program	23249.50

ARTICLE 1. DRIVING OFFENSES

Section	
23100.	Application of chapter.
23101.	Renumbered.
23101.5.	Repealed.
23102.	Renumbered.
23102.1.	Repealed.
23102.2.	Renumbered.
23102.3.	Renumbered.
23102.4.	Renumbered.
23102.5.	Repealed.
23102.6.	Repealed.
23103.	Reckless driving.
23103.5.	Acceptance of guilty or nolo contendere plea to violation of § 23103 in place of charge for violation of § 23152; statement by prosecution; duty of court; violations; effect.
23104.	Reckless driving; bodily injury; great bodily injury and prior conviction.
23105.	Conviction for reckless driving; injuries to another; penalties.
23106.	Repealed.
23107.	Renumbered.
23108.	Repealed.
23109.	Speed contests and exhibitions of speed.
23109.1.	Motor vehicle speed contests; injuries to another; penalties.
23109.2.	Arrest of persons engaged in speed contests or reckless driving; removal and seizure of vehicles; impoundment of vehicles; storage hearing; release of impounded vehicles; liability for towing and storage charges.
23109.5.	Speed contests; prior offenses; effect on punishment.
23110.	Throwing substance at vehicles.
23111.	Throwing substances on highways or adjoining areas.
23112.	Throwing, depositing, or dumping matter on highway.
23112.5.	Dumping, spilling, or releasing hazardous material or waste on highway; notification; penalty.
23112.7.	Illegal dumping of waste matter or harmful waste matter; impoundment; civil forfeiture.
23113.	Removal of material from highway.
23114.	Spilling loads on highway; cargo area; equipment; covering of transported material.
23115.	Rubbish vehicles.
23116.	Pickup or flatbed motor truck; transportation in back; section application.
23116.1.	Inoperative.
23117.	Transportation of animals; enclosure or restraint requirements.
23118.	Vehicle used in violation of code governing repossessors; seizure; release; notice and hearing; liability.
23120.	Temple width of glasses.
23121 to 23122.5.	Renumbered.
23123.	Driving a motor vehicle while using a wireless telephone; penalty; exceptions.

Section
23123.5. Driving motor vehicle while writing, sending or reading text-based communication; exceptions; penalty.
23123.6. Renumbered.
23124.   Driving motor vehicle while using wireless telephone or electronic wireless communications device; minor drivers; penalty; enforcement; exceptions.
23125.   School bus or transit vehicles; prohibition upon use of wireless telephones during operation; exceptions.
23126.   Renumbered.
23127.   Trails and paths.
23128.   Snowmobiles.
23129.   Camper mounted on motor vehicle; exit requirements.
23130, 23130.5. Repealed.
23135.   Motorized bicycles; modifications.

§ 23100. Application of chapter

The provisions of this chapter apply to vehicles upon the highways and elsewhere throughout the State unless expressly provided otherwise. *(Stats.1959, c. 3, p. 1707, § 23100.)*

Cross References

Definitions,
  Highway, see Vehicle Code §§ 360, 591, 592.
  Vehicle, see Vehicle Code § 670.

§ 23101. Renumbered § 23153 and amended by Stats. 1981, c. 940, p. 3566, § 10

§ 23101.5. Repealed by Stats.1971, c. 1530, p. 3027, § 13, operative May 3, 1972

§ 23102. Renumbered § 23152 and amended by Stats. 1981, c. 940, p. 3567, § 12

§ 23102.1. Repealed by Stats.1981, c. 940, p. 3567, § 14

§ 23102.2. Renumbered § 23208 and amended by Stats.1981, c. 940, p. 3567, § 15

§ 23102.3. Renumbered § 23205 and amended by Stats.1981, c. 940, p. 3567, § 16

§ 23102.4. Renumbered § 23209 and amended by Stats.1981, c. 940, p. 3568, § 17

§ 23102.5. Repealed by Stats.1971, c. 1530, p. 3027, § 14, operative May 3, 1972

§ 23102.6. Repealed by Stats.1982, c. 53, p. 171, § 23, eff. Feb. 18, 1982

§ 23103. Reckless driving

(a) A person who drives a vehicle upon a highway in willful or wanton disregard for the safety of persons or property is guilty of reckless driving.

(b) A person who drives a vehicle in an offstreet parking facility, as defined in subdivision (c) of Section 12500, in willful or wanton disregard for the safety of persons or property is guilty of reckless driving.

(c) Except as otherwise provided in Section 40008, persons convicted of the offense of reckless driving shall be punished by imprisonment in a county jail for not less than five days nor more than 90 days or by a fine of not less than one hundred forty-five dollars ($145) nor more than one thousand dollars ($1,000), or by both that fine and imprisonment, except as provided in Section 23104 or 23105. *(Added by Stats.1978, c. 790, p. 2535, § 5.5, eff. Sept. 18, 1978, operative July 1, 1980. Amended by Stats.1980, c. 276, p. 552, § 8, eff. June 30, 1980; Stats. 1980, c. 661, p. 1850, § 9; Stats.1981, c. 155, p. 960, § 1; Stats.1982, c. 331, p. 1472, § 2, eff. June 30, 1982; Stats.1983, c. 1092, § 393, eff. Sept. 27, 1983, operative Jan. 1, 1984; Stats.1985, c. 160, § 1; Stats.1991, c. 928 (A.B.1886), § 30.5, eff. Oct. 14, 1991; Stats.2001, c. 739 (A.B.1707), § 19; Stats.2007, c. 682 (A.B.430), § 16; Stats.2010, c. 685 (A.B.2479), § 2.)*

Cross References

Advisory statement to be given by court to person convicted of a violation of this section, see Vehicle Code § 23593.
Applicability of this section to trolley coaches, see Vehicle Code § 21051.
Arraignment or plea and sentencing in certain misdemeanors, presence of defendant, see Penal Code § 977.
Arrest of persons engaged in speed contests or reckless driving, removal and seizure of vehicles, see Vehicle Code § 23109.2.
Chemical blood, breath or urine tests, see Vehicle Code § 13353.
Conviction of violation of § 23152 within five years after two violations of §§ 23152, 23153 or 23103 as specified in § 23103.5, see Vehicle Code § 23546.
Conviction of violation of § 23152 within five years of three or more violations of §§ 23152, 23153 or 23103 as specified in § 23103.5, see Vehicle Code § 23550.
Conviction of violation of this section as a ground for cancelling, suspending or revoking license to teach driving, see Vehicle Code § 11110.
Deposit in special account for each conviction under this section, see Penal Code § 1463.14.
Driver's license, suspension or revocation,
  Court, see Vehicle Code § 13200.
  Department, see Vehicle Code §§ 13350, 13361.
  Driving after suspension or revocation, see Vehicle Code § 14601.
Driving privileges, suspension or delay, restricted driving privileges imposed on showing of critical need to drive, see Vehicle Code § 13353.8.
Driving under influence of alcoholic beverages, see Vehicle Code §§ 23152, 23153.
Driving under the influence, arrest of person with prior DUI conviction, impoundment of vehicle, see Vehicle Code § 22651.10.
Guilty plea, see Vehicle Code § 41610.
Immunity from criminal prosecution under specified minor consumption provisions, inapplicability to this section, see Business and Professions Code § 25667.
Investigation by the department, see Vehicle Code § 13800 et seq.

Medical assistance exception to controlled substance possession and related offenses, persons experiencing drug-related overdose, no exception to laws prohibiting actions made dangerous by controlled substance use, see Health and Safety Code § 11376.5.

Penalties, public offenses, fines in misdemeanor cases for violations pertaining to passing school buildings or grounds, see Vehicle Code § 42011.

Prior convictions under §§ 23103, 23152 or 23153, effect on sentencing and driving privileges, see Vehicle Code § 23622.

Procedure on arrest for violation of this section, see Vehicle Code § 40303.

Public offenses, State Amnesty Program, not applicable to parking violations and violations of this section, see Vehicle Code § 42008.7.

Records available to courts and law enforcement officials, incidents under certain DWI and homicide laws, period of time records must be available, see Vehicle Code § 1808.

Refusal to submit to alcohol testing under DUI laws, calculation of prior convictions, certain foreign convictions recognized, see Vehicle Code §§ 13353, 13353.1 and 13353.3.

Subsequent convictions, grounds for suspension of license, see Vehicle Code § 13361.

Suspension or revocation of driving privilege for a violation of this section, notice by personal service, see Vehicle Code § 13106.

Traffic violation point count, see Vehicle Code § 12810.

Traffic violator schools, suspension or revocation of license for violation of this section, see Vehicle Code § 11215.

Violation as misdemeanor, see Vehicle Code § 40000.15.

Violation of this section, relinquishment of motor vehicle to convicted minor, see Penal Code § 193.8.

§ 23103.5. Acceptance of guilty or nolo contendere plea to violation of § 23103 in place of charge for violation of § 23152; statement by prosecution; duty of court; violations; effect

(a) If the prosecution agrees to a plea of guilty or nolo contendere to a charge of a violation of Section 23103 in satisfaction of, or as a substitute for, an original charge of a violation of Section 23152, the prosecution shall state for the record a factual basis for the satisfaction or substitution, including whether or not there had been consumption of an alcoholic beverage or ingestion or administration of a drug, or both, by the defendant in connection with the offense. The statement shall set forth the facts that show whether or not there was a consumption of an alcoholic beverage or the ingestion or administration of a drug by the defendant in connection with the offense.

(b) The court shall advise the defendant, prior to the acceptance of the plea offered pursuant to a factual statement pursuant to subdivision (a), of the consequences of a conviction of a violation of Section 23103 as set forth in subdivision (c).

(c) If the court accepts the defendant's plea of guilty or nolo contendere to a charge of a violation of Section 23103 and the prosecutor's statement under subdivision (a) states that there was consumption of an alcoholic beverage or the ingestion or administration of a drug by the defendant in connection with the offense, the result-

ing conviction shall be a prior offense for the purposes of Section 23540, 23546, 23550, 23560, 23566, or 23622, as specified in those sections.

(d) The court shall notify the Department of Motor Vehicles of each conviction of Section 23103 that is required under this section to be a prior offense for purposes of Section 23540, 23546, 23550, 23560, 23566, or 23622.

(e) Except as provided in paragraph (1) of subdivision (f), if the court places the defendant on probation for a conviction of Section 23103 that is required under this section to be a prior offense for purposes of Section 23540, 23546, 23550, 23560, 23566, or 23622, the court shall order the defendant to enroll in an alcohol and drug education program licensed under Chapter 9 (commencing with Section 11836) of Part 2 of Division 10.5 of the Health and Safety Code and complete, at a minimum, the educational component of that program, as a condition of probation. If compelling circumstances exist that mitigate against including the education component in the order, the court may make an affirmative finding to that effect. The court shall state the compelling circumstances and the affirmative finding on the record, and may, in these cases, exclude the educational component from the order.

(f)(1) If the court places on probation a defendant convicted of a violation of Section 23103 that is required under this section to be a prior offense for purposes of Section 23540, 23546, 23550, 23560, 23566, or 23622, and that offense occurred within 10 years of a separate conviction of a violation of Section 23103, as specified in this section, or within 10 years of a conviction of a violation of Section 23152 or 23153, the court shall order the defendant to participate for nine months or longer, as ordered by the court, in a program licensed under Chapter 9 (commencing with Section 11836) of Part 2 of Division 10.5 of the Health and Safety Code that consists of at least 60 hours of program activities, including education, group counseling, and individual interview sessions.

(2) The court shall revoke the person's probation, except for good cause shown, for the failure to enroll in, participate in, or complete a program specified in paragraph (1).

(g) The Department of Motor Vehicles shall include in its annual report to the Legislature under Section 1821 an evaluation of the effectiveness of the programs described in subdivisions (e) and (f) as to treating persons convicted of violating Section 23103. *(Added by Stats.1981, c. 941, p. 3587, § 5. Amended by Stats.1982, c. 53, p. 171, § 24, eff. Feb. 18, 1982; Stats.1988, c. 939, § 1, operative July 1, 1989; Stats.1988, c. 1273, § 2, operative July 1, 1989; Stats.1998, c. 118 (S.B.1186), § 11.9, operative July 1, 1999; Stats.1998, c. 487 (S.B.1176), § 3; Stats.1998, c. 487 (S.B.1176), § 4, operative July 1, 1999; Stats.2008, c. 103 (A.B.2802), § 2.)*

Cross References

Advisory statement to be given by court to person convicted of a violation of this section, see Vehicle Code § 23593.

Arraignment, presence of defendant, see Penal Code § 977.

Challenging constitutional validity of separate conviction, see Vehicle Code § 41403.

Chemical blood, breath or urine tests, see Vehicle Code § 13353.

Conviction of violation of § 23152 within five years after two violations of §§ 23152, 23153 or 23103 as specified in § 23103.5, see Vehicle Code § 23546.

Conviction of violation of § 23152 within five years of three or more violations of §§ 23152, 23153 or 23103 as specified in § 23103.5, see Vehicle Code § 23550.

Driving privileges, suspension or delay, restricted driving privileges imposed on showing of critical need to drive, see Vehicle Code § 13353.8.

Driving under the influence, arrest of person with prior DUI conviction, impoundment of vehicle, see Vehicle Code § 22651.10.

Immunity from criminal prosecution under specified minor consumption provisions, inapplicability to this section, see Business and Professions Code § 25667.

Investigation for driver's license suspension or revocation, three convictions in three years under this or other specified sections, see Vehicle Code § 13800.

Mandatory participation in alcohol and drug problem assessment program for conviction of violation of this section, see Vehicle Code § 23647 et seq.

Medical assistance exception to controlled substance possession and related offenses, persons experiencing drug-related overdose, no exception to laws prohibiting actions made dangerous by controlled substance use, see Health and Safety Code § 11376.5.

Prior convictions under §§ 23103, 23152 or 23153, effect on sentencing and driving privileges, see Vehicle Code § 23622.

Refusal to submit to alcohol testing under DUI laws, calculation of prior convictions, certain foreign convictions recognized, see Vehicle Code §§ 13353, 13353.1 and 13353.3.

Santa Barbara County emergency medical services, penalty assessment, application to this section, see Government Code § 76104.1.

§ 23104. Reckless driving; bodily injury; great bodily injury and prior conviction

(a) Except as provided in subdivision (b), whenever reckless driving of a vehicle proximately causes bodily injury to a person other than the driver, the person driving the vehicle shall, upon conviction thereof, be punished by imprisonment in the county jail for not less than 30 days nor more than six months or by a fine of not less than two hundred twenty dollars ($220) nor more than one thousand dollars ($1,000), or by both the fine and imprisonment.

(b) A person convicted of reckless driving that proximately causes great bodily injury, as defined in Section 12022.7 of the Penal Code, to a person other than the driver, who previously has been convicted of a violation of Section 23103, 23104, 23105, 23109, 23109.1, 23152, or 23153, shall be punished by imprisonment pursuant to subdivision (h) of Section 1170 of the Penal Code, by imprisonment in the county jail for not less than 30 days

nor more than six months or by a fine of not less than two hundred twenty dollars ($220) nor more than one thousand dollars ($1,000) or by both the fine and imprisonment. *(Added by Stats.1978, c. 790, p. 2535, § 6.5, eff. Sept. 18, 1978, operative July 1, 1980. Amended by Stats.1980, c. 276, p. 553, § 10, eff. June 30, 1980; Stats.1980, c. 661, p. 1851, § 12; Stats.1981, c. 155, p. 960, § 3; Stats.1982, c. 331, p. 1632, § 3, eff. June 30, 1982; Stats.1983, c. 1092, § 394, eff. Sept. 27, 1983, operative Jan. 1, 1984; Stats.1983, c. 965, § 1; Stats.1984, c. 216, § 11; Stats.2007, c. 682 (A.B.430), § 17; Stats.2011, c. 15 (A.B.109), § 609, eff. April 4, 2011, operative Oct. 1, 2011.)*

Cross References

Applicability of this section to trolley coaches, see Vehicle Code § 21051.

Conviction of a violation of this section as a ground for cancelling, suspending or revoking license to teach driving, see Vehicle Code § 11110.

Deposit in special account for each conviction under this section, see Penal Code § 1463.14.

Driver's license, suspension or revocation,
  By court, see Vehicle Code §§ 13200, 13201.
  By department, see Vehicle Code §§ 13350, 13361.
  Driving after suspension or revocation, see Vehicle Code § 14601.

Guilty plea, see Vehicle Code § 41610.

Investigation by the department, see Vehicle Code § 13800 et seq.

Manslaughter in driving of a vehicle, see Penal Code § 192.

Penalties, public offenses, fines in misdemeanor cases for violations pertaining to passing school buildings or grounds, see Vehicle Code § 42011.

Procedure on arrest for violation of this section, see Vehicle Code § 40303.

Public offenses, State Amnesty Program, not applicable to parking violations and violations of this section, see Vehicle Code § 42008.7.

Subsequent convictions, grounds for suspension of license, see Vehicle Code § 13361.

Suspension or revocation of driving privilege for a violation of this section, notice by personal service, see Vehicle Code § 13106.

Traffic violation point count, see Vehicle Code § 12810.

Traffic violators schools, suspension or revocation of license for violation of this section, see Vehicle Code § 11215.

Violation as misdemeanor, see Vehicle Code § 40000.15.

§ 23105. Conviction for reckless driving; injuries to another; penalties

(a) A person convicted of reckless driving in violation of Section 23103 that proximately causes one or more of the injuries specified in subdivision (b) to a person other than the driver, shall be punished by imprisonment pursuant to subdivision (h) of Section 1170 of the Penal Code, or by imprisonment in a county jail for not less than 30 days nor more than six months, or by a fine of not less than two hundred twenty dollars ($220) nor more than one thousand dollars ($1,000), or by both that fine and imprisonment.

(b) This section applies to all of the following injuries:

(1) A loss of consciousness.

(2) A concussion.

(3) A bone fracture.

(4) A protracted loss or impairment of function of a bodily member or organ.

(5) A wound requiring extensive suturing.

(6) A serious disfigurement.

(7) Brain injury.

(8) Paralysis.

(c) This section does not preclude or prohibit prosecution under any other provision of law. *(Added by Stats.2006, c. 432 (A.B.2190), § 1. Amended by Stats. 2011, c. 15 (A.B.109), § 610, eff. April 4, 2011, operative Oct. 1, 2011.)*

Cross References

Applicability of this section to trolley coaches, see Vehicle Code § 21051.

Conviction of a violation of this section as a ground for cancelling, suspending or revoking license to teach driving, see Vehicle Code § 11110.

Motor vehicle speed contests, injuries to another, see Vehicle Code § 23109.1.

Public offenses, State Amnesty Program, not applicable to parking violations and violations of this section, see Vehicle Code § 42008.7.

Traffic violator schools, suspension or revocation of license for violation of this section, see Vehicle Code § 11215.

§ 23106. Repealed by Stats.1981, c. 940, p. 3569, §§ 20, 21

§ 23107. Renumbered § 23201 and amended by Stats. 1981, c. 940, p. 3569, § 22

§ 23108. Repealed by Stats.1971, c. 1530, p. 3028, § 20, operative May 3, 1972

§ 23109. Speed contests and exhibitions of speed

(a) A person shall not engage in a motor vehicle speed contest on a highway. As used in this section, a motor vehicle speed contest includes a motor vehicle race against another vehicle, a clock, or other timing device. For purposes of this section, an event in which the time to cover a prescribed route of more than 20 miles is measured, but where the vehicle does not exceed the speed limits, is not a speed contest.

(b) A person shall not aid or abet in any motor vehicle speed contest on any highway.

(c) A person shall not engage in a motor vehicle exhibition of speed on a highway, and a person shall not aid or abet in a motor vehicle exhibition of speed on any highway.

(d) A person shall not, for the purpose of facilitating or aiding or as an incident to any motor vehicle speed contest or exhibition upon a highway, in any manner obstruct or place a barricade or obstruction or assist or participate in placing a barricade or obstruction upon any highway.

(e)(1) A person convicted of a violation of subdivision (a) shall be punished by imprisonment in a county jail for not less than 24 hours nor more than 90 days or by a fine of not less than three hundred fifty-five dollars ($355) nor more than one thousand dollars ($1,000), or by both that fine and imprisonment. That person shall also be required to perform 40 hours of community service. The court may order the privilege to operate a motor vehicle suspended for 90 days to six months, as provided in paragraph (8) of subdivision (a) of Section 13352. The person's privilege to operate a motor vehicle may be restricted for 90 days to six months to necessary travel to and from that person's place of employment and, if driving a motor vehicle is necessary to perform the duties of the person's employment, restricted to driving in that person's scope of employment. This subdivision does not interfere with the court's power to grant probation in a suitable case.

(2) If a person is convicted of a violation of subdivision (a) and that violation proximately causes bodily injury to a person other than the driver, the person convicted shall be punished by imprisonment in a county jail for not less than 30 days nor more than six months or by a fine of not less than five hundred dollars ($500) nor more than one thousand dollars ($1,000), or by both that fine and imprisonment.

(f)(1) If a person is convicted of a violation of subdivision (a) for an offense that occurred within five years of the date of a prior offense that resulted in a conviction of a violation of subdivision (a), that person shall be punished by imprisonment in a county jail for not less than four days nor more than six months, and by a fine of not less than five hundred dollars ($500) nor more than one thousand dollars ($1,000).

(2) If the perpetration of the most recent offense within the five-year period described in paragraph (1) proximately causes bodily injury to a person other than the driver, a person convicted of that second violation shall be imprisoned in a county jail for not less than 30 days nor more than six months and by a fine of not less than five hundred dollars ($500) nor more than one thousand dollars ($1,000).

(3) If the perpetration of the most recent offense within the five-year period described in paragraph (1) proximately causes serious bodily injury, as defined in paragraph (4) of subdivision (f) of Section 243 of the Penal Code, to a person other than the driver, a person convicted of that second violation shall be imprisoned in the state prison, or in a county jail for not less than 30 days nor more than one year, and by a fine of not less than five hundred dollars ($500) nor more than one thousand dollars ($1,000).

(4) The court shall order the privilege to operate a motor vehicle of a person convicted under paragraph (1), (2), or (3) suspended for a period of six months, as provided in paragraph (9) of subdivision (a) of Section 13352. In lieu of the suspension, the person's privilege to operate a motor vehicle may be restricted for six months

to necessary travel to and from that person's place of employment and, if driving a motor vehicle is necessary to perform the duties of the person's employment, restricted to driving in that person's scope of employment.

(5) This subdivision does not interfere with the court's power to grant probation in a suitable case.

(g) If the court grants probation to a person subject to punishment under subdivision (f), in addition to subdivision (f) and any other terms and conditions imposed by the court, which may include a fine, the court shall impose as a condition of probation that the person be confined in a county jail for not less than 48 hours nor more than six months. The court shall order the person's privilege to operate a motor vehicle to be suspended for a period of six months, as provided in paragraph (9) of subdivision (a) of Section 13352 or restricted pursuant to subdivision (f).

(h) If a person is convicted of a violation of subdivision (a) and the vehicle used in the violation is registered to that person, the vehicle may be impounded at the registered owner's expense for not less than one day nor more than 30 days.

(i) A person who violates subdivision (b), (c), or (d) shall upon conviction of that violation be punished by imprisonment in a county jail for not more than 90 days, by a fine of not more than five hundred dollars ($500), or by both that fine and imprisonment.

(j) If a person's privilege to operate a motor vehicle is restricted by a court pursuant to this section, the court shall clearly mark the restriction and the dates of the restriction on that person's driver's license and promptly notify the Department of Motor Vehicles of the terms of the restriction in a manner prescribed by the department. The Department of Motor Vehicles shall place that restriction in the person's records in the Department of Motor Vehicles and enter the restriction on a license subsequently issued by the Department of Motor Vehicles to that person during the period of the restriction.

(k) The court may order that a person convicted under this section, who is to be punished by imprisonment in a county jail, be imprisoned on days other than days of regular employment of the person, as determined by the court.

(*l*) This section shall be known and may be cited as the Louis Friend Memorial Act. (*Stats.1959, c. 3, p. 1709, § 23109. Amended by Stats.1967, c. 607, p. 1956, § 1; Stats.1983, c. 935, § 1; Stats.1983, c. 1092, § 395, eff. Sept. 27, 1983, operative Jan. 1, 1984; Stats.1983, c. 953, § 2.5; Stats.1984, c. 216, § 12; Stats.2004, c. 595 (S.B.1541), § 2; Stats.2005, c. 475 (A.B.1325), § 1; Stats.2006, c. 538 (S.B.1852), § 661; Stats.2009, c. 193 (S.B.598), § 3, operative July 1, 2010; Stats.2010, c. 301 (A.B.1601), § 2; Stats.2011, c. 15 (A.B.109), § 611, eff. April 4, 2011, operative Oct. 1, 2011; Stats.2011, c. 39 (A.B.117), § 64, eff. June 30, 2011, operative Oct. 1, 2011.)*

722

Cross References

Highway defined, see Vehicle Code §§ 360, 591, 592.

Influence of alcoholic beverage or drug, suspension or revocation of driving privileges, see Vehicle Code § 13352.

Penalties, public offenses, fines in misdemeanor cases for violations pertaining to passing school buildings or grounds, see Vehicle Code § 42011.

Private parking facilities, application of section, see Vehicle Code § 21107.8.

Procedure on arrest for violation of this section, see Vehicle Code § 40303.

Removal of vehicles used in motor vehicle speed contests in violation of this section, removal by peace officers or specified employees, see Vehicle Code § 22651.6.

Revocation or suspension of driver's license for speeding, see Vehicle Code § 13200.

Revocation or suspension of license for violation of this section, see Vehicle Code § 13352.

Speed laws, see Vehicle Code § 22349 et seq.

Testimony based on speed trap, applicability of provisions to violations of this section, see Vehicle Code § 40804.

Traffic violation point count, violation of this section, see Vehicle Code § 12810.

Uniform of traffic officer investigating violations of this section, see Vehicle Code § 40800.

Violation as misdemeanor, see Vehicle Code § 40000.15.

§ 23109.1. Motor vehicle speed contests; injuries to another; penalties

(a) A person convicted of engaging in a motor vehicle speed contest in violation of subdivision (a) of Section 23109 that proximately causes one or more of the injuries specified in subdivision (b) to a person other than the driver, shall be punished by imprisonment pursuant to subdivision (h) of Section 1170 of the Penal Code, or by imprisonment in a county jail for not less than 30 days nor more than six months, or by a fine of not less than five hundred dollars ($500) nor more than one thousand dollars ($1,000), or by both that fine and imprisonment.

(b) This section applies to all of the following injuries:

(1) A loss of consciousness.

(2) A concussion.

(3) A bone fracture.

(4) A protracted loss or impairment of function of a bodily member or organ.

(5) A wound requiring extensive suturing.

(6) A serious disfigurement.

(7) Brain injury.

(8) Paralysis.

(c) This section does not preclude or prohibit prosecution under any other provision of law. (*Added by Stats.2006, c. 432 (A.B.2190), § 2. Amended by Stats. 2011, c. 15 (A.B.109), § 612, eff. April 4, 2011, operative Oct. 1, 2011.)*

Cross References

Conviction for reckless driving, injuries to another, see Vehicle Code § 23105.

Traffic violation point count, violation of this section, see Vehicle Code § 12810.

§ 23109.2. Arrest of persons engaged in speed contests or reckless driving; removal and seizure of vehicles; impoundment of vehicles; storage hearing; release of impounded vehicles; liability for towing and storage charges

(a)(1) Whenever a peace officer determines that a person was engaged in any of the activities set forth in paragraph (2), the peace officer may immediately arrest and take into custody that person and may cause the removal and seizure of the motor vehicle used in that offense in accordance with Chapter 10 (commencing with Section 22650). A motor vehicle so seized may be impounded for not more than 30 days.

(2)(A) A motor vehicle speed contest, as described in subdivision (a) of Section 23109.

(B) Reckless driving on a highway, as described in subdivision (a) of Section 23103.

(C) Reckless driving in an offstreet parking facility, as described in subdivision (b) of Section 23103.

(D) Exhibition of speed on a highway, as described in subdivision (c) of Section 23109.

(b) The registered and legal owner of a vehicle removed and seized under subdivision (a) or their agents shall be provided the opportunity for a storage hearing to determine the validity of the storage in accordance with Section 22852.

(c)(1) Notwithstanding Chapter 10 (commencing with Section 22650) or any other provision of law, an impounding agency shall release a motor vehicle to the registered owner or his or her agent prior to the conclusion of the impoundment period described in subdivision (a) under any of the following circumstances:

(A) If the vehicle is a stolen vehicle.

(B) If the person alleged to have been engaged in the motor vehicle speed contest, as described in subdivision (a), was not authorized by the registered owner of the motor vehicle to operate the motor vehicle at the time of the commission of the offense.

(C) If the registered owner of the vehicle was neither the driver nor a passenger of the vehicle at the time of the alleged violation pursuant to subdivision (a), or was unaware that the driver was using the vehicle to engage in any of the activities described in subdivision (a).

(D) If the legal owner or registered owner of the vehicle is a rental car agency.

(E) If, prior to the conclusion of the impoundment period, a citation or notice is dismissed under Section 40500, criminal charges are not filed by the district attorney because of a lack of evidence, or the charges are otherwise dismissed by the court.

(2) A vehicle shall be released pursuant to this subdivision only if the registered owner or his or her agent presents a currently valid driver's license to operate the vehicle and proof of current vehicle registration, or if ordered by a court.

(3) If, pursuant to subparagraph (E) of paragraph (1) a motor vehicle is released prior to the conclusion of the impoundment period, neither the person charged with a violation of subdivision (a) of Section 23109 nor the registered owner of the motor vehicle is responsible for towing and storage charges nor shall the motor vehicle be sold to satisfy those charges.

(d) A vehicle seized and removed under subdivision (a) shall be released to the legal owner of the vehicle, or the legal owner's agent, on or before the 30th day of impoundment if all of the following conditions are met:

(1) The legal owner is a motor vehicle dealer, bank, credit union, acceptance corporation, or other licensed financial institution legally operating in this state, or is another person, not the registered owner, holding a security interest in the vehicle.

(2) The legal owner or the legal owner's agent pays all towing and storage fees related to the impoundment of the vehicle. No lien sale processing fees shall be charged to a legal owner who redeems the vehicle on or before the 15th day of impoundment.

(3) The legal owner or the legal owner's agent presents foreclosure documents or an affidavit of repossession for the vehicle.

(e)(1) The registered owner or his or her agent is responsible for all towing and storage charges related to the impoundment, and any administrative charges authorized under Section 22850.5.

(2) Notwithstanding paragraph (1), if the person convicted of engaging in the activities set forth in paragraph (2) of subdivision (a) was not authorized by the registered owner of the motor vehicle to operate the motor vehicle at the time of the commission of the offense, the court shall order the convicted person to reimburse the registered owner for any towing and storage charges related to the impoundment, and any administrative charges authorized under Section 22850.5 incurred by the registered owner to obtain possession of the vehicle, unless the court finds that the person convicted does not have the ability to pay all or part of those charges.

(3) If the vehicle is a rental vehicle, the rental car agency may require the person to whom the vehicle was rented to pay all towing and storage charges related to the impoundment and any administrative charges authorized under Section 22850.5 incurred by the rental car agency in connection with obtaining possession of the vehicle.

(4) The owner is not liable for any towing and storage charges related to the impoundment if acquittal or dismissal occurs.

(5) The vehicle may not be sold prior to the defendant's conviction.

(6) The impounding agency is responsible for the actual costs incurred by the towing agency as a result of

the impoundment should the registered owner be absolved of liability for those charges pursuant to paragraph (3) of subdivision (c). Notwithstanding this provision, nothing shall prohibit impounding agencies from making prior payment arrangements to satisfy this requirement.

(f) Any period when a vehicle is subjected to storage under this section shall be included as part of the period of impoundment ordered by the court under subdivision (h) of Section 23109. *(Added by Stats.2007, c. 727 (S.B.67), § 3, eff. Oct. 14, 2007.)*

§ 23109.5. Speed contests; prior offenses; effect on punishment

(a) In any case charging a violation of subdivision (a) of Section 23109 and where the offense occurs within five years of one or more prior offenses which resulted in conviction of violation of subdivision (a) of Section 23109, the court shall not strike any prior conviction of those offenses for purposes of sentencing in order to avoid imposing, as part of the sentence or term of probation, the minimum time of imprisonment, as provided in subdivision (f) of Section 23109, or for purposes of avoiding revocation, suspension, or restriction of the privilege to operate a motor vehicle, as provided in Section 13352 or 23109.

(b) In any case charging a violation of subdivision (a) of Section 23109, the court shall obtain a copy of the driving record of the person charged from the Department of Motor Vehicles and may obtain any records from the Department of Justice or any other source to determine if one or more prior convictions of the person for violation of subdivision (a) of Section 23109 have occurred within five years of the charged offense. *(Added by Stats.1983, c. 953, § 3.)*

Cross References

Destruction of court records, notice, retention periods, see Government Code § 68152.

§ 23110. Throwing substance at vehicles

(a) Any person who throws any substance at a vehicle or any occupant thereof on a highway is guilty of a misdemeanor.

(b) Any person who with intent to do great bodily injury maliciously and willfully throws or projects any rock, brick, bottle, metal or other missile, or projects any other substance capable of doing serious bodily harm at such vehicle or occupant thereof is guilty of a felony and upon conviction shall be punished by imprisonment in the state prison. *(Stats.1959, c. 3, p. 1709, § 23110. Amended by Stats.1976, c. 1139, p. 5173, § 341, operative July 1, 1977; Stats.1976, c. 1119, p. 5023, § 2; Stats.2011, c. 15 (A.B.109), § 613, eff. April 4, 2011, operative Oct. 1, 2011; Stats.2011, c. 39 (A.B.117), § 65, eff. June 30, 2011, operative Oct. 1, 2011.)*

Cross References

Applicability of this section to trolley coaches, see Vehicle Code § 21051.

724

Misdemeanor and felony defined, see Penal Code § 17.
Punishment for misdemeanors, see Vehicle Code § 42002.
Shooting on public highways, see Penal Code § 374c.
Throwing substances upon highway likely to injure persons, animals or vehicles, see Penal Code § 588a.
Violation as misdemeanor, see Vehicle Code § 40000.15.

§ 23111. Throwing substances on highways or adjoining areas

No person in any vehicle and no pedestrian shall throw or discharge from or upon any road or highway or adjoining area, public or private, any lighted or nonlighted cigarette, cigar, match, or any flaming or glowing substance. This section shall be known as the Paul Buzzo Act. *(Stats.1959, c. 3, p. 1709, § 23111. Amended by Stats.1963, c. 2038, p. 4267, § 30; Stats.1965, c. 474, p. 1778, § 1; Stats.1965, c. 1261, p. 3137, § 1; Stats.1970, c. 1548, p. 3151, § 8.)*

Cross References

Definitions,
   Highway, see Vehicle Code §§ 360, 591, 592.
   Private road or driveway, see Vehicle Code § 490.
Forfeiture of bail, see Vehicle Code § 40512.
Litter violations, disposition of fines and forfeitures, see Penal Code § 1463.9.
Littering or dumping on highways, see Penal Code § 374.3.
Optional bail forfeiture, see Vehicle Code § 40512.5.
Punishment for littering violations, see Vehicle Code § 42001.7.
Safety roadside rest, refuse disposal, see Streets and Highways Code § 224.
Similar provision, see Health and Safety Code § 13002.
Throwing substances upon highway likely to injure persons, animals or vehicles, see Penal Code § 588a.
Warning signs, see Streets and Highways Code § 101.6.

§ 23112. Throwing, depositing, or dumping matter on highway

(a) No person shall throw or deposit, nor shall the registered owner or the driver, if such owner is not then present in the vehicle, aid or abet in the throwing or depositing upon any highway any bottle, can, garbage, glass, nail, offal, paper, wire, any substance likely to injure or damage traffic using the highway, or any noisome, nauseous, or offensive matter of any kind.

(b) No person shall place, deposit, or dump, or cause to be placed, deposited, or dumped, any rocks, refuse, garbage, or dirt in or upon any highway, including any portion of the right-of-way thereof, without the consent of the state or local agency having jurisdiction over the highway. *(Stats.1959, c. 3, p. 1709, § 23112. Amended by Stats.1959, c. 40, p. 1896, § 2; Stats.1965, c. 1261, p. 3137, § 2; Stats.1970, c. 62, p. 77, § 1; Stats.1976, c. 213, p. 399, § 2; Stats.1980, c. 74, p. 190, § 4.)*

Cross References

Forfeiture of bail, see Vehicle Code § 40512.
Highway defined, see Vehicle Code §§ 360, 591, 592.
Litter violations, disposition of fines and forfeitures, see Penal Code § 1463.9.
Littering or dumping on highways, see Penal Code § 374.3.
Optional bail forfeiture, see Vehicle Code § 40512.5.

Punishment for littering violations, see Vehicle Code § 42001.7.

Right-of-way defined, see Vehicle Code § 525.

Safety roadside rest, refuse disposal, see Streets and Highways Code § 224.

Throwing substances upon highway likely to injure persons, animals or vehicles, see Penal Code § 588a.

§ 23112.5. Dumping, spilling, or releasing hazardous material or waste on highway; notification; penalty

(a) Any person who dumps, spills, or causes the release of hazardous material, as defined by Section 353, or hazardous waste, as defined by Section 25117 of the Health and Safety Code, upon any highway shall notify the Department of the California Highway Patrol or the agency having traffic jurisdiction for that highway of the dump, spill, or release, as soon as the person has knowledge of the dump, spill, or release and notification is possible. Upon receiving notification pursuant to this section, the Department of the California Highway Patrol shall, as soon as possible, notify the * * * Office of Emergency Services of the dump, spill, or release, except for petroleum spills of less than 42 gallons from vehicular fuel tanks.

(b) Any person who is convicted of a violation of this section shall be punished by a mandatory fine of not less than two thousand dollars ($2,000). *(Added by Stats. 1985, c. 646, § 1. Amended by Stats.1990, c. 429 (A.B. 3904), § 1; Stats.1994, c. 1214 (A.B.3404), § 8; Stats. 2010, c. 618 (A.B.2791), § 294; Stats.2013, c. 352 (A.B. 1317), § 525, eff. Sept. 26, 2013, operative July 1, 2013.)*

§ 23112.7. Illegal dumping of waste matter or harmful waste matter; impoundment; civil forfeiture

(a)(1) A motor vehicle used for illegal dumping of waste matter on public or private property is subject to impoundment pursuant to subdivision (c).

(2) A motor vehicle used for illegal dumping of harmful waste matter on public or private property is subject to impoundment and civil forfeiture pursuant to subdivision (d).

(b) For the purposes of this section, the following terms have the following meanings:

(1) "Illegal dumping" means the willful or intentional depositing, dropping, dumping, placing, or throwing of any waste matter onto public or private property that is not expressly designated for the purpose of disposal of waste matter. "Illegal dumping" does not include the discarding of small quantities of waste matter related to consumer goods and that are reasonably understood to be ordinarily carried on or about the body of a living person, including, but not limited to, beverage containers and closures, packaging, wrappers, wastepaper, newspaper, magazines, or other similar waste matter that escapes or is allowed to escape from a container, receptacle, or package.

(2) "Waste matter" means any form of tangible matter described by any of the following:

(A) All forms of garbage, refuse, rubbish, recyclable materials, and solid waste.

(B) Dirt, soil, rock, decomposed rock, gravel, sand, or other aggregate material dumped or deposited as refuse.

(C) Abandoned or discarded furniture; or commercial, industrial, or agricultural machinery, apparatus, structure, or other container; or a piece, portion, or part of these items.

(D) All forms of liquid waste not otherwise defined in or deemed to fall within the purview of Section 25117 of the Health and Safety Code, including, but not limited to, water-based or oil-based paints, chemical solutions, water contaminated with any substance rendering it unusable for irrigation or construction, oils, fuels, and other petroleum distillates or byproducts.

(E) Any form of biological waste not otherwise designated by law as hazardous waste, including, but not limited to, body parts, carcasses, and any associated container, enclosure, or wrapping material used to dispose these matters.

(F) A physical substance used as an ingredient in any process, now known or hereafter developed or devised, to manufacture a controlled substance specified in Section 11054, 11055, 11056, 11057, or 11058 of the Health and Safety Code, or that is a byproduct or result of the manufacturing process of the controlled substance.

(3) "Harmful waste matter" is a hazardous substance as defined in Section 374.8 of the Penal Code; a hazardous waste as defined in Section 25117 of the Health and Safety Code; waste that, pursuant to Division 30 (commencing with Section 40000) of the Public Resources Code, cannot be disposed in a municipal solid waste landfill without special handling, processing, or treatment; or waste matter in excess of one cubic yard.

(c)(1) Whenever a person, who has one or more prior convictions of Section 374.3 or 374.8 of the Penal Code that are not infractions, is convicted of a misdemeanor violation of Section 374.3 of the Penal Code, or of a violation of Section 374.8 of the Penal Code, for illegally dumping waste matter or harmful waste matter that is committed while driving a motor vehicle of which he or she is the registered owner of the vehicle, or is the registered owner's agent or employee, the court at the time of sentencing may order the motor vehicle impounded for a period of not more than six months.

(2) In determining the impoundment period imposed pursuant to paragraph (1), the court shall consider both of the following factors:

(A) The size and nature of the waste matter dumped.

(B) Whether the dumping occurred for a business purpose.

(3) The cost of keeping the vehicle is a lien on the vehicle pursuant to Chapter 6.5 (commencing with Section 3067) of Title 14 of Part 4 of Division 3 of the Civil Code.

(4) Notwithstanding paragraph (1), a vehicle impounded pursuant to this subdivision shall be released to the legal owner or his or her agent pursuant to subdivision (b) of Section 23592.

(5) The impounding agency shall not be liable to the registered owner for the release of the vehicle to the legal owner or his or her agent when made in compliance with paragraph (4).

(6) This subdivision does not apply if there is a community property interest in the vehicle that is owned by a person other than the defendant and the vehicle is the only vehicle available to the defendant's immediate family that may be operated on the highway with a class A, class B, or class C driver's license.

(d)(1) Notwithstanding Section 86 of the Code of Civil Procedure and any other provision of law otherwise prescribing the jurisdiction of the court based upon the value of the property involved, whenever a person, who has two or more prior convictions of Section 374.3 or 374.8 of the Penal Code that are not infractions, is charged with a misdemeanor violation of Section 374.3 of the Penal Code, or of a violation of Section 374.8 of the Penal Code, for illegally dumping harmful waste matter, the court with jurisdiction over the offense may, upon a motion of the prosecutor or the county counsel in a criminal action, declare a motor vehicle if used by the defendant in the commission of the violation, to be a nuisance, and upon conviction order the vehicle sold pursuant to Section 23596, if the person is the registered owner of the vehicle or the registered owner's employee or agent.

(2) The proceeds of the sale of the vehicle pursuant to this subdivision shall be distributed and used in decreasing order of priority, as follows:

(A) To satisfy all costs of the sale, including costs incurred with respect to the taking and keeping of the vehicle pending sale.

(B) To the legal owner in an amount to satisfy the indebtedness owed to the legal owner remaining as of the date of the sale, including accrued interest or finance charges and delinquency charges.

(C) To recover the costs made, incurred, or associated with the enforcement of this section, the abatement of waste matter, and the deterrence of illegal dumping.

(3) A vehicle shall not be sold pursuant to this subdivision in either of the following circumstances:

(A) The vehicle is owned by the employer or principal of the defendant and the use of the vehicle was made without the employer's or principal's knowledge and consent, and did not provide a direct benefit to the employer's or principal's business.

(B) There is a community property interest in the vehicle that is owned by a person other than the defendant and the vehicle is the only vehicle available to the defendant's immediate family that may be operated on the highway with a class A, class B, or class C driver's license. *(Added by Stats.2006, c. 765 (A.B.2253), § 1.)*

Cross References

Infractions, see Penal Code § 16.
Misdemeanor, definition and penalties, see Penal Code §§ 17, 19, 19.2.

§ 23113. Removal of material from highway

(a) Any person who drops, dumps, deposits, places, or throws, or causes or permits to be dropped, dumped, deposited, placed, or thrown, upon any highway or street any material described in Section 23112 or in subdivision (d) of Section 23114 shall immediately remove the material or cause the material to be removed.

(b) If the person fails to comply with subdivision (a), the governmental agency responsible for the maintenance of the street or highway on which the material has been deposited may remove the material and collect, by civil action, if necessary, the actual cost of the removal operation in addition to any other damages authorized by law from the person made responsible under subdivision (a).

(c) A member of the Department of the California Highway Patrol may direct a responsible party to remove the aggregate material described in subdivision (d) of Section 23114 from a highway when that material has escaped or been released from a vehicle.

(d) Notwithstanding any other provision of law, a government agency described in subdivision (b), the Department of the California Highway Patrol, or the employees or officers of those agencies, may not be held liable for any damage to material, to cargo, or to personal property caused by a negligent act or omission of the employee or officer when the employee or officer is acting within the scope and purpose of subdivision (b) or (c). Nothing in this subdivision affects liability for purposes of establishing gross negligence or willful misconduct. This subdivision applies to the negligent performance of a ministerial act, and does not affect liability under any provision of law, including liability, if any, derived from the failure to preserve evidence in a civil or criminal action. *(Stats.1959, c. 3, p. 1709, § 23113. Amended by Stats.1963, c. 1668, p. 3257, § 1; Stats.1965, c. 552, p. 1879, § 1; Stats.1988, c. 1486, § 2; Stats.1989, c. 1360, § 158; Stats.1989, c. 125, § 1, eff. July 12, 1989; Stats.1999, c. 421 (S.B.681), § 2.)*

Cross References

Forfeiture of bail, see Vehicle Code § 40512.
Highway defined, see Vehicle Code §§ 360, 591, 592.
Litter violations, disposition of fines and forfeitures, see Penal Code § 1463.9.
Optional bail forfeiture, see Vehicle Code § 40512.5.
Punishment for littering violations, see Vehicle Code § 42001.7.

Street defined, see Vehicle Code §§ 590, 591.

§ 23114. Spilling loads on highway; cargo area; equipment; covering of transported material

(a) Except as provided in Subpart I (commencing with Section 393.100) of Title 49 of the Code of Federal Regulations related to hay and straw, a vehicle shall not be driven or moved on any highway unless the vehicle is so constructed, covered, or loaded as to prevent any of its contents or load other than clear water or feathers from live birds from dropping, sifting, leaking, blowing, spilling, or otherwise escaping from the vehicle.

(b)(1) Aggregate material shall only be carried in the cargo area of a vehicle. The cargo area shall not contain any holes, cracks, or openings through which that material may escape, regardless of the degree to which the vehicle is loaded, except as provided in paragraph (2).

(2) Every vehicle used to transport aggregate materials, regardless of the degree to which the vehicle is loaded, shall be equipped with all of the following:

(A) Properly functioning seals on any openings used to empty the load, including, but not limited to, bottom dump release gates and tailgates.

(B) Splash flaps behind every tire, or set of tires, regardless of the position on the truck, truck tractor, or trailer.

(C) Center flaps at a location to the rear of each bottom dump release gate as to trucks or trailers equipped with bottom dump release gates. The center flap may be positioned directly behind the bottom dump release gate and in front of the rear axle of the vehicle, or it may be positioned to the rear of the rear axle in line with the splash flaps required behind the tires. The width of the center flap may extend not more than one inch from one sidewall to the opposite sidewall of the inside tires and shall extend to within five inches of the pavement surface, and may be not less than 24 inches from the bottom edge to the top edge of that center flap.

(D) Fenders starting at the splash flap with the leading edge of the fenders extending forward at least six inches beyond the center of the axle that cover the tops of tires not already covered by the truck, truck tractor, or trailer body.

(E) Complete enclosures on all vertical sides of the cargo area, including, but not limited to, tailgates.

(F) Shed boards designed to prevent aggregate materials from being deposited on the vehicle body during top loading.

(c) Vehicles comprised of full rigid enclosures are exempt only from subparagraphs (C) and (F) of paragraph (2) of subdivision (b).

(d) For purposes of this section, "aggregate material" means rock fragments, pebbles, sand, dirt, gravel, cobbles, crushed base, asphalt, and other similar materials.

(e)(1) In addition to subdivisions (a) and (b), a vehicle may not transport any aggregate material upon a highway unless the material is covered.

(2) Vehicles transporting loads composed entirely of asphalt material are exempt only from the provisions of this section requiring that loads be covered.

(3) Vehicles transporting loads composed entirely of petroleum coke material are not required to cover their loads if they are loaded using safety procedures, specialized equipment, and a chemical surfactant designed to prevent materials from blowing, spilling, or otherwise escaping from the vehicle.

(4) Vehicles transporting loads of aggregate materials are not required to cover their loads if the load, where it contacts the sides, front, and back of the cargo container area, remains six inches from the upper edge of the container area, and if the load does not extend, at its peak, above any part of the upper edge of the cargo container area.

(f) A person who provides a location for vehicles to be loaded with an aggregate material or other material shall provide a location for vehicle operators to comply with this section before entering a highway.

(1) A person is exempt from the requirements of this subdivision if the location that he or she provides for vehicles to be loaded with the materials described in this subdivision has 100 yards or less between the scale houses where the trucks carrying aggregate material are weighed and the point of egress to a public road.

(2) A driver of a vehicle loaded with aggregate material leaving locations exempted from the requirements of this subdivision is authorized to operate on public roads only until that driver is able to safely cover the load at a site near the location's point of egress to the public road. Except as provided under paragraph (4) of subdivision (e), an uncovered vehicle described in this paragraph may not operate more than 200 yards from the point of egress to the public road. *(Stats.1959, c. 3, p. 1709, § 23114. Amended by Stats.1961, c. 713, p. 1953, § 1; Stats.1965, c. 455, p. 1765, § 1; Stats.1988, c. 1486, § 3; Stats.1989, c. 125, § 2, eff. July 12, 1989; Stats.1989, c. 533, § 12; Stats.2002, c. 673 (S.B.1530), § 1; Stats.2004, c. 518 (A.B.2201), § 4; Stats.2008, c. 250 (A.B.2714), § 1.)*

Cross References

Damage to highway, weight or size of vehicle, see Vehicle Code § 17302.

§ 23115. Rubbish vehicles

(a) No vehicle transporting garbage, swill, used cans or bottles, wastepapers, waste cardboard, ashes, refuse, trash, or rubbish, or any noisome, nauseous, or offensive matter, or anything being transported for disposal or recycling shall be driven or moved upon any highway unless the load is totally covered in a manner that will prevent the load or any part of the load from spilling or falling from the vehicle.

(b) Subdivision (a) does not prohibit a rubbish vehicle from being without cover while in the process of acquiring its load if no law, administrative regulation, or local ordinance requires that it be covered in those circumstances.

(c) Vehicles transporting wastepaper, waste cardboard, or used cans or bottles, are in compliance with subdivision (a) if appropriate binders including, but not limited to, bands, wires, straps, or netting are used to prevent the load, or any part of the load, from spilling or falling from the vehicle.

(d) This section does not apply to any vehicle engaged in transporting wet waste fruit or vegetable matter, or waste products to or from a food processing establishment. *(Stats.1959, c. 3, p. 1709, § 23115. Amended by Stats.1975, c. 1166, p. 2884, § 1; Stats.1988, c. 1486, § 4, operative Sept. 1, 1990; Stats.2001, c. 279 (S.B.624), § 1.)*

Cross References

Definitions,
  Highway, see Vehicle Code §§ 360, 591, 592.
  Vehicle, see Vehicle Code § 670.

§ 23116. Pickup or flatbed motor truck; transportation in back; section application

(a) No person driving a pickup truck or a flatbed motortruck on a highway shall transport any person in or on the back of the truck.

(b) No person shall ride in or on the back of a truck or flatbed motortruck being driven on a highway.

(c) Subdivisions (a) and (b) do not apply if the person in the back of the truck is secured with a restraint system. The restraint system shall meet or exceed the federal motor vehicle safety standards published in Sections 571.207, 571.209, and 571.210 of Title 49 of the Code of Federal Regulations.

(d) Subdivisions (a), (b), and (c) do not apply to any person transporting one or more persons in the back of a truck or flatbed motortruck owned by a farmer or rancher, if that vehicle is used exclusively within the boundaries of lands owned or managed by that farmer or rancher, including the incidental use of that vehicle on not more than one mile of highway between one part of the farm or ranch to another part of that farm or ranch.

(e) Subdivisions (a), (b), and (c) do not apply if the person in the back of the truck or the flatbed is being transported in an emergency response situation by a public agency or pursuant to the direction or authority of a public agency.

As used in this subdivision, "emergency response situation" means instances in which necessary measures are needed in order to prevent injury or death to persons or to prevent, confine, or mitigate damage or destruction to property.

(f) Subdivisions (a) and (b) do not apply if the person in the back of the truck or flatbed motortruck is being transported in a parade that is supervised by a law

enforcement agency and the speed of the truck while in the parade does not exceed eight miles per hour. *(Added by Stats.1982, c. 1275, p. 4709, § 1. Amended by Stats.1984, c. 128, § 1; Stats.1993, c. 895 (A.B.153), § 1; Stats.1995, c. 766 (S.B.726), § 35; Stats.2000, c. 308 (A.B.602), § 2.)*

§ 23116.1. Inoperative

§ 23117. Transportation of animals; enclosure or restraint requirements

(a) No person driving a motor vehicle shall transport any animal in the back of the vehicle in a space intended for any load on the vehicle on a highway unless the space is enclosed or has side and tail racks to a height of at least 46 inches extending vertically from the floor, the vehicle has installed means of preventing the animal from being discharged, or the animal is cross tethered to the vehicle, or is protected by a secured container or cage, in a manner which will prevent the animal from being thrown, falling, or jumping from the vehicle.

(b) This section does not apply to any of the following:

(1) The transportation of livestock.

(2) The transportation of a dog whose owner either owns or is employed by a ranching or farming operation who is traveling on a road in a rural area or who is traveling to and from a livestock auction.

(3) The transportation of a dog for purposes associated with ranching or farming. *(Added by Stats.1987, c. 224, § 1.)*

§ 23118. Vehicle used in violation of code governing repossessors; seizure; release; notice and hearing; liability

(a)(1) A magistrate presented with the affidavit of a peace officer establishing reasonable cause to believe that a vehicle, described by vehicle type and license number, is being used or operated in violation of Section 7502.1 of the Business and Professions Code shall issue a warrant or order authorizing any peace officer to immediately seize and cause the removal of the vehicle.

(2) The warrant or court order may be entered into a computerized database.

(3) Any vehicle so impounded may be impounded until such time as the owner of the property, or the person in possession of the property at the time of the impoundment, produces proof of licensure pursuant to Chapter 11 (commencing with Section 7500) of Division 3 of the Business and Professions Code, or proof of an exemption from licensure pursuant to Section 7500.2 or 7500.3 of the Business and Professions Code.

(4) The impounding agency, within two working days of impoundment, shall send a notice by certified mail, return receipt requested, to the legal owner of the vehicle, at an address obtained from the department, informing the owner that the vehicle has been impounded and providing the owner with a copy of the warrant or

court order. Failure to notify the legal owner within two working days shall prohibit the impounding agency from charging for more than 15 days impoundment when a legal owner redeems the impounded vehicle. The law enforcement agency shall be open to issue a release to the registered owner or legal owner, or the agent of either, whenever the agency is open to serve the public for regular, nonemergency business.

(b)(1) An impounding agency shall release a vehicle to the registered owner or his or her agent prior to the end of the impoundment period and without the permission of the magistrate authorizing the vehicle's seizure under any of the following circumstances:

(A) When the vehicle is a stolen vehicle.

(B) When the vehicle was seized under this section for an offense that does not authorize the seizure of the vehicle.

(2) No vehicle may be released under this subdivision, except upon presentation of the registered owner's or agent's currently valid license to operate the vehicle, and proof of current vehicle registration, or upon order of the court.

(c)(1) Whenever a vehicle is impounded under this section, the magistrate ordering the storage shall provide the vehicle's registered and legal owners of record, or their agents, with the opportunity for a poststorage hearing to determine the validity of the storage.

(2) A notice of the storage shall be mailed or personally delivered to the registered and legal owners within 48 hours after issuance of the warrant or court order, excluding weekends and holidays, by the person or agency executing the warrant or court order, and shall include all of the following information:

(A) The name, address, and telephone number of the agency providing the notice.

(B) The location of the place of storage and a description of the vehicle, which shall include, if available, the name or make, the manufacturer, the license plate number, and the mileage of the vehicle.

(C) A copy of the warrant or court order and the peace officer's affidavit, as described in subdivision (a).

(D) A statement that, in order to receive their poststorage hearing, the owners, or their agents, are required to request the hearing from the magistrate issuing the warrant or court order in person, in writing, or by telephone, within 10 days of the date of the notice.

(3) The poststorage hearing shall be conducted within two court days after receipt of the request for the hearing.

(4) At the hearing, the magistrate may order the vehicle released if he or she finds any of the circumstances described in subdivision (b) or (e) that allow release of a vehicle by the impounding agency.

(5) Failure of either the registered or legal owner, or his or her agent, to request, or to attend, a scheduled hearing satisfies the poststorage hearing requirement.

(6) The agency employing the peace officer who caused the magistrate to issue the warrant or court order shall be responsible for the costs incurred for towing and storage if it is determined in the poststorage hearing that reasonable grounds for the storage are not established.

(d) The registered owner or his or her agent is responsible for all towing and storage charges related to the impoundment, and any administrative charges authorized under Section 22850.5.

(e) A vehicle removed and seized under subdivision (a) shall be released to the legal owner of the vehicle or the legal owner's agent prior to the end of the impoundment period and without the permission of the magistrate authorizing the seizure of the vehicle if all of the following conditions are met:

(1) The legal owner is a motor vehicle dealer, bank, credit union, acceptance corporation, or other licensed financial institution legally operating in this state or is another person, not the registered owner, holding a security interest in the vehicle.

(2)(A) The legal owner or the legal owner's agent pays all towing and storage fees related to the seizure of the vehicle. Except as specifically authorized by this subdivision, no other fees shall be charged to the legal owner or the agent of the legal owner. No lien sale processing fees shall be charged to the legal owner who redeems the vehicle prior to the 15th day of impoundment. Neither the impounding authority nor any person having possession of the vehicle shall collect from the legal owner of the type specified in paragraph (1), or the legal owner's agent any administrative charges imposed pursuant to Section 22850.5 unless the legal owner voluntarily requested a poststorage hearing.

(B) A person operating or in charge of a storage facility where vehicles are stored pursuant to this section shall accept a valid bank credit card or cash for payment of towing, storage, and related fees by a legal or registered owner or the owner's agent claiming the vehicle. A credit card shall be in the name of the person presenting the card. "Credit card" means "credit card" as defined in subdivision (a) of Section 1747.02 of the Civil Code, except, for the purposes of this section, credit card does not include a credit card issued by a retail seller.

(C) A person operating or in charge of a storage facility described in subparagraph (B) who violates subparagraph (B) shall be civilly liable to the owner of the vehicle or to the person who tendered the fees for four times the amount of the towing, storage, and related fees, but not to exceed five hundred dollars ($500).

(D) A person operating or in charge of the storage facility shall have sufficient funds on the premises of the primary storage facility during normal business hours to accommodate, and make change in, a reasonable monetary transaction.

(E) Credit charges for towing and storage services shall comply with Section 1748.1 of the Civil Code. Law enforcement agencies may include the costs of providing

729

for payment by credit when making agreements with towing companies on rates.

(3)(A) The legal owner or the legal owner's agent presents to the law enforcement agency or impounding agency, or any person acting on behalf of those agencies, a copy of the assignment, as defined in subdivision (b) of Section 7500.1 of the Business and Professions Code; a release from the one responsible governmental agency, only if required by the agency; a government-issued photographic identification card; and any one of the following as determined by the legal owner or the legal owner's agent: a certificate of repossession for the vehicle, a security agreement for the vehicle, or title, whether paper or electronic, showing proof of legal ownership for the vehicle. The law enforcement agency, impounding agency, or any other governmental agency, or any person acting on behalf of those agencies, shall not require the presentation of any other documents.

(B) The legal owner or the legal owner's agent presents to the person in possession of the vehicle, or any person acting on behalf of the person in possession, a copy of the assignment, as defined in subdivision (b) of Section 7500.1 of the Business and Professions Code; a release from the one responsible governmental agency, only if required by the agency; a government-issued photographic identification card; and any one of the following as determined by the legal owner or the legal owner's agent: a certificate of repossession for the vehicle, a security agreement for the vehicle, or title, whether paper or electronic, showing proof of legal ownership for the vehicle. The person in possession of the vehicle, or any person acting on behalf of the person in possession, shall not require the presentation of any other documents.

(C) All presented documents may be originals, photocopies, or facsimile copies, or may be transmitted electronically. The law enforcement agency, impounding agency, or any person in possession of the vehicle, or anyone acting on behalf of them, shall not require a document to be notarized. The law enforcement agency, impounding agency, or any person acting on behalf of those agencies, may require the agent of the legal owner to produce a photocopy or facsimile copy of its repossession agency license or registration issued pursuant to Chapter 11 (commencing with Section 7500) of Division 3 of the Business and Professions Code, or to demonstrate, to the satisfaction of the law enforcement agency, impounding agency, or any person in possession of the vehicle, or anyone acting on behalf of them, that the agent is exempt from licensure pursuant to Section 7500.2 or 7500.3 of the Business and Professions Code.

(D) No administrative costs authorized under subdivision (a) of Section 22850.5 shall be charged to the legal owner of the type specified in paragraph (1), who redeems the vehicle unless the legal owner voluntarily requests a poststorage hearing. No city, county, city and county, or state agency shall require a legal owner or a legal owner's agent to request a poststorage hearing as a

requirement for release of the vehicle to the legal owner or the legal owner's agent. The law enforcement agency, impounding agency, or any other governmental agency, or any person acting on behalf of those agencies, shall not require any documents other than those specified in this paragraph. The law enforcement agency, impounding agency, or other governmental agency, or any person acting on behalf of those agencies, may not require any documents to be notarized. The legal owner or the legal owner's agent shall be given a copy of any documents he or she is required to sign, except for a vehicle evidentiary hold logbook. The law enforcement agency, impounding agency, or any person acting on behalf of those agencies, or any person in possession of the vehicle, may photocopy and retain the copies of any documents presented by the legal owner or legal owner's agent.

(4) A failure by a storage facility to comply with any applicable conditions set forth in this subdivision shall not affect the right of the legal owner or the legal owner's agent to retrieve the vehicle, provided all conditions required of the legal owner or legal owner's agent under this subdivision are satisfied.

(f)(1) A legal owner or the legal owner's agent that obtains release of the vehicle pursuant to subdivision (e) shall not release the vehicle to the registered owner of the vehicle or the person who was listed as the registered owner when the vehicle was impounded or the person in possession of the vehicle at the time of the impound or any agents of the registered owner until the termination of the impoundment period.

(2) The legal owner or the legal owner's agent shall not relinquish the vehicle to the registered owner or the person who was listed as the registered owner when the vehicle was impounded until the registered owner or that owner's agent presents his or her valid driver's license or valid temporary driver's license to the legal owner or the legal owner's agent. The legal owner or the legal owner's agent or the person in possession of the vehicle shall make every reasonable effort to ensure that the licenses presented are valid and possession of the vehicle will not be given to the driver who was involved in the original impound proceeding until the expiration of the impoundment period.

(3) Prior to relinquishing the vehicle, the legal owner may require the registered owner to pay all towing and storage charges related to the impoundment and the administrative charges authorized under Section 22850.5 that were incurred by the legal owner in connection with obtaining the custody of the vehicle.

(4) Any legal owner who knowingly releases or causes the release of a vehicle to a registered owner or the person in possession of the vehicle at the time of the impound or any agent of the registered owner in violation of this subdivision shall be guilty of a misdemeanor and subject to a fine in the amount of two thousand dollars ($2,000) in addition to any other penalties established by law.

(5) The legal owner, registered owner, or person in possession of the vehicle shall not change or attempt to change the name of the legal owner or the registered owner on the records of the department until the vehicle is released from the impound.

(g) Notwithstanding any other provision of this section, the registered owner and not the legal owner shall remain responsible for any towing and storage charges related to the impoundment and the administrative charges authorized under Section 22850.5 and any parking fines, penalties, and administrative fees incurred by the registered owner.

(h) The law enforcement agency and the impounding agency, including any storage facility acting on behalf of the law enforcement agency or impounding agency, shall comply with this section and shall not be liable to the registered owner for the improper release of the vehicle to the legal owner or the legal owner's agent provided the release complies with the provisions of this section. The legal owner shall indemnify and hold harmless a storage facility from any claims arising out of the release of the vehicle to the legal owner or the legal owner's agent and from any damage to the vehicle after its release, including the reasonable costs associated with defending any such claims. A law enforcement agency shall not refuse to issue a release to a legal owner or the agent of a legal owner on the grounds that it previously issued a release. *(Added by Stats.2009, c. 322 (A.B.515), § 11.)*

§ 23120. Temple width of glasses

No person shall operate a motor vehicle while wearing glasses having a temple width of one-half inch or more if any part of such temple extends below the horizontal center of the lens so as to interfere with lateral vision. *(Added by Stats.1959, c. 531, p. 2498, § 1.)*

§§ 23121 to 23122.5. Renumbered §§ 23220 to 23223 and amended by Stats.1981, c. 940, p. 3569, §§ 23 to 26

§ 23123. Driving a motor vehicle while using a wireless telephone; penalty; exceptions

(a) A person shall not drive a motor vehicle while using a wireless telephone unless that telephone is specifically designed and configured to allow hands-free listening and talking, and is used in that manner while driving.

(b) A violation of this section is an infraction punishable by a base fine of twenty dollars ($20) for a first offense and fifty dollars ($50) for each subsequent offense.

(c) This section does not apply to a person using a wireless telephone for emergency purposes, including, but not limited to, an emergency call to a law enforcement agency, health care provider, fire department, or other emergency services agency or entity.

(d) This section does not apply to an emergency services professional using a wireless telephone while operating an authorized emergency vehicle, as defined in Section 165, in the course and scope of his or her duties.

(e) This section does not apply to a person driving a schoolbus or transit vehicle that is subject to Section 23125.

(f) This section does not apply to a person while driving a motor vehicle on private property.

(g) This section shall become operative on July 1, 2011. *(Added by Stats.2006, c. 290 (S.B.1613), § 5, operative July 1, 2011. Amended by Stats.2007, c. 214 (S.B.33), § 3, operative July 1, 2011.)*

Cross References

Conviction of violation of this section, giving of violation points, see Vehicle Code § 12810.3.

Suspension or revocation of license for driving under the influence or engaging in speed contests or exhibitions of speed, reinstatement conditions, see Vehicle Code § 13352.

§ 23123.5. Driving motor vehicle while writing, sending or reading text-based communication; exceptions; penalty

(a) A person shall not drive a motor vehicle while using an electronic wireless communications device to write, send, or read a text-based communication, unless the electronic wireless communications device is specifically designed and configured to allow voice-operated and hands-free operation to dictate, send, or listen to a text-based communication, and it is used in that manner while driving.

(b) As used in this section "write, send, or read a text-based communication" means using an electronic wireless communications device to manually communicate with any person using a text-based communication, including, but not limited to, communications referred to as a text message, instant message, or electronic mail.

(c) For purposes of this section, a person shall not be deemed to be writing, reading, or sending a text-based communication if the person reads, selects, or enters a telephone number or name in an electronic wireless communications device for the purpose of making or receiving a telephone call or if a person otherwise activates or deactivates a feature or function on an electronic wireless communications device.

(d) A violation of this section is an infraction punishable by a base fine of twenty dollars ($20) for a first offense and fifty dollars ($50) for each subsequent offense.

(e) This section does not apply to an emergency services professional using an electronic wireless communications device while operating an authorized emergency vehicle, as defined in Section 165, in the course and scope of his or her duties. *(Added by Stats.2008, c. 270 (S.B.28), § 2. Amended by Stats.2012, c. 92 (A.B.1536), § 1.)*

Driving commercial motor vehicle while using electronic wireless communication device to write, send, or read text-based communications, defined as serious traffic violation, see Vehicle Code § 15210.

§ 23123.6.   Renumbered § 23226 and amended by Stats.1981, c. 940, p. 3570, § 29

§ 23124.   Driving motor vehicle while using wireless telephone or electronic wireless communications device; minor drivers; penalty; enforcement; exceptions

(a) This section applies to a person under the age of 18 years.

(b) Notwithstanding Sections 23123 and 23123.5, a person described in subdivision (a) shall not drive a motor vehicle while using a wireless telephone or an electronic wireless communications device, even if equipped with a hands-free device * * *.

(c) A violation of this section is an infraction punishable by a base fine of twenty dollars ($20) for a first offense and fifty dollars ($50) for each subsequent offense.

(d) A law enforcement officer shall not stop a vehicle for the sole purpose of determining whether the driver is violating subdivision (b).

(e) Subdivision (d) does not prohibit a law enforcement officer from stopping a vehicle for a violation of Section 23123 or 23123.5.

(f) This section does not apply to a person using a wireless telephone or a mobile service device for emergency purposes, including, but not limited to, an emergency call to a law enforcement agency, health care provider, fire department, or other emergency services agency or entity.

(g) For the purposes of this section, "* * * electronic wireless communications device" includes, but is not limited to, a broadband personal communication device, specialized mobile radio device, handheld device or laptop computer with mobile data access, pager, and two-way messaging device.

* * *   *(Added by Stats.2007, c. 214 (S.B.33), § 4, operative July 1, 2008. Amended by Stats.2013, c. 754 (S.B.194), § 1.)*

Issuance and renewal of licenses, violation points, see Vehicle Code § 12810.3.

§ 23125.   School bus or transit vehicles; prohibition upon use of wireless telephones during operation; exceptions

(a) A person may not drive a schoolbus or transit vehicle, as defined in subdivision (g) of Section 99247 of the Public Utilities Code, while using a wireless telephone.

732

(b) This section does not apply to a driver using a wireless telephone for work-related purposes, or for emergency purposes, including, but not limited to, an emergency call to a law enforcement agency, health care provider, fire department, or other emergency service agency or entity.

(c) Notwithstanding any other provision of law, a violation of subdivision (a) does not constitute a serious traffic violation within the meaning of subdivision (i) of Section 15210. *(Added by Stats.2004, c. 505 (A.B.2785), § 1.)*

§ 23126.   Renumbered § 23155 and amended by Stats. 1981, c. 940, p. 3570, § 31

§ 23127.   Trails and paths

No person shall operate an unauthorized motor vehicle on any state, county, city, private, or district hiking or horseback riding trail or bicycle path that is clearly marked by an authorized agent or owner with signs at all entrances and exits and at intervals of not more than one mile indicating no unauthorized motor vehicles are permitted on the hiking or horseback riding trail or bicycle path, except bicycle paths which are contiguous or adjacent to a roadway dedicated solely to motor vehicle use.

For the purpose of this section "unauthorized motor vehicle" means any motor vehicle that is driven upon a hiking or horseback riding trail or bicycle path without the written permission of an agent or the owner of the trail or path.

This section does not apply to the operation of an authorized emergency or maintenance vehicle on a hiking or horseback riding trail or bicycle path whenever necessary in furtherance of the purpose for which the vehicle has been classed as an authorized emergency vehicle. Any person who violates this section is guilty of a misdemeanor. *(Added by Stats.1965, c. 1559, p. 3650, § 1. Amended by Stats.1973, c. 951, p. 1790, § 1.)*

Authorized emergency vehicle, see Vehicle Code § 165.
Motorized bicycles, prohibited operation, see Vehicle Code § 21207.5.
Punishment for violation of this section, see Vehicle Code § 42001.

§ 23128.   Snowmobiles

It is unlawful for any person to operate a snowmobile in the following manner:

(a) On a highway except as provided in Section 38025.

(b) In a careless or negligent manner so as to endanger a person or property.

(c) For the purpose of pursuing deer or other game mammal with intent to harass such animals.

(d) For the purpose of violating Section 602 of the Penal Code. *(Formerly § 23337, added by Stats.1969, c. 1075, p. 2064, § 9. Renumbered § 23128 and amended by*

Stats.1971, c. 438, p. 909, § 194, operative May 3, 1972. Amended by Stats.1972, c. 973, p. 1759, § 17, eff. Aug. 16, 1972.)

Cross References

Snowmobile defined, see Vehicle Code § 557.

§ 23129. Camper mounted on motor vehicle; exit requirements

No person shall drive a motor vehicle upon which is mounted a camper containing any passengers unless there is at least one unobstructed exit capable of being opened from both the interior and exterior of such camper. *(Added by Stats.1972, c. 432, p. 797, § 1.)*

Cross References

Camper defined, see Vehicle Code § 243.

§§ 23130, 23130.5. Repealed by Stats.2001, c. 92 (S.B. 1081), §§ 1, 2

§ 23135. Motorized bicycles; modifications

It is unlawful for any person to operate upon a highway any vehicle which was originally manufactured as a motorized bicycle, as defined in Section 406, and which has been modified in such a manner that it no longer conforms to the definition of a motorized bicycle. *(Added by Stats.1978, c. 421, p. 1320, § 3.)*

Cross References

Punishment for violations, see Vehicle Code § 42001.9.

ARTICLE 1.3. OFFENSES BY PERSONS UNDER 21 YEARS OF AGE INVOLVING ALCOHOL

Section
23136. Blood alcohol concentration of .01 or greater; implied consent to testing; failure to submit to or complete testing.
23137 to 23139. Repealed.

Cross References

Data and monitoring system to track violations under this article, legislative intent, see Vehicle Code § 1822.

§ 23136. Blood alcohol concentration of .01 or greater; implied consent to testing; failure to submit to or complete testing

(a) Notwithstanding Sections 23152 and 23153, it is unlawful for a person under the age of 21 years who has a blood-alcohol concentration of 0.01 percent or greater, as measured by a preliminary alcohol screening test or other chemical test, to drive a vehicle. However, this section shall not be a bar to prosecution under Section 23152 or 23153 or any other provision of law.

(b) A person shall be found to be in violation of subdivision (a) if the person was, at the time of driving, under the age of 21 years, and the trier of fact finds that the person had consumed an alcoholic beverage and was driving a vehicle with a blood-alcohol concentration of 0.01 percent or greater, as measured by a preliminary alcohol screening test or other chemical test.

(c)(1) Any person under the age of 21 years who drives a motor vehicle is deemed to have given his or her consent to a preliminary alcohol screening test or other chemical test for the purpose of determining the presence of alcohol in the person, if lawfully detained for an alleged violation of subdivision (a).

(2) The testing shall be incidental to a lawful detention and administered at the direction of a peace officer having reasonable cause to believe the person was driving a motor vehicle in violation of subdivision (a).

(3) The person shall be told that his or her failure to submit to, or the failure to complete, a preliminary alcohol screening test or other chemical test as requested will result in the suspension or revocation of the person's privilege to operate a motor vehicle for a period of one year to three years, as provided in Section 13353.1. *(Added by Stats.1993, c. 899 (S.B.689), § 11. Amended by Stats.1994, c. 938 (S.B.1295), § 13, eff. Sept. 28, 1994; Stats.1996, c. 10 (A.B.1869), § 18, eff. Feb. 9, 1996.)*

Cross References

Driving privileges, suspension or delay, restricted driving privileges imposed on showing of critical need to drive, see Vehicle Code § 13353.8.
Santa Barbara County emergency medical services, penalty assessment, application to this section, see Government Code § 76104.1.

§§ 23137 to 23139. Repealed by Stats.1998, c. 118 (S.B.1186), §§ 11.11 to 13, operative July 1, 1999

ARTICLE 1.5. JUVENILE OFFENSES INVOLVING ALCOHOL

Section
23140. Persons under 21 years of age; blood-alcohol concentration of .05 or more; driving vehicle prohibited; abstract of record.

Cross References

Data and monitoring system to track violations under this article, legislative intent, see Vehicle Code § 1822.

§ 23140. Persons under 21 years of age; blood-alcohol concentration of .05 or more; driving vehicle prohibited; abstract of record

(a) It is unlawful for a person under the age of 21 years who has 0.05 percent or more, by weight, of alcohol in his or her blood to drive a vehicle.

(b) A person may be found to be in violation of subdivision (a) if the person was, at the time of driving, under the age of 21 years and under the influence of, or affected by, an alcoholic beverage regardless of whether a chemical test was made to determine that person's blood-alcohol concentration and if the trier of fact finds that the person had consumed an alcoholic beverage and was driving a vehicle while having a concentration of 0.05 percent or more, by weight, of alcohol in his or her blood.

(c) Notwithstanding any provision of law to the contrary, upon a finding that a person has violated this section, the clerk of the court shall prepare within 10 days after the finding and immediately forward to the department an abstract of the record of the court in which the finding is made. That abstract shall be a public record and available for public inspection in the same manner as other records reported under Section 1803. *(Added by Stats.1986, c. 1105, § 1. Amended by Stats.1989, c. 1465, § 5; Stats.1994, c. 938 (S.B.1295), § 16, eff. Sept. 28, 1994; Stats.2007, c. 263 (A.B.310), § 32.)*

Law Revision Commission Comments

2007 Amendment

Subdivision (c) of Section 23140 is amended to delete unnecessary language authorizing the judge to substitute for the clerk if there is no clerk. See Code Civ. Proc. § 167 (judge may perform any act court clerk may perform); Gov't Code §§ 69840–69848 (duties of clerk of superior court), 71620(b) (executive or administrative officer has authority of clerk of court). [35 Cal.L.Rev.Comm. Reports 219 (2007)].

Cross References

Driving privileges, suspension or delay, restricted driving privileges imposed on showing of critical need to drive, see Vehicle Code § 13353.8.

Driving under the influence, arrest of person with prior DUI conviction, impoundment of vehicle, see Vehicle Code § 22651.10.

Gross vehicular manslaughter while intoxicated, see Penal Code § 191.5.

Immediate removal and seizure of vehicle driven by repeat offender, storage and impoundment, vehicle owner's rights and responsibilities, see Vehicle Code § 14602.8.

Juvenile offenders, programs of supervision, see Welfare and Institutions Code § 654.1.

Records available to courts and law enforcement officials, incidents under certain DWI and homicide laws, period of time records must be available, see Vehicle Code § 1808.

Refusal to submit to alcohol testing under DUI laws, calculation of prior convictions, certain foreign convictions recognized, see Vehicle Code §§ 13353, 13353.1 and 13353.3.

Santa Barbara County emergency medical services, penalty assessment, application to this section, see Government Code § 76104.1.

Search warrants, grounds for issuance, see Penal Code § 1524.

Violation of this section, relinquishment of motor vehicle to convicted minor, see Penal Code § 193.8.

Violations of this section, punishment, see Vehicle Code § 42001.25.

ARTICLE 1.7. YOUTHFUL DRUNK DRIVER VISITATION PROGRAM [REPEALED]

Section
23141 to 23147. Repealed.

§§ 23141 to 23147. Repealed by Stats.1998, c. 118 (S.B.1186), §§ 14 to 24.5, operative July 1, 1999

ARTICLE 2. OFFENSES INVOLVING ALCOHOL AND DRUGS

Section
23151. Renumbered.
23152. Driving under influence; blood alcohol percentage; presumptions.
23153. Driving under the influence and causing bodily injury to another person; blood alcohol percentage; presumptions.
23154. Persons on probation for driving under the influence; operation of motor vehicle with blood-alcohol percentage of .01 percent or greater prohibited; use of preliminary alcohol screening test.
23155, 23156. Repealed.
23157. Renumbered.
23157.5. Repealed.
23158. Administration of tests; additional tests by person tested; disclosure of results; immunity from liability of medical personnel.
23158.2 to 23159.5. Repealed.
23160. Renumbered.
23161. Renumbered.
23165. Repealed.
23166. Repealed.
23166.1. Repealed.
23167. Repealed.
23168. Repealed.
23170 to 23176. Repealed.
23180. Repealed.
23181 to 23185. Repealed.
23186. Renumbered.
23186.1. Repealed.
23187. Repealed.
23190 to 23197. Repealed.
23198. Repealed.
23199 to 23202. Repealed.
23203. Renumbered.
23204. Renumbered.
23205. Repealed.
23205.1. Repealed.
23206 to 23212. Repealed.
23213. Social rehabilitation facility patient or resident; registered motor vehicle on or near premises.
23215. Departmental enforcement of § 23152 provisions.
23216. Express application of provisions of §§ 2, 6, 7, and 10; references to renumbered sections; construction of other references; retroactive effect of section.
23217. Legislative findings and declarations; repeat offenders of prohibition against driving under influence of alcohol or drugs; sequence of convictions not to affect enhancement of punishment for prior offenses; application of section.
23220. Drinking while driving a motor vehicle up any highway; lands.
23221. Drinking in motor vehicle upon highway.
23222. Possession of open container containing alcoholic beverage or marijuana while driving a motor vehicle; penalty.
23223. Possession of opened container in a motor vehicle.
23224. Possession of alcoholic beverage in vehicle; persons under 21; penalties.
23225. Storage of opened container.

Section

23226. Keeping open container in passenger compartment of motor vehicle; exceptions.

23229. Possession of alcoholic beverage in for-hire vehicles; exceptions.

23229.1. Application of prohibition against possession or storage of opened container to driver providing prearranged transportation services as a charter-party carrier of passengers while transporting passenger under 21; forwarding record of conviction to Public Utilities Commission.

Cross References

Commercial motor vehicle drivers, sanctions, see Vehicle Code § 15300.

Data and monitoring system to track violations under this article, legislative intent, see Vehicle Code § 1822.

Driving following restriction of driving privilege pursuant to this article, see Vehicle Code § 14601.2.

§ 23151. Renumbered § 109 and amended by Stats. 1982, c. 53, § 25, eff. Feb. 18, 1982

§ 23152. Driving under influence; blood alcohol percentage; presumptions

(a) It is unlawful for a person who is under the influence of any alcoholic beverage to drive a vehicle.

(b) It is unlawful for a person who has 0.08 percent or more, by weight, of alcohol in his or her blood to drive a vehicle.

For purposes of this article and Section 34501.16, percent, by weight, of alcohol in a person's blood is based upon grams of alcohol per 100 milliliters of blood or grams of alcohol per 210 liters of breath.

In any prosecution under this subdivision, it is a rebuttable presumption that the person had 0.08 percent or more, by weight, of alcohol in his or her blood at the time of driving the vehicle if the person had 0.08 percent or more, by weight, of alcohol in his or her blood at the time of the performance of a chemical test within three hours after the driving.

(c) It is unlawful for a person who is addicted to the use of any drug to drive a vehicle. This subdivision shall not apply to a person who is participating in a narcotic treatment program approved pursuant to Article 3 (commencing with Section 11875) of Chapter 1 of Part 3 of Division 10.5 of the Health and Safety Code.

(d) It is unlawful for a person who has 0.04 percent or more, by weight, of alcohol in his or her blood to drive a commercial motor vehicle, as defined in Section 15210.

In any prosecution under this subdivision, it is a rebuttable presumption that the person had 0.04 percent or more, by weight, of alcohol in his or her blood at the time of driving the vehicle if the person had 0.04 percent or more, by weight, of alcohol in his or her blood at the time of the performance of a chemical test within three hours after the driving.

(e) It is unlawful for a person who is under the influence of any drug to drive a vehicle.

(f) It is unlawful for a person who is under the combined influence of any alcoholic beverage and drug to drive a vehicle.

(g) This section shall become operative on January 1, 2014. *(Added by Stats.1989, c. 1114, § 25, operative Jan. 1, 1992. Amended by Stats.1992, c. 974 (S.B.1600), § 16, eff. Sept. 28, 1992; Stats.1995, c. 455 (A.B.1113), § 31, eff. Sept. 5, 1995; Stats.2012, c. 753 (A.B.2552), § 2, operative Jan. 1, 2014.)*

Cross References

Advisory statement to be given by court to person convicted of a violation of this section, see Vehicle Code § 23593.

Alcohol and drug problem assessment program, violator participation, sentencing, and assessment upon fine, see Vehicle Code § 23646 et seq.

Alcoholic beverages in vehicles, see Vehicle Code § 23220 et seq.

Applicability of this section to trolley coaches, see Vehicle Code § 21051.

Arraignment or plea and sentencing in certain misdemeanors, presence of defendant, see Penal Code § 977.

Arrest without warrant, see Vehicle Code § 40300.5.

Board of Pilot Commissioners, participation in pull-notice system, purpose of participation, periodic reports from Department of Motor Vehicles, notification of termination of pilot's license, removal from training program, fee exemption, board action based on reports, see Harbors and Navigation Code § 1178.5.

Challenging constitutional validity of separate conviction, see Vehicle Code § 41403.

Chemical blood, breath or urine tests, see Vehicle Code §§ 13353, 13354.

Chemical tests as evidence, see Vehicle Code § 23610.

Commercial motor vehicles,
First time violations, see Vehicle Code § 15300.
Multiple violations, see Vehicle Code § 15302.

Coroner's inquiry into deaths, see Government Code § 27491.25.

County alcohol and drug problem assessment programs; mandatory participation for convicted violators of this section, see Vehicle Code §§ 23646, 23647.

Crime of violence, within act for indemnification of victims of crime, see Government Code § 13960.

Defense of drug use to violations, see Vehicle Code § 23630.

Drivers license revocation, conviction of driver under eighteen, see Vehicle Code § 13352.3.

Driving privileges, suspension or delay, restricted driving privileges imposed on showing of critical need to drive, see Vehicle Code § 13353.8.

Driving school or instructor, revocation or suspension of license for violation of this section, see Vehicle Code § 11110.

Driving under the influence, arrest of person with prior DUI conviction, impoundment of vehicle, see Vehicle Code § 22651.10.

Gross vehicular manslaughter while intoxicated, see Penal Code § 191.5.

Guilty plea, see Vehicle Code § 41610.

Immediate removal and seizure of vehicle driven by repeat offender, storage and impoundment, vehicle owner's rights and responsibilities, see Vehicle Code § 14602.8.

Immunity from criminal prosecution under specified minor consumption provisions, inapplicability to this section, see Business and Professions Code § 25667.

Impoundment of vehicle of registered owner convicted under this section, see Vehicle Code § 23594.

Influence of alcoholic beverage or drug, suspension or revocation of driving privileges, see Vehicle Code § 13352.

Juvenile offenders, programs of supervision, see Welfare and Institutions Code § 654.1.

Juveniles with blood-alcohol concentrations of 0.05 or more, driving violations, participation in rehabilitation programs, see Vehicle Code § 23504.

Medical assistance exception to controlled substance possession and related offenses, persons experiencing drug-related overdose, no exception to laws prohibiting actions made dangerous by controlled substance use, see Health and Safety Code § 11376.5.

Penalties, public offenses, fines in misdemeanor cases for violations pertaining to passing school buildings or grounds, see Vehicle Code § 42011.

Persons certified as consenting to participation in programs, see Vehicle Code § 13352.5.

Persons certified or granted probation on conviction of driving under the influence of alcohol or drugs or combined influence on certain conditions, restriction, revocation or suspension of driving privilege, consent to participation in treatment program, see Vehicle Code § 13352.5.

Please Don't Drink and Drive memorial signs, requests for and duration of placement, exception for a party to an accident convicted or determined to be mentally incompetent under this section, see Streets and Highways Code § 101.10.

Presentence investigation and assessment, see Vehicle Code § 23655.

Presumptions, see Evidence Code § 600 et seq.

Prior convictions under §§ 23103, 23152 or 23153, effect on sentencing and driving privileges, see Vehicle Code § 23622.

Procedure on arrest for violation of this section, see Vehicle Code § 40302.

Public offenses, State Amnesty Program, not applicable to parking violations and violations of this section, see Vehicle Code § 42008.7.

Records available to courts and law enforcement officials, incidents under certain DWI and homicide laws, period of time records must be available, see Vehicle Code § 1808.

Refusal to submit to alcohol testing under DUI laws, calculation of prior convictions, certain foreign convictions recognized, see Vehicle Code §§ 13353, 13353.1 and 13353.3.

Restricted driver's license, application of this section, see Vehicle Code § 13352.2.

Santa Barbara County emergency medical services, penalty assessment, application to this section, see Government Code § 76104.1.

Search warrants, grounds for issuance, see Penal Code § 1524.

Surrender of driver's license to court, see Vehicle Code § 13550.

Suspension or revocation of driving privilege for a violation of this section, notice by personal service, see Vehicle Code § 13106.

Suspension or revocation of license,

    Generally, see Vehicle Code § 13352.

    Alcohol-related accident within five years of vehicular manslaughter, see Vehicle Code § 13954.

    Driver license compact, see Vehicle Code § 15000 et seq.

    Driving after suspension or revocation, see Vehicle Code § 14601.2.

    Investigation by department, three convictions in three years under this or other specified statutes, see Vehicle Code § 13800.

    Prior convictions, record, see Vehicle Code § 13209.

Traffic violation point count, violation of this section, see Vehicle Code § 12810.

Traffic violators schools, suspension or revocation of license for violation of this section, see Vehicle Code § 11215.

Vehicular homicide, see Penal Code § 192.

Violation as misdemeanor, see Vehicle Code § 40000.15.

Violation of this section, relinquishment of motor vehicle to convicted minor, see Penal Code § 193.8.

Youthful drunk driver visitation program, see Vehicle Code § 23509 et seq.

§ 23153. Driving under the influence and causing bodily injury to another person; blood alcohol percentage; presumptions

(a) It is unlawful for a person, while under the influence of any alcoholic beverage to drive a vehicle and concurrently do any act forbidden by law, or neglect any duty imposed by law in driving the vehicle, which act or neglect proximately causes bodily injury to any person other than the driver.

(b) It is unlawful for a person, while having 0.08 percent or more, by weight, of alcohol in his or her blood to drive a vehicle and concurrently do any act forbidden by law, or neglect any duty imposed by law in driving the vehicle, which act or neglect proximately causes bodily injury to any person other than the driver.

In any prosecution under this subdivision, it is a rebuttable presumption that the person had 0.08 percent or more, by weight, of alcohol in his or her blood at the time of driving the vehicle if the person had 0.08 percent or more, by weight, of alcohol in his or her blood at the time of the performance of a chemical test within three hours after driving.

(c) In proving the person neglected any duty imposed by law in driving the vehicle, it is not necessary to prove that any specific section of this code was violated.

(d) It is unlawful for a person, while having 0.04 percent or more, by weight, of alcohol in his or her blood to drive a commercial motor vehicle, as defined in Section 15210, and concurrently to do any act forbidden by law or neglect any duty imposed by law in driving the vehicle, which act or neglect proximately causes bodily injury to any person other than the driver.

In any prosecution under this subdivision, it is a rebuttable presumption that the person had 0.04 percent or more, by weight, of alcohol in his or her blood at the time of driving the vehicle if the person had 0.04 percent or more, by weight, of alcohol in his or her blood at the time of performance of a chemical test within three hours after driving.

(e) It is unlawful for a person, while under the influence of any drug, to drive a vehicle and concurrently do any act forbidden by law, or neglect any duty imposed by law in driving the vehicle, which act or neglect proximately causes bodily injury to any person other than the driver.

(f) It is unlawful for a person, while under the combined influence of any alcoholic beverage and drug, to drive a vehicle and concurrently do any act forbidden by law, or neglect any duty imposed by law in driving the vehicle, which act or neglect proximately causes bodily injury to any person other than the driver.

(g) This section shall become operative on January 1, 2014. *(Added by Stats.1989, c. 1114, § 30, operative Jan. 1, 1992. Amended by Stats.1992, c. 974 (S.B.1600), § 18, eff. Sept. 28, 1992; Stats.2012, c. 753 (A.B.2552), § 5, operative Jan. 1, 2014.)*

Cross References

Advisory statement to be given by court to person convicted of a violation of this section, see Vehicle Code § 23593.

Alcohol and drug problem assessment program, violator participation, sentencing, and assessment upon fine, see Vehicle Code § 23646 et seq.

Alcoholic beverages in vehicles, see Vehicle Code § 23220 et seq.

Applicability of this section to trolley coaches, see Vehicle Code § 21051.

Arraignment or plea and sentencing in certain misdemeanors, presence of defendant, see Penal Code § 977.

Arrest without warrant, see Vehicle Code § 40300.5.

Board of Pilot Commissioners, participation in pull-notice system, purpose of participation, periodic reports from Department of Motor Vehicles, notification of termination of pilot's license, removal from training program, fee exemption, board action based on reports, see Harbors and Navigation Code § 1178.5.

Challenging constitutional validity of separate conviction, see Vehicle Code § 41403.

Chemical blood, breath or urine tests, see Vehicle Code §§ 13353, 13354.

Chemical tests as evidence, see Vehicle Code § 23610.

Commercial motor vehicles,
  First time violations, see Vehicle Code § 15300.
  Multiple violations, see Vehicle Code § 15302.

Conviction of vehicular manslaughter as conviction of violation of this section, see Vehicle Code § 13350.5.

Conviction of violation of specified subdivisions of Penal Code § 192 to be deemed conviction of violation of this section, see Vehicle Code § 13350.5.

Coroner's inquiry into deaths, see Government Code § 27491.25.

County alcohol and drug problem assessment programs; mandatory participation for convicted violators of this section, see Vehicle Code §§ 23646, 23647.

Crime of violence, within act for indemnification of victims of crime, see Government Code § 13960.

Defense of drug use to violations, see Vehicle Code § 23630.

Deposit in special account for each conviction under this section, see Penal Code § 1463.14.

Drivers license revocation, conviction of driver under eighteen, see Vehicle Code § 13352.3.

Driving privileges, suspension or delay, restricted driving privileges imposed on showing of critical need to drive, see Vehicle Code § 13353.8.

Driving schools and driving instructors, revocation or suspension of license for violation of this section, see Vehicle Code § 11110.

Driving under the influence, arrest of person with prior DUI conviction, impoundment of vehicle, see Vehicle Code § 22651.10.

Felony defined, see Penal Code § 17.

Gross vehicular manslaughter while intoxicated, see Penal Code § 191.5.

Guilty plea, see Vehicle Code § 41610.

Immediate removal and seizure of vehicle driven by repeat offender, storage and impoundment, vehicle owner's rights and responsibilities, see Vehicle Code § 14602.8.

Immunity from criminal prosecution under specified minor consumption provisions, inapplicability to this section, see Business and Professions Code § 25667.

Impoundment of vehicle of registered owner convicted under this section, see Vehicle Code § 23594.

Influence of alcoholic beverage or drug, suspension or revocation of driving privileges, see Vehicle Code § 13352.

Injury to guest by intoxicated driver, see Vehicle Code § 17158.

Juveniles with blood-alcohol concentrations of 0.05 or more, driving violations, participation in rehabilitation programs, see Vehicle Code § 23504.

Manslaughter, negligent homicide by vehicle, see Penal Code § 192.

Medical assistance exception to controlled substance possession and related offenses, persons experiencing drug-related overdose, no exception to laws prohibiting actions made dangerous by controlled substance use, see Health and Safety Code § 11376.5.

Nuisance, sale or other disposition of motor vehicle driven by defendant, see Vehicle Code § 23596.

Penalties, public offenses, fines in misdemeanor cases for violations pertaining to passing school buildings or grounds, see Vehicle Code § 42011.

Please Don't Drink and Drive memorial signs, requests for and duration of placement, exception for a party to an accident convicted or determined to be mentally incompetent under this section, see Streets and Highways Code § 101.10.

Presentence investigation and assessment, see Vehicle Code § 23655.

Prior convictions under §§ 23103, 23152 or 23153, effect on sentencing and driving privileges, see Vehicle Code § 23622.

Public offenses, State Amnesty Program, not applicable to parking violations and violations of this section, see Vehicle Code § 42008.7.

Records available to courts and law enforcement officials, incidents under certain DWI and homicide laws, period of time records must be available, see Vehicle Code § 1808.

Refusal to submit to alcohol testing under DUI laws, calculation of prior convictions, certain foreign convictions recognized, see Vehicle Code §§ 13353, 13353.1 and 13353.3.

Release on own recognizance, report, violation of this section, see Penal Code § 1318.1.

Santa Barbara County emergency medical services, penalty assessment, application to this section, see Government Code § 76104.1.

Search warrants, grounds for issuance, see Penal Code § 1524.

Suspension or revocation of driving privilege for a violation of this section, notice by personal service, see Vehicle Code § 13106.

Suspension or revocation of license,
  Generally, see Vehicle Code § 13350.
  Alcohol-related accident within five years of vehicular manslaughter, see Vehicle Code § 13954.
  Driver license compact, see Vehicle Code § 15000 et seq.
  Driving after suspension or revocation, see Vehicle Code § 14601.2.
  Driving under the influence or engaging in speed contests or exhibitions of speed, reinstatement conditions, see Vehicle Code § 13352.

Investigation by department, three convictions in three years under this or other specified sections, see Vehicle Code § 13800.

Prior convictions, record, see Vehicle Code § 13209.

Traffic violation point count, violation of this section, see Vehicle Code § 12810.

Traffic violators schools, suspension or revocation of license for violation of this section, see Vehicle Code § 11215.

Violation of this section, relinquishment of motor vehicle to convicted minor, see Penal Code § 193.8.

§ 23154. Persons on probation for driving under the influence; operation of motor vehicle with blood-alcohol percentage of .01 percent or greater prohibited; use of preliminary alcohol screening test

(a) It is unlawful for a person who is on probation for a violation of Section 23152 or 23153 to operate a motor vehicle at any time with a blood-alcohol concentration of 0.01 percent or greater, as measured by a preliminary alcohol screening test or other chemical test.

(b) A person may be found to be in violation of subdivision (a) if the person was, at the time of driving, on probation for a violation of Section 23152 or 23153, and the trier of fact finds that the person had consumed an alcoholic beverage and was driving a vehicle with a blood-alcohol concentration of 0.01 percent or greater, as measured by a preliminary alcohol screening test or other chemical test.

(c)(1) A person who is on probation for a violation of Section 23152 or 23153 who drives a motor vehicle is deemed to have given his or her consent to a preliminary alcohol screening test or other chemical test for the purpose of determining the presence of alcohol in the person, if lawfully detained for an alleged violation of subdivision (a).

(2) The testing shall be incidental to a lawful detention and administered at the direction of a peace officer having reasonable cause to believe the person is driving a motor vehicle in violation of subdivision (a).

(3) The person shall be told that his or her failure to submit to, or the failure to complete, a preliminary alcohol screening test or other chemical test as requested will result in the suspension or revocation of the person's privilege to operate a motor vehicle for a period of one year to three years, as provided in Section 13353.1. *(Added by Stats.2007, c. 749 (A.B.1165), § 5, operative Jan. 1, 2009.)*

Cross References

Drivers' licenses, review of suspension or revocation order, see Vehicle Code § 13557.

§§ 23155, 23156. Repealed by Stats.1998, c. 118 (S.B. 1186), §§ 26, 27, operative July 1, 1999

§ 23157. Renumbered Vehicle Code § 23612 by Stats. 1999, c. 22 (S.B.24), § 18.4, eff. May 26, 1999, operative July 1, 1999

§ 23157.5. Repealed by Stats.1998, c. 118 (S.B.1186), § 29, operative July 1, 1999

§ 23158. Administration of tests; additional tests by person tested; disclosure of results; immunity from liability of medical personnel

(a) Notwithstanding any other provision of law, only a licensed physician and surgeon, registered nurse, licensed vocational nurse, duly licensed clinical laboratory scientist or clinical laboratory bioanalyst, a person who has been issued a "certified phlebotomy technician" certificate pursuant to Section 1246 of the Business and Professions Code, unlicensed laboratory personnel regulated pursuant to Sections 1242, 1242.5, and 1246 of the Business and Professions Code, or certified paramedic acting at the request of a peace officer may withdraw blood for the purpose of determining the alcoholic content therein. This limitation does not apply to the taking of breath specimens. An emergency call for paramedic services takes precedence over a peace officer's request for a paramedic to withdraw blood for determining its alcoholic content. A certified paramedic shall not withdraw blood for this purpose unless authorized by his or her employer to do so.

(b) The person tested may, at his or her own expense, have a licensed physician and surgeon, registered nurse, licensed vocational nurse, duly licensed clinical laboratory scientist or clinical laboratory bioanalyst, person who has been issued a "certified phlebotomy technician" certificate pursuant to Section 1246 of the Business and Professions Code, unlicensed laboratory personnel regulated pursuant to Sections 1242, 1242.5, and 1246 of the Business and Professions Code, or any other person of his or her own choosing administer a test in addition to any test administered at the direction of a peace officer for the purpose of determining the amount of alcohol in the person's blood at the time alleged as shown by chemical analysis of his or her blood, breath, or urine. The failure or inability to obtain an additional test by a person does not preclude the admissibility in evidence of the test taken at the direction of a peace officer.

(c) Upon the request of the person tested, full information concerning the test taken at the direction of the peace officer shall be made available to the person or the person's attorney.

(d) Notwithstanding any other provision of law, no licensed physician and surgeon, registered nurse, licensed vocational nurse, duly licensed clinical laboratory scientist or clinical laboratory bioanalyst, person who has been issued a "certified phlebotomy technician" certificate pursuant to Section 1246 of the Business and Professions Code, unlicensed laboratory personnel regulated pursuant to Sections 1242, 1242.5, and 1246 of the Business and Professions Code, or certified paramedic, or hospital, laboratory, or clinic employing or utilizing the services of the licensed physician and surgeon, registered nurse, licensed vocational nurse, duly licensed clinical laboratory scientist or clinical laboratory bioanalyst, person who has been issued a "certified phlebotomy technician" certificate pursuant to Section 1246 of the Business and Professions Code, unlicensed laboratory personnel regulated pursuant to Sections 1242, 1242.5, and 1246 of the Business and Professions Code, or certified paramedic, owning or leasing the premises on which tests are performed, shall incur any civil or criminal liability as a result of the administering of a blood test in a reasonable manner in a hospital, clinical laboratory, medical clinic environment, jail, or law enforcement facility, according to accepted venipuncture practices, without violence by the person administering the test, and when requested in writing by a peace officer to administer the test.

(e) Notwithstanding any other provision of law, a person who has been issued a "certified phlebotomy technician" certificate pursuant to Section 1246 of the Business and Professions Code and who is authorized by this section to draw blood at the request and in the presence of a peace officer for purposes of determining its alcoholic content, may do so in a jail, law enforcement facility, or medical facility, with general supervision. The "certified phlebotomy technician" shall draw blood following the policies and procedures approved by a physician and surgeon licensed under Chapter 5 (commencing with Section 2000) of Division 2 of the Business and Professions Code, appropriate to the location where the blood is being drawn and in accordance with state regulations.

(f) The Certified Phlebotomy Technician I or II shall carry a current, valid identification card issued by the State Department of Health Services, attesting to the technician's name, certificate type, and effective dates of certification, when performing blood withdrawals.

(g) As used in this section, "general supervision" means that the supervisor of the technician is licensed under the Business and Professions Code as a physician and surgeon, physician assistant, clinical laboratory bioanalyst, registered nurse, or clinical laboratory scientist, and reviews the competency of the technician before the technician may perform blood withdrawals without direct supervision, and on an annual basis thereafter. The supervisor is also required to review the work of the technician at least once a month to ensure compliance with venipuncture policies, procedures, and regulations. The supervisor, or another person licensed as a physician and surgeon, physician assistant, clinical laboratory bioanalyst, registered nurse, or clinical laboratory scientist, shall be accessible to the location where the technician is working to provide onsite, telephone, or electronic consultation, within 30 minutes when needed.

(h) Nothing in this section shall be construed as requiring the certified phlebotomy technician who is authorized to withdraw blood by this section at the request and in the presence of a peace officer for purposes of determining alcoholic content to be associated with a clinical laboratory or to be directly supervised after competency has been established.

(i) If the test given under Section 23612 is a chemical test of urine, the person tested shall be given such privacy in the taking of the urine specimen as will ensure the accuracy of the specimen and, at the same time, maintain the dignity of the individual involved.

(j) The department, in cooperation with the State Department of Health Services or any other appropriate agency, shall adopt uniform standards for the withdrawal, handling, and preservation of blood samples prior to analysis.

(k) As used in this section, "certified paramedic" does not include any employee of a fire department.

(l) Consent, waiver of liability, or the offering to, acceptance by, or refusal of consent or waiver of liability by the person on whom a test is administered, is not an issue or relevant to the immunity from liability for medical or law enforcement personnel or other facilities designated under subdivision (d). *(Formerly § 13354, added by Stats.1972, c. 188 p. 406, § 2, operative July 1, 1973. Amended by Stats.1978, c. 554, p. 1728, § 1; Stats.1981, c. 939, p. 3558, § 8; Stats.1982, c. 1339, p. 4982, § 9, eff. Sept. 24, 1982. Renumbered § 23158 and amended by Stats.1985, c. 735, § 4. Amended by Stats. 1989, c. 80, § 1; Stats.1998, c. 118 (S.B.1186), § 30, operative July 1, 1999; Stats.2004, c. 14 (A.B.371), § 2, eff. Feb. 11, 2004.)*

§§ 23158.2 to 23159.5. Repealed by Stats.1998, c. 118 (S.B.1186), §§ 30.5 to 33, operative July 1, 1999

§ 23160. Renumbered Vehicle Code § 23536 and amended by Stats.1999, c. 22 (S.B.24), § 19, eff. May 26, 1999, operative July 1, 1999

§ 23161. Renumbered Vehicle Code § 23538 and amended by Stats.1999, c. 22 (S.B.24), § 20, eff. May 26, 1999, operative July 1, 1999

§ 23165. Repealed by Stats.1998, c. 118 (S.B.1186), § 36, operative July 1, 1999

§ 23166. Renumbered Vehicle Code § 23542 and amended by Stats.1999, c. 22 (S.B.24), § 21, eff. May 26, 1999, operative July 1, 1999

§ 23166.1. Repealed by Stats.1984, c. 1725, § 1.4, eff. Jan. 1, 1988

§ 23167. Repealed by Stats.1998, c. 756 (A.B.762), § 14, operative July 1, 1999

§ 23168. Repealed by Stats.1993, c. 1244 (S.B.126), § 20

§§ 23170 to 23176. Repealed by Stats.1998, c. 118 (S.B.1186), §§ 39 to 42, operative July 1, 1999

§ 23180. Repealed by Stats.1998, c. 118 (S.B.1186), § 43, operative July 1, 1999

§§ 23181 to 23185. Repealed by Stats.1998, c. 118 (S.B.1186), §§ 44 to 46, operative July 1, 1999

§ 23186. Renumbered Vehicle Code § 23562 and amended by Stats.1999, c. 22 (S.B.24), § 22, eff. May 26, 1999, operative July 1, 1999

§ 23186.1. Repealed by Stats.1984, c. 1725, § 4, operative Jan. 1, 1988

§ 23187. Repealed by Stats.1998, c. 756 (A.B.762), § 16, operative July 1, 1999

§§ 23190 to 23197. Repealed by Stats.1998, c. 118 (S.B.1186), §§ 49 to 55, operative July 1, 1999

§ 23198. Repealed by Stats.1999, c. 22 (S.B.24), § 18.1, eff. May 26, 1999, operative July 1, 1999

§§ 23199 to 23202. Repealed by Stats.1998, c. 118 (S.B.1186), §§ 57 to 60, operative July 1, 1999

§ 23203. Renumbered Vehicle Code § 23662 and amended by Stats.1999, c. 22 (S.B.24), § 23, eff. May 26, 1999, operative July 1, 1999

§ 23204. Renumbered Vehicle Code § 23660 and amended by Stats.1999, c. 22 (S.B.24), § 24, eff. May 26, 1999, operative July 1, 1999

§ 23205. Repealed by Stats.1998, c. 118 (S.B.1186), § 63, operative July 1, 1999

§ 23205.1. Repealed by Stats.1984, c. 1725, § 6, operative Jan. 1, 1988

§§ 23206 to 23212. Repealed by Stats.1998, c. 118 (S.B.1186), §§ 64 to 72, operative July 1, 1999

§ 23213. Social rehabilitation facility patient or resident; registered motor vehicle on or near premises

No patient or other person residing in a social rehabilitation facility licensed pursuant to Chapter 3 (commencing with Section 1500) of Division 2 of the Health and Safety Code for the rehabilitation of persons who have abused alcohol or drugs, shall have a motor vehicle registered in the name of that patient or person on or near the premises of that facility unless the patient or person has an operator's license issued pursuant to this code which is not suspended or revoked. *(Added by Stats.1982, c. 1339, p. 4993, § 30, eff. Sept. 24, 1982.)*

§ 23215. Departmental enforcement of § 23152 provisions

The department may, but shall not be required to, provide patrol or enforce the provisions of Section 23152 for offenses which occur other than upon a highway. *(Added by Stats.1981, c. 940, p. 3571, § 32.)*

§ 23216. Express application of provisions of §§ 2, 6, 7, and 10; references to renumbered sections; construction of other references; retroactive effect of section

(a) The provisions of Sections 2, 6, 7, and 10 expressly apply to the provisions of this article, and, further, for any recidivist or enhancement purpose, reference to an offense by section number is a reference to the provisions contained in that section, insofar as they were renumbered by Chapter 940 of the Statutes of 1981 without substantive change, and those provisions shall be construed as restatements and continuations thereof and not as new enactments.

(b) Any reference in the provisions of this code to a separate violation of Section 23152 shall include a separate offense under Section 23102 or 23105, as those sections read prior to January 1, 1982.

(c) Any reference in the provisions of the Vehicle Code to a separate violation of Section 23153 shall include a separate offense under Section 23101 or 23106 as those sections read prior to January 1, 1982.

(d) The provisions of this section are to be given retroactive effect. *(Added by Stats.1984, c. 1205, § 13.)*

§ 23217. Legislative findings and declarations; repeat offenders of prohibition against driving under influence of alcohol or drugs; sequence of convictions not to affect enhancement of punishment for prior offenses; application of section

The Legislature finds and declares that some repeat offenders of the prohibition against driving under the influence of alcohol or drugs, when they are addicted or when they have too much alcohol in their systems, may be escaping the intent of the Legislature to punish the offender with progressively greater severity if the offense is repeated one or more times within a 10–year period. This situation may occur when a conviction for a subsequent offense occurs before a conviction is obtained on an earlier offense.

The Legislature further finds and declares that the timing of court proceedings should not permit a person to avoid aggravated mandatory minimum penalties for multiple separate offenses occurring within a 10–year period. It is the intent of the Legislature to provide that a person be subject to enhanced mandatory minimum penalties for multiple offenses within a period of 10 years, regardless of whether the convictions are obtained in the same sequence as the offenses had been committed.

Nothing in this section requires consideration of judgment of conviction in a separate proceeding that is entered after the judgment in the present proceeding, except as it relates to violation of probation.

Nothing in this section or the amendments to Section 23540, 23546, 23550, 23560, 23566, 23622, or 23640 made by Chapter 1205 of the Statutes of 1984 affects the penalty for a violation of Section 23152 or 23153 occurring prior to January 1, 1985. *(Added by Stats.1984, c.*

1205, § 14. Amended by Stats.1986, c. 1117, § 13; Stats.1998, c. 118 (S.B.1186), § 72.5, operative July 1, 1999; Stats.2004, c. 550 (S.B.1694), § 11.)

§ 23220. Drinking while driving a motor vehicle up any highway; lands

(a) No person shall drink any alcoholic beverage while driving a motor vehicle upon any highway or on any lands described in subdivision (b).

(b) As used in subdivision (a), "lands" means those lands to which the Chappie–Z'berg Off–Highway Motor Vehicle Law of 1971 (Division 16.5 (commencing with Section 38000)) applies as to off-highway motor vehicles, as described in Section 38001. (Formerly § 23121, added by Stats.1961, c. 1903, p. 4010, § 1. Amended by Stats. 1979, c. 363, p. 1228, § 2. Renumbered § 23220 and amended by Stats.1981, c. 940, p. 3569, § 23. Amended by Stats.1998, c. 384 (S.B.1639), § 1, eff. Aug. 24, 1998.)

Cross References

Driving while under the influence of alcoholic beverage or drugs, see Vehicle Code §§ 23152, 23153.

Exceptions to application of this section, see Vehicle Code § 23229.

Penalties, public offenses, fines in misdemeanor cases for violations pertaining to passing school buildings or grounds, see Vehicle Code § 42011.

Person under the influence of intoxicating liquor, drug, controlled substance or toluene in public place as disorderly person, see Penal Code § 647.

§ 23221. Drinking in motor vehicle upon highway

(a) No driver shall drink any alcoholic beverage while in a motor vehicle upon a highway.

(b) No passenger shall drink any alcoholic beverage while in a motor vehicle upon a highway. (Formerly § 23121.5, added by Stats.1979, c. 363, p. 1228, § 3. Renumbered § 23221 and amended by Stats.1981, c. 940, p. 3569, § 24. Amended by Stats.1999, c. 723 (A.B.194), § 2.)

Cross References

Driving while under the influence of alcohol or drugs, see Vehicle Code §§ 23152, 23153.

Exceptions to application of this section, see Vehicle Code § 23229.

Motor vehicle defined, see Vehicle Code § 415.

Penalties, public offenses, fines in misdemeanor cases for violations pertaining to passing school buildings or grounds, see Vehicle Code § 42011.

Person under the influence of intoxicating liquor, drug, controlled substance or toluene in public place as disorderly person, see Penal Code § 647.

§ 23222. Possession of open container containing alcoholic beverage or marijuana while driving a motor vehicle; penalty

(a) No person shall have in his or her possession on his or her person, while driving a motor vehicle upon a highway or on lands, as described in subdivision (b) of Section 23220, any bottle, can, or other receptacle, containing any alcoholic beverage which has been opened, or a seal broken, or the contents of which have been partially removed.

(b) Except as authorized by law, every person who possesses, while driving a motor vehicle upon a highway or on lands, as described in subdivision (b) of Section 23220, not more than one avoirdupois ounce of marijuana, other than concentrated cannabis as defined by Section 11006.5 of the Health and Safety Code, is guilty of an infraction punishable by a fine of not more than one hundred dollars ($100). (Formerly § 23122, added by Stats.1961, c. 1903, p. 4010, § 2. Amended by Stats.1968, c. 238, p. 549, § 1; Stats.1979, c. 363, p. 1228, § 4. Renumbered § 23222 and amended by Stats.1981, c. 940, p. 3569, § 25. Amended by Stats.1983, c. 1005, § 1; Stats.1998, c. 384 (S.B.1639), § 2, eff. Aug. 24, 1998; Stats.2010, c. 708 (S.B.1449), § 2.)

Cross References

Alcoholic beverage defined, see Business and Professions Code § 23004.

Driving while under the influence of alcoholic beverages or drugs, see Vehicle Code §§ 23152, 23153.

Exceptions to application of this section, see Vehicle Code § 23229.

Investigation for driver's license suspension or revocation, three convictions in three years under this or other specified sections, see Vehicle Code § 13800.

Misdemeanor, marijuana possession, see Vehicle Code § 40000.15.

Motor vehicle defined, see Vehicle Code § 415.

Penalties, public offenses, fines in misdemeanor cases for violations pertaining to passing school buildings or grounds, see Vehicle Code § 42011.

Person under the influence of intoxicating liquor, drug, controlled substance or toluene in public place as disorderly person, see Penal Code § 647.

Special proceedings in narcotics and drug abuse cases, application to violation of this section, see Penal Code § 1000.

§ 23223. Possession of opened container in a motor vehicle

(a) No driver shall have in his or her possession, while in a motor vehicle upon a highway or on lands, as described in subdivision (b) of Section 23220, any bottle, can, or other receptacle, containing any alcoholic beverage that has been opened, or a seal broken, or the contents of which have been partially removed.

(b) No passenger shall have in his or her possession, while in a motor vehicle upon a highway or on lands, as described in subdivision (b) of Section 23220, any bottle, can, or other receptacle containing any alcoholic beverage that has been opened or a seal broken, or the contents of which have been partially removed. (Formerly § 23122.5, added by Stats.1979, c. 363, p. 1228, § 5. Renumbered § 23223 and amended by Stats.1981, c. 940, p. 3569, § 26. Amended by Stats.1998, c. 384 (S.B.1639), § 3, eff. Aug. 24, 1998; Stats.1999, c. 723 (A.B.194), § 3.)

Cross References

Penalties, public offenses, fines in misdemeanor cases for violations pertaining to passing school buildings or grounds, see Vehicle Code § 42011.

Third or subsequent violations of provisions relating to storage and possession of open containers by driver operating under valid certificate or permit pursuant to Passenger Charter-party Carriers' Act, misdemeanor, see Vehicle Code § 40000.20.

§ 23224. Possession of alcoholic beverage in vehicle; persons under 21; penalties

(a) No person under the age of 21 years shall knowingly drive any motor vehicle carrying any alcoholic beverage, unless the person is accompanied by a parent, responsible adult relative, any other adult designated by the parent, or legal guardian for the purpose of transportation of an alcoholic beverage, or is employed by a licensee under the Alcoholic Beverage Control Act (Division 9 (commencing with Section 23000) of the Business and Professions Code), and is driving the motor vehicle during regular hours and in the course of the person's employment. If the driver was unaccompanied, he or she shall have a complete defense if he or she was following, in a timely manner, the reasonable instructions of his or her parent, legal guardian, responsible adult relative, or adult designee relating to disposition of the alcoholic beverage.

(b) No passenger in any motor vehicle who is under the age of 21 years shall knowingly possess or have under that person's control any alcoholic beverage, unless the passenger is accompanied by a parent, legal guardian, responsible adult relative, any other adult designated by the parent, or legal guardian for the purpose of transportation of an alcoholic beverage, or is employed by a licensee under the Alcoholic Beverage Control Act (Division 9 (commencing with Section 23000) of the Business and Professions Code), and possession or control is during regular hours and in the course of the passenger's employment. If the passenger was unaccompanied, he or she shall have a complete defense if he or she was following, in a timely manner, the reasonable instructions of his or her parent, legal guardian, responsible adult relative or adult designee relating to disposition of the alcoholic beverage.

(c) If the vehicle used in any violation of subdivision (a) or (b) is registered to an offender who is under the age of 21 years, the vehicle may be impounded at the owner's expense for not less than one day nor more than 30 days for each violation.

(d) Any person under 21 years of age convicted of a violation of this section is subject to Section 13202.5.

(e) Any person convicted for a violation of subdivision (a) or (b) is guilty of a misdemeanor and shall be punished upon conviction by a fine of not more than one thousand dollars ($1,000) or by imprisonment in the county jail for not more than six months, or by both that fine and imprisonment. *(Formerly § 23123.5, added by Stats.1965, c. 1662, p. 3772, § 2. Amended by Stats.1972,*

c. 881, p. 1559, § 2. Renumbered § 23224 and amended by Stats.1981, c. 940, p. 3569, § 28. Amended by Stats. 1990, c. 1697 (S.B.2635), § 6; Stats.1996, c. 690 (A.B. 2000), § 1.)

Cross References

Alcoholic beverage defined, see Business and Professions Code § 23004.

Driving while under the influence of alcoholic beverages or drugs, see Vehicle Code §§ 23152, 23153.

Investigation for driver's license suspension or revocation, three convictions in three years under this or other specified sections, see Vehicle Code § 13800.

Penalties, public offenses, fines in misdemeanor cases for violations pertaining to passing school buildings or grounds, see Vehicle Code § 42011.

Procedure to remove and store vehicles, see Vehicle Code § 22850 et seq.

§ 23225. Storage of opened container

(a)(1) It is unlawful for the registered owner of any motor vehicle to keep in a motor vehicle, when the vehicle is upon any highway or on lands, as described in subdivision (b) of Section 23220, any bottle, can, or other receptacle containing any alcoholic beverage that has been opened, or a seal broken, or the contents of which have been partially removed, unless the container is kept in the trunk of the vehicle.

(2) If the vehicle is not equipped with a trunk and is not an off-highway motor vehicle subject to identification, as defined in Section 38012, the bottle, can, or other receptacle described in paragraph (1) shall be kept in some other area of the vehicle that is not normally occupied by the driver or passengers. For the purposes of this paragraph, a utility compartment or glove compartment shall be deemed to be within the area occupied by the driver and passengers.

(3) If the vehicle is not equipped with a trunk and is an off-highway motor vehicle subject to identification, as defined in subdivision (a) of Section 38012, the bottle, can, or other receptacle described in paragraph (1) shall be kept in a locked container. As used in this paragraph, "locked container" means a secure container that is fully enclosed and locked by a padlock, key lock, combination lock, or similar locking device.

(b) Subdivision (a) is also applicable to a driver of a motor vehicle if the registered owner is not present in the vehicle.

(c) This section shall not apply to the living quarters of a housecar or camper. *(Formerly § 23123, added by Stats.1961, c. 1903, p. 4010, § 3. Amended by Stats.1968, c. 238, p. 549, § 2. Renumbered § 23225 and amended by Stats.1981, c. 940, p. 3569, § 27. Amended by Stats.1998, c. 384 (S.B.1639), § 4, eff. Aug. 24, 1998; Stats.1999, c. 723 (A.B.194), § 4.)*

Cross References

Alcoholic beverage defined, see Business and Professions Code § 23004.

Camper defined, see Vehicle Code § 243.

Driving while under the influence of alcoholic beverages or drugs, see Vehicle Code §§ 23152, 23153.

Exceptions to application of this section, see Vehicle Code § 23229.

House car defined, see Vehicle Code § 362.

Motor vehicle defined, see Vehicle Code § 415.

Penalties, public offenses, fines in misdemeanor cases for violations pertaining to passing school buildings or grounds, see Vehicle Code § 42011.

Third or subsequent violations of provisions relating to storage and possession of open containers by driver operating under valid certificate or permit pursuant to Passenger Charter-party Carriers' Act, misdemeanor, see Vehicle Code § 40000.20.

Violation of this section by driver of limousine or officer, agent or employee of charter-party carrier of passengers, penalties, see Public Utilities Code § 5384.5.

§ 23226. Keeping open container in passenger compartment of motor vehicle; exceptions

(a) It is unlawful for any driver to keep in the passenger compartment of a motor vehicle, when the vehicle is upon any highway or on lands, as described in subdivision (b) of Section 23220, any bottle, can, or other receptacle containing any alcoholic beverage that has been opened, or a seal broken, or the contents of which have been partially removed.

(b) It is unlawful for any passenger to keep in the passenger compartment of a motor vehicle, when the vehicle is upon any highway or on lands, as described in subdivision (b) of Section 23220, any bottle, can, or other receptacle containing any alcoholic beverage that has been opened or a seal broken, or the contents of which have been partially removed.

(c) This section shall not apply to the living quarters of a housecar or camper. *(Formerly § 23123.6, added by Stats.1979, c. 363, p. 1228, § 6. Renumbered § 23226 and amended by Stats.1981, c. 940, p. 3570, § 29. Amended by Stats.1998, c. 384 (S.B.1639), § 5, eff. Aug. 24, 1998; Stats.1999, c. 723 (A.B.194), § 5.)*

Cross References

Penalties, public offenses, fines in misdemeanor cases for violations pertaining to passing school buildings or grounds, see Vehicle Code § 42011.

§ 23229. Possession of alcoholic beverage in for-hire vehicles; exceptions

(a) Except as provided in Section 23229.1, Sections 23221 and 23223 do not apply to passengers in any bus, taxicab, or limousine for hire licensed to transport passengers pursuant to the Public Utilities Code or proper local authority, or the living quarters of a housecar or camper.

(b) Except as provided in Section 23229.1, Section 23225 does not apply to the driver or owner of a bus, taxicab, or limousine for hire licensed to transport passengers pursuant to the Public Utilities Code or proper local authority.

(c) This section shall become operative on July 1, 1989. *(Added by Stats.1988, c. 1105, § 7, operative July 1, 1989.)*

§ 23229.1. Application of prohibition against possession or storage of opened container to driver providing prearranged transportation services as a charter-party carrier of passengers while transporting passenger under 21; forwarding record of conviction to Public Utilities Commission

(a) Subject to subdivision (b), Sections 23223 and 23225 apply to any driver providing transportation services on a prearranged basis as a charter-party carrier of passengers, as defined in Section 5360 of the Public Utilities Code, when the driver of the vehicle transports any passenger under 21 years of age and fails to comply with the requirements of Section 5384.1 of the Public Utilities Code.

(b) For purposes of subdivision (a), it is not a violation of Section 23225 for any driver providing transportation services on a prearranged basis as a charter-party carrier of passengers that is licensed pursuant to the Public Utilities Code to keep any bottle, can, or other receptacle containing any alcoholic beverage in a locked utility compartment within the area occupied by the driver and passengers.

(c) In addition to the requirements of Section 1803, every clerk of a court in which any driver in subdivision (a) was convicted of a violation of Section 23225 shall prepare within 10 days after conviction, and immediately forward to the Public Utilities Commission at its office in San Francisco, an abstract of the record of the court covering the case in which the person was convicted. If sentencing is not pronounced in conjunction with the conviction, the abstract shall be forwarded to the commission within 10 days after sentencing, and the abstract shall be certified, by the person required to prepare it, to be true and correct. For the purposes of this subdivision, a forfeiture of bail is equivalent to a conviction. *(Added by Stats.1988, c. 1105, § 8, operative July 1, 1989. Amended by Stats.2007, c. 263 (A.B.310), § 33; Stats.2012, c. 461 (A.B.45), § 6.)*

Law Revision Commission Comments

2007 Amendment

Subdivision (c) of Section 23229.1 is amended to delete unnecessary language authorizing the judge to substitute for the clerk if there is no clerk. See Code Civ. Proc. § 167 (judge may perform any act court clerk may perform); Gov't Code §§ 69840–69848 (duties of clerk of superior court), 71620(b) (executive or administrative officer has authority of clerk of court).

Subdivision (c) is also amended to make a stylistic revision. Subdivision (d) is deleted as obsolete. [35 Cal.L.Rev.Comm. Reports 219 (2007)].

ARTICLE 3. ALCOHOL REHABILITATION FACILITIES [REPEALED]

§§ 23230 to 23234. Repealed by Stats.1984, c. 1725, § 7, operative Jan. 1, 1988

ARTICLE 4. IGNITION INTERLOCK DEVICE

Section
23235.   Renumbered.
23236 to 23240.   Repealed.
23240.2, 23240.5.   Repealed.
23241 to 23244.   Repealed.
23244.5.   Repealed.
23245.   Repealed.
23246.   Renumbered.
23247.   Prohibited activities regarding persons whose driving
              privileges have been restricted pursuant to Section
              13352, 23575, or 23700; punishment; defenses.
23248.   Repealed.
23249.   Repealed.
23249.1.   Repealed.
23249.2 to 23249.4.   Repealed.

§ 23235. Renumbered Vehicle Code § 13386 and amended by Stats.1999, c. 22 (S.B.24), § 25, eff. May 26, 1999, operative July 1, 1999

§§ 23236 to 23240. Repealed by Stats.1994, c. 1237 (A.B.2639), § 2, eff. Sept. 30, 1994

§§ 23240.2, 23240.5. Repealed by Stats.1986, c. 1108, § 5, operative Jan. 1, 1990

§§ 23241 to 23244. Repealed by Stats.1994, c. 1237 (A.B.2639), § 2, eff. Sept. 30, 1994

§ 23244.5. Repealed by Stats.1986, c. 1108, § 5, operative Jan. 1, 1990

§ 23245. Repealed by Stats.1994, c. 1237 (A.B.2639), § 2, eff. Sept. 30, 1994

§ 23246. Renumbered Vehicle Code § 23575 and amended by Stats.1999, c. 22 (S.B.24), § 27, eff. May 26, 1999, operative July 1, 1999

§ 23247. Prohibited activities regarding persons whose driving privileges have been restricted pursuant to Section 13352, 23575, or 23700; punishment; defenses

(a) It is unlawful for a person to knowingly rent, lease, or lend a motor vehicle to another person known to have had his or her driving privilege restricted as provided in Section 13352, 23575, or 23700, unless the vehicle is equipped with a functioning, certified ignition interlock device. A person, whose driving privilege is restricted pursuant to Section 13352, 23575, or 23700 shall notify any other person who rents, leases, or loans a motor vehicle to him or her of the driving restriction imposed under that section.

(b) It is unlawful for any person whose driving privilege is restricted pursuant to Section 13352, 23575, or 23700 to request or solicit any other person to blow into an ignition interlock device or to start a motor vehicle equipped with the device for the purpose of providing the person so restricted with an operable motor vehicle.

(c) It is unlawful to blow into an ignition interlock device or to start a motor vehicle equipped with the device for the purpose of providing an operable motor vehicle to a person whose driving privilege is restricted pursuant to Section 13352, 23575, or 23700.

(d) It is unlawful to remove, bypass, or tamper with, an ignition interlock device.

(e) It is unlawful for any person whose driving privilege is restricted pursuant to Section 13352, 23575, or 23700 to operate any vehicle not equipped with a functioning ignition interlock device.

(f) Any person convicted of a violation of this section shall be punished by imprisonment in the county jail for not more than six months or by a fine of not more than five thousand dollars ($5,000), or by both that fine and imprisonment.

(g)(1) If any person whose driving privilege is restricted pursuant to Section 13352 is convicted of a violation of subdivision (e), the court shall notify the Department of Motor Vehicles, which shall immediately terminate the restriction and shall suspend or revoke the person's driving privilege for the remaining period of the originating suspension or revocation and until all reinstatement requirements in Section 13352 are met.

(2) If any person who is restricted pursuant to subdivision (a) or (l) of Section 23575 or Section 23700 is convicted of a violation of subdivision (e), the department shall suspend the person's driving privilege for one year from the date of the conviction.

(h) Notwithstanding any other provision of law, if a vehicle in which an ignition interlock device has been installed is impounded, the manufacturer or installer of the device shall have the right to remove the device from the vehicle during normal business hours. No charge shall be imposed for the removal of the device nor shall the manufacturer or installer be liable for any removal, towing, impoundment, storage, release, or administrative costs or penalties associated with the impoundment. Upon request, the person seeking to remove the device shall present documentation to justify removal of the device from the vehicle. Any damage to the vehicle resulting from the removal of the device is the responsibility of the person removing it. *(Added by Stats.1992, c. 694 (A.B.2851), § 2, operative July 1, 1993. Amended by Stats.1993, c. 1244 (S.B.126), § 26; Stats.1994, c. 1237 (A.B.2639), § 5, eff. Sept. 30, 1994; Stats.1998, c. 118 (S.B.1186), § 74.5, operative July 1, 1999; Stats.1998, c. 756 (A.B.762), § 22, operative July 1, 1999; Stats.1999, c. 22 (S.B.24), § 28, eff. May 26, 1999, operative July 1, 1999; Stats.2010, c. 30 (S.B.895), § 3, eff. June 22, 2010.)*

Cross References

Out of state residents, expiration of suspension or revocation period, see Vehicle Code § 13353.5.

§ 23248. Repealed by Stats.1998, c. 118 (S.B.1186), § 75, operative July 1, 1999

§ 23249. Repealed by Stats.2003, c. 468 (S.B.851), § 28, operative Jan. 1, 2005

§ 23249.1. Repealed by Stats.2003, c. 468 (S.B.851), § 29

§§ 23249.2 to 23249.4. Repealed by Stats.1986, c. 1108, § 5, operative Jan. 1, 1990

ARTICLE 4.5.   INSTALLATION OF IGNITION INTERLOCK DEVICES [REPEALED]

ARTICLE 5.   ALCOHOL AND DRUG PROBLEM ASSESSMENT PROGRAM

Section
23249.50. Legislative findings and intent.
23249.51. Repealed.
23249.52. Renumbered.
23249.53. Renumbered.
23249.54. Renumbered.
23249.55. Renumbered.
23249.56. Repealed.
23249.57, 23249.58. Repealed.

§ 23249.50. Legislative findings and intent

(a) The Legislature finds and declares all of the following:

(1) Driving under the influence of an alcoholic beverage or a drug is a serious problem, constituting the largest group of misdemeanor violations in many counties.

(2) Studies of first offenders have found that more than half of first offenders are alcoholics or problem drinkers. There are higher percentages of problem drinkers among second offenders than among first offenders.

(3) As the link between the health and legal aspects of the problem has become recognized, the courts have sought more information on a presentence basis in determining the appropriate sentence.

(4) Laws relating to driving under the influence of an alcoholic beverage or a drug allow the courts to order a presentence investigation to determine whether a person can benefit from an education, training, or treatment program. The Legislature thus finds that, to adequately assess whether an individual arrested for driving under the influence of an alcoholic beverage or a drug is chemically dependent, it is important to develop and implement screening programs in order to continue to address the problem of driving under the influence of alcoholic beverages or drugs in the state.

(b) It is therefore the intent of the Legislature to establish an additional procedure to assist the courts in the use of presentence investigations of individuals convicted of driving under the influence of an alcoholic beverage or a drug and to enable the courts to make appropriate dispositions in these cases. As part of this process, the courts should obtain and consider a presentence investigation report detailing the defendant's driving and criminal record, and, where possible, an alcohol or drug problem assessment report. In all cases, an alcohol or drug problem assessment report should be completed by qualified personnel prior to the determination of an education or treatment plan and subsequent sentencing by the courts. *(Added by Stats.1988, c. 160, § 183.)*

§ 23249.51. Repealed by Stats.1989, c. 1360, § 159

§ 23249.52. Renumbered Vehicle Code § 23646 and amended by Stats.1999, c. 22 (S.B.24), § 29, eff. May 26, 1999, operative July 1, 1999

§ 23249.53. Renumbered Vehicle Code § 23647 and amended by Stats.1999, c. 22 (S.B.24), § 30, eff. May 26, 1999, operative July 1, 1999

§ 23249.54. Renumbered Vehicle Code § 23648 and amended by Stats.1999, c. 22 (S.B.24), § 32, eff. May 26, 1999, operative July 1, 1999

§ 23249.55. Renumbered Vehicle Code § 23649 and amended by Stats.1999, c. 22 (S.B.24), § 33, eff. May 26, 1999, operative July 1, 1999

§ 23249.56. Repealed by Stats.1998, c. 118 (S.B.1186), § 81, operative July 1, 1999

§§ 23249.57, 23249.58. Repealed by Stats.1998, c. 656 (A.B.1916), §§ 9, 10

CHAPTER 13.   VEHICULAR CROSSINGS AND TOLL HIGHWAYS

Article	Section
1. General Provisions	23250
2. Towing on Vehicular Crossings	23270
3. Tolls and Other Charges	23300
4. Special Traffic Regulations	23330

ARTICLE 1.   GENERAL PROVISIONS

Section
23250. Application of chapter.
23251. Authority of California Highway Patrol; temporary arrangements made by private operators of toll highways; reimbursement.
23252. Authority of department of transportation personnel.
23253. Obedience to officers.
23254. "Vehicular crossing".
23255. "Approach".

§ 23250. Application of chapter

All of the provisions of this code not inconsistent with the provisions of this chapter shall be applicable to vehicular crossings and toll highways. This chapter shall control over any provision of this code inconsistent with this chapter. *(Stats.1959, c. 3, p. 1710, § 23250. Amend-*

745

ed by Stats.1996, c. 1154 (A.B.3020), § 72, eff. Sept. 30, 1996.)

§ 23251. Authority of California Highway Patrol; temporary arrangements made by private operators of toll highways; reimbursement

(a) The Department of the California Highway Patrol shall provide for proper and adequate policing of all toll highways and all vehicular crossings to ensure the enforcement thereon of this code and of any other law relating to the use and operation of vehicles upon toll highways, highways or vehicular crossings, and of the rules and regulations of the Department of Transportation in respect thereto, and to cooperate with the Department of Transportation to the end that vehicular crossings be operated at all times in a manner as to carry traffic efficiently. The authority of the Department of the California Highway Patrol is exclusive except as to the authority conferred by law upon the Department of Transportation in respect to vehicular crossings.

(b) Notwithstanding subdivision (a), a private operator of a toll highway may make temporary arrangements, not to exceed 30 days, for traffic law enforcement services with an agency that employs peace officers as described in Section 830.1 of the Penal Code, if the Department of the California Highway Patrol cannot fulfill its responsibilities as described in this section, as determined by the Secretary of the Business, Transportation and Housing Agency.

(c) The services provided by the Department of the California Highway Patrol for all toll highways that are operated by a private entity shall be reimbursed pursuant to Section 30809.1 of the Streets and Highways Code. If the private operator of a toll highway and the Department of the California Highway Patrol reach an impasse in negotiating an agreement for reimbursement, the Secretary of the Business, Transportation and Housing Agency shall assist in resolving the impasse. (Stats.1959, c. 3, p. 1710, § 23251. Amended by Stats.1974, c. 545, p. 1332, § 218; Stats.1992, c. 1241 (S.B.1615), § 23.)

§ 23252. Authority of department of transportation personnel

The chief of toll services, captains, lieutenants, and sergeants employed by the Department of Transportation shall have the powers and authority of peace officers as listed in Section 830.4 of the Penal Code while so employed on any vehicular crossing or as may be neces-

sary to the performance of their duties while not upon such vehicular crossing. Captains, lieutenants, and sergeants so employed shall wear, while on duty, a uniform which shall be distinctly different from that of the California Highway Patrol, to be specified by the Director of Transportation. (Stats.1959, c. 3, p. 1710, § 23252. Amended by Stats.1968, c. 1222, p. 2330, § 75.5; Stats. 1974, c. 545, p. 1332, § 219.)

§ 23253. Obedience to officers

All persons in, or upon, any toll highway or vehicular crossing shall at all times comply with any lawful order, signal, or direction by voice or hand of any member of the California Highway Patrol or an employee of the Department of Transportation who is a peace officer. (Stats. 1959, c. 3, p. 1710, § 23253. Amended by Stats.1974, c. 545, p. 1332, § 220; Stats.1992, c. 1241 (S.B.1615), § 24.)

§ 23254. "Vehicular crossing"

A "vehicular crossing" is any toll bridge or toll highway crossing and the approaches thereto, constructed or acquired by the Department of Transportation under the provisions of the California Toll Bridge Authority Act.[1] (Stats.1959, c. 3, p. 1710, § 23254. Amended by Stats. 1974, c. 545, p. 1333, § 221.)

[1] Streets and Highways Code § 30000 et seq.

§ 23255. "Approach"

An "approach" is that portion of a state highway leading to or from a toll bridge or toll highway crossing which lies between one end of the bridge or crossing and the nearest intersection of a highway with the state highway. A ramp or other structure designed exclusively for use in connection with a toll bridge or toll highway crossing shall not be deemed an intersecting highway but is a part of the approach. (Stats.1959, c. 3, p. 1710, § 23255.)

Cross References

Definitions,
  Highway, see Vehicle Code § 360.
  Intersection, see Vehicle Code § 365.
Tolls and other charges, see Vehicle Code § 23300 et seq.

ARTICLE 2. TOWING ON VEHICULAR CROSSINGS

Section
23270. Unauthorized towing; maximum towing fee; permits.
23271. Towing service; maintenance on each vehicular crossing; rates.
23272. Disposition of towed vehicles; charges for fuel.
23273. Inapplicability of tow car requirements.

§ 23270. Unauthorized towing; maximum towing fee; permits

(a) No person shall commence to tow any vehicle or other object on any vehicular crossing unless authorized to do so by the Department of Transportation and unless the towing is done by means of a tow truck as defined in Section 615. No person, other than a member of the California Highway Patrol or an employee of the Department of Transportation, shall, by means of pushing with another vehicle, propel any vehicle or object on a vehicular crossing. No person, other than an employee of the Department of Transportation, shall, on any vehicular crossing, tow any vehicle or other object except a vehicle or object constructed and designed to be towed by a vehicle of a type similar to that being used for this purpose.

(b) The California Transportation Commission shall, by regulation, establish the maximum towing fee which may be charged by any person authorized to tow a vehicle pursuant to subdivision (a). No authorized person shall charge a fee for towing a vehicle which is in excess of the maximum fee established by the California Transportation Commission.

(c) The Director of Transportation may grant a special permit to any person to tow any vehicle or object over and completely across any vehicular crossing when in his or her judgment the towing vehicle is so constructed and equipped that the vehicle or object can be towed across the vehicular crossing without endangering persons or property and without interrupting the orderly traffic across the vehicular crossing.

(d) The prohibitions of this section shall apply only on those vehicular crossings upon which a towing service is maintained by the Department of Transportation. *(Stats. 1959, c. 3, p. 1711, § 23270. Amended by Stats.1969, c. 221, p. 551, § 1; Stats.1972, c. 510, p. 889, § 1; Stats. 1974, c. 545, p. 1333, § 222; Stats.1980, c. 622, p. 1707, § 4; Stats.1990, c. 216 (S.B.2510), § 119.)*

Cross References

Tow truck requirements, see Vehicle Code §§ 22513, 23273, 24605, 25253, 27700, 27907.

§ 23271. Towing service; maintenance on each vehicular crossing; rates

A towing service may be maintained on each vehicular crossing by the Department of Transportation, and the department may furnish such service as is necessary to permit the orderly flow of traffic upon such crossing. The Department of Transportation may prescribe and collect reasonable rates for towing services furnished. *(Stats.1959, c. 3, p. 1711, § 23271. Amended by Stats. 1974, c. 545, p. 1333, § 223; Stats.1974, c. 1053, p. 2271, § 1.)*

§ 23272. Disposition of towed vehicles; charges for fuel

When any vehicle or object on any vehicular crossing, upon which towing service is maintained, is stopped for any reason and is obstructing or may obstruct traffic, the vehicle or object shall be towed by the towing service either to the nearest property of the Department of Transportation designated for the parking or storing of vehicles, or to a suitable parking location on a public street or highway and thereupon left in the custody of the owner or operator of the vehicle or object, or his agent, or, if no owner, operator, or agent is present, or if an owner, operator, or agent so requests, to a public garage or off-street parking facility. The department may prescribe the limits within which the towing service shall be operated.

Notwithstanding the foregoing provisions, the department may furnish and deliver fuel to vehicles, the supply of which is exhausted, or change tires, and may charge a reasonable sum for the services and materials furnished or, if the department deems it safe and advisable, and the owner or operator of the vehicle or object so requests, it may be towed from the vehicular crossing. *(Stats.1959, c. 3, p. 1711, § 23272. Amended by Stats.1974, c. 545, p. 1333, § 224; Stats.1980, c. 622, p. 1707, § 5; Stats.1982, c. 681, p. 2812, § 85.)*

§ 23273. Inapplicability of tow car requirements

Sections 24605, 25253, 27700, and 27907 do not apply to vehicles operated by the Department of Transportation pursuant to this article. *(Stats.1959, c. 3, p. 1712, § 23273. Amended by Stats.1961, c. 58, p. 1011, § 43, eff. March 31, 1961; Stats.1971, c. 438, p. 909, § 193, operative May 3, 1972; Stats.1974, c. 545, p. 1334, § 225.)*

Cross References

Rules of the road, exemption of authorized emergency vehicles, see Vehicle Code § 21055.

ARTICLE 3. TOLLS AND OTHER CHARGES

Section
23300. Signs.
23301. Toll on crossings.
23301.5. Emergency vehicles; exemption from tolls.
23301.8. Pay-by-plate toll payment; public information.
23302. Failure to pay tolls; transponder or other electronic toll payment device; prima facie evidence.
23302.5. Evasion of tolls.
23303. Liens.

§ 23300. Signs

The Department of Transportation shall erect appropriate signs at each entrance to a vehicular crossing to notify traffic that it is entering upon a vehicular crossing. *(Stats.1959, c. 3, p. 1712, § 23300. Amended by Stats. 1974, c. 545, p. 1334, § 226.)*

Cross References

Highway signs, markers or warning notices, failure to observe, misdemeanor, see Vehicle Code §§ 21367, 40000.14.
Vehicular crossing defined, see Vehicle Code § 23254.

§ 23301. Toll on crossings

Except as provided in Section 23301.5, each vehicle that enters into or upon a vehicular crossing immediately becomes liable for those tolls and other charges as may from time to time be prescribed by the California Transportation Commission. *(Stats.1959, c. 3, p. 1712, § 23301. Amended by Stats.1980, c. 622, p. 1708, § 6; Stats.2009, c. 425 (A.B.254), § 1.)*

Cross References

Toll bridges, toll roads, and toll ferries, see Streets and Highways Code § 30800 et seq.

§ 23301.5. Emergency vehicles; exemption from tolls

(a) An authorized emergency vehicle is exempt from any requirement to pay a toll or other charge on a vehicular crossing, toll highway, or high-occupancy toll (HOT) lane, including the requirements of Section 23301, if all of the following conditions are satisfied:

(1) The authorized emergency vehicle is properly displaying an exempt California license plate, and is properly identified or marked as an authorized emergency vehicle, including, but not limited to, displaying an external surface-mounted red warning light, blue warning light, or both, and displaying public agency identification, including, but not limited to, "Fire Department," "Sheriff," or "Police."

(2)(A) The vehicle is being driven while responding to or returning from an urgent or emergency call, engaged in an urgent or emergency response, or engaging in a fire station coverage assignment directly related to an emergency response.

(B) For purposes of this paragraph, an "urgent" response or call means an incident or circumstance that requires an immediate response to a public safety-related incident, but does not warrant the use of emergency warning lights. "Urgent" does not include any personal use, commuting, training, or administrative uses.

(C) Notwithstanding subparagraph (A), an authorized emergency vehicle, when returning from an urgent or emergency call, or from being engaged in an urgent or emergency response, or from engaging in a fire station coverage assignment directly related to an emergency response, shall not be exempt from any requirement to pay a toll or other charge imposed while traveling on a high-occupancy toll (HOT) lane.

(3) The driver of the vehicle determines that the use of the toll facility shall likely improve the availability or response and arrival time of the authorized emergency vehicle and its delivery of essential public safety services.

(b) If the operator of a toll facility elects to send a bill or invoice to the public agency for the use of the toll facility by an authorized emergency vehicle, exempt pursuant to subdivision (a), the fire chief, police chief, county sheriff, head of the public agency, or his or her designee, is authorized to certify in writing that the authorized emergency vehicle was responding to or returning from an emergency call or response and is exempt from the payment of the toll or other charge in accordance with this section. The letter shall be accepted by the toll operator in lieu of payment and is a public document.

(c) An authorized emergency vehicle that does not comply with this section is not exempt from the requirement to pay a toll or other charge on a toll highway, vehicular crossing, or high-occupancy toll (HOT) lane. Upon information and belief of the toll operator that an authorized emergency vehicle is not in compliance with this section, the fire chief, police chief, county sheriff, head of the public agency, or his or her designee, upon the written request of the owner or operator of the toll facility, shall provide or otherwise make accessible to the toll operator the dispatch records or log books relevant to the time period when the vehicle was in use on the toll highway, vehicular crossing, or high-occupancy toll (HOT) lane.

(d) Nothing in this section shall prohibit or amend an agreement entered into between the owner or operator of a toll facility and a local emergency service provider that establishes mutually agreed upon terms for the use of the toll facility by the emergency service provider. This section shall not prohibit the owner or operator of a toll facility from having a policy that meets or exceeds this section. If at any time an emergency service provider or the owner or operator of a toll facility opts to terminate an agreement regarding the payment and processing of tolls or other charges, this section shall apply to the emergency service provider and the toll facility. An agreement between an emergency service provider and the owner or operator of a toll facility does not exempt other emergency service providers not named in the original agreement and the toll facility from the requirements of this section when those other emergency service providers use a toll facility in the jurisdiction of the owner or operator of the toll facility.

(e) Sections 23302 and 23302.5 do not apply to authorized emergency vehicles exempt pursuant to this section.

(f) As used in this section, "toll facility" includes a toll road, high-occupancy toll (HOT) lane, toll bridge, toll highway, a vehicular crossing for which payment of a toll or charge is required, or any other toll facility. *(Added by Stats.2009, c. 425 (A.B.254), § 2.)*

§ 23301.8. Pay-by-plate toll payment; public information

Where an issuing agency permits pay-by-plate toll payment as described in subdivision (e) of Section 23302, it shall communicate, as practicable, the pay-by-plate toll amount in the same manner as it communicates other toll payment methods. The issuing agency shall provide publicly available information on how pay-by-plate toll payment works, including the toll amount, process for payment, and period of time a vehicle has to resolve the payment before an issuing agency may process the trip as a violation under Section 40255. Communication of this information may include the Department of Transportation's approved signage, posting of information on the issuing agency's Internet Web site, media advertising, public meeting or disclosure as required by the issuing agency's policies, or other methods of communication. Except where the issuing agency has an agreement with a vehicle owner that specifies in advance any administrative fees that will be imposed on the owner for pay-by-plate toll payment, administrative costs shall be incorporated into the pay-by-plate toll amount, and no additional administrative costs shall be added above the posted pay-by-plate toll amount. *(Added by Stats.2009, c. 459 (A.B.628), § 1.)*

§ 23302. Failure to pay tolls; transponder or other electronic toll payment device; prima facie evidence

(a)(1) It is unlawful for a driver to fail to pay tolls or other charges on any vehicular crossing or toll highway. Except as otherwise provided in subdivision (b), (c), or (d), it is prima facie evidence of a violation of this section for a person to drive a vehicle onto any vehicular crossing or toll highway without either lawful money of the United States in the driver's immediate possession in an amount sufficient to pay the prescribed tolls or other charges due from that driver or a transponder or other electronic toll payment device associated with a valid Automatic Vehicle Identification account with a balance sufficient to pay those tolls.

(2) Except as specified in paragraph (3), if a transponder or other electronic toll payment device is used to pay tolls or other charges due, the device shall be located in or on the vehicle in a location so as to be visible for the purpose of enforcement at all times when the vehicle is located on the vehicular crossing or toll highway. Where required by the operator of a vehicular crossing or toll highway, this requirement applies even if the operator offers free travel or nontoll accounts to certain classes of users.

(3) If a motorcyclist uses a transponder or other electronic toll payment device to lawfully enter a vehicle crossing or toll highway, the motorcyclist shall use any one of the following methods as long as the transponder or device is able to be read by the toll operator's detection equipment:

(A) Place the transponder or other electronic toll payment device in the motorcyclist's pocket.

(B) Place the transponder or other electronic toll payment device inside a cycle net that drapes over the gas tank of the motorcycle.

(C) Mount the transponder or other electronic toll payment device on license plate devices provided by the toll operator, if the toll operator provides those devices.

(D) Keep the transponder or other electronic toll payment device in the glove or storage compartment of the motorcycle.

(E) Mount the transponder or other electronic toll payment device on the windshield of the motorcycle.

(b) For vehicular crossings and toll highways that use electronic toll collection as the only method of paying tolls or other charges, it is prima facie evidence of a violation of this section for a driver to drive a vehicle onto the vehicular crossing or toll highway without a transponder or other electronic toll payment device associated with a valid Automatic Vehicle Identification account with a balance sufficient to pay those tolls.

(c) For vehicular crossings and toll highways where the issuing agency, as defined in Section 40250, permits pay-by-plate payment of tolls and other charges, in accordance with policies adopted by the issuing agency, it is prima facie evidence of a violation of this section for a driver to drive a vehicle onto the vehicular crossing or toll highway without at least one of the following:

(1) Lawful money of the United States in the driver's immediate possession in an amount sufficient to pay the prescribed tolls or other charges due from that person.

(2) A transponder or other electronic toll payment device associated with a valid Automatic Vehicle Identification account with a balance sufficient to pay those tolls.

(3) Valid vehicle license plates properly attached pursuant to Section 4850.5 or 5200 to the vehicle in which that driver enters onto the vehicular crossing or toll highway.

(d) For vehicular crossings and toll highways where the issuing agency, as defined in Section 40250, permits pay-by-plate payment of tolls and other charges in accordance with policies adopted by the issuing agency, and where electronic toll collection is the only other method of paying tolls or other charges, it is prima facie evidence of a violation of this section for a driver to drive a vehicle onto the vehicular crossing or toll highway without either a transponder or other electronic toll payment device associated with a valid Automatic Vehicle Identification account with a balance sufficient to pay those tolls or valid vehicle license plates properly attached to the vehicle pursuant to Section 4850.5 or 5200 in which that driver enters onto the vehicular crossing or toll highway.

(e) As used in this article, "pay-by-plate toll payment" means an issuing agency's use of on-road vehicle license plate identification recognition technology to accept payment of tolls in accordance with policies adopted by the issuing agency.

(f) This section does not require an issuing agency to offer pay-by-plate toll processing as a method for paying tolls. *(Stats.1959, c. 3, p. 1712, § 23302. Amended by Stats.1993, c. 1292 (S.B.274), § 15; Stats.1995, c. 739 (A.B.1223), § 6; Stats.1996, c. 1154 (A.B.3020), § 73, eff. Sept. 30, 1996; Stats.2009, c. 459 (A.B.628), § 2; Stats. 2012, c. 81 (A.B.1890), § 1.)*

Cross References

Electronic toll collection system, transportation agencies prohibited from using personally identifiable information obtained from nonsubscribers for marketing activities, exception for toll-related products or services contained in notice of toll evasion pursuant to this section, see Streets and Highways Code § 31490.

Statute making one fact prima facie evidence of another fact, see Evidence Code § 602.

§ 23302.5. Evasion of tolls

(a) No person shall evade or attempt to evade the payment of tolls or other charges on any vehicular crossing or toll highway.

(b) A violation of subdivision (a) is subject to civil penalties and is neither an infraction nor a public offense, as defined in Section 15 of the Penal Code. The enforcement of those civil penalties shall be governed by the civil administrative procedures set forth in Article 4 (commencing with Section 40250) of Chapter 1 of Division 17. *(Added by Stats.1995, c. 739 (A.B.1223), § 7.)*

§ 23303. Liens

The Department of Transportation shall have a lien and may enforce such lien, as provided in Chapter 6.5 (commencing with Section 3067) of Title 14 of Part 4 of Division 3 of the Civil Code, for all tolls and charges provided by this chapter. *(Stats.1959, c. 3, p. 1712, § 23303. Amended by Stats.1974, c. 545, p. 1334, § 227.)*

ARTICLE 4.   SPECIAL TRAFFIC REGULATIONS

Section
23330.   Animals and vehicles.
23331.   Pedestrians.
23332.   Trespass prohibited.
23333.   Stopping and parking.
23334.   Adoption of traffic rules.
23335.   Publication of traffic rules.
23336.   Violation of rules and regulations.
23337.   Renumbered.

§ 23330. Animals and vehicles

Except where a special permit has been obtained from the Department of Transportation under the provisions of Article 6 (commencing with Section 35780) of Chapter 5 of Division 15, none of the following shall be permitted on any vehicular crossing:

(a) Animals while being led or driven, even though tethered or harnessed.

(b) Bicycles, motorized bicycles, or motorized scooters, unless the department by signs indicates that bicycles,

motorized bicycles, or motorized scooters, or any combination thereof, are permitted upon all or any portion of the vehicular crossing.

(c) Vehicles having a total width of vehicle or load exceeding 102 inches.

(d) Vehicles carrying items prohibited by regulations promulgated by the Department of Transportation. *(Stats.1959, c. 3, p. 1712, § 23330. Amended by Stats. 1972, c. 437, p. 802, § 1; Stats.1974, c. 545, p. 1334, § 228; Stats.1975, c. 987, p. 2331, § 8; Stats.1978, c. 611, p. 2050, § 1; Stats.1999, c. 722 (S.B.441), § 8.)*

Cross References

Bicycle defined, see Vehicle Code § 231.
Motorized bicycle, see Vehicle Code §§ 406, 4020.
Transportation of explosives, see Vehicle Code § 31600 et seq.

§ 23331. Pedestrians

Pedestrians shall not be permitted upon any vehicular crossing, unless unobstructed sidewalks of more than three feet in width are constructed and maintained and signs indicating that pedestrians are permitted are in place. *(Stats.1959, c. 3, p. 1712, § 23331.)*

Cross References

Pedestrian defined, see Vehicle Code § 467.
Sidewalk defined, see Vehicle Code § 555.

§ 23332. Trespass prohibited

It is unlawful for any person to be upon any portion of a vehicular crossing which is not intended for public use without the permission of the Department of Transportation. This section does not apply to a person engaged in the operation, maintenance, or repair of a vehicular crossing or any facility thereon nor to any person attempting to effect a rescue. *(Stats.1959, c. 3, p. 1712, § 23332. Amended by Stats.1974, c. 545, p. 1334, § 229.)*

Cross References

Procedure on arrest for violation of this section, see Vehicle Code § 40303.
Violation as misdemeanor, punishment, see Vehicle Code §§ 40000.15, 42001.

§ 23333. Stopping and parking

No vehicle shall stop, stand, or be parked in or upon any vehicular crossing except:

(a) When necessary to avoid injury or damage to persons or property.

(b) When necessary for the repair, maintenance or operation of a publicly owned toll bridge.

(c) In compliance with the direction of a member of the California Highway Patrol or an employee of the Department of Transportation who is a peace officer or with the direction of a sign or signal.

(d) In such places as may be designated by the Director of Transportation. *(Stats.1959, c. 3, p. 1713, § 23333. Amended by Stats.1974, c. 545, p. 1335, § 230.)*

Cross References

Stopping, standing or parking, generally, see Vehicle Code § 22500 et seq.

§ 23334. Adoption of traffic rules

The Department of Transportation may adopt rules and regulations not inconsistent with this chapter for the control of traffic on any vehicular crossing to aid and insure the safe and orderly flow of traffic, and shall, so far as practicable, notify the public of the rules and regulations by signs on the vehicular crossing. *(Stats.1959, c. 3, p. 1713, § 23334. Amended by Stats.1974, c. 545, p. 1335, § 231.)*

§ 23335. Publication of traffic rules

The Department of Transportation shall cause to be published and made available to the public at the toll gates of each vehicular crossing copies of those traffic laws and rules and regulations particularly applicable thereto. *(Stats.1959, c. 3, p. 1713, § 23335. Amended by Stats.1974, c. 545, p. 1335, § 232.)*

§ 23336. Violation of rules and regulations

It is unlawful to violate any rules or regulations adopted under Section 23334, notice of which has been given either by a sign on a vehicular crossing or by publication as provided in Section 23335. *(Stats.1959, c. 3, p. 1713, § 23336.)*

Cross References

Violations, punishment, see Vehicle Code § 42001 et seq.

§ 23337. Renumbered § 23128 and amended by Stats. 1971, c. 438, p. 909, § 194, operative May 3, 1972

CHAPTER 14. PARKWAYS [REPEALED]

§§ 23340 to 23343. Repealed by Stats.1982, c. 681, p. 2812, § 86

Division 11.5

SENTENCING FOR DRIVING WHILE UNDER THE INFLUENCE

Chapter	Section
1. Court-Imposed Penalties: Persons Less Than 21 Years of Age	23500
2. Court Penalties	23530
3. Probation	23600
4. Procedures	23610
5. Ignition Interlock Devices	23700

Cross References

Juvenile court, option of not requiring a mandatory appearance for infractions contained in the Vehicle Code, exception for infractions specified in this Division, see Penal Code § 853.6a.

CHAPTER 1. COURT–IMPOSED PENALTIES: PERSONS LESS THAN 21 YEARS OF AGE

Article	Section
1. General Provisions	23500
2. Penalties for a Violation of Section 23140	23502
3. Youthful Drunk Driver Visitation Program	23509
4. Penalties for a Violation of Section 23152 or 23153	23520

ARTICLE 1. GENERAL PROVISIONS

Section
23500. Application of chapter.

§ 23500. Application of chapter

This chapter applies to the imposition of penalties and sanctions by the courts on persons who were less than 21 years of age at the time of the commission of the driving while under the influence offenses described in Chapter 12 (commencing with Section 23100) of Division 11. *(Added by Stats.1998, c. 118 (S.B.1186), § 84, operative July 1, 1999.)*

ARTICLE 2. PENALTIES FOR A VIOLATION OF SECTION 23140

Section
23502. Driving-under-the-influence program; required attendance.
23504 to 23508. Repealed.

§ 23502. Driving-under-the-influence program; required attendance

(a) Notwithstanding any other provision of law, if a person who is at least 18 years of age is convicted of a first violation of Section 23140, in addition to any penalties, the court shall order the person to attend a program licensed under Section 11836 of the Health and Safety Code, subject to a fee schedule developed under paragraph (2) of subdivision (b) of Section 11837.4 of the Health and Safety Code.

(b) The attendance in a licensed driving-under-the-influence program required under subdivision (a) shall be as follows:

(1) If, within 10 years of the current violation of Section 23140, the person has not been convicted of a separate violation of Section 23140, 23152, or 23153, or of Section 23103, with a plea of guilty under Section 23103.5, or of Section 655 of the Harbors and Navigation Code, or of Section 191.5 of, or subdivision (a) of Section 192.5 of, the Penal Code, the person shall complete, at a minimum, the education component of that licensed driving-under-the-influence program.

(2) If the person does not meet the requirements of paragraph (1), the person shall complete, at a minimum, the program described in paragraph (1) of subdivision (c) of Section 11837 of the Health and Safety Code.

(c) The person's privilege to operate a motor vehicle shall be suspended by the department as required under Section 13352.6, and the court shall require the person to surrender his or her driver's license to the court in accordance with Section 13550.

(d) The court shall advise the person at the time of sentencing that the driving privilege will not be restored until the person has provided the department with proof satisfactory to the department that the person has successfully completed the driving-under-the-influence program required under this section. *(Added by Stats.2000, c. 1063 (A.B.803), § 4. Amended by Stats.2004, c. 550 (S.B.1694), § 12; Stats.2007, c. 747 (A.B.678), § 32.)*

§§ 23504 to 23508. Repealed by Stats.2000, c. 1063 (A.B.803), § 3

ARTICLE 3. YOUTHFUL DRUNK DRIVER VISITATION PROGRAM

Section
23509. Short title of article.
23510. Legislative findings and declarations.
23512. Program.
23514. Violation of specified alcohol related offenses; participation in program as term and condition of probation; age preference; abstinence requirement.
23516. Suitability of defendant or ward; appropriateness of program.
23517. Supervised visitations; places to visit; coordination through substance abuse counselors; counseling sessions; termination.

Section
23518.   Personal conference or written report or letter after visitation.
23518.5.   Civil immunity.

§ 23509. Short title of article

This article shall be known and may be cited as the "Youthful Drunk Driver Visitation Program Act." *(Added by Stats.1998, c. 118 (S.B.1186), § 84, operative July 1, 1999.)*

§ 23510. Legislative findings and declarations

The Legislature finds and declares all of the following:

(a) Young drivers often do not realize the consequences of drinking alcohol or ingesting any other drugs, whether legal or not, and driving a motor vehicle while their physical capabilities to drive safely are impaired by those substances.

(b) Young drivers who use alcohol or other drugs are likely to become dependent on those substances and prompt intervention is needed to protect other persons, as well as the young driver, from death or serious injury.

(c) The conviction of a young driver for driving under the influence of an alcoholic beverage, a drug, or both, identifies that person as a risk to the health and safety of others, as well as that young driver, because of the young driver's inability to control his or her conduct.

(d) It has been demonstrated that close observation of the effects on others of alcohol and other drugs, both chronic and acute, by a young driver convicted of driving under the influence has a marked effect on recidivism and should therefore be encouraged by the courts, prehospital emergency medical care personnel, and other officials charged with cleaning up the carnage and wreckage caused by drunk drivers.

(e) The program prescribed in this article provides guidelines for the operation of an intensive program to discourage recidivism by convicted young drunk drivers. *(Added by Stats.1998, c. 118 (S.B.1186), § 84, operative July 1, 1999.)*

§ 23512. Program

For the purposes of this article, "program" means the Youthful Drunk Driver Visitation Program prescribed in this article. *(Added by Stats.1998, c. 118 (S.B.1186), § 84, operative July 1, 1999.)*

§ 23514. Violation of specified alcohol related offenses; participation in program as term and condition of probation; age preference; abstinence requirement

(a) If a person is found to be in violation of Section 23140, is convicted of, or is adjudged a ward of the juvenile court for, a violation of Section 21200.5, 23140, or 23152 punishable under Section 23536, or Section 23220, 23221, or 23222, subdivision (a) or (b) of Section 23224, or Section 23225 or 23226, and is granted probation, the court may order, with the consent of the defendant or ward, as a term and condition of probation

in addition to any other term and condition required or authorized by law, that the defendant or ward participate in the program.

(b) The court shall give preference for participation in the program to defendants or wards who were less than 21 years of age at the time of the offense if the facilities of the program in the jurisdiction are limited to fewer than the number of defendants or wards eligible and consenting to participate.

(c) The court shall require that the defendant or ward not drink any alcoholic beverage at all before reaching the age of 21 years and not use illegal drugs. *(Added by Stats.1998, c. 118 (S.B.1186), § 84, operative July 1, 1999.)*

§ 23516. Suitability of defendant or ward; appropriateness of program

The court shall investigate and consult with the defendant or ward, defendant's or ward's counsel, if any, and any proposed supervisor of a visitation under the program, and the court may consult with any other person whom the court finds may be of value, including, but not limited to, the defendant's or ward's parents or other family members, in order to ascertain that the defendant or ward is suitable for the program, that the visitation will be educational and meaningful to the defendant or ward, and that there are no physical, emotional, or mental reasons to believe the program would not be appropriate or would cause any injury to the defendant or ward. *(Added by Stats.1998, c. 118 (S.B.1186), § 84, operative July 1, 1999.)*

§ 23517. Supervised visitations; places to visit; coordination through substance abuse counselors; counseling sessions; termination

(a) To the extent that personnel and facilities are made available to the court, the court may include a requirement for supervised visitation by the defendant or ward to all, or any, of the following:

(1) A trauma facility, as defined in Section 1798.160 of the Health and Safety Code, a base hospital designated pursuant to Section 1798.100 or 1798.101 of the Health and Safety Code, or a general acute care hospital having a basic emergency medical services special permit issued pursuant to subdivision (c) of Section 1277 of the Health and Safety Code that regularly receives victims of vehicle accidents, between the hours of 10 p.m. and 2 a.m. on a Friday or Saturday night to observe appropriate victims of vehicle accidents involving drinking drivers, under the supervision of any of the following:

(A) A registered nurse trained in providing emergency trauma care or prehospital advanced life support.

(B) An emergency room physician.

(C) An emergency medical technician-paramedic or an emergency medical technician II.

(2) A facility that cares for advanced alcoholics, such as a chemical dependency recovery hospital, as defined in Section 1250.3 of the Health and Safety Code, to observe

persons in the terminal stages of alcoholism or drug abuse, under the supervision of appropriately licensed medical personnel.

(3) If approved by the county coroner, the county coroner's office or the county morgue to observe appropriate victims of vehicle accidents involving drinking drivers, under the supervision of the coroner or a deputy coroner.

(b) As used in this section, "appropriate victims" means victims whose condition is determined by the visitation supervisor to demonstrate the results of accidents involving drinking drivers without being excessively gruesome or traumatic to the probationer.

(c) If persons trained in counseling or substance abuse are made available to the court, the court may coordinate the visitation program or the visitations at any facility designated in subdivision (a) through those persons.

(d) Any visitation shall include, before any observation of victims or disabled persons by the probationer, a comprehensive counseling session with the visitation supervisor at which the supervisor shall explain and discuss the experiences which may be encountered during the visitation in order to ascertain whether the visitation is appropriate for the probationer.

(e) If at any time, whether before or during a visitation, the supervisor of the probationer determines that the visitation may be or is traumatic or otherwise inappropriate for the probationer, or is uncertain whether the visitation may be traumatic or inappropriate, the visitation shall be terminated without prejudice to the probationer. *(Added by Stats.1998, c. 118 (S.B.1186), § 84, operative July 1, 1999.)*

§ 23518. Personal conference or written report or letter after visitation

(a) The program may include a personal conference after the visitations described in Section 23517 between the sentencing judge or judicial officer or the person responsible for coordinating the program for the judicial district and the probationer, his or her counsel, and, if available, the probationer's parents to discuss the experiences of the visitation and how those experiences may impact the probationer's future conduct.

(b) If a personal conference described in subdivision (a) is not practicable, because of the probationer's absence from the jurisdiction, conflicting time schedules, or other reasons, the program should provide for a written report or letter by the probationer to the court discussing the experiences and their impact on the probationer. *(Added by Stats.1998, c. 118 (S.B.1186), § 84, operative July 1, 1999.)*

§ 23518.5. Civil immunity

The county, a court, any facility visited pursuant to the program, the agents, employees, or independent contractors of the court, county, or facility visited pursuant to the program, and any person supervising a probationer during the visitation, is not liable for any civil damages resulting from injury to the probationer, or civil damages caused by the probationer, during, or from any activities relating to, the visitation, except for willful or grossly negligent acts intended to, or reasonably expected to result in, that injury or damage and except for workers' compensation for the probationer as prescribed by law if the probationer performs community service at the facility as an additional term or condition of probation. *(Added by Stats.1998, c. 118 (S.B.1186), § 84, operative July 1, 1999.)*

ARTICLE 4. PENALTIES FOR A VIOLATION OF SECTION 23152 OR 23153

Section
23520. Juvenile offenders; first drug or alcohol offense; alcohol or drug education program requirement; expenses and fees; waiver; application of section.
23521. Finding of another jurisdiction as conviction of violation of §§ 23152 and 23153.
23522. Repealed.
23524. Repealed.

§ 23520. Juvenile offenders; first drug or alcohol offense; alcohol or drug education program requirement; expenses and fees; waiver; application of section

(a) Whenever, in any county specified in subdivision (b), a judge of a juvenile court, a juvenile hearing officer, or referee of a juvenile court finds that a person has committed a first violation of Section 23152 or 23153, the person shall be required to participate in and successfully complete an alcohol or drug education program, or both of those programs, as designated by the court. The expense of the person's attendance in the program shall be paid by the person's parents or guardian so long as the person is under the age of 18 years, and shall be paid by the person thereafter. However, in approving the program, each county shall require the program to provide for the payment of the fee for the program in installments by any person who cannot afford to pay the full fee at the commencement of the program and shall require the program to provide for the waiver of the fee for any person who is indigent, as determined by criteria for indigency established by the board of supervisors. Whenever it can be done without substantial additional cost, each county shall require that the program be provided for juveniles at a separate location from, or at a different time of day than, alcohol and drug education programs for adults.

(b) This section applies only in those counties that have one or more alcohol or drug education programs certified by the county alcohol program administrator and approved by the board of supervisors. *(Added by Stats. 1998, c. 118 (S.B.1186), § 84, operative July 1, 1999. Amended by Stats.2003, c. 149 (S.B.79), § 85.)*

Subdivision (a) of Section 23520 is amended to reflect the redesignation of traffic hearing officers as juvenile hearing officers. See 1997 Cal. Stat. ch. 679. [33 Cal.L.Rev.Comm. Reports 259 (2003)].

§ 23521. Finding of another jurisdiction as conviction of violation of §§ 23152 and 23153

(a) Any finding of a juvenile court judge, juvenile hearing officer, or referee of a juvenile court of a commission of an offense in any state, territory, possession of the United States, the District of Columbia, the Commonwealth of Puerto Rico, or the Dominion of Canada that, if committed in this state, would be a violation of Section 23152, is a conviction of a violation of Section 23152 for the purposes of Sections 13352, 13352.3, 13352.4, and 13352.5, and the finding of a juvenile court judge, juvenile hearing officer, or referee of a juvenile court of a commission of an offense that, if committed in this state, would be a violation of Section 23153 is a conviction of a violation of Section 23153 for the purposes of Sections 13352 and 13352.3.

(b) This section shall become operative on September 20, 2005. *(Added by Stats.1998, c. 118 (S.B.1186), § 84, operative July 1, 1999. Amended by Stats.2002, c. 545 (S.B.1852), § 18; Stats.2003, c. 149 (S.B.79), § 86; Stats. 2004, c. 551 (S.B.1697), § 14, operative Sept. 20, 2005.)*

Section 23521 is amended to reflect the redesignation of traffic hearing officers as juvenile hearing officers. See 1997 Cal. Stat. ch. 679. [33 Cal.L.Rev.Comm. Reports 259 (2003)].

§ 23522. Repealed by Stats.1999, c. 22 (S.B.24), § 35, eff. May 26, 1999, operative July 1, 1999

§ 23524. Repealed by Stats.1999, c. 22 (S.B.24), § 35.2, eff. May 26, 1999, operative July 1, 1999

CHAPTER 2. COURT PENALTIES

Article	Section
1. General Provisions	23530
2. Penalties for a Violation of Section 23152	23536
3. Penalties for a Violation of Section 23153	23554
4. Additional Punishments	23572
5. Additional Penalties and Sanctions	23575
6. Additional Court-Imposed Orders and Directions	23590
7. Alternative to Alcohol or Drug Education Program	23598

ARTICLE 1. GENERAL PROVISIONS

Section
23530. Application of chapter.

§ 23530. Application of chapter

This chapter applies to the imposition of penalties, sanctions, and probation upon persons convicted of violating driving while under the influence offenses that are set forth in Chapter 12 (commencing with Section 23100) of Division 11. *(Added by Stats.1998, c. 118 (S.B.1186), § 84, operative July 1, 1999.)*

ARTICLE 2. PENALTIES FOR A VIOLATION OF SECTION 23152

Section
23536.   Conviction of first violation of § 23152; punishment.
23538.   Conditions of probation for first time offense.
23540.   Second offense; punishment.
23542.   Conditions of probation for second offense.
23546.   Third offense; punishment.
23548.   Conditions of probation for third offense.
23550.   Multiple offenses within 10 years; punishment; habitual traffic offender designation.
23550.5. Additional public offense for multiple driving under the influence violations within 10 years; punishment; habitual traffic offender designation.
23552.   Additional conditions of probation for multiple offenses; condition upon restoration of driving privilege.

§ 23536. Conviction of first violation of § 23152; punishment

(a) If a person is convicted of a first violation of Section 23152, that person shall be punished by imprisonment in the county jail for not less than 96 hours, at least 48 hours of which shall be continuous, nor more than six months, and by a fine of not less than three hundred ninety dollars ($390), nor more than one thousand dollars ($1,000).

(b) The court shall order that a person punished under subdivision (a), who is to be punished by imprisonment in the county jail, be imprisoned on days other than days of regular employment of the person, as determined by the court. If the court determines that 48 hours of continuous imprisonment would interfere with the person's work schedule, the court shall allow the person to serve the imprisonment whenever the person is normally scheduled for time off from work. The court may make this determination based upon a representation from the defendant's attorney or upon an affidavit or testimony from the defendant.

(c) The person's privilege to operate a motor vehicle shall be suspended by the department under paragraph (1) of subdivision (a) of Section 13352 or Section 13352.1. The court shall require the person to surrender the driver's license to the court in accordance with Section 13550.

(d) Whenever, when considering the circumstances taken as a whole, the court determines that the person punished under this section would present a traffic safety or public safety risk if authorized to operate a motor vehicle during the period of suspension imposed under paragraph (1) of subdivision (a) of Section 13352 or Section 13352.1, the court may disallow the issuance of a restricted driver's license required under Section 13352.4.

(Formerly § 23160, added by Stats.1981, c. 940, p. 3571, § 32. Amended by Stats.1982, c. 53, p. 174, § 29, eff. Feb. 18, 1982; Stats.1982, c. 331, p. 1632, § 4, eff. June 30, 1982; Stats.1982, c. 1339, § 15, eff. Sept. 24, 1982; Stats.1984, c. 216, § 13; Stats.1990, c. 286 (A.B.3009), § 1; Stats.1998, c. 756 (A.B.762), § 11, operative July 1, 1999. Renumbered § 23536 and amended by Stats.1999, c. 22 (S.B.24), § 19, eff. May 26, 1999, operative July 1, 1999. Amended by Stats.2002, c. 545 (S.B.1852), § 19; Stats. 2004, c. 551 (S.B.1697), § 15, operative Sept. 20, 2005; Stats.2006, c. 692 (S.B.1756), § 5.)

Cross References

Alcohol and drug problem assessment program, violator participation, sentencing, and assessment upon fine, see Vehicle Code § 23646 et seq.

Alcoholic beverages in vehicles, see Vehicle Code § 23220 et seq.

Applicability of this section to trolley coaches, see Vehicle Code § 21051.

Arrest without warrant, see Vehicle Code § 40300.5.

Challenging constitutional validity of separate conviction, see Vehicle Code § 41403.

Chemical blood, breath or urine tests, see Vehicle Code §§ 13353, 13354.

Chemical tests as evidence, see Vehicle Code § 23610.

Conviction of violation of specified subdivisions of Penal Code § 192 to be deemed conviction of violation of specified DUI provisions, see Vehicle Code § 13350.5.

Coroner's inquiry into deaths, see Government Code § 27491.25.

County alcohol and drug problem assessment programs; mandatory participation for convicted violators of this section, see Vehicle Code §§ 23646, 23647.

Crime of violence, within act for indemnification of victims of crime, see Government Code § 13960.

Defense of drug use to violations, see Vehicle Code § 23630.

Deposit in special account for each conviction under DUI provisions, see Penal Code § 1463.14.

Drivers license revocation, conviction of driver under eighteen, see Vehicle Code § 13352.3.

Driving school or instructor, revocation or suspension of license for violation of this section, see Vehicle Code § 11110.

Gross vehicular manslaughter while intoxicated, see Penal Code § 191.5.

Guilty plea, see Vehicle Code § 41610.

Impoundment of vehicle of registered owner convicted under this section, see Vehicle Code § 23594.

Influence of alcoholic beverage or drug, suspension or revocation of driving privileges, see Vehicle Code § 13352.

Injury to guest by intoxicated driver, see Vehicle Code § 17158.

Juvenile offenders, programs of supervision, see Welfare and Institutions Code § 654.1.

Juveniles with blood-alcohol concentrations of 0.05 or more, driving violations, participation in rehabilitation programs, see Vehicle Code § 23504.

Manslaughter, negligent homicide by vehicle, see Penal Code § 192.

Nuisance, sale or other disposition of motor vehicle driven by defendant, see Vehicle Code § 23596.

Persons certified or granted probation on conviction of driving under the influence of alcohol or drugs or combined influence on certain conditions, restriction, revocation or suspension of driving privilege, consent to participation in treatment program, see Vehicle Code § 13352.5.

Please Don't Drink and Drive memorial signs, requests for and duration of placement, exception for a party to an accident convicted or determined to be mentally incompetent under this section, see Streets and Highways Code § 101.10.

Presentence investigation and assessment, see Vehicle Code § 23655.

Presumptions, see Evidence Code § 600 et seq.

Prior convictions under sections 23103, 23152 or 23153, effect on sentencing and driving privileges, see Vehicle Code § 23622.

Procedure on arrest for violation of this section, see Vehicle Code § 40302.

Records available to courts and law enforcement officials, incidents under certain DWI and homicide laws, period of time records must be available, see Vehicle Code § 1808.

Refusal to submit to alcohol testing under DUI laws, calculation of prior convictions, certain foreign convictions recognized, see Vehicle Code §§ 13353, 13353.1 and 13353.3.

Surrender of driver's license to court, see Vehicle Code § 13550.

Suspension or revocation of driving privilege for a violation of this section, notice by personal service, see Vehicle Code § 13106.

Suspension or revocation of license,
 Generally, see Vehicle Code § 13352.
 Alcohol-related accident within five years of vehicular manslaughter, see Vehicle Code § 13954.
 Driver license compact, see Vehicle Code § 15000 et seq.
 Driving after suspension or revocation, see Vehicle Code § 14601.2.
 Investigation by department, three convictions in three years under this or other specified statutes, see Vehicle Code § 13800.
 Prior convictions, record, see Vehicle Code § 13209.

Traffic violation point count, violation of this section, see Vehicle Code § 12810.

Traffic violators schools, suspension or revocation of license for violation of this section, see Vehicle Code § 11215.

Vehicular homicide, see Penal Code § 192.

Violation as misdemeanor, see Vehicle Code § 40000.15.

Violation of this section, relinquishment of motor vehicle to convicted minor, see Penal Code § 193.8.

Youthful drunk driver visitation program, see Vehicle Code § 23509 et seq.

§ 23538. Conditions of probation for first time offense

(a)(1) If the court grants probation to person punished under Section 23536, in addition to the provisions of Section 23600 and any other terms and conditions imposed by the court, the court shall impose as a condition of probation that the person pay a fine of at least three hundred ninety dollars ($390), but not more than one thousand dollars ($1,000). The court may also impose, as a condition of probation, that the person be confined in a county jail for at least 48 hours, but not more than six months.

(2) The person's privilege to operate a motor vehicle shall be suspended by the department under paragraph (1) of subdivision (a) of Section 13352 or Section 13352.1. The court shall require the person to surrender the

driver's license to the court in accordance with Section 13550.

(3) Whenever, when considering the circumstances taken as a whole, the court determines that the person punished under this section would present a traffic safety or public safety risk if authorized to operate a motor vehicle during the period of suspension imposed under paragraph (1) of subdivision (a) of Section 13352 or Section 13352.1, the court may disallow the issuance of a restricted driver's license required under Section 13352.4.

(b) In any county where the board of supervisors has approved, and the State Department of * * * Health Care Services has licensed, a program or programs described in Section 11837.3 of the Health and Safety Code, the court shall also impose as a condition of probation that the driver shall enroll and participate in, and successfully complete a driving-under-the- influence program, licensed pursuant to Section 11836 of the Health and Safety Code, in the driver's county of residence or employment, as designated by the court. For the purposes of this subdivision, enrollment in, participation in, and completion of an approved program shall be subsequent to the date of the current violation. Credit may not be given for any program activities completed prior to the date of the current violation.

(1) The court shall refer a first offender whose blood-alcohol concentration was less than 0.20 percent, by weight, to participate for at least three months or longer, as ordered by the court, in a licensed program that consists of at least 30 hours of program activities, including those education, group counseling, and individual interview sessions described in Chapter 9 (commencing with Section 11836) of Part 2 of Division 10.5 of the Health and Safety Code.

(2) The court shall refer a first offender whose blood-alcohol concentration was 0.20 percent or more, by weight, or who refused to take a chemical test, to participate for at least nine months or longer, as ordered by the court, in a licensed program that consists of at least 60 hours of program activities, including those education, group counseling, and individual interview sessions described in Chapter 9 (commencing with Section 11836) of Part 2 of Division 10.5 of the Health and Safety Code.

(3) The court shall advise the person at the time of sentencing that the driving privilege shall not be restored until proof satisfactory to the department of successful completion of a driving-under-the-influence program of the length required under this code that is licensed pursuant to Section 11836 of the Health and Safety Code has been received in the department's headquarters.

(c)(1) The court shall revoke the person's probation pursuant to Section 23602, except for good cause shown, for the failure to enroll in, participate in, or complete a program specified in subdivision (b).

(2) The court, in establishing reporting requirements, shall consult with the county alcohol program administrator. The county alcohol program administrator shall

758

coordinate the reporting requirements with the department and with the State Department of * * * Health Care Services. That reporting shall ensure that all persons who, after being ordered to attend and complete a program, may be identified for either (A) failure to enroll in, or failure to successfully complete, the program, or (B) successful completion of the program as ordered. *(Added by Stats.2004, c. 551 (S.B.1697), § 16.5, operative Sept. 20, 2005. Amended by Stats.2005, c. 164 (A.B.1353), § 3; Stats.2006, c. 692 (S.B.1756), § 6; Stats.2013, c. 22 (A.B.75), § 87, eff. June 27, 2013, operative July 1, 2013.)*

Cross References

County alcohol and drug problem assessment programs; mandatory participation for convicted violators of this section, see Vehicle Code § 23646.

Drug treatment programs, referral of first offenders, see Health and Safety Code § 11837.

Influence of alcoholic beverage or drug, suspension or revocation of driving privileges, see Vehicle Code § 13352.

Presentence investigation, see Vehicle Code § 23655.

§ 23540. Second offense; punishment

(a) If a person is convicted of a violation of Section 23152 and the offense occurred within 10 years of a separate violation of Section 23103, as specified in Section 23103.5, 23152, or 23153, that resulted in a conviction, that person shall be punished by imprisonment in the county jail for not less than 90 days nor more than one year and by a fine of not less than three hundred ninety dollars ($390) nor more than one thousand dollars ($1,000). The person's privilege to operate a motor vehicle shall be suspended by the department pursuant to paragraph (3) of subdivision (a) of Section 13352. The court shall require the person to surrender the driver's license to the court in accordance with Section 13550.

(b) Whenever, when considering the circumstances taken as a whole, the court determines that the person punished under this section would present a traffic safety or public safety risk if authorized to operate a motor vehicle during the period of suspension imposed under paragraph (3) of subdivision (a) of Section 13352, the court may disallow the issuance of a restricted driver's license required under Section 13352.5.

(c) This section shall become operative on September 20, 2005. *(Added by Stats.2004, c. 551 (S.B.1697), § 17.5, operative Sept. 20, 2005.)*

Cross References

Alcohol and drug problem assessment program, violator participation, sentencing, and assessment upon fine, see Vehicle Code § 23646 et seq.

Alcoholic beverages in vehicles, see Vehicle Code § 23220 et seq.

Applicability of this section to trolley coaches, see Vehicle Code § 21051.

Arrest without warrant, see Vehicle Code § 40300.5.

Challenging constitutional validity of separate conviction, see Vehicle Code § 41403.

Chemical blood, breath or urine tests, see Vehicle Code §§ 13353, 13354.

Chemical tests as evidence, see Vehicle Code § 23610.

Conviction of violation of specified subdivisions of Penal Code § 192 to be deemed conviction of violation of specified DUI provisions, see Vehicle Code § 13350.5.

Coroner's inquiry into deaths, see Government Code § 27491.25.

County alcohol and drug problem assessment programs; mandatory participation for convicted violators of this section, see Vehicle Code §§ 23646, 23647.

Crime of violence, within act for indemnification of victims of crime, see Government Code § 13960.

Defense of drug use to violations, see Vehicle Code § 23630.

Deposit in special account for each conviction under DUI provisions, see Penal Code § 1463.14.

Drivers license revocation, conviction of driver under eighteen, see Vehicle Code § 13352.3.

Driving school or instructor, revocation or suspension of license for violation of this section, see Vehicle Code § 11110.

Gross vehicular manslaughter while intoxicated, see Penal Code § 191.5.

Guilty plea, see Vehicle Code § 41610.

Impoundment of vehicle of registered owner convicted under this section, see Vehicle Code § 23594.

Influence of alcoholic beverage or drug, suspension or revocation of driving privileges, see Vehicle Code § 13352.

Injury to guest by intoxicated driver, see Vehicle Code § 17158.

Juvenile offenders, programs of supervision, see Welfare and Institutions Code § 654.1.

Juveniles with blood-alcohol concentrations of 0.05 or more, driving violations, participation in rehabilitation programs, see Vehicle Code § 23504.

Manslaughter, negligent homicide by vehicle, see Penal Code § 192.

Nuisance, sale or other disposition of motor vehicle driven by defendant, see Vehicle Code § 23596.

Persons certified or granted probation on conviction of driving under the influence of alcohol or drugs or combined influence on certain conditions, restriction, revocation or suspension of driving privilege, consent to participation in treatment program, see Vehicle Code § 13352.5.

Please Don't Drink and Drive memorial signs, requests for and duration of placement, exception for a party to an accident convicted or determined to be mentally incompetent under this section, see Streets and Highways Code § 101.10.

Presentence investigation and assessment, see Vehicle Code § 23655.

Presumptions, see Evidence Code § 600 et seq.

Prior convictions under sections 23103, 23152 or 23153, effect on sentencing and driving privileges, see Vehicle Code § 23622.

Procedure on arrest for violation of this section, see Vehicle Code § 40302.

Records available to courts and law enforcement officials, incidents under certain DWI and homicide laws, period of time records must be available, see Vehicle Code § 1808.

Refusal to submit to alcohol testing under DUI laws, calculation of prior convictions, certain foreign convictions recognized, see Vehicle Code §§ 13353, 13353.1 and 13353.3.

Restricted driver's license, application of this section, see Vehicle Code § 13352.2.

Surrender of driver's license to court, see Vehicle Code § 13550.

Suspension or revocation of driving privilege for a violation of this section, notice by personal service, see Vehicle Code § 13106.

Suspension or revocation of license,
  Generally, see Vehicle Code § 13352.

Alcohol-related accident within five years of vehicular manslaughter, see Vehicle Code § 13954.

Driver license compact, see Vehicle Code § 15000 et seq.

Driving after suspension or revocation, see Vehicle Code § 14601.2.

Investigation by department, three convictions in three years under this or other specified statutes, see Vehicle Code 13800.

Prior convictions, record, see Vehicle Code § 13209.

Traffic violation point count, violation of this section, see Vehicle Code § 12810.

Traffic violators schools, suspension or revocation of license for violation of this section, see Vehicle Code § 11215.

Vehicular homicide, see Penal Code § 192.

Violation as misdemeanor, see Vehicle Code § 40000.15.

Violation of this section, relinquishment of motor vehicle to convicted minor, see Penal Code § 193.8.

Youthful drunk driver visitation program, see Vehicle Code § 23509 et seq.

§ 23542. Conditions of probation for second offense

(a)(1) If the court grants probation to a person punished under Section 23540, in addition to the provisions of Section 23600 and any other terms and conditions imposed by the court, the court shall impose as conditions of probation that the person be confined in county jail and fined under either of the following:

(A) For at least 10 days, but not more than one year, and pay a fine of at least three hundred ninety dollars ($390), but not more than one thousand dollars ($1,000).

(B) For at least 96 hours, but not more than one year, and pay a fine of at least three hundred ninety dollars ($390), but not more than one thousand dollars ($1,000). A sentence of 96 hours of confinement shall be served in two increments consisting of a continuous 48 hours each. The two 48–hour increments may be served nonconsecutively.

(2) The person's privilege to operate a motor vehicle shall be suspended by the department under paragraph (3) of subdivision (a) of Section 13352. The court shall require the person to surrender the driver's license to the court in accordance with Section 13550.

(b) In addition to the conditions specified in subdivision (a), the court shall require the person to do either of the following:

(1) Enroll and participate, for at least 18 months subsequent to the date of the underlying violation and in a manner satisfactory to the court, in a driving-under-the-influence program licensed pursuant to Section 11836 of the Health and Safety Code, as designated by the court. The person shall complete the entire program subsequent to, and shall not be given any credit for any program activities completed prior to, the date of the current violation. The program shall provide for persons who cannot afford the program fee pursuant to paragraph (2) of subdivision (b) of Section 11837.4 of the Health and Safety Code in order to enable those persons to participate.

759

(2) Enroll and participate, for at least 30 months subsequent to the date of the underlying violation and in a manner satisfactory to the court, in a driving-under-the-influence program licensed pursuant to Section 11836 of the Health and Safety Code. The person shall complete the entire program subsequent to, and shall not be given any credit for any program activities completed prior to, the date of the current violation.

(c) The court shall advise the person at the time of sentencing that the driving privilege shall not be restored until proof satisfactory to the Department of Motor Vehicles of successful completion of a driving-under-the-influence program of the length required under this code licensed pursuant to Section 11836 of the Health and Safety Code has been received in the department's headquarters.

(d) Whenever, when considering the circumstances taken as a whole, the court determines that the person punished under this section would present a traffic safety or public safety risk if authorized to operate a motor vehicle during the period of suspension imposed under paragraph (3) of subdivision (a) of Section 13352, the court may disallow the issuance of a restricted driver's license required under Section 13352.5.

(e) This section shall become operative on September 20, 2005. *(Added by Stats.2004, c. 551 (S.B.1697), § 18.5, operative Sept. 20, 2005.)*

Cross References

Persons certified or granted probation on conviction or driving under the influence of alcohol or drugs or combined influence on certain conditions, restriction, revocation or suspension of driving privilege, consent to participation in treatment program, see Vehicle Code § 13352.5.
Presentence investigation, see Vehicle Code § 23655.
Restricted driver's license, application of this section, see Vehicle Code § 13352.2.

§ 23544. Editorial Note

Stats.1998, c. 118 (S.B.1186), provided for repeal of § 23167 and addition of this similar section. Stats.1998, c. 756 (A.B.762), § 14 re-pealed § 23167, operative July 1, 1999. Section affected by two or more acts at the same session of the legislature, see Government Code § 9605.

§ 23546. Third offense; punishment

(a) If a person is convicted of a violation of Section 23152 and the offense occurred within 10 years of two separate violations of Section 23103, as specified in Section 23103.5, 23152, or 23153, or any combination thereof, that resulted in convictions, that person shall be punished by imprisonment in the county jail for not less than 120 days nor more than one year and by a fine of not less than three hundred ninety dollars ($390) nor more than one thousand dollars ($1,000). The person's privilege to operate a motor vehicle shall be revoked by the Department of Motor Vehicles as required in paragraph (5) of subdivision (a) of Section 13352. The court shall

require the person to surrender his or her driver's license to the court in accordance with Section 13550.

(b) A person convicted of a violation of Section 23152 punishable under this section shall be designated as a habitual traffic offender for a period of three years, subsequent to the conviction. The person shall be advised of this designation pursuant to subdivision (b) of Section 13350. *(Added by Stats.1998, c. 118 (S.B.1186), § 84, operative July 1, 1999. Amended by Stats.1999, c. 22 (S.B.24), § 34, eff. May 26, 1999, operative July 1, 1999; Stats.2002, c. 545 (S.B.1852), § 23; Stats.2004, c. 550 (S.B.1694), § 14.)*

Cross References

Alcohol and drug problem assessment program, violator participation, sentencing, and assessment upon fine, see Vehicle Code § 23646 et seq.
Alcoholic beverages in vehicles, see Vehicle Code § 23220 et seq.
Applicability of this section to trolley coaches, see Vehicle Code § 21051.
Arrest without warrant, see Vehicle Code § 40300.5.
Challenging constitutional validity of separate conviction, see Vehicle Code § 41403.
Chemical blood, breath or urine tests, see Vehicle Code §§ 13353, 13354.
Chemical tests as evidence, see Vehicle Code § 23610.
Conviction of violation of specified subdivisions of Penal Code § 192 to be deemed conviction of violation of specified DUI provisions, see Vehicle Code § 13350.5.
Coroner's inquiry into deaths, see Government Code § 27491.25.
County alcohol and drug problem assessment programs; mandatory participation for convicted violators of this section, see Vehicle Code §§ 23646, 23647.
Crime of violence, within act for indemnification of victims of crime, see Government Code § 13960.
Defense of drug use to violations, see Vehicle Code § 23630.
Deposit in special account for each conviction under DUI provisions, see Penal Code § 1463.14.
Drivers license revocation, conviction of driver under eighteen, see Vehicle Code § 13352.3.
Driving school or instructor, revocation or suspension of license for violation of this section, see Vehicle Code § 11110.
Gross vehicular manslaughter while intoxicated, see Penal Code § 191.5.
Guilty plea, see Vehicle Code § 41610.
Impoundment of vehicle of registered owner convicted under this section, see Vehicle Code § 23594.
Influence of alcoholic beverage or drug, suspension or revocation of driving privileges, see Vehicle Code § 13352.
Injury to guest by intoxicated driver, see Vehicle Code § 17158.
Juvenile offenders, programs of supervision, see Welfare and Institutions Code § 654.1.
Juveniles with blood-alcohol concentrations of 0.05 or more, driving violations, participation in rehabilitation programs, see Vehicle Code § 23504.
Manslaughter, negligent homicide by vehicle, see Penal Code § 192.
Nuisance, sale or other disposition of motor vehicle driven by defendant, see Vehicle Code § 23596.

Persons certified or granted probation on conviction of driving under the influence of alcohol or drugs or combined influence on certain conditions, restriction, revocation or suspension of driving privilege, consent to participation in treatment program, see Vehicle Code § 13352.5.

Please Don't Drink and Drive memorial signs, requests for and duration of placement, exception for a party to an accident convicted or determined to be mentally incompetent under this section, see Streets and Highways Code § 101.10.

Presentence investigation and assessment, see Vehicle Code § 23655.

Presumptions, see Evidence Code § 600 et seq.

Prior convictions under sections 23103, 23152 or 23153, effect on sentencing and driving privileges, see Vehicle Code § 23622.

Procedure on arrest for violation of this section, see Vehicle Code § 40302.

Records available to courts and law enforcement officials, incidents under certain DWI and homicide laws, period of time records must be available, see Vehicle Code § 1808.

Refusal to submit to alcohol testing under DUI laws, calculation of prior convictions, certain foreign convictions recognized, see Vehicle Code §§ 13353, 13353.1 and 13353.3.

Surrender of driver's license to court, see Vehicle Code § 13550.

Suspension or revocation of driving privilege for a violation of this section, notice by personal service, see Vehicle Code § 13106.

Suspension or revocation of license,

Generally, see Vehicle Code § 13352.

Alcohol-related accident within five years of vehicular manslaughter, see Vehicle Code § 13954.

Driver license compact, see Vehicle Code § 15000 et seq.

Driving after suspension or revocation, see Vehicle Code § 14601.2.

Investigation by department, three convictions in three years under this or other specified statutes, see Vehicle Code 13800.

Prior convictions, record, see Vehicle Code § 13209.

Traffic violation point count, violation of this section, see Vehicle Code § 12810.

Traffic violators schools, suspension or revocation of license for violation of this section, see Vehicle Code § 11215.

Vehicular homicide, see Penal Code § 192.

Violation as misdemeanor, see Vehicle Code § 40000.15.

Violation of this section, relinquishment of motor vehicle to convicted minor, see Penal Code § 193.8.

Youthful drunk driver visitation program, see Vehicle Code § 23509 et seq.

§ 23548. Conditions of probation for third offense

(a)(1) If the court grants probation to any person punished under Section 23546, in addition to the provisions of Section 23600 and any other terms and conditions imposed by the court, the court shall impose as conditions of probation that the person be confined in the county jail for at least 120 days but not more than one year and pay a fine of at least three hundred ninety dollars ($390) but not more than one thousand dollars ($1,000).

(2) The person's privilege to operate a motor vehicle shall be revoked by the department under paragraph (5) of subdivision (a) of Section 13352. The court shall require the person to surrender the driver's license to the court in accordance with Section 13550.

(b) In addition to subdivision (a), if the court grants probation to any person punished under Section 23546, the court may order as a condition of probation that the person participate, for at least 30 months subsequent to the underlying conviction and in a manner satisfactory to the court, in a driving-under-the-influence program licensed pursuant to Section 11836 of the Health and Safety Code. In lieu of the minimum term of imprisonment specified in subdivision (a), the court shall impose as a condition of probation under this subdivision that the person be confined in the county jail for at least 30 days but not more than one year. The court shall not order the treatment prescribed by this subdivision unless the person makes a specific request and shows good cause for the order, whether or not the person has previously completed a treatment program pursuant to paragraph (4) of subdivision (b) of Section 23542 or paragraph (4) of subdivision (b) of Section 23562. In order to enable all required persons to participate, each person shall pay the program costs commensurate with the person's ability to pay as determined pursuant to Section 11837.4 of the Health and Safety Code. No condition of probation required pursuant to this subdivision is a basis for reducing any other probation requirement in this section or Section 23600 or for avoiding the mandatory license revocation provisions of paragraph (5) of subdivision (a) of Section 13352.

(c) In addition to the provisions of Section 23600 and subdivision (a), if the court grants probation to any person punished under Section 23546 who has not previously completed a treatment program pursuant to paragraph (4) of subdivision (b) of Section 23542 or paragraph (4) of subdivision (b) of Section 23562, and unless the person is ordered to participate in and complete a driving-under-the-influence program under subdivision (b), the court shall impose as a condition of probation that the person, subsequent to the date of the current violation, enroll and participate, for at least 18 months and in a manner satisfactory to the court, in a driving-under-the-influence program licensed pursuant to Section 11836 of the Health and Safety Code, as designated by the court. The person shall complete the entire program subsequent to, and shall not be given any credit for program activities completed prior to, the date of the current violation. Any person who has previously completed a 12-month or 18-month program licensed pursuant to Section 11836 of the Health and Safety Code shall not be eligible for referral pursuant to this subdivision unless a 30-month licensed driving-under-the-influence program is not available for referral in the county of the person's residence or employment. The program shall provide for persons who cannot afford the program fee pursuant to paragraph (2) of subdivision (b) of Section 11837.4 of the Health and Safety Code in order to enable those persons to participate. No condition of probation required pursuant to this subdivision is a basis for reducing any other probation requirement in this section or Section 23600 or for avoiding the mandatory license revocation provisions of paragraph (5) of subdivision (a) of Section 13352.

(d) The court shall advise the person at the time of sentencing that the driving privilege may not be restored until the person provides proof satisfactory to the department of successful completion of a driving-under-the-influence program of the length required under this code that is licensed pursuant to Section 11836 of the Health and Safety Code.

(e) This section shall become operative on September 20, 2005. *(Added by Stats.1998, c. 118 (S.B.1186), § 84, operative July 1, 1999. Amended by Stats.2002, c. 545 (S.B.1852), § 24; Stats.2004, c. 551 (S.B.1697), § 19, operative Sept. 20, 2005.)*

Cross References

Conviction for driving under the influence or engaging in speed contests or exhibitions of speed, suspension or revocation of license, eligibility for restricted license, reinstatement conditions, see Vehicle Code § 13352.

§ 23550. Multiple offenses within 10 years; punishment; habitual traffic offender designation

(a) If a person is convicted of a violation of Section 23152 and the offense occurred within 10 years of three or more separate violations of Section 23103, as specified in Section 23103.5, or Section 23152 or 23153, or any combination thereof, that resulted in convictions, that person shall be punished by imprisonment pursuant to subdivision (h) of Section 1170 of the Penal Code, or in a county jail for not less than 180 days nor more than one year, and by a fine of not less than three hundred ninety dollars ($390) nor more than one thousand dollars ($1,000). The person's privilege to operate a motor vehicle shall be revoked by the Department of Motor Vehicles pursuant to paragraph (7) of subdivision (a) of Section 13352. The court shall require the person to surrender the driver's license to the court in accordance with Section 13550.

(b) A person convicted of a violation of Section 23152 punishable under this section shall be designated as a habitual traffic offender for a period of three years, subsequent to the conviction. The person shall be advised of this designation pursuant to subdivision (b) of Section 13350. *(Added by Stats.1998, c. 118 (S.B.1186), § 84, operative July 1, 1999. Amended by Stats.1999, c. 22 (S.B.24), § 34.2, eff. May 26, 1999, operative July 1, 1999; Stats.2002, c. 545 (S.B.1852), § 25; Stats.2004, c. 550 (S.B.1694), § 15; Stats.2009, c. 193 (S.B.598), § 4, operative July 1, 2010; Stats.2010, c. 301 (A.B.1601), § 3; Stats.2011, c. 15 (A.B.109), § 614, eff. April 4, 2011, operative Oct. 1, 2011.)*

Cross References

Alcohol and drug problem assessment program, violator participation, sentencing, and assessment upon fine, see Vehicle Code § 23646 et seq.
Alcoholic beverages in vehicles, see Vehicle Code § 23220 et seq.

Applicability of this section to trolley coaches, see Vehicle Code § 21051.
Arrest without warrant, see Vehicle Code § 40300.5.
Challenging constitutional validity of separate conviction, see Vehicle Code § 41403.
Chemical blood, breath or urine tests, see Vehicle Code §§ 13353, 13354.
Chemical tests as evidence, see Vehicle Code § 23610.
Conviction of violation of specified subdivisions of Penal Code § 192 to be deemed conviction of violation of specified DUI provisions, see Vehicle Code § 13350.5.
Coroner's inquiry into deaths, see Government Code § 27491.25.
County alcohol and drug problem assessment programs; mandatory participation for convicted violators of this section, see Vehicle Code §§ 23646, 23647.
Crime of violence, within act for indemnification of victims of crime, see Government Code § 13960.
Defense of drug use to violations, see Vehicle Code § 23630.
Deposit in special account for each conviction under DUI provisions, see Penal Code § 1463.14.
Drivers license revocation, conviction of driver under eighteen, see Vehicle Code § 13352.3.
Driving school or instructor, revocation or suspension of license for violation of this section, see Vehicle Code § 11110.
Gross vehicular manslaughter while intoxicated, see Penal Code § 191.5.
Guilty plea, see Vehicle Code § 41610.
Impoundment of vehicle of registered owner convicted under this section, see Vehicle Code § 23594.
Influence of alcoholic beverage or drug, suspension or revocation of driving privileges, see Vehicle Code § 13352.
Injury to guest by intoxicated driver, see Vehicle Code § 17158.
Juvenile offenders, programs of supervision, see Welfare and Institutions Code § 654.1.
Juveniles with blood-alcohol concentrations of 0.05 or more, driving violations, participation in rehabilitation programs, see Vehicle Code § 23504.
Manslaughter, negligent homicide by vehicle, see Penal Code § 192.
Nuisance, sale or other disposition of motor vehicle driven by defendant, see Vehicle Code § 23596.
Persons certified or granted probation on conviction of driving under the influence of alcohol or drugs or combined influence on certain conditions, restriction, revocation or suspension of driving privilege, consent to participation in treatment program, see Vehicle Code § 13352.5.
Please Don't Drink and Drive memorial signs, requests for and duration of placement, exception for a party to an accident convicted or determined to be mentally incompetent under this section, see Streets and Highways Code § 101.10.
Presentence investigation and assessment, see Vehicle Code § 23655.
Presumptions, see Evidence Code § 600 et seq.
Prior convictions under sections 23103, 23152 or 23153, effect on sentencing and driving privileges, see Vehicle Code § 23622.
Procedure on arrest for violation of this section, see Vehicle Code § 40302.
Records available to courts and law enforcement officials, incidents under certain DWI and homicide laws, period of time records must be available, see Vehicle Code § 1808.
Refusal to submit to alcohol testing under DUI laws, calculation of prior convictions, certain foreign convictions recognized, see Vehicle Code §§ 13353, 13353.1 and 13353.3.
Surrender of driver's license to court, see Vehicle Code § 13550.

Suspension or revocation of driving privilege for a violation of this section, notice by personal service, see Vehicle Code § 13106.

Suspension or revocation of license,
Generally, see Vehicle Code § 13352.
Alcohol-related accident within five years of vehicular manslaughter, see Vehicle Code § 13954.
Driver license compact, see Vehicle Code § 15000 et seq.
Driving after suspension or revocation, see Vehicle Code § 14601.2.
Investigation by department, three convictions in three years under this or other specified statutes, see Vehicle Code 13800.
Prior convictions, record, see Vehicle Code § 13209.
Traffic violation point count, violation of this section, see Vehicle Code § 12810.
Traffic violators schools, suspension or revocation of license for violation of this section, see Vehicle Code § 11215.
Vehicular homicide, see Penal Code § 192.
Violation as misdemeanor, see Vehicle Code § 40000.15.
Violation of this section, relinquishment of motor vehicle to convicted minor, see Penal Code § 193.8.
Youthful drunk driver visitation program, see Vehicle Code § 23509 et seq.

§ 23550.5. Additional public offense for multiple driving under the influence violations within 10 years; punishment; habitual traffic offender designation

(a) A person is guilty of a public offense, punishable by imprisonment in the state prison or confinement in a county jail for not more than one year and by a fine of not less than three hundred ninety dollars ($390) nor more than one thousand dollars ($1,000) if that person is convicted of a violation of Section 23152 or 23153, and the offense occurred within 10 years of any of the following:

(1) A prior violation of Section 23152 that was punished as a felony under Section 23550 or this section, or both, or under former Section 23175 or former Section 23175.5, or both.

(2) A prior violation of Section 23153 that was punished as a felony.

(3) A prior violation of paragraph (1) of subdivision (c) of Section 192 of the Penal Code that was punished as a felony.

(b) Each person who, having previously been convicted of a violation of subdivision (a) of Section 191.5 of the Penal Code, a felony violation of subdivision (b) of Section 191.5, or a violation of subdivision (a) of Section 192.5 of the Penal Code, is subsequently convicted of a violation of Section 23152 or 23153 is guilty of a public offense punishable by imprisonment in the state prison or confinement in a county jail for not more than one year and by a fine of not less than three hundred ninety dollars ($390) nor more than one thousand dollars ($1,000).

(c) The privilege to operate a motor vehicle of a person convicted of a violation that is punishable under subdivision (a) or (b) shall be revoked by the department under paragraph (7) of subdivision (a) of Section 13352, unless paragraph (6) of subdivision (a) of Section 13352 is also applicable, in which case the privilege shall be revoked under that provision. The court shall require the person to surrender the driver's license to the court in accordance with Section 13550.

(d) A person convicted of a violation of Section 23152 or 23153 that is punishable under this section shall be designated as a habitual traffic offender for a period of three years, subsequent to the conviction. The person shall be advised of this designation under subdivision (b) of Section 13350. *(Added by Stats.1998, c. 118 (S.B. 1186), § 84, operative July 1, 1999. Amended by Stats. 1999, c. 22 (S.B.24), § 34.6, eff. May 26, 1999, operative July 1, 1999; Stats.1999, c. 706 (A.B.1236), § 14, eff. Oct. 10, 1999; Stats.2001, c. 849 (A.B.1078), § 1; Stats.2002, c. 545 (S.B.1852), § 26; Stats.2007, c. 747 (A.B.678), § 33; Stats.2009, c. 193 (S.B.598), § 5, operative July 1, 2010; Stats.2010, c. 301 (A.B.1601), § 4.)*

Cross References

Alcohol and drug problem assessment program, violator participation, sentencing, and assessment upon fine, see Vehicle Code § 23646 et seq.
Alcoholic beverages in vehicles, see Vehicle Code § 23220 et seq.
Applicability of this section to trolley coaches, see Vehicle Code § 21051.
Arrest without warrant, see Vehicle Code § 40300.5.
Challenging constitutional validity of separate conviction, see Vehicle Code § 41403.
Chemical blood, breath or urine tests, see Vehicle Code §§ 13353, 13354.
Chemical tests as evidence, see Vehicle Code § 23610.
Conviction of violation of specified subdivisions of Penal Code § 192 to be deemed conviction of violation of specified DUI provisions, see Vehicle Code § 13350.5.
Coroner's inquiry into deaths, see Government Code § 27491.25.
County alcohol and drug problem assessment programs; mandatory participation for convicted violators of this section, see Vehicle Code §§ 23646, 23647.
Crime of violence, within act for indemnification of victims of crime, see Government Code § 13960.
Defense of drug use to violations, see Vehicle Code § 23630.
Deposit in special account for each conviction under DUI provisions, see Penal Code § 1463.14.
Drivers license revocation, conviction of driver under eighteen, see Vehicle Code § 13352.3.
Driving school or instructor, revocation or suspension of license for violation of this section, see Vehicle Code § 11110.
Gross vehicular manslaughter while intoxicated, see Penal Code § 191.5.
Guilty plea, see Vehicle Code § 41610.
Impoundment of vehicle of registered owner convicted under this section, see Vehicle Code § 23594.
Influence of alcoholic beverage or drug, suspension or revocation of driving privileges, see Vehicle Code § 13352.
Injury to guest by intoxicated driver, see Vehicle Code § 17158.
Juvenile offenders, programs of supervision, see Welfare and Institutions Code § 654.1.
Juveniles with blood-alcohol concentrations of 0.05 or more, driving violations, participation in rehabilitation programs, see Vehicle Code § 23504.

Manslaughter, negligent homicide by vehicle, see Penal Code § 192.

Nuisance, sale or other disposition of motor vehicle driven by defendant, see Vehicle Code § 23596.

Persons certified or granted probation on conviction of driving under the influence of alcohol or drugs or combined influence on certain conditions, restriction, revocation or suspension of driving privilege, consent to participation in treatment program, see Vehicle Code § 13352.5.

Please Don't Drink and Drive memorial signs, requests for and duration of placement, exception for a party to an accident convicted or determined to be mentally incompetent under this section, see Streets and Highways Code § 101.10.

Presentence investigation and assessment, see Vehicle Code § 23655.

Presumptions, see Evidence Code § 600 et seq.

Prior convictions under sections 23103, 23152 or 23153, effect on sentencing and driving privileges, see Vehicle Code § 23622.

Procedure on arrest for violation of this section, see Vehicle Code § 40302.

Records available to courts and law enforcement officials, incidents under certain DWI and homicide laws, period of time records must be available, see Vehicle Code § 1808.

Records open to public inspection, criminal records, see Vehicle Code § 1808.

Refusal to submit to alcohol testing under DUI laws, calculation of prior convictions, certain foreign convictions recognized, see Vehicle Code §§ 13353, 13353.1 and 13353.3.

Surrender of driver's license to court, see Vehicle Code § 13550.

Suspension or revocation of driving privilege for a violation of this section, notice by personal service, see Vehicle Code § 13106.

Suspension or revocation of license,

Generally, see Vehicle Code § 13352.

Alcohol-related accident within five years of vehicular manslaughter, see Vehicle Code § 13954.

Driver license compact, see Vehicle Code § 15000 et seq.

Driving after suspension or revocation, see Vehicle Code § 14601.2.

Investigation by department, three convictions in three years under this or other specified statutes, see Vehicle Code 13800.

Prior convictions, record, see Vehicle Code § 13209.

Traffic violation point count, violation of this section, see Vehicle Code § 12810.

Traffic violators schools, suspension or revocation of license for violation of this section, see Vehicle Code § 11215.

Vehicular homicide, see Penal Code § 192.

Violation as misdemeanor, see Vehicle Code § 40000.15.

Violation of this section, relinquishment of motor vehicle to convicted minor, see Penal Code § 193.8.

Youthful drunk driver visitation program, see Vehicle Code § 23509 et seq.

§ 23552. Additional conditions of probation for multiple offenses; condition upon restoration of driving privilege

(a)(1) If the court grants probation to a person punished under Section 23550, in addition to the provisions of Section 23600 and any other terms and conditions imposed by the court, the court shall impose as conditions of probation that the person be confined in a county jail for at least 180 days but not more than one year and pay a fine of at least three hundred ninety dollars ($390) but not more than one thousand dollars ($1,000).

(2) The person's privilege to operate a motor vehicle shall be revoked by the department under paragraph (7) of subdivision (a) of Section 13352. The court shall require the person to surrender the driver's license to the court in accordance with Section 13550.

(b) In addition to subdivision (a), if the court grants probation to any person punished under Section 23550, the court may order as a condition of probation that the person participate, for at least 30 months subsequent to the underlying conviction and in a manner satisfactory to the court, in a driving-under-the-influence program licensed pursuant to Section 11836 of the Health and Safety Code. In lieu of the minimum term of imprisonment in subdivision (a), the court shall impose as a condition of probation under this subdivision that the person be confined in the county jail for at least 30 days but not more than one year. The court shall not order the treatment prescribed by this subdivision unless the person makes a specific request and shows good cause for the order, whether or not the person has previously completed a treatment program pursuant to subdivision (b) of Section 23542 or paragraph (4) of subdivision (b) of Section 23562. In order to enable all required persons to participate, each person shall pay the program costs commensurate with the person's ability to pay as determined pursuant to Section 11837.4 of the Health and Safety Code. No condition of probation required pursuant to this subdivision is a basis for reducing any other probation requirement in this section or Section 23600 or for avoiding the mandatory license revocation provisions of paragraph (7) of subdivision (a) of Section 13352.

(c) In addition to Section 23600 and subdivision (a), if the court grants probation to any person punished under Section 23550 who has not previously completed a treatment program pursuant to subdivision (b) of Section 23542 or paragraph (4) of subdivision (b) of Section 23562, and unless the person is ordered to participate in, and complete, a program under subdivision (b), the court shall impose as a condition of probation that the person, subsequent to the date of the current violation, enroll in and participate, for at least 18 months and in a manner satisfactory to the court, in a driving-under-the- influence program licensed pursuant to Section 11836 of the Health and Safety Code, as designated by the court. The person shall complete the entire program subsequent to, and shall not be given any credit for program activities completed prior to, the date of the current violation. A person who has previously completed a 12–month or 18– month driving-under-the- influence program licensed pursuant to Section 11836 of the Health and Safety Code shall not be eligible for referral pursuant to this subdivision unless a 30–month driving-under-the-influence program licensed pursuant to Section 11836 of the Health and Safety Code is not available for referral in the county of the person's residence or employment. A condition of probation required pursuant to this subdivision is not a basis for reducing any other probation requirement in this section or Section 23600 or for avoiding the mandatory license revocation provisions of paragraph (7) of subdivision (a) of Section 13352.

(d) The court shall advise the person at the time of sentencing that the driving privilege may not be restored until the person provides proof satisfactory to the department of successful completion of a driving-under-the-influence program of the length required under this code that is licensed pursuant to Section 11836 of the Health and Safety Code. *(Added by Stats.1998, c. 118 (S.B.1186), § 84, operative July 1, 1999. Amended by Stats.1999, c. 22 (S.B.24), § 35.7, eff. May 26, 1999, operative July 1, 1999; Stats.2002, c. 545 (S.B.1852), § 27; Stats.2004, c. 551 (S.B.1697), § 20, operative Sept. 20, 2005; Stats.2009, c. 193 (S.B.598), § 6, operative July 1, 2010; Stats.2010, c. 301 (A.B.1601), § 5.)*

ARTICLE 3. PENALTIES FOR A VIOLATION OF SECTION 23153

Section
23554. First offense; punishment.
23556. Conditions of probation for first offense.
23558. Causing bodily injury or death to more than one victim while driving in violation of specified sections; felony convictions; enhancement of punishment.
23560. Second offense; punishment.
23562. Conditions of probation for second offense.
23566. Three or more convictions; punishment; habitual traffic offender designation; order for participation in alcohol or drug program.
23568. Additional conditions of probation for persons punished under § 23566.

§ 23554. First offense; punishment

If any person is convicted of a first violation of Section 23153, that person shall be punished by imprisonment in the state prison, or in a county jail for not less than 90 days nor more than one year, and by a fine of not less than three hundred ninety dollars ($390) nor more than one thousand dollars ($1,000). The person's privilege to operate a motor vehicle shall be suspended by the Department of Motor Vehicles pursuant to paragraph (2) of subdivision (a) of Section 13352. The court shall require the person to surrender the driver's license to the court in accordance with Section 13550. *(Added by Stats.1998, c. 118 (S.B.1186), § 84, operative July 1, 1999. Amended by Stats.2002, c. 545 (S.B.1852), § 28.)*

Cross References

Alcohol and drug problem assessment program, violator participation, sentencing, and assessment upon fine, see Vehicle Code § 23646 et seq.
Alcoholic beverages in vehicles, see Vehicle Code § 23220 et seq.
Applicability of this section to trolley coaches, see Vehicle Code § 21051.
Arrest without warrant, see Vehicle Code § 40300.5.

Challenging constitutional validity of separate conviction, see Vehicle Code § 41403.
Chemical blood, breath or urine tests, see Vehicle Code §§ 13353, 13354.
Chemical tests as evidence, see Vehicle Code § 23610.
Conviction of violation of specified subdivisions of Penal Code § 192 to be deemed conviction of violation of specified DUI provisions, see Vehicle Code § 13350.5.
Coroner's inquiry into deaths, see Government Code § 27491.25.
County alcohol and drug problem assessment programs; mandatory participation for convicted violators of this section, see Vehicle Code §§ 23646, 23647.
Crime of violence, within act for indemnification of victims of crime, see Government Code § 13960.
Defense of drug use to violations, see Vehicle Code § 23630.
Deposit in special account for each conviction under DUI provisions, see Penal Code § 1463.14.
Drivers license revocation, conviction of driver under eighteen, see Vehicle Code § 13352.3.
Driving school or instructor, revocation or suspension of license for violation of this section, see Vehicle Code § 11110.
Gross vehicular manslaughter while intoxicated, see Penal Code § 191.5.
Guilty plea, see Vehicle Code § 41610.
Impoundment of vehicle of registered owner convicted under this section, see Vehicle Code § 23594.
Influence of alcoholic beverage or drug, suspension or revocation of driving privileges, see Vehicle Code § 13352.
Injury to guest by intoxicated driver, see Vehicle Code § 17158.
Juvenile offenders, programs of supervision, see Welfare and Institutions Code § 654.1.
Juveniles with blood-alcohol concentrations of 0.05 or more, driving violations, participation in rehabilitation programs, see Vehicle Code § 23504.
Manslaughter, negligent homicide by vehicle, see Penal Code § 192.
Nuisance, sale or other disposition of motor vehicle driven by defendant, see Vehicle Code § 23596.
Persons certified or granted probation on conviction of driving under the influence of alcohol or drugs or combined influence on certain conditions, restriction, revocation or suspension of driving privilege, consent to participation in treatment program, see Vehicle Code § 13352.5.
Please Don't Drink and Drive memorial signs, requests for and duration of placement, exception for a party to an accident convicted or determined to be mentally incompetent under this section, see Streets and Highways Code § 101.10.
Presentence investigation and assessment, see Vehicle Code § 23655.
Presumptions, see Evidence Code § 600 et seq.
Prior convictions under sections 23103, 23152 or 23153, effect on sentencing and driving privileges, see Vehicle Code § 23622.
Procedure on arrest for violation of this section, see Vehicle Code § 40302.
Records available to courts and law enforcement officials, incidents under certain DWI and homicide laws, period of time records must be available, see Vehicle Code § 1808.
Refusal to submit to alcohol testing under DUI laws, calculation of prior convictions, certain foreign convictions recognized, see Vehicle Code §§ 13353, 13353.1 and 13353.3.
Surrender of driver's license to court, see Vehicle Code § 13550.
Suspension or revocation of driving privilege for a violation of this section, notice by personal service, see Vehicle Code § 13106.

Suspension or revocation of license,
  Generally, see Vehicle Code § 13352.
  Alcohol-related accident within five years of vehicular man-
    slaughter, see Vehicle Code § 13954.
  Driver license compact, see Vehicle Code § 15000 et seq.
  Driving after suspension or revocation, see Vehicle Code
    § 14601.2.
  Investigation by department, three convictions in three years
    under this or other specified statutes, see Vehicle Code
    13800.
  Prior convictions, record, see Vehicle Code § 13209.
  Traffic violation point count, violation of this section, see
    Vehicle Code § 12810.
  Traffic violators schools, suspension or revocation of license for
    violation of this section, see Vehicle Code § 11215.
  Vehicular homicide, see Penal Code § 192.
  Violation as misdemeanor, see Vehicle Code § 40000.15.
  Violation of this section, relinquishment of motor vehicle to
    convicted minor, see Penal Code § 193.8.
  Youthful drunk driver visitation program, see Vehicle Code
    § 23509 et seq.

§ 23556. Conditions of probation for first offense

(a)(1) If the court grants probation to any person punished under Section 23554, in addition to the provisions of Section 23600 and any other terms and conditions imposed by the court, the court shall impose as a condition of probation that the person be confined in the county jail for at least five days but not more than one year and pay a fine of at least three hundred ninety dollars ($390) but not more than one thousand dollars ($1,000).

(2) The person's privilege to operate a motor vehicle shall be suspended by the department under paragraph (2) of subdivision (a) of Section 13352. The court shall require the person to surrender the driver's license to the court in accordance with Section 13550.

(b)(1) In a county where the county alcohol program administrator has certified, and the board of supervisors has approved, a program or programs, the court shall also impose as a condition of probation that the driver shall participate in, and successfully complete, an alcohol and other drug education and counseling program, established pursuant to Section 11837.3 of the Health and Safety Code, as designated by the court.

(2) In any county where the board of supervisors has approved and the State Department of * * * Health Care Services has licensed an alcohol and other drug education and counseling program, the court shall also impose as a condition of probation that the driver enroll in, participate in, and successfully complete, a driving-under-the-influence program licensed pursuant to Section 11836 of the Health and Safety Code, in the driver's county of residence or employment, as designated by the court. For the purposes of this paragraph, enrollment in, participation in, and completion of, an approved program shall be subsequent to the date of the current violation. Credit may not be given to any program activities completed prior to the date of the current violation.

766

(3) The court shall refer a first offender whose blood-alcohol concentration was less than 0.20 percent, by weight, to participate for three months or longer, as ordered by the court, in a licensed program that consists of at least 30 hours of program activities, including those education, group counseling, and individual interview sessions described in Chapter 9 (commencing with Section 11836) of Part 2 of Division 10.5 of the Health and Safety Code.

(4) The court shall refer a first offender whose blood-alcohol concentration was 0.20 percent or more, by weight, or who refused to take a chemical test, to participate for nine months or longer, as ordered by the court, in a licensed program that consists of at least 60 hours of program activities, including those education, group counseling, and individual interview sessions described in Chapter 9 (commencing with Section 11836) of Part 2 of Division 10.5 of the Health and Safety Code.

(c)(1) The court shall revoke the person's probation pursuant to Section 23602, except for good cause shown, for the failure to enroll in, participate in, or complete a program specified in subdivision (b).

(2) The court, in establishing reporting requirements, shall consult with the county alcohol program administrator. The county alcohol program administrator shall coordinate the reporting requirements with the department and with the State Department of * * * Health Care Services. That reporting shall ensure that all persons who, after being ordered to attend and complete a program, may be identified for either (A) failure to enroll in, or failure to successfully complete, the program, or (B) successful completion of the program as ordered.

(d) The court shall advise the person at the time of sentencing that the driving privilege shall not be restored until the person has provided proof satisfactory to the department of successful completion of a driving-under-the-influence program of the length required under this code that is licensed pursuant to Section 11836 of the Health and Safety Code.

(e) This section shall become operative on September 20, 2005. *(Added by Stats.1998, c. 118 (S.B.1186), § 84, operative July 1, 1999. Amended by Stats.2002, c. 545 (S.B.1852), § 29; Stats.2004, c. 551 (S.B.1697), § 21, operative Sept. 20, 2005; Stats.2005, c. 164 (A.B.1353), § 4; Stats.2013, c. 22 (A.B.75), § 88, eff. June 27, 2013, operative July 1, 2013.)*

Cross References

County alcohol and drug problem assessment programs; mandatory participation for convicted violators of this section, see Vehicle Code § 23646.

§ 23558. Causing bodily injury or death to more than one victim while driving in violation of specified sections; felony convictions; enhancement of punishment

A person who proximately causes bodily injury or death to more than one victim in any one instance of driving in violation of Section 23153 of this code or in violation of Section 191.5 of, or subdivision (a) of Section 192.5 of, the Penal Code, shall, upon a felony conviction, and notwithstanding subdivision (g) of Section 1170.1 of the Penal Code, receive an enhancement of one year in the state prison for each additional injured victim. The enhanced sentence provided for in this section shall not be imposed unless the fact of the bodily injury to each additional victim is charged in the accusatory pleading and admitted or found to be true by the trier of fact. The maximum number of one year enhancements that may be imposed pursuant to this section is three.

Notwithstanding any other provision of law, the court may strike the enhancements provided in this section if it determines that there are circumstances in mitigation of the additional punishment and states on the record its reasons for striking the additional punishment. *(Added by Stats.1998, c. 118 (S.B.1186), § 84, operative July 1, 1999. Amended by Stats.1999, c. 706 (A.B.1236), § 15, eff. Oct. 10, 1999; Stats.2007, c. 747 (A.B.678), § 34.)*

§ 23560. Second offense; punishment

If a person is convicted of a violation of Section 23153 and the offense occurred within 10 years of a separate violation of Section 23103, as specified in Section 23103.5, 23152, or 23153 that resulted in a conviction, that person shall be punished by imprisonment in the state prison, or in a county jail for not less than 120 days nor more than one year, and by a fine of not less than three hundred ninety dollars ($390) nor more than five thousand dollars ($5,000). The person's privilege to operate a motor vehicle shall be revoked by the Department of Motor Vehicles pursuant to paragraph (4) of subdivision (a) of Section 13352. The court shall require the person to surrender the driver's license to the court in accordance with Section 13550. *(Added by Stats.1998, c. 118 (S.B. 1186), § 84, operative July 1, 1999. Amended by Stats. 2002, c. 545 (S.B.1852), § 30; Stats.2004, c. 550 (S.B. 1694), § 16.)*

Cross References

Alcohol and drug problem assessment program, violator participation, sentencing, and assessment upon fine, see Vehicle Code § 23646 et seq.

Alcoholic beverages in vehicles, see Vehicle Code § 23220 et seq.

Applicability of this section to trolley coaches, see Vehicle Code § 21051.

Arrest without warrant, see Vehicle Code § 40300.5.

Challenging constitutional validity of separate conviction, see Vehicle Code § 41403.

Chemical blood, breath or urine tests, see Vehicle Code §§ 13353, 13354.

Chemical tests as evidence, see Vehicle Code § 23610.

Conviction of violation of specified subdivisions of Penal Code § 192 to be deemed conviction of violation of specified DUI provisions, see Vehicle Code § 13350.5.

Coroner's inquiry into deaths, see Government Code § 27491.25.

County alcohol and drug problem assessment programs; mandatory participation for convicted violators of this section, see Vehicle Code §§ 23646, 23647.

Crime of violence, within act for indemnification of victims of crime, see Government Code § 13960.

Defense of drug use to violations, see Vehicle Code § 23630.

Deposit in special account for each conviction under DUI provisions, see Penal Code § 1463.14.

Drivers license revocation, conviction of driver under eighteen, see Vehicle Code § 13352.3.

Driving school or instructor, revocation or suspension of license for violation of this section, see Vehicle Code § 11110.

Gross vehicular manslaughter while intoxicated, see Penal Code § 191.5.

Guilty plea, see Vehicle Code § 41610.

Impoundment of vehicle of registered owner convicted under this section, see Vehicle Code § 23594.

Influence of alcoholic beverage or drug, suspension or revocation of driving privileges, see Vehicle Code § 13352.

Injury to guest by intoxicated driver, see Vehicle Code § 17158.

Juvenile offenders, programs of supervision, see Welfare and Institutions Code § 654.1.

Juveniles with blood-alcohol concentrations of 0.05 or more, driving violations, participation in rehabilitation programs, see Vehicle Code § 23504.

Manslaughter, negligent homicide by vehicle, see Penal Code § 192.

Nuisance, sale or other disposition of motor vehicle driven by defendant, see Vehicle Code § 23596.

Persons certified or granted probation on conviction of driving under the influence of alcohol or drugs or combined influence on certain conditions, restriction, revocation or suspension of driving privilege, consent to participation in treatment program, see Vehicle Code § 13352.5.

Please Don't Drink and Drive memorial signs, requests for and duration of placement, exception for a party to an accident convicted or determined to be mentally incompetent under this section, see Streets and Highways Code § 101.10.

Presentence investigation and assessment, see Vehicle Code § 23655.

Presumptions, see Evidence Code § 600 et seq.

Prior convictions under sections 23103, 23152 or 23153, effect on sentencing and driving privileges, see Vehicle Code § 23622.

Procedure on arrest for violation of this section, see Vehicle Code § 40302.

Records available to courts and law enforcement officials, incidents under certain DWI and homicide laws, period of time records must be available, see Vehicle Code § 1808.

Refusal to submit to alcohol testing under DUI laws, calculation of prior convictions, certain foreign convictions recognized, see Vehicle Code §§ 13353, 13353.1 and 13353.3.

Surrender of driver's license to court, see Vehicle Code § 13550.

Suspension or revocation of driving privilege for a violation of this section, notice by personal service, see Vehicle Code § 13106.

Suspension or revocation of license,

Generally, see Vehicle Code § 13352.

Alcohol-related accident within five years of vehicular manslaughter, see Vehicle Code § 13954.

Driver license compact, see Vehicle Code § 15000 et seq.

Driving after suspension or revocation, see Vehicle Code § 14601.2.

Investigation by department, three convictions in three years under this or other specified statutes, see Vehicle Code 13800.

Prior convictions, record, see Vehicle Code § 13209.

Traffic violation point count, violation of this section, see Vehicle Code § 12810.

Traffic violators schools, suspension or revocation of license for violation of this section, see Vehicle Code § 11215.

Vehicular homicide, see Penal Code § 192.

Violation as misdemeanor, see Vehicle Code § 40000.15.

Violation of this section, relinquishment of motor vehicle to convicted minor, see Penal Code § 193.8.

Youthful drunk driver visitation program, see Vehicle Code § 23509 et seq.

§ 23562. Conditions of probation for second offense

If the court grants probation to a person punished under Section 23560, in addition to the provisions of Section 23600 and any other terms and conditions imposed by the court, the court shall impose as conditions of probation that the person be subject to either subdivision (a) or (b), as follows:

(a) Be confined in the county jail for at least 120 days and pay a fine of at least three hundred ninety dollars ($390), but not more than five thousand dollars ($5,000). The person's privilege to operate a motor vehicle shall be revoked by the department under paragraph (4) of subdivision (a) of Section 13352. The court shall require the person to surrender the driver's license to the court in accordance with Section 13550.

(b) All of the following apply:

(1) Be confined in the county jail for at least 30 days, but not more than one year.

(2) Pay a fine of at least three hundred ninety dollars ($390), but not more than one thousand dollars ($1,000).

(3) The privilege to operate a motor vehicle shall be revoked by the department under paragraph (4) of subdivision (a) of Section 13352. The court shall require the person to surrender the driver's license to the court in accordance with Section 13550.

(4) Either of the following:

(A) Enroll and participate, for at least 18 months subsequent to the date of the underlying violation and in a manner satisfactory to the court, in a driving-under-the-influence program licensed pursuant to Section 11836 of the Health and Safety Code, if available in the county of the person's residence or employment, as designated by the court. The person shall complete the entire program subsequent to, and shall not be given any credit for program activities completed prior to, the date of the current violation. The program shall provide for persons who cannot afford the program fee pursuant to paragraph (2) of subdivision (b) of Section 11837.4 of the Health and Safety Code in order to enable those persons to participate.

(B) Enroll and participate, for at least 30 months subsequent to the date of the underlying violation and in a manner satisfactory to the court, in a driving-under-the-influence program licensed pursuant to Section 11836 of the Health and Safety Code, if available in the county of the person's residence or employment. The person shall complete the entire program subsequent to, and shall not be given any credit for program activities completed prior to, the date of the current violation.

(c) The court shall advise the person at the time of sentencing that the driving privilege shall not be restored until the person has provided proof satisfactory to the department of successful completion of a driving-under-the-influence program of the length required under this code that is licensed pursuant to Section 11836 of the Health and Safety Code.

(d) This section shall become operative on September 20, 2005. *(Formerly § 23186, added by Stats.1981, c. 940, p. 3571, § 32. Amended by Stats.1982, c. 53, p. 177, § 38, eff. Feb. 18, 1982; Stats.1982, c. 1338, p. 4972, § 11, operative July 1, 1983; Stats.1982, c. 1339, p. 4990, § 25, eff. Sept. 24, 1982; Stats.1982, c. 1339, p. 4991, § 26, eff. Sept. 24, 1982, operative July 1, 1983; Stats.1984, c. 667, p. 3, § 17, operative July 1, 1985; Stats.1987, c. 214, § 4; Stats.1989, c. 803, § 8; Stats.1991, c. 990 (S.B.713), § 4, eff. Oct. 14, 1991; Stats.1992, c. 974 (S.B.1600), § 23, eff. Sept. 28, 1992; Stats.1993, c. 272 (A.B.301), § 48, eff. Aug. 2, 1993; Stats.1997, c. 493 (S.B.1177), § 4; Stats.1998, c. 756 (A.B.762), § 15, operative July 1, 1999. Renumbered § 23562 and amended by Stats.1999, c.22 (S.B.24), § 22, eff. May 26, 1999, operative July 1, 1999. Amended by Stats.2002, c. 545 (S.B.1852), § 31; Stats.2004, c. 551 (S.B.1697), § 22, operative Sept. 20, 2005.)*

Cross References

Conviction for driving under the influence or engaging in speed contests or exhibitions of speed, suspension or revocation of license, eligibility for restricted license, reinstatement conditions, see Vehicle Code § 13352.

Persons certified or granted probation on conviction or driving under the influence of alcohol or drugs or combined influence on certain conditions, restriction, revocation or suspension of driving privilege, consent to participation in treatment program, see Vehicle Code § 13352.5.

Presentence investigation, see Vehicle Code § 23655.

§ 23564. Editorial Note

Operative Effect

Stats.1998, c. 118 (S.B.1186), provided for repeal of § 23187 and addition of this similar section. Stats.1998, c. 756 (A.B.762), § 16, repealed § 23187, operative July 1, 1999. Section affected by two or more acts at the same session of the legislature, see Government Code § 9605.

§ 23566. Three or more convictions; punishment; habitual traffic offender designation; order for participation in alcohol or drug program

(a) If a person is convicted of a violation of Section 23153 and the offense occurred within 10 years of two or more separate violations of Section 23103, as specified in Section 23103.5, or Section 23152 or 23153, or any combination of these violations, that resulted in convictions, that person shall be punished by imprisonment in the state prison for a term of two, three, or four years and by a fine of not less than one thousand fifteen dollars ($1,015) nor more than five thousand dollars ($5,000). The person's privilege to operate a motor vehicle shall be revoked by the Department of Motor Vehicles pursuant to paragraph (6) of subdivision (a) of Section 13352. The court shall require the person to surrender the driver's license to the court in accordance with Section 13550.

(b) If a person is convicted of a violation of Section 23153, and the act or neglect proximately causes great bodily injury, as defined in Section 12022.7 of the Penal Code, to any person other than the driver, and the offense occurred within 10 years of two or more separate violations of Section 23103, as specified in Section 23103.5, or Section 23152 or 23153, or any combination of these violations, that resulted in convictions, that person shall be punished by imprisonment in the state prison for a term of two, three, or four years and by a fine of not less than one thousand fifteen dollars ($1,015) nor more than five thousand dollars ($5,000). The person's privilege to operate a motor vehicle shall be revoked by the Department of Motor Vehicles pursuant to paragraph (6) of subdivision (a) of Section 13352. The court shall require the person to surrender the driver's license to the court in accordance with Section 13550.

(c) If a person is convicted under subdivision (b), and the offense for which the person is convicted occurred within 10 years of four or more separate violations of Section 23103, as specified in Section 23103.5, or Section 23152 or 23153, or any combination of these violations, that resulted in convictions, that person shall, in addition and consecutive to the sentences imposed under subdivision (b), be punished by an additional term of imprisonment in the state prison for three years.

The enhancement allegation provided in this subdivision shall be pleaded and proved as provided by law.

(d) A person convicted of Section 23153 punishable under this section shall be designated as a habitual traffic offender for a period of three years, subsequent to the conviction. The person shall be advised of this designation pursuant to subdivision (b) of Section 13350.

(e) A person confined in state prison under this section shall be ordered by the court to participate in an alcohol or drug program, or both, that is available at the prison during the person's confinement. Completion of an alcohol or drug program under this section does not meet the program completion requirement of paragraph (6) of subdivision (a) of Section 13352, unless the drug or alcohol program is licensed under Section 11836 of the Health and Safety Code, or is a program specified in Section 8001 of the Penal Code. *(Added by Stats.1998, c. 118 (S.B.1186), § 84, operative July 1, 1999. Amended by Stats.1999, c. 22 (S.B.24), § 36, eff. May 26, 1999, operative July 1, 1999; Stats.2002, c. 545 (S.B.1852), § 32; Stats. 2004, c. 550 (S.B.1694), § 17; Stats.2009, c. 193 (S.B.598),*

§ 7, operative July 1, 2010; Stats.2010, c. 301 (A.B.1601), § 6.)

Cross References

Suspension or revocation of license for driving under the influence or engaging in speed contests or exhibitions of speed, reinstatement conditions, see Vehicle Code § 13352.

§ 23568. Additional conditions of probation for persons punished under § 23566

(a) If the court grants probation to a person punished under Section 23566, in addition to the provisions of Section 23600 and any other terms and conditions imposed by the court, the court shall impose as conditions of probation that the person be confined in the county jail for at least one year, that the person pay a fine of at least three hundred ninety dollars ($390) but not more than five thousand dollars ($5,000), and that the person make restitution or reparation pursuant to Section 1203.1 of the Penal Code. The person's privilege to operate a motor vehicle shall be revoked by the department under paragraph (6) of subdivision (a) of Section 13352. The court shall require the person to surrender the driver's license to the court in accordance with Section 13550.

(b) In addition to Section 23600 and subdivision (a), if the court grants probation to a person punished under Section 23566, the court shall impose as a condition of probation that the person enroll in and complete, subsequent to the date of the underlying violation and in a manner satisfactory to the court, an 18–month driving-under-the-influence program licensed pursuant to Section 11836 of the Health and Safety Code or, if available in the county of the person's residence or employment, a 30–month driving-under-the-influence program licensed pursuant to Section 11836 of the Health and Safety Code, as designated by the court. The person shall complete the entire program subsequent to, and shall not be given any credit for program activities completed prior to, the date of the current violation. In lieu of the minimum term of imprisonment in subdivision (a), the court shall impose as a minimum condition of probation under this subdivision that the person be confined in the county jail for at least 30 days but not more than one year. Except as provided in this subdivision, if the court grants probation under this section, the court shall order the treatment prescribed by this subdivision, whether or not the person has previously completed a treatment program pursuant to subdivision (b) of Section 23542 or paragraph (4) of subdivision (b) of Section 23562. In order to enable all required persons to participate, each person shall pay the program costs commensurate with the person's ability to pay as determined pursuant to Section 11837.4 of the Health and Safety Code. No condition of probation required pursuant to this subdivision is a basis for reducing any other probation requirement in this section or Section 23600 or for avoiding the mandatory license revocation provisions of paragraph (6) of subdivision (a) of Section 13352.

(c) The court shall advise the person at the time of sentencing that the driving privilege may not be restored until the person provides proof satisfactory to the department of successful completion of a driving-under-the-influence program of the length required under this code that is licensed pursuant to Section 11836 of the Health and Safety Code. *(Added by Stats.1998, c. 118 (S.B.1186), § 84, operative July 1, 1999. Amended by Stats.1999, c. 22 (S.B.24), § 37, eff. May 26, 1999, operative July 1, 1999; Stats.2002, c. 545 (S.B.1852), § 33; Stats.2004, c. 551 (S.B.1697), § 23, operative Sept. 20, 2005; Stats.2009, c. 193 (S.B.598), § 8, operative July 1, 2010; Stats.2010, c. 301 (A.B.1601), § 7.)*

Cross References

Suspension or revocation of license for driving under the influence or engaging in speed contests or exhibitions of speed, reinstatement conditions, see Vehicle Code § 13352.

ARTICLE 4.   ADDITIONAL PUNISHMENTS

Section
23572.   Conviction of violation of § 23152; minor in vehicle; enhanced punishment.
23573.   Violations necessitating ignition interlock device; installation and maintenance; license restriction; exemptions; failure to comply.

§ 23572.   Conviction of violation of § 23152; minor in vehicle; enhanced punishment

(a) If any person is convicted of a violation of Section 23152 and a minor under 14 years of age was a passenger in the vehicle at the time of the offense, the court shall impose the following penalties in addition to any other penalty prescribed:

(1) If the person is convicted of a violation of Section 23152 punishable under Section 23536, the punishment shall be enhanced by an imprisonment of 48 continuous hours in the county jail, whether or not probation is granted, no part of which shall be stayed.

(2) If a person is convicted of a violation of Section 23152 punishable under Section 23540, the punishment shall be enhanced by an imprisonment of 10 days in the county jail, whether or not probation is granted, no part of which may be stayed.

(3) If a person is convicted of a violation of Section 23152 punishable under Section 23546, the punishment shall be enhanced by an imprisonment of 30 days in the county jail, whether or not probation is granted, no part of which may be stayed.

(4) If a person is convicted of a violation of Section 23152 which is punished as a misdemeanor under Section 23550, the punishment shall be enhanced by an imprisonment of 90 days in the county jail, whether or not probation is granted, no part of which may be stayed.

(b) The driving of a vehicle in which a minor under 14 years of age was a passenger shall be pled and proven.

(c) No punishment enhancement shall be imposed pursuant to this section if the person is also convicted of a violation of Section 273a of the Penal Code arising out of the same facts and incident. *(Added by Stats.1998, c. 118 (S.B.1186), § 84, operative July 1, 1999. Amended by Stats.1999, c. 22 (S.B.24), § 38, eff. May 26, 1999, operative July 1, 1999.)*

Cross References

Alcohol and drug problem assessment program, violator participation, sentencing, and assessment upon fine, see Vehicle Code § 23646 et seq.
Alcoholic beverages in vehicles, see Vehicle Code § 23220 et seq.
Applicability of this section to trolley coaches, see Vehicle Code § 21051.
Arrest without warrant, see Vehicle Code § 40300.5.
Challenging constitutional validity of separate conviction, see Vehicle Code § 41403.
Chemical blood, breath or urine tests, see Vehicle Code §§ 13353, 13354.
Chemical tests as evidence, see Vehicle Code § 23610.
Conviction of violation of specified subdivisions of Penal Code § 192 to be deemed conviction of violation of specified DUI provisions, see Vehicle Code § 13350.5.
Coroner's inquiry into deaths, see Government Code § 27491.25.
County alcohol and drug problem assessment programs; mandatory participation for convicted violators of this section, see Vehicle Code §§ 23646, 23647.
Crime of violence, within act for indemnification of victims of crime, see Government Code § 13960.
Defense of drug use to violations, see Vehicle Code § 23630.
Deposit in special account for each conviction under DUI provisions, see Penal Code § 1463.14.
Drivers license revocation, conviction of driver under eighteen, see Vehicle Code § 13352.3.
Driving school or instructor, revocation or suspension of license for violation of this section, see Vehicle Code § 11110.
Gross vehicular manslaughter while intoxicated, see Penal Code § 191.5.
Guilty plea, see Vehicle Code § 41610.
Impoundment of vehicle of registered owner convicted under this section, see Vehicle Code § 23594.
Influence of alcoholic beverage or drug, suspension or revocation of driving privileges, see Vehicle Code § 13352.
Injury to guest by intoxicated driver, see Vehicle Code § 17158.
Juvenile offenders, programs of supervision, see Welfare and Institutions Code § 654.1.
Juveniles with blood-alcohol concentrations of 0.05 or more, driving violations, participation in rehabilitation programs, see Vehicle Code § 23504.
Manslaughter, negligent homicide by vehicle, see Penal Code § 192.
Nuisance, sale or other disposition of motor vehicle driven by defendant, see Vehicle Code § 23596.
Persons certified or granted probation on conviction of driving under the influence of alcohol or drugs or combined influence on certain conditions, restriction, revocation or suspension of driving privilege, consent to participation in treatment program, see Vehicle Code § 13352.5.
Please Don't Drink and Drive memorial signs, requests for and duration of placement, exception for a party to an accident convicted or determined to be mentally incompetent under this section, see Streets and Highways Code § 101.10.

Presentence investigation and assessment, see Vehicle Code § 23655.

Presumptions, see Evidence Code § 600 et seq.

Prior convictions under sections 23103, 23152 or 23153, effect on sentencing and driving privileges, see Vehicle Code § 23622.

Procedure on arrest for violation of this section, see Vehicle Code § 40302.

Records available to courts and law enforcement officials, incidents under certain DWI and homicide laws, period of time records must be available, see Vehicle Code § 1808.

Refusal to submit to alcohol testing under DUI laws, calculation of prior convictions, certain foreign convictions recognized, see Vehicle Code §§ 13353, 13353.1 and 13353.3.

Surrender of driver's license to court, see Vehicle Code § 13550.

Suspension or revocation of driving privilege for a violation of this section, notice by personal service, see Vehicle Code § 13106.

Suspension or revocation of license,

Generally, see Vehicle Code § 13352.

Alcohol-related accident within five years of vehicular manslaughter, see Vehicle Code § 13954.

Driver license compact, see Vehicle Code § 15000 et seq.

Driving after suspension or revocation, see Vehicle Code § 14601.2.

Investigation by department, three convictions in three years under this or other specified statutes, see Vehicle Code 13800.

Prior convictions, record, see Vehicle Code § 13209.

Traffic violation point count, violation of this section, see Vehicle Code § 12810.

Traffic violators schools, suspension or revocation of license for violation of this section, see Vehicle Code § 11215.

Vehicular homicide, see Penal Code § 192.

Violation as misdemeanor, see Vehicle Code § 40000.15.

Violation of this section, relinquishment of motor vehicle to convicted minor, see Penal Code § 193.8.

Youthful drunk driver visitation program, see Vehicle Code § 23509 et seq.

§ 23573. Violations necessitating ignition interlock device; installation and maintenance; license restriction; exemptions; failure to comply

(a) The Department of Motor Vehicles, upon receipt of the court's abstract of conviction for a violation listed in subdivision (j), shall inform the convicted person of the requirements of this section and the term for which the person is required to have a certified ignition interlock device installed. The records of the department shall reflect the mandatory use of the device for the term required and the time when the device is required to be installed pursuant to this code.

(b) The department shall advise the person that installation of an ignition interlock device on a vehicle does not allow the person to drive without a valid driver's license.

(c) A person who is notified by the department pursuant to subdivision (a) shall, within 30 days of notification, complete all of the following:

(1) Arrange for each vehicle owned or operated by the person to be fitted with an ignition interlock device by a certified ignition interlock device provider under Section 13386.

(2) Notify the department and provide to the department proof of installation by submitting the "Verification of Installation" form described in paragraph (2) of subdivision (g) of Section 13386.

(3) Pay to the department a fee sufficient to cover the costs of administration of this section, including startup costs, as determined by the department.

(d) The department shall place a restriction on the driver's license record of the convicted person that states the driver is restricted to driving only vehicles equipped with a certified ignition interlock device.

(e)(1) A person who is notified by the department pursuant to subdivision (a) shall arrange for each vehicle with an ignition interlock device to be serviced by the installer at least once every 60 days in order for the installer to recalibrate and monitor the operation of the device.

(2) The installer shall notify the department if the device is removed or indicates that the person has attempted to remove, bypass, or tamper with the device, or if the person fails three or more times to comply with any requirement for the maintenance or calibration of the ignition interlock device.

(f) The department shall monitor the installation and maintenance of the ignition interlock device installed pursuant to subdivision (a).

(g)(1) A person who is notified by the department, pursuant to subdivision (a), is exempt from the requirements of subdivision (c) if all of the following circumstances occur:

(A) Within 30 days of the notification, the person certifies to the department all of the following:

(i) The person does not own a vehicle.

(ii) The person does not have access to a vehicle at his or her residence.

(iii) The person no longer has access to the vehicle being driven by the person when he or she was arrested for a violation that subsequently resulted in a conviction for a violation listed in subdivision (j).

(iv) The person acknowledges that he or she is only allowed to drive a vehicle that is fitted with an operating ignition interlock device and that he or she is required to have a valid driver's license before he or she can drive.

(v) The person is subject to the requirements of this section when he or she purchases or has access to a vehicle.

(B) The person's driver's license record has been restricted pursuant to subdivision (d).

(C) The person complies with this section immediately upon commencing ownership or operation of a vehicle subject to the required installation of an ignition interlock device.

(2) A person who has been granted an exemption pursuant to this subdivision and who subsequently drives a vehicle in violation of the exemption is subject to the

penalties of subdivision (i) in addition to any other applicable penalties in law.

(h) This section does not permit a person to drive without a valid driver's license.

(i) A person who is required under subdivision (c) to install an ignition interlock device who willfully fails to install the ignition interlock device within the time period required under subdivision (c) is guilty of a misdemeanor and shall be punished by imprisonment in the county jail for not more than six months or by a fine of not more than five thousand dollars ($5,000), or by both that fine and imprisonment.

(j) In addition to all other requirements of this code, a person convicted of any of the following violations shall be punished as follows:

(1) Upon a conviction of a violation of Section 14601.2, 14601.4, or 14601.5 subsequent to one prior conviction of a violation of Section 23103.5, 23152, or 23153, within a 10–year period, the person shall immediately install a certified ignition interlock device, pursuant to this section, in all vehicles owned or operated by that person for a term of one year.

(2) Upon a conviction of a violation of Section 14601.2, 14601.4, or 14601.5 subsequent to two prior convictions of a violation of Section 23103.5, 23152, or 23153, within a 10–year period, or one prior conviction of Section 14601.2, 14601.4, or 14601.5, within a 10–year period, the person shall immediately install a certified ignition interlock device, pursuant to this section, in all vehicles owned or operated by that person for a term of two years.

(3) Upon a conviction of a violation of Section 14601.2, 14601.4, or 14601.5 subsequent to three or more prior convictions of a violation of Section 23103.5, 23152, or 23153, within a 10–year period, or two or more prior convictions of Section 14601.2, 14601.4, or 14601.5, within a 10–year period, the person shall immediately install a certified ignition interlock device, pursuant to this section, in all vehicles owned or operated by that person for a term of three years.

(k) The department shall notify the court if a person subject to this section has failed to show proof of installation within 30 days of the department informing the person he or she is required to install a certified ignition interlock device.

(*l*) Subdivisions (j), (k), (m), (n), and (*o*) of Section 23575 apply to this section.

(m) The requirements of this section are in addition to any other requirements of law.

(n) This section shall become operative on July 1, 2009. *(Added by Stats.2008, c. 404 (S.B.1388), § 4, operative July 1, 2009.)*

ARTICLE 5. ADDITIONAL PENALTIES AND SANCTIONS

Section
23575.   Court-mandated use of ignition interlock device.
23575.1.   Ignition interlock devices; effectiveness study and report.
23576.   Motor vehicle owned by employer; exemption.
23577.   Willful refusal to submit to or failure to complete chemical test by person convicted of driving under the influence of alcohol or drugs; penalties; pleading and proof.
23578.   Conviction of violation of § 23152 or § 23153; alcohol concentration or refusal to take chemical test as special factor; penalty enhancement or probation.
23580.   Second or subsequent offense involving alcohol or drugs; minimum confinement.
23582.   Driving under the influence; addition penalty for excessive speed and reckless driving during commission of offense; additional punishment.

§ 23575. Court-mandated use of ignition interlock device

(a)(1) In addition to any other law, the court may require that a person convicted of a first offense violation of Section 23152 or 23153 install a certified ignition interlock device on any vehicle that the person owns or operates and prohibit that person from operating a motor vehicle unless that vehicle is equipped with a functioning, certified ignition interlock device. The court shall give heightened consideration to applying this sanction to a first offense violator with 0.15 percent or more, by weight, of alcohol in his or her blood at arrest, or with two or more prior moving traffic violations, or to persons who refused the chemical tests at arrest. If the court orders the ignition interlock device restriction, the term shall be determined by the court for a period not to exceed three years from the date of conviction. The court shall notify the Department of Motor Vehicles, as specified in subdivision (a) of Section 1803, of the terms of the restrictions in accordance with subdivision (a) of Section 1804. The Department of Motor Vehicles shall place the restriction in the person's records in the Department of Motor Vehicles.

(2) The court shall require a person convicted of a violation of Section 14601.2 to install an ignition interlock device on any vehicle that the person owns or operates and prohibit the person from operating a motor vehicle unless the vehicle is equipped with a functioning, certified ignition interlock device. The term of the restriction shall be determined by the court for a period not to exceed three years from the date of conviction. The court shall notify the Department of Motor Vehicles, as specified in subdivision (a) of Section 1803, of the terms of the restrictions in accordance with subdivision (a) of Section 1804. The Department of Motor Vehicles shall place the restriction in the person's records in the Department of Motor Vehicles.

(b) The court shall include on the abstract of conviction or violation submitted to the Department of Motor

Vehicles under Section 1803 or 1816 the requirement and term for the use of a certified ignition interlock device. The records of the department shall reflect mandatory use of the device for the term ordered by the court.

(c) The court shall advise the person that installation of an ignition interlock device on a vehicle does not allow the person to drive without a valid driver's license.

(d) A person whose driving privilege is restricted by the court pursuant to this section shall arrange for each vehicle with an ignition interlock device to be serviced by the installer at least once every 60 days in order for the installer to recalibrate and monitor the operation of the device. The installer shall notify the court if the device is removed or indicates that the person has attempted to remove, bypass, or tamper with the device, or if the person fails three or more times to comply with a requirement for the maintenance or calibration of the ignition interlock device. There is no obligation for the installer to notify the court if the person has complied with all of the requirements of this article.

(e) The court shall monitor the installation and maintenance of an ignition interlock device restriction ordered pursuant to subdivision (a) or (*l*). If a person fails to comply with the court order, the court shall give notice of the fact to the department pursuant to Section 40509.1.

(f)(1) If a person is convicted of a violation of Section 23152 or 23153 and the offense occurred within 10 years of one or more separate violations of Section 23152 or 23153 that resulted in a conviction, or if a person is convicted of a violation of Section 23103, as specified in Section 23103.5, and is suspended for one year under Section 13353.3, the person may apply to the Department of Motor Vehicles for a restricted driver's license pursuant to Section 13352 or 13353.3 that prohibits the person from operating a motor vehicle unless that vehicle is equipped with a functioning ignition interlock device, certified pursuant to Section 13386. The restriction shall remain in effect for at least the remaining period of the original suspension or revocation and until all reinstatement requirements in Section 13352 or 13353.4 are met.

(2) Pursuant to subdivision (g), the Department of Motor Vehicles shall immediately terminate the restriction issued pursuant to Section 13352 or 13353.3 and shall immediately suspend or revoke the privilege to operate a motor vehicle of a person who attempts to remove, bypass, or tamper with the device, who has the device removed prior to the termination date of the restriction, or who fails three or more times to comply with any requirement for the maintenance or calibration of the ignition interlock device ordered pursuant to Section 13352 or 13353.3. The privilege shall remain suspended or revoked for the remaining period of the originating suspension or revocation and until all reinstatement requirements in Section 13352 or 13353.4 are met.

(g) A person whose driving privilege is restricted by the Department of Motor Vehicles pursuant to Section 13352 or 13353.3 shall arrange for each vehicle with an ignition interlock device to be serviced by the installer at least once every 60 days in order for the installer to recalibrate the device and monitor the operation of the device. The installer shall notify the Department of Motor Vehicles if the device is removed or indicates that the person has attempted to remove, bypass, or tamper with the device, or if the person fails three or more times to comply with any requirement for the maintenance or calibration of the ignition interlock device. There is no obligation on the part of the installer to notify the department or the court if the person has complied with all of the requirements of this section.

(h) Nothing in this section permits a person to drive without a valid driver's license.

(i) The Department of Motor Vehicles shall include information along with the order of suspension or revocation for repeat offenders informing them that after a specified period of suspension or revocation has been completed, the person may either install an ignition interlock device on any vehicle that the person owns or operates or remain with a suspended or revoked driver's license.

(j) Pursuant to this section, an out-of-state resident who otherwise would qualify for an ignition interlock device restricted license in California shall be prohibited from operating a motor vehicle in California unless that vehicle is equipped with a functioning ignition interlock device. An ignition interlock device is not required to be installed on any vehicle owned by the defendant that is not driven in California.

(k) If a person has a medical problem that does not permit the person to breathe with sufficient strength to activate the device, then that person shall only have the suspension option.

(*l*) This section does not restrict a court from requiring installation of an ignition interlock device and prohibiting operation of a motor vehicle unless that vehicle is equipped with a functioning, certified ignition interlock device for a person to whom subdivision (a) or (b) does not apply. The term of the restriction shall be determined by the court for a period not to exceed three years from the date of conviction. The court shall notify the Department of Motor Vehicles, as specified in subdivision (a) of Section 1803, of the terms of the restrictions in accordance with subdivision (a) of Section 1804. The Department of Motor Vehicles shall place the restriction in the person's records in the Department of Motor Vehicles.

(m) For the purposes of this section, "vehicle" does not include a motorcycle until the state certifies an ignition interlock device that can be installed on a motorcycle. Any person subject to an ignition interlock device restriction shall not operate a motorcycle for the duration of the ignition interlock device restriction period.

(n) For the purposes of this section, "owned" means solely owned or owned in conjunction with another person or legal entity. For purposes of this section, "operates" includes operating a vehicle that is not owned by the person subject to this section.

(*o*) For the purposes of this section, "bypass" includes, but is not limited to, either of the following:

(1) A combination of failing or not taking the ignition interlock device rolling retest three consecutive times.

(2) An incidence of failing or not taking the ignition interlock device rolling retest, when not followed by an incidence of passing the ignition interlock rolling retest prior to turning off the vehicle's engine. *(Formerly § 23246, added by Stats.1992, c. 694 (A.B.2851), § 2, operative July 1, 1993. Amended by Stats.1993, c. 1244 (S.B.126), § 25; Stats.1994, c. 1237 (A.B.2639), § 4, eff. Sept. 30, 1994; Stats.1998, c. 756 (A.B.762), § 21, operative July 1, 1999. Renumbered § 23575 and amended by Stats.1999, c. 22 (S.B.24), § 27, eff. May 26, 1999, operative July 1, 1999. Amended by Stats.2000, c. 1064 (A.B.2227), § 11, eff. Sept. 30, 2000; Stats.2001, c. 473 (S.B.485), § 23; Stats.2004, c. 550 (S.B.1694), § 18; Stats.2005, c. 22 (S.B.1108), § 202; Stats.2008, c. 392 (S.B.1190), § 1; Stats.2011, c. 657 (A.B.520), § 4; Stats.2012, c. 162 (S.B.1171), § 182.)*

Cross References

Interest of justice exceptions to the statutory requirements for installation of an ignition interlock device under this section, findings, statement of reasons, see California Rules of Court, Rule 4.325.

Out of state residents, expiration of suspension or revocation period, see Vehicle Code § 13353.5.

§ 23575.1. Ignition interlock devices; effectiveness study and report

The department may undertake a study and report its findings of that study to the Legislature on or before January 1, 2013, regarding the overall effectiveness of the use of ignition interlock devices (IID) to reduce the recidivism rate of first-time violators of Section 23152 or 23153. If the department exercises this authority, the study shall focus on those drivers who actually have an IID installed in their vehicles rather than on those who are subject to a judicial order to have an IID installed. *(Added by Stats.2008, c. 392 (S.B.1190), § 2.)*

§ 23576. Motor vehicle owned by employer; exemption

(a) Notwithstanding Sections 23575 and 23700, if a person is required to operate a motor vehicle in the course and scope of his or her employment and if the vehicle is owned by the employer, the person may operate that vehicle without installation of an approved ignition interlock device if the employer has been notified by the person that the person's driving privilege has been restricted pursuant to Sections 23575 and 23700 and if the person has proof of that notification in his or her possession, or if the notice, or a facsimile copy thereof, is with the vehicle.

(b) A motor vehicle owned by a business entity that is all or partly owned or controlled by a person otherwise subject to Sections 23575 and 23700, is not a motor vehicle owned by the employer subject to the exemption in subdivision (a). *(Added by Stats.1998, c. 118 (S.B. 1186), § 84, operative July 1, 1999. Amended by Stats. 2009, c. 217 (A.B.91), § 2.)*

§ 23577. Willful refusal to submit to or failure to complete chemical test by person convicted of driving under the influence of alcohol or drugs; penalties; pleading and proof

(a) If any person is convicted of a violation of Section 23152 or 23153, and at the time of the arrest leading to that conviction that person willfully refused a peace officer's request to submit to, or willfully failed to complete, the chemical test or tests pursuant to Section 23612, the court shall impose the following penalties:

(1) If the person is convicted of a first violation of Section 23152, notwithstanding any other provision of subdivision (a) of Section 23538, the terms and conditions of probation shall include the conditions in paragraph (1) of subdivision (a) of Section 23538.

(2) If the person is convicted of a first violation of Section 23153, the punishment shall be enhanced by an imprisonment of 48 continuous hours in the county jail, whether or not probation is granted and no part of which may be stayed, unless the person is sentenced to, and incarcerated in, the state prison and the execution of that sentence is not stayed.

(3) If the person is convicted of a second violation of Section 23152, punishable under Section 23540, or a second violation of Section 23153, punishable under Section 23560, the punishment shall be enhanced by an imprisonment of 96 hours in the county jail, whether or not probation is granted and no part of which may be stayed, unless the person is sentenced to, and incarcerated in, the state prison and execution of that sentence is not stayed.

(4) If the person is convicted of a third violation of Section 23152, punishable under Section 23546, the punishment shall be enhanced by an imprisonment of 10 days in the county jail, whether or not probation is granted and no part of which may be stayed.

(5) If the person is convicted of a fourth or subsequent violation of Section 23152, punishable under Section 23550 or 23550.5, the punishment shall be enhanced by imprisonment of 18 days in the county jail, whether or not probation is granted and no part of which may be stayed.

(b) The willful refusal or failure to complete the chemical test required pursuant to Section 23612 shall be pled and proven. *(Added by Stats.1998, c. 118 (S.B.1186), § 84, operative July 1, 1999. Amended by Stats.1999, c. 22 (S.B.24), § 39, eff. May 26, 1999, operative July 1, 1999.)*

§ 23578. Conviction of violation of § 23152 or § 23153; alcohol concentration or refusal to take chemical test as special factor; penalty enhancement or probation

In addition to any other provision of this code, if a person is convicted of a violation of Section 23152 or

23153, the court shall consider a concentration of alcohol in the person's blood of 0.15 percent or more, by weight, or the refusal of the person to take a chemical test, as a special factor that may justify enhancing the penalties in sentencing, in determining whether to grant probation, and, if probation is granted, in determining additional or enhanced terms and conditions of probation. *(Added by Stats.1998, c. 118 (S.B.1186), § 84, operative July 1, 1999. Amended by Stats.2005, c. 89 (A.B.571), § 1.)*

Cross References

Alcohol and drug problem assessment program, violator participation, sentencing, and assessment upon fine, see Vehicle Code § 23646 et seq.

Alcoholic beverages in vehicles, see Vehicle Code § 23220 et seq.

Applicability of this section to trolley coaches, see Vehicle Code § 21051.

Arrest without warrant, see Vehicle Code § 40300.5.

Challenging constitutional validity of separate conviction, see Vehicle Code § 41403.

Chemical blood, breath or urine tests, see Vehicle Code §§ 13353, 13354.

Chemical tests as evidence, see Vehicle Code § 23610.

Conviction of violation of specified subdivisions of Penal Code § 192 to be deemed conviction of violation of specified DUI provisions, see Vehicle Code § 13350.5.

Coroner's inquiry into deaths, see Government Code § 27491.25.

County alcohol and drug problem assessment programs; mandatory participation for convicted violators of this section, see Vehicle Code §§ 23646, 23647.

Crime of violence, within act for indemnification of victims of crime, see Government Code § 13960.

Defense of drug use to violations, see Vehicle Code § 23630.

Deposit in special account for each conviction under DUI provisions, see Penal Code § 1463.14.

Drivers license revocation, conviction of driver under eighteen, see Vehicle Code § 13352.3.

Driving school or instructor, revocation or suspension of license for violation of this section, see Vehicle Code § 11110.

Gross vehicular manslaughter while intoxicated, see Penal Code § 191.5.

Guilty plea, see Vehicle Code § 41610.

Impoundment of vehicle of registered owner convicted under this section, see Vehicle Code § 23594.

Influence of alcoholic beverage or drug, suspension or revocation of driving privileges, see Vehicle Code § 13352.

Injury to guest by intoxicated driver, see Vehicle Code § 17158.

Juvenile offenders, programs of supervision, see Welfare and Institutions Code § 654.1.

Juveniles with blood-alcohol concentrations of 0.05 or more, driving violations, participation in rehabilitation programs, see Vehicle Code § 23504.

Manslaughter, negligent homicide by vehicle, see Penal Code § 192.

Nuisance, sale or other disposition of motor vehicle driven by defendant, see Vehicle Code § 23596.

Persons certified or granted probation on conviction of driving under the influence of alcohol or drugs or combined influence on certain conditions, restriction, revocation or suspension of driving privilege, consent to participation in treatment program, see Vehicle Code § 13352.5.

Please Don't Drink and Drive memorial signs, requests for and duration of placement, exception for a party to an accident convicted or determined to be mentally incompetent under this section, see Streets and Highways Code § 101.10.

Presentence investigation and assessment, see Vehicle Code § 23655.

Presumptions, see Evidence Code § 600 et seq.

Prior convictions under sections 23103, 23152 or 23153, effect on sentencing and driving privileges, see Vehicle Code § 23622.

Procedure on arrest for violation of this section, see Vehicle Code § 40302.

Records available to courts and law enforcement officials, incidents under certain DWI and homicide laws, period of time records must be available, see Vehicle Code § 1808.

Refusal to submit to alcohol testing under DUI laws, calculation of prior convictions, certain foreign convictions recognized, see Vehicle Code §§ 13353, 13353.1 and 13353.3.

Surrender of driver's license to court, see Vehicle Code § 13550.

Suspension or revocation of driving privilege for a violation of this section, notice by personal service, see Vehicle Code § 13106.

Suspension or revocation of license,
  Generally, see Vehicle Code § 13352.
  Alcohol-related accident within five years of vehicular manslaughter, see Vehicle Code § 13954.
  Driver license compact, see Vehicle Code § 15000 et seq.
  Driving after suspension or revocation, see Vehicle Code § 14601.2.
  Investigation by department, three convictions in three years under this or other specified statutes, see Vehicle Code 13800.
  Prior convictions, record, see Vehicle Code § 13209.

Traffic violation point count, violation of this section, see Vehicle Code § 12810.

Traffic violators schools, suspension or revocation of license for violation of this section, see Vehicle Code § 11215.

Vehicular homicide, see Penal Code § 192.

Violation as misdemeanor, see Vehicle Code § 40000.15.

Violation of this section, relinquishment of motor vehicle to convicted minor, see Penal Code § 193.8.

Youthful drunk driver visitation program, see Vehicle Code § 23509 et seq.

§ 23580. Second or subsequent offense involving alcohol or drugs; minimum confinement

(a) If any person is convicted of a violation of Section 23152 or 23153 and the offense was a second or subsequent offense punishable under Section 23540, 23546, 23550, 23550.5, 23560, or 23566, the court shall require that any term of imprisonment that is imposed include at least one period of not less than 48 consecutive hours of imprisonment or, in the alternative and notwithstanding Section 4024.2 of the Penal Code, that the person serve not less than 10 days of community service.

(b) Notwithstanding any other provision of law, except Section 2900.5 of the Penal Code, unless the court expressly finds in the circumstances that the punishment inflicted would be cruel or unusual punishment prohibited by Section 17 of Article I of the California Constitution, no court or person to whom a person is remanded for execution of sentence shall release, or permit the release of, a person from the requirements of subdivision

775

(a), including, but not limited to, any work-release program, weekend service of sentence program, diversion or treatment program, or otherwise.

(c) For the purposes of this section, "imprisonment" means confinement in a jail, in a minimum security facility, or in an inpatient rehabilitation facility, as provided in Part 1309 (commencing with Section 1309.1) of Title 23 of the Code of Federal Regulations.

(Added by Stats.1998, c. 118 (S.B.1186), § 84, operative July 1, 1999. Amended by Stats.2002, c. 664 (A.B. 3034), § 223.)

Cross References

Alcohol and drug problem assessment program, violator participation, sentencing, and assessment upon fine, see Vehicle Code § 23646 et seq.

Alcoholic beverages in vehicles, see Vehicle Code § 23220 et seq.

Applicability of this section to trolley coaches, see Vehicle Code § 21051.

Arrest without warrant, see Vehicle Code § 40300.5.

Challenging constitutional validity of separate conviction, see Vehicle Code § 41403.

Chemical blood, breath or urine tests, see Vehicle Code §§ 13353, 13354.

Chemical tests as evidence, see Vehicle Code § 23610.

Conviction of violation of specified subdivisions of Penal Code § 192 to be deemed conviction of violation of specified DUI provisions, see Vehicle Code § 13350.5.

Coroner's inquiry into deaths, see Government Code § 27491.25.

County alcohol and drug problem assessment programs; mandatory participation for convicted violators of this section, see Vehicle Code §§ 23646, 23647.

Crime of violence, within act for indemnification of victims of crime, see Government Code § 13960.

Defense of drug use to violations, see Vehicle Code § 23630.

Deposit in special account for each conviction under DUI provisions, see Penal Code § 1463.14.

Drivers license revocation, conviction of driver under eighteen, see Vehicle Code § 13352.3.

Driving school or instructor, revocation or suspension of license for violation of this section, see Vehicle Code § 11110.

Gross vehicular manslaughter while intoxicated, see Penal Code § 191.5.

Guilty plea, see Vehicle Code § 41610.

Impoundment of vehicle of registered owner convicted under this section, see Vehicle Code § 23594.

Influence of alcoholic beverage or drug, suspension or revocation of driving privileges, see Vehicle Code § 13352.

Injury to guest by intoxicated driver, see Vehicle Code § 17158.

Juvenile offenders, programs of supervision, see Welfare and Institutions Code § 654.1.

Juveniles with blood-alcohol concentrations of 0.05 or more, driving violations, participation in rehabilitation programs, see Vehicle Code § 23504.

Manslaughter, negligent homicide by vehicle, see Penal Code § 192.

Nuisance, sale or other disposition of motor vehicle driven by defendant, see Vehicle Code § 23596.

Persons certified or granted probation on conviction of driving under the influence of alcohol or drugs or combined influence on certain conditions, restriction, revocation or suspension of driving privilege, consent to participation in treatment program, see Vehicle Code § 13352.5.

Please Don't Drink and Drive memorial signs, requests for and duration of placement, exception for a party to an accident convicted or determined to be mentally incompetent under this section, see Streets and Highways Code § 101.10.

Presentence investigation and assessment, see Vehicle Code § 23655.

Presumptions, see Evidence Code § 600 et seq.

Prior convictions under sections 23103, 23152 or 23153, effect on sentencing and driving privileges, see Vehicle Code § 23622.

Procedure on arrest for violation of this section, see Vehicle Code § 40302.

Records available to courts and law enforcement officials, incidents under certain DWI and homicide laws, period of time records must be available, see Vehicle Code § 1808.

Refusal to submit to alcohol testing under DUI laws, calculation of prior convictions, certain foreign convictions recognized, see Vehicle Code §§ 13353, 13353.1 and 13353.3.

Surrender of driver's license to court, see Vehicle Code § 13550.

Suspension or revocation of driving privilege for a violation of this section, notice by personal service, see Vehicle Code § 13106.

Suspension or revocation of license,
  Generally, see Vehicle Code § 13352.
  Alcohol-related accident within five years of vehicular manslaughter, see Vehicle Code § 13954.
  Driver license compact, see Vehicle Code § 15000 et seq.
  Driving after suspension or revocation, see Vehicle Code § 14601.2.
  Investigation by department, three convictions in three years under this or other specified statutes, see Vehicle Code 13800.
  Prior convictions, record, see Vehicle Code § 13209.

Traffic violation point count, violation of this section, see Vehicle Code § 12810.

Traffic violators schools, suspension or revocation of license for violation of this section, see Vehicle Code § 11215.

Vehicular homicide, see Penal Code § 192.

Violation as misdemeanor, see Vehicle Code § 40000.15.

Violation of this section, relinquishment of motor vehicle to convicted minor, see Penal Code § 193.8.

Youthful drunk driver visitation program, see Vehicle Code § 23509 et seq.

§ 23582. Driving under the influence; addition penalty for excessive speed and reckless driving during commission of offense; additional punishment

(a) Any person who drives a vehicle 30 or more miles per hour over the maximum, prima facie, or posted speed limit on a freeway, or 20 or more miles per hour over the maximum, prima facie, or posted speed limit on any other street or highway, and in a manner prohibited by Section 23103 during the commission of a violation of Section 23152 or 23153 shall, in addition to the punishment prescribed for that person upon conviction of a violation of Section 23152 or 23153, be punished by an additional and consecutive term of 60 days in the county jail.

(b) If the court grants probation or suspends the execution of sentence, it shall require as a condition of probation or suspension that the defendant serve 60 days in the county jail, in addition and consecutive to any other sentence prescribed by this chapter.

(c) On a first conviction under this section, the court shall order the driver to participate in, and successfully complete, an alcohol or drug education and counseling program, or both an alcohol and a drug education and counseling program. Except in unusual cases where the interests of justice would be served, a finding making this section applicable to a defendant shall not be stricken pursuant to Section 1385 of the Penal Code or any other provision of law. If the court decides not to impose the additional and consecutive term, it shall specify on the court record the reasons for that order.

(d) The additional term provided in this section shall not be imposed unless the facts of driving in a manner prohibited by Section 23103 and driving the vehicle 30 or more miles per hour over the maximum, prima facie, or posted speed limit on a freeway, or 20 or more miles per hour over the maximum, prima facie, or posted speed limit on any other street or highway, are charged in the accusatory pleading and admitted or found to be true by the trier of fact. A finding of driving in that manner shall be based on facts in addition to the fact that the defendant was driving while under the influence of alcohol, any drug, or both, or with a specified percentage of alcohol in the blood. *(Added by Stats.1998, c. 118 (S.B.1186), § 84, operative July 1, 1999.)*

ARTICLE 6. ADDITIONAL COURT–IMPOSED ORDERS AND DIRECTIONS

Section
23590. Repealed.
23592. Impoundment of vehicle; specified offenses.
23593. Advisory statement to be given by court to person convicted of violation of specified sections.
23594. Impoundment of vehicle of registered owner convicted of violation of § 23152 or § 23153; prior offenses; considerations; exemption.
23596. Motor vehicle as nuisance; sale of vehicle.
23597. Ten-year revocation for person convicted of three or more separate driving under the influence offenses; application for reinstatement; conditions.

§ 23590. Repealed by Stats.1999, c. 22 (S.B.24), § 40, eff. May 26, 1999, operative July 1, 1999

§ 23592. Impoundment of vehicle; specified offenses

(a)(1) Whenever a person is convicted of any of the following offenses committed while driving a motor vehicle of which he or she is the owner, the court, at the time sentence is imposed on the person, may order the motor vehicle impounded for a period of not more than six months for a first conviction, and not more than 12 months for a second or subsequent conviction:

(A) Driving with a suspended or revoked driver's license.

(B) A violation of Section 2800.2 resulting in an accident or Section 2800.3, if either violation occurred within seven years of one or more separate convictions for a violation of any of the following:

(i) Section 23103, if the vehicle involved in the violation was driven at a speed of 100 or more miles per hour.

(ii) Section 23152.

(iii) Section 23153.

(iv) Subdivisions (a) and (b) of Section 191.5 of the Penal Code.

(v) Subdivision (c) of Section 192 of the Penal Code.

(vi) Subdivision (a) of Section 192.5 of the Penal Code.

(2) The cost of keeping the vehicle is a lien on the vehicle pursuant to Chapter 6.5 (commencing with Section 3067) of Title 14 of Part 4 of Division 3 of the Civil Code.

(b) Notwithstanding subdivision (a), a motor vehicle impounded pursuant to this section that is subject to a chattel mortgage, conditional sale contract, or lease contract shall be released by the court to the legal owner upon the filing of an affidavit by the legal owner that the chattel mortgage, conditional sale contract, or lease contract is in default and shall be delivered to the legal owner upon payment of the accrued cost of keeping the vehicle. *(Added by Stats.1998, c. 118 (S.B.1186), § 84, operative July 1, 1999. Amended by Stats.2007, c. 747 (A.B.678), § 35.)*

Cross References

Illegal dumping of waste matter, impoundment, see Vehicle Code § 23112.7.

§ 23593. Advisory statement to be given by court to person convicted of violation of specified sections

(a) The court shall advise a person convicted of a violation of Section 23103, as specified in Section 23103.5, or a violation of Section 23152 or 23153, as follows:

"You are hereby advised that being under the influence of alcohol or drugs, or both, impairs your ability to safely operate a motor vehicle. Therefore, it is extremely dangerous to human life to drive while under the influence of alcohol or drugs, or both. If you continue to drive while under the influence of alcohol or drugs, or both, and, as a result of that driving, someone is killed, you can be charged with murder."

(b) The advisory statement may be included in a plea form, if used, or the fact that the advice was given may be specified on the record.

(c) The court shall include on the abstract of the conviction or violation submitted to the department under Section 1803 or 1816, the fact that the person has been advised as required under subdivision (a). *(Added by Stats.2004, c. 502 (A.B.2173), § 1. Amended by Stats.2005, c. 279 (S.B.1107), § 24; Stats.2005, c. 22 (S.B.1108), § 203.)*

§ 23594. Impoundment of vehicle of registered owner convicted of violation of § 23152 or § 23153; prior offenses; considerations; exemption

(a) Except as provided in subdivision (b), the interest of any registered owner of a motor vehicle that has been used in the commission of a violation of Section 23152 or 23153 for which the owner was convicted, is subject to impoundment as provided in this section. Upon conviction, the court may order the vehicle impounded at the registered owner's expense for not less than one nor more than 30 days.

If the offense occurred within five years of a prior offense which resulted in conviction of a violation of Section 23152 or 23153, the prior conviction shall also be charged in the accusatory pleading and if admitted or found to be true by the jury upon a jury trial or by the court upon a court trial, the court shall, except in an unusual case where the interests of justice would best be served by not ordering impoundment, order the vehicle impounded at the registered owner's expense for not less than one nor more than 30 days.

If the offense occurred within five years of two or more prior offenses which resulted in convictions of violations of Section 23152 or 23153, the prior convictions shall also be charged in the accusatory pleading and if admitted or found to be true by the jury upon a jury trial or by the court upon a court trial, the court shall, except in an unusual case where the interests of justice would best be served by not ordering impoundment, order the vehicle impounded at the registered owner's expense for not less than one nor more than 90 days.

For the purposes of this section, the court may consider in the interests of justice factors such as whether impoundment of the vehicle would result in a loss of employment of the offender or the offender's family, impair the ability of the offender or the offender's family to attend school or obtain medical care, result in the loss of the vehicle because of inability to pay impoundment fees, or unfairly infringe upon community property rights or any other facts the court finds relevant. When no impoundment is ordered in an unusual case pursuant to this section, the court shall specify on the record and shall enter in the minutes the circumstances indicating that the interests of justice would best be served by that disposition.

(b) No vehicle which may be lawfully driven on the highway with a class C or class M driver's license, as specified in Section 12804.9, is subject to impoundment under this section if there is a community property interest in the vehicle owned by a person other than the defendant and the vehicle is the sole vehicle available to the defendant's immediate family which may be operated on the highway with a class C or class M driver's license. *(Added by Stats.1998, c. 118 (S.B.1186), § 84, operative July 1, 1999.)*

Cross References

Immediate removal and seizure of vehicle driven by repeat offender, storage and impoundment, vehicle owner's rights and responsibilities, see Vehicle Code § 14602.8.

§ 23596. Motor vehicle as nuisance; sale of vehicle

(a)(1) Upon its own motion or upon motion of the prosecutor in a criminal action for a violation of any of the following offenses, the court with jurisdiction over the offense, notwithstanding Section 86 of the Code of Civil Procedure and any other provision of law otherwise prescribing the jurisdiction of the court based upon the value of the property involved, may declare the motor vehicle driven by the defendant to be a nuisance if the defendant is the registered owner of the vehicle:

(A) A violation of Section 191.5 of, or subdivision (a) of Section 192.5 of, the Penal Code.

(B) A violation of Section 23152 that occurred within seven years of two or more separate offenses of Section 191.5 of, or subdivision (a) of Section 192.5 of, the Penal Code, or Section 23152 or 23153, or any combination thereof, that resulted in convictions.

(C) A violation of Section 23153 that occurred within seven years of one or more separate offenses of Section 191.5 of, or subdivision (a) of Section 192.5 of, the Penal Code, or Section 23152 or 23153, that resulted in convictions.

(2) The court or the prosecutor shall give notice of the motion to the defendant, and the court shall hold a hearing before a motor vehicle may be declared a nuisance under this section.

(b) Except as provided in subdivision (g), upon the conviction of the defendant and at the time of pronouncement of sentence, the court with jurisdiction over the offense shall order a vehicle declared to be a nuisance pursuant to subdivision (a) to be sold. A vehicle ordered to be sold pursuant to this subdivision shall be surrendered to the sheriff of the county or the chief of police of the city in which the violation occurred. The officer to whom the vehicle is surrendered shall promptly ascertain from the department the names and addresses of all legal and registered owners of the vehicle and, within five days of receiving that information, shall send by certified mail a notice to all legal and registered owners of the vehicle other than the defendant, at the addresses obtained from the department, informing them that the vehicle has been declared a nuisance and will be sold or otherwise disposed of pursuant to this section and of the approximate date and location of the sale or other disposition. The notice shall also inform a legal owner of its right to conduct the sale pursuant to subdivision (c).

(c) The legal owner who is a motor vehicle dealer, bank, credit union, acceptance corporation, or other licensed finance institution legally operating in this state, or the agent of that legal owner, may take possession and conduct the sale of the vehicle declared to be a nuisance if it notifies the officer to whom the vehicle is surrendered of its intent to conduct the sale within 15 days of the mailing of the notice pursuant to subdivision (b). Sale of the vehicle pursuant to this subdivision may be conducted at the time, in the manner, and on the notice usually given for the sale of repossessed or surrendered vehicles. The proceeds of a sale conducted by the legal owner shall be disposed of as provided in subdivision (e). A notice pursuant to this subdivision may be presented in person, by certified mail, by facsimile transmission, or by electronic mail. The agent of a legal owner acting pursuant to this subdivision shall be licensed, or exempt from licensure, pursuant to Chapter 11 (commencing with Section 7500) of Division 3 of the Business and Professions Code.

(d) If the legal owner or the agent of the legal owner does not notify the officer to whom the vehicle is surrendered of its intent to conduct the sale as provided in subdivision (c), the officer shall offer the vehicle for sale at public auction within 60 days of receiving the vehicle. At least 10 days but not more than 20 days prior to the sale, not counting the day of the sale, the officer shall give notice of the sale by advertising once in a newspaper of general circulation published in the city or county, as the case may be, in which the vehicle is located, that notice shall contain a description of the make, year, model, identification number, and license number of the vehicle and the date, time, and location of the sale. For motorcycles, the engine number shall also be included. If there is no newspaper of general circulation published in the county, notice shall be given by posting a notice of sale containing the information required by this subdivision in three of the most public places in the city or county in which the vehicle is located, and at the place where the vehicle is to be sold, for 10 consecutive days prior to and including the day of the sale.

(e) The proceeds of a sale conducted pursuant to this section shall be disposed of in the following priority:

(1) To satisfy the costs of the sale, including costs incurred with respect to the taking and keeping of the vehicle pending sale.

(2) To the legal owner in an amount to satisfy the indebtedness owed to the legal owner remaining as of the date of the sale, including accrued interest or finance charges and delinquency charges.

(3) To the holder of a subordinate lien or encumbrance on the vehicle to satisfy any indebtedness so secured if written notification of demand is received before distribution of the proceeds is completed. The holder of a subordinate lien or encumbrance, if requested, shall reasonably furnish reasonable proof of its interest and, unless it does so on request, is not entitled to distribution pursuant to this paragraph.

(4) To any other person who can establish an interest in the vehicle, including a community property interest, to the extent of his or her provable interest.

(5) If the vehicle was forfeited as a result of a felony violation of subdivision (a) of Section 191.5 of, or subdivision (a) of Section 192.5 of, the Penal Code, or of Section 23153 that resulted in serious bodily injury to a person other than the defendant, the balance, if any, to the city or county in which the violation occurred, to be deposited in its general fund.

(6) Except as provided in paragraph (5), the balance, if any, to the city or county in which the violation occurred, to be expended for community-based adolescent substance abuse treatment services.

The person conducting the sale shall disburse the proceeds of the sale as provided in this subdivision, and provide a written accounting regarding the disposition to all persons entitled to or claiming a share of the proceeds, within 15 days after the sale is conducted.

(f) If the vehicle to be sold under this section is not of the type that can readily be sold to the public generally, the vehicle shall be destroyed or donated to an eleemosynary institution.

(g) No vehicle shall be sold pursuant to this section in either of the following circumstances:

(1) The vehicle is stolen, unless the identity of the legal and registered owners of the vehicle cannot be reasonably ascertained.

(2) The vehicle is owned by another, or there is a community property interest in the vehicle owned by a person other than the defendant and the vehicle is the only vehicle available to the defendant's immediate family that may be operated on the highway with a class 3 or class 4 driver's license.

(h) The Legislature finds and declares it to be the public policy of this state that no policy of insurance shall afford benefits that would alleviate the financial detriment suffered by a person as a direct or indirect result of a confiscation of a vehicle pursuant to this section. *(Added by Stats.1999, c. 22 (S.B.24), § 40.4, eff. May 26, 1999, operative July 1, 1999. Amended by Stats.2007, c. 747 (A.B.678), § 36.)*

Cross References

Illegal dumping of harmful waste matter, impoundment and civil forfeiture, see Vehicle Code § 23112.7.

§ 23597. Ten-year revocation for person convicted of three or more separate driving under the influence offenses; application for reinstatement; conditions

(a) Notwithstanding Sections 13202.5, 13203, and 13352, a court may order a 10–year revocation of the driver's license of a person who has been convicted of three or more separate violations of Section 23152 or 23153, the last of which is punishable under Section 23546, 23550, 23550.5, or 23566. When making this order, the court shall consider all of the following:

(1) The person's level of remorse for the acts.

(2) The period of time that has elapsed since the person's previous convictions.

(3) The person's blood-alcohol level at the time of the violation.

(4) The person's participation in an alcohol treatment program.

(5) The person's risk to traffic or public safety.

(6) The person's ability to install a certified ignition interlock device in each motor vehicle that he or she owns or operates.

(b) Upon receipt of a duly certified abstract of the record of the court showing the court has ordered a 10–year revocation of a driver's license pursuant to this section, the department shall revoke the person's driver's license for 10 years, except as provided in subdivision (c).

(c)(1) Five years from the date of the last conviction of a violation of Section 23152 or 23153, a person whose license was revoked pursuant to subdivision (a) may apply to the department to have his or her privilege to operate a motor vehicle reinstated, subject to the condition that the person submits the "Verification of Installation" form described in paragraph (2) of subdivision (h) of Section 13386 and agrees to maintain the ignition interlock device as required under subdivision (g) of Section 23575. Notwithstanding Chapter 5 (commencing with Section 23700) or subdivision (f) of Section 23575, the ignition interlock device shall remain on the person's motor vehicle for two years following the reinstatement of the person's driving privilege pursuant to this section.

(2) The department shall reinstate the person's license pursuant to paragraph (1), if the person satisfies all of the following conditions:

(A) The person was not convicted of any drug- or alcohol-related offenses, under state law, during the driver's license revocation period.

(B) The person successfully completed a driving-under-the-influence program, licensed pursuant to Section 11836 of the Health and Safety Code, following the date of the last conviction of a violation of Section 23152 or 23153.

(C) The person was not convicted of violating Section 14601, 14601.1, 14601.2, 14601.4, or 14601.5 during the driver's license revocation period.

(3) The department shall immediately terminate the restriction issued pursuant to this section and shall immediately revoke the privilege to operate a motor vehicle of a person who attempts to remove, bypass, or tamper with the device, who has the device removed prior to the termination date of the restriction, or who fails three or more times to comply with any requirement for the maintenance or calibration of the ignition interlock device. The privilege shall remain revoked for the remaining period of the original revocation and until all reinstatement requirements are met.

(d) This section shall become operative on January 1, 2012. *(Added by Stats.2010, c. 301 (A.B.1601), § 8, operative Jan. 1, 2012.)*

ARTICLE 7. ALTERNATIVE TO ALCOHOL OR DRUG EDUCATION PROGRAM

Section
23598.   Live-in alternative to incarceration rehabilitation programs.

§ 23598. Live-in alternative to incarceration rehabilitation programs

In lieu of the alcohol or drug education program prescribed by Section 23538, 23542, 23548, 23552, 23556, 23562, or 23568, a court may impose, as a condition of probation, that the person complete, subsequent to the underlying conviction, a program specified in Section 8001 of the Penal Code, if the person consents and has been accepted into that program. Acceptance into that program shall be verified by a certification, under penalty of perjury, by the director of the program. *(Added by Stats.1998, c. 118 (S.B.1186), § 84, operative July 1, 1999.)*

CHAPTER 3. PROBATION

Section
23600.   Conviction and pronouncement of sentence for violations of § 23152 or § 23153; probation; minimum confinement or fine; violation of probation.
23601.   Convictions under § 23152 or § 23153; fine, restitution, or assessment; enforcement.
23602.   Suspended sentence and probation; violation of probation; procedure for revocation.

§ 23600. Conviction and pronouncement of sentence for violations of § 23152 or § 23153; probation; minimum confinement or fine; violation of probation

(a) If any person is convicted of a violation of Section 23152 or 23153, the court shall not stay or suspend pronouncement of sentencing, and shall pronounce sentence in conjunction with the conviction in a reasonable time, including time for receipt of any presentence investigation report ordered pursuant to Section 23655.

(b) If any person is convicted of a violation of Section 23152 or 23153 and is granted probation, the terms and conditions of probation shall include, but not be limited to, the following:

(1) Notwithstanding Section 1203a of the Penal Code, a period of probation not less than three nor more than five years; provided, however, that if the maximum sentence provided for the offense may exceed five years in the state prison, the period during which the sentence may be suspended and terms of probation enforced may be for a longer period than three years but may not exceed the maximum time for which sentence of imprisonment may be pronounced.

(2) A requirement that the person shall not drive a vehicle with any measurable amount of alcohol in his or her blood.

(3) A requirement that the person, if arrested for a violation of Section 23152 or 23153, shall not refuse to

submit to a chemical test of his or her blood, breath, or urine, pursuant to Section 23612, for the purpose of determining the alcoholic content of his or her blood.

(4) A requirement that the person shall not commit any criminal offense.

(c) The court shall not absolve a person who is convicted of a violation of Section 23152 or 23153 from the obligation of spending the minimum time in confinement, if any, or of paying the minimum fine imposed by law.

(d) In addition to any other provision of law, if any person violates paragraph (2) or (3) of subdivision (b) and the person had a blood alcohol concentration of over 0.04 percent as determined by a chemical test, the court shall revoke or terminate the person's probation as provided by Section 23602, regardless of any other proceeding, and shall only grant a new term of probation of not more than five years on the added condition that the person be confined in the county jail for not less than 48 hours for each of these violations of probation, except in unusual cases where the interests of justice would best be served if this additional condition were not imposed. *(Added by Stats.1998, c. 118 (S.B.1186), § 84, operative July 1, 1999. Amended by Stats.1999, c. 22 (S.B.24), § 40.6, eff. May 26, 1999, operative July 1, 1999.)*

§ 23601. Convictions under § 23152 or § 23153; fine, restitution, or assessment; enforcement

(a) Except as provided in subdivision (c), an order to pay any fine, restitution, or assessment, imposed as a condition of the grant of probation or as part of a judgment of conditional sentence for a violation of Section 23152 or 23153, may be enforced in the same manner provided for the enforcement of money judgments.

(b) A willful failure to pay any fine, restitution, or assessment during the term of probation is a violation of the terms and conditions of probation.

(c) If an order to pay a fine as a condition of probation is stayed, a writ of execution shall not be issued, and any failure to pay the fine is not willful, until the stay is removed. *(Added by Stats.1998, c. 118 (S.B.1186), § 84, operative July 1, 1999.)*

§ 23602. Suspended sentence and probation; violation of probation; procedure for revocation

Except as otherwise expressly provided in this code, if a person has been convicted of a violation of Section 23152 or 23153 and the court has suspended execution of the sentence for that conviction and has granted probation, and during the time of that probation, the person is found by the court to have violated a required term or condition of that probation, the court shall revoke the suspension of sentence, revoke or terminate probation, and shall proceed in the manner provided in subdivision (c) of Section 1203.2 of the Penal Code. *(Added by Stats.1998, c. 118 (S.B.1186), § 84, operative July 1, 1999. Amended by*

Stats.1999, c. 22 (S.B.24), § 41, eff. May 26, 1999, operative July 1, 1999.)

CHAPTER 4. PROCEDURES

Article		Section
1.	General Provisions	23610
2.	Prior and Separate Offenses	23620
3.	Defenses	23630
4.	Dismissal on the Record	23635
5.	Court Restrictions	23640
6.	Alcohol Assessment	23645
7.	Presentence Investigation	23655
8.	Surrender and Notification of License Restriction	23660
9.	Delayed Suspensions and Revocations	23665
10.	Conflict of Interest	23670
11.	Operative Date	23675

ARTICLE 1. GENERAL PROVISIONS

Section
23610. Blood alcohol percentages; presumptions; other evidence.
23612. Chemical, blood, breath, or urine tests.
23614. Chemical blood, breath, or urine tests; advising persons submitting to breath tests; admissibility of evidence.

§ 23610. Blood alcohol percentages; presumptions; other evidence

(a) Upon the trial of any criminal action, or preliminary proceeding in a criminal action, arising out of acts alleged to have been committed by any person while driving a vehicle while under the influence of an alcoholic beverage in violation of subdivision (a) of Section 23152 or subdivision (a) of Section 23153, the amount of alcohol in the person's blood at the time of the test as shown by chemical analysis of that person's blood, breath, or urine shall give rise to the following presumptions affecting the burden of proof:

(1) If there was at that time less than 0.05 percent, by weight, of alcohol in the person's blood, it shall be presumed that the person was not under the influence of an alcoholic beverage at the time of the alleged offense.

(2) If there was at that time 0.05 percent or more but less than 0.08 percent, by weight, of alcohol in the person's blood, that fact shall not give rise to any presumption that the person was or was not under the influence of an alcoholic beverage, but the fact may be considered with other competent evidence in determining whether the person was under the influence of an alcoholic beverage at the time of the alleged offense.

(3) If there was at that time 0.08 percent or more, by weight, of alcohol in the person's blood, it shall be presumed that the person was under the influence of an alcoholic beverage at the time of the alleged offense.

(b) Percent, by weight, of alcohol in the person's blood shall be based upon grams of alcohol per 100 milliliters of blood or grams of alcohol per 210 liters of breath.

(c) This section shall not be construed as limiting the introduction of any other competent evidence bearing upon the question of whether the person ingested any alcoholic beverage or was under the influence of an alcoholic beverage at the time of the alleged offense. *(Added by Stats.1998, c. 118 (S.B.1186), § 84, operative July 1, 1999.)*

§ 23612.   Chemical, blood, breath, or urine tests

(a)(1)(A) A person who drives a motor vehicle is deemed to have given his or her consent to chemical testing of his or her blood or breath for the purpose of determining the alcoholic content of his or her blood, if lawfully arrested for an offense allegedly committed in violation of Section 23140, 23152, or 23153. If a blood or breath test, or both, are unavailable, then paragraph (2) of subdivision (d) applies.

(B) A person who drives a motor vehicle is deemed to have given his or her consent to chemical testing of his or her blood for the purpose of determining the drug content of his or her blood, if lawfully arrested for an offense allegedly committed in violation of Section 23140, 23152, or 23153. If a blood test is unavailable, the person shall be deemed to have given his or her consent to chemical testing of his or her urine and shall submit to a urine test.

(C) The testing shall be incidental to a lawful arrest and administered at the direction of a peace officer having reasonable cause to believe the person was driving a motor vehicle in violation of Section 23140, 23152, or 23153.

(D) The person shall be told that his or her failure to submit to, or the failure to complete, the required chemical testing will result in a fine, mandatory imprisonment if the person is convicted of a violation of Section 23152 or 23153, and (i) the suspension of the person's privilege to operate a motor vehicle for a period of one year, (ii) the revocation of the person's privilege to operate a motor vehicle for a period of two years if the refusal occurs within 10 years of a separate violation of Section 23103 as specified in Section 23103.5, or of Section 23140, 23152, or 23153 of this code, or of Section 191.5 or subdivision (a) of Section 192.5 of the Penal Code that resulted in a conviction, or if the person's privilege to operate a motor vehicle has been suspended or revoked pursuant to Section 13353, 13353.1, or 13353.2 for an offense that occurred on a separate occasion, or (iii) the revocation of the person's privilege to operate a motor vehicle for a period of three years if the refusal occurs within 10 years of two or more separate violations of Section 23103 as specified in Section 23103.5, or of Section 23140, 23152, or 23153 of this code, or of Section 191.5 or subdivision (a) of Section 192.5 of the Penal Code, or any combination thereof, that resulted in convictions, or if the person's privilege to operate a motor vehicle has been suspended or revoked two or more times pursuant to Section 13353, 13353.1, or 13353.2 for offenses that occurred on separate occasions, or if there is

any combination of those convictions, administrative suspensions, or revocations.

(2)(A) If the person is lawfully arrested for driving under the influence of an alcoholic beverage, the person has the choice of whether the test shall be of his or her blood or breath and the officer shall advise the person that he or she has that choice. If the person arrested either is incapable, or states that he or she is incapable, of completing the chosen test, the person shall submit to the remaining test. If a blood or breath test, or both, are unavailable, then paragraph (2) of subdivision (d) applies.

(B) If the person is lawfully arrested for driving under the influence of any drug or the combined influence of an alcoholic beverage and any drug, the person has the choice of whether the test shall be of his or her blood or breath, and the officer shall advise the person that he or she has that choice.

(C) A person who chooses to submit to a breath test may also be requested to submit to a blood test if the officer has reasonable cause to believe that the person was driving under the influence of a drug or the combined influence of an alcoholic beverage and a drug and if the officer has a clear indication that a blood test will reveal evidence of the person being under the influence. The officer shall state in his or her report the facts upon which that belief and that clear indication are based. The officer shall advise the person that he or she is required to submit to an additional test. The person shall submit to and complete a blood test. If the person arrested is incapable of completing the blood test, the person shall submit to and complete a urine test.

(3) If the person is lawfully arrested for an offense allegedly committed in violation of Section 23140, 23152, or 23153, and, because of the need for medical treatment, the person is first transported to a medical facility where it is not feasible to administer a particular test of, or to obtain a particular sample of, the person's blood or breath, the person has the choice of those tests, including a urine test, that are available at the facility to which that person has been transported. In that case, the officer shall advise the person of those tests that are available at the medical facility and that the person's choice is limited to those tests that are available.

(4) The officer shall also advise the person that he or she does not have the right to have an attorney present before stating whether he or she will submit to a test or tests, before deciding which test or tests to take, or during administration of the test or tests chosen, and that, in the event of refusal to submit to a test or tests, the refusal may be used against him or her in a court of law.

(5) A person who is unconscious or otherwise in a condition rendering him or her incapable of refusal is deemed not to have withdrawn his or her consent and a test or tests may be administered whether or not the person is told that his or her failure to submit to, or the noncompletion of, the test or tests will result in the suspension or revocation of his or her privilege to operate a motor vehicle. A person who is dead is deemed not to

have withdrawn his or her consent and a test or tests may be administered at the direction of a peace officer.

(b) A person who is afflicted with hemophilia is exempt from the blood test required by this section, but shall submit to, and complete, a urine test.

(c) A person who is afflicted with a heart condition and is using an anticoagulant under the direction of a licensed physician and surgeon is exempt from the blood test required by this section, but shall submit to, and complete, a urine test.

(d)(1) A person lawfully arrested for an offense allegedly committed while the person was driving a motor vehicle in violation of Section 23140, 23152, or 23153 may request the arresting officer to have a chemical test made of the arrested person's blood or breath for the purpose of determining the alcoholic content of that person's blood, and, if so requested, the arresting officer shall have the test performed.

(2) If a blood or breath test is not available under subparagraph (A) of paragraph (1) of subdivision (a), or under subparagraph (A) of paragraph (2) of subdivision (a), or under paragraph (1) of this subdivision, the person shall submit to the remaining test in order to determine the percent, by weight, of alcohol in the person's blood. If both the blood and breath tests are unavailable, the person shall be deemed to have given his or her consent to chemical testing of his or her urine and shall submit to a urine test.

(e) If the person, who has been arrested for a violation of Section 23140, 23152, or 23153, refuses or fails to complete a chemical test or tests, or requests that a blood or urine test be taken, the peace officer, acting on behalf of the department, shall serve the notice of the order of suspension or revocation of the person's privilege to operate a motor vehicle personally on the arrested person. The notice shall be on a form provided by the department.

(f) If the peace officer serves the notice of the order of suspension or revocation of the person's privilege to operate a motor vehicle, the peace officer shall take possession of all driver's licenses issued by this state that are held by the person. The temporary driver's license shall be an endorsement on the notice of the order of suspension and shall be valid for 30 days from the date of arrest.

(g)(1) The peace officer shall immediately forward a copy of the completed notice of suspension or revocation form and any driver's license taken into possession under subdivision (f), with the report required by Section 13380, to the department. If the person submitted to a blood or urine test, the peace officer shall forward the results immediately to the appropriate forensic laboratory. The forensic laboratory shall forward the results of the chemical tests to the department within 15 calendar days of the date of the arrest.

(2)(A) Notwithstanding any other law, a document containing data prepared and maintained in the govern-mental forensic laboratory computerized database system that is electronically transmitted or retrieved through public or private computer networks to or by the department is the best available evidence of the chemical test results in all administrative proceedings conducted by the department. In addition, any other official record that is maintained in the governmental forensic laboratory, relates to a chemical test analysis prepared and maintained in the governmental forensic laboratory computerized database system, and is electronically transmitted and retrieved through a public or private computer network to or by the department is admissible as evidence in the department's administrative proceedings. In order to be admissible as evidence in administrative proceedings, a document described in this subparagraph shall bear a certification by the employee of the department who retrieved the document certifying that the information was received or retrieved directly from the computerized database system of a governmental forensic laboratory and that the document accurately reflects the data received or retrieved.

(B) Notwithstanding any other law, the failure of an employee of the department to certify under subparagraph (A) is not a public offense.

(h) A preliminary alcohol screening test that indicates the presence or concentration of alcohol based on a breath sample in order to establish reasonable cause to believe the person was driving a vehicle in violation of Section 23140, 23152, or 23153 is a field sobriety test and may be used by an officer as a further investigative tool.

(i) If the officer decides to use a preliminary alcohol screening test, the officer shall advise the person that he or she is requesting that person to take a preliminary alcohol screening test to assist the officer in determining if that person is under the influence of alcohol or drugs, or a combination of alcohol and drugs. The person's obligation to submit to a blood, breath, or urine test, as required by this section, for the purpose of determining the alcohol or drug content of that person's blood, is not satisfied by the person submitting to a preliminary alcohol screening test. The officer shall advise the person of that fact and of the person's right to refuse to take the preliminary alcohol screening test.

*** (Formerly § 23157, added by Stats.1992, c. 1281 (A.B.3580), § 9.7, operative July 1, 1993. Amended by Stats.1993, c. 272 (A.B.301), § 44.5, eff. Aug. 2, 1993; Stats.1993, c. 1244 (S.B.126), § 16; Stats.1994, c. 938 (S.B.1295), § 17, eff. Sept. 28, 1994; Stats.1996, c. 1154 (A.B.3020), § 70, eff. Sept. 30, 1996; Stats.1998, c. 740 (S.B.1890), § 4. Renumbered § 23612 and amended by Stats.1999, c. 22 (S.B.24), § 18.4, eff. May 26, 1999, operative July 1, 1999. Amended by Stats.1999, c. 853 (S.B.832), § 17; Stats.1999, c. 854 (S.B.1282), § 2, eff. Oct. 10, 1999; Stats.2000, c. 287 (S.B.1955), § 26; Stats. 2003, c. 254 (S.B.408), § 2; Stats.2004, c. 550 (S.B.1694), § 19; Stats.2007, c. 747 (A.B.678), § 37; Stats.2012, c. 196 (A.B.2020), § 1; Stats.2013, c. 76 (A.B.383), § 196.)

Cross References

Commercial motor vehicles, first time violations, see Vehicle
  Code § 15300.
Commercial motor vehicles, multiple violations, see Vehicle
  Code § 15302.
Search warrants, grounds for issuance, see Penal Code § 1524.

§ 23614. Chemical blood, breath, or urine tests; advising persons submitting to breath tests; admissibility of evidence

(a) In addition to the requirements of Section 23612, a person who chooses to submit to a breath test shall be advised before or after the test that the breath-testing equipment does not retain any sample of the breath and that no breath sample will be available after the test which could be analyzed later by that person or any other person.

(b) The person shall also be advised that, because no breath sample is retained, the person will be given an opportunity to provide a blood or urine sample that will be retained at no cost to the person so that there will be something retained that may be subsequently analyzed for the alcoholic content of the person's blood. If the person completes a breath test and wishes to provide a blood or urine sample to be retained, the sample shall be collected and retained in the same manner as if the person had chosen a blood or urine test initially.

(c) The person shall also be advised that the blood or urine sample may be tested by either party in any criminal prosecution. The failure of either party to perform this test shall place neither a duty upon the opposing party to perform the test nor affect the admissibility of any other evidence of the alcoholic content of the blood of the person arrested.

(d) No failure or omission to advise pursuant to this section shall affect the admissibility of any evidence of the alcoholic content of the blood of the person arrested. *(Added by Stats.1998, c. 118 (S.B.1186), § 84, operative July 1, 1999.)*

ARTICLE 2. PRIOR AND SEPARATE OFFENSES

Section
23620. Separate offenses.
23622. Violations of § 23152 or § 23153 within 10 years of
          specified offenses; effect upon sentencing.
23624. Separate conviction; challenge to constitutional valid-
          ity; use in judicial or administrative proceedings.
23626. Effect of convictions in other jurisdictions.

§ 23620. Separate offenses

(a) For the purposes of this division, Section 13352, and Chapter 12 (commencing with Section 23100) of Division 11, a separate offense that resulted in a conviction of a violation of subdivision (f) of Section 655 of the Harbors and Navigation Code or of Section 191.5 of, or subdivision (a) of Section 192.5 of, the Penal Code is a separate offense of a violation of Section 23153.

784

(b) For the purposes of this division and Chapter 12 (commencing with Section 23100) of Division 11, and Section 13352, a separate offense that resulted in a conviction of a violation of subdivision (b), (c), (d), or (e) of Section 655 of the Harbors and Navigation Code is a separate violation of Section 23152. *(Added by Stats. 1998, c. 118 (S.B.1186), § 84, operative July 1, 1999. Amended by Stats.1999, c. 724 (A.B.1650), § 43; Stats. 2007, c. 747 (A.B.678), § 38.)*

§ 23622. Violations of § 23152 or § 23153 within 10 years of specified offenses; effect upon sentencing

(a) In any case charging a violation of Section 23152 or 23153 and the offense occurred within 10 years of one or more separate violations of Section 23103, as specified in Section 23103.5, that occurred on or after January 1, 1982, 23152, or 23153, or any combination thereof, that resulted in convictions, the court shall not strike any separate conviction of those offenses for purposes of sentencing in order to avoid imposing, as part of the sentence or term of probation, the minimum time of imprisonment and the minimum fine, as provided in this chapter, or for purposes of avoiding revocation, suspension, or restriction of the privilege to operate a motor vehicle, as provided in this code.

(b) In any case charging a violation of Section 23152 or 23153, the court shall obtain a copy of the driving record of the person charged from the Department of Motor Vehicles and may obtain any records from the Department of Justice or any other source to determine if one or more separate violations of Section 23103, as specified in Section 23103.5, that occurred on or after January 1, 1982, 23152, or 23153, or any combination thereof, that resulted in convictions, have occurred within 10 years of the charged offense. The court may obtain, and accept as rebuttable evidence, a printout from the Department of Motor Vehicles of the driving record of the person charged, maintained by electronic and storage media pursuant to Section 1801 for the purpose of proving those separate violations.

(c) If any separate convictions of violations of Section 23152 or 23153 are reported to have occurred within 10 years of the charged offense, the court shall notify each court where any of the separate convictions occurred for the purpose of enforcing terms and conditions of probation pursuant to Section 23602. *(Added by Stats.1998, c. 118 (S.B.1186), § 84, operative July 1, 1999. Amended by Stats.2004, c. 550 (S.B.1694), § 20.)*

§ 23624. Separate conviction; challenge to constitutional validity; use in judicial or administrative proceedings

Only one challenge shall be permitted to the constitutionality of a separate conviction of a violation of Section 14601, 14601.2, 23152, or 23153, which was entered in a separate proceeding. When a proceeding to declare a separate judgment of conviction constitutionally invalid has been held, a determination by the court that the separate conviction is constitutional precludes any subsequent attack on constitutional grounds in a subsequent prosecution in which the same separate conviction is charged. In addition, any determination that a separate conviction is unconstitutional precludes any allegation or use of that separate conviction in any judicial or administrative proceeding, and the department shall strike that separate conviction from its records. Pursuant to Section 1803, the court shall report to the Department of Motor Vehicles any determination upholding a conviction on constitutional grounds and any determination that a conviction is unconstitutional.

This section shall not preclude a subsequent challenge to a conviction if, at a later time, a subsequent statute or appellate court decision having retroactive application affords any new basis to challenge the constitutionality of the conviction. *(Added by Stats.1998, c. 118 (S.B.1186), § 84, operative July 1, 1999.)*

§ 23626. Effect of convictions in other jurisdictions

A conviction of an offense in any state, territory, or possession of the United States, the District of Columbia, the Commonwealth of Puerto Rico, or the Dominion of Canada that, if committed in this state, would be a violation of Section 23152 or 23153 of this code, or Section 191.5 of, or subdivision (a) of Section 192.5 of, the Penal Code, is a conviction of Section 23152 or 23153 of this code, or Section 191.5 of, or subdivision (a) of Section 192.5 of, the Penal Code for the purposes of this code. *(Added by Stats.1998, c. 118 (S.B.1186), § 84, operative July 1, 1999. Amended by Stats.2007, c. 747 (A.B.678), § 39.)*

ARTICLE 3. DEFENSES

Section
23630. Legality of drug use as defense to violations.

§ 23630. Legality of drug use as defense to violations

The fact that any person charged with driving under the influence of any drug or the combined influence of alcoholic beverages and any drug in violation of Section 23152 or 23153 is, or has been entitled to use, the drug under the laws of this state shall not constitute a defense against any violation of the sections. *(Added by Stats. 1998, c. 118 (S.B.1186), § 84, operative July 1, 1999.)*

ARTICLE 4. DISMISSAL ON THE RECORD

Section
23635. Dismissal of allegation of violation of § 23152, substitution of lesser offense, or dismissal or striking of allegation of separate conviction; reasons by court and prosecution.

§ 23635. Dismissal of allegation of violation of § 23152, substitution of lesser offense, or dismissal or striking of allegation of separate conviction; reasons by court and prosecution

When an allegation of a violation of Section 23152 is dismissed by the court, an allegation of a different or lesser offense is substituted for an allegation of a violation of Section 23152, or an allegation of a separate conviction is dismissed or stricken, the court shall specify on the record its reason or reasons for the order. The court shall also specify on the record whether the dismissal, substitution, or striking was requested by the prosecution and whether the prosecution concurred in or opposed the dismissal, substitution, or striking.

When the prosecution makes a motion for a dismissal or substitution, or for the striking of a separate conviction, the prosecution shall submit a written statement which shall become part of the court record and which gives the reasons for the motion. The reasons shall include, but need not be limited to, problems of proof, the interests of justice, why another offense is more properly charged, if applicable, and any other pertinent reasons. If the reasons include the "interests of justice," the written statement shall specify all of the factors which contributed to this conclusion. *(Added by Stats.1998, c. 118 (S.B.1186), § 84, operative July 1, 1999.)*

ARTICLE 5. COURT RESTRICTIONS

Section
23640. Participation in driver improvement or treatment programs; no suspension or stay of proceedings prior to acquittal or conviction of violation of § 23152 or § 23153; effect after conviction and sentencing.

§ 23640. Participation in driver improvement or treatment programs; no suspension or stay of proceedings prior to acquittal or conviction of violation of § 23152 or § 23153; effect after conviction and sentencing

(a) In any case in which a person is charged with a violation of Section 23152 or 23153, prior to acquittal or conviction, the court shall neither suspend nor stay the proceedings for the purpose of allowing the accused person to attend or participate, nor shall the court consider dismissal of or entertain a motion to dismiss the proceedings because the accused person attends or participates during that suspension, in any one or more education, training, or treatment programs, including, but not limited to, a driver improvement program, a treatment program for persons who are habitual users of alcohol or other alcoholism program, a program designed to offer alcohol services to problem drinkers, an alcohol or drug education program, or a treatment program for persons who are habitual users of drugs or other drug-related program.

(b) This section shall not apply to any attendance or participation in any education, training, or treatment programs after conviction and sentencing, including attendance or participation in any of those programs as a condition of probation granted after conviction when permitted. *(Added by Stats.1998, c. 118 (S.B.1186), § 84, operative July 1, 1999. Amended by Stats.1999, c. 22 (S.B.24), § 42, eff. May 26, 1999, operative July 1, 1999.)*

ARTICLE 6.   ALCOHOL ASSESSMENT

Section
23645.   Alcohol abuse education and prevention penalty assessment; determination of ability to pay; annual evaluation of primary prevention programs.
23646.   County alcohol and drug problem assessment program.
23647.   Alcohol-related or drug-related driving offenses; participation in program.
23648.   Assessment report.
23649.   Fine or penalty assessment; use of moneys.
23650.   Rules and guidelines.

§ 23645.   Alcohol abuse education and prevention penalty assessment; determination of ability to pay; annual evaluation of primary prevention programs

(a) Except as otherwise provided in subdivision (c), any person convicted of a violation of Section 23152 or 23153 shall, in addition to any other fine, assessment, or imprisonment imposed pursuant to law, pay an alcohol abuse education and prevention penalty assessment in an amount not to exceed fifty dollars ($50) for deposit and distribution pursuant to Section 1463.25 of the Penal Code.

(b) The payment of the penalty assessment under this section shall be ordered upon conviction of a person of a violation of Section 23152 or 23153 irrespective of any other proceeding and, if probation is granted, the payment of the penalty assessment shall also be ordered as a condition of probation, except in unusual cases that are subject to subdivision (d) of Section 1464 of the Penal Code.

(c) The court shall determine if the defendant has the ability to pay a penalty assessment. If the court determines that the defendant has the ability to pay a penalty assessment, the court may set the amount to be paid and order the defendant to pay that sum to the county in the manner in which the court believes reasonable and compatible with the defendant's financial ability. In making a determination of whether a defendant has the ability to pay, the court shall take into account the amount of any fine imposed upon the defendant and any amount the defendant has been ordered to pay in restitution. If the court determines that the defendant does not have the ability to pay a penalty assessment, the defendant shall not be required to pay a penalty assessment.

(d) Five percent of the funds allocated to primary prevention programs to the school and the communities pursuant to subdivision (a) of Section 11802 of the Health and Safety Code shall be used to conduct an annual evaluation. The annual evaluation shall be conducted by the office of the county superintendent of schools in counties where the program is operating in a single county or in the office of the county superintendent of schools in the county designated as the lead county in counties where the program is operating as a consortium of counties. The evaluation shall contain the following:

786

(1) A needs assessment evaluation that provides specific data regarding the problem to be resolved.

(2) A written report of the planning process outlining the deliberations, considerations, and conclusions following a review of the needs assessment.

(3) An end of fiscal year accountability evaluation that will indicate the program's continuing ability to reach appropriate program beneficiaries, deliver the appropriate benefits, and use funds appropriately.

(4) An impact evaluation charged with the task of assessing the effectiveness of the program. Guidelines for the evaluation report format and the timeliness for the submission of the report shall be developed by the State Department of Education. Each county shall submit an evaluation report annually to the State Department of Education and the State Department of Education shall write and submit a report to the Legislature and Governor. *(Added by Stats.1998, c. 118 (S.B.1186), § 84, operative July 1, 1999.)*

§ 23646.   County alcohol and drug problem assessment program

(a) Each county alcohol program administrator or the administrator's designee shall develop, implement, operate, and administer an alcohol and drug problem assessment program pursuant to this article for each person described in subdivision (b). The alcohol and drug problem assessment program may include a referral and client tracking component.

(b)(1) The court shall order a person to participate in an alcohol and drug problem assessment program pursuant to this section and Sections 23647 to 23649, inclusive, and the related regulations of the State Department of * * * Health Care Services, if the person was convicted of a violation of Section 23152 or 23153 that occurred within 10 years of a separate violation of Section 23152 or 23153 that resulted in a conviction.

(2) A court may order a person convicted of a violation of Section 23152 or 23153 to attend an alcohol and drug problem assessment program pursuant to this article.

(3)(A) The court shall order a person convicted of a violation of Section 23152 or 23153 who has previously been convicted of a violation of Section 23152 or 23153 that occurred more than 10 years ago, or has been previously convicted of a violation of subdivision (f) of Section 647 of the Penal Code, to attend and complete an alcohol and drug problem assessment program under this article. In order to determine whether a previous conviction for a violation occurring more than 10 years ago exists, the court shall rely on state summary criminal history information, local summary history information, or records made available to the judge through the district attorney.

(B) If the program assessment recommends additional treatment, the court may order a person sentenced under either Section 23538 or 23556 to enroll, participate, and complete either of the programs described under paragraph (4) of subdivision (b) of Section 23542.

(c) The State Department of * * * Health Care Services shall establish minimum specifications for alcohol and other drug problem assessments and reports. *(Formerly § 23249.52, added by Stats.1988, c. 160, § 183. Amended by Stats.1998, c. 656 (A.B.1916), § 4. Renumbered § 23646 and amended by Stats.1999, c. 22 (S.B.24), § 29, eff. May 26, 1999, operative July 1, 1999. Amended by Stats.2000, c. 1064 (A.B.2227), § 12, eff. Sept. 30, 2000; Stats.2004, c. 550 (S.B.1694), § 21; Stats.2013, c. 22 (A.B.75), § 89, eff. June 27, 2013, operative July 1, 2013.)*

§ 23647. Alcohol-related or drug-related driving offenses; participation in program

(a) Any person convicted of a violation of Section 23152 or 23153 who is required to participate in a county alcohol and drug problem assessment program shall participate in that program.

(b) Any person convicted of a violation of Section 23103, as specified in Section 23103.5, in a judicial district that participates in a county alcohol and drug problem assessment program pursuant to this article, may be ordered to participate in the program. *(Formerly § 23249.53, added by Stats.1988, c. 160, § 183. Amended by Stats.1991, c. 1175 (A.B.2091), § 1; Stats.1998, c. 656 (A.B.1916), § 5. Renumbered § 23647 and amended by Stats.1999, c. 22 (S.B.24), § 30, eff. May 26, 1999, operative July 1, 1999.)*

§ 23648. Assessment report

(a) Each county shall prepare, or contract to be prepared, an alcohol and drug problem assessment report on each person described in subdivision (b) of Section 23646.

(b) The assessment report shall include, if applicable, a recommendation for any additional treatment and the duration of the treatment. The treatment shall be in addition to the education and counseling program required under Section 11837 of the Health and Safety Code. The assessment report shall be submitted to the court not more than 14 days after the date the assessment was conducted.

(c) Within 30 days of the receipt of the report, the court shall order the person to complete the recommendations set forth in the report in satisfaction of, and consistent with, the terms and conditions of probation. If the court elects not to order the completion of the recommended plan, the court shall specify on the record its reason for not adopting these recommendations.

(d) This section shall become operative on January 1, 2000. *(Formerly § 23249.54, added by Stats.1998, c. 656 (A.B.1916), § 7. Renumbered § 23648 and amended by Stats.1999, c. 22 (S.B.24), § 32, eff. May 26, 1999, operative Jan. 1, 2000.)*

§ 23649. Fine or penalty assessment; use of moneys

(a) Notwithstanding any other provision of law, in addition to any other fine or penalty assessment, there shall be levied an assessment of not more than one hundred dollars ($100) upon every fine, penalty, or forfeiture imposed and collected by the courts for a violation of Section 23152 or 23153 in any judicial district that participates in a county alcohol and drug problem assessment program. An assessment of not more than one hundred dollars ($100) shall be imposed and collected by the courts from each person convicted of a violation of Section 23103, as specified in Section 23103.5, who is ordered to participate in a county alcohol and drug problem assessment program pursuant to Section 23647.

(b) The court shall determine if the defendant has the ability to pay the assessment. If the court determines that the defendant has the ability to pay the assessment then the court may set the amount to be reimbursed and order the defendant to pay that sum to the county in the manner that the court determines is reasonable and compatible with the defendant's financial ability. In making a determination of whether a defendant has the ability to pay, the court shall take into account the amount of any fine imposed upon the defendant and any amount the defendant has been ordered to pay in restitution.

(c) Notwithstanding Section 1463 or 1464 of the Penal Code or any other provision of law, all moneys collected pursuant to this section shall be deposited in a special account in the county treasury and shall be used exclusively by the county alcohol program administrator or the administrator's designee to pay for the costs of developing, implementing, operating, maintaining, and evaluating alcohol and drug problem assessment programs.

(d) On January 15 of each year, the treasurer of each county that administers an alcohol and drug problem assessment program shall determine those moneys in the special account that were not expended during the preceding fiscal year, and shall transfer those moneys to the general fund of the county.

(e) Any moneys remaining in the special account, if and when the alcohol and drug problem assessment program is terminated, shall be transferred to the general fund of the county.

(f) The county treasurer shall annually transfer an amount of money equal to the county's administrative cost incurred pursuant to this section, as he or she shall determine, from the special account to the general fund of the county. *(Formerly § 23249.55, added by Stats.1988, c. 160, § 183. Amended by Stats.1991, c. 1175 (A.B.2091), § 3; Stats.1998, c. 656 (A.B.1916), § 8. Renumbered § 23649 and amended by Stats.1999, c. 22 (S.B.24), § 33, eff. May 26, 1999, operative July 1, 1999. Amended by Stats.2000, c. 1064 (A.B.2227), § 13, eff. Sept. 30, 2000.)*

§ 23650. Rules and guidelines

The Office of Traffic Safety shall adopt rules and guidelines to implement Sections 23646 to 23649, inclusive. *(Added by Stats.1998, c. 118 (S.B.1186), § 84, operative July 1, 1999. Amended by Stats.1999, c. 22 (S.B.24), § 43, eff. May 26, 1999, operative July 1, 1999.)*

§ 23651. Editorial Note

Stats.1998, c. 118 (S.B.1186), provided for repeal of § 23249.58 and addition of this similar section. Stats.1998, c. 656 (A.B.1916), § 10 amended § 23249.58. Section affected by two or more acts at the same session of the legislature, see Government Code § 9605.

ARTICLE 7. PRESENTENCE INVESTIGATION

Section
23655.   Convictions of § 23152 or § 23153; determination of benefit of education, training or treatment programs; conditions of probation; standard form.

§ 23655. Convictions of § 23152 or § 23153; determination of benefit of education, training or treatment programs; conditions of probation; standard form

(a) Upon any conviction of a violation of Section 23152 or 23153, any judge of the court may order a presentence investigation to determine whether a person convicted of the violation would benefit from one or more education, training, or treatment programs, and the court may order suitable education, training, or treatment for the person, in addition to imposing any penalties required by this code.

(b) In determining whether to require, as a condition of probation, the participation in a program pursuant to subdivision (b) of Section 23538, subdivision (b) of Section 23542, subdivision (b) of Section 23548, subdivision (b) of Section 23552, subdivision (b) of Section 23556, subdivision (b) of Section 23562, or subdivision (b) of Section 23568, the court may consider any relevant information about the person made available pursuant to a presentence investigation, which is permitted but not required by subdivision (a), or other screening procedure. That information shall not be furnished to the court by any person who also provides services in a privately operated, approved program or who has any direct interest in a privately operated, approved program. In addition, the court shall obtain from the Department of Motor Vehicles a copy of the person's driving record to determine whether the person is eligible to participate in an approved program.

(c) The Judicial Council shall adopt a standard form for use by all courts, defendants, and alcohol or drug education programs in certifying to the court that the person has achieved both of the following:

(1) Enrolled within the specified time period.

(2) Successfully completed any program required by Section 23538 or 23556. *(Added by Stats.1998, c. 118 (S.B.1186), § 84, operative July 1, 1999. Amended by Stats.1999, c. 22 (S.B.24), § 44, eff. May 26, 1999, operative July 1, 1999.)*

788

ARTICLE 8. SURRENDER AND NOTIFICATION OF LICENSE RESTRICTION

Section
23660.   Suspension or revocation of privilege to operate motor vehicle; surrender of license; application of section.
23662.   Department of Motor Vehicles notified of probation.

§ 23660. Suspension or revocation of privilege to operate motor vehicle; surrender of license; application of section

(a) If a person's privilege to operate a motor vehicle is required to be suspended or revoked by the department under other provisions of this code upon the conviction of an offense described in Article 2 (commencing with Section 23152) of Chapter 12 of Division 11, that person shall surrender each and every operator's license of that person to the court upon conviction. The court shall transmit the license or licenses required to be suspended or revoked to the department under Section 13550, and the court shall notify the department.

(b) This section does not apply to an administrative proceeding by the department to suspend or revoke the driving privilege of any person pursuant to other provisions of law.

(c) This section shall become operative on September 20, 2005. *(Formerly § 23204, added by Stats.1981, c. 940, p. 3571, § 32. Amended by Stats.1984, c. 1205, § 8; Stats.1986, c. 1117, § 11; Stats.1998, c. 756 (A.B.762), § 18, operative July 1, 1999. Renumbered § 23660 and amended by Stats.1999, c. 22 (S.B.24), § 24, eff. May 26, 1999, operative July 1, 1999. Amended by Stats.2004, c. 551 (S.B.1697), § 24, operative Sept. 20, 2005.)*

§ 23662. Department of Motor Vehicles notified of probation

If a person is placed on probation, the court shall promptly notify the Department of Motor Vehicles of the probation and probationary term and conditions in a manner prescribed by the department. The department shall place the fact of probation and the probationary term and conditions on the person's records in the department. *(Formerly § 23203, added by Stats.1981, c. 940, p. 3571, § 32. Amended by Stats.1984, c. 1417, § 3, operative July 1, 1985; Stats.1996, c. 124 (A.B.3470), § 131; Stats.1998, c. 756 (A.B.762), § 17, operative July 1, 1999. Renumbered § 23662 and amended by Stats.1999, c. 22 (S.B.24), § 23, eff. May 26, 1999, operative July 1, 1999.)*

ARTICLE 9. DELAYED SUSPENSIONS AND REVOCATIONS

Section
23665.   Driving under the influence; bodily injury to person other than driver; jail sentence; postponement of revocation or suspension.

§ 23665. Driving under the influence; bodily injury to person other than driver; jail sentence; postponement of revocation or suspension

(a) If a person is convicted of a violation of Section 20001, or of Section 23152 or 23153 and is sentenced to one year in a county jail or more than one year in the state prison under Section 23540, 23542, 23546, 23548, 23550, 23550.5, 23552, 23554, 23556, 23558, 23560, 23562, 23566, or 23568, the court may postpone the revocation or suspension of the person's driving privilege until the term of imprisonment is served.

(b) This section shall become operative on September 20, 2005. *(Added by Stats.1998, c. 118 (S.B.1186), § 84, operative July 1, 1999. Amended by Stats.1999, c. 22 (S.B.24), § 45, eff. May 26, 1999, operative July 1, 1999; Stats.2004, c. 551 (S.B.1697), § 25, operative Sept. 20, 2005.)*

ARTICLE 10. CONFLICT OF INTEREST

Section
23670. Referral to program in which employee of court has economic interest.

§ 23670. Referral to program in which employee of court has economic interest

A court shall not order or refer any person to any program, including an alcohol and other drug education program or a program licensed pursuant to Chapter 9 (commencing with Section 11836) of Part 2 of Division 10.5 of the Health and Safety Code, or to a provider of a program, in which any employee of the court has a direct or indirect economic interest. *(Added by Stats.1998, c. 118 (S.B.1186), § 84, operative July 1, 1999.)*

ARTICLE 11. OPERATIVE DATE

Section
23675. Operative date of Division.

§ 23675. Operative date of Division

This division shall become operative on July 1, 1999. *(Added by Stats.1998, c. 118 (S.B.1186), § 84, operative July 1, 1999.)*

CHAPTER 5. IGNITION INTERLOCK DEVICES

Section
23700. Pilot program to reduce driving under the influence offenses; establishment in Alameda, Los Angeles, Sacramento, and Tulare Counties.
23700.5. Implementation of pilot program.
23701. Report to Legislature on effectiveness of pilot program.
23702. Duration of chapter.

Repeal

For repeal of Chapter 5, see Vehicle Code § 23702.

§ 23700. Pilot program to reduce driving under the influence offenses; establishment in Alameda, Los Angeles, Sacramento, and Tulare Counties

(a) Notwithstanding any other provision of law, the Department of Motor Vehicles shall establish a pilot program in the Counties of Alameda, Los Angeles, Sacramento, and Tulare to reduce the number of first-time violations and repeat offenses of Sections 23152 and 23153, as follows:

(1) The Department of Motor Vehicles, upon receipt of the court's abstract conviction for a violation listed in paragraph (7), shall inform the convicted person of the requirements of this section, including the term for which the person is required to have a certified ignition interlock device installed. The records of the department shall reflect the mandatory use of the device for the term required and the time when the device is required to be installed by this code.

(2) The department shall advise the person that installation of an ignition interlock device on a vehicle does not allow the person to drive without a valid driver's license.

(3) Before a driver's license may be issued, reissued, or returned to a person after a suspension or revocation of that person's driving privilege that requires the installation of an ignition interlock device, a person who is notified by the department pursuant to paragraph (1) shall complete all of the following:

(A) Arrange for each vehicle owned or operated by the person to be fitted with an ignition interlock device by a certified ignition interlock device provider under Section 13386.

(B) Notify the department and provide to the department proof of installation by submitting the "Verification of Installation" form described in paragraph (2) of subdivision (g) of Section 13386.

(C) Pay the fee, determined by the department, that is sufficient to cover the costs of administration of this section.

(4) The department shall place a restriction on the driver's license record of the convicted person that states the driver is restricted to driving only vehicles equipped with a certified ignition interlock device.

(5)(A) A person who is notified by the department pursuant to paragraph (1) shall arrange for each vehicle with an ignition interlock device to be serviced by the installer at least once every 60 days in order for the installer to recalibrate and monitor the operation of the device.

(B) The installer shall notify the department if the device is removed or indicates that the person has attempted to remove, bypass, or tamper with the device, or if the person fails three or more times to comply with any requirement for the maintenance or calibration of the ignition interlock device.

(6) The department shall monitor the installation and maintenance of the ignition interlock device installed pursuant to paragraph (1).

(7) A person is required to install an ignition interlock device for the applicable term as a condition of being issued a restricted driver's license, being reissued a driver's license, or having the privilege to operate a motor vehicle reinstated subsequent to a conviction for a violation or a suspension of a person's driver's license, as follows:

(A) A person convicted of a violation of Section 23152 shall be required to install an ignition interlock device, as follows:

(i) Upon a first offense, the person shall install an ignition interlock device in all vehicles owned or operated by that person for a mandatory term of five months.

(ii) Upon a second offense, the person shall install an ignition interlock device in all vehicles owned or operated by that person for a mandatory term of 12 months.

(iii) Upon a third offense, the person shall install an ignition interlock device in all vehicles owned or operated by that person for a mandatory term of 24 months.

(iv) Upon a fourth offense or any subsequent violation, the person shall install an ignition interlock device in all vehicles owned or operated by that person for a mandatory term of 36 months.

(B) A person convicted of a violation of Section 23153 shall install an ignition interlock device, as follows:

(i) Upon a first offense, the person shall install an ignition interlock device in all vehicles owned or operated by that person for a mandatory term of 12 months.

(ii) Upon a second offense, the person shall install an ignition interlock device in all vehicles owned or operated by that person for a mandatory term of 24 months.

(iii) Upon a third offense, the person shall install an ignition interlock device in all vehicles owned or operated by that person for a mandatory term of 36 months.

(iv) Upon a fourth offense or any subsequent violation, the person shall install an ignition interlock device in all vehicles owned or operated by that person for a mandatory term of 48 months.

(C) The terms prescribed in this paragraph shall begin once a person has provided to the department proof of installation pursuant to paragraph (2) of subdivision (h) of Section 13386 and upon restoration of the driving privilege pursuant to Section 13352.

(8) A person who is notified by the department, pursuant to this subdivision, is exempt from the requirements of this subdivision if within 30 days of the notification, the person certifies to the department all of the following:

(A) The person does not own a vehicle.

(B) The person does not have access to a vehicle at his or her residence.

(C) The person no longer has access to the vehicle being driven by the person at the time he or she was arrested for a violation that subsequently resulted in a conviction for a violation listed in this subdivision.

(D) The person acknowledges that he or she is only allowed to drive a vehicle that is fitted with a functioning ignition interlock device.

(E) The person acknowledges that he or she is required to have a valid driver's license before he or she can drive.

(F) The person is subject to the requirements of this section when he or she purchases or has access to a vehicle.

(9) Subdivisions (j), (k), (m), (n), and (o) of Section 23575 apply to this section.

(10) If a person fails to comply with any of the requirements regarding ignition interlock devices, the mandatory term for which the ignition interlock device is required to be installed shall be reset by the department.

(b)(1) Every manufacturer and manufacturer's agent certified by the department to provide ignition interlock devices, under Section 13386, shall adopt the following fee schedule that provides for the payment of the costs of the ignition interlock device by offenders subject to this chapter in amounts commensurate with that person's income relative to the federal poverty level, as defined in Section 127400 of the Health and Safety Code:

(A) A person with an income at 100 percent of the federal poverty level and below is responsible for 10 percent of the cost of the ignition interlock device. The ignition interlock device provider is responsible for absorbing the cost of the ignition interlock device that is not paid by the person.

(B) A person with an income at 101 to 200 percent of the federal poverty level is responsible for 25 percent of the cost of the ignition interlock device. The ignition interlock device provider is responsible for absorbing the cost of the ignition interlock device that is not paid by the person.

(C) A person with an income at 201 to 300 percent of the federal poverty level is responsible for 50 percent of the cost of the ignition interlock device. The ignition interlock device provider is responsible for absorbing the cost of the ignition interlock device that is not paid by the person.

(D) All other offenders are responsible for 100 percent of the cost of the ignition interlock device.

(2) The cost of the ignition interlock device may only be raised annually equal to the Consumer Price Index.

(3) The offender's income may be verified by presentation of that person's current federal income tax return or three months of monthly income statements.

(c) This section does not permit a person to drive without a valid driver's license.

(d) The requirements of this section are in addition to any other requirements of law.

(e) For the purposes of this section, "vehicle" does not include a motorcycle until the state certifies an ignition interlock device that can be installed on a motorcycle. A person subject to an ignition interlock device restriction shall not operate a motorcycle for the duration of the ignition interlock device restriction period.

(f) This section shall become operative on July 1, 2010. *(Added by Stats.2009, c. 217 (A.B.91), § 3, operative July 1, 2010.)*

Repeal

For repeal of Chapter 5, see Vehicle Code § 23702.

Cross References

Motor vehicle owned by employer and driven by employee with restricted driving privileges in the course and scope of employment, exemption from ignition interlock device installation requirements, see Vehicle Code § 23576.
Prohibited activities regarding persons whose driving privileges have been restricted pursuant to this section, punishment, defenses, see Vehicle Code § 23247.

§ 23700.5. Implementation of pilot program

The department shall not implement Section 23700 if, by January 31, 2010, the department fails to obtain nonstate funds for the programming costs of the pilot program specified in Section 23700. *(Added by Stats. 2009, c. 217 (A.B.91), § 3.)*

Repeal

For repeal of Chapter 5, see Vehicle Code § 23702.

§ 23701. Report to Legislature on effectiveness of pilot program

On or before January 1, 2015, the Department of Motor Vehicles shall report to the Legislature regarding the effectiveness of the pilot program authorized under this chapter in reducing the number of first-time violations and repeat offenses of Sections 23152 and 23153 in the Counties of Alameda, Los Angeles, Sacramento, and Tulare. *(Added by Stats.2009, c. 217 (A.B.91), § 3.)*

Repeal

For repeal of Chapter 5, see Vehicle Code § 23702.

§ 23702. Duration of chapter

This chapter shall remain in effect only until January 1, 2016, and as of that date is repealed, unless a later enacted statute, that is enacted before January 1, 2016, deletes or extends that date. *(Added by Stats.2009, c. 217 (A.B.91), § 3.)*

Division 12

EQUIPMENT OF VEHICLES

Chapter	Section
1. General Provisions	24000
2. Lighting Equipment	24250
3. Brakes	26300
4. Windshields and Mirrors	26700
5. Other Equipment	27000
6. Vehicle Equipment Safety Compact [Repealed]	
7. Motor Vehicle Pollution Control Device Installation and Inspection Stations [Repealed]	

CHAPTER 1. GENERAL PROVISIONS

Section
24000.   Department.
24001.   Application of divisions.
24001.5.   Golf cart.
24002.   Unlawful operation of vehicles.
24002.5.   Farm labor vehicles; operation when presents immediate safety hazard; violations; misdemeanor.
24003.   Vehicle with unlawful lights.
24004.   Unlawful operation after notice by officer.
24005.   Sale, transfer or installment of unlawful equipment.
24005.5.   Uncertified synthetic rope or webbing strap material.
24006.   Name or trademark; instructions.
24007.   Responsibility of dealer or other person selling motor vehicle.
24007.1.   Manufacturer of equipment used in assembly of authorized emergency vehicles; reimbursement of local public fire service agencies for costs of repairs.
24007.2.   No exhaust devices: free installation for low-income elderly persons.
24007.3.   Repealed.
24007.5.   Sale by auctioneer or public agency.
24007.6.   Salvage pools; notice required by § 5900; notification that buyer obtain certificate of compliance or noncompliance and register vehicle.
24008.   Modification of vehicles.
24008.5.   Frame or body floor heights.
24009.   Manufacturer's name and gross vehicle weight rating plates or markings.
24010.   Vehicle rental responsibility.
24011.   Federal safety standard.
24011.3.   Bumper strength notice for passenger vehicles; requirements; violations; penalties.
24011.7.   Exhaust and noise emission control inspection.
24012.   Compliance with lighting equipment mounting regulations.
24013.   Statement of minimum octane number of gasoline for motor vehicle.
24013.5.   Light duty truck sales; label with pricing and other information.
24014.   Motorcycle sales: required price information.
24015.   Motorized bicycles; federal safety standards; equipment.
24016.   Motorized bicycles; manufacturing and operating criteria; tampering.

Section
24017.   Transit bus operated by motor carrier; speedometer.
24018.   Transit buses operated by motor carriers; equipment with two-way communication device allowing driver to contact motor carrier in an emergency.

Cross References

Criteria for issuing arrest warrant for violations, see Vehicle Code § 40509.5.

Enforcement of this division by air pollution control officer, exceptions, see Health and Safety Code § 40753.

Leased vehicle to meet equipment requirements, see Civil Code § 2986.5.

Notice to correct violations, see Vehicle Code § 40303.5.

§ 24000. Department

Wherever in this division the word "department" occurs, it means the Department of the California Highway Patrol. *(Stats.1959, c. 3, p. 1713, § 24000.)*

Cross References

Department defined, see Vehicle Code §§ 290, 2101, 21000.

Department of the California highway patrol, in general, see Vehicle Code § 2100 et seq.

Law enforcement, California highway patrol, see Vehicle Code § 2400.

§ 24001. Application of divisions

This division and Division 13 (commencing at Section 29000), unless otherwise provided, applies to all vehicles whether publicly or privately owned when upon the highways, including all authorized emergency vehicles. *(Stats.1959, c. 3, p. 1713, § 24001. Amended by Stats. 1959, c. 1996, p. 4632, § 29.)*

Cross References

Authorized emergency vehicle defined, see Vehicle Code § 165.

Exemption of authorized emergency vehicles from rules of the road, see Vehicle Code §§ 21055, 21056.

Flashing and colored lights, see Vehicle Code § 25250 et seq.

Issuance of emergency vehicle permits, see Vehicle Code § 2416.

§ 24001.5. Golf cart

A golf cart as defined in Section 345 shall only be subject to the provisions of this division which are applicable to a motorcycle. *(Added by Stats.1968, c. 1303, p. 2457, § 5. Amended by Stats.1969, c. 1075, p. 2064, § 10; Stats.1972, c. 973, p. 1759, § 18, eff. Aug. 16, 1972.)*

Cross References

Motorcycle,
    Authorized emergency vehicle, see Vehicle Code § 165.

Defined, see Vehicle Code § 400.

Required equipment, see Vehicle Code § 27800 et seq.

Operation of golf carts during darkness on local highways, see Vehicle Code § 21115.

§ 24002. Unlawful operation of vehicles

(a) It is unlawful to operate any vehicle or combination of vehicles which is in an unsafe condition, or which is not safely loaded, and which presents an immediate safety hazard.

(b) It is unlawful to operate any vehicle or combination of vehicles which is not equipped as provided in this code. *(Stats.1959, c. 3, p. 1713, § 24002. Amended by Stats.1992, c. 696 (A.B.1344), § 92, eff. Sept. 15, 1992.)*

Cross References

Cotton module movers, operation on state highways, conditions, see Vehicle Code § 35555.

Required equipment,

    Brake equipment, see Vehicle Code § 26301 et seq.

    Exhaust systems, see Vehicle Code § 27150 et seq.

    Horns and sirens, see Vehicle Code § 27000 et seq.

    Lighting equipment, see Vehicle Code § 24250 et seq.

    Safety belts, see Vehicle Code § 27302 et seq.

    Tires, see Vehicle Code § 27450 et seq.

    Windshields and mirrors, see Vehicle Code § 26700 et seq.

Unsafe condition, modification of vehicle, see Vehicle Code § 24008.

Vehicles incidentally operated over highway, applicability of this section, see Vehicle Code § 25802.

§ 24002.5. Farm labor vehicles; operation when presents immediate safety hazard; violations; misdemeanor

(a) No person may operate a farm labor vehicle that is in a condition that presents an immediate safety hazard or in violation of Section 24004 or 31402.

(b) A violation of this section is a misdemeanor punishable by a fine of not less than one thousand dollars ($1,000) and not more than five thousand dollars ($5,000), or both that fine and a sentence of confinement for not more than six months in the county jail. No part of any fine imposed under this section may be suspended.

(c) As used in this section, an "immediate safety hazard" is any equipment violation described in subdivision (a) of Section 31401 or Section 31405, including any violation of a regulation adopted pursuant to those provisions.

(d) Any member of the Department of the California Highway Patrol may impound a farm labor vehicle operated in violation of this section pursuant to Section 34506.4. *(Added by Stats.2000, c. 873 (A.B.2086), § 2.)*

Cross References

Farm labor vehicles subject to forfeiture as nuisance, and impounding, see Vehicle Code § 34506.5.

§ 24003. Vehicle with unlawful lights

No vehicle shall be equipped with any lamp or illuminating device not required or permitted in this code, nor shall any lamp or illuminating device be mounted inside a vehicle unless specifically permitted by this code. This section does not apply to:

(a) Interior lamps such as door, brake and instrument lamps, and map, dash, and dome lamps designed and used for the purpose of illuminating the interior of the vehicle.

(b) Lamps needed in the operation or utilization of those vehicles mentioned in Section 25801, or vehicles used by public utilities in the repair or maintenance of their service, or used only for the illumination of cargo space of a vehicle while loading or unloading.

(c) Warning lamps mounted inside an authorized emergency vehicle and meeting requirements established by the department. *(Stats.1959, c. 3, p. 1713, § 24003. Amended by Stats.1963, c. 547, p. 1427, § 1; Stats.1979, c. 723, p. 2217, § 7.)*

Cross References

Lighting equipment, see Vehicle Code § 24250 et seq.

Violations, punishment, see Vehicle Code § 42002.

§ 24004. Unlawful operation after notice by officer

No person shall operate any vehicle or combination of vehicles after notice by a peace officer, as defined in Section 830.1 or subdivision (a) of Section 830.2 of the Penal Code, that the vehicle is in an unsafe condition or is not equipped as required by this code, except as may be necessary to return the vehicle or combination of vehicles to the residence or place of business of the owner or driver or to a garage, until the vehicle and its equipment have been made to conform with the requirements of this code.

The provisions of this section shall not apply to an employee who does not know that such notice has been issued, and in such event the provisions of Section 40001 shall be applicable. *(Stats.1959, c. 3, p. 1714, § 24004. Amended by Stats.1965, c. 306, p. 1403, § 1; Stats.1979, c. 171, p. 390, § 2.)*

Cross References

Unlawful to operate vehicle in unsafe condition, see Vehicle Code § 24002.

Vehicles incidentally operated over highway, applicability of this section, see Vehicle Code § 25802.

§ 24005. Sale, transfer or installment of unlawful equipment

It is unlawful for any person to sell, offer for sale, lease, install, or replace, either for himself or as the agent or employee of another, or through such agent or employee, any glass, lighting equipment, signal devices, brakes, vacuum or pressure hose, muffler, exhaust, or any kind of equipment whatsoever for use, or with knowledge that any such equipment is intended for eventual use, in any vehicle, that is not in conformity with this code or regulations made thereunder. *(Stats.1959, c. 3, p. 1714, § 24005. Amended by Stats.1961, c. 226, p. 1245, § 1; Stats.1971, c. 734, p. 1460, § 1, operative May 3, 1972.)*

Cross References

Brake equipment, generally, see Vehicle Code § 26301 et seq.

Exhaust systems, see Vehicle Code § 27150 et seq.

Mufflers, see Vehicle Code § 27150.

Safety glazing material, see Vehicle Code §§ 26701, 26703, 26704.

Vehicle defined, see Vehicle Code § 670.

Vehicles incidentally operated over highway, applicability of this section, see Vehicle Code § 25802.

Windshields and mirrors, see Vehicle Code § 26700 et seq.

§ 24005.5. Uncertified synthetic rope or webbing strap material

It is unlawful for any person to sell or offer for sale for use on loads regulated by the department any type of synthetic fiber rope or webbing strap material unless it meets requirements established by the department. *(Added by Stats.1972, c. 466, p. 834, § 1. Amended by Stats.1979, c. 723, p. 2217, § 8.)*

§ 24006. Name or trademark; instructions

No person shall sell or offer for sale either separately or as a part of the equipment of a new motor vehicle any equipment or device subject to requirements established by the department unless the equipment or device bears thereon the trademark or name and type or model designation under requirements established by the department and is accompanied by any printed instructions which may be required by the department as to the light source to be used with lamps, any particular methods of mounting or adjustment of lamps or other devices, and any other instructions as determined by the department necessary for compliance with this code. *(Stats.1959, c. 3, p. 1714, § 24006. Amended by Stats.1967, c. 440, p. 1653, § 1, eff. June 30, 1967; Stats.1979, c. 723, p. 2217, § 9.)*

§ 24007. Responsibility of dealer or other person selling motor vehicle

(a)(1) No dealer or person holding a retail seller's permit shall sell a new or used vehicle that is not in compliance with this code and departmental regulations adopted pursuant to this code, unless the vehicle is sold to another dealer, sold for the purpose of being legally wrecked or dismantled, or sold exclusively for off-highway use.

(2) Paragraph (1) does not apply to any vehicle sold by either (A) a dismantler after being reported for dismantling pursuant to Section 11520 or (B) a salvage pool after obtaining a salvage certificate pursuant to Section 11515 or a nonrepairable vehicle certificate issued pursuant to Section 11515.2.

(3) Notwithstanding paragraph (1), the equipment requirements of this division do not apply to the sale of a leased vehicle by a dealer to a lessee if the lessee is in possession of the vehicle immediately prior to the time of the sale and the vehicle is registered in this state.

(b)(1) Except as provided in Section 24007.5, no person shall sell, or offer or deliver for sale, to the ultimate purchaser, or to any subsequent purchaser a new

or used motor vehicle, as those terms are defined in Chapter 2 (commencing with Section 39010) of Part 1 of Division 26 of the Health and Safety Code, subject to Part 5 (commencing with Section 43000) of that Division 26 which is not in compliance with that part and the rules and regulations of the State Air Resources Board, unless the vehicle is sold to a dealer or sold for the purpose of being legally wrecked or dismantled.

(2) Prior to or at the time of delivery for sale, the seller shall provide the purchaser a valid certificate of compliance or certificate of noncompliance, as appropriate, issued in accordance with Section 44015 of the Health and Safety Code.

(3) Paragraph (2) does not apply to any vehicle whose transfer of ownership and registration is described in subdivision (d) of Section 4000.1.

(4) Paragraphs (1) and (2) do not apply to any vehicle sold by either (A) a dismantler after being reported for dismantling pursuant to Section 11520 or (B) a salvage pool after obtaining a salvage certificate pursuant to Section 11515 or a nonrepairable vehicle certificate issued pursuant to Section 11515.2.

(c)(1) With each application for initial registration of a new motor vehicle or transfer of registration of a motor vehicle subject to Part 5 (commencing with Section 43000) of Division 26 of the Health and Safety Code, a dealer, the purchaser, or his or her authorized representative, shall transmit to the Department of Motor Vehicles a valid certificate of compliance or noncompliance, as appropriate, issued in accordance with Section 44015 of the Health and Safety Code.

(2) Notwithstanding paragraph (1) of this subdivision, with respect to new vehicles certified pursuant to Chapter 2 (commencing with Section 43100) of Part 5 of Division 26 of the Health and Safety Code, a dealer may transmit, in lieu of a certificate of compliance, a statement, in a form and containing information deemed necessary and appropriate by the Director of Motor Vehicles and the Executive Officer of the State Air Resources Board, to attest to the vehicle's compliance with that chapter. The statement shall be certified under penalty of perjury, and shall be signed by the dealer or the dealer's authorized representative.

(3) Paragraph (1) does not apply to a transfer of ownership and registration under any of the circumstances described in subdivision (d) of Section 4000.1. *(Stats.1959, c. 3, p. 1714, § 24007. Amended by Stats. 1965, c. 2031, p. 4612, § 11; Stats.1965, c. 2033, p. 4618, § 1; Stats.1966, 1st Ex.Sess., c. 82, p. 521, § 2; Stats.1967, c. 394, p. 1618, § 2; Stats.1968, c. 764, p. 1483, § 14; Stats.1970, c. 766, p. 1450, § 3; Stats.1971, c. 86, p. 113, § 1, operative May 3, 1972; Stats.1971, c. 1488, p. 2940, § 2, operative May 3, 1972; Stats.1972, c. 99, p. 137, § 1; Stats.1972, c. 268, p. 520, § 2; Stats.1975, c. 957, p. 2233, § 29; Stats.1976, c. 1206, p. 5493, § 17; Stats.1977, c. 1038, p. 3139, § 5, eff. Sept. 23, 1977; Stats.1984, c. 246, § 6; Stats.1987, c. 1091, § 15; Stats.1988, c. 1268, § 18.5; Stats.1988, c. 1544, § 61; Stats.1990, c. 1012 (S.B.1876),*

§ 1; Stats.1993, c. 958 (S.B.575), § 3; Stats.1994, c. 1008 (S.B.1833), § 18, operative July 1, 1995; Stats.1998, c. 517 (S.B.559), § 2; Stats.2004, c. 230 (S.B.1107), § 20, eff. Aug. 16, 2004.)

Cross References

Brakes, requirements generally, see Vehicle Code § 26301 et seq.

Lighting equipment generally, see Vehicle Code § 24250 et seq.

New vehicle defined, see Vehicle Code § 430.

Test and approval of lighting equipment, see Vehicle Code § 26100 et seq.

Used vehicle defined, see Vehicle Code § 665.

§ 24007.1.   Manufacturer of equipment used in assembly of authorized emergency vehicles; reimbursement of local public fire service agencies for costs of repairs

(a) The manufacturer of equipment used in the assembly of an authorized emergency vehicle, as defined in Section 165, used by a local public fire service agency shall, upon request of the fire department, reimburse the agency for the cost of repairs to the vehicle if (1) the repair was made to correct a manufacturer's defect, and (2) the vehicle is placed on a safety-related recall to correct that defect.

(b) A final stage equipment manufacturer is deemed to be an original equipment manufacturer in the event of a warranty dispute with a local public fire service agency regarding the failure of component parts used in the assembly of the agency's authorized emergency vehicle. As used in this section, "final stage equipment manufacturer" means the manufacturer who assembles the authorized emergency vehicle from one or more components supplied by other manufacturers.

(c) The Legislature finds and declares that local public fire service agencies of this state are entitled to safe and efficient use of their equipment, and that defects in emergency equipment, especially emergency vehicles, endanger the firefighters of California and the public they serve. It is the intent of the Legislature to ensure that these defects are repaired as expeditiously as possible and with no expense to the local public fire service agencies. (Added by Stats.1994, c. 1220 (A.B.3132), § 65, eff. Sept. 30, 1994.)

§ 24007.2.   No exhaust devices: free installation for low-income elderly persons

If a dealer, or a person holding a retail seller's permit, sells to an elderly low-income person, as defined in Section 39026.5 of the Health and Safety Code, a 1966 through 1970 model year motor vehicle which is not equipped, as required pursuant to Sections 43654 and 43656 of that code, with a certified device to control its exhaust emission of oxides of nitrogen, the dealer or such person, as the case may be, shall install the required certified device on the motor vehicle without cost to the elderly low-income person. (Added by Stats.1976, c. 231, p. 442, § 6.)

796

§ 24007.3.   Repealed by Stats.1990, c. 1563 (A.B.3243), § 61

§ 24007.5.   Sale by auctioneer or public agency

(a) (1) No auctioneer or public agency shall sell, at public auction, any vehicle specified in subdivision (a) of Section 24007, which is not in compliance with this code.

(2) Paragraph (1) does not apply to a vehicle that is sold under the conditions specified in subdivision (c), (d), (e), or (g) or is sold to a dealer or for the purpose of being wrecked or dismantled or is sold exclusively for off-highway use.

(b) Except with respect to the sale of a vehicle specified in paragraph (2) of subdivision (a), the consignor of any vehicle, specified in subdivision (b) of Section 24007, sold at public auction, shall provide the purchaser a valid certificate of compliance or certificate of noncompliance, as appropriate, issued in accordance with Section 44015 of the Health and Safety Code.

(c) Notwithstanding any other provision of this code, if, in the opinion of a public utility or public agency, the cost of repairs to a vehicle exceeds the value of the vehicle to the public utility or public agency, the public utility or public agency shall, as transferee or owner, surrender the certificates of registration, documents satisfactory to the Department of Motor Vehicles showing proof of ownership, and the license plates issued for the vehicle to the Department of Motor Vehicles. As used in this section, "public utility" means a public utility as described in Sections 218, 222, and 234 of the Public Utilities Code.

(d) The public utility or public agency having complied with subdivision (c) shall, upon sale of the vehicle, give to the purchaser a bill of sale which includes, in addition to any other required information, the last issued license plate number.

(e) (1) Subdivisions (a) and (b) do not apply to any judicial sale, including, but not limited to, a bankruptcy sale, conducted pursuant to a writ of execution or order of court.

(2) Subdivision (b) does not apply to any lien sale if the lienholder does both of the following:

(A) Gives the notice required by subdivisions (a) and (b) of Section 5900.

(B) Notifies the buyer that California law requires that the buyer obtain a certificate of compliance or noncompliance and register the vehicle with the department, and that failure to comply will result in a lien against any vehicle owned by the buyer pursuant to Section 10876 of the Revenue and Taxation Code, enforceable pursuant to Section 10877 of the Revenue and Taxation Code and Article 6 (commencing with Section 9800) of Chapter 6 of Division 3. Receipt of the notice required by this subparagraph shall be evidenced by the signature of the buyer.

(f) The exceptions in this section do not apply to any requirements for registration of a vehicle pursuant to Section 4000.1, 4000.2, or 4000.3.

(g) Except as otherwise provided in subdivision (e), any public agency or auctioneer which sells, at public auction, any vehicle specified in subdivision (b) of Section 24007, which is registered to a public agency or a public utility, shall provide each bidder with a notice in writing that a certificate of compliance is required to be obtained, certifying that the vehicle complies with Part 5 (commencing with Section 43000) of Division 26 of the Health and Safety Code, before the vehicle may be registered in this state, unless the vehicle is sold to a dealer or for the purpose of being wrecked or dismantled or is sold exclusively for off-highway use. Prior to the sale of the vehicle, a public agency or public utility shall remove the license plates from the vehicle and surrender them to the department. The purchaser of the vehicle shall be given a bill of sale which includes, in addition to any other required information, the vehicle's last issued license plate number. *(Added by Stats.1971, c. 1021, p. 1967, § 1, operative May 3, 1972. Amended by Stats.1975, c. 957, p. 2234, § 30; Stats.1987, c. 1091, § 16; Stats.1991, c. 1054 (S.B.245), § 5; Stats.1992, c. 427 (A.B.3355), § 167.)*

§ 24007.6. Salvage pools; notice required by § 5900; notification that buyer obtain certificate of compliance or noncompliance and register vehicle

Except for vehicles sold to a dealer or for the purpose of being wrecked or dismantled or sold exclusively for off-highway use, a salvage pool shall do both of the following:

(a) Give the notice required by subdivisions (a) and (b) of Section 5900.

(b) Notify the buyer that California law requires that the buyer obtain a certificate of compliance or noncompliance and to register the vehicle with the department, and that failure to comply will result in a lien against any vehicle owned by the buyer pursuant to Section 10876 of the Revenue and Taxation Code, enforceable pursuant to Section 10877 of the Revenue and Taxation Code and Article 6 (commencing with Section 9800) of Chapter 6 of Division 3. Receipt of the notice required by this paragraph shall be evidenced by the signature of the buyer. *(Added by Stats.1991, c. 996 (S.B.798), § 4.)*

§ 24008. Modification of vehicles

It is unlawful to operate any passenger vehicle, or commercial vehicle under 6,000 pounds, which has been modified from the original design so that any portion of the vehicle, other than the wheels, has less clearance from the surface of a level roadway than the clearance between the roadway and the lowermost portion of any rim of any wheel in contact with the roadway. *(Added by Stats.1959, c. 1791, p. 4272, § 1. Amended by Stats.1961, c. 1562, p. 3383, § 1; Stats.1984, c. 462, § 3.)*

Cross References
Repossession, notice of seizure, see Business and Professions Code § 7507.10.

§ 24008.5. Frame or body floor heights

(a) No person shall operate any motor vehicle with a frame height or body floor height greater than specified in subdivisions (b) and (c).

(b) The maximum frame height is as follows:

Vehicle Type	Frame Height
(1) Passenger vehicles, except housecars	23 inches
(2) All other motor vehicles, including housecars, as follows:	
Up to 4,500 pounds GVWR	27 inches
4,501 to 7,500 pounds GVWR	30 inches
7,501 to 10,000 pounds GVWR	31 inches

(c) The lowest portion of the body floor shall not be more than five inches above the top of the frame.

(d) The following definitions govern the construction of this section:

(1) "Frame" means the main longitudinal structural members of the chassis of the vehicle or, for vehicles with unitized body construction, the lowest main longitudinal structural members of the body of the vehicle.

(2) "Frame height" means the vertical distance between the ground and the lowest point on the frame, measured when the vehicle is unladen on a level surface at the lowest point on the frame midway between the front axle and the second axle on the vehicle.

(3) "GVWR" means the manufacturer's gross vehicle weight rating, as defined in Section 390, whether or not the vehicle is modified by use of parts not originally installed by the manufacturer. *(Added by Stats.1985, c. 835, § 2. Amended by Stats.1987, c. 718, § 1.)*

§ 24009. Manufacturer's name and gross vehicle weight rating plates or markings

No person shall sell or offer for sale a new motor truck, truck tractor, or bus that is not equipped with an identification plate or marking bearing the manufacturer's name and the manufacturer's gross vehicle weight rating of such vehicle. *(Added by Stats.1967, c. 1287, p. 3090, § 2.)*

Cross References
Definitions,
  Bus, see Vehicle Code § 233.
  Manufacturer's gross vehicle weight rating, see Vehicle Code § 390.
  Motor truck, see Vehicle Code § 410.
  Truck tractor, see Vehicle Code § 655.

§ 24010. Vehicle rental responsibility

(a) No person engaged in the rental of any vehicle, for periods of 30 days or less, shall rent, lease or otherwise allow the operation of such vehicle unless all of the following requirements are met:

(1) All necessary equipment required by this code and regulations adopted pursuant to this code for the operation of the vehicle upon a highway has been provided or offered to the lessee for his or her use.

(2) The vehicle conforms to all applicable federal motor vehicle safety standards established under the National Traffic and Motor Vehicle Safety Act of 1966 (15 U.S.C. Sec. 1381 et seq.) and the regulations adopted under that act.

(3) The vehicle is mechanically sound and safe to operate within the meaning of Section 24002.

(b) In order to ensure compliance with this section, the department may conduct periodic inspections, without prior notice, of the business premises of persons engaged in the rental of vehicles for periods of 30 days or less and of the vehicles themselves, for the purpose of ascertaining that the vehicles are in compliance with this section. Any vehicle which is found not in compliance shall not be rented or leased until proof of full compliance with this section is made to the satisfaction of the department.

(c) The contract or rental agreement shall include the name of the person from whom the vehicle is rented, leased or obtained, the address of that person's place of business in this state where the vehicle is rented, leased, or delivered, and a statement of any required equipment refused by the person to whom the vehicle is rented, leased, or delivered. *(Added by Stats.1967, c. 855, p. 2292, § 1. Amended by Stats.1971, c. 1536, p. 3040, § 3, operative May 3, 1972; Stats.1973, c. 88, p. 148, § 1; Stats.1990, c. 306 (A.B.4108), § 1.)*

§ 24011. Federal safety standard

Whenever a federal motor vehicle safety standard is established under federal law (49 U.S.C. Sec. 30101 et seq.), no dealer shall sell or offer for sale a vehicle to which the standard is applicable, and no person shall sell or offer for sale for use upon a vehicle an item of equipment to which the standard is applicable, unless:

(a) The vehicle or equipment conforms to the applicable federal standard.

(b) The vehicle or equipment bears thereon a certification by the manufacturer or distributor that it complies with the applicable federal standards. The certification may be in the form of a symbol prescribed in the federal standards or, if there is no federal symbol, by a symbol acceptable to the department. *(Added by Stats.1968, c. 192, p. 481, § 1. Amended by Stats.2004, c. 615 (S.B. 1233), § 29.)*

§ 24011.3. Bumper strength notice for passenger vehicles; requirements; violations; penalties

(a) Every manufacturer or importer of new passenger vehicles for sale or lease in this state, shall affix to a window or the windshield of the vehicle a notice with either of the following statements, whichever is appropriate:

(1) "This vehicle is equipped with bumpers that can withstand an impact of 2.5 miles per hour with no damage to the vehicle's body and safety systems, although the bumper and related components may sustain damage. The bumper system on this vehicle conforms to the current federal bumper standard of 2.5 miles per hour. "

(2) "This vehicle is equipped with a front bumper of a type that has been tested at an impact speed of (here specify the appropriate number) miles per hour, and a rear bumper of a type that has been tested at an impact speed of (here specify the appropriate number) miles per hour, resulting in no damage to the vehicle's body and safety systems and minimal damage to the bumper and attachment hardware. 'Minimal damage to the bumper' means minor cosmetic damage that can be repaired with the use of common repair materials and without replacing any parts. The stronger the bumper, the less likely the vehicle will require repair after a low-speed collision. This vehicle exceeds the current federal bumper standard of 2.5 miles per hour."

(b) The impact speed required to be specified in the notice pursuant to paragraph (2) of subdivision (a) is the maximum speed of impact upon the bumper of the vehicle at which the vehicle sustains no damage to the body and safety systems and only minimal damage to the bumper when subjected to the fixed barrier and pendulum impact tests, and when subjected to the corner impact test at not less than 60 percent of that maximum speed, conducted pursuant to Part 581 of Title 49 of the Code of Federal Regulations.

(c)(1) A manufacturer who willfully fails to affix the notice required by subdivision (a), or willfully misstates any information in the notice, is guilty of a misdemeanor, which shall be punishable by a fine of not more than five hundred dollars ($500). Each failure or misstatement is a separate offense.

(2) A person who willfully defaces, alters, or removes the notice required by subdivision (a) prior to the delivery of the vehicle, to which the notice is required to be affixed, to the registered owner or lessee is guilty of a misdemeanor, which shall be punishable by a fine of not more than five hundred dollars ($500). Each willful defacement, alteration, or removal is a separate offense.

(d) For purposes of this section, the following terms have the following meanings:

(1) "Manufacturer" is any person engaged in the manufacture or assembly of new passenger vehicles for distribution or sale, and includes an importer of new passenger vehicles for distribution or sale and any person who acts for, or is under the control of, a manufacturer in connection with the distribution or sale of new passenger vehicles.

(2) "Passenger vehicle" means, notwithstanding Section 465, a motor vehicle subject to impact testing conducted pursuant to Part 581 of Title 49 of the Code of Federal Regulations.

798

(3) "No damage" means that, when a passenger vehicle is subjected to impact testing, conducted pursuant to the conditions and test procedures of Sections 581.6 and 581.7 of Part 581 of Title 49 of the Code of Federal Regulations, the vehicle sustains no damage to the body and safety systems.

(4) For purposes of paragraph (2) of subdivision (a) and subdivision (b), "minimal damage to the bumper and attachment hardware" means damage that can be repaired with the use of common repair materials and without replacing any parts. In addition, not later than 30 minutes after completion of each pendulum or barrier impact test, the bumper face bar shall have no permanent deviation greater than three-quarters of one inch from its original contour and position relative to the vehicle frame and no permanent deviation greater than three-eighths of one inch from its original contour on areas of contact with the barrier face or impact ridge of the pendulum test device, measured from a straight line connecting the bumper contours adjoining the contact area.

(e) The notice required by this section may be included in any notice or label required by federal law to be affixed to a window or windshield of the vehicle. *(Added by Stats.1991, c. 1219 (S.B.265), § 1. Amended by Stats.2006, c. 538 (S.B.1852), § 662.)*

§ 24011.7. Exhaust and noise emission control inspection

(a) Nothing in Chapter 20.4 (commencing with Section 9889.50) of Division 3 of the Business and Professions Code, shall be construed as having any effect on the existing inspection program conducted by the department. Rather, it is the intent of the Legislature that such program continue and that a cooperative relationship between the department and the Department of Consumer Affairs be established, under which the department can inform the Department of Consumer Affairs of the results and experiences of the department in order to provide data on exhaust and noise emission control device tampering and performance deterioration following mandatory inspections. *(Added by Stats.1973, c. 1154, p. 2400, § 5.)*

§ 24012. Compliance with lighting equipment mounting regulations

All lighting equipment or devices subject to requirements established by the department shall comply with the engineering requirements and specifications, including mounting and aiming instructions, determined and publicized by the department. *(Formerly § 25953, enacted by Stats.1959, c. 3, p. 1729. Renumbered § 24012 and amended by Stats.1969, c. 341, p. 717, § 7; Stats.1979, c. 723, p. 2217, § 10.)*

Cross References

Cotton module movers, operation on state highways, conditions, see Vehicle Code § 35555.
Implements of husbandry, applicability of this section, see Vehicle Code § 36500.

Lighting during darkness, see Vehicle Code § 24250.
Lighting equipment defined, see Vehicle Code § 375.
Mandatory signal devices, see Vehicle Code § 24950.
Special construction and maintenance equipment, see Vehicle Code § 25801.
Special mobile equipment, applicability of this section, see Vehicle Code § 25800.

§ 24013. Statement of minimum octane number of gasoline for motor vehicle

No new motor vehicle shall be sold unless the seller provides the buyer with a statement of the minimum octane number of the gasoline for such vehicle.

As used in this section "octane number" means the octane number of the gasoline adopted by the Federal Trade Commission, and if the Federal Trade Commission does not adopt an octane number, then the American Society for Testing Materials research octane number of the gasoline as defined by Section 20710 of the Business and Professions Code. *(Added by Stats.1971, c. 711, p. 1378, § 3, operative Jan. 1, 1972.)*

§ 24013.5. Light duty truck sales; label with pricing and other information

(a) No dealer shall sell, offer for sale, or display for sale any new light duty truck with a manufacturer's gross vehicle weight rating of 8,500 pounds or less unless there is securely affixed to the windshield or side window of the light duty truck a label on which the manufacturer has endorsed clearly, distinctly, and legibly, true and correct entries disclosing the following information concerning the light duty truck:

(1) The make, model, and serial or identification number or numbers.

(2) The retail price of the light duty truck as suggested by the manufacturer.

(3) The retail delivered price, as suggested by the manufacturer, for each accessory or item of optional equipment which is physically attached to the light duty truck at the time of its delivery to the dealer and which is not included within the price of the light duty truck as stated pursuant to paragraph (2).

(4) The amount charged, if any, to the dealer for the transportation of the light duty truck to the location at which it is delivered to the dealer.

(5) The total of the amounts specified pursuant to paragraphs (2), (3), and (4).

(b) Subdivision (a) applies to every light duty truck sold, offered for sale, or displayed in California which is manufactured on or after September 1, 1988. *(Added by Stats.1987, c. 418, § 2.)*

Cross References

Licensed dealer violations relating to this section's requirements, see Vehicle Code § 11712.5.

§ 24014. Motorcycle sales: required price information

(a) No dealer shall sell, offer for sale, or display, any new, assembled motorcycle on its premises, unless there is securely attached to its handlebar a label, approved by the Department of Motor Vehicles, furnished by the manufacturer, on which the manufacturer shall clearly indicate the following:

(1) The recommended retail price of the motorcycle.

(2) The recommended price for each accessory or item of optional equipment physically attached to the motorcycle at the time of its delivery to the dealer.

(b) The dealer shall clearly indicate on the label, furnished by the manufacturer, the following:

(1) The amount charged, if any, over and above the suggested retail price for transportation to the dealership.

(2) The amount charged, if any, for the assembly, preparation, or both, of the motorcycle.

(3) The amount charged, if any, for each dealer added accessory or item of optional equipment.

(4) The total recommended retail price of the vehicle which shall be the aggregate value of paragraphs (1) and (2) of subdivision (a) and paragraphs (1), (2) and (3) of subdivision (b). *(Added by Stats.1974, c. 1089, p. 2315, § 2. Amended by Stats.1978, c. 623, p. 2076, § 1.)*

Cross References

Motorcycle defined, see Vehicle Code § 400.
Motorcycle sales, required price information, see Vehicle Code § 11712.5.

§ 24015. Motorized bicycles; federal safety standards; equipment

(a) Motorized bicycles shall comply with those federal motor vehicle safety standards established under the National Traffic and Motor Vehicle Safety Act of 1966 (15 U.S.C., Sec. 1381, et seq.) [1] which are applicable to a motor-driven cycle, as that term is defined in such federal standards. Such standards include, but are not limited to, provisions requiring a headlamp, taillamp, stoplamp, side and rear reflex reflectors, and adequate brakes.

(b) In addition to equipment required in subdivision (a), all motorized bicycles operated upon a highway shall be equipped with a mirror as required in subdivision (a) of Section 26709, a horn as required in Section 27000, and an adequate muffler as required in subdivision (a) of Section 27150.

(c) Except as provided in subdivisions (a) and (b), none of the provisions of this chapter relating to motorcycles and motor-driven cycles, as defined in this code, shall apply to a motorized bicycle. *(Added by Stats.1975, c. 987, p. 2332, § 9. Amended by Stats.1978, c. 421, p. 1320, § 4.)*

[1] 15 U.S.C.A. § 1381 et seq.

Cross References

Motorized bicycle defined, see Vehicle Code § 406.

§ 24016. Motorized bicycles; manufacturing and operating criteria; tampering

(a) A motorized bicycle described in subdivision (b) of Section 406 shall meet the following criteria:

(1) Comply with the equipment and manufacturing requirements for bicycles adopted by the Consumer Product Safety Commission (16 C.F.R. 1512.1, et seq.) or the requirements adopted by the National Highway Traffic Safety Administration (49 C.F.R. 571.1, et seq.) in accordance with the National Traffic and Motor Vehicle Safety Act of 1966 (15 U.S.C. Sec. 1381, et seq.) for motor driven cycles.

(2) Operate in a manner so that the electric motor is disengaged or ceases to function when the brakes are applied, or operate in a manner such that the motor is engaged through a switch or mechanism that, when released, will cause the electric motor to disengage or cease to function.

(b) All of the following apply to a motorized bicycle described in subdivision (b) of Section 406:

(1) No person shall operate a motorized bicycle unless the person is wearing a properly fitted and fastened bicycle helmet that meets the standards described in Section 21212.

(2) A person operating a motorized bicycle is subject to Sections 21200 and 21200.5.

(3) A person operating a motorized bicycle is not subject to the provisions of this code relating to financial responsibility, driver's licenses, registration, and license plate requirements, and a motorized bicycle is not a motor vehicle.

(4) A motorized bicycle shall only be operated by a person 16 years of age or older.

(5) Every manufacturer of a motorized bicycle shall certify that it complies with the equipment and manufacturing requirements for bicycles adopted by the Consumer Product Safety Commission (16 C.F.R. 1512.1, et seq.).

(c) No person shall tamper with or modify a motorized bicycle described in subdivision (b) of Section 406 so as to increase the speed capability of the bicycle. *(Added by Stats.1995, c. 804 (A.B.1501), § 3.)*

§ 24017. Transit bus operated by motor carrier; speedometer

A transit bus operated by a motor carrier, whether the motor carrier is a private company or a public agency, that provides public transportation services shall be equipped with a speedometer that shall be maintained in good working order. *(Added by Stats.2011, c. 341 (S.B. 565), § 5.)*

§ 24018. Transit buses operated by motor carriers; equipment with two-way communication device allowing driver to contact motor carrier in an emergency

(a) Every transit bus operated by a motor carrier, whether that motor carrier is a private company or a public agency, that provides public transportation services shall be equipped with a two-way communication device that enables the driver to contact the motor carrier in the event of an emergency. The two-way communication devices shall be maintained in good working order.

(b) For the purposes of this section, "two-way communication device" is a radio, cellular telephone, or other similar device permitting communication between the transit bus driver and personnel responsible for the safety of operations of the motor carrier, including, but not limited to, the motor carrier's dispatcher.

(c) This section does not apply to buses operated by a school district or on behalf of a school district.

(d) The commissioner shall upon request grant a nonrenewable one year extension to any motor carrier to comply with the requirements of this section.

(e) Nothing in this section shall require a motor carrier to replace an existing two-way communication device that currently meets the requirements of this section. *(Added by Stats.2002, c. 937 (A.B.629), § 3.)*

CHAPTER 2. LIGHTING EQUIPMENT

Article	Section
1. General Provisions	24250
2. Headlamps and Auxiliary Lamps	24400
3. Rear Lighting Equipment	24600
4. Parking Lamps	24800
5. Signal Lamps and Devices	24950
6. Side and Fender Lighting Equipment	25100
7. Flashing and Colored Lights	25250
8. Warning Lights and Devices	25300
9. Commercial and Common Carrier Vehicles	25350
10. Diffused Lights	25400
11. Acetylene Lamps	25450
12. Reflectorizing Material	25500
13. Headlamps on Motorcycles and Motor-Driven Cycles	25650
14. Vehicles Exempted	25800
15. Light Restrictions and Mounting	25950
16. Equipment Testing	26100

ARTICLE 1.   GENERAL PROVISIONS

Section
24250. Lighting during darkness.
24251. Lighting distance requirement.
24252. Lighting equipment requirements.
24253. Taillamps which remain lighted.
24254. Mounting height.
24255. Illuminating devices on vehicles to supplement driver's visibility of roadway; operation of system.

Cross References

Cotton module movers, operation on state highways, conditions, see Vehicle Code § 35555.

§ 24250. Lighting during darkness

During darkness, a vehicle shall be equipped with lighted lighting equipment as required for the vehicle by this chapter. *(Stats.1959, c. 3, p. 1714, § 24250.)*

Cross References

Darkness defined, see Vehicle Code § 280.

Flashing and colored lights, see Vehicle Code §§ 25250 et seq., 25950.
Implements of husbandry, applicability of this section, see Vehicle Code § 36500.
Sale, lease and installation of unlawful lighting devices prohibited, see Vehicle Code § 24005.
Special construction and maintenance equipment, applicability of this section, see Vehicle Code § 25801.
Special mobile equipment, applicability of this section, see Vehicle Code § 25800.
Vehicles incidentally operated over highway, applicability of this section, see Vehicle Code § 25802.

§ 24251. Lighting distance requirement

Any requirement in this chapter as to the distance from which any lighting equipment shall render a person or vehicle visible or within which any lighting equipment shall be visible shall apply during darkness, directly ahead upon a straight, level unlighted highway, and under normal atmospheric conditions, unless a different time, direction, or condition is expressly stated. *(Stats.1959, c. 3, p. 1714, § 24251.)*

Cross References

Darkness defined, see Vehicle Code § 280.
Flashing and colored lights, see Vehicle Code § 25250 et seq.
Implements of husbandry, applicability of this section, see Vehicle Code § 36500.
Special construction and maintenance equipment, applicability of this section, see Vehicle Code § 25801.
Special mobile equipment, applicability of this section, see Vehicle Code § 25800.
Vehicles incidentally operated over highway, applicability of this section, see Vehicle Code § 25802.

§ 24252. Lighting equipment requirements

(a) All lighting equipment of a required type installed on a vehicle shall at all times be maintained in good working order. Lamps shall be equipped with bulbs of the correct voltage rating corresponding to the nominal voltage at the lamp socket.

(b) The voltage at any tail, stop, license plate, side marker or clearance lamp socket on a vehicle shall not be less than 85 percent of the design voltage of the bulb. Voltage tests shall be conducted with the engine operating.

(c) Two or more lamp or reflector functions may be combined, provided each function subject to requirements established by the department meets such requirements.

(1) No turn signal lamp may be combined optically with a stoplamp unless the stoplamp is extinguished when the turn signal is flashing.

(2) No clearance lamp may be combined optically with any taillamp or identification lamp. *(Stats.1959, c. 3, p. 1714, § 24252. Amended by Stats.1965, c. 1276, p. 3161, § 1; Stats.1968, c. 980, p. 1866, § 2; Stats.1979, c. 723, p. 2217, § 11.)*

Lighting equipment defined, see Vehicle Code § 375.

§ 24253.   Taillamps which remain lighted

(a) All motor vehicles manufactured and first registered after January 1, 1970, shall be equipped so all taillamps are capable of remaining lighted for a period of at least one-quarter hour with the engine inoperative. This requirement shall be complied with by an energy storing system which is recharged by energy produced by the vehicle.

(b) All motorcycles manufactured and first registered after January 1, 1971, shall be equipped so all taillamps, when turned on, will remain lighted automatically for a period of at least one-quarter hour if the engine stops. *(Added by Stats.1967, c. 544, p. 1892, § 1.   Amended by Stats.1970, c. 217, p. 470, § 1.)*

§ 24254.   Mounting height

Whenever a requirement is declared as to the mounted height of lamps or reflectors, the height shall be measured from the center of the lamp or reflector to the level surface upon which the vehicle stands when it is without a load. *(Formerly § 25952, enacted by Stats.1959, c. 3, p. 1729.   Renumbered § 24254 and amended by Stats.1969, c. 341, p. 716, § 5.)*

Fog lights, see Vehicle Code § 24403.
Headlamps on motor vehicles, see Vehicle Code § 24400.
Implements of husbandry, applicability of this section, see Vehicle Code § 36500.
Special construction and maintenance equipment, applicability of this section, see Vehicle Code § 25801.
Special mobile equipment, applicability of this section, see Vehicle Code § 25800.

§ 24255.   Illuminating devices on vehicles to supplement driver's visibility of roadway; operation of system

(a) A vehicle may be equipped with a system to supplement the driver's visibility of the roadway to the front or rear of the vehicle during darkness.   This system may incorporate an illuminating device that emits radiation predominantly in the infrared region of the electromagnetic spectrum and a display monitor to provide an image visible to the driver of the vehicle.   The system, or any portion of it, shall not obstruct the vision of the driver, and shall not emit any glaring light visible in any direction or to any person.   The illuminating device may be mounted inside the vehicle, if it is constructed and mounted so as to prevent any direct or reflected light, other than a monitorial indicator emitted from the device, from being visible to the driver.

(b) The system shall be operated only with the headlamps lighted.   An illuminating device for the system shall be interlocked with the headlamp switch so that it is operable only when the headlamps are lighted.

(c)(1) No part of the illuminating device may be physically or optically combined with any other required or permitted lighting device.

(2) The illuminating device may be installed within a housing containing other required or permitted lighting devices, if the function of the other devices is not impaired thereby.   *(Added by Stats.2004, c. 198 (S.B. 1236), § 2.)*

Equipment of vehicles, light restrictions, color or lamps and reflectors, see Vehicle Code § 25950.

ARTICLE 2.   HEADLAMPS AND AUXILIARY LAMPS

Section
24400.   Headlamps on motor vehicles; inclement weather.
24401.   Dimmed lights on parked vehicles.
24402.   Auxiliary driving and passing lamps.
24403.   Fog lamps.
24404.   Spotlamps.
24405.   Maximum number of lamps.
24406.   Multiple beams.
24407.   Upper and lower beam.
24408.   Beam indicator.
24409.   Use of multiple beams.
24410.   Single beams.
24411.   Auxiliary lamps; off-highway use.

§ 24400.   Headlamps on motor vehicles; inclement weather

(a) A motor vehicle, other than a motorcycle, shall be equipped with at least two headlamps, with at least one on each side of the front of the vehicle, and, except as to vehicles registered prior to January 1, 1930, they shall be located directly above or in advance of the front axle of the vehicle.   The headlamps and every light source in any headlamp unit shall be located at a height of not more than 54 inches nor less than 22 inches.

(b) A motor vehicle, other than a motorcycle, shall be operated during darkness, or inclement weather, or both, with at least two lighted headlamps that comply with subdivision (a).

(c) As used in subdivision (b), "inclement weather" is a weather condition that is either of the following:

(1) A condition that prevents a driver of a motor vehicle from clearly discerning a person or another motor vehicle on the highway from a distance of 1,000 feet.

(2) A condition requiring the windshield wipers to be in continuous use due to rain, mist, snow, fog, or other precipitation or atmospheric moisture.   *(Added by Stats. 2004, c. 415 (A.B.1854), § 2, operative July 1, 2005. Amended by Stats.2006, c. 311 (S.B.1586), § 9; Stats.2010, c. 491 (S.B.1318), § 43.)*

Acetylene headlamps, see Vehicle Code § 25450 et seq.
Auxiliary driving and passing lamps, see Vehicle Code § 24402.

Beam indicator, see Vehicle Code § 24408.
Color of lights, see Vehicle Code § 25950.
Definitions,
Axle, see Vehicle Code § 230.
Darkness, see Vehicle Code § 280.
Motor vehicle, see Vehicle Code § 415.
Motorcycle and motor-driven cycle, see Vehicle Code §§ 400, 405.
Flashing and colored lights, see Vehicle Code § 25250 et seq.
Implements of husbandry,
Application of section when implements operated at night, see Vehicle Code § 36505.
Application of this section, see Vehicle Code § 36500.
Lamps on parked vehicles, see Vehicle Code § 24802.
Maximum number of lamps, see Vehicle Code § 24405.
Measurement of height, see Vehicle Code § 24254.
Motorcycle headlamps, see Vehicle Code §§ 25650, 25650.5.
Prohibitions on spotlamps, see Vehicle Code § 24404.
Special construction and maintenance equipment, applicability of this section, see Vehicle Code § 25801.
Special mobile equipment, applicability of this section, see Vehicle Code § 25800.
Test and approval of lighting equipment in general, see Vehicle Code § 26100 et seq.
Use of fog lamps, see Vehicle Code § 24403.
Use of single and multiple beam lighting equipment, see Vehicle Code §§ 24409, 24410.
Vehicles incidentally operated over highway, applicability of this section, see Vehicle Code § 25802.

§ 24401. Dimmed lights on parked vehicles

Whenever any motor vehicle is parked or standing upon a highway any headlamp that is lighted shall be dimmed or on the lower beam. *(Stats.1959, c. 3, p. 1715, § 24401.)*

Cross References

Implements of husbandry, applicability of this section, see Vehicle Code § 36500.
Lamps on parked vehicles, see Vehicle Code § 24802.
Parking lamps, see Vehicle Code § 24800 et seq.
Special construction and maintenance equipment, applicability of this section, see Vehicle Code § 25801.
Special mobile equipment, applicability of this section, see Vehicle Code § 25800.
Stopping, standing and parking vehicles, see Vehicle Code § 22500 et seq.
Vehicles incidentally operated over highway, applicability of this section, see Vehicle Code § 25802.

§ 24402. Auxiliary driving and passing lamps

(a) Any motor vehicle may be equipped with not to exceed two auxiliary driving lamps mounted on the front at a height of not less than 16 inches nor more than 42 inches. Driving lamps are lamps designed for supplementing the upper beam from headlamps and may not be lighted with the lower beam.

(b) Any motor vehicle may be equipped with not to exceed two auxiliary passing lamps mounted on the front at a height of not less than 24 inches nor more than 42 inches. Passing lamps are lamps designed for supplementing the lower beam from headlamps and may also be

lighted with the upper beam. *(Stats.1959, c. 3, p. 1715, § 24402.)*

Cross References

Implements of husbandry, applicability of this section, see Vehicle Code § 36500.
Special construction and maintenance equipment, applicability of this section, see Vehicle Code § 25801.
Special mobile equipment, applicability of this section, see Vehicle Code § 25800.
Vehicles incidentally operated over highway, applicability of this section, see Vehicle Code § 25802.

§ 24403. Fog lamps

(a) A motor vehicle may be equipped with not more than two foglamps that may be used with, but may not be used in substitution of, headlamps.

(b) On a motor vehicle other than a motorcycle, the foglamps authorized under this section shall be mounted on the front at a height of not less than 12 inches nor more than 30 inches and aimed so that when the vehicle is not loaded none of the high-intensity portion of the light to the left of the center of the vehicle projects higher than a level of four inches below the level of the center of the lamp from which it comes, for a distance of 25 feet in front of the vehicle.

(c) On a motorcycle, the foglamps authorized under this section shall be mounted on the front at a height of not less than 12 inches nor more than 40 inches and aimed so that when the vehicle is not loaded none of the high-intensity portion of the light to the left of the center of the vehicle projects higher than a level of four inches below the level of the center of the lamp from which it comes, for a distance of 25 feet in front of the vehicle. *(Stats.1959, c. 3, p. 1715, § 24403. Amended by Stats. 1961, c. 58, p. 1011, § 44, eff. March 31, 1961; Stats.1969, c. 341, p. 715, § 1; Stats.2003, c. 451 (A.B.1718), § 20.)*

Cross References

Approved lighting equipment, see Vehicle Code § 375.
Headlamps on motor vehicles, see Vehicle Code § 24400.
Implements of husbandry, applicability of this section, see Vehicle Code § 36500.
Measurement of height, see Vehicle Code § 24254.
Special construction and maintenance equipment, applicability of this section, see Vehicle Code § 25801.
Special mobile equipment, applicability of this section, see Vehicle Code § 25800.
Test and approval of lighting equipment, see Vehicle Code § 26100 et seq.
Vehicles incidentally operated over highway, applicability of this section, see Vehicle Code § 25802.

§ 24404. Spotlamps

(a) A motor vehicle may be equipped with not to exceed two white spotlamps, which shall not be used in substitution of headlamps.

(b) No spotlamp shall be equipped with any lamp source exceeding 32 standard candlepower or 30 watts nor project any glaring light into the eyes of an approaching driver.

(c) Every spotlamp shall be so directed when in use: That no portion of the main substantially parallel beam of light will strike the roadway to the left of the prolongation of the left side line of the vehicle.

That the top of the beam will not strike the roadway at a distance in excess of 300 feet from the vehicle.

(d) This section does not apply to spotlamps on authorized emergency vehicles.

(e) No spotlamp when in use shall be directed so as to illuminate any other moving vehicle. *(Stats.1959, c. 3, p. 1715, § 24404. Amended by Stats.1959, c. 403, p. 2336, § 2; Stats.1959, c. 1996, p. 4632, § 29.5; Stats.1967, c. 544, p. 1893, § 2.)*

Cross References

Authorized emergency vehicle defined, see Vehicle Code § 165.
Implements of husbandry, applicability of this section, see Vehicle Code § 36500.
Special construction and maintenance equipment, applicability of this section, see Vehicle Code § 25801.
Special mobile equipment, applicability of this section, see Vehicle Code § 25800.
Vehicles incidentally operated over highway, applicability of this section, see Vehicle Code § 25802.

§ 24405.   Maximum number of lamps

(a) Not more than four lamps of the following types showing to the front of a vehicle may be lighted at any one time:

(1) Headlamps.

(2) Auxiliary driving or passing lamps.

(3) Fog lamps.

(4) Warning lamps.

(5) Spot lamps.

(6) Gaseous discharge lamps specified in Section 25258.

(b) For the purpose of this section each pair of a dual headlamp system shall be considered as one lamp.

(c) Subdivision (a) does not apply to any authorized emergency vehicle. *(Stats.1959, c. 3, p. 1716, § 24405. Amended by Stats.1963, c. 547, p. 1427, § 2; Stats.1965, c. 1313, p. 3199, § 2; Stats.1970, c. 174, p. 426, § 1; Stats.1976, c. 234, p. 444, § 1.)*

Cross References

Authorized emergency vehicle defined, see Vehicle Code § 165.

§ 24406.   Multiple beams

Except as otherwise provided, the headlamps, or other auxiliary driving lamps, or a combination thereof, on a motor vehicle during darkness shall be so arranged that the driver may select at will between distributions of light projected to different elevations, and the lamps may, in addition, be so arranged that the selection can be made automatically. *(Stats.1959, c. 3, p. 1716, § 24406.)*

Cross References

Beam indicator, see Vehicle Code § 24408.
Darkness defined, see Vehicle Code § 280.

§ 24407.   Upper and lower beam

Multiple-beam road lighting equipment shall be designed and aimed as follows:

(a) There shall be an uppermost distribution of light, or composite beam, so aimed and of such intensity as to reveal persons and vehicles at a distance of at least 350 feet ahead for all conditions of loading.

(b) There shall be a lowermost distribution of light, or composite beam so aimed and of sufficient intensity to reveal a person or vehicle at a distance of at least 100 feet ahead.   On a straight level road under any condition of loading none of the high intensity portion of the beam shall be directed to strike the eyes of an approaching driver. *(Stats.1959, c. 3, p. 1716, § 24407. Amended by Stats.1963, c. 547, p. 1427, § 3.)*

§ 24408.   Beam indicator

(a) Every new motor vehicle registered in this state after January 1, 1940, which has multiple-beam road lighting equipment shall be equipped with a beam indicator, which shall be lighted whenever the uppermost distribution of light from the headlamps is in use, and shall not otherwise be lighted.

(b) The indicator shall be so designed and located that when lighted it will be readily visible without glare to the driver of the vehicle so equipped.   Any such lamp on the exterior of the vehicle shall have a light source not exceeding two candlepower, and the light shall not show to the front or sides of the vehicle. *(Stats.1959, c. 3, p. 1716, § 24408. Amended by Stats.1965, c. 1124, p. 2772, § 1; Stats.1970, c. 422, p. 834, § 1.)*

§ 24409.   Use of multiple beams

Whenever a motor vehicle is being operated during darkness, the driver shall use a distribution of light, or composite beam, directed high enough and of sufficient intensity to reveal persons and vehicles at a safe distance in advance of the vehicle, subject to the following requirements and limitations:

(a) Whenever the driver of a vehicle approaches an oncoming vehicle within 500 feet, he shall use a distribution of light or composite beam so aimed that the glaring rays are not projected into the eyes of the oncoming driver.

The lowermost distribution of light specified in this article shall be deemed to avoid glare at all times regardless of road contour.

(b) Whenever the driver of a vehicle follows another vehicle within 300 feet to the rear, he shall use the lowermost distribution of light specified in this article. *(Stats.1959, c. 3, p. 1716, § 24409. Amended by Stats. 1963, c. 547, p. 1427, § 4; Stats.1965, c. 37, p. 915, § 1.)*

Cross References

Darkness defined, see Vehicle Code § 280.

§ 24410. Single beams

Headlamps arranged to provide a single distribution of light not supplemented by auxiliary driving lamps are permitted on motor vehicles manufactured and sold prior to September 19, 1940, in lieu of multiple-beam road lighting equipment if the single distribution of light complies with the following requirements and limitations:

(a) The headlamps shall be so aimed that when the vehicle is not loaded none of the high-intensity portion of the light shall at a distance of 25 feet ahead project higher than a level of five inches below the level of the center of the lamp from which it comes, and in no case higher than 42 inches above the level on which the vehicle stands at a distance of 75 feet ahead.

(b) The intensity shall be sufficient to reveal persons and vehicles at a distance of at least 200 feet. *(Stats.1959, c. 3, p. 1716, § 24410.)*

§ 24411. Auxiliary lamps; off-highway use

Notwithstanding any other provision of law, a vehicle may be equipped with not more than eight lamps for use as headlamps while the vehicle is operated or driven off the highway. The lamps shall be mounted at a height of not less than 16 inches from the ground, or more than 12 inches above the top of the passenger compartment, at any place between the front of the vehicle and a line lying on a point 40 inches to the rear of the seat occupied by the driver, shall be wired independently of all other lighting circuits, and, whenever the vehicle is operated or driven upon a highway, shall be covered or hooded with an opaque hood or cover, and turned off. *(Added by Stats.1975, c. 860, p. 1931, § 1. Amended by Stats.1979, c. 723, p. 2218, § 12; Stats.1980, c. 399, p. 783, § 3, eff. July 11, 1980; Stats.1986, c. 149, § 1.)*

ARTICLE 3. REAR LIGHTING EQUIPMENT

Section
24600. Taillamps generally.
24601. Lamp.
24602. Fog taillamps.
24603. Stoplamps.
24604. Lamp or flag on projections.
24605. Tow trucks, automobile dismantler's tow vehicle and towed vehicle.
24606. Backup lamps.
24607. Reflectors.
24608. Reflectors on front and sides.
24609. Vehicle reflectors.
24610. Multiple-unit truck reflector.
24611. Reflective sheeting or reflectors on sides and rear.
24612. Trailers, semitrailers, and motor trucks; conspicuity system.
24615. Slow moving vehicle emblem.
24616. Rear-facing auxiliary lamps.
24617. Yield right–of–way signs on transit buses.

Cross References

Cotton module movers, operation on state highways, conditions, see Vehicle Code § 35555.
Implements of husbandry, applicability of this Article, see Vehicle Code § 36500.
Special mobile equipment, applicability of this Article, see Vehicle Code § 25800.

§ 24600. Taillamps generally

During darkness every motor vehicle which is not in combination with any other vehicle and every vehicle at the end of a combination of vehicles shall be equipped with lighted taillamps mounted on the rear as follows:

(a) Every vehicle shall be equipped with one or more taillamps.

(b) Every vehicle, other than a motorcycle, manufactured and first registered on or after January 1, 1958, shall be equipped with not less than two taillamps, except that trailers and semitrailers manufactured after July 23, 1973, which are less than 30 inches wide, may be equipped with one taillamp which shall be mounted at or near the vertical centerline of the vehicles. If a vehicle is equipped with two taillamps, they shall be mounted as specified in subdivision (d).

(c) Every vehicle or vehicle at the end of a combination of vehicles, subject to subdivision (a) of Section 22406 shall be equipped with not less than two taillamps.

(d) When two taillamps are required, at least one shall be mounted at the left and one at the right side respectively at the same level.

(e) Taillamps shall be red in color and shall be plainly visible from all distances within 500 feet to the rear except that taillamps on vehicles manufactured after January 1, 1969, shall be plainly visible from all distances within 1,000 feet to the rear.

(f) Taillamps on vehicles manufactured on or after January 1, 1969, shall be mounted not lower than 15 inches nor higher than 72 inches, except that a tow truck, in addition to being equipped with the required taillamps, may also be equipped with two taillamps which may be mounted not lower than 15 inches nor higher than the maximum allowable vehicle height and as far forward as the rearmost portion of the driver's seat in the rearmost position. The additional taillamps on a tow truck shall be lighted whenever the headlamps are lighted. *(Added by Stats.1968, c. 980, p. 1867, § 4. Amended by Stats.1969, c. 341, p. 715, § 2; Stats.1970, c. 923, p. 1676, § 5; Stats.1974, c. 635, p. 1488, § 2; Stats.1976, c. 154, p. 248, § 2; Stats.1988, c. 924, § 11.)*

Cross References

Color of lights, see Vehicle Code § 25950.
Definitions,
   Darkness, see Vehicle Code § 280.
   Motor vehicle, see Vehicle Code § 415.
   Trailer coach, see Vehicle Code § 635.
   Vehicle, see Vehicle Code § 670.
Special construction and maintenance equipment, applicability of this section, see Vehicle Code § 25801.

Special mobile equipment, applicability of this section, see
    Vehicle Code § 25800.
Test and approval of lighting equipment and signal devices, see
    Vehicle Code § 26100 et seq.
Vehicles incidentally operated over highway, applicability of this
    section, see Vehicle Code § 25802.

§ 24601. Lamp

Either the taillamp or a separate lamp shall be so
constructed and placed as to illuminate with a white light
the rear license plate during darkness and render it
clearly legible from a distance of 50 feet to the rear.
When the rear license plate is illuminated by a lamp other
than a required taillamp, the two lamps shall be turned on
or off only by the same control switch at all times.
*(Stats.1959, c. 3, p. 1717, § 24601. Amended by Stats.
1965, c. 1313, p. 3200, § 4.)*

Cross References

Special construction and maintenance equipment, applicability
    of this section, see Vehicle Code § 25801.
Test and approval of lighting equipment, see Vehicle Code
    § 26100 et seq.
Vehicles incidentally operated over highway, applicability of this
    section, see Vehicle Code § 25802.

§ 24602. Fog taillamps

(a) A vehicle may be equipped with not more than two
red fog taillamps mounted on the rear which may be
lighted, in addition to the required taillamps, only when
atmospheric conditions, such as fog, rain, snow, smoke, or
dust, reduce the daytime or nighttime visibility of other
vehicles to less than 500 feet.

(b) The lamps authorized under subdivision (a) shall
be installed as follows:

(1) When two lamps are installed, one shall be mounted at the left side and one at the right side at the same
level and as close as practical to the sides. When one
lamp is installed, it shall be mounted as close as practical
to the left side or on the center of the vehicle.

(2) The lamps shall be mounted not lower than 12
inches nor higher than 60 inches.

(3) The edge of the lens of the lamp shall be no closer
than four inches from the edge of the lens of any
stoplamp.

(4) The lamps shall be wired so they can be turned on
only when the headlamps are on and shall have a switch
that allows them to be turned off when the headlamps are
on.

(5) A nonflashing amber pilot light that is lighted when
the lamps are turned on shall be mounted in a location
readily visible to the driver. *(Added by Stats.1977, c. 800,
p. 2451, § 2, eff. Sept. 14, 1977. Amended by Stats.1980, c.
350, p. 695, § 1; Stats.2004, c. 615 (S.B.1233), § 30;
Stats.2005, c. 270 (S.B.731), § 11.)*

§ 24603. Stoplamps

Every motor vehicle that is not in combination with any
other vehicle and every vehicle at the end of a combina-

tion of vehicles shall at all times be equipped with
stoplamps mounted on the rear as follows:

(a) Every such vehicle shall be equipped with one or
more stoplamps.

(b) Every such vehicle, other than a motorcycle, manufactured and first registered on or after January 1, 1958,
shall be equipped with two stoplamps, except that trailers
and semitrailers manufactured after July 23, 1973, which
are less than 30 inches wide, may be equipped with one
stoplamp which shall be mounted at or near the vertical
centerline of the trailer. If such vehicle is equipped with
two stoplamps, they shall be mounted as specified in
subdivision (d).

(c) Except as provided in subdivision (h), stoplamps on
vehicles manufactured on or after January 1, 1969, shall
be mounted not lower than 15 inches nor higher than 72
inches, except that a tow truck or a repossessor's tow
vehicle, in addition to being equipped with the required
stoplamps, may also be equipped with two stoplamps
which may be mounted not lower than 15 inches nor
higher than the maximum allowable vehicle height and as
far forward as the rearmost portion of the driver's seat in
the rearmost position.

(d) Where two stoplamps are required, at least one
shall be mounted at the left and one at the right side,
respectively, at the same level.

(e) Stoplamps on vehicles manufactured on or after
January 1, 1979, shall emit a red light. Stoplamps on
vehicles manufactured before January 1, 1979, shall emit
a red or yellow light. All stoplamps shall be plainly
visible and understandable from a distance of 300 feet to
the rear both during normal sunlight and at nighttime,
except that stoplamps on a vehicle of a size required to be
equipped with clearance lamps shall be visible from a
distance of 500 feet during those times.

(f) Stoplamps shall be activated upon application of
the service (foot) brake and the hand control head for air,
vacuum, or electric brakes. In addition, all stoplamps
may be activated by a mechanical device designed to
function only upon sudden release of the accelerator
while the vehicle is in motion. Stoplamps on vehicles
equipped with a manual transmission may be manually
activated by a mechanical device when the vehicle is
downshifted if the device is automatically rendered inoperative while the vehicle is accelerating.

(g) Any vehicle may be equipped with supplemental
stoplamps mounted to the rear of the rearmost portion of
the driver's seat in its rearmost position in addition to the
lamps required to be mounted on the rear of the vehicle.
Supplemental stoplamps installed after January 1, 1979,
shall be red in color and mounted not lower than 15
inches above the roadway. The supplemental stoplamp
on that side of a vehicle toward which a turn will be made
may flash as part of the supplemental turn signal lamp.

A supplemental stoplamp may be mounted inside the
rear window of a vehicle, if it is mounted at the centerline
of the vehicle and is constructed and mounted so as to

prevent any light, other than a monitorial indicator emitted from the device, either direct or reflected, from being visible to the driver.

(h) Any supplemental stoplamp installed after January 1, 1987, shall comply with Federal Motor Vehicle Safety Standard No. 108 (49 C.F.R. 571.108). Any vehicle equipped with a stoplamp that complies with the federal motor vehicle safety standards applicable to that make and model vehicle shall conform to that applicable safety standard unless modified to comply with the federal motor vehicle safety standard designated in this subdivision. *(Added by Stats.1968, c. 980, p. 1868, § 7. Amended by Stats.1969, c. 341, p. 715, § 3; Stats.1973, c. 774, p. 1388, § 3, eff. Sept. 25, 1973; Stats.1974, c. 635, p. 1488, § 3; Stats.1976, c. 154, p. 249, § 3; Stats.1977, c. 287, p. 1183, § 2; Stats.1978, c. 252, p. 533, § 3, eff. June 16, 1978; Stats.1979, c. 723, p. 2218, § 13; Stats.1981, c. 738, p. 2897, § 1; Stats.1984, c. 64, § 1; Stats.1986, c. 1184, § 1; Stats.1988, c. 924, § 12; Stats.2009, c. 307 (S.B.821), § 108.)*

Cross References

Deceleration warning lights, see Vehicle Code § 25251.5.
Motorcycle defined, see Vehicle Code § 400.
Semitrailer defined, see Vehicle Code § 550.
Special construction and maintenance equipment, applicability of this section, see Vehicle Code § 25801.
Taillamps, see Vehicle Code § 24600 et seq.
Trailer defined, see Vehicle Code § 630.
Vehicles incidentally operated over highway, applicability of this section, see Vehicle Code § 25802.

§ 24604. Lamp or flag on projections

Whenever the load upon any vehicle extends, or whenever any integral part of any vehicle projects, to the rear four feet or more beyond the rear of the vehicle, as measured from the taillamps, there shall be displayed at the extreme end of the load or projecting part of the vehicle during darkness, in addition to the required taillamp, two red lights with a bulb rated not in excess of six candlepower plainly visible from a distance of at least 500 feet to the sides and rear. At any other time there shall be displayed at the extreme end of the load or projecting part of the vehicle a solid red or fluorescent orange flag or cloth not less than 12 inches square. *(Stats.1959, c. 3, p. 1718, § 24604. Amended by Stats. 1959, c. 1996, p. 4633, § 31; Stats.1965, c. 1313, p. 3200, § 6; Stats.1998, c. 828 (S.B.1637), § 18; Stats.2000, c. 1035 (S.B.1403), § 28.)*

Cross References

Color of lights, see Vehicle Code § 25950.
Darkness defined, see Vehicle Code § 280.
Flashing and colored lights, see Vehicle Code § 25250 et seq.
Projecting load on left side of vehicle, see Vehicle Code § 25103.
Regulations governing size, weight and load, see Vehicle Code § 35000 et seq.
Special construction and maintenance equipment, applicability of this section, see Vehicle Code § 25801.

Vehicles incidentally operated over highway, applicability of this section, see Vehicle Code § 25802.

§ 24605. Tow trucks, automobile dismantler's tow vehicle and towed vehicle

(a) A tow truck or an automobile dismantler's tow vehicle used to tow a vehicle shall be equipped with and carry a taillamp, a stoplamp, and turn signal lamps for use on the rear of a towed vehicle.

(b) Whenever a tow truck or an automobile dismantler's tow vehicle is towing a vehicle and a stoplamp and turn signal lamps cannot be lighted and displayed on the rear of the towed vehicle, the operator of the tow truck or the automobile dismantler's tow vehicle shall display to the rear a stoplamp and turn signal lamps mounted on the towed vehicle, except as provided in subdivision (c). During darkness, if a taillamp on the towed vehicle cannot be lighted, the operator of the tow truck or the automobile dismantler's tow vehicle shall display to the rear a taillamp mounted on the towed vehicle. No other lighting equipment need be displayed on the towed vehicle.

(c) Whenever any motor vehicle is towing another motor vehicle, stoplamps and turn signal lamps are not required on the towed motor vehicle, but only if a stoplamp and a turn signal lamp on each side of the rear of the towing vehicle is plainly visible to the rear of the towed vehicle. This subdivision does not apply to driveaway-towaway operations. *(Stats.1959, c. 3, p. 1718, § 24605. Amended by Stats.1961, c. 1933, p. 4083, § 1; Stats.1965, c. 34, p. 913, § 1; Stats.1977, c. 287, p. 1184, § 3; Stats.1985, c. 710, § 3; Stats.1988, c. 924, § 13; Stats.2009, c. 322 (A.B.515), § 12.)*

Cross References

Driveaway-towaway operation defined, see Vehicle Code § 303.
Parking of utility vehicles, see Vehicle Code § 22512.
Rules of the road, exemption of authorized emergency vehicles, see Vehicle Code § 21055.
Test and approval of lighting equipment, see Vehicle Code § 26100 et seq.
Tow truck defined, see Vehicle Code § 615.
Towing and loading equipment, see Vehicle Code § 29000 et seq.
Vehicles operated by department of transportation, inapplicability of this section, see Vehicle Code § 23273.

§ 24606. Backup lamps

(a) Every motor vehicle, other than a motorcycle, of a type subject to registration and manufactured on and after January 1, 1969, shall be equipped with one or more backup lamps either separately or in combination with another lamp. Any vehicle may be equipped with backup lamps.

(b) Backup lamps shall be so directed as to project a white light illuminating the highway to the rear of the vehicle for a distance not to exceed 75 feet. A backup lamp may project incidental red, amber, or white light through reflectors or lenses that are adjacent or close to, or a part of, the lamp assembly.

(c) Backup lamps shall not be lighted except when the vehicle is about to be or is backing or except in conjunction with a lighting system which activates the lights for a temporary period after the ignition system is turned off.

(d) Any motor vehicle may be equipped with a lamp emitting white light on each side near or on the rear of the vehicle which is designed to provide supplemental illumination in an area to the side and rear not lighted by the backup lamps. These lamps shall be lighted only with the backup lamps. *(Stats.1959, c. 3, p. 1718, § 24606. Amended by Stats.1961, c. 159, p. 1164, § 2; Stats.1965, c. 315, p. 1414, § 1; Stats.1967, c. 544, p. 1893, § 3; Stats.1968, c. 980, p. 1869, § 8; Stats.1981, c. 813, p. 3158, § 17.)*

Cross References

Special construction and maintenance equipment, applicability of this section, see Vehicle Code § 25801.
Vehicles incidentally operated over highway, applicability of this section, see Vehicle Code § 25802.

§ 24607. Reflectors

Every vehicle subject to registration under this code shall at all times be equipped with red reflectors mounted on the rear as follows:

(a) Every vehicle shall be equipped with at least one reflector so maintained as to be plainly visible at night from all distances within 350 to 100 feet from the vehicle when directly in front of the lawful upper headlamp beams.

(b) Every vehicle, other than a motorcycle or a low-speed vehicle, manufactured and first registered on or after January 1, 1965, shall be equipped with at least two reflectors meeting the visibility requirements of subdivision (a), except that trailers and semitrailers manufactured after July 23, 1973, that are less than 30 inches wide, may be equipped with one reflector which shall be mounted at or near the vertical centerline of the trailer. If the vehicle is equipped with two reflectors, they shall be mounted as specified in subdivision (d).

(c) Every motortruck having an unladen weight of more than 5,000 pounds, every trailer coach, every camp trailer, every vehicle, or vehicle at the end of a combination of vehicles, subject to subdivision (a) of Section 22406, and every vehicle 80 or more inches in width manufactured on or after January 1, 1969, shall be equipped with at least two reflectors maintained so as to be plainly visible at night from all distances within 600 feet to 100 feet from the vehicle when directly in front of lawful upper headlamp beams.

(d) When more than one reflector is required, at least one shall be mounted at the left side and one at the right side, respectively, at the same level. Required reflectors shall be mounted not lower than 15 inches nor higher than 60 inches, except that a tow truck, in addition to being equipped with the required reflectors, may also be equipped with two reflectors which may be mounted not

lower than 15 inches nor higher than the maximum allowable vehicle height and as far forward as the rearmost portion of the driver's seat in the rearmost position. Additional reflectors of a type meeting requirements established by the department may be mounted at any height.

(e) Reflectors on truck tractors may be mounted on the rear of the cab. Any reflector installed on a vehicle as part of its original equipment prior to January 1, 1941, need not meet the requirements of the department provided it meets the visibility requirements of subdivision (a).

(f) Area reflectorizing material may be used in lieu of the reflectors required or permitted in subdivisions (a), (b), (c), (d), and (e), provided each installation is of sufficient size to meet the photometric requirement for those reflectors. *(Added by Stats.1968, c. 980, p. 1869, § 10. Amended by Stats.1971, c. 1536, p. 3043, § 4, operative May 3, 1972; Stats.1974, c. 635, p. 1489, § 4; Stats.1975, c. 854, p. 1919, § 1; Stats.1976, c. 154, p. 250, § 4; Stats.1979, c. 723, p. 2219, § 14; Stats.1990, c. 216 (S.B.2510), § 120; Stats.1995, c. 766 (S.B.726), § 36; Stats.1999, c. 140 (S.B.186), § 7.)*

Cross References

Bicycle reflectors, see Vehicle Code § 21201.
Definitions,
    Camp trailer, see Vehicle Code § 242.
    Motor truck, see Vehicle Code § 410.
    Motorcycle, see Vehicle Code § 400.
    Semitrailer, see Vehicle Code § 550.
    Trailer, see Vehicle Code § 630.
    Trailer coach, see Vehicle Code § 635.
    Truck tractor, see Vehicle Code § 655.
Mounting height of lamps and reflectors, see Vehicle Code § 24254.
Registration in general, see Vehicle Code § 4000 et seq.
Special construction and maintenance equipment, applicability of this section, see Vehicle Code § 25801.
Test and approval of lighting equipment and signal devices, see Vehicle Code § 26100 et seq.
Vehicles incidentally operated over highway, applicability of this section, see Vehicle Code § 25802.

§ 24608. Reflectors on front and sides

(a) Motortrucks, trailers, semitrailers, and buses 80 or more inches in width manufactured on or after January 1, 1968, shall be equipped with an amber reflector on each side at the front and a red reflector on each side at the rear. Any vehicle may be so equipped.

(b) Motortrucks, trailers, semitrailers, housecars, and buses 80 or more inches in width and 30 or more feet in length manufactured on or after January 1, 1968, shall be equipped with an amber reflector mounted on each side at the approximate midpoint of the vehicle. Any such vehicle manufactured prior to January 1, 1968, may be so equipped.

(c) Required reflectors on the sides of vehicles shall be mounted not lower than 15 inches nor higher than 60 inches. Additional reflectors of a type meeting requirements established by the department may be mounted at any height.

(d) Reflectors required or permitted in subdivisions (a) and (b) shall be so maintained as to be plainly visible at night from all distances within 600 feet to 100 feet from the vehicle when directly in front of lawful upper headlamp beams.

(e) Area reflectorizing material may be used in lieu of the reflectors required or permitted in subdivisions (a) and (b), provided each installation is of sufficient size to meet the photometric requirement for such reflectors. *(Added by Stats.1968, c. 980, p. 1870, § 12. Amended by Stats.1970, c. 422, p. 834, § 2; Stats.1975, c. 854, p. 1919, § 2; Stats.1979, c. 723, p. 2220, § 15.)*

Cross References
Definitions,
    Bus, see Vehicle Code § 233.
    House car, see Vehicle Code § 362.
    Motor truck, see Vehicle Code § 410.
    Semitrailer, see Vehicle Code § 550.
    Trailer coach, see Vehicle Code § 635.
    Vehicle, see Vehicle Code § 670.
Special construction and maintenance equipment, applicability of this section, see Vehicle Code § 25801.
Vehicles incidentally operated over highway, applicability of this section, see Vehicle Code § 25802.

§ 24609. Vehicle reflectors

(a) A vehicle may be equipped with white or amber reflectors that are mounted on the front of the vehicle at a height of 15 inches or more, but not more than 60 inches from the ground.

(b) A schoolbus may be equipped with a set of two devices, with each device in the set consisting of an amber reflector integrated into the lens of an amber light that is otherwise permitted under this code, if the set is mounted with one device on the left side and one on the right side of the vehicle, and with each device at the same level. *(Added by Stats.1969, c. 341, p. 716, § 4. Amended by Stats.2003, c. 594 (S.B.315), § 44.)*

Cross References
Special construction and maintenance equipment, applicability of this section, see Vehicle Code § 25801.
Vehicles incidentally operated over highway, applicability of this section, see Vehicle Code § 25802.

§ 24610. Multiple-unit truck reflector

A reflector placed on vehicles under Section 24609 which is of the button or other multiple-unit type shall contain not less than seven units with a total of not less than three square inches of reflecting surface. The red reflectors required may be separate units or a part of the red taillamps, but in either event the reflector and taillamps shall comply with all of the requirements of Sections 24600, 24602, and 24609, and any reflector constituting an integral part of a taillamp shall comply with all photometric requirements applicable to a separate reflector. *(Stats.1959, c. 3, p. 1719, § 24610.*

Amended by Stats.1959, c. 1996, p. 4633, § 32; Stats.1965, c. 1313, p. 3201, § 8.)

Cross References
Special construction and maintenance equipment, applicability of this section, see Vehicle Code § 25801.
Test and approval of lighting equipment, see Vehicle Code § 26100 et seq.
Vehicle defined, see Vehicle Code § 670.
Vehicles incidentally operated over highway, applicability of this section, see Vehicle Code § 25802.

§ 24611. Reflective sheeting or reflectors on sides and rear

Trailers that are equipped with red and white reflective sheeting or reflectors on both the sides and rear and displayed in accordance with federal Motor Vehicle Safety Standard regulations (49 C.F.R. 571.108) for trailers with a width of 80 inches or more and having a gross vehicle weight rating of over 10,000 pounds need not be equipped with the reflectors required by Section 24607 or 24608. *(Added by Stats.1995, c. 766 (S.B.726), § 37.)*

§ 24612. Trailers, semitrailers, and motor trucks; conspicuity system

(a) All trailers and semitrailers having an overall width of 80 inches or more and a gross vehicle weight rating of more than 10,000 pounds, and manufactured on or after December 1, 1993, except those designed exclusively for living or office use, and all truck tractors manufactured on or after July 1, 1997, shall be equipped with the conspicuity system specified in federal Motor Vehicle Safety Standard No. 108 (49 C.F.R. 571.108). The conspicuity system shall consist of either retroreflective sheeting or reflex reflectors, or a combination of retroreflective sheeting and reflex reflectors, as specified in the federal standard applicable on the date of manufacture of the vehicle.

(b) Any trailer, semitrailer, or motor truck having an overall width of 80 inches or more and manufactured prior to December 1, 1993, and any truck tractor manufactured prior to July 1, 1997, may be equipped with the conspicuity system described in subdivision (a). *(Added by Stats.2001, c. 825 (S.B.290), § 17.)*

§ 24615. Slow moving vehicle emblem

It is unlawful to operate upon a public highway any vehicle or combination of vehicles, which is designed to be and is operated at a speed of 25 miles per hour or less, unless the rearmost vehicle displays a "slow-moving vehicle emblem," except upon vehicles used by a utility, whether publicly or privately owned, for the construction, maintenance, or repair of its own facilities or upon vehicles used by highway authorities or bridge or highway districts in highway maintenance, inspection, survey, or construction work, while such vehicle is engaged in work at the jobsite upon a highway. Any other vehicle or combination of vehicles, when operated at a speed of 25 miles per hour or less, may display such emblem. The emblem shall be mounted on the rear of the vehicle, base down, and at a height of not less than three nor more than five feet from ground to base. Such emblem shall consist of a truncated equilateral triangle having a minimum height of 14 inches with a red reflective border not less than 1¾ inches in width and a fluorescent orange center.

This emblem shall not be displayed except as permitted or required by this section. *(Added by Stats.1969, c. 949, p. 1895, § 1. Amended by Stats.1971, c. 287, p. 593, § 1, operative May 3, 1972.)*

Cross References

Amber turn signals, use as warning lights, see Vehicle Code § 25251.1.

Implements of husbandry, applicability of this section, see Vehicle Code § 36500.

§ 24616. Rear-facing auxiliary lamps

(a) A motor vehicle may be equipped with one or two rear-facing auxiliary lamps. For the purposes of this section, a rear-facing auxiliary lamp is a lamp that is mounted on the vehicle facing rearward. That lamp shall meet the photometric and performance requirements of the Society of Automotive Engineers Standard J1424 for cargo lamps.

(b) A rear-facing auxiliary lamp may project only a white light, with the main cone of light projecting both rearward and downward. The main cone of light shall illuminate the road surface or ground immediately rearward of a line parallel to the rear of the vehicle for a distance not greater than 50 feet. The main cone of light may not project to the front or sides of the vehicle.

(c) A rear-facing auxiliary lamp may be activated only when the vehicle is stopped. A vehicle equipped with a rear-facing auxiliary lamp shall also be equipped with a system that allows activation of the lamp only when the vehicle is in the "park" setting, if the vehicle is equipped with an automatic transmission, or in the "neutral" setting with the parking brake engaged, if the vehicle is equipped with a manual transmission.

(d) A vehicle equipped with a rear-facing auxiliary lamp may have an activation switch accessible to the operator from the rear of the vehicle. *(Added by Stats.2001, c. 739 (A.B.1707), § 20.)*

§ 24617. Yield right–of–way signs on transit buses

(a) A transit bus may be authorized to be equipped with a yield right-of-way sign on the left rear of the bus. The yield right-of-way sign may flash simultaneously with the rear turn signal lamps, but is not required to do so. The sign shall be both of the following:

(1) Designed to warn a person operating a motor vehicle approaching the rear of the bus that the bus is entering traffic.

(2) Illuminated by a red flashing light when the bus is signaling in preparation for entering a traffic lane after having stopped to receive or discharge passengers.

(b) This section does not require a transit agency to install the yield right-of-way sign described in subdivision (a).

(c) This section does not relieve the driver of a transit bus from the duty to drive the bus with due regard for the safety of all persons and property. This section does not exempt the driver of a transit bus from Section 21804.

(d) This section applies only to the Santa Cruz Metropolitan Transit District and the Santa Clara Valley Transportation Authority, if the governing board of the applicable entity approves a resolution, after a public hearing on the issue, requesting that this section be made applicable to it.

(e) A participating transit agency shall undertake a public education program to encourage motorists to yield to a transit bus when the sign specified in subdivision (a) is activated. *(Added by Stats.2007, c. 451 (A.B.1492), § 1. Amended by Stats.2008, c. 179 (S.B.1498), § 222.)*

ARTICLE 4. PARKING LAMPS

Section
24800. Lighted parking lamps.
24801. Parking lamps.
24802. Lamps on parked vehicle.
24803. Repealed.

Cross References

Cotton module movers, operation on state highways, conditions, see Vehicle Code § 35555.

Implements of husbandry, applicability of this Article, see Vehicle Code § 36500.

Special construction and maintenance equipment, applicability of this Article, see Vehicle Code § 25801.

Special mobile equipment, applicability of this Article, see Vehicle Code § 25800.

Vehicles incidentally operated over highway, applicability of this Article, see Vehicle Code § 25802.

§ 24800. Lighted parking lamps

No vehicle shall be driven at any time with the parking lamps lighted except when the lamps are being used as turn signal lamps or when the headlamps are also lighted. *(Stats.1959, c. 3, p. 1719, § 24800. Amended by Stats. 1961, c. 58, p. 1011, § 45, eff. March 31, 1961.)*

§ 24801. Parking lamps

Parking lamps are those lamps permitted by Section 25106, or any lamps mounted on the front of a vehicle, designed to be displayed primarily when the vehicle is parked. *(Stats.1959, c. 3, p. 1719, § 24801.)*

§ 24802. Lamps on parked vehicle

No lights need be displayed upon a vehicle which is:

(a) Parked off the roadway and not in a hazardous position on the highway; or

(b) Parked with a wheel within 18 inches of a curb; or

(c) Parked within a business or residence district with a wheel within 18 inches of a curb or edge of the roadway.

(Stats.1959, c. 3, p. 1719, § 24802. Amended by Stats. 1961, c. 639, p. 1847, § 1; Stats.1977, c. 620, p. 2098, § 2.)

Cross References

Business district defined, see Vehicle Code § 235.
Dimmed lights on parked vehicles, see Vehicle Code § 24401.
Prohibition of stopping, standing or parking, see Vehicle Code § 22500 et seq.
Public grounds, driving upon restricted, see Vehicle Code § 21113.
Residence district defined, see Vehicle Code § 515.

§ 24803. Repealed by Stats.1961, c. 639, p. 1847, § 2

ARTICLE 5. SIGNAL LAMPS AND DEVICES

Section
24950. Turn signal system required.
24951. Turn signal system.
24952. Requirement of signals.
24953. Lamps of turn signals.
24954. Repealed.

Cross References

Cotton module movers, operation on state highways, conditions, see Vehicle Code § 35555.
Implements of husbandry, applicability of this Article, see Vehicle Code § 36500.
Special construction and maintenance equipment, applicability of this Article, see Vehicle Code § 25801.
Special mobile equipment, applicability of this Article, see Vehicle Code § 25800.
Vehicles incidentally operated over highway, applicability of this Article, see Vehicle Code § 25802.

§ 24950. Turn signal system required

Whenever any motor vehicle is towing a trailer coach or a camp trailer the combination of vehicles shall be equipped with a lamp-type turn signal system. *(Stats. 1959, c. 3, p. 1720, § 24950. Amended by Stats.1965, c. 1012, p. 2643, § 2; Stats.1971, c. 1536, p. 3044, § 5, operative May 3, 1972.)*

Cross References

Definitions,
  Camp trailer, see Vehicle Code § 242.
  Semitrailer, see Vehicle Code § 550.
  Trailer, see Vehicle Code § 630.
  Trailer coach, see Vehicle Code § 635.
Mounting regulations, see Vehicle Code § 24012.

§ 24951. Turn signal system

(a) Any vehicle may be equipped with a lamp-type turn signal system capable of clearly indicating any intention to turn either to the right or to the left.

(b) The following vehicles shall be equipped with a lamp-type turn signal system meeting the requirements of this chapter.

(1) Motortrucks, truck tractors, buses and passenger vehicles, other than motorcycles, manufactured and first registered on or after January 1, 1958.

(2) Trailers and semitrailers manufactured and first registered between December 31, 1957, and January 1, 1969, having a gross weight of 6,000 pounds or more.

(3) Trailers and semitrailers 80 or more inches in width manufactured on or after January 1, 1969.

(4) Motorcycles manufactured and first registered on or after January 1, 1973, except motor-driven cycles whose speed attainable in one mile is 30 miles per hour or less.

The requirements of this subdivision shall not apply to special mobile equipment, or auxiliary dollies.

(c) Turn signal lamps on vehicles manufactured on or after January 1, 1969, shall be mounted not lower than 15 inches. *(Stats.1959, c. 3, p. 1720, § 24951. Amended by Stats.1959, c. 1996, p. 4633, § 32.5; Stats.1961, c. 118, p. 1128, § 2; Stats.1963, c. 292, p. 1059, § 4; Stats.1965, c. 1012, p. 2643, § 3; Stats.1967, c. 859, p. 2300, § 2; Stats.1968, c. 980, p. 1870, § 14; Stats.1973, c. 135, p. 370, § 1; Stats.1975, c. 475, p. 984, § 1.)*

Cross References

Definitions,
  Auxiliary dolly, see Vehicle Code § 225.
  Bus, see Vehicle Code § 233.
  Motor truck, see Vehicle Code § 410.
  Motor-driven cycle, see Vehicle Code § 405.
  Motorcycle, see Vehicle Code § 400.
  Passenger vehicle, see Vehicle Code § 465.
  Semitrailer, see Vehicle Code § 550.
  Special mobile equipment, see Vehicle Code § 575.
  Trailer, see Vehicle Code § 630.
  Truck tractor, see Vehicle Code § 655.
Rear lighting equipment, see Vehicle Code § 24600 et seq.

§ 24952. Requirement of signals

A lamp-type turn signal shall be plainly visible and understandable in normal sunlight and at nighttime from a distance of at least 300 feet to the front and rear of the vehicle, except that turn signal lamps on vehicles of a size required to be equipped with clearance lamps shall be visible from a distance of 500 feet during such times. *(Stats.1959, c. 3, p. 1720, § 24952. Amended by Stats. 1965, c. 1012, p. 2644, § 4.)*

§ 24953. Lamps of turn signals

(a) Any turn signal system used to give a signal of intention to turn right or left shall project a flashing white or amber light visible to the front and a flashing red or amber light visible to the rear.

(b) Side–mounted turn signal lamps projecting a flashing amber light to either side may be used to supplement the front and rear turn signals. Side–mounted turn signal lamps mounted to the rear of the center of the vehicle may project a flashing red light no part of which shall be visible from the front.

(c) In addition to any required turn signal lamps, any vehicle may be equipped with supplemental rear turn signal lamps mounted to the rear of the rearmost portion of the driver's seat in its rearmost position.

(d) In addition to any required or authorized turn signal lamps, any vehicle may be equipped with supplemental rear turn signal lamps that are mounted on, or are an integral portion of, the outside rearview mirrors, so long as the lamps flash simultaneously with the rear turn signal lamps, the light emitted from the lamps is projected only to the rear of the vehicle and is not visible to the driver under normal operating conditions, except for a visual indicator designed to allow monitoring of lamp operation, and the lamps do not project a glaring light. *(Stats.1959, c. 3, p. 1720, § 24953. Amended by Stats. 1963, c. 223, p. 964, § 2; Stats.1972, c. 203, p. 425, § 1; Stats.1979, c. 723, p. 2220, § 16; Stats.1994, c. 207 (A.B.2827), § 2, eff. July 18, 1994; Stats.1997, c. 945 (A.B.1561), § 22.)*

§ 24954. Repealed by Stats.1965, c. 1012, p. 2644, § 5

ARTICLE 6.   SIDE AND FENDER LIGHTING EQUIPMENT

Section
25100.   Clearance and side-marker lamps.
25100.1.   Clearance lamps; ambulances.
25101.   Repealed.
25102.   Lamps on sides of vehicles.
25102.5.   Schoolbuses; lamps on sides; regulations.
25103.   Projecting load.
25104.   Wide vehicles.
25105.   Courtesy lamps; door-mounted lamps/reflectors; exterior lamps.
25106.   Cowl or fender lamps; side-marker or combination clearance and side-marker lamps.
25107.   Cornering lamps on fenders.
25108.   Pilot indicators; data monitors.
25109.   Running lamps.
25110.   Utility flood and loading lamps.

Cross References

Cotton module movers, operation on state highways, conditions, see Vehicle Code § 35555.
Implements of husbandry, applicability of this Article, see Vehicle Code § 36500.
Special construction and maintenance equipment, applicability of this Article, see Vehicle Code § 25801.
Special mobile equipment, applicability of this Article, see Vehicle Code § 25800.
Vehicles incidentally operated over highway, applicability of this Article, see Vehicle Code § 25802.

§ 25100.   Clearance and side-marker lamps

(a) Except as provided in subdivisions (b) and (d), every vehicle 80 inches or more in overall width shall be equipped during darkness as follows:

(1) At least one amber clearance lamp on each side mounted on a forward-facing portion of the vehicle and visible from the front and at least one red clearance lamp on each side mounted on a rearward-facing portion of the vehicle and visible from the rear.

(2) At least one amber side-marker lamp on each side near the front and at least one red side-marker lamp on each side near the rear.

(3) At least one amber side-marker lamp on each side at or near the center on trailers and semitrailers 30 feet or more in length and which are manufactured and first registered after January 1, 1962. Any such vehicle manufactured and first registered prior to January 1, 1962, may be so equipped.

(4) At least one amber side-marker lamp mounted at approximate midpoint of housecars, motortrucks, and buses 30 or more feet in length and manufactured on or after January 1, 1969. Any such vehicle manufactured prior to January 1, 1969, may be so equipped.

(5) Combination clearance and side-marker lamps mounted as side-marker lamps and meeting the visibility requirements for both types of lamps may be used in lieu of required individual clearance or side-marker lamps.

(b) The following vehicles when 80 inches or more in overall width and not equipped as provided in subdivision (a) shall be equipped during darkness as follows:

(1) Truck tractors shall be equipped with at least one amber clearance lamp on each side on the front of the cab or sleeper and may be equipped with amber side-marker lamps on each side.

(2) Truck tractors manufactured on or after January 1, 1969, shall be equipped with one amber side-marker lamp on each side near the front.

(3) Pole or pipe dollies, or logging dollies, shall be equipped with at least one combination clearance and side-marker lamp on each side showing red to the front, side, and rear.

(4) Vehicles, except truck tractors, which are 80 inches or more in width over a distance not exceeding three feet from front to rear shall be equipped with at least one amber combination clearance lamp and side-marker lamp on each side visible from the front, side, and rear if the projection is near the front of the vehicle and at least one red lamp if the projection is near the rear of the vehicle.

(5) Towing motor vehicles engaged in driveaway-towaway operations shall be equipped with at least one amber clearance lamp at each side on the front and at least one amber side-marker lamp on each side near the front.

(6) Towed motor vehicles engaged in driveaway-towaway operations shall be equipped with at least one amber side-marker lamp on each side of intermediate vehicles, and the rearmost vehicle shall be equipped with at least one red side-marker lamp on each side and at least one red clearance lamp on each side on the rear.

(7) Trailers and semitrailers designed for transporting single boats in a cradle-type mounting and for launching the boat from the rear of the trailer need not be equipped with front and rear clearance lamps provided amber clearance lamps showing to the front and red clearance lamps showing to the rear are located on each side at or

near the midpoint between the front and rear of the trailer to indicate the extreme width of the trailer.

(c) Loads extending beyond the side of a vehicle where the overall width of the vehicle and load is 80 inches or more shall be equipped with an amber combination clearance and side-marker lamp on the side at the front and a red combination clearance and side-marker lamp on the side at the rear. In lieu of the foregoing requirement, projecting loads not exceeding three feet from front to rear at the extreme width shall be equipped with at least one amber combination clearance and side-marker lamp on the side visible from the front, side, and rear if the projection is near the front of the vehicle and at least one red lamp if the projection is near the rear of the vehicle.

(d) Clearance and side-marker lamps are not required on auxiliary dollies or on passenger vehicles other than a housecar.

(e) Clearance lamps shall be visible from all distances between 500 feet and 50 feet to the front or rear of the vehicle, and side-marker lamps shall be visible from all distances between 500 feet and 50 feet to the side of the vehicle.

(f) Clearance lamps shall, so far as is practicable, be mounted to indicate the extreme width of the vehicle. Side-marker lamps shall be mounted not lower than 15 inches on vehicles manufactured on and after January 1, 1968. Combination clearance and side-marker lamps required on loads shall be mounted so the lenses project to the outer extremity of the vehicle or load. *(Added by Stats.1961, c. 1989, p. 4186, § 4. Amended by Stats.1963, c. 78, p. 704, § 1; Stats.1963, c. 292, p. 1061, § 5; Stats.1965, c. 1313, p. 3201, § 9; Stats.1968, c. 980, p. 1870, § 15; Stats.1970, c. 422, p. 835, § 3; Stats.1975, c. 854, p. 1920, § 3; Stats.1976, c. 900, p. 2070, § 1; Stats.1981, c. 714, p. 2799, § 446.)*

Cross References

Buses, crime alarm lights, see Vehicle Code § 25275.5.
Color of lights, see Vehicle Code § 25950.
Definitions,
 Auxiliary dolly, see Vehicle Code § 225.
 Bus, see Vehicle Code § 233.
 House car, see Vehicle Code § 362.
 Logging dolly, see Vehicle Code § 378.
 Pole or pipe dolly, see Vehicle Code § 475.
 Semitrailer, see Vehicle Code § 550.
 Trailer, see Vehicle Code § 630.
 Trailer coach, see Vehicle Code § 635.
 Truck tractor, see Vehicle Code § 655.
Flashing and colored lights, see Vehicle Code § 25250 et seq.
Implements of husbandry operated at night, applicability of section, see Vehicle Code § 36505.
Mounting height of lamps and reflectors, see Vehicle Code § 24254.
Passenger common carriers, see Vehicle Code § 25350.
Special construction and maintenance equipment, applicability of this Article, see Vehicle Code § 25801.
Test and approval of lamps, lamp equipment and signal devices, see Vehicle Code § 26100 et seq.

Vehicles incidentally operated over highway, applicability of this section, see Vehicle Code § 25802.

§ 25100.1. Clearance lamps; ambulances

Notwithstanding any other provisions of this code, an ambulance may be equipped with clearance and side-marker lamps. *(Added by Stats.1975, c. 616, p. 1344, § 1.)*

§ 25101. Repealed by Stats.1974, c. 635, p. 1490, § 5

§ 25102. Lamps on sides of vehicles

In addition to the lamps otherwise permitted by this chapter, any motor vehicle may be equipped with lamps on the sides thereof, visible from the side of the vehicle but not from the front or rear thereof, which lamps, together with mountings or receptacles, shall be set into depressions or recesses in the body of the vehicle and shall not protrude beyond or outside the body of the vehicle. The light source in each of the lamps shall not exceed two candlepower and shall emit diffused light of any color, except that the color red is permitted only on authorized emergency vehicles. *(Stats.1959, c. 3, p. 1721, § 25102.)*

Cross References

Authorized emergency vehicle defined, see Vehicle Code § 165.

§ 25102.5. Schoolbuses; lamps on sides; regulations

(a) A schoolbus may be equipped with lamps mounted so as to be visible from the sides of the bus which may be lighted, in addition to other required lights, when, and only when, atmospheric conditions such as fog, rain, snow, smoke, or dust, reduce the visibility of other vehicles to less than 500 feet.

(b) The type and mounting requirements of such lamps shall be established by regulations adopted by the department. The regulations shall be adopted by January 1, 1980. *(Added by Stats.1978, c. 543, p. 1705, § 1. Amended by Stats.1979, c. 723, p. 2220, § 17.)*

Cross References

Schoolbus defined, see Vehicle Code § 545.

§ 25103. Projecting load

Whenever the load upon any vehicle extends from the left side of the vehicle one foot or more, there shall be displayed at the extreme left side of the load during darkness:

(a) An amber lamp plainly visible for 300 feet to the front and rear of the vehicle.

(b) An amber lamp at the front visible for 300 feet to the front and a red lamp at the rear plainly visible for 300 feet to the rear of the vehicle if the projecting load exceeds 120 inches in length.

The lamp shall not contain a bulb rated in excess of six candlepower. *(Stats.1959, c. 3, p. 1721, § 25103. Amended by Stats.1981, c. 774, p. 3022, § 1.)*

Color of lights upon vehicles, see Vehicle Code § 25950.
Flashing and colored lights, see Vehicle Code § 25250 et seq.
Red lights, requirements, see Vehicle Code § 24604.
Size, weight and load, see Vehicle Code § 35000 et seq.

§ 25104. Wide vehicles

Any vehicle or equipment that requires a permit issued pursuant to Article 6 (commencing with Section 35780) of Chapter 5 of Division 15 because it is wider than permitted under Chapter 2 (commencing with Section 35100) of Division 15 shall display a solid red or fluorescent orange flag or cloth not less than 12 inches square at the extreme left front and left rear of the vehicle or equipment, if the vehicle or equipment is being operated other than during darkness. *(Stats.1959, c. 3, p. 1721, § 25104. Amended by Stats.1994, c. 675 (S.B.1741), § 8; Stats.1998, c. 828 (S.B.1637), § 19.)*

Red flag on projecting load, see Vehicle Code § 25803.
Size, weight, and load of vehicles, see Vehicle Code § 35000 et seq.
Special mobile equipment defined, see Vehicle Code § 575.

§ 25105. Courtesy lamps; door-mounted lamps/reflectors; exterior lamps

(a) Any motor vehicle may be equipped with running board or door-mounted courtesy lamps. The bulbs in the lamps shall not exceed six standard candlepower and shall emit either a green or white light without glare. The beams of the lamps shall not be visible to the front or rear of the vehicle.

(b) Any motor vehicle may be equipped with inside door-mounted red lamps or red reflectorizing devices or material visible to the rear of the vehicle when the doors are open. The bulbs in the lamps shall not exceed six standard candlepower.

(c) Any motor vehicle may be equipped with exterior lamps for the purpose of lighting the entrances and exits of the vehicles, which lamps may be lighted only when the vehicles are not in motion. The lamp source of the exterior lamps shall not exceed 32 standard candlepower, or 30 watts, nor project any glaring light into the eyes of an approaching driver. *(Stats.1959, c. 3, p. 1721, § 25105. Amended by Stats.1965, c. 314, p. 1414, § 1; Stats.1967, c. 443, p. 1654, § 1; Stats.1977, c. 287, p. 1184, § 4; Stats.1995, c. 348 (A.B.1597), § 1.)*

Definitions,
Bus, see Vehicle Code § 233.
Camper, see Vehicle Code § 243.
House car, see Vehicle Code § 362.
Lighting equipment, see Vehicle Code § 24250 et seq.

Reflectorizing material, see Vehicle Code § 25500.

§ 25106. Cowl or fender lamps; side-marker or combination clearance and side-marker lamps

(a) Any motor vehicle may be equipped with lighted white or amber cowl or fender lamps on the front. Any vehicle may be equipped with not more than one amber side lamp on each side near the front, nor more than one red side lamp on each side near the rear. The light source of each such lamp shall not exceed four standard candlepower.

(b) Lamps meeting requirements established by the department for side-marker or combination clearance and side-marker lamps may be installed on the sides of vehicles at any location, but any lamp installed within 24 inches of the rear of the vehicle shall be red, and any lamp installed at any other location shall be amber. *(Added by Stats.1967, c. 728, p. 2103, § 2. Amended by Stats.1970, c. 422, p. 837, § 3.5; Stats.1975, c. 854, p. 1921, § 4; Stats.1978, c. 252, p. 534, § 4, eff. June 16, 1978; Stats.1979, c. 723, p. 2221, § 18.)*

Flashing side lamps authorized, see Vehicle Code § 25251.
Parking lamps, see Vehicle Code § 24801.

§ 25107. Cornering lamps on fenders

Any motor vehicle may be equipped with not more than two cornering lamps designed and of sufficient intensity for the purpose of revealing objects only in the direction of turn while the vehicle is turning or while the turn signal lamps are operating to signal an intention to turn. The lamps shall be designed so that no glaring light is projected into the eyes of an approaching driver. *(Stats.1959, c. 3, p. 1722, § 25107. Amended by Stats. 1961, c. 159, p. 1164, § 3; Stats.1965, c. 1313, p. 3202, § 10.)*

Approval of modifying devices, see Vehicle Code § 26101.

§ 25108. Pilot indicators; data monitors

(a) Any motor vehicle may be equipped with not more than two amber turn-signal pilot indicators mounted on the exterior. The light output from any indicator shall not exceed five candlepower unless a provision is made for operating the indicator at reduced intensity during darkness in which event the light output shall not exceed five candlepower during darkness or 15 candlepower at any other time. The center of the beam shall be projected toward the driver.

(b) Any vehicle may be equipped with pilot indicators visible from the front to monitor the functioning or condition of parts essential to the operation of the vehicle or of equipment attached to the vehicle that is necessary for protection of the cargo or load. The pilot indicators shall be steady-burning, having a projected lighted lens area of not more than three-quarters of a square inch and have a light output of not more than five candlepower. The pilot indicator may be of any color except red.

(c) Other exterior pilot indicators of any color may be used for monitoring exterior lighting devices, provided that the area of each indicator is less than 0.20 square inches, the intensity of each indicator does not exceed 0.10 candlepower, and the color red is not visible to the front.

(d) Any towed vehicle may be equipped with an exterior-mounted indicator lamp used only to indicate the functional status of an antilock braking system providing that either of the following conditions are met:

(1) The indicator lamp complies with the applicable requirements of the federal motor vehicle safety standards.

(2) The indicator lamp is designed and located so that it will be readily visible, with the assistance of a rearview mirror if necessary, to the driver of the towing motor vehicle and the indicator lamp has a light source not exceeding five candlepower. The light shall not show to the sides or rear of the vehicle and the indicator lamp may emit any color except red.

(e)(1) Notwithstanding any other provision of law, any motor vehicle may be equipped with not more than two exterior-lighted data monitors that transmit information to the driver of the vehicle regarding the efficient or safe operation, or both the efficient and safe operation, of the vehicle.

(2) Data monitors shall comply with all of the following conditions:

(A) Be mounted to the vehicle in a manner so that they are readily visible to the driver of the vehicle when the driver is seated in the normal driving position. Data monitors shall not be designed to convey information to any person other than the driver of the vehicle.

(B) Be limited in size to not more than two square inches of lighted area each.

(C) Not emit a light brighter than reasonably necessary to convey the intended information.

(D) Not project a glaring light to the driver or, to other motorists, or to any other person.

(3) Data monitors may incorporate flashing or changing elements only as necessary to convey the intended information. Data monitors shall not resemble any official traffic-control device or required lighting device or be combined with any required lighting device.

(4) Data monitors may display any color, except that the color red shall not be visible to the front of the vehicle. *(Added by Stats.1961, c. 159, p. 1164, § 4. Amended by Stats.1963, c. 223, p. 964, § 3; Stats.1967, c. 440, p. 1653, § 2, eff. June 30, 1967; Stats.1980, c. 349, p. 695, § 1; Stats.1983, c. 142, § 170; Stats.1994, c. 675 (S.B.1741), § 9; Stats.1998, c. 938 (S.B.1754), § 3; Stats. 2001, c. 739 (A.B.1707), § 21.)*

§ 25109. Running lamps

Any motor vehicle may be equipped with two white or amber running lamps mounted on the front, one at each side, which shall not be lighted during darkness except while the motor vehicle is parked. *(Added by Stats.1965, c. 858, p. 2461, § 2.)*

§ 25110. Utility flood and loading lamps

(a) The following vehicles may be equipped with utility flood or loading lamps mounted on the rear, and sides, that project a white light illuminating an area to the side or rear of the vehicle for a distance not to exceed 75 feet at the level of the roadway:

(1) Tow trucks that are used to tow disabled vehicles may display utility floodlights, but only during the period of preparation for towing at the location from which a disabled vehicle is to be towed.

(2) Ambulances used to respond to emergency calls may display utility flood and loading lights, but only at the scene of an emergency or while loading or unloading patients.

(3) Firefighting equipment designed and operated exclusively as such may display utility floodlamps only at the scene of an emergency.

(4) Vehicles used by law enforcement agencies or organizations engaged in the detoxification of alcoholics may display utility flood or loading lights when loading or unloading persons under the influence of intoxicants for transportation to detoxification centers or places of incarceration.

(5) Vehicles used by law enforcement agencies for mobile blood alcohol testing, drug evaluation, or field sobriety testing.

(6) Vehicles used by publicly or privately owned public utilities may display utility flood or loading lights when engaged in emergency roadside repair of electric, gas, telephone, telegraph, water, or sewer facilities.

(b) Lamps permitted under subdivision (a) shall not be lighted during darkness, except while the vehicle is parked, nor project any glaring light into the eyes of an approaching driver. *(Added by Stats.1975, c. 551, p. 1125, § 1. Amended by Stats.1981, c. 518, p. 1878, § 1; Stats.1988, c. 924, § 14; Stats.1996, c. 124 (A.B.3470), § 132.)*

Cross References

Tow truck defined, see Vehicle Code § 615.

ARTICLE 7. FLASHING AND COLORED LIGHTS

Section
25250.   Flashing lights.
25251.   Permitted flashing lights.
25251.1. Implements of husbandry displaying slow moving vehicle emblems.

815

Section

25251.2. Motorcycles; modulation of upper beam of head-lamp.
25251.3. Turn signal warning lights: civil liability.
25251.4. Theft alarm system.
25251.5. Deceleration warning lights.
25252. Warning lights on authorized emergency vehicles.
25252.5. Flashing headlamps on authorized emergency vehicle.
25253. Warning lights on tow trucks used to tow disabled vehicles.
25253.1. Automobile dismantler's tow vehicle; flashing amber warning lamps.
25254. Warning lights on vehicles operated by personnel of marshal's department.
25255. Repealed.
25256. Warning lights on highway maintenance vehicles.
25257. Schoolbus; amber warning light and flashing red light signal systems and stop signal arm as equipment.
25257.2. Schoolbus used for transportation of developmentally disabled persons; use of amber and flashing red light signal systems and stop signal arm restricted.
25257.5. Backing maneuver for schoolbus; flashing turn signal lamps.
25257.7. Schoolbuses; white strobe lights.
25258. Authorized emergency vehicles; additional lights.
25258.1. Repealed.
25259. Additional warning lights on authorized emergency vehicles.
25259.1. Disaster service worker vehicles; training; treatment of lights not in use.
25259.5. Emergency response or disaster service vehicles owned or leased and operated by American National Red Cross.
25260. Warning lights on public utility vehicles and public transit vehicles assisting disabled district buses.
25260.1. Warning lights on vehicles engaged in oil or gas pipeline activities.
25260.3. Warning lights on personnel aerial lift vehicle.
25260.4. Warning lights on hazardous substance spill response vehicles.
25261. Warning lights on county vehicles.
25262. Armored cars.
25263. Warning lights on house towing trucks.
25264. Warning lights on coroner vehicles.
25265. Warning lights on sanitation district repair vehicles.
25266. Warning lights on vehicles engaged in aqueduct, levee, or stream measurement work.
25267. Warning lights on pest abatement vehicles.
25268. Use of flashing amber warning light.
25269. Use of red warning light.
25270. Warning lights on pilot cars and related vehicles.
25270.5. Warning lights on vehicles herding livestock.
25271. Warning lights on pet ambulances.
25271.5. Flashing or revolving amber warning lights on animal control law enforcement vehicle.
25272. Warning lights on rural mail vehicles.
25273. Warning lights on school district vehicles.
25274. Warning lights on cable television company vehicles.
25275. Warning lamp on trucks with long loads.
25275.5. Buses; crime alarm lights.
25276. Warning lights on vehicles transporting individuals who have intellectual or physical disabilities.
25277. Warning lights on vehicles enforcing parking laws.

Section

25278. Warning lights; land surveyor or civil engineer vehicle; civil liability.
25279. Warning lights on private security agency vehicles.
25280. Warning lights on garbage or rubbish vehicles.
25281. Warning lights; water tender vehicle.
25282. Contractors; construction company vehicles; amber warning lights; use or absence as basis for civil actions.

§ 25250. Flashing lights

Flashing lights are prohibited on vehicles except as otherwise permitted. *(Stats.1959, c. 3, p. 1722, § 25250. Amended by Stats.1963, c. 223, p. 964, § 4.)*

§ 25251. Permitted flashing lights

(a) Flashing lights are permitted on vehicles as follows:

(1) To indicate an intention to turn or move to the right or left upon a roadway, turn signal lamps and turn signal exterior pilot indicator lamps and side lamps permitted under Section 25106 may be flashed on the side of a vehicle toward which the turn or movement is to be made.

(2) When disabled or parked off the roadway but within 10 feet of the roadway, or when approaching, stopped at, or departing from, a railroad grade crossing, turn signal lamps may be flashed as warning lights if the front turn signal lamps at each side are being flashed simultaneously and the rear turn signal lamps at each side are being flashed simultaneously.

(3) To warn other motorists of accidents or hazards on a roadway, turn signal lamps may be flashed as warning lights while the vehicle is approaching, overtaking, or passing the accident or hazard on the roadway if the front turn signal lamps at each side are being flashed simultaneously and the rear turn signal lamps at each side are being flashed simultaneously.

(4) For use on authorized emergency vehicles.

(5) To warn other motorists of a funeral procession, turn signal lamps may be flashed as warning lights on all vehicles actually engaged in a funeral procession, if the front turn signal lamps at each side are being flashed simultaneously and the rear turn signal lamps at each side are being flashed simultaneously.

(b) Turn signal lamps shall be flashed as warning lights whenever a vehicle is disabled upon the roadway and the vehicle is equipped with a device to automatically activate the front turn signal lamps at each side to flash simultaneously and the rear turn signal lamps at each side to flash simultaneously, if the device and the turn signal lamps were not rendered inoperative by the event which caused the vehicle to be disabled.

(c) Side lamps permitted under Section 25106 and used in conjunction with turn signal lamps may be flashed with the turn signal lamps as part of the warning light system, as provided in paragraphs (2) and (3) of subdivision (a).

(d) Required or permitted lamps on a trailer or semitrailer may flash when the trailer or semitrailer has broken away from the towing vehicle and the connection between the vehicles is broken.

(e) Hazard warning lights, as permitted by paragraphs (2) and (3) of subdivision (a) may be flashed in a repeating series of short and long flashes when the driver is in need of help. *(Stats.1959, c. 3, p. 1722, § 25251. Amended by Stats.1959, c. 1996, p. 4633, § 33; Stats.1961, c. 58, p. 1011, § 46; Stats.1961, c. 159, p. 1164, § 5; Stats.1961, c. 653, p. 1861, § 29; Stats.1963, c. 223, p. 964, § 5; Stats.1965, c. 1125, p. 2772, § 1; Stats.1970, c. 422, p. 837, § 4; Stats.1972, c. 203, p. 425, § 2; Stats.1977, c. 445, p. 1482, § 1; Stats.1981, c. 774, p. 3022, § 2; Stats.1983, c. 410, § 1; Stats.1984, c. 121, § 1; Stats.1986, c. 256, § 2; Stats.1997, c. 945 (A.B.1561), § 23.)*

Cross References

Authorized emergency vehicle defined, see Vehicle Code § 165.
Definitions,
    Lighting equipment, see Vehicle Code § 375.
    Motor vehicle, see Vehicle Code § 415.
    Tow truck, see Vehicle Code § 615.
    Vehicle, see Vehicle Code § 670.
Diffused lights, see Vehicle Code § 25400 et seq.
Highway maintenance vehicles, warning lights, see Vehicle Code § 25256.
Mounting and light restrictions, see Vehicle Code § 25950 et seq.
Pest abatement vehicles, warning lights, see Vehicle Code § 25267.
Tow trucks, warning lights, see Vehicle Code § 25253.

§ 25251.1. Implements of husbandry displaying slow moving vehicle emblems

Any implement of husbandry displaying a slow moving vehicle emblem, as defined in Section 24615, and being operated at a speed of 25 miles per hour or less, may be equipped with double-faced amber turn signals which may be flashed simultaneously as warning lights. *(Added by Stats.1978, c. 252, p. 534, § 5, eff. June 16, 1978.)*

§ 25251.2. Motorcycles; modulation of upper beam of headlamp

Any motorcycle may be equipped with a means of modulating the upper beam of the headlamp between a high and a lower brightness at a rate of 200 to 280 flashes per minute. Such headlamps shall not be so modulated during darkness. *(Added by Stats.1980, c. 35, p. 94, § 1, eff. March 7, 1980.)*

§ 25251.3. Turn signal warning lights: civil liability

No civil liability shall attach to any person for the use or nonuse of turn signal lamps in the manner permitted by paragraph (3) or (5) of subdivision (a) of Section 25251, except for such civil liability as would attach for the use or nonuse of any other device required by this article or Article 8 (commencing with Section 25300). *(Added by Stats.1977, c. 445, p. 1483, § 3. Amended by Stats.1983, c. 410, § 2.)*

§ 25251.4. Theft alarm system

Any motor vehicle may also be equipped with a theft alarm system which flashes any of the lights required or permitted on the motor vehicle and which operates as specified in Article 13 (commencing with Section 28085) of Chapter 5 of this division. *(Added by Stats.1977, c. 993, p. 2982, § 1.)*

§ 25251.5. Deceleration warning lights

(a) Any motor vehicle may also be equipped with a system in which an amber light is center mounted on the rear of a vehicle to communicate a component of deceleration of the vehicle, and which light pulses in a controlled fashion at a rate which varies exponentially with a component of deceleration.

(b) Any motor vehicle may be equipped with two amber lamps on the rear of the vehicle which operate simultaneously with not more than four flashes within four seconds after the accelerator pedal is in the deceleration position and which are not lighted at any other time. The lamps shall be mounted at the same height, with one lamp located on each side of the vertical centerline of the vehicle, not higher than the bottom of the rear window, or if the vehicle has no rear window, not higher than 60 inches. The light output from each of the lamps shall not exceed 200 candlepower at any angle horizontal or above. The amber lamps may be used either separately or in combination with another lamp.

(c) Any stoplamp or supplemental stoplamp required or permitted by Section 24603 may be equipped so as to flash not more than four times within the first four seconds after actuation by application of the brakes. *(Formerly § 25251.1, added by Stats.1972, c. 740, p. 1330, § 1. Amended by Stats.1974, c. 574, p. 1394, § 1, eff. Aug. 30, 1974. Renumbered § 25251.5 and amended by Stats. 1977, c. 445, p. 1483, § 2. Amended by Stats.1982, c. 261, p. 840, § 1; Stats.1983, c. 410, § 3.)*

§ 25252. Warning lights on authorized emergency vehicles

Every authorized emergency vehicle shall be equipped with at least one steady burning red warning lamp visible from at least 1,000 feet to the front of the vehicle to be used as provided in this code.

In addition, authorized emergency vehicles may display revolving, flashing, or steady red warning lights to the front, sides or rear of the vehicles. *(Stats.1959, c. 3, p. 1722, § 25252. Amended by Stats.1961, c. 653, p. 1861, § 30, operative Jan. 1, 1962; Stats.1974, c. 635, p. 1490, § 6.)*

Cross References

Authorized emergency vehicle defined, see Vehicle Code § 165.
Exemptions, see Vehicle Code § 21055.
State vehicle fleet, development and adoption of specifications and standards for passenger cars and light-duty trucks, see Public Resources Code § 25722.5.

§ 25252.5. Flashing headlamps on authorized emergency vehicle

(a) Every authorized emergency vehicle may be equipped with a system which flashes the upper-beam headlamps of the vehicle with the flashes occurring alternately from the front headlamp on one side of the vehicle to the front headlamp on the other side of the vehicle. The flashing of the headlamps shall consist only of upper-beam flashing, and not the flashing of any other light beam.

(b) "Upper-beam headlamp," as used in this section, means a headlamp or that part of a headlamp which projects a distribution of light, or composite beam, so aimed and of such intensity as to reveal persons and vehicles at a distance of at least 350 feet ahead for all conditions of loading.

(c) The system provided for in subdivision (a) shall only be used when an authorized emergency vehicle is being operated pursuant to Section 21055. *(Added by Stats.1970, c. 681, p. 1310, § 1. Amended by Stats.1972, c. 203, p. 425, § 3; Stats.1979, c. 723, p. 2221, § 19; Stats.1983, c. 1017, § 4.)*

Cross References

Authorized emergency vehicle defined, see Vehicle Code § 165.

§ 25253. Warning lights on tow trucks used to tow disabled vehicles

(a) Tow trucks used to tow disabled vehicles shall be equipped with flashing amber warning lamps. This subdivision does not apply to a tractor-trailer combination.

(b) Tow trucks may display flashing amber warning lamps while providing service to a disabled vehicle. A flashing amber warning lamp upon a tow truck may be displayed to the rear when the tow truck is towing a vehicle and moving at a speed slower than the normal flow of traffic.

(c) A tow truck shall not display flashing amber warning lamps on a freeway except when an unusual traffic hazard or extreme hazard exists.

(Stats.1959, c. 3, p. 1722, § 25253. Amended by Stats.1961, c. 653, p. 1861, § 31, operative Jan. 1, 1962; Stats.1980, c. 399, p. 783, § 4, eff. July 11, 1980; Stats. 1981, c. 774, p. 3023, § 3; Stats.1988, c. 924, § 15; Stats.1995, c. 404 (S.B.240), § 9; Stats.2006, c. 375 (S.B.1610), § 3; Stats.2009, c. 33 (S.B.159), § 2.)

Cross References

Approved lighting equipment defined, see Vehicle Code § 375.
Parking of utility vehicles, see Vehicle Code § 22512.
Required equipment for tow trucks, see Vehicle Code § 27700.
Rules of the road, exemption of authorized emergency vehicles, see Vehicle Code § 21055.
Test and approval of lighting equipment, see Vehicle Code § 26100 et seq.
Tow truck defined, see Vehicle Code § 615.
Towing equipment, see Vehicle Code § 29000 et seq.

818

Vehicles operated by department of transportation, inapplicability of this section, see Vehicle Code § 23273.

§ 25253.1. Automobile dismantler's tow vehicle; flashing amber warning lamps

An automobile dismantler's tow vehicle used to tow a disabled vehicle may be equipped with flashing amber warning lamps.

A flashing amber warning lamp upon an automobile dismantler's tow vehicle may be displayed to the rear when the automobile dismantler's tow vehicle is towing a vehicle and moving at a speed slower than the normal flow of traffic. *(Added by Stats.1985, c. 710, § 4.)*

§ 25254. Warning lights on vehicles operated by personnel of marshal's department

In any county with a population of 250,000 or more persons, publicly owned vehicles operated by peace officer personnel of a marshal's department, when actually being used in the enforcement of the orders of any court, including, but not limited to, the transportation of prisoners, may display flashing amber warning lights to the rear when such vehicles are necessarily parked upon a roadway and such parking constitutes a hazard to other motorists. *(Added by Stats.1973, c. 401, p. 868, § 1. Amended by Stats.1974, c. 934, p. 1948, § 1.)*

§ 25255. Repealed by Stats.1961, c. 653, p. 1861, § 33, operative Jan. 1, 1962

§ 25256. Warning lights on highway maintenance vehicles

Vehicles used by highway authorities or bridge and highway districts, and vehicles of duly authorized representatives thereof, used in highway maintenance, inspection, survey or construction work may display flashing amber warning lights to the front, sides or rear when such vehicles are parked or working on the highway. *(Stats. 1959, c. 3, p. 1723, § 25256. Amended by Stats.1961, c. 653, p. 1861, § 34, operative Jan. 1, 1962; Stats.1967, c. 544, p. 1893, § 4.)*

Cross References

Special construction equipment defined, see Vehicle Code § 565.

§ 25257. Schoolbus; amber warning light and flashing red light signal systems and stop signal arm as equipment

(a) Every schoolbus, when operated for the transportation of schoolchildren, shall be equipped with a flashing red light signal system.

(b) (1) Every schoolbus manufactured on or after September 1, 1992, shall also be equipped with a stop signal arm. Any schoolbus manufactured before September 1, 1992, may be equipped with a stop signal arm.

(2) Any schoolbus manufactured on or after July 1, 1993, shall also be equipped with an amber warning light system, in addition to the flashing red light signal system.

Any schoolbus manufactured before July 1, 1993, may be equipped with an amber warning light system.

(3) On or before September 1, 1992, the department shall adopt regulations governing the specifications, installation, and use of stop signal arms, to comply with federal standards.

(4) A "stop signal arm" is a device that can be extended outward from the side of a schoolbus to provide a signal to other motorists not to pass the bus because it has stopped to load or unload passengers, that is manufactured pursuant to the specifications of Federal Motor Vehicle Safety Standard No. 131, issued on April 25, 1991. *(Stats.1959, c. 3, p. 1723, § 25257. Amended by Stats.1992, c. 624 (A.B.3144), § 7, eff. Sept. 14, 1992.)*

Cross References

Lettering, see Vehicle Code § 27906.
Operation of signals while unloading or stopping, see Vehicle Code § 22112.
Schoolbus defined, see Vehicle Code § 545.
Special stops, see Vehicle Code § 22454.

§ 25257.2. Schoolbus used for transportation of developmentally disabled persons; use of amber and flashing red light signal systems and stop signal arm restricted

If a schoolbus is used for the transportation of persons of any age who are developmentally disabled, as defined by the Lanterman Developmental Disabilities Services Act (Division 4.5 (commencing with Section 4500) of the Welfare and Institutions Code), the amber light signal system, flashing red light signal system, and stop signal arm shall not be used other than as required by Sections 22112 and 22454. *(Added by Stats.1986, c. 678, § 2. Amended by Stats.1992, c. 624 (A.B.3144), § 8, eff. Sept. 14, 1992.)*

§ 25257.5. Backing maneuver for schoolbus; flashing turn signal lamps

To warn other motorists or pedestrians on a roadway during a backing maneuver, the operator of a schoolbus may flash turn signal lamps if the front turn signal lamps at each side are flashed simultaneously and the rear signal lamps at each side are flashed simultaneously. *(Added by Stats.1984, c. 127, § 1.)*

§ 25257.7. Schoolbuses; white strobe lights

(a) A schoolbus may be equipped with a white strobe light mounted so as to be visible from the front, sides, or rear of the bus. The strobe light may only be lighted when visibility is reduced to 500 feet or less due to atmospheric conditions including, but not limited to, fog, rain, snow, smoke, or dust. Reduced visibility due to atmospheric conditions does not include the time of darkness from one-half hour after sunset to one-half hour before sunrise.

(b) The type and mounting requirements of strobe lights authorized by subdivision (a) shall be established by regulations adopted by the department by April 1, 1991.

No schoolbus shall be equipped with a strobe light until the regulations are adopted. *(Added by Stats.1990, c. 169 (S.B.1814), § 1, eff. June 22, 1990.)*

§ 25258. Authorized emergency vehicles; additional lights

(a) An authorized emergency vehicle operating under the conditions specified in Section 21055 may display a flashing white light from a gaseous discharge lamp designed and used for the purpose of controlling official traffic control signals.

(b) An authorized emergency vehicle used by a peace officer, as defined in Section 830.1 of, subdivision (a), (b), (c), (d), (e), (f), (g), or (i) of Section 830.2 of, subdivision (n) of Section 830.3 of, subdivision (b) of Section 830.31 of, subdivision (a) or (b) of Section 830.32 of, Section 830.33 of, subdivision (a) of Section 830.36 of, subdivision (a) of Section 830.4 of, or Section 830.6 of, the Penal Code, in the performance of the peace officer's duties, may, in addition, display a steady or flashing blue warning light visible from the front, sides, or rear of the vehicle.

(c) Except as provided in subdivision (a), a vehicle shall not be equipped with a device that emits any illumination or radiation that is designed or used for the purpose of controlling official traffic control signals. *(Stats.1959, c. 3, p. 1723, § 25258. Amended by Stats. 1967, c. 1037, p. 2639, § 1; Stats.1974, c. 255, p. 473, § 1; Stats.1979, c. 723, p. 2221, § 20; Stats.1981, c. 1112, p. 4341, § 2; Stats.1982, c. 954, p. 3446, § 2; Stats.1987, c. 429, § 2; Stats.1989, c. 245, § 1; Stats.1989, c. 1165, § 48; Stats.1990, c. 82 (S.B.655), § 18, eff. May 3, 1990; Stats.1990, c. 1695 (S.B.2140), § 13; Stats.1991, c. 13 (A.B.37), § 54, eff. Feb. 13, 1991; Stats.1996, c. 1154 (A.B.3020), § 74, eff. Sept. 30, 1996; Stats.1997, c. 945 (A.B.1561), § 24; Stats.1998, c. 828 (S.B.1637), § 20; Stats.2004, c. 198 (S.B.1236), § 3; Stats.2010, c. 618 (A.B.2791), § 295.)*

Cross References

Authorized emergency vehicles defined, see Vehicle Code § 165.
Diffused nonglaring light, exception as to color, see Vehicle Code § 25400.
Nonliability for injury caused by operation or nonoperation of traffic control signals controlled by an emergency vehicle, see Government Code § 830.9.
Traffic control signal changing devices, priority of emergency vehicle over bus, see Vehicle Code § 25352.

§ 25258.1. Repealed by Stats.1996, c. 1154 (A.B.3020), § 75, eff. Sept. 30, 1996

§ 25259. Additional warning lights on authorized emergency vehicles

(a) Any authorized emergency vehicle may display flashing amber warning lights to the front, sides, or rear.

(b) A vehicle operated by a police or traffic officer while in the actual performance of his or her duties may display steady burning or flashing white lights to either side mounted above the roofline of the vehicle.

(c) Any authorized emergency vehicle may display not more than two flashing white warning lights to the front mounted above the roofline of the vehicle and not more than two flashing white warning lights to the front mounted below the roofline of the vehicle. These lamps may be in addition to the flashing headlamps permitted under Section 25252.5. *(Stats.1959, c. 3, p. 1723, § 25259. Amended by Stats.1959, c. 974, p. 3004, § 1; Stats.1961, c. 653, p. 1861, § 35; Stats.1965, c. 1357, p. 3250, § 1; Stats.1978, c. 252, p. 534, § 6, eff. June 16, 1978; Stats.1979, c. 723, p. 2221, § 21; Stats.1991, c. 13 (A.B.37), § 55, eff. Feb. 13, 1991; Stats.1997, c. 945 (A.B.1561), § 25.)*

Cross References

Authorized emergency vehicle defined, see Vehicle Code § 165.

§ 25259.1. Disaster service worker vehicles; training; treatment of lights not in use

(a) Any vehicle operated by a disaster service worker who has received training in accordance with subdivision (b) and used by that worker in the performance of emergency or disaster services ordered by lawful authority during a state of war emergency, a state of emergency, or a local emergency, as those terms are defined in Section 8558 of the Government Code, may display flashing amber warning lights to the front, sides, or rear while at the scene of the emergency or disaster.

(b) Any disaster service worker operating a vehicle that displays flashing amber warning lights shall receive a training course from the public agency, disaster council, or emergency organization described in Section 3101 of the Government Code concerning the safe operation of the use of flashing amber warning lights prior to operating a vehicle that displays flashing amber warning lights.

(c) A person operating a vehicle that is authorized to display flashing amber warning lights under this section shall either completely cover or remove those lights when the lights are not in use. *(Added by Stats.1997, c. 144 (A.B.924), § 1.)*

§ 25259.5. Emergency response or disaster service vehicles owned or leased and operated by American National Red Cross

An emergency response or disaster service vehicle owned or leased and operated by the American National Red Cross, or any chapter or branch thereof, and equipped and clearly marked as a Red Cross emergency service or disaster service vehicle, may display flashing amber warning lights to the front, sides, or rear of the vehicle while at the scene of an emergency or disaster operation. Vehicles not used on emergency response shall not be included. *(Added by Stats.1986, c. 178, § 1. Amended by Stats.1997, c. 144 (A.B.924), § 2.)*

§ 25260. Warning lights on public utility vehicles and public transit vehicles assisting disabled district buses

(a) Public utility vehicles, and vehicles of duly authorized representatives of a public utility, actually engaged in

the construction, removal, maintenance, or inspection of public utility facilities, including the cutting or trimming of trees immediately adjacent thereto, may display flashing amber warning lights to the front, sides, or rear when necessarily parked on a highway or when moving at a speed slower than the normal flow of traffic.

(b) Vehicles owned by public transit operators which provide assistance to a disabled district bus may display flashing amber warning lights to the front, sides, or rear when necessarily parked on a highway. *(Stats.1959, c. 3, p. 1723, § 25260. Amended by Stats.1961, c. 653, p. 1862, § 36; Stats.1963, c. 656, p. 1646, § 1; Stats.1965, c. 1352, p. 3244, § 1; Stats.1980, c. 399, p. 783, § 5, eff. July 11, 1980.)*

Cross References

Vehicles incidentally operated over highway, applicability of this section, see Vehicle Code § 25802.

§ 25260.1. Warning lights on vehicles engaged in oil or gas pipeline activities

Vehicles actually engaged in the construction, removal, maintenance, or inspection of any oil or gas pipeline may display flashing amber warning lights to the front, sides, or rear when necessarily parked on a highway or when necessarily moving at a speed slower than the normal flow of traffic and only in accordance with Section 25268. *(Added by Stats.1978, c. 120, p. 289, § 1.)*

§ 25260.3. Warning lights on personnel aerial lift vehicle

Any vehicle having personnel aerial lift equipment, actually engaged in the construction, removal, maintenance or inspection of any building, structure, or appurtenances thereto, including the cutting or trimming of trees immediately adjacent thereto, may display flashing amber warning lights to the front, sides, or rear when necessarily parked on a highway or when moving at a speed slower than the normal flow of the traffic. *(Added by Stats.1976, c. 334, p. 917, § 1.)*

§ 25260.4. Warning lights on hazardous substance spill response vehicles

Any hazardous substance spill response vehicle, under contract to the Department of Transportation for the cleanup of hazardous substance spills, may display flashing amber warning lights to the front, sides, or rear of the vehicle while it is engaged in the actual cleanup of the spill. The warning lights shall be removed or covered with opaque material whenever the vehicle is not actually engaged in the cleanup of a hazardous substance at the scene of the spill. *(Added by Stats.1984, c. 887, § 1, eff. Sept. 5, 1984.)*

§ 25261. Warning lights on county vehicles

Vehicles used by a county or county department of agriculture and vehicles of duly authorized representatives thereof, actually engaged in weed control or pest detection, may display flashing amber warning lights to the front, sides, or rear when necessarily parked on a highway or when moving at a speed slower than the normal flow of traffic. *(Added by Stats.1969, c. 218, p. 548, § 1.)*

Cross References

Equipment provisions, applicability, see Vehicle Code § 24001.

§ 25262. Armored cars

An armored car may be equipped with red lights which may be used while resisting armed robbery. At all other times the red lights shall not be lighted. The authority to use red lights granted by this section does not constitute an armored car an authorized emergency vehicle, and all other provisions of this code applicable to drivers of vehicles apply to drivers of armored cars. *(Stats.1959, c. 3, p. 1723, § 25262. Amended by Stats.1969, c. 9, p. 63, § 5, eff. March 6, 1969.)*

Cross References

Armored car defined, see Vehicle Code § 115.
Authorized emergency vehicle defined, see Vehicle Code § 165.
License required to operate, see Vehicle Code § 21713.
Offenses, see Vehicle Code § 40000.1 et seq.
Penalties, see Vehicle Code § 42000 et seq.
Sirens on armored car, see Vehicle Code § 27003.

§ 25263. Warning lights on house towing trucks

Trucks actually engaged in the towing of houses or buildings upon any highway may display flashing amber warning lights to the front, sides or rear on the vehicle or load. *(Stats.1959, c. 3, p. 1723, § 25263. Amended by Stats.1961, c. 653, p. 1862, § 38, operative Jan. 1, 1962.)*

§ 25264. Warning lights on coroner vehicles

Any motor vehicle operated by a coroner, or by a deputy coroner, and which is at the scene of any violent highway death, may display flashing amber warning lights to the front or rear. *(Added by Stats.1961, c. 653, p. 1862, § 40, operative Jan. 1, 1962.)*

Cross References

Duties of coroner, generally, see Government Code § 27460 et seq.

§ 25265. Warning lights on sanitation district repair vehicles

Repair vehicles of sanitary districts or county sanitation districts necessarily parked other than adjacent to the curb in a highway for purposes of repairing district facilities, may display flashing amber warning lights to the front, sides or rear, but these lights shall not be lighted when the vehicle is in motion. *(Added by Stats.1959, c. 809, p. 2819, § 1. Amended by Stats.1961, c. 653, p. 1862, § 41, operative Jan. 1, 1962.)*

§ 25266. Warning lights on vehicles engaged in aqueduct, levee, or stream measurement work

Vehicles owned by the state and operated by officers or employees of the state who are actually engaged in aqueduct or levee construction, maintenance, patrol, or inspection, or in stream measurement work, may display flashing amber warning lights to the front, sides and rear when parked on the traveled roadway so as to partially obstruct the free flow of traffic, or when moving at a speed slower than the normal flow of traffic. *(Added by Stats.1959, c. 1501, p. 3792, § 1. Amended by Stats.1961, c. 653, p. 1862, § 42, operative Jan. 1, 1962; Stats.1973, c. 763, p. 1374, § 1.)*

§ 25267. Warning lights on pest abatement vehicles

Vehicles used by mosquito abatement districts or pest abatement districts when dispersing insecticides may display flashing amber warning lights to the front or rear while the vehicles are parked or working on the highway. *(Added by Stats.1961, c. 653, p. 1862, § 43, operative Jan. 1, 1962.)*

§ 25268. Use of flashing amber warning light

No person shall display a flashing amber warning light on a vehicle as permitted by this code except when an unusual traffic hazard exists. *(Added by Stats.1961, c. 653, p. 1862, § 44, operative Jan. 1, 1962.)*

§ 25269. Use of red warning light

No person shall display a flashing or steady burning red warning light on a vehicle except as permitted by Section 21055 or when an extreme hazard exists. *(Added by Stats.1961, c. 653, p. 1862, § 45, operative Jan. 1, 1962.)*

§ 25270. Warning lights on pilot cars and related vehicles

Any pilot car required by the permit referred to in Section 35780 or 35790, or any vehicle or combination of vehicles subject to the permit if specified in the permit, shall be equipped with flashing amber warning lights to the front, sides or rear. The pilot car and any vehicles required by the permit to have flashing amber warning lights, shall display the flashing amber warning lights while actually engaged in the movement described in the permit. The warning lamps shall be removed or covered with opaque material whenever the pilot car is not escorting the movement described in the permit. *(Added by Stats.1961, c. 653, p. 1862, § 46, operative Jan. 1, 1962. Amended by Stats.1973, c. 64, p. 106, § 1; Stats.1981, c. 774, p. 3023, § 4; Stats.1988, c. 460, § 1.)*

§ 25270.5. Warning lights on vehicles herding livestock

Any motor vehicle engaged in, or aiding in, the herding of livestock along or across a public roadway may display flashing amber warning lights to the front, sides, or rear of the vehicle while it is stopped in the roadway near the livestock or is proceeding with the livestock along the roadway. *(Added by Stats.1974, c. 1145, p. 2436, § 1. Amended by Stats.1975, c. 391, p. 869, § 1; Stats.1977, c. 287, p. 1184, § 5.)*

821

§ 25271. Warning lights on pet ambulances

Any publicly owned vehicle or any vehicle operated by a corporation incorporated under Part 4 (commencing with Section 10400) of Division 2 of Title 1 of the Corporations Code for the purpose of the prevention of cruelty to animals, when used for removing dead animals, injured animals, or loose livestock, may, display flashing amber warning lights to the front or rear when necessarily parked on the roadway or when moving at a speed slower than the normal flow of traffic. *(Added by Stats.1961, c. 653, p. 1863, § 47, operative Jan. 1, 1962.)*

§ 25271.5. Flashing or revolving amber warning lights on animal control law enforcement vehicle

Any publicly owned vehicle used for the enforcement of animal control laws contained in a statute, local ordinance, or regulation may display flashing or revolving amber warning lights to the front, sides, or rear of the vehicle when actually engaged in the enforcement of those laws and when necessarily parked on a roadway or moving at a speed slower than the normal flow of traffic. *(Added by Stats.1985, c. 131, § 1.)*

§ 25272. Warning lights on rural mail vehicles

A motor vehicle used by a rural mail carrier may display flashing amber warning lights to the front and rear of the vehicle while the vehicle is necessarily stopped or stopping upon a roadway for the delivery of United States mail. *(Added by Stats.1961, c. 653, p. 1863, § 48, operative Jan. 1, 1962.)*

§ 25273. Warning lights on school district vehicles

Any motor vehicle owned and operated by a school district with an average daily attendance in excess of 400,000 while being used to measure the distance from school to a school pupil's residence may display a flashing amber warning light to the rear of the vehicle when moving at a speed substantially slower than the normal flow of traffic. *(Added by Stats.1963, c. 404, p. 1212, § 1.)*

§ 25274. Warning lights on cable television company vehicles

Any vehicle owned by a cable television company and operated by employees, or duly authorized representatives, of a cable television company, when actually engaged in the construction, removal, maintenance or inspection of cable television facilities, including but not limited to, the cutting or trimming of trees immediately adjacent thereto, may display flashing amber warning lights to the front, sides, or rear when necessarily parked on a highway or when moving at a speed slower than the normal flow of traffic.

For the purposes of this section, "cable television company" means any person engaged in the business of transmitting television programs by cable to subscribers for a fee. *(Added by Stats.1972, c. 406, p. 728, § 1.)*

§ 25275. Warning lamp on trucks with long loads

Any truck or truck tractor which is primarily used in the transportation of loads specified in subdivision (a) of Section 35414, may be equipped with a flashing amber warning lamp. Such lamp may be displayed to the front, sides, or rear of the combination only when its length exceeds 75 feet and when an unusual traffic hazard exists. *(Added by Stats.1973, c. 64, p. 107, § 2.)*

§ 25275.5. Buses; crime alarm lights

Any bus operated either by a public agency or under the authority of a certificate of public convenience and necessity issued by the Public Utilities Commission may be equipped with a system of crime alarm lights. The system of crime alarm lights shall consist of the installation of additional lamp sources, not exceeding 32 standard candlepower or 30 watts, in the front and rear clearance lamps required or permitted by Section 25100. Such lamps shall be operated by a flasher unit or units that are not audible inside the bus. When actuated, both rear crime alarm lights shall flash simultaneously and both front crime alarm lights shall flash simultaneously. Crime alarm lights shall be actuated only when a crime is in progress on board the bus or has recently been committed on board the bus. *(Added by Stats.1975, c. 777, p. 1798, § 1. Amended by Stats.1979, c. 723, p. 2222, § 22.)*

§ 25276. Warning lights on vehicles transporting individuals who have intellectual or physical disabilities

(a) A motor vehicle designed for carrying more than eight persons, including the driver, owned by a private, nonprofit organization that provides training or other activities for persons who have intellectual or physical disabilities, or both, and that is certified by the Department of Rehabilitation or licensed by the State Department of Developmental Services, with respect to the providing of this training or other activities, may be equipped with a flashing amber light signal system.

(b) A motor vehicle, described in subdivision (a), may, while actually engaged in the transportation of persons described in subdivision (a) to or from a training or activity center operated by the organization, display the flashing amber lights of the system when necessarily parked upon a highway and in the process of loading or unloading persons.

(c) Subdivisions (a) and (b) apply to a motor vehicle that is rented, leased, or chartered by the organization. *(Added by Stats.1975, c. 683, p. 1627, § 1. Amended by Stats.2004, c. 404 (S.B.1725), § 19; Stats.2012, c. 448 (A.B.2370), § 45; Stats.2012, c. 457 (S.B.1381), § 45.)*

§ 25277. Warning lights on vehicles enforcing parking laws

Any vehicle used by any police department, sheriff's office, or other governmental agency for the purpose of enforcing parking laws contained in the Vehicle Code or in a local ordinance or regulation may display flashing or revolving amber warning lights to the front, sides, or rear of the vehicle when actually engaged in the enforcement of such laws and when either necessarily stopped on a street, or when moving at a speed slower than the normal flow of traffic. *(Added by Stats.1976, c. 234, p. 444, § 2.)*

§ 25278. Warning lights; land surveyor or civil engineer vehicle; civil liability

Any vehicle owned or operated by a land surveyor or civil engineer licensed to practice in this state may display flashing amber warning lights to the front, sides, or rear, if the vehicle is engaged in any phase of a project that requires surveying or surveying related activities to be performed on a highway, or in the vicinity of a highway, and the vehicle is parked on the highway or moving at a speed lower than the normal flow of traffic. The use of, or absence of, amber warning lights as authorized in this section shall not serve as the basis for any civil action, a defense to a civil action, or establish negligence as a matter of law or negligence per se for comparative fault purposes. *(Added by Stats.1994, c. 207 (A.B.2827), § 3, eff. July 18, 1994. Amended by Stats.1995, c. 91 (S.B.975), § 181.)*

§ 25279. Warning lights on private security agency vehicles

(a) Vehicles owned and operated by private security agencies and utilized exclusively on privately owned and maintained roads to which this code is made applicable by local ordinance or resolution, may display flashing amber warning lights to the front, sides, or rear, while being operated in response to emergency calls for the immediate preservation of life or property.

(b)(1) Vehicles owned by a private security agency and operated by personnel who are registered with the Department of Consumer Affairs under Article 3 (commencing with Section 7582) of Chapter 11.5 of Division 3 of the Business and Professions Code may be equipped with a flashing amber warning light system while the vehicle is operated on a highway, if the vehicle is in compliance with Section 27605 and is distinctively marked with the words "PRIVATE SECURITY" or "SECURITY PATROL" on the rear and both sides of the vehicle in a size that is legible from a distance of not less than 50 feet.

(2) The flashing amber warning light system authorized under paragraph (1) shall not be activated while the vehicle is on the highway, unless otherwise directed by a peace officer, as defined in Chapter 4.5 (commencing with Section 830) of Title 3 of Part 2 of the Penal Code.

(c) A peace officer may order that the flashing amber warning light system of a vehicle that is found to be in violation of this section be immediately removed at the place of business of the vehicle's owner or a garage.

(d) A flashing amber warning light system shall not be installed on a vehicle that has been found to be in violation of this section, unless written authorization is obtained from the Commissioner of the California Highway Patrol. *(Added by Stats.1979, c. 178, p. 397, § 1, eff. June 29, 1979. Amended by Stats.1996, c. 1154 (A.B. 3020), § 76, eff. Sept. 30, 1996.)*

§ 25280. Warning lights on garbage or rubbish vehicles

Vehicles operated by a local public entity, or pursuant to a permit, license, contract, or franchise with a local public entity, and used to collect and transport garbage, rubbish, or refuse may display flashing amber warning lights to the front, sides, or rear while stopped upon a street and actually engaged in the collection of garbage, rubbish, or refuse, or while moving between stops at a speed not greater than 10 miles per hour. *(Added by Stats.1981, c. 280, p. 1398, § 1.)*

§ 25281. Warning lights; water tender vehicle

A privately owned or operated water tender vehicle, when used exclusively for contract emergency services provided to any public agency, may display flashing amber warning lights to the front, sides, or rear of the vehicle when necessarily parked on a highway or other public road, blocking or partially blocking a highway or other public road, traveling at a speed slower than the normal flow of traffic, or crossing or entering a highway or other public road. The flashing amber lights shall not be displayed when the water tender vehicle is traveling to or from an emergency at the normal speed and flow of traffic, except when the vehicle is traveling in escort with a fire engine or other authorized emergency vehicle. The lights shall be covered with an opaque material when not being displayed. *(Added by Stats.1994, c. 207 (A.B.2827), § 4, eff. July 18, 1994.)*

§ 25282. Contractors; construction company vehicles; amber warning lights; use or absence as basis for civil actions

Any vehicle owned or operated by a contractor or a construction company licensed to operate in this state pursuant to the Business and Professions Code may display flashing amber warning lights to the front, sides, or rear, if the vehicle is engaged in any phase of a construction project performed on a highway, or in the vicinity of a highway, and the vehicle is parked on the highway or moving at a speed lower than the normal flow of traffic. The use of, or absence of, amber warning lights as authorized in this section shall not serve as the basis for any civil action, a defense to civil action, or establish negligence as a matter of law or negligence per se for comparative fault purposes. *(Added by Stats.1996, c. 10 (A.B.1869), § 21, eff. Feb. 9, 1996.)*

ARTICLE 8.   WARNING LIGHTS AND DEVICES

Section
25300.   Emergency reflectors; emergency warning signs or banners; disabled or parked vehicles.
25301.   Utility and public utility vehicles.
25302 to 25304.   Repealed.
25305.   Use of fusees.

Cross References

Test and approval of lighting equipment, see Vehicle Code § 26100 et seq.

§ 25300. Emergency reflectors; emergency warning signs or banners; disabled or parked vehicles

(a) Every vehicle which, if operated during darkness, would be subject to the provisions of Section 25100, and every truck tractor, irrespective of width, shall at all times be equipped with at least three red emergency reflectors. The reflectors need be carried by only one vehicle in a combination.

All reflectors shall be maintained in good working condition.

(b) When any such vehicle is disabled on the roadway during darkness, reflectors of the type specified in subdivision (a) shall be immediately placed as follows:

(1) One at the traffic side of the disabled vehicle, not more than 10 feet to the front or rear thereof;

(2) One at a distance of approximately 100 feet to the rear of the disabled vehicle in the center of the traffic lane occupied by such vehicle; and

(3) One at a distance of approximately 100 feet to the front of the disabled vehicle in the center of the traffic lane occupied by such vehicle.

(4) If disablement of any such vehicle occurs within 500 feet of a curve, crest of a hill, or other obstruction to view, the driver shall so place the reflectors in that direction as to afford ample warning to other users of the highway, but in no case less than 100 nor more than 500 feet from the disabled vehicle.

(5) If disablement of the vehicle occurs upon any roadway of a divided or one-way highway, the driver shall place one reflector at a distance of approximately 200 feet and one such reflector at a distance of approximately 100 feet to the rear of the vehicle in the center of the lane occupied by the stopped vehicle, and one such reflector at the traffic side of the vehicle not more than 10 feet to the rear of the vehicle.

(c) When any such vehicle is disabled or parked off the roadway but within 10 feet thereof during darkness, warning reflectors of the type specified in subdivision (a) shall be immediately placed by the driver as follows: one at a distance of approximately 200 feet and one at a distance of approximately 100 feet to the rear of the vehicle, and one at the traffic side of the vehicle not more than 10 feet to the rear of the vehicle. The reflectors shall, if possible, be placed between the edge of the roadway and the vehicle, but in no event less than two feet to the left of the widest portion of the vehicle or load thereon.

(d) Until the reflectors required by this section can be placed properly, the requirements of this section may be complied with temporarily by either placing lighted red fusees in the required locations or by use of turn signal lamps, but only if front turn signal lamps at each side are being flashed simultaneously and rear turn signal lamps at each side are being flashed simultaneously.

(e) The reflectors shall be displayed continuously during darkness while the vehicle remains disabled upon the roadway or parked or disabled within 10 feet thereof.

(f) Subdivisions (b), (c), (d), and (e) do not apply to a vehicle under either of the following circumstances:

(1) Parked in a legal position within the corporate limits of any city.

(2) Parked in a legal position upon a roadway bounded by adjacent curbs.

(g) In addition to the reflectors specified in subdivision (a), an emergency warning sign or banner may be attached to a vehicle which is disabled upon the roadway or which is parked or disabled within 10 feet of a roadway. *(Stats.1959, c. 3, p. 1724, § 25300. Amended by Stats.1963, c. 143, p. 815, § 1; Stats.1965, c. 1125, p. 2772, § 2; Stats.1967, c. 372, p. 1599, § 1; Stats.1977, c. 287, p. 1184, § 6; Stats.1981, c. 774, p. 3023, § 5.)*

Cross References

Definitions,
    Commercial vehicle, see Vehicle Code § 260.
    Motor truck, see Vehicle Code § 410.
    Roadway, see Vehicle Code § 530.
    Semi-trailer, see Vehicle Code § 550.
    Trailer, see Vehicle Code § 630.
    Trailer coach, see Vehicle Code § 635.
    Truck tractor, see Vehicle Code § 655.
    Unladen weight, see Vehicle Code § 660.
Lighting during darkness, see Vehicle Code § 24250.
Parking of utility vehicles, see Vehicle Code § 22512.
Reflectorizing material, see Vehicle Code § 25500.
Reflectors on front and sides, see Vehicle Code § 24608.
Regulations governing color of lights, see Vehicle Code § 25950.
Rules of the road, exemption of authorized emergency vehicles, see Vehicle Code § 21055.
Size of identification signs, see Vehicle Code § 25350.
Special restrictions on lamps and reflectors, see Vehicle Code § 25950 et seq.
Taillamps, see Vehicle Code § 24600 et seq.
Test and approval of equipment and signal devices, see Vehicle Code § 26100 et seq.
Warning lights on tow trucks, see Vehicle Code § 25253.

§ 25301. Utility and public utility vehicles

When utility or public utility vehicles are parked, stopped or standing at the site of work as described in Section 22512, warning devices shall be displayed as follows:

(a) During daylight warning devices shall consist of either:

A warning flag or barricade striping on the front and rear of the vehicle.

A warning flag, sign, or barrier on the highway not more than 50 feet in advance of the vehicle and not more than 50 feet to the rear thereof, except that in zones where the speed limit is in excess of 25 miles per hour the

50-foot distance may be increased up to 500 feet from the vehicle as circumstances may warrant.

(b) During darkness the warning devices shall consist of either:

One or more flashing amber warning lights on the vehicle giving warning to approaching traffic from each direction.

A warning light, flare, fusee, or reflector on the highway not more than 50 feet in advance of the vehicle and not more than 50 feet to the rear thereof, except that in zones where the speed limit is in excess of 25 miles per hour the 50-foot distance may be increased up to 500 feet from the vehicle where circumstances may warrant.

(c) The provisions of subdivision (a) or (b) do not prevent the display of both types of the warning devices during daylight or darkness.

(d) During either daylight or darkness, no warning device is necessary if the vehicle is equipped with the flashing warning lights visible to approaching traffic from each direction as provided in subdivision (b). *(Stats. 1959, c. 3, p. 1724, § 25301. Amended by Stats.1959, c. 1996, p. 4634, § 33.5; Stats.1961, c. 653, p. 1863, § 49, operative Jan. 1, 1962.)*

Cross References

Authorized emergency vehicle, see Vehicle Code § 165.
Local regulation of state highways, see Vehicle Code § 22501.
Parking of utility vehicles, see Vehicle Code § 22512.
Regulation on color of lamps and reflectors, see Vehicle Code § 25950.
Rules of the road, exemption of authorized emergency vehicles, see Vehicle Code § 21055.
Special restriction on lamps and reflectors, see Vehicle Code § 25950 et seq.
Speed limit when persons at work, see Vehicle Code § 22362.
Taillamps, see Vehicle Code § 24600 et seq.
Warning lights on public utility vehicles, see Vehicle Code §§ 25260, 25260.1.

§§ 25302 to 25304. Repealed by Stats.1965, c. 34, p. 914, §§ 2 to 4

§ 25305. Use of fusees

(a) No person shall place, deposit, or display upon or adjacent to any highway any lighted fusee, except as a warning to approaching vehicular traffic or railroad trains, or both, of an existing hazard upon or adjacent to the highway or highway-railroad crossing.

(b) It is unlawful to use any fusee which produces other than a red light. The provisions of this subdivision shall not apply to any railroad, as defined in Section 229 of the Public Utilities Code. *(Added by Stats.1971, c. 84, p. 112, § 2, operative May 3, 1972.)*

ARTICLE 9. COMMERCIAL AND COMMON CARRIER VEHICLES

Section
25350.   Identification lamps and signs.

Section
25351.   Identification lamps.
25352.   Traffic control signal changing devices.
25353.   Illuminated signs on buses.
25353.1. Buses operated by City of Santa Monica's publicly owned transit system; illuminated signs that display advertising; conditions; operation as dynamic message signs; report on adverse impacts; limit on number of buses.
25354.   University of California, Irvine's public transport system; illuminated signs displaying advertisements; conditions; pilot program.

Cross References

Commercial vehicle defined, see Vehicle Code § 260.
Common carrier defined, see Civil Code § 2168; Public Utilities Code § 211 et seq.
Cotton module movers, operation on state highways, conditions, see Vehicle Code § 35555.
Implements of husbandry, applicability of this Article, see Vehicle Code § 36500.
Special construction and maintenance equipment, applicability of this Article, see Vehicle Code § 25801.
Special mobile equipment, applicability of this Article, see Vehicle Code § 25800.
Vehicles incidentally operated over highway, applicability of this Article, see Vehicle Code § 25802.

§ 25350. Identification lamps and signs

Any passenger common carrier motor vehicle manufactured prior to January 1, 1968, may be equipped with green identification lamps. Any bus may be equipped with an illuminated termini sign, an illuminated identification sign, or any combination thereof, which shall not project any glaring light. Internally illuminated termini signs, identification signs, or any combination thereof, meeting the requirements of Section 25400 may be mounted inside a bus. Any commercial vehicle, other than a passenger common carrier motor vehicle, may be equipped with an illuminated identification sign upon the front thereof which shall not exceed 24 inches in length or 8 inches in width and which emits diffused white light without glare. *(Stats.1959, c. 3, p. 1725, § 25350. Amended by Stats.1963, c. 152, p. 820, § 1; Stats.1968, c. 980, p. 1872, § 16; Stats.1981, c. 813, p. 3158, § 18.)*

Cross References

Bus defined, see Vehicle Code § 233.
Commercial vehicle defined, see Vehicle Code § 260.
Identification signs, see Vehicle Code § 27900 et seq.

§ 25351. Identification lamps

(a) A commercial vehicle and, except as provided in subdivision (d), any other vehicle 80 or more inches in width may be equipped with identification lamps mounted on the front or rear. No part of any such lamps or their mountings on the front of a motor vehicle shall extend below the top of the windshield.

(b) Identification lamps on such vehicles manufactured prior to January 1, 1968, may exhibit either amber, green, or white light to the front and red light to the rear.

825

(c) Identification lamps on such vehicles manufactured on or after January 1, 1968, may exhibit only amber light to the front and red light to the rear.

(d) Identification lamps are not permitted on passenger vehicles, except housecars and ambulances, regardless of width. *(Stats.1959, c. 3, p. 1725, § 25351. Amended by Stats.1963, c. 152, p. 821, § 2; Stats.1968, c. 980, p. 1872, § 17; Stats.1970, c. 422, p. 837, § 5; Stats.1975, c. 616, p. 1344, § 2; Stats.1975, c. 854, p. 1922, § 6.)*

Cross References

Commercial vehicle defined, see Vehicle Code § 260.
House car defined, see Vehicle Code § 362.
Passenger vehicle defined, see Vehicle Code § 465.

§ 25352. Traffic control signal changing devices

Any bus operated by a publicly owned transit system on regularly scheduled service may be equipped with a device capable of sending a signal that interrupts or changes the sequence patterns of an official traffic control signal, under the following conditions:

(a) If such a device is a flashing gaseous discharge lamp, such lamp shall not emit a visible light exceeding an average of 0.0003 candela per flash of any color measured at a distance of 10 feet.

(b) Such device shall not be installed or used unless and until authorized on specific routes by either the Department of Transportation pursuant to Section 21350 or local authorities pursuant to Section 21351.

(c) Any bus or system operating under the conditions specified herein shall allow emergency vehicles operating pursuant to Section 25258 or 21055 to have priority in changing the sequence patterns of an official traffic control signal. *(Added by Stats.1977, c. 805, p. 2457, § 2. Amended by Stats.1979, c. 723, p. 2222, § 23; Stats.1980, c. 399, p. 783, § 6, eff. July 11, 1980.)*

§ 25353. Illuminated signs on buses

(a) Notwithstanding Sections 25400 and 25950, a bus operated by a publicly owned transit system on regularly scheduled service may be equipped with illuminated signs that include destination signs, route-number signs, run-number signs, public service announcement signs, or a combination thereof, visible from any direction of the vehicle, that emit any light color, other than the color red emitted from forward-facing signs, pursuant to the following conditions:

(1) Each illuminated sign shall emit diffused nonglaring light.

(2) Each illuminated sign shall be limited in size to a display area of not greater than 720 square inches.

(3) Each illuminated sign shall not resemble nor be installed in a position that interferes with the visibility or effectiveness of a required lamp, reflector, or other device upon the vehicle.

(4) Each illuminated sign shall display information directly related to public transit service, including, but not limited to, route number, destination description, run number, and public service announcements.

(5) The mixing of individually colored light emitting diode elements, including red, is allowed as long as the emitted color formed by the combination of light emitting diode elements is not red.

(b)(1) An illuminated sign may be operated as a dynamic message sign in a paging or streaming mode.

(2) The following definitions shall govern the construction of paragraph (1):

(A) "Paging," meaning character elements or other information presented for a period of time and then disappearing all at once before the same or new elements are presented, is permitted if the display time of each message is between 2.7 and 10 seconds. Blanking times between each message shall be between 0.5 and 25 seconds.

(B) "Streaming," meaning character elements or other information moving smoothly and continuously across the display, is permitted if the character movement time, from one end of the display to the other, is at least 2.7 seconds, and the movement time of the entire message does not exceed 10 seconds.

(c) A regulation adopted pursuant to this section shall comply with applicable federal law, including, but not limited to, the federal Americans with Disabilities Act of 1990 (42 U.S.C. Sec. 12101 et seq.). *(Added by Stats. 2006, c. 881 (S.B.1726), § 2.)*

Cross References

Lighting equipment defined, see Vehicle Code § 375.

§ 25353.1. Buses operated by City of Santa Monica's publicly owned transit system; illuminated signs that display advertising; conditions; operation as dynamic message signs; report on adverse impacts; limit on number of buses

(a) Notwithstanding Sections 25400 and 25950, a bus operated by the City of Santa Monica's publicly owned transit system, on regularly scheduled service, in addition to the illuminated signs described in section 25353, may also be equipped with illuminated signs that display advertising and that emit any light color, if all of the following conditions are met:

(1) Each illuminated sign displaying advertising shall emit diffused nonglaring light.

(2) Each illuminated sign displaying advertising shall be limited in size to a display area of not greater than 4,464 square inches.

(3) Each illuminated sign displaying advertising shall not resemble nor be installed in a position that interferes with the visibility or effectiveness of a required lamp, reflector, or other device upon the vehicle.

(4) Each illuminated sign displaying advertising shall only be placed on one or both sides of the vehicle, and shall not be placed in a forward-facing or rear-facing position, and no more than one such sign shall be placed on either side of any single vehicle.

(5) The mixing of individually colored light emitting diode elements, including red, is allowed in each illuminated sign displaying advertising as long as the emitted color formed by the combination of light emitting diode elements is not red.

(b)(1) An illuminated sign displaying advertising may be operated as a dynamic message sign in a paging or streaming mode. However, the electronic message sign display shall remain static while a bus is operating on a freeway as defined in Section 257 of the Streets and Highways Code.

(2) The following definitions shall govern the construction of paragraph (1):

(A) "Paging," meaning character elements or other information presented for a period of time and then disappearing all at once before the same or new elements are presented, is permitted if the display time of each message is between 2.7 and 10 seconds. Blanking times between each message shall be between 0.5 and 25 seconds.

(B) "Streaming," meaning character elements or other information moving smoothly and continuously across the display, is permitted if the character movement time, from one end of the display to the other, is at least 2.7 seconds, and the movement time of the entire message does not exceed 10 seconds.

(c) By July 1, 2016, the City of Santa Monica shall submit to the Legislature and to the department a report on the incidence of adverse impacts on roadway and pedestrian safety due to the utilization of illuminated signs on transit buses displaying advertising pursuant to this section, if any. The report shall be the product of a collaborative effort by Santa Monica law enforcement and transit officials, other local law enforcement officials in whose jurisdictions Santa Monica transit vehicles operate, and the department.

(d) The City of Santa Monica's publicly owned transit system may, pursuant to subdivision (a), operate up to 25 buses with illuminated signs displaying advertising for two years, after which time the city may increase the number of buses with the signs to up to 30.

(e) This section shall remain in effect only until January 1, 2017, and as of that date is repealed, unless a later enacted statute, that is enacted before January 1, 2017, deletes or extends that date. *(Added by Stats.2011, c. 529 (A.B.607), § 3.)*

Repeal

For repeal of this section, see its terms.

Cross References

Lighting equipment defined to include illuminated signs utilized pursuant to this section, see Vehicle Code § 375.

§ 25354. University of California, Irvine's public transport system; illuminated signs displaying advertisements; conditions; pilot program

(a) Notwithstanding Sections 25400 and 25950, and except as provided in subdivision (c), a bus operated by the University of California, Irvine's public transport system on regularly scheduled service, in addition to the illuminated signs described in Section 25353, may also be equipped with illuminated signs that display advertising and that emit any light color, if all of the following conditions are met:

(1) Each illuminated sign displaying advertising emits diffused nonglaring light.

(2) Each illuminated sign displaying advertising is limited in size to a display area of not greater than 4,464 square inches.

(3) Each illuminated sign displaying advertising does not resemble, and is not installed in a position that interferes with the visibility or effectiveness of, a required lamp, reflector, or other device upon the vehicle.

(4) Each illuminated sign displaying advertising is only placed on one or both sides of the vehicle, and is not placed in a forward-facing or rear-facing position, and no more than one such sign is placed on either side of any single vehicle.

(5) The mixing of individually colored light emitting diode elements, including red, is allowed in each illuminated sign displaying advertising as long as the emitted color formed by the combination of light emitting diode elements is not red.

(b)(1) An illuminated sign displaying advertising may be operated as a dynamic message sign in a paging or streaming mode. However, the electronic message sign display shall remain static while a bus is operating on a freeway, as that term is defined in Section 257 of the Streets and Highways Code.

(2) The following definitions shall govern the construction of paragraph (1):

(A) "Paging," meaning character elements or other information that is presented for a period of time and then disappears all at once before the same or new elements are presented, is permitted if the display time of each message is between 2.7 and 10 seconds. Blanking times between each message shall be between 0.5 and 25 seconds.

(B) "Streaming," meaning character elements or other information moving smoothly and continuously across the display, is permitted if the character movement time, from one end of the display to the other, is at least 2.7 seconds, and the movement time of the entire message does not exceed 10 seconds.

(c) On or before March 1, 2014, the University of California, Irvine, if it elects to implement a pilot program pursuant to this section, shall determine whether the City of Santa Monica has at least 12 transit buses equipped with illuminated signs that are operational pursuant to Section 25353.1. The University of California, Irvine, may implement the pilot program authorized by this section only if it determines that the City of Santa Monica has less than 12 transit buses equipped with illuminated signs that are operational pursuant to Section 25353.1.

(d) If the University of California, Irvine implements the pilot program pursuant to this section, it shall submit a report to the Legislature and the department on the incidence of adverse impacts on roadway and pedestrian safety due to the utilization of illuminated signs on transit buses displaying advertising pursuant to this section, if any, by July 1, 2018. The report shall be the product of a collaborative effort between university law enforcement and transit officials, other law enforcement officials in whose jurisdictions the university's transit vehicles operate, and the department. The report shall be submitted in compliance with Section 9795 of the Government Code.

(e) The University of California, Irvine's public transport system may, pursuant to subdivision (a), operate up to 25 buses with illuminated signs displaying advertising for two years, after which time the city may increase the number of buses with the signs to up to 30.

(f) This section shall remain in effect only until January 1, 2019, and as of that date is repealed, unless a later enacted statute, that is enacted before January 1, 2019, deletes or extends that date. *(Added by Stats.2013, c. 133 (A.B.541), § 1.)*

Repeal

For repeal of this section, see its terms.

ARTICLE 10.   DIFFUSED LIGHTS

Section
25400.   Lighting requirements.
25401.   Diffused lights resembling signs.

§ 25400.   Lighting requirements

(a) Any vehicle may be equipped with a lamp or device on the exterior of the vehicle that emits a diffused nonglaring light of not more than 0.05 candela per square inch of area.

(b) Any diffused nonglaring light shall not display red to the front, but may display other colors. A diffused nonglaring light shall not resemble nor be installed within 12 inches or in such position as to interfere with the visibility or effectiveness of any required lamp, reflector, or other device upon the vehicle.

(c) A diffused nonglaring lamp or device, other than a display sign authorized by subdivision (d), shall be limited in size to an area of 720 square inches and where any lease, rental, or donation is involved the installation of the lamp or device shall be limited to those vehicles operated either primarily within business or residential districts or municipalities, or between business districts, residential districts, and municipalities in close proximity.

(d) An internally illuminated sign emitting not more than 0.25 candela per square inch and possessing copy which does not contain a white background may be

displayed on each side, but not on the front or rear, of a trolley coach or of a bus being operated in urban or suburban service as described in Section 35107 of this code. *(Stats.1959, c. 3, p. 1726, § 25400. Amended by Stats.1963, c. 547, p. 1428, § 5; Stats.1968, c. 144, p. 364, § 1; Stats.1968, c. 582, p. 1249, § 1, eff. July 16, 1968.)*

Cross References

Approval of modifying devices, see Vehicle Code § 26101.
Illuminated signs on buses, see Vehicle Code § 25353.
University of California Irvine's public transport system, illuminated signs displaying advertisements, conditions, see Vehicle Code § 25354.

§ 25401.   Diffused lights resembling signs

No diffused nonglaring light on a vehicle shall resemble any official traffic control device. *(Stats.1959, c. 3, p. 1726, § 25401.)*

Cross References

Official traffic control device defined, see Vehicle Code § 440.

ARTICLE 11.   ACETYLENE LAMPS

Section
25450.   Acetylene lamps.
25451.   Motorcycles.
25452.   Glare of lights.

Cross References

Cotton module movers, operation on state highways, conditions, see Vehicle Code § 35555.
Implements of husbandry, applicability of this Article, see Vehicle Code § 36500.
Special construction and maintenance equipment, applicability of this Article, see Vehicle Code § 25801.
Special mobile equipment, applicability of this Article, see Vehicle Code § 25800.
Vehicles incidentally operated over highway, applicability of this Article, see Vehicle Code § 25802.

§ 25450.   Acetylene lamps

Any motor vehicle, other than a motorcycle, equipped with lighted acetylene headlamps complies with the provisions of this code concerning lighted headlamps when it has two lighted acetylene headlamps of approximately equal candlepower mounted upon the front of the motor vehicle and fitted with clear plane glass fronts and bright six-inch spherical mirrors and standard acetylene five-eighths or three-quarters foot burners, not more and not less, projecting sufficient light ahead to reveal any vehicle, person or substantial object upon the roadway within 200 feet. *(Stats.1959, c. 3, p. 1726, § 25450.)*

Cross References

Definitions,
    Motor vehicle, see Vehicle Code § 415.
    Motor-driven cycle, see Vehicle Code § 405.
    Motorcycle, see Vehicle Code § 400.
Exemption of special mobile equipment, see Vehicle Code § 25800.
Headlamps, motor vehicles, see Vehicle Code § 24400.

Lighting equipment, see Vehicle Code § 24250 et seq.

Test and approval of lamp or lighting device before sale or use, see Vehicle Code § 26100 et seq.

§ 25451. Motorcycles

Any motorcycle equipped with one lighted acetylene headlamp complies with the provisions of this code concerning lighted headlamps on motorcycles when the acetylene headlamp is fitted with a clear plane glass front and a bright six-inch spherical mirror and a standard acetylene one-half or five-eighths foot burner, projecting sufficient light ahead to reveal any vehicle, person, or substantial object upon the roadway within a distance of 115 feet. *(Stats.1959, c. 3, p. 1726, § 25451.)*

Cross References

Headlamps,
  Motor-driven cycles, see Vehicle Code § 25651.
  Motorcycles, see Vehicle Code §§ 25650, 25650.5.
Lighting equipment, see Vehicle Code § 24250 et seq.
Motor-driven cycle defined, see Vehicle Code § 405.
Motorcycle defined, see Vehicle Code § 400.
Test, approval and inspection of lighting equipment and signal devices, see Vehicle Code § 26100 et seq.

§ 25452. Glare of lights

No acetylene lamp shall emit any glaring light. *(Stats. 1959, c. 3, p. 1726, § 25452.)*

ARTICLE 12. REFLECTORIZING MATERIAL

Section
25500. Use of reflectorizing material.
25501, 25502. Repealed.

Cross References

Implements of husbandry, applicability of this Article, see Vehicle Code § 36500.
Special construction and maintenance equipment, applicability of this Article, see Vehicle Code § 25801.
Special mobile equipment, applicability of this Article, see Vehicle Code § 25800.
Vehicles incidentally operated over highway, applicability of this Article, see Vehicle Code § 25802.

§ 25500. Use of reflectorizing material

(a) Area reflectorizing material may be displayed on any vehicle, provided: the color red is not displayed on the front; designs do not tend to distort the length or width of the vehicle; and designs do not resemble official traffic control devices, except that alternate striping resembling a barricade pattern may be used.

No vehicle shall be equipped with area reflectorizing material contrary to these provisions.

(b) The provisions of this section shall not apply to license plate stickers or tabs affixed to license plates as authorized by the Department of Motor Vehicles. *(Stats. 1959, c. 3, p. 1726, § 25500. Amended by Stats.1961, c. 58, p. 1012, § 47, effective March 31, 1961; Stats.1961, c. 1320, p. 3099, § 1; Stats.1967, c. 106, p. 1023, § 1, eff.*

May 9, 1967; Stats.1970, c. 422, p. 837, § 6; Stats.1971, c. 1536, p. 3044, § 7, operative May 3, 1972.)

§§ 25501, 25502. Repealed by Stats.1967, c. 106, p. 1024, §§ 2, 3, eff. May 9, 1967

ARTICLE 13. HEADLAMPS ON MOTORCYCLES AND MOTOR–DRIVEN CYCLES

Section
25650. Headlights on motorcycles.
25650.5. Motorcycles manufactured and first registered after 1977; motorcycles used as emergency vehicles.
25651. Headlamps on motor-driven cycles.
25652. Repealed.

Cross References

Implements of husbandry, applicability of this Article, see Vehicle Code § 36500.
Special construction and maintenance equipment, applicability of this Article, see Vehicle Code § 25801.
Special mobile equipment, applicability of this Article, see Vehicle Code § 25800.
Vehicles incidentally operated over highway, applicability of this Article, see Vehicle Code § 25802.

§ 25650. Headlights on motorcycles

Every motorcycle during darkness shall be equipped with at least one and not more than two lighted headlamps which shall conform to the requirements and limitations of this division. *(Stats.1959, c. 3, p. 1727, § 25650.)*

Cross References

Alternate acetylene lamps, see Vehicle Code § 25451.
Darkness defined, see Vehicle Code § 280.
Motorcycle defined, see Vehicle Code § 400.
Regulations governing color of lamps and reflectors, see Vehicle Code § 25950.
Sale, lease and installation of unlawful equipment prohibited, see Vehicle Code § 24005.
Test and approval of lamps, lamp equipment and signal devices, see Vehicle Code § 26100 et seq.

§ 25650.5. Motorcycles manufactured and first registered after 1977; motorcycles used as emergency vehicles

Every motorcycle manufactured and first registered on and after January 1, 1978, shall be equipped with at least one and not more than two headlamps which automatically turn on when the engine of the motorcycle is started and which remain lighted as long as the engine is running. This section does not preclude equipping motorcycles used as authorized emergency vehicles with a switch to be used to turn off the headlamp during emergency situations or when the light would interfere with law enforcement, if the switch is removed prior to resale of the motorcycle. *(Added by Stats.1972, c. 201, p. 424, § 1. Amended by Stats.1978, c. 252, p. 535, § 7, eff. June 16, 1978; Stats.1984, c. 247, § 3.)*

§ 25651. Headlamps on motor-driven cycles

The headlamp upon a motor-driven cycle may be of the single-beam or multiple-beam type, but in either event, when the vehicle is operated during darkness, the headlamp shall comply with the requirements and limitations as follows:

(a) The headlamp shall be of sufficient intensity to reveal a person or a vehicle at a distance of not less than 100 feet when the motor-driven cycle is operated at any speed less than 25 miles per hour and at a distance of not less than 200 feet when operated at a speed of 25 to not exceeding 35 miles per hour, and at a distance of 300 feet when operated at a speed greater than 35 miles per hour.

(b) In the event the motor-driven cycle is equipped with a multiple-beam headlamp, the upper beam shall meet the minimum requirements set forth above and the lowermost beam shall meet the requirements applicable to a lowermost distribution of light as set forth in subdivision (b) of Section 24407.

(c) In the event the motor-driven cycle is equipped with a single-beam lamp, it shall be so aimed that when the vehicle is loaded none of the high intensity portion of light, at a distance of 25 feet ahead, shall project higher than the level of the center of the lamp from which it comes. *(Stats.1959, c. 3, p. 1727, § 25651. Amended by Stats.1959, c. 1996, p. 4635, § 35.)*

Cross References

Alternate acetylene lamps, see Vehicle Code § 25451.
Darkness defined, see Vehicle Code § 280.
Headlamps on motorcycles, see Vehicle Code §§ 25650, 25650.5.
Lighting equipment on motor-driven cycles, see Vehicle Code § 25803.
Motorcycle and motor-driven cycle defined, see Vehicle Code §§ 400, 405.
Rules governing color of lamps and reflectors, see Vehicle Code § 25950.
Test and approval of lamps, lamp equipment and signal devices, see Vehicle Code § 26100 et seq.
Time when vehicles are to be equipped with lighted lamps, see Vehicle Code § 24250.
Use of single and multiple beam lighting equipment, see Vehicle Code §§ 24409, 24410.

§ 25652. Repealed by Stats.1963, c. 479, p. 1338, § 3

ARTICLE 14. VEHICLES EXEMPTED

Section
25800.　Special mobile equipment.
25801.　Special construction and maintenance equipment.
25802.　Vehicles incidentally operated over highway.
25803.　Lamps on other vehicles.
25804.　Historical vehicles' lighting equipment.
25805.　Lamps on forklift trucks.
25806.　Ambulances or firetrucks; warning lamps and sirens.

§ 25800. Special mobile equipment

The provisions of Sections 24012, 24250, 24251, 24400 to 24404, inclusive, and Articles 3 (commencing with Section 24600), 4 (commencing with Section 24800), 5 (commencing with Section 24950), 6 (commencing with Section 25100), 9 (commencing with Section 25350), 11 (commencing with Section 25450), and 13 (commencing with Section 25650), shall not apply to special mobile equipment. Such equipment shall be subject to the provisions of Sections 24254, 25803, and 25950, and Article 12 (commencing with Section 25500). *(Stats. 1959, c. 3, p. 1728, § 25800. Amended by Stats.1959, c. 1996, p. 4635, § 36; Stats.1963, c. 2149, p. 4487, § 15; Stats.1972, c. 618, p. 1150, § 147.)*

Cross References

Implements of husbandry defined, see Vehicle Code § 36000.
Special mobile equipment defined, see Vehicle Code § 575.

§ 25801. Special construction and maintenance equipment

The provisions of Sections 24012, 24250, 24251, 24254, 24400 to 24404, inclusive, 24600 to 24604, inclusive, 24606 to 24610, inclusive, Section 25950, and Articles 4 (commencing with Section 24800), 5 (commencing with Section 24950), 6 (commencing with Section 25100), 9 (commencing with Section 25350), 11 (commencing with Section 25450), 12 (commencing with Section 25500), and 13 (commencing with Section 25650) and shall not apply to special construction or maintenance equipment, nor to motortrucks equipped with snow removal or sanding devices, but shall apply to motortrucks and automobiles used independently of such equipment.

The provisions of Section 25803 shall be applicable to such equipment. *(Stats.1959, c. 3, p. 1728, § 25801. Amended by Stats.1961, c. 1659, p. 3627, § 9; Stats.1972, c. 618, p. 1150, § 148.)*

Cross References

Special construction equipment defined, see Vehicle Code § 565.
Vehicles with unlawful lights, see Vehicle Code § 24003.

§ 25802. Vehicles incidentally operated over highway

Sections 24002, 24005, 24012, 24250, 24251, 24400 to 24404, inclusive, 24600 to 24604, inclusive, 24606 to 24610, inclusive, Article 4 (commencing with Section 24800), Article 5 (commencing with Section 24950), Article 6 (commencing with Section 25100), Article 9 (commencing with Section 25350), Article 11 (commencing with Section 25450), and Article 13 (commencing with Section 25650) of Chapter 2 of this division, Chapter 3 (commencing with Section 26301), Chapter 4 (commencing with Section 26700), and Chapter 5 (commencing with Section 27000) of this division, and Chapter 2 (commencing with Section 29200), Chapter 3 (commencing with Section 29800), Chapter 4 (commencing with Section 30800), and Chapter 5 (commencing with Section 31301) of Division 13 do not apply to logging vehicles or any vehicle of a type subject to registration under this code that is not designed, used, or maintained for the transportation of persons or property and that is operated or moved over a highway only incidentally; but any such vehicle shall be subject to Sections 2800, 2806, 24004, 25260, 25803, 25950, 25952, 26457, 27454, 27602, 31500, and 40150, and to Article 12 (commencing with Section 25500) of Chapter 2 of this division. *(Stats.1959, c. 3, p. 1728, § 25802. Amended by Stats.1961, c. 119, p. 1129, § 1; Stats.1970, c. 923, p. 1677, § 7; Stats.1975, c. 517, p. 1083, § 5; Stats.1979, c. 373, p. 1384, § 326; Stats.1996, c. 124 (A.B.3470), § 133.)*

§ 25803. Lamps on other vehicles

(a) All vehicles not otherwise required to be equipped with headlamps, rear lights, or reflectors by this chapter shall, if operated on a highway during darkness, be equipped with a lamp exhibiting a red light visible from a distance of 500 feet to the rear of the vehicle. In addition, all of these vehicles operated alone or as the first vehicle in a combination of vehicles, shall be equipped with at least one lighted lamp exhibiting a white light visible from a distance of 500 feet to the front of the vehicle.

(b) A vehicle shall also be equipped with an amber reflector on the front near the left side and a red reflector on the rear near the left side. The reflectors shall be mounted on the vehicle not lower than 16 inches nor higher than 60 inches above the ground and so designed and maintained as to be visible during darkness from all distances within 500 feet from the vehicle when directly in front of a motor vehicle displaying lawful lighted headlamps undimmed.

(c) In addition, if a vehicle described in subdivision (a) or the load thereon has a total outside width in excess of 100 inches there shall be displayed during darkness at the left outer extremity at least one amber light visible under normal atmospheric conditions from a distance of 500 feet to the front, sides, and rear. At all other times there shall be displayed at the left outer extremity a solid red or fluorescent orange flag or cloth not less than 12 inches square. *(Stats.1959, c. 3, p. 1728, § 25803. Amended by Stats.1959, c. 958, p. 2988, § 1; Stats.1978, c. 252, p. 535, § 8, eff. June 16, 1978; Stats.1998, c. 828 (S.B.1637), § 21; Stats.2004, c. 183 (A.B.3082), § 354.)*

Cross References

Approval of modifying devices, see Vehicle Code § 26101.
Implements of husbandry, application of this section, see Vehicle Code § 36500.
Mounting height of lamps and reflectors, see Vehicle Code § 24254.
Rear lighting equipment, see Vehicle Code § 24600 et seq.
Reflectorizing material, see Vehicle Code § 25500.
Regulations governing color of lamps and reflectors, see Vehicle Code § 25256 et seq.
Special mobile equipment, applicability of this section, see Vehicle Code § 25800.
Test and approval of lamps, lamp equipment and signal devices, see Vehicle Code § 26100 et seq.

§ 25804. Historical vehicles' lighting equipment

Notwithstanding any other provision of this code, original lighting equipment installed on a vehicle manu-factured prior to January 1, 1946, need not meet the requirements established by the department when the vehicle is used primarily for the purpose of historical exhibition. *(Added by Stats.1967, c. 594, p. 1938, § 1. Amended by Stats.1973, c. 706, p. 1283, § 1; Stats.1979, c. 723, p. 2222, § 24.)*

Cross References

Lighting equipment defined, see Vehicle Code § 375.

§ 25805. Lamps on forklift trucks

Notwithstanding any other provision of this article, a forklift truck which is towed upon the highway at the end of a combination of vehicles shall at all times be equipped with at least one stop lamp mounted upon the rear of the vehicle and shall be equipped with lamp-type turn signals. Such vehicle shall, during the hours of darkness, be equipped with at least one taillamp and one red reflector mounted upon the rear of the vehicle and shall be equipped with clearance lamps if the vehicle is 80 or more inches in width. *(Added by Stats.1969, c. 132, p. 283, § 1.)*

§ 25806. Ambulances or firetrucks; warning lamps and sirens

Sections 24003 and 27002 shall not apply to the installation of warning lamps and sirens on ambulances or firetrucks which are used solely for demonstration purposes in the sales work of a licensed dealer, distributor, or vehicle manufacturer and shall not apply to ambulances or firetrucks being operated on a highway solely for the purpose of delivery from the licensee to a purchaser. Warning lamps shall be removed or covered with opaque material and the siren controls disabled whenever the vehicle is upon a highway. *(Added by Stats.1982, c. 217, p. 731, § 1.)*

ARTICLE 15. LIGHT RESTRICTIONS AND MOUNTING

Section
25950. Color of lamps and reflectors; infrared region of electromagnetic spectrum.
25951. Direction of beam.
25952. Lamps and reflectors on loads.
25953. Renumbered.

§ 25950. Color of lamps and reflectors; infrared region of electromagnetic spectrum

This section applies to the color of lamps and to any reflector exhibiting or reflecting perceptible light of 0.05 candela or more per foot-candle of incident illumination. Unless provided otherwise, the color of lamps and reflectors upon a vehicle shall be as follows:

(a) The emitted light from all lamps and the reflected light from all reflectors, visible from in front of a vehicle, shall be white or yellow, except as follows:

(1) Rear side marker lamps required by Section 25100 may show red to the front.

831

(2) The color of foglamps described in Section 24403 may be in the color spectrum from white to yellow.

(3) An illuminating device, as permitted under Section 24255, shall emit radiation predominantly in the infrared region of the electromagnetic spectrum. Any incidental visible light projecting to the front of the vehicle shall be predominantly yellow to white. Any incidental visible light projecting to the rear of the vehicle shall be predominantly red. Any incidental visible light from an illuminating device, as permitted under Section 24255, shall not resemble any other required or permitted lighting device or official traffic control device.

(b) The emitted light from all lamps and the reflected light from all reflectors, visible from the rear of a vehicle, shall be red except as follows:

(1) Stoplamps on vehicles manufactured before January 1, 1979, may show yellow to the rear.

(2) Turn signal lamps may show yellow to the rear.

(3) Front side marker lamps required by Section 25100 may show yellow to the rear.

(4) Backup lamps shall show white to the rear.

(5) The rearward facing portion of a front-mounted double- faced turn signal lamp may show amber to the rear while the headlamps or parking lamps are lighted, if the intensity of the light emitted is not greater than the parking lamps and the turn signal function is not impaired.

(6) A reflector meeting the requirements of, and installed in accordance with, Section 24611 shall be red or white, or both.

(c) All lamps and reflectors visible from the front, sides, or rear of a vehicle, except headlamps, may have any unlighted color, provided the emitted light from all lamps or reflected light from all reflectors complies with the required color. Except for backup lamps, the entire effective projected luminous area of lamps visible from the rear or mounted on the sides near the rear of a vehicle shall be covered by an inner lens of the required color when the unlighted color differs from the required emitted light color. Taillamps, stoplamps, and turn signal lamps that are visible to the rear may be white when unlighted on vehicles manufactured before January 1, 1974. *(Added by Stats.1979, c. 723, p. 2222, § 24.5. Amended by Stats.1980, c. 399, p. 784, § 7, eff. July 11, 1980; Stats.1994, c. 1220 (A.B.3132), § 66, eff. Sept. 30, 1994; Stats.1995, c. 766 (S.B.726), § 38; Stats.2004, c. 198 (S.B.1236), § 4.)*

Cross References

Illuminated signs on buses, see Vehicle Code § 25353.
Implements of husbandry, applicability of this section, see Vehicle Code § 36500.
Special construction and maintenance equipment, applicability of this section, see Vehicle Code § 25801.
Special mobile equipment, applicability of this section, see Vehicle Code § 25800.

University of California Irvine's public transport system, illuminated signs displaying advertisements, conditions, see Vehicle Code § 25354.
Vehicles incidentally operated over highway, applicability of this section, see Vehicle Code § 25802.

§ 25951. Direction of beam

Any lighted lamp or device upon a motor vehicle other than headlamps, spotlamps, signal lamps, or auxiliary driving lamps, warning lamps which projects a beam of light of an intensity greater than 300 candlepower shall be so directed that no part of the beam will strike the level of the roadway at a distance of more than 75 feet from the vehicle. *(Stats.1959, c. 3, p. 1729, § 25951. Amended by Stats.1965, c. 1313, p. 3203, § 12.)*

§ 25952. Lamps and reflectors on loads

(a) Lamps, reflectors, and area reflectorizing material of a type required or permitted on a vehicle may be mounted on a load carried by the vehicle in lieu of, or in addition to, such equipment on the vehicle. Such equipment shall be mounted on the load in a manner that would comply with the requirements of this code and regulations adopted pursuant to this code if the load were an integral part of the vehicle.

(b) Lamps on vehicles carried as a load shall not be lighted unless such lamps are mounted in accordance with subdivision (a). *(Added by Stats.1969, c. 341, p. 716, § 6.)*

Cross References

Vehicles incidentally operated over highway applicability of this section, see Vehicle Code § 25802.

§ 25953. Renumbered § 24012 and amended by Stats. 1969, c. 341, p. 717, § 7

ARTICLE 16. EQUIPMENT TESTING

Section
26100. Lighting equipment, safety glazing material, or other device not in compliance with testing requirements; sale or use prohibited; exception.
26101. Device intended to modify lighting equipment, safety glazing material, or other device not in compliance with testing requirements; sale or use prohibited; exception.
26102. Subsequent regulations; application to equipment installed after effective date.
26103. Standards and specifications; regulations; adoption and enforcement; pre-emption of federal standards.
26104. Tests; necessity prior to sale; proof of compliance with standards.
26105. Purchase and test by department.
26106. Permit for experimental purposes.
26107 to 26119. Repealed.

§ 26100. Lighting equipment, safety glazing material, or other device not in compliance with testing requirements; sale or use prohibited; exception

(a) A person shall not sell or offer for sale for use upon or as part of the equipment of a vehicle any lighting equipment, safety glazing material, or other device that does not meet the provisions of Section 26104.

(b) A person shall not use upon a vehicle, and a person shall not drive a vehicle upon a highway that is equipped with, any lighting equipment, safety glazing material, or other device that is not in compliance with Section 26104.

(c) This section does not apply to a taillamp or stop lamp in use on or prior to December 1, 1935. *(Added by Stats.1979, c. 723, p. 2223, § 26. Amended by Stats.2010, c. 491 (S.B.1318), § 44.)*

Cross References

Lighting equipment,
   Defined, see Vehicle Code § 375.
   Requirements, see Vehicle Code § 24250 et seq.
Method of signalling, see Vehicle Code § 22110.
Safety glazing material defined, see Vehicle Code § 535.
Vehicle defined, see Vehicle Code § 670.

§ 26101. Device intended to modify lighting equipment, safety glazing material, or other device not in compliance with testing requirements; sale or use prohibited; exception

(a) A person shall not sell or offer for sale for use upon or as part of the equipment of a vehicle any device that is intended to modify the original design or performance of any lighting equipment, safety glazing material, or other device, unless the modifying device meets the provisions of Section 26104.

(b) A person shall not use upon a vehicle, and a person shall not drive a vehicle upon a highway that has installed a device that is intended to modify the original design or performance of a lighting, safety glazing material, or other device, unless the modifying device complies with Section 26104.

(c) This section does not apply to a taillamp or stop lamp in use on or prior to December 1, 1935, or to lamps installed on authorized emergency vehicles. *(Added by Stats.1979, c. 723, p. 2223, § 26. Amended by Stats.1997, c. 945 (A.B.1561), § 26; Stats.2010, c. 491 (S.B.1318), § 45.)*

Cross References

Lighting equipment,
   Generally, see Vehicle Code § 24250 et seq.
   Defined, see Vehicle Code § 375.
Safety glazing material defined, see Vehicle Code § 535.

§ 26102. Subsequent regulations; application to equipment installed after effective date

In the event any equipment in actual use meets the requirements of this code or a department regulation adopted pursuant to this code, a subsequent regulation shall not require the replacement of the equipment and shall be applicable only to equipment installed after the effective date of the regulation. *(Added by Stats.1979, c. 723, p. 2223, § 26.)*

§ 26103. Standards and specifications; regulations; adoption and enforcement; pre-emption of federal standards

(a) The department may adopt and enforce regulations establishing standards and specifications for lighting equipment listed in Section 375 and for safety belts, safety glazing material, safety helmets, sirens, tire traction devices, bunk stakes, and synthetic binders. The standards and specifications may include installation and aiming requirements.

(b) If there exists a Federal Motor Vehicle Safety Standard adopted pursuant to the National Traffic and Motor Vehicle Safety Act of 1966 (15 U.S.C. 1381 et seq.) covering the same aspect of performance of a device, the provisions of that standard shall prevail over provisions of this code or regulations adopted pursuant to this code. Lamps, devices, and equipment certified by the manufacturer to meet applicable federal motor vehicle safety standards as original equipment on new vehicles and the identical replacements for those items need not be certified to the department. *(Added by Stats.1979, c. 723, p. 2223, § 26. Amended by Stats.1990, c. 71 (A.B.2498), § 2, eff. May 1, 1990.)*

Cross References

Department of the California highway patrol, see Vehicle Code § 2100 et seq.
Safety glazing material defined, see Vehicle Code § 535.
Tire traction devices defined, see Vehicle Code § 605.

§ 26104. Tests; necessity prior to sale; proof of compliance with standards

(a) Every manufacturer who sells, offers for sale, or manufactures for use upon a vehicle devices subject to requirements established by the department shall, before the device is offered for sale, have laboratory test data showing compliance with such requirements. Tests may be conducted by the manufacturer.

(b) The department may at any time request from the manufacturer a copy of the test data showing proof of compliance of any device with the requirements established by the department and additional evidence that due care was exercised in maintaining compliance during production. If the manufacturer fails to provide such proof of compliance within 30 days of notice from the department, the department may prohibit the sale of the device in this state until acceptable proof of compliance is received by the department. *(Added by Stats.1979, c. 723, p. 2223, § 26. Amended by Stats.1980, c. 399, p. 784, § 8, eff. July 11, 1980.)*

Cross References

Device modifying lighting equipment, safety glazing, or other device that is not in compliance with section, sale or use, see Vehicle Code § 26101.
Lighting equipment defined, see Vehicle Code § 375.
Lighting equipment, safety glazing, or other device that is not in compliance with section, sale or use, see Vehicle Code § 26100.

§ 26105. Purchase and test by department

The department may purchase any equipment sold for use on vehicles and test or retest the same as to conformance with the requirements of this code and department regulations adopted pursuant to this code and any expense incurred in such purchase and test shall be a legal charge against the Motor Vehicle Fund. *(Added by Stats.1979, c. 723, p. 2223, § 26.)*

§ 26106. Permit for experimental purposes

The department may issue a permit for the use of equipment for experimental purposes. The use of such equipment under the permit is not a violation of this code. *(Added by Stats.1979, c. 723, p. 2223, § 26.)*

§§ 26107 to 26119. Repealed by Stats.1979, c. 723, p. 2223, § 25

CHAPTER 3. BRAKES

Article	Section
1. Brake Requirements	26300
2. Operation of Brakes	26450
3. Airbrakes	26500
4. Vacuum Brakes	26520

ARTICLE 1. BRAKE REQUIREMENTS

Section
26300.   Repealed.
26301.   Motor vehicles over seven tons.
26301.5. Emergency brake systems.
26302.   Trailers.
26303.   Trailer coaches and camp trailers.
26304.   Breakaway brakes.
26305.   Auxiliary or tow dollies.
26306.   Repealed.
26307.   Forklift truck brakes.
26308 to 26310.   Repealed.
26311.   Service brakes on all wheels.

§ 26300. Repealed by Stats.1965, c. 443, p. 1750, § 1

§ 26301. Motor vehicles over seven tons

Any motor vehicle first registered in this state after January 1, 1940, shall be equipped with power brakes if its gross weight exceeds 14,000 pounds, except that any such vehicle having a gross weight of less than 18,000 pounds may, in lieu of power brakes, be equipped with two-stage hydraulic actuators of a type designed to increase braking effect of its brakes. *(Stats.1959, c. 3, p.*

834

1733, § 26301.   Amended by Stats.1982, c. 789, p. 3057, § 1.)

§ 26301.5. Emergency brake systems

Every passenger vehicle manufactured and first registered after January 1, 1973, except motorcycles, shall be equipped with an emergency brake system so constructed that rupture or leakage-type failure of any single pressure component of the service brake system, except structural failures of the brake master cylinder body or effectiveness indicator body, shall not result in complete loss of function of the vehicle's brakes when force on the brake pedal is continued. *(Added by Stats.1971, c. 1110, p. 2123, § 1, operative May 3, 1972.)*

§ 26302. Trailers

(a) Every trailer or semitrailer, manufactured and first registered after January 1, 1940, and having a gross weight of 6,000 pounds or more and which is operated at a speed of 20 miles per hour or over shall be equipped with brakes.

(b) Every trailer or semitrailer manufactured and first registered after January 1, 1966, and having a gross weight of 3,000 pounds or more shall be equipped with brakes on at least two wheels.

(c) Every trailer or semitrailer manufactured after January 1, 1982, and equipped with air brakes shall be equipped with brakes on all wheels.

(d) Brakes required on trailers or semitrailers shall be adequate, supplemental to the brakes on the towing vehicle, to enable the combination of vehicles to comply with the stopping distance requirements of Section 26454.

(e) The provisions of this section shall not apply to any vehicle being used to support the boom or mast attached to a mobile crane or shovel. *(Stats.1959, c. 3, p. 1733, § 26302.   Amended by Stats.1965, c. 444, p. 1752, § 1; Stats.1967, c. 373, p. 1600, § 1; Stats.1981, c. 774, p. 3024, § 6.)*

§ 26303. Trailer coaches and camp trailers

Every trailer coach and every camp trailer having a gross weight of 1,500 pounds or more, but exclusive of passengers, shall be equipped with brakes on at least two wheels which are adequate, supplemental to the brakes on the towing vehicle, to enable the combination of vehicles to comply with the stopping distance requirements of Section 26454. *(Stats.1959, c. 3, p. 1733, § 26303. Amended by Stats.1961, c. 409, p. 946, § 1; Stats.1965, c. 444, p. 1752, § 2; Stats.1971, c. 1536, p. 3044, § 8, operative May 3, 1972.)*

Cross References

Camp trailer defined, see Vehicle Code § 242.
Trailer coach defined, see Vehicle Code § 635.

§ 26304. Breakaway brakes

(a) Power brakes on any trailer or semitrailer manufactured after December 31, 1955, operated over public highways and required to be equipped with brakes shall be designed to be automatically applied upon breakaway from the towing vehicle and shall be capable of stopping and holding such vehicle stationary for not less than 15 minutes.

(b) Every new truck or truck tractor manufactured after December 31, 1955, operated over public highways and used in towing a vehicle shall be equipped with service brakes capable of stopping the truck or truck tractor in the event of breakaway of the towed vehicle. *(Stats.1959, c. 3, p. 1733, § 26304. Amended by Stats. 1963, c. 208, p. 946, § 1; Stats.1972, c. 733, p. 1323, § 1.)*

Cross References

Definitions,
  Power brakes, see Vehicle Code § 480.
  Semitrailer defined, see Vehicle Code § 550.
  Trailer defined, see Vehicle Code § 630.
  Truck tractor, see Vehicle Code § 655.

§ 26305. Auxiliary or tow dollies

Any auxiliary dolly or tow dolly may be equipped with brakes. *(Stats.1959, c. 3, p. 1733, § 26305. Amended by Stats.1983, c. 708, § 9.)*

Cross References

Auxiliary dolly defined, see Vehicle Code § 225.

§ 26306. Repealed by Stats.1965, c. 439, p. 1748, § 1

§ 26307. Forklift truck brakes

No forklift truck manufactured after January 1, 1970, shall be towed behind another vehicle unless it is equipped with brakes on the wheels of the rearmost axle when the forklift truck is in the towing position, which brakes shall be adequate, supplemental to the brakes on the towing vehicle, to enable the combination of vehicles to comply with the stopping distance requirements of Section 26454. *(Added by Stats.1969, c. 132, p. 283, § 2.)*

§§ 26308 to 26310. Repealed by Stats.1963, c. 496, p. 1351, § 1; Stats.1967, c. 411, p. 1630, §§ 2, 3

§ 26311. Service brakes on all wheels

(a) Every motor vehicle shall be equipped with service brakes on all wheels, except as follows:

(1) Trucks and truck tractors manufactured before January 1, 1982, having three or more axles need not have brakes on the front wheels, except when such vehicles are equipped with at least two steerable axles, the wheels of one such axle need not be equipped with brakes.

(2) Any vehicle being towed in a driveaway-towaway operation.

(3) Any vehicle manufactured prior to 1930.

(4) Any two-axle truck tractor manufactured prior to 1964.

(5) Any sidecar attached to a motorcycle.

(6) Any motorcycle manufactured prior to 1966. Such motorcycle shall be equipped with brakes on at least one wheel.

(b) Any bus, truck, or truck tractor may be equipped with a manual or automatic means for reducing the braking effort on the front wheels. The manual means shall be used only when operating under adverse road conditions, such as wet, snowy, or icy roads.

(c) Vehicles and combinations of vehicles exempted in subdivisions (a) and (b) from the requirements of brakes on all wheels shall comply with the stopping distance requirements of Section 26454. *(Added by Stats.1963, c. 208, p. 947, § 2. Amended by Stats.1965, c. 439, p. 1748, § 2; Stats.1981, c. 774, p. 3025, § 7.)*

Cross References

Definitions,
  Motor vehicle, see Vehicle Code § 415.
  Motorcycle, see Vehicle Code § 400.
Operation of brakes, requirements, see Vehicle Code § 26450.

ARTICLE 2. OPERATION OF BRAKES

Section
26450. Required brake system.
26451. Parking brake system.
26452. Brakes after engine failure.
26453. Conditions of brakes.
26454. Control and stopping requirements.
26455. Determination of vehicle weight.
26456. Stopping tests.
26457. Exemptions.
26458. Power brake; single control.
26458.5. Trailers; use of additional brake control.

Cross References

Brake requirements of trailers, see Vehicle Code § 26302.
Brakes on trailer coaches, and camp trailers, see Vehicle Code § 26303.
Breakaway brakes, see Vehicle Code § 26304.
Cotton module movers, operation on state highways, conditions, see Vehicle Code § 35555.
Dealer's responsibility, see Vehicle Code § 24007.
Forklift truck brakes, see Vehicle Code § 26307.
Service brakes on all wheels, see Vehicle Code § 26311.

§ 26450. Required brake system

Every motor vehicle shall be equipped with a service brake system and every motor vehicle, other than a motorcycle, shall be equipped with a parking brake

835

system. Both the service brake and parking brake shall be separately applied.

If the two systems are connected in any way, they shall be so constructed that failure of any one part, except failure in the drums, brakeshoes, or other mechanical parts of the wheel brake assemblies, shall not leave the motor vehicle without operative brakes. *(Stats.1959, c. 3, p. 1734, § 26450. Amended by Stats.1963, c. 208, p. 947, § 3; Stats.1965, c. 443, p. 1750, § 2; Stats.1967, c. 369, p. 1597, § 1.)*

§ 26451. Parking brake system

The parking brake system of every motor vehicle shall comply with the following requirements:

(a) The parking brake shall be adequate to hold the vehicle or combination of vehicles stationary on any grade on which it is operated under all conditions of loading on a surface free from snow, ice or loose material. In any event the parking brake shall be capable of locking the braked wheels to the limit of traction.

(b) The parking brake shall be applied either by the driver's muscular efforts, by spring action, or by other energy which is isolated and used exclusively for the operation of the parking brake or the combination parking brake and emergency stopping system.

(c) The parking brake shall be held in the applied position solely by mechanical means. *(Stats.1959, c. 3, p. 1734, § 26451. Amended by Stats.1963, c. 208, p. 947, § 4; Stats.1965, c. 443, p. 1751, § 3; Stats.1967, c. 1427, p. 3355, § 1; Stats.1981, c. 774, p. 3025, § 8.)*

§ 26452. Brakes after engine failure

All motor vehicles shall be so equipped as to permit application of the brakes at least once for the purpose of bringing the vehicle to a stop within the legal stopping distance after the engine has become inoperative. *(Stats. 1959, c. 3, p. 1734, § 26452.)*

Cross References

Stopping distance requirements, see Vehicle Code § 26454.

§ 26453. Conditions of brakes

All brakes and component parts thereof shall be maintained in good condition and in good working order. The brakes shall be so adjusted as to operate as equally as practicable with respect to the wheels on opposite sides of the vehicle. *(Stats.1959 c. 3, p. 1734, § 26453. Amended by Stats.1959, c. 675, p. 2646, § 1; Stats.1959, c. 2183, p. 5307, § 1.)*

§ 26454. Control and stopping requirements

(a) The service brakes of every motor vehicle or combination of vehicles shall be adequate to control the movement of and to stop and hold such vehicle or combination of vehicles under all conditions of loading on any grade on which it is operated.

(b) Every motor vehicle or combination of vehicles, at any time and under all conditions of loading, shall, upon application of the service brake, be capable of stopping from an initial speed of 20 miles per hour according to the following requirements:

	Maximum Stopping Distance (feet)
(1) Any passenger vehicle	25
(2) Any single motor vehicle with a manufacturer's gross vehicle weight rating of less than 10,000 lbs.	30
(3) Any combination of vehicles consisting of a passenger vehicle or any motor vehicle with a manufacturer's gross vehicle weight rating of less than 10,000 lbs. in combination with any trailer, semitrailer or trailer coach	40
(4) Any single motor vehicle with a manufacturer's gross vehicle weight rating of 10,000 lbs. or more or any bus	40
(5) All other combinations of vehicles	50

(Stats.1959, c. 3, p. 1734, § 26454. Amended by Stats. 1965, c. 443, p. 1751, § 4.)

Cross References

Definitions,
  Motor vehicle, see Vehicle Code § 415.
  Semitrailer, see Vehicle Code § 550.
  Trailer, see Vehicle Code § 630.
  Trailer coach, see Vehicle Code § 635.
  Vehicle, see Vehicle Code § 670.
Implements of husbandry, nonapplicability of section, see Vehicle Code § 36510.

§ 26455. Determination of vehicle weight

In respect to any motor vehicle designed, used or maintained primarily for the transportation of property which is not equipped with a plate or marker showing the manufacturer's gross vehicle weight rating, for purposes of stopping distance requirements, the weight of a vehicle shall be determined as follows:

(a) Any motor vehicle having less than six wheels is the equivalent of a vehicle having a manufacturer's gross vehicle weight rating of less than 10,000 pounds.

(b) Any motor vehicle having six wheels or more is the equivalent of a vehicle having a manufacturer's gross vehicle weight rating of 10,000 pounds or more. *(Stats. 1959, c. 3, p. 1735, § 26455.)*

§ 26456. Stopping tests

Stopping distance requirement tests shall be conducted on a substantially level, dry, smooth, hard-surfaced road that is free from loose material and where the grade does not exceed plus or minus 1 percent. Stopping distance shall be measured from the instant brake controls are moved and from an initial speed of approximately 20 miles per hour. No test of brake performance shall be made upon a highway at a speed in excess of 25 miles per hour. *(Stats.1959, c. 3, p. 1735, § 26456.)*

§ 26457. Exemptions

Special mobile equipment, logging vehicles, equipment operated under special permit, and any chassis without body or load are not subject to stopping distance requirements, but if any such vehicle or equipment cannot be stopped within 32 feet from an initial speed of 15 miles per hour, it shall not be operated at a speed in excess of that permitting a stop in 32 feet. *(Stats.1959, c. 3, p. 1735, § 26457. Amended by Stats.1963, c. 2149, p. 4488, § 17; Stats.1975, c. 517, p. 1083, § 6.)*

Cross References

Special mobile equipment defined, see Vehicle Code § 575.
Vehicles incidentally operated over highway, applicability of this section, see Vehicle Code § 25802.

§ 26458. Power brake; single control

(a) The braking system on every motor vehicle used to tow another vehicle shall be so arranged that one control on the towing vehicle shall, when applied, operate all the service brakes on the power unit and combination of vehicles when either or both of the following conditions exist:

(1) The towing vehicle is required to be equipped with power brakes.

(2) The towed vehicle is required to be equipped with brakes and is equipped with power brakes.

(b) Subdivision (a) shall not be construed to prohibit motor vehicles from being equipped with an additional control to be used to operate the brakes on the trailer or trailers.

(c) Subdivision (a) does not apply to any of the following combinations of vehicles, if the combination of vehicles meets the stopping distance requirements of Section 26454:

(1) Vehicles engaged in driveaway-towaway operations.

(2) Disabled vehicles, while being towed.

(3) Towed motor vehicles.

(4) Trailers equipped with inertially controlled brakes which are designed to be applied automatically upon breakaway from the towing vehicle and which are capable of stopping and holding the trailer stationary for not less than 15 minutes. *(Added by Stats.1963, c. 207, p. 946, § 2. Amended by Stats.1965, c. 186, p. 1152, § 2; Stats.1975, c. 397, p. 874, § 1; Stats.1991, c. 121 (A.B. 430), § 1.)*

Cross References

Driveaway—towaway operation defined, see Vehicle Code § 303.
Power brake, see Vehicle Code § 480.

§ 26458.5. Trailers; use of additional brake control

Pursuant to Section 26458, whenever a motor vehicle is equipped with an additional control to operate the brakes on a trailer, that control shall not be used in lieu of the service brake control, except in the case of failure of the service brake system. *(Added by Stats.1989, c. 316, § 1.)*

ARTICLE 3. AIRBRAKES

Section
26500. Repealed.
26502. Adjustment and use of special devices.
26503. Safety valve.
26504. Air governor.
26505. Pressure gauge.
26506. Warning device.
26507. Check valve.
26508. Emergency stopping system.

Cross References

Cotton module movers, operation on state highways, conditions, see Vehicle Code § 35555.

§ 26500. Repealed by Stats.1963, c. 207, p. 946, § 3

§ 26502. Adjustment and use of special devices

(a) Airbrakes of every motor vehicle and combination of vehicles shall be so adjusted and maintained as to be capable of providing full service brake application at all times except as provided in subdivision (b) of Section 26311. A full service brake application shall deliver to all brake chambers not less than 90 percent of the air reservoir pressure remaining with the brakes applied.

(b) The department may by regulation authorize the use of special devices or systems to automatically reduce the maximum air pressure delivered to the brake chambers in order to compensate for load variation and to obtain balanced braking. Permitted systems shall be of the fail safe type and shall not increase the vehicle stopping distance. *(Added by Stats.1965, c. 1789, p. 4126, § 2.)*

§ 26503. Safety valve

Every motor vehicle equipped with airbrakes or equipped to operate airbrakes on towed vehicles shall be equipped with a standard type safety valve which shall be installed so as to have an uninterrupted connection with the air reservoir or tank. It shall be adjusted and maintained so that it will open and discharge the air system under any condition at a pressure of not to exceed 150 pounds per square inch and close and reseat itself at a point above the maximum air governor setting. The department may by regulation prescribe a higher maximum opening pressure for air pressure systems designed for, and capable of safely operating with, pressure safety valves with a higher opening pressure. *(Added by Stats. 1959, c. 455, p. 2392, § 1. Amended by Stats.1963, c. 207, p. 946, § 4; Stats.1965, c. 186, p. 1152, § 3; Stats.1967, c. 1578, p. 3780, § 1.)*

Cross References

Emergency stopping system, see Vehicle Code § 26508.

§ 26504. Air governor

The air governor cut-in and cut-out pressures of every motor vehicle equipped with airbrakes or equipped to operate airbrakes on towed vehicles shall be adjusted so that the maximum pressure in the air system and the minimum cut-in pressure shall be within limits prescribed by the department. In adopting regulations specifying such pressures the department shall consider the safe operating capacities of the various airbrake systems which are now or may be used on motor vehicles and shall be guided by the designed capabilities of those systems. *(Added by Stats.1959, c. 740, p. 2729, § 1. Amended by Stats.1967, c. 1578, p. 3780, § 2.)*

§ 26505. Pressure gauge

A motor vehicle equipped with airbrakes or equipped to operate airbrakes on towed vehicles shall be equipped with a pressure gauge of reliable and satisfactory construction and maintained in an efficient working condition, accurate within 10 percent of the actual air reservoir pressure, and visible and legible to a person when seated in the driving position. *(Added by Stats.1959, c. 454, p. 2392, § 1, operative Jan. 1, 1960. Amended by Stats.1961, c. 48, p. 988, § 1; Stats.1967, c. 1578, p. 3780, § 3; Stats.2010, c. 491 (S.B.1318), § 46.)*

§ 26506. Warning device

(a) Every motor vehicle airbrake system used to operate the brakes on a motor vehicle or on a towed vehicle shall be equipped with a low air pressure warning device that complies with either the requirements set forth in the Federal Motor Vehicle Safety Standards in effect at the time of manufacture or the requirements of subdivision (b).

(b) The device shall be readily visible or audible to the driver and shall give a satisfactory continuous warning when the air supply pressure drops below a fixed pressure, which shall be not more than 75 pounds per square inch nor less than 55 pounds per square inch with the engine running. A gauge indicating pressure shall not satisfy this requirement. *(Added by Stats.1959, c. 419, p. 2359, § 1, operative Jan. 1, 1960. Amended by Stats.1965, c. 440, p. 1748, § 1; Stats.1992, c. 1241 (S.B.1615), § 25.)*

§ 26507. Check valve

A check valve shall be installed and properly maintained in the air supply piping of every motor vehicle equipped with airbrakes, either between the air compressor and the first reservoir or tank immediately adjacent to the air intake of said reservoir, or between No. 1 reservoir (wet tank) and No. 2 reservoir (dry tank) immediately adjacent to the air intake of the No. 2 reservoir; provided, that the air supply for the brakes is not drawn from the No. 1 reservoir and that the No. 1 and No. 2 reservoirs are connected by only one pipeline. *(Added by Stats.1959, c. 510, p. 2473, § 2.)*

§ 26508. Emergency stopping system

Every vehicle or combination of vehicles using compressed air at the wheels for applying the service brakes shall be equipped with an emergency stopping system meeting the requirements of this section and capable of

838

stopping the vehicle or combination of vehicles in the event of failure in the service brake air system as follows:

(a) Every motor vehicle operated either singly or in a combination of vehicles and every towed vehicle shall be equipped with an emergency stopping system.

(b) Motor vehicles used to tow vehicles which use compressed air at the wheels for applying the service brakes shall be equipped with a device or devices with both a manual and automatic means of actuating the emergency stopping system on the towed vehicle as follows:

(1) The automatic device shall operate automatically in the event of reduction of the service brake air supply of the towing vehicle to a fixed pressure which shall be not lower than 20 pounds per square inch nor higher than 45 pounds per square inch.

(2) The manual device shall be readily operable by a person seated in the driver's seat, with its emergency position or method of operation clearly indicated. In no instance may the manual means be so arranged as to permit its use to prevent operation of the automatic means.

(c) Motor vehicles manufactured prior to 1964 shall be deemed to be in compliance with subdivisions (e) and (f) when equipped with axle-by-axle protected airbrakes using a separate air tank system for each of at least two axles, provided that each system independently meets all other requirements of this section. Each system shall be capable of being manually applied, released, and reapplied from the driver's seat but shall not be capable of being released from the driver's seat after any reapplication unless there is available a means which can be applied from the driver's seat to stop and hold the vehicle or combination of vehicles.

(d) Towed vehicles shall be deemed to be in compliance with this section when:

(1) The towed vehicle is equipped with a no-bleed-back relay-emergency valve or equivalent device, so designed that the supply reservoir used to provide air for the brakes is safeguarded against backflow of air from the reservoir through the supply line,

(2) The brakes are applied automatically and promptly upon breakaway from the towing vehicle and maintain application for at least 15 minutes, and

(3) The combination of vehicles is capable of stopping within the distance and under the conditions specified in subdivisions (k) and (*l*).

(e) If the service brake system and the emergency stopping system are connected in any way, they shall be so constructed that a failure or malfunction in any one part of either system, including brake chamber diaphragm failure but not including failure in the drums, brakeshoes, or other mechanical parts of the wheel brake assemblies, shall not leave the vehicle without one operative stopping system capable of complying with the performance requirements in subdivision (k).

(f) Every emergency stopping system shall be designed so that it is capable of being manually applied, released, and reapplied by a person seated in the driver's seat. The system shall be designed so that it cannot be released from the driver's seat after any reapplication unless immediate further application can be made from the driver's seat to stop and hold the vehicle or combination of vehicles. The emergency stopping system may also be applied automatically.

(g) No vehicle or combination of vehicles upon failure of the service brake air system shall be driven on a highway under its own power except to the extent necessary to move the vehicles off the roadway to the nearest place of safety.

(h) No vehicle or combination of vehicles shall be equipped with an emergency stopping system that creates a hazard on the highway, or increases the service brake stopping distance of a vehicle or combination of vehicles, or interferes in any way with the application of the service brakes on any vehicle or combination of vehicles.

(i) Any energy-storing device which is a part of the emergency stopping system shall be designed so that it is recharged or reset from the course of compressed air or other energy produced by the vehicle, except that energy to release the emergency stopping system may be produced by the driver's muscular effort from the driver's seat. No device shall be used which can be set to prevent automatic delivery of air to protected air supply reservoirs of motor vehicle emergency stopping systems when air is available in the service brake air supply system.

(j) Any vehicle manufactured on or after January 1, 1964, which uses axle-by-axle protected airbrakes as the emergency stopping system shall use a separate air tank system for each axle, except that motor vehicles equipped with a dual or tandem treadle valve system need have no more than two protected air tanks in such system, one for each valve.

(k) Every motor vehicle or combination of vehicles, at all times and under all conditions of loading, upon application of the emergency stopping system, shall be capable of:

(1) Developing a stopping force that is not less than the percentage of its gross weight tabulated herein for its classification.

(2) Decelerating in a stop from 20 miles per hour at not less than the feet per second per second tabulated herein for its classification, and

(3) Stopping from a speed of 20 miles per hour in not more than the distance tabulated herein for its classification, such distance to be measured from the point at which movement of the emergency stopping system control begins.

EMERGENCY STOPPING SYSTEM REQUIREMENTS

Classification of vehicle and combination of vehicles	Stopping force as a percentage of gross vehicle or combination weight	Deceleration in feet per second per second	Stopping distance in feet
A Single-motor vehicles	16.7	5.5	90
B Combination of vehicles	19.0	6.0	90
C Single-motor vehicle with 3 or more axles manufactured prior to 1964 . .	12.1	4.0	120

(*l*) Tests for deceleration and stopping distance shall be made on a substantially level, dry, smooth, hard surface that is free from loose material and where the grade does not exceed plus or minus 1 percent. No test of emergency stopping system performance shall be made upon a highway at a speed in excess of 25 miles per hour.

(m) The provisions of this section shall not apply to:

(1) Auxiliary dollies, special mobile equipment, or special construction equipment.

(2) Motor vehicles which are operated in a driveaway-towaway operation and not registered in this state.

(3) Disabled vehicles when being towed.

(4) Vehicles which are operated under a one-trip permit as provided in Section 4003.

(5) Vehicles which because of unladen width, length, height or weight may not be moved upon the highway without the permit specified in Section 35780.

(n) The emergency stopping system requirements specified in subdivision (k) shall not apply to a vehicle or combination of vehicles being operated under a special weight permit nor to any overweight authorized emergency vehicle operated under the provisions of Section 35002.

(*o*) Every owner or lessee shall instruct and require that the driver be thoroughly familiar with the requirements of this section. The driver of a vehicle or combination of vehicles required to comply with the requirements of this section shall be able to demonstrate the application and release of the emergency system on the vehicle and each vehicle in the combination. (*Added by Stats.1963, c. 496, p. 1351, § 2. Amended by Stats. 1965, c. 594, p. 1928, § 1; Stats.1967, c. 1578, p. 3780, § 4.*)

ARTICLE 4. VACUUM BRAKES

Section
26520. Vacuum gauge.
26521. Warning device.
26522. Check valve.

§ 26520. Vacuum gauge

Motor vehicles required to be equipped with power brakes and which are equipped with vacuum or vacuum-assisted brakes shall be equipped with a properly maintained vacuum gauge of reliable and satisfactory construction, accurate within 10 percent of the actual vacuum in

839

the supply reservoir, and visible and legible to the driver at all times.

This section shall not apply to a two-axle motor truck operated singly. *(Added by Stats.1963, c. 386, p. 1194, § 1.)*

Cross References

Definitions,
  Motor truck, see Vehicle Code § 410.
  Power brake, see Vehicle Code § 480.

§ 26521.   Warning device

Motor vehicles required to be equipped with power brakes and equipped with vacuum or vacuum-assisted brakes and motor vehicles used to tow vehicles equipped with vacuum brakes or vacuum-assisted brakes shall be equipped with either an audible or visible warning signal to indicate readily to the driver when the vacuum drops to eight inches of mercury and less. A vacuum gauge shall not be deemed to meet this requirement.

This section shall not apply to a two-axle motor truck operated singly nor to any motor vehicle manufactured prior to 1964. *(Added by Stats.1963, c. 386, p. 1194, § 1.)*

Cross References

Definitions,
  Motor truck, see Vehicle Code § 410.
  Power brake, see Vehicle Code § 480.

§ 26522.   Check valve

Vehicles required to be equipped with power brakes and equipped with vacuum or vacuum-assisted brakes shall have a check valve installed and properly maintained in the vacuum system between the source of vacuum and the vacuum reserve. *(Added by Stats.1963, c. 386, p. 1194, § 1.)*

Cross References

Power brake defined, see Vehicle Code § 480.

CHAPTER 4.   WINDSHIELDS AND MIRRORS

Section
26700.   Windshields; exceptions.
26701.   Safety glazing material.
26702.   Repealed.
26703.   Replacement of glazing material.
26704.   Safety glazing material defined.
26705.   Motorcycle windshields.
26706.   Windshield wipers.
26707.   Condition and use of windshield wipers.
26708.   Material obstructing or reducing driver's view; exceptions; installation, affixation or application of transparent material.
26708.2.   Requirements for sun screening devices.
26708.5.   Transparent materials; tinted safety glass.
26708.7.   Window tinting or glazing; vehicles used by peace officers; exemptions from California law.
26709.   Mirrors.
26710.   Defective windshields and rear windows.

Section
26711.   Eyeshades on bus or trolley coach.
26712.   Defroster required.

§ 26700.   Windshields; exceptions

(a) Except as provided in subdivision (b), a passenger vehicle, other than a motorcycle, and every bus, motor-truck or truck tractor, and every firetruck, fire engine or other fire apparatus, whether publicly or privately owned, shall be equipped with an adequate windshield.

(b) Subdivision (a) does not apply to any vehicle issued identification plates pursuant to Section 5004 which was not required to be equipped with a windshield at the time it was first sold or registered under the laws of this state, another state, or foreign jurisdiction. *(Stats.1959, c. 3, p. 1735, § 26700. Amended by Stats.1959, c. 1635, p. 4006, § 1; Stats.1963, c. 2149, p. 4488, § 18; Stats.1967, c. 379, p. 1604, § 1; Stats.1983, c. 222, § 1.)*

Cross References

Defective windshields and rear windows, see Vehicle Code § 26710.
Definitions,
  Bus, see Vehicle Code § 233.
  Motor truck, see Vehicle Code § 410.
  Motorcycle, see Vehicle Code § 400.
  Passenger vehicle, see Vehicle Code § 465.
  Truck tractor, see Vehicle Code § 655.
Stickers on windshields or windows, see Vehicle Code § 26708.
Vehicles incidentally operated over highway, nonapplicability of this section, see Vehicle Code § 25802.

§ 26701.   Safety glazing material

(a) No person shall sell, offer for sale, or operate any motor vehicle, except a motorcycle, manufactured after January 1, 1936, unless it is equipped with safety glazing material wherever glazing materials are used in interior partitions, doors, windows, windshields, auxiliary wind deflectors or openings in the roof.

(b) No person shall sell or offer for sale any camper manufactured after January 1, 1968, nor shall any person operate a motor vehicle registered in this state which is equipped with that camper, unless the camper is equipped with safety glazing materials wherever glazing materials are used in outside windows and doors, interior partitions, and openings in the roof.

(c) No person shall operate a motorcycle manufactured after January 1, 1969, equipped with a windshield containing glazing material unless it is safety glazing material.

(d) No person shall sell, offer for sale, or operate any motor vehicle equipped with red, blue, or amber translucent aftermarket material in any partitions, windows, windshields, or wind deflectors.

(e) No person shall sell, offer for sale, or operate any trailer coach manufactured after January 1, 1977, that is capable of being towed with a fifth-wheel device unless the trailer coach is equipped with safety glazing materials wherever glazing materials are used in windows or doors, interior partitions, and openings in the roof. *(Stats.1959, c. 3, p. 1735, § 26701. Amended by Stats.1965, c. 335, p. 1442, § 1; Stats.1967, c. 1268, p. 3073, § 3; Stats.1968, c. 980, p. 1873, § 20; Stats.1968, c. 1469, p. 2938, § 5; Stats.1976, c. 900, p. 2072, § 2; Stats.1993, c. 540 (A.B. 1849), § 2.)*

Cross References

Definitions,
　Camper, see Vehicle Code § 243.
　Motorcycle and motor-driven cycle, see Vehicle Code §§ 400, 405.
　Safety glazing material, see Vehicle Code §§ 535, 26704.
　Trailer coach, see Vehicle Code § 635.
Motorcycle windshields, see Vehicle Code § 26705.
Violations, see Vehicle Code § 40000.1 et seq.

§ 26702. Repealed by Stats.1967, c. 1268, p. 3073, § 4

§ 26703. Replacement of glazing material

(a) No person shall replace any glazing materials used in interior partitions, doors, windows, or openings in the roof in any motor vehicle, in the outside windows, doors, interior partitions, or openings in the roof of any camper, or in windows, doors, interior partitions, or openings in the roof of a trailer coach capable of being towed with a fifth-wheel device, with any glazing material other than safety glazing material.

(b) No person shall replace any glazing material used in the windshield, rear window, auxiliary wind deflectors, or windows to the left and right of the driver with any material other than safety glazing material. *(Stats.1959, c. 3, p. 1736, § 26703. Amended by Stats.1965, c. 335, p. 1442, § 2; Stats.1967, c. 1268, p. 3073, § 5; Stats.1968, c. 980, p. 1874, § 21; Stats.1976, c. 900, p. 2072, § 3.)*

Cross References

Camper defined, see Vehicle Code § 243.
Safety glazing material defined, see Vehicle Code §§ 535, 26704.
Trailer coach defined, see Vehicle Code § 635.

§ 26704. Safety glazing material defined

Wherever the term "safety glazing material" is used in this article, it means safety glazing material of a type meeting requirements established by the department. *(Added by Stats.1979, c. 723, p. 2224, § 28.)*

Cross References

Safety glazing material defined, see Vehicle Code § 535.

§ 26705. Motorcycle windshields

On or after January 1, 1969, no person shall sell or offer for sale for use upon or as part of the equipment of a motorcycle any motorcycle windshield unless the glazing material used therein is safety glazing material. *(Added by Stats.1968, c. 980, p. 1874, § 21.6; Stats.1968, c. 1469, p. 2938, § 7.)*

Cross References

Motorcycle and motor-driven cycle defined, see Vehicle Code §§ 400, 405.

Safety glazing material defined, see Vehicle Code §§ 535, 26704.

§ 26706. Windshield wipers

(a) Every motor vehicle, except motorcycles, equipped with a windshield shall also be equipped with a self-operating windshield wiper.

(b) Every new motor vehicle first registered after December 31, 1949, except motorcycles, shall be equipped with two such windshield wipers, one mounted on the right half and one on the left half of the windshield, except that any motor vehicle may be equipped with a single wiper so long as it meets the wiped area requirements in Federal Motor Vehicle Safety Standards Governing Windshield Wiping and Washing Systems.

(c) This section does not apply to snow removal equipment equipped with adequate manually operated windshield wipers. *(Stats.1959, c. 3, p. 1736, § 26706. Amended by Stats.1959, c. 1635, p. 4006, § 2; Stats.1963, c. 2149, p. 4488, § 19; Stats.1978, c. 196, p. 435, § 1.)*

Cross References

Applicability of this section to trolley coaches, see Vehicle Code § 21051.
Motorcycle defined, see Vehicle Code § 400.

§ 26707. Condition and use of windshield wipers

Windshield wipers required by this code shall be maintained in good operating condition and shall provide clear vision through the windshield for the driver. Wipers shall be operated under conditions of fog, snow, or rain and shall be capable of effectively clearing the windshield under all ordinary storm or load conditions while the vehicle is in operation. *(Stats.1959, c. 3, p. 1736, § 26707.)*

Cross References

Applicability of this section to trolley coaches, see Vehicle Code § 21051.

§ 26708. Material obstructing or reducing driver's view; exceptions; installation, affixation or application of transparent material

(a)(1) A person shall not drive any motor vehicle with any object or material placed, displayed, installed, affixed, or applied upon the windshield or side or rear windows.

(2) A person shall not drive any motor vehicle with any object or material placed, displayed, installed, affixed, or applied in or upon the vehicle that obstructs or reduces the driver's clear view through the windshield or side windows.

(3) This subdivision applies to a person driving a motor vehicle with the driver's clear vision through the windshield, or side or rear windows, obstructed by snow or ice.

(b) This section does not apply to any of the following:

(1) Rearview mirrors.

841

(2) Adjustable nontransparent sunvisors that are mounted forward of the side windows and are not attached to the glass.

(3) Signs, stickers, or other materials that are displayed in a seven-inch square in the lower corner of the windshield farthest removed from the driver, signs, stickers, or other materials that are displayed in a seven-inch square in the lower corner of the rear window farthest removed from the driver, or signs, stickers, or other materials that are displayed in a five-inch square in the lower corner of the windshield nearest the driver.

(4) Side windows that are to the rear of the driver.

(5) Direction, destination, or terminus signs upon a passenger common carrier motor vehicle or a schoolbus, if those signs do not interfere with the driver's clear view of approaching traffic.

(6) Rear window wiper motor.

(7) Rear trunk lid handle or hinges.

(8) The rear window or windows, if the motor vehicle is equipped with outside mirrors on both the left- and right-hand sides of the vehicle that are so located as to reflect to the driver a view of the highway through each mirror for a distance of at least 200 feet to the rear of the vehicle.

(9) A clear, transparent lens affixed to the side window opposite the driver on a vehicle greater than 80 inches in width and that occupies an area not exceeding 50 square inches of the lowest corner toward the rear of that window and that provides the driver with a wide-angle view through the lens.

(10) Sun screening devices meeting the requirements of Section 26708.2 installed on the side windows on either side of the vehicle's front seat, if the driver or a passenger in the front seat has in his or her possession a letter or other document signed by a licensed physician and surgeon certifying that the person must be shaded from the sun due to a medical condition, or has in his or her possession a letter or other document signed by a licensed optometrist certifying that the person must be shaded from the sun due to a visual condition. The devices authorized by this paragraph shall not be used during darkness.

(11) An electronic communication device affixed to the center uppermost portion of the interior of a windshield within an area that is not greater than five inches square, if the device provides either of the following:

(A) The capability for enforcement facilities of the Department of the California Highway Patrol to communicate with a vehicle equipped with the device.

(B) The capability for electronic toll and traffic management on public or private roads or facilities.

(12) A portable Global Positioning System (GPS), which may be mounted in a seven-inch square in the lower corner of the windshield farthest removed from the driver or in a five-inch square in the lower corner of the windshield nearest to the driver and outside of an airbag

deployment zone, if the system is used only for door-to-door navigation while the motor vehicle is being operated.

(13)(A) A video event recorder with the capability of monitoring driver performance to improve driver safety, which may be mounted in a seven-inch square in the lower corner of the windshield farthest removed from the driver, in a five-inch square in the lower corner of the windshield nearest to the driver and outside of an airbag deployment zone, or in a five-inch square mounted to the center uppermost portion of the interior of the windshield. As used in this section, "video event recorder" means a video recorder that continuously records in a digital loop, recording audio, video, and G–force levels, but saves video only when triggered by an unusual motion or crash or when operated by the driver to monitor driver performance.

(B) A vehicle equipped with a video event recorder shall have a notice posted in a visible location which states that a passenger's conversation may be recorded.

(C) Video event recorders shall store no more than 30 seconds before and after a triggering event.

(D) The registered owner or lessee of the vehicle may disable the device.

(E) The data recorded to the device is the property of the registered owner or lessee of the vehicle.

(F) When a person is driving for hire as an employee in a vehicle with a video event recorder, the person's employer shall provide unedited copies of the recordings upon the request of the employee or the employee's representative. These copies shall be provided free of charge to the employee and within five days of the request.

(14)(A) A video event recorder in a commercial motor vehicle with the capability of monitoring driver performance to improve driver safety, which may be mounted no more than two inches below the upper edge of the area swept by the windshield wipers, and outside the driver's sight lines to the road and highway signs and signals. Subparagraphs (B) to (F), inclusive, of paragraph (13) apply to the exemption provided by this paragraph.

(B) Except as provided in subparagraph (C), subparagraph (A) shall become inoperative on the following dates, whichever date is later:

(i) The date that the Department of the California Highway Patrol determines is the expiration date of the exemption from the requirements of paragraph (1) of subdivision (e) of Section 393.60 of Title 49 of the Code of Federal Regulations, as renewed in the notice of the Federal Motor Carrier Safety Administration on pages 21791 and 21792 of Volume 76 of the Federal Register (April 18, 2011).

(ii) The date that the Department of the California Highway Patrol determines is the expiration date for a subsequent renewal of an exemption specified in clause (i).

(C) Notwithstanding subparagraph (B), subparagraph (A) shall become operative on the date that the Department of the California Highway Patrol determines is the effective date of regulations revising paragraph (1) of subdivision (e) of Section 393.60 of Title 49 of the Code of Federal Regulations to allow the placement of a video event recorder at the top of the windshield on a commercial motor vehicle.

(c) Notwithstanding subdivision (a), transparent material may be installed, affixed, or applied to the topmost portion of the windshield if the following conditions apply:

(1) The bottom edge of the material is at least 29 inches above the undepressed driver's seat when measured from a point five inches in front of the bottom of the backrest with the driver's seat in its rearmost and lowermost position with the vehicle on a level surface.

(2) The material is not red or amber in color.

(3) There is no opaque lettering on the material and any other lettering does not affect primary colors or distort vision through the windshield.

(4) The material does not reflect sunlight or headlight glare into the eyes of occupants of oncoming or following vehicles to any greater extent than the windshield without the material.

(d) Notwithstanding subdivision (a), clear, colorless, and transparent material may be installed, affixed, or applied to the front side windows, located to the immediate left and right of the front seat if the following conditions are met:

(1) The material has a minimum visible light transmittance of 88 percent.

(2) The window glazing with the material applied meets all requirements of Federal Motor Vehicle Safety Standard No. 205 (49 C.F.R. 571.205), including the specified minimum light transmittance of 70 percent and the abrasion resistance of AS–14 glazing, as specified in that federal standard.

(3) The material is designed and manufactured to enhance the ability of the existing window glass to block the sun's harmful ultraviolet A rays.

(4) The driver has in his or her possession, or within the vehicle, a certificate signed by the installing company certifying that the windows with the material installed meet the requirements of this subdivision and the certificate identifies the installing company and the material's manufacturer by full name and street address, or, if the material was installed by the vehicle owner, a certificate signed by the material's manufacturer certifying that the windows with the material installed according to manufacturer's instructions meet the requirements of this subdivision and the certificate identifies the material's manufacturer by full name and street address.

(5) If the material described in this subdivision tears or bubbles, or is otherwise worn to prohibit clear vision, it shall be removed or replaced. *(Stats.1959, c. 3, p. 1736,*

§ 26708. Amended by Stats.1961, c. 1196, p. 2931, § 1; Stats.1965, c. 2031, p. 4613, § 12, eff. July 23, 1965; Stats.1967, c. 546, p. 1894, § 1; Stats.1968, c. 178, p. 403, § 2; Stats.1972, c. 528, p. 912, § 1; Stats.1976, c. 843, p. 1923, § 3; Stats.1978, c. 222, p. 473, § 1; Stats.1978, c. 500, p. 1641, § 2; Stats.1981, c. 770, p. 3015, § 1; Stats.1982, c. 635, p. 2644, § 1; Stats.1983, c. 632, § 1; Stats.1984, c. 74, § 1; Stats.1987, c. 552, § 1; Stats.1989, c. 533, § 13; Stats.1996, c. 1154 (A.B.3020), § 77, eff. Sept. 30, 1996; Stats.1998, c. 476 (A.B.2320), § 1; Stats. 2008, c. 413 (S.B.1567), § 1; Stats.2009, c. 140 (A.B. 1164), § 181; Stats.2010, c. 458 (A.B.1942), § 1; Stats. 2012, c. 375 (A.B.2477), § 2.)

Cross References

Applicability of this section to trolley coaches, see Vehicle Code § 21051.

§ 26708.2. Requirements for sun screening devices

Sun screening devices permitted by paragraph (10) of subdivision (b) of Section 26708 shall meet the following requirements:

(a) The devices shall be held in place by means allowing ready removal from the window area, such as a frame, a rigid material with temporary fasteners, or a flexible roller shade.

(b) Devices utilizing transparent material shall be green, gray, or a neutral smoke in color and shall have a luminous transmittance of not less than 35 percent.

(c) Devices utilizing nontransparent louvers or other alternating patterns of opaque and open sections shall have an essentially uniform pattern over the entire surface, except for framing and supports. At least 35 percent of the device area shall be open and no individual louver or opaque section shall have a projected vertical dimension exceeding $\frac{3}{16}$ inch.

(d) The devices shall not have a reflective quality exceeding 35 percent on either the inner or outer surface. *(Added by Stats.1984, c. 74, § 2.)*

§ 26708.5. Transparent materials; tinted safety glass

(a) No person shall place, install, affix, or apply any transparent material upon the windshield, or side or rear windows, of any motor vehicle if the material alters the color or reduces the light transmittance of the windshield or side or rear windows, except as provided in subdivision (b), (c), or (d) of Section 26708.

(b) Tinted safety glass may be installed in a vehicle if (1) the glass complies with motor vehicle safety standards of the United States Department of Transportation for safety glazing materials, and (2) the glass is installed in a location permitted by those standards for the particular type of glass used. *(Added by Stats.1972, c. 528, p. 912, § 2. Amended by Stats.1981, c. 714, p. 2801, § 447; Stats.1984, c. 210, § 1; Stats.1998, c. 476 (A.B.2320), § 2.)*

§ 26708.7. Window tinting or glazing; vehicles used by peace officers; exemptions from California law

Notwithstanding any other law, a vehicle operated and owned or leased by a federal, state, or local agency, department, or district, that employs peace officers, as defined by Chapter 4.5 (commencing with Section 830) of Title 3 of Part 2 of the Penal Code, for use by those peace officers in the performance of their duties, is exempt from California law, and regulations adopted pursuant thereto, prohibiting or limiting material that may be placed, displayed, installed, affixed, or applied to the side or rear windows, commonly referred to as window tinting or glazing. *(Added by Stats.2012, c. 171 (A.B.2660), § 1.)*

§ 26709. Mirrors

(a) Every motor vehicle registered in a foreign jurisdiction and every motorcycle subject to registration in this state shall be equipped with a mirror so located as to reflect to the driver a view of the highway for a distance of at least 200 feet to the rear of such vehicle.

Every motor vehicle subject to registration in this state, except a motorcycle, shall be equipped with not less than two such mirrors, including one affixed to the left-hand side.

(b) The following described types of motor vehicles, of a type subject to registration, shall be equipped with mirrors on both the left- and right-hand sides of the vehicle so located as to reflect to the driver a view of the highway through each mirror for a distance of at least 200 feet to the rear of such vehicle:

(1) A motor vehicle so constructed or loaded as to obstruct the driver's view to the rear.

(2) A motor vehicle towing a vehicle and the towed vehicle or load thereon obstructs the driver's view to the rear.

(3) A bus or trolley coach.

(c) The provisions of subdivision (b) shall not apply to a passenger vehicle when the load obstructing the driver's view consists of passengers. *(Stats.1959, c. 3, p. 1737, § 26709. Amended by Stats.1959, c. 1019, § 3042, § 1; Stats.1961, c. 1381, p. 3155, § 1; Stats.1963, c. 480, p. 1338, § 1; Stats.1965, c. 1312, p. 3198, § 1; Stats.1967, c. 548, p. 1896, § 1, operative Jan. 1, 1968; Stats.1970, c. 74, p. 87, § 1.)*

Cross References

Motorized bicycles, federal safety standards for equipment, see Vehicle Code § 24015.
Street rod vehicles, non-exemption from equipment requirements, see Vehicle Code § 5004.6.
Vehicles of historic value, see Vehicle Code § 5004.

§ 26710. Defective windshields and rear windows

It is unlawful to operate any motor vehicle upon a highway when the windshield or rear window is in such a defective condition as to impair the driver's vision either to the front or rear.

In the event any windshield or rear window fails to comply with this code the officer making the inspection shall direct the driver to make the windshield and rear window conform to the requirements of this code within 48 hours. The officer may also arrest the driver and give him notice to appear and further require the driver or the owner of the vehicle to produce in court satisfactory evidence that the windshield or rear window has been made to conform to the requirements of this code. *(Stats.1959, c. 3, p. 1737, § 26710.)*

Cross References

Authority of highway patrol and police to inspect vehicles, see Vehicle Code §§ 2804, 2806.

§ 26711. Eyeshades on bus or trolley coach

Every bus or trolley coach, except those first registered prior to January 1, 1960, and engaged in urban and suburban service as defined in Section 35107, shall be equipped with movable eyeshades of sufficient size to shade the eyes of the operator of a bus or trolley coach while it is being driven facing the sun. *(Added by Stats.1961, c. 1381, p. 3155, § 2. Amended by Stats.1963, c. 661, p. 1651, § 1.)*

Cross References

Bus defined, see Vehicle Code § 233.
Trolley coach defined, see Vehicle Code § 650.

§ 26712. Defroster required

Every passenger vehicle used or maintained for the transportation of persons for hire, compensation, or profit shall be equipped with a defrosting device which is adequate to remove snow, ice, frost, fog, or internal moisture from the windshield. *(Added by Stats.1965, c. 1601, p. 3693, § 1.)*

CHAPTER 5. OTHER EQUIPMENT

Article		Section
1.	Horns, Sirens, and Amplification Devices	27000
2.	Exhaust Systems	27150
2.5.	Noise Limits	27200
3.	Safety Belts and Inflatable Restraint Systems	27300
3.2.	Child Passenger Seat Restraints [Repealed]	
3.3.	Child Safety Belt and Passenger Restraint Requirements	27360
3.4.	Emergency Exits for Charter–Party Carriers of Passengers	27375
3.5.	Headsets and Earplugs	27400
4.	Tires	27450
5.	Fenders, Ornaments, and Television	27600
6.	Tow Trucks	27700
7.	Motorcycles	27800
8.	Signs	27900
9.	Refrigeration Equipment	28000
10.	Odometers	28050
11.	Fire Extinguishers	28060
11.5.	Bumpers	28070
12.	Camper Signaling Devices	28080

Article	Section
13. Theft Alarm System	28085
14. Cellular Telephones	28090
15. Pilot Cars	28100
16. Methanol or Ethanol Fueled Vehicles	28110
17. Jamming Devices	28150

ARTICLE 1. HORNS, SIRENS, AND AMPLIFICATION DEVICES

Section
27000. Horns or warning devices on motor vehicle or authorized emergency vehicle; automatic back-up audible alarm and rear-view camera on refuse or garbage truck; automatic back-up audible alarm on construction vehicle.
27001. Use of horns; theft alarm system.
27002. Sirens.
27003. Sirens on armored cars.
27007. Outside sound amplification systems; exemptions.

§ 27000. Horns or warning devices on motor vehicle or authorized emergency vehicle; automatic back-up audible alarm and rear-view camera on refuse or garbage truck; automatic back-up audible alarm on construction vehicle

(a) A motor vehicle, when operated upon a highway, shall be equipped with a horn in good working order and capable of emitting sound audible under normal conditions from a distance of not less than 200 feet, but no horn shall emit an unreasonably loud or harsh sound. An authorized emergency vehicle may be equipped with, and use in conjunction with the siren on that vehicle, an air horn that emits sounds that do not comply with the requirements of this section.

(b) A refuse or garbage truck shall be equipped with an automatic backup audible alarm that sounds on backing and is capable of emitting sound audible under normal conditions from a distance of not less than 100 feet or shall be equipped with an automatic backup device that is in good working order, located at the rear of the vehicle and that immediately applies the service brake of the vehicle on contact by the vehicle with any obstruction to the rear. The backup device or alarm shall also be capable of operating automatically when the vehicle is in neutral or a forward gear but rolls backward.

(c) A refuse or garbage truck, except a vehicle, known as a rolloff vehicle, that is used for the express purpose of transporting waste containers such as open boxes or compactors, purchased after January 1, 2010, shall also be equipped with a functioning camera providing a video display for the driver that enhances or supplements the driver's view behind the truck for the purpose of safely maneuvering the truck.

(d)(1) A construction vehicle with a gross vehicle weight rating (GVWR) in excess of 14,000 pounds that operates at, or transports construction or industrial materials to and from, a mine or construction site, or both, shall be equipped with an automatic backup audible alarm that sounds on backing and is capable of emitting sound audible under normal conditions from a distance of not less than 200 feet.

(2) As used in this subdivision, "construction vehicle" includes, but is not limited to, all of the following:

(A) A vehicle designed to transport concrete, cement, clay, limestone, aggregate material as defined in subdivision (d) of Section 23114, or other similar construction or industrial material, including a transfer truck or a tractor trailer combination used exclusively to pull bottom dump, end dump, or side dump trailers.

(B) A vehicle that is a concrete mixer truck, a truck with a concrete placing boom, a water tank truck, a single engine crane with a load rating of 35 tons or more, or a tractor that exclusively pulls a low-boy trailer. *(Stats. 1959, c. 3, p. 1737, § 27000. Amended by Stats.1965, c. 1015, p. 2650, § 1; Stats.1982, c. 926, p. 3379, § 1, eff. Sept. 13, 1982; Stats.1983, c. 1144, § 8, eff. Sept. 28, 1983; Stats.1997, c. 945 (A.B.1561), § 27; Stats.2005, c. 166 (A.B.1637), § 2; Stats.2011, c. 235 (S.B.341), § 1.)*

Cross References

Authorized emergency vehicle defined, see Vehicle Code § 165.
Camper passenger signaling device, see Vehicle Code § 28080.
Motorized bicycles, federal safety standards for equipment, see Vehicle Code § 24015.
Passing, audible signal of overtaking vehicle, see Vehicle Code § 21753.
Police and traffic officers' use of siren, see Vehicle Code § 21057.
Right-of-way, see Vehicle Code § 21806.
Vehicles incidentally operated over highway, nonapplicability of this section, see Vehicle Code § 25802.
Violation of refuse or garbage truck provisions of this section, see Vehicle Code § 42001.20.

§ 27001. Use of horns; theft alarm system

(a) The driver of a motor vehicle when reasonably necessary to insure safe operation shall give audible warning with his horn.

(b) The horn shall not otherwise be used, except as a theft alarm system which operates as specified in Article 13 (commencing with Section 28085) of this chapter. *(Stats.1959, c. 3, p. 1737, § 27001. Amended by Stats. 1977, c. 993, p. 2982, § 2.)*

§ 27002. Sirens

No vehicle, except an authorized emergency vehicle, shall be equipped with, nor shall any person use upon a vehicle any siren except that an authorized emergency vehicle shall be equipped with a siren meeting requirements established by the department. *(Stats.1959, c. 3, p. 1737, § 27002. Amended by Stats.1961, c. 653, p. 1863, § 50, operative Jan. 1, 1962; Stats.1979, c. 723, p. 2224, § 29.)*

Cross References

Authorized emergency vehicle, see Vehicle Code § 165.
Speed of escorts, see Vehicle Code § 21057.

Traffic laws, exemption of authorized emergency vehicles, see Vehicle Code §§ 21055, 21056.

§ 27003.   Sirens on armored cars

An armored car may be equipped with a siren which may be used while resisting armed robbery. At all other times, the siren shall not be sounded. The authority to use a siren granted by this section does not constitute an armored car an authorized emergency vehicle, and all other provisions of this code applicable to drivers of vehicles apply to drivers of armored cars. *(Stats.1959, c. 3, p. 1737, § 27003.)*

Cross References

Armored car defined, see Vehicle Code § 115.
Authorized emergency vehicle defined, see Vehicle Code § 165.
Horns or warning devices, see Vehicle Code § 27000.
Lighting equipment on armored cars, see Vehicle Code § 25262.
Prohibition against use of siren, see Vehicle Code § 21057.

§ 27007.   Outside sound amplification systems; exemptions

No driver of a vehicle shall operate, or permit the operation of, any sound amplification system which can be heard outside the vehicle from 50 or more feet when the vehicle is being operated upon a highway, unless that system is being operated to request assistance or warn of a hazardous situation.

This section does not apply to authorized emergency vehicles or vehicles operated by gas, electric, communications, or water utilities. This section does not apply to the sound systems of vehicles used for advertising, or in parades, political or other special events, except that the use of sound systems on those vehicles may be prohibited by a local authority by ordinance or resolution. *(Added by Stats.1978, c. 1306, p. 4294, § 2. Amended by Stats. 1989, c. 538, § 1.)*

ARTICLE 2.   EXHAUST SYSTEMS

Section
27150.   Adequate muffler required.
27150.1.   Sale of exhaust systems; misdemeanor.
27150.2.   Stations providing referee functions; testing of vehicular exhaust systems; certificates of compliance; fee charge for certification.
27150.3.   Modification of vehicle exhaust system; whistle-tips.
27150.4.   Repealed.
27150.5.   Sale of non-complying exhaust system.
27150.6.   Repealed.
27150.7.   Dismissal of prosecution.
27150.8.   Repealed.
27151.   Modification of exhaust systems.
27152.   Exhaust pipes.
27152.5.   Repealed.
27153.   Exhaust products.
27153.5.   January 1, 1971, motor vehicle exhaust standards.
27154.   Gases and fumes.
27155.   Fuel tank caps.
27156.   Gross polluters; air pollution control devices; fines.
27156.1.   Auxiliary gasoline fuel tanks.
27156.2.   Authorized emergency vehicles; exemption.

Section
27156.3.   Motor vehicle pollution control devices; exempted vehicles.
27156.5.   Repealed.
27157.   Vehicle pollution emission regulations.
27157.5.   Vehicle pollution emission standards; 1955 through 1965 model year motor vehicles.
27158.   Certificates of compliance; vehicle inspection.
27158.5.   Certificates of compliance; 1955 through 1965 model year motor vehicles.
27159.   Removal of heavy-duty diesel motor vehicles from service for failure to comply under Health & S.C. § 44011.6; towing and storage fees.
27160, 27161.   Repealed.

§ 27150.   Adequate muffler required

(a) Every motor vehicle subject to registration shall at all times be equipped with an adequate muffler in constant operation and properly maintained to prevent any excessive or unusual noise, and no muffler or exhaust system shall be equipped with a cutout, bypass, or similar device.

(b) Except as provided in Division 16.5 (commencing with Section 38000) with respect to off-highway motor vehicles subject to identification, every passenger vehicle operated off the highways shall at all times be equipped with an adequate muffler in constant operation and properly maintained so as to meet the requirements of Article 2.5 (commencing with Section 27200), and no muffler or exhaust system shall be equipped with a cutout, bypass, or similar device.

(c) The provisions of subdivision (b) shall not be applicable to passenger vehicles being operated off the highways in an organized racing or competitive event conducted under the auspices of a recognized sanctioning body or by permit issued by the local governmental authority having jurisdiction. *(Stats.1959, c. 3, p. 1737, § 27150. Amended by Stats.1971, c. 714, p. 1385, § 1, operative May 3, 1972; Stats.1971, c. 735, p. 1461, § 1, operative May 3, 1972; Stats.1971, c. 952, p. 1858, § 2, operative May 3, 1972; Stats.1971, c. 1816, p. 3925, § 8, eff. Dec. 22, 1971, operative May 3, 1972; Stats.1972, c. 973, p. 1759, § 19, eff. Aug. 16, 1972; Stats.1977, c. 579, p. 1919, § 188; Stats.1977, c. 558, p. 1784, § 1.)*

Cross References

Motorized bicycles, federal safety standards for equipment, see Vehicle Code § 24015.
Muffler defined, see Vehicle Code § 425.
Street rod vehicles, non-exemption from equipment requirements, see Vehicle Code § 5004.6.
Vehicles of historic value, exemptions, see Vehicle Code § 5004.
Vehicles subject to registration, see Vehicle Code § 4000 et seq.

§ 27150.1.   Sale of exhaust systems; misdemeanor

No person engaged in a business that involves the selling of motor vehicle exhaust systems, or parts thereof, including, but not limited to, mufflers, shall offer for sale, sell, or install, a motor vehicle exhaust system, or part thereof, including, but not limited to, a muffler, unless it meets the regulations and standards applicable pursuant to this article. Motor vehicle exhaust systems or parts thereof include, but are not limited to, nonoriginal exhaust equipment.

A violation of this section is a misdemeanor. *(Added by Stats.1971, c. 1769, p. 3823, § 1, operative May 3, 1972. Amended by Stats.1973, c. 610, p. 1131, § 1; Stats.2001, c. 92 (S.B.1081), § 3; Stats.2002, c. 569 (S.B.1420), § 2.)*

Cross References

Muffler defined, see Vehicle Code § 425.
Violation as misdemeanor, see Vehicle Code § 40000.15.

§ 27150.2. Stations providing referee functions; testing of vehicular exhaust systems; certificates of compliance; fee charge for certification

(a) Stations providing referee functions pursuant to Section 44036 of the Health and Safety Code shall provide for the testing of vehicular exhaust systems and the issuance of certificates of compliance only for those vehicles that have received a citation for a violation of Section 27150 or 27151.

(b) A certificate of compliance for a vehicular exhaust system shall be issued pursuant to subdivision (a) if the vehicle complies with Sections 27150 and 27151. Exhaust systems installed on motor vehicles, other than motorcycles, with a manufacturer's gross vehicle weight rating of less than 6,000 pounds comply with Sections 27150 and 27151 if they emit no more than 95 dbA when tested in accordance with Society of Automotive Engineers Standard J1169 May 1998.

(c) An exhaust system certificate of compliance issued pursuant to subdivision (a) shall identify, to the extent possible, the make, model, year, license number, and vehicle identification number of the vehicle tested, and the make and model of the exhaust system installed on the vehicle.

(d) The station shall charge a fee for the exhaust system certificate of compliance issued pursuant to subdivision (a). The fee charged shall be calculated to recover the costs incurred by the Department of Consumer Affairs to implement this section. The fees charged by the station shall be deposited in the Vehicle Inspection and Repair Fund established by Section 44062 of the Health and Safety Code.

(e) Vehicular exhaust systems are exempt from the requirements of Sections 27150 and 27151 if compliance with those sections, or the regulations adopted pursuant thereto, would cause an unreasonable hardship without resulting in a sufficient corresponding benefit with respect to noise level control. *(Added by Stats.1971, c. 1769, p. 3823, § 2, operative May 3, 1972. Amended by Stats.2001, c. 92 (S.B.1081), § 4; Stats.2002, c. 569 (S.B.1420), § 3.)*

Cross References

Vehicular air pollution control, licensing of smog check stations, technicians, inspection of vehicles by referees, see Health and Safety Code § 44014.

§ 27150.3. Modification of vehicle exhaust system; whistle-tips

(a) A person may not modify the exhaust system of a motor vehicle with a whistle-tip.

(b) A person may not operate a motor vehicle if that vehicle's exhaust system is modified in violation of subdivision (a).

(c) A person may not engage in the business of installing a whistle-tip onto a motor vehicle's exhaust system.

(d) For purposes of subdivisions (a) and (c), a "whistle-tip" is a device that is applied to, or is a modification of, a motor vehicle's exhaust pipe for the sole purpose of creating a high-pitched or shrieking noise when the motor vehicle is operated. *(Added by Stats.2003, c. 432 (A.B. 377), § 1.)*

Cross References

Penalties and disposition of fees and fines, infractions and special misdemeanors, see Vehicle Code § 42001.

§ 27150.4. Repealed by Stats.2001, c. 92 (S.B.1081), § 6

§ 27150.5. Sale of non-complying exhaust system

Any person holding a retail seller's permit who sells or installs an exhaust system, or part thereof, including, but not limited to, a muffler, in violation of Section 27150.1 or 27150.2 or the regulations adopted pursuant thereto, shall thereafter be required to install an exhaust system, or part thereof, including, but not limited to, a muffler, which is in compliance with such regulations upon demand of the purchaser or registered owner of the vehicle concerned, or to reimburse the purchaser or registered owner for the expense of replacement and installation of an exhaust system, or part thereof, including, but not limited to, a muffler, which is in compliance, at the election of such purchaser or registered owner. *(Added by Stats.1971, c. 1769, p. 3824, § 5, operative May 3, 1972.)*

§ 27150.6. Repealed by Stats.2001, c. 92 (S.B.1081), § 7

§ 27150.7. Dismissal of prosecution

A court may dismiss any action in which a person is prosecuted for operating a vehicle in violation of Section 27150 or 27151 if a certificate of compliance has been issued by a station pursuant to Section 27150.2, or if the defendant had reasonable grounds to believe that the exhaust system was in good working order and had reasonable grounds to believe that the vehicle was not operated in violation of Section 27150 or 27151. *(Added by Stats.1971, c. 1769, p. 3824, § 7, operative May 3, 1972. Amended by Stats.2001, c. 92 (S.B.1081), § 8; Stats.2002, c. 569 (S.B.1420), § 4.)*

§ 27150.8. Repealed by Stats.2001, c. 92 (S.B.1081), § 9

§ 27151. Modification of exhaust systems

(a) No person shall modify the exhaust system of a motor vehicle in a manner which will amplify or increase the noise emitted by the motor of the vehicle so that the vehicle is not in compliance with the provisions of Section 27150 or exceeds the noise limits established for the type of vehicle in Article 2.5 (commencing with Section 27200). No person shall operate a motor vehicle with an exhaust system so modified.

(b) For the purposes of exhaust systems installed on motor vehicles with a manufacturer's gross vehicle weight rating of less than 6,000 pounds, other than motorcycles, a sound level of 95 dbA or less, when tested in accordance with Society of Automotive Engineers Standard J1169 May 1998, complies with this section. Motor vehicle exhaust systems or parts thereof include, but are not limited to, nonoriginal exhaust equipment. *(Stats. 1959, c. 3, p. 1737, § 27151. Amended by Stats.1971, c. 503, p. 995, § 1, operative May 3, 1972; Stats.1980, c. 382, p. 759, § 1; Stats.2001, c. 92 (S.B.1081), § 10.)*

Cross References

Muffler defined, see Vehicle Code § 425.

§ 27152. Exhaust pipes

The exhaust gases from a motor vehicle shall not be directed to the side of the vehicle between 2 feet and 11 feet above the ground. *(Stats.1959, c. 3, p. 1738, § 27152.)*

§ 27152.5. Repealed by Stats.1992, c. 628 (S.B.1518), § 1

§ 27153. Exhaust products

No motor vehicle shall be operated in a manner resulting in the escape of excessive smoke, flame, gas, oil, or fuel residue.

The provisions of this section apply to motor vehicles of the United States or its agencies, to the extent authorized by federal law. *(Stats.1959, c. 3, p. 1738, § 27153. Amended by Stats.1971, c. 739, p. 1465, § 5, operative May 3, 1972.)*

Cross References

Repair assistance program, eligibility, owners meeting certain income guidelines and issued a notice under this section, see Health and Safety Code § 44062.1.

§ 27153.5. January 1, 1971, motor vehicle exhaust standards

(a) No motor vehicle first sold or registered as a new motor vehicle on or after January 1, 1971, shall discharge into the atmosphere at elevation of less than 4,000 feet any air contaminant for a period of more than 10 seconds which is:

(1) As dark or darker in shade as that designated as No. 1 on the Ringelmann Chart, as published by the United States Bureau of Mines, or

848

(2) Of such opacity as to obscure an observer's view to a degree equal to or greater than does smoke described in paragraph (1) of this subdivision.

(b) No motor vehicle first sold or registered prior to January 1, 1971, shall discharge into the atmosphere at elevation of less than 4,000 feet any air contaminant for a period of more than 10 seconds which is:

(1) As dark or darker in shade than that designated as No. 2 on the Ringelmann Chart, as published by the United States Bureau of Mines, or

(2) Of such opacity as to obscure an observer's view to a degree equal to or greater than does smoke described in paragraph (1) of this subdivision.

(c) The provisions of this section apply to motor vehicles of the United States or its agencies, to the extent authorized by federal law. *(Added by Stats.1968, c. 764, p. 1483, § 15. Amended by Stats.1971, c. 739, p. 1465, § 6, operative May 3, 1972; Stats.1973, c. 216, p. 596, § 1.)*

Cross References

Repair assistance program, eligibility, owners meeting certain income guidelines and issued a notice under this section, see Health and Safety Code § 44062.1.

§ 27154. Gases and fumes

The cab of any motor vehicle shall be reasonably tight against the penetration of gases and fumes from the engine or exhaust system. The exhaust system, including the manifold, muffler, and exhaust pipes shall be so constructed as to be capable of being maintained and shall be maintained in a reasonably gastight condition. *(Stats.1959, c. 3, p. 1738, § 27154.)*

§ 27155. Fuel tank caps

No motor vehicle shall be operated or parked upon any highway unless the filling spout for the fuel tank is closed by a cap or cover of noncombustible material. *(Stats. 1959, c. 3, p. 1738, § 27155. Amended by Stats.1965, c. 453, p. 1764, § 1.)*

§ 27156. Gross polluters; air pollution control devices; fines

(a) No person shall operate or leave standing upon a highway a motor vehicle that is a gross polluter, as defined in Section 39032.5 of the Health and Safety Code.

(b) No person shall operate or leave standing upon a highway a motor vehicle that is required to be equipped with a motor vehicle pollution control device under Part 5 (commencing with Section 43000) of Division 26 of the Health and Safety Code or any other certified motor vehicle pollution control device required by any other state law or any rule or regulation adopted pursuant to that law, or required to be equipped with a motor vehicle pollution control device pursuant to the National Emission Standards Act (42 U.S.C. Secs. 7521 to 7550, inclusive) and the standards and regulations adopted pursuant to that federal act, unless the motor vehicle is equipped with the required motor vehicle pollution control device that is correctly installed and in operating condition. No person shall disconnect, modify, or alter any such required device.

(c) No person shall install, sell, offer for sale, or advertise any device, apparatus, or mechanism intended for use with, or as a part of, a required motor vehicle pollution control device or system that alters or modifies the original design or performance of the motor vehicle pollution control device or system.

(d) If the court finds that a person has willfully violated this section, the court shall impose the maximum fine that may be imposed in the case, and no part of the fine may be suspended.

(e) "Willfully," as used in this section, has the same meaning as the meaning of that word prescribed in Section 7 of the Penal Code.

(f) No person shall operate a vehicle after notice by a traffic officer that the vehicle is not equipped with the required certified motor vehicle pollution control device correctly installed in operating condition, except as may be necessary to return the vehicle to the residence or place of business of the owner or driver or to a garage, until the vehicle has been properly equipped with such a device.

(g) The notice to appear issued or complaint filed for a violation of this section shall require that the person to whom the notice to appear is issued, or against whom the complaint is filed, produce proof of correction pursuant to Section 40150 or proof of exemption pursuant to Section 4000.1 or 4000.2.

(h) This section shall not apply to an alteration, modification, or modifying device, apparatus, or mechanism found by resolution of the State Air Resources Board to do either of the following:

(1) Not to reduce the effectiveness of a required motor vehicle pollution control device.

(2) To result in emissions from the modified or altered vehicle that are at levels that comply with existing state or federal standards for that model-year of the vehicle being modified or converted.

(i) Aftermarket and performance parts with valid State Air Resources Board Executive Orders may be sold and installed concurrent with a motorcycle's transfer to an ultimate purchaser.

(j) This section applies to motor vehicles of the United States or its agencies, to the extent authorized by federal law. *(Added by Stats.1960, Ex.Sess., c. 23, p. 351, § 3.5. Amended by Stats.1963, c. 2028, p. 4172, § 3; Stats.1965, c. 2031, p. 4613, § 13, eff. July 23, 1965; Stats.1968, c. 49, p. 195, § 10, eff. April 25, 1968; Stats.1968, c. 1207, p. 2288, § 1; Stats.1969, c. 9, p. 64, § 6, eff. March 6, 1969; Stats.1969, c. 622, p. 1260, § 3, eff. July 28, 1969; Stats.1969, c. 1253, p. 2452, § 4, eff. Aug. 31, 1969; Stats.1970, c. 331, p. 728, § 1; Stats.1971, c. 739, p. 1466, § 7, operative May 3, 1972; Stats.1972, c. 503, p. 876, § 3;*

Stats.1975, c. 957, p. 2234, § 31; Stats.1976, c. 231, p. 442, § 7; Stats.1994, c. 27 (A.B.2018), § 62, eff. March 30, 1994; Stats.2007, c. 325 (A.B.829), § 1.)

Cross References

Effect of revocation, suspension or restriction of certification after vehicle equipped with device, see Health and Safety Code § 43643.

Exemption of vehicle modified to use fuel other than gasoline or diesel prior to August 31, 1969, see Health and Safety Code § 43005.

Gross polluter, defined, see Health and Safety Code § 39032.5.

Penalties for violations of this section, see Health and Safety Code § 43008.6.

§ 27156.1. Auxiliary gasoline fuel tanks

The installation, prior to January 1, 1974, of an auxiliary gasoline fuel tank for use on a 1973 or earlier model year motor vehicle, which vehicle is required, pursuant to Part 5 (commencing with Section 43000) of Division 26 of the Health and Safety Code or the National Emission Standards Act (42 U.S.C., Secs. 1857f–1 to 1857f–7,[1] inclusive), to be equipped with a fuel system evaporative loss control device, shall not be deemed a violation of Section 27156 of this code. As used in this section, the term "auxiliary gasoline fuel tank," has the same meaning as defined in subdivision (b) of Section 43834 of the Health and Safety Code. *(Added by Stats.1973, c. 836, p. 1500, § 3, eff. Sept. 25, 1973. Amended by Stats.1975, c. 957, p. 2235, § 32.)*

[1] See 42 U.S.C.A. §§ 7521 et seq., 7541 et seq.

§ 27156.2. Authorized emergency vehicles; exemption

Notwithstanding any other provision of law, any publicly owned authorized emergency vehicle operated by a peace officer, as defined in Section 830 of the Penal Code, any authorized emergency vehicle, as defined in Section 165 and used for fighting fires or responding to emergency fire calls pursuant to paragraph (2) of subdivision (b) or pursuant to subdivision (c) or (d) of that section, and any publicly owned authorized emergency vehicle used by an emergency medical technician-paramedic, as defined in Section 1797.84 of the Health and Safety Code, is exempt from requirements imposed pursuant to California law and the regulations adopted pursuant thereto for motor vehicle pollution control devices. *(Added by Stats.1981, c. 595, p. 2307, § 1.)*

§ 27156.3. Motor vehicle pollution control devices; exempted vehicles

Notwithstanding any other provision of law, any motor vehicle of mosquito abatement, vector control, or pest abatement districts or agencies, any authorized emergency vehicle as defined in Section 165, except subdivision (f) thereof, and any ambulance used by a private entity under contract with a public agency, is exempt from requirements imposed pursuant to California law and the regulations adopted pursuant thereto for motor vehicle pollution control devices. *(Formerly § 27156.2, added by Stats.1981, c. 669, p. 2459, § 1, eff. Sept. 23, 1981.*

Renumbered § 27156.3 and amended by Stats.1982, c. 466, p. 2058, § 116.)

Cross References

Application of nonvehicular emissions regulations to this section, see Health and Safety Code § 41514.

§ 27156.5. Repealed by Stats.1965, c. 2031, p. 4613, § 13.5

§ 27157. Vehicle pollution emission regulations

The State Air Resources Board, after consultation with, and pursuant to the recommendations of, the commissioner, shall adopt such reasonable regulations as it determines are necessary for the public health and safety regarding the maximum allowable emissions of pollutants from vehicles upon a highway. Such regulations shall apply only to vehicles required by Part 5 (commencing with Section 43000) of Division 26 of the Health and Safety Code or any federal law or regulation to be equipped with devices or systems to control emission of pollutants from the exhaust and shall not be stricter than the emission standards required of that model year motor vehicle when first manufactured. *(Added by Stats.1970, c. 1295, p. 2400, § 13. Amended by Stats.1979, c. 373, p. 1384, § 327.)*

Cross References

Compliance with standards, see Health and Safety Code § 43009.
Exemption from enforcement powers of air pollution control officers, see Health and Safety Code § 40753.

§ 27157.5. Vehicle pollution emission standards; 1955 through 1965 model year motor vehicles

The State Air Resources Board, after consultation with, and pursuant to the recommendations of, the commissioner, shall adopt such reasonable standards as it determines are necessary for the public health and safety for the emission of air pollutants from the exhaust of motor vehicles of 1955 through 1965 model years. These standards shall be based on the normal emissions of such cars when the timing and carburetor are in proper adjustment and the spark plugs are in proper operating condition. *(Added by Stats.1971, c. 1095, p. 2076, § 2, operative May 3, 1972.)*

Cross References

Compliance with standards, see Health and Safety Code § 43009.
Exemption from enforcement powers of air pollution control officers, see Health and Safety Code § 40753.

§ 27158. Certificates of compliance; vehicle inspection

After notice by a traffic officer that a vehicle does not comply with any regulation adopted pursuant to Section 27157, no person shall operate, and no owner shall permit the operation of, such vehicle for more than 30 days thereafter unless a certificate of compliance has been issued for such vehicle in accordance with the provisions

850

of Section 9889.18 of the Business and Professions Code or unless the department has checked the vehicle and determined that the vehicle has been made to comply with such regulation adopted pursuant to Section 27157. A certificate of compliance issued for such vehicle shall, for a period of one year from date of issue, constitute proof of compliance with any regulations adopted pursuant to Section 27157 provided that no required pollution control device has been disconnected, modified, or altered or has been adjusted by other than a licensed installer in a licensed motor vehicle pollution control device installation and inspection station subsequent to the issuance of the certificate of compliance. The provisions of this section shall apply to the United States and its agencies to the extent authorized by federal law. *(Added by Stats.1970, c. 1295, p. 2400, § 14. Amended by Stats.1971, c. 739, p. 1467, § 8, operative May 3, 1972; Stats.1971, c. 1578, p. 3182, § 8, operative May 3, 1972; Stats.1974, c. 769, p. 1690, § 1.)*

Cross References

Exemption from enforcement powers of air pollution control officers, see Health and Safety Code § 40753.

§ 27158.5. Certificates of compliance; 1955 through 1965 model year motor vehicles

After notice by a traffic officer that a motor vehicle does not comply with any standard adopted pursuant to Section 27157.5, no person shall operate, and no owner shall permit the operation of, such motor vehicle for more than 30 days thereafter unless a certificate of compliance has been issued for such vehicle in accordance with the provisions of Section 9889.18 of the Business and Professions Code or unless the department has checked the vehicle and determined that the vehicle has been made to comply with such standard adopted pursuant to Section 27157.5. A certificate of compliance issued for such vehicle shall, for a period of one year from date of issue, constitute proof of compliance with the standards determined pursuant to Section 27157.5. *(Added by Stats.1971, c. 1095, p. 2076, § 3, operative May 3, 1972. Amended by Stats.1971, c. 1578, p. 3182, § 9, operative May 3, 1972; Stats.1974, c. 769, p. 1691, § 2.)*

Cross References

Exemption from enforcement powers of air pollution control officers, see Health and Safety Code § 40753.

§ 27159. Removal of heavy-duty diesel motor vehicles from service for failure to comply under Health & S.C. § 44011.6; towing and storage fees

Any uniformed member of the California Highway Patrol may order a vehicle stored when it is located within the territorial limits in which the member may act if requested by a representative of the State Air Resources Board to remove the vehicle from service pursuant to subdivision (f) of Section 44011.6 of the Health and Safety Code. All towing and storage fees for a vehicle removed under this section shall be paid by the owner. *(Added by Stats.1990, c. 1433 (S.B.1874), § 24.)*

§§ 27160, 27161. Repealed by Stats.1975, c. 83, p. 151, §§ 1, 2

ARTICLE 2.5. NOISE LIMITS

Section
27200. Vehicle registration and sale prohibitions.
27201. Pre-1970 motorcycle limit.
27202. Motorcycle limits.
27202.1. Motorcycle exhaust system labels; penalties; proof of correction; scope.
27203. Snowmobile limit.
27204. Vehicles with gross vehicle weight ratings over 6,000, over 8,500, and over 10,000 pounds.
27204.5, 27205. Repealed.
27206. Limits for other vehicles.
27207. Limit for vehicles exceeding 10,000 pounds gross vehicle weight and equipped with governor.

Cross References

Equipment of vehicles, regulations governing exhaust systems, see Vehicle Code § 27150.2.[1]

§ 27200. Vehicle registration and sale prohibitions

(a) The Department of Motor Vehicles shall not register on a dealer's report of sale a new motor vehicle, except an off-highway motor vehicle subject to identification as provided in Division 16.5 (commencing with Section 38000), which produces a maximum noise exceeding the applicable noise limit at a distance of 50 feet from the centerline of travel under test procedures established by the Department of the California Highway Patrol.

(b) The Department of Motor Vehicles may accept a dealer's certificate as proof of compliance with this article.

(c) Test procedures for compliance with this article shall be established by the Department of the California Highway Patrol, taking into consideration the test procedures of the Society of Automotive Engineers.

(d) No person shall sell or offer for sale a new motor vehicle, except an off-highway motor vehicle subject to identification as provided in Division 16.5 (commencing with Section 38000), which produces a maximum noise exceeding the applicable noise limit specified in this article, and for which noise emission standards or regulations have not been adopted by the Administrator of the Environmental Protection Agency pursuant to the Noise Control Act of 1972 (P.L. 92–574).[1]

(e) No person shall sell or offer for sale a new motor vehicle, except an off-highway motor vehicle subject to identification as provided in Division 16.5 (commencing with Section 38000), which produces noise that exceeds or in any way violates the noise emission standards or regulations adopted for such a motor vehicle by the Administrator of the Environmental Protection Agency pursuant to the Noise Control Act of 1972 (P.L. 92–574).

(f) As used in this section, the term "register" is equivalent to the term "licensing" as used in Section 6(e)(2) of the Noise Control Act of 1972 (P.L. 92–574;

Title 42, United States Code, Section 4905(e)(2)).[2]
(Added by Stats.1975, c. 83, p. 151, § 3. Amended by Stats.1977, c. 558, p. 1784, § 2.)

[1] 42 U.S.C.A. §§ 4901 to 4918.
[2] 42 U.S.C.A. § 4905(e)(2).

Cross References

Modification of exhaust systems, see Vehicle Code § 27151.

§ 27201. Pre-1970 motorcycle limit

For the purposes of Section 27200, the noise limit of 92 dbA shall apply to any motorcycle manufactured before 1970. *(Added by Stats.1975, c. 83, p. 151, § 3.)*

§ 27202. Motorcycle limits

For the purposes of Section 27200, the following noise limits shall apply to any motorcycle, other than a motor-driven cycle, manufactured:

(1) After 1969, and before 1973 . . . . 88 dbA
(2) After 1972, and before 1975 . . . . 86 dbA
(3) After 1974, and before 1986 . . . . 83 dbA
(4) After 1985 . . . . 80 dbA

(Added by Stats.1975, c. 83, p. 151, § 3. Amended by Stats.1976, c. 464, p. 1202, § 1; Stats.1980, c. 358, p. 709, § 1; Stats.1981, c. 81, p. 197, § 1; Stats.1982, c. 356, p. 1672, § 1.)

Cross References

Motorcycle defined, see Vehicle Code § 400.

§ 27202.1. Motorcycle exhaust system labels; penalties; proof of correction; scope

(a) Notwithstanding any other law, a person shall not park, use, or operate a motorcycle, registered in the State of California, that does not bear the required applicable federal Environmental Protection Agency exhaust system label pursuant to Subparts D (commencing with Section 205.150) and E (commencing with Section 205.164) of Part 205 of Title 40 of the Code of Federal Regulations. A violation of this section shall be considered a mechanical violation and a peace officer shall not stop a motorcycle solely on a suspicion of a violation of this section. A peace officer shall cite a violation of this section as a secondary infraction.

(b) A violation of this section is punishable as follows:

(1) For a first conviction, by a fine of not less than fifty dollars ($50), nor more than one hundred dollars ($100).

(2) For a second or subsequent conviction, by a fine of not less than one hundred dollars ($100), nor more than two hundred fifty dollars ($250).

(c)(1) The notice to appear issued or complaint filed for a violation of this section shall require that the person to whom the notice to appear is issued, or against whom the complaint is filed, produce proof of correction pursuant to Section 40150.

(2) Upon producing proof of correction to the satisfaction of the court, the court may dismiss the penalty

851

imposed pursuant to subdivision (b) for a first violation of this section.

(d)(1) This section is applicable to a person operating a motorcycle that is manufactured on or after January 1, 2013, or a motorcycle with aftermarket exhaust system equipment that is manufactured on or after January 1, 2013.

(2) Penalties imposed pursuant to this section are in addition to penalties imposed pursuant to any other applicable laws or regulations.

(3) This section does not supersede, negate, or otherwise alter any other applicable laws or regulations. *(Added by Stats.2010, c. 407 (S.B.435), § 1.)*

§ 27203. Snowmobile limit

For the purposes of Section 27200, the noise limit of 82 dbA shall apply to any snowmobile manufactured after 1972. *(Added by Stats.1975, c. 83, p. 152, § 3.)*

Cross References

Snowmobile defined, see Vehicle Code § 557.

§ 27204. Vehicles with gross vehicle weight ratings over 6,000, over 8,500, and over 10,000 pounds

For the purposes of Section 27200, the following noise limits shall apply to any motor vehicle within the specified manufacturer's gross vehicle weight rating and date of manufacture:

GVWR—Pounds	Date of Manufacture	Noise Limit— dbA
Over 6,000	after 1967 and before 1973	88
Over 6,000	after 1972 and before 1975	86
Over 6,000	after 1974 and before 1978	83
Over 8,500	after 1977 and before 1982	83
Over 6,000 but not over 8,500	after 1977	80
Over 8,500 but not over 10,000	after 1981	80
Over 10,000	after 1981 and before 1988	83
Over 10,000	after 1987	80

(Added by Stats.1982, c. 793, p. 3072, § 2. Amended by Stats.1985, c. 274, § 1.)

§§ 27204.5, 27205. Repealed by Stats.1982, c. 793, p. 3072, §§ 3, 4

§ 27206. Limits for other vehicles

For the purposes of Section 27200, the following noise limits shall apply to any other motor vehicle, not specified in this article, manufactured:

(1) After 1967, and before 1973 . . . . 86 dbA
(2) After 1972, and before 1975 . . . . 84 dbA
(3) After 1974 . . . . 80 dbA

(Formerly § 27205, added by Stats.1975, c. 83, p. 151, § 3. Renumbered § 27206 and amended by Stats.1977, c. 558, p. 1785, § 4.)

§ 27207. Limit for vehicles exceeding 10,000 pounds gross vehicle weight and equipped with governor

No motor vehicle with a gross vehicle weight rating of more than 10,000 pounds and equipped with an engine speed governor shall produce a sound level exceeding 88 dbA, measured on an open site at a distance of 50 feet from the longitudinal centerline of the vehicle, when its engine is accelerated from idle with wide open throttle to governed speed with the vehicle stationary, transmission in neutral, and clutch, if any, engaged. Test procedures for compliance with this section shall be established by the department, taking into consideration the procedures of the United States Department of Transportation. The procedures may provide for measuring at other distances, in which case the measurement shall be corrected so as to provide for measurements equivalent to the noise limit established by this section measured at 50 feet. *(Added by Stats.1977, c. 558, p. 1786, § 6. Amended by Stats. 1996, c. 124 (A.B.3470), § 134.)*

ARTICLE 3.   SAFETY BELTS AND INFLATABLE RESTRAINT SYSTEMS

Section
27300, 27301.   Repealed.
27302.   Compliance with requirements.
27303.   Repealed.
27304.   Driver training vehicles.
27305.   Firefighting vehicles.
27309.   Repealed.
27314.   Used passenger vehicles.
27314.5.   Sale of used passenger vehicles; warning regarding failure to install and use shoulder harnesses with lap belts.
27315.   Motor Vehicle Safety Act; mandatory use of seatbelts; violations; penalties; application; partial conditional inoperation.
27315.1.   Persons in fully enclosed three-wheeled motor vehicles; vehicle length, width, and weight restrictions.
27315.3.   Law enforcement agencies; maintenance of safety belts; violations.
27315.5.   Agency safety belt policy.
27316.   Schoolbuses purchased or leased for use in California; requirement of equipping all designated seating positions with a combination pelvic and upper torso passenger restraint; conditions; failure to use or improper use; legislative intent.
27316.5.   School pupil activity buses; requirement of equipping all designated seating positions with combination pelvic and upper torso passenger restraints; failure to use or improper use.
27317.   Modification of a vehicle's computer or supplemental restraint system; distribution or sale of previously deployed airbag; penalties.

§§ 27300, 27301. Repealed by Stats.1968, c. 980, p. 1874, §§ 22, 23

§ 27302. Compliance with requirements

No person shall sell or offer for sale any seatbelt or attachments thereto for use in a vehicle unless it complies with requirements established by the department. *(Stats. 1959, c. 3, p. 1738, § 27302. Amended by Stats.1968, c. 980, p. 1875, § 32; Stats.1979, c. 723, p. 2224, § 30.)*

§ 27303. Repealed by Stats.1968, c. 980, p. 1874, § 25

§ 27304. Driver training vehicles

All vehicles owned and utilized in driver training by a driver training school licensed under the provisions of Chapter 1 (commencing with Section 11100) of Division 5 or in a course in automobile driver training in any secondary school maintained under the Education Code shall be equipped with a seatbelt for the driver and each passenger. Such seatbelt shall comply with requirements established by the department.

It shall be unlawful for any driver or passenger to operate or ride in such a vehicle while it is being operated for the purposes of driver training, unless such person is utilizing an installed seatbelt in the proper manner. *(Added by Stats.1961, c. 1329, p. 3108, § 1. Amended by Stats.1968, c. 742, p. 1446, § 1; Stats.1972, c. 618, p. 1151, § 149; Stats.1979, c. 723, p. 2225, § 31.)*

§ 27305. Firefighting vehicles

All publicly owned firefighting vehicles designed for and used in responding to emergency fire calls and in combating fires shall be equipped with seatbelts for each seat utilized by personnel when such vehicles are being operated. Such seatbelts shall comply with requirements established by the department. *(Added by Stats.1963, c. 1691, p. 3321, § 1. Amended by Stats.1968, c. 980, p. 1875, § 33; Stats.1979, c. 723, p. 2225, § 32.)*

§ 27309. Repealed by Stats.1968, c. 980, p. 1874, § 27

§ 27314. Used passenger vehicles

(a) No dealer shall sell or offer for sale any used passenger vehicle that was manufactured on or after January 1, 1962, other than a motorcycle, unless it is equipped with at least two seatbelts which are installed for the use of persons in the front seat of the vehicle.

(b) No dealer shall sell or offer for sale any used passenger vehicle manufactured on or after January 1, 1968, other than a motorcycle, unless it is equipped with seatbelts for each seating position.

(c) Seatbelts required in subdivisions (a) and (b) shall comply with regulations established by the department.

(d) The requirements of this section shall not apply to sales to dealers, automobile dismantlers, or junk dealers. *(Added by Stats.1967, c. 430, p. 1644, § 1. Amended by Stats.1968, c. 980, p. 1876, § 34; Stats.1979, c. 723, p. 2225, § 33.)*

§ 27314.5. Sale of used passenger vehicles; warning regarding failure to install and use shoulder harnesses with lap belts

(a)(1) Subject to paragraph (3), no dealer shall sell or offer for sale any used passenger vehicle of a model year of 1972 to 1990, inclusive, unless there is affixed to the window of the left front door or, if there is no window, to another suitable location so that it may be seen and read by a person standing outside the vehicle at that location, a notice, printed in 14–point type, which reads as follows:

"WARNING: While use of all seat belts reduces the chance of ejection, failure to install and use shoulder harnesses with lap belts can result in serious or fatal injuries in some crashes. Lap-only belts increase the chance of head and neck injury by allowing the upper torso to move unrestrained in a crash and increase the chance of spinal column and abdominal injuries by concentrating excessive force on the lower torso. Because children carry a disproportionate amount of body weight above the waist, they are more likely to sustain those injuries. Shoulder harnesses may be available that can be retrofitted in this vehicle. For more information call the Auto Safety Hotline at 1–800–424–9393."

(2) The notice shall remain affixed to the vehicle pursuant to paragraph (1) at all times that the vehicle is for sale.

(3) The notice is not required to be affixed to any vehicle equipped with both a lap belt and a shoulder harness for the driver and one passenger in the front seat of the vehicle and for at least two passengers in the rear seat of the vehicle.

(b)(1) In addition to the requirements of subdivision (a), and subject to paragraph (3) and subdivision (c), the dealer shall affix, to one rear seat lap belt buckle of every used passenger vehicle of a model year of 1972 to 1990, inclusive, that has a rear seat, a notice, printed in 10–point type, that reads as follows:

"WARNING: While use of all seat belts reduces the chance of ejection, failure to install and use shoulder harnesses with lap belts can result in serious or fatal injuries in some crashes. Shoulder harnesses may be available that can be retrofitted in this vehicle. For more information, call the Auto Safety Hotline at 1–800–424–9393."

(2) The notice shall remain affixed to the vehicle pursuant to paragraph (1) at all times that the vehicle is for sale.

(3) The message is not required to be affixed to any vehicle either equipped with both a lap belt and a shoulder harness for at least two passengers in the rear seat or having no rear seat lap belts.

(c) A dealer is not in violation of subdivision (b) unless a private nonprofit entity has furnished a supply of the appropriate notices suitable for affixing as required free

853

of charge or, having requested a resupply of notices, has not received the resupply.

(d) The department shall furnish, to a nonprofit private entity for purposes of this section, for a fee not to exceed its costs in so furnishing, at least once every six months, a list of all licensed dealers who sell used passenger vehicles. *(Added by Stats.1992, c. 562 (A.B. 1751), § 2. Amended by Stats.1997, c. 619 (S.B.506), § 11.)*

§ 27315.   Motor Vehicle Safety Act;   mandatory use of seatbelts; violations; penalties; application; partial conditional inoperation

(a) The Legislature finds that a mandatory seatbelt law will contribute to reducing highway deaths and injuries by encouraging greater usage of existing manual seatbelts, that automatic crash protection systems that require no action by vehicle occupants offer the best hope of reducing deaths and injuries, and that encouraging the use of manual safety belts is only a partial remedy for addressing this major cause of death and injury. The Legislature declares that the enactment of this section is intended to be compatible with support for federal motor vehicle safety standards requiring automatic crash protection systems and should not be used in any manner to rescind federal requirements for installation of automatic restraints in new cars.

(b) This section shall be known and may be cited as the Motor Vehicle Safety Act.

(c)(1) As used in this section, "motor vehicle" means a passenger vehicle, a motortruck, or a truck tractor, but does not include a motorcycle.

(2) For purposes of this section, a "motor vehicle" also means a farm labor vehicle, regardless of the date of certification under Section 31401.

(d)(1) A person shall not operate a motor vehicle on a highway unless that person and all passengers 16 years of age or over are properly restrained by a safety belt. This paragraph does not apply to the operator of a taxicab, as defined in Section 27908, when the taxicab is driven on a city street and is engaged in the transportation of a fare-paying passenger. The safety belt requirement established by this paragraph is the minimum safety standard applicable to employees being transported in a motor vehicle. This paragraph does not preempt more stringent or restrictive standards imposed by the Labor Code or another state or federal regulation regarding the transportation of employees in a motor vehicle.

(2) For purposes of this section the phrase, "properly restrained by a safety belt" means that the lower (lap) portion of the belt crosses the hips or upper thighs of the occupant and the upper (shoulder) portion of the belt, if present, crosses the chest in front of the occupant.

(3) The operator of a limousine for hire or the operator of an authorized emergency vehicle, as defined in subdivision (a) of Section 165, shall not operate the limousine for hire or authorized emergency vehicle unless

854

the operator and any passengers eight years of age or over in the front seat, are properly restrained by a safety belt.

(4) The operator of a taxicab shall not operate the taxicab unless any passengers eight years of age or over in the front seat, are properly restrained by a safety belt.

(e) A person 16 years of age or over shall not be a passenger in a motor vehicle on a highway unless that person is properly restrained by a safety belt. This subdivision does not apply to a passenger in a sleeper berth, as defined in subdivision (x) of Section 1201 of Title 13 of the California Code of Regulations.

(f) An owner of a motor vehicle, including an owner or operator of a taxicab, as defined in Section 27908, or a limousine for hire, operated on a highway shall maintain safety belts in good working order for the use of the occupants of the vehicle. The safety belts shall conform to motor vehicle safety standards established by the United States Department of Transportation. This subdivision, however, does not require installation or maintenance of safety belts if it is not required by the laws of the United States applicable to the vehicle at the time of its initial sale.

(g) This section does not apply to a passenger or operator with a physically disabling condition or medical condition that would prevent appropriate restraint in a safety belt, if the condition is duly certified by a licensed physician and surgeon or by a licensed chiropractor who shall state the nature of the condition, as well as the reason the restraint is inappropriate. This section also does not apply to a public employee, if the public employee is in an authorized emergency vehicle as defined in paragraph (1) of subdivision (b) of Section 165, or to a passenger in a seat behind the front seat of an authorized emergency vehicle as defined in paragraph (1) of subdivision (b) of Section 165 operated by the public employee, unless required by the agency employing the public employee.

(h) Notwithstanding subdivision (a) of Section 42001, a violation of subdivision (d), (e), or (f) is an infraction punishable by a fine of not more than twenty dollars ($20) for a first offense, and a fine of not more than fifty dollars ($50) for each subsequent offense. In lieu of the fine and any penalty assessment or court costs, the court, pursuant to Section 42005, may order that a person convicted of a first offense attend a school for traffic violators or another court-approved program in which the proper use of safety belts is demonstrated.

(i) In a civil action, a violation of subdivision (d), (e), or (f), or information of a violation of subdivision (h), does not establish negligence as a matter of law or negligence per se for comparative fault purposes, but negligence may be proven as a fact without regard to the violation.

(j) If the United States Secretary of Transportation fails to adopt safety standards for manual safety belt systems by September 1, 1989, a motor vehicle manufactured after that date for sale or sold in this state shall not be registered unless it contains a manual safety belt system that meets the performance standards applicable to automatic crash protection devices adopted by the United States Secretary of Transportation pursuant to Federal Motor Vehicle Safety Standard No. 208 (49 C.F.R. 571.208) as in effect on January 1, 1985.

(k) A motor vehicle offered for original sale in this state that has been manufactured on or after September 1, 1989, shall comply with the automatic restraint requirements of Section S4.1.2.1 of Federal Motor Vehicle Safety Standard No. 208 (49 C.F.R. 571.208), as published in Volume 49 of the Federal Register, No. 138, page 29009. An automobile manufacturer that sells or delivers a motor vehicle subject to this subdivision, and fails to comply with this subdivision, shall be punished by a fine of not more than five hundred dollars ($500) for each sale or delivery of a noncomplying motor vehicle.

(*l*) Compliance with subdivision (j) or (k) by a manufacturer shall be made by self-certification in the same manner as self-certification is accomplished under federal law.

(m) This section does not apply to a person actually engaged in delivery of newspapers to customers along the person's route if the person is properly restrained by a safety belt prior to commencing and subsequent to completing delivery on the route.

(n) This section does not apply to a person actually engaged in collection and delivery activities as a rural delivery carrier for the United States Postal Service if the person is properly restrained by a safety belt prior to stopping at the first box and subsequent to stopping at the last box on the route.

(o) This section does not apply to a driver actually engaged in the collection of solid waste or recyclable materials along that driver's collection route if the driver is properly restrained by a safety belt prior to commencing and subsequent to completing the collection route.

(p) Subdivisions (d), (e), (f), (g), and (h) shall become inoperative immediately upon the date that the United States Secretary of Transportation, or his or her delegate, determines to rescind the portion of the Federal Motor Vehicle Safety Standard No. 208 (49 C.F.R. 571.208) that requires the installation of automatic restraints in new motor vehicles, except that those subdivisions shall not become inoperative if the secretary's decision to rescind that Standard No. 208 is not based, in any respect, on the enactment or continued operation of those subdivisions. *(Added by Stats.1992, c. 122 (A.B.338), § 2, operative Jan. 1, 1996. Amended by Stats.1994, c. 1101 (S.B.2004), § 2, operative Jan. 1, 1996; Stats.1995, c. 365 (A.B.1400), § 1, operative Jan. 1, 1996; Stats.1996, c. 1154 (A.B.3020), § 78, eff. Sept. 30, 1996; Stats.1997, c. 153 (A.B.1278), § 1; Stats.1998, c. 471 (A.B.2062), § 1; Stats.1998, c. 877 (A.B.2132), § 67.5; Stats.1999, c. 557 (A.B.1165), § 3, eff. Sept. 29, 1999; Stats.2003, c. 521 (A.B.1625), § 1; Stats. 2004, c. 420 (A.B.2139), § 1; Stats.2008, c. 179 (S.B. 1498), § 223; Stats.2011, c. 474 (S.B.929), § 1.)*

Cross References

Children under eight years of age, obligation of parent, legal guardian, or driver not to transport in motor vehicle unless secured in rear seat child passenger restraint system, see Vehicle Code § 27360.

Traffic violation point count, convictions under this section, see Vehicle Code § 12810.2.

§ 27315.1. Persons in fully enclosed three-wheeled motor vehicles; vehicle length, width, and weight restrictions

Section 27315 applies to any person in a fully enclosed three-wheeled motor vehicle that is not less than seven feet in length and not less than four feet in width, and has an unladen weight of 900 pounds or more. *(Added by Stats.1997, c. 710 (A.B.1029), § 2.)*

§ 27315.3. Law enforcement agencies; maintenance of safety belts; violations

(a) As used in this section, "passenger motor vehicle" means a passenger vehicle as defined in Section 465 and a motortruck as defined in Section 410 of less than 6,001 pounds unladen weight, but does not include a motorcycle as defined in Section 400.

(b) Every sheriff's department and city police department and the Department of the California Highway Patrol shall maintain safety belts in good working order for the use of occupants of a vehicle that it operates on a highway for the purpose of patrol. The safety belts shall conform to motor vehicle safety standards established by the United States Department of Transportation. This subdivision does not, however, require installation or maintenance of safety belts where not required by the laws of the United States applicable to the vehicle at the time of its initial sale.

(c) Notwithstanding subdivision (a) of Section 42001, a violation of subdivision (b) is an infraction punishable by a fine, including all penalty assessments and court costs imposed on the convicted department, of not more than twenty dollars ($20) for a first offense, and a fine, including all penalty assessments and court costs imposed on the convicted department, of not more than fifty dollars ($50) for each subsequent offense.

(d)(1) For a violation of subdivision (b), in addition to the fines provided for pursuant to subdivision (c) and the penalty assessments provided for pursuant to Section 1464 of the Penal Code, an additional penalty assessment of two dollars ($2) shall be levied for a first offense, and an additional penalty assessment of five dollars ($5) shall be levied for any subsequent offense.

(2) All money collected pursuant to this subdivision shall be utilized in accordance with Section 1464 of the Penal Code.

(e) In a civil action, a violation of subdivision (b) or information of a violation of subdivision (c) shall not establish negligence as a matter of law or negligence per se for comparative fault purposes, but negligence may be proven as a fact without regard to the violation.

(f) Subdivisions (b) and (c) shall become inoperative immediately upon the date that the Secretary of the United States Department of Transportation, or his or her delegate, determines to rescind the portion of the Federal Motor Vehicle Safety Standard No. 208 (49 C.F.R. 571.208) that requires the installation of automatic restraints in new passenger motor vehicles, except that those subdivisions shall not become inoperative if the secretary's decision to rescind Standard No. 208 is not based, in any respect, on the enactment or continued operation of those subdivisions or subdivisions (d) to (h), inclusive, of Section 27315. *(Added by Stats.1990, c. 33 (S.B.1372), § 2, eff. March 26, 1990. Amended by Stats. 2011, c. 474 (S.B.929), § 2.)*

Operative Effect

For inoperative date of some provisions of this section, see its terms.

§ 27315.5. Agency safety belt policy

All law enforcement agencies shall, not later than January 1, 1991, establish a policy and issue an order, in writing, which states whether or not their officers are required to wear seat belts. When a law enforcement agency is developing a safety belt policy, the agency shall consider the officer's safety, comfort, and convenience. *(Added by Stats.1990, c. 33 (S.B.1372), § 3, eff. March 26, 1990.)*

§ 27316. Schoolbuses purchased or leased for use in California; requirement of equipping all designated seating positions with a combination pelvic and upper torso passenger restraint; conditions; failure to use or improper use; legislative intent

(a) Unless specifically prohibited by the National Highway Transportation Safety Administration, all schoolbuses purchased or leased for use in California shall be equipped at all designated seating positions with a combination pelvic and upper torso passenger restraint system, if the schoolbus is either of the following:

(1) Type 1, as defined in paragraph (1) of subdivision (b) of Section 1201 of Title 13 of the California Code of Regulations, and is manufactured on or after July 1, 2005.

(2) Type 2, as defined in paragraph (2) of subdivision (b) of Section 1201 of Title 13 of the California Code of Regulations, and is manufactured on or after July 1, 2004.

(b) For purposes of this section, a "passenger restraint system" means any of the following:

(1) A restraint system that is in compliance with Federal Motor Vehicle Safety Standard 209, for a type 2 seatbelt assembly, and with Federal Motor Vehicle Safety Standard 210, as those standards were in effect on the date the schoolbus was manufactured.

(2) A restraint system certified by the schoolbus manufacturer that is in compliance with Federal Motor Vehicle Safety Standard 222 and incorporates a type 2 lap/shoulder restraint system.

(c) No person, school district, or organization, with respect to a schoolbus equipped with passenger restraint systems pursuant to this section, may be charged for a violation of this code or any regulation adopted thereunder requiring a passenger to use a passenger restraint system, if a passenger on the schoolbus fails to use or improperly uses the passenger restraint system.

(d) It is the intent of the Legislature, in implementing this section, that school pupil transportation providers work to prioritize the allocation of schoolbuses purchased, leased, or contracted for on or after July 1, 2004, for type 2 schoolbuses, or on or after July 1, 2005, for type 1 schoolbuses, to ensure that elementary level schoolbus passengers receive first priority for new schoolbuses whenever feasible. *(Added by Stats.1999, c. 648 (A.B.15), § 4. Amended by Stats.2001, c. 581 (S.B.568), § 2.)*

§ 27316.5. School pupil activity buses; requirement of equipping all designated seating positions with combination pelvic and upper torso passenger restraints; failure to use or improper use

(a) Unless specifically prohibited by the National Highway Transportation Safety Administration, all type 2 school pupil activity buses, manufactured on or after July 1, 2004, purchased or leased for use in California shall be equipped at all designated seating positions with a combination pelvic and upper torso passenger restraint system.

(b) For purposes of this section, a "passenger restraint system" is either of the following:

(1) A restraint system that is in compliance with Federal Motor Vehicle Safety Standard 209, for a type 2 seatbelt assembly, and with Federal Motor Vehicle Safety Standard 210, as those standards were in effect on the date that the school pupil activity bus was manufactured.

(2) A restraint system certified by the school pupil activity bus manufacturer that is in compliance with Federal Motor Vehicle Safety Standard 222 and incorporates a type 2 lap-shoulder restraint system.

(c) No person, school district, or organization, with respect to a type 2 school pupil activity bus equipped with passenger restraint systems pursuant to this section, may be charged for a violation of this code or any regulation adopted thereunder requiring a passenger to use a passenger restraint system, if a passenger on the school pupil activity bus fails to use or improperly uses the passenger restraint system. *(Added by Stats.2002, c. 360 (A.B.2681), § 2.)*

Cross References

Passenger restraint systems, school pupil activity buses, regulations mandating use, see Education Code § 38047.6.

§ 27317. Modification of a vehicle's computer or supplemental restraint system; distribution or sale of previously deployed airbag; penalties

A person who installs, reinstalls, rewires, tampers with, alters, or modifies for compensation, a vehicle's computer system or supplemental restraint system, including, but not limited to, the supplemental restraint system's on-board system performance indicators, so that it falsely indicates the supplemental restraint system is in proper working order, or who knowingly distributes or sells a previously deployed air bag or previously deployed air bag component that will no longer meet the original equipment manufacturing form or function for proper operation, is guilty of a misdemeanor punishable by a fine of up to five thousand dollars ($5,000) or by imprisonment in a county jail for up to one year, or by both the fine and imprisonment. *(Added by Stats.1999, c. 449 (A.B.1471), § 2. Amended by Stats.2012, c. 97 (A.B. 1854), § 1.)*

ARTICLE 3.2. CHILD PASSENGER SEAT RESTRAINTS [REPEALED]

§§ 27350 to 27356. Repealed by Stats.1982, c. 573, p. 2532, § 1, operative Jan. 1, 1984

ARTICLE 3.3. CHILD SAFETY BELT AND PASSENGER RESTRAINT REQUIREMENTS

Section
27360.   Children under eight years of age; obligation of parent, legal guardian, or driver not to transport in motor vehicle unless secured in rear seat child passenger restraint system; exception for driver if parent or legal guardian is present and not driving.
27360.5. Children eight years of age but under sixteen years of age; obligation of parent, legal guardian, or driver not to transport in motor vehicle unless secured in child passenger restraint system or safety belt; exception for driver if parent or legal guardian is present and not driving.
27360.6. Conviction under Section 27360 or 27360.5; penalties for first offense; penalties for second or subsequent conviction; allocation of fines collected.
27361.   Stopping of vehicles believed to be in violation; notice to appear.
27362.   Sale or installation of nonconforming child restraint system; violations; punishment; allocation of fines.
27362.1. Prohibition against sale or offer for sale of child passenger restraint system in use during a motor vehicle accident.
27363.   Exemption permitted due to child's physical unfitness, medical condition, or size; additional exceptions.
27363.5. Hospitals, clinics, and birthing centers; duty to provide and discuss information on current child passenger restraint systems law; duty to provide and discuss information on child passenger restraint system assistance; immunity from liability.
27364.   Legislative intent.
27365.   Car rental agencies; posting of law; exception; restraint systems rental; violations.
27366.   Child passenger restraints; information dissemination.
27368.   Child passengers; three-wheeled motor vehicles; vehicle length, height, and weight restrictions.

§ 27360. Children under eight years of age; obligation of parent, legal guardian, or driver not to transport in motor vehicle unless secured in rear seat child passenger restraint system; exception for driver if parent or legal guardian is present and not driving

(a) Except as provided in Section 27363 a parent, legal guardian, or driver shall not transport on a highway in a motor vehicle, as defined in paragraph (1) of subdivision (3) of Section 27315, a child or ward who is under eight years of age, without properly securing that child in a rear seat in an appropriate child passenger restraint system meeting applicable federal motor vehicle safety standards.

(b) Subdivision (a) does not apply to a driver if the parent or legal guardian of the child is also present in the motor vehicle and is not the driver. *(Added by Stats.2011, c. 474 (S.B.929), § 4.)*

Cross References

Traffic violation point counts, allocation of points, see Vehicle Code § 12810.

§ 27360.5. Children eight years of age but under sixteen years of age; obligation of parent, legal guardian, or driver not to transport in motor vehicle unless secured in child passenger restraint system or safety belt; exception for driver if parent or legal guardian is present and not driving

(a) A parent, legal guardian, or driver shall not transport on a highway in a motor vehicle, as defined in paragraph (1) of subdivision (c) of Section 27315, a child or ward who is eight years of age or older, but less than 16 years of age, without properly securing that child or ward in an appropriate child passenger restraint system or safety belt meeting applicable federal motor vehicle safety standards.

(b) Subdivision (a) does not apply to a driver if the parent or legal guardian of the child is also present in the motor vehicle and is not the driver. *(Added by Stats.2011, c. 474 (S.B.929), § 6.)*

Cross References

Signs posted at day care centers, contents, requirements concerning child passenger restraint system under this section, see Health and Safety Code § 1596.95.
Traffic violation point counts, allocation of points, see Vehicle Code § 12810.

§ 27360.6. Conviction under Section 27360 or 27360.5; penalties for first offense; penalties for second or subsequent conviction; allocation of fines collected

(a)(1) For a conviction under Section 27360 or 27360.5, a first offense is punishable by a fine of one hundred dollars ($100), except that the court may reduce or waive the fine if the defendant establishes to the satisfaction of the court that he or she is economically disadvantaged, and the court, instead, refers the defendant to a community education program that includes, but is not limited to, education on the proper installation and use of a child passenger restraint system for children of all ages, and provides certification to the court of completion of that program. Upon completion of the program, the defendant shall provide proof of participation in the program. If an education program on the proper installation and use of a child passenger restraint system is not available within 50 miles of the residence of the defendant, the requirement to participate in that program shall be waived. If the fine is paid, waived, or reduced, the court shall report the conviction to the department pursuant to Section 1803.

(2) The court may require a defendant described under paragraph (1) to attend an education program that includes demonstration of proper installation and use of a child passenger restraint system and provides certification to the court that the defendant has presented for inspection a child passenger restraint system that meets applicable federal safety standards.

(b)(1) A second or subsequent conviction under Section 27360 or 27360.5 is punishable by a fine of two hundred fifty dollars ($250), no part of which may be waived by the court, except that the court may reduce or waive the fine if the defendant establishes to the satisfaction of the court that he or she is economically disadvantaged, and the court, instead refers the defendant to a community education program that includes, but is not limited to, education on the proper installation and use of child passenger restraint systems for children of all ages, and provides certification to the court of completion of that program. Upon completion of the program, the defendant shall provide proof of participation in the program. If an education program on the proper installation and use of a child passenger restraint system is not available within 50 miles of the residence of the defendant, the requirement to participate in that program shall be waived. If the fine is paid, waived, or reduced, the court shall report the conviction to the department pursuant to Section 1803.

(2) The court may require a defendant described under paragraph (1) to attend an education program that includes demonstration of proper installation and use of a child passenger restraint system and provides certification to the court that the defendant has presented for inspection a child passenger restraint system that meets applicable federal safety standards.

(c) Notwithstanding any other law, the fines collected under this section shall be allocated as follows:

(1)(A) Sixty percent to health departments of local jurisdictions where the violation occurred, to be used for a community education and assistance program that includes, but is not limited to, demonstration of the proper installation and use of child passenger restraint systems for children of all ages and assistance to economi-

cally disadvantaged families in obtaining a restraint system through a low-cost purchase or loan. The county or city health department shall designate a coordinator to facilitate the creation of a special account and to develop a relationship with the court system to facilitate the transfer of funds to the program. The county or city may contract for the implementation of the program. Prior to obtaining possession of a child passenger restraint system pursuant to this subdivision, a person shall attend an education program that includes demonstration of proper installation and use of a child passenger restraint system.

(B) As the proceeds from fines become available, county or city health departments shall prepare and maintain a listing of all child passenger restraint low-cost purchase or loaner programs in their counties, including a semiannual verification that all programs listed are in existence. Each county or city shall forward the listing to the Office of Traffic Safety in the Business, Transportation and Housing Agency and the courts, birthing centers, community child health and disability prevention programs, county clinics, prenatal clinics, women, infants, and children programs, and county hospitals in that county, who shall make the listing available to the public. The Office of Traffic Safety shall maintain a listing of all of the programs in the state.

(2) Twenty-five percent to the county or city for the administration of the community education program.

(3) Fifteen percent to the city, to be deposited in its general fund except that, if the violation occurred in an unincorporated area, this amount shall be allocated to the county for purposes of paragraph (1). *(Added by Stats. 2011, c. 474 (S.B.929), § 7.)*

§ 27361. Stopping of vehicles believed to be in violation; notice to appear

A law enforcement officer reasonably suspecting a violation of Section 27360 or 27360.5, or both of those sections, may stop a vehicle transporting a child appearing to the officer to be within the age specified in Section 27360 or 27360.5. The officer may issue a notice to appear for a violation of Section 27360 or 27360.5. *(Added by Stats.1982, c. 839, p. 3165, § 2. Amended by Stats.2000, c. 675 (S.B.567), § 7; Stats.2004, c. 420 (A.B.2139), § 4; Stats.2011, c. 474 (S.B.929), § 8.)*

§ 27362. Sale or installation of nonconforming child restraint system; violations; punishment; allocation of fines

(a) A manufacturer, wholesaler, or retailer shall not sell, offer for sale, or install in a motor vehicle, a child passenger restraint system that does not conform to all applicable federal motor vehicle safety standards on the date of manufacture. Responsibility for compliance with this section shall rest with the individual selling the system, offering the system for sale, or installing the system. A person who violates this section is guilty of a misdemeanor and shall be punished as follows:

(1) Upon a first conviction, by a fine not exceeding four hundred dollars ($400), or by imprisonment in a county jail for a period of not more than 90 days, or both.

(2) Upon a second or subsequent conviction, by a fine not exceeding one thousand dollars ($1,000), or by imprisonment in a county jail for a period of not more than 180 days, or both.

(b) The fines collected for a violation of this section shall be allocated as follows:

(1)(A) Sixty percent to the county or city health department where the violation occurred, to be used for a child passenger restraint low-cost purchase or loaner program which shall include, but not be limited to, education on the proper installation and use of a child passenger restraint system. The county health department shall designate a coordinator to facilitate the creation of a special account and to develop a relationship with the superior court to facilitate the transfer of funds to the program. The county may contract for the implementation of the program. Prior to obtaining possession of a child passenger restraint system pursuant to this section, a person shall receive information relating to the importance of utilizing that system.

(B) As the proceeds from fines become available, county health departments shall prepare and maintain a listing of all child passenger restraint low-cost purchase or loaner programs in their counties, including a semiannual verification that all programs listed are in existence. Each county shall forward the listing to the Office of Traffic Safety in the Business, Transportation and Housing Agency and the courts, birthing centers, community child health and disability prevention programs, and county hospitals in that county, who shall make the listing available to the public. The Office of Traffic Safety shall maintain a listing of all of the programs in the state.

(2) Twenty-five percent to the county for the administration of the program.

(3) Fifteen percent to the city, to be deposited in its general fund except that, if the violation occurred in an unincorporated area, this amount shall be allocated to the county for purposes of paragraph (1). *(Added by Stats. 1982, c. 839, p. 3165, § 2. Amended by Stats.1990, c. 33 (S.B.1372), § 5, eff. March 26, 1990; Stats.1991, c. 1223 (S.B.1073), § 4; Stats.1995, c. 512 (S.B.503), § 7; Stats. 2002, c. 784 (S.B.1316), § 601; Stats.2004, c. 420 (A.B. 2139), § 5; Stats.2005, c. 22 (S.B.1108), § 204.)*

Law Revision Commission Comments

2002 Amendment

Subdivision (b)(1) of Section 27362 is amended to reflect unification of the municipal and superior courts pursuant to Article VI, Section 5(e), of the California Constitution. [32 Cal.L.Rev.Comm. Reports 542 (2002)].

§ 27362.1. Prohibition against sale or offer for sale of child passenger restraint system in use during a motor vehicle accident

(a) No individual may sell or offer for sale a child passenger restraint system that was in use by a child during an accident involving a motor vehicle.

(b) A violation of this section shall be punished by a fine of one hundred dollars ($100). *(Added by Stats.2002, c. 703 (A.B.1902), § 2.)*

Cross References

Insurance coverage for replacement of child passenger restraint system, see Insurance Code § 11580.011.

§ 27363. Exemption permitted due to child's physical unfitness, medical condition, or size; additional exceptions

(a) The court may exempt from the requirements of this article any class of child by age, weight, or size if it is determined that the use of a child passenger restraint system would be impractical by reason of physical unfitness, medical condition, or size. The court may require satisfactory proof of the child's physical unfitness, medical condition, or size and that an appropriate special needs child passenger restraint system is not available.

(b) In case of a life-threatening emergency, or when a child is being transported in an authorized emergency vehicle, if there is no child passenger restraint system available, a child may be transported without the use of that system, but the child shall be secured by a seatbelt.

(c) A child weighing more than 40 pounds may be transported in the backseat of a vehicle while wearing only a lap safety belt when the backseat of the vehicle is not equipped with a combination lap and shoulder safety belt.

(d) Notwithstanding Section 27360, a child or ward under eight years of age who is four feet nine inches in height or taller may be properly restrained by a safety belt, as defined in paragraph (2) of subdivision (d) of Section 27315, rather than by a child passenger restraint system.

(e) Notwithstanding Section 27360, a child or ward under eight years of age may ride properly secured in an appropriate child passenger restraint system meeting applicable federal motor vehicle safety standards in the front seat of a motor vehicle under any of the following circumstances:

(1) There is no rear seat.

(2) The rear seats are side-facing jump seats.

(3) The rear seats are rear-facing seats.

(4) The child passenger restraint system cannot be installed properly in the rear seat.

(5) All rear seats are already occupied by children seven years of age or under.

(6) Medical reasons necessitate that the child or ward not ride in the rear seat. The court may require satisfactory proof of the child's medical condition.

(f) Notwithstanding subdivision (e), a child shall not be transported in a rear-facing child passenger restraint system in the front seat of a motor vehicle that is equipped with an active frontal passenger airbag. *(Added by Stats.2000, c. 675 (S.B.567), § 9, operative Jan. 1, 2002. Amended by Stats.2001, c. 84 (S.B.42), § 5, eff. July 19, 2001, operative Jan. 1, 2002; Stats.2011, c. 474 (S.B.929), § 9.)*

§ 27363.5. Hospitals, clinics, and birthing centers; duty to provide and discuss information on current child passenger restraint systems law; duty to provide and discuss information on child passenger restraint system assistance; immunity from liability

(a) A public or private hospital, clinic, or birthing center shall, at the time of the discharge of a child, provide to and discuss with the parents or the person to whom the child is released, if the child is under eight years of age, information on the current law requiring child passenger restraint systems, safety belts, and the transportation of children in rear seats.

(b) A public or private hospital, clinic, or birthing center shall also provide to and discuss with the parent or person to whom the child is released, if the child is under eight years of age, contact information to direct the person to an Internet Web site or other contact that could provide, at no cost or low cost, information and assistance relating to child passenger restraint system requirements, installation, and inspection. Pursuant to this subdivision, the hospital, clinic, or birthing center does not have any additional obligation to provide patients with any assistance relating to child passenger restraint systems, other than providing the contact information as set forth in this subdivision. This contact information may include the following:

(1) Call 1–866–SEAT–CHECK or visit www.seatcheck.org to find a nearby location.

(2) The telephone number of the local office of the Department of the California Highway Patrol.

(3) The Internet Web site for the National Highway Traffic Safety Administration's Child Safety Seat Inspection Station Locator.

(4) The Internet Web site for the State Department of Public Health's child passenger restraint system safety inspection locator.

(c) A public or private hospital, clinic, or birthing center shall not be responsible for the failure of the parent or person to whom the child is released to properly transport the child. *(Added by Stats.2000, c. 675 (S.B.567), § 11, operative Jan. 1, 2002. Amended by Stats.2011, c. 474 (S.B.929), § 10; Stats.2012, c. 185 (A.B.1452), § 2.)*

§ 27364. Legislative intent

(a) It is the intent of the Legislature, in enacting this article, to insure that children, who are, because of their tender years, helpless dependent passengers, are provided with the safest transportation possible.

(b) It is the further intent of the Legislature to stress and communicate to all drivers in this state the importance of using child passenger restraint systems.

(c) Nothing in this article shall be construed to extend application of these provisions to a class of children other than the class of children herein specified. *(Added by Stats.1982, c. 839, p. 3165, § 2. Amended by Stats.1995, c. 512 (S.B.503), § 9.)*

§ 27365. Car rental agencies; posting of law; exception; restraint systems rental; violations

(a)(1) A car rental agency in California shall inform each of its customers of Section 27360 by posting, in a place conspicuous to the public in each established place of business of the agency, a notice not smaller than 15 by 20 inches which states the following:

"CALIFORNIA LAW REQUIRES ALL CHILDREN UNDER 8 YEARS OF AGE TO BE TRANSPORTED IN THE REAR SEAT OF THE VEHICLE IN A CHILD RESTRAINT SYSTEM. THIS AGENCY IS REQUIRED TO PROVIDE FOR RENTAL OF A CHILD RESTRAINT SYSTEM IF YOU DO NOT HAVE A CHILD RESTRAINT SYSTEM YOURSELF."

(2) The posted notice specified in paragraph (1) is not required if the car rental agency's place of business is located in a hotel that has a business policy prohibiting the posting of signs or notices in any area of the hotel. In that case, a car rental agency shall furnish a written notice to each customer that contains the same information as required for the posted notice.

(b) Every car rental agency in California shall have available for, and shall, upon request, provide for rental to, adults traveling with children under eight years of age, child passenger restraint systems that are certified by the manufacturer to meet applicable federal motor vehicle safety standards for use by children, are in good and safe condition, with no missing original parts, and are not older than five years.

(c) A violation of this section is an infraction punishable by a fine of one hundred dollars ($100). *(Added by Stats.2000, c. 675 (S.B.567), § 13, operative Jan. 1, 2002. Amended by Stats.2001, c. 84 (S.B.42), § 6, eff. July 19, 2001, operative Jan. 1, 2002; Stats.2004, c. 420 (A.B.2139), § 6; Stats.2011, c. 474 (S.B.929), § 11.)*

§ 27366. Child passenger restraints; information dissemination

(a) The department shall do the following:

(1) Prepare and disseminate materials for the purpose of educating the public about the importance of using passenger restraints for infants and children under 15

years of age. These materials shall include, but are not limited to, audiovisual aids and written materials that explain the effects of motor vehicle accidents on infants and children and the reduction in risk of injury or death as a result of the utilization of passenger restraints for infants and children.

(2) As funding is available, produce and administer a billboard campaign stressing the importance of utilizing child passenger restraint systems and instructing the public on where to obtain those systems.

(b) The department, the Office of Traffic Safety, and the State Department of Health Services shall meet annually to coordinate, share information about, and outline the programs that each organization is pursuing in the area of child passenger restraint systems. *(Added by Stats.1995, c. 512 (S.B.503), § 10.)*

§ **27368. Child passengers; three-wheeled motor vehicles; vehicle length, height, and weight restrictions**

This article applies to child passengers in a fully enclosed three-wheeled motor vehicle that is not less than seven feet in length and not less than four feet in width, and has an unladen weight of 900 pounds or more. *(Added by Stats.1997, c. 710 (A.B.1029), § 3.)*

ARTICLE 3.4. EMERGENCY EXITS FOR CHARTER–PARTY CARRIERS OF PASSENGERS

Section
27375. Limousines; emergency exits; unlocking of doors; duties of owner or operator; application of provisions.

§ **27375. Limousines; emergency exits; unlocking of doors; duties of owner or operator; application of provisions**

(a) Any person who operates a limousine, as defined in subdivision (i) of Section 5371.4 of the Public Utilities Code, in any city, county, or city and county, that has been modified or extended for purposes of increasing vehicle length in an amount sufficient to accommodate additional passengers shall ensure that the vehicle has at least two rear side doors and one or two rear windows, as specified in paragraph (1), that the rear seat passengers or all passengers of the vehicle may open from the inside of the vehicle in case of any fire or other emergency that may require the immediate exit of the passengers of the vehicle. A limousine subject to this section shall be equipped with both of the following:

(1)(A) Except as provided in subparagraph (B), at least two rear push-out windows that are accessible to all passengers. At least one push-out window shall be located on each side of the vehicle, unless the design of the limousine precludes the installation of a push-out window on one side of the vehicle, in which case the second push-out window shall instead be located in the roof of the vehicle.

(B) If the design of the limousine precludes the installation of even one push-out window on a side of the vehicle, one push-out window shall instead be located in the roof of the vehicle.

(C) The Department of the California Highway Patrol shall establish, by regulation, standards to ensure that window exits are operable and sufficient in emergency situations for limousine passengers. The department shall ensure that these regulations comply with any applicable federal motor vehicle safety standards.

(2) At least two rear side doors that are accessible to all passengers and that may be opened manually by any passenger. At least one rear side door shall be located on each side of the vehicle. For vehicles modified or extended for purposes of increasing vehicle length in an amount sufficient to accommodate additional passengers on or after July 1, 2015, at least one of these side doors shall be located near the driver's compartment and another near the back of the vehicle. These side doors shall comply with any applicable federal motor vehicle safety standards as deemed necessary by the Department of the California Highway Patrol.

(b) In the case of any fire or other emergency that requires the immediate exit of the passengers from the limousine, the driver of the limousine shall unlock the doors so that the rear side doors can be opened by the passengers from the inside of the vehicle.

(c) An owner or operator of a limousine shall do all of the following:

(1) Instruct all passengers on the safety features of the vehicle prior to the beginning of any trip, including, but not limited to, instructions for lowering the partition between the driver and passenger compartments and for communicating with the driver by the use of an intercom or other onboard or wireless device.

(2) Disclose to the contracting party and the passengers whether the limousine meets the safety requirements described in this section.

(3) If paragraph (3) of subdivision (d) applies, the owner or operator of a limousine shall further disclose to the contracting party and the passengers that the limousine does not meet the safety requirements required in subdivision (a) regarding vehicle escape options because of its exempt status, and therefore may pose a greater risk to passengers should emergency escape be necessary.

(d)(1) Subdivision (a) shall apply to all limousines modified or extended for purposes of increasing vehicle length in an amount sufficient to accommodate additional passengers on or after July 1, 2015.

(2) Subdivision (a) shall, beginning January 1, 2016, apply to all limousines that were modified or extended for purposes of increasing vehicle length in an amount sufficient to accommodate additional passengers prior to July 1, 2015.

(3) Except as provided in paragraph (4), subdivision (a) shall not apply to any limousine manufactured prior to

1970 and that has an active transportation charter-party carrier (TCP) number as of August 15, 2013.

(4) Subdivision (a) shall apply to any limousine manufactured prior to 1970 if it is modified or extended for the purpose of increasing vehicle length in an amount sufficient to accommodate additional passengers after August 15, 2013. *(Added by Stats.2013, c. 752 (S.B.109), § 2.)*

ARTICLE 3.5.   HEADSETS AND EARPLUGS

Section
27400.   Wearing of headsets, earplugs or hearing protectors.

§ 27400.   Wearing of headsets, earplugs or hearing protectors

A person operating a motor vehicle or bicycle may not wear a headset covering, or earplugs in, both ears.   This prohibition does not apply to any of the following:

(a) A person operating authorized emergency vehicles, as defined in Section 165.

(b) A person engaged in the operation of either special construction equipment or equipment for use in the maintenance of any highway.

(c) A person engaged in the operation of refuse collection equipment who is wearing a safety headset or safety earplugs.

(d) A person wearing personal hearing protectors in the form of earplugs or molds that are specifically designed to attenuate injurious noise levels.   The plugs or molds shall be designed in a manner so as to not inhibit the wearer's ability to hear a siren or horn from an emergency vehicle or a horn from another motor vehicle.

(e) A person using a prosthetic device that aids the hard of hearing. *(Added by Stats.1973, c. 87, p. 148, § 1. Amended by Stats.1975, c. 495, p. 1021, § 1; Stats.1977, c. 348, p. 1317, § 1; Stats.1980, c. 107, p. 248, § 1, eff. May 20, 1980; Stats.1982, c. 542, p. 2478, § 1, eff. Aug. 18, 1982; Stats.1985, c. 736, § 2; Stats.2003, c. 594 (S.B.315), § 45.)*

ARTICLE 4.   TIRES

Section
27450.   Thickness of solid tire.
27451.   Measurement of solid tire.
27452.   Condition of solid tire.
27453.   Dual solid tires.
27454.   Protuberances on tires.
27455.   Inner tubes.
27459.   Tire chains or snow-tread tires;   manufacturer's markings on snow-tread tires.
27459.5.   Sale, lease, installation or replacement of tire traction devices.
27459.6.   Repealed.
27460.   Four-wheel drive vehicles.
27460.5.   Sale of recut or regrooved tires.
27461.   Use of recut or regrooved tires.
27465.   Tread depth of pneumatic tires.

Section
27500.   Pneumatic tire standard regulations.
27501.   Pneumatic tires which do not conform to regulations.
27502.   Sale of tires not conforming to noise standards prohibited.
27503.   Adoption of regulations;   noise standards for tires.
27504.   Repealed.

§ 27450.   Thickness of solid tire

When any vehicle is equipped with any solid tire, the solid tire shall have a minimum thickness of resilient rubber as follows:

(a) If the width of the tire is three inches but less than six inches, one inch thick.

(b) If the width of the tire is six inches but not more than nine inches, 1¼ inches thick.

(c) If the width of the tire is more than nine inches, 1½ inches thick. *(Stats.1959, c. 3, p. 1738, § 27450.)*

Cross References

Metal tire defined, see Vehicle Code § 395.
Pneumatic tire defined, see Vehicle Code § 485.
Pneumatic tires, width of vehicle, restrictions, see Vehicle Code § 35101.
Solid tire, see Vehicle Code § 560.
Speed laws, see Vehicle Code §§ 22409, 22410.
Transporting explosives, requirements, see Vehicle Code § 31610.

§ 27451.   Measurement of solid tire

The rubber of a solid tire shall be measured between the surface of the roadway and the nearest metal part of the base flange to which the tire is attached at the point where the concentrated weight of the vehicle bears upon the surface of the roadway. *(Stats.1959, c. 3, p. 1738, § 27451.)*

Cross References

Solid tire defined, see Vehicle Code § 560.
Speed laws, see Vehicle Code §§ 22409, 22410.

§ 27452.   Condition of solid tire

The required thickness of rubber shall extend evenly around the entire periphery of the tire.   The entire solid tire shall be securely attached to the channel base and shall be without flat spots or bumpy rubber. *(Stats.1959, c. 3, p. 1739, § 27452.)*

§ 27453.   Dual solid tires

There shall not be an average difference greater than ⅛ inch between the outside diameters of each single tire composing a dual solid rubber tire. *(Stats.1959, c. 3, p. 1739, § 27453.)*

Cross References

Solid tire defined, see Vehicle Code § 560.

§ 27454.   Protuberances on tires

A tire on a vehicle upon a highway shall not have on its periphery any block, stud, flange, cleat, ridge, bead, or any other protuberance of metal or wood that projects beyond the tread of the traction surface of the tire.

This section does not apply to any of the following:

(a) Tire traction devices of reasonable size used to prevent skidding when upon wet surfaces or when upon snow or ice.

(b) Pneumatic tires that have embedded therein wire not to exceed 0.075 of an inch in diameter and that are constructed so that under no conditions will the percentage of metal in contact with the roadway exceed 5 percent of the total tire area in contact with the roadway, except that during the first 1,000 miles of use or operation of the tire, the metal in contact with the roadway may exceed 5 percent of the tire area in contact with the roadway, but shall in no event exceed 20 percent of the area.

(c) Vehicles operated upon unimproved roadways when necessary in the construction or repair of highways.

(d) Traction engines or tractors when operated under the conditions of a permit first obtained from the Department of Transportation.

(e)(1) Pneumatic tires containing metal-type studs of tungsten carbide or other suitable material that are inserted or constructed so that under no condition will the number of studs or the percentage of metal in contact with the roadway exceed 3 percent of the total tire area in contact with the roadway, between November 1 and April 30 of each year. A vehicle may be equipped year-round with tires that have studs that retract pneumatically or mechanically when not in use, if the studs are retracted between May 1 and October 31 of each year. A tire on a vehicle shall not be worn to a point at which the studs protrude beyond the tire tread when retracted.

(2) The commissioner, after consultation with the Department of Transportation, may extend the period during which the studded pneumatic tires may be used with studs deployed or inserted in areas of the state for the protection of the public because of adverse weather conditions.

(f) Pneumatic tires used on an authorized emergency vehicle, as defined in Section 165, containing metal-type studs of tungsten carbide or other suitable material, if the studs are inserted or constructed so that under no conditions will the number of studs or the percentage of metal in contact with the roadway exceed 3 percent of the total tire area in contact with the roadway. Notwithstanding subdivision (e), authorized emergency vehicles are permitted the unrestricted use of studded pneumatic tires throughout the year. *(Stats.1959, c. 3, p. 1739, § 2754. Amended by Stats.1967, c. 704, p. 2078, § 1, eff. July 12, 1967; Stats.1969, c. 169, p. 420, § 1, eff. June 10, 1969; Stats.1974, c. 545, p. 1335, § 233; Stats.1975, c. 72, p. 136, § 1, eff. May 13, 1975; Stats.1976, c. 70, p. 104, § 1, eff. March 27, 1976; Stats.1978, c. 190, p. 431, § 1, eff. June 2, 1978; Stats.1979, c. 364, p. 1230, § 3; Stats.1981, c. 653, p. 2432, § 1, eff. Sept. 23, 1981; Stats.1982, c. 703, p. 2854, § 1, eff. Sept. 8, 1982; Stats.1983, c. 212, § 1; Stats.1990, c. 71 (A.B.2498), § 3,* eff. May 1, 1990; Stats.1998, c. 828 (S.B.1637), § 22; Stats.2008, c. 220 (A.B.1971), § 1.)*

Cross References

Metal tire defined, see Vehicle Code § 395,
Pneumatic tire defined, see Vehicle Code § 485.
Solid tire, see Vehicle Code § 560.
Speed laws, see Vehicle Code §§ 22409, 22410.
Tire traction devices defined, see Vehicle Code § 605.
Vehicles operated incidentally over highway, see Vehicle Code § 25802.

§ 27455. Inner tubes

(a) On and after January 1, 1975, no person shall sell or offer for sale an inner tube for use in a radial tire unless, at the time of manufacture, the tube valve stem is colored red or is distinctly marked in accordance with rules and regulations adopted by the department, taking into consideration the recommendations of manufacturers of inner tubes.

(b) No person shall install an inner tube in a radial tire unless the inner tube is designed for use in a radial tire. *(Added by Stats.1973, c. 741, p. 1338, § 1, eff. Sept. 25, 1973.)*

§ 27459. Tire chains or snow-tread tires; manufacturer's markings on snow-tread tires

No person shall operate any motor vehicle, trailer or semitrailer upon any portion of a highway without tire traction devices when that portion of the highway is signed for the requirement of tire traction devices. In any case where a passenger vehicle or motortruck having an unladen weight of 6,000 pounds or less may be required by the Department of Transportation or local authorities to be equipped with tire traction devices, the devices shall be placed on at least two drive wheels, or the department or local authorities may provide, in the alternative, that the vehicle may be equipped with snow-tread tires on at least two drive wheels when the weather and surface conditions at the time are such that the stopping, tractive, and cornering abilities of the snow-tread tires are adequate. The snow-tread tires shall be of a type and design manufactured for use on snow as a replacement for tire chains or tire traction devices, shall be in good condition, and shall bear the marking of M-S, M/S, or other marking indicating that the tire was manufactured for use on snow, or, in the case of tires purchased before January 1, 1987, shall either bear the markings or, in the opinion of the inspecting officer, comply with the tread pattern requirements of Section 558. *(Added by Stats.1959, c. 1572, p. 3902, § 1. Amended by Stats.1961, c. 26, p. 932, § 2; Stats.1963, c. 430, p. 1250, § 1; Stats.1967, c. 374, p. 1601, § 1; Stats.1970, c. 424, p. 839, § 1; Stats.1972, c. 281, p. 555, § 1; Stats.1974, c. 545, p. 1336, § 234; Stats.1974, c. 591, p. 1411, § 1; Stats.1986, c. 325, § 1; Stats.1990, c. 71 (A.B.2498), § 4, eff. May 1, 1990.)*

Cross References

Snow-tread tire defined, see Vehicle Code § 558.

Tire traction devices defined, see Vehicle Code § 605.

§ 27459.5. Sale, lease, installation or replacement of tire traction devices

(a) No person shall sell, offer for sale, lease, install, or replace on a vehicle for use on a highway, any tire traction devices which are not in compliance with requirements specified in Section 605.

(b) Every manufacturer who sells, offers for sale, or manufactures for use upon a vehicle, tire traction devices subject to the requirements of Section 605 shall, before the device is offered for sale, have laboratory test data showing compliance with those requirements. Tests may be conducted by the manufacturer. *(Added by Stats.1990, c. 71 (A.B.2498), § 5, eff. May 1, 1990.)*

Cross References

Tire traction devices defined, see Vehicle Code § 605.

§ 27459.6. Repealed by Stats.1990, c. 71 (A.B.2498), § 6, eff. May 1, 1990

§ 27460. Four-wheel drive vehicles

Any passenger vehicle or motortruck having an unladen weight of 6,500 pounds or less and operated and equipped with four-wheel drive and with snow-tread tires on all four drive wheels may be operated upon any portion of a highway without tire traction devices, notwithstanding the fact that the highway is signed for the requirement of those devices and provided that tire traction devices for at least one set of drive wheels are carried in or upon the vehicle. The snow-tread tires shall meet the requirements specified in Section 27459, and the vehicle shall not, when so operated, tow another vehicle except as may be necessary to move a disabled vehicle from the roadway.

No person shall use those tires on four-wheel drive vehicles in place of tire traction devices whenever weather and roadway conditions at the time are such that the stopping, tractive, and cornering abilities of the tires are not adequate or whenever the Department of Transportation or local authorities, in their respective jurisdictions, place signs prohibiting their operation unless equipped with tire traction devices. *(Added by Stats.1965, c. 600, p. 1934, § 1. Amended by Stats.1974, c. 545, p. 1336, § 235; Stats.1974, c. 591, p. 1412, § 2; Stats.1990, c. 71 (A.B. 2498), § 7, eff. May 1, 1990.)*

Cross References

Snow-tread tire defined, see Vehicle Code § 558.
Tire Traction devices defined, see Vehicle Code § 605.

§ 27460.5. Sale of recut or regrooved tires

No person shall knowingly sell or offer or expose for sale any motor vehicle tire except a commercial vehicle tire, or any motor vehicle equipped with any tire except a commercial vehicle tire, which has been recut or regrooved. For purposes of this section a recut or regrooved tire is an unretreaded or unrecapped tire into

864

which new grooves have been cut or burned. *(Added by Stats.1965, c. 1518, p. 3612, § 1.)*

§ 27461. Use of recut or regrooved tires

No person shall cause or permit the operation of and no driver shall knowingly operate any motor vehicle except a commercial vehicle, on any street or highway, which is equipped with one or more recut or regrooved tires. For purposes of this section a recut or regrooved tire is an unretreaded or unrecapped tire into which new grooves have been cut or burned. *(Added by Stats.1965, c. 1518, p. 3612, § 2.)*

Cross References

Commercial vehicle defined, see Vehicle Code § 260.

§ 27465. Tread depth of pneumatic tires

(a) No dealer or person holding a retail seller's permit shall sell, offer for sale, expose for sale, or install on a vehicle axle for use on a highway, a pneumatic tire when the tire has less than the tread depth specified in subdivision (b). This subdivision does not apply to any person who installs on a vehicle, as part of an emergency service rendered to a disabled vehicle upon a highway, a spare tire with which the disabled vehicle was equipped.

(b) No person shall use on a highway a pneumatic tire on a vehicle axle when the tire has less than the following tread depth, except when temporarily installed on a disabled vehicle as specified in subdivision (a):

(1) One thirty-second ($\frac{1}{32}$) of an inch tread depth in any two adjacent grooves at any location of the tire, except as provided in paragraphs (2) and (3).

(2) Four thirty-second ($\frac{4}{32}$) of an inch tread depth at all points in all major grooves on a tire on the steering axle of any motor vehicle specified in Section 34500, and two thirty-second ($\frac{2}{32}$) of an inch tread depth at all points in all major grooves on all other tires on the axles of these vehicles.

(3) Six thirty-second ($\frac{6}{32}$) of an inch tread depth at all points in all major grooves on snow tires used in lieu of tire traction devices in posted tire traction device control areas.

(c) The measurement of tread depth shall not be made where tie bars, humps, or fillets are located.

(d) The requirements of this section shall not apply to implements of husbandry.

(e) The department, if it determines that such action is appropriate and in keeping with reasonable safety requirements, may adopt regulations establishing more stringent tread depth requirements than those specified in this section for those vehicles defined in Sections 322 and 545, and may adopt regulations establishing tread depth requirements different from those specified in this section for those vehicles listed in Section 34500. *(Added by Stats.1970, c. 216, p. 469, § 2. Amended by Stats.1971, c. 510, p. 1005, § 4, operative May 3, 1972; Stats.1976, c. 70, p. 105, § 2, eff. March 27, 1976; Stats.1977, c. 77, p.*

483, § 1, eff. May 26, 1977; Stats.1977, c. 733, p. 2324, § 1; Stats.1980, c. 676, p. 2025, § 313; Stats.1984, c. 1567, § 1; Stats.1990, c. 71 (A.B.2498), § 8, eff. May 1, 1990.)

Cross References

Pneumatic tire defined, see Vehicle Code § 485.
Tire tread defined, see Vehicle Code § 610.

§ 27500. Pneumatic tire standard regulations

(a) The department may adopt regulations relating to standards for pneumatic tires of a vehicle type as it determines necessary to provide for public safety.

(b) In adopting these regulations, the department shall consider as evidence of generally accepted standards, the rules and regulations which have been adopted by the Federal Highway Administration and Rubber Manufacturers Assocation [1]. *(Added by Stats.1965, c. 1619, p. 3706, § 1. Amended by Stats.1970, c. 216, p. 469, § 3.)*

[1] So in enrolled bill.

Cross References

Pneumatic tire defined, see Vehicle Code § 485.

§ 27501. Pneumatic tires which do not conform to regulations

(a) No dealer or person holding a retail seller's permit shall sell, offer for sale, expose for sale, or install on a vehicle for use on a highway, a pneumatic tire which is not in compliance with regulations adopted pursuant to Section 27500. This subdivision shall not apply to any person who installs on a vehicle, as part of an emergency service rendered to a vehicle upon a highway, a spare tire with which such disabled vehicle was equipped.

(b) No person shall use on a highway a pneumatic tire which is not in conformance with such regulations. *(Added by Stats.1970, c. 216, p. 469, § 4. Amended by Stats.1971, c. 510, p. 1006, § 5, operative May 3, 1972; Stats.1976, c. 70, p. 105, § 3, eff. March 27, 1976.)*

§ 27502. Sale of tires not conforming to noise standards prohibited

No dealer or person holding a retail seller's permit shall sell, offer for sale, expose for sale, or install on a vehicle for use on a highway, a tire which is not in compliance with regulations adopted pursuant to Section 27503. *(Added by Stats.1971, c. 1197, p. 2293, § 1, operative May 3, 1972.)*

§ 27503. Adoption of regulations; noise standards for tires

(a) The commissioner, after public hearings, shall adopt regulations setting noise standards for pneumatic tires. Such standards shall be the lowest level of noise consistent with economic and technological feasibility and with public safety as stated in the regulations adopted pursuant to Section 27500. Such standards may be adopted for each tire-vehicle type combination. The regulations may require the manufacturer to prove to the commissioner that the tire meets the standards, subject to

such inspection as the commissioner prescribes. The regulations shall be filed with the Legislature eight months after the federal study on tire noise is available, and shall become operative one year after such filing.

(b) It is the intent of the Legislature in enacting this section that the commissioner shall consider recommendations of the United States Department of Transportation before developing independent standards for tire noise. *(Added by Stats.1971, c. 1197, p. 2293, § 2, operative May 3, 1972.)*

Cross References

Pneumatic tire defined, see Vehicle Code § 485.

§ 27504. Repealed by Stats.1979, c. 723, p. 2225, § 35

ARTICLE 5. FENDERS, ORNAMENTS, AND TELEVISION

Section
27600. Fenders and mudguards.
27601. Repealed.
27602. Television receiver, video monitor, or television or video screen, or similar means of displaying broadcast or signal.
27603. Color required for former schoolbus.
27604. Law enforcement vehicles; repainting on sale.
27605. Vehicle painted as law enforcement vehicle; prohibited ownership; exceptions.
27606. Light bar or facsimile; prohibited equipment.
27607. Light bar or facsimile; application to certain vehicles.

§ 27600. Fenders and mudguards

No person shall operate any motor vehicle having three or more wheels, any trailer, or semitrailer unless equipped with fenders, covers, or devices, including flaps or splash aprons, or unless the body of the vehicle or attachments thereto afford adequate protection to effectively minimize the spray or splash of water or mud to the rear of the vehicle and all such equipment or such body or attachments thereto shall be at least as wide as the tire tread. This section does not apply to those vehicles exempt from registration, trailers and semitrailers having an unladen weight of under 1,500 pounds, or any vehicles manufactured and first registered prior to January 1, 1971, having an unladen weight of under 1,500 pounds. *(Stats.1959, c. 3, p. 1739, § 27600. Amended by Stats. 1970, c. 215, p. 468, § 1.)*

Cross References

Street rod vehicles, non-exemption from equipment requirements, see Vehicle Code § 5004.6.
Vehicles of historic value, see Vehicle Code § 5004.

§ 27601. Repealed by Stats.1994, c. 270 (A.B.3326), § 54

§ 27602. Television receiver, video monitor, or television or video screen, or similar means of displaying broadcast or signal

(a) A person shall not drive a motor vehicle if a television receiver, a video monitor, or a television or video screen, or any other similar means of visually displaying a television broadcast or video signal that produces entertainment or business applications, is operating and is located in the motor vehicle at a point forward of the back of the driver's seat, or is operating and the monitor, screen, or display is visible to the driver while driving the motor vehicle.

(b) Subdivision (a) does not apply to the following equipment when installed in a vehicle:

(1) A vehicle information display.

(2) A global positioning display.

(3) A mapping display.

(4) A visual display used to enhance or supplement the driver's view forward, behind, or to the sides of a motor vehicle for the purpose of maneuvering the vehicle.

(5) A television receiver, video monitor, television or video screen, or any other similar means of visually displaying a television broadcast or video signal, if that equipment satisfies one of the following requirements:

(A) The equipment has an interlock device that, when the motor vehicle is driven, disables the equipment for all uses except as a visual display as described in paragraphs (1) to (4), inclusive.

(B) The equipment is designed, operated, and configured in a manner that prevents the driver of the motor vehicle from viewing the television broadcast or video signal while operating the vehicle in a safe and reasonable manner.

(6) A mobile digital terminal that is fitted with an opaque covering that does not allow the driver to view any part of the display while driving, even though the terminal may be operating, installed in a vehicle that is owned or operated by any of the following:

(A) An electrical corporation, as defined in Section 218 of the Public Utilities Code.

(B) A gas corporation, as defined in Section 222 of the Public Utilities Code.

(C) A sewer system corporation, as defined in Section 230.6 of the Public Utilities Code.

(D) A telephone corporation, as defined in Section 234 of the Public Utilities Code.

(E) A water corporation, as defined in Section 241 of the Public Utilities Code.

(F) A local publicly owned electric utility, as defined in Section 224.3 of the Public Utilities Code.

(G) A city, joint powers agency, or special district, if that local entity uses the vehicle solely in the provision of sewer service, gas service, water service, or wastewater service.

(c) Subdivision (a) does not apply to a mobile digital terminal installed in an authorized emergency vehicle or to a motor vehicle providing emergency road service or roadside assistance.

(d) Subdivision (a) does not apply to a mobile digital terminal installed in a vehicle when the vehicle is deployed in an emergency to respond to an interruption or impending interruption of electrical, natural gas, telephone, sewer, water, or wastewater service, and the vehicle is owned or operated by any of the following:

(1) An electrical corporation, as defined in Section 218 of the Public Utilities Code.

(2) A gas corporation, as defined in Section 222 of the Public Utilities Code.

(3) A sewer system corporation, as defined in Section 230.6 of the Public Utilities Code.

(4) A telephone corporation, as defined in Section 234 of the Public Utilities Code.

(5) A water corporation, as defined in Section 241 of the Public Utilities Code.

(6) A local publicly owned electric utility, as defined in Section 224.3 of the Public Utilities Code.

(7) A city, joint powers agency, or special district, if that local entity uses the vehicle solely in the provision of sewer service, gas service, water service, or wastewater service. *(Stats.1959, c. 3, p. 1739, § 27602. Amended by Stats.1980, c. 107, p. 248, § 2, eff. May 20, 1980; Stats. 2003, c. 303 (A.B.301), § 1; Stats.2004, c. 615 (S.B.1233), § 31; Stats.2009, c. 73 (A.B.62), § 1; Stats.2009, c. 229 (A.B.282), § 6.5; Stats.2010, c. 328 (S.B.1330), § 231.)*

Cross References

Vehicles incidentally operated over highway, applicability of this section, see Vehicle Code § 25802.

§ 27603. Color required for former schoolbus

When a motor vehicle formerly used as a schoolbus is sold to any person and is used exclusively for purposes other than the transportation of pupils pursuant to Article 3 (commencing with Section 39830) of Chapter 5 of Part 23 of the Education Code, it shall be painted by the purchaser a color different than that prescribed by the Department of the California Highway Patrol for schoolbuses before it is operated on any street or highway other than to have the vehicle painted or moved to a place of storage.

The provisions of this section shall not apply where the ownership of a schoolbus is transferred to a nonprofit organization under a contractual arrangement under which the ownership is required to be retransferred to the original owner within 90 days of the date of the original transfer. *(Added by Stats.1959, c. 84, p. 1941, § 1. Amended by Stats.1961, c. 1369, p. 3144, § 1; Stats.1977, c. 406, p. 1416, § 10, eff. Aug. 27, 1977; Stats.1980, c. 676, p. 2025, § 314.)*

Cross References

Schoolbus defined, see Vehicle Code § 545.

§ 27604. Law enforcement vehicles; repainting on sale

When a motor vehicle, painted, as required by Section 40800, and formerly used in the enforcement of the provisions of Division 10 (commencing with Section 20000) or 11 (commencing with Section 21000), is sold to any person and is used for purposes other than law enforcement, the vehicle shall be painted or partially painted by the seller or agency formerly using such vehicle so that it will no longer resemble a vehicle complying with Section 40800 and any insignia or other marking of the vehicle identifying it as a traffic law enforcement vehicle shall be removed by the seller or agency formerly using such vehicle before it shall be operated on any street or highway, other than to have the vehicle moved to be painted or to a place of storage.

The provisions of this section do not apply to former law enforcement vehicles, without insignia, which are painted one solid color, or which are used exclusively for movie or television production and display signs stating "movie car" prominently on the doors, or which are motorcycles, as defined in Section 400, without insignia. *(Added by Stats.1979, c. 689, p. 2159, § 1. Amended by Stats.1981, c. 340, p. 1498, § 1.)*

§ 27605. Vehicle painted as law enforcement vehicle; prohibited ownership; exceptions

No person shall own or operate a motor vehicle painted in the manner described in Section 40800 to resemble a motor vehicle used by a peace officer or traffic officer on duty for the primary purpose of enforcing the provisions of Division 10 (commencing with Section 20000) or Division 11 (commencing with Section 21000) pursuant to Section 40800.

The provisions of this section shall not apply to vehicles which are painted one solid color or to vehicles first registered on or before January 1, 1979. These provisions shall not apply to vehicles which are any of the following:

(a) Owned by vehicle manufacturers or dealers.

(b) Used by law enforcement agencies in the enforcement of the provisions of Division 10 (commencing with Section 20000) or Division 11 (commencing with Section 21000).

(c) Owned by persons or companies who use the vehicles exclusively for movie or television production and display signs stating "movie car" prominently on the doors.

(d) Owned by persons or companies who use the vehicles exclusively for funeral escort purposes.

(e) Motorcycles, as defined in Section 400, without insignia. *(Added by Stats.1979, c. 689, p. 2159, § 2. Amended by Stats.1980, c. 412, p. 814, § 1; Stats.1981, c. 340, p. 1499, § 2.)*

§ 27606. Light bar or facsimile; prohibited equipment

(a) No person shall own or operate a motor vehicle which is equipped with a light bar, or facsimile thereof, to resemble a motor vehicle used by a peace officer or traffic officer while on duty within that jurisdiction for the primary purpose of enforcing Division 10 (commencing with Section 20000) or Division 11 (commencing with Section 21000) pursuant to Section 40800.

(b) For purposes of this section the following definitions apply:

(1) A "light bar" means any light or device affixed to or mounted upon the roof of a vehicle and extending the width of the roof, or a substantial portion thereof, which emits amber, red, or blue, or any combination of those lights.

(2) A "facsimile of a light bar" is any device designed or contrived to resemble a light bar regardless of the degree of light emission or lack thereof. *(Added by Stats.1986, c. 759, § 1.)*

§ 27607. Light bar or facsimile; application to certain vehicles

(a) Section 27606 does not apply to vehicles owned or used by persons licensed pursuant to Article 3.1 (commencing with Section 7540) or Article 3.2 (commencing with Section 7544) of Chapter 11.5 of, or Chapter 11.6 (commencing with Section 7590) of, Division 3 of the Business and Professions Code in the performance of their duties under those provisions.

(b) This section does not authorize those persons described in subdivision (a) to equip a vehicle with a light bar if prohibited by other provisions of existing law or regulation. *(Added by Stats.1986, c. 759, § 2.)*

ARTICLE 6. TOW TRUCKS

Section
27700. Required equipment.

§ 27700. Required equipment

(a) Tow trucks shall be equipped with and carry all of the following:

(1) One or more brooms, and the driver of the tow truck engaged to remove a disabled vehicle from the scene of an accident shall remove all glass and debris deposited upon the roadway by the disabled vehicle which is to be towed.

(2) One or more shovels, and whenever practical the tow truck driver engaged to remove any disabled vehicle shall spread dirt upon that portion of the roadway where oil or grease has been deposited by the disabled vehicle.

(3) One or more fire extinguishers of the dry chemical or carbon dioxide type with an aggregate rating of at least 4–B, C units and bearing the approval of a laboratory nationally recognized as properly equipped to make the approval.

(b) A person licensed as a repossession agency pursuant to Chapter 11 (commencing with Section 7500) of Division 3 of the Business and Professions Code is exempt from this section. *(Stats.1959, c. 3, p. 1740, § 27700. Amended by Stats.1961, c. 529, p. 1632, § 1; Stats.1988, c. 924, § 17.)*

Cross References

Definitions,
  Roadway, see Vehicle Code § 530.
  Tow truck, see Vehicle Code § 615.
Lighting equipment for tow cars, see Vehicle Code § 24605.
Parking of utility vehicles, see Vehicle Code § 22512.
Rules of the road, exemption of authorized emergency vehicles, see Vehicle Code § 21055.
Schoolbus, fire extinguisher, see Education Code § 39838.
Vehicles operated by department of transportation, inapplicability of this section, see Vehicle Code § 23273.

ARTICLE 7. MOTORCYCLES

Section
27800. Passengers; equipment and usage.
27801. Required position of equipment.
27802. Safety helmets; specifications and standards; motorcyclists and motorized bicyclists.
27803. Safety helmets; required use by drivers and passengers on motorcycles, motor-driven cycles or motorized bicycles; legislative intent.

§ 27800. Passengers; equipment and usage

It is unlawful for a driver of a motorcycle or a motorized bicycle to carry any other person thereon, except on a seat securely fastened to the machine at the rear of the driver and provided with footrests, or in a sidecar attached to a motorcycle and designed for the purpose of carrying a passenger. Every passenger on a motorcycle or a motorized bicycle shall keep his feet on the footrests while such vehicle is in motion. *(Stats.1959, c. 3, p. 1740, § 27800. Amended by Stats.1968, c. 1469, p. 2938, § 8; Stats.1978, c. 421, p. 1320, § 5.)*

Cross References

Motorcycle and motor-driven cycle defined, see Vehicle Code §§ 400, 405.
Motorized bicycle defined, see Vehicle Code § 406.

§ 27801. Required position of equipment

A person shall not drive a two-wheel motorcycle that is equipped with either of the following:

(a) A seat so positioned that the driver, when sitting astride the seat, cannot reach the ground with his or her feet.

(b) Handlebars so positioned that the hands of the driver, when upon the grips, are more than six inches above his or her shoulder height when sitting astride the seat. *(Added by Stats.1968, c. 1469, p. 2938, § 10. Amended by Stats.1971, c. 207, p. 271, § 1, operative May 3, 1972; Stats.2004, c. 280 (A.B.2844), § 1.)*

Cross References

Motorcycle defined, see Vehicle Code § 400.

§ 27802. Safety helmets; specifications and standards; motorcyclists and motorized bicyclists

(a) The department may adopt reasonable regulations establishing specifications and standards for safety helmets offered for sale, or sold, for use by drivers and passengers of motorcycles and motorized bicycles as it determines are necessary for the safety of those drivers and passengers. The regulations shall include, but are not limited to, the requirements imposed by Federal Motor Vehicle Safety Standard No. 218 (49 C.F.R. Sec. 571.218) and may include compliance with that federal standard by incorporation of its requirements by reference. Each helmet sold or offered for sale for use by drivers and passengers of motorcycles and motorized bicycles shall be conspicuously labeled in accordance with the federal standard which shall constitute the manufacturer's certification that the helmet conforms to the applicable federal motor vehicle safety standards.

(b) No person shall sell, or offer for sale, for use by a driver or passenger of a motorcycle or motorized bicycle any safety helmet which is not of a type meeting requirements established by the department. *(Added by Stats.1970, c. 159, p. 404, § 1. Amended by Stats.1977, c. 655, p. 2171, § 1; Stats.1979, c. 723, p. 2225, § 36; Stats.1985, c. 163, § 1.)*

Cross References

All-terrain vehicles on public lands, helmet requirement, see Vehicle Code § 38505.
Motorcycle defined, see Vehicle Code § 400.
Motorized bicycle defined, see Vehicle Code § 406.
Safety helmets, operation of recreational off-highway vehicles, see Vehicle Code § 38601.

§ 27803. Safety helmets; required use by drivers and passengers on motorcycles, motor-driven cycles or motorized bicycles; legislative intent

(a) A driver and any passenger shall wear a safety helmet meeting requirements established pursuant to Section 27802 when riding on a motorcycle, motor-driven cycle, or motorized bicycle.

(b) It is unlawful to operate a motorcycle, motor-driven cycle, or motorized bicycle if the driver or any passenger is not wearing a safety helmet as required by subdivision (a).

(c) It is unlawful to ride as a passenger on a motorcycle, motor-driven cycles, or motorized bicycle if the driver or any passenger is not wearing a safety helmet as required by subdivision (a).

(d) This section applies to persons who are riding on motorcycles, motor-driven cycles, or motorized bicycles operated on the highways.

(e) For the purposes of this section, "wear a safety helmet" or "wearing a safety helmet" means having a safety helmet meeting the requirements of Section 27802 on the person's head that is fastened with the helmet straps and that is of a size that fits the wearing person's head securely without excessive lateral or vertical movement.

(f) This section does not apply to a person operating, or riding as a passenger in, a fully enclosed three-wheeled motor vehicle that is not less than seven feet in length and not less than four feet in width, and has an unladen weight of 900 pounds or more, if the vehicle meets or exceeds all of the requirements of this code, the Federal Motor Vehicle Safety Standards, and the rules and regulations adopted by the United States Department of Transportation and the National Highway Traffic Safety Administration.

(g) In enacting this section, it is the intent of the Legislature to ensure that all persons are provided with an additional safety benefit while operating or riding a motorcycle, motor-driven cycle, or motorized bicycle. *(Added by Stats.1984, c. 987, § 1. Amended by Stats.1991, c. 32 (A.B.7), § 1; Stats.1997, c. 710 (A.B.1029), § 4.)*

ARTICLE 8. SIGNS

Section
27900. Identification required.
27901. Name and trademark.
27902. Exemption.
27903. Vehicles transporting specified dangerous substances; display of placards or markings; exemptions.
27904. Pilot cars; signs showing owner or operator.
27904.5. Pilot cars; "oversize" signs.
27905. Fire departments.
27906. School buses.
27906.5. Youth bus.
27907. Tow trucks, repossessor's tow vehicles or automobile dismantler's tow vehicles.
27908. Taxicab signs.
27909. Vehicles carrying or fueled by liquified petroleum gas or natural gas.
27910. Enforcement of Commercial Vehicle Registration Act of 2001; study; recommendations.

§ 27900. Identification required

(a) Every motor vehicle or combination of vehicles used to carry the property of others for hire or used to carry passengers for hire, any truck or truck tractor having three or more axles or any truck tractor with a semitrailer, and all commercial motor vehicles, as defined in subdivision (c) of Section 34601, shall have displayed on both sides of each vehicle or on both sides of one of the vehicles in each combination of vehicles the name or trademark of the person under whose authority the vehicle or combination of vehicles is being operated.

(b) A vehicle or combination of vehicles listed in subdivision (a) that is operated under a rental agreement with a term of not more than 30 calendar days shall meet all of the following requirements:

(1) Have displayed on both sides of each vehicle or on both sides of one of the vehicles in each combination of vehicles the name or trademark of the lessor.

(2) Have displayed on both sides of each vehicle or on both sides of one of the vehicles in each combination of vehicles any of the following numbers issued to the lessor:

(A) The carrier identification number issued by the United States Department of Transportation.

(B) A valid operating authority number.

(C) A valid motor carrier of property number.

(3)(A) Have in the vehicle or combination of vehicles a copy of the rental agreement entered into by the lessor and the vehicle operator.

(B) The rental agreement shall be available for inspection immediately upon the request of any authorized employee of the department or any regularly employed and salaried police officer or deputy sheriff, or any reserve police officer or reserve deputy sheriff listed in Section 830.6 of the Penal Code.

(C) If the rented vehicle or combination of vehicles is operated in conjunction with a commercial enterprise, the rental agreement shall include the operator's carrier identification number or motor carrier of property permit number.

(c) A vehicle or combination of vehicles that is in compliance with Section 390.21 of Title 49 of the Code of Federal Regulations shall be deemed to be in compliance with subdivision (b).

(d) All names, trademarks, and other identifiers for companies no longer in business, no longer operating with the same name, or no longer operating under the same operating authority, shall be removed from or covered over on every motor vehicle or combination of vehicles listed in subdivision (a), within 60 days from the change of company ownership or operation. Those vehicles or combinations of vehicles shall be remarked pursuant to subdivision (a) before they may be operated on the highways. *(Stats.1959, c. 3, p. 1740, § 27900. Amended by Stats.1961, c. 210, p. 1220, §1; Stats.1987, c. 563, § 1; Stats.1998, c. 380 (S.B.1491), § 1; Stats.2003, c. 292 (A.B.1436), § 9.)*

Cross References

Criminal procedure, deputized or appointed peace officers, see Penal Code § 830.6.
Semitrailer defined, see Vehicle Code § 550.
Truck tractor defined, see Vehicle Code § 655.

§ 27901. Name and trademark

The display of the name or trademark shall be in letters in sharp contrast to the background and shall be of such size, shape, and color as to be readily legible during daylight hours from a distance of 50 feet.

This section does not prohibit additional displays not inconsistent with this article. *(Stats.1959, c. 3, p. 1740, § 27901.)*

§ 27902. Exemption

Section 27900 does not apply to any motor vehicle having an unladen weight of 6,000 pounds or less or to any vehicle towed by such motor vehicles, or to any motor vehicle operating under manufacturers, dealers, or transporters special plates, or to any motor vehicle operated by a passenger stage corporation subject to the jurisdiction of the Public Utilities Commission. *(Stats.1959, c. 3, p. 1740, § 27902. Amended by Stats.1961, c. 58, p. 1012, § 48; Stats.1963, c. 1021, p. 2293, § 1.)*

§ 27903. Vehicles transporting specified dangerous substances; display of placards or markings; exemptions

(a) Subject to Section 114765 of the Health and Safety Code, any vehicle transporting any explosive, blasting agent, flammable liquid, flammable solid, oxidizing material, corrosive, compressed gas, poison, radioactive material, or other hazardous materials, of the type and in quantities that require the display of placards or markings on the vehicle exterior by the United States Department of Transportation regulations (49 C. F.R., Parts 172, 173, and 177), shall display the placards and markings in the manner and under conditions prescribed by those regulations of the United States Department of Transportation.

(b) This section does not apply to the following:

(1) Any vehicle transporting not more than 20 pounds of smokeless powder or not more than five pounds of black sporting powder or any combination thereof.

(2) An authorized emergency vehicle as defined in paragraph (1) of subdivision (b) of Section 165, operated by a peace officer as defined in Sections 830.1 and 830.2 of the Penal Code, when transportation is required within the scope and course of law enforcement explosives detection or removal duties, provided one of the following conditions applies:

(A) The law enforcement agency operating the vehicle complies with regulations adopted by the California Highway Patrol pursuant to subdivision (b) of Section 34501, notwithstanding Section 34500 and subdivision (a) of Section 34501.

(B) The peace officer possesses an exemption issued by the commissioner, who may require additional transportation restrictions as deemed appropriate. *(Stats. 1959, c. 3, p. 1740, § 27903. Amended by Stats.1959, c. 1810, p. 4309, § 1; Stats.1961, c. 58, p. 1012, § 49, eff. March 31, 1961; Stats.1961, c. 1705, p. 3686, § 2; Stats.1963, c. 827, p. 2026, § 1; Stats.1967, c. 1498, p. 3504, § 1; Stats.1972, c. 618, p. 1151, § 150; Stats.1973, c. 1119, p. 2284, § 1; Stats.1980, c. 875, p. 2747, § 4; Stats.1996, c. 1023 (S.B.1497), § 426, eff. Sept. 29, 1996; Stats.2002, c. 241 (A.B.2276), § 1, eff. Aug. 26, 2002.)*

Cross References

Compliance with lawful orders and lawful out-of-service orders of peace officers or other enforcement officers, unlawful violations by drivers transporting hazardous materials in commercial motor vehicle required to display placard pursuant to this section, see Vehicle Code § 2800.

License requirements, see Vehicle Code § 32000.5.

Liquefied petroleum gas defined, see Vehicle Code § 380.

Permits authorizing transportation of explosives, see Health and Safety Code § 12101.

Signs on vehicles transporting explosives, see Health and Safety Code § 12089.

Transportation of hazardous material, inspections, equipment on vehicles, compliance with laws and regulations and exemptions, see Vehicle Code § 32001.

Use of reflectorizing material, see Vehicle Code § 25500.

§ 27904. Pilot cars; signs showing owner or operator

There shall be displayed in a conspicuous place on both the right and left sides of a pilot car a sign showing the name of the company which owns or operates the pilot car. The name shall contrast with the background and shall be of a size, shape, and color as to be readily legible during daylight hours from a distance of 50 feet. Additional markings which do not interfere with the legibility of the name may also be displayed. *(Added by Stats.1982, c. 568, p. 2524, § 2. Amended by Stats.1988, c. 460, § 2.)*

§ 27904.5. Pilot cars; "oversize" signs

Subject to Section 35783.5, a pilot car shall display neat, clean, and legible signs containing the word "OVERSIZE." The words "OVERSIZE LOAD," "WIDE LOAD," or "LONG LOAD" may be substituted as applicable. The sign shall be a minimum of 48 inches above the ground and shall be legible at 45 degrees from either side when read from the front or rear. The sign shall have a bright yellow background with a minimum projected area of 440 square inches. The lettering shall be black with a 1–inch minimum brush stroke width and a 6–inch minimum letter height. *(Added by Stats.1988, c. 460, § 3.)*

§ 27905. Fire departments

It is unlawful to display on a vehicle any sign with the words "fire" or "fire department" thereon, except on vehicles owned and operated by a regularly organized fire department, fire district, forestry service, or the State Fire Marshal's Office, and on the privately owned vehicles of any regular member of any such fire departments. *(Stats.1959, c. 3, p. 1741, § 27905.)*

Cross References

Authorized emergency vehicle defined, see Vehicle Code § 165.

§ 27906. School buses

(a) Every schoolbus, while being used for the transportation of school pupils at or below the 12th-grade level shall bear upon the front and rear of the bus a plainly visible sign containing the word "schoolbus" in letters not less than eight inches in height. The letters on schoolbus signs shall be of proportionate width.

Except as provided in subdivision (b), no other vehicle shall display a sign containing the word "schoolbus."

(b) Notwithstanding subdivision (a), a schoolbus which is also used to transport persons of any age who are developmentally disabled, as defined by the Lanterman

Developmental Disabilities Services Act (Division 4.5 (commencing with Section 4500) of the Welfare and Institutions Code), may display a sign containing the word "schoolbus" while transporting those persons to or from vocational, prevocational, or work training centers sponsored by the State Department of Developmental Services.

(c) Every schoolbus, when operated for the transportation of school pupils at or below the 12th-grade level, shall bear upon the rear of the bus, below the rear windows, a plainly visible sign containing the words "Stop When Red Lights Flash" in letters not less than six inches in height. The letters on schoolbus signs shall be of proportionate width. *(Stats.1959, c. 3, p. 1741, § 27906. Amended by Stats.1968, c. 1076, p. 2083, § 1; Stats.1986, c. 678, § 3.)*

Cross References

Lighting equipment for school bus, see Vehicle Code § 25257.
Schoolbus defined, see Vehicle Code § 545.

§ 27906.5. Youth bus

Every youth bus, when operated for the transportation of school pupils, shall bear, upon the front and rear of the youth bus, a plainly visible sign containing the words "YOUTH BUS" in letters not less than eight inches in height. The letters on youth bus signs shall be of proportionate width and the letters shall be in sharp contrast to the background. *(Added by Stats.1982, c. 383, p. 1713, § 6, eff. July 4, 1982.)*

§ 27907. Tow trucks, repossessor's tow vehicles or automobile dismantler's tow vehicles

There shall be displayed in a conspicuous place on both the right and left side of a tow truck, a repossessor's tow vehicle, or an automobile dismantler's tow vehicle used to tow or carry vehicles a sign showing the name of the company or the owner or operator of the tow truck or tow vehicle. The sign shall also contain the business address and telephone number of the owner or driver. The letters and numbers of the sign shall not be less than 2 inches in height and shall be in contrast to the color of the background upon which they are placed.

A person licensed as a repossession agency pursuant to Chapter 11 (commencing with Section 7500) of Division 3 of the Business and Professions Code, or a registrant of the agency, may use the license number issued to the agency by the Department of Consumer Affairs in lieu of a name, business address, and telephone number. *(Stats. 1959, c. 3, p. 1741, § 27907. Amended by Stats.1985, c. 710, § 5; Stats.1988, c. 924, § 18; Stats.1993, c. 479 (A.B.1113), § 3; Stats.1999, c. 456 (S.B.378), § 16.)*

Cross References

Parking of utility vehicles, see Vehicle Code § 22512.
Rules of the road, exemption of authorized emergency vehicles, see Vehicle Code § 21055.
Tow truck defined, see Vehicle Code § 615.

Vehicles operated by department of transportation, inapplicability of this section, see Vehicle Code § 23273.

§ 27908. Taxicab signs

(a) In every taxicab operated in this state there shall be a sign of heavy material, not smaller than 6 inches by 4 inches, or such other size as the agency regulating the operation of the taxicab provides for other notices or signs required to be in every taxicab, securely attached and clearly displayed in view of the passenger at all times, providing in letters as large as the size of the sign will reasonably allow, all of the following information:

(1) The name, address, and telephone number of the agency regulating the operation of the taxicab.

(2) The name, address, and telephone number of the firm licensed or controlled by the agency regulating the operation of the taxicab.

(b) In the event more than one local regulatory agency has jurisdiction over the operation of the taxicab, the notice required by paragraph (1) of subdivision (a) shall provide the name, address, and telephone number of the agency having jurisdiction in the area where the taxicab operator conducts its greatest volume of business; or, if this cannot readily be ascertained, the agency having jurisdiction in the area where the taxicab operator maintains its offices or primary place of business, provided that the operator conducts a substantial volume of business in such area; or, if neither of the foregoing provisions apply, any agency having jurisdiction of an area where the taxicab operator conducts a substantial volume of business.

(c) As used in this section, "taxicab" means a passenger vehicle designed for carrying not more than eight persons, excluding the driver, and used to carry passengers for hire. "Taxicab" shall not include a charter-party carrier of passengers within the meaning of the Passenger Charter-party Carriers' Act, Chapter 8 (commencing with Section 5351) of Division 2 of the Public Utilities Code. *(Added by Stats.1973, c. 1158, p. 2405, § 1.)*

§ 27909. Vehicles carrying or fueled by liquified petroleum gas or natural gas

Any vehicle which carries liquefied petroleum gas fuel or natural gas, in a tank attached to a vehicle, in any concealed area, including trunks, compartments, or under the vehicle, shall display on the exterior of the vehicle the letters "CNG," "LNG," or "LPG," whichever type fuel is utilized, in block letters at least one inch high. The letters shall be of contrasting color and shall be placed as near as possible to the area of the location of the tank. Any vehicle fueled by liquefied petroleum gas fuel or by natural gas may also comply with this section by displaying on each side of the vehicle words or letters at least 0.25 inch high indicating that the vehicle is fueled by liquefied petroleum gas or natural gas. It is unlawful to dispense liquefied petroleum gas fuel or natural gas into any tank in a concealed area of any vehicle registered in California, unless the vehicle complies with the requirements of this section. *(Added by Stats.1981, c. 770, p. 3016, § 2. Amended by Stats.1982, c. 214, p. 728, § 1; Stats.1983, c. 142, § 171.)*

§ 27910. Enforcement of Commercial Vehicle Registration Act of 2001; study; recommendations

The Department of the California Highway Patrol shall initiate a 12–month study to determine an effective means to enforce the provisions of the Commercial Vehicle Registration Act of 2001. The Department of the California Highway Patrol, after consultation with representatives from the Department of Transportation, the Board of Equalization, the Department of Motor Vehicles, and the commercial vehicle industry, shall provide, on or before July 1, 2003, recommendations to the Legislature for actions to be taken to ensure compliance with that act. *(Added by Stats.2000, c. 861 (S.B. 2084), § 55, eff. Sept. 29, 2000.)*

ARTICLE 9. REFRIGERATION EQUIPMENT

Section
28000.   Refrigerator vans.

§ 28000. Refrigerator vans

Every refrigerator van equipped with one or more doors designed to lock automatically upon closure shall have at least one door which can be opened from inside the van as an emergency means of exit.

For the purposes of this article, "refrigerator van" means any motor truck, semitrailer, or trailer, with a fully enclosed cargo body having an enclosed volume of 15 cubic feet or more, which utilizes a mechanical refrigeration system to reduce the temperature within the enclosed portion of the vehicle to 32 degrees Fahrenheit or less, or which provides refrigeration by the use of dry ice. *(Added by Stats.1961, c. 1335, p. 314, § 1.)*

ARTICLE 10. ODOMETERS

Section
28050.   True mileage driven.
28050.5. Operation with nonfunctional odometer prohibited.
28051.   Unlawful to alter indicated mileage.
28051.5. Device to turn back or reset odometer.
28052.   New motor vehicle warranty; mileage.
28053.   Service, repair, or replacement; mileage adjustment; doorframe notice.

§ 28050. True mileage driven

It is unlawful for any person to advertise for sale, to sell, to use, or to install on any part of a motor vehicle or on an odometer in a motor vehicle any device which causes the odometer to register any mileage other than the true mileage driven. For the purposes of this section the true mileage driven is that mileage driven by the car as registered by the odometer within the manufacturer's designed tolerance. *(Added by Stats.1967, c. 1109, p. 2754, § 1.)*

872

§ 28050.5. Operation with nonfunctional odometer prohibited

It is unlawful for any person with the intent to defraud to operate a motor vehicle on any street or highway knowing that the odometer of such vehicle is disconnected or nonfunctional. *(Added by Stats.1967, c. 1210, p. 2754, § 1.)*

§ 28051. Unlawful to alter indicated mileage

It is unlawful for any person to disconnect, turn back, advance, or reset the odometer of any motor vehicle with the intent to alter the number of miles indicated on the odometer gauge. *(Added by Stats.1967, c. 1210, p. 2754, § 2. Amended by Stats.1968, c. 1216, p. 2295, § 1; Stats.1969, c. 111, p. 250, § 1; Stats.1973, c. 774, p. 1388, § 4, eff. Sept. 25, 1973.)*

§ 28051.5. Device to turn back or reset odometer

It is unlawful for any person to advertise for sale, to sell, or to use, any device designed primarily for the purpose of turning back or resetting the odometer of any motor vehicle to reduce the number of miles indicated on the odometer gauge. *(Added by Stats.1970, c. 841, p. 1576, § 1.)*

§ 28052. New motor vehicle warranty; mileage

If a manufacturer, distributor, or dealer of a new motor vehicle makes any warranty to the purchaser of, and with respect to, a new motor vehicle which is based on the amount of miles that the motor vehicle is driven, only those miles which the motor vehicle has been driven on and after the date that the motor vehicle has first been sold as new to the purchaser shall be considered for purposes of the warranty.

The mileage indicated upon the odometer of the motor vehicle on the date that the motor vehicle is first sold as new to the purchaser shall, for purposes of the warranty, be the mileage upon which the warranty shall commence.

Nothing in this section shall be construed to relieve any person of any criminal punishment to which he would otherwise be subject under Section 28051.

The provisions of this section shall apply only to motor vehicles which are sold on or after the effective date of this section. *(Added by Stats.1969, c. 111, p. 250, § 2.)*

§ 28053. Service, repair, or replacement; mileage adjustment; doorframe notice

(a) Nothing in this article prevents the service, repair, or replacement of an odometer, if the mileage indicated thereon remains the same as before the service, repair, or replacement. If the odometer is incapable of registering the same mileage as before the service, repair, or replacement, the odometer shall be adjusted to read zero and a notice in writing shall be attached to the left doorframe of the vehicle by the person performing the service, repair, or replacement specifying the mileage prior to the service, repair, or replacement of the odometer and the date on which it was serviced, repaired, or replaced.

(b) No person shall fail to adjust an odometer or affix a notice regarding the adjustment as required by subdivision (a).

(c) No person shall, with intent to defraud, remove or alter any notice affixed to a vehicle pursuant to subdivision (a). *(Added by Stats.1987, c. 130, § 2.)*

ARTICLE 11. FIRE EXTINGUISHERS

Section
28060. Recreational vehicles and campers.

§ 28060. Recreational vehicles and campers

(a) No person shall sell or offer for sale a new recreational vehicle or new camper which is equipped with cooking equipment or heating equipment, and no dealer or person holding a retail seller's permit shall sell or offer for sale a used recreational vehicle or a used camper which is equipped with cooking or heating equipment, unless such new or used vehicle or new or used camper is equipped with at least one fire extinguisher, filled and ready for use, of the dry chemical or carbon dioxide type with an aggregate rating of at least 4–B:C units, which meets the requirements specified in Section 13162 of the Health and Safety Code.

(b) The operator of a recreational vehicle, or a vehicle to which a camper is attached, which recreational vehicle or camper is equipped with a fire extinguisher as required by subdivision (a), shall carry such fire extinguisher in such recreational vehicle or camper and shall maintain the fire extinguisher in an efficient operating condition.

(c) As used in this section:

(1) "Cooking equipment" means a device designed for cooking which utilizes combustible material, including, but not limited to, materials such as charcoal or any flammable gas or liquid, and "heating equipment" means a device designed for heating which utilizes combustible material, including, but not limited to, materials such as charcoal or any flammable gas or liquid.

(2) "Recreational vehicle" has the same meaning as defined in Section 18010.5 of the Health and Safety Code. *(Added by Stats.1972, c. 392, p. 715, § 1.)*

Cross References
Camper defined, see Vehicle Code § 243.

ARTICLE 11.5. BUMPERS

Section
28070. Passenger vehicle.
28071. Passenger vehicle bumper requirements.

§ 28070. Passenger vehicle

As used in this article, "passenger vehicle" means "passenger vehicle" as defined in Section 34710. *(Added by Stats.1972, c. 272, p. 547, § 1.)*

§ 28071. Passenger vehicle bumper requirements

Every passenger vehicle registered in this state shall be equipped with a front bumper and with a rear bumper. As used in this section, "bumper" means any device designed and intended by a manufacturer to prevent the front or rear of the body of the vehicle from coming into contact with any other motor vehicle. This section shall not apply to any passenger vehicle that is required to be equipped with an energy absorption system pursuant to either state or federal law, or to any passenger vehicle which was not equipped with a front or rear bumper, or both, at the time that it was first sold and registered under the laws of this or any other state or foreign jurisdiction. *(Added by Stats.1972, c. 272, p. 547, § 1. Amended by Stats.1973, c. 451, p. 917, § 1.)*

ARTICLE 12. CAMPER SIGNALING DEVICES

Section
28080. Camper passenger signaling device.
28081. When signaling device not required.

§ 28080. Camper passenger signaling device

(a) Every motor vehicle upon which a camper is mounted shall be equipped with an audible or visual signaling device which can be activated from inside the camper and which is constructed so as to allow any person inside the camper to gain the attention of the driver of the motor vehicle. In no event shall a horn, as required by Section 27000, be used to comply with this subdivision.

(b) No person shall drive a motor vehicle upon which is mounted a camper containing any passenger unless the motor vehicle is equipped as required by subdivision (a). *(Added by Stats.1973, c. 292, p. 700, § 1, operative Jan. 1, 1975.)*

§ 28081. When signaling device not required

The provisions of Section 28080 shall not apply to either of the following:

(a) Any motor vehicle upon which a camper is mounted if a person is able to move between the cab portion of the motor vehicle and the camper.

(b) Any motor vehicle upon which a camper is mounted, which motor vehicle is equipped with a sliding or removable rear window which can be opened or removed by a person inside such camper. *(Added by Stats.1973, c. 292, p. 700, § 1, operative Jan. 1, 1975.)*

ARTICLE 13. THEFT ALARM SYSTEM

Section
28085. Authorized systems.

§ 28085. Authorized systems

Any motor vehicle may be equipped with a theft alarm system which flashes the lights of the vehicle, or sounds an audible signal, or both, and which operates as follows:

(a) The system may flash any of the lights required or permitted on the vehicle.

(b) The system may sound an audible signal.

(c) No vehicle shall be equipped with a theft alarm system which emits the sound of a siren. *(Added by Stats.1977, c. 993, p. 2982, § 3. Amended by Stats.1994, c. 516 (A.B.2860), § 1.)*

Cross References

Flashing and colored lights, equipment with theft alarm system, see Vehicle Code § 25251.4.
Use of horns, see Vehicle Code § 27001.

ARTICLE 14. CELLULAR TELEPHONES

Section
28090. Rented vehicles; instructions for operation of cellular telephones.

§ 28090. Rented vehicles; instructions for operation of cellular telephones

Every renter of a motor vehicle with cellular radio telephone equipment shall provide the person who rents the motor vehicle with written operating instructions concerning the safe use of the equipment. The equipment shall also be clearly labeled with operating instructions concerning the safe use of the equipment. *(Added by Stats.1987, c. 1306, § 1.)*

ARTICLE 15. PILOT CARS

Section
28100. Warning flags.
28101. Additional safety requirements.
28102. Vertical clearance measuring devices.
28103. Violations; infractions.
28104 to 28109. Repealed.

§ 28100. Warning flags

A pilot car shall display at least one red warning flag on each side of the vehicle. The flags shall be a minimum of 16 inches square, and shall be mounted so as to be visible from both the front and rear of the vehicle. The flags shall be removed or covered when the vehicle is not operating as a pilot car. *(Added by Stats.1988, c. 460, § 4.)*

874

§ 28101. Additional safety requirements

In addition to the lighting, sign, and flag requirements in Sections 25270, 27904, 27904.5, and 28100, a pilot car shall meet all of the following requirements:

(a) Be a vehicle not less than 60 inches in width.

(b) Be equipped with all of the following:

(1) One STOP/SLOW paddle.

(2) One orange vest, shirt, or jacket.

(3) One red hand flag (24 inches square).

(4) One two-way radio communication device. *(Added by Stats.1988, c. 460, § 4.)*

§ 28102. Vertical clearance measuring devices

Pilot cars equipped with vertical clearance measuring devices shall comply with Section 35252. *(Added by Stats.1988, c. 460, § 4.)*

§ 28103. Violations; infractions

It is unlawful and an infraction for any person to violate any provision of this article or to fail to have any required equipment in good working order. *(Added by Stats.1988, c. 460, § 4.)*

§§ 28104 to 28109. Repealed by Stats.1981, c. 302, p. 1432, § 1

ARTICLE 16. METHANOL OR ETHANOL FUELED VEHICLES

Section
28110. Antisiphoning device defined.
28111. 1993 and later vehicles; equipment with antisiphoning device.
28112. Exemptions from antisiphoning device requirements.
28113. Light-duty and medium-duty motor vehicles operated for compensation to transport persons; low-emission vehicle requirements.
28114. Heavy-duty vehicles operated by transit authority, etc.; compliance with emission standards.

§ 28110. Antisiphoning device defined

As used in this article, "antisiphoning device" means a device which prevents the removal by suction of fuel from a motor vehicle. *(Added by Stats.1989, c. 1301, § 1.)*

§ 28111. 1993 and later vehicles; equipment with antisiphoning device

Except as otherwise provided in Section 28112, any 1993 and later model-year vehicle which is capable of operating on methanol or ethanol and is imported into the state, or sold, purchased, leased, rented, or acquired in the state, shall be equipped with an antisiphoning device. *(Added by Stats.1989, c. 1301, § 1.)*

§ 28112. Exemptions from antisiphoning device requirements

Notwithstanding subdivision (a) of Section 28111, the State Air Resources Board may adopt regulations providing for exemptions from antisiphoning device requirements for categories of vehicles of 1993 and later model-years which it determines not susceptible to siphoning. *(Added by Stats.1989, c. 1301, § 1.)*

§ 28113. Light-duty and medium-duty motor vehicles operated for compensation to transport persons; low-emission vehicle requirements

(a) Every light-duty and medium-duty motor vehicle operated for compensation to transport persons in an air quality management district or air pollution control district, which does not meet all applicable state ambient air quality standards, shall be a low-emission vehicle, as defined by regulation of the State Air Resources Board. If the vehicle is capable of operating on more than one fuel, it shall be operated within any nonattainment area to the maximum extent practicable either on the designated clean fuel on which the low-emission vehicle was certified or on any other fuel designated by the State Air Resources Board as a substitute fuel for the designated clean fuel. Any air quality management district or air pollution control district may adopt regulations for the enforcement of this section which are consistent with regulations of the State Air Resources Board.

(b) As used in this section, "motor vehicle operated for compensation to transport persons" includes a taxi cab, bus, airport shuttle vehicle, transit authority or transit district vehicle, or a vehicle owned by a private entity providing transit service under contract with a transit district or transportation authority.

(c) As used in this section, "light-duty" has the same meaning as defined in Section 39035 of the Health and Safety Code.

(d) As used in this section, "medium-duty" has the same meaning as defined in Section 39037.5 of the Health and Safety Code.

(e) This section applies to all new light-duty motor vehicles purchased on or after January 1, 1997, and to all new medium-duty vehicles purchased on or after January 1, 1998. *(Added by Stats.1991, c. 496 (S.B.135), § 3.)*

§ 28114. Heavy-duty vehicles operated by transit authority, etc.; compliance with emission standards

(a) Every heavy-duty vehicle operated by a transit authority or transit district, or owned by a private entity providing transit service under contract with a transit district or transportation authority, and used to transport persons for compensation shall meet the emission standards adopted by the State Air Resources Board pursuant to Section 43806 of the Health and Safety Code.

(b) As used in this section, "heavy-duty" has the same meaning as defined in Section 39033 of the Health and Safety Code.

(c) This section applies to all new heavy-duty motor vehicles purchased on or after January 1, 1996, and all

new or replacement engines purchased on or after January 1, 1996, for use in heavy-duty vehicles. *(Added by Stats.1991, c. 496 (S.B.135), § 4.)*

ARTICLE 17. JAMMING DEVICES

Section
28150. Interference with radar, laser or any other electronic device used by law enforcement agencies; violation.

§ 28150. Interference with radar, laser or any other electronic device used by law enforcement agencies; violation

(a) No vehicle shall be equipped with any device that is designed for, or is capable of, jamming, scrambling, neutralizing, disabling, or otherwise interfering with radar, laser, or any other electronic device used by a law enforcement agency to measure the speed of moving objects.

(b) No person shall use, buy, possess, manufacture, sell, or otherwise distribute any device that is designed for jamming, scrambling, neutralizing, disabling, or otherwise interfering with radar, laser, or any other electronic device used by a law enforcement agency to measure the speed of moving objects.

(c) Except as provided in subdivision (d), a violation of subdivision (a) or (b) is an infraction.

(d) When a person possesses four or more devices in violation of subdivision (b), the person is guilty of a misdemeanor.

(e) Notwithstanding any other provision of law, a person who has a valid federal license for operating the devices described in this section may transport one or more of those devices if the license is carried in the vehicle transporting the device at all times when the device is being transported. *(Added by Stats.1998, c. 493 (S.B.1964), § 1.)*

CHAPTER 6. VEHICLE EQUIPMENT SAFETY COMPACT [REPEALED]

CHAPTER 7. MOTOR VEHICLE POLLUTION CONTROL DEVICE INSTALLATION AND INSPECTION STATIONS [REPEALED]

§§ 28500 to 28506. Repealed by Stats.1968, c. 1309, p. 2474, § 11, operative Jan. 1, 1969

§ 28507. Repealed by Stats.1965, c. 2031, p. 4613, § 14

§§ 28508 to 28510. Repealed by Stats.1968, c. 1309, p. 2474, § 11, operative Jan. 1, 1969

§ 28511. Repealed by Stats.1968, c. 552, p. 1219, § 2

Division 13

TOWING AND LOADING EQUIPMENT

Chapter   Section
1. Towing Equipment 29000
2. Logs and Poles [Repealed]
3. Lumber and Lumber Products [Repealed]
4. Baled Hay [Repealed]
5. Transporting Other Loads 31300

Cross References

Criteria for issuing arrest warrant for violations, see Vehicle Code § 40509.5.

Damage to highway, weight or size of vehicle, see Vehicle Code § 17302.

Law enforcement, California highway patrol, see Vehicle Code § 2400.

Notice to correct violations, see Vehicle Code § 40303.5.

Powers and duties of commissioner, see Vehicle Code § 2400.

CHAPTER 1. TOWING EQUIPMENT

Section
29000. Application of chapter.
29001. Fifth wheel connecting device.
29002. Fifth wheel locking device.
29003. Hitch, coupling device, or connection.
29004. Towing requirements.
29004.5. Recreation vehicles; safety connection; instructions.
29005. Drawbar length.
29006. Coupling of towed vehicles.
29007. Driveaway-towaway operations.
29008. Trailers or dollies supporting booms attached to truck cranes.
29009. Dollies used to support special construction equipment; inapplicability of § 29004.

§ 29000. Application of chapter

Unless specified, this chapter does not apply to tow trucks or to the drawbar or other connection between a motor vehicle and a pole or pipe dolly or logging dolly or to any lawful trailer used as a pole or pipe dolly. *(Formerly § 29004, enacted by Stats.1959, c. 3, p. 1742. Amended by Stats.1961, c. 58, p. 1012, § 50; Stats.1963, c. 292, p. 1062, § 6. Renumbered § 29000 and amended by Stats.1969, c. 338, p. 712, § 6. Amended by Stats.1988, c. 924, § 19.)*

Cross References

Definitions,
  Auxiliary dolly, see Vehicle Code § 225.
  Logging dolly, see Vehicle Code § 378.
  Pole or pipe dolly, see Vehicle Code § 475.
  Tow truck, see Vehicle Code § 615.

§ 29001. Fifth wheel connecting device

The upper and lower halves of every fifth wheel connecting device on any semitrailer and truck-tractor or auxiliary dolly shall be securely affixed to the vehicles to prevent shifting of the device on the vehicle to which it is attached. *(Formerly § 29000, enacted by Stats.1959, c. 3, p. 1741. Renumbered § 29001 and amended by Stats. 1969, c. 338, p. 712, § 1.)*

Cross References

Definitions,
  Semitrailer, see Vehicle Code § 550.
  Trailer, see Vehicle Code § 630.

§ 29002. Fifth wheel locking device

Every fifth wheel mechanism, including adapters, shall be equipped with a locking device which will not permit the upper and lower halves to be separated without the operation of a positive manual release. The manual release shall be designed, installed, and maintained so that it cannot be accidentally operated. Automatic locking devices on fifth wheels designed and constructed to be readily separable are required on any vehicle first required to be registered in this state after January 1, 1954. *(Formerly § 29001, enacted by Stats.1959, c. 3, p. 1741. Amended by Stats.1967, c. 442, p. 1654, § 1. Renumbered § 29002 and amended by Stats.1969, c. 338, p. 712, § 2.)*

§ 29003. Hitch, coupling device, or connection

(a) Every hitch or coupling device used as a means of attaching the towed and towing vehicles shall be properly and securely mounted and be structurally adequate for the weight drawn. The mounting of the hitch or coupling device on the towing and towed vehicle shall include sufficient reinforcement or bracing of the frame to provide sufficient strength and rigidity to prevent undue distortion of the frame.

(b) The drawbar, tongue, or other connection between the towing and towed vehicles shall be securely attached and structurally adequate for the weight drawn.

(c) The raised end of any motor vehicle being transported by another motor vehicle using a tow dolly shall be secured to the tow dolly by two separate chains, cables, or equivalent devices adequate to prevent shifting or separation of the towed vehicle and the tow dolly. *(Added by Stats.1969, c. 338, p. 712, § 5. Amended by Stats.1983, c. 708, § 10.)*

Cross References

Definitions,
  Drawbar, see Vehicle Code § 300.
  Tow truck, see Vehicle Code § 615.

Length of drawbar, see Vehicle Code § 29005.

§ 29004. Towing requirements

(a)(1) Except as required under paragraph (2), a towed vehicle shall be coupled to the towing vehicle by means of a safety chain, cable, or equivalent device in addition to the regular drawbar, tongue, or other connection.

(2) A vehicle towed by a tow truck shall be coupled to the tow truck by means of at least two safety chains in addition to the primary restraining system. The safety chains shall be securely affixed to the truck frame, bed, or towing equipment, independent of the towing sling, wheel lift, or under-reach towing equipment.

(3) A vehicle transported on a slide back carrier tow truck or on a trailer shall be secured by at least four tiedown chains, straps, or an equivalent device, independent of the winch or loading cable. This subdivision does not apply to vehicle bodies that are being transported in compliance with Sections 393.100 to 393.136, inclusive, of Title 49 of the Code of Federal Regulations.

(b) All safety connections and attachments shall be of sufficient strength to control the towed vehicle in the event of failure of the regular hitch, coupling device, drawbar, tongue, or other connection. All safety connections and attachments also shall have a positive means of ensuring that the safety connection or attachment does not become dislodged while in transit.

(c) No more slack may be left in a safety chain, cable, or equivalent device than is necessary to permit proper turning. When a drawbar is used as the towing connection, the safety chain, cable, or equivalent device shall be connected to the towed and towing vehicle and to the drawbar so as to prevent the drawbar from dropping to the ground if the drawbar fails.

(d) Subdivision (a) does not apply to a semitrailer having a connecting device composed of a fifth wheel and kingpin assembly, and does not apply to a towed motor vehicle when steered by a person who holds a license for the type of vehicle being towed.

(e) For purposes of this section, a "tow truck" includes both of the following:

(1) A repossessor's tow vehicle, as defined in subdivision (b) of Section 615.

(2) An automobile dismantler's tow vehicle, as defined in subdivision (c) of Section 615.

(f) A vehicle towed by a repossessor's tow vehicle, as defined in subdivision (b) of Section 615, is exempt from the multisafety chain requirement of paragraph (2) of subdivision (a) so long as the vehicle is not towed more than one mile on a public highway and is secured by one safety chain. *(Added by Stats.1969, c. 338, p. 712, § 7. Amended by Stats.1988, c. 924, § 20; Stats.1992, c. 1241 (S.B.1615), § 26; Stats.1999, c. 724 (A.B.1650), § 45; Stats.2009, c. 322 (A.B.515), § 13; Stats.2010, c. 491 (S.B.1318), § 47; Stats.2011, c. 296 (A.B.1023), § 308; Stats.2012, c. 769 (A.B.2679), § 39.)*

878

Cross References

Definitions,
    Drawbar, see Vehicle Code § 300.
    Tow truck, see Vehicle Code § 615.
Length of drawbar, see Vehicle Code § 29005.

§ 29004.5. Recreation vehicles; safety connection; instructions

No recreational vehicle, as described in Section 18010.5 of the Health and Safety Code, designed to be towed, shall be manufactured for sale in this state, sold, offered for sale, leased, or rented unless it is equipped with a safety connection in compliance with Section 29004 with breaking strength which equals or exceeds the gross weight of the towed vehicle. The retail seller, renter, or lessor shall supply instructions to the purchaser, renter, or lessee of such recreational vehicle on proper methods of making the connection between the towed and towing vehicles. Nothing in this section shall, however, require a lessor of a recreational vehicle to supply to the lessee of such vehicle the required instructions if such vehicle is sold to the lessor by a third party and such third party or the agent of the third party delivers possession of the vehicle to the lessee. In such case, such third party shall supply to the lessee the required instructions. *(Added by Stats.1978, c. 932, p. 2906, § 1.)*

§ 29005. Drawbar length

When one vehicle is towing another, the drawbar or other connection shall not exceed 15 feet. *(Added by Stats.1961, c. 58, p. 1012, § 50.1, eff. March 31, 1961.)*

Cross References

Drawbar, see Vehicle Code § 300.

§ 29006. Coupling of towed vehicles

(a) No person shall operate a vehicle towing another motor vehicle upon a freeway unless the towing vehicle is coupled to the towed vehicle by a rigid structure attached securely to both vehicles by nonrigid means.

(b) The requirements of subdivision (a) are not applicable to a vehicle towing a motor vehicle which has been disabled and is being towed from the point of disablement to the nearest and most accessible exit from the freeway. *(Added by Stats.1970, c. 334, p. 731, § 1.)*

§ 29007. Driveaway-towaway operations

The requirements of Section 29004 shall not apply to vehicles engaged in driveaway-towaway operations if all the following conditions are met:

(a) The towed vehicle has one end supported by the towing vehicle.

(b) The towed vehicle is secured to the towing vehicle by a device designed and constructed as to be readily demountable and to perform the functions of a fifth-wheel-type connection.

(c) The fifth-wheel-type connection device is securely affixed to the vehicles to prevent shifting of the device on the vehicles to which it is attached.

(d) The fifth-wheel-type connection device provides a means of variation of inclination between the towing and towed vehicle due to vertical curvatures of the highway. Such means shall not depend upon either the looseness or deformation of the connection or the vehicles to provide for such variation. *(Added by Stats.1975, c. 470, p. 975, § 1.)*

Cross References

Driveaway-towaway operation defined, see Vehicle Code § 303.

§ 29008. Trailers or dollies supporting booms attached to truck cranes

Sections 29004 and 29005 shall not apply to trailers or dollies used to support booms attached to truck cranes if the following conditions are met:

(a) The trailer or dolly is connected to the boom by a pin, coupling device, or fifth wheel assembly.

(b) The trailer is secured to the boom with a chain, cable, or equivalent device of sufficient strength to control the trailer or dolly in case of failure of the connection consisting of a pin, coupling device, or fifth wheel assembly. *(Added by Stats.1979, c. 132, p. 319, § 1. Amended by Stats.2006, c. 538 (S.B.1852), § 664.)*

§ 29009. Dollies used to support special construction equipment; inapplicability of § 29004

The requirements of Section 29004 do not apply to a dolly used to support a portion of special construction equipment, as defined in Section 565, which, due to its size or weight is being operated under the authority of a permit issued by the Department of Transportation, if the dolly is secured to the construction equipment, and the construction equipment is secured to the towing vehicle, by chain, cable, or equivalent devices of sufficient strength to control the construction equipment and dolly. *(Added by Stats.1988, c. 907, § 3.)*

CHAPTER 2. LOGS AND POLES [REPEALED]

§§ 29200, 29201. Repealed by Stats.2006, c. 288 (A.B. 3011), § 7

§§ 29350 to 29366. Repealed by Stats.1965, c. 1266, p. 3140, § 1, operative July 1, 1966

§§ 29550 to 29554. Repealed by Stats.1965, c. 1266, p. 3140, § 1, operative July 1, 1966

CHAPTER 3. LUMBER AND LUMBER PRODUCTS [REPEALED]

§ 29800. Repealed by Stats.2006, c. 288 (A.B.3011), § 8

§§ 29801 to 29805. Repealed by Stats.1965, c. 1266, p. 3141, § 3, operative July 1, 1966

§§ 30050 to 30070. Repealed by Stats.1965, c. 1266, p. 3141, § 3, operative July 1, 1966

§§ 30350 to 30360. Repealed by Stats.1965, c. 1266, p. 3141, § 3, operative July 1, 1966

§§ 30550 to 30559. Repealed by Stats.1965, c. 1266, p. 3141, § 3, operative July 1, 1966

CHAPTER 4. BALED HAY [REPEALED]

Cross References

Vehicles incidentally operated over highway, nonapplicability of this chapter, see Vehicle Code § 25802.

§§ 30800, 30801. Repealed by Stats.2006, c. 288 (A.B. 3011), § 9

§§ 30900 to 30904. Repealed by Stats.1961, c. 1712, p. 3708, § 1, eff. July 1, 1962

§§ 31000 to 31011. Repealed by Stats.1959, c. 494, p. 2431, § 2; Stats.1961, c. 1712, p. 3708, § 1, eff. July 1, 1962

CHAPTER 5. TRANSPORTING OTHER LOADS

Article	Section
1. Hazardous Materials	31300
2. Vehicles Transporting Workmen	31400
3. Trailers [Repealed]	
4. Metal and Metal Products [Repealed]	
5. Baled Cotton, Paper and Jute [Repealed]	
6. Boxes [Repealed]	
7. Tank Containers	31540
8. Waste Tires	31560

Cross References

Vehicles incidentally operated over highway, nonapplicability of this chapter, see Vehicle Code § 25802.

ARTICLE 1. HAZARDOUS MATERIALS

Section
31300. Repealed.
31301. Transportation of explosive substance, flammable liquid, or liquefied petroleum or poisonous gas through Caldecott Tunnel; restrictions; operative effect.
31302. Repealed.
31303. Highway transportation of hazardous materials or waste requiring display of placards or markings; route; attending vehicles and parking; waste hauler transportation safety plan; deviation from route; operative effect.
31304. Highway transportation of hazardous materials or waste requiring display of placards or markings; restrictions or prohibitions; deviation.

Section
31305. Written petitions from parties affected by restrictions
or prohibitions; preemption of restrictions or prohibitions; written petitions from parties affected by
preemptions; hearings; operative effect.
31306. List of restricted or prohibited highways; operative
effect.
31307. Violations; misdemeanors; penalties.
31308. Exemption from code; operative effect.
31309. Vehicles displaying hazardous materials placards;
regulatory compliance.

§ 31300. Repealed by Stats.1990, c. 429 (A.B.3904), § 2

§ 31301. Transportation of explosive substance, flammable liquid, or liquefied petroleum or poisonous gas through Caldecott Tunnel; restrictions; operative effect

(a) No person shall transport any explosive substance, flammable liquid, liquefied petroleum gas or poisonous gas in a tank truck, trailer, or semitrailer through the Caldecott Tunnel located on State Highway, Route 24, near the Alameda-Contra Costa County boundary, connecting Oakland with Contra Costa County in the East Bay area at any time other than between the hours of 3 a.m. to 5 a.m.

(b) The Department of Transportation may, in compliance with the requirements of Article 1 (commencing with Section 22400) of Division 11, determine and declare a reduced speed limit, lower than the maximum speed of 55 miles per hour, found most appropriate for traffic safety between the hours of 3 a.m. and 5 a.m.

(c) Nothing in this section shall be construed as a limitation or restriction on the power of the Department of Transportation, conferred by any other provision of law, to adopt regulations with regard to the movement of vehicles, including, but not limited to, tank truck vehicles transporting any cargo specified under subdivision (a) through the Caldecott Tunnel.

If, pursuant to any such other law, the Department of Transportation adopts or amends regulations after the effective date of this section, which adopted or amended regulations govern the movement of vehicles subject to subdivision (a), then on the operative date of those regulations, this section shall no longer be operative. *(Added by Stats.1982, c. 1140, p. 4107, § 1, eff. Sept. 20, 1982.)*

§ 31302. Repealed by Stats.1988, c. 1384, § 2, eff. Jan. 1, 1992

§ 31303. Highway transportation of hazardous materials or waste requiring display of placards or markings; route; attending vehicles and parking; waste hauler transportation safety plan; deviation from route; operative effect

(a) The provisions of this section apply to the highway transportation of hazardous materials and hazardous waste for which the display of placards or markings is required pursuant to Section 27903. This section does

not apply to hazardous materials being transported on specified routes pursuant to Section 31616 or 33000.

(b) Unless restricted or prohibited pursuant to Section 31304, the transportation shall be on state or interstate highways which offer the least overall transit time whenever practicable.

(c) The transporter shall avoid, whenever practicable, congested thoroughfares, places where crowds are assembled, and residence districts as defined in Section 515.

(d) Vehicles used for the transportation shall not be left unattended or parked overnight in a residence district as defined in Section 515.

(e) When transporting hazardous waste pursuant to Section 25169.3 of the Health and Safety Code, all provisions of the waste hauler transportation safety plan, as approved by the Department of Toxic Substances Control, shall be complied with.

(f) Transportation which deviates from the routes required by this section shall not be excused on the basis of operating convenience.

(g) Notwithstanding subdivisions (b) and (c), vehicles engaged in the transportation may also use any of the following highways:

(1) Highways which provide necessary access to local pickup or delivery points consistent with safe vehicle operation.

(2) Highways which provide reasonable access to fuel, repairs, rest, or food facilities that are designed and intended to accommodate commercial vehicle parking, when that access is consistent with safe vehicle operation and when the facility is within one-half road mile of points of entry or exit from the state or interstate highway being used.

(3) Highways restricted or prohibited pursuant to this section when no other lawful alternative exists.

(h) This section shall become operative on January 1, 1987. *(Added by Stats.1985, c. 814, § 2, operative Jan. 1, 1987. Amended by Gov.Reorg.Plan. No. 1 of 1991, § 189, eff. July 17, 1991.)*

Cross References

Misdemeanor, see Vehicle Code § 40000.19; Penal Code §§ 19, 19.2.

Overnight parking of vehicles, see Vehicle Code § 22507.5.

§ 31304. Highway transportation of hazardous materials or waste requiring display of placards or markings; restrictions or prohibitions; deviation

(a) The transportation of hazardous materials and hazardous waste for which the display of placards or markings is required pursuant to Section 27903 may be restricted or prohibited, by the Department of the California Highway Patrol, after consultation with the Department of Transportation, with regard to state or interstate highways, or by a city or county by ordinance or resolution, after formal notice to the Department of the California Highway Patrol and with the concurrence of their appropriate transportation planning agency defined in Section 29532 of the Government Code, with regard to specified highways under their control, if all of the following requirements are met:

(1) The respective highway is appreciably less safe than a reasonable alternate highway as determined by using either of the following criteria:

(A) The "Guidelines for Applying Criteria to Designate Routes for Transporting Hazardous Materials" prepared by the Federal Highway Administration (FHWA A–IP–80–15).

(B) The Department of the California Highway Patrol or the city or county, whichever has jurisdiction pursuant to subdivision (a), determines that the respective highway is located within the watershed of a drinking water reservoir which meets all of the following requirements:

(i) The reservoir is owned or operated by a public water system, as defined in Section 116275 of the Health and Safety Code.

(ii) The reservoir has a capacity of at least 10,000 acre feet.

(iii) The reservoir directly serves a water treatment plant, as defined in Section 116275 of the Health and Safety Code.

(iv) The reservoir is impounded by a dam, as defined in Section 6002 of the Water Code.

(v) The reservoir's shoreline is located within 500 feet of the highway.

(2) The restriction or prohibition on the use of the highway pursuant to this section is not precluded or preempted by federal law.

(3) The restriction or prohibition does not eliminate necessary access to local pickup or delivery points consistent with safe vehicle operation; does not eliminate reasonable access to fuel, repairs, rest, or food facilities that are designed and intended to accommodate commercial vehicle parking, when that access is consistent with safe vehicle operation and when the facility is within one-half road mile of points of entry or exit from the state or interstate highway being used; or does not restrict or prohibit the use of highways when no other lawful alternative exists.

(4) Written concurrence has been obtained from affected surrounding jurisdictions, including, but not limited to, state agencies, counties, cities, special districts, or other political subdivisions of the state, that the proposed restriction or prohibition is not incompatible with through transportation. If written concurrence is not granted by one of the affected surrounding jurisdictions, that action may be appealed to the appropriate transportation planning agency for final resolution.

(5) The highway is posted by the agency responsible for highway signs on that highway in conformity with standards of the Department of Transportation.

(6) A list of the routes restricted or prohibited is submitted to the Department of the California Highway Patrol.

(7) The highway is included in a list of highways restricted or prohibited pursuant to this section which is published by the Department of the California Highway Patrol and is available to interested parties for not less than 14 days.

(b) Notwithstanding any prohibition or restriction adopted pursuant to subdivision (a), deviation from restricted or prohibited routes is authorized in an emergency or other special circumstances with the concurrence of a member of the agency having traffic law enforcement authority for the highway. *(Added by Stats. 1985, c. 814, § 3, operative Jan. 1, 1987. Amended by Stats.1987, c. 1049, § 1; Stats.2002, c. 104 (A.B.2687), § 1.)*

§ 31305. Written petitions from parties affected by restrictions or prohibitions; preemption of restrictions or prohibitions; written petitions from parties affected by preemptions; hearings; operative effect

(a) Upon receipt of a written petition from a local jurisdiction or motor carrier adversely affected by a restriction or prohibition adopted pursuant to Section 31304, the Department of the California Highway Patrol may preempt any local restriction or prohibition that, in its opinion, is not compatible with reasonable and necessary access or the use of highways when no other lawful alternative exists as provided for in paragraph (3) of subdivision (a) of that section, or through transportation as provided for in paragraph (4) of subdivision (a) of that section.

(b) Upon receipt of a written petition from a local jurisdiction or motor carrier adversely affected by a preemption issued pursuant to subdivision (a), the Department of the California Highway Patrol, after holding a public hearing, shall render a decision upholding or denying the petition.

(c) This section shall become operative on January 1, 1987. *(Added by Stats.1985, c. 814, § 4, operative Jan. 1, 1987.)*

§ 31306. List of restricted or prohibited highways; operative effect

(a) A list of highways restricted or prohibited pursuant to subdivision (a) of Section 31304 shall be published or updated by the Department of the California Highway Patrol semiannually.

(b) This section shall become operative on January 1, 1987. *(Added by Stats.1985, c. 814, § 5, operative Jan. 1, 1987.)*

§ 31307. Violations; misdemeanors; penalties

(a) It is unlawful for the owner of any vehicle or the authorized agent of the owner to drive, or to direct or knowingly permit the driving of, the vehicle in violation of

Section 31303 or 31304. Violation of any of these sections is a misdemeanor punishable as follows:

(1) For a first violation, a fine not exceeding five hundred dollars ($500), imprisonment in the county jail not exceeding 60 days, or both the fine and imprisonment.

(2) For a second violation within a 12–month period, a fine not exceeding one thousand dollars ($1,000), imprisonment in the county jail not exceeding 60 days, or both the fine and imprisonment.

(3) For a third or subsequent violation within a 12–month period, a fine not exceeding two thousand five hundred dollars ($2,500), imprisonment in the county jail not exceeding 120 days, or both the fine and imprisonment.

(b) Additionally, upon recommendation of the Department of the California Highway Patrol, three or more violations of these sections constitute grounds for suspension or revocation of registration, or denial of an application for registration under Section 25163 of the Health and Safety Code by the Department of Toxic Substances Control. Proceedings in these cases shall be subject to Chapter 5 (commencing with Section 11500) of Part 1 of Division 3 of Title 2 of the Government Code.

(c) This section shall become operative on January 1, 1987. *(Added by Stats.1985, c. 814, § 6, operative Jan. 1, 1987. Amended by Gov.Reorg.Plan No. 1 of 1991, § 190, eff. July 17, 1991.)*

§ 31308. Exemption from code; operative effect

(a) Nothing contained in Section 31303 or 31304 shall be deemed to exempt any person subject to these sections from other provisions of this code.

(b) This section shall become operative on January 1, 1987. *(Added by Stats.1985, c. 814, § 7, operative Jan. 1, 1987.)*

§ 31309. Vehicles displaying hazardous materials placards; regulatory compliance

Notwithstanding Section 34500 and subdivision (a) of Section 34501, the transportation of hazardous materials in a manner requiring that placards be displayed on the transporting vehicle pursuant to Section 27903, shall comply with regulations adopted by the California Highway Patrol pursuant to subdivision (b) of Section 34501. *(Added by Stats.1990, c. 429 (A.B.3904), § 3.)*

ARTICLE 2. VEHICLES TRANSPORTING WORKMEN

Section
31400. Trucks used to transport workmen.
31401. Farm labor vehicles.
31401.5. Display stickers for farm labor vehicles.
31402. Operation of unsafe farm labor vehicle for repairs.
31403. Mechanic's certification of farm labor vehicle.
31404. Farm labor vehicle; misdemeanor; penalties.
31405. Seatbelt assemblies for farm labor vehicles.

Section
31406. Federal Regulations compliance; passenger seating positions; seating system.
31407. Tools, equipment, or materials; attachment to the vehicle.
31408. Operation of farm labor vehicles on highways; headlamps.
31409. Public transit system vehicle; compliance with specified farm labor vehicle provisions.

§ 31400. Trucks used to transport workmen

Trucks used primarily or regularly for the transportation of workmen shall be:

(a) Equipped with seats securely fastened to the vehicle.

(b) Equipped, if a motortruck, with a railing or other suitable enclosure on the sides and end of the vehicle not less than 46 inches above the floor of the vehicle.

(c) Equipped with steps, stirrups, or other equivalent devices so placed and arranged that the vehicle may be safely mounted and dismounted. *(Added by Stats.1968, c. 1019, p. 1971, § 2, operative July 1, 1969.)*

Cross References
Motor truck defined, see Vehicle Code § 410.
Railroad crossings, special stops, see Vehicle Code § 22452.

§ 31401. Farm labor vehicles

(a) The department shall adopt regulations designed to promote the safe operation of farm labor vehicles described in Section 322, including, but not limited to, vehicular design, equipment, passenger safety, and seating.

(b) The department shall inspect every farm labor vehicle described in Section 322 at least once annually to ascertain whether its construction, design, and equipment comply with all provisions of law. No person shall drive any farm labor vehicle described in Section 322 unless there is displayed therein a certificate issued by the department stating that on a stated day, which shall be within 13 months of the date of operation, an authorized employee of the department inspected the vehicle and found on the date of inspection the vehicle complied with applicable regulations relating to construction, design, and equipment. The commissioner shall provide by rule or regulation for the issuance and display of distinctive inspection certificates.

(c) The department may inspect any vehicle subject to these regulations in maintenance facilities, terminals, labor camps, or other private property of the vehicle owner or the farm labor contractor to insure compliance with the provisions of this code and regulations adopted pursuant to this section.

(d) The owner of any farm labor vehicle or any farm labor contractor, as defined in Section 1682 of the Labor Code, who rents a farm labor vehicle or who otherwise uses a farm labor vehicle to transport individuals is responsible for the inspection required under subdivision (b).

(e) An owner of any farm labor vehicle or any farm labor contractor who operates a farm labor vehicle under the circumstances described in subdivision (d) may not operate that vehicle unless the vehicle has a current certificate described in subdivision (b).

(f) It is unlawful to violate any provision of these regulations or this section. *(Added by Stats.1968, c. 1019, p. 1971, § 2, operative July 1, 1969. Amended by Stats. 1969, c. 9, p. 64, § 7, eff. March 6, 1969, operative July 1, 1969; Stats.1974, c. 1447, p. 3161, § 6, eff. Sept. 26, 1974; Stats.1980, c. 676, p. 2026, § 315; Stats.1999, c. 556 (A.B.555), § 3, eff. Sept. 29, 1999.)*

§ 31401.5. Display stickers for farm labor vehicles

(a) The department shall develop, by regulation, specifications for a display sticker that shall be clearly displayed on every farm labor vehicle. This display sticker shall list the inspection certification date pursuant to this section and the "800" telephone reporting system required by Section 2429.

(b) The regulations of the department shall require every owner or operator of a farm labor vehicle to request the scheduling of the inspection required under subdivision (b) of Section 31401 as follows:

(1) The owner or operator of a farm labor vehicle that has a current inspection certificate pursuant to Section 31401 shall make the request for inspection not later than four weeks prior to the expiration date of the certificate.

(2) The owner or operator of a farm labor vehicle required to have its initial inspection shall make the request for inspection not later than three business days prior to the requested date.

(c) In no event shall the owner or operator of a farm labor vehicle allow the operation of a farm labor vehicle without the proper certification requirements specified under Section 31401. *(Added by Stats.1999, c. 557 (A.B.1165), § 4, eff. Sept. 29, 1999.)*

§ 31402. Operation of unsafe farm labor vehicle for repairs

(a) No person may operate any farm labor vehicle except as may be necessary to return the unladen vehicle or combination of vehicles to the residence or place of business of the owner or driver, or to a garage, after notice by the department to the owner that the vehicle is in an unsafe condition or is not equipped as required by this code, or any regulations adopted thereunder, until the vehicle and its equipment have been made to conform with the requirements of this code, or any regulations adopted thereunder, and approved by the department.

(b)(1) A person who operates a farm labor vehicle in violation of this section while the vehicle is in a condition that presents an immediate safety hazard is guilty of a misdemeanor punishable by a fine of not less than one thousand dollars ($1,000) and not more than five thousand dollars ($5,000), or both that fine and a sentence of confinement for not more than six months in the county

jail. No part of any fine imposed under this subdivision may be suspended.

(2) As used in this subdivision, an "immediate safety hazard" is any equipment violation described in subdivision (a) of Section 31401 or Section 31405, including any violation of a regulation adopted pursuant to that provision or those provisions.

(c) Any member of the Department of the California Highway Patrol may impound a farm labor vehicle operated in violation of this section pursuant to Section 34506.4. A farm labor vehicle shall not be impounded unless a member of that department determines that a person has failed to comply with subdivision (a) or a person fails to comply with a lawful out-of-service order, as described in subdivision (b) of Section 2800. *(Added by Stats.1974, c. 1447, p. 3161, § 7, eff. Sept. 26, 1974. Amended by Stats.1980, c. 676, p. 2026, § 316; Stats.2000, c. 873 (A.B.2086), § 3.)*

Cross References

Farm labor vehicles subject to forfeiture as nuisance, and impounding, see Vehicle Code § 34506.5.

§ 31403. Mechanic's certification of farm labor vehicle

A farm labor vehicle known to an owner, farm labor contractor, or driver, to be unsafe, or not equipped as required by this code, or any regulations adopted thereunder, shall not be used for transporting any passengers until it is examined and repaired or equipped as required by this code, or any regulations adopted thereunder, and certified by a competent mechanic to be safe and lawfully equipped. *(Added by Stats.1974, c. 1447, p. 3161, § 8, eff. Sept. 26, 1974.)*

§ 31404. Farm labor vehicle; misdemeanor; penalties

Any person who operates, or any owner or farm labor contractor who knowingly allows the operation of, a farm labor vehicle in violation of subdivision (b) or (d) of Section 31401 or Section 31402 or 31403 is guilty of a misdemeanor. When a person has been convicted of willfully violating those provisions, the person shall, in addition, be fined not less than one thousand dollars ($1,000) for each violation, and no part of the fine may be suspended. If passengers are in the vehicle at the time of the violation, the person shall, in addition, be fined five hundred dollars ($500) for each passenger, not to exceed a total of five thousand dollars ($5,000) for each violation, and no part of this fine may be suspended. As used in this section, the terms "knowingly" and "willfully" have the same meaning as prescribed in Section 7 of the Penal Code. *(Added by Stats.1988, c. 613, § 1. Amended by Stats.1999, c. 556 (A.B.555), § 4, eff. Sept. 29, 1999.)*

§ 31405. Seatbelt assemblies for farm labor vehicles

(a) Except as authorized under paragraph (1) of subdivision (e), every farm labor vehicle issued an inspection certificate under Section 31401 shall be equipped at each passenger position with a Type 1 or Type 2 seatbelt assembly, conforming to the specifications set forth in

883

Section 571.209 of Title 49 of the Code of Federal Regulations, that is anchored to the vehicle in a manner that conforms to the specifications of Section 571.210 of Title 49 of the Code of Federal Regulations.

(b) Except as authorized under paragraph (1) of subdivision (e), the department may not issue an initial inspection certificate under Section 31401 to any farm labor vehicle that is not equipped with a seatbelt assembly at each passenger position, as described in subdivision (a).

(c) The owner of a farm labor vehicle shall maintain all seatbelt assemblies and seatbelt assembly anchorages required under this section in good working order for the use of passengers.

(d) Except as authorized under paragraph (1) of subdivision (e) or subdivision (d) of Section 23116, no person may operate a farm labor vehicle on a highway unless that person and all passengers are properly restrained by a seatbelt assembly that conforms to this section.

(e)(1) Until January 1, 2007, this section does not apply to a farm labor vehicle that meets the definition in subdivision (a) of Section 233, meets all state and federal standards for safety and construction, and is not currently required to have seatbelts.

(2) On or after January 1, 2007, any farm labor vehicle that meets the conditions set forth in paragraph (1) shall be equipped at each passenger position with a seatbelt assembly as described in subdivision (a), unless exempted from this requirement under the regulations promulgated under Section 31401.

(f) The department shall adopt regulations to implement this section. *(Added by Stats.1999, c. 557 (A.B. 1165), § 5, eff. Sept. 29, 1999. Amended by Stats.2000, c. 308 (A.B.602), § 3.)*

§ 31406. Federal Regulations compliance; passenger seating positions; seating system

(a) No person may be transported in a farm labor vehicle that does not have all passenger seating positions in compliance with Section 571.207 of Title 49 of the Code of Federal Regulations, as that provision exists now or may hereafter be amended.

(b) No person may install a seat or seating system in a farm labor vehicle unless that seat or seating system is in compliance with Section 571.207 of Title 49 of the Code of Federal Regulations, as that provision exists now or may hereafter be amended.

(c) This section shall become operative on March 31, 2002. *(Added by Stats.2000, c. 308 (A.B.602), § 4, operative March 31, 2002.)*

§ 31407. Tools, equipment, or materials; attachment to the vehicle

All cutting tools or tools with sharp edges carried in the passenger compartment of a farm labor vehicle shall be placed in securely latched containers that are firmly

884

attached to the vehicle. All other tools, equipment, or materials carried in the passenger compartment shall be secured to the body of the vehicle to prevent their movement while the vehicle is in motion. Under no circumstances shall those tools, equipment, or materials obstruct an aisle or an emergency exit. *(Added by Stats.2000, c. 308 (A.B.602), § 5.)*

§ 31408. Operation of farm labor vehicles on highways; headlamps

No person may operate a farm labor vehicle on a highway unless both headlamps required under Section 24400 are lighted, regardless of the time of day. *(Added by Stats.1999, c. 556 (A.B.555), § 5, eff. Sept. 29, 1999.)*

§ 31409. Public transit system vehicle; compliance with specified farm labor vehicle provisions

Notwithstanding paragraph (2) of subdivision (c) of Section 322, any vehicle owned or operated by or for a public transit system that is purchased with funds appropriated pursuant to Item 2660–103–0046 of Section 2.00 of the Budget Act of 2000 (Chapter 52 of the Statutes of 2000) or pursuant to Section 5309 of Title 49 of the United States Code and is used to transport farmworkers for any farmworker transportation program shall comply with the farm labor vehicle provisions contained in, and the regulations promulgated under, this chapter, relating to the following:

(a)(1) Annual farm labor vehicle inspection and certification.

(2) Following initial certification, the inspection and certification of buses designed, used, or maintained for carrying more than 15 persons, including the driver, shall be conducted during the inspection required by subdivision (c) of Section 34501.

(b) Seatbelt installation.

(c) Illumination of headlamps.

(d) Storage and securing of tools in passenger compartments. *(Added by Stats.2000, c. 308 (A.B.602), § 6.)*

ARTICLE 3. TRAILERS [REPEALED]

§§ 31500, 31501. Repealed by Stats.2006, c. 288 (A.B. 3011), § 10

ARTICLE 4. METAL AND METAL PRODUCTS [REPEALED]

§ 31510. Repealed by Stats.2006, c. 288 (A.B.3011), § 11

ARTICLE 5. BALED COTTON, PAPER AND JUTE [REPEALED]

§ 31520. Repealed by Stats.2006, c. 288 (A.B.3011), § 12

ARTICLE 6.   BOXES [REPEALED]

§ **31530.   Repealed by Stats.2006, c. 288 (A.B.3011), § 13**

ARTICLE 7.   TANK CONTAINERS

Section
31540.   Regulations governing.

§ **31540.   Regulations governing**

(a) The department shall adopt and enforce such regulations as it determines are necessary for public safety regarding the transportation of:

(1) Freight van or tank containers which can be removed from the running gear or chassis of a truck or trailer, and

(2) Collapsible containers used to transport liquids on flatbed vehicles.

(b) It is unlawful to fail to comply with any provision of the regulations adopted by the department. *(Added by Stats.1963, c. 1580, p. 3161, § 1.   Amended by Stats.1965, c. 1266, p. 3140, § 5;   Stats.1968, c. 1192, p. 2259, § 9.3, operative Jan. 1, 1969.)*

ARTICLE 8.   WASTE TIRES

Section
31560.   Vehicle operators;   transporting waste tires;   registration;   violation;   penalty.

§ **31560.   Vehicle operators;   transporting waste tires; registration;   violation;   penalty**

(a) A person operating a vehicle, or combination of vehicles, in the transportation of 10 or more used tires or waste tires, or a combination of used tires and waste tires totaling 10 or more, as defined in Section 42950 of the Public Resources Code, shall be registered with the California Integrated Waste Management Board, unless specifically exempted, as provided in Chapter 19 (commencing with Section 42950) of Part 3 of Division 30 of the Public Resources Code and in regulations adopted by the board to implement that chapter.

(b) It is unlawful and constitutes an infraction for a person engaged in the transportation of 10 or more used tires or waste tires, or a combination of used tires and waste tires totaling 10 or more, to violate a provision of this article or Section 42951 of the Public Resources Code. *(Added by Stats.1996, c. 304 (A.B.2108), § 5. Amended by Stats.2002, c. 625 (S.B.649), § 23, eff. Sept. 17, 2002;   Stats.2008, c. 696 (S.B.1781), § 31, eff. Sept. 30, 2008.)*

Division 14

TRANSPORTATION OF EXPLOSIVES

Section
31600. Explosives defined.
31601. Application of division.
31602. License; routes to be used.
31603 to 31606. Repealed.
31607. Inspection of vehicles transporting explosives.
31608. Scope of inspection.
31609. Record of inspection.
31610. Requirements in respect to equipment.
31611. Instructions to drivers.
31612. Shipping instructions.
31613. Certain cargoes prohibited.
31614. Traffic laws applicable to transportation of explosives.
31615. Application of other vehicle code provisions.
31616. Designation of routes.
31616.5. Regulations; review by office of administrative law; time.
31617. Emergency changes.
31618. Violation.
31619. Smokeless powder.
31620. Waiver or suspension of requirement.

Cross References

High explosives, regulation, see Health and Safety Code § 12000 et seq.
License to transport explosives, see Vehicle Code §§ 2531, 2532.
Railroad crossings, special stops for motor trucks carrying explosives, see Vehicle Code § 22452.
Violation of division a misdemeanor, see Vehicle Code § 40000.19.

§ 31600. Explosives defined

For the purposes of this division "explosive" or "explosives" means any substance, or combination of substances, the primary or common purpose of which is detonation or rapid combustion and which is capable of a relatively instantaneous or rapid release of gas and heat. "Explosive" or "explosives" includes, but is not necessarily limited to, explosives as defined in Section 12000 of the Health and Safety Code, and any of the following:

(a) Dynamite, nitroglycerine, picric acid, lead azide, fulminate of mercury, black powder, smokeless powder, propellant explosives, detonating primers, blasting caps, commercial boosters, ammonium nitrate-fuel oil mixture (blasting agent), or any explosives as defined in Section 841 of Title 18 of the United States Code and published pursuant to Section 555.23 of Title 27 of the Code of Federal Regulations, when transported in a combined load with any explosive, as defined in this section.

(b) Substances determined to be division 1.1, 1.2, 1.3, or 1.6 explosives as classified by the United States Department of Transportation.

(c) "Explosive" or "explosives" does not include small arms ammunition or any other division 1.4 explosive.

(d) This division shall not apply to special fireworks classified by the United States Department of Transportation as division 1.2 or 1.3 explosives when those special fireworks are regulated by and in conformance with Part 2 (commencing with Section 12500) of Division 11 of the Health and Safety Code.

(e) Nothing in this chapter supersedes any regulations for the transportation of hazardous materials as defined in Section 2402.7 or as regulated in Division 14.1 (commencing with Section 32000). (*Stats.1959, c. 3, p. 1752, § 31600. Amended by Stats.1965, c. 1500, p. 3524, § 12; Stats.1967, c. 251, p. 1399, § 2; Stats.1967, c. 1498, p. 3504, § 4; Stats.1970, c. 923, p. 1677, § 8; Stats.1970, c. 1315, p. 2446, § 2.5; Stats.1970, c. 1421, p. 2709, § 33, eff. Sept. 18, 1970; Stats.1970, c. 1425, p. 2725, § 33, eff. Sept. 18, 1970; Stats.1971, c. 754, p. 1497, § 1, operative May 3, 1972; Stats.1977, c. 825, p. 2495, § 7; Stats.1981, c. 912, p. 3452, § 5, eff. Sept. 28, 1981; Stats.1998, c. 478 (A.B. 2372), § 6; Stats.2004, c. 247 (A.B.1232), § 17, eff. Aug. 23, 2004.*)

Cross References

Ordinances governing explosives, see Health and Safety Code § 12002.
Permit to transport explosives, record, see Health and Safety Code § 12122.

§ 31601. Application of division

(a) This division shall apply to the operation of any motor vehicle on any highway, and to the operation and parking of any vehicle on any property designated pursuant to this division as a safe stopping place for the purpose of transporting any explosive in any amount when the transportation is rendered as a delivery service or for hire, or in any other event for the purpose of transporting any explosive or a combined load of any explosive and ammonium nitrate-fuel oil mixture (blasting agent) in an amount in excess of 1,000 pounds. The transportation of quantities of explosives of 1,000 pounds or less, or other than on a public highway, is governed by Division 11 (commencing at Section 12000) of the Health and Safety Code. Notwithstanding other provisions of this section, a license required by Section 31602 may be used to transport quantities of less than 1,000 pounds of explosives if all other requirements of this division are met.

(b) It is the legislative intention in enacting this division and with particular reference to requiring licenses for transportation of explosives as set forth herein that such provisions shall apply uniformly throughout the State of California and that such license to be obtained from the Department of the California Highway Patrol, as provided in Chapter 2.5 (commencing with Section

887

2500) of Division 2, shall be in lieu of any requirement for any license to be obtained by any such owner from any local authority within the state. *(Stats.1959, c. 3, p. 1752, § 31601. Amended by Stats.1965, c. 1500, p. 3524, § 13; Stats.1967, c. 1498, p. 3505, § 5; Stats.1968, c. 1309, p. 2474, § 12, operative Jan. 1, 1969; Stats.1971, c. 754, p. 1498, § 2, operative May 3, 1972; Stats.1981, c. 912, p. 3453, § 6, eff. Sept. 28, 1981.)*

§ 31602. License; routes to be used

(a) It is a misdemeanor for any owner of a vehicle to drive or permit the driving of the vehicle on any public highway for the purpose of transporting any explosive as defined herein and within the scope of Section 31601 unless the owner then holds a valid license for the transportation of explosives as provided in this division, except such persons as are expressly exempted in this division.

(b) It is a misdemeanor for the owner, or authorized agent of the owner, of any vehicle transporting explosives to drive, or to permit the driving of the vehicle, or for the driver to drive such vehicle, upon any public highway, not designated in regulations adopted by the Department of the California Highway Patrol as a route for the transportation of explosives, unless the use of the highway is required to permit delivery of, or the loading of, explosives at a point not on a highway designated as a route for the transportation of explosives, or unless the use of the highway is required to permit the vehicle to proceed to, and return from, a point designated as an inspection stop pursuant to this division.

(c) It is a misdemeanor for the driver of any vehicle transporting explosives to stop at any place not designated as a safe stopping place unless the vehicle is disabled or except when necessary to avoid conflict with other traffic or to comply with the orders of a peace officer or an official traffic control device. A safe stopping place is any location designated by the Department of the California Highway Patrol where the driver may stop for food, fuel or other necessary reasons and any location designated by the Department of the California Highway Patrol as a safe parking place, a safe stopping place, or as an inspection stop for purposes of this division.

(d) In the event the owner of a vehicle leases the same to be used in the transportation of explosives for which a license is required, the lessee shall be deemed the owner for the purposes of this division. *(Stats.1959, c. 3, p. 1753, § 31602. Amended by Stats.1959, c. 1671, p. 4057, § 7, eff. July 8, 1959, operative Sept. 18, 1959; Stats.1968, c. 1309, p. 2474, § 13, operative Jan. 1, 1969; Stats.1970, c. 1315, p. 2446, § 3.)*

Cross References

Department of California Highway Patrol, see Vehicle Code
     § 2100 et seq.
Punishment for misdemeanors, see Vehicle Code § 42002.

888

Traffic violation point count, violation of this section, see
     Vehicle Code § 12810.

§§ 31603 to 31606.   Repealed by Stats.1968, c. 1309, p. 2475, §§ 14 to 17, operative Jan. 1, 1969

§ 31607.   Inspection of vehicles transporting explosives

(a) Any person operating or permitting the operation of a vehicle or combination of vehicles used in the transportation of explosives and subject to this division shall make or cause to be made an inspection of every said vehicle or combination of vehicles as hereinafter set forth.

(b) Such inspection as called for in Section 31608 shall be made immediately preceding the actual transportation of explosives by the vehicle and whenever there is an interchange of any vehicle operating in combination with any other vehicle in the transportation of explosives.

(c) Inspection of tires and brakes shall also be made en route at suitable intervals, off the roadway, at inspection stops established by the Department of the California Highway Patrol, at regular stops, terminal points, or driver-change points. *(Stats.1959, c. 3, p. 1754, § 31607. Amended by Stats.1961, c. 228, p. 1246, § 1.)*

Cross References

Department of California Highway Patrol, see Vehicle Code
     § 2100 et seq.

§ 31608.   Scope of inspection

The inspection of a vehicle required under subdivision (b) of Section 31607 shall include inspection of the following:

(a) Brakes and the brake system.

(b) The ignition and lighting systems.

(c) All tires on the equipment.

(d) All supplemental equipment as required by Section 31610. *(Stats.1959, c. 3, p. 1755, § 31608. Amended by Stats.1959, c. 1996, p. 4636, § 42.)*

§ 31609.   Record of inspection

Every person operating a vehicle or combination of vehicles in the transportation of explosives subject to this division shall complete a record of every inspection which is required under Sections 31607 and 31608 in such form as approved by the Department of the California Highway Patrol showing the time and place of every inspection. The person making the inspection shall certify the fact in the record. The forms may be based upon the type used by the United States Department of Transportation. The record of every inspection shall be made at the time such inspection is conducted.

The driver of the vehicle shall display the record upon demand of any member of the California Highway Patrol or any police officer of a city who is on duty for the exclusive or main purpose of enforcing the provisions of this code. *(Stats.1959, c. 3, p. 1755, § 31609. Amended by Stats.1967, c. 1498, p. 3506, § 6; Stats.1970, c. 1315, p. 2447, § 4.)*

Cross References

Department of California Highway Patrol, see Vehicle Code § 2100 et seq.

§ 31610.   Requirements in respect to equipment

Every vehicle or combination of vehicles used in the transportation of explosives and subject to this division, in addition to any other equipment required by law, shall be equipped and maintained as required by this section.

(a) Brakes and the brake system shall be maintained in good and safe operating condition.

(b) The ignition and lighting systems shall be maintained in good operating condition.

(c) All tires shall be in good condition, properly matched and inflated. Except as may be necessary to cause immediate replacement, no vehicle shall be driven unless all tires in actual use on the vehicle are properly inflated.

(d) Fire extinguishers and other safety equipment prescribed by regulations adopted by the department pursuant to subdivision (f) of Section 34500 and Section 34501 shall be carried in each vehicle or combination of vehicles.

(e) No flare, fusee, oil lantern, or any signal device producing a flame shall be carried upon any vehicle or combination of vehicles. *(Stats.1959, c. 3, p. 1755, § 31610. Amended by Stats.1959, c. 1996, p. 4636, § 43; Stats.1967, c. 1498, p. 3506, § 7; Stats.1971, c. 754, p. 1499, § 3, operative May 3, 1972.)*

Cross References

Schoolbus, fire extinguisher, see Education Code § 39838.

§ 31611.   Instructions to drivers

Every owner of a vehicle used in the transportation of explosives and subject to this division shall make available in each vehicle the latest map showing the routes which are to be used for the transportation of explosives which has been furnished for the vehicle by the Department of the California Highway Patrol and a list of the safe stopping places prescribed by the regulations of the Department of the California Highway Patrol for vehicles transporting explosives. The owner shall require that the driver be thoroughly familiar with the provisions of this division before operating any vehicle in the transportation of explosives. *(Stats.1959, c. 3, p. 1755, § 31611. Amended by Stats.1959, c. 1671, p. 4058, § 7.5, eff. July 8, 1959, operative Sept. 18, 1959; Stats.1970, c. 1315, p. 2447, § 5; Stats.1971, c. 754, p. 1499, § 4, operative May 3, 1972.)*

Cross References

Department of California Highway Patrol, see Vehicle Code § 2100 et seq.

§ 31612.   Shipping instructions

Persons operating vehicles, or combinations of vehicles, in the transportation of explosives and subject to this division, shall not accept any explosives for transportation unless the shipment is accompanied by a bill of lading or other shipping paper supplied by the shipper, showing the kind of explosives and bearing a statement that they have been packaged, labeled and marked in accordance with regulations of the United States Department of Transportation, and the bill of lading or other shipping paper shall be carried in the vehicle while en route and shall be displayed upon demand of any member of the California Highway Patrol or any police officer of a city who is on duty for the exclusive or main purpose of enforcing the provisions of this code. *(Stats.1959, c. 3, p. 1756, § 31612. Amended by Stats.1970, c. 1315, p. 2448, § 6.)*

§ 31613.   Certain cargoes prohibited

There shall not be included in any cargo of explosives any flammable liquids, acids, or corrosive liquids, oxidizers, or combustible materials, other than the explosives themselves, which may have such characteristics. Blasting caps or detonators shall not be transported upon the same vehicle with other explosives, nor shall electric blasting caps be transported upon any vehicle equipped with a radio transmitter. The foregoing provisions of this section shall be subject to such exceptions as are permitted by the United States Department of Transportation loading chart for cargoes of explosives. *(Stats.1959, c. 3, p. 1756, § 31613. Amended by Stats.1970, c. 1315, p. 2448, § 7.)*

§ 31614.   Traffic laws applicable to transportation of explosives

The following provisions shall apply to any vehicle transporting explosives subject to this division:

(a) When transporting explosives through or into a city or any other congested area for which a route has not been designated by the Department of the California Highway Patrol, drivers shall follow such routes as may be prescribed or established by local authorities.

(b) Where routes are not prescribed by local authority, every driver of a vehicle transporting explosives shall avoid, so far as practicable, and, where feasible, by prearrangement of routes, driving into or through congested thoroughfares, places where crowds are assembled, streetcar tracks, tunnels, viaducts, and dangerous crossings.

(c) No driver or other person in charge of any vehicle on any public or private property shall permit any explosive to be loaded into, or on, or to be unloaded from any motor vehicle with the engine running, and, whenever any loading operation is in progress, the parking brake on the motor vehicle shall be securely set and all reasonable precautions taken to prevent movement of the motor vehicle during loading or unloading.

(d) No driver or other person in charge of such vehicle shall operate or permit the operation of any vehicle transporting explosives unless all of that portion of the lading which consists of explosives is contained entirely within the body of the motor vehicle or within the horizontal outline thereof, without overhang or projection of any part of the load, and if such motor vehicle has a tailboard or tailgate it shall be closed and secured in place during such transportation.

(e) Every motor vehicle transporting explosives shall have either a closed body or have the explosive cargo covered with a fire- and water-resistant tarpaulin, and in either event, care shall be taken to protect the load from moisture and sparks. Subject to other exceptions as are permitted by the United States Department of Transportation regulations, explosives may be transported on flat-bed vehicles if the explosive portion of the load on each vehicle is packed in fire- and water-resistant containers or covered with a fire- and water-resistant tarpaulin.

(f) No person shall operate any vehicle transporting explosives past any fire of any kind burning on or near the highway until the driver ascertains that such passing can be made with safety.

(g) No motor vehicle transporting explosives shall be left unattended upon any street or highway except in extreme emergency. The vehicle shall be deemed attended whenever a driver or person in charge thereof is in or upon the vehicle or is in a position to observe the vehicle at all times. The driver or person in charge of a vehicle transporting explosives may, however, leave the vehicle unattended at any place designated as a safe parking place on the list of safe stopping places prepared by the Department of the California Highway Patrol unless conditions exist, which are known to the driver, which make it unreasonable to do so.

(h) No driver or other person shall smoke or light any match or otherwise have or produce any fire or flame while in, upon, or near any vehicle transporting explosives.

(i) No person shall transport any explosives in a passenger vehicle, or bus, which is subject to this division. *(Stats.1959, c. 3, p. 1756, § 31614. Amended by Stats. 1959, c. 1671, § 8, eff. July 8, 1959, operative Sept. 18, 1959; Stats.1965, c. 69, p. 949, § 4; Stats.1967, c. 78, p. 978, § 12; Stats.1967, c. 1498, p. 3507, § 8; Stats.1970, c. 1315, p. 2448, § 8; Stats.1971, c. 754, p. 1499, § 5, operative May 3, 1972.)*

Cross References

Department of California Highway Patrol, see Vehicle Code
    § 2100 et seq.
Maximum speed limits, see Vehicle Code § 22406.

§ 31615. Application of other vehicle code provisions

Nothing contained in this division shall be deemed to exempt any vehicle transporting explosives and subject to
890

this division, or the owner or any other person, from other provisions of this code, but all such other provisions relating to the driving and movement of vehicles, the size, weight, and equipment thereof, shall be deemed to apply as applicable to each and every vehicle engaged in transporting explosives subject to this division. *(Stats. 1959, c. 3, p. 1757, § 31615.)*

§ 31616. Designation of routes

The Department of the California Highway Patrol, after consultation with the officials having the responsibility for the prevention and suppression of fire in communities through which routes for the transporting of explosives pass, representatives of transportation companies concerned, explosives manufacturers, and the State Fire Marshal shall, by regulation, designate the routes in this state which are to be used for the transportation of explosives. The Department of the California Highway Patrol shall prepare for distribution to persons engaged in the transportation of explosives, maps which clearly indicate the routes, as established in regulations, which are to be used for the transportation of explosives. The Department of the California Highway Patrol shall prepare for distribution to persons engaged in the transportation of explosives a list of locations of required inspection stops, safe parking places, and safe stopping places and shall revise the list to keep it current. Notwithstanding any other provision of law, regulations adopted pursuant to this section shall be adopted in accordance with Chapter 3.5 (commencing with Section 11340) of Part 1 of Division 3 of Title 2 of the Government Code, except that, for the purposes of subdivision (a) of Section 11346.4 of the Government Code, the public comment period shall be 30 days, and the regulations shall become effective upon filing with the Secretary of State. *(Added by Stats.1959, c. 1671, p. 4059, § 9, eff. July 8, 1959, operative Sept. 18, 1959. Amended by Stats.1970, c. 1315, p. 2449, § 9; Stats.1988, c. 63, § 1, eff. March 30, 1988.)*

Cross References

Department of California Highway Patrol, see Vehicle Code
    § 2100 et seq.

§ 31616.5. Regulations; review by office of administrative law; time

Notwithstanding Section 11349.3 of the Government Code, the review by the Office of Administrative Law of regulations adopted pursuant to Section 31616 shall be completed within 15 days after the regulations have been submitted to the Office of Administrative Law for review. *(Added by Stats.1988, c. 63, § 2, eff. March 30, 1988.)*

§ 31617. Emergency changes

In the event of an emergency, the Department of the California Highway Patrol is authorized to suspend or change any designated route for the transportation of explosives or to temporarily designate new or additional routes for such transportation. The Department of the California Highway Patrol shall, unless the nature of the emergency makes it impracticable to do so, consult with local fire officials in the area or areas affected before making any such changes or new designations. If the changes or new designations are made before they can be discussed with those officials, the Department of the California Highway Patrol shall immediately notify the appropriate officials of his action.

The change in or new designation of routes shall not be effective for more than 90 days from the date of such action, unless the Department of the California Highway Patrol determines that the change or new designation should become permanent, in which case the Department of the California Highway Patrol shall, within the 90-day period, initiate action to make the change or new designation permanent in accordance with the provisions of Section 31616 and in which case the emergency change or designation shall remain in effect until superseded by a regulation of the Department of the California Highway Patrol. *(Added by Stats.1959, c. 1671, p. 4060, § 10, eff. July 8, 1959, operative Sept. 18, 1959. Amended by Stats.1970, c. 1315, p. 2450, § 10.)*

§ 31618. Violation

Where not specifically provided otherwise, it is a misdemeanor for any person to violate any provision of this division. Every person convicted of a misdemeanor for a violation of any of the provisions of this division shall be punished as follows:

(a) For a first violation, by a fine of not less than one thousand dollars ($1,000), or by imprisonment for not more than six months, or by both fine and imprisonment.

(b) For a second or subsequent violation, by a fine of not less than two thousand dollars ($2,000) or by imprisonment for not more than six months, or by both fine and imprisonment. *(Added by Stats.1959, c. 1671, p. 4060, § 11, eff. July 8, 1959, operative Sept. 18, 1959. Amended*

by Stats.1983, c. 1092, § 396, eff. Sept. 27, 1983, operative Jan. 1, 1984; Stats.1988, c. 1384, § 3.)

§ 31619. Smokeless powder

When not in conflict with any local ordinance pertaining to the transportation of explosives, it shall be lawful to transport smokeless powder in an amount not exceeding 100 pounds if packed in containers prescribed by the United States Department of Transportation upon a highway not designated by the Department of the California Highway Patrol as a route for the transportation of explosives. *(Added by Stats.1959, c. 1671, p. 4060, § 12, eff. July 8, 1959, operative Sept. 18, 1959. Amended by Stats.1970, c. 1315, p. 2450, § 11.)*

§ 31620. Waiver or suspension of requirement

The Department of the California Highway Patrol, upon application of any interested party, with the concurrence of the fire chief or chiefs in the area or areas affected, and if he determines that such action may be taken without jeopardizing the public safety, may suspend, or waive compliance with, the whole or any part of the requirements of this division insofar as they apply to the delivery or transportation of explosives in sparsely populated, unincorporated areas or in any area where there may be practical difficulties or unnecessary or unreasonable hardship in carrying out the provisions of this division. No person shall be charged with any crime for any violation of the provisions of this division when such a suspension or waiver by the Department of the California Highway Patrol is in effect in the area in which the alleged violation occurs. *(Added by Stats.1959, c. 1671, p. 4060, § 13, eff. July 8, 1959, operative Sept. 18, 1959. Amended by Stats.1970, c. 1315, p. 2450, § 12.)*

Division 14.1

TRANSPORTATION OF HAZARDOUS MATERIAL

Chapter	Section
1. Licensing	32000
2. Notification of Routes	32050

Cross References

Drivers licensed to transport hazardous materials, exemption from prohibition on issuing permits if display of placards required, see Health and Safety Code § 12101.

Federal definitions of hazardous materials, substances, or wastes, adoption by commissioner, see Vehicle Code § 2402.7.

Hazardous material defined, see Vehicle Code § 353.

Highway spill containment and abatement of hazardous substances, see Vehicle Code § 2450 et seq.

License for transportation of hazardous material, see Vehicle Code §§ 2531, 2532.

Used oil, refuse removal or curbside collection vehicles, exemption from this division, see Health and Safety Code § 25250.15.

Violation as misdemeanor, see Vehicle Code § 40000.19.

CHAPTER 1. LICENSING

Section
32000. Legislative intent.
32000.5. Licenses; examination and display; exemptions.
32001. Inspections; equipment on vehicles; compliance with laws and regulations; licenses; exemptions.
32002. Regulations; violations; punishment.
32002.5. Temporary suspension of licenses.
32003. Deposit and use of fees.
32004. Injunctions.
32005. Repealed.
32006. Repealed.

§ 32000. Legislative intent

It is the intent of the Legislature, by enacting this division, that the public be provided additional protection through the licensing of motor carriers transporting hazardous material. The Department of the California Highway Patrol shall be authorized to inspect and license the motor carriers with special attention directed to the negligent operators or repeat violators. *(Added by Stats. 1981, c. 860, p. 3295, § 13.)*

§ 32000.5. Licenses; examination and display; exemptions

(a) A motor carrier who directs the transportation of an explosive and a motor carrier who directs the transportation of a hazardous material, who is required to display placards pursuant to Section 27903, and a motor carrier who transports for a fee in excess of 500 pounds of hazardous materials of the type requiring placards pursuant to Section 27903, shall be licensed in accordance with this code, unless specifically exempted by this code or regulations adopted pursuant to this code. This license shall be available for examination and shall be displayed in accordance with the regulations adopted by the commissioner.

(b)(1) Except as provided in Section 32001, this division shall not apply to a person hauling only hazardous waste, as defined in Section 25115 or 25117 of the Health and Safety Code, and who is registered pursuant to subdivision (a) of Section 25163 of the Health and Safety Code or who is exempt from that registration pursuant to subdivision (b) of that section.

(2) A motor carrier that is transporting a hazardous waste and is required to display placards pursuant to Section 27903 shall comply with all provisions of Section 32001 except paragraph (3) of subdivision (c) of that section.

(c) This division does not apply to implements of husbandry, as defined in Section 36000.

(d) This division does not apply to the hauling of division 1.3 explosives classified as special fireworks or to division 1.4 explosives classified as common fireworks by the United States Department of Transportation if those fireworks are transported by a motor carrier under the authority of, and in conformance with, a license issued to the motor carrier by the State Fire Marshal pursuant to Part 2 (commencing with Section 12500) of Division 11 of the Health and Safety Code. In that case, a copy of the license shall be carried in the vehicle and presented to a peace officer upon request.

(e)(1) The department shall not issue a license to transport hazardous materials to a motor carrier unless each terminal from which hazardous materials carrying vehicles are operated is in compliance with Section 34501.12 and is currently rated satisfactory.

(2) The department shall adopt rules and regulations that provide for a temporary license to transport hazardous materials for a carrier who, within the previous three years, has not been issued an unsatisfactory rating as a result of an inspection conducted pursuant to Section 34501, 34501.12, or 34520.

(3) It is the intent of the Legislature that a carrier's license to transport hazardous materials should not be unreasonably hindered as a result of the department's verification and issuance process.

(f) This section does not prevent the department from issuing a new or initial license to transport hazardous materials to a motor carrier that applies for a license to transport hazardous materials and that, within the previous three years, has been issued an unsatisfactory rating as a result of an inspection conducted pursuant to Section 34501, 34501.12, or 34520, if the motor carrier has corrected the unsatisfactory rating before applying for the license to transport hazardous materials. *(Added by*

Stats.1981, c. 860, p. 3295, § 13. Amended by Stats.1982, c. 533, p. 2464, § 1; Stats.1982, c. 1255, p. 4603, § 5.5; Stats.1982, c. 1273, p. 4705, § 21; Stats.1983, c. 661, § 1; Stats.1998, c. 478 (A.B.2372), § 7; Stats.2002, c. 610 (S.B.1257), § 3; Stats.2007, c. 514 (A.B.1612), § 1; Stats.2009, c. 111 (A.B.463), § 1.)

§ 32001. Inspections; equipment on vehicles; compliance with laws and regulations; licenses; exemptions

(a)(1) Any authorized employee of the department may inspect any sealed or unsealed vehicle, container, or shipment subject to this division in maintenance facilities, terminals, or other public or private property to ascertain the quantity and kind of hazardous material and to ensure compliance with the provisions of this code and regulations adopted pursuant to this code.

(2) If a seal is opened for inspection, the department shall reseal any vehicle, container, or shipment prior to further transportation.

(b) Unless specifically stated, nothing contained in this division shall be deemed to exempt any vehicle transporting a hazardous material subject to this division or the operator or any other person from other provisions of this code.

(c) No motor carrier shall direct the transportation of any shipment of a hazardous material in any vehicle unless all of the following are complied with:

(1) The vehicle is equipped as required by this code and applicable regulations adopted pursuant to law.

(2) The shipment complies with laws and regulations pertaining to the shipment or transportation of hazardous material.

(3) The motor carrier holds a valid license for the transportation of hazardous materials.

(4)(A) A vehicle or combination of vehicles required to display placards pursuant to Section 27903 is equipped with a two-way communication device, maintained in good working order, that enables the driver to contact the personnel responsible for the safety operations of the motor carrier in the event of an emergency.

(B) For the purposes of this section, "two-way communication device" means a radio, cellular telephone, or other similar device that permits communication between the driver and personnel responsible for the safety operations of the motor carrier.

(5)(A) The enclosed cargo body, when the display of placards is required pursuant to Section 27903, shall be locked and remain locked during transit of the hazardous materials so as to prevent any unauthorized entry and shall be opened only during loading, unloading, or at the direction of a peace officer, an authorized employee of the department, or a person authorized pursuant to Section 25185 of the Health and Safety Code.

(B) A driver transporting hazardous material in a locked cargo body shall verify that all locks are in place if

894

the vehicle has been left unattended for any length of time. Each driver shall make a notation in his or her log book of the time and date that the verification occurred.

(C) For the purposes of this section, "cargo body" means a fully enclosed area that is an integral part of the vehicle and designed to encapsulate the entire load, such as a van body or an intermodal freight container, and does not mean a tank or flatbed type of vehicle.

(d) The commissioner may issue exemptions from the provisions of this section.

(e) Nothing in this section shall limit the ability of other state or local agencies to carry out their regulatory, enforcement, or emergency response duties under other provisions of law. (Added by Stats.1981, c. 860, p. 3295, § 13. Amended by Stats.2002, c. 610 (S.B.1257), § 4.)

§ 32002. Regulations; violations; punishment

(a) The commissioner may adopt any regulations that are necessary to administer this division. It is a misdemeanor for any motor carrier to violate this division or regulations adopted pursuant to this division.

(b) Notwithstanding subdivision (a), it is unlawful for the motor carrier or the person who directs the driver to operate a vehicle transporting hazardous material, when that transportation requires a license pursuant to this division, to cause the operation of the vehicle unless the motor carrier holds a valid license for the transportation of hazardous materials. A violation of this subdivision shall be punished as follows:

(1) For a first violation, by a fine of not less than two thousand dollars ($2,000).

(2) For a second or subsequent violation, by a fine of not less than four thousand dollars ($4,000). (Added by Stats.1981, c. 860, p. 3295, § 13. Amended by Stats.1988, c. 1384, § 4.)

§ 32002.5. Temporary suspension of licenses

(a) The commissioner may temporarily suspend a license to haul hazardous material prior to any hearing, when, in the commissioner's opinion, the action is necessary to prevent an imminent and substantial danger to the public health. The commissioner shall notify the holder of the license of the temporary suspension and the effective date thereof and, at the same time, shall serve the person with an accusation. Upon receipt of a notice of defense to the accusation, the commissioner shall set the matter for a hearing which shall be held as soon as possible, but not later than 10 days after receipt of the notice of defense. The temporary suspension shall remain in effect until the hearing is completed and the commissioner has made a final determination on the merits, which, in any event, shall be made within 10 days after the completion of the hearing. If the determination is not transmitted within 10 days after the hearing is completed, the temporary suspension is of no further effect.

(b) The commissioner shall suspend a license to transport hazardous material of a person or motorcarrier, for a period of at least 90 days but not more than 180 days, if the holder of the license permits the transportation of fissile class III shipments or highway route controlled quantity radioactive materials, as defined in Subpart I (commencing with Section 173.401) of Part 173 of Title 49 of the Code of Federal Regulations, by a person who does not possess a license of the appropriate class and an attached radioactive materials driver's certificate or an endorsement issued under Article 6 (commencing with Section 15275) of Chapter 7 of Division 6. *(Added by Stats.1981, c. 860, p. 3297, § 13. Amended by Stats.1983, c. 893, § 6, operative July 1, 1984; Stats.1992, c. 1241 (S.B.1615), § 27; Stats.1992, c. 1243 (A.B.3090), § 92, eff. Sept. 30, 1992.)*

§ 32003. Deposit and use of fees

(a) All fees collected by the department pursuant to the issuance or renewal of a license for the transportation of hazardous material shall be deposited in the Motor Vehicle Account of the State Transportation Fund.

(b) All moneys collected from these fees shall be used for the support of the hazardous materials inspection and licensing program of the department upon appropriation therefor by the Legislature. *(Added by Stats.1981, c. 860, p. 3295, § 13.)*

§ 32004. Injunctions

Any violation of any provision of this division may be enjoined in a civil action brought by the Attorney General in the name of the people of the State of California, upon request of the department, except that it shall not be necessary to show lack of adequate remedy at law or to show irreparable damage or loss. *(Added by Stats.1981, c. 860, p. 3295, § 13.)*

§ 32005. Repealed by Stats.2004, c. 193 (S.B.111), § 198

Law Revision Commission Comments

2004 Repeal

Section 32005 is repealed as obsolete. The required report was to be completed by January 1, 1983. [33 Cal.L.Rev.Comm. Reports 497 (2004)].

§ 32006. Repealed by Stats.1986, c. 434, § 3

CHAPTER 2. NOTIFICATION OF ROUTES

Section
32050. Advance notification of shipments required; conflicts with federal law; definitions.
32051. Advance notification; contents; forms.
32052. Time of notification; notification of change in schedule or route or cancellation of shipment.
32053. Violations; civil penalties.

§ 32050. Advance notification of shipments required; conflicts with federal law; definitions

(a) Prior to the transport of anhydrous hydrazine, methylhydrazine, dimethylhydrazine, Aerozine 50, fuming nitric acid, liquid fluorine, or nitrogen tetroxide in bulk packaging, except when that packaging contains only residue, outside the confines of a facility where that material was used or stored, or prior to the delivery of that bulk material to a carrier for transport, each carrier shall provide advance notification, in writing, of the shipment, to the department, which, in turn, shall notify the sheriff of each county and police chief of each city in which is located the proposed route. Notification shall be made through the Department of Justice's California Law Enforcement Telecommunications System. The sheriffs and police chiefs shall, in turn, make timely notification to the fire chiefs within their respective jurisdictions through a mutually agreed upon communications system.

(b) Subdivision (a) applies only to the extent that it does not conflict with federal law.

(c) For the purposes of this section, the following definitions apply:

(1) "Bulk packaging" has the same meaning as defined in Section 171.8 of Title 49 of the Code of Federal Regulations.

(2) "Fire chief" means the fire chief of each county and city fire department and the fire chief of each fire protection district serving a population greater than 15,000 in which is located the proposed route. This paragraph does not apply to any fire chief of a fire department or fire protection district that is composed of 50 percent or more volunteer firefighters.

(3) "Residue" has the same meaning as defined in Section 171.8 of Title 49 of the Code of Federal Regulations. *(Added by Stats.1988, c. 1222, § 2. Amended by Stats.1996, c. 124 (A.B.3470), § 135.)*

Cross References

Designation of routes, transportation of inhalation hazards composed of chemical rocket propellants, see Vehicle Code § 32102.

§ 32051. Advance notification; contents; forms

(a) Each advance notification required by Section 32050 shall contain all of the following information:

(1) The name, address, and emergency telephone number of the manufacturer, shipper, carrier, and receiver of the shipment.

(2) A current copy of a material data safety sheet, as designated by the department, regarding the material.

(3) If the shipment is originating within California, the point of origin of the shipment and the 48–hour period during which departure of the shipment is estimated to occur, the destination of the shipment within California, and the 48–hour period during which the shipment is estimated to arrive.

(4) If the shipment is originating outside of California, the point of origin of the shipment and the 48–hour period during which the shipment is estimated to arrive at the state boundary, the destination of the shipment within California, and the 48–hour period during which the shipment is estimated to arrive.

(5) A telephone number and address for current shipment information.

(b) The department shall design a standard notification form to include all of the information specified in subdivision (a) and shall make these forms available by April 1, 1989. *(Added by Stats.1988, c. 1222, § 2.)*

§ 32052. Time of notification; notification of change in schedule or route or cancellation of shipment

(a) The notification required by Section 32050 shall reach the department at least 72 hours before the beginning of the 48–hour period during which departure of the shipment of any material designated in Section 32050 is estimated to occur, and the department shall notify the sheriffs and the police chiefs as specified in subdivision (a) of Section 32050 at least 36 hours before the beginning of the 48–hour departure period specified in subdivision (a) of Section 32051, who shall notify the fire chiefs, as provided in Section 32050. A copy of the notification shall be retained by the department for three years.

(b) The carrier shall also notify, by telephone or telegram, the department if there are any changes in the scheduling of a shipment, in the routes to be used for shipment, or any cancellation of a shipment. The department shall, in turn, notify the sheriffs and the police chiefs specified in subdivision (a) of Section 32050 that would be affected by these changes in the scheduling of a shipment, in the routes to be used for a shipment, or the cancellation of a shipment, who shall notify the fire chiefs, as provided in Section 32050. The department shall maintain for three years a record of each telegram and telephonic notification. *(Added by Stats.1988, c. 1222, § 2.)*

§ 32053. Violations; civil penalties

(a) Any carrier who violates Section 32050, 32051, or 32052, in addition to any other penalty provided by law, is subject to a civil penalty of not less than five hundred dollars ($500) or more than one thousand dollars ($1,000) for each violation. For purposes of this section, each day of a continuing violation is a separate violation.

(b) When establishing the amount of the civil penalty, the court shall consider, in addition to other relevant circumstances, all of the following:

(1) The extent of the harm caused by the violation.

(2) The persistence of the violation.

(3) The number of prior violations by the same violator.

(4) The deterrent value of the penalty based on the financial resources of the violator. *(Added by Stats.1988, c. 1222, § 2.)*

Division 14.3

TRANSPORTATION OF INHALATION HAZARDS

Section
32100. Legislative intent.
32100.5. Application of division.
32101. Definitions.
32102. Regulations; violations; designation of routes; maps; inspection stops; Vandenberg Air Force Base.
32103. Map and list of inspection stops and safe stopping places available in vehicle; driver familiarity; operative date of section.
32104. Driving on undesignated routes; stopping at undesignated places; operative date of section.
32105. Driving into heavily populated or congested areas; unattended vehicles; inspections; records; operative date of section.
32106. Equipment and maintenance of vehicles.
32107. Breathing apparatus; communication equipment.
32108. Repealed.
32109. Application of other code provisions.

§ 32100. Legislative intent

It is the intent of the Legislature, in enacting this division, to create a special category of inhalation hazards and poison gases and to establish special safeguards for their transportation.

These materials are highly toxic, spread rapidly, and require rapid and widespread evacuation if there is loss of containment or a fire. For these reasons, the Legislature intends to more rigorously restrict and otherwise control the transportation of these materials. *(Added by Stats. 1988, c. 1384, § 5.)*

§ 32100.5. Application of division

This division applies to the transportation of inhalation hazards in bulk packaging, except when that packaging contains only residue. *(Added by Stats.1988, c. 1384, § 5.)*

§ 32101. Definitions

As used in this division:

(a) "Inhalation hazard" means any material defined as "Poison A" pursuant to Section 173.326 of Title 49 of the Code of Federal Regulations or for which a "Poison–Inhalation Hazard" or "Inhalation Hazard" shipping paper description is required pursuant to Section 172.203 of Title 49 of the Code of Federal Regulations.

(b) "Bulk packaging" means the same as defined in Section 171.8 of Title 49 of the Code of Federal Regulations.

(c) "Residue" means the same as defined in Section 171.8 of Title 49 of the Code of Federal Regulations.

(d) "Inspection stop" means any location designated as such in regulations adopted pursuant to this division or any safe stopping place.

(e) "Safe parking place" means any loading or unloading facility or motor carrier terminal where the driver may safely and lawfully park and leave the vehicle unattended when authorized by the owner or person in charge of the facility or terminal.

(f) "Safe stopping place" means any place designated by the department pursuant to this division where a driver may stop for food, fuel, or any other necessary reason, provided the vehicle is attended at all times. A vehicle is "attended" when the driver or person in charge of it is awake and occupies any part of it except the sleeper berth, or is within 100 feet of the vehicle and has an unobstructed view of it. *(Added by Stats.1988, c. 1384, § 5.)*

§ 32102. Regulations; violations; designation of routes; maps; inspection stops; Vandenberg Air Force Base

(a) The department may adopt any regulations that are necessary to administer this division. It is a misdemeanor for any person to violate this division or regulations adopted pursuant to this division.

(b) The department shall, by regulation, designate through routes in this state which are to be used for the transportation of inhalation hazards. The department may also designate separate through routes for the transportation of inhalation hazards composed of any chemical rocket propellant specified in Section 32050. The Department of Transportation shall assist the department in developing the recommended routes. The department shall hold public hearings in each field operation division of the department in which are located proposed routes. In recommending the through routes, the department shall do both of the following:

(1) Perform a risk assessment which shall include, but not be limited to, consideration of the population density, capabilities of the emergency response personnel near the proposed routes, and the safety of the roadways.

(2) Consult with officials having the responsibility for the prevention and suppression of fire in communities in which are located the proposed routes, the representatives of persons engaged in the transportation of inhalation hazards, manufacturers of inhalation hazards, and the State Fire Marshal.

(c) The department shall prepare for distribution to persons engaged in the transportation of inhalation hazards maps which clearly indicate the routes which are to be used for the transportation of inhalation hazards.

(d) The department shall prepare for distribution to persons engaged in the transportation of inhalation hazards a list of locations of required inspection stops and

897

safe stopping places and shall revise the list to keep it current.

(e) Until other routes are designated by the department for the transportation of chemical rocket propellants pursuant to subdivision (b), the designated through routes for the transportation of chemical rocket propellants to Vandenberg Air Force Base shall be those routes designated in the letter of agreement between the department and the United States Department of the Air Force executed in 1992. *(Added by Stats.1988, c. 1384, § 5. Amended by Stats.1992, c. 516 (S.B.1991), § 1.)*

§ 32103. Map and list of inspection stops and safe stopping places available in vehicle; driver familiarity; operative date of section

(a) Every motor carrier shall make available in each vehicle used in the transportation of inhalation hazards the latest map showing the routes to be used for the transportation of inhalation hazards and a list of the safe stopping places and inspection stops for vehicles transporting inhalation hazards as prescribed by regulations of the department. The carrier shall require that the driver be thoroughly familiar with this division before operating any vehicle in the transportation of inhalation hazards.

(b) This section shall become operative on January 1, 1992. *(Added by Stats.1988, c. 1384, § 5, operative Jan. 1, 1992.)*

§ 32104. Driving on undesignated routes; stopping at undesignated places; operative date of section

(a) It is unlawful for the motor carrier or its authorized agent to drive or to permit the driving of any vehicle transporting inhalation hazards, or for the driver to drive the vehicle, upon any public highway not designated in regulations adopted by the department as a route for the transportation of inhalation hazards. This subdivision shall not apply when the use of the highway is required (1) to permit delivery of, or the loading of, inhalation hazards at a point not on a highway designated as a route for the transportation of inhalation hazards, or (2) to permit the vehicle to proceed to, and return from, an inspection stop, safe stopping place, or safe parking place.

(b) It is unlawful for the driver of any vehicle transporting inhalation hazards to stop at any place other than a safe stopping place, safe parking place, or an inspection stop unless the vehicle is disabled or except when necessary to avoid conflict with other traffic or to comply with the orders of a peace officer or an official traffic control device.

(c) This section shall become operative on January 1, 1992. *(Added by Stats.1988, c. 1384, § 5, operative Jan. 1, 1992.)*

§ 32105. Driving into heavily populated or congested areas; unattended vehicles; inspections; records; operative date of section

(a) Unless there is no practicable alternative, every driver of a vehicle transporting inhalation hazards shall

avoid, by prearrangement of routes, driving into or through heavily populated areas, congested thoroughfares, or places where crowds are assembled. Operating convenience is not a basis for determining whether it is practicable to operate a vehicle in accordance with this subdivision.

(b) No vehicle transporting inhalation hazards shall be left unattended upon any street or highway.

(c) Inspection of the following items of equipment shall be made immediately preceding the actual transportation of an inhalation hazard:

(1) Brakes and the brake system.

(2) Steering, connection devices, and lighting systems.

(3) All tires.

(4) All supplemental equipment as required by Section 32106.

(d) En route inspection of tires and brakes on vehicles transporting inhalation hazards shall be performed at the following locations:

(1) At an inspection stop at least every four hours or 150 miles traveled, whichever occurs first, or as close thereto as is practicable, depending upon the proximity of those inspection stops.

(2) Regardless of elapsed time or miles traveled, at the top of and prior to descending any grade upon which the Department of Transportation has declared a speed limit for trucks of less than 55 miles per hour as provided by Section 22407. The inspection shall be made off the roadway.

(3) Regardless of elapsed time or miles traveled, at any location designated in regulations of the department as a required inspection stop.

(e)(1) Every person operating a vehicle transporting an inhalation hazard shall complete a record of every inspection which is required pursuant to this section in the form approved by the department showing the time and place of every inspection.

(2) The record of every inspection shall be made at the time the inspection is conducted.

(3) The person making the inspection shall certify the fact in the record.

(f) This section shall become operative on January 1, 1992. *(Added by Stats.1988, c. 1384, § 5, operative Jan. 1, 1992.)*

§ 32106. Equipment and maintenance of vehicles

Every vehicle used in the transportation of an inhalation hazard, in addition to any other equipment required by law, shall be equipped and maintained as required by this section.

(a) Brakes and the brake system shall be maintained in good and safe operating condition.

(b) Steering, connection devices, and lighting systems shall be maintained in good operating condition.

(c) All tires shall be in good condition, properly matched and inflated. Except as may be necessary to cause immediate replacement, no vehicle shall be driven unless all tires in actual use on the vehicle are properly inflated.

(d) Fire extinguishers and other safety equipment prescribed by regulations adopted by the department pursuant to Section 34501 shall be carried in each vehicle or combination of vehicles. *(Added by Stats.1988, c. 1384, § 5.)*

§ 32107. Breathing apparatus; communication equipment

Every vehicle, or combination of vehicles, transporting an inhalation hazard shall contain a self-contained breathing apparatus and equipment capable of immediate communication with emergency personnel. *(Added by Stats.1988, c. 1384, § 5.)*

§ 32108. Repealed by Stats.1996, c. 10 (A.B.1869), § 22, eff. Feb. 9, 1996

§ 32109. Application of other code provisions

Nothing in this division exempts any vehicle transporting inhalation hazards and subject to this division, or the owner or any other person, from other provisions of this code. All those other provisions relating to the driving and movement of vehicles, and the size, weight and equipment thereof, shall apply as applicable to each and every vehicle engaged in transporting inhalation hazards subject to this division. *(Added by Stats.1988, c. 1384, § 5.)*

Division 14.5

TRANSPORTATION OF RADIOACTIVE MATERIALS

Section
33000. Regulations.
33001. Repealed.
33002. Notification; persons to be notified; contents; time; record; violations; penalties.

Cross References

Department of California Highway Patrol, see Vehicle Code § 2100 et seq.

Federal definitions of hazardous materials, substances, or wastes, adoption by commissioner, see Vehicle Code § 2402.7.

Hazardous material defined, see Vehicle Code § 353.

Highway spill containment and abatement of hazardous substances, see Vehicle Code § 2450 et seq.

License for transportation of hazardous material, see Vehicle Code §§ 2531, 2532.

Violation of division a misdemeanor, see Vehicle Code § 40000.19.

§ 33000. Regulations

Subject to the provisions of Section 114765 of the Health and Safety Code, the Department of the California Highway Patrol, after consulting with the State Department of Health Services, shall adopt regulations specifying the time that shipments may occur and the routes that are to be used in the transportation of cargoes of hazardous radioactive materials, as are defined in regulations of the State Department of Health Services. *(Added by Stats.1980, c. 875, p. 2747, § 6. Amended by Stats.1996, c. 1023 (S.B.1497), § 427, eff. Sept. 29, 1996.)*

§ 33001. Repealed by Stats.1961, c. 1705, p. 3687, § 6

§ 33002. Notification; persons to be notified; contents; time; record; violations; penalties

(a) Prior to the transport of any hazardous radioactive materials containing cargoes of commercially produced, spent radioactive fuel outside the confines of a facility where that material was used or stored, or prior to the delivery of these materials to a carrier for transport, each carrier shall provide advance notification, in writing, of the shipment to the Department of the California Highway Patrol, which, in turn, shall notify all of the following persons:

(1) The fire chiefs of each city and county fire department and the fire chiefs of each fire protection district serving a population greater than 15,000, which city, county, or fire protection district is located along the proposed route. The Department of the California Highway Patrol, however, shall notify only those fire chiefs who have requested, in writing, to be so notified. A fire chief may revoke this request, in writing, at any time.

This paragraph does not apply to any fire chief of a fire department or fire protection district that is composed of 50 percent or more volunteer firefighters.

(2) The police chiefs of each city where surface transportation would occur along the proposed route.

(b) Subdivision (a) applies only to the extent that it does not conflict with federal law.

(c) Each advance notification shall contain the following information:

(1) The name, address, and telephone number of the shipper, carrier, and receiver of the shipment.

(2) If the shipment originates within California, the point of origin of the shipment and the 48–hour period during which departure of the shipment is estimated to occur, the destination of the shipment within California, and the 48–hour period during which the shipment is estimated to arrive.

(3) If the shipment originates outside of California, the point of origin of the shipment and the 48–hour period during which the shipment is estimated to arrive at state boundaries, the destination of the shipment within California, and the 48–hour period during which the shipment is estimated to arrive.

(4) A telephone number and address for current shipment information.

(d) The Department of the California Highway Patrol shall design a standard notification form to include all of the information specified in subdivision (c) and shall make these forms available by April 1, 1984.

(e) The notification is required to reach the Department of the California Highway Patrol at least 72 hours before the beginning of the 48–hour period during which departure of the shipment is estimated to occur, and the Department of the California Highway Patrol shall notify the fire chiefs who have requested notification and the police chiefs specified in subdivision (a) at least 36 hours before the beginning of this 48–hour period. A copy of the notification shall be retained by the Department of the California Highway Patrol for three years.

(f) The carrier shall also notify, by telephone or telegram, the Department of the California Highway Patrol if there are any changes in the scheduling of a shipment, in the routes to be used for a shipment, or any cancellation of a shipment. The Department of the California Highway Patrol shall, in turn, notify the fire chiefs who have requested notification and the police chiefs specified in subdivision (a) who would be affected by these changes in the scheduling of a shipment, in the routes to be used for a shipment, or the cancellation of a shipment. The Department of the California Highway

901

Patrol shall maintain for three years a record of each telegram and telephonic notification.

(g) Any person or agency that receives any information pursuant to this section shall not disseminate or reveal this information to any other person, state agency, city, county, or local agency unless the person or agency determines that disseminating or revealing this information is necessary to protect the public health and safety or the environment.

(h) The Governor shall appoint the fire chiefs eligible to request notification, as specified in paragraph (1) of subdivision (a), as the designated representatives of the Governor pursuant to paragraph (1) of subsection (c) of Section 73.21 of Title 10 of the Code of Federal Regulations for the purpose of receiving information classified as safeguards information pursuant to Part 73 of Title 10 of the Code of Federal Regulations.

(i) Any carrier who violates this section, in addition to any penalty provided by law, is subject to a civil penalty of not more than five hundred dollars ($500) for each violation. For purposes of this section, each day of a continuing violation is a separate and distinct violation.

When establishing the amount of civil liability pursuant to this subdivision, the court shall consider, in addition to other relevant circumstances, the following:

(1) The extent of the harm caused by the violation.

(2) The persistence of the violation.

(3) The number of prior violations by the same violator.

(4) The deterrent value of the penalty based on the financial resources of the violator. *(Added by Stats.1983, c. 1093, § 2. Amended by Stats.1996, c. 124 (A.B.3470), § 136.)*

Division 14.7

FLAMMABLE AND COMBUSTIBLE LIQUIDS

Article   Section
1. **Administration** 34000
2. **Regulations** 34019
3. **Registration [Repealed]**
4. **Enforcement** 34060
5. **Violations** 34100
6. **Reciprocity [Repealed]**

ARTICLE 1. ADMINISTRATION

Section
34000.   Legislative intent.
34001.   Application of division.
34001.1. Repealed.
34002.   Legislative policy.
34003.   Definitions.
34004.   Application of division.
34005.   Trap wagons and spray rigs.
34006.   Wine and alcoholic aqueous solutions.
34007 to 34016. Repealed.

Cross References

Federal definitions of hazardous materials, substances, or wastes, adoption by commissioner, see Vehicle Code § 2402.7.

Hazardous material defined, see Vehicle Code § 353.

Highway spill containment and abatement of hazardous substances, see Vehicle Code § 2450 et seq.

License for transportation of hazardous material, see Vehicle Code §§ 2531, 2532.

Vapor recovery systems on tanks of tank vehicles, state air resources board's regulations to be consistent with state fire marshal's regulations, see Health and Safety Code § 41962.

Violation of division a misdemeanor, see Vehicle Code § 40000.19.

§ 34000. Legislative intent

It is the intent of the Legislature to provide additional protection to the public and reduce the risk of possible hazards in the highway transportation of hazardous waste and of flammable and combustible liquids in tank vehicles. It is further the intent of the Legislature that the Department of the California Highway Patrol shall place as a high priority the random inspection of cargo tanks and hazardous waste transport vehicles and containers for compliance with this code. *(Added by Stats.1982, c. 1255, p. 4604, § 6. Amended by Stats.1983, c. 661, § 2; Stats.1996, c. 539 (A.B.2201), § 28.)*

§ 34001. Application of division

The provisions of this division refer to vehicles having a cargo tank and to hazardous waste transport vehicles and containers, as defined in Section 25167.4 of the Health and Safety Code, that are operating on highways within this state. *(Added by Stats.1967, c. 1106, p. 2749, § 3. Amended by Stats.1997, c. 945 (A.B.1561), § 28.)*

§ 34001.1. Repealed by Stats.1986, c. 434, § 4

§ 34002. Legislative policy

(a) It is the legislative intention that the regulations adopted by the commissioner pursuant to this division shall apply uniformly throughout the State of California, and no state agency, city, city and county, county, or other political subdivision of this state, including, but not limited to, a chartered city, city and county, or county, shall adopt or enforce any ordinance or regulation which is inconsistent with this division.

(b) No other state agency, city, city and county, county, or other public agency of this state, including, but not limited to, a chartered city, city and county, or county, shall enforce any provisions regarding the design and construction of any cargo tank subject to this division, regardless of the location of the cargo tank, or the area of operation of the cargo tank, within this state. *(Added by Stats.1967, c. 1106, p. 2749, § 3. Amended by Stats.1982, c. 1255, p. 4604, § 8; Stats.1983, c. 661, § 3.)*

Cross References

Vapor recovery systems on tanks of tank vehicles, compliance with emission standards, see Health and Safety Code § 41962.

§ 34003. Definitions

As used in this division:

(a) "Cargo tank" means any tank having a volumetric capacity in excess of 120 gallons that is used for the transportation of flammable liquids or combustible liquids. "Cargo tank" includes pumps, meters, valves, fittings, piping, and other appurtenances attached to a tank vehicle and used in connection with the flammable liquids or combustible liquids being transported in the cargo tank except that the volumetric capacity refers to the capacity of the container portion of a cargo tank.

"Cargo tank" does not include any of the following:

(1) Any tank used only to carry fuel necessary for the operation of the vehicle or any equipment of the vehicle.

(2) Any tank containing not more than 120 gallons of residue. For purposes of this paragraph, "residue" means the liquid material remaining after a tank has been unloaded to the maximum extent practicable through the normal discharge opening.

(3) Any intermodal portable tank, meeting United States Department of Transportation IM 101 or IM 102 Specification transported as part of an interstate shipment when operated within a 25-mile radius of its ocean port or railroad terminal loading or unloading facility.

(4) Any tank meeting the requirements of Title 49 of the Code of Federal Regulations, with a volumetric capacity of less than 500 gallons used to transport flammable or combustible liquids, except a portable tank used to transport an inhalation hazard as defined in subdivision (a) of Section 32101.

(5) Any tank designated by the United States Department of Transportation as a "single trip container" or "nonreusable container," marked and used as such, with a volumetric capacity of less than 500 gallons.

(6) Any vehicle that is registered in any other state and is used for refueling aircraft while operating in this state pursuant to a contract with this state or the United States for the conduct of fire suppression or other emergency-related activities.

(b) "Tank vehicle" means any truck, trailer, or semi-trailer equipped with a cargo tank which is used for the transportation of flammable liquids or combustible liquids within this state.

(c) "Flammable liquids" and "combustible liquids" mean those liquids as defined by the regulations adopted by the commissioner pursuant to Section 2402.7. *(Added by Stats.1967, c. 1106, p. 2749, § 3. Amended by Stats. 1977, c. 825, p. 2496, § 9; Stats.1982, c. 466, p. 2058, § 117; Stats.1990, c. 429 (A.B.3904), § 4; Stats.1992, c. 1243 (A.B.3090), § 93, eff. Sept. 30, 1992.)*

Cross References
Sign designating cargo of tank vehicle, see Vehicle Code
§ 27903.

§ 34004. Application of division

The provisions of this division shall apply equally to new as well as existing cargo tanks. *(Added by Stats.1967, c. 1106, p. 2749, § 3.)*

§ 34005. Trap wagons and spray rigs

The provisions of this division shall not apply to a trap wagon or spray rig when empty or when transporting not more than 1,000 gallons of flammable liquids or combustible liquids to accomplish the basic function of such vehicle. For the purpose of this section, "trap wagon" and "spray rig" have the same meaning of those terms as defined in Section 36005. *(Added by Stats.1969, c. 1214, p. 2355, § 1. Amended by Stats.1977, c. 825, p. 2496, § 10.)*

§ 34006. Wine and alcoholic aqueous solutions

The provisions of this division shall not apply to "wine," as defined by Section 23007 of the Business and Professions Code, or any other aqueous solution, having an alcoholic content less than, or equal to, 24 percent by volume. This exemption applies only if the nonalcohol portion of the aqueous solution does not fall within the definition of flammable or combustible liquid. *(Added by Stats.1978, c. 868, p. 2732, § 8.)*

§§ 34007 to 34016. Repealed by Stats.1967, c. 1106, p. 2749, § 2

ARTICLE 2. REGULATIONS

Section
34019.   Design, construction, and structural safety of cargo tanks and fire equipment; tank vehicle stability; federal standards.
34020.   Repealed.
34020.5. Regulation of tunnel travel; survey; signs.
34021.   Content of regulations.
34022.   Safety standards.
34023.   Repealed.
34024.   Regulations; administrative procedure act.

§ 34019. Design, construction, and structural safety of cargo tanks and fire equipment; tank vehicle stability; federal standards

(a) The commissioner shall adopt reasonable regulations with respect to the following:

(1) The design, construction, and structural safety of cargo tanks and fire auxiliary equipment.

(2) To the extent permitted by federal law, the stability of tank vehicles.

(b) For intrastate shipments in this state, the commissioner shall, as soon as feasible, incorporate any new United States Department of Transportation standards concerning interstate shipments. *(Added by Stats.1982, c. 1255, p. 4605, § 9. Amended by Stats.1983, c. 661, § 4; Stats.1991, c. 1043 (S.B.123), § 2.)*

§ 34020. Repealed by Stats.1996, c. 539 (A.B.2201), § 29

§ 34020.5. Regulation of tunnel travel; survey; signs

(a) The Department of Transportation, after consultation with the Department of the California Highway Patrol, the State Fire Marshal, and affected local agencies, and following a public hearing subject to Section 21109.5, may regulate the time when tank vehicles may travel through a tunnel on state highways.

(b) In evaluating the use of a tunnel on a state highway, the Department of Transportation shall conduct a traffic and engineering survey which includes an analysis of the relative risks to public safety in determining the feasibility of reasonable alternative routes.

(c) For the purposes of this section, a tunnel is a horizontal passage enclosed on the sides and top containing a roadway of a length of not less than 300 feet.

(d) No prohibition or restriction adopted pursuant to this section shall be effective until appropriate signs have been posted giving notice thereof to drivers approaching the tunnel. *(Added by Stats.1982, c. 1255, p. 4605, § 12.)*

§ 34021. Content of regulations

The regulations adopted by the commissioner shall make reasonable allowances for cargo tanks in existence when the regulations become effective. No allowance shall, however, be made for any cargo tank which because of its design or construction constitutes a distinct hazard to life or property. *(Added by Stats.1967, c. 1106, p. 2749,*

§ 3.   Amended by Stats.1982, c. 1255, p. 4605, § 13; Stats.1983, c. 661, § 5.)

§ 34022.   Safety standards

In adopting the regulations, the commissioner shall consider, as evidence of generally accepted safety standards, the publications of the National Fire Protection Association and the United States Department of Transportation. (Added by Stats.1967, c. 1106, p. 2749, § 3. Amended by Stats.1973, c. 78, p. 139, § 19; Stats.1982, c. 1255, p. 4605, § 14; Stats.1983, c. 661, § 6.)

§ 34023.   Repealed by Stats.1992, c. 1243 (A.B.3090), § 94, eff. Sept. 30, 1992

§ 34024.   Regulations; administrative procedure act

The regulations adopted by the commissioner pursuant to this division shall be adopted, amended, and repealed in accordance with Chapter 3.5 (commencing with Section 11340) of Part 1 of Division 3 of Title 2 of the Government Code. (Added by Stats.1967, c. 1106, p. 2749, § 3. Amended by Stats.1982, c. 1255, p. 4606, § 16; Stats.1983, c. 661, § 8; Stats.1985, c. 106, § 166.)

ARTICLE 3.   REGISTRATION [REPEALED]

§§ 34040 to 34045.5.   Repealed by Stats.1996, c. 539 (A.B.2201), § 30

§§ 34046, 34047.   Repealed by Stats.1982, c. 1255, p. 4607, §§ 24, 25

§§ 34048 to 34050.   Repealed by Stats.1996, c. 539 (A.B.2201), § 30

ARTICLE 4.   ENFORCEMENT

Section
34060.   Inspection.
34060.5. Testing.
34061.   Inspections report.
34062, 34063.   Repealed.
34064.   Inspection permitted.

§ 34060.   Inspection

The commissioner shall provide for the establishment, operation, and enforcement of random on- and off-highway inspections of cargo tanks and hazardous waste transport vehicles and containers. The commissioner shall also provide training in the inspection of cargo tanks and hazardous waste transport vehicles and containers to employees of the department whose primary duties include the enforcement of laws and regulations relating to commercial vehicles and who, thereafter, are required to perform random inspections of cargo tanks and hazardous waste transport vehicles and containers to determine whether or not the cargo tanks and hazardous waste transport vehicles and containers are designed, constructed, and maintained in accordance with the regulations adopted by the commissioner pursuant to this

code and Chapter 6.5 (commencing with Section 25100) of Division 20 of the Health and Safety Code. (Added by Stats.1967, c. 1106, p. 2749, § 3. Amended by Stats.1982, c. 1255, p. 4607, § 28; Stats.1983, c. 661, § 10; Stats.1996, c. 539 (A.B.2201), § 31; Stats.1997, c. 945 (A.B.1561), § 29.)

§ 34060.5.   Testing

Any required pressure, vacuum, or hydrostatic testing of a cargo tank shall be performed, or be caused to be performed, by the carrier, operator, or consultant who shall certify in writing that the cargo tank meets the requirements of the United States Department of Transportation, the State Air Resources Board, and the commissioner. An authorized representative of the department may observe or require these tests. Records of these certifications shall be maintained at the carrier's place of business. (Added by Stats.1982, c. 1255, p. 4608, § 29. Amended by Stats.1983, c. 661, § 11.)

§ 34061.   Inspections report

The department shall compile data and annually publish a report relating to the level of cargo tank and hazardous waste transport vehicle and container inspections conducted during the previous year. The data included in the report shall include, but need not be limited to, all of the following:

(a) The number of inspections conducted.

(b) The number of violations recorded.

(c) The number of on-highway incidents involving cargo tanks and hazardous waste transport vehicles and containers that were reported to the * * * Office of Emergency Services under Section 8574.17 of the Government Code. (Added by Stats.1996, c. 539 (A.B.2201), § 33. Amended by Stats.2010, c. 618 (A.B.2791), § 296; Stats.2013, c. 352 (A.B.1317), § 526, eff. Sept. 26, 2013, operative July 1, 2013.)

§§ 34062, 34063.   Repealed by Stats.1996, c. 539 (A.B.2201), §§ 34, 35

§ 34064.   Inspection permitted

Any duly authorized employee of the department may inspect cargo tanks and hazardous waste transport vehicles and containers, or the appurtenances and equipment thereof, in terminals, yards, or similar places, as often as may be necessary for the purpose of ascertaining and causing to be corrected any conditions likely to cause damage to any personal or real property or injury or death to any person or animal or any violation of the provisions or intent of this division. Any duly authorized employee of the department may enter upon private property to conduct those inspections. The owner, lessee, bailee, manager, or operator of that property shall permit any duly authorized employee of the department to enter the property and inspect cargo tanks and hazardous waste transport vehicles and containers for the purpose stated in this division. (Added by Stats.1967, c.

1106, p. 2749, § 3. Amended by Stats.1982, c. 1255, p. 4609, § 33; Stats.1996, c. 539 (A.B.2201), § 36.)

ARTICLE 5. VIOLATIONS

Section
34100.   Violations.
34101, 34101.5. Repealed.
34102.   Renumbered.

§ 34100. Violations

A violation of this division or of any regulation adopted by the commissioner pursuant to this division is a misdemeanor. No person shall operate a tank vehicle upon a highway in violation of this division or of any regulation adopted by the commissioner pursuant to this division. *(Formerly § 34102, added by Stats.1967, c. 1106, p. 2749, § 3. Amended by Stats.1982, c. 1255, p. 4609, § 36; Stats.1983, c. 661, § 15. Renumbered § 34100 and amended by Stats.1996, c. 539, (A.B.2201), § 40.)*

§§ 34101, 34101.5. Repealed by Stats.1996, c. 539 (A.B. 2201), §§ 38, 39

§ 34102. Renumbered Vehicle Code § 34100 and amended by Stats.1996, c. 539 (A.B.2201), § 40

ARTICLE 6.   RECIPROCITY [REPEALED]

§§ 34120, 34121. Repealed by Stats.1996, c. 539 (A.B. 2201), § 41

Division 14.8

SAFETY REGULATIONS

Section

34500.   Vehicles to which applicable.

34500.1.   Regulation of tour buses.

34500.2.   Emergency vehicles; inspection during emergencies.

34500.3.   Cargo securement standards; exemptions.

34500.5.   Commercial motor vehicle; definition.

34501.   Adoption of regulations; inspection of vehicles and records; installation and use of wheelchair lifts; transportation of hazardous materials.

34501.1.   Manufacturers and distributors of wheelchair lifts; certificate of compliance.

34501.2.   Carriers; hours-of-service; maximum on-duty time limits; emergencies.

34501.3.   Schedules necessitating unlawful speeds or exceeding hours of service requirements; logbook reflecting travel requiring excessive speed; presumption that driver exceeded speed limit; violations; penalties.

34501.4.   Inability to produce driver's logbook; presumption of violation of hours of service limitations.

34501.5.   Schoolbus safety regulations.

34501.6.   Schoolbuses; procedures for limiting operation due to reduced visibility.

34501.7.   Regulations for construction, testing, or certification of wheelchair lifts used on buses; review of costs; operative date of section.

34501.8.   General public paratransit vehicle; annual inspection; display of certificates; fees; operative date of section.

34501.9.   Wage rates; effect of this division and regulations under this division.

34501.10.   Registration of location of log books and other required driver records.

34501.12.   Biennial Inspection of Terminals Program (BIT).

34501.12.   Basic Inspection of Terminals program (BIT).

34501.13.   Schoolbus maintenance facility or terminal; inspection; unsatisfactory rating; notification of school board.

34501.14.   Grape gondola inspections; applicability of section.

34501.15.   Commercial drivers; blood alcohol of .01 percent or more; 24-hour period out of service; operative date and duration of section.

34501.16.   Commercial drivers; employer-provided information on blood alcohol percentage provisions; duration of section.

34501.17.   Paratransit vehicles; regular inspections and maintenance; minimum requirements; documentation.

34501.18.   Report to department from motor carrier regularly employing more than 20 full-time drivers whenever it replaces more than half within 30–day period; department inspection; terms defined.

34502.   Safety standards.

34503.   Legislative intent: uniform regulation.

34504.   Enforcement.

34505.   Inspection of tour buses; correction of defects; records of inspections.

34505.1.   Suspension, denial or revocation of operating authority for tour buses; grounds; notice and hearing.

34505.5.   Vehicle inspections; elements; operation of defective vehicles; records of inspections.

34505.5.   Vehicle inspections; elements; operation of defective vehicles; records of inspections.

34505.6.   Vehicles described in § 34500; motor carriers of property; household goods carriers; suspension, denial, or revocation of permit or operating authority; grounds; notice and hearing.

34505.6.   Vehicles described in § 34500; motor carriers of property; household goods carriers; suspension, denial, or revocation of permit or operating authority; grounds; notice and hearing.

34505.7.   Private carriers of passengers; written recommendation of suspension; grounds; records; notice; staffing at Mexican border.

34505.9.   Intermodal roadability inspection program; conditions; program components; records; citation for violation; reinspection; carrier's and driver's rights and duties.

34505.10.   Dispatch and pay records; motor carriers contracting or subcontracting transportation for other carriers.

34506.   Violations: misdemeanors.

34506.3.   Violations: infractions.

34506.4.   Unsafe vehicles; removal from highway; towing and storage fees.

34506.5.   Farm labor vehicles subject to forfeiture as nuisance; driven on highways; impounding.

34507.   Display of identifying symbol.

34507.5.   Carrier identification numbers; application; display; application of section; exceptions; companies no longer in operating; disposal of vehicles and numbers.

34507.6.   Exempt operators of charter-party carriers; carrier identification numbers; application; display.

34508.   Additional regulations: school buses.

34508.5.   Repealed.

34509.   Vanpool vehicles.

34510.   Vehicles transporting hazardous material; shipping papers; display.

34510.5.   Brokers of construction trucking services furnishing or hiring transportation services; surety bond required; evidence of bond; violations, penalties; rebuttable presumption in civil actions; exceptions; definition.

34511.   Violations; injunction.

34513.   Rules and regulations relating to tour buses.

34514.   Roadside safety inspections; funds.

34515.   Maintenance facility or terminal.

34515.   Maintenance facility or terminal.

34516.   Prohibition of use of motor vehicle for transportation of food products for human consumption if used to transport solid waste or hazardous substances; violations; misdemeanor; avoidance of liability.

Section

34517.   Commercial motor vehicles from another country; operation outside designated Commercial Zone restricted; violation; penalty; enforcement.

34518.   Operation without or in violation of certificate of registration.

34520.   Compliance with federal drug and alcohol regulations; preemployment test for controlled substances and alcohol use; placement on duty; test results and other records; penalties; exemptions.

34520.3.   School transportation vehicles; federal drug and alcohol testing requirements.

34520.5.   Employers of paratransit vehicle drivers; paratransit vehicle drivers; compliance with federal drug-testing requirements.

Cross References

Department of California Highway Patrol, see Vehicle Code § 2100 et seq.

Failure to comply with this division, contracts to administer motor carriers of property permit act and impose fines, see Vehicle Code § 34605.

Notice to correct violations, see Vehicle Code § 40303.5.

Violations of this division relating to motor carriers of property, additional sanctions, see Vehicle Code § 34670.

§ 34500.   Vehicles to which applicable

The department shall regulate the safe operation of the following vehicles:

(a) Motortrucks of three or more axles that are more than 10,000 pounds gross vehicle weight rating.

(b) Truck tractors.

(c) Buses, schoolbuses, school pupil activity buses, youth buses, farm labor vehicles, and general public paratransit vehicles.

(d) Trailers and semitrailers designed or used for the transportation of more than 10 persons, and the towing motor vehicle.

(e) Trailers and semitrailers, pole or pipe dollies, auxiliary dollies, and logging dollies used in combination with vehicles listed in subdivision (a), (b), (c), or (d). This subdivision does not include camp trailers, trailer coaches, and utility trailers.

(f) A combination of a motortruck and a vehicle or vehicles set forth in subdivision (e) that exceeds 40 feet in length when coupled together.

(g) A truck, or a combination of a truck and any other vehicle, transporting hazardous materials.

(h) Manufactured homes that, when moved upon the highway, are required to be moved pursuant to a permit as specified in Section 35780 or 35790.

(i) A park trailer, as described in Section 18009.3 of the Health and Safety Code, that, when moved upon a highway, is required to be moved pursuant to a permit pursuant to Section 35780.

(j) Any other motortruck not specified in subdivisions (a) to (h), inclusive, or subdivision (k), that is regulated by the Department of Motor Vehicles, Public Utilities Commission, or United States Secretary of the Department of Transportation, but only for matters relating to hours of service and logbooks of drivers.

(k) A commercial motor vehicle with a gross vehicle weight rating of 26,001 or more pounds or a commercial motor vehicle of any gross vehicle weight rating towing a vehicle described in subdivision (e) with a gross vehicle weight rating of more than 10,000 pounds, except combinations including camp trailers, trailer coaches, or utility trailers. For purposes of this subdivision, the term "commercial motor vehicle" has the meaning defined in subdivision (b) of Section 15210. *(Added by Stats.1987, c. 986, § 5.5, operative July 1, 1988. Amended by Stats.1990, c. 429 (A.B.3904), § 5; Stats.1991, c. 298 (A.B.964), § 1; Stats.1992, c. 1243 (A.B.3090), § 96, eff. Sept. 30, 1992; Stats.1993, c. 272 (A.B.301), § 50, eff. Aug. 2, 1993; Stats.1995, c. 766 (S.B.726), § 39; Stats.1999, c. 724 (A.B.1650), § 46; Stats.2000, c. 566 (A.B.1912), § 7; Stats.2006, c. 288 (A.B.3011), § 14.)*

Cross References

Age of drivers of vehicles defined in this section, see Vehicle Code § 12515.

Definitions,
   Auxiliary dolly, see Vehicle Code § 225.
   Bus, see Vehicle Code § 233.
   Logging dolly, see Vehicle Code § 378.
   Motor truck, see Vehicle Code § 410.
   Pole or pipe dolly, see Vehicle Code § 475.
   Schoolbus, see Vehicle Code § 545.
   Semitrailer, see Vehicle Code § 550.
   Trailer, see Vehicle Code § 630.
   Truck tractor, see Vehicle Code § 655.

Equipment requirements, transportation of explosives, see Vehicle Code § 31610.

Fleet owners licensed as inspection and maintenance stations, see Vehicle Code § 2525 et seq.

§ 34500.1.   Regulation of tour buses

In addition to the duties imposed by Section 34500, the department shall regulate the safe operation of tour buses. *(Added by Stats.1986, c. 1306, § 13.)*

§ 34500.2.   Emergency vehicles; inspection during emergencies

No additional inspection shall be required under this division on any vehicle which is owned and operated by a public agency and is used for responding to and returning from an emergency, as defined in subdivision (c) of Section 35002, during the duration of the emergency, as determined by the public agency, if an inspection pursuant to Section 1215 of Title 13 of the California Code of Regulations has been completed on the vehicle within the past 24 hours. Any vehicle used in responding to an emergency shall be inspected immediately upon the termination of the emergency. *(Added by Stats.1990, c. 899 (A.B.3424), § 1, eff. Sept. 14, 1990.)*

§ 34500.3.   Cargo securement standards; exemptions

(a) The department shall adopt rules and regulations that are designed to promote the safe operation of vehicles, regarding cargo securement standards. The regulations adopted pursuant to this section shall be consistent with the securement regulations adopted by the United States Department of Transportation in Part 393 (commencing with Section 393. 1) of Title 49 of the Code of Federal Regulations, as those regulations now exist or are amended in the future.

(b) Regulations adopted pursuant to subdivision (a) do not apply to the transportation of a pole on a pole dolly by a public utility company or a local public agency engaged in the business of supplying electricity or telephone service, by the Department of Transportation, or by a licensed contractor in the performance of work for a public utility company, a local agency, or the Department of Transportation, when the transportation is between storage yards or between a storage yard and job location where the pole is to be used. However, no more than nine poles shall be transported on a dolly if any of those poles exceeds a length of 30 feet. If poles 30 feet or less are transported by a pole or pipe dolly, no more than 18 poles shall be transported. A pole shall be adequately secured when being transported on a dolly, to prevent shifting or spilling of a load.

(c) Regulations adopted pursuant to subdivision (a) do not apply to a farmer transporting his or her own hay or straw, incidental to his or her farming operation, if that transportation requires that the farmer use a highway, except that this subdivision does not relieve the farmer from loading and securing the hay or straw in a safe manner. *(Added by Stats.2006, c. 288 (A.B.3011), § 15.)*

§ 34500.5. Commercial motor vehicle; definition

For purposes of this division, the term "commercial motor vehicle" has the same meaning as defined in subdivision (b) of Section 15210. *(Added by Stats.1997, c. 945 (A.B.1561), § 30.)*

§ 34501. Adoption of regulations; inspection of vehicles and records; installation and use of wheelchair lifts; transportation of hazardous materials

(a)(1) The department shall adopt reasonable rules and regulations that, in the judgment of the department, are designed to promote the safe operation of vehicles described in Section 34500, regarding, but not limited to, controlled substances and alcohol testing of drivers by motor carriers, hours of service of drivers, equipment, fuel containers, fueling operations, inspection, maintenance, recordkeeping, accident reports, and drawbridges. The rules and regulations shall not, however, be applicable to schoolbuses, which shall be subject to rules and regulations adopted pursuant to Section 34501.5.

The rules and regulations shall exempt local law enforcement agencies, within a single county, engaged in the transportation of inmates or prisoners when those agencies maintain other motor vehicle operations records which furnish hours of service information on drivers which are in substantial compliance with the rules and regulations. This exemption does not apply to any local law enforcement agency engaged in the transportation of inmates or prisoners outside the county in which the agency is located, if that agency would otherwise be required, by existing law, to maintain driving logs.

(2) The department may adopt rules and regulations relating to commercial vehicle safety inspection and out-of-service criteria. In adopting the rules and regulations, the commissioner may consider the commercial vehicle safety inspection and out-of-service criteria adopted by organizations such as the Commercial Vehicle Safety Alliance, other intergovernmental safety group, or the United States Department of Transportation. The commissioner may provide departmental representatives to that alliance or other organization for the purpose of promoting the continued improvement and refinement of compatible nationwide commercial vehicle safety inspection and out-of-service criteria.

(3) The commissioner shall appoint a committee of 15 members, consisting of representatives of industry subject to the regulations to be adopted pursuant to this section, to act in an advisory capacity to the department, and the department shall cooperate and confer with the advisory committee so appointed. The commissioner shall appoint a separate committee to advise the department on rules and regulations concerning wheelchair lifts for installation and use on buses, consisting of persons who use the wheelchair lifts, representatives of transit districts, representatives of designers or manufacturers of wheelchairs and wheelchair lifts, and representatives of the Department of Transportation.

(4) The department may inspect any vehicles in maintenance facilities or terminals, as well as any records relating to the dispatch of vehicles or drivers, and the pay of drivers, to assure compliance with this code and regulations adopted pursuant to this section.

(b) The department, using the definitions adopted pursuant to Section 2402.7, shall adopt regulations for the transportation of hazardous materials in this state, except the transportation of materials which are subject to other provisions of this code, that the department determines are reasonably necessary to ensure the safety of persons and property using the highways. The regulations may include provisions governing the filling, marking, packing, labeling, and assembly of, and containers that may be used for, hazardous materials shipments, and the manner by which the shipper attests that the shipments are correctly identified and in proper condition for transport.

(c) At least once every 13 months, the department shall inspect every maintenance facility or terminal of any person who at any time operates any bus. If the bus operation includes more than 100 buses, the inspection shall be without prior notice.

(d) The commissioner shall adopt and enforce regulations which will make the public or private users of any bus aware of the operator's last safety rating.

(e) It is unlawful and constitutes a misdemeanor for any person to operate any bus without the inspection specified in subdivision (c) having been conducted.

(f) The department may adopt regulations restricting or prohibiting the movement of any vehicle from a maintenance facility or terminal if the vehicle is found in violation of this code or regulations adopted pursuant to this section. *(Added by Stats.1986, c. 969, § 3, operative July 1, 1987. Amended by Stats.1987, c. 56, § 174; Stats.1987, c. 726, § 8, operative July 1, 1988; Stats.1991, c. 177 (A.B.539), § 1; Stats.1994, c. 832 (S.B.2034), § 2; Stats.1998, c. 380 (S.B.1491), § 2.)*

Cross References

Employer responsibilities, commercial vehicle safety, self employment as driver, see Vehicle Code § 15242.

Equipment requirements, transportation of explosives, see Vehicle Code § 31610.

Licenses, examination and display, exemptions, see Vehicle Code § 32000.5.

Maintenance of driving logs, punishment, see Vehicle Code § 42001.3.

Vehicles transporting specified dangerous substances, display of placards or markings, exemptions, see Vehicle Code § 27903.

§ 34501.1. Manufacturers and distributors of wheelchair lifts; certificate of compliance

A manufacturer or distributor of wheelchair lifts for buses, schoolbuses, youth buses, and general public transit vehicles, regardless of capacity, shall, prior to the distribution of the wheelchair lift model in California, provide to the Department of the California Highway Patrol proof of certification from an independent laboratory or registered mechanical engineer of this state that the wheelchair lift model complies with the California and any federal law and the regulations adopted pursuant thereto. *(Added by Stats.1989, c. 428, § 1.)*

§ 34501.2. Carriers; hours-of-service; maximum on-duty time limits; emergencies

(a) The regulations adopted under Section 34501 for vehicles engaged in interstate or intrastate commerce shall establish hours-of-service regulations for drivers of those vehicles that are consistent with the hours-of-service regulations adopted by the United States Department of Transportation in Part 395 of Title 49 of the Code of Federal Regulations, as those regulations now exist or are hereafter amended.

(b) The regulations adopted under Section 34501 for vehicles engaged in intrastate commerce that are not transporting hazardous substances or hazardous waste, as those terms are defined by regulations in Section 171.8 of Title 49 of the Code of Federal Regulations, as those regulations now exist or are hereafter amended, shall have the following exceptions:

(1) The maximum driving time within a work period shall be 12 hours for a driver of a truck or truck tractor, except for a driver of a tank vehicle with a capacity of more than 500 gallons transporting flammable liquid, who

shall not drive for more than 10 hours within a work period.

(2) A motor carrier shall not permit or require a driver to drive, nor shall any driver drive, for any period after having been on duty for 80 hours in any consecutive eight days.

(3) A driver employed by an electrical corporation, as defined in Section 218 of the Public Utilities Code, a gas corporation, as defined in Section 222 of that code, a telephone corporation, as defined in Section 234 of that code, a water corporation, as defined in Section 241 of that code, or a public water district as defined in Section 20200 of the Water Code, is exempt from all hours-of-service regulations while operating a public utility or public water district vehicle.

(4) Any other exceptions applicable to drivers assigned to governmental fire suppression and prevention, as determined by the department.

(5) A driver employed by a law enforcement agency, as defined in Section 390.3(f)(2) of Title 49 of the Code of Federal Regulations, as that section now exists or is hereafter amended, during an emergency or to restore the public peace.

(c) The regulations adopted under Section 34501 for vehicles engaged in the transportation of farm products in intrastate commerce shall include all of the following provisions:

(1) A driver employed by an agricultural carrier, including a carrier holding a seasonal permit, or by a private carrier, when transporting farm products from the field to the first point of processing or packing, shall not drive for any period after having been on duty 16 hours or more following eight consecutive hours off duty and shall not drive for any period after having been on duty for 112 hours in any consecutive eight-day period, except that a driver transporting special situation farm products from the field to the first point of processing or packing, or transporting livestock from pasture to pasture, may be permitted, during one period of not more than 28 consecutive days or a combination of two periods totaling not more than 28 days in a calendar year, to drive for not more than 12 hours during any workday of not more than 16 hours. A driver who thereby exceeds the driving time limits specified in paragraph (2) of subdivision (b) shall maintain a driver's record of duty status, and shall keep a duplicate copy in his or her possession when driving a vehicle subject to this chapter. These records shall be presented immediately upon request by any authorized employee of the department, or any police officer or deputy sheriff.

(2) Upon the request of the Director of Food and Agriculture, the commissioner may, for good cause, temporarily waive the maximum on-duty time limits applicable to any eight-day period when an emergency exists due to inclement weather, natural disaster, or an adverse economic condition that threatens to disrupt the orderly movement of farm products during harvest for the

duration of the emergency. For purposes of this paragraph, an emergency does not include a strike or labor dispute.

(3) For purposes of this subdivision, the following terms have the following meanings:

(A) "Farm products" means every agricultural, horticultural, viticultural, or vegetable product of the soil, honey and beeswax, oilseeds, poultry, livestock, milk, or timber.

(B) "First point of processing or packing" means a location where farm products are dried, canned, extracted, fermented, distilled, frozen, ginned, eviscerated, pasteurized, packed, packaged, bottled, conditioned, or otherwise manufactured, processed, or preserved for distribution in wholesale or retail markets.

(C) "Special situation farm products" means fruit, tomatoes, sugar beets, grains, wine grapes, grape concentrate, cotton, or nuts. *(Added by Stats.1984, c. 779, § 4. Amended by Stats.1990, c. 429 (A.B.3904), § 6; Stats. 1991, c. 928 (A.B.1886), § 32, eff. Oct. 14, 1991; Stats. 1991, c. 1043 (S.B.123), § 4; Stats.1992, c. 1144 (A.B. 2417), § 2; Stats.1993, c. 208 (A.B.1187), § 1; Stats.1995, c. 102 (S.B.253), § 1; Stats.2000, c. 787 (S.B.1404), § 24; Stats.2009, c. 200 (S.B.734), § 15.)*

§ 34501.3. Schedules necessitating unlawful speeds or exceeding hours of service requirements; logbook reflecting travel requiring excessive speed; presumption that driver exceeded speed limit; violations; penalties

(a) No motor carrier shall schedule a run or permit or require the operation of any motor vehicle subject to this division between points within a period of time which would do either of the following:

(1) Necessitate the vehicle being operated at speeds greater than those prescribed by this code.

(2) Require the driver of the vehicle to exceed the applicable maximum hours of service.

(b) A logbook of a driver, which reflects a trip or trips between points within a period of time which would have necessitated excessive speed to complete, shall give rise to a rebuttable presumption that the driver exceeded the lawful speed limit.

(c) For a violation of paragraph (2) of subdivision (a), a first offense is punishable by a fine of not more than one thousand dollars ($1,000), a second offense by a fine of not more than two thousand five hundred dollars ($2,500), and a third or subsequent offense by a fine of not more than five thousand dollars ($5,000). *(Added by Stats.1986, c. 1306, § 14. Amended by Stats.1991, c. 392 (S.B.1226), § 1.)*

§ 34501.4. Inability to produce driver's logbook; presumption of violation of hours of service limitations

Any driver subject to the hours of service limitations and logbook requirements of this division, who is unable to produce upon request of a representative of the department any driver's logbook or is only able to produce an incomplete driver's log book for the prior 24–hour period, is rebuttably presumed to be in violation of the hours of service limitations in Sections 34501 and 34501.2. *(Added by Stats.1986, c. 1306, § 15.)*

§ 34501.5. Schoolbus safety regulations

(a) The Department of the California Highway Patrol shall adopt reasonable rules and regulations which, in the judgment of the department, are designed to promote the safe operation of vehicles described in Sections 39830 and 82321 of the Education Code and Sections 545 and 34500 of this code. The Commissioner of the California Highway Patrol shall appoint a committee of 11 members to act in an advisory capacity when developing and adopting regulations affecting school pupil transportation buses and school pupil transportation operations. The advisory committee shall consist of 11 members appointed as follows:

(1) One member of the State Department of Education.

(2) One member of the Department of Motor Vehicles.

(3) One member of the Department of the California Highway Patrol.

(4) One member who is employed as a schoolbus driver.

(5) One member of the Office of Traffic Safety in the Business, Transportation and Housing Agency.

(6) Two members who are schoolbus contractors, one of whom shall be from an urban area of the state and one of whom shall be from a rural area of the state, as determined by the department.

(7) Two members who are representatives of school districts, one of whom shall be from an urban area of the state and one of whom shall be from a rural area of the state, as determined by the department.

(8) One professionally licensed member of the American Academy of Pediatrics.

(9) One member representing school pupil transportation operations other than schoolbus operations.

(b) The department shall cooperate and confer with the advisory committee appointed pursuant to this section prior to adopting rules or regulations affecting school pupil transportation buses and school pupil transportation operations. *(Added by Stats.1977, c. 406, p. 1417, § 11.5, eff. Aug. 27, 1977. Amended by Stats.1983, c. 142, § 172; Stats.1999, c. 1008 (S.B.533), § 13; Stats.2005, c. 677 (S.B.512), § 50, eff. Oct. 7, 2005.)*

§ 34501.6. Schoolbuses; procedures for limiting operation due to reduced visibility

The governing board of a local educational agency that provides for the transportation of pupils shall adopt procedures that limit the operation of schoolbuses when atmospheric conditions reduce visibility on the roadway to 200 feet or less during regular home-to-school transportation service. Operational policies for school activity trips shall give schoolbus drivers discretionary authority to discontinue schoolbus operation if the driver determines that it is unsafe to continue operation because of reduced visibility. *(Added by Stats.1992, c. 624 (A.B. 3144), § 9, eff. Sept. 14, 1992.)*

§ 34501.7. Regulations for construction, testing, or certification of wheelchair lifts used on buses; review of costs; operative date of section

(a) Any rules or regulations adopted pursuant to Section 34501 for the construction, testing, or certification of wheelchair lifts for installation and use on buses shall take into consideration the costs of implementing the regulations and shall be reviewed and brought up to date by the department annually.

(b) This section shall become operative on July 1, 1987. *(Added by Stats.1986, c. 969, § 4, operative July 1, 1987.)*

§ 34501.8. General public paratransit vehicle; annual inspection; display of certificates; fees; operative date of section

(a) The Department of the California Highway Patrol shall inspect every general public paratransit vehicle, as defined in Section 336, at least once each year to certify that its condition complies with all provisions of law, including being equipped with a fire extinguisher, first-aid kit, and three-point tie downs for transporting wheelchair passengers.

(b) On or after July 1, 1989, no person shall drive any general public paratransit vehicle unless there is displayed therein a certificate issued by the Department of the California Highway Patrol stating that on a certain date, which shall be within 13 months of the date of operation, an authorized employee of the Department of the California Highway Patrol inspected the general public paratransit vehicle and found that on the date of inspection the general public paratransit vehicle complied with the applicable provisions of state law. The Commissioner of the California Highway Patrol shall provide, by rule or regulation, for the issuance and display of distinctive inspection certificates.

(c) The Commissioner of the California Highway Patrol shall determine a fee and method of collection for the annual inspection of general public paratransit vehicles. The fee, established by regulation, shall be sufficient to cover the cost to the department for general public paratransit vehicle inspections. All fees received shall be deposited in the Motor Vehicle Account in the State Transportation Fund.

This section shall become operative January 1, 1989. *(Added by Stats.1987, c. 986, § 6, operative July 1, 1988. Amended by Stats.1988, c. 683, § 5, eff. Aug. 27, 1988, operative Jan. 1, 1989.)*

§ 34501.9. Wage rates; effect of this division and regulations under this division

(a) Nothing in this division or the regulations adopted under this division is intended to, or shall, affect the rate of payment of wages, including, but not limited to, regular, premium, or overtime rates, paid to any person whether for on-duty hours or driving hours or otherwise.

(b) Nothing in this division or the regulations adopted under this division is intended to, or shall, affect the regulations adopted pursuant to other provisions of law concerning the rate or rates of payment of wages by any other public agency, including, but not limited to, the Industrial Welfare Commission or the Division of Labor Standards Enforcement of the Department of Industrial Relations. *(Added by Stats.1987, c. 70, § 2. Amended by Stats.1987, c. 747, § 2.5.)*

§ 34501.10. Registration of location of log books and other required driver records

The employer of any person required to keep log books, records of physical examination, and other driver records as may be required by the Department of the California Highway Patrol, the Department of Motor Vehicles, the Department of Toxic Substances Control, or the State Department of Health Services, shall register with the Department of the California Highway Patrol the address where the log books and other records are available for inspection. *(Added by Stats.1988, c. 1452, § 3. Amended by Gov.Reorg.Plan No. 1 of 1991, § 191, eff. July 17, 1991.)*

§ 34501.12. Biennial Inspection of Terminals Program (BIT)

Section operative until Jan. 1, 2016. See, also, section operative Jan. 1, 2016.

(a) Notwithstanding Section 408, as used in this section and Sections 34505.5 and 34505.6, "motor carrier" means the registered owner of a vehicle described in subdivision (a), (b), (e), (f), or (g) of Section 34500, except in the following circumstances:

(1) The registered owner leases the vehicle to another person for a term of more than four months. If the lease is for more than four months, the lessee is the motor carrier.

(2) The registered owner operates the vehicle exclusively under the authority and direction of another person. If the operation is exclusively under the authority and direction of another person, that other person may assume the responsibilities as the motor carrier. If not so assumed, the registered owner is the motor carrier. A person who assumes the motor carrier responsibilities of another pursuant to subdivision (b) shall provide to that other person whose motor carrier responsibility is so assumed, a completed copy of a departmental form documenting that assumption, stating the period for which responsibility is assumed, and signed by an agent of the assuming person. A legible copy shall be carried in each vehicle or combination of vehicles operated on the

highway during the period for which responsibility is assumed. That copy shall be presented upon request by an authorized employee of the department. The original completed departmental form documenting the assumption shall be provided to the department within 30 days of the assumption. If the assumption of responsibility is terminated, the person who had assumed responsibility shall so notify the department in writing within 30 days of the termination.

(b)(1) A motor carrier may combine two or more terminals that are not subject to an unsatisfactory compliance rating within the last 36 months for purposes of the inspection required by subdivision (d), subject to all of the following conditions:

(A) The carrier identifies to the department, in writing, each terminal proposed to be included in the combination of terminals for purposes of this subdivision prior to an inspection of the designated terminal pursuant to subdivision (d).

(B) The carrier provides the department, prior to the inspection of the designated terminal pursuant to subdivision (d), a written listing of all its vehicles of a type subject to subdivision (a), (b), (e), (f), or (g) of Section 34500 that are based at each of the terminals combined for purposes of this subdivision. The listing shall specify the number of vehicles of each type at each terminal.

(C) The carrier provides to the department during the inspection all maintenance, records and driver records and a representative sample of vehicles based at each of the terminals included within the combination of terminals.

(2) If the carrier fails to provide the maintenance records, driver records, and representative sample of vehicles pursuant to subparagraph (C) of paragraph (1), the department shall assign the carrier an unsatisfactory terminal rating and require a reinspection to be conducted pursuant to subdivision (h).

(3) For purposes of this subdivision, the following terms have the following meanings:

(A) "Driver records" includes pull notice system records, driver proficiency records, and driver timekeeping records.

(B) "Maintenance records" includes all required maintenance, lubrication, and repair records and drivers' daily vehicle condition reports.

(C) "Representative sample" means the following, applied separately to the carrier's fleet of motortrucks and truck tractors and its fleet of trailers:

Fleet Size	Representative Sample
1 or 2	All
3 to 8	3
9 to 15	4
16 to 25	6
26 to 50	9
51 to 90	14
91 or more	20

(c) Each motor carrier who, in this state, directs the operation of, or maintains, a vehicle of a type described in subdivision (a) shall designate one or more terminals, as defined in Section 34515, in this state where vehicles can be inspected by the department pursuant to paragraph (4) of subdivision (a) of Section 34501 and where vehicle inspection and maintenance records and driver records will be made available for inspection.

(d)(1) The department shall inspect, at least every 25 months, every terminal, as defined in Section 34515, of a motor carrier who, at any time, operates a vehicle described in subdivision (a).

(2) The department shall place an inspection priority on those terminals operating vehicles listed in subdivision (g) of Section 34500.

(3) As used in this section and in Sections 34505.5 and 34505.6, subdivision (f) of Section 34500 includes only those combinations where the gross vehicle weight rating * * * of the towing vehicle exceeds 10,000 pounds, but does not include a pickup truck, and subdivision (g) of Section 34500 includes only those vehicles transporting hazardous material for which the display of placards is required pursuant to Section 27903, a license is required pursuant to Section 32000.5, or for which hazardous waste transporter registration is required pursuant to Section 25163 of the Health and Safety Code. Historical vehicles, as described in Section 5004, vehicles that display special identification plates in accordance with Section 5011, implements of husbandry and farm vehicles, as defined in Chapter 1 (commencing with Section 36000) of Division 16, and vehicles owned or operated by an agency of the federal government are not subject to this section or to Sections 34505.5 and 34505.6.

(e)(1) It is the responsibility of the motor carrier to schedule with the department the inspection required by subdivision (d). The motor carrier shall submit an application form supplied by the department, accompanied by the required fee contained in paragraph (2), for each terminal the motor carrier operates. This fee shall be submitted within 30 days of establishing a terminal. All fees submitted under paragraph (2) are nonrefundable.

(2)(A) The fee for each terminal is set forth in the following table:

Terminal fleet size	Required fee per terminal
1	$ 270
2	375
3 to 8	510
9 to 15	615
16 to 25	800
26 to 50	1,040
51 to 90	1,165
91 or more	1,870

(B) In addition to the fee specified in subparagraph (A), the motor carrier shall submit an additional fee of three hundred fifty dollars ($350) for each of its terminals not previously inspected under the section.

(3) Except as provided in paragraph (5), the inspection term for each inspected terminal of a motor carrier shall expire 25 months from the date the terminal receives a satisfactory compliance rating, as specified in subdivision (h). Applications and fees for subsequent inspections shall be submitted not earlier than nine months and not later than seven months before the expiration of the motor carrier's then current inspection term. If the motor carrier has submitted the inspection application and the required accompanying fees, but the department is unable to complete the inspection within the 25–month inspection period, then no additional fee shall be required for the inspection requested in the original application.

(4) All fees collected pursuant to this subdivision, including delinquence fees, shall be deposited in the Motor Vehicle Account in the State Transportation Fund. An amount equal to the fees collected shall be available for appropriation by the Legislature from the Motor Vehicle Account to the department for the purpose of conducting truck terminal inspections and for the additional roadside safety inspections required by Section 34514.

(5) To avoid the scheduling of a renewal terminal inspection pursuant to this section during a carrier's seasonal peak business periods, the current inspection term of a terminal that has paid all required fees and has been rated satisfactory in its last inspection may be reduced by not more than nine months if a written request is submitted by the carrier to the department at least four months prior to the desired inspection month, or at the time of payment of renewal inspection fees in compliance with paragraph (3), whichever date is earlier. A motor carrier may request this adjustment of the inspection term during any inspection cycle. A request made pursuant to this paragraph shall not result in a fee proration and does not relieve the carrier from the requirements of paragraph (3).

(6) Failure to pay a fee required by this section, within the appropriate timeframe, shall result in additional delinquent fees as follows:

(A) For a delinquency period of more than 30 days and less than one year, the penalty is 60 percent of the required fee.

(B) For a delinquency period of one to two years, the penalty is 80 percent of the required fee.

(C) For a delinquency period of more than two years, the penalty is 160 percent of the required fee.

(7) Federal, state, and local public entities are exempt from the fee requirement of this section.

(f) It is unlawful for a motor carrier to operate a vehicle subject to this section without having submitted an inspection application and the required fees to the department as required by subdivision (e) or (h).

(g)(1) It is unlawful for a motor carrier to operate a vehicle subject to this section after submitting an inspection application to the department, without the inspection described in subdivision (d) having been performed and a safety compliance report having been issued to the motor carrier within the 25–month inspection period or within 60 days immediately preceding the inspection period.

(2) It is unlawful for a motor carrier to contract or subcontract with, or otherwise engage the services of, another motor carrier, subject to this section, unless the contracted motor carrier has complied with this section. A motor carrier shall not contract or subcontract with, or otherwise engage the services of, another motor carrier until the contracted motor carrier provides certification of compliance with this section. This certification shall be completed in writing by the contracted motor carrier. The certification, or a copy thereof, shall be maintained by each involved party for the duration of the contract or the period of service plus two years, and shall be presented for inspection immediately upon the request of an authorized employee of the department.

(h)(1) An inspected terminal that receives an unsatisfactory compliance rating shall be reinspected within 120 days after the issuance of the unsatisfactory compliance rating.

(2) A terminal's first required reinspection under this subdivision shall be without charge unless one or more of the following is established:

(A) The motor carrier's operation presented an imminent danger to public safety.

(B) The motor carrier was not in compliance with the requirement to enroll all drivers in the pull notice program pursuant to Section 1808.1.

(C) The motor carrier failed to provide all required records and vehicles for a consolidated inspection pursuant to subdivision (b).

(3) If the unsatisfactory rating was assigned for any of the reasons set forth in paragraph (2), the carrier shall submit the required fee as provided in paragraph (4).

(4) Applications for reinspection pursuant to paragraph (3) or for second and subsequent consecutive reinspections under this subdivision shall be accompanied by the fee specified in paragraph (2) of subdivision (e) and shall be filed within 60 days of issuance of the unsatisfactory compliance rating. The reinspection fee is nonrefundable.

(5) When a motor carrier's Motor Carrier of Property Permit or Public Utilities Commission operating authority is suspended as a result of an unsatisfactory compliance rating, the department shall not conduct a reinspection for permit or authority reinstatement until requested to do so by the Department of Motor Vehicles or the Public Utilities Commission, as appropriate.

(i) It is the intent of the Legislature that the department make its best efforts to inspect terminals within the resources provided. In the interest of the state, the Commissioner of the California Highway Patrol may extend for a period, not to exceed six months, the inspection terms beginning prior to July 1, 1990.

(j) Except as provided in paragraph (5), to encourage motor carriers to attain continuous satisfactory compliance ratings, the department may establish and implement an incentive program consisting of the following:

(1) After the second consecutive satisfactory compliance rating assigned to a motor carrier terminal as a result of an inspection conducted pursuant to subdivision (d), and after each consecutive satisfactory compliance rating thereafter, an appropriate certificate, denoting the number of consecutive satisfactory ratings, shall be awarded to the terminal, unless the terminal has received an unsatisfactory compliance rating as a result of an inspection conducted in the interim between the consecutive inspections conducted under subdivision (d), or the motor carrier is rated unsatisfactory by the department following a controlled substances and alcohol testing program inspection. The certificate authorized under this paragraph shall not be awarded for performance in the administrative review authorized under paragraph (2). However, the certificate shall include a reference to any administrative reviews conducted during the period of consecutive satisfactory compliance ratings.

(2) Unless the department's evaluation of the motor carrier's safety record indicates a declining level of compliance, a terminal that has attained two consecutive satisfactory compliance ratings assigned following inspections conducted pursuant to subdivision (d) is eligible for an administrative review in lieu of the next required inspection, unless the terminal has received an unsatisfactory compliance rating as a result of an inspection conducted in the interim between the consecutive inspections conducted under subdivision (d). An administrative review shall consist of all of the following:

(A) A signed request by a terminal management representative requesting the administrative review in lieu of the required inspection containing a promise to continue to maintain a satisfactory level of compliance for the next 25–month inspection term.

(B) A review with a terminal management representative of the carrier's record as contained in the department's files. If a terminal has been authorized a second consecutive administrative review, the review required under this subparagraph is optional, and may be omitted at the carrier's request.

(C) Absent any cogent reasons to the contrary, upon completion of the requirements of subparagraphs (A) and (B), the safety compliance rating assigned during the last required inspection shall be extended for 25 months.

(3) Not more than two administrative reviews may be conducted consecutively. At the completion of the 25–month inspection term following a second administrative review, a terminal inspection shall be conducted pursuant to subdivision (d). If this inspection results in a satisfactory compliance rating, the terminal shall again be eligible for an administrative review in lieu of the next required inspection. If the succession of satisfactory ratings is interrupted by a rating of other than satisfactory, irrespective of the reason for the inspection, the terminal shall again attain two consecutive satisfactory ratings to become eligible for an administrative review.

(4) As a condition for receiving the administrative reviews authorized under this subdivision in lieu of inspections, and in order to ensure that compliance levels remain satisfactory, the motor carrier shall agree to accept random, unannounced inspections by the department.

(5) Notwithstanding paragraphs (1) to (4), inclusive, a motor carrier of hazardous materials shall not be granted administrative review pursuant to this subdivision in lieu of a terminal inspection pursuant to subdivision (d) at any terminal from which hazardous materials carrying vehicles identified by paragraph (3) of subdivision (d) are operated.

(k) This section shall be known and may be cited as the Biennial Inspection of Terminals Program or BIT.

(*l*) The department shall, on or before January 1, 2016, adopt regulations establishing a performance-based truck terminal inspection priority selection system.

(m) This section shall remain in effect only until January 1, 2016, and as of that date is repealed, unless a later enacted statute, that is enacted before January 1, 2016, deletes or extends that date. *(Added by Stats.1988, c. 1586, § 6. Amended by Stats.1989, c. 1216, § 10, eff. Oct. 1, 1989; Stats.1991, c. 13 (A.B.37), § 58, eff. Feb. 13, 1991; Stats.1991, c. 928 (A.B.1886), § 33, eff. Oct. 14, 1991; Stats.1992, c. 1243 (A.B.3090), § 97, eff. Sept. 30, 1992; Stats.1994, c. 58 (A.B.1633), § 2, eff. April 26, 1994; Stats.1996, c. 1154 (A.B.3020), § 80, eff. Sept. 30, 1996; Stats.1997, c. 210 (A.B.1257), § 1; Stats.1998, c. 877 (A.B.2132), § 68; Stats.1999, c. 1008 (S.B.533), § 14; Stats.2002, c. 610 (S.B.1257), § 5; Stats.2003, c. 729 (A.B.1238), § 3; Stats.2004, c. 518 (A.B.2201), § 5; Stats.2005, c. 400 (A.B.1031), § 1; Stats.2007, c. 173 (S.B.79), § 10, eff. Aug. 24, 2007; Stats.2007, c. 514 (A.B.1612), § 2; Stats.2013, c. 500 (A.B.529), § 5.)*

Repeal

For repeal of this section, see its terms.

Cross References

Licenses, examination and display, exemptions, see Vehicle Code § 32000.5.
Motor carrier permits,
  Applications, fees and contents, see Vehicle Code § 34621.
  Necessity of registration and issuance of permits, prohibited use of carrier services without permit or certification, see Vehicle Code § 34620.

§ 34501.12. Basic Inspection of Terminals program (BIT)

Section operative Jan. 1, 2016. See, also, section operative until Jan. 1, 2016.

(a) Vehicles and the operation thereof, subject to this section, are those described in subdivision (a), (b), (e), (f), (g), (j), or (k) of Section 34500.

(b) It is unlawful for a motor carrier to operate any vehicle of a type described in subdivision (a) without identifying to the department all terminals, as defined in Section 34515, in this state where vehicles may be inspected by the department pursuant to paragraph (4) of subdivision (a) of Section 34501 and where vehicle inspection and maintenance records and driver records will be made available for inspection. Motor carriers shall make vehicles and records available for inspection upon request by an authorized representative of the department. If a motor carrier fails to provide vehicles and records, an unsatisfactory terminal rating shall be issued by the department.

(1) The number of vehicles that will be selected for inspection by the department at a terminal shall be based on terminal fleet size and applied separately to a terminal fleet of power units and trailers, according to the following schedule:

Fleet Size	Representative Sample
1 or 2	All
3 to 8	3
9 to 15	4
16 to 25	6
26 to 50	9
51 to 90	14
91 or more	20

(2) The lessor of any vehicle described in subdivision (a) shall make vehicles available for inspection upon request of an authorized representative of the department in the course of inspecting the terminal of the lessee. This section does not affect whether the lessor or driver provided by the lessor is an employee of the authorized carrier lessee, and compliance with this section and its attendant administrative requirements does not imply an employee-employer relationship.

(c)(1) The department may inspect any terminal, as defined in Section 34515, of a motor carrier who, at any time, operates any vehicle described in subdivision (a).

(2) The department shall adopt rules and regulations establishing a performance-based truck terminal inspection selection priority system. In adopting the system's rules and regulations, the department shall incorporate methodologies consistent with those used by the Federal Motor Carrier Safety Administration, including those related to the quantitative analysis of safety-related motor carrier performance data, collected during the course of

inspection or enforcement contact by authorized representatives of the department or any authorized federal, state, or local safety official, in categories, including, but not limited to, driver fatigue, driver fitness, vehicle maintenance, and controlled substances and alcohol use. The department shall also incorporate other safety-related motor carrier performance data in this system, including citations and accident information. The department shall create a database to include all performance-based data specified in this section that shall be updated in a manner to provide real-time information to the department on motor carrier performance. The department shall prioritize for selection those motor carrier terminals never previously inspected by the department, those identified by the inspection priority selection system, and those terminals operating vehicles listed in subdivision (g) of Section 34500. The department is not required to inspect a terminal subject to inspection pursuant to this section more often than once every six years, if a terminal receives a satisfactory compliance rating as the result of a terminal inspection conducted by the department pursuant to this section or Section 34501, or if the department has not received notification by the system of a motor carrier operating while exceeding the threshold of the inspection selection priority system. Any motor carrier that is inspected and receives less than a satisfactory compliance rating, or that falls below the threshold of the selection priority system, shall be subject to periodic inquiries and inspections as outlined in subdivision (f), and these inquiries and inspections shall be based on the severity of the violations.

(3) As used in this section and Section 34505.6, subdivision (f) of Section 34500 includes only those combinations where the gross vehicle weight rating of the towing vehicle exceeds 10,000 pounds, but does not include a pickup truck or any combination never operated in commercial use, and subdivision (g) of Section 34500 includes only those vehicles transporting hazardous material for which the display of placards is required pursuant to Section 27903, a license is required pursuant to Section 32000.5, or for which hazardous waste transporter registration is required pursuant to Section 25163 of the Health and Safety Code. Notwithstanding Section 5014.1, vehicles that display special identification plates in accordance with Section 5011, historical vehicles, as described in Section 5004, implements of husbandry and farm vehicles, as defined in Chapter 1 (commencing with Section 36000) of Division 16, and vehicles owned or operated by an agency of the federal government are not subject to this section or Section 34505.6.

(d) It is unlawful for a motor carrier to operate, or cause to be operated, any vehicle which is subject to this section, Section 34520, or Division 14.85 (commencing with Section 34600), unless the motor carrier is knowledgeable of, and in compliance with, all applicable statutes and regulations.

(e) It is unlawful for a motor carrier to contract or subcontract with, or otherwise engage the services of, another motor carrier, subject to this section, unless the contracted motor carrier has complied with subdivision (d). A motor carrier shall not contract or subcontract with, or otherwise engage the services of, another motor carrier until the contracted motor carrier provides certification of compliance with subdivision (d). This certification shall be completed in writing by the contracted motor carrier in a manner prescribed by the department. The certification, or a copy of the certification, shall be maintained by each involved party for the duration of the contract or the period of service plus two years, and shall be presented for inspection immediately upon the request of an authorized employee of the department. The certifications required by this subdivision and subdivision (b) of 34620 may be combined.

(f)(1) An inspected terminal that receives an unsatisfactory compliance rating shall be reinspected by the department within 120 days after the issuance of the unsatisfactory compliance rating.

(2) When a motor carrier's Motor Carrier of Property Permit or Public Utilities Commission operating authority is suspended as a result of an unsatisfactory compliance rating, the department shall not conduct a reinspection for permit or authority reinstatement until requested to do so by the Department of Motor Vehicles or the Public Utilities Commission, as appropriate.

(g) A motor carrier issued an unsatisfactory terminal rating may request a review of the rating within five business days of receipt of the notification of the rating. The department shall conduct and evaluate the review within 10 business days of the request.

(h) The department shall publish performance-based inspection completion data and make the data available for public review.

(i) This section shall be known, and may be cited, as the Basic Inspection of Terminals program or BIT program.

(j) This section shall become operative on January 1, 2016. *(Added by Stats.2013, c. 500 (A.B.529), § 6, operative Jan. 1, 2016.)*

Cross References

Licenses, examination and display, exemptions, see Vehicle Code § 32000.5.
Motor carrier permits,
  Applications, fees and contents, see Vehicle Code § 34621.
  Necessity of registration and issuance of permits, prohibited use of carrier services without permit or certification, see Vehicle Code § 34620.

§ 34501.13. Schoolbus maintenance facility or terminal; inspection; unsatisfactory rating; notification of school board

If the inspection of a carrier facility, maintenance facility, or terminal of any person who operates a schoolbus results in an unsatisfactory terminal rating by

the department, the department shall notify the school board of the district that is responsible for the terminal. *(Added by Stats.1989, c. 359, § 4. Amended by Stats.1999, c. 1007 (S.B.532), § 24.5.)*

§ 34501.14. Grape gondola inspections; applicability of section

(a) Notwithstanding Section 34501.12, for purposes of this division, safety inspections of grape gondolas are governed by this section.

(b) Every registered owner of a grape gondola shall submit an application and the fee specified in subdivision (g) to the department for the initial inspection required by this section. The initial application shall be submitted on or before July 1, 1993. The inspection term for a grape gondola shall expire 25 months from the date the department conducts the inspection, and issues a certificate indicating the gondola has passed the inspection, and every 25 months thereafter. Applications and fees for subsequent inspections and certificates shall be submitted not later than seven months before the expiration of the then current inspection term. If the registered owner has submitted the inspection application and the required accompanying fees, but the department is unable to complete the inspection within the 25-month inspection period, then no additional fee shall be required for the inspection requested in the original application.

(c) On and after July 1, 1993, no person may operate any grape gondola without having submitted an inspection application and the required fees to the department as required by this section.

(d) On and after January 1, 1995, no person may operate any grape gondola, without the inspection described in subdivision (e) having been performed and a certificate having been issued to the owner.

(e) The safety inspection undertaken pursuant to this section shall be limited to an inspection of the brake system, steering, lights, connections, wheels and tires, frame, and suspension.

(f) For purposes of undertaking the inspection of grape gondolas under this section, the department shall schedule all inspections at one central location during a continuous eight-week period every odd-numbered year with at least two days of each week during that eight-week period devoted to the actual inspection. If the gondola does not pass its first inspection, it may be reinspected during the eight-week period at no additional cost.

(g) Fees shall be established by the department in an amount equal to the actual costs incurred by the department in carrying out this section, but not to exceed twenty-five dollars ($25) for each inspection or reinspection.

(h) As used in this section, "grape gondola" means a motor vehicle which has been permanently altered and is attached to a grape tank by two means. The first mean is by use of a kingpin on the trunk which is centered through a turntable assembly on the tank. The second

917

means of attachment is through the use of a pair of horizontal crossarms between the drive axle and the rear tank axle. The tank is designed to pivot off of the chassis on two support arms during dumping, and is further designed to be specifically compatible with dumping facilities of the wineries.

(i) This section only applies to a grape gondola that is used under all of the following conditions:

(1) For 60 days or less during any calendar year.

(2) For not more than 500 miles in any calendar year.

(3) Only for the transportation of grapes. *(Added by Stats.1992, c. 724 (A.B.2326), § 1.)*

Cross References

Violations, misdemeanors, see Vehicle Code §§ 40000.22, 40000.26.

§ 34501.15. Commercial drivers; blood alcohol of .01 percent or more; 24-hour period out of service; operative date and duration of section

(a) The regulations adopted pursuant to Section 34501 shall require that any driver of a commercial motor vehicle, as defined in Section 15210, be ordered out of service for 24 hours if the driver is found to have 0.01 percent or more, by weight, of alcohol in his or her blood.

(b) This section shall become operative on January 1, 1992, and shall remain operative until the director determines that federal regulations adopted pursuant to the Commercial Motor Vehicle Safety Act of 1986 (49 U.S.C. Sec. 2701 et seq.) contained in that act and Section 391.15 of Title 49 of the Code of Federal Regulations do not require the state to order the operator of a commercial vehicle out of service for 24 hours when the operator has a measurable concentration of alcohol in his or her blood.

(c) The director shall submit a notice of the determination under subdivision (b) to the Secretary of State, and this section shall be repealed upon the receipt of that notice. *(Added by Stats.1989, c. 1114, § 40, operative Jan. 1, 1992.)*

Repeal

Section 34501.15 is repealed by its terms upon receipt of specified notice.

§ 34501.16. Commercial drivers; employer-provided information on blood alcohol percentage provisions; duration of section

(a) Every employer of a commercial driver shall provide information to that employee at the time of hiring and to all employed commercial drivers annually, concerning all of the following:

(1) The prohibition against driving a commercial motor vehicle with over 0.04 percent or more, by weight, alcohol in his or her blood on and after January 1, 1992.

(2) The requirement to be placed out of service for 24 hours if the person's blood-alcohol concentration is tested

to be 0.01 percent or more, by weight, on and after January 1, 1992.

(b) The Department of Motor Vehicles shall include the information prescribed in subdivision (a), together with information concerning the alcohol concentration in a person's blood resulting from consumption of alcoholic beverages, in each publication of the commercial driver's handbook published after January 1, 1990.

(c) This section shall remain operative until the director determines that federal regulations adopted pursuant to the Commercial Motor Vehicle Safety Act of 1986 (49 U.S.C. Sec. 2701 et seq.) do not require the state to implement the prohibitions and requirements in paragraphs (1) and (2) of subdivision (a).

(d) The director shall submit a notice of the determination under subdivision (c) to the Secretary of State, and this section shall be repealed upon the receipt of that notice. *(Added by Stats.1989, c. 1114, § 41.)*

Repeal

Section 34501.16 is repealed by its terms upon receipt of specified notice.

§ 34501.17. Paratransit vehicles; regular inspections and maintenance; minimum requirements; documentation

(a) All paratransit vehicles shall be regularly and systematically inspected, maintained, and lubricated by the owner or operator in accordance with the manufacturer's recommendations, or more often if necessary to ensure the safe operating condition of the vehicle. The maintenance shall include, at a minimum, in-depth inspection of the vehicle's brake system, steering components, lighting system, and wheels and tires, to be performed at intervals in accordance with the manufacturer's recommendations.

(b) All owners or operators of paratransit vehicles shall document each systematic inspection, maintenance, and lubrication and repair performed for each vehicle subject to this section. Required records shall include service performed, the name of the person performing the service, the date that the service was performed, and the odometer reading of the vehicle at the time of the service. The records shall be maintained for the period that the vehicle is in service at the place of business in this state of the owner or operator of the vehicle, and shall be presented upon demand to any authorized representative of the department. The odometer of a paratransit vehicle shall be maintained in proper working order. *(Added by Stats.1998, c. 241 (A.B.1634), § 3.)*

§ 34501.18. Report to department from motor carrier regularly employing more than 20 full-time drivers whenever it replaces more than half within 30–day period; department inspection; terms defined

(a) Every motor carrier regularly employing more than 20 full-time drivers shall report to the department whenever it replaces more than half of its drivers within a

30–day period. Within 21 days of receipt of that report, the department shall inspect the motor carrier to ensure that the motor carrier is complying with all safety of operations requirements, including, but not limited to, controlled substances testing and hours-of-service regulations. The reporting requirement of this subdivision does not apply to a motor carrier who, through normal seasonal fluctuations in the business operations of the carrier, or through termination of a contract for transportation services, other than a collective bargaining agreement, replaces drivers in one geographical location with drivers in another geographical location.

(b) For the purposes of subdivision (a), "employing" means having an employer-employee relationship with a driver or contracting with an owner-operator, as described in Section 34624, to provide transportation services for more than 30 days within the previous year.

(c) For the purposes of subdivision (a), "full-time" means that the driver is on-duty with the motor carrier for an average of 30 hours or more per week during the course of his or her employment or contract with the motor carrier. *(Added by Stats.2001, c. 789 (A.B.1262), § 1.)*

§ 34502. Safety standards

In adopting rules and regulations, the Department of the California Highway Patrol shall consider as evidence of generally accepted safety standards the rules and regulations which have been adopted by the Public Utilities Commission. *(Added by Stats.1963, c. 2148, p. 4484, § 8.)*

Cross References

Public Utilities Commission, see Public Utilities Code § 301 et seq.

§ 34503. Legislative intent: uniform regulation

It is the legislative intention in enacting this division that the rules and regulations adopted by the Department of the California Highway Patrol pursuant to this division shall apply uniformly throughout the State of California, and no state agency, city, city and county, county, or other political subdivision of this State, including, but not limited to, a chartered city, city and county, or county, shall adopt or enforce any ordinance or regulation which is inconsistent with the rules and regulations adopted by the department pursuant to this division. *(Added by Stats.1963, c. 2148, p. 4484, § 8.)*

§ 34504. Enforcement

The Department of the California Highway Patrol shall enforce the rules and regulations adopted pursuant to Section 34501. Rules and regulations adopted pursuant to Section 34501 shall become effective on March 1, 1965. *(Added by Stats.1963, c. 2148, p. 4485, § 8.)*

§ 34505. Inspection of tour buses; correction of defects; records of inspections

(a) Tour bus operators shall, in addition to the systematic inspection, maintenance, and lubrication services required of all motor carriers, require each tour bus to be inspected at least every 45 days, or more often if necessary to ensure safe operation. This inspection shall include, but not be limited to, all of the following:

(1) Brake adjustment.

(2) Brake system components and leaks.

(3) Steering and suspension systems.

(4) Tires and wheels.

(b) A tour bus shall not be used to transport passengers until all defects listed during the inspection conducted pursuant to subdivision (a) have been corrected and attested to by the signature of the operator's authorized representative.

(c) Records of inspections conducted pursuant to subdivision (a) shall be kept at the operator's maintenance facility or terminal where the tour bus is regularly garaged. The records shall be retained by the operator for one year, and shall be made available for inspection upon request by any authorized employee of the department. Each record shall include, but not be limited to, all of the following:

(1) Identification of the vehicle, including make, model, license number, or other means of positive identification.

(2) Date and nature of each inspection and any repair performed.

(3) Signature of operator's authorized representative attesting to the inspection and to the completion of all required repairs.

(4) Company vehicle number. *(Added by Stats.1986, c. 1306, § 16.)*

§ 34505.1. Suspension, denial or revocation of operating authority for tour buses; grounds; notice and hearing

(a) Upon determining that a tour bus operator has either (1) failed to maintain any vehicle used in transportation for compensation in a safe operating condition or to comply with the Vehicle Code or with regulations contained in Title 13 of the California Code of Regulations relative to motor carrier safety, and, in the department's opinion, that failure presents an imminent danger to public safety or constitutes such a consistent failure as to justify a recommendation to the Public Utilities Commission or the Interstate Commerce Commission or (2) failed to enroll all drivers in the pull notice system as required by Section 1808.1, the department shall recommend to the Public Utilities Commission that the carrier's operating authority be suspended, denied, or revoked, or to the federal Highway Administration Office of Motor Carriers, that appropriate administrative action be taken against the carrier's Interstate Commerce Commission operating authority, whichever is appropriate. For purposes of this subdivision, two consecutive unsatisfactory compliance ratings for an inspected terminal assigned because the tour bus operator failed to comply with the periodic report requirements of Section 1808.1 or the cancellation of the operator's enrollment by the Department of Motor Vehicles for nonpayment of required fees is a consistent failure. However, when recommending denial of an application for new or renewal authority, the department need not conclude that the carrier's failure presents an imminent danger to public safety or that it constitutes a consistent failure. The department need only conclude that the carrier's compliance with the safety-related matters described in paragraph (1) of subdivision (a) is sufficiently unsatisfactory to justify a recommendation for denial. The department shall retain a record, by operator, of every recommendation made pursuant to this section.

(b) Before transmitting a recommendation pursuant to subdivision (a), the department shall notify the carrier in writing of all of the following:

(1) That the department has determined that the carrier's safety record is unsatisfactory, furnishing a copy of any documentation or summary of any other evidence supporting the determination.

(2) That the determination may result in a suspension, revocation, or denial of the carrier's operating authority by the California Public Utilities Commission or the Interstate Commerce Commission.

(3) That the carrier may request a review of the determination by the department within five days of its receipt of the notice required under this subdivision. If a review is requested by the carrier, the department shall conduct and evaluate that review prior to transmitting any notification pursuant to subdivision (a). *(Added by Stats.1986, c. 1306, § 17. Amended by Stats.1989, c. 1216, § 11, eff. Oct. 1, 1989; Stats.1991, c. 928 (A.B.1886), § 34, eff. Oct. 14, 1991; Stats.1993, c. 272 (A.B.301), § 51, eff. Aug. 2, 1993.)*

§ 34505.5. Vehicle inspections; elements; operation of defective vehicles; records of inspections

Section operative until Jan. 1, 2016. See, also, section operative Jan. 1, 2016.

(a) Every motor carrier operating any vehicle described in subdivision (a), (b), (e), (f), or (g) of Section 34500, except those vehicles exempted under Section 34501.12, shall, as a part of the systematic inspection, maintenance, and lubrication services required of all motor carriers, require the vehicle or vehicles for which it is responsible pursuant to Section 34501.12 to be inspected at least every 90 days, or more often if necessary to ensure safe operation. Vehicles which are out of service for periods greater than 90 calendar days are not required to be inspected at 90-day intervals if they are inspected before operation on the highway. This inspection shall include, but not be limited to, all of the following:

(1) Brake adjustment.

(2) Brake system components and leaks.

(3) Steering and suspension systems.

(4) Tires and wheels.

(5) Vehicle connecting devices.

(b) No vehicle subject to this section shall be operated on the highway other than to a place of repair until all defects listed during the inspection conducted pursuant to subdivision (a) have been corrected and attested to by the signature of the motor carrier's authorized representative.

(c) Records of inspections conducted pursuant to subdivision (a) shall be kept at the motor carrier's terminals, as designated in accordance with Section 34501.12. The records shall be retained by the motor carrier for two years, and shall be made available for inspection upon request by any authorized employee of the department. Each record shall include, but not be limited to, all of the following:

(1) Identification of the vehicle, including make, model, license number, company vehicle number, or other means of positive identification.

(2) Date and nature of each inspection and any repair performed.

(3) Signature of the motor carrier's authorized representative attesting to the inspection and to the completion of all required repairs.

(d) Printouts of inspection and maintenance records maintained in computer systems shall be accepted in lieu of signed inspection or repair records if the printouts include the information required in paragraphs (1) and (2) of subdivision (c).

(e) Notwithstanding subdivisions (a) to (d), inclusive, records of 90-day inspections need not be retained in California for interstate vehicles which are not physically based in California. However, when these vehicles are present in California, they are subject to inspection by the department. If the inspection results indicate maintenance program deficiencies, the department may require the motor carrier to produce the maintenance records or copies of those records for inspection within 10 working days.

(f) This section shall remain in effect only until January 1, 2016, and as of that date is repealed, unless a later enacted statute, that is enacted before January 1, 2016, deletes or extends that date. *(Added by Stats.1988, c. 1586, § 7, operative July 1, 1989. Amended by Stats. 1989, c. 1216, § 11.5, eff. Oct. 1, 1989; Stats.1992, c. 1243 (A.B.3090), § 98, eff. Sept. 30, 1992; Stats.1994, c. 58 (A.B.1633), § 3, eff. April 26, 1994; Stats.2013, c. 500 (A.B.529), § 7.)*

Repeal

For repeal of this section, see its terms.

§ 34505.5. Vehicle inspections; elements; operation of defective vehicles; records of inspections

Section operative Jan. 1, 2016. See, also, section operative until Jan. 1, 2016.

(a) Every motor carrier operating any vehicle described in subdivision (a), (b), (e), (f), (g), (j), or (k) of Section 34500, except those vehicles exempted under Section 34501.12, shall, as a part of the systematic inspection, maintenance, and lubrication services required of all motor carriers, require the vehicle or vehicles for which it is responsible pursuant to Section 34501.12 to be inspected at least every 90 days, or more often if necessary to ensure safe operation. Vehicles which are out of service for periods greater than 90 calendar days are not required to be inspected at 90–day intervals if they are inspected before operation on the highway. This inspection shall include, but not be limited to, all of the following:

(1) Brake adjustment.

(2) Brake system components and leaks.

(3) Steering and suspension systems.

(4) Tires and wheels.

(5) Vehicle connecting devices.

(b) No vehicle subject to this section shall be operated on the highway other than to a place of repair until all defects listed during the inspection conducted pursuant to subdivision (a) have been corrected and attested to by the signature of the motor carrier's authorized representative.

(c) Records of inspections conducted pursuant to subdivision (a) shall be kept at the motor carrier's terminals, as designated in accordance with Section 34501.12. The records shall be retained by the motor carrier for two years, and shall be made available for inspection upon request by any authorized employee of the department. Each record shall include, but not be limited to, all of the following:

(1) Identification of the vehicle, including make, model, license number, company vehicle number, or other means of positive identification.

(2) Date and nature of each inspection and any repair performed.

(3) Signature of the motor carrier's authorized representative attesting to the inspection and to the completion of all required repairs.

(d) Printouts of inspection and maintenance records maintained in computer systems shall be accepted in lieu of signed inspection or repair records if the printouts include the information required in paragraphs (1) and (2) of subdivision (c).

(e) Notwithstanding subdivisions (a) to (d), inclusive, records of 90–day inspections need not be retained in California for interstate vehicles which are not physically based in California. However, when these vehicles are present in California, they are subject to inspection by the department. If the inspection results indicate maintenance program deficiencies, the department may require the motor carrier to produce the maintenance records or copies of those records for inspection within 10 working days.

(f) This section shall become operative on January 1, 2016. *(Added by Stats.2013, c. 500 (A.B.529), § 8, operative Jan. 1, 2016.)*

§ 34505.6. Vehicles described in § 34500; motor carriers of property; household goods carriers; suspension, denial, or revocation of permit or operating authority; grounds; notice and hearing

Section operative until Jan. 1, 2016. See, also, section operative Jan. 1, 2016.

(a) Upon determining that a motor carrier of property who is operating any vehicle described in subdivision (a), (b), (e), (f), (g), or (k) of Section 34500, or any motortruck of two or more axles that is more than 10,000 pounds gross vehicle weight rating, on a public highway, has done any of the following, the department shall recommend that the Department of Motor Vehicles suspend or revoke the carrier's motor carrier permit, or for interstate operators, the department shall recommend to the Federal Motor Carrier Safety Administration that appropriate administrative action be taken against the carrier:

(1) Failed to maintain any vehicle of a type described above in a safe operating condition or to comply with the Vehicle Code or with applicable regulations contained in Title 13 of the California Code of Regulations, and, in the department's opinion, that failure presents an imminent danger to public safety or constitutes a consistent failure so as to justify a suspension or revocation of the motor carrier's motor carrier permit.

(2) Failed to enroll all drivers in the pull-notice system as required by Section 1808.1.

(3) Failed to submit any application or pay any fee required by subdivision (e) or (h) of Section 34501.12 within the timeframes set forth in that section.

(b) Upon determining that a household goods carrier, or a household goods carrier transporting used office, store, or institution furniture and fixtures under its household goods carrier permit issued under Section 5137 of the Public Utilities Code, operating any vehicle described in subdivision (a), (b), (e), (f), (g), or (k) of Section 34500 on a public highway has done any of the following, the department shall recommend that the Public Utilities Commission deny, suspend, or revoke the carrier's operating authority, or for interstate operators, the department shall recommend to the Federal Motor Carrier Safety Administration that appropriate administrative action be taken against the carrier:

(1) Failed to maintain any vehicle used in transportation for compensation in a safe operating condition or to comply with the Vehicle Code or with applicable regulations contained in Title 13 of the California Code of

Regulations, and, in the department's opinion, that failure presents an imminent danger to public safety or constitutes a consistent failure so as to justify a suspension, revocation, or denial of the motor carrier's operating authority.

(2) Failed to enroll all drivers in the pull-notice system as required by Section 1808.1.

(3) Failed to submit any application or pay any fee required by subdivision (e) or (h) of Section 34501.12 within the timeframes set forth in that section.

(c) For purposes of this section, two consecutive unsatisfactory compliance ratings for an inspected terminal assigned because the motor carrier failed to comply with the periodic report requirements of Section 1808.1 or the cancellation of the carrier's enrollment by the Department of Motor Vehicles for the nonpayment of required fees is a consistent failure. The department shall retain a record, by operator, of every recommendation made pursuant to this section.

(d) Before transmitting a recommendation pursuant to subdivision (a), the department shall notify the carrier in writing of all of the following:

(1) That the department has determined that the carrier's safety record or compliance with Section 1808.1 or subdivision (e) or (h) of Section 34501.12 is unsatisfactory, furnishing a copy of any documentation or summary of any other evidence supporting the determination.

(2) That the determination may result in a suspension, revocation, or denial of the carrier's motor carrier permit by the Department of Motor Vehicles, suspension, revocation, of the motor carrier's operating authority by the California Public Utilities Commission, or administrative action by the Federal Motor Carrier Safety Administration.

(3) That the carrier may request a review of the determination by the department within five days of its receipt of the notice required under this subdivision. If a review pursuant to this paragraph is requested by the carrier, the department shall conduct and evaluate that review prior to transmitting any notification pursuant to subdivision (a) or (b).

(e) Upon receipt of a written recommendation from the department that a motor carrier permit or operating authority be suspended, revoked, or denied, the Department of Motor Vehicles or Public Utilities Commission, as appropriate, shall, pending a hearing in the matter pursuant to Section 34623 or appropriate Public Utilities Commission authority, suspend the motor carrier permit or operating authority. The written recommendation shall specifically indicate compliance with subdivision (d).

(f) This section shall remain in effect only until January 1, 2016, and as of that date is repealed, unless a later enacted statute, that is enacted before January 1, 2016, deletes or extends that date. *(Added by Stats.1988, c. 1586, § 8, operative Jan. 1, 1990. Amended by Stats. 1989, c. 1216, § 12, eff. Oct. 1, 1989; Stats.1991, c. 928 (A.B.1886), § 35, eff. Oct. 14, 1991; Stats.1993, c. 272*

922

(A.B.301), § 52, eff. Aug. 2, 1993; Stats.1994, c. 58 (A.B.1633), § 4, eff. April 26, 1994; Stats.1996, c. 1042 (A.B.1683), § 51, eff. Sept. 29, 1996; Stats.1997, c. 652 (A.B.1518), § 11; Stats.1999, c. 1005 (A.B.1658), § 97; Stats.1999, c. 1006 (A.B.957), § 2; Stats.2000, c. 860 (A.B.2908), § 9; Stats.2013, c. 500 (A.B.529), § 9.)

Repeal

For repeal of this section, see its terms.

§ 34505.6. Vehicles described in § 34500; motor carriers of property; household goods carriers; suspension, denial, or revocation of permit or operating authority; grounds; notice and hearing

Section operative Jan. 1, 2016. See, also, section operative until Jan. 1, 2016.

(a) Upon determining that a motor carrier of property who is operating any vehicle described in subdivision (a), (b), (e), (f), (g), (j), or (k) of Section 34500, or any motortruck of two or more axles that is more than 10,000 pounds gross vehicle weight rating, on a public highway, has done either of the following, the department shall recommend that the Department of Motor Vehicles suspend or revoke the carrier's motor carrier permit, or, for interstate operators, the department shall recommend to the Federal Motor Carrier Safety Administration that appropriate administrative action be taken against the carrier:

(1) Failed to maintain any vehicle of a type described above in a safe operating condition or to comply with the Vehicle Code or with applicable regulations contained in Title 13 of the California Code of Regulations, and, in the department's opinion, that failure presents an imminent danger to public safety or constitutes a consistent failure so as to justify a suspension or revocation of the motor carrier's motor carrier permit.

(2) Failed to enroll all drivers in the pull-notice system as required by Section 1808.1.

(b) Upon determining that a household goods carrier, or a household goods carrier transporting used office, store, or institution furniture and fixtures under its household goods carrier permit issued under Section 5137 of the Public Utilities Code, operating any vehicle described in subdivision (a), (b), (e), (f), (g), (j), or (k) of Section 34500 on a public highway, has done either of the following, the department shall recommend that the Public Utilities Commission deny, suspend, or revoke the carrier's operating authority, or, for interstate operators, the department shall recommend to the Federal Motor Carrier Safety Administration that appropriate administrative action be taken against the carrier:

(1) Failed to maintain any vehicle used in transportation for compensation in a safe operating condition or to comply with the Vehicle Code or with applicable regulations contained in Title 13 of the California Code of Regulations, and, in the department's opinion, that failure presents an imminent danger to public safety or

constitutes a consistent failure so as to justify a suspension, revocation, or denial of the motor carrier's operating authority.

(2) Failed to enroll all drivers in the pull-notice system as required by Section 1808.1.

(c) For purposes of this section, two consecutive unsatisfactory compliance ratings for an inspected terminal assigned because the motor carrier failed to comply with the periodic report requirements of Section 1808.1 or the cancellation of the carrier's enrollment by the Department of Motor Vehicles for the nonpayment of required fees is a consistent failure. The department shall retain a record, by operator, of every recommendation made pursuant to this section.

(d) Before transmitting a recommendation pursuant to subdivision (a), the department shall notify the carrier in writing of all of the following:

(1) That the department has determined that the carrier's safety record or compliance with Section 1808.1 is unsatisfactory, furnishing a copy of any documentation or summary of any other evidence supporting the determination.

(2) That the determination may result in a suspension, revocation, or denial of the carrier's motor carrier permit by the Department of Motor Vehicles, suspension, revocation, of the motor carrier's operating authority by the California Public Utilities Commission, or administrative action by the Federal Motor Carrier Safety Administration.

(3) That the carrier may request a review of the determination by the department within five days of its receipt of the notice required under this subdivision. If a review pursuant to this paragraph is requested by the carrier, the department shall conduct and evaluate that review prior to transmitting any notification pursuant to subdivision (a) or (b).

(e) Upon receipt of a written recommendation from the department that a motor carrier permit or operating authority be suspended, revoked, or denied, the Department of Motor Vehicles or Public Utilities Commission, as appropriate, shall, pending a hearing in the matter pursuant to Section 34623 or appropriate Public Utilities Commission authority, suspend the motor carrier permit or operating authority. The written recommendation shall specifically indicate compliance with subdivision (d).

(f) This section shall become operative on January 1, 2016. *(Added by Stats.2013, c. 500 (A.B.529), § 10, operative Jan. 1, 2016.)*

§ 34505.7. **Private carriers of passengers; written recommendation of suspension; grounds; records; notice; staffing at Mexican border**

(a) Upon determining that a private carrier of passengers, as defined in Section 4001 of the Public Utilities Code, has either (1) failed to maintain any vehicle of the carrier in a safe operating condition or to comply with the Vehicle Code or with regulations contained in Title 13 of the California Code of Regulations relative to motor carrier safety, and, in the department's opinion, the failure presents an imminent danger to public safety or constitutes such a consistent failure as to justify a recommendation to the Public Utilities Commission, or (2) failed to enroll all drivers in the pull notice system as required by Section 1808.1, the department shall make a written recommendation to the Public Utilities Commission that the carrier's registration be suspended. Two consecutive unsatisfactory terminal ratings assigned for failure to comply with the periodic report requirements in Section 1808.1, or cancellation of an employer's enrollment by the Department of Motor Vehicles for nonpayment of fees, constitutes a consistent failure. The department shall retain a record, by operator, of every recommendation made pursuant to this section.

(b) Before transmitting a recommendation pursuant to subdivision (a), the department shall give written notice to the carrier of all of the following:

(1) That the department has determined that the carrier's safety record is unsatisfactory, furnishing a copy of any documentation or summary of any other evidence supporting the determination.

(2) That the determination may result in a suspension or revocation of the carrier's registration by the California Public Utilities Commission.

(3) That the carrier may request a review of the determination by the department within five days of its receipt of the notice required by this subdivision. If a review pursuant to this paragraph is requested by the carrier, the department shall conduct and evaluate that review prior to transmitting any notification pursuant to subdivision (a).

(c) Commercial vehicle inspection facilities along the border of Mexico, including those in Calexico and Otay Mesa, shall be staffed at all times by a California Highway Patrol inspector whenever those facilities are open to the public. The California Highway Patrol shall also assign, as staffing permits, a commercial inspector to control truck traffic entering the United States at the Tecate border crossing. *(Added by Stats.1991, c. 1144 (S.B. 1227), § 6. Amended by Stats.1996, c. 1042 (A.B.1683), § 52, eff. Sept. 29, 1996.)*

§ 34505.9. **Intermodal roadability inspection program; conditions; program components; records; citation for violation; reinspection; carrier's and driver's rights and duties**

(a) An ocean marine terminal that receives and dispatches intermodal chassis may conduct the intermodal roadability inspection program, as described in this section, in lieu of the inspection required by Section 34505.5, if the terminal meets all of the following conditions:

(1) More than 1,000 chassis are based at the ocean marine terminal.

(2) The ocean marine terminal, following the two most recent consecutive inspections required by Section 34501.12, has received satisfactory compliance ratings, and the terminal has received no unsatisfactory compliance ratings as a result of any inspection conducted in the interim between the consecutive inspections conducted under Section 34501.12.

(3) Each intermodal chassis exiting the ocean marine terminal shall have a current decal and supporting documentation in accordance with Section 396.17 of Title 49 of the Code of Federal Regulations.

(4) The ocean marine terminal's intermodal roadability inspection program shall consist of all of the following:

(A) Each time an intermodal chassis is released from the ocean marine terminal, the chassis shall be inspected. The inspection shall include, but not be limited to, brake adjustment, brake system components and leaks, suspension systems, tires and wheels, vehicle connecting devices, and lights and electrical system, and shall include a visual inspection of the chassis to determine that it has not been tampered with.

(B) Each inspection shall be recorded on a daily roadability inspection report that shall include, but not be limited to, all of the following:

(i) Positive identification of the intermodal chassis, including company identification number and vehicle license plate number.

(ii) Date and nature of each inspection.

(iii) Signature, under penalty of perjury, of the ocean marine terminal operator or an authorized representative that the inspection has been performed.

(iv) The inspector shall affix a green tag to a chassis that has passed inspection and a red tag to a chassis that has failed inspection. The tag shall contain the name of the inspector and the date and time that the inspection was completed and shall be placed in a conspicuous location so that it may be viewed from the rear of the vehicle. The tag shall be provided by the marine terminal operator and shall meet specifications determined by the Department of the California Highway Patrol. The provisions of this subparagraph shall also be applicable to an intermodal chassis inspected by a marine terminal operator pursuant to Section 34505.5.

(C) Records of each inspection conducted pursuant to subparagraph (A) shall be retained for 90 days at the ocean marine terminal at which each chassis is based and shall be made available upon request by any authorized employee of the department.

(D) Defects noted on any intermodal chassis shall be repaired, and the repairs shall be recorded on the intermodal chassis maintenance file, before the intermodal chassis is released from the control of the ocean marine terminal. No vehicle subject to this section shall be released to a motor carrier or operated on the highway other than to a place of repair until all defects listed during the inspection conducted pursuant to subpara-

graph (A) have been corrected and attested to by the signature of the operator's authorized representative.

(E) Records of maintenance or repairs performed pursuant to the inspection in subparagraph (A) shall be maintained at the ocean marine terminal for two years and shall be made available upon request of the department. Repair records may be retained in a computer system if printouts of those records are provided to the department upon request.

(F) Individuals performing ocean marine terminal roadability inspections pursuant to this section shall be qualified, at a minimum, as set forth in Section 396.19 of Title 49 of the Code of Federal Regulations. Evidence of each inspector's qualification shall be retained by the ocean marine terminal operator for the period during which the inspector is performing intermodal roadability inspections.

(b) The records maintained pursuant to paragraphs (C) and (E) of subdivision (a) and Section 34505.5 shall be made available during normal business hours to any motor carrier or driver or the authorized representative thereof who has been engaged to transport an intermodal container on a chassis inspected pursuant to this section or Section 34505.5 from the ocean marine terminal.

(c) Any citation issued for the violation of any state or federal law related to the defective condition of an intermodal chassis subject to inspection pursuant to this section or Section 34505.5, that is not owned by that motor carrier or commercial driver, shall be issued to the entity responsible for the inspection and maintenance of the intermodal chassis, unless the officer determines that the defective condition of the intermodal chassis was caused by the failure of the driver to operate a commercial motor vehicle in a safe manner.

(d) Any provision contained in a contract between the registered owner or lessee of an intermodal chassis subject to inspection pursuant to this section, or any other entity responsible for the inspection and maintenance of the intermodal chassis, and any motor carrier or any contract between a motor carrier and another motor carrier engaged to transport an intermodal container on a chassis subject to inspection pursuant to this section that contains a hold harmless or indemnity clause concerning defects in the physical condition of that chassis shall be void as against public policy. This subdivision shall not apply to damage to the intermodal chassis caused by the negligent or willful failure of the motor carrier to operate a commercial motor vehicle in a safe manner.

(e) Following a terminal inspection in which the department determines that an operator of an ocean marine terminal has failed to comply with the requirements of this section, the department shall conduct a reinspection within 120 days as specified in subdivision (h) of Section 34501.12. If the terminal fails the reinspection, the department shall direct the operator to comply with the requirements of Section 34505.5 until eligibility to utilize the inspection program described in this section is reestablished pursuant to subdivision (a). If any inspection results in an unsatisfactory rating due to conditions presenting an imminent danger to the public safety or due to the operator's repeated failure to inspect and repair intermodal chassis pursuant to this section, the department shall immediately forward a recommendation to the Department of Motor Vehicles to suspend the operator's motor carrier property permit, and forward a recommendation to the Federal Motor Carrier Safety Administration for administrative or other action deemed necessary against the carrier's interstate operating authority, pursuant to Section 34505.6 or 34505.7.

(f) Any driver who believes that an intermodal chassis is in an unsafe operating condition may request that the chassis be reinspected by the entity responsible for the inspection and maintenance of the chassis pursuant to this section or Section 34505.5. The request for reinspection, any corrective action taken, or the reason why corrective action was not taken shall be recorded in the intermodal chassis maintenance file.

(g) No commercial driver shall be threatened, coerced, or otherwise retaliated against by any ocean marine terminal operator for contacting a law enforcement agency with regard to the physical condition of an intermodal chassis or for requesting that the intermodal chassis be reinspected or repaired.

(h) For the purposes of this section, the following definitions shall apply:

(1) "Intermodal chassis" means a trailer designed to carry intermodal freight containers.

(2) "Ocean marine terminal" means a terminal, as defined in Section 34515, located at a port facility that engages in the loading and unloading of the cargo of oceangoing vessels.

(i) Nothing in this section shall relieve a commercial driver or commercial motor carrier of any duty imposed by state or federal law related to the safe operation of a commercial motor vehicle.

(j) Nothing in this section shall affect the rights, duties, and obligations set forth in Section 2802 of the Labor Code. *(Added by Stats.1998, c. 340 (A.B.346), § 1, eff. Aug. 24, 1998. Amended by Stats.2000, c. 135 (A.B.2539), § 163; Stats.2002, c. 897 (S.B.1507), § 1.)*

Cross References

Intermodal marine equipment provider or terminal operator, regulation, see Business and Professions Code § 22928.

§ 34505.10. Dispatch and pay records; motor carriers contracting or subcontracting transportation for other carriers

Motor carriers who contract or subcontract transportation service for other motor carriers shall retain all required records relating to the dispatch of vehicles and drivers and the pay of drivers that are not required to be retained by the carrier for whom the contracted or subcontracted service is performed. *(Added by Stats. 1997, c. 652 (A.B.1518), § 12.)*

§ 34506. Violations: misdemeanors

It is a misdemeanor to fail to comply with any rule or regulation adopted by the Department of the California Highway Patrol pursuant to Section 34501, 34501.5, 34508, or 34513 regarding any of the following:

(a) Hours of service of drivers.

(b) Hazardous material transportation.

(c) Schoolbus construction, design, color, equipment, maintenance, or operation.

(d) Youth bus equipment, maintenance, or operation.

(e) Tour bus equipment, maintenance, or operation.

(f) Equipment, maintenance, or operation of any vehicle described in subdivision (a), (b), (c), (d), (e), (f), or (g) of Section 34500.

(g) Equipment, maintenance, or operation of any school pupil activity bus. *(Added by Stats.1963, c. 2148, p. 4485, § 8. Amended by Stats.1968, c. 1192, p. 2259, § 9.4; Stats.1969, c. 9, p. 65, § 8, eff. March 6, 1969; Stats.1971, c. 1178, p. 2245, § 1, operative May 3, 1972; Stats.1977, c. 406, p. 1418, § 12, eff. Aug. 27, 1977; Stats.1981, c. 774, p. 3026, § 10; Stats.1982, c. 383, p. 1713, § 8, eff. July 4, 1982; Stats.1986, c. 1306, § 18; Stats.1988, c. 1586, § 9, operative July 1, 1989; Stats.1990, c. 429 (A.B.3904), § 7; Stats.1991, c. 928 (A.B.1886), § 36, eff. Oct. 14, 1991.)*

Cross References

Certain violations as misdemeanors, see Vehicle Code § 40000.21.
Drivers' hours of service, punishment for violation of regulations, see Vehicle Code § 42001.3.

§ 34506.3. Violations: infractions

Except as otherwise provided in this division, it is an infraction to fail to comply with any rule or regulation adopted by the department pursuant to this division. *(Added by Stats.1977, c. 406, p. 1418, § 12.5, eff. Aug. 27, 1977. Amended by Stats.1991, c. 298 (A.B.964), § 2.)*

Cross References

Maintenance of driving logs, punishment, see Vehicle Code § 42001.3.

§ 34506.4. Unsafe vehicles; removal from highway; towing and storage fees

(a) Any member of the Department of the California Highway Patrol may remove from the highway and have placed in a storage facility, any vehicle described in subdivision (a) of Section 22406, subdivision (g) of Section 34500, and any motortruck with a gross vehicle weight rating of more than 10,000 pounds, which is in an unsafe condition.

(b) Any member of the Department of the California Highway Patrol may impound any farm labor vehicle operated in violation of subdivision (b) of Section 2800, subdivision (a) of Section 24002.5, or subdivision (a) of Section 31402, subject to the following requirements:

(1) A farm labor vehicle impounded for a first violation of subdivision (b) of Section 2800, subdivision (a) of Section 24002.5, or subdivision (a) of Section 31402 may be released within 24 hours upon delivery to the impounding authority of satisfactory proof that the vehicle will be legally moved or transported to a place of repair.

(2) A farm labor vehicle shall be impounded for not less than 10 days for a second violation of subdivision (b) of Section 2800, subdivision (a) of Section 24002.5, or subdivision (a) of Section 31402, or any combination of two of those provisions, if the original equipment or maintenance violation has not been repaired to comply with existing law. The farm labor vehicle shall be released after 10 days upon delivery to the impounding authority of satisfactory proof that the vehicle has been repaired to comply with existing law, or upon delivery to the impounding agency of satisfactory proof that the vehicle will be lawfully moved or transported to a place of repair.

(3) A farm labor vehicle shall be impounded for not less than 30 days for a third or subsequent violation of subdivision (b) of Section 2800, subdivision (a) of Section 24002.5, or subdivision (a) of Section 31402, or any combination of three or more of those provisions, if the original equipment or maintenance violation has not been repaired to comply with existing law. The farm labor vehicle shall be released after 30 days upon delivery to the impounding authority of satisfactory proof that the vehicle has been repaired to comply with existing law, or upon delivery to the impounding agency of satisfactory proof that the vehicle will be lawfully moved or transported to a place of repair.

(c) All towing and storage fees for a vehicle removed under this section shall be paid by the owner. *(Added by Stats.1988, c. 1452, § 4. Amended by Stats.1991, c. 13 (A.B.37), § 59, eff. Feb. 13, 1991; Stats.2000, c. 873 (A.B.2086), § 4.)*

Cross References
Farm labor vehicles, operation when presents immediate safety hazard, violations and penalties, see Vehicle Code § 24002.5.

§ 34506.5. Farm labor vehicles subject to forfeiture as nuisance; driven on highways; impounding

(a) A farm labor vehicle is subject to forfeiture as a nuisance if it is driven on a highway in violation of subdivision (b) of Section 2800, subdivision (a) of Section 24002.5, or subdivision (a) of Section 31402 and has been impounded for a second or subsequent time pursuant to paragraph (3) of subdivision (b) of Section 34506.4.

(b)(1) A registered or legal owner of record at the time of impoundment may request a hearing to determine the validity of the impoundment pursuant to paragraph (1) or (2) of subdivision (n) of Section 14607.6.

(2) If it is determined that the necessary repairs had been completed and the farm labor vehicle complied with existing laws at the time of impoundment, the agency

926

employing the person who directed the impoundment shall be responsible for the costs incurred for towing and storage.

(c) Procedures established in subdivisions (e), (f), (g), (h), (i), (j), (k), (*l*), (*o*), (p), (q), (r), (t), (u), and (v) of Section 14607.6 shall be utilized for the forfeiture of an impounded farm labor vehicle. *(Added by Stats.2000, c. 873 (A.B.2086), § 5.)*

§ 34507. Display of identifying symbol

To assist the department in enforcing this division, a vehicle that is subject to this division and to the jurisdiction, control, and regulation of the Department of Motor Vehicles, the Public Utilities Commission, or the United States Secretary of the Department of Transportation shall have displayed prominently a distinctive identifying symbol as required by Section 34507.5. *(Added by Stats.1975, c. 396, p. 874, § 1. Amended by Stats.1978, c. 66, p. 184, § 1, eff. March 29, 1978; Stats.1984, c. 1715, § 7; Stats.2006, c. 288 (A.B.3011), § 16.)*

Cross References
Public Utilities Commission, see Public Utilities Code § 301 et seq.

§ 34507.5. Carrier identification numbers; application; display; application of section; exceptions; companies no longer in operating; disposal of vehicles and numbers

(a) A motor carrier, as defined in Section 408, a motor carrier of property, and a for-hire motor carrier of property, as defined in Section 34601, shall obtain a carrier identification number from the department. Application for a carrier identification number shall be on a form furnished by the department. Information provided in connection with an application for a carrier identification number shall be updated by a motor carrier upon request from the department.

(b) The carrier identification number assigned to the motor carrier under whose operating authority or motor carrier permit the vehicle or combination of vehicles is being operated shall be displayed on both sides of each vehicle, or on both sides of at least one motor vehicle in each combination of the following vehicles:

(1) Each vehicle set forth in Section 34500.

(2) A motortruck of two or more axles that is more than 10,000 pounds gross vehicle weight rating.

(3) Any other motortruck or motor vehicle used to transport property for compensation.

(c) A vehicle or combination of vehicles listed in subdivision (b) that is operated under a rental agreement with a term of not more than 30 calendar days shall meet all of the following requirements:

(1) Have displayed on both sides of each vehicle or on both sides of one of the vehicles in each combination of vehicles the name or trademark of the lessor.

(2) Have displayed on both sides of each vehicle or on both sides of one of the vehicles in each combination of vehicles any of the following numbers issued to the lessor:

(A) The carrier identification number issued by the United States Department of Transportation.

(B) A valid operating authority number.

(C) A valid motor carrier of property number.

(3)(A) Have in the vehicle or combination of vehicles a copy of the rental agreement entered into by the lessor and the vehicle operator.

(B) The rental agreement shall be available for inspection immediately upon the request of an authorized employee of the department, a regularly employed and salaried police officer or deputy sheriff, or a reserve police officer or reserve deputy sheriff listed pursuant to Section 830.6 of the Penal Code.

(C) If the rented vehicle or combination of vehicles is operated in conjunction with a commercial enterprise, the rental agreement shall include the operator's carrier identification number or motor carrier of property permit number.

(d) A vehicle or combination of vehicles that is in compliance with Section 390.21 of Title 49 of the Code of Federal Regulations shall be deemed to be in compliance with subdivision (c).

(e) This section does not apply to any of the following vehicles:

(1) A vehicle described in subdivision (f) of Section 34500, that is operated by a private carrier as defined in subdivision (d) of Section 34601, if the gross vehicle weight rating of the towing vehicle is 10,000 pounds or less, or the towing vehicle is a pickup truck, as defined in Section 471. This exception does not apply to a vehicle combination described in subdivision (k) of Section 34500.

(2) A vehicle described in subdivision (g) of Section 34500, that is operated by a private carrier as defined in subdivision (d) of Section 34601, if the hazardous material transportation does not require the display of placards pursuant to Section 27903, a license pursuant to Section 32000.5, or hazardous waste hauler registration pursuant to Section 25163 of the Health and Safety Code.

(3) A historical vehicle, as described in Section 5004, and * * * a vehicle that displays special identification plates in accordance with Section 5011.

(4) An implement of husbandry as defined in Chapter 1 (commencing with Section 36000) of Division 16.

(5) A vehicle owned or operated by an agency of the federal government.

(6) A pickup truck, as defined in Section 471, and a two- axle daily rental truck with a gross vehicle weight rating of less than 26,001 pounds, when operated in noncommercial use.

(f) Subdivision (b) does not apply to the following:

(1) A vehicle that displays a valid identification number assigned by the United States Secretary of the Department of Transportation.

(2) A vehicle that is regulated by, and that displays a valid operating authority number issued by, the Public Utilities Commission, including a household goods carrier as defined in Section 5109 of the Public Utilities Code.

(3) A for-hire motor carrier of passengers.

(g) The display of the carrier identification number shall be in sharp contrast to the background, and shall be of a size, shape, and color that it is readily legible during daylight hours from a distance of 50 feet.

(h) The carrier identification number for a company no longer in business, no longer operating with the same name, or no longer operating under the same operating authority, identification number, or motor carrier permit shall be removed before sale, transfer, or other disposal of a vehicle marked pursuant to this section. *(Added by Stats.1988, c. 229, § 1; Stats.1988, c. 907, § 4. Amended by Stats.1989, c. 1216, § 13, eff. Oct. 1, 1989; Stats.1991, c. 13 (A.B.37), § 60, eff. Feb. 13, 1991; Stats.1992, c. 1243 (A.B.3090), § 99, eff. Sept. 30, 1992; Stats.1997, c. 652 (A.B.1518), § 13; Stats.1998, c. 380 (S.B.1491), § 3; Stats.2003, c. 292 (A.B.1436), § 10; Stats.2006, c. 288 (A.B.3011), § 17.)*

Cross References

Criminal procedure, deputized or appointed peace officers, see Penal Code § 830.6.

Itemized invoice for towing and storage charges, inclusion of carrier identification number, see Vehicle Code § 22651.07.

§ 34507.6. Exempt operators of charter-party carriers; carrier identification numbers; application; display

(a) Every operator of transportation service which is exempt from regulation as a charter-party carrier of passengers pursuant to subdivision (k) or (*l*) of Section 5353 of the Public Utilities Code, and which furnishes that transportation service in a bus, shall obtain a carrier identification number from the Department of the California Highway Patrol. Application for a carrier identification number shall be on a form furnished by the Department of the California Highway Patrol.

(b)(1) The carrier identification number so obtained by the operator shall be displayed on both sides of each bus used in that transportation service.

(2) The display of the carrier identification number shall be in sharp contrast to the background, and shall be of a size, shape, and color as to be readily legible during daylight hours from a distance of at least 50 feet.

(3) The carrier identification number shall be removed before the sale, transfer, or other disposal of the bus. *(Added by Stats.1988, c. 1039, § 2.)*

§ 34508. Additional regulations: school buses

The Department of the California Highway Patrol shall adopt and enforce rules and regulations relating to the equipment, maintenance, construction, design, color, and operation of schoolbuses. *(Added by Stats.1977, c. 406, p. 1418, § 13, eff. Aug. 27, 1977. Amended by Stats.1981, c. 774, p. 3026, § 11.)*

Cross References

Schoolbus defined, see Vehicle Code § 545.

§ 34508.5. Repealed by Stats.2004, c. 193 (S.B.111), § 199

Law Revision Commission Comments

2004 Repeal

Section 34508.5 is repealed as obsolete. The required report was to be completed by July 1, 1993. [33 Cal.L.Rev.Comm. Reports 497 (2004)].

§ 34509. Vanpool vehicles

Vanpool vehicles, as defined in Section 668, and vanpool vehicles when used for purposes other than traveling to and from a work location and transporting not more than 10 persons including the driver, shall be exempt from the regulations adopted pursuant to Section 34501, except that the following shall apply:

(a) The vanpool vehicle shall be equipped with an operable fire extinguisher which is of the dry chemical or carbon dioxide type with an aggregate rating of at least 4-B:C and which is securely mounted and readily accessible.

(b) The vanpool vehicle shall be equipped with a first aid kit, conforming to the minimum requirements for schoolbuses. First aid kits shall be readily visible, accessible, and plainly marked "First Aid Kit."

(c) The vanpool vehicle shall be regularly and systematically inspected, maintained, and lubricated in accordance with the manufacturer's recommendations, or more often if necessary to ensure the safe operating condition of the vehicle. The maintenance shall include, as a minimum, an in-depth inspection of the vehicle's brake system, steering components, lighting system, and wheels and tires, to be performed at intervals of not more than every six months or 6,000 miles, whichever occurs first.

(d) Operators of vanpool vehicles shall document each systematic inspection, maintenance, and lubrication and repair performed for each vehicle under their control. Required records shall include services performed, the person performing the service, the date, and the mileage on the vehicle at the time of the repair. The records shall be maintained with the vehicle for one year, and shall be presented upon demand to any authorized representative of the California Highway Patrol.

(e) Vanpool vehicles being operated pursuant to the exemptions specified in this section shall display, upon the rear and sides of the vehicle, a sign or placard, clearly visible and discernable for a distance of not less than 50 feet, indicating that the vehicle is being used as a vanpool vehicle. *(Added by Stats.1982, c. 46, p. 142, § 11.)*

928

§ 34510. Vehicles transporting hazardous material; shipping papers; display

Persons operating vehicles, or combinations of vehicles, in the transportation of hazardous material and subject to this division, shall carry in the vehicle while en route any shipping papers required to accompany the vehicle in accordance with regulations adopted pursuant to Section 2402. The bill of lading or other shipping paper shall be displayed upon demand of any member of the California Highway Patrol or any police officer of a city who is on duty for the exclusive or main purpose of enforcing the provisions of this code.

(Added by Stats.1981, c. 912, p. 3454, § 8, eff. Sept. 28, 1981. Amended by Stats.1993, c. 757 (S.B.619), § 3; Stats.1998, c. 877 (A.B.2132), § 69; Stats.2001, c. 504 (A.B.1280), § 8.)

§ 34510.5. Brokers of construction trucking services furnishing or hiring transportation services; surety bond required; evidence of bond; violations, penalties; rebuttable presumption in civil actions; exceptions; definition

(a)(1) A broker of construction trucking services, as defined in Section 3322 of the Civil Code, shall not furnish construction transportation services to any construction project unless it has secured a surety bond of not less than fifteen thousand dollars ($15,000) executed by an admitted surety insurer. The surety bond shall ensure the payment of the claims of a contracted motor carrier of property in dump truck equipment if the broker fails to pay the contracted motor carrier within the time period specified in paragraph (1) of subdivision (a) of Section 3322 of the Civil Code.

(2)(A) A broker of construction trucking services annually shall provide written evidence of the broker's valid surety bond to a third-party nonprofit organization that is related to the industry and regularly maintains a published database of bonded brokers or post a current copy of the surety bond on the broker's Internet Web site.

(B) When a copy of a surety bond is provided to a third-party nonprofit organization, the broker shall notify the third-party nonprofit organization if at any time the surety bond is cancelled or expired. When a copy of the surety bond is posted on the broker's Internet Web site, the broker shall remove the copy of the surety bond from his or her Internet Web site if at any time the surety bond is cancelled or expired.

(C) A third-party nonprofit organization shall not charge a broker for posting evidence of a valid surety bond or limit the posting of the bond only to the organization's members.

(D) A third-party nonprofit organization shall not be liable for any damages caused by the publication of any information provided pursuant to this paragraph that is erroneous or outdated.

(b) A broker of construction trucking services shall not hire, or otherwise engage the services of, a motor carrier of property to furnish construction transportation services unless the broker provides, prior to the commencement of work each calendar year, written evidence of the broker's valid surety bond to any person that hires, or otherwise engages the services of, the broker to furnish construction transportation services and also to the hired motor carrier of property.

(c) A broker of construction trucking services who furnishes construction transportation services in violation of this section is guilty of a misdemeanor and subject to a fine of up to five thousand dollars ($5,000).

(d) In any civil action brought against a broker of construction trucking services by a motor carrier of property in dump truck equipment with whom the broker contracted during any period of time in which the broker did not have a surety bond in violation of this section, the failure to have the bond shall create a rebuttable presumption that the broker failed to pay to the motor carrier the amount due and owing.

(e) For purposes of this section, "a broker of construction trucking services" does not include a facility that meets all the following requirements:

(1) Arranges for transportation services of its product.

(2) Primarily handles raw materials to produce a new product.

(3) Is a rock product operation (such as an "aggregate" operation), a hot mixing asphalt plant, or a concrete, concrete product, or Portland cement product manufacturing facility.

(4) Does not accept a fee for the arrangement.

(f) For the purposes of this section, "written evidence of the broker's valid surety bond" includes a copy of the surety bond, a certificate of insurance, a continuation certificate, or other similar documentation originally issued from the surety that includes the surety's and broker's name, the bond number, and the effective and expiration dates of the bond. *(Added by Stats.2010, c. 429 (A.B.145), § 1. Amended by Stats.2012, c. 490 (S.B.1092), § 1; Stats.2013, c. 76 (A.B.383), § 197.)*

§ 34511. Violations; injunction

Any violation of any provision of this division or regulation adopted pursuant thereto may be enjoined in a civil action brought by the Attorney General in the name of the people of the State of California, upon request of the department, except that it shall not be necessary to show lack of adequate remedy at law or to show irreparable damage or loss.

The department may not submit a request for civil action and the Attorney General may not bring action pursuant to this section unless the person charged with a violation of this division or regulation adopted pursuant thereto fails to take corrective action after being notified of the violation by the department, in writing, on at least two occasions over a 60-day period. Prior to the submission of the department's request for civil action, the person charged shall receive, at his or her request, a departmental hearing on the matter and the department's request for civil action shall be forwarded by the department to, and approved by, the Commissioner of the California Highway Patrol. *(Added by Stats.1982, c. 789, p. 3057, § 3.)*

§ 34513. Rules and regulations relating to tour buses

The department shall adopt rules and regulations relating to the equipment and maintenance of tour buses. *(Added by Stats.1986, c. 1306, § 19.)*

§ 34514. Roadside safety inspections; funds

(a) Beginning with the 1990–91 fiscal year, the department shall, upon appropriation of the requisite funds by the Legislature, annually conduct additional roadside vehicle safety inspections of vehicles described in Section 34501.12. These roadside inspections shall be in addition to the maintenance facility and terminal inspections required by that section, and over and above the number of roadside vehicle safety inspections conducted during the 1987–88 fiscal year.

(b) It is the intent of the Legislature that, beginning with the 1990–91 fiscal year, funds are to be appropriated to the department annually, for the purposes of subdivision (a), from the Motor Vehicle Account in the State Transportation Fund, to the extent that sufficient funds are collected pursuant to Section 34501.12. *(Added by Stats.1988, c. 1596, § 1. Amended by Stats.1992, c. 1243 (A.B.3090), § 100, eff. Sept. 30, 1992.)*

§ 34515. Maintenance facility or terminal

Section operative until Jan. 1, 2016. See, also, section operative Jan. 1, 2016.

(a) As used in this division and in regulations adopted pursuant to this division, "maintenance facility or terminal" means any place or places where a vehicle of a type listed in Section 34500 is regularly garaged or maintained, or from which it is operated or dispatched. "Maintenance facility or terminal" may include a private business or residence.

(b) For the purpose of the inspections required by Section 34501.12, "terminal" means the location or locations in this state that are designated by a motor carrier, where subject vehicles may be inspected by the department pursuant to paragraph (4) of subdivision (a) of Section 34501, and where vehicle maintenance and inspection records and drivers' records will be made available for inspection.

(c) This section shall remain in effect only until January 1, 2016, and as of that date is repealed, unless a later enacted statute, that is enacted before January 1, 2016, deletes or extends that date. *(Added by Stats.1988, c. 1596, § 2. Amended by Stats.1989, c. 1216, § 14, eff. Oct. 1, 1989; Stats.1992, c. 1243 (A.B.3090), § 101, eff. Sept. 30, 1992; Stats.2011, c. 296 (A.B.1023), § 309; Stats.2013, c. 500 (A.B.529), § 11.)*

§ 34515. Maintenance facility or terminal

Section operative Jan. 1, 2016. See, also, section operative until Jan. 1, 2016.

(a) As used in this division and in regulations adopted pursuant to this division, "maintenance facility or terminal" means any place or places where a vehicle of a type listed in Section 34500 is regularly garaged or maintained, or from which it is operated or dispatched. "Maintenance facility or terminal" includes a private business or residence.

(b) For the purpose of the inspections conducted pursuant to Section 34501.12, "terminal" means the location or locations in this state that are designated by a motor carrier, where subject vehicles may be inspected by the department and where vehicle maintenance and inspection records and drivers' records will be made available for inspection.

(c) This section shall become operative on January 1, 2016. *(Added by Stats.2013, c. 500 (A.B.529), § 12, operative Jan. 1, 2016.)*

§ 34516. Prohibition of use of motor vehicle for transportation of food products for human consumption if used to transport solid waste or hazardous substances; violations; misdemeanor; avoidance of liability

(a) No person shall use or arrange for the use of a refrigerated motor vehicle, tank truck, dry van, or other motor vehicle, to provide transportation of food products for human consumption if the vehicle has been used to transport solid waste destined for landfills, or if precluded from use in accordance with subdivision (c).

(b) A violation of this section is a misdemeanor.

(c) If, pursuant to a federal statute having the same purposes as the act which added this section to the Public Utilities Code during the 1990 portion of the 1989–90 Regular Session, the United States Secretary of Transportation publishes a list of categories of solid waste or hazardous substances which he or she determines make food unsafe as a result of having been transported in a refrigerated motor vehicle, tank truck, dry van, or other motor vehicle also used to transport food products for human consumption, subdivisions (a) and (b) apply to those substances.

(d) A person or corporation charged with a violation of this section may avoid liability upon a showing by clear and convincing evidence that the transportation alleged to violate this section did not in fact endanger the public health, due to the specific protective or remedial actions taken by the person or corporation charged. *(Added by Stats.1990, c. 1685 (A.B.2568), § 12.)*

930

§ 34517. Commercial motor vehicles from another country; operation outside designated Commercial Zone restricted; violation; penalty; enforcement

(a) With respect to a commercial motor vehicle from another country, a person shall not operate the vehicle outside the boundaries of a designated commercial zone unless the required operating authority from the United States Secretary of the Department of Transportation has first been obtained.

(b) A violation of subdivision (a) is an infraction punishable by a fine of one thousand dollars ($1,000).

(c) Notwithstanding subdivision (b), a peace officer, as defined in Chapter 4.5 (commencing with Section 830) of Title 3 of Part 2 of the Penal Code, shall issue a citation for a violation of subdivision (a) to the driver of the vehicle and order the driver of the vehicle to return the vehicle to its country of origin. The peace officer may impound a vehicle cited pursuant to this section and its cargo until the citation and all charges related to the impoundment are cleared. The impoundment charges are the responsibility of the vehicle's owner.

(d) As used in this section, "designated commercial zone" means a commercial zone, as defined in Part 372 (commencing with Section 372.101) of Title 49 of the Code of Federal Regulations. *(Added by Stats.1991, c. 707 (A.B.1355), § 2. Amended by Stats.2006, c. 288 (A.B.3011), § 18.)*

Cross References

Peace officer authorized to impound vehicle and its cargo pursuant to this section, see Vehicle Code § 22651.4.

§ 34518. Operation without or in violation of certificate of registration

(a) A foreign motor carrier or foreign private motor carrier required to have a certificate of registration issued by the United States Secretary of the Department of Transportation pursuant to Part 368 (commencing with Section 368.1), or required to be registered pursuant to Part 365 (commencing with Section 365.101), of Title 49 of the Code of Federal Regulations shall not do any of the following:

(1) Operate in this state without the required certificate in the vehicle.

(2) Operate beyond the limitations or restrictions specified in the certificate as issued.

(3) Refuse to show the certificate upon request of a peace officer.

(4) Provide point-to-point transportation services, including express delivery services, within the United States for goods other than international cargo.

(b) A motor carrier required to be registered with the United States Secretary of the Department of Transportation pursuant to Section 13902 of Title 49 of the United States Code, Part 365 (commencing with Section 365.101), Part 390 (commencing with Section 390.1), or

Section 392.9a of Title 49 of the Code of Federal Regulations shall not do any of the following:

(1) Operate in this state without the required registration.

(2) Operate beyond the limitations or restrictions specified in its registration.

(3) Operate in this state without the required operating authority.

(c) A violation of subdivision (a) or (b) is an infraction punishable by a fine of one thousand dollars ($1,000).

(d) A member of the Department of the California Highway Patrol may impound a vehicle operated in violation of subdivision (a) or (b) and its cargo, until the citation and all charges related to the impoundment are cleared. The impoundment charges are the responsibility of the vehicle's owner.

(e)(1) A motor carrier granted permanent operating authority pursuant to subdivision (a) shall not operate a vehicle on a highway, unless the vehicle is inspected by a Commercial Vehicle Safety Alliance-certified inspector every three months and displays a current safety inspection decal attesting to the successful completion of those inspections for at least three years after receiving permanent operating authority.

(2) Paragraph (1) does not apply to a motor carrier granted authority to operate solely in a commercial zone on the United States–Mexico International Border.

(f) As used in this section "limitations" or "restrictions" include definitions of "commercial zones," "municipality," "contiguous municipalities," "unincorporated area," and "terminal areas," in Part 372 (commencing with Section 372.101) of Title 49 of the Code of Federal Regulations. *(Formerly § 6855, added by Stats.1985, c. 1162, § 2. Renumbered § 34518 and amended by Stats. 2006, c. 288 (A.B.3011), § 2. Amended by Stats.2010, c. 491 (S.B.1318), § 48.)*

Cross References

Impounding of commercial vehicles from another country, see Vehicle Code § 22651.4.

§ 34520. Compliance with federal drug and alcohol regulations; preemployment test for controlled substances and alcohol use; placement on duty; test results and other records; penalties; exemptions

(a) Motor carriers and drivers shall comply with the controlled substances and alcohol use, transportation, and testing requirements of the United States Secretary of Transportation as set forth in Part 382 (commencing with Section 382.101) of, and Sections 392.5(a)(1) and 392.5(a)(3) of, Title 49 of the Code of Federal Regulations.

(b)(1) A motor carrier shall make available for inspection, upon the request of an authorized employee of the department, copies of all results and other records pertaining to controlled substances and alcohol use and testing conducted pursuant to federal law, as specified in

subdivision (a), including those records contained in individual driver qualification files.

(2) For the purposes of complying with the return-to-duty alcohol or controlled substances test requirements, or both, of Section 382.309 of Title 49 of the Code of Federal Regulations and the followup alcohol or controlled substances test requirements, or both, of Section 382.311 of that title, the department may use those test results to monitor drivers who are motor carriers.

(3) Evidence derived from a positive test result in the possession of a motor carrier shall not be admissible in a criminal prosecution concerning unlawful possession, sale, or distribution of controlled substances.

(c) A drug or alcohol testing consortium, as defined in Section 382.107 of Title 49 of the Code of Federal Regulations, shall mail a copy of all drug and alcohol positive test result summaries to the department within three days of the test. This requirement applies only to drug and alcohol positive tests of those drivers employed by motor carriers who operate terminals within this state.

(d) A transit agency receiving federal financial assistance under Section 3, 9, or 18 of the Federal Transit Act, or under Section 103(e)(4) of Title 23 of the United States Code, shall comply with the controlled substances and alcohol use and testing requirements of the United States Secretary of Transportation as set forth in Part 655 (commencing with Section 655.1) of Title 49 of the Code of Federal Regulations.

(e) The owner-operator shall notify all other motor carriers with whom he or she is under contract when the owner-operator has met the requirements of subdivision (c) of Section 15242. Notwithstanding subdivision (i), a violation of this subdivision is an infraction.

(f) Except as provided in Section 382.301 of Title 49 of the Code of Federal Regulations, an applicant for employment as a commercial driver or an owner-operator seeking to provide transportation services and meeting the requirements of subdivision (b) of Section 34624, may not be placed on duty by a motor carrier until a preemployment test for controlled substances and alcohol use meeting the requirements of the federal regulations referenced in subdivision (a) have been completed and a negative test result has been reported.

(g) An applicant for employment as a commercial driver or an owner-operator, seeking to provide transportation services and meeting the requirements of subdivision (b) of Section 34624, may not be placed on duty by a motor carrier until the motor carrier has completed a full investigation of the driver's employment history meeting the requirements of the federal regulations cited under subdivision (a). Every motor carrier, whether making or receiving inquiries concerning a driver's history, shall document all activities it has taken to comply with this subdivision.

(h) A motor carrier that utilizes a preemployment screening service to review applications is in compliance with the employer duties under subdivisions (e) and (f) if the preemployment screening services that are provided satisfy the requirements of state and federal law and the motor carrier abides by any findings that would, under federal law, disqualify an applicant from operating a commercial vehicle.

(i) It is a misdemeanor punishable by imprisonment in the county jail for six months and a fine not to exceed five thousand dollars ($5,000), or by both the imprisonment and fine, for a person to willfully violate this section. As used in this subdivision, "willfully" has the same meaning as defined in Section 7 of the Penal Code.

(j) This section does not apply to a peace officer, as defined in Section 830.1 or 830.2 of the Penal Code, who is authorized to drive vehicles described in Section 34500, or to a firefighter, as defined in subdivision (f) of Section 15250.6, who is authorized to operate firefighting equipment as defined in subdivision (g) of Section 15250.6, if that peace officer or firefighter is participating in a substance abuse detection program within the scope of his or her employment. *(Added by Stats.1994, c. 832 (S.B.2034), § 3. Amended by Stats.1995, c. 405 (S.B.46), § 5; Stats.1999, c. 724 (A.B.1650), § 47; Stats.2001, c. 298 (S.B.871), § 3; Stats.2002, c. 774 (S.B.2079), § 4, eff. Sept. 21, 2002; Stats.2008, c. 368 (A.B.2742), § 2.)*

Cross References

Damages for wrongs, measure of damages, recovery of treble damages, see Civil Code § 3333.7.
Licenses, examination and display, exemptions, see Vehicle Code § 32000.5.
Motor carrier permits, applications, fees and contents, see Vehicle Code § 34621.
Suspension of motor carrier permit of motor carrier of property, grounds, see Vehicle Code § 34623.

§ 34520.3. School transportation vehicles; federal drug and alcohol testing requirements

(a) For the purposes of this section, a "school transportation vehicle" is a vehicle that is not a schoolbus, school pupil activity bus, or youth bus, and is used by a school district or county office of education for the primary purpose of transporting children.

(b) A school district or county office of education that employs drivers to drive a school transportation vehicle, and the driver of those vehicles, who are not otherwise required to participate in a testing program of the United States Secretary of Transportation, shall participate in a program that is consistent with the controlled substances and alcohol use and testing requirements of the United States Secretary of Transportation that apply to school-bus drivers and are set forth in Part 382 (commencing with Section 382.101) of, and Sections 392.5(a)(1) and (3) of, Title 49 of the Code of Federal Regulations.

(c) It is the intent of the Legislature that this section be implemented in a manner that does not require a school district or county office of education to administer a program for drivers of school transportation vehicles that imposes controlled substance and alcohol use and testing requirements greater than those applicable to school bus drivers under existing law. *(Added by Stats. 2005, c. 324 (A.B.1052), § 1.)*

§ 34520.5. Employers of paratransit vehicle drivers; paratransit vehicle drivers; compliance with federal drug-testing requirements

(a) All employers of drivers who operate paratransit vehicles, and the drivers of those vehicles, who are not otherwise required to participate in a testing program of the United States Secretary of Transportation, shall participate in a program consistent with the controlled substances and alcohol use and testing requirements of the United States Secretary of Transportation as set forth in Part 382 (commencing with Section 382.101), Part 653 (commencing with Section 653.1), or Part 654 (commencing with Section 654.1) of Title 49 of the Code of Federal Regulations.

(b) Section 34520 is applicable to any controlled substances or alcohol testing program undertaken under this section.

(c) The employer of a paratransit vehicle driver shall participate in the pull notice system defined in Section 1808.1. *(Added by Stats.1998, c. 241 (A.B.1634), § 4. Amended by Stats.1999, c. 1007 (S.B.532), § 25.)*

Division 14.85

MOTOR CARRIERS OF PROPERTY PERMIT ACT

Chapter   **Section**
1. General Provisions and Definitions 34600
2. Motor Carrier Permits 34620
3. Insurance 34630
4. Workers' Compensation 34640
5. Identification 34650
6. Fines and Penalties 34660

Cross References

Apportioned registration, operation of a vehicle or a fleet for which apportioned registration has been suspended, see Vehicle Code § 8104.

License to act as registration service,
    Generally, see Vehicle Code § 11400.
    Grounds for refusal, suspension, revocation, or cancellation, see Vehicle Code § 11405.

Payment by broker of construction trucking services of transportation charges submitted by motor carrier of property in dump truck equipment, see Civil Code § 3322.

"Registration service" defined to include persons engaged in the business of soliciting or receiving applications for motor carrier permits, see Vehicle Code § 505.2.

Violations of this division, offense, see Vehicle Code § 40000.22.

CHAPTER 1. GENERAL PROVISIONS AND DEFINITIONS

Section
34600. Short title.
34601. Motor carrier of property; for-hire motor carrier of property; commercial motor vehicle; private carrier; definitions.
34601. Motor carrier of property; for-hire motor carrier of property; commercial motor vehicle; private carrier; definitions.
34602. "Fund" defined.
34603. Development and enforcement of division; use of records from specified agencies.
34604. Rules and regulations; adoption.
34605. Contracts to administer division and impose fines; deposit of fees.
34606. Repealed.

§ 34600. Short title

This division shall be known and may be cited as the Motor Carriers of Property Permit Act. *(Added by Stats.1996, c. 1042 (A.B.1683), § 53, eff. Sept. 29, 1996.)*

§ 34601. Motor carrier of property; for-hire motor carrier of property; commercial motor vehicle; private carrier; definitions

Section operative until Jan. 1, 2016. See, also, section operative Jan. 1, 2016.

(a) As used in this division, "motor carrier of property" means any person who operates any commercial motor vehicle as defined in subdivision (c). "Motor carrier of property" does not include a household goods carrier, as defined in Section 5109 of the Public Utilities Code, a household goods carrier transporting used office, store, and institution furniture and fixtures under its household goods carrier permit pursuant to Section 5137 of the Public Utilities Code, persons providing only transportation of passengers, or a passenger stage corporation transporting baggage and express upon a passenger vehicle incidental to the transportation of passengers.

(b) As used in this division, "for-hire motor carrier of property" means a motor carrier of property as defined in subdivision (a) who transports property for compensation.

(c)(1) As used in this division, except as provided in paragraph (2), a "commercial motor vehicle" means any self-propelled vehicle listed in subdivisions (a), (b), (f), (g), and (k) of Section 34500, any motortruck of two or more axles that is more than 10,000 pounds gross vehicle weight rating, and any other motor vehicle used to transport property for compensation.

(2) As used in this division, "commercial motor vehicle" does not include any of the following:

(A) Vehicles identified in subdivision (f) of Section 34500, if the gross vehicle weight rating of the towing vehicle is 10,000 pounds or less.

(B) Vehicles identified in subdivision (g) of Section 34500, if the hazardous material transportation does not require the display of placards under Section 27903, a license under Section 32000.5, or a hazardous waste transporter registration under Section 25163 of the Health and Safety Code, and the vehicle is not operated in commercial use.

(C) Vehicles operated by a household goods carrier, as defined in Section 5109 of the Public Utilities Code, under the household goods carrier permit pursuant to Section 5137 of that code.

(D) Vehicles operated by a household goods carrier to transport used office, store, and institution furniture and fixtures under its household goods carrier permit pursuant to Section 5137 of the Public Utilities Code.

(E) Pickup trucks as defined in Section 471, if the conditions in subparagraphs (A) and (B) are also met.

(F) Two-axle daily rental trucks with a gross vehicle weight rating of less than 26,001 pounds, when operated in noncommercial use.

(G) Motortrucks or two-axle truck tractors, with a gross vehicle weight rating of less than 26,001 pounds, * * * operated solely to tow a camp trailer, trailer coach, fifth-wheel travel trailer, trailer designed to transport watercraft, or utility trailer. Vehicle combinations described in this subparagraph are not subject to Section 27900, 34501.12, or 34507.5.

(H) Motortrucks or two-axle truck tractors, with a gross vehicle weight rating of less than 16,001 pounds, operated singly in noncommercial use.

(d) For purposes of this chapter, "private carrier" means a motor carrier of property, who transports only his or her own property, including, but not limited to, the delivery of goods sold by that carrier.

(e) This section shall remain in effect only until January 1, 2016, and as of that date is repealed, unless a later enacted statute, that is enacted before January 1, 2016, deletes or extends that date. *(Added by Stats.1996, c. 1042 (A.B.1683), § 53, eff. Sept. 29, 1996. Amended by Stats.1997, c. 652 (A.B.1518), § 14; Stats.1999, c. 1005 (A.B.1658), § 98; Stats.1999, c. 1008 (S.B.533), § 15.5; Stats.2000, c. 787 (S.B.1404), § 25; Stats.2013, c. 392 (A.B.501), § 5; Stats.2013, c. 500 (A.B.529), § 13.5.)*

Repeal

For repeal of this section, see its terms.

§ 34601. Motor carrier of property; for-hire motor carrier of property; commercial motor vehicle; private carrier; definitions

Section operative Jan. 1, 2016. See, also, section operative until Jan. 1, 2016.

(a) As used in this division, "motor carrier of property" means any person who operates any commercial motor vehicle as defined in subdivision (c). "Motor carrier of property" does not include a household goods carrier, as defined in Section 5109 of the Public Utilities Code, a household goods carrier transporting used office, store, and institution furniture and fixtures under its household goods carrier permit pursuant to Section 5137 of the Public Utilities Code, persons providing only transportation of passengers, or a passenger stage corporation transporting baggage and express upon a passenger vehicle incidental to the transportation of passengers.

(b) As used in this division, "for-hire motor carrier of property" means a motor carrier of property as defined in subdivision (a) who transports property for compensation.

(c)(1) As used in this division, except as provided in paragraph (2), a "commercial motor vehicle" means any self-propelled vehicle listed in subdivisions (a), (b), (f), (g), and (k) of Section 34500, any motortruck of two or more axles that is more than 10,000 pounds gross vehicle weight rating, and any other motor vehicle used to transport property for compensation.

(2) As used in this division, "commercial motor vehicle" does not include any of the following:

(A) Vehicles identified in subdivision (f) of Section 34500, if the gross vehicle weight rating of the towing vehicle is 10,000 pounds or less.

(B) Vehicles identified in subdivision (g) of Section 34500, if the hazardous material transportation does not require the display of placards under Section 27903, a license under Section 32000.5, or a hazardous waste transporter registration under Section 25163 of the Health and Safety Code, and the vehicle is not operated in commercial use.

(C) Vehicles operated by a household goods carrier, as defined in Section 5109 of the Public Utilities Code, under the household goods carrier permit pursuant to Section 5137 of that code.

(D) Vehicles operated by a household goods carrier to transport used office, store, and institution furniture and fixtures under its household goods carrier permit pursuant to Section 5137 of the Public Utilities Code.

(E) Pickup trucks as defined in Section 471, if the conditions in subparagraphs (A) and (B) are also met.

(F) Two-axle daily rental trucks with a gross vehicle weight rating of less than 26,001 pounds, when operated in noncommercial use.

(G) Vehicles never operated in commercial use, including motortrucks or two-axle truck tractors, with a gross vehicle weight rating of less than 26,001 pounds, when operated singly, or, when used to tow a camp trailer, trailer coach, fifth-wheel travel trailer, trailer designed to transport watercraft, or a utility trailer, never operated in commercial use. Vehicle combinations described in this subparagraph are not subject to Section 27900, 34501.12, or 34507.5.

(d) For purposes of this chapter, "private carrier" means a motor carrier of property, who transports only his or her own property, including, but not limited to, the delivery of goods sold by that carrier.

(e) This section shall become operative on January 1, 2016. *(Added by Stats.2013, c. 500 (A.B.529), § 14, operative Jan. 1, 2016.)*

§ 34602. "Fund" defined

As used in this division, "fund" means the Motor Vehicle Account in the State Transportation Fund. *(Added by Stats.1996, c. 1042 (A.B.1683), § 53, eff. Sept. 29, 1996. Amended by Stats.2002, c. 805 (A.B.2996), § 22, eff. Sept. 23, 2002, operative July 1, 2003.)*

§ 34603. Development and enforcement of division; use of records from specified agencies

The Department of the California Highway Patrol, the Public Utilities Commission, and the State Board of Equalization shall furnish, upon request, whatever information from their records may be required to assist the department in the effective development and enforcement of this division. *(Added by Stats.1996, c. 1042 (A.B.1683), § 53, eff. Sept. 29, 1996.)*

§ 34604. Rules and regulations; adoption

The department may adopt reasonable rules and regulations necessary to administer this division. The department may also adopt rules and regulations necessary to administer civil sanction proceedings and impose fines for failure to comply with Division 14.8 (commencing with Section 34500), or this division, or regulations adopted pursuant to this code. *(Added by Stats.1996, c. 1042 (A.B.1683), § 53, eff. Sept. 29, 1996.)*

§ 34605. Contracts to administer division and impose fines; deposit of fees

(a) The department may contract with the Office of Administrative Hearings to administer proceedings and impose fines for failure to comply with Division 14.8 (commencing with Section 34500), or this division, or regulations adopted pursuant to this code.

(b) The department and the California Highway Patrol may also contract with the Public Utilities Commission to administer this division in a manner described by the contract, or if permitted by the Department of Motor Vehicles, in a manner as existed on January 1, 1996. This temporary authority shall be terminated on December 31, 1997.

(c) All fees collected under this contract shall be deposited in the Motor Vehicle Account in the State Transportation Fund. *(Added by Stats.1996, c. 1042 (A.B.1683), § 53, eff. Sept. 29, 1996. Amended by Stats. 2002, c. 805 (A.B.2996), § 23, eff. Sept. 23, 2002, operative July 1, 2003.)*

§ 34606. Repealed by Stats.2013, c. 500 (A.B.529), § 15

CHAPTER 2. MOTOR CARRIER PERMITS

Section

34620. Necessity of registration; issuance of permit; prohibited use of carrier services without permit or certification; copies; inspections; retrieval and release of vehicle utilizing tow truck; necessity of providing and maintaining motor carrier permit; inapplicability to person licensed under Collateral Recovery Act.
34621. Applications; fees; contents.
34622. Exempt vehicles; application of chapter.
34623. Safety regulations; jurisdiction; suspension of permit; nature of suspension; grounds; notice; hearing; reinstatement.
34623. Safety regulations; jurisdiction; suspension of permit; nature of suspension; grounds; notice; hearing; reinstatement.
34623.1. Tax delinquencies; suspension of permit.
34623.5. Reinstatement fee.
34624. Owner-operator classification; suspension of driving privilege; suspension of permit.

§ 34620. Necessity of registration; issuance of permit; prohibited use of carrier services without permit or certification; copies; inspections; retrieval and release of vehicle utilizing tow truck; necessity of providing and maintaining motor carrier permit; inapplicability to person licensed under Collateral Recovery Act

(a) Except as provided in subdivision (b) and Section 34622, a motor carrier of property shall not operate a commercial motor vehicle on any public highway in this state, unless it has complied with Section 34507.5 and has registered with the department its carrier identification number authorized or assigned thereunder, and holds a valid motor carrier permit issued to that motor carrier by the department. The department shall issue a motor carrier permit upon the carrier's written request, compliance with Sections 34507.5, 34630, and 34640, and subdivisions (e) and (h) of Section 34501.12 for motor carriers listed in that section, and the payment of the fee required by this chapter.

(b) A person shall not contract with, or otherwise engage the services of, a motor carrier of property, unless that motor carrier holds a valid motor carrier of property permit issued by the department. A motor carrier of property or broker of construction trucking services, as defined in Section 3322 of the Civil Code, shall not contract or subcontract with, or otherwise engage the services of, a motor carrier of property, until the contracted motor carrier of property provides certification in the manner prescribed by this section, of compliance with subdivision (a). This certification shall be completed by the contracted motor carrier of property and shall include a provision requiring the contracted motor carrier of property to immediately notify the person to whom they are contracted if the contracted motor carrier of property's permit is suspended or revoked. A copy of the contracted motor carrier of property's permit shall accompany the required certificate. The Department of the California Highway Patrol shall, by regulation, prescribe the format for the certificate and may make available an optional specific form for that purpose. The certificate, or a copy thereof, shall be maintained by each involved party for the duration of the contract or period of service plus two years, and shall be presented for inspection at the location designated by each carrier under Section 34501.10, immediately upon the request of an authorized employee of the Department of the California Highway Patrol.

(c)(1) A motor carrier of property shall not retrieve a vehicle through the use of a tow truck, as defined in subdivision (a) of Section 615, from the premises of another motor carrier of property until the retrieving motor carrier provides a copy of its motor carrier permit to the releasing motor carrier.

(2) A motor carrier of property shall not release a vehicle to another motor carrier of property utilizing a tow truck, as defined in subdivision (a) of Section 615, until the releasing motor carrier obtains a copy of the motor carrier permit from the retrieving motor carrier. The motor carrier releasing the vehicle shall maintain a copy of the motor carrier permit for a period of two years after the transaction, and, upon the request of an authorized employee of the Department of the California Highway Patrol, shall immediately present the permit for inspection at the location designated by the releasing motor carrier under Section 34501.10.

(3) This subdivision does not apply to a person licensed pursuant to the Collateral Recovery Act (Chapter 11 (commencing with Section 7500) of Division 3 of the Business and Professions Code). *(Added by Stats.1996, c. 1042 (A.B.1683), § 53, eff. Sept. 29, 1996. Amended by Stats.1997, c. 652 (A.B.1518), § 15; Stats.2003, c. 729 (A.B.1238), § 4; Stats.2004, c. 183 (A.B.3082), § 356; Stats.2010, c. 429 (A.B.145), § 2; Stats.2013, c. 96 (A.B. 306), § 1.)*

§ 34621. Applications; fees; contents

(a) The fee required by Section 7232 of the Revenue and Taxation Code shall be paid to the department upon initial application for a motor carrier permit and for annual renewal.

(b) An application for an original or a renewal motor carrier permit shall contain all of the following information:

(1) The full name of the motor carrier; any fictitious name under which it is doing business; address, both physical and mailing; and business telephone number.

(2) Status as individual, partnership, owner-operator, or corporation, and officers of corporation and all partners.

(3) Name, address, and driver's license number of owner-operator.

(4) California carrier number, number of commercial motor vehicles in fleet, interstate or intrastate operations, State Board of Equalization, federal Department of Transportation or the Federal Motor Carrier Safety Administration number, as applicable.

(5) Transporter or not a transporter of hazardous materials or petroleum.

(6) Evidence of financial responsibility.

(7) Evidence of workman's compensation coverage, if applicable.

(8) Carrier certification of enrollment in the biennial inspection of terminals (BIT) program under subdivisions (e) and (h) of Section 34501.12, unless otherwise exempted.

(9) Carrier certification of enrollment in a controlled substance and alcohol use and testing (CSAT) program required under Section 34520, unless otherwise exempted.

(10) Any other information necessary to enable the department to determine whether the applicant is entitled to a permit. *(Added by Stats.1996, c. 1042 (A.B.1683), § 53, eff. Sept. 29, 1996. Amended by Stats.1997, c. 652 (A.B.1518), § 16; Stats.2003, c. 729 (A.B.1238), § 5; Stats.2007, c. 66 (A.B.1513), § 2.)*

§ 34622. Exempt vehicles; application of chapter

This chapter does not apply to any of the following:

(a) Vehicles described in Section 5004 or 5011, and those that are exempt from vehicle registration fees.

(b) A household goods carrier transporting used office, store, and institution furniture and fixtures under its household goods carrier permit pursuant to Section 5137 of the Public Utilities Code. *(Added by Stats.1996, c. 1042 (A.B.1683), § 53, eff. Sept. 29, 1996. Amended by Stats.1997, c. 945 (A.B.1561), § 31; Stats.1999, c. 1005 (A.B.1658), § 100; Stats.2013, c. 500 (A.B.529), § 16.)*

§ 34623. Safety regulations; jurisdiction; suspension of permit; nature of suspension; grounds; notice; hearing; reinstatement

Section operative until Jan. 1, 2016. See, also, section operative Jan. 1, 2016.

(a) The Department of the California Highway Patrol has exclusive jurisdiction for the regulation of safety of operation of motor carriers of property.

(b) The motor carrier permit of a motor carrier of property may be suspended for failure to do any of the following:

(1) Maintain any vehicle of the carrier in a safe operating condition or to comply with this code or with applicable regulations contained in Title 13 of the California Code of Regulations, if that failure is either a consistent failure or presents an imminent danger to public safety.

(2) Enroll all drivers in the pull notice system as required by Section 1808.1.

(3) Submit any application or pay any fee required by subdivision (e) or (h) of Section 34501.12 within the timeframes set forth in that section.

(c) The motor carrier permit of a motor carrier of property shall be suspended for failure to either (1) comply with the requirements of federal law described in subdivision (a) of Section 34520 of the Vehicle Code, or (2) make copies of results and other records available as required by subdivision (b) of that section. The suspension shall be as follows:

(1) For a serious violation, which is a willful failure to perform substance abuse testing in accordance with state or federal law:

(A) For a first offense, a mandatory five-day suspension.

(B) For a second offense within three years of a first offense, a mandatory three-month suspension.

(C) For a third offense within three years of a first offense, a mandatory one-year suspension.

(2) For a nonserious violation, the time recommended to the department by the Department of the California Highway Patrol.

(3) For the purposes of this subdivision, "willful failure" means any of the following:

(A) An intentional and uncorrected failure to have a controlled substances and alcohol testing program in place.

(B) An intentional and uncorrected failure to enroll an employed driver into the controlled substances and alcohol testing program.

(C) A knowing use of a medically disqualified driver, including the failure to remove the driver from safety-sensitive duties upon notification of the medical disqualification.

(D) An attempt to conceal legal deficiencies in the motor carrier's controlled substances and alcohol testing program.

(d) The department, pending a hearing in the matter pursuant to subdivision (f), may suspend a carrier's permit.

(e)(1) A motor carrier whose motor carrier permit is suspended pursuant to subdivision (b) may obtain a reinspection of its terminal and vehicles by the Department of the California Highway Patrol by submitting a written request for reinstatement to the department and paying a reinstatement fee as required by Section 34623.5.

(2) A motor carrier whose motor carrier permit is suspended for failure to submit any application or to pay any fee required by Section 34501.12 shall present proof of having submitted that application or have paid that fee to the Department of the California Highway Patrol before applying for reinstatement of its motor carrier permit.

(3) The department shall deposit all reinstatement fees collected from motor carriers of property pursuant to this section in the fund. Upon receipt of the fee, the department shall forward a request to the Department of the California Highway Patrol, which shall perform a reinspection within a reasonable time, or shall verify receipt of the application or fee or both the application and fee. Following the term of a suspension imposed under Section 34670, the department shall reinstate a carrier's motor carrier permit suspended under subdivision (b) upon notification by the Department of the California Highway Patrol that the carrier's safety compliance has improved to the satisfaction of the Department of the California Highway Patrol, or that the required application or fees have been received by the Department of the California Highway Patrol, unless the permit is suspended for another reason or has been revoked.

(f) Whenever the department suspends the permit of any carrier pursuant to subdivision (b), (c), or paragraph (3) of subdivision (i), the department shall furnish the carrier with written notice of the suspension and shall provide for a hearing within a reasonable time, not to exceed 21 days, after a written request is filed with the department. At the hearing, the carrier shall show cause why the suspension should not be continued. Following the hearing, the department may terminate the suspension, continue the suspension in effect, or revoke the permit. The department may revoke the permit of any carrier suspended pursuant to subdivision (b) at any time that is 90 days or more after its suspension if the carrier

has not filed a written request for a hearing with the department or has failed to submit a request for reinstatement pursuant to subdivision (e).

(g) Notwithstanding any other provision of this code, no hearing shall be provided when the suspension of the motor carrier permit is based solely upon the failure of the motor carrier to maintain satisfactory proof of financial responsibility as required by this code, or failure of the motor carrier to submit an application or to pay fees required by Section 34501.12.

(h) A motor carrier of property may not operate a commercial motor vehicle on any public highway in this state during any period its motor carrier of property permit is suspended pursuant to this division.

(i)(1) A motor carrier of property whose motor carrier permit is suspended pursuant to this section or Section 34505.6, which suspension is based wholly or in part on the failure of the motor carrier to maintain any vehicle in safe operating condition, may not lease, or otherwise allow, another motor carrier to operate the vehicles of the carrier subject to the suspension, during the period of the suspension.

(2) A motor carrier of property may not knowingly lease, operate, dispatch, or otherwise utilize any vehicle from a motor carrier of property whose motor carrier permit is suspended, which suspension is based wholly or in part on the failure of the motor carrier to maintain any vehicle in safe operating condition.

(3) The department may immediately suspend the motor carrier permit of any motor carrier that the department determines to be in violation of paragraph (2).

(j) This section shall remain in effect only until January 1, 2016, and as of that date is repealed, unless a later enacted statute, that is enacted before January 1, 2016, deletes or extends that date. *(Added by Stats.1996, c. 1042 (A.B.1683), § 53, eff. Sept. 29, 1996. Amended by Stats.1997, c. 652 (A.B.1518), § 17; Stats.1999, c. 1006 (A.B.957), § 3; Stats.2001, c. 298 (S.B.871), § 4; Stats. 2002, c. 774 (S.B.2079), § 5, eff. Sept. 21, 2002; Stats. 2013, c. 500 (A.B.529), § 17.)*

Repeal

For repeal of this section, see its terms.

Cross References

Damages for wrongs, measure of damages, recovery of treble damages, see Civil Code § 3333.7.
Safety regulations, compliance with federal drug and alcohol regulations, drug and alcohol testing, see Vehicle Code § 34520.

§ 34623. Safety regulations; jurisdiction; suspension of permit; nature of suspension; grounds; notice; hearing; reinstatement

Section operative Jan. 1, 2016. See, also, section operative until Jan. 1, 2016.

(a) The Department of the California Highway Patrol has exclusive jurisdiction for the regulation of safety of operation of motor carriers of property.

(b) The motor carrier permit of a motor carrier of property may be suspended for failure to do either of the following:

(1) Maintain any vehicle of the carrier in a safe operating condition or to comply with this code or with applicable regulations contained in Title 13 of the California Code of Regulations, if that failure is either a consistent failure or presents an imminent danger to public safety.

(2) Enroll all drivers in the pull-notice system as required by Section 1808.1.

(c) The motor carrier permit of a motor carrier of property shall be suspended for failure to either (1) comply with the requirements of federal law described in subdivision (a) of Section 34520 of the Vehicle Code, or (2) make copies of results and other records available as required by subdivision (b) of that section. The suspension shall be as follows:

(1) For a serious violation, which is a willful failure to perform substance abuse testing in accordance with state or federal law:

(A) For a first offense, a mandatory five-day suspension.

(B) For a second offense within three years of a first offense, a mandatory three-month suspension.

(C) For a third offense within three years of a first offense, a mandatory one-year suspension.

(2) For a nonserious violation, the time recommended to the department by the Department of the California Highway Patrol.

(3) For the purposes of this subdivision, "willful failure" means any of the following:

(A) An intentional and uncorrected failure to have a controlled substances and alcohol testing program in place.

(B) An intentional and uncorrected failure to enroll an employed driver into the controlled substances and alcohol testing program.

(C) A knowing use of a medically disqualified driver, including the failure to remove the driver from safety-sensitive duties upon notification of the medical disqualification.

(D) An attempt to conceal legal deficiencies in the motor carrier's controlled substances and alcohol testing program.

(d) The department, pending a hearing in the matter pursuant to subdivision (f), may suspend a carrier's permit.

(e)(1) A motor carrier whose motor carrier permit is suspended pursuant to subdivision (b) may obtain a reinspection of its terminal and vehicles by the Department of the California Highway Patrol by submitting a

written request for reinstatement to the department and paying a reinstatement fee as required by Section 34623.5.

(2) The department shall deposit all reinstatement fees collected from motor carriers of property pursuant to this section in the fund. Upon receipt of the fee, the department shall forward a request to the Department of the California Highway Patrol, which shall perform a reinspection within a reasonable time, or shall verify receipt of the application or fee or both the application and fee. Following the term of a suspension imposed under Section 34670, the department shall reinstate a carrier's motor carrier permit suspended under subdivision (b) upon notification by the Department of the California Highway Patrol that the carrier's safety compliance has improved to the satisfaction of the Department of the California Highway Patrol, unless the permit is suspended for another reason or has been revoked.

(f) Whenever the department suspends the permit of any carrier pursuant to subdivision (b), (c), or paragraph (3) of subdivision (i), the department shall furnish the carrier with written notice of the suspension and shall provide for a hearing within a reasonable time, not to exceed 21 days, after a written request is filed with the department. At the hearing, the carrier shall show cause why the suspension should not be continued. Following the hearing, the department may terminate the suspension, continue the suspension in effect, or revoke the permit. The department may revoke the permit of any carrier suspended pursuant to subdivision (b) at any time that is 90 days or more after its suspension if the carrier has not filed a written request for a hearing with the department or has failed to submit a request for reinstatement pursuant to subdivision (e).

(g) Notwithstanding any other provision of this code, a hearing shall not be provided if the suspension of the motor carrier permit is based solely upon the failure of the motor carrier to maintain satisfactory proof of financial responsibility as required by this code.

(h) A motor carrier of property may not operate a commercial motor vehicle on any public highway in this state during any period its motor carrier of property permit is suspended pursuant to this division.

(i)(1) A motor carrier of property whose motor carrier permit is suspended pursuant to this section or Section 34505.6, which suspension is based wholly or in part on the failure of the motor carrier to maintain any vehicle in safe operating condition, may not lease, or otherwise allow, another motor carrier to operate the vehicles of the carrier subject to the suspension, during the period of the suspension.

(2) A motor carrier of property may not knowingly lease, operate, dispatch, or otherwise utilize any vehicle from a motor carrier of property whose motor carrier permit is suspended, which suspension is based wholly or in part on the failure of the motor carrier to maintain any vehicle in safe operating condition.

(3) The department may immediately suspend the motor carrier permit of any motor carrier that the department determines to be in violation of paragraph (2).

(j) This section shall become operative on January 1, 2016. *(Added by Stats.2013, c. 500 (A.B.529), § 18, operative Jan. 1, 2016.)*

Cross References

Damages for wrongs, measure of damages, recovery of treble damages, see Civil Code § 3333.7.

Safety regulations, compliance with federal drug and alcohol regulations, drug and alcohol testing, see Vehicle Code § 34520.

§ 34623.1. Tax delinquencies; suspension of permit

The motor carrier permit of a licensee may be suspended pursuant to Section 494.5 of the Business and Professions Code if a licensee's name is included on a certified list of tax delinquencies provided by the State Board of Equalization or the Franchise Tax Board pursuant to Section 7063 or Section 19195, respectively of the Revenue and Taxation Code. *(Added by Stats.2011, c. 455 (A.B.1424), § 17.)*

§ 34623.5. Reinstatement fee

Except as provided under subdivision (c) of Section 34630 and subdivision (d) of Section 34640, before a permit may be reissued after a suspension is terminated, there shall, in addition to any other fees required by this code, be paid to the department a fee of one hundred fifty dollars ($150). *(Added by Stats.1996, c. 1042 (A.B. 1683), § 53, eff. Sept. 29, 1996. Amended by Stats.2007, c. 58 (A.B.913), § 1.)*

§ 34624. Owner-operator classification; suspension of driving privilege; suspension of permit

(a) The department shall establish a classification of motor carrier of property known as owner-operators.

(b) As used in this section and in Sections 1808.1 and 34501.12, an owner-operator is a person who meets all of the following requirements:

(1) Holds a class A or class B driver's license or a class C license with a hazardous materials endorsement.

(2) Owns, leases, or otherwise operates not more than one power unit and not more than three towed vehicles.

(3) Is required to obtain a permit as a motor carrier of property by the department under this division.

(c)(1) As used in this section, "power unit" is a motor vehicle described in subdivision (a), (b), (g), (f), or (k) of Section 34500, or a motortruck of two or more axles that is more than 10,000 pounds gross vehicle weight rating, but does not include those vehicles operated by household goods carriers, as defined in Section 5109 of the Public Utilities Code or persons providing transportation of passengers. A "towed vehicle" is a nonmotorized vehicle described in subdivision (d), (e), (f), (g), or (k) of that section.

(2) As used in this section, subdivision (f) of Section 34500 includes only those combinations where the gross vehicle weight rating of the towing vehicle exceeds 11,500 pounds, and subdivision (g) of Section 34500 includes only those vehicles transporting hazardous materials for which the display of placards is required pursuant to Section 27903, a license is required pursuant to Section 32000.5, or for which a hazardous waste transporter registration is required pursuant to Section 25163 of the Health and Safety Code.

(d) The department, upon suspending or revoking the driving privilege of an owner-operator shall also suspend the owner-operator's motor carrier permit, unless the owner-operator, within 15 days, shows good cause why the permit should not be suspended.

(e) Every motor carrier who is within the classification established by this section is responsible for notifying all other motor carriers with whom he or she is under contract when the status of the motor carrier changes so that he or she is no longer within the classification established by this section.

(f) This section shall not be construed to change the definition of "employer," "employee," or "independent contractor" for any other purpose. *(Added by Stats.1996, c. 1042 (A.B.1683), § 53, eff. Sept. 29, 1996. Amended by Stats.1997, c. 652 (A.B.1518), § 18; Stats.2002, c. 774 (S.B.2079), § 6, eff. Sept. 21, 2002.)*

Cross References

Employer responsibilities, commercial vehicle safety, self employment as driver, see Vehicle Code § 15242.

Report to department from motor carrier regularly employing more than 20 full-time drivers whenever it replaces more than half within 30–day period, see Vehicle Code § 34501.18.

Safety regulations, compliance with federal drug and alcohol regulations, drug and alcohol testing, see Vehicle Code § 34520.

CHAPTER 3. INSURANCE

Section

34630. Proof of financial responsibility; certificate of insurance or surety bond; cancellation restrictions; lapse or termination; suspension of permit.

34631. Evidence of proof of financial responsibility; deposits with department.

34631.5. Liability protection; evidence; emergency moves.

34632. List of vehicles; periodic reporting; failure to obtain insurance coverage; penalty.

34633. Carriers with fleets of 20 or more vehicles; reporting of employee and driver classifications and compensation; notice to workers' compensation administrator.

34634. False statements of workers' compensation insurance coverage; judgments pursuant to uninsured employers fund; penalties; hearing.

§ 34630. Proof of financial responsibility; certificate of insurance or surety bond; cancellation restrictions; lapse or termination; suspension of permit

(a) A motor carrier permit shall not be granted to any motor carrier of property until there is filed with the department proof of financial responsibility in the form of a currently effective certificate of insurance, issued by a company licensed to write that insurance in this state or by a nonadmitted insurer subject to Section 1763 of the Insurance Code, if the policy represented by the certificate meets the minimum insurance requirements contained in Section 34631.5. The certificate of insurance or surety bond shall provide coverage with respect to the operation, maintenance, or use of any vehicle for which a permit is required, although the vehicle may not be specifically described in the policy, or a bond of surety issued by a company licensed to write surety bonds in this state, or written evidence of self-insurance by providing the self-insured number granted by the department on a form approved by the department.

(b) Proof of financial responsibility shall be continued in effect during the active life of the motor carrier permit. The certificate of insurance shall not be cancelable on less than 30 days' written notice from the insurer to the department except in the event of cessation of operations as a permitted motor carrier of property.

(c) Whenever the department determines or is notified that the certificate of insurance or surety bond of a motor carrier of property will lapse or be terminated, the department shall suspend the carrier's permit effective on the date of lapse or termination unless the carrier provides evidence of valid insurance coverage pursuant to subdivision (a).

(1) If the carrier's permit is suspended, the carrier shall pay a reinstatement fee as set forth in Section 34623.5, and prior to conducting on-highway operations, present proof of financial responsibility pursuant to subdivision (a) in order to have the permit reinstated.

(2) If the evidence provided by the carrier of valid insurance coverage pursuant to subdivision (a) demonstrates that a lapse in coverage for the carrier's operation did not occur, the reinstatement fee shall be waived. *(Added by Stats.1996, c. 1042 (A.B.1683), § 53, eff. Sept. 29, 1996. Amended by Stats.2007, c. 58 (A.B.913), § 2.)*

Cross References

Reinstatement fee after termination of suspension, see Vehicle Code §§ 34623.5, 34671.

§ 34631. Evidence of proof of financial responsibility; deposits with department

The proof of financial responsibility required under Section 34630 shall be evidenced by the deposit with the department, covering each vehicle used or to be used under the motor carrier permit applied for, of one of the following:

(a) A certificate of insurance, issued by a company licensed to write insurance in this state, or by a nonadmit-

ted insurer subject to Section 1763 of the Insurance Code, if the policies represented by the certificate comply with Section 34630 and the rules promulgated by the department pursuant to Section 34604.

(b) A bond of a surety company licensed to write surety bonds in the state.

(c) Evidence of qualification of the carrier as a self-insurer as provided for in subdivision (a) of Section 34630. However, any certificate of self-insurance granted to a motor carrier of property shall be limited to serve as proof of financial responsibility under paragraphs (1) and (2) of subdivision (a) of Section 34631.5 minimum limits only and shall not be acceptable as proof of financial responsibility for the coverage required pursuant to paragraph (3) or (4) of subdivision (a) of Section 34631.5.

(d) Evidence on a form that indicates that coverage is provided by a charitable risk pool operating under Section 5005.1 of the Corporations Code, if the registered owner of the vehicle is a nonprofit organization that is exempt from taxation under paragraph (3) of subsection (c) of Section 501 of the United States Internal Revenue Code. The form shall include all of the following:

(1) The name and address of the motor carrier.

(2) The name and address of the charitable risk pool providing the policy for the motor carrier.

(3) The policy number, effective date, and liability limits of the policy.

(4) A statement from the charitable risk pool that the policy meets the requirements of Section 34631.5. *(Added by Stats.1996, c. 1042 (A.B.1683), § 53, eff. Sept. 29, 1996. Amended by Stats.1997, c. 652 (A.B.1518), § 19; Stats.2002, c. 758 (A.B.3024), § 15.)*

§ 34631.5. Liability protection; evidence; emergency moves

(a)(1) Every motor carrier of property as defined in Section 34601, except those subject to paragraph (2), (3), or (4), shall provide and thereafter continue in effect adequate protection against liability imposed by law upon those carriers for the payment of damages in the amount of a combined single limit of not less than seven hundred fifty thousand dollars ($750,000) on account of bodily injuries to, or death of, one or more persons, or damage to or destruction of, property other than property being transported by the carrier for any shipper or consignee whether the property of one or more than one claimant in any one accident.

(2) Every motor carrier of property, as defined in Section 34601, who operates only vehicles under 10,000 pounds GVWR and who does not transport any commodity subject to paragraph (3) or (4), shall provide and thereafter continue in effect adequate protection against liability imposed by law for the payment of damages caused by bodily injuries to or the death of any person; or for damage to or destruction of property of others, other than property being transported by the carrier, in

an amount not less than three hundred thousand dollars ($300,000).

(3) Every intrastate motor carrier of property, as defined in Section 34601, who transports petroleum products in bulk, including waste petroleum and waste petroleum products, shall provide and thereafter continue in effect adequate protection against liability imposed by law upon the carrier for the payment of damages for personal bodily injuries (including death resulting therefrom) in the amount of not less than five hundred thousand dollars ($500,000) on account of bodily injuries to, or death of, one person; and protection against a total liability of those carriers on account of bodily injuries to, or death of more than one person as a result of any one accident, but subject to the same limitation for each person in the amount of not less than one million dollars ($1,000,000); and protection in an amount of not less than two hundred thousand dollars ($200,000) for one accident resulting in damage to or destruction to property other than property being transported by the carrier for any shipper or consignee, whether the property of one or more than one claimant; or a combined single limit in the amount of not less than one million two hundred thousand dollars ($1,200,000) on account of bodily injuries to, or death of, one or more persons or damage to or destruction of property, or both, other than property being transported by the carrier for any shipper or consignee whether the property of one or more than one claimant in any one accident.

(4) Except as provided in paragraph (3), every motor carrier of property, as defined in Section 34601, that transports any hazardous material, as defined by Section 353, shall provide and thereafter continue in effect adequate protection against liability imposed by law on those carriers for the payment of damages for personal injury or death, and damage to or destruction of property, in amounts of not less than the minimum levels of financial responsibility specified for carriers of hazardous materials by the United States Department of Transportation in Part 387 (commencing with Section 387.1) of Title 49 of the Code of Federal Regulations. The applicable minimum levels of financial responsibility required are as follows:

Commodity Transported:	Combined Single Limit Coverage
(A) Oil listed in Section 172.101 of Title 49 of the Code of Federal Regulations; or hazardous waste, hazardous materials and hazardous substances defined in Section 171.8 of Title 49 of the Code of Federal Regulations and listed in Section 172.101 of Title 49 of the Code of Federal Regulations, but not mentioned in subparagraph (C) or (D).	$1,000,000
(B) Hazardous waste as defined in Section 25117 of the Health and Safety Code and in Article 1 (commencing with Section 66261.1) of Chapter 11 of	

Commodity Transported:	Combined Single Limit Coverage
Division 4.5 of Title 22 of the California Code of Regulations, but not mentioned in subparagraph (C) or (D).	$1,000,000
(C) Hazardous substances, as defined in Section 171.8 of Title 49 of the Code of Federal Regulations, or liquefied compressed gas or compressed gas, transported in cargo tanks, portable tanks, or hopper-type vehicle with capacities in excess of 3,500 water gallons.	$5,000,000
(D) Any quantity of division 1.1, 1.2, or 1.3 explosives; any quantity of poison gas (Poison A); or highway route controlled quantity radioactive materials as defined in Section 173.403 of Title 49 of the Code of Federal Regulations.	$5,000,000

(b)(1) The protection required under subdivision (a) shall be evidenced by the deposit with the department, covering each vehicle used or to be used in conducting the service performed by each motor carrier of property, an authorized certificate of public liability and property damage insurance, issued by a company licensed to write the insurance in the State of California, or by a nonadmitted insurer subject to Section 1763 of the Insurance Code.

(2) The protection required under subdivision (a) by every motor carrier of property engaged in interstate or foreign transportation of property in or through California, shall be evidenced by the filing and acceptance of a department authorized certificate of insurance, or qualification as a self-insurer as may be authorized by law.

(3) A certificate of insurance, evidencing the protection, shall not be cancelable on less than 30 days' written notice to the department, the notice to commence to run from the date notice is actually received at the office of the department in Sacramento.

(4) Every insurance certificate or equivalent protection to the public shall contain a provision that the certificate or equivalent protection shall remain in full force and effect until canceled in the manner provided by paragraph (3).

(5) Upon cancellation of an insurance certificate or the cancellation of equivalent protection authorized by the Department of Motor Vehicles, the motor carrier permit of any motor carrier of property, shall stand suspended immediately upon the effective date of the cancellations.

(6) No carrier shall engage in any operation on any public highway of this state during the suspension of its permit.

(7) No motor carrier of property, whose permit has been suspended under paragraph (5) shall resume operations unless and until the carrier has filed an insurance certificate or equivalent protection in effect at the time and that meets the standards set forth in this section.

941

The operative rights of the complying carriers shall be reinstated from suspension upon the filing of an insurance certificate or equivalent protection.

(8) In order to expedite the processing of insurance filings by the department, each insurance filing made should contain the insured's California carrier number, if known, in the upper right corner of the certificate.

(c)(1) Notwithstanding any other provision of law, the operator of a for-hire tow truck who is in compliance with subdivision (a) may perform emergency moves, irrespective of the load carried aboard the vehicle being moved.

(2) For the purposes of paragraph (1), an "emergency move" is limited to one or more of the following activities:

(A) Removal of a disabled or damaged vehicle or combination of vehicles from a highway.

(B) Removal of a vehicle or combination of vehicles from public or private property following a traffic collision.

(C) Removal of a vehicle or combination of vehicles from public or private property to protect public health, safety, or property.

(D) Removal of a vehicle or combination of vehicles from any location for impound or storage, at the direction of a peace officer.

(3) The authority granted under paragraph (1) applies only to the first one-way carriage of property from the scene of the emergency to the nearest safe location. Any subsequent move of that property shall be subject to subdivision (a), including, but not limited to, a requirement that the for-hire tow truck operator have a level of liability protection that is adequate for the commodity being transported by the towed vehicle or combination of vehicles.

(4) Any transportation of property by an operator of an operator of a for-hire tow truck that is not an emergency move, as authorized under paragraph (1), shall be subject to subdivision (a), including, but not limited to, a requirement that the for-hire tow truck operator have a level of liability protection that is adequate for the commodity being transported by the towed vehicle or combination of vehicles. *(Added by Stats.1996, c. 1042 (A.B.1683), § 53, eff. Sept. 29, 1996. Amended by Stats.1997, c. 652 (A.B.1518), § 20; Stats. 1998, c. 478 (A.B.2372), § 8; Stats.1998, c. 877 (A.B. 2132), § 70.5; Stats.1999, c. 724 (A.B.1650), § 48.)*

§ 34632. List of vehicles; periodic reporting; failure to obtain insurance coverage; penalty

(a) Every motor carrier of property shall furnish the department annually, as specified by the department, a list, prepared under oath, of all vehicles, described in Section 34601, used in transportation during the preceding year.

(b) If the carrier's insurer informs the department that the carrier has failed to obtain insurance coverage for any vehicle reported on the list, the department shall, in addition to any other applicable penalty provided in this division, suspend the carrier's permit. *(Added by Stats. 1996, c. 1042 (A.B.1683), § 53, eff. Sept. 29, 1996.)*

§ 34633. Carriers with fleets of 20 or more vehicles; reporting of employee and driver classifications and compensation; notice to workers' compensation administrator

Every motor carrier of property with a carrier fleet of 20 or more commercial motor vehicles as defined in Section 34601 shall, under oath, file annually a report with the department indicating the number, classification, and compensation of all employees and owner-operator drivers hired or engaged during the reporting period. The department shall submit a copy of the report to the administrator of the corporation's workers' compensation self-insurance plan if the corporation is self-insured, or to the carrier's workers' compensation insurer if the carrier's workers' compensation protection is provided by a policy or policies of insurance. *(Added by Stats.1996, c. 1042 (A.B.1683), § 53, eff. Sept. 29, 1996.)*

§ 34634. False statements of workers' compensation insurance coverage; judgments pursuant to uninsured employers fund; penalties; hearing

(a) Upon receipt of a stop order issued by the Director of Industrial Relations pursuant to Section 3710.1 of the Labor Code, the department shall determine whether the motor carrier of property has filed a false statement relative to workers' compensation insurance coverage, in violation of statute, or rules or orders of the department. If, after notice and opportunity to be heard, the department determines that there has been a violation of statute, or rules or orders of the department, the department shall, in addition to any other applicable penalty provided in this division, suspend the carrier's permit.

(b) Upon notification from the Director of Industrial Relations that a final judgment has been entered against any motor carrier of property as a result of an award having been made to an employee pursuant to Section 3716.2 of the Labor Code, the department shall, 30 days from the date the carrier is mailed the notice pursuant to subdivision (c), revoke the carrier's permit unless the judgment has been satisfied or has been discharged in accordance with the bankruptcy laws of the United States or the carrier requests a hearing pursuant to subdivision (c).

(c) Within seven days of notification from the Director of Industrial Relations that a final judgment has been entered against any motor carrier of property as a result of an award having been made to an employee pursuant to Section 3716.2 of the Labor Code, the department shall furnish to the carrier named in the final judgment written notice of the right to a hearing regarding the revocation of the permit and the procedure to follow to request a hearing. The notice shall state that the department is required to revoke the carrier's permit pursuant to subdivision (b) after 30 days from the date the notice is mailed unless the carrier provides proof that the judgment is satisfied or has been discharged in accordance with the bankruptcy laws of the United States and the department has been so notified seven days prior to the conclusion of the 30–day waiting period. The carrier may request a hearing within 10 days from the date the notice is sent by the department. The request for the hearing shall stay the revocation. The hearing shall be held within 30 days of the receipt of the request. If the department finds that an unsatisfied judgment exists concerning a debt arising under Section 3717 of the Labor Code, the department shall immediately revoke the carrier's permit. *(Added by Stats.1996, c. 1042 (A.B.1683), § 53, eff. Sept. 29, 1996.)*

CHAPTER 4. WORKERS' COMPENSATION

Section
34640. Required filings; cancellation notice; notification of changes; lapse or termination; reinstatement; fee.

§ 34640. Required filings; cancellation notice; notification of changes; lapse or termination; reinstatement; fee

(a) A motor carrier permit shall not be granted to any motor carrier of property until one of the following is filed with the department:

(1) A certificate of workers' compensation coverage for its employees issued by an admitted insurer.

(2) A certification of consent to self-insure issued by the Director of Industrial Relations, and the identity of the administrator of the carrier's workers' compensation self-insurance plan.

(3) A statement, under penalty of perjury, stating that, in its operations as a motor carrier of property, it does not employ any person in any manner so as to become subject to the workers' compensation laws of this state.

(b) The workers' compensation certified under paragraph (1) of subdivision (a) shall be effective until canceled. The insurer shall provide to the motor carrier of property and to the department a notice of cancellation not less than 30 days in advance of the effective date.

(c) If, after filing the statement described in paragraph (3) of subdivision (a), the carrier becomes subject to the workers' compensation laws of this state, the carrier shall promptly notify the department that the carrier is withdrawing its statement under paragraph (3) of subdivision (a), and shall simultaneously file the certificate described in either paragraph (1) or (2) of subdivision (a).

(d) Whenever the department determines or is notified that the certificate of workers' compensation insurance or certification to self-insure a motor carrier of property will lapse or be terminated, the department shall suspend the carrier's permit effective on the date of the lapse or termination, unless the motor carrier provides evidence of valid insurance coverage pursuant to subdivision (a).

(1) If the carrier's permit is suspended, the carrier shall pay a reinstatement fee as set forth in Section 34671, and prior to conducting on-highway operations, present proof of valid insurance coverage pursuant to subdivision (a) in order to have the permit reinstated.

(2) If the evidence provided by the carrier of valid insurance coverage pursuant to subdivision (a) demonstrates that a lapse in coverage for the carrier's operation did not occur, the reinstatement fee shall be waived. *(Added by Stats.1996, c. 1042 (A.B.1683), § 53, eff. Sept. 29, 1996. Amended by Stats.2007, c. 58 (A.B.913), § 3.)*

Cross References

Reinstatement fee after termination of suspension, see Vehicle Code §§ 34623.5, 34671.

CHAPTER 5. IDENTIFICATION

Section
34650. Repealed.

§ 34650. Repealed by Stats.1997, c. 652 (A.B.1518), § 21

CHAPTER 6. FINES AND PENALTIES

Section
34660. Operation following suspension of permit; offense; punishment; injunctions; impoundment of vehicles; towing and storage charges.
34661. Violations of division; offense; punishment.
34670. Violations of safety regulations; additional sanctions.
34671. Reinstatement; fee; requirements.
34672. Payments by dishonored checks; restitution; cancellation of permit.

§ 34660. Operation following suspension of permit; offense; punishment; injunctions; impoundment of vehicles; towing and storage charges

(a) A motor carrier of property, after its motor carrier permit has been suspended by the department, who continues to operate as a motor carrier, either independently or for another motor carrier, is guilty of a misdemeanor, punishable by a fine of not more than two thousand five hundred dollars ($2,500), or by imprisonment in the county jail for not more than three months, or by both that fine and imprisonment.

(b) Each violation of this section is a separate and distinct offense, and, in the case of a continuing violation, each day's continuance of operation as a carrier in violation of this section is a separate and distinct offense.

(c) Upon finding that a motor carrier of property is willfully violating this section after being advised that it is not operating in compliance with the laws of this state, the court may issue an injunction to stop the carrier's continued operation.

(d) A member of the Department of the California Highway Patrol may impound a vehicle or combination of vehicles operated by a motor carrier of property, when the vehicle or combination of vehicles is found upon a highway, any public lands, or an offstreet parking facility and the motor carrier is found to be in violation of this section or of subdivision (a) of Section 34620. For purposes of this subdivision, the vehicle shall be released to the registered owner or authorized agent only after the registered owner or authorized agent furnishes the Department of the California Highway Patrol with proof of current registration, a currently valid driver's license of the appropriate class to operate the vehicle or combination of vehicles, and proof of compliance with this division. The registered owner or authorized agent is responsible for all towing and storage charges related to the impoundment. *(Added by Stats.1996, c. 1042 (A.B. 1683), § 53, eff. Sept. 29, 1996. Amended by Stats.1997, c. 652 (A.B.1518), § 22.)*

§ 34661. Violations of division; offense; punishment

Any person or corporation who violates any provision of this division is guilty of a misdemeanor, punishable by a fine of not more than two thousand five hundred dollars ($2,500), or by imprisonment in the county jail for not more than three months, or by both that fine and imprisonment. *(Added by Stats.1996, c. 1042 (A.B.1683), § 53, eff. Sept. 29, 1996.)*

§ 34670. Violations of safety regulations; additional sanctions

Any violation of Division 14.8 (commencing with Section 34500) or any violation that results in a suspension or revocation of the motor carrier permit pursuant to Section 34505.6 or 34623, or subdivision (d) of Section 34624, in addition to any other penalties, shall be sanctioned as follows:

(a) If there have been no prior sanctions imposed on the permitholder, the permit shall be suspended for 30 days.

(b) If the permit had been suspended once prior in the previous 36 months, the permit shall be suspended for 60 days.

(c) If the permit had been previously suspended two or more times in the previous 36 months, the permit shall be suspended for 90 days, and a fine of one thousand five hundred dollars ($1,500) shall be imposed. *(Added by Stats.1996, c. 1042 (A.B.1683), § 53, eff. Sept. 29, 1996. Amended by Stats.1997, c. 652 (A.B.1518), § 23.)*

§ 34671. Reinstatement; fee; requirements

Except as provided under subdivision (c) of Section 34630 and subdivision (d) of Section 34640, a motor carrier permit suspended or revoked under the provisions of this code shall not be reinstated until a fee of one hundred fifty dollars ($150) has been paid, and the motor carrier permitholder has met all requirements for the issuance of a permit. *(Added by Stats.1996, c. 1042 (A.B.1683), § 53, eff. Sept. 29, 1996. Amended by Stats. 2007, c. 58 (A.B.913), § 4.)*

§ 34672. Payments by dishonored checks; restitution; cancellation of permit

If a motor carrier permit is paid for by a check that is dishonored by the bank, the permit shall be canceled. The department shall notify the carrier that the check was dishonored and that the permit will be canceled 30 days from the date of notification if the applicant does not make restitution. If the applicant does not make restitution for the dishonored check, and pay the dishonored check fee within 30 days of the notice, the application for a motor carrier permit shall be canceled. *(Added by Stats.1996, c. 1042 (A.B.1683), § 53, eff. Sept. 29, 1996. Amended by Stats.2001, c. 825 (S.B.290), § 18.)*

Division 14.9

MOTOR VEHICLE DAMAGE CONTROL

Chapter	Section
1. Short Title	34700
2. General Provisions and Definitions	34710
3. Departmental Action	34725

CHAPTER 1. SHORT TITLE

Section
34700. Short title.

§ 34700. Short title

This division may be cited as the Greene-Harmer Motor Vehicle Damage Control Act. *(Added by Stats. 1971, c. 598, p. 1202, § 1, operative May 3, 1972.)*

CHAPTER 2. GENERAL PROVISIONS AND DEFINITIONS

Section
34710. Passenger vehicle defined.
34715. Energy-absorption system.

§ 34710. Passenger vehicle defined

As used in this division, "passenger vehicle" means any motor vehicle defined in Section 465, except any of the following motor vehicles:

(a) Motorcycles.

(b) Housecars.

(c) Specially constructed vehicles.

(d) Motor vehicles equipped with four-wheel drive.

(e) Motor vehicles constructed on a truck chassis.

(f) Motor vehicles operated for hire, compensation, or profit.

(g) Makes of motor vehicles of a model year manufactured or sold in California in quantities of less than 2,000 units for each such model year.

(h) Motor vehicles designed and constructed by the manufacturer of such vehicles, for off-highway use, as determined by the Department of Motor Vehicles. *(Added by Stats.1971, c. 598, p. 1202, § 1, operative May 3, 1972. Amended by Stats.1973, c. 451, p. 917, § 2; Stats.1974, c. 635, p. 1490, § 7.)*

Cross References

Application of definition, see Vehicle Code § 28070.
House car defined, see Vehicle Code § 362.
Motorcycle defined, see Vehicle Code § 400.

§ 34715. Energy-absorption system

No new passenger vehicle, except a passenger vehicle certified by its manufacturer as having been manufactured prior to September 1, 1973, shall be sold or registered on and after September 1, 1973, unless it has a manufacturer's warranty that it is equipped with an appropriate energy-absorption system that meets the requirement for energy absorption systems set by the National Highway Traffic Safety Administration. *(Added by Stats.1971, c. 598, p. 1202, § 1, operative May 3, 1972. Amended by Stats.1977, c. 880, p. 2650, § 2.)*

Cross References

Bumpers on passenger vehicles, see Vehicle Code § 28070 et seq.

CHAPTER 3. DEPARTMENTAL ACTION

Section
34725. Injunction for violations.

§ 34725. Injunction for violations

Any violation of any provisions of this division may be enjoined in a civil action brought by the Attorney General in the name of the people of the State of California, upon request of the Department of Motor Vehicles, except that it shall not be necessary to show lack of adequate remedy at law or to show irreparable damage or loss. *(Added by Stats.1971, c. 598, p. 1202, § 1, operative May 3, 1972.)*

Division 15

SIZE, WEIGHT AND LOAD

Chapter	Section
1. General Provisions	35000
2. Width	35100
3. Height	35250
4. Length	35400
5. Weight	35550
6. Multistate Highway Transportation Agreement [Repealed]	

Cross References

Trailer defined, application to this division, see Vehicle Code § 630.

CHAPTER 1. GENERAL PROVISIONS

Section

35000. Division refers to vehicles upon highways.

35001. Snow removal devices.

35002. Authorized emergency vehicles; applicability of division; liability.

35003. Booms, masts, machinery, and other equipment.

Cross References

Criteria for issuing arrest warrant for violations, see Vehicle Code § 40509.5.

Power to act by ordinance as power to act by resolution, see Vehicle Code § 32.

Violating weight restrictions, see Vehicle Code § 42030 et seq.

§ 35000. Division refers to vehicles upon highways

The provisions of this division refer exclusively to the size and weight of, and loads upon, vehicles when operated upon the highways. *(Stats.1959, c. 3, p. 1757, § 35000.)*

Cross References

Applicability of this section to trolley coaches, see Vehicle Code § 21051.

Damage to highway, weight or size of vehicle, see Vehicle Code § 17302.

Highway defined, see Vehicle Code § 360.

Law enforcement, California highway patrol, see Vehicle Code § 2400.

§ 35001. Snow removal devices

The provisions of this division, except those requiring a permit for overweight loads, do not apply to motor trucks equipped with snow removal devices. *(Stats.1959, c. 3, p. 1757, § 35001.)*

Cross References

Applicability of this section to trolley coaches, see Vehicle Code § 21051.

Damage to highway, weight or size of vehicle, see Vehicle Code § 17302.

Motor truck defined, see Vehicle Code § 410.

Permits for increased size and weight, see Vehicle Code § 35780 et seq.

§ 35002. Authorized emergency vehicles; applicability of division; liability

(a)(1) This division does not apply to an authorized emergency vehicle owned or operated by a governmental agency while being used in responding to and returning from emergency fire calls, while being moved from place to place in anticipation of emergency fire calls, when used during training in any fire service application or during fire prevention activities, or when vehicles ordinarily used for those purposes are necessarily transported for vehicle maintenance, repair, or service. This subdivision only applies to vehicles purchased prior to January 1, 1994. Vehicles purchased on January 1, 1992, to and including December 31, 1993, shall meet the applicable requirements of Standards 1901 to 1904, inclusive, of the National Fire Protection Association, as those standards were in effect on December 31, 1991.

(2) All vehicles described in paragraph (1) first purchased on or after January 1, 1994, shall comply with the applicable permit requirements adopted by the Department of Transportation.

(3) For purposes of this section, "purchased" means the date that the operating agency enters into a contract to purchase the vehicle.

(b) All vehicles described in subdivision (a) purchased on or after January 1, 1994, shall meet the following requirements:

(1) It shall be the responsibility of the manufacturer to provide a gross axle weight rating (GAWR), gross combined weight rating (GCWR), and gross vehicle weight rating (GVWR), adequate to carry a full water tank with the allowance for personnel and miscellaneous equipment, including hose load, shown in the table below:

	Personnel	Misc. Equipment
Pumpers	1,200 lbs.	2,000 lbs.
Light attack apparatus	600 lbs.	900 lbs.
Water towers	1,200 lbs.	1,500 lbs.
Aerial platforms with ground ladders	1,200 lbs.	2,500 lbs.
Aerial ladders with ground ladders	1,200 lbs.	2,500 lbs.

Fire apparatus shall be weighed and certified by the manufacturer to determine compliance with the table above prior to acceptance by the purchaser. Apparatus and chassis manufacturers shall furnish certification of the gross vehicle weight rating (GVWR), gross combined weight rating (GCWR), and gross axle weight rating (GAWR) on a nameplate affixed to the apparatus.

(2) A fire apparatus exceeding 31,000 pounds gross vehicle weight rating (GVWR) shall be equipped with a retarder.

(3) For purposes of this section, a "fire apparatus" is a vehicle designed, maintained, and used under emergency conditions to transport personnel and equipment, or for the suppression of fires or mitigation of other hazardous situations, consistent with the 2009 edition of Standard 1901 of the National Fire Protection Association.

(4) Notwithstanding the weight exemption provided for in Chapter 7 of Division 2 of Title 21 of the California Code of Regulations, effective on July 2, 2010, nor any other provision of law, a fire apparatus vehicle is prohibited from towing or hauling any other vehicle or equipment while operating under an overweight permit.

(5) This chapter and Chapter 7 of Division 2 of Title 21 of the California Code of Regulations do not limit the discretion of the department or a local government to deny an application for an overweight permit on the basis of good cause.

(c) A vehicle owned, operated, or rented by a public agency that is being used in responding to or returning from an emergency, may be operated as required, if a reasonable effort is first made by the agency to obtain verbal permission from an authorized officer or employee of the agency having jurisdiction of the highways used, and, upon termination of the emergency, when the vehicle is returning from the site of the emergency, the public agency either obtains a permit at the location of the emergency or makes a reasonable effort to obtain verbal permission from an authorized officer or employee of the agency having jurisdiction of the highways used, and obtains a written permit for that use pursuant to Section 35780 not later than three days after the date of the emergency. As used in this subdivision, "emergency" means a condition that poses an imminent threat of loss of property or a hazard to life, as determined by the public agency charged with responsibility to respond thereto.

(d) A governmental agency operating an authorized emergency vehicle or other vehicle subject to this section is liable to the governmental agency having jurisdiction of a state or county highway for the damage to the highway or a highway structure caused by the operation of the vehicle of a size or weight of vehicle or load exceeding that specified in this division. The cost of repair of the damage is a proper charge against the support fund of the governmental agency operating the oversize or overweight vehicle.

(e) Neither the state nor an agency thereof is liable for damage to a highway or highway structure caused by vehicles operated, pursuant to this section, by or on behalf of a local authority or any other local governmental entity. *(Stats.1959, c. 3, p. 1757, § 35002. Amended by Stats.1961, c. 653, p. 1864, § 51, operative Jan. 1, 1962; Stats.1965, c. 1608, p. 3699, § 1; Stats.1982, c. 827, p. 3137, § 1, eff. Sept. 10, 1982; Stats.1984, c. 1110, § 1; Stats.1989, c. 1337, § 3; Stats.1990, c. 899 (A.B.3424),*

948

§ 2, eff. Sept. 14, 1990; Stats.1991, c. 648 (S.B.880), § 2; Stats.1992, c. 1243 (A.B.3090), § 102, eff. Sept. 30, 1992; Stats.1994, c. 1220 (A.B.3132), § 68, eff. Sept. 30, 1994; Stats.2010, c. 487 (S.B.1220), § 1, eff. Sept. 29, 2010.)

Cross References

Authorized emergency vehicle defined, see Vehicle Code § 165.
Retarder defined, see Vehicle Code § 521.

§ 35003. Booms, masts, machinery, and other equipment

For the purpose of this division, booms, masts, machinery or other equipment which is not attendant to the efficient operation of the body of the vehicle but which may be attached to the body or chassis or connected with the driving mechanism, shall be regarded as a load. *(Added by Stats.1968, c. 12, p. 157, § 1.)*

CHAPTER 2.　WIDTH

Section
35100.　　Outside width; safety devices; local ordinances.
35100.1.　Outside width; metric equivalent.
35100.5.　Cotton module movers; width.
35101.　　Pneumatic tires.
35102.　　Loose loads.
35103.　　Exceeding maximum width for vehicle; appurtenance; definitions; use of an appurtenance.
35104.　　Vehicles limited to 120-inch width.
35105.　　Chartered cities.
35106.　　Motor coaches and buses.
35106.5.　Repealed.
35107.　　Urban and suburban service defined.
35108.　　Repealed.
35109.　　Projecting lights, mirrors or devices.
35110.　　Projecting equipment.
35111.　　Loads on passenger vehicles.
35112.　　Repealed.
35114 to 35117.　Repealed.

Cross References

Nonapplicability of chapter to,
　Automatic bale wagons, see Vehicle Code § 36606.
　Implements of husbandry, see Vehicle Code § 36600.
Trailers, semitrailers, lift carriers, and tip-bed trailers transporting implements of husbandry, see Vehicle Code § 36605.

§ 35100. Outside width; safety devices; local ordinances

(a) The total outside width of any vehicle or its load shall not exceed 102 inches, except as otherwise provided in this chapter.

(b) Notwithstanding any other provision of law, safety devices which the Secretary of Transportation determines to be necessary for the safe and efficient operation of motor vehicles shall not be included in the calculation of width as specified in subdivision (a).

(c) Any city or county may, by ordinance, prohibit a combination of vehicles of a total width in excess of 96 inches upon highways under its jurisdiction. The ordinance shall not be effective until appropriate signs are erected indicating the streets affected. *(Stats.1959, c. 3, p. 1758, § 35100. Amended by Stats.1974, c. 972, p. 2022, § 1; Stats.1982, c. 827, p. 3137, § 2, eff. Sept. 10, 1982; Stats.1983, c. 145, § 1.5, eff. June 28, 1983; Stats.1988, c. 1452, § 5.)*

§ 35100.1. Outside width; metric equivalent

For purposes of subdivision (a) of Section 35100, the following apply:

(a) The metric equivalent of 102 inches, 2.6 meters, meets the requirement of Section 35100.

(b) The width measurement of any vehicle with side walls shall be made from the outside wall of the two opposite sides of the vehicle. *(Added by Stats.1988, c. 1452, § 6.)*

§ 35100.5. Cotton module movers; width

The total outside width of a cotton module mover operated on the highways pursuant to Section 35555 and the load thereon shall not exceed 130 inches in width. However, a county board of supervisors, with respect to any or all county highways within its jurisdiction or any portion thereof, may by resolution prohibit or limit the operation of cotton module movers exceeding the maximum width specified in Section 35100. *(Added by Stats.1984, c. 270, § 3, eff. July 3, 1984.)*

§ 35101. Pneumatic tires

When any vehicle is equipped with pneumatic tires, the maximum width from the outside of one wheel and tire to the outside of the opposite outer wheel and tire shall not exceed 108 inches, but the outside width of the body of the vehicle or the load thereon shall not exceed 102 inches.

Vehicles manufactured, reconstructed, or modified after the effective date of amendments to this section enacted during the 1983 portion of the 1983–84 Regular Session of the Legislature, to utilize the 102 inch maximum width dimension, shall be equipped with axles, tires, and wheels of sufficient width to adequately and safely stabilize the vehicle. The Department of the California Highway Patrol shall conduct tests relating to the dynamic stability of vehicles utilizing body widths over 96 inches, up to and including 102 inches, to determine the necessity for establishing performance standards under the authority of Section 34500. Such standards if established shall be consistent with width standards established by or under the authority of the United States Department of

Transportation. *(Stats.1959, c. 3, p. 1758, § 35101. Amended by Stats.1983, c. 145, § 2, eff. June 28, 1983.)*

§ 35102. Loose loads

When any vehicle carries a load of loosely piled agricultural products such as hay, straw, or leguminous plants in bulk but not crated, baled, boxed, or sacked, such load of loosely piled material and any loading racks retaining the same shall not exceed 120 inches in width. *(Stats.1959, c. 3, p. 1758, § 35102.)*

§ 35103. Exceeding maximum width for vehicle; appurtenance; definitions; use of an appurtenance

(a) A vehicle used for recreational purposes may exceed the maximum width established under Section 35100 if the excess width is attributable to an appurtenance, excluding a safety device, that does not exceed six inches beyond either sidewall of the vehicle.

(b) For the purposes of subdivision (a), an appurtenance is an integral part of a vehicle and includes, but is not limited to, awnings, grab handles, lighting equipment, cameras, and vents. An appurtenance may not be used as a load carrying device. *(Added by Stats.2003, c. 222 (A.B.1662), § 3.)*

§ 35104. Vehicles limited to 120-inch width

The limitations as to width do not apply to the following vehicles except that these vehicles shall not exceed a width of 120 inches:

(a) Special mobile equipment.

(b) Special construction or highway maintenance equipment.

(c) Motor vehicles designed for, and used exclusively to, haul feed for livestock that are exempted from registration by subdivision (c) of Section 36102, except when operated on a highway during darkness. *(Stats. 1959, c. 3, p. 1758, § 35104. Amended by Stats.1959, c. 958, p. 2989, § 3; Stats.1961, c. 1659, p. 3627, § 10; Stats.1963, c. 209, p. 950, § 11, eff. April 29, 1963; Stats.1963, c. 2149, p. 4488, § 21; Stats.1982, c. 827, p. 3137, § 4, eff. Sept. 10, 1982; Stats.1984, c. 1021, § 1.)*

Special mobile equipment defined, see Vehicle Code § 575.

§ 35105.   Chartered cities

Any city organized under a freeholders' charter may by ordinance permit a total outside width of vehicle and load in excess of the limits set forth in Sections 35100, 35101, 35102, 35104, and 35106 when the vehicle is used exclusively within the boundary limits of the city. *(Stats. 1959, c. 3, p. 1758, § 35105. Amended by Stats.1983, c. 145, § 4, eff. June 28, 1983.)*

Cross References

Applicability of this section to trolley coaches, see Vehicle Code § 21051.
Damage to highway, weight or size of vehicle, see Vehicle Code § 17302.
Lighting equipment of wide vehicles, see Vehicle Code § 25104.
Special permits for increased size or weight, see Vehicle Code § 35780 et seq.

§ 35106.   Motor coaches and buses

(a) Motor coaches or buses may have a maximum width not exceeding 102 inches.

(b) Notwithstanding subdivision (a), motor coaches or buses operated under the jurisdiction of the Public Utilities Commission in urban or suburban service may have a maximum outside width not exceeding 104 inches, when approved by order of the Public Utilities Commission for use on routes designated by it. Motor coaches or buses operated by common carriers of passengers for hire in urban or suburban service and not under the jurisdiction of the Public Utilities Commission may have a maximum outside width not exceeding 104 inches.

(Added by Stats.1999, c. 724 (A.B.1650), § 50, operative Jan. 1, 2002. Amended by Stats.2006, c. 538 (S.B. 1852), § 665.)

Cross References

Applicability of this section to trolley coaches, see Vehicle Code § 21051.
Bus defined, see Vehicle Code § 233.
Damage to highway, weight or size of vehicle, see Vehicle Code § 17302.
Lighting equipment of wide vehicles, see Vehicle Code § 25104.

§ 35106.5.   Repealed by Stats.1983, c. 145, § 5, eff. June 28, 1983

§ 35107.   Urban and suburban service defined

"Urban and suburban service" means a service performed in urban or suburban areas, or between municipalities in close proximity, except that:

(a) The one-way route mileage of the service shall not be more than 50 miles.

(b) Designated motor coach routes over state highways outside limits of incorporated cities where the one-way route mileage is over 25 miles, but does not exceed 50 miles, shall be approved by the Department of Transportation. *(Stats.1959, c. 3, p. 1758, § 35107. Amended by Stats.1974, c. 545, p. 1337, § 239.)*

Cross References

Lighting equipment of wide vehicles, see Vehicle Code § 25104.

§ 35108.   Repealed by Stats.1983, c. 145, § 6, eff. June 28, 1983

§ 35109.   Projecting lights, mirrors or devices

Lights, mirrors, or devices which are required to be mounted upon a vehicle under this code may extend beyond the permissible width of the vehicle to a distance not exceeding 10 inches on each side of the vehicle. *(Stats.1959, c. 3, p. 1759, § 35109. Amended by Stats. 1963, c. 1666, p. 3209, § 1; Stats.1983, c. 145, § 7, eff. June 28, 1983.)*

Cross References

Permits for overwidth manufactured homes, see Vehicle Code § 35790.
Required lighting equipment, see Vehicle Code § 24250 et seq.

§ 35110.   Projecting equipment

(a) Door handles, hinges, cable cinchers, chain binders, aerodynamic devices, and holders for the display of placards warning of hazardous materials may extend three inches on each side of the vehicle.

(b) For purposes of this section, "aerodynamic devices" means devices using technologies that minimize drag and improve airflow over an entire tractor-trailer vehicle. These include gap fairings that reduce turbulence between the tractor and trailer, side skirts that minimize wind under the trailer, and rear fairings that reduce turbulence and pressure drop at the rear of the trailer, provided that these devices shall not adversely impact the vehicle's swept width and turning characteristics and that the primary purpose of the device is not for advertising. *(Stats.1959, c. 3, p. 1759, § 35110. Amended by Stats.1977, c. 38, p. 415, § 1, eff. May 6, 1977; Stats.1983, c. 145, § 8, eff. June 28, 1983; Stats.2012, c. 727 (S.B.12), § 1.)*

Cross References

Permits for overwidth manufactured homes, see Vehicle Code § 35790.

§ 35111.   Loads on passenger vehicles

No passenger vehicle shall be operated on any highway with any load carried thereon extending beyond the line of the fenders on its left side or more than six inches beyond the line of the fenders on its right side. *(Stats. 1959, c. 3, p. 1759, § 35111. Amended by Stats.1961, c. 120, p. 1129, § 1.)*

Cross References

Applicability of this section to trolley coaches, see Vehicle Code § 21051.
Length of loads, see Vehicle Code § 35406.
Passenger vehicle defined, see Vehicle Code § 465.

§ 35112.   Repealed by Stats.1983, c. 145, § 9, eff. June 28, 1983

§§ 35114 to 35117. Repealed by Stats.1983, c. 145, §§ 10 to 13, eff. June 28, 1983

CHAPTER 3. HEIGHT

Section
35250. Maximum vehicle or load height; exceptions.
35251. Hydraulic boom or mast; restraining.
35252. Pilot cars.

§ 35250. Maximum vehicle or load height; exceptions

No vehicle or load shall exceed a height of 14 feet measured from the surface upon which the vehicle stands, except that a double-deck bus may not exceed a height of 14 feet, 3 inches. Any vehicle or load which exceeds a height of 13 feet, 6 inches, shall only be operated on those highways where deemed to be safe by the owner of the vehicle or the entity operating the bus. *(Stats.1959, c. 3, p. 1760, § 35250. Amended by Stats.1963, c. 2149, p. 4488, § 22; Stats.1969, c. 827, p. 1655, § 1; Stats.1971, c. 1708, p. 3647, § 1, operative May 3, 1972; Stats.1975, c. 240, p. 630, § 1; Stats.1984, c. 849, § 1; Stats.1984, c. 1287, § 1, eff. Sept. 19, 1984.)*

Cross References

Damage to highway, weight or size of vehicle, see Vehicle Code § 17302.
Implement of husbandry defined, see Vehicle Code §§ 36000, 36005.
Implements of husbandry, height exemption, applicability of section, see Vehicle Code § 36610.
Length of loads, see Vehicle Code § 35406.
Manufactured homes exceeding height specifications, permits authorizing exemption, see Vehicle Code § 35790.6.

§ 35251. Hydraulic boom or mast; restraining

(a) A boom or mast which is designed to be raised and lowered by hydraulic mechanisms and which is a constituent part of or an attachment to a vehicle or machine, shall be securely chained or otherwise restrained to ensure compliance with Section 35250 while the vehicle or machine is being transported as a load or driven upon any highway.

(b) Subdivision (a) does not apply when the configuration and design of the hydraulic boom effectively restrain the movement of the boom during transit. *(Added by Stats.1985, c. 695, § 1. Amended by Stats.1994, c. 704 (S.B.1699), § 21.)*

§ 35252. Pilot cars

(a) A pilot car may operate a vertical clearance measuring device with a height in excess of 14 feet when escorting a permitted overheight load. The pilot car may also operate the vertical clearance measuring device when surveying a route for a permitted overheight load.

(b) Any vertical measuring device used by a pilot car shall be designed and operated so as to avoid any damages to overhead structures. The measuring device shall be securely affixed to the pilot car, and shall be operated in a manner that does not create a hazard to surrounding traffic.

(c) The operator of the pilot car shall not reduce the vehicle's speed more than 20 miles per hour below the posted speed limit on the roadway to measure overhead clearance, nor exit the vehicle to measure the clearance of overhead structures from a vantage point on or above the roadway. *(Added by Stats.1988, c. 460, § 5.)*

CHAPTER 4. LENGTH

Section
35400. Restrictions on length; exceptions; transporting bicycles; Route Review Committee; establishment, jurisdiction, and membership; legislative intent.
35400.5. Exception: Cotton module mover.
35400.6. Fifth-wheel travel trailers under specified lengths; exception from length restrictions of Section 35400; delivery documents to include necessary registration information.
35400.7. Alameda-Contra Costa Transit District; bicycle racks on buses.
35400.8. Sacramento Regional Transit District; bicycle racks on buses; route review committee; report to legislative committees.
35400.9. Gold Coast Transit (GCT); bicycle racks on buses; route review committee; report to legislative committees.
35401. Maximum total length of combination of vehicles coupled together; exceptions.
35401.1. Operation of certain combinations of vehicles on highways under local jurisdiction.
35401.3. Combination of vehicles designed to transport motor vehicles or boats; maximum length.
35401.5. Combination of vehicles; exemption from limitations; conditions; access to terminals or facilities; carriers of household goods; special permits for motorsports use.
35401.7. Application of limitations of access to licensed carriers of livestock on State Highway Route 101; conditions.
35401.8. Repealed.
35402. Extension devices.
35403. Safety devices.
35404. Prohibiting highway use; vehicle size.
35405. Repealed.
35406. Loads.
35407. Booms and masts.
35407.5. Booms or masts of certain log loaders; exemption from front-end extension limit; conditions.
35408. Front bumper.
35409. Frontmounted platform.
35410. Projections to the rear.
35411. Combination of vehicles.
35412. Repealed.
35413. Repealed.
35414. Dollies or semitrailers transporting poles, pipes, etc.; exemption from limitations.
35415. Repealed.
35416. Renumbered.
35417. Repealed.

Nonapplicability of chapter to implements of husbandry, see Vehicle Code § 36615.

§ 35400. Restrictions on length; exceptions; transporting bicycles; Route Review Committee; establishment, jurisdiction, and membership; legislative intent

(a) A vehicle may not exceed a length of 40 feet.

(b) This section does not apply to any of the following:

(1) A vehicle used in a combination of vehicles when the excess length is caused by auxiliary parts, equipment, or machinery not used as space to carry any part of the load, except that the combination of vehicles shall not exceed the length provided for combination vehicles.

(2) A vehicle, when the excess length is caused by any parts necessary to comply with the fender and mudguard regulations of this code.

(3)(A) An articulated bus or articulated trolley coach that does not exceed a length of 60 feet.

(B) An articulated bus or articulated trolley coach described in subparagraph (A) may be equipped with a folding device attached to the front of the bus or trolley if the device is designed and used exclusively for transporting bicycles. The device, including any bicycles transported thereon, shall be mounted in a manner that does not materially affect efficiency or visibility of vehicle safety equipment, and shall not extend more than 36 inches from the front body of the bus or trolley coach when fully deployed. The handlebars of a bicycle that is transported on a device described in this subparagraph shall not extend more than 42 inches from the front of the bus.

(4) A semitrailer while being towed by a motortruck or truck tractor, if the distance from the kingpin to the rearmost axle of the semitrailer does not exceed 40 feet for semitrailers having two or more axles, or 38 feet for semitrailers having one axle if the semitrailer does not, exclusive of attachments, extend forward of the rear of the cab of the motortruck or truck tractor.

(5) A bus or house car when the excess length is caused by the projection of a front safety bumper or a rear safety bumper, or both. The safety bumper shall not cause the length of the vehicle to exceed the maximum legal limit by more than one foot in the front and one foot in the rear. For the purposes of this chapter, "safety bumper" means any device that is fitted on an existing bumper or which replaces the bumper and is constructed, treated, or manufactured to absorb energy upon impact.

(6) A schoolbus, when the excess length is caused by the projection of a crossing control arm. For the purposes of this chapter, "crossing control arm" means an extendable and retractable device fitted to the front of a schoolbus that is designed to impede movement of pupils exiting the schoolbus directly in front of the schoolbus so that pupils are visible to the driver while they are moving in front of the schoolbus. An operator of a schoolbus

shall not extend a crossing control arm while the schoolbus is in motion. Except when activated, a crossing control arm shall not cause the maximum length of the schoolbus to be extended by more than 10 inches, inclusive of any front safety bumper. Use of a crossing control arm by the operator of a schoolbus does not, in and of itself, fulfill his or her responsibility to ensure the safety of students crossing a highway or private road pursuant to Section 22112.

(7) A bus, when the excess length is caused by a device, located in front of the front axle, for lifting wheelchairs into the bus. That device shall not cause the length of the bus to be extended by more than 18 inches, inclusive of any front safety bumper.

(8) A bus, when the excess length is caused by a device attached to the rear of the bus designed and used exclusively for the transporting of bicycles. This device may be up to 10 feet in length, if the device, along with any other device permitted pursuant to this section, does not cause the total length of the bus, including any device or load, to exceed 50 feet.

(9) A bus operated by a public agency or a passenger stage corporation, as defined in Section 226 of the Public Utilities Code, used in transit system service, other than a schoolbus, when the excess length is caused by a folding device attached to the front of the bus which is designed and used exclusively for transporting bicycles. The device, including any bicycles transported thereon, shall be mounted in a manner that does not materially affect efficiency or visibility of vehicle safety equipment, and shall not extend more than 36 inches from the front body of the bus when fully deployed. The handlebars of a bicycle that is transported on a device described in this paragraph shall not extend more than 42 inches from the front of the bus. A device described in this paragraph may not be used on a bus that, exclusive of the device, exceeds 40 feet in length or on a bus having a device attached to the rear of the bus pursuant to paragraph (8).

(10)(A) A bus of a length of up to 45 feet when operating on those highways specified in subdivision (a) of Section 35401.5. The Department of Transportation or local authorities, with respect to highways under their respective jurisdictions, may not deny reasonable access to a bus of a length of up to 45 feet between the highways specified in subdivision (a) of Section 35401.5 and points of loading and unloading for motor carriers of passengers as required by the federal Intermodal Surface Transportation Efficiency Act of 1991 (P.L. 102–240).

(B) A bus operated by a public agency and on those highways specified in subparagraph (A) may be equipped with a folding device attached to the front of the bus that is designed and used exclusively for transporting bicycles. The device, including all bicycles transported thereon, may be mounted in a manner that does not materially affect efficiency or visibility of vehicle safety equipment, and may not extend more than 36 inches from the front body of the bus when fully deployed. The handlebars of a bicycle that is transported on a device described in this subparagraph may not extend more than 42 inches from the front of the bus. The total length of the bus, including the folding device or load, may not exceed 48.5 feet. A Route Review Committee, established under this subparagraph, shall review the routes where a public agency proposes to operate a 45–foot bus equipped with a front mounted bicycle rack. The Route Review Committee shall be comprised of one member from the public agency appointed by the general manager of the public agency; one member who is a traffic engineer and is employed and selected by the public agency that has jurisdiction over the largest proportional share of routes among all affected agencies; and one member appointed by the labor organization that is the exclusive representative of the bus drivers of the public agency. If there is no exclusive representative of the bus drivers, a bus driver member shall be chosen by a majority vote of the bus drivers employed by the agency. The members of the Route Review Committee shall be selected not more than 30 days after receipt of a public agency proposal to equip a 45–foot bus with a front mounted bicycle rack. The review shall include a field review of the proposed routes. The purpose of the Route Review Committee is to ensure the safe operation of a 45–foot bus that is equipped with a front mounted bicycle rack. The Route Review Committee, by a unanimous vote, shall make a determination of which routes are suitable for the safe operation of a 45–foot bus that is equipped with a front mounted bicycle rack. These determinations shall be consistent with the operating requirements specified in subparagraph (A). It is the intent of the Legislature that the field review required under this subparagraph include consultation with traffic engineers from affected public agencies that have jurisdiction over segments of the route or routes under review, to ensure coordination with all effected state and local public road agencies that may potentially be impacted due to the operation of a 45–foot bus with a front mounted bicycle rack.

(11)(A) A house car of a length of up to 45 feet when operating on the National System of Interstate and Defense Highways or when using those portions of federal aid primary system highways that have been qualified by the United States Secretary of Transportation for that use, or when using routes appropriately identified by the Department of Transportation or local authorities, with respect to highways under their respective jurisdictions.

(B) A house car described in subparagraph (A) may be operated on a highway that provides reasonable access to facilities for purposes limited to fuel, food, and lodging when that access is consistent with the safe operation of the vehicle and when the facility is within one road mile of identified points of ingress and egress to or from highways specified in subparagraph (A) for use by that vehicle.

(C) As used in this paragraph and paragraph (10), "reasonable access" means access substantially similar to that authorized for combinations of vehicles pursuant to subdivision (c) of Section 35401.5.

(D) Any access route established by a local authority pursuant to subdivision (d) of Section 35401.5 is open for access by a house car of a length of up to 45 feet. In addition, local authorities may establish a process whereby access to services by house cars of a length of up to 45 feet may be applied for upon a route not previously established as an access route. The denial of a request for access to services shall be only on the basis of safety and an engineering analysis of the proposed access route. In lieu of processing an access application, local authorities, with respect to highways under their jurisdiction, may provide signing, mapping, or a listing of highways, as necessary, to indicate the use of these specific routes by a house car of a length of up to 45 feet.

(c) The Legislature, by increasing the maximum permissible kingpin to rearmost axle distance to 40 feet effective January 1, 1987, as provided in paragraph (4) of subdivision (b), does not intend this action to be considered a precedent for any future increases in truck size and length limitations.

(d) Any transit bus equipped with a folding device installed on or after January 1, 1999, that is permitted under subparagraph (B) of paragraph (3) of subdivision (b) or under paragraph (9) of subdivision (b) shall be additionally equipped with any of the following:

(1) An indicator light that is visible to the driver and is activated whenever the folding device is in an extended position.

(2) Any other device or mechanism that provides notice to the driver that the folding device is in an extended position.

(3) A mechanism that causes the folding device to retract automatically from an extended position.

(e)(1) A person may not improperly or unsafely mount a bicycle on a device described in subparagraph (B) of paragraph (3) of subdivision (b), or in paragraph (9) or (10) of subdivision (b).

(2) Notwithstanding subdivision (a) of Section 23114 or subdivision (a) of Section 24002 or any other provision of law, when a bicycle is improperly or unsafely loaded by a passenger onto a transit bus, the passenger, and not the driver, is liable for any violation of this code that is attributable to the improper or unlawful loading of the bicycle. *(Added by Stats.1978, c. 64, p. 180, § 1.5, eff. March 24, 1978, operative Jan. 1, 1980. Amended by Stats.1980, c. 847, p. 2641, § 2; Stats.1981, c. 82, p. 197, § 1; Stats.1986, c. 1378, § 1; Stats.1987, c. 74, § 1; Stats.1991, c. 151 (A.B.226), § 1, eff. July 23, 1991; Stats.1992, c. 391 (A.B.2670), § 1; Stats.1995, c. 766 (S.B.726), § 40; Stats.1998, c. 560 (A.B.1851), § 1; Stats. 2000, c. 860 (A.B.2908), § 10; Stats.2001, c. 658 (A.B.67), § 6, eff. Oct. 10, 2001; Stats.2002, c. 78 (A.B.1765), § 1; Stats.2003, c. 468 (S.B.851), § 30; Stats.2003, c. 399 (A.B.1409), § 1.)*

Damage to highway, weight or size of vehicle, see Vehicle Code
    § 17302.
Definitions,
    Bus, see Vehicle Code § 233.
    Semitrailer, see Vehicle Code § 550.
    Vehicle, see Vehicle Code § 670.
Fenders and mudguards, see Vehicle Code § 27600.

§ 35400.5.   Exception: Cotton module mover

Subdivision (a) of Section 35400 does not apply to a motortruck used solely as a cotton module mover and which does not exceed 48 feet in length. *(Added by Stats.1976, c. 93, p. 151, § 1, eff. April 2, 1976. Amended by Stats.1984, c. 270, § 4, eff. July 3, 1984.)*

§ 35400.6.   Fifth-wheel travel trailers under specified lengths; exception from length restrictions of Section 35400; delivery documents to include necessary registration information

(a) Subdivision (a) of Section 35400 does not apply to a fifth-wheel travel trailer that does not exceed the following lengths:

(1) Forty-eight feet in length from the foremost point of the trailer to the rear extremity of the trailer.

(2)(A) For a fifth-wheel travel trailer with a single axle, 38 feet in length from the kingpin to the rearmost axle.

(B) For a fifth-wheel travel trailer with two or more axles, 40 feet in length from the kingpin to the rearmost axle.

(b) A manufacturer of a fifth-wheel travel trailer described by subdivision (a) shall include in the delivery documents the information necessary to register that fifth-wheel travel trailer, including its overall length pursuant to paragraph (1) of subdivision (a) and a declaration that its length is in compliance with subparagraph (A) or subparagraph (B) of paragraph (2) of subdivision (a). The dealer may reject acceptance of the fifth-wheel travel trailer if this documentation is not provided. *(Added by Stats.2013, c. 548 (A.B.64), § 1.)*

§ 35400.7.   Alameda-Contra Costa Transit District; bicycle racks on buses

(a) Notwithstanding Section 35400, the Alameda–Contra Costa Transit District created pursuant to Part 1 (commencing with Section 24501) of Division 10 of the Public Utilities Code may install a folding device attached to the front of a bus that is designed and used exclusively for transporting bicycles if the following conditions are met:

(1) The device does not extend more than 40 inches from the front body of the bus when fully deployed.

(2) The device, including all bicycles transported thereon, is mounted in a manner that does not materially affect efficiency or visibility of vehicle safety equipment.

(3) The handlebars of a bicycle that is transported on a device described in this subdivision does not extend more than 46 inches from the front of the bus.

(b)(1) The Alameda–Contra Costa Transit District shall establish a route review committee prior to the installation of the initial folding device, pursuant to subdivision (a), on a bus that is 45 feet in length. The purpose of the committee is to ensure the safe operation of a 45–foot bus that is equipped with a front-mounted bicycle rack.

(2) The committee established pursuant to this subdivision shall perform an initial review of the routes on which the district proposes to operate a 45–foot bus equipped with a front-mounted bicycle rack. The review shall include a field review of the proposed routes. It is the intent of the Legislature that the field review required under this paragraph include consultation with traffic engineers from affected public agencies that have jurisdiction over segments of the route or routes under review, to ensure coordination with all affected state and local public road agencies that may potentially be impacted due to the operation of a 45–foot bus with a front-mounted bicycle rack.

(3) By unanimous vote of all voting members, the committee shall make a determination of the routes that are suitable for the safe operation of a 45–foot bus that is equipped with a front-mounted bicycle rack.

(4) Upon any proposal to make substantive changes or additions to approved routes, those changes shall be subject to review and certification pursuant to paragraph (2) prior to being approved by the committee.

(5) The members of the committee shall be selected not more than 30 days after receipt of the district proposal to equip a 45–foot bus with a front-mounted bicycle rack and shall be comprised of the following members:

(A) One member from the district who shall be appointed by the district's general manager and who shall be a voting member of the committee.

(B) One member who is a traffic engineer selected by the district and who shall be a voting member of the committee.

(C) One member appointed by the labor organization that is the exclusive representative of the busdrivers of the district. If there is no exclusive representative of the busdrivers, a busdriver member shall be chosen by a majority vote of the busdrivers employed by the district. This member shall be a voting member of the committee.

(D) One member appointed by the governing board who shall be a representative of the bicycling community and who shall reside in the district. This member shall be a nonvoting member of the committee.

(c) If a folding device is installed pursuant to subdivision (a), the Alameda–Contra Costa Transit District shall submit a report to the Assembly Committee on Transportation and the Senate Committee on Transportation and

Housing on or before December 31, 2014. The report shall include a summary of any incidents where the size of the folding devices was a factor, and a summary of the mobility improvements these folding devices provide. *(Added by Stats.2009, c. 369 (A.B.652), § 1.)*

§ 35400.8. Sacramento Regional Transit District; bicycle racks on buses; route review committee; report to legislative committees

(a) Notwithstanding Section 35400, the Sacramento Regional Transit District, created pursuant to Article 1 (commencing with Section 6500) of Chapter 5 of Division 7 of Title 1 of the Government Code as a joint powers agency, may install a folding device attached to the front of a bus that is designed and used exclusively for transporting bicycles if the following conditions are met:

(1) The device does not extend more than 40 inches from the front body of the bus when fully deployed.

(2) The device, including all bicycles transported on the device, is mounted in a manner that does not materially affect efficiency or visibility of vehicle safety equipment.

(3) The handlebars of a bicycle that is transported on a device described in this subdivision do not extend more than 46 inches from the front of the bus.

(b) For purposes of this section, "district" means the Sacramento Regional Transit District.

(c)(1) The district shall establish a route review committee prior to the installation of the initial folding device, pursuant to subdivision (a), on a bus that is 45 feet in length. The purpose of the committee is to ensure the safe operation of a 45–foot bus that is equipped with a front-mounted bicycle rack.

(2) The committee established pursuant to this subdivision shall perform an initial review of the routes on which the district proposes to operate a 45–foot bus equipped with a front-mounted bicycle rack. The review shall include a field review of the proposed routes, including consultation with licensed traffic engineers from affected public agencies that have jurisdiction over segments of the route or routes under review in order to ensure coordination with all affected state and local public road agencies that may potentially be impacted due to the operation of a 45–foot bus with a front-mounted bicycle rack.

(3)(A) By unanimous vote of all members, the committee shall make a determination of the routes that are suitable for the safe operation of a 45–foot bus that is equipped with a front-mounted bicycle rack.

(B) Before conducting a vote pursuant to subparagraph (A), the committee shall obtain certification approved by a licensed traffic engineer that all proposed routes are safe for travel by 45–foot buses equipped with the bicycle racks specified in subdivision (a).

(4) Upon any proposal to make substantive changes to additions to approved routes, those changes shall be subject to review and certification pursuant to paragraph (2) prior to being approved by the committee.

(5) The members of the committee shall be selected not more than 30 days after receipt of the district's proposal to equip a 45–foot bus with a front-mounted bicycle rack and shall be comprised of the following members:

(A) One member from the district who shall be appointed by the district's general manager and who shall be a voting member of the committee.

(B) One member who is a licensed traffic engineer selected by the governing board of the district and who shall be a voting member of the committee.

(C) One member appointed by the labor organization that is the exclusive representative of the busdrivers of the district. This member shall be a voting member of the committee.

(D) One member appointed by the governing board of the district who shall be a representative of the bicycling community and who shall reside within the area of the district jurisdiction. This member shall be a nonvoting member of the committee.

(d) If a folding device is installed pursuant to subdivision (a), the district shall submit a report in compliance with Section 9795 of the Government Code to the Assembly Committee on Transportation and the Senate Committee on Transportation and Housing on or before December 31, 2018. The report shall include a summary of any vehicular or traffic incidents where the size of the folding device was a factor, and a summary of the mobility improvements that these folding devices provide. *(Added by Stats.2013, c. 95 (A.B.206), § 1.)*

§ 35400.9. Gold Coast Transit (GCT); bicycle racks on buses; route review committee; report to legislative committees

(a) Notwithstanding Section 35400, Gold Coast Transit (GCT), created pursuant to Article 1 (commencing with Section 6500) of Chapter 5 of Division 7 of Title 1 of the Government Code as a joint powers agency, may install a folding device attached to the front of a bus that is designed and used exclusively for transporting bicycles if all of the following conditions are met:

(1) The device does not extend more than 40 inches from the front body of the bus when fully deployed.

(2) The device, including all bicycles transported on the device, is mounted in a manner that does not materially affect efficiency or visibility of vehicle safety equipment.

(3) The handlebars of a bicycle that is transported on a device described in this subdivision do not extend more than 46 inches from the front of the bus.

(b)(1) GCT shall establish a route review committee prior to the installation of the initial folding device, pursuant to subdivision (a), on a bus that is 45 feet in length. The purpose of the committee is to ensure the safe operation of a 45–foot bus that is equipped with a front-mounted bicycle rack.

(2) The committee established pursuant to this subdivision shall perform an initial review of the routes on which GCT proposes to operate a 45–foot bus equipped with a front-mounted bicycle rack. The review shall include a field review of the proposed routes. It is the intent of the Legislature that the field review required under this paragraph include consultation with licensed traffic engineers from affected public agencies that have jurisdiction over segments of the route or routes under review, to ensure coordination with all affected state and local public road agencies that may potentially be impacted due to the operation of a 45–foot bus with a front-mounted bicycle rack.

(3)(A) By unanimous vote of all voting members, the committee shall make a determination of the routes that are suitable for the safe operation of a 45–foot bus that is equipped with a front-mounted bicycle rack.

(B) Before conducting a vote pursuant to subparagraph (A), the committee shall obtain certification approved by a licensed traffic engineer that all proposed routes are safe for travel by 45 foot buses equipped with the bicycle racks specified in subdivision (a).

(4) Upon any proposal to make substantive changes or additions to approved routes, those changes shall be subject to review and certification pursuant to paragraph (2) prior to being approved by the committee.

(5) The members of the committee shall be selected not more than 30 days after receipt of the GCT proposal to equip a 45–foot bus with a front-mounted bicycle rack and shall be comprised of the following members:

(A) One member from GCT who shall be appointed by GCT's general manager and who shall be a voting member of the committee.

(B) One member who is a licensed traffic engineer selected by the governing board of GCT and who shall be a voting member of the committee.

(C) One member appointed by the labor organization that is the exclusive representative of the busdrivers of GCT. If there is no exclusive representative of the busdrivers, a busdriver member shall be chosen by a majority vote of the busdrivers employed by GCT. This member shall be a voting member of the committee.

(D) One member appointed by the governing board of GCT who shall be a representative of the bicycling community and who shall reside within the area of GCT's jurisdiction. This member shall be a nonvoting member of the committee.

(c) If a folding device is installed pursuant to subdivision (a), GCT shall submit a report in compliance with Section 9795 of the Government Code to the Assembly Committee on Transportation and the Senate Committee on Transportation and Housing on or before December 31, 2017. The report shall include a summary of any vehicular or traffic incidents where the size of the folding

956

devices was a factor, and a summary of the mobility improvements that these folding devices provide. *(Added by Stats.2012, c. 376 (A.B.2488), § 1.)*

§ 35401. Maximum total length of combination of vehicles coupled together; exceptions

(a) Except as provided in subdivisions (b), (c), and (d), a combination of vehicles coupled together, including attachments, may not exceed a total length of 65 feet.

(b)(1) A combination of vehicles coupled together, including attachments, that consists of a truck tractor, a semitrailer, and a semitrailer or trailer, may not exceed a total length of 75 feet, if the length of neither the semitrailers nor the trailer in the combination of vehicles exceeds 28 feet 6 inches.

(2) A B–train assembly is excluded from the measurement of semitrailer length when used between the first and second semitrailers of a truck tractor-semitrailer-semitrailer combination of vehicles. However, if there is no second semitrailer mounted to the B–train assembly, it shall be included in the length measurement of the semitrailer to which it is attached.

(c)(1) A tow truck in combination with a single disabled vehicle or a single abandoned vehicle that is authorized to travel on the highways by this chapter is exempt from subdivision (a) when operating under a valid annual transportation permit.

(2) A tow truck, in combination with a disabled or abandoned combination of vehicles that are authorized to travel on the highways by this chapter, is exempt from subdivision (a) when operating under a valid annual transportation permit and within a 100–mile radius of the location specified in the permit.

(3) A tow truck may exceed the 100–mile radius restriction imposed under paragraph (2) if a single trip permit is obtained from the Department of Transportation.

(d) A city or county may, by ordinance, prohibit a combination of vehicles of a total length in excess of 60 feet upon highways under its respective jurisdiction. The ordinance may not be effective until appropriate signs are erected indicating either the streets affected by the ordinance or the streets not affected, as the local authority determines will best serve to give notice of the ordinance.

(e) A city or county, upon a determination that a highway or portion of highway under its jurisdiction cannot, in consideration of public safety, sustain the operation of trailers or semitrailers of the maximum kingpin to rearmost axle distances permitted under Section 35400, may, by ordinance, establish lesser distances consistent with the maximum distances that the highway or highway portion can sustain, except that a city or county may not restrict the kingpin to rearmost axle measurement to less than 38 feet on those highways or highway portions. A city or county considering the adoption of an ordinance shall consider, but not be limited to, consideration of, all of the following:

(1) A comparison of the operating characteristics of the vehicles to be limited as compared to operating characteristics of other vehicles regulated by this code.

(2) Actual traffic volume.

(3) Frequency of accidents.

(4) Any other relevant data.

In addition, the city or county may appoint an advisory committee consisting of local representatives of those interests that are likely to be affected and shall consider the recommendations of the advisory committee in adopting the ordinance. The ordinance may not be effective until appropriate signs are erected indicating the highways or highway portions affected by the ordinance.

This subdivision shall only become operative upon the adoption of an enabling ordinance by a city or county.

(f) Whenever, in the judgment of the Department of Transportation, a state highway cannot, in consideration of public safety, sustain the operation of trailers or semitrailers of the maximum kingpin to rearmost axle distances permitted under Section 35400, the director, in consultation with the Department of the California Highway Patrol, shall compile data on total traffic volume, frequency of use by vehicles covered by this subdivision, accidents involving these vehicles, and other relevant data to assess whether these vehicles are a threat to public safety and should be excluded from the highway or highway segment. The study, containing the conclusions and recommendations of the director, shall be submitted to the Secretary of the Business, Transportation and Housing Agency. Unless otherwise notified by the secretary, the director shall hold public hearings in accordance with the procedures set forth in Article 3 (commencing with Section 35650) of Chapter 5 for the purpose of determining the maximum kingpin to rear axle length, which shall be not less than 38 feet, that the highway or highway segment can sustain without unreasonable threat to the safety of the public. Upon the basis of the findings, the Director of Transportation shall declare in writing the maximum kingpin to rear axle lengths which can be maintained with safety upon the highway. Following the declaration of maximum lengths as provided by this subdivision, the Department of Transportation shall erect suitable signs at each end of the affected portion of the highway and at any other points that the Department of Transportation determines to be necessary to give adequate notice of the length limits.

The Department of Transportation, in consultation with the Department of the California Highway Patrol, shall compile traffic volume, geometric, and other relevant data, to assess the maximum kingpin to rearmost axle distance of vehicle combinations appropriate for those state highways or portion of highways, affected by this section, that cannot safely accommodate trailers or semitrailers of the maximum kingpin to rearmost axle

distances permitted under Section 35400. The department shall erect suitable signs appropriately restricting truck travel on those highways, or portions of highways.

(g) This section shall become operative on January 1, 2010. *(Added by Stats.2006, c. 450 (S.B.1237), § 2, operative Jan. 1, 2009. Amended by Stats.2008, c. 394 (S.B.1228), § 2.)*

Cross References

"B-train assembly" defined, see Vehicle Code § 230.5.
"Semitrailer" defined, see Vehicle Code § 550.
"Truck tractor" defined, see Vehicle Code § 655.

§ 35401.1. Operation of certain combinations of vehicles on highways under local jurisdiction

A combination of vehicles operated pursuant to Section 35400 or 35401 with a kingpin to rearmost axle measurement of greater than 38 feet but not more than 40 feet may be operated on those highways under the jurisdiction of local authorities only where it is deemed to be safe by the owner of the vehicle or the person operating the vehicle and where its operation is not specifically prohibited by local ordinance pursuant to subdivision (d) of Section 35401. *(Added by Stats.1986, c. 1378, § 3.)*

§ 35401.3. Combination of vehicles designed to transport motor vehicles or boats; maximum length

(a) Notwithstanding subdivisions (a) and (b) of Section 35401, a combination of vehicles designed and used to transport motor vehicles, camper units, or boats, which consists of a motortruck and stinger-steered semitrailer, shall be allowed a length of up to 70 feet if the kingpin is at least 3 feet behind the rear drive axle of the motortruck. This combination shall not be subject to subdivision (a) of Section 35411, but the load upon the rear vehicle of the combination shall not extend more than 6 feet 6 inches beyond the allowable length of the vehicle.

(b) A combination of vehicles designed and used to transport motor vehicles, camper units, or boats, which consists of a motortruck and stinger-steered semitrailer, shall be allowed a length of up to 75 feet if all of the following conditions are maintained:

(1) The distance from the steering axle to the rear drive axle of the motortruck does not exceed 24 feet.

(2) The kingpin is at least 5 feet behind the rear drive axle of the motortruck.

(3) The distance from the kingpin to the rear axle of the semitrailer does not exceed 34 feet except that the distance from the kingpin to the rear axle of a triple axle semitrailer does not exceed 36 feet.

This combination shall not be subject to subdivision (a) of Section 35411, but the load upon the rear vehicle of the combination shall not extend more than 6 feet 6 inches beyond the allowable length of the vehicle. *(Added by Stats.1986, c. 736, § 1. Amended by Stats.1991, c. 13 (A.B.37), § 62, eff. Feb. 13, 1991; Stats.1992, c. 70*

(S.B.1302), § 1; Stats.1998, c. 340 (A.B.346), § 2, eff. Aug. 24, 1998; Stats.2000, c. 860 (A.B.2908), § 11.)

§ 35401.5. Combination of vehicles; exemption from limitations; conditions; access to terminals or facilities; carriers of household goods; special permits for motorsports use

(a) A combination of vehicles consisting of a truck tractor and semitrailer, or of a truck tractor, semitrailer, and trailer, is not subject to the limitations of Sections 35400 and 35401, when operating on the Dwight D. Eisenhower National System of Interstate and Defense Highways or when using those portions of federal-aid primary system highways that have been qualified by the United States Secretary of Transportation for that use, or when using routes appropriately identified by the Department of Transportation or local authorities as provided in subdivision (c) or (d), if all of the following conditions are met:

(1) The length of the semitrailer in exclusive combination with a truck tractor does not exceed 48 feet. A semitrailer not more than 53 feet in length shall satisfy this requirement when configured with two or more rear axles, the rearmost of which is located 40 feet or less from the kingpin or when configured with a single axle which is located 38 feet or less from the kingpin. For purposes of this paragraph, a motortruck used in combination with a semitrailer, when that combination of vehicles is engaged solely in the transportation of motor vehicles, camper units, or boats, is considered to be a truck tractor.

(2) Neither the length of the semitrailer nor the length of the trailer when simultaneously in combination with a truck tractor exceeds 28 feet 6 inches.

(b) Subdivisions (b), (d), and (e) of Section 35402 do not apply to combinations of vehicles operated subject to the exemptions provided by this section.

(c) Combinations of vehicles operated pursuant to subdivision (a) may also use highways not specified in subdivision (a) that provide reasonable access to terminals and facilities for purposes limited to fuel, food, lodging, and repair when that access is consistent with the safe operation of the combinations of vehicles and when the facility is within one road mile of identified points of ingress and egress to or from highways specified in subdivision (a) for use by those combinations of vehicles.

(d) The Department of Transportation or local authorities may establish a process whereby access to terminals or services may be applied for upon a route not previously established as an access route. The denial of a request for access to terminals and services shall be only on the basis of safety and an engineering analysis of the proposed access route. If a written request for access has been properly submitted and has not been acted upon within 90 days of receipt by the department or the appropriate local agency, the access shall be deemed automatically approved. Thereafter, the route shall be deemed open for access by all other vehicles of the same type regardless of ownership. In lieu of processing an access application, the Department of Transportation or local authorities with respect to highways under their respective jurisdictions may provide signing, mapping, or a listing of highways as necessary to indicate the use of specific routes as terminal access routes. For purposes of this subdivision, "terminal" means either of the following:

(1) A facility where freight originates, terminates, or is handled in the transportation process.

(2) A facility where a motor carrier maintains operating facilities.

(e) Nothing in subdivision (c) or (d) authorizes state or local agencies to require permits of terminal operators or to charge terminal operators fees for the purpose of attaining access for vehicles described in this section.

(f) Notwithstanding subdivision (d), the limitations of access specified in that subdivision do not apply to licensed carriers of household goods when directly enroute to or from a point of loading or unloading of household goods, if travel on highways other than those specified in subdivision (a) is necessary and incidental to the shipment of the household goods.

(g)(1) Notwithstanding Sections 35400 and 35401, a combination of vehicles consisting of a truck tractor semitrailer combination with a kingpin to rearmost axle measurement limit of not more than 46 feet, a trailer length of not more than 56 feet, and used exclusively or primarily in connection with motorsports, may operate on the routes identified in subdivision (a) as well as on any other routes authorized for that purpose by the Department of Transportation in consultation with the Department of the California Highway Patrol. As used in this subdivision, "motorsports" means an event, and all activities leading up to that event, including, but not limited to, administration, testing, practice, promotion, and merchandising, that is sanctioned under the auspices of the member organizations of the Automobile Competition Committee for the United States.

(2)(A) The Department of Transportation shall conduct a field test of the tractor truck semitrailer combination authorized under paragraph (1) for motorsport trucks with a trailer length of 56 feet to evaluate their performance on various segments of the National Network and transition routes. The Department of Transportation shall, no later than January 1, 2014, submit a report to the Legislature in compliance with Section 9795 of the Government Code that includes the results of the field test and a recommendation, in consultation with the Department of the California Highway Patrol, as to whether the 56 foot trailer length should be reauthorized.

(B) Notwithstanding Section 10231.5 of the Government Code, the requirement for submitting a report under this paragraph is inoperative on January 1, 2018.

(3) This subdivision shall remain in effect only until January 1, 2016, and as of that date is repealed, unless a later enacted statute, that is enacted before January 1, 2016, deletes or extends that date.

(h) The Legislature finds and declares both of the following:

(1) In authorizing the use of 53–foot semitrailers, it is the intent of the Legislature to conform with Section 31111(b)(1)(C) of Title 49 of the United States Code by permitting the continued use of semitrailers of the dimensions as those that were in actual and legal use on December 1, 1982, and does not intend this action to be a precedent for future increases in the parameters of any of those vehicles that would adversely affect the turning maneuverability of vehicle combinations.

(2) In authorizing the department to issue special transportation permits for motorsports, it is the intent of the Legislature to conform with Section 31111(b)(1)(F) of Title 49 of the United States Code. It is also the intent of the Legislature that this action not be a precedent for future increases in the distance from the kingpin to the rearmost axle of semitrailers and trailers that would adversely affect the turning maneuverability of vehicle combinations. *(Added by Stats.1983, c. 145, § 16, eff. June 28, 1983. Amended by Stats.1984, c. 542, § 4; Stats.1984, c. 1287, § 3, eff. Sept. 19, 1984; Stats.1986, c. 1378, § 4; Stats.1987, c. 146, § 2, eff. July 9, 1987; Stats.1992, c. 391 (A.B.2670), § 2; Stats.1996, c. 353 (S.B.1463), § 1; Stats.1998, c. 340 (A.B.346), § 3, eff. Aug. 24, 1998; Stats.2000, c. 860 (A.B.2908), § 12; Stats.2012, c. 292 (S.B.1174), § 1.)*

§ 35401.7. Application of limitations of access to licensed carriers of livestock on State Highway Route 101; conditions

(a) The limitations of access specified in subdivision (d) of Section 35401.5 do not apply to licensed carriers of livestock when those carriers are directly en route to or from a point of loading or unloading of livestock on those portions of State Highway Route 101 located in the Counties of Del Norte, Humboldt, and Mendocino from its junction with State Highway Route 1 near Leggett north to the Oregon border, if the travel is necessary and incidental to the shipment of the livestock.

(b) The exemption allowed under this section does not apply unless all of the following conditions are met:

(1) The length of the truck tractor, in combination with the semitrailer used to transport the livestock, does not exceed a total of 70 feet.

(2) The distance from the kingpin to the rearmost axle of the semitrailer does not exceed 43 feet.

(3) The length of the semitrailer does not exceed a total of 48 feet.

(c) The exemption allowed under this section does not apply to travel conducted on the day prior to, or on the day of, any federally recognized holiday.

(d) This section shall remain in effect only until January 1, 2015, and as of that date is repealed, unless a later enacted statute, that is enacted before January 1, 2015, deletes or extends that date.

(e)(1) If prior to January 1, 2012, the Director of Transportation determines that the only adjustment to State Highway Route 101 possible to accommodate the truck sizes allowed to travel on portions of State Highway Route 101, pursuant to subdivisions (a) and (b) is the removal of any tree that has a diameter of 42 inches or greater, measured outside the bark, at 12 inches above ground on the side adjacent to the highest ground level, the director shall notify the Secretary of State of that determination.

(2) If prior to January 1, 2015, the Director of Transportation determines that safety improvements to the portion of State Highway Route 101 described in subdivision (a) have resulted in the reclassification of the entire segment as a terminal access route pursuant to subdivision (d) of Section 35401.5, the director shall notify the Secretary of State of that determination.

(3) The notice required under paragraph (1) or (2) shall state that it is being made pursuant to this section.

(4) This section is repealed on the date the Secretary of State receives either of the notices described in this subdivision. *(Added by Stats.1999, c. 911 (A.B.1474), § 3. Amended by Stats.2001, c. 413 (A.B.220), § 1; Stats.2003, c. 188 (S.B.127), § 1; Stats.2004, c. 183 (A.B.3082), § 357; Stats.2006, c. 449 (S.B.1224), § 1; Stats.2007, c. 440 (S.B.773), § 1; Stats.2011, c. 172 (A.B.349), § 1.)*

Repeal

For repeal of this section, see its terms.

§ 35401.8. Repealed by Stats.2002, c. 442 (A.B.2051), § 1, operative Jan. 1, 2007

§ 35402. Extension devices

(a) Any extension or device, including any adjustable axle added to the front or rear of a vehicle, used to increase the carrying capacity of a vehicle shall be included in measuring the length of a vehicle, except that a drawbar shall not be included in measuring the length of a vehicle but shall be included in measuring the overall length of a combination of vehicles.

(b) Notwithstanding subdivision (a), extensions of not more than 18 inches in length on each end of a vehicle or combination of vehicles used exclusively to transport vehicles shall not be included in measuring the length of a vehicle or combination of vehicles when the vehicles are loaded.

(c) Notwithstanding subdivision (a), an extension of not more than 18 inches in length on the last trailer in a combination of vehicles transporting loads shall not be included in measuring the length of a vehicle or combination of vehicles when the vehicles are loaded. Additionally, an extension of not more than 18 inches in length on the front of the first trailer in a combination of vehicles transporting loads shall not be included in measuring the length of a vehicle or combination of vehicles when the vehicles are loaded and on highways, other than those highways designated by the United States Department of Transportation as national network routes.

(d) Notwithstanding subdivision (a), any extension or device which is not used to carry any load and which does not exceed three feet in length, added to the rear of a vehicle, and is used exclusively for pushing the vehicle or a combination of vehicles, which vehicle or combination of vehicles is designed and used exclusively to transport earth, sand, gravel, and similar materials, shall be included in measuring the length of the vehicle but shall not be included in measuring the overall length of the combination of vehicles.

(e) Notwithstanding subdivision (a), a truck semitrailer combination, but not a truck tractor and semitrailer combination, may use a sliding fifth wheel, or a truck tractor, semitrailer, trailer, and a truck-trailer combination may use a sliding drawbar, to extend the length of the combination by not more than 2 feet 6 inches while traveling 35 miles per hour or less on any highway, except a freeway. These provisions shall apply, however, to freeway onramps and offramps and freeway connectors. The sliding fifth wheel or drawbar when extended shall not be included in measuring the overall length of the combination of vehicles if the pivot point of the semitrailer connection is more than two feet to the rear of the center of the rearmost axle of the motortruck or if the distance from the pivot point to the center of the rearmost axle of the semitrailer does not exceed 34 feet.

Combinations of vehicles permitted by this subdivision shall be in compliance with the weight limits provided in Article 1 (commencing with Section 35550) of Chapter 5 whenever any drawbar or sliding fifth wheel is extended, contracted, or in any intermediate position as provided for by this subdivision. *(Stats.1959, c. 3, p. 1760, § 35402. Amended by Stats.1967, c. 1280, p. 3083, § 2; Stats.1974, c. 1117, p. 2399, § 1; Stats.1978, c. 481, p. 1607, § 1; Stats.1981, c. 54, p. 105, § 1; Stats.1981, c. 314, p. 1454, § 1; Stats.1999, c. 181 (A.B.1489), § 1; Stats.2000, c. 860 (A.B.2908), § 13.)*

Cross References

Drawbar defined, see Vehicle Code § 300.

§ 35403. Safety devices

Safety devices which are required to be mounted upon a vehicle pursuant to provisions of this code, may extend beyond the permissible length of a vehicle, or a combination of vehicles, to a distance not exceeding 10 inches. *(Added by Stats.1974, c. 1117, p. 2399, § 2.)*

§ 35404. Prohibiting highway use; vehicle size

Any county having a population in excess of 4,000,000 and having within its limits a natural island with an area in excess of 20,000 acres may, by ordinance, prohibit the use of any highway or lane, hereafter established in unincorporated area thereon, (1) by any vehicle exceeding an overall length of 170 inches and an overall width of 65 inches, or (2) by any such vehicle and all vehicles driven by internal combustion engines. Notwithstanding

960

the provisions of Section 906 of the Streets and Highways Code, no such ordinance shall be enacted unless the board of supervisors shall have theretofore adopted, by a four-fifths vote, a resolution determining that the public convenience and necessity require that such highway or lane have a width of 35 feet or less and a roadway width of 22 feet or less.

Any ordinance enacted pursuant to this section shall be subject to Sections 35718 to 35720, inclusive, of this code and shall not apply to authorized emergency vehicles. *(Added by Stats.1969, c. 723, p. 1454, § 1.)*

§ 35405. Repealed by Stats.1967, c. 1280, p. 3084, § 5

§ 35406. Loads

(a) Except as provided in subdivision (b), the load upon any vehicle operated alone, or the load upon the front vehicle of a combination of vehicles, shall not extend more than three feet beyond the foremost part of the front tires of the vehicle or the front bumper of the vehicle, if it is equipped with a front bumper.

(b) When the load is composed solely of vehicles, the load upon the front vehicle of a combination of vehicles shall not extend more than four feet beyond the foremost part of the front tires of the vehicle or the front bumper of the vehicle, if it is equipped with a front bumper. *(Stats.1959, c. 3, p. 1760, § 35406. Amended by Stats. 1972, c. 434, p. 798, § 1.)*

Cross References

Width of projecting equipment, see Vehicle Code § 35110.

§ 35407. Booms and masts

Section 35406 does not apply to the booms or masts of shovels, cranes or water well drilling and servicing equipment carried upon a motor vehicle if the following conditions are met:

(a) The booms or masts shall not extend more than two-thirds of the wheelbase beyond the front tires of such vehicle.

(b) The projecting structure or attachments thereto shall be securely held in place to prevent dropping or swaying.

(c) No part of the structure which extends beyond the front tires shall be less than seven feet from the roadway.

(d) The driver's vision shall not be impaired by the projecting or supporting structure. *(Stats.1959, c. 3, p. 1761, § 35407. Amended by Stats.1959, c. 816, p. 2835, § 1.)*

§ 35407.5. Booms or masts of certain log loaders; exemption from front-end extension limit; conditions

Section 35406 and subdivisions (a) and (d) of Section 35407 do not apply to the booms or masts of a self-propelled heel-boom log loader first sold in this state prior to January 1, 1988, if all of the following conditions are met:

(a) A system of mirrors or other view enhancements permits the driver to see in any area blocked from view.

(b) The log loader is operated together with a four wheeled lead vehicle which remains a reasonable distance ahead to guide the movement of the log loader.

(c) Two-way radio communication equipment is maintained in good working condition on the log loader and the pilot car, and is used between those vehicles during movement upon any highway. *(Added by Stats.1988, c. 550, § 1.)*

§ 35408. Front bumper

In no event shall a front bumper on a motor vehicle be constructed or installed so as to project more than two feet forward of the foremost part of either the fenders or cab structure or radiator, whichever extends farthest toward the front of such vehicle. *(Stats.1959, c. 3, p. 1761, § 35408.)*

§ 35409. Frontmounted platform

(a) Any motor vehicle used for the purpose of taking photographs, motion pictures, or television pictures or for teaching safe driving may be equipped with a dismountable platform or other device extending forward of either the fenders or cab structure or radiator, whichever extends farthest toward the front of such vehicle, for a distance not exceeding five feet while such vehicle is in use for such purpose.

(b) Any device used for the sole purpose of teaching safe driving, as provided in subdivision (a), shall be of a type authorized by the Department of the California Highway Patrol and the Department of Motor Vehicles. *(Stats.1959, c. 3, p. 1761, § 35409. Amended by Stats. 1976, c. 775, p. 1816, § 1; Stats.1979, c. 723, p. 2226, § 37.)*

§ 35410. Projections to the rear

The load upon any motor vehicle alone or an independent load only upon a trailer or semitrailer shall not extend to the rear beyond the last point of support for a greater distance than that equal to two-thirds of the length of the wheelbase of the vehicle carrying such load, except that the wheelbase of a semitrailer shall be considered as the distance between the rearmost axle of the towing vehicle and the rearmost axle of the semitrailer. *(Stats.1959, c. 3, p. 1761, § 35410.)*

Cross References

Axle defined, see Vehicle Code § 230.
Semitrailer defined, see Vehicle Code § 550.
Trailer defined, see Vehicle Code § 630.

§ 35411. Combination of vehicles

(a) Except as provided in subdivision (b), the load upon any combination of vehicles shall not exceed 75 feet measured from the front extremity of the front vehicle or load to the rear extremity of the last vehicle or load.

(b) The load upon any combination of vehicles operating pursuant to Section 35401 or 35401.5, when the overall length of the combination of vehicles exceeds 75 feet, shall be confined within the exterior dimensions of the vehicles. *(Stats.1959, c. 3, p. 1761, § 35411. Amended by Stats.1963, c. 209, p. 950, § 12, eff. April 29, 1963; Stats.1983, c. 145, § 17, eff. June 28, 1983.)*

§ 35412. Repealed by Stats.1961, c. 58, p. 1015, § 66.5, eff. March 31, 1961

§ 35413. Repealed by Stats.1979, c. 723, p. 2226, § 38

§ 35414. Dollies or semitrailers transporting poles, pipes, etc.; exemption from limitations

(a) Except where a load can be transported consistent with the limitations on vehicle and load length specified in other sections of this chapter, the limitations of this chapter as to length of vehicles do not apply when only poles, timbers, pipes, integral structural materials, or single unit component parts, including, but not limited to, missile components, aircraft assemblies, drilling equipment, and tanks not exceeding 80 feet in length are being transported upon any of the following:

(1) Upon a pole or pipe dolly or otherwise lawful trailer used as a pole or pipe dolly in connection with a motor vehicle.

(2) Upon a semitrailer, except for the limitations provided in Section 35410.

(3) Upon a semitrailer and a pole or pipe dolly used in connection with a truck tractor to haul flexible integral structural material.

(b) Poles and the tools and materials incidental to the work to be performed may be transported on a pole or pipe dolly or otherwise lawful semitrailer used as a pole or pipe dolly, transporting not more than three poles not exceeding 80 feet in length and when used by public utility companies or local public agencies engaged in the business of supplying electricity or telephone service, by the Department of Transportation, or by a licensed contractor in the performance of work for a utility, the department, or a local public agency, when such transportation is between a storage yard and job location where such tools and materials are to be used, in which event the limitations of this chapter as to length of vehicles and loads shall not apply. *(Stats.1959, c. 3, p. 1761, § 35414. Amended by Stats.1959, c. 1996, p. 4637, § 44; Stats.1961, c. 1846, p. 3929, § 2; Stats.1963, c. 1045, p. 2342, § 1; Stats.1968, c. 1360, p. 2598, § 1; Stats.1974, c. 545, p. 1337, § 240; Stats.1979, c. 685, p. 2149, § 2; Stats.1984, c. 1287, § 4, eff. Sept. 19, 1984; Stats.1998, c. 135 (A.B. 1719), § 1, eff. July 13, 1998.)*

Cross References

Damage to highway, weight or size of vehicle, see Vehicle Code § 17302.
Implements of husbandry defined, see Vehicle Code §§ 36000, 36005.
Pole or pipe dolly defined, see Vehicle Code § 475.

Semitrailer defined, see Vehicle Code § 550.

Trailer defined, see Vehicle Code § 630.

Warning lamp on trucks with long loads, see Vehicle Code § 25275.

§ 35415. Repealed by Stats.1963, c. 2149, p. 4488, § 23

§ 35416. Renumbered § 36620 and amended by Stats. 1963, c. 2149, p. 4488, § 23.5

§ 35417. Repealed by Stats.1974, c. 479, p. 1112, § 3

CHAPTER 5. WEIGHT

Article		Section
1.	Axle Limits	35550
1.5.	Intermodal Weight Determination Program	35580
2.	Tire Limits	35600
3.	Limit Changes on State Highways	35650
4.	Local Authorities	35700
5.	Bridges and Other Structures	35750
6.	Permits and Agreements	35780

ARTICLE 1. AXLE LIMITS

Section

35550. Maximum weight on single axle or wheels.

35551. Computation of allowable gross weight.

35551.5. Alternative method of computation; combinations of vehicles containing trailers or semitrailers.

35552. Vehicles transporting logs.

35552.5. Repealed.

35553. Exemptions.

35554. Gross weight limit for bus axle; transit buses.

35554. Gross weight limit for bus axle; transit buses.

35555. Cotton module movers or truck tractor pulling a semitrailer that is a cotton module mover; application of weight limitations; operation on state highway; national network routes.

35557. Inspection of vehicle weight certificates; admission in criminal or civil proceedings.

35558. Axle weight scale at loading facility; request to weigh load being transported.

35559. Repealed.

Cross References

Extension devices for vehicles, see Vehicle Code § 35402.

Violation of chapter a misdemeanor, exception, see Vehicle Code § 40000.23.

§ 35550. Maximum weight on single axle or wheels

(a) The gross weight imposed upon the highway by the wheels on any one axle of a vehicle shall not exceed 20,000 pounds and the gross weight upon any one wheel, or wheels, supporting one end of an axle, and resting upon the roadway, shall not exceed 10,500 pounds.

(b) The gross weight limit provided for weight bearing upon any one wheel, or wheels, supporting one end of an axle shall not apply to vehicles the loads of which consist of livestock.

(c) The maximum wheel load is the lesser of the following:

962

(1) The load limit established by the tire manufacturer, as molded on at least one sidewall of the tire.

(2) A load of 620 pounds per lateral inch of tire width, as determined by the manufacturer's rated tire width as molded on at least one sidewall of the tire for all axles except the steering axle, in which case paragraph (1) applies. *(Stats.1959, c. 3, p. 1762, § 35550. Amended by Stats.1959, c. 268, p. 2169, § 1; Stats.1970, c. 831, p. 1564, § 2; Stats.1971, c. 169, p. 222, § 1, operative May 3, 1972; Stats.1975, c. 132, p. 254, § 1; Stats.1975, c. 651, p. 1409, § 1; Stats.1976, c. 48, p. 79, § 1, eff. March 17, 1976; Stats.1979, c. 519, p. 1701, § 1; Stats.1987, c. 718, § 2; Stats.1989, c. 632, § 1; Stats.1996, c. 1154 (A.B.3020), § 82, eff. Sept. 30, 1996.)*

Cross References

Applicability of this section to trolley coaches, see Vehicle Code § 21051.

Axle, definition of, see Vehicle Code § 230.

Computation of allowable gross weight, see Vehicle Code § 35551.

Excess weights one offense, see Vehicle Code § 42031.

Gross weights per inch on solid and metal tires, see Vehicle Code §§ 35600, 35601.

Hauling of saw logs, see Vehicle Code § 35785.

Manufactured homes, permit to move, compliance with this section, see Vehicle Code § 35790.

Special permits, see Vehicle Code § 35780 et seq.

Weight limitations on bridges and other structures, see Vehicle Code § 35750 et seq.

§ 35551. Computation of allowable gross weight

(a) Except as otherwise provided in this section or Section 35551.5, the total gross weight in pounds imposed on the highway by any group of two or more consecutive axles shall not exceed that given for the respective distance in the following table:

Distance in feet between the extremes of any group of 2 or more consecutive axles	2 axles	3 axles	4 axles	5 axles	6 axles
4	34,000	34,000	34,000	34,000	34,000
5	34,000	34,000	34,000	34,000	34,000
6	34,000	34,000	34,000	34,000	34,000
7	34,000	34,000	34,000	34,000	34,000
8	34,000	34,000	34,000	34,000	34,000
9	39,000	42,500	42,500	42,500	42,500
10	40,000	43,500	43,500	43,500	43,500
11	40,000	44,000	44,000	44,000	44,000
12	40,000	45,000	50,000	50,000	50,000
13	40,000	45,500	50,500	50,500	50,500
14	40,000	46,500	51,500	51,500	51,500
15	40,000	47,000	52,000	52,000	52,000
16	40,000	48,000	52,500	52,500	52,500
17	40,000	48,500	53,500	53,500	53,500
18	40,000	49,500	54,000	54,000	54,000
19	40,000	50,000	54,500	54,500	54,500
20	40,000	51,000	55,500	55,500	55,500
21	40,000	51,500	56,000	56,000	56,000
22	40,000	52,500	56,500	56,500	56,500
23	40,000	53,000	57,500	57,500	57,500
24	40,000	54,000	58,000	58,000	58,000
25	40,000	54,500	58,500	58,500	58,500
26	40,000	55,500	59,500	59,500	59,500
27	40,000	56,000	60,000	60,000	60,000

Distance in feet between the extremes of any group of 2 or more consecutive axles	2 axles	3 axles	4 axles	5 axles	6 axles
28	40,000	57,000	60,500	60,500	60,500
29	40,000	57,500	61,500	61,500	61,500
30	40,000	58,500	62,000	62,000	62,000
31	40,000	59,000	62,500	62,500	62,500
32	40,000	60,000	63,500	63,500	63,500
33	40,000	60,000	64,000	64,000	64,000
34	40,000	60,000	64,500	64,500	64,500
35	40,000	60,000	65,500	65,500	65,500
36	40,000	60,000	66,000	66,000	66,000
37	40,000	60,000	66,500	66,500	66,500
38	40,000	60,000	67,500	67,500	67,500
39	40,000	60,000	68,000	68,000	68,000
40	40,000	60,000	68,500	70,000	70,000
41	40,000	60,000	69,500	72,000	72,000
42	40,000	60,000	70,000	73,280	73,280
43	40,000	60,000	70,500	73,280	73,280
44	40,000	60,000	71,500	73,280	73,280
45	40,000	60,000	72,000	76,000	80,000
46	40,000	60,000	72,500	76,500	80,000
47	40,000	60,000	73,500	77,500	80,000
48	40,000	60,000	74,000	78,000	80,000
49	40,000	60,000	74,500	78,500	80,000
50	40,000	60,000	75,500	79,000	80,000
51	40,000	60,000	76,000	80,000	80,000
52	40,000	60,000	76,500	80,000	80,000
53	40,000	60,000	77,500	80,000	80,000
54	40,000	60,000	78,000	80,000	80,000
55	40,000	60,000	78,500	80,000	80,000
56	40,000	60,000	79,500	80,000	80,000
57	40,000	60,000	80,000	80,000	80,000
58	40,000	60,000	80,000	80,000	80,000
59	40,000	60,000	80,000	80,000	80,000
60	40,000	60,000	80,000	80,000	80,000

(b) In addition to the weights specified in subdivision (a), two consecutive sets of tandem axles may carry a gross weight of 34,000 pounds each if the overall distance between the first and last axles of the consecutive sets of tandem axles is 36 feet or more. The gross weight of each set of tandem axles shall not exceed 34,000 pounds and the gross weight of the two consecutive sets of tandem axles shall not exceed 68,000 pounds.

(c) The distance between axles shall be measured to the nearest whole foot. When a fraction is exactly six inches, the next larger whole foot shall be used.

(d) Nothing contained in this section shall affect the right to prohibit the use of any highway or any bridge or other structure thereon in the manner and to the extent specified in Article 4 (commencing with Section 35700) and Article 5 (commencing with Section 35750) of this chapter.

(e) The gross weight limits expressed by this section and Section 35550 shall include all enforcement tolerances. *(Added by Stats.1981, c. 467, p. 1721, § 2, eff. Sept. 13, 1981, operative Dec. 31, 1984. Amended by Stats.1982, c. 827, p. 3139, § 13, eff. Sept. 10, 1982.)*

Cross References

Applicability of this section to trolley coaches, see Vehicle Code § 21051.

Axle defined, see Vehicle Code § 230.

Hauling of saw logs, see Vehicle Code § 35785.

Manufactured homes, permit to move, compliance with this section, see Vehicle Code § 35790.

§ 35551.5. Alternative method of computation; combinations of vehicles containing trailers or semitrailers

(a) The provisions of this section shall apply only to combinations of vehicles which contain a trailer or semitrailer. Each vehicle in such combination of vehicles, and every such combination of vehicles, shall comply with either Section 35551 or with subdivisions (b), (c), and (d) of this section.

(b) The gross weight imposed upon the highway by the wheels on any one axle of a vehicle shall not exceed 18,000 pounds and the gross weight upon any one wheel, or wheels, supporting one end of an axle and resting upon the roadway, shall not exceed 9,500 pounds, except that the gross weight imposed upon the highway by the wheels on any front steering axle of a motor vehicle shall not exceed 12,500 pounds. The gross weight limit provided for weight bearing upon any one wheel, or wheels, supporting one end of an axle shall not apply to vehicles the loads of which consist of livestock. The following vehicles are exempt from the front axle weight limits specified in this subdivision:

(1) Trucks transporting vehicles.

(2) Trucks transporting livestock.

(3) Dump trucks.

(4) Cranes.

(5) Buses.

(6) Transit mix concrete or cement trucks, and trucks that mix concrete or cement at, or adjacent to, a jobsite.

(7) Motor vehicles that are not commercial vehicles.

(8) Vehicles operated by any public utility furnishing electricity, gas, water, or telephone service.

(9) Trucks or truck tractors with a front axle at least four feet to the rear of the foremost part of the truck or truck tractor, not including the front bumper.

(10) Trucks transporting garbage, rubbish, or refuse.

(11) Trucks equipped with a fifth wheel when towing a semitrailer.

(12) Tank trucks which have a cargo capacity of at least 1,500 gallons.

(13) Trucks transporting bulk grains or bulk livestock feed.

(c) The total gross weight with load imposed on the highway by any group of two or more consecutive axles of a vehicle in such combination of vehicles or of such combination of vehicles where the distance between the first and last axles of the two or more consecutive axles is 18 feet or less shall not exceed that given for the respective distance in the following table:

Distance in feet between first and last axles of group	Allowed load in pounds on group of axles
4	32,000
5	32,000
6	32,200
7	32,900
8	33,600
9	34,300
10	35,000
11	35,700
12	36,400
13	37,100
14	43,200
15	44,000
16	44,800
17	45,600
18	46,400

(d) The total gross weight with load imposed on the highway by any vehicle in such combination of vehicles or of such combination of vehicles where the distance between the first and last axles is more than 18 feet shall not exceed that given for the respective distances in the following table:

Distance in feet	Allowed load in pounds
19	47,200
20	48,000
21	48,800
22	49,600
23	50,400
24	51,200
25	55,250
26	56,100
27	56,950
28	57,800
29	58,650
30	59,500
31	60,350
32	61,200
33	62,050
34	62,900
35	63,750
36	64,600
37	65,450
38	66,300
39	68,000
40	70,000
41	72,000
42	73,280
43	73,280
44	73,280
45	73,280
46	73,280
47	73,280
48	73,280
49	73,280
50	73,280
51	73,280
52	73,600
53	74,400
54	75,200
55	76,000
56 or over	76,800

(e) The distance between axles shall be measured to the nearest whole foot. When a fraction is exactly six inches, the next larger whole foot shall be used.

(f) The gross weight limits expressed by this section shall include all enforcement tolerances.

(g) Nothing in this section shall affect the right to prohibit the use of any highway or any bridge or other structure thereon in the manner and to the extent specified in Article 4 (commencing with Section 35700) and Article 5 (commencing with Section 35750) of Chapter 5 of Division 15.

(h) The Legislature, in enacting this section, does not intend to increase, and this section shall not be construed to allow, statutory weights any greater than existed prior to January 1, 1976. *(Added by Stats.1980, c. 784, p. 2379, § 4.)*

Cross References

Definitions,
  Axle, see Vehicle Code § 230.
  Bus, see Vehicle Code § 233.
  Commercial vehicle, see Vehicle Code § 260.
  Semitrailer, see Vehicle Code § 550.
  Trailer, see Vehicle Code § 630.
  Truck tractor, see Vehicle Code § 655.

§ 35552. Vehicles transporting logs

(a) This section applies only to trucks and vehicle combinations while transporting loads composed solely of logs.

(b) One set of tandem axles of such a truck or vehicle combination shall be deemed to be in compliance with Section 35551 if the total gross weight of 34,000 pounds on such a set that is permitted by Section 35551 is not exceeded by more than 1,500 pounds. In addition, such a truck and vehicle combination that has two consecutive sets of tandem axles shall be deemed to be in compliance with Section 35551 if such consecutive sets of tandem axles do not carry a combined total gross weight of more than 69,000 pounds, if the total gross weight on any one such set does not exceed 35,500 pounds, and if the overall distance between the first and last axle of such consecutive sets of tandem axles is 34 feet or more. All such truck and vehicle combinations shall be subject to all other provisions of Section 35551 or any other provision made applicable to the total gross weight of such a truck or vehicle combination in lieu of Section 35551.

(c) The gross weight limits expressed in this section shall include all enforcement tolerances.

(d) If any total gross weight permitted by this section is exceeded, the allowed weight in pounds set forth in subdivision (a) of Section 35551 shall be the maximum permitted weight for purposes of determining the amount of fine for such violation as specified in the table in Section 42030; except that, whenever the violation is for exceeding the total gross weight for two consecutive sets of tandem axles, and if the overall distance between the first and last axle of such sets is 34 feet or more, the allowed weight on the two consecutive sets shall be 68,000 pounds.

(e) This section shall have no application to highways which are a part of the National System of Interstate and Defense Highways (as referred to in subdivision (a) of Section 108 of the Federal-aid Highway Act of 1956).[1]

This section may be cited as the Christensen-Belotti Act. *(Stats.1959, c. 3, p. 1763, § 35552. Amended by Stats.1959, c. 63, p. 1926, § 1; Stats.1961, c. 1266, p. 3044, § 1; Stats.1975, c. 651, p. 1411, § 4; Stats.1976, c. 249, p. 519, § 1, eff. June 21, 1976.)*

[1] 23 U.S.C.A. § 101.

§ 35552.5. Repealed by Stats.1975, c. 651, p. 1412, § 5

§ 35553. Exemptions

The provisions of this article shall not apply to any vehicle in the immediate vicinity of an unloading or loading area while actually preparing for or in the process of unloading or loading, provided any overload is incidental to and necessitated by such action; and provided that such action does not occur on a bridge or highway structure.

This section shall have no application to highways which are a part of the national system of interstate and defense highways (as referred to in subdivision (a) of Section 108 of the Federal-aid Highway Act of 1956) [1]. *(Added by Stats.1965, c. 537, p. 1867, § 3. Amended by Stats.1972, c. 733, p. 1323, § 2.)*

[1] 23 U.S.C.A. § 108(a).

§ 35554. Gross weight limit for bus axle; transit buses

Section operative until Jan. 1, 2015. See, also, section operative Jan. 1, 2015.

(a)(1) Notwithstanding Section 35550, the gross weight on any one axle of a bus shall not exceed 20,500 pounds.

(2) A transit bus procured through a solicitation process pursuant to which a solicitation was issued before January 1, 2013, or though a solicitation process pursuant to subdivision (d) is not subject to this subdivision.

(b) A transit bus is not subject to Section 35550.

(c) A transit bus shall not operate on the Dwight D. Eisenhower System of Interstate and Defense Highways in excess of the weight limitation for transit buses specified in federal law.

(d)(1) A publicly owned or operated transit system or an operator of a transit system under contract with a publicly owned or operated transit system shall not procure, through a solicitation process pursuant to which a solicitation is issued on or after January 1, 2013, a transit bus whose weight on any single axle exceeds 20,500 pounds except as follows:

(A) It may procure and operate a new bus exceeding 20,500 pounds that is of the same or lesser weight than the bus it is replacing.

(B) It may procure and operate a new transit bus exceeding 20,500 pounds in order to incorporate a new fleet class into its inventory if its governing board adopts a finding at a public hearing that the fleet class expansion or change in fleet classes is necessary to address a need to serve a new or existing market pursuant to its most recently adopted short-range transit plan, or to meet a federal, state, or regional statutory or regulatory requirement, and includes a consideration of vehicle needs and fleet size.

(2) If the governing board of the publicly owned or operated transit system holds a public hearing to consider a procurement made pursuant to subparagraph (A) or (B) of paragraph (1), the board shall provide written notice to those cities and counties on whose roads the bus would travel of the public hearing at which this procurement is to be considered and shall place in the public record any comment of concern the board receives about the procurement.

(3) For purposes of this subdivision "fleet class" means a group of transit buses designated by a publicly owned or operated transit system or an operator under contract with a publicly owned or operated transit system that owns those transit buses, if the transit buses have a combination of two or more of the following similar defining characteristics:

(A) Length.

(B) Seating capacity.

(C) Number of axles.

(D) Fuel or power system.

(E) Width.

(F) Structure.

(G) Equipment package.

(e) This section shall remain in effect only until January 1, 2015, and as of that date is repealed, unless a later enacted statute, that is enacted before January 1, 2015, deletes or extends that date. *(Added by Stats.1975, c. 651, p. 1412, § 6. Amended by Stats.1982, c. 827, p. 3140, § 14, eff. Sept. 10, 1982; Stats.2012, c. 771 (A.B. 1706), § 3.)*

Repeal

For repeal of this section, see its terms.

§ 35554. Gross weight limit for bus axle; transit buses

Section operative Jan. 1, 2015. See, also, section operative until Jan. 1, 2015.

(a)(1) Notwithstanding Section 35550, the gross weight on any one axle of a bus shall not exceed 20,500 pounds.

(2) A transit bus procured through a solicitation process pursuant to which a solicitation was issued before January 1, 2013, is not subject to this subdivision.

(b) A transit bus is not subject to Section 35550.

(c) This section shall become operative on January 1, 2015. *(Added by Stats.2012, c. 771 (A.B.1706), § 4, operative Jan. 1, 2015.)*

§ 35555. Cotton module movers or truck tractor pulling a semitrailer that is a cotton module mover; application of weight limitations; operation on state highway; national network routes

(a) During the period commencing September 15 of each year and ending March 15 of the following year, the weight limitations of Section 35551 do not apply to any cotton module mover or any truck tractor pulling a semitrailer that is a cotton module mover, when operated as follows:

(1) Laterally across a state highway at grade of the state highway.

(2) Upon any county highway within the Counties of Butte, Colusa, Fresno, Glenn, Imperial, Kern, Kings, Madera, Merced, Riverside, Sacramento, San Benito, San Bernardino, San Joaquin, Stanislaus, Sutter, Tehama, Tulare, Yolo, and Yuba, except as prohibited or limited on county highways or portions thereof by resolution of the county board of supervisors having jurisdiction.

(b) A cotton module mover may be operated upon a state highway within the counties and during the period set forth in subdivision (a) if all of the following are met:

(1) The operator is in possession of a driver's license of the class required for operation of the mover.

(2) The mover is operated in compliance with Sections 24002 and 24012; Article 1 (commencing with Section 24250) of, Article 3 (commencing with Section 24600) of, Article 4 (commencing with Section 24800) of, Article 5 (commencing with Section 24950) of, Article 6 (commencing with 25100) of, Article 9 (commencing with 25350) of, Article 11 (commencing with 25450) of, Chapter 2 of Division 12; and Article 2 (commencing with 26450) and Article 3 (commencing with 26502) of Chapter 3 of Division 12.

(3) The mover does not exceed the maximum allowable gross axle weight for tandem axles set forth in Section 35551 by more than 6,000 pounds.

(4) The operator of a mover that exceeds the maximum allowable gross axle weight for tandem axle vehicles as set forth in Section 35551 shall possess a commercial driver's license as defined in subdivision (a) of Section 15210.

(c) This section does not apply to those highways designated by the United States Department of Transportation as national network routes. *(Added by Stats.1980, c. 1147, p. 3712, § 1, eff. Sept. 29, 1980. Amended by Stats.1981, c. 131, p. 881, § 1, eff. June 30, 1981; Stats. 1984, c. 270, § 5, eff. July 3, 1984; Stats.1985, c. 106, § 167; Stats.1989, c. 1361, § 1, eff. Oct. 2, 1989; Stats. 1996, c. 323 (A.B.2244), § 1, eff. July 29, 1996; Stats.2001, c. 497 (S.B.964), § 1, eff. Oct. 4, 2001.)*

966

§ 35557. Inspection of vehicle weight certificates; admission in criminal or civil proceedings

(a) Only upon request to, and approval by, and in accordance with regulations adopted by, the Director of Food and Agriculture, all of the following are available for inspection by district attorneys and are subject to legal process for admission in any criminal or civil proceeding arising out of a violation of this chapter:

(1) Vehicle weight certificates issued on or after January 1, 1984, pursuant to Chapter 7 (commencing with Section 12700), Chapter 7.3 (commencing with Section 12740), and Chapter 7.7 (commencing with Section 12770) of Division 5 of the Business and Professions Code.

(2) Other records of vehicle weight relating to those certificates.

(3) Copies of those certificates and records.

(b) All certificates, records, and copies thereof, issued before January 1, 1984, shall not be available for inspection and are not admissible in any criminal or civil proceedings arising out of a violation of this chapter. *(Added by Stats.1983, c. 1319, § 1.)*

§ 35558. Axle weight scale at loading facility; request to weigh load being transported

Any person or business which has an axle weight scale at its loading facilities shall, upon the request of the driver, weigh any load being transported for that person or business before the vehicle leaves the loading facility. In a port facility, this requirement only applies if the scale is located in outbound lanes. The request to weigh shall be based upon a reasonable assumption that the load is overweight. *(Added by Stats.1990, c. 217 (A.B.1683), § 1.)*

§ 35559. Repealed by Stats.2001, c. 504 (A.B.1280), § 9

ARTICLE 1.5. INTERMODAL WEIGHT DETERMINATION PROGRAM

Section
35580. Legislative findings and declarations.
35581. Plan for implementation of scale facilities at major intermodal terminals; development; inclusions; submission to legislature; exemptions.

§ 35580. Legislative findings and declarations

(a) The Legislature finds and declares that a substantial number of container trailers using California highways exceed weight limitations authorized for California highways. Intermodal container trailers are containers which have been unloaded from ships or trains and placed on truck chassis, or are piggyback trailers unloaded from trains, for subsequent transport upon the highways. Container trailers are usually loaded by shippers in other states or foreign countries where gross and axle weight restrictions imposed by this code are of no concern to the loader. These loading practices often result in overweight vehicles traveling on California highways, which contributes to highway deterioration.

(b) The Legislature further finds and declares that the continued growth of intermodal transportation within the United States and the Pacific Rim makes it important for California to initiate a program to allow intermodal freight to be weighed at major terminal locations prior to operation on the highways, to ensure that these vehicles are within the established weight limits. The Legislature finds that the imposition of heavy fines and assessments is one means of reducing the number of overweight vehicles on the highways. A more effective, and preferable, alternative is to assure that intermodal container trailers are properly loaded at the outset by the party responsible for loading goods into the container trailer, so that vehicles meet weight requirements prior to their operation on the highways. *(Added by Stats.1988, c. 865, § 1.)*

§ 35581. Plan for implementation of scale facilities at major intermodal terminals; development; inclusions; submission to legislature; exemptions

(a) The Department of Transportation, in cooperation with the Department of the California Highway Patrol, shall develop a plan for implementing or identifying new or existing scale facilities at major intermodal terminals which may serve as intermodal weighing facilities for weighing commercial vehicles which transport intermodal freight, prior to their entry onto any highway which is not specifically exempted from weight limitations by a local authority. The plan shall include consideration of options for financing the construction of required intermodal weighing facilities. The plan shall be submitted to the Legislature not later than August 1, 1989.

(b) The Department of Transportation may enter into agreements with local authorities or private entities to provide for exemption from weight restrictions for short distance movement to an intermodal weighing facility.

(Added by Stats.1988, c. 865, § 1. Amended by Stats.1990, c. 1455 (S.B.2374), § 28; Stats.1993, c. 272 (A.B.301), § 53, eff. Aug. 2, 1993; Stats.2001, c. 745 (S.B.1191), § 229, eff. Oct. 12, 2001.)

ARTICLE 2. TIRE LIMITS

Section
35600. Solid tires.
35601. Metal tires.

§ 35600. Solid tires

The gross weight upon a solid tire upon a vehicle shall not exceed 600 pounds upon any inch of the channel base width of such tire. *(Stats.1959, c. 3, p. 1764, § 35600.)*

Cross References

Solid tire defined, see Vehicle Code § 560.

§ 35601. Metal tires

The gross weight of any vehicle and load resting upon any metal tire in contact with the roadway shall not

exceed 500 pounds upon any inch of the width of such tire but this limitation shall not apply to traction engines or tractors, the propulsive power of which is not exerted through wheels resting upon the roadway but by means of a flexible band or chain, known as a movable track, when the portions of the movable tracks in contact with the surface of the roadway present plane surfaces. *(Stats. 1959, c. 3, p. 1764, § 35601.)*

Cross References

Metal tire defined, see Vehicle Code § 395.

ARTICLE 3. LIMIT CHANGES ON STATE HIGHWAYS

Section
35650. Increases.
35651. Decreases.
35652. Notice of hearing.
35653. Hearing.
35654. Erection of signs.
35655. Violation of decreased restriction.
35655.5. Interstate 580 from Oakland to San Leandro; vehicle weight restriction.
35655.6. State Route 2 from La Canada Flintridge to Los Angeles County; vehicle weight restriction.

Cross References

Department of Transportation, see Government Code § 14000 et seq.

§ 35650. Increases

The Department of Transportation, whenever it determines after an engineering investigation that any highway under its jurisdiction will with safety to itself sustain vehicles and loads weighing more than the maximum weight limits set forth in this code, shall have authority to declare and to fix a weight limit for the highway greater than the maximum weight limit set forth in this code. Thereafter it shall be lawful to operate or move vehicles and loads of a gross weight upon the highways designated, equal to but not in excess of the maximum weight limit fixed by the department. *(Stats.1959, c. 3, p. 1764, § 35650. Amended by Stats.1974, c. 545, p. 1338, § 241.)*

§ 35651. Decreases

Whenever in the judgment of the Department of Transportation any state highway will not with safety to itself sustain the maximum weights permitted under this code for the highway, the department shall determine, after a public hearing, the maximum weight which the highway will sustain. *(Stats.1959, c. 3, p. 1764, § 35651. Amended by Stats.1974, c. 545, p. 1338, § 242.)*

§ 35652. Notice of hearing

The Department of Transportation shall give notice of the time and place of the hearing by posting a notice in the county seat of each county in which any affected portion of the highway is located and shall also post copies of the notice at intervals of not more than one mile along said highway and a notice at each end of the affected portion thereof. Notice of the hearing shall be given for not less than 10 days and the hearing shall be had at the county seat of the county in which the affected highway is situated or at some other place convenient to the portion of the highway affected. *(Stats.1959, c. 3, p. 1764, § 35652. Amended by Stats.1974, c. 545, p. 1338, § 243.)*

§ 35653. Hearing

The hearing shall be conducted by one or more engineers appointed by the Director of Transportation. The engineers shall hear all evidence presented at the time and place mentioned in the notice and shall report findings made in writing to the Director of Transportation. Upon the basis of the findings, the Director of Transportation shall declare in writing the maximum weight which can be maintained with safety upon the state highway. In no event shall the weight be less than 16,000 pounds. *(Stats.1959, c. 3, p. 1765, § 35653. Amended by Stats.1974, c. 545, p. 1338, § 244.)*

§ 35654. Erection of signs

Following the declaration of maximum weight as provided in this article, the Department of Transportation shall erect suitable signs at each end of the affected portion of the highway and at such other points as the department deems necessary to give adequate notice of the weight limits. *(Stats.1959, c. 3, p. 1765, § 35654. Amended by Stats.1974, c. 545, p. 1338, § 245.)*

Cross References

Weight violations, penalty, see Vehicle Code § 42030 et seq.

§ 35655. Violation of decreased restriction

(a) No person shall drive a vehicle on any state highway when the weight of the vehicle and load is greater than the maximum weight which the highway will sustain. Violations of this subdivision shall be punished in accordance with the schedule of fines set forth in Section 42030.

(b) Upon the trial of any person charged with a violation with respect to signs erected under Section 35654, proof of the determination and the maximum weight by the Department of Transportation and the existence of the signs constitutes prima facie evidence of the maximum weight which the state highway will sustain. *(Stats.1959, c. 3, p. 1765, § 35655. Amended by Stats. 1974, c. 545, p. 1338, § 246; Stats.1984, c. 542, § 5.)*

Cross References

Damage to highway, weight or size of vehicle, see Vehicle Code § 17302.

§ 35655.5. Interstate 580 from Oakland to San Leandro; vehicle weight restriction

(a) Notwithstanding this article or any other provision of law, no vehicle, as described in Sections 410 and 655, with a gross weight of 9,000 pounds or more, shall be operated on the segment of Interstate Route 580 (I–580)

that is located between Grand Avenue in the City of Oakland and the city limits of the City of San Leandro. This subdivision does not apply to passenger buses or paratransit vehicles.

(b) The Department of Transportation shall erect suitable signs at each end of the portion of highway described in subdivision (a) and at any other points that the department deems necessary to give adequate notice of the weight limit imposed under this section. *(Added by Stats.2000, c. 212 (A.B.500), § 1.)*

§ 35655.6. State Route 2 from La Canada Flintridge to Los Angeles County; vehicle weight restriction

(a) Except as provided in subdivision (b), a person shall not drive a commercial vehicle with three or more axles, or a gross vehicle weight or a combined gross weight of 9,000 pounds or more, on the segment of State Route 2 (SR–2) that is located between Interstate Route 210 (I–210) in the City of La Canada Flintridge and County Route N4 (Big Pine Highway) in the County of Los Angeles.

(b) Subdivision (a) does not apply to any of the following vehicles:

(1) An authorized emergency vehicle.

(2) A vehicle operated by a publicly or privately owned public utility.

(3) A vehicle operated by a government agency.

(4) A transit bus servicing facilities accessible only from that portion of State Route 2 specified in subdivision (a).

(5) A tow truck providing assistance to a vehicle that is accessible only from that portion of State Route 2 specified in subdivision (a).

(6) A commercial vehicle making deliveries to or from, or servicing, property that is either of the following:

(A) Located within the city limits of the City of La Canada Flintridge.

(B) Is accessible only from the portion of State Route 2 specified in subdivision (a).

(7) A commercial vehicle involved in a motion picture, commercial, or television production conducting motion picture, commercial, or television production activities in areas that are accessible only from that portion of State Route 2 specified in subdivision (a).

(c) A person who violates this section shall, upon conviction, be punished by a fine pursuant to subdivision (a) of Section 42030 or one thousand dollars ($1,000), whichever is greater.

(d) The Department of Transportation shall erect suitable signs at each end of the portion of State Route 2 specified in subdivision (a) and any other points that the department deems necessary to give adequate notice of the prohibition pursuant to this section. *(Added by Stats.2009, c. 147 (A.B.1361), § 1, eff. Aug. 6, 2009.)*

ARTICLE 4. LOCAL AUTHORITIES

Section
35700. Increases.
35700.5. Terminal Island Freeway; special permit; criteria.
35701. Decreases by cities or counties; exceptions.
35702. Approval of ordinance.
35703. Commercial vehicles.
35704. Public utility construction or repair vehicle.
35705. Highway user tax funds, expenditure on city streets.
35706. Unimproved county highways.
35707. Improved county highways.
35708. Ordinances subject to approval.
35709. Hearing.
35710. Signs on unimproved county highways.
35711. Delivery routes.
35712. Highways closed to commercial vehicles.
35713. Signs; alternate route.
35714. Exemptions.
35715. Highway restriction; Nevada county.
35715.1. Prohibition of Old Priest Grade in Tuolumne County; weight restrictions; effectiveness of adopted ordinances.
35716. Licensed contractors and highway carriers.
35717. Defective roadways.
35718. Signing required.
35719. Intercounty streets.
35720. Vehicles exempt.
35721. Notice and hearing.
35722. Route 85 corridor; proposed ordinance.
35723. Repealed.

§ 35700. Increases

(a) The legislative body of any county or city may by ordinance permit the operation and moving of vehicles and loads upon highways under their respective jurisdictions of a maximum gross weight in excess of the maximum gross weight of vehicles and loads specified in this code.

(b) This section does not apply to state highways. *(Stats.1959, c. 3, p. 1765, § 35700.)*

Cross References

Local authorities defined, see Vehicle Code § 385.
Reduction of weight limits by cities, see Vehicle Code § 35701.
State highway system, generally, see Streets and Highways Code § 230 et seq.

§ 35700.5. Terminal Island Freeway; special permit; criteria

(a) The Department of Transportation, upon adoption of an ordinance or resolution that is in conformance with the provisions of this section by the City of Carson, the City of Long Beach, and the City of Los Angeles, covering designated routes, may issue a special permit to the operator of a vehicle, combination of vehicles, or mobile equipment, permitting the operation and movement of the vehicle, combination, or equipment, and its load, on the 3.66–mile portion of State Route 47 and State Route 103 known as the Terminal Island Freeway, between Willow Street in the City of Long Beach and Terminal Island in the City of Long Beach and the City of Los Angeles, and on the 2.4–mile portion of State Highway Route 1, that is between Sanford Avenue in the City of Los Angeles and Harbor Avenue in the City of Long Beach, if the vehicle, combination, or equipment meets all of the following criteria:

(1) The vehicle, combination of vehicles, or mobile equipment is used to transport intermodal cargo containers that are moving in international commerce.

(2) The vehicle, combination of vehicles, or mobile equipment, in combination with its load, has a maximum gross weight in excess of the maximum gross weight limit of vehicles and loads specified in this chapter, but does not exceed 95,000 pounds gross vehicle weight.

(3)(A) The vehicle, combination of vehicles, or mobile equipment conforms to the axle weight limits specified in Section 35550.

(B) The vehicle, combination of vehicles, or mobile equipment conforms to the axle weight limits in Section 35551, except as specified in subparagraph (C).

(C) Vehicles, combinations of vehicles, or mobile equipment that impose more than 80,000 pounds total gross weight on the highway by any group of two or more consecutive axles, exceed 60 feet in length between the extremes of any group of two or more consecutive axles, or have more than six axles shall conform to weight limits that shall be determined by the Department of Transportation.

(b) The permit issued by the Department of Transportation shall be required to authorize the operation or movement of a vehicle, combination of vehicles, or mobile equipment described in subdivision (a). The permit shall not authorize the movement of hazardous materials or hazardous wastes, as those terms are defined by local, state, and federal law. The following criteria shall be included in the application for the permit:

(1) A description of the loads and vehicles to be operated under the permit.

(2) An agreement wherein each applicant agrees to be responsible for all injuries to persons and for all damage to real or personal property of the state and others directly caused by or resulting from the operation of the applicant's vehicles or combination of vehicles under the conditions of the permit. The applicant shall agree to hold harmless and indemnify the state and all its agents for all costs or claims arising out of or caused by the movement of vehicles or combination of vehicles under the conditions of the permit.

(3) The applicant shall provide proof of financial responsibility that covers the movement of the shipment as described in subdivision (a). The insurance shall meet the minimum requirements established by law.

(4) An agreement to carry a copy of the permit in the vehicle at all times and furnish the copy upon request of an employee of the Department of the California Highway Patrol or the Department of Transportation.

(5) An agreement to place an indicia, developed by the Department of Transportation, in consultation with the

Department of the California Highway Patrol, upon the vehicle identifying it as a vehicle possibly operating under this section. The indicia shall be displayed in the lower right area of the front windshield of the power unit. The Department of Transportation may charge a fee to cover the cost of producing and issuing this indicia.

(c) The permit issued pursuant to subdivision (a) shall be valid for one year. The permit may be canceled by the Department of Transportation for any of the following reasons:

(1) The failure of the applicant to maintain any of the conditions required pursuant to subdivision (b).

(2) The failure of the applicant to maintain a satisfactory rating, as required by Section 34501.12.

(3) A determination by the Department of Transportation that there is sufficient cause to cancel the permit because the continued movement of the applicant's vehicles under the permit would jeopardize the safety of the motorists on the roadway or result in undue damage to the highways listed in this section.

(d) This section does not authorize an applicant or holder of a special permit under subdivision (a) to operate a vehicle or combination of vehicles in excess of the maximum gross weight limit of vehicles and loads specified in this chapter outside of the designated corridors identified in subdivision (a). A violation of this subdivision shall result in the revocation of the permit.

(e) The Department of Transportation may charge a fee to cover the cost of issuing a permit pursuant to subdivision (a). *(Added by Stats.1994, c. 1037 (A.B.2438), § 1. Amended by Stats.1997, c. 358 (S.B.839), § 1; Stats.2002, c. 229 (S.B.2072), § 1; Stats.2011, c. 298 (A.B.1128), § 2.)*

§ 35701. Decreases by cities or counties; exceptions

(a) Any city, or county for a residence district, may, by ordinance, prohibit the use of a street by any commercial vehicle or by any vehicle exceeding a maximum gross weight limit, except with respect to any vehicle which is subject to Sections 1031 to 1036, inclusive, of the Public Utilities Code, and except with respect to vehicles used for the collection and transportation of garbage, rubbish, or refuse using traditionally used routes in San Diego County when the solid waste management plan prepared under Section 66780.1 of the Government Code is amended to designate each traditionally used route used for the purpose of transporting garbage, rubbish, or refuse which intersects with a local or regional arterial circulation route contained within a city or county's traffic circulation element and which provides access to a solid waste disposal site.

(b) The ordinance shall not be effective until appropriate signs are erected indicating either the streets affected by the ordinance or the streets not affected, as the local authority determines will best serve to give notice of the ordinance.

970

(c) No ordinance adopted pursuant to this section after November 10, 1969, shall apply to any state highway which is included in the National System of Interstate and Defense Highways, except an ordinance which has been approved by a two-thirds vote of the California Transportation Commission.

(d) The solid waste management plan prepared under Section 66780.1 of the Government Code by San Diego County may designate the traditionally used routes.

(e) "Traditionally used route," for purposes of this section, means any street used for a period of one year or more as access to or from a solid waste disposal site. *(Stats.1959, c. 3, p. 1765, § 35701. Amended by Stats. 1969, c. 1365, p. 2791, § 3; Stats.1980, c. 622, p. 1708, § 7; Stats.1982, c. 681, p. 2812, § 87; Stats.1986, c. 1378, § 5; Stats.1987, c. 616, § 1.)*

Cross References

Commercial vehicle defined, see Vehicle Code § 260.
Reduction of weight limits by counties, see Vehicle Code § 35706.
Street defined, see Vehicle Code § 590.
Weight limits, see Vehicle Code § 35550 et seq.

§ 35702. Approval of ordinance

No ordinance proposed under Section 35701 is effective with respect to any highway which is not under the exclusive jurisdiction of the local authority enacting the ordinance, or, in the case of any state highway, until the ordinance has been submitted by the governing body of the local authority to, and approved in writing by, the Department of Transportation. In submitting a proposed ordinance to the department for approval, the governing body of the local authority shall designate therein, an alternate route for the use of vehicles, which route shall remain unrestricted by any local regulation as to weight limits or types of vehicles so long as the ordinance proposed shall remain in effect. The approval of the proposed ordinance by the Department of Transportation shall constitute an approval by it of the alternate route so designated. *(Stats.1959, c. 3, p. 1765, § 35702. Amended by Stats.1969, c. 1365, p. 2792, § 4; Stats.1974, c. 545, p. 1339, § 247; Stats.1980, c. 622, p. 1708, § 8; Stats.1998, c. 877 (A.B.2132), § 71.)*

Cross References

Definitions,
  Highway, see Vehicle Code § 360.
  Local authorities, see Vehicle Code § 385.

§ 35703. Commercial vehicles

No ordinance adopted pursuant to Section 35701 shall prohibit any commercial vehicles coming from an unrestricted street having ingress and egress by direct route to and from a restricted street when necessary for the purpose of making pickups or deliveries of goods, wares, and merchandise from or to any building or structure located on the restricted street or for the purpose of delivering materials to be used in the actual and bona fide repair, alteration, remodeling, or construction of any building or structure upon the restricted street for which a building permit has previously been obtained. *(Stats. 1959, c. 3, p. 1766, § 35703.)*

Cross References

Definitions,
    Commercial vehicle, see Vehicle Code § 260.
    Street, see Vehicle Code § 590.

§ 35704. Public utility construction or repair vehicle

No ordinance adopted pursuant to Section 35701 to decrease weight limits shall apply to any vehicle owned by a public utility or a licensed contractor while necessarily in use in the construction, installation, or repair of any public utility. *(Stats.1959, c. 3, p. 1766, § 35704. Amended by Stats.1959, c. 307, p. 2216, § 2; Stats.1987, c. 371, § 1.)*

§ 35705. Highway user tax funds, expenditure on city streets

Section 35701 shall not be applicable to any city street on which money from the State Highway Account in the State Transportation Fund has been or is used for construction or maintenance except in such cases as the legislative body of the city, after notice and hearing, determines to reduce weight limits on such streets. Notice of the hearing shall be published as provided in Section 6064 of the Government Code. The notice shall advise all interested parties that they may submit written and oral objections to the proposed action and shall designate a time and place for presentation of such objections. The time for submission of objections shall not expire, and the hearing may not be held, less than 60 days after the first publication of notice. The hearing shall be held before the legislative body of the city. All objections shall be considered and interested parties shall be afforded an adequate opportunity to be heard in respect to their objections. *(Stats.1959, c. 3, p. 1766, § 35705. Amended by Stats.1974, c. 545, p. 1339, § 248.)*

§ 35706. Unimproved county highways

Boards of supervisors in their respective counties may by ordinance reduce the permissible weight of vehicles and loads upon unimproved county highways or upon county bridges. *(Stats.1959, c. 3, p. 1766, § 35706.)*

Cross References

County highways, generally, see Streets and Highways Code
    § 900 et seq.

§ 35707. Improved county highways

Boards of supervisors in their respective counties may by ordinance reduce the permissible weights upon improved highways only which by reason of deterioration will be destroyed unless the weight limits are reduced, but no such reduction shall extend for a period of more than 90 days unless actual repair of the highway is begun within that time and thereafter continuously carried on to completion.

For the purposes of this section, an improved county highway means a highway paved with cement concrete or asphaltic concrete, or a highway with a roadway of hard surface not less than four inches thick made up of a mixture of rock, sand, or gravel bound together by an artificial binder other than natural soil. *(Stats.1959, c. 3, p. 1766, § 35707.)*

Cross References

County highways, generally, see Streets and Highways Code
    § 900 et seq.

§ 35708. Ordinances subject to approval

In the event any person protests in writing to the clerk of the board of supervisors within 15 days after the adoption of an ordinance reducing the permissible gross weight upon an improved highway, the reduction in weight shall not become final until the Department of Transportation after a hearing approves the action of the board of supervisors in making such reduction. *(Stats. 1959, c. 3, p. 1767, § 35708. Amended by Stats.1974, c. 545, p. 1339, § 249.)*

§ 35709. Hearing

The hearing shall be held in the county in which the highway is located within 25 days after a request therefor, and shall be conducted by one or more engineers of the Department of Transportation to be designated by the Director of Transportation. The engineers shall hear all evidence presented and report their findings in writing to the director. Such director shall, upon the basis of the findings, declare in writing the approval or disapproval of the reduction. *(Stats.1959, c. 3, p. 1767, § 35709. Amended by Stats.1974, c. 545, p. 1340, § 250.)*

§ 35710. Signs on unimproved county highways

Whenever any weight limit different from those specified in this code is fixed in accordance with Section 35706 or 35707, the board of supervisors shall cause signs indicating the weight so fixed to be erected at all entrances to the highway upon which the permissible gross weight is altered. *(Stats.1959, c. 3, p. 1767, § 35710.)*

§ 35711. Delivery routes

No ordinance adopted pursuant to Section 35706 or 35707 or 35712 shall prohibit any commercial vehicle from using any county highway by direct route to or from a state highway for the purpose of delivering or loading for transportation goods, wares, or merchandise. *(Stats. 1959, c. 3, p. 1767, § 35711. Amended by Stats.1969, c. 1598, p. 3252, § 1.)*

Cross References

Commercial vehicle defined, see Vehicle Code § 260.

§ 35712. Highways closed to commercial vehicles

(a) Any county may, by ordinance, prohibit the use of any highway located in an unincorporated residential or

971

subdivision area by any commercial vehicle exceeding a gross weight of 14,000 pounds.

(b) Any county of the third class, as defined by Section 28024 of the Government Code, or of the ninth class, as defined by Section 28030 of the Government Code, may, by ordinance, prohibit the use of any highway located in an unincorporated residential or subdivision area by any commercial vehicle exceeding a gross weight of 5,000 pounds.

(c) This section does not apply to a vehicle operated by, or on behalf of, a public utility in connection with the installation, operation, maintenance, or repair of its facilities.

(Stats.1959, c. 3, p. 1767, § 35712. Amended by Stats.1967, c. 1042, p. 2648, § 1; Stats.1969, c. 1365, p. 2793, § 7; Stats.1969, c. 1598, p. 3253, § 3; Stats.1980, c. 622, p. 1708, § 9; Stats.1982, c. 681, p. 2813, § 88; Stats.1998, c. 877 (A.B.2132), § 72.)

Cross References

Commercial vehicle defined, see Vehicle Code § 260.

§ 35713. Signs; alternate route

No ordinance closing a highway under Section 35712 or 35715 is effective until appropriate signs are erected indicating either the highways affected by the ordinance or the highways not affected as the county may determine will best serve to give notice of the ordinance, nor shall any ordinance be effective with respect to any county highway unless the board of supervisors designates in the ordinance an alternate route for the use of the vehicles which shall remain unrestricted by any local regulation as to commercial vehicles so long as the ordinance proposed shall remain in effect. *(Stats.1959, c. 3, p. 1767, § 35713. Amended by Stats.1959, c. 1996, p. 4637, § 45; Stats.1975, c. 660, p. 1426, § 1, eff. Sept. 10, 1975.)*

Cross References

Commercial vehicle defined, see Vehicle Code § 260.

§ 35714. Exemptions

No ordinance adopted pursuant to Section 35712 shall be effective with respect to:

(a) Any vehicle which is subject to the provisions of Article 2 (commencing with Section 1031) of Chapter 5 of Part 1 of Division 1 of the Public Utilities Code.

(b) Any highway, any portion of which is also under the jurisdiction of a city, unless the consent of the governing body of the city is first obtained.

(c) Any commercial vehicle coming from an unrestricted highway having ingress and egress by direct route to and from the restricted highway when necessary for the purpose of making pickups or deliveries of goods, wares, and merchandise from or to any building or structure located on the restricted highway or for the purpose of delivering materials to be used in the actual and bona fide repair, alteration, remodeling, or construction of any

972

building or structure upon the restricted highway for which a building permit has previously been obtained.

(d) The operation of ambulances or hearses.

(e) Any vehicle owned, operated, controlled, or used by a public utility in connection with the construction, installation, operation, maintenance, or repair of any public utility facilities.

(f) Any state highway, until the proposed ordinance has been submitted by the board of supervisors of the county to and approved in writing by the Department of Transportation. In submitting a proposed ordinance to the department for approval, the board of supervisors shall designate therein, an alternate route for the use of the vehicles which shall remain unrestricted by any local regulation as to commercial vehicles so long as the ordinance proposed shall remain in effect. The approval of the proposed ordinance by the Department of Transportation shall constitute an approval by the department of the alternate route so designated.

(g) Vehicles operated as an incident to any industrial, commercial or agricultural enterprise conducted within the boundaries of the unincorporated residential subdivision area. *(Stats.1959, c. 3, p. 1767, § 35714. Amended by Stats.1959, c. 1996, p. 4637, § 46; Stats.1967, c. 1042, p. 2649, § 2; Stats.1969, c. 1365, p. 2793, § 6; Stats.1974, c. 545, p. 1340, § 251; Stats.1980, c. 622, p. 1709, § 10; Stats.1998, c. 877 (A.B.2132), § 73.)*

Cross References

Commercial vehicle defined, see Vehicle Code § 260.
Through highway defined, see Vehicle Code § 600.

§ 35715. Highway restriction; Nevada county

(a) The County of Nevada may by ordinance prohibit the use of Northwoods Boulevard in such county by any commercial vehicle exceeding a gross weight specified in the ordinance.

(b) No ordinance adopted pursuant to this section shall be effective with respect to:

(1) Any commercial vehicle coming from an unrestricted highway having ingress and egress by direct route to and from the restricted highway when necessary for the purpose of making pickups or deliveries of goods, wares, and merchandise from or to any building or structure located on the restricted highway or for the purpose of delivering materials to be used in the actual and bona fide repair, alteration, remodeling, or construction of any building or structure upon the restricted highway for which a building permit has previously been obtained.

(2) The operation of ambulances or hearses.

(3) Any vehicle owned, operated, controlled, or used by a public utility in connection with the construction, installation, operation, maintenance, or repair of any public utility facilities. *(Added by Stats.1975, c. 660, p. 1426, § 1.5, eff. Sept. 10, 1975.)*

§ 35715.1. Prohibition of Old Priest Grade in Tuolumne County; weight restrictions; effectiveness of adopted ordinances

(a) The County of Tuolumne may by ordinance prohibit the use of Old Priest Grade in that county by a vehicle or combination of vehicles that exceeds a weight limit of 7,500 pounds or more. The weight limit shall be determined by the County Board of Supervisors and specified in the ordinance.

(b) An ordinance adopted pursuant to this section is not effective with respect to the following:

(1) A vehicle or combination of vehicles coming from an unrestricted highway having ingress and egress by direct route to and from the restricted highway when necessary for the purpose of making pickups or deliveries of goods, wares, and merchandise from or to any building or structure located on the restricted highway or for the purpose of delivering materials to be used in the actual and bona fide repair, alteration, remodeling, or construction of a building or structure upon the restricted highway for which a building permit has previously been obtained.

(2) The operation of ambulances, hearses, or vehicles providing emergency roadside services or roadside assistance.

(3) A vehicle or combination of vehicles owned, operated, controlled, or used by a public utility in connection with the construction, installation, operation, maintenance, or repair of a public utility facility. *(Added by Stats.2003, c. 15 (A.B.582), § 1.)*

§ 35716. Licensed contractors and highway carriers

No ordinance adopted by a city to decrease weight limits shall apply to any vehicle owned, leased, operated or controlled by any licensed contractor while necessarily in use in the construction, maintenance, or repair of a public works project, or by any highway carrier regulated by the Public Utilities Commission while transporting any materials to or from a public works project, when the bids were opened prior to the adoption of the ordinance unless an alternate direct route is provided substantially within and by the city enacting the ordinance. *(Added by Stats.1959, c. 307, p. 2217, § 3. Amended by Stats.1965, c. 971, p. 2589, § 1; Stats.1969, c. 393, p. 925, § 1.)*

Cross References

Public Utilities Commission, see Public Utilities Code § 301 et seq.
Vehicle defined, see Vehicle Code § 670.

§ 35717. Defective roadways

Notwithstanding any provision to the contrary, any county may by ordinance prohibit the use of any street, road or highway by any commercial vehicle exceeding a maximum gross weight of 14,000 pounds if, by accepted engineering standards, the street, road or highway cannot support such vehicle. *(Added by Stats.1959, c. 1732, p. 4181, § 1.)*

Cross References

Commercial vehicle defined, see Vehicle Code § 260.

§ 35718. Signing required

No ordinance adopted pursuant to Section 35717 shall be effective until appropriate signs are erected indicating either the streets, roads or highways affected by the ordinance or the streets, roads or highways not affected, as the board of supervisors may determine will best serve to give notice of the ordinance. *(Added by Stats.1959, c. 1732, p. 4182, § 2.)*

§ 35719. Intercounty streets

No ordinance adopted pursuant to Section 35717 shall be effective with respect to any street, road or highway which connects with, or is a continuation of, any street, road or highway of an adjoining county unless the board of supervisors of each county in which the street, road or highway is a through highway, by concurrent action and like limitation, prohibit the use of such street, road or highway pursuant to this section. *(Added by Stats.1959, c. 1732, p. 4182, § 3.)*

Cross References

Through highway defined, see Vehicle Code § 600.

§ 35720. Vehicles exempt

No ordinance adopted pursuant to Section 35717 shall be effective with respect to:

(a) Any vehicle which is subject to the provisions of Article 2 (commencing with Section 1031) of Chapter 5 of Part 1 of Division 1 of the Public Utilities Code or any farm labor vehicle.

(b) Any street, road or highway which is not under the exclusive jurisdiction of the board of supervisors enacting such ordinance, except as otherwise provided in Section 35719, or, in the case of any state highway, until such proposed ordinance has been submitted by the board of supervisors to and approved in writing by the Department of Transportation. In submitting such a proposed ordinance to the department for approval, the board of supervisors shall designate therein, an alternate route or routes for the use of such vehicles which shall remain unrestricted by any local regulation as to weight limits or types of vehicles so long as the ordinance proposed shall remain in effect. The approval of such proposed ordinances by the Department of Transportation shall constitute an approval by the department of such alternate route or routes so designated.

(c) Any commercial vehicle coming from an unrestricted street, road or highway having ingress and egress by direct route to and from such restricted streets, roads, and highways when necessary for the purpose of making pickups or deliveries of goods, wares and merchandise from or to any building or structure located on such restricted streets, roads or highways or for the purpose of delivering materials to be used in the actual and bona fide repair, alteration, remodeling or construction of any

973

building or structure upon such restricted street, road or highway for which a building permit, if required, has previously been obtained therefor, or vehicles, machinery, or construction equipment used in connection with, the construction, repair or maintenance of such restricted street or public work projects located thereon.

(d) Any vehicle operated as an incident to any industrial, commercial, or agricultural enterprise conducted upon any such street, road, or highway.

(e) Any vehicle owned, operated, controlled, or used by a public utility or licensed contractor in connection with the construction, installation, operation, maintenance, or repair of any public utility facilities or public works projects.

(f) The operation of ambulances or hearses. *(Added by Stats.1959, c. 1732, p. 4182, § 4. Amended by Stats. 1974, c. 545, p. 1340, § 252; Stats.1980, c. 676, p. 2026, § 317.)*

Cross References

Commercial vehicle defined, see Vehicle Code § 260.
Farm labor vehicle defined, see Vehicle Code § 322.
Through highway defined, see Vehicle Code § 600.

§ 35721. Notice and hearing

No ordinance shall be adopted pursuant to Section 35717 except upon notice and hearing in the manner prescribed in this section.

Notice of hearing shall be published as prescribed in Section 6064 of the Government Code. The notice shall advise all interested parties that they may submit written or oral objections to the proposed action and shall designate a time and place for presentation of such objections. The time for submission of objections shall not expire, and the hearing may not be held, less than 60 days after the first publication of notice. The hearing shall be held before the board of supervisors and interested parties shall be afforded an adequate opportunity to be heard with respect to their objections. *(Added by Stats.1959, c. 1732, p. 4183, § 5.)*

§ 35722. Route 85 corridor; proposed ordinance

Prior to the execution of freeway agreements for State Highway Route 85 in Santa Clara County, with the concurrence of each city within the highway corridor, the Board of Supervisors of the County of Santa Clara may, after a public hearing, adopt a proposed ordinance imposing a maximum gross truck weight limit of 9,000 pounds on Route 85 from State Highway Route 280 in Cupertino south and east to State Highway Route 101 in San Jose, and submit the proposed ordinance to the Department of Transportation for approval.

Upon approval of the proposed ordinance by the department, this weight limit shall be stipulated in the applicable freeway agreements with the local entities in the Route 85 corridor.

If the proposed ordinance is approved by the department, the weight limit shall become effective upon

opening of any portion of the new Route 85 freeway corridor as defined in this section, and the department shall post appropriate signs, similar to the signs on State Highway Route 580 in Oakland. Except as otherwise provided in this section, this article shall be applicable to an ordinance adopted pursuant to this section. *(Added by Stats.1987, c. 1250, § 1.)*

§ 35723. Repealed by Stats.1975, c. 651, p. 1412, § 8

ARTICLE 5. BRIDGES AND OTHER STRUCTURES

Section
35750. Decreases.
35751. Investigation and hearing.
35752. Maximum weights; signs.
35753. Violation of decreased restrictions.
35754. Maximum weights on bridges under local jurisdiction.
35755. Maximum weights on state highway bridges.

§ 35750. Decreases

(a) The Department of Transportation may, in the manner provided in Section 35751, determine the maximum weight of vehicle and load, lower than the maximum weight otherwise permitted under this code which a bridge or other structure with safety to itself will sustain.

(b) The city council or the board of supervisors of a city or county with a population of 1,100,000 or more, as determined by the 1970 federal decennial census, may, in the manner provided in Section 35751, determine the maximum weight of vehicle and load, lower than the maximum weight otherwise permitted under this code which a bridge or other structure under its jurisdiction with safety to itself will sustain. *(Stats.1959, c. 3, p. 1768, § 35750. Amended by Stats.1972, c. 597, p. 1058, § 1; Stats.1974, c. 545, p. 1341, § 253.)*

Cross References

Applicability of this section to trolley coaches, see Vehicle Code § 21051.

§ 35751. Investigation and hearing

(a) The Department of Transportation or the city council or board of supervisors of a city or county with a population of 1,100,000 or more, as determined by the 1970 federal decennial census, as the case may be, shall make an engineering investigation and hold a public hearing whenever such a determination appears necessary.

(b) Notice of the time and place of the hearing shall be posted upon the bridge or other structure at least five days before the date fixed for the hearing. Upon the basis of the investigation and all evidence presented at the hearing, the department or the city council or board of supervisors, as the case may be, shall determine by order in writing the maximum weight of vehicle and load which the bridge or other structure with safety to itself will sustain.

(c) With respect to any bridge or other structure not under its jurisdiction, the department shall not proceed under subdivisions (a) and (b) unless it first receives a request to do so from the city council or the board of supervisors having jurisdiction over the bridge or other structure. *(Stats.1959, c. 3, p. 1768, § 35751. Amended by Stats.1972, c. 597, p. 1058, § 2; Stats.1974, c. 545, p. 1342, § 254.)*

Cross References

Applicability of this section to trolley coaches, see Vehicle Code § 21051.

§ 35752. Maximum weights; signs

Thereupon, the authority having jurisdiction over the bridge or other structure shall erect and maintain suitable signs specifying the maximum weight so determined, at a distance of not more than 500 feet from each end of the bridge or other structure or any approach thereto.

The standards and specifications for such signs shall be established in accordance with Section 21400 of this code. *(Stats.1959, c. 3, p. 1769, § 35752. Amended by Stats. 1963, c. 148, p. 818, § 1; Stats.1969, c. 1033, p. 2011, § 3.)*

Cross References

Weight violations, penalty, see Vehicle Code § 42030 et seq.

§ 35753. Violation of decreased restrictions

(a) No person shall drive a vehicle over any bridge, causeway, viaduct, trestle, or dam constituting a part of a highway when the weight of the vehicle and load thereon is greater than the maximum weight which the bridge or other structure with safety to itself will sustain. Violations of this subdivision shall be punished in accordance with the schedule of fines set forth in Section 42030.

(b) Upon the trial of any person charged with a violation with respect to a weight restriction sign erected pursuant to Section 35752, proof of the determination of the maximum weight by the Department of Transportation and the existence of the weight restriction signs constitute prima facie evidence of the maximum weight which the bridge or other structure with safety to itself will sustain. *(Stats.1959, c. 3, p. 1769, § 35753. Amended by Stats.1984, c. 542, § 6.)*

Cross References

Applicability of this section to trolley coaches, see Vehicle Code § 21051.
Prima facie evidence, see Evidence Code § 602.

§ 35754. Maximum weights on bridges under local jurisdiction

Whenever, in the opinion of a local authority, a bridge under its jurisdiction is in a dangerous or weak condition, it may temporarily erect suitable signs at all entrances to such bridge specifying the maximum weight which it believes the bridge with safety to itself will sustain. The maximum weight limit so fixed and posted shall remain in effect for not more than 90 days. *(Stats.1959, c. 3, p.*

1769, § 35754. Amended by Stats.1972, c. 597, p. 1059, § 3.)

Cross References

Local authorities defined, see Vehicle Code § 385.

§ 35755. Maximum weights on state highway bridges

Whenever a state highway bridge is in a dangerous or weak condition, the Department of Transportation may temporarily erect suitable signs at all entrances to such bridge specifying the maximum weight which the bridge may safely sustain. Under no circumstances shall the maximum weight limit so fixed and posted pursuant to this section remain in effect for more than 90 days. *(Added by Stats.1968, c. 1063, p. 2063, § 1. Amended by Stats.1974, c. 545, p. 1342, § 255.)*

ARTICLE 6. PERMITS AND AGREEMENTS

Section

35780.	Permits for variances; processes for application and issuance.
35780.3.	Persons qualified for issuance of park trailer permit.
35780.5.	Special permit to operate or move vehicles transporting trusses or wall panels lying in horizontal position.
35781.	Application form; permit form.
35782.	Withholding or restricting permit; bond; proof of financial responsibility.
35783.	Possession of permit.
35783.5.	Warning signs.
35784.	Violation of permit.
35784.5.	Conviction of transporting extralegal load or causing, directing, or driving vehicle without permit; punishment; excess weight, additional fine.
35785.	Hauling of saw logs.
35786.	Use of truck booster power units.
35787.	Issuance of truck booster power unit permit.
35788.	Agreement for transporting overloads.
35789.	Building mover's notice to railroad.
35789.5.	Legislative findings and declaration; movement of manufactured homes.
35790.	Overwidth manufactured homes; annual or special permits.
35790.1.	Additional conditions and specifications.
35790.4.	Legislative findings and declaration.
35790.5.	Vehicles carrying units of manufactured home; exemption from length limitations.
35790.6.	Manufactured homes exceeding height specifications; permits authorizing exemption.
35791.	Single permit.
35792 to 35794.	Repealed.
35795.	Permit fees.
35796.	Delegation by local authorities to road commissioner.

Cross References

Department of Transportation, see Government Code § 14000 et seq.
Identification plates, issuance to manufacturer or dealer, see Vehicle Code § 5016.5.

Local authorities defined, see Vehicle Code § 385.

§ 35780. Permits for variances; processes for application and issuance

(a) The Department of Transportation or local authorities, with respect to highways under their respective jurisdictions, may, at their discretion upon application and if good cause appears, issue a special permit authorizing the applicant:

(1) To operate or move a vehicle or combination of vehicles or special mobile equipment of a size or weight of vehicle or load exceeding the maximum specified in this code.

(2) To use corrugations on the periphery of the movable tracks on a traction engine or tractor, the propulsive power of which is not exerted through wheels resting upon the roadway but by means of a flexible band or chain.

(3) Under emergency conditions, to operate or move a type of vehicle otherwise prohibited hereunder, upon any highway under the jurisdiction of the party granting the permit and for the maintenance of which the party is responsible.

(4) To operate or move a vehicle or combination of vehicles transporting loads composed of logs only for the purpose of crossing a highway from one private property to another without complying with any or all of the equipment requirements of Division 12 (commencing with Section 24000) and Division 13 (commencing with Section 29000). These crossings shall be as near to a right angle to the roadway as is practical and shall not include any travel parallel to the roadway. The Department of Transportation shall determine standards and conditions upon which permits shall be issued and any permit not in compliance with those standards and conditions shall be invalid, except that a permit may contain more restrictive conditions if the issuing authority deems it appropriate.

(b) Under conditions prescribed by the Department of Transportation or the local authority, the Department of Transportation or local authority may accept applications made by, and issue permits directly to, an applicant or permit service by any of the following processes:

(1) In writing.

(2) By an authorized facsimile process.

(3) Through an authorized computer and modem connection. *(Stats.1959, c. 3, p. 1769, § 35780. Amended by Stats.1961, c. 912, p. 2534, § 1; Stats.1974, c. 545, p. 1342, § 256; Stats.1989, c. 201, § 1; Stats.1990, c. 1388 (S.B.2842), § 1; Stats.1992, c. 391 (A.B.2670), § 3.)*

Cross References

Animals and certain vehicles not permitted on certain crossings, exception, see Vehicle Code § 23330.
Applicability of safety regulations, see Vehicle Code § 34500.
Authority of highway patrol to inspect vehicles, see Vehicle Code § 2804.

Farm vehicles exempt from registration, see Vehicle Code § 36101.
Increased weight limits, see Vehicle Code § 35650.
Prohibiting further movement of oversized vehicle until permit obtained, see Vehicle Code § 2803.
Registration exemptions for automatic bale wagons and feed hauling vehicles, see Vehicle Code § 36102.
Special mobile equipment defined, see Vehicle Code § 575.
Warning lights on pilot cars and related vehicles, see Vehicle Code § 25270.

§ 35780.3. Persons qualified for issuance of park trailer permit

A permit issued under Section 35780 for the movement of a park trailer, as described in Section 18009.3 of the Health and Safety Code, shall not be issued except to transporters, or licensed manufacturers and dealers. *(Added by Stats.1986, c. 1078, § 11, eff. Sept. 24, 1986, operative Jan. 1, 1987. Amended by Stats.1993, c. 272 (A.B.301), § 54, eff. Aug. 2, 1993; Stats.2000, c. 566 (A.B.1912), § 8.)*

§ 35780.5. Special permit to operate or move vehicles transporting trusses or wall panels lying in horizontal position

(a) Notwithstanding Section 320.5, the Department of Transportation or a local authority, with respect to highways under their respective jurisdictions, may, upon application, issue a special permit authorizing the applicant to operate or move a vehicle carrying a load, lying in the horizontal position, of stacked trusses or wall panels that are used as single width components in the manufacture of a finished product, that exceeds the maximum width specified by this code, if the load does not exceed 12 feet in width and the permittee complies with the regulations of the Department of Transportation or a local authority, as the case may be, governing the transportation of these loads.

(b) Under conditions prescribed by the Department of Transportation or the local authority, the Department of Transportation or local authority may accept applications and issue permits directly to an applicant or permit service, by any of the following processes:

(1) In writing.

(2) By an authorized facsimile process.

(3) Through an authorized computer and modem connection.

(c) The special permit allowed pursuant to this section shall, under conditions prescribed by the Department of Transportation or a local authority, be granted on either a per trip or annual basis.

(d) As used in this section, "truss" means a designed and manufactured assemblage of structural elements typically arranged in a triangle or combination of triangles to form a rigid framework and used as a structural support in buildings.

(e) As used in this section, "wall panel" means a designed and manufactured assemblage of structural elements constructed in the same manner as site-built walls to form a rigid framework and used as a structural support in buildings, which may have attached various types of sheathing products including wood structural panels, foam panels, and gypsum board that do not exceed more than one foot beyond the main structural elements. *(Added by Stats.2007, c. 514 (A.B.1612), § 3.)*

§ 35781. Application form; permit form

The Department of Transportation shall develop a standard application form and a standard permit form for the application for, and the issuance of, a permit. The standard permit form may be used as the standard application form. The application for a permit shall specifically describe the vehicle and load to be operated or moved and the particular highways over which permit to operate is requested, and whether the permit is requested for a single trip or for continuous operation. Local authorities shall use the standard application form and the standard permit form developed by the Department of Transportation. The standard application form and the standard permit form shall be developed in cooperation with representatives of local government and the commercial trucking industry. *(Stats.1959, c. 3, p. 1770, § 35781. Amended by Stats.1989, c. 206, § 1; Stats.1996, c. 464 (A.B.2027), § 1.)*

Cross References

Prohibition of animals and certain vehicles on vehicular crossings, exception, see Vehicle Code § 23330.

§ 35782. Withholding or restricting permit; bond; proof of financial responsibility

(a) The Department of Transportation or a local authority may issue or withhold the permit at its discretion, or, if the permit is issued, do any of the following when necessary to protect against injury to the road, foundations, surfaces, or structures:

(1) Limit the number of trips.

(2) Establish seasonal or other time limitations within which the vehicle or vehicles described may be operated on the highways indicated.

(3) Otherwise limit or prescribe conditions of operation of the vehicle.

(b) The Department of Transportation or a local authority may not require the posting of a bond as a condition of the issuance of a permit, except that a requirement of extra insurance or other financial security may be imposed as a condition for a permit for unusually large or heavy loads that pose a substantial risk to public facilities.

(c) Except as provided in subdivision (b), the Department of Transportation or a local authority may not require proof of financial responsibility in an amount greater than that required for compliance with Section 16500.5 as a condition of the permit, and shall accept evidence of financial responsibility that complies with Section 16020. *(Stats.1959, c. 3, p. 1770, § 35782.*

Amended by Stats.1974, c. 545, p. 1343, § 257; Stats.1990, c. 938 (A.B.4228), § 1; Stats.1996, c. 124 (A.B.3470), § 137.)

Cross References

Prohibition of animals and certain vehicles on vehicular crossings, exception, see Vehicle Code § 23330.

§ 35783. Possession of permit

Every permit shall be carried in the vehicle or combination of vehicles to which it refers and shall be open to inspection of any peace officer, traffic officer, authorized agent of the Department of Transportation, or any other officer or employee charged with the care or protection of such highways. *(Stats.1959, c. 3, p. 1770, § 35783. Amended by Stats.1974, c. 545, p. 1343, § 258.)*

Cross References

Prohibition of animals and certain vehicles on vehicular crossings, exception, see Vehicle Code § 23330.

§ 35783.5. Warning signs

Warning signs required by the terms of a permit shall either be removed from the vehicle or covered from the view of other motorists whenever the vehicle is operating without the load that required the permit. *(Added by Stats.1978, c. 287, p. 579, § 4.)*

§ 35784. Violation of permit

(a) Except as provided in subdivision (b), it is unlawful for any person to violate any of the terms or conditions of any special permit.

(b) In an incorporated city where compliance with the route described in a special permit would result in a violation of local traffic regulations, the permittee may detour from the prescribed route to avoid violating the local traffic regulations if the permittee returns as soon as possible to the prescribed route. A detour under this subdivision shall be made only on nonresidential streets.

(c) If a violation under subdivision (a) consists of an extralegal load not being on the route described in the special permit, and the violation is directly caused by the action of an employee under the supervision of, or by the action of any independent contractor working for, a permittee subject to this section, the employee or independent contractor causing the violation is guilty of a misdemeanor. This subdivision applies only if the employee or independent contractor has been provided written direction on the route to travel and has not been directed to take a different route by a peace officer.

(d) The guilt of an employee or independent contractor under subdivision (c) shall not extend to the permittee employing that person unless the permittee is separately responsible for an action causing the violation.

(e) A violation of equipment requirements contained in Division 12 (commencing with Section 24000), by any person operating a pilot car shall not be considered a violation of any terms or conditions of a special permit under subdivision (a).

(f) (1) Any person convicted of a violation of the terms and conditions of a special permit shall be punished by a fine not exceeding five hundred dollars ($500) or by imprisonment in the county jail for a period not exceeding six months, or by both that fine and imprisonment.

(2) In addition, if the violation involves weight in excess of that authorized by the permit, an additional fine shall be levied as specified in Section 42030 on the amount of weight in excess of the amount authorized by the permit. *(Stats.1959, c. 3, p. 1770, § 35784. Amended by Stats.1963, c. 994, p. 2256, § 1; Stats.1968, c. 1192, p. 2259, § 10, operative Jan. 1, 1969; Stats.1983, c. 145, § 18, eff. June 28, 1983; Stats.1984, c. 542, § 7; Stats.1988, c. 460, § 6.)*

Cross References

Prohibition of animals and certain vehicles on vehicular crossings, exception, see Vehicle Code § 23330.
Punishment for violations, see Vehicle Code § 42001 et seq.
Violation as misdemeanor, see Vehicle Code § 40000.23.

§ 35784.5. Conviction of transporting extralegal load or causing, directing, or driving vehicle without permit; punishment; excess weight, additional fine

(a) Any person convicted of transporting an extralegal load on a highway, or causing or directing the operation of or driving on a highway any vehicle or combination of vehicles for which a permit is required pursuant to this article, without having obtained a permit issued in accordance with this article, shall be punished by a fine not exceeding five hundred dollars ($500) or by imprisonment in the county jail for a period not exceeding six months, or by both that fine and imprisonment.

(b) If the violation involves excess weight, an additional fine shall be levied as specified in Section 42030 on the amount of weight in excess of that authorized pursuant to this chapter. *(Added by Stats.1984, c. 542, § 8.)*

Cross References

Violation as misdemeanor, see Vehicle Code § 40000.23.

§ 35785. Hauling of saw logs

(a) The axle weight limitations imposed in Sections 35550 and 35551 shall not apply to the transportation of a single saw log which does not exceed 8 feet in diameter and 21 feet in length or 6 feet in diameter and 33 feet in length, if such log is hauled on a combination of vehicles consisting of a three-axle truck and a two-axle logging dolly under permit issued by the Department of Transportation or by local authorities with respect to highways under their respective jurisdictions. Such permit may be granted for not more than thirty (30) days and may be revocable upon notice by the department or local authorities, as the case may be.

(b) When so transported, the vehicle shall not be operated over any bridge or causeway at a speed of more than 15 miles per hour or on the highway at more than 25 miles per hour, on routes designated in the permit. Diameter measurements of the logs shall be made on the large end. *(Stats.1959, c. 3, p. 1770, § 35785. Amended by Stats.1961, c. 1149, p. 2893, § 1; Stats.1963, c. 292, p. 291, § 8; Stats.1974, c. 545, p. 1343, § 259.)*

Cross References

Weight limitations on bridges and other structures, see Vehicle Code § 35750 et seq.

§ 35786. Use of truck booster power units

Truck booster power units may be used to aid in propelling or moving any motor truck or lawful combination of motor vehicles upon a highway upon an ascending or descending grade, subject to the following conditions:

(a) A permit for such operation must be obtained as provided in this article.

(b) The truck booster power unit shall be operated only on such highways and at such times and according to such conditions and requirements as may be specified in the permit. *(Stats.1959, c. 3, p. 1771, § 35786.)*

§ 35787. Issuance of truck booster power unit permit

The Department of Transportation or local authority, as the case may be, shall issue a truck booster power unit permit only if in its opinion the proposed operation would not tend to endanger the traveling public or to damage the highway, bridge or any highway structure.

The Department of Transportation and local authorities, in issuing a permit, may make such conditions and requirements as in their opinion are necessary or desirable for the safety of the traveling public and of the highway, including bridges and other highway structures. *(Stats.1959, c. 3, p. 1771, § 35787. Amended by Stats. 1974, c. 545, p. 1343, § 260.)*

§ 35788. Agreement for transporting overloads

Upon application to the Director of Transportation for permission to use and operate on highways private or contract vehicles for the purpose of hauling loads which weigh in excess of the maximum load weight limits, the director may enter into an agreement with the applicant, permitting such overloads, specifying protective restrictions and providing for the payment of a financial contribution for the issuance of such permission, except that the overload shall not exceed 25 percent of the maximum load weight limitation, in pounds, set forth in this code. The agreement shall not permit the applicant to transport such excess weight loads on highways for distances exceeding 75 miles. All contributions received by the Department of Transportation shall be used for the construction, improvement, or maintenance of the highway designated in the permission to operate overweight loads. Sections 188 and 188.8 of the Streets and Highways Code does not apply to contributions received pursuant to this section, and any expenditures of the contributions by the department shall not be credited against amounts required to be expended pursuant to Sections 188 and 188.8 of the Streets and Highways Code.

978

This section does not apply to highways which are a part of the National System of Interstate and Defense Highways. *(Stats.1959, c. 3, p. 1771, § 35788. Amended by Stats.1965, c. 182, p. 1149, § 1; Stats.1974, c. 545, p. 1344, § 261; Stats.1982, c. 827, p. 3141, § 16, eff. Sept. 10, 1982.)*

§ 35789.   Building mover's notice to railroad

Any housemoving contractor or other person who by contract or otherwise moves or transports a dwelling house or other building across railroad tracks shall furnish to the division or district superintendent of the railroad company operating such tracks written notice of intention to make such movement at least 36 hours prior to doing so. The written notice of intention to make such a movement shall contain the name of the street, highway or road over which such dwelling house or other building will be moved across the railroad tracks, the approximate time of day such movement will be made and such other information as may be necessary to enable the railroad company to take precautionary measures to avoid a collision by a train with such dwelling house or other building. *(Formerly § 25789, enacted by Stats.1959, c. 3, p. 1771, § 25789. Renumbered § 35789 and amended by Stats.1959, c. 1996, p. 4638, § 47.)*

§ 35789.5.   Legislative findings and declaration; movement of manufactured homes

(a) The Legislature finds and declares all of the following:

(1) Current restrictions on the movement on the highways of manufactured homes in excess of 14 feet in width has caused the closure of some manufactured housing manufacturing facilities, that have, in turn, relocated to other states in order to compete with interstate commerce.

(2) Those restrictions on the movement of manufactured homes could cause the closure of at least three more manufacturing facilities within the next 12 months, thereby laying off some 500 employees, while at the same time those manufacturing facilities relocate to other states.

(3) The Department of Transportation has a policy allowing permitted loads in excess of 14 feet in width for the general trucking industry and the boating industry.

(4) The Legislature supports allowing the movement on the highways of manufactured homes in excess of 14 feet in width, with appropriate safeguards, because this policy will result in both of the following:

(A) Enable the manufactured housing industry to produce homes for export to other states, thereby keeping jobs within the state and benefiting the state's economy.

(B) Permit the building of manufactured homes with eaves, which provide structural and aesthetic benefits to the homes.

(b) The Legislature further finds and declares that allowing the movement on the highways of manufactured homes that are 16 feet in width, with appropriate safeguards, will benefit the state's economy and will allow production of more affordable and aesthetic manufactured homes. *(Added by Stats.1980, c. 1150, p. 3789, § 11. Amended by Stats.1996, c. 278 (A.B.420), § 1.)*

§ 35790.   Overwidth manufactured homes; annual or special permits

(a) The Department of Transportation or local authorities with respect to highways under their respective jurisdictions may, upon application in writing and if good cause appears, issue a special or annual permit in writing authorizing the applicant to move any manufactured home in excess of the maximum width but not exceeding 14 feet in total width, exclusive of lights and devices provided for in Sections 35109 and 35110, upon any highway under the jurisdiction of the party granting the permit.

(b) A public agency, in the exercise of its discretion in granting permits for the movement of overwidth manufactured homes, and in considering the individual circumstances of each case, may use merchandising or relocation of residence as a basis for movement for good cause.

(c)(1) The application for a special permit shall specifically describe the manufactured home to be moved and the particular highways over which the permit to operate is requested.

(2) The application for an annual permit shall specifically describe the power unit to be used to tow the overwidth manufactured homes and the particular highways over which the permit to operate is requested. The annual permit shall be subject to all of the conditions of this section and any additional conditions imposed by the public agency.

(d) The Department of Transportation or local authority may establish seasonal or other time limitations within which a manufactured home may be moved on the highways indicated, and may require an undertaking or other security as it deems necessary to protect the highways and bridges from injury or to provide indemnity for any injury resulting from the operation.

(e) Permits for the movement of manufactured homes under this section shall not be issued except to transporters or licensed manufacturers and dealers and only under the following conditions:

(1) The manufactured home for which the permit is issued shall comply with Sections 35550 and 35551.

(2) In the case of a permit issued on an individual or repetitive trip basis, the applicant has first received the approval of a city or county if the trip will include movement on streets or highways under the jurisdiction of the city or county. The application for such a permit shall indicate the complete route of the proposed move and shall specify all cities and counties that have approved the move. This paragraph shall not be construed

to require the Department of Transportation to verify the information provided by an applicant with respect to movement on streets or highways under local jurisdiction.

(3) It is a violation of any permit, which is issued by the Department of Transportation and authorizes a move only on a state highway, for that move to be extended to a street or highway under the jurisdiction of a city or county unless the move has been approved by the city or county.

(f) The Department of Transportation, in cooperation with the Department of the California Highway Patrol, or the local authority may establish additional reasonable permit regulations as they may deem necessary in the interest of public safety, which regulations shall be consistent with this section.

(g) Every permit, the consent form or forms as required by Section 18099.5 of the Health and Safety Code, and a copy of the tax clearance certificate, certificate of origin, or dealer's notice of transfer, when the certificate or notice is required to be issued, shall be carried in the manufactured home or power unit to which it refers and shall be open to inspection by any peace officer or traffic officer, any authorized agent of the Department of Transportation, or any other officer or employee charged with the care and protection of the highways.

(h) It is unlawful for any person to violate any of the terms or conditions of any permit. *(Stats.1959, c. 3, p. 1772, § 35790. Amended by Stats.1959, c. 1778, p. 4261, § 1; Stats.1961, c. 1149, p. 2894, § 2; Stats.1963, c. 4, p. 609, § 1; Stats.1968, c. 1192, p. 2259, § 10.3, operative Jan. 1, 1969; Stats.1974, c. 545, p. 1344, § 262; Stats.1979, c. 194, p. 431, § 10; Stats.1980, c. 315, p. 646, § 1; Stats.1980, c. 1150, p. 3789, § 12; Stats.1981, c. 975, p. 3797, § 44; Stats.1982, c. 40, p. 85, § 12, eff. Feb. 17, 1982; Stats.1982, c. 827, p. 3141, § 17, eff. Sept. 10, 1982; Stats.1983, c. 1124, § 51, operative July 1, 1984; Stats. 1996, c. 124 (A.B.3470), § 138.)*

Cross References

Applicability of safety regulations, see Vehicle Code § 34500.
Warning lights on pilot cars and related vehicles, see Vehicle Code § 25270.

§ 35790.1.   Additional conditions and specifications

In addition to the requirements and conditions contained in Section 35790 and notwithstanding any other provision of law, all of the following conditions and specifications shall be complied with to move any manufactured home, as defined in Section 18007 of the Health and Safety Code, that is in excess of 14 feet in total width, but not exceeding 16 feet in total width, exclusive of lights and devices provided for in Sections 35109 and 35110, upon any highway under the jurisdiction of the entity granting the permit:

(a) For the purposes of width requirements under this code, the overall width of manufactured housing specified in this section shall be the overall width, including roof overhang, eaves, window shades, porch roofs, or any other part of the manufactured house that cannot be 980

removed for the purposes of transporting upon any highway.

(b) Unless otherwise exempted under this code, all combinations of motor vehicles and manufactured housing shall be equipped with service brakes on all wheels. Service brakes required under this subdivision shall be adequate, supplemental to the brakes on the towing vehicle, to enable the combination of vehicles to comply with the stopping distance requirements of Section 26454.

(c) In addition to the requirements contained in Section 26304, the breakaway brake device on any manufactured housing unit equipped with electric brakes shall be powered by a wet cell rechargeable battery that is of the same voltage rating as the brakes and has sufficient charge to hold the brakes applied for not less than 15 minutes.

(d) Notwithstanding any other provision of this code, the weight imposed upon any tire, wheel, axle, drawbar, hitch, or other suspension component on a manufactured housing unit shall not exceed the manufacturer's maximum weight rating for the item or component.

(e) In addition to the requirements in subdivision (d), the maximum allowable weight upon one manufactured housing unit axle shall not exceed 6,000 pounds, and the maximum allowable weight upon one manufactured housing unit wheel shall not exceed 3,000 pounds.

(f) Manufactured housing unit tires shall be free from defects, have at least $\frac{2}{32}$ of an inch tread depth, as determined by tire tread wear indicators, and shall comply with specifications and requirements contained in Section 3280.904(b)(8) of Title 24 of the Code of Federal Regulations.

(g) Manufactured housing unit manufacturers shall provide transporters with a certification of compliance document, certifying the manufactured housing unit complies with the specifications and requirements contained in subdivisions (d), (e), and (f). Each certification of compliance document shall identify, by serial or identification number, the specific manufactured housing unit being transported and shall be signed by a representative of the manufacturer. Each transporter of manufactured housing units shall have in his or her immediate possession a copy of the certification of compliance document and shall make the document available upon request by any member of the Department of the California Highway Patrol, any authorized employee of the Department of Transportation, or any regularly employed and salaried municipal police officer or deputy sheriff.

(h) Manufactured housing unit dealers shall provide transporters with a certification of compliance document, specifying that all modifications, equipment additions, or loading changes by the dealer have not exceeded the gross vehicle weight rating of the manufactured housing unit or the axle and wheel requirements contained in subdivisions (d), (e), and (f). Each certification of compliance document shall identify, by serial or identification number, the specific manufactured housing unit being transported and shall be signed by a representative of the dealer. Each transporter of manufactured housing units shall have in his or her immediate possession a copy of the certification of compliance document and shall make the document available upon request by any member of the Department of the California Highway Patrol, any authorized employee of the Department of Transportation, any regularly employed and salaried municipal police officer or deputy sheriff, or any reserve police officer or reserve deputy sheriff listed under Section 830.6 of the Penal Code.

(i) Transporters of manufactured housing units shall not transport any additional load in, or upon, the manufactured housing unit that has not been certified by the manufactured housing unit's manufacturer or dealer.

(j) Every hitch, coupling device, drawbar, or other connections between the towing unit and the towed manufactured housing unit shall be securely attached and shall comply with Subpart J of Part 3280 of Title 24 of the Code of Federal Regulations.

(k) Manufactured housing units shall be equipped with an identification plate, specifying the manufacturer's name, the manufactured housing unit's serial number, the gross vehicle weight rating of the manufactured housing unit, and the gross weight of the cargo that may be transported in or upon the manufactured housing unit without exceeding the gross vehicle weight rating. The identification plate shall be permanently attached to the manufactured housing unit and shall be positioned adjacent to, and meet the same specifications and requirements applicable to, the certification label required by Subpart A of Part 3280 of Title 24 of the Code of Federal Regulations.

(*l*) Manufactured housing units shall be subject to all lighting requirements contained in Sections 24603, 24607, 24608, and 24951. When transported during darkness, manufactured housing units shall additionally be subject to Sections 24600 and 25100.

(m) Manufactured housing units shall have all open sides covered by plywood, hard board, or other rigid material, or by other suitable plastics or flexible material. Plastic or flexible side coverings shall not billow or flap in excess of six inches in any one place. Units that are opened on both sides may be transported empty with no side coverings.

(n) Transporters of manufactured housing units shall make available all permits, licenses, certificates, forms, and any other relative document required for the transportation of manufactured housing upon request by any member of the Department of the California Highway Patrol, any authorized employee of the Department of Transportation, any regularly employed and salaried municipal police officer or deputy sheriff, or any reserve police officer or reserve deputy sheriff listed under Section 830.6 of the Penal Code.

(*o*) The Department of Transportation, in cooperation with the Department of the California Highway Patrol, or the local authority, shall require pilot car or special escort services for the movement of any manufactured housing unit pursuant to this section, and may establish additional reasonable permit regulations, including special routing requirements, as necessary in the interest of public safety and consistent with this section.

(p) The Department of Transportation shall not issue a permit to move a manufactured home that is in excess of 14 feet in total width unless that department determines that all of the conditions and specifications set forth in this section have been met. *(Added by Stats.1996, c. 278 (A.B.420), § 2. Amended by Stats.2000, c. 135 (A.B.2539), § 164; Stats.2003, c. 292 (A.B.1436), § 11.)*

Cross References

Criminal procedure, deputized or appointed peace officers, see Penal Code § 830.6.

§ 35790.4. Legislative findings and declaration

The Legislature finds and declares that current restrictions on the movement of combinations of manufactured homes have unduly restricted the ability of the California manufactured housing industry to meet the needs of the consumer in this state.

The Legislature further finds and declares that the improved movement of manufactured homes, with appropriate safeguards, will benefit the state's economy and will allow production of more affordable and aesthetic manufactured homes. *(Added by Stats.1984, c. 1312, § 1.)*

§ 35790.5. Vehicles carrying units of manufactured home; exemption from length limitations

(a) A permit issued pursuant to Section 35790 may authorize an exemption from length limitations otherwise applicable to vehicles and combinations of vehicles for the transportation of more than one unit of a manufactured home if all of the following conditions are met:

(1) The units are parts of a manufactured home that, when completed, connect two or more modular units.

(2) The units are mounted or loaded on a single vehicle or chassis in a manner so that their narrowest dimension represents the loaded width on the highway.

(3) The units are loaded in tandem only with respect to length, and the dimension from the front of the forward unit to the rear of the last unit does not exceed the length of vehicles in combination that would otherwise be permitted under this section.

(b) Applications for permits issued pursuant to this section shall specifically describe the manufactured home units to be moved and shall include a written statement of good cause satisfying the requirements of this section.

(c) Permits, other than annual permits, issued pursuant to this section shall describe the particular highways over which the permit is valid and shall be subject to all of the conditions of this article and any additional conditions imposed by the public agency issuing the permit. *(Added by Stats.1984, c. 1312, § 2.)*

§ 35790.6. Manufactured homes exceeding height specifications; permits authorizing exemption

A permit issued pursuant to Section 35780 or 35790 may authorize an exemption from the height limitations in Section 35250 for manufactured homes, including manufactured homes with a height in excess of 15 feet, measured from the surface upon which the vehicle stands, if the proposed route can accommodate the vehicle. *(Added by Stats.1986, c. 350, § 2, eff. July 15, 1986.)*

§ 35791. Single permit

The Department of Transportation and any local authority may, with respect to such highways as may be agreed upon under their respective jurisdictions which traverse any area within the boundaries of the local authority, contract for the issuance by either authority of a single permit authorizing the operation or movement of a vehicle or a combination of vehicles or special mobile equipment in the same manner as if each authority had issued separate permits pursuant to Section 35780. *(Added by Stats.1959, c. 2006, p. 4647, § 1. Amended by Stats.1974, c. 545, p. 1345, § 263.)*

§§ 35792 to 35794. Repealed by Stats.1985, c. 88, §§ 1 to 3

§ 35795. Permit fees

(a)(1) The Department of Transportation may charge a fee for the issuance of permits pursuant to this article.

(2) The fee established by the Department of Transportation pursuant to this section shall be established by a regulation adopted pursuant to Chapter 4.5 (commencing with Section 11371) of Part 1 of Division 3 of Title 2 of the Government Code, and shall be calculated to produce a total estimated revenue that is not more than the estimated total cost to that department for administering this article.

(3) Special services necessitated by unusually large or heavy loads requiring engineering investigations, or other services, may be billed separately for each permit.

(4) The funds collected by the Department of Transportation pursuant to this subdivision shall be deposited in the State Highway Account in the State Transportation Fund.

(b)(1) Local authorities may charge a fee for the issuance of permits pursuant to this article. However, the fee established by a local authority pursuant to this section shall be established by ordinance or resolution adopted after notice and hearing. The fee shall be

calculated to produce a total estimated revenue that is not more than the estimated total cost incurred by the local authority in administering its authority under this article and shall not exceed the fee developed by the Department of Transportation pursuant to subdivision (a). The fee for the issuance of permits shall be developed in consultation with representatives of local government and the commercial trucking industry. Notice of the hearing shall be by publication as provided in Section 6064 of the Government Code. The hearing shall be held before the legislative body of the local authority. All objections shall be considered and interested parties shall be afforded an adequate opportunity to be heard in respect to their objections.

(2) Special services necessitated by unusually large or heavy loads requiring engineering investigations, escorts, tree trimming, or other services, excluding services necessary to provide the notification required under this section and services that are within the scope of the local authority's ordinary duty to provide, shall be billed separately for each permit.

(3) For purposes of determining whether, under paragraph (2), special services are necessitated by an unusually large or heavy load, a local authority shall be governed by the criteria set forth in subdivision (b) of Section 1411.3 of Title 21 of the California Code of Regulations.

(c) Nothing in this section shall limit or restrict the application of Section 35782. *(Added by Stats.1969, c. 1150, p. 2239, § 1. Amended by Stats.1974, c. 545, p. 1346, § 267; Stats.1979, c. 883, p. 3069, § 1; Stats.1989, c. 206, § 2; Stats.1996, c. 464 (A.B.2027), § 2; Stats.2006, c. 242 (S.B.372), § 1.)*

§ 35796. Delegation by local authorities to road commissioner

Any or all of the powers granted to local authorities in this article may, by ordinance or resolution, be delegated by such local authorities to the road commissioner or to such other local official as may be performing functions substantially the same as a road commissioner in the county or municipality enacting such ordinance or resolution. *(Added by Stats.1971, c. 380, p. 745, § 1, operative May 3, 1972.)*

CHAPTER 6. MULTISTATE HIGHWAY TRANSPORTATION AGREEMENT [REPEALED]

§§ 35900 to 35908. Repealed by Stats.1998, c. 828 (S.B.1637), § 24

Division 16

IMPLEMENTS OF HUSBANDRY

Chapter	Section
1. Definitions	36000
2. Registration of Implements of Husbandry	36100
3. Drivers' Licenses	36300
4. Speed Laws	36400
5. Equipment of Implements of Husbandry	36500
6. Size, Weight and Load of Implements of Husbandry	36600
7. Other Requirements	36700
8. General Provisions	36800

CHAPTER 1. DEFINITIONS

Section
36000. Implement of husbandry defined.
36005. Implements of husbandry exemplified.
36010. Farm trailer defined.
36011. Automatic bale wagon defined.
36012. Cotton module mover.
36015. Farm tractor used for towing.
36016. Trap wagon.
36017. Empty bins, pallets, and tiedown straps not considered loads.

Cross References

Notice to correct violations, see Vehicle Code § 40303.5.

§ 36000. Implement of husbandry defined

An "implement of husbandry" is a vehicle which is used exclusively in the conduct of agricultural operations.

An implement of husbandry does not include a vehicle if its existing design is primarily for the transportation of persons or property on a highway, unless specifically designated as such by some other provision of this code. *(Added by Stats.1963, c. 2149, p. 4489, § 24. Amended by Stats.1986, c. 973, § 4.)*

Cross References

Air pollution control districts, California Air Pollution Control Officers Association, development of clearinghouse for control measures and strategies, see Health and Safety Code § 40731.

Air resources, application of this definition, see Health and Safety Code § 39034.

Enforcement of chapter, see Vehicle Code § 2400.

Exemption from use fuel tax, see Revenue and Taxation Code § 8652.

Implements of husbandry defined for property taxation assessment, see Revenue and Taxation Code § 411.

License not required to drive, see Vehicle Code § 12501.

Licenses for transportation of hazardous materials, application of section, see Vehicle Code § 32000.5.

Pollution, agricultural sources of pollution, regulation, see Health and Safety Code § 39011.5.

Registration of implements of husbandry, see Vehicle Code § 36100 et seq.

§ 36005. Implements of husbandry exemplified

An implement of husbandry includes, but is not limited to, all of the following:

(a) A lift carrier or other vehicle designed and used exclusively for the lifting and carrying of implements of husbandry or tools used exclusively for the production or harvesting of agricultural products, when operated or moved upon a highway.

(b) A trailer of the tip-bed type when used exclusively in the transportation of other implements of husbandry or tools used exclusively for the production or harvesting of agricultural products.

(c) A trailer or semitrailer having no bed, and designed and used solely for transporting a hay loader or swather.

(d) A spray or fertilizer applicator rig used exclusively for spraying or fertilizing in the conduct of agricultural operations. This subdivision does not apply to anhydrous ammonia fertilizer applicator rigs which have a transportation capacity in excess of 500 gallons.

(e)(1) A trailer or semitrailer that has a maximum transportation capacity in excess of 500 gallons, but not more than 1,000 gallons, used exclusively for the transportation and application of anhydrous ammonia, if the vehicle is either equipped with operating brakes or is towed upon a highway by a motortruck that is assigned a manufacturer's gross vehicle weight rating of ¾ ton or more.

(2) These vehicles are subject to Section 24603 if the stoplamps of the towing vehicle are not clearly visible.

(3) For purposes of this subdivision, a combination of vehicles is limited to two vehicles in tandem.

(f) A nurse rig or equipment auxiliary to the use of and designed or modified for the fueling, repairing, or loading of an applicator rig or an airplane used for the dusting, spraying, fertilizing, or seeding of crops.

(g) A row duster.

(h) A wagon or van used exclusively for carrying products of farming from one part of a farm to another part thereof, or from one farm to another farm, and used solely for agricultural purposes, including any van used in harvesting alfalfa or cotton, which is only incidentally operated or moved on a highway as a trailer.

(i) A wagon or portable house on wheels used solely by shepherds as a permanent residence in connection with sheep raising operations and moved from one part of a ranch to another part thereof or from one ranch to

983

another ranch, which is only incidentally operated or moved on a highway as a trailer.

(j) Notwithstanding subdivision (f) of Section 36101, a trap wagon, as defined in Section 36016, moved from one part of a ranch to another part of the same ranch or from one ranch to another, which is only operated or moved on a highway incidental to agricultural operations. The fuel tank or tanks of the trap wagon shall not exceed 1,000 gallons total capacity.

(k) Any vehicle that is operated upon a highway only for the purpose of transporting agricultural products and is in no event operated along a highway for a total distance greater than one mile from the point of origin of the trip.

(*l*) A portable honey-extracting trailer or semitrailer.

(m) A fertilizer nurse tank or trailer that is not self-propelled and which is moved unladen on the highway and auxiliary to the use of a spray or fertilizer applicator rig.

(n) Any cotton trailer when used on the highways for the exclusive purpose of transporting cotton from a farm to a cotton gin, and returning the empty trailer to such farm, except that Section 5014 shall apply to such trailers.

(*o*) A truck tractor or truck tractor and semitrailer combination specified in this subdivision which is owned by a farmer and operated on the highways, (1) only incidental to a farming operation, (2) not for compensation, and (3) for a distance of not more than two miles (on the highway) each way. This subdivision applies only to truck tractors with a manufacturer's gross vehicle weight rating over 10,000 pounds that are equipped with all-wheel drive and off-highway traction tires on all wheels, and only to semitrailers used in combination with such a truck tractor and exclusively in production or harvesting of tomatoes. The vehicles specified in this subdivision shall not be operated in excess of 25 miles per hour on the highways.

(p) An all-terrain or utility-terrain vehicle used exclusively in agricultural operations. *(Added by Stats.1963, c. 2149, p. 4489, § 24. Amended by Stats.1971, c. 1135, p. 2149, § 1, operative May 3, 1972; Stats.1976, c. 584, p. 1423, § 1, eff. Aug. 25, 1976; Stats.1984, c. 270, § 6, eff. July 3, 1984; Stats.1984, c. 1077, § 10, operative July 1, 1985; Stats.1986, c. 973, § 5; Stats.2010, c. 110 (S.B. 1229), § 1; Stats.2012, c. 168 (A.B.2111), § 3.)*

Cross References

Definitions,
  Semitrailer, see Vehicle Code § 550.
  Trailer, see Vehicle Code § 630.

§ 36010. Farm trailer defined

A "farm trailer" is either of the following:

(a) A trailer or semitrailer owned and operated by a farmer in the conduct of agricultural operations, and used exclusively to transport agricultural products upon the highway to the point of first handling and return.

(b) A trailer or semitrailer equipped with rollers on the bed, with a frame not taller than 10 inches high, and with a gross vehicle weight rating of 10,000 pounds or less, that is owned, rented, or leased by a farmer and operated by that farmer in the conduct of agricultural operations, used exclusively to transport fruit and vegetables upon the highway to the point of first handling and return, and that was manufactured and in use prior to January 1, 1997. These vehicles may also be operated on the highways without a load for the purposes of delivering a rented or leased vehicle to the renting or leasing farmer's farm, or returning empty to the owner's premises. *(Added by Stats.1963, c. 2149, p. 4490, § 24. Amended by Stats.1969, c. 697, p. 1363, § 3; Stats.1996, c. 650 (A.B.2417), § 2; Stats.2000, c. 861 (S.B.2084), § 56, eff. Sept. 29, 2000.)*

Cross References

Registration exemption, see Vehicle Code § 36109.

§ 36011. Automatic bale wagon defined

An "automatic bale wagon" is a motor vehicle capable of transporting property on a highway and equipped with apparatus specifically designed to pick up single bales of hay or straw from a field and to load and unload baled hay or straw. *(Added by Stats.1977, c. 627, p. 2116, § 1.)*

§ 36012. Cotton module mover

A "cotton module mover" is a motortruck, semitrailer, or a truck tractor, in combination with a semitrailer, that is equipped with a self-loading bed and is designed and used exclusively to transport field manufactured cotton modules to a cotton gin. *(Added by Stats.1986, c. 973, § 6. Amended by Stats.1997, c. 641 (A.B.777), § 1.)*

§ 36015. Farm tractor used for towing

"Implement of husbandry" includes any farm tractor, otherwise an implement of husbandry used upon a highway to draw a farm trailer carrying farm produce, or to draw any trailer or semitrailer carrying other implements of husbandry, between farms, or from a farm to a processing or handling point and returning with or without the trailer. *(Added by Stats.1963, c. 2149, p. 4490, § 24.)*

Cross References

Nonexemption of farm tractors from lighting requirements, see
  Vehicle Code § 36505.

§ 36016. Trap wagon

A "trap wagon" is a trailer or semitrailer used exclusively in the conduct of agricultural operations to fuel, service, or repair implements of husbandry. A trap wagon may be equipped with tools, spare parts, lubricating supplies, or fuel tanks. *(Added by Stats.1986, c. 973, § 7.)*

§ 36017. Empty bins, pallets, and tiedown straps not considered loads

For the exclusive purpose of this division, empty bins, pallets, and tiedown straps shall not be considered a load when transported within the parameters of agricultural operations. Any farm trailer or other vehicle transporting these items shall continue to be regulated pursuant to this division. The total outside width of any of the transported items shall not exceed 102 inches. *(Added by Stats.1986, c. 973, § 8.)*

CHAPTER 2. REGISTRATION OF IMPLEMENTS OF HUSBANDRY

Section
36100. Implements of husbandry exempt.
36101. Farm vehicles.
36102. Bale wagons and feed hauling vehicle; exemption.
36105. Other trailers exempt.
36106. Repealed.
36109. Farm trailers.
36110. Repealed.
36112. Repealed.
36115. Identification plates.
36115.5 to 36125. Repealed.
36130. Applications for identification plates; renewals.

§ 36100. Implements of husbandry exempt

Implements of husbandry which are only incidentally operated or moved over a highway and implements of husbandry listed in Section 36005 or 36015 are exempt from registration. *(Added by Stats.1963, c. 2149, p. 4490, § 24.)*

Cross References

Implements of husbandry, definition, see Vehicle Code § 36000.

§ 36101. Farm vehicles

The following farm vehicles are exempt from registration, if they have and display an identification plate as specified in Section 5014, and the vehicles shall not be deemed to be implements of husbandry and they shall be subject to all equipment and device requirements as if registered:

(a) A motor vehicle of a size so as to require a permit under Section 35780 owned and operated by a farmer, designed and used exclusively for carrying, or returning empty from carrying, feed and seed products of farming, and used on a highway between one part of a farm to another part of that farm or from one farm to another farm.

(b) A vehicle equipped with a water tank owned by a farmer and used exclusively to service his or her own implements of husbandry.

(c) A water tank truck that is owned by a farmer, not operated for compensation, and used extensively in the conduct of agricultural operations, when used exclusively (1) for sprinkling water on dirt roads providing access to agricultural fields or (2) transportation of water for irrigation of crops or trees.

(d)(1) A cotton module mover, as defined in Section 36012.

(2) In order to maintain the exemption from registration granted under this subdivision for a truck tractor, when combined with a semitrailer, the owner of that truck tractor shall not operate it during the exemption period in any manner other than as a cotton module mover, as defined in Section 36012, and shall do all of the following:

(A) Register the vehicle with the department before operating it as a commercial motor vehicle.

(B) Apply to the department on a yearly basis for any renewal of the exemption from registration.

(3) Exemption from registration under this subdivision does not exempt a truck tractor, when combined with a semitrailer, operating as a cotton module mover pursuant to Section 36012 and this subdivision from the applicable safety requirements of this code or any regulation adopted pursuant to any statute, including, but not limited to, equipment standards, driver licensing requirements, maximum driving and on-duty hours provisions, log book requirements, drug and alcohol testing, maintenance of vehicles, and any driver or vehicle standards specified in Division 14.8 (commencing with Section 34500).

(4) Truck tractors exempt from registration under this subdivision are subject to the fees imposed under Sections 9250, 9250.8, and 9250.13, and to any other vehicle fees that are imposed by statute on or after January 1, 1998, that are deposited in the Motor Vehicle Account.

(e) A trailer that is equipped with a plenum chamber for the drying of agricultural commodities.

(f) Except as provided in subdivision (j) of Section 36005, a trap wagon, as defined in Section 36016, that is equipped with a fuel tank or tanks. The fuel tank or tanks shall not exceed 3,000 gallons total capacity.

(g) A forklift truck, operated by a farmer not for compensation. For purposes of this section, a hay-squeeze shall be deemed a forklift.

(h) A truck tractor or truck tractor and semitrailer combination specified in this subdivision that is owned by a farmer and operated on the highways only incidental to a farming operation and not for compensation. This subdivision applies only to truck tractors with a manufacturer's gross vehicle weight rating over 10,000 pounds that are equipped with all-wheel drive and off-highway traction tires on all wheels, and only to semitrailers used in combination with that truck tractor and exclusively in the production or harvesting of melons. The vehicles specified in this subdivision shall not be operated in excess of 25 miles per hour on the highways.

The Commissioner of the California Highway Patrol may, by regulation, prohibit the vehicles specified in this subdivision from operating on specific routes. These vehicles shall not be operated laden on the highway for more than two miles from the point of origin and shall not be operated for more than 30 miles unladen on the highway from the point of origin. These vehicles shall not be operated for more than 15 miles unladen on the highway from the point of origin, unless accompanied by an escort vehicle to the front, and an escort vehicle to the rear.

(i) A motor vehicle specifically designed for, and used exclusively in, an agricultural operation for purposes of carrying, or returning empty from carrying, silage that is operated by a farmer, an employee of the farmer, or a contracted employee of the farmer between one part of a farm to another part of that farm or from one farm to another farm, on a highway for a distance not to exceed 20 miles from the point of origin of the trip. This subdivision does not include a vehicle that is used for the transportation of silage for retail sales.

For the purposes of this subdivision, "silage" includes field corn, sorghum, grass, legumes, cereals, or cereal mixes, either green or mature, converted into feed for livestock. *(Added by Stats.1972, c. 176, p. 396, § 1. Amended by Stats.1974, c. 217, p. 414, § 1, eff. May 7, 1974; Stats.1980, c. 791, p. 2400, § 1; Stats.1981, c. 50, p. 98, § 1; Stats.1981, c. 774, p. 3026, § 12; Stats.1983, c. 428, § 1; Stats.1984, c. 270, § 7, eff. July 3, 1984; Stats.1984, c. 1077, § 11, operative July 1, 1985; Stats. 1986, c. 973, § 9; Stats.1988, c. 877, § 4; Stats.1990, c. 1360 (S.B.1510), § 48; Stats.1996, c. 114 (S.B.1435), § 1; Stats.1997, c. 641 (A.B.777), § 2; Stats.1998, c. 877 (A.B.2132), § 74.)*

§ 36102. Bale wagons and feed hauling vehicle; exemption

The following vehicles are exempt from registration if they have and display identification plates, as specified in Section 5014; and these vehicles, except when operated pursuant to subdivision (k) of Section 36005, shall not be deemed to be implements of husbandry and they shall be subject to all equipment and device requirements as if registered:

(a) An automatic bale wagon operated unladen on a highway.

(b) An automatic bale wagon when transporting baled hay or straw for a distance of not more than five continuous road miles on a highway from one parcel of property owned, leased, or controlled by a farmer to another parcel of property owned, leased, or controlled by such farmer.

(c) A motor vehicle which is designed for, and used exclusively to, haul feed for livestock and which is owned and operated exclusively by a farmer or an employee of a farmer. A vehicle exempted by this subdivision may be operated only on those highways that are maintained by local authorities, only pursuant to a permit issued as provided in Section 35780 by the local authority having jurisdiction over the highways used, and only for a distance of not more than five continuous road miles from one parcel of property owned, leased, or controlled

986

by the farmer to another parcel of property owned, leased, or controlled by the farmer. This subdivision does not apply to transportation for compensation. *(Added by Stats.1977, c. 627, p. 2116, § 2. Amended by Stats.1984, c. 1021, § 2; Stats.1984, c. 1077, § 12.5, operative July 1, 1985.)*

Cross References

Automatic bale wagon defined, see Vehicle Code § 36011.
Drivers' licenses for implements of husbandry, see Vehicle Code §§ 36300, 36305.
Width limit, see Vehicle Code § 36606.

§ 36105. Other trailers exempt

A trailer or semitrailer owned and used exclusively by a farmer to haul his or her own implements of husbandry, portable sanitary facility, shade trailer, or tools used exclusively for the production or harvesting of agricultural products is exempt from registration. *(Added by Stats.1963, c. 2149, p. 4490, § 24. Amended by Stats.1969, c. 808, § 1; Stats.2012, c. 168 (A.B.2111), § 4.)*

Cross References

Implements of husbandry defined, see Vehicle Code § 36000.
Trailer defined, see Vehicle Code § 630.

§ 36106. Repealed by Stats.1972, c. 176, p. 396, § 2

§ 36109. Farm trailers

"Farm trailers," as defined in Section 36010, having a gross weight of 10,000 pounds or less, are exempt from registration except that Section 5014 shall apply to such trailers. *(Added by Stats.1974, c. 217, p. 415, § 2, eff. May 7, 1974. Amended by Stats.1984, c. 1077, § 13, operative July 1, 1985; Stats.2000, c. 861 (S.B.2084), § 57, eff. Sept. 29, 2000.)*

§ 36110. Repealed by Stats.1973, c. 889, p. 1658, § 57, eff. Sept. 28, 1973, operative Dec. 1, 1974

§ 36112. Repealed by Stats.1972, c. 176, p. 396, § 4

§ 36115. Identification plates

(a) Any person who owns an implement of husbandry which is exempt from registration may obtain an identification plate as provided in Section 5014 for the implement.

(b) The department shall issue an identification plate as applied for to any manufacturer or dealer of an implement of husbandry which is exempt from registration as provided in Section 5016.5. That manufacturer or dealer may obtain more than one plate. *(Added by Stats.1963, c. 2149, p. 4490, § 24. Amended by Stats.1970, c. 405, p. 817, § 6; Stats.1984, c. 1077, § 14, operative July 1, 1985.)*

Cross References

Implements of husbandry defined, see Vehicle Code § 36000.

Implements of husbandry exempt from registration, see Vehicle Code § 36100.

§§ 36115.5 to 36125. Repealed by Stats.1984, c. 1077, §§ 15, 16, 17, operative July 1, 1985

§ 36130. Applications for identification plates; renewals

(a) On and after January 1, 1986, original applications for identification plates on vehicles specified in Division 16 (commencing with Section 36000) shall be submitted pursuant to Section 5014 or Section 5016.5.

(b) Effective January 1, 1986, identification plates that expired on December 31, 1983, shall not be eligible for renewal. Applicants shall apply for identification plates pursuant to Section 5014 or Section 5016.5.

(c) Commencing with 1987 renewals, all expiring identification plates are canceled and owners of vehicles defined in Division 16 (commencing with Section 36000), that are required to display these plates, shall submit applications pursuant to Section 5014 or Section 5016.5. *(Added by Stats.1984, c. 1077, § 19, operative July 1, 1985.)*

CHAPTER 3. DRIVERS' LICENSES

Section
36300. Implement of husbandry operation.
36305. Class C driver's license; necessity.

§ 36300. Implement of husbandry operation

Any person, while driving or operating an implement of husbandry incidentally operated or moved over a highway is not required to obtain a driver's license; except that the driver of any farm tractor while being used to draw a farm trailer carrying farm produce between farms or from a farm to a processing or handling point and return, and the driver of an automatic bale wagon which is being operated as specified in Section 36102, but is not being operated as provided in subdivision (k) of Section 36005, shall be in possession of a driver's license of the appropriate class other than a junior permit. *(Added by Stats.1963, c. 2149, p. 4491, § 24. Amended by Stats.1969, c. 697, p. 1364, § 5; Stats.1977, c. 627, p. 2117, § 4.)*

Cross References

Automatic bale wagon defined, see Vehicle Code § 36011.
Implement of husbandry defined, see Vehicle Code § 36000.
Persons exempt from requirements for drivers' licenses, see Vehicle Code § 12501.

§ 36305. Class C driver's license; necessity

The driver of any implement of husbandry shall possess a valid class C driver's license when operating a combination of vehicles at a speed in excess of 25 miles per hour or towing any implement of husbandry as specified in subdivision (d), (e), or (j) of Section 36005. *(Added by Stats.1986, c. 973, § 10. Amended by Stats.1993, c. 272 (A.B.301), § 55, eff. Aug. 2, 1993.)*

CHAPTER 4. SPEED LAWS

Section
36400. Lift-carrier limit.

§ 36400. Lift-carrier limit

No person shall move or drive a lift-carrier or other vehicle designed and used exclusively for the lifting and carrying of implements of husbandry or tools used exclusively for the production or harvesting of agricultural products at a speed in excess of 35 miles per hour. *(Added by Stats.1963, c. 2149, p. 4491, § 24. Amended by Stats.1971, c. 1135, p. 2150, § 2, operative May 3, 1972.)*

Cross References

Implements of husbandry defined, see Vehicle Code § 36000.

CHAPTER 5. EQUIPMENT OF IMPLEMENTS OF HUSBANDRY

Section
36500. Exemptions and requirements.
36505. Lighting requirements.
36508. New implement of husbandry.
36509. Flashing amber lights; red flags.
36510. Stopping distance requirements.
36515. Windshield exemption.
36520. Windshield wiper exemption.

§ 36500. Exemptions and requirements

The provisions of Sections 24012, 24250, 24251, 24400 to 24404, inclusive, and Articles 3 (commencing with Section 24600), 4 (commencing with Section 24800), 5 (commencing with Section 24950), 6 (commencing with Section 25100), 9 (commencing with Section 25350), 11 (commencing with Section 25450), and 13 (commencing with Section 25650) of Chapter 2 of Division 12 shall not apply to implements of husbandry. Such vehicles shall be subject to the provisions of Sections 24254, 24615, 25803, and 25950, and Article 12 (commencing with Section 25500) of Chapter 2 of Division 12. *(Added by Stats.1963, c. 2149, p. 4491, § 24. Amended by Stats.1969, c. 949, p. 1895, § 2; Stats.1972, c. 618, p. 1151, § 151.)*

§ 36505. Lighting requirements

Farm tractors as defined in Section 36015, and trailers displaying an identification plate, as provided for in Section 36115 or 36130, when operated during darkness shall not be exempted from the provisions of Sections 24400 and 25100. *(Added by Stats.1963, c. 2149, p. 4491, § 24. Amended by Stats.1996, c. 124 (A.B.3470), § 139.)*

§ 36508. New implement of husbandry

After July 1, 1970, no new implement of husbandry designed or intended by the manufacturer to be operated or moved at a speed not in excess of 25 miles per hour shall be sold in this state unless it is equipped by the manufacturer with a slow-moving vehicle emblem as prescribed by Section 24615, and such an emblem shall thereafter be displayed and maintained on such implement of husbandry while the implement is able to be operated upon a public highway. *(Added by Stats.1967, c. 380, p. 1604, § 1. Amended by Stats.1969, c. 632, p. 1283, § 2; Stats.1969, c. 949, p. 1895, § 3.)*

Cross References

Display of slow-moving vehicle emblem, see Vehicle Code § 24615.

§ 36509.   Flashing amber lights; red flags

(a) An implement of husbandry, a farm vehicle, or any vehicle escorting or towing an implement of husbandry or farm vehicle, may display flashing amber warning lamps or flashing amber turn signals:

(1) When the vehicle is required to display a "slow moving vehicle" emblem as defined in Section 24615.

(2) When the width, length, height, or speed of the vehicle may cause a hazard to other traffic on the highway.

(b) An implement of husbandry, a farm vehicle, or any vehicle towing an implement of husbandry or farm vehicle, when the load upon the vehicle exceeds 120 inches in width, shall display either:

(1) Flashing amber warning lamps.

(2) Flashing amber turn signals.

(3) During daylight hours, red flags, each of which shall be not less than 16 inches square, mounted at the left and right outer extremities of the vehicle or load whichever has the greater horizontal dimension. *(Added by Stats.1986, c. 973, § 11.)*

§ 36510.   Stopping distance requirements

Implements of husbandry are not subject to stopping distance requirements contained in Section 26454, but if any such vehicle cannot be stopped within 32 feet from an initial speed of 15 miles per hour, it shall not be operated at a speed in excess of that permitting a stop in 32 feet. *(Added by Stats.1963, c. 2149, p. 4492, § 24.)*

§ 36515.   Windshield exemption

The provisions of Section 26700 relating to windshields shall not apply to implements of husbandry. *(Added by Stats.1963, c. 2149, p. 4492, § 24.)*

§ 36520.   Windshield wiper exemption

The provisions of Section 26706 relating to windshield wipers shall not apply to implements of husbandry. *(Added by Stats.1963, c. 2149, p. 4492, § 24.)*

CHAPTER 6.   SIZE, WEIGHT AND LOAD OF IMPLEMENTS OF HUSBANDRY

Section
36600.   Width exemptions and limitations.
36605.   Width limitations for certain vehicles.
36606.   Automatic bale wagon: width exemptions and limitations.
36610.   Height exemption; transporting vehicle; writing.

Section
36615.   Length exemption.
36620.   Repealed.
36625.   Towing more than one vehicle.
36626.   Towing two cotton trailers.
36627.   Towing two almond trailers.

§ 36600.   Width exemptions and limitations

(a) The limitations as to width as set forth in Chapter 2 (commencing with Section 35100) of Division 15 do not apply to implements of husbandry incidentally operated, transported, towed, or otherwise moved over a highway.

(b) Notwithstanding subdivision (a), when an implement of husbandry is transported or moved over a highway which is a part of the National System of Interstate and Defense Highways (as referred to in Section 108 of the Federal-aid Highway Act of 1956)[1] as a load on another vehicle, if the load exceeds 102 inches in width, the vehicle and load shall not be operated for a distance in excess of 25 miles from the point of origin of the trip. The operator of the transporting vehicle shall be a farmer or a person regularly employed by a farmer or farm corporation, and the operator transporting the load shall have in his or her immediate possession a writing signed by the farmer or farm corporation agent which states the origin and destination of the trip.

(c) Notwithstanding subdivision (a), when an implement of husbandry is transported or moved over any other highway as a load on another vehicle, if the load exceeds 120 inches in width, the vehicle and load shall not be operated for a distance in excess of 25 miles from the point of origin of the trip. The operator of the transporting vehicle shall be a farmer or a person employed by a farmer or farm corporation, and the operator transporting the load shall have in his or her immediate possession a writing signed by the farmer or farm corporation agent which states the origin and destination of the trip. *(Added by Stats.1963, c. 2149, p. 4492, § 24. Amended by Stats.1970, c. 76, p. 89, § 1; Stats.1982, c. 686, p. 2820, § 1; Stats.1986, c. 973, § 12; Stats.1988, c. 103, § 1, eff. May 11, 1988.)*

[1] See 23 U.S.C.A. § 101 et seq.

Cross References

Damage to highway, weight or size of vehicle, see Vehicle Code § 17302.
Implements of husbandry defined, see Vehicle Code §§ 36000, 36005.
Lighting equipment of wide vehicles, see Vehicle Code § 25104.

§ 36605.   Width limitations for certain vehicles

The limitations as to width, as set forth in Chapter 2 (commencing with Section 35100) of Division 15, do not apply to any trailer or semitrailer, including lift carriers and tip-bed trailers, used exclusively for the transportation of implements of husbandry or tools used exclusively for the production or harvesting of agricultural products by farmers or implement dealers, except as follows:

(1) With respect to any trailer or semitrailer transporting a grain-harvesting combine, that vehicle shall not exceed a width of 144 inches.

(2) With respect to any other vehicle described in this section, that vehicle, or the load on that vehicle when that load consists of tools, shall not exceed a width of 120 inches.

(3) With respect to any trailer or semitrailer described in subdivision (c) of Section 36005, that vehicle, when towed upon a highway shall not exceed a width of 174 inches and shall be subject to subdivisions (b) and (c) of Section 36600. *(Added by Stats.1963, c. 2149, p. 4492, § 24. Amended by Stats.1971, c. 1135, p. 2150, § 3, operative May 3, 1972; Stats.1975, c. 120, p. 194, § 1, eff. June 14, 1975; Stats.1982, c. 827, p. 3142, § 18, eff. Sept. 10, 1982; Stats.1986, c. 973, § 13.)*

§ 36606. Automatic bale wagon: width exemptions and limitations

(a) The limitations as to width, as set forth in Chapter 2 (commencing with Section 35100) of Division 15, do not apply to automatic bale wagons while operated as specified in Section 36102, except that such vehicles or the load thereon may not exceed 120 inches in width.

(b) This section shall have no application to highways which are a part of the National System of Interstate and Defense Highways (as referred to in subdivision (a) of Section 108 of the Federal-Aid Highway Act of 1956). *(Added by Stats.1977, c. 627, p. 2117, § 5.)*

Cross References
Automatic bale wagon defined, see Vehicle Code § 36011.

§ 36610. Height exemption; transporting vehicle; writing

(a) The limitations as to height of vehicles contained in Chapter 3 (commencing with Section 35250) of Division 15 do not apply to implements of husbandry incidentally operated, transported, towed, or otherwise moved over a highway.

(b) Notwithstanding subdivision (a), when an implement of husbandry is transported or moved over a highway as a load on another vehicle and the load exceeds 14 feet in height, the vehicle and load shall not be operated for a distance in excess of 25 miles from the point of origin of the trip. The operator of the transporting vehicle shall be a farmer or a person regularly employed by a farmer or farm corporation, and the operator transporting the vehicle shall have in his or her immediate possession a writing signed by the farmer or farm corporation agent which states the origin and destination of the trip. *(Added by Stats.1963, c. 2149, p. 4492, § 24. Amended by Stats.1982, c. 686, p. 2820, § 2.)*

§ 36615. Length exemption

The limitations as to length of vehicles contained in Chapter 4 (commencing with Section 35400) do not apply to implements of husbandry operated or moved over a highway incidental to agricultural operations. Notwith-

standing Section 36626, when an implement of husbandry is operated in a combination of vehicles that exceeds the length requirements of Section 35401, the combination is limited to two vehicles in tandem. *(Added by Stats.1963, c. 2149, p. 4492, § 24. Amended by Stats.1986, c. 973, § 14.)*

Cross References
Damage to highway, weight or size of vehicle, see Vehicle Code § 17302.
Height exemption, implements of husbandry, see Vehicle Code § 36610.
Implement of husbandry defined, see Vehicle Code §§ 36000, 36005.

§ 36620. Repealed by Stats.1976, c. 1079, p. 4890, § 92

§ 36625. Towing more than one vehicle

The provisions of Section 21715 do not apply to any vehicle drawing or towing unladen implements of husbandry. *(Added by Stats.1963, c. 2149, p. 4492, § 24.)*

§ 36626. Towing two cotton trailers

Notwithstanding the provisions of Section 21715, a motor truck with an unladen weight of not less than 3,500 pounds and a gross weight of not less than 4,200 pounds may tow a combination of two cotton trailers operated on the highways for the exclusive purpose of transporting cotton from a farm to a cotton gin and returning the empty trailers to such farm. Extra weight or ballast may be added to meet the requirements of this section and shall be in the form of 100-pound bags of sand. *(Added by Stats.1963, c. 2004, p. 4083, § 2.)*

§ 36627. Towing two almond trailers

Notwithstanding the provisions of Section 21715, a motortruck with an unladen weight of not less than 3,500 pounds and a gross weight of not less than 4,200 pounds may tow a combination of two almond trailers operated on the highways for the exclusive purpose of transporting almonds from a farm to an almond huller and returning the empty trailers to such farm. Extra weight or ballast may be added to meet the requirements of this section and shall be in the form of 100-pound bags of sand. *(Added by Stats.1973, c. 293, p. 701, § 1.)*

CHAPTER 7. OTHER REQUIREMENTS

Section
36700. Application of other provisions.
36705. Automatic bale wagon: operation during darkness.

§ 36700. Application of other provisions

All implements of husbandry, farm trailers or any other vehicles subject to the provisions of this division, and any owner, operator or driver of such vehicles, shall also comply with and be subject to all other provisions of this code which are not in conflict with the specific provisions contained in this division. *(Added by Stats.1963, c. 2149, p. 4493, § 24.)*

§ 36705. Automatic bale wagon: operation during darkness

No automatic bale wagon exceeding 96 inches in width or carrying a load in excess of 100 inches in width may be

989

operated on any highway during darkness. *(Added by Stats.1977, c. 627, p. 2118, § 7.)*

CHAPTER 8.   GENERAL PROVISIONS

Section
36800.   Application of division.

§ 36800.   Application of division

The provisions of this division, unless otherwise provided, apply to all vehicles, whether publicly or privately owned, when upon the highways.   *(Added by Stats.1963, c. 2149, p. 4493, § 24.)*

Division 16.5

OFF–HIGHWAY VEHICLES

Chapter	Section
1. General Provisions	38000
2. Registration of Off-Highway Vehicles; Original and Renewal of Identification; Issuance of Certificates of Ownership	38010
3. Transfer of Title or Interest [Renumbered]	
4. Identification Fees [Renumbered]	
5. Off-Highway Vehicle Operating Rules	38280
6. Equipment of Off–Highway Vehicles	38325
7. All–Terrain Vehicles	38500
8. Recreational Off–Highway Vehicles	38600

Cross References

Enforcement of off-highway motor vehicle use and equipment, see Public Resources Code § 5090.32.

Off–Highway Vehicle Trust Fund, transfer of money, see Revenue and Taxation Code § 8352.6.

Sale of specified vehicles, presumption of sale at retail, rebuttal by taking resale certificate, additional contents of resale certificate, see Revenue and Taxation Code § 6092.5.

Tangible personal property, due dates for use taxes imposed for storage, use or other consumption of property, see Revenue and Taxation Code § 6451.5.

Violation of license provisions, see Vehicle Code §§ 14601 to 14601.5.

CHAPTER 1. GENERAL PROVISIONS

Section
38000. Short title.
38001. Applicability of provisions.
38006. Off-highway motor vehicle defined.
38007. Course of instruction.

Cross References

Disposition of off-highway vehicle fines and forfeitures, see Vehicle Code § 42204.

Exemption of gross receipts for occasional sales of vehicles required to be identified under this division from taxes, see Revenue and Taxation Code § 6367.

Exemption of gross receipts of sales of vehicles,
  Vessels or aircraft from use tax, see Revenue and Taxation Code § 6281.
  Vessels or aircraft required to be identified under this division from sales tax, see Revenue and Taxation Code § 6283.

Notice to correct violations, see Vehicle Code § 40303.5.

Payment of sales tax on sale of vehicle subject to this division by retailer not subject to § 11615.5, see Revenue and Taxation Code § 6293.

Retailer defined to include person subject to identification under this division, Sales and Use Tax Law, see Revenue and Taxation Code § 6275.

State park system and state vehicular recreation area and trial system, enforcement of this division, see Public Resources Code § 5008.

Transfer of money from Motor Vehicle Fuel Account to Off-Highway Vehicle Fund, see Revenue and Taxation Code § 8352.6.

Vehicle defined to include off-highway motor vehicles, Sales and Use Tax Law, see Revenue and Taxation Code § 6272.

Vehicle registration and sale prohibitions, see Vehicle Code § 27200.

§ 38000. Short title

This division may be cited as the Chappie-Z'berg Off-Highway Motor Vehicle Law of 1971. *(Added by Stats. 1971, c. 1816, p. 3925, § 9, eff. Dec. 22, 1971, operative July 1, 1972.)*

Cross References

Report of conviction to department, see Vehicle Code § 1803.

§ 38001. Applicability of provisions

(a) Except as otherwise provided, this division applies to off-highway motor vehicles, as defined in Section 38006, on lands, other than a highway, that are open and accessible to the public, including any land acquired, developed, operated, or maintained, in whole or in part, with money from the Off–Highway Vehicle Trust Fund, except private lands under the immediate control of the owner or his or her agent where permission is required and has been granted to operate a motor vehicle. For purposes of this division, the term "highway" does not include fire trails, logging roads, service roads regardless of surface composition, or other roughly graded trails and roads upon which vehicular travel by the public is permitted.

(b) Privately owned and maintained parking facilities that are generally open to the public are exempt from this division, unless the facilities are specifically declared subject to this division by the procedure specified in Section 21107.8. *(Added by Stats.1976, c. 1093, p. 4942, § 5. Amended by Stats.1982, c. 994, p. 3625, § 13; Stats.1986, c. 1009, § 4; Stats.2002, c. 563 (A.B.2274), § 37.)*

Cross References

Applicability of emission control equipment regulations, see Vehicle Code § 38397.

§ 38006. Off-highway motor vehicle defined

As used in this division, an "off-highway motor vehicle" is any of the following:

(a) A motor vehicle subject to the provisions of subdivision (a) of Section 38010.

(b) A motor vehicle registered under Section 4000, when such motor vehicle is operated on land to which this division has application.

(c) A motor vehicle owned or operated by a nonresident of this state, whether or not such motor vehicle is identified or registered in a foreign jurisdiction, when such motor vehicle is operated on lands to which this division has application. *(Added by Stats.1976, c. 1093, p. 4942, § 6.)*

Cross References

Equipment of off-highway motor vehicles, applicability of provisions, see Vehicle Code § 38325.

Mufflers and exhaust systems, see Vehicle Code § 38365.

§ 38007. Course of instruction

The Off–Highway Motor Vehicle Recreation Division of the Department of Parks and Recreation shall adopt courses of instruction in off-highway motor vehicle safety, operation, and principles of environmental preservation by January 1, 2005. For this purpose the division shall consult with the Department of the California Highway Patrol and other public and private agencies or organizations. The division shall make this course of instruction available directly, through contractual agreement, or through volunteers authorized by the division to conduct a course of instruction. *(Added by Stats.1976, c. 1093, p. 4942, § 6.5. Amended by Stats.2002, c. 563 (A.B.2274), § 38.)*

Cross References

Department of California Highway Patrol, see Vehicle Code § 2100 et seq.

CHAPTER 2. REGISTRATION OF OFF–HIGHWAY VEHICLES; ORIGINAL AND RENEWAL OF IDENTIFICATION; ISSUANCE OF CERTIFICATES OF OWNERSHIP

Article	Section
1. Motor Vehicles Subject to Identification	38010
2. Original Identification	38040
3. Evidences of Identification	38070
4. Renewal of Identification	38110
5. Refusal of Identification	38145
6. Identification Plate or Device	38160
7. Dismantling of Off-Highway Motor Vehicles	38180
8. Transfers of Title or Interest	38195
9. Identification Fees	38225
10. Off-Highway Vehicle Fund Expenditures [Repealed]	

ARTICLE 1. MOTOR VEHICLES SUBJECT TO IDENTIFICATION

Section
38010. Identification plate or device; issuance and display; exemptions.
38012. Definitions.
38013. Identification, identification certificate defined.
38014. Closed course defined.
38020. Identification required; riding in violation of seasons.
38021. Exemption; special permit.
38022. Motorcycles; transportation on highway.
38025. Operation on highway.
38026. Highway providing connecting link to off-highway motor vehicle uses; designation for combined use;

Section
    conditions; proposals; approval by commissioner of highway patrol.
38026.1. County of Inyo highway use pilot project.
38026.5. Operation of off-highway motor vehicle on combined-use highway; prohibited acts.
38027. Motor-driven cycles; movement adjacent to a roadway; designation of access routes leading to off-highway parks for operation of vehicles.
38030. Off-highway vehicles delivered to dealer.

§ 38010. Identification plate or device; issuance and display; exemptions

(a) Except as otherwise provided in subdivision (b), every motor vehicle specified in Section 38012 that is not registered under this code because it is to be operated or used exclusively off the highways, except as provided in this division, shall be issued and display an identification plate or device issued by the department.

(b) Subdivision (a) does not apply to any of the following:

(1) Motor vehicles specifically exempted from registration under this code, including, but not limited to, motor vehicles exempted pursuant to Sections 4006, 4010, 4012, 4013, 4015, 4018, and 4019.

(2) Implements of husbandry.

(3) Motor vehicles owned by the state, or any county, city, district, or political subdivision of the state, or the United States.

(4) Motor vehicles owned or operated by, or operated under contract with a utility, whether privately or publicly owned, when used as specified in Section 22512.

(5) Special construction equipment described in Section 565, regardless of whether those motor vehicles are used in connection with highway or railroad work.

(6) A motor vehicle with a currently valid special permit issued under Section 38087.5 that is owned or operated by a nonresident of this state and the vehicle is not identified or registered in a foreign jurisdiction. For the purposes of this paragraph, a person who holds a valid driver's license issued by a foreign jurisdiction is presumed to be a nonresident.

(7) Commercial vehicles weighing more than 6,000 pounds unladen.

(8) Any motorcycle manufactured in the year 1942 or prior.

(9) Four–wheeled motor vehicles operated solely in organized racing or competitive events upon a closed course when those events are conducted under the auspices of a recognized sanctioning body or by permit issued by the local governmental authority having jurisdiction.

(10) A motor vehicle with a currently valid identification or registration permit issued by another state. *(Added by Stats.1971, c. 1816, p. 3925, § 9, eff. Dec. 22, 1971, operative July 1, 1972. Amended by Stats.1972, c. 973, p. 1760, § 21, eff. Aug. 16, 1972; Stats.1973, c. 78, p.*

139, § 22; Stats.1973, c. 974, p. 1873, § 1, operative July 1, 1974; Stats.1974, c. 377, p. 936, § 1, eff. June 30, 1974, operative July 1, 1974; Stats.1975, c. 1050, p. 2483, § 2; Stats.1987, c. 513, § 1; Stats.1996, c. 124 (A.B.3470), § 140; Stats.1996, c. 572 (S.B.2079), § 1; Stats.1999, c. 1008 (S.B.533), § 16.)

Cross References

Advertisement of used vehicle as certified, see Vehicle Code § 11713.18.

Consideration for assignment of conditional sale contract, see Civil Code § 2982.10.

Definitions,
    Commercial vehicle, see Vehicle Code § 260.
    Motorcycle, see Vehicle Code § 400.

Disclosure of additional charges for goods or services, see Vehicle Code § 11713.19.

Entry of motor vehicle into federal or state wilderness area, public offense and penalties, see Vehicle COde § 38301.3.

Formalities of conditional sale contracts, see Civil Code § 2982.

Motor vehicle sold or leased by new motor vehicle dealer, electronic registration, exceptions, see Vehicle Code § 4456.4.

Notice to vehicle credit applicant of consumer credit score, see Vehicle Code § 11713.20.

Off-highway vehicles, operation by peace officers on highways in emergency response situations, see Vehicle Code § 38025.

Used vehicles, NMVTIS vehicle history report required, requirements for junk or salvage automobile, exceptions, see Vehicle Code § 11713.26.

Violation of local ordinance prohibiting entry into mountain fire district, see Vehicle Code § 38301.5.

§ 38012. Definitions

(a) As used in this division, "off-highway motor vehicle subject to identification" means a motor vehicle subject to subdivision (a) of Section 38010.

(b) As used in this division, "off-highway motor vehicle" includes, but is not limited to, the following:

(1) A motorcycle or motor-driven cycle, except for any motorcycle that is eligible for a special transportation identification device issued pursuant to Section 38088.

(2) A snowmobile or other vehicle designed to travel over snow or ice, as defined in Section 557.

(3) A motor vehicle commonly referred to as a sand buggy, dune buggy, or all-terrain vehicle.

(4) A motor vehicle commonly referred to as a jeep.

(5) A recreational off-highway vehicle as defined in Section 500. *(Added by Stats.1971, c. 1816, p. 3926, § 9, eff. Dec. 22, 1971, operative July 1, 1972. Amended by Stats.1973, c. 974, p. 1873, § 2, operative July 1, 1974; Stats.1974, c. 377, p. 937, § 2, eff. June 30, 1974, operative July 1, 1974; Stats.1975, c. 1050, p. 2483, § 3; Stats.2012, c. 165 (A.B.1595), § 2.)*

Cross References

Exemption from driver's license, see Vehicle Code § 12501.

§ 38013. Identification, identification certificate defined

Unless otherwise provided, the terms "identification" and "identification certificate" shall have the same meaning as the terms "registration" and "registration card," respectively, as used in Division 3 (commencing with Section 4000). *(Added by Stats.1971, c. 1816, p. 3926, § 9, eff. Dec. 22, 1971, operative July 1, 1972.)*

§ 38014. Closed course defined

As used in this division, "closed course" includes, but is not limited to, a speedway, racetrack, or a prescribed and defined route of travel on or off a highway that is closed to all motor vehicles other than those of participants. A closed course is one which is not available at any time for vehicular access by the general public. *(Added by Stats. 1975, c. 1050, p. 2484, § 4.)*

§ 38020. Identification required; riding in violation of seasons

Except as otherwise provided in this division, no person shall operate, transport, or leave standing any off-highway motor vehicle subject to identification under this code which is not registered under the provisions of Division 3 (commencing with Section 4000), unless it is identified under the provisions of this chapter. A violation of this section is an infraction. Riding in violation of seasons established by Section 2412(f) and 2415 of Title 13 of the California Code of Regulations constitutes a violation of this section. This section shall not apply to the operation, transportation, or leaving standing of an off-highway vehicle pursuant to a valid special permit. *(Added by Stats.1971, c. 1816, p. 3926, § 9, eff. Dec. 22, 1971, operative July 1, 1972. Amended by Stats.1976, c. 1093, p. 4942, § 7; Stats.1986, c. 1009, § 5; Stats.2004, c. 908 (A.B.2666), § 20.)*

Cross References

Punishment for violation of section, see Vehicle Code § 42001.10.

§ 38021. Exemption; special permit

(a) A manufacturer, dealer, or distributor, or his agent, owning or lawfully possessing any off-highway motor vehicle of a type otherwise required to be identified hereunder may operate or use such vehicle without an identification certificate and plate or device upon condition that each such vehicle is accompanied by a special permit issued to the manufacturer, dealer, or distributor as provided in this division.

(b) Persons licensed pursuant to Article 1 (commencing with Section 11700) of Chapter 4 of Division 5 need not obtain such a permit provided the vehicle is operated or used under special plates issued to the licensee. *(Added by Stats.1972, c. 973, p. 1761, § 22, eff. Aug. 16, 1972. Amended by Stats.1976, c. 1093, p. 4943, § 8.)*

§ 38022. Motorcycles; transportation on highway

Notwithstanding the provisions of Section 4000, motorcycles issued a special transportation identification device pursuant to Section 38088 may be transported upon a highway to and from a closed course. *(Added by Stats.1975, c. 1050, p. 2484, § 5.)*

§ 38025. Operation on highway

In accordance with subdivision (c) of Section 4000, a motor vehicle issued a plate or device pursuant to Section 38160 may be operated or driven upon a highway but only as follows:

(a) On a two-lane highway, only to cross the highway at an angle of approximately 90 degrees to the direction of the roadway and at a place where a quick and safe crossing may be made, or only when the roadway is not maintained by snow removal equipment and is closed to motor vehicles that are subject to registration pursuant to Division 3 (commencing with Section 4000), or only to cross a highway in the manner specified in subdivision (b).

(b) With respect to the crossing of a highway having more than two lanes, or a highway having limited access, a motor vehicle may cross a highway but only at a place designated by the Department of Transportation or local authorities with respect to a highway under their respective jurisdictions as a place where a motor vehicle, or specified types of motor vehicle, may cross a highway, and a vehicle shall cross the highway only at that designated place and only in a quick and safe manner.

(c) The Department of Transportation and local authorities with respect to a highway under their respective jurisdictions may designate, by the erection of an appropriate sign of a type approved by the Department of Transportation, a place where a motor vehicle, or specified type of motor vehicle, may cross a highway having more than two lanes or having limited access.

(d) A motor vehicle identified pursuant to Section 38010 may be towed upon a highway, but not driven, if the vehicle displays a plate or device issued pursuant to Section 38160.

(e) A motorcycle identified pursuant to Section 38010 may be pushed upon a highway, but not ridden, if the motorcycle has displayed upon it a plate or device issued pursuant to Section 38160.

(f) A peace officer, as defined in Chapter 4.5 (commencing with Section 830) of Title 3 of Part 2 of the Penal Code, may operate or drive an off-highway vehicle identified pursuant to Section 38010 upon a highway in an emergency response situation. *(Added by Stats.1971, c. 1816, p. 3926, § 9, eff. Dec. 22, 1971, operative July 1, 1972. Amended by Stats.1972, c. 973, p. 1761, § 23, eff. Aug. 16, 1972; Stats.1973, c. 825, p. 1473, § 1; Stats.1974, c. 947, p. 1977, § 1; Stats.1987, c. 44, § 2; Stats.2003, c. 135 (S.B.637), § 1.)*

Cross References

Exemption from driver's license, see Vehicle Code § 12501.
Snowmobiles, unlawful operation, see Vehicle Code § 23128.

§ 38026. Highway providing connecting link to off-highway motor vehicle uses; designation for combined use; conditions; proposals; approval by commissioner of highway patrol

(a) In addition to Section 38025 and after complying with subdivision (c) of this section, if a local authority, an agency of the federal government, or the Director of Parks and Recreation finds that a highway, or a portion of a highway, under the jurisdiction of the authority, agency, or the director, as the case may be, is located in a manner that provides a connecting link between off-highway motor vehicle trail segments, between an off-highway motor vehicle recreational use area and necessary service facilities, or between lodging facilities and an off-highway motor vehicle recreational facility and if it is found that the highway is designed and constructed so as to safely permit the use of regular vehicular traffic and also the driving of off-highway motor vehicles on that highway, the local authority, by resolution or ordinance, agency of the federal government, or the Director of Parks and Recreation, as the case may be, may designate that highway, or a portion of a highway, for combined use and shall prescribe rules and regulations therefor. A highway, or portion of a highway, shall not be so designated for a distance of more than three miles, except as provided in Section 38026.1. A freeway shall not be designated under this section.

(b) The Off–Highway Motor Vehicle Recreation Commission may propose highway segments for consideration by local authorities, an agency of the federal government, or the Director of Parks and Recreation for combined use.

(c) Prior to designating a highway or portion of a highway on the motion of the local authority, an agency of the federal government, or the Director of Parks and Recreation, or as a recommendation of the Off–Highway Motor Vehicle Recreation Commission, a local authority, an agency of the federal government, or the Director of Parks and Recreation shall notify the Commissioner of the California Highway Patrol, and shall not designate any segment pursuant to subdivision (a) which, in the opinion of the commissioner, would create a potential traffic safety hazard.

(d)(1) A designation of a highway, or a portion of a highway, under subdivision (a) shall become effective upon the erection of appropriate signs of a type approved by the Department of Transportation on and along the highway, or portion of the highway.

(2) The cost of the signs shall be reimbursed from the Off–Highway Vehicle Trust Fund, when appropriated by the Legislature, or by expenditure of funds from a grant or cooperative agreement made pursuant to Section 5090. 50 of the Public Resources Code. *(Added by Stats.1985, c. 676, § 1. Amended by Stats.1987, c. 44, § 3; Stats. 2002, c. 563 (A.B.2274), § 39; Stats.2011, c. 532 (A.B. 628), § 3.)*

§ 38026.1. County of Inyo highway use pilot project

(a) Except as provided in subdivision (e), the County of Inyo may establish a pilot project to designate combined-use highways on unincorporated county roads in the county for no more than 10 miles so that the combined-use highways can be used to link existing off-highway motor vehicle trails and trailheads on federal

Bureau of Land Management or United States Forest Service lands, and to link off-highway motor vehicle recreational-use areas with necessary service and lodging facilities, in order to provide a unified system of trails for off-highway motor vehicles, preserve traffic safety, improve natural resource protection, reduce off-highway vehicle trespass on private land, and minimize impacts on county residents.

(b) The pilot project shall do all of the following:

(1) Prescribe a procedure for highway, road, or route selection and designation. The procedure shall be approved by a vote of a majority of the Inyo County Board of Supervisors.

(2) Prescribe a procedure for the county to remove a combined-use designation, including a designation that is removed as a result of the conclusion of the pilot program.

(3) In cooperation with the Department of Transportation, establish uniform specifications and symbols for signs, markers, and traffic control devices to control off-highway motor vehicles, including, but not limited to, the following:

(A) Devices to warn of dangerous conditions, obstacles, or hazards.

(B) Designations of the right-of-way for regular vehicular traffic and off-highway motor vehicles.

(C) A description of the nature and destination of the off-highway motor vehicle trail.

(D) Warning signs for pedestrians and motorists of the presence of off-highway motor vehicle traffic.

(4) Require that off-highway motor vehicles subject to the pilot project meet the safety requirements of federal and state law regarding proper drivers' licensing, helmet usage, and the requirements pursuant to Section 38026.5.

(5) Prohibit off-highway motor vehicles from traveling faster than 35 miles per hour on highways designated under this section.

(6) Include an opportunity for public comment at a public hearing held by the county in order to evaluate the pilot project.

(c) The pilot project may include use of a state highway, subject to the approval of the Department of Transportation, or any crossing of a highway designated pursuant to Section 38025.

(d)(1) By selecting and designating a highway for combined use pursuant to this section, the County of Inyo agrees to defend and indemnify the state against any and all claims, including legal defense and liability arising from a claim, for any safety-related losses or injuries arising or resulting from use by off-highway motor vehicles of a highway designated as a combined-use highway by the Inyo County Board of Supervisors pursuant to this section.

(2) This subdivision does not alter the requirements of subdivision (e).

(e) The County of Inyo shall not designate a highway for combined use pursuant to this section unless the Commissioner of the Department of the California Highway Patrol finds that designating the highway for combined use would not create a potential traffic safety hazard.

(f) Not later than January 1, 2016, the County of Inyo, in consultation with the Department of the California Highway Patrol, the Department of Transportation, and the Department of Parks and Recreation, shall prepare and submit to the Legislature a report evaluating the pilot project, and containing both of the following:

(1) A description of the road segments designated to allow combined use for over three miles, as approved or adopted by a majority vote of the members of the Inyo County Board of Supervisors.

(2) An evaluation of the overall safety and effectiveness of the pilot project, including its impact on traffic flows, safety, off-highway vehicle usage on existing trails, incursions into areas not designated for off-highway vehicle usage, and nonmotorized recreation.

(3) A description of the public comments received at a public hearing held by the county in regards to an evaluation of the pilot project.

(g)(1) A report submitted pursuant to subdivision (f) shall be submitted in compliance with Section 9795 of the Government Code.

(2) This section shall remain in effect only until January 1, 2017, and as of that date is repealed, unless a later enacted statute, that is enacted before January 1, 2017, deletes or extends that date. *(Added by Stats.2011, c. 532 (A.B.628), § 4.)*

Repeal

For repeal of this section, see its terms.

§ 38026.5. Operation of off-highway motor vehicle on combined-use highway; prohibited acts

(a) In accordance with subdivision (c) of Section 4000, a motor vehicle issued a plate or device pursuant to Section 38160 may be operated or driven on a local highway, or a portion of the local highway, that is designated pursuant to Section 38026 or 38026.1 if the operation is in conformance with this code and the vehicle complies with off-highway vehicle equipment requirements specified in this division.

(b) Notwithstanding subdivision (a), it is unlawful for a person using an off-highway vehicle on a combined-use highway to do any of the following:

(1) Operate an off-highway motor vehicle on the highway during the hours of darkness.

(2) Operate a vehicle on the highway that does not have an operational stoplight.

(3) Operate a vehicle on the highway that does not have rubber tires.

(4) Operate a vehicle without a valid driver's license of the appropriate class for the vehicle operation in possession.

(5) Operate a vehicle on the highway without complying with Article 2 (commencing with Section 16020) of Chapter 1 of Division 7. *(Added by Stats.1985, c. 676, § 2. Amended by Stats.1987, c. 44, § 4; Stats.2011, c. 532 (A.B.628), § 5.)*

§ 38027. Motor-driven cycles; movement adjacent to a roadway; designation of access routes leading to off-highway parks for operation of vehicles

Motor-driven cycles issued a plate or device pursuant to Section 38160 may be moved, by nonmechanical means only, adjacent to a roadway, in such a manner so as to not interfere with traffic upon the highway, only for the purpose of gaining access to, or returning from, areas designed for the operation of off-highway vehicles, when no other route is available. The Department of Transportation or local authority may designate access routes leading to off-highway parks as suitable for the operation of off-highway vehicles, if such access routes are available to the general public only for pedestrian and off-highway motor vehicle travel. *(Added by Stats.1971, c. 1816, p. 3926, § 9, eff. Dec. 22, 1971, operative July 1, 1972. Amended by Stats.1976, c. 1093, p. 4943, § 9.)*

§ 38030. Off-highway vehicles delivered to dealer

Notwithstanding the provisions of Section 38020, an unidentified off-highway motor vehicle subject to identification may be left standing upon a highway or public or private property adjacent to the place of business of a dealer of such motor vehicles when done so in connection with the loading and unloading or storage of such vehicles to be used in the dealer's business, unless already prohibited by law. *(Added by Stats.1971, c. 1816, p. 3927, § 9, eff. Dec. 22, 1971, operative July 1, 1972. Amended by Stats.1973, c. 78, p. 140, § 23.)*

ARTICLE 2. ORIGINAL IDENTIFICATION

Section
38040. Application for identification.
38041. Application for identification; motorcycle.
38045. Co-ownership of off-highway vehicle.
38050. Undertaking or bond.
38055. Return and surrender of bond or undertaking.
38060. Change of address.

§ 38040. Application for identification

Application for the original identification of a motor vehicle, other than a motorcycle, required to be identified pursuant to this division shall be made by the owner to the department upon the appropriate form furnished by it and shall contain all of the following:

(a) The true, full name, business or residence and mailing address, and the driver's license or identification card number, if any, of the owner and the legal owner, if any.

996

(b) The name of the county in which the owner resides.

(c) A description of the vehicle, including the following, insofar as it may exist:

(1) The make, model, and type of body.

(2) The vehicle identification number or any other number as may be required by the department.

(d) Information as may reasonably be required by the department to enable it to determine whether the vehicle is lawfully entitled to identification. *(Added by Stats. 1971, c. 1816, p. 3927, § 9, eff. Dec. 22, 1971, operative July 1, 1972. Amended by Stats.1975, c. 389, p. 867, § 7; Stats.1976, c. 1093, p. 4943, § 10; Stats.1989, c. 1213, § 15; Stats.1994, c. 1221 (S.B.1758), § 18.)*

§ 38041. Application for identification; motorcycle

Application for the original identification of a motorcycle shall be made by the owner to the department upon the appropriate form furnished by it, and shall contain:

(a) The true, full name, business or residence and mailing address, and the driver's license or identification card number, if any, of the owner and the legal owner, if any.

(b) The name of the county in which the owner resides.

(c) A description of the motorcycle including the following data insofar as it may exist:

(1) The make and type of body.

(2) The motor and frame numbers recorded exactly as stamped on the engine and frame, respectively, by the manufacturer, and any other identifying number of the motorcycle as may be required by the department.

(3) The date first sold by a manufacturer or dealer to a consumer.

(d) Such information as may reasonably be required by the department to enable it to determine whether the vehicle is lawfully entitled to identification.

(e) The department shall maintain a cross-index file of motor and frame numbers identified with it.

The application shall be accompanied by a tracing, tape lift, or photograph of the motor or frame numbers, or where the facsimile of the motor or frame numbers cannot be obtained, a verification of the numbers shall be required. *(Added by Stats.1976, c. 1093, p. 4943, § 11. Amended by Stats.1989, c. 1213, § 16; Stats.1994, c. 1221 (S.B.1758), § 19.)*

Cross References

Motorcycle defined, see Vehicle Code § 400.

§ 38045. Co-ownership of off-highway vehicle

Ownership of title to an off-highway motor vehicle subject to identification under this division may be held by two (or more) coowners as provided in Section 682 of the Civil Code, except that:

(a) A vehicle may be identified in the names of two (or more) persons as coowners in the alternative by the use of the word "or." A vehicle so identified in the alternative shall be deemed to be held in joint tenancy. Each coowner shall be deemed to have granted to the other coowners the absolute right to dispose of the title and interest in the vehicle. Upon the death of a coowner, the interest of the decedent shall pass to the survivor as though title or interest in the vehicle was held in joint tenancy, unless a contrary intention is set forth in writing upon the application for identification.

(b) A vehicle may be identified in the names of two (or more) persons as coowners in the alternative by the use of the word "or" and if declared in writing upon the application for identification by the applicants to be community property, or tenancy in common, shall grant to each coowner the absolute power to transfer the title or interest of the other coowners only during the lifetime of such coowners.

(c) A vehicle may be identified in the names of two (or more) persons as coowners in the conjunctive by the use of the word "and" and shall thereafter require the signature of each coowner or his personal representative to transfer title to the vehicle, except where title to the vehicle is set forth in joint tenancy, the signature of each coowner or his personal representative shall be required only during the lifetime of the coowners, and upon death of a coowner title shall pass to the surviving coowner.

(d) The department may adopt suitable abbreviations to appear upon the certificate of identification and certificate of ownership to designate the manner in which title to the vehicle is held if set forth by the coowners upon the application for identification. *(Added by Stats. 1971, c. 1816, p. 3927, § 9, eff. Dec. 22, 1971, operative July 1, 1972.)*

§ 38050. Undertaking or bond

In the absence of the regularly required supporting evidence of ownership upon application for identification or transfer of a vehicle, the department may accept an undertaking or bond which shall be conditioned to protect the department and all officers and employees thereof and any subsequent purchaser of the vehicle, any person acquiring a lien or security interest thereon, or the successor in interest of such purchaser or person against any loss or damage on account of any defect in or undisclosed claim upon the right, title, and interest of the applicant or other person in and to the vehicle. *(Added by Stats.1971, c. 1816, p. 3928, § 9, eff. Dec. 22, 1971, operative July 1, 1972.)*

§ 38055. Return and surrender of bond or undertaking

In the event the vehicle is no longer identified in this state and the currently valid certificate of ownership is surrendered to the department, the bond or undertaking shall be returned and surrendered at the end of three years or prior thereto. *(Added by Stats.1971, c. 1816, p.*

3928, § 9, eff. Dec. 22, 1971, operative July 1, 1972. Amended by Stats.1982, c. 517, p. 2430, § 402.)

Law Revision Commission Comments
1982 Amendment

Section 38055 is amended to delete provisions duplicated in the Bond and Undertaking Law. See Code Civ. Proc. §§ 996.410 (enforcement of liability on bond) and 996.470 (limitation on liability of surety). [16 Cal.L.Rev.Comm. Reports 501 (1981)].

§ 38060. Change of address

(a) Whenever any person, after making application for identification of an off-highway motor vehicle subject to identification, or after the identification either as owner or legal owner, moves or acquires a new address different from the address shown in the application or upon the certificate of ownership or identification certificate, that person shall, within 10 days thereafter, notify the department of his or her old and new addresses.

(b) Any owner having notified the department as required in subdivision (a), shall immediately mark out the former on the face of the certificate and write with pen and ink or type the new on the face of the certificate immediately below the former address and initial the entry. *(Added by Stats.1971, c. 1816, p. 3928, § 9, eff. Dec. 22, 1971, operative July 1, 1972. Amended by Stats.1976, c. 552, p. 1392, § 6; Stats.1982, c. 466, p. 2059, § 118.)*

ARTICLE 3. EVIDENCES OF IDENTIFICATION

Section
38070. Issuance of certificate of ownership and identification certificate.
38075. Contents of certificate of identification.
38076. Contents of certificate of ownership.
38080. Copies of report-of-sale form and identification devices; use and display.
38085. Identification certificate kept with vehicle.
38087. Special permits for manufacturers, dealers, and distributors.
38087.5. Non-residents; special permits; issuance by parks and recreation department.
38088. Motorcycle used in racing.
38090. Stolen, lost or damaged identification plates and certificate.
38095. Stolen, lost or damaged certificate of ownership.
38100. Applicability of registration provisions.

§ 38070. Issuance of certificate of ownership and identification certificate

The department, upon identifying an off-highway motor vehicle subject to identification, shall issue a certificate of ownership to the legal owner and an identification certificate to the owner, or both to the owner if there is no legal owner. *(Added by Stats.1971, c. 1816, p. 3925, § 9, eff. Dec. 22, 1971, operative July 1, 1972. Amended by Stats.1972, c. 973, p. 1762, § 24, eff. Aug. 16, 1972; Stats.1976, c. 1093, p. 4944, § 12.)*

§ 38075. Contents of certificate of identification

(a) The identification certificate shall contain upon the face thereof the date issued, the name and residence or business or mailing address of the owner and of the legal owner, if any, the identification number to the vehicle, and a description of the vehicle as complete as that required in the application for the identification of a vehicle.

(b) The director may modify the form, arrangement, and information appearing on the face of the identification certificate and may provide for standardization and abbreviation of fictitious or firm names thereon whenever he finds that the efficiency of the department will be promoted thereby, except that general delivery or post office box numbers shall not be permitted as the address of the identified owner unless there is no other address. *(Added by Stats.1971, c. 1816, p. 3929, § 9, eff. Dec. 22, 1971, operative July 1, 1972. Amended by Stats.1989, c. 1213, § 17.)*

§ 38076. Contents of certificate of ownership

The certificate of ownership shall contain:

(a) Not less than the information required upon the face of the identification certificate.

(b) Provision for notice to the department of a transfer of the title or interest of the owner or legal owner.

(c) Provision for application for transfer of identification by the transferee. *(Added by Stats.1971, c. 1816, p. 3929, § 9, eff. Dec. 22, 1971, operative July 1, 1972.)*

§ 38080. Copies of report-of-sale form and identification devices; use and display

(a) The department may authorize, under Section 4456, dealers licensed under Article 1 (commencing with Section 11700) of Chapter 4 of Division 5 to use numbered copies of the report-of-sale form and corresponding temporary identification devices upon off-highway motor vehicles subject to identification that they sell.

(b) Off–highway motor vehicles subject to identification that are purchased from dealers not required to be licensed under Article 1 (commencing with Section 11700) of Chapter 4 of Division 5, or that are specially constructed by the owner or owners, may be operated off-highway, as provided by this division, without an identification plate or device or identification certificate, provided a receipt or other suitable device issued by the department is displayed upon the vehicle evidencing an application has been made and appropriate fees paid pursuant to this division, until the identification plate or device and identification certificate are received from the department. *(Added by Stats.1971, c. 1816, p. 3929, § 9, eff. Dec. 22, 1971, operative July 1, 1972. Amended by Stats.1996, c. 124 (A.B.3470), § 141.)*

§ 38085. Identification certificate kept with vehicle

(a) Every owner upon receipt of an identification certificate shall maintain the same or a facsimile copy

thereof with the vehicle for which it is issued at all times when the vehicle is operated or transported.

(b) The provisions of this section do not apply when an identification certificate is removed from the vehicle for the purpose of application for renewal or transfer of identification. *(Added by Stats.1971, c. 1816, p. 3929, § 9, eff. Dec. 22, 1971, operative July 1, 1972. Amended by Stats.1976, c. 1093, p. 4944, § 12.5; Stats.1988, c. 1268, § 19.)*

§ 38087. Special permits for manufacturers, dealers, and distributors

(a) Upon payment of the fees specified in Section 38231, the department may issue to manufacturers, dealers, distributors, or their agents, a special permit to operate or use for the purpose of delivery, demonstration, or display, off-highway motor vehicles otherwise required to be identified under this division.

(b) Special permits issued pursuant to this section shall expire at midnight on the 30th day of June in the second calendar year following the year of issuance of such permit. *(Added by Stats.1972, c. 973, p. 1762, § 25, eff. Aug. 16, 1972. Amended by Stats.1974, c. 947, p. 1978, § 2; Stats.1976, c. 1093, p. 4944, § 13.)*

Cross References

Dealer defined, see Vehicle Code § 285.
Special permit fees, see Vehicle Code § 38231.

§ 38087.5. Non-residents; special permits; issuance by parks and recreation department

(a) Upon payment of the fee specified in Section 38231.5, the Department of Parks and Recreation may issue to a nonresident of this state a special permit to operate an off-highway motor vehicle otherwise required to be identified under this chapter.

(b) Special permits issued under this section shall expire on December 31 in the year of their issuance. *(Added by Stats.1996, c. 572 (S.B.2079), § 2.)*

§ 38088. Motorcycle used in racing

(a) Upon payment of the fee specified in Section 38232, the department shall issue to the owner of a motorcycle, which the owner has certified as being used exclusively in racing events on a closed course, a special transportation identification device for the purpose of identifying the motorcycle while it is being transported upon a highway to and from racing events on a closed course. Such device may be either a plate or a sticker, whichever is determined by the department to be the most appropriate.

(b) Such device is nonrenewable, nontransferrable, and becomes invalid when the vehicle for which it was issued is sold or dismantled.

(c) A certificate of ownership may not be issued in conjunction with a special transportation identification device. *(Added by Stats.1975, c. 1050, p. 2484, § 6.)*

Motorcycle defined, see Vehicle Code § 400.

Off-highway motor vehicle defined, see Vehicle Code §§ 38006, 38012.

Special transportation identification fee, see Vehicle Code § 38232.

Transportation of motorcycles on highway, see Vehicle Code § 38022.

§ 38090. Stolen, lost or damaged identification plates and certificate

If any identification certificate or identification plate or device is stolen, lost, mutilated or illegible, the owner of the vehicle for which the same was issued, as shown by the records of the department, shall immediately make application for and may, upon furnishing information satisfactory to the department, obtain a duplicate or substitute or a new identification under a new number, as determined to be most advisable by the department. An application for a duplicate identification certificate is not required in conjunction with any other application. *(Added by Stats.1971, c. 1816, p. 3929, § 9, eff. Dec. 22, 1971, operative July 1, 1972. Amended by Stats.1988, c. 1268, § 20.)*

§ 38095. Stolen, lost or damaged certificate of ownership

If any certificate of ownership is stolen, lost, mutilated or illegible, the legal owner or, if none, the owner of the vehicle for which the same was issued as shown by the records of the department shall immediately make application for and may, upon furnishing information satisfactory to the department, obtain a duplicate. *(Added by Stats.1971, c. 1816, p. 3930, § 9, eff. Dec. 22, 1971, operative July 1, 1972.)*

§ 38100. Applicability of registration provisions

The provisions of Sections 4458, 4460, 4461, 4462, 4463, and 4464 shall be fully applicable to motor vehicles identified under this division and the terms "identification" and "identification certificate" shall have the same meaning as the terms "registration" and "registration card," respectively, as used in those sections. *(Added by Stats.1971, c. 1816, p. 3930, § 9, eff. Dec. 22, 1971, operative July 1, 1972. Amended by Stats.1976, c. 1093, p. 4944, § 14.)*

ARTICLE 4. RENEWAL OF IDENTIFICATION

Section
38110. Certificates of ownership.
38115. Expiration date.
38120. Application for renewal.
38121. Certificate of nonoperation; fee; renewal of identification.
38122. Repealed.
38125. Stolen or embezzled vehicles.
38130. Operation pending renewal.
38135. Validation of certificate.

§ 38110. Certificates of ownership

Certificates of ownership shall not be renewed but shall remain valid until suspended, revoked, or canceled by the department for cause or upon transfer of any interest shown therein. *(Added by Stats.1971, c. 1816, p. 3930, § 9, eff. Dec. 22, 1971, operative July 1, 1972.)*

§ 38115. Expiration date

Every motor vehicle identification and identification certificate issued pursuant to this division shall expire at midnight on the 30th day of June in the second calendar year following the year of issuance of such certificate. The department may upon payment of the proper fees renew such identification. *(Added by Stats.1971, c. 1816, p. 3930, § 9, eff. Dec. 22, 1971, operative July 1, 1972. Amended by Stats.1972, c. 973, p. 1762, § 26, eff. Aug. 16, 1972; Stats.1974, c. 947, p. 1978, § 3; Stats.1976, c. 1093, p. 4944, § 15.)*

§ 38120. Application for renewal

(a) Application for renewal of identification of off-highway motor vehicles subject to identification shall be made by the owner not later than midnight of the 30th day of June of the expiration year. The application shall contain the true, full name and driver's license or identification card number, if any, of the owner.

(b) Whenever any application for identification or transfer of ownership of an off-highway motor vehicle subject to identification is filed with the department between June 1 and June 30 of the year of expiration, the application shall be accompanied by the full renewal fees in addition to any other fees then due and payable.

(c) Whenever an application for identification or transfer of ownership of an off-highway motor vehicle subject to identification is filed with the department between January 1 and May 31 of the year of expiration, the application may be accompanied by full renewal fees in addition to any other fees then due and payable, which renewal fees shall be for the two-year period following June 30th of the year in which paid. *(Added by Stats. 1971, c. 1816, p. 3930, § 9, eff. Dec. 22, 1971, operative July 1, 1972. Amended by Stats.1974, c. 947, p. 1978, § 4, operative March 10, 1975; Stats.1976, c. 1093, p. 4945, § 16; Stats.1994, c. 1221 (S.B.1758), § 20.)*

Application for transfer, see Vehicle Code § 38205.

§ 38121. Certificate of nonoperation; fee; renewal of identification

(a) Prior to the expiration of the identification of an off-highway motor vehicle, if that identification is not to be renewed prior to its expiration, the owner of the vehicle shall file, under penalty of perjury, a certification that the vehicle will not be operated, used, or transported on public property or private property in a manner so as to subject the vehicle to identification during the subsequent identification period without first making an application for identification of the vehicle, including full payment of all fees. The certification of nonoperation is valid until the identification is renewed under subdivision (c).

(b) Each certification of nonoperation filed pursuant to subdivision (a) shall be accompanied by a filing fee of fifteen dollars ($15).

(c) An application for renewal of identification, whether or not accompanied by an application for transfer of title to, or any interest in, the vehicle, shall be submitted to the department with payment of the required fees for the current identification period and without penalty for delinquent payment of fees imposed under this code if the department receives the application on or before the date the vehicle is first operated, used, or transported on public property or private property in a manner so as to subject the vehicle to identification and certification of nonoperation required pursuant to subdivision (a).

(d) A certification of nonoperation is not required to be filed pursuant to subdivision (a) for a vehicle on which the identification expires while being held as inventory by a dealer or lessor-retailer. *(Added by Stats.1990, c. 1352 (A.B.2912), § 16, eff. Sept. 27, 1990, operative June 30, 1990. Amended by Stats.2003, c. 719 (S.B.1055), § 27.)*

Cross References

Base fee amounts, adjustment of fees, see Vehicle Code § 1678.

§ 38122. Repealed by Stats.1990, c. 1352 (A.B.2912), § 18, operative Jan. 1, 1995

§ 38125. Stolen or embezzled vehicles

Whenever by reason of the theft or embezzlement of an off-highway motor vehicle subject to identification the owner or legal owner is not in possession of the vehicle at the time penalties accrue for failure to obtain identification, or renewal thereof, the owner or legal owner may secure the identification or renewal of the identification of the vehicle within 20 days after its recovery upon filing an affidavit setting forth the circumstances of the theft or embezzlement if the theft or embezzlement of the vehicle has been reported pursuant to provisions of this code, without penalty for delinquent payment of fees imposed under this division. *(Added by Stats.1971, c. 1816, p. 3930, § 9, eff. Dec. 22, 1971, operative July 1, 1972. Amended by Stats.1974, c. 947, p. 1978, § 6, operative March 10, 1975.)*

§ 38130. Operation pending renewal

When application for identification of an off-highway motor vehicle subject to identification has been made as required by this division, the vehicle may be operated pursuant to this division until the new indicia of current identification have been received from the department on condition that there be displayed on the vehicle the identification plate or device and validating device, if any, issued to the vehicle for the previous identification term. *(Added by Stats.1971, c. 1816, p. 3930, § 9, eff. Dec. 22, 1971, operative July 1, 1972.)*

§ 38135. Validation of certificate

The department may, upon renewing of an identification of off-highway motor vehicles subject to identification, issue a new identification certificate or may endorse or authorize the endorsement of a receipt or validation upon payment of the required fees. The receipt or validation to be stamped upon the identification certificate last issued for the vehicle during the preceding period, or upon a potential identification certificate issued near the close of the preceding period, which identification certificate so endorsed or validated shall constitute the identification certificate for the ensuing two-year period. If the identification certificate and potential identification certificate are unavailable, a fee as specified in Section 38260 shall not be paid. *(Added by Stats.1971, c. 1816, p. 3931, § 9, eff. Dec. 22, 1971, operative July 1, 1972. Amended by Stats.1988, c. 1268, § 21.)*

ARTICLE 5. REFUSAL OF IDENTIFICATION

Section
38145. Grounds requiring refusal of identification.
38150. Grounds permitting refusal of identification.

§ 38145. Grounds requiring refusal of identification

The department shall refuse the identification or renewal or transfer of identification of an off-highway motor vehicle subject to identification upon any of the following grounds:

(a) That the application contains any false or fraudulent statement.

(b) That the required fee has not been paid. *(Added by Stats.1971, c. 1816, p. 3931, § 9, eff. Dec. 22, 1971, operative July 1, 1972.)*

§ 38150. Grounds permitting refusal of identification

The department may refuse the identification or renewal or transfer of identification of an off-highway motor vehicle subject to identification in any of the following circumstances:

(a) If the department is satisfied that the applicant is not entitled thereto under this code.

(b) If the applicant has failed to furnish the department with information required in the application or reasonable additional information required by the department.

(c) If the department determines that the applicant has made or permitted unlawful use of any identification certificate, certificate of ownership, identification plates, or other identifying indicia. *(Added by Stats.1971, c. 1816, p. 3931, § 9, eff. Dec. 22, 1971, operative July 1, 1972. Amended by Stats.1976, c. 1093, p. 4945, § 18.)*

ARTICLE 6. IDENTIFICATION PLATE OR DEVICE

Section
38160. Issuance of identification plates.
38165. Design of identification plates; report for improvements.
38170. Display of identification plates.

§ 38160. Issuance of identification plates

The department, upon identifying an off-highway motor vehicle subject to identification, shall issue to the owner a suitable identification plate or device which is capable of being attached to the vehicle in such a manner so as to not endanger the operator or passengers of the vehicle, and which shall identify the vehicle for which it is issued for the period of its validity. *(Added by Stats.1971, c. 1816, p. 3931, § 9, eff. Dec. 22, 1971, operative July 1, 1972.)*

Cross References

Movement of motor-driven cycles adjacent to a roadway, see Vehicle Code § 38027.
Off-highway vehicles, operation on highway, conditions, see Vehicle Code § 38025.
Operation of motorcycles on highway, see Vehicle Code § 38025.

§ 38165. Design of identification plates; report for improvements

(a) The department shall determine the size, color, and letters or number of the plate or device issued pursuant to this division and the life of the series of plate or device issued, but in no event less than six years. The design of the plate or device shall have the identification number as the most prominent feature of the device. During the intervening identification periods for which the plate or device is issued, the department shall issue a tab, sticker, or other suitable device to indicate the term for which such plate or device will be valid.

(b) On or before July 1, 2009, the department, in conjunction with the Division of Off–Highway Motor Vehicle Recreation of the Department of Parks and Recreation, shall report to the Assembly Committee on Water, Parks and Wildlife and the Senate Committee on Natural Resources and Water, regarding recommendations to improve the identification of off-highway motor vehicles. At a minimum, the report shall examine the benefits and challenges of all of the following:

(1) Using multiple identification stickers for each vehicle.

(2) Using large-print identifying numbers or letters.

(3) Various identifying devices, such as license plates and stickers.

(4) Requiring license plates or other device alternatives for certain off-highway vehicle types.

(5) Including a unique number for special nonresident permits issued under Section 38087.5.

(c) In preparing the report, the department and the Division of Off–Highway Motor Vehicle Recreation shall work with vehicle manufacturers to evaluate feasibility. *(Added by Stats.1971, c. 1816, p. 3931, § 9, eff. Dec. 22, 1971, operative July 1, 1972. Amended by Stats.2007, c. 541 (S.B.742), § 23.)*

§ 38170. Display of identification plates

(a) Every off-highway motor vehicle subject to identification shall have displayed upon it the identification number assigned to the vehicle for which it is issued, together with the word "California" or the abbreviation "CAL" and the year number for which it is issued or a suitable device issued by the department for validation purposes, which device shall contain the year for which it is issued.

(b) The identification plate or device shall at all times be securely fastened to the vehicle for which it is issued and shall be mounted or affixed in a position to be clearly visible, and shall be maintained in a condition so as to be clearly legible. No covering shall be used on the identification plate or device.

(c) All identification plates or devices issued on or after January 1, 1996, shall be displayed as follows:

(1) On the left fork leg of a motorcycle, either horizontal or vertical, and shall be visible from the left side of the motorcycle.

(2) On the left quadrant of the metal frame member of sand rails, rail-type buggies, and dune buggies, visible from the rear of the vehicle.

(3) On the left rear quadrant on permanent plastic or metal frame members of all-terrain vehicles, visible to outside inspections.

(4) On the left tunnel on the back quadrant of snowmobiles. *(Added by Stats.1971, c. 1816, p. 3932, § 9, eff. Dec. 22, 1971, operative July 1, 1972. Amended by Stats.1972, c. 973, p. 1763, § 28, eff. Aug. 16, 1972; Stats.1994, c. 14 (A.B.982), § 1.)*

ARTICLE 7. DISMANTLING OF OFF–HIGHWAY MOTOR VEHICLES

Section
38180. Application of other provisions pertaining to dismantling of vehicles.
38185. Subsequent identification of previously dismantled or salvaged vehicles.

§ 38180. Application of other provisions pertaining to dismantling of vehicles

Chapter 3 (commencing with Section 11500) of Division 5 shall be applicable to off-highway motor vehicles subject to identification, except as provided in this article. *(Added by Stats.1971, c. 1816, p. 3932, § 9, eff. Dec. 22, 1971, operative July 1, 1972.)*

§ 38185. Subsequent identification of previously dismantled or salvaged vehicles

No off-highway motor vehicle subject to identification which has been reported dismantled or sold as salvage may be subsequently identified until it has been inspected by the department. *(Added by Stats.1971, c. 1816, p. 3932, § 9, eff. Dec. 22, 1971, operative July 1, 1972.)*

ARTICLE 8.   TRANSFERS OF
TITLE OR INTEREST

Section
38195.   Transfer of title to off-highway vehicles.
38200.   Notice of transfer by dealers.
38205.   Application for transfer.
38210.   Notice of transfer to dealer not required.
38211.   Payment of use tax.

§ 38195.   Transfer of title to off-highway vehicles

The provisions of Chapter 2 (commencing with Section 5600) of Division 3 shall be applicable to off-highway motor vehicles subject to identification, and the terms "registration," "registration card," and "registered" as used therein, shall apply to the terms "identification," "identification certificate," and "identified," respectively, except that Sections 5901, 5902, 5903, 5904, 5906, and 6052 shall not apply. *(Added by Stats.1971, c. 1816, p. 3932, § 9, eff. Dec. 22, 1971, operative July 1, 1972.)*

§ 38200.   Notice of transfer by dealers

(a) Every licensed dealer upon transferring by sale, lease, or otherwise any off-highway motor vehicle subject to identification, whether new or used, of a type subject to identification under this division, shall, not later than the end of the fifth calendar day thereafter, not counting the day of sale, lease, or other transfer, give written notice of the transfer to the department upon an appropriate form provided by it; but a dealer need not give the notice when selling or transferring a new unidentified off-highway motor vehicle subject to identification to another dealer.

A "sale" shall be deemed completed and consummated when the purchaser of that vehicle has paid the purchase price, or, in lieu thereof, has signed a purchase contract or security agreement, and taken physical possession or delivery of that vehicle.

(b) Every dealer of off-highway motor vehicles subject to identification who is not licensed with the department, and who engages only in the sale of vehicles of a type not properly equipped for operation upon the highway and that are restricted to off-highway operation or use, shall comply with the provisions of Section 5900, or such regulations as the director determines are necessary to carry out the provisions of this division. *(Added by Stats.1971, c. 1816, p. 3932, § 9, eff. Dec. 22, 1971, operative July 1, 1972. Amended by Stats.1975, c. 440, p. 936, § 1.)*

Cross References

Dealer defined, see Vehicle Code § 285.
Manufacturers, transporters and dealers, license suspension or revocation for violation of this section, see Vehicle Code § 11705.

§ 38205.   Application for transfer

Whenever any person has received as transferee a properly endorsed certificate of ownership, he or she shall, within 10 days thereafter, endorse the ownership certificate as required and forward the ownership certificate with the proper transfer fee and, if required under Section 38120, any other fee due and thereby make application for transfer of identification. The certificate of ownership shall contain a space for the applicant's driver's license or identification card number, and the applicant shall furnish that number, if any, in the space provided. *(Added by Stats.1971, c. 1816, p. 3933, § 9, eff. Dec. 22, 1971, operative July 1, 1972. Amended by Stats.1988, c. 1268, § 22; Stats.1994, c. 1221 (S.B.1758), § 21.)*

Cross References

Waiver of penalties and registration fees, see Vehicle Code § 38247.

§ 38210.   Notice of transfer to dealer not required

When the transferee of an off-highway motor vehicle subject to identification is a dealer who holds such vehicle for resale, the dealer is not required to make application for transfer, but upon transferring his title or interest to another person he shall comply with this division. *(Added by Stats.1971, c. 1816, p. 3933, § 9, eff. Dec. 22, 1971, operative July 1, 1972.)*

§ 38211.   Payment of use tax

(a) The department shall withhold identification of or the transfer of ownership of any vehicle subject to identification under this division until the applicant pays to the department the use tax measured by the sales price of the vehicle as required by the Sales and Use Tax Law, together with penalty, if any, unless the purchaser presents evidence on a form prescribed by the State Board of Equalization that sales tax will be paid by the seller or that use tax has been collected by the seller or that the State Board of Equalization finds that no use tax is due. If the applicant so desires, he may pay the use tax and penalty, if any, to the department so as to secure immediate action upon his application for identification or transfer of ownership, and thereafter he may apply through the Department of Motor Vehicles to the State Board of Equalization under the provisions of the Sales and Use Tax Law for a refund of the amount so paid.

(b) The department shall transmit to the State Board of Equalization all collections of use tax and penalty made under this section. This transmittal shall be made at least monthly, accompanied by a schedule in such form as the department and board may prescribe.

(c) The State Board of Equalization shall reimburse the department for its costs incurred in carrying out the provisions of this section. Such reimbursement shall be effected under agreement between the agencies, approved by the Department of Finance.

(d) In computing any use tax or penalty thereon under the provisions of this section dollar fractions shall be disregarded in the manner specified in Section 9559 of this code. Payment of tax and penalty on this basis shall be deemed full compliance with the requirements of the Sales and Use Tax Law insofar as they are applicable to the use of vehicles to which this section relates. *(Added by Stats.1971, c. 1816, p. 3933, § 9, eff. Dec. 22, 1971, operative July 1, 1972.)*

Cross References

Payment of use tax by purchasers of off-highway vehicle from certain retailers, see Revenue and Taxation Code § 6293.

ARTICLE 9. IDENTIFICATION FEES

Section
38225.   Service fee.
38225.4.   Issuance or renewal of identification fee.
38225.5.   Fee to offset costs of increasing uniformed field
            strength of highway patrol.
38230.   Additional fee; in lieu of tax.
38231.   Fees for special permits.
38231.5.   Non-resident special permit; parks and recreation
            department; vendors.
38232.   Fee; special transportation identification.
38235.   Report and deposit of fees.
38240.   Allocation and use of fees.
38240.1.   Repealed.
38240.5.   Repealed.
38241.   Repealed.
38245.   Delinquency of fees.
38246.   Penalties.
38247.   Waiver of penalties and registration fees.
38250.   Delinquency of transfer fees.
38255.   Transfer application and fees.
38260.   Fees for duplicate certificates, plates, stickers, or
            devices.
38265.   Penalty fee for delinquency.

§ 38225. Service fee

(a) A service fee of seven dollars ($7) shall be paid to the department for the issuance or renewal of identification of off-highway motor vehicles subject to identification, except as expressly exempted under this division.

(b) In addition to the service fee required by subdivision (a), a special fee of thirty-three dollars ($33) shall be paid at the time of payment of the service fee for the issuance or renewal of an identification plate or device.

(c) All money transferred pursuant to Section 8352.6 of the Revenue and Taxation Code, all fees received by the department pursuant to subdivision (b), and all day use, overnight use, or annual or biennial use fees for state vehicular recreation areas received by the Department of Parks and Recreation shall be deposited in the Off–Highway Vehicle Trust Fund, which is hereby created.

There shall be a separate reporting of special fee revenues by vehicle type, including four-wheeled vehicles, all-terrain vehicles, motorcycles, and snowmobiles. All money shall be deposited in the fund, and, upon appropriation by the Legislature, shall be allocated according to Section 5090.61 of the Public Resources Code.

(d) Any money temporarily transferred by the Legislature from the Off–Highway Vehicle Trust Fund to the General Fund shall be reimbursed, without interest, by the Legislature within two fiscal years of the transfer.

(e) This section shall remain in effect only until January 1, 2018, and as of that date is repealed, unless a later enacted statute, that is enacted before January 1, 2018, deletes or extends that date. Any unencumbered funds remaining in the Off–Highway Vehicle Trust Fund on January 1, 2018, shall be transferred to the General Fund. *(Added by Stats.1982, c. 994, p. 3626, § 15, operative Jan. 1, 1988. Amended by Stats.1985, c. 1248, § 2, operative Jan. 1, 1988; Stats.1987, c. 1027, § 27, operative Jan. 1, 1993; Stats.1990, c. 954 (A.B.2549), § 3; Stats.1992, c. 701 (S.B.1565), § 64, eff. Sept. 15, 1992; Stats.1992, c. 964 (S.B.1282), § 7, operative Jan. 1, 1998; Stats.1995, c. 970 (S.B.383), § 4, operative Jan. 1, 2003; Stats.1996, c. 202 (A.B.3495), § 7, eff. July 22, 1996, operative Jan. 1, 2003; Stats.2001, c. 227 (A.B.723), § 3, operative Jan. 1, 2007; Stats.2006, c. 77 (A.B.1803), § 58, eff. July 18, 2006, operative Jan. 1, 2008; Stats.2007, c. 541 (S.B.742), § 24.)*

Repeal

For repeal of this section, see its terms.

§ 38225.4. Issuance or renewal of identification fee

In addition to the service fees specified in subdivision (a) of Section 38225, as amended by Section 6 of Chapter 964 of the Statutes of 1992, a fee of three dollars ($3) shall be paid at the time of issuance or renewal of identification of off-highway motor vehicles subject to identification, except as expressly exempted under this division. The department shall deposit the fee received under this section in the Motor Vehicle Account in the State Transportation Fund. The money deposited in the account pursuant to this section shall be available, upon appropriation by the Legislature, for expenditure to offset the costs of maintaining the uniformed field strength of the Department of the California Highway Patrol. *(Added by Stats.1994, c. 1197 (A.B.3080), § 3. Amended by Stats.2003, c. 719 (S.B.1055), § 29.)*

Cross References

Base fee amounts, adjustment of fees, see Vehicle Code § 1678.

§ 38225.5. Fee to offset costs of increasing uniformed field strength of highway patrol

In addition to the service fees specified in Section 38225, a fee of three dollars ($3) shall be paid at the time of issuance or renewal of identification of off-highway vehicles subject to identification, except as expressly exempted under this division. The department shall

1003

deposit the fee received under this section in the Motor Vehicle Account in the State Transportation Fund. The money deposited in the account pursuant to this section shall be available, upon appropriation by the Legislature, for expenditure to offset the costs of increasing the uniformed field strength of the Department of the California Highway Patrol beyond its 1994 staffing level and those costs associated with maintaining this new level of uniformed field strength and carrying out those duties specified in subdivision (a) of Section 830.2 of the Penal Code. *(Added by Stats.1994, c. 1196 (A.B.2949), § 2. Amended by Stats.2003, c. 719 (S.B.1055), § 30.)*

Cross References

Base fee amounts, adjustment of fees, see Vehicle Code § 1678.

§ 38230.   Additional fee; in lieu of tax

In addition to the fees imposed by Section 38225, there shall be paid a four-dollar ($4) fee for the issuance or renewal of identification for every off-highway motor vehicle subject to identification. The fee imposed by this section is in lieu of all taxes according to value levied for state or local purposes. *(Added by Stats.1971, c. 1816, p. 3934, § 9, eff. Dec. 22, 1971, operative July 1, 1972.)*

§ 38231.   Fees for special permits

The fees for a special permit issued under Section 38087 shall be the prevailing identification fees as set forth in Sections 38225 and 38230 and shall be deposited and distributed as are identification fees under this chapter. *(Added by Stats.1972, c. 973, p. 1763, § 30, eff. Aug. 16, 1972.)*

§ 38231.5.   Non-resident special permit; parks and recreation department; vendors

(a) The fee for a special permit issued under Section 38087.5 shall be not less than twenty dollars ($20), as established by the Department of Parks and Recreation. The Department of Parks and Recreation may adjust the special permit fee for a permit issued to a nonresident of this state under Section 38087.5, as necessary, to recover the costs of this program. After deducting its administrative and vendor costs, the Department of Parks and Recreation shall deposit the fees received under this section in the Off–Highway Vehicle Trust Fund. Money in the fund shall be allocated, upon appropriation, as provided in Sections 5090.50 and 5090.64 of the Public Resources Code.

(b) The Department of Parks and Recreation shall print the special permits required by Section 38087.5 and shall supervise the sale of those permits throughout the state.

(c) The Department of Parks and Recreation shall either distribute and sell the special permits directly or contract with vendors according to rules and regulations established by that department. The vendors shall receive a commission in an amount not to exceed 5 percent of the fee imposed pursuant to subdivision (a) for each special permit sold. The Department of Parks and

Recreation may solicit the participation of qualified retail commercial enterprises engaged in the sale or rental of off-highway vehicles, equipment, accessories, or supplies to act as authorized vendors of the special permits and may authorize local and federal agencies that provide off-highway vehicle opportunities to act as authorized vendors of the special permits. *(Added by Stats.1996, c. 572 (S.B.2079), § 3. Amended by Stats.2002, c. 563 (A.B. 2274), § 41.)*

§ 38232.   Fee; special transportation identification

A special fee of fifteen dollars ($15) shall be paid to the department for the issuance of a special transportation identification device issued pursuant to Section 38088 and shall be deposited in the Motor Vehicle Account in the Transportation Tax Fund. The fee is in lieu of the fees provided in Section 38225. *(Added by Stats.1975, c. 1050, p. 2484, § 7. Amended by Stats.2003, c. 719 (S.B.1055), § 31.)*

Cross References

Base fee amounts, adjustment of fees, see Vehicle Code § 1678.

§ 38235.   Report and deposit of fees

All money collected by the department under Section 38230 shall be reported monthly to the Controller and at the same time be deposited in the State Treasury to the credit of the Off–Highway License Fee Fund, which is hereby created. *(Added by Stats.1971, c. 1816, p. 3934, § 9, eff. Dec. 22, 1971, operative July 1, 1972. Amended by Stats.1994, c. 1004 (A.B.3717), § 7; Stats.1995, c. 403 (A.B.728), § 2; Stats.1995, c. 970 (S.B.383), § 5.)*

§ 38240.   Allocation and use of fees

(a) The Controller shall allocate the fees collected under Section 38230 in July and January of each fiscal year to cities and counties based upon the proportional estimated off-highway motor vehicle use and related activity within the respective jurisdictions pursuant to the report described in subdivision (d) of Section 5090.15 of the Public Resources Code.

(b) The funds collected under Section 38230 shall be used for the purposes set forth in Sections 5090.50 and 5090.64 of the Public Resources Code.

(c) In addition to the purposes set forth in subdivision (b), funds received by a city or county pursuant to this section may be expended for facilities located outside the limits of the city or county if both of the following conditions are met:

(1) The funds are expended for the purposes of acquiring, developing, and constructing trails, areas, or other facilities for the use of off-highway motor vehicles.

(2) The funds are expended pursuant to an agreement with the city in which the facility is located or with the county in which the facility is located if the facility is located in an unincorporated territory.

(d) This section shall become operative on January 1, 2006. *(Added by Stats.2004, c. 908 (A.B.2666), § 22, operative Jan. 1, 2006.)*

§ 38240.1. Repealed by Stats.2002, c. 563 (A.B.2274), § 43

§ 38240.5. Repealed by Stats.2006, c. 78 (A.B.1805), § 7, operative Jan. 1, 2008

§ 38241. Repealed by Stats.2004, c. 908 (A.B.2666), § 23, operative Jan. 1, 2006

§ 38245. Delinquency of fees

Whenever an off-highway motor vehicle subject to identification is operated or transported in this state without the fees required by this division having first been paid, the fee is delinquent. *(Added by Stats.1971, c. 1816, p. 3934, § 9, eff. Dec. 22, 1971, operative July 1, 1972. Amended by Stats.1973, c. 974, p. 1874, § 4, operative July 1, 1974.)*

§ 38246. Penalties

(a) A penalty shall be added upon any application for renewal of identification made on or after the day following the expiration date, except as provided in Section 4605, 38121, or 38247.

(b) If the fee specified in subdivision (a) or (b) of Section 38255 is not paid within 10 days after the fee becomes delinquent, a penalty shall be assessed.

(c) If renewal fee penalties have not accrued and the ownership of the vehicle is transferred, the transferee has 20 days from the date of transfer to pay the identification fees that become due without payment of any penalties that would otherwise be required under subdivision (a) or to file a certificate of nonoperation pursuant to subdivision (a) of Section 38121, if the vehicle will not be operated, used, or transported on public property or private property in a manner so as to subject the vehicle to identification during the subsequent identification period without first making application for identification of the vehicle, including full payment of all fees.

(d) Except as otherwise provided in this section, if any fee is not paid within 20 days after the fee becomes delinquent, a penalty shall be assessed. *(Added by Stats.1972, c. 973, p. 1764, § 31, eff. Aug. 16, 1972. Amended by Stats.1974, c. 947, p. 1979, § 7, operative March 10, 1975; Stats.1975, c. 440, p. 937, § 2; Stats.1976, c. 935, p. 2143, § 7; Stats.1978, c. 380, p. 1204, § 146; Stats.1990, c. 1352 (A.B.2912), § 19, eff. Sept. 27, 1990, operative June 30, 1990; Stats.1999, c. 1008 (S.B.533), § 17.)*

§ 38247. Waiver of penalties and registration fees

(a) When a transferee or purchaser of a vehicle applies for transfer of identification, as provided in Section 38205, and it is determined by the department that penalties accrued prior to the purchase of the vehicle, and that the transferee or purchaser was not cognizant of the nonpayment of the fees for identification for the current or prior identification years, the department may waive the identification penalties upon payment of the fees for identification due.

(b) Other provisions of this code notwithstanding, the director may at his discretion investigate into the circumstances of any application for identification to ascertain if penalties had accrued through no fault or intent of the owner. Provided such circumstances prevail, the director may waive any penalties upon payment of the fees for identification then due.

(c) When a transferee or purchaser of a vehicle applies for transfer of identification of a vehicle, and it is determined by the department that fees for identification of the vehicle for any year are unpaid and due, that such fees became due prior to the purchase of the vehicle by the transferee or purchaser and that the transferee or purchaser was not cognizant of the fact that such fees were unpaid and due, the department may waive such fees and any penalty thereon when the identification fees due for the vehicle for the current year are paid.

(d) Upon the transfer of a vehicle for which fees for identification and any penalties thereon are unpaid and due, such fees and penalties are, notwithstanding the provisions of Article 6 (commencing with Section 9800) of this chapter, the personal debt of the transferor of the vehicle who did not pay such fees and penalties when they became due or accrued. Such fees and penalties may be collected by the department in an appropriate civil action if the department has waived such fees and penalties pursuant to subdivision (c). *(Added by Stats.1976, c. 935, p. 2143, § 8.)*

§ 38250. Delinquency of transfer fees

Whenever any person has received as transferee a properly endorsed certificate of ownership and the transfer fee has not been paid as required by this division within 10 days, the fee is delinquent. *(Added by Stats. 1971, c. 1816, p. 3934, § 9, eff. Dec. 22, 1971, operative July 1, 1972. Amended by Stats.1988, c. 1268, § 23.)*

§ 38255. Transfer application and fees

Upon application for transfer of ownership or any interest of an owner, or legal owner in or to any off-highway motor vehicle identified under this division, there shall be paid the following fees:

(a) For a transfer by the owner $15
(b) For a transfer by the legal owner $15
(c) When application is presented showing a transfer
    by both the owner and legal owner $15

(Added by Stats.1971, c. 1816, p. 3934, § 9, eff. Dec. 22, 1971, operative July 1, 1972. Amended by Stats.1982, c. 1273, p. 4705, § 22; Stats.1987, c. 651, § 1; Stats.2003, c. 719 (S.B.1055), § 32.)

Cross References

Base fee amounts, adjustment of fees, see Vehicle Code § 1678.

§ 38260.   Fees for duplicate certificates, plates, stickers, or devices

Upon application for a duplicate ownership certificate or identification certificate, or a duplicate or substitute identification plate or device, or any other tabs, stickers, or devices, there shall be paid a fee in the amount of fifteen dollars ($15). *(Added by Stats.1971, c. 1816, p. 3935, § 9, eff. Dec. 22, 1971, operative July 1, 1972. Amended by Stats.2003, c. 719 (S.B.1055), § 33.)*

Cross References

Base fee amounts, adjustment of fees, see Vehicle Code § 1678.

§ 38265.   Penalty fee for delinquency

(a) The penalty for delinquency in respect to any transfer shall be fifteen dollars ($15), and shall apply only to the last transfer.

(b) The penalty for delinquency in respect to the fees imposed by Sections 38225 and 38230 shall be equal to one-half the fee after it has been computed. *(Added by Stats.1971, c. 1816, p. 3935, § 9, eff. Dec. 22, 1971. Amended by Stats.1973, c. 974, p. 1874, § 5; Stats.1974, c. 947, p. 1979, § 8, operative March 10, 1975; Stats.1988, c. 1268, § 24; Stats.2003, c. 719 (S.B.1055), § 34.)*

Cross References

Base fee amounts, adjustment of fees, see Vehicle Code § 1678.

ARTICLE 10.   OFF–HIGHWAY VEHICLE FUND EXPENDITURES [REPEALED]

§§ 38270 to 38273.   Repealed by Stats.1980, c. 846, p. 2640, § 5

§ 38275.   Repealed by Stats.1976, c. 1093, p. 4947, § 24

CHAPTER 3.   TRANSFER OF TITLE OR INTEREST [RENUMBERED]

CHAPTER 4.   IDENTIFICATION FEES [RENUMBERED]

CHAPTER 5.   OFF–HIGHWAY VEHICLE OPERATING RULES

Article	Section
1. Traffic Signs, Signals, and Markings	38280
2. Operating Controls	38304
3. Speed Laws	38305
4. Turning and Starting	38312
5. Reckless Driving	38316
6. Littering and Environmental Protection	38319

ARTICLE 1.   TRAFFIC SIGNS, SIGNALS, AND MARKINGS

Section
38280.   Federal, state, and local authority.
38285.   Conformity to uniform standards.
38286.   Organized racing events.
38300.   Unlawful to disobey sign, signal, or traffic control device.
38301.   Unlawful to violate special regulations; penalties.
38301.3. Entry of motor vehicle into federal or state wilderness area; public offense; penalties.
38301.5. Violation of local ordinance prohibiting entry into mountain fire district; punishment.
38302.   Unlawful to place unauthorized signs.

§ 38280.   Federal, state, and local authority

Federal, state, or local authorities having jurisdiction over public lands may place or cause to be placed and maintained, such appropriate signs, signals and other traffic control devices as may be necessary to properly indicate and carry out any provision of law or any duly adopted regulation of such governmental authority or to warn or guide traffic. *(Added by Stats.1976, c. 1093, p. 4947, § 26.)*

§ 38285.   Conformity to uniform standards

Only those signs, signals, markings, or devices that conform to the uniform standards and specifications adopted by the Department of Parks and Recreation, with the approval of the Off-Highway Motor Vehicle Recreation Commission, shall be placed as provided in Section 38280.

Special signs, signals, markings, or devices may be used on a temporary basis for purposes of directing traffic on and at sanctioned events conducted on public lands with permission of the agency having administrative jurisdiction over such lands. *(Added by Stats.1976, c. 1093, p. 4947, § 26.   Amended by Stats.1984, c. 729, § 1.)*

§ 38286.   Organized racing events

The provisions of Article 3 (commencing with Section 38305), Article 4 (commencing with Section 38312), Article 5 (commencing with Section 38316), Section 38319 of this chapter, and subdivision (h) of Section 38370 shall not apply to a motor vehicle being operated in an organized racing event that is conducted under the auspices of a recognized sanctioning body or by permit issued by the governmental authority having jurisdiction. *(Added by Stats.1976, c. 1093, p. 4947, § 26.   Amended by Stats.2002, c. 563 (A.B.2274), § 44.)*

§ 38300.   Unlawful to disobey sign, signal, or traffic control device

It is unlawful for the driver of any vehicle to disobey any sign, signal, or traffic control device placed or maintained pursuant to Section 38280. *(Added by Stats. 1976, c. 1093, p. 4947, § 26.)*

§ 38301. Unlawful to violate special regulations; penalties

(a) It is unlawful to operate a vehicle in violation of special regulations which have been promulgated by the governmental agency having jurisdiction over public lands, including, but not limited to, regulations governing access, routes of travel, plants, wildlife, wildlife habitat, water resources, and historical sites.

(b) A person who operates a motor vehicle in an area closed to that vehicle is guilty of a public offense and shall be punished as follows:

(1) Except as provided in paragraphs (2) and (3), the offense is an infraction punishable by a fine not exceeding fifty dollars ($50).

(2) For a second offense committed within seven years after a prior violation for which there was a conviction punishable under paragraph (1), the offense is an infraction punishable by a fine not exceeding seventy-five dollars ($75).

(3) For a third or subsequent offense committed within seven years after two or more prior violations for which there were convictions punishable under this section, the offense is punishable by a fine not exceeding one hundred fifty dollars ($150). In addition to the fine, the court may assess costs sufficient to repair property damage resulting from the violation. *(Added by Stats. 1976, c. 1093, p. 4947, § 26. Amended by Stats.2007, c. 541 (S.B.742), § 25.)*

Cross References

Drivers' licenses, issuance and renewal, traffic violation point counts, see Vehicle Code § 12810.

§ 38301.3. Entry of motor vehicle into federal or state wilderness area; public offense; penalties

Notwithstanding subdivision (d) of Section 5008 of the Public Resources Code, or any other provision of state law, and to the extent authorized under federal law, a person who violates a state or federal regulation that prohibits entry of a motor vehicle into all or portions of an area designated as a federal or state wilderness area is guilty of a public offense and shall be punished as follows:

(a) Except as provided in subdivisions (b) and (c), the offense is an infraction punishable by a fine not exceeding one hundred fifty dollars ($150).

(b) For a second offense committed within seven years after a prior violation for which there was a conviction punishable under subdivision (a), the offense is an infraction punishable by a fine not exceeding two hundred twenty-five dollars ($225).

(c)(1) For a third or subsequent offense committed within seven years after two or more prior violations for which there were convictions punishable under this section, the offense is a misdemeanor punishable by a fine not exceeding three hundred dollars ($300) or by imprisonment in the county jail not exceeding 90 days, or by both that fine and imprisonment.

(2) In addition to the fine imposed under paragraph (1), the court may order impoundment of the vehicle used in the offense under the following conditions:

(A) The person convicted under this subdivision is the owner of the vehicle.

(B) The vehicle is subject to Section 4000 or 38010.

(3) The period of impoundment imposed pursuant to this subdivision shall be not less than one day nor more than 30 days. The impoundment shall be at the owner's expense. *(Added by Stats.2005, c. 571 (A.B.1086), § 4.)*

Cross References

Point count determination for violations under this section, see Vehicle Code § 12810.

Recordkeeping requirements for violations under this section, see Vehicle Code § 1807.

Violations under this section not exempted from reporting requirement, see Vehicle Code § 1803.

§ 38301.5. Violation of local ordinance prohibiting entry into mountain fire district; punishment

Every person convicted of violating a local ordinance which is adopted by a city with a population over 2,000,000 persons pursuant to Section 38301 and which prohibits entry into all or portions of an area designated by ordinance as a mountain fire district shall be punished as follows:

(a) Except as provided in subdivisions (b) and (c), the offense is an infraction punishable by a fine not exceeding one hundred fifty dollars ($150).

(b) For a second offense committed within one year of a prior violation for which there was a conviction punishable under subdivision (a), the offense is punishable as an infraction by a fine not exceeding two hundred fifty dollars ($250).

(c)(1) For a third or subsequent offense committed within one year of two or more prior violations for which there were convictions punishable under this section, the offense is punishable as a misdemeanor by a fine not exceeding one thousand dollars ($1,000) or by imprisonment in the county jail not exceeding 90 days, or by both that fine and imprisonment. Additionally, the court may order impoundment of the vehicle used in the offense under the following conditions:

(A) The person convicted under this subdivision is the owner of the vehicle.

(B) The vehicle is subject to Section 38010.

(2) The period of impoundment imposed pursuant to this subdivision shall be not less than one day nor more than 30 days. The impoundment shall be at the owner's expense. *(Added by Stats.1984, c. 1015, § 1.)*

Cross References

Drivers' licenses, issuance and renewal, traffic violation point counts, see Vehicle Code § 12810.

Violation as misdemeanor, see Vehicle Code § 40000.24.

§ 38302.　Unlawful to place unauthorized signs

It is unlawful for any person to place or erect any sign, signal, or traffic control device for off-highway traffic upon public lands unless authorized by law. *(Added by Stats.1976, c. 1093, p. 4947, § 26.)*

ARTICLE 2.　OPERATING CONTROLS

Section
38304.　Ability to reach and operate controls.
38304.1.　Children under fourteen years of age; permission to operate off-highway vehicles prohibited; penalties.

§ 38304.　Ability to reach and operate controls

The operator of an off-highway motor vehicle shall be able to reach and operate all controls necessary to safely operate the vehicle. *(Added by Stats.1976, c. 1093, p. 4947, § 26.)*

§ 38304.1.　Children under fourteen years of age; permission to operate off-highway vehicles prohibited; penalties

(a) Neither a parent or guardian of a child who is under 14 years of age, nor an adult who is authorized by the parent or guardian to supervise that child, shall grant permission to, or knowingly allow, that child to operate an off-highway motor vehicle in a manner that violates Section 38304.

(b) A person convicted of a violation of subdivision (a) is punishable as follows:

(1) For a first conviction, the court shall impose a fine of thirty-five dollars ($35).

(2) For a second conviction, a fine of not less than thirty-five dollars ($35) nor more than fifty dollars ($50).

(3) For a third or any subsequent conviction, a fine of not less than fifty dollars ($50) nor more than seventy-five dollars ($75). *(Added by Stats.2009, c. 414 (A.B.134), § 3.)*

Cross References

Drivers' licenses, issuance and renewal, traffic violation point counts, see Vehicle Code § 12810.

ARTICLE 3.　SPEED LAWS

Section
38305.　Basic speed law.
38310.　Prima facie speed limit.

§ 38305.　Basic speed law

No person shall drive an off-highway motor vehicle at a speed greater than is reasonable or prudent and in no event at a speed which endangers the safety of other persons or property. *(Added by Stats.1976, c. 1093, p. 4947, § 26.)*

1008

§ 38310.　Prima facie speed limit

The prima facie speed limit within 50 feet of any campground, campsite, or concentration of people or animals shall be 15 miles per hour unless changed as authorized by this code and, if so changed, only when signs have been erected giving notice thereof. *(Added by Stats.1976, c. 1093, p. 4947, § 26.)*

ARTICLE 4.　TURNING AND STARTING

Section
38312.　Starting parked vehicles.
38314.　Turning movements.

Cross References

Exemption of authorized emergency vehicles, see Vehicle Code § 21055.

§ 38312.　Starting parked vehicles

No person shall place in motion an off-highway motor vehicle that is stopped, standing, or parked until such movement can be made with reasonable safety. *(Added by Stats.1976, c. 1093, p. 4947, § 26.)*

§ 38314.　Turning movements

No person shall turn an off-highway motor vehicle from a direct course or move right or left until such movement can be made with reasonable safety. *(Added by Stats.1976, c. 1093, p. 4947, § 26.)*

ARTICLE 5.　RECKLESS DRIVING

Section
38316.　Reckless driving.
38317.　Reckless driving causing bodily injury.
38318.　Throwing substances at off-highway motor vehicles.
38318.5.　Malicious removal or alteration of safety or guidance signs; placement of cable, chain or rope.

Cross References

Violation as misdemeanor, see Vehicle Code § 40000.24.

§ 38316.　Reckless driving

(a) It is unlawful for any person to drive any off-highway motor vehicle with a willful and wanton disregard for the safety of other persons or property.

(b) Any person who violates this section shall, upon conviction thereof, be punished by imprisonment in the county jail for not less than five days nor more than 90 days or by fine of not less than fifty dollars ($50) nor more than five hundred dollars ($500) or by both such fine and imprisonment, except as provided in Section 38317. *(Added by Stats.1976, c. 1093, p. 4947, § 26. Amended by Stats.1983, c. 1092, § 397, eff. Sept. 27, 1983, operative Jan. 1, 1984.)*

§ 38317.　Reckless driving causing bodily injury

Whenever reckless driving of an off-highway motor vehicle proximately causes bodily injury to any person, the person driving the vehicle shall, upon conviction thereof, be punished by imprisonment in the county jail for not less than 30 days nor more than six months or by fine of not less than one hundred dollars ($100) nor more than one thousand dollars ($1,000) or by both such fine and imprisonment. *(Added by Stats.1976, c. 1093, p. 4947, § 26. Amended by Stats.1983, c. 1092, § 398, eff. Sept. 27, 1983, operative Jan. 1, 1984.)*

§ 38318. Throwing substances at off-highway motor vehicles

(a) Any person who throws any substance at an off-highway motor vehicle or occupant thereof is guilty of a misdemeanor and shall be punished pursuant to Section 42002 by a fine of not more than one thousand dollars ($1,000) or by imprisonment in the county jail for not more than six months, or by both the fine and imprisonment.

(b) Any person who, with intent to do great bodily injury, maliciously and willfully throws or projects any rock, brick, bottle, metal, or other missile, projects any other substance capable of doing serious bodily harm, or discharges a firearm at an off-highway motor vehicle or occupant thereof is guilty of a felony. *(Added by Stats.1976, c. 1093, p. 4947, § 26. Amended by Stats.1984, c. 729, § 1.5.)*

§ 38318.5. Malicious removal or alteration of safety or guidance signs; placement of cable, chain or rope

(a) Any person who maliciously removes or alters trail, danger, or directional markers or signs provided for the safety or guidance of off-highway motor vehicles is guilty of a misdemeanor and shall be punished pursuant to Section 42002 by a fine of not more than one thousand dollars ($1,000) or by imprisonment in the county jail for not more than six months, or by both the fine and imprisonment.

(b) Any person who, with intent to do great bodily injury (1) proximately causes great bodily injury to any person as a result of acts prohibited by subdivision (a), or (2) erects or places any cable, chain, rope, fishing line, or other similar material which is unmarked or intentionally placed, or both, for malicious purpose is guilty of a felony.

(c) Any person convicted under subdivision (a) or (b) shall, if the violation proximately causes one or more adverse environmental impacts, also be liable in civil damages for the cost of mitigation, restoration, or repair thereof, in addition to any other liability imposed by law. *(Added by Stats.1976, c. 1093, p. 4947, § 26. Amended by Stats.1984, c. 729, § 2; Stats.1985, c. 1322, § 1.)*

ARTICLE 6. LITTERING AND ENVIRONMENTAL PROTECTION

Section
38319. Operation causing damage.
38320. Throwing, depositing, or dumping matter.
38321. Removal of material.

Violation as misdemeanor, see Vehicle Code § 40000.24.

§ 38319. Operation causing damage

No person shall operate, nor shall an owner permit the operation of, an off-highway motor vehicle in a manner likely to cause malicious or unnecessary damage to the land, wildlife, wildlife habitat or vegetative resources. *(Added by Stats.1976, c. 1093, p. 4947, § 26.)*

§ 38320. Throwing, depositing, or dumping matter

(a) No person shall throw or deposit, nor shall the registered owner or the driver, if such owner is not then present in the vehicle, aid or abet in the throwing or depositing, upon any area, public or private, any bottle, can, garbage, glass, nail, offal, paper, wire, any substance likely to injure or kill wild or domestic animal or plant life or damage traffic using such area, or any noisome, nauseous or offensive matter of any kind.

(b) No person shall place, deposit or dump, or cause to be placed, deposited or dumped, any rocks or dirt in or upon any area, public or private, without the consent of the property owner or public agency having jurisdiction over the area.

(c) Any person who violates this section shall, upon conviction thereof, be punished by a fine of not less than fifty dollars ($50). No part of such fine shall be suspended. The court may permit the fine required by this section to be paid in installments if the court determines that the defendant is unable to pay the fine in one lump sum. *(Added by Stats.1976, c. 1093, p. 4947, § 26. Amended by Stats.1983, c. 1092, § 399, eff. Sept. 27, 1983, operative Jan. 1, 1984.)*

Violation as misdemeanor, see Vehicle Code § 40000.24.

§ 38321. Removal of material

(a) Any person who drops, dumps, deposits, places, or throws, or causes or permits to be dropped, dumped, deposited, placed, or thrown, upon any area, any material described in Section 38320, shall immediately remove the material or cause it to be removed.

(b) If such person fails to comply with the provisions of this section, the governmental agency responsible for the maintenance of the area, or the property owner of the land on which the material has been deposited, may remove such material and collect, by civil action, if necessary, the actual cost of the removal operation in addition to any other damages authorized by law from the person who did not comply with the requirements of this section. *(Added by Stats.1976, c. 1093, p. 4947, § 26.)*

CHAPTER 6. EQUIPMENT OF OFF–HIGHWAY VEHICLES

Article   **Section**
1. General Provisions 38325

Article	Section
2. Lighting Equipment	38335
3. Brakes	38355
4. Equipment	38365
5. Emission Control Equipment	38390

ARTICLE 1.   GENERAL PROVISIONS

Section
38325.   Applicability of provisions.
38330.   Vehicle not equipped or unsafe.

§ 38325.   Applicability of provisions

The provisions of this chapter shall apply to all off-highway motor vehicles, as defined in Section 38006, when operated in areas in which this division has application. *(Added by Stats.1976, c. 1093, p. 4950, § 28.)*

§ 38330.   Vehicle not equipped or unsafe

It is unlawful to operate any vehicle or combination of vehicles which is in an unsafe condition, which is not equipped as required by this chapter or the equipment regulations of the governmental agency having jurisdiction over public lands, or which is not safely loaded. *(Added by Stats.1976, c. 1093, p. 4950, § 28.)*

ARTICLE 2.   LIGHTING EQUIPMENT

Section
38335.   Headlamps.
38345.   Taillamps.
38346.   Warning lights.

§ 38335.   Headlamps

When operated from one-half hour after sunset to one-half hour before sunrise, each motor vehicle shall be equipped with at least one lighted white headlamp directed toward the front of the vehicle. Such lamp shall be of an intensity sufficient to reveal persons and vehicles at a distance of at least 200 feet. *(Added by Stats.1976, c. 1093, p. 4950, § 28.)*

§ 38345.   Taillamps

When operated from one-half hour after sunset to one-half hour before sunrise, each motor vehicle which is not in combination with any other vehicle shall be equipped with at least one lighted red taillamp which shall be clearly visible from the rear.

(a) Every such vehicle or vehicles at the end of a combination of vehicles shall be equipped with one lighted red taillamp when operated from one-half hour after sunset to one-half hour before sunrise. *(Added by Stats.1976, c. 1093, p. 4950, § 28.)*

§ 38346.   Warning lights

A person shall not display a flashing or steady burning red or blue warning light on an off-highway motor vehicle except as permitted by Section 21055 or when an extreme hazard exists. *(Added by Stats.2004, c. 908 (A.B.2666), § 24.)*

ARTICLE 3.   BRAKES

Section
38355.   Service brakes required.

§ 38355.   Service brakes required

(a) Except as provided in subdivision (b), every motor vehicle shall be equipped with a service brake system which is in good working order and adequate to control the movement of, and to stop and hold to the limit of traction of, such vehicle or combination of vehicles under all conditions of loading and upon any grade on which it is operated.

(b) Any motor vehicle, such as an air-cushioned vehicle, which is unable to comply with the requirements of this section due to the method of operation, is exempt, if the operator is able to exercise safe control over the movement of such vehicle. *(Added by Stats.1976, c. 1093, p. 4950, § 28.)*

ARTICLE 4.   EQUIPMENT

Section
38365.   Mufflers and exhaust systems.
38366.   Spark arresters.
38370.   Noise limits.
38375.   Sirens.
38380.   Additional equipment.

§ 38365.   Mufflers and exhaust systems

(a) Every off-highway motor vehicle, as defined in Section 38006, shall at all times be equipped with an adequate muffler in constant operation and properly maintained so as to meet the requirements of Section 38370, and no muffler or exhaust system shall be equipped with a cutout, bypass, or similar device.

(b) The provisions of subdivision (a) shall not be applicable to vehicles being operated off the highways in an organized racing or competitive event upon a closed course or in a hill climb or drag race, which is conducted under the auspices of a recognized sanctioning body or by permit issued by the local governmental authority having jurisdiction. *(Added by Stats.1976, c. 1093, p. 4950, § 28.)*

§ 38366.   Spark arresters

(a) Notwithstanding Section 4442 of the Public Resources Code, and except for vehicles with mufflers as provided in Article 2 (commencing with Section 27150) of Chapter 5 of Division 12, no person shall use, operate, or allow to be used or operated, any off-highway motor vehicle, as defined in Section 38006, on any forest-covered land, brush-covered land, or grass-covered land unless the vehicle is equipped with a spark arrester maintained in effective working order.

(b) A spark arrester affixed to the exhaust system of a vehicle subject to this section shall not be placed or mounted in such a manner as to allow flames or heat from the exhaust system to ignite any flammable material.

(c) A spark arrester is a device constructed of non-flammable materials specifically for the purpose of removing and retaining carbon and other flammable particles over 0.0232 of an inch in size from the exhaust flow of an internal combustion engine or which is qualified and rated by the United States Forest Service.

(d) Subdivision (a) shall not be applicable to vehicles being operated off the highway in an organized racing or competitive event upon a closed course, which is conducted under the auspices of a recognized sanctioning body and by permit issued by the fire protection authority having jurisdiction. *(Added by Stats.1987, c. 1027, § 28.)*

§ 38370. Noise limits

(a) The Department of Motor Vehicles shall not identify any new off-highway motor vehicle, which is subject to identification and which produces a maximum noise level that exceeds the following noise limit, at a distance of 50 feet from the centerline of travel, under test procedures established by the Department of the California Highway Patrol.

(1) Any such vehicle manufactured before January 1, 1973 . . . . 92 dBA
(2) Any such vehicle manufactured on or after January 1, 1973, and before January 1, 1975 . . . . 88 dBA
(3) Any such vehicle manufactured on or after January 1, 1975, and before January 1, 1986 . . . . 86 dBA
(4) Any such vehicle manufactured on or after January 1, 1986 . . . . 82 dBA

(b) The department may accept a dealer's certificate as proof of compliance with this section.

(c) Test procedures for compliance with this section shall be established by the Department of the California Highway Patrol, taking into consideration the test procedures of the Society of Automotive Engineers.

(d) No person shall sell or offer for sale any new off-highway motor vehicle which is subject to identification and which produces a maximum noise level that exceeds the noise limits in subdivision (a), and for which noise emission standards or regulations have not been adopted by the Administrator of the Environmental Protection Agency pursuant to the Federal Noise Control Act of 1972 (P.L. 92–574).[1]

(e) No person shall sell or offer for sale any new off-highway motor vehicle which is subject to identification and which produces a noise level that exceeds, or in any way violates, the noise emission standards or regulations adopted for such a motor vehicle by the Administrator of the Environmental Protection Agency pursuant to the Federal Noise Control Act of 1972 (P.L. 92–574).[2]

(f) As used in this section, the term "identify" is equivalent to the term "licensing" as used in Section 6(e)(2) of the Federal Noise Control Act of 1972 (P.L. 92–574).

(g) Any off-highway motor vehicle, when operating pursuant to Section 38001, shall at all times be equipped with a silencer, or other device, which limits noise emissions to not more than 101 dBA if manufactured on or after January 1, 1975, or 105 dBA if manufactured before January 1, 1975, when measured from a distance of 20 inches using test procedures established by the Society of Automotive Engineers under Standard J–1287. This subdivision shall only be operative until January 1, 2003.

(h) On and after January 1, 2003, off-highway motor vehicles, when operating pursuant to Section 38001, shall at all times be equipped with a silencer, or other device, which limits noise emissions.

(1) Noise emissions of competition off-highway vehicles manufactured on or after January 1, 1998, shall be limited to not more than 96 dBA, and if manufactured prior to January 1, 1998, to not more than 101 dBA, when measured from a distance of 20 inches using test procedures established by the Society of Automotive Engineers under Standard J–1287, as applicable. Noise emissions of all other off-highway vehicles shall be limited to not more than 96 dBA if manufactured on or after January 1, 1986, and not more than 101 dBA if manufactured prior to January 1, 1986, when measured from a distance of 20 inches using test procedures established by the Society of Automotive Engineers under Standard J–1287, as applicable.

(2) The Off–Highway Motor Vehicle Recreation Division of the Department of Parks and Recreation shall evaluate and reassess the dates specified in paragraph (1) and include the findings and recommendations in the noise report required in subdivision *(o)* of Section 5090.32 of the Public Resources Code.

(i) Off-highway vehicle manufacturers or their agents prior to the sale to the general public in California of any new off-highway vehicle model manufactured after January 1, 2003, shall provide to the Off–Highway Motor Vehicle Recreation Division of the California Department of Parks and Recreation rpm data needed to conduct the J–1287 test, where applicable. *(Added by Stats.1976, c. 1093, p. 4950, § 28. Amended by Stats.1988, c. 815, § 1; Stats.1989, c. 533, § 14; Stats.2002, c. 563 (A.B.2274), § 45; Stats.2004, c. 908 (A.B.2666), § 25.)*

[1] 42 U.S.C.A. § 4901 et seq.
[2] 42 U.S.C.A. § 4905(e)(2).

Cross References

Department of California Highway Patrol, see Vehicle Code § 2100 et seq.

§ 38375. Sirens

(a) An off-highway motor vehicle, except an authorized emergency vehicle, shall not be equipped with a siren.

(b) A person driving an off-highway motor vehicle, except the driver of an authorized emergency vehicle as permitted by Section 21055, shall not use a siren. *(Added by Stats.2004, c. 908 (A.B.2666), § 26.)*

§ 38380.　Additional equipment

(a) Because of specialized conditions such as fire hazard, public safety or other circumstances, any local authority, or state or federal agencies having control over public lands may require that vehicles being operated off highway be equipped with additional equipment.

(b) When such additional equipment is required in a specific location, the governmental agency having jurisdiction over that location shall insure that such regulations are posted in a manner that operators of off-highway motor vehicles using those locations will be aware of the special requirements. *(Added by Stats.1976, c. 1093, p. 4950, § 28.)*

ARTICLE 5.　EMISSION CONTROL EQUIPMENT

Section
38390.　Pollution control device.
38391.　Modification devices.
38392.　Imposition of penalty for willful violation.
38393.　Operation after notice.
38394.　Proof of correction.
38395.　Modification devices; exceptions to prohibition.
38396.　Federally owned off-highway vehicles.
38397.　Applicability.

§ 38390.　Pollution control device

No person shall operate or maintain in a condition of readiness for operation any off-highway motor vehicle which is required to be equipped with a motor vehicle pollution control device under Part 5 (commencing with Section 43000) of Division 26 of the Health and Safety Code or with any other certified motor vehicle pollution control device required by any other state law or any rule or regulation adopted pursuant to such law, or required to be equipped with a motor vehicle pollution control device pursuant to the Clean Air Act (42 U.S.C. 1857 et seq.)[1] and the standards and regulations promulgated thereunder, unless it is equipped with the required motor vehicle pollution control device which is correctly installed and in operating condition. No person shall disconnect, modify, or alter any such required device. Notwithstanding Section 43107 of the Health and Safety Code, this section shall apply only to off-highway motor vehicles of the 1978 or later model year. *(Added by Stats.1976, c. 1093, p. 4950, § 28.)*

[1] Transferred; see, now, 42 U.S.C.A. § 7401 et seq.

§ 38391.　Modification devices

No person shall install, sell, offer for sale, or advertise any device, apparatus, or mechanism intended for use with, or as a part of, any required off-highway motor vehicle pollution control device or system which alters or modifies the original design or performance of any such motor vehicle pollution control device or system. *(Added by Stats.1976, c. 1093, p. 4950, § 28.)*

§ 38392.　Imposition of penalty for willful violation

When the court finds that a person has willfully violated any provision of this article, such person shall be fined the maximum amount that may be imposed for such an offense, and no part of the fine may be suspended.

"Willfully", as used in this section, has the same meaning as the meaning of that word prescribed in Section 7 of the Penal Code. *(Added by Stats.1976, c. 1093, p. 4950, § 28.)*

§ 38393.　Operation after notice

No person shall operate an off-highway motor vehicle after notice by a traffic officer or other authorized public officer that such vehicle is not equipped with the required certified motor vehicle pollution control device correctly installed in operating condition, except as may be necessary to return the vehicle to the residence or place of business of the owner or driver or to a garage, until the vehicle has been properly equipped with such a device. *(Added by Stats.1976, c. 1093, p. 4950, § 28.)*

§ 38394.　Proof of correction

The notice to appear issued or complaint filed for a violation of any provision of this article shall require that the person to whom the notice to appear is issued or against whom the complaint is filed produce proof of correction pursuant to Section 40150. *(Added by Stats. 1976, c. 1093, p. 4950, § 28.)*

§ 38395.　Modification devices; exceptions to prohibition

This article shall not apply to an alteration, modification, or modifying device, apparatus, or mechanism found by resolution of the State Air Resources Board either:

(a) To not reduce the effectiveness of any required off-highway motor vehicle pollution control device; or

(b) To result in emissions from any such modified or altered off-highway vehicle which are at levels which comply with existing state or federal standards for that model year of the vehicle being modified or converted. *(Added by Stats.1976, c. 1093, p. 4950, § 28.)*

§ 38396.　Federally owned off-highway vehicles

The provisions of this article apply to off-highway motor vehicles of the United States or its agencies, to the extent authorized by federal law. *(Added by Stats.1976, c. 1093, p. 4950, § 28.)*

§ 38397.　Applicability

Except as provided in Section 38390, this article shall be applicable to all off-highway motor vehicles, whether or not subject to identification pursuant to this division and without limitation by the exceptions contained in Section 38001, and to all off-highway motor vehicles operated or maintained in a condition of readiness for operation on private or public property. *(Added by Stats.1976, c. 1093, p. 4950, § 28.)*

CHAPTER 7. ALL–TERRAIN VEHICLES

Section
38500. Off-highway vehicle safety education committee; membership.
38500.1. Duties of committee.
38501. All-terrain vehicle safety certificate; fees.
38502. Monitoring of training organizations and instructors.
38503. Minors under age 18; conditions of operation of vehicle.
38504. Minors under age 14; conditions of operation of vehicle.
38504.1. Minors under age 14; operation of all-terrain vehicle in manner that violates § 38504; parent, guardian or supervising adult; punishment.
38504.2. Minors under age 14; attendance and completion of all-terrain vehicle safety training course accompanied by person who violated § 38504.1.
38505. Helmets.
38506. Passengers.

§ 38500. Off-highway vehicle safety education committee; membership

The Off-Highway Vehicle Safety Education Committee is hereby established. The committee consists of the Commissioner of the California Highway Patrol, the Deputy Director of Parks and Recreation for Off-Highway Vehicles, the Director of Motor Vehicles, or their designees, and a member of the Off-Highway Motor Vehicle Recreation Commission appointed by the members of the commission. The committee shall receive staff assistance in its operations from the Off-Highway Motor Vehicle Recreation Division in the Department of Parks and Recreation. *(Added by Stats.1987, c. 881, § 37.)*

§ 38500.1. Duties of committee

The Off-Highway Vehicle Safety Education Committee shall meet periodically to perform all of the following:

(a) Develop minimum criteria for certification as an approved all-terrain vehicle safety training organization. The criteria shall include, but not be limited to, the following:

(1) Curriculum and materials for training instructors to teach all-terrain vehicle operation and safety.

(2) Curriculum and materials for training all-terrain vehicle safety.

(3) Curriculum for teaching responsible use of off-highway vehicles with respect to environmental considerations, private property restrictions, off-highway vehicle operating laws, including noise and spark arrestor laws, and prohibitions against operating off-highway vehicles under the influence of alcohol or drugs.

(4) Record keeping and insurance requirements to satisfy the requirements of Sections 11103.1 and 11108.

(b) Upon presentation to the committee of a proposed program by an applicant to become an approved all-terrain vehicle safety training organization, the committee shall determine whether the applicant's program meets the minimum criteria and, if approved, shall recommend the organization for licensing pursuant to Section 11105.6. *(Added by Stats.1987, c. 881, § 37.)*

§ 38501. All-terrain vehicle safety certificate; fees

(a) An all-terrain vehicle safety training organization, commencing on January 1, 1989, shall issue an all-terrain vehicle safety certificate furnished by the department to any individual who successfully completes a course of instruction in all-terrain vehicle operation and safety as approved and certified by the Off-Highway Vehicle Safety Education Committee.

(b) The department shall charge a fee not to exceed three dollars ($3) for each all-terrain vehicle safety certificate issued by an all-terrain vehicle safety training organization to each person completing a course of instruction from an all-terrain vehicle safety instructor using the approved course of instruction of the all-terrain vehicle safety training organization. The amount of the fee shall be determined by the department and shall be sufficient to defray the actual costs incurred by the department for administering and monitoring this program.

(c) An all-terrain vehicle safety training organization shall not charge a fee in excess of the fee charged by the department pursuant to subdivision (b) for furnishing an all-terrain vehicle safety certificate. An organization may charge a fee not to exceed three dollars ($3) in addition to the fee charged by the department for the issuance of a duplicate certificate and shall provide a duplicate certificate if requested by the person who completed the course. *(Added by Stats.1987, c. 881, § 37.)*

§ 38502. Monitoring of training organizations and instructors

The department, on and after July 1, 1988, may monitor any all-terrain vehicle safety training organization or any all-terrain vehicle safety instructor without advance notice. The monitoring may include, but is not limited to, the instruction provided, business practices, and records required by Section 11108. *(Added by Stats.1987, c. 881, § 37.)*

§ 38503. Minors under age 18; conditions of operation of vehicle

No person under the age of 18 years, on and after January 1, 1990, shall operate an all-terrain vehicle on public lands of this state unless the person satisfies one of the following conditions:

(a) The person is taking a prescribed safety training course under the direct supervision of a certified all-terrain vehicle safety instructor.

(b) The person is under the direct supervision of an adult who has in their possession an appropriate safety certificate issued by this state, or issued under the authority of another state.

(c) The person has in possession an appropriate safety certificate issued by this state or issued under the authority of another state. *(Added by Stats.1987, c. 881, § 37.)*

§ 38504. Minors under age 14; conditions of operation of vehicle

No person under 14 years of age, on and after January 1, 1990, shall operate an all-terrain vehicle on public lands of this state unless the person satisfies one of the conditions set forth in Section 38503 and, in addition, is accompanied by and under the direct supervision of a parent or guardian or is accompanied by and under the direct supervision of an adult who is authorized by the parent or guardian. *(Added by Stats.1987, c. 881, § 37.)*

§ 38504.1. Minors under age 14; operation of all-terrain vehicle in manner that violates § 38504; parent, guardian or supervising adult; punishment

(a) Neither a parent or guardian of a child who is under 14 years of age, nor an adult who is authorized by the parent or guardian to supervise that child shall grant permission to, or knowingly allow, that child to operate an all-terrain vehicle in a manner that violates Section 38504.

(b) A person convicted of a violation of subdivision (a) is punishable as follows:

(1) For a first conviction, the court shall either impose a fine of one hundred twenty-five dollars ($125) or order the person to take or retake and complete an all-terrain vehicle safety training course pursuant to Section 38501. If ordered to take or retake and complete the safety training course, the person shall provide the court a copy of the all-terrain vehicles safety certificate issued as a result of that completion.

(2) For a second conviction, a fine of not less than one hundred twenty-five dollars ($125) nor more than two hundred fifty dollars ($250).

(3) For a third or any subsequent conviction, a fine of not less than two hundred fifty dollars ($250) nor more than five hundred dollars ($500). *(Added by Stats.2006, c. 195 (A.B.2755), § 1.)*

Cross References

Drivers' licenses, issuance and renewal, traffic violation point counts, see Vehicle Code § 12810.

§ 38504.2. Minors under age 14; attendance and completion of all-terrain vehicle safety training course accompanied by person who violated § 38504.1

If a person under 14 years of age was not properly supervised or accompanied in accordance with Section 38504, and the parent or guardian of that child or the adult who was authorized by the parent or guardian to supervise or accompany that child is in violation of Section 38504.1, upon a conviction pursuant to Section 38504, the court may order that child to attend and complete the all-terrain vehicle safety training course accompanied by the person who violated Section 38504.1. If so ordered, the child under 14 years of age shall

provide the court a copy of the all-terrain vehicles safety certificate issued as a result of that completion. *(Added by Stats.2006, c. 195 (A.B.2755), § 2.)*

§ 38505. Helmets

No person, on and after January 1, 1989, shall operate, ride, or be otherwise propelled on an all-terrain vehicle on public lands unless the person wears a safety helmet meeting requirements established for motorcycles and motorized bicycles, pursuant to Section 27802. *(Added by Stats.1987, c. 881, § 37. Amended by Stats.1988, c. 165, § 2.)*

§ 38506. Passengers

No operator of an all-terrain vehicle may carry a passenger when operating on public lands.

However, the operator of an all-terrain vehicle, that is designed for operation off of the highway by an operator with no more than one passenger, may carry a passenger when operating on public lands. *(Added by Stats.1987, c. 881, § 37. Amended by Stats.2003, c. 252 (S.B.232), § 2.)*

CHAPTER 8. RECREATIONAL OFF–HIGHWAY VEHICLES

Section
38600. Operation of vehicle; minimum age; parent or guardian supervision.
38601. Safety helmets.
38602. Seatbelt and shoulder belt; safety harness.
38603. Occupying of separate seat location not designed or provided for passengers.
38604. Operation of vehicle with passenger; occupant hand-hold design.

§ 38600. Operation of vehicle; minimum age; parent or guardian supervision

A person operating a recreational off-highway vehicle shall be at least 16 years of age, or be directly supervised in the vehicle by a parent or guardian or by an adult authorized by the parent or guardian. *(Added by Stats. 2012, c. 165 (A.B.1595), § 3.)*

§ 38601. Safety helmets

A person shall not operate, or allow a passenger in, a recreational off-highway vehicle unless the person and the passenger are wearing safety helmets meeting the requirements established for motorcycles and motorized bicycles pursuant to Section 27802. *(Added by Stats.2012, c. 165 (A.B.1595), § 3.)*

§ 38602. Seatbelt and shoulder belt; safety harness

A person operating, and any passenger in, a recreational off-highway vehicle shall wear a seatbelt and shoulder belt or safety harness that is properly fastened when the vehicle is in motion. *(Added by Stats.2012, c. 165 (A.B.1595), § 3.)*

§ 38603. Occupying of separate seat location not designed or provided for passengers

(a) A person operating a recreational off-highway vehicle with a model year of 2014 or later shall not allow a passenger to occupy a separate seat location not designed and provided by the manufacturer for a passenger.

* * *

(b) Seats that are installed in a separate seat location not designed and provided by the manufacturer for a passenger in vehicles with model year of 2013 or earlier may be occupied by a passenger if the occupant of the seat is fully contained inside of the vehicle's rollover protection structure at all times while the vehicle is being operated. *(Added by Stats.2012, c. 165 (A.B.1595), § 3. Amended by Stats.2012, c. 529 (A.B.1266), § 1, eff. Sept. 25, 2012, operative July 1, 2013; Stats.2013, c. 179 (S.B.234), § 1, eff. Aug. 27, 2013.)*

§ 38604. Operation of vehicle with passenger; occupant handhold design

(a) A person operating a recreational off-highway vehicle shall not ride with a passenger, unless the passenger, while seated upright with his or her back against the seatback, can grasp the occupant handhold with the seatbelt and shoulder belt or safety harness properly fastened.

(b) For purposes of this chapter, "occupant handhold" means any factory or aftermarket device grasped by an occupant to provide support and to assist in keeping arms and hands within the recreational off-highway vehicle. The steering wheel shall be considered an occupant handhold for the recreational off-highway vehicle operator.

(c) Occupant handholds shall be designed to allow the recreational off-highway vehicle passenger to exit the vehicle without interference from the handholds. *(Added by Stats.2012, c. 165 (A.B.1595), § 3. Amended by Stats.2012, c. 529 (A.B.1266), § 2, eff. Sept. 25, 2012, operative Jan. 1, 2013; Stats.2013, c. 179 (S.B.234), § 2, eff. Aug. 27, 2013.)*

Division 16.6

AUTONOMOUS VEHICLES

Section

38750. Definitions; testing of autonomous vehicle; application for operation of autonomous vehicle on public roads; regulations; application of other law; disclosure to purchaser.

§ 38750. Definitions; testing of autonomous vehicle; application for operation of autonomous vehicle on public roads; regulations; application of other law; disclosure to purchaser

(a) For purposes of this division, the following definitions apply:

(1) "Autonomous technology" means technology that has the capability to drive a vehicle without the active physical control or monitoring by a human operator.

(2)(A) "Autonomous vehicle" means any vehicle equipped with autonomous technology that has been integrated into that vehicle.

(B) An autonomous vehicle does not include a vehicle that is equipped with one or more collision avoidance systems, including, but not limited to, electronic blind spot assistance, automated emergency braking systems, park assist, adaptive cruise control, lane keep assist, lane departure warning, traffic jam and queuing assist, or other similar systems that enhance safety or provide driver assistance, but are not capable, collectively or singularly, of driving the vehicle without the active control or monitoring of a human operator.

(3) "Department" means the Department of Motor Vehicles.

(4) An "operator" of an autonomous vehicle is the person who is seated in the driver's seat, or if there is no person in the driver's seat, causes the autonomous technology to engage.

(5) A "manufacturer" of autonomous technology is the person as defined in Section 470 that originally manufactures a vehicle and equips autonomous technology on the originally completed vehicle or, in the case of a vehicle not originally equipped with autonomous technology by the vehicle manufacturer, the person that modifies the vehicle by installing autonomous technology to convert it to an autonomous vehicle after the vehicle was originally manufactured.

(b) An autonomous vehicle may be operated on public roads for testing purposes by a driver who possesses the proper class of license for the type of vehicle being operated if all of the following requirements are met:

(1) The autonomous vehicle is being operated on roads in this state solely by employees, contractors, or other persons designated by the manufacturer of the autonomous technology.

(2) The driver shall be seated in the driver's seat, monitoring the safe operation of the autonomous vehicle, and capable of taking over immediate manual control of the autonomous vehicle in the event of an autonomous technology failure or other emergency.

(3) Prior to the start of testing in this state, the manufacturer performing the testing shall obtain an instrument of insurance, surety bond, or proof of self-insurance in the amount of five million dollars ($5,000,000), and shall provide evidence of the insurance, surety bond, or self-insurance to the department in the form and manner required by the department pursuant to the regulations adopted pursuant to subdivision (d).

(c) Except as provided in subdivision (b), an autonomous vehicle shall not be operated on public roads until the manufacturer submits an application to the department, and that application is approved by the department pursuant to the regulations adopted pursuant to subdivision (d). The application shall contain, at a minimum, all of the following certifications:

(1) A certification by the manufacturer that the autonomous technology satisfies all of the following requirements:

(A) The autonomous vehicle has a mechanism to engage and disengage the autonomous technology that is easily accessible to the operator.

(B) The autonomous vehicle has a visual indicator inside the cabin to indicate when the autonomous technology is engaged.

(C) The autonomous vehicle has a system to safely alert the operator if an autonomous technology failure is detected while the autonomous technology is engaged, and when an alert is given, the system shall do either of the following:

(i) Require the operator to take control of the autonomous vehicle.

(ii) If the operator does not or is unable to take control of the autonomous vehicle, the autonomous vehicle shall be capable of coming to a complete stop.

(D) The autonomous vehicle shall allow the operator to take control in multiple manners, including, without limitation, through the use of the brake, the accelerator pedal, or the steering wheel, and it shall alert the operator that the autonomous technology has been disengaged.

(E) The autonomous vehicle's autonomous technology meets Federal Motor Vehicle Safety Standards for the vehicle's model year and all other applicable safety standards and performance requirements set forth in state and federal law and the regulations promulgated pursuant to those laws.

(F) The autonomous technology does not make inoperative any Federal Motor Vehicle Safety Standards for the vehicle's model year and all other applicable safety standards and performance requirements set forth in state and federal law and the regulations promulgated pursuant to those laws.

(G) The autonomous vehicle has a separate mechanism, in addition to, and separate from, any other mechanism required by law, to capture and store the autonomous technology sensor data for at least 30 seconds before a collision occurs between the autonomous vehicle and another vehicle, object, or natural person while the vehicle is operating in autonomous mode. The autonomous technology sensor data shall be captured and stored in a read-only format by the mechanism so that the data is retained until extracted from the mechanism by an external device capable of downloading and storing the data. The data shall be preserved for three years after the date of the collision.

(2) A certification that the manufacturer has tested the autonomous technology on public roads and has complied with the testing standards, if any, established by the department pursuant to subdivision (d).

(3) A certification that the manufacturer will maintain a surety bond, or proof of self-insurance as specified in regulations adopted by the department pursuant to subdivision (d), in an amount of five million dollars ($5,000,000).

(d)(1) As soon as practicable, but no later than January 1, 2015, the department shall adopt regulations setting forth requirements for the submission of evidence of insurance, surety bond, or self-insurance required by subdivision (b), and the submission and approval of an application to operate an autonomous vehicle pursuant to subdivision (c).

(2) The regulations shall include any testing, equipment, and performance standards, in addition to those established for purposes of subdivision (b), that the department concludes are necessary to ensure the safe operation of autonomous vehicles on public roads, with or without the presence of a driver inside the vehicle. In developing these regulations, the department may consult with the Department of the California Highway Patrol, the Institute of Transportation Studies at the University of California, or any other entity identified by the department that has expertise in automotive technology, automotive safety, and autonomous system design.

(3) The department may establish additional requirements by the adoption of regulations, which it determines, in consultation with the Department of the California Highway Patrol, are necessary to ensure the safe operation of autonomous vehicles on public roads, including, but not limited to, regulations regarding the

aggregate number of deployments of autonomous vehicles on public roads, special rules for the registration of autonomous vehicles, new license requirements for operators of autonomous vehicles, and rules for revocation, suspension, or denial of any license or any approval issued pursuant to this division.

(4) The department shall hold public hearings on the adoption of any regulation applicable to the operation of an autonomous vehicle without the presence of a driver inside the vehicle.

(e)(1) The department shall approve an application submitted by a manufacturer pursuant to subdivision (c) if it finds that the applicant has submitted all information and completed testing necessary to satisfy the department that the autonomous vehicles are safe to operate on public roads and the applicant has complied with all requirements specified in the regulations adopted by the department pursuant to subdivision (d).

(2) Notwithstanding paragraph (1), if the application seeks approval for autonomous vehicles capable of operating without the presence of a driver inside the vehicle, the department may impose additional requirements it deems necessary to ensure the safe operation of those vehicles, and may require the presence of a driver in the driver's seat of the vehicle if it determines, based on its review pursuant to paragraph (1), that such a requirement is necessary to ensure the safe operation of those vehicles on public roads. The department shall notify the Legislature of the receipt of an application from a manufacturer seeking approval to operate an autonomous vehicle capable of operating without the presence of a driver inside the vehicle and approval of the application. Approval of the application shall be effective no sooner than 180 days after the date the application is submitted.

(f) Nothing in this division shall limit or expand the existing authority to operate autonomous vehicles on public roads, until 120 days after the department adopts the regulations required by paragraph (1) of subdivision (d).

(g) Federal regulations promulgated by the National Highway Traffic Safety Administration shall supersede the provisions of this division when found to be in conflict with any other state law or regulation.

(h) The manufacturer of the autonomous technology installed on a vehicle shall provide a written disclosure to the purchaser of an autonomous vehicle that describes what information is collected by the autonomous technology equipped on the vehicle. The department may promulgate regulations to assess a fee upon a manufacturer that submits an application pursuant to subdivision (c) to operate autonomous vehicles on public roads in an amount necessary to recover all costs reasonably incurred by the department. *(Added by Stats.2012, c. 570 (S.B. 1298), § 2.)*

Division 16.7

REGISTRATION AND LICENSING OF BICYCLES

Section
39000. Definitions.
39001. License and registration form.
39002. License requirements; violations.
39003. Issuance of licenses and registration forms.
39004. Fees.
39005. Records.
39006. Information required upon retail sale.
39007. Serial numbers.
39008. Recordation of transfer.
39009. Notification of change of address; duplicate license or registration form.
39010. Repealed.
39011. Fines: Limitation.
39012. Repealed.
39013. Repealed.

Cross References

Notice to correct violations, see Vehicle Code § 40303.5.

§ 39000. Definitions

"Bicycle", for the purposes of this division, means any device upon which a person may ride, which is propelled by human power through a system of belts, chains, or gears having either two or three wheels (one of which is at least 20 inches in diameter) or having a frame size of at least 14 inches, or having four or more wheels. *(Added by Stats.1974, c. 971, p. 2019, § 5, eff. Sept. 20, 1974. Amended by Stats.1975, c. 188, p. 542, § 1; Stats.1975, c. 1250, p. 3220, § 2; Stats.1978, c. 421, p. 1321, § 6.)*

§ 39001. License and registration form

(a) The department shall procure and distribute bicycle license indicia and registration forms to all counties and cities which have adopted a bicycle licensing ordinance or resolution. Those counties and cities shall issue the indicia and registration form to the owner of any new bicycle, and may, upon request of the owner, issue an indicia and registration form to the owner of any bicycle which complies with Section 39007.

The department shall charge and collect a fee, not to exceed the cost of procuring and distributing the license indicia and registration form, for each bicycle license indicia and registration form issued. All fees collected pursuant to this section shall be deposited in the Motor Vehicle Account in the State Transportation Fund. Those fees are hereby continuously appropriated from the account for use by the department to defray costs to procure and distribute the bicycle license indicia and registration forms.

(b) The director shall design the bicycle license indicia and registration form described in subdivision (a), and shall establish procedures for the distribution of the indicia and registration form to counties and cities. The indicia shall be adhesive, durable, flexible, and of a size to permit it to be affixed to the front of the seat tube of the bicycle frame. Each indicia shall bear a unique license number and shall be permanently assigned to a bicycle. Each registration form shall comply with Section 39005.

(c) Bicycle licenses shall be renewed uniformly throughout the state on January 1 of the third year following the year of registration. Renewal of a bicycle license shall be indicated by a supplementary adhesive device affixed parallel to, and above or below, the indicia, with the expiration date showing. *(Added by Stats.1974, c. 971, p. 2019, § 5, eff. Sept. 20, 1974. Amended by Stats.1975, c. 188, p. 543, § 2; Stats.1975, c. 1250, p. 3220, § 3; Stats.1985, c. 488, § 1; Stats.1988, c. 1268, § 25, operative July 1, 1989.)*

§ 39002. License requirements; violations

(a) A city or county, which adopts a bicycle licensing ordinance or resolution, may provide in the ordinance or resolution that no resident shall operate any bicycle, as specified in the ordinance, on any street, road, highway, or other public property within the jurisdiction of the city or county, as the case may be, unless the bicycle is licensed in accordance with this division.

(b) It is unlawful for any person to tamper with, destroy, mutilate, or alter any license indicia or registration form, or to remove, alter, or mutilate the serial number, or the identifying marks of a licensing agency's identifying symbol, on any bicycle frame licensed under this division. *(Added by Stats.1974, c. 971, p. 2020, § 5, eff. Sept. 20, 1974. Amended by Stats.1975, c. 188, p. 543, § 3; Stats.1975, c. 1250, p. 3221, § 4; Stats.1985, c. 488, § 2; Stats.1996, c. 674 (S.B.515), § 8.)*

§ 39003. Issuance of licenses and registration forms

If a city or county has or adopts a bicycle licensing ordinance or resolution, indicia and a copy of the registration form obtained from the department shall be issued to the owner by the city or county or other licensing agency designated by it. *(Added by Stats.1974, c. 971, p. 2020, § 5, eff. Sept. 20, 1974. Amended by Stats.1975, c. 188, p. 542, § 4; Stats.1975, c. 1250, p. 3221, § 5.)*

§ 39004. Fees

Each licensing agency, by ordinance or resolution, may adopt rules and regulations for the collection of license fees. Revenues from license fees shall be retained by the licensing city or county and shall be used for the support of such bicycle ordinance or resolution, and may be used to reimburse retailers for services rendered. In addition, fees collected shall be used to improve bicycle safety programs and establish bicycle facilities, including bicycle paths and lanes, within the limits of the jurisdiction.

The fees required to be paid pursuant to this division are as follows:

(a) For each new bicycle license and registration certificate, the sum shall not exceed four dollars ($4) per year or any portion thereof.

(b) For each transfer of registration certificate, the sum shall not exceed two dollars ($2).

(c) For each replacement of a bicycle license or registration certificate, the sum shall not exceed two dollars ($2).

(d) For each bicycle license renewal, the sum shall not exceed two dollars ($2) per year. *(Added by Stats.1974, c. 971, p. 2020, § 5, eff. Sept. 20, 1974. Amended by Stats.1975, c. 188, p. 543, § 5; Stats.1975, c. 1250, p. 3221, § 6; Stats.1999, c. 277 (A.B.134), § 4.)*

§ 39005.　Records

Cities and counties having a bicycle licensing ordinance or resolution shall maintain records of each bicycle registered. Such records shall include, but not be limited to, the license number, the serial number of the bicycle, the make and type, of the bicycle, and the name and address of the licensee.

Records shall be maintained by the licensing agency during the period of validity of the license or until notification that the bicycle is no longer to be operated. *(Added by Stats.1974, c. 971, p. 2020, § 5, eff. Sept. 20, 1974. Amended by Stats.1975, c. 188, p. 544, § 6; Stats.1975, c. 1250, p. 3221, § 7.)*

§ 39006.　Information required upon retail sale

(a) Each bicycle retailer and each bicycle dealer shall supply to each purchaser a preregistration form provided by the licensing agency and shall include, on the sales check or receipt given to the purchaser, a record of the following information: name of retailer, address of retailer, year and make of the bicycle, serial number of the bicycle if delivered to the purchaser in an assembled state, general description of the bicycle, name of purchaser, and address of purchaser. A copy of the preregistration form shall be filled out and forwarded by the purchaser to the appropriate licensing agency within 10 days from the date of sale.

(b) For the purposes of this division, a bicycle dealer is any person who sells, gives away, buys, or takes in trade for the purpose of resale, more than five bicycles in any one calendar year, whether or not such bicycles are owned by such person. "Bicycle dealer" also includes agents or employees of such person. *(Added by Stats. 1974, c. 971, p. 2020, § 5, eff. Sept. 20, 1974. Amended by Stats.1975, c. 1250, p. 3222, § 8.)*

§ 39007.　Serial numbers

After December 31, 1976, no bicycle retailer shall sell any new bicycle in this state unless such bicycle has legibly

1020

and permanently stamped or cast on its frame a serial number, no less than one-eighth inch in size, and unique to the particular bicycle of each manufacturer. The serial number only shall be stamped or cast in the head of the frame, either side of the seat tube, the toeplate, or the bottom sprocket (crank) housing. *(Added by Stats.1974, c. 971, p. 2020, § 5, eff. Sept. 20, 1974. Amended by Stats.1975, c. 188, p. 544, § 7; Stats.1975, c. 1250, p. 3222, § 9.)*

§ 39008.　Recordation of transfer

(a) Whenever any person sells or otherwise disposes of a bicycle, he shall endorse upon the registration certificate previously issued for such bicycle a written transfer of same, setting forth the name, address, telephone number of the transferee, date of transfer, and signature of the transferrer, and shall deliver the registration certificate, so endorsed, to the licensing agency within 10 days.

(b) Any person who purchases or otherwise acquires possession of a bicycle shall, within 10 days of taking possession, apply for the transfer of license to his own name. Cities and counties may establish rules and regulations to govern and enforce the provisions of this section. *(Added by Stats.1974, c. 971, p. 2020, § 5, eff. Sept. 20, 1974. Amended by Stats.1975, c. 188, p. 544, § 8; Stats.1975, c. 1250, p. 3222, § 10.)*

§ 39009.　Notification of change of address; duplicate license or registration form

(a) Whenever the owner of a bicycle licensed pursuant to an ordinance or resolution of a city or county changes his address, he shall within 10 days notify the appropriate licensing agency of the old and new address.

(b) In the event that any bicycle license indicia or registration form issued pursuant to the provisions of this division is lost, stolen, or mutilated, the licensee of such bicycle shall immediately notify the licensing agency, and, within 10 days after such notification, shall apply to the licensing agency for a duplicate license indicia or registration form. Thereupon, the licensing agency shall issue to such licensee a replacement indicia or registration form upon payment to the licensing agency of the appropriate fee. *(Added by Stats.1974, c. 971, p. 2021, § 5, eff. Sept. 20, 1974. Amended by Stats.1975, c. 188, p. 544, § 9; Stats.1975, c. 1250, p. 3222, § 11.)*

§ 39010.　Repealed by Stats.1982, c. 681, p. 2813, § 89

§ 39011.　Fines: Limitation

No fine imposed for any violation of an ordinance or resolution, which is adopted pursuant to this division, shall exceed ten dollars ($10). *(Added by Stats.1974, c. 971, p. 2021, § 5, eff. Sept. 20, 1974. Amended by Stats.1983, c. 1092, § 400, eff. Sept. 27, 1983, operative Jan. 1, 1984.)*

§ 39012.　Repealed by Stats.1996, c. 674 (S.B.515), § 9

§ 39013.   Repealed by Stats.1980, c. 1070, p. 3420, § 2

Division 16.8

LICENSING OF BICYCLES [REPEALED]

§§ 39100 to 39118.   Repealed by Stats.1974, c. 971, p.
2021, § 6, eff. Sept. 20, 1974

Division 17

OFFENSES AND PROSECUTION

Chapter		Section
1.	**Offenses**	40000
2.	**Procedure on Arrests**	40300
2.5.	**Administrative Adjudication of Traffic Safety Violations [Repealed]**	
3.	**Illegal Evidence**	40800
3.5.	**Evidence**	40900
4.	**Presumptions**	41100
5.	**Defenses**	41400
6.	**Nonprosecution of Violations**	41500
7.	**Arrest Quotas**	41600
8.	**Consolidated Disposition**	41610

CHAPTER 1. OFFENSES

Article		Section
1.	Violation of Code	40000
2.	Procedure on Equipment and Registration Violations	40150
3.	Procedure on Parking Violations	40200
3.5.	Procedure on Video Imaging of Parking Violations Occurring in Transit–Only Lanes	40240
3.6.	Procedure on Photo Enforcement and Digital Photographing of Parking Violations During Street Sweeping	40245
4.	Procedure on Toll Evasion Violations	40250

ARTICLE 1. VIOLATION OF CODE

Section
40000. Repealed.
40000.1. Infractions.
40000.3. Felonies and offenses punishable either as felonies or misdemeanor violation of court order punishable as contempt.
40000.5. Misdemeanors.
40000.6. Misdemeanor.
40000.61. Misdemeanor; unauthorized disclosure of department records.
40000.65. Misdemeanors; emergency road service.
40000.7. Misdemeanors.
40000.70. Notification of on-highway hazardous spill.
40000.77. Misdemeanors; transportation of pupils.
40000.8. Misdemeanors; vessels.
40000.9. Misdemeanors.
40000.11. Misdemeanors.
40000.13. Misdemeanors.
40000.13. Misdemeanors.
40000.14. Failure to obey person or control devices at site of construction, maintenance or repair; penalties.
40000.15. Misdemeanors.
40000.16. Escape of materials from vehicle; offense.
40000.18. Misdemeanors.
40000.19. Misdemeanors.
40000.20. Third or subsequent violations of provisions relating to storage and possession of open containers by driver operating under valid certificate or

Section
permit pursuant to Passenger Charter-party Carriers' Act; misdemeanor.
40000.21. Misdemeanors.
40000.22. Misdemeanors; inspections; violations of Motor Carriers of Property Permit Act.
40000.22. Misdemeanors; inspections; violations of Motor Carriers of Property Permit Act.
40000.23. Misdemeanors.
40000.24. Misdemeanors.
40000.25. Misdemeanors.
40000.26. Misdemeanors; failure to submit to inspection.
40000.28. Misdemeanor; three or more violations.
40001. Owner, lessee, or any other person; codefendant; rebuttable presumption.
40002. Prosecution of persons owning or controlling vehicles.
40002.1. Notice of noncompliance or subsequent adjudication; transmittal to department; warrant of arrest.
40003. Prosecution of employees.
40004. Period for commencement of criminal actions.
40005. Employer's failure.
40006. Towing unregistered disabled vehicle; infraction.
40007. Application of other statutory provisions applicable to acts violating Division 5.
40008. Intent to capture image, recording or impression for a commercial purpose; endangerment of minor.

Cross References

Applicability of this code,
  Emergency vehicles, see Vehicle Code § 21055 et seq.
  Physicians, see Vehicle Code § 21058.
  Public vehicles, see Vehicle Code § 21052 et seq.
  Riding animals, see Vehicle Code § 21050.
  Trolley coaches, see Vehicle Code § 21051.
Commissioner of California highway patrol, duty of administration and enforcement, see Vehicle Code § 2400.
Death or personal injury cases, see Vehicle Code § 20001.
False evidences of registration, see Vehicle Code § 4463.
Felonies,
  Driving under influence of liquor, see Vehicle Code § 23153.
  Theft and unlawful driving or taking of a vehicle, see Vehicle Code § 10851.
Felony and misdemeanor defined, see Penal Code § 17.
Infractions, see Penal Code §§ 16, 17, 19.6, 19.7, 1042.5.
Misdemeanors,
  Driving vehicle which exceeds size, weight, and load limitations, see Vehicle Code § 40001.
  Failure or refusal to stop and submit vehicle to be weighed, see Vehicle Code § 2802.
  Refusal to stop and submit to a test of equipment, see Vehicle Code §§ 2806, 40150.
  Unlawful use or tampering with vehicles by bailee, see Vehicle Code § 10854.
Operation of vehicles without evidences of registration, see Vehicle Code § 4000.
Person, definition, see Vehicle Code § 470.

Punishment,
    Felony, see Penal Code § 18.
    Infractions, see Vehicle Code § 42001; Penal Code § 19.6.
    Misdemeanor, see Penal Code §§ 19.2, 19.4.
    Special misdemeanors, see Vehicle Code § 42001.
Punishment for infractions and special misdemeanors, see Vehicle Code § 42001.
Test and approval of lamps, lamp equipment and signal devices, see Vehicle Code § 26100 et seq.
Violations of this code as negligence, see Vehicle Code § 40830.

§ 40000. Repealed by Stats.1971, c. 1178, p. 2245, § 2, operative May 3, 1972

§ 40000.1. Infractions

Except as otherwise provided in this article, it is unlawful and constitutes an infraction for any person to violate, or fail to comply with any provision of this code, or any local ordinance adopted pursuant to this code. *(Added by Stats.1971, c. 1178, p. 2245, § 3, operative May 3, 1972.)*

Cross References

Infractions, see Penal Code § 19.6 et seq.
Leaving a child unsupervised inside a motor vehicle, prosecution, see Vehicle Code § 15620.
Person defined, see Vehicle Code § 470.

§ 40000.3. Felonies and offenses punishable either as felonies or misdemeanor violation of court order punishable as contempt

A violation expressly declared to be a felony, or a public offense which is punishable, in the discretion of the court, either as a felony or misdemeanor, or a willful violation of a court order which is punishable as contempt pursuant to subdivision (a) of Section 42003, is not an infraction. *(Added by Stats.1971, c. 1178, p. 2245, § 4, operative May 3, 1972. Amended by Stats.1973, c. 1162, p. 2419, § 1.5.)*

§ 40000.5. Misdemeanors

A violation of any of the following provisions shall constitute a misdemeanor, and not an infraction:

Section 20, relating to false statements.

Section 27, relating to impersonating a member of the California Highway Patrol.

Section 31, relating to giving false information.

Paragraph (3) of subdivision (a), or subdivision (b), or both, of Section 221, relating to proper evidence of clearance for dismantling. *(Added by Stats.1971, c. 1178, p. 2245, § 5, operative May 3, 1972. Amended by Stats. 1976, c. 937, p. 2146, § 3; Stats.1999, c. 316 (A.B.342), § 3.)*

§ 40000.6. Misdemeanor

A violation of any of the following is a misdemeanor and not an infraction:

(a) Subdivision (b) of Section 1808.1, relating to enrollment in the pull notice system.

(b) Subdivision (f) of Section 1808.1, relating to employment of disqualified drivers. *(Added by Stats.1986, c. 1306, § 20. Amended by Stats.1987, c. 726, § 9, operative July 1, 1988; Stats.1988, c. 1586, § 10, operative Jan. 1, 1990; Stats.1991, c. 928 (A.B.1886), § 37, eff. Oct. 14, 1991.)*

§ 40000.61. Misdemeanor; unauthorized disclosure of department records

A violation of Section 1808.45, relating to unauthorized disclosure of department records, is a misdemeanor, and not an infraction. *(Added by Stats.1989, c. 1213, § 18.)*

§ 40000.65. Misdemeanors; emergency road service

A violation of Section 2430.5 or 2432, relating to emergency road service, is a misdemeanor and not an infraction. *(Added by Stats.1991, c. 488 (A.B.123), § 9.)*

§ 40000.7. Misdemeanors

(a) A violation of any of the following provisions is a misdemeanor, and not an infraction:

(1) Section 2416, relating to regulations for emergency vehicles.

(2) Section 2800, relating to failure to obey an officer's lawful order or submit to a lawful inspection.

(3) Section 2800.1, relating to fleeing from a peace officer.

(4) Section 2801, relating to failure to obey a firefighter's lawful order.

(5) Section 2803, relating to unlawful vehicle or load.

(6) Section 2813, relating to stopping for inspection.

(7) Subdivisions (b), (c), and (d) of Section 4461 and subdivisions (b) and (c) of Section 4463, relating to disabled person placards and disabled person and disabled veteran license plates.

(8) Section 4462.5, relating to deceptive or false evidence of vehicle registration.

(9) Section 4463.5, relating to deceptive or facsimile license plates.

(10) Section 5500, relating to the surrender of registration documents and license plates before dismantling may begin.

(11) Section 5506, relating to the sale of a total loss salvage vehicle, or of a vehicle reported for dismantling by a salvage vehicle rebuilder.

(12) Section 5753, relating to delivery of certificates of ownership and registration when committed by a dealer or any person while a dealer within the preceding 12 months.

(13) Section 5901, relating to dealers and lessor-retailers giving notice.

(14) Section 5901.1, relating to lessors giving notice and failure to pay fee.

(15) Section 8802, relating to the return of canceled, suspended, or revoked certificates of ownership, registra-

tion cards, or license plates, when committed by any person with intent to defraud.

(16) Section 8803, relating to return of canceled, suspended, or revoked documents and license plates of a dealer, manufacturer, remanufacturer, transporter, dismantler, or salesman.

(b) This section shall become operative on January 1, 2001. *(Added by Stats.1996, c. 697 (A.B.2852), § 4, operative Jan. 1, 2001. Amended by Stats.2002, c. 670 (S.B.1331), § 10; Stats.2010, c. 709 (S.B.1062), § 26.)*

Cross References

Infractions, see Penal Code § 19.6 et seq.
Misdemeanor, see Penal Code §§ 19, 19.2.

§ 40000.70. Notification of on-highway hazardous spill

A violation of Section 23112.5, relating to notification of an on-highway hazardous material or hazardous waste spill, is a misdemeanor and not an infraction. *(Added by Stats.1990, c. 429 (A.B.3904), § 10.)*

§ 40000.77. Misdemeanors; transportation of pupils

A violation of Article 7 (commencing with Section 2570) of Chapter 2.5 of Division 2, relating to transportation of school pupils, is a misdemeanor, and not an infraction. *(Added by Stats.1990, c. 1563 (A.B.3243), § 62.)*

§ 40000.8. Misdemeanors; vessels

A violation of any of the following provisions is a misdemeanor, and not an infraction:

Section 9872, relating to the registration of vessels.

Section 9872.1, relating to unidentified vessels. *(Added by Stats.1972, c. 618, p. 1151, § 152. Amended by Stats.1991, c. 922 (A.B.1201), § 7.)*

Cross References

Infractions, see Penal Code § 19.6 et seq.
Misdemeanor, see Penal Code §§ 19, 19.2.

§ 40000.9. Misdemeanors

A violation of any of the following provisions shall constitute a misdemeanor, and not an infraction:

Section 10501, relating to false report of vehicle theft.

Sections 10750 and 10751, relating to altered or defaced vehicle identifying numbers.

Section 10851.5, relating to theft of binder chains.

Sections 10852 and 10853, relating to injuring or tampering with a vehicle.

Section 10854, relating to unlawful use of stored vehicle. *(Added by Stats.1971, c. 1178, p. 2246, § 7, operative May 3, 1972.)*

Cross References

Infractions, see Penal Code § 19.6 et seq.

Misdemeanor, see Penal Code §§ 19, 19.2.

§ 40000.11. Misdemeanors

A violation of any of the following provisions is a misdemeanor, and not an infraction:

(a) Division 5 (commencing with Section 11100), relating to occupational licensing and business regulations.

(b) Section 12500, subdivision (a), relating to unlicensed drivers.

(c) Section 12515, subdivision (b), relating to persons under 21 years of age driving, and the employment of those persons to drive, vehicles engaged in interstate commerce or transporting hazardous substances or wastes.

(d) Section 12517, relating to a special driver's certificate to operate a schoolbus or school pupil activity bus.

(e) Section 12517.45, relating to a special driver's certificate and vehicle inspection for the transportation of pupils to or from school-related activities by a passenger charter-party carrier as defined in subdivision (k) of Section 545.

(f) Section 12519, subdivision (a), relating to a special driver's certificate to operate a farm labor vehicle.

(g) Section 12520, relating to a special driver's certificate to operate a tow truck.

(h) Section 12804, subdivision (d), relating to medical certificates.

(i) Section 12951, subdivision (b), relating to refusal to display license.

(j) Section 13004, relating to unlawful use of an identification card.

(k) Section 13004.1, relating to identification documents.

(*l*) Sections 14601, 14601.1, 14601.2, and 14601.5, relating to driving with a suspended or revoked driver's license.

(m) Section 14604, relating to unlawful use of a vehicle.

(n) Section 14610, relating to unlawful use of a driver's license.

(*o*) Section 14610.1, relating to identification documents.

(p) Section 15501, relating to use of false or fraudulent license by a minor. *(Added by Stats.1971, c. 1178, p. 2246, § 8, operative May 3, 1972. Amended by Stats.1981, c. 940, p. 3581, § 43; Stats.1982, c. 1233, p. 4547, § 3; Stats.1984, c. 779, § 5; Stats.1990, c. 170 (S.B.1873), § 3; Stats.1991, c. 488 (A.B.123), § 8; Stats.1994, c. 1221 (S.B.1758), § 22; Stats.1995, c. 101 (S.B.317), § 5; Stats. 1995, c. 922 (S.B.833), § 7; Stats.2008, c. 649 (A.B.830), § 5.)*

Cross References

Infractions, see Penal Code § 19.6 et seq.
Misdemeanor, see Penal Code §§ 19, 19.2.

Unlawful to drive unless licensed, see Vehicle Code § 12500.
Violation of license provisions, see Vehicle Code § 14600 et seq.

§ 40000.13.   Misdemeanors

Section operative until the date that the Secretary of State receives notice from the Director of Transportation as described in § 5205.5. See, also, section operative on the date such notice is received.

A violation of any of the following provisions is a misdemeanor, and not an infraction:

(a) Section 16560, relating to interstate highway carriers.

(b) Sections 20002 and 20003, relating to duties at accidents.

(c) Section 21200.5, relating to riding a bicycle while under the influence of an alcoholic beverage or any drug.

(d) Subdivision (b) of Section 21651, relating to wrong-way driving on divided highways.

(e) Subdivision (c) of Section 21655.9, relating to illegal use of decals, labels, or other identifiers.

(f) Section 22520.5, a second or subsequent conviction of an offense relating to vending on or near freeways.

(g) Section 22520.6, a second or subsequent conviction of an offense relating to roadside rest areas and vista points.

(h) This section shall remain in effect only until the date that the Secretary of State receives the notice from the Director of Transportation as described in Section 5205.5, and as of that date is repealed. *(Added by Stats.1971, c. 1178, p. 2246, § 9, operative May 3, 1972. Amended by Stats.1980, c. 680, p. 2064, § 3; Stats.1981, c. 936, p. 3540, § 2; Stats.1981, c. 937, p. 3541, § 3; Stats.1983, c. 275, § 4, eff. July 15, 1983; Stats.1984, c. 487, § 2; Stats.1985, c. 1013, § 4; Stats.1988, c. 765, § 3; Stats.1999, c. 330 (A.B.71), § 4; Stats.2006, c. 614 (A.B. 2600), § 5; Stats.2010, c. 37 (A.B.1500), § 3; Stats.2010, c. 215 (S.B.535), § 3.)*

Repeal

For repeal of this section, see its terms.

Cross References

Infractions, see Penal Code § 19.6 et seq.
Misdemeanor, see Penal Code §§ 19, 19.2.

§ 40000.13.   Misdemeanors

Section operative on the date that the Secretary of State receives notice from the Director of Transportation as described in § 5205.5. See, also, section operative until the date such notice is received.

A violation of any of the following provisions is a misdemeanor, and not an infraction:

(a) Section 16560, relating to interstate highway carriers.

(b) Sections 20002 and 20003, relating to duties at accidents.

(c) Section 21200.5, relating to riding a bicycle while under the influence of an alcoholic beverage or any drug.

(d) Subdivision (b) of Section 21651, relating to wrong- way driving on divided highways.

(e) Section 22520.5, a second or subsequent conviction of an offense relating to vending on or near freeways.

(f) Section 22520.6, a second or subsequent conviction of an offense relating to roadside rest areas and vista points.

(g) This section shall become operative on the date that the Secretary of State receives the notice from the Director of Transportation as described in Section 5205.5. *(Added by Stats.1999, c. 330 (A.B.71), § 5, operative Jan. 1, 2008. Amended by Stats.2006, c. 614 (A.B.2600), § 6, operative Jan. 1, 2011; Stats.2010, c. 215 (S.B.535), § 4, operative contingent.)*

§ 40000.14.   Failure to obey person or control devices at site of construction, maintenance or repair; penalties

A violation of subdivision (b) or (c) of Section 21367 is an infraction, except as follows:

(a) A willful violation is a misdemeanor.

(b) A willful violation committed in a manner exhibiting a wanton disregard for the safety of persons is a misdemeanor punishable by imprisonment in the county jail for not more than one year. *(Added by Stats.1986, c. 748, § 3.)*

§ 40000.15.   Misdemeanors

A violation of any of the following provisions shall constitute a misdemeanor, and not an infraction:

Subdivision (g), (j), (k), (l), or (m) of Section 22658, relating to unlawfully towed or stored vehicles.

Sections 23103 and 23104, relating to reckless driving.

Section 23109, relating to speed contests or exhibitions.

Subdivision (a) of Section 23110, relating to throwing at vehicles.

Section 23152, relating to driving under the influence.

Subdivision (b) of Section 23222, relating to possession of marijuana.

Subdivision (a) or (b) of Section 23224, relating to persons under 21 years of age knowingly driving, or being a passenger in, a motor vehicle carrying any alcoholic beverage.

Section 23253, relating to directions on toll highways or vehicular crossings.

Section 23332, relating to trespassing.

Section 24002.5, relating to unlawful operation of a farm vehicle.

Section 24011.3, relating to vehicle bumper strength notices.

Section 27150.1, relating to sale of exhaust systems.

Section 27362, relating to child passenger seat restraints.

Section 28050, relating to true mileage driven.

Section 28050.5, relating to nonfunctional odometers.

Section 28051, relating to resetting odometers.

Section 28051.5, relating to devices to reset odometers.

Subdivision (d) of Section 28150, relating to possessing four or more jamming devices. *(Added by Stats.1971, c. 1178, p. 2246, § 10, operative May 3, 1972. Amended by Stats.1973, c. 610, p. 1131, § 2; Stats.1973, c. 1162, p. 2420, § 6; Stats.1980, c. 313, p. 644, § 1; Stats.1981, c. 939, p. 3560, § 12; Stats.1981, c. 940, p. 3582, § 44; Stats.1983, c. 1005, § 2; Stats.1986, c. 1108, § 6; Stats. 1983, c. 1005, § 2, operative Jan. 1, 1990; Stats.1990, c. 33 (S.B.1372), § 8, eff. March 26, 1990; Stats.1990, c. 1403 (A.B.2040), § 7, eff. Sept. 28, 1990; Stats.1991, c. 1219 (S.B.265), § 2; Stats.1996, c. 690 (A.B.2000), § 2; Stats. 1998, c. 493 (S.B.1964), § 2; Stats.1999, c. 83 (S.B.966), § 190; Stats.2000, c. 873 (A.B.2086), § 6; Stats.2006, c. 609 (A.B.2210), § 6.)*

Cross References

Infractions, see Penal Code § 19.6 et seq.
Misdemeanor, definition and penalties, see Penal Code §§ 17, 19, 19.2.

§ 40000.16. Escape of materials from vehicle; offense

A second or subsequent violation of Section 23114, relating to preventing the escape of materials from vehicles, occurring within two years of a prior violation of that section is a misdemeanor, and not an infraction. *(Added by Stats.1988, c. 1486, § 5. Amended by Stats. 1997, c. 945 (A.B.1561), § 32.)*

§ 40000.18. Misdemeanors

A violation of subdivision (b) of Section 31401 or Section 31402 or 31403, relating to farm labor vehicles, is a misdemeanor and not an infraction. *(Added by Stats. 1988, c. 613, § 2.)*

§ 40000.19. Misdemeanors

A violation of any of the following provisions is a misdemeanor, and not an infraction:

(a) Section 31303, relating to transportation of hazardous waste.

(b) Division 14 (commencing with Section 31600), relating to transportation of explosives.

(c) Division 14.1 (commencing with Section 32000), relating to the transportation of hazardous material.

(d) Division 14.3 (commencing with Section 32100), relating to transportation of inhalation hazards.

(e) Division 14.5 (commencing with Section 33000), relating to transportation of radioactive materials.

(f) Division 14.7 (commencing with Section 34001), relating to flammable liquids. *(Added by Stats.1971, c. 1178, p. 2247, § 11, operative May 3, 1972. Amended by Stats.1981, c. 860, p. 3298, § 14; Stats.1984, c. 1683, § 3; Stats.1988, c. 1384, § 6.)*

Cross References

Infractions, see Penal Code § 19.6 et seq.
Misdemeanor, see Penal Code §§ 19, 19.2.

§ 40000.20. Third or subsequent violations of provisions relating to storage and possession of open containers by driver operating under valid certificate or permit pursuant to Passenger Charter-party Carriers' Act; misdemeanor

A third or subsequent violation of Section 23225, relating to the storage of an opened container of an alcoholic beverage, or Section 23223, relating to the possession of an open container of an alcoholic beverage, by a driver of a vehicle used to provide transportation services on a prearranged basis, operating under a valid certificate or permit pursuant to the Passenger Charter-party Carriers' Act (Chapter 8 (commencing with Section 5351) of Division 2 of the Public Utilities Code), is a misdemeanor. *(Added by Stats.2012, c. 461 (A.B.45), § 7. Amended by Stats.2013, c. 76 (A.B.383), § 198.)*

§ 40000.21. Misdemeanors

A violation of any of the following provisions is a misdemeanor, and not an infraction:

(a) Subdivision (a) of Section 34506, relating to the hours of service of drivers.

(b) Subdivision (b) of Section 34506, relating to the transportation of hazardous materials.

(c) Subdivision (c) of Section 34506, relating to school-buses.

(d) Subdivision (d) of Section 34506, relating to youth buses.

(e) Section 34505 or subdivision (e) of Section 34506, relating to tour buses.

(f) Section 34505.5 or subdivision (f) of Section 34506, relating to vehicles described in subdivisions (a) to (g), inclusive, of Section 34500.

(g) Subdivision (a) of Section 34501.3, relating to unlawful scheduling of runs by motor carriers.

(h) Subdivision (g) of Section 34506, relating to school pupil activity buses.

(i) Subparagraph (D) of paragraph (4) of subdivision (a) of Section 34505.9, relating to intermodal chassis. *(Added by Stats.1971, c. 1178, p. 2247, § 12, operative May 3, 1972. Amended by Stats.1977, c. 406, p. 1418, § 14, eff. Aug. 27, 1977; Stats.1982, c. 383, p. 1714, § 9, eff. July 4, 1982; Stats.1986, c. 1306, § 21; Stats.1988, c. 1586, § 11; Stats.1990, c. 429 (A.B.3904), § 9; Stats.1991, c. 928 (A.B.1886), § 38, eff. Oct. 14, 1991; Stats.1994, c. 58 (A.B.1633), § 6, eff. April 26, 1994; Stats.1998, c. 340 (A.B.346), § 4, eff. Aug. 24, 1998.)*

Cross References

Infractions, see Penal Code § 19.6 et seq.

Misdemeanor, see Penal Code §§ 19, 19.2.

§ 40000.22. Misdemeanors; inspections; violations of Motor Carriers of Property Permit Act

Section operative until Jan. 1, 2016. See, also, section operative Jan. 1, 2016.

(a) A violation of subdivision (e) of Section 34501, subdivision (f) of Section 34501.12, or subdivision (c) of Section 34501.14, relating to applications for inspections, is a misdemeanor and not an infraction.

(b) A violation of Division 14.85 (commencing with Section 34600), relating to motor carriers of property, is a misdemeanor and not an infraction.

(c) This section shall remain in effect only until January 1, 2016, and as of that date is repealed, unless a later enacted statute, that is enacted before January 1, 2016, deletes or extends that date. *(Added by Stats.1988, c. 1586, § 13, operative July 1, 1989. Amended by Stats.1992, c. 724 (A.B.2326), § 2; Stats.1992, c. 1243 (A.B.3090), § 103, eff. Sept. 30, 1992; Stats.1992, c. 1243 (A.B.3090), § 106.1, eff. Sept. 30, 1992, operative Jan. 1, 1993; Stats.1996, c. 1042 (A.B.1683), § 54, eff. Sept. 29, 1996; Stats.2013, c. 500 (A.B.529), § 19.)*

Repeal

For repeal of this section, see its terms.

§ 40000.22. Misdemeanors; inspections; violations of Motor Carriers of Property Permit Act

Section operative Jan. 1, 2016. See, also, section operative until Jan. 1, 2016.

(a) A violation of subdivision (e) of Section 34501, subdivision (b) or (d) of Section 34501.12, or subdivision (c) of Section 34501.14, relating to applications for inspections, is a misdemeanor and not an infraction.

(b) A violation of Division 14.85 (commencing with Section 34600), relating to motor carriers of property, is a misdemeanor and not an infraction.

(c) This section shall become operative on January 1, 2016. *(Added by Stats.2013, c. 500 (A.B.529), § 20, operative Jan. 1, 2016.)*

§ 40000.23. Misdemeanors

A violation of any of the following provisions is a misdemeanor, and not an infraction:

(a) Paragraph (1) of subdivision (c) of Section 35784, relating to special permit violations.

(b) Subdivision (a) of Section 35784.5 relating to extralegal loads and operation of vehicles without a special permit.

(c) Other provisions of Chapter 5 (commencing with Section 35550) of Division 15, which relate to weight restrictions, except in cases of weight violations where the amount of excess weight is less than 4,501 pounds. *(Added by Stats.1971, c. 1178, p. 2247, § 13, operative May 3, 1972. Amended by Stats.1984, c. 542, § 9.)*

Infractions, see Penal Code § 19.6 et seq.
Misdemeanor, see Penal Code §§ 19, 19.2.

§ 40000.24. Misdemeanors

A violation of any of the following provisions shall constitute a misdemeanor and not an infraction:

(a) Subdivision (c) of Section 38301.5, relating to unauthorized operation of a vehicle within a mountain fire district.

(b) Section 38316, relating to reckless driving.

(c) Section 38317, relating to reckless driving with injury.

(d) Subdivision (a) of Section 38318 or subdivision (a) of Section 38318.5, relating to off-highway vehicles.

(e) Section 38319, relating to protection of the environment.

(f) Section 38320, relating to the depositing of matter. *(Added by Stats.1976, c. 1093, p. 4953, § 29. Amended by Stats.1984, c. 729, § 3; Stats.1984, c. 1015, § 3.)*

§ 40000.25. Misdemeanors

A violation of any of the following provisions shall constitute a misdemeanor, and not an infraction:

Section 40005, relating to owner's responsibility.

Section 40504, relating to false signatures.

Section 40508, relating to failure to appear or to pay fine.

Section 40519, relating to failure to appear.

Section 40614, relating to use of a fictitious name.

Section 40616, relating to a willful violation of a notice to correct.

Section 42005, relating to failure to attend traffic school. *(Added by Stats.1971, c. 1178, p. 2247, § 14, operative May 3, 1972. Amended by Stats.1973, c. 1162, p. 2419, § 3; Stats.1978, c. 1350, p. 4478, § 1, operative July 1, 1979.)*

Infractions, see Penal Code § 19.6 et seq.
Misdemeanor, see Penal Code §§ 19, 19.2.

§ 40000.26. Misdemeanors; failure to submit to inspection

A violation of subdivision (g) of Section 34501.12 or subdivision (d) of Section 34501.14, relating to inspections, is a misdemeanor and not an infraction. *(Added by Stats.1988, c. 1586, § 13.5, operative Jan. 1, 1992. Amended by Stats.1992, c. 724 (A.B.2326), § 3; Stats. 1992, c. 1243 (A.B.3090), § 107, eff. Sept. 30, 1992; Stats.1992, c. 1243 (A.B.3090), § 107.1, eff. Sept. 30, 1992, operative Jan. 1, 1993.)*

§ 40000.28. Misdemeanor; three or more violations

Any offense which would otherwise be an infraction is a misdemeanor if a defendant has been convicted of three or more violations of this code or any local ordinance adopted pursuant to this code within the 12-month period immediately preceding the commission of the offense and such prior convictions are admitted by the defendant or alleged in the accusatory pleading. For this purpose, a bail forfeiture shall be deemed to be a conviction of the offense charged.

This section shall have no application to violations by pedestrians. *(Added by Stats.1973, c. 1162, p. 2419, § 4. Amended by Stats.1975, c. 635, p. 1379, § 1.)*

§ 40001. Owner, lessee, or any other person; codefendant; rebuttable presumption

(a) It is unlawful for the owner, or any other person, employing or otherwise directing the driver of any vehicle to cause the operation of the vehicle upon a highway in any manner contrary to law.

(b) It is unlawful for an owner to request, cause, or permit the operation of any vehicle that is any of the following:

(1) Not registered or for which any fee has not been paid under this code.

(2) Not equipped as required in this code.

(3) Not in compliance with the size, weight, or load provisions of this code.

(4) Not in compliance with the regulations promulgated pursuant to this code, or with applicable city or county ordinances adopted pursuant to this code.

(5) Not in compliance with the provisions of Part 5 (commencing with Section 43000) of Division 26 of the Health and Safety Code and the rules and regulations of the State Air Resources Board.

(c) Any employer who violates an out-of-service order, that complies with Section 396.9 of Title 49 of the Code of Federal Regulations, or who knowingly requires or permits a driver to violate or fail to comply with that out-of-service order, is guilty of a misdemeanor.

(d) An employer who is convicted of allowing, permitting, requiring, or authorizing a driver to operate a commercial motor vehicle in violation of any statute or regulation pertaining to a railroad-highway grade crossing is subject to a fine of not more than ten thousand dollars ($10,000).

(e) Whenever a violation is chargeable to the owner or lessee of a vehicle pursuant to subdivision (a) or (b), the driver shall not be arrested or cited for the violation unless the vehicle is registered in a state or country other than California, or unless the violation is for an offense that is clearly within the responsibility of the driver.

(f) Whenever the owner, or lessee, or any other person is prosecuted for a violation pursuant to this section, the court may, on the request of the defendant, take appropriate steps to make the driver of the vehicle, or any other person who directs the loading, maintenance, or operation of the vehicle, a codefendant. However, the court may make the driver a codefendant only if the driver is

the owner or lessee of the vehicle, or the driver is an employee or a contractor of the defendant who requested the court to make the driver a codefendant. If the codefendant is held solely responsible and found guilty, the court may dismiss the charge against the defendant.

(g) In any prosecution under this section, it is a rebuttable presumption that any person who gives false or erroneous information in a written certification of actual gross cargo weight has directed, requested, caused, or permitted the operation of a vehicle in a manner contrary to law in violation of subdivision (a) or (b), or both. *(Stats.1959, c. 3, p. 1773, § 40001. Amended by Stats. 1961, c. 58, p. 1015, § 66.6; Stats.1963, c. 1322, p. 2843, § 1; Stats.1965, c. 2031, p. 4616, § 16, eff. July 23, 1965; Stats.1965, c. 2032, p. 4617, § 1; Stats.1968, c. 49, p. 197, § 15, eff. April 25, 1968; Stats.1979, c. 373, p. 1384, § 328; Stats.1984, c. 981, § 2, operative July 1, 1985; Stats.1989, c. 533, § 15; Stats.1993, c. 647 (S.B.952), § 3; Stats.1993, c. 757 (S.B.619), § 5; Stats.1999, c. 724 (A.B.1650), § 51; Stats.2001, c. 504 (A.B.1280), § 10; Stats.2004, c. 193 (S.B.111), § 200.)*

Law Revision Commission Comments
2004 Amendment

Section 40001 is amended to delete reference to an obsolete reporting requirement. The required report was to be completed by January 1, 1988. [33 Cal.L.Rev.Comm. Reports 498 (2004)].

Cross References

Applicability of this section to trolley coaches, see Vehicle Code § 21051.

Driving while under the influence of alcohol or drugs as felony or misdemeanor, see Vehicle Code §§ 23152, 23153.

Equipment testing, see Vehicle Code § 26100 et seq.

Highway defined, see Vehicle Code § 360.

Limitation on driving hours, see Vehicle Code § 21702.

Miscellaneous rules as to traffic laws, generally, see Vehicle Code § 21000 et seq.

Notice of offense under this section, time notice complete, see Vehicle Code § 23.

Parking violations, see Vehicle Code § 40200 et seq.

Reckless driving, punishment for, see Vehicle Code §§ 23103, 23104.

Registration indices and records, generally, see Vehicle Code § 1800 et seq.

Speed laws in general, limitations with respect to, see Vehicle Code § 22349 et seq.

Theft of vehicles, see Vehicle Code § 10851.

Traffic violation point count and negligent operation defined, see Vehicle Code § 12810.

Vehicular homicide, see Penal Code § 192.

Violations of,
   Additional and accessory equipment regulations, see Vehicle Code § 27000 et seq.
   Traffic laws, see Vehicle Code § 21000 et seq.
   Vehicular crossing regulations, see Vehicle Code § 23250 et seq.

Weight violations, penalty, see Vehicle Code § 42030 et seq.

§ 40002. Prosecution of persons owning or controlling vehicles

(a)(1) If there is a violation of Section 40001, an owner or any other person subject to Section 40001, who was not driving the vehicle involved in the violation, may be mailed a written notice to appear. An exact and legible duplicate copy of that notice when filed with the court, in lieu of a verified complaint, is a complaint to which the defendant may plead "guilty."

(2) If, however, the defendant fails to appear in court or does not deposit lawful bail, or pleads other than "guilty" of the offense charged, a verified complaint shall be filed which shall be deemed to be an original complaint, and thereafter proceedings shall be had as provided by law, except that a defendant may, by an agreement in writing, subscribed by the defendant and filed with the court, waive the filing of a verified complaint and elect that the prosecution may proceed upon a written notice to appear.

(3) A verified complaint pursuant to paragraph (2) shall include a paragraph that informs the person that unless he or she appears in the court designated in the complaint within 21 days after being given the complaint and answers the charge, renewal of registration of the vehicle involved in the offense may be precluded by the department, or a warrant of arrest may be issued against him or her.

(b)(1) If a person mailed a notice to appear pursuant to paragraph (1) of subdivision (a) fails to appear in court or deposit bail, a warrant of arrest shall not be issued based on the notice to appear, even if that notice is verified. An arrest warrant may be issued only after a verified complaint pursuant to paragraph (2) of subdivision (a) is given the person and the person fails to appear in court to answer that complaint.

(2) If a person mailed a notice to appear pursuant to paragraph (1) of subdivision (a) fails to appear in court or deposit bail, the court may give by mail to the person a notice of noncompliance. A notice of noncompliance shall include a paragraph that informs the person that unless he or she appears in the court designated in the notice to appear within 21 days after being given by mail the notice of noncompliance and answers the charge on the notice to appear, or pays the applicable fine and penalties if an appearance is not required, renewal of registration of the vehicle involved in the offense may be precluded by the department.

(c) A verified complaint filed pursuant to this section shall conform to Chapter 2 (commencing with Section 948) of Title 5 of Part 2 of the Penal Code.

(d)(1) The giving by mail of a notice to appear pursuant to paragraph (1) of subdivision (a) or a notice of noncompliance pursuant to paragraph (2) of subdivision (b) shall be done in a manner prescribed by Section 22.

(2) The verified complaint pursuant to paragraph (2) of subdivision (a) shall be given in a manner prescribed by Section 22. *(Added by Stats.2007, c. 452 (A.B.1464), § 3. Amended by Stats.2008, c. 179 (S.B.1498), § 224; Stats. 2008, c. 699 (S.B.1241), § 26; Stats.2010, c. 328 (S.B. 1330), § 232.)*

Execution of warrants on behalf of local peace officers by highway patrol, expenses of, see Vehicle Code § 40516.
Service of warrants, authority of members of highway patrol with respect to, see Vehicle Code § 2411.

§ 40002.1. Notice of noncompliance or subsequent adjudication; transmittal to department; warrant of arrest

(a) Whenever a person has failed to appear in the court designated in the notice to appear or a verified complaint specified in Section 40002, following personal service of the notice of noncompliance or deposit in the mail pursuant to Section 22, the magistrate or clerk of the court may give notice of that fact to the department.

(b) Whenever the matter is adjudicated, including a dismissal of the charges upon forfeiture of bail or otherwise, the magistrate or clerk of the court hearing the matter shall immediately do all of the following:

(1) Endorse a certificate to that effect.

(2) Provide the person or the person's attorney with a copy of the certificate .

(3) Transmit a copy of the certificate to the department.

(c) A notice of noncompliance shall not be transmitted to the department pursuant to subdivision (a) if a warrant of arrest has been issued on the same offense pursuant to subdivision (b) of Section 40002. A warrant of arrest shall not be issued pursuant to subdivision (b) of Section 40002 if a notice of noncompliance has been transmitted to the department on the same offense pursuant to this section, except that, when a notice has been received by the court pursuant to subdivision (c) of Section 4766 or recalled by motion of the court, a warrant may then be issued. *(Added by Stats.1984, c. 981, § 4, operative July 1, 1985. Amended by Stats.1998, c. 877 (A.B.2132), § 75; Stats.2007, c. 452 (A.B.1464), § 4.)*

§ 40003. Prosecution of employees

Whenever an employee is prosecuted for a violation of any provision of this code, or regulations promulgated pursuant to this code, relating to the size, weight, registration, equipment, or loading of a vehicle while operating a vehicle he was employed to operate, and which is owned by his employer, the court shall on the request of the employee take appropriate proceedings to make the owner of the vehicle a codefendant. In the event it is found that the employee had reasonable grounds to believe that the vehicle operated by him as an employee did not violate such provisions, and in the event the owner is found guilty under the provisions of Section 40001, the court may dismiss the charges against the employee.

In those cases in which the charges against the employee are dismissed, the abstract of the record of the court required by Section 1803 shall clearly indicate that such charges were dismissed and that the owner of the vehicle was found guilty under Section 40001. *(Stats.*

1959, c. 3, p. 1773, § 40003. Amended by Stats.1963, c. 950, p. 2205, § 1; Stats.1967, c. 819, p. 2245, § 1.)

Cross References

Applicability of this section to trolley coaches, see Vehicle Code § 21051.

§ 40004. Period for commencement of criminal actions

(a) The period for commencing criminal action against any person having filed or caused to be filed any false, fictitious, altered, forged or counterfeit document with the Department of Motor Vehicles or the Department of the California Highway Patrol shall, if the offense is a misdemeanor, expire one year from time of discovery of such act.

(b) The period for commencing criminal action against any person having filed or caused to be filed any false, fictitious, altered, forged or counterfeit document with the Department of Motor Vehicles or the Department of the California Highway Patrol shall, if the offense is a felony, expire three years from time of discovery of such act.

(c) The time allowed for commencing criminal proceedings as provided in subdivisions (a) and (b) of this section shall not extend beyond five years from the date of commission of the act. *(Added by Stats.1968, c. 1192, p. 2262, § 12, operative Jan. 1, 1969.)*

§ 40005. Employer's failure

Whenever a driver is cited for a violation of any provision of this code, or regulations promulgated pursuant to this code, relating to the size, weight, equipment, registration, fees, or loading of a vehicle, while operating a vehicle he was employed or otherwise directed to operate, and which is not owned by him, and the driver gives the citation to the owner or any other person referred to in Section 40001, if the owner or other person undertakes to answer the charge or otherwise to cause its disposition without any further action by the driver and then fails to act in accordance with the undertaking as a consequence of which a warrant is issued for the arrest of the driver, the owner or other person is guilty of a misdemeanor. *(Added by Stats.1965, c. 294, p. 1292, § 1.)*

Cross References

Violation a misdemeanor, see Vehicle Code § 40000.25.

§ 40006. Towing unregistered disabled vehicle; infraction

Whenever a disabled vehicle, being taken to a repair shop, garage, or other place of storage, is being towed upon a highway by a tow car and the vehicle is determined to be in violation of subdivision (a) of Section 4000, the violation shall be charged as prescribed in Section 40001. *(Added by Stats.1979, c. 152, p. 349, § 1.)*

§ 40007. Application of other statutory provisions applicable to acts violating Division 5

Division 5 (commencing with Section 11100) does not preclude the application of any other statutory provision which is applicable to any act violating any provision of Division 5. *(Added by Stats.1985, c. 93, § 1.)*

§ 40008. Intent to capture image, recording or impression for a commercial purpose; endangerment of minor

(a) Notwithstanding any other provision of law, except as otherwise provided in subdivision (c), any person who violates Section 21701, 21703, or 23103, with the intent to capture any type of visual image, sound recording, or other physical impression of another person for a commercial purpose, is guilty of a misdemeanor and not an infraction and shall be punished by imprisonment in a county jail for not more than six months and by a fine of not more than two thousand five hundred dollars ($2,500).

(b) Notwithstanding any other provision of law, except as otherwise provided in subdivision (c), any person who violates Section 21701, 21703, or 23103, with the intent to capture any type of visual image, sound recording, or other physical impression of another person for a commercial purpose and who causes a minor child or children to be placed in a situation in which the child's person or health is endangered, is guilty of a misdemeanor and not an infraction and shall be punished by imprisonment in a county jail for not more than one year and by a fine of not more than five thousand dollars ($5,000).

(c) Pursuant to Section 654 of the Penal Code, an act or omission described in subdivision (a) or (b) that is punishable in different ways by different provisions of law shall be punished under the provision that provides for the longest potential term of imprisonment, but in no case shall the act or omission be punished under more than one provision. An acquittal or conviction and sentence under any one provision bars a prosecution for the same act or omission under any other provision. *(Added by Stats.2010, c. 685 (A.B.2479), § 3.)*

ARTICLE 2. PROCEDURE ON EQUIPMENT AND REGISTRATION VIOLATIONS

Section
40150. Proof of correction.
40151. Lighting equipment.
40152. Proof of registration or reduction to junk.
40153. Repealed.

§ 40150. Proof of correction

Whenever any vehicle or combination of vehicles is found to be in an unsafe mechanical condition or is not equipped as required by this code, and a notice to appear is issued or a complaint filed for such violation, the notice to appear or the complaint may require that the person to whom the notice to appear is issued or against whom the complaint is filed shall produce in court satisfactory evidence that the vehicle or its equipment has been made to conform with the requirements of this code. *(Stats. 1959, c. 3, p. 1774, § 40150. Amended by Stats.1961, c. 1728, p. 3738, § 1.)*

Cross References

Disposition of traffic violation hearing for minors, see Welfare and Institutions Code § 258.
Equipment regulations, see Vehicle Code § 24000 et seq.
Inspection of vehicles and equipment, see Vehicle Code §§ 2804, 2806.
Obedience to peace officers, see Vehicle Code § 2800.
Proof of correction of emission control equipment for off-highway motor vehicles, see Vehicle Code § 38394.
Vehicles incidentally operated over highway, applicability of this section, see Vehicle Code § 25802.

§ 40151. Lighting equipment

(a) Whenever any lighting equipment or device does not meet requirements established by the Department of the California Highway Patrol, the officer making the inspection shall direct the driver to remove the lighting equipment or device within 24 hours.

(b) Whenever any lighting equipment or device meets requirements established by the department but by reason of faulty adjustment or otherwise fails to comply with this code, the officer making the inspection shall direct the driver to make it comply with this code within 48 hours. *(Stats.1959, c. 3, p. 1774, § 40151. Amended by Stats.1979, c. 723, p. 2226, § 39.)*

Cross References

Inspection of vehicles and equipment, see Vehicle Code §§ 2804, 2806.
Lighting regulations, see Vehicle Code § 24250 et seq.
Obedience to peace officers, see Vehicle Code § 2800.

§ 40152. Proof of registration or reduction to junk

(a) Whenever any vehicle or combination of vehicles is found to be not registered as required by this code, and a notice to appear is issued or a complaint is filed for that violation, the person to whom the notice to appear is issued or against whom the complaint is filed shall produce in court satisfactory evidence that the vehicle or combination of vehicles has been registered or has had the appropriate fees paid, or has been reduced to junk, to conform with the requirements of this code. The court shall not dismiss the offense until that evidence is produced.

(b) A four-day, nonresident commercial trip permit of the type authorized in Section 4004 may not be accepted as evidence of registration compliance as required in subdivision (a) of this section. *(Added by Stats.1980, c. 544, p. 1500, § 4. Amended by Stats.1981, c. 245, p. 1298, § 4; Stats.1988, c. 1008, § 4; Stats.1996, c. 1154 (A.B. 3020), § 83, eff. Sept. 30, 1996.)*

§ 40153. Repealed by Stats.1992, c. 258 (S.B.133), § 3

ARTICLE 3.   PROCEDURE ON PARKING VIOLATIONS

Section
40200.   Application of article.
40200.1.   Notice of parking violation and notice to appear for same violation.
40200.2.   Repealed.
40200.3.   Deposit and transfer of amounts collected by processing agency; report; public record.
40200.4.   Deposit of sums due county; transfer of processing function; counties with contracts to process violations; law governing; prohibition on termination of court employees.
40200.5.   Contract for processing notices of violations; minority business participation; distribution of amounts collected; provision of qualified examiners or administrative hearing providers.
40200.6.   Processing agency; contracts for processing notices of violations; policies and procedures; oversight; complaint resolution.
40200.7.   Repealed.
40200.8.   Parking citations; recall of hold on vehicle registration; notice to department.
40202.   Notice of violation attached to vehicle; contents; filing; alteration or destruction prior to filing; cancellation of violation; corrections.
40203.   Notice of amount of parking penalty; payment by mail; procedures to contest notice of violation.
40203.5.   Parking penalties; late payment penalties; minimum and maximum penalties; suspension of penalty; installment payments.
40203.6.   Additional assessments.
40204.   Termination of proceedings on receipt of penalty by authorized person.
40205.   Contest of parking violation; procedure of processing agency.
40206.   Service or mailing of notice of delinquent violation.
40206.5.   Copy of original notice of violation; fee; cancellation upon failure of vehicle to match description.
40207.   Contents of notice of delinquent violation.
40207.   Contents of notice of delinquent violation.
40208.   Affidavit of nonliability; information and instructions.
40209.   Affidavit of nonliability; proof of written lease or rental of vehicle; notice of delinquent violation; proceedings against rentee or lessee.
40210.   Affidavit of nonliability; evidence of prior sale or transfer and delivery of vehicle to purchaser; cancellation of notice of delinquent violation; proceedings against owner; collection of penalties from person having ownership on date of alleged violation.
40211.   Deposit of penalty with authorized person; processing agency procedures; termination of proceedings.
40215.   Review of notice of parking violation; initial review by issuing agency; administrative hearing; process; application of section to certain agencies.
40219.   Repealed.
40220.   Collection of unpaid parking penalty; options of processing agency; application.
40221.   Civil judgment; filing; prerequisites.
40222.   Termination of processing agency proceedings on notice of delinquent violation.
40223.   Repealed.

Section

40224. Limitation of actions; tolling until return or recall of notice of delinquent violation.

40225. Equipment violation; entry on notice of parking violation; civil penalty; allocation.

40226. Cancellation of citation for failure to display a disabled placard; fees.

40230. Review; filing of appeal; notice; evidence; fee.

Cross References

Additional penalties on fines for criminal offenses for support of emergency medical services, see Government Code § 76000.5.

Additional state-only penalty, levy and collection, deposit into DNA Identification Fund, see Government Code § 76104.7.

County penalties, additional penalties on fines for criminal offenses, see Government Code § 76000.

DNA Fingerprint, Unsolved Crime and Innocence Protection Act, purpose, deposits of funds, and reports, see Government Code § 76104.6.

Local regulations, public grounds, enforcement of conditions or regulations upon persons who park or leave vehicles standing, see Vehicle Code § 21113.

Santa Barbara County emergency medical services, penalty assessment, see Government Code § 76104.1.

State court construction penalty, levy and collection, see Government Code § 70372.

§ 40200. Application of article

(a) Any violation of any regulation that is not a misdemeanor governing the standing or parking of a vehicle under this code, under any federal statute or regulation, or under any ordinance enacted by local authorities is subject to a civil penalty. The enforcement of those civil penalties shall be governed by the civil administrative procedures set forth in this article.

(b) Except as provided in Section 40209, the registered owner and driver, rentee, or lessee of a vehicle cited for any violation of any regulation governing the parking of a vehicle under this code, under any federal statute or regulation, or under any ordinance enacted by a local authority shall be jointly liable for parking penalties imposed under this article, unless the owner can show that the vehicle was used without consent of that person, express or implied. An owner who pays any parking penalty, civil judgment, costs, or administrative fees pursuant to this article shall have the right to recover the same from the driver, rentee, or lessee.

(c) The driver of a vehicle who is not the owner thereof but who uses or operates the vehicle with the express or implied permission of the owner shall be considered the agent of the owner to receive notices of parking violations served in accordance with this article and may contest the notice of violation. *(Added by Stats.1986, c. 939, § 15. Amended by Stats.1992, c. 1244 (A.B.408), § 7, operative July 1, 1993; Stats.1993, c. 1093 (A.B.780), § 3.)*

Cross References

Emergency Medical Air Transportation Act, penalty assessment, exclusion for violations under this article, see Government Code § 76000.10.

§ 40200.1. Notice of parking violation and notice to appear for same violation

A person shall not be subject to both a notice of parking violation and a notice to appear for the same violation. *(Added by Stats.2009, c. 415 (A.B.144), § 5.)*

§ 40200.2. Repealed by Stats.1992, c. 1244 (A.B.408), § 9, operative July 1, 1993

§ 40200.3. Deposit and transfer of amounts collected by processing agency; report; public record

(a) All parking penalties collected by the processing agency, which may be the issuing agency, including process service fees and fees and collection costs related to civil debt collection, shall be deposited to the account of the issuing agency, except that those sums attributable to the issuance of a notice of parking violation by a peace officer of the Department of the California Highway Patrol shall be deposited in the account in the jurisdiction where the violation occurred, and except those sums payable to a county pursuant to Chapter 12 (commencing with Section 76000) of Title 8 of the Government Code and that portion of any parking penalty which is attributable to an increase in the parking bail amount effective between September 16, 1988, and July 1, 1992, inclusive, pursuant to Section 1463.28 of the Penal Code. Those funds attributable to this increase in bail shall be transferred to the county treasurer and deposited in the general fund. Any increase in parking penalties effective after July 1, 1992, shall accrue to the benefit of the issuing agency.

(b) The processing agency shall prepare a report at the end of each fiscal year setting forth the number of cases processed, and all sums received and distributed, together with any other information that may be required by the issuing agency or the Controller. This report is a public record and shall be delivered to each issuing agency. Copies shall be made available, upon request, to the county auditor, the Controller, and the grand jury. *(Added by Stats.1992, c. 1244 (A.B.408), § 10.2, operative July 1, 1993. Amended by Stats.1993, c. 1093 (A.B.780), § 4; Gov.Reorg.Plan No. 1 of 1995, § 70, eff. July 12, 1995; Stats.1995, c. 734 (A.B.1228), § 3; Stats.1996, c. 305 (A.B.3103), § 72.)*

§ 40200.4. Deposit of sums due county; transfer of processing function; counties with contracts to process violations; law governing; prohibition on termination of court employees

(a) The processing agency shall deposit with the county treasurer all sums due the county as the result of processing a parking violation not later than 45 calendar days after the last day of the month in which the parking penalty was received.

(b) Except as provided in subdivisions (c) and (d), if a court within a county has been processing notices of parking violations and notices of delinquent parking violations for a city, a district, or any other issuing agency, the issuing agency and the county shall provide in an agreement for the orderly transfer of the processing activity as soon as possible but not later than January 1, 1994. The agreement shall permit the court to phase out, and the issuing agency to phase in, or transfer, personnel, equipment, and facilities that may have been acquired or need to be acquired in contemplation of a long-term commitment to processing of notices of parking violations and notices of delinquent parking violations for the issuing agency under this article. The court shall transfer the processing function for parking citations issued by the Department of the California Highway Patrol to the processing agency in the city or county where the violation occurred.

(c) If Contra Costa County or San Mateo County, or a court in either county, had a contract in effect on January 1, 1992, to process notices of parking violations and notices of delinquent parking violations for a city, district, or other issuing agency within the particular county or counties, the county may continue to provide those services to the issuing agencies pursuant to the terms of the contract and any amendments thereto, to and including June 30, 1996, after which Section 40200.5 shall govern any contracts entered into for these services.

(d) San Francisco Municipal Court employees engaged in processing notices of parking violations and the positions of those employees shall be transferred to equivalent civil service positions in the City and County of San Francisco.

(e) No court employee shall be terminated or otherwise released from employment as a result of the transfer of processing notices of parking violations and notices of delinquent parking violations from the courts to the issuing agencies.

(f) As used in this article, "parking penalty" includes the fine authorized by law, including assessments authorized by this article, any late payment penalty, and costs of collection as provided by law. *(Added by Stats.1986, c. 939, § 15. Amended by Stats.1992, c. 1244 (A.B.408), § 11, operative July 1, 1993; Stats.1993, c. 1093 (A.B.780), § 5; Gov.Reorg.Plan No. 1 of 1995, § 71, eff. July 12, 1995; Stats.1995, c. 734 (A.B.1228), § 4; Stats.1996, c. 305 (A.B.3103), § 73.)*

§ 40200.5. Contract for processing notices of violations; minority business participation; distribution of amounts collected; provision of qualified examiners or administrative hearing providers

(a) Except as provided in subdivision (c) of Section 40200.4, an issuing agency may elect to contract with the county, with a private vendor, or with any other city or county processing agency, other than the Department of the California Highway Patrol or other state law enforcement agency, within the county, with the consent of that

other entity, for the processing of notices of parking violations and notices of delinquent parking violations, prior to filing with the court pursuant to Section 40230.

If an issuing agency contracts with a private vendor for processing services, it shall give special consideration to minority business enterprise participation in providing those services. For purposes of this subdivision, "special consideration" has the same meaning as specified in subdivision (c) of Section 14838 of the Government Code, as it relates to small business preference.

(b) A contract entered pursuant to subdivision (a) shall provide for monthly distribution of amounts collected between the parties, except those amounts payable to a county pursuant to Chapter 12 (commencing with Section 76000) of Title 8 of the Government Code and amounts payable to the Department of Motor Vehicles pursuant to Section 4763 of this code.

(c) If a contract entered into pursuant to subdivision (a) includes the provision of qualified examiners or administrative hearing providers, the contract shall be based on either a fixed monthly rate or on the number of notices processed and shall not include incentives for the processing entity based on the number of notices upheld or denied or the amount of fines collected. *(Added by Stats.1986, c. 939, § 15. Amended by Stats.1992, c. 1244 (A.B.408), § 12, operative July 15, 1993; Stats.1993, c. 1093 (A.B.780), § 6; Gov.Reorg.Plan No. 1 of 1995, § 72, eff. July 12, 1995; Stats.1996, c. 305 (A.B.3103), § 74; Stats.2008, c. 13 (A.B.602), § 1.)*

§ 40200.6. Processing agency; contracts for processing notices of violations; policies and procedures; oversight; complaint resolution

(a) If a contract is entered into pursuant to Section 40200.5, for the purposes of this article, "processing agency" means the contracting party responsible for the processing of the notices of parking violations and notices of delinquent parking violations.

(b) The governing body of the issuing agency shall establish written policies and procedures pursuant to which the contracting party shall provide services.

(c) The issuing agency shall be responsible for all actions taken by contracting parties and shall exercise effective oversight over the parties. "Effective oversight" includes, at a minimum, an annual review of the services of the processing agency and a review of complaints made by motorists using the services of the processing agency. The issuing agency shall establish procedures to investigate and resolve complaints by motorists about any processing agency.

(d) Subdivision (c) does not apply to an issuing agency that is a law enforcement agency if the issuing agency does not also act as the processing agency. *(Added by Stats.1986, c. 939, § 15. Amended by Stats.1995, c. 734 (A.B.1228), § 5.)*

§ 40200.7. Repealed by Stats.1995, c. 734 (A.B.1228), § 6

§ 40200.8. Parking citations; recall of hold on vehicle registration; notice to department

The parking processing agency shall notify the department and recall any hold on the registration of a vehicle that it filed with the department in connection with a parking citation if the processing agency is awarded a civil judgment for the citation pursuant to subdivision (b) or (c) of Section 40220, or if the processing agency has granted a review of the issuance of the citation pursuant to Section 40200.7 or Section 40215. *(Added by Stats. 1995, c. 766 (S.B.726), § 41.)*

§ 40202. Notice of violation attached to vehicle; contents; filing; alteration or destruction prior to filing; cancellation of violation; corrections

(a) If a vehicle is unattended during the time of the violation, the peace officer or person authorized to enforce parking laws and regulations shall securely attach to the vehicle a notice of parking violation setting forth the violation, including reference to the section of this code or of the Public Resources Code, the local ordinance, or the federal statute or regulation so violated; the date; the approximate time thereof; the location where the violation occurred; a statement printed on the notice indicating that the date of payment is required to be made not later than 21 calendar days from the date of citation issuance; and the procedure for the registered owner, lessee, or rentee to deposit the parking penalty or, pursuant to Section 40215, contest the citation. The notice of parking violation shall also set forth the vehicle license number and registration expiration date if they are visible, the last four digits of the vehicle identification number, if that number is readable through the windshield, the color of the vehicle, and, if possible, the make of the vehicle. The notice of parking violation, or copy thereof, shall be considered a record kept in the ordinary course of business of the issuing agency and the processing agency and shall be prima facie evidence of the facts contained therein.

(b) The notice of parking violation shall be served by attaching it to the vehicle either under the windshield wiper or in another conspicuous place upon the vehicle so as to be easily observed by the person in charge of the vehicle upon the return of that person.

(c) Once the issuing officer has prepared the notice of parking violation and has attached it to the vehicle as provided in subdivisions (a) and (b), the officer shall file the notice with the processing agency. Any person, including the issuing officer and any member of the officer's department or agency, or any peace officer who alters, conceals, modifies, nullifies, or destroys, or causes to be altered, concealed, modified, nullified, or destroyed the face of the remaining original or any copy of a citation that was retained by the officer, for any reason, before it is filed with the processing agency or with a person authorized to receive the deposit of the parking penalty, is guilty of a misdemeanor.

(d) If, during the issuance of a notice of parking violation, without regard to whether the vehicle was initially attended or unattended, the vehicle is driven away prior to attaching the notice to the vehicle, the issuing officer shall file the notice with the processing agency. The processing agency shall mail, within 15 calendar days of issuance of the notice of parking violation, a copy of the notice of parking violation or transmit an electronic facsimile of the notice to the registered owner.

(e) If, within 21 days after the notice of parking violation is attached to the vehicle, the issuing officer or the issuing agency determines that, in the interest of justice, the notice of parking violation should be canceled, the issuing agency, pursuant to subdivision (a) of Section 40215, shall cancel the notice of parking violation or, if the issuing agency has contracted with a processing agency, shall notify the processing agency to cancel the notice of parking violation pursuant to subdivision (a) of Section 40215. The reason for the cancellation shall be set forth in writing.

If, after a copy of the notice of parking violation is attached to the vehicle, the issuing officer determines that there is incorrect data on the notice, including, but not limited to, the date or time, the issuing officer may indicate in writing, on a form attached to the original notice, the necessary correction to allow for the timely entry of the notice on the processing agency's data system. A copy of the correction shall be mailed to the registered owner of the vehicle.

(f) Under no circumstances shall a personal relationship with any officer, public official, or law enforcement agency be grounds for cancellation. *(Added by Stats. 1986, c. 939, § 15. Amended by Stats.1987, c. 72, § 3, eff. June 30, 1987; Stats.1990, c. 1004 (A.B.3261), § 1; Stats.1992, c. 1243 (A.B.3090), § 108, eff. Sept. 30, 1992; Stats.1992, c. 1244 (A.B.408), § 15, operative July 1, 1993; Stats.1993, c. 1093 (A.B.780), § 8; Stats.1993, c. 1292 (S.B.274), § 17; Stats.1995, c. 734 (A.B.1228), § 7; Stats. 1996, c. 1156 (A.B.3157), § 6; Stats.1998, c. 885 (A.B. 1730), § 3.)*

Cross References

Trial by written declaration, see Vehicle Code § 40902.

§ 40203. Notice of amount of parking penalty; payment by mail; procedures to contest notice of violation

The notice of parking violation shall be accompanied by a written notice of the amount of the parking penalty due for that violation, the address of the person authorized to receive a deposit of the parking penalty, a statement in bold print that payments of the parking penalty for the parking violation may be sent through the mail, and instructions on obtaining information on the procedures to contest the notice of parking violation. *(Added by Stats.1986, c. 939, § 15. Amended by Stats. 1995, c. 734 (A.B.1228), § 8.)*

§ 40203.5. Parking penalties; late payment penalties; minimum and maximum penalties; suspension of penalty; installment payments

(a) The schedule of parking penalties for parking violations and late payment penalties shall be established by the governing body of the jurisdiction where the notice of violation is issued. To the extent possible, issuing agencies within the same county shall standardize parking penalties.

(b) Parking penalties under this article shall be collected as civil penalties.

(c)(1) Notwithstanding subdivision (a) the penalty for a violation of Section 22507.8 or an ordinance or resolution adopted pursuant to Section 22511.57 shall be not less than two hundred fifty dollars ($250) and not more than one thousand dollars ($1,000).

(2) The issuing agency may suspend the imposition of the penalty in paragraph (1), if the violator, at the time of the offense, possesses but failed to display a valid special identification license plate issued pursuant to Section 5007 or a distinguishing placard issued pursuant to Section 22511.55 or 22511.59.

(3) A penalty imposed pursuant to this subdivision may be paid in installments if the issuing agency determines that the violator is unable to pay the entire amount in one payment. *(Added by Stats.1986, c. 939, § 15. Amended by Stats.1990, c. 203 (S.B.1944), § 1; Stats.1991, c. 329 (A.B.2170), § 1; Stats.1992, c. 1244 (A.B.408), § 16, operative July 1, 1993; Stats.1995, c. 734 (A.B.1228), § 9; Stats.2009, c. 415 (A.B.144), § 6.)*

§ 40203.6. Additional assessments

(a) In addition to an assessment levied pursuant to any other law, an additional assessment equal to 10 percent of the penalty established pursuant to Section 40203.5 shall be imposed by the governing body of the jurisdiction where the notice of parking violation is issued for a civil violation of any of the following:

(1) Subdivisions (b), (c), and (d) of Section 4461.

(2) Subdivision (c) of Section 4463.

(3) Section 22507.8.

(4) An ordinance or resolution adopted pursuant to Section 22511.57.

(5) Section 22522.

(b) An assessment imposed pursuant to this section shall be deposited with the city or county where the violation occurred. *(Added by Stats.2009, c. 415 (A.B. 144), § 7.)*

§ 40204. Termination of proceedings on receipt of penalty by authorized person

If the parking penalty is received by the person authorized to receive the deposit of the parking penalty and there is no contest as to that parking violation, the proceedings under this article shall terminate. *(Added by*

Stats.1986, c. 939, § 15. Amended by Stats.1992, c. 1244 (A.B.408), § 17, operative July 1, 1993.)

§ 40205. Contest of parking violation; procedure of processing agency

If a person contests the parking violation, the processing agency shall proceed in accordance with Section 40215. *(Added by Stats.1986, c. 939, § 15. Amended by Stats.1992, c. 1244 (A.B.408), § 18, operative July 1, 1993.)*

§ 40206. Service or mailing of notice of delinquent violation

(a) If the payment of the parking penalty is not received by the person authorized to receive a deposit of the parking penalty by the date fixed on the notice of parking violation under Section 40202, the processing agency shall deliver to the registered owner a notice of delinquent parking violation.

(b) Delivery of a notice of delinquent parking violation under this section may be made by personal service or by first-class mail addressed to the registered owner, as shown on records of the Department of Motor Vehicles. *(Added by Stats.1986, c. 939, § 15. Amended by Stats. 1992, c. 1244 (A.B.408), § 19, operative July 1, 1993.)*

Cross References

Trial by written declaration, see Vehicle Code § 40902.

§ 40206.5. Copy of original notice of violation; fee; cancellation upon failure of vehicle to match description

(a) Within 15 days of a request, by mail or in person, the processing agency shall mail or otherwise provide to any person who has received a notice of delinquent parking violation, or his or her agent, a photostatic copy of the original notice of parking violation or an electronically produced facsimile of the original notice of parking violation. The issuing agency may charge a fee sufficient to recover the actual cost of providing the copy, not to exceed two dollars ($2). Until the issuing agency complies with a request for a copy of the original notice of parking violation, the processing agency may not proceed pursuant to subdivision (i) of Section 22651, Section 22651.7, or Section 40220.

(b) If the description of the vehicle on the notice of parking violation does not substantially match the corresponding information on the registration card for that vehicle and the processing agency is satisfied that the vehicle has not been incorrectly described due to the intentional switching of license plates, the processing agency shall, on written request of the person cancel the notice of parking violation without the necessity of an appearance by that person.

(c) For purposes of this section, a copy of the notice of parking violation may be a photostatic copy or an electronically produced facsimile. *(Added by Stats.1986, c. 939, § 15. Amended by Stats.1989, c. 502, § 2; Stats.1992, c. 1244 (A.B.408), § 20, operative July 1, 1993; Stats.1993, c. 1093 (A.B.780), § 9.)*

§ 40207. Contents of notice of delinquent violation

Section operative until Jan. 1, 2016. See, also, section operative Jan. 1, 2016.

(a) The notice of delinquent parking violation shall contain the information specified in subdivision (a) of Section 40202, subdivision (a) of Section 40241, or subdivision (a) of Section 40248, as applicable, and Section 40203, and, additionally shall contain a notice to the registered owner that, unless the registered owner pays the parking penalty or contests the citation within 21 calendar days from the date of issuance of the citation or 14 calendar days after the mailing of the notice of delinquent parking violation or completes and files an affidavit of nonliability that complies with Section 40208 or 40209, the renewal of the vehicle registration shall be contingent upon compliance with the notice of delinquent parking violation. If the registered owner, by appearance or by mail, makes payment to the processing agency within 21 calendar days from the date of issuance of the citation or 14 calendar days after the mailing of the notice of delinquent parking violation, the parking penalty shall consist solely of the amount of the original penalty. Additional fees, assessments, or other charges shall not be added.

(b) This section shall remain in effect only until January 1, 2016, and as of that date is repealed, unless a later enacted statute, that is enacted before January 1, 2016, deletes or extends that date. *(Added by Stats.1986, c. 939, § 15. Amended by Stats.1989, c. 750, § 2; Stats.1992, c. 1244 (A.B.408), § 21, operative July 1, 1993; Stats.1995, c. 734 (A.B.1228), § 10; Stats.1996, c. 1156 (A.B.3157), § 7; Stats.2007, c. 377 (A.B.101), § 1; Stats. 2010, c. 471 (A.B.2567), § 1; Stats.2011, c. 325 (A.B. 1041), § 1.)*

Repeal

For repeal of this section, see its terms.

§ 40207. Contents of notice of delinquent violation

Section operative Jan. 1, 2016. See, also, section operative until Jan. 1, 2016.

(a) The notice of delinquent parking violation shall contain the information specified in subdivision (a) of Section 40202 or subdivision (a) of Section 40248, as applicable, and Section 40203, and, additionally shall contain a notice to the registered owner that, unless the registered owner pays the parking penalty or contests the citation within 21 calendar days from the date of issuance of the citation or 14 calendar days after the mailing of the notice of delinquent parking violation or completes and files an affidavit of nonliability that complies with Section 40208 or 40209, the renewal of the vehicle registration shall be contingent upon compliance with the notice of delinquent parking violation. If the registered owner, by appearance or by mail, makes payment to the processing agency within 21 calendar days from the date of issuance of the citation or 14 calendar days after the mailing of the notice of delinquent parking violation, the parking penal-

ty shall consist solely of the amount of the original penalty. Additional fees, assessments, or other charges shall not be added.

(b) This section shall become operative on January 1, 2016. *(Added by Stats.2007, c. 377 (A.B.101), § 2, operative Jan. 1, 2012. Amended by Stats.2010, c. 471 (A.B.2567), § 2, operative Jan. 1, 2012; Stats.2011, c. 325 (A.B.1041), § 2, operative Jan. 1, 2016.)*

§ 40208. Affidavit of nonliability; information and instructions

The notice of delinquent parking violation shall contain, or be accompanied with, an affidavit of nonliability and information of what constitutes nonliability, information as to the effect of executing the affidavit, and instructions for returning the affidavit to the issuing agency. *(Added by Stats.1986, c. 939, § 15.)*

§ 40209. Affidavit of nonliability; proof of written lease or rental of vehicle; notice of delinquent violation; proceedings against rentee or lessee

If the affidavit of nonliability is returned to the processing agency within 30 calendar days of the mailing of the notice of delinquent parking violation together with the proof of a written lease or rental agreement between a bona fide rental or leasing company, and its customer which identifies the rentee or lessee and provides the driver's license number, name, and address of the rentee or lessee, the processing agency shall serve or mail to the rentee or lessee identified in the affidavit of nonliability a notice of delinquent parking violation. If payment is not received within 21 calendar days from the date of issuance of the citation or 14 calendar days after the mailing of the notice of delinquent parking violation, the processing agency may proceed against the rentee or lessee pursuant to Section 40220. *(Added by Stats.1986, c. 939, § 15. Amended by Stats.1989, c. 750, § 3; Stats.1992, c. 1244 (A.B.408), § 22, operative July 1, 1993; Stats.1995, c. 734 (A.B.1228), § 11; Stats.1996, c. 1156 (A.B.3157), § 8.)*

§ 40210. Affidavit of nonliability; evidence of prior sale or transfer and delivery of vehicle to purchaser; cancellation of notice of delinquent violation; proceedings against owner; collection of penalties from person having ownership on date of alleged violation

(a) If the affidavit of nonliability is returned and indicates that the registered owner served has made a bona fide sale or transfer of the vehicle and has delivered possession of the vehicle to the purchaser prior to the date of the alleged violation, the processing agency shall obtain verification from the department that the registered owner has complied with Section 5602.

(b) If the registered owner has complied with Section 5602, the processing agency shall cancel the notice of delinquent parking violation or violations with respect to the registered owner.

(c) If the registered owner has not complied with Section 5602, the processing agency shall inform the registered owner that the citation shall be paid in full or contested pursuant to Section 40215 unless the registered owner delivers evidence within 15 days of the notice that establishes that the transfer of ownership and possession of the vehicle occurred prior to the date of the alleged violation. If the registered owner does not comply with this notice, the processing agency shall proceed pursuant to Section 40220. If the registered owner delivers the evidence within 15 days of the notice, the processing agency shall cancel the notice of delinquent parking violation or violations with respect to the registered owner.

(d) For purposes of subdivision (c), evidence sufficient to establish that the transfer of ownership and possession occurred prior to the date of the alleged violation or violations shall include, but is not limited to, a copy of the executed agreement showing the date of the transfer of vehicle ownership.

(e) This section does not limit or impair the ability or the right of the processing agency to pursue the collection of delinquent parking penalties from the person having ownership and possession of the vehicle on the date the alleged violation occurred. *(Added by Stats.1986, c. 939, § 15. Amended by Stats.1992, c. 1244 (A.B.408), § 23, operative July 1, 1993; Stats.1995, c. 734 (A.B.1228), § 12; Stats.2008, c. 741 (A.B.2401), § 3.)*

§ 40211. Deposit of penalty with authorized person; processing agency procedures; termination of proceedings

(a) If the registered owner, or an agent of the registered owner, or a rentee or lessee who was served with the notice of delinquent parking violation pursuant to Section 40206 or Section 40209, or any other person who presents the notice of parking violation or notice of delinquent parking violation after the notice of delinquent parking violation has been issued for delivery under Section 40206, deposits the parking penalty with a person authorized to receive it, the processing agency shall do both of the following:

(1) Deliver a copy of one of the following: the notice of delinquent parking violation issued under Section 40206; a true and correct abstract containing the information set forth in the notice of parking violation if the citation was issued electronically; or an electronically reproduced listing of the citation information presented in a notice of delinquent parking violation to the person and record the name, address, and driver's license number of the person actually given the copy in the records of the issuing agency.

For the purposes of this paragraph, a copy of the notice of delinquent parking violation may be a photostatic copy.

(2) Determine whether the notice of delinquent parking violation has been filed with the department pursuant

to subdivision (b) of Section 40220 or a civil judgment has been entered pursuant to Section 40220.

(b) If the notice of delinquent parking violation has not been filed with the department or judgment entered and payment of the parking penalty, including any applicable assessments, is received, the proceedings under this article shall terminate.

(c) If the notice of delinquent parking violation has been filed with the department, has been returned under subdivision (b) or (c) of Section 4760 or Section 4764, and payment of the parking penalty together with the administrative service fee of the processing agency for costs of service and any applicable assessments is received, the proceedings under this article shall terminate.

(d) If the notice of delinquent parking violation has been filed with the department and has not been returned under Section 4760, 4762, and 4764, and payment of the parking penalty for, and any applicable costs of, service in connection with civil debt collection, is received by the processing agency, the processing agency shall do all of the following:

(1) Deliver a certificate of payment to the registered owner, the agent, the lessee, or the rentee or other person making the payment.

(2) Immediately transmit the payment information to the department in the manner prescribed by the department.

(3) Terminate proceedings on the notice of delinquent parking violation.

(4) Transmit for deposit all parking penalties and assessments in accordance with law. *(Added by Stats. 1986, c. 939, § 15. Amended by Stats.1989, c. 750, § 4; Stats.1992, c. 1244 (A.B.408), § 24, operative July 1, 1993; Stats.1995, c. 734 (A.B.1228), § 13.)*

§ 40215. Review of notice of parking violation; initial review by issuing agency; administrative hearing; process; application of section to certain agencies

(a) For a period of 21 calendar days from the issuance of a notice of parking violation or 14 calendar days from the mailing of a notice of delinquent parking violation, exclusive of any days from the day the processing agency receives a request for a copy or facsimile of the original notice of parking violation pursuant to Section 40206.5 and the day the processing agency complies with the request, a person may request an initial review of the notice by the issuing agency. The request may be made by telephone, in writing, or in person. There shall be no charge for this review. If, following the initial review, the issuing agency is satisfied that the violation did not occur, that the registered owner was not responsible for the violation, or that extenuating circumstances make dismissal of the citation appropriate in the interest of justice, the issuing agency shall cancel the notice of parking violation or notice of delinquent parking violation. The issuing agency shall advise the processing agency, if any, of the cancellation. The issuing agency or the processing agency shall mail the results of the initial review to the person contesting the notice, and, if following that review, cancellation of the notice does not occur, include a reason for that denial, notification of the ability to request an administrative hearing, and notice of the procedure adopted pursuant to subdivision (b) for waiving prepayment of the parking penalty based upon an inability to pay.

(b) If the person is dissatisfied with the results of the initial review, the person may request an administrative hearing of the violation no later than 21 calendar days following the mailing of the results of the issuing agency's initial review. The request may be made by telephone, in writing, or in person. The person requesting an administrative hearing shall deposit the amount of the parking penalty with the processing agency. The issuing agency shall adopt a written procedure to allow a person to request an administrative hearing without payment of the parking penalty upon satisfactory proof of an inability to pay the amount due. After January 1, 1996, an administrative hearing shall be held within 90 calendar days following the receipt of a request for an administrative hearing, excluding time tolled pursuant to this article. The person requesting the hearing may request one continuance, not to exceed 21 calendar days.

(c) The administrative hearing process shall include the following:

(1) The person requesting a hearing shall have the choice of a hearing by mail or in person. An in-person hearing shall be conducted within the jurisdiction of the issuing agency. If an issuing agency contracts with an administrative provider, hearings shall be held within the jurisdiction of the issuing agency or within the county of the issuing agency.

(2) If the person requesting a hearing is a minor, that person shall be permitted to appear at a hearing or admit responsibility for the parking violation without the necessity of the appointment of a guardian. The processing agency may proceed against the minor in the same manner as against an adult.

(3) The administrative hearing shall be conducted in accordance with written procedures established by the issuing agency and approved by the governing body or chief executive officer of the issuing agency. The hearing shall provide an independent, objective, fair, and impartial review of contested parking violations.

(4)(A) The issuing agency's governing body or chief executive officer shall appoint or contract with qualified examiners or administrative hearing providers that employ qualified examiners to conduct the administrative hearings. Examiners shall demonstrate those qualifications, training, and objectivity necessary to conduct a fair and impartial review. An examiner shall not be employed, managed, or controlled by a person whose primary duties are parking enforcement or parking citation, processing, collection, or issuance. The examiner shall be separate and independent from the citation collection or processing function. An examiner's contin-

ued employment, performance evaluation, compensation, and benefits shall not, directly or indirectly, be linked to the amount of fines collected by the examiner.

(B) Examiners shall have a minimum of 20 hours of training. The examiner is responsible for the costs of the training. The issuing agency may reimburse the examiner for those costs. Training may be provided through (i) an accredited college or university, (ii) a program conducted by the Commission on Peace Officer Standards and Training, (iii) American Arbitration Association or a similar established organization, or (iv) through any program approved by the governing board of the issuing agency, including a program developed and provided by, or for, the agency. Training programs may include topics relevant to the administrative hearing, including, but not limited to, applicable laws and regulations, parking enforcement procedures, due process, evaluation of evidence, hearing procedures, and effective oral and written communication. Upon the approval of the governing board of the issuing agency, up to 12 hours of relevant experience may be substituted for up to 12 hours of training. In addition, up to eight hours of the training requirements described in this subparagraph may be credited to an individual, at the discretion of the governing board of the issuing agency, based upon training programs or courses described in (i) to (iv), inclusive, that the individual attended within the last five years.

(5) The officer or person who issues a notice of parking violation shall not be required to participate in an administrative hearing. The issuing agency shall not be required to produce any evidence other than the notice of parking violation or copy thereof and information received from the Department of Motor Vehicles identifying the registered owner of the vehicle. The documentation in proper form shall be prima facie evidence of the violation.

(6) The examiner's decision following the administrative hearing may be personally delivered to the person by the examiner or sent by first-class mail, and, if the notice is not cancelled, include a written reason for that denial.

(7) Following a determination by the examiner that a person has committed the violation, the examiner may, consistent with the written guidelines established by the issuing agency, allow payment of the parking penalty in installments, or an issuing agency may allow for deferred payment or allow for payments in installments, if the person provides evidence satisfactory to the examiner or the issuing agency, as the case may be, of an inability to pay the parking penalty in full. If authorized by the governing board of the issuing agency, the examiner may permit the performance of community service in lieu of payment of a parking penalty.

(d) The provisions of this section relating to the administrative appeal process do not apply to an issuing agency that is a law enforcement agency if the issuing agency does not also act as the processing agency. *(Added by Stats.1995, c. 734 (A.B.1228), § 15. Amended by Stats.2002, c. 640 (A.B.1314), § 4; Stats.2008, c. 13 (A.B.602), § 2; Stats.2009, c. 200 (S.B.734), § 16.)*

Cross References

Notice of parking violation, contents, procedure to contest, see Vehicle Code § 40248.

§ 40219. Repealed by Stats.1987, c. 852, § 4

§ 40220. Collection of unpaid parking penalty; options of processing agency; application

Except as otherwise provided in Sections 40221 and 40222, the processing agency shall proceed under only one of the following options in order to collect an unpaid parking penalty:

(a) File an itemization of unpaid parking penalties and service fees with the department for collection with the registration of the vehicle pursuant to Section 4760.

(b) If more than four hundred dollars ($400) in unpaid penalties and fees have been accrued by any person or registered owner, proof thereof may be filed with the court with the same effect as a civil judgment. Execution may be levied and other measures may be taken for the collection of the judgment as are authorized for the collection of an unpaid civil judgment entered against a defendant in an action on a debtor. The court may assess costs against a judgment debtor to be paid upon satisfaction of the judgment. The processing agency shall send a notice by first-class mail to the person or registered owner indicating that a judgment shall be entered for the unpaid penalties, fees, and costs and that, after 21 calendar days from the date of the mailing of the notice, the judgment shall have the same effect as an entry of judgment against a judgment debtor. The person or registered owner shall also be notified at that time that execution may be levied against his or her assets, liens may be placed against his or her property, his or her wages may be garnisheed, and other steps may be taken to satisfy the judgment. If a judgment is rendered for the processing agency, that agency may contract with a collection agency to collect the amount of that judgment.

Notwithstanding any other provision of law, the processing agency shall pay the established first paper civil filing fee at the time an entry of civil judgment is requested.

(c) If the registration of the vehicle has not been renewed for 60 days beyond the renewal date, and the citation has not been collected by the department pursuant to Section 4760, file proof of unpaid penalties and fees with the court with the same effect as a civil judgment as provided in subdivision (b).

(d) This section does not apply to a registered owner of a vehicle if the citation was issued prior to the registered owner taking possession of the vehicle and the department has notified the processing agency pursuant to Section 4764. *(Added by Stats.1986, c. 939, § 15. Amended by Stats.1987, c. 852, § 5; Stats.1991, c. 329*

1040

(A.B.2170), § 2; Stats.1992, c. 1244 (A.B.408), § 27, operative July 1, 1993; Stats.1995, c. 734 (A.B.1228), § 16; Stats.2008, c. 741 (A.B.2401), § 4.)

§ 40221. Civil judgment; filing; prerequisites

The processing agency shall not file a civil judgment with the court relating to a parking violation which has been filed with the department unless the processing agency has determined that the registration of the vehicle has not been renewed for 60 days beyond the renewal date and the citation has not been collected by the department pursuant to Section 4760. *(Added by Stats. 1986, c. 939, § 15. Amended by Stats.1992, c. 1244 (A.B.408), § 28, operative July 1, 1993.)*

§ 40222. Termination of processing agency proceedings on notice of delinquent violation

The processing agency shall terminate proceedings on a notice of a delinquent parking violation or violations in all of the following cases:

(a) Upon receipt of collected penalties and administrative fees remitted by the department under Section 4762 for that notice of delinquent parking violation or violations. The termination under this subdivision is by satisfaction of the parking penalty or penalties.

(b) If the notice of a delinquent parking violation or violations was returned to the processing agency pursuant to Section 4764 and five years have elapsed since the date of the last violation. The termination under this subdivision is by the running of a statute of limitation of proceedings.

(c) The processing agency receives information, that it shall verify with the department, that the penalty or penalties have been paid to the department pursuant to Section 4762.

(d)(1) If the registered owner of the vehicle provides proof to the processing agency that he or she was not the registered owner on the date of the violation.

(2) This subdivision does not limit or impair the ability or the right of the processing agency to pursue the collection of a delinquent parking violation or violations from the person who was the registered owner or lessee of the vehicle on the date of the violation. *(Added by Stats.1986, c. 939, § 15. Amended by Stats.2008, c. 741 (A.B.2401), § 5.)*

§ 40223. Repealed by Stats.1993, c. 1093 (A.B.780), § 11

§ 40224. Limitation of actions; tolling until return or recall of notice of delinquent violation

The time limitation provided by law for commencement of a civil action for a violation specified in Section 40200 shall be tolled from and after the date a notice of delinquent parking violation is filed with the department pursuant to subdivision (b) of Section 40220 until the notice is returned to the processing agency under subdivision (b) of Section 4760 or Section 4762 or 4764 or is recalled by the processing agency pursuant to subdivision (d) of Section 40211. *(Added by Stats.1986, c. 939, § 15. Amended by Stats.1992, c. 1244 (A.B.408), § 29, operative July 1, 1993; Stats.1995, c. 734 (A.B.1228), § 17.)*

§ 40225. Equipment violation; entry on notice of parking violation; civil penalty; allocation

(a) An equipment violation entered on the notice of parking violation attached to the vehicle under Section 40203 shall be processed in accordance with this article. All of the violations entered on the notice of parking violation shall be noticed in the notice of delinquent parking violation delivered pursuant to Section 40206, together with the amount of civil penalty.

(b) Whether or not a vehicle is in violation of any regulation governing the standing or parking of a vehicle but is in violation of subdivision (a) of Section 5204, a person authorized to enforce parking laws and regulations shall issue a written notice of parking violation, setting forth the alleged violation. The violation shall be processed pursuant to this section.

(c) The civil penalty for each equipment violation, including failure to properly display a license plate, is the amount established for the violation in the Uniform Bail and Penalty Schedule, as adopted by the Judicial Council, except that upon proof of the correction to the processing agency, the penalty shall be reduced to ten dollars ($10). The reduction provided for in this subdivision involving failure to properly display license plates shall only apply if, at the time of the violation, valid license plates were issued for that vehicle in accordance with this code. The civil penalty for each violation of Section 5204 is the amount established for the violation in the Uniform Bail and Penalty Schedule, as adopted by the Judicial Council, except that upon proof of the correction to the processing agency, the penalty shall be reduced to ten dollars ($10).

(d) Fifty percent of any penalty collected pursuant to this section for registration or equipment violations by a processing agency shall be paid to the county for remittance to the State Treasurer and the remaining 50 percent shall be retained by the issuing agency and processing agency subject to the terms of the contract described in Section 40200.5.

(e) Subdivisions (a) and (b) do not preclude the recording of a violation of subdivision (a) or (b) of Section 4000 on a notice of parking violation or the adjudication of that violation under the civil process set forth in this article. *(Added by Stats.1986, c. 939, § 15. Amended by Stats.1989, c. 729, § 2, operative July 1, 1990; Stats.1992, c. 1244 (A.B.408), § 30, operative July 1, 1993; Stats.1993, c. 1093 (A.B.780), § 12; Stats.1996, c. 1154 (A.B.3020), § 84, eff. Sept. 30, 1996; Stats.1998, c. 885 (A.B.1730), § 4.)*

§ 40226. Cancellation of citation for failure to display a disabled placard; fees

An issuing agency may, in lieu of collecting a fine for a citation for failure to display a disabled placard, charge an administrative fee not to exceed twenty-five dollars ($25) to process cancellation of a citation in any case where the individual who received the citation can show proof that he or she had been issued a valid placard at the time the citation was received. *(Added by Stats.2002, c. 640 (A.B.1314), § 5.)*

§ 40230. Review; filing of appeal; notice; evidence; fee

(a) Within 30 calendar days after the mailing or personal delivery of the final decision described in subdivision (b) of Section 40215, the contestant may seek review by filing an appeal to be heard by the superior court where the same shall be heard de novo, except that the contents of the processing agency's file in the case shall be received in evidence. A copy of the notice of parking violation or, if the citation was issued electronically, a true and correct abstract containing the information set forth in the notice of parking violation shall be admitted into evidence as prima facie evidence of the facts stated therein. A copy of the notice of appeal shall be served in person or by first-class mail upon the processing agency by the contestant. For purposes of computing the 30-calendar-day period, Section 1013 of the Code of Civil Procedure shall be applicable. A proceeding under this subdivision is a limited civil case.

(b) The fee for filing the notice of appeal is as provided in Section 70615 of the Government Code. The court shall request that the processing agency's file on the case be forwarded to the court, to be received within 15 calendar days of the request. The court shall notify the contestant of the appearance date by mail or personal delivery. The court shall retain the fee under Section 70615 of the Government Code regardless of the outcome of the appeal. If the court finds in favor of the contestant, the amount of the fee shall be reimbursed to the contestant by the processing agency. Any deposit of parking penalty shall be refunded by the processing agency in accordance with the judgment of the court.

(c) The conduct of the appeal under this section is a subordinate judicial duty that may be performed by traffic trial commissioners and other subordinate judicial officials at the direction of the presiding judge of the court.

(d) If no notice of appeal of the processing agency's decision is filed within the period set forth in subdivision (a), the decision shall be deemed final.

(e) If the parking penalty has not been deposited and the decision is against the contestant, the processing agency shall, after the decision becomes final, proceed to collect the penalty pursuant to Section 40220. *(Added by Stats.1992, c. 1244 (A.B.408), § 33, operative July 1, 1993. Amended by Stats.1993, c. 1093 (A.B.780), § 13; Stats. 1995, c. 734 (A.B.1228), § 18; Stats.1998, c. 931 (S.B. 2139), § 459, eff. Sept. 28, 1998; Stats.2005, c. 75 (A.B. 145), § 152, eff. July 19, 2005, operative Jan. 1, 2006; Stats.2007, c. 738 (A.B.1248), § 43.)*

Law Revision Commission Comments

1998 Amendment

Section 40230 is amended to accommodate unification of the municipal and superior courts in a county. Cal. Const. art. VI, § 5(e). The section is also amended to reflect elimination of the justice court. Cal. Const. art. VI, §§ 1, 5(b).

A limited civil case is within the original jurisdiction of the municipal court or of the superior court in a county in which there is no municipal court. Cal. Const. art. VI, 10 (superior court jurisdiction); Code Civ. Proc. §§ 85, 85.1 (limited civil cases). See also Code Civ. Proc. §§ 91, 904.2, 1085 (trial procedures and writ and appellate jurisdiction for limited civil cases). [28 Cal.L.Rev.Comm. Reports 51 (1998)].

Cross References

Notice of parking violation, contents, procedure for court review, see Vehicle Code § 40248.

Organization and government of courts, collection of fees and fines pursuant to this section, deposits, see Government Code § 68085.1.

ARTICLE 3.5. PROCEDURE ON VIDEO IMAGING OF PARKING VIOLATIONS OCCURRING IN TRANSIT–ONLY LANES

Section
40240.   Automated forward facing parking control devices; video imaging of parking violations.
40241.   Notice of parking violation.
40242.   Parking enforcement pilot program; evaluation.
40243.   Duration of article.

Repeal

For repeal of Article 3.5, see Vehicle Code § 40243.

§ 40240. Automated forward facing parking control devices; video imaging of parking violations

(a) The City and County of San Francisco may install automated forward facing parking control devices on city-owned public transit vehicles, as defined by Section 99211 of the Public Utilities Code, for the purpose of video imaging of parking violations occurring in transit-only traffic lanes. Citations shall be issued only for violations captured during the posted hours of operation for a transit-only traffic lane. The devices shall be angled and focused so as to capture video images of parking violations and not unnecessarily capture identifying images of other drivers, vehicles, and pedestrians. The devices shall record the date and time of the violation at the same time as the video images are captured.

(b) Prior to issuing notices of parking violations pursuant to subdivision (a) of Section 40241, the City and County of San Francisco shall commence a program to issue only warning notices for 30 days. The City and County of San Francisco shall also make a public announcement of the program at least 30 days prior to commencement of issuing notices of parking violations.

(c) A designated employee of the City and County of San Francisco, who is qualified by the city and county to issue parking citations, shall review video image recordings for the purpose of determining whether a parking violation occurred in a transit-only traffic lane. A violation of a statute, regulation, or ordinance governing vehicle parking under this code, under a federal or state statute or regulation, or under an ordinance enacted by the City and County of San Francisco occurring in a transit-only traffic lane observed by the designated employee in the recordings is subject to a civil penalty.

(d) The registered owner shall be permitted to review the video image evidence of the alleged violation during normal business hours at no cost.

(e)(1) Except as it may be included in court records described in Section 68152 of the Government Code, or as provided in paragraph (2), the video image evidence may be retained for up to six months from the date the information was first obtained, or 60 days after final disposition of the citation, whichever date is later, after which time the information shall be destroyed.

(2) Notwithstanding Section 26202.6 of the Government Code, video image evidence from forward facing automated enforcement devices that does not contain evidence of a parking violation occurring in a transit-only traffic lane shall be destroyed within 15 days after the information was first obtained.

(f) Notwithstanding Section 6253 of the Government Code, or any other provision of law, the video image records are confidential. Public agencies shall use and allow access to these records only for the purposes authorized by this article.

(g) For purposes of this article, "local agency" means the City and County of San Francisco.

(h) For purposes of this article, "transit-only traffic lane" means any designated transit-only lane on which use is restricted to mass transit vehicles, or other designated vehicles including taxis and vanpools, during posted times. *(Added by Stats.2007, c. 377 (A.B.101), § 3. Amended by Stats.2008, c. 179 (S.B.1498), § 225; Stats. 2011, c. 325 (A.B.1041), § 3; Stats.2012, c. 162 (S.B. 1171), § 183.)*

Repeal

For repeal of Article 3.5, see Vehicle Code § 40243.

Cross References

Inspection of public records, exemptions from disclosure, automated forward facing parking control devices, video imaging records, see Government Code § 6276.04.

§ 40241. Notice of parking violation

(a) A designated employee of the local agency shall issue a notice of a parking violation to the registered owner of a vehicle within 15 calendar days of the date of the violation. The notice of violation shall set forth the violation of a statute, regulation, or ordinance governing vehicle parking under this code, under a federal or state statute or regulation, or under an ordinance enacted by the City and County of San Francisco occurring in a transit-only traffic lane, a statement indicating that payment is required within 21 calendar days from the date of citation issuance, and the procedure for the registered owner, lessee, or rentee to deposit the parking penalty or contest the citation pursuant to Section 40215. The notice of a parking violation shall also set forth the date, time, and location of the violation, the vehicle license number, registration expiration date if visible, the color of the vehicle, and, if possible, the make of the vehicle. The notice of parking violation, or copy of the notice, shall be considered a record kept in the ordinary course of business of the City and County of San Francisco and shall be prima facie evidence of the facts contained in the notice. The City and County of San Francisco shall send information regarding the process for requesting review of the video image evidence along with the notice of parking violation.

(b) The notice of parking violation shall be served by depositing the notice in the United States mail to the registered owner's last known address listed with the Department of Motor Vehicles. Proof of mailing demonstrating that the notice of parking violation was mailed to that address shall be maintained by the local agency. If the registered owner, by appearance or by mail, makes payment to the processing agency or contests the violation within either 21 calendar days from the date of mailing of the citation, or 14 calendar days after the mailing of the notice of delinquent parking violation, the parking penalty shall consist solely of the amount of the original penalty.

(c) If, within 21 days after the notice of parking violation is issued, the local agency determines that, in the interest of justice, the notice of parking violation should be canceled, the local agency shall cancel the notice of parking violation pursuant to subdivision (a) of Section 40215. The reason for the cancellation shall be set forth in writing.

(d) Following an initial review by the local agency, and an administrative hearing, pursuant to Section 40215, a contestant may seek court review by filing an appeal pursuant to Section 40230.

(e) The City and County of San Francisco may contract with a private vendor for the processing of notices of parking violations and notices of delinquent violations. The City and County of San Francisco shall maintain overall control and supervision of the program. *(Added by Stats.2007, c. 377 (A.B.101), § 3.)*

Repeal

For repeal of Article 3.5, see Vehicle Code § 40243.

§ 40242. Parking enforcement pilot program; evaluation

If the City and County of San Francisco implements a parking enforcement pilot program pursuant to this article, no later than March 1, 2015, the City and County of San Francisco shall provide to the transportation and judiciary committees of the Legislature an evaluation of the pilot program's effectiveness and impact on privacy in

compliance with Section 9795 of the Government Code. *(Added by Stats.2007, c. 377 (A.B.101), § 3. Amended by Stats.2011, c. 325 (A.B.1041), § 4.)*

Repeal

For repeal of Article 3.5, see Vehicle Code § 40243.

§ 40243. Duration of article

This article shall remain in effect only until January 1, 2016, and as of that date is repealed, unless a later enacted statute, that is enacted before January 1, 2016, deletes or extends that date. *(Added by Stats.2007, c. 377 (A.B.101), § 3. Amended by Stats.2011, c. 325 (A.B. 1041), § 5.)*

ARTICLE 3.6. PROCEDURE ON PHOTO ENFORCEMENT AND DIGITAL PHOTOGRAPHING OF PARKING VIOLATIONS DURING STREET SWEEPING

Section
40245. Legislative findings and declarations.
40246. Definitions.
40247. Automated parking enforcement system on street-sweepers for purpose of digital photography of street-sweeping parking violations in street-sweeping parking lanes; installation and operation; citations; 30-day warning period; review of photographs; retention and destruction; confidentiality.
40248. Notice of parking violation; contents; considered business record and prima facie evidence; service; procedure to contest; court review; contracting with private vendor for processing.
40249. Report to Senate and Assembly Committees on Judiciary and Senate Committee on Transportation and Housing; contents.
40249.5. Duration of article.

Repeal

For repeal of Article 3.6, see Vehicle Code § 40249.5.

§ 40245. Legislative findings and declarations

(a) The Legislature finds and declares all of the following:

(1) Streetsweepers operating throughout our nation and the world remove from streets and roads unnecessary pollutants, contaminants, chemicals, trash, and debris, which provides significant environmental and sanitation benefits, thereby protecting the environment and contributing to the health of people in communities worldwide.

(2) Each year, illegally parked private cars, trucks, and service vehicles on local streets and roads disrupt full street sweeping of as many as three parking spaces per illegally parked vehicle, resulting in significant debris, grease, oil, and other pollutants being needlessly washed into the stormwater drains.

(3) A major benefit of street sweeping, especially in more urbanized areas with higher areas of paving, is that

by capturing pollutants before they are made soluble by rainwater, the need for stormwater treatment practices, which can be very costly when compared to collecting pollutants before they become soluble, may be reduced.

(4) According to an analysis by the District of Columbia Department of Public Works, an average of 10 pounds of oil and grease, three pounds of nitrogen and phosphorus, and up to two pounds of heavy metals are typically removed per mile swept of local streets and roads through street sweeping.

(5) According to an August 2004 technical report on "Trash Best Management Practices" submitted by the County of Los Angeles Department of Public Works, street sweeping and stricter enforcement of no parking regulations should "be utilized to the maximum extent practicable" to help prevent trash, litter, and other harmful pollutants from getting into the stormwater drain system.

(6) According to a July 2007 technical report titled "Trash Total Maximum Daily Loads for the Los Angeles River Watershed," stormwater drain discharges are the "primary source of trash" in the waterbodies of the Los Angeles River Watershed, whereby unswept street litter is washed through the storm drain sewers into the Los Angeles River, the Estuary, the beaches at Long Beach, and the Pacific Ocean.

(7) In August 2007, after extensive studies, public meetings, and economic benefit analysis, the Los Angeles Regional Water Quality Control Board adopted a phased-in goal of "zero" discharges of manmade trash in the Los Angeles River Watershed by 2016, a goal that was subsequently approved by the State Water Resources Control Board in April 2008 and the United States Environmental Protection Agency in July 2008.

(8) Cities such as Chicago and Washington D.C. already utilize automated parking enforcement systems mounted on their local public agency-owned or local public agency-operated streetsweepers to enforce existing regulations and improve compliance with street-sweeping regulations, which benefits the environment by helping reduce waste and pollutants from entering stormwater drain systems.

(b) It is the intent of the Legislature that a citation shall be issued, under the provisions of this article, only for violations captured during the designated hours of operation for a street-sweeping parking lane. It is also the intent of the Legislature that a citation shall not be issued, under the provisions of this article, for a vehicle that is parked on the street during the designated hours of operation for a street-sweeping parking lane when the vehicle is parked on the street after the street has been cleaned by a streetsweeper.

(c) It is also the intent of the Legislature that this article shall provide a single statewide standard for the use of camera enforcement technology on streetsweepers to help ensure continuity in program implementation and enforcement by local public agencies that desire to implement camera enforcement systems, including prohibiting the use of information read from license plates for any other purpose, establishing appropriate context supporting the violation that ensures individual privacy is maintained, and ensuring confidential data is disposed of properly, adequately, and safely after final disposition.

(d) Therefore, it is the intent of the Legislature to allow local public agency-owned or local public agency-operated streetsweepers to utilize automated parking enforcement systems for the purpose of digital photographing of street-sweeping parking violations for vehicles that are illegally parked during the designated hours of operation in a street-sweeping parking lane, thus serving the public interest by benefiting the environment, improving water quality, decreasing stormwater drain runoff, and helping reduce ongoing habitat deterioration. *(Added by Stats.2010, c. 471 (A.B.2567), § 3.)*

Repeal

For repeal of Article 3.6, see Vehicle Code § 40249.5.

§ 40246. **Definitions**

For the purposes of this article, the following terms have the following meanings:

(a) "Local public agency" means a city, county, city and county, district, or joint powers authority.

(b) "Streetsweeper" means a mechanical vehicle that cleans streets and roads, utilizing a broom, conveyor belt, vacuum, or regenerative-air mechanism, among other mechanisms, to loosen, carry, and collect debris, dust, grease, oil, metals, and other pollutants from streets and roads.

(c) "Street–sweeping parking lane" means the land designated as a parking area on any street or road routinely cleaned by streetsweepers during designated hours of operation as indicated on schedule signs designated on both sides of the street or road. *(Added by Stats.2010, c. 471 (A.B.2567), § 3.)*

Repeal

For repeal of Article 3.6, see Vehicle Code § 40249.5.

§ 40247. **Automated parking enforcement system on streetsweepers for purpose of digital photography of street-sweeping parking violations in street-sweeping parking lanes; installation and operation; citations; 30-day warning period; review of photographs; retention and destruction; confidentiality**

(a) A local public agency may install and operate an automated parking enforcement system on local public agency-owned or local public agency-operated streetsweepers for the purpose of digital photographing of street-sweeping parking violations occurring in street-sweeping parking lanes. The equipment shall be angled and focused so as to capture digital photographs of license plates on vehicles violating designated street-sweeping regulations and shall not unnecessarily capture identifying photographs of other drivers, vehicles, or pedestrians. The equipment shall only capture digital photographs when the automated parking enforcement system detects the occurrence of a parking infraction. The equipment shall record the date and time the violation was captured onto the photograph. Any information read from a license plate at a location or at a time not designated for streetsweeping shall be destroyed by the close of the next business day. Notwithstanding subdivision (e) of Section 40248, only a local public agency may operate an automated parking enforcement system.

(1) A citation shall be issued only for violations captured during the designated hours of operation for a street-sweeping parking lane.

(2) A citation shall not be issued, under the provisions of this article, for a vehicle that is parked on the street during the designated hours of operation for a street-sweeping parking lane when the vehicle is parked on the street after the street has been cleaned by a streetsweeper.

(b) At least 30 days prior to issuing notices of parking violations pursuant to subdivision (a) of Section 40248, a local public agency utilizing an automated parking enforcement system pursuant to this article shall make a public announcement of the automated parking enforcement system and shall only issue warning notices during this 30–day period. This subdivision does not affect the authority of a local public agency to issue notices of parking violations through a manual system before, during, or after the 30–day warning period in this subdivision.

(c) A designated employee for the local public agency, who is qualified by the local public agency to issue parking citations, shall review digital photographs for the purpose of determining whether a parking violation occurred in a street-sweeping parking lane. A violation of a statute, regulation, or ordinance governing parking under this code, under a federal or state statute or regulation, or under an ordinance enacted by the local public agency occurring in a street-sweeping parking lane observed by the designated employee in the photographs is subject to a civil penalty.

(d)(1) Except as it may be included in court records described in Section 68152 of the Government Code, or as provided in paragraph (2), the digital photograph evidence may be retained for up to six months from the date the information was first obtained, or 90 days after final disposition of the citation, whichever date is sooner, after which time the information shall be destroyed in a manner that shall preserve the confidentiality of any person included in the record or information.

(2) Notwithstanding Section 26202.6 of the Government Code, digital photographs from automated parking enforcement systems that do not contain evidence of a parking violation occurring in a street-sweeping parking lane shall be destroyed within 15 days after the information was first obtained in a manner that shall preserve the confidentiality of any person included in the information.

(e) Notwithstanding Section 6253 of the Government Code, or any other provision of law, the digital photographs made, and any information read from license plates, by an automated parking enforcement system shall be confidential. Local public agencies shall use and allow access to these photographs and license plate readings only for the purposes authorized by this article. *(Added by Stats.2010, c. 471 (A.B.2567), § 3.)*

Repeal

For repeal of Article 3.6, see Vehicle Code § 40249.5.

§ 40248. Notice of parking violation; contents; considered business record and prima facie evidence; service; procedure to contest; court review; contracting with private vendor for processing

(a) A designated employee for the local public agency shall issue a notice of a parking violation to the registered owner of a vehicle within 15 calendar days of the date of the violation. The notice of violation shall set forth the violation of a statute, regulation, or ordinance governing vehicle parking under this code, under a federal or state statute or regulation, or under an ordinance enacted by the local public agency occurring in a street-sweeping parking lane, a statement indicating that payment is required within 21 calendar days from the date of citation issuance, and the procedure for the registered owner to deposit the parking penalty or contest the citation pursuant to Section 40215. The notice of a parking violation shall also set forth the date, time, and location of the violation, the vehicle license number, registration expiration date if visible, the color of the vehicle, and, if possible, the make of the vehicle. The notice of parking violation shall include a copy of the digital photograph evidence. Except as provided in paragraph (1) of subdivision (d) of Section 40247, the notice of parking violation, or copy of the notice, shall be considered a record kept in the ordinary course of business of the local public agency and shall be prima facie evidence of the facts contained in the notice.

(b) The notice of parking violation shall be served by depositing the notice in the United States Postal Service to the registered owner's last known address listed with the Department of Motor Vehicles. Confidential information obtained from the Department of Motor Vehicles for the administration or enforcement of this article shall be held confidential, and may not be used for any other purpose. Proof of mailing demonstrating that the notice of parking violation was mailed to that address shall be maintained by the local public agency. If the registered owner, by appearance or by mail, makes payment to the processing agency or contests the violation within either 21 calendar days from the date of mailing of the citation, or 14 calendar days after the mailing of the notice of delinquent parking violation, the parking penalty shall consist solely of the amount of the original penalty.

1045

(c) The local public agency shall allow a person to contest a notice of parking violation pursuant to Section 40215.

(d) Following an initial review by the local public agency, and an administrative hearing, pursuant to Section 40215, a contestant may seek court review by filing an appeal pursuant to Section 40230.

(e) The local public agency may contract with a private vendor for the processing of notices of parking violations and notices of delinquent violations, if the local public agency maintains overall control and supervision of the automated parking enforcement system. *(Added by Stats. 2010, c. 471 (A.B.2567), § 3.)*

Repeal

For repeal of Article 3.6, see Vehicle Code § 40249.5.

§ 40249. Report to Senate and Assembly Committees on Judiciary and Senate Committee on Transportation and Housing; contents

By January 1, 2015, a local public agency that utilizes an automated parking enforcement system pursuant to this article shall collect and report to the Senate and Assembly Committees on Judiciary, the Senate Committee on Transportation and Housing, and the Assembly Committee on Transportation, all of the following data:

(a) Number of citations issued for parking violations.

(b) Number of violations contested, and the final disposition of those violations.

(c) Number and percentage of photographs recorded from which notices of parking violations were issued.

(d) Number and percentage of photographs recorded from which no notices of parking violations were recorded.

(e) A summary of any instances in which a person or entity requested a photograph for a purpose unrelated to this article, including information regarding the purpose for which the photograph was requested, whether or not the local public agency provided the photograph, and, if the public agency provided the photograph, to whom the photograph was provided.

(f) The specific procedures that were used for the destruction of license plate readings pursuant to subdivision (a) of Section 40247 and the photographs pursuant to subdivision (d) of Section 40247.

(g) An evaluation of the overall effectiveness of the program.

(h) An evaluation of the privacy implications of the system, including a summary of any privacy-related complaints about the system. *(Added by Stats. 2010, c. 471 (A.B.2567), § 3.)*

Repeal

For repeal of Article 3.6, see Vehicle Code § 40249.5.

§ 40249.5. Duration of article

This article shall remain in effect only until January 1, 2016, and as of that date is repealed, unless a later enacted statute, that is enacted before January 1, 2016, deletes or extends that date. *(Added by Stats. 2010, c. 471 (A.B.2567), § 3.)*

ARTICLE 4. PROCEDURE ON TOLL EVASION VIOLATIONS

Section

40250.	Civil penalties; parties liable; application of article.
40251.	Deposit of toll evasion penalties and fees.
40252.	Issuing agencies may contract for processing of notices of toll evasion violations.
40253.	Processing agencies.
40254.	Notice of toll evasion violations; timeliness; repeat violators; contents.
40255.	Right to contest notice; administrative procedures.
40256.	Appeals.
40257.	Accompanying notice of penalty; contents; payment by mail.
40258.	Penalty schedule.
40259.	Termination of proceedings after payment.
40260.	Delivery of notice of delinquent violation after failure to pay penalty.
40261.	Request for photostatic copy or electronically produced facsimile of original notice; cancellation of notice when vehicle description inconsistent with registration records.
40262.	Information required in notice of delinquent violation.
40262.5.	Failure to pay penalty; liability of registered owner.
40263.	Affidavit of nonliability.
40264.	Return of affidavit; rental agreement or lease.
40265.	Return of affidavit; sale or transfer of vehicle; evidence of transfer.
40266.	Processing of payment of penalties.
40267.	Unpaid toll evasion penalties; collection options.
40268.	Filing of civil judgment.
40269.	Termination of proceedings by processing agency.
40270.	Notice of noncollection; cancellation of notice of delinquency.
40271.	Commencement of civil action; limitations period; tolling.
40272.	Civil liability under § 23302.5 not a conviction or part of driving record or insurance coverage.
40273.	Confidentiality of information obtained from automated devices.

§ 40250. Civil penalties; parties liable; application of article

(a) Except where otherwise specifically provided, a violation of a statute, regulation, or ordinance governing the evasion of tolls on toll facilities under this code, under a federal or state statute or regulation, or under an ordinance enacted by a local authority including a joint powers authority, or a district organized pursuant to Part 3 (commencing with Section 27000) of Division 16 of the Streets and Highways Code is subject to a civil penalty. The enforcement of a civil penalty is governed by the civil administrative procedures set forth in this article.

(b) Except as provided in Section 40264, the registered owner, driver, rentee, or lessee of a vehicle cited for a toll evasion violation of a toll facility, under an applicable statute, regulation, or ordinance shall be jointly and severally liable for the toll evasion penalty imposed under this article, unless the owner can show that the vehicle was used without the express or implied consent of that person. A person who pays a toll evasion penalty, a civil judgment, costs, or administrative fees pursuant to this article has the right to recover the same from the driver, rentee, or lessee.

(c) The driver of a vehicle who is not the vehicle owner but who uses or operates the vehicle with the express or implied permission of the owner is the agent of the owner to receive a notice of a toll evasion violation served in accordance with this article and may contest the notice of violation.

(d) If the driver of the vehicle is in violation of a statute, regulation, or ordinance governing toll evasion violations, and if the driver is arrested pursuant to Article 1 (commencing with Section 40300) of Chapter 2, this article does not apply.

(e) For the purposes of this article, the following definitions apply:

(1) "Issuing agency" is an entity, public or private, authorized to collect tolls.

(2) "Registered owner" is either of the following:

(A) A person described in Section 505.

(B) A person registered as the owner of the vehicle by the appropriate agency or authority of another state, the District of Columbia, or a territory or possession of the United States. *(Added by Stats.1995, c. 739 (A.B.1223), § 8. Amended by Stats.2007, c. 150 (S.B.124), § 1, eff. July 27, 2007.)*

§ 40251. Deposit of toll evasion penalties and fees

All toll evasion penalties collected by the processing agency, as defined in Section 40253, including all administrative fees, process service fees, and fees and collection costs related to civil debt collection, shall be deposited to the account of the issuing agency, except that those sums attributable to the issuance of a toll evasion violation by a member of the California Highway Patrol shall be deposited in accordance with Article 1 (commencing with Section 42200) of Chapter 2 of Division 18 in the city or county where the violation occurred. At the end of each fiscal year, the issuing agencies of facilities which have been developed pursuant to Section 143 of the Streets and Highways Code shall deposit in the State Highway Account in the State Transportation Fund any amounts collected under Section 40253 in excess of the sum of the unpaid toll, administrative fees, other costs incurred by the issuing agency that are related to toll evasion, process service fees, and fees and collection costs related to civil debt collection. *(Added by Stats.1995, c. 739 (A.B.1223), § 8.)*

§ 40252. Issuing agencies may contract for processing of notices of toll evasion violations

(a) An issuing agency may elect to contract with the state, the county, a local authority, or a district organized pursuant to Part 3 (commencing with Section 27000) of Division 16 of the Streets and Highways Code, or with a private vendor, for the processing of notices of toll evasion violations and notices of delinquent toll evasion violations, prior to filing with the court pursuant to Section 40256.

(b) As used in this article, "toll evasion penalty" includes, but is not limited to, any late payment penalty, administrative fee, fine, assessment, and costs of collection as provided by law. *(Added by Stats.1995, c. 739 (A.B.1223), § 8.)*

§ 40253. Processing agencies

If a contract is entered into pursuant to Section 40252, for the purpose of this article, "processing agency" means the party responsible for the processing of the notices of toll evasions and notices of delinquent toll evasions. Absent such contract, "processing agency" shall be synonymous with "issuing agency." *(Added by Stats.1995, c. 739 (A.B.1223), § 8.)*

§ 40254. Notice of toll evasion violations; timeliness; repeat violators; contents

(a) If a vehicle is found, by automated devices, by visual observation, or otherwise, to have evaded tolls on any toll road or toll bridge, and subdivision (d) of Section 40250 does not apply, an issuing agency or a processing agency, as the case may be, shall, within 21 days of the violation, forward to the registered owner a notice of toll evasion violation setting forth the violation, including reference to the section violated, the approximate time thereof, and the location where the violation occurred. If accurate information concerning the identity and address of the registered owner is not available to the processing agency within 21 days of the violation, the processing agency shall have an additional 45 calendar days to obtain such information and forward the notice of toll evasion violation. Where the registered owner is a repeat violator, the processing agency shall forward the notice of toll evasion violation within 90 calendar days of the violation. "Repeat violator" means any registered owner for whom more than five violations have been issued pursuant to this section in any calendar month within the preceding 12-month period. The notice of toll evasion violation shall also set forth the following:

(1) The vehicle license plate number.

(2) If practicable, the registration expiration date and the make of the vehicle.

(3) A clear and concise explanation of the procedures for contesting the violation and appealing an adverse decision pursuant to Sections 40255 and 40256.

(b) Once the authorized person has notified the processing agency of a toll evasion violation, the processing agency shall prepare and forward the notice of violation to the registered owner of the vehicle cited for the violation. Any person, including the authorized person and any member of the person's department or agency, or any peace officer who, with intent to prejudice, damage, or defraud, is found guilty of altering, concealing, modifying, nullifying, or destroying, or causing to be altered, concealed, modified, nullified, or destroyed, the face of the original or any copy of a notice that was retained by the authorized person before it is filed with the processing agency or with a person authorized to receive the deposit of the toll evasion violation is guilty of a misdemeanor.

(c) If, after a copy of the notice of toll evasion violation has been sent to the registered owner, the issuing person determines that, due to a failure of proof of apparent violation, the notice of toll evasion violation should be dismissed, the issuing agency may recommend, in writing, that the charges be dismissed. The recommendation shall cite the reasons for the recommendation and shall be filed with the processing agency.

(d) If the processing agency makes a finding that there are grounds for dismissal, the notice of toll evasion violation shall be canceled pursuant to Section 40255.

(e) Under no circumstances shall a personal relationship with any law enforcement officer, public official, law enforcement agency, processing agency or toll operating agency or entity be grounds for dismissal of the violation.

The processing agency shall use its best efforts to obtain accurate information concerning the identity and address of the registered owner for the purpose of forwarding a notice of toll evasion violation pursuant to subdivision (a). *(Added by Stats.1995, c. 739 (A.B.1223), § 8. Amended by Stats.1996, c. 1154 (A.B.3020), § 85, eff. Sept. 30, 1996; Stats.2002, c. 184 (A.B.2299), § 1.)*

§ 40255. **Right to contest notice; administrative procedures**

(a) Within 21 days from the issuance of the notice of toll evasion violation, or within 15 days from the mailing of the notice of delinquent toll evasion, whichever occurs later, a person may contest a notice of toll evasion violation or a notice of delinquent toll evasion. In that case, the processing agency shall do the following:

(1) The processing agency shall either investigate with its own records and staff or request that the issuing agency investigate the circumstances of the notice with respect to the contestant's written explanation of reasons for contesting the toll evasion violation. If, based upon the results of that investigation, the processing agency is satisfied that the violation did not occur or that the registered owner was not responsible for the violation, the processing agency shall cancel the notice of toll evasion violation and make an adequate record of the reasons for canceling the notice. The processing agency shall mail the results of the investigation to the person who contested the notice of toll evasion violation or the notice of delinquent toll evasion violation.

(2) If the person contesting a notice of toll evasion violation or notice of delinquent toll evasion violation is not satisfied with the results of the investigation provided for in paragraph (1), the person may, within 15 days of the mailing of the results of the investigation, deposit the amount of the toll evasion penalty and request an administrative review. After January 1, 1996, an administrative hearing shall be held within 90 calendar days following the receipt of a request for an administrative hearing, excluding any time tolled pursuant to this article. The person requesting the hearing may request one continuance, not to exceed 21 calendar days.

(b) The administrative review procedure shall consist of the following:

(1) The person requesting an administrative review shall indicate to the processing agency his or her election for a review by mail or personal conference.

(2) If the person requesting an administrative review is a minor, that person shall be permitted to appear at an administrative review or admit responsibility for a toll evasion violation without the necessity of the appointment of a guardian. The processing agency may proceed against that person in the same manner as if that person were an adult.

(3)(A) The administrative review shall be conducted before a reviewer designated to conduct the review by the issuing agency's governing body or chief executive officer. In the case of violations on facilities developed pursuant to Section 143 of the Streets and Highways Code, the processing agency shall contract with a public agency or a private entity that has no financial interest in the facility for the provision of administrative review services pursuant to this subdivision. The costs of those administrative review services shall be included in the administrative fees authorized by this article.

(B) In addition to any other requirements of employment, a reviewer shall demonstrate those qualifications, training, and objectivity prescribed by the issuing agency's governing body or chief executive as are necessary and which are consistent with the duties and responsibilities set forth in this article.

(C) The examiner's continued employment, performance evaluation, compensation, and benefits shall not be directly or indirectly linked to the amount of fines collected by the examiner.

(4) The officer or person authorized to issue a notice of toll evasion violation shall not be required to participate in an administrative review. The issuing agency shall not be required to produce any evidence other than the notice of toll evasion violation or copy thereof, information received from the department identifying the registered owner of the vehicle, and a statement under penalty of perjury from the person reporting the violation. The documentation in proper form shall be considered prima facie evidence of the violation.

(5) For a toll evasion violation that occurs on a vehicular crossing or toll highway where the issuing

agency allows pay-by-plate toll payment, as defined in subdivision (e) of Section 23302, the officer or person authorized to issue a notice of toll evasion violation shall not be required to participate in an administrative review. The issuing agency shall not be required to produce any evidence other than the notice of toll evasion violation or copy thereof, information received from the department identifying the registered owner of the vehicle, and a statement from the officer or person authorized to issue a notice of toll evasion that the tolls or other charges and any applicable fee was not paid in accordance with the issuing agency's policies for pay-by-plate toll payment. Any officer or person who knowingly provides false information pursuant to this paragraph shall be subject to a civil penalty for each violation in the minimum amount of two hundred fifty dollars ($250) up to a maximum amount of two thousand five hundred dollars ($2,500). An action for a civil penalty may be brought by any public prosecutor in the name of the people of the State of California. The documentation in proper form shall be considered prima facie evidence of the violation.

(6) The review shall be conducted in accordance with the written procedure established by the processing agency which shall ensure fair and impartial review of contested toll evasion violations. The agency's final decision may be delivered personally or by first-class mail. *(Added by Stats.1995, c. 739 (A.B.1223), § 8. Amended by Stats.2009, c. 459 (A.B.628), § 3.)*

Cross References

Pay-by-plate toll payments, grace periods, public information, see Vehicle Code § 23301.8.

§ 40256. Appeals

(a) Within 20 days after the mailing of the final decision described in subdivision (b) of Section 40255, the contestant may seek review by filing an appeal to the superior court, where the same shall be heard de novo, except that the contents of the processing agency's file in the case on appeal shall be received in evidence. A copy of the notice of toll evasion violation shall be admitted into evidence as prima facie evidence of the facts stated therein. A copy of the notice of appeal shall be served in person or by first-class mail upon the processing agency by the contestant. For purposes of computing the 20–day period, Section 1013 of the Code of Civil Procedure shall be applicable. A proceeding under this subdivision is a limited civil case.

(b) Notwithstanding Section 72055 of the Government Code, the fee for filing the notice of appeal shall be twenty-five dollars ($25). If the appellant prevails, this fee, together with any deposit of toll evasion penalty, shall be promptly refunded by the processing agency in accordance with the judgment of the court.

(c) The conduct of the hearing on appeal under this section is a subordinate judicial duty which may be performed by commissioners and other subordinate judicial officials at the direction of the presiding judge of the court.

(d) If no notice of appeal of the processing agency's decision is filed within the period set forth in subdivision (a), the decision shall be deemed final.

(e) If the toll evasion penalty has not been deposited and the decision is adverse to the contestant, the processing agency may, promptly after the decision becomes final, proceed to collect the penalty under Section 40267. *(Added by Stats.1995, c. 739 (A.B.1223), § 8. Amended by Stats.1998, c. 931 (S.B.2139), § 460, eff. Sept. 28, 1998; Stats.2002, c. 784 (S.B.1316), § 602.)*

Law Revision Commission Comments
1998 Amendment

Section 40256 is amended to accommodate unification of the municipal and superior courts in a county. Cal. Const. art. VI, § 5(e). The section is also amended to reflect elimination of the justice court. Cal. Const. art. VI, §§ 1, 5(b).

A limited civil case is within the original jurisdiction of the municipal court or of the superior court in a county in which there is no municipal court. Cal. Const. art. VI, 10 (superior court jurisdiction); Code Civ. Proc. §§ 85, 85.1 (limited civil cases). See also Code Civ. Proc. §§ 91, 904.2, 1085 (trial procedures and writ and appellate jurisdiction for limited civil cases). [28 Cal.L.Rev.Comm. Reports 51 (1998)].

2002 Amendment

Subdivision (a) of Section 40256 is amended to reflect unification of the municipal and superior courts pursuant to Article VI, Section 5(e), of the California Constitution.

Subdivision (b) is amended to make clear that the fee for seeking review pursuant to this section is the amount specified in this section ($25), not the usual fee for filing the first paper in a limited civil case. [32 Cal.L.Rev.Comm. Reports 543 (2002)].

§ 40257. Accompanying notice of penalty; contents; payment by mail

The notice of toll evasion violation shall be accompanied by a written notice of the toll evasion penalty due for that violation and the address of the person authorized to receive a deposit of the toll evasion penalty, to whom payments may be sent, and a statement in bold print that payments of the toll evasion penalty for the toll evasion violation may be sent through the mail. *(Added by Stats.1995, c. 739 (A.B.1223), § 8.)*

§ 40258. Penalty schedule

(a) The schedule of toll evasion penalties for toll evasion violations shall be limited to one hundred dollars ($100) for the first violation, two hundred fifty dollars ($250) for a second violation within one year, and five hundred dollars ($500) for each additional violation within one year.

(b) Toll evasion penalties under this article shall be collected as civil penalties. *(Added by Stats.1995, c. 739 (A.B.1223), § 8.)*

§ 40259. Termination of proceedings after payment

If the toll evasion penalty is received by the person authorized to receive the deposit of the toll evasion penalty and there is no contest as to that toll evasion violation, the proceedings under this article shall terminate. *(Added by Stats.1995, c. 739 (A.B.1223), § 8.)*

§ 40260. Delivery of notice of delinquent violation after failure to pay penalty

(a) If the payment of the toll evasion penalty is not received by the person authorized to receive a deposit of the toll evasion penalty by the time and date fixed for appearance on the notice of toll evasion violation under Section 40254, the processing agency shall serve or mail to the registered owner a notice of delinquent toll evasion violation.

(b) Delivery of a notice of delinquent toll evasion violation under this section may be made by personal service or by first-class mail addressed to the registered owner. *(Added by Stats.1995, c. 739 (A.B.1223), § 8.)*

§ 40261. Request for photostatic copy or electronically produced facsimile of original notice; cancellation of notice when vehicle description inconsistent with registration records

(a) Within 10 days from the mailing of a notice of delinquent toll evasion violation, any person or his or her agent, may request by mail or in person a photostatic copy or an electronically produced facsimile of the original notice of toll evasion violation. The issuing agency may charge a fee sufficient to recover the actual cost of providing the copy, not to exceed two dollars ($2). Within 15 days of the request, the processing agency shall mail or otherwise provide the copy. Until the issuing agency complies with a request for a copy of the original notice of toll evasion violation, the processing agency may not proceed pursuant to subdivision (i) of Section 22651, or Section 22651.7 or 40267.

(b) If the description of the vehicle on the notice of toll evasion violation does not match the department's corresponding vehicle registration record, the processing agency may, on written request of the person, cancel the notice of toll evasion violation without the necessity of an appearance by that person. *(Added by Stats.1995, c. 739 (A.B.1223), § 8.)*

§ 40262. Information required in notice of delinquent violation

The notice of delinquent toll evasion violation shall contain the information specified in Section 40254 and, additionally shall contain a notice to the registered owner that, unless the registered owner pays the toll evasion penalty or contests the notice within 15 days after mailing of the notice of delinquent toll evasion violation or completes and files an affidavit of nonliability which complies with Section 40263 or 40264, the renewal of the vehicle registration shall be contingent upon compliance with the notice of delinquent toll evasion violation. If the registered owner, by appearance or by mail, makes payment to the processing agency within 15 days of the mailing of the notice of delinquent toll evasion violation, the toll evasion penalty shall consist of the amount of the original penalty without any additional administrative

fees or charges. *(Added by Stats.1995, c. 739 (A.B.1223), § 8.)*

§ 40262.5. Failure to pay penalty; liability of registered owner

If the registered owner fails to pay the toll evasion penalty, as required in Section 40262, or fails to contest the violation, as provided in Section 40255, the registered owner shall be deemed liable for the violation by operation of law, and the toll evasion penalty and any administrative fees or charges shall be considered a debt due and owing the issuing agency by the registered owner. *(Added by Stats.1995, c. 739 (A.B.1223), § 8.)*

§ 40263. Affidavit of nonliability

The notice of delinquent toll evasion violation shall contain, or be accompanied with, an affidavit of nonliability and information of what constitutes nonliability, information as to the effect of executing the affidavit, and instructions for returning the affidavit to the issuing agency. *(Added by Stats.1995, c. 739 (A.B.1223), § 8.)*

§ 40264. Return of affidavit; rental agreement or lease

If the affidavit of nonliability is returned to the agency within 30 days of the mailing of the notice of toll evasion violation together with the proof of a written rental agreement or lease between a bona fide renting or leasing company and its customer which identifies the rentee or lessee and provides the driver's license number, name, and address of the rentee or lessee, the processing agency shall serve or mail to the rentee or lessee identified in the affidavit of nonliability a notice of delinquent toll evasion violation. If payment is not received within 15 days of the mailing of the notice of delinquent toll evasion violation, the processing agency may proceed against the rentee or lessee pursuant to Section 40267. *(Added by Stats.1995, c. 739 (A.B.1223), § 8.)*

Cross References

Toll evasion violations, civil penalties and parties liable, see Vehicle Code § 40250.

§ 40265. Return of affidavit; sale or transfer of vehicle; evidence of transfer

(a) If the affidavit of nonliability is returned and indicates that the registered owner served has made a bona fide sale or transfer of the vehicle and has delivered possession of the vehicle to the purchaser prior to the date of the alleged violation, the processing agency shall obtain verification from the department that the registered owner has complied with subdivision (b) of Section 5602.

(b) If the registered owner has complied with subdivision (b) of Section 5602, the processing agency shall cancel the notice of toll evasion violation with respect to the registered owner.

(c) If the registered owner has not complied with subdivision (b) of Section 5602, the processing agency shall inform the registered owner that the notice shall be paid in full or contested pursuant to Section 40255 unless the registered owner delivers evidence within 15 days of the notice that establishes that the transfer of ownership and possession of the vehicle occurred prior to the date of the alleged violation. If the registered owner does not comply with this notice, the processing agency shall proceed pursuant to Section 40220. If the registered owner delivers the evidence within 15 days of the notice, the processing agency shall cancel the notice of delinquent toll evasion violation or violations with respect to the registered owner.

(d) For purposes of subdivision (c), evidence sufficient to establish that the transfer of ownership and possession occurred prior to the date of the alleged violation or violations shall include, but is not limited to, a copy of the executed agreement showing the date of the transfer of vehicle ownership.

(e) This section does not limit or impair the ability or the right of the processing agency to pursue the collection of delinquent toll evasion penalties from the person having ownership and possession of the vehicle on the date the alleged violation occurred. *(Added by Stats. 1995, c. 739 (A.B.1223), § 8. Amended by Stats.2008, c. 741 (A.B.2401), § 6.)*

§ 40266. Processing of payment of penalties

(a) If the registered owner, or an agent of the registered owner, or a rentee or lessee who was served with the notice of delinquent toll evasion violation pursuant to Section 40260 or 40264, or any other person who presents the notice of toll evasion violation or notice of delinquent toll evasion violation after the notice of delinquent toll evasion violation has been issued for delivery under Section 40260, deposits that toll evasion violation penalty with a person authorized to receive it, the processing agency shall do both of the following:

(1) Deliver a copy of the notice of delinquent toll evasion violation issued under Section 40260, or a listing of the notice information presented in a notice of delinquent toll evasion violation to the person and record the name, address, and driver's license number of the person actually given the copy in the records of the issuing agency.

For the purposes of this paragraph, a copy of the notice of delinquent toll evasion violation may be a photostatic copy.

(2) Determine whether the notice of delinquent toll evasion violation has been filed with the department pursuant to subdivision (b) of Section 40267 or a civil judgment has been entered pursuant to Section 40267.

(b) If the notice of delinquent toll evasion violation has not been filed with the department or judgment entered and payment of the toll evasion penalty and any applicable assessments is received, the proceedings under this article shall terminate.

(c) If the notice of delinquent toll evasion violation has been filed with the department, has been returned to the processing agency pursuant to subdivision (b) or (c) of Section 4770 or pursuant to Section 4774, and payment of the toll evasion penalty together with the administrative service fee of the processing agency for costs of service and any applicable assessment is received, the proceedings under this article shall terminate.

(d) If the notice of delinquent toll evasion violation has been filed with the department and has not been returned to the processing agency pursuant to Section 4770, 4772, or 4774, and payment of the toll evasion penalty together with the administrative fee of the department established under Section 4773, and administrative service fee of the issuing agency for costs of service, and any applicable assessments is received by the processing agency, the processing agency shall do all of the following:

(1) Immediately transmit the payment information to the department in the manner prescribed by the department.

(2) Terminate proceedings on the notice of delinquent toll evasion violation.

(3) Transmit for deposit all toll evasion penalties and assessments in accordance with law. *(Added by Stats. 1995, c. 739 (A.B.1223), § 8.)*

§ 40267. Unpaid toll evasion penalties; collection options

Except as otherwise provided in Sections 40268 and 40269, the processing agency shall proceed under one or more of the following options to collect an unpaid toll evasion penalty:

(a) The processing agency may file an itemization of unpaid toll evasion penalties and administrative and service fees with the department for collection with the registration of the vehicle pursuant to Section 4770.

(b)(1) If more than four hundred dollars ($400) in unpaid penalties and fees have been accrued by a person or registered owner, the processing agency may file proof of that fact with the court with the same effect as a civil judgment. Execution may be levied and other measures may be taken for the collection of the judgment as are authorized for the collection of an unpaid civil judgment entered against a defendant in an action on a debt. The court may assess costs against a judgment debtor to be paid upon satisfaction of the judgment. The processing agency shall send a notice by first-class mail to the person or registered owner indicating that a judgment shall be entered for the unpaid penalties, fees, and costs and that, after 30 days from the date of the mailing of the notice, the judgment shall have the same effect as an entry of judgment against a judgment debtor. The person or registered owner shall also be notified at that time that execution may be levied against his or her assets, liens may be placed against his or her property, his or her wages may be garnished, and other steps may be taken to satisfy the judgment. The filing fee plus any costs of collection shall be added to the judgment amount.

1051

(2) Notwithstanding any other provision of law, the processing agency shall pay the established first paper civil filing fee, if required by law, at the time an entry of civil judgment is requested.

(c) If the registration of the vehicle has not been renewed for 60 days beyond the renewal date, and the notice has not been collected by the department pursuant to Section 4770, the processing agency may file proof of unpaid penalties and fees with the court with the same effect as a civil judgment as provided in subdivision (b), except that if the amount of the unpaid penalties and fees is not more than four hundred dollars ($400), the filing fee shall be collectible by the court from the debtor.

(d) The issuing agency may contract with a collection agency to collect unpaid toll evasion penalties, fees, and charges.

(e) This section does not apply to the registered owner of a vehicle if the toll evasion violation occurred prior to the registered owner taking possession of the vehicle and the department has notified the processing agency pursuant to Section 4774. *(Added by Stats.1995, c. 739 (A.B.1223), § 8. Amended by Stats.2008, c. 741 (A.B. 2401), § 7.)*

§ 40268. Filing of civil judgment

The processing agency shall not file a civil judgment with the court relating to a toll evasion violation which has been filed with the department unless the processing agency has determined that the registration of the vehicle has not been renewed for 60 days beyond the renewal date and the notice has not been collected by the department pursuant to Section 4770. *(Added by Stats. 1995, c. 739 (A.B.1223), § 8.)*

§ 40269. Termination of proceedings by processing agency

(a) The processing agency shall terminate proceedings on the notice of a delinquent toll evasion violation in any of the following cases:

(1) Upon receipt of collected penalties and administrative fees remitted by the department under Section 4772 for that notice of delinquent toll evasion violation. The termination under this subdivision is by satisfaction of the toll evasion penalty.

(2) If the notice of delinquent toll evasion violation was returned to the processing agency pursuant to Section 4774 and five years have elapsed since the date of the violation. The termination under this subdivision is by the running of a statute of limitation of proceedings.

(3) The processing agency receives information, which it shall verify with the department, that the penalty has been paid to the department pursuant to Section 4772.

(4) If the registered owner of the vehicle provides proof to the processing agency that he or she was not the registered owner on the date of the toll evasion violation.

(b) This section does not limit or impair the ability or the right of the processing agency to pursue the collection of delinquent toll evasion penalties from the person who was the registered owner or lessee of the vehicle on the date of the alleged toll evasion violation. *(Added by Stats.1995, c. 739 (A.B.1223), § 8. Amended by Stats. 2008, c. 741 (A.B.2401), § 8.)*

§ 40270. Notice of noncollection; cancellation of notice of delinquency

If the notice of delinquent toll evasion violation is filed with the department pursuant to subdivision (b) of Section 40267 and the department returns the notice of delinquent toll evasion violation by notice of noncollection pursuant to subdivision (b) of Section 4770 or Section 4774, the processing agency may cancel the notice of delinquent toll evasion violation. *(Added by Stats. 1995, c. 739 (A.B.1223), § 8.)*

§ 40271. Commencement of civil action; limitations period; tolling

The time limitation provided by law for commencement of a civil action for a violation specified in Section 40250 shall be tolled from and after the date a notice of delinquent toll evasion violation is filed with the department pursuant to subdivision (b) of Section 40267 until the notice is returned to the processing agency under subdivision (b) of Section 4770, or Section 4772 or 4774, or is recalled by the processing agency pursuant to subdivision (b) of Section 40255. *(Added by Stats.1995, c. 739 (A.B.1223), § 8.)*

§ 40272. Civil liability under § 23302.5 not a conviction or part of driving record or insurance coverage

Notwithstanding any other provision of law, an imposition of civil liability for a violation of Section 23302.5 shall not be deemed a conviction of a driver, rentee, lessee, or registered owner and shall not be made part of the driving record of the person upon whom that liability is imposed, nor shall it be used for insurance purposes in connection with the provision of motor vehicle insurance coverage. *(Added by Stats.1995, c. 739 (A.B.1223), § 8.)*

§ 40273. Confidentiality of information obtained from automated devices

Any information obtained pursuant to this article through the use of automated devices shall not be used for any purpose other than to identify, and obtain the mailing address information of, either of the following:

(a) Toll evasion violators, to facilitate the serving of notices of toll evasion violations and notices of delinquent toll evasion violations.

(b) Persons entering a vehicular crossing and toll highway where pay-by-plate toll payment, as defined in Section 23302, is permitted by the toll operator to facilitate the collection of tolls. *(Added by Stats.1995, c. 739 (A.B.1223), § 8. Amended by Stats.2009, c. 459 (A.B.628), § 4.)*

CHAPTER 2. PROCEDURE ON ARRESTS

Article	Section
1. Arrests	40300
2. Release Upon Promise to Appear	40500
3. Notice of Violation	40600
4. Notice to Correct Violation	40610

Cross References

Accusatory pleadings in electronic form, conditions for authorization, and notice to appear, see Penal Code § 959.1.

ARTICLE 1. ARRESTS

Section
40300. Application of chapter.
40300.2. Commercial motor vehicles; indication on complaints or notices.
40300.5. Arrest without warrant.
40300.6. Liberal interpretation of § 40300.5 required.
40301. Procedure.
40302. Mandatory appearance.
40302.5. Traffic infraction cases; custody of person under age 18.
40303. Optional appearance before a magistrate; procedure for contesting charge on basis that person charged is other than person issued notice to appear.
40303.5. Notice to correct violations; offenses; conditions.
40304. Discretionary procedure.
40304.5. Failure to appear on citation for parking offense or traffic infraction; deposit of bail; booking, photographing, fingerprinting and arrest record; requirements.
40305. Offense by nonresident; procedure where charge is contested on basis that charged person is other than person issued notice to appear.
40305.5. Nonresidents; offenses while driving commercially registered motor vehicles; guaranteed traffic arrest bail bond certificate in lieu of proceedings; contents; procedures where charge is contested by charged person claiming to be other than person issued notice to appear.
40306. Misdemeanor and infraction procedure before magistrate.
40307. Magistrate unavailable.
40308. Repealed.
40309. Mailing of parking penalty payment.
40309.5. Repealed.
40310. Adoption of uniform traffic penalty schedule; maximum penalty; notice of assessment; payment.
40311. Arraignment for other violations.
40312. Payment of fines; receipts; arrest for outstanding warrants prohibited.
40313. Notice of reexamination issued arrested person; notation and record.

Cross References

Safety roadside rests, refuse disposal violations, see Streets and Highways Code § 224.

Toll evasion violations, civil penalties and parties liable, see Vehicle Code § 40250.

§ 40300. Application of chapter

The provisions of this chapter shall govern all peace officers in making arrests for violations of this code without a warrant for offenses committed in their presence, but the procedure prescribed herein shall not otherwise be exclusive of any other method prescribed by law for the arrest and prosecution of a person for an offense of like grade. *(Stats.1959, c. 3, p. 1774, § 40300.)*

Cross References

Arrest without warrant by peace officer, see Penal Code §§ 836, 849.

Powers and duties of peace officers generally, see Penal Code § 830 et seq.

§ 40300.2. Commercial motor vehicles; indication on complaints or notices

Whenever a person is arrested for a violation of this code, or a violation of any other statute required to be reported under Section 1803, the written complaint, notice to appear in court, or other notice of violation, shall indicate whether the vehicle involved in the offense is a commercial motor vehicle, as defined in subdivision (b) of Section 15210. *(Added by Stats.1988, c. 1509, § 10.)*

§ 40300.5. Arrest without warrant

In addition to the authority to make an arrest without a warrant pursuant to paragraph (1) of subdivision (a) of Section 836 of the Penal Code, a peace officer may, without a warrant, arrest a person when the officer has reasonable cause to believe that the person had been driving while under the influence of an alcoholic beverage or any drug, or under the combined influence of an alcoholic beverage and any drug when any of the following exists:

(a) The person is involved in a traffic accident.

(b) The person is observed in or about a vehicle that is obstructing a roadway.

(c) The person will not be apprehended unless immediately arrested.

(d) The person may cause injury to himself or herself or damage property unless immediately arrested.

(e) The person may destroy or conceal evidence of the crime unless immediately arrested. *(Added by Stats.1969, c. 956, p. 1904, § 1. Amended by Stats.1977, c. 16, p. 28, § 1; Stats.1982, c. 53, p. 179, § 42, eff. Feb. 18, 1982; Stats.1984, c. 722, § 1; Stats.1996, c. 1078 (S.B.1379), § 6.)*

Cross References

Driving while under the influence of alcohol or drugs, see Vehicle Code §§ 23152, 23153.

Peace officers, arrest without warrant, see Penal Code § 836.

§ 40300.6. Liberal interpretation of § 40300.5 required

Section 40300.5 shall be liberally interpreted to further safe roads and the control of driving while under the influence of an alcoholic beverage or any drug in order to permit arrests to be made pursuant to that section within a reasonable time and distance away from the scene of a traffic accident.

The enactment of this section during the 1985–86 Regular Session of the Legislature does not constitute a change in, but is declaratory of, the existing law. *(Added by Stats.1986, c. 584, § 1.)*

§ 40301. Procedure

Except as provided in this chapter, whenever a person is arrested for any violation of this code declared to be a felony, he shall be dealt with in like manner as upon arrest for the commission of any other felony. *(Stats. 1959, c. 3, p. 1774, § 40301.)*

Cross References

Driving offenses, see Vehicle Code § 23103 et seq.
Felony defined, see Penal Code § 17.

§ 40302. Mandatory appearance

Whenever any person is arrested for any violation of this code, not declared to be a felony, the arrested person shall be taken without unnecessary delay before a magistrate within the county in which the offense charged is alleged to have been committed and who has jurisdiction of the offense and is nearest or most accessible with reference to the place where the arrest is made in any of the following cases:

(a) When the person arrested fails to present his driver's license or other satisfactory evidence of his identity for examination.

(b) When the person arrested refuses to give his written promise to appear in court.

(c) When the person arrested demands an immediate appearance before a magistrate.

(d) When the person arrested is charged with violating Section 23152. *(Stats.1959, c. 3, p. 1774, § 40302. Amended by Stats.1963, c. 1341, p. 2864, § 1; Stats.1968, c. 647, p. 1332, § 1; Stats.1971, c. 1530, p. 3028, § 21, operative May 3, 1972; Stats.1982, c. 53, p. 179, § 43, eff. Feb. 18, 1982.)*

Cross References

Acceptance of bail by magistrate's clerk or officer in charge of jail, see Vehicle Code § 40307.
Driving offenses, see Vehicle Code § 23103 et seq.
Infractions, release procedures, see Penal Code § 853.5.
Option of arresting officer to take person immediately before magistrate, see Vehicle Code § 40303.
Reasons for nonrelease after arrest, see Penal Code § 853.6.

§ 40302.5. Traffic infraction cases; custody of person under age 18

Whenever any person under the age of 18 years is taken into custody in connection with any traffic infraction case, and he is not taken directly before a magistrate, he shall be delivered to the custody of the probation officer. Unless sooner released, the probation officer shall keep the minor in the juvenile hall pending his appearance before a magistrate. When a minor is cited for an offense not involving the driving of a motor vehicle, the minor shall not be taken into custody

pursuant to subdivision (a) of Section 40302 solely for failure to present a driver's license. *(Added by Stats.1980, c. 1299, p. 4389, § 2.)*

§ 40303. Optional appearance before a magistrate; procedure for contesting charge on basis that person charged is other than person issued notice to appear

(a) Whenever a person is arrested for any of the offenses listed in subdivision (b) and the arresting officer is not required to take the person without unnecessary delay before a magistrate, the arrested person shall, in the judgment of the arresting officer, either be given a 10 days' notice to appear, or be taken without unnecessary delay before a magistrate within the county in which the offense charged is alleged to have been committed and who has jurisdiction of the offense and is nearest or most accessible with reference to the place where the arrest is made. The officer may require that the arrested person, if he or she does not have satisfactory identification, place a right thumbprint, or a left thumbprint or fingerprint if the person has a missing or disfigured right thumb, on the 10 days' notice to appear when a 10 days' notice is provided. Except for law enforcement purposes relating to the identity of the arrestee, a person or entity shall not sell, give away, allow the distribution of, include in a database, or create a database with, this print.

(b) Subdivision (a) applies to the following offenses:

(1) Section 10852 or 10853, relating to injuring or tampering with a vehicle.

(2) Section 23103 or 23104, relating to reckless driving.

(3) Subdivision (a) of Section 2800, insofar as it relates to a failure or refusal of the driver of a vehicle to stop and submit to an inspection or test of the lights upon the vehicle pursuant to Section 2804, that is punishable as a misdemeanor.

(4) Subdivision (a) of Section 2800, insofar as it relates to a failure or refusal of the driver of a vehicle to stop and submit to a brake test that is punishable as a misdemeanor.

(5) Subdivision (a) of Section 2800, relating to the refusal to submit vehicle and load to an inspection, measurement, or weighing as prescribed in Section 2802 or a refusal to adjust the load or obtain a permit as prescribed in Section 2803.

(6) Subdivision (a) of Section 2800, insofar as it relates to a driver who continues to drive after being lawfully ordered not to drive by a member of the Department of the California Highway Patrol for violating the driver's hours of service or driver's log regulations adopted pursuant to subdivision (a) of Section 34501.

(7) Subdivision (b), (c), or (d) of Section 2800, relating to a failure or refusal to comply with a lawful out-of-service order.

(8) Section 20002 or 20003, relating to duties in the event of an accident.

(9) Section 23109, relating to participating in a speed contest or exhibition of speed.

(10) Section 14601, 14601.1, 14601.2, or 14601.5, relating to driving while the privilege to operate a motor vehicle is suspended or revoked.

(11) When the person arrested has attempted to evade arrest.

(12) Section 23332, relating to persons upon vehicular crossings.

(13) Section 2813, relating to the refusal to stop and submit a vehicle to an inspection of its size, weight, and equipment.

(14) Section 21461.5, insofar as it relates to a pedestrian who, after being cited for a violation of Section 21461.5, is, within 24 hours, again found upon the freeway in violation of Section 21461.5 and thereafter refuses to leave the freeway after being lawfully ordered to do so by a peace officer and after having been informed that his or her failure to leave could result in his or her arrest.

(15) Subdivision (a) of Section 2800, insofar as it relates to a pedestrian who, after having been cited for a violation of subdivision (a) of Section 2800 for failure to obey a lawful order of a peace officer issued pursuant to Section 21962, is within 24 hours again found upon the bridge or overpass and thereafter refuses to leave after being lawfully ordered to do so by a peace officer and after having been informed that his or her failure to leave could result in his or her arrest.

(16) Section 21200.5, relating to riding a bicycle while under the influence of an alcoholic beverage or a drug.

(17) Section 21221.5, relating to operating a motorized scooter while under the influence of an alcoholic beverage or a drug.

(c)(1) A person contesting a charge by claiming under penalty of perjury not to be the person issued the notice to appear may choose to submit a right thumbprint, or a left thumbprint if the person has a missing or disfigured right thumb, to the issuing court through his or her local law enforcement agency for comparison with the one placed on the notice to appear. A local law enforcement agency providing this service may charge the requester no more than the actual costs. The issuing court may refer the thumbprint submitted and the notice to appear to the prosecuting attorney for comparison of the thumbprints. When there is no thumbprint or fingerprint on the notice to appear, or when the comparison of thumbprints is inconclusive, the court shall refer the notice to appear or copy thereof back to the issuing agency for further investigation, unless the court finds that referral is not in the interest of justice.

(2) Upon initiation of the investigation or comparison process by referral of the court, the court shall continue the case and the speedy trial period shall be tolled for 45 days.

(3) Upon receipt of the issuing agency's or prosecuting attorney's response, the court may make a finding of factual innocence pursuant to Section 530.6 of the Penal Code if the court determines that there is insufficient evidence that the person cited is the person charged and shall immediately notify the Department of Motor Vehicles of its determination. If the Department of Motor Vehicles determines the citation or citations in question formed the basis of a suspension or revocation of the person's driving privilege, the department shall immediately set aside the action.

(4) If the prosecuting attorney or issuing agency fails to respond to a court referral within 45 days, the court shall make a finding of factual innocence pursuant to Section 530.6 of the Penal Code, unless the court finds that a finding of factual innocence is not in the interest of justice.

(5) The citation or notice to appear may be held by the prosecuting attorney or issuing agency for future adjudication should the arrestee who received the citation or notice to appear be found. *(Stats.1959, c. 3, p. 1775, § 40303. Amended by Stats.1959, c. 1996, p. 4639, § 48.5; Stats.1961, c. 63, p. 1034, § 1; Stats.1967, c. 236, p. 1372, § 7; Stats.1967, c. 253, p. 1403, § 8; Stats.1967, c. 607, p. 1957, § 2; Stats.1968, c. 1195, p. 2270, § 6; Stats.1969, c. 517, p. 1126, § 1; Stats.1975, c. 759, p. 1770, § 1; Stats.1976, c. 1082, p. 4905, § 1; Stats.1980, c. 680, p. 2064, § 4; Stats.1981, c. 675, p. 2470, § 3; Stats.1982, c. 53, p. 179, § 44, eff. Feb. 18, 1982; Stats.1985, c. 1013, § 5; Stats.1992, c. 468 (A.B.2617), § 2; Stats.1999, c. 724 (A.B.1650), § 52; Stats.2000, c. 860 (A.B.2908), § 14; Stats.2003, c. 467 (S.B.752), § 4; Stats.2006, c. 288 (A.B.3011), § 19.)*

Cross References

Acceptance of bail by magistrate's clerk or officer in charge of jail, see Vehicle Code § 40307.

Infractions, release procedures, see Penal Code § 853.5.

Reasons for nonrelease after arrest, see Penal Code § 853.6.

§ 40303.5. Notice to correct violations; offenses; conditions

Whenever any person is arrested for any of the following offenses, the arresting officer shall permit the arrested person to execute a notice containing a promise to correct the violation in accordance with the provisions of Section 40610 unless the arresting officer finds that any of the disqualifying conditions specified in subdivision (b) of Section 40610 exist:

(a) Any registration infraction set forth in Division 3 (commencing with Section 4000).

(b) Any driver's license infraction set forth in Division 6 (commencing with Section 12500), and subdivision (a) of Section 12951, relating to possession of driver's license.

(c) Section 21201, relating to bicycle equipment.

(d) Any infraction involving equipment set forth in Division 12 (commencing with Section 24000), Division 13 (commencing with Section 29000), Division 14.8 (commencing with Section 34500), Division 16 (commencing with Section 36000), Division 16.5 (commencing with Section 38000), and Division 16.7 (commencing with Section 39000). *(Added by Stats.1978, c. 1350, p. 4479, § 2, operative July 1, 1979. Amended by Stats.1979, c. 71, p. 173, § 1, eff. May 19, 1979; Stats.1981, c. 774, p. 3026, § 13; Stats.1984, c. 915, § 1, operative July 1, 1985; Stats.1989, c. 729, § 3, operative July 1, 1990; Stats.1992, c. 258 (S.B.133), § 4.)*

Cross References

Dismissal of charge on proof of correction, see Vehicle Code § 40522.

Nonresident defined, see Vehicle Code § 435.

Notice to appear, dismissal upon proof of correction, see Vehicle Code § 40522.

§ 40304. Discretionary procedure

Whenever any person is arrested by any member of the California Highway Patrol for any violation of any state law regulating the operation of vehicles or the use of the highways declared to be a misdemeanor but which offense is not specified in this code, he shall, in the judgment of the arresting officer, either be given a 10-day notice to appear in the manner provided in this chapter or be taken without unnecessary delay before a magistrate within the county in which the offense charged is alleged to have been committed and who has jurisdiction of the offense and is nearest or most accessible with reference to the place where the arrest is made, or, upon demand of the person arrested, before a magistrate in the judicial district in which the offense is alleged to have been committed. *(Stats.1959, c. 3, p. 1775, § 40304.)*

Cross References

Misdemeanor defined, see Penal Code § 17.

§ 40304.5. Failure to appear on citation for parking offense or traffic infraction; deposit of bail; booking, photographing, fingerprinting and arrest record; requirements

Notwithstanding any other provision of law, whenever any person is taken into custody for bail to be collected on two or fewer outstanding warrants for failure to appear on a citation for a parking offense or a traffic infraction, the person shall be provided the opportunity immediately to post bail, and shall not be booked, photographed, or fingerprinted, nor shall an arrest record be made, when the amount of bail required to be paid on the warrant may be ascertained by reference to the face thereof or to a fixed schedule of bail, unless and until all of the following requirements have been exhausted:

(a) If the person has sufficient cash in his or her possession, that person shall be given the opportunity immediately to post bail with the person in charge of the jail or his or her designee.

(b) If the person does not have sufficient cash in his or her possession, that person shall be informed of his or her rights and given the opportunity to do all of the following:

(1) Make not less than three completed telephone calls to obtain bail. The person shall be permitted the use of

1056

the police or sheriff's department telephone to make not less than three completed local or collect long-distance telephone calls to obtain bail.

(2) Have not less than three hours in which to arrange for the deposit of bail. *(Added by Stats.1984, c. 35, § 3, eff. March 8, 1984, operative March 31, 1984.)*

§ 40305. Offense by nonresident; procedure where charge is contested on basis that charged person is other than person issued notice to appear

(a) Whenever a nonresident is arrested for violating any section of this code while driving a motor vehicle and does not furnish satisfactory evidence of identity and an address within this state at which he or she can be located, he or she may, in the discretion of the arresting officer, be taken immediately before a magistrate within the county where the offense charged is alleged to have been committed, and who has jurisdiction over the offense and is nearest or most accessible with reference to the place where the arrest is made. If the magistrate is not available at the time of the arrest and the arrested person is not taken before any other person authorized to receive a deposit of bail, and if the arresting officer does not have the authority or is not required to take the arrested person before a magistrate or other person authorized to receive a deposit of bail by some other provision of law, the officer may require the arrested person, if he or she has no satisfactory identification, to place a right thumbprint, or a left thumbprint or fingerprint if the person has a missing or disfigured right thumb, on the notice to appear as provided in Article 2 (commencing with Section 40500).

Except for law enforcement purposes relating to the identity of the arrestee, no person or entity may sell, give away, allow the distribution of, include in a database, or create a database with, this print.

(b)(1) A person contesting a charge by claiming under penalty of perjury not to be the person issued the notice to appear may choose to submit a right thumbprint, or a left thumbprint if the person has a missing or disfigured right thumb, to the issuing court through his or her local law enforcement agency for comparison with the one placed on the notice to appear. A local law enforcement agency providing this service may charge the requester no more than the actual costs. The issuing court may refer the thumbprint submitted and the notice to appear to the prosecuting attorney for comparison of the thumbprints. When there is no thumbprint or fingerprint on the notice to appear, or when the comparison of thumbprints is inconclusive, the court shall refer the notice to appear or copy thereof back to the issuing agency for further investigation, unless the court finds that referral is not in the interest of justice.

(2) Upon initiation of the investigation or comparison process by referral of the court, the court shall continue the case and the speedy trial period shall be tolled for 45 days.

(3) Upon receipt of the issuing agency's or prosecuting attorney's response, the court may make a finding of factual innocence pursuant to Section 530.6 of the Penal Code if the court determines that there is insufficient evidence that the person cited is the person charged and shall immediately notify the Department of Motor Vehicles of its determination. If the Department of Motor Vehicles determines the citation or citations in question formed the basis of a suspension or revocation of the person's driving privilege, the department shall immediately set aside the action.

(4) If the prosecuting attorney or issuing agency fails to respond to a court referral within 45 days, the court shall make a finding of factual innocence pursuant to Section 530.6 of the Penal Code, unless the court determines that a finding of factual innocence is not in the interest of justice.

(5) The citation or notice to appear may be held by the prosecuting attorney or issuing agency for future adjudication should the arrestee who received the citation or notice to appear be found. *(Stats.1959, c. 3, p. 1776, § 40305. Amended by Stats.1961, c. 314, p. 1357, § 1; Stats.2003, c. 467 (S.B.752), § 5.)*

Cross References

Bail, generally, see Penal Code § 1268 et seq.
Infractions, release procedures, see Penal Code § 853.5.
Nonresident defined, see Vehicle Code § 435.

§ 40305.5. Nonresidents; offenses while driving commercially registered motor vehicles; guaranteed traffic arrest bail bond certificate in lieu of proceedings; contents; procedures where charge is contested by charged person claiming to be other than person issued notice to appear

(a) If a nonresident is arrested for violating this code while driving a commercially registered motor vehicle, excluding house cars, with an unladen weight of 7,000 pounds or more, and does not furnish satisfactory evidence of identity and an address within this state at which he or she can be located, the arresting officer may, in lieu of the procedures set forth in Section 40305, accept a guaranteed traffic arrest bail bond certificate, and the nonresident shall be released from custody upon giving a written promise to appear as provided in Article 2 (commencing with Section 40500). The officer may require the arrested person, if he or she has no satisfactory identification, to place a right thumbprint, or a left thumbprint or fingerprint if the person has a missing or disfigured right thumb, on the notice to appear as provided in Article 2 (commencing with Section 45000). Except for law enforcement purposes relating to the identity of the arrestee, a person or entity shall not sell, give away, allow the distribution of, include in a database, or create a database with, this print.

(b) Every guaranteed traffic arrest bail bond certificate shall contain all of the following information:

(1) The name and address of the surety and of the issuer, if other than the surety.

(2) The name, address, driver's license number and signature of the individual covered by the certificate.

(3) The maximum amount guaranteed.

(4) Exclusions from coverage.

(5) A statement that the issuing company guarantees the appearance of a person to whom a guaranteed traffic arrest bail bond certificate is issued and, in the event of the failure of the person to appear in court at the time of trial, the issuing company shall pay any fine or forfeiture imposed on the person, not to exceed the amount stated on the certificate.

(6) The expiration date of the certificate.

(c) A guaranteed traffic arrest bail bond certificate may be issued by a surety admitted in this state. The certificate may also be issued by an association of motor carriers if all of the following conditions are met:

(1) The association is incorporated, or authorized to do business, in this state.

(2) The association is covered by a guaranteed traffic arrest bail bond issued by a surety admitted in this state.

(3) The association agrees to pay fines or bail assessed against the guaranteed traffic arrest bail bond certificate.

(4) The surety guarantees payment of fines or bail assessed against the guaranteed traffic arrest bail bond certificates issued by the association.

(d) The arresting officer shall file the guaranteed traffic arrest bail bond certificate with the notice to appear required to be filed by Section 40506.

(e) A "guaranteed traffic arrest bail bond certificate" is a document that guarantees the payment of fines or bail assessed against an individual for violation of this code, except driving while under the influence of alcohol or drugs, driving without a license or driving with a suspended or revoked license, operating a motor vehicle without the permission of the owner, or any violation punishable as a felony.

(f) A "guaranteed traffic arrest bail bond" is a bond issued by a surety guaranteeing the obligations of the issuer of guaranteed traffic arrest bail bond certificates. The bond shall be in the amount of fifty thousand dollars ($50,000) and shall be filed with the Secretary of State. Any court in this state may assess against the surety the amount of covered fines or bail that the issuer of a guaranteed traffic arrest bail bond certificate fails to pay.

(g)(1) A person contesting a charge by claiming under penalty of perjury not to be the person issued the notice to appear may choose to submit a right thumbprint, or a left thumbprint if the person has a missing or disfigured right thumb, to the issuing court through his or her local law enforcement agency for comparison with the one placed on the notice to appear. A local law enforcement agency providing this service may charge the requester no more than the actual costs. The issuing court may refer

1057

the thumbprint submitted and the notice to appear to the prosecuting attorney for comparison of the thumbprints. If there is no thumbprint or fingerprint on the notice to appear or the comparison of thumbprints is inconclusive, the court shall refer the notice to appear or copy of the notice to appear back to the issuing agency for further investigation, unless the court finds that referral is not in the interest of justice.

(2) Upon initiation of the investigation or comparison process by referral of the court, the court shall continue the case and the speedy trial period shall be tolled for 45 days.

(3) Upon receipt of the issuing agency's or prosecuting attorney's response, the court may make a finding of factual innocence pursuant to Section 530.6 of the Penal Code if the court determines that there is insufficient evidence that the person cited is the person charged and shall immediately notify the Department of Motor Vehicles of its determination. If the Department of Motor Vehicles determines the citation or citations in question formed the basis of a suspension or revocation of the person's driving privilege, the department shall immediately set aside the action.

(4) If the prosecuting attorney or issuing agency fails to respond to a court referral within 45 days, the court shall make a finding of factual innocence pursuant to Section 530.6 of the Penal Code, unless the court determines that a finding of factual innocence is not in the interest of justice.

(5) The citation or notice to appear may be held by the prosecuting attorney or issuing agency for future adjudication should the arrestee who received the citation or notice to appear be found. *(Added by Stats.1982, c. 1394, p. 5309, § 3. Amended by Stats.2003, c. 467 (S.B.752), § 6; Stats.2011, c. 296 (A.B.1023), § 310.)*

Cross References

Infractions, release procedures, see Penal Code § 853.5.

§ 40306. Misdemeanor and infraction procedure before magistrate

(a) Whenever a person is arrested for a misdemeanor or an infraction and is taken before a magistrate, the arresting officer shall file with the magistrate a complaint stating the offense with which the person is charged.

(b) The person taken before a magistrate shall be entitled to at least five days continuance of his case in which to plead and prepare for trial and the person shall not be required to plead or be tried within the five days unless he waives such time in writing or in open court.

(c) The person taken before a magistrate shall thereupon be released from custody upon his own recognizance or upon such bail as the magistrate may fix. *(Stats.1959, c. 3, p. 1776, § 40306. Amended by Stats. 1968, c. 1192, p. 2262, § 13, operative Jan. 1, 1969.)*

1058

§ 40307. Magistrate unavailable

(a) When an arresting officer attempts to take a person arrested for a misdemeanor or infraction of this code before a magistrate and the magistrate or person authorized to act for him or her is not available, the arresting officer shall take the person arrested, without unnecessary delay, before one of the following:

(1) The clerk of the magistrate, who shall admit the person to bail for the full amount set for the offense in a schedule fixed as provided in Section 1269b of the Penal Code.

(2) The officer in charge of the most accessible county or city jail or other place of detention within the county, who shall admit the person to bail for the full amount set for the offense in a schedule fixed as provided in Section 1269b of the Penal Code or may, in lieu of bail, release the person on his or her written promise to appear as provided in subdivisions (a) to (f), inclusive, of Section 853.6 of the Penal Code.

(b) Whenever a person is taken into custody pursuant to subdivision (a) of Section 40302 and is arrested for a misdemeanor or infraction of this code pertaining to the operation of a motor vehicle, the officer in charge of the most accessible county or city jail or other place of detention within the county may detain the person arrested for a reasonable period of time, not to exceed two hours, in order to verify his or her identity. *(Stats. 1959, c. 3, p. 1776, § 40307. Amended by Stats.1968, c. 1192, p. 2262, § 14, operative Jan. 1, 1969; Stats.1970, c. 753, p. 1433, § 1; Stats.1971, c. 1528, p. 3019, § 1, operative May 3, 1972; Stats.1974, c. 593, p. 1419, § 1; Stats.2007, c. 738 (A.B.1248), § 44.)*

Cross References

Bail, generally, see Penal Code § 1268 et seq.

§ 40308. Repealed by Stats.1959, c. 1996, p. 4640, § 49

§ 40309. Mailing of parking penalty payment

Whenever a notice of parking violation is issued in accordance with Sections 40202 and 40203, or a notice of delinquent parking violation is issued pursuant to Section 40206, the amount fixed as a parking penalty for the violation charged may be forwarded by United States mail to the person authorized to receive a deposit of the parking penalty. Payment of a parking penalty forwarded by mail is effective only when actually received, and the presumption that a letter duly directed and mailed was received does not apply. Section 40512 is applicable to a parking penalty posted pursuant to this section. *(Added by Stats.1960, 1st Ex.Sess., c. 40, p. 384, § 1. Amended by Stats.1986, c. 939, § 16.)*

§ 40309.5. Repealed by Stats.1986, c. 939, § 17

§ 40310. Adoption of uniform traffic penalty schedule; maximum penalty; notice of assessment; payment

The Judicial Council shall annually adopt a uniform traffic penalty schedule which shall be applicable to all nonparking infractions specified in this code, unless in a particular case before the court the judge or authorized hearing officer specifies a different penalty. No penalty shall be established for any infraction in an amount, exclusive of any additional penalty levied pursuant to Section 1464 of the Penal Code, in excess of the amount of the maximum fine pursuant to Section 42001 or 42001.5, and penalties shall be set without regard to residence. In case a traffic penalty is not paid within 20 days following mailing of a notice that the penalty has been assessed, a late charge shall be due in the amount of 50 percent of total initial penalty.

In establishing a uniform traffic penalty schedule, the Judicial Council shall classify the offenses into four or fewer penalty categories, according to the severity of offenses, so as to permit convenient notice and payment of the scheduled penalty. *(Added by Stats.1980, c. 618, p. 1702, § 2. Amended by Stats.1986, c. 953, § 13; Stats. 1992, c. 696 (A.B.1344), § 93, eff. Sept. 15, 1992.)*

Cross References

Penalties, public offenses, fines in misdemeanor cases for violations pertaining to passing school buildings or grounds, see Vehicle Code § 42011.

§ 40311. Arraignment for other violations

Whenever a person is arrested under authority of a warrant, the court to which such person is taken shall, with his consent, have jurisdiction to arraign him at that time for any other alleged violation of this code or an ordinance relating to traffic offenses for which he has been issued a written notice to appear in court, notwithstanding the fact that the time for appearance specified in such notice has not yet arrived. *(Added by Stats.1959, c. 977, p. 3006, § 1.)*

§ 40312. Payment of fines; receipts; arrest for outstanding warrants prohibited

A peace officer shall not arrest, on the basis of an outstanding warrant arising from a violation of this code, any person who presents to the peace officer a receipt, from a proper official of the court, indicating that the person has paid the fine for the violation that caused the warrant to be issued. The receipt shall contain sufficient information to identify the name and number of the court issuing the receipt, the date the case was adjudicated or the fine was paid, the case number or docket number, and the violations disposed of. *(Added by Stats.1982, c. 290, p. 930, § 1.)*

§ 40313. Notice of reexamination issued arrested person; notation and record

If a notice of reexamination was issued pursuant to Section 21061, the record of arrest for the traffic violation, or any notice to appear issued under this article, or both, shall include a notation indicating that the notice of reexamination was issued to the arrested person and the driver's license record maintained by the department shall contain a record of the notice of reexamination.

The record of the notice of reexamination shall be considered confidential by the department pursuant to Section 1808.5. *(Added by Stats.1986, c. 304, § 5, operative July 1, 1987.)*

ARTICLE 2. RELEASE UPON PROMISE TO APPEAR

Section
40500. Notice to appear; form; bail; delivery; alteration or destruction of notice before filing; arresting agency recommendation that case be dismissed; contest of charge by charged person claiming to be other than person issued notice to appear.
40501. Time to appear.
40502. Place to appear.
40502.1. Repealed.
40503. Speed charge.
40504. Delivery of notice; promise to appear; evidence of identification; use of false or fictitious name; procedure for contest of charge where charged person claims to be other than person issued notice to appear.
40505. Copy of notice.
40506. Filing copies.
40506.5. Request for continuance; authorization.
40507. Appearance by counsel.
40508. Promise to appear; fine payment; court order condition; violations; driver's license impoundment.
40508.5. Violations of promises to appear or specified court orders; assessments.
40508.6. Administrative assessments for costs; record of prior convictions for vehicle code violations; notice of attachments or restrictions of drivers license or automobile registration.
40509. Notice of violations; certification of satisfaction; application of section.
40509.1. Notice of willful failure to comply with certain court orders.
40509.5. Notice of violations; criteria for arrest warrants; election by court to notify; application of section; exception.
40510. Deposit of bail or parking penalty; payment by personal check; agency policy.
40510.5. Payment and forfeiture of bail; circumstances.
40511. Fixing bail.
40512. Forfeiture of bail; guaranteed traffic arrest bail bond certificates.
40512.5. Optional bail forfeiture.
40512.6. Failure to submit proof of completion of traffic violators school; forfeiture of bail.
40513. Filing of notice in lieu of complaint.
40514. Issuance of warrant.
40515. Issuance of warrant for violation of promise to appear or continuance of promise to appear.
40516. Expense to departments.
40517. Repealed.
40518. Certain violations recorded by automated traffic enforcement system; notice to appear; contents; notice of nonliability; form; dismissal.
40519. Trial scheduling; written not guilty plea.
40520. Automatic enforcement system violation; notice to appear; affidavit of nonliability.
40521. Forfeiture of bail; payment of assessments.

Section
40522.   Notice; registration, license or mechanical violations; dismissal on proof of correction.

Cross References

Conduct of hearing upon copy of notice to appear in lieu of
petition where minor is charged with traffic offense, see
Welfare and Institutions Code § 257.
Immobilization of vehicles, notice to appear, see Vehicle Code
§ 22651.7.
Nonresidents, offenses while driving commercially registered
motor vehicles, guaranteed traffic arrest bail bond certifi-
cate in lieu of proceedings, see Vehicle Code § 40305.5.
Notice of violation, reasonable cause for issuance, see Vehicle
Code § 40600.
Offense by nonresident, see Vehicle Code § 40305.
Registration, license or mechanical violations, conditions for use,
see Vehicle Code § 40610.

**§ 40500.   Notice to appear; form; bail; delivery; alter-
ation or destruction of notice before filing; arresting
agency recommendation that case be dismissed;
contest of charge by charged person claiming to be
other than person issued notice to appear**

(a) Whenever a person is arrested for any violation of
this code not declared to be a felony, or for a violation of
an ordinance of a city or county relating to traffic offenses
and he or she is not immediately taken before a
magistrate, as provided in this chapter, the arresting
officer shall prepare in triplicate a written notice to
appear in court or before a person authorized to receive a
deposit of bail, containing the name and address of the
person, the license number of his or her vehicle, if any,
the name and address, when available, of the registered
owner or lessee of the vehicle, the offense charged and
the time and place when and where he or she shall
appear. If the arrestee does not have a driver's license or
other satisfactory evidence of identity in his or her
possession, the officer may require the arrestee to place a
right thumbprint, or a left thumbprint or fingerprint if the
person has a missing or disfigured right thumb, on the
notice to appear. Except for law enforcement purposes
relating to the identity of the arrestee, no person or entity
may sell, give away, allow the distribution of, include in a
database, or create a database with, this print.

(b) The Judicial Council shall prescribe the form of
the notice to appear.

(c) Nothing in this section requires the law enforcement agency or the arresting officer issuing the notice to
appear to inform any person arrested pursuant to this
section of the amount of bail required to be deposited for
the offense charged.

(d) Once the arresting officer has prepared the written
notice to appear, and has delivered a copy to the arrested
person, the officer shall deliver the remaining original
and all copies of the notice to appear as provided by
Section 40506.

Any person, including the arresting officer and any
member of the officer's department or agency, or any
peace officer, who alters, conceals, modifies, nullifies, or

1060

destroys, or causes to be altered, concealed, modified,
nullified, or destroyed, the face side of the remaining
original or any copy of a citation that was retained by the
officer, for any reason, before it is filed with the
magistrate or with a person authorized by the magistrate
or judge to receive a deposit of bail, is guilty of a
misdemeanor.

If, after an arrested person has signed and received a
copy of a notice to appear, the arresting officer or other
officer of the issuing agency, determines that, in the
interest of justice, the citation or notice should be
dismissed, the arresting agency may recommend, in
writing, to the magistrate or judge that the case be
dismissed. The recommendation shall cite the reasons
for the recommendation and be filed with the court.

If the magistrate or judge makes a finding that there
are grounds for dismissal, the finding shall be entered on
the record and the infraction or misdemeanor dismissed.

Under no circumstances shall a personal relationship
with any officer, public official, or law enforcement
agency be grounds for dismissal.

(e)(1) A person contesting a charge by claiming under
penalty of perjury not to be the person issued the notice
to appear may choose to submit a right thumbprint, or a
left thumbprint if the person has a missing or disfigured
right thumb, to the issuing court through his or her local
law enforcement agency for comparison with the one
placed on the notice to appear. A local law enforcement
agency providing this service may charge the requester no
more than the actual costs. The issuing court may refer
the thumbprint submitted and the notice to appear to the
prosecuting attorney for comparison of the thumbprints.
When there is no thumbprint or fingerprint on the notice
to appear, or when the comparison of thumbprints is
inconclusive, the court shall refer the notice to appear or
copy thereof back to the issuing agency for further
investigation, unless the court determines that referral is
not in the interest of justice.

(2) Upon initiation of the investigation or comparison
process by referral of the court, the court shall continue
the case and the speedy trial period shall be tolled for 45
days.

(3) Upon receipt of the issuing agency's or prosecuting
attorney's response, the court may make a finding of
factual innocence pursuant to Section 530.6 of the Penal
Code if the court determines that there is insufficient
evidence that the person cited is the person charged and
shall immediately notify the Department of Motor Vehicles of its determination. If the Department of Motor
Vehicles determines the citation or citations in question
formed the basis of a suspension or revocation of the
person's driving privilege, the department shall immediately set aside the action.

(4) If the prosecuting attorney or issuing agency fails
to respond to a court referral within 45 days, the court
shall make a finding of factual innocence pursuant to
Section 530.6 of the Penal Code, unless the court

determines that a finding of factual innocence is not in the interest of justice.

(5) The citation or notice to appear may be held by the prosecuting attorney or issuing agency for future adjudication should the arrestee who received the citation or notice to appear be found. *(Stats.1959, c. 3, p. 1777, § 40500. Amended by Stats.1961, c. 58, p. 1016, § 68; Stats.1965, c. 1052, p. 2691, § 1, operative July 1, 1966; Stats.1975, c. 1257, p. 3295, § 1; Stats.1987, c. 72, § 4, eff. June 30, 1987; Stats.1995, c. 93 (A.B.219), § 3; Stats. 2003, c. 467 (S.B.752), § 7.)*

Cross References

Acceptance by municipal court commissioner or traffic referee, see Government Code § 72304.

Arrest of persons engaged in speed contests or reckless driving, removal and seizure of vehicles, see Vehicle Code § 23109.2.

Bail, generally, see Penal Code § 1268 et seq.

Driving under the influence, arrest of person with prior DUI conviction, impoundment of vehicle, see Vehicle Code § 22651.10.

Inapplicability of forfeiture of bail provisions of Penal Code to cases arising under this section, see Penal Code § 1306.1.

Procedure for bail of nonresidents, see Vehicle Code § 40305.

Procedure on equipment violations, see Vehicle Code § 40150 et seq.

Trials, documentary evidence of infractions, see Vehicle Code § 40901.

Trials by written declaration, see Vehicle Code § 40902.

§ 40501. Time to appear

(a) The time specified in the notice to appear shall be a specific date which is at least 21 days after the arrest, except that the court having jurisdiction over the offense charged may authorize the arresting officer to specify on the notice that an appearance may be made before the time specified.

(b) In the case of juveniles, the court having jurisdiction over the offense charged may require the arresting officer to indicate on the notice "to be notified" rather than specifying a specific date pursuant to subdivision (a). *(Stats.1959, c. 3, p. 1777, § 40501. Amended by Stats. 1985, c. 1289, § 2; Stats.1986, c. 557, § 1, eff. Aug. 22, 1986.)*

§ 40502. Place to appear

The place specified in the notice to appear shall be any of the following:

(a) Before a magistrate within the county in which the offense charged is alleged to have been committed and who has jurisdiction of the offense and is nearest or most accessible with reference to the place where the arrest is made.

(b) Upon demand of the person arrested, before a judge or other magistrate having jurisdiction of the offense at the county seat of the county in which the offense is alleged to have been committed. This subdivision applies only if the person arrested resides, or the person's principal place of employment is located, closer to the county seat than to the magistrate nearest or most accessible to the place where the arrest is made.

(c) Before a person authorized to receive a deposit of bail.

The clerk and deputy clerks of the superior court are persons authorized to receive bail in accordance with a schedule of bail approved by the judges of that court.

(d) Before the juvenile court, a juvenile court referee, or a juvenile hearing officer within the county in which the offense charged is alleged to have been committed, if the person arrested appears to be under the age of 18 years. The juvenile court shall by order designate the proper person before whom the appearance is to be made.

In a county that has implemented the provisions of Section 603.5 of the Welfare and Institutions Code, if the offense alleged to have been committed by a minor is classified as an infraction under this code, or is a violation of a local ordinance involving the driving, parking, or operation of a motor vehicle, the citation shall be issued as provided in subdivision (a), (b), or (c); provided, however, that if the citation combines an infraction and a misdemeanor, the place specified shall be as provided in subdivision (d).

If the place specified in the notice to appear is within a county where a department of the superior court is to hold a night session within a period of not more than 10 days after the arrest, the notice to appear shall contain, in addition to the above, a statement notifying the person arrested that the person may appear before a night session of the court. *(Stats.1959, c. 3, p. 1777, § 40502. Amended by Stats.1961, c. 1616, p. 3508, § 6; Stats.1965, c. 1704, p. 3837, § 2; Stats.1965, c. 1705, p. 3838, § 2; Stats.1980, c. 1299, p. 4390, § 3; Stats.1984, c. 400, § 1; Stats.1998, c. 931 (S.B.2139), § 461, eff. Sept. 28, 1998; Stats.2002, c. 784 (S.B.1316), § 603; Stats.2003, c. 149 (S.B.79), § 87.)*

Law Revision Commission Comments
1998 Amendment

Section 40502 is amended to accommodate unification of the municipal and superior courts in a county. Cal. Const. art. VI, § 5(e). *Cf.* Penal Code § 808 (magistrates). In a county in which there is no municipal court, the relevant geographical unit is the county rather than judicial district. *Cf.* Code Civ. Proc. § 38 & Comment ("judicial district" defined). The section is also amended to reflect elimination of the justice court. Cal. Const. art. VI, §§ 1, 5(b). [28 Cal.L.Rev.Comm. Reports 51 (1998)].

2002 Amendment

Section 40502 is amended to reflect unification of the municipal and superior courts pursuant to Article VI, Section 5(e), of the California Constitution. *Cf.* Code Civ. Proc. § 38 (judicial district). [32 Cal.L.Rev.Comm. Reports 544 (2002)].

2003 Amendment

Subdivision (b) of Section 40502 is amended to reflect unification of the municipal and superior courts pursuant to former Section 5(e) of Article VI of the California Constitution.

Subdivision (d) is amended to reflect the redesignation of traffic hearing officers as juvenile hearing officers. See 1997 Cal. Stat. ch. 679. [33 Cal.L.Rev.Comm. Reports 261 (2003)].

Cross References

Minors charged with traffic offense, conduct of hearing on written notice to appear, see Welfare and Institutions Code § 257.

Municipal court commissioner or traffic referee, power to fix bail and endorse it on notice for appearance, see Government Code § 72304.

Renewal of license, refusal for failure to appear in court, see Vehicle Code § 12808.

§ 40502.1. Repealed by Stats.1998, c. 356 (A.B.635), § 2, operative Jan. 1, 2002

§ 40503. Speed charge

Every notice to appear or notice of violation and every complaint or information charging a violation of any provision of this code regulating the speed of vehicles upon a highway shall specify the approximate speed at which the defendant is alleged to have driven and exactly the prima facie or maximum speed limit applicable to the highway at the time and place of the alleged offense and shall state any other speed limit alleged to have been exceeded if applicable to the particular type of vehicle or combination of vehicles operated by the defendant. *(Stats.1959, c. 3, p. 1777, § 40503. Amended by Stats. 1961, c. 917, p. 2544, § 1; Stats.1969, c. 1056, p. 2039, § 1.)*

Cross References

Speed laws in general, see Vehicle Code § 22349 et seq.

§ 40504. Delivery of notice; promise to appear; evidence of identification; use of false or fictitious name; procedure for contest of charge where charged person claims to be other than person issued notice to appear

(a) The officer shall deliver one copy of the notice to appear to the arrested person and the arrested person in order to secure release must give his or her written promise to appear in court or before a person authorized to receive a deposit of bail by signing two copies of the notice which shall be retained by the officer, and the officer may require the arrested person, if this person has no satisfactory identification, to place a right thumbprint, or a left thumbprint or fingerprint if the person has a missing or disfigured right thumb, on the notice to appear. Thereupon, the arresting officer shall forthwith release the person arrested from custody. Except for law enforcement purposes relating to the identity of the arrestee, no person or entity may sell, give away, allow the distribution of, include in a database, or create a database with, this print.

(b) Any person who signs a written promise to appear with a false or fictitious name is guilty of a misdemeanor regardless of the disposition of the charge upon which he or she was originally arrested.

(c)(1) A person contesting a charge by claiming under penalty of perjury not to be the person issued the notice to appear may choose to submit a right thumbprint, or a left thumbprint if the person has a missing or disfigured right thumb, to the issuing court through his or her local law enforcement agency for comparison with the one placed on the notice to appear. A local law enforcement agency providing this service may charge the requester no more than the actual costs. The issuing court may refer the thumbprint submitted and the notice to appear to the prosecuting attorney for comparison of the thumbprints. When there is no thumbprint or fingerprint on the notice to appear, or when the comparison of thumbprints is inconclusive, the court shall refer the notice to appear or copy thereof back to the issuing agency for further investigation, unless the court finds that referral is not in the interest of justice.

(2) Upon initiation of the investigation or comparison process by referral of the court, the court shall continue the case and the speedy trial period shall be tolled for 45 days.

(3) Upon receipt of the issuing agency's or prosecuting attorney's response, the court may make a finding of factual innocence pursuant to Section 530.6 of the Penal Code if the court determines that there is insufficient evidence that the person cited is the person charged and shall immediately notify the Department of Motor Vehicles of its determination. If the Department of Motor Vehicles determines the citation or citations in question formed the basis of a suspension or revocation of the person's driving privilege, the department shall immediately set aside the action.

(4) If the prosecuting attorney or issuing agency fails to respond to a court referral within 45 days, the court shall make a finding of factual innocence pursuant to Section 530.6 of the Penal Code, unless the court finds that a finding of factual innocence is not in the interest of justice.

(5) The citation or notice to appear may be held by the prosecuting attorney or issuing agency for future adjudication should the arrestee who received the citation or notice to appear be found. *(Stats.1959, c. 3, p. 1777, § 40504. Amended by Stats.1963, c. 802, p. 1833, § 1; Stats.1995, c. 93 (A.B.219), § 4; Stats.2003, c. 467 (S.B. 752), § 8.)*

Cross References

Violation a misdemeanor, see Vehicle Code § 40000.25.

§ 40505. Copy of notice

Whenever any traffic or police officer delivers a notice to appear or notice of violation charging an offense under this code to any person, it shall include all information set forth upon the copy of the notice filed with a magistrate and no traffic or police officer shall set forth on any notice filed with a magistrate or attach thereto or accompany the notice with any written statement giving information or containing allegations which have not been delivered to the person receiving the notice to appear or notice of violation. *(Stats.1959, c. 3, p. 1778, § 40505. Amended by Stats.1969, c. 1056, p. 2039, § 2.)*

Cross References

Misdemeanor defined, see Penal Code § 17.

§ 40506. Filing copies

The officer shall, as soon as practicable, file a copy of the notice with the magistrate or before a person authorized by the magistrate or judge to receive a deposit of bail specified therein, and a copy with the commissioner, chief of police, sheriff or other superior officer of the arresting officer. *(Stats.1959, c. 3, p. 1778, § 40506.)*

Cross References

Nonresidents, offenses while driving commercially registered motor vehicles, guaranteed traffic arrest bail bond certificate in lieu of proceedings, see Vehicle Code § 40305.5.

§ 40506.5. Request for continuance; authorization

Prior to the date upon which the defendant promised to appear and without depositing bail, the defendant may request a continuance of the written promise to appear. A judge of the superior court may authorize the clerk to grant the continuance. *(Added by Stats.1979, c. 235, p. 489, § 1. Amended by Stats.1998, c. 931 (S.B.2139), § 462, eff. Sept. 28, 1998; Stats.2002, c. 784 (S.B.1316), § 604.)*

Law Revision Commission Comments

1998 Amendment

Section 40506.5 is amended to accommodate unification of the municipal and superior courts in a county. Cal. Const. art. VI, § 5(e). The section is also amended to reflect elimination of the justice court. Cal. Const. art. VI, 1, 5(b). [28 Cal.L.Rev.Comm. Reports 51 (1998)].

2002 Amendment

Section 40506.5 is amended to reflect unification of the municipal and superior courts pursuant to Article VI, Section 5(e), of the California Constitution. [32 Cal.L.Rev.Comm. Reports 545 (2002)].

§ 40507. Appearance by counsel

A written promise to appear in court may be complied with by an appearance by counsel. *(Stats.1959, c. 3, p. 1778, § 40507.)*

Cross References

Appearance defined, see Code of Civil Procedure § 1014.

§ 40508. Promise to appear; fine payment; court order condition; violations; driver's license impoundment

(a) A person willfully violating his or her written promise to appear or a lawfully granted continuance of his or her promise to appear in court or before a person authorized to receive a deposit of bail is guilty of a misdemeanor regardless of the disposition of the charge upon which he or she was originally arrested.

(b) A person willfully failing to pay bail in installments as agreed to under Section 40510.5 or a lawfully imposed fine for a violation of a provision of this code or a local ordinance adopted pursuant to this code within the time authorized by the court and without lawful excuse having been presented to the court on or before the date the bail or fine is due is guilty of a misdemeanor regardless of the full payment of the bail or fine after that time.

(c) A person willfully failing to comply with a condition of a court order for a violation of this code, other than for failure to appear or failure to pay a fine, is guilty of a misdemeanor, regardless of his or her subsequent compliance with the order.

(d) If a person convicted of an infraction fails to pay bail in installments as agreed to under Section 40510.5, or a fine or an installment thereof, within the time authorized by the court, the court may, except as otherwise provided in this subdivision, impound the person's driver's license and order the person not to drive for a period not to exceed 30 days. Before returning the license to the person, the court shall endorse on the reverse side of the license that the person was ordered not to drive, the period for which that order was made, and the name of the court making the order. If a defendant with a class C or M driver's license satisfies the court that impounding his or her driver's license and ordering the defendant not to drive will affect his or her livelihood, the court shall order that the person limit his or her driving for a period not to exceed 30 days to driving that is essential in the court's determination to the person's employment, including the person's driving to and from his or her place of employment if other means of transportation are not reasonably available. The court shall provide for the endorsement of the limitation on the person's license. The impounding of the license and ordering the person not to drive or the order limiting the person's driving does not constitute a suspension of the license, but a violation of the order constitutes contempt of court. *(Stats.1959, c. 3, p. 1778, § 40508. Amended by Stats. 1961, c. 1653, p. 3608, § 2; Stats.1968, c. 1192, p. 2262, § 15, operative Jan. 1, 1969; Stats.1979, c. 235, p. 489, § 2; Stats.1987, c. 726, § 10, operative July 1, 1988; Stats.1993, c. 272 (A.B.301), § 56, eff. Aug. 2, 1993; Stats.1993, c. 909 (S.B.15), § 16; Stats.2003, c. 451 (A.B.1718), § 21; Stats. 2007, c. 738 (A.B.1248), § 45.)*

Cross References

Bail, payment and forfeiture, see Vehicle Code § 40510.5.
Continuance, see Vehicle Code § 40506.5.
Misdemeanor defined, see Penal Code § 17.
Public offenses, State Amnesty Program, eligible violations of this section, see Vehicle Code § 42008.7.
Refusal to appear, denial of license for, see Vehicle Code § 12807.
Renewal of license, checking record for failure to appear in court, see Vehicle Code § 12808.
Suspension of driver's license for violation of section, see Vehicle Code § 13365.

Violation a misdemeanor, see Vehicle Code § 40000.25.

§ 40508.5.   Violations of promises to appear or specified court orders; assessments

(a) In addition to the fees authorized or required by any other provision of law, a county may, by resolution of the board of supervisors, require the courts of that county to impose an assessment of fifteen dollars ($15) upon every person who violates his or her written promise to appear or a lawfully granted continuance of his or her promise to appear in court or before a person authorized to receive a deposit of bail, or who otherwise fails to comply with any valid court order for a violation of any provision of this code or local ordinance adopted pursuant to this code. This assessment shall apply whether or not a violation of Section 40508 is concurrently charged or a warrant of arrest is issued pursuant to Section 40515.

(b) The courts subject to subdivision (a) shall increase the bail schedule amounts to reflect the amount of the assessment imposed by this section.

(c) If bail is returned, the amount of the assessment shall also be returned, but only if the person did not violate his or her promise to appear or citation following a lawfully granted continuance.

(d) The clerk of the court shall deposit the amounts collected under this section in the county treasury. All money so deposited shall be used first for the development and operation of an automated county warrant system. If sufficient funds are available after appropriate expenditures to develop, modernize, and maintain the automated warrant system, a county may use the balance to fund a warrant service task force for the purpose of serving all bench warrants within the county. *(Added by Stats.1986, c. 151, § 2. Amended by Stats.1992, c. 696 (A.B.1344), § 94, eff. Sept. 15, 1992; Stats.1996, c. 578 (A.B.2069), § 2; Stats.2002, c. 148 (S.B.1754), § 2.)*

Cross References

Violations of promises to appear, assessments, use of funds for automated county warrant system, see Penal Code § 853.7a.

§ 40508.6.   Administrative assessments for costs; record of prior convictions for vehicle code violations; notice of attachments or restrictions of drivers license or automobile registration

The superior court in any county may establish administrative assessments, not to exceed ten dollars ($10), for clerical and administrative costs incurred for the following activities:

(a) An assessment for the cost of recording and maintaining a record of the defendant's prior convictions for violations of this code. The assessment shall be payable at the time of payment of a fine or when bail is forfeited for any subsequent violations of this code other than parking, pedestrian, or bicycle violations.

(b) An assessment for all defendants whose driver's license or automobile registration is attached or restricted pursuant to Section 40509 or 40509.5, to cover the cost of

notifying the Department of Motor Vehicles of the attachment or restriction. *(Added by Stats.1991, c. 651 (S.B.757), § 3. Amended by Stats.1998, c. 931 (S.B.2139), § 463, eff. Sept. 28, 1998; Stats.2002, c. 784 (S.B.1316), § 604.5.)*

Law Revision Commission Comments
1998 Amendment

Section 40508.6 is amended to reflect elimination of the justice court. Cal. Const. art. VI, §§ 1, 5(b). [28 Cal.L.Rev.Comm. Reports 51 (1998)].

2002 Amendment

Section 40508.6 is amended to reflect unification of the municipal and superior courts pursuant to Article VI, Section 5(e), of the California Constitution.

The section is also amended to reflect enactment of the Trial Court Funding Act. See Gov't Code § 77001 (local trial court management).

Cross References

Carry over of unexpended funds by trial courts, funds excluded from calculation of amount authorized to be carried over commencing June 30, 2014, see Government Code § 77203.

§ 40509.   Notice of violations; certification of satisfaction; application of section

(a) Except as required under subdivision (c) of Section 40509.5, if any person has violated a written promise to appear or a lawfully granted continuance of his or her promise to appear in court or before the person authorized to receive a deposit of bail, or violated an order to appear in court, including, but not limited to, a written notice to appear issued in accordance with Section 40518, the magistrate or clerk of the court may give notice of the failure to appear to the department for any violation of this code, or any violation that can be heard by a juvenile traffic hearing referee pursuant to Section 256 of the Welfare and Institutions Code, or any violation of any other statute relating to the safe operation of a vehicle, except violations not required to be reported pursuant to paragraphs (1), (2), (3), (6), and (7) of subdivision (b) of Section 1803. If thereafter the case in which the promise was given is adjudicated or the person who has violated the court order appears in court or otherwise satisfies the order of the court, the magistrate or clerk of the court hearing the case shall sign and file with the department a certificate to that effect.

(b) If any person has willfully failed to pay a lawfully imposed fine within the time authorized by the court or to pay a fine pursuant to subdivision (a) of Section 42003, the magistrate or clerk of the court may give notice of the fact to the department for any violation, except violations not required to be reported pursuant to paragraphs (1), (2), (3), (6), and (7) of subdivision (b) of Section 1803. If thereafter the fine is fully paid, the magistrate or clerk of the court shall issue and file with the department a certificate showing that the fine has been paid.

(c)(1) Notwithstanding subdivisions (a) and (b), the court may notify the department of the total amount of bail, fines, assessments, and fees authorized or required by this code, including Section 40508.5, which are unpaid by any person.

(2) Once a court has established the amount of bail, fines, assessments, and fees, and notified the department, the court shall not further enhance or modify that amount.

(3) This subdivision applies only to violations of this code that do not require a mandatory court appearance, are not contested by the defendant, and do not require proof of correction certified by the court.

(d) With respect to a violation of this code, this section is applicable to any court which has not elected to be subject to the notice requirements of subdivision (b) of Section 40509.5.

(e) Any violation subject to Section 40001, which is the responsibility of the owner of the vehicle, shall not be reported under this section. *(Stats.1959, c. 3, p. 1778, § 40509. Amended by Stats.1961, c. 1653, p. 3608, § 3; Stats.1967, c. 593, p. 1937, § 1; Stats.1968, c. 1192, p. 2262, § 15.5, operative Jan. 1, 1969; Stats.1971, c. 1532, p. 3037, § 3, operative May 3, 1972; Stats.1979, c. 235, p. 490, § 3; Stats.1981, c. 584, p. 2250, § 3, operative July 1, 1982; Stats.1984, c. 858, § 2, operative July 1, 1985; Stats.1985, c. 1008, § 4; Stats.1986, c. 953, § 14; Stats. 1989, c. 126, § 1; Stats.1990, c. 472 (S.B.1826), § 2; Stats.1991, c. 13 (A.B.37), § 63, eff. Feb. 13, 1991; Stats.1991, c. 651 (S.B.757), § 4; Stats.1992, c. 40 (A.B. 2098), § 1; Stats.1993, c. 158 (A.B.392), § 22, eff. July 21, 1993; Stats.1994, c. 1216 (S.B.1802), § 6; Stats.1996, c. 224 (S.B.1579), § 5; Stats.1998, c. 877 (A.B.2132), § 76; Stats.2007, c. 738 (A.B.1248), § 46.)*

Cross References

Continuance, see Vehicle Code § 40506.5.

Guilty plea to traffic infraction or misdemeanor, see Vehicle Code § 41610.

Lien on vehicles, notice of failure to appear or failure to pay fine, see Vehicle Code § 14911.

Record of license applicant for conviction of traffic violations and traffic accidents, see Vehicle Code § 12808.

Refusal to appear, denial of license for, see Vehicle Code § 12807.

§ 40509.1. Notice of willful failure to comply with certain court orders

If any person has willfully failed to comply with a court order, except a failure to appear, to pay a fine, or to attend traffic violator school, which was issued for a violation of this code, the magistrate or clerk of the court may give notice of the fact to the department. *(Added by Stats.1993, c. 158 (A.B.392), § 22.5, eff. July 21, 1993. Amended by Stats.1998, c. 877 (A.B.2132), § 77.)*

§ 40509.5. Notice of violations; criteria for arrest warrants; election by court to notify; application of section; exception

(a) Except as required under subdivision (c), if, with respect to an offense described in subdivision (e), a person has violated his or her written promise to appear or a lawfully granted continuance of his or her promise to appear in court or before the person authorized to receive a deposit of bail, or violated an order to appear in court, including, but not limited to, a written notice to appear issued in accordance with Section 40518, the magistrate or clerk of the court may give notice of the failure to appear to the department for a violation of this code, a violation that can be heard by a juvenile traffic hearing referee pursuant to Section 256 of the Welfare and Institutions Code, or a violation of any other statute relating to the safe operation of a vehicle, except violations not required to be reported pursuant to paragraphs (1), (2), (3), (6), and (7) of subdivision (b) of Section 1803. If thereafter the case in which the promise was given is adjudicated or the person who has violated the court order appears in court and satisfies the order of the court, the magistrate or clerk of the court hearing the case shall sign and file with the department a certificate to that effect.

(b) If, with respect to an offense described in subdivision (e), a person has willfully failed to pay a lawfully imposed fine, or bail in installments as agreed to under Section 40510.5, within the time authorized by the court or to pay a fine pursuant to subdivision (a) of Section 42003, the magistrate or clerk of the court may give notice of the fact to the department for a violation, except violations not required to be reported pursuant to paragraphs (1), (2), (3), (6), and (7) of subdivision (b) of Section 1803. If thereafter the fine or bail is fully paid, the magistrate or clerk of the court shall issue and file with the department a certificate showing that the fine or bail has been paid.

(c) If a person charged with a violation of Section 23152 or 23153, or Section 191.5 of the Penal Code, or subdivision (a) of Section 192.5 of that code has violated a lawfully granted continuance of his or her promise to appear in court or is released from custody on his or her own recognizance and fails to appear in court or before the person authorized to receive a deposit of bail, or violated an order to appear in court, the magistrate or clerk of the court shall give notice to the department of the failure to appear. If thereafter the case in which the notice was given is adjudicated or the person who has violated the court order appears in court or otherwise satisfies the order of the court, the magistrate or clerk of the court hearing the case shall prepare and forward to the department a certificate to that effect.

(d) Except as required under subdivision (c), the court shall mail a courtesy warning notice to the defendant by first-class mail at the address shown on the notice to appear, at least 10 days before sending a notice to the department under this section.

(e) If the court notifies the department of a failure to appear or pay a fine or bail pursuant to subdivision (a) or (b), no arrest warrant shall be issued for an alleged violation of subdivision (a) or (b) of Section 40508, unless one of the following criteria is met:

(1) The alleged underlying offense is a misdemeanor or felony.

(2) The alleged underlying offense is a violation of any provision of Division 12 (commencing with Section 24000), Division 13 (commencing with Section 29000), or Division 15 (commencing with Section 35000), required to be reported pursuant to Section 1803.

(3) The driver's record does not show that the defendant has a valid California driver's license.

(4) The driver's record shows an unresolved charge that the defendant is in violation of his or her written promise to appear for one or more other alleged violations of the law.

(f) Except as required under subdivision (c), in addition to the proceedings described in this section, the court may elect to notify the department pursuant to subdivision (c) of Section 40509.

(g) This section is applicable to courts that have elected to provide notice pursuant to subdivision (b). The method of commencing or terminating an election to proceed under this section shall be prescribed by the department.

(h) A violation subject to Section 40001, that is the responsibility of the owner of the vehicle, shall not be reported under this section. *(Added by Stats.1984, c. 858, § 3, operative July 1, 1985. Amended by Stats.1985, c. 1008, § 5; Stats.1989, c. 126, § 2; Stats.1990, c. 472 (S.B.1826), § 3; Stats.1991, c. 13 (A.B.37), § 64, eff. Feb. 13, 1991; Stats.1991, c. 651 (S.B.757), § 5; Stats.1992, c. 40 (A.B.2098), § 2; Stats.1992, c. 1243 (A.B.3090), § 109, eff. Sept. 30, 1992; Stats.1993, c. 158 (A.B.392), § 23, eff. July 21, 1993; Stats.1996, c. 224 (S.B.1579), § 6; Stats. 1998, c. 828 (S.B.1637), § 25; Stats.1998, c. 877 (A.B. 2132), § 78.5; Stats.2007, c. 738 (A.B.1248), § 47; Stats. 2007, c. 747 (A.B.678), § 40.5.)*

Cross References

Lien on vehicles, notice of failure to appear or failure to pay fine, see Vehicle Code § 14911.

§ 40510. Deposit of bail or parking penalty; payment by personal check; agency policy

(a) Prior to the date upon which a defendant promised to appear, or prior to the expiration of any lawful continuance of that date, or upon receipt of information that an action has been filed and prior to the scheduled court date, the defendant may deposit bail with the magistrate or the person authorized to receive a deposit of bail.

(b) For any offense which is not declared to be a felony, a deposit of bail or a penalty may be by a personal check meeting the criteria established in accordance with subdivision (c).

(c) Each court, sheriff, or other agency which regularly accepts deposits of bail or penalties, shall adopt a written policy governing the acceptance of personal checks in payment of bail or penalty deposits. The policy shall

permit clerks and other appropriate officers to accept personal checks under conditions which tend to assure the validity of the checks.

(d) The written policy governing the acceptance of personal checks adopted pursuant to subdivision (c) shall provide that the payee of the deposit made by personal check shall be the agency accepting the deposit. *(Stats. 1959, c. 3, p. 1778, § 40510. Amended by Stats.1970, c. 299, p. 572, § 1; Stats.1979, c. 235, p. 490, § 4; Stats. 1979, c. 951, p. 3278, § 1; Stats.1981, c. 775, p. 3029, § 3; Stats.1984, c. 481, § 4; Stats.1986, c. 939, § 18; Stats. 1992, c. 1244 (A.B.408), § 34, operative July 1, 1993.)*

§ 40510.5. Payment and forfeiture of bail; circumstances

(a) The clerk of the court may accept a payment and forfeiture of at least 10 percent of the total bail amount for each infraction violation of this code prior to the date on which the defendant promised to appear, or prior to the expiration of any lawful continuance of that date, or upon receipt of information that an action has been filed and prior to the scheduled court date, if all of the following circumstances exist:

(1) The defendant is charged with an infraction violation of this code or an infraction violation of an ordinance adopted pursuant to this code.

(2) The defendant submits proof of correction, when proof of correction is mandatory for a correctable offense.

(3) The offense does not require an appearance in court.

(4) The defendant signs a written agreement to pay and forfeit the remainder of the required bail according to an installment schedule as agreed upon with the court. The Judicial Council shall prescribe the form of the agreement for payment and forfeiture of bail in installments for infraction violations.

(b) When a clerk accepts an agreement for payment and forfeiture of bail in installments, the clerk shall continue the appearance date of the defendant to the date to complete payment and forfeiture of bail in the agreement.

(c) Except for subdivisions (b) and (c) of Section 1269b and Section 1305.1, the provisions of Chapter 1 (commencing with Section 1268) of Title 10 of Part 2 of the Penal Code do not apply to an agreement to pay and forfeit bail in installments under this section.

(d) For the purposes of reporting violations of this code to the department under Section 1803, the date that the defendant signs an agreement to pay and forfeit bail in installments shall be reported as the date of conviction.

(e) When the defendant fails to make an installment payment according to an agreement under subdivision (a) above, the court may charge a failure to appear or pay under Section 40508 and impose a civil assessment as provided in Section 1214.1 of the Penal Code or issue an arrest warrant for a failure to appear.

(f) Payment of a bail amount under this section is forfeited when collected and shall be distributed by the court in the same manner as other fines, penalties, and forfeitures collected for infractions.

(g) The defendant shall pay to the clerk of the court or the collecting agency a fee for the processing of install-ment accounts. This fee shall equal the administrative and clerical costs, as determined by the board of supervi-sors or by the court, except that the fee shall not exceed thirty-five dollars ($35). *(Added by Stats.2007, c. 738 (A.B.1248), § 48. Amended by Stats.2010, c. 720 (S.B. 857), § 36, eff. Oct. 19, 2010.)*

§ 40511. Fixing bail

If bail has not been previously fixed and approved by the judges of the court in accordance with a schedule of bail, the magistrate shall fix the amount of bail which in his judgment, in accordance with Section 1275 of the Penal Code, will be reasonable and sufficient for the appearance of the defendant and shall endorse upon the notice a statement signed by him in the form set forth in Section 815a of the Penal Code. *(Stats.1959, c. 3, p. 1778, § 40511.)*

Cross References

Authority of municipal court commissioner or traffic referee to accept bail, see Government Code § 72304.

§ 40512. Forfeiture of bail; guaranteed traffic arrest bail bond certificates

(a)(1) Except as specified in paragraph (2) and subdi-vision (b), if at the time the case is called for arraignment before the magistrate the defendant does not appear, either in person or by counsel, the magistrate may declare the bail forfeited and may, in his or her discretion, order that no further proceedings be had in the case, unless the defendant has been charged with a violation of Section 23111 or 23112, or subdivision (a) of Section 23113, and he or she has been previously convicted of the same offense, except if the magistrate finds that undue hard-ship will be imposed upon the defendant by requiring him or her to appear, the magistrate may declare the bail forfeited and order that no further proceedings shall be had in the case.

(2) If the defendant has posted surety bail and the magistrate has ordered the bail forfeited and that no further proceedings shall be had in the case, the bail retains the right to obtain relief from the forfeiture as provided in Section 1305 of the Penal Code if the amount of the bond, money, or property deposited exceeds seven hundred dollars ($700).

(b)(1) If, at the time the case is called for a compliance appearance before the magistrate, the defendant has entered into a bail installment agreement pursuant to Section 40510.5 but has not made an installment payment as agreed and does not appear, either in person or by counsel, the court may continue the arraignment to a date beyond the last agreed upon installment payment, issue a

warrant of arrest, or impose a civil assessment as provid-ed in Section 1214.1 of the Penal Code for the failure to appear.

(2) If, at the time the case is called for a compliance appearance before the magistrate, the defendant has paid all required bail funds and the defendant does not appear, either in person or by counsel, the court may order that no further proceedings shall be had in the case, unless the defendant has been charged with a violation of Section 23111 or 23112, or subdivision (a) of Section 23113, and he or she has been previously convicted of the same offense, except that if the magistrate finds that undue hardship will be imposed upon the defendant by requiring him or her to appear, the magistrate may order that no further proceedings shall be had in the case.

(c) Upon the making of the order that no further proceedings shall be had, all sums deposited as bail shall be paid into the city or county treasury, as the case may be.

(d) If a guaranteed traffic arrest bail bond certificate has been filed, the clerk of the court shall bill the issuer for the amount of bail fixed by the uniform countywide schedule of bail required under subdivision (c) of Section 1269b of the Penal Code.

(e) Upon presentation by a court of the bill for a fine or bail assessed against an individual covered by a guaranteed traffic arrest bail bond certificate, the issuer shall pay to the court the amount of the fine or forfeited bail that is within the maximum amount guaranteed by the terms of the certificate.

(f) The court shall return the guaranteed traffic arrest bail bond certificate to the issuer upon receipt of payment in accordance with subdivision (d). *(Stats.1959, c. 3, p. 1778, § 40512. Amended by Stats.1970, c. 1548, p. 3151, § 9; Stats.1982, c. 1394, p. 5310, § 4; Stats.1993, c. 524 (A.B.734), § 6; Stats.2006, c. 538 (S.B.1852), § 666; Stats.2007, c. 738 (A.B.1248), § 49.)*

Cross References

Equivalent of conviction, see Vehicle Code §§ 1803, 13103.
Inapplicability of forfeiture of bail provisions of Penal Code to cases arising under § 40500, see Penal Code § 1306.1.

§ 40512.5. Optional bail forfeiture

(a) Except as specified in subdivision (b), if at the time the case is called for trial the defendant does not appear, either in person or by counsel, and has not requested in writing that the trial proceed in his or her absence, the court may declare the bail forfeited and may, in its discretion, order that no further proceedings be had in the case, or the court may act pursuant to Section 1043 of the Penal Code. However, if the defendant has been charged with a violation of Section 23111 or 23112, or subdivision (a) of Section 23113, and he or she has been previously convicted of a violation of the same section, the court may declare the bail forfeited, but shall issue a bench warrant for the arrest of the person charged, except if the magistrate finds that undue hardship will be imposed upon the defendant by requiring him or her to appear, the magistrate may declare the bail forfeited and order that no further proceedings shall be had in the case.

(b) If the defendant has posted surety bail and the magistrate has ordered the bail forfeited and that no further proceedings shall be had in the case, the bail retains the right to obtain relief from the forfeiture as provided in Section 1305 of the Penal Code if the amount of the bond, money, or property deposited exceeds seven hundred dollars ($700). *(Added by Stats.1968, c. 1109, p. 2123, § 1. Amended by Stats.1970, c. 1548, p. 3151, § 10; Stats.1993, c. 524 (A.B.734), § 7.)*

§ 40512.6. Failure to submit proof of completion of traffic violators school; forfeiture of bail

(a) If a defendant who elects or is ordered to attend a traffic violator school in accordance with Section 42005 and has paid the full traffic violator school bail amount required under Section 42007 fails to successfully complete the program within the time ordered by the court or any extension thereof, the court may, following notice to the defendant, order that the fee paid by the defendant be converted to bail and declare the bail forfeited. The bail forfeiture under this section shall be distributed as provided by Section 42007. Upon forfeiture of the bail, the court may order that no further proceedings shall be had in the case.

(b) This section shall become operative on July 1, 2011. *(Added by Stats.2010, c. 599 (A.B.2499), § 11.5, operative July 1, 2011.)*

Cross References

State surcharge on state penalty imposed on fines, penalties, or forfeitures imposed and collected by the courts for offenses involving Vehicle Code violations, exceptions, see Penal Code § 1465.7.

§ 40513. Filing of notice in lieu of complaint

(a) Whenever written notice to appear has been prepared, delivered, and filed with the court, an exact and legible duplicate copy of the notice when filed with the magistrate, in lieu of a verified complaint, shall constitute a complaint to which the defendant may plead "guilty" or "nolo contendere."

If, however, the defendant violates his or her promise to appear in court or does not deposit lawful bail, or pleads other than "guilty" or "nolo contendere" to the offense charged, a complaint shall be filed that shall conform to Chapter 2 (commencing with Section 948) of Title 5 of Part 2 of the Penal Code, which shall be deemed to be an original complaint, and thereafter

proceedings shall be had as provided by law, except that a defendant may, by an agreement in writing, subscribed by him or her and filed with the court, waive the filing of a verified complaint and elect that the prosecution may proceed upon a written notice to appear.

(b) Notwithstanding subdivision (a), whenever the written notice to appear has been prepared on a form approved by the Judicial Council, an exact and legible duplicate copy of the notice when filed with the magistrate shall constitute a complaint to which the defendant may enter a plea and, if the notice to appear is verified, upon which a warrant may be issued. If the notice to appear is not verified, the defendant may, at the time of arraignment, request that a verified complaint be filed. In the case of an infraction violation in which the defendant is a minor, the defendant may enter a plea at the arraignment upon a written notice to appear. Notwithstanding any other provision of law, in the case of an infraction violation, no consent of the minor is required prior to conducting the hearing upon a written notice to appear. *(Stats.1959, c. 3, p. 1778, § 40513. Amended by Stats.1959, c. 606, p. 2591, § 6; Stats.1963, c. 325, p. 1111, § 1; Stats.1965, c. 1190, p. 3006, § 1; Stats.1968, c. 906, p. 1697, § 2; Stats.1996, c. 124 (A.B.3470), § 143; Stats. 1997, c. 17 (S.B.947), § 145; Stats.2001, c. 830 (S.B.940), § 1.)*

Cross References

Notice to appear in criminal actions excluded from municipal court indexing requirements, see Government Code § 71280.3.
Records of indexes of actions in municipal courts inapplicable to this section, see Government Code § 71280.3.

§ 40514. Issuance of warrant

No warrant shall issue on the charge for the arrest of a person who has given his written promise to appear in court or before a person authorized to receive a deposit of bail, unless he has violated the promise, the lawfully granted continuance of his promise, or has failed to deposit bail, to appear for arraignment, trial or judgment, or to comply with the terms and provisions of the judgment, as required by law. *(Stats.1959, c. 3, p. 1779, § 40514. Amended by Stats.1979, c. 235, p. 491, § 5.)*

Cross References

Arrest on failure to post bond, see Vehicle Code § 40515.

§ 40515. Issuance of warrant for violation of promise to appear or continuance of promise to appear

(a) When a person signs a written promise to appear or is granted a continuance of his or her promise to appear at the time and place specified in the written promise to appear or the continuance thereof, and has not posted full bail or has failed to pay an installment of bail as agreed to under Section 40510.5, the magistrate may issue and have delivered for execution a warrant for his or her arrest within 20 days after his or her failure to appear before the magistrate or pay an installment of bail as agreed, or if the person promises to appear before an officer authorized to accept bail other than a magistrate and fails to do so on or before the date on which he or she promised to appear, then, within 20 days after the delivery of the written promise to appear by the officer to a magistrate having jurisdiction over the offense.

(b) When the person violates his or her promise to appear before an officer authorized to receive bail other than a magistrate, the officer shall immediately deliver to a magistrate having jurisdiction over the offense charged the written promise to appear and the complaint, if any, filed by the arresting officer. *(Stats.1959, c. 3, p. 1779, § 40515. Amended by Stats.1968, c. 831, p. 1603, § 1; Stats.1971, c. 1042, p. 1998, § 1, operative May 3, 1972; Stats.1979, c. 235, p. 491, § 6; Stats.2007, c. 738 (A.B. 1248), § 51.)*

Cross References

Bail, generally, see Penal Code § 1268 et seq.

§ 40516. Expense to departments

(a) The expenses incurred by the Department of the California Highway Patrol and the Department of Motor Vehicles in executing any warrant issued as a result of a notice to appear issued by a member of the California Highway Patrol shall be a legal charge against the city or county in which jurisdiction the warrant was issued except where the commissioner authorizes the acceptance of a warrant for execution within 30 days of the date of its issuance.

(b) The commissioner or director shall certify to the Controller the cost of executing warrants on behalf of each city or county under this section. The departments shall be reimbursed for costs as provided in Section 11004.5 of the Revenue and Taxation Code.

(c) The peace officer to whom a warrant has been delivered for execution, upon demand, shall transfer the warrant, if it has not been executed within 30 days of the date of its issuance, to any member of the California Highway Patrol or to the Department of Motor Vehicles for execution. *(Stats.1959, c. 3, p. 1779, § 40516. Amended by Stats.1959, c. 1996, p. 4640, § 52.)*

Cross References

County charges, generally, see Government Code § 29600 et seq.
Deduction from allocations of amounts chargeable to each city and county under this section, see Revenue and Taxation Code § 11004.5.
Police authority of members of highway patrol, see Vehicle Code § 2409.

Service of warrants by highway patrol, see Vehicle Code § 2411.

§ 40517. Repealed by Stats.1994, c. 1220 (A.B.3132), § 69, eff. Sept. 30, 1994

§ 40518. Certain violations recorded by automated traffic enforcement system; notice to appear; contents; notice of nonliability; form; dismissal

(a) Whenever a written notice to appear has been issued by a peace officer or by a qualified employee of a law enforcement agency on a form approved by the Judicial Council for an alleged violation of Section 22451, or, based on an alleged violation of Section 21453, 21455, or 22101 recorded by an automated traffic enforcement system pursuant to Section 21455.5 or 22451, and delivered by mail within 15 days of the alleged violation to the current address of the registered owner of the vehicle on file with the department, with a certificate of mailing obtained as evidence of service, an exact and legible duplicate copy of the notice when filed with the magistrate shall constitute a complaint to which the defendant may enter a plea. Preparation and delivery of a notice to appear pursuant to this section is not an arrest.

(b)(1) A notice to appear shall contain the name and address of the person, the license plate number of the person's vehicle, the violation charged, including a description of the offense, and the time and place when, and where, the person may appear in court or before a person authorized to receive a deposit of bail. The time specified shall be at least 10 days after the notice to appear is delivered. If, after the notice to appear has been issued, the citing peace officer or qualified employee of a law enforcement agency determines that, in the interest of justice, the citation or notice should be dismissed, the citing agency may recommend, in writing, to the magistrate or the judge that the case be dismissed. The recommendation shall cite the reasons for the recommendation and be filed with the court. If the magistrate or judge makes a finding that there are grounds for dismissal, the finding shall be entered on the record and the infraction dismissed.

(2) A notice to appear shall also contain all of the following information:

(A) The methods by which the registered owner of the vehicle or the alleged violator may view and discuss with the issuing agency, both by telephone and in person, the evidence used to substantiate the violation.

(B) The contact information of the issuing agency.

(c)(1) This section and Section 40520 do not preclude the issuing agency or the manufacturer or supplier of the automated traffic enforcement system from mailing a notice of nonliability to the registered owner of the vehicle or the alleged violator prior to issuing a notice to appear. The notice of nonliability shall be substantively identical to the following form:

VEHICLE CODE

COURTESY NOTICE: THIS IS NOT A TICKET

[insert name of jurisdiction]
PHOTO ENFORCEMENT PROGRAM
Agency Address:

<Name>
<Address>
<City State, Zip>

VIOLATION #							
ADDRESS			CITY			STATE	ZIP
COLOR	YEAR	MAKE	MODEL	STYLE	LICENSE PLATE	STATE	
MONTH	DAY	YEAR	TIME				
LOCATION			VEHICLE SPEED		POSTED SPEED		
Statute			Violation Description				
Officer's Name			Badge #				

SCENE A

SCENE B

ZOOM FACE

ZOOM PLATE

Certificate of Mailing

I, (name_of_mailer), of_____, do certify that I am over 18 years old and not a party to the above entitled case. On (Print_Date) I placed this Notice in an envelope addressed to the registered owner or lessee as shown above, sealed it and deposited the envelope in a United States Postal Service receptacle located in (city, state). In the ordinary course of business, the envelope is sealed, affixed with proper postage and mailed. I declare under the penalty of perjury under the laws of the State of California that the foregoing is true and correct.

Dated:

Signature of Mailer

(Code of Civil Procedure 1013a (3), 2015.5)

COURTESY NOTICE: THIS IS NOT A TICKET
[Insert agency name]
INSTRUCTION PAGE

The Reason You Received This Notice:
A vehicle registered in your name was photographed failing to stop for an official red light traffic control signal. This is a violation of the State of California Vehicle Code Section 21453(a) or (c) pursuant to Section 21455.5

You are encouraged to view the video of this violation and to respond to this notice. You may make an appointment to view the evidence by calling the [insert agency name] at (000) 000-0000. During this viewing, an officer or qualified employee will show you a high quality video and still images depicting the violation in greater detail than the printed photos in this notice.

You can also view the video online at www 0000000000.

The video is available online for 60 days from the date of violation. After 60 days an appointment must be made with [insert agency name].

DO NOT CALL THE COURT REGARDING THIS NOTICE. For additional questions contact the Photo Enforcement Program at (000) 000-0000.

Tear Here   Tear Here   Tear Here

NOTICE OF NON-LIABILITY

IF YOU WERE NOT THE DRIVER/OWNER
Violation #: <<Enter #>>   Last Issued To: <<Enter Name>>

[Insert agency name]

CHECK ONE: ☐ The person named below was the driver of the vehicle.
☐ I sold the vehicle prior to the violation date to the person named below.
☐ I have never owned this vehicle or license plate.

CHECK ONE: ☐ I am an individual.
☐ I am a car rental or leasing company.

Print Actual Driver/New Owner's Name: _____   Driver's License/ID No.: _____

Address: _____   Issued in the State of: _____

City, State, ZIP Code: _____   Date of Birth: _____

Gender: _____ Hair Color: _____ Eye Color: _____ Height: _____ Weight: _____

DECLARATION
I CERTIFY THAT THE FOREGOING IS TRUE AND CORRECT

Signature _____   Print Name _____

Your Telephone Number ( ) _____ - _____   Date _____

---

(2) The form specified in paragraph (1) may be translated to other languages.

(d) A manufacturer or supplier of an automated traffic enforcement system or the governmental agency operating the system shall not alter the notice to appear or any other form approved by the Judicial Council. If a form is found to have been materially altered, the citation based on the altered form may be dismissed. *(Added by Stats.1994, c. 1216 (S.B.1802), § 7. Amended by Stats. 1995, c. 922 (S.B.833), § 8; Stats.1998, c. 54 (S.B.1136), § 6; Stats.2012, c. 735 (S.B.1303), § 4.)*

Cross References

Evidence,
Printed representation of computer-generated information, see EVID Code § 1552.
Printed representation of video or digital images, see EVID Code § 1553.

Offenses, automated traffic enforcement system, requirements, use of printed representation as evidence, confidentiality and retention of records, review of alleged violation by registered owner, manufacturers and suppliers, duties and contract limitations, see VEHICLE Code § 21455.5.

§ 40519. Trial scheduling; written not guilty plea

(a) Any person who has received a written notice to appear for an infraction may, prior to the time at which the person is required to appear, make a deposit and declare the intention to plead not guilty to the clerk of the court named in the notice to appear. The deposit shall be in the amount of bail established pursuant to Section 1269b of the Penal Code, together with any assessment required by Section 42006 of this code or Section 1464 of the Penal Code, for the offense charged, and shall be used for the purpose of guaranteeing the appearance of the defendant at the time and place scheduled by the clerk for arraignment and for trial, and to apply toward the payment of any fine or assessment prescribed by the court in the event of conviction. The case shall thereupon be set for arraignment and trial on the same date, unless the defendant requests separate arraignment. A deposit of bail under this section does not constitute entry of a plea or a court appearance. A plea of not guilty under this section must be made in court at the arraignment.

(b) Any person who has received a written notice to appear may, prior to the time at which the person is required to appear, plead not guilty in writing in lieu of appearing in person. The written plea shall be directed to the court named in the notice to appear and, if mailed, shall be sent by certified or registered mail postmarked not later than five days prior to the day upon which appearance is required. The written plea and request to the court or city agency shall be accompanied by a deposit consisting of the amount of bail established pursuant to Section 1269b of the Penal Code, together with any assessment required by Section 42006 of this code or Section 1464 of the Penal Code, for that offense, which amount shall be used for the purpose of guaranteeing the appearance of the defendant at the time and place set by the court for trial and to apply toward the payment of any fine or assessment prescribed by the court in the event of conviction. Upon receipt of the plea and deposit, the case shall be set for arraignment and trial on the same date, unless the defendant requests separate arraignment. Thereafter, the case shall be conducted in the same manner as if the defendant had appeared in person, had made his or her plea in open court, and had deposited that sum as bail. The court or the clerk of the court shall notify the accused of the time and place of trial by first-class mail postmarked at least 10 days prior to the time set for the trial. Any person using this procedure shall be deemed to have waived the right to be tried within the statutory period.

(c) Any person using the procedure set forth in subdivision (a) or (b) shall be deemed to have given a written promise to appear at the time designated by the court for trial, and failure to appear at the trial shall constitute a misdemeanor. *(Added by Stats.1975, c. 1257, p. 3296, § 3. Amended by Stats.1983, c. 210, § 1; Stats.1986, c. 631, § 1; Stats.1986, c. 953, § 15.5; Stats. 1987, c. 852, § 7; Stats.1992, c. 1244 (A.B.408), § 35, operative July 1, 1993; Stats.2009, c. 35 (S.B.174), § 30.)*

Cross References

Violation a misdemeanor, see Vehicle Code § 40000.25.

§ 40520. Automatic enforcement system violation; notice to appear; affidavit of nonliability

(a) A notice to appear issued pursuant to Section 40518 for an alleged violation recorded by an automatic enforcement system shall contain, or be accompanied by, an affidavit of nonliability and information as to what constitutes nonliability, information as to the effect of executing the affidavit, and instructions for returning the affidavit to the issuing agency.

(b)(1) If a notice to appear is sent to a car rental or leasing company, as the registered owner of the vehicle, the company may return the notice of nonliability pursuant to paragraph (2), if the violation occurred when the vehicle was either leased or rented and operated by a person other than an employee of the rental or leasing company.

(2) If the affidavit of nonliability is returned to the issuing agency by the registered owner within 30 days of the mailing of the notice to appear together with the proof of a written rental agreement or lease between a bona fide renting or leasing company and its customer and that agreement identifies the renter or lessee and provides the driver's license number, name, and address of the renter or lessee, the agency shall cancel the notice for the registered owner to appear and shall, instead, issue a notice to appear to the renter or lessee identified in the affidavit of nonliability.

(c) Nothing in this section precludes an issuing agency from establishing a procedure whereby registered owners, other than bona fide renting and leasing companies, may execute an affidavit of nonliability if the registered owner identifies the person who was the driver of the vehicle at the time of the alleged violation and whereby the issuing agency issues a notice to appear to that person. *(Added by Stats.1998, c. 828 (S.B.1637), § 26.)*

§ 40521. Forfeiture of bail; payment of assessments

(a) Except when personal appearance is required by the bail schedule established under Section 1269b of the Penal Code, a person to whom a notice to appear has been issued under Section 40500, who intends to forfeit bail and to pay any assessment may forward by United States mail the full amount fixed as bail, together with the appropriate amount of any assessment, to the person authorized to receive a deposit of bail. The amounts may be paid in the form of a personal check which meets the criteria established pursuant to subdivision (c) of Section 40510, or a bank cashier's check or a money order. Bail and any assessment shall be paid not later than the day of appearance set forth in the notice to appear or prior to the expiration of any lawful continuance of that date.

(b) Bail forwarded by mail is effective only when the funds are actually received.

(c) Paragraph (1) of subdivision (a) of Section 40512 is applicable to bail paid pursuant to this section. Upon the making of the order pursuant to Section 40512 that no further proceedings be had, the amount paid as bail shall be paid into the city or county treasury, as the case may be, and the assessment shall be transmitted to the State Treasury in the manner provided in Section 1464 of the Penal Code. *(Added by Stats.1976, c. 127, p. 204, § 1, operative Jan. 1, 1978. Amended by Stats.1980, c. 561, p. 1548, § 7; Stats.1981, c. 775, p. 3029, § 4; Stats.1986, c. 939, § 19; Stats.1986, c. 953, § 16; Stats.1992, c. 1244 (A.B.408), § 36, operative July 1, 1993; Stats.2007, c. 738 (A.B.1248), § 52.)*

§ 40522. Notice; registration, license or mechanical violations; dismissal on proof of correction

Whenever a person is arrested for violations specified in Section 40303.5 and none of the disqualifying conditions set forth in subdivision (b) of Section 40610 exist, and the officer issues a notice to appear, the notice shall specify the offense charged and note in a form approved by the Judicial Council that the charge shall be dismissed on proof of correction. If the arrested person presents, by mail or in person, proof of correction, as prescribed in Section 40616, on or before the date on which the person promised to appear, the court shall dismiss the violation or violations charged pursuant to Section 40303.5. *(Added by Stats.1979, c. 71, p. 173, § 3, eff. May 19, 1979. Amended by Stats.1979, c. 874, p. 3045, § 1, eff. Sept. 22, 1979; Stats.1984, c. 915, § 2, operative July 1, 1985; Stats.1985, c. 898, § 1; Stats.1989, c. 729, § 4, operative July 1, 1990; Stats.1991, c. 1168 (A.B.2142), § 8, eff. Oct. 14, 1991; Stats.1992, c. 258 (S.B.133), § 5.)*

ARTICLE 3. NOTICE OF VIOLATION

Section
40600. Notice to appear; reasonable cause for issuance.
40601 to 40603. Repealed.
40604. Issuance of warrant.

§ 40600. Notice to appear; reasonable cause for issuance

(a) Notwithstanding any other provision of law, a peace officer who has successfully completed a course or courses of instruction, approved by the Commission on Peace Officer Standards and Training, in the investigation of traffic accidents may prepare, in triplicate, on a form approved by the Judicial Council, a written notice to appear when the peace officer has reasonable cause to believe that any person involved in a traffic accident has violated a provision of this code not declared to be a felony or a local ordinance and the violation was a factor in the occurrence of the traffic accident.

(b) A notice to appear shall contain the name and address of the person, the license number of the person's vehicle, if any, the name and address, when available, of the registered owner or lessee of the vehicle, the offense charged, and the time and place when and where the person may appear in court or before a person authorized to receive a deposit of bail. The time specified shall be at least 10 days after the notice to appear is delivered.

(c) The preparation and delivery of a notice to appear pursuant to this section is not an arrest.

(d) For purposes of this article, a peace officer has reasonable cause to issue a written notice to appear if, as a result of the officer's investigation, the officer has evidence, either testimonial or real, or a combination of testimonial and real, that would be sufficient to issue a written notice to appear if the officer had personally witnessed the events investigated.

(e) As used in this section, "peace officer" means any person specified under Section 830.1 or 830.2 of the Penal Code, or any reserve police officer or reserve deputy sheriff listed in Section 830.6 of the Penal Code, with the exception of members of the California National Guard.

(f) A written notice to appear prepared on a form approved by the Judicial Council and issued pursuant to this section shall be accepted by any court. *(Added by Stats.1974, c. 794, p. 1737, § 2. Amended by Stats.1975, c. 525, p. 1091, § 1; Stats.1978, c. 722, p. 2253, § 2; Stats.1979, c. 229, p. 483, § 4; Stats.1987, c. 191, § 1; Stats.1992, c. 1242 (S.B.602), § 5; Stats.1996, c. 1155 (S.B.1587), § 8; Stats.2003, c. 292 (A.B.1436), § 12.)*

Cross References

Criminal procedure, deputized or appointed peace officers, see Penal Code § 830.6.

§§ 40601 to 40603. Repealed by Stats.1992, c. 1242 (S.B.602), §§ 6 to 8

§ 40604. Issuance of warrant

(a) If the person charged with the offense has not signed a promise to appear, no warrant for arrest may be issued following the filing of the written notice to appear issued pursuant to Section 40600, until 15 days after a notice of the filing has been served upon the person by personal delivery or by mail, addressed to the person at the address shown in the accident report.

(b) The notice shall contain the name and address of the person, the license number of the vehicle involved, the name and address, when available, of the registered owner or lessee of the vehicle, the offense shown on the written notice to appear, and the approximate time of the commission of the offense. The notice shall inform the person that, unless he or she appears in the court designated in the notice within 10 days after the service of the notice and answers the charges, a warrant will be issued for his or her arrest.

(c) Proof of service shall be made by the affidavit of any person over 18 years of age making the service showing the time, place, and manner of service and facts showing that the service was made in accordance with this section. If service is made by mail, no warrant for arrest may be issued until 14 days after the deposit of the notice of filing in the mail. *(Added by Stats.1974, c. 794, p. 1738, § 4. Amended by Stats.1992, c. 1242 (S.B.602), § 9; Stats.1992, c. 1243 (A.B.3090), § 107.7, eff. Sept. 30, 1992, operative Jan. 1, 1993.)*

ARTICLE 4. NOTICE TO CORRECT VIOLATION

Section
40610. Registration, license, safety certificate, or mechanical violations; conditions for use; proof of corrections.
40611. Transaction fee upon proof of correction of alleged violation.
40612. Copies; delivery to violators.

1073

Section
40614.   False or fictitious names; signatures; misdemeanor.
40616.   Failure to correct; proof of correction; misdemeanor.
40618.   Failure to receive proof of correction; delivery of signed promise; certification; complaint; warrant.

§ 40610.   Registration, license, safety certificate, or mechanical violations; conditions for use; proof of corrections

(a)(1) Except as provided in paragraph (2), if, after an arrest, accident investigation, or other law enforcement action, it appears that a violation has occurred involving a registration, license, all-terrain vehicle safety certificate, or mechanical requirement of this code, and none of the disqualifying conditions set forth in subdivision (b) exist and the investigating officer decides to take enforcement action, the officer shall prepare, in triplicate, and the violator shall sign, a written notice containing the violator's promise to correct the alleged violation and to deliver proof of correction of the violation to the issuing agency.

(2) If any person is arrested for a violation of Section 4454, and none of the disqualifying conditions set forth in subdivision (b) exist, the arresting officer shall prepare, in triplicate, and the violator shall sign, a written notice containing the violator's promise to correct the alleged violation and to deliver proof of correction of the violation to the issuing agency. In lieu of issuing a notice to correct violation pursuant to this section, the officer may issue a notice to appear, as specified in Section 40522.

(b) Pursuant to subdivision (a), a notice to correct violation shall be issued as provided in this section or a notice to appear shall be issued as provided in Section 40522, unless the officer finds any of the following:

(1) Evidence of fraud or persistent neglect.

(2) The violation presents an immediate safety hazard.

(3) The violator does not agree to, or cannot, promptly correct the violation.

(c) If any of the conditions set forth in subdivision (b) exist, the procedures specified in this section or Section 40522 are inapplicable, and the officer may take other appropriate enforcement action.

(d) Except as otherwise provided in subdivision (a), the notice to correct violation shall be on a form approved by the Judicial Council and, in addition to the owner's or operator's address and identifying information, shall contain an estimate of the reasonable time required for correction and proof of correction of the particular defect, not to exceed 30 days, or 90 days for the all-terrain vehicle safety certificate. *(Added by Stats. 1978, c. 1350, p. 4479, § 3, operative July 1, 1979. Amended by Stats.1979, c. 71, p. 173, § 2, eff. May 19, 1979; Stats.1980, c. 399, p. 785, § 9, eff. July 11, 1980; Stats.1982, c. 466, p. 2059, § 119; Stats.1982, c. 402, p. 1739, § 2; Stats.1984, c. 915, § 3, operative July 1, 1985; Stats.1985, c. 898, § 2; Stats.1989, c. 729, § 5, operative July 1, 1990; Stats.1991, c. 90 (A.B.1297), § 71, eff. June*
1074

30, 1991; Stats.1992, c. 258 (S.B.133), § 6; Stats.2004, c. 908 (A.B.2666), § 27.)

Cross References

Arrest for certain offenses, notice to correct, see Vehicle Code § 40303.5.
Dismissal of charge on proof of correction, see Vehicle Code § 40522.
Notice to appear, dismissal upon proof of correction, see Vehicle Code § 40522.

§ 40611.   Transaction fee upon proof of correction of alleged violation

(a) Upon proof of correction of an alleged violation of Section 12500 or 12951, or any violation cited pursuant to Section 40610, or upon submission of evidence of financial responsibility pursuant to subdivision (e) of Section 16028, the clerk shall collect a twenty-five-dollar ($25) transaction fee for each violation. The fees shall be deposited by the clerk in accordance with Section 68084 of the Government Code.

(b)(1) For each citation, ten dollars ($10) shall be allocated monthly as follows:

(A) Thirty-three percent shall be transferred to the local governmental entity in whose jurisdiction the citation was issued for deposit in the general fund of the entity.

(B) Thirty-four percent shall be transferred to the State Treasury for deposit in the State Penalty Fund established by Section 1464 of the Penal Code.

(C) Thirty-three percent shall be deposited in the county general fund.

(2) The remainder of the fees collected on each citation shall be deposited in the Immediate and Critical Needs Account of the State Court Facilities Construction Fund, established in Section 70371.5 of the Government Code.

(c) No fee shall be imposed pursuant to this section if the violation notice is processed only by the issuing agency and no record of the action is transmitted to the court. *(Added by Stats.1991, c. 90 (A.B.1297), § 72, eff. June 30, 1991. Amended by Stats.1991, c. 189 (A.B.544), § 42, eff. July 29, 1991; Stats.1991, c. 613 (A.B.195), § 11; Stats.1992, c. 427 (A.B.3355), § 168; Stats.1994, c. 704 (S.B.1699), § 23; Stats.1996, c. 1126 (A.B.650), § 16, operative Jan. 1, 1997; Stats.1999, c. 880 (S.B.652), § 21; Stats.2008, c. 311 (S.B.1407), § 30.)*

§ 40612.   Copies; delivery to violators

An exact, legible copy of the notice to correct shall be delivered to the alleged violator at the time he or she signs such notice. *(Added by Stats.1978, c. 1350, p. 4479, § 3, operative July 1, 1979.)*

§ 40614.   False or fictitious names; signatures; misdemeanor

Any person who signs a notice to correct or a certificate of correction with a false or fictitious name is guilty of a misdemeanor. *(Added by Stats.1978, c. 1350, p. 4479, § 3, operative July 1, 1979.)*

Cross References

Violation as misdemeanor, see Vehicle Code § 40000.25.

§ 40616. Failure to correct; proof of correction; misdemeanor

Any person willfully violating a written promise to correct or willfully failing to deliver proof of correction of violation is guilty of a misdemeanor. Proof of correction may consist of a certification by an authorized representative of one of the following agencies that the alleged violation has been corrected:

(a) Brake, lamp, smog device, or muffler violations may be certified as corrected by any station licensed to inspect and certify for the violation pursuant to Article 8 (commencing with Section 9889.15) of Chapter 20.3 of Division 3 of the Business and Professions Code and Section 27150.2.

(b) Driver license and registration violations may be certified as corrected by the Department of Motor Vehicles or by any clerk or deputy clerk of a court.

(c) Any violation may be certified as corrected by a police department, the California Highway Patrol, sheriff, marshal, or other law enforcement agency regularly engaged in enforcement of the Vehicle Code. *(Added by Stats.1978, c. 1350, p. 4479, § 3, operative July 1, 1979. Amended by Stats.1983, c. 361, § 1.)*

Cross References

Dismissal of charge on proof of correction, see Vehicle Code § 40522.
Notice to appear, dismissal upon proof of correction, see Vehicle Code § 40522.
Violation as misdemeanor, see Vehicle Code § 40000.25.

§ 40618. Failure to receive proof of correction; delivery of signed promise; certification; complaint; warrant

Whenever proof of correction of violation is not received by the issuing agency in accordance with Section 40610, the issuing agency may deliver the signed promise to the court having jurisdiction of the violation with a certification that no proof of correction has been received. If prepared on a form approved by the Judicial Council, the promise under Section 40610, together with the certification under this section, shall constitute a complaint to which the defendant may enter a plea, and upon which a warrant may be issued if the complaint is verified. *(Added by Stats.1978, c. 1350, p. 4479, § 3, operative July 1, 1979.)*

CHAPTER 2.5. ADMINISTRATIVE ADJUDICATION OF TRAFFIC SAFETY VIOLATIONS [REPEALED]

§§ 40650 to 40762. Repealed by Stats.1983, c. 1116, § 8, operative Jan. 1, 1986

CHAPTER 3. ILLEGAL EVIDENCE

Article	Section
1. Prosecutions Under Code	40800
2. Civil Actions	40830

ARTICLE 1. PROSECUTIONS UNDER CODE

Section
40800.	Vehicle and uniform used by officers.
40801.	Speed trap prohibition.
40802.	Speed trap defined.
40802.5.	Repealed.
40803.	Speed trap evidence.
40804.	Testimony based on speed trap.
40805.	Admission of speed trap evidence.
40806.	Police reports.
40807.	Use of evidence regarding departmental action.
40808.	Effect of constitutional right to truth-in-evidence provision.

§ 40800. Vehicle and uniform used by officers

(a) A traffic officer on duty for the exclusive or main purpose of enforcing the provisions of Division 10 (commencing with Section 20000) or 11 (commencing with Section 21000) shall wear a full distinctive uniform, and if the officer while on duty uses a motor vehicle, it must be painted a distinctive color specified by the commissioner.

(b) This section does not apply to an officer assigned exclusively to the duty of investigating and securing evidence in reference to the theft of a vehicle or failure of a person to stop in the event of an accident or violation of Section 23109 or 23109.1 or in reference to a felony charge, or to an officer engaged in serving a warrant when the officer is not engaged in patrolling the highways for the purpose of enforcing the traffic laws. *(Stats.1959, c. 3, p. 1780, § 40800. Amended by Stats.1961, c. 202, p. 1212, § 2; Stats.2007, c. 682 (A.B.430), § 18.)*

Cross References

Officers as witnesses, competency, see Vehicle Code § 40804.
Powers and duties of director, generally, see Vehicle Code § 1650 et seq.
Prohibited ownership of vehicle painted as law enforcement vehicle, see Vehicle Code § 27605.
Repainting on sale of law enforcement vehicles, see Vehicle Code § 27604.
Unauthorized wearing of uniforms, misdemeanor, see Military and Veterans Code § 422.
Wearing of uniforms, see Vehicle Code § 2261.

§ 40801. Speed trap prohibition

No peace officer or other person shall use a speed trap in arresting, or participating or assisting in the arrest of, any person for any alleged violation of this code nor shall any speed trap be used in securing evidence as to the speed of any vehicle for the purpose of an arrest or prosecution under this code. *(Stats.1959, c. 3, p. 1780, § 40801.)*

§ 40802. Speed trap defined

(a) A "speed trap" is either of the following:

(1) A particular section of a highway measured as to distance and with boundaries marked, designated, or otherwise determined in order that the speed of a vehicle may be calculated by securing the time it takes the vehicle to travel the known distance.

(2) A particular section of a highway with a prima facie speed limit that is provided by this code or by local ordinance under subparagraph (A) of paragraph (2) of subdivision (a) of Section 22352, or established under Section 22354, 22357, 22358, or 22358.3, if that prima facie speed limit is not justified by an engineering and traffic survey conducted within five years prior to the date of the alleged violation, and enforcement of the speed limit involves the use of radar or any other electronic device that measures the speed of moving objects. This paragraph does not apply to a local street, road, or school zone.

(b)(1) For purposes of this section, a local street or road is one that is functionally classified as " local" on the "California Road System Maps," that are approved by the Federal Highway Administration and maintained by the Department of Transportation. When a street or road does not appear on the "California Road System Maps," it may be defined as a "local street or road" if it primarily provides access to abutting residential property and meets the following three conditions:

(A) Roadway width of not more than 40 feet.

(B) Not more than one-half of a mile of uninterrupted length. Interruptions shall include official traffic control signals as defined in Section 445.

(C) Not more than one traffic lane in each direction.

(2) For purposes of this section, "school zone" means that area approaching or passing a school building or the grounds thereof that is contiguous to a highway and on which is posted a standard "SCHOOL" warning sign, while children are going to or leaving the school either during school hours or during the noon recess period. "School zone" also includes the area approaching or passing any school grounds that are not separated from the highway by a fence, gate, or other physical barrier while the grounds are in use by children if that highway is posted with a standard "SCHOOL" warning sign.

(c)(1) When all of the following criteria are met, paragraph (2) of this subdivision shall be applicable and subdivision (a) shall not be applicable:

(A) When radar is used, the arresting officer has successfully completed a radar operator course of not less than 24 hours on the use of police traffic radar, and the course was approved and certified by the Commission on Peace Officer Standards and Training.

(B) When laser or any other electronic device is used to measure the speed of moving objects, the arresting officer has successfully completed the training required in subparagraph (A) and an additional training course of

not less than two hours approved and certified by the Commission on Peace Officer Standards and Training.

(C)(i) The prosecution proved that the arresting officer complied with subparagraphs (A) and (B) and that an engineering and traffic survey has been conducted in accordance with subparagraph (B) of paragraph (2). The prosecution proved that, prior to the officer issuing the notice to appear, the arresting officer established that the radar, laser, or other electronic device conformed to the requirements of subparagraph (D).

(ii) The prosecution proved the speed of the accused was unsafe for the conditions present at the time of alleged violation unless the citation was for a violation of Section 22349, 22356, or 22406.

(D) The radar, laser, or other electronic device used to measure the speed of the accused meets or exceeds the minimal operational standards of the National Traffic Highway Safety Administration, and has been calibrated within the three years prior to the date of the alleged violation by an independent certified laser or radar repair and testing or calibration facility.

(2) A "speed trap" is either of the following:

(A) A particular section of a highway measured as to distance and with boundaries marked, designated, or otherwise determined in order that the speed of a vehicle may be calculated by securing the time it takes the vehicle to travel the known distance.

(B)(i) A particular section of a highway or state highway with a prima facie speed limit that is provided by this code or by local ordinance under subparagraph (A) of paragraph (2) of subdivision (a) of Section 22352, or established under Section 22354, 22357, 22358, or 22358.3, if that prima facie speed limit is not justified by an engineering and traffic survey conducted within one of the following time periods, prior to the date of the alleged violation, and enforcement of the speed limit involves the use of radar or any other electronic device that measures the speed of moving objects:

(I) Except as specified in subclause (II), seven years.

(II) If an engineering and traffic survey was conducted more than seven years prior to the date of the alleged violation, and a registered engineer evaluates the section of the highway and determines that no significant changes in roadway or traffic conditions have occurred, including, but not limited to, changes in adjoining property or land use, roadway width, or traffic volume, 10 years.

(ii) This subparagraph does not apply to a local street, road, or school zone. *(Added by Stats.1995, c. 315 (S.B.574), § 2, operative Jan. 1, 1999. Amended by Stats.1996, c. 124 (A.B.3470), § 145, operative Jan. 1, 1999; Stats.1996, c. 104 (S.B.2006), § 2, operative Jan. 1, 1999; Stats.1998, c. 1037 (A.B.2222), § 1; Stats.1999, c. 1008 (S.B.533), § 18; Stats.2000, c. 521 (A.B.280), § 3; Stats.2010, c. 491 (S.B.1318), § 49.)*

§ 40802.5. Repealed by Stats.1996, c. 124 (A.B.3470), § 146, operative Jan. 1, 1999

§ 40803. Speed trap evidence

(a) No evidence as to the speed of a vehicle upon a highway shall be admitted in any court upon the trial of any person in any prosecution under this code upon a charge involving the speed of a vehicle when the evidence is based upon or obtained from or by the maintenance or use of a speedtrap.

(b) In any prosecution under this code of a charge involving the speed of a vehicle, where enforcement involves the use of radar or other electronic devices which measure the speed of moving objects, the prosecution shall establish, as part of its prima facie case, that the evidence or testimony presented is not based upon a speedtrap as defined in paragraph (2) of subdivision (a) of Section 40802.

(c) When a traffic and engineering survey is required pursuant to paragraph (2) of subdivision (a) of Section 40802, evidence that a traffic and engineering survey has been conducted within five years of the date of the alleged violation or evidence that the offense was committed on a local street or road as defined in paragraph (2) of subdivision (a) of Section 40802 shall constitute a prima facie case that the evidence or testimony is not based upon a speedtrap as defined in paragraph (2) of subdivision (a) of Section 40802. *(Stats.1959, c. 3, p. 1781, § 40803. Amended by Stats.1981, c. 357, p. 1530, § 3; Stats.1991, c. 459 (S.B.733), § 3; Stats.1992, c. 538, (A.B.3659), § 1; Stats.1996, c. 124 (A.B.3470), § 147.)*

§ 40804. Testimony based on speed trap

(a) In any prosecution under this code upon a charge involving the speed of a vehicle, an officer or other person shall be incompetent as a witness if the testimony is based upon or obtained from or by the maintenance or use of a speed trap.

(b) An officer arresting, or participating or assisting in the arrest of, a person so charged while on duty for the exclusive or main purpose of enforcing the provisions of Divisions 10 (commencing with Section 20000) and 11 (commencing with Section 21000) is incompetent as a witness if at the time of that arrest he was not wearing a distinctive uniform, or was using a motor vehicle not painted the distinctive color specified by the commissioner.

(c) This section does not apply to an officer assigned exclusively to the duty of investigating and securing evidence in reference to the theft of a vehicle or failure of a person to stop in the event of an accident or violation of Section 23109 or 23109.1 or in reference to a felony charge or to an officer engaged in serving a warrant when the officer is not engaged in patrolling the highways for the purpose of enforcing the traffic laws. *(Stats.1959, c. 3, p. 1781, § 40804. Amended by Stats.1961, c. 58, p. 1016, § 69, eff. March 31, 1961; Stats.1978, c. 84, p. 219, § 1; Stats.2007, c. 682 (A.B.430), § 19.)*

Cross References

Color of vehicles and uniform used by enforcement officers, see Vehicle Code § 40800.
Speed trap prohibited, see Vehicle Code § 40801.

§ 40805. Admission of speed trap evidence

Every court shall be without jurisdiction to render a judgment of conviction against any person for a violation of this code involving the speed of a vehicle if the court admits any evidence or testimony secured in violation of, or which is inadmissible under this article. *(Stats.1959, c. 3, p. 1781, § 40805.)*

§ 40806. Police reports

In the event a defendant charged with an offense under this code pleads guilty, the trial court shall not at any time prior to pronouncing sentence receive or consider any report, verbal or written, of any police or traffic officer or witness of the offense without fully informing the defendant of all statements in the report or statement of witnesses, or without giving the defendant an opportunity to make answer thereto or to produce witnesses in rebuttal, and for such purpose the court shall grant a continuance before pronouncing sentence if requested by the defendant. *(Stats.1959, c. 3, p. 1781, § 40806.)*

§ 40807. Use of evidence regarding departmental action

No record of any action taken by the department against a person's privilege to operate a motor vehicle, nor any testimony regarding the proceedings at, or concerning, or produced at, any hearing held in connection with such action, shall be admissible as evidence in any court in any criminal action.

No provision of this section shall in any way limit the admissibility of such records or testimony as is necessary to enforce the provisions of this code relating to operating a motor vehicle without a valid driver's license or when the driving privilege is suspended or revoked, the admissibility of such records or testimony in any prosecution for failure to disclose any matter at such a hearing when required by law to do so, or the admissibility of such records and testimony when introduced solely for the purpose of impeaching the credibility of a witness. *(Added by Stats.1977, c. 804, p. 2454, § 4.)*

§ 40808. Effect of constitutional right to truth-in-evidence provision

Subdivision (d) of Section 28 of Article I of the California Constitution shall not be construed as abrogating the evidentiary provisions of this article. *(Added by Stats.1992, c. 538, (A.B.3659), § 2.)*

ARTICLE 2. CIVIL ACTIONS

Section
40830. Effect of convictions.
40831. Effect of speed conviction.
40832. Suspension or revocation of driving privilege.

Section
40833.   Report or action of department as evidence.
40834.   Effect of conviction.

§ 40830.   Effect of convictions

In either of the following circumstances a violation of any provision of this code does not establish negligence as a matter of law, but in any civil action under either of the circumstances negligence must be proved as a fact without regard to the violation. The circumstances under which this section applies are either:

(a) Where violation of the provision was required by a law of the federal government or by any rule, regulation, directive or order of any agency of the federal government, the violation of which is subject to penalty under an act of Congress or by any valid order of military authority.

(b) Where violation of the provision was required in order to comply with any regulation, directive, or order of the Governor promulgated under the California Emergency Services Act. *(Stats.1959, c. 3, p. 1781, § 40830. Amended by Stats.1971, c. 438, p. 909, § 195, operative May 3, 1972.)*

§ 40831.   Effect of speed conviction

In any civil action proof of speed in excess of any prima facie limit declared in Section 22352 at a particular time and place does not establish negligence as a matter of law but in all such actions it shall be necessary to establish as a fact that the operation of a vehicle at the excess speed constituted negligence. *(Stats. 1959, c. 3, p. 1782, § 40831.)*

Cross References

Applicability of this section to trolley coaches, see Vehicle Code § 21051.
Negligent operator defined, see Vehicle Code § 12810.
Rules of the road, exemption of authorized emergency vehicles, see Vehicle Code § 21055.
Speed charge to be specified, see Vehicle Code § 40503.
Speed laws, see Vehicle Code § 22349 et seq.

§ 40832.   Suspension or revocation of driving privilege

No record of the suspension or revocation of the privilege to operate a motor vehicle by the department, nor any testimony of or concerning or produced at the hearing terminating in the suspension or revocation, shall be admissible as evidence in any court in any civil action. *(Stats.1959, c. 3, p. 1782, § 40832.)*

Cross References

Revocation and suspension of license by a court, see Vehicle Code § 13200 et seq.

§ 40833.   Report or action of department as evidence

Neither the report required by Sections 16000, 16001, 16002, or 16003, the action taken by the department pursuant to Chapter 1 of Division 7 (commencing at Section 16000), the findings, if any, of the department upon which action is based, nor the security filed as provided in that chapter shall be referred to in any way, or be any evidence of the negligence or due care of any party, at the trial of any action at law to recover damages. *(Stats.1959, c. 3, p. 1782, § 40833.)*

§ 40834.   Effect of conviction

A judgment of conviction for any violation of this code or of any local ordinance relating to the operation of a motor vehicle or a finding reported under Section 1816 shall not be res judicata or constitute a collateral estoppel of any issue determined therein in any subsequent civil action. *(Added by Stats.1963, c. 1530, p. 3116, § 1.)*

CHAPTER 3.5.   EVIDENCE

Section
40900.   Electronic verification of vehicle ownership.
40901.   Trials; infractions; rules.
40902.   Trial by written declaration; adoption of rules and forms; introduction of evidence; trial de novo.
40903.   Failure to appear; evidence.

§ 40900.   Electronic verification of vehicle ownership

Notwithstanding any other provision of law, a verification by telegraph, teletype, facsimile transmission, or any other electronic device, from the department, of ownership of a vehicle registered pursuant to this code, is admissible in evidence as proof of ownership of the vehicle in any proceeding involving a parking violation of this code, or any local parking ordinance adopted pursuant to this code. *(Added by Stats.1973, c. 616, p. 1141, § 1. Amended by Stats.1991, c. 13 (A.B.37), § 65, eff. Feb. 13, 1991.)*

§ 40901.   Trials; infractions; rules

(a) A court, pursuant to this section, may by rule provide for the trial of any alleged infraction involving a violation of this code or any local ordinance adopted pursuant to this code.

(b) The rules governing the trials may provide for testimony and other relevant evidence to be introduced in the form of a notice to appear issued pursuant to Section 40500 and, notwithstanding Division 10 (commencing with Section 1200) of the Evidence Code, a business record or receipt.

(c) Prior to the entry of a waiver of constitutional right pursuant to any rules adopted under this section, the court shall inform the defendant in writing of the nature of the proceedings and of his or her right to confront and cross-examine witnesses, to subpoena witnesses on his or her behalf, and to hire counsel at his or her own expense. The court shall ascertain that the defendant knowingly and voluntarily waives his or her right to be confronted by the witnesses against him or her, to subpoena witnesses in his or her behalf, and to hire counsel on his or her behalf before proceeding.

(d) In any jurisdiction with a non-English speaking population exceeding 5 percent of the total population of the jurisdiction in any one language, a written explanation of the procedures and rights under this section shall be available in that language.

(e) Except as set forth above, nothing contained herein shall be interpreted to permit the submission of evidence other than in accordance with the law, nor to prevent courts from adopting other rules to provide for trials in accordance with the law. *(Added by Stats.1976, c. 1232, p. 5549, § 1. Amended by Stats.1996, c. 124 (A.B.3470), § 148.)*

§ 40902. Trial by written declaration; adoption of rules and forms; introduction of evidence; trial de novo

(a)(1) The court, pursuant to this section, shall, by rule, provide that the defendant may elect to have a trial by written declaration upon any alleged infraction, as charged by the citing officer, involving a violation of this code or any local ordinance adopted pursuant to this code, other than an infraction cited pursuant to Article 2 (commencing with Section 23152) of Chapter 12 of Division 11.

(2) The Judicial Council may adopt rules and forms governing trials by declaration in accordance with this section. Any rule or form adopted by the Judicial Council pursuant to this paragraph shall supersede any local rule of a court adopted pursuant to paragraph (1).

(b) If the defendant elects to have a trial by written declaration, the defendant shall, at the time of submitting that declaration, submit bail in the amount established in the uniform traffic penalty schedule pursuant to Section 40310. If the defendant is found not guilty or if the charges are otherwise dismissed, the amount of the bail shall be promptly refunded to the defendant.

(c) Notwithstanding Division 10 (commencing with Section 1200) of the Evidence Code, the rules governing trials by written declaration may provide for testimony and other relevant evidence to be introduced in the form of a notice to appear issued pursuant to Section 40500, a business record or receipt, a sworn declaration of the arresting officer, or a written statement or letter signed by the defendant.

(d) If the defendant is dissatisfied with a decision of the court in a proceeding pursuant to this section, the defendant shall be granted a trial de novo. *(Added by Stats.1978, c. 1282, p. 4187, § 1. Amended by Stats.1983, c. 345, § 1; Stats.1988, c. 91, § 1; Stats.1993, c. 488 (A.B.1398), § 1; Stats.1998, c. 265 (S.B.1813), § 1.)*

§ 40903. Failure to appear; evidence

(a) Any person who fails to appear as provided by law may be deemed to have elected to have a trial by written declaration upon any alleged infraction, as charged by the citing officer, involving a violation of this code or any local ordinance adopted pursuant to this code.

(b) Notwithstanding Division 10 (commencing with Section 1200) of the Evidence Code, testimony and other relevant evidence may be introduced in the form of a notice to appear issued pursuant to Section 40500, a notice of parking violation issued pursuant to Section 40202, a notice of delinquent parking violation issued pursuant to Section 40206, a business record or receipt, a sworn declaration of the arresting officer, or a written statement or letter signed by the defendant. *(Added by Stats.1992, c. 696 (A.B.1344), § 95, eff. Sept. 15, 1992.)*

CHAPTER 4. PRESUMPTIONS

Section
41100.   Speed restriction signs.
41101.   Official signs and traffic control devices.
41102.   Repealed.
41103.   Repealed.
41103.2.   Repealed.
41103.5.   Repealed.
41104.   Train of vehicles.

§ 41100. Speed restriction signs

In any action involving the question of unlawful speed of a vehicle upon a highway which has been signposted with speed restriction signs of a type complying with the requirements of this code, it shall be presumed that existing facts authorize the erection of the signs and that the prima facie speed limit on the highway is the limit stated on the signs. This presumption may be rebutted. *(Stats.1959, c. 3, p. 1782, § 41100.)*

Cross References

Business and residential areas defined, see Vehicle Code §§ 235, 515.
Presumptions and inferences,
    Generally, see Evidence Code § 600 et seq.
    Burden of producing evidence, see Evidence Code § 630 et seq.
    Burden of proof, see Evidence Code § 660 et seq.
Signs restricting speed, see Vehicle Code §§ 21357, 21359.
Speed laws generally, see Vehicle Code § 22349 et seq.
Statute making one fact prima facie evidence of another, see Evidence Code § 602.

§ 41101. Official signs and traffic control devices

(a) Whenever a traffic sign or traffic control device is placed in a position approximately conforming to the requirements of this code, it shall be presumed to have been placed by the official act or direction of lawful authority, unless the contrary is established by competent evidence.

(b) Any sign or traffic control device placed pursuant to this code and purporting to conform to the lawful requirements pertaining to it shall be presumed to comply with the requirements of this code unless the contrary is established by competent evidence. *(Stats.1959, c. 3, p. 1782, § 41101.)*

Cross References

Presumption of regular performance of official duty, see Evidence Code § 664.

Traffic signs, signals, and markings, see Vehicle Code § 21350 et seq.

§ 41102. Repealed by Stats.1992, c. 1244 (A.B.408), § 37, operative July 1, 1993

§ 41103. Repealed by Stats.1986, c. 939, § 21

§ 41103.2. Repealed by Stats.1986, c. 939, § 22

§ 41103.5. Repealed by Stats.1986, c. 939, § 23

§ 41104. Train of vehicles

In any case, involving an accident or otherwise, where any rear component of a train of vehicles fails to follow substantially in the path of the towing vehicle while moving upon a highway, the vehicle shall be presumed to have been operated in violation of Section 21711. *(Added by Stats.1959, c. 44, p. 1902, § 4.)*

CHAPTER 5. DEFENSES

Section
41400. Prior conviction or acquittal.
41401. Federal law.
41402. Emergency Services Act.
41403. Challenging constitutional validity of separate convictions; procedure; burden of proof; hearing at time of sentencing.

§ 41400. Prior conviction or acquittal

Whenever any person is charged with a violation of this code, it is a sufficient defense to such charge if it appears that in a criminal prosecution in another state or by the Federal Government, founded upon the act or omission in respect to which he is on trial, he has been convicted or acquitted. *(Stats.1959, c. 3, p. 1783, § 41400.)*

Cross References

Double jeopardy, prohibition against, see Const. Art. 1, § 15, Penal Code §§ 687, 1023.
Foreign conviction or acquittal, defense, see Penal Code § 656.

§ 41401. Federal law

No person shall be prosecuted for a violation of any provision of this code if the violation was required by a law of the federal government, by any rule, regulation, directive or order of any agency of the federal government, the violation of which is subject to penalty under an act of Congress, or by any valid order of military authority. *(Stats.1959, c. 3, p. 1784, § 41401. Amended by Stats.1973, c. 78, p. 140, § 24.)*

§ 41402. Emergency Services Act

No person shall be prosecuted for a violation of any provision of this code when violation of such provision is required in order to comply with any regulation, directive, or order of the Governor promulgated under the California Emergency Services Act. *(Stats.1959, c. 3, p. 1784, § 41402. Amended by Stats.1971, c. 438, p. 909, § 196, operative May 3, 1972.)*

Cross References

California Emergency Service Act, see Government Code § 8550 et seq.

§ 41403. Challenging constitutional validity of separate convictions; procedure; burden of proof; hearing at time of sentencing

(a) In any proceedings to have a judgment of conviction of a violation of Section 14601, 14601.1, 14601.2, 23152, or 23153, or Section 23103 as specified in Section 23103.5, which was entered in a separate proceeding, declared invalid on constitutional grounds, the defendant shall state in writing and with specificity wherein the defendant was deprived of the defendant's constitutional rights, which statement shall be filed with the clerk of the court and a copy served on the court that rendered that judgment and on the prosecuting attorney in the present proceedings at least five court days prior to the hearing thereon.

(b) Except as provided in subdivision (c), the court shall, prior to the trial of any pending criminal action against the defendant wherein the separate conviction is charged as such, hold a hearing, outside of the presence of the jury, in order to determine the constitutional validity of the charged separate conviction issue. At the hearing the procedure, the burden of proof, and the burden of producing evidence shall be as follows:

(1) The prosecution shall initially have the burden of producing evidence of the separate conviction sufficient to justify a finding that the defendant has suffered that separate conviction.

(2) After the production of evidence required by paragraph (1), the defendant then has the burden of proof by a preponderance of the evidence that the defendant's constitutional rights were infringed in the separate proceeding at issue. If the separate conviction sought to be invalidated is based upon a plea of guilty or nolo contendere, the defendant shall provide the court with evidence of the prior plea, including the court docket, written waivers of constitutional rights executed by the defendant, and transcripts of the relevant court proceedings at the time of the entry of the defendant's plea. These records shall be provided to the defendant without cost to him or her, when the defendant is represented by the public defender or counsel appointed pursuant to Section 987.2 of the Penal Code.

(3) If the defendant bears this burden successfully, the prosecution shall have the right to produce evidence in rebuttal.

(4) The court shall make a finding on the basis of the evidence thus produced and shall strike from the accusatory pleading any separate conviction found to be constitutionally invalid.

(c) If the defendant fails to comply with the notice requirement of subdivision (a) or fails to produce the evidence required by paragraph (2) of subdivision (b), the court shall hear the motion at the time of sentencing in lieu of continuing the trial, unless good cause is shown for failure to provide notice pursuant to subdivision (a) or produce the evidence required by paragraph (2) of subdivision (b), in which case the court shall grant a continuance of the trial for a reasonable period. The procedure, burden of proof, and burden of producing evidence as provided in subdivision (b) shall apply regardless of when the motion is heard. *(Formerly § 23102.2, added by Stats.1973, c. 1128, p. 2296, § 4. Amended by Stats.1977, c. 186, p. 705, § 1. Renumbered § 23208 and amended by Stats.1981, c. 940, p. 3567, § 15. Amended by Stats.1984, c. 1205, § 10. Renumbered § 41403 and amended by Stats.1984, c. 1585, § 2. Amended by Stats.1995, c. 83 (A.B.232), § 1.)*

CHAPTER 6. NONPROSECUTION OF VIOLATIONS

Section
41500. Non-felony offenses of persons in custody.
41501. Continuance; attendance at licensed school for traffic violators, licensed driving school, or court approved program of driving instruction; conviction held confidential.
41501. Continuance; attendance at licensed school for traffic violators, licensed driving school, or court approved program of driving instruction; conviction held confidential.

§ 41500. Non-felony offenses of persons in custody

(a) No person shall be subject to prosecution for any nonfelony offense arising out of the operation of a motor vehicle or violation of this code as a pedestrian which is pending against him at the time of his commitment to the custody of the Director of Corrections or the Department of the Youth Authority.

(b) Notwithstanding any other provisions of law to the contrary, no driver's license shall be suspended or re-voked, nor shall the issuance or renewal of a license be refused as a result of a pending nonfelony offense occurring prior to the time a person was committed to the custody of the Director of Corrections or the Department of the Youth Authority or as a result of a notice received by the department pursuant to subdivision (a) of Section 40509 when the offense which gave rise to the notice occurred prior to the time a person was committed to the custody of the Director of Corrections or the Department of the Youth Authority.

(c) The department shall remove from its records any notice received by it pursuant to subdivision (a) of Section 40509 upon receipt of satisfactory evidence that a person was committed to the custody of the Director of Corrections or the Department of the Youth Authority after the offense which gave rise to the notice occurred.

(d) The provisions of this section shall not apply to any nonfelony offense wherein the department is required by this code to immediately revoke or suspend the privilege of any person to drive a motor vehicle upon receipt of a duly certified abstract of the record of any court showing

that the person has been convicted of that nonfelony offense.

(e) The provisions of subdivisions (a), (b), and (c) do not apply to any offense committed by a person while he is temporarily released from custody pursuant to law or while he is on parole.

(f) The provisions of subdivisions (a), (b), and (c) do not apply if the pending offense is a violation of Section 23103, 23152, or 23153. *(Added by Stats.1970, c. 1163, p. 2066, § 2. Amended by Stats.1972, c. 1073, p. 2009, § 1; Stats.1975, c. 545, p. 1111, § 1; Stats.1992, c. 950 (A.B. 3569), § 1.)*

Cross References
Director of Corrections, see Penal Code § 5050 et seq.
Record of license applicant for conviction of traffic violations and traffic accidents, see Vehicle Code § 12808.
Youth Authority, see Welfare and Institutions Code § 1700 et seq.

§ 41501. Continuance; attendance at licensed school for traffic violators, licensed driving school, or court approved program of driving instruction; conviction held confidential

Section added by Stats.2010, c. 216 (A.B.2144), § 12.5, operative July 1, 2011. See, also, another section of the same number, added by Stats.2010, c. 599 (A.B.2499), § 12.5, operative July 1, 2011.

(a) After a deposit of bail and bail forfeiture, a plea of guilty or no contest, or a conviction, the court may order a continuance of a proceeding against a person, who receives a notice to appear in court for a violation of a statute relating to the safe operation of a vehicle, in consideration for successful completion of a course of instruction at a licensed school for traffic violators, a licensed driving school, or any other court-approved program of driving instruction, and pursuant to Section 1803.5 or 42005, the court may order that the conviction be held confidential by the department according to Section 1808.7.

(b) Subdivision (a) does not apply to a person who receives a notice to appear as to, or is otherwise charged with, a violation of an offense described in subdivisions (a) to (e), inclusive, of Section 12810.

(c) This section shall become operative on July 1, 2011. *(Added by Stats.2010, c. 216 (A.B.2144), § 12.5, operative July 1, 2011.)*

Cross References
Additional fee imposed for maintenance of funding for court security upon conviction for criminal offense involving violations of Vehicle Code, exceptions, see Penal Code § 1465.8.
Occupational licensing, traffic violator schools, duties of Judicial Council, see Vehicle Code § 11205.4.

§ 41501. Continuance; attendance at licensed school for traffic violators, licensed driving school, or court approved program of driving instruction; conviction held confidential

Section added by Stats.2010, c. 599 (A.B.2499), § 12.5, operative July 1, 2011. See, also, another section of the same number added by Stats.2010, c. 216 (A.B.2144), § 12.5, operative July 1, 2011.

(a) After a deposit of bail and bail forfeiture, a plea of guilty or no contest, or a conviction, the court may order a continuance of a proceeding against a person, who receives a notice to appear in court for a violation of a statute relating to the safe operation of a vehicle, in consideration for successful completion of a course of instruction at a licensed school for traffic violators and pursuant to Section 1803.5 or 42005, the court may order that the conviction be held confidential by the department in accordance with Section 1808.7. The court shall notify a person that only one conviction within 18 months will be held confidential.

(b) Subdivision (a) does not apply to a person who receives a notice to appear as to, or is otherwise charged with, a violation of an offense described in subdivisions (a) to (e), inclusive, of Section 12810.

(c) This section shall become operative on July 1, 2011. *(Added by Stats.2010, c. 599 (A.B.2499), § 12.5, operative July 1, 2011. Amended by Stats.2011, c. 296 (A.B.1023), § 311.)*

Cross References

Additional fee imposed for maintenance of funding for court security upon conviction for criminal offense involving violations of Vehicle Code, exceptions, see Penal Code § 1465.8.

Occupational licensing, traffic violator schools, duties of Judicial Council, see Vehicle Code § 11205.4.

CHAPTER 7.   ARREST QUOTAS

Section
41600.   Arrest quota defined.
41601.   Citation defined.
41601.5.   Agency defined.
41602.   Arrest quota prohibited.
41603.   Evaluation of peace officer's or parking enforcement officer's performance.

§ 41600.   Arrest quota defined

For purposes of this chapter, "arrest quota" means any requirement regarding the number of arrests made, or the number of citations issued, by a peace officer, or parking enforcement employee, or the proportion of those arrests made and citations issued by a peace officer or parking enforcement employee, relative to the arrests made and citations issued by another peace officer or parking enforcement employee, or group of officers or employees. *(Added by Stats.1976, c. 1111, p. 5001, § 1. Amended by Stats.2002, c. 105 (S.B.2069), § 1.)*

§ 41601.   Citation defined

For purposes of this chapter, "citation" means a notice to appear, notice of violation, or notice of parking violation. *(Added by Stats.1976, c. 1111, p. 5001, § 1.)*

§ 41601.5.   Agency defined

For purposes of this chapter, "agency" includes the Regents of the University of California. *(Added by Stats.2002, c. 105 (S.B.2069), § 2.)*

§ 41602.   Arrest quota prohibited

No state or local agency employing peace officers or parking enforcement employees engaged in the enforcement of this code or any local ordinance adopted pursuant to this code, may establish any policy requiring any peace officer or parking enforcement employees to meet an arrest quota. *(Added by Stats.1976, c. 1111, p. 5001, § 1. Amended by Stats.2002, c. 105 (S.B.2069), § 3.)*

§ 41603.   Evaluation of peace officer's or parking enforcement officer's performance

No state or local agency employing peace officers or parking enforcement employees engaged in the enforcement of this code shall use the number of arrests or citations issued by a peace officer or parking enforcement employees as the sole criterion for promotion, demotion, dismissal, or the earning of any benefit provided by the agency. Those arrests or citations, and their ultimate dispositions, may only be considered in evaluating the overall performance of a peace officer or parking enforcement employees. An evaluation may include, but shall not be limited to, criteria such as attendance, punctuality, work safety, complaints by citizens, commendations, demeanor, formal training, and professional judgment. *(Added by Stats.1976, c. 1111, p. 5001, § 1. Amended by Stats.1977, c. 579, p. 1920, § 189; Stats.1979, c. 373, p. 1385, § 329; Stats.2002, c. 105 (S.B.2069), § 4.)*

CHAPTER 8.   CONSOLIDATED DISPOSITION

Section
41610.   Guilty plea to traffic infraction or misdemeanor; election to enter guilty plea for consolidated disposition of other charged offenses; procedure; exceptions.

§ 41610.   Guilty plea to traffic infraction or misdemeanor; election to enter guilty plea for consolidated disposition of other charged offenses; procedure; exceptions

(a) Whenever a person who is in custody enters a guilty plea to an infraction or misdemeanor under this code and there is outstanding any warrant of arrest for a violation of this code or a local ordinance adopted pursuant to this code that is filed in any court within the same county, the defendant may elect to enter a guilty plea to any of these charged offenses of which the court has a record, except offenses specified in subdivision (b). The court shall sentence the defendant for each of the offenses for which a guilty plea has been entered pursuant to this section, and shall notify the appropriate court or department in each affected judicial district of the disposition. After receiving that notice of disposition, the court in which each complaint was filed shall prepare and transmit to the department any certification required by applicable provisions of Section 40509 as if the court had heard the case.

(b) Subdivision (a) does not authorize entry of a guilty plea as specified in that subdivision to an offense for which a notice of parking violation has been issued, nor to any offense specified in Section 14601.2, 14601.3, 20002, 23103, 23104, 23105, 23152, or 23153, subdivision (a) of Section 14601, or subdivision (a) of Section 14601.1. *(Added by Stats.1983, c. 989, § 1. Amended by Stats.2007, c. 682 (A.B.430), § 20.)*

Division 18

PENALTIES AND DISPOSITION OF FEES, FINES, AND FORFEITURES

Chapter		Section
1.	Penalties	42000
2.	Disposition of Fees, Fines, and Forfeitures	42200
3.	Motor Vehicle Account	42270

CHAPTER 1. PENALTIES

Article		Section
1.	Public Offenses	42000
2.	Weight Violations	42030
3.	Driver Training Penalty Assessments [Repealed]	

ARTICLE 1. PUBLIC OFFENSES

Section
42000. Felony.
42000.1. Speeding in excess of 100 miles per hour; fine.
42000.5. Buses, motor trucks or truck tractors; speed limit violations.
42001. Infractions and special misdemeanors.
42001.1. Conviction of infraction for violation of §§ 2815, 22526; punishment.
42001.2. Violations of § 27153.5; subsequent violations of § 27153.
42001.3. Maintenance of driving logs; violations of truck and school bus safety regulations; punishment.
42001.4. Transportation of animals; failure to enclose or restrain.
42001.5. Parking in disabled person's space.
42001.6. Parking in zero-emission vehicle (ZEV) space.
42001.7. Littering.
42001.8. Vehicle registration offenses.
42001.9. Violations of section 23135.
42001.10. Violations of § 38020.
42001.11. Violations of sections 21655.5 or 21655.8.
42001.12. Failure to yield right-of-way to emergency vehicles; punishment.
42001.13. Penalty for person convicted of infraction for violation of § 22507.8; suspension of penalty; payment of fine.
42001.14. Disconnecting, modifying, or altering required pollution control devices; punishment.
42001.15. Violations of sections relating to steady red circular or arrow signals; lane use control signals; illuminated flashing red traffic signal; fines.
42001.16. Railroad grade crossing violations.
42001.17. Conviction under § 21951; fines.
42001.18. Conviction under § 21971; fines.
42001.19. Conviction under § 21070; fines.
42001.20. Violation of section relating to warning devices on certain refuse or garbage trucks.
42001.25. Violations of § 23140.
42002. General misdemeanors.
42002.1. Failure to stop and submit to inspection of equipment or for an unsafe condition endangering a person; punishment.

Section
42002.1. Misdemeanor violation of §§ 2800, 2801, or 2803; punishment.
42002.1. Misdemeanor convictions relating to a failure to stop and submit to inspection of equipment or an unsafe condition endangering a person.
42002.4. Purchase, sale, receipt or possession of vehicles or components with removed or altered serial or identification numbers; punishment.
42002.5. Violations of §§ 10852 or 10853 involving vehicle modified for use of disabled person; penalties.
42003. Payment of fines and costs.
42004. Determination of penalty.
42004.5. 24-hour suspension of sentence.
42005. Traffic violator schools; courts may permit or require attendance; conviction records not confidential; convictions not added to violation point counts; commercial motor vehicle drivers ineligible; other violations rendering operators ineligible; choice of school; failure to attend as misdemeanor.
42005.1. Participation in study of traffic violator schools in lieu of attendance.
42005.2. Repealed.
42005.3. Driver awareness or education program participation; traffic violations; application of section to diversion programs for minors.
42005.5. Attendance at school for traffic violators; computation of average daily attendance.
42006. Night court assessment.
42007. Uniform fee for traffic violator school.
42007.1. Amount of fee collected pursuant to subd. (a) of § 42007; allocation of fees assessed pursuant to subd. (c) of § 11208.
42007.3. Traffic violator school for infraction violations relating to steady red circular or arrow signal; lane use control signals; illuminated flashing red traffic signal; allocation of fees.
42007.4. Use of fees collected from persons attending traffic violator school as a result of railroad grade crossing violations.
42007.5. Repealed.
42008. County amnesty program for delinquent fines and bail; implementation and application; amount; effect of payment under program; deposit of funds.
42008.1. Repealed.
42008.5. Amnesty program.
42008.7. State amnesty program.
42009. Violations within highway construction or maintenance area.
42010. Offenses committed within Safety Enhancement–Double Fine Zones.
42011. Repealed.

§ 42000. Felony

Unless a different penalty is expressly provided by this code, every person convicted of a felony for a violation of

1085

any provision of this code shall be punished by a fine of not less than one thousand dollars ($1,000) or more than ten thousand dollars ($10,000), or by imprisonment pursuant to subdivision (h) of Section 1170 of the Penal Code, or by both such fine and imprisonment. *(Stats. 1959, c. 3, p. 1784, § 42000. Amended by Stats.1976, c. 1139, p. 5173, § 342, operative July 1, 1977; Stats.1983, c. 1092, § 401, eff. Sept. 27, 1983, operative Jan. 1, 1984; Stats.2011, c. 15 (A.B.109), § 615, eff. April 4, 2011, operative Oct. 1, 2011.)*

Cross References

Felony defined, see Penal Code § 17.
Punishment for felony, see Penal Code § 18.

§ 42000.1. Speeding in excess of 100 miles per hour; fine

Notwithstanding Section 42001, every person convicted of an infraction for a violation described in subdivision (b) of Section 22348 shall be punished by a fine not exceeding five hundred dollars ($500). *(Added by Stats. 1983, c. 980, § 4.)*

§ 42000.5. Buses, motor trucks or truck tractors; speed limit violations

Every person convicted of an infraction for a violation of Section 22350, 22406, or 22407 while operating a bus, motor truck, or truck tractor having three or more axles, or any motor truck or truck tractor drawing any other vehicle, shall be punished by a fine not exceeding one hundred dollars ($100) for a first conviction, except that if the person has exceeded the specified speed limit by 10 miles per hour or more, the fine shall not exceed two hundred dollars ($200) for a first conviction, and not exceeding three hundred dollars ($300) for a second or subsequent conviction. *(Added by Stats.1987, c. 1170, § 1. Amended by Stats.1989, c. 980, § 1.)*

§ 42001. Infractions and special misdemeanors

(a) Except as provided in this code, a person convicted of an infraction for a violation of this code or of a local ordinance adopted pursuant to this code shall be punished as follows:

(1) By a fine not exceeding one hundred dollars ($100).

(2) For a second infraction occurring within one year of a prior infraction that resulted in a conviction, a fine not exceeding two hundred dollars ($200).

(3) For a third or subsequent infraction occurring within one year of two or more prior infractions that resulted in convictions, a fine not exceeding two hundred fifty dollars ($250).

(b) A pedestrian convicted of an infraction for a violation of this code or any local ordinance adopted pursuant to this code shall be punished by a fine not exceeding fifty dollars ($50).

(c) A person convicted of a violation of subdivision (a) or (b) of Section 27150.3 shall be punished by a fine of two hundred fifty dollars ($250), and a person convicted of a violation of subdivision (c) of Section 27150.3 shall be punished by a fine of one thousand dollars ($1,000).

(d) Notwithstanding any other provision of law, a local public entity that employs peace officers, as designated under Chapter 4.5 (commencing with Section 830) of Title 3 of Part 2 of the Penal Code, the California State University, and the University of California may, by ordinance or resolution, establish a schedule of fines applicable to infractions committed by bicyclists within its jurisdiction. A fine, including all penalty assessments and court costs, established pursuant to this subdivision shall not exceed the maximum fine, including penalty assessment and court costs, otherwise authorized by this code for that violation. If a bicycle fine schedule is adopted, it shall be used by the courts having jurisdiction over the area within which the ordinance or resolution is applicable instead of the fines, including penalty assessments and court costs, otherwise applicable under this code. *(Stats.1959, c. 3, p. 1784, § 42001. Amended by Stats.1961, c. 1974, p. 4164, § 1; Stats.1965, c. 1123, p. 2771, § 1; Stats.1968, c. 1192, p. 2264, § 16, operative Jan. 1, 1969; Stats.1970, c. 1431, p. 2778, § 7; Stats.1973, c. 1162, p. 2420, § 5; Stats.1975, c. 635, p. 1379, § 2; Stats.1977, c. 1104, p. 3527, § 2; Stats.1978, c. 421, p. 1321, § 7; Stats.1978, c. 626, p. 2078, § 3; Stats.1979, c. 373, p. 1385, § 330; Stats.1983, c. 1092, § 402, eff. Sept. 27, 1983, operative Jan. 1, 1984; Stats.1983, c. 619, § 1; Stats.1984, c. 69, § 2, eff. April 5, 1984; Stats.1984, c. 396, § 1; Stats.1984, c. 508, § 2; Stats.1985, c. 1126, § 7, eff. Sept. 28, 1985, operative April 1, 1986; Stats.1987, c. 1170, § 2; Stats.1988, c. 504, § 5, eff. Aug. 22, 1988; Stats.1988, c. 1054, § 4; Stats.1988, c. 1544, § 62; Stats.1991, c. 13 (A.B.37), § 66, eff. Feb. 13, 1991; Stats.1993, c. 307 (A.B.669), § 1; Stats.1997, c. 852 (A.B.1191), § 3; Stats. 1999, c. 841 (A.B.923), § 4; Stats.2000, c. 833 (A.B.2522), § 13; Stats.2003, c. 432 (A.B.377), § 2; Stats.2003, c. 555 (A.B.327), § 7.5; Stats.2004, c. 338 (A.B.340), § 2; Stats. 2004, c. 391 (S.B.1085), § 2; Stats.2005, c. 166 (A.B. 1637), § 3; Stats.2006, c. 538 (S.B.1852), § 667; Stats. 2006, c. 898 (S.B.1021), § 4; Stats.2006, c. 899 (A.B. 2752), § 2; Stats.2006, c. 900 (A.B.1850), § 3.)*

Cross References

Family day care homes, licensees to sign statement showing no conviction of crimes other than traffic infractions under this section, see Health and Safety Code § 1597.59.
Infractions under automotive repair act, application of this section, see Business and Professions Code § 9889.21.
Maximum penalty for infractions, residence, see Vehicle Code § 40310.
Misdemeanor defined, see Penal Code § 17.
Punishments,
  Infractions, see Penal Code § 19.6.
  Misdemeanors, see Penal Code §§ 19.2, 19.4.
School safety patrol traffic signals, disregarding, see Education Code § 49307.

Traffic referees, powers and duties, see Government Code § 72401.

§ 42001.1. Conviction of infraction for violation of §§ 2815, 22526; punishment

(a) Every person convicted of an infraction for a violation of Section 2815 or a violation of subdivision (a) or (b) of Section 22526 at an intersection posted pursuant to subdivision (d) of Section 22526 shall be punished as follows:

(1) For a first conviction, a fine of not less than fifty dollars ($50) nor more than one hundred dollars ($100).

(2) For a second conviction within a period of one year, a fine of not less than one hundred dollars ($100) nor more than two hundred dollars ($200).

(3) For a third or any subsequent conviction within a period of two years, a fine of not less than two hundred fifty dollars ($250) nor more than five hundred dollars ($500).

(b) In addition to the fine specified in subdivision (a), the court may order the department to suspend the driver's license for up to 30 days of any person convicted of a third or any subsequent conviction of Section 2815 within a period of two years, and the department shall suspend the license for the period of time so ordered. *(Added by Stats.1984, c. 69, § 4, eff. April 5, 1984. Amended by Stats.1987, c. 739, § 2; Stats.1999, c. 724 (A.B.1650), § 53; Stats.2005, c. 716 (A.B.1067), § 7.)*

Cross References

Anti–Gridlock Act of 1987, see Vehicle Code § 22526.
Obstructing railroad track, punishment, see Penal Code § 218.1.
Rail transit related traffic violations, county populations greater than 500,000, punishment, see Penal Code § 369b.

§ 42001.2. Violations of § 27153.5; subsequent violations of § 27153

(a) A person convicted of an infraction for a violation of Section 27153.5 with a motor vehicle having a manufacturer's maximum gross vehicle weight rating of 6,001 or more pounds is punishable by a fine for the first offense of not less than two hundred fifty dollars ($250) and not more than two thousand five hundred dollars ($2,500), and for a second or subsequent offense within one year of not less than five hundred dollars ($500) and not more than five thousand dollars ($5,000).

(b) A person convicted of an infraction for a second or subsequent violation of Section 27153, or a second or subsequent violation of 27153.5, with a motor vehicle having a manufacturer's maximum gross vehicle weight rating of less than 6,001 pounds, is punishable by a fine of not less than one hundred thirty-five dollars ($135) nor more than two hundred eighty-five dollars ($285).

(c) Notwithstanding Section 40616, the penalties in subdivision (b) apply when a person is guilty of willfully violating a written promise to correct, or willfully failing to deliver proof of correction, as prescribed in Section 40616, when an offense described in subdivision (b) was the violation for which the notice to correct was issued and the person was previously convicted of the same offense, except that costs of repair shall be limited to those specified in Section 44017 of the Health and Safety Code.

(d) Notwithstanding any other provision of law and subject to Section 1463.15 of the Penal Code, revenues collected from fines and forfeitures imposed under this section shall be allocated as follows: 15 percent to the county in which the prosecution is conducted, 10 percent to the prosecuting agency, 25 percent to the enforcement agency, except the Department of the California Highway Patrol, and 50 percent to the air quality management district or air pollution control district in which the infraction occurred, to be used for programs to regulate or control emissions from vehicular sources of air pollution. If the enforcement agency is the Department of the California Highway Patrol, the revenues shall be allocated 25 percent to the county in which the prosecution is conducted, 25 percent to the prosecuting agency, and 50 percent to the air quality management district or air pollution control district in which the infraction occurred. If no prosecuting agency is involved, the revenues that would otherwise be allocated to the prosecuting agency shall instead be allocated to the air quality management district or air pollution control district in which the infraction occurred.

(e) For the purposes of subdivisions (a), (b), and (c), a second or subsequent offense does not include an offense involving a different motor vehicle. *(Added by Stats.1988, c. 1544, § 63. Amended by Stats.1990, c. 367 (A.B.911), § 1; Stats.1991, c. 928 (A.B.1886), § 39, eff. Oct. 14, 1991; Stats.1992, c. 1243 (A.B.3090), § 110, eff. Sept. 30, 1992; Stats.2003, c. 482 (S.B.708), § 4.)*

§ 42001.3. Maintenance of driving logs; violations of truck and school bus safety regulations; punishment

(a) Violations of Section 34506.3, with respect to any regulation adopted under Section 34501 relative to the maintenance of driving logs, shall be punishable by a fine of not more than five hundred dollars ($500).

(b) Violations of subdivision (a) of Section 34506, with respect to any regulation adopted under Section 34501 relative to drivers' hours of service, shall be punishable by a fine of not less than five hundred dollars ($500) nor more than one thousand dollars ($1,000). In addition, the violations may be punishable by imprisonment in the county jail for not more than six months. *(Added by Stats.1983, c. 619, § 2. Amended by Stats.1988, c. 631, § 1.)*

§ 42001.4. Transportation of animals; failure to enclose or restrain

Every person convicted of an infraction for violation of Section 23117 shall be punished as follows:

(a) By a fine of not less than fifty dollars ($50) nor more than one hundred dollars ($100).

(b) For a second infraction occurring within one year of a prior infraction which resulted in a conviction, a fine of not less than seventy-five dollars ($75) nor more than two hundred dollars ($200).

(c) For a third or any subsequent infraction occurring within one year of two or more prior infractions which resulted in convictions, a fine of not less than one hundred dollars ($100) nor more than two hundred fifty dollars ($250). *(Added by Stats.1987, c. 224, § 2.)*

§ 42001.5. Parking in disabled person's space

(a) A person convicted of an infraction for a violation of subdivision (i) or (*l*) of Section 22500, or of Section 22522, shall be punished by a fine of not less than two hundred fifty dollars ($250).

(b) No part of any fine imposed under this section may be suspended, except the court may suspend that portion of the fine above one hundred dollars ($100).

(c) A fine imposed under this section may be paid in installments if the court determines that the defendant is unable to pay the entire amount in one payment. *(Added by Stats.1970, c. 1431, p. 2778, § 8. Amended by Stats. 1977, c. 590, p. 1956, § 2; Stats.1982, c. 975, p. 3497, § 11; Stats.1986, c. 328, § 3; Stats.1988, c. 1008, § 5; Stats.1991, c. 630 (A.B.1346), § 2; Stats.1992, c. 785 (A.B.2289), § 4; Stats.1992, c. 1243 (A.B.3090), § 111, eff. Sept. 30, 1992; Stats.1992, c. 1243 (A.B.3090), § 111.1, eff. Sept. 30, 1992, operative Jan. 1, 1993; Stats.1994, c. 221 (S.B.1378), § 4, operative July 1, 1995; Stats.1994, c. 1149 (A.B.2878), § 12; Stats.2003, c. 555 (A.B.327), § 8.)*

Cross References

Disposition of fines, see Penal Code § 1463.20.
Maximum penalty for infractions, residence, see Vehicle Code § 40310.

§ 42001.6. Parking in zero-emission vehicle (ZEV) space

Every person convicted of an infraction for a violation of Section 22511.1 is punishable by a fine of one hundred dollars ($100).

No part of any fine imposed shall be suspended, except the court may suspend that portion of the fine above twenty-five dollars ($25) for a violation of Section 22511.1 if the person convicted possessed at the time of the offense, but failed to display, a valid zero-emission vehicle decal identification issued pursuant to <u>subdivision</u> (a) * * * of Section 5205.5. The fine may be paid in installments if the court determines that the defendant is unable to pay the entire amount in one payment. *(Added by Stats.2002, c. 640 (A.B.1314), § 6. Amended by Stats.2013, c. 414 (S.B.286), § 4.)*

§ 42001.7. Littering

(a) Every person convicted of a violation of Section 23111 or 23112, or subdivision (a) of Section 23113, shall be punished by a mandatory fine of not less than one hundred dollars ($100) nor more than one thousand

dollars ($1,000) upon a first conviction, by a mandatory fine of not less than five hundred dollars ($500) nor more than one thousand dollars ($1,000) upon a second conviction, and by a mandatory fine of not less than seven hundred fifty dollars ($750) nor more than one thousand dollars ($1,000) upon a third or subsequent conviction.

In no case may the court order imprisonment in the county jail for a violation punishable under this subdivision, unless imprisonment is ordered pursuant to Section 166 of the Penal Code.

(b) The court shall, in addition to the fines imposed pursuant to subdivision (a), order the offender to pick up litter or clean up graffiti at a time and place within the jurisdiction of the court as follows:

(1) For a first conviction punished pursuant to subdivision (a), the court shall require the offender to pick up litter or clean up graffiti for not less than eight hours.

(2) For a second conviction punished pursuant to subdivision (a), the court shall require the offender to pick up litter or clean up graffiti for not less than 16 hours.

(3) For a third or subsequent conviction punished pursuant to subdivision (a), the court shall require the offender to pick up litter or clean up graffiti for not less than 24 hours.

(c) It is the intent of the Legislature that persons convicted of highway littering be required to bear the penalty for their actions. Therefore, the court may not suspend the mandatory fines required by subdivision (a) except in unusual cases where the interest of justice would best be served by suspension of the fine. If the court suspends imposition of any fine required by subdivision (a), it shall, as a condition of that suspension, require the offender to pick up litter or clean up graffiti at a time and place within the jurisdiction of the court for not less than eight hours for every one hundred dollars ($100) of fine suspended. The court may not suspend the order to pick up litter or clean up graffiti required by this subdivision or subdivision (b) except in unusual cases where the interest of justice would best be served by suspension of that order. *(Added by Stats.1970, c. 1548, p. 3152, § 11. Amended by Stats.1983, c. 1092, § 403, eff. Sept. 27, 1983, operative Jan. 1, 1984; Stats.1987, c. 133, § 6; Stats.1990, c. 982 (A.B.4229), § 1.)*

§ 42001.8. Vehicle registration offenses

Every person convicted of an infraction for a violation of Section 4000 shall be punished by a fine of not less than fifty dollars ($50) and not more than two hundred fifty dollars ($250). *(Added by Stats.1985, c. 1126, § 8, eff. Sept. 28, 1985, operative April 1, 1986.)*

§ 42001.9. Violations of section 23135

Every person convicted of an infraction for a violation of Section 23135 shall be punished by a fine of fifty dollars ($50). *(Added by Stats.1978, c. 421, p. 1321, § 8.)*

§ 42001.10. Violations of § 38020

Every person convicted for a violation of Section 38020 shall be punished by a fine of not less than fifty dollars ($50) for a first offense, and not more than two hundred fifty dollars ($250) for every subsequent offense. *(Formerly § 42001.9, added by Stats.1986, c. 1009, § 6. Amended by Stats.1987, c. 56, § 175; Stats.1987, c. 1027, § 29. Renumbered § 42001.10 by Stats.1988, c. 160, § 184.)*

§ 42001.11. Violations of sections 21655.5 or 21655.8

Every person convicted of an infraction for a violation of Section 21655.5 or 21655.8 shall be punished as follows:

(a) For a first conviction, a fine of not less than one hundred dollars ($100), nor more than one hundred fifty dollars ($150).

(b) For a second conviction within a period of one year, a fine of not less than one hundred fifty dollars ($150), nor more than two hundred dollars ($200).

(c) For a third or any subsequent conviction within a period of two years, a fine of not less than two hundred fifty dollars ($250), nor more than five hundred dollars ($500). *(Added by Stats.1988, c. 1054, § 5.)*

§ 42001.12. Failure to yield right-of-way to emergency vehicles; punishment

Every person convicted of an infraction for a violation of Section 21806 shall be punished as follows:

(a) For a first conviction, by a fine of not less than one hundred dollars ($100) nor more than two hundred fifty dollars ($250).

(b) For a second conviction within one year, by a fine of not less than one hundred fifty dollars ($150) nor more than five hundred dollars ($500).

(c) For a third or any subsequent conviction within three years, by a fine of not less than two hundred fifty dollars ($250) nor more than five hundred dollars ($500). *(Added by Stats.1991, c. 13 (A.B.37), § 67, eff. Feb. 13, 1991.)*

Cross References

Failure to yield right-of-way to emergency vehicles, see Vehicle Code § 21806.

§ 42001.13. Penalty for person convicted of infraction for violation of § 22507.8; suspension of penalty; payment of fine

(a) A person who commits a violation of Section 22507.8 is subject to either a civil notice of parking violation pursuant to Article 3 (commencing with Section 40200) of Chapter 1 of Division 17 or a criminal notice to appear.

(b) If a notice to appear is issued and upon conviction of an infraction for a violation of Section 22507.8, a person shall be punished as follows:

(1) A fine of not less than two hundred fifty dollars ($250) and not more than five hundred dollars ($500) for the first offense.

(2) A fine of not less than five hundred dollars ($500) and not more than seven hundred fifty dollars ($750) for the second offense.

(3) A fine of not less than seven hundred fifty dollars ($750) and not more than one thousand dollars ($1,000) for three or more offenses.

(c) The court may suspend the imposition of the fine if the person convicted possessed at the time of the offense, but failed to display, a valid special identification license plate issued pursuant to Section 5007 or a distinguishing placard issued pursuant to Section 22511.55 or 22511.59.

(d) A fine imposed under this section may be paid in installments if the court determines that the defendant is unable to pay the entire amount in one payment. *(Added by Stats.2003, c. 555 (A.B.327), § 9. Amended by Stats. 2007, c. 413 (A.B.1531), § 6; Stats.2009, c. 415 (A.B.144), § 8; Stats.2010, c. 328 (S.B.1330), § 233.)*

Cross References

Additional fines imposed for violation of disabled parking restrictions, see Penal Code § 1465.6.

Designation of parking for disabled persons and veterans, display of fine on parking space sign, see Vehicle Code § 22511.7.

Fines imposed and collected for violation of disabled parking restrictions, see Penal Code § 1465.5.

Issuance and renewal of disabled parking placards, penalty printing requirements, see Vehicle Code §§ 22511.55 and 22511.59.

Offstreet parking, designation of parking for disabled persons and veterans, display of fine on parking space sign, see Vehicle Code § 22511.8.

Parking facilities for physically handicapped persons and disabled veterans, display of fine on parking space sign, see Government Code § 14679.

Penalties for infractions and special misdemeanors, application of this section, see Vehicle Code § 42001.

§ 42001.14. Disconnecting, modifying, or altering required pollution control devices; punishment

(a) Every person convicted of an infraction for the offense of disconnecting, modifying, or altering a required pollution control device in violation of Section 27156 shall be punished as follows:

(1) For a first conviction, by a fine of not less than fifty dollars ($50), nor more than one hundred dollars ($100).

(2) For a second or subsequent conviction, by a fine of not less than one hundred dollars ($100), nor more than two hundred fifty dollars ($250).

(b)(1) The fines collected under subdivision (a) shall be allocated pursuant to subdivision (d) of Section 42001.2.

(2) The amounts allocated pursuant to paragraph (1) to the air pollution control district or air quality management district in which the infraction occurred shall first be allocated to the State Air Resources Board and the Bureau of Automotive Repair to pay the costs of the state

board and the bureau under Article 8 (commencing with Section 44080) of Chapter 5 of Part 5 of Division 26 of the Health and Safety Code.

(3) The funds collected under subdivision (a) which are not required for purposes of paragraph (2) shall be used for the enforcement of Section 27156 or for the implementation of Article 8 (commencing with Section 44080) of Chapter 5 of Part 5 of Division 26 of the Health and Safety Code. *(Added by Stats.1992, c. 972 (S.B.1404), § 3.)*

§ 42001.15. Violations of sections relating to steady red circular or arrow signals; lane use control signals; illuminated flashing red traffic signal; fines

Every person convicted of an infraction for a violation of subdivision (a) or (c) of Section 21453, subdivision (c) of Section 21454, or subdivision (a) of Section 21457 shall be punished by a fine of one hundred dollars ($100). *(Added by Stats.1997, c. 852 (A.B.1191), § 4.)*

§ 42001.16. Railroad grade crossing violations

(a) Every person convicted of an infraction for a violation of subdivision (c) of Section 21752, subdivision (c) of Section 22526, or Section 22450, involving railroad grade crossings, or Section 22451 or 22452 shall be punished as follows:

(1) For the first infraction, by a fine of one hundred dollars ($100).

(2) For a second infraction of any of the offenses described in this subdivision occurring within one year of a prior infraction that resulted in a conviction, by a fine not exceeding two hundred dollars ($200).

(3) For a third or any subsequent infraction of any of the offenses described in this subdivision occurring within one year of two or more prior infractions that resulted in convictions, by a fine not exceeding two hundred fifty dollars ($250).

(b) In addition to the fine imposed pursuant to subdivision (a), a court, in a county in which Section 369b of the Penal Code applies, may require the person to attend a traffic school as described in Section 369b of the Penal Code. *(Added by Stats.1999, c. 841 (A.B.923), § 5. Amended by Stats.2005, c. 716 (A.B.1067), § 8.)*

§ 42001.17. Conviction under § 21951; fines

Notwithstanding any other provision of law, every person convicted of an infraction for a violation of Section 21951 shall be punished as follows:

(a) For the first infraction, by a fine of one hundred dollars ($100).

(b) For a second infraction for a violation of Section 21951 occurring within one year of a prior infraction of violating of that section that resulted in a conviction, by a

fine not exceeding two hundred dollars ($200), as provided in paragraph (2) of subdivision (a) of Section 42001.

(c) For a third or any subsequent infraction for a violation of Section 21951 occurring within one year of two or more prior infractions of violating that section that resulted in convictions, by a fine not exceeding two hundred fifty dollars ($250), as provided in paragraph (3) of subdivision (a) of Section 42001. *(Added by Stats.2000, c. 833 (A.B.2522), § 14.)*

§ 42001.18. Conviction under § 21971; fines

Notwithstanding any other provision of law, every person convicted of an infraction for a violation of Section 21971 shall be punished as follows:

(a) For the first infraction, by a fine of two hundred twenty dollars ($220).

(b) For a second infraction for a violation of Section 21971 occurring within one year of a prior violation of that section that resulted in a conviction, by a fine of three hundred twenty dollars ($320).

(c) For a third or any subsequent infraction for a violation of Section 21971 occurring within one year of two or more prior infractions of violating that section that resulted in convictions by a fine of three hundred seventy dollars ($370). *(Added by Stats.2000, c. 833 (A.B.2522), § 15.)*

§ 42001.19. Conviction under § 21070; fines

Notwithstanding any other provision of law, a person convicted of a violation of Section 21070 is punishable, as follows:

(a) For a violation involving bodily injury, by a fine of seventy dollars ($70).

(b) For a violation involving great bodily injury, as defined in Section 12022.7 of the Penal Code, by a fine of ninety-five dollars ($95). *(Added by Stats.2006, c. 898 (S.B.1021), § 5.)*

§ 42001.20. Violation of section relating to warning devices on certain refuse or garbage trucks

Notwithstanding any other provision of law, a person who violates subdivision (b) or (c) of Section 27000 is punishable as follows:

(a) By a fine of one hundred fifty dollars ($150).

(b) For a second infraction occurring within one year of a prior infraction that resulted in a conviction, a fine not exceeding two hundred dollars ($200).

(c) For a third or any subsequent infraction occurring within one year of two or more prior infractions that resulted in convictions, a fine, not exceeding two hundred fifty dollars ($250). *(Added by Stats.2005, c. 166 (A.B. 1637), § 4.)*

§ 42001.25. Violations of § 23140

Notwithstanding any other provision of law, a person who violates Section 23140 is punishable as follows:

(a) By a fine of one hundred dollars ($100).

(b) For a second infraction occurring within one year of a prior infraction that resulted in a conviction, a fine of two hundred dollars ($200).

(c) For a third or any subsequent infraction occurring within one year of two or more prior infractions that resulted in convictions, a fine of three hundred dollars ($300). *(Added by Stats.2006, c. 899 (A.B.2752), § 3.)*

§ 42002. General misdemeanors

Unless a different penalty is expressly provided by this code, every person convicted of a misdemeanor for a violation of any of the provisions of this code shall be punished by a fine of not exceeding one thousand dollars ($1,000) or by imprisonment in the county jail for not exceeding six months, or by both such fine and imprisonment. *(Stats.1959, c. 3, p. 1785, § 42002. Amended by Stats.1983, c. 1092, § 404, eff. Sept. 27, 1983, operative Jan. 1, 1984.)*

Cross References

Applicability of this section to trolley coaches, see Vehicle Code § 21051.
Fines, disabled parking restrictions, see Penal Code § 1465.6.
Parking lots, failure to post charges and closing hour, see Vehicle Code § 22950.
Safety roadside rests, refuse disposal violations, see Streets and Highways Code § 224.
Unauthorized wearing of uniforms of California highway patrol, see Vehicle Code § 2261.

§ 42002.1. Failure to stop and submit to inspection of equipment or for an unsafe condition endangering a person; punishment

Section as added by Stats.2006, c. 898 (S.B. 1021), § 6. See, also, other sections of the same number, added by Stats.2006, c. 899 (A.B.2752), § 4, and Stats.2006, c. 900 (A.B.1850), § 4.

A person convicted of a misdemeanor violation of Section 2800, 2801, or 2803, insofar as it affects a failure to stop and submit to inspection of equipment or for an unsafe condition endangering a person, shall be punished as follows:

(a) By a fine not exceeding fifty dollars ($50) or imprisonment in the county jail not exceeding five days.

(b) For a second conviction within a period of one year, a fine not exceeding one hundred dollars ($100) or imprisonment in the county jail not exceeding 10 days, or both that fine and imprisonment.

(c) For a third or a subsequent conviction within a period of one year, a fine not exceeding five hundred dollars ($500) or imprisonment in the county jail not exceeding six months, or both that fine and imprisonment. *(Added by Stats.2006, c. 898 (S.B.1021), § 6.)*

Cross References

Fulfillment of conditions of probation for the entire period of probation, dismissal of charges, see Penal Code § 1203.4.
Misdemeanor, definition, penalties, see Penal Code §§ 17, 19 and 19.2.

§ 42002.1. Misdemeanor violation of §§ 2800, 2801, or 2803; punishment

Section as added by Stats.2006, c. 899 (A.B. 2752), § 4. See, also, other sections of the same number, added by Stats.2006, c. 898 (S.B.1021), § 6, and Stats.2006, c. 900 (A.B.1850), § 4.

A person convicted of a misdemeanor violation of Section 2800, 2801, or 2803, insofar as it affects a failure to stop and submit to inspection of equipment or for an unsafe condition endangering a person, is punishable as follows:

(a) By a fine not exceeding fifty dollars ($50) or imprisonment in the county jail not exceeding five days.

(b) For a second conviction within a period of one year, a fine not exceeding one hundred dollars ($100) or imprisonment in the county jail not exceeding 10 days, or both that fine and imprisonment.

(c) For a third or a subsequent conviction within a period of one year, a fine not exceeding five hundred dollars ($500) or imprisonment in the county jail not exceeding six months, or both that fine and imprisonment. *(Added by Stats.2006, c. 899 (A.B.2752), § 4.)*

Cross References

Fulfillment of conditions of probation for the entire period of probation, dismissal of charges, see Penal Code § 1203.4.
Misdemeanor, definition and penalties, see Penal Code §§ 17, 19 and 19.2.

§ 42002.1. Misdemeanor convictions relating to a failure to stop and submit to inspection of equipment or an unsafe condition endangering a person

Section as added by Stats.2006, c. 900 (A.B. 1850), § 4. See, also, other sections of the same number, added by Stats.2006, c. 898 (S.B.1021), § 6, and Stats.2006, c. 899 (A.B.2752), § 4.

A person convicted of a misdemeanor violation of Section 2800, 2801, or 2803, insofar as it affects a failure to stop and submit to inspection of equipment or for an unsafe condition endangering a person, shall be punished as follows:

(a) By a fine not exceeding fifty dollars ($50) or imprisonment in the county jail not exceeding five days.

(b) For a second conviction within a period of one year, a fine not exceeding one hundred dollars ($100) or imprisonment in the county jail not exceeding 10 days, or both that fine and imprisonment.

(c) For a third or a subsequent conviction within a period of one year, a fine not exceeding five hundred dollars ($500) or imprisonment in the county jail not exceeding six months, or both that fine and imprisonment. *(Added by Stats.2006, c. 900 (A.B.1850), § 4.)*

Cross References

Fulfillment of conditions of probation for the entire period of probation, dismissal of charges, see Penal Code § 1203.4.

§ 42002.4. Purchase, sale, receipt or possession of vehicles or components with removed or altered serial or identification numbers; punishment

A violation of Section 10751 shall be punished by imprisonment in the county jail not exceeding six months if the value of the property does not exceed nine hundred fifty dollars ($950), and by imprisonment in the county jail not exceeding one year if the value of the property is more than nine hundred fifty dollars ($950). *(Added by Stats.1990, c. 408 (A.B.3483), § 2. Amended by Stats. 2009–2010, 3rd Ex.Sess., c. 28 (S.B.18), § 55, eff. Jan. 25, 2010.)*

§ 42002.5. Violations of §§ 10852 or 10853 involving vehicle modified for use of disabled person; penalties

Notwithstanding Section 42002, every person convicted of a violation of Section 10852 or 10853 involving a vehicle that has been modified for the use of a disabled veteran or any other disabled person and that displays a special identification license plate issued pursuant to Section 5007 or a distinguishing placard issued pursuant to Section 22511.55 or 22511.59, if those facts are known or should reasonably have been known to the person, shall be punished by a fine of not more than two thousand dollars ($2,000) or by imprisonment in the county jail for not more than one year, or by both the fine and imprisonment. *(Added by Stats.1986, c. 1214, § 2. Amended by Stats.1994, c. 1149 (A.B.2878), § 13.)*

§ 42003. Payment of fines and costs

(a) A judgment that a person convicted of an infraction be punished by a fine may also provide for the payment to be made within a specified time or in specified installments. A judgment granting a defendant time to pay the fine shall order that if the defendant fails to pay the fine or any installment thereof on the date that it is due, he or she shall appear in court on that date for further proceedings. Willful violation of the order is punishable as contempt.

(b) A judgment that a person convicted of any other violation of this code be punished by a fine may also order, adjudge, and decree that the person be imprisoned until the fine is satisfied. In all of these cases, the judgment shall specify the extent of the imprisonment which shall not exceed one day for every thirty dollars ($30) of the fine, nor extend in this case beyond the term for which the defendant might be sentenced to imprisonment for the offense of which he or she was convicted.

(c) In any case when a person appears before a traffic referee or judge of the superior court for adjudication of a violation of this code, the court, upon request of the defendant, shall consider the defendant's ability to pay. Consideration of a defendant's ability to pay may include his or her future earning capacity. A defendant shall bear the burden of demonstrating lack of his or her ability to pay. Express findings by the court as to the factors bearing on the amount of the fine shall not be required. The reasonable cost of these services and of probation shall not exceed the amount determined to be the actual average cost thereof. The court shall order the defendant to appear before a county officer designated by the court to make an inquiry into the ability of the defendant to pay all or a portion of those costs or the court or traffic referee may make this determination at a hearing. At that hearing, the defendant shall be entitled to have, but shall not be limited to, the opportunity to be heard in person, to present witnesses and other documentary evidence, to confront and cross-examine adverse witnesses, to disclosure of the evidence against him or her, and to a written statement of the findings of the court or the county officer. If the court determines that the defendant has the ability to pay all or part of the costs, the court shall set the amount to be reimbursed and order the defendant to pay that sum to the county in the manner in which the court believes reasonable and compatible with the defendant's financial ability; or, with the consent of a defendant who is placed on probation, the court shall order the probation officer to set the amount of payment, which shall not exceed the maximum amount set by the court, and the manner in which the payment shall be made to the county. In making a determination of whether a defendant has the ability to pay, the court shall take into account the amount of any fine imposed upon the defendant and any amount the defendant has been ordered to pay in restitution.

The court may hold additional hearings during the probationary period. If practicable, the court or the probation officer shall order payments to be made on a monthly basis. Execution may be issued on the order in the same manner as a judgment in a civil action. The order to pay all or part of the costs shall not be enforced by contempt.

A payment schedule for reimbursement of the costs of presentence investigation based on income shall be developed by the probation department of each county and approved by the presiding judge of the superior court.

(d) The term "ability to pay" means the overall capability of the defendant to reimburse the costs, or a portion of the costs, of conducting the presentence investigation, preparing the presentence report, and probation, and includes, but is not limited to, all of the following regarding the defendant:

(1) Present financial position.

(2) Reasonably discernible future financial position. In no event shall the court consider a period of more than six months from the date of the hearing for purposes of determining reasonably discernible future financial position.

(3) Likelihood that the defendant will be able to obtain employment within the six-month period from the date of the hearing.

(4) Any other factors that may bear upon the defendant's financial capability to reimburse the county for the costs.

(e) At any time during the pendency of the judgment rendered according to the terms of this section, a defendant against whom a judgment has been rendered may petition the rendering court to modify or vacate its previous judgment on the grounds of a change of circumstances with regard to the defendant's ability to pay the judgment. The court shall advise the defendant of this right at the time of rendering of the judgment. *(Stats.1959, c. 3, p. 1785, § 42003. Amended by Stats. 1968, c. 1192, p. 2264, § 17, operative Jan. 1, 1969; Stats.1971, c. 1532, p. 3037, § 4, operative May 3, 1972; Stats.1976, c. 1045, p. 4666, § 4; Stats.1993, c. 674 (A.B.708), § 1; Stats.1996, c. 124 (A.B.3470), § 149; Stats.1996, c. 1077 (A.B.2898), § 30; Stats.2002, c. 784 (S.B.1316), § 605.)*

Law Revision Commission Comments

2002 Amendment

Subdivision (c) of Section 42003 is amended to reflect unification of the municipal and superior courts pursuant to Article VI, Section 5(e), of the California Constitution. [32 Cal.L.Rev.Comm. Reports 546 (2002)].

Cross References

Deposit of bail, parking violations, see Vehicle Code § 40509.
Felonies and offenses punishable either as felonies or misdemeanor violation of court order punishable as contempt, see Vehicle Code § 40000.3.
Notice of violations to department, courtesy warning notice, criteria for arrest warrant issuance, see Vehicle Code § 40509.5.
Suspension of driver's license for violation of section, see Vehicle Code § 13365.
Violation a misdemeanor, see Vehicle Code § 40000.25.

§ 42004. Determination of penalty

For the purpose of determining the penalty to be imposed pursuant to this code, the court may consider a written report from the Department of Motor Vehicles containing information from its records showing prior convictions; and the communication is prima facie evidence of such convictions, if the defendant admits them, regardless of whether or not the complaint commencing the proceedings has alleged prior convictions.

For the purpose of this chapter a prior bail forfeiture shall be deemed to be a conviction of the offense charged. *(Added by Stats.1968, c. 1192, p. 2265, § 19, operative Jan. 1, 1969.)*

Cross References

Forfeiture of bail, see Penal Code §§ 1269b, 1305 et seq.
Report of accident or conviction, see Vehicle Code § 1806.

Report of court action, see Vehicle Code § 1803.

§ 42004.5. 24-hour suspension of sentence

Upon conviction of any violation of any provision of this code, other than a felony violation and except this section, execution of sentence of imprisonment in the county jail shall be suspended, at the request of the convicted person, for a period of 24 hours, unless the judge determines that the person would not return. If, prior to the end of such period, the person does not deliver himself into custody for commencement of the execution of such sentence, his failure to appear shall constitute a misdemeanor. *(Added by Stats.1973, c. 1184, p. 2470, § 1.)*

§ 42005. Traffic violator schools; courts may permit or require attendance; conviction records not confidential; convictions not added to violation point counts; commercial motor vehicle drivers ineligible; other violations rendering operators ineligible; choice of school; failure to attend as misdemeanor

(a) Except as otherwise provided in this section, after a deposit of the fee under Section 42007 or bail, a plea of guilty or no contest, or a conviction, a court may order or permit a person who holds a noncommercial class C, class M1, or class M2 driver's license who pleads guilty or who pleads no contest or who is convicted of a traffic offense to attend a traffic violator school licensed pursuant to Chapter 1.5 (commencing with Section 11200) of Division 5.

(b) To the extent the court is in conformance with Title 49 of the Code of Federal Regulations, and except as otherwise provided in this section, the court may, after deposit of the fee under Section 42007 or bail, order or permit a person who holds a class A, class B, or commercial class C driver's license, who pleads guilty or no contest or is convicted of a traffic offense, to complete a course of instruction at a licensed traffic violator school if the person was operating a vehicle requiring only a class C license, or a class M license. The court may not order that the record of conviction be kept confidential. However, the conviction shall not be added to a violation point count for purposes of determining whether a driver is presumed to be a negligent operator under Section 12810.5.

(c) The court shall not order that a conviction of an offense be kept confidential according to Section 1808.7, order or permit avoidance of consideration of violation point counts under subdivision (b), or permit a person, regardless of the driver's license class, to complete a program at a licensed traffic violator school in lieu of adjudicating an offense if any of the following applies to the offense:

(1) It occurred in a commercial motor vehicle, as defined in subdivision (b) of Section 15210.

(2) Is a violation of Section 20001, 20002, 23103, 23104, 23105, 23140, 23152, or 23153, or of Section 23103, as specified in Section 23103.5.

1093

(3) It is a violation described in subdivision (d) or (e) of Section 12810.

(d) A person ordered to attend a traffic violator school pursuant to subdivision (a) or (b) may choose the traffic violator school the person will attend. The court shall provide to each person subject to that order or referral the department's current list of licensed traffic violator schools.

(e) A person who willfully fails to comply with a court order to attend traffic violator school is guilty of a misdemeanor.

(Added by Stats.2010, c. 599 (A.B.2499), § 13.5, operative July 1, 2011. Amended by Stats.2012, c. 302 (A.B.1888), § 2.)

Cross References

Additional fee imposed for maintenance of funding for court security upon conviction for criminal offense involving violations of Vehicle Code, exceptions, see Penal Code § 1465.8.

Child passenger restraint violators, see Vehicle Code § 27360 et seq.

General misdemeanors, see Vehicle Code § 42002.

Occupational licensing, traffic violator schools, duties of Judicial Council, see Vehicle Code § 11205.4.

Traffic violator school defined, see Vehicle Code § 626.

Violation a misdemeanor, see Vehicle Code § 40000.25

§ 42005.1. Participation in study of traffic violator schools in lieu of attendance

The court may order a person designated to attend a traffic violator school to instead participate in a study of traffic violator schools licensed pursuant to Chapter 1.5 (commencing with Section 11200) of Division 5. The person's participation in that study constitutes attending a licensed traffic violator school program. *(Added by Stats.1990, c. 1354 (A.B.2999), § 1. Amended by Stats. 2010, c. 599 (A.B.2499), § 13.7.)*

§ 42005.2. Repealed by Stats.2010, c. 599 (A.B.2499), § 14, operative Jan. 1, 2013

§ 42005.3. Driver awareness or education program participation; traffic violations; application of section to diversion programs for minors

Operative January 1, 1993, no local authority may allow a person who is alleged to have committed a traffic offense in violation of this code or an ordinance or resolution adopted under this code, to participate in a driver awareness or education program or in any other diversion program as an alternative to the procedure required to be followed under this code for alleged violations of this code.

This section does not apply to diversion programs for minors who commit infractions not involving a motor vehicle for which no fee is charged. *(Added by Stats.1992, c. 1199 (A.B.2409), § 13, eff. Sept. 30, 1992.)*

§ 42005.5. Attendance at school for traffic violators; computation of average daily attendance

Notwithstanding Section 46300 or 84500 of the Education Code or any other provision of law, on and after September 1, 1985, attendance at a school for traffic violators permitted or ordered pursuant to Section 41501 or 42005 shall not be included in computing the average daily attendance of any school district, community college district, or other public educational institution for purposes of allocation of state funds. *(Added by Stats.1985, c. 959, § 1. Amended by Stats.2010, c. 599 (A.B.2499), § 15.)*

§ 42006. Night court assessment

(a) Except as provided in subdivision (c), there may be levied a special assessment in an amount equal to one dollar ($1) for every fine, forfeiture, and traffic violator school fee imposed and collected by any court that conducts a night or weekend session of the court, on all offenses involving a violation of a section of this code or any local ordinance adopted pursuant to this code, except offenses relating to parking.

(b) When a person makes a deposit of bail for an offense to which this section applies, in a case in which the person is required to appear in a court that conducts a night or weekend session, the person making the deposit shall also deposit a sufficient amount to include the assessment prescribed in this section for forfeited bail. If bail is forfeited, the amount of the assessment shall be transmitted by the clerk of the court to the county treasury for disposition as prescribed by subdivision (d).

(c) If a court conducts night or weekend sessions at two or more locations, the court may do either of the following:

(1) Levy assessments only on those persons who are required to appear at the location where night or weekend sessions are held.

(2) Levy assessments on persons who have the option to appear at a location where night or weekend court sessions are held and that is within 25 miles of the location of the court where the person is otherwise required to appear.

(d) After a determination by the court of the amount of the assessment due, the clerk of the court shall collect the amount and transmit it as provided in subdivision (g).

(e) In any case where a person convicted of any offense to which this section applies is imprisoned until the fine is satisfied, the court shall waive the penalty assessment.

(f) As used in subdivisions (g) and (h), the following terms have the following meanings:

(1) "Court Facilities Trust Fund" means the fund established by Section 70352 of the Government Code.

(2) "Location" means a court facility holding night or weekend sessions under this section.

(3) "Transfer of responsibility" means the transfer of responsibility for court facilities from the counties to the state pursuant to Chapter 5.7 (commencing with Section 70301) of Title 8 of the Government Code.

(g)(1) If transfer of responsibility for a location has occurred, the clerk shall collect any assessment imposed pursuant to subdivision (c) and transmit it to the Court Facilities Trust Fund. Moneys deposited pursuant to this subdivision shall be used for any purpose provided by subdivision (b) of Section 70352 of the Government Code.

(2) If transfer of responsibility for a location has not occurred, the clerk shall collect any assessment imposed pursuant to subdivision (c) and transmit it to the county treasury to be deposited in the night court session fund, and the moneys in the fund shall be expended by the county for maintaining courts for which transfer of responsibility has not occurred and that have night or weekend sessions for traffic offenses.

(h)(1) The county treasurer of each county shall transfer from the night court session fund to the Court Facilities Trust Fund an amount that is the same percentage of the night court session fund as of January 1, 2009, as the square footage of locations for which transfer of responsibility has occurred on or before January 1, 2009, is to the total square footage of locations.

(2) For locations for which transfer of responsibility occurs after January 1, 2009, the county treasurer shall, at the time of transfer of any location, transfer from the night court session fund to the Court Facilities Trust Fund an amount that is the same percentage of the night court session fund as the square footage of the location for which transfer of responsibility is occurring is to the sum of the square footage of locations for which transfer of responsibility has not occurred and the square footage of the location being transferred.

(3) Upon the transfer of responsibility for all locations, the county treasurer shall transfer to the Court Facilities Trust Fund any amount remaining in the night court session fund.

(4) Any expenditures made from the fund for a purpose other than those specified in paragraph (2) of subdivision (g) shall be repaid to the state for deposit in the Court Facilities Trust Fund. *(Added by Stats.1965, c. 1705, p. 3839, § 3. Amended by Stats.1970, c. 1009, p. 1816, § 3; Stats.1973, c. 739, p. 1332, § 1; Stats.1974, c. 181, p. 367, § 4; Stats.1974, c. 1265, p. 2745, § 1; Stats.1981, c. 362, p. 1539, § 4; Stats.1982, c. 900, p. 3329, § 1; Stats.1991, c. 613 (A.B.195), § 12; Stats.2007, c. 738 (A.B.1248), § 53; Stats.2008, c. 218 (A.B.1949), § 7.)*

Cross References

Trial scheduling, written not guilty pleas, see Vehicle Code § 40519.

§ 42007. Uniform fee for traffic violator school

(a)(1) The clerk of the court shall collect a fee from every person who is ordered or permitted to attend a traffic violator school pursuant to Section 41501 or 42005 in an amount equal to the total bail set forth for the eligible offense on the uniform countywide bail schedule. As used in this subdivision, "total bail" means the amount established pursuant to Section 1269b of the Penal Code in accordance with the Uniform Bail and Penalty Schedule adopted by the Judicial Council, including all assessments, surcharges, and penalty amounts. Where multiple offenses are charged in a single notice to appear, the "total bail" is the amount applicable for the greater of the qualifying offenses. However, the court may determine a lesser fee under this subdivision upon a showing that the defendant is unable to pay the full amount.

The fee shall not include the cost, or any part thereof, of traffic safety instruction offered by a traffic violator school.

(2) The clerk may accept from a defendant who is ordered or permitted to attend traffic violator school a payment of at least 10 percent of the fee required by paragraph (1) upon filing a written agreement by the defendant to pay the remainder of the fee according to an installment payment schedule of no more than 90 days as agreed upon with the court. The Judicial Council shall prescribe the form of the agreement for payment of the fee in installments. When the defendant signs the Judicial Council form for payment of the fee in installments, the court shall continue the case to the date in the agreement to complete payment of the fee and submit the certificate of completion of traffic violator school to the court. The clerk shall collect a fee of up to thirty-five dollars ($35) to cover administrative and clerical costs for processing an installment payment of the traffic violator school fee under this paragraph.

(3) If a defendant fails to make an installment payment of the fee according to an installment agreement, the court may convert the fee to bail, declare it forfeited, and report the forfeiture as a conviction under Section 1803. The court may also charge a failure to pay under Section 40508 and impose a civil assessment as provided in Section 1214.1 of the Penal Code or issue an arrest warrant for a failure to pay. For the purposes of reporting a conviction under this subdivision to the department under Section 1803, the date that the court declares the bail forfeited shall be reported as the date of conviction.

(b) Revenues derived from the fee collected under this section shall be deposited in accordance with Section 68084 of the Government Code in the general fund of the county and, as may be applicable, distributed as follows:

(1) In any county in which a fund is established pursuant to Section 76100 or 76101 of the Government Code, the sum of one dollar ($1) for each fund so established shall be deposited with the county treasurer and placed in that fund.

(2) In any county that has established a Maddy Emergency Medical Services Fund pursuant to Section 1797.98a of the Health and Safety Code, an amount equal to the sum of each two dollars ($2) for every seven dollars

($7) that would have been collected pursuant to Section 76000 of the Government Code and, commencing January 1, 2009, an amount equal to the sum of each two dollars ($2) for every ten dollars ($10) that would have been collected pursuant to Section 76000.5 of the Government Code with respect to those counties to which that section is applicable shall be deposited in that fund. Nothing in the act that added this paragraph shall be interpreted in a manner that would result in either of the following:

(A) The utilization of penalty assessment funds that had been set aside, on or before January 1, 2000, to finance debt service on a capital facility that existed before January 1, 2000.

(B) The reduction of the availability of penalty assessment revenues that had been pledged, on or before January 1, 2000, as a means of financing a facility which was approved by a county board of supervisors, but on January 1, 2000, is not under construction.

(3) The amount of the fee that is attributable to Section 70372 of the Government Code shall be transferred pursuant to subdivision (f) of that section.

(c) For fees resulting from city arrests, an amount equal to the amount of base fines that would have been deposited in the treasury of the appropriate city pursuant to paragraph (3) of subdivision (b) of Section 1463.001 of the Penal Code shall be deposited in the treasury of the appropriate city.

(d) The clerk of the court, in a county that offers traffic school shall include in any courtesy notice mailed to a defendant for an offense that qualifies for traffic school attendance the following statement:

NOTICE: If you are eligible and decide not to attend traffic school your automobile insurance may be adversely affected. For drivers with a noncommercial driver's license, one conviction in any 18–month period will be held confidential and not show on your driving record if you complete a traffic violator school program. For drivers with a commercial driver's license, one conviction in any 18–month period will show on your driving record without a violation point if you complete a traffic violator school program.

(e) Notwithstanding any other provision of law, a county that has established a Maddy Emergency Medical Services Fund pursuant to Section 1797. 98a of the Health and Safety Code shall not be held liable for having deposited into the fund, prior to January 1, 2009, an amount equal to two dollars ($2) for every ten dollars ($10) that would have been collected pursuant to Section 76000.5 of the Government Code from revenues derived from traffic violator school fees collected pursuant to this section. *(Added by Stats.1976, c. 1205, p. 5487, § 1. Amended by Stats.1981, c. 362, p. 1539, § 5; Stats.1985, c. 396, § 24, eff. July 30, 1985; Stats.1985, c. 1289, § 4; Stats.1987, c. 775, § 1; Stats.1990, c. 1354 (A.B.2999),*

1096

§ 4; Stats.1991, c. 90 (A.B.1297), § 73, eff. June 30, 1991; Stats.1991, c. 189 (A.B.544), § 43, eff. July 29, 1991; Stats.1991, c. 1168 (A.B.2142), § 9, eff. Oct. 14, 1991; Stats.1997, c. 850 (A.B.233), § 59; Stats.1999, c. 679 (S.B.623), § 2; Stats.2003, c. 592 (S.B.256), § 26; Stats. 2004, c. 193 (S.B.111), § 201; Stats.2007, c. 738 (A.B. 1248), § 54; Stats.2008, c. 511 (A.B.3076), § 1, eff. Sept. 28, 2008; Stats.2010, c. 599 (A.B.2499), § 16; Stats.2010, c. 720 (S.B.857), § 37, eff. Oct. 19, 2010; Stats.2011, c. 341 (S.B.565), § 6; Stats.2013, c. 523 (S.B.788), § 31.)

Cross References

Additional fee imposed for maintenance of funding for court security upon conviction for criminal offense involving violations of Vehicle Code, exceptions, see Penal Code § 1465.8.

Court facility funding, assessments on criminal convictions, see Government Code § 1463.

Maddy Emergency Medical Services Fund, report to Legislature on implementation and status, see Health and Safety Code § 1797.98b.

Occupational licensing, traffic violator schools, duties of Judicial Council, see Vehicle Code § 11205.4.

State surcharge on state penalty imposed on fines, penalties, or forfeitures imposed and collected by the courts for offenses involving Vehicle Code violations, exceptions, see Penal Code § 1465.7.

§ 42007.1. Amount of fee collected pursuant to subd. (a) of § 42007; allocation of fees assessed pursuant to subd. (c) of § 11208

(a) The amount collected by the clerk pursuant to subdivision (a) of Section 42007 shall be in an amount equal to the total bail set forth for the eligible offense on the uniform countywide bail schedule plus a forty-nine-dollar ($49) fee, and a fee determined by the department to be sufficient to defray the cost of routine monitoring of traffic violator school instruction pursuant to subdivision (c) of Section 11208, and a fee, if any, established by the court pursuant to subdivision (c) of Section 11205.2 to defray the costs incurred by a traffic assistance program.

(b) Notwithstanding subdivision (b) of Section 42007, the revenue from the forty-nine-dollar ($49) fee collected under this section shall be deposited in the county general fund. Fifty-one percent of the amount collected under this section and deposited into the county general fund shall be transmitted therefrom monthly to the Controller for deposit in the Immediate and Critical Needs Account of the State Court Facilities Construction Fund, established in Section 70371.5 of the Government Code.

(c) The fee assessed pursuant to subdivision (c) of Section 11208 shall be allocated to the department to defray the costs of monitoring traffic violator school instruction. *(Added by Stats.1997, c. 850 (A.B.233), § 60. Amended by Stats.2008, c. 311 (S.B.1407), § 31; Stats. 2010, c. 599 (A.B.2499), § 17.)*

§ 42007.3. Traffic violator school for infraction violations relating to steady red circular or arrow signal; lane use control signals; illuminated flashing red traffic signal; allocation of fees

(a) Notwithstanding Section 42007, revenues derived from fees collected under Section 42007 from each person required or permitted to attend traffic violator school pursuant to Section 41501 or 42005 as a result of a violation of subdivision (a) or (c) of Section 21453, subdivision (c) of Section 21454, or subdivision (a) of Section 21457 shall be allocated as follows:

(1) The first 30 percent of the amount collected shall be allocated to the general fund of the city or county in which the offense occurred.

(2) The balance of the amount collected shall be deposited by the county treasurer under Section 42007.

(b) This section does not apply to the additional forty-nine-dollar ($49) court administrative fee assessed pursuant to subdivision (c) of Section 11208 collected under subdivision (a) of Section 42007.1. *(Added by Stats.1997, c. 852 (A.B.1191), § 5. Amended by Stats.2010, c. 599 (A.B.2499), § 18.)*

§ 42007.4. Use of fees collected from persons attending traffic violator school as a result of railroad grade crossing violations

(a) Notwithstanding Section 42007, revenues derived from fees collected under Section 42007 from each person required or permitted to attend traffic violator school pursuant to Section 369b of the Penal Code as a result of a violation of subdivision (c) of Section 21752, involving railroad grade crossings, or Section 22451 or 22452 shall be allocated as follows:

(1) If the offense occurred in an area where a transit district or transportation commission established under Division 12 (commencing with Section 130000) of the Public Utilities Code provides rail transportation, the first 30 percent of the amount collected shall be allocated to the general fund of that transit district or transportation commission to be used only for public safety and public education purposes relating to railroad grade crossings.

(2) If there is no transit district or transportation commission providing rail transportation in the area where the offense occurred, the first 30 percent of the amount collected shall be allocated to the general fund of the county in which the offense occurred, to be used only for public safety and public education purposes relating to railroad grade crossings.

(3) The balance of the amount collected shall be deposited by the county treasurer under Section 1463 of the Penal Code.

(4) A transit district, transportation commission, or a county that is allocated funds pursuant to paragraph (1) or (2) shall provide public safety and public education relating to railroad grade crossings only to the extent that those purposes are funded by the allocations provided pursuant to paragraph (1) or (2).

(b) This section does not apply to the additional forty-nine-dollar ($49) court administrative fee assessed pursuant to subdivision (c) of Section 11208 collected under subdivision (a) of Section 42007.1. *(Added by Stats.1999, c. 841 (A.B.923), § 6. Amended by Stats.2010, c. 599 (A.B.2499), § 19.)*

§ 42007.5. Repealed by Stats.2011, c. 268 (A.B.412), § 3, operative Jan. 1, 2014

§ 42008. County amnesty program for delinquent fines and bail; implementation and application; amount; effect of payment under program; deposit of funds

(a) Any county may operate an amnesty program for delinquent fines and bail imposed for an infraction or misdemeanor violation of the Vehicle Code, except parking violations of the Vehicle Code and violations of Section 23103, 23104, 23152, or 23153. The program shall be implemented by the courts in accordance with Judicial Council guidelines, and shall apply to infraction or misdemeanor violations of the Vehicle Code, except parking violations, upon which a fine or bail was delinquent on or before April 1, 1991.

(b) Under the amnesty program, any person owing a fine or bail due on or before April 1, 1991, that was imposed for an infraction or misdemeanor violation of the Vehicle Code, except violations of Section 23103, 23104, 23152, or 23153 or parking violations, may pay to the superior court the amount scheduled by the court, which shall be either (1) 70 percent of the total fine or bail or (2) the amount of one hundred dollars ($100) for an infraction or five hundred dollars ($500) for a misdemeanor. This amount shall be accepted by the court in full satisfaction of the delinquent fine or bail.

(c) No criminal action shall be brought against any person for a delinquent fine or bail paid under this amnesty program and no other additional penalties shall be assessed for the late payment of the fine or bail made under the amnesty program.

(d) Notwithstanding Section 1463 of the Penal Code, the total amount of funds collected by the courts pursuant to the amnesty program created by this section shall be deposited in the county treasury. *(Added by Stats.1991, c. 90 (A.B.1297), § 74, eff. June 30, 1991. Amended by Stats.1991, c. 189 (A.B.544), § 44, eff. July 29, 1991; Stats.1991, c. 1168 (A.B.2142), § 10, eff. Oct. 14, 1991; Stats.1992, c. 696 (A.B.1344), § 96, eff. Sept. 15, 1992; Stats.1998, c. 931 (S.B.2139), § 464, eff. Sept. 28, 1998; Stats.2002, c. 784 (S.B.1316), § 606.)*

Law Revision Commission Comments

1998 Amendment

Section 42008 is amended to accommodate unification of the municipal and superior courts in a county. Cal. Const. art. VI, § 5(e). The section is also amended to reflect elimination of the justice court. Cal. Const. art. VI, §§ 1, 5(b).

The phrase "of the Penal Code" was inadvertently omitted from subdivision (d) when originally enacted. [28 Cal.L.Rev. Comm. Reports 51 (1998)].

2002 Amendment

Subdivision (b) of Section 42008 is amended to reflect unification of the municipal and superior courts pursuant to Article VI, Section 5(e), of the California Constitution. [32 Cal.L.Rev.Comm. Reports 548 (2002)].

§ 42008.1. Repealed by Stats.1993, c. 1299 (S.B.149), § 1, operative Jan. 1, 1997

§ 42008.5. Amnesty program

(a) A county may establish a one-time amnesty program for fines and bail that have been delinquent for not less than six months as of the date upon which the program commences and were imposed for an infraction or misdemeanor violation of this code, except parking violations of this code and violations of Section 23103, 23104, 23105, 23152, or 23153.

(b) A person owing a fine or bail that is eligible for amnesty under the program may pay to the superior or juvenile court the amount scheduled by the court, that shall be accepted by the court in full satisfaction of the delinquent fine or bail and shall be either of the following:

(1) Seventy percent of the total fine or bail.

(2) The amount of one hundred dollars ($100) for an infraction or five hundred dollars ($500) for a misdemeanor.

(c) The amnesty program shall be implemented by the courts of the county on a one-time basis and conducted in accordance with Judicial Council guidelines for a period of not less than 120 days. The program shall operate not longer than six months from the date the court initiates the program.

(d) No criminal action shall be brought against a person for a delinquent fine or bail paid under the amnesty program and no other additional penalties, except as provided in Section 1214.1 of the Penal Code, shall be assessed for the late payment of the fine or bail made under the amnesty program.

(e) Notwithstanding Section 1463 of the Penal Code, the total amount of funds collected by the courts pursuant to the amnesty program shall be deposited in the county treasury until 150 percent of the cost of operating the program, excluding capital expenditures, have been so deposited. Thereafter, 37 percent of the amount of the delinquent fines and bail deposited in the county treasury shall be distributed by the county pursuant to Section 1464 of the Penal Code, 26 percent of the amount deposited shall be distributed by the county pursuant to Article 2 (commencing with Section 76100) of Chapter 12 of Title 8 of the Government Code, and the remaining 37 percent of the amount deposited shall be retained by the county.

(f) The deposit of fines and bails in the county treasury as described in subdivision (e) is limited to the amnesty program described in this section, and it is the intent of the Legislature that it shall not be considered a precedent with respect to affecting programs that receive funding pursuant to Section 1463 of the Penal Code.

(g) Each county participating in the program shall file, not later than six months after the termination of the program, a written report with the Assembly Committee on Judiciary and the Senate Committee on Judiciary.

The report shall summarize the amount of money collected, operating costs of the program, distribution of funds collected, and when possible, how the funds were expended. *(Added by Stats.1996, c. 742 (A.B.3095), § 1, eff. Sept. 23, 1996. Amended by Stats.2002, c. 784 (S.B.1316), § 607; Stats.2007, c. 682 (A.B.430), § 21.)*

Law Revision Commission Comments
2002 Amendment

Subdivision (b) of Section 42008.5 is amended to reflect unification of the municipal and superior courts pursuant to Article VI, Section 5(e), of the California Constitution. [32 Cal.L.Rev.Comm. Reports 549 (2002)].

§ 42008.7. State amnesty program

(a) The State of California continues to face a fiscal and economic crisis affecting the State Budget and the overall state economy. In light of this crisis, a one-time infraction amnesty program would do the following:

(1) Provide relief to individuals who have found themselves in violation of a court-ordered obligation because they are financially unable to pay traffic bail or fines.

(2) Provide increased revenue at a time when revenue is scarce by encouraging payment of old fines that have remained unpaid.

(3) Allow courts and counties to resolve older delinquent cases and focus limited resources on collecting on more recent cases.

(b) A one-time amnesty program for fines and bail meeting the eligibility requirements set forth in subdivision (e) shall be established in each county. Unless agreed otherwise by the court and the county in writing, the government entities that are responsible for the collection of delinquent court-ordered debt shall be responsible for implementation of the amnesty program as to that debt, maintaining the same division of responsibility in place with respect to the collection of court-ordered debt under subdivision (b) of Section 1463.010 of the Penal Code.

(c) As used in this section, the term "fine" or "bail" refers to the total amounts due in connection with a specific violation, which include, but are not limited to, the following:

(1) Base fine or bail, as established by court order, by statute, or by the court's bail schedule.

(2) Penalty assessments imposed pursuant to Section 1464 of the Penal Code and Sections 70372, 76000, 76000.5, 76104.6, and 76104.7 of the Government Code.

(3) Civil assessment imposed pursuant to Section 1214.1 of the Penal Code.

(4) State surcharge imposed pursuant to Section 1465.7 of the Penal Code.

(5) Court security fee imposed pursuant to Section 1465.8 of the Penal Code.

(d) In addition to and at the same time as the mandatory one-time amnesty program is established pursuant to subdivision (b), the court and the county may jointly agree to extend that amnesty program to fines and bail imposed for a misdemeanor violation of this code and a violation of Section 853.7 of the Penal Code added to the misdemeanor case otherwise subject to the amnesty. The amnesty program authorized pursuant to this subdivision shall not apply to parking violations and violations of Section 23103, 23104, 23105, 23152, or 23153 of this code.

(e) Violations are only eligible for amnesty if paragraph (1), (2), or (3) applies and the requirements of paragraphs (4), (5), and (6) are met:

(1) The violation is an infraction violation filed with the court.

(2) It is a violation of subdivision (a) or (b) of Section 40508, or a violation of Section 853.7 of the Penal Code added to the case subject to paragraph (1).

(3) The violation is a misdemeanor violation filed with the court to which subdivision (d) applies.

(4) The due date for payment of the fine or bail was on or before January 1, 2009.

(5) The defendant does not owe victim restitution on any case within the county.

(6) There are no outstanding misdemeanor or felony warrants for the defendant within the county, except for misdemeanor warrants for misdemeanor violations authorized by the court and the county pursuant to subdivision (d).

(f) Each amnesty program shall accept, in full satisfaction of any eligible fine or bail, 50 percent of the fine or bail amount, as defined in subdivision (c) of this section. Payment of a fine or bail under an amnesty program implemented pursuant to this section shall be accepted beginning January 1, 2012, and ending June 30, 2012. The Judicial Council shall adopt guidelines for the amnesty program no later than November 1, 2011, and each program shall be conducted in accordance with Judicial Council guidelines.

(g) No criminal action shall be brought against a person for a delinquent fine or bail paid under the amnesty program.

(h) The total amount of funds collected under the amnesty program shall as soon as practical after receipt thereof be deposited in the county treasury or the account established under Section 77009 of the Government Code. Any unreimbursed costs of operating the amnesty program, excluding capital expenditures, may be deducted from the revenues collected under the amnesty program by the court or the county that incurred the expense of operating the program. Notwithstanding Section 1203.1d of the Penal Code, the remaining revenues collected under the amnesty program shall be distributed on a pro rata basis in the same manner as a partial payment distributed pursuant to Section 1462.5 of the Penal Code.

(i) Each court or county implementing an amnesty program shall file, not later than September 30, 2012, a written report with the Judicial Council, on a form approved by the Judicial Council. The report shall include information about the number of cases resolved, the amount of money collected, and the operating costs of the amnesty program. Notwithstanding Section 10231.5 of the Government Code, on or before December 31, 2012, the Judicial Council shall submit a report to the Legislature summarizing the information provided by each court or county. *(Added by Stats.2010, c. 720 (S.B.857), § 38, eff. Oct. 19, 2010. Amended by Stats. 2011, c. 662 (A.B.1358), § 1.)*

§ 42009. Violations within highway construction or maintenance area

(a) For an offense specified in subdivision (b), committed by the driver of a vehicle within a highway construction or maintenance area, during any time when traffic is regulated or restricted through or around that area pursuant to Section 21367, or when the highway construction or maintenance is actually being performed in the area by workers acting in their official capacity, the fine, in a misdemeanor case, shall be double the amount otherwise prescribed. In an infraction case, the fine shall be one category higher than the penalty otherwise prescribed by the uniform traffic penalty schedule established pursuant to Section 40310.

(b) A violation of the following is an offense that is subject to subdivision (a):

(1) Section 21367, relating to regulation of traffic at a construction site.

(2) Article 3 (commencing with Section 21450) of Chapter 2 of Division 11, relating to obedience to traffic devices.

(3) Chapter 3 (commencing with Section 21650) of Division 11, relating to driving, overtaking, and passing.

(4) Chapter 4 (commencing with Section 21800) of Division 11, relating to yielding the right-of-way.

(5) Chapter 6 (commencing with Section 22100) of Division 11, relating to turning and stopping and turn signals.

(6) Chapter 7 (commencing with Section 22348) of Division 11, relating to speed limits.

(7) Chapter 8 (commencing with Section 22450) of Division 11, relating to special traffic stops.

(8) Section 23103, relating to reckless driving.

(9) Section 23104 or 23105, relating to reckless driving which results in bodily injury to another.

(10) Section 23109 or 23109.1, relating to speed contests.

(11) Section 23152, relating to driving under the influence of alcohol or a controlled substance, or a violation of Section 23103, as specified in Section 23103.5, relating to alcohol-related reckless driving.

(12) Section 23153, relating to driving under the influence of alcohol or a controlled substance, which results in bodily injury to another.

(13) Section 23154, relating to convicted drunk drivers operating a motor vehicle with a blood-alcohol concentration of 0.01 percent or greater.

(14) Section 23220, relating to drinking while driving.

(15) Section 23221, relating to drinking in a motor vehicle while on the highway.

(16) Section 23222, relating to driving while possessing an open alcoholic beverage container.

(17) Section 23223, relating to being in a vehicle on the highway while possessing an open alcoholic beverage container.

(18) Section 23224, relating to being a driver or passenger under the age of 21 possessing an open alcoholic beverage container.

(19) Section 23225, relating to being the owner or driver of a vehicle in which there is an open alcoholic beverage container.

(20) Section 23226, relating to being a passenger in a vehicle in which there is an open alcoholic beverage container.

(c) This section applies only when construction or maintenance work is actually being performed by workers, and there are work zone traffic control devices, traffic controls or warning signs, or any combination of those, to notify motorists and pedestrians of construction or maintenance workers in the area. *(Added by Stats.1993, c. 674 (A.B.708), § 2. Amended by Stats.2007, c. 682 (A.B.430), § 22; Stats.2007, c. 749 (A.B.1165), § 6.5, operative Jan. 1, 2009.)*

§ 42010. Offenses committed within Safety Enhancement–Double Fine Zones

(a) For an offense specified in subdivision (b) that is committed by the driver of a vehicle within an area that has been designated as a Safety Enhancement–Double Fine Zone pursuant to Section 97 and following of the Streets and Highways Code, the fine, in a misdemeanor case, shall be double the amount otherwise prescribed, and, in an infraction case, the fine shall be one category higher than the penalty otherwise prescribed by the uniform traffic penalty schedule established pursuant to Section 40310.

(b) A violation of the following is an offense that is subject to subdivision (a):

(1) Chapter 3 (commencing with Section 21650) of Division 11, relating to driving, overtaking, and passing.

(2) Chapter 7 (commencing with Section 22348) of Division 11, relating to speed limits.

(3) Section 23103, relating to reckless driving.

(4) Section 23104 or 23105, relating to reckless driving that results in bodily injury to another.

(5) Section 23109 or 23109.1, relating to speed contests.

(6) Section 23152, relating to driving under the influence of alcohol or a controlled substance, or a violation of Section 23103, as specified in Section 23103.5, relating to alcohol-related reckless driving.

(7) Section 23153, relating to driving under the influence of alcohol or a controlled substance, which results in bodily injury to another.

(8) Section 23154, relating to convicted drunk drivers operating a motor vehicle with a blood-alcohol concentration of 0.01 percent or greater.

(9) Section 23220, relating to drinking while driving.

(10) Section 23221, relating to drinking in a motor vehicle while on the highway.

(11) Section 23222, relating to driving while possessing an open alcoholic beverage container.

(12) Section 23223, relating to being in a vehicle on the highway while possessing an open alcoholic beverage container.

(13) Section 23224, relating to being a driver or passenger under 21 years of age possessing an open alcoholic beverage container.

(14) Section 23225, relating to being the owner or driver of a vehicle in which there is an open alcoholic beverage container.

(15) Section 23226, relating to being a passenger in a vehicle in which there is an open alcoholic beverage container.

(c) This section applies only when traffic controls or warning signs have been placed pursuant to Section 97 or 97.1 of the Streets and Highways Code.

(d)(1) Notwithstanding any other provision of law, the enhanced fine imposed pursuant to this section shall be based only on the base fine imposed for the underlying offense and shall not include any other enhancements imposed pursuant to law.

(2) Notwithstanding any other provision of law, any additional penalty, forfeiture, or assessment imposed by any other statute shall be based on the amount of the base fine before enhancement or doubling and shall not be based on the amount of the enhanced fine imposed pursuant to this section. *(Added by Stats.2006, c. 179 (S.B.3), § 3. Amended by Stats.2007, c. 682 (A.B.430), § 23; Stats.2007, c. 749 (A.B.1165), § 7.5, operative Jan. 1, 2009.)*

Cross References

Designation of Safety Enhancement-Double Fine Zones, see Streets and Highways Code § 97.

Vasco Road Safety Enhancement–Double Fine Zone, requirements, limitation of liability, see Streets and Highways Code § 97.4.

§ 42011. Repealed by Stats.2003, c. 62 (S.B.600), § 309, operative Jan. 1, 2007

ARTICLE 2. WEIGHT VIOLATIONS

Section
42030.   Penalties.
42030.1.   Penalties for violations.
42031.   Weight and axle or wheel weight.
42032.   Excessive weight violation convictions; ownership or
            operation of vehicles used for collection of gar-
            bage, etc.; penalties.

Cross References

Penalties for infractions, exception for provisions of this Article,
    see Vehicle Code § 42001.

§ 42030. Penalties

(a) Every person convicted of a violation of any weight limitation provision of Division 15 (commencing with Section 35000), and every person convicted of a violation of Section 21461 with respect to signs provided pursuant to Section 35654 or 35752, and every person convicted of a violation of Section 40001 for requiring the operation of a vehicle upon a highway in violation of any provision referred to in this section shall be punished by a fine which equals the amounts specified in the following table:

Pounds of excess weight	Fine
0- 1,000	$ 20
1,001- 1,500	30
1,501- 2,000	40
2,001- 2,500	55
2,501- 3,000	85
3,001- 3,500	105
3,501- 4,000	125
4,001- 4,500	145
4,501- 5,000	175
5,001- 6,000	.04 each lb.
6,001- 7,000	.06 each lb.
7,001- 8,000	.08 each lb.
8,001-10,000	.15 each lb.
10,001 and over	.20 each lb.

(b) No part of the penalties prescribed by this section shall be suspended for a conviction of any of the following:

(1) Section 40001 for requiring operation of a vehicle upon a highway in violation of any provision referred to in this section.

(2) Any provision referred to in this section when the amount of the weight exceeds 4,000 pounds.

(3) Any provision referred to in this section when a second or subsequent conviction of a violation thereof occurs within three years immediately preceding the violation charged.

(c) However, notwithstanding any other provision of this section, the court shall exercise discretion with respect to the imposition of the fine under this section for excess weight not exceeding 1,000 pounds if the load of the vehicle cited consisted entirely of field-loaded, unprocessed bulk agricultural or forest products or livestock being transported from the field to the first point of processing or handling.

(d) Notwithstanding any other provision of this section, the court may exercise discretion with respect to the imposition of the fine under this section if any applicable local permit was obtained prior to the court hearing and, at the time of issuance of the notice to appear, the motor carrier was transporting construction equipment or materials and a valid extra-legal load permit from the Department of Transportation was in effect. *(Stats.1959, c. 3, p. 1785, § 42030. Amended by Stats.1971, c. 259, p. 415, § 2, operative May 3, 1972; Stats.1983, c. 145, § 19, eff. June 28, 1983; Stats.1984, c. 542, § 10; Stats.1996, c. 456 (A.B.2345), § 1.)*

Cross References

Axle weight limits, see Vehicle Code § 35550.
Computation of allowable gross weight, see Vehicle Code § 35551.
State Route 2 from La Canada Flintridge to Los Angeles County, vehicle weight restriction, see Vehicle Code § 35655.6.
Vehicles transporting logs, see Vehicle Code § 35552.
Violation of decreased restrictions, see Vehicle Code § 35753.
Violation of special permit, see Vehicle Code § 35784.

§ 42030.1. Penalties for violations

(a) Every person convicted of a violation of any declared gross vehicle weight limitation provision of this code, shall be punished by a fine that equals the amounts specified in the following table:

Pounds in Excess of the Declared Gross Vehicle Weight	Fine
1,001–1,500	$ 250
1,501–2,000	300
2,001–2,500	350
2,501–3,000	400
3,001–3,500	450
3,501–4,000	500
4,001–4,500	550
4,501–5,000	600
5,001–6,000	700
6,001–7,000	800
7,001–8,000	900
8,001–10,000	1,000
10,001 and over	2,000

(b) No part of the penalties prescribed by this section shall be suspended for a conviction of any of the following:

(1) Section 40001 for requiring operation of a vehicle upon a highway in violation of any provision referred to in this section.

(2) Any provision referred to in this section when a second or subsequent conviction of a violation thereof occurs within three years immediately preceding the violation charged. *(Added by Stats.2000, c. 861 (S.B. 2084), § 58, eff. Sept. 29, 2000.)*

§ 42031. Weight and axle or wheel weight

Whenever the gross weight and any axle or wheel weight of a vehicle are in excess of the limits prescribed in this code, the excess weights shall be deemed one offense in violation of this code. *(Stats.1959, c. 3, p. 1786, § 42031.)*

Cross References

Applicability of this section to trolley coaches, see Vehicle Code § 21051.

Axle weight limits, see Vehicle Code § 35550.

§ 42032. Excessive weight violation convictions; ownership or operation of vehicles used for collection of garbage, etc.; penalties

(a) In addition to any other fines and penalties, any local public agency which owns or operates vehicles used for the collection of garbage, refuse, or rubbish and which has, within any 90-day period, been convicted an excessive number of times for operating those vehicles in violation of any of the weight limitations set forth in Chapter 5 (commencing with Section 35550) of Division 15, taking into consideration the total number of trip routes for those vehicles which are normally scheduled in the same 90-day period, may be assessed a civil penalty not to exceed two thousand five hundred dollars ($2,500) for each violation. Nothing in this section affects the legal standards, proof requirements, or penalty provisions of any other provision of the law.

(b) The penalties imposed by this section shall be assessed and recovered in a civil action brought by the Attorney General or by any district attorney or city attorney. Prior to undertaking a civil action, a reasonable effort for informal resolution of the problem of excessive violations shall be made by the applicable attorney. Penalties recovered shall be paid to the Treasurer for deposit in the State Highway Account in the State Transportation Fund and used, upon appropriation, for purposes of highway maintenance. *(Added by Stats.1990, c. 88 (A.B.776), § 1.)*

ARTICLE 3. DRIVER TRAINING PENALTY ASSESSMENTS [REPEALED]

§§ 42050 to 42053. Repealed by Stats.1981, c. 166, p. 972, §§ 11 to 14, eff. July 12, 1981

CHAPTER 2. DISPOSITION OF FEES, FINES, AND FORFEITURES

Article	Section
1. Fines and Forfeitures	42200
2. Refund of Fees and Penalties	42230

ARTICLE 1. FINES AND FORFEITURES

Section
42200. Disposition by cities.
42201. Disposition by county.

Section
42201.1. Reimbursement to state for construction of platform scales and vehicle inspection facilities.
42201.5. Disposition of infraction fines and forfeitures.
42201.6. Refund of bail deposits; multiple or duplicate deposits; interest.
42202. Disobedience by officials.
42203. Disposition of fines and forfeitures for violations on certain county owned premises.
42204. Disposition of off-highway vehicle fines and forfeitures.
42205. Disposition of weight fees for commercial vehicles.

§ 42200. Disposition by cities

(a) Of the total amount of fines and forfeitures received by a city under Section 1463 of the Penal Code that proportion which is represented by fines and forfeitures collected from any person charged with a misdemeanor under this code following arrest by an officer employed by a city, shall be paid into the treasury of the city and deposited in a special fund to be known as the "Traffic Safety Fund," and shall be used exclusively for official traffic control devices, the maintenance thereof, equipment and supplies for traffic law enforcement and traffic accident prevention, and for the maintenance, improvement, or construction of public streets, bridges, and culverts within the city, but the fund shall not be used to pay the compensation of traffic or other police officers. The fund may be used to pay the compensation of school crossing guards who are not regular full-time members of the police department of the city.

(b) For purposes of this section, "city" includes any city, city and county, district, including any enterprise special district, community service district, or county service area engaged in police protection activities as reported to the Controller for inclusion in the 1989–90 edition of the Financial Transactions Report Concerning Special Districts under the heading of Police Protection and Public Safety, authority, or other local agency (other than a county) which employs persons authorized to make arrests or to issue notices to appear or notices of violation which may be filed in court. *(Stats.1959, c. 3, p. 1787, § 42200. Amended by Stats.1995, c. 285 (A.B.433), § 2.)*

Cross References

Misdemeanor defined, see Penal Code § 17.
Municipal and justice courts, disposition of fines in, see Government Code § 71006.
Reimbursement of school districts employing school crossing guards from funds collected pursuant to this section, see Education Code § 45451.

§ 42201. Disposition by county

(a) Of the total amount of fines and forfeitures received by a county under Section 1463.001 of the Penal Code, fines and forfeitures collected from any person charged with a misdemeanor under this code following arrest by any officer employed by the state or by the county shall be paid into the general fund of the county. However, the board of supervisors of the county may, by resolution, provide that a portion thereof be transferred into the road fund of the county.

(b) The board of supervisors of a county may enter into a contract with the Department of the California Highway Patrol for the purpose of providing adequate protection for school pupils who are required to cross heavily traveled streets, highways, and roadways in the unincorporated areas of the county. When requested, the Department of the California Highway Patrol may provide such service and the county shall reimburse the state for salaries and wages of crossing guards furnished by the Department of the California Highway Patrol pursuant to such contract, including any necessary retirement and general administrative costs and expenses in connection therewith, and may pay the costs thereof from amounts deposited in the road fund pursuant to this section.

(c) Fines and forfeitures received by a county under Section 1463.001 of the Penal Code may be used to pay the compensation of school crossing guards and necessary equipment costs and administrative costs.

(d) When requested by any county which had in effect on June 30, 1979, a contract with the Department of the California Highway Patrol, to provide protection for school pupils at school crossings, the department upon request of a county shall continue to administer such school crossing program until June 30, 1980. The county shall reimburse the Department of the California Highway Patrol for general administrative costs and expenses in connection therewith, except that, effective January 1, 1980, the crossing guards shall be furnished to the California Highway Patrol and such crossing guards shall be employees of the county, the county superintendent of schools, the affected school districts, or both the superintendent and the affected school districts, at the option of the board of supervisors of the county. Any salaries and wages of crossing guards, including necessary retirement and equipment costs and any administrative costs shall be paid or reimbursed by the county from amounts deposited in the road fund pursuant to this section.

(e) The board of supervisors may adopt standards for the provision of school crossing guards. The board has final authority over the total cost of the school crossing guard program of any agency to be paid or reimbursed from amounts deposited in the road fund pursuant to this section. The board of supervisors may specify that a designated county officer, employee, or commissioner is to hire school crossing guards, or, in the alternative, the board may specify that any school district crossing guard program in unincorporated areas shall be maintained by the school districts desiring the program. *(Stats.1959, c. 3, p. 1788, § 42201. Amended by Stats.1961, c. 801, p. 2066, § 15; Stats.1965, c. 60, p. 941, § 1, eff. April 9, 1965; Stats.1968, c. 538, p. 1199, § 2; Stats.1970, c. 1248, p. 2241, § 1, eff. Sept. 16, 1970; Stats.1978, c. 295, p. 619, § 3, eff. June 27, 1978; Stats.1979, c. 1039, p. 3617, § 1, eff. Sept. 26, 1979; Stats.1994, c. 308 (A.B.2544), § 34, eff. July 21, 1994.)*

Cross References

Highway funds, generally, see Streets and Highways Code §§ 1580, 2150.

Municipal and justice courts, disposition of fines and forfeitures in, see Government Code § 71006.

Reimbursement of school districts employing school crossing guards from funds collected pursuant to this section, see Education Code § 45451.

Road fund, see Streets and Highways Code § 1622.

§ 42201.1. Reimbursement to state for construction of platform scales and vehicle inspection facilities

Fines and forfeitures received by a county under Section 1463 of the Penal Code may be used to reimburse the state for the construction of platform scales and vehicle inspection facilities in the county. *(Added by Stats.1985, c. 407, § 1, eff. July 30, 1985.)*

§ 42201.5. Disposition of infraction fines and forfeitures

Fines, forfeitures, and deposits of bail collected as a result of a charge or conviction of an infraction shall be deposited and distributed in the same manner as fines, forfeitures, and deposits of bail collected from a person charged with or convicted of a misdemeanor. *(Added by Stats.1968, c. 1192, p. 2265, § 22, operative Jan. 1, 1969.)*

§ 42201.6. Refund of bail deposits; multiple or duplicate deposits; interest

(a) A deposit of bail received with respect to an infraction violation of this code, or any local ordinance adopted pursuant to this code, including, but not limited to, a violation involving the standing or parking of a vehicle, shall be refunded by the agency which issued the notice of violation or the court within 30 days of a cancellation, dismissal, or finding of not guilty of the offense charged.

(b) Multiple or duplicate deposits of bail or parking penalty shall be identified by the court or agency and refunded within 30 days of identification.

(c) Any amount to be refunded in accordance with subdivision (a) or (b) shall accrue interest, at the rate specified in Section 3289 of the Civil Code, on and after the 60th day of a cancellation, dismissal, or finding of not guilty or identification of multiple or duplicate deposits, and shall be refunded as soon as possible thereafter along with accrued interest. *(Added by Stats.1985, c. 1289, § 5. Amended by Stats.1989, c. 290, § 1.)*

§ 42202. Disobedience by officials

Failure, refusal, or neglect on the part of any judicial or other officer or employee receiving or having custody of any fine or forfeiture mentioned in this article either before or after deposit in the respective fund to comply with the foregoing provisions of this article is misconduct in office and ground for removal therefrom. *(Stats.1959, c. 3, p. 1788, § 42202.)*

§ 42203. Disposition of fines and forfeitures for violations on certain county owned premises

Notwithstanding Section 42201 or 42201.5, 50 percent of all fines and forfeitures collected in a superior court upon conviction or upon the forfeiture of bail for violations of any provisions of the Vehicle Code, or of any local ordinance or resolution, relating to stopping, standing, or parking a vehicle, that have occurred upon the premises of facilities physically located in such county, but which are owned by another county, which other county furnishes law enforcement personnel for the premises, shall be transmitted pursuant to this section to the county which owns the facilities upon which the violations occurred. The court receiving such moneys shall, once each month, transmit such moneys received in the preceding month to the county treasurer of the county in which the court is located. Once each month in which the county treasurer receives such moneys, the county treasurer shall transmit to the county which owns such facilities an amount equal to 50 percent thereof. The county owning such facilities shall, upon receipt of such moneys from the superior court of the county in which the facilities are physically located, deposit such moneys in its county treasury for use solely in meeting traffic control and law enforcement expenses on the premises upon which the violations occurred.

This section shall not apply when the county in which such facilities are located performs all law enforcement functions with respect to such facilities. *(Added by Stats.1970, c. 449, p. 898, § 3. Amended by Stats.1998, c. 931 (S.B.2139), § 465, eff. Sept. 28, 1998; Stats.2002, c. 784 (S.B.1316), § 608.)*

Law Revision Commission Comments
1998 Amendment

Section 42203 is amended to accommodate unification of the municipal and superior courts in a county. Cal. Const. art. VI, § 5(e). The section is also amended to reflect elimination of the justice court. Cal. Const. art. VI, 1, 5(b). [28 Cal.L.Rev.Comm. Reports 51 (1998)].

2002 Amendment

Section 42203 is amended to reflect unification of the municipal and superior courts pursuant to Article VI, Section 5(e), of the California Constitution. [32 Cal.L.Rev.Comm. Reports 550 (2002)].

Cross References

Municipal and justice courts, disposition of fines and forfeitures in, see Government Code § 71006.

§ 42204. Disposition of off-highway vehicle fines and forfeitures

Notwithstanding any other provisions of law, all fines and forfeitures collected for violations of Division 16.5 (commencing with Section 38000) shall be deposited in the appropriate fund in the county where the violation occurred and distributed in the same manner as specified in Section 42201.5, and shall be used for enforcing laws related to the operation of off-highway motor vehicles.

(Added by Stats.1971, c. 1816, p. 3936, § 10, eff. Dec. 22, 1971, operative July 1, 1972. Amended by Stats.1973, c. 974, p. 1874, § 6; Stats.1978, c. 380, p. 1205, § 147; Stats.1982, c. 994, p. 3626, § 16; Stats.2002, c. 563 (A.B.2274), § 46.)

§ 42205. Disposition of weight fees for commercial vehicles

(a) Notwithstanding Chapter 3 (commencing with Section 42270), the department shall file, at least monthly with the Controller, a report of money received by the department pursuant to Section 9400 for the previous month and shall, at the same time, remit all money so reported to the Treasurer. On order of the Controller, the Treasurer shall deposit all money so remitted into the State Highway Account in the State Transportation Fund, or directly into the Transportation Debt Service Fund as provided in paragraph (2) of subdivision (c) of Section 9400.4, as applicable.

(b) The Legislature shall appropriate from the State Highway Account in the State Transportation Fund to the department and the Franchise Tax Board amounts equal to the costs incurred by each in performing their duties pursuant to Article 3 (commencing with Section 9400) of Chapter 6 of Division 3. The applicable amounts shall be determined so that the appropriate costs for registration and weight fee collection activities are appropriated between the recipients of revenues in proportion to the revenues that would have been received individually by those recipients if the total fee imposed under the Vehicle License Fee Law (Part 5 (commencing with Section 10701) of Division 2 of the Revenue and Taxation Code) was 2 percent of the market value of a vehicle. The remainder of the funds collected under Section 9400 and deposited in the account, other than the direct deposits to the Transportation Debt Service Fund referenced in subdivision (a), may be appropriated to the Department of Transportation, the Department of the California Highway Patrol, and the Department of Motor Vehicles for the purposes authorized under Section 3 of Article XIX of the California Constitution. *(Added by Stats.1981, c. 541, p. 2185, § 38, eff. Sept. 17, 1981, operative Jan. 1, 1982. Amended by Stats.1984, c. 123, § 2; Stats.1994, c. 1243 (S.B.1805), § 77.5, eff. Sept. 30, 1994, operative Jan. 1, 1994; Stats.1996, c. 10 (A.B.1869), § 23, eff. Feb. 9, 1996; Stats.1999, c. 85 (A.B.1660), § 2; Stats.2004, c. 211 (S.B.1096), § 42, eff. Aug. 5, 2004; Stats.2013, c. 35 (S.B.85), § 15, eff. June 27, 2013.)*

Cross References

State Highway Account revenues derived from weight fees, use of revenues to make remaining authorized bond debt service reimbursement and loans to the General Fund, see Streets and Highways Code § 2103.

Transportation Debt Service Fund, creation, use of moneys, Transportation Bond Direct Payment Account, state covenant regarding alteration, amendment, or restriction of specified provisions relating to transfer of weight fees, transfers to General Fund, see Government Code § 16965.

ARTICLE 2. REFUND OF FEES AND PENALTIES

Section
42230. Return after rejection of application.
42231. Erroneous collection of fees.
42232. Application for refund.
42233. Refund procedures.
42234. Repealed.
42235. Late application for refund.

§ 42230. Return after rejection of application

Whenever any application made under this code is accompanied by any fee, except an application for an occupational license accompanied by a fee as specified in Section 9262, 9262.5, 11309, or 11820, or an application for a duplicate driver's license, as required by law, and the application is refused or rejected, the fees shall be returned to the applicant, except that, whenever any application is made for the first set of special plates under subdivision (a) of Section 9262 and the application is refused or rejected, the fee for the special plates only shall be returned to the applicant or, when application is made for the first set of special plates under subdivision (1) of Section 9264 and the application is refused or rejected, the fee for the special plates shall be returned to the applicant. *(Stats.1959, c. 3, p. 1788, § 42230. Amended by Stats.1959, c. 1015, p. 3037, § 1; Stats.1961, c. 1615, p. 3458, § 36; Stats.1963, c. 142, p. 814, § 1; Stats.1967, c. 1064, p. 2694, § 4; Stats.1980, c. 608, p. 1680, § 10; Stats.1996, c. 124 (A.B.3470), § 150.)*

Cross References

Applicability of this section to trolley coaches, see Vehicle Code § 21051.

Department of California highway patrol, see Vehicle Code § 2100 et seq.

Grounds for refusal of license, see Vehicle Code § 12805 et seq.

Procedure for refund, see Vehicle Code § 42231 et seq.

Similar provision, see Revenue and Taxation Code § 10901.

§ 42231. Erroneous collection of fees

Whenever any application is made under this code and the application is accompanied by any fee which is excessive or not legally due, or whenever the department in consequence of any error either of fact or of law as to the proper amount of any fee or any penalty thereon or as to the necessity of obtaining any privilege under this code collects any fee or penalty which is excessive, erroneous, or not legally due, the person who has paid the erroneous or excessive fee or penalty, or his agent on his behalf, may apply for and receive a refund of the amount thereof as provided in this article, or the department may refund the same within three years after the date of the payment or collection. *(Stats.1959, c. 3, p. 1788, § 42231. Amended by Stats.1961, c. 20, p. 579, § 2.)*

Cross References

Applicability of this section to trolley coaches, see Vehicle Code § 21051.

Disposition of overpayments of fees less than $10, see Government Code § 16302.1.

§ 42232. Application for refund

The application for refund shall be presented to the department in a format prescribed by the department within three years from the date of payment of the erroneous or excessive fee or penalty and shall identify the payment made and state the grounds upon which it is claimed that the payment was excessive or erroneous. *(Stats.1959, c. 3, p. 1778, § 42232. Amended by Stats. 1961, c. 20, p. 579, § 3; Stats.2000, c. 787 (S.B.1404), § 26.)*

Cross References

Applicability of this section to trolley coaches, see Vehicle Code § 21051.

§ 42233. Refund procedures

(a) Whenever any fee or penalty subject to refund under Section 42231 after application therefor has not been paid into the State Treasury, the department shall refund the fee or penalty.

(b) Whenever any fee or penalty subject to refund under Section 42231 after application therefor or Section 10901 of the Revenue and Taxation Code has been paid into the State Treasury to the credit, in whole or in part, of the Motor Vehicle License Fee Account in the Transportation Tax Fund (hereafter referred to in this section as the Motor Vehicle License Fee Account), or to the credit, in whole or in part, of the Motor Vehicle Account in the State Transportation Fund (hereafter referred to in this section as the Motor Vehicle Account), the department shall prepare a claim setting forth the facts pertaining to the fee or penalty sought to be refunded, and the State Controller shall draw his warrant upon the account or accounts to which the fee or penalty was credited. In lieu of filing claims for refund against both the Motor Vehicle Account and the Motor Vehicle License Fee Account when an amount has been determined to be due from both accounts, the director may file a single claim with the State Controller, drawn against the Motor Vehicle Account covering the amount of both refunds, and the State Controller shall thereupon draw his warrant on the Motor Vehicle Account. At least quarterly, the director shall certify to the State Controller the amounts paid from the Motor Vehicle Account which are properly chargeable to the Motor Vehicle License Fee Account supported by such detail as the State Controller may require. Upon order of the State Controller, the amounts so required shall be transferred from the Motor Vehicle License Fee Account to the credit of the Motor Vehicle Account.

(c) This section is an appropriation of any and all amounts necessary to refund and repay any excessive or erroneous fees and penalties collected under this code, and the procedure prescribed in this article for refunds shall be deemed a compliance with the requirements of the Government Code relating to the refund of excessive

1105

or erroneous fees or penalties. *(Stats.1959, c. 3, p. 1789, § 42233. Amended by Stats.1974, c. 545, p. 1346, § 268; Stats.1978, c. 669, p. 2158, § 10.)*

Cross References

Applicability of this section to trolley coaches, see Vehicle Code § 21051.

Disposition of overpayments of $10 or less by state agencies, see Government Code § 16302.1.

Refunds in general, see Government Code § 13140 et seq.

§ 42234. Repealed by Stats.1990, c. 1352 (A.B.2912), § 20

§ 42235. Late application for refund

Whenever the department collects any fee which is excessive or not legally due and application for the refund of the fee is not filed within the time prescribed by law because the applicant failed to receive from the department a certificate of registration for the vehicle upon which the refund of fee is sought, the director shall have the power to authorize the payment of a refund in such a case upon a proper showing by the applicant that the delay in applying for the refund was due to the failure to receive the certificate of registration within the statutory period allowed for making application for refund of fees. *(Stats.1959, c. 3, p. 1789, § 42235.)*

CHAPTER 3. MOTOR VEHICLE ACCOUNT

Section

42270.	Report and deposit of money.
42271.	Motor vehicle account; creation; support and operation of departments.
42271.5.	Repealed.
42272.	Motor Vehicle Account; transfer to General Fund; loan.
42273.	Transfer of balance.
42274.	Repealed.
42275.	Advance transfer.
42276.	Quadrennial report on fee studies.
42277.	Automobile driver training; prohibition against use of funds.

Cross References

Disposition of weight fees for commercial vehicles, see Vehicle Code § 42205.

§ 42270. Report and deposit of money

(a) The Department of Motor Vehicles and the Department of the California Highway Patrol each shall file, at least monthly with the Controller, a report of money received by the department covering all fees for applications accepted by the department and all other moneys received by the department under this code and, at the same time, shall remit all money so reported to the Treasurer. On order of the Controller, the Treasurer shall deposit in the Motor Vehicle Account in the State Transportation Fund, into which is merged the Motor Vehicle Account in the Transportation Tax Fund, all moneys so reported and remitted.

Any reference in any law or regulation to the Motor Vehicle Fund, or to the Motor Vehicle Account in the Transportation Tax Fund, shall be deemed to refer to the Motor Vehicle Account in the State Transportation Fund, which is created by subdivision (a) of Section 42271.

(b) The amount of any penalties collected by the department pursuant to Sections 9553 and 9554 of this code and Sections 10770 and 10854 of the Revenue and Taxation Code shall, for purposes of subdivision (a), be deemed to be a percentage of the weight fee, registration fee, and vehicle license fee obtained when applying the total of these fees collected, excluding use tax, against the individual weight fees, registration fees, and vehicle license fees collected on each application. Penalties which cannot be allocated in accordance with this subdivision shall be allocated according to subdivision (c).

(c) The amount of any penalties collected by the department, as provided in Sections 9553 and 9554 of this code and Sections 10770 and 10854 of the Revenue and Taxation Code which cannot be allocated in accordance with subdivision (b), shall, for the purposes of subdivision (a), be deemed to be a percentage of the total fees allocated under this section and under Section 11001 of the Revenue and Taxation Code equal to that percentage of the ratio based on the fees previously allocated under this section and under Section 11001 of the Revenue and Taxation Code in the fiscal year preceding the calendar year for which the penalties are to be allocated. That ratio shall be reevaluated periodically and shall be adjusted to reflect any change in the fee structure that may be provided in this code or in Part 5 (commencing with Section 10701) of Division 2 of the Revenue and Taxation Code.

(d) Whenever any fee paid to the department has not been allocated within one year of the date of collection, the fee shall be allocated to the Motor Vehicle License Fee Account in the Transportation Tax Fund, and the Motor Vehicle Account and the State Highway Account in the State Transportation Fund, in proportion to the revenue allocated to those accounts by the department in the previous fiscal year. *(Stats.1959, c. 3, p. 1790, § 42270. Amended by Stats.1971, c. 1243, p. 2436, § 20, operative Jan. 1, 1972; Stats.1973, c. 889, p. 1658, § 59, eff. Sept. 28, 1973, operative March 10, 1975; Stats.1974, c. 1330, p. 2898, § 30, eff. Sept. 26, 1974, operative March 8, 1976; Stats.1978, c. 669, p. 2159, § 11; Stats.1984, c. 123, § 3; Stats.1986, c. 248, § 242; Stats.1986, c. 693, § 1.)*

Cross References

Department of California Highway Patrol, see Vehicle Code § 2100 et seq.

Disposition of fees, fines and forfeitures, see Vehicle Code § 42200 et seq.

Proceeds from sale to enforce lien for vehicle fees, taxes, and penalties, see Vehicle Code § 9802.

§ 42271. Motor vehicle account; creation; support and operation of departments

(a) The Motor Vehicle Account in the State Transportation Fund is hereby created.

(b) The moneys deposited to the credit of the Motor Vehicle Account in the State Transportation Fund which are appropriated in the Budget Act or any other appropriation act for the support of or expenditure by the Department of Motor Vehicles shall be expended by the department in carrying out the provisions of this code and in enforcing any other laws relating to vehicles or the use of highways.

Regularly employed peace officers of the department may, when authorized by the director, expend such sums as authorized for the purchase of counterfeit, false, forged, or fictitious certificates of ownership, registration card, certificate, license or special plate or permit, or driver's license provided for by this code as evidence, or for expenditures related to the procurement of such evidence, or for expenditures made to investigate other violations of laws administered by the department. When approved by the director, the identity of a peace officer who submits a claim need not be disclosed if the disclosure might materially prejudice the investigation.

The sums so expended shall be repaid to the peace officer making the expenditure upon claims approved by the director. The claims, when approved, shall be paid out of funds appropriated or made available by law for the support of the department.

(c) The moneys deposited to the credit of the Motor Vehicle Account in the State Transportation Fund which are appropriated in the Budget Act or any other appropriation act for the support of or expenditure by the Department of the California Highway Patrol shall be expended by the department in carrying out the provisions of this code and in enforcing any other laws relating to vehicles or the use of highways. The Department of the California Highway Patrol may draw, without at the time furnishing vouchers and itemized statements, sums not to exceed in the aggregate one hundred thousand dollars ($100,000), the sums so drawn to be used as a revolving fund where cash advances are necessary. At the close of each fiscal year, the moneys so drawn shall be accounted for and substantiated by vouchers and itemized statements submitted to and audited by the State Controller. *(Stats.1959, c. 3, p. 1790, § 42271. Amended by Stats.1959, c. 2080, p. 4812, § 1; Stats.1961, c. 180, p. 1184, § 1; Stats.1969, c. 833, p. 1665, § 1, eff. Aug. 26, 1969; Stats.1971, c. 1243, p. 2437, § 21, operative Jan. 1, 1972; Stats.1974, c. 545, p. 1347, § 269; Stats.1978, c. 669, p. 2159, § 12.)*

Cross References

Department of California Highway Patrol, see Vehicle Code § 2100 et seq.
Disposition of fees, fines and forfeitures, see Vehicle Code § 42200 et seq.

§ 42271.5. Repealed by Stats.1999, c. 85 (A.B.1660), § 7, operative June 30, 2000

§ 42272. Motor Vehicle Account; transfer to General Fund; loan

For the 2012–13 fiscal year, upon order of the Director of Finance, the Controller shall transfer four hundred thirty-two million two hundred thousand dollars ($432,200,000) from the Motor Vehicle Account to the General Fund as a loan, provided that the loan shall be repaid. The Director of Finance shall order the repayment by the Controller of that four hundred thirty-two million two hundred thousand dollars ($432,200,000) to the Motor Vehicle Account no later than June 30, 2016. *(Added by Stats.2012, c. 22 (A.B.1465), § 8, eff. June 27, 2012.)*

§ 42273. Transfer of balance

By the 10th day of each calendar month, the balance remaining to the credit of the Motor Vehicle Account in the State Transportation Fund at the close of business on the last day of the preceding calendar month, after payments of refunds and administration and enforcement, that is not needed for immediate use from the Motor Vehicle Account shall, on order of the State Controller, be transferred to the credit of the State Highway Account in the State Transportation Fund. *(Stats.1959, c. 3, p. 1790, § 42273. Amended by Stats. 1971, c. 1243, p. 2438, § 22, operative May 3, 1972; Stats.1978, c. 669, p. 2160, § 14.)*

§ 42274. Repealed by Stats.1971, c. 1243, p. 2438, § 23, operative Jan. 1, 1972

§ 42275. Advance transfer

Notwithstanding Section 42273, the State Controller may, after at least 15 days' prior notice, transfer back to the Motor Vehicle Account in the State Transportation Fund amounts transferred to the State Highway Account in the State Transportation Fund pursuant to that section to pay costs incurred against other appropriations from the Motor Vehicle Account. *(Added by Stats.1969, c. 1437, p. 2946, § 1. Amended by Stats.1974, c. 545, p. 1348, § 271; Stats.1978, c. 669, p. 2160, § 15.)*

§ 42276. Quadrennial report on fee studies

Not later than January 10, 1985, and not later than January 10th of each four-year period thereafter, the Secretary of the Business, Transportation and Housing Agency shall submit a report to the Legislature on a study of the fees imposed under this code, including any finding or recommendation on changes in the fees necessary to generate sufficient revenues for the Motor Vehicle Account in the State Transportation Fund to finance those operations of state government to be financed from those revenues. *(Added by Stats.1981, c. 541, p. 2185, § 39, eff. Sept. 17, 1981, operative Jan. 1, 1982.)*

§ 42277. Automobile driver training; prohibition against use of funds

No money in the Motor Vehicle Account in the State Transportation Fund may be expended for automobile driver training. *(Added by Stats.1984, c. 94, § 1.)*

CALIFORNIA VEHICLE CODE
VIOLATIONS TABLE

This table is intended to be used as a reference tool only. It does not carry the force and effect of codified law. It is not provided to replace the enacted provisions of the California Vehicle Code, but is to be used in conjunction with that Code. See the provisions of the California Vehicle Code for all codified law questions.

Types of Violations
C – Civil
F – Felony
I – Infraction
M – Misdemeanor

Types of convictions received for violation of certain sections of the General Provisions of the Vehicle Code.		
Type	**VC Section**	**Violation**
M	20	False statements, in documents filed with DMV or CHP.
I	25(a)	Unlawful advertising by person, as DMV or CHP.
I	25(b)	Unlawful advertising by holder of occupational license, as DMV or CHP.
I	25.5	False representation as employee of DMV.
M	27	Impersonating member of CHP.
I	28(a)	Repossessor, notify local police or sheriffs of taking possession of a vehicle within one hour.
I	28(c)	Repossessor to notify local police or sheriff within one hour of taking possession of a vehicle.
M	31	False information, given orally or in writing.
I	545.1(b)	Driver shall escort pupils as required by subdivision (d) of Section 22112.

VEHICLE VIOLATIONS TABLE

Type	VC Section	Violation
		Types of convictions received for violation of certain sections of Division 2 of the Vehicle Code.
M	1808.1(a)	Employers of prospective drivers of hazardous material, ambulances, farm labor vehicles, youth buses, specified limousines for hire, and paratransit required to obtain report of current driving record and maintain report until receipt of pull notice system reports.
M	1808.1(b)	Employers of above-listed drivers to request participation in pull notice system.
I	1808.1(c)	Employers of above-listed drivers enrolled in Electronic Pull Notice program to obtain a pull notice report every 12 months.
I	1808.1(d)	Employers failure to notify DMV to discontinue enrollment in pull-notice system upon driver termination.
I	1808.1(e)	If drivers are, owners/ operators/ family/ volunteers to be enrolled in pull notice system.
M	1808.1(f)	Employment of driver after notice of conviction of driving offense.
I	1808.1(h)(3)	Failure of specified Board of Pilot Commissioners and its Port Agent to participate in pull-notice system.
I	1808.1(j)	Failure of an employer to be in possession of a casual drivers record as recorded by the Department.
I	1808.1(k)	Employers to obtain current driving record only for above-listed casual drivers (excluding those requiring passenger transportation endorsement).
I	1808.1(n)	Failure to show taxicab pull-notice report to an authorized representative.
I	1808.21(a)	Unlawful release of confidential and suppressed records.
M	1808.22(c)	Misuse of confidential records by an attorney.
I	1808.23(d)	Vehicle manufacturers not to release residential addresses for marketing or soliciting.
M	1808.45	Unauthorized disclosure of information from any DMV record or use of false representation to obtain information.
I	1808.46	Prescribes penalties for obtaining confidential information utilizing false representations or distribution of that information to unauthorized individuals.
I	2261	Unauthorized wearing of CHP or similar type uniform.

VEHICLE VIOLATIONS TABLE

I	2402.6(b)	Violation of fuel system or container regulations.
I	2402.6(c)	Violation of fuel system or container regulations.
M	2416(c)	Misuse of authorized emergency vehicle permit.
I	2418.5	Emergency ambulance must be equipped with resuscitator.
M	2430.5(a)	Employer involved in freeway service patrol operations to obtain and maintain applicant's tow truck driver certificate. (Effective July 1, 1992)
M	2430.5(b)	Employer involved in freeway service patrol operations to obtain and maintain certificates for all tow truck driver employees. (Effective July 1, 1992)
M	2430.5(c)	Employer involved in freeway service patrol operations to maintain categorized list of tow truck driver as specified.
M	2430.5(d)	Employer involved in freeway service patrol operations to remove tow truck driver from freeway service patrol operations upon notice of arrest or conviction.
M	2432	Tow truck driver involved in freeway service patrol operations providing false information. CHP rotation tow truck operator to notify of arrest/conviction.
M	2432(b)	Failure of tow truck driver involved in freeway service patrol operations to notify employer of arrest or conviction. ·
I	2436.3(a)	Employer involved in freeway service patrol operations to obtain carrier ID number for display on each tow truck operating freeway service patrol (Effective July 1, 1992)
I	2436.3(b)	Operating a tow truck involved in freeway service patrol operations with a suspended ID number.
I	2436.3(c)	Removal of ID number from tow truck involved in freeway service patrol operations upon sale/transfer or other disposition.
M	2462(a)	Renderer of kitchen grease, record and maintain specified information.
M	2462(b)	Transporter of kitchen grease, record and maintain specified information.
M	2464	Renderers and transporters of kitchen grease, records maintained at place of business, presented upon demand of peace officer.
M	2468(a)	Failure of licensed renderer to keep written records of inedible kitchen grease.
M	2468(b)	Failure of licensed renderer or registered transporter to exhibit required record or destruction of required record.
M/F	2470	Transporter of kitchen grease, required to be registered with Department of Food and Agriculture, possess valid certificate.
M/F	2472	Transporting inedible kitchen grease without a certificate.
M/F	2474	Steal, misappropriate, contaminate or damage inedible kitchen grease.
M/F	2476	Knowingly receive stolen inedible kitchen grease.
I	2504	Violation of regulations governing ambulances, armored cars is an infraction.
I	2510(b)	Operating vehicle as ambulance without CHP inspection.
I	2525.2	Licensed fleet owners shall comply with regulations.
I	2525.6	Fleet owner, inspection and maintenance station placing sticker on vehicle not part of fleet.
I	2525.10	Stickers, unlawful to place on vehicle which does not comply with equipment requirements.

VEHICLE VIOLATIONS TABLE

I	2545	Licenses issued by CHP. License to be surrendered upon suspension or revocation.
M	2572(b)	Requires a valid license for the transportation of school pupils.
M	2800(a)	Refusal to obey peace officer.
M	2800(b)(1)	Failure to obey an out-of-service order including violations of Title 49 of the Code of Federal Regulations issued by any peace officer or authorized employee of the California Highway Patrol.
M	2800(b)(2)	Hazardous materials driver in a commercial motor vehicle displaying a placard pursuant to section 27903 violating VC Section 2800(b)(1).
M	2800(b)(3)	Driver of vehicle designed to transport 16 or more passengers, including the driver, violating VCSection 2800(b)(1).
M	2800(d)	Failure to obey an out-of-service order including violations of Title 49 of the Code of Federal Regulations issued by any peace officer or commercial vehicle inspector.
M	2800.1(a)	Attempt to evade pursuing peace officer's motor vehicle.
M	2800.1(b)	Attempt to evade pursuing peace officer's bicycle.
M/F	2800.2(a)	Attempt to evade a pursuing peace officer in a reckless manner.
M/F	2800.3	Attempt to evade a pursuing peace officer causing injury.
M	2800.4	Driving on a highway in a direction opposite to that in which traffic lawfully moves while fleeing under 2800.1 VC.
M	2801	Lawful order or direction, failure to obey fireman's.
M	2803(a)	Refusal to adjust load or obtain special permit.
M	2803(b)	Weight certificate or bill of lading, shall submit to officer.
I	2807(b)	School bus, display CHP inspection certificate.
I	2807.1(b)	Other motor vehicles transporting pupils, display CHP inspection certificate.
I	2807.2	Failure to retain record of inspection on file for review by CHP upon request.display of appropriate certificate verifying inspection.
I	2807.3(b)	Operation of youth bus without display of appropriate certificate verifying inspection.
I	2810.1(b)	Rented commercial vehicle, refusal to submit to inspection by traffic officer relative transportation of household goods.
M	2813	Commercial vehicle, stop and submit for signposted inspection.
M	2813.5(b)	Commercial vehicle, unauthorized inspection sticker.
I	2814	Passenger vehicle, stop and submit for signposted inspection.
I	2814.2(a)	Failure to stop and submit to a sobriety checkpoint.
I	2815	School crossing guard, failure to obey.
I	2816	Unlawful to load or unload children from a youth bus upon a highway where children must cross unless traffic is controlled by a traffic officer or signal.
I	2817	Disregarding signal or direction of a peace officer escorting a funeral procession.
I	2818	Traversing an electronic beacon, flare, or cone pattern established by public safety personnel.

VEHICLE VIOLATIONS TABLE

Types of convictions received for violation of certain sections of Division 3 of the Vehicle Code.

Type	VC Section	Violation
I	4000(a)(1)	Vehicle on highway or off-street parking facility unregistered or with additional fees due; exceptions.
I	4000(b)	Vehicle on highway registered in violation of air pollution control regulations; exceptions.
I	4000.4(a)	Unregistered California based vehicle.
I	4000.5(a)	An autoette shall be registered.
I	4000.5(b)	Autoette license plate shall be removed and returned to if removed from an island, as described.
I	4000.6(d)	Commercial vehicles exceeding declared gross vehicle weight.
I	4001	Failure to register exempt vehicles and display license plate bearing distinguishing marks indicating exemption.
I	4004(a)	Commercial trip permit, identify vehicle, complete prior to operation, inaccessible from inside cab, valid.
I	4152.5	Upon expiration of home state license plates of a foreign vehicle, owner must make application for California registration within 20 days; exceptions.
I	4159	Change of address, notify DMV within 10 days. Replacement of motorcycle engines not required to destroy casings.
I	4160	Change of address, owner to change on registration slip.
I	4161(a)	Motor change, notify DMV within 10 days.
I	4301	Evidence of foreign registration, applicant to surrender.
I	4453.6	Failure of lessor of vehicle to furnish name and address of lessee upon demand of a peace officer.
I	4454(a)	Registration card, shall maintain the same or a facsimile copy thereof with the vehicle for which issued.
I	4455	Foreign commercial vehicle, carry temporary permit in vehicle at all times.
M	4456.4	Failure of new motor vehicle dealer to electronically

		register sold or leased vehicles.
M	4456.5	Misrepresenting a dealer document processing fee as a government fee.
I	4457	Plates, tabs, certificates; obtain new when lost, mutilated, or illegible.
I	4458	Plates, both lost or stolen, registered owner must notify police and apply for duplicates through DMV.
I	4459	Certificate of ownership, owner obtain duplicate when lost or mutilated.
C/M	4461(a)	Evidences of registration, lending or allowing improper use.
C/M	4461(b)	Disabled person placard, lending or allowing improper use.
C/M	4461(c)	Disabled person placard, improper use or display of cancelled or revoked placard.
C/M	4461(d)	Vehicle displaying disabled plates shall not be parked in disabled stall unless transporting disabled person.
I	4462(a)	Evidences of registration, present to officer for examination.
I	4462(b)	Evidences of registration, presenting for wrong vehicle.
M	4462(c)	Unlawful possession of registration card, identification card, temporary receipt, certification of ownership, license plate, or validation tab.
M	4462.5	Presenting or displaying false evidences of registration with the intent to avoid registration fees.
F	4463(a)	False evidences of registration, California or foreign, with intent to defraud.
M	4463(b)	Forges or counterfeits disabled person placard.
C/M	4463(c)	Displays a forged or counterfeit disabled persons placard.
M	4463(d)	Disabled person, lending placard.
I	4463(e)	Forged or counterfit Clean Air Sticker.
M	4463.5(a)	Facsimile license plates, unlawful manufacture or sale.
I	4464	Altered license plate, displayed upon vehicle.
I	5011	Special construction, mobile, cemetery equipment, trailer, semi-trailer, and logging vehicle, shall display ID plate issued pursuant to Section 5014 VC and Section 5014.1 VC.
I	5011.5	Charter Party Carrier-operated limousine, display special license plate required by Section 5385.6 PUC.
I	5017	Identification plate, attach to vehicle for which issued, surrender upon sale or destruction of vehicle.
I	5018	Transfer ownership of equipment, logging vehicle, or implement of husbandry, transfer of ownership within 10 days.
I	5030	Motorized bicycle required to display special license plate.
I	5032	Operation of motorized bicycle without applying for a

VEHICLE VIOLATIONS TABLE

		license plate within 5 days.
I	5035	Motorized bicycle using license plate on another motorized bicycle.
I	5037(a)	Motorized bicycle sold on or after July 1, 1981, on a highway without assigned plates.
I	5037(b)	Motorized bicycle sold prior to July 1, 1981, on a highway without assigned plates after January 1, 1982.
I	5109	Environmental license plates. Notify DMV upon transfer of plates.
I	5200(a)	License plates; two on a vehicle, one in front and one in the rear.
I	5200(b)	License plates; only one issue shall be attached to the rear unless issued to a truck tractor and then to be displayed in accordance with Section 4850.5 VC.
I	5201(a)	License plates, securely attached and clearly visible. Rear plate 12 to 60 inches high. Characters on plate must be upright and displayed from left to right.
I	5201(a)(6)(A)	The rear license plate on a dump bed motortruck equipped with a trailing, load bearing swing axle shall be mounted more than 12 inches, but not more than 107 inches, from the ground.
I	5201(b)	License plates clearly visible. No covering may be used on license plates, with certain exceptions.
I	5201(c)	License plates, prohibits casing, shield, frame, border, product, or other device which obstructs or impairs the recognition of the license plate.
I	5201.1(a)	Selling a product that obscures or is intended to obscure a license plate.
I	5201.1(b)	Operating a vehicle with a product or device that violates VC Section 5201.1(a).
I	5201.1(c)	Altering a license plate to avoid visual or electronic capture of the license plate or its characters.
I	5202	License plates, operating vehicle without proper display of.
I	5204(a)	Current month and year tabs, attached to rear license plate, except on truck tractor to front plate.
I	5206	Partial year registration, shall display certificate or insignia.
I	5302(d)	Display of name, trademark, or logo of company required on both sides of a vehicle.
I	5352	Trailer coach, current registration required, on or off highway.
M	5500(a)	Dismantling of a vehicle, person in possession surrender ownership and registration documents to DMV.
M	5506	Salvage Vehicle Rebuilder reselling vehicle without certification of inspection from CHP or DMV.
I	5604	Insurance coverage, dealer to notify purchaser.
M	5753(a)	Failure of commercial dealer to deliver certificate of ownership and registration card to transferee.

VEHICLE VIOLATIONS TABLE

I	5753(c)(1)	Certificate of ownership, upon receiving payment in full, shall deliver the vehicle's certificate of ownership to the transferee within 15 business days.
I	5753(c)(2)	Certificate of ownership, delivered to lessee within 15 days of receiving payment in full for the purchase.
I	5753(d)	Certificate of ownership shall be signed by the legal owner or lessor reflecting transfer of ownership.
C	5753(e)	Provides civil penalties for failing to comply with the provisions of subdivisions (c) and (d).
M	5753(f)	Failure of licensed dealer upon written request to disclose pertinent information.
I	5900(a)	Transfer of ownership, owner to notify DMV within 5 days.
I	5900(b)	Transfer of ownership, owner notify DMV of mileage.
I	5900(c)	Transfer of ownership, person in possession of vehicle. Notify DMV of mileage. If sold or transferred through wholesale auction owner to supply dealer with information.
M	5901(a)	Transfer of ownership, dealer notify DMV.
M	5901(b)	Transfer of ownership, dealer notify DMV of mileage.
M	5901(c)	Transfer of ownership, person in possession of vehicle notify DMV of mileage.
I	5902	Transfer of ownership, transferee notify DMV within 10 days. Certificate to include DL/ID number.
I	5906.5(a)	Transfer of vehicles, no application required, transferee notify DMV of vehicle mileage.
I	5906.5(b)	Transfer of vehicle, no application required, person in possession notify DMV of vehicle mileage.
I	6700.3(a)	Filing with DMV for nonresident commuter indicia.
I	6700.4	Display of nonresident commuter indicia and identification card carried with vehicle.
I	8057(a)	Apportioned registration, fleet records to be maintained for 3 years after the close of the registration year, cost and weight records for 4 years after the vehicle was deleted.
I/M	8802	Evidence of registration, surrender when canceled, suspended or revoked. Misdemeanor with intent to defraud.
M	8803	Dealer, salesman, manufacturer, remanufacturer, transporter or dismantler, surrender licenses when canceled, suspended or revoked.
M	8804	Resident registering vehicle in a foreign jurisdiction.
I	9102.5(b)	Contract school bus, display of permit.
I	9400	Commercial vehicle weight fees due, 10,000 pounds or less.
I	9400.1(f)(4)	Proper display of gross vehicle weight decals.
I	9400.1(f)(5)	Weight decal must reflect proper gross vehicle weight reported to the department.

VEHICLE VIOLATIONS TABLE

I	9406	Alterations increasing weight fee, failure to report.
I	9564(b)	Scrap metal processor submit documents and certificate of title.
I	9564(c)	Reconstruction of vehicle delivered to scrap metal processor.

Types of convictions received for violation of certain sections of Division 3.5 of the Vehicle Code.

Type	VC Section	Violation
I	9850	Undocumented vessels shall be numbered prior to operation on waters.
I	9853.2	Undocumented vessels, display of required numbers.
I	9853.4(b)	Improper use of sticker, tab or device on vessel.
I	9853.8	Undocumented vessels: compliance with emissions standards.
I	9854	Out of state registration; make application within 30 days.
I	9865	Holder of a certificate of number, notify department within 15 days of change of address.
I	9866	Improper display of number on vessel.
I	9872	Defacing, destroying vessel number prohibited.
M	9872.1(a)	Buy, sell, offer for sell, receive, or possess vessel with missing, defaced, or altered hull identification number.
I	9901	Transfer of ownership, notify DMV within 10 days.
I	9910	Transfer of ownership, required delivery and endorsement.
I	9911	Transfer of ownership, notify DMV within 5 days.
I	9912	Dealer notify DMV upon transfer of ownership.

Types of convictions received for violation of certain sections of Division 3.6 of the Vehicle Code.

Type	VC Section	Violation
I	9951(a)	Manufacturers of new motor vehicles disclosure of "event data recorders" (EDR's) , and "sensing and diagnostic modules (SDM'S).
I	9952	Unlawful to publish, offer for sale, sell, advertisement, brochure or manual in violation 9950.
M	9953	If new motor vehicle cannot be operated with tire chains, manufacturer shall so indicate in owner's manual or other written material. Provide franchised new motor vehicle dealers with a list of affected vehicle models.

VEHICLE VIOLATIONS TABLE

Types of convictions received for violation of certain sections of Division 4 of the Vehicle Code.

Type	VC Section	Violation
I	10500(a)	Stolen vehicle or plates, police forward report to DOJ immediately.
M	10501(a)	False report of vehicle theft, with intent to deceive.
M/F	10501(b)	Repeat offense of false report of vehicle theft, with intent to deceive.
I	10502(b)	Report of embezzled vehicle, owner notify CHP upon recovery.
I	10551	Stolen undocumented vessel, police notify DMV of theft and immediately upon recovery.
I	10552	False report of theft of undocumented vessel.
I	10650(a)	Towing service, shall keep written record of stored vehicles.
I	10650(b)	Towing service, specific data on written records.
I	10650(c)	Towing service, records kept for one year.
I	10650(d)	Towing service, statement of disposition upon termination of storage.
I	10653	Garage or repair shop notify sheriff or police of bullet marks within 24 hours.
I	10654	Renter of private building used as a private garage, notify sheriff or police of storage within 24 hours.
I	10655	Stored vehicles, keeper maintain records, make required reports.
M	10750(a)	Vehicle identifying numbers; altering, defacing or replacing.
M	10751(a)	Vehicle and component identifying numbers; knowingly buy, sell or possess vehicle with such numbers removed, altered, defaced.
M/F	10752(a)	Fraudulent acquisition or disposition of manufactures serial or identification number.
M/F	10752(b)	Fraudulent acquisition or disposition of CHP or DMV identification number.
M/F	10801	No person shall own or operate a chop shop.
M/F	10802	Vehicle identification numbers: alteration, obliteration, defacement, or forgery.
M/F	10803(a)	Vehicles and components: buy to resell knowing vehicle

		identification numbers have been defaced, counterfeited or obliterated.
M/F	10803(b)	Possession of vehicles or components with intent to sell knowing vehicle identification numbers have been defaced, counterfeited or obliterated.
M/F	10851(a)	Auto theft, permanently or temporarily deprive owner of possession.
F	10851(b)	Prescribes punishment for theft of ambulance, law enforcement or fire vehicle on an emergency call or vehicle displaying disabled plate or placard modified for use by a disabled person.
M	10851.5	Theft of binder chains, permanently or temporarily deprive the owner of possession.
M	10852	Injuring or tampering, with vehicle or contents.
M	10853	Unattended vehicle, tampering with mechanism or setting in motion.
M	10854	Stored vehicle, unlawful use by keeper.

VEHICLE VIOLATIONS TABLE

	Types of convictions received for violation of certain sections of Division 5 of the Vehicle Code.	
Type	**VC Section**	**Violation**
M	11100(a)	Driver training school operator, unlicensed.
M	11103	Driving school operator and independent instructor, maintain required insurance.
M	11103.1	All-terrain vehicle training organization-required insurance.
M	11108(a)	Driving school operator and independent instructor, maintain specified records.
M	11108(b)	Retain records for 3 years.
M	11108(c)	Surrender records upon termination of activities.
M	11108(d)	ATV safety training organization, maintain records for safety instructors.
M	11108(e)	ATV instructor, report information to ATV training organization. ATV organization, report information to Department.
M	11108.5(a)	School owner, report change of ownership within 10 days.
M	11108.5(b)	School owner, immediately notify DMV of change of location.
M	11108.5(c)	School owner and instructor, report change of residence within five days.
M	11109	Driving school operator and independent instructor, maintain vehicles in safe condition.
M	11110	Driving schools, unlawful acts. (Use appropriate subsection.)
M	11200(a)	No person shall own, operate, or give instruction in a traffic violator school without a valid license issued by DMV.
M	11200 (b)	Traffic violator school to obtain signature on specified consumer disclosure statement.
M	11202.5(a)	No person shall operate a traffic violator school without a valid license issued by DMV.
M	11206(a)	No person shall act as a traffic violator school instructor without a valid license issued by DMV.
M	11212(a)	Failing to maintain prescribed records for traffic violator schools.

VEHICLE VIOLATIONS TABLE

M	11212(b)	Traffic violator schools, retain records for 3 years.
M	11212(c)	Traffic violator schools, surrender records upon termination of activities.
M	11212(d)	Traffic violator school to use student's address for school administrative purposes only.
M	11213(a)	Traffic violator school owner shall notify DMV within 10 days of any change of ownership.
M	11213(b)	Traffic violator school owner shall immediately notify DMV upon changing the location of the school's place of business.
M	11213(c)	Traffic violator school operator/instructor notify of change of address within 5 days.
M	11300	Acting as a vehicle verifier without proper permit.
M	11302.2(a)	Vehicle verifiers, notify DMV of address change within 10 days.
M	11307(a)	Failure of vehicle verifier to maintain a record of each verification made.
M	11307(b)	Failure of vehicle verifier to submit records to peace officer.
M	11400	Requires the licensing of a registration service.
M	11406(a)	Registration service maintain business records with specified information.
M	11406(c)	Registration service, provide customer with transaction document.
M	11406(d)	Failure of registration service to display sign that it is not a branch of DMV or to so inform customer.
M	11406.5	When customer fails to submit documents or fees to a registration service, the registration service shall return everything pertaining to the transaction to the customer's last known address (within 60 days) by registered mail.
M	11411	If a registration service ceases operation, the owner shall immediately notify the department and send all records, transaction documents, receipts, and fees to the department.
M	11500	Auto dismantler, unlicensed.
M	11513(a)	Auto dismantler, failure to notify DMV of address change.
M	11514(a)	Auto dismantler, failure to display signs.
M	11515(a)	Salvage vehicle, insurance company forwards certificate of ownership and license plates to DMV, within 10 days of loss settlement.
M	11515(b)	Salvage vehicle retained, insurance company notification to DMV; owner forwards certificate of ownership and license plates to DMV.
I/M	11515(c)	Salvage vehicle, failure of owner to forward the certificate of ownership and license plates to DMV within 10 days.
M	11515(d)	Salvage vehicle, failure of self-insurer to forward certificate of ownership and license plates to DMV within 10 days.
M	11515(e)	Salvage vehicle, failure to deliver salvage certificate to purchaser within 10 days of purchase.
M	11515.1(a)	A salvage pool shall sell a vehicle only with a salvage certificate except pursuant to subdivision (f) of Section 11515, or as provided in subdivision (b) of this section.
M	11515.1(b)	A salvage pool shall sell a vehicle only with a nonrepairable vehicle certificate except pursuant to subdivision (f) of Section 11515.2, or

		as provided in subdivision (a) of this section.
M	11515.2(a)	Nonrepairable vehicle, insurance company forwards certificate of ownership and license plates to DMV, within 10 days of loss settlement.
M	11515.2(b)	Nonrepairable vehicle retained, insurance company notification to DMV; owner forwards certificate of ownership and license plates to DMV.
I/M	11515.2(c)	Nonrepairable vehicle, failure of owner to forward the certificate of ownership and license plates to DMV within 10 days.
M	11515.2(d)	Nonrepairable vehicle, failure of self-insurer to forward certificate of ownership and license plates to DMV within 10 days.
M	11515.2(e)	Nonrepairable vehicle, failure to deliver nonrepairable vehicle certificate to purchaser within 10 days of purchase.
M	11516(c)	Auto dismantler, failure to maintain registration with special plates.
M	11520(a)	Licensed auto dismantler, notify DMV and DOJ within five days, (1) wait 10 days before dismantling vehicle. Surrender license plates and ownership papers. Maintain business records.
M	11521	Auto dismantler, failure to indicate license or permit number issued by the department in advertisement.
M	11540(a)	Salvage pool, maintenance of records; failure to notify DMV.
M	11540(b)	Salvage pool, submission of license plates to DMV prior to disposition and maintenance of record of license plates for two years.
M	11614	Lessor-Retailer, unlawful acts (use appropriate subsection).
M	11614.1	Lessor-Retailer, unlawful advertising practices (use appropriate subsection).
M	11615(a)	Lessor-Retailer, delivery of vehicle not meeting equipment requirements.
M	11615(b)	Lessor-Retailer, failure to deliver properly endorsed certificate of ownership.
M	11615(c)	Lessor-Retailer, noncompliance with Revenue and Taxation or Rules and Regulations.
M	11615(d)	Lessor-Retailer, taking a vehicle in trade for a vehicle sold.
M	11615(e)	Lessor-Retailer, sale of a vehicle not previously leased, bailed, or rented.
M	11615(f)	Makes it unlawful for a lessor-retailer to display a vehicle for sale at a location other than an established place of business authorized by DMV.
M	11700	Dealer, manufacturer, manufacturer branch, remanufacturer, remanufacturer branch, distributor, distributor branch, or transporter, unlicensed.
M	11700.3	Aid and abet a person violating occupational licensing laws in Chapter 4 of Division 5.
M	11709(a)	Dealer, display adequate business sign.
M	11709(c)	Dealer, display identification sign or device at exhibits.
M	11709.1	Requires dealers who sell used cars to post a sign indicating that the prospective buyer may have a vehicle inspected by a third party.

VEHICLE VIOLATIONS TABLE

M	11709.2	Dealers to post a sign indicating "No Cooling-Off Period" for sale and lease contracts.
M	11709.3	Motor vehicle dealers to display in showroom a listing of each vehicle advertised for sale under specified conditions.
M	11709.4	Failure of a dealer to payoff trade in vehicle in 21 calendar days.
M	11712(a)	Dealer, change of place of business.
M	11712(b)	Dealer, change of franchise.
M	11712.5(a)	Dealer, sale of motorcycle without display of dealer's charges affixed.
M	11712.5(b)	Dealer, sale of light truck without display of required information.
M	11713(a)	Dealer, misleading advertising.
M	11713(b)	Dealer, advertising vehicle not actually for sale.
M	11713(c)	Dealer, failing to withdraw advertising within 48 hours of sale.
M	11713(d)	Dealer, representing used vehicle as new.
M	11713(e)	Dealer, operating without valid bond.
M	11713(f)	Dealer, failing to maintain established place of business.
M	11713(g)	Dealer, falsely adding licensing or transfer fees to selling price.
M	11713(h)	Dealer, employing unlicensed salesmen or failing to report to DMV employment or termination of a salesman within 10 days.
M	11713(i)	Dealer, delivering new vehicle illegally equipped.
M	11713(j)	Dealer, misuse, or permit unlawful use of special plates.
M	11713(k)	Dealer, advertise no down payment when in fact required.
M	11713(l)	Dealer, involved in sale of private vehicle without paying sales tax.
M	11713(m)	Dealer, permitting misuse of license or books.
M	11713(n)	Dealer, disconnecting or resetting odometer.
M	11713(o)	Prohibits the sale of a previously unregistered vehicle without disclosing in writing the date that the manufacturer's or distributor's warranty commenced.
M	11713(p)	Provides that no licensee shall accept a deposit unless the vehicle is present at the dealer's premises or available to the dealer directly from the manufacturer or distributor at the time the dealer accepts the deposit.
M	11713(q)	Prohibits consignment of a new vehicle for sale to another dealer.
M	11713(r)	Requires dealers to display vehicles for sale at an established place of business authorized by the department for that dealer.
M	11713(s)	Dealer, use a picture in advertising the price of a vehicle that depicts a different year, make, or model of vehicle.
M	11713(t)	Dealer, fail to disclose in advertisement previous specified use of vehicle.
M	11713.1(a)	Advertising vehicle for sale without properly identifying same.
M	11713.1(b)	Advertising total price of vehicle for sale without including total costs (exceptions).
M	11713.1(c)	Failure to disclose that taxes, charges, and fees will be added to the advertised price in advertisement of vehicle sale.
M	11713.1(d)	Dealer preparation charges being represented as a government fee.

VEHICLE VIOLATIONS TABLE

M	11713.1(e)	Failure to sell vehicle at the advertised total price. Advertised vehicles shall be sold at or below the advertised total price, with statutorily permitted exclusions, regardless of whether the purchaser has knowledge of the advertised total price.
M	11713.1(f)	Advertising vehicle for sale or selling vehicle when dealer does not hold franchise.
M	11713.1(g)	Sale of park trailer without notification that movement must be under permit.
M	11713.1(h)	Advertising free merchandise, services, or gifts contingent on the purchase of a vehicle.
M	11713.1(i)	Advertising vehicles with intent not to supply reasonably expected demand, unless advertisement discloses the number of vehicles in stock at the advertised price. The actual phrase that states the number of vehicles in stock at the advertised price shall be printed in the same type, color, and size used for the advertised price.
M	11713.1(j)	Use of the term "rebate" or similar words in advertisement without expressing dollar amount.
M	11713.1(k)	Require a person to pay a higher price for a vehicle for receiving advertised credit terms.
M	11713.1(l)	Advertise guaranteed trade-in allowance unless the guarantee is provided by manufacturer or distributor.
M	11713.1(m)	Misrepresent the authority of a salesperson or agent to negotiate the final terms of a transaction.
M	11713.1(n)	Use prohibited terms that refer to dealer's cost for a vehicle in an advertisement or advertise that the selling price of a vehicle is above, below, or at invoice price or dealer cost except during face to face negotiations and in advertisements to commercial purchasers.
M	11713.1(o)	Violate any law prohibiting bait and switch advertising.
M	11713.1(p)	Make any untrue statement indicating that a vehicle is equipped with all factory optional equipment the manufacturer offers.
M	11713.1(q)	Supplemental stickers, must clearly disclose that price is the dealer's asking price not the manufacturer's suggested retail price.
M	11713.1(r)	Advertise any underselling claim without recent survey to substantiate claim.
M	11713.1(s)	Advertise any incentive offer which the dealer is required to contribute to the cost of the incentive, without disclosing that dealer participation may affect consumer cost.
M	11713.1(t)	Offer for sale used vehicles unless there is a Federal Trade Commissions Buyers guide affixed to the vehicle.
M	11713.1(u)	Dealer failure to disclose to franchisor the name of purchaser, date of sale, and vehicle identification number of new vehicle sold or intentional submission of false purchaser or date.
M	11713.1(v)	Vehicle sale contracts must disclose whether vehicle sold is new or used.
M	11713.1(w)	Use of simulated check in advertisement for lease or sale of vehicle.
M	11713.1(x)	Failure to disclose on face of new vehicle contract whether transaction is subject to a fee received by an autobroker and, if so, the autobroker's name.

1123

VEHICLE VIOLATIONS TABLE

M	11713.1(y)	A dealer selling or leasing a new motor vehicle after October 1, 2012 without a contractual agreement with the DMV pursuant to VC Section 1685.
M	11713.26(a)	Displaying or offering for sale a retail or used vehicle without obtaining a NMVTIS vehicle history report for that vehicle.
M	11713.26(b)(1)	Failure to properly post the disclosure of a junked or salvaged vehicle.
M	11713.26(b)(2)	Failure to provide NMVTIS vehicle history report to purchaser prior to sale, upon request.
M	11713.3(a)	Manufacturer and distributor, refuse or fail to deliver upon an order from a dealer, new vehicles, parts and accessories.
M	11713.3(b)	Manufacturer and distributor, to prevent by contract or otherwise any change in the capital structure of a dealership.
M	11713.3(c)	Manufacturer and distributor, to require or prevent a dealer from changing the executive management of a dealership.
M	11713.3(d)	Manufacturer and distributor, to require or prevent a dealer from transferring interest in the dealership between officers, partners, stockholders, etc.
M	11713.3(e)	Manufacturer and distributor, preventing a dealer from receiving reasonable compensation for the value of the franchised business.
M	11713.3(f)	Manufacturer and distributor, obtaining money, goods or services from persons with whom the dealer does business.
M	11713.3(g)	Manufacturer and distributor, requiring a dealer to submit to arbitration between any person other than the board.
M	11713.3(g)(1)(A)	Modifying or disclaiming a duty or obligation of a manufacturer, manufacturer branch, distributor, distributor branch, or representative, or a right or privilege of a dealer.
M	11713.3(g)(1)(B)	Limiting or constraining the right of a dealer to file, pursue, or submit evidence connected with a protest before the board.
M	11713.3(g)(1)(C)	Requiring a dealer to terminate a franchise.
M	11713.3(g)(1)(D)	Requiring arbitration between manufacturer or distributor, with a dealer, without the written consent of all parties.
M	11713.3(h)	Manufacturer and distributor, increasing prices of motor vehicles which a dealer has ordered for a private retail consumer.
M	11713.3(i)	Manufacturer and distributor, failure to pay a dealer for a new vehicle of a prior year model, which is in a dealer's inventory when the new models are introduced.
M	11713.3(j)	Manufacturer and distributor, denying the heirs the right of ownership upon the death of the owner of the dealership.
M	11713.3(k)	Manufacturer and distributor, offering any inducement to persons purchasing new motor vehicles for the state or any political subdivision.
M	11713.3(l)	Manufacturer and distributor, to modify or refuse to renew a franchise.
M	11713.3(m)	Manufacturer and distributor, employing a person as a representative who has not been licensed.
M	11713.3(n)	Manufacturer and distributor, denying any dealer the right of free association with any other dealer for any lawful purpose.
M	11713.3(o)	Manufacturer and distributor, competing with a dealer in the

		relevant market area.
M	11713.3(p)	Manufacturer and distributor, unfairly discriminating among its franchises re: warranty reimbursement.
M	11713.3(q)	Manufacturer and distributor, selling vehicles to persons not licensed.
M	11713.3(r)	Manufacturer or distributor of park trailer, failure to affix identification number.
M	11713.3(s)	Manufacturer and distributor dishonoring a warranty, rebate, or other incentive to the public because the sale was arranged or negotiated by an autobroker.
M	11713.3(t)	Manufacturer and distributor, exercising any right requiring a franchisee to release the franchised business to the franchisor.
M	11713.3(u)	Manufacturer and distributor, unfairly discriminating in favor of a dealership owned or controlled by a manufacturer or distributor.
M	11713.3(v)	Manufacturer and distributor, unauthorized use or modification of dealer computer records.
M	11713.3(x)(1)	Unfairly discriminating against a franchisee selling a service contract, debt cancellation agreement, maintenance agreement, or similar product not approved by the maufacturer or distributor.
M	11713.5(a)	Dealer, misrepresentation of the model year of a vehicle.
M	11713.5(b)	Dealer, ordering change of the model year of a vehicle.
M	11713.5(c)	Dealer, unlawful to sell housecar manufactured in 2 stages unless buyer informed.
M	11713.6(a)	Dealer must disclose in writing to buyer, if so stated by the manufacturer, that the vehicle may not be operated with tire chains.
M	11713.6(c)	Prior to sale or lease, dealer shall present disclosure statement for signature and provide a copy of the signed disclosure.
M	11713.8(a)	Remanufacturer, failure to report vehicle identification number.
M	11713.8(b)	Remanufacturer, failure to die stamp assigned VIN on frame.
M	11713.8(c)	Remanufacturer, failure to disclose vehicle is remanufactured.
M	11713.8(d)	Remanufacturer, failure to remove trade name of original manufacturer.
M	11713.8(e)	Remanufacturer, failure to maintain for 3 years bills of sale or invoices for parts.
M	11713.8(f)	Remanufacturer, failure to maintain for 3 years proof vehicle was dismantled when frame used in a remanufactured vehicle.
M	11713.8(g)	Remanufacturer, failure to disclose on VIN plate, vehicle remanufactured and includes used parts.
M	11713.8(h)	Remanufacturer, failure to disclose to dealer, vehicle remanufactured and includes used parts.
M	11713.9(a)	Display for sale motor vehicle with engine not labeled as specified.
M	11713.10	Failure to disclose to purchaser of a low-speed vehicle its maximum speed and the potential risks of driving one.
M	11713.11(a)	Dealer advertising auction event to disclose in advertisement the date, location, whether attendance fee is charged, amount of attendance fee (if any), name and number of auctioning dealer, whether a buyer's fee will be charged, and the amount of buyer's fee or formula used to calculate it.

VEHICLE VIOLATIONS TABLE

M	11713.11(b)	Dealer advertising auction event to disclose in advertisement of vehicle seized by a federal, state, or local public agency or authority the number of asset seizures and total number of vehicles to be auctioned.
M	11713.11(c)	Auctioning dealer; fail to identify vehicle seized by a federal, state, or local public agency or authority, before bidding begins on the vehicle.
M	11713.11(d)	Dealer including costs in the total price of an auctioned vehicle, except those specified.
M	11713.11(e)	Dealer charging a buyer's fee when conducting an auction unless a prescribed disclosure is given.
M	11713.11(f)	Dealer auctioning vehicles, failure to comply with dealer licensing and operating provisions of the Vehicle Code and specified auctioneer laws in the Civil Code, Commercial Code, Penal Code, and laws administered by State Board of Equalization.
M	11713.12(a)	Lemon Law decal: manufacturer shall affix to left front door frame of "Lemon Law Buyback" vehicle or in a location designated by the DMV.
M	11713.12(b)	Person removing or altering decal affixed pursuant to subdivision (a).
M	11713.13(a)	Preventing or attempting to prevent by contract to otherwise, a dealer from adding, or maintaining a sales or service operation for another line make of vehicles at the same or expanded facility.
M	11713.13(b)	Requiring a dealer to establish or maintain exclusive facilities, personnel, or display space if the imposition would be unreasonable in light of existing circumstances, including economic conditions.
M	11713.13(c)	Requiring a dealer to make material alterations, expansion, or addition to any dealership facility, unless the required alteration, expansion, or addition is reasonable in light of all existing circumstances, including economic conditions.
M	11713.15(a)	Temporary branch licenses; dealer shall submit to DMV a manufacturer's written authorization with specified information.
M	11713.15(b)	Advertising and promotional materials for the sale of recreational vehicles at temporary locations shall contain name and established place of business and identify used vehicles as such.
M	11713.15(c)	Recreational vehicle dealer at temporary branch site provide buyer a written statement disclosing identity and established business location, or if none, so state.
M	11713.16(a)	Advertise used vehicle without disclosing it as such.
M	11713.16(b)	Use "on approved credit" or similar term inconspicuously or abbreviated.
M	11713.16(c)	Advertise "unpaid balance" or similar term except conspicuously and in proximity to advertised balance.
M	11713.16(d)	Advertise credit terms in violation of specified Federal Regulations.
M	11713.16(e)	Advertise total vehicle sale price that reflects deduction for rebate.
M	11713.16(f)	Advertise "everyone financed" or similar term if untrue.
M	11713.16(g)	Advertise false amount of down payment.
M	11713.16(h)	Advertise price of a new vehicle which has less than standard equipment.

VEHICLE VIOLATIONS TABLE

M	11713.16(i)	Fail to make required disclosures in advertising.
M	11713.17(a)	Dealer, delivery of vehicle without license plate bracket.
M	11713.17(b)	Manufacturer, failure to equip vehicle with bracket to secure license plates.
M	11713.18	Dealer, advertise for sale or sell a used vehicle as "certified" under specified conditions.
M	11713.19	Dealer, add charges to the contract for any goods or services without previously disclosing to the consumer the goods and services to be added and obtaining the consumer's consent. Inflate the amount of an installment payment or down payment or extend the maturity of a sale or lease contract for the purpose of disguising the actual charges for goods or services to be added by the dealer to the contract.
M	11713.20	Dealer, who obtains a credit score from a prospective customer for use in a credit application for the purchase of a motor vehicle must provide a specified disclosure in writing regarding consumer rights applicable to the credit application process.
M	11713.21(a)	Dealer failure to offer buyer of used vehicle a contract cancellation option.
M	11713.21(b)	Contract cancellation option agreement; document form and content.
M	11713.21(c)	Dealer failure to cancel contract pursuant to cancellation option agreement and provide buyer with full refund.
M	11713.22	Failure or refusal to provide a recreational vehicle dealer with a written "recreational vehicle franchise" pursuant to section 331.3.
M	11713.23	Selling a new recreational vehicle without a "recreational vehicle franchise" pursuant to section 331.3.
M	11713.25(a)	Computer vendor, unauthorized use or modification of dealer computer records; failure to maintain safeguards over dealer computer records.
M	11714(b)	Dealer selling at retail at a location not posted.
M	11714(c)	Wholesale dealer selling at retail.
M	11715(f)	Manufacturer, remanufacturer, or dealer, failure to maintain registration with special plates.
M	11725(a)	License plates to DMV prior to transporting or driving to foreign jurisdiction with intent to register or sell.
M	11725(b)	License plates to DMV prior to delivery for export to foreign jurisdiction outside the U.S.
M	11729(a)	When the owner is not an Occupational Licensee, requires dealers to execute a prescribed consignment agreement when accepting possession of a vehicle for the purpose of selling the vehicle for the owner and paying the owner or his or her designee from the proceeds of the sale.
M	11729(b)	Prescribes contents of consignment agreement to be used by dealers conducting auction sales on behalf of fleet owners.
M	11730	Requires any dealer engaging in consignments to execute a prescribed consignment agreement containing specified terms, phrases, conditions, and disclosures. (Use appropriate subsection.)
M	11735(a)	Engaging in brokering without obtaining autobroker endorsement and paying required fee.

M	11735(c)	Autobroker log must contain specified information.
M	11736(a)	Failure to execute written brokering agreement and to provide copies to consumer and selling dealer.
M	11736(b)	Accepting purchase deposit from consumer that exceeds 2.5 percent of selling price of vehicle.
M	11736(c)	Failing to refund purchase money or deposit upon demand by consumer prior to completed sale.
M	11736(d)	Failing to cancel brokering agreement and refund money to consumer when final price exceeds price in broker agreement, when vehicle delivered is not as described, or when agreement expires.
M	11736(e)	Acting as seller and autobroker in the same transaction.
M	11736(f)	Failure to disclose whether autobroker receives a fee from the selling dealer and, if so, the dollar amount of the fee.
M	11736(g)	Failure to record specified information in autobroker log.
M	11736(h)	Failure to maintain copy of executed autobroker agreement and related notices and documents for at least 3 years.
M	11736(i)	Failure to advise consumer that refund will be made if vehicle is not obtained or service orally contracted is not provided.
M	11737(a)	Dealer must deposit purchase money from broker sales in trust account.
M	11737(b)	Brokering dealer prohibited from encumbering trust account except in payment to a selling dealer or to make refunds.
M	11737(d)	Brokering dealer must serve as trustee of trust account.
M	11737(e)	Broker trust accounts must be maintained in bank, savings and loan, or credit union regulated by the state or federal government.
M	11738	Specifies contents and print size of brokering agreement. (Use appropriate subsection.)
M	11739	Selling dealer, not autobroker, must apply for title and registration, secure manufacturer's warranty, and apply for manufacturer's rebates and incentives for the purchaser.
M	11800	Salesman; unlicensed or having license suspended, revoked, invalid or expired.
M	11806(a)	Salesman-outstanding unsatisfied judgement.
M	11806(b)	Salesmen-failure to pay over funds or property to dealer.
M	11806(c)	Salesman-failure to return vehicle to dealer upon termination of employment.
M	11806(d)	Salesman-a cause for refusal, suspension or revocation exists under Section 11302 to 11909.
M	11806(e)	Salesman-purchase or sale without using dealer's report.
M	11806(f)	Salesman-representing more than one dealer.
M	11806(g)	Salesman-failure to comply with Section 11812.
M	11806(h)	Salesman-while licensed as a managerial employee committed wrongful acts causing suspension or revocation of the license.
M	11806(i)	DMV may refuse to issue or suspend or revoke a license to an applicant who has acted as a dealer when that person was not acting on behalf of a dealer.
M	11812(a)	Failure to post a Salesman's license or true and exact copy in

VEHICLE VIOLATIONS TABLE

		conspicuous place.
M	11812(b)	Failure to display Salesman's license or true and exact copy continuously and to return it when employment is terminated and destroying all copies.
M	11812(c)	Vehicle salesman, failure to notify DMV within 5 days of residence address change.
M	11819(a)	Lending Salesman's license.
M	11819(b)	Displaying license issued to another.
M	11819(c)	Failure to surrender license.
M	11819(d)	Permitting use of license.
M	11819(e)	Unauthorized duplication of salesperson's license.
M	11900	Representative, unlicensed.
M	11950(a)	Failure of a buy-here-pay-here automotive dealer to affix a label on a used vehicle stating the "Reasonable Market Value" of that vehicle.
M	11950(b)	Failure of a buy–here–pay–here automotive dealer to provide prospective buyer of used vehicle a copy of any information obtained to determine the reasonable market value of that vehicle
M	12001(a)	Failure to provide customer with an invoice which identifies by brand name parts installed.
M	12001(b)	Failure to provide customer with an invoice which identifies used parts installed.
M	12002	Manufacturing, installing, or selling a defective vehicle part as defined by the National Traffic and Motor Vehicle Safety Act of 1966.
M	12110(a)	Unlawful to pay or receive compensation from a towing service for arranging or requesting tow truck service.
M	12120	Sale of vehicle other than by dealer or registered owner.

VEHICLE VIOLATIONS TABLE

	Types of convictions received for violation of certain sections of Division 6 of the Vehicle Code.	
Type	**VC Section**	**Violation**
M	12500(a)	Driver, unlicensed.
I	12500(b)	Requires the driver of a motorcycle to be licensed.
I	12500(c)	Prohibits operation of a vehicle in or upon any offstreet parking facility unless the individual is licensed.
I	12500(d)	Prohibits the operation of vehicles if not properly licensed.
I	12500(e)	Operation of motorized scooter in violation of emission requirements.
I	12502(b)	Nonresident driver, medical certificate required.
I	12502(c)	Nonresident driver, shall comply with any restriction of the medical certificate issued to that nonresident.
I	12509(d)	Person with instruction permit shall not drive motor vehicle unless a under the immediate supervision of a valid California licensed driver, who must occupy a position within the driver's compartment.
I	12509(e)	Operating a government owned vehicle with a permit while not under the instruction of the California National Guard.
I	12509.5(a)	Person with instruction permit shall not drive a motorcycle unless successfully completing a motorcyclist safety program.
I	12509.5(c)	Person with instruction permit shall not drive a motorcycle during darkness, on a freeway, or with a passenger.
I	12511	Driver's license, possession of more than one.
I	12515(a)	Minor under 18 employed for purpose of driving.
M	12515(b)	Driver under 21 operating or employed to operate interstate commerce or hazardous substance vehicle.
I	12516	School bus driver, under 18.
M	12517(a)	School bus driver must possess both driver's license and certificate.

VEHICLE VIOLATIONS TABLE

M	12517(b)	School pupil activity bus driver must possess both driver's license and certificate.
M	12517.45	Transporting school pupils pursuant to section 545 without appropriate license, certification, or parental authorization.
I	12517.5(a)	Operating a paratransit vehicle without valid, appropriate license.
I	12517.5(b)	Operating a paratransit vehicle without proper training.
M	12519(a)	Farm labor vehicle, endorsed driver's license required.
M	12520(a)	Operation of tow truck involved in freeway service patrol operations without valid California driver's license and tow truck driver certificate.
I	12521(a)	Tour bus operator, use safety belts.
I	12521(b)	Tour bus operator, report accidents.
I	12522(a)	Schoolbus or youth bus driver, first aid qualification.
I	12523(a)	Youth bus operator, driver's license, appropriate class.
I	12523(d)	Youth bus operator-Use seat belt, refrain from smoking, report any accidents to CHP.
I	12523.5(a)	General public paratransit operator, driver's license, appropriate class and certificate.
I	12523.5(d)	General public paratransit operator; use seatbelts, refrain from smoking, report accidents.
I	12523.6(a)	Driver of disabled, drivers license appropriate class and endorsement.
I	12523.6(d)	Driver of disabled, shall not employ without appropriate class and endorsement.
I	12524(a)	Radioactive materials driver's certificate required.
I	12804.6(a)	Transit bus operator, possess appropriate certificate.
I	12804.6(f)	Transit bus, employer permitting person to drive without a valid certificate on file in employee records.
M	12804.9	Persons applying for house car endorsements required to complete instructional course and demonstrate specified skills.
M	12804.10	Class C drivers may operate house cars up to 40 feet in length.
I	12804.11	Operating firefighting equipment without a proper endorsement or license issued by the Department.
I/M	12804.15	Driver of 'house car' must possess appropriate class of driver's license, including endorsement if required.
I	12814.6(b)(1)(A)	Provisional DL drive between 11:00 p.m. and 5:00 a.m.
I	12814.6(b)(1)(B)	Provisional DL transport passengers under 20 years old.
I	12815(a)	Driver's license, lost or mutilated, obtain duplicate, destroy original if found.
I	12950	Signature of Licensee.Failure to sign usual signature.
I	12950(a)	Failure to sign driver's license with usual signature.
I	12951(a)	Driver's license, not in possession.
M	12951(b)	Driver's license, refusal to present to officer.

VEHICLE VIOLATIONS TABLE

I	12952	Driver's license, display to court.
I	13003(a)	ID card; obtain duplicate if lost, stolen, mutilated, or name change.
I	13003(b)	ID card; surrender to DMV within 10 days after notification by DMV or law enforcement that document is mutilated.
M	13004(a)	ID card display or possession of, cancelled, altered, fictitious, fraudulently obtained.
M	13004(b)	ID card, lending or permitting another to use.
M	13004(c)	ID card, displaying another's.
M	13004(d)	ID card, permitting unlawful use.
M	13004(e)	To do any act forbidden by this article.
M	13004(f)	ID card, reproducing or possession of facsimile.
M	13004(g)	ID card, unauthorized alteration.
M	13004.1(a)	Prohibits the manufacture or sale of an identification document which is substantially similar to a driver's license, or that purports to confer the same privileges, as the drivers' license issued by the Department.
I	13007	ID card holder notify DMV change of address within 10 days.
I	13007.5	Unlawful for applicant to knowingly declare to DMV that no birth certificate exists when, in fact, a birth certificate does exist.
I	14600(a)	Change of address, notify DMV within 10 days. (DL)
I	14600(b)	Present change-of-address document to a peace officer. (DL)
M	14601(a)	Driving when driver's license suspended or revoked for reckless driving, negligent or incompetent driving acts.
M	14601.1(a)	Driving when driver's license suspended or revoked for offenses not related to driving ability.
M	14601.2(a)	Driving when driver's license suspended or revoked for driving under the influence of alcohol, drug, or combination.
M	14601.2(b)	Restricted license for alcohol and drug offenses, disobeying restrictions.
M	14601.3(a)	Driver's license suspended or revoked-Habitual traffic offender.
M	14601.4(a)	Driving while license suspended or revoked pursuant to Section 14601.2 and causing an injury collision.
M	14601.5	Driver's license suspended or revoked-chemical test refusal. (Use appropriate subsection.)
M	14602.8(g)(4)	Legal owner knowingly releasing or causing the release of an impounded vehicle to a registered owner in violation of this subdivision.
I	14603	Restricted license, disobeying restrictions.
M	14604(a)	Motor vehicle owner, unlawful to loan to unlicensed driver. Must make reasonable effort to determine license status of person to whom car is loaned.

VEHICLE VIOLATIONS TABLE

I	14605(a)	Parking lot attendant, unlicensed.
I	14605(b)	Parking lot attendant, employing unlicensed.
I	14606(a)	Unlicensed person, employing, hiring, or knowingly permitting to drive.
I	14606(b)	Failure of employer to report a person's failure to qualify to operate a commercial motor vehicle to DMV within 10 days.
I	14606(c)	Failure of employer to obtain a copy of the driver medical certification, and retain certification as part of a driver qualification file.
I	14607	Person cause or permit own child, ward, or employee under the age of 18 to drive unless licensed.
I	14608(a)(1)	Renting motor vehicle to unlicensed person
I	14608(a)(2)	Failure of a person renting a vehicle to another to inspect the driver license along with comparing the signature or photograph prior to releasing a vehicle.
I	14609(a)	Renting motor vehicle, maintain proper records.
I	14609(b)	Renting motor vehicle to unlicensed person, maintain proper records.
M	14610(a)(1)	Makes it unlawful to display or possess any cancelled, revoked, suspended, fictitious, fraudulently altered, or fraudulently obtained driver's license.
M	14610(a)(2)	Makes it unlawful to lend a driver's license to any person.
M	14610(a)(3)	Makes it unlawful for a person to represent as their license one that was not issued to them.
M	14610(a)(4)	Makes it unlawful to fail or refuse to surrender to DMV any driver's license which has been suspended, revoked or cancelled.
M	14610(a)(5)	Makes it unlawful to permit any unlawful use of a driver's license.
M	14610(a)(6)	Makes it unlawful to do any act forbidden or fail to perform any act required by this division.
M	14610(a)(7)	Makes it unlawful to photograph, photostat, duplicate, or in any way reproduce any driver's license or facsimile so that it could be mistaken for a valid license.
M	14610(a)(8)	Makes it unlawful to alter any driver's license in any manner not authorized by the Vehicle Code.
M	14610.1(a)	Prohibits the manufacture or sale of an identification document which is substantially similar to a driver's license, or that purports to confer the same privileges, as the drivers' license issued by the Department.
I/M	14610.5(a)	Sale or distribution of crib sheet on DMV driver's license examination; impersonation of a driver's license applicant.
M	14610.7	Knowingly assist an illegal alien in obtaining a driver's license.
I	14611	Knowingly directing hauling of radioactive materials by person not possessing certificate.
I	15220	Commercial motor vehicle driver shall report any out-of-

VEHICLE VIOLATIONS TABLE

		state conviction involving the safe operation of a motor vehicle to DMV within 30 days.
I	15222	Commercial motor vehicle driver shall report any conviction involving the safe operation of motor vehicle to his or her employer within 30 days.
I	15224	Commercial motor vehicle driver shall notify employer of suspended or revoked driver's license before the end of business day following the action.
I	15226	Driver placed out-of-service for violation of Federal Motor Carrier Safety Regulations shall report to his or her employer within 24 hours.
I	15228	Driver placed out-of-service for violation of Federal Motor Vehicle Safety Regulations shall report to DMV within 30 days.
I	15230	Each person who applies for employment as a driver of a commercial motor vehicle shall provide employer with required information.
I	15240(a)	Employer knowingly allows a driver to drive a commercial motor vehicle with a suspended or revoked driving privilege. Out-of-service order applicable when driver/commercial motor carrier found in violation of railroad-highway grade crossing laws.
I	15240(b)	Employer knowingly allows a driver with more than one driver's license to operate a commercial motor vehicle.
I	15250(a)	Person operating commercial motor vehicle shall have in his or her immediate possession valid commercial driver's license of appropriate class.
I	15250.5(a)	Requires a person operating firefighting equipment to possess a valid driver's license for the appropriate class.
I	15250.6(a)	Operation of firefighting equipment. Driver shall have in immediate possession driver license of appropriate class.
I	15275(a)	Person operating a commercial motor vehicle shall have an endorsement, as required by the CHP.
M	15278(a)	Requires an endorsement to operate certain commercial vehicles.
M	15312	Commercial drivers prohibited from operating vehicle for specified time due to a violation of railroad grade crossing regulations.

Types of convictions received for violation of certain sections of Division 6.5 of the Vehicle Code.		
Type	**VC Section**	**Violation**
I	15500	Minor without driver's license, purchasing or obtaining motor vehicle.
M	15501	Driver's license, minor presenting false license for leasing or purchasing of car.

Types of convictions received for violation of certain sections of Division 6.7 of the Vehicle Code.

Type	VC Section	Violation
I	15620	Children six (6) and under alone in vehicle when significant risk to health/safety exists.

Types of convictions received for violation of certain sections of Division 7 of the Vehicle Code.

Type	VC Section	Violation
I	16000	SR-1 report, within 10 days of reportable on-highway or off-highway accident.
I	16002	Employer's report, within 10 days. Driver's of publicly owned/operated transit vehicles to report collisions within 10 days of their occurrence and maintain records of such collisions.
I	16003	Driver incapable, owner shall file report.
I	16020(a)	Driver and owner must maintain a form of financial responsibility and shall carry evidence of financial responsibility in the vehicle at all times. Name of insurance company and policy number required for proper evidence of financial responsibility when requested.
I	16020.3	Vanpool vehicle, employer must maintain proof of financial responsibility.
I	16025(a)	Exchange of information, including evidence of financial responsibility, at the scene of an accident.
I	16028(a)	Display proof of financial responsibility when requested by a peace officer or traffic investigator when involved in an accident.
I	16028(c)	Display proof of financial responsibility when requested by a peace officer when involved in an accident.
I	16030(a)	Providing false evidence of financial responsibility.
I	16050.5	Owner shall furnish driver involved in reportable accident of his/her insurance information.
I	16054	Requires the owner of an insured vehicle to furnish insurance information to an individual involved in an accident while operating the vehicle with the owner's permission.
I	16457(a)	Driving a motor vehicle not covered by a certificate of insurance when proof of ability to respond in damages is required.
I	16502	Commercial passenger vehicle, owner to maintain proof of ability to respond.
M	16560	Interstate highway carriers, failure to comply with P.U.C. regulations.

VEHICLE VIOLATIONS TABLE

	Types of convictions received for violation of certain sections of Division 10 of the Vehicle Code.	
Type	**VC Section**	**Violation**
F	20001(a)	Hit-run, injury or death, immediate report of fatal.
M	20002(a)	Hit-run, property damage, including vehicles. Driver required to immediately stop vehicle involved in property damage only collision at the nearest location which will not impede traffic or otherwise jeopardize the safety of other motorists.
M	20002(b)	Hit-run, property damage, by runaway vehicle.
M	20003(a)	Driver involved in accident resulting in injury or death shall provide information.
M	20003(b)	Driver involved in accident resulting in injury or death shall present drivers license.
I	20006	Driver without license present other evidence of identification.
I	20008(a)	Accidents, injury or fatal, written report within 24 hours.
I	20008(b)	Common carrier file report by 10th of following month.
I	20010	Accident report, passenger comply when driver unable.
I	20011	Coroner's report, all M.V. fatals to CHP by 10th of following month.

VEHICLE VIOLATIONS TABLE

Type	VC Section	Violation
		Types of convictions received for violation of certain sections of Division of the Vehicle Code.
I	21070	Public Offense: Unsafe Operation of Motor Vehicle.
I	21100.3	Failure to obey traffic direction of local authority.
I	21106(b)	Crosswalk, use of where prohibited by sign.
I	21113(a)	School or public grounds, trespassing on with vehicle, animal, bicycle, skateboard, motorized bicycle, or roller skates.
I	21116(a)	Unlawful to drive upon roadway on a levee, canal bank, pipeline right-of-way or natural waterline course.
M	21200.5	Riding a bicycle while under the influence of alcohol, drugs, or both.
I	21201(a)	Bicycle, single wheel brake required.
I	21201(b)	Bicycle, handlebars no higher than operator's shoulders.
I	21201(c)	Bicycle: rider unable to support in an upright position with at least one foot on the ground.
I	21201(d)	Bicycle illumination, devices required while riding upon a highway, sidewalk, or a bikeway. White or Yellow reflectors may be worn on a shoe or ankle as an option to the pedals.
I	21201.3(b)	Steady or flashing blue light on bicycle.
I	21201.5(a)	Sale of unapproved, reflex reflector, or reflectorized tire.
I	21201.5(b)	Sale of bicycle without required reflectors on pedals and sides.
I	21202(a)	Bicyclist, failure to use right edge of roadway.
I	21203	Bicyclist, hitching ride on other vehicle.
I	21204(a)	Bicyclist, riding on other than permanent seat and/or passenger riding on other than permanent seat, unless the bicycle was designed by the manufacturer to be ridden without a seat.
I	21204(b)	Bicyclist, permitting passenger on other than a permanent seat; minor passenger not retained in seat.
I	21205	Bicyclist, unable to keep at least one hand free to use on handlebars.
I	21207.5	Operation of motorized bicycle upon bikeway, equestrian, hiking or recreational trail without proper authority.

VEHICLE VIOLATIONS TABLE

I	21208(a)	Failure to ride in a bicycle lane.
I	21208(b)	Bicyclist shall not leave bike lane until reasonably safe.
I	21209(a)	Driving in bicycle lane. Except as provided.
I	21210	Bicycle lying on its side on a sidewalk.
I	21211(a)	Standing, stopping, sitting, or loitering on a Class I bikeway. Tow trucks exempt from prohibition of blocking bikeway when engaged in towing a vehicle.
I	21211(b)	Placing or parking any bicycle, vehicle, or object upon a Class I bikeway which impedes the movement of a bicyclist.
I	21212(a)	Person under 18 operating or riding as passenger on a bicycle, nonmotorized scooter, or skateboard or wear in-line roller skates or roller skates without wearing an approved helmet.
I	21212(c)	Sale of safety helmet not meeting applicable safety standards.
M	21221.5	Riding a motorized scooter while under the influence of alcohol, drugs, or both.
I	21223	Motorized scooter, during darkness headlight, red reflector to the rear, and side reflectors required.
I	21226(b)	Violation of motorized scooter muffler equipment requirements.
I	21226(d)	Violation of motorized scooter exhaust/noise level requirements or operation with modified exhaust.
I	21228(a)	Motorized scooter, failure to ride as close as practicable to the right hand curb or right edge of the roadway.
I	21229(a)	Motorized scooter, failure to ride within an established bicycle lane.
I	21229(b)	Prohibits the operator of a motorized scooter to exit a bicycle lane without signaling.
I	21235(a)	Operating a motorized scooter unless it is equipped with a brake.
I	21235(b)	Operating a motorized scooter on a highway with a posted speed limit in excess of 25 miles per hour unless the motorized scooter is operated within a bicycle lane.
I	21235(c)	Operating a motorized scooter without wearing a properly fitted and fastened bicycle helmet.
I	21235(d)	Operating a motorized scooter when the operator is under 16 years of age.
I	21235(e)	Operating a motorized scooter with any passengers in addition to the operator.
I	21235(f)	Operating a motorized scooter carrying any package, bundle, or article that prevents the operator from keeping at least one hand upon the handlebars.
I	21235(g)	Operating a motorized scooter upon a sidewalk.
I	21235(h)	Operating a motorized scooter on a roadway with handlebars above the operator's shoulders.
I	21235(i)	Leaving a motorized scooter lying on its side on any sidewalk, or parking a motorized scooter on a sidewalk so that it blocks pedestrian traffic.
I	21235(j)	Attaching a motorized scooter or the operator while on the roadway, by any means, to any other vehicle on the roadway.
I	21260(a)	Prohibits a low-speed vehicle from being operated on any roadway with a speed limit in excess of 35 miles per hour except when the

		roadway is being crossed.
I	21281(a)	Electric personal assistive mobility device, shall be equipped with front, rear, and side reflectors.
I	21281(b)	Electric personal assistive mobility device, equipped with a system to bring the device to a controlled stop.
I	21281(c)	Electric personal assistive mobility device, equipped with a lamp emitting a white light while in motion during darkness.
I	21281(d)	Electric personal assistive mobility device, equipped with a sound emitting device activated by the operator to alert nearby persons.
I	21281.5(a)	Unsafe operation of an electric personal assistive mobility device.
I	21281.5(b)	Unsafe operation of an electric personal assistive mobility device, speed that endangers the safety of persons or property.
I	21281.5(c)	Unsafe operation of an electric personal assistive mobility device, wanton disregard for the safety of persons or property.
I	21281.5(d)	Unsafe operation of an electric personal assistive mobility device, failure to yield to a pedestrian.
I	21367(b)	Department of Transportation, disobeying traffic control at construction site.
I	21367(c)	Failure to obey warning devices at construction site.
I	21451(a)	Circular green signal, shall proceed but shall yield to vehicles and pedestrians lawfully within intersection.
I	21451(b)	Green arrow, shall enter intersection only to make movement indicated.
I	21451(c)	Pedestrians facing circular green, may proceed but must yield to vehicles lawfully within the intersection.
I	21451(d)	Pedestrian facing green arrow shall not enter roadway.
I	21452(b)	Failure of pedestrian to properly respond to signal of yellow light or arrow.
I	21453	Red or Stop, vehicles stop at limit line or X-walk. When making right turn at a red light/stop sign driver required to yield to any vehicle approaching so closely as to constitute an immediate hazard.
I	21453(b)	After stopping, may turn right, or turn left from a one-way street to a one-way street, (unless sign posted) but shall yield to pedestrians and traffic on cross street.
I	21453(c)	Red arrow, driver shall not enter intersection to make indicated movement.
I	21453(d)	Pedestrian facing circular red or red arrow, shall not enter roadway.
I	21454(c)	Lane use control signal, steady red, driver shall not enter or use.
I	21454(d)	Lane use control signal, flashing yellow, driver may use only for making left turn to or from the highway.
I	21455	Official traffic control signal erected at other than an intersection, shall stop at sign, crosswalk, limit line, or if none, at the signal.
I	21456(a)	"Walk" pedestrian failure to yield right-of-way to vehicles already in crosswalk.
I	21456(b)	"Don't walk" or "wait" or "upraised hand", pedestrian crossing against.
I	21457(a)	Flashing Red, failing to stop for.

VEHICLE VIOLATIONS TABLE

I	21457(b)	Flashing Yellow, proceed only with caution.
I	21460(a)	Double solid lines, driving to left of, except driveway, intersection, or U-turn.
I	21460(b)	Parallel solid white lines, crossing except as permitted.
I	21460(c)	Solid-broken lines, driving to the left when solid line placed on the right.
I	21460.5(c)	Two-way left turn lane, driving in, or turning from through lane.
I	21461(a)	Traffic control sign, failure to obey regulatory provisions.
I	21461.5	Pedestrian, failure to obey any sign or signal.
I	21462	Traffic control signals, all traffic (Sec. 620) to obey.
I	21463	Traffic signals, illegal operation.
I	21464(a)	Signs, signals, markers, or motorist call boxes, damaging, removing, or attaching material to.
I	21464(b)	Person using or unauthorized vehicle equipped with signal changing device.
I	21464(c)	Possessing, manufacturing, installing, selling, or distriuting equipment described in section (b) of this code.
M/F	21464(d)	Violation of (a) (b), or (c) of VC Section 21464 that results in injury or death.
I	21464(e)	Willful interference with traffic device or willful use, possession, or distribution of traffic interference device not resulting in injury.
I	21465	Traffic devices, display of unauthorized.
I	21466	Blinding lights, displayed toward highway.
I	21466.5	Display of light source impairing vision of drivers.
I	21650	Right half of roadway, failure to drive on.
I	21650.1	Bicycle on roadway or shoulder required to be operated in same direction as motor vehicles.
I	21651(a)	Divided highways, driving over, upon or across dividing section; left or semicircular U-turn except through marked opening.
M	21651(b)	Driving the wrong way on a divided highway.
M/F	21651(c)	Driving the wrong way on a divided highway which causes injury or death.
I	21652	Service road, entering or leaving adjacent highway from other than lawful opening.
I	21654(a)	Slower vehicle, in left lane(s).
I	21655(b)	Certain vehicles (22406) using left lane(s), or passing in lane other than adjacent to right lane. Trailer buses allowed in HOV lane.
I	21655.5(b)	Failure to obey sign posted preferential traffic lane(s); exceptions - motorcycles, mass transit buses, and paratransit vehicles.
I	21655.8(a)	Crossing over double yellow lines to enter or exit a preferential use traffic lane.
I	21655.9(b)	No person shall drive a vehicle described in 5205.5 unless the proper decal, label, or other identifier is displayed
M	21655.9(c)	No person shall operate or own a vehicle displaying a decal, label, or other identifier as described in 5205.5, if that decal, label, or other identifier is not assigned to that vehicle.

VEHICLE VIOLATIONS TABLE

I	21656	Slow vehicle, failure to use signposted turnout or safe area.
I	21657	One-way street, highway, driving against traffic.
I	21658(a)	Laned roadways (2 or more lanes in direction of travel), straddling or changing when unsafe.
I	21658(b)	Designate lanes, failure to obey signs.
I	21659	3-lane highway, driving in far left lane, or using center lane when unsafe.
I	21660	Meeting vehicles, failure to pass to right, and/or yield half of roadway.
I	21661	Descending narrow grade, yield to ascending vehicle.
I	21662	Mountain driving, hold motor vehicle under control.
I	21662(a)	Mountain driving, drive as near the right edge as possible.
I	21662(b)	Mountain driving, roadway with insufficient width, driver to give audible warning where view obstructed within 200 feet.
I	21663	Driving on sidewalk, except when permitted.
I	21664	Exiting or entering a freeway at other than a designated on-ramp or off-ramp.
I	21700	Obstructing driver's view or control, by passengers or load.
I	21700.5	Operation of bus with school pupils standing in city of San Diego.
I	21701	Interfering with driver's control of vehicle.
M	21702(a)	Driving Hours-Persons, not to exceed 10 hours.
M	21702(b)	Driving Hours-Property, not to exceed 12 hours.
I	21703	Following Too Closely, not reasonable and prudent.
I	21704(a)	Distance between trucks, 300 feet on 2-lane highway.
I	21705	Caravans, maintain at least 100 feet distance between vehicles.
I	21706	Authorized emergency vehicles, following within 300 feet.
I	21706.5(b)	A person shall not operate a vehicle in an unsafe manner within an emergency incident zone.
I	21707	Fire area, operating vehicle within the block or 300 feet.
I	21708	Fire hoses, driving over unprotected.
I	21709	Safety zone, driving through.
I	21710	Coasting, in neutral on downgrade.
I	21711	Towed vehicle, whipping, swerving or failing to track properly.
I	21712(a)	Permitting person to ride where unlawful.
I	21712(b)	Unlawful riding on portion not intended for passengers or load.
I	21712(c)	Person driving a motor vehicle shall not knowingly permit a person to ride in the trunk of that motor vehicle.
I	21712(d)	A person shall not ride in the trunk of a vehicle.
I	21712(g)	Permitting riding in trailer coach or trailer carrying vessel unlawful.
I	21712(h)	Unlawful towing of bicycle, skis, sled, etc.
M	21713	Privately owned armored car, operated without CHP license.
I	21714(a)	Operating a fully enclosed 3-wheel motor vehicle described in 27803(f) adjacent to lane markings.
I	21714(b)	Operating fully enclosed 3-wheel motor vehicle described in 27803

VEHICLE VIOLATIONS TABLE

		(f) in any lane established under 21655.5 between vehicles.
I	21715(a)	Passenger vehicle towing more than one other vehicle. (See 36625 and 36626 for exceptions.)
I	21715(b)	Motor vehicle under 4,000 pounds towing any vehicle over 6,000 pounds.
I	21716	Operating golf cart in speed zone above 25 mph.
I	21717	Motor vehicle turning across a bicycle lane.
I	21718(a)	Stopping or parking on freeway having full access and no crossing grades.
I	21720	Pocket bike, shall not be operated on a sidewalk, roadway, or any part of a highway, or on a bikeway, bicycle path or trail, equestrian trail, hiking or recreational trail, or on public lands open to off-highway motor vehicle use.
I	21750	Overtaking vehicle, failure to pass safely to left.
I	21751	Overtaking vehicle, passing without sufficient clearance.
I	21752(a)	Driving left of center, when view limited by curve or hill crest.
I	21752(b)	Driving left of center, when view limited approaching bridge, viaduct or tunnel.
I	21752(c)	Driving left of center, traversing any RR crossing.
I	21752(d)	Driving left of center, traversing any intersection.
I	21753	Overtaken vehicle, not moving to right on audible signal, or increasing speed.
I	21754	Passing on right, when unlawful.
I	21755(a)	Passing on right, when unsafe, or on shoulder.
I	21756(a)	Passing streetcar when receiving or discharging passengers.
I	21756(b)	Passing streetcar at unsafe speed.
I	21756(c)	Passing trolley coach at unsafe speed.
I	21757	Passing streetcar on left.
I	21758	Passing too slowly on grade (10 mph faster, complete pass 1/4 mile).
I	21759	Passing animals, stop or reduce speed as necessary.
I	21800(a)	Uncontrolled intersection, yield to first vehicle within.
I	21800(b)	Uncontrolled intersection, yield to vehicle on right.
I	21800(c)	Intersection controlled from all sides (4-way stop), yield to vehicle on right.
I	21800(d)(1)	Driver shall stop at intersection with inoperative signals.
I	21800(d)(2)	Two vehicles at intersection with inoperative signals; driver on left yield right-of-way.
I	21801(a)	Left turns or U-turns yield until reasonably safe.
I	21801(b)	Failure to yield, turning vehicle having yielded (lane by lane).
I	21802(a)	Entering through highway, yield until reasonably safe.
I	21802(b)	Failure to yield, by vehicle not a hazard.
I	21803(a)	Yield signs, yield until reasonably safe.
I	21803(b)	Failure to yield, by vehicle not a hazard.
I	21804(a)	Public or private property, yield to approaching traffic so close as to

		constitute an immediate hazard.
I	21804(b)	Failure to yield, by vehicle not a hazard.
I	21805(b)	Equestrian crossings, failure to yield by driver.
I	21805(c)	Horseback rider proceeding into path of vehicle.
I	21806(a)	Emergency vehicles, other driver failing to yield.
I	21806(b)	Emergency vehicles, motorman failing to yield.
I	21806(c)	Emergency vehicles, pedestrian failing to yield.
I	21807	Driving authorized emergency vehicle without due regard for safety of persons and property.
I	21809(a)	A person driving on a freeway approaching a stopped emergency vehicle, tow truck, or marked Department of Transportation vehicle with its emergency or flashing amber warning lights on, if in an immediately adjacent lane, must change to an adjacent lane or slow to a prudent speed.
I	21950(a)	Crosswalks, failure to yield to pedestrians within.
I	21950(b)	Crosswalk, pedestrian running in front of vehicle.
I	21950(c)	Failure to exercise due care and reduce speed of the vehicle for pedestrians.
I	21951	Crosswalk, overtaking and passing vehicle stopped for pedestrian within.
I	21952	Sidewalk, failure to yield to pedestrian on.
I	21953	Pedestrian yield, if protected crossing available.
I	21954(a)	Pedestrian yield, upon roadway outside crosswalk.
I	21955	Jaywalking, between signal controlled intersections.
I	21956	Walking on roadway, other than pedestrian's left edge.
I	21957	Hitchhiking, while standing in roadway.
I	21959	Skiing, tobogganing, on or across highway interfering with traffic.
I	21960(a)	Violation of freeway or expressway use restrictions by pedestrian, motor-driven cycle, motorized bicycle, or motorized scooter.
M	21963	Fail to yield right of way to blind pedestrian.
I	21964	Other than blind person carrying white cane.
I	21966	Pedestrian in a bicycle lane where pedestrian facility.
I	21968	Motorized skateboard on highway, bikeway, or trail.
I	21970(a)	Stopping unnecessarily and blocking a marked or unmarked crosswalk or sidewalk.
I	22100(a)	Right turn at intersection, improper position.
I	22100(b)	Left turn at intersection, improper position.
I	22100.5	U-turn at traffic signal, only from left lane.
I	22101(d)	Required or prohibited turn, failure to obey official sign.
I	22102	U-turn in business district, other than from extreme left-hand lane at an intersection or opening in divided highway.
I	22103	U-turn in residence district, vehicle approaching within 200 feet.
I	22104	U-turn at fire station, in front of or using entrance.
I	22105	U-turn, vision obstructed within 200 feet.

I	22106	Starting or backing when unsafe.
I	22107	Unsafe turn, and/or without signalling.
I	22108	Turning without signalling last 100 feet.
I	22109	Stopping suddenly without signalling.
I	22110	Signals shall be given by signal lamp, unless a vehicle is not required to be and is not equipped with turn signals. Vehicles not required to be and not equipped with turn signals shall give a hand and arm signal.
I	22111(a)	Left turn hand signal, improperly given.
I	22111(b)	Right turn hand signal, improperly given.
I	22111(c)	Stop hand signal, improperly given.
I	22112(a)	Schoolbus driver shall activate amber warning light system 200 feet prior to stop. Driver shall deactivate amber system upon stop. Driver shall activate flashing red light system and stop signal arm when the bus is stopped for loading and unloading pupils.
I	22112(b)	Schoolbus driver, stop to load or unload pupils only at designated schoolbus stops.
I	22112(c)	Schoolbus driver, when required, ensure the flashing red signal system and stop signal arm are activated and it is safe to enter or exit the schoolbus.
I	22112(d)	Schoolbus driver, escort pupil with hand held stop sign, require all pupils to walk in front of bus, ensure all pupils and pedestrians are a safe distance from the bus before departing.
I	22112(e)	Schoolbus driver, may not activate the amber warning light system at specified locations, except where pupils must cross the highway.
I	22112(f)	Activation of either the amber warning light system or the flashing red light system at a location determined by the CHP as necessary.
I	22348(b)	Driving in excess of 100 mph.
I	22348(c)	Vehicle subject to 22406 using left lane(s) or passing in lane other than lane immediately adjacent to right lane.
I	22349(a)	Exceeding 65 mph maximum speed limit.
I	22349(b)	Exceeding 55 mph speed limit on a two-lane undivided highway.
I	22350	Unsafe speed for prevailing conditions (use for all prima facie limits).
I	22356(b)	Exceeding the maximum speed limit, as specified.
I	22400(a)	Minimum speed, impeding normal flow of traffic.
I	22400(b)	Minimum speed, below signposted limit.
I	22405(a)	Unsafe speed (signposted) for condition of bridge, structure, tube or tunnel.
I	22406(a)	55 mph limit, truck or truck tractor (3 axle or any combo).
I	22406(b)	55 mph limit, passenger car, or bus, towing any vehicle.
I	22406(c)	55 mph limit, schoolbus with pupils.
I	22406(d)	55 mph limit, farm labor vehicle transporting passengers.
I	22406(e)	55 mph limit, any vehicle transporting explosives.
I	22406(f)	55 mph limit, trailer bus.
M	22406.1	Operating a commercial vehicle, as defined, upon a highway at a

VEHICLE VIOLATIONS TABLE

		speed exceeding 15 mph over the established maximum speed limit.
I	22406.5	Speeding or reckless driving, tank vehicles transporting more than 500 gallons of flammable liquid.
I	22407	Truck speed on downgrade, exceeding posted limit 10,000 lbs. or over.
I	22409	Solid tire vehicle, speed restricted by weight.
I	22410	Metal tire, vehicle exceeding 6 mph.
I	22411	No person shall operate a motorized scooter at a speed in excess of 15 miles per hour.
I	22450(a)	Stop sign, failure to stop at limit line, crosswalk, or entrance to intersection.
I	22450(b)	Stop sign at railroad crossing, stop at a limit line, first track or entrance to railroad grade crossing.
I	22451(a)	RR crossing, vehicle or pedestrian fails to stop for signal device or closely approaching train.
I	22451(b)	RR crossing, driver or pedestrian proceeding through a closed crossing gate.
I	22452(b)	Railroad crossing, certain vehicles, including farm labor vehicles and any school bus transporting pupils, must stop.
I	22454(a)	Passing school bus, stop when red lights flashing.
I	22455(a)	Failure to bring a commercial vehicle to a complete stop and lawfully parked while engaged in vending from the vehicle.
I	22456(d)	Ice cream truck shall be equipped while vending in residential areas with legible signs.
I	22456(e)	A person may not vend from an ice cream truck that is stopped, parked, or standing on any public street, alley or highway as specified.
C	22500(a)	Parking unlawfully, within intersection.
C	22500(b)	Parking unlawfully, on crosswalk.
C	22500(c)	Parking unlawfully, adjacent to safety zone.
C	22500(d)	Parking unlawfully, within 15 feet of fire station driveway.
C	22500(e)	Parking unlawfully, blocking any driveway.
C	22500(f)	Parking unlawfully, on a sidewalk.
C	22500(g)	Parking unlawfully, blocking excavation.
C	22500(h)	Parking unlawfully, double parking.
I/C	22500(i)	Parking unlawfully, in posted bus loading zone.
I	22500(j)	Parking unlawfully, in tube or tunnel.
I	22500(k)	Parking upon any bridge, unless posted to permit.
I/C	22500(l)	Parking unlawfully, blocking sidewalk wheelchair access.
I/C	22500.1	Parking unlawfully, in a fire lane.
C	22502(a)	Park parallel on right, and/or within 18" if curbed; motorcycle, one wheel at curb.
C	22502(e)	Parking on one-way streets-parallel parking on left permitted within 18" of curb except upon divided highways.
I	22504(a)	Stopping or parking, on roadway outside city limits.

VEHICLE VIOLATIONS TABLE

I	22504(c)(1)	A school bus stop is not permitted where there is not a clear view of the stop from at least 200 feet in each direction or from at least 500 feet on a highway with a speed greater than 25 MPH.
I	22505(b)	Stop, park, or leave standing on state highway where sign posted.
I/C	22507.8(a)	Parking in spaces, on public streets or public or privately owned off-street parking facilities designated for handicapped prohibited.
I/C	22507.8(b)	Obstruct or block designated handicapped parking space, except as provided.
I/C	22507.8(c)	Makes it unlawful to park on the lines marking the boundaries of a parking stall or space designated for disabled persons or an area designated for the loading and unloading of vehicles.
C	22510(a)	Parking in snow areas, where sign posted by local jurisdictions.
C	22510(c)	Parking in snow areas where sign posted by Caltrans.
I/C	22511.1(a)	Parking in a space designated for vehicle connected for electronic charging purposes.
C	22511.1(b)	Block parking space designated for clean air vehicles.
I	22511.56	Failure to present identification and evidence of issuance of placard to peace officer upon request.
M	22513(b)	Tow truck, unauthorized stop at accident or for disabled to solicit services.
M	22513(c)	Tow truck, unauthorized moving of vehicle
C	22514	Fire hydrant, parking unattended vehicle within 15 feet.
C	22515(a)	Unattended motor vehicle, motor running and/or brakes not set.
C	22515(b)	Unattended vehicle, wheels not blocked, and/or not set.
I	22516	Locked vehicle, with person who cannot escape.
I	22517	Vehicle doors, opening to traffic when unsafe, leaving open.
I	22520.5(a)	Person who solicits, displays, sells, or vends within the freeway right-of-way.
M	22520.5(a)	Person who solicits, displays, sells, or vends within the freeway right-of-way. Second offense.
I	22520.6(a)	Person who solicits, displays, sells, or vends within a highway rest area or vista point.
M	22520.6(a)	Person who solicits, displays, sells, or vends within a highway rest area or vista point. Second offense.
C	22521	Unlawful to park within 7 1/2 ft. of railroad track.
I	22522	Parking within 3 feet of a sidewalk access ramp.
I	22523(a)	Abandoning vehicle on highway.
I	22523(b)	Abandoning vehicle on public or private property.
I	22526(a)	Entering intersection without sufficient space to clear intersection.
I	22526(b)	Driver making left turn, facing yellow traffic signal, entering an intersection without sufficient space to clear intersection.
I	22526(c)	Entering railroad without sufficient space to clear the railroad. Driver's prohibited from traversing railroad crossings unless vehicle's undercarriage has sufficient clearance to cross intersection.
I	22526(d)	Entering railroad or rail transit crossing without sufficient space to clear the crossing and to accommodate the vehicle driven and any

VEHICLE VIOLATIONS TABLE

		railway vehicle.
I	22650	Unauthorized removal of unattended vehicle from highway.
C	22651.07	Failure of a towing company to properly post or provide copies of a "Towing Fees and Access Notice".
I	22651.7(b)	Immobilization of vehicle by unauthorized person.
I	22651.1	Persons operating storage facility, where vehicles are stored pursuant to Section 22651, shall accept a valid credit card or cash for payment of towing and storage fees.
I	22658(e)(2)	Property owner or agent's responsibility for vehicle removal.
M	22658(g)	Tow company shall immediately and unconditionally release a vehicle not yet removed from private property.
M	22658(i)(1)(B)	Towing operator shall make available for inspection CHP approved rate to law enforcement, Attorney General, district attorney, or city attorney.
M	22658(j)(2)	Excessive towing, service, or storage charge.
M	22658(k)(1)	Storage facility refusing to accept a valid credit card as payment.
M	22658(k)(2)	Storage facility shall conspicuously display advising all valid credit cards and cash are acceptable means of payment.
M	22658(l)	Tow company shall maintain the original written authorization.
M	22658(m)	Failure of a tow company to provide proper notification to law enforcement.
I	22658.1(a)	Tow company failure to notify property owner of damage sustained, including fence, while removing vehicle.
I	22951	Parking lot operator, patron's vehicle on street or alley.
I	22952(a)	Parking lot operator, having vehicle removed within 24 hours.
I	22952(b)	Parking lot operator, having vehicle removed for nonpayment when no pay facilities available.
I	22953(a)	Towing of a vehicle parked in a no cost privately owned off- street parking facility within one hour of the vehicle being parked, prohibited
M	23103(a)	Reckless driving, no injury.
M	23103(b)	Reckless driving, off-street parking facility.
M	23104(a)	Reckless driving, causing bodily injury.
F	23104(b)	Reckless driving, causing great bodily injury with specified prior convictions.
M	23105(a)	Reckless driving, with specific injury (refer to code).
M	23109(a)	Speed contest, engage in.
M	23109(b)	Speed contest, aid or abet.
M	23109(c)	Exhibition of speed, engaged aid or abet.
M	23109(d)	Speed contest, blocking or obstructing highway.
M	23109(e)(2)	Engaging in a speed contest, causing specific injury.
M/F	23109(f)(3)	Repeat violation of 23109 (a) (b) (c) (d) or (f) within 5 years causing serious bodily injury.
M/F	23109.1	Engaging in a speed contest resulting in specific injury.
M	23110(a)	Throwing substance at vehicle.

VEHICLE VIOLATIONS TABLE

F	23110(b)	Throwing missile with intent to do serious bodily harm.
I	23111	Lighted substance, throwing on highway.
I	23112(a)	Litterbug, depositing glass or trash on highway.
I	23112(b)	Litterbug, depositing rocks or dirt anywhere on right of way.
M	23112.5(a)	Hazardous material spill, notification to CHP.
I	23113(a)	Failure to remove spilled material immediately.
I/M	23114(a)	Spilling load, other than loose hay and straw, clear water, and feathers from live birds.
I/M	23114(b)	Aggregate material, failure to comply with equipment requirements.
M	23114(e)	Aggregate material, failure to cover load.
I/M	23114(f)	Failure to provide a location for operators to cover load.
I	23115(a)	Rubbish vehicle, transporting specified garbage, cover required to prevent spilling load.
I	23116(a)	Unlawful to transport person in back of motor truck.
I	23116(b)	Unlawful to ride in back of motor truck.
I	23117(a)	Unrestrained animal in space intended for load.
I	23120	Obstructed side-vision, by wide earpiece on glasses.
I	23123(a)	Wireless telephone, person prohibited from operating motor vehicle while using wireless telephone without a hands free device, with exceptions. (Effective July 1, 2008)
I	23123.5(a)	A person shall not drive a motor vehicle while using an electronic wireless communications device to write, send, or read a text–based communication, unless it is designed and configured for voice–operated and hands–free operation.
I	23124(b)	Wireless telephone, person under 18 prohibited from operating motor vehicle while using a wireless telephone or mobile service device. This is a secondary violation. (Effective July 1, 2008)
I	23125(a)	Driving school bus or transit vehicle while using wireless phone.
M	23127	Riding, bicycle path or hiking trail, unauthorized motor vehicle on.
I	23128(a)	Snowmobile, operating on highway except in crossing.
I	23128(b)	Snowmobile, careless or negligent operation.
I	23128(c)	Snowmobile, pursuing game animal with intent to harass.
I	23128(d)	Snowmobile, operating for purpose of violating 602 P.C.
I	23129	Operation of vehicle with camper with obstructed or inoperable exits in which persons are riding.
I	23135	Operating motorized bicycle modified to no longer conform to definition.
I	23136(a)	Minor driving with a BAC of .01% or greater.
I	23140(a)	Minor driving with BAC of .05% or more.
M	23152(a)	Under influence of alcohol, drug, or combination, while driving a vehicle.
M	23152(b)	Driving with a BAC of .08% or more.
M	23152(c)	Addict except when in an approved treatment program.
M	23152(d)	Commercial Driver, driving a commercial vehicle with a BAC of .04% or more.

VEHICLE VIOLATIONS TABLE

F	23153(a)	Driving under the influence of alcohol, drug, or combination, causing injury or death to another.
F	23153(b)	Driving with a BAC of .08% or more causing injury or death to another.
F	23153(d)	Commercial Driver, driving with a BAC of .04% or more causing injury or death to another.
I	23154(a)	Prohibits a person who is on probation for DUI to operate a motor vehicle with a BAC of .01 percent or greater.
I	23213	Unlawful for patient or person residing at a social rehabilitation facility to have a motor vehicle registered in their name on or near the rehabilitation facility.
I	23220(a)	Drinking alcoholic beverage while driving a motor vehicle on highway.
I	23221(a)	No driver shall drink an alcoholic beverage in a motor vehicle on a highway.
I	23221(b)	No passenger shall drink an alcoholic beverage in a motor vehicle on a highway.
I	23222(a)	Alcohol, personal possession of an opened container while driving a motor vehicle.
I	23222(b)	Marijuana, possession of less than one ounce while driving a motor vehicle.
I	23223(a)	No driver shall have in possession an alcoholic beverage in a motor vehicle on a highway.
I	23223(b)	No passenger shall have in possession an alcoholic beverage in a motor vehicle on a highway.
M	23224(a)	Driver under 21, knowingly operating vehicle carrying alcohol.
M	23224(b)	Passenger under 21, personal possession of alcohol in motor vehicle.
I	23225(a)(1)	Owner or driver allowing opened container in passenger area.
I	23225(b)	Driver allowing opened container in passenger area, registered owner not present.
I	23226(a)	No driver shall allow alcoholic beverages in passenger compartment, living quarters of campers and housecars exempted.
I	23226(b)	No passenger shall allow alcoholic beverages in passenger compartment, living quarters of campers and housecars exempted.
M	23229.1(a)	Violating Public Utilities Code section 5384.1.
M	23247(a)	Ignition interlock device, renting, leasing, or lending motor vehicle. (Operative 7/1/93)
M	23247(b)	Ignition interlock device, soliciting another person to start vehicle. (Operative 7/1/93)
M	23247(c)	Ignition interlock device, activating vehicle for driver. (Operative 7/1/93)
M	23247(d)	Ignition interlock device, tampering with or circumventing operation of. (Operative 7/1/93)
M	23247(e)	Operation of vehicle which has been prohibited by a court order.
M	23253	Vehicular crossing or toll highway: failure to obey officer's lawful order.
I	23270(a)	Vehicular crossing: unauthorized towing or pushing.

VEHICLE VIOLATIONS TABLE

I	23270(b)	Charging excessive fee for towing on vehicular crossing.
I	23302(a)	Vehicular crossing or toll highway: refusing to pay toll charge
I	23302(a)(3)	Failure of motorcyclist to properly place or display transponder for payment of toll fees.
I	23302(b)	Failure to display transponder on specified vehicle crossing or toll highway.
I	23302(c)	Pay by plate vehicular crossing or toll highway, failure to have valid vehicle license plates and/or full monetary or electronic payment.
I	23302(d)	Pay by plate, electronic (only) vehicular crossing or toll highway, failure to have valid license plates and/or transponder or other electronic device payment in full.
C	23302.5(a)	Vehicular crossing or toll highway: evading toll charge.
I	23330	Vehicular crossing: (a) unauthorized use by animals, (b) bicycles, motorized bicycles, motorized scooters, (c) overwidth vehicles, (d) carrying items prohibited by the Department of Transportation.
I	23331	Vehicular crossing: unauthorized use by pedestrians.
M	23332	Vehicular crossing: person in unauthorized area.
I	23333	Vehicular crossing: unauthorized standing or parking.
I	23336	Vehicular crossing: failure to obey any sign or regulation.
M/F	23550.5(a)	Driving under the influence, within 10 years of prior felony DUI.

VEHICLE VIOLATIONS TABLE

Types of convictions received for violation of certain sections of Division 12 of the Vehicle Code.		

Type	VC Section	Violation
I	24002(a)	Unsafe condition of vehicle, load or equipment presenting immediate safety hazard.
I	24002(b)	Vehicle not properly equipped.
M	24002.5	Unsafe condition of a farm labor vehicle that presents an immediate safety hazard.
I	24003	Unlawful lights, other than those required or permitted.
I	24004	Unlawful operation, after notice by peace officer.
I	24005	Unlawful equipment, selling, offering for sale, installing or replacing with.
I	24005.5	Sale of synthetic rope or webbing not certified to CHP.
I	24006	Unapproved equipment, selling or offering for sale.
I	24007(a)	Dealer selling vehicle not in compliance with code.
I	24007(b)	Any person selling vehicle not in compliance with smog requirements.
I	24007.5(a)	Auctioneer, or public agency, vehicle not in compliance with code.
I	24007.5(b)	Auctioneer, or public agency, notify bidder that certificate of compliance required.
I	24007.5(c)	Auctioneer, or public agency, surrender certificates of registration and ownership, and plates to DMV.
I	24007.5(d)	Auctioneer, or public agency, provide bill of sale and license plate number.
I	24008	Passenger vehicle or commercial vehicle under 6,000 lbs., clearance modified to less than rim height.
I	24008.5(a)	Maximum frame height of vehicle less than 10,000 pounds, operation prohibited.
I	24009	Dealer, sale of new truck, truck tractor or bus without ID plate and GVW rating.
I	24010(a)	Vehicle rental; necessary equipment, conform to safety standards mechanically safe and sound.
I	24010(b)	Vehicle rental; vehicle not in compliance.

I	24010(c)	Vehicle rental agreement to include specified information.
I	24011	Sale of vehicle or equipment not in compliance with federal standards or not properly marked.
M	24011.3(a)	Manufacturer sticker affixed to passenger vehicle-bumper strength notice.
I	24012	Lighting equipment or devices, failure to comply with mounting requirements.
I	24013	Seller to inform buyer of minimum fuel octane rating.
I	24013.5(a)	Light duty trucks, dealers not affixing pricing information.
I	24014(a)	Dealer offering motorcycle for sale without label indicating price.
I	24014(b)	Dealer offering motorcycle for sale without specified information on label.
I	24015(a)	Motorized bicycle: comply with National Motor Vehicle Act.
I	24015(b)	Motorized bicycle: mirror and muffler.
I	24016(b)(1)	Motorized bicycle; operation without properly fitted and fastened bicycle helmet.
I	24016(b)(4)	Motorized bicycle; operation by person under 16 years of age.
I	24016(b)(5)	Motorized bicycle; manufacturer shall certify compliance with equipment and manufacturing requirements for bicycles.
I	24016(c)	Motorized bicycle; tampering with or modifying to increase speed capability.
I	24017	Public transit bus, shall be equipped with a working speedometer.
I	24018(a)	Public transit bus, shall be equipped with a two-way communication device.
I	24250	Driving without lights during darkness.
I	24252(a)	Lighting equipment of required type, maintain in good working order.
I	24252(b)	Voltage of required lamps to be 85% of design voltage.
I	24252(c)	Combined lamps, reflectors shall meet department specifications. (1) Turn signal shall not be combined with stop lamp. (Certain exceptions.) (2) Clearance lamps shall not be combined with tail or identification lamps.
I	24253(a)	Adequate battery required on motor vehicle first registered after 1/1/70.
I	24253(b)	Adequate battery required on motorcycles first registered after 1/1/70.
I	24255(a)	Infrared lighting equipment violation.
I	24255(b)	Operation of infrared lighting system without use of headlights.
I	24400(a)	Equipped with headlamps, height 22 to 54 inches.
	24400(b)	Operated during darkness, inclement weather, or both.
I	24401	Parked vehicle, with lights on high beam.
I	24402(a)	Auxiliary driving lamps; two maximum, height 16 to 42 inches. Cannot be lighted with lower beam.
I	24402(b)	Auxiliary passing lamps; two maximum, height 24 to 42 inches.
I	24403	Fog lamps on vehicles other than motorcycle, number 2, height 12

		to 30 inches, properly adjusted. On motorcycle height of 12 to 40 inches, properly adjusted.
I	24404(a)	Spotlamps, number 2, not substituted for headlamps, white only.
I	24404(b)	Spotlamps, exceeding 32 c.p. or glaring light ahead.
I	24404(c)	Spotlamps, improper use on highway.
I	24404(e)	Spotlamps, directed to illuminate moving vehicle.
I	24405(a)	Forward lamps, not to exceed 4 lighted.
I	24406	Dimmer switch, driver unable to select proper light distribution.
I	24407(a)	High beam, project at least 350 feet.
I	24407(b)	Low beam, project at least 100 feet without glare.
I	24408(a)	High beam indicator required.
I	24408(b)	Readily visible, not to exceed 2 c.p. or show to front or sides when on exterior.
I	24409(a)	Failure to dim, within 500 feet of approaching vehicle.
I	24409(b)	Failure to dim, within 300 feet of overtaken vehicle.
I	24410(a)	Single beam, proper adjustment.
I	24410(b)	Single beam, project at least 200 feet.
I	24411	Off-highway lamps: more than allowed, not mounted properly, not covered, or used when operated on the highway.
I	24600(a)	Taillamp-one required all such vehicles.
I	24600(b)	Taillamp-two all vehicles manufactured after 1/1/58, except motorcycles, trailers and semitrailers less than 30 inches wide.
I	24600(c)	Taillamp-two all vehicles subject to 22406a.
I	24600(d)	Taillamp-when two required, must have one on left, one on right side at same level.
I	24600(e)	Taillamp-red, visible 500 ft., vehicle manufactured after 1/1/69 visible 1,000 ft.
I	24600(f)	Taillamp-must be mounted 15 to 72 inches on vehicles manufactured after 1/1/69. Additional lamps allowed on tow truck masts.
I	24601	License plate light, render clearly visible from 50 feet.
I	24602(a)	Not more than 2 red fog taillamps mounted on rear when visibility less than 500 feet.
I	24602(b)	Fog taillamps; mounted as close as practical to sides, between 15 and 60 inches, 4 inches from stoplamp, wired properly, with switch, with nonflashing amber pilot light.
I	24603(a)	Stoplamps-every vehicle must be equipped with one or more.
I	24603(b)	Stop lamps-two required, vehicles manufactured after 1/1/58 (except motorcycles, trailers and semitrailers less than 30 inches wide).
I	24603(c)	Stoplamps-mounted 15 to 72 inches on vehicles manufactured after 1/1/69. Additional lamps allowed on tow truck masts.
I	24603(d)	Stoplamps-when two required one must be on left, one on right at same level.
I	24603(e)	Stoplamps-red or amber, visible 300 ft., vehicles of size requiring clearance lamps must be visible 500 ft.

VEHICLE VIOLATIONS TABLE

I	24603(f)	Must be activated by foot brakes and by hand valve for power brakes. May be activated by sudden release of accelerator. Manual transmission; mechanical device to activate stoplamps.
I	24603(g)	Supplemental stoplamps installed after January 1, 1979, shall be red and mounted not lower than 15 inches above roadway.
I	24604	Projecting load, 4 feet to rear, 2 red lights at night, 12" red or fluorescent orange flag otherwise.
I	24605(a)	Tow truck or dismantler's tow vehicle, carry stop and taillamp with extension cord.
I	24605(b)	Tow truck or dismantler's tow vehicle, display tail and stop lamp on rear of disabled vehicle.
I	24606(a)	Backup lamp required on vehicles subject to registration manufactured after 1/1/69.
I	24606(b)	Backup lamp white only, beam not over 75 ft. to rear.
I	24606(c)	Backup lamp used other than when backing.
I	24606(d)	Vehicle may be equipped with supplemental backup lamps, lighted only with backup lights.
I	24607(a)	Reflectors, every vehicle must have one, visible 350 to 100 ft. with upper beams.
I	24607(b)	Reflectors, every vehicle manufactured and first registered after 1/1/65, except motorcycles, low speed vehicles, trailers and semitrailers less than 30 inches wide, must have two.
I	24607(c)	Reflectors, motortruck with unladen weight of 5,000 lbs., trailer coach, vehicle at end of combination, vehicles 80 inches or more wide manufactured after 1/1/69, must have two visible 600 ft. to 100 ft. with upper beams.
I	24607(d)	Reflectors, when more than one required, one must be on right, one on left at same level. Additional reflectors may be mounted at any height. Additional reflectors allowed on tow cars.
I	24608(a)	Reflectors, motortrucks, semitrailers, buses 80" wide manufactured after 1/1/68, must have amber reflector on each side at front, red reflector on each side at rear.
I	24608(b)	Reflectors, such vehicles 30 ft. or more in length shall have amber reflector on each side at midpoint.
I	24608(c)	Reflectors, on sides must be mounted 15 to 60 inches. Additional reflectors may be mounted at any height.
I	24608(d)	Reflectors required or permitted by (a) and (b) must be visible 600 ft. to 1,000 ft. with upper beam.
I	24609	Reflectors, white or amber on front to be mounted 15 to 60 inches. Reflectors/lights amber in color on a school bus, mounted on the left and right sides at equal height.
I	24610	Reflectors, button type to contain not less than 7 units with total area of not less than 3 sq. inches.
I	24612	Trailers/semitrailers of specified width/weight to be equipped with conspicuity system pursuant to federal Motor Vehicle Safety Standard No. 108 (49 C.F.R. 571.108).
I	24615	Slow-moving vehicle emblem, vehicles designed and operated 25 mph or less.
I	24616	Vehicles allowed one/two rear-facing auxiliary lamps meeting specified lamp/mounting standards.

VEHICLE VIOLATIONS TABLE

I	24800	Parking lights, driving with, unless headlamps also lighted.
I	24950	Trailer coach, turn signal lamps required.
I	24951(b)(1)	Turn signals required, passenger vehicles, trucks, truck tractors, buses manufactured and first registered after 1/1/58.
I	24951(b)(2)	Turn signals required, trailers and semitrailers manufactured and first registered between 12/31/57 and 1/1/69.
I	24951(b)(3)	Turn signals required, trailers and semitrailers 80 inches or more in width manufactured after 1/1/69.
I	24951(b)(4)	Turn signals required on motorcycles manufactured and first registered after 1/1/73. Except motor- driven cycles whose speed attainable in one mile is 30 mph or less.
I	24951(c)	Turn signals on vehicles manufactured after 1/1/69, 15-inch minimum height.
I	24952	Turn signal lamps, clearly visible 300 feet front and rear (500 feet for vehicles with clearance lamps).
I	24953(a)	Turn signal lamps, white or amber to front, red or amber to rear.
I	24953(b)	Side-mounted turn signals, mounted to rear of center must be red.
I	24953(d)	Side-view mirror-mounted turnsignals: Must flash in unison with car mounted signals, must be visible only from the rear and not visible to the driver, except for visual indicator.
I	25100(a)	Vehicle over 80 inches: (1) clearance lamps; 1 amber each side on front, 1 red each side on rear. (2) Side-marker lamps; 1 amber each side near front, 1 red each side near rear. (3) 1 amber each side near center if trailer over 30 feet. (4) 1 amber sidemarker midpoint of multipurpose passenger vehicles, motor trucks, buses 30 ft. in length manufactured after 1/1/69.
I	25100(b)	Vehicle over 80 inches not equipped under (a): (1) Truck tractor, 1 amber clearance lamp each side on front of cab or sleeper, amber side-marker lamps OK on sides. (2) Truck tractor manufactured and first registered after 1/1/69, one amber side marker on each side near front. (3) Pole or logging dolly, 1 red combination clearance and side-marker lamp each side. (4) Vehicles (except tractors) over 80 inches for 3 feet or less: if near front, 1 amber combination lamp each side; if near rear, 1 red combination lamp each side. (5) Driveaway-towaway towing vehicle: 1 amber clearance lamp each side on front, 1 amber side- marker lamp each side near front. (6) driveaway- towaway towed vehicle: 1 amber side-marker each side of intermediate vehicles; 1 red side-marker lamp each side and 1 red clearance lamp near each side on rearmost vehicle.
I	25100(c)	Loads over 80 inches extending beyond side: 1 amber combination lamp on side at front and red combination lamp on side at rear. If projecting load not over 3 feet front to rear: 1 amber combination lamp on side if load near front, 1 red combination lamp on side if near rear of vehicle.
I	25100(e)	Visibility requirements.
I	25100(f)	Mounting requirements-required positions.
I	25102	Side lamps, recessed, not to exceed 2 c.p. or use color red.
I	25103(a)	Projecting load to left, amber light to front and rear.
I	25103(b)	Projecting load to left, amber light to front, red light to rear if projection exceeds 120 inches.

VEHICLE VIOLATIONS TABLE

I	25104	Overwidth vehicles, display 12 inch red or fluorescent orange flag, left front and rear.
I	25105(a)	Running board lamps, 6 c.p., white or green without glare.
I	25105(b)	Door-mounted lamps or reflectors, 6 c.p., red.
I	25105(c)	Entrance/exit exterior lamps lighted only when vehicle motionless, lamp not to exceed 32 c.p. or 30 watts.
I	25106(a)	Front cowl or fender lamps, white or amber; 1 amber side lamp near front, 1 red side lamp near rear, 4 c.p. maximum.
I	25106(b)	Lamps installed within 24 inches of rear shall be red; all other locations amber.
I	25107	Cornering lamps, not over 2, to reveal objects while turning.
I	25108(a)	Exterior signal indicator lamps, amber, properly mounted, not exceeding 5 c.p., at night or 15 c.p. day.
I	25108(b)	Pilot indicators; steady burning, lighted lens area of not more than 3/4 of an inch, no more than 5 c.p., and not red.
I	25108(d)	Tow vehicle equipped with exterior mounted pilot lamp for antilock braking system; readily visible, not more than 5 c.p., shall not show to sides or rear, not red. Lamp for antilock braking system shall not allow to show to sides, must comply with FMVSS.
I	25109	Running lamps, 2 on front, white or amber, not lighted at night.
I	25110(b)	Utility flood or loading lamps. Improper use of such devices.
I	25250	Flashing lights prohibited, exceptions listed.
I	25251(b)	Disabled vehicle on roadway, failure to activate flashing signal lamps.
I	25252	Authorized emergency vehicle, red lamp required.
I	25252.5(a)	Authorized emergency vehicles-flashing headlamps prohibited during darkness.
I	25252.5(c)	Flashing headlamps permitted only (1) during emergency call or when in pursuit; (2)when red warning light displayed and siren is sounded.
I	25253(a)	Tow trucks, flashing amber warning lights required; exemptions.
I	25253(c)	A tow truck shall not display flashing amber warning lights unless an unusual traffic hazard or extreme hazard exists.
I	25254	Marshal's cars: misuse of flashing amber warning lamp.
I	25257(a)	Schoolbus, flashing red signal system required.
I	25257(b)(1)	Schoolbus manufactured on or after 9/1/92, stop signal arm required.
I	25257(b)(2)	Schoolbus manufactured on or after 7/1/93, amber warning light system required.
I	25257.2	Schoolbus transporting developmentally disabled, unlawful use of flashing red light signal, amber light signal system, and stop signal arm.
I	25259(c)	Authorized emergency vehicles-not more than 2 flashing white lights to the front mounted above roofline and 2 below roofline.
I	25259.1(c)	Disaster service worker, must cover or remove flashing amber lights when not in use.
I	25259.5	American National Red Cross, flashing amber warning lights on other than emergency or disaster service vehicles.

VEHICLE VIOLATIONS TABLE

I	25260.4	Amber warning lights on hazardous substance spill response vehicle must be covered when not engaged in a cleanup.
I	25262	Armored cars, misuse of red light.
I	25265	Warning lights on sanitation vehicles not to be lighted when vehicle in motion.
I	25266	State aqueduct vehicle: misuse of flashing amber warning lamp.
I	25268	Flashing amber warning lights, improper use.
I	25269	Red warning lights, improper use.
I	25270	Pilot cars and vehicles: improper use of or failure to cover amber warning lamps.
I	25270.5	Livestock herding vehicles, misuse of flashing amber warning lamps.
I	25275	Improper display of amber flashing lights on truck tractor in the absence of unusual traffic hazard.
I	25275.5	Improper use of flashing crime lights by bus driver.
I	25276(a)	Improper use of warning lamps by vehicle used to transport handicapped or mentally retarded.
I	25279(b)	Private security vehicle; misuse of flashing amber lights; distinctively marked on rear and two sides.
I	25279(d)	Private security vehicle; flashing amber warning system installed without written authorization of CHP.
I	25281	Water tender vehicles; misuse of flashing amber lights.
I	25300(a)	Warning devices required on vehicles subject to 25100 and any truck tractor.
I	25300(b)	Display, when truck or any trailer disabled on roadway.
I	25300(c)	Display, when parked or disabled within 10 ft. of roadway during darkness.
I	25300(e)	Display continuously during darkness, if disabled on roadway or parked within 10 ft.
I	25301(a)	Utility vehicles, failure to display proper warning devices during daylight.
I	25301(b)	Utility vehicles, failure to display proper warning device during darkness.
I	25305(a)	Fusee used on highway.
I	25305(b)	Unlawful to use other than red fusee.
I	25350	Noncompliance with Vehicle Code Standards for illuminated identification signs.
I	25351(a)	Commercial vehicles and vehicles 80 inches or more in width; ID lamps front or rear but front not below windshield.
I	25351(b)	Vehicles manufactured prior to 1/1/68; ID lamps amber, green or white to front; red to rear.
I	25351(c)	ID lamps, vehicles manufactured after 1/1/68, may exhibit only amber to front and red to rear.
I	25351(d)	ID lamps unlawful on passenger vehicles.
I	25352(a)	Devices affecting traffic control signals on buses visible light not to exceed an average of .0003 candela per flash.
I	25352(b)	Public transit bus using signal sequence changing device on other

		than authorized routes.
I	25352(c)	Failure to give emergency vehicles priority in changing traffic control signals.
I	25353(a)	Public transit buses, light and sign regulations.
I	25353.1	City of Santa Monica public transit buses light and sign violations.
I	25400(a)	Exterior lamp or device not to emit light of more than .05 candela per square inch of area.
I	25400(b)	Diffused light, no red to front or interference with required lamps.
I	25400(c)	Diffused light, 720 sq. inches maximum, rental use limited.
I	25400(d)	Internally illuminated sign, no white background.
I	25401	Diffused light on vehicle, resembling official traffic control device.
I	25452	Acetylene headlamps, emitting glaring light.
I	25500(a)	Reflectorizing material, resembling or conflicting with any warning device or signal.
I	25650	Motorcycle's headlamps, one required, two permitted.
I	25650.5	Motorcycle have lighted headlamp if manufactured after 1/1/78.
I	25651(a)	Motor driven cycle headlamps, reveal person 100 ft. \@ 25 mph, 200 ft. up to 35 mph, 300 ft. over 35 mph.
I	25651(c)	Motor driven cycle, single beam headlamp adjustment.
I	25803(a)	All other vehicles, display white light front, red to rear, visible 500 ft.
I	25803(b)	All other vehicles, also display reflectors, amber left front and red left rear, height 16 to 60 inches, visible 500 feet.
I	25803(c)	All other vehicles over 100 inch width, display on left extremity amber light at night, a red flag otherwise.
I	25805	Forklift trucks, not equipped with required lights when towed upon highway.
I	25950(a)	Front lights and reflectors, white or amber unless specifically permitted.
I	25950(b)	Rear lights and reflectors, red unless specifically permitted.
I	25951	Front lights, adjustment of beam for other than driving lights.
I	25952(a)	Lamps, reflectors on load, failure to comply with mounting regulations.
I	25952(b)	Lamps on vehicle carried as load unlawfully lighted.
I	26100(a)	Lighting equipment or devices, selling or using unapproved type.
I	26100(b)	Driving with lighting equipment or devices of an unapproved type.
I	26101(a)	Lights or devices, selling or using unapproved modifying devices.
I	26101(b)	Lights or devices, operating a vehicle while using unapproved modifying devices.
I	26301	Power brakes required on new motor vehicles 14,000 lbs. Two stage actuators less than 18,000 lbs.
I	26301.5	Passenger vehicles manufactured after 1/1/73, except motorcycles, required to have dual master cylinder.
I	26302(a)	Brakes required on semi trailer over 6,000 gross.
I	26302(b)	Brakes required on semi or trailer over 3,000 gross manufactured after Jan. 1, 1966.

VEHICLE VIOLATIONS TABLE

I	26302(c)	Brakes required on all wheels of trailer or semitrailer manufactured after January 1, 1982, and equipped with air brakes.
I	26302(d)	Brakes on trailers or semitrailers must be adequate to supplement brakes on towing vehicle.
I	26303	Brakes required, in trailer coaches over 1,500 gross.
I	26304(a)	Breakaway device, required on certain trailers or semitrailers.
I	26304(b)	Breakaway device, required for trucks or truck tractors in combination.
I	26307	Brakes required on forklift truck manufactured after 1/1/70, when towed upon highway.
I	26311(a)	Brakes required on all wheels of motor vehicles; exceptions.
I	26311(b)	Reduced braking to front wheels by manual means permitted only under adverse weather conditions.
I	26450	Brake systems, both service and parking required on motor vehicles.
I	26451(a)	Parking brake, adequate for load and grade.
I.	26451(b)	Parking brake, separate means of application.
I	26451(c)	Parking brake held solely by mechanical means.
I	26452	Brakes on motor vehicle, adequate to stop vehicle after motor failure.
I	26453	Brake system defective, not in good working order or proper adjustment.
I	26454(a)	Service brakes, adequate for load and grade.
I	26454(b)	Service brake stopping distance requirements: (1) Passenger vehicle, 25 ft. \@ 20 mph. (2) Single vehicle under 10,000 lbs., or any bus, 30 ft. \@ 20 mph. (3) Vehicles in (1) or (2) in combination, 40 ft. \@ 20 mph. (4) Single vehicle over 10,000 lbs. or any bus, 40 ft. \@ 20 mph. (5) All other combinations, 50 ft. \@ 20 mph.
I	26456	Brake tests in excess of 25 mph prohibited.
I	26457	Certain vehicles, 32 ft. \@ 15 mph, or not exceed speed permitting stop within 32 ft.
I	26458(a)	Single control, if motor vehicle or combo required to be equipped with power brakes.
I	26458.5	Additional control to operate the brakes on a trailer shall not be used in lieu of the service brake.
I	26502(a)	Airbrakes capable of full service application, deliver 90 percent of reservoir pressure.
I	26503	Safety valve, properly installed, adjusted and maintained.
I	26504	Air governor, adjust within CHP regulations.
I	26505	Pressure gauge required, maintain good condition, legible at all times.
I	26506(a)	Airbrakes, required warning system.
I	26506(b)	Airbrake warning device readily visible or audible with continuous warning.
I	26507	Check valve, properly installed and properly maintained.
I	26508	Vehicles using compressed air to apply service brakes shall meet

VEHICLE VIOLATIONS TABLE

		following requirements: a. Motor or towed vehicle, must have emergency stopping system. b. Motor vehicle combo, both manual and automatic means to actuate emergency system of towed vehicle. e. Service brake and emergency system: failure of 1 system not to affect other. f. Emergency system, manually applied, released, and reapplied from driver's seat. g. Service brake air failure, vehicle not to be driven. h. Emergency system, must not increase stopping distance, nor interfere with service brake operation. i. Energy-storing device, operating requirements. j. Axle-by-axle protection system, separate air tank each axle or each valve. k. Stopping distance requirements. o. Owner instruct driver-driver able to demonstrate operation.
I	26520	Vacuum gauge, accurate and visible.
I	26521	Warning device, audible or visible, operate 8 inches mercury.
I	26522	Check valve, between vacuum source and reserve.
I	26700(a)	Windshields, required on passenger vehicle, trucks and fire apparatus.
I	26701(a)	Safety glazing material, required wherever glass is used.
I	26701(b)	Safety glazing material in campers, manufactured Jan. 1, 1968. Also in internal partitions and openings in the roof.
I	26701(c)	Safety glazing material, MC windshields manufactured after 1-1-69
I	26701(d)	Prohibits red, blue or amber translucent aftermarket material in partitions, windows, windshields of motor vehicles.
I	26701(e)	Safety glazing material in windows, doors, interior partitions, openings in roof of towed trailer coach.
I	26703(a)	Safety glazing material, replacing with other than.
I	26703(b)	Safety glazing material, replacing with anything other than.
I	26705	Motorcycle windshield, after 1/1/69, unlawful to sell unless contains safety glazing material.
I	26706(a)	Windshield wipers, required on all motor vehicles (except motorcycles).
I	26706(b)	Windshield wipers, two required vehicle first registered January 1, 1950.
I	26707	Windshield wipers, maintain good condition, use when necessary.
I	26708(a)(1)	A person shall not drive any motor vehicle with any object or material placed, displayed, installed, affixed, or applied upon the windshield or side or rear windows.
I	26708(a)(2)	A person shall not drive any motor vehicle with any object or material placed, displayed, installed, affixed, or applied in or upon the vehicle that obstructs or reduces the driver's clear view through the windshield or side windows.
I	26708(a)(3)	A person shall not drive any motor vehicle when the driver's clear vision through the windshield, side or rear windows, are obstructed by snow or ice.
I	26708(b)(13)(B)	Failure to post notice in of video recording in visible location.
I	26708(b)(13)(C)	Storing more that 30 seconds of video either before or after a

		triggering event.
I	26708(b)(13)(F)	Failure to provide unedited copies to employees/representatives free of charge within 5 days of request
I	26708.2	Sunscreen devices shall be removable.
I	26708.5	Application of transparent material to windows.
I	26709(a)	Rear view mirror, required on all motor vehicles subject to registration; two on motor vehicle subject to Calif. registration, with one on lefthand side.
I	26709(b)	Two side-view mirrors, required on certain vehicles or combos.
I	26710	Defective windshield or rear window, impairing driver's view, correct within 48 hours.
I	26711	Sun visor required on bus or trolley coach, except pre-60 in urban service.
I	26712	Adequate defroster required, for-hire passenger vehicle.
I	27000(a)	Horn required in good working order, audible within 200 feet but shall not emit unreasonably harsh or loud sound.
I	27000(b)	Garbage and refuse trucks, equipped with automatic backup alarm that sounds immediately upon backing or equipped with an automatic backup device that immediately applies the service brake on contact with any obstruction to the rear.
I	27000(d)(1)	Construction vehicle with a (GVWR) in excess of 14,000 pounds must be equipped with automatic backup audible alarm that sounds on backing up.
I	27001(a)	Shall use horn when reasonably necessary.
I	27001(b)	Use of horn, only as reasonably necessary.
I	27002	Siren, vehicle illegally equipped with or used on, or unapproved type.
I	27003	Armored car, misuse of siren.
I	27007	Outside speakers, except to warn of hazard or request assistance.
I	27150(a)	Mufflers, vehicle subject to registration not equipped with, or emitting excessive noise.
I	27150(b)	Mufflers, off-highway passenger vehicle not equipped with, or emitting excessive noise. Exceptions.
M	27150.1	Exhaust system, sale, offering for sale, or installing system, including non-original exhaust equipment, not in compliance with CHP regulation.
M	27150.1	Exhaust system, sale, offering for sale, or installing system, including non-original exhaust equipment, not in compliance with regulations and standards.
I	27150.3	"Whistle-tips", shall not operate/modify exhaust system with a whistle tip, nor engage in the business of installing a whistle tip onto an exhaust system.
I	27151	Exhaust systems, modified to exceed 95 decibels (vehicles under 6000 GVWR, except motorcycles). Exhaust system, modified to amplify or increase noise (vehicles 6000 GVWR & above, and motorcycles).
I	27152	Exhaust pipes, directed to side between 2 to 11 ft.
I	27153	Exhaust products, excessive smoke, flame or residue.

VEHICLE VIOLATIONS TABLE

I	27153.5(a)	New vehicle registered after 1/1/71, cannot discharge from exhaust more than 10 seconds. (1) Excess of No. 1 on Ringelmann chart. (2) Smoke equal to opacity of No. 1 Ringelmann.
I	27153.5(b)	Vehicle sold prior to 1/1/71, limited to (1) No. 2 on Ringelmann chart. (2) Smoke equal to opacity of No. 2 Ringelmann.
I	27154	Exhaust system, not maintained in gas tight condition.
I	27155	Fuel tank caps required, of noncombustible material.
I	27156(a)	Gross Polluter, operated or left standing on a highway.
I	27156(b)	Smog Device, vehicle not equipped with device when required, or device has been disconnected or modified.
I	27156(c)	Smog device; shall not install, sell, offer for sale, or advertise any device which modifies pollution control device or system.
I	27156(f)	Smog Device, continued operation in violation after notice by peace officer.
I	27158	Motor vehicle smog device unlawful to operate after 30 days following notification by traffic officer. (Except 1955-1965 year models)
I	27158.5	Motor vehicle smog device, unlawful to operate after 30 days following notice by peace officer (1955-1965 year model vehicles only).
I	27200(d)	No person shall sell or offer for sale a motor vehicle not in compliance with noise standards.
I	27200(e)	No person shall sell or offer for sale a motor vehicle not in compliance with noise standards.
I	27202.1	A person shall not park, use, or operate a motorcycle registered in this state that does not bear the federal exhaust system label. Applicable to motorcycles manufactured on or after January 1, 2013.
I	27302	Safety belts, selling approved type.
I	27304	Driver training vehicle, seat belts not installed or not in use.
I	27305	Firefighting vehicles, publicly owned, seat belts for all personnel.
I	27314(a)	Dealer, selling 1962 or later used car without safety belts.
I	27314(b)	Dealer selling 1968 vehicle without belt for each passenger position.
I	27314(c)	Seatbelts to comply with CHP regulations.
I	27314.5(a)	Dealer selling or offering for sale 1972 to 1990 vehicle without seatbelt warning affixed to vehicle.
I	27314.5(b)	Dealer to affix notice, if supplied as specified, to rear seat lap belt of used 1972 to 1990 model vehicles.
I	27315(d)(1)	Driver not seatbelted.
I	27315(d)(3)	Driver of limousine and emergency vehicle, operator and passengers are properly seatbelted.
I	27315(d)(4)	Driver of taxicab shall not operate vehicle unless all front seat passengers are properly seat belted.
I	27315(e)	Passenger over 16 years restrained by safety belt.
I	27315(f)	Motor vehicle safety belts maintained in good working order.
I	27315.3(b)	Requires law enforcement agencies to maintain safety belts in good working order.

I	27316.5(a)	Type II School Pupil Activity Bus shall be equipped with passenger restraint system at all seating positions.
M	27317	No person shall install, reinstall, rewire, tamper with, alter or modify a vehicle computer system or supplemental restraint system to falsely indicate that it is in working order, or distribute or sell any previously deployed air bag.
I	27360(a)	Unlawful for a parent, legal guardian, or driver to permit a child less than eight years old to be transported by a vehicle without a child passenger restraint system, and requires the child to be secured in the rear seat except specified circumstances.
I	27360(b)	Makes it unlawful for any driver to transport a child by vehicle without a child passenger seat restraint system not applicable to driver if parent or guardian present.
I	27360.5	Children less than 6 years of age and who weighs 60 pounds transported upon a highway, in a motor vehicle, without proper child restraint system.
I	27360.5(a)	Children between the ages 8 and 16 years of age transported upon a highway, in a motor vehicle, without proper child restraint system.
M	27362(a)	Selling an unimproved child passenger seat restraint system.
I	27362.1(a)	No person shall sell or offer for sell a child passenger restraint system that was in use during a traffic collision.
M	27363.5(a)	Hospitals, clinics, and birthing centers are required to provide to the parents or to the person whom a child is released, information on child passenger restraint systems, safety belts, and the transportation of children in rear seats if a released child is less than eight years of age.
I	27365(a)	Rental car agencies required to inform customers of child restraint requirements.
I	27365(b)	Car rental agencies to provide child passenger restraint system.
I	27400	Wearing headset which covers both ears.
I	27450(a)	Solid tire, 3 to 6 inches wide, thickness one inch.
I	27450(b)	Solid tire, 6 to 9 inches wide, thickness 11/4 inch.
I	27450(c)	Solid tire, over 9 inches wide, thickness 11/2 inches.
I	27452	Solid tire, even thickness without flat spots, securely attached.
I	27453	Dual solid tires, diameters not to exceed 1/8 inch variance.
I	27454	Projection on tires, metal studs, cleats or flanges prohibited. (Snow studs O.K. first day of November through last day of April.)
I	27455(a)	Selling unauthorized inner tube for use in a radial tire.
I	27455(b)	Installing unauthorized inner tube for use in a radial tire.
I	27459	Tire chains or snow-tread tires required when signposted; exceptions.
I	27459.5(a)	Selling, leasing, installing or replacing unauthorized tire chains.
I	27460	4-wheel drive with snow tires in lieu of chains, operated under adverse roadway conditions or when posted to require chains.
I	27460.5	Regrooved tire, selling passenger type tire or vehicle so equipped.
I	27461	Regrooved tire, operating or permitting use on highway, except on commercial vehicle.
I	27465(a)	Dealers, selling, installing tires with less than 1/32 inch tread.

VEHICLE VIOLATIONS TABLE

I	27465(b)	Use of tire in chain control area with less than 6/32 inch tread. Use of ties on motor vehicles specified in 34500 with less than 4/32 or 2/32 inch of tread.
I	27501(a)	Dealers, retail sellers prohibited from selling, installing tire not conforming with CHP regulations.
I	27501(b)	No person shall use tire not in conformance with CHP regulations.
I	27502	Dealers, retail sellers prohibited from selling, installing tire not in compliance with CHP tire noise regulations.
I	27600	Mudguards required on vehicles subject to registration over 1500 lbs.
I	27602(a)	Operation of motor vehicle containing unauthorized video screen or TV monitor within view of driver.
I	27603	Former school bus, not repainted a different color, except 90 day transfer.
I	27604	Resale of police vehicles, removal of marking required.
I	27605	Operation of a vehicle painted in the same manner as a police vehicle described in Section 40800 prohibited.
I	27606(a)	Light bar or facsimile, owning or operating vehicle to resemble law enforcement vehicle.
I	27700(a)	Tow trucks; carry broom, shovel, and fire extinguisher.
I	27800	Motorcycle or motorized bicycle passenger, not provided with seat and footrests. Passenger not using footrests.
I	27801(a)	Motorcycle seat, operator unable to reach ground with feet.
I	27801(b)	Motorcycle handlebars, grips at or above shoulder height.
I	27802(b)	Sale of motorcycle safety helmets not meeting federal requirements prohibited.
I	27803(a)	Driver and passenger, wear approved helmet when riding on a motorcycle, motor-driven cycle, or motorized bicycle.
I	27803(b)	Unlawful to operate a motorcycle, motor-driven cycle, or motorized bicycle if driver or passenger is not wearing a safety helmet.
I	27803(c)	Unlawful to ride as a passenger on a motorcycle, motor-driven cycle, or motorized bicycle if driver or any passenger is not wearing a safety helmet.
I	27900(a)	For hire vehicles, or 3-axle truck or tractor, or tractor-semi combination, not displaying identifying name on both sides.
I	27900(b)	Identifying names, change within 60 days of changing ownership.
I	27901	For hire vehicles, name or trade mark not readily legible.
I	27903	Hazardous cargo, not displaying signs in accordance with Health and Safety Code.
I	27904	Pilot cars, must display company name on both sides of the car.
I	27904.5	Pilot cars, shall display signs containing the word "oversize" or acceptable substitute, as required by permit.
I	27905	Fire or Fire Department signs, on other than authorized vehicle.
I	27906(a)	Schoolbus shall bear word "schoolbus" in letters 8 inches high or greater on front and rear.
I	27906(c)	Schoolbus, shall bear on rear below window sign with words "Stop When Red Lights Flash" 6 inches high or greater.

I	27906.5	Youth bus, transporting school pupils, signed front and rear with "youth bus," eight inches in height.
I	27907	Tow trucks, not displaying identifying information on both sides.
I	27908(a)	Operating taxicab without proper display of interior sign and information.
I	27909	Vehicle using liquefied petroleum gas: shall display letters "CNG, LNG, or LPG," one inch high near tank. Unlawful to dispense LPG into tank not marked.
I	28000	Refrigerator van, emergency exit required.
M	28050	Odometer alteration device, sell, offer for sale, install or use.
M	28050.5	Odometer defective, operation with fraudulent intent.
M	28051	Odometer, disconnected, advanced or turned back.
M	28051.5	Odometer, advertising for sale device designed to reset odometer.
I	28053(b)	Odometer repair, failure to adjust or affix notice.
I	28053(c)	Odometer notice affixed, remove or alter with intent to defraud.
I	28060(a)	Sale of recreational vehicle with cooking equipment without fire extinguisher.
I	28060(b)	Operator of a recreational vehicle or vehicle with camper shall carry and maintain fire extinguisher.
I	28071	Passenger vehicles required to be equipped with bumpers, exception.
I	28080(a)	Camper required to have passenger signaling device.
I	28080(b)	Driving a vehicle with a camper which does not have a visual or audible signalling device.
I	28085(c)	Vehicle theft alarm emitting sound of siren.
I	28090	Cellular telephone, failure of motor vehicle renter to provide written instructions.
I	28100	Pilot car, display at least one flag (as specified) on each side of the vehicle. Remove when not operating as a pilot car.
I	28101(a)	Pilot car, less than 60 inches in width.
I	28101(b)	Pilot car, equipped as specified.
I	28103	Pilot cars, failure to comply with provisions or equipment requirements.
I	28111	Any 1993 or later model-year vehicle which is capable of operating on methanol or ethanol shall be equipped with an antisiphoning device.
I	28150(a)	Vehicle equipped with radar jamming device.
I	28150(b)	Possession of radar jamming device.
M	28150(d)	Possession of four or more radar jamming devices.

VEHICLE VIOLATIONS TABLE

Types of convictions received for violation of certain sections of Division 13 of the Vehicle Code.

Type	VC Section	Violation
I	29001	Fifth wheel halves, not securely attached to vehicle.
I	29002	Fifth wheel, locking device inoperable or defective
I	29003(a)	Hitch or coupling structurally inadequate or improperly mounted.
I	29003(b)	Drawbar or other connection, improperly attached or structurally inadequate.
I	29003(c)	Tow dolly, raised end of towed vehicle improperly secured.
I	29004(a)	Every towed vehicle shall be couple to towing vehicle using a safety chain or equivalent device in addition to regular connection.
I	29004(b)	Safety connection must be of sufficient strength to control towed vehicle.
I	29004(c)	Safety chain or equivalent device, no more slack than necessary.
I	29004.5	Recreational vehicle: sold, manufactured without safety chain.
I	29005	Length of drawbar or connection, not to exceed 15 feet.
I	29006(a)	Towing on freeway prohibited unless coupled by rigid device.
I	29200(c)	Logs and poles, transporting in violation of CHP regulations.
I	29201	Logs and poles exempt from CHP regulations required to be safely loaded.
I	29800(c)	Lumber and lumber products, transporting in violation of CHP regulations.
I	30800(b)	Baled hay and straw, transporting in violation of CHP regulations.
I	31301(a)	Transporting explosive, flammable, petroleum or poisonous gas through the Caldecott Tunnel except between 3 a.m. to 5 a.m.
M	31303(b)	Transportation of hazardous waste on most direct route.
M	31303(c)	Hazardous waste transporter to avoid congestion, crowds, and residential districts.
M	31303(d)	Hazardous waste transport vehicles not to be left unattended.
M	31303(e)	Hazardous waste transporter; comply with provisions of transportation safety plan.
M	31304	No person shall transport specified hazardous materials near a

VEHICLE VIOLATIONS TABLE

		reservoir owned or operated by a public water system or near a reservoir that directly serves a water treatment plant.
M	31307(a)	Owner or agent direct or permit the driving of a vehicle in violation of 31303 or 31304.
I	31400(a)	Workmen on trucks used regularly, seats securely mounted.
I	31400(b)	Workmen on trucks, side and end railing at least 46 inches high.
I	31400(c)	Workmen on trucks, steps or stirrups required.
M	31401(b)	Operating farm labor vehicle without required certificate.
I	31401(d)	Farm labor buses and trucks-violation of CHP regulations.
I	31401(f)	Farm labor buses and trucks-violation of CHP regulations.
M	31402	Operation of farm labor vehicle after notification that it is in an unsafe condition or not equipped as required.
M	31403	Owner or operator transporting passengers in farm labor bus which is in an unsafe condition or not equipped as required.
I	31405(d)	No person may operate a farm labor vehicle on a highway unless the driver and all passengers are properly restrained by a seatbelt.
I	31406(a)	Transportation of passengers in farm labor vehicle with a seating system that is noncompliant with the Vehicle Code.
I	31406(b)	Installation of seat or seating system in farm labor vehicle that is not compliant with Vehicle Code.
I	31047	Farm labor vehicle in motion with sharp tool unsecured or blocking aisle or exit.
I	31408	No person may operate a farm labor vehicle on a highway unless both headlamps required under existing law are lighted, regardless of the time of day.
I	31501	Rails and chocks, for logging dolly, securely attached.
M	34501.3(a)	Motor Carrier requiring driver to exceed maximum hours of service.
I	31510(d)	Loads of metal products, in violation of CHP regulations.
I	31520(b)	Baled cotton, paper or jute, violation of CHP regulations.
I	31530(b)	Empty wooden boxes, transporting in violation of CHP regulations.
I	31540(b)	Removable freight van or tank containers, violation of CHP regulations.
I	31560	Person operating a vehicle or combination of vehicles in the transportation of 10 or more used tires or waste tires, or a combination of used and waste tires totaling 10 or more shall be registered with the California Integrated Waste Management Board, unless specifically exempted.
I	31560(a)	Person operating a vehicle or combination of vehicles while transporting waste tires, shall be registered with the California Integrated Waste Management Board, unless specifically exempted.

VEHICLE VIOLATIONS TABLE

Type	VC Section	Violation
		Types of convictions received for violation of certain sections of Division 14 of the Vehicle Code.
Type	VC Section	Violation
M	31602(a)	License required, to engage in such transportation.
M	31602(b)	Operating (or owner permitting) explosive vehicles outside designated routes.
M	31602(c)	Stopping at other than designated safe stopping place.
M	31607(a)	Inspection required, prior to transporting and other places.
M	31609	Record of inspection, maintain and display on demand.
M	31610	Required equipment, maintained in good order.
M	31610(a)	Vehicles transporting explosives; brakes and brake system maintained in good working order.
M	31610(b)	Vehicles transporting explosives; ignition and lighting maintained in good working order.
M	31610(c)	Vehicles transporting explosives; tires in good condition and properly inflated.
M	31610(d)	Vehicles transporting explosives; carry fire extinguishers.
M	31610(e)	Vehicles transporting explosives; shall not carry flame producing signal device.
M	31611	Owner supply map of routes, safe stopping places, and summary.
M	31611	Owner of vehicle used in the transportation of explosives, make route map available in every vehicle.
M	31612	Shipping instructions, carry and display on demand.
M	31613	Prohibited cargo; flammable or corrosive fluid, combustible material, detonators, etc.
M	31614(a)	Prescribed route through city.
M	31614(b)	Avoid congested areas.
M	31614(c)	Motor off and brakes set when loading or unloading.
M	31614(d)	Load contained entirely within body.
M	31614(e)	Load enclosed or covered.
M	31614(f)	Care in passing fire.

Type	VC Section	Violation
M	31614(g)	Vehicle unattended.
M	31614(h)	Smoking or open flame around vehicle.
M	31614(i)	Explosives in passenger vehicle subject to regulations.

VEHICLE VIOLATIONS TABLE

Types of convictions received for violation of certain sections of Division 14.1 of the Vehicle Code.

Type	VC Section	Violation
M	32000.5(a)	Hazardous material, licensed, displayed.
M	32000.5(d)	Fireworks transportation; carry copy of license and present to peace officer upon request.
M	32001(c)	Hazardous material, motor carrier directing transportation.
M	32002(a)	Hazardous material, violate provisions of Div. 14.1, or regulations.
M	32002(b)	Hazardous material transportation, valid license.

Types of convictions received for violation of certain sections of Division 14.3 of the Vehicle Code.

Type	VC Section	Violation
M	32103(a)	Inhalation hazard transporter, must have latest map showing routes, safe stopping places, and inspection stops.
M	32104(a)	Inhalation hazard transporter, driving on other than designated route.
M	32104(b)	Inhalation hazard transporter, stopping or parking except where permitted.
M	32105(a)	Inhalation hazard transporter, avoid listed areas, when possible.
M	32105(b)	Inhalation hazard transporter, vehicle left unattended on highway.
M	32105(c)	Inhalation hazard transporter, perform required inspection preceding transportation.
M	32105(d)	Inhalation hazard transporter, perform required inspections at designated locations.
M	32105(e)	Inhalation hazard transporters, maintain record of every inspection.
M	32106(a)	Vehicles transporting inhalation hazard; brakes maintained in good condition.
M	32106(b)	Vehicles transporting inhalation hazard; steering and lighting system maintained in good condition.
M	32106(c)	Vehicles transporting inhalation hazard; tires in good condition, matched, and inflated.
M	32106(d)	Vehicles transporting inhalation hazard; carry fire extinguishers as required.
M	32107	Inhalation hazard transporter, must have self-contained breathing apparatus and communication equipment.

Types of convictions received for violation of certain sections of Division 14.5 of the Vehicle Code.

Type	VC Section	Violation
C	33002	Notification to the CHP required prior to the transportation of any hazardous radioactive materials.

VEHICLE VIOLATIONS TABLE

Types of convictions received for violation of certain sections of Division 14.8 of the Vehicle Code.		
Type	**VC Section**	**Violation**
I	34500.3	Noncompliance with CHP cargo regulations.
M	34501(e)	Bus terminal or maintenance facility, bus operation without CHP inspection.
I	34501.1	Manufacturers and distributors of wheelchair lifts shall submit proof of safety certification to the CHP.
I	34501.2(b)(1)	Driving hours and duty status.
I	34501.2(b)(2)	Motor carrier requiring driver to exceed maximum hours of service.
I	34501.2(c)(1)	Driving hours and duty status, agricultural drivers.
M	34501.3(a)	Schedule necessitating unlawful speeds.
I	34501.4	Failure to produce complete driver's logbook for the last 24-hour period.
I	34501.8(b)	General public paratransit vehicle, operation without required inspection certificate.
M	34501.12(e)	Motor carrier, failure to submit application and fees for original and subsequent inspection.
M	34501.12(f)	Motor carrier, operating without having submitted inspection application and fees.
M	34501.12(g)	Motor carrier operating any vehicle without inspection performed and safety compliance report issued within the prescribed period.
M	34501.12(h)	Failure to apply for reinspection.
M	34501.14(b)	Failure to apply for grape gondola inspection.
M	34501.14(c)	Operation of grape gondola without being inspected and certified.
M	34501.14(d)	Operation of grape gondola without being inspected and certified.
I	34501.17(a)	Failure to inspect, maintain or lubricate paratransit vehicle.
I	34501.17(b)	Failure to document inspection and maintenance

		information; maintain records at place of business; present documentation to CHP; maintain odometer of paratransit vehicle.
M	34501.18	Motor carriers employing more than 20 full-time drivers required to report to CHP when more than half of their drivers are replaced within a 30-day period.
M	34505(a)	Tour bus required to be inspected every 45 days.
M	34505(b)	Tour bus not to be operated until defects corrected.
M	34505(c)	Tour bus records of inspection to be retained in garage where tour bus kept for 1 year and include specified information.
M	34505.5(a)	Motor carrier inspect vehicles every 90 days.
M	34505.5(b)	All defects noted must be repaired prior to operation.
M	34505.5(c)	Records must be maintained at motor carrier's terminal, include specified information, and retained for 2 years.
I	34505.9(g)	Ocean marine terminal operator, threaten, coerce, or retaliate against any driver.
M	34505.10	Motor carriers failure to retain required records of contracted transportation service.
M	34506(a)	Driving hours, failure to comply.
M	34506(b)	Hazardous materials, failure to comply.
M	34506(c)	Schoolbus construction, design, color, equipment, maintenance, or operation, failure to comply.
M	34506(d)	Provides a penalty for failing to comply with regulations regarding youth bus equipment, maintenance or operation.
M	34506(e)	Provides a penalty for failing to comply with regulations regarding tour bus equipment, maintenance or operation.
M	34506(f)	Commercial vehicles, failure to comply with any equipment, maintenance, or operation regulation.
M	34506(g)	School pupil activity bus; equipment, maintenance or operation.
I	34506.3	Failure to comply with any rule or regulation pursuant to Division 14.8.
I	34507	Failure of motor carrier subject to PUC or ICC to have such identifying number or symbol displayed on vehicle.
I	34507.5(a)	Motor carrier, must make application for a carrier identification number unless exempted.
I	34507.5(b)	Motor carrier, failure to display carrier identification number.
I	34507.5(e)	Identification number shall be legible from a distance of 50 feet.
I	34507.5(h)	When no longer in business, identification markings shall be removed.
I	34507.6(a)	Bus carrier identification number, shall obtain from CHP.
I	34507.6(b)	Bus carrier identification number, properly displayed.
I	34509(a)	Vanpool vehicle, equipped with fire extinguisher
I	34509(b)	Vanpool vehicle, equipped with first aid kit.

VEHICLE VIOLATIONS TABLE

I	34509(c)	Vanpool vehicle, properly inspected and maintained.
I	34509(d)	Vanpool vehicle, inspections must be documented and maintained with vehicle for one year, present to any authorized representative of the CHP.
I	34509(e)	Proper display, identifying as a vanpool vehicle.
I	34510(a)	Vehicles transporting hazardous material subject to Division 14.8 shall carry shipping papers, including bill of lading, and must display to officer upon demand.
I	34510(b)	Intermodal transportation vehicles with cargo weight exceeding 10,000 lbs. shall carry certificate of actual gross cargo weight and description of container contents; must display to officer upon demand.
M	34510.5(a)(1)	Failure of broker of construction truck services to secure a surety bond while providing services.
M	34510.5(a)(2)(A)	Failure of broker to annually provide written evidence of valid surety bond to third party, or post current copy on broker's website.
M	34510.5(a)(2)(B)	Failure of broker to notify third-party nonprofit when surety bond is cancelled or expired, or to remove it from their website.
M	34510.5(b)	Broker hiring a motor carrier without providing written evidence of valid surety bond.
M	34516(a)	Prohibits the use of certain vehicles to transport food products for human consumption if the vehicles have been used to transport solid waste.
I	34517(a)	Prohibits operation outside boundaries of designated commercial zone of vehicle from another county without prior approval of the United States Department of Transportation.
I	34518(a)	Foreign motor vehicle, operation without certificate.
I	34518(b)	Foreign motor vehicle, operating beyond limitations or restrictions of certificate.
I	34518(c)	Foreign motor carrier shall not operate a vehicle unless inspected by a Commercial Vehicle Safety Alliance inspector every three months.
M	34520(e)	Motor carriers and drivers must comply with federal drug and alcohol use testing requirements, including pre-employment testing.
M	34520(a)	Motor carriers and drivers comply with federal drug and alcohol use and testing requirements.
M	34520(b)	Motor carrier make available copies of results and records of drug and alcohol use and testing.
M	34520(c)	Testing consortium mail positive drug and alcohol test results summaries to the California Highway Patrol within 3 days of test.
I	34520(e)	Owner-operator shall notify contracted motor carriers when the requirements of Section 15242 VC have been met.
M	34520(f)	Owner-operator placed on duty by a motor carrier before preemployment drug and alcohol test has been

VEHICLE VIOLATIONS TABLE

		completed.
I	34520.3	School transportation vehicle driver must participate in a program that is consistent with the federal controlled substance and alcohol use testing requirements that apply to school bus drivers.
I	34520.5(a)	Failure of employer of driver of paratransit vehicle to participate in federal drug and alcohol testing program.
I	34520.5(c)	Failure of employer of paratransit vehicle to participate in pull notice program.
M	34620(a)	Motor Carrier of Property, operating without registering its carrier identification number with the DMV or failing to posses a valid motor carrier permit issued by DMV.
M	34620(b)	Contracting or subcontracting with motor carrier of property without certification, or contracting by a broker of construction services without certification.
M	34623(c)	Motor carrier permits shall be suspended for failure to comply with federal law described in Section 34520.
M	34623(g)	Motor carrier of property operating when permit suspended.
M	34623(h)	Motor carrier of property who is suspended for the failure to maintain any vehicle in safe operating condition, may not operate the vehicles of the carrier subject to the suspension, during the period of the suspension.
M	34660(a)	Motor carrier of property continuing to operate after permit suspended by DMV.

Types of convictions received for violation of certain sections of Division 14.9 of the Vehicle Code.		
Type	**VC Section**	**Violation**
I	34715(a)	Sale of passenger vehicle manufactured after 9/1/73 without warranty of energy absorption system.

VEHICLE VIOLATIONS TABLE

Types of convictions received for violation of certain sections of Division 15 of the Vehicle Code.		
Type	**VC Section**	**Violation**
I	35100(a)	Limitations on width.
I	35100.5	Cotton module mover width 130 inches.
I	35101	Width, 108 inches to outside of pneumatic tires.
I	35102	Loose agricultural products, 120 inches.
I	35103(a)	Maximum width due to appurtenance extending beyond six inches from either side wall.
I	35104	Special mobile or construction equipment, not to exceed 120 inches.
I	35106(a)	Motor coaches and buses, maximum width 102 inches.
I	35106(b)	Specified motor coaches and buses, maximum width 104 inches.
I	35109	Required devices, 10 inches each side, not to exceed 120 inches total width.
I	35110(a)	Specified equipment projecting more than three inches beyond the side of a vehicle.
I	35111	Passenger vehicles, projecting load to left, or over 6 inches to right.
I	35250	Height, vehicle or load exceeding 14 feet.
I	35251(a)	Boom or mast with hydraulic mechanism secured by chain while vehicle being transported.
I	35252(b)	Pilot car; vertical measuring device securely attached with no damage to overhead structures and no hazard to surrounding traffic.
I	35252(c)	Pilot car operator; shall not slow 20 mph below speed limit or exit vehicle to measure clearance.
I	35400(a)	Length, single vehicle 40 feet (exception for housecars).
I	35400(b)(6)	An operator of a schoolbus shall not extend a crossing control arm while the schoolbus is in motion.
I	35400(e)	Properly mount bicycle on front of bus or trolley.
I	35401(a)	Length of combinations, 65 feet, exceptions.
I	35401(b)	Length of combinations, 75 feet, exceptions.

VEHICLE VIOLATIONS TABLE

I	35401.5(g)	A motorsports trailer exceeding the 56 foot maximum length.
I	35401.8(a)	Length of combinations, 75 feet, exceptions for transportation of agricultural biomass.
I	35401.8(b)	Transportation of agricultural biomass with 75 feet combination limited to specified counties.
I	35401.8(c)	Transportation of agricultural biomass with 75 feet combination prohibited on national network routes.
I	35406(a)	Load to front, not over 3 feet (with exceptions).
I	35406(b)	Load of motor vehicles, not to extend over 4 feet to front.
I	35408	Front bumper, not to extend over 2 feet forward.
I	35410	Projections to rear, not to exceed 2/3 wheelbase.
I	35411(a)	Length of combination and load, 75 feet (except poles or pipes).
I	35411(b)	Load shall be contained within the exterior dimensions of the vehicle, when the combination of vehicle exceeds 75 feet.
M[1]	35550(a)	Weight on axle, 20,000 lbs.; one end of axle, 10,500 lbs.; Steering axle motor vehicle, 12,500 lbs.
M[1]	35551(a)	Exceeding allowable weights for consecutive axles.
M[1]	35551.5	Exceeding allowable weight limits for consecutive axles (alternate method). (Use appropriate subsection.)
M[1]	35554	Weight on any one axle of a bus shall not exceed 20,500 lbs., if the bus procurement process was initiated before January 1, 2013.
M	35600	Solid tires, weight not to exceed 600 lbs. per inch of base width.
M	35601	Metal tires, not to exceed 500 lbs. per inch of base width.
M	35655(a)	Load restriction on state highway, exceeding posted limit.
I	35655.6(a)	A person shall not drive a commercial vehicle with three or more axles, or a gross vehicle weight or a combined gross weight of 9,000 lbs. or more, on the segment of SR-2 between I-210 in the City of La Canada Flintridge and County Route N4 (Big Pine Highway) in the County of Los Angeles.
M	35753(a)	Weight limit on bridges, exceeding posted limit.
M	35783	Special permit, carry and display upon demand.
I	35783.5	Warning signs removed or covered.
M	35784(a)	Special permit (size, weight, etc.), violation of terms.
M	35784(c)	Extra legal load, not on prescribed route.
M	35784.5(a)	Extra legal load, transporting without permit.
M	35785(b)	Single saw log under permit, 15 mph on bridge, 25 mph on highway.
M	35786(b)	Truck booster power unit operating in violation of permit.
M	35789	House mover, notify R.R. 36 hours before crossing.
M	35790(g)	Overwidth manufactured home, permit to be carried in manufactured home or power unit.
M	35790(h)	Violating terms of permit.
I	35790.1(b)	Combinations of motor vehicles and manufactured housing shall be equipped with adequate service brakes on towing vehicle.
I	35790.1(c)	Breakaway device on manufactured housing unit shall be equipped

		with electric brakes powered by wet cell rechargeable battery.
M	35790.1(d)	Weight imposed upon any tire, wheel, axle, drawbar, hitch, or other suspension component on manufactured housing unit shall not exceed manufacturer's maximum weight rating for the item or component.
M	35790.1(e)	Maximum allowable weight on one housing unit axle shall not exceed 6000 pounds.Maximum allowable weight on one housing unit wheel shall not exceed 3000 pounds.
I	35790.1(f)	Manufactured housing unit tires shall be free from defects and have at least 2/32 of an inch tread depth.
M	35790.1(g)	Manufacturers shall provide transporters with a certification of compliance.Transporters shall make documents available to the CHP, DOT, municipal police officer, or deputy sheriff, including reserves.
M	35790.1(h)	Manufactured housing unit dealers shall provide transporters with certification of compliance document.Transporters shall make documentation available to CHP, DOT, and any municipal police officer or deputy sheriff, including reserves.
I	35790.1(i)	Transporters of manufactured housing units shall not transport any additional load in or upon unit that has not been certified.
I	35790.1(j)	Every hitch, coupling device, drawbar, or other connection shall be securely attached.
I	35790.1(k)	Manufactured housing units shall be equipped with an identification plate, and shall be positioned properly.
I	35790.1(m)	Manufactured housing units shall be equipped with proper side coverings.
M	35790.1(n)	Transporters shall make available all required documentation available to CHP, DOT, any municipal police officer or deputy sheriff including reserves.

[1] NOTE: Violation of this VC section is a misdemeanor only if the amount of weight in violation exceeds 4,500 pounds. Otherwise, it is an infraction. See VC Section 40000.23 (c).

VEHICLE VIOLATIONS TABLE

Types of convictions received for violation of certain sections of Division 16 of the Vehicle Code.		
Type	VC Section	Violation
I	36300	Driver of farm tractor required to possess license of proper class.
I	36305	Implement of husbandry, driver towing or operating combination of vehicles in excess of 25 mph, not possessing valid Class 3 driver's license.
I	36400	Lift-carrier, 35 mph speed limit.
I	36508	Slow-moving vehicle emblem, display of, on implements of husbandry only.
I	36509(b)	Implement of husbandry or farm vehicle towing loads exceeding 120 inches in width, not displaying flashing amber signals or red flags.
I	36510	Implement of husbandry stopping distance, 32 ft. \@ 15 mph, or speed permitting stop within 32 ft.
I	36600(b)	Implements of husbandry on federal highway, operating in excess of 25 miles from point of origin; operator not a farmer or farm employee; operator does not possess written origin and destination.
I	36600(c)	Implement of husbandry on highway, operating in excess of 25 miles from point of origin; operator not a farmer or farm employee; operator does not possess written origin and destination.
I	36605	Trailers and lift-carriers used exclusively, width not to exceed 120 inches. Trailers transporting grain harvesters not to exceed 144 inches.
I	36705	Operation of automatic bale wagon exceeding 96 inches in width, or carrying a load in excess of 100 inches during darkness.

VEHICLE VIOLATIONS TABLE

Types of convictions received for violation of certain sections of Division 16.5 of the Vehicle Code.		
Type	**VC Section**	**Violation**
I	38010(a)	Vehicles not registered and used exclusively off-highway required to display ID plate. Exceptions.
I	38020	Off-highway vehicles, not registered, required to be identified.
I	38026.5(b)	Prohibited operation of off-highway vehicles on designated highways.
I	38027	Off-highway vehicles moved by non-mechanical means.
I	38060(a)	Change of address, notify DMV within 10 days.
I	38060(b)	Change of address, owner to change on certificate.
I	38085(a)	Identification certificate, owner maintain with vehicle.
I	38090	ID certificate or plates, stolen, lost, mutilated, or illegible, owner immediately apply for duplicate.
I	38095	Certificate of ownership, stolen, lost, mutilated, or illegible, owner immediately apply for duplicate.
I	38170(a)	ID plate required to be displayed.
I	38170(b)	ID plate, securely attached and clearly visible. No covering.
I	38170(c)	ID plates, properly displayed
I	38200(a)	Transfer of ownership, dealer notify DMV.
I	38200(b)	Unlicensed dealer of off-highway vehicles immediately notify DMV of change of ownership.
I	38205	Transfer of ownership, transferee notify DMV within 10 days.
I	38300	Failure to obey any sign, signal, or traffic control device.
I	38301	Unlawful to violate special regulations
I	38302	Unlawful to erect any sign, signal, or traffic control device unless authorized by law.
I	38304	Operator unable to reach or operate all vehicle controls.
I	38304.1	Neither a parent or guardian of a child who is under 14

VEHICLE VIOLATIONS TABLE

		years of age, nor an adult who is authorized by the parent or guardian to supervise that child, shall grant permission to, or knowingly allow, that child to operate an off-highway motor vehicle in a manner that violates CVC Section 38304.
I	38305	Off-highway prima facie speed limit.
I	38310	Speed limit within 50 feet of people or animals.
I	38312	Unsafe start.
I	38314	Unsafe turning movement.
M	38316(a)	Reckless driving, willful and wanton disregard for safety of persons or property.
M	38317	Reckless driving, causing injury.
M	38318(a)	Throwing a substance at an off-highway motor vehicle or occupant.
F	38318(b)	Throwing a substance, with intent to do great bodily injury.
M	38318.5(a)	Maliciously removes or alters trail, danger, or directional markers.
F	38318.5(b)	Maliciously with the intent to do great bodily harm, erects or places chain, cable, rope, etc.
M	38319	Illegal to operate or own vehicle which is operated in a manner which harms the environment.
M	38320(a)	Litterbugging
M	38320(b)	Illegal dumping.
I	38330	Unsafe vehicle; condition.
I	38335	One lighted headlamp required during darkness.
I	38345	One lighted red tail lamp required during darkness.
I	38355(a)	Service brake required on off-highway vehicles.
I	38365(a)	Adequate mufflers required on off-highway vehicles.
I	38366(a)	Spark arrester required.
I	38370	Persons selling/offering new off-highway vehicle subject to identification which produces maximum allowable noise.
I	38370(b)(1)	Noise limits.
I	38370(g)	Off-highway vehicle required to have silencer to limit noise emissions.
I	38375(a)	Off-highway vehicle equipped with siren.
I	38375(b)	Use of siren while driving an off-highway motor vehicle.
I	38380	Additional equipment requirements.
I	38390	Illegal to operate an off-highway vehicle without emission control equipment.
I	38391	Illegal to offer, or sell, off-highway vehicles without emission control equipment.
I	38393	Illegal to operate an off-highway vehicle after notification by a traffic officer that the vehicle is not equipped with a proper smog device.

I	38503	Person under 18 years of age operating all-terrain vehicle on public lands without safety certificate.
I	38504	Person under 14 years of age operating all-terrain vehicle on public lands without being under the supervision of an adult.
I	38504.1(a)	Parent or guardian of a person under 14 years of age allowed to operate all-terrain vehicle on public land without being under the supervision of an adult.
I	38505	All-terrain vehicle, must wear safety helmet when operating or riding on public lands.
I	38506	No operator of an all-terrain vehicle shall carry a passenger when operating on public lands except under specific circumstances.
I	38600	Person under 16 yrs. of age operating a recreational off-highway vehicle, unless directly supervised by parent or guardian, or authorized adult.
I	38601	Person operating, or allowing any passenger in, a recreational off-highway vehicle without wearing safety helmets.
I	38602	Person operating, or any passenger in a recreational off-highway vehicle not wearing a seatbelt, shoulder belt, or safety harness when the vehicle is in motion.
I	38603	Person operating a recreational off-highway vehicle, allowing a passenger to occupy a seat not designed and provided by the manufacturer.
I	38604	Person operating a recreational off-highway vehicle with a passenger who, when seated upright, with their back against the seatback, cannot grasp the occupant handhold while the seatbelt and shoulder belt or safety harness are properly fastened.
I	38750(b)(2)	Operating autonomous vehicle while not seated in the driver's seat, monitoring the safe operation, and capable of taking immediate control.
M	38750(b)(3)	Autonomous vehicle manufacturer testing without license or insurance.
I	38750(c)	Operating an autonomous vehicle on public roads without an approved DMV application.

Types of convictions received for violation of certain sections of Division 16.7 of the Vehicle Code.

Type	VC Section	Violation
I	39002(a)	Operation of unlicensed bicycle where license required.
I	39002(b)	Tampering, mutilating or altering bicycle license indicia, registration forms, bicycle serial numbers or identifying mark on bicycle frame.
I	39006(a)	Bicycle retailer to provide bicycle ID information.
I	39007	Sale of bicycle after 12/31/76 without ID number stamped in frame.
I	39008(a)	Failure to notify licensing agency of sale of bicycle, within 10 days.
I	39008(b)	Failure of owner to apply for transfer of license, within 10 days.
I	39009(a)	Failure to notify within ten days of address change.
I	39009(b)	Bicycle license indicia or registration form lost, stolen, or mutilated; immediately notify licensing agency and apply for duplicate within 10 days.

VEHICLE VIOLATIONS TABLE

Types of convictions received for violation of certain sections of Division 17 of the Vehicle Code.		
Type	**VC Section**	**Violation**
M	40000.7	Salvage vehicle rebuilder, failing to provide buyer with CHP inspection report or DMV verification form.
M	40000.11	Occupational or drivers license violation pursuant to section 545.
M	40000.20	A third or subsequent offense of Section 23223 VC or Section 23225 VC by a transportation services driver.
I	40001(a)	Owner, or person directing driver, causing unlawful operation on highway; including railroad-highway grade crossing.
I	40001(b)	Owner requesting or permitting operation of vehicle which: (1) Is unregistered or has fees due. (2) Is not equipped as required. (3) Does not comply with size, weight or loading requirements. (4) Does not comply with administrative regulations. (5) Does not comply with smog device requirements.
M	40005	Owner, or person directing driver, failure to dispose of driver's citation after agreement.
M	40008(a)	Violating VC Sections 21701, 21703, or 23103 with the intent to get a visual image, sound recording, or other physical impression of another person for a commercial purpose.
M	40008(b)	Violating VC Sections 21701, 21703, or 23103 with the intent to get a visual image, sound recording, or other physical impression of another person for a commercial purpose and endangering the person or health of a minor child or children.
M	40254(b)	Notice of toll evasion violation: law enforcement or processing agency personnel tampering with notice.
M	40500	Persons who alter, conceals, modifies, nullifies, or destroys citation before it is filed with magistrate.
M	40504(b)	False signature, given on written notice to appear.
I	40505	Traffic Officer failing to include all court information on violator's copy of citation.
M	40508(a)	Failure to appear, after signing citation or court continuance.

M	40508(b)	Failure to pay installment fine for violation of Div. 11.
M	40508(c)	Failure to comply with condition of a court order.
M	40519(b)	Failure to appear, written plea.
M	40614	Signing a notice to correct or a certificate of correction with a false or fictitious name.
M	40616	Willful violation of a written promise to correct or willfully failing to deliver proof of correction.

VEHICLE VIOLATIONS TABLE

Types of convictions received for violation of certain sections of Division 18 of the Vehicle Code.		
Type	**VC Section**	**Violation**
M	42005(e)	Failure to attend traffic school.
C	42032	Authorizes assessment of a civil penalty against local public agencies operating garbage/refuse/rubbish collection vehicles that continuously violate weight limits.

INDEX TO

VEHICLE CODE

ABANDONED OR UNCLAIMED PROPERTY
Animals, this index
Auctions and auctioneers, highway patrol, **Veh 2415**
Highway Patrol, this index
Motor Vehicles, this index
Parks, this index
Traffic Rules and Regulations, this index
Vessels,
  Termination of certificates of number and ownership, **Veh 9864**
  Undocumented vessels, notice to assessor, **Veh 9869**

ABANDONED VEHICLE ABATEMENT
Definitions, funds, **Veh 22710**

ABANDONED VESSELS
Notice, assessors, **Veh 9869**
Termination, certificates of number and ownership, **Veh 9864**

ABATEMENT
Graffiti, abatement program, **Veh 13202.6**
Motor vehicles,
  Abandoned, wrecked, local ordinances, **Veh 22660 et seq.**
  Parked or standing, **Veh 22650 et seq.**
Nuisance, this index
Traffic signs and signals, **Veh 21467**

ABATEMENT OF ACTIONS OR PROCEEDINGS
Motor vehicles, accidents, continuation of action against personal representative, **Veh 17452**

ABETTORS
Accomplices and Accessories, generally, this index

ABILITY TO PAY
Definitions, traffic judgments, **Veh 42003**

ABILITY TO RESPOND IN DAMAGES
Definitions, motor vehicle insurance, **Veh 102**

ABODE
Domicile and Residence, generally, this index

ABSENCE AND ABSENTEES
Drivers licenses,
  Armed forces, **Veh 12817**
  Renewal, **Veh 12814**
Motor vehicles, drivers licenses,
  Armed forces, **Veh 12817**

ABSENCE AND ABSENTEES—Cont'd
Motor vehicles, drivers licenses—Cont'd
  Renewal, **Veh 12814**
Truants. Schools and School Districts, this index

ABSENTEES
Absence and Absentees, generally, this index

ABUSE
Children and Minors, this index

ACADEMIES
Private Schools, generally, this index

ACCESSORIES
Accomplices and Accessories, generally, this index

ACCIDENTS
Abstracts, court records, **Veh 1803 et seq.**
Arrest,
  Driving under influence of intoxicating liquor or drugs, arrest without warrant, **Veh 40300.5**
  Option of officer to take arrested person before magistrate, **Veh 40303**
Buses, this index
Carriers, this index
Confidential reports, **Veh 16005, 20012, 20014**
Coroners vehicles, lights, **Veh 25264**
Crimes and offenses, failure of driver to stop, **Veh 20001, 20002**
Death,
  Information and aid by driver, **Veh 20003**
  Reports, **Veh 20008**
Debris, removal, expense, **Veh 17300 et seq.**
Disclosure, reports, **Veh 20012**
Driverless vehicle, **Veh 20002**
Drivers, exchange of information, **Veh 16025**
Driving hours, limitation, **Veh 21702**
Driving schools and instructors, **Veh 11103**
Driving under influence of intoxicating liquor or drugs, arrest without warrant, **Veh 40300.5**
Drugs, driving under influence of, arrest without warrant, **Veh 40300.5**
Drunken driving, arrest without warrant, **Veh 40300.5**
Duty of driver to stop, **Veh 20001**
Evidence. Reports, post

ACCIDENTS—Cont'd
Expenses, removal of debris, **Veh 17300 et seq.**
Glass and debris, removal, **Veh 27700**
Highway Patrol, this index
Hit and run, **Veh 20000 et seq.**
Identification, driver, exhibit of evidence, **Veh 20006**
Impounding vehicle for investigation, **Veh 22655**
Information and aid by driver, **Veh 20003**
  Striking unattended vehicle, **Veh 20002**
Information exchanges, **Veh 20002**
Insurance, generally, this index
Law enforcement vehicles, **Veh 5003**
License applications of minors, civil liability, persons signing, **Veh 17700 et seq.**
Mass Transit, this index
Medical or surgical treatment, **Veh 20003, 20016**
Minors, license application, civil liability, person signing, **Veh 17700 et seq.**
Motor Carriers, this index
Motor vehicles. Traffic Rules and Regulations, this index
Notice,
  Correction of violations, **Veh 40610 et seq.**
  Striking unattended vehicle, contents, **Veh 20002**
  Traffic violations, **Veh 40600**
Option of officer to take arrested person before magistrate, **Veh 40303**
Personal Injuries, generally, this index
Physical incapability of driver to make report, duty of owner, **Veh 16003**
Presumptions, train of vehicles, **Veh 41104**
Process, service, **Veh 17450 et seq.**
Property damage,
  Duty of driver, **Veh 20002**
  Option of officer to take arrested person before magistrate, **Veh 40303**
Records and recordation, exempt vehicles, **Veh 5003**
Removal of glass and debris, **Veh 27700**
Reports, **Veh 20000 et seq.**
  Abstracts, court records, **Veh 1803 et seq.**
  Buses, **Veh 16002**
  Confidential or privileged information, **Veh 16005, 20012, 20014**
  Death or injuries, **Veh 20008**
  Disclosure, **Veh 20012**
  Evidence, **Veh 20013, 40833**
  Forms, **Veh 2407**

I–1

ACCIDENTS—Cont'd
Reports—Cont'd
  Highway Patrol, this index
  Hit and run, **Veh 20000 et seq.**
  Mass transit, **Veh 16002**
  Motor Carriers, this index
  Physical incapacity to make, **Veh 16003**
  Police,
    Confidential use, **Veh 20014**
    Death or injuries, **Veh 20008**
  Prejudice, **Veh 20012**
  Supplemental reports, motor carriers, **Veh 20009**
  Suspension of driving privilege, **Veh 16004**
  Time, **Veh 20008**
  Traffic Rules and Regulations, this index
  Transit systems, **Veh 16002**
Runaway vehicle, **Veh 20002**
Security deposit following accident, evidence, **Veh 40833**
Service of process, **Veh 17450 et seq.**
Sheriffs, this index
Tow car drivers, duties, **Veh 27700**
Traffic Rules and Regulations, this index
Traffic safety fund, use to prevent, **Veh 42200**
Traffic safety program, **Veh 2900 et seq.**
Train of vehicles, presumption of violation, **Veh 41104**
Transit systems, reports, **Veh 16002**
Transportation, injured persons, **Veh 20016**
Unattended vehicle, **Veh 20002**
Workers Compensation, generally, this index
Youth buses, reports, **Veh 12523**

ACCOMPLICES AND ACCESSORIES
Motor Vehicles, this index
Speed contest or exhibition on highway, arrest, procedure, **Veh 40303**
Theft, motor vehicles, **Veh 10851**
Traffic rules and regulations, speed contests, **Veh 23109**

ACCOUNTS AND ACCOUNTING
County Controllers, generally, this index
Gold Star Family license plate account, **Veh 5157**
Motor Vehicles, this index
State highway account. Highways and Roads, this index
State Treasury, this index

ACCUSEDS COUNSEL
Counsel for accused. Crimes and Offenses, this index

ACETYLENE LAMPS
Motor vehicles, **Veh 25450 et seq.**

ACIDS
Air Pollution, generally, this index
Explosives, transportation with, **Veh 31613**

ACKNOWLEDGMENTS
Motor vehicles, documents, **Veh 19**

ACTIONS AND PROCEEDINGS
Administrative Law and Procedure, generally, this index
Appeal and Review, generally, this index
Cause of action, definitions, financial responsibility, motor vehicles insurance, **Veh 16251**
Colleges and Universities, this index
Commencement of actions. Limitation of Actions, generally, this index
Compromise and Settlement, generally, this index
Contempt, generally, this index
Costs, generally, this index
Damages, generally, this index
Decrees. Judgments and Decrees, generally, this index
Driving schools,
  Actions upon licensees bond or deposit, **Veh 11102.1**
  Appointment of agent for service of process, **Veh 11102**
Evidence, generally, this index
Highways and Roads, this index
Judgments and Decrees, generally, this index
Limitation of Actions, generally, this index
Motor Carriers, this index
Motor Vehicles, this index
Municipal Courts, generally, this index
Negligence, generally, this index
Nuisance, generally, this index
Off highway vehicles, littering, **Veh 38321**
Privileges and Immunities, generally, this index
Probate Proceedings, generally, this index
Process, generally, this index
Seatbelts, mandatory, **Veh 27315**
Service of process. Process, this index
Small Claims Courts, generally, this index
Smog impact fees, motor vehicles, foreign states, **Veh 1673.4**
Statute of limitations. Limitation of Actions, generally, this index
Stay of proceedings. Supersedeas or Stay, generally, this index
Subpoenas, generally, this index
Summons. Process, this index
Supersedeas or Stay, generally, this index
Time. Limitation of Actions, generally, this index
Toll evasion, **Veh 40250 et seq.**
Torts, generally, this index
Traffic Rules and Regulations, this index

ACTIVITY BUSES
School Buses, this index

ACTS OF GOD
Traffic rules and regulations, limitation on driving hours, exemption, **Veh 21702**

AD VALOREM TAXES
Taxation, generally, this index

ADAMS LAW
Generally, **Veh 13386, 14601.2 et seq.**

ADDICTS
Drug Addicts, generally, this index

ADDRESS
Bicycles, change of address, notice to licensing agency, **Veh 39009**
City council members, confidentiality, **Veh 1808.4**
Confidential or privileged information, home addresses, designated persons, **Veh 1808.4**
County supervisors boards, confidentiality, **Veh 1808.4**
Court officers and employees, confidential or privileged information, **Veh 1808.4**
Crimes and Offenses, this index
Designated persons, **Veh 1808.4**
  Home addresses, parole hearings board, parole hearings division, youthful offender parole board, **Veh 1808.6**
District attorneys, confidentiality, **Veh 1808.4**
Drivers licenses, change of address, **Veh 14600**
Federal prosecutors, confidentiality, **Veh 1808.4**
Highway patrol, nonsworn personnel, confidentiality, **Veh 1808.4**
Home addresses, confidential information, designated personnel, parole hearings board, parole hearings division, youthful offender parole board, **Veh 1808.6**
Husband and wife, confidentiality, **Veh 1808.4**
Judges, this index
Juvenile Delinquents and Dependents, this index
Marriage, this index
Motor vehicle insurance, confidential or privileged information, records and recordation, **Veh 1808.22**
Motor Vehicles, this index
Municipal attorneys, confidentiality, **Veh 1808.4**
Municipal council members, confidentiality, **Veh 1808.4**
National park service rangers, confidentiality, **Veh 1808.4**
Peace Officers, this index
Police, this index
Police dispatchers, disclosure, **Veh 1808.4**
Public defenders, confidential or privileged information, **Veh 1808.4**
Public employer attorneys, confidentiality, **Veh 1808.4**
Request for information, motor vehicles, **Veh 1810**
Social Workers, this index
State officers and employees,
  Designated persons, confidential or privileged information, **Veh 1808.4**
  Home addresses, confidentiality, **Veh 1808.4**

ADJOINING STATES
Foreign States, generally, this index

ADJUSTABLE AXLE
Motor vehicles, devices to increase length, inclusion in measurement, **Veh 35402**

ADMINISTRATIVE LAW AND PROCEDURE
Highway patrol, rules and regulations, **Veh 2402**
Motor vehicle department, sale of registration information, **Veh 1810**
Registration, sale of information, motor vehicles, **Veh 1810**
Sales, motor vehicle registration information, **Veh 1810**

ADMINISTRATIVE PROCEDURE ACT
Administrative Law and Procedure, generally, this index

ADMINISTRATORS
Executors and administrators. Probate Proceedings, this index

ADMISSIBILITY OF EVIDENCE
Evidence, generally, this index

ADULTS
Aged Persons, generally, this index

ADVANCES AND ADVANCEMENTS
Highway patrol, uniforms, **Veh 2260**

ADVERSE OR PECUNIARY INTEREST
Attorneys, this index
Driving under the influence, alcohol education and treatment programs, **Veh 23670**
Towing, vehicles, kickbacks to public entities, **Veh 12110, 13351.85**
Traffic rules and regulations, driving under the influence, alcohol education and treatment programs, **Veh 23670**

ADVERTISEMENTS
Autobrokers, **Veh 11713**
Billboards. Outdoor Advertising, generally, this index
Buses, this index
Definitions, motor vehicles, sales, **Veh 11713.1**
Driving schools and instructors, false advertising, **Veh 11110**
Highways and roads. Outdoor Advertising, generally, this index
Mobile billboard advertising displays, traffic rules and regulations, **Veh 21100**
Impounding, **Veh 22651**
Mobilehomes and Mobilehome Parks, this index
Motor Vehicles, this index
Motor vehicles department, message display systems, contracts, **Veh 1656.5**
Odometers for motor vehicles, device for resetting, **Veh 28051.5**
Outdoor Advertising, generally, this index
Recreational Vehicles, this index
Trademarks, generally, this index

ADVERTISEMENTS—Cont'd
Traffic rules and regulations, mobile billboard advertising displays, **Veh 21100**
Impounding, **Veh 22651**

ADVISORY BOARDS AND COMMISSIONS
School buses, **Veh 34501.5**
Traffic safety program, **Veh 2903**

ADVISORY COMMITTEES
Motorcycle safety, **Veh 2932**

AERONAUTICS
Aircraft, generally, this index

AEROPLANES
Aircraft, generally, this index

AFFIDAVITS
Application for registration of new vehicle not within state, **Veh 4152**
Motions, vacation or setting aside prior judgment drunk driving conviction, **Veh 41403**
Motor Vehicles, this index
Release of impounded vehicle to legal owner, **Veh 14602**

AFFILIATES
Definitions, motor vehicles, engine manufacturer different from vehicle manufacturer, **Veh 9980**

AFFIRMATIONS
Oaths and Affirmations, generally, this index

AGE
Aged Persons, generally, this index
Bicycles, motorized, operation, **Veh 24016**
Drivers licenses. Motor Vehicles, this index
Driving instructors, **Veh 11104**
Driving schools, operators, **Veh 11102.5**
Highway patrol, officers and employees, **Veh 2256**
Motor Vehicles, this index
Motorized bicycles, operation, **Veh 24016**
School bus driver, **Veh 12516**

AGED PERSONS
Drivers licenses, renewal, **Veh 12814**
Driving schools, courses for mature drivers, **Veh 1675 et seq.**
Electric carts, sidewalk use, age 50 or older, local regulations, **Veh 21114.5**
Guardian and Ward, generally, this index
Mature driver improvement courses, **Veh 1675 et seq.**
Paratransit Vehicles, generally, this index
Sidewalks, electric carts, use, age 50 or older, local regulations, **Veh 21114.5**

AGENCY
Definitions, arrest, quotas, peace officers, **Veh 41601.5**
Local Agencies, generally, this index
Public Agencies, generally, this index

AGENT FOR SERVICE OF PROCESS
Process, this index

AGENTS
Government agencies. Public Agencies, generally, this index
Insurance Agents, Solicitors or Brokers, generally, this index
Motor Vehicles, this index
Process, this index
Public Agencies, generally, this index
State Agencies, generally, this index

AGREEMENTS
Contracts, generally, this index

AGRICULTURAL COMMODITIES
Agricultural Products, generally, this index

AGRICULTURAL LABOR AND EMPLOYMENT
Buses,
  Certificates and certification, farm labor contractors, education, **Veh 2429.5**
  Equipment, inspection, **Veh 31401**
  Fines and penalties, farm labor contractors, **Veh 31404**
  Lights and lighting, farm labor contractors, **Veh 31408**
  Speed limits, **Veh 22406 et seq.**
  Tires, tread depth requirements, **Veh 27465**
Certificates and certification. Motor vehicles, post
Definitions, farm labor vehicles, **Veh 322**
Farm labor vehicles. Motor vehicles, generally, post
Fines and penalties, motor vehicles, farm labor contractors, **Veh 31404**
Mass transit, farm labor vehicles, **Veh 31409**
Motor vehicles,
  Buses, generally, ante
  Cargo area, **Veh 23116**
  Certificates and certification, **Veh 12519**
    Farm labor contractors, education, **Veh 2429.5**
    Hearings, certificates, **Veh 14100.1**
    Inspection and inspectors, **Veh 31401.5**
  Definitions, **Veh 322**
  Driver education course, **Veh 12519**
  Drivers licenses, **Veh 12519**
  Driving of unsafe vehicle, **Veh 31402, 31403**
  Fines and penalties, farm labor contractors, **Veh 31404**
  Inspection and inspectors, **Veh 31401**
    Certificates and certification, **Veh 31401.5**
  Lights and lighting, farm labor contractors, **Veh 31408**
  Mass transit, **Veh 31409**
  Mechanics certification of vehicle, **Veh 31403**
  Railroad crossings, **Veh 22452**
  Registration,
    Cards, **Veh 4453.2**

AGRICULTURAL

**AGRICULTURAL LABOR AND EMPLOY-
MENT**—Cont'd

Motor vehicles—Cont'd
Registration—Cont'd
Renewal, **Veh 4154**
Repair of unsafe vehicle, **Veh 31402,
31403**
Seatbelts, **Veh 31405**
Seats, **Veh 31406**
Tools, **Veh 31407**
Traffic rules and regulations, generally,
post
Unsafe farm labor vehicles, repairs, **Veh
31402**
Portable sanitary facility, motor carriers
exempt from registration, **Veh 36105**
Registration. Motor vehicles, ante
Seatbelts, **Veh 31405**
Seats, motor vehicles, **Veh 31406**
Shade trailers, registration, exemptions,
Veh 36105
Tools, motor vehicles, **Veh 31407**
Traffic rules and regulations,
Distance between vehicles, **Veh 21704**
Railroad crossings, **Veh 22452**
Slow moving vehicles, designated lanes,
Veh 21655
Speed limits, **Veh 22406, 22407**
Transportation. Motor vehicles, general-
ly, ante

**AGRICULTURAL MACHINERY AND EQUIP-
MENT**

Generally, **Veh 36000 et seq., 36500 et
seq.**
Agricultural water well boring rig, defini-
tions, **Veh 105**
Almond trailers, towing, weight limita-
tions, **Veh 36627**
Application for identification plate, **Veh
36130**
Application of laws, **Veh 36700, 36800**
Automatic bale wagons,
Definitions, **Veh 36011**
Exemption, registration, **Veh 36102**
Identification plates, **Veh 36102**
Licenses, operation, **Veh 36300**
Operation, licenses, **Veh 36300**
Registration, exemption, **Veh 36102**
Width, **Veh 36606, 36705**
Cancellation, identification plates, **Veh
36130**
Cargo area, passengers, **Veh 23116**
Cargo tanks, flammable liquid transporta-
tion, registration exemption, **Veh
34005**
Certificates and certification,
Agricultural hazardous material trans-
portation, driver certification pro-
gram, **Veh 12804.2**
Endorsement certificates, **Veh 13369**
Permanent trailer identification plates,
Veh 5016, 5017
Chauffeurs licenses, **Veh 12519**
Combinations of vehicles,
Drivers licenses, **Veh 36305**

**AGRICULTURAL MACHINERY AND EQUIP-
MENT**—Cont'd

Combinations of vehicles—Cont'd
Length exemptions and limitations, **Veh
36615**
Combines, grain harvesting, widths, **Veh
36605**
Cotton Module Mover, generally, this in-
dex
Cotton trailers, **Veh 12804.7**
Towing, weight of motor truck, **Veh
36626**
Crimes and offenses, safety, **Veh 24002.5,
31402, 40000.15, 40000.18**
Dangerous substances, driver certification
program, **Veh 12804.2**
Darkness, lighting requirements, **Veh
36505**
Definitions, **Veh 36000 et seq.**
Dirt road sprinkler trucks, registration, ex-
emption, **Veh 36101**
Drivers licenses, **Veh 36300**
Certificates and certification, farm labor
contractors, education, **Veh 2429.5**
Combinations of vehicles, **Veh 36305**
Farm labor vehicles, **Veh 12519**
Hazardous materials transportation,
driver certification program, **Veh
12804.2**
Towing implements of husbandry, **Veh
36305**
Drugs and medicine, tests, exemptions,
Veh 40000.15
Emblems, slow moving vehicle emblem,
Veh 24615
Display, **Veh 36508**
Empty load, continuation of exemption,
Veh 36017
Exemptions, **Veh 36615 et seq.**
Equipment and devices, **Veh 36500 et
seq.**
Hazardous materials transportation li-
censes, **Veh 32000.5**
Height of vehicles, **Veh 36610**
Inspection and inspectors, **Veh 40000.15**
Length exemption and limitations, **Veh
36615 et seq.**
Registration, **Veh 36100 et seq.**
Safety, crimes and offenses, **Veh 31402**
Towing more than one vehicle, **Veh
36625**
Width exemptions and limitations, **Veh
36600, 36605**
Expenses and expenditures, impounding,
Veh 34506.5
Feed and seed vehicles, oversized permits,
registration, exemption, **Veh 36101**
Feed haulers, registration exemptions, **Veh
36102**
Fees,
Farm labor vehicle certificates, **Veh
12519**
Identification plates, **Veh 5014**
Adjustments, **Veh 1678**
Owners and ownership, transfer, **Veh
5018, 9261, 9261.1**

**AGRICULTURAL MACHINERY AND EQUIP-
MENT**—Cont'd

Fees—Cont'd
Owners and ownership, transfer
—Cont'd
Adjustments, **Veh 1678**
Fines and penalties,
Inspection violations, **Veh 31404**
Safety, **Veh 24002.5, 31402**
Flags, display, **Veh 36509**
Flammable liquids,
Agricultural hazardous materials trans-
portation, driver certification pro-
gram, **Veh 12804.2**
Transported in cargo tanks, registration
exemption, **Veh 34005**
Forfeitures, nuisances, **Veh 34506.5**
Forklift trucks, registration exemption,
Veh 36101
Grain harvesting combines, widths, **Veh
36605**
Hazardous materials transportation licens-
es, exemptions, **Veh 32000.5**
Hazardous substances and waste, transpor-
tation, driver certification program,
Veh 12804.2
Hearings, impounding, **Veh 34506.5**
Height limitations, exemption, **Veh 36610**
Identification plates, **Veh 36115 et seq.**
Application, **Veh 36130**
Cancellation, **Veh 36130**
Fees, registration, exemption, **Veh 36101**
Renewal, **Veh 36130**
Impounding,
Hearings, **Veh 34506.5**
Safety, crimes and offenses, **Veh
24002.5, 31402**
Time, **Veh 34506.4**
Insignia, slow moving vehicle, display, **Veh
36508**
Inspection and inspectors, **Veh 31401**
Crimes and offenses, violations, **Veh
31404**
Exemptions, **Veh 40000.15**
Farm labor vehicles, certificates and
certification, **Veh 31401.5**
Fines and penalties, violations, **Veh
31404**
State patrol, stolen equipment, **Veh
2805**
Irrigating water truck, registration, exemp-
tion, **Veh 36101**
Length, exemptions and limitations, **Veh
36615 et seq.**
License plates, **Veh 5014 et seq.**
Licenses and permits, livestock feed haul-
ers, **Veh 36102**
Lift carriers,
Speed, **Veh 36400**
Width limitations, **Veh 36605**
Lights and lighting, **Veh 36505**
Farm labor vehicles, **Veh 31408**
Implements of husbandry,
Double faced amber turn signals,
warning lights, **Veh 25251.1**
Flashing amber lights, **Veh 36509**

AGRICULTURAL MACHINERY AND EQUIP-MENT—Cont'd

Livestock feed haulers, registration exemptions, **Veh 36102**

Loads and loading, limitations, **Veh 36600 et seq.**

Motor vehicles. Agricultural Labor and Employment, this index

Nuisance, forfeitures, **Veh 34506.5**

Off highway vehicles subject to identification, **Veh 38000 et seq.**

Oversize feed and seed vehicles, registration, exemption, **Veh 36101**

Owners and ownership, transfer, **Veh 5018, 9261, 9261.1**

Adjustments, **Veh 1678**

Passengers,
Cargo area, **Veh 23116**
Seats, **Veh 31406**

Penalties. Fines and penalties, generally, ante

Permanent trailer identification plates, **Veh 5015 et seq.**

Person operating, license, exemption, **Veh 12501**

Plates. Identification plates, generally, ante

Portable sanitary facility, motor carriers exempt from registration, **Veh 36105**

Public policy, inspection and inspectors, exemptions, **Veh 40000.15**

Red flags, display, **Veh 36509**

Registration, **Veh 36100 et seq.**

Renewal, identification plates, **Veh 36130**

Repairs, impounding, release, **Veh 34506.4**

Safety, **Veh 31401 et seq.**
Crimes and offenses, ante
Fines and penalties, **Veh 24002.5**
Violations, **Veh 31404**
Impounding, ante
Passengers, cargo area, **Veh 23116**
Seatbelts, **Veh 31405**
Seats, **Veh 31406**
Tools, **Veh 31407**

Seatbelts, **Veh 31405**

Seats, motor vehicles, **Veh 31406**

Second and subsequent offenses, safety, impounding, time, **Veh 34506.4**

Semitrailers,
Registration exemption, **Veh 36101**
Width limitations, **Veh 36605**

Shade trailers, registration, exemptions, **Veh 36105**

Silage, registration, exemption, **Veh 36101**

Size limitations, **Veh 36600 et seq.**

Slow moving vehicle emblem, display, **Veh 24615, 36508**

Specific roads and highways, prohibiting operation on, **Veh 36101**

Speed laws, **Veh 22406 et seq., 36400**
National system of interstate and defense highways, **Veh 36600**

Spray rig, flammable liquids transported in cargo tanks, registration exemption, **Veh 34005**

Stopping distance, exemption, **Veh 36510**

AGRICULTURAL MACHINERY AND EQUIP-MENT—Cont'd

Storage, impounding, expenses and expenditures, **Veh 34506.5**

Tests, drugs and medicine, exemptions, **Veh 40000.15**

Time, impounding, safety, crimes and offenses, **Veh 34506.4**

Tip bed trailers, width limitations, **Veh 36605**

Tires, tread depth requirement, exemption, **Veh 27465**

Tools, motor vehicles, **Veh 31407**

Towing,
Almond trailers, weight limitations, **Veh 36627**
Drivers licenses, **Veh 36305**
Farm tractors used for, **Veh 36015**
Several vehicles, exemption, **Veh 36625**

Trailers,
Definitions, **Veh 36010**
Fees, transfers, **Veh 1678, 9261, 9261.1**
License plates, **Veh 5014 et seq.**
Plenum chamber, registration, exemption, **Veh 36101**
Registration, exemption, **Veh 36109**
Transfers, fees, **Veh 1678, 9261, 9261.1**
Width limitations, **Veh 36605**

Transporting water truck, registration, exemption, **Veh 36101**

Trap wagon,
Flammable liquids transported in cargo tanks, registration exemption, **Veh 34005**
Registration exemption, **Veh 36101**

Truck tractors, registration exemption, **Veh 36101**

Turn signals, **Veh 22110**
Implements of husbandry, **Veh 25251.1**

Warning lights, implements of husbandry, **Veh 25251.1**

Water tank carrying vehicle, registration, exemption, **Veh 36101**

Weight limit exemptions, **Veh 35720**

Width, exemptions and limitations, **Veh 36600, 36605**

Windshield wipers, exemption, **Veh 36520**

Windshields, exemptions, **Veh 36515**

AGRICULTURAL PRODUCTS

Air Pollution, generally, this index

Definitions, motor carriers, hours of service, **Veh 34501.2**

Grapes and Grapevines, generally, this index

Highway patrol, vehicle transporting, inspection of bills of lading, **Veh 2810**

Motor carriers,
Hours of service, **Veh 34501.2**
Inspection, **Veh 2810**

Silage, motor vehicles, registration, exemption, **Veh 36101**

Traffic rules and regulations,
Loose loads, **Veh 35102**
Width of loads, **Veh 35102**

AGRICULTURAL SPRAYING AND DUSTING

Flammable liquids transported in cargo tanks, registration exemption, **Veh 34005**

Spray rig, flammable liquids transported in cargo tanks, registration exemption, **Veh 34005**

AGRICULTURAL VEHICLES

Agricultural Machinery and Equipment, generally, this index

AGRICULTURAL WATER WELL BORING RIG

Definitions, motor vehicles, **Veh 105**

Weight fees, exemption, **Veh 9405**

AGRICULTURE

Animals, generally, this index

Dangerous substances, transportation, driver certification program, **Veh 12804.2**

Employment. Agricultural Labor and Employment, generally, this index

Grapes and Grapevines, generally, this index

Hazardous Substances and Waste, this index

Labor and employment. Agricultural Labor and Employment, generally, this index

Livestock. Animals, generally, this index

Machinery. Agricultural Machinery and Equipment, generally, this index

Products. Agricultural Products, generally, this index

AIDERS AND ABETTORS

Accomplices and Accessories, generally, this index

AIR BAGS

Motor Vehicles, this index

AIR BRAKES

Motor Vehicles, this index

AIR COMPRESSORS

Special highway construction equipment, **Veh 565**

AIR DRILLS

Special highway construction equipment, **Veh 565**

AIR FORCE

Military Forces, generally, this index

AIR GOVERNOR

Motor vehicles, airbrakes, **Veh 26504**

AIR POLLUTION

Actions and proceedings. Motor vehicles, post

Advanced technology partial zero emission vehicles, decals, **Veh 5205.5**

Air basins. South coast air quality management district, generally, post

Automobiles. Motor vehicles, generally, post

AIR POLLUTION—Cont'd

Brands, marks and labels, motor vehicles, low emission vehicles, **Veh 5205.5, 21655.9, 40000.13**

Buses, low emission vehicles, **Veh 28113**

Cars. Motor vehicles, generally, post

Certificate of compliance. Motor vehicles, post

Certified devices. Motor vehicles, post

Commercial vehicles. Motor carriers, generally, post

Control districts. South coast air quality management district, generally, post

Counties,
Control districts. South coast air quality management district, generally, post
Speed limits, south coast air quality management district, **Veh 22365**

Crimes and offenses,
Motor vehicles, post
Smog impact fees, motor vehicles, foreign states, **Veh 1673.6**

Dealers. Motor vehicles, post

Decals. Motor vehicles, post

Emissions,
Foreign commercial vehicles, inspection and inspectors, **Veh 2418.1**
Motor carriers, post
Motor vehicles, post
Motorized scooters, **Veh 12500**
Specially constructed vehicles, inspection and inspectors, registration, **Veh 4750.1**

Enhanced advanced technology partial zero emission vehicles, decals, **Veh 5205.5, 21655.9**

Exemptions,
Collector vehicles, inspection and inspectors, **Veh 4000.1**
Inspection and inspectors, collector vehicles, **Veh 4000.1**
Motor vehicles, post

Fees. South coast air quality management district, post

Fines and penalties. Motor vehicles, post

Foreign countries, commercial vehicles, Inspection and inspectors, emissions, **Veh 2418.1**
Standards, **Veh 2418**

Foreign states. Motor vehicles, post

Gross polluters,
Crimes and offenses, **Veh 27156**
Motor vehicles, post

Hybrid vehicles, decals, **Veh 5205.5**

Identity and identification. Motor vehicles, post

Inherently low emission vehicles, decals, **Veh 5205.5**

Inspection and inspectors. Motor vehicles, post

Limitation of actions, motor vehicles, smog impact fees, foreign states, **Veh 1673.4**

AIR POLLUTION—Cont'd

Los Angeles County. South coast air quality management district, generally, post

Low emission vehicles. Motor vehicles, post

Misdemeanors. Crimes and offenses, generally, ante

Motor carriers,
Emissions, foreign countries, inspection and inspectors, **Veh 2418.1**
Inspection and inspectors, **Veh 2418.1, 2802**
Registration, refusal, **Veh 4755**
Standards, **Veh 2418**

Motor vehicles, **Veh 27153 et seq.**
Actions and proceedings, smog impact fees, foreign states, **Veh 1673.4**
Advanced technology partial zero emission vehicles, decals, **Veh 5205.5**
Aged persons, control devices, installation, costs, **Veh 24007.2**
Alteration or modification of control devices, **Veh 27156**
Antisiphoning devices, methanol, ethanol fuel, **Veh 28110 et seq.**
Biannual motor vehicle inspection program, urban nonattainment areas, certificate of compliance, issuance, **Veh 4000.3**
Brands, marks and labels, low emission vehicles, **Veh 5205.5, 21655.9, 40000.13**
Certificate of compliance, **Veh 27158**
Inspection, urban nonattainment areas, issuance, **Veh 4000.3**
Temporary registration, **Veh 4156**
Fees, **Veh 9257.5**
Certified devices,
Aged, low income persons, installation, dealers, **Veh 24007.2**
Installation, aged, low income persons, dealers, **Veh 24007.2**
Standing or operating vehicle on highway, **Veh 27156**
Used, **Veh 27158.5**
Crimes and offenses, **Veh 40001 et seq.**
Disconnecting, modifying or altering control devices, **Veh 42001.14**
Low emission vehicles, decals, **Veh 21655.9, 40000.13**
Smog impact fees, foreign states, **Veh 1673.6**
Dealers, statements of effectiveness, control devices, **Veh 24007**
Decals, low emission vehicles, **Veh 5205.5, 21655.9, 40000.13**
Devices, **Veh 27156**
Alteration, **Veh 42001.14**
Alteration of vehicle, **Veh 27156**
Certified device, standing or operating vehicle on highway, used, **Veh 27158.5**
Dealers, certificates, **Veh 24007**

AIR POLLUTION—Cont'd

Motor vehicles—Cont'd
Devices—Cont'd
Emission control equipment, application of law, exemptions, **Veh 38395**
Licenses and permits, revocation or suspension, **Veh 2540 et seq.**
Off highway vehicles, **Veh 38390 et seq.**
Application of law, **Veh 38395, 38396, 38397**
Fines and penalties, **Veh 38392**
Improper device, notice of violation, **Veh 38393**
Refusal of registration, **Veh 4750**
Registration, **Veh 4000.1**
Vehicles previously registered out of state, **Veh 4000.2**
Statements of effectiveness, dealers, **Veh 24007**
Disconnection of device, **Veh 27156**
Emergency vehicles, control devices, **Veh 27156.2, 27156.3**
Emissions,
Aged persons, low income, installation, dealers, **Veh 24007.2**
Equipment, **Veh 27150 et seq.**
National Emission Standards Act controlling, **Veh 27156**
New vehicles, **Veh 27153.5**
Enhanced advanced technology partial zero emission vehicles, decals, **Veh 5205.5, 21655.9**
Environmental license plate fund, **Veh 5100 et seq.**
Evaporative loss control devices, gas tanks, installation, **Veh 27156.1**
Exemptions, altered or modified vehicle, **Veh 27156**
Federally owned vehicles, **Veh 2814, 27153 et seq.**
Fines and penalties,
Collection and deposit, **Veh 9250.18**
Control devices, **Veh 27156**
Disconnecting, modifying or altering control devices, **Veh 42001.14**
Emission standards or test procedures, **Veh 42001.14**
Gross polluters, operating or leaving on roadway, **Veh 27156**
Low emission vehicles, decals, **Veh 21655.9, 40000.13**
Foreign states,
Registration, **Veh 4000.2**
Smog impact fees, **Veh 1673 et seq.**
Gross polluters, crimes and offenses, **Veh 27156**
High occupancy vehicle lanes, **Veh 21655.5**
Hybrid vehicles, decals, **Veh 5205.5**
Identity and identification, operation on highways, **Veh 27156**
Inherently low emission vehicles, decals, **Veh 5205.5**

AIR POLLUTION—Cont'd
Motor vehicles—Cont'd
Inspection and inspectors,
Checkpoints, **Veh 2814.1**
Collector vehicles, exemptions, **Veh 4000.1**
Pretests, **Veh 4000.3**
Installation of certified devices, aged, low income persons, dealers, **Veh 24007.2**
Limitation of actions, smog impact fees, foreign states, **Veh 1673.4**
Liquefied petroleum gas propulsion systems, regulation violations, infractions, **Veh 2402.6**
Low emission vehicles,
Brands, marks and labels, **Veh 5205.5, 21655.9, 40000.13**
Decals, **Veh 5205.5, 21655.9, 40000.13**
Modification of device or vehicle, **Veh 27156**
National Emission Standards Act, control devices, **Veh 27156**
Natural gas propulsion systems, regulation violations, infractions, **Veh 2402.6**
New vehicles,
Notice, smog indexing program information, **Veh 1667**
Registration, smog indexing program information, **Veh 1667**
Smog indexing program, information, **Veh 1667**
Notice,
Pretests, **Veh 4000.3**
Smog impact fees, foreign states, **Veh 1673.2, 1673.4, 1673.7**
Off highway vehicles, emission control equipment, **Veh 38390 et seq.**
Application of law, **Veh 38396**
Exemptions, **Veh 38395**
Fines and penalties, **Veh 38392**
Improper device, notice, **Veh 38393**
Notice to appear, proof of correction, **Veh 38394**
Operation of vehicle to prevent excessive pollutant escape, **Veh 27153**
Operation without certification after notice, used cars, **Veh 27158.5**
Perjury, smog impact fees, foreign states, **Veh 1673.6**
Pretests, **Veh 4000.3**
Prevention of penetration into cab of vehicle, **Veh 27154**
Refunds, smog impact fees, foreign states, **Veh 1673 et seq.**
Registration, **Veh 4000**
Actions and proceedings, smog impact fees, foreign states, **Veh 1673.4**
Certificates of compliance or noncompliance, **Veh 4000.1, 4000.2**
Crimes and offenses, smog impact fees, foreign states, **Veh 1673.6**

AIR POLLUTION—Cont'd
Motor vehicles—Cont'd
Registration—Cont'd
Fees,
Smog impact fees, foreign states, **Veh 1673 et seq.**
South coast air quality management district, **Veh 9250.11**
Foreign states, smog impact fees, **Veh 1673 et seq.**
Limitation of actions, smog impact fees, foreign states, **Veh 1673.4**
Notice, smog impact fees, foreign states, **Veh 1673.2, 1673.4, 1673.7**
Perjury, smog impact fees, foreign states, **Veh 1673.6**
Previous registration outside state, **Veh 4000.2**
Refunds, smog impact fees, foreign states, **Veh 1673 et seq.**
Small claims courts, smog impact fees, foreign states, **Veh 1673.4**
Smog impact fees, foreign states, **Veh 1673 et seq.**
Statement subject to perjury, transfer of title, exemption from emission standards test, **Veh 5751.5**
Transfer of title, certificates of compliance or noncompliance, emission standards, **Veh 4000.1, 4000.2**
Sales, nonconforming vehicles, **Veh 24007.5**
Small claims courts, smog impact fees, foreign states, **Veh 1673.4**
Smog impact fees, foreign states, **Veh 1673 et seq.**
Specially constructed vehicles, inspection and inspectors, registration, **Veh 4750.1**
Standards, **Veh 27153.5, 27156**
National Emissions Standards Act, **Veh 27156**
Used vehicles, **Veh 27157.5**
Statements of effectiveness, control devices, dealers, **Veh 24007**
Super ultralow emission vehicles, decals, **Veh 5205.5, 21655.9, 40000.13**
Tests, pretests, **Veh 4000.3**
Transfer of ownership, lessors of vehicles, **Veh 4000.1**
Transitional zero emission vehicles, decals, **Veh 5205.5**
Ultralow emission vehicles, decals, **Veh 4463, 5205.5, 21655.9, 40000.13**
United States vehicles, **Veh 2814, 27153 et seq.**
Used vehicles,
Operation after notice, **Veh 27158.5**
Standards, **Veh 27157.5**
Wilfully, definitions, crimes and offenses, gross polluters, **Veh 27156**
Motorcycles,
Aftermarket parts, **Veh 27156**
Checkpoints, emissions, **Veh 2814.1**
Motorized scooters, emissions, **Veh 12500**

AIR POLLUTION—Cont'd
Municipalities, speed limits, south coast air quality management district, **Veh 22365**
New vehicles. Motor vehicles, ante
Notice. Motor vehicles, ante
Off highway vehicles. Motor vehicles, ante
Offenses. Crimes and offenses, generally, ante
Orange County. South coast air quality management district, generally, post
Perjury, motor vehicles, smog impact fees, foreign states, **Veh 1673.6**
Registration,
Motor vehicles, ante
Transfer of title, statements, exemptions from emission test requirements, **Veh 5751.5**
Riverside County. South coast air quality management district, generally, post
Rules and regulations, fees, San Joaquin Valley unified air pollution control district, motor vehicle surcharge, **Veh 9250.16**
Sales. Motor vehicles, ante
San Bernardino County. South coast air quality management district, generally, post
Small claims courts, motor vehicles, smog impact fees, foreign states, **Veh 1673.4**
Smog impact fees, motor vehicles, foreign states, **Veh 1673 et seq.**
Smog index, program, information, **Veh 1667**
South coast air quality management district,
Accounting procedures, fees, **Veh 9250.11**
Fees, surcharges, **Veh 9250.11**
Municipalities, speed limits, **Veh 22365**
Speed limits, **Veh 22365**
Surcharges, fees, **Veh 9250.11**
Southern California air pollution control district. South coast air quality management district, generally, ante
Standards. Motor vehicles, ante
Statements of effectiveness, motor vehicle dealers, control devices, **Veh 24007**
Super ultralow emission vehicles, decals, **Veh 5205.5, 21655.9, 40000.13**
Tests. Motor vehicles, ante
Transit districts, heavy duty vehicles, emission standards, **Veh 28114**
Transitional zero emission vehicles, decals, **Veh 5205.5**
Transportation. Motor vehicles, generally, ante
Ultralow emission vehicles, decals, **Veh 4463, 5205.5, 21655.9, 40000.13**
Used vehicles. Motor vehicles, ante
Vehicles. Motor vehicles, generally, ante
Ventura County. South coast air quality management district, generally, ante

AIR QUALITY MANAGEMENT DISTRICTS
Sacramento metropolitan air quality management district, motor vehicles, registration, surcharge, **Veh 9250.2**

AIRCRAFT
Airports and Landing Fields, generally, this index
Assemblies, motor vehicle length limitation exemption, **Veh 35414**
Highway patrol, **Veh 2267**
Landing fields. Airports and Landing Fields, generally, this index
Noise Pollution, generally, this index
Refueling vehicles, registration, exemption, **Veh 4021**
Traffic rules and regulations, taxiing on local streets or county highways, **Veh 21114**

AIRPORTS AND LANDING FIELDS
Aircraft refueling vehicles, registration, exemption, **Veh 4021**
Animals, traffic regulations, **Veh 21113**
Bicycles, riding or parking on grounds, **Veh 21113**
Motor vehicles,
Aircraft refueling vehicles, registration, exemption, **Veh 4021**
Municipal airport regulations, **Veh 21113**
Shuttle vehicles, low emission vehicles, **Veh 28113**
Motorized bicycles, riding or parking on public grounds, **Veh 21113**
Private roads, local regulation, **Veh 21108**
Roller skates, riding or parking on public grounds, **Veh 21113**
Shuttle vehicles, low emission vehicles, **Veh 28113**
Skateboards, riding or parking on public grounds, **Veh 21113**
Traffic rules and regulations,
Local streets, taxiing, **Veh 21114**
Municipal airports, **Veh 21113**
Private roads, local authorities, **Veh 21108**

ALAMEDA CONTRA COSTA TRANSIT DISTRICT
Transit Districts, this index

ALAMEDA COUNTY
Highways and roads, high occupancy vehicles, exclusive or preferential use, **Veh 21655.6**

ALARM COMPANY OPERATORS
Light bars, motor vehicles, **Veh 27607**
Motor vehicles, light bars, **Veh 27607**

ALARMS
Buses, crime alarm lights, **Veh 25275.5**
Motor Vehicles, this index

ALCOHOLIC BEVERAGE CONTROL DEPARTMENT
Alcoholic Beverages, generally, this index

ALCOHOLIC BEVERAGES
Alcoholics and Alcoholism, generally, this index
Automobiles. Motor vehicles, generally, post
Boats and boating,
Drivers license suspension, **Veh 13202.5**
Reports, violations, **Veh 1803**
Checkpoints, sobriety checkpoints, traffic rules and regulations, **Veh 2814.2**
Children and minors,
Drivers license delay, restriction, suspension or revocation, designated violations, **Veh 13202.5**
Motor vehicles, post
Possession, **Veh 23224, 40000.15**
Consumption, limousine for hire passengers, exemption, **Veh 23229**
Definitions, motor vehicles, **Veh 109**
Designated driver program, information sheet, **Veh 2426**
Drivers licenses. Motor vehicles, post
Driving school operator or instructor, conviction, cancellation, license, **Veh 11110**
Driving under the influence. Traffic Rules and Regulations, this index
Limousines, this index
Minors. Children and minors, generally, ante
Motor vehicles,
Alcohol and drug problem assessment program, **Veh 23249.50**
Blood alcohol concentration table published in handbook, drivers license examination, **Veh 1666**
Children and minors, **Veh 23140**
Containing beverages, operation by persons under 21 years, **Veh 23224, 40000.15**
Drivers licenses, revocation or suspension, **Veh 13202.5**
Children and minors, **Veh 23224**
Driving under the influence, **Veh 13352 et seq.**
Traffic Rules and Regulations, this index
Violations, drivers license delay, restriction, suspension or revocation, **Veh 13202.5**
Possession,
Children and minors, **Veh 23224, 40000.15**
Limousines for hire, passengers, exemptions, **Veh 23229**
Problem assessment program, motor vehicle drivers, **Veh 23249.50**
Schools and School Districts, this index
Sobriety checkpoints, traffic rules and regulations, **Veh 2814.2**
Traffic Rules and Regulations, this index
Vehicles. Motor vehicles, generally, ante

ALCOHOLICS AND ALCOHOLISM
Checkpoints, sobriety checkpoints, **Veh 2814.2**

ALCOHOLICS AND ALCOHOLISM—Cont'd
Detoxification vehicles, utility flood or loading lamps, **Veh 25110**
Drivers licenses, **Veh 12806**
Driving under the influence. Traffic Rules and Regulations, this index
Education, driving under the influence, **Veh 23502, 23520, 23538, 23542 et seq., 23640 et seq., 23670**
Flood or loading lamps, detoxification vehicle, **Veh 25110**
Motor vehicles,
Assessment program, **Veh 23249.50**
Drivers licenses, **Veh 12806**
Rehabilitation center residents, **Veh 23213**
Problem assessment program, motor vehicle drivers, **Veh 23249.50**
Radioactive materials, transportation, drivers certificates, denial, **Veh 12524**
Rehabilitation programs, motor vehicles, rehab center residents, **Veh 23213**
Sobriety checkpoints, **Veh 2814.2**
Treatment, driving under the influence, **Veh 23538, 23542 et seq., 23640 et seq., 23670**
Children and minors, **Veh 23520**
Vehicles, detoxification vehicles, utility flood or loading lamps, **Veh 25110**

ALIAS
Assumed or Fictitious Names, generally, this index

ALIENS
Children and minors, deferred action for childhood arrivals. Immigration, this index
Deferred action for childhood arrivals. Immigration, this index
Deportation, drivers licenses, **Veh 12801.7**
Drivers licenses. Motor Vehicles, this index
Identification cards, deportation, **Veh 12801.7**
Motor Vehicles, this index

ALKALI MALLOW
Weeds, generally, this index

ALLEYS
Streets and Alleys, generally, this index

ALMONDS
Trailers, towing, weight limitations, **Veh 36627**

ALPHA PARTICLES
Atomic Energy, generally, this index

ALTERATION OF INSTRUMENTS
Operators and chauffeurs licenses, **Veh 14610**

ALTERNATIVE FUEL VEHICLES
Motor Vehicles, this index

AMBASSADORS AND CONSULS
Motor vehicles, drivers licenses, exemptions, Veh 12502

AMBER
Definitions, motor vehicle equipment, **Veh 112**

AMBER LIGHTS
Motor Vehicles, this index

AMBRIZ, STEVE ACT
Generally, **Veh 13385**

AMBULANCES
Cardiopulmonary resuscitation, liability for attempts, rescue teams, **Veh 165.5**
Certificates and certification. Drivers, post
Clearance and side marker lamps, equipment, **Veh 25100.1**
Definitions, **Veh 165**
Demonstrators, warning lamps and sirens, **Veh 25806**
Dispatchers, emergency medical dispatcher training, **Veh 2422**
Drivers, certificates and certification, **Veh 2512, 12527**
  Refusal, suspension or revocation, **Veh 13372 et seq.**
Earplugs, wearing while operating, **Veh 27400**
Emergency ambulance, definitions, resuscitation equipment, **Veh 2418.5**
Emergency medical dispatchers, training, **Veh 2422**
Emergency medical training, drivers, **Veh 12527**
Equipment,
  Clearance and side marker lamps, **Veh 25100.1**
  Identification lamps, **Veh 25351**
  Warning lamps and sirens, demonstrators or delivery to purchaser, **Veh 25806**
Exemptions,
  Drivers, emergency medical training, **Veh 12527**
  Fees, **Veh 9104**
  Pollution control devices, **Veh 27156.2, 27156.3**
Fees,
  Drivers certification, **Veh 2512**
  Exemptions, **Veh 9104**
Handbooks for drivers, **Veh 2512**
Hazardous substances and waste, signs and signals, exemptions, **Veh 27903**
Headsets, wearing while operating, **Veh 27400**
Hearings, drivers, certificates, refusal, suspension or revocation, **Veh 13374**
Identification lamps, **Veh 25351**
Indians, fees, exemptions, **Veh 9104.2**
Inspection and inspectors, licenses and permits, **Veh 2510**
Licenses and permits, **Veh 2416**
  Eligibility, **Veh 2511**

AMBULANCES—Cont'd
Licenses and permits—Cont'd
  Privately owned and operated ambulances, **Veh 2500 et seq.**
  Regulations, **Veh 2512**
  Revocation or suspension, **Veh 2417, 2512, 2540 et seq.**
Lights and lighting,
  Utility flood or loading lamps, **Veh 25110**
  Warning lamps and sirens, demonstrators or delivery to purchaser, **Veh 25806**
Limitation of actions, revocation of licenses, **Veh 2547**
Motor vehicle accidents, transportation of injured persons, expenses, liability of public employees, **Veh 20016**
Owners and ownership, changes, licenses and permits, **Veh 2503**
Peace officers, emergency vehicles, **Veh 165**
Pet ambulances, warning lights, **Veh 25271**
Pollution control devices, **Veh 27156.2, 27156.3**
Privately owned ambulances, transportation of medical supplies, lifesaving equipment or personnel, emergency vehicle status, **Veh 2416**
Public officers and employees, liability for expenses, **Veh 20016**
Qualifications, drivers, **Veh 2512**
Rescue teams, liability for resuscitation attempts, **Veh 165.5**
Resuscitator, **Veh 2418.5**
Rules and regulations, **Veh 2512**
Safety headsets, wearing while operating, **Veh 27400**
Sirens and warning lamps, demonstrators or delivery to purchaser, **Veh 25806**
Statute of limitations, revocation of licenses, **Veh 2547**
Theft, **Veh 10851**
Time, licenses and permits, staggered renewals, **Veh 2505**
Training,
  Drivers, emergency medical training, **Veh 12527**
  Rescue teams, **Veh 165.5**
Utility flood or loading lamps, **Veh 25110**
Volunteers, drivers, emergency medical training, exemptions, **Veh 12527**
Warning lamps and sirens, demonstrators or delivery to purchaser, **Veh 25806**
Weight limit exemption, **Veh 35714, 35720**

AMIDONE
Drug Addicts, generally, this index

AMMONIUM NITRATE
Fertilizers, this index

AMMUNITION
Motor vehicles, bullet marks, reports, **Veh 10653**

AMNESTY
Motor vehicles, registration, fees, specially constructed vehicles, inspection and inspectors, emissions, **Veh 4750.1**
Traffic rules and regulations, fines and penalties, **Veh 42008.5, 42008.7**

AMPHIBIOUS VEHICLES
Certificate of ownership, issuance, **Veh 9872.5**
Definitions, certificate of ownership, **Veh 9872.5**

AMPLIFICATION DEVICES
Motor vehicles, **Veh 27007**

ANATOMICAL GIFTS
Motor vehicles,
  Drivers licenses, **Veh 12811**
    Information, **Veh 1672**
    Stickers, **Veh 1672.5**
  Identification cards, **Veh 12811, 13005**
    Information, **Veh 1672**
    Stickers, **Veh 1672.5**

ANIMAL CONTROL
Enforcement vehicles, amber warning lights, **Veh 25271.5**

ANIMAL DISEASES
Medical waste. Hazardous Substances and Waste, this index

ANIMALS
Abandoned or unclaimed property,
  Drivers handbook, **Veh 1656.3**
    Drivers licenses, examiners and examinations, **Veh 1666.5**
    Traffic signs and signals, crimes and offenses, **Veh 21376**
Airports and landing fields, traffic regulations, **Veh 21113**
Ambulances, warning lights on pet ambulances, **Veh 25271**
Carriers. Livestock carriers, generally, post
Colleges and universities, traffic regulations, **Veh 21113**
Commuter rail system, traffic regulations, **Veh 21113**
County parks, traffic regulations, **Veh 21113**
Crossings, signs, **Veh 21364**
Drivers or riders, application of traffic laws, **Veh 21050**
Education, traffic rules and regulations, **Veh 21113**
Exemptions, livestock carriers, access, **Veh 35401.7**
Fences, generally, this index
Fish and Game, generally, this index
Game. Fish and Game, generally, this index
Harbor districts, traffic regulations, **Veh 21113**
Hospitals, traffic regulations, **Veh 21113**
Licenses and permits, livestock carriers, studies, **Veh 35401.7**

ANIMALS—Cont'd
Livestock carriers,
Access, exemptions, **Veh 35401.7**
Drivers licenses, restricted, towing, **Veh 12804.14**
Exemptions, access, **Veh 35401.7**
Licenses and permits, studies, **Veh 35401.7**
Reports, access, exemptions, **Veh 35401.7**
Towing, restricted drivers licenses, **Veh 12804.14**
Medical waste. Hazardous Substances and Waste, this index
Motor carriers,
Field loaded livestock, weight limitations, penalties, **Veh 42030**
Inspection, **Veh 2810**
Livestock carriers, generally, ante
Motor vehicles,
Herding, flashing amber lights, **Veh 25270.5**
Towing, restricted drivers licenses, **Veh 12804.14**
Transporting, restraints, **Veh 23117, 42001.4**
Municipal airports, traffic regulations, **Veh 21113**
Noise Pollution, generally, this index
Obedience to traffic signals, person in charge, **Veh 21462**
Open livestock range, signs, **Veh 21365**
Parks, this index
Rapid transit districts, traffic regulations, **Veh 21113**
Reports, livestock carriers, access, exemptions, **Veh 35401.7**
Riding, application of traffic laws, **Veh 21050**
Schools and School Districts, this index
State parks, traffic regulations, **Veh 21113**
Towing, restricted drivers licenses, **Veh 12804.14**
Traffic Rules and Regulations, this index
Traffic Signs and Signals, this index
Transit districts, traffic regulations, **Veh 21113**
Transportation,
Livestock carriers, generally, ante
Truck axle weight limitations, **Veh 35551.5**
Wild animals and birds. Fish and Game, generally, this index

ANSWER
Pleadings, this index

ANTIGRIDLOCK ACT
Generally, **Veh 22526**

ANTIQUE CARS
Historic Vehicles, generally, this index

ANTISIPHONING DEVICE
Definitions, motor vehicles, **Veh 28110**

ANTITERRORISM FUND
Generally, **Veh 5066**

APARTMENT HOUSES
Business structures, definitions, motor vehicles, **Veh 240**

APPARATUS
Machinery and Equipment, generally, this index

APPEAL AND REVIEW
Drivers licenses. Motor Vehicles, this index
Driving school operator and instructor, cancellation, license, **Veh 11111**
Highways and Roads, this index
Motor Vehicles, this index
Parking, San Francisco City and County, buses, videotape, transit only traffic lanes, **Veh 40241**
Stay. Supersedeas or Stay, generally, this index
Supersedeas or Stay, generally, this index
Traffic rules and regulations, parking, San Francisco City and County, buses, videotape, transit only traffic lanes, **Veh 40241**

APPEARANCE
Children and Minors, this index
Parking violations, motor vehicles, **Veh 40230**
Traffic Rules and Regulations, this index

APPRAISAL AND APPRAISERS
Motor vehicles, abandoned vehicles, **Veh 22855**

APPROPRIATE VICTIMS
Definitions, youthful drunk driver visitation program, **Veh 23517**

AQUATIC ORGANISMS
Fish and Game, generally, this index

AQUEDUCTS
Vehicles used in construction, maintenance, patrol of inspection, flashing amber lights, **Veh 25266**

ARBITRATION AND AWARD
Motor Vehicles, this index

ARM SIGNALS
Traffic signs and signals, turning, **Veh 22110, 22111**

ARMED FORCES
Military Forces, generally, this index

ARMORED CARS
Definitions, **Veh 115**
Inspection and inspectors, licenses and permits, **Veh 2510**
Licenses and permits, **Veh 2500 et seq., 21713**
Eligibility, **Veh 2511**
Revocation or suspension, **Veh 2540 et seq.**
Rules and regulations, **Veh 2512**
Lights and lighting, red light, robbery, use while resisting, **Veh 25262**

ARMORED CARS—Cont'd
Limitation of actions, revocation of license, **Veh 2547**
Owners and ownership, changes, licenses and permits, **Veh 2503**
Red lights, **Veh 25262**
Sirens, **Veh 27003**
Resisting armed robbery, **Veh 27003**
Statute of limitations, revocation of license, **Veh 2547**
Time, licenses and permits, staggered renewals, **Veh 2505**
Traffic rules and regulations, licenses, **Veh 21713**

ARMS
Weapons, generally, this index

ARMY
Military Forces, generally, this index

ARRAIGNMENT
Bail, generally, this index
Closed circuit television, infractions or misdemeanors, Placer County, **Veh 40502.1**
Motor Vehicles, this index
Placer County, closed circuit television, infractions or misdemeanors, **Veh 40502.1**
Television and radio, closed circuit television, infractions or misdemeanors, Placer County, **Veh 40502.1**
Traffic Rules and Regulations, this index

ARREST
Children and Minors, this index
Colleges and Universities, this index
Contempt, generally, this index
Counties, this index
Evasion of arrest, motorists, option of officer to take arrested person before magistrate, **Veh 40303**
Fines and penalties, receipts, **Veh 40312**
Fingerprints and Fingerprinting, generally, this index
Highway Patrol, this index
Infractions, this index
Licenses and permits, producing drivers license, **Veh 12951**
Pedestrians, refusal to leave freeway, overpass or highway, **Veh 40303**
Production of drivers license in court, **Veh 12951**
Quotas, peace officers, **Veh 41600 et seq.**
Receipts, fines paid, **Veh 40312**
Searches and Seizures, generally, this index
Thumbprints, **Veh 40500, 40504**
Traffic Rules and Regulations, this index
Warrants. Traffic Rules and Regulations, this index

ARREST QUOTAS
Definitions, peace officers, **Veh 41600**

ARROWS
Traffic Signs and Signals, this index

ART AND ARTISTS
Motor vehicles, special license plates, **Veh 5074**

ASPHALT
Spreaders, special highway construction equipment, **Veh 565**

ASSAULT AND BATTERY
Motor vehicles, used as deadly weapon, driver license revocation, **Veh 13351.5**
Traffic Rules and Regulations, this index
Weapons, drivers licenses, revocation, **Veh 13351.5**

ASSEMBLY
Traffic rules and regulations, local regulations, **Veh 21100 et seq.**

ASSESSMENTS
Driver and peace officer training, vehicle code violations, night court assessments, **Veh 42006**
Motor Vehicles, this index
Traffic Rules and Regulations, this index

ASSIGNMENTS
Motor Vehicles, this index

ASSISTIVE DEVICES
Handicapped Persons, this index

ASSOCIATIONS AND SOCIETIES
Badges, Emblems and Insignia, generally, this index
Business structures, definitions, motor vehicles, **Veh 240**
Cemetery associations. Cemeteries and Dead Bodies, generally, this index
Charities, generally, this index
Definitions, business structures, motor vehicles, **Veh 240**
Highway patrol department, membership fees, joining, **Veh 2114**
Motor vehicles department, membership fees, joining, **Veh 1658**
Religious Organizations and Societies, generally, this index

ASSUMED OR FICTITIOUS NAMES
Automobile dismantlers, license revocation, **Veh 11509**
Motor Vehicles, this index
Notice, correction of violations, false or fictitious name, **Veh 40614**
Traffic rules and regulations, arrested persons, promise to appear, **Veh 40504**

ASYLUMS
Mentally Ill Persons, generally, this index

ATHLETICS
Golf Carts, generally, this index

ATOMIC ENERGY
Confidential or privileged information, spent radioactive fuel, transportation, notice, **Veh 33002**
Motor carriers,
Signs, display, **Veh 27903**

ATOMIC ENERGY—Cont'd
Motor carriers—Cont'd
Transporting, **Veh 33000**
Spent radioactive fuel, notice, **Veh 33002**
Notice, transportation of spent radioactive fuel, **Veh 33002**
Signs on vehicles carrying radioactive materials, **Veh 27903**
Transportation,
Markings, **Veh 27903**
Rules and regulations, time and routes, **Veh 33000**

ATOMIC WAR
War and Civil Defense, generally, this index

ATTEMPTS
Fines and penalties, disabled person placards, motor vehicles, **Veh 4463.3**
Motor vehicles, flight from peace officers, **Veh 2800.1 et seq., 13201**

ATTORNEY FEES
Motor Vehicles, this index

ATTORNEY GENERAL
Address, home address, confidential, **Veh 1808.4**
Confidential and privileged information, home address, **Veh 1808.4**
Motor vehicles, records and recordation, access, **Veh 1810.5**

ATTORNEYS
Accident reports, disclosure by department of highway patrol or law enforcement agency, **Veh 20012**
Adverse or pecuniary interest, disclosure, **Veh 1808.46**
Affidavits, generally, this index
Attorney General, generally, this index
Child abuse cases, county counsels, addresses, confidentiality, **Veh 1808.4**
Confidential or privileged information, disclosure, **Veh 1808.46**
Counsel for accused. Crimes and Offenses, this index
District Attorneys, generally, this index
Fines and penalties, confidential information, disclosure, **Veh 1808.46**
Indigent persons. Public Defenders, generally, this index
Judges, generally, this index
Motor Vehicles, this index
Municipal Attorneys, generally, this index
Public employers, attorneys for, home addresses, confidentiality, **Veh 1808.4**
Right to counsel, counsel for accused. Crimes and Offenses, this index
Traffic offenses, appearance, sufficiency under written promise, **Veh 40507**

ATTRACTIVE NUISANCE
Nuisance, generally, this index

AUCTIONS AND AUCTIONEERS
Abandoned or Unclaimed Property, this index
Dealers, definitions, motor vehicles, **Veh 286**
Highway patrol, unclaimed property, **Veh 2415**
Motor Vehicles, this index

AUDITS AND AUDITORS
County Auditors, generally, this index
Motor Carriers, this index
Motor Vehicles, this index
Recreational Vehicles, this index
Traffic rules and regulations, handicapped persons, parking, placards, **Veh 1825**

AUSTRIAN FIELD CRESS
Weeds, generally, this index

AUTHORITIES
Cemetery authority. Cemeteries and Dead Bodies, generally, this index
Housing Authorities, generally, this index
Juvenile Facilities Division, generally, this index

AUTHORIZED DRIVER
Definitions, drivers licenses, **Veh 40000.11**

AUTHORIZED EMERGENCY VEHICLES
Emergency Vehicles, generally, this index

AUTOETTES
Generally, **Veh 175**
Registration, **Veh 4000.5**

AUTOMATED ENFORCEMENT SYSTEMS
Traffic Signs and Signals, this index

AUTOMATIC BALE WAGONS
Agricultural Machinery and Equipment, this index
Definitions, **Veh 36011**

AUTOMATIC VEHICLE IDENTIFICATION SYSTEMS
Toll roads and bridges. Highways and Roads, this index

AUTOMOBILE DISMANTLERS TOW VEHICLE
Definitions, **Veh 615**

AUTOMOBILE INSURANCE
Motor Vehicle Insurance, generally, this index

AUTOMOBILES
Generally, **Veh 1 et seq.**
Motor Vehicles, generally, this index

AUTOMOTIVE REPAIR FACILITIES
Motor Vehicle Repair Dealers, generally, this index

AUTONOMOUS VEHICLES
Generally, **Veh 38750 et seq.**

AUXILIARY DOLLIES
Motor Carriers, this index

AVENUES
Streets and Alleys, generally, this index

AVERAGE DAILY ATTENDANCE
Community colleges and districts. Colleges and Universities, this index
Schools and School Districts, this index

AVIATION
Aircraft, generally, this index

AVOIRDUPOIS WEIGHT
Weights and Measures, generally, this index

AWNINGS
Recreational vehicles, width, **Veh 35103**

AXLES
Motor Vehicles, this index

B TRAIN ASSEMBLY
Definitions, motor vehicles, **Veh 230.5**

BABIES
Children and Minors, generally, this index

BACKGROUND CHECKS
Criminal History Information, generally, this index

BACKING VEHICLES
Traffic rules and regulations, **Veh 22106**

BACKUP LAMPS
Motor vehicles, **Veh 24606**

BAD CHECKS
Negotiable Instruments, this index

BADGES, EMBLEMS AND INSIGNIA
Agricultural machinery and equipment, slow moving vehicle emblem, display, **Veh 24615, 36508**
Handicapped parking, special enforcement units, **Veh 22507.9**
Highway Patrol, this index
Law enforcement vehicles, removal, sale or nonlaw enforcement use, **Veh 27604**
Motor carriers, weight fees, certificates, **Veh 5206**
Motor vehicles,
  Police cars, removal on sale or nonlaw enforcement use, **Veh 27604**
  Reflectorizing material, use, **Veh 25500**
Motorcycles, former police vehicles, exemption, **Veh 27604**
Physicians and surgeons, vehicles, exemption from traffic regulation, **Veh 21058**

BAIL
Commercially registered motor vehicle, guaranteed traffic bail bond certificate, nonresidents, **Veh 40305.5**
Definitions, traffic rules and regulations, amnesty, **Veh 42008.7**
Forfeitures, traffic violator schools,
  Installment payments, fees, **Veh 42007**
  Proof of completion, **Veh 40512.6**

BAIL—Cont'd
Guaranteed traffic arrest bail bond certificate, nonresidents, **Veh 40305.5**
Impounding, motor vehicles, **Veh 22651**
Infractions, this index
Interest, refunds, traffic rules and regulations, **Veh 42201.6**
Motor vehicles,
  Guaranteed traffic arrest bail bond certificate, nonresidents, **Veh 40305.5**
  Impounding, **Veh 22651**
Nonresidents, guaranteed traffic arrest bail bond certificate, **Veh 40305.5**
Solid Waste, this index
Traffic Rules and Regulations, this index
Traffic Violator Schools, this index

BAILMENT
Bills of Lading, generally, this index
Motor Vehicles, this index

BANK DEPOSITS AND COLLECTIONS
Abandoned or Unclaimed Property, generally, this index
Unclaimed property. Abandoned or Unclaimed Property, generally, this index

BANKRUPTCY
Motor vehicles, consumer protection, recovery corporation, **Veh 12200 et seq.**

BANKS AND BANKING
Abandoned or Unclaimed Property, generally, this index
Bills and notes. Negotiable Instruments, generally, this index
Dealers, definitions, motor vehicles, **Veh 286**
Motor vehicles, address, confidential or privileged information, records and recordation, **Veh 1808.22**
Negotiable Instruments, generally, this index
Unclaimed property. Abandoned or Unclaimed Property, generally, this index

BANNERS
Motor vehicles, disabled vehicles, **Veh 25300**

BARRICADES
Traffic Rules and Regulations, this index

BEADS
Motor vehicle tires, protuberances, **Veh 27454**

BEAM INDICATOR
Motor vehicle equipment, requirement, **Veh 24408**

BELOTTI CHRISTENSEN ACT
Logging trucks, **Veh 35552**

BENEVOLENT ASSOCIATIONS OR CORPORATIONS
Insurance, generally, this index

BEQUESTS
Gifts, Devises and Bequests, generally, this index

BETA PARTICLES
Atomic Energy, generally, this index

BEVERAGES
Alcoholic Beverages, generally, this index

BIAS AND PREJUDICE
Motor vehicle accident reports, **Veh 20012**

BICYCLE LICENSE FUND
Deposit of license fees, **Veh 39001**

BICYCLES
Address, change, notice to licensing agency, **Veh 39009**
Age, motorized bicycles, operation, **Veh 24016**
Alcoholic beverages, driving while intoxicated, **Veh 40000.13, 40303**
Alteration, license indicia, registration forms, serial numbers or identification marks, crimes and offenses, **Veh 39002**
Assembled bicycles delivered to purchaser, preregistration forms, **Veh 39006**
Bicycle lanes. Lanes, generally, post
Bicycle license fund, deposit of license fees, **Veh 39001**
Bikeways,
  Crossings, **Veh 231.6**
  Electric personal assistive mobility devices, **Veh 21280 et seq.**
  Lights and lighting, **Veh 21201**
  Local authorities, **Veh 21207**
  Motorized scooters, rules of the road, **Veh 21230**
  Motorized skateboards, **Veh 21968**
  Obstruction, **Veh 21211**
  Personal assistive mobility devices, **Veh 21280 et seq.**
  Reflectors, **Veh 21201**
  Skateboards, motorized skateboards, **Veh 21968**
  Tow trucks, obstruction, **Veh 21211**
Blocking bicycle lanes, **Veh 21211**
Brakes, equipment, **Veh 21201**
Brands, marks and labels, helmets, **Veh 21212**
Buses, this index
Carrying articles, **Veh 21205**
Children and minors, motorized bicycles, instruction permits, **Veh 12509.5**
Consumer product safety commission regulations, reflectors, **Veh 21201.5**
Costs, schedule of costs, infractions, **Veh 42001**
Counties, this index
Crimes and offenses, **Veh 39002**
  Tampering, destruction or mutilation, license indicia, registration forms, serial numbers, **Veh 39002**
Dealers, information supplied to purchaser, preregistration forms, **Veh 39006**

BICYCLES—Cont'd
Definitions, **Veh 231**
   Licenses, **Veh 39000**
      Operation on roadways, **Veh 21200**
Disclosure, insurance, **Veh 406**
Earplugs, **Veh 27400**
Emergencies, peace officers, traffic rules and regulations, exemptions, **Veh 21200**
Equipment, **Veh 21201**
   Notice to correct, crimes and offenses, **Veh 40303.5**
   Reflectors, **Veh 21201, 21201.5**
Exemption, registration, motorized bicycles, **Veh 4020**
Expiration date, licenses, **Veh 39001**
Facilities, **Veh 39001**
   Disposition of license fees, **Veh 39004**
Fees,
   Licenses, **Veh 39001, 39004**
   Registration certificates, **Veh 39004**
Fines and penalties,
   Driving while intoxicated, **Veh 21200**
   Helmets, bicyclist use, **Veh 21212**
   Licenses, **Veh 39011**
   Registration, **Veh 39011**
   Schedules, establishment, **Veh 42001**
Forms, registration forms, **Veh 39001 et seq.**
Freeways, this index
Hand signals, **Veh 22111**
Handlebars, riders, **Veh 21204**
Headsets, **Veh 27400**
Helmets,
   Motorized bicycles, post
   Use, bicyclists and passengers, **Veh 21212**
Hiking trails, motorized bicycles, **Veh 21207.5**
Hitching rides on vehicles, **Veh 21203**
Indicia for licenses, design, issuance, **Veh 39001, 39003**
Instruction permits, motorized bicycles, **Veh 12509.5**
Insurance, disclosure, **Veh 406**
Lanes, **Veh 21207 et seq.**
   Blocking, **Veh 21211**
   Motor vehicles, driving in bicycle lane, restrictions, **Veh 21209**
   Motorized bicycles, **Veh 21207.5**
      Speed, **Veh 21209**
   Motorized scooters, rules of the road, **Veh 21229**
   Obstruction, **Veh 21211**
   Parking, **Veh 21211**
   Pedestrians, **Veh 21966**
   Permitted movements from lanes, **Veh 21208**
   Public utility vehicles, **Veh 22512**
   Speed, **Veh 21209**
Left side of road, **Veh 21202**
License plates, motorized bicycles, **Veh 5030 et seq.**
Licenses and permits, **Veh 21206, 39000 et seq.**
Lights and lighting, **Veh 21201**

BICYCLES—Cont'd
Local authorities, regulation, **Veh 21206, 21207**
Mopeds, definitions, **Veh 406**
Motor Driven Cycles, generally, this index
Motor vehicles, bicycle lanes, driving motor vehicle in, restrictions, **Veh 21209**
Motorized bicycles,
   Age, operation, **Veh 24016**
   Attachment to other vehicles, **Veh 21203, 21712**
   Brakes, **Veh 24015**
   Children and minors, instruction permits, **Veh 12509.5**
   Definitions, **Veh 406**
   Drivers licenses, **Veh 12500 et seq., 12509**
      Examiners and examinations, exemptions, **Veh 12804.9**
   Equipment and manufacturing requirements, **Veh 24016**
   Footrests, passengers, **Veh 27800**
   Freeways, **Veh 21960**
      Drivers licenses, **Veh 12500 et seq.**
      Instruction permits, **Veh 12509.5**
   Headlights, **Veh 25650 et seq.**
   Helmets, **Veh 27802**
      Adoption and enforcement of standards and specifications, **Veh 26103**
      Wearing regulations, drivers and passengers, **Veh 27803**
   Instruction permits, **Veh 12509.5**
   Lanes, **Veh 21207.5**
      Speed, **Veh 21209**
   Lights, **Veh 24015**
   Modification, operation on highway following nonconforming modification, **Veh 23135**
   Motorized Scooters, generally, this index
   Mufflers, **Veh 24015**
   Nighttime, instruction permits, **Veh 12509.5**
   Operation, **Veh 24016**
      On bicycle path, **Veh 21207.5**
   Public grounds, riding or parking, **Veh 21113**
   Reflectors, **Veh 24015**
   Registration, **Veh 4020, 5030 et seq.**
   Safety standards, **Veh 24015**
   Seats, passengers, **Veh 27800**
   Tampering, **Veh 24016**
   Towing, **Veh 21712**
   Traffic Rules and Regulations, this index
   Vehicular crossings, **Veh 23330**
Motorized Scooters, generally, this index
Municipalities, this index
Mutilation, license indicia or registration forms, serial numbers or identification marks, **Veh 39002**
Nighttime, motorized bicycles, instruction permits, **Veh 12509.5**

BICYCLES—Cont'd
Notice,
   Change of address, notice to licensing agency, **Veh 39009**
   Sales, notice to licensing agency, **Veh 39008**
   Unauthorized vehicles, **Veh 23127**
Obstructing bicycle lanes, **Veh 21211**
Overtaking and passing, **Veh 21750 et seq., 21760**
Parking, **Veh 21210**
   Blocking lanes, **Veh 21211**
Passengers, seats, **Veh 21204**
Paths. Bikeways, generally, ante
Peace officers, traffic rules and regulations, exemptions, **Veh 21200**
Pedicabs,
   Definitions, **Veh 467.5**
   Traffic rules and regulations, **Veh 21100, 21200**
Penalties. Fines and penalties, generally, ante
Preregistration forms, **Veh 39006**
Prosthetic devices, **Veh 27400**
Public grounds, riding or parking, **Veh 21113**
Public utility vehicles, obstructing lanes, **Veh 22512**
Pursuit, peace officers, traffic rules and regulations, exemptions, **Veh 21200**
Radios, headsets or earplugs, **Veh 27400**
Records and recordation,
   Registered bicycles, **Veh 39005**
   Retailers, information supplied to purchasers, **Veh 39006**
Recreational trails, motorized bicycles, **Veh 21207.5**
Reflectors, **Veh 21201, 21201.5**
Registration certificates, endorsement upon sale, **Veh 39008**
Registration forms, **Veh 39001 et seq.**
   Duplicates, **Veh 39009**
Removal, serial numbers or identification marks, crimes and offenses, **Veh 39002**
Renewal of licenses, **Veh 39001**
   Fees, **Veh 39004**
Rescue, peace officers, traffic rules and regulations, exemptions, **Veh 21200**
Riders, **Veh 21204**
   Motor vehicles, towing, **Veh 21712**
Right of way, **Veh 21804**
Right side of road, **Veh 21202**
Right turns, **Veh 21202**
Road rage. Traffic Rules and Regulations, this index
Routes. Bikeways, generally, ante
Rules and regulations, **Veh 21113**
Safety,
   Helmets, motorized bicycles, **Veh 27802**
      Wearing regulations, drivers and passengers, **Veh 27803**
   Programs, disposition of license fees, **Veh 39004**
Sales,
   Bicycle helmets, **Veh 21212**

BICYCLES—Cont'd

Sales—Cont'd

Endorsement, registration certificates, **Veh 39008**

Notice to licensing agency, **Veh 39008**

Records, information supplied by retailer to purchaser, **Veh 39006**

Reflectors, **Veh 21201.5**

Registration certificates, endorsement, **Veh 39008**

Serial number, **Veh 39007**

Schedules, fines and costs, bicycle infractions, **Veh 42001**

Schools and School Districts, this index

Seats, passengers, **Veh 21204**

Serial numbers,

Records and recordation, **Veh 39005**

Removal or mutilation, **Veh 39002**

Retailers, information supplied to purchaser, **Veh 39006**

Sales by retailers, **Veh 39007**

Records, information supplied to purchaser, **Veh 39006**

Shoulder of road, powers and duties, **Veh 21200**

Sidewalks,

Lights and lighting, **Veh 21201**

Local regulations, **Veh 21100**

Speed, motorized bicycle lanes, **Veh 21209**

Standards, bicycle helmets, **Veh 21212**

Stopping, blocking lanes, **Veh 21211**

Street Railways, this index

Streets and alleys,

Bicycle lanes, **Veh 21207**

Exits, driver warnings, **Veh 21356.5**

Tampering,

License indicia or registration form, crimes and offenses, **Veh 39002**

Motorized bicycles, **Veh 24016**

Tires, reflectorized tires, **Veh 21201.5**

Tow trucks, bikeways, obstruction, **Veh 21211**

Traffic Rules and Regulations, this index

Traffic safety program, **Veh 2900 et seq.**

Traffic signs and signals, **Veh 21450**

Traffic actuated signals, **Veh 21450.5**

Traffic violator schools, right of way, courses of study, **Veh 11219.3**

Trails. Bikeways, generally, ante

Transfer,

Endorsement of registration certificates, **Veh 39008**

Licenses, **Veh 39008**

Transit Districts, this index

BIDS AND BIDDING

Highway patrol, unclaimed property sale, **Veh 2415**

Motor Vehicles, this index

BIENNIAL INSPECTION OF TERMINALS PROGRAM

Generally, **Veh 34501.12**

BIKEWAYS

Bicycles, this index

BILLBOARDS

Outdoor Advertising, generally, this index

BILLS

Negotiable Instruments, generally, this index

BILLS OF EXCHANGE

Negotiable Instruments, generally, this index

BILLS OF LADING

Explosives, vehicle transporting, **Veh 31612**

Hazardous substances haulers, **Veh 34510**

Inspection and inspectors, **Veh 2810**

Load removal, traffic officers, **Veh 2803**

Traffic officers, load removal, **Veh 2803**

Transportation,

Explosives, motor carriers, **Veh 31612**

Timber and lumber, inspection, **Veh 2810**

BILLY

Weapons, generally, this index

BIOANALYSTS

Clinical Laboratories, this index

BIRTH

Drivers license, renewal on birth date, **Veh 12816**

Midwives, generally, this index

BIRTH CERTIFICATES

Vital Statistics, this index

BIT

Biennial inspection of terminals program, motor carriers, **Veh 34501.12**

BITUMINOUS MIXERS

Special highway construction equipment, **Veh 565**

BLACK POWDER

Explosives, generally, this index

BLACKJACKS

Weapons, generally, this index

BLANK CARTRIDGES

Fireworks, generally, this index

BLANK FORMS

Forms, generally, this index

BLASTING CAPS

Explosives, generally, this index

BLIGHTED AREAS

Housing Authorities, generally, this index

BLIND INTERSECTION LAW

Generally, **Veh 22352**

BLIND PERSONS

Crimes and offenses, right of way, **Veh 21963**

Definitions, traffic rules and regulations, **Veh 21965**

BLIND PERSONS—Cont'd

Fines and penalties, right of way, **Veh 21963**

Motor Vehicles, this index

Right of way, **Veh 21963 et seq.**

Traffic rules and regulations, right of way, **Veh 21963 et seq.**

Veterans, motor vehicle fees, exemptions, **Veh 9105**

White canes,

Carrying, persons other than blind, **Veh 21964**

Right of way, **Veh 21963 et seq.**

BLINDING LIGHTS

Motor vehicle spotlamps, **Veh 24404**

BLOCKS

Motor vehicle tire, protuberances, **Veh 27454**

BLOOD

Medical waste. Hazardous Substances and Waste, this index

BLOOD TESTS

Clinical Laboratories, this index

Driving under the influence. Traffic Rules and Regulations, this index

Emergency Medical Technicians, this index

Motor vehicles, alcohol concentration table, handbooks, drivers licenses, examinations and examiners, **Veh 1666**

Nurses, this index

Privileges and immunities, alcoholic content, **Veh 23158**

Vocational Nursing, this index

BLUE LIGHTS

Emergency Vehicles, this index

BLUEWEED

Weeds, generally, this index

BOARD OF DIRECTORS

Directors, generally, this index

BOARD OF SUPERVISORS

County Supervisors Boards, generally, this index

BOARDS AND COMMISSIONS

Administrative Law and Procedure, generally, this index

Buildings. Public Buildings and Works, generally, this index

County Supervisors Boards, generally, this index

Court Commissioners, generally, this index

Economic auto theft, claims board, **Veh 10902**

Motor Vehicles, this index

New motor vehicle board. Motor Vehicles Department, this index

Parole Hearings Board, generally, this index

Public Agencies, generally, this index

BOARDS AND COMMISSIONS—Cont'd
Supervisors, county board of. County Supervisors Boards, generally, this index

BOATS AND BOATING
Additional fees, certificates of number, **Veh 9853, 9853.6**
Alcoholic Beverages, this index
Assessors,
Numbers, change of ownership, **Veh 9856**
Registration information, **Veh 9869**
Assignment, title or interest in vessel, **Veh 9906**
Bonds (officers and fiduciaries), transfer of title of interest, **Veh 9923, 9924**
Brands, marks and labels, engines, **Veh 9853.7**
Builder hull identification number, **Veh 9871, 9872**
Registration, renewal, **Veh 9871.5**
Cancellation, certificates or registration, **Veh 9874**
Canoes, number or registration, **Veh 9873**
Certificates of number, **Veh 9850 et seq.**
Additional fees, **Veh 9853, 9853.6**
Address change, **Veh 9865**
Agent for issuance, **Veh 9858, 9859**
Applications, **Veh 9853 et seq.**
Cancellation, **Veh 9874**
Change of owner, **Veh 9855**
Documentary preparation charges, **Veh 9858.1**
Duplicate, fee, **Veh 9867**
Engines, emissions, **Veh 9852.9, 9853.7**
Exemptions, **Veh 9873**
Expiration, **Veh 9861**
Fees, **Veh 9853, 9853.6**
State, preferred claim to, **Veh 9859**
Involuntary transfer of title or interest, **Veh 9915**
Lost certificate, replacement on transfer of title, **Veh 9917**
Nondelivery on transfer of title, **Veh 9910**
Renewal, **Veh 9860, 9862**
Revocation or suspension, **Veh 9874**
Temporary certificate,
Agent for issuance, **Veh 9858, 9859**
Dealer, **Veh 9856**
Suspension, cancellation or revocation, **Veh 9874**
Termination upon abandonment, of vessel, **Veh 9864**
Transfer of title or interest, undocumented vessel, **Veh 9900 et seq.**
Transfer to dealer, **Veh 9856**
Certificates of ownership, **Veh 9850 et seq.**
Agent for issuance, **Veh 9858, 9859**
Cancellation, **Veh 9874**
Change of owner, **Veh 9855**
Duplicate, fee, **Veh 9867**
Fees, state, preferred claim to, **Veh 9859**
Involuntary transfer of title or interest, **Veh 9915**
Lost certificate, replacement on transfer of title, **Veh 9917**

BOATS AND BOATING—Cont'd
Certificates of ownership—Cont'd
Nondelivery on transfer of title, **Veh 9910**
Replacing lost or destroyed certificate, **Veh 9909**
Revocation, **Veh 9874**
Security interest, perfecting, **Veh 9919 et seq.**
Suspension, **Veh 9874**
Termination upon abandonment of vessel, **Veh 9864**
Transfer of title or interest, undocumented vessel, **Veh 9900 et seq.**
Transfer to dealer, **Veh 9856**
Charges and rates, documentary preparation charge, **Veh 9858.1**
Charitable corporations, fee exemption, **Veh 9870**
Crimes and offenses,
Certificates of number or ownership, nondelivery on transfer of title, **Veh 9910**
Drivers license suspension, **Veh 13202.5**
Numbering and registration, **Veh 9875**
Reports, operating under the influence of alcohol or drugs, **Veh 1803**
Unidentified vessels, **Veh 40000.8**
Dealers,
Notice of sale, **Veh 9912**
Trailers, sales, licenses, **Veh 11709**
Transfers, **Veh 9856**
Death, owner, transfer of title or interest, **Veh 9852.5**
Definitions, registration and transfer of vessels, **Veh 9840**
Delinquent taxes, undocumented vessels, title or interest transfer prerequisite, **Veh 9900**
Destruction, undocumented vessels,
Notice to assessor, **Veh 9869**
Termination of certificates of number and ownership, **Veh 9864**
Dismantling, termination of certificates of number and ownership, **Veh 9864**
Display,
Stickers, **Veh 9853.4**
Vessel number, **Veh 9866**
Documentary preparation charges, **Veh 9858.1**
Drivers license suspension, alcohol and drug violations, **Veh 13202.5**
Drugs and medicine,
Drivers license suspension, **Veh 13202.5**
Reports of violations, **Veh 1803**
Embezzlement of vessel, reporting, **Veh 10553, 10554**
Engines, brands, marks and labels, **Veh 9853.7**
Exemptions,
Fees, nonprofit corporations, **Veh 9870**
Numbering or registration, **Veh 9873**
Fairs and expositions, trailers, sales, licenses, **Veh 11709**
Federal numbering system, conformity with, **Veh 9857**

BOATS AND BOATING—Cont'd
Federal registration, **Veh 9854**
Fees,
Additional fees, certificates of number, **Veh 9853, 9853.6**
Certificates of number, **Veh 9853, 9853.6**
Change of ownership, **Veh 9855**
Disposition, **Veh 9863, 9868**
Documentary preparation, **Veh 9858.1**
Duplicate of certificates, **Veh 9867**
Exemption, nonprofit corporations, **Veh 9870**
Nonpayment, **Veh 9874**
Quagga mussels, infestation prevention fee, registration, **Veh 9853, 9860**
Renewal, certificate of number, **Veh 9860**
Late renewal, **Veh 9862**
Transfer of title or interest, **Veh 9901**
Transfers to dealer, **Veh 9856**
Zebra mussels, infestation prevention fee, registration, **Veh 9853, 9860**
Felonies. Crimes and offenses, generally, ante
Fines and penalties,
Fractional parts of dollar, **Veh 9862.5**
Registration and numbering, **Veh 9875**
Fish and Game, this index
Foreign registration, application for number, **Veh 9854**
Foreign ships,
Certificates of number, fees, **Veh 9853, 9853.6**
Number, exemption, **Veh 9873**
Fraud,
Certificates or registration, **Veh 9874**
Theft reports, **Veh 10552**
Hearings, altered identification numbers, impoundment, **Veh 9872.1**
Historical interest, vessels, special plaques identifying, **Veh 9853.5**
Impoundment, altered identification numbers, **Veh 9872.1**
Infractions, registration and numbering violations, **Veh 9875**
Inspection and inspectors, identification, **Veh 9845**
Investigations and investigators, identification, **Veh 9845**
Involuntary transfer of title or interest, **Veh 9915**
Junking undocumented vessel, termination of certificates of number and ownership, **Veh 9864**
Leases, certificates of number, **Veh 9853.3**
Legal owner, definitions, registration and transfer, **Veh 9840**
Lifeboats, number or registration, exemption, **Veh 9873**
Misdemeanors. Crimes and offenses, generally, ante
Noise Pollution, generally, this index
Nonprofit corporations, fee exemptions, **Veh 9870**

BOATS AND BOATING—Cont'd

Notice,
Abandoned vessels, **Veh 9864**
Altered identification numbers, **Veh 9872.1**
Assessor, change of ownership, **Veh 9856**
Reported theft or recovery, **Veh 10551.5**
Sale or transfer of title or interest, **Veh 9911**
Tax delinquencies, withholding registration renewal, **Veh 9880**
Transfer of title or interest, **Veh 9911 et seq.**
Numbers and numbering, **Veh 9850 et seq.**
Builder hull identification number, **Veh 9871, 9872**
Registration, renewal, **Veh 9871.5**
Certificates of number, generally, ante
Crimes and offenses, **Veh 9875**
Display of number, **Veh 9866**
Exemptions, **Veh 9873**
Offenses. Crimes and offenses, generally, ante
Owner, definitions, registration and transfer, **Veh 9840**
Paddle boats, registration and numbering, **Veh 9873**
Peace Officers, this index
Plaques, historical interest, **Veh 9853.5**
Pollution, **Veh 9853.5**
Possession, altered identification numbers, **Veh 9872.1**
Quagga mussels, infestation prevention fee, registration, **Veh 9853, 9860**
Rates and charges, documentary preparation charges, **Veh 9858.1**
Records and recordation, stolen or embezzled vessel, **Veh 10554**
Registered owner, registration and transfer, **Veh 9840**
Registration, **Veh 9840 et seq., 9850 et seq.**
Certificates of number, generally, ante
Crimes and offenses, **Veh 9875**
Exemptions, **Veh 9873**
Hull identification numbers, registration renewal, **Veh 9871.5**
Quagga mussels, infestation prevention fee, **Veh 9853, 9860**
Tax delinquencies, notice, withholding renewal, **Veh 9880**
Time for waiting, **Veh 1669**
Zebra mussels, infestation prevention fee, **Veh 9853, 9860**
Reports,
Operating under the influence of alcohol or drugs, **Veh 1803**
Stolen vessels, **Veh 10550 et seq.**
Violations, **Veh 1803**
Revocation, certificates or registration, **Veh 9874**
Rowboats, registration and numbering, **Veh 9873**
Sales,
Altered identification numbers, **Veh 9872.1**

BOATS AND BOATING—Cont'd

Sales—Cont'd
Transfer of title or interest, generally, post
Sales and Use Taxes, this index
Security interest,
Perfecting, **Veh 9919 et seq.**
Satisfaction, **Veh 9913, 9914**
State of principal use, definitions, registration and transfer, **Veh 9840**
Stickers, **Veh 9853.4**
Suspension, cancellation or revocation, **Veh 9874**
Stolen vessels, reports, **Veh 10550 et seq.**
Suspension, certificates or registration, **Veh 9874**
Tags, engines, **Veh 9853.7**
Tax assessors, registration information, **Veh 9869**
Tax delinquencies, withholding registration renewal, notice, **Veh 9880**
Temporary certificate. Certificates of number, ante
Theft, reports, stolen vessels, **Veh 10550 et seq.**
Title to property,
Registration, transfers, **Veh 9840 et seq.**
Transfer of title or interest, undocumented vessels, **Veh 9900 et seq.**
Trailers,
Carrying riders, **Veh 21712**
Clearance lamps, **Veh 25100**
Dealers,
Definitions, **Veh 286**
Licenses, **Veh 11709**
Transfer of title or interest, **Veh 9840 et seq., 9900 et seq.**
Bond or undertaking, **Veh 9923, 9924**
Notice, **Veh 9911, 9912**
Transporters, length, **Veh 35401.3, 35401.5**
Undocumented vessel, definitions, registration and transfer, **Veh 9840**
Use, definitions, registration and transfer, **Veh 9840**
Use taxes. Sales and Use Taxes, this index
Vessel, definitions, registration and transfer, **Veh 9840**
Waters of this state, registration and transfer, **Veh 9840**
Wrecking, undocumented vessel, termination of certificates of number and ownership, **Veh 9864**
Zebra mussels, infestation prevention fee, registration, **Veh 9853, 9860**

BODILY INJURY

Personal Injuries, generally, this index

BOILERS

Ships and Shipping, generally, this index

BONDS

Employees. Bonds (Officers and Fiduciaries), generally, this index
Fiduciaries. Bonds (Officers and Fiduciaries), generally, this index

BONDS—Cont'd

Official bonds. Bonds (Officers and Fiduciaries), generally, this index

BONDS (OFFICERS AND FIDUCIARIES)

All terrain vehicles, dealers, licenses and permits, **Veh 11710**
Boats and Boating, this index
Brokers, motor carriers, construction, **Veh 34510.5**
Construction, this index
Driving schools, **Veh 11102, 11102.1**
Lessor retailer, **Veh 11612**
Motor Carriers, this index
Motor Vehicles, this index
Motor vehicles department, applicant to examine records, **Veh 1814, 1815**
Motorcycles, dealers, **Veh 11710**
Remanufacturers, motor vehicles, **Veh 11710**
Ships and Shipping, this index
Traffic rules and regulations, permits for exceeding size, weight, protection of highways and bridges, **Veh 35782**
Traffic Violator Schools, this index

BOOKS AND PAPERS

Evidence, generally, this index
Highway patrol, possession and control, **Veh 2104**

BOOMS

Motor carried shovels or cranes, length, **Veh 35407**
Motor vehicles, load defined, **Veh 35003**

BOOSTER POWER UNITS

Trucks, permits, **Veh 35786, 35787**

BOOTS

Highway patrol, **Veh 2267**

BOULEVARDS

Northwoods boulevard, Nevada County ordinances, commercial vehicle weights, **Veh 35715**

BOUNDARIES

Business and residential districts, speed signs, **Veh 21358**
Traffic control, boundary line streets, **Veh 21105**

BOURBON

Alcoholic Beverages, generally, this index

BOY SCOUTS

Fee exemption, boat and vessel registration, **Veh 9870**

BOYS

Children and Minors, generally, this index

BRADY JARED TEEN DRIVER SAFETY ACT

Generally, **Veh 12814.6**

BRAKES

Bicycles, **Veh 21201**
Motor Carriers, this index
Motor Vehicles, this index

BRAKES—Cont'd
Motorcycles, service brakes, **Veh 26311**
Motorized bicycles, **Veh 24015**
Traffic Rules and Regulations, this index

BRANCH OFFICES
Mobilehomes, sales, used mobilehomes, **Veh 11709**
Motor Vehicles, this index
Recreational vehicles, franchises, **Veh 3072**

BRANDS, MARKS AND LABELS
Air pollution, motor vehicles, low emission vehicles, **Veh 5205.5, 21655.9, 40000.13**
Bicycle helmets, **Veh 21212**
Boats and boating, engines, **Veh 9853.7**
Explosives, statement, motor carriers, **Veh 31612**
Motor Vehicles, this index
Motorcycles, price information, **Veh 24014**
Ocean marine terminals, intermodal roadability inspection program, **Veh 34505.9**
Service marks. Trademarks, generally, this index
Trademarks, generally, this index

BRASS KNUCKLES
Weapons, generally, this index

BREAKAWAY BRAKES
Trucks, trailers or semitrailers, **Veh 26304**

BREATH TESTS
Driving under the influence. Traffic Rules and Regulations, this index

BRIBERY AND CORRUPTION
Motor vehicles, towing, kickbacks, **Veh 12110, 13351.85**
Towing, motor vehicles, kickbacks, **Veh 12110, 13351.85**

BRICKS
Motor vehicles, throwing or discharging at vehicle or occupant, **Veh 23110**

BRIDGE AND HIGHWAY DISTRICTS
Highway and Bridge Districts, generally, this index

BRIDGES
Highways and Roads, this index
Toll roads and bridges. Highways and Roads, this index

BRIDLE PATHS AND TRAILS
Traffic rules and regulations,
    Right of way, **Veh 21805**
    Unauthorized vehicles, riding and hiking trails, **Veh 23127**

BROADCASTS
Television and Radio, generally, this index

BROKERS
Bonds (officers and fiduciaries), motor carriers, construction, **Veh 34510.5**

BROKERS—Cont'd
Crimes and offenses, motor carriers, construction, bonds (officers and fiduciaries), **Veh 34510.5**
Definitions, motor vehicles, **Veh 232.5**
Fines and penalties, motor carriers, construction, bonds (officers and fiduciaries), **Veh 34510.5**
Insurance Agents, Solicitors or Brokers, generally, this index
Motor carriers, construction, bonds (officers and fiduciaries), **Veh 34510.5**
Motor Vehicles, this index

BROOMS
Motor vehicles, tow truck equipment, **Veh 27700**

BUCKET LOADERS
Special highway construction equipment, **Veh 565**

BUILDING STANDARDS
Contractors, generally, this index

BUILDINGS
Advertisements. Outdoor Advertising, generally, this index
Business structures, definitions, motor vehicles, **Veh 240**
Contractors, generally, this index
Correctional Institutions, generally, this index
Defacement, vandalism, **Veh 13202.6**
Fires and Fire Protection, generally, this index
Highway patrol, erecting, **Veh 2405**
Hospitals, generally, this index
Housing, generally, this index
Motor vehicles department, acquisition, **Veh 1654**
Outdoor Advertising, generally, this index
Prisons. Correctional Institutions, generally, this index
Public Buildings and Works, generally, this index
Railroad tracks, mover transporting, notice, sites, **Veh 35789**
Traffic rules and regulations, movers transporting across railroad tracks, notice, **Veh 35789**
Trucks towing, warning lights, **Veh 25263**
Vandalism, defacement of property, **Veh 13202.6**

BULBS
Lights and Lighting, generally, this index

BULLS
Animals, generally, this index

BUMPERS
Definitions, length of buses, **Veh 35400**
Motor Vehicles, this index

BUNK STAKES
Standards and specifications, adoption and enforcement, **Veh 26103**

BURDEN OF PROOF
Evidence, this index

BUREAUS
Motor vehicles, license plates, special plates, **Veh 5151 et seq.**

BURIAL
Cemeteries and Dead Bodies, generally, this index

BURIAL PARK
Cemeteries and Dead Bodies, generally, this index

BURNING
Fires and Fire Protection, generally, this index

BUSES
Accidents, reports, **Veh 16002**
Activity buses. School Buses, this index
Advertisements,
    Illuminated signs, Santa Monica, **Veh 25353.1**
    Lighted display signs, **Veh 25400**
Agricultural Labor and Employment, this index
Air Pollution, this index
Alameda Contra Costa transit district, bicycles, transportation, length, **Veh 35400.7**
Alarms, crime alarm lights, **Veh 25275.5**
Axle limits, weight, **Veh 35551.5**
Bicycles, length, **Veh 35400, 35400.9**
    Alameda Contra Costa transit district, **Veh 35400.7**
    Sacramento City and County, **Veh 35400.8**
Brakes, stopping distance requirements, **Veh 26454**
Cellular phones, **Veh 24018**
Certificates and certification,
    Transit bus drivers, **Veh 12804.6**
    Wheelchair lifts,
        Rules and regulations, **Veh 34501.7**
        Safety certification, **Veh 34501.1**
Clearance and side marker lamps, **Veh 25100**
Colleges and Universities, this index
Color, former school buses, **Veh 27603**
Committees, bicycles, transportation, length, Alameda Contra Costa transit district, **Veh 35400.7**
Community colleges and districts. Colleges and Universities, this index
Costs, wheelchair lifts, installation cost, **Veh 34501.7**
Crimes and offenses,
    Alarm lights, **Veh 25275.5**
    Driving log violations, **Veh 42001.3**
    Inspection, maintenance facilities or terminals, **Veh 40000.22**
Definitions, **Veh 233**
    Illuminated signs, **Veh 25353**
    Safety bumper, length, **Veh 35400**
    Two way communication devices, **Veh 24018**

BUSES

BUSES—Cont'd
Definitions—Cont'd
Urban and suburban service, **Veh 35107**
Destination signs, windows, obstruction of view, **Veh 26708**
Direction signs, windows, obstruction of view, **Veh 26708**
Display signs, lights, **Veh 25400**
Double deck buses, height, **Veh 35250**
Drivers, hours, limitation, **Veh 21702**
Driving logs, violations, crimes, **Veh 42001.3**
Emergencies, two way communication devices, **Veh 24018**
Equipment, **Veh 26709**
Exterior lamps, entrances and exists, **Veh 25105**
Exemptions, weight fees, **Veh 9107**
Explosives, transportation, **Veh 31614**
Exterior lamps, entrances and exits, **Veh 25105**
Eyeshades, windshield, **Veh 26711**
Farm labor, vehicles, equipment, inspection, **Veh 31401**
Fees,
Temporary operating authority, out of state buses, **Veh 4007**
Weight fees, exemptions, **Veh 9107**
Financial responsibility, **Veh 16500 et seq.**
Identification numbers, evidence, **Veh 16020**
Fines and penalties,
Inspection violations, **Veh 34501**
Log book violations, **Veh 42001.3**
Speeding violations, **Veh 42000.5**
Folding devices, bicycles, transportation, length, **Veh 35400, 35400.9**
Alameda Contra Costa transit district, **Veh 35400.7**
Foreign countries, temporary operating authority, **Veh 4007**
Foreign states, temporary operating authority, out of state buses, **Veh 4007**
Handicapped persons, wheelchair lifts, rules and regulations, **Veh 34501.7**
Height, double deck buses, **Veh 35250**
Hours of driving, limitation, **Veh 21702**
House cars, length, **Veh 35400**
Identity and identification,
Financial responsibility, evidence, **Veh 16020**
Lights and signs, **Veh 25350, 25351**
Passenger charter party carriers, exempt vehicles, **Veh 34507.6**
Illuminated signs, **Veh 25353**
Santa Monica, advertisements, **Veh 25353.1**
University of California, Irvine, **Veh 25354**
Inspection, maintenance facilities or terminals, **Veh 34501**
Crimes, **Veh 40000.22**
Insurance, **Veh 16500 et seq.**
Financial responsibility, identification numbers, evidence, **Veh 16020**
Internally illuminated signs, **Veh 25400**

BUSES—Cont'd
Interstate highways, width, **Veh 35106**
Lamps, exterior, entrances and exists, **Veh 25105**
Left side, right of way, yielding, signs and signals, **Veh 24617**
Length, **Veh 35400**
Bicycles, ante
Licenses and permits, temporary operating authority, out of state buses, **Veh 4007**
Lights and lighting,
Crime alarm lights, **Veh 25275.5**
Display signs, **Veh 25400**
Exterior lamps, entrances and exists, **Veh 25105**
Flashing amber lights, nonprofit organizations, handicapped or mentally retarded persons, **Veh 25276**
Illuminated signs, generally, ante
Right of way, yielding, signs and signals, **Veh 24617**
Side marker lights, **Veh 25100**
Turn signal system, **Veh 24951 et seq.**
Maintenance facilities, inspection, **Veh 34501**
Crimes, **Veh 40000.22**
Mirrors, equipment, **Veh 26709**
Misdemeanors. Crimes and offenses, generally, ante
Offenses. Crimes and offenses, generally, ante
Operating authority, out of state buses, temporary authority, **Veh 4007**
Painting, former school buses, **Veh 27603**
Paratransit Vehicles, generally, this index
Parking, San Francisco City and County, videotape, transit only traffic lanes, **Veh 40240 et seq.**
Penalties. Fines and penalties, generally, ante
Radios, **Veh 24018**
Reflectors, **Veh 24607 et seq.**
Registration, suspension, financial responsibility, **Veh 16503**
Reports,
Accidents, **Veh 16002**
Bicycles, transportation, length, Alameda Contra Costa transit district, **Veh 35400.7**
Width, ski carrying devices, **Veh 35106**
Right of way, yielding, signs and signals, **Veh 24617**
Route review committee, bicycles, transportation, **Veh 35400**
Routes, bicycles, transportation, length, **Veh 35400.9**
Rules and regulations, wheelchair lifts, **Veh 34501.7**
Sacramento City and County, this index
Safety, **Veh 34500 et seq.**
Tour buses, crimes and offenses, **Veh 40000.21**
Wheelchair lifting devices, safety certification, **Veh 34501.1**
Safety bumper, definitions, **Veh 35400**
Sales, identification plates, **Veh 24009**

BUSES—Cont'd
Santa Clara valley transportation authority, right of way, yielding, signs and signals, **Veh 24617**
Santa Cruz metropolitan transit district, right of way, yielding, signs and signals, **Veh 24617**
Santa Monica, illuminated signs, advertisements, **Veh 25353.1**
School Buses, generally, this index
Semaphore changing devices, **Veh 25352**
Service brakes, stopping distance requirements, **Veh 26454**
Sex offenses, drivers, license revocation, **Veh 13369 et seq.**
Side marker lights, **Veh 25100**
Signal lamps and devices, turn signal system, **Veh 24951 et seq.**
Signs and signals,
Illuminated signs, generally, ante
Lights, **Veh 25400**
Right of way, yielding, **Veh 24617**
Termini signs, **Veh 25350**
Windows, obstruction of view, **Veh 26708**
Skiing, width, equipment carrying devices, **Veh 35106**
Speeding, fines and penalties, **Veh 42000.5**
Stands, **Veh 21112**
Stopping distance, service brakes, **Veh 26454**
Stops, van pools, **Veh 22525**
Studies, width, ski carrying devices, **Veh 35106**
Telecommunications, emergencies, **Veh 24018**
Television and radio, **Veh 24018**
Temporary operating authority, out of state buses, **Veh 4007**
Terminals,
Inspection, **Veh 34501**
Crimes, **Veh 40000.22**
Signs, windows, obstruction, **Veh 26708**
Tour buses,
Brake adjustment, inspections, **Veh 34505**
Camps, drivers licenses, **Veh 15250.3**
Crimes and offenses, **Veh 40000.21**
Drivers licenses, revocation or suspension, **Veh 1808.1**
Driving records, reports, **Veh 40000.6**
Equipment, maintenance, **Veh 34506**
Rules and regulations, noncompliance, **Veh 34506**
Definitions, **Veh 612**
Drivers licenses, reports, crimes, **Veh 40000.6**
Driving record, reports, **Veh 1808.1**
Inspection and inspectors, **Veh 34505**
Terminals, operating authority, **Veh 34505.1**
Licenses and permits,
Driving record, reports, **Veh 1808.1**
Revocation or suspension, **Veh 34505.1**
Reports, **Veh 1808.1**

BUSES—Cont'd

Tour buses—Cont'd

Operators, duties, **Veh 12521**

Preventive maintenance instruction guide, **Veh 2807.2**

Records and recordation,

Drivers, crimes and offenses, **Veh 40000.6**

Inspection and inspectors, **Veh 34505**

Unsatisfactory inspections, terminals, **Veh 34505.1**

Reports,

Drivers licenses, crimes and offenses, **Veh 40000.6**

Driving record, **Veh 1808.1**

Rules and regulations, equipment, maintenance, **Veh 34513**

Safety inspections, **Veh 34505**

Safety regulations, **Veh 34500.1**

School Buses, this index

Steering, inspection and inspectors, **Veh 34505**

Terminal, operating authority, revocation or suspension, **Veh 34505.1**

Wheels, inspection and inspectors, **Veh 34505**

Traffic Rules and Regulations, this index

Traffic Signs and Signals, this index

Trailer buses, regulation and definition, **Veh 636**

Training, youth bus drivers, **Veh 2423**

Transit buses, speedometers, **Veh 24017**

Transit Districts, generally, this index

Turn signal system, **Veh 24951 et seq.**

Two way communication devices, **Veh 24018**

University of California, Irvine, illuminated signs, **Veh 25354**

Weights and measures,

Axle limits, **Veh 35550, 35551.5**

Exemptions, **Veh 35720**

Fees, exemptions, **Veh 9107**

Wheelchairs, lifting devices,

Located in front of front axle, exemption from length requirement, **Veh 35400**

Rules and regulations, **Veh 34501.7**

Safety certification, **Veh 34501.1**

Width, **Veh 35106, 35107**

Windshields, **Veh 26700**

Yielding, right of way, signs and signals, **Veh 24617**

Youth Buses, generally, this index

BUSINESS AND COMMERCE

Assumed or Fictitious Names, generally, this index

Business license taxes. Taxation, this index

Corporations, generally, this index

Definitions, motor vehicles, **Veh 234**

Licenses and permits,

Business license taxes. Taxation, this index

Tow trucks, cities, cities and counties, **Veh 12111**

BUSINESS AND COMMERCE—Cont'd

Motor vehicle registration, data base, accessing, commercial use, **Veh 1810.7**

Motor vehicles, registration, foreign business established within this state, **Veh 6702**

Trademarks, generally, this index

BUSINESS CORPORATIONS

Corporations, generally, this index

BUSINESS DAY

Definitions, motor vehicles, private property, removal, **Veh 22658**

BUSINESS DISTRICT

Definitions, motor vehicles, **Veh 235, 240**

U turns, intersections, **Veh 22102**

BUSINESS LICENSE TAXES

Taxation, this index

BUSINESS REPRESENTATIVE

Definitions, motor vehicles, **Veh 236**

BUSINESS TAXES

Taxation, generally, this index

BUTTONS

Badges, Emblems and Insignia, generally, this index

BYPASSES

Motor vehicles, exhaust system, **Veh 27150**

CABLE TELEVISION

Vehicles, flashing amber warning lights, **Veh 25274**

CABLES

Motor carriers, towed vehicle coupling, **Veh 29004**

Motor vehicles, maximum width of body and cable cinchers, **Veh 35110**

Towed vehicle coupled to towing vehicle, **Veh 29003**

Off highway vehicles, placing in position to do bodily injury, **Veh 38318.5**

Telecommunications, generally, this index

CABS

Motor vehicles, requisites to prevent penetration of gases and fumes, **Veh 27154**

Taxicabs, generally, this index

CADAVERS

Cemeteries and Dead Bodies, generally, this index

CAL H.E.A.T. (CALIFORNIANS HELP ELIMINATE AUTO THEFT) PROGRAM

Generally, **Veh 10902**

CALDECOTT TUNNEL

Explosive or flammable liquids, hauling by truck, **Veh 31301**

CALIFORNIA STATE UNIVERSITY

Colleges and Universities, this index

CALL BOXES

Freeways, this index

CAMELTHORN

Weeds, generally, this index

CAMERAS

Photography and Pictures, generally, this index

CAMP TRAILERS

Brakes, **Veh 26303**

Definitions, **Veh 242**

Passengers, towing passengers in trailer, **Veh 21712**

Reflectors, **Veh 24607**

Safety regulations, **Veh 34500 et seq.**

Traffic rules and regulations,

Length, **Veh 35400.6**

Towing passengers, **Veh 21712**

Turn signals, **Veh 24950**

CAMPERS

Commercial vehicles, towing, weight fees, **Veh 9400, 9401**

Communication device between camper and cab, **Veh 28080**

Definitions, **Veh 243**

Exits, **Veh 23129**

Exterior lamps, **Veh 25105**

Exterior lamps, entrances and exits, **Veh 25105**

Fire extinguishers, **Veh 28060**

Lamps, exterior, entrances and exits, **Veh 25105**

Passenger signaling devices, **Veh 28080, 28081**

Registration, **Veh 5350 et seq.**

Rules and regulations, **Veh 38000 et seq.**

Safety glazing materials, equipment, **Veh 26701 et seq.**

Towing, weight fees, exemption, vehicles manufactured before designated time, **Veh 9401**

Traffic rules and regulations,

Distances between vehicles, exemption, **Veh 21704**

Exits, **Veh 23129**

Intoxicating liquors, occupants drinking or possessing opened containers, **Veh 23229**

Transporters, length, **Veh 35401.3, 35401.5**

Transporters, length, **Veh 35401.3, 35401.5**

Weight fees, **Veh 9400 et seq.**

CAMPS AND CAMPING

Buses, tours, drivers licenses, **Veh 15250.3**

Drivers licenses, tour buses, **Veh 15250.3**

Juvenile day centers, ranches and camps. Juvenile Institutions and Schools, this index

Mobilehomes and Mobilehome Parks, generally, this index

Tour buses, drivers licenses, **Veh 15250.3**

CANADA
Drivers licenses, conviction of offenses, suspension or revocation of privilege, **Veh 13363**
Driving under the influence. Traffic Rules and Regulations, this index
Motor vehicles,
Drivers licenses, revocation or suspension, **Veh 13352**
Out of service orders, failure to comply, **Veh 2800**

CANADA THISTLE
Weeds, generally, this index

CANALS
Motor vehicle operation restrictions on banks, **Veh 21116**

CANYONS
Traffic rules and regulations, mountain driving, warnings, **Veh 21662**

CAR COMPANIES
Railroads, generally, this index

CAR INSURANCE
Motor Vehicle Insurance, generally, this index

CAR POOLS
Motor Vehicles, this index

CAR SHARE VEHICLE PROGRAM
Parking, exclusive use spaces, **Veh 22507.1**

CARAVANS
Traffic rules and regulations, spacing, **Veh 21705**

CARBON
Air Pollution, generally, this index

CARBON MONOXIDE
Air Pollution, generally, this index

CARDS
Identification Cards, generally, this index
Medical information cards, drivers licenses, **Veh 12811.1**
Motor Vehicles, this index

CARGO TANKS
Motor Carriers, this index

CARGO THEFT INTERDICTION PROGRAM
Fees, **Veh 9400**

CARRIERS
Accidents, reports, highway patrol, **Veh 20008, 20009**
Bills of Lading, generally, this index
Boats and Boating, generally, this index
Buses, generally, this index
Campers, towing, weight fees, **Veh 9400, 9401**
Financial responsibility, **Veh 16500 et seq.**
Highway carriers. Motor Carriers, generally, this index
Household Goods Carriers, generally, this index

CARRIERS—Cont'd
Limousines, generally, this index
Livestock carriers. Animals, this index
Marine carriers. Ships and Shipping, generally, this index
Motor Carriers, generally, this index
Moving companies. Household Goods Carriers, generally, this index
Railroads, generally, this index
School Buses, generally, this index
Ships and Shipping, generally, this index
Street Railways, generally, this index
Supplemental reports, accidents, **Veh 20009**
Tour buses. Buses, this index
Traffic Rules and Regulations, this index
Water carriers. Ships and Shipping, generally, this index
Weight fees, campers, towing, **Veh 9400, 9401**

CARRYALL
Definitions, motor vehicles, **Veh 245**
Special highway construction equipment, **Veh 565**

CARS
Motor Vehicles, generally, this index

CARSON CITY
Traffic rules and regulations, overweight vehicles, special permits, **Veh 35700.5**

CARTS
Golf Carts, generally, this index

CASUAL DRIVERS
Definitions, driving record, **Veh 1808.1**

CATERPILLAR TRACTORS
Special highway construction equipment, **Veh 565**

CATTLE
Animals, generally, this index

CAUSES OF ACTION
Actions and Proceedings, generally, this index

CAUSEWAYS
Traffic Rules and Regulations, this index

CAUTION
Definitions, traffic signals, **Veh 21452**

CAUTION LIGHTS
Traffic control signals, **Veh 21452**

CELLULAR RADIO TELEPHONES
Wireless telecommunications. Telecommunications, this index

CEMENT MIXERS
Construction, backup devices or alarms, **Veh 27000**

CEMETERIES AND DEAD BODIES
Anatomical Gifts, generally, this index
Coroners, generally, this index
Funeral Processions, generally, this index

CEMETERIES AND DEAD BODIES—Cont'd
Gifts, devises and bequests. Anatomical Gifts, generally, this index
Licenses and permits, equipment, license plates, **Veh 5011, 5014 et seq.**
Motor vehicles,
Equipment, license plates, **Veh 4155, 5011**
Fees, **Veh 1678, 9261, 9261.1**
Identification cards and plates, **Veh 5015 et seq.**
Registration,
Exemption, **Veh 4012**
Fees, **Veh 1678, 9261, 9261.1**
Registration, exemption, vehicle used in maintenance, **Veh 4012**

CEMETERY ASSOCIATIONS
Cemeteries and Dead Bodies, generally, this index

CEMETERY AUTHORITY
Cemeteries and Dead Bodies, generally, this index

CEMETERY CORPORATIONS
Cemeteries and Dead Bodies, generally, this index

CEMETERY DISTRICTS
Cemeteries and Dead Bodies, generally, this index

CENSUS
Identification cards, verification of age, **Veh 13007.5**

CERTIFICATES AND CERTIFICATION
Agricultural Machinery and Equipment, this index
Birth certificates. Vital Statistics, this index
Boats and boating, engines, brands, marks and labels, **Veh 9853.7**
Buses, this index
Driving schools, mature driver improvement courses, **Veh 1675 et seq.**
Highway Patrol, this index
Ignition interlock devices, **Veh 13386**
Limousines, this index
Medical certificates, motor vehicles, drivers licenses, nonresidents, **Veh 12502**
Mentally Retarded and Developmentally Disabled Persons, this index
Motor Carriers, this index
Motor Vehicle Insurance, this index
Motor Vehicles, this index
Ownership without registration, motor vehicles, **Veh 4452**
Paratransit Vehicles, this index
Recreational vehicles, sales, temporary branch license, **Veh 11713.15**
School Buses, this index
Tow truck drivers, **Veh 2430 et seq.**
Traffic Rules and Regulations, this index
Traffic Violator Schools, this index
Trailers, permanent trailer identification plates, **Veh 5014.1, 5016**

CERTIFICATES AND CERTIFICATION
  —Cont'd
Violations, corrections, **Veh 40616**
Weights and Measures, this index
Youth Buses, this index

CERTIFICATES OF COMPLIANCE
Definitions, motor vehicles, **Veh 246**

CERTIFICATES OF NUMBER
Boats and Boating, this index
Ships and Shipping, this index

CERTIFICATES OF OWNERSHIP
Boats and Boating, this index
Ships and Shipping, this index

CERTIFICATES OF TITLE
Mobilehomes and Mobilehome Parks, this
  index
Motor Vehicles, this index

CERTIFICATION
Certificates and Certification, generally,
  this index

CERTIFIED DEVICES
Motor vehicles. Air Pollution, this index

**CERTIFIED RECORD OF PERMANENT EX-
  PORTATION**
Definitions, vehicles, inspection and can-
  cellation of titles, **Veh 6161**

CHAINS
Motor Carriers, this index
Motor Vehicles, this index
Off highway vehicles, placing in position
  to do bodily injury, **Veh 38318.5**

CHANCELLORS
Community colleges and districts. Colleges and Universities, this index

CHANGE
Modification or Change, generally, this index

**CHAPPIE ZBERG OFF HIGHWAY MOTOR
  VEHICLE LAW**
Generally, **Veh 38000 et seq.**

CHARACTER AND REPUTATION
Automobile dismantlers, license qualifications, **Veh 11504**

CHARITIES
Boats and boating, fee exemption, non-
  profit corporations, **Veh 9870**
Motor vehicle insurance, charitable risk
  pools, financial responsibility, **Veh
  16054.2**
Motor vehicles,
  Dealers, exclusions, **Veh 286**
  Gifts, devises and bequests, records and
    recordation, **Veh 1660**
Records and recordation, motor vehicles,
  gifts, devises and bequests, **Veh 1660**
Ships and shipping, fee exemption, non-
  profit corporations, **Veh 9870**

**CHARTER PARTY CARRIERS OF PASSEN-
  GERS**
Limousines, generally, this index

CHARTS
Maps and Plats, generally, this index

CHATTEL MORTGAGES
Motor Vehicles, this index

CHAUFFEURS LICENSES
Generally, **Veh 12500 et seq.**
Drivers licenses. Motor Vehicles, this in-
  dex

CHECK VALVE
Motor vehicle vacuum brakes, **Veh 26522**

CHECKS
Negotiable Instruments, this index

CHEMICAL ENGINEERS
Engineers, generally, this index

CHEMICALLY DEPENDENT PERSONS
Alcoholics and Alcoholism, generally, this
  index
Drug Addicts, generally, this index

CHEMICALS, CHEMISTRY AND CHEMISTS
Hazardous Substances and Waste, generally, this index

CHICO STATE COLLEGE
Colleges and Universities, generally, this
  index

CHIEF OF FIRE DEPARTMENT
Firefighters and Fire Departments, this
  index

CHIEF OF POLICE
Police, this index

CHILD PROTECTIVE AGENCIES
Impudent negligence, agency workers,
  privileges and immunities, signing and
  verification of application of minor
  for drivers license, **Veh 17707**
Workers, drivers licenses, signing and verification of application for minors license, **Veh 17701**
  Privileges and immunities, **Veh 17707**

CHILDREN AND MINORS
Abuse,
  Child Protective Agencies, generally,
    this index
  Investigations and investigators, ad-
    dresses, confidentiality, **Veh 1808.4**
Alcoholic Beverages, this index
Appearance, motor vehicle violations, ar-
  rest, **Veh 40502**
Applications, drivers licenses, civil liability
  of persons signing, **Veh 17700 et seq.**
Arrest, motor vehicle violations, arrest,
  appearance, **Veh 40502**
Bicycle helmet violations, parent and mi-
  nor joint fine liability, **Veh 21212**
Bicycles, motorized bicycles, instruction
  permits, **Veh 12509.5**

CHILDREN AND MINORS—Cont'd
Birth certificates. Vital Statistics, this in-
  dex
Camps and Camping, generally, this index
Cigarettes and cigars,
  Motor vehicles, highways, **Veh 23111**
  Sales, reports, **Veh 1817**
Civil liability, persons signing drivers li-
  cense applications of minors, **Veh
  17700 et seq.**
Crimes and offenses,
  Buses, **Veh 2816**
  Defacing property,
    Delay or suspension of driving privi-
      leges, **Veh 13202.6**
    Suspension or delay of driving privi-
      leges, **Veh 13202.6**
  Juvenile Delinquents and Dependents,
    generally, this index
  Youth buses, loading or leaving, **Veh
    2816**
Custody. Marriage, this index
Defacement of property, delay or suspen-
  sion of driving privileges, **Veh 13202.6**
Definitions, motor vehicles, **Veh 17700**
Dependent children. Juvenile Delin-
  quents and Dependents, generally,
  this index
Driver education. Schools and School
  Districts, this index
Drivers licenses. Motor Vehicles, this in-
  dex
Driving schools, provisional licenses, **Veh
  12814.6**
Driving under the influence. Traffic
  Rules and Regulations, this index
Drugs and Medicine, this index
Exemplary damages, persons signing driv-
  ers license applications, **Veh 17709**
Fines and penalties,
  Bicycle helmet violations, joint liability,
    parent and minor, **Veh 21212**
  Defacement of property, delay or sus-
    pension of driving privileges, **Veh
    13202.6**
  Driving under the influence, **Veh 23500
    et seq.**
  Vandalism, defacement of property, sus-
    pension or delay of driving privi-
    leges, **Veh 13202.6**
Guardian and Ward, generally, this index
Hospitals, vehicle passenger restraint sys-
  tems, information upon discharge,
  Veh 27363.5
Ice cream trucks, vending, **Veh 22456**
Infractions, motor vehicles, arrest, appear-
  ance, **Veh 40502**
Investigations and investigators. Abuse,
  ante
Juvenile Delinquents and Dependents,
  generally, this index
Marriage, this index
Medical care and treatment. Midwives,
  generally, this index
Midwives, generally, this index

CHILDREN AND MINORS—Cont'd

Miscreant child. Juvenile Delinquents and Dependents, generally, this index

Motor carriers, driving for hire, **Veh 12515**

Motor Vehicles, this index

Motorcycles, instruction permits, **Veh 12509.5**

Motorized bicycles, instruction permits, **Veh 12509.5**

Motorized scooters, instruction permits, **Veh 12509.5**

Neglected child. Juvenile Delinquents and Dependents, generally, this index

Off highway vehicles, **Veh 38503 et seq.**

Controls, ability to reach and operate, crimes and offenses, **Veh 38304.1**

Offenses. Crimes and offenses, generally, ante

Peace officers, surviving children, death in line of duty, addresses, confidentiality, **Veh 1808.4**

Penalties. Fines and penalties, generally, ante

Persons signing drivers license applications, civil liability, **Veh 17700 et seq.**

Police, this index

Purchase or lease of vehicle without drivers license, **Veh 15500**

Sales. Cigarettes and cigars, ante

Schools and School Districts, generally, this index

Seatbelts, motor vehicles, **Veh 27360 et seq.**

Point system, **Veh 12810**

Telecommunications, this index

Torts, drivers license, person signing, **Veh 17700 et seq.**

Traffic Rules and Regulations, this index

Traffic signs and signals, deaf children, **Veh 21351.7**

Truants. Schools and School Districts, this index

Vandalism,

Defacing property, delay or suspension of driving privileges, **Veh 13202.6**

Suspension or delay of driving privileges, **Veh 13202.6**

Vending, ice cream trucks, **Veh 22456**

Youth buses, loading or leaving, crimes, **Veh 2816**

CHIROPRACTORS

Motor vehicles,

Disabled veterans, license fees, exemptions, certificates and certification, **Veh 9105**

Handicapped persons, parking, placards, certificates and certification, **Veh 22511.55, 22511.59**

License plates, handicapped persons, certificates and certification, **Veh 5007**

CHOOSE CLEAN CARS ACT

Generally, **Veh 5205.5**

CHOP SHOPS

Generally, **Veh 10801 et seq.**

Motor Vehicles, this index

CHRISTENSEN BELOTTI ACT

Motor vehicles, axle weight limits, transporting logs, **Veh 35552**

CHURCHES

Religious Organizations and Societies, generally, this index

CIGARETTES AND CIGARS

Children and Minors, this index

Littering, **Veh 23111**

Motor vehicles, throwing from vehicle, **Veh 23111**

Reports, **Veh 1817**

Paul Buzzo Act, **Veh 23111**

CIRCULARS

Advertisements, generally, this index

CITATIONS

Definitions, peace officer arrest quota, **Veh 41601**

Ocean marine terminals, intermodal roadability inspection program, **Veh 34505.9**

Process, generally, this index

Traffic Rules and Regulations, this index

University of California, quotas, police, **Veh 41600 et seq.**

CITIES AND COUNTIES

Consolidated Cities and Counties, generally, this index

CITIES AND TOWNS

Municipalities, generally, this index

CITIZENS AND CITIZENSHIP

Drivers licenses, evidence, **Veh 12801.5**

Highway patrol, qualifications, **Veh 2267**

Motor vehicles, drivers licenses, evidence, **Veh 12801.5**

CITIZENS BAND RADIO

Motor vehicles, special plates, **Veh 5020, 5021**

CITIZENSHIP

Citizens and Citizenship, generally, this index

CITY

Municipalities, generally, this index

CITY ATTORNEYS

Municipal Attorneys, generally, this index

CITY COUNCIL

Municipal Council, generally, this index

CITY COURTS

Municipal Courts, generally, this index

CITY JAILS

Jails, generally, this index

CITY OFFICERS AND EMPLOYEES

Municipal Officers and Employees, generally, this index

CIVIL ACTIONS

Actions and Proceedings, generally, this index

CIVIL AIR PATROL

Motor vehicles, fees, exemptions, **Veh 9106**

CIVIL DEFENSE

War and Civil Defense, generally, this index

CIVIL ENGINEERS

Engineers, generally, this index

CIVIL MARRIAGE

Marriage, generally, this index

CIVIL PENALTIES

Fines and Penalties, generally, this index

CIVIL PROCESS

Process, generally, this index

CLASSIC CARS

Historic Vehicles, generally, this index

CLASSIFIED EMPLOYEES

School Officers and Employees, this index

CLEANUP

Hazardous Substances and Waste, this index

CLEARANCE

Traffic Rules and Regulations, this index

CLEARANCE AND SIDE MARKER LAMPS

Vehicles 80 inches or more in width, equipment, **Veh 25100**

CLEARANCE LIGHTS

Generally, **Veh 25100 et seq.**

Motor Vehicles, this index

CLEATS

Motor vehicle tires, protuberances, **Veh 27454**

CLERKS

County Clerks, generally, this index

CLERKS OF COURTS

Traffic rules and regulations, bail, infraction or misdemeanor cases, **Veh 40307**

CLINICAL LABORATORIES

Bioanalysts,

Blood samples, drunken driving tests, administration, **Veh 23158**

Drunken driving, blood tests, **Veh 23158**

Blood tests, bioanalysts, drunken driving tests, administration, **Veh 23158**

Certified phlebotomy technicians, driving under the influence, blood tests, **Veh 23158**

CLINICAL LABORATORIES—Cont'd

Phlebotomy technicians, driving under the influence, blood tests, **Veh 23158**

Technicians, certified phlebotomy technicians, driving under the influence, blood tests, **Veh 23158**

CLINICS

Laboratories. Clinical Laboratories, generally, this index

Medical waste. Hazardous Substances and Waste, this index

CLOSED CIRCUIT TELEVISION

Crimes and offenses, arraignment, Placer County, **Veh 40502.1**

Placer County, crimes and offenses, arraignment, **Veh 40502.1**

CLOSED COURSE

Definitions, off highway vehicle registration, **Veh 38014**

CLOSING

Highways and Roads, this index

Streets and Alleys, this index

CLUBS

Business structures, definitions, motor vehicles, **Veh 240**

Motor Clubs, generally, this index

Weapons, generally, this index

COACH BUSES

Trona unified school district, inspection, **Veh 545.5**

COCKTAIL LOUNGES

Alcoholic Beverages, generally, this index

COLLAPSIBLE CONTAINERS

Motor carriers, flatbed vehicle, loads and loading, **Veh 31540**

COLLATERAL ESTOPPEL

Drivers licenses, revocation or suspension,
Administrative review, **Veh 13558**
Judicial review, **Veh 13559**

Motor vehicle offenses, conviction, civil actions, **Veh 40834**

COLLECTORS

Definitions, historic vehicles, **Veh 5051**

COLLEGES AND UNIVERSITIES

Actions and proceedings, parking lots and facilities, address, disclosure, **Veh 1808.25**

Animals, traffic regulations, **Veh 21113**

Arrest, University of California, quotas, police, **Veh 41600 et seq.**

Average daily attendance. Community colleges and districts, post

Bicycles, **Veh 21113**

Buses,
Community colleges and districts, post
University of California, Irvine, illuminated signs, **Veh 25354**

COLLEGES AND UNIVERSITIES—Cont'd

California State University,
Bicycle infractions, costs and fines schedule, establishment, **Veh 42001**
Costs, bicycle infractions, schedules, **Veh 42001**
Fines and penalties, bicycle infractions, schedule establishment, **Veh 42001**
President, motor vehicles, special license plates, **Veh 5002.6**
Traffic rules and regulations, **Veh 21113**

Chancellors. Community colleges and districts, post

Citations, University of California, quotas, police, **Veh 41600 et seq.**

Community colleges and districts,
Average daily attendance, traffic offender school, **Veh 42005.5**
Buses,
Exemptions, **Veh 545.1**
School buses, authority for operation, **Veh 545**
Chancellors, motor vehicles, special license plates, **Veh 5002.6**
Exemptions,
Buses, **Veh 545.1**
School buses, **Veh 545.1**
Motor vehicles, activated alarm devices, removal, **Veh 22651.5**
President, motor vehicles, special license plates, **Veh 5002.6**
School buses, exemptions, **Veh 545.1**
Traffic violator school, average daily attendance, inclusion, **Veh 42005.5**

Confidential or privileged information, parking lots and facilities, address, disclosure, **Veh 1808.25**

Continuing Education, generally, this index

Contracts, records and recordation, addresses, parking enforcement, disclosure, **Veh 1808.25**

Costs,
California State University, ante
University of California, post

Directional signs, freeways, **Veh 21375**

Driver training,
Exemptions, **Veh 11101**
Traffic rules and regulations, local authorities closing street, **Veh 21101**

Exemptions. Community colleges and districts, ante

Fines and penalties,
California State University, ante
University of California, post

Freeway directional signs, **Veh 21375**

Full time equivalent student, average daily attendance. Community colleges and districts, ante

Funds, memorial scholarship fund, September 11, 2001, **Veh 5066**

Junior colleges. Community colleges and districts, generally, ante

Motor vehicles,
Activated alarm devices, removal, **Veh 22651**

COLLEGES AND UNIVERSITIES—Cont'd

Motor vehicles—Cont'd
Addresses, parking enforcement, records and recordation, disclosure, **Veh 1808.25**
Confidential or privileged information, address, parking lots and facilities, **Veh 1808.25**
Fees, exemption, **Veh 9102**
Hit and run vehicles, removal for inspection, **Veh 22655**
License plates,
Commemorative special license plates, **Veh 5024**
Special plates, chancellors or presidents, **Veh 5002.6**
Police, abandoned or unclaimed property, removal, **Veh 22669**
Railroad right of way, removal of vehicle, **Veh 22656**
Records and recordation, addresses, parking enforcement, disclosure, **Veh 1808.25**
Removal, **Veh 22651**
Hit and run vehicle inspection, **Veh 22655**
Removal of vehicles from private property after accident, **Veh 22653**
Residence addresses, parking enforcement, records and recordation, disclosure, **Veh 1808.25**
Tort liability, **Veh 17000 et seq.**

Motorized bicycles, **Veh 21113**

Parking lots and facilities, addresses, records and recordation, disclosure, **Veh 1808.25**

Police,
Abandoned vehicles, appraisals, **Veh 22855**
Removal of abandoned vehicles from private property after accident, **Veh 22653**
University of California, post

President,
California State University, ante
Community colleges and districts, ante
University of California, post

Quotas, University of California, arrest, police, **Veh 41600 et seq.**

Roller skates, **Veh 21113**

Skateboards, **Veh 21113**

State university. California State University, generally, ante

Torts, motor vehicles, **Veh 17000 et seq.**

Traffic Rules and Regulations, this index

Traffic signs and signals, directional signs, **Veh 21375**

University of California,
Abandoned or unclaimed property, motor vehicles, accidents, removal, **Veh 22653**
Arrest, quotas, police, **Veh 41600 et seq.**
Bicycle infractions, costs and fines schedule, establishment, **Veh 42001**
Buses, Irvine, illuminated signs, **Veh 25354**

COLLEGES AND UNIVERSITIES—Cont'd
University of California—Cont'd
Citations, quotas, police, **Veh 41600 et seq.**
Costs, bicycle infractions, schedule establishment, **Veh 42001**
Fines and penalties, bicycle violations, fines schedule establishment, **Veh 42001**
Irvine, buses, illuminated signs, **Veh 25354**
Police,
Arrest, quotas, **Veh 41600 et seq.**
Quotas, arrest, **Veh 41600 et seq.**
Removal of abandoned vehicle from private property after accident, **Veh 22653**
President, motor vehicles, special license plates, **Veh 5002.6**
Quotas, arrest, police, **Veh 41600 et seq.**
Traffic rules and regulations, **Veh 21113**

COLLIER PORTER ACT
Vehicle weight limits, **Veh 35551**

COLLISIONS
Accidents, generally, this index

COLLUSION
Fraud, generally, this index

COLORS AND COLORING
Curbs, parking regulations, **Veh 21458**
Fire lane signs, **Veh 22500.1**
Handicapped persons, parking, exclusive use spaces, designation, **Veh 21458, 22511.7, 22511.8, 22511.9**
Motor vehicles, traffic officers, distinctive uniform and vehicle, **Veh 40800, 40804**
Parking, handicapped persons, exclusive use spaces, designation, **Veh 21458, 22511.7, 22511.8, 22511.9**
School Buses, this index

COMBAT
War and Civil Defense, generally, this index

COMBINATIONS OF VEHICLES
Traffic Rules and Regulations, this index

COMBUSTIBLE LIQUIDS
Definitions, motor vehicle load, **Veh 34003**

COMBUSTIBLES
Air Pollution, generally, this index
Explosives, generally, this index
Motor Carriers, this index

COMMANDING OFFICERS
Military Forces, this index

COMMERCE
Business and Commerce, generally, this index

COMMERCIAL BOOSTERS
Definition, explosives, **Veh 31600**

COMMERCIAL BOOSTERS—Cont'd
Regulations, motor carriers, transportation, **Veh 31600 et seq.**

COMMERCIAL BUILDINGS
Buildings, generally, this index

COMMERCIAL COACHES
Mobilehomes and Mobilehome Parks, generally, this index
Traffic rules and regulations, width, **Veh 35789.5**

COMMERCIAL PAPER
Negotiable Instruments, generally, this index

COMMERCIAL PURCHASER
Definitions, motor vehicles, **Veh 11713.1**

COMMERCIAL VEHICLES
Motor Vehicles, this index

COMMERCIAL VESSELS
Ships and Shipping, generally, this index

COMMERCIALS
Advertisements, generally, this index

COMMITTEES
Buses, bicycles, transportation, length, Alameda Contra Costa transit district, **Veh 35400.7**
Motor vehicles, house cars, safety, **Veh 2429.3**
Off highway vehicle safety education committee, **Veh 38500 et seq.**
Social Security, generally, this index

COMMON CARRIERS
Carriers, generally, this index
Marine carriers. Ships and Shipping, generally, this index
Motor Carriers, generally, this index
Railroads, generally, this index

COMMON SCHOOL DISTRICTS
Schools and School Districts, generally, this index

COMMUNICATIONS
Telecommunications, generally, this index
Television and Radio, generally, this index

COMMUNITY BASED ORGANIZATIONS
Nonprofit Organizations, generally, this index

COMMUNITY COLLEGES AND DISTRICTS
Colleges and Universities, this index

COMMUNITY PROPERTY
Motor Vehicles, this index

COMMUNITY SERVICE
Defacement of property, **Veh 13202.6**
Definitions, defacement of property, persons aged 13 to 21, **Veh 13202.6**
Motor Vehicles, this index
Traffic signs and signals, interference with, sentence, **Veh 21464**

COMMUTERS
Car pools. Motor Vehicles, this index
Vanpooling, generally, this index

COMPACTS
Drivers License Compact, **Veh 15000 et seq.**

COMPENSATION AND SALARIES
Handicapped parking, special enforcement units, **Veh 22507.9**
Highway Patrol, this index
Motor vehicle dealers, interference, **Veh 11713.2, 11713.3**
Motor Vehicles, this index
Motor vehicles department, officers and employees, **Veh 1507**
Recreational vehicles, delivery, preparation, obligations, franchises, **Veh 3074**
School Officers and Employees, this index
Towing, vehicles, kickbacks, **Veh 12110, 13351.85**
Workers Compensation, generally, this index

COMPETITION
Motor Vehicles, this index

COMPLAINTS
Crimes and Offenses, this index
Motor Vehicles, this index
Traffic Rules and Regulations, this index
Traffic violator schools, reports, **Veh 11208.5**

COMPRESSED AIR
Motor vehicles, air brakes, **Veh 26502 et seq.**

COMPRESSED GAS
Signs and signals, vehicles, **Veh 27903**

COMPROMISE AND SETTLEMENT
Driving schools, **Veh 11218**
Fines and penalties, **Veh 11111.5**
Highways and roads, damages, **Veh 17300**
Motor Vehicle Insurance, this index
Motor vehicle lessor retailers, **Veh 11613.5**
Motor Vehicles, this index
Traffic violator schools, accusation against licensee, **Veh 11218**
Vehicle verifiers, fines and penalties, **Veh 11302.5**

COMPUTERS
E mail. Electronic Mail, generally, this index
Electronic Mail, generally, this index
Motor vehicles, dealers, records and recordation, privacy, **Veh 11713.3, 11713.25**

CONCEALED WEAPONS
Weapons, this index

CONCRETE MIXERS
Construction, backup devices or alarms, **Veh 27000**

CONDITIONAL SALES
Affidavit, release of impounded vehicle, **Veh 14602**
Motor Vehicles, this index

CONDOMINIUMS
Motor vehicles, common interest property, removal, **Veh 22658**

CONFIDENTIAL OR PRIVILEGED INFORMATION
Accidents, reports, **Veh 16005, 20012, 20014**
Address, this index
Attorneys, this index
Colleges and Universities, this index
Corrections and Rehabilitation Department, this index
Court officers and employees, address, **Veh 1808.4**
Disclosure, generally, this index
District Attorneys, this index
Electricity, this index
Home addresses, designated persons, **Veh 1808.4**
Parole hearings division, youthful offender parole board, parole hearings board, **Veh 1808.6**
Judges, this index
Juvenile Delinquents and Dependents, this index
Legislature, this index
Marriage, this index
Motor vehicle department, records, **Veh 1808.4**
Motor Vehicle Insurance, this index
Motor Vehicles, this index
Parole hearings division, designated personnel, home addresses, **Veh 1808.6**
Peace Officers, this index
Public Defenders, this index
Public Utilities, this index
Radioactive materials, spent fuel, transportation, notice, **Veh 33002**
Social workers, address, **Veh 1808.4**
Tow truck drivers, certification, **Veh 2431**
Traffic Rules and Regulations, this index
Traffic signs and signals, automated enforcement systems, photographic records, **Veh 21455.5**
Traffic Violator Schools, this index
Youthful offender parole board, designated personnel, home addresses, **Veh 1808.6**

CONFISCATION
Searches and Seizures, generally, this index

CONFLAGRATION
Fires and Fire Protection, generally, this index

CONFLICT OF INTEREST
Adverse or Pecuniary Interest, generally, this index

CONGESTION
Highways and Roads, this index

CONGRESS
Motor vehicles, special plates, fees, **Veh 5002.8**

CONGRESSIONAL MEDAL OF HONOR
Motor Vehicles, this index

CONSCIOUSNESS
Drivers licenses, fainting spells, persons subject to, **Veh 12806**

CONSERVATION
Fish and Game, generally, this index
Pollution, generally, this index

CONSERVATION DEPARTMENT
Forests and Forestry, generally, this index

CONSERVATORS AND CONSERVATORSHIPS
Motor vehicles, accident reports, disclosure, **Veh 20012**

CONSERVATORS OF THE PEACE
Peace Officers, generally, this index

CONSIGNMENT
Definitions, motor vehicle dealers, **Veh 266**
Motor vehicles, dealers, agreements, **Veh 11729, 11730**

CONSOLIDATED CITIES AND COUNTIES
Airports and Landing Fields, generally, this index
Firefighters and Fire Departments, generally, this index
Handicapped persons, parking, special enforcement units, **Veh 22507.9**
Housing, generally, this index
Housing Authorities, generally, this index
Jails, generally, this index
Landing fields. Airports and Landing Fields, generally, this index
Manufactured housing, private roads, ordinances, **Veh 21107.9**
Mobilehomes and mobilehome parks, private roads, ordinances, **Veh 21107.9**
Motor vehicles, prostitution, impounding, ordinances, **Veh 22659.5**
Ordinances, this index
Parking Meters, generally, this index
Parks, generally, this index
Police, generally, this index
San Francisco City and County, generally, this index
Taxation, tow trucks, business license tax, **Veh 12111**
Tow trucks, business license tax, **Veh 12111**

CONSPICUITY SYSTEM
Motor carriers, retroreflective sheeting, **Veh 24612**

CONSTABLES
Arrest, generally, this index

CONSTABLES—Cont'd
Process, generally, this index
Service of process. Process, this index
Sheriffs, generally, this index

CONSTITUTION OF CALIFORNIA
Municipalities. Taxation, generally, this index

CONSTRUCTION
Bonds (officers and fiduciaries), motor carriers, **Veh 34510.5**
Contractors, generally, this index
Courthouses, this index
Equipment, special equipment, inspection, state patrol, stolen vehicles, **Veh 2805**
Highways and Roads, this index
Machinery and Equipment, this index
Motor Carriers, this index
Motor vehicles, backup devices or alarms, **Veh 27000**
Traffic Rules and Regulations, this index
Traffic Signs and Signals, this index

CONSTRUCTION VEHICLES
Definitions, backup devices or alarms, **Veh 27000**

CONSUMER AFFAIRS DEPARTMENT
Automotive repairs bureau. Motor Vehicle Repair Dealers, generally, this index
Motor Vehicle Repair Dealers, generally, this index

CONSUMER MOTOR VEHICLE RECOVERY CORPORATION
Generally, **Veh 12200 et seq.**

CONSUMER PROTECTION
Motor Vehicles, this index
Traffic violator schools, disclosure, **Veh 11200**

CONSUMERS
Definitions, motor vehicles, consumer protection, recovery corporation, **Veh 12200**

CONTAINERS
Brands, Marks and Labels, generally, this index
Explosives, this index
Fuel, this index
Labels. Brands, Marks and Labels, generally, this index
Motor Carriers, this index
Motor vehicles, throwing or discharging bottles at vehicle or occupant, **Veh 23110**
Tanks, generally, this index

CONTAMINATION
Air Pollution, generally, this index

CONTEMPT
Motor vehicles, violations, infractions, Failure to pay fine, **Veh 42003**

CONTEMPT—Cont'd

Motor vehicles, violations, infractions
—Cont'd
  Impoundment of drivers license and or-
    dering person not to drive, **Veh
    40508**
  Traffic rules and regulations, infractions,
    impoundment of drivers license, fail-
    ure to pay fine, **Veh 40508**

CONTESTS

Traffic rules and regulations, speed contests, highways, **Veh 23109**
  Impoundment of vehicle, **Veh 22651.6**

CONTINUANCE

Traffic safety violations, written promise
  to appear, **Veh 40506.5**
Trial, this index
Written promise to appear, traffic offenses, **Veh 40506.5**

CONTINUING EDUCATION

Driving school instructors, in lieu of license renewal examination, **Veh
  11105.1**
Motor vehicles, dealers, **Veh 11704.5**
Traffic violator schools, **Veh 11204**

CONTRA COSTA COUNTY

Contracts, parking violations notices, processing, **Veh 40200.4**
Parking violations notices processing, contracts, **Veh 40200.4**

CONTRABAND

Weapons, generally, this index

CONTRACTORS

Railroad tracks, transporting dwelling
  house or building, notice, **Veh 35789**
Traffic rules and regulations, weight of
  vehicles, exemption, **Veh 35704, 35716**

CONTRACTS

Adverse or Pecuniary Interest, generally,
  this index
Colleges and Universities, this index
Conflict of interest. Adverse or Pecuniary
  Interest, generally, this index
Contra Costa County, this index
Fraud, generally, this index
Freeways, this index
Highway Patrol, this index
Malibu, state highway route 1, traffic rules
  and regulations, **Veh 2400.6**
Mobilehomes and Mobilehome Parks, this
  index
Motor Carriers, this index
Motor Vehicles, this index
Motor Vehicles Department, this index
Motorcycle safety program, **Veh 2933**
Personal interest. Adverse or Pecuniary
  Interest, generally, this index
Recreational Vehicles, this index
Traffic Rules and Regulations, this index

CONTRACTS—Cont'd

Traffic signs and signals, automatic enforcement systems, manufacturers
  and manufacturing, **Veh 21455.5,
  21455.6**

CONTRIBUTIONS

Gifts, Devises and Bequests, generally, this
  index

CONTROLLED SUBSTANCES

Drugs and Medicine, generally, this index

CONTROLLER

County Controllers, generally, this index

CONVERSION

Embezzlement, generally, this index

CONVICTS

Correctional Institutions, generally, this
  index
Jails, generally, this index

CORN

Agricultural Products, generally, this index

CORNERING LIGHTS

Definitions, motor vehicles, **Veh 375**
Motor vehicle equipment, **Veh 25107**

CORONERS

Drunk driver visitation program (youth),
  Veh 23517
Motor vehicles,
  Flashing and colored lights, **Veh 25264**
  Reports of death, **Veh 20011**
Youthful drunk driver visitation program,
  Veh 23517

CORPORATION TAXES

Delinquency, motor carriers, licenses and
  permits, revocation or suspension,
  Veh 34623.1
Motor carriers, licenses and permits, delinquent taxes, revocation or suspension, **Veh 34623.1**

CORPORATIONS

Assumed or Fictitious Names, generally,
  this index
Automobile dismantlers, cancellation of li-
  censes, **Veh 11518**
Carriers, generally, this index
Cemetery corporations. Cemeteries and
  Dead Bodies, generally, this index
Charities, generally, this index
Colleges and Universities, generally, this
  index
Driving schools, license, **Veh 11107**
Insurance companies. Insurance, general-
  ly, this index
Motor vehicles, sales by owner or repre-
  sentative, application of law, **Veh
  12121**
Names. Assumed or Fictitious Names,
  generally, this index
Nonprofit Corporations, generally, this in-
  dex

CORPORATIONS—Cont'd

Public Benefit Corporations, generally,
  this index
Public Utilities, generally, this index
Railroads, generally, this index
Religious Organizations and Societies,
  generally, this index
Sole corporations. Religious Organizations and Societies, generally, this index
Traffic violator schools, refusal to issue
  license, **Veh 11211**
Universities. Colleges and Universities,
  generally, this index
Utilities. Public Utilities, generally, this
  index

CORPSE

Cemeteries and Dead Bodies, generally,
  this index

CORRECTIONAL INSTITUTIONS

Commitment of prisoner, traffic violations,
  prosecution, **Veh 41500**
Industrial education, motor vehicles, resto-
  ration and rebuilding, **Veh 22711**
Jails, generally, this index
Juvenile Delinquents and Dependents,
  generally, this index
Juvenile Facilities Division, generally, this
  index
Labor and employment, motor vehicles,
  restoration and rebuilding, **Veh 22711**
Mandatory supervision. Parole and Pro-
  bation, generally, this index
Motor vehicles,
  Drivers licenses, revocation or suspen-
    sion, **Veh 41500**
  Former inmates, **Veh 12808**
  Restoration and rebuilding, inmates,
    Veh 22711
  Special license plates, **Veh 5001**
  Violations, nonprosecution of prisoners,
    Veh 41500
Parole and Probation, generally, this index
Traffic violations, prosecution after com-
  mitment, **Veh 41500**
Vocational education, motor vehicles, res-
  toration and rebuilding, **Veh 22711**

**CORRECTIONS AND REHABILITATION DE-
PARTMENT**

Confidential or privileged information,
  home addresses, designated personnel, **Veh 1808.6**
Deputy director, parole hearings division,
  home addresses, confidential information, **Veh 1808.6**
Juvenile Facilities Division, generally, this
  index
Parole hearings division, home addresses,
  designated personnel, confidential information, **Veh 1808.6**

CORRIDORS

Highways and Roads, this index

CORRUPTION
Bribery and Corruption, generally, this index

COSTS
California State University. Colleges and Universities, this index
Freeways, emergency call boxes, reimbursement, **Veh 2421.5**
Motor Vehicles, this index
Taxicabs, impounding, **Veh 21100.4**
Toll roads and bridges, evasion, **Veh 40250 et seq.**
Traffic Rules and Regulations, this index

COTTON
Trailers. Cotton Trailers, generally, this index

COTTON MODULE MOVER
Definitions, agricultural machinery and equipment, **Veh 36012**
Length, **Veh 35400.5**
Registration, exemption, **Veh 36101**
Weight, **Veh 35555**
Width, **Veh 35100.5**

COTTON TRAILERS
Fees, transfers, **Veh 1678, 9261, 9261.1**
License plates, **Veh 5014 et seq.**
Towing, **Veh 36626**
Transfers, fees, **Veh 1678, 9261, 9261.1**

COUNCILS
Municipal Council, generally, this index

COUNSEL
Attorneys, generally, this index

COUNSEL FOR ACCUSED
Crimes and Offenses, this index

COUNTERFEITING
Motor Vehicles, this index

COUNTIES
Agents. County Officers and Employees, generally, this index
Air Pollution, this index
Alcoholism and drug abuse programs, motor vehicle drivers, **Veh 23249.50**
Arrest, quotas, peace officers, **Veh 41600 et seq.**
Attorneys. District Attorneys, generally, this index
Audits and auditors. County Auditors, generally, this index
Automobiles. Motor vehicles, generally, post
Bicycles, licenses and permits, **Veh 39000 et seq.**
Boards and commissions,
 County Supervisors Boards, generally, this index
 Supervisors. County Supervisors Boards, generally, this index
Bridge and highway districts. Highway and Bridge Districts, generally, this index

COUNTIES—Cont'd
Cities and counties. Consolidated Cities and Counties, generally, this index
Civil defense. War and Civil Defense, generally, this index
Clerks. County Clerks, generally, this index
Commercial vehicles. Motor vehicles, post
Consolidated Cities and Counties, generally, this index
Controller. County Controllers, generally, this index
Convicts. Jails, generally, this index
Coroners, generally, this index
Correctional institutions. Jails, generally, this index
Definitions, motor vehicles, **Veh 270**
District Attorneys, generally, this index
Elections, generally, this index
Employees. County Officers and Employees, generally, this index
Fees. Motor vehicles, post
Financial statements and reports, motor vehicles, registration, fees, **Veh 9250.14**
Fines and penalties, disposition, county owning premises on which traffic violation occurred, **Veh 42203**
Firefighters and Fire Departments, generally, this index
Funds,
 Night court session funds, assessments, traffic rules and regulations, **Veh 42006**
 Treasurers. County Treasurers, generally, this index
Handicapped persons, parking, special enforcement units, **Veh 22507.9**
Highways and Roads, this index
Hours of service records, law enforcement agencies, transportation of inmates or prisoners, exemption, **Veh 34501**
Housing, generally, this index
Housing Authorities, generally, this index
Jails, generally, this index
Juvenile halls. Juvenile Institutions and Schools, this index
Labor and employment. County Officers and Employees, generally, this index
Law enforcement agencies, hours of service records, transportation of inmates or prisoners, exemption, **Veh 34501**
Legislative body. County Supervisors Boards, generally, this index
Local Agencies, generally, this index
Manufactured housing, private roads, ordinances, **Veh 21107.9**
Mobilehomes and mobilehome parks, private roads, ordinances, **Veh 21107.9**
Motor Vehicle Insurance, this index
Motor vehicles,
 Abandonment, procedures for removal and abatement, funds, **Veh 22710**

COUNTIES—Cont'd
Motor vehicles—Cont'd
 Commercial vehicles,
  Crimes and offenses, fees, **Veh 9250.14**
  Fingerprints and fingerprinting, fees, **Veh 9250.19**
  Weight regulation, **Veh 35718 et seq.**
 County, definitions, **Veh 270**
 Fees,
  Exemption, **Veh 9101**
  Registration, **Veh 9250.14**
 Financial responsibility, exemption, **Veh 16051**
 Financial statements and reports, registration, fees, **Veh 9250.14**
 Fines and forfeitures, disposition, **Veh 42201**
 Marshals department vehicles, flashing amber warning lights, **Veh 25254**
 Off highway vehicles, **Veh 38000 et seq.**
 Prostitution, impounding, ordinances, **Veh 22659.5**
 Registration, **Veh 4155**
 Reports, registration, fingerprints and fingerprinting, fees, **Veh 9250.19**
 Revocation or suspension, registration, fees, **Veh 9250.14**
 Special license plates, **Veh 5001**
 Tort liability, **Veh 17000 et seq.**
Motorized scooters, powers and duties, **Veh 21225**
National defense. War and Civil Defense, generally, this index
Night court session funds, assessments, traffic rules and regulations, **Veh 42006**
Officers and employees. County Officers and Employees, generally, this index
Ordinances, this index
Parking Meters, generally, this index
Parks, this index
Placer County, generally, this index
Prisoners. Jails, generally, this index
Records and recordation, law enforcement agencies, hours of service records, transportation of inmates or prisoners, exemption, **Veh 34501**
Reports, motor vehicles, registration, fingerprints and fingerprinting, fees, **Veh 9250.19**
Rescue, generally, this index
Sheriffs, generally, this index
Supervisors. County Supervisors Boards, generally, this index
Taxation, generally, this index
Torts, motor vehicles, **Veh 17000 et seq.**
Traffic Rules and Regulations, this index
Traffic signs and signals,
 Bridges, weight, **Veh 35754**
 Buildings, driveways and paths, **Veh 21113**
 Weight, reduction, **Veh 35710**
Treasurers. County Treasurers, generally, this index
Vehicles. Motor vehicles, generally, ante

COUNTIES

COUNTIES—Cont'd
War and Civil Defense, generally, this index

COUNTIES OF FIRST CLASS
Los Angeles County, generally, this index

COUNTY AUDITORS
License plates, regular series, **Veh 5002.7**
Motor vehicles, regular series license plates, **Veh 5002.7**
Regular series, license plates, **Veh 5002.7**

COUNTY BOARDS OF SUPERVISORS
County Supervisors Boards, generally, this index

COUNTY CLERKS
Motor vehicle insurance, traffic violator schools, notice, **Veh 42007**
Notice, traffic violator schools, motor vehicle insurance, **Veh 42007**
Traffic violator schools, motor vehicle insurance, notice, **Veh 42007**

COUNTY CONTROLLERS
License plates, regular series, **Veh 5002.7**
Motor vehicles, regular series license plates, **Veh 5002.7**
Regular series, license plates, **Veh 5002.7**

COUNTY CORONERS
Coroners, generally, this index

COUNTY EMPLOYEES
County Officers and Employees, generally, this index

COUNTY ENGINEERS
County highways. Highways and Roads, this index

COUNTY FIRE PROTECTION DISTRICTS
Fires and Fire Protection, generally, this index

COUNTY FLOOD CONTROL DISTRICTS
Motor vehicles, size and weight limitations, exemptions, emergency use, **Veh 35002**

COUNTY FUNDS
County Treasurers, generally, this index

COUNTY HIGHWAYS
Highways and Roads, this index

COUNTY INSTITUTIONS
Traffic control, animal or vehicle, stopping or standing on driveways, **Veh 21113**

COUNTY JAILS
Jails, generally, this index

COUNTY OFFICERS AND EMPLOYEES
Attorneys. District Attorneys, generally, this index
Auditors. County Auditors, generally, this index
Boards and commissions. County Supervisors Boards, generally, this index

COUNTY OFFICERS AND EMPLOYEES —Cont'd
Clerks. County Clerks, generally, this index
Controller. County Controllers, generally, this index
District Attorneys, generally, this index
Impounding,
    Motor vehicles, authority, **Veh 22651**
    Parked or standing vehicles, **Veh 22654**
Motor vehicles,
    Impounding, authority, **Veh 22651**
    Removal, parked or standing vehicles, **Veh 22654**
Sheriffs, generally, this index
Supervisors. County Supervisors Boards, generally, this index
Treasurers. County Treasurers, generally, this index

COUNTY PARKS
Counties. Parks, this index

COUNTY PEACE OFFICERS
Arrest quotas, **Veh 41600 et seq.**

COUNTY SUPERVISORS BOARDS
Addresses, board members, confidentiality, **Veh 1808.4**
Confidential or privileged information, home addresses, board members, **Veh 1808.4**
Home addresses, board members, confidentiality, **Veh 1808.4**
License plates, regular series, **Veh 5002.7**
Members, addresses, confidentiality, **Veh 1808.4**
Motor vehicles, regular series license plates, **Veh 5002.7**
Regular series license plates, **Veh 5002.7**

COUNTY TREASURERS
License plates, regular series, **Veh 5002.7**
Motor vehicles, regular series license plates, **Veh 5002.7**
Regular series, license plates, **Veh 5002.7**

COUPLING
Motor vehicles, towing equipment, **Veh 29002 et seq.**

COURT COMMISSIONERS
Address, home address, confidential, **Veh 1808.4**
Confidential or privileged information, home address, **Veh 1808.4**
Home address, confidential, **Veh 1808.4**
Husband and wife, address, confidential, **Veh 1808.4**

COURT OFFICERS AND EMPLOYEES
Address, confidential or privileged information, **Veh 1808.4**
Confidential or privileged information, address, **Veh 1808.4**
Court Commissioners, generally, this index

COURT ORDERS
Orders of Court, generally, this index

COURTESY LAMPS
Motor vehicle equipment, **Veh 25105**

COURTHOUSES
Construction, funds, traffic violator schools, fees, deposit, **Veh 42007.1**
Trust funds, night court, assessments, traffic rules and regulations, **Veh 42006**

COURTS
Accident reports, failure to file, **Veh 1805**
Appeal and Review, generally, this index
Bicycle infractions costs and fines schedules, use, **Veh 42001**
City courts. Municipal Courts, generally, this index
Commissioners. Court Commissioners, generally, this index
Contempt, generally, this index
Costs, generally, this index
Dealers, definitions, motor vehicles, **Veh 286**
Exhibits, generally, this index
Guardian and Ward, generally, this index
Judges, generally, this index
Judgments and Decrees, generally, this index
Motor Vehicles, this index
Municipal Courts, generally, this index
Orders of Court, generally, this index
Small Claims Courts, generally, this index
Subpoenas, generally, this index

COURTS OF APPEAL
Appeal and Review, generally, this index

COURTS OF RECORD
Judges, generally, this index

COWL LAMPS
Motor vehicles, **Veh 25106**

COWS
Animals, generally, this index

CRANES
Axle weight limitations, **Veh 35551.5**
Construction, backup devices or alarms, **Veh 27000**
Motor vehicles used to support boom or mast,
    Brakes, exemption, **Veh 26302**
    Length, **Veh 35407**
Traffic Rules and Regulations, this index

CREDIT
Motor Vehicles, this index

CREDIT CARDS
Definitions, taxicabs, impounding, **Veh 21100.4**
Motor Vehicles, this index

CRIMES AND OFFENSES
Abettors. Accomplices and Accessories, generally, this index
Abuse. Children and Minors, this index
Accidents, this index
Accomplices and Accessories, generally, this index

CRIMES AND OFFENSES—Cont'd

Address,

Confidentiality, public officers and employees, **Veh 1808.4**

Disclosure, motor vehicles department records, designated persons, **Veh 1808.4**

Agricultural Machinery and Equipment, this index

Aiders and abettors. Accomplices and Accessories, generally, this index

Air Pollution, this index

Ambulances, theft, **Veh 10851**

Armored cars,

Licenses and permits, **Veh 21713**

Use of red lights, violation, **Veh 25262**

Arraignment, generally, this index

Arrest, generally, this index

Attempts, generally, this index

Automobile dismantlers, license revocation, **Veh 11509**

Background checks. Criminal History Information, generally, this index

Bad checks. Negotiable Instruments, this index

Bail, generally, this index

Bicycles, this index

Blind Persons, this index

Boats and Boating, this index

Bribery and Corruption, generally, this index

Brokers, motor carriers, construction, bonds (officers and fiduciaries), **Veh 34510.5**

Buses, this index

Children and Minors, this index

Chop shops, **Veh 10801 et seq.**

Climbing into vehicle with intent to commit, **Veh 10853**

Closed Circuit Television, this index

Commercial vehicles, inspection, **Veh 2813**

Complaints, failure to correct violations, **Veh 40618**

Contempt, generally, this index

Conviction of crime. Traffic Rules and Regulations, this index

Correctional Institutions, generally, this index

Corruption. Bribery and Corruption, generally, this index

Counsel for accused, motor vehicle operators, chemical tests, driving under influence of alcohol or drugs, **Veh 13353**

Defacing, generally, this index

Destruction or damaging of property. Malicious Mischief, generally, this index

Disabled person placards, **Veh 4461, 4463**

Fines and penalties, **Veh 4463.3**

Discharging children, youth buses, **Veh 2816**

Disclosure,

Address, ante

CRIMES AND OFFENSES—Cont'd

Disclosure—Cont'd

Motor vehicles department records, addresses, designated persons, **Veh 1808.4**

District Attorneys, generally, this index

Drivers licenses. Motor Vehicles, this index

Driving Schools, this index

Driving under the influence. Traffic Rules and Regulations, this index

Embezzlement, generally, this index

Equipment, notice to correct violations, proof of correction, **Veh 40616**

Failure to stop at accident involving property damages, **Veh 20002**

False Personation, generally, this index

False representation. Fraud, generally, this index

Farm labor vehicles, drivers certificates, **Veh 40000.11**

Fines and Penalties, generally, this index

Fingerprints and Fingerprinting, generally, this index

Fire department vehicles, theft, **Veh 10851**

Firearms. Weapons, this index

Firefighters and Fire Departments, this index

Fraud, generally, this index

Funeral processions, peace officers signals and directions, disregarding, **Veh 2817**

Grapes and Grapevines, this index

Guilty plea. Traffic Rules and Regulations, this index

Habitual criminals. Second and subsequent offenses, generally, post

Handicapped Persons, this index

Hazardous Substances and Waste, this index

Hazardous Waste Haulers, this index

Highways and Roads, this index

Hit and Run Drivers, generally, this index

Homicide, generally, this index

Housing, this index

Identification Cards, this index

Impersonation. False Personation, generally, this index

Indigent persons. Public Defenders, generally, this index

Infractions, generally, this index

Inhalation hazards, transportation, **Veh 32104, 40000.19**

Jails, generally, this index

Juvenile Delinquents and Dependents, generally, this index

Juvenile Institutions and Schools, generally, this index

Larceny. Theft, generally, this index

Law Enforcement, this index

Lessor retailers, **Veh 11614 et seq., 40000.7**

Light duty trucks, itemized price stickers, **Veh 11712.5, 24013.5**

Loading children, youth buses, **Veh 2816**

Local detention facilities. Jails, generally, this index

Malicious Mischief, generally, this index

CRIMES AND OFFENSES—Cont'd

Mandatory supervision. Parole and Probation, generally, this index

Manslaughter. Homicide, this index

Marijuana. Drugs and Medicine, this index

Minors. Children and Minors, this index

Mobilehomes and Mobilehome Parks, this index

Motor Carriers, this index

Motor Vehicle Repair Dealers, this index

Motor Vehicle Service Stations, this index

Motor Vehicles, this index

Motorcycles, this index

Motorized scooters, pocket bikes, **Veh 21720**

Murder. Homicide, generally, this index

Nolo Contendere, generally, this index

Notice, correct violations, **Veh 40303.5**

Failure to correct, complaint, **Veh 40618**

Proof of correction, **Veh 40616**

Nuisance, generally, this index

Off highway vehicles. Motor Vehicles, this index

Parole and Probation, generally, this index

Peace Officers, this index

Penalties. Fines and Penalties, generally, this index

Placer County, closed circuit television, testimony or appearance for arraignment, **Veh 40502.1**

Pleas. Nolo Contendere, generally, this index

Pocket bikes, **Veh 21720**

Police, this index

Presentence investigations,

Driving under the influence, **Veh 23655**

Traffic Rules and Regulations, this index

Principal and accessory. Accomplices and Accessories, generally, this index

Prisoners. Jails, generally, this index

Probable Cause, generally, this index

Probation. Parole and Probation, generally, this index

Proof of correction of violations, **Veh 40616**

Public Defenders, generally, this index

Railroad Crossings, this index

Recidivists. Second and subsequent offenses, generally, post

Reckless driving, great bodily injury, **Veh 23104**

Records and recordation. Criminal History Information, generally, this index

Remanufactured vehicles, **Veh 11713.8**

Renderers, inedible grease, records and recordation, **Veh 2468 et seq.**

Roadside rest areas, rules and regulations, violations, **Veh 22520.6**

School Buses, this index

Searches and Seizures, generally, this index

Second and subsequent offenses,

Decals, motorcycles, exhaust systems, noise pollution, **Veh 27202.1**

CRIMES

CRIMES AND OFFENSES—Cont'd

Second and subsequent offenses—Cont'd

Drivers licenses, **Veh 12951**

Driving under the influence, **Veh 23540, 23560, 41403**

Alcohol and drug problem assessment program, **Veh 23646 et seq.**

Habitual traffic offenders, **Veh 14601.3**

Marijuana, motor vehicles, possession while operating, **Veh 23222**

Motor Vehicles, this index

Motorcycles, exhaust systems, noise pollution, decals, **Veh 27202.1**

Roadside rest areas, vista points, violations, **Veh 22520.6**

Speed contests on highways, **Veh 23109**

Speeding, **Veh 13355, 22348**

Traffic Rules and Regulations, this index

Weapons, this index

Sex Offenders, generally, this index

Ships and Shipping, this index

Smog impact fees, motor vehicles, foreign states, **Veh 1673.6**

Snowmobiles, operation, **Veh 23128**

Supersedeas or Stay, generally, this index

Taxicabs, this index

Theft, generally, this index

Thumbprints, **Veh 40500, 40504**

Time, impounding, agricultural machinery and equipment, safety, **Veh 34506.4**

Traffic Rules and Regulations, this index

Traffic Signs and Signals, this index

Traffic violator schools, **Veh 11200 et seq.**

Failure to attend, court orders, **Veh 42005**

Vandalism, generally, this index

Vista points, highways and roads, rules and regulations, **Veh 22520.6**

Warrants, issuance, failure to correct violations, **Veh 40618**

Weapons, this index

Wireless telecommunications. Telecommunications, this index

Youth Buses, this index

CRIMINAL HISTORY INFORMATION

Mentally Retarded and Developmentally Disabled Persons, this index

Motor Vehicles, this index

Paratransit vehicles, drivers, certificates and certification, **Veh 12517.3**

School buses, drivers certificates, **Veh 12517.3**

Tow trucks, **Veh 2430.3, 2432.3**

Youth buses, drivers, certificates and certification, **Veh 12517.3**

CRIMINAL INVESTIGATORS

Addresses, confidentiality, **Veh 1808.4**

CRIMINAL PROCEDURE

Crimes and Offenses, generally, this index

CRIPPLED PERSONS

Handicapped Persons, generally, this index

CROPS

Agricultural Products, generally, this index

CROSSINGS

Railroad Crossings, generally, this index

Traffic Rules and Regulations, this index

Traffic Signs and Signals, this index

CROSSWALKS

Schools and School Districts, this index

Traffic Rules and Regulations, this index

Traffic Signs and Signals, this index

CRUDE OIL

Oil and Gas, generally, this index

CRUISING

Definitions, traffic control points, **Veh 21100**

Traffic rules and regulations, **Veh 21100**

CRUSTACEANS

Shellfish, generally, this index

CULVERTS

Traffic safety fund, use for construction, **Veh 42200**

CURBS AND GUTTERS

Parking regulations, coloring, **Veh 21458**

Traffic Rules and Regulations, this index

Traffic Signs and Signals, this index

CURVES

Traffic Rules and Regulations, this index

DAGGERS

Weapons, generally, this index

DAIRIES AND DAIRY PRODUCTS

Ice cream, vending trucks, **Veh 22456**

DAMAGES

Exemplary damages,

Children and minors, drivers licenses, applications, **Veh 17709**

Motor vehicles,

Minors, drivers licenses, person signing license, **Veh 17709**

Torts, **Veh 17151**

Signatories of drivers license applications for minors, **Veh 17709**

Highways and Roads, this index

Indemnity, generally, this index

Joint and Several Liability, generally, this index

Mitigation, off highway vehicles, **Veh 38318.5**

Motor Vehicles, this index

Off highway vehicles, **Veh 38318.5**

Privileges and Immunities, generally, this index

Removal of vehicles from private property without written authorization, towing companies, **Veh 22658**

Signatories, drivers license applications of minors, **Veh 17700 et seq.**

Taxicabs, impounding, **Veh 21100.4**

Torts, generally, this index

DAMAGES—Cont'd

Towing of vehicles, damage to vehicle, **Veh 22658**

Traffic Rules and Regulations, this index

DANGEROUS WEAPONS

Weapons, generally, this index

DANGERS

Motor carriers, signs and signals, display, **Veh 27903**

Transportation, agricultural hazardous materials, **Veh 12804.2**

DARKNESS

Definitions, motor vehicles, **Veh 280**

Motor vehicles, sunscreening devices, use, **Veh 26708**

DATA MONITORS

Motor vehicles, **Veh 25108**

DAY CAMPS

Camps and Camping, generally, this index

DAYGO BOMBS

Fireworks, generally, this index

DAYS

Definitions, motor vehicles, forfeitures, unlicensed drivers, **Veh 14607.6**

DEAD BODIES

Cemeteries and Dead Bodies, generally, this index

DEADLY WEAPONS

Weapons, generally, this index

DEAF AND MUTE PERSONS

Traffic signs and signals, children, **Veh 21351.7**

DEATH

Accidents, this index

Anatomical Gifts, generally, this index

Boats and Boating, this index

Commercial passenger vehicles, ability to respond in damages, **Veh 16500**

Coroners, generally, this index

Driving school operator, certificate of convenience, **Veh 11105**

Failure of driver to stop, revocation of license, **Veh 13350**

Firefighters and Fire Departments, this index

Highway Patrol, this index

Homicide, generally, this index

Information and aid by driver, accidents, **Veh 20003**

Insurance, generally, this index

Investigation. Coroners, generally, this index

Motor Vehicles, this index

Murder. Homicide, generally, this index

Parents, cancellation of drivers license, **Veh 17712**

Peace Officers, this index

Police, this index

Probate Proceedings, generally, this index

DEATH—Cont'd
Traffic violator school licensees, temporary license, **Veh 11204**

DECALS
Motor Vehicles, this index
Motorcycles, exhaust systems, noise pollution, crimes and offenses, **Veh 27202.1**

DECEDENTS ESTATES
Probate Proceedings, generally, this index

DECEIT
Fraud, generally, this index

DECELERATION LIGHTS
Generally, **Veh 25251.5**

DECEPTION
Fraud, generally, this index

DECREES
Judgments and Decrees, generally, this index

DEER
Fish and Game, this index

DEFACING
Driving privilege, suspension, **Veh 13202.6**
Motor vehicle identification numbers, **Veh 10802**
Paints and Painting, this index
Restrictions, driving privileges, **Veh 13202.6**
Revocation or suspension, driving privilege, **Veh 13202.6**
Traffic control devices, **Veh 21464**
Vehicle identification number, **Veh 10802**

DEFALCATION
Embezzlement, generally, this index

DEFAULT
Motor Vehicles, this index

DEFECTIVE WINDSHIELD ACT
Generally, **Veh 26710**

DEFENSE HIGHWAYS
Interstate highways. Highways and Roads, this index

DEFERRED ACTION FOR CHILDHOOD ARRIVALS
Immigration, this index

DEFINITIONS
Words and Phrases, generally, this index

DEFROSTERS
Motor vehicles, equipment, **Veh 26712**

DELINQUENT CHILDREN
Juvenile Delinquents and Dependents, generally, this index

DELINQUENT TAXES
Income Tax—State, this index
Sales and Use Taxes, this index

DEMEROL
Drug Addicts, generally, this index

DEMONSTRATION PROGRAMS
Highways and Roads, this index

DENTISTS AND DENTISTRY
Medical waste. Hazardous Substances and Waste, this index

DENVER BOOTS
Traffic rules and regulations, scofflaws, **Veh 22651.7**

DEPARTMENTS
Administrative Law and Procedure, generally, this index
Definitions,
Highway patrol, equipment of vehicles, **Veh 24000**
Motor vehicles, **Veh 290, 291**
Autonomous vehicles, **Veh 38750**

DEPENDENT CHILDREN
Juvenile Delinquents and Dependents, generally, this index

DEPENDENTS
Juvenile Delinquents and Dependents, generally, this index

DEPORTATION
Aliens, this index

DEPOSITS
Emergency medical services funds, **Veh 42007**
Inspection fees, youth bus inspection fees, **Veh 2807.3**
Motor Vehicles, this index
Off highway vehicle fund, **Veh 42204**
Traffic violator schools, in lieu of bond, **Veh 11203**
Youth bus inspection fees, **Veh 2807.3**

DESCENT AND DISTRIBUTION
Probate Proceedings, generally, this index
Succession, generally, this index

DESERTION
Juvenile Delinquents and Dependents, generally, this index

DESIGNS AND DESIGNERS
Highways and Roads, this index

DESTINY NICOLE STOUT MEMORIAL ACT
Generally, **Veh 22456**

DESTROYED PROPERTY
Lost or Destroyed Property, generally, this index

DESTRUCTIVE DEVICES
Explosives, generally, this index

DETENTION FACILITIES
Juvenile Institutions and Schools, generally, this index

DETONATING PRIMERS
Explosives, generally, this index

DETOURS
Highways and Roads, this index

DETOXIFICATION VEHICLES
Lamps, **Veh 25110**

DEVELOPMENTAL DISABILITIES
Mentally Retarded and Developmentally Disabled Persons, generally, this index

DEVELOPMENTALLY DISABLED PERSONS
Mentally Retarded and Developmentally Disabled Persons, generally, this index

DEVISES AND DEVISEES
Gifts, Devises and Bequests, generally, this index

DIAGNOSTIC LABORATORIES
Laboratories, generally, this index

DIAL A RIDE
Paratransit Vehicles, generally, this index

DIESEL FUEL TAX
Licenses and permits, foreign vehicles, **Veh 2400**

DIFFUSED LIGHTS
Motor equipment, **Veh 25400, 25401**

DIKES
Levees and Flood Control, generally, this index

DILAUDID
Drug Addicts, generally, this index

DIMMING LIGHTS
Approaching vehicles, **Veh 24409**

DIRECTORS
Consumer motor vehicle recovery corporation, **Veh 12202**
Definitions, motor vehicles, **Veh 295**
Motor Vehicles Department, this index
New motor vehicle board, **Veh 3014**

DIRKS
Weapons, generally, this index

DIRT
Tow cars, shovel to spread dirt on oil or grease deposited by disabled vehicle, **Veh 27700**
Traffic rules and regulations, highway dumping, **Veh 23112, 23113**

DISABLED PERSON PLACARD
Definitions, motor vehicles, **Veh 4461, 4463**

DISABLED PERSONS
Definitions, parking, **Veh 295.5**
Handicapped Persons, generally, this index

DISABLED VEHICLES
Motor Carriers, this index

DISABLED

DISABLED VETERANS
Veterans, this index

DISASTERS
Highways and Roads, this index
Rules and regulations, removal of parked
or standing vehicles, **Veh 22654**
War and Civil Defense, generally, this index

DISCHARGE
Hospitals, this index
Military Forces, this index

DISCLOSURE
Bicycles, insurance, **Veh 406**
Crimes and Offenses, this index
Electricity, this index
Highways and roads, toll roads and
bridges, pay by plate toll payment,
Veh 23301.8
Insurance, this index
Junk and junk dealers, NMVTIS (national
motor vehicle title information sys-
tem), history, reports, **Veh 11713.26**
Motor Vehicle Insurance, this index
Motor Vehicles, this index
Motor Vehicles Department, this index
Motorized scooters, manufacturers and
manufacturing, **Veh 407.5**
Public Utilities, this index
Remanufactured vehicles, **Veh 11713.7**
Sheriffs, this index

DISCRIMINATION
Definitions, motor vehicles, franchises,
Veh 11713.3
Motor Vehicles, this index
Traffic violators schools, handicapped per-
sons, **Veh 11216.2**

DISEASES
Housing Authorities, generally, this index

DISGUISES
Vehicle identification numbers, **Veh 10802**

DISMANTLERS
Generally, **Veh 11500 et seq.**
Motor Vehicles, this index

DISMISSAL AND NONSUIT
Motor vehicles, prosecution of employees,
record, **Veh 40003**
Traffic Rules and Regulations, this index

DISPATCHERS
Police, this index

DISTANCE
Motor vehicle lighting equipment, visibility
requirement, **Veh 24251**

DISTANCE BETWEEN VEHICLES
Traffic Rules and Regulations, this index

DISTILLED SPIRITS
Alcoholic Beverages, generally, this index

DISTINCTIVE COLOR ACT
Traffic officers, **Veh 40800**

DISTRIBUTION OF DECEDENTS ESTATES
Succession, generally, this index

DISTRIBUTORS
Motor Vehicles, this index
Motorcycles, licenses with general distin-
guishing number, **Veh 11701**
Snowmobiles, licenses with general distin-
guishing number, **Veh 11701**

DISTRICT ATTORNEYS
Addresses, confidentiality, **Veh 1808.4**
Confidential or privileged information, addresses, **Veh 1808.4**
Definitions, motor vehicles, forfeitures,
unlicensed drivers, **Veh 14607.6**
Husband and wife, address, confidentiality, **Veh 1808.4**
Investigations and investigators, motor vehicles, confidential and privileged information, records and recordation,
address of investigator, **Veh 1808.2**
Motor Vehicles, this index

DISTRICT OF COLUMBIA
Motor vehicle violations, drivers license
revocation or suspension, **Veh 13352**

DISTRICTS
Bridges. Highway and Bridge Districts,
generally, this index
Community colleges and districts. Col-
leges and Universities, this index
Definitions, buses, bicycles, length, Sacra-
mento City and County, **Veh 35400.8**
Harbor Districts, generally, this index
Health Care Districts, generally, this index
Highway and Bridge Districts, generally,
this index
Local Agencies, generally, this index
Mosquito Abatement or Vector Control
Districts, generally, this index
Motor Vehicles, this index
Officers and employees. Social Security,
generally, this index
Schools and School Districts, generally,
this index
Traffic laws, applicability to official vehi-
cles, **Veh 21052**
Traffic safety program, participation, **Veh
2909, 2910**
Transit Districts, generally, this index
Vector control districts. Mosquito Abate-
ment or Vector Control Districts,
generally, this index

DITCHERS
Special highway construction equipment,
Veh 565

DIVIDED HIGHWAYS
Highways and Roads, this index

DIVISIONS
Juvenile Facilities Division, generally, this
index
Motor vehicles, license plates, special
plates, **Veh 5151 et seq.**

DOCTORS
Physicians and Surgeons, generally, this
index

DOCUMENTED VESSEL
Definitions, registration and transfer of
vessel, **Veh 9840**

DOCUMENTS OF TITLE
Bills of Lading, generally, this index

DODDER
Weeds, generally, this index

DOGS
Motor vehicles, transporting, restraining,
Veh 23117, 42001.4

DOLLIES
Definitions, motor vehicles, **Veh 225**
Permanent trailer identification plates,
certificates and certification, **Veh
5014.1**
Registration, **Veh 4000**
Weight fees, **Veh 9400**
Weight fees, **Veh 9400**

DOMESTIC ANIMALS
Animals, generally, this index

DOMESTIC CORPORATIONS
Corporations, generally, this index

DOMESTIC INSURERS
Insurance, generally, this index

DOMESTIC VIOLENCE
Motor vehicles, license plates, new plates,
Veh 4467

DOMICILE AND RESIDENCE
Definitions, motor vehicles, registration,
Veh 516
Highway patrol, commissioner, **Veh 2107**
Mentally Retarded and Developmentally
Disabled Persons, this index
Motor vehicle insurance, address, confi-
dential or privileged information, rec-
ords and recordation, **Veh 1808.22**
Motor Vehicles, this index
Police dispatchers, disclosure, **Veh 1808.4**

DOMINION OF CANADA
Canada, generally, this index

DONATIONS
Gifts, Devises and Bequests, generally, this
index

DONATIVE TRANSFERS
Gifts, Devises and Bequests, generally, this
index

DOORS
Motor Vehicles, this index
Traffic control, opening, restrictions, **Veh
22517**

DOWN PAYMENTS
Motor Vehicles, this index

DRAG RACING
Generally, **Veh 23109 et seq.**
Traffic Rules and Regulations, this index

DRAGLINES
Special highway construction equipment, definitions, **Veh 565**

DRAWBARS
Definitions, motor vehicles, **Veh 300**
Motor Carriers, this index
Motor Vehicles, this index

DRILLS AND DRILLING
Equipment, motor vehicle length limitation exemption, **Veh 35414**

DRINKS
Alcoholic Beverages, generally, this index

DRIVEAWAY TOWAWAY OPERATION
Accidents, **Veh 20002**
Definitions, motor vehicles, **Veh 303**

DRIVER EDUCATION
Schools and School Districts, this index

DRIVER IMPROVEMENT PROGRAMS
Traffic Rules and Regulations, this index

DRIVER TRAINING
Colleges and Universities, this index
Driving Schools, generally, this index
Traffic Rules and Regulations, this index

DRIVERS
Definitions, motor vehicles, **Veh 305**

DRIVERS LICENSE ACT
Generally, **Veh 12500 et seq.**

DRIVERS LICENSE COMPACT
Generally, **Veh 15000 et seq.**

DRIVERS LICENSES
Generally, **Veh 12500 et seq.**
Motor Vehicles, this index

DRIVEWAYS
Bicycles, **Veh 21113**
Parking in front of private driveways, owners and lessees, permits, **Veh 22507.2**
Roller skates, **Veh 21113**
Skateboards, **Veh 21113**

DRIVING RECORD HISTORY
Definitions, motor vehicles, drivers license revocation or suspension, **Veh 14601.3**

DRIVING RULES
Generally, **Veh 21000 et seq.**
Traffic Rules and Regulations, generally, this index

DRIVING SCHOOLS
Generally, **Veh 11100 et seq.**
Accreditation, **Veh 11100.5**
Actions against licensees, bonds or deposits, **Veh 11102.1**
Actions and proceedings, agent for service of process, **Veh 11102**

DRIVING SCHOOLS—Cont'd
Age,
Instructors, **Veh 11104**
Operators, **Veh 11102.5**
Aged persons, courses for mature drivers, **Veh 1675 et seq.**
Agent for service of process, **Veh 11102**
Aggressive driving, courses of study, **Veh 11113**
Bonds (officers and fiduciaries), **Veh 11102, 11102.1, 11110**
License cancellation, **Veh 11110.2**
Certificates and certification,
All terrain vehicles, licensed safety instructors, **Veh 11100.1**
Mature driver improvement courses, **Veh 1675 et seq.**
Certificates of convenience, death of operator, **Veh 11105**
Certification, **Veh 11100.5**
Change in ownership or location, notice, **Veh 11108.5**
Character and reputation. Licenses and permits, post
Charters, suspension or cancellation, license cancellation, **Veh 11110.2**
Children and minors,
Instruction permits, **Veh 12509**
Provisional licenses, **Veh 12814.6**
Civil liability for damages, student license, **Veh 12650**
Colleges and universities, exemptions, **Veh 11101**
Commercial vehicles, licensing standards, **Veh 11113.5**
Compromise and settlement, **Veh 11218**
Fines and penalties, **Veh 11111.5**
Continuing education, instructors, in lieu of license renewal examination, **Veh 11105.1**
Corporate status of licensee, change, license cancellation, **Veh 11110.2**
Courses of study, **Veh 11113**
Standards, **Veh 11113.5**
Crimes and offenses, **Veh 11110**
Application of law, **Veh 40007**
License suspension, revocation, **Veh 11110.7**
Licenses, **Veh 40000.11**
Revocation, **Veh 11107, 11110**
Dealers, exemptions, **Veh 11101**
Death of operator, certificate of convenience, **Veh 11105**
Definition, **Veh 310.6**
Racing vehicle, **Veh 11101**
Deposits, licensees, return, **Veh 11102.1**
Deposits in lieu of bonds, **Veh 11102.1**
Descent and distribution, license, **Veh 11105**
Division, types of businesses, **Veh 1670**
Drivers licenses,
Completion of course, **Veh 12509**
Condition of probation, **Veh 14250.5**
Instructor, **Veh 11104**
Reinstatement, **Veh 13368**
Student licenses, **Veh 12650 et seq.**

DRIVING SCHOOLS—Cont'd
Driving instructor, definitions, **Veh 310.4**
Driving school operator, definitions, **Veh 310.8**
Driving school owner, definitions, **Veh 311**
Drugs, driving under influence of, cancellation, suspension or revocation of license, **Veh 11110**
Drunken driving, revocation of license, **Veh 11110**
Educational institutions, application of law, **Veh 11101**
Equipment, **Veh 11102**
Rules and regulations, **Veh 11113**
Seatbelts, **Veh 27304**
Examinations and examiners, **Veh 11104**
Fee, **Veh 11102**
License renewal, **Veh 11105**
Exemptions, **Veh 11101**
False personation, license revocation, **Veh 11110**
Fees, **Veh 11105.2**
Examination, **Veh 11102**
Instructors license, **Veh 11104**
Licenses and permits, suspension, reinstatement, **Veh 11111**
Student licenses, **Veh 12660**
Fines and penalties,
Application of law, **Veh 40007**
Compromise and settlement, **Veh 11111.5**
Forms, license applications, **Veh 11104.6**
Fraud,
Cancellation of license, **Veh 11110**
Revocation of license, **Veh 11107**
Student licenses, disciplinary action, **Veh 12660**
Handicapped persons,
Instructors, licenses and permits, **Veh 11104**
Licenses and permits, revocation, **Veh 11110**
Hazardous radioactive materials, drivers certificates, **Veh 12524**
Hearing,
License refused, **Veh 11112**
License revocation or suspension, **Veh 11110, 11111**
Independent driving instructor, license, **Veh 11105.5**
Inspection of records, **Veh 11108**
Instruction permits, **Veh 12509**
Instructors,
Change in address, notice, **Veh 11108.5**
Character and reputation, **Veh 11104.5**
Failure to renew license, **Veh 11105.3**
Handicapped persons, licenses and permits, **Veh 11104**
Licenses, **Veh 11113.5**
Certificate, **Veh 11105.1**
Insurance, **Veh 11103**
Investigation fees, **Veh 11102**
Licenses and permits, **Veh 11100 et seq.**
All terrain vehicles, safety instructors, **Veh 11100.1**

DRIVING

DRIVING SCHOOLS—Cont'd
Licenses and permits—Cont'd
Cancellation, **Veh 11110, 11110.2,
11110.5**
Reinstatement, **Veh 11110.5**
Certificate,
Corporate charters, suspension or
cancellation, **Veh 11110.2**
Issuance by department, **Veh 11105**
Notice of hearing, **Veh 11111**
Refusal to issue, grounds, **Veh 11107**
Temporary permits, **Veh 11106**
Character and reputation, **Veh 11104.5**
Revocation, **Veh 11110**
Crimes and offenses, **Veh 40000.11**
Suspension, revocation, **Veh 11110.7**
Deposits, return, **Veh 11102.1**
Drivers licenses, generally, ante
Driving while under influence of drugs,
Veh 11110
Exemptions, **Veh 11101**
Failure to renew, **Veh 11105.3**
Fees, **Veh 11105.2**
Reinstatement, **Veh 11111**
Forms, applications, **Veh 11104.6**
Handicapped persons, instructors, **Veh
11104**
Independent instructor, **Veh 11105.5**
Instructors, **Veh 11100, 11104**
License certificate, **Veh 11105.1**
Issuance, **Veh 11105**
Moral turpitude, license suspension,
revocation, **Veh 11110.7**
Nolo contendere,
Conviction, suspension or revocation,
Veh 11110
Refusal to issue license, **Veh 11107**
Operators, **Veh 11105**
Permitting use by nonlicensed person,
Veh 11110
Record, person instructed, **Veh 11108**
Reexamination, **Veh 11114**
Refusal to issue, **Veh 11107**
Hearing, **Veh 11112**
Renewal, **Veh 11105**
Failure to renew, **Veh 11105.3**
Instructors, **Veh 11105.1**
Standards, **Veh 11113.5**
Suspension or revocation,
Causes, **Veh 11110.1**
Crimes and offenses, **Veh 11110.7**
Fraudulent student licenses, **Veh
12660**
Reexamination, failure to submit, **Veh
11114**
Temporary permit, **Veh 11106**
Temporary suspension, hearings, **Veh
11111**
Time, renewal, **Veh 11105**
Instructors, **Veh 11105.1**
Traffic violator schools, **Veh 11200 et
seq.**
Machinery and equipment. Equipment,
generally, ante
Mature driver improvement courses, **Veh
1675 et seq.**

DRIVING SCHOOLS—Cont'd
Motor Vehicle Insurance, this index
Nolo contendere,
Conviction of crime, refusal to issue
license, **Veh 11107**
Licenses, suspension or revocation, **Veh
11110**
Nonprofit corporations or organizations,
exemptions, **Veh 11101**
Notice,
Cancellation, suspension or revocation
of license, **Veh 11111**
Change in ownership or location of
school, **Veh 11108.5, 11110.2**
License revocation or suspension, **Veh
11110**
Off highway vehicles,
Records and recordation, inspection,
Veh 11108
Safety instructors,
Licenses, **Veh 11100.1**
Qualifications, **Veh 11104.3**
Safety training organizations,
Insurance, **Veh 11103.1**
Qualifications, licenses, **Veh 11105.6**
Offenses. Crimes and offenses, generally,
ante
Office, place of business, **Veh 1670, 1671**
Operators, **Veh 11102.5**
Change in address, notice, **Veh 11108.5**
Character and reputation, **Veh 11104.5**
Failure to renew license, **Veh 11105.3**
Licenses, **Veh 11105**
Perjury, workers compensation, compli-
ance, **Veh 11103.2**
Permits. Licenses and permits, generally,
ante
Place of business, **Veh 11102**
Abandonment, license cancellation, **Veh
11110.2**
Probationary license, **Veh 11105**
Procedure, refusal to issue license, **Veh
11107**
Process,
Agent for service of process, appoint-
ment, **Veh 11102**
New address or termination of business,
Veh 11111.2
Public schools, application of law, **Veh
11101**
Qualifications, **Veh 11102**
Instructor, **Veh 11104**
Racing vehicle, exemption, **Veh 11101**
Radioactive materials, drivers certificates,
Veh 12524
Records and recordation, **Veh 11108**
Failure to keep, **Veh 11110**
Service of process, **Veh 11102**
Reexamination of licensees, **Veh 11114**
Renewal of license, **Veh 11105**
Reports, student license programs, **Veh
12660**
Return to licensee, bond or deposit, **Veh
11102.1**

DRIVING SCHOOLS—Cont'd
Revocation or suspension of license, **Veh
11107, 11110**
Instructor, **Veh 11104**
Road rage, courses of study, **Veh 11113**
Rules and regulations, **Veh 11113**
Safe mechanical condition of vehicles, **Veh
11109**
Salesmen, exemptions, **Veh 11101**
Seatbelts, **Veh 27304**
Service of process,
Appointment of agent for service of
process, **Veh 11102**
New address or termination of business,
Veh 11111.2
Settlement and compromise, fines and
penalties, **Veh 11111.5**
Solicitation of business, **Veh 11110**
Standards, **Veh 1659**
Licensing, **Veh 11113.5**
Student licenses, **Veh 12650 et seq.**
Temporary permit, **Veh 11106**
Tests, applicant for license, interference
with, **Veh 21701**
Time, licenses and permits, renewal, **Veh
11105**
Instructors, **Veh 11105.1**
Traffic rules and regulations, interference
with driver or mechanism, exemption,
Veh 21701
Traffic safety program, **Veh 2900 et seq.**
Traffic Violator Schools, generally, this in-
dex
Tuition, mature driver improvement
courses, **Veh 1676**
Two or more types of businesses, division
between, **Veh 1670**
Unsafe driving, permitting, **Veh 11110**
Unsafe manner or contrary to safe driving
practices, operation of vehicle, cancel-
lation, suspension or revocation of li-
cense, **Veh 11110**
Violators schools. Traffic Violator
Schools, generally, this index
Workers compensation, **Veh 11103.2**

DRIVING UNDER THE INFLUENCE
Generally, **Veh 23152 et seq.**
Traffic Rules and Regulations, this index

DRIVING WITH PERMISSION ACT
Generally, **Veh 17150 et seq.**

DRUG ABUSE
Drug Addicts, generally, this index

DRUG ADDICTS
Drivers licenses, **Veh 12806, 12809**
Driving under the influence. Traffic
Rules and Regulations, this index
Motor vehicles, drivers licenses, refusal,
Veh 12809

DRUGS AND MEDICINE
Abuse,
Addicts. Drug Addicts, generally, this
index
Drug Addicts, generally, this index

DRUGS AND MEDICINE—Cont'd

Activity buses, drivers certificates, revocation, **Veh 13376**

Addicts. Drug Addicts, generally, this index

Agricultural machinery and equipment, tests, exemptions, **Veh 40000.15**

Boats and Boating, this index

Cannabis sativa. Marijuana, generally, post

Children and minors, drivers license delay, restriction, suspension or revocation, **Veh 13202.5**

Crimes and offenses,
  Marijuana, post
  Second and subsequent offenses. Marijuana, post

Definitions, Vehicle Code, **Veh 312**

Drivers licenses. Motor Vehicles, this index

Driving under the influence. Traffic Rules and Regulations, this index

Fines and penalties,
  Marijuana, post
  Motor vehicles, marijuana, possession while operating, **Veh 23222**

First aid, school bus driver, qualifications, **Veh 12522**

Hazardous Substances and Waste, generally, this index

Hemp. Marijuana, generally, post

Indian hemp. Marijuana, generally, post

Marijuana,
  Crimes and offenses, motor vehicles, possession while driving, **Veh 23222**
  Fines and penalties, motor vehicles, possession while operating, **Veh 23222**
  Motor vehicles, possession while driving, **Veh 23222**
  Off highway vehicles, possession, **Veh 23222**
  Possession, motor vehicles, operation, **Veh 23222**
  Second and subsequent offenses, motor vehicles, possession of marijuana while operating, **Veh 23222**

Mentally Retarded and Developmentally Disabled Persons, this index

Motor Carriers, this index

Motor Vehicles, this index

Paratransit vehicles, drivers,
  Certificates and certification, revocation, **Veh 13376**
  Tests and testing, **Veh 34520.5**

Possession,
  Marijuana, ante
  Motor vehicles, possession of marijuana, **Veh 23222**

School buses, drivers certificates, revocation, **Veh 13376**

Schools and School Districts, this index

Tests,
  Exemptions, agricultural machinery and equipment, **Veh 40000.15**
  Paratransit vehicles, drivers, **Veh 34520.5**

DRUGS AND MEDICINE—Cont'd

Youth buses, driver certificates, revocation, **Veh 13376**

DRUNKEN DRIVING

Generally, **Veh 23152 et seq.**

DUAL SOLID TIRES

Motor vehicles, outside diameters, **Veh 27453**

DUMP TRUCKS

Motor Carriers, this index

DUMPS AND DUMPING

Hazardous Substances and Waste, this index

Junk and Junk Dealers, generally, this index

DUNE BUGGY

Definitions, off highway motor vehicles, **Veh 38012**

Identification plates, display, **Veh 38170**

Place of business, posting, signs and licenses, application of law, **Veh 11709**

Rules and regulations, **Veh 38000 et seq.**

DURESS OR COERCION

Motor vehicles, dealers, **Veh 11713.1, 11713.2**

DUST

Air Pollution, generally, this index

Highways, closing, menace to public health or safety, **Veh 2812**

School buses, additional lights, reduced visibility, **Veh 25102.5**

DWELLINGS

Housing, generally, this index

DYNAMITE

Explosives, generally, this index

E MAIL

Electronic Mail, generally, this index

EARNINGS

Compensation and Salaries, generally, this index

EARPLUGS

Bicycles, **Veh 27400**

Motor vehicles, wearing while operating, **Veh 27400**

ECOLOGICAL RESERVES

Definitions, highway access, **Veh 21117**

Highways and roads, access, local authority control, **Veh 21117**

ECOLOGY

Environment, generally, this index

ECONOMIC AUTOMOBILE THEFT

Definitions, **Veh 10901**
  Prevention, **Veh 10901**

ECONOMIC POISONS

Peace officers, pesticide spillage or release reports, **Veh 20017**

EDUCATION

Alcoholics and Alcoholism, this index

Anatomical Gifts, generally, this index

Animals, traffic regulations, **Veh 21113**

Colleges and Universities, generally, this index

Continuing Education, generally, this index

Driving Schools, generally, this index

Motor Vehicles, this index

Records and recordation, motor vehicles, gifts, devises and bequests, **Veh 1660**

Schools and School Districts, generally, this index

Traffic Rules and Regulations, this index

Training, generally, this index

EDUCATIONAL PERSONNEL

School Officers and Employees, generally, this index

EIGHT HUNDRED (800) NUMBERS

Telecommunications, this index

ELDERLY PERSONS

Aged Persons, generally, this index

ELECTIONS

Registration of voters,
  Address, change, notice, **Veh 12950**
  Drivers licenses, notice, **Veh 1679**

Notice,
  Change of address, **Veh 12950**
  Drivers licenses, **Veh 1679**

ELECTORS

Elections, generally, this index

ELECTRIC CARTS

Traffic rules and regulations, local authorities, **Veh 21114.5**

ELECTRIC PERSONAL ASSISTIVE MOBILITY DEVICES

Generally, **Veh 21280 et seq.**

ELECTRIC VEHICLES

Motor Vehicles, this index

ELECTRICITY

Confidential or privileged information, electric vehicles, registration, access, **Veh 1808.23**

Disclosure, electric vehicles, registration, confidential or privileged information, **Veh 1808.23**

Motor Vehicles, this index

ELECTRONIC COMMUNICATIONS

Telecommunications, generally, this index

ELECTRONIC DEVICES AND EQUIPMENT

Motor vehicles, license plates, **Veh 4853**

Traffic rules and regulations, parking violations, proof of ownership, verification, **Veh 40900**

ELECTRONIC MAIL

Motor vehicles,
  Infractions, **Veh 23123.5**

ELECTRONIC MAIL—Cont'd
Motor vehicles—Cont'd
  Tow trucks, private property, removal,
    Veh 22658
Traffic rules and regulations, infractions,
  Veh 23123.5

ELECTRONIC RECORDING
Motor Vehicles, this index

ELECTRONIC SIGNATURES
Signatures, this index

ELECTRONIC TRANSMISSIONS
Motor vehicle insurance, coverage, **Veh 16058**
Motor vehicles, documents, **Veh 1801.1**

ELEEMOSYNARY INSTITUTIONS
Charities, generally, this index
Public Benefit Corporations, generally,
  this index

ELEMENTARY SCHOOLS
Schools and School Districts, generally,
  this index

ELEVATED RAILROADS
Transit Districts, generally, this index

EMBANKMENTS
Levees and Flood Control, generally, this
  index

EMBEZZLEMENT
Boats, reporting, **Veh 10553, 10554**
Motor Vehicles, this index
Ships, reporting, **Veh 10553, 10554**
Traffic rules and regulations, removal of
  parked or standing vehicles, **Veh 22650 et seq.**

EMBLEMENTS
Agricultural Products, generally, this index

EMBLEMS
Badges, Emblems and Insignia, generally,
  this index

EMERGENCIES
Bicycles, peace officers, traffic rules and
  regulations, exemptions, **Veh 21200**
Buses, two way communication devices,
  Veh 24018
Closing, highways, **Veh 2812**
Freeways, this index
Highway patrol,
  Directing traffic, **Veh 2410**
  Transfer, **Veh 2255**
Highways and Roads, this index
Levees and Flood Control, this index
Limousines, exits, **Veh 27375**
Medical Care and Treatment, this index
Medical dispatchers, training, highway pa-
  trol, **Veh 2422**
Motor Carriers, this index
Motor Vehicles, this index
Motorist aid system, freeways, **Veh 2421.5**
Off highway vehicles, peace officers, **Veh 38025**

EMERGENCIES—Cont'd
Peace Officers, this index
Permits, traffic rules and regulations, ex-
  ceeding maximum size, weight limita-
  tions, **Veh 35780 et seq.**
Physicians and Surgeons, this index
Police, this index
Public Buildings and Works, this index
Rescue, generally, this index
State Agencies, this index
Traffic Rules and Regulations, this index
Traffic safety program, **Veh 2900 et seq.**
Traffic Signs and Signals, this index

**EMERGENCY MEDICAL SERVICES AU-
THORITY**
Guidelines, emergency medical dispatcher
  training, **Veh 2422**

EMERGENCY MEDICAL SERVICES FUNDS
Deposits, **Veh 42007**

EMERGENCY MEDICAL TECHNICIANS
Blood tests, driving while intoxicated, **Veh 23158**
Emergency vehicles, pollution control de-
  vices, **Veh 27156.2, 27156.3**
Pollution control devices, emergency vehi-
  cles, **Veh 27156.2, 27156.3**

EMERGENCY MOVE
Definitions, motor carriers, **Veh 34631.5**

EMERGENCY ROAD SERVICE
Definitions, tow truck driver certification,
  Veh 2430.1

EMERGENCY ROADSIDE ASSISTANCE
Generally, **Veh 2435 et seq.**

EMERGENCY SERVICES
Highway Patrol, this index

EMERGENCY VEHICLES
Ambulances, generally, this index
Applicability of traffic laws, **Veh 21052**
Arbitrary exercise of privileges, traffic law
  exemptions, **Veh 21056**
Blue lights,
  Highway patrol, **Veh 25258**
  Police departments, **Veh 25258**
  Sheriffs departments, **Veh 25258**
Civil liability, exemptions, **Veh 17004**
Colored lights, **Veh 25252**
  Authorized vehicles, **Veh 25252, 25258, 25259**
  Blue lights, generally, ante
  Coroners vehicles, **Veh 25264**
  Pet ambulances, **Veh 25271**
  Red warning light, **Veh 25252, 25269**
  Revolving and warning lights, **Veh 25252**
  Side lamps, **Veh 25102**
Coroner, warning lights, **Veh 25264**
Definitions, **Veh 165**
Display of white light, **Veh 25258**
Due care, duty of driver or operator, **Veh 21056**
Earplugs, wearing while operating, **Veh 27400**

EMERGENCY VEHICLES—Cont'd
Exemptions,
  Civil liability, **Veh 17004**
  Pollution control devices, **Veh 27156.2, 27156.3**
  Spotlamps, **Veh 24404**
  Toll roads and bridges, rates and
    charges, vehicular crossings, **Veh 23301.5**
  Traffic rules and regulations, **Veh 21052, 21055, 21056**
Financial responsibility, exemptions, **Veh 16051**
Fire protection, pollution control devices,
  Veh 27156.2
Flashing lights, **Veh 25252**
  Authorized vehicles, **Veh 25252, 25252.5, 25258, 25259**
  Coroners vehicles, **Veh 25264**
  Permitted, **Veh 25251**
  Pet ambulances, **Veh 25271**
  White light, controlling traffic signals,
    Veh 25258
Gaseous discharge lamp, controlling traffic
  signals, **Veh 25258**
Restrictions, **Veh 24405**
Hazardous substances and waste,
  Signs and signals, exemptions, **Veh 27903**
  Spill response vehicles, warning lights,
    Veh 25260.4
Headsets, wearing while operating, **Veh 27400**
Highway patrol, blue light display, **Veh 25258**
Highways and Roads, this index
Horns or warning devices, **Veh 27000 et seq.**
Licenses and permits, **Veh 2416**
  Suspension or revocation, **Veh 2417**
Lights and lighting,
  Colored lights, generally, ante
  Flashing lights, generally, ante
  Gaseous discharge, controlling traffic
    signals, **Veh 25258**
  Highway patrol, blue lights, **Veh 25258**
  Interior warning lamps, **Veh 24003**
  Pet ambulances, **Veh 25271**
  Restrictions on number, **Veh 24405**
  Side lamps, **Veh 25102**
  Spotlamps, exemption, **Veh 24404**
  Warning lights, **Veh 25252, 25258, 25259, 25264, 25268, 25269**
Manufacturers defect correction, expense
  reimbursement, **Veh 24007.1**
Medical technician paramedic use, pollu-
  tion control devices, **Veh 27156.2, 27156.3**
Pet ambulances, warning lights, **Veh 25271**
Police, blue light display, **Veh 25258**
Pollution control devices, **Veh 27156.2, 27156.3**
Privately owned ambulances, transporta-
  tion of medical supplies, lifesaving
  equipment or personnel, **Veh 2416**
Red lights, side lamps, **Veh 25102**

EMERGENCY VEHICLES—Cont'd
Red warning lamp, **Veh 25252**
    Use authorized, **Veh 25269**
Resuscitation equipment, **Veh 2418.5**
Revolving red warning lights, **Veh 25252**
Safety headsets, wearing while operating, **Veh 27400**
Semaphore changing devices, **Veh 21464**
Sheriffs, blue light display, **Veh 25258**
Side lamps, red lights, **Veh 25102**
Signs and signals, privately owned ambulances, transportation of medical supplies, lifesaving equipment or personnel, **Veh 2416**
Sirens, **Veh 27002**
    Standards and specifications, adoption and enforcement, **Veh 26103**
Spot lamps, **Veh 24404**
Studded tires, **Veh 27454**
Toll roads and bridges, exemptions, rates and charges, vehicular crossings, **Veh 23301.5**
Traffic Rules and Regulations, this index
Traffic safety program, **Veh 2900 et seq.**
Traffic signs and signals, gaseous discharge lamp, **Veh 25258**
Warning lights, **Veh 25252, 25258, 25259, 25264, 25268, 25269**
White light, gaseous discharge lamp, controlling traffic signals, **Veh 25258**
White warning lights, authorized vehicles, **Veh 25259**

EMISSIONS
Air Pollution, this index

EMOLUMENTS
Compensation and Salaries, generally, this index

EMPLOYEES
Labor and Employment, generally, this index
Public Officers and Employees, generally, this index

EMPLOYERS
Definitions,
    Emergency roadside assistance, **Veh 2436**
    Tow truck driver certification, **Veh 2430.1**
Labor and Employment, generally, this index

EMPLOYMENT
Labor and Employment, generally, this index

ENCLOSURES
Fences, generally, this index

ENCUMBRANCES
Liens and Incumbrances, generally, this index

ENDORSEMENT
Motor Vehicles, this index

ENEMY ATTACK
War and Civil Defense, generally, this index

ENERGY
Motor Vehicle Fuel, generally, this index
Vanpooling, generally, this index

ENGAGED IN A BUSINESS
Definitions, station wagons, weight fees, **Veh 9404**

ENGINEERING AND TRAFFIC SURVEY
Definitions, motor vehicles, **Veh 627**

ENGINEERS
Amber flashing warning lights, civil engineer vehicles, **Veh 25278**
Flashing amber warning lights, civil engineer vehicles, **Veh 25278**
Land surveyors. Surveys and Surveyors, generally, this index
Lights and lighting, flashing amber warning lights, civil engineer vehicles, **Veh 25278**
Motor vehicles, civil engineer vehicles, flashing amber warning lights, **Veh 25278**
Railroads, this index
Surveys and Surveyors, generally, this index
Warning lights, amber flashing warning lights, civil engineer vehicles, **Veh 25278**

ENGINES
Motor Vehicles, this index

ENGLISH LANGUAGE
Drivers licenses, inability to read or understand, refusal to issue or renew, **Veh 12805**
Motor vehicle reports and notices, **Veh 9**
Traffic rules and regulations, **Veh 1656**
Vehicle Code, publication, **Veh 1656**

ENGRAVERS AND ENGRAVING
Motor vehicles,
    Drivers licenses, **Veh 12800.5, 12811**
    Identification cards, **Veh 13005, 13005.3, 13005.5**

ENTOMBMENT
Cemeteries and Dead Bodies, generally, this index

ENVIRONMENT
Air Pollution, generally, this index
Funds, motor vehicle license plates, **Veh 5100 et seq.**
Hazardous Substances and Waste, generally, this index
Highways and Roads, this index
Internet, license plates, orders, **Veh 5112**
License plates, environmental design, **Veh 5075**
Motor Vehicles, this index
Off highway vehicles, **Veh 38319 et seq.**
Pollution, generally, this index

ENVIRONMENTAL LICENSE PLATE FUND
Generally, **Veh 5100 et seq.**

EPILEPSY
Drivers licenses, denial, **Veh 12806**

EQUESTRIAN CROSSINGS
Traffic signs and signals, **Veh 21805**

EQUESTRIAN TRAILS
Motorized skateboards, **Veh 21968**

EQUIPMENT
Machinery and Equipment, generally, this index

EQUIPMENT RENTAL YARDS
Motor vehicles, inspections, stolen vehicles, **Veh 2805**

ESCAPE
Traffic officers, point system, **Veh 12810**

ESCHEAT
Highway patrol, abandoned or unclaimed property, **Veh 2415**
Motor vehicle financial responsibility, security deposit, **Veh 16027**

ESCORT VEHICLES
Traffic Rules and Regulations, this index

ESTATES
Probate Proceedings, generally, this index

ESTATES OF DECEDENTS
Probate Proceedings, generally, this index

ESTOPPEL
Collateral Estoppel, generally, this index

ETHANOL FUEL
Antisiphoning devices, motor vehicles, **Veh 28110 et seq.**

EVASION OF TOLLS
Generally, **Veh 4770 et seq., 40250 et seq.**

EVIDENCE
Affidavits, generally, this index
Burden of proof,
    Driving while under influence, judgment or conviction valid on constitutional grounds, **Veh 41403**
    Motor Vehicles, this index
Driving under the influence. Traffic Rules and Regulations, this index
Electronically stored motor vehicle data, original document status, **Veh 1801**
Exhibits, generally, this index
Ignition interlock devices, driving under the influence, **Veh 23575**
Insurance, this index
Motor Carriers, this index
Motor Vehicles, this index
Presumptions,
    Automobile dismantlers, possession of stolen vehicle, **Veh 11511**
    Habitual traffic offenders, drivers license revocation or suspension, knowledge, **Veh 14601.3**

EVIDENCE—Cont'd
Presumptions, drivers—Cont'd
  Motor Carriers, this index
Prisoner of war status, special motor vehicle license plates, **Veh 5101.5**
Privileges and Immunities, generally, this index
Probable Cause, generally, this index
Traffic Rules and Regulations, this index
Writing, notice, motor vehicles, accidents, probable cause, **Veh 40600**

EVIDENCE OF FINANCIAL RESPONSIBILITY
Definitions, drivers license examination, **Veh 12804.9**

EXCAVATIONS
Traffic rules and regulations, stopping, standing or parking vehicles, **Veh 22500**

EXCHANGE, BILLS OF
Negotiable Instruments, generally, this index

EXECUTIVE DEPARTMENT
Attorney General, generally, this index
Justice Department, generally, this index
State Agencies, generally, this index

EXECUTORS AND ADMINISTRATORS
Probate Proceedings, this index

EXEMPLARY DAMAGES
Damages, this index

EXEMPTIONS
Agricultural Machinery and Equipment, this index
Air Pollution, this index
All terrain vehicles, dealers, licenses and permits, **Veh 11704.5, 11723**
Ambulances, pollution control devices, **Veh 27156.2, 27156.3**
Animals, this index
Boats and Boating, this index
Driving schools, **Veh 11101**
Emergency Vehicles, this index
Factory built housing, length limitations, **Veh 35790.5**
Firefighters and Fire Departments, this index
Fires and Fire Protection, this index
Ignition interlock devices, **Veh 23575**
Indians, this index
Licenses and Permits, this index
Manufactured housing. Housing, this index
Medical transportation vehicles, emergencies, pollution control devices, **Veh 27156.2, 27156.3**
Mobilehomes and Mobilehome Parks, this index
Mosquito abatement or vector control districts, motor vehicles, pollution control devices, **Veh 27156.3**
Motor Carriers, this index
Motor Vehicles, this index
Motorcycles, this index

EXEMPTIONS—Cont'd
Parking lots and facilities, park and ride lots, alternative fuel vehicles, **Veh 22518**
Peace Officers, this index
Pest abatement districts, motor vehicles, pollution control devices, **Veh 27156.2, 27156.3**
Pollution control devices, motor vehicles, **Veh 27156.2, 27156.3**
School Buses, this index
Ships and Shipping, this index
Traffic Rules and Regulations, this index

EXHAUST SYSTEMS
  Generally, **Veh 27150 et seq.**
Motor Vehicles, this index

EXHIBITS
Motor vehicles, speed contest on highway, **Veh 23109, 40303**
  Impoundment of vehicle, **Veh 22651.6**

EXITS
Alleys, driver warnings, pedestrians and bicyclists, **Veh 21356.5**
Campers, **Veh 23129**
Limousines, emergencies, **Veh 27375**

EXPERIMENTS
Motor vehicles, equipment use, permits, **Veh 26106**

EXPLOSIVES
Automobiles. Motor vehicles, generally, post
Caldecott tunnel, transportation, **Veh 31301**
Cargo container equipment, explosives transportation, **Veh 655**
Containers,
  Motor carriers, **Veh 31614**
  Transportation,
    Cargo container equipment, **Veh 655**
    Statement, **Veh 31612**
Definitions, blasting caps, **Veh 31600**
Detonators, motor carriers, mixed cargo, **Veh 31613**
Display of signs, on transporting vehicles, **Veh 27903**
Fire protection, vehicles transporting explosives, **Veh 31614**
Fireworks, generally, this index
Highways and roads,
  Public menace, closing, **Veh 2812**
  Transportation, **Veh 31600 et seq.**
Inspection and inspectors, motor carriers, **Veh 31602, 31607 et seq.**
  Stopping locations, **Veh 31616**
Licenses and permits, transportation,
  Cargo container equipment, **Veh 655**
  Staggered license renewals, **Veh 2505**
Mixed cargoes, **Veh 31613**
Motor carriers, transportation regulation, **Veh 31600 et seq.**

EXPLOSIVES—Cont'd
Motor vehicles,
  Adoption of United States department of transportation definitions relating to explosives, **Veh 2402.7**
  Crimes and offenses, **Veh 32002, 40000.19**
  Hazardous material, definitions, **Veh 353**
  Licenses and permits, **Veh 32000 et seq.**
    Transportation of explosives, **Veh 2501**
  Owners and ownership, changes, licenses, **Veh 2503**
Parking. Traffic Rules and Regulations, this index
Signs on vehicles carrying, **Veh 27903**
Traffic Rules and Regulations, this index
Transportation, **Veh 31600 et seq.**
  Caldecott tunnel, **Veh 31301**
  Cargo container equipment, **Veh 655**
  Exception, **Veh 31619**
  Licenses and permits, staggered renewals, **Veh 2505**
  Point system, drivers license, **Veh 12810**
Tunnels, this index
Vehicles. Motor vehicles, generally, ante

EXPORTS AND IMPORTS
Dealers, definitions, motor vehicles, **Veh 286**
Definitions, vehicles, inspection and cancellation of titles, **Veh 6161**
Motor Vehicles, this index
Vehicle parts or motor vehicles with altered identification numbers, **Veh 10803**

EXPRESSWAYS
Freeways, generally, this index

EXSERVICEMEN
Veterans, generally, this index

EXTINGUISHERS
Fire Extinguishers, generally, this index

EXTRALEGAL LOAD
Definitions, **Veh 320.5**

EYEGLASSES
Motor vehicle operators, temple width of glasses, **Veh 23120**

EYES AND EYESIGHT
Blind Persons, generally, this index
Drivers licenses, **Veh 12805**
  Examiners and examinations, **Veh 1674 et seq.**
Motor vehicles, drivers licenses, **Veh 12805**
  Examiners and examinations, **Veh 1674 et seq.**
Optometrists, generally, this index
Tests, drivers licenses, **Veh 1674 et seq.**

EYESHADES
Buses and trolley coaches, **Veh 26711**

FABRICS
Fires and Fire Protection, generally, this index

FACSIMILES
Motor vehicle salesmens licenses, **Veh 11819**
Signatures, this index

FACTORIES
Manufacturers and Manufacturing, generally, this index

FAIL SAFE SYSTEM
Motor vehicles, air brakes, **Veh 26502**

FAINTING
Persons subject to, drivers licenses, **Veh 12806**

FAIRS AND EXPOSITIONS
Motor vehicles, exemption from registration, **Veh 4003**

FALSE ADVERTISING
Advertisements, generally, this index

FALSE NAMES
Assumed or Fictitious Names, generally, this index

FALSE PERSONATION
Drivers licenses, refusal, **Veh 12809**
Driving schools and driving instructors, license, cancellation, revocation and suspension, **Veh 11110**
Highway patrol, **Veh 27, 2261, 40000.5**
Motor Vehicles, this index

FALSE REPRESENTATIONS
Fraud, generally, this index

FALSE STATEMENTS
Fraud, generally, this index

FAMILY
Children and Minors, generally, this index
Definitions, motor vehicles, license plates, special plates,
    Congressional Medal of Honor, **Veh 5101.6**
    Military forces, decorations for valor, **Veh 5101.4**
    Prisoners of war, **Veh 5101.5**
    Purple Heart recipients, **Veh 5101.8**
Marriage, generally, this index

FAMILY MEMBERS
Definitions, motor vehicles, franchises, sales, **Veh 11713.3**

FAMILY PURPOSE DOCTRINE
Motor vehicles, **Veh 17708**
    Damages, **Veh 17709**

FARM LABOR
Agricultural Labor and Employment, generally, this index

FARM MACHINERY AND EQUIPMENT
Agricultural Machinery and Equipment, generally, this index

FARM PRODUCTS
Agricultural Products, generally, this index

FARM TRACTORS
Agricultural Machinery and Equipment, generally, this index

FATHER AND CHILD
Children and Minors, generally, this index

FAX MACHINES
Traffic rules and regulations, parking violations, proof of ownership, verification, **Veh 40900**

FEDERAL AID
Traffic safety program, **Veh 2907**

FEDERAL GOVERNMENT
United States, generally, this index

FEDERAL LANDS
United States, this index

FEDERAL LAW
Motor Vehicles, this index

FEDERAL OLD AGE AND SURVIVORS INSURANCE
Social Security, generally, this index

FEDERAL PROSECUTORS
Addresses, confidentiality, **Veh 1808.4**

FEDERAL SOCIAL SECURITY
Social Security, generally, this index

FELONIES
Crimes and Offenses, generally, this index

FENCES
Advertisements. Outdoor Advertising, generally, this index
Highways and Roads, this index
Motor vehicles, tow trucks, damage, notice, **Veh 22658.1**
Outdoor Advertising, generally, this index
Tow trucks, damage, notice, **Veh 22658.1**
Traffic officers, report of damages, **Veh 2811**

FENDERS
Motor Vehicles, this index

FERMENTED LIQUIDS
Alcoholic Beverages, generally, this index

FERRIES
Toll ferries, evasion of tolls, **Veh 4770 et seq., 40250 et seq.**

FERTILIZERS
Ammonium nitrate, motor carriers, **Veh 31600 et seq.**

FICTITIOUS BUSINESS NAMES
Assumed or Fictitious Names, generally, this index

FICTITIOUS DOCUMENTS
Motor vehicle documents, limitation of actions, **Veh 40004**

FICTITIOUS NAMES
Assumed or Fictitious Names, generally, this index

FIDELITY BONDS
Bonds (Officers and Fiduciaries), generally, this index

FIDUCIARIES
Autobrokers, **Veh 11737**
Bonds (Officers and Fiduciaries), generally, this index
Embezzlement, generally, this index
Executors and administrators. Probate Proceedings, this index
Guardian and Ward, generally, this index
Motor vehicles, autobrokers, **Veh 11737**

FIELD BINDWEED
Weeds, generally, this index

FIELD CROPS
Agricultural Products, generally, this index

FILLING STATIONS
Motor Vehicle Service Stations, generally, this index

FINAL JUDGMENTS, DECREES AND ORDERS
Judgments and Decrees, generally, this index

FINANCE CHARGE
Motor Vehicles, this index

FINANCE COMPANIES
Dealers, definitions, motor vehicles, **Veh 286**

FINANCIAL INTEREST
Adverse or Pecuniary Interest, generally, this index

FINANCIAL RESPONSIBILITY
Buses, this index
Motor Vehicle Insurance, this index

FINANCIAL STATEMENTS AND REPORTS
Counties, this index
Motor vehicles, counties, registration, fees, **Veh 9250.14**

FINANCING AGENCY
Sales, this index

FINES AND PENALTIES
Accidents, failure of driver to stop, **Veh 20001**
Agricultural Labor and Employment, this index
Agricultural Machinery and Equipment, this index
Air Pollution, this index
Armored car,
    Driver, use of red lights, violation, **Veh 25262**

FINES

FINES AND PENALTIES—Cont'd

Armored car—Cont'd
Licenses and permits, **Veh 21713**
Arrest, this index
Attempts, this index
Attorneys, this index
Bicycles, this index
Blind Persons, this index
Boats and Boating, this index
Bribery and Corruption, generally, this index
Brokers, motor carriers, construction, bonds (officers and fiduciaries), **Veh 34510.5**
Buses, this index
Children and Minors, this index
Chop shops, **Veh 10801 et seq.**
Colleges and Universities, this index
Corruption. Bribery and Corruption, generally, this index
Counties, this index
Decals, motorcycles, exhaust systems, noise pollution, **Veh 27202.1**
Definitions, traffic rules and regulations, amnesty, **Veh 42008.7**
Disabled person placards, **Veh 4461**
Motor vehicles, **Veh 4463, 4463.3**
Drag racing, **Veh 23109 et seq.**
Driving Schools, this index
Driving under the influence. Traffic Rules and Regulations, this index
Drugs and Medicine, this index
Exemplary damages. Damages, this index
False disabled person placards, motor vehicles, **Veh 4463.3**
Flight from peace officers, motor vehicles, **Veh 2800.1 et seq., 13201**
Guardian and Ward, this index
Hazardous Substances and Waste, this index
Highways and Roads, this index
Jails, generally, this index
Kitchen Grease, this index
Marijuana. Drugs and Medicine, this index
Motor Carriers, this index
Motor vehicle fund, claims for refunds, **Veh 42233**
Motor Vehicle Insurance, this index
Motor Vehicle Repair Dealers, this index
Motor Vehicle Service Stations, this index
Motor Vehicles, this index
Motorcycles, exhaust systems, noise pollution, decals, **Veh 27202.1**
Motorized scooters, pocket bikes, **Veh 21721**
Noise pollution, motorcycles, exhaust systems, decals, **Veh 27202.1**
Parking. Traffic Rules and Regulations, this index
Payment, receipts, traffic violations, **Veh 40312**
Pocket bikes, **Veh 21721**
Police, this index
Radioactive materials, spent fuel, transportation, **Veh 33002**

FINES AND PENALTIES—Cont'd

Railroad Crossings, this index
Reckless driving, great bodily injury, **Veh 23104**
Renderers, inedible grease, records and recordation, **Veh 2468, 2478**
Sales and Use Taxes, this index
School Buses, this index
Schools and School Districts, this index
Second and subsequent offenses. Crimes and Offenses, this index
Sheriffs, this index
Ships and Shipping, this index
Solid Waste, this index
Speeding, **Veh 42000.1**
Taxicabs, this index
Toll roads and bridges. Highways and Roads, this index
Traffic Rules and Regulations, this index
Traffic Signs and Signals, this index
Traffic violator schools, stipulated penalties, accusation against licensee, **Veh 11218**
University of California. Colleges and Universities, this index
Use tax. Sales and Use Taxes, this index
Vehicle verifiers, compromise and settlement, **Veh 11302.5**
Veterans, this index
Wireless telecommunications. Telecommunications, this index

FINGERPRINTS AND FINGERPRINTING

Drivers licenses, **Veh 12800**
Local law enforcement identification programs, funding, motor vehicle registration fees, **Veh 9250.19**
Mentally retarded and developmentally disabled persons, transportation, drivers, **Veh 12523.6**
Motor Vehicles, this index
Paratransit vehicles, drivers, certificates and certification, **Veh 12517.3**
School buses, drivers certificates, **Veh 12517.3**
Thumbprints, generally, this index
Tow trucks, **Veh 2432.3**
Drivers, certification, **Veh 2431**
Youth buses, drivers, certificates and certification, **Veh 12517.3**

FINISHING MACHINES

Special highway construction equipment, **Veh 565**

FIRE APPARATUS

Definitions, emergency vehicles, **Veh 35002**

FIRE BALLOONS

Fireworks, generally, this index

FIRE DEPARTMENTS

Firefighters and Fire Departments, generally, this index

FIRE EXTINGUISHERS

Campers, **Veh 28060**

FIRE EXTINGUISHERS—Cont'd

Motor carriers, explosives transports, **Veh 31610**
Motor Vehicles, this index
Recreational vehicles, **Veh 28060**
Tow trucks, equipment, **Veh 27700**
Vanpooling, **Veh 34509**

FIRE HYDRANTS

Traffic control, removal of illegally parked vehicle preventing access by fire fighting equipment to, **Veh 22651**

FIRE LANES

Vehicles stopping, parking or standing, **Veh 22500.1**

FIRE MARSHAL

State Fire Marshal, generally, this index

FIRE NUISANCE

Fires and Fire Protection, generally, this index

FIREARMS

Weapons, generally, this index

FIRECRACKERS

Fireworks, generally, this index

FIREFIGHTERS AND FIRE DEPARTMENTS

Chief of fire department,
Hazardous substances and waste, route notification, **Veh 32050 et seq.**
Radioactive materials, transportation, notice, **Veh 33002**
Crimes and offenses,
Failure to obey order, **Veh 40000.7**
Vehicles, theft, **Veh 10851**
Death, special license plates, transfer to surviving spouse, **Veh 5101.2**
Drivers licenses, **Veh 12804.11**
Examinations and examiners, **Veh 12804.9**
Earplugs, motor vehicle operations, **Veh 27400**
Emergency Vehicles, generally, this index
Endorsement, drivers licenses, **Veh 12804.11**
Equipment, definitions, drivers licenses, **Veh 12804.11**
Exemptions, traffic rules and regulations, **Veh 21055**
Fees, motor vehicles, driving record, reports, **Veh 1808.1**
Hazardous substances and waste, motor vehicles, signs and signals, exemptions, **Veh 27903**
Indians, motor vehicles, fees, exemptions, **Veh 9104.2**
License plates, **Veh 5101.2**
Motor vehicles,
Accidents, transportation of injured person, **Veh 20016**
Drivers licenses, **Veh 12804.11**
Examinations and examiners, **Veh 12804.9**
Driving record, reports, fees, **Veh 1808.1**
Earplugs or headsets, **Veh 27400**

FIREFIGHTERS AND FIRE DEPARTMENTS
—Cont'd
Motor vehicles—Cont'd
Emergency vehicles, **Veh 165**
Permits, **Veh 2416**
Fees, exemptions, **Veh 9102, 9104**
Financial responsibility, exemptions,
Veh 16051
Flashing lights, headlamps, **Veh 25252.5**
Following emergency vehicles, **Veh
21706**
Hazardous substances and waste, signs
and signals, exemptions, **Veh 27903**
Headlamps, flashing, **Veh 25252.5**
Indians, fees, exemptions, **Veh 9104.2**
License plates, **Veh 5101.2**
Licenses, **Veh 2416**
Obedience to orders, **Veh 2801**
Crimes and offenses, **Veh 40000.7**
Red lights and sirens, **Veh 30**
Registration, exemption, **Veh 4015**
Seatbelts, **Veh 27305**
Signs, **Veh 27905**
Special license plates, **Veh 5101.2**
Theft, **Veh 10851**
Tort liability, **Veh 17004, 17004.5**
Traffic rules and regulations, generally,
post
Utility flood or loading lamps, **Veh
25110**
Warning lamps and sirens, demonstra-
tors, **Veh 25806**
Width of vehicle or load, exemptions,
Veh 35002
Orders, signal or direction of member,
failure or refusal to comply, **Veh 2801**
Red lights and sirens, public policy, **Veh
30**
Rescue, generally, this index
Safety headsets, motor vehicle operation,
Veh 27400
Signs on vehicle, display, **Veh 27905**
Stations, traffic rules and regulations, **Veh
22104**
Theft, motor vehicles, **Veh 10851**
Tiller operators, drivers licenses, **Veh
12804.11**
Traffic rules and regulations,
Chemical hose, crossing or damage, **Veh
21708**
Crossing fire hoses, **Veh 21708**
Driving or operation in fire areas, **Veh
21707**
Exemptions, emergency vehicles, **Veh
21055**
Fire hoses, crossing or damage, **Veh
21708**
Following emergency vehicles, **Veh
21706**
Hydrants, stopping or parking, **Veh
22514**
Obedience to orders, **Veh 2801**
Removal of parked or standing vehicles,
Veh 22650 et seq.
Station, turning in approaches, **Veh
22104**

FIREFIGHTERS AND FIRE DEPARTMENTS
—Cont'd
Traffic rules and regulations—Cont'd
Stopping, standing or parking vehicle,
Veh 22500
Turning near fire stations, **Veh 22104**
U turns near fire stations, **Veh 22104**
Width of vehicle or load, exemptions,
Veh 35002
Transportation, person injured in accident,
Veh 20016
Vehicles. Motor vehicles, generally, ante
Volunteer firefighters and fire depart-
ments, motor vehicles,
Fees, exemption, **Veh 9104**
Obedience to orders, **Veh 2801**

FIREFIGHTERS MEMORIAL
Deposits, **Veh 5101.2**

FIREFIGHTING EQUIPMENT
Definitions, drivers licenses, **Veh 12804.11**

FIRES AND FIRE PROTECTION
Air Pollution, generally, this index
Attorneys, authorized emergency vehicles,
civil liability, **Veh 17004**
Cargo tank vehicles, safety devices, **Veh
34019**
Emergency Vehicles, generally, this index
Exemptions, emergency vehicles, pollution
control devices, **Veh 27156.2, 27156.3**
Explosives, generally, this index
Extinguishers. Fire Extinguishers, gener-
ally, this index
Fire areas, traffic rules and regulations,
emergency situations, **Veh 21707**
Fire Extinguishers, generally, this index
Fireworks, generally, this index
Hazards, private property, **Veh 23111**
Highway patrolmen, directing, traffic, **Veh
2410**
Highways and roads, closing, menace to
public health or safety, **Veh 2812**
Machinery and equipment,
Defects, manufacturers and manufactur-
ing, **Veh 24007.1**
Exemptions, registration, **Veh 4015**
Fire Extinguishers, generally, this index
Manufacturers and manufacturing, de-
fects, **Veh 24007.1**
Registration, exemptions, **Veh 4015**
Sirens and warning lamps, **Veh 25806**
Warning lamps and sirens, **Veh 25806**
Windshields, **Veh 26700**
Manufacturers and manufacturing, emer-
gency vehicles, defects, **Veh 24007.1**
Motor carriers,
Cargo tank vehicles, fire safety devices,
Veh 34019
Operation of vehicles transporting ex-
plosives, burning on or near high-
way, **Veh 31614**
Motor vehicles,
Emergency Vehicles, generally, this in-
dex

FIRES AND FIRE PROTECTION—Cont'd
Motor vehicles—Cont'd
Flaming or glowing substance, throwing
or discharging, permits, **Veh 2416**
Throwing substances from vehicle, re-
ports, **Veh 1817**
Pollution control devices, emergency vehi-
cles, **Veh 27156.2, 27156.3**
Repairs, emergency vehicles, manufactur-
ers defect correction, expense reim-
bursement, **Veh 24007.1**
Rules and regulations, cargo tank vehicles,
safety devices, **Veh 34019**
Solid Waste, this index

FIREWORKS
Commercial vehicles, drivers licenses, revocation or suspension, **Veh 15301**
Motor carriers, licenses and permits, revocation or suspension, **Veh 15301**
Transportation, motor carriers, **Veh
32000.5**

FIRST AID
Equipment highway patrol vehicle, **Veh
2406**
Kits, vanpooling, **Veh 34509**
Schools and School Districts, this index
Youth buses, courses of instruction, driv-
ers, **Veh 12522**

**FIRST POINT OF PROCESSING OR PACK-
ING**
Definitions, motor carriers, hours of ser-
vice, **Veh 34501.2**

FIRST STAGE MANUFACTURERS
Definitions, house cars, **Veh 11930**

FISH AND GAME
Boats and boating,
Quagga mussels, infestation prevention
fee, registration, **Veh 9853, 9860**
Zebra mussels, infestation prevention
fee, registration, **Veh 9853, 9860**
Crustaceans. Shellfish, generally, this in-
dex
Deer, snowmobiles, pursing and harassing,
Veh 23128
Lines, off highway vehicles, placing in po-
sition to do bodily harm, **Veh 38318.5**
Livestock. Animals, generally, this index
Mussels. Shellfish, this index
Off highway vehicles, malicious damage,
Veh 38319 et seq.
Quagga mussels, infestation prevention
fee, boats and boating, registration,
Veh 9853, 9860
Shellfish, generally, this index
Snowmobiles, pursuing and harassing
game animals, **Veh 23128**
Wildlife areas, abandoned vehicles, re-
moval, **Veh 22667**
Zebra mussels, infestation prevention fee,
boats and boating, registration, **Veh
9853, 9860**

FISHING
Fish and Game, generally, this index

FLAGMEN
Railroad crossings, train signals, **Veh 22451**

FLAGS
Explosives, vehicle transporting, **Veh 31610**
Motor Carriers, this index
Public utility vehicle, warning devices, **Veh 25301**
Traffic Rules and Regulations, this index

FLAMMABLE LIQUIDS
Definitions, motor vehicle load, **Veh 34003**
Motor Carriers, this index
Traffic Rules and Regulations, this index

FLASHING LIGHTS
Definitions, motor vehicles, **Veh 375**

FLATBED TRUCKS
Clearance lamps, mounting, **Veh 25100**

FLEET VEHICLES
Motor Vehicles, this index

FLEXIBLE STRUCTURAL MATERIALS
Motor carriers, load length limitations, **Veh 35414**

FLIES
Mosquito Abatement or Vector Control Districts, generally, this index

FLIGHT
Motor vehicles, **Veh 2800.1 et seq., 13201**

FLOOD CONTROL
Levees and Flood Control, generally, this index

FLOOD PREVENTION
Levees and Flood Control, generally, this index

FLOODS AND FLOODING
Control. Levees and Flood Control, generally, this index
Flood control. Levees and Flood Control, generally, this index
Levees and Flood Control, generally, this index

FOG
School buses additional lights, **Veh 25102.5**

FOG LAMPS
Motor Vehicles, this index

FOLLOWING VEHICLES
Traffic Rules and Regulations, this index

FOOD
Agricultural Products, generally, this index
Fish and Game, generally, this index
Grapes and Grapevines, generally, this index
Grease. Kitchen Grease, generally, this index

FOOD—Cont'd
Ice cream. Dairies and Dairy Products, this index
Inedible grease. Kitchen Grease, generally, this index
Kitchen Grease, generally, this index
Motor Carriers, this index
Shellfish, generally, this index

FOOTRESTS
Motorcycles or motorized bicycles, **Veh 27800**

FOR HIRE
Definitions, paratransit vehicles, **Veh 462**

FOR HIRE VEHICLES
Taxicabs, generally, this index

FORCE AND VIOLENCE
Motor vehicles, dealers, notice, repossessors and repossession, assignments, **Veh 11724**
Road rage. Traffic Rules and Regulations, this index

FORECLOSURE
Taxicabs, impounding, **Veh 21100.4**

FOREIGN CORPORATIONS
Motor vehicles, registration requirements, established place of business within state, **Veh 6702**

FOREIGN COUNTRIES
Air Pollution, this index
Buses, temporary operating authority, **Veh 4007**
Canada, generally, this index
Exports and Imports, generally, this index
Motor Carriers, this index
Motor vehicle insurance, financial responsibility, denial of entry, **Veh 16502**
Motor Vehicles, this index

FOREIGN JURISDICTION
Definitions, motor vehicles, **Veh 325**

FOREIGN SHIPS
Boats and Boating, this index
Ships and Shipping, this index

FOREIGN STATES
Buses, temporary operating authority, out of state buses, **Veh 4007**
Driving under the influence. Traffic Rules and Regulations, this index
Handicapped persons, parking exemptions, **Veh 22511.5**
Motor Carriers, this index
Motor Vehicles, this index
Peace officers, license plates, reciprocity, **Veh 5001.5**
Sales and Use Taxes, this index
Traffic Rules and Regulations, this index
Use taxes. Sales and Use Taxes, this index

FOREIGN VEHICLES
Definitions, **Veh 330**

FOREIGN VEHICLES—Cont'd
Motor Carriers, this index

FOREST FIRES
Flaming substance, throwing from vehicle, reports, **Veh 1817**
Motor vehicles, throwing flaming substances from, **Veh 1817**

FOREST PRODUCTS
Timber and Lumber, generally, this index

FORESTERS
Hazardous substances and waste, motor vehicles, signs and signals, exemptions, **Veh 27903**
Motor vehicles, hazardous substances and waste, signs and signals, exemptions, **Veh 27903**

FORESTRY AND FIRE PROTECTION DEPARTMENT
State Fire Marshal, generally, this index

FORESTS AND FORESTRY
Lumber. Timber and Lumber, generally, this index
Motor vehicles,
  Irrigation and irrigation districts, machinery and equipment, inspection and inspectors, **Veh 2810.2**
  Signs, **Veh 27905**
Signs on forestry service vehicles, display, **Veh 27905**
State forest, motor vehicles, irrigation and irrigation districts, machinery and equipment, inspection and inspectors, **Veh 2810.2**
Timber and Lumber, generally, this index

FORFEITURES
Agricultural machinery and equipment, nuisance, **Veh 34506.5**
Bail, this index
Motor Vehicles, this index
Nuisance, agricultural machinery and equipment, **Veh 34506.5**
Traffic Rules and Regulations, this index

FORGERY
Drivers licenses, **Veh 14610**
Motor Vehicles, this index

FORKLIFT TRUCKS
Motor Carriers, this index

FORMER JEOPARDY
Motor vehicles offenses, prosecution for code violations, **Veh 41400**
Traffic rules and regulations, prosecutions for code violations, **Veh 41400**

FORMS
Automobile dismantlers, license application, **Veh 11504**
Bicycles, registration forms, **Veh 39001 et seq.**
Department of motor vehicles, abstract of conviction record, **Veh 1804**

FORMS—Cont'd
Highway patrol, accident reports, preparation and supply, **Veh 2407**
Motor Vehicles, this index
Motor Vehicles Department, this index
Traffic Rules and Regulations, this index

FOUNDATIONS
Charities, generally, this index

FOUNDRIES
Manufacturers and Manufacturing, generally, this index

FOUR WHEEL DRIVE VEHICLES
Motor Vehicles, this index

FRANCHISES
Motor Vehicles, this index
Recreational Vehicles, this index

FRAUD
Automobile dismantlers, license revocation, **Veh 11509**
Birth certificates, declaration as to existence, identification cards, **Veh 13007.5**
Boats and Boating, this index
Definitions,
 Lessor retailers, **Veh 11613**
 Motor vehicles, license revocation, **Veh 11705**
Drivers licenses. Motor Vehicles, this index
Driving Schools, this index
Education programs, motor vehicle insurance, **Veh 10904**
False report of theft of vehicle, **Veh 10501**
Leases, this index
Motor Carriers, this index
Motor Vehicle Insurance, this index
Motor Vehicles, this index
Ships and Shipping, this index
Traffic rules and regulations, handicapped persons, certification, **Veh 22511.58**
Vehicle identification numbers, falsifying, **Veh 10802**

FREEWAY SERVICE PATROL
Definitions,
 Emergency roadside assistance, **Veh 2436**
 Tow truck driver certification, **Veh 2430.1**

FREEWAYS
Authorities, service authority, emergencies, **Veh 2421.5**
Bicycles,
 Motorized bicycles, **Veh 21960**
 Restrictions, **Veh 21960**
Billboards. Outdoor Advertising, generally, this index
Call boxes, **Veh 2421.5**
Central dispatching services, emergency motorist aid system, **Veh 2421.5**
Colleges and universities, directional signs, **Veh 21375**

FREEWAYS—Cont'd
Contracts,
 Emergency call boxes, **Veh 2421.5**
 Service authority, emergencies, **Veh 2421.5**
Costs, emergency call boxes, reimbursement, **Veh 2421.5**
Definitions, **Veh 332**
 Counties, **Veh 314**
Disabled vehicles, **Veh 21960**
 Removal, **Veh 22654**
Disasters, removal of parked or standing vehicles, **Veh 22654**
Dispatching services, emergency motorist aid system, **Veh 2421.5**
Drivers licenses, instruction permits, **Veh 12509**
Emergencies,
 Motorist aid system, **Veh 2421.5**
 Service authority, **Veh 2421.5**
Emergency roadside assistance, **Veh 2435 et seq.**
Entering, ramps, **Veh 21664**
Exiting, ramps, **Veh 21664**
Fees, emergencies, **Veh 9250.10**
High occupancy vehicle lanes. Highways and Roads, this index
Impounding vehicles, **Veh 22651**
 Sale, satisfaction of lien, **Veh 22851.1**
Jurisdiction, **Veh 2400**
Long Beach, overweight vehicles, special permits, **Veh 35700.5**
Los Angeles, overweight vehicles, special permits, **Veh 35700.5**
Motor driven cycles, restrictions, **Veh 21960**
Motorcycles, instruction permits, **Veh 12509.5**
Motorist aid system, emergencies, **Veh 2421.5**
Motorized bicycles, **Veh 21960**
 Instruction permits, **Veh 12509.5**
Motorized scooters, **Veh 21960**
 Instruction permits, **Veh 12509.5**
Nonmotorized transportation facilities, restrictions, **Veh 21960**
Notice,
 Disabled vehicles, removal, **Veh 22654**
 Restrictions on use, **Veh 21960**
Off or on ramps, **Veh 21664**
On or off ramps, **Veh 21664**
Outdoor Advertising, generally, this index
Parking, **Veh 21718**
 Transportation corridor parking facilities, **Veh 22518**
Pedestrians,
 Arrest, refusal to leave freeway, **Veh 40303**
 Disabled vehicles, **Veh 21960**
 Restrictions, **Veh 21960**
Ramps, exiting or entering, **Veh 21664**
Reimbursement, emergency call boxes, costs, **Veh 2421.5**
Reports, San Bernardino freeway, high occupancy vehicle lanes, **Veh 21655.12**
Restriction of use, **Veh 21960**

FREEWAYS—Cont'd
San Bernardino freeway, high occupancy vehicle lanes, **Veh 21655.12**
Service authority, emergencies, **Veh 2421.5**
Signs and signals,
 Colleges and universities, location indicators, **Veh 21375**
 Notice of restrictions on use, **Veh 21960**
Speed limits, **Veh 22355, 22356**
Standing vehicles, **Veh 21718**
Stopping, **Veh 21718**
Terminal Island freeway, overweight vehicles, special permits, **Veh 35700.5**
Tow bars, **Veh 29006**
Tow trucks,
 Driver certification, **Veh 2430 et seq.**
 Stopping or parking, **Veh 22513**
Traffic Rules and Regulations, generally, this index
Traffic Signs and Signals, this index

FREIGHT VAN OR TANK CONTAINER
Traffic rules and regulations, loads and loading, **Veh 31540**

FRIEND MEMORIAL ACT
Generally, **Veh 23109**

FRUITS
Grapes and Grapevines, generally, this index

FUEL
Containers, motor carriers, safety regulations, **Veh 34500 et seq.**
Motor Vehicle Fuel, generally, this index
Motor vehicles,
 Air pollution control devices, alteration of modification, **Veh 27156**
 Operation to prevent excessive escape, **Veh 27153**

FULL FAITH AND CREDIT
Foreign certificates of title, motor vehicles, **Veh 4304**
Motor vehicles, foreign certificates of title, **Veh 4304**

FULMINATE OF MERCURY
Explosives, generally, this index

FUMES
Air Pollution, generally, this index
Motor vehicles, prevention of penetration into cab, **Veh 27154**

FUNDS
Abandoned vehicle trust fund, **Veh 9250.7**
 Expenditure, **Veh 22710**
Antiterrorism fund, **Veh 5066**
Colleges and Universities, this index
Counties, this index
Environment, this index
Firefighters memorial fund, deposits, **Veh 5101.2**
Memorial scholarship fund, September 11, 2001, **Veh 5066**
Motor Carriers, this index
Motor Vehicles, this index

FUNDS—Cont'd
Off highway license fee fund, **Veh 38235**
Specialized license plate fund, **Veh 5157**
State Treasury, generally, this index
Terrorism, this index
Traffic Rules and Regulations, this index
Traffic safety fund, **Veh 42200**
Traffic safety program fund, **Veh 2906 et seq.**

FUNERAL PROCESSIONS
Flashing lights, **Veh 25251**
Peace officers, signs and signals, disregarding, **Veh 2817**
Traffic rules and regulations, local regulations, **Veh 21100, 21100.7**

FUNERALS
Escort vehicles, color, regulation, **Veh 27605**
Highway patrol, out of state attendance, **Veh 2421**

FURLOUGHS
Work furloughs. Jails, this index

FURNITURE
Household Goods Carriers, generally, this index

FUSEES
Motor Vehicles, this index

GAME
Fish and Game, generally, this index

GAME BIRDS
Fish and Game, generally, this index

GAMMA RAYS
Atomic Energy, generally, this index

GANTRY TRUCKS
Definitions, **Veh 335**

GARAGES
Buildings, rental of private building for use as garage, **Veh 10654**
Definitions, **Veh 340**
Equipment requirements of vehicle, returning to garage for, **Veh 24004**
Highway patrol, inspection, motor vehicles, **Veh 2805**
Inspection,
  Stolen vehicle, **Veh 2805**
  Vehicle for registration and title, **Veh 1655, 10656**
Landlord and tenant, rental of private building, **Veh 10654**
Liens and incumbrances, towage and keeping vehicle removed from highway, **Veh 22851**
  Lien sales, actions for despoliation of evidence, immunity, **Veh 22856**
Private garage,
  Definitions, **Veh 10654**
  Rental of a private building, report, **Veh 10654**
  Stored vehicles, reports, **Veh 10654**

GARAGES—Cont'd
Privileges and immunities, towed vehicles, lien sales, despoliation of evidence, **Veh 22856**
Records and recordation, stored vehicles, **Veh 10650 et seq.**
Removal of parked or standing vehicles, **Veh 22650 et seq.**
Rental of private building for use as garage, report, **Veh 10654**
Repairs, motor vehicles, exemption from registration, **Veh 4003**
Reports,
  Rental of private building as garage, **Veh 10654**
  Stored vehicle, **Veh 10652**
  Vehicle showing bullet marks, **Veh 10653**
Traffic rules and regulations, removal of parked or standing vehicles, **Veh 22650 et seq.**
Wreckers, stored vehicles, failure or refusal to keep, **Veh 10655**

GARBAGE AND REFUSE
Solid Waste, generally, this index

GAS
Air Pollution, generally, this index
Oil and Gas, generally, this index

GAS COMPANIES
Oil and Gas, generally, this index

GAS STATIONS
Motor Vehicle Service Stations, generally, this index

GASEOUS DISCHARGE LAMP
Emergency vehicles, controlling traffic signals, **Veh 25258**

GASOLINE
Fuel octane number, new vehicles, sales, **Veh 24013**
Liquefied Petroleum Gas, generally, this index

GASOLINE STATIONS
Motor Vehicle Service Stations, generally, this index

GATES
Streets and alleys, local ordinances or resolutions, **Veh 21102.1**
Traffic rules and regulations,
  Railroad crossings, stopping vehicle, **Veh 22451**
  Restricting access, **Veh 21101.6**

GENERAL ASSEMBLY
Legislature, generally, this index

GENERAL CORPORATION LAW
Corporations, generally, this index

GENERAL ELECTIONS
Elections, generally, this index

GENERAL FUND
State Treasury, this index

GENERAL NONPROFIT CORPORATION LAW
Nonprofit Corporations, generally, this index

GENERAL PUBLIC PARATRANSIT VEHICLES
Paratransit Vehicles, generally, this index

GENERAL SALES TAX
Sales and Use Taxes, generally, this index

GENERAL SESSIONS
Legislature, generally, this index

GIFTS, DEVISES AND BEQUESTS
Anatomical Gifts, generally, this index
Charities, generally, this index
Motor Vehicles, this index
Probate Proceedings, generally, this index
Towing, vehicles, kickbacks, **Veh 12110, 13351.85**
Traffic rules and regulations, overloaded vehicles, agreement for use, **Veh 35788**

GIN
Alcoholic Beverages, generally, this index

GIRL SCOUTS
Boat and vessel registration, fee exemption, **Veh 9870**

GIRLS
Children and Minors, generally, this index

GLASS
Motor Vehicles, this index
Tow cars, removal from roadway, **Veh 27700**

GLAZING MATERIAL
Motorcycle windshield, safety material, **Veh 26701, 26705**

GLOBAL POSITIONING SYSTEM
Motor vehicles, windshields, obstruction of view, **Veh 26708**

GO
Definitions, traffic devices, **Veh 21451**

GOLD STAR FAMILIES
Motor vehicles, special plates, **Veh 5156, 5157**

GOLF CARTS
Definitions, **Veh 345**
Equipment requirements, **Veh 24001.5**
Highways and Roads, this index
Registration exemption, **Veh 4019**
Speed limits and other operating standards, **Veh 21115**
Traffic Rules and Regulations, this index

GOODS, WARES AND MERCHANDISE
Motor vehicles, dealers, rates and charges, disclosure, **Veh 11713.19**

GOVERNMENTAL AGENCIES
Public Agencies, generally, this index

GOVERNMENTAL AGENCIES LIABILITY LAW (OPERATION OF MOTOR VEHICLES)
Generally, **Veh 17000 et seq.**

GOVERNOR
Appointments,
    Fire chiefs, spent radioactive fuel, transportation, eligibility for notice, **Veh 33002**
    Highway safety representative, **Veh 2901**

GRADE CROSSINGS
Railroad Crossings, generally, this index

GRADES AND GRADING
Traffic Rules and Regulations, this index

GRAFFITI
Abatement, **Veh 13202.6**
Removal, penalty for littering, **Veh 42001.7**

GRAIN
Agricultural Products, generally, this index

GRANDPARENTS AND GRANDCHILDREN
Drivers licenses, signing and verification of application for minors license, **Veh 17701**

GRAPE GONDOLAS
Inspection and certification, **Veh 34501.14**
    Crimes and offenses, **Veh 40000.22, 40000.26**

GRAPES AND GRAPEVINES
Crimes and offenses, grape gondolas inspection and certification, **Veh 40000.22, 40000.26**
Grape gondolas, inspection and certification, **Veh 34501.14**
    Crimes and offenses, **Veh 40000.22, 40000.26**
Inspection and inspectors, grape gondolas, **Veh 34501.14**
    Crimes and offenses, **Veh 40000.22, 40000.26**

GRATUITIES
Gifts, Devises and Bequests, generally, this index

GRAVES
Cemeteries and Dead Bodies, generally, this index

GRAVEYARDS
Cemeteries and Dead Bodies, generally, this index

GREASE
Kitchen Grease, generally, this index
Tow car driver to spread dirt over roadway, **Veh 27700**

GREAT BODILY INJURY
Definitions, **Veh 27700**

GREEN
Definitions, traffic devices, **Veh 21451**

GREENE HARMER MOTOR VEHICLE DAMAGE CONTROL ACT
Generally, **Veh 34700 et seq.**

GRIME
Air Pollution, generally, this index

GROSS POLLUTERS
Air Pollution, this index

GROWING CROPS
Agricultural Products, generally, this index

GUARANTEED TRAFFIC ARREST BAIL BOND
Definitions, nonresidents, **Veh 40305.5**

GUARDIAN AND WARD
Bicycle helmet violations, joint liability for fine, **Veh 21212**
Cancellation of minors drivers license on death, **Veh 17712**
Fines and penalties, bicycle helmet violations, joint liability, guardian and minor, **Veh 21212**
Motor Vehicles, this index
Signing and verification, application for minors drivers license, **Veh 17701**

GUARDRAILS
Damages, tort liability, **Veh 17300 et seq.**

GUESTS
Motorcycle passenger, **Veh 27800**

GUIDELINES
Peace Officers, this index

GUIDEPOSTS
Highways and Roads, this index
Traffic Signs and Signals, this index

GUN POWDER
Explosives, generally, this index

GUNS
Weapons, generally, this index

HABIT FORMING DRUGS
Drug Addicts, generally, this index
Drugs and Medicine, generally, this index

HABITUAL CRIMINALS
Second and subsequent offenses. Crimes and Offenses, this index

HABITUAL TRAFFIC OFFENDERS
Traffic Rules and Regulations, this index

HALLS
Juvenile halls. Juvenile Institutions and Schools, this index

HALOGETON
Weeds, generally, this index

HAM RADIO OPERATORS
Motor vehicles, license plates, **Veh 5005**

HAND AND ARM SIGNALS
Traffic signs and signals, turning vehicle, **Veh 22110, 22111**

HANDGUNS
Weapons, generally, this index

HANDICAPPED PERSONS
Assistive devices, parking, **Veh 22511.85**
Blind Persons, generally, this index
Buses, this index
Cities and counties. Consolidated Cities and Counties, this index
Consolidated Cities and Counties, this index
Counties, this index
Crimes and offenses, theft of vehicles, enhanced sentences, **Veh 10851, 42002.5**
Death, parking placard, use, **Veh 22511.57, 22652.6**
Definitions, parking, **Veh 295.5**
Disabled veterans. Veterans, this index
Driving schools, instructors, licenses and permits, **Veh 11104**
    Revocation, **Veh 11110**
Electric carts, sidewalk use, local regulation, **Veh 21114.5**
Guardian and Ward, generally, this index
Insurance, this index
Labor and employment, parking, special enforcement units, **Veh 22507.9**
Lost parking placard, use, **Veh 22511.57, 22652.6**
Motor Vehicles, this index
Paratransit Vehicles, generally, this index
Parking. Traffic Rules and Regulations, this index
Parking Lots and Facilities, this index
Police, this index
Sidewalks,
    Access ramp, vehicle parking restrictions, **Veh 22522**
    Electric carts, use, local regulation, **Veh 21114.5**
Stolen parking placard, use, **Veh 22511.57, 22652.6**
Traffic Rules and Regulations, this index
Traffic Signs and Signals, this index
Traffic violators schools, accommodation, **Veh 11202**
Wheelchairs, generally, this index

HANDLEBARS
Motorcycles, position of equipment, **Veh 27801**

HARBOR DISTRICTS
Animals, parking, **Veh 21113**
Bicycles, **Veh 21113**
Motorized bicycles, **Veh 21113**
Parking regulations, **Veh 21113**
Roller skates, **Veh 21113**
Skateboards, **Veh 21113**
Traffic rules and regulations, **Veh 21113**

HARBORS AND PORTS
Districts. Harbor Districts, generally, this index

HARBORS AND PORTS—Cont'd
Harbor Districts, generally, this index

HARRISON NARCOTIC ACT
Drugs and Medicine, generally, this index

HARVESTING
Equipment. Agricultural Machinery and Equipment, generally, this index

HARVESTING EQUIPMENT
Agricultural Machinery and Equipment, generally, this index

HAULING
Hazardous Waste Haulers, generally, this index

HAVE A HEART, BE A STAR, HELP OUR KIDS
Motor vehicle license plates, **Veh 5072**

HAWKERS AND PEDDLERS
Sales and Use Taxes, generally, this index

HAY
Motor carriers, loading and securement, **Veh 34500.3**

HAZARDOUS MATERIALS
Hazardous Substances and Waste, generally, this index

HAZARDOUS SUBSTANCES AND WASTE
Age, transportation, drivers, **Veh 12515, 40000.11**
Agriculture, transportation, driver certification program, **Veh 12804.2**
Ambulances, signs and signals, exemptions, **Veh 27903**
Atomic Energy, generally, this index
Cleanup, spill response vehicles, warning lights, **Veh 25260.4**
Crimes and offenses,
Inhalation hazards, transportation, **Veh 32104, 40000.19**
Spills, highways, notice, **Veh 40000.70**
Definitions,
Highway spill containment and abatement, **Veh 2452**
Transportation, route notification, **Veh 32050**
Direct route, transportation, **Veh 31303**
Driver certification, transportation, agricultural materials transportation, **Veh 12804.2**
Dumps and dumping, highways and roads, notice, **Veh 23112.5**
Emergency vehicles,
Signs and signals, exemptions, **Veh 27903**
Spill response vehicles, warning lights, **Veh 25260.4**
Enforcement. Medical waste, post
Fines and penalties,
Highways and roads, spills, **Veh 23112.5**
Transportation, route notification, **Veh 32050 et seq.**

HAZARDOUS SUBSTANCES AND WASTE —Cont'd
Fire chiefs, route notification, **Veh 32050 et seq.**
Firefighters and Fire Departments, this index
Foresters, motor vehicles, signs and signals, exemptions, **Veh 27903**
Haulers. Hazardous Waste Haulers, generally, this index
Highway Patrol, this index
Highways and Roads, this index
Inhalation hazards, transportation, traffic rules and regulations, **Veh 32100 et seq.**
Licenses and permits,
Staggered licenses, transportation, **Veh 2505**
Transportation, post
Lights and lighting, spill response vehicles, warning lights, **Veh 25260.4**
Littering, highways and roads, notice, fines, **Veh 23112.5**
Marshals, motor vehicles, signs and signals, exemptions, **Veh 27903**
Medical waste, enforcement, **Veh 2401.1**
Motor Carriers, this index
Motor Vehicles, this index
Notice,
Highways and roads, spills, **Veh 23112.5**
Radioactive materials, spent fuel, transportation, **Veh 33002**
Spills, highways and roads, offenses, **Veh 40000.70**
Transportation, routes, **Veh 32050 et seq.**
Offenses. Crimes and offenses, generally, ante
Peace officers, motor vehicles, signs and signals, exemptions, **Veh 27903**
Pesticides, generally, this index
Police, motor vehicles, signs and signals, exemptions, **Veh 27903**
Police chiefs, route notification, **Veh 32050 et seq.**
Radioactive waste. Atomic Energy, generally, this index
Railroad crossings, traffic rules and regulations, **Veh 22452**
Registration, hauling, **Veh 31303**
Sheriffs,
Motor vehicles, signs and signals, exemptions, **Veh 27903**
Routes, notification, **Veh 32050 et seq.**
Spills,
Highways and roads, notice, **Veh 23112.5**
Crimes and offenses, **Veh 40000.70**
Response vehicles, warning lights, **Veh 25260.4**
Time, transportation, route notification, **Veh 32050 et seq.**
Traffic Rules and Regulations, this index
Transportation, **Veh 31303**
Certificates and certification, **Veh 13369**
Revocation, **Veh 14100.1**

HAZARDOUS SUBSTANCES AND WASTE —Cont'd
Transportation—Cont'd
Crimes and offenses, spills, **Veh 40000.70**
Criminal conviction records, abstract form, **Veh 1804**
Driver certification, agricultural hazardous materials transportation, **Veh 12804.2**
Endorsement revocation, **Veh 13369**
Inhalation hazards, **Veh 32100 et seq.**
Licenses and permits, **Veh 2531, 2532**
Staggered renewals, **Veh 2505**
Poison gases, **Veh 32100 et seq.**
Spills, crimes and offenses, **Veh 40000.70**
Traffic rules and regulations, **Veh 31309**

HAZARDOUS SUBSTANCES HAULERS
Hazardous Waste Haulers, generally, this index

HAZARDOUS SUBSTANCES HIGHWAY SPILL CONTAINMENT AND ABATEMENT ACT
Generally, **Veh 2450 et seq.**

HAZARDOUS WASTE
Hazardous Substances and Waste, generally, this index

HAZARDOUS WASTE HAULERS
Generally, **Veh 31303**
Bills of lading, **Veh 34510**
Cities, congested areas, requirements, **Veh 31303**
Combustible liquids, **Veh 34001 et seq.**
Crimes and offenses, **Veh 31303**
Certain restricted and prohibited routes, use, **Veh 31307**
Direct route, **Veh 31303**
Fines and penalties, traffic rules and regulations, **Veh 31303**
Flammable liquids, **Veh 34001 et seq.**
Highways and roads,
Direct routes, **Veh 31303**
Restrictions or prohibitions, **Veh 31304 et seq.**
Licenses and permits, **Veh 2501**
Motor vehicles, age, **Veh 12515, 40000.11**
Notice, atomic energy, spent radioactive fuel, transportation, **Veh 33002**
Parking, rules and regulations, **Veh 31303**
Registration,
Prohibited or restricted routes, use, suspension or revocation of registration, **Veh 31307**
Requirements, **Veh 31303**
Route notification, **Veh 32050 et seq.**
Shipping papers, **Veh 34510**
Traffic rules and regulations, **Veh 31303**
Water supply, highways and roads, restrictions or prohibitions, **Veh 31304**

HEADLIGHTS
Motor Vehicles, this index

HEADLIGHTS—Cont'd
Motorcycles, flashing headlamps, **Veh 25251.2**
Motorized bicycles, **Veh 24015**

HEADQUARTERS
Highway patrol, establishment, **Veh 2404**

HEADSETS
Bicycles, **Veh 27400**
Motor vehicles, wearing while operating, **Veh 27400**

HEALTH AND SANITATION
Cemeteries and Dead Bodies, generally, this index
Dead bodies. Cemeteries and Dead Bodies, generally, this index
Drugs and Medicine, generally, this index
Environmental license plate fund, **Veh 5100 et seq.**
Hazardous Substances and Waste, generally, this index
Health Care Districts, generally, this index
Hospitals, generally, this index
Housing Authorities, generally, this index
Medical waste. Hazardous Substances and Waste, this index
Medicine. Drugs and Medicine, generally, this index
Mosquito Abatement or Vector Control Districts, generally, this index
Pest Abatement Districts, generally, this index
Portable sanitary facility, motor carriers exempt from registration, **Veh 36105**
Solid Waste, generally, this index

HEALTH CARE DISTRICTS
Bicycles, **Veh 21113**
Motorized bicycles, **Veh 21113**
Roller skates, **Veh 21113**
Skateboards, **Veh 21113**
Traffic rules and regulations, public grounds, local regulation, **Veh 21113**

HEALTH CARE PROVIDERS
Midwives, generally, this index
Nurses, generally, this index
Physicians and Surgeons, generally, this index

HEALTH FACILITIES
Hospitals, generally, this index
Medical waste. Hazardous Substances and Waste, this index
Nurses, generally, this index
Physician Assistants, generally, this index

HEARSES
Weight limit exemptions, **Veh 35720**

HEART DISEASE
Motor vehicles, blood tests, driving under influence of alcohol or drugs, **Veh 13353**

HEAVY DUTY
Definitions, transit district vehicles, emission standards, **Veh 28114**

HEAVY VEHICLE TAX
Motor vehicles, nonpayment of tax, refusal of registration, **Veh 4750**

HEIGHT
Traffic Rules and Regulations, this index

HELMETS
Bicycles, use, bicyclists and passengers, **Veh 21212**
Motorcycles, this index
Motorized scooters, **Veh 21235**
Standards and specifications, adoption and enforcement, **Veh 26103**
Traffic Rules and Regulations, this index

HEMOPHILIA
Driving under the influence, blood tests, exemption, **Veh 23612**
Motor vehicles, blood tests, driving under influence of alcohol or drugs, **Veh 13353**

HIGH BEAM HEADLAMPS
Motor vehicles, dimming for approaching vehicles, **Veh 24409**

HIGH EXPLOSIVES
Explosives, generally, this index

HIGH OCCUPANCY VEHICLE LANES
Highways and Roads, this index

HIGH SCHOOLS OR SECONDARY SCHOOLS
Driver education. Schools and School Districts, this index
Peace officers, flight from, **Veh 2800.1 et seq.**
School Buses, generally, this index

HIGHER EDUCATION
Colleges and Universities, generally, this index

HIGHWAY ACCOUNT
Transportation fund. State Treasury, this index

HIGHWAY AND BRIDGE DISTRICTS
Motor vehicles,
Colored lights, **Veh 25256**
Flashing lights, **Veh 25256**
Lights and lighting, flashing and colored lights, **Veh 25256**
Warning lights, **Veh 25256**
Traffic rules and regulations, **Veh 21113**

HIGHWAY CARRIERS
Motor Carriers, generally, this index

HIGHWAY LITTER ACT
Generally, **Veh 23111 et seq.**

HIGHWAY PATROL
Generally, **Veh 2100 et seq.**

HIGHWAY PATROL—Cont'd
Abandoned or unclaimed property, **Veh 2414, 2415**
Appraisals, **Veh 22855**
Removal, **Veh 22669**
From private property after accident, **Veh 22653**
Rules and regulations, **Veh 22666**
Accidents, reports,
Confidential use, **Veh 20014**
Coroners, **Veh 20011**
Death or personal injuries, **Veh 20004, 20008**
Investigations, **Veh 2412**
Disclosure, **Veh 20012**
Forms, preparation and supply, **Veh 2407**
Notice, **Veh 20002**
Tabulation and analysis, **Veh 2408**
Administrative Procedure Act, rules and regulations, **Veh 2402**
Advances, uniforms, **Veh 2260**
Age, officers and employees, **Veh 2256**
Aircraft, **Veh 2267**
Application of law, Government Code, **Veh 2105**
Appointments from promotional eligible lists, **Veh 2251**
Arrest, discretionary procedures, **Veh 40304**
Assignment of member for service outside county of appointment, **Veh 2255**
Assistance, disabled motorist, **Veh 20018 et seq.**
Associations, membership fees, **Veh 2114**
Auctions, sale of unclaimed property, **Veh 2415**
Authorized emergency vehicles,
Permit, **Veh 2416**
Use by member, display of blue light, **Veh 25258**
Badges, emblems and insignia, **Veh 2257, 2258**
Marksmanship, **Veh 2264**
Bids and bidding, sale of unclaimed property, **Veh 2415**
Bills of lading, vehicle transporting timber, inspection, **Veh 2810**
Blue light, authorized emergency vehicle, **Veh 25258**
Boards and commissions. Commissioner, generally, post
Books and papers, possession and control, **Veh 2104**
Boots, **Veh 2267**
Branch offices, establishment, **Veh 2403**
Buildings, acquisition, **Veh 2405**
Bulletproof vests, **Veh 2259.5**
CAL H.E.A.T. (Californians help eliminate auto theft) program, **Veh 10902**
California highway patrol, definitions, **Veh 2102**
Captain, appointment from promotional eligible lists, **Veh 2251**
Certificates and certification, school buses, **Veh 2807**

HIGHWAY

HIGHWAY PATROL—Cont'd

Citizens and citizenship, qualifications, **Veh 2267**

Claims board, economic auto theft, **Veh 10902**

Closing highway, public health or safety, **Veh 2812**

Commissioner,
Administrative and enforcement duties, **Veh 2400 et seq.**
Assistants,
Appointment, **Veh 2110**
Duties, **Veh 2111**
Promotional eligible list, **Veh 2251**
Chief administrative officer, **Veh 2112**
Powers and duties, **Veh 2113**
Definitions, **Veh 265**
Powers and duties, **Veh 2108, 2400 et seq.**
Statewide vehicle theft investigation and apprehension coordinator, designation, **Veh 2413**

Common carriers, accident reports, **Veh 20009**

Drivers, **Veh 20008**

Communications operators, compensation and salaries, **Veh 2266**

Compensation and salaries,
Communications operators, **Veh 2266**
Deductions for uniforms, **Veh 2260**
Sale of unclaimed property, **Veh 2415**

Confidential or privileged information,
Officers and employees, motor carrier specialist 1, addresses, **Veh 1808.4**
Radioactive materials, transportation, notice, **Veh 33002**

Contracts,
Emergency road services, **Veh 2424**
Supplemental traffic patrol services, **Veh 2410.5**
Towing agreements, **Veh 2424**
Training schools, **Veh 2262**

Counties, service outside county, **Veh 2255**

Crude oil, inspection, **Veh 2810**

Day and night patrol, **Veh 2401**

Death,
Investigation, accidents, **Veh 2412**
Report, **Veh 20004**

Definitions, **Veh 2101**
Department, **Veh 21000**
Equipment of vehicles, **Veh 24000**
Rules of the road, **Veh 21000**

Disability, records, examination, **Veh 2254**

Disabled motorist, assistance, **Veh 20018 et seq.**

Display, blue light, authorized emergency vehicle used by member, **Veh 25258**

Districts, creation, **Veh 2403**

Domicile and residence, commissioner, **Veh 2107**

Education. Training, generally, post

Emergency medical dispatchers, training, **Veh 2422**

Emergency services, **Veh 2108**
Directing traffic, **Veh 2410**
First aid equipment, **Veh 2406**

HIGHWAY PATROL—Cont'd

Emergency services—Cont'd
Road services, contracts, **Veh 2424**
Service outside county, **Veh 2255**

Emergency vehicles, blue light, **Veh 25258**

Escheat, abandoned or unclaimed property, **Veh 2415**

Examinations,
Promotional, **Veh 2251**
Specialized positions, open competitive examinations, **Veh 2252**

Expenses and expenditures,
Change in uniform regulations, **Veh 2265**
Unclaimed property sale, **Veh 2415**

False personation, **Veh 27, 2261, 40000.5**

Farm produce, vehicle transporting, inspection, **Veh 2810**

Fences, report of damages, **Veh 2811**

Field tests, accident prevention, **Veh 2408**

Fires, directing traffic, **Veh 2410, 21707**

First aid equipment, **Veh 2406**

Flares, replacement, **Veh 2419**

Following emergency vehicles, **Veh 21706**

Forms,
Accident reports, preparation and supply, **Veh 2407**
Radioactive materials, transportation, notice, **Veh 33002**

Garages, inspection, motor vehicles, **Veh 2805**

Guidelines, pursuit, **Veh 17004.7**

Hazardous radioactive materials, transportation, notice, **Veh 33002**

Hazardous substances and waste, **Veh 2401.1**
Motor vehicles, signs and signals, exemptions, **Veh 27903**

Head of department, **Veh 2105**

Headquarters, establishment, **Veh 2404**

Impersonation, **Veh 27, 2261**

Industrial disability cases, disputes, **Veh 2254**

Information, associations for dissemination of information, membership, **Veh 2114**

Injured patrolmen, limited duty positions, **Veh 2268**

Injuries, examination of records, **Veh 2254**

Inspection and inspectors,
Appointment from promotional eligible lists, **Veh 2251**
Injury and disability records, **Veh 2254**
Kitchen grease, transporters, **Veh 2810**
Motor carriers drivers records, **Veh 34501**
Motor vehicle or equipment, **Veh 2804, 2805**
School buses, **Veh 2807**

Investigations and investigators, accidents resulting in personal injuries or death, **Veh 2412**

Jurisdiction, **Veh 2108**

Kitchen grease, transporters, inspection and inspectors, **Veh 2810**

Law governing, **Veh 2105**

HIGHWAY PATROL—Cont'd

Leased property, **Veh 2405**

License plates, inspection, **Veh 2804**

Licenses and permits, **Veh 2500 et seq.**
Authorized emergency vehicle, **Veh 2416**

Lieutenant, appointment from promotional eligible list, **Veh 2251**

Limited duty positions, assignments, **Veh 2268**

Livestock, vehicle transporting, inspection, **Veh 2810**

Loaded vehicles, inspection to determine legality of possession, **Veh 2810**

Loads, rope or strap material, certification, **Veh 24005.5**

Location of patrol area, **Veh 2255**

Lost or stolen property, disposition, **Veh 2414, 2415**

Machinery and equipment,
First aid equipment, **Veh 2406**
Possession and control, **Veh 2104**
Repairs, costs, **Veh 2259**

Main offices, **Veh 2106**

Marksmanship badges, **Veh 2264**

Medical dispatchers, emergency medical dispatchers, training, **Veh 2422**

Motor vehicle account, **Veh 42270 et seq.**

Motor vehicles,
Abandoned or unclaimed property, removal, **Veh 22669**
Hazardous substances and waste, signs and signals, exemptions, **Veh 27903**
Leased vehicles, investigations, name of lessee, **Veh 4453.6**
Off highway motor vehicles, identification fees,
Adjustments, **Veh 1678**
Maintaining uniformed field strength, **Veh 38225.4**
Registration and renewal fees, maintaining uniformed field strength, **Veh 9250.9**
Removal, **Veh 22659**
Hit and run accidents, **Veh 22655**
Left at scene of accident, **Veh 22653**
Railroad right of way, **Veh 22656**
Theft, statewide vehicle theft investigation and apprehension coordinator, **Veh 2413**

Motorcycles, **Veh 2267**
Safety program, **Veh 2930 et seq.**

Nonsworn personnel, addresses, confidentiality, **Veh 1808.4**

Notice,
Radioactive materials,
Spent fuel, transportation, **Veh 33002**
Transporting, **Veh 33002**
Stolen or embezzled vehicle, **Veh 10503**
Striking unattended vehicle, **Veh 20002**
Written notice, motor vehicle violations as cause of accident, **Veh 40600**

Nuisance, prohibited sign, signal, removal, **Veh 21467**

HIGHWAY PATROL—Cont'd
Off highway motor vehicles, identification fees,
  Adjustments, **Veh 1678**
  Maintaining uniformed field strength, **Veh 38225.4**
Officers and employees,
  Motor carrier specialist 1, addresses, confidentiality, **Veh 1808.4**
  Protective services, costs, **Veh 2428**
  Reports, additional officers, **Veh 9250.13**
Offices,
  Main office at Sacramento, **Veh 2106**
  Possession and control, **Veh 2104**
Oil and gas, inspection, **Veh 2810**
Organization of department, **Veh 2109**
Out of state funerals, peace officers, **Veh 2421**
Parked or abandoned vehicles, removal, state owned, rented or protected property, **Veh 22659**
Parking lots, motor vehicles, inspection, **Veh 2805**
Patrol districts, creation, **Veh 2403**
Personal injuries,
  Accidents, investigations, **Veh 2412**
  Records, **Veh 2254**
Petroleum products, inspection, **Veh 2810**
Police department, accidents resulting in injuries or death, report, **Veh 20008**
Policies, pursuit, **Veh 17004.7**
Possession of records and property, **Veh 2104**
Poultry, vehicle transporting, inspection, **Veh 2810**
Powers, duties, jurisdiction and responsibility, **Veh 2108**
Privileges and immunities, pursuit, **Veh 17004.7**
Promotional examinations, **Veh 2251**
Property, possession and control, **Veh 2104**
Protective services,
  State officers and employees, costs, **Veh 2428**
  State property, costs, **Veh 2428**
Public buildings and works,
  Costs, **Veh 2428**
  Protective services, costs, **Veh 2428**
Pursuit, **Veh 17004.7**
  Reports, **Veh 14602.1**
Qualifications, citizenship, **Veh 2267**
Radioactive materials, transporting, notice, **Veh 33002**
Real estate, purchase or lease, **Veh 2405**
Receiving stolen goods, disposition, **Veh 2414, 2415**
Records and recordation,
  Examination, industrial disability disputes, **Veh 2254**
  Possession and control, **Veh 2104**
  Radioactive materials, transportation, notice, **Veh 33002**
Registration card, inspection, **Veh 2804**

HIGHWAY PATROL—Cont'd
Removal,
  Abandoned vehicles from private property after accident, **Veh 22653**
  Motor vehicles, powers, **Veh 22659**
  Parked or standing vehicles, **Veh 22650 et seq.**
Repair of uniforms, expenses, **Veh 2259**
Repair shops, inspection, **Veh 2805**
Reports,
  Accidents, ante
  Emergency medical dispatcher training, **Veh 2422**
  Officers and employees, additional officers, **Veh 9250.13**
  Pursuit, **Veh 14602.1**
  Stolen vehicles, **Veh 10500 et seq.**
  Stored or parked vehicles, **Veh 10652**
  Towing agreements, **Veh 2424**
Rules and regulations, **Veh 2402**
Sacramento, city of, main office, **Veh 2106**
Sale, lost, stolen or abandoned property, **Veh 2415**
Scales, weighing motor vehicles, certification, **Veh 2809**
School buses,
  Inspection for construction, equipment, **Veh 2807**
  Stops, unincorporated areas, approval, **Veh 22504**
School for training, **Veh 2262**
Sergeant, appointment from promotional, eligible list, **Veh 2251**
Shooting practice and firearms instructions, **Veh 2263**
Special peace officers, transfer of powers and duties, state police division, **Veh 2250.1**
Specialized positions, open competitive examinations, **Veh 2252**
Standards, pursuit, **Veh 17004.7**
State agencies, protective services, costs, **Veh 2428**
State compensation insurance fund, industrial dispute, examination of record, **Veh 2254**
State treasury, protective services fund, **Veh 2428**
Stolen vehicles, reports, **Veh 10500 et seq.**
Storage charges, abandoned property, **Veh 2414**
Stretcher and emergency first aid equipment, **Veh 2406**
Substations, establishment, **Veh 2404**
Successor to former division of enforcement, **Veh 2103**
Supplemental traffic patrol services, contracts, **Veh 2410.5**
Termination of employment, citizenship, **Veh 2267**
Theaters and shows, uniforms, **Veh 2261**
Timber products, inspection of vehicle transporting, **Veh 2810**
Toll roads and bridges, vehicular crossings, authority, **Veh 23251**
Tour buses, safe operation, **Veh 34500.1**

HIGHWAY PATROL—Cont'd
Towing agreements, **Veh 2424**
Traffic officers, members and membership, **Veh 625**
Traffic Rules and Regulations, generally, this index
Training,
  Contracts, **Veh 2262**
  Emergency medical dispatchers, **Veh 2422**
  Pursuit, **Veh 17004.7**
Transfer, warrant of arrest for execution, **Veh 40516**
Transfer of powers and duties, state police division, **Veh 2250.1**
Transportation, injured persons, **Veh 2406**
Traveling expenses, out of state funerals, **Veh 2421**
Unclaimed property, disposition, **Veh 2414, 2415**
Uniforms, **Veh 2259 et seq.**
  Bulletproof vests, **Veh 2259.5**
  Change in regulations, **Veh 2265**
  Furnishing, **Veh 2260**
  Repairs, costs, **Veh 2259**
  Unauthorized wearing, **Veh 2261**
Vests, bulletproof, **Veh 2259.5**
Visibility limitations, restricted highway use, **Veh 2812.5**
Warrants, authority to serve, **Veh 2411**
Weapons,
  Marksmanship badges, **Veh 2264**
  Training, **Veh 2263**
Wearing apparel. Uniforms, generally, ante
Workers compensation, **Veh 2253**
  Records, inspection, **Veh 2254**
Written notice, motor vehicle violation as cause of accident, probable cause, **Veh 40600**

HIGHWAYS AND ROADS
Access, ecological reserve areas, local authority control, **Veh 21117**
Accidents. Traffic Rules and Regulations, this index
Accounts and accounting. State highway account, generally, post
Actions and proceedings,
  Claims, damages to highways, **Veh 17300 et seq.**
  Damages, **Veh 17300 et seq.**
  Motor vehicles, damage to roads or bridges, **Veh 17300 et seq.**
  Toll roads and bridges, post
Advertisements. Outdoor Advertising, generally, this index
Aggressive driving, road rage. Traffic Rules and Regulations, this index
Agricultural machinery and equipment, prohibiting from specific routes, **Veh 36101**
Alameda County, this index
Appeal and review, toll evasion violations, **Veh 40255, 40256**
Appurtenances, wilfully or negligently damaging, **Veh 17300 et seq.**

HIGHWAYS

HIGHWAYS AND ROADS—Cont'd

Assault and battery, road rage. Traffic Rules and Regulations, this index

Assistance, disabled motorist, law enforcement officers, **Veh 20018 et seq.**

Automatic vehicle identification systems. Toll roads and bridges, post

Bicycles, generally, this index

Billboards. Outdoor Advertising, generally, this index

Boundary line highways,
Local authorities, traffic rules and regulations, **Veh 21105**
Speed limits, **Veh 22359**

Bridge and highway districts. Highway and Bridge Districts, generally, this index

Bridges,
Actions, damages, **Veh 17300 et seq.**
County highways, weight limits, **Veh 35706 et seq., 35754**
Damages,
Illegal operation, driving, liability, **Veh 17301**
Joint liability of motor vehicle owner and driver for, **Veh 17302**
Tort liability, **Veh 17300 et seq.**
Dangerous or weakened condition, posting maximum weight, **Veh 35755**
Debris, removal after accident or damages, **Veh 17300 et seq.**
Detours,
Damaged highways, expenses and expenditures, **Veh 17300 et seq.**
Signs and signals, **Veh 21363**
Hauling saw logs, speed, **Veh 35785**
Highway and Bridge Districts, generally, this index
Joint and several liability of motor vehicle owner for damages, **Veh 17301**
Joint liability of motor vehicle owner and driver for damages, **Veh 17302**
Manufactured housing, **Veh 35790**
Negligence, damages, tort liability, **Veh 17300 et seq.**
Pedestrian facilities, refusal to leave, arrest, **Veh 40303**
Pedestrians, local regulation, **Veh 21109**
Speed, hauling logs over, **Veh 35785**
Toll roads and bridges, generally, post
Traffic Rules and Regulations, this index
Traffic safety fund, construction, **Veh 42200**
Traffic Signs and Signals, this index
Vertical clearance measuring devices, pilot cars, **Veh 35252**
Weight limits, **Veh 35750 et seq.**

Causeways, hauling saw logs, speed, **Veh 35785**

Chemical rocket propellants, transportation, route designation, **Veh 32102**

Closing, emergencies, **Veh 2812**

Combined use highways, off highway vehicles, **Veh 38026**
Inyo County, **Veh 38026.1**

HIGHWAYS AND ROADS—Cont'd

Compromise and settlement, damage to highway, **Veh 17300**

Congestion, San Mateo County, managers and management, **Veh 9250.5**

Construction, improvement and repair,
Equipment. Construction or maintenance equipment, generally, ante
Funds. State highway account, generally, post
State highway account, generally, post
Traffic safety program, **Veh 2900 et seq.**
Zone, code violations, **Veh 42009**

Construction or maintenance equipment,
Aerial lift equipped vehicles, amber warning lights, **Veh 25260.3**
Drivers licenses, **Veh 12521**
Examinations, drivers licenses, **Veh 12521**
Fees,
Identification plates, **Veh 9261, 9261.1**
Adjustments, **Veh 1678**
Special construction equipment certificates, **Veh 12521**
Flashing and colored lights, **Veh 25256**
Identification plates, **Veh 4155**
Fees, **Veh 1678, 9261, 9261.1**
Lighting equipment, exemption, **Veh 25801**
Oil and gas pipelines, flashing amber lights, **Veh 25260.1**
Road rollers, **Veh 565**
Special equipment, **Veh 570**
Certificates, **Veh 12521**
Definitions, **Veh 565, 570**
Drivers license, **Veh 12521**
Identification plates and cards, **Veh 5011 et seq.**
Inspection, stolen vehicles, **Veh 2805**
License plates, **Veh 5011**
Lights and lighting, **Veh 25801**
Movement, manufacturer or dealer, **Veh 5016.5**
Registration, exemption, **Veh 4010**
Tires, **Veh 27454**
Width, **Veh 35104**

Continuing cross highways, intersection with terminated highway, right of way, **Veh 21800**

Corridors,
Parking, facilities, **Veh 22518**
State highways, post

County highways,
Bridges, ante
Cotton module movers, weights, **Veh 35555**
Ice and Snow, generally, this index
Inyo County, combined use highways, off highway vehicles, **Veh 38026.1**
Sidewalks, generally, this index
Signs and signals. Traffic Signs and Signals, generally, this index
Snow. Ice and Snow, generally, this index
Traffic Signs and Signals, generally, this index

HIGHWAYS AND ROADS—Cont'd

County highways—Cont'd
Vehicle length, regulation, **Veh 35401**
Weight limits, **Veh 35700 et seq.**

County roads. County highways, generally, ante

Crimes and offenses,
Divided highways, **Veh 21651**
Fines and penalties, generally, post

Crossings. Railroad Crossings, generally, this index

Damages,
Detours, cost of providing, **Veh 17300 et seq.**
Illegal operation, of vehicle, liability, **Veh 17301**
Joint liability of motor vehicle owner and driver for, **Veh 17302**
Tort liability, **Veh 17300 et seq.**

Debris,
Removal after accident or damages, **Veh 17300 et seq.**
Tow car drivers, duty to remove, **Veh 27700**

Defective roads, weight limits, **Veh 35717**

Definitions, **Veh 360, 591**
Hazardous substances, spill containment and abatement, **Veh 2452**
Motor vehicles, **Veh 360, 591, 592**
National forest lands, **Veh 592**
Vehicle Code, **Veh 527**

Demonstration programs, combined use highways, off highway vehicles, Inyo County, **Veh 38026.1**

Designs and designers, traffic safety program, **Veh 2900 et seq.**

Detours,
Expenses of providing detours for damaged highway, **Veh 17300 et seq.**
Signs, location, **Veh 21363**
Traffic rules and regulations, special size and weight permittees, **Veh 35784**

Disabled motorist, assistance, law enforcement officers, **Veh 20018 et seq.**

Disasters, removal of parked or standing vehicles, **Veh 22654**

Disclosure, toll roads and bridges, pay by plate toll payment, **Veh 23301.8**

Divided highways,
Crimes and offenses, **Veh 21651**
Traffic Rules and Regulations, this index
Traffic Signs and Signals, this index

Divisions, highways, employee, transportation, person injured in accident, **Veh 20016**

Double fine zones, **Veh 42010**

Drivers License Compact, **Veh 15000 et seq.**

Dumping, **Veh 23112**

Ecological reserves, access, local authority control, **Veh 21117**

Electric personal assistive mobility devices, **Veh 21280 et seq.**

HIGHWAYS AND ROADS—Cont'd
Emergencies,
  Closing, **Veh 2812**
  Contracts, service authority, **Veh 2421.5**
  Motorist aid system, dispatching services, **Veh 2421.5**
Emergency vehicles,
  Political subdivisions, liability for highway damage, **Veh 35002**
  Toll roads and bridges, exemptions, **Veh 23301.5**
Environment,
  Ecological reserves, access, **Veh 21117**
  Hazardous substance spill containment and abatement, **Veh 2450 et seq.**
  Sensitive areas, access, local authorities, **Veh 21117**
Equipment. Construction or maintenance equipment, generally, ante
Evasion of tolls, **Veh 40250 et seq.**
Exclusive use, **Veh 21655.6**
Exemptions. Toll roads and bridges, post
Explosives, this index
Expressways. Freeways, generally, this index
Fees. Construction or maintenance equipment, ante
Fences, damages, reports, **Veh 2811**
Fines and penalties,
  Double fine zones, **Veh 42010**
  Hazardous substances and waste, dumps or spills, notice, **Veh 23112.5**
  Safety enhancement double fine zones, **Veh 42010**
  Toll roads and bridges, post
Fires and Fire Protection, this index
Flammable liquids, transportation, **Veh 34001 et seq.**
Freeways, generally, this index
Funds,
  State highway account, generally, post
  Transportation fund. State Treasury, this index
Glass and debris, tow car drivers, duty to remove, **Veh 27700**
Golf carts,
  Crossings, **Veh 21115.1**
  Local authorities, **Veh 21115**
Grade crossings. Railroad Crossings, generally, this index
Guideposts, traffic control, injury, removal, **Veh 21464**
Hazardous substances and waste,
  Chemical rocket propellants, transportation, route designation, **Veh 32102**
  Fines and penalties, notice, **Veh 23112.5**
  Haulers, traffic rules and regulations, **Veh 31303**
  Inhalation hazards, route designation, **Veh 32102 et seq.**
  Notice,
    Fines and penalties, **Veh 23112.5**
    Routes, **Veh 32050 et seq.**
  Poison gases, route designation, **Veh 32102 et seq.**

HIGHWAYS AND ROADS—Cont'd
Hazardous substances and waste—Cont'd
  Restrictions or prohibitions, **Veh 31304 et seq.**
  Routes, notification, **Veh 32050 et seq.**
  Spills,
    Containment and abatement, **Veh 2450 et seq.**
    Notice, fines, **Veh 23112.5**
  Transportation, direct routes, **Veh 31303**
  Water supply, restrictions or prohibitions, **Veh 31304**
High occupancy vehicle lanes, **Veh 21655.5 et seq.**
  Automatic vehicle identification systems, hybrid vehicles, **Veh 5205.5**
  Emergency vehicles, **Veh 21655.8, 21806**
  Enhanced advanced technology partial zero emission vehicles, decals, **Veh 5205.5, 21655.9**
  Fines and penalties, **Veh 42001.11**
  Hybrid vehicles, decals, **Veh 5205.5, 21655.9**
  Low emission vehicles, decals, **Veh 5205.5, 21655.9**
  San Bernardino freeway, **Veh 21655.12**
Highway fund. State highway account, generally, post
Housing, this index
HOV lanes. High occupancy vehicle lanes, generally, ante
Ice and Snow, generally, this index
Ice cream trucks, vending, **Veh 22456**
Information, toll roads and bridges, pay by plate toll payment, **Veh 23301.8**
Inhalation hazards, transportation, route designation, **Veh 32102 et seq.**
Intersections, terminating highway, intersection with continuing cross highway, right of way, **Veh 21800**
Interstate highways,
  Billboards. Outdoor Advertising, generally, this index
  Buses, width, **Veh 35106**
  Outdoor Advertising, generally, this index
Inyo County, combined use highways, off highway vehicles, **Veh 38026.1**
Joint and several liability of motor vehicle owner for damages, **Veh 17301**
Joint liability of motor vehicle owner and driver for damages to, **Veh 17302**
Limitation of actions, toll evasion, **Veh 40271**
Lists, hazardous substances and waste, routes where restricted or prohibited, **Veh 31306**
Local Agencies, this index
Local authorities,
  Action on claims for damages, **Veh 17300**
  Bicycle lanes, **Veh 21207**
  Ecological reserves, access, local control, **Veh 21117**
  Weights of vehicles, powers, **Veh 35700 et seq.**

HIGHWAYS AND ROADS—Cont'd
Machinery and equipment. Construction or maintenance equipment, generally, ante
Maintenance equipment. Construction or maintenance equipment, generally, ante
Manufactured housing,
  Permits, **Veh 35790**
  Private roads, **Veh 21107.9**
Mass Transit, this index
Mobilehomes and Mobilehome Parks, this index
Motorized scooters, pocket bikes, **Veh 21720**
Motorized skateboards, **Veh 21968**
Mountain highways, **Veh 21662**
  Coasting down grade in neutral, **Veh 21710**
  Driving on right hand edge, **Veh 21662**
  Horn warning, **Veh 21662**
  Traffic Rules and Regulations, this index
Municipalities, vehicle length, regulation, **Veh 35401**
Negligence, damages, tort liability, **Veh 17300 et seq.**
Nighttime, patrols, **Veh 2401**
Notice,
  Closing, **Veh 2812**
  Hazardous substances and waste, Routes, **Veh 32050 et seq.**
  Substance spills, **Veh 2453**
  Temporary closures, **Veh 21101.4**
  Toll evasion violations, **Veh 40254 et seq.**
Off highway vehicles, combined use highways, **Veh 38026**
  Inyo County, **Veh 38026.1**
Oil and gas,
  Closing, poisonous gas menace to public health or safety, **Veh 2812**
  Poisonous gas, menace to public health or safety, closing, **Veh 2812**
Oil or grease deposits, tow car driver, duties, **Veh 27700**
Oil well production service unit, vehicle incidentally operated or moved on highway, **Veh 450**
One way streets, parking, **Veh 22502**
Outdoor Advertising, generally, this index
Paratransit vehicles, high occupancy vehicle lanes, **Veh 21655.5**
Parking Lots and Facilities, this index
Parks, speed limit, local authorities, **Veh 22358.3**
Patrol of highways, **Veh 2401**
Paul Buzzo Act, **Veh 23111**
Pay by plate toll payment, **Veh 23302**
  Information, **Veh 23301.8**
Penalties. Fines and penalties, generally, ante
Personal assistive mobility devices, **Veh 21280 et seq.**
Pocket bikes, **Veh 21720**

HIGHWAYS

HIGHWAYS AND ROADS—Cont'd

Poisonous gas,
  Closing, **Veh 2812**
  Route designation, **Veh 32102 et seq.**
Political subdivisions, temporary closure,
  Veh 21101.4
Preferential use, **Veh 21655.6**
Private roads,
  Manufactured housing, **Veh 21107.9**
  Mobilehomes and mobilehome parks,
    Veh 21107.9
  Traffic Rules and Regulations, this index
  Traffic Signs and Signals, this index
Proceedings. Actions and proceedings,
  generally, ante
Punishment. Fines and penalties, gener-
  ally, ante
Railroad Crossings, generally, this index
Railroads, generally, this index
Rates and charges. Toll roads and
  bridges, post
Right of way, definitions, motor vehicles,
  Veh 525
Road districts. Highway and Bridge Dis-
  tricts, generally, this index
Road rage. Traffic Rules and Regula-
  tions, this index
Roadside rest areas, rules and regulations,
  Veh 22520.6
Roadway, definitions, motor vehicles, **Veh
  530**
Rocket propellants, transportation, route
  designation, **Veh 32102**
Roller skating, local regulation, **Veh 21969**
Routes, hazardous substances and waste,
  notification, **Veh 32050 et seq.**
Rules and regulations. Traffic Rules and
  Regulations, generally, this index
Safe Streets Act, **Veh 14607.4 et seq.**
  Publicity, **Veh 1664**
Safety, liability for costs, **Veh 17300**
Safety enhancement double fine zones,
  Veh 42010
Sales, roadside rest areas, **Veh 22520.5**
San Mateo County, congestion, managers
  and management, **Veh 9250.5**
Santa Clara County, this index
Service roads. State highways, post
Settlement, claims for damages, **Veh 17300**
Sidewalks, generally, this index
Signs and signals,
  Outdoor Advertising, generally, this in-
    dex
  Traffic Signs and Signals, generally, this
    index
Size of vehicle, counties over 4,000,000,
  Veh 35404
Skateboards,
  Motorized skateboards, **Veh 21968**
  Rules and regulations, **Veh 21967**
Snow. Ice and Snow, generally, this index
Snowmobile operation, **Veh 23128**
Solid waste,
  Local agencies, rules and regulations,
    deposits, **Veh 21100**

HIGHWAYS AND ROADS—Cont'd

Solid waste—Cont'd
  Removal, liability, **Veh 17300 et seq.**
Special equipment. Construction or
  maintenance equipment, ante
Speed contest or exhibition on, punish-
  ment, **Veh 23109**
  Impoundment of vehicle, **Veh 22651.6**
Speed traps, **Veh 40801 et seq.**
Spills, hazardous substances and waste,
  notice, **Veh 23112.5**
State highway account,
  Deposits, **Veh 42270**
  Transfers, **Veh 42205, 42271, 42275**
  Weight limit decreases, streets using
    funds for construction, **Veh 35705**
State highway fund. State highway ac-
  count, generally, ante
State highway route 1, Malibu, traffic rules
  and regulations, **Veh 2400.6**
State highways,
  Abandoned vehicles, removal and
    abatement priorities, **Veh 22667**
  Bridges, generally, ante
  Bus stops, van pools, **Veh 22525**
  Construction, improvement and repair,
    Funds. State highway account, gen-
      erally, ante
    State highway account, generally, ante
  Corridors, parking, facilities, **Veh 22518**
  Cotton module movers, weights, **Veh
    35555**
  Freeways, generally, this index
  Fringe parking facilities, **Veh 22518**
  Funds. State highway account, general-
    ly, ante
  High occupancy vehicle lanes, generally,
    ante
  Ice and Snow, generally, this index
  Outdoor Advertising, generally, this in-
    dex
  Railroads, generally, this index
  Removal, abandoned vehicles, **Veh
    22667**
  Route 85, Santa Clara County, weights,
    Veh 35722
  Santa Clara County, route 85, weights,
    Veh 35722
  Service roads, entering or leaving high-
    way, **Veh 21652**
  Sidewalks, generally, this index
  Snow. Ice and Snow, generally, this
    index
  Streets and Alleys, this index
  Toll roads and bridges, generally, post
  Traffic Rules and Regulations, this in-
    dex
  Traffic Signs and Signals, this index
  Transportation fund. State Treasury,
    this index
  Tunnels, cargo tank vehicles, **Veh
    34020.5**
  Van pools, bus stops, **Veh 22525**
  Weight limits of motor vehicles,
    changes, **Veh 35650 et seq.**

HIGHWAYS AND ROADS—Cont'd

Suits. Actions and proceedings, generally,
  ante
Terminating highways, intersection with
  continuing cross highway, right of
  way, **Veh 21800**
Time, toll roads and bridges, evasion, no-
  tice, **Veh 40254**
Toll ferries. Ferries, this index
Toll roads and bridges,
  Actions and proceedings, evasion of
    tolls, **Veh 40250 et seq.**
  Affidavits, nonliability, evasion of tolls,
    Veh 40263 et seq.
  Appeal and review, evasion violations,
    Veh 40255, 40256
  Automatic vehicle identification ac-
    count, **Veh 23302**
    Pay by plate toll payment, informa-
      tion, **Veh 23301.8**
  Automatic vehicle identification sys-
    tems, hybrid vehicles, **Veh 5205.5**
  Costs, evasion of tolls, **Veh 40250 et seq.**
  Disclosure, pay by plate toll payment,
    Veh 23301.8
  Electronic collection, **Veh 23302**
  Emergency vehicles, exemptions, **Veh
    23301.5**
  Enhanced advanced technology partial
    zero emission vehicles, rates and
    charges, **Veh 5205.5**
  Evasion of tolls, **Veh 4770 et seq., 40250
    et seq.**
  Exemptions, emergency vehicles, **Veh
    23301.5**
  Expenses, state patrol, enforcement ser-
    vices, reimbursement, **Veh 23251**
  Fines and penalties, evasion of tolls,
    Veh 4770 et seq., 40250 et seq.
  Highway and Bridge Districts, generally,
    this index
  Hybrid vehicles, rates and charges, **Veh
    5205.5**
  Information, pay by plate toll payment,
    Veh 23301.8
  Joint and several liability, evasion of
    tolls, **Veh 40250**
  Limitation of actions, evasion of tolls,
    Veh 40271
  Low emission vehicles, rates and
    charges, **Veh 5205.5**
  Motorcycles, electronic collection, **Veh
    23302**
  Nonliability, affidavits, evasion of tolls,
    Veh 40263 et seq.
  Nonpayment, evasion of tolls, registra-
    tion, refusal, **Veh 4770 et seq.**
  Notice, evasion violations, **Veh 40254 et
    seq.**
  Pay by plate toll payment, **Veh 23302**
    Information, **Veh 23301.8**
  Rates and charges,
    Low emission vehicles, **Veh 5205.5**
    Towing services, **Veh 23271, 23272**
    Vehicular crossings, **Veh 23301 et seq.**

HIGHWAYS AND ROADS—Cont'd
Toll roads and bridges—Cont'd
Registration of vehicle, refusal, nonpayment, toll evasion penalties, **Veh 4770 et seq.**
State patrol, enforcement services, reimbursement, **Veh 23251**
Time, evasion, notice, **Veh 40254**
Towing vehicles, **Veh 23270 et seq.**
Tools. Construction or maintenance equipment, generally, ante
Tort liability, damages, **Veh 17300 et seq.**
Traffic Rules and Regulations, generally, this index
Traffic safety program, **Veh 2900 et seq.**
Traffic Signs and Signals, generally, this index
Transportation fund. State Treasury, this index
Traps, speed traps, **Veh 40801 et seq.**
Tuolumne County, Old Priest Grade, weights, **Veh 35715.1**
Users tax fund, street name signs, payment of expenses, **Veh 21366**
Van pools, bus stops, state highways, utilizing, **Veh 22525**
Vending, ice cream trucks, **Veh 22456**
Vista points, rules and regulations, **Veh 22520.6**

HIKING TRAILS
Motorized skateboards, **Veh 21968**
Traffic rules and regulations, unauthorized vehicles, **Veh 23127**

HINGES
Motor vehicles, maximum width of body and hinges, **Veh 35110**

HISTORIC VEHICLES
Generally, **Veh 5050 et seq.**
Abandoned or unclaimed property, abatement and removal, local ordinance, reconstruction, **Veh 22661**
Definitions, **Veh 5052**
Emissions control devices, exemptions, **Veh 4000.1, 4000.2**
License plates, special plates, **Veh 5004, 5004.1**
Lighting and signaling equipment, exhibition vehicles, **Veh 25804**
Motorcycles, license plates, **Veh 5004.5**
Parts car, definitions, **Veh 5051**
Special interest vehicle, definitions, **Veh 5051**
Storage, **Veh 5052**

HISTORICAL LANDMARKS, MARKERS AND MONUMENTS
Boats, plaques, **Veh 9853.5**
Injury, removal, **Veh 21464**
Traffic Signs and Signals, this index

HIT AND RUN DRIVERS
Generally, **Veh 20000 et seq.**
Arrest, **Veh 40303**
Deaths, accident, **Veh 20001**

HIT AND RUN DRIVERS—Cont'd
Drivers License Compact, **Veh 15000 et seq.**
Fines and penalties, **Veh 20001, 20002, 42001**
Investigating offices, official uniform and vehicle, exemption, **Veh 40800, 40804**
Optional appearance before magistrate, **Veh 40303**
Personal injuries, **Veh 20001**
Point count, **Veh 12810**
Property damage, **Veh 20002**
Option of officer to take arrested person before magistrate, **Veh 40303**
Removal of vehicle from highway for inspection, **Veh 22655**
Revocation of license, **Veh 13350**
Sentence and punishment, **Veh 20001, 20002**
Suspension of license, **Veh 13201, 13361**
Traffic officers investigating, exemption from uniform and vehicle requirements, **Veh 40800**
Traffic violator schools, continuance, attendance, exemptions, **Veh 41501**

HITCHES
Motor carriers, towing equipment, **Veh 29003, 29004**
Motor vehicles, towing units, **Veh 29002**

HITCHHIKING
Traffic Rules and Regulations, this index

HOARY CRESS
Weeds, generally, this index

HOMELAND SECURITY
War and Civil Defense, generally, this index

HOMES
Housing, generally, this index

HOMICIDE
Advisory statements, motor vehicles, driving under the influence, **Veh 23593**
Driving under the influence, motor vehicles, advisory statements, **Veh 23593**
Manslaughter,
Motor vehicles, revocation of license, **Veh 13351**
Vehicular manslaughter,
Point system, drivers licenses, **Veh 12810**
Subsequent accidents, alcoholic beverages, **Veh 13954**
Motor vehicles,
Driving under the influence, advisory statements, **Veh 23593**
License revocation or suspension, **Veh 13350**
Subsequent accident, alcohol related, **Veh 13954**
Statements, driving under the influence, advisory statements, **Veh 23593**
Traffic control devices or signs, death caused in act of defacing, **Veh 21464**

HORNS AND SIRENS
Motor Vehicles, this index

HORSE NETTLE
Weeds, generally, this index

HORSEBACK RIDING
Traffic Rules and Regulations, this index

HORSEDRAWN VEHICLES
Traffic rules and regulations, overtaking and passing, **Veh 21759**

HORSELESS CARRIAGES
Abandoned or unclaimed property, abatement and removal of public nuisance, local ordinance, reconstruction, **Veh 22661**
Historic exhibits, lighting equipment, **Veh 25804**
Vehicles of historic value, special license plates, **Veh 5004**

HORSEPOWER
Motor vehicle advertising, **Veh 9950, 9952**

HORSES
Traffic rules and regulations,
Horseback rider, yielding right of way to, **Veh 21805**
Passing animals, **Veh 21759**

HOSES
Motor vehicles, nonconforming equipment, sales, **Veh 24005**

HOSPITAL DISTRICTS
Health Care Districts, generally, this index

HOSPITALS
Ambulances, generally, this index
Bicycles, **Veh 21113**
Children and Minors, this index
Discharge, children and minors, vehicle passenger restraint systems, information, **Veh 27363.5**
Districts. Health Care Districts, generally, this index
Driving while intoxicated, blood tests, administration, **Veh 23158**
Drugs and Medicine, generally, this index
Drunk driver visitation program (youth), **Veh 23517**
Information, child passenger restraint systems, motor vehicles, discussion upon discharge, **Veh 27363.5**
Internet, child passenger restraint systems, motor vehicles, information, **Veh 27363.5**
Medical waste. Hazardous Substances and Waste, this index
Medicine. Drugs and Medicine, generally, this index
Motor vehicles, child passenger restraint systems, information upon discharge, **Veh 27363.5**
Motorized bicycles, **Veh 21113**
Newborn children. Children and Minors, this index

HOSPITALS—Cont'd
Nurses, generally, this index
Physician Assistants, generally, this index
Roller skates, **Veh 21113**
Skateboards, **Veh 21113**
Tests, drunken driving, administration, **Veh 23158**
Transportation, **Veh 20003, 20016**
Youthful drunk driver visitation program, **Veh 23517**

HOTELS
Business structures, definitions, motor vehicles, **Veh 240**

HOURS
Drivers licenses, restrictions, **Veh 12812**
Labor and Employment, this index

HOURS OF LABOR
Labor and Employment, this index

HOUSE CARS
Motor Vehicles, this index

HOUSE TOWING TRUCKS
Lights and lighting, warning lights, **Veh 25263**

HOUSE TRAILERS
Mobilehomes and Mobilehome Parks, generally, this index

HOUSEHOLD GOODS CARRIERS
Commercial vehicles, violations, **Veh 2810.1**
Exemptions, permits, **Veh 34622**
Financial responsibility, identification numbers, evidence, **Veh 16020**
Identity and identification, financial responsibility, evidence, **Veh 16020**
Infractions, commercial vehicles, **Veh 2810.1**
Inspection and inspectors, commercial vehicles, violations, **Veh 2810.1**
Insurance, financial responsibility, identification numbers, evidence, **Veh 16020**
Operating authority, denial, suspension or revocation, safety regulations, **Veh 34505.6**
Permits, exemptions, **Veh 34622**
Probable cause, stops, commercial vehicles, **Veh 2810.1**
Safety regulations, violations, suspension of permit, **Veh 34505.6**
Stops, probable cause, commercial vehicles, **Veh 2810.1**

HOUSING
Construction. Manufactured housing, generally, post
Contractors, generally, this index
Crimes and offenses, defacement of property, **Veh 13202.6**
Defacement of property, **Veh 13202.6**
Definitions, vessels, **Veh 9840**
Exemptions. Manufactured housing, post
Factory built housing. Manufactured housing, generally, post

HOUSING—Cont'd
Highways and roads, manufactured housing, private roads, **Veh 21107.9**
Licenses and permits. Manufactured housing, post
Manufactured housing,
Combinations of homes, transportation, **Veh 35790.4, 35790.5**
Consolidated cities and counties, private roads, ordinances, **Veh 21107.9**
Counties, private roads, ordinances, **Veh 21107.9**
Exemptions, length limitations, **Veh 35790.5**
Hearings, private roads, **Veh 21107.9**
Highways and roads,
Licenses, **Veh 35790**
Private roads, **Veh 21107.9**
Instructions, escrow, highways and roads, **Veh 35790**
Length limitations, exemptions, **Veh 35790.4, 35790.5**
Licenses and permits, transportation, **Veh 35790.5**
Mobilehomes and Mobilehome Parks, generally, this index
Notice, private roads, **Veh 21107.9**
Ordinances, private roads, **Veh 21107.9**
Oversize vehicles, **Veh 35790.4, 35790.5**
Petitions, private roads, **Veh 21107.9**
Private roads, **Veh 21107.9**
Speed, private roads, **Veh 21107.9**
Traffic rules and regulations,
Length limitations, **Veh 35790.4, 35790.5**
Width, **Veh 35789.5, 35790, 35790.1**
Mobilehomes and Mobilehome Parks, generally, this index
Modular housing. Manufactured housing, generally, ante
Notice. Manufactured housing, ante
Prefabricated housing. Manufactured housing, generally, ante
Railroad tracks, movers, notice, **Veh 35789**
Traffic rules and regulations,
Housing projects, local authorities, **Veh 21111**
Manufactured housing, ante
Movers, railroad tracks, notice, **Veh 35789**
Trucks, towing, warning lights, **Veh 25263**
Vandalism, **Veh 13202.6**

HOUSING AND COMMUNITY DEVELOPMENT DEPARTMENT
Mobilehomes and Mobilehome Parks, generally, this index

HOUSING AUTHORITIES
Definitions, traffic rules and regulations, **Veh 21113**
Los Angeles County, traffic rules and regulations, **Veh 21113**
Motor vehicles, traffic rules and regulations, **Veh 21113**
Traffic rules and regulations, **Veh 21113**

HUMAN REMAINS
Cemeteries and Dead Bodies, generally, this index

HUMBOLDT COUNTY
Abandoned vehicle trust fund, allocation, **Veh 22710**
Motor vehicles, abandoned vehicle trust fund, allocation, **Veh 22710**

HUMBOLDT STATE COLLEGE
Colleges and Universities, generally, this index

HUNTERS AND HUNTING
Fish and Game, generally, this index

HUSBAND AND WIFE
Marriage, generally, this index

HYBRID VEHICLES
Motor Vehicles, this index

HYDRAULIC ACTUATORS
Motor vehicles, equipment in lieu of power brakes, **Veh 26301**

HYDROCARBON SUBSTANCES
Oil and Gas, generally, this index

ICE AND SNOW
Lighting and signalling equipment, exemption of special construction and maintenance equipment, **Veh 25801**
Parking, **Veh 22510**
Removal, machinery and equipment,
Exemption from size, weight and load provisions, **Veh 35001**
Windshield wipers, self operating, necessity, **Veh 26706**
School buses, additional lights, reduced visibility, **Veh 25102.5**
Special highway construction and maintenance equipment, lights and lighting, exemption, **Veh 25801**
Speed restrictions, **Veh 22363**
Traffic Rules and Regulations, this index
Windows, obstruction, **Veh 26708**
Windshield wipers, **Veh 26706**

ICE CREAM
Dairies and Dairy Products, this index

IDENTIFIABLE VEHICLE COMPONENT
Definitions, motor vehicle theft, **Veh 2805**

IDENTIFICATION CARDS
Aliens, this index
Birth certificates, verification of age, **Veh 13007.5**
Crimes and offenses, sale or manufacture, similar documents, **Veh 13004.1**
Motor Vehicles, this index
Time for waiting, **Veh 1669**
United States census, verification of age, **Veh 13007.5**

IDENTIFICATION LAMP
Commercial and common carrier vehicles, **Veh 25350, 25351**

IDENTIFICATION PLATES
Agricultural Machinery and Equipment, this index

IDENTITY AND IDENTIFICATION
Arrest. Traffic Rules and Regulations, this index
Buses, this index
Cards. Identification Cards, generally, this index
Driver involved in collision to inform others, **Veh 20003 et seq.**
False Personation, generally, this index
Fingerprints and Fingerprinting, generally, this index
Household Goods Carriers, this index
Intermodal chassis, ocean marine terminals, intermodal roadability inspection program, **Veh 34505.9**
Motor Carriers, this index
Motor Vehicles, this index
Motorcycle registration, motor and vehicle identification numbers, **Veh 4150.2**
Motorists, appearance before magistrate when failing to offer evidence, **Veh 40302**
  Nonresident, arrest, **Veh 40305**
Park trailers, numbers, **Veh 11713.3**
Thumbprints, generally, this index
Traffic violator, detention to determine identity, **Veh 40307**

IGNITION INTERLOCK DEVICES
Driving under the influence. Traffic Rules and Regulations, this index
Motor Vehicles, this index

ILLITERATE PERSONS
Drivers licenses, **Veh 12805**

ILLNESS
Motor vehicles,
  Family members, junior permits, **Veh 12513**
  Operator, removal of vehicle, **Veh 22651**

IMMEDIATE SAFETY HAZARD
Definitions, agricultural machinery and equipment, **Veh 24002.5, 31402**

IMMEDIATELY
Definitions, driving under the influence,
  Notice, suspension order, **Veh 13382**
  Reports, **Veh 13380**
    Children and minors, **Veh 13388**

IMMIGRATION
Deferred action for childhood arrivals, motor vehicles,
  Drivers licenses, **Veh 12801.6**
  Identification cards, **Veh 13001**

IMMUNITIES
Privileges and Immunities, generally, this index

IMPERSONATION
False Personation, generally, this index

IMPLEMENTS
Machinery and Equipment, generally, this index

IMPLEMENTS OF HUSBANDRY
Agricultural Machinery and Equipment, generally, this index

IMPORTS
Exports and Imports, generally, this index

IMPOSTERS
False Personation, generally, this index

IMPOUNDING
Agricultural Machinery and Equipment, this index
Limousines, **Veh 14602.9**
Motor Carriers, this index
Taxicabs, **Veh 21100.4**
Traffic Rules and Regulations, this index

IMPRISONMENT
Correctional Institutions, generally, this index
Crimes and Offenses, generally, this index
Definitions, driving under the influence, second and subsequent offenses, **Veh 23580**
Fines and Penalties, generally, this index

IMPROVEMENT DISTRICTS
Local Agencies, generally, this index

IMPUTED NEGLIGENCE
Negligence, this index

IN LINE SKATING
Helmets, children and minors, **Veh 21212**

INCENTIVES
Motor Vehicles, this index
Recreational vehicles, franchises, **Veh 3076**

INCLOSURES
Fences, generally, this index

INCOME TAX—STATE
Delinquent taxes, motor carriers, licenses and permits, revocation or suspension, **Veh 34623.1**
Motor carriers, licenses and permits, delinquent taxes, revocation or suspension, **Veh 34623.1**

INCOMPETENT OPERATOR
Definitions, traffic rules, **Veh 12809**

INCOMPETENT PERSONS
Alcoholics and Alcoholism, generally, this index
Drug Addicts, generally, this index
Guardian and Ward, generally, this index
Mentally Ill Persons, generally, this index
Mentally Retarded and Developmentally Disabled Persons, generally, this index

INCORPORATED TOWNS
Municipalities, generally, this index

INCORRIGIBLE CHILDREN
Juvenile Delinquents and Dependents, generally, this index

INCUMBRANCES
Liens and Incumbrances, generally, this index

INDEMNITY
Motor carriers, ocean marine terminals, intermodal roadability inspection program, **Veh 34505.9**
Ocean marine terminals, intermodal roadability inspection program, **Veh 34505.9**
Personal Injuries, this index
Taxicabs, impounding, **Veh 21100.4**
Traffic rules and regulations, injury from operation under permit, increased size, weight, **Veh 35782**

INDIANS
Ambulances, fees, exemptions, **Veh 9104.2**
Exemptions, motor vehicles, license fees, **Veh 9104.5**
Firefighters and fire departments, motor vehicles, fees, exemptions, **Veh 9104.2**
Motor vehicles, license fees, exemptions, **Veh 9104.5**
Mutual aid agreements, firefighters and fire departments, motor vehicles, fees, exemptions, **Veh 9104.2**

INDICATORS
Motor vehicles, pilot indicators, **Veh 25108**

INDICTMENT AND INFORMATION
Arraignment, generally, this index
Motor vehicles, speed charges, **Veh 40503**
Traffic rules and regulations, speed violations, **Veh 40503**

INDIGENT PERSONS
Housing Authorities, generally, this index
Motor Vehicles, this index
Public Defenders, generally, this index

INDUSTRIAL COMPENSATION LAW
Workers Compensation, generally, this index

INDUSTRIAL PLANTS
Manufacturers and Manufacturing, generally, this index

INDUSTRIAL RELATIONS DEPARTMENT
Housing, generally, this index
Labor and Employment, generally, this index
Mobilehomes and Mobilehome Parks, generally, this index

INDUSTRIAL WASTE
Solid Waste, generally, this index

INDUSTRY
Manufacturers and Manufacturing, generally, this index

INEDIBLE

INEDIBLE KITCHEN GREASE
Kitchen Grease, generally, this index

INFANTS
Children and Minors, generally, this index

INFLAMMABLE LIQUIDS
Motor Carriers, this index

INFORMATION
Disclosure, generally, this index
Highways and Roads, this index
Hospitals, this index
Motor Vehicle Insurance, this index
Motor Vehicles, this index
Traffic Rules and Regulations, this index

INFORMATION TECHNOLOGY
Telecommunications, generally, this index

INFRACTIONS
Acceptance, bail, **Veh 40307**
Arrest, **Veh 40306**
Bail, **Veh 40307**
 Check as, motor vehicle infractions, **Veh 40510**
 Collection, disposition, **Veh 42201.5**
 Magistrates, unavailable, **Veh 40307**
Boats and Boating, this index
Certificate of adjudication, failure to appear or pay fine, **Veh 40509**
Children and minors, arrest, appearance, **Veh 40502**
Complaint, **Veh 40306**
Contempt, impounding license and ordering person not to drive, **Veh 40508**
Definitions, **Veh 40000.1, 40000.3**
Disposition of fines, **Veh 42201.5**
Drivers licenses, impoundment, **Veh 40508**
Failure to appear,
 Certificate of adjudication, **Veh 40509**
 Written promise, violation of, **Veh 42003**
Impoundment of licenses, **Veh 40508**
Liquefied petroleum gas propulsion systems, regulation violations, **Veh 2402.6**
Motor Carriers, this index
Motor vehicle advertisements, horsepower, **Veh 9952**
Motor Vehicles, this index
Natural gas propulsion systems, regulation violations, **Veh 2402.6**
Night court assessments, **Veh 42006**
Payment of fines, **Veh 42003**
Records and recordation, prior conviction, reports, **Veh 42004**
Release, recognizance, motor vehicle violations, **Veh 40307**
Reports, prior convictions, **Veh 42004**
School buses, safety violations, **Veh 34506.3**
Second and subsequent offenses, reports, **Veh 42004**
Traffic Rules and Regulations, this index
Traffic violator schools,
 Court ordered attendance, **Veh 42005**
 Failure to attend, offenses, **Veh 42005**

INFRACTIONS—Cont'd
Waiver, continuation for preparation of defense, **Veh 40306**

INFRARED TRANSMITTERS
Traffic signs and signals, crimes and offenses, **Veh 21464**

INHALATION HAZARDS
Definitions, transportation by motor carriers, **Veh 34501.6**
Transportation, traffic rules and regulations, **Veh 32100 et seq.**

INHERITANCE
Succession, generally, this index

INJUNCTION
Motor Carriers, this index
Motor Vehicles, this index

INJURIES
Personal Injuries, generally, this index

INMATES
Correctional Institutions, generally, this index
Jails, generally, this index

INSANE PERSONS
Mentally Ill Persons, generally, this index

INSECT PESTS AND PLANT DISEASES
Mosquito Abatement or Vector Control Districts, generally, this index

INSIGNIA
Badges, Emblems and Insignia, generally, this index

INSPECTION AND INSPECTORS
Agricultural Machinery and Equipment, this index
Bills of lading, vehicle transporting timber products, livestock, **Veh 2810**
Boats and Boating, this index
Buses, youth buses, **Veh 2807.3**
Commercial vehicles, **Veh 2813**
Explosives, this index
Farm labor vehicles, design, equipment, **Veh 31401**
Flammable liquids cargo tanks, motor carriers, **Veh 34060 et seq.**
Grapes and Grapevines, this index
Highway Patrol, this index
Household Goods Carriers, this index
Kitchen grease, rendering plants, transporters, **Veh 2466, 2810**
Limousines, this index
Motor Carriers, this index
Motor Vehicles, this index
Ocean marine terminals, intermodal roadability inspection program, **Veh 34505.9**
Oil and Gas, this index
Paratransit vehicles, **Veh 34501.17**
 Safety, **Veh 34501.8**
Police, this index
Records and Recordation, this index
School Buses, this index

INSPECTION AND INSPECTORS—Cont'd
Ships and Shipping, this index
State department of motor vehicles, record, **Veh 1808**
Tour buses, preventive maintenance guide, **Veh 2807.2**
Traffic Rules and Regulations, this index
Traffic safety program, **Veh 2900 et seq.**
Vanpooling, safety, **Veh 34509**
Weights and Measures, this index
Youth buses, **Veh 2807.3**

INSTALLATION
Keys. Locksmiths, generally, this index
Locksmiths, generally, this index
Motor Vehicles, this index

INSTALLMENT PAYMENTS
Traffic rules and regulations, bail, forfeitures, infractions, **Veh 40510.5, 40512**
Traffic violator schools, fees, **Veh 42007**

INSTRUCTORS
Driving Schools, this index

INSTRUMENTS
Negotiable Instruments, generally, this index

INSURANCE
Agents. Insurance Agents, Solicitors or Brokers, generally, this index
Automobiles. Motor Vehicle Insurance, generally, this index
Bicycles, disclosure, **Veh 406**
Brokers. Insurance Agents, Solicitors or Brokers, generally, this index
Buses, this index
Dealers, definitions, motor vehicles, **Veh 286**
Disclosure, bicycles, **Veh 406**
Driving schools and instructors, **Veh 11103**
Evidence, driving schools and instructors, **Veh 11103**
Handicapped persons, parking, special enforcement units, **Veh 22507.9**
Household Goods Carriers, this index
Liability insurance. Motor Vehicle Insurance, generally, this index
Motor Carriers, this index
Motor Clubs, generally, this index
Motor Vehicle Insurance, generally, this index
No fault vehicle insurance. Motor Vehicle Insurance, generally, this index
Old age and survivors insurance. Social Security, generally, this index
Policies. Motor Vehicle Insurance, this index
Self insurance. Motor Vehicle Insurance, this index
Solicitors. Insurance Agents, Solicitors or Brokers, generally, this index
Vehicles. Motor Vehicle Insurance, generally, this index

INSURANCE AGENTS, SOLICITORS OR BROKERS
Motor vehicle insurance,
  Certificates of title, duplicates, **Veh 4466**
  Fraud, accidents, failure to prove financial responsibility, **Veh 16000.8**
  License plates, duplicates, **Veh 4466**
  Revocation or suspension, licenses and permits, fraud, accidents, failure to prove financial responsibility, **Veh 16000.8**

INSURANCE COMMISSIONER
Insurance, generally, this index

INSURANCE COMPANIES
Insurance, generally, this index

INSURANCE DEPARTMENT
Insurance, generally, this index

INSURERS
Insurance, generally, this index

INTELLECTUAL DISABILITY
Mentally Retarded and Developmentally Disabled Persons, generally, this index

INTEMPERANCE
Alcoholics and Alcoholism, generally, this index

INTENTIONAL AND MALICIOUS DESTRUCTION OF PROPERTY
Vandalism, generally, this index

INTENTIONAL TORTS
Torts, generally, this index

INTERCITY RAIL TRANSPORTATION
Railroads, generally, this index

INTEREST
Bail, this index
Motor carriers, registration, fees, apportionment, foreign states, **Veh 8058**

INTERMODAL CHASSIS
Definitions, ocean marine terminals, intermodal roadability inspection program, **Veh 34505.9**

INTERNATIONAL REGISTRATION PLAN
Motor Vehicles, this index

INTERNET
Electronic Mail, generally, this index
Environment, this index
Hospitals, child passenger restraint systems, motor vehicles, information, **Veh 27363.5**
Motor vehicles, identification cards, renewal, **Veh 13002.1**

INTERSECTIONS
Definitions, **Veh 365**
Traffic Rules and Regulations, this index
Traffic Signs and Signals, this index

INTERSTATE AND FOREIGN HIGHWAY CARRIERS
Motor Carriers, this index

INTERSTATE COMMERCE
Motor Carriers, this index
Traffic rules and regulations, violation required by regulation, defense, **Veh 41401**

INTERSTATE HIGHWAYS
Highways and Roads, this index

INTERURBAN RAILROADS
Grade crossings. Railroad Crossings, generally, this index
Railroad Crossings, generally, this index

INTESTATE SUCCESSION
Succession, generally, this index

INTOXICATING LIQUORS
Alcoholic Beverages, generally, this index

INTOXICATION
Alcoholics and Alcoholism, generally, this index

INVALIDS
Handicapped Persons, generally, this index

INVASION
War and Civil Defense, generally, this index

INYO COUNTY
Highways and roads, combined use highways, off highway vehicles, **Veh 38026.1**

IONIZING RADIATION
Atomic Energy, generally, this index

IRRIGATION AND IRRIGATION DISTRICTS
Motor vehicles, machinery and equipment, public lands, inspection and inspectors, **Veh 2810.2**

ISLANDS
Counties over 4,000,000, vehicle size, restricting use, **Veh 35404**
Traffic rules and regulations, island cities, **Veh 21100.5**

ISONIPECAINE
Drug Addicts, generally, this index

ISSUE
Children and Minors, generally, this index

ISSUES, PROOF AND VARIANCE
Evidence, generally, this index

ISSUING AGENCY
Definitions, toll evasion, **Veh 40250**

ITALIAN THISTLE
Weeds, generally, this index

JAILS
Motor vehicles, bail, infractions, **Veh 40307**

JAILS—Cont'd
Officers and employees, addresses, confidentiality, **Veh 1808.4**
Work furloughs, driving under the influence, **Veh 23536, 23580**

JAMMING DEVICES (SPEED)
Motor vehicles, **Veh 28150, 40000.15**

JEEPS
Traffic Rules and Regulations, this index

JOHNSON GRASS
Weeds, generally, this index

JOINT AND SEVERAL LIABILITY
Damages to highways or bridges, **Veh 17301, 17302**
Persons signing drivers license application of minors, **Veh 17707**
Toll evasion, **Veh 40250**

JOINT POWERS AGREEMENTS
Commuter rail system, traffic rules and regulations, **Veh 21113**

JOINT TENANTS
Motor Vehicles, this index

JOY RIDING LAW
Generally, **Veh 10851**

JUDGES
Address, home address, confidential, **Veh 1808.4**
Confidential or privileged information, home address, **Veh 1808.4**
Drivers license, display on request, **Veh 12952**
Home address, confidential, **Veh 1808.4**
Husband and wife, address, confidentiality, **Veh 1808.4**
Judgments and Decrees, generally, this index
Misconduct in office, traffic violations, failure to report, **Veh 1805**
Orders of Court, generally, this index

JUDGMENTS AND DECREES
Appeal and Review, generally, this index
Compromise and Settlement, generally, this index
Definitions, financial responsibility, motor vehicle insurance, **Veh 16250**
Lessor retailers, revocation or suspension of license, **Veh 11604**
Motor Vehicles, this index
Offer of judgment. Compromise and Settlement, generally, this index
Small Claims Courts, this index
Speeding violations, speed trap evidence, **Veh 40805**
Supersedeas or Stay, generally, this index
Traffic offenses, arrest warrants, issuance for failure to comply, **Veh 40514**
Traffic Rules and Regulations, this index

JUDGMENTS AND DECREES—Cont'd
Vacating or setting aside,
Driving while intoxicated, proceedings to declare invalid on constitutional grounds, **Veh 41403**
Motions, driving while intoxicated, **Veh 41403**

JUDICIAL DISTRICTS
Judges, generally, this index

JUDICIAL REVIEW
Appeal and Review, generally, this index

JUDICIAL SALES
Dealers, definitions, motor vehicles, **Veh 286**

JUNIOR COLLEGES
Community colleges and districts. Colleges and Universities, this index

JUNIOR PERMITS
Motor vehicles, drivers licenses, **Veh 12513**

JUNK AND JUNK DEALERS
Disclosure, NMVTIS (national motor vehicle title information system), history, reports, **Veh 11713.26**
Inspections and inspectors, motor vehicles, title, **Veh 1655**
NMVTIS (national motor vehicle title information system), history, reports, disclosure, **Veh 11713.26**
Ships, junking undocumented vessel, termination of certificates of number and ownership, **Veh 9864**

JURY
Contempt, generally, this index

JUSTICE COURTS
Claims courts. Small Claims Courts, generally, this index
Small Claims Courts, generally, this index

JUSTICE DEPARTMENT
Addresses, attorneys, confidentiality, **Veh 1808.4**
Attorney General, generally, this index
Confidential or privileged information, attorneys, addresses, **Veh 1808.4**
Juvenile Delinquents and Dependents, generally, this index
Notice, removal of vehicles from highway for storage, **Veh 22854**
Reports,
Stolen vehicles, **Veh 10500 et seq.**
Stored or parked vehicles, **Veh 10652**
Stolen vehicle system, **Veh 10500 et seq.**
Stolen vehicles, reports, **Veh 10500 et seq.**

JUSTICES
Judges, generally, this index

JUVENILE COURTS
Juvenile Delinquents and Dependents, generally, this index

JUVENILE DAY CENTERS, RANCHES AND CAMPS
Juvenile Institutions and Schools, this index

JUVENILE DELINQUENTS AND DEPENDENTS
Abuse. Children and Minors, this index
Address, halls, camps, ranches and homes, personnel, confidentiality, **Veh 1808.4**
Child Protective Agencies, generally, this index
Confidential or privileged information, personnel, detention halls, **Veh 1808.4**
Defacement of property, delay or suspension of driving privileges, **Veh 13202.6**
Detention facilities. Juvenile Institutions and Schools, generally, this index
Drivers licenses, revocation or suspension, Defacing property with paint or liquid, **Veh 13202.6**
Probation, **Veh 13203**
Driving under the influence, **Veh 13352.3**
Guardian and Ward, generally, this index
Junior permits, motor vehicles, wards of court, **Veh 12513**
Juvenile day centers, ranches and camps. Juvenile Institutions and Schools, this index
Juvenile halls. Juvenile Institutions and Schools, this index
Juvenile Institutions and Schools, generally, this index
Motor Vehicles, this index
Parole and probation,
Boards and commissions. Parole Hearings Board, generally, this index
Hearings board. Parole Hearings Board, generally, this index
Parole Hearings Board, generally, this index
Reports, traffic offenses, **Veh 1816**
Speeding, **Veh 13355**
Traffic Rules and Regulations, this index
Truants. Schools and School Districts, this index
Vandalism, defacing property with paint or liquid, delay or suspension of driving privileges, **Veh 13202.6**

JUVENILE FACILITIES DIVISION
Detention facilities. Juvenile Institutions and Schools, generally, this index
Drivers licenses, suspension or revocation, juveniles committed to youth authority, **Veh 41500**
Juvenile day centers, ranches and camps. Juvenile Institutions and Schools, this index
Juvenile Delinquents and Dependents, generally, this index
Juvenile Institutions and Schools, generally, this index
Motor vehicles, special license plates, **Veh 5001**
Peace officers,
Addresses, confidentiality, **Veh 1808.4**

JUVENILE FACILITIES DIVISION—Cont'd
Peace officers—Cont'd
Husband and wife, addresses, confidentiality, **Veh 1808.4**

JUVENILE HALLS
Juvenile Institutions and Schools, this index

JUVENILE INSTITUTIONS AND SCHOOLS
Juvenile day centers, ranches and camps, nonsworn personnel, addresses, confidentiality, **Veh 1808.4**
Juvenile halls, nonsworn personnel, addresses, confidentiality, **Veh 1808.4**
Officers and employees, addresses, confidentiality, **Veh 1808.4**

JUVENILE PROBATION OFFICERS
Drivers licenses, signing and verification of application for minors license, **Veh 17701**
Privileges and immunities, **Veh 17707**

KAITLYNS LAW
Motor vehicles, unattended children, **Veh 15600 et seq.**

KERN COUNTY STATE COLLEGE
Colleges and Universities, generally, this index

KEYS
Locksmiths, generally, this index
Motor Vehicles, this index

KICKBACKS
Vehicles, towing, public entities, **Veh 12110, 13351.85**

KILLING
Homicide, generally, this index

KITCHEN GREASE
Fines and penalties, records and recordation, **Veh 2468, 2478**
Highway patrol, inspection and inspectors, transporters, **Veh 2810**
Inspection and inspectors, rendering plants, transporters, **Veh 2466, 2810**
Records and recordation, **Veh 2460 et seq.**
Registration, transportation, **Veh 2470, 2472**
Theft, **Veh 2474**
Transportation, registration, **Veh 2460 et seq.**

KLAMATH WEED
Weeds, generally, this index

KNIVES
Weapons, generally, this index

KNOWLEDGE
Notice, generally, this index

KNUCKLES
Weapons, generally, this index

LABELS
Brands, Marks and Labels, generally, this index

LABOR AND EMPLOYMENT
Agricultural Labor and Employment, generally, this index
Cancellation of minors drivers license, death of parent or guardian, **Veh 17712**
Compensation and Salaries, generally, this index
Correctional Institutions, this index
Director of motor vehicles, appointment, **Veh 1507**
Drivers licenses. Motor Vehicles, this index
Driving under the influence,
  Drivers licenses, restrictions, **Veh 23538, 23542, 23562**
  Work release programs, **Veh 23536, 23580**
Firefighters and Fire Departments, generally, this index
Handicapped Persons, this index
Hours of labor,
  Motor carriers, hours of service of drivers, safety regulations, **Veh 34500 et seq.**
  Traffic rules and regulations, driving, limitation, **Veh 21702**
Licenses and permits, drivers licenses, restrictions, driving under the influence, **Veh 23538, 23542, 23562**
Motor Vehicles, this index
Municipal Officers and Employees, generally, this index
Police, this index
Public Buildings and Works, generally, this index
Salaries. Compensation and Salaries, generally, this index
Tort liability, drivers license of minor employee, signing, **Veh 17706 et seq.**
Wages. Compensation and Salaries, generally, this index
Workers Compensation, generally, this index

LABORATORIES
Blood tests, drunken driving, administration of tests, **Veh 23158**
Clinical Laboratories, generally, this index
Medical waste. Hazardous Substances and Waste, this index
Motor vehicle lighting equipment, tests, **Veh 26103 et seq.**
Unlicensed laboratory personnel, drunken driving test, administration, **Veh 23158**

LAKES AND PONDS
Fish and Game, generally, this index

LAMPS
Clearance and side market lamps, vehicles 80 inches or more in width, **Veh 25100**

LAMPS—Cont'd
Cowl or fender, motor vehicles, equipment, **Veh 25106**
Lights and Lighting, generally, this index

LAND
Definitions, drinking, motor vehicles, **Veh 23220**
Real Estate, generally, this index

LAND SURVEYORS
Surveys and Surveyors, generally, this index

LANDFILLS
Solid Waste, generally, this index

LANDING FIELDS
Airports and Landing Fields, generally, this index

LANES
Streets and Alleys, generally, this index
Traffic Rules and Regulations, this index
Traffic Signs and Signals, this index

LANGUAGE
English Language, generally, this index

LANTERNS
Lights and Lighting, generally, this index

LARCENY
Theft, generally, this index

LASERS
Motor vehicles, jamming devices, speed, **Veh 28150, 40000.15**

LAW
Legislature, generally, this index
Ordinances, generally, this index

LAW ENFORCEMENT
Crimes and offenses,
  Motor vehicles, theft, **Veh 10851**
  Vehicles, theft, **Veh 10851**
Disabled motorists, assistance, **Veh 20018 et seq.**
Employed drivers, hours of service regulations, exceptions, **Veh 34501.2**
Fingerprint identification programs (local), funding, motor vehicle registration fees, **Veh 9250.19**
Guidelines, pursuit, **Veh 17004.7**
Hours of service records, transportation, inmates or prisoners, exemption, **Veh 34501**
Marshals, generally, this index
Motor vehicles, records and recordation, access, **Veh 1810.5**
Peace Officers, generally, this index
Police, generally, this index
Policies, pursuit, **Veh 17004.7**
Privileges and immunities, pursuit, **Veh 17004.7**
Pursuit, **Veh 17004.7**
Records and recordation, hours of service, transportation, inmates or prisoners, exemption, **Veh 34501**

LAW ENFORCEMENT—Cont'd
Sheriffs, generally, this index
Standards, pursuit, **Veh 17004.7**
Theft, vehicles, **Veh 10851**
Training, pursuit, **Veh 17004.7**
Transportation, inmates or prisoners, hours of service records, exemption, **Veh 34501**
Vehicles, theft, **Veh 10851**

LAW OF THE ROAD
Generally, **Veh 21000 et seq.**
Traffic Rules and Regulations, generally, this index

LAWYERS
Attorneys, generally, this index

LEAFY SPURGE
Weeds, generally, this index

LEAKAGE
Traffic rules and regulations, spilling load or contents on highways, **Veh 23114**

LEASES
Fraud, lessor retailers, licensed suspension or revocation, **Veh 11613**
Highway patrol, acquisition of property, **Veh 2405**
Motor Carriers, this index
Motor Vehicle Insurance, this index
Motor Vehicles, this index
School Buses, this index
Ships and Shipping, this index

LEAVING SCENE OF ACCIDENT
Hit and Run Drivers, generally, this index

LEFT LANE
Traffic Rules and Regulations, this index

LEFT TURNS
Traffic Rules and Regulations, this index
Traffic Signs and Signals, this index

LEGACIES AND LEGATEES
Gifts, Devises and Bequests, generally, this index
Probate Proceedings, generally, this index

LEGAL ASSISTANCE
Attorneys, generally, this index

LEGAL OWNERS
Definitions,
  Motor vehicles, **Veh 370**
  Registration and transfer of vessels, **Veh 9840**

LEGAL SERVICES
Attorney General, generally, this index
Attorneys, generally, this index
District Attorneys, generally, this index

LEGEND DRUGS
Drugs and Medicine, generally, this index

LEGISLATURE
Address, home address, confidential, **Veh 1808.4**

LEGISLATURE

LEGISLATURE—Cont'd
Confidential or privileged information, home address, **Veh 1808.4**
Home address, confidential, **Veh 1808.4**
Husband and wife, address, confidentiality, **Veh 1808.4**
License plates, motor vehicles, **Veh 5002.5**
Motor vehicles, special license plates, **Veh 5002.5, 5002.8**
Reports, diplomatic drivers license holders, accident and violations frequency, **Veh 12502**
Special plates, **Veh 5002.5**

LEMON LAW BUYBACK
Generally, **Veh 11713.12**

LENGTH
Buses, this index
House cars, **Veh 35400**
Motor carriers,
  Inspection, **Veh 2802**
  Reloading, **Veh 2803**
Traffic Rules and Regulations, this index
Trolley coaches, **Veh 35400**

LESSEE
Definitions, leasing contracts, **Veh 371**
Parking in front of private driveway, permits, **Veh 22507.2**

LESSOR
Definitions, motor vehicle leasing, **Veh 372**

LESSOR RETAILERS
Generally, **Veh 11600 et seq.**
Motor Vehicles, this index

LEVEES AND FLOOD CONTROL
Construction vehicles, flashing amber lights, **Veh 25266**
Emergencies, motor vehicles, size and weight limitation exemptions, **Veh 35002**
Inspection vehicles, flashing amber lights, **Veh 25266**
Maintenance vehicles, flashing amber lights, **Veh 25266**
Motor vehicles,
  Emergency use, size and weight limitation exemptions, **Veh 35002**
  Restrictions, operation, **Veh 21116**
  State levee maintenance vehicles, warning lights, **Veh 25266**
Patrol vehicles, flashing amber lights, **Veh 25266**

LEVELING GRADERS
Special highway construction equipment, definitions, **Veh 565**

LIABILITY INSURANCE
Motor Vehicle Insurance, generally, this index

LIBRARIES
Traffic rules and regulations, distribution, **Veh 1656**
Vehicle Code, distribution, **Veh 1656**

LICENSE PLATES
Generally, **Veh 4850 et seq.**
Motor Vehicles, this index

LICENSED RENDERERS
Definitions, inedible kitchen grease, **Veh 2460**

LICENSED VOCATIONAL NURSES
Vocational Nursing, generally, this index

LICENSES AND PERMITS
Ambulances, this index
Animals, this index
Armored Cars, this index
Bicycles, this index
Buses, this index
Business and Commerce, this index
Cemeteries and Dead Bodies, this index
Commercial vehicles, local authorities, **Veh 16501**
Diesel Fuel Tax, this index
Drivers licenses. Motor Vehicles, this index
Driving Schools, this index
Electric carts, sidewalk use, disabled persons or persons age 50 or older, **Veh 21114.5**
Emergency Vehicles, this index
Exemptions, foreign commercial vehicle licensed in another state, **Veh 8001**
Explosives, this index
Fees, parking in front of private driveways, owners or lessees, permit fees, **Veh 22507.2**
Fire department, emergency vehicles, **Veh 2416**
Foreign commercial vehicles, **Veh 8001**
Hazardous Substances and Waste, this index
Highway patrol, general provisions, **Veh 2500 et seq.**
Housing, this index
Labor and Employment, this index
Lessor retailers, motor vehicles, **Veh 11600 et seq.**
Limousines, this index
Manufactured housing. Housing, this index
Military Forces, this index
Mobilehomes and Mobilehome Parks, this index
Motor Carriers, this index
Motor Vehicles, this index
Motorcycles, this index
Original drivers license, definitions, **Veh 455**
Park trailers, movement, **Veh 35780.3**
Parking in front of private driveways, owners and lessees, **Veh 22507.2**
Police, emergency vehicles, **Veh 2416**
Private driveways, parking in front of, owners and lessees, **Veh 22507.2**
Privately owned ambulances, transportation of medical supplies, lifesaving equipment or personnel, emergency vehicle status, **Veh 2416**

LICENSES AND PERMITS—Cont'd
Recreational Vehicles, this index
Remanufacturers, motor vehicles, **Veh 11700 et seq.**
Repossessors and Repossession, this index
School Buses, this index
Taxicabs, this index
Tow trucks, local authorities, **Veh 21100 et seq.**
Traffic Rules and Regulations, this index
Traffic Violator Schools, this index
Veterans, this index

LIENS AND INCUMBRANCES
Garages, this index
Motor carriers, fees, **Veh 9800 et seq.**
Motor Vehicle Service Stations, this index
Motor Vehicles, this index
Motorcyclist safety fund, **Veh 2934**
Registration, foreign vehicles, **Veh 4307**
Stored removed vehicles, traffic rules and regulations, sale to satisfy lien, **Veh 22851.1**
Traffic Rules and Regulations, this index

LIFEBOATS
Boats and Boating, this index
Ships and Shipping, this index

LIFESAVING DEVICES AND SERVICES
Emergency vehicles, definitions, **Veh 165**
Motor vehicles, red lights and sirens, **Veh 30**

LIFT CARRIERS
Agricultural machinery and equipment,
  Speed limit, **Veh 36400**
  Width limitations, **Veh 36605**

LIGHT DUTY
Definitions, low emission vehicles, **Veh 28113**

LIGHT DUTY MOTOR VEHICLES
Motor Vehicles, this index

LIGHTING PLANTS
Special highway construction equipment, definitions, **Veh 565**

LIGHTS AND LIGHTING
Agricultural Machinery and Equipment, this index
Amber lights, flashing lights, garbage trucks, **Veh 25280**
Bicycles, **Veh 21201**
  Equipment, **Veh 21201**
Buses, this index
Emergency Vehicles, this index
Garbage trucks, flashing lights, **Veh 25280**
Hazardous substances and waste, spill response vehicles, warning lights, **Veh 25260.4**
Mobilehomes and Mobilehome Parks, this index
Motor Carriers, this index
Motor Vehicles, this index
Motorcycles, this index
Off highway vehicles, **Veh 38335 et seq.**

LIGHTS AND LIGHTING—Cont'd

Police vehicles, blue warning lights, **Veh 25258**

Recreational vehicles, width, **Veh 35103**

School Buses, this index

Traffic Rules and Regulations, this index

Traffic Signs and Signals, this index

Trolley coaches, display signs, **Veh 25400**

LIMIT LINE

Definitions, motor vehicles, **Veh 377**

LIMITATION OF ACTIONS

Air Pollution, this index

Ambulances, licenses and permits, revocation or suspension, **Veh 2547**

Armored cars, licenses and permits, revocation or suspension, **Veh 2547**

Highways and Roads, this index

Motor Vehicles, this index

Smog impact fees, motor vehicles, foreign states, **Veh 1673.4**

Toll evasion, **Veh 40271**

Traffic Rules and Regulations, this index

LIMITATION OF PROSECUTIONS

Parking, violations, **Veh 40224**

LIMOUSINES

Alcoholic beverages, **Veh 23229.1**

Passengers possessing or consuming, **Veh 23229**

Certificates and certification, endorsement, **Veh 13369**

Display, special license plates, **Veh 5011.5**

Drivers licenses, reports, **Veh 1808.1**

Emergencies, exits, **Veh 27375**

Exemptions, carrier identification numbers, **Veh 34507.6**

Exits, emergencies, **Veh 27375**

Hearings, refusal, **Veh 14100.1**

Impounding, **Veh 14602.9**

Inspection and inspectors, preventive maintenance, **Veh 2807.2**

License plates,
Display, special plates, **Veh 5011.5**
Livery, **Veh 5011.9**
Memorandum of understanding, **Veh 5011.6**

Licenses and permits,
Revocation or suspension, **Veh 13369**
Reports, **Veh 1808.1**
Traffic violations, reports, **Veh 1803 et seq.**

Livery plates, **Veh 5011.9**

Memorandum of understanding, special license plates, **Veh 5011.6**

Numbers, exempt vehicles, identity and identification, **Veh 34507.6**

Permits. Licenses and permits, generally, ante

Plates. License plates, generally, ante

Rules and regulations, machinery and equipment, maintenance, **Veh 34513**

Safety,
Inspection and inspectors, **Veh 34505**
Rules and regulations, **Veh 34500.1**

Seatbelts, mandatory, **Veh 27315**

LIMOUSINES—Cont'd

Special license plates,
Display, **Veh 5011.5**
Memorandum of understanding, **Veh 5011.6**

Steering, inspection and inspectors, **Veh 34505**

Tour buses. Buses, this index

Wheels, inspection and inspectors, **Veh 34505**

LINES

Fish and Game, this index

LIQUEFIED PETROLEUM GAS

Concealed tanks, block letters indicating fuel, display on vehicle, **Veh 27909**

Definitions, motor vehicles, **Veh 380**

Motor vehicles, filling stations, posting safety regulations, **Veh 2402.6**

Traffic Rules and Regulations, this index

Transportation, Caldecott tunnel, **Veh 31301**

LIQUIDS

Defacement, suspension or delay of driving privileges, **Veh 13202.6**

LIQUOR

Alcoholic Beverages, generally, this index

LISTS

Mail and Mailing, this index

Motor Vehicles, this index

Traffic violator schools, **Veh 11205**

LITTER

Solid Waste, generally, this index

LIVESTOCK

Animals, generally, this index

LIVESTOCK CARRIERS

Animals, this index

LOADS AND LOADING

Agricultural machinery and equipment, **Veh 36600 et seq.**

Bills of lading, inspection, **Veh 2810**

Traffic Rules and Regulations, this index

LOANS

Disabled person placards, motor vehicles,
Crimes and offenses, **Veh 4461**
Fines and penalties, **Veh 4461.5**

Motor Vehicles, this index

Schools and School Districts, this index

State Treasury, this index

LOCAL AGENCIES

Arrest quotas, peace officers, **Veh 41600 et seq.**

Cities and counties. Consolidated Cities and Counties, generally, this index

Consolidated Cities and Counties, generally, this index

Definitions, parking, buses, videotape, transit only traffic lanes, **Veh 40240**

Electric carts, sidewalk use, local regulation, **Veh 21114.5**

LOCAL AGENCIES—Cont'd

Highways and roads, use restrictions, **Veh 9400.7, 9400.8**

Officers and employees, electric carts, sidewalk use, local regulations, **Veh 21114.5**

Peace Officers, this index

Sidewalks, electric carts, local regulation, **Veh 21114.5**

Solid Waste, this index

Streets and alleys, use restrictions, **Veh 9400.7, 9400.8**

Traffic Rules and Regulations, this index

LOCAL AUTHORITIES

Definitions, motor vehicles, **Veh 385**

Highways and Roads, this index

Motor Vehicles, this index

Traffic Rules and Regulations, this index

LOCAL EDUCATIONAL AGENCIES

Schools and School Districts, generally, this index

LOCAL ENTITIES

Definitions, tow truck driver certification, **Veh 2430.1**

LOCAL GOVERNMENT

Political Subdivisions, generally, this index

LOCAL HOSPITAL DISTRICTS

Health Care Districts, generally, this index

LOCAL PUBLIC AGENCY

Definitions, street sweeping, parking, enforcement, **Veh 40246**

LOCAL PUBLIC ENTITIES

Bicycle infractions, costs and fines schedules, establishment, **Veh 42001**

LOCKED CONTAINERS

Definitions, open containers, motor vehicles, **Veh 23225**

LOCKS AND LOCKING

Motor carriers, fifth wheel connecting device, **Veh 29002**

LOCKSMITHS

Definitions, motor vehicles, **Veh 9954**

Liability, motor vehicles, **Veh 9954**

Motor vehicles, **Veh 9954**

LOCKUPS

Jails, generally, this index

LOG BOOK

Motor Carriers, this index

LOGGING DOLLIES

Clearance lamps, **Veh 25100**

Definitions, motor vehicles, **Veh 385.2**

Experiment, dollies carried on trucks, **Veh 35101**

License plates, permanent trailer identification plates, certificates and certification, **Veh 5014.1**

LOGGING DOLLIES—Cont'd
Permanent trailer identification plates, certificates and certification, **Veh 5014.1**
Registration, **Veh 4000 et seq.**
  Weight fees, **Veh 9400**
Safety regulations, **Veh 34500 et seq.**
Towing, weight fees, **Veh 9400**
  Exemption, vehicles manufactured before designated time, **Veh 9401**
Traffic rules and regulations, permits, weight limits, exemption, **Veh 35785**
Weight fees, **Veh 9400, 9401**

LOGGING TRUCKS ACT
Generally, **Veh 35552**

LOGGING VEHICLES
Definitions, **Veh 385.3**

LOGOS
Trademarks, generally, this index

LOGS AND LOGGING
Timber and Lumber, generally, this index

LONG BEACH
Overweight vehicles, special permits, **Veh 35700.5**
Parking, left hand parking, two way roadways, pilot programs, **Veh 22502**
Terminal Island freeway, overweight vehicles, special permits, **Veh 35700.5**
Traffic rules and regulations,
  Overweight vehicles, special permits, **Veh 35700.5**
  Parking, left hand parking, two way roadways, pilot programs, **Veh 22502**

LONG BEACH STATE COLLEGE
Colleges and Universities, generally, this index

LOS ANGELES
Licenses and permits, overweight vehicles, Terminal Island freeway, **Veh 35700.5**
Overweight vehicles, special permits, **Veh 35700.5**
Special permits, overweight vehicles, **Veh 35700.5**
State highway 101, high occupancy vehicles, exclusive or preferential use, **Veh 21655.6**
Terminal Island freeway, overweight vehicles, special permits, **Veh 35700.5**
Traffic regulations, overweight vehicles, special permits, **Veh 35700.5**

LOS ANGELES COUNTY
Funeral processions, traffic rules and regulations, **Veh 21100.7**
Housing authorities, traffic rules and regulations, **Veh 21113**
Motor Vehicle Insurance, this index
Notice, traffic rules and regulations, commercial vehicles, weights, maximum, **Veh 35655.6**

LOS ANGELES COUNTY—Cont'd
South coast air quality management district. Air Pollution, this index
Traffic rules and regulations,
  Commercial vehicles, weights, maximum, **Veh 35655.6**
  Funeral processions, **Veh 21100.7**

LOS ANGELES STATE COLLEGE OF APPLIED ARTS AND SCIENCES
Colleges and Universities, generally, this index

LOST OR DESTROYED DOCUMENTS
Drivers license, **Veh 12815**
Duplicates, drivers license, **Veh 12815**
Motor Vehicles, this index

LOST OR DESTROYED PROPERTY
Boats, undocumented vessels, termination of certificates of number and ownership, **Veh 9864**
Drivers license, duplicate, **Veh 12815**
Highway patrol, disposition, **Veh 2414, 2415**
Ships, documented vessels, termination of certificates of number and ownership, **Veh 9864**
Trailers, permanent trailer identification plates, **Veh 5017**

LOTS
Parking Lots and Facilities, generally, this index

LOUIS FRIEND MEMORIAL ACT
Generally, **Veh 23109**

LOW AND MODERATE INCOME HOUSING
Housing Authorities, generally, this index

LOW COST INSURANCE
Motor Vehicle Insurance, this index

LOW SPEED VEHICLES
Motor Vehicles, this index

LP GAS
Liquefied Petroleum Gas, generally, this index

LUMBER
Timber and Lumber, generally, this index

MACHINERY AND EQUIPMENT
Agricultural Machinery and Equipment, generally, this index
Brakes, generally, this index
Construction, special equipment, inspection by state patrol, stolen vehicles, **Veh 2805**
Cranes, generally, this index
Drilling machinery. Water Wells, this index
Fires and Fire Protection, this index
Highway Patrol, this index
Jamming devices (speed), motor vehicles, **Veh 28150, 40000.15**

MACHINERY AND EQUIPMENT—Cont'd
Lifesaving equipment, privately owned ambulances, emergency vehicle status, **Veh 2416**
Mobile cranes or shovels, motor vehicles used to support boom or mast, brakes, exemption, **Veh 26302**
Notice, violations, corrections, **Veh 40303.5**
Proof of correction of violations, **Veh 40616**
Tour buses, **Veh 34506**
Towing equipment, recreational vehicles, safety connections, **Veh 29004.5**
Youth buses, **Veh 34506**

MAGAZINES
Advertisements, generally, this index

MAGISTRATES
Clerk, acceptance of bail, **Veh 40307**
Traffic rules and regulations,
  Arrest, appearance, **Veh 40302 et seq.**
  Arrested person to be taken immediately before, **Veh 40302**

MAIL AND MAILING
Electronic Mail, generally, this index
Lists, motor vehicles, records, sale, **Veh 1810 et seq.**
Motor Vehicles, this index
Motor vehicles department, message display systems, contracts, **Veh 1656.5**
Traffic Rules and Regulations, this index

MAIL CARRIERS
Motor vehicles, rural carriers, flashing amber lights, **Veh 25272**

MAINTENANCE
Facilities, motor carriers, safety regulations, **Veh 34500 et seq.**
Safety regulations, motor carriers, **Veh 34500 et seq.**
School buses, rules and regulations, **Veh 34508**
Tour buses, **Veh 34506**
Vanpooling, **Veh 34509**
Youth buses, **Veh 34506**

MALIBU
State highway route 1, traffic rules and regulations, **Veh 2400.6**
Traffic rules and regulations, state highway route 1, **Veh 2400.6**

MALICIOUS DESTRUCTION OF PROPERTY
Vandalism, generally, this index

MALICIOUS MISCHIEF
Delay or suspension of driving privileges, **Veh 13202.6**
Driving privileges,
  Delay or suspension, **Veh 13202.6**
  Revocation or suspension, **Veh 13202.6**
Motor Vehicles, this index
Restrictions, driving privileges, **Veh 13202.6**

MALICIOUS MISCHIEF—Cont'd
Revocation or suspension, driving privileges, **Veh 13202.6**
Suspension of driving privileges, **Veh 13202.6**

MALPRACTICE
Emergency vehicle rescue teams, resuscitation attempts, **Veh 165.5**
Resuscitation attempts, emergency vehicle rescue teams, **Veh 165.5**

MAMMALS
Fish and Game, generally, this index

MANDATORY SUPERVISION
Parole and Probation, generally, this index

MANIFOLDS
Motor vehicles, construction and maintenance in reasonably gastight condition, **Veh 27154**

MANSLAUGHTER
Homicide, this index

MANUFACTURED HOUSING
Housing, this index

MANUFACTURERS AND MANUFACTURING
Definitions, motor vehicles,
　Autonomous vehicles, **Veh 38750**
　Bumpers, notice, **Veh 24011.3**
Emergency fire vehicles, manufacturers defect correction, repair expense reimbursement, **Veh 24007.1**
Machinery and equipment, special construction equipment, license plates, **Veh 5016.5**
Motor Vehicles, this index
Motorized scooters, disclosure, **Veh 407.5**
　Pocket bikes, **Veh 9955**
Noise Pollution, generally, this index
Numbers or marks upon new vehicles, **Veh 10750**
Recreational vehicles, franchises, contracts, **Veh 11713.22, 11713.23**
Trailer coaches, registration, **Veh 5353**

MANUFACTURING
Manufacturers and Manufacturing, generally, this index

MAPS AND PLATS
Inhalation hazards, transportation, route designation, **Veh 32102, 32103**
Motor carriers, explosives, transportation routes, **Veh 31611, 31616**
Poison gas, transportation, route designation, **Veh 32102, 32103**

MARIJUANA
Drugs and Medicine, this index

MARINE CARRIERS
Ships and Shipping, generally, this index

MARINE CORPS
Military Forces, generally, this index

MARINE TERMINALS
Intermodal roadability inspection program, **Veh 34505.9**

MARINES
Military Forces, generally, this index

MARKERS AND MARKING
Explosives, transportation, statement, **Veh 31612**
Traffic Signs and Signals, this index

MARKET
Markets and Marketing, generally, this index

MARKETING
Markets and Marketing, generally, this index

MARKETS AND MARKETING
Commercial vehicles, special interest license plates, **Veh 5060**
Motor vehicles, special license plates, limitations, **Veh 5060**
Motorcycles, special interest license plates, **Veh 5060**
Special license plates, limitations, **Veh 5060**
Trailers, special interest license plates, **Veh 5060**

MARKS
Brands, Marks and Labels, generally, this index
Trademarks, generally, this index

MARKS BADHAM ENVIRONMENTAL PROTECTION AND RESEARCH ACT
Motor vehicles, environmental license plates, **Veh 5100 et seq.**

MARRIAGE
Address, confidential or privileged information, **Veh 1808.4**
Children and minors,
　Custody,
　　Motor vehicles, infraction violations, **Veh 40302.5**
　　Traffic infraction cases, **Veh 40302.5**
Drivers license, signature, tort liability, **Veh 17702**
Confidential or privileged information, addresses, **Veh 1808.4**
Drivers licenses, military forces, absence and absentees, expiration, **Veh 12817**
Military Forces, this index
Motor vehicles,
　Minors drivers license, person signing, tort liability, **Veh 17700 et seq.**
　Tort liability, **Veh 17150.5**
Peace Officers, this index
Police dispatchers, address, telephone number, disclosure, **Veh 1808.4**
Torts, motor vehicles, **Veh 17150.5**

MARSHALS
Deputies and assistants,
　Emergency vehicle permits, **Veh 2416**

MARSHALS—Cont'd
Deputies and assistants—Cont'd
　Motor vehicles, emergency vehicle permits, **Veh 2416**
　Vehicles, emergency vehicle permits, **Veh 2416**
Emergency vehicles, permits, **Veh 2416**
Hazardous Substances and Waste, this index
Motor vehicles,
　Emergency vehicles, permits, **Veh 2416**
　Hazardous substances and waste, signs and signals, exemptions, **Veh 27903**
State Fire Marshal, generally, this index
Vehicles, emergency vehicle permits, **Veh 2416**

MASS TRANSIT
Accidents,
　Investigations, **Veh 2400 et seq.**
　Reports, **Veh 16002**
Agricultural machinery and equipment, farm labor vehicles, **Veh 31409**
Automated rail crossing enforcement system, rail transit, **Veh 21362.5**
Breakdowns, high occupancy vehicle lanes, **Veh 21655.5**
Buses, generally, this index
Districts. Transit Districts, generally, this index
Emergencies, high occupancy vehicle lanes, **Veh 21655.5**
High occupancy vehicle lanes, transit vehicles, emergencies or breakdowns, **Veh 21655.5**
Highways and roads, guideways, licenses and permits, **Veh 21655.7**
Paratransit Vehicles, generally, this index
Parking, San Francisco City and County, videotape, transit only traffic lanes, **Veh 40240 et seq.**
Parking lots and facilities, state highways, **Veh 22518**
Railroads, generally, this index
Reports, accidents, **Veh 16002**
Traffic rules and regulations,
　Cellular radio telephones, **Veh 23125**
　Parking, San Francisco City and County, videotape, transit only traffic lanes, **Veh 40240 et seq.**
Transit Districts, generally, this index
Vanpooling, generally, this index

MASS TRANSIT VEHICLES
Definitions, high occupancy vehicle lanes, **Veh 21655.5**

MASTER AND SERVANT
Labor and Employment, generally, this index

MASTS
Motor carried shovels or cranes, length, **Veh 35407**
Motor vehicles, load defined, **Veh 35003**

MDA
Drugs and Medicine, generally, this index

MEASUREMENTS

MEASUREMENTS
Weights and Measures, generally, this index

MEATS
Fish and Game, generally, this index
Game. Fish and Game, generally, this index

MECHANICAL ENGINEERS
Engineers, generally, this index

MECHANICS
Motor Vehicle Repair Dealers, generally, this index
School buses, endorsements, drivers licenses, **Veh 12517, 15275.1**

MEDICAL CARE AND TREATMENT
Anatomical Gifts, generally, this index
Certificates and certification, motor vehicles, drivers licenses, nonresidents, **Veh 12502**
Definitions, rescue team, emergency vehicles, liability, resuscitation attempts, **Veh 165.5**
Drivers licenses. Motor vehicles, post
Drug Addicts, generally, this index
Drugs and Medicine, generally, this index
Emergencies, rescue teams, resuscitation, **Veh 165.5**
First Aid, generally, this index
Health Care Districts, generally, this index
Hospitals, generally, this index
Midwives, generally, this index
Motor vehicles,
    Accidents, transportation of injured persons, **Veh 20016**
    Drivers licenses,
        Certificates and certification, Nonresidents, **Veh 12502**
        Officers and employees, disqualification on reexamination, **Veh 14606**
        House cars, endorsement, applications, **Veh 12804.10, 12804.15**
        Information cards, **Veh 12811.1**
        Revocation or suspension, restricted licenses, **Veh 16077, 16078**
    Injured persons, **Veh 20003**
Narcotics. Drug Addicts, generally, this index
Physician Assistants, generally, this index
Physicians and Surgeons, generally, this index
Rescue teams, emergency vehicles, liability, resuscitation attempts, **Veh 165.5**
Research. Anatomical Gifts, generally, this index
Supplies, transportation, privately owned ambulances, emergency vehicle status, **Veh 2416**
Training, rescue teams, **Veh 165.5**
Volunteers, rescue team, emergency vehicles, liability, resuscitation attempts, **Veh 165.5**

MEDICAL EXAMINERS
Coroners, generally, this index

MEDICAL INFORMATION CARDS
Drivers licenses, **Veh 12811.1**

MEDICAL LABORATORIES
Clinical Laboratories, generally, this index

MEDICAL PRACTICE ACT
Physicians and Surgeons, generally, this index

MEDICAL TECHNICIANS
Emergency vehicles, pollution control devices, **Veh 27156.2, 27156.3**

MEDICAL WASTE
Hazardous Substances and Waste, this index

MEDICINE
Drugs and Medicine, generally, this index

MEDITERRANEAN SAGE
Weeds, generally, this index

MEDIUM DUTY
Definitions, low emission vehicles, **Veh 28113**

MEMORANDUM OF UNDERSTANDING
Limousines, special license plates, **Veh 5011.6**

MEMORIAL SCHOLARSHIP FUND
September 11, 2001, **Veh 5066**

MENTAL HEALTH
Mentally Ill Persons, generally, this index

MENTAL INSTITUTIONS
Mentally Ill Persons, generally, this index
Mentally Retarded and Developmentally Disabled Persons, generally, this index

MENTALLY ILL PERSONS
Drivers licenses,
    Denial, **Veh 12805**
    Revocation or suspension, **Veh 13556**
        Application of law, **Veh 14904**
Guardian and Ward, generally, this index
Motor vehicles,
    Investigations, drivers, **Veh 13953**
    Records, confidential information, **Veh 1808.5**
Social Workers, this index

MENTALLY RETARDED AND DEVELOPMENTALLY DISABLED PERSONS
Automobiles. Motor vehicles, generally, post
Certificates and certification, transportation, drivers, **Veh 12523.6**
Criminal history information, transportation, drivers, certification, **Veh 12523.6**
Domicile and residence, transportation, drivers, **Veh 12523.6**

MENTALLY RETARDED AND DEVELOPMENTALLY DISABLED PERSONS—Cont'd
Drivers licenses,
    Revocation or suspension, **Veh 13556**
        Application of law, **Veh 14904**
    Transportation of persons, certification, **Veh 12523.6**
Drugs and medicine, transportation, drivers, certificates and certification, revocation, **Veh 13376**
Fingerprints and fingerprinting, transportation, drivers, **Veh 12523.6**
Guardian and Ward, generally, this index
Motor vehicles,
    Drivers licenses, generally, ante
    Flashing amber lights, nonprofit organizations, **Veh 25276**
    Investigations of drivers, **Veh 13953**
    Paratransit Vehicles, generally, this index
    Records, confidential information, **Veh 1808.5**
    Transportation, generally, post
Paratransit Vehicles, generally, this index
School buses,
    Flashing lights, **Veh 25257.2**
    Stop signal arm, **Veh 25257.2**
    Stop signs, **Veh 27906**
Transportation,
    Certificates and certification, drivers, **Veh 12523.6**
    Criminal history information, drivers, certification, **Veh 12523.6**
    Drivers, licensure and certification, **Veh 12523.6**
    Drugs and medicine, drivers, certificates and certification, revocation, **Veh 13376**
Vehicles. Motor vehicles, generally, ante

MESSAGES
Telecommunications, generally, this index

METAL KNUCKLES
Weapons, generally, this index

METAL STUDS
Tires, **Veh 27454**

METAL TIRES
Definitions, **Veh 395**
Traffic rules and regulations, gross weight limitations, **Veh 35601**

METERS
Parking Meters, generally, this index

METHANOL FUEL
Antisiphoning devices, motor vehicles, **Veh 28110 et seq.**

METRIC SYSTEM
Weights and Measures, this index

METROLOGICAL STANDARDS
Weights and Measures, generally, this index

MEXICO
Motor Carriers, this index
Motor vehicles, out of service orders, failure to comply, **Veh 2800**
Registration and commercial safety inspections, vehicles, **Veh 2404.5**

MIDGET AUTOS
Dealers, definitions, motor vehicles, **Veh 286**

MIDWIVES
Motor vehicles,
Disabled veterans, license fees, exemptions, certificates and certification, **Veh 9105**
Handicapped persons,
License plates, certificates and certification, **Veh 5007**
Parking, placards, certificates and certification, **Veh 22511.55, 22511.59**
Veterans, license fees, exemptions, certificates and certification, **Veh 9105**
License plates, handicapped persons, certificates and certification, **Veh 5007**

MILEAGE
Motor Vehicles, this index

MILITARY DEPARTMENT
Military Forces, generally, this index

MILITARY FORCES
Absence and absentees. Commanding officers, post
Chemical rocket propellants, transportation, route designation, **Veh 32102**
Commanding officers, absence and absentees, drivers licenses, **Veh 12817**
Commercial vehicles, drivers licenses, **Veh 1651.3**
Examiners and examinations, hazardous substances and waste, endorsements, **Veh 15250**
Discharge, motor vehicle registration, person entering state following discharge, **Veh 6703**
Drivers licenses. Motor vehicles, post
Licenses and permits, commercial drivers licenses, **Veh 1651.3**
Exemptions, **Veh 15250**
Marriage,
Drivers licenses, absence and absentees, expiration, **Veh 12817**
Motor vehicles, registration, exemptions, **Veh 6701**
Motor vehicles,
Commercial vehicles, drivers licenses, examiners and examinations, hazardous substances and waste, endorsements, **Veh 15250**
Drivers licenses,
Absent persons, **Veh 12817**
Commercial vehicles, **Veh 1651.3**
Exemptions, **Veh 15250**

MILITARY FORCES—Cont'd
Motor vehicles—Cont'd
Drivers licenses—Cont'd
Marriage, absence and absentees, expiration, **Veh 12817**
Nonresident minors, **Veh 12518**
Emergency vehicles, permits, **Veh 2416**
License plates, decorations for valor, **Veh 5101.4**
National guard, post
Nonresident minor, operating vehicle within state, **Veh 12518**
Prisoners of war, post
Registration,
Exemptions,
Discharge, entry into state, **Veh 6703**
Fees, reinstatement, financial responsibility, **Veh 4000.38**
Renewal, fines and penalties, waiver, **Veh 9560**
National guard,
Drivers licenses, **Veh 12814.7**
Instruction permits, motor vehicles, **Veh 12509**
Motor vehicles,
Drivers licenses, **Veh 12814.7**
Instruction permits, **Veh 12509**
Police, escorts, sirens and speed, **Veh 21057**
Prisoners of war, motor vehicles,
License fees, exemptions, **Veh 9105**
Special license plates, **Veh 5101.5**
Registration. Motor vehicles, ante
Traffic rules and regulations,
Escorting vehicles, siren and speed, **Veh 21057**
Violation required by order of military authority, defenses, **Veh 41401**
Veterans, generally, this index

MILLS
Manufacturers and Manufacturing, generally, this index

MINES AND MINERALS
Motor carriers, construction, backup devices or alarms, **Veh 27000**
Motor vehicles, construction, backup devices or alarms, **Veh 27000**
Oil and Gas, generally, this index

MINIBIKES
Dealers, definitions, motor vehicles, **Veh 286**

MINORITY, WOMEN, OR DISABLED VETERAN BUSINESSES
Parking violations, processing contracts, **Veh 40200.5**

MINORS
Children and Minors, generally, this index

MIRRORS
Motor vehicles, **Veh 26709**
Motorcycles, **Veh 26709**

MISAPPROPRIATION OF FUNDS
Embezzlement, generally, this index

MISBRANDED
Brands, Marks and Labels, generally, this index

MISCREANT CHILDREN
Juvenile Delinquents and Dependents, generally, this index

MISDEMEANORS
Crimes and Offenses, generally, this index

MISREPRESENTATION
Fraud, generally, this index

MISSILES
Carriers, length limitation, exemption for components, **Veh 35414**
Motor vehicles, throwing or discharging at vehicle or occupant, **Veh 23110**

MITIGATION
Damages, this index

MOBILE DWELLINGS
Mobilehomes and Mobilehome Parks, generally, this index

MOBILE INFRARED TRANSMITTERS
Traffic signs and signals, crimes and offenses, **Veh 21464**

MOBILE TELECOMMUNICATIONS
Wireless telecommunications. Telecommunications, this index

MOBILEHOMES AND MOBILEHOME PARKS
Advertisements, **Veh 11713.1**
Brakes, **Veh 26303**
Operation, stopping distance, **Veh 26454 et seq.**
Branch locations, sales office, **Veh 11709**
Camp Trailers, generally, this index
Campers, towing, weight fees, **Veh 9400**
Exemption, vehicles manufactured before designated time, **Veh 9401**
Carrying permit for movement in coach, **Veh 35790**
Certificates of title,
Fines and penalties, offsets, revenue forecasts, **Veh 9554.1**
Sale of abandoned home, **Veh 5903**
Charges. Fees, generally, post
Combinations of homes, transportation, **Veh 35790.4, 35790.5**
Conditions, permits for movement, **Veh 35790**
Consolidated cities and counties, private roads, ordinances, **Veh 21107.9**
Contracts, rentals, permits for movement, terms or conditions, violations, **Veh 35790**
Counties, this index
Crimes and offenses, **Veh 11713**
Dealers,
Display models, identifying signs, **Veh 11709**
Registration, **Veh 5353**

MOBILEHOMES

MOBILEHOMES AND MOBILEHOME PARKS
—Cont'd
Definitions, **Veh 396**
  Motor vehicles, **Veh 387**
Delinquent fees, **Veh 9555**
Display units, dealers, signs and signals, **Veh 11709**
Equipment, brakes, **Veh 26303**
Exemptions,
  Length limitations, **Veh 35790.5**
  Registration, **Veh 5353**
Fees,
  Advertisements, **Veh 11713.1**
  Delinquent fees, **Veh 9555**
  Escrow fees, advertisements, **Veh 11713.1**
  Registration, post
Hearings, private roads, **Veh 21107.9**
Highways and roads,
  Private roads, **Veh 21107.9**
  Width, limitations, **Veh 35790**
Lamp type turn signal system, **Veh 24950**
Length limitations, exemptions, **Veh 35790.4, 35790.5**
Licenses and permits,
  Business history requirements, **Veh 11703, 11704**
  Overwidth coaches, movement, **Veh 35790**
  Transportation, **Veh 35790.5**
Lights and lighting, signal lamp or device, when towing, **Veh 24950**
Limitations on movements upon highways, **Veh 35790**
  Registration, **Veh 5353**
Model homes, display, sign identifying dealer, **Veh 11709**
Moving, width, **Veh 35790**
Municipalities, this index
Nonresidents, registration, **Veh 5353, 5354**
Notice, private roads, **Veh 21107.9**
Occupational licenses. Licenses and permits, generally, ante
Ordinances, private roads, **Veh 21107.9**
Oversize vehicles, **Veh 35790.4, 35790.5**
Overwidth permits, **Veh 35790**
Owners and ownership. Sales, generally, post
Park Trailers, generally, this index
Permits. Licenses and permits, generally, ante
Petitions, private roads, **Veh 21107.9**
Private roads, **Veh 21107.9**
Public agencies, permit for movement of overwidth coaches, **Veh 35790**
Purchases. Sales, generally, post
Rates and charges. Fees, generally, ante
Records and recordation, stored vehicles, **Veh 10650 et seq.**
Registration, **Veh 5350 et seq.**
  Fees, **Veh 9250, 9250.1**
    Delinquency, **Veh 9555**
  Fines and penalties, offsets, revenue forecasts, **Veh 9554.1**
  Reregistration, abandoned homes after sale, **Veh 5903**

MOBILEHOMES AND MOBILEHOME PARKS
—Cont'd
Registration cards, sale of abandoned home, **Veh 5903**
Reports,
  Parked vehicles, **Veh 10652**
  Recreational vehicles stored, **Veh 10658**
Safety, glazing materials, **Veh 26701**
Sales,
  Abandonment, reregistration, **Veh 5903**
  Advertisements, **Veh 11713.1**
  Used mobilehomes, post
Service brakes, stopping distance, **Veh 26454 et seq.**
Signs and signals, dealer, model homes, **Veh 11709**
Special permits, movement of coach in excess of maximum width, **Veh 35790**
Speed, private roads, **Veh 21107.9**
Stock in trade, registration, **Veh 5353**
Storage, recreational vehicles, reports, **Veh 10658**
Streets and alleys, width, limitation, **Veh 35790**
Taxation, advertisements, **Veh 11713.1**
Towing, distance, following another vehicle, **Veh 21704**
Traffic Rules and Regulations, this index
Trailer Coaches, generally, this index
Transporters, registration, **Veh 5353**
Turn signal system, **Veh 24950**
Used mobilehomes, sales, branch locations, **Veh 11709**
Width,
  Excess of maximum width, movement, **Veh 35790**
  Movement, **Veh 35790**
Wreckers, stored or parked vehicle, failure or refusal to keep, **Veh 10655**

MODELS
Mobilehomes, display, signs identifying dealers, **Veh 11709**

MODIFICATION OR CHANGE
Motor Vehicles, this index
Motorized bicycles, operation on highway following nonconforming modification, **Veh 23135**
Recreational vehicles, franchises, **Veh 3070, 3071**

MONITORING
Motor vehicles, data monitors, **Veh 25108**

MONUMENTS AND MEMORIALS
Traffic signs and signals, damages, **Veh 17300 et seq.**

MOPEDS
Motorized bicycles. Bicycles, this index
Motorized Scooters, generally, this index

MORPHINE
Drug Addicts, generally, this index

MOSQUES
Religious Organizations and Societies, generally, this index

MOSQUITO ABATEMENT OR VECTOR CONTROL DISTRICTS
Exemptions, pollution control devices, motor vehicles, **Veh 27156.3**
Motor vehicles,
  Lights and lighting, flashing or colored lights, **Veh 25267**
  Pollution control devices, **Veh 27156.3**
Pollution control devices, motor vehicles, **Veh 27156.3**

MOSQUITOES
Abatement or vector control districts. Mosquito Abatement or Vector Control Districts, generally, this index

MOTHER AND CHILD
Children and Minors, generally, this index

MOTION PICTURES
Motor vehicles, length of vehicle taking pictures, **Veh 35409**

MOTIONS
Time, driving under the influence, vacating or setting aside prior judgment, **Veh 41403**

MOTOR CARRIERS
Access, terminals, **Veh 35401.5**
  Exemptions, **Veh 35401.7**
Accidents, reports, **Veh 20008**
  Safety regulations, **Veh 34500 et seq.**
  Supplemental reports, **Veh 20009**
Acids, explosives, mixed cargo, **Veh 31613**
Actions and proceedings,
  Damage to highways or bridges, **Veh 17303**
  Safety violations, injunction, **Veh 34511**
Adapters, fifth wheel mechanism, locking device, **Veh 29002**
Aerodynamic devices, width of vehicle or load, **Veh 35110**
Affirmations, fleet vehicles, insurance, reports, **Veh 34633**
Age, drivers licenses, **Veh 12515**
Agricultural Products, this index
Air brakes, **Veh 26502 et seq.**
Air Pollution, this index
Aircraft refueling vehicles, registration, exemption, **Veh 4021**
Alcoholic beverages,
  Licenses and permits, suspension or revocation, tests, labor and employment, **Veh 34623**
  Tests, **Veh 34520**
Amber clearance lamps, **Veh 25100**
Animals, this index
Applications,
  Alcoholic beverages, tests, labor and employment, **Veh 34520**
  Drugs and medicine, tests, labor and employment, **Veh 34520**
  Identification numbers, **Veh 34507.5**
  Investigations and investigators, labor and employment, **Veh 34520**
  Permanent trailer identification plates, **Veh 5015**

MOTOR CARRIERS—Cont'd

Applications—Cont'd
Permits, **Veh 34621**
Terminal reinspections, **Veh 34501.12**
Approval, lighting and signalling equipment and devices, **Veh 26100 et seq.**
Area reflectorizing material, **Veh 25500**
Atomic Energy, this index
Audits and auditors, fleet vehicles, **Veh 5302, 8057**
Automatic locking devices on fifth wheels, **Veh 29001, 29002**
Auxiliary dollies,
Brakes, **Veh 26305**
Definitions, motor vehicles, **Veh 225**
Electrical turn signal, necessity, **Veh 24951**
Fifth wheel connecting device to be securely affixed, **Veh 29000**
New vehicles, one trip permits, **Veh 4003.5**
Registration, **Veh 4000 et seq.**
Safety chains, **Veh 29009**
Safety regulations, **Veh 34500 et seq.**
Turn signals, exemption, **Veh 24951**
Weight fees, **Veh 9400**
Auxiliary lamps, **Veh 24400 et seq.**
Backup devices or alarms, **Veh 27000**
Backup lamps, **Veh 24606**
Bad checks, permits, fees, **Veh 34672**
Banners, disabled vehicles, **Veh 25300**
Biennial inspection of terminals program, **Veh 34501.12**
Bills of Lading, generally, this index
BIT (biennial inspection of terminals program), **Veh 34501.12**
Blasting agents, adoption of United States department of transportation definitions, **Veh 2402.7**
Blasting caps, explosives, mixed cargoes, **Veh 31613**
Bonds (officers and fiduciaries),
Brokers, construction, **Veh 34510.5**
Financial responsibility, **Veh 34631**
Proof of financial responsibility, **Veh 34630**
Booster power units, permits, **Veh 35786, 35787**
Brakes, **Veh 26301 et seq.**
Air brakes, **Veh 26502 et seq.**
Explosives transports, **Veh 31610**
Forklift truck, towing, **Veh 26307**
Operation of braking system, **Veh 26450 et seq.**
Service brakes, generally, post
Trailers, **Veh 26302**
Vacuum brakes, **Veh 26520 et seq.**
Breakaway stopping system,
Airbrakes, **Veh 26508**
Towing vehicles, **Veh 26304**
Brokers, construction, bonds (officers and fiduciaries), **Veh 34510.5**
Building materials, width of vehicle or load, trusses, wall panels, **Veh 35780.5**

MOTOR CARRIERS—Cont'd

Bulk agricultural or forest products, weight restrictions, penalties, **Veh 42030**
Bunk stakes, standards and specifications, adoption and enforcement, **Veh 26103**
Buses, generally, this index
Business or residence districts, explosives, routes, **Veh 31614**
Cables, towed vehicle coupling, **Veh 29004**
Caldecott tunnel, explosives or flammable substances, transportation, **Veh 31301**
Camp tour buses, drivers licenses, **Veh 15250.3**
Cancellation, licenses and permits, bad checks, fees, **Veh 34672**
Cargo,
Passengers, **Veh 23116**
Securement, **Veh 34500.3**
Cargo tanks,
Definitions, motor vehicle load, **Veh 34003**
Fire safety devices, **Veh 34019**
Flammable liquids,
Registration, **Veh 34001 et seq.**
Tunnels, regulations, **Veh 21109**
Tests, pressure, vacuum or hydrostatic, **Veh 34060.5**
Tunnels, rules and regulations, **Veh 34020.5**
Cargo theft interdiction program, fees, **Veh 9400**
Cement mixers, construction, backup devices or alarms, **Veh 27000**
Cemetery equipment, license plates, manufacturers or dealers, **Veh 5016.5**
Certificates and certification,
Insurance policy, **Veh 34630, 34631, 34631.5**
Operation certificates, negligent operators, certificate revocation, suspension or continuance, **Veh 12812**
Permanent trailer identification plates, **Veh 5016, 5017**
Conversion, **Veh 5014.1**
Radioactive materials, drivers certificate, **Veh 12524 et seq.**
Certificates of ownership, duplicates, service fees, **Veh 9270**
Chains,
Safety chains, towing units, **Veh 29003**
Dollies, application of law, **Veh 29009**
Towed vehicles, **Veh 29004**
Change in routes, explosives, **Veh 31617**
Charitable risk pools, financial responsibility, **Veh 34631**
Check valve, vacuum brakes, **Veh 26522**
Children and minors, driving for hire, **Veh 12515**
Classification of carriers, owner operators, **Veh 34624**
Clearance and side marker lamps, **Veh 25100**
Forklift trucks, **Veh 25805**
Vehicles 80 inches or more in width, **Veh 25100**

MOTOR CARRIERS—Cont'd

Combination lighting equipment, clearance and side marker lamps, **Veh 25100**
Combustible liquids, adoption of United States department of transportation definitions, **Veh 2402.7**
Combustibles, **Veh 34001 et seq.**
Explosives, mixed cargo, **Veh 31613**
Grade crossing, stopping, **Veh 22452**
Mixed cargoes, **Veh 31613**
Signs, display, **Veh 27903**
Commercial paper, bad checks, permits, fees, **Veh 34672**
Compressed air, brake system, **Veh 26502 et seq.**
Compressed gas, signs, display, **Veh 27903**
Concrete mixers, construction, backup devices or alarms, **Veh 27000**
Congressional medal of honor recipients, registration fees, exemption, **Veh 9105**
Conspicuity system, retroreflective sheeting, **Veh 24612**
Construction,
Backup devices or alarms, **Veh 27000**
Bonds (officers and fiduciaries), **Veh 34510.5**
Containers,
Explosives, fire and water resistance, **Veh 31614**
Freight van or tank containers, loading, **Veh 31540**
Weights, intermodal terminals, scales, **Veh 35580, 35581**
Continuous satisfactory compliance ratings, truck terminal operators, incentives, **Veh 34501.12**
Contracts,
Licenses and permits,
Certification, **Veh 34620**
Enforcement, **Veh 34605**
Maintenance facilities, inspection and inspectors, certificates and certification, **Veh 34501.12**
Transportation service, records, dispatch and pay, **Veh 34505.10**
Corporation taxes, licenses and permits, delinquent taxes, revocation or suspension, **Veh 34623.1**
Corrosive liquids,
Explosives, mixed cargo, **Veh 31613**
Signs, display, **Veh 27903**
Corrosive materials, adoption of United States department of transportation definitions, **Veh 2402.7**
Cotton Module Mover, generally, this index
Coupling device, **Veh 29003**
Mounting drawbar, trailer hitch or coupling, **Veh 29002**
Court orders, occupational licenses, practices, **Veh 1651.2**
Cowl or fender lamps, equipment, **Veh 25106**
Credit, weight fees, withdrawal from service, **Veh 9408**

MOTOR

MOTOR CARRIERS—Cont'd

Crimes and offenses, **Veh 34660 et seq., 40000.22**

Cargo theft interdiction program, fees, **Veh 9400**

Construction, brokers, bonds (officers and fiduciaries), **Veh 34510.5**

Controlled substances and alcohol use, **Veh 34520**

Drivers schedules, hours, **Veh 34501.3**

Driving logs, violations, **Veh 42001.3**

Explosives, **Veh 31618**

Highway transport, **Veh 31602, 31614**

Farm labor vehicles, equipment, **Veh 31401**

Food, previous use of vehicles, **Veh 34516**

Hazardous substances and waste, post

Inhalation hazards, transportation, **Veh 32104, 40000.19**

Inspection, failure to submit, commercial vehicles, **Veh 2813**

Interstate highway carriers, **Veh 16560, 40000.13**

Maintenance facility inspections, **Veh 40000.22, 40000.26**

Operation without maintenance facility inspection application, **Veh 34501.12**

Out of service orders, **Veh 2800**

Radioactive materials, drivers certificates, **Veh 14611**

Safety inspection violations, **Veh 40000.21**

Safety regulations, **Veh 34506**

Dangerous substances, signs, display, **Veh 27903**

Dealers, license plates for special construction equipment, **Veh 5016.5**

Definitions, **Veh 260, 550, 630, 34501.12**

Funds, motor vehicle account, **Veh 34602**

Motor carrier of property, **Veh 34601 et seq.**

Power unit, owner operators, **Veh 34624**

Safety regulations, **Veh 408**

Terminal, **Veh 595**

Towed vehicle, owner operators, **Veh 34624**

Willfully, controlled substances and alcohol use, **Veh 34520**

Delinquency, fees, terminals, inspection and inspectors, **Veh 34501.12**

Delinquent taxes, licenses and permits, revocation or suspension, **Veh 34623.1**

Deposits,

Proof of financial responsibility, **Veh 34631**

Registration, additional operating areas, apportionment, foreign states, **Veh 9259.3**

Destination signs, windows, obstruction of view, **Veh 26708**

Detonators, explosives, mixed cargoes, **Veh 31613**

Devices, warning signals, **Veh 25300 et seq.**

MOTOR CARRIERS—Cont'd

Direction signs, windows, obstruction of view, **Veh 26708**

Disabled vehicles,

Fusees, warning signals and devices, **Veh 25300 et seq.**

Turn signal lamps, flashing, **Veh 25300**

Warning signals and devices, **Veh 25300 et seq.**

Dishonored checks, permits, fees, **Veh 34672**

Display,

Fleet vehicles, name, trademark or logo, **Veh 5302**

Hazardous materials transportation licenses, **Veh 32000.5**

Identification number, **Veh 34507.5**

License plates, **Veh 4850.5**

Permanent trailer identification plates, **Veh 5017**

Signs, **Veh 27900 et seq.**

Symbols or numbers, safety regulations, **Veh 34507**

Distance, following another vehicle, **Veh 21704**

Dollies. Auxiliary dollies, generally, ante

Drawbars, **Veh 29000 et seq.**

Length, towing units, **Veh 29005**

Mounting, **Veh 29002**

Provisions inapplicable, **Veh 29004**

Towing units, mounting, **Veh 29002**

Driveaway towaway operation, rules and regulations, **Veh 29007**

Drivers licenses. Licenses and permits, generally, post

Driving hours. Hours of labor, generally, post

Driving under the influence. Traffic Rules and Regulations, this index

Drugs and medicine,

Licenses and permits, suspension or revocation, tests, labor and employment, **Veh 34623**

Tests, labor and employment, **Veh 34520**

Dual solid tires, outside measurement, **Veh 27453**

Dump trucks,

Axle weight limitations, **Veh 35551.5**

Construction, backup devices or alarms, **Veh 27000**

Eight hundred (800) numbers, laborers, trucks transporting, **Veh 2429**

Electric vehicles, weight fees, **Veh 9400**

Exemption, vehicles manufactured before designated time, **Veh 9401**

Electrical turn signals, requisites, **Veh 24951**

Electronic recording devices, hours of driving, monitoring, transportation of hazardous materials, **Veh 34501.6**

Emergencies,

Agricultural carriers, hours of service, **Veh 34501.2**

Change in routes, explosives, **Veh 31617**

Removal of vehicles, **Veh 34631.5**

MOTOR CARRIERS—Cont'd

Emergencies—Cont'd

Stopping system, airbrakes, **Veh 26508**

Tow trucks, **Veh 34631.5**

Emissions. Air Pollution, this index

Employees. Officers and employees, generally, post

Employers, powers and duties, **Veh 15240, 15242**

Environmental license plates, **Veh 5101 et seq.**

Equipment, **Veh 24000 et seq.**

Brakes, **Veh 26301 et seq.**

Clearance and side marker lamps, vehicles 80 inches or more in width, **Veh 25100**

Cowl or fender lamps, **Veh 25106**

Experiments, licenses and permits, **Veh 26106**

Farm labor vehicles, **Veh 31400, 31401**

Fenders, **Veh 27600**

Inhalation hazards, transportation, **Veh 32106, 32107**

Inspection, **Veh 2806, 2813**

Laborer trucks, **Veh 31400**

Mudguards, **Veh 27600**

Operation with unsafe equipment, **Veh 24002**

Purchase of equipment for testing purposes, **Veh 26105**

Reflectors, **Veh 24607**

Front and side, **Veh 24608**

Refrigerator van, **Veh 28000**

Safety regulations, **Veh 34500 et seq.**

Signs, **Veh 27900 et seq.**

Tires, **Veh 27450 et seq.**

Towing equipment, **Veh 29000 et seq.**

Trucks transporting, **Veh 31400**

Evidence,

Brokers, construction, bonds (officers and fiduciaries), nonprofit organizations, **Veh 34510.5**

Controlled substances and alcohol use, admissibility, **Veh 34520**

Financial responsibility, **Veh 34630, 34631**

Presumptions,

Log book,

Hours of operation, **Veh 34501.4**

Speed, **Veh 34501.3**

Negligence, point system, **Veh 12810.5**

Self insurance, **Veh 34631**

Examination of books, hazardous materials transportation licenses, **Veh 32000.5**

Exemptions,

Congressional medal of honor recipients, fees, **Veh 9105**

Controlled substances and alcohol use, participation in substance abuse detection programs, **Veh 34520**

Hazardous materials transportation licenses, **Veh 32000.5**

Hours of labor, **Veh 34501.2**

Lighting equipment, **Veh 25800 et seq.**

Permits, **Veh 34622**

I–68

MOTOR CARRIERS—Cont'd

Exemptions—Cont'd

Reciprocity, **Veh 6852, 8000 et seq.**

Registration, foreign commercial vehicles, **Veh 4004**

Signs, **Veh 27902, 27903**

Veterans, disabled, fees, **Veh 9105**

Weight fees, **Veh 9107, 9410**

Vehicles manufactured before designated time, **Veh 9401**

Explosives, transportation regulation, **Veh 31600 et seq.**

Farm labor vehicles, inspection, **Veh 31401**

Federal motor vehicle safety program, apportionment, registration, foreign states, **Veh 8100 et seq.**

Fees,

Cargo theft interdiction program, **Veh 9400**

Exemptions,

Congressional medal of honor recipients, **Veh 9105**

Disabled veterans, **Veh 9105**

Fleet vehicle device, **Veh 9259**

Licenses and permits, post

Payment, **Veh 9550 et seq.**

Permanent trailer identification plates, **Veh 5014.1**

Transfers, **Veh 5016**

Radioactive materials, drivers certificates, **Veh 12524**

Registration, post

Semitrailers, transfers, **Veh 5016**

Temporary operating authority, out of state passenger carriers, **Veh 4007**

Terminal reinspections, **Veh 34501.12**

Unladen operation permits, **Veh 4004.7**

Fenders,

Equipment, **Veh 27600**

Lights and lighting, **Veh 25100 et seq.**

Fifth wheel connecting device, **Veh 29001**

Locking device, **Veh 29002**

Fifth wheels, extension devices, **Veh 35402**

Financial responsibility, **Veh 34630 et seq.**

Identification numbers, evidence, **Veh 16020**

Fines and penalties, **Veh 34660 et seq.**

Construction, brokers, bonds (officers and fiduciaries), **Veh 34510.5**

Driving log violations, **Veh 42001.3**

Explosives, **Veh 31618**

Foreign vehicles, registration, **Veh 34518**

Hazardous substances, **Veh 32002**

Interstate highway carriers, **Veh 16560**

Radioactive materials,

Drivers certificates, **Veh 14611**

Transportation, notice, **Veh 33002**

Registration, fees, apportionment, foreign states, **Veh 8058, 9553.5**

Safety regulations, **Veh 34506**

Schedules, excess hours of service, **Veh 34501.3**

Speed violations, **Veh 42000.5**

Fire extinguishers, explosives transports, **Veh 31610**

MOTOR CARRIERS—Cont'd

Fires, operation of vehicle transporting explosives, **Veh 31614**

Fireworks, **Veh 32000.5**

Licenses and permits, revocation or suspension, **Veh 15301**

Flags,

Projecting loads, **Veh 24604**

Wide vehicles, **Veh 25104**

Flammable liquids,

Caldecott tunnel, transportation, **Veh 31301**

Enforcement of law, **Veh 34060 et seq.**

Flammable substances, adoption of United States department of transportation definitions, **Veh 2402.7**

Flashing amber lights,

Side mounted turn signal lamps, **Veh 24953**

Trucks transporting poles, timbers, **Veh 25275**

Flashing lights, trailer or semitrailer breaking away from towing vehicle, **Veh 25251**

Flatbed trucks, clearance lamps, mounting, **Veh 25100**

Fleet vehicles. Motor Vehicles, this index

Follow up alcohol or controlled substances test requirements, **Veh 34520**

Food, crimes and offenses, previous use of vehicles, **Veh 34516**

Foreign countries,

Inspection and inspectors, **Veh 2418.1**

Operating outside designated commercial zones, **Veh 22651.4, 34517**

Reciprocity, **Veh 8000 et seq.**

Registration, **Veh 34518**

Standards, **Veh 2418**

Temporary operating authority, passenger carriers, **Veh 4007**

Foreign states,

Licenses and permits, display, **Veh 4455**

Reciprocity, **Veh 8000 et seq.**

Registration, post

Temporary operating authority, out of state passenger carriers, **Veh 4007**

Foreign vehicles,

Diesel fuel tax permit, **Veh 2400**

Impounding, **Veh 22651.4**

Operating outside designated commercial zones, **Veh 22651.4, 34517**

Reciprocity, **Veh 6854**

Registration, **Veh 34518**

Temporary registration, **Veh 4004**

Forklift trucks,

Brakes, **Veh 26307**

Inspection and inspectors, stolen equipment, **Veh 2805**

Lights, **Veh 25805**

Registration, exemption, **Veh 4013**

Towing, braking requirements, **Veh 26307**

Turn signals, **Veh 25805**

Weight fees, **Veh 9409**

Four wheel drive vehicles, tire, **Veh 27460**

MOTOR CARRIERS—Cont'd

Frame, reinforcement or bracing for hitch or coupling device mounting, **Veh 29003**

Fraud, workers compensation, **Veh 34634**

Freight, **Veh 31540**

Front reflectors, **Veh 24608**

Fuel containers, safety regulations, **Veh 34500 et seq.**

Funds,

Motor carriers permit fund, **Veh 34602**

Motor vehicle account, **Veh 34602**

Fusees, warning signals or devices, **Veh 25300 et seq.**

Gantry truck, definitions, **Veh 335**

Garbage and refuse, covering loads, **Veh 23114, 23115**

Gross weight, registration, **Veh 4000.6**

Gunpowder, transportation of smokeless powder, **Veh 31619**

Handicapped persons, weight fees, exemptions, **Veh 9410**

Hay, loading and securement, **Veh 34500.3**

Hazardous substances and waste, **Veh 32000 et seq.**

Adoption of United States department of transportation definitions, **Veh 2402.7**

Crimes and offenses, **Veh 32002, 34506, 40000.19**

Food transportation, previous use of vehicle, **Veh 34516**

Placards, **Veh 2800**

Definitions, **Veh 353**

Drivers, certificates and certification, **Veh 12804.2**

Exemptions, licenses, **Veh 32000.5**

Hours of driving, electronic recording devices, priority, **Veh 34501.6**

Inhalation hazards, transportation, **Veh 32100 et seq.**

Inspection and inspectors, **Veh 32000 et seq.**

Liability insurance, **Veh 34631.5**

Licenses and permits, **Veh 2501 et seq., 32000 et seq.**

Position, **Veh 5201**

Placards, crimes and offenses, **Veh 2800**

Poison gases, transportation, **Veh 32100 et seq.**

Radioactive materials, **Veh 12524 et seq.**

Fines and penalties, **Veh 14611**

Signs, display, **Veh 27903**

Transportation, **Veh 1808.1, 12524, 14611**

Notice, **Veh 33002**

Removal of vehicles, emergencies, **Veh 34631.5**

Safety regulations, **Veh 34500 et seq.**

Signs, display, **Veh 27903**

Hazardous Waste Haulers, generally, this index

Headlamps, **Veh 24400 et seq.**

Hearings,

Hazardous materials transportation licenses, suspension, **Veh 32002**

MOTOR

MOTOR CARRIERS—Cont'd
Hearings—Cont'd
Permits, suspension, **Veh 34623**
Workers compensation, suspension or revocation, permit, **Veh 34634**
Height. Traffic Rules and Regulations, this index
Hitches. Drawbars, generally, ante
Hold harmless, ocean marine terminals, intermodal roadability inspection program, **Veh 34505.9**
Hours of labor, **Veh 34500 et seq.**
Crimes and offenses, **Veh 40000.21**
Electronic recording devices, priorities, hazardous substances, **Veh 34501.6**
Fines and penalties, **Veh 42001.3**
Foreign commercial vehicles, **Veh 2418**
Limitation, **Veh 21702, 34506**
Log books, presumptions, **Veh 34501.4**
Schedules, **Veh 34501.3**
Violations, procedure, **Veh 40303**
House cars, length, **Veh 35400**
House towing trucks, warning lights, **Veh 25263**
Household Goods Carriers, generally, this index
Hydraulic actuators in lieu of power brakes, **Veh 26301**
Hydraulic booms or masts, restraint, **Veh 35251**
Hydrostatic tests, cargo tank vehicles, **Veh 34060.5**
Identification lamp, commercial vehicles, **Veh 25350, 25351**
Identity and identification,
Fleet vehicles, **Veh 5302**
Numbers and numbering, **Veh 34507.5**
Charter party carriers, exemptions, **Veh 34507.6**
Financial responsibility, evidence, **Veh 16020**
Registration, **Veh 34620**
Signs and signals, **Veh 27900 et seq.**
Display, safety regulations, **Veh 34507**
Hazardous materials, transportation, **Veh 27903**
Illuminated identification signs, **Veh 25350**
Impounding,
Foreign carriers, **Veh 2418, 22651.4, 34517**
Registration, **Veh 34518**
Operation after suspension, **Veh 34660**
Income tax—state, licenses and permits, delinquent taxes, revocation or suspension, **Veh 34623.1**
Incumbrances, fees, **Veh 9800 et seq.**
Indemnity, ocean marine terminals, intermodal roadability inspection program, **Veh 34505.9**
Industrial materials, construction, backup devices or alarms, **Veh 27000**
Inflammable liquids,
Explosives, mixed cargo, **Veh 31613**
Signs, display, **Veh 27903**
Transportation, **Veh 34001 et seq.**

MOTOR CARRIERS—Cont'd
Infractions,
Registration, post
Speed, **Veh 22406.1**
Inhalation hazards, transportation, **Veh 32100 et seq.**
Injunction,
Hazardous materials transportation, **Veh 32004**
Occupational licenses, practices, **Veh 1651.2**
Operation after suspension, **Veh 34660**
Safety regulations, violations, **Veh 34511**
Insignia, prior registration, temporary use, **Veh 9710**
Inspection and inspectors,
Bills of lading, **Veh 2810**
Controlled substances and alcohol use, **Veh 34520**
Drivers records, highway patrol, **Veh 34501**
Equipment, **Veh 2806**
Explosives,
Highway transportation, **Veh 31602, 31607 et seq.**
Stopping locations, **Veh 31616**
Farm labor vehicles, **Veh 31401**
Fees, maintenance facility inspections, **Veh 34501.12**
Flammable liquid cargo tanks, **Veh 34060 et seq.**
Foreign vehicles, safety, **Veh 2418.1, 34518**
Hazardous substances and waste, **Veh 32000 et seq.**
Inhalation hazards, transportation, **Veh 32105**
Interim inspections, **Veh 34501.12**
Intermodal roadability inspection program, ocean marine terminals, **Veh 34505.9**
Legal possession of products, **Veh 2810**
Loads, **Veh 2802**
Maintenance facilities, **Veh 34501.12**
Ocean marine terminals, intermodal roadability inspection program, **Veh 34505.9**
Officers and employees, replacement, **Veh 34501.18**
Owner operators, preventive maintenance guide, **Veh 2807.2**
Registration, gross weight, **Veh 4000.6**
Reinspection,
Ocean marine terminals, intermodal roadability inspection program, **Veh 34505.9**
Unsatisfactory initial check, **Veh 34501.12**
Reinstatement, registration, suspension for safety or pull notice system violations, **Veh 34505.7**
Roadside vehicle safety inspections, **Veh 34514**
Safety, **Veh 34500 et seq.**
Scales and weighing instruments, **Veh 2809**

MOTOR CARRIERS—Cont'd
Inspection and inspectors—Cont'd
Scales and weighing instruments —Cont'd
Fines and forfeitures, **Veh 42201.1**
Semitrailers, registration, gross weight, **Veh 4000.6**
Stations, fines and forfeitures, **Veh 42201.1**
Terminal first required reinspection, charges, **Veh 34501.12**
Tour buses, **Veh 34505**
Weights, exemption from registration, **Veh 4002**
Instructions to drivers, explosives, **Veh 31611**
Insurance, **Veh 34630 et seq.**
Financial responsibility, identification numbers, evidence, **Veh 16020**
Foreign commercial vehicles, standards, **Veh 2418**
Self insurance, **Veh 34631**
Interest, registration, fees, apportionment, foreign states, **Veh 8058**
Interim inspections, **Veh 34501.12**
Intermodal containers, terminals, scales, **Veh 35580, 35581**
Intermodal roadability inspection program, ocean marine terminals, **Veh 34505.9**
International registration plan, **Veh 8052**
Fees, apportionment, **Veh 9250.15**
Interstate and foreign highway carriers, crimes and offenses, **Veh 16560**
Interstate commerce,
Hours of driving, **Veh 34501.2**
Registration, **Veh 4303**
Intracity vehicles, weight fees, exemptions, **Veh 9107**
Intrastate carriers, hours of driving, **Veh 34501.2**
Investigations and investigators, applications, labor and employment, **Veh 34520**
Irritating materials, adoption of United States department of transportation definitions, **Veh 2402.7**
Jurisdiction, safe operation, **Veh 34623**
Labor and employment. Officers and employees, generally, post
Lamp on projecting loads, **Veh 24604, 25103**
Lamp type turn signal system, **Veh 24951 et seq.**
Lanterns, warning signals and devices, equipment, **Veh 25300**
Larceny, inspection to prevent theft, **Veh 2810**
Law enforcement agencies, driver employment, hours of service regulations, **Veh 34501.2**
Leases,
Identification signs, **Veh 27900, 34507.5**
Registration, **Veh 6853**
Length. Traffic Rules and Regulations, this index

MOTOR CARRIERS—Cont'd

License plates,
Fleet vehicles, fees, **Veh 9259**
Mounting, **Veh 4850.5, 5201**
Prior registration, temporary use, **Veh 9710**
Rear plate, mounting, **Veh 5201**
Special construction equipment, manufacturers or dealers, **Veh 5016.5**
Licenses and permits, **Veh 34600 et seq.**
Alcoholic beverages, suspension or revocation, tests, labor and employment, **Veh 34623**
Booster power units, **Veh 35786, 35787**
Camp tour buses, **Veh 15250.3**
Combination vehicles, special permits, **Veh 35401.5**
Contracts, certification, **Veh 34620**
Drugs and medicine, suspension or revocation, tests, labor and employment, **Veh 34623**
Environmental license plates, **Veh 5101 et seq.**
Exemptions, **Veh 34622**
Disabled veterans, fees, **Veh 9105**
Explosives, highway transport, **Veh 31601, 31602**
Fees, **Veh 34621**
Disabled veterans exemption, **Veh 9105**
Dishonored checks, **Veh 34672**
Hazardous material transportation licenses, disposition of fees, **Veh 32003**
Hazardous substances, **Veh 2502**
Reinstatement, **Veh 34623, 34623.5, 34671**
Insurance, lapse, **Veh 34630**
Workers compensation, lapse, **Veh 34640**
Unladen operation permits, **Veh 4004.7**
Fireworks, revocation or suspension, **Veh 15301**
Fleet owner inspection and maintenance stations, staggered renewals, **Veh 2505**
Foreign vehicles, display, **Veh 4455**
Hazardous substances and waste, ante
Manufactured housing, oversize width, movements, **Veh 35790**
Notice, suspension, **Veh 34623**
Ocean marine terminals, intermodal roadability inspection program, suspension or revocation, **Veh 34505.9**
Overloaded vehicle, **Veh 2803**
Violation procedure, **Veh 40303**
Radioactive materials, transportation, **Veh 12524 et seq.**
Registration services, **Veh 11400 et seq.**
Reinstatement, **Veh 34623, 34671**
Restricted drivers licenses, **Veh 13352**
Revocation or suspension, **Veh 34623**
Delinquent taxes, collection, **Veh 34623.1**

MOTOR CARRIERS—Cont'd

Licenses and permits—Cont'd
Revocation or suspension—Cont'd
Driving under the influence, **Veh 13366.5**
Fireworks, **Veh 15301**
Hazardous substances, **Veh 2531, 2540**
Temporary suspension, **Veh 32002.5**
Insurance, **Veh 34631.5, 34632**
Ocean marine terminals, intermodal roadability inspection program, **Veh 34505.9**
Radioactive materials, **Veh 32002.5**
Registration services, **Veh 11405**
Workers compensation, hearings, **Veh 34634**
Special moving permits, pilot cars, flashing or colored lights, **Veh 25270**
Special permits, motorsports, length, **Veh 35401.5**
Subcontracts, certification, **Veh 34620**
Temporary operating authority, out of state passenger carriers, **Veh 4007**
Truck booster power units, **Veh 35786, 35787**
Unladen operation permits, **Veh 4004.7**
Liens and incumbrances, fees, **Veh 9800 et seq.**
Lights and lighting, **Veh 24250 et seq.**
Approval, equipment and devices, **Veh 26100 et seq.**
Auxiliary lamps, **Veh 24400 et seq.**
Electrical turn signal, **Veh 24951**
Exemptions, **Veh 25800 et seq.**
Flashing lights, trailer or semitrailer breaking away from towing vehicle, **Veh 25251**
Forklift trucks, **Veh 25805**
Garbage trucks, flashing lights, **Veh 25280**
Headlamps and auxiliary lamps, **Veh 24400 et seq.**
House towing trucks, warning lights, **Veh 25263**
Identification lamps and signs, **Veh 25350, 25351**
Mounting lights, **Veh 25950 et seq.**
Parking lamps, **Veh 24800 et seq.**
Pilot lights, **Veh 25108**
Poles, timbers, trucks transporting, flashing amber lights, **Veh 25275**
Projecting loads, **Veh 25103**
Rear lighting equipment, generally, post
Reflectorizing material, **Veh 25500**
Reflectors, forklift trucks, **Veh 25805**
Restrictions and mounting, **Veh 25950 et seq.**
Side lighting equipment, **Veh 25100 et seq.**
Signal lamps and devices, **Veh 24950 et seq.**
Snow removal or sanding devices, exemption, **Veh 25801**
Tail lamps, **Veh 24600 et seq.**
Forklift truck being towed, **Veh 25805**

MOTOR CARRIERS—Cont'd

Lights and lighting—Cont'd
Testing and approval, **Veh 26100 et seq.**
Warning signals, **Veh 25300 et seq.**
Limitation, hours of driving, **Veh 21702, 34506**
Lists, **Veh 34632**
Livestock carriers. Animals, this index
Loads and loading. Traffic Rules and Regulations, this index
Locking devices on fifth wheels, **Veh 29001 et seq.**
Log book,
Availability for inspection, **Veh 34501.10**
Driving logs, violation, fines, **Veh 42001.3**
Hours of operation, presumption, **Veh 34501.4**
Speed, presumption, **Veh 34501.3**
Logging Dollies, generally, this index
Logos, fleet vehicles, **Veh 5302**
Logs, trucks transporting, flashing amber warning lights, **Veh 25275**
Lost or destroyed property, semitrailers, permanent trailer identification plates, **Veh 5017**
Low air pressure warning device, vehicles equipped with airbrakes, **Veh 26506**
Machinery and equipment. Equipment, generally, ante
Maintenance facilities or terminals, safety regulations, **Veh 34500 et seq.**
Maintenance of vehicles,
Foreign commercial vehicles, standards, **Veh 2418**
Records, **Veh 34501.12**
Manual release, fifth wheel mechanism, **Veh 29002**
Manufacturers, special construction equipment, license plates, **Veh 5016.5**
Maps and charts, explosives, transportation routes, **Veh 31611, 31616**
Mexico,
Inspection and inspectors, safety and pollution, **Veh 2418.1**
Standards, safety and pollution, **Veh 2418**
Mines and minerals, construction, backup devices or alarms, **Veh 27000**
Mirrors, equipment, **Veh 26709**
Mixed cargoes, explosives, **Veh 31613**
Mobile crane or shovel, brakes of vehicle used to support boom or mast, **Veh 26302**
Motor vehicle account, **Veh 34602**
Motor vehicle insurance. Insurance, generally, ante
Motorsports, length, special permits, **Veh 35401.5**
Moving companies. Household Goods Carriers, generally, this index
Mudguard, equipment, **Veh 27600**
Multiple unit truck reflectors, **Veh 24610**
Names,
Fleet vehicles, **Veh 5302**
Removal, **Veh 27900**

MOTOR

MOTOR CARRIERS—Cont'd
Names—Cont'd
Signs, **Veh 27900 et seq.**
New registration, fees, surrender of weight fees, **Veh 9408**
Noise limits, **Veh 27150.1 et seq.**
Nonflammable gas, adoption of United States department of transportation definitions, **Veh 2402.7**
Nonprofit organizations,
Brokers, construction, bonds (officers and fiduciaries), evidence, **Veh 34510.5**
Charitable risk pools, financial responsibility, **Veh 34631**
Nonresidents,
Leases, registration, **Veh 6853**
Registration, **Veh 6850 et seq.**
Notice,
Insurance certificate, cancellation, **Veh 34630**
Licenses and permits,
Fees, bad checks, **Veh 34672**
Suspension, **Veh 34623**
Radioactive materials, transportation of spent fuel, **Veh 33002**
Suspension or revocation of permit, hazardous substances, temporary license suspension, **Veh 32002.5**
Workers compensation, awards, **Veh 34634**
Numbers and numbering. Identity and identification, ante
Oaths and affirmations, fleet vehicles, insurance, reports, **Veh 34633**
Ocean marine terminals, intermodal roadability inspection program, **Veh 34505.9**
Offenses. Crimes and offenses, generally, ante
Officers and employees,
Eight hundred (800) numbers, **Veh 2429**
Equipment, **Veh 31400**
Explosives, training, **Veh 31611**
Powers and duties, **Veh 15240, 15242**
Reports, replacement, **Veh 34501.18**
Trucks transporting, eight hundred (800) numbers, **Veh 2429**
Workmen, trucks transporting, equipment, **Veh 31400**
One trip permits,
Fees, **Veh 9258.5**
New trailers or semitrailers, **Veh 4003.5**
Operating authority,
Denial, suspension or revocation, safety inspection violations, **Veh 34505.1, 34505.6**
Out-of state passenger carriers, temporary authority, **Veh 4007**
Operation certificates, negligent operators, certificate revocation, suspension or continuance, **Veh 12812**
Operation of braking system, **Veh 26450 et seq.**
Orders, stop orders, workers compensation, **Veh 34634**

MOTOR CARRIERS—Cont'd
Orders of court, occupational licenses, practices, **Veh 1651.2**
Organic peroxides, adoption of United States department of transportation definitions, **Veh 2402.7**
Out of service orders,
Crimes and offenses, **Veh 2800**
Registration, revocation or suspension, **Veh 8800**
Overhang, explosive loads, **Veh 31614**
Owner operators, **Veh 34624**
Oxidizers,
Adoption of United States department of transportation definitions, **Veh 2402.7**
Explosives, mixed cargoes, **Veh 31613**
Oxidizing material, signs, display, **Veh 27903**
Parked vehicles, warning signals and devices, **Veh 25300 et seq.**
Parking lamps, **Veh 24800 et seq.**
Partial year registration, **Veh 9700 et seq.**
Weight fees, **Veh 9407, 9700 et seq.**
Passenger common carrier, identification lamp and signs, **Veh 25350**
Payment of fees, **Veh 9550 et seq.**
Weight fees quarterly payment, **Veh 9700 et seq.**
Peace officers, employed drivers, hours of service regulations, exception, **Veh 34501.2**
Penalties. Fines and penalties, generally, ante
Permanent trailer identification plates, **Veh 5011, 5014.1 et seq.**
Permit fund, **Veh 34602**
Permits. Licenses and permits, generally, ante
Petroleum and petroleum products, intrastate carriers, liability insurance, **Veh 34631.5**
Physical examination records, availability for inspection, **Veh 34501.10**
Pilot cars, lights and lighting, flashing or colored lights, **Veh 25270**
Pilot light indicators, parts functioning checks, **Veh 25108**
Pipes, trucks transporting, flashing amber warning lights, **Veh 25275**
Placards, hazardous substances and waste, crimes and offenses, **Veh 2800**
Platform scales, inspection facilities, fines and forfeitures, **Veh 42201.1**
Point system,
Negligent drivers, prima facie presumption, **Veh 12810.5**
Presumption of negligence, **Veh 12810.5**
Poison gases, transportation, **Veh 32100 et seq.**
Poisons,
Adoption of United States department of transportation definitions, **Veh 2402.7**
Signs, display, **Veh 27903**

MOTOR CARRIERS—Cont'd
Pole or pipe dollies,
Flashing amber warning lights, **Veh 25275**
Securement, **Veh 34500.3**
Police,
Employed drivers, hours of service regulations, exception, **Veh 34501.2**
Inspection of loads, **Veh 2802**
Portable sanitary facility, exemption from registration, **Veh 36105**
Pot torches, truck tractors, equipment, **Veh 25300**
Poultry and poultry products, inspection, **Veh 2810**
Powder, transportation of smokeless powder, **Veh 31619**
Power brakes, **Veh 26301 et seq.**
Power units, truck booster power units, permits, **Veh 35786, 35787**
Pressure tests, cargo tank vehicles, **Veh 34060.5**
Presumptions. Evidence, ante
Preventive maintenance inspection guide, owner operators, **Veh 2807.2**
Projecting load, flag or lamp, **Veh 24604, 25103**
Proof of financial responsibility, reciprocity, **Veh 6854**
Proration, weight fees, **Veh 9407**
Pull notice system violations, registration suspension, **Veh 34505.7**
Radioactive materials. Hazardous substances and waste, ante
Radios, equipment, carrying electric blasting caps, **Veh 31613**
Random on and off highway inspections, flammable liquids cargo tanks, **Veh 34060 et seq.**
Rear lighting equipment, **Veh 24600 et seq.**
Clearance lamps, **Veh 25100**
Commercial vehicles, **Veh 25351**
Forklift trucks, **Veh 25805**
Side marker lamps, **Veh 25100**
Reciprocity, **Veh 6852, 8000 et seq.**
Exemptions, **Veh 8001**
International registration plan, fees, apportionment, **Veh 9250.15**
Registration, foreign commercial vehicles, **Veh 6854**
Temporary registration, foreign commercial vehicles, **Veh 4004**
Records and recordation,
Alcohol use, inspections, **Veh 34520**
Contracts, transportation service, dispatch and pay, **Veh 34505.10**
Controlled substances and alcohol use, inspection, **Veh 34520**
Drivers,
Availability for inspection, **Veh 34501.10**
Time and pay, inspection by highway patrol, **Veh 34501**
Fleet vehicles, **Veh 8057**

I–72

MOTOR CARRIERS—Cont'd

Records and recordation—Cont'd
Inspection,
Highway patrol, **Veh 34501**
Vehicle transporting explosives, **Veh 31609**
Permits, **Veh 34603**
Registration services, **Veh 11406**
Safety regulations, **Veh 34500 et seq.**
Subcontracts, transportation service, dispatch and pay, **Veh 34505.10**
Recycling, covering loads, **Veh 23115**
Red clearance lamps, **Veh 25100**
Red emergency reflectors, equipment, **Veh 25300 et seq.**
Red flags,
Excessive width, **Veh 25803**
Explosives, transporting vehicles, **Veh 31610**
Loads, projecting, **Veh 24604**
Wide vehicles, display, **Veh 25104**
Reflectorizing material, **Veh 25500**
Reflectors, **Veh 24607 et seq., 25300 et seq.**
Forklift trucks, **Veh 25805**
Registration, **Veh 4000 et seq.**
Additional operating areas, deposits, apportionment, foreign states, **Veh 9259.3**
Air pollution, refusal, **Veh 4755**
Aircraft refueling vehicles, exemption, **Veh 4021**
Commercial vehicles, gross weight, **Veh 4000.6**
Cotton module mover, exemption, **Veh 36101**
Deposits, additional operating areas, apportionment, foreign states, **Veh 9259.3**
Expiration date, **Veh 1651.5**
Fees, **Veh 9250 et seq., 9250.1**
Apportionment, foreign states, Delinquency, **Veh 8058, 9553.5**
Federal motor vehicle safety program, **Veh 8102**
Fines and penalties, fees, apportionment, foreign states, **Veh 8058, 9553.5**
Fleet vehicles, **Veh 5301 et seq.**
Foreign states, **Veh 4004, 6850 et seq., 34518**
Apportionment, **Veh 8050 et seq.**
Federal motor vehicle safety program, **Veh 8100 et seq.**
Identification, **Veh 34620**
Numbers and numbering, **Veh 34507.5**
Infractions,
Foreign vehicles, **Veh 34518**
Waste tire haulers, **Veh 31560**
Interest, fees, apportionment, foreign states, **Veh 8058**
Leased vehicles, **Veh 6853**
Liens and encumbrances, **Veh 9800 et seq.**
Partial year registration, **Veh 9700 et seq.**

MOTOR CARRIERS—Cont'd

Registration—Cont'd
Partial year registration—Cont'd
Weight fees, **Veh 9407, 9700 et seq.**
Reciprocity, **Veh 6854, 8000 et seq.**
Records and recordation, registration services, **Veh 11406**
Reinstatement,
Federal motor vehicle safety program, **Veh 8102**
Suspension for safety or pull notice system violations, **Veh 34505.7**
Renewal,
Additional weight fees, **Veh 9702**
Adjustments, **Veh 1678**
Weight fees, **Veh 9704**
Revocation or suspension, **Veh 8800**
Apportionment, foreign states, federal motor vehicle safety program, **Veh 8102 et seq.**
Safety or pull notice system violations, **Veh 34505.7**
Service fees, **Veh 9270**
Services, **Veh 11400 et seq.**
Telecommunications, fees, apportionment, foreign states, **Veh 9259.5**
Temporary use of prior registration, **Veh 9710**
Time for waiting, **Veh 1669**
Transfers, service fees, **Veh 9270**
Unladen operation permits, **Veh 4004.7**
Waste tire haulers, infractions, **Veh 31560**
Weight fees, **Veh 9400**
Year round registration, **Veh 1651.5**
Reinspection, ocean marine terminals, intermodal roadability inspection program, **Veh 34505.9**
Reinstatement. Registration, ante
Removal of vehicles, emergencies, **Veh 34631.5**
Renewal. Registration, ante
Rental vehicles, identification signs, **Veh 27900, 34507.5**
Reports,
Accidents, ante
Flammable liquids cargo tanks, **Veh 34061**
Fleet vehicles, insurance, **Veh 34633**
Officers and employees, replacement, **Veh 34501.18**
Tour bus, driving record, **Veh 1808.1**
Retroreflective sheeting, conspicuity system, **Veh 24612**
Return to duty alcohol or controlled substances test requirements, **Veh 34520**
Revocation or suspension,
Licenses and permits, ante
Registration, ante
Roadside vehicle safety inspections, **Veh 34514**
Routes, explosives, **Veh 31614 et seq.**
Rules and regulations, permits, **Veh 34604**

MOTOR CARRIERS—Cont'd

Safety, **Veh 34500 et seq.**
Federal motor vehicle safety program, apportionment, registration, foreign states, **Veh 8100 et seq.**
Foreign commercial vehicles,
Inspection and inspectors, **Veh 2418.1**
Standards, **Veh 2418**
Foreign vehicles, inspection and inspectors, **Veh 34518**
Glazing materials, windshields, **Veh 26701 et seq.**
Inspections, **Veh 2806**
Suspension, registration, **Veh 34505.7**
Safety belts, **Veh 27315**
Safety chains,
Dollies, application of law, **Veh 29009**
Towed vehicle, exception, **Veh 29003**
Towed vehicles coupling, **Veh 29004**
Sales,
Testing equipment prior to sale, **Veh 26104**
Without identification plates, **Veh 24009**
Sales and Use Taxes, this index
Satisfactory compliance ratings, terminal operators, incentives, **Veh 34501.12**
Scales, inspection, **Veh 2809**
Schedules, unlawful speed, **Veh 34501.3**
Scheduling,
Renewal of terminal inspections, **Veh 34501.12**
Unlawful runs, crimes and offenses, **Veh 40000.21**
School Buses, generally, this index
Seatbelts, **Veh 27315**
Securement, cargo, **Veh 34500.3**
Self insurance, evidence, **Veh 34631**
Service brakes,
Emergency stopping system, **Veh 26508**
Stopping distance, **Veh 26454 et seq.**
Trucks and truck tractors, **Veh 26311**
Service fees, registration, **Veh 9270**
Shade trailers, registration, exemptions, **Veh 36105**
Shipping instructions, explosives, **Veh 31612**
Side lighting equipment, **Veh 25100 et seq.**
Side mounted turn signal lamps, flashing amber lights, **Veh 24953**
Side reflectors, **Veh 24608**
Signal lamps and devices, **Veh 24950 et seq.**
Signs and signals, **Veh 27900 et seq.**
Disabled vehicle, **Veh 25300**
Identification numbers, **Veh 34507.5**
Identity and identification, ante
Termini signs, **Veh 25350**
Size. Traffic Rules and Regulations, this index
Slack, towed vehicle safety chain, cable or equivalent device, **Veh 29004**
Smoking, explosives, **Veh 31614**
Snow tires, **Veh 27459**
Solid tires, **Veh 27450 et seq.**
Solid Waste, this index

MOTOR

MOTOR CARRIERS—Cont'd

Sparsely populated areas, explosives transportation, waiver of provisions, **Veh 31620**

Special construction equipment, license plates, manufacturers or dealers, **Veh 5016.5**

Special mobile equipment,
  License plates, manufacturers or dealers, **Veh 5016.5**
  Turn signal, exemption, **Veh 24951**

Special permits, motorsports, length, **Veh 35401.5**

Specialized transportation services, exemptions, weight fees, **Veh 9107**

Speed. Traffic Rules and Regulations, this index

Splash aprons, mudguards, **Veh 27600**

Spray rig, flammable liquids transported in cargo tanks, registration exemption, **Veh 34005**

Standards, foreign commercial vehicles, **Veh 2418**

Statement of nonemployment, workers compensation, **Veh 34640**

Stop orders, workers compensation, **Veh 34634**

Stopping distance, braking system operation, **Veh 26454 et seq.**

Straw, securement, **Veh 34500.3**

Subcontracts,
  Permits, certification, **Veh 34620**
  Transportation service, records, dispatch and pay, **Veh 34505.10**

Tail board or tail gate, closing, vehicle transporting explosives, **Veh 31614**

Tail lamps, **Veh 24600 et seq.**
  Forklift trucks, **Veh 25805**

Tank containers, loads and loading, **Veh 31540**

Tank vehicles,
  Axle weight limitations, **Veh 35551.5**
  Flammable liquids, registration, **Veh 34001 et seq.**

Tarpaulins, explosives loads, **Veh 31614**

Tax collection, licenses and permits, delinquent taxes, revocation or suspension, **Veh 34623.1**

Taxation, apportionment, foreign states, **Veh 8050 et seq.**
  Federal motor vehicle safety program, **Veh 8100 et seq.**

Telecommunications,
  Eight hundred (800) numbers, laborers, trucks transporting, **Veh 2429**
  Registration, fees, apportionment, foreign states, **Veh 9259.5**

Temporary operating authority, out of state passenger carriers, **Veh 4007**

Temporary registration, foreign commercial vehicles, **Veh 4004**

Terminals,
  Access, **Veh 35401.5**
  Definitions, **Veh 595**
  Hazardous materials transportation licenses, **Veh 32000.5**

MOTOR CARRIERS—Cont'd

Terminals—Cont'd
  Livestock carriers, access, exemptions, **Veh 35401.7**
  Maintenance facilities, safety regulations, **Veh 34500 et seq.**
  Safety regulations, **Veh 34500 et seq.**

Termini signs,
  Common carrier passenger vehicles, **Veh 25350**
  Windows, obstruction of view, **Veh 26708**

Tests,
  Cargo tank vehicles, pressure, vacuum or hydrostatic tests, **Veh 34060.5**
  Controlled substances and alcohol use, **Veh 34520**
  Inspection for equipment violations, **Veh 2813**
  Lighting and signalling devices, **Veh 26100 et seq.**

Theft, this index

Timber and Lumber, this index

Time, bad checks, licenses and permits, restitution, **Veh 34672**

Tires, **Veh 27450 et seq.**
  Explosives transports, **Veh 31610**
  Traction devices, **Veh 27454, 27459 et seq.**
  Tread depth requirements, adoption of regulations, **Veh 27465**
  Waste tires, haulers, nonregistration, infraction, **Veh 31560**

Torches, pot torches, equipment, **Veh 25300**

Tour buses. Buses, this index

Tow dollies, brakes, **Veh 26305**

Towing, **Veh 29000 et seq.**
  Breakaway brakes, **Veh 26304**
  Emergencies, **Veh 34631.5**
  Forklift trucks, **Veh 25805**
  Licenses and permits, **Veh 34620**
  Service brakes, **Veh 26304, 26311**

Trademarks,
  Fines and penalties, **Veh 27900 et seq.**
  Fleet vehicles, **Veh 5302**
  Removal, **Veh 27900**
  Signs, **Veh 27900 et seq.**

Traffic Rules and Regulations, this index

Trailer Coaches, generally, this index

Trailer hitches. Drawbars, generally, ante

Transfer of ownership,
  Fees, fleet vehicles, **Veh 9259**
  Semitrailers, permanent trailer identification plates, **Veh 5017**

Transit buses, speedometers, **Veh 24017**

Transportation of people, safety regulation, **Veh 34500 et seq.**

Trap wagon, flammable liquids transported in cargo tanks, registration exemption, **Veh 34005**

Trip permits, one trip permits, new trailers or semitrailers, **Veh 4003.5**

Truck booster power units, permits, **Veh 35786, 35787**

MOTOR CARRIERS—Cont'd

Trusses, width of vehicle or load, stacks, **Veh 35780.5**

Turn signals, **Veh 24950 et seq.**
  Disabled vehicles, flashing, **Veh 25300**
  Forklift truck, **Veh 25805**

Turning, towed vehicle safety chain, cable or equivalent device, slack, **Veh 29004**

Unattended vehicle, explosives, **Veh 31614**

Unladen operation permits, **Veh 4004.7**

Vacuum brakes, **Veh 26520 et seq.**

Vacuum tests, cargo tank vehicles, **Veh 34060.5**

Van or tank containers, loads and loading, **Veh 31540**

Vanpooling, generally, this index

Visibility,
  Clearance lamps, **Veh 25100**
  Turn signal, lamps, **Veh 24952**

Waiver of provisions, explosives, **Veh 31620**

Wall panels, width of vehicle or load, stacks, **Veh 35780.5**

Warning signals and devices, **Veh 25300 et seq.**

Waste petroleum, liability insurance, **Veh 34631.5**

Waste tire haulers, registration, infractions, **Veh 31560**

Weights and measures. Traffic Rules and Regulations, this index

Width. Traffic Rules and Regulations, this index

Windshields, **Veh 26700 et seq.**

Withdrawal from service, weight fees, **Veh 9408**

Workers compensation,
  Certificates, filing, **Veh 34640**
  Statement of nonemployment, **Veh 34640**
  Stop orders, **Veh 34634**

Workmen, trucks transporting,
  Eight hundred (800) numbers, **Veh 2429**
  Equipment, **Veh 31400**

Year round registration, **Veh 1651.5**

MOTOR CARRIERS SAFETY IMPROVEMENT FUND

Cargo theft interdiction program, fees, **Veh 9400**

MOTOR CLUBS

Dealers, definitions, motor vehicles, **Veh 286**

Definitions, dealers, **Veh 286**

Emergency roadside assistance, **Veh 2435 et seq.**

Registration of motor vehicles, validation, **Veh 4610**

Tow truck drivers, certification, **Veh 2430 et seq.**

MOTOR DRIVEN CYCLES

Definitions, **Veh 405**

Freeways, restrictions, **Veh 21960**

Headlights, **Veh 25650 et seq.**

MOTOR DRIVEN CYCLES—Cont'd

Helmets, wearing regulations, drivers and passengers, **Veh 27803**

Lighting equipment, **Veh 25802**

Motorized Scooters, generally, this index

Off highway vehicles subject to identification, movement by nonmechanical means, **Veh 38027**

Place of business, posting, signs and licenses, application of law, **Veh 11709**

Rules and regulations, **Veh 38000 et seq.**

Traffic rules and regulations, restrictions, **Veh 21960**

Turn signals, exception, **Veh 24951**

MOTOR FUEL

Motor Vehicle Fuel, generally, this index

MOTOR GRADERS

Special highway construction equipment, definitions, **Veh 565**

MOTOR OIL

Tow car drivers, duty to remove, **Veh 27700**

MOTOR SCOOTERS

Motorized Scooters, generally, this index

MOTOR VEHICLE DRIVERS LICENSING ACT

Generally, **Veh 12500 et seq.**

MOTOR VEHICLE FINANCIAL RESPONSIBILITY ACT

Generally, **Veh 16000 et seq.**

MOTOR VEHICLE FUEL

Antisiphoning devices, methanol, ethanol fuel, **Veh 28110 et seq.**

Clean fuel vehicles, license plates, **Veh 5062**

Liquified petroleum gas, block letters indicating, display, vehicle having concealed tanks, **Veh 27909**

Natural gas, block letters indicating use, display, vehicles having concealed tanks, **Veh 27909**

Octane number, motor vehicle sales, **Veh 24013**

Tank caps, **Veh 27155**

MOTOR VEHICLE FUEL TAX

Transportation fund. State Treasury, this index

MOTOR VEHICLE INSURANCE

Address, confidential or privileged information, records and recordation, **Veh 1808.22**

Agents. Insurance Agents, Solicitors or Brokers, this index

Bonds (officers and fiduciaries). Financial responsibility, post

Brokers. Insurance Agents, Solicitors or Brokers, this index

Buses, **Veh 16500 et seq.**

CAL H.E.A.T. (Help Eliminate Auto Theft), **Veh 10902**

MOTOR VEHICLE INSURANCE—Cont'd

Certificates and certification,

Financial responsibility, post

Proof of ability to respond in damages, cancellation, substitution, **Veh 16483**

Self insurance, proof of financial responsibility, **Veh 16052, 16053**

Certificates of title, duplicates, **Veh 4466**

Charities, charitable risk pools, financial responsibility, **Veh 16054.2**

Children and minors. Financial responsibility, post

Clubs. Motor Clubs, generally, this index

Commercial vehicles,

Ability to respond in damages, **Veh 16500, 16500.5**

Financial responsibility, post

Compromise and settlement,

Total loss salvage vehicles, salvage certificates, **Veh 11515, 11568**

Uninsured motorists, reduction, **Veh 17200 et seq.**

Compulsory financial responsibility. Financial responsibility, generally, post

Confidential or privileged information, **Veh 16005**

Address, records and recordation, **Veh 1808.22**

Domicile and residence, address, records and recordation, **Veh 1808.22**

Policies, **Veh 1808.24**

Protection, **Veh 1808.46**

Counties,

Application of law, financial responsibility, **Veh 16056.1**

Low cost insurance, financial responsibility,

Application of law, **Veh 16056.1**

Exemptions, **Veh 16020.2**

Coverage, electronic transmissions, **Veh 16058**

Crimes and offenses. Fraud, generally, post

Dealers, physical damage insurance, notice, **Veh 5604.5**

Definitions, financial responsibility, **Veh 16450**

Deposits. Financial responsibility, post

Disclosure,

Confidential or privileged information, address, attorneys, records and recordation, **Veh 1808.22**

Motorized scooters, **Veh 407.5**

Domicile and residence, address, confidential or privileged information, records and recordation, **Veh 1808.22**

Drivers licenses, revocation or suspension, financial responsibility, insurance coverage, proof, **Veh 16431**

Fraud, **Veh 16000.8**

Driving schools, **Veh 12660**

All terrain vehicles, **Veh 11103.1**

Safety training organizations, **Veh 11103.1**

Instructors, **Veh 11103**

MOTOR VEHICLE INSURANCE—Cont'd

Electronic transmissions, coverage, **Veh 16058**

Evidence. Financial responsibility, post

Exemptions. Financial responsibility, post

Fees, financial responsibility, judgment creditors,

Installment payments, **Veh 16379**

Register of actions, **Veh 16373**

Financial responsibility, **Veh 16000 et seq.**

Accidents, **Veh 16028**

Exchange of information between drivers, **Veh 16025**

Failure to prove existence, fraudulent acts of agent or broker, **Veh 16000.8**

Affidavit of insurers liability, **Veh 16375**

Agents, accidents, fraud, **Veh 16000.8**

Alternate procedure, evidence, **Veh 16058**

Appearance, evidence, **Veh 16028**

Bonds (officers and fiduciaries),

Cancellation, **Veh 16480 et seq.**

Commercial passenger vehicles, **Veh 16500**

Commercial vehicles, **Veh 16500.5**

Confidential or privileged information, **Veh 1808.22, 1808.24**

Proof of financial responsibility, **Veh 16054**

Surety company, **Veh 16434**

Brokers, accidents, fraud, **Veh 16000.8**

Buses, **Veh 16500 et seq.**

Police power, **Veh 16501**

Cause of action, definitions, **Veh 16251**

Certificates and certification,

Cancellation, **Veh 16433, 16480**

Carrier, **Veh 16431**

Notice, cancellation, **Veh 16433**

Self insurance, **Veh 16436**

Certified copies, judgments and decrees, register of actions, **Veh 16373**

Charitable risk pools, **Veh 16054.2**

Children and minors, **Veh 17702 et seq.**

Failure of proof, **Veh 17704**

Commercial vehicles, **Veh 16500 et seq.**

Liability coverage, **Veh 16500.5**

Registration, **Veh 4000.37, 4000.38, 4750**

Company authorized to do business in state, **Veh 16056**

Confidential or privileged information, bonds (officers and fiduciaries), **Veh 1808.24**

Records and recordation, **Veh 1808.22**

Counties, low cost insurance, application of law, **Veh 16056.1**

Crimes and offenses, fraud, **Veh 16030**

Damages, ability to pay, **Veh 16430 et seq.**

Deposits,

Cancellation, **Veh 16480 et seq.**

Substitution, **Veh 16483**

Commercial passenger vehicles, **Veh 16500**

Commercial vehicles, **Veh 16500.5**

MOTOR

MOTOR VEHICLE INSURANCE—Cont'd
Financial responsibility—Cont'd
Deposits—Cont'd
Disposition, **Veh 16378**
Proof of financial responsibility, **Veh 16054.2**
Drivers licenses, revocation or suspension, **Veh 13352**
Insurance coverage, proof, **Veh 16431**
Driving under the influence,
Reinstatement, **Veh 13352.6**
Restrictions, **Veh 13352.5**
Driving while privilege suspended, **Veh 16070 et seq., 16370 et seq.**
Failure to report accident, **Veh 16004**
Erroneous information, actions based on, **Veh 16074**
Establishing proof, **Veh 16050**
Evidence, **Veh 16020, 16028 et seq.**
Ability to pay damages, **Veh 16430 et seq.**
Alternate procedure, **Veh 16058**
Bonds, **Veh 16054, 16055**
Charitable risk pools, **Veh 16054.2**
Insurance or bond coverage, **Veh 16055**
Liability insurance, **Veh 16054, 16055**
Self insurance, **Veh 16052**
State or municipal ownership, **Veh 16051**
Exchange of information, accidents, between drivers, **Veh 16025**
Exemptions, **Veh 16051**
Driving in course of employment, **Veh 16073**
Low cost insurance, **Veh 16020.2**
Failure of proof to respond to damages, **Veh 16484**
Failure to prove, summary of penalty provisions, **Veh 1656.2**
Fees, judgment creditors,
Installment payments, **Veh 16379**
Register of actions, **Veh 16373**
Fines and penalties, **Veh 16029**
Fraud, **Veh 16030**
Fleet vehicles, registration, **Veh 4000.37 et seq., 4750**
Foreign countries, denial of entry, **Veh 16502**
Foreign states, suspension of drivers license, **Veh 16071**
Fraud,
Accidents, agent or broker, **Veh 16000.8**
Evidence, **Veh 16030**
Good time period, release of proof to respond to damages, **Veh 16480 et seq.**
Governmental agencies, **Veh 17000 et seq.**
Hearings, suspension of driving privileges, **Veh 16075**
Identification numbers, motor carriers, evidence, **Veh 16020**
Impoundment, **Veh 16029**

MOTOR VEHICLE INSURANCE—Cont'd
Financial responsibility—Cont'd
Incapacity of driver, accident report, **Veh 16003**
Installment payments, judgments, **Veh 16379 et seq.**
Labor and employment, **Veh 16028**
Los Angeles County, exemptions, **Veh 16020.1**
Low cost insurance,
Application of law, **Veh 16056.1**
Los Angeles County, pilot programs, **Veh 16020.1**
Medical treatment, suspended license, restricted license, **Veh 16077, 16078**
Mental health treatment, suspended license, restricted license, **Veh 16077**
Mobile electronic devices, evidence, **Veh 16028**
Motor vehicle liability policy, definitions, **Veh 16450**
Motorized scooters, application of law, **Veh 21224**
Nonresident minors certificate, **Veh 12504**
Nonresidents, **Veh 16056, 16431**
Judgment, **Veh 16376**
Notice,
Appearance, **Veh 16028**
Cancellation of liability policy, certificate of insurance, contents, **Veh 16433**
Coverage not in effect at time of accident, **Veh 16055, 16057**
Driving privileges, termination of suspension, **Veh 16076**
Intent to suspend driving privileges, **Veh 16070, 16075**
Operation of vehicles not covered by certificate of ownership, **Veh 16457**
Operators policy, **Veh 16452**
Owners policy, **Veh 16451**
Peace officers, evidence, **Veh 16028**
Policy provisions, **Veh 16453**
Political subdivisions, **Veh 16021**
Privileges and immunities, evidence, **Veh 16033**
Proof of financial responsibility, **Veh 16050 et seq.**
Suspension upon failure to establish proof, **Veh 16070 et seq.**
Records and recordation, confidential or privileged information, bonds (officers and fiduciaries), **Veh 1808.22**
Register of actions, **Veh 16373**
Registration, **Veh 4000.37 et seq., 4750**
Suspension, **Veh 16070 et seq., 16370 et seq.**
Reports of accidents, **Veh 16000 et seq.**
Requirements, **Veh 16430 et seq.**
Restoration of driving privileges, **Veh 16482**
Restricted driving privilege eligibility, **Veh 13352**

MOTOR VEHICLE INSURANCE—Cont'd
Financial responsibility—Cont'd
Satisfaction of judgment, exemption, **Veh 16053**
Second and subsequent offenses, **Veh 16029**
Security, **Veh 16020 et seq.**
Self insurance, generally, post
State, **Veh 16021, 17000 et seq.**
Accident reports, **Veh 16000 et seq.**
Stored vehicles, **Veh 16455**
Submitting evidence, **Veh 16055**
Suspensions, **Veh 16070 et seq.**
Fraud, **Veh 16030**
Unsatisfied judgments, **Veh 16250, 16251, 16370 et seq.**
Taxicabs, **Veh 16500 et seq.**
Telecommunications, electronic verification, **Veh 16058.1**
Termination of driving privilege suspension, **Veh 16076**
Time, accident reports, **Veh 16000**
Traffic collision investigators, evidence, **Veh 16028**
Uninsured motor vehicle, definitions, **Veh 16000.7**
Uninsured owners, judgments, settlements, reduction, **Veh 17200 et seq.**
United States, **Veh 16021**
Unsatisfied judgment, suspensions, **Veh 16250, 16251, 16370 et seq.**
Verification,
Electronic verification, **Veh 16058.1**
Mobile electronic devices, **Veh 16028**
Law enforcement agencies, provision of information, **Veh 4750.4**
Waiver, proof of ability to respond in damages, **Veh 16480**
Workers compensation, **Veh 16454**
Fines and penalties,
Confidential or privileged information, Disclosure, **Veh 1808.46**
Records and recordation, **Veh 1808.22**
Financial responsibility, ante
Fleet vehicles, financial responsibility, registration, **Veh 4000.37 et seq., 4750**
Foreign commercial vehicles, standards, **Veh 2418**
Foreign countries, financial responsibility, denial of entry, **Veh 16502**
Fraud,
Accidents, financial responsibility, **Veh 16000.8**
Drivers licenses, revocation or suspension, **Veh 13201**
Education program, **Veh 10904**
Financial responsibility, ante
Hearings, suspension of driving privileges, financial responsibility, **Veh 16075**
Information, furnishing to nonowner driver, **Veh 16050.5**
Insurance Agents, Solicitors or Brokers, this index
Leases, notice, **Veh 5604**
License plates, duplicates, **Veh 4466**

MOTOR VEHICLE INSURANCE—Cont'd

Lienholders, application for transfer of ownership, certificate, exemption, **Veh 5752**

Los Angeles County, financial responsibility, exemptions, **Veh 16020.1**

Low cost insurance,
Counties, ante
Notice, **Veh 4000.38**

Mobile electronic devices, financial responsibility, evidence, **Veh 16028**

Motor Clubs, generally, this index

Motor Vehicle Financial Responsibility Act. Financial responsibility, generally, ante

Motorized Scooters, this index

Nonprofit organizations, charitable risk pools, financial responsibility, **Veh 16054.2**

Nonrepairable vehicles, total loss settlements, **Veh 11515.2**

Notice,
Financial responsibility, ante
Low cost insurance, ante
Motorized scooters, coverage, **Veh 407.5**

Operators policy, financial responsibility, **Veh 16452**

Owners policy, financial responsibility, **Veh 16451**

Physical damage coverage, dealers, policies, notice, **Veh 5604.5**

Policies,
Confidential or privileged information, **Veh 1808.24**
Financial responsibility, **Veh 16453**

Political subdivisions,
Accident reports, **Veh 16000 et seq.**
Financial responsibility, **Veh 16021**
Accident reports, **Veh 16000 et seq.**

Privileged information. Confidential or privileged information, generally, ante

Proof of ability to respond in damages, **Veh 16430 et seq.**

Proof of financial responsibility. Financial responsibility, ante

Registration. Financial responsibility, ante

Reports, electronic transmissions, **Veh 16058**

Sale of vehicles, application of law, **Veh 12121**

Salvage certificates, total loss salvage vehicles, **Veh 11515**
Compromise and settlement, **Veh 11568**

Self insurance, **Veh 16021, 16052, 16053**
Total loss salvage vehicles, **Veh 11515, 11568**

Settlement. Compromise and settlement, generally, ante

State, financial responsibility, **Veh 16021**

Stored vehicles, coverage, **Veh 22524.5**

Subrogation, uninsured owners, judgments, settlements, reduction, **Veh 17202**

Taxicabs, **Veh 16500 et seq.**

MOTOR VEHICLE INSURANCE—Cont'd

Telecommunications, financial responsibility, electronic verification, **Veh 16058.1**

Termination, reports, **Veh 16058**

Time,
Financial responsibility, ante
Satisfaction of judgment, **Veh 16377**

Total loss salvage vehicles,
Compromise and settlement, salvage certificates, **Veh 11568**
Salvage certificates, **Veh 11515**

Towed vehicles, coverage, **Veh 22524.5**

Traffic Rules and Regulations, generally, this index

Transfer of title or interest, notice, **Veh 5604**

Uninsured motorists, reduction of judgment or settlement, failure to procure insurance, **Veh 17200 et seq.**

United States, financial responsibility, **Veh 16021**
Accident reports, **Veh 16000 et seq.**

Verification. Financial responsibility, ante

MOTOR VEHICLE OPERATOR FOR COMPENSATION TO TRANSPORT PERSONS

Definitions, low emission vehicles, **Veh 28113**

MOTOR VEHICLE OWNERS LIABILITY ACT

Generally, **Veh 17150**

MOTOR VEHICLE REPAIR DEALERS

Crimes and offenses, towing services, kickbacks, **Veh 12110, 13351.85**

Fines and penalties, towing services, kickbacks, **Veh 12110, 13351.85**

Kickbacks, towing services, **Veh 12110, 13351.85**

MOTOR VEHICLE SERVICE STATIONS

Crimes and offenses, towing services, kickbacks, **Veh 12110, 13351.85**

Equipment requirements, vehicles returning for unlawful operation, **Veh 24004**

Fines and penalties, towing services, kickbacks, **Veh 12110, 13351.85**

Kickbacks, towing services, **Veh 12110, 13351.85**

Liens and incumbrances, towage and keeping vehicles removed from highway, **Veh 22851**
Sales, actions for despoliation of evidence, privileges and immunities, **Veh 22856**

Motor Vehicle Fuel, generally, this index

Privileges and immunities, towed vehicles, lien sales, actions for despoliation of evidence, **Veh 22851**

Traffic rules and regulations, removal of parked or standing vehicles, **Veh 22650 et seq.**

MOTOR VEHICLE SPEED CONTEST

Definitions, crimes and offenses, **Veh 23109**

MOTOR VEHICLE THEFT PREVENTION ACT

Generally, **Veh 10900 et seq.**

MOTOR VEHICLES

Generally, **Veh 1 et seq.**

Abandoned or unclaimed property, **Veh 22523 et seq.**

Abandoned vehicle trust fund, expenditure, **Veh 22710**

Appraisal and appraisers, **Veh 22855**

Contracts, removal, local authorities, **Veh 22671**

Correctional institutions, delivery to, **Veh 22711**

Dismantlers, cancellation of license, **Veh 11518**

Disposition, **Veh 22851 et seq.**
Public agencies, **Veh 22851.3**

Estimated value, liens and incumbrances, **Veh 22670**

Fines and penalties, **Veh 22523**

Hazards, immobilized vehicles, **Veh 22669**

Highway Patrol, this index

Impounding. Traffic Rules and Regulations, this index

Infractions, failure to redeem after impound, **Veh 22523**

Liens and incumbrances,
Estimated value, **Veh 22670**
Impounded vehicle, **Veh 22851.1**

Local authority, contracts, removal, **Veh 22671**

Local ordinances, removal and abatement procedures, **Veh 22660 et seq.**

National law enforcement telecommunication system, storage, notice, **Veh 22854.5**

Public agencies,
Appraisal, lien sales, **Veh 22670**
Removal of vehicles, **Veh 22851.3**

Release, registration, **Veh 22651**

Removal,
Establishing funds, **Veh 22710**
Highway patrol or police, **Veh 22651.05, 22669**
Junk vehicles, disposal, **Veh 22851.3**
Local ordinances, **Veh 22660 et seq.**
Parked or standing vehicles, **Veh 22650 et seq.**
Private property, vehicles left at scene of accident, **Veh 22653**

Security deposit under financial responsibility, **Veh 16027**

Service authorities, removal, **Veh 22710**

Storage, **Veh 22850 et seq.**
Vehicles used in fleeing peace officers, **Veh 22655.3**

Value of vehicle, **Veh 22851.2**

Vehicles used to flee or elude peace officers, **Veh 22655.3**

Abandoned vehicle trust fund, **Veh 9250.7**
Expenditures, **Veh 22710**

MOTOR VEHICLES—Cont'd

Abatement, abandoned or wrecked vehicles, local ordinances, **Veh 22660 et seq.**

Absent persons, drivers licenses, renewal, **Veh 12814**

Abstracts, accidents, inspection and inspectors, **Veh 1808**

Accidents. Traffic Rules and Regulations, this index

Accomplices and accessories,

Larceny, **Veh 10851**

License revocation, special licenses, **Veh 2542**

Accounts and accounting,

Autobrokers, trust accounts, **Veh 11737**

Gold Star Family license plate account, **Veh 5157**

Trust accounts, autobrokers, **Veh 11737**

Acknowledgments, **Veh 19**

Actions and proceedings, **Veh 40830 et seq.**

Accident reports, evidence, **Veh 20013**

Arbitration and award, generally, post

Bond pending registration, **Veh 4158**

Certificates of title, transfer, **Veh 5753**

Civil actions, **Veh 40830 et seq.**

Consumer protection, recovery corporation, **Veh 12210**

Crimes and offenses, generally, post

Dealers, post

Enforcement of liens, **Veh 9803, 9804**

Evidence, generally, post

Franchises, **Veh 3065 et seq.**

Highway or bridge damage, **Veh 17300 et seq.**

Leases, post

Limitation of actions, generally, post

Nonresidents, service of process, **Veh 17450 et seq.**

Off highway vehicles, littering, **Veh 38321**

Pending actions, **Veh 4**

Recovery corporation, consumer protection, **Veh 12210**

Registration,

Recovery on bond or undertaking, **Veh 4158**

Smog impact fees, foreign states, **Veh 1673.4**

Safety violations, injunction, **Veh 34511**

Seat belts, use, establishing negligence, **Veh 27315**

Smog impact fees, registration, foreign states, **Veh 1673.4**

Address,

Attorneys,

Confidential or privileged information, records and recordation, **Veh 1808.22**

Disclosure, **Veh 1808.4**

Banks and banking, confidential or privileged information, records and recordation, **Veh 1808.22**

Change,

Notice, responsibility, **Veh 13106**

MOTOR VEHICLES—Cont'd

Address—Cont'd

Change—Cont'd

Registration, **Veh 4159, 4160**

Confidential or privileged information, records and recordation, **Veh 1808.21 et seq.**

Disclosure, attorneys, **Veh 1808.4**

Drivers, accident scene information exchange, **Veh 20002**

Financial institutions, confidential or privileged information, records and recordation, **Veh 1808.22**

Off highway vehicle subject to identification, change of address, **Veh 38060**

Records and recordation, confidential or privileged information, **Veh 1808.21 et seq.**

Inspectors and investigators, **Veh 1808.2**

Reports, change of address, vehicle verifiers, **Veh 11302.2**

Salespersons, notice, change, **Veh 11812**

Wholesale vehicle auctions, dealer report, **Veh 4456**

Adjudication certificate, noncompliance notices, registration, **Veh 4766**

Adjustment, brakes, **Veh 26453**

Administrative service charge, noncompliance notices, registration, **Veh 4766**

Admissibility of evidence. Evidence, generally, post

Advanced technology partial zero emission vehicles, decals, **Veh 5205.5**

Advertisements,

Autobrokers, **Veh 11713**

Fees, **Veh 11713.1**

Bait and switch, **Veh 11713.1**

Dealers, post

Dealers cost and invoice price claims, **Veh 11713.1**

Dismantlers, occupational license or permit number, **Veh 11521**

Document preparation charges, **Veh 11713.1**

Duress or coercion, **Veh 11713.1**

Engine manufacturer different from vehicle manufacturer, **Veh 9981**

Exemptions, sales, **Veh 11713.1**

False advertising, **Veh 11713**

Dealers, **Veh 11713**

Fees, **Veh 11713.1**

Finance charges, **Veh 11713.1**

Horsepower ratings, **Veh 9950, 9952**

Invoice, dealer invoice, or wholesale price, **Veh 11713.1**

Lessor retailers, **Veh 11614, 11614.1**

Number of vehicles available at advertised price, **Veh 11713.1**

Official connection with state authorities, **Veh 25**

Rebates, **Veh 11713.16**

Removal of advertising vehicles, **Veh 22651.2**

MOTOR VEHICLES—Cont'd

Advertisements—Cont'd

Sales,

Identification, **Veh 11713.1**

Removal of vehicles, **Veh 22651.9**

Simulated checks, **Veh 11713.1**

Used vehicles, certificates and certification, **Veh 11713.18**

Aerial lift equipment, amber warning lights, **Veh 25260.3**

Affidavits,

Certificate of title without registration, **Veh 4452**

Drivers licenses, aliens, **Veh 12801**

Fees, payment by mail, **Veh 9557**

Notice, **Veh 24**

Registration,

Unregistered vehicle, **Veh 6052**

Vehicle outside state, **Veh 4152**

Service of process on nonresidents, **Veh 17456**

Theft, renewal of registration, **Veh 4605**

Affiliates, definitions, engine manufacturer different from vehicle manufacturer, **Veh 9980**

Age,

Drivers licenses, post

Driving for hire, **Veh 12515**

Hazardous substances, waste, transportation, **Veh 12515, 40000.11**

Vehicle age, pollution control devices, **Veh 4000.1, 4000.2**

Aged persons,

Identification cards, post

Paratransit Vehicles, generally, this index

Agents,

Operation of vehicle, liability of owner, **Veh 40001 et seq.**

Service of process,

Nonresidents, **Veh 17450 et seq.**

Registration services, **Veh 11403**

Agreements. Contracts, generally, post

Agricultural Labor and Employment, this index

Agricultural work location, inspection, stolen vehicles, **Veh 2805**

Air bags,

Previous deployment, installation, **Veh 27317**

Salvaged vehicles, **Veh 5505**

Air brakes. Brakes, post

Air cushioned vehicles, brakes, exemption, **Veh 38355**

Air governor, airbrakes, **Veh 26504**

Air Pollution, this index

Aircraft refueling vehicles, registration, exemption, **Veh 4021**

Airports and Landing Fields, this index

Alarm company operators, light bars, **Veh 27607**

Alarms,

Activated devices, impoundment, **Veh 22651.5**

Airbrakes, driver warning device, **Veh 26506**

MOTOR VEHICLES—Cont'd
Alarms—Cont'd
Theft, **Veh 25251.4, 28085**
Alcoholic Beverages, this index
Alcoholics and Alcoholism, this index
Aliens,
Deferred action for childhood arrivals, Drivers licenses, **Veh 12801.6**
Identification cards, **Veh 13001**
Deportation, drivers licenses, **Veh 12801.7**
Drivers licenses, post
Registration exemptions, **Veh 6700.2**
All terrain vehicles. Off highway vehicles, generally, post
Alley, definitions, **Veh 110**
Alteration,
Drivers licenses, **Veh 14610**
Evidences of registration, **Veh 4463**
Identification cards, **Veh 13004**
Lemon Law buyback decals, **Veh 11713.12**
Vehicle numbers, **Veh 10750, 10751**
Weight fees, **Veh 9406**
Alternative fuel vehicles, park and ride lots, exemptions, **Veh 22518**
Amber glazing material, equipment, **Veh 26701**
Amber lights, **Veh 25251.5**
Aerial lift equipped vehicles, **Veh 25260.3**
Animal control, enforcement vehicles, flashing, revolving, **Veh 25271.5**
Clearance lamps, **Veh 25100**
Deceleration lights, **Veh 25251.5**
Flashing lights,
Aerial lift equipped vehicles, **Veh 25260.3**
Animals, herding, **Veh 25270.5**
Aqueduct or levee construction, maintenance, control or inspection, **Veh 25266**
Cable television vehicles, **Veh 25274**
Civil engineer vehicles, **Veh 25278**
Land surveyor vehicles, **Veh 25278**
Marshals department vehicles, **Veh 25254**
Nonprofit organizations, transporting handicapped or mentally retarded persons, **Veh 25276**
Special moving permits, **Veh 25270**
Unusual traffic hazards, **Veh 25268**
Water tender vehicles, **Veh 25281**
Hazardous substance spill response vehicles, **Veh 25260.4**
Implements of husbandry, **Veh 25251.1**
Light bars, **Veh 27606, 27607**
Oil and gas pipelines, construction and maintenance, flashing lights, **Veh 25260.1**
Pest detection, **Veh 25261**
Tow trucks, **Veh 25253**
Visibility from front of vehicle, **Veh 25950**
Weed control, **Veh 25261**
Amber reflectors, **Veh 24608, 24609**

MOTOR VEHICLES—Cont'd
Ambulances, generally, this index
Amnesty, registration, fees, specially constructed vehicles, inspection and inspectors, emissions, **Veh 4750.1**
Amount of bail, fixing by magistrate, **Veh 40511**
Amplification devices, **Veh 27007**
Anatomical Gifts, this index
Animal control, enforcement vehicles, amber warning lights, **Veh 25271.5**
Animals, this index
Antique vehicles. Historic Vehicles, generally, this index
Antisiphoning devices, methanol, ethanol fuels, **Veh 28110 et seq.**
Appeal and review,
Consumer protection, recovery corporation, **Veh 12209**
Drivers licenses, post
Enforcement of liens, **Veh 9803, 9804**
Franchises, post
Limitation of actions, **Veh 14401**
New vehicles, filing fee, **Veh 3050.5**
Recovery corporation, consumer protection, **Veh 12209**
Appearance. Drivers licenses, post
Application of law, **Veh 10**
Engines, manufacturer different from vehicle manufacturer, **Veh 9982, 11713.9**
Low speed vehicles, **Veh 21251**
Applications,
Dismantlers, licenses and permits, **Veh 11504**
Drivers licenses, post
False statements, **Veh 1652**
Filing, **Veh 1653**
Grape gondolas inspection and certification, **Veh 34501.14**
Identification cards,
Anatomical gifts, **Veh 12811**
Citizens and citizenship, evidence, **Veh 12801.5**
Motorized bicycles, registration, **Veh 5031 et seq.**
Refund, fees or penalties, limitations, **Veh 42232**
Registration, post
Approaching vehicles, dimming lights, **Veh 24409**
Approval, equipment and devices, **Veh 26100 et seq.**
Aqueduct construction maintenance, control or inspection vehicles, state, warning lights, **Veh 25266**
Arbitration and award,
Branch distributors, **Veh 3050**
Dealers, **Veh 3050, 11713.2, 11713.3**
Area reflectorizing material, **Veh 24607, 25500**
Load, mounted on, **Veh 25952**
Armored Cars, generally, this index
Arraignment,
Failure to appear,
Forfeiture of bail, **Veh 40512**

MOTOR VEHICLES—Cont'd
Arraignment—Cont'd
Failure to appear—Cont'd
Warrant for arrest, **Veh 40514**
Jurisdiction of other violations, **Veh 40311**
Arrest. Traffic Rules and Regulations, this index
Art and artists, special license plates, **Veh 5074**
Assault and battery. Traffic Rules and Regulations, this index
Assessments,
Alcohol and drug programs, **Veh 23249.50**
Fines and penalties, post
Assignments, **Veh 5603**
Dealers,
Force and violence, notice, repossessors and repossession, **Veh 11724**
Requiring prospective assent, **Veh 11713.2, 11713.3**
Franchises, approval, **Veh 11713.2, 11713.3**
Special penalty assessment. Fines and penalties, post
Associations and societies, private property, removal, **Veh 22658**
Assumed or fictitious names, **Veh 20, 40000.25**
Arrested person, promise to appear, **Veh 40504**
Dealers and manufacturers, license revocation, **Veh 11705**
Drivers licenses, **Veh 14610**
Refusal, **Veh 12809**
Identification cards, issuance, renewal, **Veh 13000.1**
Registration, seizure of document, **Veh 4460**
Registration card, **Veh 4453**
Atomic energy. Radioactive materials, generally, post
Attempts,
Evade arrest, optional appearance before magistrate, **Veh 40303**
Flight from peace officers, **Veh 2800.1 et seq., 13201**
Attorney fees,
Certificates of title, transfer, **Veh 5753**
Consumer protection, recovery corporation, **Veh 12210**
Excessive storage charges, **Veh 10652.5**
Franchises, sales, **Veh 11713.3**
Licenses and permits, willful failure to comply with law, **Veh 11726**
New vehicles, discovery, investigations and investigators, **Veh 3050.2**
Recovery corporation, consumer protection, **Veh 12210**
Attorney general, records and recordation, access, **Veh 1810.5**
Attorneys,
Accident reports, disclosure, **Veh 20012**

MOTOR VEHICLES—Cont'd
Attorneys—Cont'd
Address,
Confidential or privileged information, records and recordation, **Veh 1808.22**
Disclosure, **Veh 1808.4**
Appearance, sufficiency under written promise, **Veh 40507**
Confidential or privileged information, address, records and recordation, **Veh 1808.22**
Auctions and auctioneers,
Consignment, dealers, contracts, **Veh 11729**
Dealers, post
Fees, dealers, **Veh 11713.11**
Repossessed vehicles, renewal fees payment, penalties waiver, **Veh 9561**
Sales, equipment, **Veh 24007.5**
Wholesale motor vehicle auctions, **Veh 6100 et seq.**
Dealers, reporting, **Veh 4456**
Audits and auditors,
Fleet vehicles, registration, **Veh 5302**
Franchises, post
Handicapped persons, parking, placards, **Veh 1825**
Authorization, private property, removal, **Veh 22658**
Auto brokers. Brokers, generally, post
Auto buying service, definitions, **Veh 166**
Autoettes, **Veh 175**
Registration, **Veh 4000.5**
Automated rail crossing enforcement system, traffic rules and regulations, **Veh 21362.5**
Automatic locking devices on fifth wheels, **Veh 29001**
Automobile dismantlers. Dismantlers, generally, post
Autonomous vehicles, **Veh 38750 et seq.**
Auxiliary dollies. Motor Carriers, this index
Auxiliary gas tank evaporative loss control devices, installation, **Veh 27156.1**
Auxiliary lamps, **Veh 24400 et seq.**
Rear lamps, **Veh 24616**
Axles,
Definitions, **Veh 230**
Tire tread depth, **Veh 27465**
Weight restrictions, **Veh 35550 et seq.**
B train assembly, definitions, **Veh 230.5**
Backup devices or alarms, **Veh 27000**
Backup lamps, **Veh 24606**
Bad checks,
Dealers and manufacturers, license revocation, **Veh 11705**
Payment of fees, **Veh 9558**
Fines and penalties, suspension of drivers license, **Veh 13364**
Bail. Traffic Rules and Regulations, this index
Bailment,
Return, **Veh 10855**
Tampering by bailee, **Veh 10854**

MOTOR VEHICLES—Cont'd
Bailment—Cont'd
Tampering by bailee—Cont'd
Fines and penalties, **Veh 40000.9**
Tort liability, **Veh 17150 et seq.**
Unlawful use, **Veh 10854**
Bankruptcy, consumer protection, recovery corporation, **Veh 12200 et seq.**
Banks and Banking, this index
Banners, disabled vehicles, **Veh 25300**
Barricade stripping, reflectorized materials, **Veh 25500**
Based in state, presumption, registration, **Veh 4000.4**
Bead, protuberances on tires, **Veh 27454**
Beam distance, lighting requisites, **Veh 25951**
Beam indicator, equipment, **Veh 24408**
Bias or prejudice, accident reports, **Veh 20012**
Bicycles,
Lanes, restrictions, **Veh 21209**
Reports, violations, **Veh 1803 et seq.**
Bids and bidding,
Drivers licenses, identification cards, processing, **Veh 12811, 13005**
License plate manufacturer, **Veh 4850**
Reflectorized license plates, **Veh 4850**
Binder chains,
Projecting equipment, **Veh 35110**
Theft, **Veh 4000, 10851.5, 40000.9**
Blasting agents, adoption of United States department of transportation definitions, **Veh 2402.7**
Blind persons,
Leases, conditions, **Veh 14608**
Veterans, fees, exemptions, **Veh 9105**
Blinding light, spotlamps, **Veh 24404**
Block, protuberances on tires, **Veh 27454**
Block letters, liquefied petroleum gas, display, **Veh 27909**
Blood tests, alcohol concentration table, handbooks, drivers licenses, examinations and examiners, **Veh 1666**
Blue glazing material, equipment, **Veh 26701**
Blue warning lights, police and sheriff vehicles, **Veh 25258**
Boards and commissions,
Definitions, **Veh 232**
License plates, special plates, **Veh 5151 et seq.**
New motor vehicle board, **Veh 3000 et seq.**
Boat trailers, clearance lamps, **Veh 25100**
Bodily injuries, accidents,
Crimes and offenses, **Veh 21070**
Fines and penalties, **Veh 42001.19**
Body floor height, ground clearance, **Veh 24008.5**
Bonds (officers and fiduciaries),
Commercial requester accounts, records and recordation, **Veh 1810.2**
Dealers, post
Driver training school, **Veh 11102**
Examination of records, **Veh 1814, 1815**

MOTOR VEHICLES—Cont'd
Bonds (officers and fiduciaries)—Cont'd
Lessor retailers, **Veh 11612**
Manufacturers and manufacturing, post
Off highway vehicles subject to identification, original identification application, **Veh 38050, 38055**
Registration, **Veh 4157**
Actions, **Veh 4158**
Registration services, **Veh 11401, 11402**
Remanufacturer, **Veh 11710**
Title to foreign vehicle, **Veh 4307**
Transporters, post
Booms, hydraulic booms, restraint, **Veh 35251**
Brackets, license plates, **Veh 11713.17**
Brady Jared Teen Driver Safety Act, **Veh 12814.6**
Brakes, **Veh 26301 et seq.**
Adjusting stations, licensing, **Veh 2501 et seq.**
Air brakes, **Veh 26502 et seq.**
Definitions, **Veh 108**
Parking brakes, **Veh 26451**
Towed vehicles, **Veh 26503 et seq.**
Arrest, failure or refusal of driver to stop for test, **Veh 40303**
Emergency brakes, **Veh 26301.5**
Lights, **Veh 24003**
Manipulation, unattended vehicle, **Veh 10853**
Motorized scooters, **Veh 21235**
Nonconforming equipment, sales, **Veh 24005**
Off highway vehicles, **Veh 38355**
Operation of braking system, **Veh 26450 et seq.**
Pilot indicators, towed vehicles, antilock braking systems, **Veh 25108**
Power brake, definitions, **Veh 480**
Service brakes, **Veh 26311**
Emergency stopping system, **Veh 26508**
Operation of braking system, **Veh 26450**
Stopping distance, **Veh 26454 et seq.**
Stoplamps, actuating, **Veh 24603**
Towed vehicles, pilot indicators, antilock braking systems, **Veh 25108**
Trailers, use in lieu of service brake control, **Veh 26458.5**
Unattended vehicles, setting brakes, **Veh 22515**
Vacuum brakes, **Veh 26520 et seq.**
Vandalism, **Veh 10853**
Branch offices,
Dealers, post
Licenses, fees, **Veh 11723**
Brands, marks and labels,
Clean air stickers, forgery, counterfeiting, **Veh 4463**
Engines, manufacturer different from vehicle manufacturer, **Veh 9980 et seq., 11713.9**
Fleet vehicles, **Veh 5302**

MOTOR VEHICLES—Cont'd
Brands, marks and labels—Cont'd
Low emission vehicles, **Veh 5205.5, 21655.9, 40000.13**
Forgery, counterfeiting, **Veh 4463**
Pilot vehicles, **Veh 27904, 27904.5**
Breakaway brakes,
Airbrakes, **Veh 26508**
Towing vehicles, **Veh 26304**
Brochures, horsepower ratings, **Veh 9950, 9952**
Brokers,
Advertisements, **Veh 11713**
Crimes and offenses, **Veh 11736**
Disclosure, fees, **Veh 11713.1**
Rebates, incentives, warranties, **Veh 11713.3**
Registration,
Dealers, **Veh 11735**
Fees, **Veh 9262**
Trust accounts, **Veh 11737**
Bulbs, voltage, **Veh 24252**
Bullet marks, reports, **Veh 10653**
Bumper strength notices, **Veh 24011.3**
Crimes and offenses, **Veh 40000.15**
Bumpers,
Damage control, **Veh 34700 et seq.**
Definitions, **Veh 28071**
Exemptions, **Veh 28071**
Length, front bumper, **Veh 35408**
Passenger vehicles, **Veh 28070**
Safety bumpers, definitions, **Veh 35400**
Burden of proof. Evidence, post
Bureaus, license plates, special plates, **Veh 5151 et seq.**
Buses, generally, this index
Business district, definitions, **Veh 235, 240**
Buybacks, dealers and manufacturers, **Veh 11713.12**
Bypass, exhaust system, **Veh 27150**
Cab, prevention of penetration of gases and fumes, **Veh 27154**
Cable television vehicles, flashing amber warning lights, **Veh 25274**
Cables, off highway vehicles, placing in position to do bodily injury, **Veh 38318.5**
CAL H.E.A.T. (Help Eliminate Auto Theft), **Veh 10902**
Cameramen, license plates, **Veh 5008**
Camp tour buses, drivers licenses, **Veh 15250.3**
Camp Trailers, generally, this index
Campers, generally, this index
Canada,
Convictions, drivers license revocation or suspension, **Veh 13352**
Out of service orders, failure to comply, **Veh 2800**
Canal banks, operation restrictions, **Veh 21116**
Cancellation,
Dismantlers licenses, **Veh 11518**
Drivers licenses, post
Franchises, **Veh 11713.13**

MOTOR VEHICLES—Cont'd
Cancellation—Cont'd
Handicapped persons, parking placards, **Veh 22511.56**
Identification cards, **Veh 13008**
Leases, **Veh 11709.2**
Licenses and permits, **Veh 11822**
Parking placards, handicapped persons, **Veh 22511.56**
Registration, post
Salesmens license, failure or refusal to surrender license, **Veh 11819**
Capacity, carrying capacity, extension to increase, **Veh 35402**
Capped fuel tank, **Veh 27155**
Car pools,
High occupancy vehicle lanes, **Veh 21655.5**
Parking, exclusive use spaces, **Veh 22507.1**
Vanpooling, generally, this index
Weight, fees, exemption, **Veh 9107**
Cards,
Counterfeit, evidence procurement, **Veh 42271**
Medical information cards, drivers licenses, **Veh 12811.1**
Registration, post
Cargo,
Lamps, **Veh 24616**
Theft, weights and measures, interdiction, fees, **Veh 9400.1**
Carriers. Motor Carriers, generally, this index
Carryall, definitions, **Veh 245**
CB radios, special license plates, **Veh 5020, 5021**
Cement mixers, construction, backup devices or alarms, **Veh 27000**
Cemeteries and Dead Bodies, this index
Certificates and certification,
Adjudication, failure to appear in court or pay fine, **Veh 40509**
Agricultural labor and employment, farm labor contractors, education, **Veh 2429.5**
Appearance, drivers license, reinstatement, renewal, **Veh 12807, 13365**
Arrest warrant execution, costs, **Veh 40516**
Autobroker registration, **Veh 11735**
Certificates of title, generally, post
Commercial vehicles, registration, gross weight, **Veh 4150.1**
Convenience, executors and administrators, dealers, **Veh 11720**
Counterfeiting, evidence procurement, **Veh 42271**
Dealers, post
Drivers licenses, post
Exhaust systems, post
Federal motor vehicles safety standard compliance, **Veh 24011**
Fees,
Nonoperation, **Veh 4604 et seq.**
Adjustments, **Veh 1678**

MOTOR VEHICLES—Cont'd
Certificates and certification—Cont'd
Fees—Cont'd
School pupil activity buses, **Veh 12517**
Title to property, **Veh 5753**
Transfer, unavailability, **Veh 9255.5, 9867.5**
Fictitious or false, evidence procurement, **Veh 42271**
Fines and penalties, certificate of payment, **Veh 40509**
Drivers license,
Reinstatement, **Veh 13365**
Renewal or issuance, **Veh 12807**
Forgery, evidence procurement, **Veh 42271**
Grape gondolas, inspection certification, **Veh 34501.14**
Handicapped persons,
Fraud, **Veh 22511.58**
Parking exemptions, **Veh 22511.55**
Ignition interlock devices, **Veh 13386**
Lessor retailers death, continuation of business by heirs or personal representatives, **Veh 11608**
License plate destruction, delivery, dismantler, **Veh 11520**
Medical certificates, nonresidents, drivers licenses, **Veh 12502**
Nonoperation, **Veh 4604 et seq.**
Certificates, off highway vehicles, **Veh 38246**
Delinquency penalties, filing of certificates, **Veh 4604.5**
Dismantlers, **Veh 9269**
Off highway vehicles, **Veh 38121**
Partial year, **Veh 4604.2**
Registration, **Veh 4604**
Commercial vehicles, partial year registration, **Veh 9407**
Expiration, fines and penalties, **Veh 4604.5**
Renewal fee penalties, **Veh 9553**
Nonrepairable vehicle certificates, **Veh 24007**
Definitions, **Veh 432**
Ownership without registration, **Veh 4452**
Paratransit vehicles, drivers, **Veh 12523.5**
Proof of notice, **Veh 24**
Radioactive materials, transportation, drivers, **Veh 12524 et seq.**
Revocation or suspension, ignition interlock devices, **Veh 13386**
Rope or strap material, regulations, **Veh 24005.5**
Salvaged vehicles, total loss salvage vehicles, **Veh 11515, 11568**
Scales and weighing instruments, inspection, **Veh 2809**
School bus operation, **Veh 12517**
School pupil activity buses, operation, **Veh 12517**
Seatbelts, **Veh 27315**

MOTOR VEHICLES—Cont'd
Certificates and certification—Cont'd
Semitrailers, permanent trailer identification plates, **Veh 5017**
Specially constructed vehicles, registration, **Veh 4750.1**
Total loss salvage vehicles, salvage certificates, **Veh 11515, 11568**
Tow truck drivers, **Veh 2430 et seq.**
Transfer, unavailability, fees, **Veh 9255.5**
Used vehicles, sales, **Veh 11713.18**
Youth buses, **Veh 12523**
Certificates of compliance, definitions, **Veh 246**
Certificates of endorsement, **Veh 13369 et seq.**
Certificates of title, **Veh 4450 et seq.**
Abbreviations, manner of transfer of interest, **Veh 5600.5**
Acceptance, consent to service of process, **Veh 17459**
Actions and proceedings, transfer, **Veh 5753**
Amphibious vehicles, **Veh 9872.5**
Applications, social security numbers, drivers license numbers, **Veh 1653.5**
Assignment, **Veh 5603**
Attorney fees, transfer, **Veh 5753**
Cancellation, suspension or revocation, **Veh 8800, 8802**
Exported vehicles, **Veh 6160 et seq.**
Publicly owned vehicles, **Veh 4155**
Copies, **Veh 4466**
Costs, transfer, actions and proceedings, **Veh 5753**
Counterfeit, evidence procurement, **Veh 42271**
Crimes and offenses, **Veh 4462, 40000.7**
Cancelled, suspended or revoked certificate, **Veh 8800, 40000.7**
Evidence, **Veh 6150 et seq.**
Damages, transfer, **Veh 5753**
Dealers, post
Destruction or mutilation, duplicates, **Veh 4466**
Dismantlers,
Duplicates, **Veh 4466**
Surrender, **Veh 5500, 5501**
Duplicates, **Veh 4466**
Fees, **Veh 9265**
Adjustments, **Veh 1678**
Electronic lien and title program, **Veh 4450.5**
Engine numbers, **Veh 4161 et seq.**
Evidence, criminal proceedings, **Veh 6150 et seq.**
Exported vehicles, inspection and cancellation, **Veh 6160 et seq.**
Fees, transfer, **Veh 5753, 9255.3**
Fictitious or false, evidence procurement, **Veh 42271**
Fines and penalties, offsets, basing on revenue forecasts, **Veh 9554.1**
Foreign countries, duplicates, **Veh 4466**

MOTOR VEHICLES—Cont'd
Certificates of title—Cont'd
Foreign states,
Bonds (officers and fiduciaries), **Veh 4307**
Duplicates, **Veh 4466**
Full faith and credit, **Veh 4304**
Retention, **Veh 4303**
Validity, **Veh 4305**
Forgery, **Veh 4463**
Evidence procurement, **Veh 42271**
Forms, **Veh 1652, 4451**
Fraud, cancellation, **Veh 8800**
Identity and identification, applicants for copies, **Veh 4466**
Leases, **Veh 4453.5, 5753**
Licensed registration service, duplicates, **Veh 4466**
Liens and incumbrances,
Electronic lien and title program, **Veh 4450.5**
Foreign states, **Veh 4306**
Full faith and credit, **Veh 4304**
Notarized signatures, lienholders, **Veh 5752**
Loans to unauthorized persons, **Veh 4461**
Lost or stolen, **Veh 4459**
Motor vehicle insurance, duplicates, **Veh 4466**
Mutilation or destruction, duplicates, **Veh 4466**
New engine or motor, **Veh 4161**
Nonrepairable vehicles, **Veh 6050, 11515.2**
Nonresidents, exemptions, **Veh 6700 et seq.**
Notice, transfer of interest, nonpayment, **Veh 5911**
Odometer disclosure statement, **Veh 4451**
Off highway vehicles, post
Publicly owned vehicles, **Veh 4155**
Registration,
Electronic lien and title program, **Veh 4450.5**
Foreign vehicles, surrender, **Veh 4301**
Issuance without registration, **Veh 4452**
Refusal, **Veh 4750 et seq.**
Service fee, **Veh 9254**
Adjustments, **Veh 1678**
Renewal, **Veh 4600**
Revocation, return of documents to department, **Veh 8802, 8803**
Sales, **Veh 4456**
Salvaged vehicles, pools, duplicates, **Veh 4466**
Security interest, **Veh 6300 et seq.**
Release, delivery, **Veh 5753**
Seizure by police, **Veh 4460**
Social security numbers, applications, **Veh 1653.5**
Stolen, lost, mutilated or illegible, **Veh 4459**

MOTOR VEHICLES—Cont'd
Certificates of title—Cont'd
Stopping vehicle to inspect certificate, **Veh 1655**
Substitution, **Veh 4466**
Surrender,
Transfer of interest, **Veh 5902**
Vehicle no longer registered in state, **Veh 4158**
Theft, duplicates, **Veh 4466**
Transfer, **Veh 5600 et seq., 6050 et seq.**
Actions and proceedings, **Veh 5753**
Application, **Veh 5902**
Attorney fees, **Veh 5753**
Certificate unavailable, **Veh 5911**
Costs, actions and proceedings, **Veh 5753**
Damages, **Veh 5753**
Fees, **Veh 5753, 9255, 9255.3**
Notice, **Veh 5900 et seq.**
Refusal, **Veh 4750 et seq.**
Signatures, **Veh 5750 et seq.**
Unlawful possession, **Veh 4462, 40000.7**
Unregistered vehicle, **Veh 6052**
Certified or registered mail. Mail and mailing, post
Certified record of permanent exportation, definitions, **Veh 6161**
Chains,
Binder chains, theft, **Veh 10851.5, 40000.9**
Maximum width of body and chain binders, **Veh 35110**
New vehicles unable to use, notice, **Veh 9953**
Off highway vehicles, placing in position to do bodily injury, **Veh 38318.5**
Safety chains, towing, **Veh 29003**
Tire traction devices, generally, post
Change. Modification or change, generally, post
Change of name, replacement of licenses, **Veh 2503**
Chappie Zberg Off Highway Motor Vehicle Law, **Veh 38000 et seq.**
Charities, this index
Chassis,
House cars, disclosure, manufacturers and manufacturing, **Veh 11713.5**
Stopping distance, exemptions, **Veh 26457**
Chattel mortgages,
Affidavits, release of impounded vehicle, **Veh 14602**
Repossession, notice, **Veh 28**
Security interest, generally, post
Transfer of title or interest, notice, **Veh 5908**
Chauffeurs licenses. Drivers licenses, generally, post
Check valve on brakes, vacuum brakes, **Veh 26522**
Checkpoints,
Air pollution, emissions, **Veh 2814.1**
Sobriety checkpoints, **Veh 2814.2**
Checks, payment of fees, **Veh 9558**

MOTOR VEHICLES—Cont'd
Child health and safety programs, special license plates to support, **Veh 5072**
Children and minors,
Accident reports, disclosure, **Veh 20012**
Alcoholic Beverages, this index
Bail, appearance before juvenile court or officer, **Veh 40502**
Cards, identification cards, **Veh 13000 et seq.**
Cellular radio telephones, crimes and offenses, **Veh 23124**
Crimes and offenses,
Passenger restraint systems, **Veh 27360.6**
Unattended children, **Veh 15620**
Drivers licenses, post
Driving under the influence. Traffic Rules and Regulations, this index
Emancipated minors, drivers licenses, tort liability, **Veh 17705**
Family purpose doctrine, **Veh 17708**
Fines and penalties,
Passenger restraint systems, **Veh 27360.6**
Unattended children, **Veh 15620, 15630**
Identification cards, **Veh 13000 et seq.**
Instruction permits, **Veh 12509**
Junior permits, **Veh 12513**
Juvenile court wards, junior permits, **Veh 12513**
Juvenile delinquents and dependents, generally, post
Labor and employment, post
Leases, post
Nonresidents, post
Off highway vehicles, **Veh 38503 et seq., 38600**
Controls, ability to reach and operate, crimes and offenses, **Veh 38304.1**
Passenger restraint systems, **Veh 27360 et seq.**
Photography and pictures, sound recordings, endangerment, **Veh 40008**
Rental agencies, passenger restraint systems, notice, **Veh 27365**
Reports, violations, **Veh 1816**
Seatbelts, **Veh 27360 et seq.**
Point system, **Veh 12810**
Seats, car seats, **Veh 27360 et seq.**
Point system, **Veh 12810**
Spouse, signing drivers license, tort liability, **Veh 17702**
Telecommunications, cellular radio telephones, crimes and offenses, **Veh 23124**
Unattended children, **Veh 15600 et seq.**
Unlicensed drivers, permitting to drive, **Veh 14607**
Wards of juvenile court, junior permits, **Veh 12513**
Chiropractors, this index
Chop shops, **Veh 10801 et seq.**
Definitions, motor vehicles, **Veh 250**
Cigarettes and Cigars, this index

MOTOR VEHICLES—Cont'd
Citation, owner or lessee chargeable, citation of driver, **Veh 40001**
Citizens and citizenship, drivers licenses, evidence, **Veh 12801.5**
Citizens band radio, special license plates, **Veh 5020, 5021**
Civil air patrol, fees, exemptions, **Veh 9106**
Civil engineer vehicles, flashing amber warning lights, **Veh 25278**
Civil liability, **Veh 17000 et seq.**
Turn signal lamps, **Veh 25251.3**
Claims. Actions and proceedings, generally, ante
Class D radios, special license plates, **Veh 5020, 5021**
Classic cars. Historic Vehicles, generally, this index
Clean air stickers, forgery, counterfeiting, **Veh 4463**
Clean fuel vehicles, license plates, **Veh 5062**
Clearance, modification of vehicles, **Veh 24008**
Clearance lights, **Veh 25100 et seq.**
Definitions, **Veh 375**
Turn signals on vehicles equipped, visibility, **Veh 24952**
Cleats, protuberances on tires, **Veh 27454**
Clubs, registration, validation of card, **Veh 4610**
CNG, liquefied petroleum gas, natural gas, concealed tanks, block letters, **Veh 27909**
Coasting down grade in neutral, **Veh 21710**
Code violations required by federal rule or regulation, defenses, **Veh 41401**
Codefendants, operators and owners, **Veh 40001 et seq.**
Employees, size or weight violations, **Veh 40003**
Collateral estoppel, civil actions, conviction, **Veh 40834**
Collection of fees, **Veh 14910**
Collector vehicles, air pollution, inspection and inspectors, exemptions, **Veh 4000.1**
Colleges and Universities, this index
Collisions, accidents. Traffic Rules and Regulations, this index
Color of vehicle,
Police, arrest, speed, **Veh 40804**
Traffic officers, distinctive uniform and vehicle, **Veh 40800**
Colored lights, **Veh 25250 et seq., 25950**
Backup lamps, **Veh 24606**
Turn signals, flashing white or amber lights, **Veh 24953**
Combination lighting equipment,
Backup lamps, **Veh 24606**
Clearance and side marker lamps, **Veh 25100**
Stoplamps, **Veh 24603**
Combined functions, lamps or reflectors, **Veh 24252**

MOTOR VEHICLES—Cont'd
Combustibles,
Crimes and offenses, **Veh 34001 et seq.**
Signs and signals, **Veh 27903**
Commercial requester accounts, records and recordation, **Veh 1810.2**
Accidents, reports, **Veh 1810.3**
Commercial vehicles,
Abstracts, commercial vehicles involved in criminal offenses, **Veh 1804**
Aliens, drivers licenses, limitations, **Veh 12801.10**
Cargo theft interdiction program, fees, **Veh 9400.1, 9400.3**
Certificates and certification, registration, gross weight, **Veh 4150.1**
Collection, delinquent registration fees, **Veh 9800**
Congressional medal of honor recipients, fees, exemptions, **Veh 9105**
Counties, this index
Credit, weight fees, withdrawal from service, **Veh 9408**
Crimes and offenses,
Counties, fees, **Veh 9250.14**
Drivers licenses,
Revocation or suspension, **Veh 15311, 15320**
Sanctions, **Veh 15300 et seq.**
Safety inspection stickers, **Veh 2813.5, 40000.7**
Vehicles involved in, notice to motor vehicle department, **Veh 1803**
Criminal history information, drivers licenses, **Veh 15215**
Decals, weights and measures, **Veh 9400.1**
Definitions, **Veh 260**
Safety program, **Veh 15210**
Delinquent registration fees, collection, **Veh 9800**
Disqualification, drivers licenses, hazards, **Veh 15325**
Dollies, towing, weight fees, **Veh 9400**
Exemption, **Veh 9401**
Domicile and residence, drivers licenses, **Veh 12505**
Driver notification requirements, **Veh 15220 et seq.**
Drivers licenses, **Veh 15250 et seq.**
Aliens, limitations, **Veh 12801.10**
Criminal history information, **Veh 15215**
Disqualification, hazards, **Veh 15325**
Domicile and residence, **Veh 12505**
Driving under the influence, revocation or suspension, **Veh 13557**
Endorsements, **Veh 15275, 15278**
Hazardous substances and waste, **Veh 15250**
School buses, **Veh 15275.1, 15278**
Examiners and examinations, hazardous substances and waste, endorsements, **Veh 15250**
Fireworks, revocation or suspension, **Veh 15301**

MOTOR

MOTOR VEHICLES—Cont'd
Commercial vehicles—Cont'd
Drivers licenses—Cont'd
Fraud, **Veh 15309**
Hazardous substances and waste, Endorsements, **Veh 15250**
Nonresidents, **Veh 12502**
Hazards, disqualification, **Veh 15325**
Military forces, **Veh 1651.3**
Examiners and examinations, hazardous substances and waste, endorsements, **Veh 15250**
Nonresidents, exemptions, **Veh 12502**
Notice, **Veh 15220 et seq.**
Reciprocity, **Veh 12505**
Revocation or suspension, **Veh 15326**
Revocation or suspension,
Crimes and offenses, **Veh 15311, 15320**
Driving under the influence, **Veh 13353, 13557**
Fireworks, **Veh 15301**
Reciprocity, **Veh 15326**
Sanctions, license violations, **Veh 15300 et seq.**
School buses, endorsements, **Veh 15275.1, 15278**
Driving under the influence. Traffic Rules and Regulations, this index
Emergencies, freeways, fees, **Veh 9250.10**
Employers, powers and duties, **Veh 15240, 15242**
Environmental license plates, **Veh 5101 et seq.**
Exemptions,
Drivers licenses, military forces, **Veh 15250**
Fees, veterans, **Veh 9105**
Fees,
Cargo theft interdiction program, **Veh 9400.1, 9400.3**
Decals, weights and measures, **Veh 9400.1**
Delinquent registration fees, collection, **Veh 9800**
Special interest license plates, **Veh 5060**
Trip permits, foreign states, **Veh 9260**
Financial responsibility, **Veh 16500.5**
Registration, **Veh 4000.37 et seq., 4750**
Financial statements and reports, special interest license plates, **Veh 5060**
Fines and penalties,
Out of service orders, **Veh 15311.1**
Railroad crossings, **Veh 15312.1**
Safety inspection stickers, **Veh 2813.5, 40000.7**
Weights and measures, **Veh 4000.6**
Fireworks, drivers licenses, revocation or suspension, **Veh 15301**
Foreign countries, standards, safety and pollution, **Veh 2418**

MOTOR VEHICLES—Cont'd
Commercial vehicles—Cont'd
Foreign states, registration, **Veh 4004**
Fraud, drivers licenses, **Veh 15309**
Freeways, emergencies, fees, **Veh 9250.10**
Funds, special interest license plates, **Veh 5060**
Gross weight,
Crimes and offenses, **Veh 42030.1**
Registration, **Veh 4000.6, 4150.1, 9554.2**
Guaranteed traffic arrest bail bond certificate, nonresidents, **Veh 40305.5**
Hazardous substances and waste, drivers licenses,
Endorsements, **Veh 15250**
Nonresidents, **Veh 12502**
Hazards, drivers licenses, disqualification, **Veh 15325**
Household goods carriers, violations, **Veh 2810.1**
Ice cream trucks, vending, **Veh 22456**
Identification lamp, **Veh 25350, 25351**
Infractions,
Household goods carriers, **Veh 2810.1**
Weights and measures, **Veh 4000.6**
Inspection and inspectors, **Veh 2813**
Household goods carriers, violations, **Veh 2810.1**
Registration, **Veh 4000.6**
Safety inspection stickers, **Veh 2813.5, 40000.7**
Interstate registration, apportionment of fees, **Veh 9250.15**
Labor and employment, powers and duties, **Veh 15240, 15242**
License plates, special interest plates, **Veh 5060**
Licenses and permits, trip permits, foreign states, **Veh 4004**
Lighting equipment, **Veh 25350, 25351**
Markets and marketing, special interest license plates, **Veh 5060**
Mexico, standards, safety and pollution, **Veh 2418**
Military forces, drivers licenses,
Examiners and examinations, hazardous substances and waste, endorsements, **Veh 15250**
Exemptions, **Veh 15250**
Motor Vehicle Insurance, this index
Notice, special interest license plates, **Veh 5060**
Out of service orders, fines and penalties, **Veh 15311.1**
Partial year registration, **Veh 9700 et seq.**
Weight fees, **Veh 9407**
Permanent trailer identification plates, tabs, **Veh 5204**
Probable cause, stops, household goods carriers, violations, **Veh 2810.1**
Promotions, special interest license plates, **Veh 5060**

MOTOR VEHICLES—Cont'd
Commercial vehicles—Cont'd
Railroad crossings,
Fines and penalties, **Veh 15312.1, 40001**
Sanctions, **Veh 15312**
Reciprocity, drivers licenses, **Veh 12505**
Revocation or suspension, **Veh 15326**
Registration, **Veh 4000.6**
Fees, renewal, **Veh 9250.8**
Adjustments, **Veh 1678**
Financial responsibility, **Veh 4000.37 et seq., 4750**
Foreign states, **Veh 4004**
Partial year registration, **Veh 9700 et seq.**
Weight fees, **Veh 9407**
Renewal, fees, **Veh 9250.8**
Adjustments, **Veh 1678**
Studies, **Veh 27910**
Transfer, **Veh 5902**
Trip permits, foreign states, **Veh 4004**
Weight fees, **Veh 9400.1**
Reports, registration, gross weight, **Veh 4150.1**
Revocation or suspension, drivers licenses, reciprocity, **Veh 15326**
Safety inspection stickers, **Veh 2813.5, 40000.7**
Safety program, **Veh 15200 et seq.**
Sanctions, drivers licenses, **Veh 15300 et seq.**
Service fees, **Veh 9250.7**
Stops, traffic officers, household goods carriers, violations, **Veh 2810.1**
Theft, cargo theft interdiction program, fees, **Veh 9400.1, 9400.3**
Traffic Rules and Regulations, this index
Traffic Signs and Signals, this index
Traffic violator schools, **Veh 42005**
Trip permits, foreign states, **Veh 4004**
Fees, **Veh 9260**
Trip tickets, **Veh 9800**
Veterans, fees, exemption, **Veh 9105**
Video event recorders, windshields, **Veh 26708**
Violations, notification when commercial vehicle involved, **Veh 40300.2**
Withdrawal from service, weight fees, credit, **Veh 9408**
Commissions. Boards and commissions, generally, ante
Committees, house cars, safety, **Veh 2429.3**
Common carriers. Motor Carriers, generally, this index
Community colleges and districts. Colleges and Universities, this index
Community property,
Impounding, driving under the influence, **Veh 23594**
Nuisance vehicles, driving under the influence, **Veh 23596**
Prostitution, nuisance, impounding, exemptions, **Veh 22659.5**

I–84

MOTOR VEHICLES—Cont'd
Community property—Cont'd
Registration, **Veh 4150.5**
Transfer of title or interest, **Veh 5600.5**
Community service,
Drivers licenses, sale or manufacture, similar documents, **Veh 14610.1**
Identification cards, sale or manufacture, similar documents, **Veh 13004.1**
Provisional licensees, **Veh 12814.6**
Commuter rail system, traffic rules and regulations, **Veh 21113**
Compensation and salaries, dealers, interference, **Veh 11713.2, 11713.3**
Competency of driver, investigation by department, **Veh 13800 et seq.**
Competition,
Additional franchises, **Veh 3063**
Dealer and manufacturer, **Veh 11713.2, 11713.3**
Complaints,
Delivery to magistrate on violation to promise to appear, **Veh 40515**
Filing, notice to appear, **Veh 40513**
Infractions, **Veh 40306**
Notice to appear, **Veh 40513**
Parking violations, notice to appear, **Veh 40513**
Plea of accused, **Veh 40513**
Prosecution of persons owning or controlling vehicles, **Veh 40002**
Speed charge, **Veh 40503**
Waiver, filing of verified complaint, **Veh 40513**
Compliance with regulations, lighting and signalling equipment, testing and approval, **Veh 26100 et seq.**
Component parts for passenger motor vehicles, definitions, **Veh 5505**
Compressed air, brake system, **Veh 26502 et seq.**
Compromise and settlement,
Highway or bridge damage, **Veh 17300 et seq.**
New vehicles, mandatory settlement conference, **Veh 3050.4**
Tort claims, **Veh 17155**
Computers, dealers, records and recordation, privacy, **Veh 11713.3, 11713.25**
Concealed weapons, children and minors, drivers licenses, **Veh 13202.4**
Concrete mixers, construction, backup devices or alarms, **Veh 27000**
Conditional sales,
Cancellation option agreements, used vehicles, **Veh 11713.21**
Disclosure, **Veh 11709.2**
Cancellation period, **Veh 11709.2**
Cooling off period, **Veh 11709.2**
Dealers bond, coverage, **Veh 11722**
Documents, limitation of actions, **Veh 40004**
Finance charge, advertisements, **Veh 11713.1**

MOTOR VEHICLES—Cont'd
Conditional sales—Cont'd
Leases, cancellation option agreements, used vehicles, restocking fees, **Veh 11713.21**
Repossessors and repossession, notice, **Veh 28**
Crimes and offenses, **Veh 28**
Security interest, generally, post
Transfers, notice, **Veh 5908**
Used vehicles, cancellation option agreements, **Veh 11713.21**
Disclosure, **Veh 11709.2**
Conditions, broker agreements, **Veh 11738**
Condominiums, this index
Confidential or privileged information,
Accident reports, **Veh 16005, 20012, 20014**
Departmental use, **Veh 20014**
Address, records and recordation, **Veh 1808.21 et seq.**
Attorneys, address, records and recordation, **Veh 1808.22**
Banks and banking, address, records and recordation, **Veh 1808.22**
Colleges and universities, address, parking lots and facilities, **Veh 1808.25**
Drivers licenses, post
Electric vehicles, registration, access, **Veh 1808.23**
Financial institutions, address, records and recordation, **Veh 1808.22**
Police vehicles, license plates, **Veh 5003**
Records and recordation, **Veh 1808, 1808.45 et seq.**
Commercial requester accounts, **Veh 1810.2**
Convictions, **Veh 40000.61**
Dealer registration, **Veh 1808.23**
Evidence, continued confidentiality, eligibility, **Veh 1808.9**
Fines and penalties, **Veh 1808.22**
Inspectors and investigators, address, **Veh 1808.2**
Manufacturers recall, exemption, **Veh 1808.23**
Protection of confidentiality, **Veh 1808.47**
Residence addresses, **Veh 1808.21 et seq.**
Traffic violator schools, **Veh 1808.10, 42005**
Confiscation, disabled person parking placards, **Veh 22511.56**
Conformity with requirements of code, equipment, **Veh 24004**
Congressional Medal of Honor,
Fees, exemptions, **Veh 9105**
Special identification plates, **Veh 5101.6**
Consent,
Abandoned or unclaimed property, **Veh 22523**
Dealers, computers, records and recordation, privacy, **Veh 11713.25**
Nonresidents, service of process, **Veh 17451 et seq.**

MOTOR VEHICLES—Cont'd
Conservators and conservatorships, accident reports, disclosure, **Veh 20012**
Consignment sales,
Consumer protection, recovery corporation, **Veh 12200 et seq.**
Dealers, agreements, **Veh 11729, 11730**
Consolidated Cities and Counties, this index
Constitutionally exempt vehicles, fees, **Veh 9103**
Construction,
Backup devices or alarms, **Veh 27000**
Inspection and inspectors, stolen vehicles, **Veh 2805**
Construction of statutes, **Veh 2, 6, 12 et seq.**
Construction or maintenance equipment. Highways and Roads, this index
Constructive total loss, license fee credit or refund, adjustments, **Veh 1678**
Consumer, definitions, autobroker registration, **Veh 11735**
Consumer protection,
Internet web site, **Veh 1656.4**
Recovery corporation, **Veh 12200 et seq.**
Fees, **Veh 4456.3**
Contempt, infractions, failure to pay fine, **Veh 42003**
Impoundment drivers license, **Veh 40508**
Contests, speed, removal, **Veh 22651**
Continuance. Traffic Rules and Regulations, this index
Continuation of existing law, **Veh 2**
Continuous trips, registration, exemption, **Veh 4003**
Contracts,
Conditional sales, generally, ante
Consignment agreements, dealers, **Veh 11729, 11730**
Dealers, duress or coercion, **Veh 11713.1**
Drivers licenses, identification cards, processing, **Veh 13005**
Engine manufacturer different from vehicle manufacturer, disclosure in sales contract, **Veh 9981**
Inspection and inspectors, **Veh 2420.5**
Reflectorized license plates, manufacturing, **Veh 4850**
Removal, local authority, **Veh 22671**
Control requirements, brakes, **Veh 26454 et seq.**
Controlled substances. Drugs and medicine, generally, post
Conviction of crime. Crimes and offenses, post
Cooling off period, lease or purchase contracts, **Veh 11709.2**
Coownership,
Off highway vehicles subject to identification, **Veh 38045**
Registration, **Veh 4150.5**
Transfer of title or interest, **Veh 5600.5**

MOTOR

MOTOR VEHICLES—Cont'd

Copies,
House car warranties, provision to buyers by dealers, **Veh 11931**
Notice of transfer, display by dealer, **Veh 11715**
Off highway vehicles, post
Records, furnishing without charge to counties, **Veh 1812**
Cornering lamps, amber color, **Veh 25107**
Coroners, this index
Corporations, this index
Correctional Institutions, this index
Corrosive materials, adoption of United States department of transportation definitions, **Veh 2402.7**
Costs,
Arrest, issuance of warrant, certification, **Veh 40516**
Assessments, penalties, night court, **Veh 42006**
Certificates of title, transfer, actions and proceedings, **Veh 5753**
Consumer protection, recovery corporation, **Veh 12210**
Dealers, bond recovery action, **Veh 11710.2**
Disposition, liens and incumbrances, **Veh 22851.12**
Franchises, sales, **Veh 11713.3**
Impounding, repossessors and repossession, **Veh 23118**
New vehicles, discovery, investigations and investigators, **Veh 3050.2**
Night court assessments, **Veh 42006**
Offenses, arrest warrants, certification, **Veh 40516**
Recovery corporation, consumer protection, **Veh 12210**
Reports, night court assessment, **Veh 42006**
Seatbelts, **Veh 27315**
Cotton Trailers, generally, this index
Counterfeiting, **Veh 40004**
Certificates of ownership, **Veh 4463**
Evidence procurement, **Veh 42271**
Disabled person placards, **Veh 4463**
Fines and penalties, **Veh 4463.3**
Drivers licenses, **Veh 12811**
Evidence procurement, **Veh 42271**
Evidences of registration, **Veh 4463**
Identification card, **Veh 13004**
Identification numbers, **Veh 10802**
Licenses or permits, evidence procurement, **Veh 42271**
Limitation of actions, **Veh 40004**
Registration card, evidence procurement, **Veh 42271**
Counties, this index
County Officers and Employees, this index
County sanitation districts, repair vehicles, warning lights, **Veh 25265**
County Supervisors Boards, this index
Couplings, mounting draw bar or trailer hitch, **Veh 29002**

MOTOR VEHICLES—Cont'd

Courses of instruction, off highway vehicles, **Veh 38007**
Courtesy lamps, **Veh 25105**
Courts,
Abstracts, electronic transmission, **Veh 1801**
Accident reports, disclosure, **Veh 20013**
Records, **Veh 1802**
Registration, deferring approval, **Veh 6051**
Cowl or fender lamps, equipment, **Veh 25106**
Cranes, brakes or vehicles used to support boom or mast, **Veh 26302**
Credit,
Commercial vehicles, weight fees, withdrawal from service, **Veh 9408**
Dealers, trade ins, discharge, **Veh 11709.4**
Credit cards,
Driving under the influence, second and subsequent offenses, impoundment, **Veh 14602.8**
Private property, removal, payment, **Veh 22658**
Repossessors and repossession, **Veh 23118**
Towing, storage, **Veh 22651.1, 22658**
Credit scores, dealers, notice, **Veh 11713.20**
Crimes and offenses, **Veh 42000 et seq.**
Abstract of conviction, license plate number, **Veh 1818**
Address, confidential or privileged information, records and recordation, **Veh 1808.22**
Advertising, horsepower ratings, **Veh 9950, 9952**
Air bags, previous deployment, installation, **Veh 27317**
Air pollution control devices, **Veh 27156**
Aliens, drivers licenses, discrimination, **Veh 12801.9**
Application of law, **Veh 40007**
Armed forces, violations required by order of military authority, **Veh 41401**
Armored car, use of red lights, violation, **Veh 25262**
Arraignment, generally, ante
Assault and battery,
Road rage. Traffic Rules and Regulations, this index
Weapons, drivers licenses, revocation or suspension, **Veh 13351.5**
Attempts, flight from peace officers, **Veh 2800.1 et seq., 13201**
Autobrokers, **Veh 11736**
Bailee, misuse, **Veh 40000.9**
Bodily injury, accidents, **Veh 21070**
Cancellation, suspension or revocation of registration, **Veh 8800**
Certificates of title, ante
Children and minors,
Passenger restraint systems, **Veh 27360.6, 40000.15**

MOTOR VEHICLES—Cont'd

Crimes and offenses—Cont'd
Children and minors—Cont'd
Unattended children, **Veh 15620**
Chop shops, **Veh 10801 et seq.**
Codefendants,
Drivers or operators, **Veh 40001 et seq.**
Owners, employees, size or weight violation, **Veh 40003**
Commercial vehicles, ante
Complaint,
Filing, **Veh 40513**
Persons owning or controlling vehicles, **Veh 40002**
Confidential or privileged information,
Disclosure, **Veh 1808.45**
Records, convictions, **Veh 40000.61**
Continuance,
Before sentencing, rebuttal of police or traffic officer reports, **Veh 40806**
Defendants written promise to appear, **Veh 40506.5, 40508**
Conviction, definitions, **Veh 13103**
Conviction of crime,
Evidence, generally, post
License numbers, abstracts, **Veh 1818**
Counterfeiting, generally, ante
Court orders, failure to comply, **Veh 40508**
Crib sheets or impersonating applicant, **Veh 14610.5**
Habitual traffic offender, **Veh 14610.5**
Dealers, post
Defacing property, delay or suspension of privileges, **Veh 13202.6**
Defenses, code violation prosecution, **Veh 41400 et seq.**
Disabled person placards, **Veh 4461, 4463, 4463.3**
Fines and penalties, **Veh 4461.5**
Dismantlers, post
Dismissal of charges, employees, abstract of records, **Veh 40003**
Distributor branch, licenses and permits, **Veh 11700**
Domicile and residence, address, confidential or privileged information, records and recordation, **Veh 1808.22**
Double jeopardy, defenses, **Veh 41400**
Drivers licenses, post
Driving while privilege suspended, **Veh 14601.2**
Driving with specified blood alcohol level, **Veh 40000.15**
Drugs and medicine, generally, post
Embezzlement, generally, post
Emergency Services Act, violation required by governors order or directive, **Veh 41402**
Emergency vehicles, permits, **Veh 2416**
Employees, size or weight violations, **Veh 40003, 40005**

MOTOR VEHICLES—Cont'd
Crimes and offenses—Cont'd
Employers failing to dispose of charges against employees, **Veh 40005**
Equipment, **Veh 40150**
Operation without, **Veh 40001**
Evasion of fees and taxes, residents, **Veh 8804**
Evidence, generally, post
Evidences of registration, **Veh 4463**
Exhaust systems violating noise regulations or standards, business of selling or installing, **Veh 27150.1**
False impersonation, members of highway patrol, **Veh 40000.5**
False information to peace officer, **Veh 31, 40000.5**
False or fictitious names, promise to appear of arrested person, **Veh 40504**
False representation by individual as department of motor vehicles employee, **Veh 25.5**
False statements, **Veh 20, 40000.5**
Applications or documents, **Veh 1652**
Farm labor vehicles, equipment, **Veh 31401**
Federal agencies, violations required by regulations, **Veh 41401**
Federal laws, violation of code, defenses, **Veh 41401**
Fees, operation without payment, **Veh 40001**
Fictitious names, use, **Veh 40000.25**
Filing complaint or notice to appear, **Veh 40002, 40513**
Fines and penalties, generally, post
Firemen, failure to obey orders, **Veh 40000.7**
Flight from peace officers, **Veh 2800.1 et seq., 13201, 40000.7**
Foreign certificates of title, **Veh 4305**
Forgery, generally, post
Former jeopardy, **Veh 41400**
Fraud, generally, post
Grape gondolas inspections, **Veh 40000.22, 40000.26**
Gross polluters, operating or leaving on roadway, **Veh 27156**
Guilty plea, **Veh 40513**
Complaint or notice to appear, **Veh 40002**
Highway construction zones, **Veh 42009**
Identification cards, post
Ignition interlock devices, **Veh 23247**
Impounding. Traffic Rules and Regulations, this index
Inflatable restraint systems, previous deployment, installation, **Veh 27317**
Infractions, generally, post
Injuring or tampering with vehicle, **Veh 40000.9**
Inspection and inspectors, post
Interstate commerce commission, violations required by regulations, **Veh 41401**

MOTOR VEHICLES—Cont'd
Crimes and offenses—Cont'd
Investigations and investigators, **Veh 2805**
Officers, official uniform and vehicle, exemptions, **Veh 40804**
Joint defendants, **Veh 40001 et seq.**
Jurisdiction,
Arraignment on other offenses, **Veh 40311**
Speed traps, **Veh 40805**
Lamp and brake testing stations, **Veh 40000.11**
Larceny. Theft, generally, post
Leases, post
Leaving scene of accident, **Veh 20001 et seq.**
Lessor retailers, **Veh 11614 et seq.**
License plates, post
Licenses and permits, post
Liens and incumbrances, fraud, **Veh 22852.5**
Mail and mailing, written plea, **Veh 40519**
Malicious mischief, **Veh 40000.9**
Manufacturer branch, licenses and permits, **Veh 11700**
Manufacturers and manufacturing, post
Marijuana, possession while operating, **Veh 23222, 40000.15**
Mobilehomes and mobilehome parks, violations, **Veh 11713**
Names, fictitious names, **Veh 40000.25**
Nolo contendere plea, **Veh 40513**
Noncompliance notices, failure to renew registration, **Veh 4766**
Notice, appearance, **Veh 40002**
Notice to correct violations, **Veh 40610 et seq.**
Issuance, **Veh 40303.5**
Willful violations, **Veh 40000.25**
Numbers, altering or defacing identification numbers, **Veh 40000.9**
Odometers, **Veh 11713, 28050 et seq.**
Off highway vehicles, post
Orders, failure to obey lawful order, **Veh 40000.7**
Operation contrary to law, **Veh 40001**
Out of service orders, **Veh 40001, 40303**
Parts, **Veh 12003, 40000.11**
Breaking or removing, **Veh 40000.9**
Peace officers,
Flight from, **Veh 2800.1 et seq., 13201, 40000.7**
Willful flight or attempt to elude, **Veh 2800.1**
Death or bodily injury, **Veh 2800.2**
Pleading, written plea, mailing, **Veh 40519**
Point system, suspension or revocation of drivers license, **Veh 12810**
Possession, delivery after transferring title of interest, transferors liability for anothers driving, **Veh 5602**
Private property, removal, **Veh 22658**

MOTOR VEHICLES—Cont'd
Crimes and offenses—Cont'd
Promise to appear in court, violation, **Veh 40508, 42003**
Property damage, leaving scene of accident, **Veh 20002**
Rear windows, defective condition, **Veh 26710**
Records and recordation, prior convictions, reports, **Veh 42004**
Registration, post
Remanufactured vehicles, **Veh 11713.8**
Reports, **Veh 1803 et seq.**
Repossession, notice, **Veh 28**
Residents, evasion of fees and taxes, **Veh 8804**
Road rage. Traffic Rules and Regulations, this index
Rules of road, violations, **Veh 40000.15**
Runaway vehicles, failure to report, **Veh 20002**
Safety inspection stickers, commercial vehicles, **Veh 2813.5, 40000.7**
Salespersons, post
Seatbelts, **Veh 27315**
Children and minors, **Veh 27360.6**
Second and subsequent offenses,
Air pollution control devices, modified vehicles, **Veh 27156**
Drivers licenses, post
False report of theft, **Veh 10501**
Impounding vehicles, **Veh 14602**
Infractions, **Veh 42001**
Inspection and inspectors, failure to stop and submit, **Veh 42002.1**
Off highway vehicles, post
Reports, department informational reports, **Veh 42004**
Seatbelts, children and minors, **Veh 27360.6**
Speed or reckless driving, drivers license suspension, **Veh 13200**
Theft, **Veh 10851**
False reports, **Veh 10501**
Vending, **Veh 22520.5, 40000.13**
Weight limitations, violations, **Veh 42030**
Sentence and punishment, inspection and inspectors, failure to stop and submit, **Veh 42002.1**
Serial numbers, acquisition, possession or sale to prejudice, damage or defraud, **Veh 10752**
Signatures, false signatures, **Veh 40000.25**
Siren and flashing red light, willful disregard, peace officers, **Veh 2800.1**
Slow moving vehicles, **Veh 24615**
Smog impact fees, registration, foreign states, **Veh 1673.6**
Speed traps, **Veh 40801 et seq.**
Storage, **Veh 40000.9**
Rates and charges, **Veh 22658**
Striking unattended vehicle, failure to stop or comply with requirements, **Veh 20002**

MOTOR

MOTOR VEHICLES—Cont'd
Crimes and offenses—Cont'd
Supplemental restraint systems, tampering, **Veh 27317**
Suspended drivers, violations, **Veh 40000.11**
Tampering with vehicle, **Veh 40000.9**
Bailee, **Veh 10854**
Theft, generally, post
Towing, post
Traffic officers investigating, uniform and color of vehicle, **Veh 40800**
Traffic Rules and Regulations, this index
Traffic Violator Schools, generally, this index
Transfer of title or interest, criminal liability for anothers driving, **Veh 5602**
Transporters, post
Transporting vehicle to foreign country, removing license plates, **Veh 11725**
Unattended children, **Veh 15620**
United States, violations required by federal law, **Veh 41401**
Unlawful use, owners responsibilities, **Veh 40000.11**
Vandalism, delay or suspension of driving privileges, **Veh 13202.6**
Vehicle bumper strength notices, **Veh 40000.15**
Vehicles resembling law enforcement vehicles, **Veh 27605**
Vending on freeways, second or subsequent offenses, **Veh 22520.5, 40000.13**
Weight violation, **Veh 42030, 42031**
Evidence, admissibility, **Veh 35557**
Windshields, defective condition, **Veh 26710**
Written pleas, mailing, **Veh 40519**
Written promise to appear in court, violations, continuance, **Veh 40506.5, 40508**
Wrong way driving, **Veh 40000.13**
Criminal history information,
Commercial vehicles, drivers licenses, **Veh 15215**
Tow trucks, **Veh 2430.3**
Cross walks, definitions, **Veh 275**
Crossings,
Arrest, **Veh 40303**
Highways and roads, registration, exemptions, **Veh 4006**
Cruising, regulation, **Veh 21100**
Cutout, exhaust system, **Veh 27150**
Daily commuters,
Definitions, nonresident, **Veh 435.5**
Registration exemption, **Veh 6700.2 et seq.**
Damage control, **Veh 34700 et seq.**
Removal from private property, **Veh 22658**
Damages,
Arrest, procedure, **Veh 40303**
Certificates of title, transfer, **Veh 5753**

MOTOR VEHICLES—Cont'd
Damages—Cont'd
Children and minors, person signing drivers license, **Veh 17709, 17714**
Dealers, disclosure, **Veh 9990 et seq.**
Family purpose doctrine, **Veh 17708**
Impounding,
Driving under the influence, second and subsequent offenses, **Veh 14602.8**
Repossessors and repossession, **Veh 23118**
Injuring or tampering with vehicle, arrest, procedure, **Veh 40303**
Licenses and permits, willful failure to comply with law, **Veh 11726**
Odometers, replacement, **Veh 28051**
Off highway vehicles, post
Responding in, proof, negligent operators, filing, **Veh 12810.5**
Sales, disclosure, **Veh 9990 et seq.**
Theft, **Veh 10850 et seq.**
Tort liability, **Veh 17000 et seq.**
Signing minors drivers license, **Veh 17709, 17714**
Towing, fees, notice, **Veh 22651**
Transportation of injured persons, **Veh 20016**
Darkness, definitions, **Veh 280**
Data monitors, **Veh 25108**
Daytime, running lamps, **Veh 25109**
Deadly weapon, use as, drivers licenses, revocation, **Veh 13351.5**
Dealers,
Abandonment of business, cancellation of license, **Veh 11721**
Accomplices and accessories, **Veh 11700.3**
Accounts and accounting, disclosure, authorizations, **Veh 11703.4**
Actions and proceedings, **Veh 3050**
Auctions and auctioneers, purchasers, rights, **Veh 11713.14**
Bond recovery, **Veh 11710.2**
Fraud, **Veh 11711**
Licenses and permits, **Veh 11711.3**
Additional dealership within market area, **Veh 3062**
Advertisements, **Veh 11713, 11713.1, 11713.16**
Auctions, **Veh 11713.11**
Showrooms, display, **Veh 11709.3**
Affidavits, transfer of title or interest without required supporting documents, **Veh 4456**
Air Pollution, this index
Arbitration and award, **Veh 11713.2, 11713.3**
Assignments, force and violence, notice, repossessors and repossession, **Veh 11724**
Auctions and auctioneers,
Advertisements, **Veh 11713.11**
Consignment, contracts, **Veh 11729**
Purchasers, rights, **Veh 11713.14**

MOTOR VEHICLES—Cont'd
Dealers—Cont'd
Auctions and auctioneers—Cont'd
Wholesale motor vehicle auctions, **Veh 6100 et seq.**
Authorizations, disclosure, financial records, **Veh 11703.4**
Bankruptcy, consumer protection, recovery corporation, **Veh 12200 et seq.**
Benefits from transactions, receipt by manufacturers, **Veh 11713.3**
Bonds (officers and fiduciaries), **Veh 11710**
Deposits in lieu of bond, release or refund, **Veh 11710.2**
Failure to file, cancellation of license, **Veh 11721**
Failure to keep in effect, **Veh 11713**
Inadequate bond, cancellation of license, **Veh 11721**
Protection of interest, **Veh 11722**
Release or refund, **Veh 11710.2**
Transfer of title or interest without required supporting documents, **Veh 4456**
Wholesalers, **Veh 11710.1**
Branch offices,
Licenses, display, **Veh 11709**
Mobile homes, exemption, **Veh 5353**
Operation without license, **Veh 11713**
Brands, marks and labels, engine manufacturer different from vehicle manufacturer, **Veh 11713.9**
Buy here pay here, used vehicles, **Veh 241, 241.1**
Cancellation,
Franchises, **Veh 11713.13**
Lease or purchase contracts, **Veh 11709.2**
Capital structure, change, contracts, **Veh 11713.2, 11713.3**
Cash transactions, reports, **Veh 11713**
Certificates and certification,
Federal motor vehicle safety standard compliance, **Veh 24011**
Noise compliance, new vehicles, registration, **Veh 27200**
Ownership and registration, delivery, crimes and offenses, **Veh 40000.7**
Certificates of public convenience and necessity, executors and administrators, **Veh 11720**
Certificates of title,
Delivery, **Veh 40000.7**
Duplicates, **Veh 4466**
Electronic lien and title program, **Veh 4450.5**
Chains, new vehicles, inability to use, failure to disclose, crimes and offenses, **Veh 11713.6**
Change in list, notice to department, **Veh 11704**
Change of place of business, **Veh 11712**
Charities, exclusions, **Veh 286**

MOTOR VEHICLES—Cont'd
Dealers—Cont'd
Compensation and salaries, interference, **Veh 11713.2, 11713.3**
Competition from manufacturer, **Veh 11713.2, 11713.3**
Compliance with law, refusal of registration, **Veh 4751**
Computers, records and recordation, privacy, **Veh 11713.3, 11713.25**
Consent, computers, records and recordation, privacy, **Veh 11713.25**
Consignment contracts, **Veh 11729, 11730**
Consumer protection, recovery corporation, **Veh 12200 et seq.**
Fees, **Veh 4456.3**
Continuing education, **Veh 11704.5**
Contracts, consignment sales, **Veh 11729, 11730**
Cooling off period, lease or purchase contracts, **Veh 11709.2**
Corporate charters, suspension or cancellation, cancellation of license, **Veh 11721**
Credit scores, notice, **Veh 11713.20**
Crimes and offenses, **Veh 40000.11**
Certificates of ownership and registration, delivery, **Veh 40000.7**
Licenses and permits, **Veh 11700, 40000.11**
Qualifications, **Veh 11703**
New vehicles, inability to use tire chains, failure to disclose, **Veh 11713.6**
Notice, sales, **Veh 40000.7**
Return of documents and license plates, **Veh 40000.7**
Damages, disclosure, **Veh 9990 et seq.**
Death, rights of widows and heirs, **Veh 11713.2, 11713.3**
Debt cancellation agreements, discrimination, **Veh 11713.3**
Definitions, **Veh 285, 286**
Franchises, satellite warranty facilities, **Veh 3062**
Delivery and preparation, violation of provisions, suspension or revocation of license, **Veh 11705**
Deposits, availability of vehicle, **Veh 11713**
Disclosure,
Damages, **Veh 9990 et seq.**
Financial records, authorizations, **Veh 11703.4**
Low speed vehicles, **Veh 11713.10, 21252**
New vehicles, inability to use chains, **Veh 11713.6**
Repurchased vehicles, **Veh 11713.12**
Used vehicles, NMVTIS (national motor vehicle title information system), history, reports, **Veh 11713.26**
Discrimination, service contracts, **Veh 11713.3**

MOTOR VEHICLES—Cont'd
Dealers—Cont'd
Dismantlers, status as, **Veh 286**
Display,
Advertisements, showrooms, **Veh 11709.3**
Vehicles made by manufacturer different from engine manufacturer, **Veh 11713.9**
Disputes,
Arbitration and award, **Veh 11713.2, 11713.3**
Franchisee and franchisor, **Veh 3050**
Distributors, competition, **Veh 11713.3**
Division, types of businesses, **Veh 1670**
Down payment,
False representation, **Veh 11713**
Goods or services, rates and charges, **Veh 11713.19**
Driveaway towaway operations, generally, post
Driving schools, exemptions, **Veh 11101**
Duress or coercion, **Veh 11713.1**
Education, **Veh 11704.5**
Exclusions, **Veh 286**
Electronic lien and title program, **Veh 4450.5**
Electronic processing, registration, **Veh 4456.4**
Fees, **Veh 4456.5**
Endorsement, **Veh 11700.2**
Engines, manufacturer different from vehicle manufacturer, vehicles displayed or offered for sale, **Veh 11713.9**
Equipment, duties, **Veh 24007, 24009**
Established place of business, definitions, **Veh 320**
Examinations, **Veh 11704.5**
Executive management, requiring change, **Veh 11713.2**
Executors and administrators, certificate of convenience, **Veh 11720**
Exemptions,
Continuing education, **Veh 11704.5**
Examination, **Veh 11704.5**
False advertising, **Veh 11713**
Federal motor vehicle safety standard compliance, certificate, **Veh 24011**
Federal trade commission, buyers guide, **Veh 11713.1**
Fees,
Administrative service fees, noncompliance of registration or ownership, transfer provisions, **Veh 4456.1**
Consumer protection, recovery corporation, **Veh 4456.3**
Documents, processing, **Veh 4456.5**
Examination, **Veh 11704.5**
Excess payment, purchaser, **Veh 11713.3, 11713.4**
Failure to pay, **Veh 11711**
New vehicle dealers, **Veh 3016**
Payment, **Veh 9550 et seq.**

MOTOR VEHICLES—Cont'd
Dealers—Cont'd
Fees—Cont'd
Recovery corporation, consumer protection, **Veh 4456.3**
Service of process, **Veh 11710**
Fines and penalties, **Veh 11728**
Compromise and settlement, **Veh 11707**
Failure to pay, **Veh 11711**
Licenses and permits, late renewal, **Veh 11717**
Place of business, sales elsewhere, **Veh 11728**
Registration or transfer of ownership on behalf of purchaser, noncompliance, **Veh 4456.1**
Report of sale, **Veh 4456, 4456.1**
Force and violence, notice, repossessors and repossession, assignments, **Veh 11724**
Franchises, generally, post
Fraud, **Veh 11711**
Free association with other dealers, **Veh 11713.2, 11713.3**
Goods, wares and merchandise, rates and charges, disclosure, **Veh 11713.19**
House cars, safety, **Veh 2429.3**
Identification plates, special equipment, **Veh 5016 et seq.**
Inspections and inspectors, offices, records, **Veh 1670**
Installment payments, goods or services, rates and charges, **Veh 11713.19**
Insurance, notice, **Veh 5604, 5604.5**
Invoice, advertisements, **Veh 11713.1**
Labels, engine manufacturer different from vehicle manufacturer, **Veh 11713.9**
Labor and employment, salespersons, notice, **Veh 11713**
Leases, trade ins, discharge, **Veh 11709.4**
Lemon Law buyback, **Veh 11713.12**
License plates,
Automatic cancellation, **Veh 11721**
Duplicates, **Veh 4466**
Excess payment, purchaser, **Veh 11713.3, 11713.4**
Expiration, **Veh 11717**
Fees, **Veh 9262, 9550**
Renewals, **Veh 9262.5**
Identification, special equipment, **Veh 5016 et seq.**
Operation of vehicles under special plates, **Veh 11715**
Renewal, **Veh 11717**
Fees, **Veh 9262.5**
Special plates, **Veh 11714 et seq.**
Fees, **Veh 9262**
Transfer of interest, operation of vehicle without, **Veh 5906**
Unauthorized use, **Veh 11713**
Licenses and permits, **Veh 11700 et seq.**
Actions and proceedings, **Veh 11711.3**

MOTOR

MOTOR VEHICLES—Cont'd
Dealers—Cont'd
Licenses and permits—Cont'd
Application, **Veh 11701**
Form, **Veh 11704**
Automatic cancellation, **Veh 11721**
Cancellation,
Return to department, **Veh 8803**
Temporary permit, **Veh 11719**
Vehicles in possession, **Veh 11700**
Crimes and offenses, **Veh 40000.11**
Display, **Veh 11709**
Exemption, **Veh 4002**
Nonresident dealers, importation or exportation of vehicles, **Veh 11700.1**
Fines and penalties, late renewal, **Veh 11717**
Issuance, **Veh 11702, 11714**
Lessor retailer, **Veh 11600 et seq.**
Probationary license, **Veh 11718**
Reapplication, **Veh 11703.3**
Refusal, **Veh 11703**
Additional grounds, **Veh 11703.1**
Procedure, **Veh 11708**
Revocation or suspension, **Veh 11705**
Consignment sales, **Veh 11729**
Vehicles in possession, **Veh 11700**
Security interest, **Veh 11711.3**
Temporary permit, **Veh 11719**
Cancellation, **Veh 11719**
Temporary suspension, **Veh 11706**
Unsatisfied final judgments, denial, **Veh 11703.2**
Vessels, trailers, **Veh 11709**
Wholesalers selling retail, **Veh 11714**
Liens and incumbrances,
Electronic lien and title program, **Veh 4450.5**
Enforcement, **Veh 9801**
Line makes, sales, **Veh 11713.13**
Franchises, **Veh 11713.1**
Lists, advertisements, showrooms, **Veh 11709.3**
Low speed vehicles, **Veh 11713.10, 21252**
Manufacturers and manufacturing, competition, **Veh 11713.3**
Mobile homes, branch offices, **Veh 5353**
Model change allowance, failure to pay, **Veh 11713.3**
Modification of franchise, **Veh 11713.3**
Motorized bicycles, registration, **Veh 5039**
New car dealer license fee, **Veh 11723**
New motor vehicle board, **Veh 3000 et seq.**
Decision involving disputes between franchisee and franchisor, participating, **Veh 3050**
New vehicles, generally, post
NMVTIS (national motor vehicle title information system), used vehicles, history, reports, disclosure, **Veh 11713.26**

MOTOR VEHICLES—Cont'd
Dealers—Cont'd
Nonprofit organizations, exclusions, **Veh 286**
Nonrenewal, franchises, **Veh 11713.13**
Nonresidents, licensure exemption, importation and exportation of vehicles, **Veh 11700.1**
Notice,
Additional dealership or relocation of existing dealership, **Veh 3062**
Advertisements, showrooms, **Veh 11709.3**
Cooling off period, lease or purchase contracts, **Veh 11709.2**
Force and violence, repossessors and repossession, assignments, **Veh 11724**
Inspection, prospective purchasers right, **Veh 11709.1**
Repurchased vehicles, **Veh 11713.12**
Salespersons, employment termination, **Veh 11713**
Transfer, display of copy, **Veh 11715**
Violations, **Veh 40000.7**
Numbered copies of report of sale, **Veh 4456**
Odometers,
Crimes and offenses, **Veh 11713**
Disconnection or replacement, **Veh 28051**
New car warranty, mileage, **Veh 28052**
Resetting, **Veh 11713**
Off highway vehicles, post
Office, place of business, **Veh 1670, 1671**
Park trailers, disclosure, moving requirements, **Veh 11713.1**
Physical damage insurance, notice, **Veh 5604.5**
Place of business,
Offering vehicle for sale other than, **Veh 11713**
Signs, **Veh 11709**
Pollution control device installation and inspection certificate, **Veh 24007**
Posted location, sales away from, **Veh 11714**
Prices, increase without notice, **Veh 11713.2, 11713.3**
Priorities and preferences,
Claims of state, **Veh 11711**
Fraud, claims against dealers and salesmen, **Veh 11711**
Privacy, records and recordation, **Veh 11713.3, 11713.25**
Private party vehicle markets, **Veh 12101 et seq.**
Procuring change in ownership, **Veh 11713.2, 11713.3**
Protest, additional dealership or relocation of existing dealership, **Veh 3062**
Rebates, advertisements, **Veh 11713.16**

MOTOR VEHICLES—Cont'd
Dealers—Cont'd
Records and recordation,
Disclosure, authorizations, **Veh 11703.4**
Privacy, **Veh 11713.3, 11713.25**
Recovery corporation, consumer protection, **Veh 12200 et seq.**
Fees, **Veh 4456.3**
Registration,
Application on behalf of purchaser, **Veh 4456**
Autobrokers, **Veh 11735**
Confidential record access, **Veh 1808.23**
Electronic lien and title program, **Veh 4450.5**
Electronic processing, **Veh 4456.4**
Fees, **Veh 4456.5**
Exemption, **Veh 4002**
Fees, **Veh 9262**
Pro rated, **Veh 11713**
Fines and penalties, noncompliance, **Veh 4456.1**
Religious organizations and societies, exclusions, **Veh 286**
Relocation of franchise, **Veh 3062, 11713.3**
Notice, **Veh 3062**
Repairs. Motor Vehicle Repair Dealers, generally, this index
Report of sale, **Veh 4456**
Cash transactions, **Veh 11713**
Failure to comply, **Veh 4456.1**
Repossessors and repossession, force and violence, notice, assignments, **Veh 11724**
Repurchased vehicles, notice, **Veh 11713.12**
Restitution, licenses and permits, denial, **Veh 11703.2**
Retail sales by wholesalers, **Veh 11714**
Sales and use taxes, failure to pay, **Veh 11713**
Salespersons, generally, post
Seatbelts, used vehicles, **Veh 27314**
Security,
Licenses and permits, **Veh 11711.3**
Transfer of title, **Veh 5907**
Service contracts, discrimination, **Veh 11713.3**
Service of process, **Veh 11710**
Place of business closed, registered mail, **Veh 11712**
Services, rates and charges, disclosure, **Veh 11713.19**
Signs and devices on place of business, **Veh 11709**
Special plates, **Veh 11714 et seq.**
Statements of effectiveness, pollution control devices, **Veh 24007**
Termination, franchises, **Veh 11713.13**
Tire chains, new vehicles, inability to use, failure to disclose, **Veh 11713.6**
Tire standards, compliance, **Veh 27501, 27502**

MOTOR VEHICLES—Cont'd
Dealers—Cont'd
Trade ins, credit, discharge, **Veh 11709.4**
Transfer of title or interest,
Bonds (officers and fiduciaries), **Veh 4456**
Excess payment by purchaser, **Veh 11713.3, 11713.4**
Fines and penalties, **Veh 4456.1**
Notice, **Veh 5901 et seq.**
Operation without transfer, **Veh 5906**
Two or more types of businesses, division between, **Veh 1670**
Unloaded vehicles, registration, exemption, **Veh 4016**
Used vehicles,
Certificates and certification, **Veh 11713.18**
Continuing education, **Veh 11704.5**
Education, **Veh 11704.5**
Equipment, **Veh 24007**
Secondhand tires, **Veh 27465**
Examinations and examiners, **Veh 11704.5**
NMVTIS (national motor vehicle title information system), history, reports, disclosure, **Veh 11713.26**
Tire standards, compliance with, **Veh 27501**
Valuation, **Veh 11950**
Vehicle standing on highway, registration, **Veh 4016**
Videotape, house cars, safety, **Veh 2429.3**
Warranties,
Copies and lists, provision to house car buyers, **Veh 11931**
Failure to honor, **Veh 11713**
Violation of provisions, suspension or revocation of licenses, **Veh 11705**
Wholesale motor vehicle auctions, **Veh 6100 et seq.**
Reports, **Veh 4456**
Wholesalers, bonds (officers and fiduciaries), **Veh 11710.1**
Worn tires, sale, **Veh 27465**
Death,
Coroners report, **Veh 20011**
Damages, **Veh 17151**
Dealers,
Certificate of convenience, **Veh 11720**
Rights of widows and heirs, **Veh 11713.2, 11713.3**
Duty of driver, **Veh 20003**
Investigations, **Veh 2412**
Nonresidents, service of process, **Veh 17452**
Person signing minors drivers license, cancellation of license, **Veh 17712**
Tort liability, **Veh 17000 et seq.**
Traffic safety program, **Veh 2900 et seq.**
Transfer of title or interest, **Veh 5910**
Wrongful death, **Veh 17000 et seq.**
Debris, accidents, removal by tow truck operator, **Veh 27700**

MOTOR VEHICLES—Cont'd
Decals,
Clean air stickers, forgery, counterfeiting, **Veh 4463**
Fleet vehicles, weights and measures, **Veh 9400.1**
Lemon Law buyback, **Veh 11713.12**
Low emission vehicles, **Veh 5205.5, 21655.9, 40000.13**
Forgery, counterfeiting, **Veh 4463**
Special interests, **Veh 5060**
Veterans organizations, license plates, special plates, **Veh 5068.1**
Wheelchairs, lifts, carriers, license plates, obstructions, **Veh 5201**
Zero emission electric vehicles, parking, designated spaces, **Veh 22511, 22511.1, 42001.6**
Deceit. Fraud, generally, post
Deceleration lights, **Veh 25251.5**
Declaration of forfeiture, bail, failure to appear,
Arraignment, **Veh 40512**
Trial, **Veh 40512.5**
Declaration that vehicle will not be permanently located outside United States, definitions, **Veh 6161**
Decrees. Judgments and decrees, generally, post
Default, unsatisfied judgments, accidents, **Veh 16381**
Defective parts, manufacturer and sale, **Veh 12000 et seq.**
Defenses, prosecutions for code violations, **Veh 41400 et seq.**
Deferred action for childhood arrivals, aliens,
Drivers licenses, **Veh 12801.6**
Identification cards, **Veh 13001**
Definitions, **Veh 100 et seq., 415, 670**
Affiliates, engine manufacturer different from vehicle manufacturer, **Veh 9980**
Auto buying service, **Veh 166**
Autobroker, **Veh 166**
Autoettes, **Veh 175**
Automobile driver training, **Veh 223**
Brokering, **Veh 232.5**
Consumer, autobroker registration, **Veh 11735**
Drivers licenses, post
Economic automobile theft, prevention, **Veh 10901**
Exported vehicles, **Veh 6161**
Fees, exemptions, **Veh 9105**
First stage and second stage manufacturers, house cars, **Veh 11930**
Fraud, license revocations, **Veh 11705**
Infraction, **Veh 40000.1, 40000.3**
Keys, information, **Veh 9954**
Liquified petroleum gas, **Veh 380**
Maintenance facilities, inspection, **Veh 34501.12**
Minors, **Veh 17700**
Motor vehicle bumper strength notices, **Veh 24011.3**

MOTOR VEHICLES—Cont'd
Definitions—Cont'd
Nonresident daily commuter, registration exemption, **Veh 435.5**
Passenger vehicles, damage control, **Veh 34710**
Remanufactured vehicle, **Veh 507.5**
Remanufacturer, **Veh 507.8**
Ridesharing, **Veh 522**
Seatbelts, **Veh 27315**
Tire tread, **Veh 610**
Total loss salvage vehicles, **Veh 544**
Upper beam headlamp, emergency vehicles, **Veh 25252.5**
Vanpool vehicle, **Veh 668**
Vehicle verifier, **Veh 675.5**
Defrosters, equipment, **Veh 26712**
Delegation of powers, **Veh 8**
Delinquent fees. Fees, post
Delivery of vehicles not ordered by dealers, **Veh 11713.1**
Demand, arrest, appearance, **Veh 40302, 40304, 40502**
Dents, service contracts, **Veh 12800 et seq.**
Deposits,
Bail, **Veh 40510**
Off highway vehicle fund, **Veh 42204**
Descent and distribution,
Dealership, **Veh 11713.2, 11713.3**
Notice, **Veh 5910**
Designated driver program, information sheet, **Veh 2426**
Destruction,
Handicapped persons, parking placards, **Veh 22511.56**
License plates, post
Diffused lights, **Veh 25400, 25401**
Dimming lights,
Approaching vehicles, **Veh 24409**
Parked or standing vehicles, **Veh 24401**
Direction of beam, lamps or devices, **Veh 25951**
Directors. Motor Vehicles Department, this index
Disabled motorist, assistance, law enforcement agencies, **Veh 20018 et seq.**
Disabled persons. Handicapped persons, generally, post
Disabled vehicles,
Abandoned vehicles, removal, **Veh 22650 et seq.**
Assistance, **Veh 20018 et seq.**
Brakes, stopping distance requirement, **Veh 26458**
Flashing lights, **Veh 25251**
Freeways, pedestrians, **Veh 21960**
Fusees, warning signals and devices, **Veh 25300 et seq.**
Rear lamps, **Veh 24605**
Registration, exemptions, **Veh 4002**
Removal, parked or standing vehicles, **Veh 22650 et seq.**
State highways, parking, **Veh 22505**
Tail lamps, **Veh 24605**
Tire tread depth, **Veh 27465**
Towing, generally, post

MOTOR

MOTOR VEHICLES—Cont'd
Disabled vehicles—Cont'd
Turn signals, flashing, **Veh 25251, 25300**
Unincorporated areas, parking, exemptions, **Veh 22504**
Warning signals and devices, **Veh 25300 et seq.**
Disabled veterans,
Fees, exemptions, **Veh 9105**
License plates, **Veh 5007, 5007.5**
Offstreet parking facilities, removal of unauthorized vehicles, civil liability, **Veh 22652.5**
Parking placards, **Veh 22511.5 et seq.**
Fees, **Veh 9105**
Special plates, **Veh 5007, 5007.5**
Disaster areas, special permits, **Veh 4005**
Disaster service vehicles, warning lights, **Veh 25259.1, 25259.5**
Disciplinary actions, licenses revocation, special licenses, **Veh 2544**
Disclosure,
Address, attorneys, **Veh 1808.4**
Advertisements, autobrokers, **Veh 11713**
Autobroker fees, **Veh 11713.1**
Broker agreements, **Veh 11738**
Confidential or privileged information, **Veh 1808.45 et seq.**
Address, attorneys, records and recordation, **Veh 1808.22**
Credit scores, dealers, **Veh 11713.20**
Dealers, ante
Drivers licenses, post
Electric vehicles, registration, confidential or privileged information, **Veh 1808.23**
Event data recorders, **Veh 9951**
Low speed vehicles, sales, **Veh 11713.10, 21252**
New vehicles unable to use chains, **Veh 11713.6**
Recording devices, **Veh 9951**
Remanufactured vehicles, **Veh 11713.7**
Repurchased vehicles, dealers or manufacturers, **Veh 11713.12**
Sales, damages, **Veh 9990 et seq.**
Salvaged vehicles, NMVTIS (national motor vehicle title information system), history, reports, sales, **Veh 11713.26**
Sensing and diagnostic modules, **Veh 9951**
Total loss salvage vehicles, sales, **Veh 11515, 11568**
Disconnection of odometer, **Veh 28050.5, 28051**
Discovery, new vehicles, investigations, **Veh 3050.1, 3050.2**
Discrimination,
Dealers, service contracts, **Veh 11713.3**
Drivers licenses, aliens, crimes and offenses, **Veh 12801.9**
Franchises, **Veh 11713.2, 11713.3**
Sales, **Veh 11713.1**

MOTOR VEHICLES—Cont'd
Dishonored checks, payment of fees, fines and penalties, suspension of license, **Veh 13364**
Dismantlers, **Veh 4014, 11500 et seq.**
Abandoned vehicles, notice, **Veh 22851.2**
Abandonment of property, cancellation of license, **Veh 11518**
Advertisements, occupational license or permit number, **Veh 11521**
Applications, licenses and permits, **Veh 11504**
Business records, **Veh 11520**
Certificate of convenience, executors and administrators, **Veh 11517**
Certificates of title,
Duplicates, **Veh 4466**
Surrender, **Veh 5500, 5501**
Change in ownership, **Veh 11504**
Compromise and settlement, fines and penalties, **Veh 11509.1**
Crimes and offenses, **Veh 5500, 11520, 40000.11**
License revocation, **Veh 11509**
Suspension, refusal to issue, **Veh 11503.5**
Return of documents and license plates, **Veh 40000.7**
Surrender of certificates of title, license plates and registration cards, **Veh 40000.7**
Dealers, status as, **Veh 286**
Definitions, **Veh 220, 221**
Delinquent fees, **Veh 9552**
Division, types of businesses, **Veh 1670**
Documents of ownership and license plates, delivery, motor vehicle department, **Veh 11520**
Dollies, registration, **Veh 4014**
Executors and administrators, certificate of convenience, **Veh 11517**
Exemptions, licenses and permits, **Veh 221**
Fees,
Investigation fees, **Veh 9263**
License revocation, **Veh 11509**
Licenses and permits, **Veh 11504**
Payment, **Veh 9551**
Filing notice of acquisition, **Veh 11520**
Fines and penalties, **Veh 5500, 11520**
Compromise and settlement, **Veh 11509.1**
Licenses and permits, late renewal, **Veh 11508**
Stipulated penalty without hearing or appeal, **Veh 11509.1**
Fraud, registration of vehicles, **Veh 11509**
Hearing,
Refusal of department to issue license, **Veh 11512**
Revocation or suspension of license, **Veh 11509**
Inspection and inspectors, **Veh 5505, 9271**

MOTOR VEHICLES—Cont'd
Dismantlers—Cont'd
Inspection and inspectors—Cont'd
Offices, records, **Veh 1670**
Investigations,
Duties of department, **Veh 1662**
Fees, **Veh 9263**
License plates,
Delivery, **Veh 11520**
Duplicates, **Veh 4466**
Surrender, **Veh 5500, 5501**
Licenses and permits, **Veh 11500 et seq.**
Advertisements, occupational license or permit number, **Veh 11521**
Application, **Veh 11501**
Forms, **Veh 11504**
Automatic cancellation, **Veh 11518**
Cancellation, **Veh 11507, 11518**
Crimes and offenses, **Veh 11503.5**
Exemptions, **Veh 221**
Expiration, **Veh 11508**
Fees, **Veh 9262**
Fines and penalties, late renewal, **Veh 11508**
Issuance, **Veh 11505**
Mental health treatment, **Veh 16077**
Moral turpitude, crimes involving, **Veh 11503.5**
Reapplication, **Veh 11509.5**
Refusal, **Veh 11502 et seq.**
Renewal, **Veh 11508**
Restricted license, **Veh 11506**
Revocation or suspension, **Veh 8800, 11503, 11509**
Possession of stolen vehicle, **Veh 11511**
Return of documents to department, **Veh 8803**
Temporary suspension, **Veh 11510**
Temporary permits, **Veh 11507**
Cancellation, **Veh 11507**
Nonoperation certificate, exemption from, **Veh 11511**
Notice,
Abandoned vehicles, disposition, **Veh 22660**
Acquisition, **Veh 11520**
Alleged violations, **Veh 1662**
Change in ownership, **Veh 11504**
Refusal of license, **Veh 11512**
Revocation or suspension of license, **Veh 11509**
Off highway vehicles subject to identification, **Veh 38180, 38185**
Office, place of business, **Veh 1670, 1671**
Partially dismantled stolen vehicle, rebuttable presumption, **Veh 11511**
Place of business, definition, **Veh 320**
Portable dolly for rendering assistance, registration, **Veh 4014**
Possession of vehicles, reports, **Veh 11520**
Rebuttable presumption, partially dismantled stolen vehicle, **Veh 11511**

MOTOR VEHICLES—Cont'd
Dismantlers—Cont'd
Records, maintenance of business records, **Veh 11520**
Registration, **Veh 11519**
Exemption, **Veh 4002**
Fees, **Veh 9263**
Local ordinances, **Veh 22660 et seq.**
Surrender, **Veh 5500, 5501**
Removal of vehicles, **Veh 22650 et seq.**
Notice, **Veh 22660**
Renewal, licenses, **Veh 11508**
Reports,
Possession of vehicle, **Veh 11520**
Stored vehicles, **Veh 10656**
Scrap metal processing facilities, exemptions, **Veh 221**
Signs and signals, tow vehicles, **Veh 27907**
Special plates, **Veh 11502 et seq., 11516 et seq.**
Fees, **Veh 9262**
Stipulated penalties, agreement, **Veh 11509.1**
Stolen vehicles,
Inspection of lots, **Veh 2805**
Possession, **Veh 11511**
Title to property, investigations and investigators, **Veh 1655**
Tow vehicles, signs and signals, **Veh 27907**
Two or more types of businesses, division between, **Veh 1670**
Zoning, dismantling area, **Veh 1671**
Display,
Block letters indicating liquefied petroleum gas or natural gas fuel use, concealed tanks, **Veh 27909**
Dealers, ante
Disabled person placards, **Veh 4463**
Fines and penalties, **Veh 4463.3**
Drivers licenses, post
Engine manufacturer different from vehicle manufacturer, **Veh 11713.9**
Fleet vehicles, name, trademark or logo, **Veh 5302**
License plates, post
Licenses and permits,
Dealers, **Veh 11715**
Salesmans license as belonging to another, **Veh 11819**
Nonresident daily commuter, identification, card, **Veh 6700.4**
Notice of transfer, dealers, **Veh 11715**
Disposition,
Abandoned or unclaimed property, **Veh 22851 et seq.**
Fines and forfeitures, **Veh 42200 et seq.**
Liens and incumbrances, **Veh 22851 et seq.**
Disqualification, commercial vehicles, drivers licenses, hazards, **Veh 15325**
Distance, lighting equipment visibility, **Veh 24251**
Distinctive uniform and vehicle, arresting speed violators, **Veh 40804**

MOTOR VEHICLES—Cont'd
Distributors,
Accomplices and accessories, **Veh 11700.3**
Change in list, notice to department, **Veh 11704**
Coercion of dealers, **Veh 11713.2**
Competition with dealers, **Veh 11713.2, 11713.3**
Crimes and offenses, licenses and permits, **Veh 11700**
Dealers, competition, **Veh 11713.3**
Definitions, **Veh 296**
Delinquent fees, **Veh 9552**
Delivery and preparation obligation, suspension or revocation of license for violations, **Veh 11705**
Division, types of businesses, **Veh 1670**
Duress or coercion, **Veh 11713.1**
Established place of business, definitions, **Veh 320**
Fees,
License and special plates, **Veh 9262**
Time of payment, **Veh 9550**
Fines and penalties, compromise and settlement, **Veh 11707**
Franchises, generally, post
Inspections and inspectors, offices, records, **Veh 1670**
License plates,
Operation without, **Veh 11716**
Special plates, **Veh 11715**
Licenses and permits, **Veh 11700 et seq.**
Damages, **Veh 11726**
Fees, **Veh 11723**
Forms, **Veh 11704**
Plates, fees, **Veh 9262**
Reapplication, **Veh 11703.3**
Refusal to issue, **Veh 11702 et seq.**
Hearing, **Veh 11708**
Special plates, **Veh 11714 et seq.**
Suspension or revocation, **Veh 11703.1**
Grounds, **Veh 11705**
Notice and hearing, **Veh 11705**
Temporary suspension, **Veh 11706**
Territorial area, **Veh 11727**
Temporary permits, **Veh 11719**
Unsatisfied final judgments, denial, **Veh 11703.2**
New vehicles, generally, post
Off highway vehicles, operation without identification certificate, **Veh 38021**
Office, place of business, **Veh 1670, 1671**
Registration, exemptions, **Veh 4002**
Restitution, licenses and permits, denial, **Veh 11703.2**
Special plates, fees, **Veh 9262**
Subsidiaries, dealers, competition, **Veh 11713.3**
Supplying dealers, powers and duties, **Veh 11713.2, 11713.3**
Two or more types of businesses, division between, **Veh 1670**
Warranties, failure to honor, **Veh 11713**

MOTOR VEHICLES—Cont'd
Distributors—Cont'd
Warranty agreements, suspension or revocation of license and permit, **Veh 11705**
District attorneys,
Inspectors or investigators, confidential or privileged information, records and recordation, address, **Veh 1808.2**
Records and recordation, access, **Veh 1810.5**
District of Columbia, convictions, drivers license revocation or suspension, **Veh 13352**
Districts, off highway vehicles, identification, **Veh 38000 et seq.**
Diversion programs, alternative disposition for offenders, **Veh 42005.3**
Divisions, license plates, special plates, **Veh 5151 et seq.**
Documents,
Conditional sales, ante
Electronic transmissions, **Veh 1801.1**
Dogs, transporting, restraining, **Veh 23117, 42001.4**
Dollies,
Definitions, **Veh 225**
Dismantlers, registration, **Veh 4014**
Domestic violence, license plates, new plates, **Veh 4467**
Domicile and residence,
Address, confidentiality, **Veh 1808.21 et seq.**
Commercial vehicles, drivers licenses, **Veh 12505**
Drivers licenses, **Veh 12505**
Evasion of fees and taxes, crimes and offenses, **Veh 8804**
Nonresidents, generally, post
Presumption, use of vehicle in state, **Veh 4000.4**
Registration,
Multiple county use of vehicle, **Veh 4004.5**
Vehicle not within state, **Veh 4152**
Registration card, **Veh 4453**
Resident, definitions, **Veh 516**
Door frames, Lemon Law buyback decals, **Veh 11713.12**
Door mounted reflectorizing devices or material, **Veh 25105**
Doors,
Lights and lighting, interior lamps, **Veh 24003**
Opening on moving traffic, **Veh 22517**
Reflectorizing devices or material, **Veh 25105**
Replacement of glazing material, safety material, **Veh 26703**
Width, maximum width of body and door handles, **Veh 35110**
Double jeopardy, defenses to prosecution for code violations, **Veh 41400**

MOTOR

MOTOR VEHICLES—Cont'd

Down payments,
Dealers, goods or services, rates and charges, **Veh 11713.19**
Used vehicles, cancellation option agreements, conditional sales, **Veh 11713.21**
Drawbars,
Definitions, **Veh 300**
Length of vehicle,
Measurement, **Veh 35402**
Towing units, **Veh 29005**
Mounting, **Veh 29002**
Towing units, **Veh 29002, 29004**
Length of bar or connection, **Veh 29005**
Driveaway towaway operations,
Brakes, power brakes, single control, **Veh 26458**
Clearance and side marker lamps, **Veh 25100**
Definitions, **Veh 303**
Lights and lighting, exemptions, **Veh 24605**
Power brakes, single control, **Veh 26458**
Service brakes, **Veh 26311**
Side marker lamps, **Veh 25100**
Tail lamps, exemptions, **Veh 24605**
Driver, definitions, **Veh 305**
Driver awareness or education programs, alternative disposition for offenders, **Veh 42005.3**
Driver education and training. Driving Schools, generally, this index
Driverless vehicles, **Veh 38750 et seq.**
Runaway vehicles, **Veh 16001**
Drivers handbook, contents, **Veh 1656.3**
Drivers licenses, **Veh 12500 et seq.**
Absent persons,
Armed forces, **Veh 12817**
Renewal, **Veh 12814**
Acceptance, consent to service of process, **Veh 17460**
Accident without drivers license, identification of driver, **Veh 20006**
Accompanying licensed driver, instruction permits, **Veh 12509**
Address, change, **Veh 14600**
Notice, responsibility, **Veh 13106**
Administrative hearings, driving while intoxicated, **Veh 13353**
Affidavits, aliens, **Veh 12801**
Age, **Veh 12504 et seq., 12509, 14607**
Driving for hire, **Veh 12515**
Extension, licenses, **Veh 12814.5**
Grounds for denial, **Veh 12805**
Hazardous substances, waste, transportation, **Veh 12515, 40000.11**
Minimum, **Veh 12512**
Proof of age, **Veh 12800.5**
Provisional license, demonstration program, **Veh 12814.6**
Qualifications, **Veh 12805 et seq.**
Verification, **Veh 12802**
Aged persons, renewal, **Veh 12814**
Mail and mailing, **Veh 12814.5**

MOTOR VEHICLES—Cont'd
Drivers licenses—Cont'd

Agricultural Machinery and Equipment, this index
Alcoholic Beverages, this index
Alcoholics, **Veh 12806**
Aliens, **Veh 12801 et seq.**
Commercial vehicles, limitations, **Veh 12801.10**
Deferred action for childhood arrivals, **Veh 12801.6**
Discrimination, **Veh 12801.9**
Alteration, **Veh 14610**
Amphetamine, addiction, revocation, **Veh 13351**
Anatomical Gifts, this index
Appeal and review, **Veh 14400**
Administrative review, **Veh 13557, 13558**
Aliens, deportation, **Veh 12801.7**
Hearing, **Veh 14105.5**
Judicial review, **Veh 13559**
Suspension or revocation, **Veh 14105, 14401**
Notice, **Veh 14401**
Appearance, failure to appear, **Veh 12807, 12808**
Suspension or revocation, **Veh 13365**
Applications,
Anatomical gifts, **Veh 12811**
Citizens and citizenship, evidence, **Veh 12801.5**
Civil liability, person signing, **Veh 17700 et seq.**
Contents, **Veh 12800**
Driving under the influence, declarations, **Veh 13385**
Fingerprints, **Veh 12800**
Identity and identification, **Veh 12801**
Instruction permits, **Veh 12509**
Legal residency, evidence, **Veh 12801.5**
Public inspection of records, **Veh 1808**
Renewal, **Veh 12814, 12816**
Signature and verification, **Veh 12802**
Social security numbers, **Veh 1653.5, 12800, 12801**
Student license, **Veh 12650**
Arrest. Traffic Rules and Regulations, this index
Assault with deadly weapon, revocation, **Veh 13351.5**
Assumed or fictitious names, **Veh 14610**
Aunts, signing and verification of application for minors license, **Veh 17701**
Bids and bidding, processing, **Veh 12811**
Birth date, anniversary, expiration, **Veh 12816**
Blood tests, **Veh 13353**
Alcohol concentration table published in handbook, examination questions, **Veh 1666**
Boating violations, suspension of license, **Veh 13202.5**

MOTOR VEHICLES—Cont'd
Drivers licenses—Cont'd

Breath tests, driving under influence of alcohol or drugs, **Veh 13353, 13353.1**
Children and minors, **Veh 23136**
Camp tour buses, **Veh 15250.3**
Canadian convictions, revocation or suspension, **Veh 13352**
Cancellation,
Aliens, deportation, **Veh 12801.7**
Application, higher class vehicles, **Veh 13100**
Capacity, evidence of incapacity, definitions, **Veh 21061**
Causing serious bodily injury, revocation or suspension, **Veh 13351**
Certificates and certification,
Bulk liquid load transportation, abstract form, **Veh 1804**
Hazardous waste transportation, driver certification, agricultural hazardous materials transportation, **Veh 12804.2**
Medical certificates, nonresidents, **Veh 12502**
Reinstatement of license, appearance or payment of fine, **Veh 12807, 13365**
Suspension or revocation, negligent driving, **Veh 12812**
Youth bus operators, **Veh 12523**
Certified mail, revocation or suspension, notice, **Veh 13106**
Change of address, notice, **Veh 14600**
Change of name, fees, **Veh 14901**
Adjustments, **Veh 1678**
Checking record for traffic violations, **Veh 12808**
Chemical tests, driving under the influence, **Veh 13380 et seq., 23612, 23614**
Child protective services worker, signing and verification of application for minors license, **Veh 17701**
Children and minors, **Veh 15500, 15501**
Administrative review, revocation or suspension, **Veh 13558**
Application, signing and verifying by parents, **Veh 17701**
Cancellation, **Veh 17712**
Junior permits, **Veh 12514**
Cards, identification cards, **Veh 13000 et seq.**
Change of class of vehicle minor permitted to operate, consent, **Veh 12804.5**
Chauffeurs license, **Veh 12515**
Civil liability, person signing license applications, **Veh 17700 et seq.**
Concealed weapons, suspension, **Veh 13202.4**
Consent, change of class of vehicle minor permitted to operate, **Veh 12804.5**

MOTOR VEHICLES—Cont'd
Drivers licenses—Cont'd
Children and minors—Cont'd
Court supervised rehabilitation program, transportation, junior permits, **Veh 12513**
Delay of privileges, defacing property, **Veh 13202.6**
Duplicate license,
Conditions precedent, **Veh 12815**
Signing and verification of application by parents, **Veh 17701**
Employment programs, junior permits, wards of juvenile courts, **Veh 12513**
False license, use, **Veh 40000.11**
Guardians, signing and verifying application, **Veh 17701**
Identification cards, **Veh 13000 et seq.**
Instruction permits, **Veh 12509**
Intoxicating liquors, suspension for possession or transporting, **Veh 23224**
Junior permits, **Veh 12513**
Revocation, duration, **Veh 12514**
Juvenile courts, junior permits for wards of court, **Veh 12513**
Liability, transfer of acceptance, **Veh 11712**
Nonresidents, **Veh 12504**
Permitting unlicensed minor to drive, **Veh 14607**
Person signing application, tort liability, **Veh 17700 et seq.**
Provisional licenses, **Veh 12814.6**
Restricted licenses,
Alcohol or drug violations, **Veh 13202.5**
Concealed weapons, **Veh 13202.4**
Driving under the influence, **Veh 13353.8**
Revocation or suspension,
Alcohol or drug violations, **Veh 13202.5**
Death of parent, guardian or employer, **Veh 17712**
Defacing property, **Veh 13202.6**
Financial responsibility, **Veh 17704**
Sentence, **Veh 13367**
School bus operation, restriction, **Veh 12516**
Signature and verification of application, **Veh 12802, 17701**
Civil liability of person signing, **Veh 17700 et seq.**
Junior permit, **Veh 12513**
Student licenses, **Veh 12650 et seq.**
Transfer of tort liability, **Veh 17712**
Vandalism, delay of driving privileges, **Veh 13202.6**
Work programs, junior permits, wards of juvenile courts, **Veh 12513**
Citizens and citizenship, evidence, **Veh 12801.5**
Civil liability for damages, student license, **Veh 12650**

MOTOR VEHICLES—Cont'd
Drivers licenses—Cont'd
Classification of vehicles, **Veh 12804.14**
Examiners and examinations, **Veh 12804.9**
Colors and coloring, children and minors, **Veh 12814.6**
Commercial vehicles, ante
Community service,
Provisional licensees, **Veh 12814.6**
Sale or manufacture, similar documents, **Veh 14610.1**
Compact, **Veh 15000 et seq.**
Concurrent suspensions, **Veh 13353**
Confidential or privileged information,
Examinations, **Veh 12804.8**
Records and recordation, **Veh 1807.5, 1808.9**
Consciousness, persons subject to loss of, **Veh 12806**
Contents, **Veh 12811**
Continuance in effect, armed forces, **Veh 12817**
Contracts for processing, bids and bidding, **Veh 12811**
Contributions, anatomical gifts, registry, **Veh 12811**
Controlled substances, driving while under influence of, suspension, **Veh 13352 et seq.**
Correctional Institutions, this index
Counterfeiting, **Veh 12811, 14610**
Evidence procurement, **Veh 42271**
Courts, production at request of judge, **Veh 12952**
Crimes and offenses, **Veh 13201, 40000.11**
Altering, falsifying or forging, **Veh 14610**
Assault with deadly weapon, revocation, **Veh 13351.5**
Crib sheets or impersonating applicant, **Veh 14610.5**
Department, revocation, **Veh 13350**
Equivalents of conviction, **Veh 13103**
Failure to display, **Veh 40000.11**
Habitual traffic offender, **Veh 14601.3**
Notice to correct violations, **Veh 40610 et seq.**
Obtaining licenses for unauthorized persons, **Veh 14610.7**
Provisional licensees, **Veh 12814.6**
Similar documents, **Veh 14610.1**
Damages, responding in, submitting proof, negligent drivers, **Veh 12810.5**
Definitions, **Veh 310**
Fraudulent license, **Veh 14610**
Diplomats, exemptions, **Veh 12502**
Disability, denial, **Veh 12805**
Disclosure, social security numbers, **Veh 12801**
Diseases, denial, **Veh 12805**
Display, **Veh 12951**
Cancellation, **Veh 14610**
Failure to display, **Veh 40000.11**

MOTOR VEHICLES—Cont'd
Drivers licenses—Cont'd
Display—Cont'd
Request of magistrate or judge, **Veh 12952**
District of Columbia, convictions, revocation or suspension, **Veh 13352**
Domicile and residents, **Veh 12505**
Driving Schools, this index
Driving under the influence. Traffic Rules and Regulations, this index
Driving while privilege suspended, **Veh 14601 et seq.**
Driving under the influence, **Veh 14601.5**
Impounding vehicle, **Veh 14602, 14602.5, 14602.6**
Off highway vehicles, **Veh 14601 et seq.**
Point system, **Veh 12810**
Sentence and punishment, service of sentence on weekends, **Veh 14601.8**
Drug addicts, **Veh 12806**
Revocation or suspension, **Veh 13201, 13202, 13351**
Drugs and medicine,
Driving under the influence, revocation or suspension, **Veh 13352 et seq.**
Investigations and investigators, **Veh 13800**
Possession, crimes and offenses, **Veh 12809, 13202**
Revocation or suspension, **Veh 13201**
Duplicates,
Children and minors,
Conditions precedent, **Veh 12815**
Person signing, tort liability, **Veh 17701**
Fees, **Veh 9265, 14901**
Adjustments, **Veh 1678**
Lost, destroyed or mutilated license, **Veh 12815**
Name change, **Veh 12815**
Unlawful to make, **Veh 14610**
Duty of inquiry, owners, permitting use, **Veh 14604, 40000.11**
Electronic recordation, hearing proceedings, **Veh 14104.2**
Electronic signatures, **Veh 12950, 12950.5**
Employment, transportation facilities inadequate, junior permit, **Veh 12513**
Endorsement,
Firefighters and fire departments, **Veh 12804.11**
Hazardous substances and waste, commercial vehicles, **Veh 15250**
House cars, **Veh 12804.10**
English language, understanding, **Veh 12805**
Engraved pictures, **Veh 12800.5, 12811**
Epileptics, denial, **Veh 12806**
Erroneous issuance,
Cancellation, **Veh 13100**

MOTOR

MOTOR VEHICLES—Cont'd
Drivers licenses—Cont'd
Erroneous issuance—Cont'd
Surrender, **Veh 13362**
Evidence, **Veh 14103, 14106**
Hearings, **Veh 14104.7**
Incapacity, definitions, **Veh 21061**
Record of revocation or suspension, **Veh 40832**
Examiners and examinations, **Veh 12804.9**
Animals, abandoned or unclaimed property, **Veh 1666.5**
Applicant, **Veh 12803**
Blood alcohol concentration table published in handbook, **Veh 1666**
Children and minors, unattended children, **Veh 15632**
Confidential or privileged information, **Veh 12804.8**
Crib sheets, **Veh 273, 14610.5**
Discretion of department, **Veh 12814**
Eluding peace officers, **Veh 1666.1**
Eyes and eyesight, **Veh 1674 et seq.**
Grounds for denial, **Veh 12805 et seq.**
House cars, endorsement, **Veh 12804.10, 12804.15**
Impersonating applicant, **Veh 14610.5**
Peace officers, pursuit, **Veh 1666.1**
Pedestrians, **Veh 1666**
Pursuit, peace officers, **Veh 1666.1**
Special construction equipment, **Veh 12521**
Termination of suspension, mental or physical condition, **Veh 13102**
Training, **Veh 1674.4**
Unattended children, **Veh 15632**
Vision, **Veh 1674 et seq.**
Waiver, **Veh 12814**
Youth bus operators, **Veh 12523**
Exemptions, **Veh 12501 et seq.**
Nonresidents, **Veh 12502**
Exhibit, personal injury accident, **Veh 20003**
Expiration, **Veh 12816**
Armed forces, **Veh 12817**
Extension, **Veh 12814**
Limited term license, **Veh 12508**
Mail and mailing, **Veh 12814.5**
Eyes and eyesight, **Veh 12805**
Examiners and examinations, **Veh 1674 et seq.**
Facsimiles, **Veh 14610**
Failure to present license or evidence of identity, arrest, **Veh 40302**
False personation, **Veh 12809, 14610**
False statement, surrender, **Veh 13362**
Farm labor vehicles, **Veh 12519**
Feebleminded person, denial, **Veh 12805**
Fees, **Veh 14900 et seq.**
Adjustments, **Veh 1678**
Dishonored check in payment, suspension of license, **Veh 13364**
Extension of licenses, adjustments, **Veh 1678**

MOTOR VEHICLES—Cont'd
Drivers licenses—Cont'd
Fees—Cont'd
House cars, endorsement, **Veh 12804.15**
Renewal, **Veh 12816**
Restoration after suspension, **Veh 14905**
Revocation or suspension of license, notice, **Veh 14906**
Special construction equipment, **Veh 12521**
Felonies, commission with motor vehicles, revocation or suspension of license, **Veh 13350**
Fictitious names, **Veh 12809**
Evidence procurement, **Veh 42271**
Financial responsibility, revocation or suspension, **Veh 13352, 13352.1**
Fines and penalties,
Certificate of payment, reinstatement or renewal, **Veh 12807, 13365**
Defacing property, delay or suspension of driving privileges, **Veh 13202.6**
Dishonored checks, payment with, suspension of license, **Veh 13364**
Driving while privilege suspended, **Veh 14601 et seq.**
Habitual traffic offender, **Veh 14601.3**
Provisional licensees, **Veh 12814.6**
Sale or manufacture, similar documents, **Veh 14610.1**
Vandalism, delay or suspension of driving privileges, **Veh 13202.6**
Fingerprints, application, **Veh 12800**
Firefighters and fire departments, **Veh 12804.11**
Examinations and examiners, **Veh 12804.9**
Flammable liquids, driver certification, **Veh 12804.2**
Flight from peace officers, suspension, **Veh 2800.1 et seq., 13201**
Forgery, **Veh 14610**
Evidence procurement, **Veh 42271**
Forms, **Veh 1652**
Anatomical gifts, registry, **Veh 12811**
Fraud,
Children and minors, **Veh 15501, 40000.11**
Display or possession of license fraudulently altered or obtained, **Veh 14610**
Insurance or liability claims, revocation or suspension, **Veh 13201**
Refusal to issue or renew, **Veh 12809**
Unlawful or fraudulent use, **Veh 13800, 14610**
Freeways, instruction permits, **Veh 12509**
Grandparent, signing and verification of application for minors license, **Veh 17701**

MOTOR VEHICLES—Cont'd
Drivers licenses—Cont'd
Guardian and ward,
Application for cancellation, **Veh 17712**
Consent, change of class of vehicle minor permitted to operate, **Veh 12804.5**
Signatures, torts, liability, **Veh 17700 et seq.**
Habitual drunkards, denial, **Veh 12806**
Habitual truants, revocation or suspension, **Veh 13202.7**
Handicapped persons, suspension, duration, **Veh 13556**
Hardship permits,
Defacing property, **Veh 13202.6**
Driving while intoxicated, **Veh 13353.4**
Hazardous substances and waste, post
Hearings, **Veh 13558, 13950 et seq., 14100 et seq.**
Impoundment, revoked, suspended, driving without, **Veh 14602.6**
Hit and run drivers, revocation, **Veh 13350**
Hours of employment, **Veh 12812**
House cars, endorsement, **Veh 12804.10**
Identification cards, generally, post
Identity and identification, **Veh 12800.7**
Applications, **Veh 12801**
Ignition interlock devices,
Driving while privilege suspended, **Veh 14601 et seq.**
Restricted drivers licenses, **Veh 13352, 13353.3**
Illiterate persons, **Veh 12805**
Illness, family member, junior permit, **Veh 12513**
Implements of husbandry, person operating, exemption, **Veh 12501**
Implied consent, driving under the influence, tests, **Veh 13353, 13384, 23136, 23612**
Impoundment, infractions, failure to pay fine, **Veh 40508**
Incompetent persons, examinations to detect, studies, **Veh 12804.8**
Information, failure to furnish, refusal to issue or renew, **Veh 12809**
Infractions, impoundment for failure to pay fine, **Veh 40508**
Insane persons, denial, **Veh 12805**
Inspection of records, **Veh 1808**
Instruction permits, **Veh 12509, 12513, 12514**
Provisional licenses, **Veh 12814.6**
Interstate Compact, **Veh 15000 et seq.**
Inventory, depletion, **Veh 1672.3**
Investigations, **Veh 13800 et seq.**
Consideration of frequent use of vehicles by chauffeurs, **Veh 13802**
Hearings, **Veh 14100 et seq.**
Issuance, **Veh 12800 et seq.**
Review, **Veh 14400**
Junior permits, **Veh 12513**

MOTOR VEHICLES—Cont'd
Drivers licenses—Cont'd
Junior permits—Cont'd
Revocation or suspension, **Veh 12514**
Juvenile delinquents and dependents, revocation or suspension, **Veh 13101 et seq.**
Juvenile facilities division, **Veh 41500**
Labor and employment,
Junior permits, **Veh 12513**
Medical certificate, **Veh 14606**
Restricted license, **Veh 12812**
Lapses of consciousness, condition causing, denial, **Veh 12806**
Law enforcement officers, revocation or suspension, access to records, **Veh 1803.4**
Leases, **Veh 14604, 14608, 40000.11**
Legal residency, evidence, **Veh 12801.5**
Limitation of actions, appeals from suspension or revocation, **Veh 14401**
Limited term, **Veh 12508**
Livestock trailers, towing, restricted licenses, **Veh 12804.14**
Loans to another, **Veh 14610**
Lost, destroyed or mutilated, **Veh 12815**
Mail and mailing,
Alcohol consumption information, **Veh 1666**
Appeal, **Veh 14105.5**
Renewal, **Veh 12814.5**
Manslaughter, **Veh 13361**
Revocation, **Veh 13351**
Manufacture and sale, substantial similarity, **Veh 14610.1**
Marriage, military forces, absence and absentees, expiration, **Veh 12817**
Mechanical recordation, hearing proceedings, **Veh 14104.2**
Medical Care and Treatment, this index
Mentally deficient and mentally ill persons, **Veh 12805**
Military Forces, this index
Modification or change,
Parole and probation, **Veh 14251**
Revocation or suspension, notice, **Veh 13202.5**
Motorcycles, this index
Motorized bicycles, **Veh 12509**
Multiple licenses, **Veh 12511**
Mutilation, surrender, **Veh 12815**
Narcotics, revocation, **Veh 13202**
National guard, **Veh 12814.7**
Instruction permits, **Veh 12509**
Necessity of hearing, **Veh 14101**
Negligence, **Veh 12809**
Point count, determination, **Veh 12810**
Presumptions, **Veh 12810**
Refusal to issue or renew, **Veh 12809**
Respond in damages, proof of ability, filing, **Veh 12810.5**
Restricted license, **Veh 12812**
Nolo contendere, revocation or suspension, **Veh 13103**

MOTOR VEHICLES—Cont'd
Drivers licenses—Cont'd
Nonresidents, **Veh 1810 et seq., 12502, 12503**
Exemption, **Veh 12502**
Medical certificates, **Veh 12502**
Minors, **Veh 12504**
Armed forces, **Veh 12518**
Necessity, **Veh 12503**
Revocation or suspension, **Veh 13363, 13552**
Application of law, **Veh 13205**
Unsatisfied judgment, **Veh 16376**
Notice, **Veh 13950 et seq.**
Aliens, **Veh 12801.9**
Deportation, **Veh 12801.7**
Appeal and review, **Veh 14105.5**
Revocation or suspension, **Veh 14401**
Appearance, reinstatement, **Veh 13365**
Change of address, **Veh 14600**
Children and minors, driving while under the influence of drugs or alcohol, **Veh 12802.5**
Correct violations, **Veh 40303.5, 40610 et seq.**
Driving under the influence, restrictions, **Veh 23662**
Fines and penalties, payment, issuance or renewal, **Veh 12807**
Inventory, depletion, **Veh 1672.3**
License purpose, **Veh 12800.5**
Licensees granted extensions, major code changes affecting traffic laws, **Veh 12814.5**
Mutilation, surrender, **Veh 12815**
Probation, **Veh 13953**
Reexamination, **Veh 13801, 21061**
Registration of voters, **Veh 1679**
Small claims courts, unsatisfied judgments, suspension, **Veh 16370.5**
Suspension of license, dishonored check in payment for fees or fines, **Veh 13364**
Notice of order of suspension or revocation, removal of vehicle, **Veh 22651**
Numbers and numbering,
Accidents, information, exchange, **Veh 20002**
Registration, certificates of title, applications, **Veh 1653.5**
Off highway vehicles, driving while privilege suspended, **Veh 14601 et seq.**
Off street parking facilities,
Attendant, **Veh 14605**
Vehicle operations, license prerequisite, **Veh 12500**
One license in possession, **Veh 12511**
Operation of vehicle,
Off street parking, **Veh 14605**
Without license, **Veh 12500, 40000.11**
Orders at hearings, change or setting aside by department, **Veh 14103, 14106**

MOTOR VEHICLES—Cont'd
Drivers licenses—Cont'd
Owners, duty to determine before permitting use, **Veh 14604, 40000.11**
Paratransit vehicles, **Veh 12517.5**
Parking facility attendant, **Veh 14605**
Parole and probation, **Veh 14250 et seq.**
Conditions, notice, **Veh 13953**
Driving after suspension of license, condition, **Veh 14601 et seq.**
Juvenile court, revocation or suspension of privilege to operate as condition, **Veh 13203**
Notice, **Veh 13950 et seq.**
Restricted license, **Veh 12812, 13352**
Revocation or suspension privilege to operate as condition, **Veh 13203**
Termination, suspension or revocation, **Veh 13555**
Terms and conditions, **Veh 13953**
Peace officers,
Pursuit, examiners and examinations, **Veh 1666.1**
Revocation or suspension, access to records, **Veh 1803.4**
Permitting unlicensed person to drive, **Veh 14606, 14607**
Persons age eighteen to twenty one, revocation or suspension, driving under the influence, **Veh 13352.6**
Education, **Veh 23502**
Photographs, **Veh 12800.5, 12811, 14610**
Physical condition, suspension, duration, **Veh 13556**
Application of law, **Veh 14904**
Physical examinations, **Veh 12804.9, 12814**
School bus drivers, **Veh 12517.2**
Point system, **Veh 12810**
Poison transportation, agricultural hazardous materials transportation, driver certification, **Veh 12804.2**
Police, presentation for examination, **Veh 12951**
Possession, **Veh 12951**
Cancellation, **Veh 14610**
More than one license, **Veh 12511**
Presumption of knowledge, revocation or suspension,
Habitual traffic offenders, **Veh 14601.3**
Notice, certified mail, **Veh 13106**
Prior convictions, record, **Veh 13209**
Private property, employers vehicle, application of law, **Veh 14601**
Privileges and immunities, anatomical gift stickers, false or inaccurate information, **Veh 12811**
Probation officers, signing and verification of application for minors license, **Veh 17701**
Procedure, suspension or revocation, **Veh 13550 et seq.**
Production in court, **Veh 12952**
Proof of ability to respond in damages, negligent drivers, **Veh 12810.5**

MOTOR VEHICLES—Cont'd
Drivers licenses—Cont'd
Prostitution, revocation or suspension, **Veh 13201.5**
Provisional licenses, **Veh 12814.6**
Puerto Rico, convictions, revocation or suspension, **Veh 13352**
Pupils, school bus transporting, **Veh 12516, 12517**
Pursuit, peace officers, examiners and examinations, **Veh 1666.1**
Qualifications, **Veh 12805 et seq.**
Radioactive materials, drivers certificates, **Veh 12524 et seq., 14611**
Railroad engineers or crew members, train accidents or violations, citation against or furnishing license, **Veh 12953**
Railway grade crossing, failure to stop, suspension, **Veh 13201**
Recidivism tracking system, persons driving while intoxicated, **Veh 1821**
Reciprocity, **Veh 15000 et seq.**
Reckless driving, suspension, **Veh 13200, 13201, 13361**
Recommendations, revocation or suspension, **Veh 13208**
Records and recordation,
Confidential or privileged information, **Veh 1807.5, 1808.9**
Hearings, recoding, **Veh 12505**
Public inspection, **Veh 1807.5, 1808**
Reexamination, notice, **Veh 21062, 40313**
Rental, **Veh 14609**
Revocation or suspension, law enforcement officers, access, **Veh 1803.4**
Traffic violations, destruction, time, **Veh 12808**
Reexamination, **Veh 12818, 13800 et seq., 21061**
Alternative procedure, **Veh 13953**
Failure to take, revocation or suspension, **Veh 12819**
Hearings, **Veh 14100 et seq.**
Alternative procedure, **Veh 13953**
Notice, **Veh 13950 et seq.**
Records and recordation, **Veh 21062, 40313**
Refusal, chemical, breath or urine tests, **Veh 13353**
Children and minors, fines and penalties, **Veh 13353.1**
Refusal to issue or renew, **Veh 12805 et seq.**
Hearings, **Veh 14100 et seq.**
Notice, **Veh 13951, 13952**
Registration of voters. Elections, this index
Registration services, **Veh 11400 et seq.**
Reinstatement,
Aliens, deportation, **Veh 12801.7**
Driving under the influence, persons age eighteen to twenty one, **Veh 13352.6**

MOTOR VEHICLES—Cont'd
Drivers licenses—Cont'd
Reinstatement—Cont'd
Fees, **Veh 14904**
Former inmates of correctional institutions, **Veh 12808**
Insurer liable to pay accident judgment, **Veh 16375**
Renewal, **Veh 12800 et seq.**
Ability to respond to damages, **Veh 13350**
After revocation, **Veh 13351**
Aliens, deportation, **Veh 12801.7**
Application, **Veh 12814, 12816**
Certificate,
Blood alcohol concentration information, inclusion in mailing, **Veh 1666**
Payment of fine or appearance, **Veh 12807**
Driving under the influence, declarations, **Veh 13385**
Extension, **Veh 12814**
Fees, **Veh 14900**
Adjustments, **Veh 1678**
Hearings, **Veh 14100 et seq.**
Mail, renewal by, **Veh 12814.5**
Notice, **Veh 13951, 13952**
Operating privilege, **Veh 13351**
Summary of penalty provisions, failure to report accident or prove financial responsibility, **Veh 1656.2**
Reopening questions by department at hearings, **Veh 14103, 14106**
Reports,
Anatomical gifts, registry, **Veh 12811**
Diplomats, exemptions, **Veh 12502**
Driving under the influence, chemical tests, revocation or suspension, **Veh 13380, 13388, 23612**
Legislative reports, **Veh 12814, 12814.5**
Medical certificate of employee, reexamination failure of employee, **Veh 14606**
Revocation or suspension, tour buses, **Veh 1808.1**
Resident, definitions, **Veh 516**
Responding in damages, proof of ability, filing, **Veh 12810.5**
Restricted licenses, **Veh 12812, 12813, 13352, 13353.7**
Alcohol or drug violations, **Veh 13202.5, 13353.2 et seq.**
Ignition interlock devices, installation, **Veh 13352**
Authority of department, **Veh 12813**
Children and minors,
Alcohol or drug violations, **Veh 13202.5**
Concealed weapons, **Veh 13202.4**
Driving under the influence, **Veh 13353.8**
Delay, defacing property, **Veh 13202.6**

MOTOR VEHICLES—Cont'd
Drivers licenses—Cont'd
Restricted licenses—Cont'd
Driving under the influence, **Veh 13352.5, 13353.2 et seq.**
Second and subsequent offenses, **Veh 23540**
Livestock trailers, towing, **Veh 12804.14**
Mental health treatment, **Veh 16077**
Operation in violation of restricted license, **Veh 14603**
Prostitution, convictions, **Veh 13201.5**
Second and subsequent offenses, driving under the influence, **Veh 23540**
Violations, suspension or revocation, **Veh 13360**
Revocation or suspension, **Veh 13100 et seq., 14601.2**
Accident report, failure, **Veh 16004**
Accidents,
Failure of driver to stop, **Veh 13201, 13350, 13361**
Prior conviction for vehicular manslaughter involving alcohol, **Veh 13954**
Affidavits, acknowledging, **Veh 13350**
Alcohol or drug abuse education programs, **Veh 13352 et seq.**
Alcohol or drug violations, **Veh 13202.5**
Driving while suspended, minimum sentence, **Veh 14601.4**
Appeal and review,
Administrative review, **Veh 13557, 13558**
Judicial review, **Veh 13559**
Limitation of actions, **Veh 14401**
Notice, **Veh 14401**
Appearance, failure to appear, **Veh 13365**
Armed forces, member, **Veh 12817**
Arrest,
Driving after, **Veh 14602.6**
Procedure, **Veh 40303**
Assault with deadly weapon, **Veh 13351.5**
Authorization, **Veh 13100**
Canada, convictions, **Veh 13352**
Chemical tests, driving under the influence, **Veh 13380 et seq., 23612, 23614**
Children and minors, driving under the influence,
Refusal to submit to tests, **Veh 13353.1**
Reissuance, fees, **Veh 13392**
Concealed weapons, children and minors, **Veh 13202.4**
Concurrent suspensions, **Veh 13353**
Conditions, reinstatement, **Veh 13368**
Controlled substances, offense, **Veh 13202**
Convicts serving prison sentences, **Veh 41500**

MOTOR VEHICLES—Cont'd
Drivers licenses—Cont'd
  Revocation or suspension—Cont'd
    Court, Veh 13200 et seq.
    Court orders,
      Failure to comply, Veh 13365.5
      Noncompliance, Veh 13365.2
    Deadly weapon, use of vehicle as, Veh 13351.5
    Defacing property, Veh 13202.6
    Definitions, Veh 13100 et seq.
    Delay,
      Driving privilege exercise, defacing property, Veh 13202.6
      Driving under the influence, Veh 23665
    Department, Veh 13350 et seq.
    Discretionary suspension, Veh 13556
    District of Columbia, convictions, Veh 13352
    Driving under the influence, Veh 13201, 13352 et seq., 13380 et seq., 14601.5, 23536 et seq., 23562, 23612, 23660, 23665
      Children and minors, Veh 23136
      Driving while suspended, minimum sentence, Veh 14601.4
      Ignition interlock devices, Veh 23247 et seq.
      Prior conviction, vehicular manslaughter, Veh 13954
      Reinstatement, Veh 13353.4
      Second and subsequent offenses, Veh 23597
    Driving while privilege suspended, impounding, Veh 14602.5, 14602.6
    Drug addicts, Veh 13201
      Rehabilitation, Veh 13352.5
    Emergency driving, Veh 14601.2
    Evidence,
      Civil actions, Veh 40832
      Presumption of knowledge, Veh 13106, 14601.1 et seq.
    Failure of proof to respond to damages, Veh 16484
    Failure to surrender, Veh 13362
    Fees,
      Children and minors, driving under the influence, reissuance, Veh 13392
      Dishonored checks, Veh 13364
      Judgments, failure to satisfy, documents filed, Veh 16370.7
      Notice, Veh 14906
    Felony, commission with motor vehicle, Veh 13350
    Financial responsibility, Veh 13352, 13352.1
    Fines and penalties,
      Driving under the influence, Veh 14601.5
      Driving while privilege suspended, Veh 14601.2
    Flight from peace officers, Veh 2800.1 et seq., 13201

MOTOR VEHICLES—Cont'd
Drivers licenses—Cont'd
  Revocation or suspension—Cont'd
    Forfeitures, vehicles, Veh 14607.4 et seq.
    Fraudulent insurance or liability claims, Veh 13201
    Grounds, Veh 13359, 13361
    Guilty, beginning upon plea, finding or verdict of guilty, Veh 13366
    Habitual offenders, Veh 13350, 14601.3
    Habitual truants, Veh 13202.7
    Hardship permits, driving while intoxicated, Veh 13353.4
    Hearings, Veh 13558, 13950 et seq., 14100 et seq.
    House cars, endorsement, Veh 12804.15
    Impounding vehicle, Veh 14602.6
    Investigations by department, Veh 13800 et seq.
      Conditions, recommendation, Veh 13208
    Judgments, failure to satisfy, Veh 16370 et seq.
      Small claims judgments, Veh 16370.5
    Junior permits, Veh 12514
    Juvenile courts, Veh 13352
    Juvenile delinquents and dependents, Veh 13100 et seq.
      Juvenile facilities division, Veh 41500
      Probation, Veh 13203
    Knowledge, presumptions, Veh 14601.3
    Limitation of actions, appeals, Veh 14401
    Limitation on power of court, Veh 13203
    Manslaughter, Veh 13351, 13361
    Meaning, Veh 13102
    Medical treatment, restricted license, Veh 16077
    Mental condition, Veh 13102
    Narcotic drugs, Veh 13202, 13351
    Nolo contendere, conviction under plea, Veh 13103
    Nonresidents, Veh 13205
      Driving while under influence of alcohol or drugs, Veh 13353.5
      Privilege to operate, Veh 13552
    Notice, Veh 13106, 13950 et seq., 14601.1 et seq.
      Appeal and review, Veh 14401
      Certified mail, Veh 13106
      Children and minors, driving while intoxicated, Veh 13353.1
      Conviction in another state, Veh 13363
      Court orders, failure to comply, Veh 13365.5, 40509, 40509.1
      Driving under the influence, Veh 13380 et seq., 23662

MOTOR VEHICLES—Cont'd
Drivers licenses—Cont'd
  Revocation or suspension—Cont'd
    Notice—Cont'd
      Driving while intoxicated, Veh 13353
      Fees, Veh 14906
      Law enforcement officers, Veh 1803.4
      Mail and mailing, Veh 13106
      Small claims courts, unsatisfied judgments, Veh 16370.5
    Option of officer to take arrested person before magistrate, Veh 40303
    Orders of court,
      Failure to comply, Veh 13365.5
      Noncompliance, Veh 13365.2
    Parole convict, Veh 41500
    Period on suspension by department, Veh 13556
    Persons age eighteen to twenty one, driving under the influence, Veh 13352.6
      Education, Veh 23502
    Physical condition, Veh 13556
      Application of law, Veh 14904
    Point system, Veh 12810
    Possession or display unlawful, Veh 14610
    Presumption of knowledge, Veh 13106, 14601.1 et seq.
      Certified mail, Veh 13106
      Habitual traffic offenders, Veh 14601.3
    Probation, Veh 13203, 14250 et seq.
      Termination, Veh 13555
    Procedure, Veh 13550 et seq.
    Process, service, notice, Veh 13106
    Prostitution, Veh 13201.5
    Provisional licenses, Veh 12814.6
    Public inspection of records, Veh 1808
    Puerto Rico, convictions, Veh 13352
    Railway grade crossing, failure to stop, Veh 13201
    Reckless driving, Veh 13201, 13361
    Recommendations by court, Veh 13208
    Record, Veh 13206
      Law enforcement officers, access, Veh 1803.4
    Reexamination of licensee, Veh 12818
      Alternative procedure, Veh 13953
      Failure to submit, Veh 12819, 13801
      Hearing, revocation or suspension without, Veh 13953
    Refusal, chemical blood, breath or urine tests, Veh 13353
      Children and minors, Veh 13353.1
    Refusal to issue or renew, Veh 12807
    Reinstatement, Veh 13353.4
      Fees, Veh 14904, 14905
      Financial responsibility, Veh 13352, 13352.1
    Renewal, ability to respond to damages, Veh 13350

MOTOR VEHICLES—Cont'd
Drivers licenses—Cont'd
Revocation or suspension—Cont'd
Reports, driving under the influence, chemical tests, **Veh 13380, 13388, 23612**
Request by person assigning and verifying minors application, **Veh 17711**
Responding in damages, submitting proof, negligent drivers, **Veh 12810.5**
Restricted licenses,
Driving while intoxicated, **Veh 13353.2 et seq.**
Medical treatment, **Veh 16077**
Restrictions, violations, **Veh 13360**
Retention of license by court, **Veh 13206**
Return of license to driver, **Veh 13207**
Review, **Veh 14400**
Road rage, **Veh 13210, 13351.8**
School buses, stopping, **Veh 22454.5**
School crossing guard, disregarding, infraction conviction, **Veh 42001.1**
Second and subsequent offenses, alcohol related convictions, **Veh 13954**
Service of process, notice, **Veh 13106**
Small claims judgment unsatisfied, **Veh 16370.5**
Speed contests, **Veh 23109**
Speed violations, **Veh 13200, 13200.5, 13355**
Stay, **Veh 14100**
Student license, **Veh 12653**
Subpoenas, hearings, **Veh 14104.5**
Surrender, **Veh 13206, 13207, 13550, 13551**
Driving under the influence, **Veh 23660**
Termination, mental or physical condition, examination, **Veh 13102**
Tour buses, reports, **Veh 1808.1**
Tow trucks, kickbacks, **Veh 12110, 13351.85**
Truants, habitual truants, **Veh 13202.7**
United States territories or possessions, convictions, **Veh 13352**
Unlawful acts, **Veh 14610**
Unsatisfied judgments, **Veh 16374**
Vandalism, **Veh 13202.6**
Violations, **Veh 40000.11**
Weapons, concealed, children, **Veh 13202.4**
Road rage, revocation or suspension, **Veh 13210, 13351.8**
Sales,
Information, **Veh 1810 et seq.**
Photography and pictures, **Veh 12800.5**
Similar documents, **Veh 14610.1**
Salespersons, license qualifications, **Veh 11802**
School Buses, this index

MOTOR VEHICLES—Cont'd
Drivers licenses—Cont'd
Schools, student licenses, **Veh 12650 et seq.**
Second and subsequent offenses,
Alcohol related convictions, **Veh 13954**
Driving after suspension or revocation, **Veh 14601 et seq.**
Drunken driving, **Veh 13352, 13954**
Revocation, **Veh 13351**
Sibling over age 18, signing and verification of application for minors license, **Veh 17701**
Signatures, **Veh 12802, 12811, 12950**
Applications of minors, civil liability of person signing, **Veh 17700 et seq.**
Comparison on rental of vehicle, **Veh 14608**
Junior permit, **Veh 12513**
Statement of consent, student licenses, **Veh 12650**
Social security numbers, **Veh 1653.5, 12801**
Special construction equipment, **Veh 12521**
Special restricted license, **Veh 12813**
Speed contests, revocation or suspension, **Veh 23109**
Speed violation, suspension, **Veh 13200, 13200.5, 13355**
Stickers, anatomical gifts, **Veh 1672.5**
Student licenses, **Veh 12513, 12650 et seq.**
Studies,
Incompetent persons, examinations to screen, **Veh 12804.8**
License extensions, effects, **Veh 12814.5**
Summary, fines and penalties, failure to report accident or prove financial responsibility, **Veh 1656.2**
Surrender, **Veh 13362**
Cancellation, **Veh 13100, 13551**
Court, **Veh 13202.5**
Driving under the influence, **Veh 23660**
Failure to surrender, **Veh 14610**
Mutilation, **Veh 12815**
Original license on recovery of lost, destroyed or mutilated license, **Veh 12815**
Revocation or suspension, **Veh 13206, 13207, 13550, 13551, 14610**
Student license, **Veh 12653**
Temporary licenses, **Veh 12506**
Children and minors, driving under the influence, **Veh 13388**
Driving under the influence, parole and probation, **Veh 13389**
Rules and regulations, **Veh 12801.8**
Term of renewal, **Veh 12816**
Termination without prejudice, **Veh 13100**

MOTOR VEHICLES—Cont'd
Drivers licenses—Cont'd
Tests, chemical, driving under the influence, **Veh 13380 et seq., 23612, 23614**
Theft, suspension or revocation, **Veh 13357**
Third and subsequent offenses, school buses, stopping, **Veh 22454.5**
Time, **Veh 1669**
Instruction permits, **Veh 12509**
Junior permits, **Veh 12514**
Limited term license, **Veh 12508**
Revocation or suspension, **Veh 13366**
Student license, **Veh 12652**
Tour buses, violations, revocation or suspension, reports, **Veh 1808.1**
Tow trucks, revocation or suspension, kickbacks, **Veh 12110, 13351.85**
Towing livestock trailers, restricted licenses, **Veh 12804.14**
Traffic Rules and Regulations, this index
Traffic safety program, **Veh 2900 et seq.**
Traffic signs and signals, qualifications, **Veh 12805**
Treatment programs, driving under the influence, participation in lieu of execution of sentence, **Veh 13352.5**
Truants, habitual truants, revocation or suspension, **Veh 13202.7**
Unattended vehicles, release, **Veh 22651**
Uncles, signing and verification of application for minors license, **Veh 17701**
United States, officer or employee, exemption, **Veh 12501**
United States territories or possessions, convictions, drivers license revocation or suspension, **Veh 13352**
Unlawful use, **Veh 13800, 40000.11**
Unlicensed nonresident, **Veh 12503**
Urine tests, driving under influence of alcohol or drugs, **Veh 13353**
Validity, signature, **Veh 12950**
Vandalism, delay or suspension of privileges, **Veh 13202.6**
Veterans,
Benefits, applications, **Veh 12811**
Expiration date, **Veh 12817**
Violations, **Veh 14600 et seq.**
Violator schools, **Veh 11200 et seq.**
Vision tests, **Veh 1674 et seq.**
Waiver, **Veh 12814**
Right to hearing, **Veh 14103**
Weapons, this index
Withdrawal of probationary license, **Veh 14252**
Work permits, driving under the influence, **Veh 23538, 23562**
Youth Buses, this index
Driving Schools, generally, this index
Driving under the influence. Traffic Rules and Regulations, this index
Driving while privilege suspended. Drivers licenses, ante

MOTOR VEHICLES—Cont'd
Drug Addicts, this index
Drug and alcohol problem assessment program, **Veh 23249.50**
Drug rehabilitation centers, residents, **Veh 23213**
Drugs and medicine,
  Confidential records, **Veh 1808.5**
  Data and monitoring system, persons driving under influence, **Veh 1821**
  Drivers licenses, ante
  Driving under the influence. Traffic Rules and Regulations, this index
  Investigation, violations, **Veh 13800**
  Marijuana, possession while operating, **Veh 23222**
  Paratransit vehicles, drivers, testing, **Veh 34520.5**
  Possession, conviction of offense, **Veh 12809, 13202**
    Investigation, **Veh 13800**
  Problem assessment program, **Veh 23249.50**
  Records and recordation, **Veh 1803**
    Confidential or privileged information, **Veh 1807.5, 1808.5**
    Repeat offenders, use, conviction of offense, **Veh 13800**
  Reports, **Veh 1803**
  Tests,
    Exemptions, agricultural machinery and equipment, **Veh 40000.15**
    Paratransit vehicles, drivers, **Veh 34520.5**
    Use, conviction of offense, **Veh 12809, 13202**
    Investigation, **Veh 13800**
Dual solid tires, outside measurement, **Veh 27453**
Dune Buggy, generally, this index
Duplicates,
  Certificates of title, ante
  Drivers licenses, ante
  License plates, post
  Registration card or license plate, **Veh 4457 et seq.**
  Salesmens licenses, **Veh 11819**
Duress or coercion, dealers, **Veh 11713.1**
Earplugs, wearing while operating, **Veh 27400**
Economic automobile theft, definitions, prevention, **Veh 10901**
Education,
  Children and minors, passenger restraint systems, **Veh 27360.6**
  Dealers, ante
  Fees, exemptions, **Veh 9102**
  Gifts, devises and bequests, records and recordation, **Veh 1660**
  House cars, **Veh 2429.3**
  Seatbelts, children and minors, **Veh 27360.6**
  Unattended children, **Veh 15620, 15630, 15632**
Eight hundred (800) numbers, trucks transporting workmen, **Veh 2429**

MOTOR VEHICLES—Cont'd
Electric personal assistive mobility devices, **Veh 21280 et seq.**
Electric vehicles,
  Campers, towing, weight fees, **Veh 9400**
    Exemptions, **Veh 9401**
  Parking lots and facilities, designated spaces, **Veh 22511, 22511.1, 42001.6**
  Registration, confidential or privileged information, access, **Veh 1808.23**
  Weight fees, **Veh 9400**
    Exemptions, **Veh 9401**
Electricity,
  Lights and lighting, **Veh 24250 et seq.**
  Turn signals, **Veh 24951**
Electronic communication devices, **Veh 26708**
Electronic devices and equipment, license plates, **Veh 4853**
Electronic lien and title program, **Veh 4450.5**
Electronic mail,
  Infractions, **Veh 23123.5**
  Tow trucks, private property, removal, **Veh 22658**
Electronic recording,
  Accidents, reports, **Veh 1806**
  Drivers licenses, hearings, **Veh 14104.2**
  Records and recordation, **Veh 1801**
Electronic signatures,
  Documents, electronic transmissions, **Veh 1801.1**
  Drivers licenses, **Veh 12950, 12950.5**
Electronic transmissions, documents, **Veh 1801.1**
Eluding peace officers, crimes and offenses, **Veh 2800.1 et seq., 13201**
Emancipated minors, drivers licenses, tort liability, **Veh 17705**
Embezzlement,
  Failure to return leased vehicles, **Veh 10855**
  Registration, renewal, **Veh 4605**
  Removal of parked or standing vehicles, **Veh 22650 et seq.**
  Reports, **Veh 10500 et seq.**
Emergencies, **Veh 40830, 41402**
  Disaster service vehicles, warning lights, **Veh 25259.1, 25259.5**
  Motorist aid system, freeways, **Veh 2421.5**
  Off highway vehicles, peace officers, **Veh 38025**
  Political subdivisions, size and weight limitation exemption, **Veh 35002**
    Inspections, **Veh 34500.2**
  Red lights and sirens, **Veh 30**
  Stopping,
    Airbrakes, **Veh 26508**
    Combination parking brake and emergency stopping system, **Veh 26451**
Emergency roadside services, **Veh 2430 et seq.**
  Unregistered vehicles, towing, liability, **Veh 4000**

MOTOR VEHICLES—Cont'd
Emergency Vehicles, generally, this index
Emissions. Air Pollution, this index
Employer sponsored ridesharing. Car pools, generally, ante
Employment. Labor and employment, generally, post
Endorsement,
  Brokers, **Veh 11700.2**
  Dealers, **Veh 11700.2**
  Drivers licenses, ante
  Hazardous substances and waste, commercial vehicles, drivers licenses, **Veh 15250**
  House cars, drivers licenses, **Veh 12804.10**
  Transfer of title or interest, **Veh 5600 et seq.**
Energy absorption system, **Veh 34700 et seq.**
  Warranties, compliance with federal standards, **Veh 34715**
Energy storing system,
  Airbrakes, **Veh 26508**
  Taillamps, **Veh 24253**
Enforcement of law, **Veh 2400 et seq.**
Engineering and traffic survey, definitions, **Veh 627**
Engines,
  Brakes, operation in case of engine failure, **Veh 26452**
  House cars, manufacture in two or more stages, **Veh 11713.5**
  Installation, **Veh 4163**
    Filing fees, **Veh 9257**
  Manufacturer different from a vehicle manufacturer, **Veh 9980 et seq., 11713.9**
  Notice, new engine and number, **Veh 4161**
  Numbers, **Veh 4161 et seq.**
    Alteration, **Veh 10750, 10751**
  Stolen or embezzled vehicle report, **Veh 10504**
  Transfers, **Veh 4163**
English language, notices and reports, **Veh 9**
Engraved pictures,
  Drivers licenses, **Veh 12800.5, 12811**
  Identification cards, **Veh 13005, 13005.3, 13005.5**
Enhanced advanced technology partial zero emission vehicles, decals, **Veh 5205.5, 21655.9**
Environment, license plates, **Veh 5067, 5075, 5100 et seq.**
Equipment, **Veh 24000 et seq., 25106**
  Alarms, generally, ante
  Antisiphoning devices, ethanol, methanol fuel, **Veh 28110 et seq.**
  Arrest, refusal to stop for inspection, **Veh 40303**
  Axles, generally, ante
  Brakes, generally, ante
  Bumpers, generally, ante

MOTOR VEHICLES—Cont'd
Equipment—Cont'd
Campers,
  Communication device between camper and cab, **Veh 28080**
  Passenger signaling devices, **Veh 28080, 28081**
Chains, generally, ante
Clearance and side marker lamps, vehicles 80 inches or more in length, **Veh 25100**
Color, lamps, **Veh 25106**
Correcting defective equipment, appearance, **Veh 40150**
Cowl or fender lamps, **Veh 25106**
Crimes and offenses, **Veh 40001, 40150**
Data monitors, **Veh 25108**
Doors, generally, ante
Drawbars, generally, ante
Engines, generally, ante
Event data recorders, **Veh 9951**
Exhaust systems, generally, post
Experiments, licenses and permits, **Veh 26106**
Explosives, **Veh 31610**
Farm labor vehicles, **Veh 31400, 31401**
Fenders, generally, post
Fines and penalties, inspection and inspectors, failure to stop, **Veh 42002.1**
Fire extinguishers, recreational vehicles or campers, **Veh 28060**
Fog lamps, generally, post
Glass, generally, post
Horns and sirens, generally, post
Ignition interlock devices, generally, post
Illuminating devices, **Veh 24255**
  Colors and coloring, **Veh 25950**
Inflatable restraint systems, previous deployment, installation, **Veh 27317**
Inspection and inspectors, **Veh 2804, 2806, 2814**
  Arrest, procedure, **Veh 40303**
  Fines and penalties, failure to stop, **Veh 42002.1**
Leases, post
Licenses and permits, experimental use, **Veh 26106**
Lights and lighting, generally, post
Modification or change, **Veh 24008**
  Lighting and signalling equipment, **Veh 26101**
Motorized scooters, **Veh 21223, 21224, 21235**
Off highway vehicles, post
Operation without required equipment, **Veh 24002, 40001**
Parts, generally, post
Purchase of equipment for testing purposes, **Veh 26105**
Rear lamps, generally, post
Recording devices, **Veh 9951**
Recreational vehicles or campers, fire extinguishers, **Veh 28060**

MOTOR VEHICLES—Cont'd
Equipment—Cont'd
Reflectors,
  Front and side, **Veh 24608**
  Red, rear mounting, **Veh 24607**
Rental vehicles, **Veh 24010**
Retesting, **Veh 26105**
Safe driving, teaching devices, dismountable platforms, **Veh 35409**
Safety, refusal of registration, **Veh 4751**
Seatbelts, generally, post
Seats, generally, post
Second and subsequent offenses, inspection and inspectors, failure to stop and submit, **Veh 42002.1**
Sensing and diagnostic modules, **Veh 9951**
Sentence and punishment, inspection and inspectors, failure to stop and submit, **Veh 42002.1**
Special mobile equipment, generally, post
Sunscreening devices, **Veh 26708, 26708.2**
Television and radio, **Veh 27602**
Testing, **Veh 26100 et seq.**
Theft alarm systems, **Veh 25251.4, 28085**
Tinted safety glass, **Veh 26708.5**
Tire traction devices, generally, post
Tires, generally, post
Transparent materials, windshields, **Veh 26708**
Unsafe mechanical condition,
  Fines and penalties, **Veh 42002.1**
  Revocation of license, **Veh 8800**
  Towing vehicle, **Veh 34506.4**
  Unlawful operation, **Veh 24002**
Videotape, **Veh 27602**
Windows, generally, post
Equipment rental yards, inspection, stolen vehicles, **Veh 2805**
Erroneous collection of fees or penalties, refunds, limitations, **Veh 42231, 42232**
Escape from peace officers, crimes and offenses, **Veh 2800.1 et seq., 13201**
Escheat, security deposits under financial responsibility, **Veh 16027**
Escort vehicles, pilot cars, **Veh 472, 27904**
Essential parts, definitions, **Veh 315**
Established place of business, definitions, **Veh 320**
Estimates, liens and incumbrances, abandoned or unclaimed property, **Veh 22670**
Estoppel, dealers, requiring prospective assent, **Veh 11713.2, 11713.3**
Etiologic agents, adoption of United States department of transportation definitions, **Veh 2402.7**
Evading arrest, optional appearance before magistrate, **Veh 40303**
Evasion of fees and taxes, crimes and offenses, **Veh 8804**
Event data recorders, **Veh 9951**

MOTOR VEHICLES—Cont'd
Evidence, **Veh 40800 et seq.**
Abandoned or unclaimed property, presumption, **Veh 22524**
Burden of proof,
  Franchises, post
  Identity and identification, alteration, **Veh 10751**
Certificate of title, criminal proceedings, **Veh 6150 et seq.**
Civil actions, **Veh 40830 et seq.**
Code prosecution, **Veh 40800 et seq.**
Collateral estoppel, civil actions, **Veh 40834**
Confidentiality, records, designated persons, **Veh 1808.9**
Continuance before sentencing, rebuttal of police or traffic officer report, **Veh 40806**
Defective windshield and rear window, nonconforming equipment, **Veh 26710**
Defenses, code violation prosecution, **Veh 41400 et seq.**
Department informational reports, prior convictions, **Veh 42004**
Departmental finding, reports, **Veh 40833**
Disaster Act, inadmissibility, conviction for violation under governors orders or directives, **Veh 40830**
Documents, electronic transmissions, **Veh 1801.1**
Double jeopardy, **Veh 41400**
Drivers licenses, ante
Effect of conviction, civil actions, **Veh 40834**
Electronic transmissions, documents, **Veh 1801.1**
Electronically stored records, original document status, **Veh 1801**
Emergency Services Act, inadmissibility, conviction for violation under governors order or directives, **Veh 40830**
Federal authority, violations under, inadmissibility of convictions, **Veh 40830**
Financial responsibility, accident scene information exchange, **Veh 20002**
Findings of department, reports, **Veh 40833**
Forfeitures, unlicensed drivers, **Veh 14607.6**
Franchises, post
Guilty plea, police reports, **Veh 40806**
Hearing, revocation or suspension of driving privilege, **Veh 40832**
Identification cards, applications, **Veh 13000**
Identity and identification, alteration, **Veh 10751**
Illegal evidence, **Veh 40800 et seq.**
Impounding for evidence, **Veh 22655.5**
Incapacity, drivers licenses, **Veh 21061**

MOTOR VEHICLES—Cont'd
Evidence—Cont'd
Incompetency, obtained by maintenance or use of speed traps or failure to wear uniform, **Veh 40804**
Jurisdictional offenses, speed traps, **Veh 40805**
Negligence,
Departmental findings, reports, **Veh 40833**
Drivers, proof of ability to respond in damages, **Veh 12810.5**
Prima facie presumption, **Veh 12810.5**
Responding in damages, proof of ability, negligent drivers, **Veh 12810.5**
Speed violation, **Veh 40831**
Violations under state or federal authority, **Veh 40830**
Negligence actions, **Veh 40830, 40831**
Nonconforming equipment, defective windshield and rear window, **Veh 26710**
Notice, **Veh 24**
Off highway vehicles, evidences of identification, **Veh 38070 et seq.**
Proof of ownership, verification, **Veh 40900**
Police reports, guilty plea, **Veh 40806**
Presumptions, **Veh 41100 et seq.**
Abandoned or unclaimed property, **Veh 22524**
Drivers licenses, revocation or suspension, notice, **Veh 13106**
Driving after suspension of license, **Veh 14601, 14601.1**
Embezzlement, failure to return leased vehicle, **Veh 10855**
Negligent operation, **Veh 12810**
Prima facie presumption, **Veh 12810.5**
Residency, **Veh 516**
Drivers license purposes, rebuttability, **Veh 12505**
Speed, **Veh 41100**
Towing Vehicle Operators Violation Law, **Veh 41104**
Train of vehicles, failure to follow path of towing vehicle, **Veh 41104**
Prisoner of war status, special license plates, **Veh 5101.5**
Prosecutions under code, **Veh 40800 et seq.**
Purchase by peace officers, repayments, **Veh 42271**
Rebuttal evidence, police reports, **Veh 40806**
Record of license suspension or revocation, **Veh 40807**
Registration, post
Reports,
Accidents, civil actions, **Veh 1806, 20013, 40833**
Police reports on guilty plea, **Veh 40806**
Prior convictions, **Veh 42004**

MOTOR VEHICLES—Cont'd
Evidence—Cont'd
Res judicata, civil actions, **Veh 40834**
Residency, drivers license purposes, **Veh 12505**
Return of stolen vehicle retained as evidence, **Veh 6171, 6172**
Revocation or suspension of driving privilege, record, **Veh 40832**
Second and subsequent offenses, informational reports, **Veh 42004**
Security file, **Veh 40833**
Speed, **Veh 40831, 41100**
Traps, **Veh 40801 et seq.**
Towing vehicle operators violation of law, presumption, **Veh 41104**
Traffic officers,
Distinctive uniform and vehicle, **Veh 40800**
Reports, rebuttal, **Veh 40806**
Train of vehicles failure to follow path of towing vehicle, **Veh 41104**
United States, conviction for violation of code required by federal law, inadmissibility, **Veh 40830**
Weight violations, admissibility, **Veh 35557**
Examiners and examinations,
Dealers, **Veh 11704.5**
Drivers licenses, ante
Paratransit vehicles, drivers certificates, **Veh 12523.5**
Studies concerning, **Veh 12804.8**
Excessive fees or penalties, refunds, limitations, **Veh 42231, 42232**
Excessive towing charges, **Veh 22658**
Excessive width, lights and lighting, exemption, **Veh 25803**
Exclusive use of highways, high occupancy vehicles, **Veh 21655.6**
Exemplary damages,
Children and minors, drivers license, person signing license, **Veh 17709**
Torts, **Veh 17151**
Exemptions,
Advertisements, sales, **Veh 11713.1**
Air pollution, inspection and inspectors, collector vehicles, **Veh 4000.1**
Ambulances, pollution control devices, **Veh 27156.2, 27156.3**
Brakes, stopping distance requirements, **Veh 26457**
Bumpers, **Veh 28071**
Certificate of compliance or noncompliance, air pollution emission standards, transfer of title or interest, **Veh 4000.1**
Signed statement, no modification of system, **Veh 5751.5**
Child passenger restraint systems, **Veh 27363**
Collector vehicles, air pollution, inspection and inspectors, **Veh 4000.1**
Commercial vehicles, drivers licenses, military forces, **Veh 15250**

MOTOR VEHICLES—Cont'd
Exemptions—Cont'd
Daily commuters, nonresidents, registration, **Veh 6700.2 et seq.**
Dealers, ante
Drivers licenses, **Veh 12501 et seq.**
Driving under influence of alcohol or drugs, tests, **Veh 13353**
Emergency vehicles, pollution control devices, **Veh 27156.2, 27156.3**
Equipment, **Veh 25800 et seq.**
Highway construction or maintenance equipment, lights, **Veh 25801**
Inspection and inspectors, agricultural machinery and equipment, **Veh 40000.15**
Lamp requirements of exempt vehicles, **Veh 25803**
License fees, post
Licenses and permits, **Veh 4002 et seq.**
Lighting equipment, **Veh 25800 et seq.**
New vehicles, rules and regulations, **Veh 3051**
Nonresidents, **Veh 6700 et seq.**
Drivers licenses, **Veh 12502**
Off highway vehicles, identification plate or device, **Veh 38010 et seq.**
Official uniform and vehicle, investigating officers, **Veh 40804**
Pest abatement districts, pollution control devices, **Veh 27156.3**
Pollution control devices, **Veh 4000.1, 27156.2, 27156.3**
Publicly owned construction equipment, service charges, **Veh 9261**
Registration, post
Scrap metal processors, vehicle identification number, **Veh 10751**
Seatbelts, **Veh 27315**
Special mobile equipment, lights, **Veh 25800**
Station wagons, weight fees, **Veh 9404**
Stopping distance requirements, **Veh 26457**
Tire tread depth, **Veh 27465**
Tow trucks, length, **Veh 35401**
Traffic officers, distinctive uniform and vehicle, **Veh 40800**
Trailer coaches, registration, **Veh 5353**
Vector control districts, pollution control devices, **Veh 27156.3**
Vehicle verifier, **Veh 675.6**
Vehicles incidently operated or moved over highway, lights and lighting, **Veh 25802**
Weight fees, **Veh 9400**
Vehicles manufactured before designated time, **Veh 9401**
Exhaust systems, **Veh 27150 et seq.**
Certificates and certification, compliance, **Veh 27150.2**
Crimes and offenses, **Veh 40000.15**
Cutouts or bypasses, **Veh 27150**
Definitions, **Veh 425**
Fees, certificates and certification, compliance, **Veh 27150.2**

MOTOR VEHICLES—Cont'd
Exhaust systems—Cont'd
  Identity and identification, certificates and certification, compliance, **Veh 27150.2**
  Inspection, **Veh 24011.7**
  Modification or change,
    Noise, **Veh 27151**
    Whistle tips, **Veh 27150.3**
  Noise standards, **Veh 27150.1 et seq.**
  Nonconforming equipment, sale, transfer, **Veh 24005**
  Off highway vehicles, **Veh 27150, 38365**
  Operation of vehicle to prevent escape of exhaust products, **Veh 27153**
  Report of court action, modification of exhaust systems, **Veh 1803**
  Whistle tips, **Veh 27150.3**
Expenses and expenditures, arrest, issuance of warrant, **Veh 40516**
Experiments, permits, equipment use, **Veh 26106**
Expiration date, registration card, **Veh 4601**
Explosives, this index
Exports and imports,
  Altered identification numbers, **Veh 10803**
  Definitions, **Veh 6161**
  Inspection and cancellation of titles, **Veh 6160 et seq.**
Extension of time. Time, post
Eyes and eyesight, drivers licenses, **Veh 12805**
  Examiners and examinations, **Veh 1674 et seq.**
Factory equipment, advertisements, **Veh 11713.1**
Fail safe systems, air brakes, **Veh 26502**
Fainting spells, persons subject to, drivers licenses, denial, **Veh 12806**
Fair credit reporting, electronic records, **Veh 1806.5**
Fairs and expositions, exemption from registration, **Veh 4003**
False advertising,
  Dealers, **Veh 11713**
  Salespersons, **Veh 11806**
False personation,
  Arrested person, release on promise to appear, **Veh 40504**
  Drivers licenses, **Veh 14610**
    Examinations, impersonating applicant, **Veh 14610.5**
  Evidence procurement, **Veh 42271**
  Identification cards, issuance, renewal, **Veh 13000.1**
  Individual representing self as department of motor vehicles employee, **Veh 25.5**
  Member of highway patrol, **Veh 40000.5**
False reports, theft, **Veh 10501**
False statements. Fraud, generally, post
Family. License plates, post
Family purpose doctrine, **Veh 17708**
  Damages, **Veh 17709**

MOTOR VEHICLES—Cont'd
Farm vehicles. Agricultural Machinery and Equipment, generally, this index
Federal fair credit reporting, electronic records, **Veh 1806.5**
Federal law,
  Defenses, **Veh 41401**
  Evidence of convictions, **Veh 40830**
  Registration, information, **Veh 4465**
Federal motor vehicle safety standards, certificates and certification, **Veh 24011**
Fees,
  Accepting fees, refunds, **Veh 42231, 42232**
  Advertisements, **Veh 11713.1**
  Amount less than one dollar, **Veh 9559**
  Appeal and review, revocation or suspension, **Veh 14907**
  Application for refund, limitations, **Veh 42232**
  Auctions and auctioneers, dealers, **Veh 11713.11**
  Autobrokers, disclosure, **Veh 11713.1**
  Certificates and certification, ante
  Collection, **Veh 14910**
  Commercial vehicles, ante
  Computation, **Veh 9559**
  Congressional medal of honor recipients, exemption, **Veh 9105**
  Continuous trips, **Veh 4003**
  Copies of records, **Veh 1812**
  Correction of violations, **Veh 40611**
  Crimes and offenses,
    Evasion of payment, **Veh 8804**
    Operation without payment, **Veh 40001**
  Dealers, ante
  Delinquent fees, **Veh 9552 et seq.**
    Mailing, **Veh 9557**
    Payment by repossessor, **Veh 9561**
  Disabled veterans, parking placards, **Veh 9105**
  Dishonored checks, payment with, suspension of drivers licenses, **Veh 13364**
  Dismantlers, ante
  Drivers licenses, ante
  Employees,
    Arrest, employer failure to answer charges, **Veh 40005**
    Codefendants, owners, **Veh 40003**
    Dismissal of charges, abstract of records, **Veh 40003**
    Employers failure to answer charges, **Veh 40005**
  Erroneous collection, refunds, **Veh 42231, 42232**
  Exemptions, publicly owned vehicles, **Veh 9103**
  Exhaust systems, certificates and certification, compliance, **Veh 27150.2**
  Failure to pay, cancellation of registration, **Veh 8800**
  Farm labor vehicle certificates, **Veh 12519**

MOTOR VEHICLES—Cont'd
Fees—Cont'd
  Fines and penalties, waiver, **Veh 9562**
  Fleet owner inspection and maintenance stations, stickers, **Veh 2525.12**
  Fleet vehicles, registration, **Veh 5304 et seq.**
  Grape gondolas inspection and certification, **Veh 34501.14**
  Handicapped persons, parking placards, **Veh 22511.55**
  Identification cards, **Veh 14902**
    Adjustments, **Veh 1678**
  Inspection and inspectors, **Veh 9255.2**
    Total loss salvaged and dismantled vehicles, **Veh 5505, 9271**
  Lessor retailers,
    Licenses and permits, **Veh 9262**
    Recovery corporation, consumer protection, **Veh 4456.3**
  License fees, generally, post
  License plates, post
  Liens and incumbrances, post
  Limitation of actions, erroneous fee collections, **Veh 42231, 42232**
  Littering, nuisance, impounding, **Veh 22659.5**
  Local vehicle license fee surcharge, **Veh 9250.12**
  Mailing lists, **Veh 1810, 1811**
  Manufacturers and manufacturing, post
  Mistaken collection, refunds, **Veh 42231, 42232**
  New vehicle dealers, **Veh 3016**
  New vehicles, filing of appeal, protest or petition, **Veh 3050.5**
  Noncompliance notices, administrative service charges, **Veh 4766**
  Nonoperation certificates, filing, **Veh 4604 et seq.**
    Adjustments, **Veh 1678**
  Nonresident daily commuters, identification cards, **Veh 6700.25**
    Adjustments, **Veh 1678**
  Off highway vehicles, post
  Operation without payment, **Veh 40001**
  Paratransit vehicles, certificates, drivers, **Veh 12523.5**
  Parking placards, disabled veterans, **Veh 9105**
  Payment, **Veh 9550 et seq.**
    Checks, **Veh 9558**
  Personal property, storage, **Veh 22851**
  Photographers license plates, **Veh 5008**
  Private party vehicle markets, **Veh 12102**
  Prostitution, nuisance, impounding, **Veh 22659.5**
  Reflectorized license plates, **Veh 4850**
  Refunds, **Veh 42230 et seq.**
  Refusal of registration, **Veh 4750**
  Registration, post
  Rejection of applications, refunds, **Veh 42230**
  Reregistration, **Veh 6050**

MOTOR VEHICLES—Cont'd
Fees—Cont'd
Residents, evasion of payment, **Veh 8804**
Revocation or suspension, appeal and review, **Veh 14907**
Salvage certificates, **Veh 11515, 11568**
Adjustments, **Veh 1678**
Security interest, registration, **Veh 6300**
Service fees, generally, post
Service of process on director for non-residents, **Veh 17454**
Skill test, **Veh 14900, 14900.1**
Adjustments, **Veh 1678**
Special construction equipment certificates, **Veh 12521**
Station wagons, exemption from weight fees, **Veh 9404**
Storage, **Veh 10652.5**
Notice, **Veh 22651**
Title to property, post
Transfer, post
Transporters, post
Vehicle Code, copies, **Veh 1656**
Vehicle registered outside state, **Veh 9252**
Adjustments, **Veh 1678**
Veterans organizations, license plates, special plates, **Veh 5068, 5069**
Youth buses, drivers certificates, **Veh 12523**
Fences, tow trucks, damage, notice, **Veh 22658.1**
Fenders, **Veh 27600**
Cornering lamps, **Veh 25107**
Lights and lighting, **Veh 25100 et seq.**
Fictitious documents, limitation of actions, **Veh 40004**
Fictitious names. Assumed or fictitious names, generally, ante
Fiduciaries, autobrokers, **Veh 11737**
Field test, accident prevention, **Veh 2408**
Fifth wheel travel trailers, connecting device to be securely affixed, **Veh 29000**
Filing,
Arrest, copies of notice to appear, **Veh 40506**
Complaint,
Notice to appear in court, **Veh 40513**
Prosecution of persons owning or controlling vehicles, **Veh 40002**
Counterfeit or fictitious documents, limitation of actions, **Veh 40004**
Documents, electronic transmissions, **Veh 1801.1**
Electronic transmissions, documents, **Veh 1801.1**
Notice to appear, prosecution of persons owning or controlling vehicles, **Veh 40002**
Finance charge,
Advertisements, **Veh 11713.1**
Conditional sales, ante
Financial institutions, address, confidential or privileged information, records and recordation, **Veh 1808.22**

MOTOR VEHICLES—Cont'd
Financial responsibility. Motor Vehicle Insurance, this index
Financial statements and reports, registration, fees, **Veh 9250.14**
Financing agency, bonds (officers and fiduciaries), priorities and preferences, **Veh 11722**
Findings of fact, actions and proceedings, departmental findings, **Veh 40833**
Fines and penalties, **Veh 40000.1 et seq., 42001**
Abandoned vehicles, **Veh 22523**
Additional assessment, disabled person parking violations, **Veh 4461.3**
Air bags, previous deployment, installation, **Veh 27317**
Air pollution control devices, **Veh 27156**
Application for refund, limitations, **Veh 42232**
Application of law, **Veh 40007**
Armored car, red lights, **Veh 25262**
Assessments, night court, **Veh 42006**
Binder chains, theft, **Veh 10851.5**
Bodily injury, **Veh 42001.19**
Bumper strength notices, **Veh 24011.3, 40000.15**
Certificates and certification, ante
Children and minors,
Passenger restraint systems, **Veh 27360.6**
Unattended children, **Veh 15620, 15630**
Chop shops, **Veh 10801 et seq.**
Clean air stickers, forgery, counterfeiting, **Veh 4463**
Commercial vehicles, ante
Compromise and settlement, manufacturers, transporters, dealers and salesmen, **Veh 11707**
Computation of penalty in amounts of less than one dollar, **Veh 9559**
Confidential or privileged information,
Disclosure, **Veh 1808.45, 1808.46**
Records and recordation, **Veh 1808.22**
Contempt, failure to pay fine, **Veh 42003**
Counties, disposition, **Veh 42201**
Dealers, ante
Defacing property, suspension or delay of driving privileges, **Veh 13202.6**
Delinquent fees, **Veh 9553, 9554**
Payment by repossessor, **Veh 9561**
Delinquent renewal, registration, **Veh 9553 et seq.**
Dishonored checks, payment with, suspension of drivers license, **Veh 13364**
Dismantlers, ante
Disposition, **Veh 42200 et seq.**
County owning premises on which violations occur, **Veh 42203**
Drivers licenses, ante
Driving after suspension of license, **Veh 14601 et seq.**
Driving without permission, **Veh 10854**

MOTOR VEHICLES—Cont'd
Fines and penalties—Cont'd
Erroneous collection, refunds, **Veh 42231, 42232**
Excessive penalties, refunds, **Veh 42231, 42232**
Failure to pay, **Veh 40000.25**
Liens and incumbrances, **Veh 14911**
Fees, waiver, **Veh 9562**
Felony convictions, **Veh 42000**
Flight from peace officers, **Veh 2800.1 et seq., 13201**
Foreign registered auxiliary dolly, semi-trailer, or trailer, liens, **Veh 9800**
General misdemeanors, **Veh 42002**
Great bodily injury, **Veh 42001.19**
Guilty plea, consideration of police reports, **Veh 40806**
Habitual traffic offenders, **Veh 14601.3**
Handicapped persons, post
Highway construction zones, **Veh 42009**
Hit and run drivers, **Veh 20001, 20002**
Identification cards, sale or manufacture, similar documents, **Veh 13004.1**
Identifying marks on vehicles, alteration or destruction, **Veh 42002.4**
Ignition interlock devices, **Veh 23247**
Impounding. Traffic Rules and Regulations, this index
Inflatable restraint systems, previous deployment, installation, **Veh 27317**
Infractions, post
Inspection and inspectors, failure to stop, **Veh 42002.1**
Judgment ordering payment or imprisonment, **Veh 42003**
Leaving scene of accident, **Veh 20001**
Lessor retailers, licenses and permits, late renewal, **Veh 11620**
License plates, obstructions, **Veh 5201.1**
Liens, **Veh 9800 et seq.**
Limitation of actions, erroneous collection of penalties, **Veh 42231, 42232**
Local agencies, parking violations, remission of funds, **Veh 4762**
Log books, failure to maintain, **Veh 42001.3**
Manufacturers and manufacturing, post
Marijuana, possession while operating, **Veh 23222**
Mistaken collection, refunds, **Veh 42231, 42232**
Night court assessment, **Veh 42006**
Nonoperation certificates, delinquent filing, **Veh 4604.5**
Off highway vehicles, post
Official misconduct, deposit of funds, **Veh 42202**
Passenger restraint systems, children and minors, accidents, sales, **Veh 27362.1**
Payment of fines, **Veh 42003**
Penalty assessments, night court assessments, **Veh 42006**
Private property, removal, **Veh 22658**

MOTOR

MOTOR VEHICLES—Cont'd

Fines and penalties—Cont'd

Property damage, leaving scene of accident, **Veh 20002**

Provisional licensees, **Veh 12814.6**

Public offenses, **Veh 42000 et seq.**

Radioactive materials, drivers certificates, **Veh 14611**

Records and recordation,

Confidential or privileged information, **Veh 1808.22**

Prior convictions, **Veh 42004**

Refunds, **Veh 42230 et seq.**

Registration, post

Rental agencies, children and minors, passenger restraint systems, **Veh 27365**

Reports, prior convictions, **Veh 42004**

Safety belt systems, sales, failure to comply, **Veh 27315**

Seatbelts, **Veh 27315**

Children and minors, **Veh 27360.6**

Second and subsequent offenses,

Special misdemeanors, **Veh 42001**

Weight limits, violation, **Veh 42030**

Semitrailers, liens, **Veh 9800**

Serial numbers, alteration or destruction, **Veh 42002.4**

Special misdemeanors, **Veh 42001**

Special penalty assessment, night court assessment, **Veh 42006**

Speed contests, **Veh 23109, 23109.1**

Impoundment of vehicle, **Veh 22651.6**

Storage facility owners, refusal to accept vehicle owner credit card, **Veh 22658**

Striking unattended vehicle, failure to stop or comply with requirements, **Veh 20002**

Summary, failure to report accident or prove financial responsibility, **Veh 1656.2**

Supplemental restraint systems, tampering, **Veh 27317**

Suspension or revocation, person without drivers license, **Veh 13553**

Theft, post

Traffic safety fund, disposition, **Veh 42200**

Traffic violators schools, order to attend, **Veh 42005**

Trailers, liens, **Veh 9800**

Transfers, delinquent fees, **Veh 9553.7**

Transmittal of fees by mail, **Veh 9557**

Unattended children, **Veh 15620, 15630**

Unsafe mechanical condition of equipment, **Veh 42002.1**

Vandalism, delay or suspension of driving privileges, **Veh 13202.6**

Veterans, parking, **Veh 42001.13**

Violation or failure to comply with provisions of code, **Veh 42002 et seq.**

Waiver, penalties, auction of repossessed vehicles, renewal fees payment, **Veh 9561**

Weight violations, **Veh 42030, 42031**

MOTOR VEHICLES—Cont'd

Fingerprints and fingerprinting,

Department of, **Veh 1668**

Drivers licenses, **Veh 12800**

Local law enforcement identification programs, registration fees, **Veh 9250.19**

Registration service license application, **Veh 11401**

Fire extinguishers,

Explosives transports, **Veh 31610**

Recreational vehicles and campers, **Veh 28060**

Tow truck equipment, **Veh 27700**

Vanpooling, **Veh 34509**

Firearms. Weapons, this index

Firefighters and Fire Departments, this index

Fires and Fire Protection, this index

Fireworks, commercial vehicles, drivers licenses, revocation or suspension, **Veh 15301**

First stage manufacturers, definitions, house cars, **Veh 11930**

Fitness, unfit vehicles, revocation of license, **Veh 8800**

Fixing bail, magistrate, **Veh 40511**

Flags. Traffic Rules and Regulations, this index

Flammable liquids, **Veh 34001 et seq.**

Flammables, reports, **Veh 1817**

Flange, protuberances on tires, **Veh 27454**

Flares,

Accidents, replacement, **Veh 2419**

Public utility vehicle, **Veh 25301**

Flashing lights. Lights and lighting, post

Fleet vehicles,

Apportioned registration, **Veh 8054, 8057**

Devices, fees, **Veh 9259**

Financial responsibility, registration, **Veh 4000.37, 4000.38, 4750**

Inspection and maintenance stations, **Veh 2525 et seq.**

Notice, **Veh 2800**

Licenses and permits, **Veh 2501, 2505**

Owners and ownership, changes, licenses, **Veh 2503**

Registration, **Veh 5301 et seq.**

Apportionment, liens, enforcement, **Veh 8200 et seq.**

Financial responsibility, **Veh 4000.37 et seq., 4750**

Reports, insurance, **Veh 34633**

Weights and measures, decals, **Veh 9400.1**

Flight from peace officers, crimes and offenses, **Veh 2800.1 et seq., 13201**

Floats, exemption from registration, **Veh 4003**

Fog lamps, **Veh 24403**

Definitions, **Veh 375**

Lighting with other lamps, **Veh 24405**

Taillamps, **Veh 375, 24602**

For sale signs, removal of vehicle, **Veh 22651.9**

MOTOR VEHICLES—Cont'd

Force and violence, dealers, notice, repossessors and repossession, assignments, **Veh 11724**

Foreclosure, liens and incumbrances, **Veh 9801 et seq.**

Foreign countries,

Certificates of title, duplicates, **Veh 4466**

Driving convictions, revocation of license, **Veh 13363**

License plates, post

Removal of parked or standing vehicles, **Veh 22650 et seq.**

Foreign jurisdiction, definitions, **Veh 325**

Foreign purchasers, in transit permits, **Veh 6700.1**

Foreign states,

Certificates of title, ante

Commercial vehicles,

Display of permit, **Veh 4455**

Trip permits, fees, **Veh 9260**

Conviction of traffic offense in foreign state, drivers license revocation, **Veh 13363**

Disabled person placards, **Veh 4463**

Fines and penalties, **Veh 4463.3**

Drivers license, revocation, notice, **Veh 13552**

Exemptions, nonresident, **Veh 6700 et seq.**

False evidence of registration, **Veh 4463**

License plates, post

Liens and incumbrances, registration, **Veh 4306**

Out of service orders, failure to comply, **Veh 2800**

Owner or lessee chargeable, arrest or citation of driver, **Veh 40001**

Refunds, registration, smog impact fees, **Veh 1673 et seq.**

Registration, post

Removal of parked or standing vehicles, **Veh 22650 et seq.**

Notice, **Veh 22853**

Sales and use taxes, registration, **Veh 4300.5**

Service of process, **Veh 17459, 17460, 17461**

Smog impact fees, registration, **Veh 1673 et seq.**

Temporary registration, **Veh 4004**

Title to property in doubt, bond, **Veh 4307**

Foresters, hazardous substances and waste, signs and signals, exemptions, **Veh 27903**

Forests and forestry, irrigation and irrigation districts, machinery and equipment, inspection and inspectors, **Veh 2810.2**

Forfeitures,

Assessments, special penalties, night court assessments, **Veh 42006**

Counties, disposition, **Veh 42201**

Disposition, **Veh 42200 et seq.**

I–106

MOTOR VEHICLES—Cont'd
Forfeitures—Cont'd
Driving after suspension or revocation, **Veh 14607.4 et seq.**
Evidence, unlicensed drivers, **Veh 14607.6**
Infractions, disposition, **Veh 42201.5**
Liens and incumbrances, **Veh 9800 et seq.**
Night court assessments, **Veh 42006**
Notice, unlicensed drivers, **Veh 14607.6, 14607.8**
Official misconduct, deposit of funds, **Veh 42202**
Penalty assessments, night court assessments, **Veh 42006**
Safe Streets Act, **Veh 14607.4 et seq.**
Special penalty assessment, night court assessment, **Veh 42006**
Traffic safety funds, deposits, **Veh 42200**
Forgery,
Certificate of ownership, **Veh 4463**
Evidence procurement, **Veh 42271**
Drivers licenses, evidence, **Veh 42271**
Evidence, **Veh 42271**
Registration, **Veh 4463**
Foreign certificates of title, **Veh 4305**
Handicapped persons, placards, **Veh 4463**
Fines and penalties, **Veh 4463.3**
Identification cards, **Veh 13004**
Limitation of actions, **Veh 40004**
Registration card, evidence, **Veh 42271**
Vehicle identification numbers, **Veh 10802**
Former jeopardy, code violation prosecutions, **Veh 41400**
Forms,
Accident reports, **Veh 1804, 2407, 16000**
Broker agreements, **Veh 11738**
Dealers license application, **Veh 11704**
Franchises, termination, notice, **Veh 3060**
House cars, manufacture in two or more stages, **Veh 11713.5**
Identification cards, **Veh 13005, 13005.5**
Juvenile traffic offenders, reports, **Veh 1816**
License plates, **Veh 4851**
Licenses and permits, **Veh 1652, 11704**
Ambulances and armored cars, **Veh 2502**
Nonresident daily commuters, identification card application, **Veh 6700.3**
Private party vehicle markets, **Veh 12104**
Registration application, **Veh 4150**
Uniform notice to correct violations, **Veh 40610**
Wholesale vehicle auctions, dealer reporting forms, **Veh 4456**
Four wheel drive vehicles, tires, **Veh 27460**
Frame, ground clearance, **Veh 24008.5**
Franchisee, definitions, **Veh 331.1**

MOTOR VEHICLES—Cont'd
Franchises,
Actions and proceedings, **Veh 3065 et seq.**
Additional dealerships, **Veh 3062, 3063**
Administrative appeal, termination, **Veh 3060**
Appeal and review, **Veh 3068**
Incentives, **Veh 3065.1**
Application of law, **Veh 3069**
Assets, sales, **Veh 11713.3**
Assignments, approval, **Veh 11713.2, 11713.3**
Attorney fees, sales, **Veh 11713.3**
Audits and auditors,
Incentives, **Veh 3065.1**
Warranties, **Veh 3065**
Burden of proof,
Incentives, **Veh 3065.1**
Warranties, **Veh 3065**
Cancellation, **Veh 3060 et seq., 11713.13**
Competition, **Veh 11713.3**
Costs, sales, **Veh 11713.3**
Definitions, **Veh 331**
Disclosure, **Veh 11713.1**
Discrimination, **Veh 11713.2, 11713.3**
Disputes, decision, **Veh 3067**
Evidence,
Incentives, **Veh 3065.1**
Warranties, **Veh 3065**
Failure to conduct customary sales, service, termination, **Veh 3060**
Forms, notice, termination, **Veh 3060**
Fraud,
Evidence, **Veh 3066**
Incentives, **Veh 3065.1**
Termination, **Veh 3060**
Warranties, **Veh 3065**
Hearings, **Veh 3060 et seq.**
Incentives, **Veh 3065.1**
Insolvency, termination, **Veh 3060**
Investments, **Veh 3061**
Limitation of actions,
Incentives, **Veh 3065.1**
Warranties, **Veh 3065**
Modification, **Veh 3060 et seq.**
Nonrenewal, **Veh 11713.13**
Notice,
Additional dealerships, **Veh 3062**
Assets, sales, **Veh 11713.3**
Incentives, **Veh 3065.1**
Relocation, **Veh 3062**
Satellite warranty facilities, **Veh 3062**
Termination, **Veh 3060**
Warranties, **Veh 3065**
Powers and duties, **Veh 3064**
Product liability, **Veh 3064**
Protests, **Veh 3050, 3060**
Additional dealerships, **Veh 3062**
Incentives, **Veh 3065.1**
Participation, **Veh 3066**
Relocation, **Veh 3062**
Warranties, **Veh 3065**
Relocation, **Veh 3062, 3063**
Renewal, refusal, **Veh 11713.2, 11713.3**
Replacement, **Veh 3060 et seq.**

MOTOR VEHICLES—Cont'd
Franchises—Cont'd
Sales, **Veh 11713.3**
Satellite warranty facilities, **Veh 3062**
Termination, **Veh 3060 et seq., 11713.13**
Threats, cancellation, **Veh 11713.1**
Warranties, **Veh 3065**
Satellite warranty facilities, **Veh 3062**
Franchisor, definitions, **Veh 331.2**
Fraud, **Veh 20, 31, 40000.5**
Advertisements, **Veh 11713**
Alteration, certificate of ownership, **Veh 4463**
Applications or documents, **Veh 1652**
Commercial vehicles, drivers licenses, **Veh 15309**
Confidential information, obtaining or disclosing, **Veh 1808.45, 1808.46**
Dealers and manufacturers, **Veh 11711**
License revocation, **Veh 11705**
Definitions, license revocation, **Veh 11705**
Drivers licenses, ante
Evidence, **Veh 42271**
Registration, **Veh 4463**
Foreign certificates of title, **Veh 4305**
Franchises, ante
Handicapped persons, certification, special parking permits, **Veh 22511.58**
Identification cards, issuance, renewal, **Veh 13000.1**
Identification or serial numbers, acquisition, possession or sale, **Veh 10752**
Lessor retailers, **Veh 11614**
Suspension or revocation of license, **Veh 11613**
License revocation, special licenses, **Veh 2541 et seq.**
Liens and incumbrances, crimes and offenses, **Veh 22852.5**
Limitation of actions, **Veh 40004**
Mileage statements, intent, **Veh 5900**
Odometers, **Veh 28050.5, 28051**
Refusal of registration, **Veh 4750**
Registration, certificate of ownership, cancellation, suspension or revocation, **Veh 8800**
Theft, **Veh 10501**
Vehicle identification numbers, falsifying, **Veh 10802**
Vehicle verifiers, **Veh 11305**
Free merchandise or gifts, promotions, **Veh 11713.1**
Freeways,
Commercial vehicles, emergencies, fees, **Veh 9250.10**
Definitions, **Veh 332**
Frequent use of vehicle, investigations of drivers, **Veh 13802**
Front bumpers, projection, restrictions, **Veh 35408**
Front end assembly, definitions, **Veh 5505**
Front lights, **Veh 25100**
Front of vehicle, reflectorized material, **Veh 25500**

MOTOR

MOTOR VEHICLES—Cont'd

Fuel. Motor Vehicle Fuel, generally, this index

Full faith and credit, foreign certificate of title, **Veh 4304**

Funds,
Abandoned vehicle trust fund, **Veh 9250.7**
Consumer protection, recovery fund, **Veh 12200 et seq.**
Off highway vehicles, post
Recovery fund, consumer protection, **Veh 12200 et seq.**
Specialized license plate fund, **Veh 5157**

Funeral escort vehicles, color, regulation, **Veh 27605**

Funeral processions, flashing lights, **Veh 25251**

Fusees,
Disabled vehicles, **Veh 25300, 25305**
Explosives, vehicle transporting, restriction, **Veh 31610**
Public utility vehicle, **Veh 25301**
Red light, warning signal, **Veh 25305**
Utility vehicles, **Veh 25301**
Warning signals or devices, **Veh 25300 et seq.**

Gantry truck, definitions, **Veh 335**

Garages, generally, this index

Garbage and refuse. Traffic Rules and Regulations, this index

Gas and oil pipelines, construction and maintenance, flashing amber lights, **Veh 25260.1**

Gas stations. Motor Vehicle Service Stations, generally, this index

Gas tanks,
Auxiliary gas tank evaporative loss control device, installation, **Veh 27156.1**
Caps, **Veh 27155**

Gasoline stations. Motor Vehicle Service Stations, generally, this index

Gauges, vacuum gauge, vacuum or vacuum assisted brakes, **Veh 26520**

Gifts, devises and bequests,
Charities, records and recordation, **Veh 1660**
Education, records and recordation, **Veh 1660**
Nonprofit organizations, records, **Veh 1660**
Religious organizations and societies, records and recordation, **Veh 1660**

Glaring lights, acetylene headlamps, **Veh 25452**

Glass,
Removal by tow truck operators, **Veh 27700**
Safety material, **Veh 26701 et seq.**
Service contracts, **Veh 12800 et seq.**
Tinted safety glass, **Veh 26708.5**
Nonconforming equipment, sales, **Veh 24005**

Global positioning system, windshields, obstruction of view, **Veh 26708**

MOTOR VEHICLES—Cont'd

Gold Star Families, special plates, **Veh 5156, 5157**

Golf Carts, generally, this index

Goods, wares and merchandise, dealers, rates and charges, disclosure, **Veh 11713.19**

Governmental tort liability, **Veh 17000 et seq.**

Grease, tow truck operator covering with dirt, **Veh 27700**

Ground clearance, frame, **Veh 24008.5**

Guaranteed traffic arrest bail bond certificate, commercial vehicles, nonresidents, **Veh 40305.5**

Guardian and ward,
Accident reports, disclosure, **Veh 20012**
Drivers licenses, ante
Sales, application of law, **Veh 12121**

Gunpowder, transportation of smokeless powder, **Veh 31619**

Habitual traffic offenders, **Veh 14601.3**
Affidavits acknowledging, **Veh 13350 et seq.**

Ham radio operators, license plates, **Veh 5005**

Handicapped persons,
Accident reports, **Veh 16003**
Incapacity, **Veh 20010**
Audits and auditors, parking, placards, **Veh 1825**
Cancellation, parking placards, **Veh 22511.56**
Destruction, parking placards, **Veh 22511.56**
Drivers licenses, suspension, duration, **Veh 13556**
Fines and penalties,
Parking, **Veh 42001.13**
Placards, **Veh 4461 et seq.**
Flashing amber lights, nonprofit organizations, **Veh 25276**
Fraud, certification, **Veh 22511.58**
Investigations, **Veh 13953**
Leasing vehicles, conditions, **Veh 14608**
License plates, post
Offstreet parking facilities, removal of unauthorized vehicles, civil liability, **Veh 22652.5**
Paratransit Vehicles, generally, this index
Parking. Traffic Rules and Regulations, this index
Records and recordation, confidential information, **Veh 1808.5**
Theft, enhanced sentences, **Veh 10851, 42002.5**
Traffic Rules and Regulations, this index
Weight fees, exemptions, **Veh 9410**

Handlebars, position of equipment, **Veh 27801**

Hardship permits. Drivers licenses, post

Hauled vehicles, registration, exemption, **Veh 4009**

MOTOR VEHICLES—Cont'd

Have a heart, be a star, help our kids license plates, **Veh 5072**

Hazardous substances and waste,
Drivers licenses,
Age, **Veh 12515, 40000.11**
Commercial vehicles, endorsements, **Veh 15250**
Driver certification, **Veh 12804.2**
Nonresidents, **Veh 12502**
Spill response vehicles, warning lights, **Veh 25260.4**
Transportation, age, drivers, **Veh 12515, 40000.11**

Hazards, turn signal lamps, **Veh 25251**

Headlights, **Veh 24400 et seq.**
Acetylene, **Veh 25450 et seq.**
Arrangement for selection between distributions of light, **Veh 24406**
Emergency vehicles, upper beam headlamps, alternate flashing, **Veh 25252.5**
Exempt vehicles, **Veh 25803**
Mounting and aiming requirements and specifications, **Veh 24012**
Off highway driving, **Veh 24411**
Parking lamps, driving while lighted, **Veh 24800**
Restriction on lighting with additional lamps, **Veh 24405**
Single distribution of light, **Veh 24410**
Upper beam, alternate flashing, emergency vehicles, **Veh 25252.5**

Headsets, wearing while operating, **Veh 27400**

Hearings,
Abatement and removal, abandoned, wrecked, local ordinances, **Veh 22660 et seq.**
Additional dealership or relocation of existing dealership, protest, **Veh 3062**
Disposition,
Liens and incumbrances, **Veh 22851.8**
Serial or identification number destroyed, **Veh 10751**
Impounding,
Release, **Veh 14602.6, 14602.7, 22850.5**
Repossessors and repossession, **Veh 23118**
Lessor retailers, revocation or suspension of license, **Veh 11605**
Littering, nuisance, impounding, **Veh 22659.5**
Poststorage hearings, **Veh 22852**
Prostitution, nuisance, impounding, **Veh 22659.5**
Removal from highway, **Veh 22650**
Revocation or suspension of licenses,
Evidence and civil actions, **Veh 40832**
Salespersons, **Veh 11806**
Subpoenas, duces tecum, **Veh 14104.5**

Heart disease, blood tests, driving under influence of alcohol or drugs, exemptions, **Veh 13353**

MOTOR VEHICLES—Cont'd

Heavy vehicle tax, nonpayment, refusal of registration, **Veh 4750**

Height. Traffic Rules and Regulations, this index

Helmets, off highway vehicles, **Veh 38601**

Hemophilia, blood tests, exemption, driving under influence of alcohol or drugs, **Veh 13353**

High beam, dimming for approaching vehicles, **Veh 24409**

High occupancy vehicles, exclusive or preferential use of highway, **Veh 21655.6**

Highway and Bridge Districts, this index

Highway authorities, flashing and colored lights, **Veh 25256**

Highway Patrol, this index

Historic Vehicles, generally, this index

Hit and Run Drivers, generally, this index

Hitch or coupling, towing, mounting, **Veh 29002**

Homicide, this index

Horns and sirens, **Veh 27000 et seq.**
  Amplification devices, **Veh 27007**
  Off highway vehicles, **Veh 38375**
  Public policy, **Veh 30**
  Removing vehicles, **Veh 22651.5**
  Standards and specifications, adoption and enforcement, **Veh 26103**
  Theft, alarms, **Veh 28085**

Horsepower ratings, advertisements, **Veh 9950, 9952**

Hoses, nonconforming equipment, sales, **Veh 24005**

House cars,
  Amber lights, **Veh 25100**
  Amber reflectors, **Veh 24608**
  Definitions, **Veh 362**
  Education, safety, **Veh 2429.3**
  Intoxicating liquors, open containers, **Veh 23225, 23229**
  Lamps, exterior, entrances and exits, **Veh 25105**
  Length, **Veh 35400**
  Misrepresentation, manufacture in two or more stages, **Veh 11713.5**
  Towing trucks, lights and lighting, warning lights, **Veh 25263**
  Warranties, dealers, list and copies, provision to purchasers, **Veh 11931**

Housing authorities, traffic rules and regulations, **Veh 21113**

Humboldt County, abandoned vehicle trust fund, allocation, **Veh 22710**

Husband and wife, tort liability, **Veh 17150.5**

Hybrid vehicles, low emission vehicles, decals, **Veh 5205.5**
  Forgery, counterfeiting, **Veh 4463**

Hydraulic actuators in lieu of power brakes, **Veh 26301**

Hydraulic booms or masts, restraint, **Veh 35251**

Ice and Snow, generally, this index

Ice cream trucks, vending, **Veh 22456**

MOTOR VEHICLES—Cont'd

Identifiable vehicle component, definitions, theft, **Veh 2805**

Identification cards, **Veh 13000 et seq.**
  Address, change, **Veh 13007**
  Age, verification, **Veh 13007.5**
  Aged persons, **Veh 13000, 13005.3**
    Fees, **Veh 14902**
  Aliens,
    Deferred action for childhood arrivals, **Veh 13001**
    Deportation, **Veh 12801.7**
  Alteration, **Veh 13004**
  Anatomical Gifts, this index
  Applications,
    Anatomical gifts, **Veh 12811**
    Citizens and citizenship, evidence, **Veh 12801.5**
  Assumed or fictitious names, issuance, renewal, **Veh 13000.1**
  Bids and bidding, processing, **Veh 13005**
  Birth certificates, fraud, **Veh 13007.5**
  Cancellation, **Veh 13008**
    Aliens, deportation, **Veh 12801.7**
  Census, verification of age, **Veh 13007.5**
  Citizens and citizenship, evidence, **Veh 12801.5**
  Community service, sale or manufacture, similar documents, **Veh 13004.1**
  Confidential or privileged information, records, **Veh 1808.9**
  Contents, **Veh 13000**
  Contributions, anatomical gifts, registry, **Veh 12811**
  Counterfeiting, **Veh 13004**
  Crimes and offenses, **Veh 4462, 40000.7, 40000.11**
    Acquisition, possession, or sale to prejudice, damage or defraud, **Veh 10752**
    Alteration, **Veh 13004**
    Obtaining cards for unauthorized persons, **Veh 14610.7**
    Sale or manufacture, similar documents, **Veh 13004.1**
  Dealers, special equipment, **Veh 5016 et seq.**
  Destruction of records, **Veh 13002**
  Documentary evidence of age and identity of applicant, **Veh 13000**
  Duplicates, **Veh 13003**
  Engraved pictures, **Veh 13005, 13005.3, 13005.5**
  Expiration, **Veh 13002**
  False personation, issuance, renewal, **Veh 13000.1**
  Fees, **Veh 14902**
    Adjustments, **Veh 1678**
  Fines and penalties, sale or manufacture, similar documents, **Veh 13004.1**
  Forgery, **Veh 13004**
  Forms, **Veh 13005**
    Anatomical gifts, registry, **Veh 12811**
  Fraud, **Veh 13004**

MOTOR VEHICLES—Cont'd

Identification cards—Cont'd
  Fraud—Cont'd
    Issuance, renewal, **Veh 13000.1**
  Indigent persons, fees, **Veh 14902**
  Internet, renewal, **Veh 13002.1**
  Invalid, surrender, **Veh 13000.1**
  Inventory, depletion, **Veh 1672.3**
  Issuance,
    Drivers licenses, **Veh 14900.5**
    Refusal, **Veh 13000.1**
  Legal residency, evidence, **Veh 12801.5**
  Mail and mailing, renewal, **Veh 13002.1**
  Manufacturers and manufacturing,
    Similar documents, **Veh 13004.1**
    Special equipment, **Veh 5016 et seq.**
  Mutilation, surrender, **Veh 13003**
  Notice,
    Inventory, depletion, **Veh 1672.3**
    Mutilation, surrender, **Veh 13003**
  Photography and pictures, sales, **Veh 13005.5**
  Production to avoid possibility of alteration or reproduction, **Veh 13005**
  Records,
    Confidentiality, **Veh 1808.9**
    Destruction, **Veh 13002**
  Renewal,
    Mail and mailing, **Veh 13002.1**
    Refusal, **Veh 13000.1**
  Reports, anatomical gifts, registry, **Veh 12811**
  Sales,
    Photography and pictures, **Veh 13005.5**
    Similar documents, **Veh 13004.1**
  Social security numbers, **Veh 1653.5**
  Special equipment, **Veh 5014 et seq.**
  Stickers, anatomical gifts, **Veh 1672.5**
  Surrender, mutilation, **Veh 13003**
  Tort liability, **Veh 13006**
  Unlawful possession, **Veh 4462, 40000.7**

Identity and identification,
  Advertisements, **Veh 11713.1**
  Alteration or destruction, **Veh 10750, 10751, 40000.9**
  Cards. Identification cards, generally, ante
  Certificates of title, applicants for copies, **Veh 4466**
  Driver, accidents, **Veh 20006**
  Drivers licenses, ante
  Exhaust systems, certificates and certification, compliance, **Veh 27150.2**
  Fee, **Veh 14902**
  Lamps, commercial vehicles and common carriers, **Veh 25350, 25351**
  License plates, applicants for duplicates, **Veh 4466**
  Marks, alteration or destruction, **Veh 10750, 10751**
    Fines and penalties, **Veh 42002.4**
  Nonresident daily commuters, registration exemption, **Veh 6700.25**

MOTOR VEHICLES—Cont'd
Identity and identification—Cont'd
Numbers and numbering,
Accident scene information exchange, **Veh 20002**
Acquisition, possession, or sale to prejudice, damage or defraud, **Veh 10752**
Alteration, counterfeiting, **Veh 10802**
Remanufactured vehicles, crimes and offenses, **Veh 11713.8**
Removal of identifying marks, fines and penalties, **Veh 42002.4**
Ignition interlock devices, **Veh 23247 et seq., 23573, 23575**
Certificates and certification, **Veh 13386**
Drivers licenses,
Driving while privilege suspended, **Veh 14601 et seq.**
Restricted licenses, **Veh 13352, 13353.3**
Driving under the influence. Traffic Rules and Regulations, this index
Revocation or suspension, certificates and certification, **Veh 13386**
Second and subsequent offenses, **Veh 14601.2**
Tampering, **Veh 13386**
Illegal evidence, **Veh 40800 et seq.**
Illegible registration card or license plate, **Veh 4457 et seq.**
Illness, family members, junior permits, **Veh 12513**
Illuminating devices, **Veh 24255**
Colors and coloring, **Veh 25950**
Illumination of other moving vehicles, spotlamps, **Veh 24404**
Immediate removal, towing, **Veh 22953**
Immigration. Aliens, generally, ante
Implements of husbandry. Agricultural Machinery and Equipment, generally, this index
Implied consent, service of process, nonresidents, **Veh 17451 et seq.**
Imports. Exports and imports, generally, ante
Impounding. Traffic Rules and Regulations, this index
Imputed negligence,
Children and minors, **Veh 17707**
Owners, **Veh 17150 et seq.**
In transit permits, foreign purchasers, **Veh 6700.1**
Inability of driver to report accident, **Veh 20010**
Incentives,
Autobrokers sales, dishonor, **Veh 11713.3**
Franchises, **Veh 3065.1**
Sales, **Veh 11713.1**
Index, records, **Veh 1800**
Indians, license fees, exemptions, **Veh 9104.5**
Indicators,
Beam indicator, equipment, **Veh 24408**
Turn signal, pilot indicator, **Veh 25108**

MOTOR VEHICLES—Cont'd
Indictment and information, speed violations, **Veh 40503**
Indigent persons, identification cards, fees, **Veh 14902**
Infants. Children and minors, generally, ante
Inflatable restraint systems, previous deployment, installation, **Veh 27317**
Information,
Accidents, exchange, **Veh 20002**
Arrest, magistrates copy, **Veh 40505**
Credit scores, dealers, **Veh 11713.20**
Keys, **Veh 9954**
Recording devices, disclosure, **Veh 9951**
Registration, post
Infractions,
Abandoned or unclaimed property, failure to redeem after impound, **Veh 22523**
Accident scene information exchange violations, **Veh 20002**
Arrests, procedure, **Veh 40306**
Assessments, special penalties, night court, **Veh 42006**
Bail, **Veh 40307, 40510, 42201.5**
Certificate of adjudication, failure to appear or pay fine, **Veh 40509**
Clean air stickers, forgery, counterfeiting, **Veh 4463**
Clerks of court, acceptance of bail, **Veh 40307**
Commercial vehicles,
Household goods carriers, **Veh 2810.1**
Weights and measures, **Veh 4000.6**
Complaint, **Veh 40306**
Contempt, impounding license and ordering person not to drive, **Veh 40508**
Definitions, **Veh 40000.1, 40000.3**
Displaying merchandise on freeway, **Veh 22520.5**
Disposition of fines and forfeitures, **Veh 42201.5**
Drivers license,
Examinations, crib sheets or impersonating applicant, **Veh 14610.5**
Impoundment, **Veh 40508**
Failure to appear, certificate of adjudication, **Veh 40509**
Fines and penalties, **Veh 42001, 42001.8**
Disposition, **Veh 42201.5**
Payment, **Veh 40508, 42003**
Forfeitures, disposition, **Veh 42201.5**
Highway construction zones, **Veh 42009**
Horse power, advertisements, **Veh 9952**
Impoundment of licenses, **Veh 40508**
Jails, acceptance of bail by officer in charge, **Veh 40307**
Judgment ordering payment of fine, **Veh 42003**
Liquefied petroleum gas propulsion systems, regulation violations, **Veh 2402.6**
Natural gas propulsion systems, regulation violations, **Veh 2402.6**

MOTOR VEHICLES—Cont'd
Infractions—Cont'd
Night court assessments, **Veh 42006**
Payment of fines, **Veh 42003**
Penalty assessments, night court assessments, **Veh 42006**
Record of prior conviction, reports, **Veh 42004**
Release on own recognizance, **Veh 40307**
Rental agencies, children and minors, passenger restraint systems, **Veh 27365**
Reports, prior convictions, **Veh 42004**
Sales on freeway, **Veh 22520.5**
Second and subsequent offenses, **Veh 42001**
Reports, **Veh 42004**
Solicitations on freeway, **Veh 22520.5**
Special penalty assessments, night court assessment, **Veh 42006**
Towing unregistered disabled vehicle, **Veh 40006**
Traffic violator schools, court order to attend, **Veh 42005**
Studies, **Veh 42005.1**
Transfer of title or interest, **Veh 5602**
Unavailability of magistrate, bail, **Veh 40307**
Violation of written promise to appear, misdemeanor, **Veh 42003**
Waiver of continuance for preparation of defense, **Veh 40306**
Waste tire haulers, failure to register, **Veh 31560**
Weights and measures, commercial vehicles, **Veh 4000.6**
Inherently low emission vehicles, decals, **Veh 5205.5**
Forgery, counterfeiting, **Veh 4463**
Injunction,
Damage control equipment, **Veh 34725**
Licenses and permits, failure to comply with law, **Veh 11726**
Occupational licenses, practices, **Veh 1651.2**
Registration, **Veh 6051**
Safety regulations, violations, **Veh 34511**
Injuring vehicle, violations, **Veh 40000.9**
Inoperative vehicles, removal, **Veh 22650 et seq.**
Insolvency, franchises, termination, **Veh 3060**
Inspection and inspectors,
Abstracts of accident reports, **Veh 1808**
Air Pollution, this index
Arrest, refusal to stop, **Veh 40303**
Collector vehicles, air pollution, exemptions, **Veh 4000.1**
Commercial vehicles, ante
Confidential and privileged information, records and recordation, address of inspector, **Veh 1808.2**
Contracts, **Veh 2420.5**
Crimes and offenses, **Veh 40000.7**

MOTOR VEHICLES—Cont'd
Inspection and inspectors—Cont'd
Crimes and offenses—Cont'd
Safety inspection stickers, commercial vehicles, **Veh 2813.5, 40000.7**
Dismantled vehicles, **Veh 5505, 9271**
Drivers licenses or registration information, **Veh 1810 et seq.**
Emissions, **Veh 2814.2**
Equipment, ante
Exemptions, agricultural machinery and equipment, **Veh 40000.15**
Exhaust and noise emission control, **Veh 24011.7**
Explosives, highway transportation, **Veh 31602, 31607 et seq.**
Failure to stop and submit, **Veh 2800, 40000.7, 42002.1**
Option of officer to take arrested person before magistrate, **Veh 40303**
Farm labors, **Veh 31401**
Fees, **Veh 9255.2**
Total loss salvaged vehicles and dismantled vehicles, **Veh 5505, 9271**
Fines and penalties, failure to stop and submit, **Veh 42002.1**
Fleet owner inspection and maintenance stations, **Veh 2525 et seq.**
Grape gondolas, **Veh 34501.14**
Hit and run accident, removal from highway for, **Veh 22655**
Information pamphlet, registration, **Veh 4000.3**
Irrigation and irrigation districts, machinery and equipment, public lands, **Veh 2810.2**
Leased vehicles, safety standards, **Veh 24010**
Lessor retailers, customers, notice, right, **Veh 11609.5**
Mechanical condition, **Veh 2814**
Paratransit vehicles, **Veh 34501.17**
Safety, **Veh 34501.8**
Private party vehicle market records, **Veh 12103**
Records and recordation, **Veh 1808**
Mileage, public inspection, **Veh 1819**
Stored vehicles, **Veh 10650**
Sales, prospective customers rights, notice, **Veh 11709.1**
Scales and weighing instruments, **Veh 2809**
Specially constructed vehicles, registration, emissions, **Veh 4750.1**
Stickers, **Veh 2420.5**
Stored vehicles, **Veh 10656**
Total loss salvaged vehicles, **Veh 5505, 9271**
Vanpooling, safety, **Veh 34509**
Windshield and rear windows, **Veh 26710**
Installation,
Defective parts, **Veh 12000 et seq.**
Engine or motor, filing fees, **Veh 9257**
Equipment not conforming with code, **Veh 24005**

MOTOR VEHICLES—Cont'd
Installation—Cont'd
Exhaust systems violating noise regulations and standards, crimes and offenses, **Veh 27150.1**
Licenses, **Veh 2501 et seq.**
Installment payments, dealers, goods or services, rates and charges, **Veh 11713.19**
Installment sales, payments, judgments, financial responsibility, **Veh 16379 et seq.**
Instant messages, infractions, **Veh 23123.5**
Institute Safety Code, glazing material standard, **Veh 26704**
Instruction for installation, lighting equipment, **Veh 24006**
Instruction permits, **Veh 12509**
Provisional licenses, **Veh 12814.6**
Instrument lamps, unauthorized equipment, **Veh 24003**
Insurance. Motor Vehicle Insurance, generally, this index
Intent, larceny, **Veh 10851**
Interest, autobroker trust accounts, **Veh 11737**
Interference with control of vehicle, photography and pictures, sound recordings, crimes and offenses, **Veh 40008**
Interior lamps, **Veh 24003**
International registration plan, commercial vehicles, fees, apportionment, **Veh 9250.15**
Internet, identification cards, renewal, **Veh 13002.1**
Intersections. Traffic Rules and Regulations, this index
Interstate commerce, fleet owner inspection and maintenance stations, **Veh 2525.4**
Interstate commerce commission, violations required by regulations, defenses, **Veh 41401**
Inventory, drivers licenses, identification cards, depletion, **Veh 1672.3**
Investigating traffic officers, distinctive uniform and vehicle, exemption, **Veh 40800, 40804**
Investigations,
Accidents, **Veh 2412**
Confidential and privileged information, records and recordation, address of investigator, **Veh 1808.2**
Dealer complaints, **Veh 3051 et seq.**
Dismantler violations, duties of department, **Veh 1662**
Dismantlers,
Fees, **Veh 9263**
License applications, **Veh 11504**
Drivers by department, **Veh 13800 et seq.**
Drivers licenses, ante
Impounding vehicles, **Veh 22655**
Lessor retailers, licensing, **Veh 11602**

MOTOR VEHICLES—Cont'd
Investigations—Cont'd
License applications, manufacturers, transporters, dealers, and salesmen, **Veh 11704**
Traffic officers, leased vehicles, name of lessee, **Veh 4453.6**
Invoice, advertisements, **Veh 11713.1**
Involuntary transfer of title or interest, notice, **Veh 5909**
Irrigation and irrigation districts, machinery and equipment, public lands, inspection and inspectors, **Veh 2810.2**
Irritating materials, adoption of United States department of transportation definitions, **Veh 2402.7**
Issuance, warrants for arrest, **Veh 40514 et seq.**
Jails, bail infraction or misdemeanor cases, **Veh 40307**
Jamming devices (speed), **Veh 28150, 40000.15**
Jeeps, places of business, display, licenses and signs, application of law, **Veh 11709**
Joint and several liability,
Damage to highways or bridges, **Veh 17301**
Family purpose doctrine, **Veh 17708**
Joint defendants, owners and operators, **Veh 4001 et seq.**
Joint tenants,
Off highway vehicles subject to identification, **Veh 38045**
Registration, **Veh 4150.5**
Transfer of title or interest, **Veh 5600.5**
Joy Riding Law, **Veh 10851**
Judgments and decrees,
Ability to pay, **Veh 42003**
Arrest warrants, issuance for failure to comply, **Veh 40514**
Code violations, **Veh 42003**
Fines and penalties, payment or imprisonment, **Veh 42003**
Leased vehicles, liens and incumbrances, delinquent fees, fines, penalties and interest, **Veh 9805**
Lessor retailers, revocation or suspension of license, **Veh 11604**
Lien enforcement, **Veh 9805 et seq.**
Salespersons, unpaid judgment, license qualifications, **Veh 11802**
Speeding violations, speed trap evidence, **Veh 40805**
Uninsured motorists, reduction, **Veh 17200 et seq.**
Unsatisfied judgments,
Financial responsibility, suspension, **Veh 16250, 16251**
Licenses and permits, suspension, **Veh 16370 et seq.**
Restoration of driving privileges, **Veh 16482**
Junior permits, **Veh 12513**
Junk and Junk Dealers, generally, this index

MOTOR

MOTOR VEHICLES—Cont'd
Jurisdiction,
  Clerk and deputy clerk, authority to receive bail, **Veh 40502**
  Crimes and offenses, ante
  Tort liability, **Veh 17152**
Juvenile delinquents and dependents,
  Alcohol offenses, **Veh 23140**
  Drivers licenses, revocation or suspension, **Veh 13100 et seq.**
    Probation, **Veh 13203**
  Junior permits, **Veh 12513**
  Reports, **Veh 1816**
Keys,
  Information, **Veh 9954**
  Replacement, **Veh 9954**
Labels. Brands, marks and labels, generally, ante
Labor and employment,
  Arrest, employers failure to answer charges, **Veh 40005**
  Charges against employees, failure of employer to dispose, **Veh 40005**
  Children and minors,
    Application for cancellation, drivers license, **Veh 17712**
    Family purpose doctrine, **Veh 17710**
    Signing drivers license, tort liability, **Veh 17706 et seq.**
  Codefendants, owners, **Veh 40003**
  Compensation and salaries, on duty hours or driving hours, **Veh 34501.9**
  Drivers licenses, ante
  Driving hours, compensation and salaries, **Veh 34501.9**
  Financial responsibility, **Veh 16002**
  Liens and incumbrances, generally, post
  Nonresident, exemptions, **Veh 6702**
  On duty hours, compensation and salaries, **Veh 34501.9**
  Trucks transporting workmen,
    Eight hundred (800) numbers, **Veh 2429**
    Equipment, **Veh 31400**
Laboratories, testing lighting equipment, **Veh 26103 et seq.**
Laboratory technicians, blood tests for drunken driving, **Veh 23158**
Lamp and brake adjusting stations, licenses, crimes and offenses, **Veh 40000.11**
Lamps. Lights and lighting, generally, post
Land surveyor vehicles, flashing amber warning lights, **Veh 25278**
Larceny. Theft, generally, post
Laser jamming devices, speed, **Veh 28150, 40000.15**
Law enforcement fingerprint identification programs (local), registration fees, **Veh 9250.19**
Law enforcement vehicles,
  Former registration, service fee for registration, **Veh 9255.1**
  Resembling, offenses, **Veh 27605**
Law of the road. Traffic Rules and Regulations, generally, this index

MOTOR VEHICLES—Cont'd
Leases,
  Abandoned or unclaimed property, removal, **Veh 22669**
  Actions and proceedings, licenses and permits, **Veh 11711.3**
  Automated enforcement systems, affidavits of nonliability, **Veh 40520**
  Blind persons, conditions for leasing, **Veh 14608**
  Bumper strength notices, **Veh 24011.3, 40000.15**
  Cancellation option agreements, conditional sales, used vehicles, restocking fees, **Veh 11713.21**
  Cancellation period, **Veh 11709.2**
  Cellular telephones, **Veh 28090**
  Certificates of title, **Veh 4453.5, 5753**
  Children and minors,
    Acquisition without drivers license, **Veh 15500**
    Passenger restraint systems, **Veh 27365**
  Codefendant, drivers or operators, **Veh 40001 et seq.**
  Conditional sales, cancellation option agreements, used vehicles, restocking fees, **Veh 11713.21**
  Conditions of contract, **Veh 24010**
  Consumer protection, recovery corporation, **Veh 12200 et seq.**
  Cooling off period, **Veh 11709.2**
  Credit scores, dealers, notice, **Veh 11713.20**
  Crimes and offenses, owner's responsibility, **Veh 40001 et seq.**
  Dealers,
    Trade ins, discharge, **Veh 11709.4**
    Transfer of interest, notice, **Veh 5901**
  Disabled persons, conditions for leasing, **Veh 14608**
  Drivers licenses, **Veh 14604, 14608, 40000.11**
  Electronic processing, registration, **Veh 4456.4**
    Fees, **Veh 4456.5**
  Environmental license plates, lessees, **Veh 5101 et seq.**
  Equipment, **Veh 24010**
    Not conforming with code, **Veh 24005**
  Failure to return, **Veh 10855**
    Stolen vehicle status, report, **Veh 10500**
  Goods, wares and merchandise, rates and charges, disclosure, **Veh 11713.19**
  Impounding, **Veh 14602, 14602.6**
    Driving under the influence, second and subsequent offenses, **Veh 14602.8**
  Inspections,
    Leasing or rental lots, stolen vehicles, **Veh 2805**
    Safety standards, compliance, **Veh 24010**
  Lessor retailers, generally, post

MOTOR VEHICLES—Cont'd
Leases—Cont'd
  Motor Vehicle Insurance, this index
  Name of lessee, police investigation, **Veh 4453.6**
  Nondrivers, records and recordation, **Veh 14609**
  Nonresident owners, **Veh 6700**
  Notice, children and minors, passenger restraint systems, **Veh 27365**
  Off highway vehicles, **Veh 38200 et seq.**
  Ownership responsibility, **Veh 40001 et seq.**
    Drivers licenses, **Veh 14604, 40000.11**
  Public operated vehicles, fees, exemptions, **Veh 9101**
  Rates and charges, impounding, release, **Veh 14602.6**
  Records and recordation, **Veh 14609**
  Recovery corporation, consumer protection, **Veh 12200 et seq.**
  Registration, post
  Reports, vehicles not returned, stolen vehicle status, **Veh 10500**
  Repossession, notice, **Veh 28**
  Restocking fees, cancellation option agreements, conditional sales, used vehicles, **Veh 11713.21**
  School buses, license plates, **Veh 5010**
  Simulated checks, advertisements, **Veh 11713.1**
  Trade ins, discharge, **Veh 11709.4**
  Transfer of title or interest, notice, **Veh 5908**
  Used vehicles, conditional sales, cancellation option agreements, restocking fees, **Veh 11713.21**
Leaving scene of accident. Hit and Run Drivers, generally, this index
Left turns. Traffic Rules and Regulations, this index
Legacy license plates, **Veh 5004.3**
Legal owner, definitions, **Veh 370**
Legal residency, drivers licenses, evidence, **Veh 12801.5**
Legislature, special license plates, **Veh 5002.5**
Lemon Law buyback, decal, **Veh 11713.12**
Length. Traffic Rules and Regulations, this index
Length of draw bar, towing units, **Veh 29005**
Lessor retailers, **Veh 11600 et seq.**
  Actions and proceedings, licenses and permits, **Veh 11711.3**
  Advertisements, **Veh 11614.1**
    Fraudulent or misleading advertising, **Veh 11614**
  Bankruptcy, consumer protection, recovery corporation, **Veh 12200 et seq.**
  Bond, **Veh 11612**
  Cancellation of license, **Veh 11617**
  Compromise and settlement, fines and penalties, **Veh 11613.5**

MOTOR VEHICLES—Cont'd

Lessor retailers—Cont'd

Consumer protection, recovery corporation, **Veh 12200 et seq.**

Fees, **Veh 4456.3**

Crimes and offenses, **Veh 11614 et seq., 40000.7**

Licenses, **Veh 11604.5**

Death, continuation of business by heirs or representatives, **Veh 11608**

Definitions, **Veh 373**

Exhaust emission control devices, registration, transfer of title or interest, **Veh 4000.1**

Expiration, license, **Veh 11620**

Federal trade commission, buyers guide, affixing to vehicle, **Veh 11614**

Fees, recovery corporation, consumer protection, **Veh 4456.3**

Fines and penalties,

Compromise and settlement, **Veh 11613.5**

Licenses and permits, late renewal, **Veh 11620**

Fraud, **Veh 11613**

Hearing, revocation or suspension of license, **Veh 11605**

Information, licensing, **Veh 11602**

Inspection and inspectors, notice, **Veh 11609.5**

License plates, renewal, **Veh 11620**

Licenses and permits, **Veh 11600 et seq.**

Actions and proceedings, **Veh 11711.3**

Crimes and offenses, **Veh 11604.5**

Fees, **Veh 9262**

Renewals, **Veh 9262.5**

Refusal to issue, **Veh 11604.1, 11604.5**

Security interest, **Veh 11711.3**

Moral turpitude, crime involving, licenses, **Veh 11604.5**

Notice,

Change of principal place of business, **Veh 11610**

Inspection rights, **Veh 11609.5**

Posting license, **Veh 11609**

Probationary license, **Veh 11606**

Process, **Veh 11610**

Rebates, fraud, **Veh 11614**

Recovery corporation, consumer protection, **Veh 12200 et seq.**

Fees, **Veh 4456.3**

Refunds, licensing or transfer of titles, **Veh 11616**

Registration, application on behalf of purchaser, **Veh 4456**

Removal, **Veh 22658**

Renewal, licenses, **Veh 11620**

Revocation or suspension, license, **Veh 11604.1 et seq.**

Security interest, licenses and permits, **Veh 11711.3**

Temporary permit, **Veh 11607**

Temporary suspension of license, **Veh 11618**

Time, license expiration, **Veh 11620**

MOTOR VEHICLES—Cont'd

Lessor retailers—Cont'd

Transfer of title or interest, registration, exhaust emission control devices, **Veh 4000.1**

Violations, suspension or revocation of license, **Veh 11613**

Letters, use of liquefied petroleum gas or natural gas fuel, display, concealed tanks, **Veh 27909**

Levees and Flood Control, this index

Liability. Damages, generally, ante

Liability insurance. Motor Vehicle Insurance, generally, this index

License fees,

Ambulances and armored cars, **Veh 2501 et seq.**

Cemetery equipment, **Veh 9261, 9261.1**

Adjustments, **Veh 1678**

Claim for refund, **Veh 42233**

Congressional Medal of Honor, exemptions, **Veh 9105**

Consumer protection, recovery corporation, **Veh 12200 et seq.**

Credit, destroyed or stolen vehicles, adjustments, **Veh 1678**

Crimes and offenses, evasion of payment, residents, **Veh 8804**

Delinquent fees, **Veh 9552 et seq.**

Mailing, **Veh 9557**

Repossession, waiver of penalty, **Veh 9561**

Transfer of registration, **Veh 9562**

Duplicates,

Fines and penalties, **Veh 42233**

Street signs, payments, **Veh 21366**

Embezzled vehicles, **Veh 4605**

Environmental license plates, **Veh 5100 et seq.**

Excess payment to dealer, **Veh 11713.3, 11713.4**

Exemptions, **Veh 11713.3, 11713.4**

Cemetery equipment, publicly owned, **Veh 9261**

Adjustments, **Veh 1678**

Congressional Medal of Honor, **Veh 9105**

Construction equipment, publicly owned, **Veh 9261**

Adjustments, **Veh 1678**

Indians, **Veh 9104.5**

Prisoners of war, **Veh 9105**

Veterans disabled on active service, **Veh 9105**

Hazardous material, transportation, **Veh 2502**

In transit permits, foreign purchasers, **Veh 6700.1**

Indians, exemptions, **Veh 9104.5**

Lessor retailers, **Veh 9262**

Renewals, **Veh 9262.5**

Motorized bicycles, **Veh 5036**

Adjustments, **Veh 1678**

New car dealers, payment, **Veh 11723**

One trip permit, **Veh 9258**

Adjustments, **Veh 1678**

MOTOR VEHICLES—Cont'd

License fees—Cont'd

Parking placards, disabled veterans, **Veh 9105**

Prisoners of war, exemptions, **Veh 9105**

Recovery corporation, consumer protection, **Veh 12200 et seq.**

Refunds, destroyed or stolen vehicles, adjustments, **Veh 1678**

Registration service licenses, **Veh 11409**

Residents, evasion of fees and taxes, **Veh 8804**

Trip permits, **Veh 9260**

License plates, **Veh 4850 et seq.**

Abandoned vehicles, removal, **Veh 22650 et seq.**

Alterations, destruction, **Veh 4463, 4464, 10750**

Amateur radio station license, special plates, **Veh 5005**

Antique cars, **Veh 5004**

Attachment to vehicle, **Veh 5200 et seq.**

Attorney general, accidents, disclosure of records, **Veh 5003**

Autoettes, **Veh 4000.5**

Automatic bale wagons, **Veh 5014 et seq.**

Blue sky license plates, clean fuel vehicles, **Veh 5062**

Boards and commissions, special plates, **Veh 5151 et seq.**

Brackets, **Veh 11713.17**

Brokered retail new motor vehicle sales, **Veh 11739**

Bureaus, special plates, **Veh 5151 et seq.**

Cancellation, suspension or revocation, **Veh 8800**

Environmental license plates, **Veh 5105**

Failure of proof to respond in damages, **Veh 16484**

Return of plates to department, **Veh 8802, 8803**

Unsatisfied judgments, **Veh 16370 et seq.**

Cards, identification card, issuance, **Veh 5016**

CB radios, special plates, **Veh 5020, 5021**

Cemetery equipment, **Veh 5011**

Time for application, **Veh 5015**

Certificate or insignia, weight fees paid on quarterly basis, **Veh 5206**

Child health and safety programs, special plates, **Veh 5072**

Chiropractors, handicapped persons, certificates and certification, **Veh 5007**

Citizens band radios, special plates, **Veh 5020, 5021**

Classic cars, **Veh 5004**

Clean fuel vehicles, **Veh 5062**

Colleges and universities, chancellors or presidents, special plates, **Veh 5002.6**

MOTOR

MOTOR VEHICLES—Cont'd
License plates—Cont'd
Collegiate commemorative reflectorized license plates, **Veh 5024**
Commemorative 1984 olympic reflectorized license plates, **Veh 5022, 5101.7**
Commercial vehicles, environmental license plates, **Veh 5101 et seq.**
Construction equipment, time for application, **Veh 5015**
Copies, **Veh 4466**
Cotton trailers, **Veh 5014 et seq.**
Counterfeiting, evidence procurement, **Veh 42271**
County auditors, regular series, **Veh 5002.7**
County controllers, regular series, **Veh 5002.7**
County supervisors boards, regular series license plates, **Veh 5002.7**
County treasurers, regular series, **Veh 5002.7**
Covering, **Veh 5201**
  Crimes and offenses, **Veh 5201.1**
Crimes and offenses, **Veh 4462, 40000.7**
  Cancellation, **Veh 8800, 40000.7**
  Deceptive or false evidence of vehicle registration, **Veh 40000.7**
  Display on vehicle other than one for which issued, **Veh 4462.5**
  Environmental display plates, attaching to vehicles, **Veh 40000.7**
  Evasion of fees on taxes, residents, **Veh 8804**
  Obstructions, **Veh 5201.1**
  Removal of plate, foreign state travel, **Veh 11725**
  Size, decorative, facsimile plates, **Veh 4463.5, 40000.7**
Dealers, ante
Decorative, similar size, crimes and offenses, **Veh 4463.5, 40000.7**
Destruction, **Veh 5017**
  Duplicates, **Veh 4466**
Dimensions, **Veh 4852**
Disabled veterans, **Veh 5007, 5007.5**
Dismantlers, ante
Display, **Veh 4155, 4851, 5200 et seq.**
  Applicable vehicles, **Veh 5204**
  Identification card, **Veh 5017**
  Publicly owned vehicles, **Veh 4155**
  Special permits issued in lieu of plates, **Veh 5202**
  Tab, sticker or other device, **Veh 5204, 5205**
  Vehicle exempt from registration fees, **Veh 4001**
  Vehicle other than one for which issued, **Veh 4462**
    Cancellation, **Veh 8800**
    Crimes and offenses, **Veh 4462.5**
Divisions, special plates, **Veh 5151 et seq.**
Domestic violence, new plates, **Veh 4467**
Duplicates, **Veh 4457, 4466**

MOTOR VEHICLES—Cont'd
License plates—Cont'd
Duplicates—Cont'd
  Fees, **Veh 9265**
    Adjustments, **Veh 1678**
Electronic devices and equipment, **Veh 4853**
Environment, **Veh 5075, 5100 et seq.**
  Special plates, **Veh 5067**
Exemptions, vehicles exempt from registration, display, **Veh 4001**
Extension of current series, **Veh 4609**
Facsimile, similar size, crimes and offenses, **Veh 4463.5, 40000.7**
Family, special plates,
  Congressional Medal of Honor, **Veh 5101.6**
  Firefighters and fire departments, **Veh 5101.2**
  Prisoners of war, **Veh 5101.5**
Farm trailers, **Veh 5014 et seq.**
Fees,
  Amateur radio station license, **Veh 5005**
  Citizens band radio, special plates, **Veh 5020, 5021**
  Commemorative 1984 olympic reflectorized license plates, **Veh 5022, 5101.7**
  Disabled persons, parking, **Veh 22511.5**
  Domestic violence, new plates, **Veh 4467**
  Duplicates, **Veh 9265**
    Adjustments, **Veh 1678**
  Environmental license plates, **Veh 5100 et seq.**
  Foreign vehicles, disposition, **Veh 4302**
  Historic vehicles, **Veh 5004, 5004.1**
  Honorary consular officer, special plates, **Veh 5006**
  Identification plate, service fee, **Veh 9261, 9261.1**
    Adjustments, **Veh 1678**
  Increase, registration expiration, **Veh 4601.5**
  Legacy license plates, **Veh 5004.3**
  Legislature, **Veh 5002.8**
  Memorial plates, September 11, 2001, **Veh 5066**
  Payment, **Veh 9550 et seq.**
  Photographer or cameraman of newspaper, **Veh 5008**
  Prisoners of war, special plates, **Veh 5101.5**
  Reduction, registration expiration, **Veh 4601.5**
  Special mobile equipment, **Veh 5014**
    Adjustments, **Veh 1678**
  Stalking, new plates, **Veh 4467**
  Substitute plates, **Veh 9265**
    Adjustments, **Veh 1678**
Fictitious or false, evidence procurement, **Veh 42271**

MOTOR VEHICLES—Cont'd
License plates—Cont'd
Financial statements and reports, special plates, **Veh 5060**
Fines and penalties,
  Obstructions, **Veh 5201.1**
  Renewal after certain date, **Veh 9553**
Firefighters, **Veh 5101.2**
Fleet vehicles, registration, **Veh 5301 et seq.**
Foreign countries,
  Duplicates, **Veh 4466**
  Honorary consular officer, **Veh 5006**
  Sales, removal, **Veh 11725**
  Taiwan, foreign organizations, **Veh 5006.5**
Foreign organizations, **Veh 5006.5**
Foreign states, **Veh 4307, 4456**
  Agreements, **Veh 5001.5**
  Disposition after registration, **Veh 4302**
  Duplicates, **Veh 4466**
  Surrender, **Veh 4301**
Forfeitures, renewal after certain date, **Veh 9553**
Forgery, evidence procurement, **Veh 42271**
Fraud, cancellation, **Veh 8800**
Funds, special plates, **Veh 5060**
Gold Star Families, special plates, **Veh 5156, 5157**
Ham radio operators, **Veh 5005**
Handicapped persons,
  Parking, **Veh 5007, 22511.5 et seq.**
    Delivery, department of motor vehicles, **Veh 11520**
    Failure to return to department, **Veh 9263**
    Loans to unauthorized persons, **Veh 4461, 4461.5**
    Wheelchairs, lifts, carriers, obstructions, **Veh 5201**
Have a heart, be a star, help our kids license plates, **Veh 5072**
Hazardous waste, tank vehicles hauling, place of display, **Veh 5201**
Historic vehicles, **Veh 5004**
Honorary consular officer, **Veh 5006**
Identity and identification, applicants for duplicates, **Veh 4466**
Illumination, **Veh 24601**
Inspection, **Veh 2804**
  Removal of covering, **Veh 5201**
Issuance, **Veh 4850 et seq.**
  Vehicles exempt from registration fees, **Veh 5001**
Judgments, unsatisfied, suspension, **Veh 16370 et seq.**
Legacy license plates, **Veh 5004.3**
Legislature, **Veh 5002.5**
  Fees, **Veh 5002.8**
Lessees, environmental license plates, **Veh 5101 et seq.**
Lessor retailers, renewal, **Veh 11620**
Licensed registration service, duplicates, **Veh 4466**

MOTOR VEHICLES—Cont'd
License plates—Cont'd
Lights and lighting, **Veh 24601**
Limousines, this index
Loan or use, **Veh 4461**
Local vehicle license fee surcharge, **Veh 9250.12**
Logging vehicles, **Veh 5014 et seq.**
Lost or stolen plates, **Veh 4457 et seq.**
  Notice, **Veh 4458**
  Off highway vehicles subject to identification, **Veh 38090, 38095**
  Reports, **Veh 10500 et seq.**
Manufacturers and manufacturing, post
Memorial plates, September 11, 2001, **Veh 5066**
Midwives, handicapped persons, certificates and certification, **Veh 5007**
Military forces, decorations for valor, special plates, **Veh 5101.4**
Model year, historic vehicles, **Veh 5004.1**
Motor Carriers, this index
Motor vehicle insurance, duplicates, **Veh 4466**
Motorcycles, this index
Motorized bicycles, **Veh 5030 et seq.**
Motorized scooters, application of law, **Veh 21224**
Mounting and position, **Veh 5201**
Mutilation or destruction, duplicates, **Veh 4466**
New vehicles, sales without plates or markings, **Veh 24009**
Newspaper photographer or cameraman, special plates, **Veh 5008**
Nonrepairable vehicles, forwarding to motor vehicle department, **Veh 11515.2**
Notice,
  Lost or stolen plates, **Veh 4458**
  Special plates, **Veh 5060**
Number of plates, **Veh 4850**
Nurse practitioners, handicapped persons, certificates and certification, **Veh 5007**
Obstructions, **Veh 5201**
  Crimes and offenses, **Veh 5201.1**
Off highway vehicles, **Veh 38010 et seq.**
Olympic games, commemorative reflectorized plates, **Veh 5022, 5101.7**
  Fees, **Veh 5023**
Operation of vehicle pending renewal of registration, **Veh 4606**
Optometrists, handicapped persons, certificates and certification, **Veh 5007**
Owner of vehicles, furnishing information, **Veh 4465**
Parking, handicapped persons, **Veh 22511.5 et seq.**
Pearl Harbor survivor plates, **Veh 5101.3**
Photographer or cameraman, newspaper, special plates, **Veh 5008**
Physician assistants, handicapped persons, certificates and certification, **Veh 5007**

MOTOR VEHICLES—Cont'd
License plates—Cont'd
Physicians and surgeons, handicapped persons, certificates and certification, **Veh 5007**
Police, post
Press photographers, **Veh 5008**
Prisoners of war, special plates, **Veh 5101.5**
Publicly owned vehicles, **Veh 4155**
Purple Heart recipients, special plates, **Veh 5101.8**
Radio station, amateur, special plates, **Veh 5005**
Rape, new plates, **Veh 4467**
Readers, data, retention, **Veh 2413**
Record, registration of exempt vehicles with series plates, **Veh 5003**
Reflective coating, **Veh 4850**
  Alterations, **Veh 5201.1**
Refunds, fees for special plates, **Veh 42230**
Refusal of registration, **Veh 4751**
Registration number, display, **Veh 4851**
Registration of foreign vehicles, surrender, **Veh 4301**
Regular series, county officers and employees, **Veh 5002.7**
Remote emission sensing devices, obstructing or impairing, **Veh 5201**
Removal of parked or standing vehicles, **Veh 22650 et seq.**
Removed plates, application of law, **Veh 5203**
Resident, definitions, **Veh 516**
Return of unexpired plates, foreign vehicles, fee, **Veh 4302**
Rules and regulations, display of stickers or devices in lieu of license plates, **Veh 5205**
Salvaged vehicles, **Veh 11540**
  Pools, duplicates, **Veh 4466**
School buses, **Veh 5010**
Seizure by police, **Veh 4460**
September 11, 2001, memorial plates, **Veh 5066**
Series, **Veh 4609**
Sexual battery, new plates, **Veh 4467**
Size, **Veh 4851**
  Decorative, facsimile plates, crimes and offenses, **Veh 4463.5, 40000.7**
Special highway construction equipment, **Veh 5011, 5014 et seq.**
  Identification plate, service fee, **Veh 1678, 9261, 9261.1**
Special mobile equipment, **Veh 5011, 5014 et seq.**
  Identification plate, service fee, **Veh 1678, 9261, 9261.1**
Special plates, **Veh 5000 et seq., 5060 et seq.**
  Application, **Veh 5060**
  Art and artists, **Veh 5074**
  Boards and commissions, **Veh 5151 et seq.**
  Bureaus, **Veh 5151 et seq.**

MOTOR VEHICLES—Cont'd
License plates—Cont'd
Special plates—Cont'd
  Change of vehicle, retaining plate, **Veh 5060**
  Citizens band radio, **Veh 5020, 5021**
  Class D radios, **Veh 5020, 5021**
  Colleges and universities, chancellors or presidents, **Veh 5002.6**
  Commemorative 1984 olympic reflectorized license plates, **Veh 5022, 5101.7**
  Congressional Medal of Honor, **Veh 5101.6**
  Counterfeiting, evidence procurement, **Veh 42271**
  Crimes and offenses, **Veh 4462, 40000.7**
  Dealers, special equipment, **Veh 5016 et seq.**
  Delinquent fees, **Veh 9552**
  Design approval, **Veh 5060**
  Disabled veterans, **Veh 5007, 5007.5**
  Discontinuance, notice, **Veh 5060**
  Dismantlers, issuance, **Veh 11516 et seq.**
  Divisions, **Veh 5151 et seq.**
  Duplicate, fees, **Veh 9265**
    Adjustments, **Veh 1678**
  Environment, **Veh 5067, 5100 et seq.**
  Exemptions, **Veh 5019**
  Family,
    Congressional Medal of Honor, **Veh 5101.6**
    Firefighters and fire departments, **Veh 5101.2**
    Prisoners of war, **Veh 5101.5**
  Fees, **Veh 5060, 9261, 9261.1, 9262**
    Adjustments, **Veh 1678**
    Art and artists, **Veh 5074**
    Delinquent fees, **Veh 9552**
    Environmental design, **Veh 5067**
    Firefighters, **Veh 5101.2**
    Memorial plates, September 11, 2001, **Veh 5066**
    Payment, **Veh 9550**
    Refund, **Veh 42230**
    State agencies, **Veh 5157**
    Transporters, **Veh 9262**
      Payment, **Veh 9550**
    Veterans organizations, **Veh 5068, 5069**
  Fictitious or false, evidence procurement, **Veh 42271**
  Financial statements and reports, **Veh 5060**
  Firefighters, **Veh 5101.2**
  Forgery,
    Alteration, **Veh 4463**
    Evidence procurement, **Veh 42271**
  Funds, **Veh 5060**
  Gold Star Families, **Veh 5156, 5157**
  Graphic design plates, **Veh 5074**
  Handicapped persons, **Veh 5007, 5007.5**

MOTOR

MOTOR VEHICLES—Cont'd
License plates—Cont'd
  Special plates—Cont'd
    Handicapped persons—Cont'd
      Loans to unauthorized persons,
        Veh 4461
    Have a heart, be a star, help our kids
      license plates, **Veh 5072**
    Historic vehicles, **Veh 5004, 5004.1**
    Honorary consular officer, **Veh 5006**
    Issuance, **Veh 5016**
    Legacy license plates, **Veh 5004.3**
    Legislature, **Veh 5002.5**
    Loan or use, **Veh 4461**
    Manufacturers and manufacturing,
      special equipment, **Veh 5016 et
      seq.**
    Marketing, limitations, **Veh 5060**
    Memorial plates, September 11, 2001,
      Veh 5066
    Military forces, decorations for valor,
      Veh 5101.4
    Minimum number, **Veh 5060**
    Model year, historic vehicles, **Veh
      5004.1**
    Motorized bicycles, **Veh 5030 et seq.**
    Notice, **Veh 5060**
    Olympic commemorative plates, fees,
      Veh 5023
    Organizations, **Veh 5060**
    Pearl Harbor survivors, **Veh 5101.3**
    Penalties, delinquent renewal, **Veh
      9553, 9554**
    Prisoners of war, **Veh 5101.5**
    Promotion, limitations, **Veh 5060**
    Public vehicles, **Veh 4155**
    Purple Heart recipients, **Veh 5101.8**
    Refunds, special interest organiza-
      tions, **Veh 5060**
    Refusal to issue, **Veh 11703**
    Registration, exemptions, **Veh 4018**
    September 11, 2001, memorial plates,
      Veh 5066
    Special highway construction equip-
      ment, **Veh 5011, 5014 et seq.**
    Special interest organizations, **Veh
      5060**
    Special mobile equipment, **Veh 5014
      et seq.**
    State agencies, **Veh 5151 et seq.**
    State departments, **Veh 5151 et seq.**
    State officers and employees, **Veh
      5151 et seq.**
    State parks environmental design,
      Veh 5161
    Surviving spouse,
      Congressional Medal of Honor,
        Veh 5101.6, 9105
      Firefighters and fire departments,
        Veh 5101.2
      Prisoners of war, **Veh 5101.5, 9105**
      Purple Heart recipients, **Veh 5101.8**
    Survivors,
      Military forces, decorations for val-
        or, **Veh 5101.4**
      Purple Heart recipients, **Veh 5101.8**

MOTOR VEHICLES—Cont'd
License plates—Cont'd
  Special plates—Cont'd
    Unlawful possession, **Veh 4462,
      40000.7**
    Veterans, **Veh 5101.6**
      Parking meters, rates and charges,
        exemptions, **Veh 22511.3**
    Veterans affairs department, **Veh
      5156**
    Veterans organizations, **Veh 5068**
      Decals, **Veh 5068.1**
    Volunteer fire fighters, **Veh 5101.2**
  Stalking, new plates, **Veh 4467**
  State agencies, special plates, **Veh 5151
    et seq.**
  State departments, special plates, **Veh
    5151 et seq.**
  State officers and employees, special
    plates, **Veh 5151 et seq.**
  State owned vehicles, pools, series
    plates, **Veh 5002**
  State parks environmental design, spe-
    cial license plates, **Veh 5161**
  Station wagons, **Veh 9404**
  Stickers, **Veh 4853, 5204**
  Stolen, lost, mutilated or illegible, **Veh
    4457**
  Substitution, **Veh 4466**
  Surrendered plates,
    Commercial vehicle, withdrawal from
      service, **Veh 9408**
    Nonconforming equipment or air pol-
      lution controls, disposal by public
      agencies, **Veh 24007.5**
  Surviving spouse, special plates,
    Congressional Medal of Honor, **Veh
      5101.6, 9105**
    Firefighters and fire departments,
      Veh 5101.2
    Prisoners of war, **Veh 5101.5, 9105**
    Purple Heart recipients, **Veh 5101.8**
  Survivors, special plates,
    Military forces, decorations for valor,
      Veh 5101.4
    Purple Heart recipients, **Veh 5101.8**
  Tabs, **Veh 4853**
    Alteration, forgery, **Veh 4463**
    Attachment, nature, **Veh 5204**
    Off highway vehicles, **Veh 38160 et
      seq.**
    Reflectorized material, **Veh 25500**
    Unlawful possession, **Veh 4462,
      40000.7**
  Taiwan, foreign organizations, **Veh
    5006.5**
  Tank vehicles hauling hazardous waste,
    place of display, **Veh 5201**
  Tax collectors, regular series, **Veh
    5002.7**
  Television photographer or cameraman,
    Veh 5008
  Theft, **Veh 4457 et seq.**
    Duplicates, **Veh 4466**
    Notice, **Veh 4458**
    Reports, **Veh 10500 et seq.**

MOTOR VEHICLES—Cont'd
License plates—Cont'd
  Tow dollies,
    Fees, **Veh 1678, 9261, 9261.1**
    Special plates, **Veh 5014 et seq.**
  Tow trucks, place of display, **Veh 5201**
    Environmental license plates, **Veh
      5105 et seq.**
  Trailers, this index
  Transfer of ownership to equipment, re-
    moval and return of identification
    plate, **Veh 5017**
  Transferred plates, application of law,
    Veh 5203
  Transporters, post
  Unlawful possession, **Veh 4462, 40000.7**
  Unlicensed vehicle, driving out of state,
    Veh 11725
  Validating devices, waiver of fees and
    penalties, **Veh 9562**
  Validation tabs, loans to unauthorized
    persons, **Veh 4461**
  Veterans, disabled veterans, parking,
    Veh 5007, 22511.5 et seq.
  Veterans affairs department, special
    plates, **Veh 5156**
  Voluntary firefighters, **Veh 5101.2**
  Wheelchairs, lifts, carriers, obstructions,
    Veh 5201
  Yosemite Foundation special plate, **Veh
    5064**
Licensed registration service, certificates
  of title, license plates, duplicates, **Veh
  4466**
Licenses and permits,
  Application of law, **Veh 2504**
  Applications, grant or refusal, **Veh 1653**
  Cancellation, **Veh 11822**
  Commercial vehicles, trip permits, for-
    eign states, **Veh 4004**
  Counterfeiting, evidence procurement,
    Veh 42271
  Crimes and offenses, **Veh 40000.11**
    Cancellation, **Veh 8800**
    Revocation, **Veh 13201**
    Salespersons, selling without license
      or permit, **Veh 11800**
    Special licenses, **Veh 2541 et seq.**
  Dealers, ante
  Disaster areas, **Veh 4005**
  Dismantlers, ante
  Distributors, ante
  Drivers licenses, generally, ante
  Duplicate licenses, **Veh 2503**
  Electronic recording, **Veh 1801**
  Emergency vehicles, **Veh 2416**
    Revocation or suspension, **Veh 2417**
  Equipment,
    Experimental use, **Veh 26106**
    Special permit, exemption, stopping
      distance requirement, **Veh 26457**
  Evidence, records of license suspension
    or revocation, **Veh 40807**
  Examination of records, **Veh 1814**
  Exemption, **Veh 4002 et seq.**

MOTOR VEHICLES—Cont'd
Licenses and permits—Cont'd
  Experimental use of equipment, Veh 26106
  Facsimile signatures, Veh 12950
  Fees. License fees, generally, ante
  Fictitious or false, evidence procurement, Veh 42271
  Fleet owner inspection and maintenance stations, Veh 2501
    Staggered renewals, Veh 2505
  Foreign commercial vehicles, display, Veh 4455
  Forgery, Veh 4463
    Evidence procurement, Veh 42271
  Forms, Veh 1652, 2502
  Hazardous materials, transportation, Veh 2501
  Impoundment, reports, Veh 1803 et seq.
  In transit permits, Veh 6700.1
  Inspection by police, Veh 4462
  Lessor retailers, ante
  License fees, generally, ante
  Loans to unauthorized persons, Veh 4461
  Local vehicle license fee surcharge, Veh 9250.12
  Lost or destroyed records, renewal, Veh 2503
  Manufacturers and manufacturing, post
  New car dealers policy and appeals board, Veh 3051
  Off highway vehicles, post
  Pilot cars, special moving permits, flashing or colored lights, Veh 25270
  Plates. License plates, generally, ante
  Probationary license, lessor retailers, Veh 11606
  Reapplication, Veh 11703.3
  Records and recordation, Veh 1800 et seq.
    Revocation or suspension, evidence, Veh 40807
  Registration, Veh 11400 et seq.
    Data base, commercial use, Veh 1810.7
  Remanufacturers, Veh 11700 et seq.
  Renewal, registration service licenses, Veh 11410
  Reports, notation, Veh 1818
  Representatives, post
  Resident, definitions, Veh 516
  Return to department, Veh 8802, 8803
  Revocation or suspension,
    Registration service licenses, Veh 11405, 11413
    Return of documents to department, Veh 8802
  Salespersons, post
  Seizure by police, Veh 4460
  Signature, Veh 12950
  Special licenses, Veh 2500 et seq.
  Special moving permit, pilot cars, flashing or colored lights, Veh 25270
  Suspension, registration service licenses, Veh 11408

MOTOR VEHICLES—Cont'd
Licenses and permits—Cont'd
  Temporary permits, Veh 4156
    Dealers, Veh 11719
    Drivers licenses, Veh 12506
    Inspection by police, Veh 4462
    Registration services, Veh 11404
  Tow trucks, local regulations, Veh 21100 et seq.
  Traffic violations, reports, Veh 1803 et seq.
  Transfer, Veh 2503
  Transporters, post
  Trip permits, commercial vehicles, foreign states, Veh 4004
    Fees, Veh 9260
  Unsatisfied judgment, suspension, Veh 16370 et seq.
  Vehicle verifiers, Veh 11300 et seq.
  Vending, Veh 22520.5
Liens and incumbrances,
  Abandoned or unclaimed property, ante
  Bond pending registration, Veh 4157
  Certificates of title, ante
  Costs, sales, Veh 22851.12
  Crimes and offenses, fraud, Veh 22852.5
  Dealers, electronic lien and title program, Veh 4450.5
  Disposition, Veh 22851 et seq.
  Electronic lien and title program, Veh 4450.5
  Enforcement, Veh 9800 et seq.
  Expenses of keeping impounded vehicle, driving while privilege suspended or revoked, Veh 14602
  Failure to appear or pay fine, Veh 14911
  Fees, Veh 9800 et seq.
    Fleet vehicles, registration, Veh 5307
  Fleet vehicles, apportionment, registration, Veh 8200 et seq.
  Foreign certificates of title, full faith and credit, Veh 4304
  Foreign liens and incumbrances, Veh 4306
  Foreign registered auxiliary dolly, semi-trailer, or trailer, Veh 9800
  Foreign vehicles, registration, Veh 4307
  Impounding, Veh 14602, 22651
    Local authorities, Veh 22851.1
  Leases, delinquent fees, fines, penalties and interest, Veh 9801
  Limitation of actions, Veh 9800
  Local authorities, impounded vehicle, Veh 22851.1
  Notice, Veh 9800 et seq.
  Nuisance, driving under the influence, Veh 23596
  Parking violations, delinquent fines and penalties, Veh 9800
  Perfecting, Veh 6300 et seq., 9800
  Refusal of registration, Veh 4751
  Registration, post
  Sales, post
  Signatures, lienholders, transfer of ownership certificate, Veh 5752

MOTOR VEHICLES—Cont'd
Liens and incumbrances—Cont'd
  Storage of vehicles, removed from highway, Veh 22851
  Towage and keeping vehicle removed from highway, Veh 22851
  Transfer certificate of title or registration card, nonpayment, notice, Veh 5911
  Transfer of title or interest, Veh 5601
Life saving vehicles, red lights and sirens, public policy, Veh 30
Light bars, Veh 27606, 27607
Light duty motor vehicles,
  Itemized price stickers, Veh 11712.5, 24013.5
  Low emission vehicles, Veh 28113
Lighting equipment, definitions, Veh 375
Lights and lighting, Veh 24250 et seq.
  Acetylene lamps, Veh 25450 et seq.
  Adjustments, compliance with direction of officer making inspection, Veh 40151
  Agricultural machinery and equipment, farm labor vehicles, Veh 31408
  Amber lights, generally, ante
  Amber reflectors, Veh 24609
  Animal control, enforcement vehicles, amber warning lights, Veh 25271.5
  Approval of equipment and devices, Veh 26100 et seq.
  Armored car, red lights, Veh 25262
  Arrest, refusal to stop and submit to inspection or test, Veh 40303
  Authorized equipment, Veh 24003
  Auxiliary lamps, Veh 24400 et seq.
    Rear lamps, Veh 24616
  Backup lamps, Veh 24606
    Color, Veh 25950
  Bars, Veh 27606, 27607
  Beam indicator, Veh 24408
  Blue lights,
    Light bars, Veh 27606, 27607
    Police and sheriff vehicles, Veh 25258
  Buses, this index
  Cargo lights, Veh 24616
  Clearance lights, generally, ante
  Colored lights, generally, ante
  Combination lighting equipment, generally, ante
  Commercial and common carrier vehicles, Veh 25350, 25351
  Construction companies, flashing amber warning lights, Veh 25282
  Contractors, flashing amber warning lights, Veh 25282
  Data monitors, Veh 25108
  Deceleration lights, Veh 25251.5
  Definitions, Veh 375
  Diffused lights, Veh 25400, 25401
  Disaster service vehicles, warning lights, Veh 25259.1
  Dual head light system as one lamp, Veh 24405
  Emergency Vehicles, this index
  Exemptions, Veh 25800 et seq.

MOTOR

MOTOR VEHICLES—Cont'd
Lights and lighting—Cont'd
Farm labor vehicles, **Veh 31408**
Fender lighting equipment, **Veh 25100 et seq.**
Flashing lights, **Veh 25250 et seq.**
Aerial lift equipped vehicles, **Veh 25260.3**
Amber lights, ante
Animal control, enforcement vehicles, **Veh 25271.5**
Civil engineer vehicles, amber warning lights, **Veh 25278**
Construction companies, **Veh 25282**
Contractors, **Veh 25282**
Disaster service vehicles, **Veh 25259.1**
Emergency vehicles, **Veh 30**
Hazardous substance spill response vehicles, **Veh 25260.4**
Livestock, herding, **Veh 25270.5**
Marshals department, **Veh 25254**
Nonprofit organizations, handicapped or mentally retarded persons, **Veh 25276**
Off highway vehicles, **Veh 38346**
Police, **Veh 25259, 25277**
Red cross disaster vehicles, **Veh 25259.5**
Special moving permits, flashing amber warning lights, **Veh 25270**
Theft alarm systems, **Veh 25251.4, 28085**
Traffic hazards, display, **Veh 25268**
Turn signal, **Veh 24953**
Fog lamps, generally, ante
Headlights, generally, ante
Height, mounted height, **Veh 24254**
Identification lamps, **Veh 25351**
Illuminating devices, **Veh 24255**
Colors and coloring, **Veh 25950**
Implements of husbandry, turn signals, warning lights, **Veh 25251.1**
Inspection,
Failure or refusal to stop, option of officer to take arrested person before magistrate, **Veh 40303**
Removal on direction of officer making, **Veh 40151**
Instruction for installation, **Veh 24006**
Interior lamps, **Veh 24003**
Laboratory testing, **Veh 26100 et seq.**
Land surveyor vehicles, amber warning lights, **Veh 25278**
Outside rear view mirror mounted turn signals, **Veh 24953**
Water tender vehicles, amber warning lights, **Veh 25281**
Load, mounted on, **Veh 25952**
Modifying devices, lighting and signalling equipment, approval and compliance prior to sale or use, **Veh 26101**
Motorized scooters, **Veh 21223, 21224**
Mounting lights, **Veh 24012, 24254, 25950 et seq.**

MOTOR VEHICLES—Cont'd
Lights and lighting—Cont'd
Multiple beam road lighting equipment, **Veh 24407 et seq.**
Nonconforming equipment, sales, **Veh 24005**
Nonglaring lights, **Veh 25400, 25401**
Off highway vehicles, **Veh 38335, 38345**
Oil and gas pipelines, construction and maintenance, flashing amber lights, **Veh 25260.1**
Parking lamps, **Veh 24800 et seq.**
Passing lights, front of vehicle, number of lighted lamps, **Veh 24405**
Pilot indicators, **Veh 25108**
Projecting loads, **Veh 25103**
Rear lamps, generally, post
Red cross disaster service vehicles, warning lights, **Veh 25259.5**
Red lights, generally, post
Reflectorizing material, **Veh 25500**
Load, mounting on, **Veh 25952**
Reflectors, generally, post
Removal on direction of officer making inspection, **Veh 40151**
Restrictions and mounting, **Veh 25950 et seq.**
Restrictions on number, **Veh 24405**
Running lamps, **Veh 25109**
Semaphore changing devices, **Veh 21464, 25352**
Sheriff vehicles, blue warning lights, **Veh 25258**
Side lighting equipment, **Veh 25100 et seq.**
Signal lamps and devices, **Veh 24950 et seq.**
Special construction and maintenance equipment, exemption, **Veh 25801**
Special mobile equipment, exemption, **Veh 25800**
Stoplamps, generally, post
Tests, **Veh 26100 et seq.**
Theft alarm systems, **Veh 25251.4, 28085**
Towing, post
Traffic Rules and Regulations, this index
Traffic safety program, **Veh 2900 et seq.**
Traffic Signs and Signals, this index
Turn signals, generally, post
Vision impairing lights, **Veh 21466.5**
Warning signals and devices, generally, post
White lights, **Veh 24606**
White reflectors, **Veh 24609**
Width, extension beyond permissible limits, **Veh 35109**
Limit line, definitions, **Veh 377**
Limitation of actions,
Counterfeit or forged documents, **Veh 40004**
Drivers license suspension or revocation, appeals, **Veh 14401**
Fees, refunds, **Veh 42231, 42232**
Registration, **Veh 42235**

MOTOR VEHICLES—Cont'd
Limitation of actions—Cont'd
Fines and penalties, refunds, **Veh 42231, 42232**
Forged or fictitious documents, **Veh 40004**
Franchises, ante
License revocation, special licenses, **Veh 2547**
Liens and incumbrances, **Veh 9800**
Nonresidents, **Veh 17463**
Pleading, written plea, waiver of right to trial within statutory period, **Veh 40519**
Refund,
Erroneous collection of fees and penalties, **Veh 42231, 42232**
Fees, registration, **Veh 42235**
Registration, post
Smog impact fees, registration, foreign states, **Veh 1673.4**
Written plea in lieu of personal appearance, waiver, **Veh 40519**
Limousines, generally, this index
Line makes, dealers, sales, **Veh 11713.13**
Franchises, **Veh 11713.1**
Liquefied Petroleum Gas, this index
Lists,
Dealers, advertisements, showrooms, **Veh 11709.3**
House car warranties, provision to buyers by dealers, **Veh 11931**
Safety glazing materials, approved types, **Veh 26704**
Littering. Solid waste, generally, post
Livery plates, limousines, **Veh 5011.9**
Livestock, herding, flashing amber lights, **Veh 25270.5**
Livestock trailers, towing, restricted drivers licenses, **Veh 12804.14**
LNG, concealed tanks, block letters designating, **Veh 27909**
Loads and loading. Traffic Rules and Regulations, this index
Loans,
Conditional sales, generally, ante
Disabled person placards, crimes and offenses, **Veh 4461**
Drivers licenses, **Veh 14610**
Foreign state owners, **Veh 6700**
License of vehicle salesman, **Veh 11819**
Registration, evidence, unauthorized persons, **Veh 4461**
Local authorities,
Contracts, removal, **Veh 22671**
Definitions, **Veh 385**
Low speed vehicles, **Veh 21266**
Local law enforcement fingerprint identification programs, registration fees, **Veh 9250.19**
Local regulations, **Veh 21100 et seq.**
Local vehicle license fee surcharge, **Veh 9250.12**
Location,
Log books, inspection and inspectors, **Veh 34501.10**

MOTOR VEHICLES—Cont'd

Location—Cont'd
Registration, **Veh 4000.4**
Locked vehicles, duties, **Veh 22516**
Locksmiths, **Veh 9954**
Log books, availability for inspection, **Veh 34501.10**
Logos, fleet vehicles, **Veh 5302**
Logs, autobroker log, **Veh 11735**
Lost or destroyed documents,
  Certificates of title,
    Sales, **Veh 5752**
    Transfer of title or interest, **Veh 5911**
  Licenses, renewal, **Veh 2503**
Lost or stolen plates. License plates, ante
Low air pressure warning devices, air-brakes, **Veh 26506**
Low emission vehicles. Air Pollution, this index
Low speed vehicles, **Veh 21115, 21115.1, 21250 et seq.**
  Application of law, **Veh 21251**
  Dealers, **Veh 11713.10, 21252**
  Definitions, **Veh 385.5, 21250**
  Disclosure, sales, **Veh 11713.10, 21252**
  Exemptions, registration, **Veh 4023**
  Local authorities, **Veh 21266**
  Operation, **Veh 21250 et seq.**
  Reflectors, **Veh 24607**
  Registration, exemptions, **Veh 4023**
  Safety, **Veh 21253, 21254**
  Sales, disclosure, **Veh 11713.10, 21252**
Lower beam, multiple beam road equipment, **Veh 24407**
LPG, concealed tanks, block letters designating, **Veh 27909**
Machinery and equipment. Equipment, generally, ante
Magistrates, arrest procedures, **Veh 40302 et seq.**
Mail and mailing,
  Certified or registered mail,
    Notice,
      Driver license revocation, suspension, **Veh 13106**
      Method of giving notice, **Veh 29**
      Nonresidents, service of process, **Veh 17454, 17455**
      Service of process on nonresidents, **Veh 17454, 17455**
  Disposition, liens and incumbrances, **Veh 22851.8**
  Drivers licenses, ante
  Fees, delinquent fees, **Veh 9557**
  Identification cards, renewal, **Veh 13002.1**
  Notice, **Veh 22, 23, 29**
    Drivers licenses, revocation or suspension, **Veh 13106**
  Pleadings,
    Personal appearance deemed to have been made, **Veh 40519**
    Written plea, **Veh 40519**
  Reports of stored vehicles, **Veh 10652**
  Service of process on nonresidents, **Veh 17454**

MOTOR VEHICLES—Cont'd

Mail and mailing—Cont'd
  Theft, notice, recovered vehicles, **Veh 10500**
Mail carriers, flashing amber lights, **Veh 25272**
Maintenance. Repairs, generally, post
Major component parts for trucks, truck type or bus type vehicles, definitions, **Veh 5505**
Malicious mischief, **Veh 10853**
  Penalty, **Veh 40000.9**
Managerial employee, definitions, licenses, **Veh 386**
Mandatory appearance before magistrate, arrest, **Veh 40302**
Manifolds, gastight condition, **Veh 27154**
Manslaughter. Homicide, this index
Manuals,
  Horsepower ratings, **Veh 9950, 9952**
  New vehicles, chains, notice, **Veh 9953**
  Recording devices, disclosure, **Veh 9951**
Manufacturers and manufacturing,
  Abandonment of business, cancellation of license, **Veh 11721**
  Accomplices and accessories, **Veh 11700.3**
  Actions and proceedings, fraud, **Veh 11711**
  Advertisements, **Veh 11713**
  Applications, licenses and permits, **Veh 11704**
  Bonds (officers and fiduciaries), **Veh 11710, 11713**
    Failure to file, licenses and permits, cancellation, **Veh 11721**
    Protection of interest, **Veh 11722**
  Bumper strength notices, **Veh 24011.3, 40000.15**
  Certificates of convenience, executors and administrators, **Veh 11720**
  Change of place of business, **Veh 11712**
  Competition, dealers, **Veh 11713.3**
  Compliance with law, refusal of registration, **Veh 4751**
  Compromise and settlement, new vehicles, mandatory settlement conference, **Veh 3050.4**
  Crimes and offenses,
    Licenses and permits, **Veh 11700, 40000.11**
    Return of documents and license plates, **Veh 40000.7**
  Dealers, competition, **Veh 11713.3**
  Defects, correction, **Veh 9975**
  Delinquent fees, **Veh 9552**
  Disclosure, repurchased vehicles, **Veh 11713.12**
  Division, types of businesses, **Veh 1670**
  Down payment, false representation, **Veh 11713**
  Driveaway towaway operations, generally, ante
  Engines, manufacturer different from vehicle manufacturer, **Veh 9980 et seq., 11713.9**

MOTOR VEHICLES—Cont'd

Manufacturers and manufacturing —Cont'd
  Equipment, tests, **Veh 26104**
  Event data recorders, **Veh 9951**
  Executors and administrators, certificates of convenience, **Veh 11720**
  False advertising, **Veh 11713**
  Federal motor vehicle safety standards, certificates and certification, **Veh 24011**
  Fees,
    Failure to pay, **Veh 11711**
    License and special plates, **Veh 9262**
    Payment, **Veh 9550 et seq.**
    Service of process, **Veh 11710**
    Time of payment, **Veh 9550**
  Fines and penalties,
    Compromise and settlement, **Veh 11707**
    Failure to pay, **Veh 11711**
  Franchises, generally, ante
  Fraud, **Veh 11711**
  House cars, misrepresentation, manufacture in two or more stages, **Veh 11713.5**
  Identification plates,
    Sale of new vehicles, **Veh 24009**
    Special equipment, **Veh 5016 et seq.**
  Inspection and inspectors, records and recordation, **Veh 1670**
  Laboratories, tests, equipment, **Veh 26104**
  Lemon Law, buybacks, decals, **Veh 11713.12**
  License plates,
    Automatic cancellation, **Veh 11721**
    Bids and bidding, **Veh 4850**
    Expiration, **Veh 11717**
    Fees, **Veh 9262**
    Identity and identification, special equipment, **Veh 5016 et seq.**
    Renewal, **Veh 11717**
    Special plates, **Veh 11714 et seq.**
    Unauthorized use, **Veh 11713**
  Licenses and permits, **Veh 11700 et seq.**
    Applications, **Veh 11701, 11704**
    Automatic cancellation, **Veh 11721**
    Cancellation,
      Return to department, **Veh 8803**
      Temporary permit, **Veh 11719**
    Crimes and offenses, **Veh 40000.11**
    Damages, **Veh 11726**
    Display, **Veh 11709**
    Fees, **Veh 11723**
    Forms, **Veh 11704**
    Issuance, **Veh 11702, 11714**
    Probationary licenses, **Veh 11718**
    Reapplication, **Veh 11703.3**
    Refusal to issue, **Veh 11702 et seq.**
    Revocation or suspension, **Veh 11703.1 et seq.**
    Territorial area, **Veh 11727**
    Temporary permits, **Veh 11719**
    Temporary suspension, **Veh 11706**

MOTOR VEHICLES—Cont'd

Manufacturers and manufacturing —Cont'd

Licenses and permits—Cont'd

Unsatisfied final judgments, denial, **Veh 11703.2**

Lighting and signalling equipment and devices, testing and approval, **Veh 26100 et seq.**

New vehicles, generally, post

Notice, repurchased vehicles, **Veh 11713.12**

Odometers,

Accuracy, **Veh 28051**

Resetting, **Veh 11713**

Off highway vehicles, identification certificates, **Veh 38021**

Office, place of business, **Veh 1670, 1671**

Operation without license, **Veh 11713**

Parts, defective parts, **Veh 12000 et seq.**

Place of business, signs, **Veh 11709**

Priorities and preferences, claims of state, **Veh 11711**

Recall of vehicles, access to confidential information, **Veh 1808.23**

Recording devices, **Veh 9951**

Reflectorized license plates, **Veh 4850**

Registration,

Exemptions, **Veh 4002**

Fees, **Veh 9262**

Remanufactured vehicles, generally, post

Repurchased vehicles, notice, **Veh 11713.12**

Restitution, licenses and permits, denial, **Veh 11703.2**

Sales and use taxes, failure to pay, **Veh 11713**

Sensing and diagnostic modules, **Veh 9951**

Service of process, **Veh 11710**

Place of business closed, registered mail, **Veh 11712**

Settlements, mandatory settlement conference, new vehicles, **Veh 3050.4**

Signs and devices on place of business, **Veh 11709**

Special plates, **Veh 11714 et seq.**

Fees, **Veh 9262**

Subsidiaries, dealers, competition, **Veh 11713.3**

Tests, equipment, **Veh 26104**

Tires, noise standards, compliance, **Veh 27503**

Warranties,

Brokered retail new motor vehicle sales, **Veh 11739**

Failure to honor, **Veh 11713**

Markets and marketing, special license plates, limitations, **Veh 5060**

Markings. Brands, marks and labels, generally, ante

Marriage, minors, drivers license, signature, tort liability, **Veh 17700 et seq.**

MOTOR VEHICLES—Cont'd

Marshals, hazardous substances and waste, signs and signals, exemptions, **Veh 27903**

Masts, hydraulic masts, restraint, **Veh 35251**

May, definitions, construction of Act, **Veh 15**

Mechanical condition, inspection, **Veh 2814**

Mechanical recordation, drivers license hearing proceedings, **Veh 14104.2**

Mechanics liens. Liens and incumbrances, generally, ante

Medical Care and Treatment, this index

Medical information cards, drivers licenses, **Veh 12811.1**

Medical transportation vehicles, emergencies, pollution control devices, **Veh 27156.2, 27156.3**

Medium duty motor vehicles, low emission vehicles, **Veh 28113**

Mental condition of persons, confidential information, **Veh 1808.5**

Mental health treatment, restricted license, **Veh 16077**

Mentally Ill Persons, this index

Mentally Retarded and Developmentally Disabled Persons, this index

Metal studs, tires, **Veh 27454**

Metal tires, definitions, **Veh 395**

Mexico, out of service orders, failure to comply, **Veh 2800**

Midwives, this index

Mileage,

Odometers, **Veh 28050 et seq.**

Records, public inspection, **Veh 1819**

Removal of vehicles from highway for storage, **Veh 22850 et seq.**

Sales, notice, **Veh 5901**

Transfer,

Notice, **Veh 5900, 5901**

Records and recordation, **Veh 5906.5**

Wholesale vehicle auctions, dealer report, **Veh 4456**

Military Forces, this index

Mines and minerals, construction, backup devices or alarms, **Veh 27000**

Minors. Children and minors, generally, ante

Mirrors, obstruction of view, signs and stickers, **Veh 26708**

Misdemeanors. Crimes and offenses, generally, ante

Misrepresentation. Fraud, generally, ante

Mistaken collection of fees or penalties, refunds, limitation, **Veh 42231, 42232**

Mobile crane or shovel, brakes of vehicle used to support boom or mast, **Veh 26302**

Mobile digital terminals, **Veh 27602**

Mobile equipment registration, fees, **Veh 1678, 9261, 9261.1**

Model year,

License plates, historic vehicles, **Veh 5004.1**

MOTOR VEHICLES—Cont'd

Model year—Cont'd

Misrepresentation, **Veh 11713.5**

Modification or change,

Drivers licenses, revocation or suspension, **Veh 13202.5**

Equipment, ante

Exhaust systems, ante

Original design, **Veh 24008**

Owners and ownership, notice, **Veh 11704**

Monitoring,

Data monitors, **Veh 25108**

Lights and lighting, pilot indicators, **Veh 25108**

Mortgages. Chattel mortgages, generally, ante

Mosquito abatement districts,

Lights and lighting, flashing or colored lights, **Veh 25267**

Pollution control devices, **Veh 27156.3**

Motion pictures, law enforcement vehicles, removal of police insignia, **Veh 27604**

Motor Clubs, generally, this index

Motor Vehicle Fuel, generally, this index

Motor Vehicle Insurance, generally, this index

Motor Vehicle Repair Dealers, generally, this index

Motorcycles, generally, this index

Motorized bicycles. Bicycles, this index

Motorized Scooters, generally, this index

Motorized skateboards, **Veh 21968**

Mudguard, equipment, **Veh 27600**

Mufflers. Exhaust systems, generally, ante

Multiple county use, registration, exemption, **Veh 4004.5**

Multiple ownership of vehicles, engine numbers, **Veh 4163**

Multiple unit truck reflector, **Veh 24610**

Multipurpose passenger vehicles, side marker lamps, **Veh 25100**

Municipal attorneys,

Photography and pictures, disclosure, **Veh 1808.51**

Records and recordation, access, **Veh 1810.5**

Municipal Officers and Employees, this index

Municipalities, this index

Mutilated registration card or license plate, **Veh 4457 et seq.**

Names,

Change of name, replacement of license, **Veh 2503**

Fleet vehicles, **Veh 5302**

Lessee of leased vehicle, police investigation, **Veh 4453.6**

Wholesale vehicle auctions, dealer report, **Veh 4456**

National guard. Military Forces, this index

National law enforcement telecommunication system, abandoned or unclaimed property, storage, notice, **Veh 22854.5**

MOTOR VEHICLES—Cont'd

Negligence, **Veh 17000 et seq.**

Dealers and manufacturers, license revocation, **Veh 11705**

Drivers licenses, ante

Emergency Services Act, compliance with governors orders or directives, **Veh 40830**

Evidence, ante

Imputed negligence, **Veh 17150 et seq.**

Children and minors, **Veh 17707**

Owner as passenger, **Veh 17158**

Removal from private property, damages, **Veh 22658**

Reports, evidence, **Veh 40833**

Seat belts, usage, establishing, **Veh 12810.2, 27315**

Torts, generally, post

New car dealer, definitions, **Veh 426**

New car lots, inspection, stolen vehicles, **Veh 2805**

New motor vehicle board. Motor Vehicles Department, this index

New vehicles,

Air Pollution, this index

Arbitration of disputes, **Veh 3050**

Attorney fees, discovery, investigations and investigators, **Veh 3050.2**

Continuance, scheduled proceedings, **Veh 3050.6**

Costs, discovery, investigations and investigators, **Veh 3050.2**

Definitions, **Veh 430**

Discovery, investigations, **Veh 3050.1, 3050.2**

Exemptions, **Veh 3051**

Exhaust emissions inspection, gasoline minimum octane number, **Veh 24013**

Exhaust standards, **Veh 27153.5**

Fees, **Veh 3016**

Filing of appeal, protest or petition, **Veh 3050.5**

Investigations, **Veh 3050**

Licenses and permits, **Veh 11700 et seq.**

Mandatory settlement conference, **Veh 3050.4**

Noise limits, **Veh 27200 et seq.**

Nondisclosure, inability to use chains, **Veh 11713.6**

Odometers, accuracy, **Veh 28051**

Proposed stipulated decisions and orders, **Veh 3050.7**

Protest, hearings, **Veh 3066**

Refusal to deliver, **Veh 11713.2, 11713.3**

Registration, **Veh 4456**

Electronic processing, **Veh 4456.4**

Fees, **Veh 4456.5**

Noise limits, dealers certificates, **Veh 27200**

Rules and regulations, **Veh 3050**

Sales, copy of preparation obligations, **Veh 3064**

Settlements, mandatory settlement conference, **Veh 3050.4**

MOTOR VEHICLES—Cont'd

New vehicles—Cont'd

Tire chains, inability to use, notice, **Veh 9953**

Transfer of title, insurance, notice, **Veh 5604**

Warranties, **Veh 3065**

Newspaper photographers, license plates, **Veh 5008**

Newsreel photographers, license plates, **Veh 5008**

Night court,

Arrest, notice to appear, **Veh 40502**

Assessments, special penalties, **Veh 42006**

Nighttime, lights and lighting, **Veh 24250 et seq., 24400, 24600 et seq.**

Noise,

Amplification devices, **Veh 27007**

Emission control, inspection, **Veh 24011.7**

Exhaust system modification, noise limits, exceeding, **Veh 27151**

Limits, **Veh 27200 et seq.**

City on island over 20,000 acres, county over 4 million, **Veh 21100.5**

Exhaust system modification, exceeding limits, **Veh 27151**

New vehicles, sales, **Veh 27200, 27204**

Off highway vehicles, **Veh 38370**

Pneumatic tires, noise standards, **Veh 27502, 27503**

Report of court action, modification of exhaust systems, **Veh 1803**

Standards, **Veh 27150.1 et seq.**

Noise Pollution, generally, this index

Nolo contendere pleas, complaint or notice to appear, **Veh 40513**

Noncompliance notice, refusal to renew registration, **Veh 4766**

Nonflammable gas, adoption of United States department of transportation definitions, **Veh 2402.7**

Nonglaring lights,

Acetylene lamps, **Veh 25452**

Requisites, **Veh 25400, 25401**

Nonoperation. Certificates and certification, ante

Nonprofit Organizations, this index

Nonrenewal, franchises, **Veh 11713.13**

Nonrepairable vehicles,

Certificates and certification, **Veh 24007**

Certificates of title, license plates, **Veh 11515.2**

Adjustments, **Veh 1678**

Definitions, **Veh 431**

License fee credit or refund, adjustments, **Veh 1678**

Nonresidents,

Accidents, service of process, **Veh 17450 et seq.**

Agent for service of process, **Veh 17450 et seq.**

Appearance, time, **Veh 17462**

MOTOR VEHICLES—Cont'd

Nonresidents—Cont'd

Arrest,

Failure to honor appearance promise, **Veh 40515**

Procedure, **Veh 40305**

Children and minors,

Armed forces, drivers licenses, **Veh 12518**

Financial responsibility, **Veh 17703 et seq.**

Operators certificate, **Veh 12504**

Person signing drivers license, tort liability, **Veh 17703**

Continuance, service of process, **Veh 17452 et seq., 17457**

Daily commuter,

Definitions, **Veh 435.5**

Registration exemptions, **Veh 6700.2 et seq.**

Dealers, license exemption, importation or exportation of vehicles, **Veh 11700.1**

Death, service of process, **Veh 17452**

Definitions, **Veh 435**

Resident, **Veh 516**

Display, daily commuters, identification card, **Veh 6700.4**

Drivers licenses, ante

Executors and administrators, service of process, **Veh 17450 et seq.**

Exemptions, **Veh 6700 et seq.**

Fees, daily commuters, identification card, **Veh 6700.25**

Adjustments, **Veh 1678**

Forms, daily commuter, identification card application, **Veh 6700.3**

Guaranteed traffic arrest bail bond certificate, commercial vehicles, **Veh 40305.5**

Identity and identification, daily commuters, registration exemption, **Veh 6700.25**

Leases, drivers license, **Veh 14608**

Limitation of actions, **Veh 17463**

Manner of serving process, **Veh 17461**

Notice, service of process, **Veh 17455**

Off highway vehicles, special permits, **Veh 38087.5, 38231.5**

Process, **Veh 17450 et seq.**

Registration, fee, **Veh 9252**

Adjustments, **Veh 1678**

Resident, definitions, **Veh 516**

Revocation of license, return of documents to department, **Veh 8802, 8803**

Service of process, **Veh 17450 et seq.**

Time, registration exemption, **Veh 6700**

Unsatisfied judgment, suspension of privileges, **Veh 16376**

Warrants, arrest of nonresident failing to honor appearance promise, **Veh 40515**

Notice,

Appeal of drivers license suspension or revocation, **Veh 14401**

MOTOR VEHICLES—Cont'd
Notice—Cont'd

Arrest, notice of offense, **Veh 40002**

Broker agreements, **Veh 11738**

Bumper strength, **Veh 24011.3, 40000.15**

Certificate of title, transfer, nonpayment, **Veh 5911**

Chains, new vehicles unable to use, **Veh 9953**

Change in ownership, manufacturers, transporters, dealers and salesmen, **Veh 11704**

Claimants, vehicle or part having serial or identification number destroyed, hearing, **Veh 10751**

Commercial vehicles, driver notification requirements, **Veh 15220 et seq.**

Consumer protection, recovery corporation, **Veh 12205 et seq.**

Continuance of written promise to appear, violation, **Veh 40509**

Credit scores, dealers, **Veh 11713.20**

Crimes and offenses, notice to appear, **Veh 40002**

Cruising, **Veh 21100**

Dealers, ante

Defects, correction, manufacturer, **Veh 9975**

Dismantlers, ante

Disposition, liens and incumbrances, **Veh 22851.8**

Drivers licenses, ante

Electronic transmission, **Veh 1801**

English language, **Veh 9**

Equipment in unsafe condition, **Veh 24004**

Foreclosure of liens, **Veh 9801**

Forfeitures, unlicensed drivers, **Veh 14607.6, 14607.8**

Franchises, ante

Identification cards, ante

Impounding, repossessors and repossession, **Veh 23118**

Injuries resulting from failure to use seatbelts, **Veh 1663**

Inspection and inspectors, prospective customers, rights, **Veh 11609.5, 11709.1**

Insurance coverage, transfer of title, **Veh 5604**

Leases, ante

Lessor retailers, change of principal place of business, **Veh 11610**

License plates, ante

Liquefied petroleum gas propulsion systems, safety regulations, **Veh 2402.6**

Littering, nuisance, impounding, **Veh 22659.5**

Manufacturers and manufacturing, transporters, dealers and salesmen, change in ownership, **Veh 11704**

Method of giving notice, **Veh 29**

Mileage, transfer and sale, **Veh 5900, 5901**

Modification of delay, restrict or suspend order, **Veh 13202.5**

MOTOR VEHICLES—Cont'd
Notice—Cont'd

National law enforcement telecommunication system, abandoned or unclaimed property, storage, **Veh 22854.5**

Natural gas propulsion systems, safety regulations, **Veh 2402.6**

New vehicles unable to use tire chains, **Veh 9953**

Nonrepairable vehicles, owner retaining possession, **Veh 11515.2**

Nuisance, driving under the influence, sales, **Veh 23596**

Odometers, replacement, **Veh 28053**

Off highway vehicles subject to identification, change of address, **Veh 38060**

Poststorage hearings, **Veh 22852**

Private property owners, removal of vehicles, **Veh 22658**

Proof of notice, **Veh 24**

Prostitution, nuisance, impounding, **Veh 22659.5**

Records and recordation, registration or drivers license, suppression, **Veh 1808.21**

Recovery corporation, consumer protection, **Veh 12205 et seq.**

Registration, post

Remanufactured vehicles, disclosure, **Veh 11713.7**

Removal, post

Rental vehicles, children and minors, passenger restraint systems, **Veh 27365**

Repossession, **Veh 28**

Repurchased vehicles, sales, dealers or manufacturers, **Veh 11713.12**

Revocation or suspension of salespersons licenses, **Veh 11806**

Sale to enforce lien, **Veh 9802**

Salvage pools, **Veh 24007.6**

Security interest, transfer of title or interest, **Veh 5905 et seq.**

Service, **Veh 22, 23**

Nonresidents, **Veh 17455**

Service of process, lien sales, inability to serve, **Veh 22851.8**

Shoulder harness use with lap belts, **Veh 1663**

Smog impact fees, foreign states, registration, **Veh 1673.2, 1673.4, 1673.7**

Storage, fees, **Veh 10652.5, 22651**

Theft, post

Towing, fees, **Veh 22651**

Transfers,
Display of copy by dealer, **Veh 11715**
Title or interest, **Veh 5900 et seq.**

Used vehicles, warning, dangers without lap belts or shoulder harnesses, **Veh 27314.5**

Violations, notice to correct, **Veh 40000.25, 40610 et seq.**

Issuance, **Veh 40303.5**

Willful violations, **Veh 40000.25**

MOTOR VEHICLES—Cont'd
Notice—Cont'd

Watercourse banks, operation restrictions, **Veh 21116**

Novation, dealers, requiring prospective assent, **Veh 11713.2, 11713.3**

Nuisance,
Abandonment, procedures for removal and abatement, funds, **Veh 22710**
Driving under the influence, **Veh 23596**
Hazardous substances and waste, illegal dumping, **Veh 23112.7**
Littering, impounding, **Veh 22659.5**
Prostitution, **Veh 22659.5**
Removal of parked or standing vehicles, local ordinances, **Veh 22650 et seq., 22660 et seq.**

Number plates. License plates, generally, ante

Numbers and numbering,
Altering or defacing, **Veh 40000.9**
Drivers licenses, ante
Identity and identification, ante
Lamps, **Veh 24405**

Nurse practitioners. Nurses, this index

Nurses, this index

Oaths and affirmations,
Administration by officers and employees, **Veh 18**
Definitions, **Veh 16**

Obliteration, vehicle identification numbers, **Veh 10802**

Obstruction of view,
Defective windshields and rear windows, **Veh 26710**
Ice and snow, windows, **Veh 26708**
Signs and stickers, **Veh 26708**

Odometers, **Veh 28050 et seq.**
Advertising, device for resetting, **Veh 28051.5**
Certificates of title, disclosure statements, **Veh 4451**
Crimes and offenses, **Veh 11713, 40000.15**
Dealers, ante
Forms, transfer, disclosure, **Veh 5600**
Mileage, record, public inspection, **Veh 1819**
New car warranty, mileage, **Veh 28052**
Notice, replacement, **Veh 28053**
Paratransit vehicles, **Veh 34501.17**
Power of attorney form, disclosure statement, **Veh 5900**
Registration, refusal, statement, **Veh 4751**
Replacement, notice, **Veh 28053**
Resetting, dealers, **Veh 11713**
Sales,
Device for resetting, **Veh 28051.5**
Statement, mileage, **Veh 5900, 5901**
Service, repair, turning to zero, **Veh 28053**
Transfer, disclosure, forms, **Veh 5600**
True mileage, **Veh 28050 et seq.**
Wholesale motor vehicle auctions, mileage, **Veh 5900, 5901**

MOTOR VEHICLES—Cont'd
Odometers—Cont'd
Zero, repair, **Veh 28053**
Off highway vehicles, **Veh 38000 et seq.,
38600 et seq.**
Access routes, parks, **Veh 38027**
Actions and proceedings, littering, **Veh
38321**
Additional equipment, **Veh 38380**
Additional fees, registration, **Veh
38225.5**
Adjustments, **Veh 1678**
Agents, dealers, manufacturers, opera-
tion without identification certifi-
cate, **Veh 38021**
Air cushioned vehicles, brakes, exemp-
tion, **Veh 38355**
Allocation of funds, **Veh 38240 et seq.**
Applicability of law, **Veh 38001**
Motor vehicle board, off highway ve-
hicles subject to identification,
Veh 3051
Application for original identification,
Veh 38040 et seq.
Application for renewal of identifica-
tion, **Veh 38110 et seq.**
Application of law, motorcycles, **Veh
3051**
Bonds, original identification applica-
tion, **Veh 38050, 38055**
Brakes, **Veh 38355**
Brush covered land, spark arresters, **Veh
38366**
Cables, placing in position to do bodily
injury, **Veh 38318.5**
Certificates and certification, nonopera-
tion certificates, **Veh 38121, 38246**
Certificates of title, **Veh 38070 et seq.**
Expiration and renewal, **Veh 38115**
Issuance, **Veh 38070**
Transfer of title or interest, **Veh
38195 et seq.**
Chains, placing in position to do bodily
injury, **Veh 38318.5**
Change of address, notice to depart-
ment, **Veh 38060**
Chappie Zberg Off Highway Motor Ve-
hicle Law, **Veh 38000 et seq.**
Children and minors, **Veh 38503 et seq.,
38600**
Controls, ability to reach and operate,
crimes and offenses, **Veh 38304.1**
Citation of law, **Veh 38000**
Combined use highways, **Veh 38026**
Inyo County, **Veh 38026.1**
Controls, ability to reach and operate,
Veh 38304
Children and minors, crimes and of-
fenses, **Veh 38304.1**
Coownership of title, **Veh 38045**
Copies, certificates, devices or plates,
Veh 38085 et seq.
Fees, **Veh 1678, 38260**
Identification certificate, **Veh 38085**
Lost or stolen certificate or identifica-
tion plate, **Veh 38090**

MOTOR VEHICLES—Cont'd
Off highway vehicles—Cont'd
Course of instruction, **Veh 38007**
Crimes and offenses, **Veh 40000.24**
Children and minors, **Veh 38504.1**
Controls, ability to reach and oper-
ate, **Veh 38304.1**
Malicious placement of cables or
chains, **Veh 38318.5**
Public lands, operation, **Veh 38301**
Wilderness areas, **Veh 38301.3**
Crossing highway, **Veh 38025**
Damages, **Veh 38318.5**
Land, wildlands, **Veh 38319 et seq.**
Public lands, operation, **Veh 38301**
Dealers,
Fees, **Veh 38225 et seq.**
Licenses and permits, **Veh 11701,
38087**
Bonds (officers and fiduciaries),
Veh 11710
Exemptions, **Veh 11704.5, 11723**
Loading or storage, **Veh 38030**
Operation without identification cer-
tificate, **Veh 38021**
Delinquent fees, identification, **Veh
38245 et seq.**
Delivery permits, manufacturers and
dealers, **Veh 38087**
Demonstration permits, manufacturers
and dealers, **Veh 38087**
Device or plate, **Veh 38160 et seq.**
Dismantling, **Veh 38180, 38185**
Display permits, manufacturers and
dealers, **Veh 38087**
Distributors, operation without identifi-
cation certificate, **Veh 38021**
Drivers licenses, **Veh 12501**
Driving while privilege suspended,
Veh 14601 et seq.
Driving Schools, this index
Driving under the influence, driving
while privilege suspended, **Veh
14601.5**
Duplicate certificates, devices or plates,
Veh 38085 et seq.
Fees, **Veh 1678, 38260**
Embezzlement, identification period ex-
tended, **Veh 38125**
Emergencies, peace officers, **Veh 38025**
Emergency vehicles, exemption from
speed limits, **Veh 21055**
Emission control equipment, **Veh 38390
et seq.**
Environmental impact, damages, **Veh
38318.5**
Equipment, **Veh 38325 et seq.**
Additional equipment, **Veh 38380**
Brakes, **Veh 38355**
Emission control equipment, **Veh
38390 et seq.**
Exhaust system, **Veh 27150, 38365**
Lights and lighting, **Veh 38335, 38345**
Mufflers, **Veh 27150, 38365**
Evidences of identification, **Veh 38070
et seq.**

MOTOR VEHICLES—Cont'd
Off highway vehicles—Cont'd
Exemptions, **Veh 38010**
Exhaust system, **Veh 27150, 38365**
Expiration of identification, **Veh 38115**
Fees,
Additional fees, **Veh 38225.5**
Adjustments, **Veh 1678**
Identification fees, **Veh 38225 et seq.**
Renewal of identification, **Veh 38120**
Special permits, nonresidents, **Veh
38231.5**
Fines and penalties,
Children and minors, **Veh 38504.1**
Controls, ability to reach and oper-
ate, **Veh 38304.1**
Delinquent fees, **Veh 1678, 38246,
38265**
Nonoperation of vehicle, **Veh 38121**
Deposits, **Veh 42204**
Driving while privilege suspended,
Veh 14601 et seq.
Emission control equipment, **Veh
38392**
Nonoperation of vehicle, **Veh 38246**
Public lands, operation, **Veh 38301**
Wilderness areas, **Veh 38301.3**
Firearms, discharging at, **Veh 38318**
Fishing line, placing in position to do
bodily injury, **Veh 38318.5**
Flashing lights, **Veh 38346**
Forest land, spark arresters, **Veh 38366**
Forfeitures, deposit, **Veh 42204**
Funds,
Allocation of fees, **Veh 38240 et seq.**
Licenses, **Veh 38235**
Off highway vehicle fund, **Veh 42204**
Grass lands, spark arresters, **Veh 38366**
Habitual traffic offenders, driving while
privilege suspended, **Veh 14601.3**
Helmets, **Veh 38601**
Identification certificates,
Fees, **Veh 38225 et seq.**
Transfer of title or interest, **Veh
38195 et seq.**
Identification plate or device, **Veh 38010
et seq., 38160 et seq.**
Impounding, wilderness areas, **Veh
38301.3**
Inventory, registration, **Veh 38121**
Inyo County, combined use highways,
Veh 38026.1
Issuance of certificates of ownership,
Veh 38070 et seq.
Issuance of identification, fees, **Veh
38225 et seq.**
Joint tenancy, **Veh 38045**
Leases, **Veh 38200 et seq.**
License plates, **Veh 38010 et seq.**
Licenses and permits,
Manufacturers, dealers, **Veh 38087**
Nonresidents, **Veh 38087.5, 38231.5**
Operation without identification cer-
tificate, **Veh 38021**
Lights and lighting, **Veh 38335, 38345**
Littering, **Veh 38320, 38321**

MOTOR

MOTOR VEHICLES—Cont'd
Off highway vehicles—Cont'd
Lost certificate of ownership, **Veh 38090, 38095**
Manufacturers,
Operation without identification certificate, **Veh 38021**
Permits, **Veh 38087**
Misdemeanors, **Veh 40000.24**
Motorcycles, this index
Mountain fire districts, **Veh 38301.5**
Mufflers, **Veh 27150, 38365**
Mutilated certificate of ownership, **Veh 38090, 38095**
New vehicles, exemptions, **Veh 3051**
Noise limitations, **Veh 38370**
Exception, **Veh 27200**
Nonoperation certificates, **Veh 38121**
Nonresidents, special permits, **Veh 38087.5, 38231.5**
Notice, change of address, **Veh 38060**
Off highway vehicle safety education committee, **Veh 38500 et seq.**
Off street public parking facilities, use, registration requirements, **Veh 4000**
Operating rules, **Veh 38280 et seq.**
Operation,
Notice, improper pollution control device, **Veh 38393**
Registration requirements, **Veh 38020**
Operation on combined use highways, **Veh 38026.5**
Original identification, **Veh 38040 et seq.**
Ownership of title, **Veh 38045**
Passengers, public lands, **Veh 38506**
Peace officers, emergencies, **Veh 38025**
Place of business, display, licenses and signs, application of law, **Veh 11709**
Plate or device, **Veh 38160 et seq.**
Pollution control equipment, **Veh 38391 et seq.**
Public lands,
Passengers, **Veh 38506**
Special regulations, **Veh 38301, 38302**
Pushing on highway, **Veh 38025**
Reckless driving, **Veh 38316, 38317**
Recreational Trails, this index
Refusal of identification, **Veh 38145, 38150**
Registration, **Veh 38010 et seq.**
Fees, **Veh 1678, 38225.5, 38232**
Identification plate or device display, registration necessity, **Veh 4000**
Nonoperation of vehicle, **Veh 38121**
Transportation to or from closed course, **Veh 38088**
Renewal,
Certificate of identification, **Veh 38115, 38150**
Fees, **Veh 38225 et seq.**
Certificates of ownership, **Veh 38110 et seq.**
Repairs, **Veh 38318.5**
Riding on highway, **Veh 38025**

MOTOR VEHICLES—Cont'd
Off highway vehicles—Cont'd
Ropes, placing in position to do bodily injury, **Veh 38318.5**
Safety instructors,
Licenses, **Veh 11100.1**
Qualifications, **Veh 11104.3**
Safety training organizations, **Veh 11103.1**
Sales, **Veh 38195 et seq.**
Salvaging and dismantling, **Veh 38180, 38185**
Seasons, **Veh 38020**
Seatbelts, **Veh 38602**
Seats, **Veh 38603**
Second and subsequent offenses,
Children and minors, **Veh 38504.1**
Controls, ability to reach and operate, **Veh 38304.1**
Public lands, operation, **Veh 38301**
Service fee, issuance or renewal of identification, **Veh 38225**
Silencers, noise pollution, **Veh 38370**
Sirens, **Veh 38375**
Spark arresters, use on forest, brush or grass covered land, **Veh 38366**
Speed limits, **Veh 38305, 38310**
Emergency vehicles, exemption, **Veh 21055**
Standing vehicles, registration requirements, **Veh 38020**
Starting, **Veh 38312**
Emergency vehicles, exemptions, **Veh 21055**
Stolen certificate of ownership, **Veh 38090, 38095**
Stolen identification plate or device, **Veh 38090**
Theft, identification period extended, **Veh 38125**
Throwing projectiles, **Veh 38318**
Title of law, **Veh 38000**
Title or interest, transfers, **Veh 38195 et seq.**
Towing on highway, **Veh 38025**
Traffic Rules and Regulations, this index
Traffic Signs and Signals, this index
Training, **Veh 38007**
Children and minors, **Veh 38504.1, 38504.2**
Transfer,
Identity and identification, refusal, **Veh 38150**
Title or interest, **Veh 38195 et seq.**
Fees, **Veh 38255**
Adjustments, **Veh 1678**
Identification period extended, **Veh 38246**
Transportation without fee payments, delinquent fees, **Veh 38245**
Transporting, registration requirements, **Veh 38020**
Turning, **Veh 38314**
Emergency vehicles, exemptions, **Veh 21055**

MOTOR VEHICLES—Cont'd
Off highway vehicles—Cont'd
Undertaking, original identification application, **Veh 38050, 38055**
Unsafe condition, **Veh 38330**
Warning signals and devices, **Veh 38346**
Weapons, discharging at vehicle or occupants, **Veh 38318**
Wilderness areas, **Veh 38301.3**
Wildlife or wildlife habitat, damages, **Veh 38319 et seq.**
Offenses. Crimes and offenses, generally, ante
Officers and employees, hiring unlicensed personnel, **Veh 11713.2, 11713.3**
Official misconduct, disposition of fines, penalties, and forfeitures, **Veh 42202**
Official traffic control device, definitions, **Veh 440**
Official traffic control signal, definitions, **Veh 445**
Oil and gas pipelines, construction, maintenance, flashing amber lights, **Veh 25260.1**
Olympic games, commemorative reflectorized license plates, **Veh 5022, 5101.7**
One trip permit, fees, **Veh 1678, 9258**
Operation in state, registration, presumption, **Veh 4000.4**
Operation rules. Traffic Rules and Regulations, generally, this index
Operators licenses. Drivers licenses, generally, ante
Optional appearance before magistrate, violators, **Veh 40303 et seq.**
Optometrists, this index
Orders,
Failure to obey lawful orders, **Veh 40000.7**
Out of service orders, crimes and offenses, **Veh 2800, 40001, 40303**
Orders of court,
Autobroker trust accounts, distribution, **Veh 11737**
Crimes and offenses, failure to comply, **Veh 40508**
Occupational licenses, practices, **Veh 1651.2**
Recording devices, disclosure, **Veh 9951**
Searches and seizures, repossessors and repossession, **Veh 23118**
Vehicle or part having serial or identification number destroyed, disposition, **Veh 10751**
Ordinances,
Abatement and removal of abandoned vehicles, **Veh 22660 et seq.**
Bail, refunds, **Veh 42201.6**
Impounding vehicles, **Veh 22850.5**
Littering, nuisance, impounding, **Veh 22659.5**
Parking, private driveways, owners or lessees, permits, **Veh 22507.2**
Prostitution, impounding, **Veh 22659.5**

MOTOR VEHICLES—Cont'd

Organic peroxides, adoption of United States department of transportation definitions, **Veh 2402.7**

Original drivers license, definitions, **Veh 455**

Original identification, off highway vehicles, **Veh 38040 et seq.**

Out of service orders,
Commercial vehicles, fines and penalties, **Veh 15311.1**
Crimes and offenses, **Veh 2800, 40001, 40303**

Over Snow Vehicles (OSV), **Veh 557**

Overtaking and passing. Traffic Rules and Regulations, this index

Owners and ownership. Title to property, generally, post

Owners manuals. Manuals, generally, ante

Oxidizers, adoption of United States department of transportation definitions, **Veh 2402.7**

Paints and painting, law enforcement, sales, **Veh 27604**

Pandering, nuisance, impounding, **Veh 22659.5**

Parades, exemption from registration, **Veh 4003**

Paraplegic veterans, fees, exemptions, **Veh 9105**

Paratransit Vehicles, generally, this index

Parent and child. Children and minors, generally, ante

Park police, abandoned or unclaimed property, removal, **Veh 22669**

Park Trailers, generally, this index

Parked vehicle, tampering, **Veh 10853**

Parking. Traffic Rules and Regulations, this index

Parking brakes, **Veh 26450, 26451**

Parking lamps, **Veh 24800 et seq.**

Parking Lots and Facilities, generally, this index

Parking placards, disabled veterans, **Veh 9105**

Parks, this index

Parole and probation,
Drivers licenses, ante
Equivalent of conviction, **Veh 13103**
Theft, **Veh 10851**

Parole hearings board, records and recordation, confidential and privileged information, address, **Veh 1808.2**

Parole officers, special license plates, **Veh 5001**

Partial year registration, **Veh 9700 et seq.**
Commercial vehicles, weight fees, **Veh 1678, 9407, 9702**

Partitions,
Replacement of glazing material, safety material, **Veh 26703**
Safety glazing material, **Veh 26701 et seq.**

Parts,
Breaking or removing, **Veh 40000.9**

MOTOR VEHICLES—Cont'd

Parts—Cont'd
Duress or coercion, **Veh 11713.1**
Installation, **Veh 12000 et seq.**
Larceny, **Veh 10852**
Purchase or sale, vehicle identification numbers, crimes and offenses, **Veh 10803**
Refusal to deliver, **Veh 11713.2, 11713.3**
Sales, post

Passenger restraint systems. Seatbelts, generally, post

Passenger stage vehicles, fees, exemptions, **Veh 9107**

Passengers,
Accident reports, **Veh 20010**
Alcoholic beverages, children transporting liquor, **Veh 23224, 40000.15**
Farm labor vehicles, seats, **Veh 31406**
Motorized scooters, **Veh 21235**
Owner as passenger, **Veh 17158**
Seatbelts, generally, post

Passing lamps, **Veh 24402 et seq.**

Payment,
Fees, **Veh 9550 et seq.**
Fines, infractions, **Veh 42003**
Impounding, **Veh 14602.6, 14602.7**
Driving under the influence, second and subsequent offenses, **Veh 14602.8**
Peace officers procuring evidence, **Veh 42271**

Peace Officers, this index

Pedestrians. Traffic Rules and Regulations, this index

Penalties. Fines and penalties, generally, ante

Pending actions, vested rights, **Veh 4**

Perfection of security interest, **Veh 6301**

Perjury, **Veh 20**
Applications or documents, **Veh 1652**
Dismantlers, licenses and permits, application, **Veh 11504**
False information to police, **Veh 31**
Registration, smog impact fees, foreign states, **Veh 1673.6**

Permits. Licenses and permits, generally, ante

Person,
Definitions, **Veh 470**
Signing childs drivers license application, tort liability, **Veh 17700 et seq.**

Personal assistive mobility devices, **Veh 21280 et seq.**

Personal injuries, accidents. Traffic Rules and Regulations, this index

Persons age eighteen to twenty one, driving under the influence, education, **Veh 13352.6, 23502**

Persons authorized by law to receive the information, definitions, records and recordation, **Veh 1807.5**

Pest detection vehicles, amber warning lights, **Veh 25261**

Petitions, new vehicles, filing fee, **Veh 3050.5**

MOTOR VEHICLES—Cont'd

Photography and pictures,
Cameras, platform, **Veh 35409**
Drivers licenses, **Veh 12800.5, 14610**
Engraved pictures, **Veh 12800.5, 12811, 13005 et seq.**
Identification cards, **Veh 13005, 13005.3, 13005.5**
Length of vehicle taking pictures, **Veh 35409**
Municipal attorneys, disclosure, **Veh 1808.51**
Parking violations, removal, **Veh 22658**
Real estate brokers and salespersons, disclosure, enforcement, **Veh 1808.51**
Reckless driving, following too closely, interference, **Veh 40008**
Sales, drivers licenses, **Veh 12800.5**
Salespersons, licenses and permits, **Veh 11819**
Subdivided lands, disclosure, enforcement, **Veh 1808.51**

Physical condition of persons, confidential information, **Veh 1808, 1808.5**

Physical examinations,
Drivers licenses, ante
Records and recordation, inspection and inspectors, **Veh 34501.10**

Physician Assistants, this index

Physicians and Surgeons, this index

Pickup trucks,
Definitions, **Veh 471**
Weight fees, **Veh 9400**

Pilot cars,
Definitions, **Veh 472**
Equipment, **Veh 28100 et seq.**
Special permit violations, **Veh 35784**
Signs and markings, requirement, **Veh 27904**
Special moving permits, warning lights, **Veh 25270**
Vertical clearance measuring devices, **Veh 35252**

Pilot indicators, turn signals, **Veh 25108**

Pilot programs,
Electronic devices and equipment, license plates, **Veh 4853**
Tow truck drivers, certification, **Veh 2430 et seq.**

Pimping, nuisance, impounding, **Veh 22659.5**

Pipelines,
Construction and maintenance, flashing amber lights, **Veh 25260.1**
Rights of way, operation restrictions, **Veh 21116**

Place to appear, arrested person, notice, **Veh 40502**

Plans and specifications, sunscreening devices, **Veh 26708.2**

Plates. License plates, generally, ante

Platforms or other devices, **Veh 35409**

MOTOR VEHICLES—Cont'd
Pleadings,
Arrest for infraction or misdemeanor, continuance of case to prepare, **Veh 40306**
Complaints, generally, ante
Mail and mailing, written plea, **Veh 40519**
Written plea in lieu of personal appearance, **Veh 40519**
Pledges, transfer of title or interest, notice, **Veh 5908**
Plug in vehicles. Electric vehicles, generally, ante
Plural number, construction of Act, **Veh 14**
Pneumatic tires. Tires, generally, post
Pocket bikes. Motorized Scooters, this index
Point system, **Veh 12810**
Poisons, adoption of United States department of transportation definitions, **Veh 2402.7**
Police,
Abandoned vehicles, removal from private property after accident, **Veh 22653**
Amber warning lights, **Veh 25277**
Blue warning lights, **Veh 25258**
Colored lights, **Veh 25259**
Crimes and offenses, vehicles resembling law enforcement motor vehicles, **Veh 27605**
Death, reports, **Veh 20004**
False information, **Veh 31**
Flashing red lights and sirens, **Veh 25259, 25277**
Flood or loading lamps, **Veh 25110**
Hazardous substances and waste, signs and signals, exemptions, **Veh 27903**
Inspection, **Veh 2806**
Leased vehicles, investigation, name of lessee, **Veh 4453.6**
License plates,
Inspection, **Veh 4462**
Seizure, **Veh 4460**
Special plates, **Veh 5001**
Confidential information, **Veh 5003**
Theft, notice, **Veh 4458**
Licenses and permits, **Veh 2416**
Lights and lighting, flashing and colored lights, **Veh 25259**
Notice of accident, **Veh 20002**
Obedience to orders, **Veh 2800**
Personal injuries, report, **Veh 20003**
Pursuit, reports, **Veh 14602.1**
Red lights and sirens, **Veh 30**
Registration, deferring approval, **Veh 6051**
Removal, **Veh 22659**
Parked or standing vehicles, **Veh 22650 et seq.**
Private property after accident, **Veh 22653**
Repainting, sale or nonlaw enforcement use, **Veh 27604**

MOTOR VEHICLES—Cont'd
Police—Cont'd
Reports,
Guilty plea, **Veh 40806**
Larceny, **Veh 10500 et seq.**
Repossession, notice, **Veh 28**
Safety belts, **Veh 27315.3**
Theft, **Veh 10851**
Top mounted lamps, **Veh 25259**
Warning lights, **Veh 25277**
Windows, tinting, glazing, **Veh 26708.7**
Political subdivisions,
Fees, exemption, **Veh 9101, 9103**
Financial responsibility, exemption, **Veh 16051**
Registration, **Veh 4155**
Tort liability, **Veh 17000 et seq.**
Pools. Salvaged vehicles, post
Portable dollies used by dismantler, registration, exemption, **Veh 4014**
Possession,
Disabled person placards, **Veh 4463**
Fines and penalties, **Veh 4463.3**
Dismantler, notice, **Veh 11520**
Drivers licenses, ante
Registration card,
Department of motor vehicles, transfer of interest, **Veh 5912**
Location, **Veh 4454**
Storage fees, **Veh 10652.5**
Transfer, criminal or tort liability, **Veh 5602**
Powder, transportation of smokeless powder, **Veh 31619**
Power brakes, **Veh 26301 et seq.**
Definitions, **Veh 480**
Power of attorney, transfer of ownership, odometer disclosure statements, **Veh 5900**
Preferential use of highway, high occupancy vehicles, **Veh 21655.6**
Presentence investigations, code violations, **Veh 42003**
Pressure gauge, airbrakes, **Veh 26505, 26506**
Pressure hoses, nonconforming equipment sales, **Veh 24005**
Presumptions. Evidence, ante
Prevention of accidents, **Veh 2408**
Prices,
Advertisements, **Veh 11713.1**
Increase without notice, **Veh 11713.2, 11713.3**
Prima facie evidence. Evidence, generally, ante
Primary use of state highways, registration, presumption, **Veh 4000.4**
Prior conviction,
Defenses to prosecution for code violations, **Veh 41400**
Traffic violations, record, **Veh 13209**
Priorities and preferences,
Dealers, claims by state, **Veh 11711**
Impounded vehicles, liens and incumbrances, **Veh 22851.1**

MOTOR VEHICLES—Cont'd
Prisoners of war. Military Forces, this index
Privacy, dealers, records and recordation, **Veh 11713.3, 11713.25**
Private buildings, storage, reports, **Veh 10654**
Private investigators, light bars, **Veh 27607**
Private party vehicle markets, **Veh 12101 et seq.**
Private patrols, light bars, **Veh 27607**
Private property, removal,
Abandoned or unclaimed property, **Veh 22523**
Damages, **Veh 22658**
Scene of accident, **Veh 22653**
Theft, **Veh 10850 et seq.**
Private road or driveway, **Veh 490**
Private schools, definitions, **Veh 492**
Privately owned ambulances, transportation of medical supplies, lifesaving equipment or personnel, emergency vehicle status, **Veh 2416**
Privileged information. Confidential or privileged information, generally, ante
Privileges and immunities,
Drivers licenses, anatomical gift stickers, false or inaccurate information, **Veh 12811**
Tort liability, **Veh 17000 et seq.**
Unregistered vehicles, towing, **Veh 4000**
Probate Proceedings, this index
Probation. Parole and probation, generally, ante
Probationary licenses,
Dealers, **Veh 11718**
Lessor retailers, **Veh 11606**
Problem assessment program, alcohol and drug use, **Veh 23249.50**
Procedure on violations, arrest, **Veh 40300 et seq.**
Proceedings. Actions and proceedings, generally, ante
Process, **Veh 24.5**
Nonresidents, **Veh 17450 et seq.**
Service of process,
Driver license revocation or suspension, notice, **Veh 13106**
Lessor retailers, **Veh 11610**
Lien sales, inability to serve, **Veh 22851.8**
Salespersons, **Veh 11812**
Torts, **Veh 17152**
Vehicle verifiers, **Veh 11302.2**
Products, exhaust products, operation to prevent escape, **Veh 27153**
Products liability, franchises, **Veh 3064**
Projecting loads. Traffic Rules and Regulations, this index
Promotions, special license plates, limitations, **Veh 5060**
Proof. Evidence, generally, ante
Proof of financial responsibility, reciprocity, **Veh 6854**
Prosecutions under code, evidence, **Veh 40800 et seq.**

MOTOR VEHICLES—Cont'd

Prostitution,
Drivers licenses, revocation or suspension, **Veh 13201.5**
Impounding, **Veh 22659.5**
Protests,
Filing fees, **Veh 3050.5**
Franchises, ante
Protuberances on tires, **Veh 27454**
Tort liability, **Veh 17000 et seq.**
Provisional drivers license, minors, **Veh 12814.6**
Public Agencies, this index
Public defenders, records and recordation, access, **Veh 1810.5**
Public Entities, this index
Public inspection of records, **Veh 1808**
Public Lands, this index
Public officers and employees,
Accidents, transportation of injured persons, **Veh 20016**
Tort liability, **Veh 17000 et seq.**
Public policy,
Red lights and sirens, **Veh 30**
Seat belts, mandatory use, **Veh 27315**
Public Utilities, this index
Publicly owned special construction equipment, registration, fees, **Veh 1678, 9261, 9261.1**
Publicly owned vehicles,
Fees, exemptions, **Veh 9101, 9103**
License plates, **Veh 4155**
Registration, revocation, **Veh 8801**
Puerto Rico, convictions, drivers license revocation or suspension, **Veh 13352**
Purchase orders. Conditional sales, generally, ante
Purchasers, transfer of title, excess payment to dealer, **Veh 11713.3, 11713.4**
Purchases. Sales, generally, post
Purple Heart recipients, special license plates, **Veh 5101.8**
Pursuit, law enforcement agencies, reports, **Veh 14602.1**
Racing vehicles,
Definitions, **Veh 286**
Mufflers, **Veh 27150**
Off highway vehicles, **Veh 38000 et seq.**
Radar jamming devices, speed, **Veh 28150, 40000.15**
Radial tires, inner tubes, **Veh 27455**
Radio. Television and radio, generally, post
Radioactive materials,
Adoption of United States department of transportation definitions, **Veh 2402.7**
Markings, **Veh 27903**
Transporting, **Veh 33000**
Railroad crossings,
Blocking, **Veh 22526**
Commercial vehicles, ante
Failure to stop, license revocation, **Veh 13201**
Safety, drivers handbook, **Veh 1656.3**
Rape, license plates, new plates, **Veh 4467**

MOTOR VEHICLES—Cont'd

Rates and charges,
Leases, ante
Littering, nuisance, impounding, **Veh 22659.5**
Prostitution, nuisance, impounding, **Veh 22659.5**
Storage, post
Towing, post
Real Estate, this index
Rear clip, definitions, **Veh 5505**
Rear lamps, **Veh 24600 et seq.**
Approval of equipment and devices, **Veh 26100 et seq.**
Auxiliary lamps, **Veh 24616**
Cargo lamps, **Veh 24616**
Clearance lamps, **Veh 25100**
Deceleration lights, **Veh 25251.5**
Energy storing system, **Veh 24253**
Exempt vehicles, **Veh 25803**
Flashing lights, **Veh 25251**
Side marker lamps, **Veh 25100**
Visible from front of vehicle, **Veh 25950**
Testing and approval, equipment, **Veh 26100 et seq.**
Rear trunk lid handle, windows, obstruction of view, **Veh 26708**
Rear windows,
Defective equipment, **Veh 26710**
Ice and snow, obstruction, **Veh 26708**
Safety glazing materials, replacement, **Veh 26703**
Rearview mirrors,
Obstruction of view, signs and stickers, **Veh 26708**
Outside rear view mirrors, turn signal mounts, use, **Veh 24953**
Reasonable cause, removal of vehicles, **Veh 22651**
Rebates,
Advertisements, **Veh 11713.1, 11713.16**
Dishonor, autobrokers sales, **Veh 11713.3**
Rebuilt or restored vehicles. Registration, post
Rebuilt parts, sales and installation, **Veh 12000 et seq.**
Recall, confidential record access, **Veh 1808.23**
Reciprocity,
Commercial vehicles, drivers licenses, **Veh 12505**
Revocation or suspension, **Veh 15326**
Drivers licenses, **Veh 15000 et seq.**
Foreign commercial vehicles,
Registration, **Veh 6854**
Temporary operation, **Veh 4004**
International registration plan, fees, apportionment, **Veh 9250.15**
Licenses, fees, **Veh 9260**
Registration, foreign commercial vehicles, **Veh 6854**
Reckless driving. Traffic Rules and Regulations, this index

MOTOR VEHICLES—Cont'd

Reconstructed vehicles, registration, **Veh 4153**
Inspection and inspectors, emissions, **Veh 4750.1**
Recording devices, **Veh 9951**
Records and recordation, **Veh 1800 et seq.**
Abstract of record, dismissal of charges, size or weight law violations, **Veh 40003**
Accidents, reports, **Veh 1810.3**
Address, confidential or privileged information, **Veh 1808.21 et seq.**
Autobroker log, **Veh 11735**
Charities, gifts, devises and bequests, **Veh 1660**
Colleges and universities, addresses, parking enforcement, disclosure, **Veh 1808.25**
Commercial requester accounts, **Veh 1810.2**
Accidents, reports, **Veh 1810.3**
Confidential or privileged information, ante
Court records, **Veh 1802**
Crimes and offenses, ante
Dealers, privacy, **Veh 11713.3, 11713.25**
Destruction, **Veh 1807**
Identification card records, **Veh 13002**
District attorneys, inspectors or investigators, confidential and privileged information, address, **Veh 1808.2**
Drivers licenses, ante
Drivers records,
Availability for inspection, **Veh 34501.10**
Staged accidents, **Veh 1806**
Driving privilege, revocation or suspension, evidence, **Veh 40832**
Education, gifts, devises and bequests, **Veh 1660**
Electronic recording, **Veh 1801**
Evidence, **Veh 1806**
Employee, prosecution for violation, dismissal, **Veh 40003**
Evidence, revocation or suspension of driving privilege, **Veh 40832**
Examination, permits, **Veh 1814**
Failure to keep, license revocation, special licenses, **Veh 2542**
Fines and penalties, confidential or privileged information, **Veh 1808.22**
Fleet vehicles, **Veh 8057**
Free records, distribution, **Veh 1812, 1813**
Handicapped persons, ante
Identification cards, destruction, **Veh 13002**
Impounding, repossessors and repossession, **Veh 23118**
Inspection and inspectors, ante
Leases, ante
License plates, exempt vehicles, **Veh 5003**
License suspension or revocation, evidence, **Veh 40807**

MOTOR

MOTOR VEHICLES—Cont'd
Records and recordation—Cont'd
Mileage,
    Public inspection, **Veh 1819**
    Transfer, **Veh 5906.5**
Motorized bicycles, identification of stolen motorized bicycles, **Veh 5038**
Nondrivers, leases to, **Veh 14609**
Nonprofit organizations, donors, **Veh 1660**
Paratransit vehicles, **Veh 34501.17**
Parole hearings board, inspectors or investigators, confidential and privileged information, address, **Veh 1808.2**
Peace officers, inspectors or investigators, address, confidential and privileged information, **Veh 1808.2**
Prior convictions, department informational reports, **Veh 42004**
Private party vehicle markets, **Veh 12103**
Public inspection, **Veh 1808**
Registration, post
Religious organizations and societies, gifts, devises and bequests, **Veh 1660**
Remanufacturers, crimes and offenses, **Veh 11713.8**
Revocation or suspension of driving privilege, evidence, **Veh 40832**
Sale of information, **Veh 1810 et seq.**
Salvage pools, **Veh 543, 11540**
Security interest, **Veh 6300 et seq.**
Service of process on nonresidents, **Veh 17458**
Stipulated vehicle release agreements, **Veh 1806.1**
Storing vehicles, **Veh 10650 et seq.**
Suppression, registration or drivers license record, **Veh 1808.21**
Towing, post
Traffic violations, destruction, time, **Veh 12808**
Vanpooling, maintenance, **Veh 34509**
Vehicle verifiers, **Veh 11307**
Recovery corporation, consumer protection, **Veh 12200 et seq.**
    Fees, **Veh 4456.3**
Recreational Vehicles, generally, this index
Recut tires, sale, **Veh 27460.5, 27461**
Red Cross vehicles, warning lights, **Veh 25259.5**
Red flag or cloth, wide vehicles, display, **Veh 25104**
Red glazing material, equipment, **Veh 26701**
Red lights,
    Clearance lamps, **Veh 25100**
    Fusees, use, **Veh 25305**
    Light bars, **Veh 27606, 27607**
    Off highway vehicles, **Veh 38345**
    Projecting loads, **Veh 24604**
    Public policy, **Veh 30**
    Side lamps, **Veh 25106, 25950**

MOTOR VEHICLES—Cont'd
Red lights—Cont'd
    Vehicles not requiring headlamps, **Veh 25803**
    Warning light, use, **Veh 25269**
Redemption, liens and incumbrances, sale, **Veh 22851.12**
Reexamination. Drivers licenses, ante
Reflectorized license plates, **Veh 4850**
Reflectors, **Veh 24607, 24608**
    Area reflectorizing material, **Veh 24607**
    Backup lamps, **Veh 24606**
    Color, **Veh 25950**
    Combined functions, lighting equipment, **Veh 24252**
    Courtesy lights, **Veh 25105**
    Definitions, **Veh 375**
    Doors, **Veh 25105**
    Emergency reflectors, **Veh 25300 et seq.**
    Exempt vehicles, **Veh 25803**
    Explosives, vehicle transporting, **Veh 31610**
    Front and side, **Veh 24608**
    Height, mounted height, **Veh 24254**
    License plates, **Veh 4850**
    Lighting equipment, **Veh 24607 et seq.**
    Load, mounted on, **Veh 25952**
    Material, **Veh 25500**
    Mounted height, **Veh 24254, 25952**
    Multiple unit truck reflector, **Veh 24610**
    Rear lamps, **Veh 24607 et seq.**
    Red, rear mounting, **Veh 24607**
    Taillamps, **Veh 24607**
    Visibility from front of vehicle, **Veh 25950**
    Wide vehicles, warning signals and devices, **Veh 25300 et seq.**
Refrigeration equipment, **Veh 28000**
Refunds,
    Fees and penalties, **Veh 42230 et seq.**
    Lessor retailers, licensing or transfer of title, **Veh 11616**
    License fees, ante
    Notice to dealers, **Veh 11713.2, 11713.3**
    Registration, post
    Security deposits, **Veh 16027**
    Smog impact fees, foreign states, registration, **Veh 1673 et seq.**
    Used vehicles, cancellation option agreements, conditional sales, **Veh 11713.21**
Refusal of identification, off highway vehicles, **Veh 38145, 38150**
Refuse collectors, safety headsets and earplugs, **Veh 27400**
Regional park districts, irrigation and irrigation districts, machinery and equipment, inspection and inspectors, **Veh 2810.2**
Register, definitions, motor vehicle noise limits, **Veh 27200**
Registered owner, definitions, **Veh 505**
Registration, **Veh 4000 et seq., 4150 et seq.**
    Abandoned vehicles, disposition, **Veh 22660**

MOTOR VEHICLES—Cont'd
Registration—Cont'd
    Abbreviation,
        Coownership, **Veh 4150.5**
        Manner of transfer of interest, **Veh 5600.5**
    Absence of ownership, bond or undertaking, **Veh 4157**
    Acceptance, consent to service of process, **Veh 17459**
    Accessing, commercial use, licenses and permits, **Veh 1810.7**
    Actions and proceedings, smog impact fees, foreign states, **Veh 1673.4**
    Additional fees, **Veh 9250.13**
        Adjustments, **Veh 1678**
    Address, change, **Veh 4159, 4160**
    Affidavits, dealers, application without required supporting documents, **Veh 4456**
    Air pollution, certificate of compliance, temporary registration, **Veh 4156**
        Fees, **Veh 9257.5**
    Aircraft refueling vehicles, **Veh 4021**
    Amnesty, fees, specially constructed vehicles, inspection and inspectors, emissions, **Veh 4750.1**
    Amphibious vehicles, certificate of ownership, **Veh 9872.5**
    Applications, **Veh 4150**
        Drivers license numbers, **Veh 1653.5**
        Fees, applications within 30 days of expiration date, **Veh 5902.5**
        Foreign vehicles, **Veh 4300**
        Refund of fees, **Veh 42235**
        Renewal, **Veh 4602**
        Social security numbers, **Veh 1653.5**
    Apportionment basis, fleet vehicles, liens, enforcement, **Veh 8200 et seq.**
    Autobrokers, **Veh 11735**
    Autoettes, **Veh 4000.5**
    Based in state, presumption, **Veh 4000.4**
    Bond pending registration, **Veh 4157, 4158**
        Application without required supporting documents, **Veh 4456**
    Bonds, registration services, **Veh 11401, 11402**
    Brokered retail new motor vehicle sales, **Veh 11739**
    Cancellation, **Veh 8800**
        Failure of proof to respond to damages, **Veh 16484**
        Permanent registration, **Veh 8801**
        Return of evidence of registration to department, **Veh 8802**
    Cards, **Veh 4450 et seq.**
        Contents, **Veh 4453**
        Crimes and offenses, **Veh 4462, 40000.7**
        Dismantlers, surrender, **Veh 5500, 5501**
        Duplicates, fees, **Veh 9265**
            Adjustments, **Veh 1678**
        Electronic devices and equipment, **Veh 4853**

MOTOR VEHICLES—Cont'd
Registration—Cont'd
Cards—Cont'd
Expiration date, **Veh 4601**
Fictitious name, **Veh 4453**
Fictitious or false, evidence procurement, **Veh 42271**
Foreign vehicles, **Veh 4456**
Forgery, **Veh 4463**
Inspection by police, **Veh 4462**
Leases, **Veh 4453.5**
Loans to unauthorized persons, **Veh 4461**
Location, **Veh 4454**
Lost or stolen card, **Veh 4457 et seq.**
New card on renewal, **Veh 4607**
Notice, transfer, nonpayment, **Veh 5911**
Operation without, report of sale form, display, **Veh 4456**
Parking violations, itemized unpaid penalties, **Veh 4761**
Renewal, **Veh 4601**
Revocation or suspension, **Veh 8800**
Seizure by police, **Veh 4460**
Surrender on transfer of interest, **Veh 5902**
Transfer of interest, **Veh 5600 et seq.**
Delivery of card, **Veh 5753**
Unlawful possession, **Veh 4462, 40000.7**
Validation, motor clubs, **Veh 4610**
Certificates of compliance or noncompliance, air pollution, **Veh 4000.1 et seq.**
Certificates of ownership, amphibious vehicles, **Veh 9872.5**
Certificates of title, ante
Change of address, **Veh 4159, 4160**
Change of engines, **Veh 4161 et seq.**
Citizens band radio, special plates, **Veh 5020, 5021**
Commercial use, data base, accessing, licenses, **Veh 1810.7**
Commercial vehicles, ante
Community property, **Veh 4150.5**
Congressional medal of honor recipients, exemptions, **Veh 9105**
Contracts, private industry, **Veh 1685**
Coownership, **Veh 4150.5**
Counties, **Veh 4155**
Fees, **Veh 9250.14**
Crimes and offenses,
Cancellation, **Veh 8800**
Dealers, delivery, **Veh 40000.7**
Evasion of fees and taxes, residents, **Veh 8804**
Fees, theft crime programs, **Veh 9250.14**
Operation of unregistered vehicle, **Veh 40001**
Smog impact fees, foreign states, **Veh 1673.6**
Daily commuters, nonresidents, exemption, **Veh 6700.2 et seq.**

MOTOR VEHICLES—Cont'd
Registration—Cont'd
Data base, accessing, commercial use, **Veh 1810.7**
Dealers, ante
Delinquent fees, transfer of registration, **Veh 9562**
Delinquent registration, lien enforcement, **Veh 9801 et seq.**
Disaster areas, special permits, **Veh 4005**
Dismantled or wrecked vehicle, cancellation, **Veh 8800**
Dismantlers, ante
Display, nonresident daily commuter, identification card, **Veh 6700.4**
Duplicates, fees, **Veh 9265**
Adjustments, **Veh 1678**
Electric vehicles, confidential or privileged information, access, **Veh 1808.23**
Electronic devices and equipment, cards, **Veh 4853**
Electronic lien and title program, **Veh 4450.5**
Electronic processing, new vehicles, **Veh 4456.4**
Fees, **Veh 4456.5**
Embezzled vehicles, renewal, **Veh 4605**
Employees violations,
Codefendants, owners, **Veh 40003**
Employers failure to answer charges, **Veh 40005**
Engine numbers, **Veh 4161 et seq.**
Evidence, **Veh 4450 et seq.**
Ownership, absence, undertaking or bond, **Veh 4157**
Primary use or based in state, presumption, **Veh 4000.4**
Exemptions, **Veh 4000 et seq.**
Aircraft refueling, **Veh 4021**
Cemetery vehicles, **Veh 4012**
Certificates or statements of compliance, air pollution emission standards, **Veh 4000.1**
Dealer vehicle standing on highway, **Veh 4016**
Dollies used by dismantlers, **Veh 4014**
Fees, reinstatement, financial responsibility, military forces, **Veh 4000.38**
Firefighting equipment, **Veh 4015**
Foreign commercial vehicles, **Veh 4004**
Forklift trucks, **Veh 4013**
Hauled vehicles, **Veh 4009**
Low speed vehicles, **Veh 4023**
Military forces, fees, reinstatement, financial responsibility, **Veh 4000.38**
Multiple county use, **Veh 4004.5**
Operation of vehicle pending registration, **Veh 4017**
Records, special license plates, **Veh 5003**

MOTOR VEHICLES—Cont'd
Registration—Cont'd
Exemptions—Cont'd
Special highway construction equipment, **Veh 4010**
Special identification plates, **Veh 4018**
Temporary installation of engine in previously registered vehicle, **Veh 4161**
Vehicle crossing highway, **Veh 4006**
Veterans, fees, **Veh 9105**
Expiration date, **Veh 1651.5, 4601, 4601.5**
Fees, **Veh 9250 et seq.**
Additional fees, **Veh 9250.13**
Adjustments, **Veh 1678**
Adjustments, **Veh 1678**
Revenue forecasts, **Veh 9551.2**
Air pollution,
Certificate of compliance, temporary registration, **Veh 9257.5**
South coast air quality management district, **Veh 9250.11**
Amnesty, specially constructed vehicles, inspection and inspectors, emissions, **Veh 4750.1**
Applications within 30 days of expiration date, **Veh 5902.5**
Citizens band radio, special plates, **Veh 5020, 5021**
Commercial vehicles, collection of delinquent fees, **Veh 9800**
Consumer protection, recovery corporation, **Veh 12200 et seq.**
Counties, **Veh 9250.14**
Crimes and offenses, operation without payment, **Veh 40001 et seq.**
Data base, commercial use, **Veh 1810.7**
Dealers, payment, **Veh 4456**
Delinquent fees, **Veh 9552**
Repossession, waiver of penalties, **Veh 9561**
Dismantling and wrecking vehicle, **Veh 9263**
Duplicate registration, payment, registration card on availability, **Veh 9706.1**
Exemptions,
Parking violations, failure to pay penalties, **Veh 4765**
Reinstatement, financial responsibility, military forces, **Veh 4000.38**
Failure to pay, cancellation, **Veh 8800**
Fingerprint identification, local law enforcement programs, **Veh 9250.19**
Fleet vehicles, **Veh 5304 et seq.**
Freeway emergencies, **Veh 9250.10**
Ham radio operators, license plates, class D radio stations, **Veh 5020**
Liens and incumbrances, **Veh 9800 et seq.**
Fleet vehicles, **Veh 5307, 8200 et seq.**

MOTOR VEHICLES—Cont'd
Registration—Cont'd
Fees—Cont'd
Local law enforcement fingerprint identification programs, **Veh 9250.19**
Nonresident daily commuters, identification card, **Veh 6700.25**
Adjustments, **Veh 1678**
Offsets, rate adjustments, revenue forecasts, **Veh 9551.2**
Operation without payment, **Veh 40001 et seq.**
Parking violations, failure to pay penalties, **Veh 4763**
Payment, **Veh 9550 et seq.**
Rate adjustments, revenue forecasts, **Veh 9551.2**
Rebuilt and restored vehicles,
After reported dismantling, **Veh 9563**
Service fee, **Veh 9255.1**
Recovery corporation, consumer protection, **Veh 12200 et seq.**
Reduction of fees, **Veh 9407**
Refunds, **Veh 42235**
Reinstatement, financial responsibility, military forces, exemptions, **Veh 4000.38**
Renewal,
Adjustments, **Veh 1678**
Due date notice, **Veh 1661**
Military forces, fines and penalties, waiver, **Veh 9560**
Repossessor, delinquent payment, waiver of penalties, **Veh 9561**
Return of unexpired license plates, foreign vehicles, **Veh 4302**
Sacramento metropolitan air quality management district, surcharge, **Veh 9250.2**
Sales, pro rated, **Veh 11713**
San Joaquin Valley unified air pollution control district, surcharge, **Veh 9250.16**
San Mateo County, **Veh 9250.5**
Service fees, **Veh 9250.7, 22710**
Smog impact fees, foreign states, **Veh 1673 et seq.**
South coast air quality management district, **Veh 9250.11**
Stolen or embezzled vehicle, **Veh 4605**
Surcharge, San Joaquin Valley unified air pollution control district, **Veh 9250.16**
Television, photographer or cameraman, **Veh 5008**
Temporary registration, air pollution, certificate of compliance, **Veh 9257.5**
Theft crime programs, **Veh 9250.14**
Transfer of title or interest of unregistered vehicle, **Veh 9255**
Veterans, exemption, **Veh 9105**
Waiver of penalty fees, **Veh 9562**

MOTOR VEHICLES—Cont'd
Registration—Cont'd
Financial responsibility, **Veh 4000.37, 4000.38, 4750**
Fines and penalties,
Delinquent renewals, **Veh 9553 et seq.**
Fleet vehicles, apportionment, liens, **Veh 8200 et seq.**
Offsets, revenue forecasts, **Veh 9554.1**
Refusal, **Veh 4760.1**
Renewal, **Veh 4760.1**
Military forces, waiver, **Veh 9560**
Fleet vehicles, ante
Foreign built cars, identification, **Veh 4453**
Foreign commercial vehicles,
Reciprocity, **Veh 6854**
Temporary registration, **Veh 4004**
Foreign countries, removing license plates, **Veh 11725**
Foreign states, **Veh 4000.2, 4002, 4152, 4300 et seq.**
Disposition of license plates, **Veh 4302**
Evidence, procurement, **Veh 42271**
Expiration date, **Veh 4152.5**
Fees, **Veh 9252**
Adjustments, **Veh 1678**
Smog impact fees, **Veh 1673 et seq.**
Liens and incumbrances, **Veh 4306**
Mirrors, **Veh 26709**
Notice, **Veh 4309**
Operation pending registration, **Veh 4017**
Reciprocity, **Veh 6854**
Refusal, return of documents, **Veh 4308**
Sales and use taxes, **Veh 4300.5**
Smog impact fees, **Veh 1673 et seq.**
Surrender of plates and documents, **Veh 4301**
Title in doubt, **Veh 4307**
Forgery, **Veh 4463**
Forms, **Veh 1652**
Nonresident daily commuters, identification card application, **Veh 6700.3**
Fraud, cancellation, **Veh 8800**
Holds, parking processing agencies, recalls, **Veh 40200.8**
Identity and identification, nonresident daily commuters, exemption, **Veh 6700.25**
Impounding, **Veh 1661, 9553**
Information, **Veh 4465**
Inspection and inspectors, renewal, **Veh 4000.3**
Sales, **Veh 1810**
Injunction, **Veh 6051**
Inspection and inspectors, **Veh 2804, 2805**
Police, **Veh 4462**
Insurance, financial responsibility, **Veh 4000.37 et seq., 4750**
Interstate commerce, **Veh 4303**

MOTOR VEHICLES—Cont'd
Registration—Cont'd
Itemization, noncompliance notice offenses, **Veh 4766**
Joint tenancy, **Veh 4150.5**
Law enforcement,
Identification, **Veh 4453**
Prior registration, service fees, **Veh 9255.1**
Leases,
Cards, **Veh 4453.5**
Electronic processing, **Veh 4456.4**
Fees, **Veh 4456.5**
Lemon Law buyback, **Veh 4453**
Lessor retailers, application without required supporting documents, **Veh 4456**
License fees, generally, ante
Licensed registration service, certificates of title, license plates, duplicates, **Veh 4466**
Liens and incumbrances,
Certificates of title, foreign states, **Veh 4304, 4306**
Electronic lien and title program, **Veh 4450.5**
Fleet vehicles, enforcement, **Veh 8200**
Limitation of actions,
Counterfeit or fictitious documents, **Veh 40004**
Fleet vehicles, apportionment, liens and incumbrances, **Veh 8201**
Smog impact fees, foreign states, **Veh 1673.4**
Loans to unauthorized persons, **Veh 4461**
Local vehicle license fee surcharge, **Veh 9250.12**
Location in state, presumption, **Veh 4000.4**
Low speed vehicles, exemptions, **Veh 4023**
Mechanically unfit or unsafe vehicle, cancellation, **Veh 8800**
Military Forces, this index
Motor clubs, endorsement of receipts, **Veh 4610**
Motor vehicle insurance, financial responsibility, **Veh 4000.37 et seq., 4750**
Motorized bicycles, **Veh 4020, 5030 et seq.**
Motorized scooters, application of law, **Veh 21224**
Municipal vehicles, **Veh 4155**
New card, renewal, **Veh 4607**
New vehicles, ante
Newspaper photographer or cameraman, **Veh 5008**
Nonrepairable vehicles, **Veh 6050**
Nonresidents, exemptions, **Veh 6700 et seq.**
Notice,
Cessation of registration service, **Veh 11411**

MOTOR VEHICLES—Cont'd
Registration—Cont'd
Notice—Cont'd
Fleet vehicles, apportionment, liens and incumbrances, **Veh 8201**
Parking violations,
Administrative fees, **Veh 4763**
Processing agencies, recalling hold, **Veh 40200.8**
Rate adjustments, revenue forecasts, **Veh 9551.2**
Renewal fee, due date, **Veh 1661**
Revocation or suspension, financial responsibility, **Veh 4000.38**
Smog impact fees, foreign states, **Veh 1673.2, 1673.4, 1673.7**
Off highway vehicles, ante
Operation of unregistered vehicles, **Veh 40001**
Out of state vehicles, air pollution emission controls, certificate of compliance or noncompliance, **Veh 4000.1**
Park trailers, cards, **Veh 4453**
Parking violations,
Failure to pay penalties, refusal to renew, **Veh 4760 et seq., 40220**
Processing agencies, recalling hold, **Veh 40200.8**
Partial year, certificate of nonoperation, **Veh 4604.2**
Partial year registration, **Veh 9700 et seq.**
Commercial vehicles, weight fees, **Veh 9407**
Pending registration, operation of vehicle, exemption, **Veh 4017**
Perjury, smog impact fees, foreign states, **Veh 1673.6**
Photographers or cameraman, vehicle, **Veh 5008**
Political subdivisions, publicly owned vehicle, **Veh 4155**
Presumptions, vehicles primary use or based in state, **Veh 4000.4**
Primary use of state highways, **Veh 4000.4**
Private industry, contracts, **Veh 1685**
Private party vehicle markets, law provisions, supply to vendor, **Veh 12104**
Public inspection of records, **Veh 1808**
Rebuilt or restored vehicles,
Identification, **Veh 4453**
Registration fees, **Veh 9563**
Service fee, **Veh 9255.1**
Reciprocity, ante
Reconstructed vehicles, **Veh 4153**
Inspection and inspectors, emissions, **Veh 4750.1**
Records and recordation, **Veh 1800 et seq.**
Cessation of registration service, **Veh 11411**
Electric vehicles, confidential or privileged information, **Veh 1808.23**
Registration services, **Veh 11406 et seq.**

MOTOR VEHICLES—Cont'd
Registration—Cont'd
Records and recordation—Cont'd
Special license plates, exempt vehicles, **Veh 5003**
Reduction of registration fees, **Veh 9407**
Refunds,
Fees, **Veh 42235**
Smog impact fees, foreign states, **Veh 1673 et seq.**
Refusal, **Veh 4750 et seq.**
Parking violations, failure to pay, **Veh 4760 et seq., 40220**
Registration year, definitions, **Veh 506**
Reinstatement, financial responsibility, **Veh 4000.38**
Remanufactured vehicles,
Application, statement, **Veh 4153**
Inspection and inspectors, emissions, **Veh 4750.1**
Removal and disposition of vehicles, **Veh 22660**
Renewal, **Veh 4600 et seq.**
Applications, **Veh 4150**
Delinquent renewal, **Veh 9556**
Extension of time, **Veh 4603**
Fees, **Veh 9250.8, 9250.9**
Freeway emergencies, **Veh 9250.10**
Military forces, fines and penalties, waiver, **Veh 9560**
Repossessed and sold vehicles, late payment, **Veh 9561.5**
Financial responsibility, **Veh 4000.37, 4750**
Fines and penalties, **Veh 9553 et seq.**
Military forces, waiver, **Veh 9560**
Inspection and inspectors, notice, **Veh 4000.3**
Insurance, financial responsibility, **Veh 4000.37, 4750**
Military forces, fines and penalties, waiver, **Veh 9560**
Motor vehicle insurance, financial responsibility, **Veh 4000.37, 4750**
Nonoperation of vehicle, **Veh 4604, 4604.5, 38246**
Off highway vehicles, **Veh 38121**
Notice, shoulder harness and lap belt use message, **Veh 1663**
Off highway vehicles, **Veh 38121, 38246**
Operation pending renewal, **Veh 4606**
Refusal to renew,
Noncompliance notice transmitted, **Veh 4766**
Parking violations, failure to pay, **Veh 4760 et seq., 40220**
Repossessed and sold vehicles, fees, late payment, **Veh 9561.5**
Stolen vehicles, **Veh 4605**
Summary, penalty provisions, failure to report accident or prove financial responsibility, **Veh 1656.2**
Time, **Veh 4603**

MOTOR VEHICLES—Cont'd
Registration—Cont'd
Reports,
Fingerprints and fingerprinting, fees, **Veh 9250.19**
Service fees, **Veh 9250.7**
Repossessors and repossession,
Renewal fees, late payment, **Veh 9561.5**
Transportation, **Veh 4022**
Resident, definitions, **Veh 516**
Revocation or suspension, **Veh 8800**
Financial responsibility, **Veh 4000.38**
Return of evidence to department, **Veh 8802**
Safety belt system, **Veh 27315**
Sale of information, **Veh 1810 et seq.**
Sales and use taxes, foreign vehicles, **Veh 4300.5**
Salvaged vehicles, **Veh 11519**
San Mateo County, fees, **Veh 9250.5**
Security interest, **Veh 6300 et seq.**
Transfer, **Veh 5908**
Seizure, fleet vehicles, apportion, liens, **Veh 8203**
Services, **Veh 11400 et seq.**
Small claims courts, smog impact fees, foreign states, **Veh 1673.4**
Smog impact fees, foreign states, **Veh 1673 et seq.**
Special license plates, exempt vehicles, **Veh 5003**
Specially constructed vehicles, **Veh 4153**
Inspection and inspectors, emissions, **Veh 4750.1**
State vehicles, **Veh 4155**
Stopping vehicle to inspect registration, **Veh 1655**
Taxicabs,
Prior use, identification, **Veh 4453**
Vehicles formerly registered as, service fee, **Veh 9255.1**
Television photographer or cameraman, vehicle, **Veh 5008**
Temporary registration, **Veh 4156**
Fees, **Veh 9260**
Air pollution, certificate of compliance, **Veh 9257.5**
Foreign vehicles, **Veh 4004**
Prior registration, **Veh 9710**
Tenancy in common, **Veh 4150.5**
Theft, programs, fees, **Veh 9250.14**
Time,
Application, foreign vehicle registration, **Veh 4152**
Nonresidents, exemption, **Veh 6700**
Return of application, corrections or additional information, **Veh 4456**
Waiting, **Veh 1669**
Title in doubt, **Veh 4307**
Toll evasion, penalties, nonpayment, **Veh 4770 et seq.**
Total loss salvage vehicles, **Veh 11519**
Transfer, **Veh 5600 et seq., 6050 et seq.**
Cards, **Veh 5911, 5912**

MOTOR

MOTOR VEHICLES—Cont'd
Registration—Cont'd
Transfer—Cont'd
Certificates of compliance, air pollution, emissions, **Veh 4000.1, 4000.2**
Delinquent fees, **Veh 9562**
Emissions, tests, exemptions, **Veh 5751.5**
Evidence of ownership, bond or undertaking, **Veh 4157**
Fleet vehicles, apportionment, liens and incumbrances, waiver, **Veh 8204**
Identification penalties, waiver, **Veh 38247**
Noncompliance notice, renewal, **Veh 4766**
Parking, fines and penalties, **Veh 4767**
Summary of penalty provisions, failure to report accident or prove financial responsibility, **Veh 1656.2**
Unregistered vehicles, **Veh 5904, 6052**
Unattended vehicles, release, **Veh 22651**
Undertaking, absence, evidence of ownership, **Veh 4157**
United States vehicles, **Veh 4155**
Unregistered vehicles, driving or moving, **Veh 4000**
Vehicle in state, **Veh 4151**
Vehicle outside state, **Veh 4152**
Vehicle verifiers, **Veh 11300 et seq.**
Waiver,
Penalties, **Veh 9562, 38247**
Renewal, fines and penalties, military forces, **Veh 9560**
Waste tire haulers, infractions, **Veh 31560**
Weight fees, **Veh 9400**
Exemption, vehicles manufactured before designated time, **Veh 9401**
Year round registration, **Veh 1651.5**
Definitions, **Veh 676**
Registration plates. License plates, generally, ante
Regrooved tires, sales, **Veh 27460.5, 27461**
Regulations. Rules and regulations, generally, post
Rehabilitation centers, drug addicts or drunkards, **Veh 23213**
Reinstatement,
Drivers licenses, ante
Registration, financial responsibility, **Veh 4000.38**
Rejection of applications return of fees, **Veh 42230**
Relatives, transfer of title or interest, registration, exhaust emission control devices, **Veh 4000.1**
Release,
Dealers, requiring prospective assent, **Veh 11713.2, 11713.3**
Impounding, **Veh 14602.6**
Repossessors and repossession, **Veh 23118**

MOTOR VEHICLES—Cont'd
Release—Cont'd
Removal, **Veh 22658**
Security interest, registration, **Veh 5905**
Tort liability, person signing minors drivers license, **Veh 17711**
Unattended vehicles, registration, **Veh 22651**
Relevant market area, definitions, **Veh 507**
Religious Organizations and Societies, this index
Remanufactured vehicles,
Accomplices and accessories, **Veh 11700.3**
Bonds (officers and fiduciaries), producers, **Veh 11710**
Crimes and offenses, **Veh 11713.8**
Disclosure, **Veh 11713.7**
Dismantlers, surrender of certificates and title, license plates and registration cards, **Veh 5500, 5501**
Division, types of businesses, **Veh 1670**
Fees, administrative services, **Veh 4456.1**
Licenses and permits, producers, **Veh 11700 et seq.**
Office, place of business, **Veh 1670, 1671**
Registration,
Applications, statement, **Veh 4153**
Inspection and inspectors, emissions, **Veh 4750.1**
Restitution, licenses and permits, denial, **Veh 11703.2**
Transporting, producers, **Veh 11715 et seq.**
Two or more types of businesses, division between, **Veh 1670**
Removal,
Abandoned or unclaimed property, ante
Advertising vehicles, **Veh 22651.2**
Civil liability, disabled persons designated parking spaces, **Veh 22652.5**
Contracts, local authorities, **Veh 22671**
Damages, **Veh 22658**
Disabled persons designated parking spaces, civil liability, **Veh 22652.5**
Disabled vehicles, transportation department employees, **Veh 22654**
Drivers licenses, revoked, suspended, driving without, **Veh 14602.6**
For sale vehicles, signs proclaiming, **Veh 22651.9**
Highway, hearings, **Veh 22650**
Highway patrol, **Veh 22651.05, 22659**
Law enforcement, volunteers, **Veh 22651.05**
Lighting equipment or device on direction of officer making inspection, **Veh 40151**
Multiple traffic offenses, **Veh 22651.2**
Notice, **Veh 22650 et seq.**
Abandoned or unclaimed property, public agencies, **Veh 22851.3**
Ordinances, **Veh 22661**
Storage, **Veh 22851 et seq.**

MOTOR VEHICLES—Cont'd
Removal—Cont'd
Parked or standing vehicles, **Veh 22650 et seq.**
Parts, **Veh 10852**
Private property, vehicles left at scene of accident, **Veh 22653**
Public agencies, **Veh 22851.3**
Sale of vehicles, signs proclaiming, **Veh 22651.9**
Searches and seizures, generally, post
Storage, hearings, **Veh 22852**
Unauthorized vehicles in disabled persons designated parking spaces, civil liability, **Veh 22652.5**
Vehicle identification numbers, **Veh 10802**
Volunteers, law enforcement, **Veh 22651.05**
Renewal,
Drivers licenses, ante
Identification cards, mail and mailing, **Veh 13002.1**
Registration, ante
Rental cars. Leases, generally, ante
Repainting, law enforcement vehicles, sale or nonlaw enforcement use, **Veh 27604**
Repair shops,
Garages, generally, this index
Motor Vehicle Repair Dealers, generally, this index
Motor Vehicle Service Stations, generally, this index
Repairs,
Brakes, **Veh 26453**
Liens and incumbrances, generally, ante
Lighting equipment, **Veh 24252**
Motor Vehicle Repair Dealers, generally, this index
Parts, **Veh 12000 et seq.**
Vanpooling, **Veh 34509**
Replacement,
Equipment not conforming with code, **Veh 24005**
Glazing materials used in doors, **Veh 26703**
Keys, **Veh 9954**
Odometers, **Veh 28051**
Reports,
Activated alarm devices, impoundment, **Veh 22651.5**
Cigarettes, throwing from vehicle, **Veh 1817**
Commercial vehicles, registration, gross weight, **Veh 4150.1**
Convictions, Drivers License Compact, **Veh 15022**
Coroners, death, **Veh 20011**
Crimes and offenses, prior convictions, **Veh 42004**
Drivers licenses, ante
Electronic devices and equipment, license plates, **Veh 4853**
Electronic transmission, **Veh 1801**
English language, **Veh 9**

I–132

MOTOR VEHICLES—Cont'd
Reports—Cont'd
Evidence, ante
Failure to file, removal from office, **Veh 1805**
Fines and penalties, prior convictions, **Veh 42004**
Historic vehicles, special plates, **Veh 5004.1**
Infractions, prior convictions, **Veh 42004**
Juvenile traffic offenders, **Veh 1816**
Leased vehicles not returned, **Veh 10500**
License notations, **Veh 1818**
Negligence actions, admissibility of reports, findings of department, **Veh 40833**
Persons throwing flaming substance from vehicles, **Veh 1817**
Police reports, evidence on guilty plea, **Veh 40806**
Pursuit by law enforcement agencies, **Veh 14602.1**
Registration,
Fees, **Veh 9250.14**
Fingerprints and fingerprinting, fees, **Veh 9250.19**
Removal of vehicle from highway for storage, **Veh 22853**
Second and subsequent offenses, department informational reports, **Veh 42004**
Service fees, **Veh 9250.7**
Stolen vehicles, **Veh 10500 et seq.**
Stored vehicles, **Veh 10650 et seq.**
Failure to report, **Veh 10655**
Theft, post
Violations, **Veh 1803 et seq.**
Wholesale vehicle auctions, dealer reporting, **Veh 4456**
Repossessors and repossession,
Conditional sales, ante
Crimes and offenses, notice, **Veh 28**
Dealers, force and violence, notice, assignments, **Veh 11724**
Delinquent fees, payment by repossessor, waiver of penalties, **Veh 9561**
Delinquent payment of fees, **Veh 9561**
Impounding vehicles, release, **Veh 14602.6, 14602.7**
Notice, **Veh 28**
Registration,
Renewal fees, late payment, **Veh 9561.5**
Transportation, **Veh 4022**
Searches and seizures, **Veh 23118**
Signs and signals, tow vehicles, **Veh 27907**
Storage, registration, transportation, **Veh 4022**
Transfer of interest, **Veh 5601**
Transportation, registration, **Veh 4022**
Representatives,
Change in list, notice to department, **Veh 11704**
Compromise and settlement, fines and penalties, **Veh 11903.5**

MOTOR VEHICLES—Cont'd
Representatives—Cont'd
Definitions, **Veh 512**
Fees, time of payment, **Veh 9550**
Fines and penalties, compromise and settlement, **Veh 11903.5**
Licenses and permits, **Veh 11900 et seq.**
Application, names of representatives, **Veh 11704**
Fees, **Veh 9262**
Payment, **Veh 11723**
Hearings, suspension or revocation, **Veh 11903**
Suspension or revocation, **Veh 11727, 11902.5**
Hearings, **Veh 11903**
Moral turpitude, crimes involving, licenses and permits, **Veh 11902, 11902.5**
Special plates, fees, **Veh 9262**
Reproduction of salesmens licenses, **Veh 11819**
Repurchased vehicles, notice, dealers or manufacturers, **Veh 11713.12**
Requirements, sunscreening devices, **Veh 26708.2**
Reregistration, **Veh 6050 et seq.**
Res judicata, civil actions, conviction, **Veh 40834**
Resale, sale of vehicles to unlicensed persons for resale, **Veh 11713.2, 11713.3**
Rescue team, liability, resuscitation attempts, **Veh 165.5**
Residence. Domicile and residence, generally, ante
Residence address, confidentiality, **Veh 1808.21 et seq.**
Residence district, definitions, **Veh 240, 515**
Resident, definitions, **Veh 516**
Restricted licenses. Drivers licenses, ante
Retailers. Lessor retailers, generally, ante
Retrofit, shoulder harnesses, used vehicles, **Veh 27314.5**
Review. Appeal and review, generally, ante
Revocation or suspension,
Commercial vehicles, drivers licenses, reciprocity, **Veh 15326**
Drivers licenses, ante
Ignition interlock devices, certificates and certification, **Veh 13386**
Privilege to operate, speed contests on highways, **Veh 23109**
Registration, ante
Salesmens license, failure or refusal to surrender license, **Veh 11819**
Ridesharing. Car pools, generally, ante
Ridges, protuberances on tires, **Veh 27454**
Right of way,
Definitions, **Veh 525**
Traffic Rules and Regulations, this index
Right turns. Traffic Rules and Regulations, this index

MOTOR VEHICLES—Cont'd
Road rage. Traffic Rules and Regulations, this index
Roadside rest area or viewpoint, removal, **Veh 22651**
Roadway, definitions, **Veh 530**
Rooms, tow truck equipment, **Veh 27700**
Rope or strap material, loads, certification, **Veh 24005.5**
Round trip, repairs, exemption from registration, **Veh 4003**
Rules and regulations,
Hazardous materials, transportation, **Veh 2532**
Pneumatic tire noise standards, **Veh 27503**
Trailer coaches, highway movement, **Veh 34500 et seq.**
Rules of the road. Traffic Rules and Regulations, generally, this index
Runaway vehicle,
Driver, financial responsibility, **Veh 16001**
Report of accidents, **Veh 20002**
Running board courtesy lamps, **Veh 25105**
Running lamps, **Veh 25109**
Rural mail carriers, flashing amber lights, **Veh 25272**
Safe Streets Act, **Veh 14607.4 et seq.**
Publicity, **Veh 1664**
Safety, **Veh 34500 et seq.**
Brady Jared Teen Driver Safety Act, **Veh 12814.6**
Commercial motor vehicle safety program, **Veh 15200 et seq.**
Defect, correction, manufacturers, **Veh 9975**
Event data recorders, disclosure, **Veh 9951**
House cars, **Veh 2429.3**
Inspection and inspectors, **Veh 2806**
Commercial vehicles, **Veh 2813.5, 40000.7**
Low speed vehicles, **Veh 21253, 21254**
Natural gas propulsion systems, **Veh 2402.6**
Recording devices, disclosure, **Veh 9951**
Refusal of registration, **Veh 4751**
Sensing and diagnostic modules, disclosure, **Veh 9951**
Teaching devices, **Veh 35409**
Unsafe vehicles, revocation of license, **Veh 8800**
Vehicles used by driving schools, **Veh 11109**
Safety belts. Seatbelts, generally, post
Safety chains, tow vehicle coupled, **Veh 29003**
Safety glazing material, **Veh 26701 et seq.**
Definitions, **Veh 535**
Testing, **Veh 26100 et seq.**
Tinted safety glass, **Veh 26708.5**
Safety valves, air brakes, **Veh 26503**
Safety zones, definitions, **Veh 540**

MOTOR

MOTOR VEHICLES—Cont'd
Sales,
Air pollution vehicle not conforming, **Veh 24007.5**
Auctions and auctioneers,
Equipment, **Veh 24007.5**
Wholesale motor vehicle auctions, **Veh 6100 et seq.**
Bumper strength notices, **Veh 24011.3, 40000.15**
Campers, fire extinguishers, **Veh 28060**
Certificate of title, **Veh 4456**
Completed, **Veh 5901**
Conditional sales, generally, ante
Consignment sales,
Consumer protection, recovery corporation, **Veh 12200 et seq.**
Dealers, contracts, **Veh 11729, 11730**
Consumer protection,
Internet web site, **Veh 1656.4**
Recovery corporation, **Veh 12200 et seq.**
Consummated, **Veh 5901**
Contracts, disclosure that engine manufacturer differed from vehicle manufacturer, **Veh 9981**
Copies of records, **Veh 1811**
Costs, liens and incumbrances, **Veh 22851.12**
Credit scores, dealers, notice, **Veh 11713.20**
Damages, disclosure, **Veh 9990 et seq.**
Dealers, generally, ante
Disabled person placards, **Veh 4463**
Fines and penalties, **Veh 4463.3**
Disclosure, damages, **Veh 9990 et seq.**
Discrimination, **Veh 11713.1**
Drivers licenses, ante
Endorsement of documents, **Veh 5750 et seq.**
Engines, disclosure that manufacturer differed from vehicle manufacturer, **Veh 9981**
Equipment, **Veh 24007**
Conforming with code, **Veh 24005, 24007.5**
Exhaust systems,
Crimes and offenses, **Veh 40000.15**
Violating noise regulations and standards, crimes and offenses, **Veh 27150.1**
Federal trade commission, buyers guide, **Veh 11614, 11713.1**
Financing agency, bonds (officers and fiduciaries), priorities and preferences, **Veh 11722**
For sale signs, removal of vehicle, **Veh 22651.9**
Foreign countries, removing license, plates, **Veh 11725**
Franchises, **Veh 11713.3**
Goods, wares and merchandise, rates and charges, disclosure, **Veh 11713.19**
Hazardous substances and waste, illegal dumping, nuisance, **Veh 23112.7**

MOTOR VEHICLES—Cont'd
Sales—Cont'd
House cars, manufacture in two or more stages, **Veh 11713.5**
Identification, **Veh 11713.1**
Ignition interlock devices, driving under the influence, **Veh 23575**
Information from records, **Veh 1810 et seq.**
Inspection, prospective customer, **Veh 11709.1**
Insurance coverage, notice, **Veh 5604, 5604.5**
Internet web site, consumer protection, **Veh 1656.4**
Leased vehicles, delinquent fees, fines, penalties and interest, **Veh 9801**
Lemon Law buyback, decal, **Veh 11713.12**
Lessor retailers, generally, ante
Liens and incumbrances, **Veh 9802 et seq., 22851.8**
Redemption, **Veh 22851.12**
Satisfaction, impounded vehicle, **Veh 22851.1**
Light duty trucks, itemized price stickers, **Veh 11712.5, 24013.5**
Lighting and signalling equipment devices, prior testing and approval, **Veh 26100 et seq.**
Low speed vehicles, disclosure, **Veh 11713.10, 21252**
Mileage, recordation, **Veh 5906.5**
Minor without drivers license, **Veh 15500**
New or used, disclosure, **Veh 11713.1**
New vehicles,
Gasoline minimum octane number, **Veh 24013**
Noise limits, **Veh 27200, 27204**
Noncomplying equipment, **Veh 26104**
Nuisance, driving under the influence, **Veh 23596**
Numbered copies of report, **Veh 4456**
Odometers, accuracy, **Veh 28050**
Off highway vehicles, **Veh 38195 et seq.**
Parts, **Veh 12000 et seq.**
Alteration, identification numbers, **Veh 10803**
Crimes and offenses, **Veh 40000.11**
Passenger restraint systems, children and minors, accidents, **Veh 27362.1**
Physical damage insurance, notice, **Veh 5604.5**
Pollution control devices installation and inspection certificate, **Veh 24007**
Private owners, application of law, **Veh 12120**
Private party vehicles markets, provisions of law, supply to vendors, **Veh 12104**
Public agencies, equipment requirements, **Veh 24007.5**
Recovery corporation, consumer protection, **Veh 12200 et seq.**

MOTOR VEHICLES—Cont'd
Sales—Cont'd
Recreational vehicles, fire extinguishers, **Veh 28060**
Recut tires, **Veh 27460.5**
Redemption, **Veh 22851.12**
Registration fees, pro rated, **Veh 11713**
Registration information, **Veh 1810**
Regrooved tires, **Veh 27460.5**
Remanufacturers, report of sale, **Veh 4456**
Removal of vehicles with signs, **Veh 22651.9**
Repurchased vehicles, notice, dealers or manufacturers, **Veh 11713.12**
Safety glazing material equipment, **Veh 26701**
Salvaged vehicles, post
Seatbelts, **Veh 27302 et seq., 27315**
Used vehicles, **Veh 27314**
Seized vehicles, alteration of identification or manufacturing number, **Veh 10751**
Stolen vehicle, dealers and manufacturers, license revocation, **Veh 11705**
Testing equipment prior to sale, **Veh 26104**
Tire traction devices, compliance, **Veh 27459.5**
Tires,
New tire standards, **Veh 27500**
Noise standards, tires complying with regulations, **Veh 27502**
Radial tires, inner tubes, **Veh 27455**
Recut or regrooved tires, **Veh 27460.5**
Secondhand, **Veh 27465**
Standards, **Veh 27500, 27501**
Title to vehicle in two or more persons, **Veh 4150.5**
Trade ins, credit, discharge, **Veh 11709.4**
Transfer of registration, fees, **Veh 9255**
Transfer of title or interest, **Veh 5600 et seq.**
Unlicensed purchasers, **Veh 11713.2, 11713.3**
Used vehicles, post
Vehicles or parts with altered identification numbers, **Veh 10803**
Wholesale vehicle auctions, **Veh 6100 et seq.**
Reports, **Veh 4456**
Sales and Use Taxes, this index
Salespersons,
Acting as dealers, **Veh 11806**
Address, change of address, notice, **Veh 11812**
Advertisements, false, **Veh 11713**
Cancellation, licenses and permits, **Veh 11822**
Compromise and settlement, fines and penalties, **Veh 11808.5**
Crimes and offenses, **Veh 40000.11**
Return of documents and license plates, **Veh 40000.7**
Selling without licenses and permits, **Veh 11800**

MOTOR VEHICLES—Cont'd
Salespersons—Cont'd
Definitions, **Veh 675**
Driving instruction, exemptions, **Veh 11101**
Employment of unlicensed salesman, **Veh 11713**
Fines and penalties,
Compromise and settlement, **Veh 11707, 11808.5**
Place of business, sales elsewhere, **Veh 11728**
Forms, license application, **Veh 11802**
Licenses and permits, **Veh 11713, 11800 et seq.**
Applications, **Veh 11802, 11806**
Cancellation, **Veh 11822**
Crimes and offenses, **Veh 40000.11**
Display of license, **Veh 11812**
Duplicate license, **Veh 11814**
Fees, **Veh 11820**
Hearings, **Veh 11806, 11808, 11810**
Issuance, **Veh 11804**
Probationary license, **Veh 11810**
Reapplication after denial, **Veh 11810**
Refusal, **Veh 11806**
Renewal, **Veh 11814**
Revocation or suspension, **Veh 11806, 11824**
Place of business, sales elsewhere, **Veh 11728**
Temporary suspension, **Veh 11810**
Unlawful use or duplication, **Veh 11819**
Process, **Veh 11812**
Service of process, **Veh 11812**
Temporary permits, **Veh 11803**
Salvage yards, **Veh 2805**
Salvaged vehicles,
Air bags, **Veh 5505**
Certificates and certification, total loss salvage vehicles, **Veh 11515, 11568**
Disclosure, NMVTIS (national motor vehicle title information system), history, reports, sales, **Veh 11713.26**
Dismantlers, generally, ante
Inspection and inspectors, **Veh 5505**
License plates, **Veh 11540**
NMVTIS (national motor vehicle title information system), sales, history, reports, disclosure, **Veh 11713.26**
Nonrepairable vehicles, salvage pool acquiring, records, **Veh 11540**
Pools,
Certificates of title, duplicates, **Veh 4466**
Definitions, **Veh 543**
License plates, duplicates, **Veh 4466**
Nonrepairable vehicle certificate, **Veh 11515.1**
Notice, **Veh 24007.6**
Salvage certificates, **Veh 11515.1**
Records and recordation, **Veh 11540**
Salvage pools, **Veh 543**
Registration, **Veh 11519**

MOTOR VEHICLES—Cont'd
Salvaged vehicles—Cont'd
Sales,
Disclosure, total loss salvage vehicles, **Veh 11515, 11568**
Inspection and inspectors, **Veh 5506**
NMVTIS (national motor vehicle title information system), history, reports, disclosure, **Veh 11713.26**
Total loss salvage vehicles, generally, post
Transfer, inspection and inspectors, **Veh 5506**
San Francisco City and County, local vehicle license fee surcharge, **Veh 9250.12**
San Mateo County, registration, fees, **Veh 9250.5**
Sand buggies, places of business, display, licenses and permits, application of law, **Veh 11709**
Sanitary districts, repair vehicles, warning lights, **Veh 25265**
Satellite warranty facilities, franchises, **Veh 3062**
Scales, inspection, **Veh 2809**
School Buses, generally, this index
Schools and School Districts, this index
Scooters. Motorized Scooters, generally, this index
Scrap metal processors,
Application of law, vehicles or parts with altered identification numbers, **Veh 10804**
Dismantled vehicles, identification numbers, **Veh 10751**
Searches and seizures,
Documents and plates, **Veh 4460**
Drivers licenses, revoked, suspended, driving without, **Veh 14602.6**
Evidence, impounding for evidence, **Veh 22655.5**
Fleet vehicles, registration, apportion, liens, **Veh 8203**
Irrigation and irrigation districts, machinery and equipment, public lands, **Veh 2810.2**
Leased vehicles, delinquent fees, fines, penalties and interest, **Veh 9801**
Liens, **Veh 9801**
Littering, nuisance, **Veh 22659.5**
Parked or standing vehicles, **Veh 22650 et seq.**
Prostitution, **Veh 22659.5**
Repossessors and repossession, **Veh 23118**
Safety belts, mandatory use, **Veh 27315**
Unlicensed drivers, vehicles, **Veh 14607.4 et seq.**
Seatbelts, **Veh 27302 et seq.**
Children and minors, ante
Crimes and offenses, point count, **Veh 12810.2**
Mandatory use, **Veh 12810.2, 27315**
Notice, shoulder harness use with lap belts, **Veh 1663**
Off highway vehicles, **Veh 38602**

MOTOR VEHICLES—Cont'd
Seatbelts—Cont'd
School Buses, this index
Standards, adoption and enforcement, **Veh 26103**
Three wheeled vehicles, application of laws, **Veh 27315.1**
Children and minors, **Veh 27368**
Used vehicles, warning notice, dangers of not having lap belts or shoulder harnesses, **Veh 27314.5**
Youth bus operators, **Veh 12523**
Seats,
Car seats, children, **Veh 27360 et seq.**
Point system, **Veh 12810**
Farm labor vehicles, **Veh 31406**
Off highway vehicles, **Veh 38603**
Second and subsequent offenses. Crimes and offenses, ante
Second stage manufacturers, definitions, house cars, **Veh 11930**
Secondhand dealers, definitions, private party vehicle markets, **Veh 12101**
Secondhand tires, sale or use, **Veh 27465**
Section headings, application of law, **Veh 7**
Secured transactions. Security interest, generally, post
Security deposits,
Following accidents, refunds, **Veh 16027**
Off highway vehicles, **Veh 38195 et seq.**
Security interest,
Bond pending registration, **Veh 4157**
Certificates of title, delivery, release, **Veh 5753**
Dealers, licenses and permits, **Veh 11711.3**
Fees, delinquent fees, payment by repossessor, **Veh 9561**
Filing fees, **Veh 9256**
Impounding, **Veh 14602 et seq.**
Repossessors and repossession, **Veh 23118**
Insurance, notice, **Veh 5604**
Lessor retailers, licenses and permits, **Veh 11711.3**
Perfecting security interest, **Veh 6300 et seq.**
Release, certificates of title, delivery, **Veh 5753**
Repossession, **Veh 5601**
Notice, **Veh 28**
Tort liability, **Veh 17156**
Transfer of title, **Veh 5905 et seq.**
Fees, **Veh 9255**
Security officers, abandoned or unclaimed property, removal, **Veh 22669**
Seizures. Searches and seizures, generally, ante
Self driving vehicles, **Veh 38750 et seq.**
Semaphore changing devices, **Veh 21464, 25352**
Semitrailers. Motor Carriers, generally, this index
Sensing and diagnostic modules, **Veh 9951**

MOTOR

MOTOR VEHICLES—Cont'd

Sentence and punishment, inspection and inspectors, failure to stop and submit, **Veh 42002.1**

Serial numbers, alteration, **Veh 10751**
Fines and penalties, **Veh 42002.4**

Service advertisements, autobrokers, **Veh 11713**

Service authorities, removal of abandoned vehicles, **Veh 22710**

Service brakes. Brakes, ante

Service contracts, dealers, discrimination, **Veh 11713.3**

Service fees,
Certificate of ownership without registration, **Veh 1678, 9254**
Dismantlers, return of identification to department, **Veh 9263**
Fleet vehicles, **Veh 1678, 9252**
Foreign state registration, **Veh 1678, 9252**
Registration, **Veh 9250.7, 22710**
Special construction equipment, **Veh 1678, 9261, 9261.1**

Service of process. Process, ante

Service stations. Motor Vehicle Service Stations, generally, this index

Services, dealers, rates and charges, disclosure, **Veh 11713.19**

Settlement. Compromise and settlement, generally, ante

Severability of acts, **Veh 5**

Sex Offenders, this index

Sexual battery, license plates, new plates, **Veh 4467**

Sheep herding, warning lights, **Veh 25270.5**

Sheriffs, this index

Shoulder harnesses, use with lap belts, notice, **Veh 1663**

Shovels, tow truck equipment, **Veh 27700**

Shredding facilities, inspection, stolen vehicles, **Veh 2805**

Side lighting equipment, **Veh 25100 et seq.**
Color visible from front of vehicle, **Veh 25950**

Side mounted turn signal lamps, flashing amber lights, **Veh 24953**

Side reflectors, **Veh 24608**

Side windows, obstruction of view, **Veh 26708**

Sidewalks, definitions, **Veh 555**

Signals. Traffic Signs and Signals, generally, this index

Signatures, **Veh 17**
Acknowledgments, **Veh 19**
Arrested persons, assumed or fictitious name on promise to appear, **Veh 40504**
Certificates of title, **Veh 5750 et seq.**
Documents, electronic transmissions, **Veh 1801.1**
Drivers licenses, ante
Duplicate certificates of title, transfer of title or interest, **Veh 5752**
False signatures, violations, **Veh 40000.25**

MOTOR VEHICLES—Cont'd

Signatures—Cont'd
Insurers, transfer of ownership certificate, lienholders, exemption, **Veh 5752**
Licenses and permits, **Veh 12950**
Lienholders, transfer of ownership certificate, **Veh 5752**
Minors drivers license application, tort liability, **Veh 17700 et seq.**
New care buyers, vehicles unable to use chains, **Veh 11713.6**
Wholesale vehicle auctions, dealer report, **Veh 4456**

Signs. Traffic Signs and Signals, generally, this index

Simulated checks, advertisements, **Veh 11713.1**

Single beam lighting equipment, **Veh 24410**

Singular number, construction of Act, **Veh 14**

Sirens. Horns and sirens, generally, ante

Size. Traffic Rules and Regulations, this index

Skateboards, motorized skateboards, **Veh 21968**

Skill test, fees, **Veh 14900, 14900.1**
Adjustments, **Veh 1678**

Slow moving vehicles. Traffic Rules and Regulations, this index

Small Claims Courts, this index

Smog impact fees, registration, foreign states, **Veh 1673 et seq.**

Smoking, youth bus operators, **Veh 12523**

Snow tires, **Veh 27459**
Definitions, **Veh 558**
Four wheel drive vehicles, **Veh 27460**

Snowmobiles, generally, this index

Sobriety checkpoints, **Veh 2814.2**

Social security numbers. Drivers licenses, ante

Sole proprietorships, transfer of title or interest, registration, exhaust emission control devices, **Veh 4000.1**

Solicitations, on freeway, infractions, **Veh 22520.5**

Solid tires, **Veh 27450 et seq.**
Definitions, **Veh 560**

Solid waste,
Accidents, removal, **Veh 27700**
Fines and penalties, **Veh 42001.7**
Nuisance, impounding, **Veh 22659.5**

Sound alarm, airbrakes, **Veh 26506**

Sound recordings, reckless driving, following too closely, interference, **Veh 40008**

Sovereign immunity, **Veh 17000 et seq.**

Special construction equipment,
Identification plates, dealers and manufacturers, **Veh 5016 et seq.**
Lighting equipment, exemption, **Veh 25801**

Special environmental design license plates, **Veh 5075**

Special interest vehicles, **Veh 5050 et seq.**

MOTOR VEHICLES—Cont'd

Special mobile equipment,
Brakes, stopping distance requirements, **Veh 26457**
Dealers identification plates, **Veh 5016 et seq.**
Definitions, **Veh 575**
Inspection,
State patrol, stolen vehicles, **Veh 2805**
Stolen vehicles, **Veh 2805**
License plates, **Veh 5011**
Licenses and permits, increased size, **Veh 35780**
Lighting equipment, exemption, **Veh 25800**
Manufacturers identification plates, **Veh 5016 et seq.**
Stopping distance requirements, exemption, **Veh 26457**
Turn signals, **Veh 24951**
Width, **Veh 35104**

Special moving permits, warning lights, **Veh 25270**

Special penalty assessments, night court assessments, **Veh 42006**

Special plates. License plates, ante

Specialized license plate fund, **Veh 5157**

Specialized transportation services, exemptions, weight fees, **Veh 9107**

Specially constructed vehicles, **Veh 4153**
Definitions, **Veh 580**
Registration, inspection and inspectors, emissions, **Veh 4750.1**

Specifications, sunscreening devices, **Veh 26708.2**

Speed. Traffic Rules and Regulations, this index

Speedometers. Odometers, generally, ante

Splash aprons, mudguards, **Veh 27600**

Spotlamps, **Veh 24404**
Restriction on lighting with other lamps, **Veh 24405**

Stalking,
License plates, new plates, **Veh 4467**
Registration or drivers license record, suppression, **Veh 1808.21**

Stalled vehicles. Disabled vehicles, generally, ante

Standards,
Energy absorption systems, federal standards, **Veh 34715**
Equipment, adoption and enforcement, **Veh 26103**
Safety glazing material, **Veh 26704**
Seatbelts, **Veh 27315**
Tires, post

State, this index

State Agencies, this index

State departments, license plates, special plates, **Veh 5151 et seq.**

State forest, irrigation and irrigation districts, machinery and equipment, inspection and inspectors, **Veh 2810.2**

State of domicile, definitions, **Veh 12505**

State Officers and Employees, this index

I–136

MOTOR VEHICLES—Cont'd

State parks. Parks, this index

State police,
Abandoned or unclaimed property, removal, **Veh 22669**
Removal of vehicles from private property after accident, **Veh 22653**

Statements of effectiveness, pollution control devices, dealers, **Veh 24007**

Station wagons,
Definitions, **Veh 585**
Exemptions, weight fees, **Veh 9404**
Fees, weight fees, **Veh 9404**
License plates, **Veh 9404**
Weight fees, exemption, **Veh 9404**

Statistics, accident reports, **Veh 2408**

Statutes of limitation. Limitation of actions, generally, ante

Stickers,
Alteration, destruction, **Veh 4463**
Anatomical gifts, drivers licenses, identification cards, **Veh 1672.5**
Commercial vehicles, safety inspection stickers, **Veh 2813.5, 40000.7**
Devices in lieu of license plates, **Veh 4853**
Unlawful possession, **Veh 4462, 40000.7**
Fleet owner inspection and maintenance stations, **Veh 2525.6**
Fleet vehicles, fees, **Veh 9259**
Inspection and inspectors, **Veh 2420.5**
Safety, **Veh 2814**
License plates, **Veh 4853, 5204**
Obstruction of windows, **Veh 26708**
Off highway vehicle identification plate or device, **Veh 38160 et seq.**
Records, **Veh 1806.1**

Stipulations,
Proposed stipulated decision and order, new vehicles, **Veh 3050.7**
Release agreements, **Veh 14607.6**

Stolen vehicles. Theft, generally, post

Stoplamps, **Veh 24603**
Approval of equipment and devices, **Veh 26100 et seq.**
Color when unlighted, **Veh 25950**
Deceleration lights, **Veh 25251.5**
Flashing lights, **Veh 25251.5**
Testing and approval of equipment, **Veh 26100 et seq.**
Towing vehicles, **Veh 24605**

Stopping. Traffic Rules and Regulations, this index

Storage, **Veh 22852**
Abandoned vehicles, **Veh 22850 et seq.**
Vehicles used in fleeing peace officers, **Veh 22655.3**
Credit cards, private property, removal, **Veh 22658**
Crimes and offenses, **Veh 40000.9**
Rates and charges, **Veh 22658**
Damages, refusal to accept credit card payment, **Veh 22651.1, 22658**

MOTOR VEHICLES—Cont'd

Storage—Cont'd
Drivers licenses, revoked, suspended, driving without, hearings, **Veh 14602.6**
Fees, **Veh 10652.5**
Notice, **Veh 22651**
Financial responsibility, insurance, **Veh 16455**
Fines and penalties, refusal to accept owners credit card, **Veh 22658**
Impounded vehicle, lien, **Veh 22851.1**
National law enforcement telecommunication system, abandoned or unclaimed property, notice, **Veh 22854.5**
Notice,
Fees, **Veh 22651**
Removal from highway, **Veh 22852, 22853**
Private buildings, reports, **Veh 10654**
Rates and charges,
Credit cards, **Veh 22651.1, 22658**
Crimes and offenses, **Veh 22658**
Liens and incumbrances, disposition, **Veh 22851.8, 22851.10**
Payment, **Veh 22651.1**
Personal property, **Veh 22851**
Removal, private property, liability, **Veh 22658**
Vehicle seized for altered identification or manufacturing numbers, **Veh 10751**
Registration,
Exemption, **Veh 4002**
Release, **Veh 22651**
Removal of parked or standing vehicles, **Veh 22650 et seq.**
Reports, **Veh 10650 et seq.**
Repossessors and repossession, registration, transportation, **Veh 4022**
Unattended vehicles, release, registration, **Veh 22651**
Unlawful use, **Veh 10854**

Strap or rope material, loads, **Veh 24005.5**

Street, definitions, **Veh 590, 591**

Street rods, definitions, **Veh 5051**

Streetsweepers,
Parking, photography and pictures, enforcement, **Veh 40245 et seq.**
Traffic rules and regulations, exemptions, **Veh 21060**

Studded tires, **Veh 27454**

Student licenses, **Veh 12650 et seq.**

Studies,
Commercial vehicles, registration, **Veh 27910**
Drivers license extensions, effects, **Veh 12814.5**

Subpoenas,
Hearings, suspension or revocation of drivers license, **Veh 14104.5**
New motor vehicle board, **Veh 3050.1 et seq.**

MOTOR VEHICLES—Cont'd

Subrogation,
Consumer protection, recovery corporation, **Veh 12210**
Tort liability, **Veh 17153**

Subscription services, recording devices, disclosure, **Veh 9951**

Substitute license plates, fees, **Veh 9265**
Adjustments, **Veh 1678**

Substitute registration card or license plate, **Veh 4457 et seq.**

Successor dealership, widows and heirs of dealer, **Veh 11713.2, 11713.3**

Sunscreening devices, **Veh 26708, 26708.2**

Super ultralow emission vehicles, decals, **Veh 5205.5, 21655.9, 40000.13**
Forgery, counterfeiting, **Veh 4463**

Supplemental restraint systems, tampering, crimes and offenses, **Veh 27317**

Supplemental sticker, **Veh 11713.1**

Supplemental stoplamps, **Veh 24603**

Suppression, registration or drivers license record, **Veh 1808.21**

Surcharge, license fees, **Veh 9250.12**

Surrender. Drivers licenses, ante

Surviving spouse. License plates, ante

Suspension. Revocation or suspension, generally, ante

Synthetic binders, standards and specifications, adoption and enforcement, **Veh 26103**

Tabs. License plates, ante

Tail lamps. Rear lamps, generally, ante

Taiwan, foreign organizations, license plates, **Veh 5006.5**

Tampering, **Veh 10852, 40000.9**
Arrest, procedure, **Veh 40303**
Ignition interlock devices, **Veh 13386, 23247**

Tank, fuel tank caps, **Veh 27155**

Tank vehicles, flammable liquids, registration, **Veh 34001 et seq.**

Taxation,
Crimes and offenses, evasion of payment, residents, **Veh 8804**
Local vehicle license fee surcharge, **Veh 9250.12**
Residents, evasion of fees and taxes, **Veh 8804**

Taxicabs, generally, this index

Telecommunications,
Eight hundred (800) numbers, trucks transporting workmen, **Veh 2429**
Mobile digital terminals, **Veh 27602**
Parking violations, **Veh 40900**
Theft, notice, recovered vehicles, **Veh 10500**
Wireless telecommunications, **Veh 28090**
Crimes and offenses, **Veh 23123**
Children and minors, **Veh 23124**
Point system, **Veh 12810.3**

Television and radio,
Advertisements, autobrokers, **Veh 11713**
Amplification devices, **Veh 27007**
Equipment, **Veh 27602**

MOTOR

MOTOR VEHICLES—Cont'd
Television and radio—Cont'd
Ham radio operators, license plates, **Veh 5005**
Length of vehicle taking pictures, **Veh 35409**
License plates, **Veh 5005**
Photographers, **Veh 5008**
Photographers, license plates, **Veh 5008**
Temporary licenses. Drivers licenses, ante
Temporary permits. Licenses and permits, ante
Temporary registration. Registration, ante
Tenancy in common,
Registration, **Veh 4150.5**
Transfer of title or interest, **Veh 5600.5**
Tent trailers. Camp Trailers, generally, this index
Terminals, inspection, stolen vehicles, **Veh 2805**
Termination, franchises, **Veh 11713.13**
Terms, broker agreements, **Veh 11738**
Testimony. Evidence, generally, ante
Tests,
Accident prevention, **Veh 2408**
Airbrakes, emergency stopping requirements, **Veh 26508**
Brakes, stopping distances, **Veh 26456**
Chemical tests, driving under the influence, drivers licenses, **Veh 13380 et seq.**, **23612, 23614**
Drugs and medicine,
Exemptions, agricultural machinery and equipment, **Veh 40000.15**
Paratransit vehicles, drivers, **Veh 34520.5**
Equipment, **Veh 26100 et seq.**
Lighting and signalling devices, **Veh 26100 et seq.**
Skill test, fees, **Veh 14900, 14900.1**
Adjustments, **Veh 1678**
Stopping distances, brakes, **Veh 26456**
Traffic safety program, **Veh 2900 et seq.**
Text messages, infractions, **Veh 23123.5**
Theft, **Veh 10500 et seq., 10850 et seq.**
Alarm systems, **Veh 25251.4, 28085**
Ambulances, **Veh 10851**
Binder chains, **Veh 10851.5, 40000.9**
CAL H.E.A.T. (Help Eliminate Auto Theft), **Veh 10902**
Cargo, weights and measures, interdiction, fees, **Veh 9400.1**
Certificates of title,
Duplicates, **Veh 4466**
Transfer of title, **Veh 5752**
Commercial vehicles, cargo theft interdiction program, fees, **Veh 9400.1, 9400.3**
Dismantlers,
Inspection of lots for stolen vehicles, **Veh 2805**
Possession of stolen vehicle, **Veh 11511**

MOTOR VEHICLES—Cont'd
Theft—Cont'd
Economic automobile theft, definitions, **Veh 10901**
Electronic file system, notice, **Veh 10504**
Evidence, return of vehicle, **Veh 6171, 6172**
False reports, **Veh 10501, 40000.9**
Fees, registration, programs, **Veh 9250.14**
Fines and penalties, **Veh 10851**
Joy riding, **Veh 10851**
Fire department vehicles, **Veh 10851**
Horns, **Veh 27001**
Identifiable vehicle component, definitions, **Veh 2805**
Investigating officers, distinctive uniform and vehicle, exemption, **Veh 40800, 40804**
Investigation, **Veh 2805**
Joy riding, **Veh 10851**
Law enforcement agency vehicles, **Veh 10851**
License fee credit or refund, adjustments, **Veh 1678**
License plates, ante
Mail and mailing, notice, recovered vehicles, **Veh 10500**
Notice, **Veh 10503**
Electronic file system, **Veh 10504**
Recovery, **Veh 10502**
Victims, **Veh 10500**
Parts, **Veh 10852**
Prevention, **Veh 10900 et seq.**
Prostitution, nuisance, impounding, exemptions, **Veh 22659.5**
Recovery, notice, **Veh 10500**
Recovery of vehicles with altered identification numbers, **Veh 10804**
Registration, renewal, **Veh 4605**
Removal of parked or standing vehicles, **Veh 22650 et seq.**
Reports, **Veh 10500 et seq.**
Counties, **Veh 9250.14**
False reports, **Veh 40000.9**
Prevention, **Veh 10901**
Return of vehicle, evidence, **Veh 6171, 6172**
Sentence and punishment, **Veh 10851**
Statewide vehicle theft investigation and apprehension coordinator, designation, **Veh 2413**
Telephones, notice, recovered vehicles, **Veh 10500**
Transfer of registration, **Veh 10504, 10505**
Victims, notice, **Veh 10500**
Thickness, solid tires, **Veh 27450 et seq.**
Threats, franchises, cancellation, **Veh 11713.1**
Three wheeled vehicles,
Helmets, application of laws, **Veh 27803**
Seat belts, application of laws, **Veh 27315.1**
Children and minors, **Veh 27368**

MOTOR VEHICLES—Cont'd
Timberland production zones, irrigation and irrigation districts, machinery and equipment, inspection and inspectors, **Veh 2810.2**
Time,
Accident reports, **Veh 16000, 20008**
Appearance, nonresidents, **Veh 17462**
Arrested person, appearance, **Veh 40501**
Drivers licenses, ante
Extension of time,
Drivers licenses, **Veh 12814, 14610**
Registration, renewal, **Veh 4603**
Salespersons, licenses and permits, **Veh 11819**
Fees, payment, **Veh 9550**
Grape gondolas inspection certificates, duration, **Veh 34501.14**
Nonresidents, registration exemption, **Veh 6700**
Provisional licensees, driving hours, **Veh 12814.6**
Registration, ante
Sale, completing, consummating, **Veh 5901**
Tinted safety glass, **Veh 26708.5**
Tire chains, new vehicles unable to use, notice, **Veh 9953**
Tire traction devices, **Veh 27454, 27459 et seq.**
Definitions, **Veh 605**
Four wheel drive vehicles, **Veh 27460**
Sales, compliance, **Veh 27459.5**
Standards and specifications, adoption and enforcement, **Veh 26103**
Tread depth, **Veh 27465**
Tire tread, definitions, **Veh 610**
Tires, **Veh 27450 et seq.**
Definitions, **Veh 485**
Explosives transports, **Veh 31610**
Federal highway administration and Rubber Manufacturers Association standards, **Veh 27500**
Maximum vehicle width, **Veh 35101**
Metal tire, definitions, **Veh 395**
Noise standards, **Veh 27502, 27503**
Radial tires, inner tubes, **Veh 27455**
Recut tires, sale or use, **Veh 27460.5, 27461**
Sales, ante
Secondhand, sale or use, **Veh 27465**
Service contracts, **Veh 12800 et seq.**
Snow tires, generally, ante
Solid tires, definitions, **Veh 460**
Standards, **Veh 27500, 27501**
New tires, **Veh 27500**
Noise standards, **Veh 27502, 27503**
Studded tires, **Veh 27454**
Tire tread, definitions, **Veh 610**
Tread depth requirements, **Veh 27465**
Tubes, radial tires, **Veh 27455**
Used, worn tires, **Veh 27465**
Waste tires, haulers, registration, **Veh 31560**
Weight limits, **Veh 35600, 35601**

MOTOR VEHICLES—Cont'd
Title to property,
Abandonment, removal of vehicles, **Veh 22650 et seq.**
Accidents, information, exchange, **Veh 20002**
Arrest, notice to appear, **Veh 40002**
Beneficiaries, forms, **Veh 4150.7, 5910.5, 5910.7**
Brokered retail new motor vehicle sales, **Veh 11739**
Certificates of title, generally, ante
Contracts, private industry, **Veh 1685**
Coownership, generally, ante
Crimes and offenses, **Veh 40000.25**
Definitions, **Veh 6161**
Drivers licenses, **Veh 14604, 40000.11**
Fees, transfer, **Veh 5018, 5902, 9255, 9255.3, 9261, 9261.1**
Adjustments, **Veh 1678**
Excess payment to dealer, **Veh 11713.3, 11713.4**
Inspection and inspectors, **Veh 2805**
Notice, **Veh 5900 et seq.**
Off highway vehicles subject to identification, **Veh 38000 et seq., 38045**
Transfer, **Veh 38195 et seq.**
Operation contrary to law, **Veh 40001**
Private industry, contracts, **Veh 1685**
Proof of ownership, parking violations, **Veh 40900**
Registration information furnished to owner, **Veh 4465**
Removal of vehicles, **Veh 22650 et seq.**
Torts, liability, **Veh 17150 et seq.**
Total loss salvage vehicles, salvage certificates, **Veh 11515, 11568**
Transfer, **Veh 5018, 5600 et seq., 9261, 9261.1**
Applications, **Veh 5902**
Dealers, vehicle registration or transfer on behalf of purchaser, **Veh 4456**
Excess payment to dealer, **Veh 11713.3, 11713.4**
Lessor retailers, vehicle registration or transfer on behalf of purchaser, **Veh 4456**
Notice, **Veh 5900 et seq.**
Off highway vehicles, **Veh 38195 et seq., 38255**
Parking, fines and penalties, **Veh 4767**
Power of attorney, odometers, disclosure, **Veh 5900**
Without registration, certificates and certification, **Veh 4452**
Toll evasion, **Veh 4770 et seq., 40250 et seq.**
Torts, **Veh 17000 et seq.**
Accident reports, disclosure of liability, **Veh 20012**
Bailee as operator, **Veh 17154**
Compromise and settlement, **Veh 17155**
Double liability, minors drivers license, signing, **Veh 17714**

MOTOR VEHICLES—Cont'd
Torts—Cont'd
Executors and administrators, **Veh 17159**
Identification cards, **Veh 13006**
Limitation of liability, **Veh 17151**
Minors drivers license, signing application, **Veh 17700 et seq.**
Owner as passenger, **Veh 17158**
Parties, **Veh 17152**
Public employees, transportation of injured persons, **Veh 20016**
Security interest, **Veh 17156**
Service of process, **Veh 17152**
Subrogation, **Veh 17153**
Transfer of title or interest, **Veh 5602**
Total loss salvage vehicles,
Inspection and inspectors, **Veh 5505, 9271**
Registration, **Veh 11519**
Salvage certificates, **Veh 11515, 11568**
Tour buses. Buses, this index
Tow dollies,
Chains, **Veh 29003**
Fees, license plates, **Veh 1678, 9261, 9261.1**
Special license plates, **Veh 5014 et seq.**
Towing, **Veh 29000 et seq.**
Abandoned or unclaimed property, **Veh 22650 et seq.**
Access, notice, **Veh 22651**
Accidents, presumptions, **Veh 41104**
Adverse or pecuniary interest, kickbacks, public entities, **Veh 12110, 13351.85**
Advertising vehicles, removal, **Veh 22651.2**
Air brakes, **Veh 26503 et seq.**
Air governor, **Veh 26504**
Almond trailers, weight limitations, **Veh 36627**
Amber lights, **Veh 25253**
Bikeways, obstructions, **Veh 21211**
Brakes, **Veh 26458**
Air brakes, **Veh 26503 et seq.**
Breakaway brakes, **Veh 26304**
Airbrakes, **Veh 26508**
Brooms, equipment, **Veh 27700**
Business license tax, **Veh 12111**
Campers, weight fees, **Veh 9400**
Exemptions, vehicles manufactured before designated time, **Veh 9401**
Carrier identification number, **Veh 2436.3**
Certificates and certification, drivers, **Veh 2430 et seq., 12520, 13377, 13378**
Clearance lamps, **Veh 25100**
Colored lights, **Veh 25253**
House towing trucks, **Veh 25263**
Combinations of passenger vehicles, **Veh 21715**
Credit cards, private property, removal, **Veh 22658**
Crimes and offenses, **Veh 40000.15**

MOTOR VEHICLES—Cont'd
Towing—Cont'd
Crimes and offenses—Cont'd
Commissions, referral fees or inducements, **Veh 12110, 13351.85**
Drivers certificates, **Veh 2432, 40000.11**
Employers, certification, **Veh 2430.5**
Identification numbers, **Veh 2436.3**
Rates and charges, **Veh 22658**
Unregistered disabled vehicles, **Veh 40006**
Criminal history information, **Veh 2430.3, 2431, 2432.3**
Crossings, vehicular crossings, **Veh 23270 et seq.**
Damages,
Fenced property, notice, **Veh 22658.1**
Private property, removal, **Veh 22658**
Debris, removal, **Veh 27700**
Dismantlers, lights and lighting, **Veh 25253.1**
Distances between vehicles, **Veh 21704**
Driveaway towaway operations, generally, ante
Drivers licenses, **Veh 12520, 13377, 13378**
Revocation or suspension, kickbacks, **Veh 12110, 13351.85**
Electronic mail, private property, removal, **Veh 22658**
Emergency roadside assistance, **Veh 2435 et seq.**
Unregistered vehicles, liability of towing driver, **Veh 4000**
Emergency stopping system, airbrakes, **Veh 26508**
Equipment, **Veh 27700**
Evidence, accidents, presumptions, **Veh 41104**
Exemptions, length, **Veh 35401**
Fees,
Certificates, drivers, **Veh 2431**
Notice, **Veh 22651**
Vehicular crossings, **Veh 23270**
Weights and measures, **Veh 9400.1**
Fenced property, damages, notice, **Veh 22658.1**
Fines and penalties, kickbacks, **Veh 12110**
Fingerprints and fingerprinting, **Veh 2432.3**
Certificates and certification, **Veh 2431**
Fire extinguishers, **Veh 27700**
Flashing lights, **Veh 25253**
Dismantlers, **Veh 25253.1**
Fleeing peace officers, **Veh 22655.3**
Following vehicles, **Veh 21704**
Freeway service patrol operations, **Veh 2435 et seq.**
Gifts, devises and bequests, public entities, kickbacks, **Veh 12110, 13351.85**
Glass, removal, **Veh 27700**
Grease, covering with dirt, **Veh 27700**
Highway patrol, agreements, **Veh 2424**

MOTOR

MOTOR VEHICLES—Cont'd
Towing—Cont'd
Immediate removal, **Veh 22953**
Impounding, kickbacks, **Veh 12110**
Improper removal of parked vehicle, **Veh 22658**
Kickbacks, public entities, **Veh 12110, 13351.85**
Lanes designated, **Veh 21655**
Length, exemptions, **Veh 35401**
Licenses and permits, **Veh 21100 et seq.**
Liens and incumbrances, **Veh 22851**
Lights and lighting,
House towing trucks, warning lights, **Veh 25263**
Pilot indicators, **Veh 25108**
Utility flood or loading lamps, **Veh 25110**
Warning lights, **Veh 25253**
Livestock trailers, restricted drivers licenses, **Veh 12804.14**
Logging dolly, weight fees, **Veh 9400**
Exemptions, vehicles manufactured before designated time, **Veh 9401**
Low air pressure warning device, brakes, **Veh 26506**
Mirrors, **Veh 26709**
Motorized scooters, **Veh 21235**
Multiple traffic or parking violations, **Veh 22651.2**
Notice,
Arrests, convictions, certification, **Veh 2430.3**
Fees, **Veh 22651**
Fenced property, damages, **Veh 22658.1**
Payment, methods, **Veh 22658**
Odometers, disconnection, **Veh 28051**
Off highway vehicles, **Veh 38025**
Offstreet facility operators, **Veh 22952**
Parking, **Veh 22513**
Offstreet facilities, **Veh 22952**
Passenger vehicle combinations, **Veh 21715**
Passengers, **Veh 21712**
Payment of charges, **Veh 22651.1**
Pilot indicators, **Veh 25108**
Portable dollies, registration, **Veh 4014**
Power brakes, single control, **Veh 26458**
Pressure gauge, airbrakes, **Veh 26505**
Presumptions, accidents, **Veh 41104**
Privileges and immunities, unregistered vehicles, **Veh 4000**
Public entities, kickbacks, **Veh 12110, 13351.85**
Rates and charges,
Crimes and offenses, **Veh 22658**
Vehicles seized for altered identification or manufacturing numbers, **Veh 10751**
Vehicular crossings, **Veh 23271, 23272**
Rear license plates, place of mounting, **Veh 5201**
Records and recordation,
Private property, removal, **Veh 22658**
Stored vehicles, **Veh 10650**

MOTOR VEHICLES—Cont'd
Towing—Cont'd
Reflectors, additional reflectors, **Veh 24607**
Removal,
Glass and debris, **Veh 27700**
Parked or standing vehicles, **Veh 22650 et seq.**
Safety valves, air brakes, **Veh 26503**
Second and subsequent offenses, kickbacks, **Veh 12110, 13351.85**
Service brakes, **Veh 26304**
Shovels, equipment, **Veh 27700**
Side marker lamps, **Veh 25100**
Signs and signals, **Veh 27907**
Single control of service brakes, **Veh 26458**
Slow moving vehicles, designated lanes, **Veh 21655**
Speed limits, **Veh 22406 et seq.**
Distances between vehicles, **Veh 21704**
Standing vehicles, **Veh 22513**
Overtaking and passing, **Veh 21809**
Stoplamps, **Veh 24603, 24605**
Stopping on highway, **Veh 22513**
Tail lamps, **Veh 24600, 24605**
Toll roads and bridges, vehicular crossings, **Veh 23270 et seq.**
Train of vehicles, swerving, **Veh 21711**
Training, freeway service patrol, **Veh 2436.7**
Turn signal lamps, **Veh 24605**
Unregistered vehicles,
Infractions, **Veh 40006**
Liability, **Veh 4000**
Unsafe equipment or vehicle, **Veh 34506.4**
Utility flood or loading lamps, **Veh 25110**
Vacuum brakes, **Veh 26520 et seq.**
Vehicular crossings, **Veh 23270 et seq.**
Vending on freeway, **Veh 22520.5**
Warning devices, vacuum brakes, **Veh 26521**
Warning lights, **Veh 25253**
Weights and measures, fees, **Veh 9400.1**
Writing, private property, removal, **Veh 22658**
Traction surface of tire, protuberances, **Veh 27454**
Tractors,
Farm tractors. Agricultural Machinery and Equipment, generally, this index
Truck tractors. Motor Carriers, generally, this index
Trade ins,
Cancellation option agreements, conditional sales, **Veh 11713.21**
Consumer protection, recovery corporation, **Veh 12200 et seq.**
Dealers, credit, discharge, **Veh 11709.4**
Trademarks, fleet vehicles, **Veh 5302**
Traffic officer,
Definitions, **Veh 625**

MOTOR VEHICLES—Cont'd
Traffic officer—Cont'd
Enforcing code provisions, distinctive uniform and vehicle, **Veh 40800**
Flashing and colored lights, **Veh 25259**
Traffic Rules and Regulations, generally, this index
Traffic safety program, **Veh 2900 et seq.**
Traffic Signs and Signals, generally, this index
Traffic Violator Schools, generally, this index
Trailer Coaches, generally, this index
Trailer hitch, mounting, **Veh 29002**
Trailers, generally, this index
Train of vehicles, accident, presumption of violation, **Veh 41104**
Training,
Disaster service vehicles, warning lights, **Veh 25259.1**
Off highway vehicles, **Veh 38007**
Children and minors, **Veh 38504.1, 38504.2**
Paratransit vehicles, drivers, **Veh 12517.5**
Transactions,
Completing, consummating, time, **Veh 5901**
Repossession, notice, **Veh 28**
Transfer,
Auctions and auctioneers, wholesale motor vehicle auctions, **Veh 6100 et seq.**
Certificates of title, ante
Dealers, display of notice, **Veh 11715**
Delinquent fees, fines and penalties, **Veh 9553.7**
Delinquent payment, lien enforcement, **Veh 9801 et seq.**
Fees,
Fines and penalties, delinquency, **Veh 9553.7**
Title, **Veh 9255.3**
Fines and penalties, delinquent fees, **Veh 9553.7**
Mileage, recordation, **Veh 5906.5**
Odometers, disclosure, forms, **Veh 5600**
Off highway vehicles, ante
Parts with altered vehicle identification numbers, **Veh 10803**
Permanent trailer identification plates, semitrailers, **Veh 5017**
Private party vehicle markets, law provisions supply to vendor, **Veh 12104**
Registration, ante
Salvaged vehicles, inspection and inspectors, **Veh 5506**
Title to property, ante
Vehicle verifiers, **Veh 11300 et seq.**
Vehicles with altered identification numbers, **Veh 10803**
Warrant of arrest for execution, **Veh 40516**
Wholesale motor vehicle auctions, **Veh 6100 et seq.**

MOTOR VEHICLES—Cont'd
Transferee, definitions, **Veh 640**
  Removal of parked or abandoned vehicles, **Veh 22669**
Transit Districts, this index
Transitional zero emission vehicles, decals, **Veh 5205.5**
Transportation of injured persons, **Veh 20016**
Transporters,
  Abandonment of business, cancellation of license, **Veh 11721**
  Accomplices and accessories, **Veh 11700.3**
  Actions and proceedings, fraud, **Veh 11711**
  Advertisements, false, **Veh 11713**
  Bonds (officers and fiduciaries), **Veh 11710**
    Failure to file, cancellation of license, **Veh 11721**
    Failure to keep in effect, **Veh 11713**
    Protection of interest, **Veh 11722**
  Branch offices,
    Licenses, display, **Veh 11709**
    Operation without license, **Veh 11713**
  Certificate of convenience, executors and administrators, **Veh 11720**
  Change of place of business, **Veh 11712**
  Crimes and offenses,
    License qualifications, **Veh 11703**
    Licenses and permits, **Veh 40000.11**
    Return of documents and license plates, **Veh 40000.7**
  Definitions, **Veh 645**
  Down payment, false representation, **Veh 11713**
  Driveaway towaway operations, generally, ante
  Executors and administrators, certificate of convenience, **Veh 11720**
  False advertising, **Veh 11713**
  Fees,
    Failure to pay, **Veh 11711**
    Payment, **Veh 9550 et seq.**
  Fines and penalties, compromise and settlement, **Veh 11707**
  Foreign countries, removing license plates, **Veh 11725**
  Fraud, **Veh 11711**
  Length, **Veh 35401.3, 35401.5**
  License plates,
    Automatic cancellation, **Veh 11721**
    Expiration, **Veh 11717**
    Operation of vehicles under special plates, **Veh 11715**
    Operation without plates, **Veh 11716**
    Renewal, **Veh 11717**
    Unauthorized use, **Veh 11713**
  Licenses and permits, **Veh 11700 et seq.**
    Application, **Veh 11701, 11704**
    Automatic cancellation, **Veh 11721**
    Cancellation, temporary permit, **Veh 11719**
    Crimes and offenses, **Veh 40000.11**
    Display, **Veh 11709**

MOTOR VEHICLES—Cont'd
Transporters—Cont'd
  Licenses and permits—Cont'd
    Reapplication, **Veh 11703.3**
    Refusal, **Veh 11703, 11703.1**
      Procedure, **Veh 11708**
    Revocation or suspension, **Veh 11705**
      Return of documents to department, **Veh 8803**
    Temporary permit, **Veh 11719**
    Temporary suspension, **Veh 11706**
    Unsatisfied final judgments, denial, **Veh 11703.2**
  New car dealer license fee, **Veh 11723**
  Odometers, resetting, **Veh 11713**
  Place of business, signs, **Veh 11709**
  Priorities and preferences, claims of state, **Veh 11711**
  Registration, fees, **Veh 9262**
  Restitution, licenses and permits, denial, **Veh 11703.2**
  Service of process, **Veh 11710**
    Place of business closed, registered mail, **Veh 11712**
  Signs and devices on place of business, **Veh 11709**
  Special plates, **Veh 11714 et seq.**
Travel trailers. Camp Trailers, generally, this index
Tree trimming, aerial lift equipped vehicles, amber warning lights, **Veh 25260.3**
Trespass, crimes and offenses, **Veh 40000.15**
Trick, fraud or device, liens and incumbrances, **Veh 22852.5**
Trip permits, commercial vehicles, foreign states, fees, **Veh 9260**
Trip tickets, commercial vehicles, **Veh 9800**
Trolley coach, definitions, **Veh 650**
Truss, definitions, **Veh 657**
Trust accounts, autobrokers, **Veh 11737**
Turn signals, **Veh 24950 et seq.**
  Civil liability, **Veh 25251.3**
  Color when unlighted, **Veh 25950**
  Disabled vehicles, flashing, **Veh 25300**
  Exemption, restriction on lighting with other lamps, **Veh 24405**
  Flashing lights, **Veh 24953, 25251**
  Implements of husbandry, **Veh 25251.1**
  Outside rear view mirrors, signals mounted on, **Veh 24953**
  Parking lamps, driving while lighted, **Veh 24800**
  Pilot indicators, **Veh 25108**
  Restriction on lighting on other lamps, exemption, **Veh 24405**
  Towing vehicles, **Veh 24605**
Turning. Traffic Rules and Regulations, this index
Turning back odometers, **Veh 28051**
Ultralow emission vehicles, decals, **Veh 4463, 5205.5, 21655.9, 40000.13**
Unattended children, **Veh 15600 et seq.**

MOTOR VEHICLES—Cont'd
Unattended vehicles,
  Manipulation of brakes, **Veh 10853**
  Stopping motor and setting brakes, **Veh 22515**
Unclaimed property. Abandoned or unclaimed property, generally, ante
Undocumented immigrants. Aliens, generally, ante
Unfair labor practices, franchises, termination, **Veh 3060**
Unfit vehicles, revocation of license, **Veh 8800**
Uniform traffic citation, form, **Veh 40508, 40513**
Uniformity of statute, **Veh 21**
United States, this index
United States territories or possessions, convictions, drivers license revocation or suspension, **Veh 13352**
Unsafe mechanical condition. Equipment, ante
Unsatisfied judgments. Judgments and decrees, ante
Upper beams, multiple beams lighting equipment, **Veh 24407**
Urine tests, accidents, death, consent, **Veh 23612**
Used car lots,
  Dismantlers, generally, ante
  Inspection,
    Stolen vehicles, **Veh 2805**
    Vehicles on lots, **Veh 10656**
  Stored vehicles, reports, **Veh 10650 et seq.**
Used parts, installation and sale, **Veh 12000 et seq.**
Used vehicles,
  Advertisements, certificates and certification, **Veh 11713.18**
  Cancellation option agreements, conditional sales, **Veh 11713.21**
    Disclosure, **Veh 11709.2**
  Certificates and certification, sales, **Veh 11713.18**
  Change of ownership, registration, **Veh 4456**
  Conditional sales, cancellation option agreements, **Veh 11713.21**
    Disclosure, **Veh 11709.2**
  Dealers, ante
  Definitions, **Veh 665**
  Disclosure, NMVTIS (national motor vehicle title information system), history, reports, **Veh 11713.26**
  Down payments, cancellation option agreements, conditional sales, **Veh 11713.21**
  Leases, conditional sales, cancellation option agreements, restocking fees, **Veh 11713.21**
  NMVTIS (national motor vehicle title information system), history, reports, disclosure, **Veh 11713.26**
  Private party vehicle markets, **Veh 12101 et seq.**

MOTOR

MOTOR VEHICLES—Cont'd

Used vehicles—Cont'd

Refunds, cancellation option agreements, conditional sales, **Veh 11713.21**

Remanufactured vehicles, generally, ante

Retrofitting vehicle with shoulder harnesses, **Veh 27314.5**

Sales,

Cancellation option agreements, **Veh 11713.21**

Disclosure, **Veh 11709.2**

Certificates and certification, **Veh 11713.18**

Seatbelts, equipment, **Veh 27314**

Seatbelts, **Veh 27314**

Notice, dangers of not having seatbelts or shoulder harnesses, warning, **Veh 27314.5**

Trade ins, generally, ante

Utility vehicles, warning signals, parked, stopped or standing vehicles, **Veh 25301**

Vacuum brakes, **Veh 26520 et seq.**

Valuation,

Abandoned or unclaimed property, **Veh 22851.2**

Dealers, used vehicles, **Veh 11950**

Vandalism, **Veh 10853**

Vanpooling, generally, this index

Vector control districts, pollution control devices, **Veh 27156.3**

Vehicle identification number, definitions, **Veh 671**

Vehicle manufacturer, definitions, **Veh 672**

Vehicle verifiers, **Veh 11300 et seq.**

Vehicles department, process, service, **Veh 24.5**

Vending,

Crimes and offenses, second or subsequent offenses, **Veh 22520.5, 40000.13**

Ice cream trucks, **Veh 22456**

Products on streets, regulation, **Veh 22455**

Vendors, definitions, private party vehicle markets, **Veh 12102**

Venue, registration services, agent for service of process, **Veh 11402**

Verifiers, **Veh 11300 et seq.**

Vested rights, pending proceedings, **Veh 4**

Veterans,

Disabled veterans, generally, ante

Drivers licenses, benefits, applications, **Veh 12811**

Fees, exemptions, **Veh 9105**

Parking, fines and penalties, **Veh 42001.13**

Prisoners of war,

License fees, exemptions, **Veh 9105**

Special license plates, **Veh 5101.5**

Veterans affairs department, license plates, special plates, **Veh 5156**

MOTOR VEHICLES—Cont'd

Veterans organizations,

Disabled veterans, parking exemptions, **Veh 22511.5 et seq.**

License plates, special plates, **Veh 5068, 5069**

Decals, **Veh 5068.1**

Video event recorders, windshields, **Veh 26708**

Videotape,

Equipment, **Veh 27602**

House cars, safety, **Veh 2429.3**

View. Obstruction of view, generally, ante

Violator schools. Traffic Violator Schools, generally, this index

Violence, dealers, notice, repossessors and repossession, assignments, **Veh 11724**

Visibility,

Clearance lamps, **Veh 25100**

Lighting equipment, **Veh 24251**

Tail lamps, **Veh 24600**

Turn signal, lamps, **Veh 24952**

Vision tests, drivers licenses, **Veh 1674 et seq.**

Voltage, lighting equipment lamp sockets, **Veh 24252**

Volunteers,

Firefighters and fire departments, special plates, **Veh 5101.2**

Law enforcement, removal, **Veh 22651.05**

Waiver,

Arrest, continuance for pleading, infraction and misdemeanor procedure, **Veh 40306**

Complaint,

Filing of verified complaint, **Veh 40513**

Persons owning or controlling vehicles, **Veh 40002**

Dealers, requiring prospective assent, **Veh 11713.2, 11713.3**

Driving test, **Veh 12814**

Filing of verified complaint, **Veh 40513**

Fines and penalties, **Veh 9562**

Limitation of actions, written pleas in lieu of personal appearance, **Veh 40519**

Pleading, written plea, waiver of right to trial within statutory period, **Veh 40519**

Registration, ante

Warning signals and devices, **Veh 25300 et seq., 27000 et seq.**

Animal control, enforcement vehicles, amber warning lights, **Veh 25271.5**

Construction companies, **Veh 25282**

Contractors, **Veh 25282**

Emergency vehicles, application of law, **Veh 24405**

Front of vehicle, number lighted, **Veh 24405**

Horns and sirens, **Veh 27000 et seq.**

Low air pressure, brakes, **Veh 26506**

Off highway vehicles, **Veh 38346**

MOTOR VEHICLES—Cont'd

Warning signals and devices—Cont'd

Oil and gas pipelines, construction and maintenance, flashing amber lights, **Veh 25260.1**

Theft alarm systems, **Veh 25251.4, 28085**

Tow trucks, **Veh 25253**

Vacuum brakes, **Veh 26521**

Wide vehicles, reflectors, **Veh 25300**

Warnings,

Penalty provisions, failure to report accident or prove financial responsibility, **Veh 1656.2**

Used vehicles, notice, absence of lap belts or shoulder harnesses, **Veh 27314.5**

Warranties,

Dealers, ante

Defects, correction, **Veh 9975**

Discrimination, **Veh 11713.2, 11713.3**

Dishonor, **Veh 11713.3**

Energy absorption systems, compliance with federal standards, **Veh 34715**

Failure to honor, **Veh 11713**

Franchises, ante

House cars, copies and lists of warranties, provision to buyers by dealers, **Veh 11931**

Lemon Law buyback, **Veh 11713.12**

Manufacturers and manufacturing, ante

New vehicles, **Veh 3065**

Odometers, mileage, **Veh 28052**

Persons incurring liability, accident reports, disclosure, **Veh 20012**

Violation of provisions by dealers, distributors, suspension or revocation of license, **Veh 11705**

Warrants, searches and seizures, repossessors and repossession, **Veh 23118**

Waste tire haulers, failure to register, infraction, **Veh 31560**

Water tender vehicles,

Definitions, **Veh 676.5**

Flashing amber warning lights, **Veh 25281**

Watercourse banks, operation restrictions, **Veh 21116**

Watering vehicles, traffic rules and regulations, exemption, **Veh 21060**

Weapons, this index

Weather, headlamps, **Veh 24400**

Weed control vehicles, amber warning lights, **Veh 25261**

Weekend service of sentence for driving after revocation, **Veh 14601.8**

Weights and measures. Traffic Rules and Regulations, this index

Wheelchairs, license plates, lifts, carriers, obstructions, **Veh 5201**

Wheels, modification of vehicles, **Veh 24008**

Whistle tips, exhaust systems, **Veh 27150.3**

White lights, **Veh 24606**

White reflectors, **Veh 24609**

MOTOR VEHICLES—Cont'd
Wholesale motor vehicle auctions, **Veh 6100 et seq.**
Dealers, reporting, **Veh 4456**
Wholesale price, advertisements, **Veh 11713.1**
Wholesalers,
Dealers, bonds (officers and fiduciaries), **Veh 11710.1**
Sales at places other than place of business, penalties and license suspensions, **Veh 11728**
Wide vehicles, reflectors, warning signals and devices, **Veh 25300**
Widows and widowers, dealers, powers and duties, **Veh 11713.2, 11713.3**
Width. Traffic Rules and Regulations, this index
Willful injury, **Veh 10852**
Wind deflectors, safety glazing material, **Veh 26701 et seq.**
Windows, **Veh 26700 et seq.**
Defective equipment, **Veh 26710**
Defrosters, **Veh 26712**
Glazing, peace officers, **Veh 26708.7**
Ice and snow, obstructions, **Veh 26708**
Obstructions, **Veh 26708**
Rear windows, generally, ante
Safety glazing material, **Veh 26701 et seq.**
Service contracts, **Veh 12800 et seq.**
Signs and stickers, obstructions, **Veh 26708**
Snow, obstruction, **Veh 26708**
Sunscreening devices, **Veh 26708, 26708.2**
Tinting, peace officers, **Veh 26708.7**
Transparent materials, installation or application, **Veh 26708, 26708.5**
Wipers, **Veh 26706, 26707**
Wire, tires, structure, **Veh 27454**
Wireless telecommunications. Telecommunications, ante
Witnesses,
Accident reports, disclosure, **Veh 20012**
Police reports, rebuttal, **Veh 40806**
Refusal of registration, **Veh 4751**
Speed traps, incompetency of officer or person assisting in arrest, **Veh 40804**
Work permits, driving under the influence, **Veh 23538, 23562**
Workers compensation, financial responsibility, **Veh 16454**
Worn tires, sale or use, **Veh 27465**
Wrecks and wreckers,
Dismantlers, generally, ante
Towing, generally, ante
Writing, tow trucks, private property, removal, **Veh 22658**
Wrong way driving, crimes and offenses, **Veh 40000.13**
Wrongful death, **Veh 17000 et seq.**
Damages, **Veh 17151**
Year round registration, **Veh 1651.5, 40000.13**

MOTOR VEHICLES—Cont'd
Yellow lamps, **Veh 25950**
Yosemite Foundation special plate, **Veh 5064**
Youth Buses, generally, this index
Zero emission electric vehicles, parking lots and facilities, designated spaces, **Veh 22511, 22511.1, 42001.6**

MOTOR VEHICLES DEPARTMENT
Generally, **Veh 1500 et seq.**
Abstracts of records of conviction, public inspection, **Veh 1808**
Accident reports, confidential use, **Veh 20012, 20014**
Accounts and accounting, motor vehicle account, **Veh 1685**
Actions, dealers bond, recovery, **Veh 11710.2**
Advertisements, message display systems, contracts, **Veh 1656.5**
Application forms, social security numbers, **Veh 1653.5, 12800**
Application of law, **Veh 1503**
Associations, membership fees, joining, **Veh 1658**
Boards and commissions. New motor vehicle board, generally, post
Bonds (officers and employees), examination of records, **Veh 1814, 1815**
Books and papers, possession and control, **Veh 1502**
Buildings, acquisition, **Veh 1654**
Certified copies of records, **Veh 1813**
Code of laws, publication, **Veh 1656**
Compensation, officers and employees, **Veh 1507**
Confidential or privileged information, addresses, **Veh 1808.4**
Consumer protection, Internet web site, **Veh 1656.4**
Contracts,
Drivers licenses, identification cards, processing, bids, **Veh 13005**
Message display systems, **Veh 1656.5**
Copies of records, sale, **Veh 1811**
Creation, **Veh 1500**
Directors,
Administrative duties, **Veh 1650**
Agent for service of process on nonresidents, **Veh 17450 et seq.**
Bond, **Veh 1504**
New motor vehicle board, **Veh 3014**
Officers and employees, **Veh 1507**
Peace officer, **Veh 1655**
Process, service, **Veh 24.5**
Disclosure, address, designated persons, **Veh 1808.4**
Employees. Officers and employees, generally, post
Environmental license plates, Internet web site, orders, **Veh 5112**
Equipment, possession and control, **Veh 1502**
Exemptions, diplomats, drivers licenses, **Veh 12502**

MOTOR VEHICLES DEPARTMENT—Cont'd
Fees,
Contracts, registration, private industry, **Veh 1685**
Fingerprint service, **Veh 1668**
Motorcycle registration, safety programs, **Veh 2935**
Publication of vehicle code, **Veh 1656**
Financial responsibility, verification, law enforcement agencies, provision of information, **Veh 4750.4**
Fingerprints and fingerprinting, **Veh 1668**
Forms,
Abstract of conviction record, **Veh 1804**
Applications, social security numbers, **Veh 1653.5, 12800**
Furnishing, **Veh 1652**
Funds, possession and control, **Veh 1502**
Home addresses, designated personnel, parole hearings board, parole hearings division, youthful offender parole board, confidential information, **Veh 1808.6**
Hours of operation, posting or publication, **Veh 1669**
Internet,
Consumer protection, **Veh 1656.4**
Environmental license plates, orders, **Veh 5112**
Investigations and investigators,
Dismantler violations, **Veh 1662**
Peace officers, **Veh 1655**
Laws governing, **Veh 1503**
Leases, **Veh 1654**
Licenses and permits, two year licenses, fees, **Veh 1665**
Mail and mailing, message display systems, contracts, **Veh 1656.5**
Message display systems, contracts, **Veh 1656.5**
Minors traffic violations, report, **Veh 1816**
Motor vehicle account, **Veh 1685**
New motor vehicle board, **Veh 3000 et seq.**
Appeal and review, **Veh 3052 et seq.**
Appointment, **Veh 3002**
Civil service, **Veh 3014**
Directors, **Veh 3014**
Funding, **Veh 3016**
Meetings, **Veh 3007**
Open to public, **Veh 3008**
Oath of office, **Veh 3004**
Office space, **Veh 3015**
Powers and duties, **Veh 3050 et seq.**
President, **Veh 3006**
Qualification of members, **Veh 3001**
Quorum, **Veh 3010**
Removal from office, **Veh 3005**
Seal, **Veh 3013**
Term of office, **Veh 3003**
Traveling expenses, **Veh 3012**
Vacancies, **Veh 3011**
Officers and employees, **Veh 1507**
False representation by individual as department employee, **Veh 25.5**
Immunity from liability, vehicle registrations, probate transfers, **Veh 5910**

MOTOR

MOTOR VEHICLES DEPARTMENT—Cont'd

Officers and employees—Cont'd

Licensing registration examiners, confidential or privileged information, addresses, **Veh 1808.4**

Offices, **Veh 1502, 1507**

Organization, **Veh 1500 et seq.**

Peace officers,

Director, registrar, investigators, **Veh 1655**

Powers of officers and directors, **Veh 1655**

Permit, examination of records, **Veh 1813, 1814**

Possession of records and property, **Veh 1502**

Posted hours of operation, **Veh 1669**

Powers and duties, **Veh 1650 et seq.**

Dismantlers, investigations, **Veh 1662**

Property,

Message display systems, contracts, **Veh 1656.5**

Possession and control, **Veh 1502**

Real estate,

Message display systems, contracts, **Veh 1656.5**

Purchase or lease, **Veh 1654**

Records and recordation, **Veh 1800 et seq.**

Confidentiality, **Veh 1808.4**

Home addresses, designated personnel, parole hearings board, parole hearings division, youthful offender parole board, **Veh 1808.6**

Law enforcement, access, **Veh 1810.5**

Possession and control, **Veh 1502**

Registrar of vehicles, peace officer, **Veh 1655**

Reports,

Contracts, registration, private industry, **Veh 1685**

Diplomatic drivers license holders, accident and violations frequency, **Veh 12502**

Rules and regulations, **Veh 1651**

Seal, certified copies of records, **Veh 1813**

Social security numbers, application forms, **Veh 1653.5, 12800**

Successor to certain state agencies, **Veh 1501**

Vendor and purchaser, message display systems, contracts, **Veh 1656.5**

MOTORBOATS

Boats and Boating, generally, this index

MOTORCADE

Traffic rules and regulations, spacing, **Veh 21705**

MOTORCYCLES

Acetylene headlamps, **Veh 25451**

Advisory committee, safety, **Veh 2932**

Aftermarket parts, air pollution, **Veh 27156**

Air Pollution, this index

MOTORCYCLES—Cont'd

Ancient motorcycles, license plates, **Veh 5004.5**

Attaching to other vehicles, **Veh 21203, 21712**

Bonds (officers and fiduciaries), dealers, **Veh 11710**

Brakes,

Service brakes, **Veh 26311**

Unattended vehicles, setting brakes, **Veh 22515**

Checkpoints, air pollution, emissions, **Veh 2814.1**

Children and minors, instruction permits, **Veh 12509.5**

Class A motorcycles, license plates, **Veh 5004.5**

Congressional medal of honor recipients, fees, exemptions, **Veh 9105**

Crimes and offenses,

Exhaust systems, noise pollution, **Veh 27150.1**

Decals, **Veh 27202.1**

Failure to display itemized price sticker, **Veh 11712.5**

Dealers, **Veh 285**

Bonds (officers and fiduciaries), **Veh 11710**

Licenses with general distinguishing number, **Veh 11701**

Notice of transfer, display, **Veh 11715**

Decals, exhaust systems, noise pollution, crimes and offenses, **Veh 27202.1**

Definitions, **Veh 400**

Dismantlers,

Business signs, **Veh 11514**

Inspection and inspectors, **Veh 5505**

Display,

Identification plates, **Veh 38170**

Notice of transfer, dealers, **Veh 11715**

Distributors, licenses with general distinguishing number, **Veh 11701**

Drivers licenses,

Highway driving, **Veh 12500 et seq.**

Instruction permits, **Veh 12509, 12509.5**

Emergency vehicles, lights and lighting, **Veh 25650.5**

Engines, registration numbers, **Veh 4161**

Environmental license plates, **Veh 5101 et seq.**

Equipment, air pollution, aftermarket parts, performance parts, **Veh 27156**

Evidence, registration, vehicle identification numbers, **Veh 4150.2**

Exemptions,

Police,

Insignia, **Veh 27604**

Paints and painting, **Veh 27605**

Prisoners of war, fees, **Veh 9105**

Veterans, fees, **Veh 9105**

Exhaust systems, noise pollution, **Veh 27150.1 et seq.**

Decals, crimes and offenses, **Veh 27202.1**

MOTORCYCLES—Cont'd

Fees,

Congressional medal of honor recipients, exemption, **Veh 9105**

Off highway vehicle registration, transportation to or from closed course, **Veh 38232**

Adjustments, **Veh 1678**

Prisoners of war, exemptions, **Veh 9105**

Registration, **Veh 9268**

Safety program, registration surcharge, **Veh 2935**

Special interest license plates, **Veh 5060**

Veterans, exemption, **Veh 9105**

Financial statements and reports, special interest license plates, **Veh 5060**

Fines and penalties, exhaust systems, noise pollution, decals, **Veh 27202.1**

Flashing lights, **Veh 25251.2**

Fog lamps, **Veh 24403**

Footrests for passengers, **Veh 27800**

Franchisees, protest hearings, rescheduling, **Veh 3066**

Freeways, instruction permits, **Veh 12509.5**

Funds, special interest license plates, **Veh 5060**

Glazing material, windshield, **Veh 26701, 26705**

Handle bars, position of equipment, **Veh 27801**

Headlamps, **Veh 25650 et seq.**

Acetylene, **Veh 25451**

Helmets, safety helmets,

Regulations establishing specifications and standards, **Veh 27802**

Standards and specifications, adoption and enforcement, **Veh 26103**

Wearing requirements, drivers and passengers, **Veh 27803**

High occupancy vehicle lanes, **Veh 21655.5**

Highway patrol, **Veh 2267**

Historic vehicles, license plates, **Veh 5004.5**

Identification plates, display, **Veh 38170**

Identity and identification, engines, replacement, registration, **Veh 4161**

Inspection and inspectors, dismantlers and salvaged vehicles, **Veh 5505**

Instruction permits, **Veh 12509, 12509.5**

Itemized price stickers, display, **Veh 11712.5, 24014**

Lanes, operation between, prohibition, **Veh 21714**

License fees, prisoners of war, exemptions, **Veh 9105**

License plates, **Veh 4852**

Ancient motorcycles, **Veh 5004.5**

Dimensions, **Veh 4852**

Environmental license plates, **Veh 5101 et seq.**

Historic motorcycles, **Veh 5004.5**

Prisoners of war, fees, **Veh 9105**

Special plates, **Veh 5060, 5061**

Environmental license plates, **Veh 5101 et seq.**

Historic motorcycles, **Veh 5004.5**

MOTORCYCLES—Cont'd
License plates—Cont'd
  Special plates—Cont'd
    State agencies, **Veh 5151 et seq.**
Licenses and permits,
  Drivers licenses, generally, ante
  Manufacturers, licenses with general
    distinguishing number, **Veh 11701**
Lights and lighting,
  Acetylene headlamps, **Veh 25451**
  Emergency vehicles, **Veh 25650.5**
  Energy storing system, taillamps, **Veh 24253**
  Fog lamps, **Veh 24403**
  Headlamps, **Veh 25650 et seq.**
  Flashing lights, **Veh 25251.2**
Major competent parts for motorcycles, definitions, **Veh 5505**
Manufacturers, licenses and permits, **Veh 11700 et seq.**
  General distinguishing number, **Veh 11701**
Markets and marketing, special interest license plates, **Veh 5060**
Minor component parts for motorcycles, definitions, **Veh 5505**
Mirrors, **Veh 26709**
Motor and frame numbers, registration, **Veh 4150.2**
Motor Driven Cycles, generally, this index
Motorized Scooters, generally, this index
Mufflers, **Veh 27150**
Multiple beam headlamp, **Veh 25651**
Nighttime, instruction permits, **Veh 12509, 12509.5**
Noise,
  Exhaust systems, decals, crimes and offenses, **Veh 27202.1**
  Limitations, **Veh 27201, 27202**
  Standards, **Veh 27150.1 et seq.**
Notice, special interest license plates, **Veh 5060**
Off highway vehicles,
  Definitions, **Veh 38012**
  Mufflers, **Veh 27150**
  Public entity employer liability, hazardous recreational activities, registration, **Veh 38088**
    Fees, **Veh 1678, 38232**
  Transportation to and from closed course, **Veh 38022**
    Fees, **Veh 1678, 38232**
    Registration, **Veh 38088**
Offenses. Crimes and offenses, generally, ante
One way streets, parking, **Veh 22502**
Operation between lanes, prohibition, **Veh 21714**
Painting, similarity to police vehicles, **Veh 27605**
Passengers on, restrictions, **Veh 27800**
Performance parts, air pollution, **Veh 27156**
Place of business, posting, signs and licenses, application of law, **Veh 11709**
Police cycles, sale, insignia, **Veh 27604**

MOTORCYCLES—Cont'd
Position of equipment, handlebars and seats, **Veh 27801**
Premier motorcyclist safety training program, **Veh 2932**
Price information, labels, **Veh 24014**
Prisoners of war, license fees, exemptions, **Veh 9105**
Promotions, special interest license plates, **Veh 5060**
Racing, mufflers, **Veh 27150**
Registration,
  Application, **Veh 4150.2**
  Engine numbers, **Veh 4161 et seq.**
  Fees, **Veh 9268**
    Safety program, **Veh 2935**
  Historic motorcycles, **Veh 5004.5**
  Off highway vehicles, transportation to and from closed course, **Veh 38088**
    Fees, **Veh 1678, 38232**
  Renewal, application, **Veh 4150.2**
  Replacement, engines, **Veh 4161**
Replacement, engines, registration, **Veh 4161**
Rider training programs, **Veh 2932**
Rules and regulations, **Veh 38000 et seq.**
Safety, **Veh 2930 et seq.**
  Helmet wearing regulations, drivers and passengers, **Veh 27803**
Safety glazing materials, windshield, **Veh 26701, 26705**
Safety helmets. Helmets, generally, ante
Sales,
  Price information, labels, **Veh 24014**
  Safety helmets, **Veh 27802**
Seats,
  Passengers, **Veh 27800**
  Position of equipment, **Veh 27801**
Second and subsequent offenses, exhaust systems, noise pollution, decals, **Veh 27202.1**
Service brakes, **Veh 26311**
Shoulders, operation on, prohibition, **Veh 21714**
Sidecars,
  Passenger, **Veh 27800**
  Service brakes, exemption, **Veh 26311**
Single beam headlamp, **Veh 25651**
Special plates. License plates, ante
State agencies, license plates, special plates, **Veh 5151 et seq.**
Stopping motor, unattended vehicles, **Veh 22515**
Streetcars, attachment to, **Veh 21203**
Taillights, energy storing system, **Veh 24253**
Toll roads and bridges, electronic collection, **Veh 23302**
Towing, **Veh 21712**
Traffic Rules and Regulations, generally, this index
Traffic signs and signals, traffic actuated signals, **Veh 21450.5**
Traffic violator schools, right of way, courses of study, **Veh 11219.3**
Training, safety, **Veh 2932**

MOTORCYCLES—Cont'd
Transfer, notice, display by dealers, **Veh 11715**
Transporters, licenses with general distinguishing, **Veh 11701**
Turn signals, **Veh 24951**
Unattended vehicles, stopping motor and setting brakes, **Veh 22515**
Vehicle identification numbers, evidence of registration, **Veh 4150.2**
Veterans, fees, exemption, **Veh 9105**
  Prisoners of war, **Veh 9105**
Windshields, safety glazing material, **Veh 26701, 26705**

MOTORCYCLIST SAFETY FUND
Generally, **Veh 2934**

MOTORIZED BICYCLES
Bicycles, this index

MOTORIZED QUADRICYCLE
Definitions, vehicle registration, **Veh 407**

MOTORIZED SCOOTERS
Generally, **Veh 21220 et seq.**
Age, operation, **Veh 21235**
Air pollution, emissions, **Veh 12500**
Application of law, **Veh 21221**
Bicycle lanes, operation, **Veh 21229**
Bicycle paths, operation, **Veh 21230**
Brakes, **Veh 21235**
  Disengaging motor, **Veh 21227**
Children and minors, instruction permits, **Veh 12509.5**
Counties, powers and duties, **Veh 21225**
Crimes and offenses, pocket bikes, **Veh 21720**
Definitions, **Veh 407.5**
Disclosure,
  Manufacturers and manufacturing, **Veh 407.5**
  Pocket bikes, stickers, **Veh 9955**
Disengaging motor, **Veh 21227**
Drivers licenses, **Veh 12500 et seq., 21235**
  Classification, **Veh 12804.9**
Driving under the influence, **Veh 21221, 21221.5, 40303**
Equipment, **Veh 21223, 21224**
Exhaust systems, **Veh 21226**
  Disclosure, manufacturers and manufacturing, **Veh 407.5**
Financial responsibility, application of law, **Veh 21224**
Fines and penalties,
  Driving under influence, **Veh 21221.5**
  Pocket bikes, **Veh 21721**
Freeways, **Veh 21960**
  Instruction permits, **Veh 12509.5**
Helmets, **Veh 21235**
Instruction permits, **Veh 12509, 12509.5, 21235**
Lanes, operation, **Veh 21228**
License plates, application of law, **Veh 21224**
Lights and lighting, **Veh 21223, 21224**
Manufacturers and manufacturing, disclosure, **Veh 407.5**

MOTORIZED

MOTORIZED SCOOTERS—Cont'd
Motor vehicle insurance,
  Disclosure, **Veh 407.5**
  Financial responsibility, application of
    law, **Veh 21224**
Mufflers, **Veh 21226**
  Disclosure, manufacturers and manufac-
    turing, **Veh 407.5**
Municipalities, powers and duties, **Veh
  21225**
Nighttime, instruction permits, **Veh
  12509.5**
Noise, **Veh 21226**
Notice, manufacturers and manufacturing,
  Veh 407.5
Operation, **Veh 21220 et seq.**
  Pocket bikes, location, **Veh 21720**
Packages, operation, **Veh 21235**
Passengers, **Veh 21235**
Pocket bikes, **Veh 473**
  Disclosure, **Veh 9955**
  Fines and penalties, **Veh 21721**
  Operation, location, **Veh 21720**
  Searches and seizures, **Veh 21721**
  Stickers, **Veh 9955**
Reflectors, **Veh 21223**
Registration, application of law, **Veh
  21224**
Rules of the road, **Veh 21228**
Searches and seizures, pocket bikes, **Veh
  21721**
Sidewalks,
  Operation, **Veh 21235**
  Pocket bikes, **Veh 21720**
Speed, **Veh 21235, 22411**
Stickers, pocket bikes, disclosure, **Veh
  9955**
Switch, disengaging motor, **Veh 21227**
Towing, **Veh 21235**
Traffic rules and regulations, pocket bikes,
  operation, location, **Veh 21720**
Turns, **Veh 21228**
Vehicular crossings, **Veh 23330**
Warnings, stickers, pocket bikes, **Veh 9955**

MOTORIZED SKATEBOARDS
Generally, **Veh 21968**

MOTORIZED TRICYCLE
Definitions, vehicle registration, **Veh 407**

MOUNTAIN HIGHWAYS
Highways and Roads, this index

MOVERS
Household Goods Carriers, generally, this
  index

MUD GUARDS
Motor vehicles, equipment, **Veh 27600**

MUFFLERS
Definitions, motor vehicles, **Veh 425**
Motorcycles, **Veh 27150**
Motorized bicycles, **Veh 24015**

MULTIPLE BEAM LIGHTING EQUIPMENT
Motor vehicles, **Veh 24407 et seq.**

MUNICIPAL AND JUSTICE COURT ACT
Municipal Courts, generally, this index

MUNICIPAL ATTORNEYS
Addresses,
  Confidentiality, **Veh 1808.4**
  Home addresses, confidentiality, **Veh
    1808.4**
Confidential or privileged information,
  Addresses, **Veh 1808.4**
  Home addresses, **Veh 1808.4**
Home addresses, confidential or privileged
  information, **Veh 1808.4**
Motor vehicles,
  Photography and pictures, disclosure,
    Veh 1808.51
  Records and recordation, access, **Veh
    1810.5**

MUNICIPAL CORPORATIONS
Municipalities, generally, this index

MUNICIPAL COUNCIL
Addresses, members, confidentiality, **Veh
  1808.4**
Confidential or privileged information, ad-
  dresses of members, confidentiality,
  Veh 1808.4
Home addresses, council members, confi-
  dentiality, **Veh 1808.4**
Members, addresses, confidentiality, **Veh
  1808.4**
Ordinances, generally, this index

MUNICIPAL COURTS
Claims courts. Small Claims Courts, gen-
  erally, this index
Night court assessments, traffic offenses,
  Veh 42006
Reports, night court assessment, traffic of-
  fenses, **Veh 42006**
San Francisco City and County, this index
Small Claims Courts, generally, this index
Subpoenas, generally, this index
Traffic rules and regulations, night court
  assessments, special penalty, **Veh
  42006**

MUNICIPAL EMPLOYEES
Municipal Officers and Employees, generally, this index

MUNICIPAL OFFICERS AND EMPLOYEES
Addresses, parking enforcement officers,
  confidentiality, **Veh 1808.4**
Attorneys. Municipal Attorneys, general-
  ly, this index
Chief of fire department. Firefighters and
  Fire Departments, this index
Chief of police. Police, this index
Confidential or privileged information,
  parking enforcement officers, home
  addresses, **Veh 1808.4**
Council. Municipal Council, generally,
  this index
Firefighters and Fire Departments, gener-
  ally, this index

**MUNICIPAL OFFICERS AND EMPLOYEES
  —Cont'd**
Home addresses, parking enforcement of-
  ficers, confidentiality, **Veh 1808.4**
Impounding,
  Motor vehicles, authority, **Veh 22651**
  Parked or standing vehicles, **Veh 22654**
Legal advisor. Municipal Attorneys, gen-
  erally, this index
Motor vehicles,
  Impounding, authority, **Veh 22651**
  Removal, parked or standing vehicles,
    Veh 22654
Parking enforcement officers, addresses,
  confidentiality, **Veh 1808.4**
Police, generally, this index

MUNICIPAL UTILITY DISTRICTS
Security officers, emergency vehicle permit, **Veh 2416**

MUNICIPALITIES
Air Pollution, this index
Airports and Landing Fields, generally,
  this index
Alleys. Streets and Alleys, generally, this
  index
Arrest, quotas, peace officers, **Veh 41600
  et seq.**
Attorneys. Municipal Attorneys, general-
  ly, this index
Bicycles, licenses, **Veh 39000 et seq.**
Business license taxes. Taxation, this in-
  dex
Cemeteries and Dead Bodies, generally,
  this index
Chartered cities. Ordinances, generally,
  this index
City council. Municipal Council, general-
  ly, this index
Civil defense. War and Civil Defense,
  generally, this index
Consolidated Cities and Counties, general-
  ly, this index
Councils. Municipal Council, generally,
  this index
Courts. Municipal Courts, generally, this
  index
Definitions,
  Motor vehicles, **Veh 255**
  Traffic safety fund, **Veh 42200**
Employees. Municipal Officers and Em-
  ployees, generally, this index
Firefighters and Fire Departments, gener-
  ally, this index
Fires and Fire Protection, generally, this
  index
Freeways, generally, this index
Governing board. Municipal Council,
  generally, this index
Highways and Roads, this index
Housing, generally, this index
Housing Authorities, generally, this index
Jails, generally, this index
Labor and employment. Municipal Offi-
  cers and Employees, generally, this
  index

MUNICIPALITIES—Cont'd
Landing fields. Airports and Landing Fields, generally, this index
Local Agencies, generally, this index
Los Angeles, generally, this index
Maps and Plats, generally, this index
Mobilehomes and mobilehome parks, private roads, ordinances, **Veh 21107.9**
Motor vehicles,
    Abandoned or unclaimed property, removal, **Veh 22669, 22710**
    Arrest warrant execution, expenses and expenditures, **Veh 40516**
    Fees, exemption, **Veh 9101, 9103**
    Financial responsibility, exemptions, **Veh 16051**
    Off highway vehicles, **Veh 38000 et seq.**
    Prostitution, impounding, ordinances, **Veh 22659.5**
    Registration, **Veh 4155**
    Special license plates, **Veh 5001**
    Tort liability, **Veh 17000 et seq.**
Motorized scooters, powers and duties, **Veh 21225**
Municipal Council, generally, this index
Municipal Officers and Employees, generally, this index
Museums, generally, this index
National defense. War and Civil Defense, generally, this index
Officers and employees. Municipal Officers and Employees, generally, this index
Ordinances, generally, this index
Parking Lots and Facilities, generally, this index
Parking Meters, generally, this index
Parks, generally, this index
Peace Officers, generally, this index
Plats. Maps and Plats, generally, this index
Police, generally, this index
Safety program, traffic safety, **Veh 2909, 2910**
San Francisco City and County, generally, this index
Schools and School Districts, generally, this index
Sidewalks, generally, this index
Streets and Alleys, generally, this index
Taxation, generally, this index
Torts, motor vehicles, **Veh 17000 et seq.**
Traffic Rules and Regulations, this index
Traffic signs and signals, buildings, **Veh 21113**
War and Civil Defense, generally, this index
Weeds, generally, this index

MURDER
Homicide, generally, this index

MUSEUMS
Confidential or privileged information, officers and employees, security officers, addresses, **Veh 1808.4**

MUSEUMS—Cont'd
Officers and employees,
    Confidential or privileged information, security officers, addresses, **Veh 1808.4**
    Security officers, addresses, confidentiality, **Veh 1808.4**
Security officers, addresses, confidentiality, **Veh 1808.4**

MUSK THISTLE
Weeds, generally, this index

MUSSELS
Shellfish, this index

MUTUAL BENEFIT CORPORATIONS
Consumer motor vehicle recovery corporation, **Veh 12200 et seq.**

NAMES
Alias. Assumed or Fictitious Names, generally, this index
Assumed or Fictitious Names, generally, this index
False or fictitious name, notice to correct violations, **Veh 40614**
Fictitious names. Assumed or Fictitious Names, generally, this index
Motor Carriers, this index
Motor Vehicles, this index
Signatures, generally, this index
Trademarks, generally, this index
Traffic Rules and Regulations, this index
Traffic Signs and Signals, this index

NARCOTIC ADDICTS
Drug Addicts, generally, this index

NARCOTICS
Drugs and Medicine, generally, this index

NATIONAL DEFENSE
War and Civil Defense, generally, this index

NATIONAL FORESTS
Highways, definitions, **Veh 592**

NATIONAL GUARD
Military Forces, this index

NATIONAL LAW ENFORCEMENT TELE-COMMUNICATION SYSTEM
Motor vehicles, abandoned or unclaimed property, storage, notice, **Veh 22854.5**

NATIONAL PARK SERVICE
Rangers, home addresses, confidentiality, **Veh 1808.4**

NATIONAL PARKS
Service rangers, addresses, confidentiality, **Veh 1808.4**

NATIONAL TRAFFIC AND MOTOR VEHICLE SAFETY ACT OF 1966
Motor vehicle dealers, conformity, **Veh 24011**
Safety glazing material requirements, **Veh 26704**

NATIVE AMERICANS
Indians, generally, this index

NATURAL GAS
Oil and Gas, generally, this index

NATURAL RESOURCES
Environment, generally, this index

NATURALIZATION
Citizens and Citizenship, generally, this index

NAVIGATION
Ships and Shipping, generally, this index

NAVY
Military Forces, generally, this index

NEGLECTED CHILDREN
Juvenile Delinquents and Dependents, generally, this index

NEGLIGENCE
Damaging streets and highways, **Veh 17300 et seq.**
Driving while intoxicated, **Veh 23153**
Highways, damaging, **Veh 17300 et seq.**
Imputed negligence,
    Motor vehicles, **Veh 17150 et seq.**
    Children and minors, **Veh 17707**
    Traffic rules and regulations, passenger for hire, failure of driver to stop at railroad crossing, **Veh 22453**
Indemnity, generally, this index
Motor Vehicles, this index
Physicians and Surgeons, this index
Seatbelts, mandatory, **Veh 27315**
Snowmobiles, operation, **Veh 23128**
Streets and alleys, damages, **Veh 17300 et seq.**
Traffic Rules and Regulations, this index

NEGLIGENT OPERATOR
Definitions, traffic rules and regulations, **Veh 12809, 12810.5**

NEGOTIABLE INSTRUMENTS
Bad checks,
    Automobile dismantlers, license revocation, **Veh 11509**
    Motor carriers, permits, fees, **Veh 34672**
    Motor Vehicles, this index
Bills of Lading, generally, this index
Checks,
    Bail, motor vehicle offenses, **Veh 40510**
    Dishonor, motor vehicle penalties and fees, **Veh 13364**
    Simulated checks, vehicle sales, **Veh 11713.1**
Motor carriers, permits, fees, bad checks, **Veh 34672**
Motor vehicles, payment of fees by check, **Veh 9558**
Simulated checks, vehicle sales, **Veh 11713.1**

NETWORKS
Telecommunications, generally, this index

NEUTRONS
Atomic Energy, generally, this index

NEVADA COUNTY
Northwoods boulevard, commercial vehicle weights, ordinances, **Veh 35715**

NEW CAR LOTS
Inspection, stolen vehicles, **Veh 2805**

NEW MOTOR VEHICLE BOARD
Motor Vehicles Department, this index

NEW MOTOR VEHICLE DEALER
Definitions, **Veh 426**

NEW VEHICLES
Definitions, **Veh 430**

NEWBORN CHILDREN
Children and Minors, generally, this index

NEWSPAPERS
Advertisements, generally, this index
License plates, photographers, special plates, **Veh 5008**
Notice, generally, this index

NIGHT COURT
Traffic offenses,
    Notice to appear, **Veh 40502**
    Penalty assessment, **Veh 42006**

NIGHTTIME
Highways and roads, patrols, **Veh 2401**
Motorcycles, instruction permits, **Veh 12509, 12509.5**
Motorized bicycles, instruction permits, **Veh 12509.5**
Motorized scooters, instruction permits, **Veh 12509.5**

NITROGEN DIOXIDE
Air Pollution, generally, this index

NITROGLYCERINE
Explosives, generally, this index

NO DAMAGE
Definitions, motor vehicle bumper strength notices, **Veh 24011.3**

NOISE
Motor Vehicles, this index
Motorcycles, this index
Motorized scooters, **Veh 21226**
Snowmobiles, limits, **Veh 27203**
Traffic Rules and Regulations, this index

NOISE POLLUTION
Freeways, generally, this index
Off highway vehicles, **Veh 38370**
Recreational trails, off highway vehicles, **Veh 38370**
Traffic rules and regulations, exhaust systems, decals, **Veh 27202.1**
Vehicles, city on island or 20,000 acres, county over 4 million, **Veh 21100.5**

NOLO CONTENDERE
Drivers licenses, conviction under plea, revocation or suspension, **Veh 13103**
Driving schools, licenses,
    Refusal to issue, **Veh 11107**
    Suspension or revocation, **Veh 11110**
Traffic Rules and Regulations, this index

NONMOTORIZED SCOOTERS
Helmets, children and minors, **Veh 21212**

NONPROFIT CHARITABLE ORGANIZATIONS
Charities, generally, this index
Nonprofit Organizations, generally, this index

NONPROFIT CORPORATIONS
Boats and boating, fee exemption, **Veh 9870**
Charities, generally, this index
Consumer motor vehicle recovery corporation, **Veh 12200 et seq.**
Motor vehicle insurance, charitable risk pools, financial responsibility, **Veh 16054.2**
Public Benefit Corporations, generally, this index
Religious Organizations and Societies, generally, this index
Ships and shipping, fee exemption, **Veh 9870**

NONPROFIT ORGANIZATIONS
Driving schools, exemptions, **Veh 11101**
Motor carriers,
    Brokers, construction, bonds (officers and fiduciaries), evidence, **Veh 34510.5**
    Charitable risk pools, financial responsibility, **Veh 34631**
Motor vehicle insurance, charitable risk pools, financial responsibility, **Veh 16054.2**
Motor vehicles,
    Dealers, exclusions, **Veh 286**
    Donors, records, **Veh 1660**
    Flashing amber lights, handicapped or mentally retarded persons, **Veh 25276**
Records and recordation, motor vehicles, donors, **Veh 1660**
Religious Organizations and Societies, generally, this index

NONPROFIT PUBLIC BENEFIT CORPORATION LAW
Public Benefit Corporations, generally, this index

NONPROFIT RELIGIOUS CORPORATIONS
Religious Organizations and Societies, generally, this index

NONPUBLIC SCHOOLS
Private Schools, generally, this index

NONREPAIRABLE VEHICLES
Motor Vehicles, this index

NONRESIDENT DAILY COMMUTER
Definitions, registration exemption, **Veh 435.5**

NONRESIDENT MOTORIST STATUTE
Generally, **Veh 17450 et seq.**

NONRESIDENTS
Arrest, **Veh 40305**
    Guaranteed traffic arrest bail bond certificate, commercial motor vehicles, **Veh 40305.5**
Bail, guaranteed traffic arrest bail bond certificate, commercial motor vehicles, **Veh 40305.5**
Definitions, motor vehicles, **Veh 435**
Driving under the influence, ignition interlock devices, **Veh 23575**
Guaranteed traffic arrest bail bond certificate, commercial motor vehicles, **Veh 40305.5**
Ignition interlock devices, driving under the influence, **Veh 23575**
Mobilehomes and Mobilehome Parks, this index
Motor Carriers, this index
Motor Vehicles, this index
Process, this index
Registration, foreign commercial vehicles, **Veh 6850 et seq.**
Traffic Rules and Regulations, this index
Trailer coaches, registration, **Veh 5354**

NONSUFFICIENT FUNDS CHECKS
Bad checks. Negotiable Instruments, this index

NORCO
Traffic rules and regulations, speed, horseback riding, **Veh 22353**

NORMAL BUSINESS HOURS
Definitions, motor vehicles, towing, **Veh 22658**

NORTHWOODS BOULEVARD
Nevada County ordinances, commercial vehicle weights, **Veh 35715**

NOTES
Negotiable Instruments, generally, this index

NOTICE
Accidents, this index
Acquisition notice, dismantlers of motor vehicles, **Veh 11520**
Assumed or Fictitious Names, this index
Atomic Energy, this index
Bicycles, this index
Boats and Boating, this index
Cargo tank vehicles, hearings, **Veh 21109.5**
Crimes and Offenses, this index
Driving Schools, this index
Freeways, this index
Hazardous Substances and Waste, this index
Highway Patrol, this index
Highways and Roads, this index

NOTICE—Cont'd
Los Angeles County, traffic rules and regulations, commercial vehicles, weights, maximum, **Veh 35655.6**
Machinery and Equipment, this index
Manufactured housing. Housing, this index
Mobilehomes and Mobilehome Parks, this index
Motor Carriers, this index
Motor Vehicle Insurance, this index
Motor Vehicles, this index
Motorized scooters, manufacturers and manufacturing, **Veh 407.5**
Peace Officers, this index
Police, this index
Radioactive materials, transportation, **Veh 33002**
Railroads, this index
Recreational Vehicles, this index
Retailers, motor vehicles, removal, **Veh 22658**
Sales, this index
Sheriffs, this index
Ships and Shipping, this index
Smog impact fees, motor vehicles, foreign states, **Veh 1673.2 et seq.**
Speed. Traffic Rules and Regulations, this index
Taxicabs, this index
Traffic Rules and Regulations, this index
Traffic Signs and Signals, this index
Traffic Violator Schools, this index
Trailers, lost or stolen plates, **Veh 4458**

NOTIFICATION
Notice, generally, this index

NOVATION
Motor vehicles, dealers, requiring prospective assent, **Veh 11713.2**

NOXIOUS WEEDS
Weeds, generally, this index

NSF CHECKS
Bad checks. Negotiable Instruments, this index

NUCLEAR ENERGY
Atomic Energy, generally, this index

NUISANCE
Abatement, traffic signs and signals, **Veh 21467**
Agricultural machinery and equipment, forfeitures, **Veh 34506.5**
Forfeitures, agricultural machinery and equipment, **Veh 34506.5**
Motor Vehicles, this index
Noise Pollution, generally, this index
Pest Abatement Districts, generally, this index
Prostitution, this index
Traffic Rules and Regulations, this index
Traffic signs and signals, abatement, **Veh 21467**
Weeds, generally, this index

NURSE PRACTITIONERS
Nurses, this index

NURSES
Blood tests, driving under the influence, **Veh 23158**
Definitions, rescue teams, emergency vehicles, liability, resuscitation attempts, **Veh 165.5**
Emergency medical services, liability, resuscitation, **Veh 165.5**
Licensed vocational nurses. Vocational Nursing, generally, this index
Midwives, generally, this index
Motor vehicles, blood tests for drunken driving, **Veh 23158**
Nurse practitioners, motor vehicles, certificates and certification,
    Disabled veterans, license fees, exemptions, **Veh 9105**
    Handicapped persons,
        License plates, **Veh 5007**
        Parking, placards, **Veh 22511.55, 22511.59**
Physician Assistants, generally, this index
Rescue teams, emergency vehicles, liability, resuscitation attempts, **Veh 165.5**
Training, rescue teams, emergency vehicles, **Veh 165.5**
Vocational Nursing, generally, this index

NUT GRASS
Weeds, generally, this index

OAKLAND
Notice, traffic rules and regulations, weights, **Veh 35655.5**
Traffic rules and regulations, weights, maximum, **Veh 35655.5**

OATHS AND AFFIRMATIONS
Affidavits, generally, this index
Definitions, motor vehicles, **Veh 16**
Motor carriers, fleet vehicles, insurance, reports, **Veh 34633**
Motor vehicles,
    Administration by officers and employees, **Veh 18**
    Definitions, **Veh 16**

OATS
Agricultural Products, generally, this index

OBLITERATION
Motor vehicle identification numbers, **Veh 10802**

OBSTETRICS AND OBSTETRICIANS
Midwives, generally, this index

OBSTRUCTING TRAFFIC
Traffic Rules and Regulations, this index

OBSTRUCTIONS
Motor vehicle windshield, signs and stickers, **Veh 26708**

ODOMETERS
Crimes and offenses, **Veh 11713**
Motor Vehicles, this index

ODORS
Air Pollution, generally, this index

OFF HIGHWAY MOTOR VEHICLE LAW
Generally, **Veh 38000 et seq.**

OFF HIGHWAY MOTORCYCLE
Definitions, **Veh 436**

OFF HIGHWAY VEHICLE SAFETY EDUCATION COMMITTEE
Generally, **Veh 38500 et seq.**

OFF HIGHWAY VEHICLES
Generally, **Veh 38000 et seq.**
Motor Vehicles, this index

OFF STREET PARKING
Parking Lots and Facilities, generally, this index

OFF STREET PARKING FACILITY
Definitions, drivers licenses, **Veh 12500**

OFFENSES
Crimes and Offenses, generally, this index

OFFICERS AND EMPLOYEES
County Officers and Employees, generally, this index
Highway Patrol, this index
Motor Carriers, this index
Municipal Officers and Employees, generally, this index
Museums, this index
Public Officers and Employees, generally, this index
Railroads, this index
State Officers and Employees, generally, this index

OFFICIAL ADVERTISEMENTS
Advertisements, generally, this index

OFFICIAL BONDS
Bonds (Officers and Fiduciaries), generally, this index

OFFICIAL MAPS
Maps and Plats, generally, this index

OFFSTREET PARKING
Parking Lots and Facilities, generally, this index

OIL AND GAS
Definitions, oil well production service unit, **Veh 450**
Highways and Roads, this index
Inspection and inspectors, motor carriers, **Veh 2810**
Motor carriers,
    Inspection, **Veh 2810**
    Signs, display, **Veh 27903**
Motor Vehicle Fuel, generally, this index

OIL AND GAS PIPELINES
Motor vehicles, construction and maintenance, flashing amber lights, **Veh 25260.1**

OIL DEPOSITS
Motor vehicle accidents, tow car drivers, duty to remove, **Veh 27700**

OIL STATIONS
Motor Vehicle Service Stations, generally, this index

OIL WELL PRODUCTION SERVICE UNIT
Definitions, **Veh 450**

OLD AGE
Aged Persons, generally, this index

OLD AGE AND SURVIVORS INSURANCE
Social Security, generally, this index

OLD PERSONS
Aged Persons, generally, this index

OLYMPIC GAMES
Commemorative reflectorized license plates, **Veh 5022, 5101.7**

ONE WAY ROADWAYS
Traffic Rules and Regulations, this index
Traffic Signs and Signals, this index

OPEN CONTAINER LAW
Motor vehicles, intoxicating liquors, **Veh 23222, 23225, 23229**

OPERATE
Definitions, ignition interlock devices, **Veh 23575**

OPERATORS
Driving Schools, this index

OPERATORS LICENSES
Generally, **Veh 12500 et seq.**
Drivers licenses. Motor Vehicles, this index

OPTOMETRISTS
Motor vehicles, certificates and certification,
Disabled veterans, license fees, exemptions, **Veh 9105**
Handicapped persons,
License plates, **Veh 5007**
Parking, placards, **Veh 22511.55, 22511.59**

ORANGE COUNTY
South coast air quality management district. Air Pollution, this index

ORANGE COUNTY STATE COLLEGE
Colleges and Universities, generally, this index

ORDERS
Firefighters and Fire Departments, this index
Motor Vehicles, this index

ORDERS OF COURT
Appeal and Review, generally, this index
Contempt, generally, this index
Judgments and Decrees, generally, this index

ORDERS OF COURT—Cont'd
Motor carriers, occupational licenses, practices, **Veh 1651.2**
Motor Vehicles, this index
Service of process. Process, this index
Taxicabs, searches and seizures, **Veh 21100.4**
Traffic Rules and Regulations, this index
Traffic violator schools, attendance, **Veh 42005**
Studies, **Veh 42005.1**

ORDINANCES
Bicycle licenses, **Veh 39000 et seq.**
Commercial vehicles,
Passenger vehicles for hire, regulation, **Veh 16501**
Street vending, **Veh 22455**
Consolidated cities and counties,
Manufactured housing, private roads, **Veh 21107.9**
Mobilehomes and mobilehome parks, private roads, **Veh 21107.9**
Motor vehicles, prostitution, impounding, **Veh 22659.5**
Counties,
Bicycle licenses, **Veh 39000 et seq.**
Manufactured housing, private roads, ordinances, **Veh 21107.9**
Mobilehomes and mobilehome parks, private roads, **Veh 21107.9**
Motor vehicles, prostitution, impounding, **Veh 22659.5**
Fire hydrants, vehicles stopping or parking, **Veh 22514**
Highways and roads, temporary closure, **Veh 21101.4**
Local vehicle license fees, surcharges, San Francisco City and County, **Veh 9250.12**
Manufactured housing, private roads, **Veh 21107.9**
Mobilehomes and Mobilehome Parks, this index
Motor Vehicles, this index
Parking in front of private driveways, owners and lessees, permits, **Veh 22507.2**
Private driveways, parking in front of, permits, **Veh 22507.2**
Roller skating, local regulation, **Veh 21969**
San Francisco City and County, local vehicle license fee surcharge, **Veh 9250.12**
Streets and Alleys, this index
Traffic Rules and Regulations, this index
Vehicles for hire, local authorities, **Veh 16501**
Vending from commercial vehicles, street vending, **Veh 22455**

ORGAN DONORS
Anatomical Gifts, generally, this index

ORGANIZATIONS
Associations and Societies, generally, this index

ORGANIZED CAMPS
Camps and Camping, generally, this index

ORGANIZED CRIME PREVENTION AND VICTIM PROTECTION ACT
Generally, **Veh 1806**

ORIGINAL DRIVERS LICENSE
Definitions, **Veh 455**

ORIGINAL IDENTIFICATION
Motor vehicles, off highway vehicles subject to identification, **Veh 38040 et seq.**

OTHER STATES
Foreign States, generally, this index

OUT OF SERVICE ORDERS
Motor vehicles,
Commercial vehicles, fines and penalties, **Veh 15311.1**
Crimes and offenses, **Veh 40001, 40303**

OUTDOOR ADVERTISING
Buses, lighted display signs, **Veh 25400**
Mobile billboard advertising displays, traffic rules and regulations, **Veh 21100**
Impounding, **Veh 22651**
Traffic rules and regulations, mobile billboard advertising displays, **Veh 21100**
Impounding, **Veh 22651**
Trolley coaches, lighted display signs, **Veh 25400**

OVERHANGING LOADS
Motor carriers, explosives, **Veh 31614**

OVERPASSES
Traffic rules and regulations, pedestrians,
Arrest, refusal to leave, **Veh 40303**
Failure to use, **Veh 21953**

OVERTAKING AND PASSING
Traffic Rules and Regulations, this index
Traffic Signs and Signals, this index

OWNED
Definitions, ignition interlock devices, **Veh 23575**

OWNER EXEMPTIONS
Definitions, motor vehicles, **Veh 461**

OWNERS AND OWNERSHIP
Title to Property, generally, this index

OWNERS LIABILITY ACT
Motor vehicles, **Veh 17150 et seq.**

OWNERS RESPONSIBILITY LAWS (MOTOR VEHICLES)
State and governmental agencies, **Veh 17000 et seq.**

OXIDIZERS
Motor carriers, explosives, mixed cargoes, **Veh 31613**

OXIDIZING
Motor carriers, signs, display, **Veh 27903**

OXYGEN
Resuscitators, emergency ambulances, **Veh 2418.5**

PADDLE BOATS
Number or registration, **Veh 9873**

PAINTS AND PAINTING
Buses formerly used as school buses, **Veh 27603**
Defacing, children and minors, delay or suspension of driving privileges, **Veh 13202.6**
Law enforcement vehicles, repainting, sale or nonlaw enforcement use, **Veh 27604**
Motorcycles,
   Insignia, former police vehicles, **Veh 27604**
   Similarity to police cycles, **Veh 27605**

PANDERING
Motor vehicles, nuisance, impounding, **Veh 22659.5**

PANTOPON
Drug Addicts, generally, this index

PAPERS
Negotiable Instruments, generally, this index

PARADES
Motor vehicles, exemption from registration, **Veh 4003**
Traffic rules and regulations, temporary closing streets, **Veh 21101**
Trucks, passengers, cargo area, **Veh 23116**

PARAMEDICS
Emergency Medical Technicians, generally, this index

PARAPLEGICS
Handicapped Persons, generally, this index

PARATRANSIT VEHICLES
Certificates and certification,
   Certificates of endorsement, **Veh 13369 et seq.**
   Drivers, **Veh 12523.5**
   Inspection, **Veh 34501.8**
Criminal history information, drivers, certificates and certification, **Veh 12517.3**
Definitions, **Veh 336, 462**
Drivers, **Veh 12517.5**
   Certificates, **Veh 12523.5**
   Criminal history information, certificates and certification, **Veh 12517.3**
   Drugs and medicine, certificates and certification, revocation, **Veh 13376**
   Fingerprints and fingerprinting, certificates and certification, **Veh 12517.3**
   Licenses, revocation, **Veh 13371**
Drug testing, **Veh 34520.5**
Drugs and medicine, drivers, certificates and certification, revocation, **Veh 13376**
Examinations, drivers certificates, **Veh 12523.5**
Fingerprints and fingerprinting, drivers, certificates and certification, **Veh 12517.3**

PARATRANSIT VEHICLES—Cont'd
High occupancy vehicle lanes, **Veh 21655.5**
Highways and roads, high occupancy vehicle lanes, **Veh 21655.5**
Inspection and inspectors, **Veh 34501.17**
   Safety, **Veh 34501.8**
Odometers, **Veh 34501.17**
Records and recordation, **Veh 34501.17**
Revocation or suspension, certificates and certification, **Veh 13370**
Safety regulations, **Veh 34500 et seq.**
School buses, **Veh 545**
Sex offenses, drivers, license revocation, **Veh 13369 et seq.**
Training, drivers, **Veh 12517.5**

PARENT AND CHILD RELATIONSHIP
Children and Minors, generally, this index

PARENTS
Children and Minors, generally, this index

PARK AND PLAYGROUND ACT OF 1909
Parks, generally, this index

PARK RANGERS
Emergency motor vehicles, permits, **Veh 2416**

PARK TRAILERS
Definitions, trailer coaches, **Veh 635**
Identification numbers, **Veh 11713.3**
Licenses and permits, movement, **Veh 35780.3**
Registration, cards, **Veh 4453**
Safety, **Veh 34500 et seq.**
Sales, disclosure, moving requirements, **Veh 11713.1**

PARKING
Freeways, this index
Lots. Parking Lots and Facilities, generally, this index
Meters. Parking Meters, generally, this index
Traffic Rules and Regulations, this index

PARKING LOTS AND FACILITIES
   Generally, **Veh 22950 et seq.**
Advertising vehicles, removal, **Veh 22651.2**
Animals, standing, **Veh 21113**
Attendants, license to operate vehicle, **Veh 14605**
Bicycles, **Veh 21113**
Civil liability, removal of unauthorized vehicles, disabled persons authorized spaces, **Veh 22652.5**
Colleges and Universities, this index
Corridor parking facilities, state highways, **Veh 22518**
Crimes and offenses, reckless driving, **Veh 23103**
Disabled persons, designated parking spaces, removal of unauthorized vehicles, civil liability, **Veh 22652.5**
Drivers licenses, **Veh 14605**
   Prerequisite, off street parking, **Veh 12500, 12501**

PARKING LOTS AND FACILITIES—Cont'd
Electric vehicles, designated spaces, **Veh 22511, 22511.1, 42001.6**
Exemptions, park and ride lots, alternative fuel vehicles, **Veh 22518**
Freeways, transportation corridor parking facilities, **Veh 22518**
Handicapped persons,
   Designated parking spaces, removal of unauthorized vehicles, civil liability, **Veh 22652.5**
   Fines and penalties, parking in handicapped persons space, **Veh 42001.5**
   Lifts or ramps, **Veh 22511.85**
Highway patrol, inspection, motor vehicles, **Veh 2805**
Highways and roads,
   Corridor parking facilities, **Veh 22518**
   Park and ride lots, **Veh 22518**
Impounding vehicles, **Veh 22658**
Inspection and inspectors, **Veh 10656**
   Stolen vehicle, **Veh 2805**
   Vehicles, registration and title, **Veh 1655**
Mobilehomes and Mobilehome Parks, generally, this index
Motorized bicycles, **Veh 21113**
Reckless driving, **Veh 23103**
Removal of vehicles, **Veh 22651.3, 22658**
   Disabled persons designated spaces, civil liability, **Veh 22652.5**
   Multiple violations, **Veh 22651.2**
Report of parked vehicle, **Veh 10652**
Roller skates, **Veh 21113**
Signs and signals, handicapped persons, local authorities, **Veh 22511.7, 22511.8**
Skateboards, **Veh 21113**
Standing vehicles, **Veh 21113**
State highways, **Veh 22518**
Stored vehicles, reports, **Veh 10650 et seq.**
Towing vehicles, multiple violations, **Veh 22651.2**
Zero emission vehicles, designated spaces, **Veh 22511, 22511.1, 42001.6**

PARKING METERS
Handicapped persons, fee exemption, **Veh 22511.5**
Inoperable parking meters, **Veh 22508.5**
Mobile devices, payment, **Veh 22508**
Veterans, license plates, special plates, rates and charges, exemptions, **Veh 22511.3**
Zones, parking meter zones, **Veh 22508**

PARKS
Abandoned or unclaimed property, motor vehicles, removal, priority, **Veh 22667**
Animals,
   State parks, post
      Traffic regulations, **Veh 21113**
Authorized emergency vehicles, peace officers, state park system, permits, **Veh 2416**
Bicycles, **Veh 21113**
Counties,
   Animals, traffic regulations, **Veh 21113**
   Bicycles, **Veh 21113**

PARKS

PARKS—Cont'd

Counties—Cont'd

Motorized bicycles, **Veh 21113**

Roller skates, **Veh 21113**

Skateboards, **Veh 21113**

Traffic rules and regulations, **Veh 21113**

Emergency vehicles, peace officers, state park system, permits, **Veh 2416**

Highways and Roads, this index

Mobilehomes and Mobilehome Parks, generally, this index

Motor vehicles,

Abandoned vehicles, priority of removal, **Veh 22669**

Irrigation and irrigation districts, machinery and equipment, inspection and inspectors, **Veh 2810.2**

State parks, post

Motorized bicycles, **Veh 21113**

Narrow streets, speed limits, **Veh 22358.3**

Off highway vehicles, access routes, **Veh 38027**

Peace officers. State parks, post

Regional park districts,

Impounding, parked or standing vehicles, **Veh 22654**

Motor vehicles, irrigation and irrigation districts, machinery and equipment, inspection and inspectors, **Veh 2810.2**

Roller skates, **Veh 21113**

Skateboards, **Veh 21113**

Speed limit,

Local authorities, **Veh 22358.3**

Narrow streets, **Veh 22358.3**

State parks,

Animals,

Standing, **Veh 21113**

Traffic regulations, **Veh 21113**

Authorized emergency vehicles, peace officers, permits, **Veh 2416**

Bicycles, **Veh 21113**

Emergency vehicles, peace officers, permits, **Veh 2416**

Motor vehicles,

Environmental design, special license plates, **Veh 5161**

Irrigation and irrigation districts, machinery and equipment, inspection and inspectors, **Veh 2810.2**

Peace officers, emergency vehicles, permits, **Veh 2416**

Motorized bicycles, **Veh 21113**

Peace officers, emergency vehicles, permits, **Veh 2416**

Roller skates, **Veh 21113**

Skateboards, **Veh 21113**

Traffic rules and regulations, **Veh 21113**

Streets, narrow streets, speed limits, **Veh 22358.3**

Traffic rules and regulations, **Veh 21113**

Speed limit, local authorities, **Veh 22358.3**

PARKS AND RECREATION DEPARTMENT

Parks, generally, this index

PARKS AND RECREATION DEPARTMENT —Cont'd

Peace officers,

Appraisal of vehicles, powers and duties, **Veh 22855**

Hit and run accidents, powers and duties, **Veh 22655**

PAROCHIAL SCHOOLS

Private Schools, generally, this index

PAROLE AND PROBATION

Addresses, home addresses, confidential information, designated parole hearings division personnel, **Veh 1808.6**

Associate chief deputy commissioners, parole hearings division, home addresses, confidential information, **Veh 1808.6**

Boards and commissions. Parole Hearings Board, generally, this index

Chief administrative hearing officer, home addresses, confidential information, **Veh 1808.6**

Deputy commissioners, parole hearings division, home addresses, confidential information, **Veh 1808.6**

Drivers licenses,

Duration of suspension or revocation, **Veh 13203**

Suspension or revocation during parole, **Veh 41500**

Hearings board. Parole Hearings Board, generally, this index

Highways and roads, littering offenses, **Veh 42001.7**

Home addresses, designated parole hearings personnel, confidential information, **Veh 1808.6**

Ignition interlock devices, certificates and certification, **Veh 13386**

Motor Vehicles, this index

Parole Hearings Board, generally, this index

Speed contests on highways, **Veh 23109**

Traffic rules and regulations, driving under influence of drugs, **Veh 14601**

PAROLE HEARINGS BOARD

Addresses,

Designated personnel, confidential information, **Veh 1808.6**

Home addresses, designated personnel, confidential information, **Veh 1808.6**

Chairperson, home addresses, confidential information, **Veh 1808.6**

Commissioners, home addresses, confidential information, **Veh 1808.6**

Confidential or privileged information, home addresses, designated personnel, **Veh 1808.6**

Deputy commissioners, home addresses, confidential information, **Veh 1808.6**

Executive director, home addresses, confidential information, **Veh 1808.6**

PAROLE HEARINGS BOARD—Cont'd

Home addresses, designated personnel, confidential information, **Veh 1808.6**

Members and membership, home addresses, confidential information, **Veh 1808.6**

Motor vehicles, inspectors, and investigators, confidential and privileged information, records and recordation, address, **Veh 1808.2**

Officers and employees, home addresses, designated personnel, confidential information, **Veh 1808.6**

Representatives, address, confidential or privileged information, **Veh 1808.6**

PARTICIPANT

Definitions, motor vehicles, consumer protection, recovery corporation, **Veh 12200**

PARTIES

Contempt, generally, this index

PARTNERSHIP

Traffic violator schools, refusal to issue license, **Veh 11211**

PASSENGER CHARTER PARTY CARRIERS

Limousines, generally, this index

Tour buses. Buses, this index

PASSENGER MOTOR VEHICLE

Definitions, **Veh 27315.3**

PASSENGER RESTRAINT SYSTEMS

Definitions, school buses, **Veh 27316, 27316.5**

PASSENGER TRANSPORTATION VEHICLE

Definitions, trailer buses, **Veh 464**

PASSENGERS

Alcoholic beverages, children transporting liquors, **Veh 23224, 40000.15**

All terrain vehicles, public lands, **Veh 38506**

Bicycles, **Veh 21204**

Campers, exits, **Veh 23129**

Commercial passenger vehicles, financial responsibility, **Veh 16500 et seq.**

Intoxicating liquors, children transporting liquors, **Veh 23224, 40000.15**

Limousines, generally, this index

Motor Vehicles, this index

Motorcycles, **Veh 27800**

Motorized bicycles, **Veh 27800**

School Buses, this index

Tour buses. Buses, this index

Traffic Rules and Regulations, this index

PASSING OFF

Fraud, generally, this index

PATHS

Traffic control, animal or vehicle, stopping, standing, schools, **Veh 21113**

PATROL

Highway Patrol, generally, this index

PATROL VEHICLES
Safety belts, **Veh 27315.3**

PATROLMEN
Police, generally, this index

PAUL BUZZO ACT
Highway litter, **Veh 23111**

PAY
Compensation and Salaries, generally, this index

PAYMENT
Fines and Penalties, this index
Installment Payments, generally, this index
Motor Vehicles, this index

PAYROLL DEDUCTIONS
Compensation and Salaries, generally, this index

PEACE OFFICERS
Address,
    Confidentiality, **Veh 1808.4**
    Retirees, confidentiality, **Veh 1808.4**
Arrest, generally, this index
Assistance, disabled motorists, **Veh 20018 et seq.**
Bicycles,
    Flight from, **Veh 2800.1 et seq.**
    Traffic rules and regulations, exemptions, **Veh 21200**
Boats and boating, theft, reports, **Veh 10550 et seq.**
Children and Minors, this index
Confidential or privileged information, address, **Veh 1808.4**
Crimes and offenses,
    Eluding peace officers, **Veh 2800.1 et seq.**
    Flight from, **Veh 40000.7**
Death, in line of duty, surviving spouse, addresses, confidential or privileged information, **Veh 1808.4**
Definitions,
    Inedible kitchen grease, **Veh 2460**
    Motor vehicle violations, written notice, **Veh 40600**
Detoxification vehicles, utility flood or loading lamps, **Veh 25110**
Disabled motorist, assistance, **Veh 20018 et seq.**
Dispatchers. Police, this index
Eluding peace officers, **Veh 2800.1 et seq.**
Emergencies, bicycles, traffic rules and regulations, exemptions, **Veh 21200**
Employed drivers, hours of service regulations, exception, **Veh 34501.2**
Equipment, utility flood or loading lamps, vehicles, **Veh 25110**
Exemptions,
    Emergency vehicles, pollution control devices, **Veh 27156.3**
    Pollution control devices, emergency vehicles, **Veh 27156.3**
Foreign States, this index
Guidelines, pursuit, **Veh 17004.7**

PEACE OFFICERS—Cont'd
Handicapped parking, special enforcement units, **Veh 22507.9**
Hazardous Substances and Waste, this index
Highway Patrol, generally, this index
Hit and run accidents, motor vehicle removal, **Veh 22655**
In line of duty. Death, ante
Investigations and investigators, motor vehicles, confidential and privileged information, records and recordation, address of investigator, **Veh 1808.2**
Juvenile Facilities Division, this index
Lights and lighting, utility flood or loading lamps, vehicles, **Veh 25110**
Local agencies, arrest quotas, **Veh 41600 et seq.**
Marriage, confidential or privileged information, address, **Veh 1808.4**
Motor vehicles, **Veh 165**
    Activated alarm devices, removal from highways, **Veh 22651.5**
    Department of, authority of officers and employees of department, **Veh 1655**
    Drivers, obedience to orders, **Veh 2800**
    Drivers licenses, revocation or suspension, access, **Veh 1803.4**
    Financial responsibility, exemptions, **Veh 16051**
    Flight from, **Veh 2800.1 et seq., 13201**
    Hazardous substances and waste, signs and signals, exemptions, **Veh 27903**
    Inspectors and investigators, confidential and privileged information, records and recordation, address, **Veh 1808.2**
    License plates, foreign states, reciprocity, **Veh 5001.5**
    Licenses and permits, **Veh 2416**
    Light bars, persons other than peace officers, **Veh 27606, 27607**
    Off highway vehicles, emergencies, **Veh 38025**
    Pollution control devices, **Veh 27156.2, 27156.3**
    Pursuit, reports, **Veh 14602.1**
    Removal of parked or standing vehicles, **Veh 22650 et seq.**
    Violations, arrest, application of law, **Veh 40300**
    Windows, tinting, glazing, **Veh 26708.7**
Motor Vehicles Department, this index
Notice,
    Stolen vehicles, **Veh 10500**
    Written notice, motor vehicle violation as cause of accident, **Veh 40600**
Off highway vehicles, emergencies, **Veh 38025**
Parks and Recreation Department, this index
Pesticides, spillage or release, reports, **Veh 20017**
Poisons, pesticide spillage or release, reports, **Veh 20017**
Police, generally, this index

PEACE OFFICERS—Cont'd
Policies, pursuit, **Veh 17004.7**
Privileges and immunities, pursuit, **Veh 17004.7**
Pursuit, **Veh 17004.7**
    Bicycles, traffic rules and regulations, exemptions, **Veh 21200**
    Drivers licenses, examiners and examinations, **Veh 1666.1**
    Eluding peace officers, **Veh 2800.1 et seq.**
    Reports, **Veh 14602.1**
    Traffic safety program, **Veh 2911**
Railroad right of way, motor vehicle removal, **Veh 22656**
Reasonable cause, removal of vehicles, **Veh 22651**
Reports,
    Pesticides, spillage or release, **Veh 20017**
    Pursuits, **Veh 14602.1**
    Stolen vessels, **Veh 10550 et seq.**
Rescue,
    Bicycles, traffic rules and regulations, exemptions, **Veh 21200**
    Emergency vehicles, **Veh 165**
School Officers and Employees, this index
Sheriffs, generally, this index
Ships and shipping, theft, reports, **Veh 10550 et seq.**
Standards, pursuit, **Veh 17004.7**
State park system, emergency vehicles, permits, **Veh 2416**
State police. Highway Patrol, generally, this index
Surviving spouse, death in line of duty, addresses, confidentiality, **Veh 1808.4**
Traffic Rules and Regulations, generally, this index
Training, pursuit, **Veh 17004.7**
Transportation, persons injured in accident, **Veh 20016**
Written notice, motor vehicle violation as cause of accident, probable cause, **Veh 40600**

PEARL HARBOR SURVIVORS
Special license plates, **Veh 5101.3**

PECUNIARY INTEREST
Adverse or Pecuniary Interest, generally, this index

PEDESTRIANS
Arrest, pedestrians zone, freeways, over passes or bridges, **Veh 40303**
Definitions, **Veh 467**
Driver training, **Veh 1666**
    Courses of study, **Veh 11113.3**
Electric personal assistive mobility devices, **Veh 21280 et seq.**
Freeways, this index
Littering, **Veh 23111**
Personal assistive mobility devices, **Veh 21280 et seq.**
Public policy, **Veh 21949**
Railroad crossings, stopping, **Veh 22451**

PEDESTRIANS—Cont'd
Right of way, **Veh 21950 et seq.**
Schools and School Districts, this index
Streets and alleys, exits, driver warnings, **Veh 21356.5**
Subways, regulation, **Veh 21109**
Traffic Rules and Regulations, this index
Traffic Signs and Signals, this index
Traffic violator schools, courses of study, **Veh 11219, 11219.3**
Transit grade crossings, stopping, **Veh 22451**
Tubes and tunnels, regulation, **Veh 21109**

PEDICABS
Definitions, **Veh 467.5**
Traffic rules and regulations, **Veh 21100, 21200**

PEN GUNS
Weapons, generally, this index

PENAL INSTITUTIONS
Correctional Institutions, generally, this index

PENALTIES
Fines and Penalties, generally, this index

PENITENTIARIES
Correctional Institutions, generally, this index

PERFORMANCE BONDS
Bonds (Officers and Fiduciaries), generally, this index

PERJURY
Air pollution, motor vehicles, smog impact fees, foreign states, **Veh 1673.6**
Motor Vehicles, this index
Smog impact fees, motor vehicles, foreign states, **Veh 1673.6**
Workers Compensation, this index

PERMANENT, SERIOUS INJURY
Definitions, hit and run drivers, **Veh 20001**

PERMISSIVE USE ACT
Motor vehicles, **Veh 17150 et seq.**

PERMITS
Licenses and Permits, generally, this index

PERSONAL ASSISTIVE MOBILITY DEVICES
Generally, **Veh 21280 et seq.**

PERSONAL INJURIES
Damages, generally, this index
Failure of driver to stop, revocation of license, **Veh 13350**
Highway Patrol, this index
Indemnity, manufactured housing, movements, **Veh 35790**
Information and aid by driver, duty, **Veh 20003**
Negligence, generally, this index
Traffic Rules and Regulations, this index
Workers Compensation, generally, this index

PERSONAL PROPERTY
Abandoned or Unclaimed Property, generally, this index
Gifts, Devises and Bequests, generally, this index
Liens and Incumbrances, generally, this index
Sales, generally, this index
Theft, generally, this index
Title to Property, generally, this index
Transfer of Property, generally, this index
Unclaimed property. Abandoned or Unclaimed Property, generally, this index

PERSONAL PROPERTY TAXATION
Sales and Use Taxes, generally, this index
Use taxes. Sales and Use Taxes, generally, this index

PERSONAL SERVICE
Service of process. Process, this index

PERSONATION
False Personation, generally, this index

PERSONS
Words and Phrases, this index

PERSONS WITH DISABILITIES
Handicapped Persons, generally, this index

PEST ABATEMENT DISTRICTS
Exemptions, pollution control devices, motor vehicles, **Veh 27156.3**
Mosquito Abatement or Vector Control Districts, generally, this index
Motor vehicles,
  Lights and lighting, flashing or colored lights, **Veh 25267**
  Pollution control devices, **Veh 27156.3**
Pollution control devices, motor vehicles, **Veh 27156.3**

PEST CONTROL
Amber lights, pest detection vehicles, **Veh 25261**
Mosquito Abatement or Vector Control Districts, generally, this index
Motor vehicles, amber warning lights, **Veh 25261**

PESTICIDE REGULATION DEPARTMENT
Pesticides, generally, this index

PESTICIDES
Peace officers, spillage or release reporting, **Veh 20017**
Poisons, release or spillage, reports, public officers and employees, **Veh 20017**
Reports, peace officers, pesticide spillage or release, **Veh 20017**
Spillage or release, reports, peace officers, **Veh 20017**

PESTS
Mosquito Abatement or Vector Control Districts, generally, this index

PETIT LARCENY
Theft, generally, this index

PETROLEUM
Oil and Gas, generally, this index

PETROLEUM ENGINEERS
Engineers, generally, this index

PETROLEUM PRODUCTS
Oil and Gas, generally, this index

PHIALS
Drugs and Medicine, generally, this index

PHILANTHROPY
Charities, generally, this index

PHOTOGRAPHY AND PICTURES
Automated rail crossing enforcement system, **Veh 21362.5**
Automatic enforcement systems, traffic signs and signals, **Veh 21455.5 et seq.**
Drivers licenses, **Veh 12800.5, 12811, 14610**
Identification cards, sales, **Veh 13005.5**
License plate,
  Application, motor vehicles, **Veh 5014**
  Special plates for photographers, **Veh 5008**
Logging vehicles, identification plate applications, **Veh 5014 et seq.**
Motor Vehicles, this index
Parking violations, removal of motor vehicles, **Veh 22658**
Railroad crossings, automated enforcement systems, **Veh 22451**
  Notice to appear, violations, **Veh 40518**
Real estate brokers and salespersons, motor vehicles, disclosure, enforcement, **Veh 1808.51**
Recreational vehicles, width, **Veh 35103**
Sales,
  Drivers licenses, **Veh 12800.5**
  Identification cards, **Veh 13005.5**
Solid waste, motor carriers, **Veh 27000**
  Fines and penalties, **Veh 42001.20**
Special license plates, cameramen, **Veh 5008**
Streetsweepers, parking, violations, enforcement, **Veh 40245 et seq.**
Subdivided lands, motor vehicles, disclosure, enforcement, **Veh 1808.51**
Traffic Rules and Regulations, this index
Traffic Signs and Signals, this index

PHOTOSTATIC COPIES
Motor vehicles salesmens licenses, **Veh 11819**

PHYLLOXERA
Grapes and Grapevines, generally, this index

PHYSICAL CONDITION
Motor vehicles, records, confidential information, **Veh 1808.5**

PHYSICAL EXAMINATIONS
Chauffeurs license, **Veh 12814**
Motor Vehicles, this index
School bus drivers, licensing, **Veh 12517.2**

PHYSICALLY HANDICAPPED PERSONS
Handicapped Persons, generally, this index

PHYSICIAN ASSISTANTS
Motor vehicles,
    Disabled veterans, license fees, exemptions, certificates and certification, **Veh 9105**
    Handicapped persons, parking, placards, certificates and certification, **Veh 22511.55, 22511.59**
    License plates, handicapped persons, certificates and certification, **Veh 5007**

PHYSICIANS AND SURGEONS
Anatomical Gifts, generally, this index
Assistants. Physician Assistants, generally, this index
Blood tests, drunken driving, administration of tests, **Veh 23158**
Certificates and certification. Motor vehicles, post
Chiropractors, generally, this index
Controlled substances. Drugs and Medicine, generally, this index
Dead bodies. Anatomical Gifts, generally, this index
Definitions, rescue teams, liability, resuscitation attempts, **Veh 165.5**
Drugs and Medicine, generally, this index
Emergencies,
    Rescue teams, resuscitation, damages, **Veh 165.5**
    Traffic rules and regulations, exemption, **Veh 21058**
Gifts, devises and bequests. Anatomical Gifts, generally, this index
Handicapped persons. Motor vehicles, post
Insignia, vehicles, exemption from traffic regulation, **Veh 21058**
Marijuana. Drugs and Medicine, this index
Medical waste. Hazardous Substances and Waste, this index
Medicine. Drugs and Medicine, generally, this index
Motor vehicles,
    Blood tests, drunken driving, **Veh 23158**
    Certificates and certification,
        Handicapped persons,
            License plates, **Veh 5007, 5007.5**
            Parking, placards, **Veh 22511.55, 22511.59**
        Sunscreening devices, **Veh 26708**
    Disabled veterans, license fees, exemptions, certificates and certification, **Veh 9105**
    Exemptions, traffic rules and regulations, **Veh 21058**
    Handicapped persons,
        License plates, **Veh 5007, 5007.5**
        Parking, placards, **Veh 22511.55, 22511.59**
    Injured persons, **Veh 20003**
        Transportation, **Veh 20016**

PHYSICIANS AND SURGEONS—Cont'd
Motor vehicles—Cont'd
    Sunscreening devices, **Veh 26708**
Narcotics. Drugs and Medicine, generally, this index
Negligence, rescue teams, emergency vehicles, resuscitation attempts, **Veh 165.5**
Physician Assistants, generally, this index
Rescue teams, emergency vehicles, liability, resuscitation attempts, **Veh 165.5**
Traffic rules and regulations, exemption, **Veh 21058**
    Intoxicating liquors, **Veh 23229**
Transportation, person injured in accident, **Veh 20016**

PICKUP TRUCKS
Definitions, **Veh 471**

PICRIC ACID
Explosives, generally, this index

PICTURES
Photography and Pictures, generally, this index

PILOT CARS
Definitions, escort vehicles, **Veh 472**
Equipment, **Veh 28100 et seq.**
    Special permit violations, **Veh 35784**
Markings and signs, **Veh 27904, 27904.5**
Motor Vehicles, this index
Traffic Rules and Regulations, this index
Vertical clearance measuring devices, **Veh 35252**

PILOT INDICATORS
Motor vehicle turn signals, **Veh 25108**

PILOT PROGRAMS
Motor vehicles,
    Electronic devices and equipment, license plates, **Veh 4853**
    Tow truck drivers, certification, **Veh 2430 et seq.**
Parking, Long Beach, left hand parking, two way roadways, **Veh 22502**
Placer County, this index
Traffic rules and regulations,
    Parking, Long Beach, left hand parking, two way roadways, **Veh 22502**
    Tow truck drivers, certification, **Veh 2430 et seq.**

PILOT VEHICLES
Lights and lighting, special moving permits, **Veh 25270**

PILOTS
Aircraft, generally, this index

PIMPS AND PIMPING
Motor vehicles, nuisance, impounding, **Veh 22659.5**

PIPE OR POLE DOLLIES
Pole or Pipe Dollies, generally, this index

PIPES AND PIPELINES
Dollies. Pole or Pipe Dollies, generally, this index
Motor vehicle operation restrictions, rights of way, **Veh 21116**
Transportation, trucks, flashing amber warning lights, **Veh 25275**

PISTOLS
Weapons, generally, this index

PLACARDS
Motor carriers, hazardous substances and waste, crimes and offenses, **Veh 2800**
Motor vehicles, maximum width, **Veh 35110**

PLACER COUNTY
Arraignment, closed circuit television, infractions or misdemeanors, **Veh 40502.1**
Closed circuit television, testimony or appearance for arraignment, infractions or misdemeanors, **Veh 40502.1**
Crimes and offenses, closed circuit television, testimony or appearance for arraignment, **Veh 40502.1**
Pilot programs, closed circuit television, testimony or appearance for arraignment, infractions or misdemeanors, **Veh 40502.1**
Television and radio, closed circuit television, testimony or appearance for arraignment, infractions or misdemeanors, **Veh 40502.1**

PLANES
Aircraft, generally, this index

PLANS AND SPECIFICATIONS
Motor vehicle sunscreening devices, **Veh 26708.2**

PLAQUES
Boats, historical interest, **Veh 9853.5**

PLATES
License plates. Motor Vehicles, this index

PLATS
Maps and Plats, generally, this index

PLEADINGS
Answer, traffic violator schools, time, **Veh 11202**
Motor Vehicles, this index
Nolo Contendere, generally, this index
Traffic Rules and Regulations, this index

POCKET BIKES
Motorized Scooters, this index

POINT SYSTEM
Traffic Rules and Regulations, this index

POISONS
Caldecott tunnel, transportation, poison gases, **Veh 31301**
Motor Carriers, this index

POISONS

POISONS—Cont'd
Pesticides, this index
Signs on vehicles transporting, **Veh 27903**
Traffic Rules and Regulations, this index

POLANCO BATES LICENSE PLATES FOR THE ARTS ACT
Generally, **Veh 5074**

POLE OR PIPE DOLLIES
Generally, **Veh 475**
Chains, safety chains, towing units, **Veh 29003**
Clearance lamps, **Veh 25100**
Commercial vehicles, towing, weight fees, **Veh 9400**
Exemption, vehicles manufactured before designated time, **Veh 9401**
Definitions, motor vehicles, **Veh 475**
Length limitations, **Veh 35414**
License plates, permanent trailer identification plates, certificates and certification, **Veh 5014.1**
Lights and lighting, clearance and side marker lamps, **Veh 25100**
Motor Carriers, this index
Permanent trailer identification plates, certificates and certification, **Veh 5014.1**
Registration, **Veh 4000 et seq.**
Weight fees, **Veh 9400**
Safety chain, towed vehicle, exception, **Veh 29003**
Safety regulations, **Veh 34500 et seq.**
Side marker lamps, **Veh 25100**
Towed vehicle, safety chains, exception, **Veh 29003**
Traffic Rules and Regulations, this index
Trucks transporting, flashing amber warning lights, **Veh 25275**
Turn signal, necessity, **Veh 24951**
Weight fees, **Veh 9400**

POLES AND WIRES
Dollies. Pole or Pipe Dollies, generally, this index
Motor carriers, flashing amber warning lights, **Veh 25275**

POLICE
Abandoned vehicles, removal from private property after accident, **Veh 22653**
Accident reports,
Confidential use, **Veh 20014**
Forms, highway patrol department to prepare and supply, **Veh 2407**
Injuries or death, **Veh 20004**
Address, disclosure, crimes and offenses, **Veh 1808.4**
Appraisal and appraisers, abandoned vehicles, **Veh 22855**
Arrest, generally, this index
Assistance, disabled motorist, **Veh 20018 et seq.**
Blood alcohol testing vehicles, utility flood or loading lamps, **Veh 25110**
Bullet marks on motor vehicle, reports, **Veh 10653**

POLICE—Cont'd
Chief of police,
Hazardous substances and waste, route notification, **Veh 32050 et seq.**
Radioactive materials, transportation, notice, **Veh 33002**
Children and minors,
Home address and telephone number disclosure, crimes and offenses, **Veh 1808.4**
Surviving children, death in line of duty, addresses, confidentiality, **Veh 1808.4**
Colleges and Universities, this index
Crimes and offenses,
Disclosure, employee home address or telephone number, **Veh 1808.4**
Vehicles, theft, **Veh 10851**
Death, in line of duty,
Address, confidentiality, **Veh 1808.4**
Surviving spouse, address, confidentiality, **Veh 1808.4**
Detoxification vehicles, flood or loading lamps, **Veh 25110**
Disclosure. Dispatchers, post
Dispatchers, disclosure, addresses, **Veh 1808.4**
Drivers licenses, presentation for examination, **Veh 12951**
Drug testing vehicles, utility flood or loading lamps, **Veh 25110**
Earplugs, wearing while operating emergency vehicle, **Veh 27400**
Emergencies, escorts, national emergency personnel and supplies, siren and speed, **Veh 21057**
Emergency vehicles, definitions, **Veh 165**
Employed drivers, hours of service regulation, exceptions, **Veh 34501.2**
Equipment, flood or loading lamps, vehicles, **Veh 25110**
Field sobriety testing vehicles, utility flood or loading lamps, **Veh 25110**
Fines and penalties, safety belts, patrol vehicles, **Veh 27315.3**
Flood or loading lamps, vehicles, **Veh 25110**
Guidelines, pursuit, **Veh 17004.7**
Handicapped persons, motor vehicles, assistance, **Veh 20018 et seq.**
Hazardous substances and waste, motor vehicles, signs and signals, exemptions, **Veh 27903**
Headsets, wearing while operating emergency vehicles, **Veh 27400**
Highway, closing, menace to public health or safety, **Veh 2812**
Highway Patrol, generally, this index
In line of duty. Death, ante
Inspection and inspectors, motor vehicle inspection, **Veh 2806**
Labor and employment, home address or telephone number disclosure, crimes and offenses, **Veh 1808.4**
License plates,
Lost or stolen, notice, **Veh 4458**

POLICE—Cont'd
License plates—Cont'd
Seizure, **Veh 4460**
Lights and lighting, flood or loading lamps, **Veh 25110**
Loading or flood lamps, vehicles, **Veh 25110**
Mobile blood alcohol testing vehicles, utility flood or loading lamps, **Veh 25110**
Motor Vehicles, this index
Motor vehicles department,
Copy of notice for arrested person to appear, filing with, **Veh 40506**
Officers and employees, peace officers, powers, **Veh 1655**
Nonsworn personnel, addresses, confidentiality, **Veh 1808.4**
Notice,
Stolen vehicles, **Veh 10500**
Striking unattended vehicle, **Veh 20002**
Written notice, motor vehicle violation as cause of accident, **Veh 40600**
Patrol vehicles, **Veh 27315.3**
Policies, pursuit, **Veh 17004.7**
Privileges and immunities, pursuit, **Veh 17004.7**
Pursuit, **Veh 17004.7**
Reports, **Veh 14602.1**
Railroads, this index
Removal of abandoned vehicles from private property after accident, **Veh 22653**
Reports,
Accident reports, generally, ante
Pursuits, **Veh 14602.1**
Stolen vehicles, **Veh 10500 et seq.**
Stored or parked vehicles, **Veh 10652**
Rescue, generally, this index
Safety belts, patrol vehicles, **Veh 27315.3**
Safety headsets, wearing while operating emergency vehicles, **Veh 27400**
Searches and Seizures, generally, this index
Sobriety testing vehicles, utility flood or loading lamps, **Veh 25110**
Spouse, home address or telephone number disclosure, crimes and offenses, **Veh 1808.4**
Standards, pursuit, **Veh 17004.7**
State Police, generally, this index
Telecommunications, number, residence, disclosure, crimes and offenses, **Veh 1808.4**
Theft, vehicles, **Veh 10851**
Traffic Officers, generally, this index
Traffic Rules and Regulations, generally, this index
Training, pursuit, **Veh 17004.7**
University of California. Colleges and Universities, this index
Utility flood or loading lamps, vehicles, **Veh 25110**
Written notice, motor vehicle violation as cause of accident, probable cause, **Veh 40600**

POLICE POWERS

Buses, financial responsibility, **Veh 16501**

Commercial passenger vehicles for hire, insurance, **Veh 16501**

Motor vehicles, dismantlers, local authorities, **Veh 11522**

POLICEMAN

Police, generally, this index

POLICIES

Motor Vehicle Insurance, this index

Public Policy, generally, this index

POLITICAL SUBDIVISIONS

Airports and Landing Fields, generally, this index

Consolidated Cities and Counties, generally, this index

Counties, generally, this index

Districts, generally, this index

Highways and Roads, this index

Landing fields. Airports and Landing Fields, generally, this index

Local Agencies, generally, this index

Motor Vehicle Insurance, this index

Motor Vehicles, this index

Municipalities, generally, this index

Parking Lots and Facilities, generally, this index

Public Buildings and Works, generally, this index

Schools and School Districts, generally, this index

Taxation, generally, this index

Traffic laws, applicability to vehicles, **Veh 21052**

Traffic safety program, participation, **Veh 2909, 2910**

POLLUTION

Air Pollution, generally, this index

Boats and Boating, this index

Control devices, emergency vehicles, **Veh 27156.2, 27156.3**

Emergency vehicles, control devices, **Veh 27156.2, 27156.3**

Exemptions, emergency vehicles, control devices, **Veh 27156.2, 27156.3**

Hazardous Substances and Waste, generally, this index

Medical technical paramedic, emergency vehicles, control devices, **Veh 27156.2, 27156.3**

Noise Pollution, generally, this index

POPULAR NAME LAWS

Adams Law, **Veh 13386, 14601.2 et seq.**

Ambriz, Steve Act, **Veh 13385**

Antigridlock Act, **Veh 22526**

Automobile Law, **Veh 1 et seq.**

Basic Speed Law (highways), **Veh 22350**

Belotti Christensen Act (logging trucks), **Veh 35552**

Biennial inspection of terminals program, **Veh 34501.12**

BIT (biennial inspection of terminals program), **Veh 34501.12**

POPULAR NAME LAWS—Cont'd

Blind Intersection Law, **Veh 22352**

Brady Jared Teen Driver Safety Act, **Veh 12814.6**

Chappie Zberg Off Highway Motor Vehicle Law, **Veh 38000 et seq.**

Choose Clean Cars Act, **Veh 5205.5**

Christensen Belotti Act (logging trucks), **Veh 35552**

Clean Food Transport Act, **Veh 34516**

Collier Porter Act (vehicle weight limits), **Veh 35551**

Compulsory financial responsibility, motor vehicles, **Veh 16000 et seq.**

Defective Windshield Act, **Veh 26710**

Destiny Nicole Stout Memorial Act, **Veh 22456**

Distinctive Color Act (traffic officers), **Veh 40800**

Drivers License Act, **Veh 12500 et seq.**

Drivers License Compact, **Veh 15000 et seq.**

Driving with Permission Act, **Veh 17150 et seq.**

Environmental Protection and Research Act, **Veh 5100 et seq.**

Financial Privacy Act,

Motor vehicles, **Veh 16000 et seq.**

Operation of vehicles,

Private owners, **Veh 17150 et seq.**

State and governmental agencies, **Veh 17000 et seq.**

Friend Memorial Act, **Veh 23109**

Governmental Agencies Liability Law (operation of motor vehicles), **Veh 17000 et seq.**

Greene Harmer Motor Vehicle Damage Control Act, **Veh 34700 et seq.**

Hazardous Substances Highway Spill Containment and Abatement Act, **Veh 2450 et seq.**

Highway Litter Act, **Veh 23111 et seq.**

Highway Spill Containment and Abatement Act, **Veh 2450 et seq.**

Hit and Run Act, **Veh 20000 et seq.**

Implied Consent Act, **Veh 13353, 23158**

Imputed Negligence Act (motor vehicles), **Veh 17150**

Jamming Devices Law, **Veh 28150, 40000.15**

Joy Riding Law, vehicles, **Veh 10851**

Kaitlyns Law, motor vehicles, unattended children, **Veh 15600 et seq.**

Lemon Law buyback, **Veh 11713.12**

Logging Trucks Act, **Veh 35552**

Louis Friend Memorial Act, **Veh 23109**

Marks Badham Environmental Protection and Research Act, **Veh 5100 et seq.**

Motor Carriers of Property Permit Act, **Veh 34600 et seq.**

Motor Vehicle Act, **Veh 1 et seq.**

Motor Vehicle Drivers License Compact, **Veh 15000 et seq.**

Motor Vehicle Drivers Licensing Act, **Veh 12500 et seq.**

POPULAR NAME LAWS—Cont'd

Motor Vehicle Financial Responsibility Act, **Veh 16000 et seq.**

Motor Vehicle Law, **Veh 1 et seq.**

Motor Vehicle Owners Liability Act, **Veh 17150**

Motor Vehicle Theft Prevention Act, **Veh 10900 et seq.**

Nonresident Motorist Statute, **Veh 17450 et seq.**

Notice Act (transfer of vehicles), **Veh 5900**

Omnibus Traffic Safety Act, **Veh 27315 et seq., 40000.15**

Organized Crime Prevention and Victim Protection Act, **Veh 1806**

Owners Responsibility Laws, motor vehicles,

Private owners, **Veh 17150 et seq.**

State and governmental agencies, **Veh 17000 et seq.**

Paul Buzzo Act, highway litter, **Veh 23111**

Pedestrians Right of Way Act, **Veh 21950 et seq.**

Permissive Use Act (motor vehicles), **Veh 17150 et seq.**

Polanco Bates License Plates for the Arts Act, **Veh 5074**

Police and Bystander Protection and Safe Pursuit Act, **Veh 14602.1**

Porter Collier Act (vehicle weight limits), **Veh 35551**

Public Employees Liability Law (operation of motor vehicles), **Veh 17000 et seq.**

Reciprocity Law (motor vehicles), **Veh 8000 et seq.**

Reckless Driving Act, **Veh 23103**

Registration Act (motor vehicles), **Veh 4000 et seq.**

Registration and License Fee Exemption Act, **Veh 4010**

Right of Way Act, **Veh 21800 et seq.**

Rosenthal blue sky license plate program, **Veh 5062**

Safe Streets Act, **Veh 14607.4 et seq.**

Publicity, **Veh 1664**

Schrade Belotti Act, **Veh 4850**

Special Equipment Registration and License Fee Exemption Act, **Veh 4010**

Speed laws, **Veh 22350 et seq.**

Speed Trap Law, **Veh 40801 et seq.**

Steve Ambriz Act, **Veh 13385**

Three Feet for Safety Act, **Veh 21760**

Traffic safety program, **Veh 2900 et seq.**

Vehicle Registration Act, **Veh 4000 et seq.**

Vehicle Weight Limits Act, **Veh 35551**

Wireless Telephone Automobile Safety Act, **Veh 12810.3, 23123**

Yield Right of Way Act, **Veh 21800 et seq.**

PORTABLE BUILDINGS

Sanitary facility, motor carriers, exemption from registration, **Veh 36105**

PORTABLE FIRE EXTINGUISHERS

Fire Extinguishers, generally, this index

PORTER COLLIER ACT
Vehicle weight limits, **Veh 35551**

POSSESSION
Alcoholic Beverages, this index
Drugs and Medicine, this index
Marijuana. Drugs and Medicine, this index
Motor Vehicles, this index
Traffic rules and regulations, open container, intoxicating liquors, **Veh 23222, 23229**

POSTAL SERVICE
United States Postal Service, generally, this index

POSTERS
Advertisements. Outdoor Advertising, generally, this index
Outdoor Advertising, generally, this index

POSTING
Traffic rules and regulations, private off street parking, **Veh 21107.8**

POSTPONEMENT
Continuance. Trial, this index

POSTSECONDARY EDUCATION
Colleges and Universities, generally, this index

POT TORCHES
Motor carriers, warning signals and devices, **Veh 25300**

POULTRY AND POULTRY PRODUCTS
Highway patrol, vehicle transporting, inspection of bills of lading, **Veh 2810**
Motor carriers, inspection, **Veh 2810**

POVERTY WEED
Weeds, generally, this index

POWDER
Explosives, generally, this index

POWER BOATS
Boats and Boating, generally, this index

POWER BRAKES
Definitions, motor vehicles, **Veh 480**

POWER SHOVEL
Special highway construction equipment, definitions, **Veh 565**

POWER UNIT
Definitions, motor carriers, owner operators, **Veh 34624**

PRACTICE OF LAW
Attorneys, generally, this index

PREGNANCY
Midwives, generally, this index

PRESENTENCE INVESTIGATIONS
Crimes and Offenses, this index

PRESS
Motor vehicles, request for information, **Veh 1810**

PRESUMPTIONS
Evidence, this index

PRICES
Motor Vehicles, this index
Motorcycles, labels, **Veh 24014**

PRIMARY NOXIOUS WEEDS
Weeds, generally, this index

PRINCIPAL AND ACCESSORY
Accomplices and Accessories, generally, this index

PRINTING
Outdoor Advertising, generally, this index

PRIORITIES AND PREFERENCES
Motor Vehicles, this index
Paramedics, emergency calls, precedence over blood test requests, **Veh 23158**

PRISONERS OF WAR
Military Forces, this index

PRISONS AND PRISONERS
Correctional Institutions, generally, this index
Jails, generally, this index

PRIVACY
Motor vehicles, dealers, records and recordation, **Veh 11713.3, 11713.25**

PRIVATE CEMETERIES
Cemeteries and Dead Bodies, generally, this index

PRIVATE CORPORATIONS
Corporations, generally, this index

PRIVATE DRIVEWAYS
Driveways, generally, this index

PRIVATE INVESTIGATORS
Light bars, motor vehicles, **Veh 27607**
Motor vehicles, light bars, **Veh 27607**

PRIVATE PARTY VEHICLE MARKETS
Generally, **Veh 12101 et seq.**

PRIVATE PROPERTY
Motor Vehicles, this index
Traffic Rules and Regulations, this index

PRIVATE ROADS
Highways and Roads, this index

PRIVATE SCHOOL BUS CONTRACTORS
Generally, **Veh 2570 et seq.**

PRIVATE SCHOOLS
Definitions, motor vehicles, **Veh 492**
Driver education, **Veh 11101**
School buses, **Veh 545**
  Definitions, **Veh 545**
  Equipment, **Veh 2808**

PRIVATE SECURITY SERVICES
Light bars, motor vehicles, **Veh 27607**
Motor vehicles, light bars, **Veh 27607**

PRIVILEGED COMMUNICATIONS
Confidential or Privileged Information, generally, this index

PRIVILEGES AND IMMUNITIES
Blood Tests, this index
Child protective services workers, drivers licenses, signing and verification of application for minors license, **Veh 17707**
Drunk driver visitation program (youth), **Veh 23518.5**
Juvenile probation officers, drivers licenses, signing and verification of application for minors license, **Veh 17707**
Law Enforcement, this index
Motor Vehicles, this index
Peace Officers, this index
Police, this index
Public agencies, drivers licenses, anatomical gift stickers, false or inaccurate information, **Veh 12811**
Public Officers and Employees, this index
Traffic rules and regulations, youthful drunk driver visitation program, **Veh 23518.5**
Youthful drunk driver visitation program, **Veh 23518.5**

PROBABLE CAUSE
Commercial vehicles, stops, household goods carriers, violations, **Veh 2810.1**
Household goods carriers, commercial vehicles, stops, violations, **Veh 2810.1**
Written notice of motor vehicle violations, **Veh 40600**

PROBATE OF WILLS
Probate Proceedings, generally, this index

PROBATE PROCEEDINGS
Administrators. Executors and administrators, generally, post
Anatomical Gifts, generally, this index
Boats and boating, transfer of title or interest, **Veh 9852.5**
Driving schools, licenses, **Veh 11105**
Executors and administrators,
  Automobile dismantlers, certificate of convenience, **Veh 11517**
  Motor vehicles,
    Dealers, certificates of convenience, **Veh 11720**
    Sales, application of law, **Veh 12121**
    Tort liability, **Veh 17150 et seq.**
    Torts, motor vehicles, **Veh 17150 et seq.**
    Traffic violator schools, death of licensee, issuance of temporary license, **Veh 11204**
Guardian and Ward, generally, this index
Letters testamentary or of administration. Executors and administrators, generally, ante

PROBATE PROCEEDINGS—Cont'd
Motor vehicles,
Accident reports, disclosure, **Veh 20012**
Dealers, **Veh 11713.3**
Executors and administrators, ante
Negligent death or injury, tort liability, **Veh 17159**
Nonresidents, service of process, **Veh 17450 et seq.**
Title, transfer, notice, **Veh 5910**
Tort liability, **Veh 17150 et seq.**
Transfer of title or interest, notice, **Veh 5910**
Personal representatives. Executors and administrators, generally, ante

PROBATION
Parole and Probation, generally, this index

PROCEEDINGS
Actions and Proceedings, generally, this index

PROCESS
Agent for service of process, traffic violation schools, **Veh 11202**
Driving schools,
Appointment of agent for service of process, **Veh 11102**
New address or termination of business, **Veh 11111.2**
Motor Vehicles, this index
Nonresidents, motor vehicles, **Veh 17450 et seq.**
Service of process,
Driving schools,
Appointment of agent, **Veh 11102**
New address or termination of business, **Veh 11111.2**
Motor Vehicles, this index
Traffic violator schools, **Veh 11202**
New address or termination of business, **Veh 11217.5**
Subpoenas, generally, this index
Summons, service of process, traffic violator schools, **Veh 11202**
Traffic violator schools,
New address or termination of business, **Veh 11217.5**
Owners, **Veh 11202**

PROCESSING AGENCY
Definitions, toll evasion, **Veh 40253**

PROCESSIONS
Parades, generally, this index
Traffic rules and regulations, local regulations, **Veh 21100**

PRODUCE
Agricultural Products, generally, this index

PRODUCERS
Agricultural Products, generally, this index

PRODUCTS LIABILITY
Motor Vehicles, this index
Recreational vehicles, franchises, **Veh 3074**

PROFESSIONAL ENGINEERS
Engineers, generally, this index

PROFESSIONS AND OCCUPATIONS
Attorneys, generally, this index
Chiropractors, generally, this index
Contractors, generally, this index
Emergency Medical Technicians, generally, this index
Engineers, generally, this index
Insurance Agents, Solicitors or Brokers, generally, this index
Locksmiths, generally, this index
Nurses, generally, this index
Optometrists, generally, this index
Physician Assistants, generally, this index
Physicians and Surgeons, generally, this index
Social Workers, generally, this index
Vocational Nursing, generally, this index

PROMISSORY NOTES
Negotiable Instruments, generally, this index

PROMOTIONS
Commercial vehicles, special interest license plates, **Veh 5060**
Motor vehicles, special license plates, limitations, **Veh 5060**
Motorcycles, special interest license plates, **Veh 5060**
Recreational vehicles, shows, **Veh 11713.15**
Special license plates, limitations, **Veh 5060**
Trailers, special interest license plates, **Veh 5060**

PROOF
Evidence, generally, this index

PROPELLANT EXPLOSIVES
Explosives, generally, this index

PROPERTY
Defacing with paint or other liquid, **Veh 13202.6**
Department of motor vehicles, possession and control, **Veh 1502**
Highway patrol department, possession and control, **Veh 2104**
Lost or Destroyed Property, generally, this index
Motor vehicles department, message display systems, contracts, **Veh 1656.5**
Real Estate, generally, this index
Title to Property, generally, this index
Transfer of Property, generally, this index
Vandalism, defacing with paint or other liquid, **Veh 13202.6**

PROPERTY DAMAGE
Damages, generally, this index

PROPERTY TAXES
Taxation, generally, this index

PROSECUTING ATTORNEYS
District Attorneys, generally, this index

PROSECUTORS
District Attorneys, generally, this index

PROSTHETIC APPLIANCES
Bicycles, **Veh 27400**

PROSTITUTION
Drivers licenses, revocation or suspension, **Veh 13201.5**
Motor Vehicles, this index
Nuisance, motor vehicles, **Veh 22659.5**

PROTECTIVE SERVICES
Highway Patrol, this index

PROTESTS
Motor Vehicles, this index

PROTONS
Atomic Energy, generally, this index

PUBLIC AGENCIES
Employees. Public Officers and Employees, generally, this index
Motor vehicles,
Air pollution, noncompliance, **Veh 24007.5**
Sales, equipment, **Veh 24007.5**
Officers and employees. Public Officers and Employees, generally, this index
Privileges and immunities, drivers licenses, anatomical gift stickers, false or inaccurate information, **Veh 12811**
Public Buildings and Works, generally, this index
Social Security, generally, this index
State Agencies, generally, this index
Traffic laws, applicability to representatives, **Veh 21054**
Traffic rules and regulations, **Veh 21113**

PUBLIC BENEFIT CORPORATIONS
Boy scouts, fees, exemptions, **Veh 9870**
Camping for children, fees, exemptions, **Veh 9870**
Girl Scouts, fees, exemptions, **Veh 9870**

PUBLIC BODIES
Political Subdivisions, generally, this index
Public Agencies, generally, this index

PUBLIC BUILDINGS AND WORKS
Accident reports, confidential use, **Veh 20014**
Defacement, delay or suspension of driving privileges, **Veh 13202.6**
Emergencies, transportation, persons injured in accidents, **Veh 20016**
Highway Patrol, this index
Motor vehicles, transportation of persons in accidents, **Veh 20016**
Protective services, highway patrol, costs, **Veh 2428**
Toll services, vehicular crossings, duties and uniform, **Veh 23252**

PUBLIC

PUBLIC BUILDINGS AND WORKS—Cont'd
Traffic control,
  Employees, toll takers on vehicular
    crossings, **Veh 23252**
  Local authorities, **Veh 21113**
Transportation by employees, persons in-
  jured in accidents, **Veh 20016**
Vandalism, delay or suspension of driving
  privileges, **Veh 13202.6**

PUBLIC DEFENDERS
Address, confidential or privileged information, **Veh 1808.4**
Confidential or privileged information, addresses, **Veh 1808.4**
Motor vehicles, records and recordation,
  access, **Veh 1810.5**

**PUBLIC EMPLOYEES LIABILITY LAW (OP-
  ERATION OF MOTOR VEHICLES)**
Generally, **Veh 17000 et seq.**

PUBLIC ENTITIES
Bicycle infractions, costs and fines schedules, establishment, **Veh 42001**
Motor vehicles, drivers licenses, anatomical gift sticker, false or inaccurate
  information, loss or injury, liability,
  Veh 12811
Officers and employees. Public Officers
  and Employees, generally, this index

PUBLIC FUNDS
Funds, generally, this index

PUBLIC HIGHWAYS
Highways and Roads, generally, this index

PUBLIC HOSPITALS
Hospitals, generally, this index

PUBLIC INSTRUCTION
Schools and School Districts, generally,
  this index

PUBLIC LANDS
Abandoned motor vehicles, removal, pri-
  ority, **Veh 22667**
All terrain vehicles, passengers, **Veh 38506**
Federal lands. United States, this index
Highway patrol, motor vehicles, removal,
  Veh 22659
Motor vehicles,
  Impounding, **Veh 22651**
  Irrigation and irrigation districts, ma-
    chinery and equipment, inspection
    and inspectors, **Veh 2810.2**
  Removal, highway patrol, **Veh 22659**
Off highway vehicles,
  Special regulations, **Veh 38301**
  Traffic signs and signals, **Veh 38302**
United States, this index

PUBLIC NOTICE
Advertisements, generally, this index
Notice, generally, this index

PUBLIC NUISANCES
Nuisance, generally, this index

PUBLIC OFFICERS AND EMPLOYEES
Accident reports, failure to file, **Veh 1805**
Bonds (Officers and Fiduciaries), general-
  ly, this index
Bribery and Corruption, generally, this in-
  dex
Confidential or privileged information, ad-
  dresses, **Veh 1808.4**
Corruption. Bribery and Corruption, gen-
  erally, this index
County Officers and Employees, generally,
  this index
Crimes and offenses. Bribery and Cor-
  ruption, generally, this index
Dealers, definitions, motor vehicles, **Veh
  286**
Elections, generally, this index
Identification cards, false or inaccurate in-
  formation, loss or injury, liability, **Veh
  13006**
Motor vehicles,
  Accidents, transportation of injured per-
    sons, **Veh 20016**
  Tort liabilities, **Veh 17000 et seq.**
Municipal Officers and Employees, gener-
  ally, this index
Official bonds. Bonds (Officers and Fidu-
  ciaries), generally, this index
Privileges and immunities, drivers licenses,
  anatomical gift stickers, false or inac-
  curate information, **Veh 12811**
School Officers and Employees, generally,
  this index
Social Security, generally, this index
State Officers and Employees, generally,
  this index
Toll roads and bridges, vehicular crossings,
  traffic rules and regulations, **Veh
  23251 et seq.**

PUBLIC POLICY
Agricultural machinery and equipment, in-
  spection and inspectors, exemptions,
  Veh 40000.15
Driver education, **Veh 1659**
Driving under influence, separate offenses,
  Veh 23217
Handicapped persons, parking, location,
  Veh 22511.10
Motor vehicles, red lights and sirens, **Veh
  30**
Pedestrians, **Veh 21949**

PUBLIC PROPERTY
Public Lands, generally, this index

PUBLIC PROSECUTORS
District Attorneys, generally, this index

PUBLIC RECORDS
Records and Recordation, generally, this
  index

PUBLIC ROADS
Highways and Roads, generally, this index

PUBLIC SAFETY
Safety, generally, this index

PUBLIC SAFETY OFFICERS
Peace Officers, generally, this index

PUBLIC SCHOOLS
Schools and School Districts, generally,
  this index

PUBLIC SERVICE CORPORATIONS
Public Utilities, generally, this index

PUBLIC TRANSIT
Mass Transit, generally, this index

PUBLIC UTILITIES
Atomic Energy, generally, this index
Bicycle lanes, blocking, utility vehicles,
  Veh 22512
Carriers, generally, this index
Confidential or privileged information,
  electric vehicles, registration, **Veh
  1808.23**
Disclosure, electric vehicles, registration,
  confidential or privileged information,
  Veh 1808.23
Electric carts, sidewalk use, local regula-
  tions, **Veh 21114.5**
Emergency plans and repairs,
  Utility flood or loading lamps, vehicles,
    Veh 25110
  Vehicles, licenses and permits, **Veh 2416**
Employees, electric carts, sidewalk use, lo-
  cal regulations, **Veh 21114.5**
Fleet vehicles, registration, **Veh 5302**
Flood or loading lamps, vehicles, **Veh
  25110**
Gas. Oil and Gas, generally, this index
Lighting and signaling equipment on vehi-
  cles, **Veh 24003**
Lights and lighting, emergency vehicles,
  utility flood or loading lamps, **Veh
  25110**
Mobile digital terminals, motor vehicles,
  Veh 27602
Motor vehicles,
  Air pollution requirements, noncompli-
    ance, **Veh 24007.5**
  Blocking bicycle lanes, **Veh 22512**
  Emergencies, licenses and permits, **Veh
    2416**
  Flags, warning sign or barrier vehicle,
    Veh 25301
  Flares or fusees, warning devices, **Veh
    25301**
  Flashing amber warning lights, **Veh
    25301**
  Fleet vehicles, registration, **Veh 5302**
  Fuses, warning devices, **Veh 25301**
  Lamps on vehicles used in repair or
    maintenance of service, **Veh 24003**
  Lights and lighting, flashing or colored
    lights, **Veh 25260**
  Mobile digital terminals, **Veh 27602**
  Reflectors, parked or standing vehicles,
    Veh 25301
  Registration, electric vehicles, confiden-
    tial or privileged information, **Veh
    1808.23**

PUBLIC UTILITIES—Cont'd
Motor vehicles—Cont'd
Traffic Rules and Regulations, this index
Warning lights, **Veh 25260**
Warning signals, parked, stopped or standing vehicle, **Veh 25301**
Natural gas. Oil and Gas, generally, this index
Officers and employees, electric carts, sidewalk use, local regulations, **Veh 21114.5**
Oil and Gas, generally, this index
Parked, stopped or standing vehicles, warning devices, **Veh 25301**
Railroads, generally, this index
Repairs, emergency repairs, vehicles, licenses and permits, **Veh 2416**
Sidewalks, electric carts, local regulations, **Veh 21114.5**
Street Railways, generally, this index
Telecommunications, generally, this index
Traffic Rules and Regulations, this index
Vehicles, flood or loading lights, **Veh 25110**
Weight limits, exemption, **Veh 35704, 35714**

PUBLIC UTILITIES COMMISSION
Explosives, generally, this index
Width, coaches or buses operated under jurisdiction of, **Veh 35106, 35107**

PUBLIC WAYS
Highways and Roads, generally, this index
Streets and Alleys, generally, this index

PUBLIC WORKS
Public Buildings and Works, generally, this index

PUBLIC WORKS DEPARTMENT
Transportation Department, generally, this index

PUBLICATION
Traffic rules and regulations, **Veh 1656**
Vehicle Code, **Veh 1656**

PUERTO RICO
Driving under the influence. Traffic Rules and Regulations, this index
Motor vehicle violations, drivers license revocation or suspension, **Veh 13352**

PUMPS AND PUMPING
Special highway construction equipment, define, **Veh 565**

PUNCTURE VINE
Weeds, generally, this index

PUNISHMENT
Crimes and Offenses, generally, this index
Fines and Penalties, generally, this index

PUPIL ACTIVITY BUSES
Certificates of endorsement, **Veh 13369 et seq.**

PUPILS
Schools and School Districts, generally, this index

PURE FOOD AND DRUG LAWS
Drugs and Medicine, generally, this index

PURPLE LOOSESTRIFE
Weeds, generally, this index

PURSUIT
Peace Officers, this index

PYROTECHNICS
Fireworks, generally, this index

QUACK GRASS
Weeds, generally, this index

QUOTA
Arrest quotas, peace officers, **Veh 41600 et seq.**

RACES AND RACING
Traffic rules and regulations, speed contest or exhibition of speed on highway, **Veh 23109**
Impoundment of vehicle, **Veh 22651.6**

RACING VEHICLES
Motor Vehicles, this index

RADAR
Motor vehicles, jamming devices, speed, **Veh 28150, 40000.15**

RADIAL TIRES
Inner tubes, **Veh 27455**

RADIO
Television and Radio, generally, this index

RADIOS
Television and Radio, generally, this index

RAIL TRANSIT SYSTEMS
Railroads, generally, this index

RAILROAD CROSSINGS
Agricultural labor and employment, motor vehicles, **Veh 22452**
Automated enforcement systems, **Veh 22451**
Notice, violations, **Veh 40518**
Automated rail crossing enforcement system, **Veh 21362.5**
Definitions, **Veh 210**
Commercial vehicles. Motor Vehicles, this index
Crimes and offenses, fines and penalties, **Veh 42001.16**
Allocation, **Veh 42007.4**
Fines and penalties, **Veh 42001.16**
Allocation, **Veh 42007.4**
Commercial vehicles, **Veh 15312.1**
Hazardous substances and waste, traffic rules and regulations, **Veh 22452**
Motor Vehicles, this index
Pedestrians, stopping, **Veh 22451**

RAILROAD CROSSINGS—Cont'd
Photography and pictures, automated enforcement systems, **Veh 21362.5, 22451**
Notice to appear, **Veh 40518**
Signs and signals. Traffic Signs and Signals, this index
Traffic Rules and Regulations, this index
Traffic Signs and Signals, this index

RAILROADS
Automated rail crossing enforcement system, **Veh 21362.5**
Building movers, movement across tracks, notice, **Veh 35789**
Containers, motor carriers, weights, scales, **Veh 35580, 35581**
Crew members, motor vehicle operators licenses, citation or furnishing, accidents or violations, **Veh 12953**
Crossings. Railroad Crossings, generally, this index
Engineers, Motor vehicle operators license, citations or furnishing, accidents or violations, **Veh 12953**
Grade crossings. Railroad Crossings, generally, this index
House movers, movement across tracks, notice, **Veh 35789**
Intermodal containers, motor carriers, weights, **Veh 35580, 35581**
Notice, building movers, movement across tracks, **Veh 35789**
Officers and employees,
Crew members, motor vehicle operators licenses, citation or furnishing, accidents or violations, **Veh 12953**
Motor vehicles, removal from right of way, **Veh 22656**
Parking vehicles, **Veh 22521**
Piggyback containers, motor carriers, weights, **Veh 35580, 35581**
Police,
Emergency vehicle permits, **Veh 2416**
Motor vehicles, removal, **Veh 22656**
Railroad Crossings, generally, this index
Removal, motor vehicles from right of way, **Veh 22656**
Right of way,
Motor vehicles, removal, **Veh 22656**
Removal of motor vehicles, **Veh 22656**
Safety, drivers handbook, **Veh 1656.3**
Separations of grade. Railroad Crossings, generally, this index
Spur tracks, traffic control, stopping, **Veh 22452**
Street Railways, generally, this index
Traffic Rules and Regulations, this index
Transit Districts, generally, this index
Transporting dwelling house or building across, notice, **Veh 35789**

RANCHES
Juvenile day centers, ranches and camps. Juvenile Institutions and Schools, this index

RAPE
Motor vehicles, license plates, new plates, **Veh 4467**

RAPID TRANSIT
Mass Transit, generally, this index
Transit Systems, generally, this index

RAPID TRANSIT DISTRICTS
Transit Districts, generally, this index

RATES AND CHARGES
Boats and boating, documentary preparation charges, **Veh 9858.1**
Motor Vehicles, this index
Parking. Traffic Rules and Regulations, this index
Toll ferries. Ferries, this index
Toll roads and bridges. Highways and Roads, this index
Traffic Rules and Regulations, this index

RAZORS
Weapons, generally, this index

REAL ESTATE
Abandoned or Unclaimed Property, generally, this index
Developments, golf carts, regulation by local authorities, **Veh 21115**
Fences, generally, this index
Forests and Forestry, generally, this index
Highway patrol, purchase or lease by commissioner, **Veh 2405**
Housing, generally, this index
Housing Authorities, generally, this index
Liens and Incumbrances, generally, this index
Motor vehicles, department of, acquisition, **Veh 1654**
Motor Vehicles Department, this index
Public Lands, generally, this index
Records and Recordation, generally, this index
Right of Way, generally, this index
State lands. Public Lands, generally, this index
Surveys and Surveyors, generally, this index
Taxation, generally, this index
Title to Property, generally, this index
Unclaimed property. Abandoned or Unclaimed Property, generally, this index

REAL ESTATE BROKERS AND SALESPERSONS
Motor vehicles, photography and pictures, disclosure, enforcement, **Veh 1808.51**
Photography and pictures, motor vehicles, disclosure, enforcement, **Veh 1808.51**

REAL PROPERTY
Real Estate, generally, this index

REAR LIGHTS
Motor vehicles, **Veh 24600 et seq.**

REAR REFLEX REFLECTORS
Motorized bicycles, **Veh 24015**

REAR WINDOWS
Motor vehicles, safety glazing material, **Veh 26703**

REASONABLE ACCESS
Definitions, length of vehicles, **Veh 35400**

REASONABLE CAUSE
Definitions, peace officers, removal of vehicles, **Veh 22651**

REBATES
Motor Vehicles, this index

RECEIPTS
Traffic violations, fines paid, **Veh 40312**

RECEIVERS AND RECEIVERSHIP
Motor vehicles, sales, application of law, **Veh 12121**

RECEIVING STOLEN GOODS
Highway patrol, disposition, **Veh 2414, 2415**

RECIDIVISM TRACKING SYSTEM
Driving under the influence, **Veh 1821**

RECIDIVISTS
Second and subsequent offenses. Crimes and Offenses, this index

RECIPROCITY
Driver License Compact, **Veh 15000 et seq.**
Motor Carriers, this index
Motor Vehicles, this index

RECIPROCITY LAW (MOTOR VEHICLES)
Generally, **Veh 8000 et seq.**

RECKLESS DRIVING
Traffic Rules and Regulations, this index

RECORDS AND RECORDATION
Bicycles, this index
Boats and Boating, this index
Charities, this index
Counties, this index
Criminal History Information, generally, this index
Disclosure, generally, this index
Dismantlers of motor vehicles, **Veh 11520**
Driving Schools, this index
Fleet vehicles in interstate commerce, apportioned registration, **Veh 8057**
Garages, stored vehicles, **Veh 10650 et seq.**
Highway Patrol, this index
Husband and wife, address, confidentiality, **Veh 1808.4**
Infractions, this index
Inspection and inspectors,
  Driving schools and instructors, **Veh 11108**
  Motor vehicle records, **Veh 1808**
Kitchen grease, inedible, **Veh 2460 et seq.**
Law Enforcement, this index
Mobilehomes and Mobilehome Parks, this index
Motor Carriers, this index

RECORDS AND RECORDATION—Cont'd
Motor Vehicles, this index
Motor Vehicles Department, this index
Ocean marine terminals, intermodal roadability inspection program, **Veh 34505.9**
Paratransit vehicles, **Veh 34501.17**
Religious Organizations and Societies, this index
Rental, vehicles, **Veh 14609**
Ships and Shipping, this index
Traffic Rules and Regulations, this index
Traffic safety program, **Veh 2900 et seq.**
Traffic Violator Schools, this index
Trailer parks, stored vehicles, **Veh 10650 et seq.**
Vanpooling, maintenance, **Veh 34509**

RECREATION AND RECREATIONAL FACILITIES
Boats and Boating, generally, this index
Camps and Camping, generally, this index
Recreational Trails, generally, this index
Skateboards, generally, this index
Skiing, generally, this index
Trails. Recreational Trails, generally, this index

RECREATIONAL TRAILER PARKS
Mobilehomes and Mobilehome Parks, generally, this index

RECREATIONAL TRAILS
Motorized skateboards, **Veh 21968**
Noise pollution, off highway vehicles, **Veh 38370**
Off highway vehicles, noise pollution, **Veh 38370**
Skateboards, motorized skateboards, **Veh 21968**

RECREATIONAL VEHICLE PARKS
Storage, reports, **Veh 10658**

RECREATIONAL VEHICLES
Advertisements, shows, **Veh 11713.15**
Appurtenances, width, **Veh 35103**
Audits and auditors, franchises,
  Incentives, **Veh 3076**
  Warranties, **Veh 3075**
Awnings, width, **Veh 35103**
Branch offices, franchises, **Veh 3072**
Cameras, width, **Veh 35103**
Camp Trailers, generally, this index
Campers, generally, this index
Cancellation, franchises, dealers, **Veh 11713.13**
Certificates and certification, sales, temporary branch license, **Veh 11713.15**
Claims, franchises,
  Incentives, **Veh 3076**
  Warranties, **Veh 3075**
Compensation and salaries, delivery, preparation, obligations, franchises, **Veh 3074**
Contracts, dealers, franchises, **Veh 11713.22, 11713.23**

RECREATIONAL VEHICLES—Cont'd
Dealers, franchises, **Veh 3070 et seq.**
   Contracts, **Veh 11713.22, 11713.23**
   Termination, **Veh 11713.13**
Delivery, obligations, franchises, **Veh 3074**
Distributors, franchises, contracts, **Veh 11713.22, 11713.23**
Establishment, franchises, **Veh 3072, 3073**
Fees, franchises, **Veh 3077**
Franchises, **Veh 3070 et seq.**
   Dealers,
      Contracts, **Veh 11713.22, 11713.23**
      Termination, **Veh 11713.13**
Grab handles, width, **Veh 35103**
Identity and identification, sales, **Veh 11713.15**
Incentives, franchises, **Veh 3076**
Licenses and permits, temporary branch license, sales, **Veh 11713.15**
Lights and lighting, width, **Veh 35103**
Manufacturers and manufacturing, franchises, contracts, **Veh 11713.22, 11713.23**
Modification or change, franchises, **Veh 3070, 3071**
Nonrenewal, franchises, dealers, **Veh 11713.13**
Notice, franchises, **Veh 3070**
   Establishment, **Veh 3072**
   Relocation, **Veh 3072**
Off highway vehicles. Motor Vehicles, this index
Park Trailers, generally, this index
Photography and pictures, width, **Veh 35103**
Products liability, franchises, **Veh 3074**
Promotions, shows, **Veh 11713.15**
Relocation, franchises, **Veh 3072, 3073**
Replacement, franchises, **Veh 3070, 3071**
Rules and regulations, **Veh 29004.5, 38000 et seq.**
Safety, connections, towed vehicles, **Veh 29004.5**
Sales,
   Franchises, contracts, **Veh 11713.23**
   Temporary branch license, **Veh 11713.15**
Shows, temporary branch license, sales, **Veh 11713.15**
Storage, mobilehome parks, **Veh 10658**
Temporary branch license, sales, **Veh 11713.15**
Termination, franchises, **Veh 3070, 3071, 11713.13**
Towing, equipment, safety connections, **Veh 29004.5**
Used vehicle sales, **Veh 11713.15**
Vents, width, **Veh 35103**
Warranties, franchises, **Veh 3075**
Width, appurtenances, **Veh 35103**

RECREATIONAL VESSELS
Boats and Boating, generally, this index

RECYCLING
Motor carriers, covering loads, **Veh 23115**
Traffic rules and regulations, covering loads, **Veh 23115**

RED CROSS
Disaster service vehicles, warning lights, **Veh 25259.5**

RED FLAGS
Motor Carriers, this index

RED LIGHTS
Traffic Rules and Regulations, this index

RED WOLF
Fish and Game, generally, this index

REFLECTORS
Bicycles, **Veh 21201.5**
   Motorized bicycles, **Veh 24015**
Definitions, motor vehicles, **Veh 375**
Motor carriers, warning signals and devices, **Veh 25300 et seq.**
Motor Vehicles, this index
Traffic Rules and Regulations, this index

REFORMATORIES
Correctional Institutions, generally, this index

REFRIGERATOR VAN
Definitions, equipment, **Veh 28000**

REFUNDS
Motor Vehicles, this index
Traffic Rules and Regulations, this index
Vehicle verifiers, permits, cash in lieu of bond, **Veh 11301.5**

REFUSE
Solid Waste, generally, this index

REGIONAL ENTITIES
Definitions, tow truck driver certification, **Veh 2430.1**

REGIONAL OR LOCAL ENTITY
Definitions,
   Child passenger restraint systems, **Veh 2430.2**
   Emergency roadside assistance, **Veh 2436**

REGIONAL PARK DISTRICTS
Parks, this index

REGISTERED NURSES
Nurses, generally, this index

REGISTERED OWNER
Definitions,
   Motor vehicles, **Veh 505**
   Registration and transfer of vessels, **Veh 9840**

REGISTERED TRANSPORTERS
Definitions, inedible kitchen grease, **Veh 2460**

REGISTRANT
Definitions, motor vehicles, **Veh 8200**

REGISTRATION
Affidavits,
   Application for registration of new vehicle not within state, **Veh 4152**

REGISTRATION—Cont'd
Affidavits—Cont'd
   Stolen or embezzled vehicles, **Veh 4605**
Agricultural machinery and equipment, **Veh 36100 et seq.**
Air Pollution, this index
Autoettes, **Veh 4000.5**
Auxiliary dolly, **Veh 4000 et seq.**
Bicycles, **Veh 39000 et seq.**
Boats and Boating, this index
Cemeteries and Dead Bodies, this index
Certificate of title issued by other state, acceptance, **Veh 4305**
Fleet vehicles, **Veh 5301 et seq.**
Full faith and credit, certificate of title issued by other states, **Veh 4304**
Golf carts, exemption, **Veh 4019**
Hazardous Substances and Waste, this index
Hazardous Waste Haulers, this index
Highway patrol, inspection, **Veh 2804, 2805**
Historic vehicles, numbers and numbering, **Veh 5004**
Kitchen grease, transporters, **Veh 2470, 2472**
Logging dolly, **Veh 4000 et seq.**
Lost or stolen vehicles, **Veh 4458**
Mobilehomes and Mobilehome Parks, this index
Motor Carriers, this index
Motor Vehicles, this index
Motorcycles, this index
New engine or motor, **Veh 4161**
Nonresidents, foreign commercial vehicles, **Veh 6850 et seq.**
Pole or pipe dolly, **Veh 4000 et seq.**
Political subdivisions, vehicles, **Veh 4155**
Portable dolly for rendering assistance, **Veh 4014**
Reconstructed vehicle, **Veh 4153**
Renewal, stolen or embezzled vehicles, **Veh 4605**
School Buses, this index
Seals, foreign vehicles, surrender, **Veh 4301**
Semitrailers, **Veh 4000 et seq.**
   Weight fees, **Veh 9400**
Ships and Shipping, this index
Specially constructed vehicle, **Veh 4153**
Stolen or embezzled vehicles, **Veh 4605**
Taxicabs, this index
Traffic Rules and Regulations, this index
Trailers, this index
Trolley coaches, application of law, **Veh 21051**
United States, vehicles, **Veh 4155**
Waste tire haulers, infractions, **Veh 31560**
Wrecking and dismantling vehicles, service fee, **Veh 9263**

REGISTRATION ACT
Vehicles, **Veh 4000 et seq.**

REGISTRATION AND LICENSE FEE EXEMPTION ACT
Special equipment, **Veh 4010**

REGISTRATION

REGISTRATION CARDS
Mobilehomes and Mobilehome Parks, this index

REGISTRATION OF VOTERS
Elections, this index

REGROOVED TIRES
Motor vehicles, sale or use, **Veh 27460.5, 27461**

REIMBURSEMENT
Freeways, emergency call boxes, costs, **Veh 2421.5**

RELATIVES
Descent and distribution. Succession, generally, this index
Motor vehicles,
  Sales, application of law, **Veh 12121**
  Transfer of title or interest, registration, exhaust emission control devices, **Veh 4000.1**
Succession, generally, this index

RELEASE
Impounded vehicle to legal owner, **Veh 14602**
Motor Vehicles, this index
Taxicabs, impounding, **Veh 21100.4**

RELIGIOUS ORGANIZATIONS AND SOCIETIES
Business structures, definitions, motor vehicles, **Veh 240**
Motor vehicles,
  Dealers, exclusions, **Veh 286**
  Gifts, devises and bequests, records and recordation, **Veh 1660**
Records and recordation, motor vehicles, gifts, devises and bequests, **Veh 1660**

REMANUFACTURED VEHICLES
Definitions, **Veh 507.5**
Motor Vehicles, this index

REMANUFACTURERS
Definitions, motor vehicles, **Veh 507.8**

REMUNERATION
Compensation and Salaries, generally, this index

RENDERING PLANTS
Kitchen Grease, generally, this index

RENT
Housing Authorities, generally, this index
Sales and Use Taxes, generally, this index

RENTAL CARS
Leases. Motor Vehicles, this index

RENTAL COMPANY
Definitions, drivers licenses, **Veh 40000.11**

RENTER
Definitions, **Veh 508**

REPLACEMENT
Motor Vehicles, this index

REPORTS
Accidents, this index
Animals, this index
Boats and Boating, this index
Buses, this index
Counties, this index
Drivers licenses, **Veh 12814**
  Extension, **Veh 12814.5**
Driving schools, student license programs, **Veh 12660**
Freeways, this index
Garages, this index
Highway Patrol, this index
Historic vehicles, license plates, special plates, **Veh 5004.1**
Justice Department, this index
Juvenile Delinquents and Dependents, this index
Legislature, this index
Mass Transit, this index
Mobilehomes and Mobilehome Parks, this index
Motor Carriers, this index
Motor Vehicle Insurance, this index
Motor Vehicles, this index
Motor Vehicles Department, this index
Municipal Courts, this index
Peace Officers, this index
Pesticides, this index
Police, this index
Sheriffs, this index
Ships and Shipping, this index
Theft, this index
Traffic Rules and Regulations, this index
Traffic violator schools, **Veh 11208.5**
Witnesses, this index
Youth buses, accidents, **Veh 12523**

REPOSSESSORS AND REPOSSESSION
Licenses and permits, motor vehicles, searches and seizures, **Veh 23118**
Motor Vehicles, this index
Taxicabs, impounding, **Veh 21100.4**

REPOSSESSORS TOW VEHICLE
Definitions, **Veh 615**

REPRESENTATION
Legislature, generally, this index

REPRESENTATIVES
Motor Vehicles, this index

REPRODUCTIONS
Motor vehicle salesmens licenses, **Veh 11819**

RES JUDICATA
Motor vehicle offenses, conviction, civil actions, **Veh 40834**
Traffic rules and regulations, civil actions, effect of conviction, **Veh 40834**

RESCUE
Bicycles, peace officers, traffic rules and regulations, exemptions, **Veh 21200**
Definitions, rescue team, emergency vehicles, liability, resuscitation attempts, **Veh 165.5**

RESCUE—Cont'd
Emergency vehicles,
  Peace officers, **Veh 165**
  Status, rescue equipment, **Veh 2416**
Peace Officers, this index
Traffic rules and regulations, bicycles, peace officers, exemptions, **Veh 21200**

RESEARCH
Accidents, cause and control, **Veh 2408**
Anatomical Gifts, generally, this index

RESEARCH LABORATORIES
Medical waste. Hazardous Substances and Waste, this index

RESIDENCE
Domicile and Residence, generally, this index

RESIDENCE DISTRICT
Definitions, motor vehicles, **Veh 240, 515**

RESIDENTIAL BUILDINGS
Housing, generally, this index

RESIDENTS
Domicile and Residence, generally, this index

RESTAURANTS
Grease. Kitchen Grease, generally, this index
Kitchen Grease, generally, this index

RESUSCITATION
Ambulances, equipment, **Veh 2418.5**

RETAIL
Retailers, generally, this index

RETAIL SALES
Definitions, motor vehicles, **Veh 520**
Sales, generally, this index

RETAIL SELLER
Retailers, generally, this index

RETAILERS
Bicycles, records, information supplied to purchasers, **Veh 39006**
Definitions, motor vehicles, notice, removal, **Veh 22658**
Motor vehicles, removal, **Veh 22658**
Notice, motor vehicles, removal, **Veh 22658**
Sales and Use Taxes, generally, this index

RETIREMENT AND PENSIONS
Social Security, generally, this index

RETROFIT
Motor vehicles, shoulder harnesses, used vehicles, **Veh 27314.5**

RETROREFLECTIVE SHEETING
Motor carriers, conspicuity system, **Veh 24612**

REVIEW
Appeal and Review, generally, this index

REVOLVERS
Weapons, generally, this index

REVOLVING RED LIGHTS
Emergency vehicles, **Veh 25252**

RIDESHARING
Car pools. Motor Vehicles, this index
Definitions, **Veh 522**
Parking, exclusive use spaces, **Veh 22507.1**
Vanpooling, generally, this index

RIDGES
Motor vehicle tires, protuberances, **Veh 27454**

RIDING
Animals, this index

RIFLES
Weapons, generally, this index

RIGHT OF WAY
Blind persons, **Veh 21963 et seq.**
Electric personal assistive mobility devices, **Veh 21281.5**
Highways and Roads, this index
Personal assistive mobility devices, **Veh 21281.5**
Railroads, this index
Traffic Rules and Regulations, this index
Traffic Signs and Signals, this index
Traffic violator schools, courses of study, **Veh 11219.3**

RIGHT SIDE OF ROADWAY
Traffic Rules and Regulations, this index

RIGHT TURNS
Generally, **Veh 22100 et seq.**
Traffic Rules and Regulations, this index

RIOT GUNS
Weapons, generally, this index

RIVERS AND STREAMS
Abandoned vehicles, removal, priorities and preferences, **Veh 22667**
Bridges. Highways and Roads, this index
Fish and Game, generally, this index
Flood control. Levees and Flood Control, generally, this index
Levees and Flood Control, generally, this index
Motor vehicles, state measurement work, warning lights, **Veh 25266**

RIVERSIDE COUNTY
South coast air quality management district. Air Pollution, this index

ROAD RAGE
Traffic Rules and Regulations, this index

ROADS
Highways and Roads, generally, this index

ROADSIDE REST AREAS
Highways and Roads, this index

ROBBERY
Armored car,
    Red lights, use in resisting armed robbery, **Veh 25262**
    Siren, used while resisting, **Veh 27003**

ROCKETS
Fireworks, generally, this index
Highways and roads, chemical rocket propellants, route designation, **Veh 32102**

ROCKS
Motor vehicles, throwing or discharging at vehicle or occupant, **Veh 23110**
Outdoor Advertising, generally, this index
Traffic rules and regulations, highway dumping, **Veh 23112, 23113**

ROLLER SKATING
Helmets, children and minors, **Veh 21212**
Traffic Rules and Regulations, this index

ROMAN CANDLES
Fireworks, generally, this index

ROSENTHAL BLUE SKY LICENSE PLATE PROGRAM
Generally, **Veh 5062**

ROUTE DEVIATED BUS SERVICE
Paratransit Vehicles, generally, this index

ROUTES
Buses, this index
Highways and Roads, this index

RUBBISH
Solid Waste, generally, this index

RULES OF EVIDENCE
Evidence, generally, this index

RULES OF NAVIGATION
Ships and Shipping, generally, this index

RULES OF THE ROAD
Generally, **Veh 21000 et seq.**
Traffic Rules and Regulations, generally, this index

RUM
Alcoholic Beverages, generally, this index

RUNAWAY VEHICLES
Generally, **Veh 20002**
Registered owner construed to be driver, **Veh 16001**

RUNNING LIGHTS
Defined motor vehicles, **Veh 375**

RURAL MAIL CARRIERS
Motor vehicles, flashing amber lights, **Veh 25272**

RUSSIAN KNAPWEED
Weeds, generally, this index

RYE
Agricultural Products, generally, this index

SACRAMENTO CITY AND COUNTY
Buses, bicycles, length, **Veh 35400.8**
Highway patrol, main office, **Veh 2106**

SACRAMENTO METROPOLITAN AIR QUALITY MANAGEMENT DISTRICT
Motor vehicles, registration, surcharge, **Veh 9250.2**

SAFE STREETS ACT
Generally, **Veh 14607.4 et seq.**
Publicity, **Veh 1664**

SAFETY
Agricultural Machinery and Equipment, this index
Buses, this index
Drivers handbook, railroads, **Veh 1656.3**
Fires and Fire Protection, generally, this index
Highways and Roads, this index
Ice cream trucks, vending, **Veh 22456**
Limousines, this index
Mobilehomes and Mobilehome Parks, this index
Motor Carriers, this index
Motor Vehicles, this index
Park trailers, **Veh 34500 et seq.**
Railroads, this index
School Buses, this index
Streets and Alleys, this index
Traffic Rules and Regulations, this index

SAFETY CHAINS
Motor carriers, towed vehicle coupling, **Veh 29004**
Motor vehicles, towed vehicle coupled to towing vehicle by, **Veh 29003**

SAFETY CONNECTIONS
Recreational vehicles, towing equipment, **Veh 29004.5**

SAFETY GLASS
Definitions, motor vehicles, **Veh 535**
Motor vehicle windshields, **Veh 26701 et seq.**
Motorcycle windshields, **Veh 26701, 26705**

SAFETY GLAZING MATERIALS
Mobilehomes, **Veh 26701**
Motor vehicles, **Veh 26701 et seq.**

SAFETY HELMETS
Standards and specifications, adoption and enforcement, **Veh 26103**

SAILBOATS
Boats and Boating, generally, this index

SAILORS
Military Forces, generally, this index

SALARIES
Compensation and Salaries, generally, this index

SALES
Bicycle helmets, **Veh 21212**
Bicycles, this index

SALES

SALES—Cont'd

Bills of Lading, generally, this index

Boats and Boating, this index

Consignment, generally, this index

Definitions, motor vehicles, **Veh 5901**

Engines or motors installed or transferred between vehicles, **Veh 4163**

Financing agency, motor vehicles, bonds (officers and fiduciaries), priorities and preferences, **Veh 11722**

Helmets, motorcycle riders, approved type, **Veh 27802**

Highway patrol, unclaimed property, **Veh 2415**

Highways and Roads, this index

Ignition interlock devices, notice, **Veh 23575**

Markets and Marketing, generally, this index

Mobilehomes and Mobilehome Parks, this index

Motor Carriers, this index

Motor Vehicles, this index

Motorcycles, this index

Notice,
  Ignition interlock devices, driving under the influence, **Veh 23575**
  Nuisance vehicles, sales, driving under the influence, **Veh 23596**

Odometers, motor vehicles, device for resetting, **Veh 28051.5**

Park trailers, disclosure, moving requirements, **Veh 11713.1**

Photography and Pictures, this index

Recreational Vehicles, this index

Retailers, generally, this index

Safety helmets, approved type for motorcycle riders, **Veh 27802**

Ships and Shipping, this index

Tax on sales. Sales and Use Taxes, generally, this index

Traffic Rules and Regulations, this index

SALES AND USE TAXES

Automobiles. Motor vehicles, generally, post

Boats and boating, **Veh 9873**
  Temporary certificate, agent for issuance, **Veh 9859**

Delinquent taxes,
  Fines and penalties, motor vehicles, off highway vehicles, **Veh 38211**
  Motor carriers, licenses and permits, revocation or suspension, **Veh 34623.1**
  Motor vehicles, off highway vehicles, **Veh 38211**

Fines and penalties,
  Delinquent taxes, ante
  Off highway vehicles subject to identification, **Veh 38211**
  Vessels, aircraft and vehicles, delinquent payments, **Veh 9862**

Foreign states, motor vehicles, registration, **Veh 4300.5**

SALES AND USE TAXES—Cont'd

Motor carriers, licenses and permits, delinquent taxes, revocation or suspension, **Veh 34623.1**

Motor vehicles, **Veh 540**
  Dealers, nonpayment, **Veh 11713**
  Delinquent taxes, off highway vehicles, **Veh 38211**
  Foreign vehicles, registration, **Veh 4300.5**
  Refusal of registration, **Veh 4750.5**
  Registration outside state, **Veh 4152**

Ships and shipping,
  Collection, **Veh 9928**
  Failure to pay, withholding certificate of number or transfer of registration, **Veh 9928**
  Fees, certificates and certification, state preferred claims, **Veh 9859**
  Temporary certificates, agents for issuance, **Veh 9859**

Vehicles. Motor vehicles, generally, ante

Vessels. Ships and shipping, generally, ante

SALES TAXES

Sales and Use Taxes, generally, this index

SALESPERSONS

Definitions, motor vehicles, **Veh 675**

Insurance Agents, Solicitors or Brokers, generally, this index

Motor Vehicles, this index

Snowmobiles, posting certificate and license, **Veh 11709**

SALVAGE

Motor vehicles, inspection of salvage pools, stolen vehicles, **Veh 2805**

SALVAGE POOL

Definitions, salvage motor vehicles, **Veh 543**

SALVAGED VEHICLES

Motor Vehicles, this index

SAMPLES

Driving under the influence, chemical tests, **Veh 23614**

SAN BERNARDINO COUNTY

South coast air quality management district. Air Pollution, this index

SAN BERNARDINO FREEWAY

High occupancy vehicle lanes, **Veh 21655.12**

SAN BERNARDINO RIVERSIDE STATE COLLEGE

Colleges and Universities, generally, this index

SAN DIEGO

School buses, children all to be seated, **Veh 21700.5**

SAN DIEGO COUNTY

Traffic rules and regulations, garbage trucks, weight limits, **Veh 35701**

SAN DIEGO STATE COLLEGE

Colleges and Universities, generally, this index

SAN FERNANDO VALLEY STATE COLLEGE

Colleges and Universities, generally, this index

SAN FRANCISCO CITY AND COUNTY

Fees, local vehicle license fee surcharge, **Veh 9250.12**

Local vehicle license fee surcharge, **Veh 9250.12**

Motor vehicles, local vehicle license fee surcharge, **Veh 9250.12**

Municipal courts, officers and employees, parking violations, notice processing employees, civil service transfers, **Veh 40200.4**

Ordinances, local vehicle license fee surcharge, **Veh 9250.12**

Parking, videotape, transit only traffic lanes, buses, **Veh 40240 et seq.**

Resolutions, local vehicle license fee surcharge, **Veh 9250.12**

Surcharges, local vehicle license fee surcharge, **Veh 9250.12**

Traffic rules and regulations, parking, videotape, transit only traffic lanes, buses, **Veh 40240 et seq.**

Transportation, local vehicle license fee surcharge, **Veh 9250.12**

SAN FRANCISCO COUNTY

San Francisco City and County, generally, this index

SAN FRANCISCO STATE COLLEGE

Colleges and Universities, generally, this index

SAN LUIS OBISPO

Traffic rules and regulations, length, combinations of vehicles, exemptions, **Veh 35401**

SAN MATEO COUNTY

Congestion, highways and roads, managers and management, **Veh 9250.5**

Contracts, parking violations notices, processing, **Veh 40200.4**

Fees, motor vehicles, registration, **Veh 9250.5**

Highways and roads, congestion, managers and management, **Veh 9250.5**

Motor vehicles, registration, fees, **Veh 9250.5**

Parking violations notices processing, contracts, **Veh 40200.4**

Registration, motor vehicles, fees, **Veh 9250.5**

Water quality, storm water, managers and management, **Veh 9250.5**

SAN MATEO COUNTY STATE COLLEGE
Colleges and Universities, generally, this index

SAN MATEO SANTA CLARA COUNTY STATE COLLEGE
Colleges and Universities, generally, this index

SAND BUGGY
Identification plates, display, **Veh 38170**
Off highway motor vehicles, definition, **Veh 38012**
Rules and regulations, **Veh 11709, 38000 et seq.**

SANDBUR GRASS
Weeds, generally, this index

SANITARIUMS
Mentally Retarded and Developmentally Disabled Persons, generally, this index

SANTA BARBARA COUNTY
Traffic rules and regulations, length, combinations of vehicles, exemptions, **Veh 35401**

SANTA CLARA COUNTY
Highways and roads, state highway route 85, weights, **Veh 35722**
State highway route 85, weights, **Veh 35722**

SANTA CLARA VALLEY TRANSPORTATION AUTHORITY
Buses, right of way, yielding, signs and signals, **Veh 24617**

SANTA CRUZ METROPOLITAN TRANSIT DISTRICT
Transit Districts, this index

SANTA MONICA
Buses, illuminated signs, advertisements, **Veh 25353.1**

SATELLITE WARRANTY FACILITY
Definitions, motor vehicles, franchises, **Veh 3062**

SAVINGS BANKS
Unclaimed property. Abandoned or Unclaimed Property, generally, this index

SAWED OFF SHOTGUNS
Weapons, generally, this index

SCALES
Weights and Measures, generally, this index

SCARIFIERS
Special highway construction equipment, definitions, **Veh 565**

SCHOOL BUILDINGS AND GROUNDS
Closing streets, local regulations, **Veh 21102, 21103**
Traffic Rules and Regulations, this index
Traffic Signs and Signals, this index

SCHOOL BUS ACCIDENT
Definitions, motor vehicles, **Veh 12517.1**

SCHOOL BUSES
Activity buses,
    Certificates and certification,
        Operation, **Veh 12517**
            Revocation or suspension, **Veh 13370**
    Crimes and offenses, drivers certificates, **Veh 40000.11, 40000.21**
    Criminal history information, drivers certificates, **Veh 12517.3**
    Drivers licenses, **Veh 12517**
    Drugs and medicine, drivers certificates, revocation, **Veh 13376**
    Fingerprints and fingerprinting, drivers certificates, **Veh 12517.3**
    Passengers, seatbelts, **Veh 27316.5**
    Reduced visibility, driver discretion to limit operation, **Veh 34501.6**
    Seatbelts, **Veh 27316.5**
Advisory committee, **Veh 34501.5**
Age, drivers licenses, **Veh 12516**
Amber lights, **Veh 22112, 25257**
    Mentally retarded and developmentally disabled persons, **Veh 25257.2**
Amber reflectors, **Veh 24609**
Backing maneuvers, warnings, **Veh 25257.5**
Certificates and certification,
    Drivers certificates, generally, post
    Inspection, **Veh 2807, 2807.1**
    Operation, **Veh 12517**
    School pupil activity buses, **Veh 12517**
    Youth buses, **Veh 2807.3**
        Driver certificates, **Veh 12523**
Certificates of endorsement, **Veh 13369 et seq.**
Coach bus, Trona unified school district, inspection, **Veh 545.5**
Colored lights, **Veh 25257**
Colors and coloring, **Veh 2808**
    Former school buses, **Veh 27603**
    Safety regulations, **Veh 34506, 34508**
Common carrier operating vehicle, exemption from definition, **Veh 545**
Community colleges and districts, exemptions, **Veh 545.1**
Consent, parents, tour buses, **Veh 12517.45**
Construction, design, **Veh 2808**
Courses of instruction, driver, first aid, **Veh 12522**
Crimes and offenses,
    Activity buses, ante
    Drivers,
        Certificates, **Veh 40000.11**
        Licenses, revocation or denial, **Veh 13369 et seq.**
        Operators, licenses, revocation or denial, **Veh 13369 et seq.**
    Private contractors, **Veh 40000.77**
    Safety regulations, equipment, construction, design and color, **Veh 34506, 40000.21**
Tour buses, **Veh 40000.11**
Youth buses, **Veh 34506, 40000.21**

SCHOOL BUSES—Cont'd
Criminal history information, drivers certificates, **Veh 12517.3**
Crossing control arms, length, **Veh 35400**
Crossing roads, children after unloading, **Veh 22112**
Definitions, **Veh 545**
Designated stops, flashing red lights, **Veh 22112**
Developmentally disabled persons. Mentally Retarded and Developmentally Disabled Persons, this index
Double parking, **Veh 22500**
Drivers,
    Certificates and certification. Drivers certificates, generally, post
    Crimes and offenses, ante
    Licenses and permits. Drivers licenses, generally, post
    Training, endorsements, drivers licenses, **Veh 12517, 15275.1**
Drivers certificates, **Veh 545, 12517.4**
    Criminal history information, **Veh 12517.3**
    Drugs and medicine, revocation, **Veh 13376**
    Fingerprints and fingerprinting, **Veh 12517.3**
    Invalidation, failure to complete first aid course, **Veh 12522**
    Possession, **Veh 12517**
    Suspension or revocation, **Veh 12806.5**
        Grounds, **Veh 13370**
    Tour buses, **Veh 12517.45**
Drivers licenses, **Veh 545**
    Age, **Veh 12516**
    Endorsements, **Veh 12517, 15275.1, 15278**
    First aid examination, **Veh 12522**
    Foreign country drivers, **Veh 12505**
    Medical examinations, **Veh 12517.2**
    Qualifications, **Veh 12517**
    Revocation, **Veh 13371**
    School pupil activity buses, **Veh 12517**
    Tour buses, **Veh 12517.45**
Drugs and medicine, drivers certificates, revocation, **Veh 13376**
Dust, additional lights, **Veh 25102.5**
Endorsements, drivers licenses, **Veh 12517, 15275.1, 15278**
Equipment, **Veh 2808**
    Colored lights, **Veh 25257**
    Crossing control arms, length, **Veh 35400**
    Inspection, **Veh 2807**
    Stop signal arm, **Veh 25257**
Escorting children across road, **Veh 22112**
Evidence, residency, driver licensing purposes, **Veh 12505**
Exemptions,
    Construction, design, **Veh 2808**
    Equipment statutes, **Veh 2808**
    Registration and weight fees, **Veh 9102.5**
    Stopping, flashing red signal lamps, **Veh 22112**

SCHOOL

SCHOOL BUSES—Cont'd

Fees,
Licenses and permits, post
Registration, post
School pupil activity buses, certificates of operation, **Veh 12517**
Temporary permits, **Veh 9266.5**
Tour buses, inspection and inspectors, **Veh 12517.45**
Fines and penalties, private contractors, **Veh 2572**
Fingerprints and fingerprinting, drivers certificates, **Veh 12517.3**
First aid examination, driver, **Veh 12522**
Flashing red light signal system, **Veh 22112, 25257**
Developmentally disabled persons, **Veh 25257.2**
Fog, additional lights, **Veh 25102.5**
Hearings, private contractors, licenses, suspension, **Veh 2573**
Infractions, safety violations, **Veh 34506.3**
Inspection and inspectors,
Certificates, **Veh 2807.1**
Construction, equipment, **Veh 2807**
Preventive maintenance guide, **Veh 2807.2**
Private contractors, **Veh 2570 et seq.**
Tour buses, **Veh 12517.45**
Trona unified school district, coach bus, **Veh 545.5**
Leases, fees, **Veh 9266**
Length, crossing control arms, **Veh 35400**
Licenses and permits,
Control reverting to lessor, **Veh 5010**
Fees, **Veh 9102.5, 9266**
Adjustments, **Veh 1678**
Private contractors, **Veh 2570, 2571**
Operate bus transporting pupils, **Veh 12516**
Private school bus contractors, **Veh 2570 et seq.**
Sex offenders, denial or revocation, **Veh 13369 et seq.**
Temporary permit, **Veh 5010, 9102.5**
Fees, **Veh 9266.5**
Lights and lighting,
Amber reflectors, **Veh 24609**
Colored lights, **Veh 25257**
Flashing or colored lights, **Veh 25257**
Impaired visibility lamps, **Veh 25102.5**
Strobe lights, **Veh 25257.7**
Limited operation, reduced visibility, **Veh 34501.6**
Loading or unloading, **Veh 22112**
Transit bus stops, **Veh 22500.5**
Youth buses, **Veh 2816**
Machinery and equipment. Equipment, generally, ante
Maintenance, rules and regulations, **Veh 34508**
Mechanics, endorsements, drivers licenses, **Veh 12517, 15275.1**
Mentally Retarded and Developmentally Disabled Persons, this index

SCHOOL BUSES—Cont'd

Offenses. Crimes and offenses, generally, ante
Overtaking and passing, stopping before, **Veh 22454**
Painting, former school buses, **Veh 27603**
Parents, consent, tour buses, **Veh 12517.45**
Parking, double parking, **Veh 22500**
Passengers, seatbelts, **Veh 27316, 27316.5**
Permits. Licenses and permits, generally, ante
Preventive maintenance inspection guide, **Veh 2807.2**
Private contractors, licensing, **Veh 2570 et seq.**
Private Schools, this index
Proration of fees, fraction of years, **Veh 9266**
Pupil activity buses,
Crimes and offenses, **Veh 40000.21**
Equipment, **Veh 34506**
Rain, additional lights, **Veh 25102.5**
Red flashing signal system, **Veh 22112, 25257**
Reduced visibility, limited operation, **Veh 34501.6**
Registration,
Fees, **Veh 9102.5, 9266**
Adjustments, **Veh 1678**
Private contractors, **Veh 2570**
School buses temporarily reverting to control of lessor, **Veh 5010**
Revocation or suspension, drivers certificates, **Veh 12806.5, 13370**
Rules and regulations, **Veh 2808, 34500 et seq.**
Equipment, construction, design and color, **Veh 34506, 34508**
Private contractors, **Veh 2572**
Safety, **Veh 34500 et seq.**
Failure to comply, **Veh 34506.3, 40000.21**
Reduced visibility, limited operation, **Veh 34501.6**
San Diego, pupils all to be seated, **Veh 21700.5**
Seatbelts, **Veh 27316, 27316.5**
Sex offenses, drivers, license revocation, **Veh 13369 et seq.**
Signs,
Display, **Veh 27906**
Windows, obstruction of view, **Veh 26708**
Smoke, additional lights, **Veh 25102.5**
Snow, additional lights, **Veh 25102.5**
Stop signal arms, **Veh 22112, 25257**
Developmentally disabled persons, **Veh 25257.2**
Stop signs, **Veh 27906**
Stopping,
Designated stops, flashing red lights, **Veh 22112**
Flashing red signal lamps, **Veh 22112**
Receiving or discharging passengers, **Veh 22454**
Strobe lights, **Veh 25257.7**

SCHOOL BUSES—Cont'd

Temporary permit, **Veh 9102.5**
Control reverting to lessor, **Veh 5010**
Fees, **Veh 9266**
Tires, tread depth requirements, adopting regulations, **Veh 27465**
Tour buses, **Veh 12517.45**
Crimes and offenses, **Veh 40000.11**
Traffic Rules and Regulations, this index
Traffic Signs and Signals, this index
Training. Drivers, ante
Transit systems, bus stops, loading or unloading, **Veh 22500.5**
Trona unified school district, coach bus, inspection, **Veh 545.5**
Turn signals, flashing, backing maneuver warnings, **Veh 25257.5**
Warnings, backing maneuvers, **Veh 25257.5**
Wheelchair lifting devices, safety certification, **Veh 34501.1**
Youth Buses, generally, this index

SCHOOL DISTRICTS

Schools and School Districts, generally, this index

SCHOOL OFFICERS AND EMPLOYEES

Classified employees, guards, pedestrian crossings, compensation, **Veh 42201**
Compensation and salaries, pedestrian crossing guards, **Veh 42201**
Driver certificates, school pupil activities or youth buses, revocation or suspension, **Veh 12806.5**
Parking, preferential parking permits, **Veh 22507**
Peace officers, blue warning lights, emergency vehicles, **Veh 25258**
Preferential parking permits, **Veh 22507**
School buses, drivers licenses, **Veh 12517.2**

SCHOOLS AND SCHOOL DISTRICTS

Absence and absentees. Truants, generally, post
Activity buses. School Buses, this index
Alcoholic beverages,
Motor vehicles, drivers, tests, **Veh 34520.3**
Transportation, drivers, tests, **Veh 34520.3**
Animals, traffic regulations, **Veh 21113**
Attendance. Truants, generally, post
Automobiles. Motor vehicles, generally, post
Average daily attendance, traffic violator schools, **Veh 42005.5**
Bicycles, **Veh 21113**
Buses. School Buses, generally, this index
Classified employees. School Officers and Employees, this index
Colleges and Universities, generally, this index
Community colleges and districts. Colleges and Universities, this index
Compensation and salaries. School Officers and Employees, this index

SCHOOLS AND SCHOOL DISTRICTS
—Cont'd

Continuing Education, generally, this index

Courses of instruction or study. Driver education, generally, post

Crosswalks, guards, traffic signal or direction, disregard, **Veh 2815, 42001.1**

Dependent children. Juvenile Institutions and Schools, generally, this index

Driver education, **Veh 1657**

  Definitions, **Veh 223**

  Drivers licenses,

    Revocation, reinstatement, **Veh 13368**

    Students, **Veh 12650 et seq.**

  Driving Schools, generally, this index

  Exemptions, **Veh 11101**

  Instruction permits, **Veh 12509**

  Instructors, drivers licenses, **Veh 11104**

  Private schools, **Veh 11101**

  Provisional licenses, **Veh 12814.6**

  Traffic rules and regulations,

    Distribution, **Veh 1656**

    Local authorities closing street, **Veh 21101**

  Traffic safety program, **Veh 2900 et seq.**

Drugs and medicine,

  Motor vehicles, drivers, tests, **Veh 34520.3**

  Transportation, drivers, tests, **Veh 34520.3**

Emergency vehicles, police and security departments, **Veh 165**

Employees. School Officers and Employees, generally, this index

Fines and penalties, school crossing guard, traffic signal or direction, disregard, **Veh 2815, 42001.1**

First aid, bus driver, qualifications, **Veh 12522**

Habitual truants. Truants, post

Highway patrol, training school, **Veh 2262**

Home to school transportation. Transportation, generally, post

Instruction permits, driver education, **Veh 12509**

Juvenile delinquents and dependents. Truants, generally, post

Juvenile Institutions and Schools, generally, this index

Kindergartens. School Buses, generally, this index

Loans, motor vehicles, ownership, **Veh 17157**

Motor vehicles,

  Activated alarm devices, removal, **Veh 22651**

  Alcoholic beverages, drivers, tests, **Veh 34520.3**

  Crossing guards, county contracts, **Veh 42201**

  Driver education, generally, ante

  Drivers, drugs and medicine, alcoholic beverages, tests, **Veh 34520.3**

  Driving Schools, generally, this index

SCHOOLS AND SCHOOL DISTRICTS
—Cont'd

Motor vehicles—Cont'd

  Drugs and medicine, drivers, tests, **Veh 34520.3**

  Emergency vehicles, school security patrols, fees, exemption, **Veh 9102**

  Gratuitous loans to district, ownership, **Veh 17157**

  Lights and lighting, warning lights, **Veh 25273**

  Measuring distances from pupils residence, warning lights, **Veh 25273**

  Tort liability, **Veh 17000 et seq.**

  Traffic safety fund, compensation of school crossing, **Veh 42200**

  Truants, habitual truants, revocation or suspension of driving privileges, **Veh 13202.7**

Motorized bicycles, **Veh 21113**

Nonpublic schools. Private Schools, generally, this index

Notice. Truants, post

Officers and employees. School Officers and Employees, generally, this index

Parochial schools. Private Schools, generally, this index

Peace officers. School Officers and Employees, this index

Pedestrians, crosswalks, guards, compensation and salaries, **Veh 42201**

Police, peace officers. School Officers and Employees, this index

Private Schools, generally, this index

Roller skates, **Veh 21113**

School Buses, generally, this index

Skateboards, **Veh 21113**

Streets and alleys, school crossing guard, traffic signal or direction, disregard, **Veh 2815, 42001.1**

Student activities drivers, revocation or suspension, certificates and certification, **Veh 12806.5**

Torts, motor vehicles, **Veh 17000 et seq.**

Tour buses. School Buses, this index

Traffic Rules and Regulations, this index

Traffic Signs and Signals, this index

Traffic Violator Schools, generally, this index

Transportation,

  Alcoholic beverages, drivers, tests, **Veh 34520.3**

  Buses. School Buses, generally, this index

  Drivers, drugs and medicine, alcoholic beverages, tests, **Veh 34520.3**

  Drugs and medicine, drivers, tests, **Veh 34520.3**

  Private school bus contractors, **Veh 2570 et seq.**

  School Buses, generally, this index

Trona unified school district, coach bus, inspection, **Veh 545.5**

Truants,

  Driving privileges, revocation or suspension, **Veh 13202.7**

SCHOOLS AND SCHOOL DISTRICTS
—Cont'd

Truants—Cont'd

  Habitual truants, motor vehicles, suspension of driving privileges, **Veh 13202.7**

  Motor vehicles, revocation or suspension, driving privileges, **Veh 13202.7**

  Notice, **Veh 13202.7**

Vehicle Code, distribution, **Veh 1656**

Vehicles. Motor vehicles, generally, ante

Work permits, driving under the influence, **Veh 23538, 23562**

Youth bus drivers, revocation or suspension of certificate, **Veh 12806.5**

SCHRADE BELOTTI ACT

Reflectorized vehicle license plates, **Veh 4850**

SCOOTERS

Motorized Scooters, generally, this index

Nonmotorized scooters, helmets, children and minors, **Veh 21212**

SCOWS

Ships and Shipping, generally, this index

SCRAP METAL AND SALVAGE MATERIAL

Dismantlers. Motor Vehicles, this index

Processing facilities, crimes and offenses, **Veh 40000.5**

Processors, identification numbers, dismantled vehicles, **Veh 10751**

SEARCH AND RESCUE

Rescue, generally, this index

SEARCHES AND SEIZURES

Motor Vehicles, this index

Motorized scooters, pocket bikes, **Veh 21721**

Pocket bikes, **Veh 21721**

Seatbelts, motor vehicles, **Veh 27315**

Taxicabs, this index

Traffic Rules and Regulations, this index

Warrants,

  Motor vehicles, repossessors and repossession, **Veh 23118**

  Taxicabs, **Veh 21100.4**

SEASONS

Traffic rules and regulations, permits to exceed maximum size, weight, **Veh 35782**

SEATBELTS

Motor Vehicles, this index

SEATS

Bicycles, passengers, **Veh 21204**

Motorcycles, passengers, **Veh 27800, 27801**

Motorized bicycles, passengers, **Veh 27800**

SECOND STAGE MANUFACTURERS

Definitions, house cars, **Veh 11930**

SECONDARY NOXIOUS WEEDS

Weeds, generally, this index

SECONDHAND GOODS AND DEALERS
Definitions, second hand dealers, private
party vehicle markets, **Veh 12101**
Junk and Junk Dealers, generally, this index

SECRETARY OF STATE
Elections, generally, this index

SECRETS AND SECRECY
Confidential or Privileged Information,
generally, this index

SECTARIAN SCHOOLS
Private Schools, generally, this index

SECURITY DEPOSITS
Motor Vehicles, this index

SECURITY INTEREST
Boats and Boating, this index
Motor Vehicles, this index
Ships and Shipping, this index

SEIZURES
Searches and Seizures, generally, this index

SEMAPHORES
Traffic Signs and Signals, this index

SEMINARIES
Colleges and Universities, generally, this
index

SEMITRAILERS
Motor Carriers, generally, this index

SENIOR CITIZENS
Aged Persons, generally, this index

SENTENCE AND PUNISHMENT
Crimes and Offenses, generally, this index
Fines and Penalties, generally, this index

SERIAL NUMBERS
Bicycles, this index

SERIOUS BODILY INJURY
Definitions, motor vehicles, flight from
peace officers, **Veh 2800.3**

SERIOUS TRAFFIC VIOLATION
Definitions, speed limits, **Veh 22406**

SERVICE BRAKES
Towing vehicles, **Veh 26304**

SERVICE MARKS
Trademarks, generally, this index

SERVICE OF PROCESS
Process, this index

SERVICE STATIONS
Motor Vehicle Service Stations, generally,
this index

SETTLEMENT
Compromise and Settlement, generally,
this index

SEVERAL LIABILITY
Joint and Several Liability, generally, this
index

SEWERS AND SEWER SYSTEMS
Lights on repair vehicles, **Veh 25265**

SEX OFFENDERS
Buses, operators, drivers licenses, revocation or denial, **Veh 13369 et seq.**
Motor vehicles, operators, drivers licenses,
revocation or denial, **Veh 13369 et
seq.**
Paratransit vehicles, operators, drivers licenses, revocation or denial, **Veh
13369 et seq.**
School buses, drivers licenses, revocation
or denial, **Veh 13369 et seq.**
Youth buses, operators, drivers licenses,
revocation or denial, **Veh 13369 et
seq.**

SEXUAL BATTERY
Motor vehicles, license plates, new plates,
Veh 4467

SEXUAL PSYCHOPATHS
Sex Offenders, generally, this index

SEXUAL RELATIONS
Sex Offenders, generally, this index

SHELLFISH
Mussels,
Quagga mussels, infestation prevention
fee, boats and boating, registration,
Veh 9853, 9860
Zebra mussels, infestation prevention
fee, boats and boating, registration,
Veh 9853, 9860
Quagga mussels, infestation prevention
fee, boats and boating, registration,
Veh 9853, 9860
Zebra mussels, infestation prevention fee,
boats and boating, registration, **Veh
9853, 9860**

SHERIFFS
Abandoned vehicles, removal from private
property after accident, **Veh 22653**
Accidents, reports, forms, **Veh 2407**
Address, disclosure, crimes and offenses,
Veh 1808.4
Appraisers, abandoned vehicles, **Veh
22855**
Arrest, generally, this index
Blue lights, authorized emergency vehi-
cles, **Veh 25258**
Children and minors, home address and
telephone number disclosure, crimes
and offenses, **Veh 1808.4**
Copies, notice for arrested person to ap-
pear, filing with, **Veh 40506**
Disclosure, home address and telephone
number, crimes and offenses, **Veh
1808.4**
Emergency vehicles, blue lights, **Veh 25258**
Fines and penalties, safety belts, patrol
vehicles, **Veh 27315.3**

SHERIFFS—Cont'd
Fire areas, direction of traffic, **Veh 21707**
Hazardous Substances and Waste, this in-
dex
Highways, closing menace to public health
or safety, **Veh 2812**
Home address, disclosure, crimes and of-
fenses, **Veh 1808.4**
Jails, generally, this index
License plates, lost or stolen, notice, **Veh
4458**
Motor vehicles,
Amber warning lights, **Veh 25277**
Blue warning lights, **Veh 25258**
Flashing lights, **Veh 25277**
Hazardous substances and waste, signs
and signals, exemptions, **Veh 27903**
Pursuit of vehicle reports, **Veh 14602.1**
Removal of parked or standing vehicles,
Veh 22650 et seq.
Windows, tinting, glazing, **Veh 26708.7**
Notice, written notice, motor vehicle viola-
tions as cause of accident, **Veh 40600**
Prisons and prisoners. Jails, generally,
this index
Process, generally, this index
Pursuit, reports, **Veh 14602.1**
Removal,
Abandoned vehicles from private prop-
erty after accident, **Veh 22653**
Vehicles from highways, employees, **Veh
22651 et seq.**
Reports,
Pursuits, **Veh 14602.1**
Stored or parked vehicles, **Veh 10652**
Safety belts, patrol vehicles, **Veh 27315.3**
Searches and Seizures, generally, this in-
dex
Spouse, home address and telephone
number disclosure, crimes and of-
fenses, **Veh 1808.4**
Telecommunications, disclosure, tele-
phone numbers, crimes and offenses,
Veh 1808.4
Vehicles, patrol, safety belts, **Veh 27315.3**
Written notice, motor vehicle violation as
cause of accident, probable cause,
Veh 40600

SHIP MANAGERS
Owners and ownership. Ships and Shipping, this index

SHIPS AND SHIPPING
Additional fees, certificates of number,
Veh 9853, 9853.6
Assessor,
Numbers, change of ownership, **Veh
9856**
Registration information, **Veh 9869**
Assignment, lien, notice, title or interest in
undocumented vessel, **Veh 9906**
Bonds (officers and fiduciaries), transfer
of title or interest, **Veh 9923, 9924**
Builders hull identification number, **Veh
9871, 9872**
Registration, renewal, **Veh 9871.5**

SHIPS AND SHIPPING—Cont'd

Cancellation, certificates or registration, **Veh 9874**

Certificates of number, **Veh 9850 et seq.**
  Additional fees, **Veh 9853, 9853.6**
  Address charge, **Veh 9865**
  Agent for issuance, **Veh 9858, 9859**
  Applications, **Veh 9853 et seq.**
  Cancellation, **Veh 9874**
  Change of owner, **Veh 9855**
  Duplicates, fee, **Veh 9867**
  Exemptions, **Veh 9873**
  Expiration, **Veh 9861**
  Fees, **Veh 9853, 9853.6**
  Renewal, **Veh 9860**
  Withholding, failure to pay use tax, **Veh 9928**

Certificates of ownership, **Veh 9850 et seq.**
  Agent for issuance, **Veh 9858, 9859**
  Cancellation, **Veh 9874**
  Change of owner, **Veh 9855**
  Duplicates, fee, **Veh 9867**
  Involuntary transfer of title or interest, **Veh 9915**
  Lost certificate, replacement on transfer of title, **Veh 9917**
  Nondelivery on transfer of title, **Veh 9910**
  Replacing lost or destroyed certificate, **Veh 9909**
  Security interest, perfecting, **Veh 9919 et seq.**
  Suspension or revocation, **Veh 9874**
  Termination upon abandonment, of undocumented vessel, **Veh 9864**
  Transfer of title or interest, undocumented vessels, **Veh 9900 et seq.**
  Transfer to dealer, **Veh 9856**

Charitable corporations, fee exemption, **Veh 9870**

Containers, motor carriers, weights, **Veh 35580, 35581**

Crimes and offenses,
  Certificates of number or ownership, nondelivery on transfer of title, **Veh 9910**
  Numbering and registration, **Veh 9875, 40000.8**
  Registration and numbering, **Veh 9875, 40000.8**
  Stolen vessels, reports, **Veh 10550 et seq.**
  Unidentified vessels, **Veh 40000.8**

Dealers,
  Notice of sale, **Veh 9912**
  Transfers, **Veh 9856**

Definitions, registration and transfer of vessels, **Veh 9840**

Delinquent taxes, undocumented vessels, title or interest transfer prerequisite, **Veh 9900**

Destruction, undocumented vessel, termination of certificates of number and ownership, **Veh 9864**

SHIPS AND SHIPPING—Cont'd

Dismantling, undocumented vessels, termination of certificates of number and ownership, **Veh 9864**

Display,
  Stickers, **Veh 9853.4**
  Vessel number, **Veh 9866**

Embezzlement of vessel, reporting, **Veh 10553, 10554**

Exemptions,
  Fees, nonprofit corporations, **Veh 9870**
  Numbering or registration, **Veh 9873**

Federal numbering system, conformity with, **Veh 9857**

Federal registration, **Veh 9854**

Fees,
  Additional fees, certificates of number, **Veh 9853, 9853.6**
  Certificates of number, **Veh 9853, 9853.6**
  Change of ownership, **Veh 9855**
  Disposition, **Veh 9863, 9868**
  Duplicate of certificates, **Veh 9867**
  Exemption, nonprofit corporations, **Veh 9870**
  Nonpayment, **Veh 9874**
  Quagga mussels, infestation prevention fee, registration, **Veh 9853, 9860**
  Renewal, certificate of number, **Veh 9860**
    Late renewal, **Veh 9862**
  State, preferred claim to, **Veh 9859**
  Transfer of title or interest, **Veh 9901**
  Transfers to dealer, **Veh 9856**
  Zebra mussels, infestation prevention fee, registration, **Veh 9853, 9860**

Fines and penalties,
  Fractional parts of dollar, **Veh 9862.5**
  Numbering and registration, **Veh 9875**

Foreign countries. Foreign ships, generally, post

Foreign ships,
  Application for number, **Veh 9854**
  Certificates of number, fees, **Veh 9853, 9853.6**
  Number or registration, exemption, **Veh 9873**

Fraud,
  Certificates or registration, **Veh 9874**
  Theft reports, **Veh 10552**

Hearings, altered identification numbers, impoundment, **Veh 9872.1**

Impoundment, altered identification numbers, **Veh 9872.1**

Infractions, registration and numbering violations, **Veh 9875**

Inspection and inspectors, identification, **Veh 9845**

Instruction, undocumented vessels, notice to assessor, **Veh 9869**

Intermodal containers, motor carriers, weights, **Veh 35580, 35581**

Investigations and investigators, identification, **Veh 9845**

SHIPS AND SHIPPING—Cont'd

Involuntary transfer of title or interest, **Veh 9915**
  Lost certificate, replacement on transfer of title, **Veh 9917**
  Nondelivery on transfer of title, **Veh 9910**
  Renewal, **Veh 9862**
  Suspension or revocation, **Veh 9874**
  Temporary certificate,
    Agent for issuance, **Veh 9858, 9859**
    Dealer, **Veh 9856**
    Suspension, cancellation or revocation, **Veh 9874**
  Transfer to dealer, **Veh 9856**
  Undocumented vessel,
    Termination upon abandonment, **Veh 9864**
    Transfer of title or interest, **Veh 9900 et seq.**

Junking, undocumented vessel, termination of certificates of number and ownership, **Veh 9864**

Leases, certificates of number, **Veh 9853.3**

Legal owner, definitions, registration and transfer, **Veh 9840**

Lifeboats, number or registration, **Veh 9873**

Noise Pollution, generally, this index

Nonprofit corporations, fee exemption, **Veh 9870**

Notice,
  Abandoned vessels, undocumented vessels, **Veh 9864**
  Altered identification numbers, **Veh 9872.1**
  Assessor, change of ownership, **Veh 9856**

Ocean marine terminals, intermodal roadability inspection program, **Veh 34505.9**

Offenses. Crimes and offenses, generally, ante

Owners and ownership,
  Beneficiary form, **Veh 9852.7, 9916.5, 9916.7**
  Certificates of ownership, generally, ante
  Definitions, registration and transfer, **Veh 9840**
  Involuntary transfer of title or interest, generally, ante

Paddle boats, number or registration, **Veh 9873**

Peace Officers, this index

Possession, altered identification numbers, **Veh 9872.1**

Quagga mussels, infestation prevention fee, registration, **Veh 9853, 9860**

Records and recordation, stolen or embezzled vessel, **Veh 10554**

Registered owner, definitions, registration and transfer, **Veh 9840**

Registration, **Veh 9840 et seq.**
  Crimes and offenses, **Veh 9875, 40000.8**
  Exemptions, **Veh 9873**

SHIPS AND SHIPPING—Cont'd

Registration—Cont'd

Hull identification numbers, registration renewal, **Veh 9871.5**

Time for waiting, **Veh 1669**

Transfer, withholding, failure to pay use tax, **Veh 9928**

Reports, stolen vessels, **Veh 10550 et seq.**

Revocation or suspension, certificates of registration, **Veh 9874**

Sales,

Altered identification numbers, **Veh 9872.1**

Notice, **Veh 9912**

Undocumented vessels, **Veh 9900 et seq.**

Sales and Use Taxes, this index

Security interest,

Perfecting, **Veh 9919 et seq.**

Satisfaction, **Veh 9913, 9914**

State of principal use, definitions, registration and transfer, **Veh 9840**

Stickers, **Veh 9853.4**

Suspension, cancellation or revocation, **Veh 9874**

Tax assessors, registration information, **Veh 9869**

Theft, reports, **Veh 10550 et seq.**

Title to property,

Certificates of ownership, generally, ante

Involuntary transfer of title or interest, generally, ante

Registration and transfer, **Veh 9840 et seq.**

Transfer of title or interest, generally, post

Toll ferries. Ferries, this index

Transfer of title or interest, **Veh 9840 et seq., 9900 et seq.**

Bond or undertaking, **Veh 9923, 9924**

Undocumented vessels, **Veh 9900 et seq.**

Withholding, failure to pay use tax, **Veh 9928**

Undocumented vessels,

Definitions, registration and transfer, **Veh 9840**

Numbering, **Veh 9850, 9854 et seq.**

United States, this index

Use, definitions, registration and transfer, **Veh 9840**

Waters of fifth state, definitions, registration and transfer, **Veh 9840**

Wrecks and wrecked property, undocumented vessel, termination of certificates of number and ownership, **Veh 9864**

Zebra mussels, infestation prevention fee, registration, **Veh 9853, 9860**

SHORT TITLES

Popular Name Laws, generally, this index

SHOTGUNS

Weapons, generally, this index

SHOVELS

Motor carriers, equipment, length of booms or masts, **Veh 35407**

Motor vehicles,

Support of boom or mast, brakes, exemption, **Veh 26302**

Tow truck equipment, **Veh 27700**

SHREDDING FACILITIES

Motor vehicles, inspection, stolen vehicles, **Veh 2805**

SIDE LIGHTING EQUIPMENT

Motor vehicles, **Veh 25100 et seq.**

SIDE MARKER LIGHTS

Definitions, motor vehicles, **Veh 375**

SIDE REFLEX REFLECTORS

Motorized bicycles, **Veh 24015**

SIDEWALKS

Bicycles,

Lights and lighting, **Veh 21201**

Local regulations, **Veh 21100**

Definitions, **Veh 555**

Electric carts, local regulation, **Veh 21114.5, 22500**

Electric personal assistive mobility devices, **Veh 21280 et seq.**

Handicapped Persons, this index

Motorized scooters, **Veh 21235**

Pocket bikes, **Veh 21720**

Motorized skateboards, **Veh 21968**

Personal assistive mobility devices, **Veh 21280 et seq.**

Pocket bikes, **Veh 21720**

Roller skating, local regulation, **Veh 21969**

Skateboards,

Motorized skateboards, **Veh 21968**

Traffic rules and regulations, **Veh 21967**

Traffic Rules and Regulations, this index

SIGHT

Eyes and Eyesight, generally, this index

SIGNALS

Signs and Signals, generally, this index

SIGNATURES

Drivers licenses, **Veh 12811, 12950**

Electronic signatures,

Drivers licenses, **Veh 12950, 12950.5**

Motor vehicles, documents, electronic transmissions, **Veh 1801.1**

Facsimiles, motor vehicles, licenses and permits, **Veh 12950**

Motor Vehicles, this index

Ocean marine terminals, intermodal roadability inspection program, **Veh 34505.9**

SIGNS AND SIGNALS

Ambulances, demonstrators using warning lamps and sirens, **Veh 25806**

Automobile dismantlers tow vehicles, **Veh 27907**

Buses, this index

SIGNS AND SIGNALS—Cont'd

Disabled vehicles, warning signals and devices, **Veh 25300 et seq.**

Emergency vehicles, privately owned ambulances, **Veh 2416**

Fire department, vehicles, display, **Veh 27905**

Fire trucks, demonstrators using warnings lamps and sirens, **Veh 25806**

Freeways, this index

Ice cream trucks, street vending, **Veh 22456**

Illuminated signs. Buses, this index

Lessor retailers, motor vehicle sales, **Veh 11609**

Mobilehomes and Mobilehome Parks, this index

Motor Carriers, this index

Outdoor Advertising, generally, this index

Privately owned ambulances, emergency vehicles, **Veh 2416**

Repossessors and repossession, tow vehicles, **Veh 27907**

School buses, **Veh 27906**

Youth buses, **Veh 27906.5**

Taxicabs, **Veh 27908**

Tow trucks, display, **Veh 27907**

Traffic Signs and Signals, generally, this index

Vanpooling, **Veh 34509**

Vending, streets and alleys, ice cream trucks, **Veh 22456**

Youth buses, **Veh 27906.5**

SIMULATION

Checks, vehicle sales, advertisements, **Veh 11713.1**

SINGLE FAMILY DWELLINGS

Housing, generally, this index

SINGLE FAMILY RESIDENTIAL HOUSING

Housing, generally, this index

SIRENS

Ambulances, demonstrators, **Veh 25806**

Emergency vehicles, **Veh 27000 et seq.**

Exemption from traffic laws, **Veh 21055**

Fire trucks, demonstrators, **Veh 25806**

Off highway vehicles, **Veh 38375**

Police and traffic officer escorts, **Veh 21057**

Traffic Rules and Regulations, this index

SISTER STATES

Foreign States, generally, this index

SIZE

Agricultural machinery and equipment, **Veh 36600 et seq.**

Commercial vehicles, inspection, **Veh 2813**

Length, generally, this index

Traffic Rules and Regulations, this index

SKATEBOARDS

Helmets, children and minors, **Veh 21212**

Motorized skateboards, **Veh 21968**

Rules and regulations, **Veh 21113**

SKATEBOARDS—Cont'd
Traffic rules and regulations, **Veh 21967, 21968**

SKIING
Buses, width, equipment carrying devices, **Veh 35106**
Crossing roadways, **Veh 21959**
Motor vehicles pulling skiers, **Veh 21712**
Traffic rules and regulations, crossing state highways, **Veh 21959**

SKIP LOADERS
Special highway construction equipment, definitions, **Veh 565**

SKY ROCKETS
Fireworks, generally, this index

SLIDES
Photography and Pictures, generally, this index

SLINGSHOTS
Weapons, generally, this index

SLOW MOVING VEHICLES
Traffic Rules and Regulations, this index
Traffic Signs and Signals, this index

SMALL CLAIMS COURTS
Air pollution, motor vehicles, smog impact fees, foreign states, **Veh 1673.4**
Judgments and decrees,
  Multiple defendants, unsatisfied judgments, drivers licenses, suspension, **Veh 16370.5**
  Operators licenses, suspension, **Veh 16370.5**
  Unsatisfied, motor vehicle accidents, operators licenses, suspension, **Veh 16370.5**
Motor vehicles,
  Accidents,
    Judgments and decrees, operators licenses, suspension, **Veh 16370.5**
    Notice, unsatisfied judgments, drivers license suspension, **Veh 16370.5**
  Registration, smog impact fees, foreign states, **Veh 1673.4**
  Satisfaction of judgments, unsatisfied judgments, notice, suspension of operating privilege, **Veh 16370.5**
  Smog impact fees, motor vehicles, foreign states, **Veh 1673.4**

SMELLS
Air Pollution, generally, this index

SMOG
Air Pollution, generally, this index

SMOG INDEX
Air Pollution, this index

SMOKE
Air Pollution, generally, this index
Highways, closing, menace to public health or safety, **Veh 2812**

SMOKE—Cont'd
Motor vehicles, operation to prevent excessive escape, **Veh 27153**
School buses, additional lights, reduced visibility, **Veh 25102.5**

SMOKING
Motor Carriers, this index
Motor Vehicles, this index
Youth bus operators, **Veh 12523**

SNOW
Ice and Snow, generally, this index

SNOW TIRES
Motor Vehicles, this index

SNOWMOBILES
Application of law, **Veh 38000 et seq.**
Careless or negligent operation, **Veh 23128**
Certificate of identification, fees, **Veh 38225**
Dealers,
  License, **Veh 11701**
    Posting, **Veh 11709**
  Special plates, **Veh 11701**
Definitions, **Veh 557**
Display, identification plates, **Veh 38170**
Distributors, license and special plates, **Veh 11701**
Fees, identification plates, **Veh 38225**
Fish and Game, this index
Highways, operation, **Veh 23128**
Identification plate,
  Display, **Veh 38170**
  Fees, **Veh 38225**
Licenses, dealers, manufacturers, **Veh 11701**
Manufacturers, license and special plates, **Veh 11701**
Negligent operation, **Veh 23128**
Noise limits, **Veh 27203**
Off highway motor vehicles, registration, **Veh 38012**
Place of business, regulations, **Veh 11709**
Salesmen, certificate and license, posting, **Veh 11709**
Special license plates, dealers, manufacturers, **Veh 11701**
Transporters, license and special plates, **Veh 11701**
Unlawful operation, **Veh 23128**

SOBRIETY CHECKPOINTS
Generally, **Veh 2814.2**

SOCIAL MEDIA
Traffic rules and regulations, infractions, **Veh 23123.5**

SOCIAL SECURITY
Numbers and numbering,
  Drivers licenses, **Veh 12800, 12801**
  Motor vehicles department, application forms, **Veh 1653.5**

SOCIAL SERVICES
Social Security, generally, this index

SOCIAL SERVICES—Cont'd
Social Workers, generally, this index

SOCIAL WORKERS
Address, confidential or privileged information, **Veh 1808.4**
Confidential or privileged information, address, **Veh 1808.4**
Mentally ill persons, address, confidential or privileged information, **Veh 1808.4**

SOCIETIES
Associations and Societies, generally, this index

SOIL
Dirt, generally, this index

SOLDIERS, SAILORS AND MARINES
Military Forces, generally, this index
Veterans, generally, this index

SOLE CORPORATIONS
Religious Organizations and Societies, generally, this index

SOLICITATION
Roadside rest areas, **Veh 22520.5**

SOLICITOR GENERAL
Attorney General, generally, this index

SOLID TIRES
Definitions, **Veh 560**

SOLID WASTE
Alarms, backup alarms, garbage trucks, **Veh 27000**
  Fines and penalties, **Veh 42001.20**
Backup devices or alarms, garbage trucks, **Veh 27000**
  Fines and penalties, **Veh 42001.20**
Bail,
  Forfeitures,
    Highways and roads, **Veh 40512**
    Second and subsequent offenses, **Veh 40512.5**
  Second and subsequent offenses, **Veh 40512.5**
Collection, local agencies, rules and regulations, deposit in streets, **Veh 21100**
Depositing in streets, rules and regulations, **Veh 21100**
Fines and penalties, **Veh 42001.7**
  Motor carriers, backup devices or alarms, **Veh 42001.20**
  Overweight vehicles, local agencies, **Veh 42032**
Fires and fire protection, **Veh 23111**
Flashing lights, garbage trucks, **Veh 25280**
Garbage trucks. Motor carriers, generally, post
Hazardous Substances and Waste, generally, this index
Highways and Roads, this index
Junk and Junk Dealers, generally, this index
License plates, garbage trucks, **Veh 5201**
Lights, garbage trucks, **Veh 25280**

SOLID WASTE—Cont'd

Local agencies,
Fines and penalties, overweight vehicles, **Veh 42032**
Overweight vehicles, fines and penalties, **Veh 42032**
Rules and regulations, deposit in streets, **Veh 21100**
Weight limitations, garbage trucks, fines and penalties, **Veh 42032**
Motor carriers,
Backup devices or alarms, **Veh 27000**
Fines and penalties, **Veh 42001.20**
Covering loads, **Veh 23115**
Fines and penalties, backup devices or alarms, **Veh 42001.20**
Flashing lights, **Veh 25280**
License plates, **Veh 5201**
Photography and pictures, **Veh 27000**
Fines and penalties, **Veh 42001.20**
Video display devices, **Veh 27000**
Fines and penalties, **Veh 42001.20**
Motor Vehicles, this index
Off highway vehicles, **Veh 38319 et seq.**
Overweight vehicles, local governments, fines and penalties, **Veh 42032**
Penalties. Fines and penalties, generally, ante
Photography and pictures, motor carriers, **Veh 27000**
Fines and penalties, **Veh 42001.20**
Probation, **Veh 42001.7**
Refuse trucks. Motor carriers, generally, ante
Second and subsequent offenses, **Veh 42001.7**
Forfeitures, **Veh 40512.5**
Streets and alleys, local agencies, rules and regulations, deposits, **Veh 21100**
Trucks. Motor carriers, generally, ante
Video display devices, motor carriers, **Veh 27000**
Fines and penalties, **Veh 42001.20**
Weight limitations, local agency vehicles, fines and penalties, **Veh 42032**

SOOT
Air Pollution, generally, this index

SOUND RECORDINGS
Motor vehicles, reckless driving, following too closely, interference, **Veh 40008**
Traffic rules and regulations, reckless driving, following too closely, interference, **Veh 40008**

SOUTH COAST AIR QUALITY MANAGEMENT DISTRICT
Air Pollution, this index

SPANISH LANGUAGE
Vehicle code publication, **Veh 1656**

SPARKLERS
Fireworks, generally, this index

SPECIAL EDUCATION
Mentally Retarded and Developmentally Disabled Persons, generally, this index

SPECIAL EQUIPMENT REGISTRATION AND LICENSE FEE EXEMPTION ACT
Generally, **Veh 4010**

SPECIAL EVENTS
Traffic rules and regulations, temporary closing of streets, **Veh 21101**

SPECIAL FIRE PROTECTION ZONES
Fires and Fire Protection, generally, this index

SPECIAL MOBILE EQUIPMENT
Definitions, **Veh 575**
Motor Vehicles, this index

SPECIAL SITUATION FARM PRODUCTS
Definitions, motor carriers, hours of service, **Veh 34501.2**

SPECIALLY CONSTRUCTED VEHICLES
Motor Vehicles, this index

SPEED
Golf carts, **Veh 21115**
Traffic Rules and Regulations, this index
Traffic Signs and Signals, this index

SPEED SWINGS
Special highway construction equipment, definitions, **Veh 565**

SPEED TRAPS
Generally, **Veh 40801 et seq.**
Definitions, **Veh 40802**

SPILLS
Hazardous Substances and Waste, this index

SPIRITOUS LIQUORS
Alcoholic Beverages, generally, this index

SPLASH APRONS
Motor vehicles, mudguards, **Veh 27600**

SPOT LAMPS
Motor vehicles, lighting equipment, **Veh 24404**

SPOTTED KNAPWEED
Weeds, generally, this index

SPOUSE
Marriage, generally, this index

SPUR TRACKS
Railroads, this index

STALKING
Motor vehicles,
License plates, new plates, **Veh 4467**
Registration or drivers license, suppression, **Veh 1808.21**

STANDARDS
Bicycle helmets, **Veh 21212**

STANDARDS—Cont'd

Driving schools, licenses, **Veh 11113.5**
Energy absorption systems, motor vehicles, federal standards, **Veh 34715**
Motor Vehicles, this index
Peace Officers, this index
Safety devices, motor vehicles, adoption and enforcement, **Veh 26103**
Tires, **Veh 27500**
Traffic signs and signals, specifications, **Veh 21400**

STANDING VEHICLES
Generally, **Veh 22500 et seq.**
Traffic Rules and Regulations, this index

STATE
Agencies. Public Agencies, generally, this index
Buildings. Public Buildings and Works, generally, this index
Civil defense. War and Civil Defense, generally, this index
Definitions, driving under the influence, nonresidents, **Veh 13353.5**
Elections, generally, this index
Emergency vehicles,
Definitions, **Veh 165**
Peace officers, **Veh 165**
Employees. State Officers and Employees, generally, this index
Foreign States, generally, this index
Forests and Forestry, this index
Funds. State Treasury, generally, this index
Highways and Roads, this index
Lands. Public Lands, generally, this index
Legislature, generally, this index
Motor vehicle insurance,
Accident reports, **Veh 16000 et seq.**
Financial responsibility, **Veh 16021**
Motor vehicles,
Emergency vehicles, **Veh 165**
Fees, exemptions, **Veh 9101, 9103**
Financial responsibility, exemption, **Veh 16051**
Levee maintenance vehicles, warning lights, **Veh 25266**
Lights and lighting, flashing or colored lights, **Veh 25266**
Off highway vehicles subject to identification, **Veh 38000 et seq.**
Pools, special license plates, **Veh 5002**
Registration, **Veh 4155**
Special license plates, **Veh 5001**
Tort liability, **Veh 17000 et seq.**
National defense. War and Civil Defense, generally, this index
Officers and employees. State Officers and Employees, generally, this index
Parks, this index
Personnel. State Officers and Employees, generally, this index
Property. Public Lands, generally, this index
Public Buildings and Works, generally, this index

STATE—Cont'd
Public Lands, generally, this index
Public Policy, generally, this index
Real estate. Public Lands, generally, this index
Right of Way, generally, this index
Rules and regulations. Motor vehicles, generally, ante
Taxation, generally, this index
Torts, motor vehicles, **Veh 17000 et seq.**
Traffic laws, applicability to state vehicles, **Veh 21052**
War and Civil Defense, generally, this index

STATE AGENCIES
Administrative Law and Procedure, generally, this index
Buildings. Public Buildings and Works, generally, this index
Definitions, motor vehicles, license plates, special plates, **Veh 5151**
Electric carts, sidewalk use, local regulation, **Veh 21114.5**
Emergencies, vehicle use, size and weight limitation exemption, **Veh 35002**
Emergency vehicles, peace officers, **Veh 165**
Employees. State Officers and Employees, generally, this index
Highway patrol, protective services, costs, **Veh 2428**
Motor vehicles,
    Emergency vehicles, **Veh 165**
    Size and weight limitation exceptions, **Veh 35002**
    License plates, special plates, **Veh 5151 et seq.**
Motorcycles, license plates, special plates, **Veh 5151 et seq.**
Officers and employees. State Officers and Employees, generally, this index
Protective services, highway patrol, costs, **Veh 2428**
Sidewalks, electric carts, local regulations, **Veh 21114.5**
State Officers and Employees, generally, this index

STATE BUILDINGS AND GROUNDS
Public Buildings and Works, generally, this index

STATE CANDIDATES
Elections, generally, this index

STATE COLLEGES
Colleges and Universities, generally, this index

STATE COMMITTEES
Committees, generally, this index

STATE DEPARTMENTS
Administrative Law and Procedure, generally, this index
Buildings. Public Buildings and Works, generally, this index

STATE DEPARTMENTS—Cont'd
Corrections and Rehabilitation Department, generally, this index
Emergency vehicles, peace officers, **Veh 165**
Employees. State Officers and Employees, generally, this index
Highway patrol department. Highway Patrol, generally, this index
Juvenile Facilities Division, generally, this index
Motor vehicles, license plates, special plates, **Veh 5151 et seq.**
Motor Vehicles Department, generally, this index
Officers and employees. State Officers and Employees, generally, this index
Public Buildings and Works, generally, this index
State Fire Marshal, generally, this index
Transportation Department, generally, this index

STATE EMPLOYEES
State Officers and Employees, generally, this index

STATE FIRE MARSHAL
Explosives, generally, this index
Fire Extinguishers, generally, this index
Fireworks, generally, this index
Flammable liquids, transportation regulation, **Veh 34001 et seq.**
Motor vehicles, signs, **Veh 27905**
Signs, display, **Veh 27905**

STATE FOREST
Forests and Forestry, this index

STATE FUNDS
State Treasury, generally, this index

STATE HIGHWAY ACCOUNT
Highways and Roads, this index

STATE HIGHWAY PATROL
Highway Patrol, generally, this index

STATE HIGHWAY ROUTE 1
Malibu, traffic rules and regulations, **Veh 2400.6**

STATE HIGHWAYS
Highways and Roads, this index

STATE HOUSING LAW
Housing, generally, this index

STATE INSTITUTIONS
Traffic control, animal or vehicle, stopping, standing, paths, grounds or driveways, **Veh 21113**

STATE LANDS
Public Lands, generally, this index

STATE OF PRINCIPAL USE
Definitions, registration and transfer of vessel, **Veh 9840**

STATE OFFICERS AND EMPLOYEES
Addresses, home addresses, confidentiality, **Veh 1808.4**
Attorney General, generally, this index
Bribery and Corruption, generally, this index
Corruption. Bribery and Corruption, generally, this index
Crimes and offenses. Bribery and Corruption, generally, this index
Electric carts, sidewalk use, local regulation, **Veh 21114.5**
Forestry. Forests and Forestry, generally, this index
Highway Patrol, generally, this index
Home addresses, confidentiality, **Veh 1808.4**
Impounding, motor vehicles, authority, **Veh 22651**
Juvenile Facilities Division, generally, this index
Licensing registration examiners, home addresses, confidentiality, **Veh 1808.4**
Motor carrier specialist 1, home addresses, confidentiality, **Veh 1808.4**
Motor vehicles,
    Impounding, authority, **Veh 22651**
    Levee maintenance, warning lights, **Veh 25266**
    License plates, special plates, **Veh 5151 et seq.**
    Street measurement work, warning lights, **Veh 25266**
Museum security officers, home addresses, confidentiality, **Veh 1808.4**
Police. State Police, generally, this index
Protective services, highway patrol, costs, **Veh 2428**
Public Agencies, generally, this index
Social Security, generally, this index
State Fire Marshal, generally, this index
State Police, generally, this index

STATE PARKS
Parks, this index

STATE PATROL
Highway Patrol, generally, this index

STATE POLICE
Abandoned vehicles, removal, **Veh 22651**
    Private property after accident, **Veh 22653**
Blue warning lights, **Veh 25258**
Highway Patrol, generally, this index
Motor vehicles,
    Abandoned or unclaimed property, removal, **Veh 22669**
    Removal of vehicles from private property after accident, **Veh 22653**
Removal of abandoned vehicles from private property after accidents, **Veh 22653**

STATE POLICY
Public Policy, generally, this index

STATE

STATE PRISONS
Correctional Institutions, generally, this index

STATE PROPERTY
Public Lands, generally, this index

STATE PUBLIC DEFENDER
Address, confidentiality, **Veh 1808.4**
Confidential and privileged information, addresses, **Veh 1808.4**

STATE TREASURER
Unclaimed property. Abandoned or Unclaimed Property, generally, this index

STATE TREASURY
Abandoned vehicle trust fund, **Veh 9250.7**
Disposition of funds, **Veh 22668**
Accounts and accounting,
  Motor vehicle account, deposits, **Veh 9255.2**
  Motor vehicle license fee account. Transportation fund, post
Antiterrorism fund, **Veh 5066**
Bicycle license fund, deposit of license fees, **Veh 39001**
Donate life California trust subaccount, **Veh 12811**
Firefighters memorial fund, deposits, **Veh 5101.2**
General fund, loans, motor vehicle account, **Veh 42272**
Gold Star Family license plate account, **Veh 5157**
Highway patrol, protective services fund, **Veh 2428**
Loans, motor vehicle account, general fund, **Veh 42272**
Memorial scholarship fund, September 11, 2001, **Veh 5066**
Motor vehicle account. Transportation fund, post
Motor vehicle license fee account. Transportation fund, post
Motorcyclist safety fund, **Veh 2934**
Protective services fund, highway patrol, **Veh 2428**
Specialized license plate fund, **Veh 5157**
State transportation fund. Transportation fund, generally, post
Transportation fund,
  Donate life California trust subaccount, **Veh 12811**
  Motor vehicle account, **Veh 3016, 42233, 42270 et seq.**
    Automobile theft prevention, **Veh 10901**
    Deposits, **Veh 9255.2, 42270**
    Donate life California trust subaccount, **Veh 12811**
    Driver training, expenditure of funds, **Veh 42277**
    Duties, **Veh 42270**
    Hazardous materials transportation license fees, deposits, **Veh 32003**

STATE TREASURY—Cont'd
Transportation fund—Cont'd
  Motor vehicle account—Cont'd
    Highway patrol, motor vehicle registration and renewal fees, **Veh 9250.9**
    Identification fees, off highway motor vehicles, **Veh 38225.4**
      Adjustments, **Veh 1678**
    Loans, general fund, **Veh 42272**
    Motor vehicles department, **Veh 1685**
    Off highway motor vehicles, identification fees, **Veh 38225.4**
      Adjustments, **Veh 1678**
    Proceeds from sale of vehicle code copies, **Veh 1656**
    Refund, fees and penalties, **Veh 42233**
    Reports, **Veh 42276**
    Transfer of funds, **Veh 42271, 42273, 42275**
    Unclaimed security deposits, **Veh 16027**
    Youth bus inspection fees, **Veh 2807.3**
  Motor vehicle license fee account, deposits, **Veh 42270**
Transportation tax fund. Transportation fund, generally, ante

STATE UNIVERSITY
California State University. Colleges and Universities, this index

STATEMENTS
Advisory statements, driving under the influence, vehicular homicide, **Veh 23593**
Driving under the influence, vehicular homicide, advisory statements, **Veh 23593**
Homicide, driving under the influence, advisory statements, **Veh 23593**
Traffic rules and regulations, driving under the influence, advisory statements, **Veh 23593**
Vehicular homicide, advisory statements, **Veh 23593**

STATEWIDE VEHICLE THEFT INVESTIGATION AND APPREHENSION COORDINATOR
Designation, **Veh 2413**

STATION WAGONS
Motor Vehicles, this index

STATIONS AND DEPOTS
Firefighters and Fire Departments, this index
Highway patrol, substations, establishment, **Veh 2404**

STATUTE OF LIMITATIONS
Limitation of Actions, generally, this index

STATUTES
Popular Name Laws, generally, this index

STAY OF PROCEEDINGS
Supersedeas or Stay, generally, this index

STEALING
Theft, generally, this index

STEAMBOATS AND STEAMSHIPS
Ships and Shipping, generally, this index

STEEL MILLS
Purchasing vehicles subject to registration, crimes and offenses, **Veh 40000.5**

STEVE AMBRIZ ACT
Generally, **Veh 13385**

STICKERS
Boats and vessels, fraud, **Veh 9874**
Motor Vehicles, this index
Pocket bikes, warnings, **Veh 9955**

STIPENDS
Compensation and Salaries, generally, this index

STIPULATIONS
Motor Vehicles, this index

STOCK
Animals, generally, this index

STOCK CORPORATIONS
Corporations, generally, this index

STOLEN PROPERTY
Theft, generally, this index

STOP LIGHTS
Definitions, motor vehicles, **Veh 375**

STOP SIGNS
Traffic Signs and Signals, this index

STOPPING
School Buses, this index
Traffic Rules and Regulations, this index

STORAGE
Agricultural machinery and equipment, impounding, expenses and expenditures, **Veh 34506.5**
Charges, motor vehicle seized for altered identification or manufacturing number, **Veh 10751**
Highway patrol, charges, abandoned or unclaimed property, **Veh 2414**
Mobilehomes and Mobilehome Parks, this index
Motor Vehicles, this index
Rental of private building as garage, **Veh 10654**
Reports, bullet marks, vehicle showing, **Veh 10653**
Taxicabs, impounding, **Veh 21100.4**
Traffic rules and regulations, removal of parked or standing vehicles, **Veh 22650 et seq.**
Wreckers,
  Failure, refusal or neglect to keep, **Veh 10655**
  Garage, repair shop or trailer park keeper, **Veh 10654**

STORES
Private roads, traffic control, ordinance, **Veh 21107.6**
Traffic rules and regulations, private roads, local regulation, **Veh 21107.6**

STORMS
Damages. Highways and Roads, this index

STP
Drugs and Medicine, generally, this index

STREET RAILWAYS
Advertising, lighted displays signs, **Veh 25400**
Application, traffic rules and regulations, trolley coaches, **Veh 21051**
Bicycles,
　Hitching rides on streetcars, **Veh 21203**
　Transportation, length, **Veh 35400**
Crossings. Railroad Crossings, generally, this index
Definitions, **Veh 650**
Display signs, lights, **Veh 25400**
Eyeshades, windshield, **Veh 26711**
Folding devices, bicycles, transportation, length, **Veh 35400**
Grade crossings. Railroad Crossings, generally, this index
Internally illuminated signs, **Veh 25400**
Length, **Veh 35400**
Lights and lighting, display signs, **Veh 25400**
Mirrors, equipment, **Veh 26709**
Motor vehicles, removal from right of way, **Veh 22656**
Peace officers, motor vehicle removal, **Veh 22656**
Railroad Crossings, generally, this index
Removal and relocation, motor vehicles from right of way, **Veh 22656**
Right of way, motor vehicles, removal, **Veh 22656**
Separation of grade. Railroad Crossings, generally, this index
Signs and signals, lighted display signs, **Veh 25400**
Traffic Rules and Regulations, this index
Warning approach signs, **Veh 21362**

STREET ROD VEHICLES
Definitions, **Veh 5051**

STREETCARS
Street Railways, generally, this index

STREETS AND ALLEYS
Access, restriction, **Veh 21101.6**
Accident reports, **Veh 20000 et seq.**
Barriers, local ordinances or resolutions, **Veh 21102.1**
Bicycles, exits, driver warnings, **Veh 21356.5**
Boundary line streets,
　Local authorities, traffic rules and regulations, **Veh 21105**
　Speed limits, **Veh 22359**

STREETS AND ALLEYS—Cont'd
Business districts, definitions, **Veh 235, 240**
Celebrations, local street closing, **Veh 21101**
Closing,
　Local regulations, **Veh 21101 et seq.**
　School grounds, protection, **Veh 21102**
Control devices, local ordinances or resolutions, **Veh 21102.1**
Crossing. Railroad Crossings, generally, this index
Debris, removal after accident or damage, **Veh 17300 et seq.**
Defective streets, weight limits, **Veh 35717**
Definitions, **Veh 590, 591**
　Motor vehicles, **Veh 110**
Detours, expenses of providing detours for damaged highway, **Veh 17300 et seq.**
Driver warnings, exits, pedestrians and bicyclists, **Veh 21356.5**
Electric personal assistive mobility devices, **Veh 21280 et seq.**
Exits, driver warnings, pedestrians and bicyclists, **Veh 21356.5**
Freeways, generally, this index
Gates,
　Local ordinances or resolutions, **Veh 21102.1**
　Placement, selective denial of access, **Veh 21101.6**
Grade crossings. Railroad Crossings, generally, this index
Ice and Snow, generally, this index
Ice cream trucks, vending, **Veh 22456**
Limited access, **Veh 21101.6**
Local Agencies, this index
Maps and Plats, generally, this index
Motorized scooters, pocket bikes, **Veh 21720**
Motorized skateboards, **Veh 21968**
Negligence, damages, tort liability, **Veh 17300 et seq.**
Ordinances,
　Gates, barriers, or other control devices, **Veh 21102.1**
　Vending from commercial vehicles on streets, **Veh 22455**
Parades, local street closing, **Veh 21101**
Parking. Traffic Rules and Regulations, this index
Parking Meters, generally, this index
Pedestrians, exits, driver warnings, **Veh 21356.5**
Personal assistive mobility devices, **Veh 21280 et seq.**
Pocket bikes, **Veh 21720**
Railroad Crossings, generally, this index
Raised pavement markers, double lines, **Veh 21460**
Resolutions, gates, barriers, or other control devices, **Veh 21102.1**
Roller skating, local regulation, **Veh 21969**
Safety, **Veh 14607.4 et seq.**
　Costs, **Veh 17300**
Schools and School Districts, this index

STREETS AND ALLEYS—Cont'd
Selective denial of access, placing gates or other devices on streets, **Veh 21101.6**
Separation of grade. Railroad Crossings, generally, this index
Sidewalks, generally, this index
Signs and signals. Traffic Signs and Signals, generally, this index
Skateboards, motorized skateboards, **Veh 21968**
Snow. Ice and Snow, generally, this index
Special events, local street closing, **Veh 21101**
State highways, weight limit decreases, streets using funds for construction, **Veh 35705**
Streetsweeping, watering vehicles, traffic rules, exemption, **Veh 21060**
Superintendent of streets. Weeds, generally, this index
Temporary closing, local authorities, **Veh 21101**
Tort liability, damages, **Veh 17300 et seq.**
Traffic Rules and Regulations, generally, this index
Traffic safety fund, construction, **Veh 42200**
Traffic Signs and Signals, generally, this index
Use restrictions, local agencies, **Veh 9400.7, 9400.8**
Vending,
　Drivers of commercial vehicles, regulations, **Veh 22455**
　Ice cream trucks, **Veh 22456**
Warnings, exits, watching for pedestrians and bicyclists, **Veh 21356.5**
Weeds, generally, this index
Wilfully or negligently damaging, liability, **Veh 17300 et seq.**

STREETSWEEPERS
Parking, photography and pictures, enforcement, **Veh 40245 et seq.**

STRUCTURAL ENGINEERS
Engineers, generally, this index

STRUCTURES
Buildings, generally, this index

STUDDED TIRES
Generally, **Veh 27454**

STUDENTS
Colleges and Universities, generally, this index
Schools and School Districts, generally, this index

STUDIES
Buses, width, ski carrying devices, **Veh 35106**
Drivers license extensions, effects, **Veh 12814.5**
Ignition interlock devices, driving under the influence, **Veh 23575.1**
Motor Vehicles, this index

SUBDIVIDED LANDS
Motor vehicles, photography and pictures, disclosure, enforcement, **Veh 1808.51**
Photography and pictures, motor vehicles, disclosure, enforcement, **Veh 1808.51**

SUBPOENAS
Contempt, generally, this index
Motor Vehicles, this index
Motor vehicles department, process, **Veh 24.5**
Service, motor vehicles department, **Veh 24.5**
Traffic rules and regulations, infractions, **Veh 40901**

SUBROGATION
Motor vehicles,
    Consumer protection, recovery corporation, **Veh 12210**
    Torts, **Veh 17153**

SUBSTANCE ABUSE
Alcoholics and Alcoholism, generally, this index
Drug Addicts, generally, this index

SUBWAYS
Traffic control, local authorities, powers, **Veh 21109**
Traffic rules and regulations, local authorities, **Veh 21109**

SUCCESSION
Boats and boating, title, transfer, **Veh 9852.5**
Driving schools, licenses, **Veh 11105**
Motor vehicles,
    Dealership, **Veh 11713.3**
    Title, transfer, notice, **Veh 5910**

SUDAN GRASS
Weeds, generally, this index

SUFFRAGE
Elections, generally, this index

SUICIDE
Investigation. Coroners, generally, this index

SUITS
Actions and Proceedings, generally, this index

SULEV
Definitions, motor vehicles, air pollution, decals, **Veh 5205.5**

SULPHUR DIOXIDE
Air Pollution, generally, this index

SUMMONS
Process, this index

SUNSCREENING DEVICES
Motor vehicles,
    Specifications and requirements, **Veh 26708.2**
    Use, **Veh 26708**

SUPER ULTRALOW EMISSION VEHICLES
Decals, **Veh 5205.5, 21655.9, 40000.13**
    Forgery, counterfeiting, **Veh 4463**

SUPERHIGHWAYS
Freeways, generally, this index

SUPERIOR COURTS
Contempt, generally, this index
Judgments and Decrees, generally, this index
Marshals, generally, this index
Probate Proceedings, generally, this index
Small Claims Courts, generally, this index
Subpoenas, generally, this index

SUPERSEDEAS OR STAY
Driving under the influence,
    Alcohol education and treatment programs, **Veh 23640**
    Sentence and punishment, **Veh 23600**
Traffic rules and regulations, driving under the influence,
    Alcohol education and treatment programs, **Veh 23640**
    Sentence and punishment, **Veh 23600**

SUPERVISORS
County Supervisors Boards, generally, this index

SUPERVISORS BOARD
County Supervisors Boards, generally, this index

SUPREME COURT
Appeal and Review, generally, this index

SURETY BONDS
Bonds (Officers and Fiduciaries), generally, this index

SURETYSHIP AND GUARANTY
Bonds (Officers and Fiduciaries), generally, this index

SURGEONS
Physicians and Surgeons, generally, this index

SURGICAL CENTER
Medical waste. Hazardous Substances and Waste, this index

SURVEYS AND SURVEYORS
Amber flashing warning lights, land surveyor vehicles, **Veh 25278**
Flashing amber warning lights, land surveyor vehicles, **Veh 25278**
Lights and lighting, land surveyor vehicles, flashing amber warning lights, **Veh 25278**
Motor vehicles, flashing amber warning lights, land surveyor vehicles, **Veh 25278**
Warning lights, flashing amber warning lights, land surveyor vehicles, **Veh 25278**

SURVIVING SPOUSE
Peace Officers, this index

SYMBOLS
Federal safety standards, certification, **Veh 24011**
Motor carriers, identifying symbols, display, **Veh 34507**

TAGS
Boats and boating, engines, **Veh 9853.7**
Licenses and Permits, generally, this index
Ocean marine terminals, intermodal roadability inspection program, **Veh 34505.9**

TAILBOARD OR TAILGATE
Motor carriers, vehicle transporting explosives, **Veh 31614**

TAILGATING
Traffic rules and regulations, **Veh 21703**
    Photography and pictures, sound recordings, crimes and offenses, **Veh 40008**

TAILLAMPS
Definitions, motor vehicles, **Veh 375**
Motorized bicycles, **Veh 24015**

TAIWAN
Motor vehicles, foreign organizations, license plates, **Veh 5006.5**

TAKING
Fish and Game, generally, this index

TAMPERING
Bicycles,
    License indicia or registration forms, crimes and offenses, **Veh 39002**
    Motorized bicycles, **Veh 24016**
Ignition interlock devices, **Veh 23247**
Motor Vehicles, this index
Motorized bicycles, **Veh 24016**

TANK VEHICLES
Definitions, motor vehicle load, **Veh 34003**
Motor Carriers, this index

TANKS
Exemptions, motor vehicle length limitation, **Veh 35414**
Motor vehicles,
    Fuel tank caps, **Veh 27155**
    Length limitation, exemption, **Veh 35414**
Traffic rules and regulations, loads and loading, **Veh 31540**
Water tanks, agricultural vehicles carrying, registration, exemption, **Veh 36101**

TARPAULINS
Explosives, vehicle transporting, **Veh 31614**

TAX ASSESSORS
Boats,
    Notice, change of ownership, **Veh 9856**
    Registration information, **Veh 9869**

TAX COLLECTION
Motor carriers, licenses and permits, delinquent taxes, revocation or suspension, **Veh 34623.1**

TAX COLLECTORS
License plates, regular series, **Veh 5002.7**
Motor vehicles, regular series license plates, **Veh 5002.7**

TAX DELINQUENCY
Boat registration renewals, notice, **Veh 9880**

TAXATION
Business license taxes, municipalities, tow trucks, **Veh 12111**
Cities and counties. Consolidated Cities and Counties, this index
Consolidated Cities and Counties, this index
Fines and penalties,
 Motor Vehicles, this index
 Sales and Use Taxes, this index
Mobilehomes and Mobilehome Parks, this index
Motor carriers, apportionment, foreign states, **Veh 8050 et seq.**
 Federal motor vehicle safety program, **Veh 8100 et seq.**
Motor Vehicles, this index
Sales and Use Taxes, generally, this index
Tow trucks, business license tax, **Veh 12111**
Use taxes. Sales and Use Taxes, generally, this index

TAXICABS
Air pollution, low emission vehicles, **Veh 28113**
Costs, impounding, **Veh 21100.4**
Crimes and offenses, impounding, **Veh 21100.4**
Damages, impounding, **Veh 21100.4**
Defrosters, **Veh 26712**
Financial responsibility, **Veh 16500 et seq.**
 Registration, suspension, **Veh 16503**
Fines and penalties, impounding, **Veh 21100.4**
Foreclosure, impounding, **Veh 21100.4**
Hearings, storage, impounding, **Veh 21100.4**
Impounding, **Veh 21100.4**
Indemnity, impounding, **Veh 21100.4**
Insurance, **Veh 16500 et seq.**
Licenses and permits, impounding, **Veh 21100.4**
Limousines, generally, this index
Notice, impounding, **Veh 21100.4**
Orders of court, searches and seizures, **Veh 21100.4**
Payment, impounding, **Veh 21100.4**
Registration,
 Impounding, release, **Veh 21100.4**
 Prior use, identification, **Veh 4453**
 Service fees, vehicles formerly operated as taxicabs, **Veh 9255.1**

TAXICABS—Cont'd
Registration—Cont'd
 Suspension, financial responsibility, **Veh 16503**
Release, impounding, **Veh 21100.4**
Repossessors and repossession, impounding, **Veh 21100.4**
Searches and seizures, **Veh 21100.4**
Seatbelts, **Veh 27315**
Signs, **Veh 27908**
Storage, impounding, **Veh 21100.4**
Traffic Rules and Regulations, this index
Warrants, searches and seizures, **Veh 21100.4**

TAXING AGENCIES
Taxation, generally, this index

TECHNICIANS
Clinical Laboratories, this index
Emergency Medical Technicians, generally, this index

TECHNOLOGY
Information technologies. Telecommunications, generally, this index

TELECOMMUNICATIONS
Buses, emergencies, **Veh 24018**
Cellular radio telephones. Wireless telecommunications, generally, post
Children and minors, motor vehicles, crimes and offenses, **Veh 23124**
Crimes and offenses. Wireless telecommunications, post
Eight hundred (800) numbers,
 Motor carriers, laborers, trucks transporting, **Veh 2429**
 Motor vehicles, trucks transporting workmen, **Veh 2429**
 Traffic rules and regulations, trucks transporting workmen, **Veh 2429**
Electronic Mail, generally, this index
Fines and penalties. Wireless telecommunications, post
Instant messages, traffic rules and regulations, infractions, **Veh 23123.5**
Mobile telecommunications. Wireless telecommunications, generally, post
Motor Carriers, this index
Motor vehicle insurance, financial responsibility, electronic verification, **Veh 16058.1**
Motor Vehicles, this index
Numbers and numbering. Eight hundred (800) numbers, generally, ante
Police, this index
Sheriffs, this index
Text messages, traffic rules and regulations, infractions, **Veh 23123.5**
Traffic Rules and Regulations, this index
Trucks transporting laborers, eight hundred (800) numbers, **Veh 2429**
Wireless telecommunications,
 Buses, **Veh 24018**
 Children and minors, motor vehicles, crimes and offenses, **Veh 23124**

TELECOMMUNICATIONS—Cont'd
Wireless telecommunications—Cont'd
 Crimes and offenses,
  Motor vehicles, **Veh 23123**
   Children and minors, **Veh 23124**
  Traffic rules and regulations, **Veh 23123**
   Children and minors, **Veh 23124**
   School buses, mass transit, **Veh 23125**
 Fines and penalties, motor vehicles, **Veh 23123**
  Children and minors, **Veh 23124**
 Mass transit, traffic rules and regulations, **Veh 23125**
 Motor Vehicles, this index
 School buses, traffic rules and regulations, **Veh 23125**
 Traffic Rules and Regulations, this index
 Transit systems, traffic rules and regulations, **Veh 23125**

TELEGRAMS
Telecommunications, generally, this index

TELEPHONES
Telecommunications, generally, this index

TELETYPE
Motor vehicles, parking violations, proof of ownership, verification, **Veh 40900**

TELEVISION AND RADIO
Arraignment, this index
Autobrokers, advertisements, **Veh 11713**
Bicycles, **Veh 27400**
Buses, **Veh 24018**
Citizens band radio, special license plates, motor vehicles, **Veh 5020, 5021**
Motor carriers, two way radio, **Veh 31613**
Motor Vehicles, this index

TEMPLES
Religious Organizations and Societies, generally, this index

TENANCY IN COMMON
Motor vehicles,
 Registration, **Veh 4150.5**
 Transfer of title or interest, **Veh 5600.5**

TENT CAMPS
Mobilehomes and Mobilehome Parks, generally, this index

TERMINAL ISLAND FREEWAY
Overweight vehicles, special permits, **Veh 35700.5**

TERMINALS
Buses, this index
Definitions, traffic rules and regulations, length of vehicles or combinations, **Veh 35401.5**
Inspection and inspectors, stolen vehicles, **Veh 2805**
Motor Carriers, this index

TERMINALS

TERMINALS—Cont'd
Ocean marine terminals, intermodal road-ability inspection program, **Veh 34505.9**

TERMINATING HIGHWAY
Definitions, uncontrolled intersections, right of way, **Veh 21800**

TERRORISM
Antiterrorism fund, **Veh 5066**
Funds, antiterrorism fund, **Veh 5066**

TESTIMONY
Evidence, generally, this index

TESTS
Drugs and Medicine, this index
Eyes and Eyesight, this index
Hospitals, this index
Laboratories, generally, this index
Motor Carriers, this index
Motor Vehicles, this index
Traffic Rules and Regulations, this index

TEXT MESSAGES
Telecommunications, this index

THEATERS AND SHOWS
Highway patrol, uniforms, **Veh 2261**

THEFT
Boats and Boating, this index
Embezzlement, generally, this index
Kitchen Grease, this index
Motor carriers,
    Cargo theft interdiction program, fees, **Veh 9400**
    Inspection to prevent larceny, **Veh 2810**
Motor Vehicles, this index
Police, this index
Reports, stolen vessels, **Veh 10550 et seq.**
Ships and Shipping, this index
Trailers, this index

THISTLE
Weeds, generally, this index

THREATS
Motor Vehicles, this index

THREE FEET FOR SAFETY ACT
Generally, **Veh 21760**

THREE WHEELED VEHICLES
Traffic Rules and Regulations, this index

THROUGH HIGHWAYS
Highways and Roads, generally, this index

THUMBPRINTS
Arrest, **Veh 40500, 40504**
Traffic rules and regulations, arrest, **Veh 40303**
    Nonresidents, **Veh 40305, 40305.5, 40500, 40504**

TIMBER AND LUMBER
Axle weight limits of vehicle transporting logs, **Veh 35552**
Christensen Belotti Act, **Veh 35552**

TIMBER AND LUMBER—Cont'd
Dollies. Logging Dollies, generally, this index
Identity and identification, plates, logging vehicles, **Veh 5014 et seq.**
Loads and loading. Traffic Rules and Regulations, this index
Logbooks, driving logs, **Veh 42001.3**
Logging Dollies, generally, this index
Logging trucks, **Veh 35552**
Logging vehicles. Motor carriers, generally, post
Motor carriers,
    Application of law, **Veh 25802**
    Exemptions, registration, **Veh 4018**
    Field loaded unprocessed bulk forest products, weight restrictions, penalties, **Veh 42030**
    Flashing amber warning lights, **Veh 25275**
    Identification plates, **Veh 5014 et seq.**
    Inspection and inspectors, **Veh 2810**
    Length limitations, **Veh 35414**
        Flashing amber warning light, **Veh 25275**
    License plates, **Veh 5011**
        Fees, **Veh 1678, 9261, 9261.1**
    Registration, exemptions, **Veh 4018**
    Speed limits, **Veh 26457**
    Stopping distance requirements, **Veh 26457**
    Weight limits, **Veh 35552**
Motor vehicles, identification cards and plates, time for application, **Veh 5015**
Traffic Rules and Regulations, this index
Transportation, inspection of bills of lading, **Veh 2810**
Vehicles. Motor carriers, generally, ante
Weight, axle weight limits, vehicle transporting logs, **Veh 35552**

TIMBER WOLF
Fish and Game, generally, this index

TIMBERLAND PRODUCTION ZONES
Motor vehicles, irrigation and irrigation districts, machinery and equipment, inspection and inspectors, **Veh 2810.2**

TIME
Agricultural machinery and equipment, safety, crimes and offenses, impounding, **Veh 34506.4**
Boats and boating, registration, time for waiting, **Veh 1669**
Crimes and Offenses, this index
Extension of time. Motor Vehicles, this index
Hazardous Substances and Waste, this index
Highways and Roads, this index
Identification cards, waiting time, **Veh 1669**
Limitation of Actions, generally, this index
Motions, this index
Motor carriers, registration or drivers license, time for waiting, **Veh 1669**

TIME—Cont'd
Motor Vehicle Insurance, this index
Motor Vehicles, this index
Nighttime, generally, this index
Ships and shipping, registration, time for waiting, **Veh 1669**
Traffic Rules and Regulations, this index

TIP BED TRAILERS
Agricultural machinery and equipment, width limits, **Veh 36605**

TIRE TRACTION DEVICES
Generally, **Veh 27459 et seq.**
Motor Vehicles, this index

TIRES
Generally, **Veh 27450 et seq.**
Motor Carriers, this index
Motor Vehicles, this index
Traffic Rules and Regulations, this index

TITLE
Definitions, exported vehicles, inspection and cancellation of titles, **Veh 6161**

TITLE TO PROPERTY
Abandoned or Unclaimed Property, generally, this index
Ambulances, changes, licenses, **Veh 2503**
Armored cars, changes, licenses, **Veh 2503**
Boats and Boating, this index
Chop shops, crimes and offenses, **Veh 10801 et seq.**
Definitions,
    Exported vehicles, inspection and cancellation of titles, **Veh 6161**
    Motor vehicles, **Veh 460**
    Vessels, registration and transfer, **Veh 9840**
Explosives, transportation, changes, licenses, **Veh 2503**
Fleet owner inspection and maintenance stations, changes, licenses, **Veh 2503**
Motor Vehicles, this index
Ships and Shipping, this index
Traffic Rules and Regulations, this index
Unclaimed property. Abandoned or Unclaimed Property, generally, this index

TITLES OF ACTS
Popular Name Laws, generally, this index

TOBACCO AND TOBACCO PRODUCTS
Cigarettes and Cigars, generally, this index

TOBOGGANING
Crossing roadways, **Veh 21959**

TOLL BRIDGE AUTHORITY
Toll roads and bridges. Highways and Roads, this index

TOLL FERRIES
Ferries, this index

TOLL HIGHWAY
Definitions, motor vehicles, **Veh 611**

TOLL ROADS AND BRIDGES
Definitions, motor vehicles, **Veh 611**
Highways and Roads, this index
Traffic Signs and Signals, this index

TORCHES
Motor carriers, warning signals and devices, **Veh 25300**

TORPEDOES
Explosives, generally, this index
Fireworks, generally, this index

TORTS
Children and Minors, this index
Colleges and Universities, this index
Counties, this index
Executors and administrators, motor vehicles, **Veh 17150 et seq.**
Highways and roads, damages, **Veh 17300 et seq.**
Labor and employment, signing drivers license of minor employee, **Veh 17706 et seq.**
Motor carriers, damage to highways or bridges, **Veh 17300 et seq.**
Motor Vehicles, this index
Municipalities, this index
Negligence, generally, this index
Owner as passenger, motor vehicles, **Veh 17158**
Personal Injuries, generally, this index
Persons signing drivers license applications for minors, **Veh 17700 et seq.**
Political subdivisions, motor vehicles, civil liability, **Veh 17000 et seq.**
Schools and School Districts, this index
Streets and alleys, damages, **Veh 17300 et seq.**

TOTAL LOSS SALVAGE VEHICLE
Definitions, **Veh 544**

TOUR BUSES
Buses, this index

TOURISTS
Directions, **Veh 21374**

TOW BARS
Freeways, **Veh 29006**

TOW DOLLIES
Motor Vehicles, this index

TOW TRUCK DRIVER
Definitions,
    Certification, **Veh 2430.1**
    Emergency roadside assistance, **Veh 2436**

TOWED VEHICLE
Definitions, motor carriers, owner operators, **Veh 34624**

TOWING
Agricultural Machinery and Equipment, this index
Motor Carriers, this index
Motor Vehicles, this index

TOWING—Cont'd
Recreational vehicles, safety connections, **Veh 29004.5**

TOWNS
Fire companies. Firefighters and Fire Departments, generally, this index

TOXIC MATERIALS
Hazardous Substances and Waste, generally, this index

TOXIC SUBSTANCES
Hazardous Substances and Waste, generally, this index

TOXIC WASTE
Hazardous Substances and Waste, generally, this index

TOY CANNON
Fireworks, generally, this index

TOY GUNS
Fireworks, generally, this index

TOYS
Bicycles, generally, this index
Fireworks, generally, this index
Motor vehicles towing toy vehicles carrying riders, **Veh 21712**

TRACKS
Railroads, generally, this index
Street Railways, generally, this index

TRACTOR DRAWN EARTH MOVING EQUIPMENT
Special highway construction equipment, definitions, **Veh 565**

TRACTOR DUMP TRAILER COMBINATION
Special highway construction equipment, definitions, **Veh 565**

TRACTORS
Farm tractors. Agricultural Machinery and Equipment, generally, this index
Motor Carriers, generally, this index
Truck tractors, definitions, **Veh 655**

TRADE AND BUSINESS
Business and Commerce, generally, this index

TRADE NAMES
Motor carriers, forms, **Veh 27900 et seq.**
Motor vehicle equipment subject to approval, **Veh 24006**

TRADEMARKS
Assumed or Fictitious Names, generally, this index
Motor Carriers, this index
Motor vehicle equipment subject to approval, **Veh 24006**
Motor vehicles, fleet vehicles, registration, **Veh 5302**
Signs, motor carriers, **Veh 27900 et seq.**

TRAFFIC
Definitions, **Veh 620**

TRAFFIC OFFICERS
Assistance, disabled motorists, **Veh 20018 et seq.**
Definitions, **Veh 625**
Disabled motorists, assistance, **Veh 20018 et seq.**
Distinctive uniforms and vehicle, **Veh 40800**
Fences, report of damages, **Veh 2811**
Inspection and inspectors, vehicle height, width, length, or weight violations, **Veh 2802**
Investigations, uniform and color of vehicle, **Veh 40800**
Loads, inspection, **Veh 2802, 2803**
Order, signal or direction, failure or refusal to comply, **Veh 2800**

TRAFFIC RULES AND REGULATIONS
Generally, **Veh 21000 et seq.**
Abandoned or unclaimed property,
    Appraisal and appraisers, **Veh 22855**
    Removal, **Veh 22650 et seq.**
        Highway patrol, **Veh 22659**
Abstract of records,
    Employees, size or weight law violations, dismissal of charges, **Veh 40003**
    Reversal of conviction, **Veh 1803.3**
Accidents, **Veh 20000 et seq., 42001**
    Abandoned vehicles, removal from private property, **Veh 22653**
    Arrest, failure to stop, **Veh 40303**
    Arrest without warrant, driving under the influence, **Veh 40300.5**
    Blood tests, death, **Veh 23158**
        Consent, **Veh 23612**
    Consent, blood and urine samples, death, **Veh 23612**
    Coroners, lights on vehicles, **Veh 25264**
    Crimes and offenses, **Veh 40000.13**
        Bodily injuries, **Veh 21070**
        Reports, evidence, **Veh 20013**
    Damages, **Veh 17151, 17300 et seq.**
    Death,
        Coroners, reports, **Veh 20011**
        Duties of driver, **Veh 20004**
        Investigations and investigators, **Veh 13800 et seq.**
        Reports, **Veh 20001, 20004**
    Diplomatic drivers license holders, reports, **Veh 12502**
    Double fine zones, **Veh 42010**
    Drivers, exchange of information, **Veh 16025**
    Drivers licenses, failure to stop, revocation or suspension, **Veh 13201, 13350, 13361**
    Driving under the influence, generally, post
    Duty to stop, **Veh 20001 et seq.**
    Event data recorders, **Veh 9951**
    Evidence, reports, **Veh 40833**

TRAFFIC

TRAFFIC RULES AND REGULATIONS
—Cont'd

Accidents—Cont'd

Failure to report, summary of penalty provisions, **Veh 1656.2**

Fault, counter report of property damage, determination, **Veh 20015**

Fines and penalties, **Veh 42001**
Bodily injuries, **Veh 42001.19**

Flares, replacement, **Veh 2419**

Fraud, motor vehicle insurance, financial responsibility, **Veh 16000.8**

Glass and debris, removal, **Veh 27700**

Hit and Run Drivers, generally, this index

Hours of driving, limitation, **Veh 21702**

Impounding vehicle for investigation, **Veh 22655**

Information, prevention, dissemination, **Veh 1809**

Inspection and inspectors, failure to stop, fines and penalties, **Veh 42002.1**

Investigations and investigators, **Veh 2400 et seq., 13800 et seq.**

Limitation on hours of driving, **Veh 21702**

Nonresidents, service of process, **Veh 17450 et seq.**

Notice, violations, **Veh 40600**

Passenger restraint systems, children and minors, sales, **Veh 27362.1**

Pedestrians, yielding right of way, **Veh 21971, 42001.18**

Point count, **Veh 12810**

Presumptions, towing, **Veh 41104**

Property damage, duties of driver, **Veh 20002**

Records and recordation, **Veh 9951**

Registration,
Exemptions, **Veh 4002**
Refusal, **Veh 4760.1**

Removal,
Glass and debris, **Veh 27700**
Private property, vehicles left at scene of accident, **Veh 22653**

Reports, **Veh 1803 et seq., 16000, 20000 et seq.**
Abstracts, inspection and inspectors, **Veh 1808**
Address, injured persons, **Veh 16000, 20003**
Attorneys, disclosure, **Veh 20012**
Confidential or privileged information, **Veh 20012**
Copies, fees, **Veh 20012**
Crimes and offenses, **Veh 40000.13**
Disclosure, **Veh 20012**
Electronic recording, **Veh 1806**
Evidence, **Veh 20013, 40833**
Electronic recording, **Veh 1806**
Failure to file, **Veh 16000**
Misfeasance, **Veh 1805**
Summary of penalty provisions, **Veh 1656.2**
Forms, **Veh 2407**

TRAFFIC RULES AND REGULATIONS
—Cont'd

Accidents—Cont'd

Reports—Cont'd
Incapacity of driver, **Veh 20010**
Inspection and inspectors, **Veh 1808**
Motor carriers, safety regulations, **Veh 34500 et seq.**
Names, injured persons, **Veh 16000, 20003**
Property damage, **Veh 20015**
Records and recordation, **Veh 1810.3**
Time, **Veh 20008**
Youth buses, **Veh 12523**

Research, **Veh 2408**

Safety enhancement double fine zones, **Veh 42010**

Security deposits,
Evidence, civil actions, **Veh 40833**
Refunds, **Veh 16027**

Sensing and diagnostic modules, **Veh 9951**

Small claims courts, unsatisfied judgments, license suspension, **Veh 16370.5**

Statistics, **Veh 2408**

Torts, **Veh 17000 et seq.**

Tow car drivers, duties, **Veh 27700**

Traffic safety fund, **Veh 42200**

Traffic safety program, **Veh 2900 et seq.**

Train of vehicles, presumptions, **Veh 41104**

Transportation of injured persons, **Veh 20016**

Turn signal lamps, **Veh 25251**

Violations, **Veh 40000.13**

Yielding right of way, pedestrians, **Veh 21971, 42001.18**

Actions and proceedings, **Veh 40830 et seq.**
Evidence, generally, post
Garbage and refuse, removal from highway, **Veh 23113**
Hearings, impounded vehicles, **Veh 22651**
Removal of garbage or refuse from highway, **Veh 23113**

Acts of God, driving hour limitations, exemption, **Veh 21702**

Addicts and addiction. Driving under the influence, generally, post

Additional driving rules, **Veh 21700 et seq.**

Adjacent curb parking, **Veh 22502**
Unincorporated areas, **Veh 22504**

Adjacent intersections, pedestrians crossing between controlled intersections, **Veh 21955**

Adjustable axle to increase length of vehicle, inclusion in measurement, **Veh 35402**

Administrative assessments, court costs coverage, violators, **Veh 40508.6**

Admissibility of evidence. Evidence, generally, post

TRAFFIC RULES AND REGULATIONS
—Cont'd

Adverse or pecuniary interest, driving under the influence, alcohol education and treatment programs, **Veh 23670**

Advertisements, mobile billboard advertising displays, **Veh 21100**
Impounding, **Veh 22651**

Advisory statements, vehicular homicide, driving under the influence, **Veh 23593**

Aerodynamic devices, width of vehicle or load, **Veh 35110**

Affidavits of nonliability, automated enforcement systems, **Veh 40520**

Aggregate materials, carrying on highways, regulation, **Veh 23113, 23114**

Aggressive driving. Road rage, generally, post

Agricultural Labor and Employment, this index

Agricultural Machinery and Equipment, generally, this index

·Agricultural Products, this index

Air pollution control, **Veh 40001 et seq.**

Aircraft, taxiing on local streets or county highways, **Veh 21114**

Airports and Landing Fields, this index

Alarm devices, activated, removing vehicle, **Veh 22651.5**

Alcohol education programs. Driving under the influence, post

Alcoholic beverages,
Children and minors, possession, **Veh 23224, 40000.15**
Designated driver program, information sheet, **Veh 2426**
Drinking in motor vehicle, **Veh 23220**
Driving under the influence, generally, post
Implied consent, chemical tests, **Veh 13353, 23136**
Occupants, **Veh 23221**
Drinking while vehicle on highway, **Veh 23221**
Open containers, **Veh 23220 et seq.**
Passengers, **Veh 23221**
Possession, **Veh 23222 et seq.**
Children and minors, **Veh 23224, 40000.15**
Containers, **Veh 23223**
Open container, **Veh 23223**
Storage, open containers, **Veh 23223**

Alcoholics and alcoholism. Driving under the influence, generally, post

All terrain vehicles, instructors, licenses, **Veh 11100.1**

Almond trailers, towing, weight limitations, **Veh 36627**

Amber warning light system, school buses, **Veh 22112, 25257**

Ambulances, generally, this index

Amnesty, fines and penalties, **Veh 42008 et seq.**

Amount of bail, fixing by magistrate, **Veh 40511**

TRAFFIC RULES AND REGULATIONS
—Cont'd

Angle parking, ordinances, **Veh 22503**

Animals, **Veh 21113**

Abandoned or unclaimed property, drivers handbook, **Veh 1656.3**

Airports, municipal airports, **Veh 21113**

Application of law to riders or drivers, **Veh 21050**

Caution in passing, **Veh 21759**

Crossings, vehicular crossings, toll roads and bridges, **Veh 23330**

Failure to obey signals, **Veh 21462**

Field loaded livestock, weight limits, penalties, **Veh 42030**

Freeways, restrictions, **Veh 21960**

Horseback riders, right of way, **Veh 21805**

Local regulation of stopping, standing, **Veh 21113**

Municipal airports, **Veh 21113**

Overtaking and passing, caution, **Veh 21759**

Right of way, equestrian crossings or bridle paths, **Veh 21805**

Stopping, **Veh 21113**

Toll roads and bridges, vehicular crossings, **Veh 23330**

Transporting, restraints, enclosures, **Veh 23117, 42001.4**

Antigridlock Act, **Veh 22526**

Appeal and review, parking, San Francisco City and County, buses, videotape, transit only traffic lanes, **Veh 40241**

Appearance, **Veh 40303 et seq.**

Attorneys, sufficiency under written promise, **Veh 40507**

Bail, person authorized to receive deposit, **Veh 40502**

Certificate of adjudication, failure to appear or pay fine, **Veh 40509**

Children and minors, infraction violations, **Veh 40502**

Complaint, filing on violation of promise to appear, **Veh 40503**

Continuance of written promise to appear, **Veh 40506.5**

Failure to appear or pay fine, **Veh 40000.25, 42004.5**

Assessments, **Veh 40508.5**

Certificate of adjudication, **Veh 40509**

Drivers license revocation, **Veh 13365**

Evidence, **Veh 40903**

Issuance of warrant, **Veh 40514, 40515**

Liens, **Veh 14911**

Trial election, evidence introduction, **Veh 40903**

Filing notice to appear, persons owning or controlling vehicles, **Veh 40002**

Information not delivered to person receiving notice, magistrates copy, **Veh 40505**

Issuance of warrant, violation of promise, **Veh 40514, 40515**

Mail and mailing, written plea, **Veh 40519**

TRAFFIC RULES AND REGULATIONS
—Cont'd

Appearance—Cont'd

Mandatory appearance before magistrate, **Veh 40302**

Nonresidents, warrant for failing to honor appearance promise, **Veh 40515**

Notice, **Veh 40500 et seq.**

Automated enforcement systems, **Veh 40518, 40520**

Cases involving traffic accidents, **Veh 40600**

Evidence, **Veh 40903**

Failure to appear, penalty, **Veh 14911**

Highway patrol members, **Veh 40304**

Identity and identification, thumbprints, **Veh 40303**

Nonresidents, **Veh 40305, 40305.5, 40500, 40504**

Rail crossing violations, automated enforcement system, **Veh 40518, 40520**

Thumbprints, **Veh 40303**

Nonresidents, **Veh 40305, 40305.5, 40500, 40504**

Written promise, failure to appear, **Veh 40509, 40509.5**

Place to appear, **Veh 40502**

Pleading, written plea, mailing, **Veh 40519**

Release on promise to appear, **Veh 40500 et seq.**

Delivery to magistrate on failure to appear, **Veh 40515**

Infractions of misdemeanors, **Veh 40306**

Nonresidents, **Veh 40305**

Time, **Veh 40501**

Unsafe mechanical condition or equipment, **Veh 40150**

Violation of promise to appear, **Veh 40508**

Warrant, issuance on violation of promise, **Veh 40514, 40515**

Written pleas, mailing, **Veh 40519**

Written promise to appear, continuance, **Veh 40506.5**

Application,

Permit, increasing size or weight of vehicle, **Veh 35781**

Refund, fees or penalties, limitations, **Veh 42232**

Application of law, **Veh 21001, 21052**

Explosives, **Veh 31614**

Motorized scooters, **Veh 21221**

Appraisal and appraisers, abandoned vehicles, **Veh 22855**

Approaches, vehicular crossings, toll highways, **Veh 23255**

Approaching entrance of highway or intersection, stopping, **Veh 22450 et seq.**

Approval,

Explosives, transportation, **Veh 31616, 31616.5**

TRAFFIC RULES AND REGULATIONS
—Cont'd

Approval—Cont'd

Local regulations, state highways, department of public works, **Veh 21104**

Armored cars, licenses, **Veh 21713**

Arraignment,

Failure to appear,

Forfeiture of bail, **Veh 40512**

Warrant for arrest, **Veh 40514**

Jurisdiction of other violations, **Veh 40311**

Scheduling, **Veh 40519**

Arrest, **Veh 40300 et seq.**

Accidents, failure to stop, **Veh 40303**

Arraignment, generally, ante

Assumed or fictitious names, promise to appear, **Veh 40504**

Attempt to evade, optional appearance before magistrate, **Veh 40303**

Attorneys, sufficiency of appearance under written promise, **Veh 40507**

Bail, generally, post

Brake test, failure or refusal of driver to stop, **Veh 40303**

Certificate of adjudication, failure to appear or pay fine, **Veh 40509**

Children and minors, infraction violations, appearance, **Veh 40502**

Citations,

Persons owning or controlling vehicles, **Veh 40002**

Uniform traffic citation, form, **Veh 40508**

Color of official vehicle, speeding offenses, **Veh 40804**

Complaint, filing, **Veh 40513**

Continuance, infraction or misdemeanor practice, **Veh 40306**

Costs, certification, **Veh 40516**

Damaging vehicles, **Veh 40303**

Delivery of notice to appear, **Veh 40504**

Information not delivered to person receiving notice, **Veh 40505**

Demand,

Appearance before magistrate, **Veh 40304**

Immediate appearance before magistrate, **Veh 40302**

Place of appearance, **Veh 40502**

Transfer of warrant delivered to peace officer for execution, **Veh 40516**

Detention, identification, delay to determine identity, **Veh 40307**

Discretionary procedures, highway patrol members, **Veh 40304**

Drag racing, impounding vehicle, **Veh 22651.6**

Drivers licenses, **Veh 12801.5**

Driving while license suspended or revoked, **Veh 40303**

Failure to present license or evidence of identity, **Veh 40302**

TRAFFIC

TRAFFIC RULES AND REGULATIONS
—Cont'd
Arrest—Cont'd
Drivers licenses—Cont'd
Violations, impounding vehicles, **Veh 22651**
Driving under the influence, post
Driving while under influence of poison, appearance before magistrate, **Veh 40302**
Employers failure to dispose of employees size or weight law violations, **Veh 40005**
Equipment violations, proof of correction, dismissal, **Veh 40522**
Evading arrest, optional appearance before magistrate, **Veh 40303**
Evidence, generally, post
Expenses to departments, **Veh 40516**
Failure to appear or pay fine,
Certificate of adjudication, **Veh 40509**
Pleadings, written pleas, **Veh 40519**
Warrants, issuance, **Veh 40514**
Written pleas, **Veh 40519**
False or fictitious name, release on promise to appear, **Veh 40504**
Felonies, **Veh 40301**
Filing,
Complaint, **Veh 40513**
Copy of notice to appear, **Veh 40506**
Forms, uniform traffic citation, **Veh 40508**
Guaranteed traffic arrest bail bond certificate, commercial vehicles, nonresidents, **Veh 40305.5**
Highway patrol members, discretionary procedure, **Veh 40304**
Hit and run drivers, **Veh 40303**
Identity and identification,
Release, delay to determine identity, **Veh 40307**
Thumbprints, **Veh 40303**
Nonresidents, **Veh 40305, 40305.5, 40500, 40504**
Information not delivered to persons receiving notice to appear, copy of notice filed with magistrate, **Veh 40505**
Infractions, **Veh 40306**
Inspection of size, weight, refusal to stop, **Veh 40303**
Issuance of warrants, **Veh 40514 et seq.**
Judgments, failure to comply with terms, issuance of warrant, **Veh 40514**
Jurisdiction of other offenses, **Veh 40311**
Light and lighting, refusal to stop and submit to inspection, **Veh 40303**
Loads and loading, refusal to submit to weighing, **Veh 40303**
Magistrate, procedure, **Veh 40302 et seq.**
Mail and mailing, written plea, **Veh 40519**
Mandatory appearance, **Veh 40302**

TRAFFIC RULES AND REGULATIONS
—Cont'd
Arrest—Cont'd
Misdemeanors, **Veh 40306**
Night court, appearance, **Veh 40502**
Nonresidents, **Veh 40305**
Warrants for failing to honor appearance promise, **Veh 40515**
Notice of offense, persons owning or controlling vehicles, **Veh 40002**
Notice to appear, **Veh 40500 et seq.**
Certificate of adjudication, willful failure to appear or pay fine, **Veh 40509**
Complaint, **Veh 40513**
Delivery of copy to person arrested, **Veh 40504**
Filing,
Complaint, **Veh 40513**
Copies, **Veh 40506**
Form, **Veh 40500**
Highway patrol members, **Veh 40304**
Information not delivered to person receiving notice, magistrates copy, **Veh 40505**
Parking violations, **Veh 40513**
Pleading, written plea, **Veh 40519**
Speed violation, **Veh 40503**
Time, **Veh 40501**
Violations involving accidents, written notice, **Veh 40604**
Willful failure to appear, certificate of adjudication, **Veh 40509**
Notice to correct violations, **Veh 40303.5**
Obstructing roadway, **Veh 40300.5**
Offenses not specified in code, highway patrol members, **Veh 40304**
Official uniform and vehicle, speeding offenses, **Veh 40804**
Optional appearance before magistrate, **Veh 40303 et seq.**
Other violations, warrants, **Veh 40311**
Outstanding warrants, failure to appear, **Veh 40304.5**
Owner or lessee,
Arrest of driver, **Veh 40001**
Notice to appear, **Veh 40002**
Peace officers, application of law, **Veh 40300**
Persons owning or controlling vehicles, **Veh 40002**
Persons to be taken immediately before magistrate, **Veh 40302**
Place to appear, notice, **Veh 40502**
Pleading,
Continuance of case to prepare, corrections or misdemeanors, **Veh 40306**
Written plea, mailing, **Veh 40519**
Poisons, driving while under influence of, mandatory appearance, **Veh 40302**
Procedure on violations, **Veh 40300 et seq.**
Quotas, **Veh 41600 et seq.**

TRAFFIC RULES AND REGULATIONS
—Cont'd
Arrest—Cont'd
Receipt for payment of fine presented to arresting officer, **Veh 40312**
Reckless driving, **Veh 40303**
Release on promise to appear, **Veh 40500 et seq.**
Assumed or fictitious name, **Veh 40504**
False or fictitious name, **Veh 40504**
Infractions, **Veh 40306**
Misdemeanors, **Veh 40306, 40508**
Nonresident, **Veh 40305**
Refusal to give promise, **Veh 40302**
Violation of promise to appear, **Veh 40508**
Written plea, mailing, **Veh 40519**
Removal of parked or standing vehicles, **Veh 22650 et seq.**
Safety belts, mandatory use, **Veh 27315**
Signatures, assumed or fictitious names, promise to appear, **Veh 40504**
Speed, post
Tampering with vehicles, **Veh 40303**
Telephone call, **Veh 40304.5**
Thumbprints, **Veh 40303**
Nonresidents, **Veh 40305, 40305.5, 40500, 40504**
Time,
Appearance, **Veh 40501**
Identification, detention to determine, **Veh 40307**
Traffic citation, forms, uniform traffic citation form, **Veh 40508**
Traffic officers, distinctive uniforms and vehicles, **Veh 40800**
Uniform of arresting officer, speeding offenses, **Veh 40804**
Uniform traffic citation, form, **Veh 40508**
Violation of promise to appear, **Veh 40508**
Waiver, time to plead, infraction and misdemeanor procedure, **Veh 40306**
Warrants,
Arraignment for other violations, **Veh 40311**
Arrest without warrant, peace officers, **Veh 40300**
Certificates and certification, costs of execution, **Veh 40516**
Consent to arraignment on other offenses, **Veh 40311**
Consolidated disposition, **Veh 41610**
Costs, certification, **Veh 40516**
Custody for outstanding warrants, posting bail or making phone call, **Veh 40304.5**
Distinctive uniform and vehicle of officers serving, exemption, **Veh 40804**
Expenses, **Veh 40516**
Failure to appear, **Veh 40514**
Failure to deposit bail, **Veh 40514, 40515**

TRAFFIC RULES AND REGULATIONS
—Cont'd
Arrest—Cont'd
Warrants—Cont'd
Issuance, **Veh 40514 et seq.**
Traffic violation causing accident, written notice, **Veh 40604**
Judgments, failure to comply with terms, **Veh 40514**
Jurisdiction of other offenses, **Veh 40311**
Municipalities, expenses and expenditures, **Veh 40516**
Nonresidents, failing to honor appearance promise, **Veh 40515**
Notice of complaint, violations involving accidents, **Veh 40604**
Notice of violation, person owning or controlling vehicle, **Veh 40002**
Official uniform and vehicle of officer serving, exemption, **Veh 40804**
Other violations, **Veh 40311**
Persons owning or controlling vehicles, **Veh 40002**
Promise to appear, **Veh 40514, 40515**
Receipts, **Veh 40312**
Reimbursement, expenses of execution, **Veh 40516**
Traffic officers serving, exemption from uniform and vehicle requirement, **Veh 40800**
Transfer for execution, **Veh 40516**
Uniform of officer serving, exemption, **Veh 40804**
Violation of promise to appear, **Veh 40514, 40515**
Windshield or rear windows, defective equipment, **Veh 26710**
Without warrant,
Driving under influence of intoxicating liquor or drugs, **Veh 40300.5**
Peace officers, **Veh 40300**
Written pleas, mailing, **Veh 40519**
Ascending vehicles, grades, yielding right of way, **Veh 21661**
Ashes. Garbage and refuse, generally, post
Assault and battery,
Deadly weapon, drivers licenses, revocation, **Veh 13351.5**
Road rage, generally, post
Assemblages on highways, local authorities, **Veh 21100 et seq.**
Assessments, **Veh 40508.5**
Administrative assessments, court costs, defendants, **Veh 40508.6**
Driving under the influence, alcohol and drug problems, **Veh 23645 et seq.**
Night courts, **Veh 42006**
Weekend courts, special assessments, **Veh 42006**
Assumed or fictitious name,
Arrested person, promise to appear, **Veh 40504**
Notice, correction of violations, **Veh 40614**

TRAFFIC RULES AND REGULATIONS
—Cont'd
Attaching to other vehicle, motorized scooters, **Veh 21235**
Attempt to evade arrest, optional appearance before magistrate, **Veh 40303**
Attorneys, appearance, sufficiency under written promise, **Veh 40507**
Audits and auditors, handicapped persons, parking, placards, **Veh 1825**
Authorities, local regulations, **Veh 21100 et seq.**
Authorization, private property, removal of vehicles, **Veh 22658**
Automated rail crossing enforcement system, **Veh 21362.5**
Definitions, **Veh 210**
Automatic vehicle identification account, Pay by plate toll payment, information, **Veh 23301.8**
Tolls, payment, **Veh 23302**
Awareness programs, alternative disposition for offenders, **Veh 42005.3**
Axle weight. Weights, post
B train assembly, semitrailer length measurement, exclusion, **Veh 35401**
Backing vehicle on highway, **Veh 22106**
Grades, yielding right of way to ascending vehicles, **Veh 21661**
Backup devices or alarms, **Veh 27000**
Badges, emblems and insignia, physicians vehicles, **Veh 21058**
Bail, **Veh 40500 et seq.**
Amnesty, **Veh 42008.7**
Counties, **Veh 42008.5**
Amount, fixing by magistrate, **Veh 40511**
Appearance, **Veh 40502**
Written promise, failure, **Veh 40509**
Arraignment, failure to appear, forfeiture of bail, **Veh 40512**
Assessments,
Failure to appear, **Veh 40508.5**
Night court assessments, **Veh 42006**
Certificate of adjudication, failure to appear or pay fine, **Veh 40509**
Check, **Veh 40510, 40521**
Clerk of magistrate, infractions and misdemeanors, **Veh 40307**
Complaint, filing on failure to deposit, **Veh 40513**
Copy of notice to appear, filing with person authorized to receive deposit, **Veh 40506**
Declaration of forfeiture, failure to appear, **Veh 40512, 40512.5**
Delinquency, amnesty, **Veh 42008.7**
Deposit, **Veh 40510, 40519**
Failure to appear or pay fine,
Certificate of adjudication, **Veh 40509**
Forfeiture, **Veh 40512, 40512.5**
Issuance of warrant, **Veh 40515**
Failure to deposit bail for offenses, warrant for arrest, **Veh 40514, 40515**
Fixing of bail by magistrate, **Veh 40511**

TRAFFIC RULES AND REGULATIONS
—Cont'd
Bail—Cont'd
Forfeitures,
Arraignment, failure to appear, **Veh 40512**
Conviction of offense charged, bail forfeiture deemed to be, **Veh 40000.28**
Equivalent of conviction, **Veh 13103**
Forwarding by mail, **Veh 40521**
Infractions,
Disposition, **Veh 42201.5**
Installment payments, **Veh 40510.5, 40512**
Night court assessment, **Veh 42006**
Release, forfeitures in excess of specified amount, **Veh 40512, 40512.5**
Reports, **Veh 1803 et seq.**
Prior conviction, **Veh 42004**
Trial, failure to appear, **Veh 40512.5**
Violators schools, proof of completion, **Veh 40512.6**
Impounded vehicles, **Veh 22651**
Infractions, post
Interest, refunds, **Veh 42201.6**
Jails,
Acceptance of bail by officer in charge, **Veh 40307**
Magistrates unavailable, **Veh 40307**
Juvenile courts or officers, appearance before, **Veh 40502**
Mail and mailing, forfeitures and penalty assessments, **Veh 40521**
Misdemeanors, **Veh 40306**
Unavailability of magistrate, **Veh 40307**
Violation of promise to appear before person authorized to receive deposit, **Veh 40508**
Night court assessments, **Veh 42006**
Nonresidents, release on promise to appear, **Veh 40305**
Optional bail forfeiture, failure to appear at trial, **Veh 40512.5**
Outstanding warrants, opportunity to post, **Veh 40304.5**
Payment, form, **Veh 40521**
Penalty assessments, night court assessments, **Veh 42006**
Personal check, **Veh 40510, 40521**
Pleadings, written plea, mailing, **Veh 40519**
Refunds, **Veh 42201.6**
Registration, refusal, **Veh 4760.1**
Release on promise to appear. Arrest, ante
Reports, prior conviction, bail forfeiture, **Veh 42004**
Special penalty assessments, night court assessment, **Veh 42006**
Statement on notice to appear, **Veh 40511**
Traffic violator schools, continuance, attendance, **Veh 41501, 42005**

TRAFFIC

TRAFFIC RULES AND REGULATIONS
—Cont'd
Bail—Cont'd
Trial,
Failure to appear, forfeitures, **Veh 40512.5**
Written declarations, **Veh 40902**
Violation of promise to appear before person authorized to receive deposit, **Veh 40508**
Warrant for arrest, failure to deposit, **Veh 40514, 40515**
Weekend courts, special assessments, **Veh 42006**
Willful failure to appear before person authorized to receive deposit, certificate of adjudication, **Veh 40509**
Written pleas, mailing, **Veh 40519**
Barricades,
Public utility vehicle, warning devices, **Veh 25301**
Reflectorizing material, designs or patterns, **Veh 25500**
Speed contests or exhibitions, **Veh 23109**
Basic Speed Law, **Veh 22350, 22362**
Beverages. Alcoholic beverages, generally, ante
Bicycles, **Veh 21113, 21200 et seq.**
Blue lights, peace officers, **Veh 21201.3**
Carrying articles, **Veh 21205**
Children and minors, **Veh 21204**
Costs schedules, infractions prosecutions, establishment, **Veh 42001**
Crossings, vehicular crossings, toll roads and bridges, **Veh 23330**
Definitions, roadway operation, **Veh 21200**
Direction of traffic, highways, **Veh 21650.1**
Driving while intoxicated, **Veh 21200.5, 40000.13**
Drug abuse, driving under the influence, **Veh 21200.5, 40000.13**
Ear plugs, **Veh 27400**
Equipment, **Veh 21201**
Exemptions, peace officers, **Veh 21200**
Fines and penalties,
Driving under the influence, **Veh 21200.5, 40000.13**
Infractions, **Veh 42001**
Overtaking and passing, **Veh 21760**
Freeways, restrictions, **Veh 21960**
Hand signals, **Veh 22111**
Handlebars, riders, **Veh 21204**
Headsets, **Veh 27400**
Helmets,
Children, **Veh 21204**
Use, bicyclists and passengers, **Veh 21212**
Highways,
Direction of traffic, **Veh 21650.1**
Side of roadway, **Veh 21650**
Hitching rides on vehicles, **Veh 21203**
Lanes, **Veh 21207 et seq., 21717**

TRAFFIC RULES AND REGULATIONS
—Cont'd
Bicycles—Cont'd
Lanes—Cont'd
Motorized scooters, rules of the road, **Veh 21229**
Pedestrians, **Veh 21966**
Separation from vehicular lanes, **Veh 21207**
Left side of road, **Veh 21202**
Licenses and permits, **Veh 21206, 39000 et seq.**
Local authorities, **Veh 21100, 21206, 21207**
Local regulation, **Veh 21206**
Motorized bicycles, required equipment, **Veh 24015**
Notice to correct violations, **Veh 40303.5**
Overtaking and passing, **Veh 21202, 21750 et seq., 21760**
Parking, **Veh 21210**
Paths,
Motorized scooters, rules of the road, **Veh 21230**
Unauthorized vehicles, **Veh 23127**
Peace officers,
Blue lights, **Veh 21201.3**
Exemptions, **Veh 21200**
Prosthetic devices, **Veh 27400**
Public property, **Veh 21113**
Radios, headsets or earplugs, **Veh 27400**
Reports of violations, **Veh 1803 et seq.**
Riding on bicycle, **Veh 21204**
Right of way, **Veh 21804**
Drivers handbook, **Veh 1656.3**
Right side of roadway, riders, **Veh 21202**
Highways, **Veh 21650**
Rights and duties of riders, **Veh 21200**
Separate lanes, **Veh 21207**
Towing bicycles carrying riders, **Veh 21712**
Vehicular crossings, toll roads and bridges, **Veh 23330**
Violations, reports, **Veh 1803 et seq.**
Bills of lading,
Explosives, **Veh 31612**
Load removal, **Veh 2803**
Blind persons, **Veh 21963 et seq.**
Death, placard cancellation or revocation, **Veh 22511.6**
Blinding lights, display, **Veh 21466**
Blocking traffic, minimum,
Speed limit, **Veh 22400**
Stopping, **Veh 22400**
Blocking wheels, parking on hills, **Veh 22509**
Blood tests,
Accidents, ante
Driving under the influence, post
Blue lights, bicycles, peace officers, **Veh 21201.3**
Boats and boating, transporters, length, **Veh 35401.3, 35401.5**
Booms or masts of shovels or cranes, length, **Veh 35407**

TRAFFIC RULES AND REGULATIONS
—Cont'd
Booster power units, trucks, permits, **Veh 35786, 35787**
Bottles. Garbage and refuse, generally, post
Boulevards, Northwoods boulevard, Nevada County ordinances, commercial vehicle weight, **Veh 35715**
Boundary line streets,
Local regulations, **Veh 21105**
Speed, **Veh 22359**
Brakes,
Arrest, failure or refusal of driver to stop for test, **Veh 40303**
Motorized scooters, **Veh 21235**
Standing vehicle, setting, **Veh 22515**
Truck tractor towing semitrailer, **Veh 35400**
Branch lines, leading to ferries, stopping at railroad crossings, **Veh 22452, 22453**
Breath tests. Driving under the influence, post
Bridges,
Approaching vehicles, left side of roadway, **Veh 21752**
Buses, stopping to load or unload passengers, **Veh 22500**
Hauling logs, speed, **Veh 35785**
Local regulation, **Veh 21109**
Ordinances, state highways, stopping, standing or parking vehicles, **Veh 22501**
Overtaking and passing, **Veh 21752**
Parking, **Veh 22500**
State highways, ordinances, **Veh 22501**
Pedestrians stopping or standing, peace officers ordering removal, **Veh 21962**
Removal, parked or standing vehicles, **Veh 22650 et seq.**
Speed limits, **Veh 22402 et seq.**
Hauling logs, **Veh 35785**
State highways, stopping, standing or parking vehicles, local regulation, **Veh 22501**
Stopping, standing or parking vehicles, **Veh 22500**
State highways, local ordinances, **Veh 22501**
Weight limits, **Veh 35750 et seq.**
Bridle Paths and Trails, this index
Broken lines, driving to left, **Veh 21460**
Building materials, width of vehicle or load, trusses, wall panels, **Veh 35780.5**
Building mover transporting across railroad tracks, notice, **Veh 35789**
Bumper strength notices, **Veh 24011.3**
Crimes and offenses, **Veh 40000.15**
Bumpers,
Front bumpers, length limitations, **Veh 35408**
Strength notices, **Veh 24011.3, 40000.15**

TRAFFIC RULES AND REGULATIONS
—Cont'd

Buses,
Axle weight, **Veh 35554**
Bicycle transportation, length, exemptions, **Veh 35400**
Alameda Contra Costa transit district, **Veh 35400.7**
Bridges, stopping to load or unload, **Veh 22500**
Crosswalks, stopping for loading or unloading, **Veh 22500**
Drawing another vehicle, speed, **Veh 22406, 22407**
Farm labor buses or trucks, speed limit, **Veh 22406, 22407**
Hours of driving, limitation, **Veh 21702**
Safety regulations, **Veh 34500 et seq.**
Intoxicating liquors, occupant drinking or possessing opened container, **Veh 23229**
Length, **Veh 35400**
Loading zones, stopping, standing or parking, **Veh 22500**
Overtaking and passing, passengers alighting or boarding, **Veh 21756**
Parking, San Francisco City and County, videotape, transit only traffic lanes, **Veh 40240 et seq.**
Public utilities commission operation, width, **Veh 35106, 35107**
Railroad crossings,
Signs, **Veh 22452.5**
Stopping, **Veh 22452**
Passengers, imputed negligence, **Veh 22453**
Right of way, yielding, signs and signals, **Veh 24617**
Stands, local regulation, **Veh 21112**
State highways, stopping for passengers, ordinances, approval, **Veh 22501**
Stopping,
Loading zones, **Veh 22500**
Railroad crossings, **Veh 22452**
Passengers, imputed negligence, **Veh 22453**
School buses, unincorporated areas, approval, **Veh 22504**
State highways, ordinances, approval, **Veh 22501**
Urban and suburban service, width, operated by common carriers of passengers, **Veh 35106, 35107**
Width, coaches or buses operated under public utilities commission, **Veh 35106, 35107**

Business or residence districts,
Commercial vehicles, parking, standing or stopping, **Veh 22502**
Divided highways, U turns, **Veh 22102**
Explosives, routes, **Veh 31614**
Intersections, U turns, **Veh 22102**
Lights on parked vehicles, **Veh 24802**
Overtaking and passing, right side, **Veh 21754**

TRAFFIC RULES AND REGULATIONS
—Cont'd

Business or residence districts—Cont'd
Parking, blocking wheels on grade, **Veh 22509**
Pedestrians, side of roadway, **Veh 21956**
Railroad crossings, stopping, **Veh 22452, 22453**
Right side, passing, **Veh 21754**
Speed, post
Stopping, railroad crossings, **Veh 22452, 22453**
Truck routes, weight limits, **Veh 35712**
Turning, intersections, **Veh 22102, 22103**
U turns, intersections, **Veh 22102, 22103**
Caldecott tunnel, explosives and flammable substances, **Veh 31301**
Cameras, motor vehicles taking pictures, length, **Veh 35409**
Camp trailers,
Length, **Veh 35400.6**
Towing trailers carrying passengers, **Veh 21712**
Campers, this index
Canada. Driving under the influence, post
Cans. Garbage and refuse, generally, post
Canyons, mountain highways, horn warning, **Veh 21662**
Car seats, children, **Veh 27360 et seq.**
Point system, **Veh 12810**
Car share vehicle program, parking, exclusive use spaces, **Veh 22507.1**
Caravan or motorcades, spacing, **Veh 21705**
Careless driving. Road rage, generally, post
Cargo tank vehicles, flammable liquids, tunnels, **Veh 21109**
Carriers,
Armored cars, licenses, **Veh 21713**
Bona fide passengers for hire, failure to stop at railroad crossing, **Veh 22453**
Booster power units, licenses and permits, **Veh 35786, 35787**
Buses, generally, ante
Clearance between trucks, school buses and tow vehicles, **Veh 21704**
Combinations of vehicles, generally, post
Distances between vehicles, **Veh 21704**
Drivers log regulations, violation procedure, **Veh 40303**
Driving hours, limitation, **Veh 21702**
Eight hundred (800) numbers, workmen, **Veh 2429**
Flammable liquids, speed limits, **Veh 22406.5**
Hours of labor, **Veh 21702**
Lengths, **Veh 35401**
Loading or unloading, common carrier or taxicab, **Veh 22500**
Local regulation of stands, **Veh 21112**
Obstructing view of driver, passengers, **Veh 21700**

TRAFFIC RULES AND REGULATIONS
—Cont'd

Carriers—Cont'd
Overtaking and passing,
Distances between vehicles, **Veh 21704**
Passengers alighting or boarding, **Veh 21756**
Railroad crossings, stopping, **Veh 22452, 22453**
Regulation of location of stands for public carriers, **Veh 21112**
Safety regulations, **Veh 34500 et seq.**
Speed, **Veh 21704, 22406, 22406.1, 22407**
Flammable liquids, **Veh 22406.5**
Stopping,
Railroad crossings, **Veh 22452, 22453**
Standing or parking vehicles, **Veh 22500**
Transporting employees, stopping at railroad crossings, **Veh 22452**
Passengers, imputed negligence, **Veh 22453**
Carrying articles, bicycle riders, **Veh 21205**
Carrying permit for increase in size or weight of vehicle, **Veh 35783**
Carson City, overweight vehicles, special permits, **Veh 35700.5**
Casualties, driving hours, exemption from limitations, **Veh 21702**
Causeways,
Hauling saw logs, speed, **Veh 35785**
Removal of parked or standing vehicles, **Veh 22650 et seq.**
Speed, hauling saw logs, **Veh 35785**
Weight of motor vehicles, restriction, **Veh 35753**
Celebrations, temporary closing of streets, local regulations, **Veh 21101**
Center lane, three lane roadway, using, **Veh 21659**
Certificates and certification,
Adjudication, failure to appear in court or pay fine, **Veh 40509**
Arrest warrant execution, costs, **Veh 40516**
Handicapped persons,
Fraud, **Veh 22511.58**
Parking exemptions, **Veh 22511.55, 22511.59**
Tow truck drivers, **Veh 2430 et seq.**
Certified weight certificate, load removal, **Veh 2803**
Change,
Major code changes, notice, drivers license extension recipients, **Veh 12814.5**
Speed limits, prima facie limits, **Veh 22352**
Changing lanes, **Veh 21658**
Chappie Zberg Off Highway Motor Vehicle Law, **Veh 38000 et seq.**
Charges. Rates and charges, generally, post

TRAFFIC

TRAFFIC RULES AND REGULATIONS
—Cont'd

Chauffeurs, hours of driving, limitation, **Veh 21702**

Check as bail, **Veh 40510**

Checkpoints,
Air pollution, emissions, **Veh 2814.1**
Sobriety checkpoints, **Veh 2814.2**

Chemical hose, driving or crossing over, **Veh 21708**

Chemical tests. Driving under the influence, post

Children and minors,
Bail, appearance before juvenile court or officer, **Veh 40502**
Cellular radio telephones, crimes and offenses, **Veh 23124**
Custody, infraction cases, **Veh 40302.5**
Driving under the influence, post
Fines and penalties, driving under the influence, **Veh 23500 et seq.**
Infractions, post
Passenger restraint systems, **Veh 27360 et seq.**
Point system, **Veh 12810**
Photography and pictures, sound recordings, endangerment, **Veh 40008**
Records and reports, **Veh 1816**
Seatbelts, **Veh 27360 et seq.**
Point system, **Veh 12810**
Telecommunications, cellular radio telephones, crimes and offenses, **Veh 23124**
Three wheeled vehicles, seat belts, application of laws, **Veh 27368**

Christensen Belotti Act, **Veh 35552**

Cigarettes or cigars, throwing lighted substance on highway, **Veh 23111**

Citations,
Arrest, ante
Forms, uniform traffic citation, **Veh 40508**
Parking, quotas, **Veh 41600 et seq.**
Persons owning or controlling vehicles, **Veh 40002**
Scofflaws, vehicle immobilization devices, **Veh 22651.7**
Seat belts, mandatory use, **Veh 27315**
Streetsweepers, parking, photography and pictures, **Veh 40245 et seq.**

City on island over 20,000 acres, county over 4,000,000, **Veh 21100.5**

Civil actions. Actions and proceedings, generally, ante

Clearance,
Caravans or motorcades, **Veh 21705**
Emergency vehicles, following, **Veh 21706**
Following vehicles, **Veh 21703**
Photography and pictures, sound recordings, **Veh 40008**
Motorcades, **Veh 21705**
Overtaking and passing, two lane highway, left side, **Veh 21751**
Passing vehicle, **Veh 21751**

TRAFFIC RULES AND REGULATIONS
—Cont'd

Clearance—Cont'd
Side marker lamps, vehicles 80 inches or more in width, **Veh 25100**
Trucks, school buses and two vehicles, **Veh 21704**

Clergymen, intoxicating liquors, Open Container Law, exemption, **Veh 23229**

Clerks of court, bail, infractions or misdemeanors, **Veh 40307**

Closing highways or streets,
Local authorities, **Veh 21101 et seq.**
Private roads, public use, **Veh 21107.5 et seq.**

Closing off fire areas, **Veh 21707**

Coasters, towing coasters carrying riders, **Veh 21712**

Coasting down grade in neutral, **Veh 21710**

Code violations required by federal rule or regulation, defense, **Veh 41401**

Codefendants, operators and owners, **Veh 40001 et seq.**

Collapsible containers, transporting liquids, on flatbed vehicles, loads and loading, **Veh 31540**

Collateral estoppel, civil actions, effect of conviction, **Veh 40834**

Colleges and universities,
Animal or vehicle, stopping, standing, driveways, paths or grounds, **Veh 21113**
Driver training programs, local authorities closing street, **Veh 21101**
Hit and run vehicles, removal for inspection, **Veh 22655**

Color of vehicle,
Police officer arresting speeding violator, **Veh 40804**
Traffic officers, duty of enforcing code provisions, distinctive uniform and vehicle, **Veh 40800**

Combinations of vehicles,
Axle weight limits, **Veh 35551, 35552**
Length, **Veh 35400 et seq.**
Licenses and permits, **Veh 35780 et seq.**
Passenger vehicles, **Veh 21715**
Weight limits, **Veh 35551.5**

Commercial establishment, private roads, local regulation, **Veh 21107.6**

Commercial vehicles,
Business districts, parking, standing or stopping, **Veh 22502**
Coaches, width, **Veh 35789.5**
Counties of third class, weight limits, **Veh 35712**
Driving under the influence, drivers licenses, revocation or suspension, **Veh 13366.5**
Exemptions,
Prohibitions or restrictions on parking or standing vehicles, street sweeping hours, **Veh 22507.6**
Weight limitations, **Veh 35714**

TRAFFIC RULES AND REGULATIONS
—Cont'd

Commercial vehicles—Cont'd
Local authorities, parking or standing, powers, **Veh 22507.5**
Partial year registration, **Veh 9700 et seq.**
Speed, serious traffic violations, **Veh 22406.1**
Stopping, standing or parking, **Veh 22502**
Traffic violator schools, **Veh 42005**
Weights,
Approaching highway in unincorporated residential subdivision, **Veh 35712**
Cargo, theft, interdiction, fees, **Veh 9400.1**
County improved highways, **Veh 35711 et seq.**
Crimes and offenses, gross weight, **Veh 4000.6, 42030.1**
Decals, **Veh 9400.1**
Declared gross weight, excess, registration, **Veh 9554.2**
Exemptions, **Veh 35714**
Fees, vehicles manufactured before designated time, **Veh 9401**
Fees, **Veh 9400 et seq.**
Partial year registration, **Veh 9407, 9700, 9704, 9706**
Additional fees, **Veh 1678, 9702**
Infractions, **Veh 4000.6**
Inspection and inspectors, **Veh 2813**
Limits, local authorities, **Veh 35703**
Maximum, Los Angeles County, **Veh 35655.6**
Northwoods boulevard, Nevada County, ordinances, **Veh 35715**
Ordinances, **Veh 35703**
Registration, **Veh 4000.6**
Declared gross weight, excess, **Veh 9554.2**
Theft, interdiction, fees, **Veh 9400.1**

Common carriers. Carriers, generally, ante

Commuter rail systems, **Veh 21113**

Compensation, school crossing guards, **Veh 42201**

Complaints,
Delivery to magistrate on violation of promise to appear, **Veh 40515**
Failure to correct, **Veh 40618**
Filing, notice to appear, **Veh 40513**
Infractions, **Veh 40306**
Notice to appear, **Veh 40513**
Parking violations, notice to appear, **Veh 40513**
Persons owning or controlling vehicles, **Veh 40513**
Plea of accused, **Veh 40513**
Prosecution of persons owning or controlling vehicles, **Veh 40002**
Railroads, automated crossing enforcement system, **Veh 40518**
Speed charge, **Veh 40503**

TRAFFIC RULES AND REGULATIONS
—Cont'd

Complaints—Cont'd

Waiver, filing of verified complaint, **Veh 40513**

Computation, limitation on driving hours, **Veh 21702**

Concrete trucks, transit mix, axle weights, **Veh 35550**

Condition of permit, exceeding maximum size, weight, **Veh 35782**

Cone patterns, traffic control, traversing, **Veh 2818**

Confidential or privileged information, Conviction, traffic violator schools, **Veh 1803.5, 1808.7**

Records and recordation, **Veh 1808**

Traffic violator schools, driving schools, **Veh 1808.7**

Streetsweepers, parking, photography and pictures, **Veh 40247**

Confiscation, disabled person parking placards, **Veh 22511.56**

Congested traffic, diversion of vehicles, **Veh 21101.2**

Consent, implied consent. Driving under the influence, post

Consolidated disposition, **Veh 41610**

Constables, direction in emergency situation, **Veh 21707**

Construction, **Veh 21367**

Driving on right side of roadway, exemptions, **Veh 21650**

Equipment, exemptions, **Veh 35104**

Speed limits, **Veh 22362**

Contempt, infractions, impoundment of drivers license, failure to pay fine, **Veh 40508**

Continuance,

Arrest of person for infraction or misdemeanor, trial, **Veh 40306**

Nonresidents, service of process, **Veh 17452 et seq.**

School for traffic violators, licensed driving school, court approved program, attendance, **Veh 41501**

Sentencing, rebuttal of police or traffic officer reports, **Veh 40806**

Traffic violations, attendance at school for traffic violators, **Veh 1803.5**

Written promise to appear, **Veh 40506.5**

Contractors,

Licensed contractors, weight limitations, exemption, **Veh 35704, 35716**

Working on roadways, speed limits, **Veh 22362**

Contracts,

Parking, post

Transporting loads, weight limitation variances, **Veh 35788**

Weight limits, variances, **Veh 35780 et seq.**

Contributions, agreements for transporting overweight loads, **Veh 35788**

Control, private roads open for public use, local regulation, **Veh 21107.5**

TRAFFIC RULES AND REGULATIONS
—Cont'd

Controlled intersections, pedestrians crossing, **Veh 21955**

Controlled substance violations, reports, **Veh 1803**

Conviction of crime, **Veh 42000 et seq.**

Confidential or privileged information, traffic violator schools, **Veh 1803.5, 1808.7**

Driving under the influence, post
Evidence, post
License number on abstract, **Veh 1818**

Reports, **Veh 1803 et seq.**

Suspension of execution of sentence, **Veh 42004.5**

Traffic violator schools, continuance, attendance, **Veh 41501, 42005**

Costs,

Administrative assessments, defendants, **Veh 40508.6**

Bicycles, helmets, failure to use, infractions, **Veh 21212**

Impounding vehicles, **Veh 22850.5**

Night court assessments, **Veh 42006**

Weekend courts, special assessments, **Veh 42006**

Counsel, chemical tests for drugs or alcohol, **Veh 13353**

Counties,

Amnesty, fines and penalties, **Veh 42008.5, 42008.7**

Bridges, weight limits, **Veh 35754**

Driving under the influence, alcohol and drug problem assessment program, **Veh 23646 et seq.**

Fines and penalties,

Amnesty, **Veh 42008.5, 42008.7**

Disposition, **Veh 42201**

Institutions, animal or vehicle, stopping, standing, paths, driveways or grounds, **Veh 21113**

Length of vehicles, regulation, **Veh 35401**

Nevada County, commercial vehicles, weight, use of Northwoods boulevard, **Veh 35715**

Off street parking facility, **Veh 21107.8**

Parks, **Veh 21113**

Third class, commercial vehicles, weight limit, **Veh 35712**

Weight restrictions, highways, **Veh 35700 et seq.**

Covering loads, rubbish vehicles, **Veh 23115**

Cowl or fender lamps, equipment, **Veh 25106**

Cranes,

Cables, placing in position to do bodily injury, off highway vehicles, **Veh 38318.5**

Crossings, school crossing guard, disobedience, **Veh 40000.7**

Emergency vehicles, **Veh 40000.7**

Exhaust system sales, **Veh 40000.15**

TRAFFIC RULES AND REGULATIONS
—Cont'd

Cranes—Cont'd

Exhibitions of speed, highways, **Veh 40000.15**

Explosives, transportation, **Veh 40000.19**

Fishing line, placing in position to do bodily injury, off highway vehicles, **Veh 38318.5**

Flammable liquids, **Veh 40000.19**

Flight from peace officers, **Veh 40000.7**

Hazardous materials, transportation, **Veh 40000.21**

Height of vehicle or load, **Veh 40000.7**

Hours of driving, limitation, **Veh 34506**

Length of vehicle or load, **Veh 40000.7**

Loads and loading, **Veh 40000.7**

Motor carried equipment, length of booms or masts, **Veh 35407**

Off highway vehicles, **Veh 40000.24**

Peace officers, flight from, **Veh 40000.7**

Ropes, placing in position to do bodily injury, off highway vehicles, **Veh 38318.5**

Schools, crossing guard, disobedience, **Veh 40000.7**

Crest of grade, overtaking and passing, **Veh 21752**

Crimes and offenses, **Veh 23100 et seq., 40000.14, 40000.15, 40001 et seq., 42000 et seq.**

Accidents, ante

Aggressive driving. Road rage, generally, post

Alcoholic beverages, generally, ante

Amnesty, counties, **Veh 42008.5, 42008.7**

Appearance, generally, ante

Application of law, **Veh 40007**

Armored cars, licenses, **Veh 21713**

Arraignment, closed circuit television, Placer County, **Veh 40502.1**

Arrest, generally, ante

Bail, generally, ante

Blind persons, right of way, **Veh 21963**

Bodily injury, accidents, **Veh 21070**

Bridges,

Pedestrians stopping or standing, peace officers ordering removal, **Veh 21962**

Weight limitations, **Veh 35753**

Cellular radio telephones, **Veh 23123 et seq.**

Child passenger restraint systems, **Veh 27362, 40000.15**

Citations, generally, ante

Closed circuit television, testimony or appearance for arraignment, Placer County, **Veh 40502.1**

Complaints, generally, ante

Contest of speed, highways, **Veh 23109**

Impoundment of vehicle, **Veh 22651.6**

Continuance before sentencing, rebuttal of police or traffic officer reports, **Veh 40806**

Continuance of written promise to appear, **Veh 40506.5**

TRAFFIC

TRAFFIC RULES AND REGULATIONS
—Cont'd
Crimes and offenses—Cont'd
Continuance of written promise to appear—Cont'd
Willful violation, **Veh 40508**
Conviction of crime, generally, ante
Court orders, failure to comply, **Veh 40508**
Crossings, vehicular crossings, violations, **Veh 23336**
Defenses, code violation prosecution, **Veh 41400 et seq.**
Disclosure, records, convictions, **Veh 1808.6**
Dismissal and nonsuit, generally, post
Divided highways, driving and operation, **Veh 21651**
Double jeopardy, defenses, **Veh 41400**
Drag racing, generally, post
Driving under the influence, generally, post
Driving while privilege suspended, **Veh 14601.2**
Driving with specified blood alcohol level, **Veh 40000.15**
Drug addicts, **Veh 23152, 23153**
Drugs. Driving under the influence, generally, post
Drunkenness. Driving under the influence, generally, post
Eluding peace officers, **Veh 2800.1 et seq.**
Employees, size or weight violations, **Veh 40003, 40005**
Employers failing to dispose of charges against employees, **Veh 40005**
Escape of materials from vehicles on highways, **Veh 40000.16**
Evidence, generally, post
Exhaust systems, noise pollution, decals, **Veh 27202.1**
Exhibitions of speed, highways, **Veh 23109**
Impoundment of vehicle, **Veh 22651.6**
Explosives, **Veh 31602, 31614, 31618**
Failure to appear, election, **Veh 40903**
False or fictitious names, promise to appear of arrested person, **Veh 40504**
Federal agencies, violations required by regulations, **Veh 41401**
Federal laws, violation of code required by, defenses, **Veh 41401**
Filing complaint or notice to appear, **Veh 40002, 40513**
Fines and penalties, generally, post
Flammable liquids, cargo tanks, registration, speed limits, **Veh 22406.5**
Flight from peace officers, **Veh 2800.1 et seq., 13201**
Following too closely, **Veh 21703**
Photography and pictures, sound recordings, **Veh 40008**

TRAFFIC RULES AND REGULATIONS
—Cont'd
Crimes and offenses—Cont'd
Foreign vehicles, owner or lessee chargeable, arrest or citation of driver, **Veh 40001**
Former jeopardy, **Veh 41400**
Forms, uniform traffic citation, **Veh 40508**
Garbage and refuse, generally, post
Guilty plea, **Veh 40513**
Complaint or notice to appear, **Veh 40002**
Equivalent of conviction, **Veh 13103**
Evidence, police reports, **Veh 40806**
Filing of complaint, **Veh 40513**
Police reports, evidence, **Veh 40806**
Traffic violator schools, continuance, **Veh 41501, 42005**
Hazardous substances and waste, transportation, **Veh 32002**
Height of vehicle or load, **Veh 40001 et seq.**
Highway construction zones, **Veh 42009**
Highway dumping, **Veh 23112, 23113**
Hiking trails, unauthorized vehicle, **Veh 23127**
Hitchhiking, **Veh 21957**
Horseback riding trails, unauthorized vehicles, **Veh 23127**
Hours of driving, limitation, **Veh 21702**
Ignition interlock devices, **Veh 13353.3, 23247, 23573, 40000.15**
Impounding, generally, post
Infractions, generally, post
Inhalation hazards, transportation, **Veh 32104, 40000.19**
Interference with driver or mechanism, **Veh 21701**
Photography and pictures, sound recordings, **Veh 40008**
Interstate commerce commission, violations required by regulations, **Veh 41401**
Investigating officers, official uniform and vehicle, exemption, **Veh 40804**
Jamming devices (speed), **Veh 28150, 40000.15**
Joint defendants, **Veh 40001 et seq.**
Laser jamming devices, speed, **Veh 28150, 40000.15**
Length of vehicle or load, **Veh 40001 et seq.**
Licenses and permits, special permit to exceed maximum size and weight limit, **Veh 35784**
Lighted substances, throwing on highway, **Veh 23111**
Limitations, driving hours, **Veh 21702**
Loads and loading, **Veh 40001 et seq.**
Mail and mailing, written plea, **Veh 40519**
Marijuana, possession while operating vehicle, **Veh 23222, 40000.15**
Mass transit, cellular radio telephones, **Veh 23125**

TRAFFIC RULES AND REGULATIONS
—Cont'd
Crimes and offenses—Cont'd
Mileage driven, **Veh 40000.15**
Names, use of fictitious names, **Veh 40000.25**
Narcotics. Driving under the influence, generally, post
Noise pollution, exhaust systems, decals, **Veh 27202.1**
Nolo contendere, generally, post
Notice,
Appearance, **Veh 40002**
Corrections, violations, **Veh 40000.25**
Odometer, **Veh 40000.15**
Open Container Law, **Veh 23222 et seq.**
Operation without required equipment, **Veh 24002**
Out of service orders, **Veh 40001, 40303**
Overpasses, pedestrians stopping or standing, peace officers ordering removal, **Veh 21962**
Owner or lessee chargeable, arrest of driver, **Veh 40001**
Owners responsibilities, **Veh 40001**
Passengers, interference or obstruction, **Veh 21700**
Pedestrians on bridges or overpasses, peace officers ordering removal, **Veh 21962**
Permit violation, exceeding maximum size and weight limits, **Veh 35784**
Placer County, closed circuit television, testimony or appearance for arraignment, **Veh 40502.1**
Pleading, written plea, mailing, **Veh 40519**
Promise to appear in court, violation, **Veh 40508, 42003**
Punishment. Sentence and punishment, generally, post
Racing, speed contests and exhibitions and on highway, **Veh 23109**
Radar jamming devices, speed, **Veh 28150, 40000.15**
Reckless driving, generally, post
Records and recordation, prior convictions, reports, **Veh 42004**
Road rage, generally, post
Safety regulations, motor carriers, **Veh 34506**
School buses, cellular radio telephones, **Veh 23125**
Second and subsequent offenses, generally, post
Sentence and punishment, generally, post
Service roads, entering or leaving highway, **Veh 21652**
Size, vehicle or load, **Veh 40001 et seq.**
Skiing across state highways, **Veh 21959**
Slow moving vehicles, right side of roadway, **Veh 21654**
Special permit for exceeding maximum size and weight limits, **Veh 35784**
Speed, post

TRAFFIC RULES AND REGULATIONS
—Cont'd
Crimes and offenses—Cont'd
Structures, weight limits, **Veh 35753**
Tank containers, loading, **Veh 31540**
Telecommunications, cellular radio telephones, **Veh 23123 et seq.**
Temporarily appointed enforcement personnel, failure to obey, **Veh 21100.3**
Throwing,
Lighted substance on highway, **Veh 23111**
Substances at vehicles, **Veh 23110, 40000.15**
Off highway vehicles, **Veh 38318**
Tobogganing across state highways, **Veh 21959**
Traffic citation forms, **Veh 40508**
Traffic Violator Schools, generally, this index
Trails, unauthorized vehicles, **Veh 23127**
Transit systems, cellular radio telephones, **Veh 23125**
Trespassing, **Veh 40000.15**
Uniform traffic citation, forms, **Veh 40508**
United States, violations required by federal law, **Veh 41401**
Unsafe condition, operation, **Veh 24002**
Vehicle bumper strength notices, **Veh 40000.15**
Visually handicapped persons, right of way, **Veh 21963**
Weights, post
Width of vehicle or load, **Veh 40000.7, 40001 et seq.**
Written pleas, mailing, **Veh 40519**
Criminal history information, tow trucks, **Veh 2430.3**
Crossing gate, railroad crossings, stopping, **Veh 22451 et seq.**
Crossings, **Veh 23250 et seq.**
Approaching, left side of roadway, **Veh 21752**
Arrest, **Veh 40303**
Equestrian crossings, designation, **Veh 21805**
Golf carts, **Veh 21115.1**
Off highway vehicles, **Veh 38025**
Pedestrians, post
Railroad crossings, generally, post
Special traffic regulations, **Veh 23330 et seq.**
Towing, **Veh 23270 et seq.**
Traffic safety fund, guards, compensation and salaries, **Veh 42200**
Vehicles carrying prohibited items, **Veh 23330**
Crosswalks,
Adjacent controlled intersections, **Veh 21955**
Blocking, **Veh 21970**
Buses stopping for loading or unloading, **Veh 22500**
Controlled intersections, **Veh 21955**

TRAFFIC RULES AND REGULATIONS
—Cont'd
Crosswalks—Cont'd
Crossing outside crosswalks, yielding right of way, **Veh 21954**
Definitions, **Veh 275**
Jaywalkers, yielding right of way, **Veh 21954**
Local regulations, **Veh 21961**
Overtaking and passing, vehicles stopped for pedestrians, **Veh 21951**
Fines and penalties, **Veh 42001.17**
Parking, **Veh 22500**
Pedestrians, post
Red lights, **Veh 21453**
Removal, **Veh 21950.5**
Right of way, pedestrians, **Veh 21950**
Outside crosswalks, **Veh 21954**
School buildings and grounds, guards, **Veh 40000.7, 42200**
Standing vehicles, **Veh 22500**
Stopping, post
Turning on red, yielding right of way, **Veh 21453**
Unmarked crosswalks, generally, post
Unnecessary stopping, delaying, pedestrians, **Veh 21950**
Cruising, **Veh 21100**
Culverts, traffic safety fund, use, **Veh 42200**
Curbs and gutters,
Parking, **Veh 22502, 22503**
Pedestrians leaving place of safety, path of vehicles, **Veh 21950**
Service roads, entering or leaving highway, **Veh 21650**
Stopping, standing or parking vehicles, **Veh 22500**
Curves,
Approaching vehicles, left side of roadway, **Veh 21752**
Mountain driving, horn warning, **Veh 21662**
Overtaking and passing, **Veh 21752**
Zoning, special downward speed zoning, **Veh 22358.5**
Damages,
Accidents, ante
Failure to stop, **Veh 42002.1**
Arrest, **Veh 40303**
Operation under permit to exceed maximum size, weight, **Veh 35782**
Towing, fees, notice, **Veh 22651**
Dangerous drugs. Driving under the influence, generally, post
Dazzling lights, display, **Veh 21466**
Death. Accidents, ante
Debris. Garbage and refuse, generally, post
Decals, noise pollution, exhaust systems, **Veh 27202.1**
Declarations,
Forfeiture of bail, failure to appear, Arraignment, **Veh 40512**
Trial, **Veh 40512.5**
Not guilty pleas, **Veh 40519**

TRAFFIC RULES AND REGULATIONS
—Cont'd
Decreases, weight limits,
Bridges and other structures, **Veh 35750 et seq.**
Local authorities, **Veh 35701**
State highways, **Veh 35651**
Defenses,
Driving under the influence, legitimate drug use, **Veh 23630**
Prosecution for code violations, **Veh 41400 et seq.**
Deficiencies, parking, impounding, sales, **Veh 22651**
Defiles, mountain highways, horn warning, **Veh 21662**
Definitions,
Cruising, traffic control points, **Veh 21100**
Hazardous substances, spill containment and abatement, **Veh 2452**
Delaying traffic, pedestrians, **Veh 21950**
Delegation of authority, local authorities, permits for variances, **Veh 35796**
Delinquency, fines and penalties, amnesty, **Veh 42008.7**
Delivery, magistrate, complaint, violation of promise to appear, **Veh 40515**
Notice to appear to person arrested, **Veh 40504**
Information not delivered person receiving notice, **Veh 40505**
Denver boots, scofflaws, **Veh 22651.7**
Department, definitions, **Veh 21000**
Deposit of bail, **Veh 40510**
Descending vehicles, yielding right of way, **Veh 21661**
Detour to avoid traffic violations, permittees, special size and weight permits, **Veh 35784**
Dimming lights, **Veh 24409**
Parked or standing vehicles, **Veh 24401**
Direction of traffic,
Bicycles, highways, **Veh 21650.1**
Flight from peace officers, **Veh 2800.4**
Dirt, highway dumping, **Veh 23112, 23113**
Disabled persons. Handicapped persons, generally, post
Disabled vehicles. Motor Vehicles, this index
Disabled veterans,
Curbs, marking for parking, **Veh 21458**
Parking, **Veh 22511.5 et seq.**
Violations, **Veh 22507.8**
Disasters, removal of parked or standing vehicles, **Veh 22654**
Discharging children, youth buses, **Veh 2816**
Disclosure. Crimes and offenses, ante
Dismantled vehicles, removal, **Veh 22650 et seq.**
Dismissal and nonsuit,
Abstract of record, **Veh 1803.3**
Weight, **Veh 40003**
Bail, refunds, **Veh 42201.6**

TRAFFIC

TRAFFIC RULES AND REGULATIONS
—Cont'd

Dismissal and nonsuit—Cont'd
Driving under the influence, **Veh 23635, 23640**
Registration or equipment violations, proof of correction, **Veh 40522**
Display,
Blinding or dazzling light, **Veh 21466**
Lighted red lamp, emergency vehicles, **Veh 21055**
Physicians and surgeons, insignia on vehicle, **Veh 21058**
Dispositions, fines and forfeitures, **Veh 42200 et seq.**
Distance between vehicles, **Veh 21703**
Caravans or motorcades, **Veh 21705**
Emergency vehicles, following, **Veh 21706**
Photography and pictures, sound recordings, crimes and offenses, **Veh 40008**
Trucks, school buses, and tow vehicles, **Veh 21704**
Distinctive uniform and vehicle, arresting speed violators, **Veh 40804**
Districts, applicability of traffic laws to vehicles, **Veh 21052**
Diversion of vehicles, congested streets or highways, **Veh 21101.2**
Diversion programs, alternative disposition for offenders, **Veh 42005.3**
Diverting congested traffic, **Veh 21101.2**
Divided highways,
Approaching vehicles, passing, **Veh 21660**
Business districts, U turns, **Veh 22102**
Crimes and offenses, **Veh 21651**
Driving or operation, **Veh 21651**
Lanes, operation in, **Veh 21658**
Overtaken vehicle, passing on right, **Veh 21754**
Passing on right, approaching vehicles, **Veh 21660**
Point system, drivers license, **Veh 12810**
Two or more lanes, driving or operation, **Veh 21658**
U turns, business districts, **Veh 22102**
Dogs, transporting, restraining, **Veh 23117, 42001.4**
Dollies, length limitations, vehicles and combination of vehicles, **Veh 35414**
Doors, opening on side of moving traffic, **Veh 22517**
Double fine zones, **Veh 42010**
Double jeopardy, defenses to prosecution for code violations, **Veh 41400**
Double parking, **Veh 22500**
Downward speed zoning, special physical conditions, **Veh 22358.5**
Drag racing, **Veh 23109 et seq., 40000.15**
Arrest, **Veh 40303**
Impoundment of vehicle, **Veh 22651.6**
Sentence and punishment, **Veh 23109.1**
Drawbars, exclusion in measuring length of vehicle, **Veh 35402**

TRAFFIC RULES AND REGULATIONS
—Cont'd

Drinking. Alcoholic beverages, generally, ante
Driver improvement programs, alternative punishment, **Veh 42005.3**
Driver instructions, explosives, **Veh 31611**
Driver training,
Closing streets, **Veh 21101**
Interference with driver or mechanism, exemptions, **Veh 21701**
Motor vehicle account, state transportation fund, expenditure of funds, **Veh 42277**
Drivers handbook, contents, **Veh 1656.3**
Drivers licenses, **Veh 12808**
Accidents, failure to stop, revocation or suspension, **Veh 13201, 13350, 13361**
Arrest, ante
Children and minors, intoxicating liquors, suspension for possession or transportation, **Veh 23224**
Compact, **Veh 15000 et seq.**
Driving under the influence, post
Examiners and examinations, interference with driver or mechanism, exemption, **Veh 21701**
Driving hours, limitation, **Veh 21702**
Driving logs, fines and penalties, **Veh 42001.3**
Driving under the influence, **Veh 4000, 23152 et seq.**
Abstract of conviction record, blood alcohol percentage, **Veh 1804**
Adverse or pecuniary interest, alcohol education and treatment programs, **Veh 23670**
Alcohol and drug problem assessment program, counties, **Veh 23646 et seq.**
Alcohol education programs, **Veh 23538, 23542 et seq., 23640 et seq., 23670**
Children and minors, **Veh 23140 et seq., 23520**
Drivers licenses,
Reinstatement, **Veh 13352, 13352.1**
Restricted licenses, **Veh 13352.4, 13353.3**
Persons age eighteen to twenty one, **Veh 13352.6, 23502**
Proof, **Veh 13352.2**
Alcohol rehabilitation pilot programs, **Veh 23166.1**
Alternative, alcohol or drug education program, **Veh 23598**
Arrest, **Veh 23166.1, 40302**
Mandatory appearance before magistrate, **Veh 40302**
Matching arrests with convictions, data and monitoring system, **Veh 1822**
Without warrant, **Veh 40300.5, 40300.6**
Assessments, alcohol and drug problems, **Veh 23645 et seq.**

TRAFFIC RULES AND REGULATIONS
—Cont'd

Driving under the influence—Cont'd
Bicycles, **Veh 21200, 21200.5, 40000.13**
Blood tests, **Veh 13353, 23158**
Abstract of conviction record, **Veh 1804**
Children and minors, **Veh 23136**
Juvenile offenses, concentration, **Veh 23140**
Motorized scooters, **Veh 21221.5**
Bodily injury, **Veh 23153**
Breath tests, **Veh 13353, 26508**
Children and minors, **Veh 13353.1, 23136**
Motorized scooters, **Veh 21221.5**
Canada,
Implied consent, **Veh 13353**
Children and minors, **Veh 13353.1**
Revocation or suspension, drivers licenses, **Veh 13353.3**
Checkpoints, **Veh 2814.2**
Chemical tests,
Drivers licenses, revocation or suspension, **Veh 13380 et seq., 23612**
Evidence, **Veh 23612**
Implied consent, **Veh 13353, 13384, 23612**
Motorized scooters, **Veh 21221.5**
Refusal, sentence and punishment, **Veh 23577, 23578**
Samples, **Veh 23614**
Children and minors, **Veh 23136**
Alcohol education and treatment programs, **Veh 23520**
Coroners, visitation program, **Veh 23517**
Drivers licenses,
Notice before issuance, **Veh 12802.5**
Restricted licenses, **Veh 13353.8**
Revocation or suspension, reissuance, fees, **Veh 13392**
Temporary licenses, **Veh 13388**
Fines and penalties, **Veh 23500 et seq., 42001.25**
Hospitals, visitation program, **Veh 23517**
Juvenile offenses involving alcohol, **Veh 23140**
Notice before issuance, **Veh 12802.5**
Passengers under age 14, enhanced sentence, **Veh 23572**
Refusal to submit to tests, **Veh 13353.1**
Restricted licenses, **Veh 13353.8**
Second and subsequent offenses, fines and penalties, **Veh 42001.25**
Tests, **Veh 13388**
Visitation program, **Veh 23509 et seq.**
Combined influence of liquor and drugs, **Veh 23152, 23153**
Treatment program, participation in lieu of suspension of driving privileges, **Veh 13352.5**

TRAFFIC RULES AND REGULATIONS
—Cont'd
Driving under the influence—Cont'd
Confidential or privileged information, records and recordation, **Veh 1807.5, 1808.5**
Constitutional challenges, separate convictions, **Veh 23624**
Conviction of crime,
Arrest, data and monitoring system, **Veh 1822**
Licenses and permits, revocation or suspension, **Veh 13550**
Vehicular homicide, advisory statements, **Veh 23593**
Counsel, right to, chemical tests, **Veh 13353**
Counties, alcohol and drug problem assessment program, **Veh 23646 et seq.**
Data and monitoring system, violations, **Veh 1821, 1822**
Death, implied consent, chemical tests, **Veh 13353**
Defenses, legitimate drug use, **Veh 23630**
Definitions, **Veh 312**
Delayed revocations and suspensions, drivers licenses, **Veh 23665**
Designated driver program, information sheet, **Veh 2426**
Dismissal of charges, **Veh 23635, 23640**
Drinking in motor vehicle, **Veh 23221**
Drivers licenses,
Commercial vehicles, revocation or suspension, **Veh 13557**
Compact, **Veh 15000 et seq.**
Declarations, **Veh 13385**
Denial, **Veh 12805**
Parole and probation, revocation or suspension, **Veh 13353.2, 13389, 13557**
Reinstatement, persons age eighteen to twenty one, **Veh 13352.6**
Restricted licenses, **Veh 13352, 13352.5, 13353.7**
Ignition interlock devices, **Veh 13353.3, 23573**
Treatment programs, **Veh 13352.4**
Revocation or suspension, **Veh 13201, 13202, 13366.5, 13380 et seq., 13550 et seq., 14601.5, 23536 et seq., 23550.5, 23612, 23660, 23665**
Driving after revocation or suspension, **Veh 14601**
Parole and probation, **Veh 13353.2**
Persons age eighteen to twenty one, **Veh 13352.6, 23502**
Point system, **Veh 12810**
Prior conviction for vehicular manslaughter involving alcohol, **Veh 13954**
Refusal to submit to tests, children and minors, **Veh 13353.1**
Reinstatement, **Veh 13353.4**

TRAFFIC RULES AND REGULATIONS
—Cont'd
Driving under the influence—Cont'd
Drivers licenses—Cont'd
Revocation or suspension—Cont'd
Second and subsequent offenses, **Veh 23597**
Temporary licenses, parole and probation, **Veh 13389**
Driving school operator or instructor, **Veh 11110**
Driving while privilege suspended, **Veh 14601 et seq.**
Education, **Veh 23538, 23542 et seq., 23640 et seq.**
Alcoholics and alcoholism, **Veh 23538, 23542 et seq., 23640 et seq., 23670**
Children and minors, **Veh 23520**
Enforcement of regulations, **Veh 23215**
Enhanced sentences, **Veh 23578**
Evidence,
Chemical tests, **Veh 23612**
Refusal, **Veh 23577**
Destroying or concealing evidence, arrest without warrant, **Veh 40300.5**
Ignition interlock devices, **Veh 13353.3, 23573, 23575**
Passengers under age 14, punishment enhancement, **Veh 23572**
Presumptions, **Veh 23152, 23153, 23610**
Speeding, enhanced sentence, **Veh 23582**
Exemptions,
Hemophiliacs, blood tests, **Veh 23612**
Ignition interlock devices, **Veh 13353.3, 23573, 23575**
Open Container Law, **Veh 23229**
Fees, ignition interlock devices, **Veh 13353.3, 23573**
Financial responsibility, **Veh 13352.4, 13352.6**
Restricted licenses, **Veh 13352.5**
Fines and penalties, **Veh 14601, 23530 et seq.**
Bicyclists, **Veh 21200**
Children and minors, **Veh 23500 et seq.**
Ignition interlock devices, **Veh 13353.3, 23573**
Motorized scooters, **Veh 21221.5**
Parole and probation, failure to pay, **Veh 23601**
Second and subsequent offenses, **Veh 23540, 23560**
First offense, fines and penalties, **Veh 14601**
Foreign states,
Implied consent, **Veh 13353**
Children and minors, **Veh 13353.1**
Revocation or suspension, drivers licenses, **Veh 13353.3**
Guilty plea, **Veh 23103.5**

TRAFFIC RULES AND REGULATIONS
—Cont'd
Driving under the influence—Cont'd
Habitual traffic offenders, **Veh 23546, 23550, 23550.5, 23566**
Hardship or restricted permits, **Veh 13353.4**
High concentrations, blood alcohol, enhanced sentence, **Veh 23578**
Homicide, advisory statements, **Veh 23593**
Ignition interlock devices, **Veh 13352, 13353.3, 23247 et seq., 23573, 23575**
Certificates and certification, **Veh 13386**
Driving while privilege suspended, **Veh 14601.2 et seq.**
Inclusion as specified restrictions, **Veh 13202.8**
Records and recordation, **Veh 23575**
Second and subsequent offenses, **Veh 14601.2 et seq., 23597**
Studies, **Veh 23575.1**
Implied consent, **Veh 13353 et seq., 23136, 23612**
Blood tests, **Veh 13353**
Chemical tests, **Veh 13384**
Impounding, **Veh 23594**
Second and subsequent offenses, **Veh 14602.8**
Investigations and investigators, **Veh 13800 et seq.**
Presentence investigations, **Veh 23655**
Judgments and decrees,
Motion to vacate or set aside prior judgment, **Veh 41403**
Nolo contendere, prior conviction based upon, setting aside, **Veh 41403**
Juvenile delinquents and dependents, **Veh 13352.3**
Labor and employment, restricted licenses, **Veh 13352.5**
Marijuana, possession while operating, **Veh 23222, 40000.15**
Matching arrests with convictions, data and monitoring system, **Veh 1822**
Medical treatment, chemical tests, **Veh 13353**
Misdemeanor driving, **Veh 40000.15**
Monitoring system, violations, **Veh 1822**
Motions, vacating or setting aside separate judgments, **Veh 41403**
Motorized scooters, **Veh 40303**
Application of law, **Veh 21221, 21221.5**
Multiple victims, enhanced sentence, **Veh 23558**
Negligence, **Veh 23153**
Nolo contendere plea, **Veh 23103.5**
Nonresidents,
Ignition interlock devices, **Veh 23575**
License suspension or revocation, termination, **Veh 13353.5**

TRAFFIC

TRAFFIC RULES AND REGULATIONS
—Cont'd

Driving under the influence—Cont'd
Notice,
Drivers licenses, restrictions, **Veh 23662**
Ignition interlock devices, **Veh 13353.3, 23573, 23575**
Nuisance vehicles, sales, **Veh 23596**
Nuisance, motor vehicles, **Veh 23596**
Occupants of vehicle drinking on highway, **Veh 23220**
Off highway vehicles, driving while privilege suspended, **Veh 14601.5**
Open Container Law, **Veh 23222 et seq.**
Owner as passenger, **Veh 17158**
Parole and probation, **Veh 23154, 23166.1, 23530 et seq., 23600 et seq.**
Alcoholics and alcoholism, treatment, **Veh 23538, 23542 et seq.**
Children and minors, **Veh 23520**
Children and minors, **Veh 23500 et seq.**
Drivers licenses, revocation or suspension, **Veh 13353.2, 13389, 13557**
Ignition interlock devices, certificates and certification, **Veh 13386**
Notice, **Veh 23662**
Temporary licenses, **Veh 13389**
Visitation program, **Veh 23509 et seq.**
Youthful drunk driver visitation program, **Veh 23509 et seq.**
Passengers under age 14, enhanced sentence, **Veh 23572**
Persons age eighteen to twenty one, **Veh 13352.6**
Fines and penalties, **Veh 23502**
Phlebotomy technicians, blood tests, **Veh 23158**
Point count, **Veh 12810**
Poisons, arrest, appearance, **Veh 40302**
Possession of opened container, **Veh 23222 et seq.**
Presentence investigations, **Veh 23655**
Presumptions, **Veh 23152 et seq., 23610**
Prior offenses, **Veh 23620 et seq.**
Records and recordation, **Veh 13209**
Problem assessment program, **Veh 23249.50**
Public policy, separate offenses, **Veh 23217**
Puerto Rico,
Implied consent, **Veh 13353**
Children and minors, **Veh 13353.1**
Revocation or suspension, drivers licenses, **Veh 13353.3**
Recidivism tracking system, **Veh 1821**
Records and recordation,
Confidential or privileged information, **Veh 1807.5**
Ignition interlock devices, **Veh 23575**
Prior convictions, **Veh 13209**
Violations, data and monitoring system, **Veh 1822**
Refusal to submit to test, **Veh 13353**

TRAFFIC RULES AND REGULATIONS
—Cont'd

Driving under the influence—Cont'd
Refusal to submit to test—Cont'd
Children and minors, **Veh 13353.1**
Reinstatement, drivers licenses, persons age eighteen to twenty one, **Veh 13352.6**
Removal of vehicles, second and subsequent offenses, **Veh 14602.8**
Repeat offenders, investigations and investigators, **Veh 13800 et seq.**
Reports,
Alcohol and drug problem assessments, **Veh 23648**
Arrests, data and monitoring system, **Veh 1822**
Chemical tests, drivers licenses, revocation or suspension, **Veh 13380, 13388, 23612**
Convictions, data and monitoring system, **Veh 1822**
Restrictions, **Veh 13352.5**
Ignition interlock devices, installation, **Veh 13352**
Sales,
Ignition interlock devices, **Veh 23575**
Nuisance vehicles, **Veh 23596**
Samples, chemical tests, **Veh 23614**
Searches and seizures, second and subsequent offenses, **Veh 14602.8**
Second and subsequent offenses, **Veh 13352.5, 23540, 23546, 23550, 23550.5, 23560, 23566**
Alcohol and drug problem assessment program, **Veh 23646 et seq.**
Children and minors, fines and penalties, **Veh 42001.25**
Drivers licenses, revocation or suspension, **Veh 23597**
Impounding vehicles, **Veh 14602.8**
Prior conviction for vehicular manslaughter involving alcohol, **Veh 13954**
Reckless driving under influence of alcohol, **Veh 23103.5**
Removal of vehicles, **Veh 14602.8**
Searches and seizures, **Veh 14602.8**
Storage, **Veh 14602.8**
Treatment, alcoholics and alcoholism, **Veh 23580**
Weekend service of sentence program, **Veh 23580**
Work release programs, **Veh 23580**
Sentence and punishment, **Veh 23530 et seq., 23600 et seq.**
Children and minors, **Veh 23500 et seq.**
Prior conviction record, **Veh 13209**
Record of prior convictions, **Veh 13209**
Separate offenses, **Veh 23620 et seq.**
Legislative intent, **Veh 23217**
Signs and signals, monuments and memorials, damages, **Veh 17300 et seq.**
Sobriety checkpoints, **Veh 2814.2**

TRAFFIC RULES AND REGULATIONS
—Cont'd

Driving under the influence—Cont'd
Speeding, enhanced sentence, **Veh 23582**
Statements, vehicular homicide, advisory statements, **Veh 23593**
Storage,
Opened container, **Veh 23225**
Second and subsequent offenses, **Veh 14602.8**
Studies, ignition interlock devices, **Veh 23575.1**
Supersedeas or stay,
Alcohol education and treatment programs, **Veh 23640**
Sentence and punishment, **Veh 23600**
Surrender, drivers licenses, **Veh 23660**
Temporary licenses, parole and probation, **Veh 13389**
Tests, **Veh 13353, 13380 et seq., 23612**
Administration of tests, **Veh 23158**
Children and minors, **Veh 13353.1, 13388, 23136**
Implied consent, **Veh 13384, 23612**
Motorized scooters, **Veh 21221.5**
Refusal, sentence and punishment, **Veh 23577, 23578**
Samples, chemical tests, **Veh 23614**
Traffic signs and signals, monuments and memorials, damages, **Veh 17300 et seq.**
Traffic violator schools, continuance, attendance, exemptions, **Veh 41501**
Treatment programs, **Veh 23538, 23542 et seq., 23640 et seq., 23670**
Children and minors, **Veh 23520**
Drivers licenses,
Reinstatement, **Veh 13352**
Restricted licenses, **Veh 13352.4, 13353.3**
Persons age 18 to 21, **Veh 13352.6, 23502**
Proof, **Veh 13352.2**
Restriction of driving privilege, **Veh 13352.5**
Vehicular homicide, advisory statements, **Veh 23593**
Violations, data and monitoring system, **Veh 1822**
Visitation, youthful drunk driver visitation program, **Veh 23509 et seq.**
Weekend service of sentence program, **Veh 23536, 23580**
Work permits, **Veh 23538, 23562**
Work release programs, **Veh 23536, 23580**
Youthful drunk driver visitation program, **Veh 23509 et seq.**
Drug addicts. Driving under the influence, generally, ante
Drugs. Driving under the influence, generally, ante
Drunken driving. Driving under the influence, generally, ante

TRAFFIC RULES AND REGULATIONS
   —Cont'd

Dumping. Garbage and refuse, generally, post

Duplicate deposits of bail, refunds, **Veh 42201.6**

Dwelling mover, transporting across railroad tracks, notice, **Veh 35789**

Dynamic stability, testing, **Veh 35101**

Earplugs, wearing while operating motor vehicle, **Veh 27400**

Education,
   Alternative disposition for offenders, **Veh 42005.3**
   Driving under the influence, ante

Educational institutions, animal or vehicle, stopping, paths, grounds, **Veh 21113**

Effect of traffic laws, **Veh 21050 et seq.**

Eight hundred (800) numbers, trucks transporting workmen, **Veh 2429**

Election of trial, failure to appear, **Veh 40903**

Electric cars. Street railways, generally, post

Electric carts, local regulations, **Veh 21100, 21114.5**

Electric personal assistive mobility devices, **Veh 21280 et seq.**

Electric vehicles, parking, designated spaces, **Veh 22511, 22511.1, 42001.6**

Electronic beacons, traversing, **Veh 2818**

Electronic mail, infractions, **Veh 23123.5**

Electronic timing devices, speed traps, burden of proof, **Veh 40803**

Elevated structures, speed, **Veh 22402 et seq.**

Eluding peace officers, **Veh 2800.1 et seq., 13201**

Embezzlement, removal of parked or standing vehicles, **Veh 22650 et seq.**

Emergencies,
   Bicycles, peace officers, exemptions, **Veh 21200**
   Closing off fire areas, **Veh 21707**
   Crossing fire hoses, **Veh 21708**
   Fire areas, restrictions, **Veh 21707**
   Obedience to traffic signals, **Veh 21462**
   Permits to operate, excessive size, weight, **Veh 35780 et seq.**
   Physicians and surgeons, exemptions, **Veh 21058**
   Traffic control, cone and flare patterns, **Veh 2818**

Emergency roadside services, **Veh 2430 et seq.**

Emergency vehicles,
   Applicability of traffic laws, **Veh 21052**
   Arbitrary exercise of privileges, **Veh 21056**
   Authorized vehicles, yielding right of way, **Veh 21806, 21807**
   Crimes and offenses, **Veh 40000.7**
   Disasters, removal of parked or standing vehicles, **Veh 22654**
   Due care, driver or operator, **Veh 21056**
   Duty of driver, **Veh 21056**

TRAFFIC RULES AND REGULATIONS
   —Cont'd

Emergency vehicles—Cont'd
   Exemptions, **Veh 21052, 21055, 21056**
      Right of way, **Veh 21807**
      Size, weight and load provision, **Veh 35002**
         Inspections, **Veh 34500.2**
   Following vehicles, **Veh 21706**
   Gaseous discharge lamp, **Veh 25258**
   High occupancy vehicle lanes, **Veh 21655.8, 21806**
   Infractions, fines and penalties, **Veh 42001.12**
   Lighted red lamps, **Veh 21055**
   Military forces, police escort vehicles, sirens and speed, **Veh 21057**
   Obstructions, removal, **Veh 22654**
   Off highway vehicles, exemptions, **Veh 21055**
   Physicians and surgeons, exemption, **Veh 21058**
   Rates and charges, toll on crossings, exemptions, **Veh 23301.5**
   Right of way, **Veh 21806, 21807**
   Siren,
      Exemption from traffic law, **Veh 21055**
      Police and traffic officers, **Veh 21057**
   Speed, escorts, police, **Veh 21057**
   Standing vehicles, overtaking and passing, **Veh 21809**
   White light, **Veh 25258**
   Yielding right of way to, **Veh 21806**

Employees. Officers and employees, generally, post

Employers, failure to dispose of charges against employees, **Veh 40005**

Enactment, **Veh 2402**

Encumbrances. Liens and incumbrances, generally, post

Enforcement, **Veh 2400 et seq.**
   Private roads open for public use, **Veh 21107.5**

Engineering surveys, speed limits, **Veh 22354 et seq.**

English language, **Veh 1656**

Enhanced sentences, driving under the influence, **Veh 23578**

Entering controlled access freeways, ramps, **Veh 21664**

Entering roadway, barriers, local authorities, **Veh 21101**

Entrance of through highways, yielding right of way, **Veh 21802**

Environment, off highway vehicles, crimes and offenses, **Veh 40000.24**

Equestrian crossings, right of way, **Veh 21805**

Equipment,
   Bicycles, **Veh 21201**
   Bumper strength notices, **Veh 24011.3, 40000.15**
   Clearance and side marker lamps, vehicles 80 inches or more in width, **Veh 25100**

TRAFFIC RULES AND REGULATIONS
   —Cont'd

Equipment—Cont'd
   Cowl or fender lamps, **Veh 25106**
   Emergency vehicles, gaseous discharge lamps, **Veh 25258**
   Lights and lighting, generally, post
   Motor carriers, safety regulations, **Veh 34500 et seq.**
   Motorized scooters, **Veh 21223, 21224, 21235**
   Notice to correct violations, **Veh 40303.5**
   Projecting, width limits, **Veh 35110**
   Public employees, application of law, **Veh 21053**
   Reflectors,
      Front and sides, **Veh 24608**
      Red, rear mounting, **Veh 24607**
   Trolley coaches, **Veh 21051**
   Violations, proof of correction, dismissal, **Veh 40522**
   Width, vehicle or load extension beyond permissible limits, **Veh 35109, 35110**

Erroneous collection of fees or penalties, refunds, limitations, **Veh 42231, 42232**

Escape from peace officers,
   Crimes and offenses, **Veh 2800.1 et seq., 13201**
   Point system, drivers license, **Veh 12810**

Escort vehicles,
   Pilot cars, **Veh 472, 27904**
   Police or traffic officers, following vehicles, **Veh 21706**

Evading arrest, optional appearance before magistrate, **Veh 40303**

Evidence, **Veh 40800 et seq.**
   Accident report, civil actions, **Veh 40833**
   Arresting officer, sworn declaration, **Veh 40903**
   Business record, receipt, **Veh 40903**
   Civil actions, **Veh 40830 et seq.**
   Code prosecution, **Veh 40800 et seq.**
   Continuance before sentencing, rebuttal of police or traffic officer report, **Veh 40806**
   Conviction of crime,
      Civil actions, inadmissibility, **Veh 40830 et seq.**
      Collateral estoppel, civil actions, **Veh 40834**
      Double jeopardy, **Veh 41400**
      Negligence,
         Inadmissibility, violations under state or federal authority, **Veh 40830**
         Speed violations, **Veh 40831**
      Res judicata, civil actions, **Veh 40834**
      Speed violations, civil actions, **Veh 40831**
   Defenses, code violation prosecution, **Veh 41400 et seq.**
   Delinquent parking violations notice, **Veh 40903**
   Department informational reports, prior convictions, **Veh 42004**

TRAFFIC

TRAFFIC RULES AND REGULATIONS
—Cont'd
Evidence—Cont'd
Departmental finding, reports, **Veh 40833**
Disaster Act, inadmissibility, conviction for violation under governors orders or directives, **Veh 40830**
Driving privilege, revocation or suspension, civil actions, **Veh 40832**
Driving under the influence, ante
Electronic speed timing devices, speeding prosecutions, **Veh 40803, 40808**
Failure to appear, **Veh 40903**
Federal authority, violations under, inadmissibility of convictions, **Veh 40830**
Findings of department, reports, **Veh 40833**
Fines and penalties, ability to pay, **Veh 42003**
Guilty plea, police reports, **Veh 40806**
Hearing, revocation or suspension of driving privilege, **Veh 40832**
Ignition interlock devices, driving under the influence, **Veh 13353.3, 23573**
Illegal evidence, **Veh 40800 et seq.**
Incompetency, obtained by maintenance or use of speed traps or failure to wear uniform, **Veh 40804**
Infractions, trial written declaration, **Veh 40902**
Letter of defendant, **Veh 40903**
Maximum speed on bridges, **Veh 22404, 22405**
Negligence, post
Notice to appear, **Veh 40903**
Owners, proof of ownership, parking violation, **Veh 40900**
Parking, notice of violation, **Veh 40903**
Parking violations, proof of ownership, **Veh 40900**
Police reports, guilty plea, **Veh 40806**
Presumptions, **Veh 41100 et seq.**
Log book, motor carriers,
Hours of operation, **Veh 34501.4**
Speed, **Veh 34501.3**
Negligent drivers, prima facie presumption, **Veh 12810.5**
Slow moving vehicles, right side of roadway, violations, **Veh 21654**
Speed, **Veh 41100**
Towing vehicle, operator violation of law, **Veh 41104**
Train of vehicles, failure to follow path of towing vehicle, **Veh 41104**
Prosecutions under code, **Veh 40800 et seq.**
Rebuttal evidence, police reports, **Veh 40806**
Receipts, **Veh 40903**
Reports,
Accidents, civil actions, **Veh 40833**
Electronic recording, **Veh 1806**

TRAFFIC RULES AND REGULATIONS
—Cont'd
Evidence—Cont'd
Reports—Cont'd
Police reports on guilty plea, **Veh 40806**
Prior convictions, **Veh 42004**
Revocation or suspension of driving privilege, record, **Veh 40832**
Second and subsequent offenses, informational reports, **Veh 42004**
Security file, **Veh 40833**
Slow moving vehicles, violations, **Veh 21654**
Speed,
Convictions, civil actions, **Veh 40831**
Excess speed, **Veh 22351**
Lawful speed, **Veh 22351**
Maximum speed on bridges, tubes, **Veh 22404, 22405**
Presumptions, **Veh 41100**
Prima facie speed limits, **Veh 22351, 22352**
Traps, **Veh 40801 et seq.**
State highway weight limits, violation of decreased restriction, **Veh 35655**
Statement of defendant, **Veh 40903**
Toll roads and bridges, crossings, evasion of toll, **Veh 23302**
Traffic officers,
Distinctive uniform and vehicle, **Veh 40800**
Reports, rebuttal, **Veh 40806**
United States, conviction for violation of code required by federal law, inadmissibility, **Veh 40830**
Written declaration, infractions, **Veh 40902**
Excavations, stopping, standing or parking vehicles, **Veh 22500**
Exceeding maximum limits, size, weight, permits, **Veh 35780 et seq.**
Excessive fees or penalties, refunds, limitations, **Veh 42231, 42232**
Exclusive use of highway, **Veh 21655.6**
Exemptions,
Axle limits, weight, **Veh 35553**
Bicycles, peace officers, **Veh 21200**
Blind persons, parking, cancellation, revocation, **Veh 22511.6**
Child passenger restraint systems, **Veh 27363**
Driving or road tests, interference with driver or mechanism, **Veh 21701**
Driving under the influence, ante
Emergency vehicles, ante
Freeways, parking and stopping, **Veh 21718**
Garbage vehicles, **Veh 21059**
Handicapped persons, parking, cancellation, revocation, **Veh 22511.6**
Ignition interlock devices, driving under the influence, **Veh 13353.3, 23573, 23575**
Intoxicating liquors, Open Container Law, **Veh 23229**

TRAFFIC RULES AND REGULATIONS
—Cont'd
Exemptions—Cont'd
Length, post
Licensed contractors, weight limits, **Veh 35704**
Loads and loading, **Veh 35001, 35002**
Local authorities, commercial vehicles, designated hours for sweeping streets, **Veh 22507.6**
Official uniform and vehicle, investigating officers, **Veh 40804**
Parking, post
Peace officers, bicycles, **Veh 21200**
Public agency representatives, **Veh 21054**
Public employees working on highway, **Veh 21053**
Public utility vehicles, weight limits, **Veh 35704**
Right side of roadway, driving and operation, **Veh 21650**
Rubbish truck, **Veh 21059**
Size, weight and load provisions, **Veh 35001, 35002**
Streetsweeper, **Veh 21060**
Timber and lumber, hauling of saw logs, weight limits, **Veh 35785**
Traffic officers, distinctive uniform and vehicle, **Veh 40800**
Unincorporated area parking, **Veh 22504**
Watering vehicles, **Veh 21060**
Weights, post
Exhaust systems, noise pollution, decals, **Veh 27202.1**
Exhibitions of speed, highways, **Veh 23109**
Impoundment of vehicle, **Veh 22651.6**
Existing conditions, regard for, speed, **Veh 22350**
Exit, traffic barriers prohibiting, local authorities, **Veh 21101**
Expenses and expenditures, arrest, issuance of warrant, **Veh 40516**
Explosives, **Veh 31600 et seq.**
Caldecott tunnel, transportation, **Veh 31301**
Crimes and offenses, **Veh 40000.19**
Crossings, vehicular crossings, toll roads or bridges, **Veh 23330**
Designated lanes, slow moving vehicles, **Veh 21655**
Distances between vehicles, **Veh 21704**
Licenses and permits, **Veh 2501 et seq.**
Motor truck carrying, grade crossing, stopping, **Veh 22452**
Parking, post
Point system, drivers license, **Veh 12810**
Railroad crossings,
Signs, **Veh 22452.5**
Stopping, **Veh 22452, 22453**
Slow moving vehicles, designated lanes, **Veh 21655**
Speed limits, **Veh 22406 et seq.**
Distance between vehicles, **Veh 21704**

TRAFFIC RULES AND REGULATIONS
—Cont'd

Extension devices, vehicles or combination of vehicles, length restrictions, **Veh 35402**

Extralegal loads, route deviations, **Veh 35784**

Eyeglasses, motorists, temple width interfering with lateral vision, **Veh 23120**

Failure to appear or pay fine,
   Appearance, ante
   Arrest, ante
   Bail, ante

Failure to obey ordinances, **Veh 21461**

False or fictitious name, arrested person, release on promise to appear, **Veh 40504**

Farm vehicles. Agricultural Machinery and Equipment, generally, this index

Federal agencies, violations required by regulations, defenses, **Veh 41401**

Federal laws, violation of code required by, defenses, **Veh 41401**

Fees,
   Accepting fees, refunds, **Veh 42231, 42232**
   Application for refund, limitations, **Veh 42232**
   Correction of violations, **Veh 40611**
   Erroneous collection, refunds, **Veh 42231, 42232**
   Height, licenses and permits, variances, **Veh 35795**
   Ignition interlock devices, driving under the influence, **Veh 13353.3, 23573**
   Length, licenses and permits, variances, **Veh 35795**
   Loads and loading, licenses and permits, variances, **Veh 35795**
   Mistaken collection, refunds, **Veh 42231, 42232**
   Monitoring reports and services of traffic violators, **Veh 11205.1**
   Parking, post
   Refunds, **Veh 42230 et seq.**
   Size, licenses and permits, variances, **Veh 35795**
   Storage, notice, **Veh 22651**
   Traffic schools, motor vehicle violators, administrative fees, **Veh 42007, 42007.1**
   Trolley coaches, application of law, **Veh 21051**
   Weights, post
   Width of vehicle or load, licenses and permits, variances, **Veh 35795**

Ferries, stopping at railroad crossing leading to, **Veh 22453**

Field test by highway patrol, **Veh 2408**

Fifth wheels, trailers,
   Length extensions, **Veh 35402**
   Towing trailers carrying passengers, **Veh 21712**

Filing,
   Arrest, copies of notice to appear, **Veh 40506**

TRAFFIC RULES AND REGULATIONS
—Cont'd

Filing—Cont'd
   Complaint or notice to appear in court, **Veh 40513**
      Persons owning or controlling vehicles, **Veh 40002**

Fines and penalties, **Veh 23100 et seq., 40000.15, 42000 et seq.**
   Ability to pay, **Veh 42003**
   Accidents, ante
   Amnesty, **Veh 42008 et seq.**
   Application for refund, limitations, **Veh 42232**
   Application of law, **Veh 40007**
   Armored cars, licenses, **Veh 21713**
   Assessments, night court, **Veh 42006**
   Bicycles, ante
   Bodily injury, **Veh 42001.19**
   Bumper strength notices, **Veh 24011.3, 40000.15**
   Categories, offense classification, uniform schedule, **Veh 40310**
   Cellular radio telephones, **Veh 23123**
      Children and minors, **Veh 23124**
   Children and minors, passenger restraint systems, **Veh 27362**
   Classification, penalty categories, **Veh 40310**
   Compensation, school crossing guards, **Veh 42201**
   Counties, ante
   Court costs, administrative assessment, **Veh 40508.6**
   Delinquency, amnesty, **Veh 42008.7**
   Deposit applied, **Veh 40519**
   Disabled person placards, loan to unauthorized persons, fines and penalties, **Veh 4461.5**
   Disposition, **Veh 42200 et seq.**
   Double fine zones, **Veh 42010**
   Drag racing, **Veh 23109.1**
   Drivers licenses, delinquent parking violations, refusal to issue or renew, **Veh 12808.1**
   Driving hours, limitation, **Veh 21702**
   Driving under the influence, ante
   Electronic mail, **Veh 23123.5**
   Eluding peace officers, **Veh 2800.1 et seq.**
   Emergency vehicles, standing vehicles, overtaking and passing, **Veh 21809**
   Erroneous collection, refunds, **Veh 42231, 42232**
   Evidence, ability to pay, **Veh 42003**
   Excessive penalties, refunds, **Veh 42231, 42232**
   Exhaust systems, noise pollution, decals, **Veh 27202.1**
   Exhibitions of speed, highways, **Veh 23109**
   Explosives, transportation, **Veh 31618**
   Failure to appear or pay, **Veh 40000.25, 40508**
      Liens and incumbrances, **Veh 14911**
   Felony convictions, **Veh 42000**

TRAFFIC RULES AND REGULATIONS
—Cont'd

Fines and penalties—Cont'd
   Firearms, discharging at vehicle or occupant, **Veh 23110**
   Flammable liquids, tank vehicles, speed limits, **Veh 22406.5**
   Flight from peace officers, **Veh 2800.1 et seq., 13201**
   General misdemeanors, **Veh 42002**
   Great bodily injury, **Veh 42001.19**
   Guilty plea, consideration of police reports, **Veh 40806**
   Handicapped persons, parking spaces, fines and penalties, **Veh 42001.5**
   Hazardous substances and waste,
      Route notification, **Veh 32053**
      Transportation, **Veh 32002**
   Highway construction zones, **Veh 42009**
   Hours of driving, limitation, **Veh 21702**
   Ignition interlock devices, driving under the influence, **Veh 13353.3, 23247, 23573**
   Impounding, generally, post
   Infractions, post
   Inspection and inspectors, failure to stop and submit, **Veh 42002.1**
   Instant messages, **Veh 23123.5**
   Jamming devices (speed), **Veh 28150, 40000.15**
   Judgment ordering payment or imprisonment, **Veh 42003**
   Laser jamming devices, speed, **Veh 28150, 40000.15**
   Late charge, **Veh 40310**
   Liens and incumbrances, failure to pay fine, **Veh 14911**
   Limitation of actions, erroneous collection of penalties, **Veh 42231, 42232**
   Limitation on driving hours, **Veh 21702**
   Littering, off highway vehicles, **Veh 38320**
   Local authorities, highways and roads, closing, **Veh 21104**
   Logbooks, **Veh 34501.3**
   Marijuana, possession while operating, **Veh 23222**
   Mistaken collection, refunds, **Veh 42231, 42232**
   Municipality, disposition of funds, **Veh 42200**
   Night court assessment, **Veh 42006**
   Notice, failure to pay, **Veh 40509.5**
   Official misconduct, deposit of funds, **Veh 42202**
   Parking, post
   Passengers, trunk, **Veh 21712**
   Payment of fines, **Veh 42003**
   Pedestrians, **Veh 42001**
   Public offenses, **Veh 42000 et seq.**
   Racing, speed contests, **Veh 23109, 23109.1**
   Radar jamming devices, speed, **Veh 28150, 40000.15**
   Radioactive materials, drivers licenses, **Veh 14611**

TRAFFIC

TRAFFIC RULES AND REGULATIONS
—Cont'd

Fines and penalties—Cont'd

Receipt for payment proscribing arrest, **Veh 40312**

Reckless driving, **Veh 23105**

Record of prior conviction, report, **Veh 42004**

Refunds, **Veh 42230 et seq.**

Registration or equipment violations, proof of correction, **Veh 40522**

Reports, prior convictions, **Veh 42004**

Running red light, **Veh 42001.15**

Safety belt use, mandatory, **Veh 27315**

Safety enhancement double fine zones, **Veh 42010**

School crossing guards, compensation, **Veh 42201**

Second and subsequent offenses,
Reports, prior convictions, **Veh 42004**
Special misdemeanors, **Veh 42001**
Weight limits, violation, **Veh 42030**

Size, special permits,
Failure to obtain, **Veh 35784.5**
Violations of terms and conditions, **Veh 35784**

Special misdemeanors, **Veh 42001**

Speed, post

Standing vehicles, emergency vehicles, overtaking and passing, **Veh 21809**

Suspension of penalty, overweight operation, **Veh 42030**

Telecommunications, cellular radio telephones, **Veh 23123**
Children and minors, **Veh 23124**

Text messages, **Veh 23123.5**

Throwing or projecting substances at vehicles, **Veh 23110**

Tow trucks, standing vehicles, overtaking and passing, **Veh 21809**

Traffic safety fund, disposition, **Veh 42200**

Transportation department, standing vehicles, overtaking and passing, **Veh 21809**

Trunk, passengers, **Veh 21712**

Uniform schedule, **Veh 40310**

Violation or failure to comply with provisions of code, **Veh 42002 et seq.**

Weekend courts, special assessments, **Veh 42006**

Weights, post

Fire areas, restriction, **Veh 21707**

Fire hazards, littering, **Veh 23111**

Fire hose, driving over, **Veh 21708**

Fire hydrants, stopping, parking or standing vehicles, **Veh 22514**
Removal, **Veh 22650 et seq.**

Fire lanes, stopping, parking or standing vehicles, **Veh 22500.1**

Fire protection, throwing lighted substance on highway, **Veh 23111**
Off highway vehicles, **Veh 38318**

Firefighters and Fire Departments, this index

Fixing bail, magistrate, **Veh 40511**

TRAFFIC RULES AND REGULATIONS
—Cont'd

Flagmen,
Railway grade crossing, speed limit, **Veh 22352**
Stopping on signal, approach of train, **Veh 22451**

Flags,
Explosives, vehicle transporting, red flag, **Veh 31610**
Projecting load, vehicles, red flag, **Veh 24604**
Public utilities, warning sign or barrier, **Veh 25301**
Red flags,
Projecting load, **Veh 24604**
Transporting explosives, **Veh 31610**
Wide vehicles, **Veh 25104**
Vehicles transporting explosives, red flag, **Veh 31610**
Wide vehicles, red flag, **Veh 25104**

Flammable liquids, **Veh 34001 et seq.**
Caldecott tunnel, **Veh 31301**
Crimes and offenses, **Veh 40000.19**
Speed limits, tank vehicles, **Veh 22406.5**
Stopping at railroad crossings, **Veh 22452**
Passengers, imputed negligence, **Veh 22453**

Flare patterns, traffic control, traversing, **Veh 2818**

Flashing lights, **Veh 25251**

Flexible structural material, load length limitations, **Veh 35414**

Flight from peace officers,
Crimes and offenses, **Veh 2800.1 et seq., 13201**
Impounding vehicles, **Veh 14602.7**
Point system, drivers licenses, **Veh 12810**

Following vehicles,
Caravan or motorcade, **Veh 21705**
Distances between trucks, school buses and tow vehicles, **Veh 21704**
Emergency vehicles, **Veh 21706**
Fire departments, distance, **Veh 21706**
Motorcades, spacing, **Veh 21705**
Overtaking and passing, generally, post
Speed, **Veh 21703**
Photography and pictures, sound recordings, **Veh 40008**
Towed vehicles swerving, **Veh 21711**

Food processing establishments, garbage and refuse, covering loads, **Veh 23115**

Force and violence. Road rage, generally, post

Foreign registered vehicles, impounding, **Veh 22651**

Foreign states,
Convictions, drivers license revocation, **Veh 13363**
Driving under the influence, ante
Parking exemptions, **Veh 22511.5**

Forest products, field loaded unprocessed bulk products, weight restrictions, penalties, **Veh 42030**

TRAFFIC RULES AND REGULATIONS
—Cont'd

Forfeitures,
Amnesty program, **Veh 42008**
Assessments, special penalties, night court assessments, **Veh 42006**
Bail, ante
Counties, disposition, **Veh 42201**
Disposition, **Veh 42200 et seq.**
Infractions, disposition, **Veh 42201.5**
Official misconduct, deposit of funds, **Veh 42202**
Special penalty assessments, night court assessment, **Veh 42006**
Traffic safety funds, deposits, **Veh 42200**
Weekend courts, special assessments, **Veh 42006**

Forms,
Notice of traffic violations involving accidents, **Veh 40600**
Reports, juvenile traffic offenders, **Veh 1816**
Standard application form, permit to increase weight, **Veh 35781**
Uniform notice to correct violations, **Veh 40610**
Uniform traffic citation, **Veh 40508**
Weight increase, application for permit, **Veh 35781**

Fraud, handicapped persons, certification, special parking permits, **Veh 22511.58**

Freight van or tank containers, transportation, **Veh 31540**

Friend Memorial Act, **Veh 23109**

Frightening animals, overtaking and passing, **Veh 21759**

Front bumpers, projection, length limitations, **Veh 35408**

Front seat, passengers interfering with driver, **Veh 21700**

Fuel containers, motor carriers, safety regulations, **Veh 34500 et seq.**

Fueling operations, motor carriers, safety regulations, **Veh 34500 et seq.**

Funds, traffic safety fund, **Veh 42200**

Funeral processions,
Local regulations, **Veh 21100, 21100.7**
Signals or directions by peace officers, disregarding, **Veh 2817**

Garages, removal of parked or standing vehicles, **Veh 22650 et seq.**

Garbage and refuse, **Veh 21100, 23112**
Action for removal, **Veh 23113**
Bikeways, **Veh 21211**
Exemption of trucks, **Veh 21059**
Fire hazards, **Veh 23111**
Food processing establishments, covering loads, **Veh 23115**
Highway dumping, **Veh 23112, 23113**
Impounding, illegal dumping, **Veh 23112.7**
Leakage of load on highways, **Veh 23114**
Lighted substances, throwing on highway, **Veh 23111**
Off highway vehicles, littering, **Veh 38320, 38321, 40000.24**

TRAFFIC RULES AND REGULATIONS
—Cont'd

Garbage and refuse—Cont'd
Removal of material, actions, **Veh 23113**
Spilling of load on highway, **Veh 23114**
Throwing lighted substance on highway,
Veh 23111
Trucks,
Exemptions, **Veh 21059**
Flashing lights, **Veh 25280**
Gates,
Railroad crossings, stopping, **Veh 22451
et seq.**
Restricting access, **Veh 21101.6**
Gear shifting, carriers stopping at railroad
crossing, **Veh 22452**
Gifts, overloaded vehicles, agreements for
use, **Veh 35788**
Glasses, operators, temple width interfer-
ing with lateral vision, **Veh 23120**
Golf carts, **Veh 21115**
Crossings, **Veh 21115.1**
Grade crossings. Railroad crossings, gen-
erally, post
Grades and grading,
Driving on left side, passing, **Veh 21752**
Left side of roadway, approaching crest,
Veh 21752
Overtaking and passing, generally, post
Parking, blocking wheels, **Veh 22509**
Slow moving vehicles, overtaking and
passing, **Veh 21758**
Special downward speed zoning, **Veh
22358.5**
Speed,
Descending, **Veh 22407**
Streets, decreasing limit, **Veh 22413**
State limits, slow moving vehicles, **Veh
22407**
Yielding right of way, **Veh 21661**
Zoning, special downward speed zoning,
Veh 22358.5
Gross weight. Weights, generally, post
Grounds of schools, animal or vehicle,
stopping or standing, **Veh 21113**
Guilty plea. Crimes and offenses, ante
Gutters. Curbs and gutters, generally,
ante
Habitual traffic offenders, **Veh 14601.3**
Affidavit acknowledging, **Veh 13350 et
seq.**
Drivers license suspension or revoca-
tion, **Veh 14601.3**
Driving under the influence, **Veh 23546,
23550, 23550.5, 23566**
Handicapped persons,
Assistive devices, parking, **Veh 22511.85**
Audits and auditors, parking, placards,
Veh 1825
Cancellation, revocation, placards, **Veh
22511.6**
Death, placards,
Cancellation or revocation, **Veh
22511.6**
Use, **Veh 22511.57**
Exemptions, **Veh 22511.5**

TRAFFIC RULES AND REGULATIONS
—Cont'd

Handicapped persons—Cont'd
Exemptions—Cont'd
Local parking or standing regulations,
Veh 22507.5
Fines and penalties, placards, failure to
display, **Veh 40226**
Fraud, certification, **Veh 22511.58**
Location, parking spaces, **Veh 22511.10,
22511.11**
Lost parking placard, use, **Veh 22511.57**
Off street parking, **Veh 22511.8**
Lifts or ramps, **Veh 22511.85**
Parking, **Veh 22511.5 et seq.**
Assistive devices, **Veh 22511.85**
Fees, temporary placards, **Veh
22511.59**
Fines and penalties, **Veh 4461.3,
40226, 42001.5, 42001.13**
Lifts or ramps, **Veh 22511.85**
Placards, **Veh 4461, 4463, 9105,
22511.5 et seq.**
Audits and auditors, **Veh 1825**
Disabled veterans, **Veh 9105**
Failure to display, **Veh 40226**
Fines and penalties, **Veh 4461.5,
4463.3**
Loans, crimes and offenses, **Veh
4461**
Lost, stolen, death, use, **Veh
22511.57**
Maximum renewal, **Veh 22511.59**
Signs and signals, **Veh 22511.95**
Local agencies, **Veh 22511.7,
22511.8**
Spaces, **Veh 21458, 22511.7 et seq.**
Temporary placards, **Veh 22511.59**
Records and recordation, permanent
disability, **Veh 22511.55, 22511.58**
Removal of vehicles from designated
stalls, **Veh 22652, 22652.5**
Special enforcement units, **Veh 22507.9**
Theft, parking placards, **Veh 22511.57**
Veterans, **Veh 9105**
Violations, **Veh 22507.8**
Harbor districts, **Veh 21113**
Hazardous substances and waste,
Crimes and offenses, **Veh 40000.19,
40000.21**
Transportation, **Veh 32002**
Explosives, **Veh 31618**
Haulers, **Veh 31303**
Impounding, illegal dumping, **Veh
23112.7**
Inhalation hazards, transportation, **Veh
32100 et seq.**
Notice, routes, **Veh 32050 et seq.**
Nuisance, illegal dumping, **Veh 23112.7**
Poison gases, transportation, **Veh 32100
et seq.**
Railroad crossings, **Veh 22452**
Routes, notification, **Veh 32050 et seq.**
Safety regulations, **Veh 34500 et seq.**
Sales, illegal dumping, nuisance, **Veh
23112.7**

TRAFFIC RULES AND REGULATIONS
—Cont'd

Hazardous substances and waste—Cont'd
Spills, containment and abatement, **Veh
2450 et seq.**
Transportation, **Veh 31309**
Headsets, wearing while operating motor
vehicle, **Veh 27400**
Hearings,
Bridge or other structure, weight limits,
Veh 35751
Cargo tank vehicles, flammable liquids,
tunnels, **Veh 21109.5**
Impounding vehicles, **Veh 22651,
22850.5**
Flight from peace officers and reck-
less driving, storage, **Veh 14602.7**
Private roads, public use, local regula-
tion, **Veh 21107.5**
Reduction of weight limits, **Veh 35705**
County improved highways, **Veh
35708, 35709**
Removal of vehicle from highway, **Veh
22650**
Revocation or suspension of driving
privilege, evidence and civil actions,
Veh 40832
Speed,
Maximum speed on bridges, tubes,
Veh 22404, 22405
State highways, increase or decrease,
Veh 22354.5
Storage, driving under the influence,
second and subsequent offenses,
Veh 14602.8
Weights, post
Heavy vehicles. Slow moving vehicles,
generally, post
Height, **Veh 35000 et seq., 35250 et seq.**
Arrest, refusal to stop for inspection,
Veh 40303
Crimes and offenses, **Veh 40000.7,
40001 et seq.**
Double deck buses, **Veh 35250**
Emergency vehicles, exemption, **Veh
35002**
Employees, violations,
Dismissal of charges, abstract record,
Veh 40003
Employer failure to answer charges,
Veh 40005
Exceeding maximum limits, special per-
mit, **Veh 35780 et seq.**
Fees, licenses and permits, variances,
Veh 35795
Frame and body floor, **Veh 24008.5**
Highway operation of vehicles, applica-
tion of law, **Veh 35000**
Inspection, arrest, procedure, **Veh 40303**
Licenses and permits, **Veh 35780 et seq.**
Manufactured housing, **Veh 35790.6**
Operation without compliance with pro-
visions, **Veh 40001 et seq.**
Snow equipment, exemption, **Veh 35001**
Special permits, variances, **Veh 35780 et
seq.**

TRAFFIC

TRAFFIC RULES AND REGULATIONS
—Cont'd
Height—Cont'd

Variances, permits, **Veh 35780 et seq.**

Helmets,

Bicyclists and passengers, use requirements, **Veh 21212**

Motorized scooters, **Veh 21235**

Three wheeled vehicles, application of laws, **Veh 27803**

Hemophiliacs, driving under the influence, blood tests, exemptions, **Veh 23612**

High beam, dimming for approaching vehicles, **Veh 24409**

High density multiple family dwelling areas, exemptions, local parking or standing regulations, **Veh 22507.5**

High occupancy vehicle lanes. Highways and Roads, this index

Highway and Bridge Districts, this index

Highway construction zone, **Veh 21367**

Code violations, **Veh 42009**

Highway maintenance or construction equipment,

Removal of unattended vehicles, **Veh 22650 et seq.**

Width restrictions, exemption, **Veh 35104**

Hiking trails, unauthorized vehicles, **Veh 23127**

Hit and Run Drivers, generally, this index

Hitchhiking, **Veh 21957**

Arrest, refusal to leave, **Veh 40303**

Bicycles, **Veh 21203**

Homes, manufactured homes, highway movement, **Veh 34500 et seq.**

Horn warning,

Defiles or canyons, **Veh 21662**

Mountain highways, **Veh 21662**

Horns, activating, vehicle removal, **Veh 22651.5**

Horseback riding,

Norco, speed, **Veh 22353**

Right of way, **Veh 21805**

Trails, unauthorized vehicles, **Veh 23127**

Horsedrawn vehicles, overtaking and passing, **Veh 21759**

Hoses, crossing fire hoses, **Veh 21708**

Hospital districts, public grounds, local regulation, **Veh 21113**

Hours of operation, motor carriers, log book, **Veh 34501.4**

Hours of service, motor carrier drivers, schedules, **Veh 34501.3**

House cars,

Intoxicating liquors, storage of opened container, **Veh 23229**

Length, **Veh 35400**

House mover transporting across railroad tracks, notice, **Veh 35789**

Housing, this index

Housing authorities, **Veh 21113**

Housing project, local authorities, **Veh 21111**

TRAFFIC RULES AND REGULATIONS
—Cont'd
Ice and snow,

Removal,

Equipment, exemptions, size, weight and load restrictions, **Veh 35001**

Parking restrictions, **Veh 22510**

Speed, restrictions, **Veh 22363**

Ice cream trucks, vending, **Veh 22456**

Identity and identification. Arrest, ante

Ignition interlock devices. Driving under the influence, ante

Illegal evidence, **Veh 40800 et seq.**

Illegal parking, removal of vehicles, **Veh 22650 et seq.**

Immediate hazard, pedestrians leaving place of safety, **Veh 21950**

Immobilization of vehicles, illegal parking, devices, **Veh 22651.7**

Impeding traffic by stopping, **Veh 22400**

Implements of husbandry. Agricultural Machinery and Equipment, generally, this index

Implied consent. Driving under the influence, ante

Impounding, **Veh 14602.6, 14602.7, 22651, 23153**

Alarm devices, parked vehicles, activation, **Veh 22651.5**

Disabled vehicles, transportation department employees, **Veh 22654**

Drivers licenses, revocation or suspension, **Veh 14602.6**

Driving under the influence, ante

Driving while license is suspended or revoked, **Veh 14602, 14602.5**

Flight from peace officers, **Veh 14602.7, 22655.3**

For sale signs, **Veh 22651.9**

Garbage and refuse, illegal dumping, **Veh 23112.7**

Hazardous substances and waste, illegal dumping, **Veh 23112.7**

Hearings,

Flight from peace officers and reckless driving, storage, **Veh 14602.7**

Release, **Veh 14602.6, 14602.7, 22850.5**

Horns and sirens, activation of devices, **Veh 22651.5**

Illegal dumping, **Veh 23112.7**

Leases, **Veh 14602**

Driving under the influence, second and subsequent offenses, **Veh 14602.8**

Liens and incumbrances, **Veh 22851.1**

Littering, **Veh 22659.5**

Names, release, **Veh 14602.8**

Notice, **Veh 22651**

Driving under the influence, second and subsequent offenses, **Veh 14602.8**

Flight from peace officers and reckless driving, **Veh 14602.7**

Off highway vehicles, wilderness areas, **Veh 38301.3**

TRAFFIC RULES AND REGULATIONS
—Cont'd
Impounding—Cont'd

Ordinances, **Veh 22850.5**

Pandering, **Veh 22659.5**

Parking, post

Pimping, **Veh 22659.5**

Prostitution, **Veh 22659.5**

Public lands, **Veh 22651**

Rates and charges, **Veh 22850.5**

Driving under the influence, second and subsequent offenses, **Veh 14602.8**

Reckless driving, **Veh 14602.7**

Registration, **Veh 1661, 9553**

Release, **Veh 14602.8, 22651**

Proof of current registration, **Veh 22850.3**

Removal of parked or standing vehicles, **Veh 22650 et seq.**

Repossessors and repossession, **Veh 23118**

Release, **Veh 14602.6, 14602.7**

Security interest, release, foreclosure, **Veh 14602.6, 14602.7**

Stolen vehicles on private property, **Veh 22653**

Storage, generally, post

Taxicabs, **Veh 21100.4**

Unlicensed drivers, **Veh 14607.6**

Warrants, flight from peace officers and reckless driving, **Veh 14602.7**

Improvements,

County highways, weights, **Veh 35707**

Right side of roadway, exemptions, **Veh 21650**

Imputed negligence, passenger for hire, failure of driver to stop at railroad crossing, **Veh 22453**

Increase of weight limits,

Local authorities, **Veh 35700**

State highways, **Veh 35650**

Incumbrances. Liens and incumbrances, generally, post

Indemnity, injury resulting from operation under permit for increase in size, weight, **Veh 35782**

Indictment and information, speed violations, **Veh 40503**

Industrial tracks, railroad crossing, stopping, **Veh 22452, 22453**

Infants. Children and minors, generally, ante

Information,

Dissemination, **Veh 1809**

Pay by plate toll payment, **Veh 23301.8**

Sale of information, **Veh 1810 et seq.**

Speed violations, **Veh 40503**

Infractions,

Amnesty, **Veh 42008.7**

Counties, **Veh 42008.5**

Animals, transporting, restraining, **Veh 42001.4**

Arraignment, closed circuit television, Placer County, **Veh 40502.1**

Arrests, procedure, **Veh 40306**

TRAFFIC RULES AND REGULATIONS
—Cont'd
Infractions—Cont'd
Assessments, special penalties, night court, **Veh 42006**
Bail, **Veh 40306, 40307, 42201.5**
Checks, **Veh 40510**
Forfeitures, installment payments, **Veh 40510.5, 40512**
Bicycles,
Fines and penalties, **Veh 42001**
Overtaking and passing, **Veh 21760**
Children and minors,
Appearance, arrest, **Veh 40502**
Custody, **Veh 40302.5**
Hearings, consent, **Veh 40513**
Pleas, notice to appear, **Veh 40513**
Clerks of court, acceptance of bail, **Veh 40307**
Closed circuit television, testimony or appearance for arraignment, Placer County, **Veh 40502.1**
Complaint, **Veh 40306**
Contempt, impounding license and ordering person not to drive, **Veh 40508**
Continuing cross highways, terminating highways, **Veh 21800**
Conviction for violation, suspension of execution of sentence, **Veh 42004.5**
Crosswalks, yielding to pedestrians, **Veh 21971, 42001.18**
Decals, noise pollution, exhaust systems, **Veh 27202.1**
Definitions, **Veh 40000.1, 40000.3**
Drivers licenses, impoundment, **Veh 40508**
Electronic mail, **Veh 23123.5**
Emergency vehicles, standing vehicles, overtaking and passing, **Veh 21809**
Exhaust systems, noise pollution, decals, **Veh 27202.1**
Failure to appear, **Veh 42004.5**
Certificate of adjudication, **Veh 40509**
Fines and penalties, **Veh 42001 et seq.**
Disposition, **Veh 42201.5**
Emergency vehicle violations, **Veh 42001.12**
Exhaust systems, noise pollution, decals, **Veh 27202.1**
Failure to pay, **Veh 40508**
Late charge, **Veh 40310**
Night courts, **Veh 42006**
Overtaking and passing, vehicles stopped for pedestrians, **Veh 42001.17**
Payment, **Veh 42003**
Uniform schedule, **Veh 40310**
Vehicles stopped for pedestrians, overtaking and passing, **Veh 42001.17**
Yielding to pedestrians, **Veh 42001.18**
Forfeitures, disposition, **Veh 42201.5**
Helmets, bicyclists and passengers, use, **Veh 21212**
Highway construction zones, **Veh 42009**

TRAFFIC RULES AND REGULATIONS
—Cont'd
Infractions—Cont'd
Instant messages, **Veh 23123.5**
Intersections, yielding to pedestrians, **Veh 21971, 42001.18**
Jails, acceptance of bail by officer in charge, **Veh 40307**
Jamming devices (speed), **Veh 28150**
Judgment ordering payment of fine, **Veh 42003**
Laser jamming devices, speed, **Veh 28150**
Magistrate unavailable, bail, **Veh 40307**
Misdemeanors, infractions deemed to be, **Veh 40000.28**
Motor carriers, speed, **Veh 22406.1**
Multiple offenses, **Veh 40000.28**
Night court assessments, **Veh 42006**
Noise pollution, exhaust systems, decals, **Veh 27202.1**
NonEnglish speakers, notice, trials and waivers of constitutional rights, **Veh 40901**
Not guilty plea, filing, **Veh 40519**
Notice, procedure and waiver of constitutional rights, **Veh 40901**
Outstanding warrants, posting bail, or making telephone call, **Veh 40304.5**
Overtaking and passing, vehicles stopped for pedestrians, fines and penalties, **Veh 42001.17**
Parking, post
Payment, fines, **Veh 42003**
Pedestrians, **Veh 42001**
Pilot cars, equipment violations, **Veh 28103**
Placer County, closed circuit television, testimony or appearance for arraignment, **Veh 40502.1**
Public defender, right to representation, prior conviction, reports, **Veh 42004**
Radar jamming devices, speed, **Veh 28150**
Release on own recognizance, **Veh 40307**
Reports, prior convictions, **Veh 42004**
Right of way, yielding to pedestrians, **Veh 21971, 42001.18**
Roadside rest areas, **Veh 22520.6**
Safety belts, mandatory use, **Veh 27315**
Second and subsequent offenses, **Veh 42001**
Reports, prior convictions, **Veh 42004**
Sidewalks, yielding to pedestrians, **Veh 21971, 42001.18**
Special penalty assessments, night court assessment, **Veh 42006**
Speed, motor carriers, **Veh 22406.1**
Standing vehicles, emergency vehicles, overtaking and passing, **Veh 21809**
Subpoenas, **Veh 40901**
Suspension of execution of sentence, **Veh 42004.5**
Text messages, **Veh 23123.5**

TRAFFIC RULES AND REGULATIONS
—Cont'd
Infractions—Cont'd
Third or subsequent offenses, fines and penalties, **Veh 42001**
Tow trucks,
Disabled vehicles, **Veh 40006**
Standing vehicles, overtaking and passing, **Veh 21809**
Transportation department, standing vehicles, overtaking and passing, **Veh 21809**
Trial, written declaration, **Veh 40902**
Unavailability of magistrate, bail, **Veh 40307**
Vehicles stopped for pedestrians, overtaking and passing, fines and penalties, **Veh 42001.17**
Violation of written promise to appear, misdemeanor, **Veh 42003**
Vista points, **Veh 22520.6**
Waiver,
Constitutional rights, notice, **Veh 40901**
Continuance for preparation of defense, **Veh 40306**
Weekend courts, special assessments, **Veh 42006**
Weights, **Veh 4000.6**
Yielding right of way, pedestrians, **Veh 21971, 42001.18**
Inhalation hazards, transportation, **Veh 32100 et seq.**
Inoperative vehicles, removal, **Veh 22650 et seq.**
Inspection and inspectors, **Veh 2806**
Arrest, refusal to stop, **Veh 40303**
Combinations of vehicles, length, exemptions, **Veh 35401**
Emergency vehicles, size, weight, load limitations, **Veh 34500.2**
Emissions, **Veh 2814.2**
Explosives, highway transportation, **Veh 31602, 31607 et seq.**
Failure to stop, fines and penalties, **Veh 42002.1**
Fines and penalties, failure to stop, **Veh 42002.1**
Inhalation hazards, transportation, **Veh 32105**
Loads, **Veh 2802, 2803**
Motor carriers, safety regulations, **Veh 34500 et seq.**
Permits for increase in size or weight, **Veh 35783**
Records, **Veh 1808**
Weights, post
Installment payments, bail, forfeitures, infractions, **Veh 40510.5, 40512**
Instant messages, infractions, **Veh 23123.5**
Instructions to drivers, explosives transports, **Veh 31611**
Interference with control of vehicle, Passengers, **Veh 21700, 21701**

TRAFFIC

TRAFFIC RULES AND REGULATIONS
—Cont'd

Interference with control of vehicle
—Cont'd
  Photography and pictures, sound recordings, crimes and offenses, **Veh 40008**
Intersections, **Veh 23250 et seq.**
  Adjacent intersections, pedestrians crossing controlled intersections, **Veh 21955**
  Animals, **Veh 23330 et seq.**
  Antigridlock Act, **Veh 22526**
  Approaching,
    Left side of roadway, **Veh 21752**
    Stopping vehicle, **Veh 22450 et seq.**
    Yield right of way sign, **Veh 21803**
  Bicycles, **Veh 23330 et seq.**
  Blocking intersections, **Veh 22526**
  Bridle paths, designation, **Veh 21805**
  Business districts, U turns, **Veh 22102**
  Crosswalks, generally, ante
  Definitions, **Veh 365, 23254**
  Driver on left yielding right of way, **Veh 21800**
  Emergency vehicles, yielding right of way, **Veh 21806, 21807**
  Enforcement of rules, **Veh 23251**
  Entrance of through highway, yielding right of way, **Veh 21802**
  Equestrian crossings, **Veh 21805**
  Jaywalkers, right of way, **Veh 21954**
  Left turn, right of way, **Veh 21801**
  Local regulation, through highways, **Veh 21101**
  Motorized bicycles, **Veh 23330 et seq.**
  Movements authorized by signals and lights, **Veh 21450 et seq.**
  Obedience to officers, **Veh 23253**
    Crimes and offenses, **Veh 40000.15**
  Ordinances, turning, **Veh 22113**
  Overtaking and passing, post
  Parking, **Veh 22500**
  Pedestrians, post
  Points, violation points, Antigridlock Act, **Veh 12810.4**
  Stopping, post
  Terminating highways, **Veh 21800**
  Towing, **Veh 23270 et seq.**
  U turns, **Veh 22100.5**
Interstate commerce commission, defenses, **Veh 41401**
Interurban streetcars. Street railways, generally, post
Intervals, **Veh 21704**
Intoxicating liquors. Alcoholic beverages, generally, ante
Investigations and investigators, presentence investigations, driving under the influence, **Veh 23655**
Issuance, warrants for arrest, **Veh 40514 et seq.**
Jails, bail infraction or misdemeanor cases, **Veh 40307**
Jamming devices (speed), **Veh 28150, 40000.15**

TRAFFIC RULES AND REGULATIONS
—Cont'd

Jaywalkers. Pedestrians, generally, post
Jeeps,
  Place of business, posting, signs and licenses, application of law, **Veh 11709**
  Rules and regulations, **Veh 38000 et seq.**
Joint defendants, owners and operators, **Veh 40001 et seq.**
Judgments and decrees,
  Ability to pay, **Veh 42003**
  Arrest warrants, issuance for failure to comply, **Veh 40514**
  Code violations, **Veh 42003**
  Driving while intoxicated,
    Conviction, constitutional invalidation, **Veh 41403**
    Motion to vacate or set aside, **Veh 41403**
  Fine and penalties, payment or reimbursement, **Veh 42003**
  Speeding violations, speed trap evidence, **Veh 40805**
Jurisdiction, arraignment on other offenses, **Veh 40311**
  Speed traps, evidence, **Veh 40805**
Juvenile delinquents and dependents,
  Alcoholic beverages, **Veh 23140**
  Driving under the influence, **Veh 13352.3**
  Reports, **Veh 1816**
  Speeding, **Veh 13355**
Labor and employment. Officers and employees, generally, post
Lanes,
  Bicycle lanes, separation, **Veh 21207**
  Changing, **Veh 21658**
  Designated lanes, overtaking or passing, **Veh 22348**
  Driving or operation, **Veh 21658**
  Highways, marked right turn lanes, **Veh 22100**
  Left lane, generally, post
  Motorized scooters, rules of the road, **Veh 21228, 21229**
  Operation between, motorcycles, prohibition, **Veh 21714**
  Right lane, generally, post
  Single lane, operation in, **Veh 21658**
  Slow moving traffic, **Veh 21655, 21658**
  Speed limits,
    Multiple lane highways, **Veh 22361**
    State highways, **Veh 22364**
  Turning from middle lane, **Veh 22100**
  Two lane highways, generally, post
  Two way turning lanes, offenses, **Veh 21460.5**
Larceny. Theft, generally, post
Laser jamming devices, speed, **Veh 28150, 40000.15**
Leakage, loads or contents on highways, **Veh 23114**

TRAFFIC RULES AND REGULATIONS
—Cont'd

Leases,
  Impounding, driving under the influence, second and subsequent offenses, **Veh 14602.8**
  Motor vehicles, automated enforcement systems, affidavits of nonliability, **Veh 40520**
Leaving place of safety, pedestrians entering path of vehicle constituting immediate hazard, **Veh 21950**
Leaving scene of accident. Hit and Run Drivers, generally, this index
Left lane,
  Bicycles, **Veh 21202**
    Overtaking and passing, **Veh 21750 et seq.**
  Double parallel lines, offenses, **Veh 21460**
  Intersections, yielding right of way, **Veh 21800**
  Overtaking and passing, **Veh 21750 et seq.**
  Parking,
    One way roadways, ordinances, **Veh 22503**
    Two way roadways, Long Beach, pilot programs, **Veh 22502**
  Pedestrians walking outside of business or residence district, **Veh 21956**
  Three lane roadway use, **Veh 21659**
Left turns, **Veh 22100**
  Alleys, right of way, **Veh 21804**
  Divided highways, **Veh 21651**
  Double lines, **Veh 21460**
  Intersections, **Veh 22100**
    Right of way, **Veh 21801**
  Lanes, turning from middle lane, **Veh 22100**
  Middle lane,
    Terminating highway, **Veh 22100**
    Three lane highway, **Veh 22100**
  Motorized scooters, rules of the road, **Veh 21228, 21229**
  Movement of vehicle, safety, **Veh 22107**
  Overtaken vehicle, passing on right, **Veh 21754**
  Parallel lines, **Veh 21460**
  Private roads or driveways, right of way, **Veh 21804**
  Red lights, **Veh 21453**
  Right of way,
    Private road or alley, **Veh 21804**
    Uncontrolled intersections, **Veh 21800**
  Right side of roadway, exemption, from driving and operation, **Veh 21650**
  Safety, movement of vehicle, **Veh 22107**
  Slow moving vehicles, designated lanes, **Veh 21655**
  Terminating highway, middle lane, **Veh 22100**
  Three lane highway, **Veh 21659**
    Middle lane, **Veh 22100**
  Two way turning lanes, **Veh 21460.5**

TRAFFIC RULES AND REGULATIONS
—Cont'd
Left turns—Cont'd
Uncontrolled intersections, right of way, **Veh 21800**
Yielding right of way, **Veh 21801**
Length, **Veh 35000 et seq., 35400 et seq.**
Adjustable axle, inclusion in measurement, **Veh 35402**
Aircraft assemblies, **Veh 35414**
Animals, livestock carriers, access, exemptions, **Veh 35401.7**
Arrest, refusal to stop for inspection, **Veh 40303**
B train assembly, measurement exclusion, **Veh 35401**
Boat transporters, **Veh 35401.3, 35401.5**
Buses, **Veh 35400**
Camp trailers, **Veh 35400.6**
Camper transporters, **Veh 35401.3, 35401.5**
Cotton module mover, **Veh 35400.5**
Crimes and offenses, **Veh 40001 et seq.**
Dollies, **Veh 35414**
Drawbar, exclusion in measuring, **Veh 35402**
Drilling equipment, **Veh 35414**
Exemptions to limitations, **Veh 35414**
Emergency vehicles, exemption, **Veh 35002**
Employees, violations,
Arrest, **Veh 40005**
Codefendants, owners, **Veh 40003**
Dismissal of charges, abstract of record, **Veh 40003**
Employer failing to answer charges, **Veh 40005**
Escort vehicles, pilot cars, **Veh 472, 27904**
Exceeding maximum limits, special permits, **Veh 35780 et seq.**
Exemptions, **Veh 35401.5, 35414**
Combinations of vehicles, **Veh 35401**
Extension devices, exclusion in measuring, **Veh 35402**
Fees, licenses and permits, variances, **Veh 35795**
Fifth wheels, length measurements, **Veh 35402**
Front bumper, projection, **Veh 35408**
Heel boom log loaders, self propelled, **Veh 35407.5**
Highway operation of vehicle, application of law, **Veh 35000**
House cars, **Veh 35400**
Inspection, arrest, **Veh 40303**
Licenses and permits, **Veh 35780 et seq.**
Special permits, motorsports, semitrailers, **Veh 35401.5**
Livestock carriers, access, exemptions, **Veh 35401.7**
Loads, **Veh 35406, 35410, 35411**
Log loaders, self propelled heel boom, **Veh 35407.5**
Missile components, **Veh 35414**

TRAFFIC RULES AND REGULATIONS
—Cont'd
Length—Cont'd
Motor carried equipment, booms or masts, **Veh 35407**
Motor truck and trailer, combinations, **Veh 35401**
Motor vehicle transporters, **Veh 35401.3, 35401.5**
Motorsports, semitrailers, special permits, **Veh 35401.5**
Notice, livestock carriers, access, exemptions, **Veh 35401.7**
Operation without compliance with provision, **Veh 40001 et seq.**
Pilot cars, **Veh 472, 27904**
Projecting loads, **Veh 35406, 35410, 35411**
Ratio of weight to length, axle limits, **Veh 35551**
Rear projections, load, **Veh 35410**
School buses, crossing control arms, **Veh 35400**
Self propelled heel boom log loaders, **Veh 35407.5**
Snow removal equipment, exemption, **Veh 35001**
Special permits,
Motorsports, semitrailers, **Veh 35401.5**
Variances, **Veh 35780 et seq.**
Tandem loads, **Veh 35414**
Tanks, **Veh 35414**
Television pictures, photographs, vehicle taking, **Veh 35409**
Trailer coaches, **Veh 35400**
Triple axle semitrailers, **Veh 35401.3**
Variances, permits, **Veh 35780 et seq.**
Letter of defendant, evidence, **Veh 40903**
Licenses and permits,
All terrain vehicles, instructors, **Veh 11100.1**
Armored cars, **Veh 21713**
Bicycles, **Veh 21206**
Booster power units, trucks, **Veh 35786, 35787**
Contractors, weight limitations, exemption, **Veh 35704, 35716**
Crossings, vehicular crossings, toll roads and bridges, **Veh 23330**
Examiners, interference with driver, **Veh 21701**
Explosives, highway transport, **Veh 31601, 31602**
Manufactured homes, moving, **Veh 35790**
Mobilehomes, overwidth permits, **Veh 35790**
Overweight vehicle, Terminal Island freeway, **Veh 35700.5**
Parking, post
Plates, removal of parked or standing vehicles, **Veh 22650 et seq.**
Power units, truck booster power units, **Veh 35786, 35787**

TRAFFIC RULES AND REGULATIONS
—Cont'd
Licenses and permits—Cont'd
Rental vehicles, local authorities, **Veh 21100**
Single permit, excessive size or weight, **Veh 35791**
Size of vehicle or load, special permit, **Veh 35780 et seq.**
Special permits, size or weight of vehicle or load, **Veh 35780 et seq.**
Terminal Island freeway, **Veh 35700.5**
Terminal Island freeway, overweight vehicles, **Veh 35700.5**
Tow trucks, local regulations, **Veh 21100 et seq.**
Truck booster power units, **Veh 35786, 35787**
Vehicular crossings, toll roads and bridges, **Veh 23330**
Violations, proof of correction, dismissal, **Veh 40522**
Weight limits, **Veh 35780 et seq.**
Width of vehicle or load, additional width, **Veh 35109**
Liens and incumbrances,
Crossings, vehicular crossings, tolls and charges, **Veh 23303**
Failure to appear or pay fine, **Veh 14911**
Parking, impounding, sales, **Veh 22651**
Storage of vehicles removed from highway, **Veh 22851, 22851.1**
Toll roads and bridges, charges, **Veh 23303**
Light bars, **Veh 27606, 27607**
Lights and lighting,
Arrest, refusal to stop and submit to inspection or test, **Veh 40303**
Bars, **Veh 27606, 27607**
Bicycles, **Veh 21201**
Peace officers, **Veh 21201.3**
Blue lights, bicycles, peace officers, **Veh 21201.3**
Colored lights, offenses, application of law, **Veh 21450**
Dimming, **Veh 24409**
Display, blinding or dazzling light, **Veh 21466**
Emergency vehicles,
Exemptions from traffic laws, **Veh 21055**
Lighted red lamp, **Veh 21055**
Right of way, **Veh 21806, 21807**
Extension beyond permissible width limits, **Veh 35109**
Flashing lights, garbage trucks, **Veh 25280**
Garbage vehicles, **Veh 21059**
Headlamp dimming, parked or standing vehicles, **Veh 24401**
Height, mounted, lamps and reflectors, **Veh 25952**
Light bars, **Veh 27606, 27607**
Motorized scooters, **Veh 21223, 21224**
Parked vehicles, **Veh 24802**
Peace officers, bicycles, **Veh 21201.3**

TRAFFIC

TRAFFIC RULES AND REGULATIONS
—Cont'd

Lights and lighting—Cont'd
Private security agency vehicles, **Veh 25279**
Removal, **Veh 22651**
Projecting loads, **Veh 25103**
Red lights, generally, post
Rubbish trucks, **Veh 21059**
Streetsweeper, watering vehicles, **Veh 21060**
Timber and lumber, transporting, flashing amber lights, **Veh 25275**
Vision impairing lights, **Veh 21466.5**
Willful flight from peace officers, **Veh 2800.1**
Limit line, definitions, motor vehicles, **Veh 377**
Limitation of actions,
Fees, refunds, **Veh 42231, 42232**
Fines and penalties, refunds, **Veh 42231, 42232**
Pleading, written plea, waiver of right to trial within statutory period, **Veh 40519**
Refunds, erroneous collection of fees and penalties, **Veh 42231, 42232**
Written plea in lieu of personal appearance, waiver, **Veh 40519**
Limitations, driving hours, **Veh 21702**
Limousine services, seat belts, **Veh 27315**
Liquefied petroleum gas,
Caldecott tunnel, **Veh 31301**
Railroad crossings, **Veh 22452**
Passengers, imputed negligence, **Veh 22453**
Liquor. Alcoholic beverages, generally, ante
Littering. Garbage and refuse, generally, ante
Livestock. Animals, generally, ante
Loads and loading, **Veh 35000 et seq.**
Arrest, inspection and inspectors, **Veh 40303**
Axle weight limit, timber and lumber, **Veh 35552**
Exemptions, **Veh 35785**
Booms, definitions, **Veh 35003**
Building materials, trusses, wall panels, **Veh 35780.5**
Certification, rope or strap material, **Veh 24005.5**
Children and minors, youth buses, **Veh 2816**
Clearance lamps, **Veh 25100 et seq.**
Collapsible containers for liquids, flatbed vehicles, **Veh 31540**
Contracts for transporting loads, overloads, **Veh 35788**
Covers, rubbish vehicles, **Veh 23115**
Crimes and offenses, **Veh 40001 et seq.**
Crossings, vehicular crossings, toll roads and bridges, **Veh 23330**
Emergency vehicles, exemption, **Veh 35002**

TRAFFIC RULES AND REGULATIONS
—Cont'd

Loads and loading—Cont'd
Employees, violations,
Arrest, employer failure to answer charges, **Veh 40005**
Codefendants, owners, **Veh 40003**
Dismissal of charges, abstract of record, **Veh 40003**
Employers failure to answer charges, **Veh 40005**
Enactment of regulations, **Veh 32**
Exceeding maximum limits, special permit, **Veh 35780 et seq.**
Explosives, **Veh 31600 et seq.**
Fees, licenses and permits, variances, **Veh 35795**
Flag on projection, **Veh 24604**
Freight van or tank container, **Veh 31540**
Garbage and refuse, covering loads, **Veh 23115**
Height, generally, ante
Inspection and inspectors, **Veh 2802**
Arrest, **Veh 40303**
Lamp on projection, **Veh 24604, 25103**
Leakage on highway, **Veh 23114**
Length limitations, **Veh 35406**
Timber and lumber, **Veh 35414**
Licenses and permits, variances, **Veh 35780 et seq.**
Logs and poles, over bridges or causeway, speed, **Veh 35785**
Machinery and equipment,
Definitions, **Veh 35003**
Operation without, **Veh 24002**
Masts, definitions, **Veh 35003**
Mixed cargoes, explosives, **Veh 31613**
Obstructing view of driver, **Veh 21700**
Overloads. Weights, generally, post
Passenger vehicles, projecting loads, **Veh 35111**
Passengers obstructing view of driver, **Veh 21700**
Permits, variances, **Veh 35780 et seq.**
Pipes, trucks transporting, flashing amber warning lights, **Veh 25275**
Poles, trucks transporting, flashing amber warning lights, **Veh 25275**
Projecting loads, generally, post
Red lights or flags, projecting loads, **Veh 24604**
Refusal to submit to weighing, option of officer to take arrested person before magistrate, **Veh 40303**
Reloading, **Veh 2803**
Violation procedure, **Veh 40303**
Removal of illegal weight, **Veh 2803**
Riding on vehicle, restriction, **Veh 21712**
Rope or strap material, certification, **Veh 24005.5**
Rubbish vehicles, covering loads, **Veh 23115**
Safe loading, **Veh 2802, 2803**
Violation procedure, **Veh 40303**
Side marker lamps, **Veh 25100**

TRAFFIC RULES AND REGULATIONS
—Cont'd

Loads and loading—Cont'd
Size, generally, post
Snow removal equipment, exemption, **Veh 35001**
Special permits, variances, **Veh 35780 et seq.**
Spilling of load on highway, **Veh 23114**
Strap or rope material, **Veh 24005.5**
Street railways, application of law, **Veh 21051**
Tank containers, **Veh 31540**
Timber and lumber, post
Trucks transporting poles, timber and lumber, flashing warning lamps, **Veh 25275**
Trucks transporting workmen, **Veh 31400**
Trusses, wall panels, width of vehicle or load, **Veh 35780.5**
Unlawful riding, **Veh 21712**
Unloading mechanism, width limitations, **Veh 35783.5**
Unsafe condition, operation without required equipment, **Veh 24002**
Van or tank containers, **Veh 31540**
Variances, permits, **Veh 35780 et seq.**
Vehicular crossings, toll roads or bridges, **Veh 23330**
Warning signs, removal of covering, **Veh 35783.5**
Weights, generally, post
Wheel loads, **Veh 35550**
Width of vehicle or load, generally, post
Youth buses, **Veh 2816**
Local agencies, **Veh 21100 et seq.**
Use restrictions, streets or highways, **Veh 9400.7, 9400.8**
Local authorities, **Veh 21100 et seq.**
Bicycles, regulation, **Veh 21206**
Closing streets, **Veh 21101**
Designation, **Veh 21101**
Gates, restricting access, **Veh 21101.6**
Low speed vehicles, **Veh 21266**
Parking, **Veh 22506 et seq.**
Pedestrian regulations, **Veh 21961**
Permits, exceeding maximum size and weight limit, **Veh 35780 et seq.**
Special permits, exceeding maximum size or weight limit, **Veh 35780 et seq.**
Delegation of authority, **Veh 35796**
Speed limits,
Adjustment, **Veh 22357 et seq.**
Prima facie limits, **Veh 22352**
Turning movements, powers, **Veh 22113**
Uniform standards, **Veh 21100.1**
Local regulations,
Gates or other devices on streets, selective denial of access, **Veh 21101.6**
Roller skating, **Veh 21969**
Use restrictions, streets or highways, **Veh 9400.7, 9400.8**
Location, handicapped persons, parking, **Veh 22511.10, 22511.11**

TRAFFIC RULES AND REGULATIONS
—Cont'd

Locked vehicles, duties, **Veh 22516**

Log loaders, length, self propelled heel boom, **Veh 35407.5**

Logbook, motor carriers,

Crimes and offenses, **Veh 34501.3**

Hours of operation, presumptions, **Veh 34501.4**

Speed, presumption, **Veh 34501.3**

Logging dollies, permits, weight limits, exemption, **Veh 35785**

Logs and logging. Timber and lumber, generally, post

Long Beach,

Parking, left hand parking, two way roadways, pilot programs, **Veh 22502**

Special permits, overweight vehicles, **Veh 35700.5**

Loose loads, agricultural products, width, **Veh 35102**

Los Angeles,

Off street parking facilities, **Veh 22950 et seq.**

Special permits, overweight vehicles, **Veh 35700.5**

Los Angeles County,

Commercial vehicles, weights, maximum, **Veh 35655.6**

Funeral processions, **Veh 21100.7**

Louis Friend Memorial Act, **Veh 23109**

Low emission vehicles, high occupancy vehicle lanes, decals, **Veh 5205.5, 21655.9**

Low speed vehicles. Motor Vehicles, this index

Lumber. Timber and lumber, generally, post

Machinery and equipment. Equipment, generally, ante

Magistrates, arrest procedures, **Veh 40302 et seq.**

Mail and mailing,

Automated rail crossing enforcement, notice to appear, **Veh 40518**

Parking violations, payment of penalties, **Veh 40309, 40521**

Pleadings, personal appearance deemed to have been made, **Veh 40519**

Maintenance and repair,

Motor carriers, safety regulations, **Veh 34500 et seq.**

Right side of roadway, exemptions, **Veh 21460**

Major code changes affecting traffic laws, notice, drivers license extension recipients, **Veh 12814.5**

Malibu, state highway route 1, **Veh 2400.6**

Mandatory appearance before magistrate, arrest, **Veh 40302**

Manufactured housing. Housing, this index

Marijuana, possession while driving, offenses, **Veh 23222, 40000.15**

TRAFFIC RULES AND REGULATIONS
—Cont'd

Marked crosswalks. Crosswalks, generally, ante

Mass transit,

Cellular radio telephones, **Veh 23125**

Parking, San Francisco City and County, videotape, transit only traffic lanes, **Veh 40240 et seq.**

Masts or booms of shovels or cranes, length, **Veh 35407**

Maximum speed limit, **Veh 22349**

Metal car in contact with highway, speed limit, **Veh 22410**

Metals and metal products, tires, gross weight limits, **Veh 35601**

Middle lane of three lane highway, turning, **Veh 22100**

Mileage, crimes and offenses, **Veh 40000.15**

Military Forces, this index

Minimum speed limit, **Veh 22400**

Minors. Children and minors, generally, ante

Mirrors, width of vehicle or load, **Veh 35109**

Misdemeanors. Crimes and offenses, generally, ante

Mistaken collection of fees or penalties, refunds, limitation, **Veh 42231, 42232**

Mobile billboard advertising displays, **Veh 21100**

Impounding, **Veh 22651**

Mobilehomes and mobilehome parks, **Veh 34500 et seq., 35790**

Drawing or towing, distance between vehicles, **Veh 21704**

Height, **Veh 35790.6**

Length, **Veh 35400, 35790.4, 35790.5**

Overwidth permits, **Veh 35790**

Passengers, **Veh 21712**

Permits for movements, powers, **Veh 35790**

Riding in, **Veh 21712**

Width, **Veh 35789.5, 35790.1**

Moderate density residential districts, speed, **Veh 22352**

Modification, major code changes, notice, drivers license recipients, **Veh 12814.5**

Motion pictures, vehicles taking, length, **Veh 35409**

Motor carriers. Carriers, generally, ante

Motor driven cycles, restrictions, **Veh 21960**

Motor trucks. Carriers, generally, ante

Motor vehicle service stations, removal of parked or standing vehicles, **Veh 22650 et seq.**

Motorcades, spacing, **Veh 21705**

Motorized bicycles, **Veh 21113**

Motorized skateboards, **Veh 21968**

Required equipment, **Veh 24015**

Motorized scooters,

Driving under the influence, **Veh 40303**

Pocket bikes, operation, location, **Veh 21720**

TRAFFIC RULES AND REGULATIONS
—Cont'd

Motorsports, semitrailers, length, special permits, **Veh 35401.5**

Mountain highways, **Veh 21662**

Coasting downgrade in neutral, **Veh 21710**

Horns, warnings, **Veh 21662**

Movement of vehicle, turning, safety, **Veh 22107**

Multiple beam lamps, dimming, **Veh 24409**

Multiple deposits of bail, refunds, **Veh 42201.6**

Multiple lane highways,

Right turns, marked lanes, **Veh 22100**

Speed limits, **Veh 22361**

Multiple unit truck reflectors, **Veh 24610**

Municipal courts, night court assessments, special penalty, **Veh 42006**

Municipal institutions, animal or vehicle, stopping, standing, paths, driveways or grounds, **Veh 21113**

Municipalities,

Applicability of traffic laws to vehicles, **Veh 21052**

Arrest warrant execution, expenses and expenditures, **Veh 40516**

Off street parking facility, **Veh 21107.8**

Vehicles, length, **Veh 35401**

Weight limitations, **Veh 35700 et seq.**

Names,

Assumed or fictitious names, **Veh 40000.25**

Notice to correct violations, **Veh 40614**

Impounding, release, **Veh 14602.8**

Narcotics. Driving under the influence, generally, ante

Narrow roadways, grades, approaching vehicles yielding right of way, **Veh 21661**

National emergencies, police escort vehicles, siren and speed, **Veh 21057**

Negligence,

Driving while intoxicated, **Veh 23153**

Evidence, **Veh 12810.5, 40833**

Seat belt violations, **Veh 12810.2**

Inadmissibility of conviction for violation under state or federal authority, **Veh 40830**

Passenger for hire, failure of driver to stop at railroad crossing, **Veh 22453**

Reports, evidence, **Veh 40833**

Speed conviction, evidence, **Veh 40831**

Negligent homicide, drivers license, compact, **Veh 15000 et seq.**

Neutral gear, coasting down grade, **Veh 21710**

Nevada County, ordinances, commercial vehicle weight, use of Northwoods boulevard, **Veh 35715**

Noise, **Veh 27200 et seq.**

Alarms and horns, activation of devices, impounding vehicles, **Veh 22651.5**

City on island over 20,000 acres, county over 4 million, **Veh 21100.5**

Exhaust systems, decals, **Veh 27202.1**

TRAFFIC

TRAFFIC RULES AND REGULATIONS
—Cont'd
Noise—Cont'd
Motorcycles, **Veh 27201, 27202**
Snowmobiles, **Veh 27203**
Nolo contendere,
Complaint or notice to appear, **Veh 40513**
Traffic violator schools, continuance, attendance, **Veh 41501, 42005**
Nonliability, affidavits, automated enforcement systems, **Veh 40520**
Nonmotorized traffic, freeways, restrictions, **Veh 21960**
Nonresidents,
Arrest, **Veh 40305**
Appearance, **Veh 40515**
Driving under the influence,
Ignition interlock devices, **Veh 23575**
License suspension or revocation, termination, **Veh 13353.5**
Norco, speed, horseback riding, **Veh 22353**
Not guilty plea, **Veh 40519**
Notice,
Appearance, ante
Arrest,
Form of notice to appear, **Veh 40500**
Notice of offense, **Veh 40002**
Continuance of written promise to appear, violation, **Veh 40509**
Correction of violation,
Arrest, **Veh 40303.5**
Failure to correct, complaint, **Veh 40618**
Form, **Veh 40610**
Proof of correction, **Veh 40616**
Willful violation, **Veh 40000.25**
Cruising, traffic control points, **Veh 21100**
Disposition, consolidated disposition, **Veh 41610**
Driving under the influence, ante
Fines and penalties, failure to pay, **Veh 40509.5**
Liens, **Veh 14911**
Hazardous substances and waste,
Route notification, **Veh 32050 et seq.**
Spills, **Veh 2453**
Hearings, cargo tank vehicles, **Veh 21109.5**
Ignition interlock devices, **Veh 13353.3, 23573**
Impounding, ante
Infractions, ante
Length, livestock carriers, access, exemptions, **Veh 35401.7**
Major code changes affecting traffic laws, drivers license extension recipients, **Veh 12814.5**
Maximum speed limit, increase, **Veh 22366**
Parking, post
Private ownership,
Exemption from local regulation, **Veh 21107.5 et seq.**
Removal of vehicles, **Veh 22658**

TRAFFIC RULES AND REGULATIONS
—Cont'd
Notice—Cont'd
Railroads, building mover transporting across tracks, **Veh 35789**
Reduction of weight limits, **Veh 35705**
Removal of vehicles,
Disabled vehicles, freeways, **Veh 22654**
Storage, **Veh 22851 et seq.**
Speed, post
Storage, fees, **Veh 22651**
Weight limits,
Bridges and other structures, **Veh 35751**
Changes on state highways, **Veh 35652**
Notice to appear. Arrest, ante
Nuisance,
Driving under the influence, **Veh 23596**
Hazardous substances and waste, illegal dumping, **Veh 23112.7**
Prohibited sign, signal, removal, **Veh 21467**
Removal of parked or standing vehicles, **Veh 22650 et seq.**
Oakland, weights, maximum, **Veh 35655.5**
Obstructing traffic,
Arrest, **Veh 40300.5**
Disabled vehicles, removal, **Veh 22654**
Minimum speed limits, **Veh 22400**
Removal of vehicle, **Veh 22654**
Speed contests or exhibitions, **Veh 23109**
Stopping, standing or parking vehicles, **Veh 22500**
Removal, **Veh 22650 et seq.**
Obstruction of driver view,
Overtaking and passing, **Veh 21752**
Passengers, **Veh 21700**
Occupants, intoxicating liquors, **Veh 23221**
Odometer, crimes and offenses, **Veh 40000.15**
Off highway vehicles, **Veh 38000 et seq., 38280 et seq.**
Damage to land, wildlife or wildlife habitat, **Veh 38319 et seq.**
Drinking, **Veh 23220**
Littering, **Veh 38320, 38321**
Marijuana, possession, **Veh 23222**
Misdemeanors, **Veh 40000.24**
Mountain fire districts, **Veh 38301.5**
Open containers, **Veh 23220 et seq.**
Operation on combined use highways, **Veh 38026.5**
Parking, emergency vehicles, exemptions, **Veh 21055**
Placing cables, rope, in position to do bodily injury, **Veh 38318.5**
Public lands, special regulations, **Veh 38301**
Racing events, **Veh 38286**
Reckless driving, post
Speed limits, **Veh 38305, 38310**
Emergency vehicles, exemption, **Veh 21055**

TRAFFIC RULES AND REGULATIONS
—Cont'd
Off highway vehicles—Cont'd
Starting, **Veh 38312**
Throwing projectiles, **Veh 38318**
Turning, **Veh 38314**
Emergency vehicles, exemptions, **Veh 21055**
Use on highway, **Veh 38025**
Wilderness areas, **Veh 38301.3**
Off street parking. Parking, post
Offal. Garbage and refuse, generally, ante
Officers and employees,
Application of law, **Veh 21052**
Governmental agencies, application of law, **Veh 21054**
Highway construction, improvement and repair, application of law, **Veh 21053**
Public agencies, representatives, application of law, **Veh 21054**
Size or weight violations,
Arrest, employers failure to answer charges, **Veh 40005**
Dismissal of charges, abstract of record, **Veh 40003**
Toll roads and bridges, vehicular crossings, **Veh 23251 et seq.**
Traffic Officers, generally, this index
Official misconduct, disposition of fines, penalties, and forfeitures, **Veh 42202**
Official traffic control device, definitions, **Veh 440**
Official traffic control signal, definitions, **Veh 445**
Official uniform and vehicle, arresting speed violators, **Veh 40804**
One way roadways,
Bicycles, **Veh 21202**
Designation of lanes or part of roadway, **Veh 21657**
Local authorities, designation, **Veh 21101**
Overtaking and passing, post
Parking, **Veh 22502**
Ordinances, **Veh 22503**
Right side of roadway, exemption from driving requirement, **Veh 21650**
Right turn from, **Veh 22100**
Streetcars, passing on left, **Veh 21757**
Three lane roadways, driving in center or left lane, **Veh 21659**
Open containers, intoxicating liquors, **Veh 23222 et seq.**
Open range, **Veh 21365**
Optional appearance before magistrate, violators, **Veh 40303 et seq.**
Orders of court,
Crimes and offenses, failure to comply, **Veh 40508**
Warrants, generally, post
Ordinances,
Fire hydrants, **Veh 22514**
Impounding vehicles, **Veh 22850.5**

TRAFFIC RULES AND REGULATIONS
—Cont'd
Ordinances—Cont'd
Nevada County, commercial vehicles, weight, use of Northwoods boulevard, **Veh 35715**
Parking, post
Roller skating, **Veh 21969**
Speed, post
Weight limits, **Veh 35702**
Out of service orders, crimes and offenses, **Veh 40001, 40303**
Outdoor advertising, mobile billboard advertising displays, **Veh 21100**
Impounding, **Veh 22651**
Overhang, explosive loads, **Veh 31614**
Overhead crossings, pedestrians,
Failure to use, **Veh 21953**
Stopping or standing, peace officers ordering removal, **Veh 21962**
Overloads. Weights, generally, post
Overtaking and passing, **Veh 21750 et seq.**
Animals, caution, **Veh 21759**
Approaching vehicle,
Crosswalk, passing vehicle stopped for pedestrians, **Veh 21951**
Fines and penalties, **Veh 42001.17**
Narrow roadways, yielding right of way, **Veh 21661**
Right side, **Veh 21660**
Ascending vehicles, yielding right of way, **Veh 21661**
Bicycles, **Veh 21202, 21750 et seq., 21760**
Bridges, **Veh 21752**
Buses, passengers alighting or boarding, **Veh 21756**
Business or residence district, passing on right, **Veh 21754**
Caravans or motorcades, **Veh 21705**
Center lane, three lane roadway, **Veh 21659**
Clearance, two lane highway, **Veh 21751**
Crest of grade, **Veh 21752**
Crosswalks, passing vehicles stopped for pedestrians, **Veh 21951**
Fines and penalties, **Veh 42001.17**
Curves, **Veh 21752**
Descending vehicles, yielding right of way, **Veh 21661**
Designated lanes, **Veh 22348**
Distances between vehicles, **Veh 21704**
Divided roadways, passing on right, **Veh 21754**
Double lines, **Veh 21460**
Double parallel solid lines, **Veh 21460**
Electric cars,
Left side, **Veh 21757**
Passengers alighting or boarding, **Veh 21756**
Horse drawn vehicles, **Veh 21759**
Intersections, **Veh 21752**
Streetcars, **Veh 21756**
Vehicles stopped for pedestrians in crosswalk, **Veh 21951**
Fines and penalties, **Veh 42001.17**

TRAFFIC RULES AND REGULATIONS
—Cont'd
Overtaking and passing—Cont'd
Interurban electric or streetcars,
Left side, **Veh 21757**
Passengers alighting or boarding, **Veh 21756**
Left hand side, **Veh 21750 et seq.**
Streetcars, **Veh 21757**
Three lane highways, **Veh 21659**
Left turn, passing on right, **Veh 21754**
Motor trucks, distances between vehicles, **Veh 21704**
Motorcades, **Veh 21705**
Motorized scooters, **Veh 21228, 21229**
Mountain driving, **Veh 21662**
Narrow roads, **Veh 21661**
Obstruction of drivers view, **Veh 21752**
One way roadways,
Exemption, driving on left, **Veh 21752**
Passing on right, **Veh 21754**
Streetcars, left side, **Veh 21757**
Overtaken vehicle, yielding, **Veh 21753**
Parallel lines, **Veh 21460**
Passengers alighting or boarding interurban electric or streetcars, **Veh 21756**
Pedestrians, **Veh 21951**
Fines and penalties, **Veh 42001.17**
Photography and pictures, sound recordings, **Veh 40008**
Railroad crossings, **Veh 21752**
Right side,
Approaching vehicles, **Veh 21660**
Conditions, **Veh 21754, 21755**
Driving and operation, **Veh 21650**
Overtaken vehicle, yielding, **Veh 21753**
Safety zones, interurban electric or streetcars, passengers alighting or boarding, **Veh 21756**
School buses, **Veh 22454**
Distances between vehicles, **Veh 21704**
Slow moving vehicles, **Veh 21654, 21754, 21758**
Designated lanes, **Veh 21655**
Turning out of highway, **Veh 21656**
Stopping,
Animals or horse drawn vehicles, **Veh 21759**
Pedestrians, fines and penalties, **Veh 42001.17**
Streetcars,
Left side, **Veh 21757**
Passengers alighting or boarding, **Veh 21756**
Three lane roadway, center lane, **Veh 21659**
Towing,
Distances between vehicles, **Veh 21704**
Swerving, **Veh 21711**
Trolley coach or bus, **Veh 21756**
Trucks, distances between vehicles, **Veh 21704**

TRAFFIC RULES AND REGULATIONS
—Cont'd
Overtaking and passing—Cont'd
Tunnels, view obstructed, **Veh 21752**
Turning out of highway, slow moving vehicles, **Veh 21656**
Two lane highway, left side, **Veh 21751**
Vehicles proceeding in opposite direction, **Veh 21660**
Vehicles proceeding in same direction, **Veh 21704, 21750 et seq.**
Vehicles stopped for pedestrians in crosswalk, **Veh 21951, 42001.17**
Viaducts, view obstructed, **Veh 21752**
View obstructed, **Veh 21752**
Yielding right of way, **Veh 21661, 21753**
Owners and ownership. Title to property, generally, post
Packages, motorized scooters, **Veh 21235**
Parades, temporary closing streets, local regulations, **Veh 21101**
Parallel lines, driving to left, **Veh 21460**
Parallel parking, curbs, **Veh 22502**
Parking, **Veh 463, 22500 et seq., 22950 et seq.**
Abandoned vehicles, removal, **Veh 22650 et seq.**
Additional curb parking, **Veh 22503**
Adjacent curbs, **Veh 22502**
Unincorporated areas, **Veh 22504**
Administrative fees, collection and disposition, **Veh 40200.3**
Administrative hearings, contesting citation, **Veh 40215**
Affidavits, nonliability, **Veh 40208 et seq.**
Airports, municipal airports, **Veh 21113**
Alarm devices, activation, removal of vehicle, **Veh 22651.5**
Alley parking, offstreet operators, **Veh 22951**
Angle parking, ordinances, **Veh 22503**
Antigridlock Act, **Veh 22526**
Appeal and review, San Francisco City and County, buses, videotape, transit only traffic lanes, **Veh 40241**
Appearance, criminal complaints, **Veh 40230**
Backing vehicle, safety, **Veh 22106**
Bail,
Deposits, **Veh 40509**
Impounded vehicles, **Veh 22651.3**
Blocking wheels, grades, **Veh 22509**
Bordering state parks, **Veh 22505**
Bridges, **Veh 22500**
State highways, ordinances, **Veh 22501**
Buses,
Loading zones, **Veh 22500**
San Francisco City and County, videotape, transit only traffic lanes, **Veh 40240 et seq.**
Business or residence districts,
Commercial vehicles, exemptions, **Veh 22502**
Grades, blocking wheels, **Veh 22509**

TRAFFIC

TRAFFIC RULES AND REGULATIONS
—Cont'd
Parking—Cont'd
Car share vehicle program, exclusive use spaces, **Veh 22507.1**
Citations, quotas, **Veh 41600 et seq.**
Collection, penalties, disposition, **Veh 40200.3**
Commercial vehicles,
Loading or unloading, **Veh 22502**
Local authorities, powers, **Veh 22507.5**
Complaints, notice to appear, **Veh 40513**
Contesting violations, **Veh 40215**
Contracts, processing agencies, violations, **Veh 40200.5, 40200.6**
Copies, notice of delinquent parking violations, **Veh 40206.5**
Corridor parking facilities, **Veh 22518**
Counties, off street parking, **Veh 21107.8**
Court enforcement, complaints, **Veh 40220, 40221, 40230**
Crimes and offenses, reports, **Veh 1803 et seq.**
Criminal complaints, court enforcement, **Veh 40230**
Crossings, vehicular crossings, toll roads and bridges, **Veh 23333**
Crosswalks, **Veh 22500**
Curbs, **Veh 22502, 22503**
Markings, **Veh 21458**
Damages, improper removal of vehicle, **Veh 22658**
Delinquent parking violations, notice, **Veh 40206, 40207**
Evidence, **Veh 40903**
Deposits, fines and penalties, **Veh 40200.3**
Disabled persons. Handicapped persons, ante
Disabled vehicles,
State highways, **Veh 22505**
Unincorporated areas, **Veh 22504**
Disabled veterans,
Curbs, marking for parking, **Veh 21458**
Parking placards, **Veh 9105**
Doors, opening on moving traffic, **Veh 22517**
Double parking, **Veh 22500**
Drivers licenses, delinquent violations, refusal to issue or renew, **Veh 12808.1**
Electric vehicles, designated spaces, **Veh 22511, 22511.1, 42001.6**
Electronically produced facsimile, delinquent parking violations, **Veh 40206.5**
Enforcement, violations, **Veh 40200 et seq.**
Streetsweepers, **Veh 40245 et seq.**
Examiners, administrative hearings, contesting citations, **Veh 40215**
Excavations, **Veh 22500**

TRAFFIC RULES AND REGULATIONS
—Cont'd
Parking—Cont'd
Exclusive use spaces,
Cardiovascular, lung and respiratory diseases, **Veh 22511.5**
Ridesharing, **Veh 22507.1**
Exemptions,
Disabled persons, **Veh 22511.5**
Local authorities, **Veh 22507**
Public utility vehicles, **Veh 22512**
Unincorporated areas, **Veh 22504**
Explosives,
Loading, **Veh 31614**
Transports, **Veh 31616**
Failure to pay penalties, refusal to renew registration, **Veh 4760 et seq.**
Fees,
Disabled person placards, **Veh 22511.55**
Meter zones, **Veh 22508**
Offstreet operators, **Veh 22952**
Parking meter zones, **Veh 22508**
Temporary placards, handicapped persons, **Veh 22511.59**
Variable fees, **Veh 22508**
Fines and penalties, **Veh 40203.5, 40203.6**
Additional assessment, disabled person parking violations, **Veh 4461.3**
Disabled person parking violations, additional assessment, **Veh 4461.3**
Electric vehicles, designated spaces, **Veh 42001.6**
Enforcement and collection, **Veh 40200 et seq.**
Failure to pay, refusal to renew registration, **Veh 4760 et seq.**
Liens and encumbrances, failure to pay penalty, **Veh 9800**
Mode of payment, **Veh 40510**
Notice, **Veh 40203**
Satisfaction prerequisite, immobilized vehicle release, **Veh 22651.7**
Veterans, **Veh 42001.13**
Zero emission electric vehicles, designated spaces, **Veh 42001.6**
Fire hydrants, **Veh 22514**
Fire lanes, **Veh 22500.1**
Fire station entrance, **Veh 22500**
Foreign states, exemptions, **Veh 22511.5**
Freeways, **Veh 21718**
Tow trucks, **Veh 22513**
Grades, blocking wheels, **Veh 22509**
Handicapped persons, ante
Hazardous waste haulers, **Veh 31303**
High density multiple family dwelling areas, exemption, **Veh 22507.5**
Hills, blocking wheels, **Veh 22509**
Horns, activation, vehicle removal, **Veh 22651.5**
Ice and snow areas, **Veh 22510**
Immobilization of vehicles, devices, **Veh 22651.7**

TRAFFIC RULES AND REGULATIONS
—Cont'd
Parking—Cont'd
Impounding, **Veh 22650 et seq.**
Liens and incumbrances, local authority, **Veh 22851.1**
Removal from offstreet parking lots, **Veh 22651.3**
Infractions,
Handicapped parking violations, **Veh 42001.5**
Outstanding warrants, bail, **Veh 40304.5**
Initial review, **Veh 40215**
Inoperable parking meters, **Veh 22508.5**
Intersections, **Veh 22500**
Joint liability for fines and penalties, **Veh 40200**
Late payment penalties, **Veh 40203.5**
Left hand parking,
One way roadways, **Veh 22503**
Two way roadways, Long Beach, pilot programs, **Veh 22502**
Licenses and permits,
Car share vehicle program, **Veh 22507.1**
Handicapped persons, exemptions, **Veh 22507.5**
Preferential parking permits, ordinances, **Veh 22507**
Private driveways, owners and lessees, **Veh 22507.2**
Ridesharing, **Veh 22507.1**
Lights and lighting,
Dimming headlamps, **Veh 24401**
Parking lamps, **Veh 24800 et seq.**
Limitation of prosecutions, **Veh 40224**
Local authorities, powers, **Veh 22503, 22506 et seq.**
Locked vehicles, **Veh 22516**
Long Beach, left hand parking, two way roadways, pilot programs, **Veh 22502**
Mail and mailing,
Bail, **Veh 40309**
Payment of penalties, **Veh 40309, 40521**
Mass transit, San Francisco City and County, videotape, transit only traffic lanes, **Veh 40240 et seq.**
Meter zones, **Veh 22508**
Minority business enterprises, violations processing contracts, **Veh 40200.5**
Mobile devices, payment, **Veh 22508**
Motorcycles,
Curb parking, **Veh 22502**
Ordinances, **Veh 22503.5**
Motorized scooters, **Veh 21225**
Municipalities, off street parking, **Veh 21107.8**
Nonliability affidavits, **Veh 40208 et seq.**
Not guilty plea, **Veh 40519**
Notice, **Veh 40202**
Appearance, **Veh 40513**
Delinquent parking violations, **Veh 40206, 40207**

TRAFFIC RULES AND REGULATIONS
—Cont'd
Parking—Cont'd
Notice—Cont'd
Evidence, **Veh 40903**
Fines and penalties, **Veh 40203**
Private off street, application of law, **Veh 21107.8**
Processing agencies, vehicle registration, **Veh 40200.8**
Removal and impoundment, offstreet parking lots, **Veh 22651.3**
San Francisco City and County, buses, videotape, transit only traffic lanes, **Veh 40240, 40241**
Streetsweepers, violations, **Veh 40248**
Obstructing traffic, **Veh 22500**
Off highway vehicles subject to identification, **Veh 38020**
Emergency vehicles, exemptions, **Veh 21055**
Off street parking, **Veh 22951**
Cities over 2,000,000, **Veh 22950**
Definitions, **Veh 4000**
Handicapped persons, lifts or ramps, **Veh 22511.85**
Ordinances, **Veh 22519**
Removal and impoundment, **Veh 22651.3**
One way roadway, **Veh 22502**
Ordinances, **Veh 22503 et seq.**
Motorcycles, **Veh 22503.5**
Offstreet parking, **Veh 22519**
Proof of ownership, evidence, **Veh 40900**
Overnight parking, commercial vehicles, **Veh 22507.5**
Owners, proof of ownership, evidence, **Veh 40900**
Parallel parking, curbs, **Veh 22502**
Payment of penalties, **Veh 40510**
Mail and mailing, **Veh 40309, 40521**
Termination of proceedings, **Veh 40204, 40211, 40222**
Photography and pictures, enforcement, streetsweepers, **Veh 40245 et seq.**
Pilot programs, Long Beach, left hand parking, two way roadways, **Veh 22502**
Points, violation points, Antigridlock Act violations, **Veh 12810.4**
Preferential parking permits, ordinances, **Veh 22507**
Private driveways, **Veh 22500**
Owners and lessees, licenses and permits, **Veh 22507.2**
Private off street parking, **Veh 21107.8**
Processing agencies,
Vehicle registration, recalling hold, **Veh 40200.8**
Violations, **Veh 40200.6**
Public utilities,
Application of law, **Veh 22512**
Warning devices, **Veh 25301**
Quotas, citations, **Veh 41600 et seq.**
Railroad tracks, **Veh 22521**

TRAFFIC RULES AND REGULATIONS
—Cont'd
Parking—Cont'd
Rates and charges,
Offstreet facilities, **Veh 22952**
Parking meter zones, **Veh 22508**
Towing or removal, offstreet facilities, **Veh 22952**
Red paint, handicapped access ramps, **Veh 22522**
Registration, refusal to renew, failure to pay, **Veh 4760 et seq., 40220**
Removal of vehicles, **Veh 22650 et seq.**
Handicapped parking spaces, **Veh 22652**
Liability, **Veh 22652.5**
Highway patrol, **Veh 22659**
Law enforcement, volunteers, **Veh 22651.05**
Offstreet facilities, **Veh 22952**
Handicapped persons spaces, **Veh 22511.8**
Parking lot operators, **Veh 22952**
Stalls designated for handicapped persons, **Veh 22652**
Stolen vehicles on private property, **Veh 22653**
Zero emission electric vehicles, designated spaces, **Veh 22511**
Reports, Long Beach, left hand parking, two way roadways, pilot programs, **Veh 22502**
Ridesharing, exclusive use spaces, **Veh 22507.1**
Runaway vehicle, accident, duty of driver, **Veh 20002**
Safety zones, **Veh 22500**
San Francisco City and County, buses, videotape, transit only traffic lanes, **Veh 40240 et seq.**
Satisfaction of penalties, prerequisite to releasing immobilized vehicle, **Veh 22651.7**
School officers and employees, preferential parking permits, **Veh 22507**
Scofflaws, immobilization devices, **Veh 22651.7**
Sidewalks, **Veh 22500**
Handicapped persons, access ramps, **Veh 22522**
Signs and signals. Traffic Signs and Signals, this index
Snow areas, **Veh 22510**
Special enforcement units, handicapped parking, **Veh 22507**
Starting vehicle on highway, safety, **Veh 22106**
State highways, **Veh 22505, 22506**
Bridges, **Veh 22500**
Local ordinances, **Veh 22501**
Corridor parking facilities, **Veh 22518**
Ordinances or resolutions, **Veh 22506**
Parking meter zones, **Veh 22508**
Streetsweepers,
Designated hours, **Veh 22507.6**

TRAFFIC RULES AND REGULATIONS
—Cont'd
Parking—Cont'd
Streetsweepers—Cont'd
Photography and pictures, enforcement, **Veh 40245 et seq.**
Temporary placards, handicapped persons, **Veh 22511.59**
Three wheeled vehicles, **Veh 22503.5**
Time, restrictions, ordinances, **Veh 22507**
Tow trucks, **Veh 22513**
Towing vehicles,
Offstreet facilities, **Veh 22952**
Rates and charges, improper removal, **Veh 22658**
Traffic Signs and Signals, this index
Transfers of processing agencies, enforcement, **Veh 40200.4**
Trial by written declaration, defendant residence distant from court, **Veh 40902**
Tubes or tunnels, **Veh 22500**
Unattended vehicles, stopping motor and setting brakes, **Veh 22515**
Unincorporated areas, **Veh 22504**
Utility vehicles, application of law, **Veh 22512**
Vehicular crossings, toll roads and bridges, **Veh 23333**
Vending, commercial vehicles, residential districts, **Veh 22455**
Veterans, this index
Violations, **Veh 40200 et seq.**
Fines and penalties, **Veh 40203.5, 40203.6**
Handicapped persons, facilities, **Veh 22507.8**
Special enforcement unit, **Veh 22507.9**
Impoundment or immobilization, satisfactory evidence, **Veh 22651.8**
Notice, **Veh 40202**
Proof of ownership, evidence, **Veh 40900**
Reports, **Veh 1803 et seq.**
San Francisco City and County, buses, videotape, transit only traffic lanes, **Veh 40240 et seq.**
Trial by written declaration, defendants residence distant from court, **Veh 40902**
Warning signals and devices, **Veh 25300 et seq.**
Wheels, blocking on grade, **Veh 22509**
Written declaration, trial by, defendant residence distant from court, **Veh 40902**
Zero emission electric vehicles, designated spaces, **Veh 22511, 22511.1, 42001.6**
Zones, parking meters zones, **Veh 22508**
Parking facilities, privately owned facilities, public parking prohibited, posting signs, **Veh 22511.8**

TRAFFIC

TRAFFIC RULES AND REGULATIONS
—Cont'd

Parks, **Veh 21113**
   Speed, **Veh 22358.3**
Parole and probation. Driving under the influence, ante
Partial year registration, commercial vehicles, weight fees, **Veh 9407, 9700 et seq.**
   Additional weight fees, adjustments, **Veh 1678**
Passenger buses or coaches, width, **Veh 35106, 35107**
Passenger vehicles,
   Combinations, **Veh 21715**
   Drawing another vehicle, speed limits, **Veh 22406, 22407**
   Grade crossings, stopping, **Veh 22452, 22452.5**
Passengers,
   Carriers, generally, ante
   Children and minors, restraint systems, **Veh 27360 et seq.**
   Doors, opening on moving traffic, **Veh 22517**
   Drinking in motor vehicle, intoxicating liquors, **Veh 23221**
   For hire, failure of driver to stop at railroad crossing, imputed negligence, **Veh 22453**
   Front seat, interference with view or obstruction of control of vehicle, **Veh 21700**
   Hours of driving, limitation, **Veh 21702**
   Interference with control of vehicle, **Veh 21700**
   Intoxicating liquors, **Veh 23221**
      Drinking on highway, **Veh 23221**
   Motorized scooters, **Veh 21235**
   Throwing substances, **Veh 23110, 23111**
   Towing trailers carrying passengers, **Veh 21712**
   Trunk, **Veh 21712**
   Unlawful riding, **Veh 21712**
Passing. Overtaking and passing, generally, ante
Paths,
   Animal or vehicle, stopping, standing, schools, **Veh 21113**
   Bicycles, separation from vehicular traffic, **Veh 21207**
Paul Buzzo Act, **Veh 23111**
Pay by plate toll payment, **Veh 23302**
   Information, **Veh 23301.8**
Payment, fines and penalties, infractions, **Veh 42003**
Pedestrians, **Veh 21950 et seq.**
   Adjacent controlled intersections, crossing, **Veh 21955**
   Approaching vehicles, overtaking and passing vehicles stopped for pedestrians, **Veh 21951**
      Fines and penalties, **Veh 42001.17**
   Arrest,
      Freeways, overpasses and bridges, **Veh 40303**

TRAFFIC RULES AND REGULATIONS
—Cont'd

Pedestrians—Cont'd
   Arrest—Cont'd
      Optional appearance before magistrate, **Veh 40303**
   Authorized emergency vehicles, duties, **Veh 21806, 21807**
   Bicycle lanes, **Veh 21966**
   Blind persons, **Veh 21963 et seq.**
   Bridges,
      Peace officers ordering removal, **Veh 21962**
      Regulation, **Veh 21109**
   Business or residence district, side of roadway, **Veh 21956**
   Crimes and offenses, reports, **Veh 1803 et seq.**
   Crossings,
      At crosswalk, local regulation, **Veh 21106**
      Between adjacent controlled intersections, **Veh 21955**
      Failure to use overhead or tunnel crossings, **Veh 21953**
      Outside crosswalks, **Veh 21954**
      Vehicular crossings, toll roads and bridges, **Veh 23331**
   Crosswalks,
      Adjacent controlled intersections, crossing, **Veh 21955**
      Blocking, **Veh 21970**
      Controlled intersections, crossing, **Veh 21955**
      Jaywalkers, **Veh 21954**
      Local regulations, **Veh 21106, 21961**
      Overtaking and passing vehicles stopped for pedestrians, **Veh 21951**
         Fines and penalties, **Veh 42001.17**
      Removal, **Veh 21950.5**
      Right of way, **Veh 21950**
   Curbs, leaving place of safety for path of vehicle, **Veh 21950**
   Definitions, **Veh 467**
   Delay, stopping, crosswalks, **Veh 21950**
   Disabled vehicles, freeways, **Veh 21960**
   Due care, duty of using, **Veh 21950**
   Duties and rights, **Veh 21950 et seq.**
   Emergency vehicles, right of way, **Veh 21806, 21807**
   Fines and penalties, infractions, **Veh 42001**
   Freeways, restrictions, **Veh 21960**
   Hitchhiking, **Veh 21957**
   Immediate hazard, leaving place of safety, **Veh 21950**
   Infractions, **Veh 42001**
   Intersections,
      Adjacent controlled intersections, crossing, **Veh 21955**
      Crossing between adjacent controlled intersections, **Veh 21955**
      Overtaking and passing vehicles stopped, **Veh 21951**
         Fines and penalties, **Veh 42001.17**

TRAFFIC RULES AND REGULATIONS
—Cont'd

Pedestrians—Cont'd
   Jaywalkers,
      Adjacent controlled intersections, crossing at crosswalk, **Veh 21955**
      Local regulations, **Veh 21961**
      Right of way, **Veh 21954**
   Leaving place of safety, path of vehicle constituting immediate hazard, **Veh 21950**
   Local regulations, **Veh 21961**
      Subways, **Veh 21109**
   Marked crosswalks, overtaking and passing vehicles stopped, **Veh 21951**
      Fines and penalties, **Veh 42001.17**
   Motorized scooters, **Veh 21235**
   Obedience to signals, **Veh 21462**
   Outside crosswalks, yielding right of way, **Veh 21954**
   Overhead crossing, failure to use, **Veh 21953**
   Overpasses, stopping or standing, peace officers ordering removal, **Veh 21962**
   Overtaking and passing, vehicles stopped for pedestrians in crosswalk, **Veh 21951**
      Fines and penalties, **Veh 42001.17**
   Prima facie speed limits, **Veh 22352**
   Public policy, **Veh 21949**
   Railroad crossings, stopping, **Veh 22451**
   Red lights, **Veh 21453**
   Residence districts, U turns, **Veh 22103**
   Right of way, **Veh 21950**
      Blind persons, **Veh 21963 et seq.**
      Crossing roadway outside crosswalks, **Veh 21954**
      Crosswalks, **Veh 21950**
      Driver on left, **Veh 21800**
      Drivers handbook, **Veh 1656.3**
      Emergency vehicles, **Veh 21806, 21807**
      Entrance of through highway, **Veh 21802**
      Intersection governed by signal, **Veh 21451**
      Jaywalkers, **Veh 21954**
      Left turns, **Veh 21801**
      Outside crosswalks, **Veh 21954**
      Overhead crossings, failure to use, **Veh 21953**
      Sidewalks, driving over or upon, **Veh 21952**
      Sign, approaching vehicles, **Veh 21803**
      Tunnel or overhead crossing, yielding, **Veh 21953**
      Visually handicapped persons, **Veh 21963 et seq.**
   Rights and duties, **Veh 21950 et seq.**
   Road rage, generally, post
   Roller skating, **Veh 21969**
   Safety program, **Veh 2900 et seq.**
   School buses, passing, **Veh 22454**

TRAFFIC RULES AND REGULATIONS
—Cont'd
Pedestrians—Cont'd
School crossing guards, nonstudent guards, disregarding instructions, fines, **Veh 42001.1**
Side of roadway, areas outside business or residence district, **Veh 21956**
Sidewalks, right of way, **Veh 21952**
Skiing across state highways, **Veh 21959**
Slow moving vehicles, left turn, **Veh 21654**
Soliciting rides, hitchhiking, **Veh 21957**
Speed, prima facie limits, **Veh 22352**
Standing vehicles, **Veh 22500**
Stopping, **Veh 22500**
    Pedestrians in crosswalk, overtaking and passing vehicles, **Veh 21951**
    Fines and penalties, **Veh 42001.17**
    Special stops, **Veh 22450 et seq.**
Stopping in crosswalk, unnecessary delay, **Veh 21950**
Streetcars, overtaking and passing, **Veh 21756**
Through highway entrances, yielding right of way, **Veh 21802**
Tobogganing across state highways, **Veh 21959**
Traffic Signs and Signals, this index
Transit grade crossings, stopping, **Veh 22451**
Tunnel crossing, failure to use, **Veh 21953**
Turning, **Veh 22100**
Turning on red, yielding right of way, **Veh 21453**
U turns,
    Business districts, **Veh 22102**
    Residence districts, **Veh 22103**
Unmarked crosswalks, overtaking and passing vehicles stopped, **Veh 21950, 21951**
    Fines and penalties, **Veh 42001.17**
Vehicular crossings, toll roads and bridges, special regulation, **Veh 23331**
Violations, reports, **Veh 1803 et seq.**
Visually handicapped persons, **Veh 21963 et seq.**
Pedicabs, **Veh 21100, 21200**
Penalties. Fines and penalties, generally, ante
Permits. Licenses and permits, generally, ante
Personal assistive mobility devices, **Veh 21280 et seq.**
Personal check as bail, **Veh 40510**
Personal injuries,
    Driving while intoxicated, **Veh 23153**
    Great bodily injury, reckless driving, punishment, **Veh 23104**
    Reckless driving, punishment, **Veh 23104**
    Removal of parked or standing vehicles, **Veh 22650 et seq.**

TRAFFIC RULES AND REGULATIONS
—Cont'd
Personal injuries—Cont'd
    Throwing or projecting substances at vehicles or occupants, **Veh 23110**
Phlebotomy technicians, driving under the influence, blood tests, **Veh 23158**
Photography and pictures,
    Automated rail crossing enforcement system, **Veh 21362.5**
    Motor vehicles taking pictures, length, **Veh 35409**
    Parking violations,
        Removal of vehicles, **Veh 22658**
        Streetsweepers, enforcement, **Veh 40245 et seq.**
    Reckless driving, following too closely, interference, **Veh 40008**
Physicians and surgeons,
    Exemption, **Veh 21058**
    Intoxicating liquors, open container, exemption, **Veh 23229**
Pilot cars,
    Definitions, **Veh 472**
    Equipment, **Veh 28100 et seq.**
        Special permit violations, **Veh 35784**
    Signs and markings, requirement, **Veh 27904, 27904.5**
    Vertical clearance measuring devices, **Veh 35252**
Pilot programs,
    Parking, Long Beach, left hand parking, two way roadways, **Veh 22502**
    Tow truck drivers, certification, **Veh 2430 et seq.**
Pipe or pole dollies. Pole or pipe dollies, generally, post
Place to appear, arrested person, notice, **Veh 40502**
Pleadings,
    Arrest for infraction or misdemeanor, continuance of case to prepare, **Veh 40306**
    Declaration of intent to plead not guilty, **Veh 40519**
    Mail and mailing, written plea, **Veh 40519**
    Not guilty plea, filing, **Veh 40519**
    Written plea in lieu of personal appearance, **Veh 40519**
Pneumatic tires, maximum width of vehicle or load, **Veh 35101**
Pocket bikes, operation, location, **Veh 21720**
Point system, **Veh 12810**
    Antigridlock Act violations, **Veh 12810.4**
    Negligent drivers, prima facie presumption, **Veh 12810.5**
    Seat belt violations, **Veh 12810.2**
    Telecommunications, cellular radio telephones, **Veh 12810.3**
Poisons,
    Caldecott tunnel, transporting poisonous gas, **Veh 31301**

TRAFFIC RULES AND REGULATIONS
—Cont'd
Poisons—Cont'd
    Driving while under influence, arrest, mandatory appearance before magistrate, **Veh 40302**
    Transportation, **Veh 32100 et seq.**
Pole or pipe dollies,
    Length, **Veh 35414**
    Trucks transporting, flashing amber warning lights, **Veh 25275**
    Turn signals, exemption of special mobile equipment or auxiliary dollies, **Veh 24951**
Poles, loading and transportation, trucks transporting, flashing amber warning lights, **Veh 25275**
Political subdivisions, applicability of traffic laws to vehicles, **Veh 21052**
Possession. Alcoholic beverages, ante
Posting, private off street parking, application of law, **Veh 21107.8**
Power units, truck booster power units, permits, **Veh 35786, 35787**
Preferential use of highway, **Veh 21655.6, 21655.8**
    Emergency vehicles, **Veh 21655.8, 21806**
    Fines and penalties, **Veh 42001.1**
Presentence investigations,
    Code violations, **Veh 42003**
    Driving under influence, **Veh 23655**
Presumptions. Evidence, ante
Prima facie evidence. Evidence, generally, ante
Prima facie speed limits. Speed, post
Prior conviction or acquittal,
    Defenses to prosecution for code violations, **Veh 41400**
    Record, **Veh 13209**
Private property,
    Removal of parked or standing vehicles, **Veh 22653**
    Throwing objects at vehicles, **Veh 23111**
Private roads,
    Airports and landing fields, local regulation, **Veh 21108**
    Application of law, local regulations, public institutions, **Veh 21113**
    Closing to public use, **Veh 21107.5 et seq.**
    Commercial establishments, local regulation, **Veh 21107.6**
    Definitions, local regulation, **Veh 21107.7**
    Entering or crossing highway, right of way, **Veh 21804**
    Fire stations,
        Stopping, standing or parking vehicles, **Veh 22500**
        U turns in driveway entrance or approaches, **Veh 22104**
    Housing projects, local regulation, **Veh 21111**
    Left turn, right of way, **Veh 21804**
    Local authorities, **Veh 21107**
    Local regulation, **Veh 21107 et seq.**

TRAFFIC

TRAFFIC RULES AND REGULATIONS
—Cont'd
Private roads—Cont'd
Notice of private ownership, exemption from local regulation, **Veh 21107.5 et seq.**
Parking, **Veh 22500**
Public institutions, application of law, local regulation, **Veh 21113**
Public use, local regulation, **Veh 21107.5**
Removal of parked or standing vehicles, **Veh 22650 et seq.**
Right of way, entering or crossing highway, **Veh 21804**
School buses, stopping, **Veh 22500**
Service roads, entering or leaving highway, **Veh 21652**
Slow moving vehicles, left turn, **Veh 21654**
Stopping, standing or parking vehicles, **Veh 22500**
Taxicabs, stopping, **Veh 22500**
U turns, fire station entrances or approaches, **Veh 22104**
Private security agency vehicles, warning lights, **Veh 25279**
Removal of vehicles, **Veh 22651**
Privately owned armored cars, licenses and permits, **Veh 21713**
Privileged information. Confidential or privileged information, generally, ante
Privileges and immunities, youthful drunk driver visitation program, **Veh 23518.5**
Procedure on violations, arrest, **Veh 40300 et seq.**
Processing agencies. Parking, ante
Processions, local regulations, **Veh 21100 et seq.**
Prohibiting use by certain vehicles, local regulations, **Veh 21101**
Projecting loads,
Clearance and side marker lamps, **Veh 25100**
Explosives, **Veh 31614**
Lamp or flag, **Veh 24604, 25103**
Length restrictions, **Veh 35406, 35410, 35411**
Red flags or cloth, **Veh 24604**
Side marker lamps, **Veh 25100**
Warning lights, **Veh 25103**
Width restrictions, **Veh 35109, 35110**
Promise to appear. Arrest, generally, ante
Proof. Evidence, generally, ante
Proof of correction of violations, **Veh 40616**
Property damage, leaving scene of accident, **Veh 20002**
Protest, reduction of weight limits on improved county highway, **Veh 35708**
Prudent regard for conditions, speed, **Veh 22350**
Public agencies, **Veh 21113**
Representatives, application of law, **Veh 21054**

TRAFFIC RULES AND REGULATIONS
—Cont'd
Public buildings and grounds, local regulation, **Veh 21113**
Public carriers, regulation of location of stands, **Veh 21112**
Public employees, application of laws, **Veh 21053**
Public lands, impounding vehicles, **Veh 22651**
Public offenses, fines and penalties, **Veh 42000 et seq.**
Public officers and employees. Officers and employees, generally, ante
Public use of private roads, local ordinance or resolutions, **Veh 21107.5, 21107.6**
Public utilities,
Stopping, standing or parking, **Veh 22512**
Exemptions, service vehicles, **Veh 22502**
Weight limits, exemption, **Veh 35704, 35714**
Public utilities commission, stopping at industrial or spur tracks, determination, **Veh 22452**
Publication, **Veh 1656**
Publicly owned machinery and equipment, application of law, **Veh 21053**
Puerto Rico. Driving under the influence, ante
Punishment. Sentence and punishment, generally, post
Pursuit, bicycles, peace officers, exemptions, **Veh 21200**
Racing. Drag racing, generally, ante
Radar,
Jamming devices, speed, **Veh 28150, 40000.15**
Speed traps, burden of proof, **Veh 40803**
Radioactive materials, crimes and offenses, **Veh 40000.19**
Railroad crossings,
Agricultural labor and employment, motor vehicles, **Veh 22452**
Antigridlock Act, **Veh 22526**
Approaching vehicles, left side of roadway, **Veh 21752**
Automated enforcement systems, **Veh 21362.5**
Notice, violations, **Veh 40518, 40520**
Blocking crossing, **Veh 22526**
Branch lines, leading to ferries, stopping, **Veh 22452, 22453**
Buses, stopping, **Veh 22452**
Passengers, imputed negligence, **Veh 22453**
Business or residence district, carriers stopping, **Veh 22452, 22453**
Carriers, stopping, **Veh 22452, 22453**
Crimes and offenses, fines and penalties, **Veh 42001.16**
Allocation, **Veh 42007.4**
Explosives, transport stopping, **Veh 22452**

TRAFFIC RULES AND REGULATIONS
—Cont'd
Railroad crossings—Cont'd
Explosives, transport stopping—Cont'd
Passengers, imputed negligence, **Veh 22453**
Fines and penalties, **Veh 42001.16**
Allocation, **Veh 42007.4**
Flammable liquids transporters, stopping, **Veh 22452**
Passengers, imputed negligence, **Veh 22453**
Flashing lights, vehicles, **Veh 25251**
Gate crossings, stopping, **Veh 22451 et seq.**
Gear shifting, carriers stopping, **Veh 22452**
Hazardous substances and waste, **Veh 22452**
Imputed negligence, passenger for hire, failure of driver to stop, **Veh 22453**
Industrial tracks, stopping, **Veh 22452, 22453**
Liquefied petroleum gas transporters, stopping, **Veh 22452**
Passengers, imputed negligence, **Veh 22453**
Local regulation, **Veh 21110**
Looking and listening, **Veh 22452, 22453**
Motor carriers, stopping, **Veh 22452, 22453**
Motor trucks transporting employees, stopping, **Veh 22452**
Passengers, imputed negligence, **Veh 22453**
Negligence, passenger for hire, failure of driver to stop, **Veh 22453**
Notice,
Automated enforcement systems, violations, **Veh 40518, 40520**
Violations, automated enforcement system, **Veh 40518**
Obstruction of crossing, **Veh 22526**
Overtaking and passing, **Veh 21752**
Passengers for hire, imputed negligence, failure of driver to stop, **Veh 22453**
Pedestrians, stopping, **Veh 22451**
Photograph, automated rail crossing enforcement system, **Veh 21362.5**
Prima facie speed limits, **Veh 22352**
Removal of vehicles, **Veh 22656**
School buses, stopping, **Veh 22452**
Imputed negligence, passengers, **Veh 22453**
Shifting gears, carriers stopping, **Veh 22452**
Special stop street required, **Veh 22450 et seq.**
Speed, prima facie limits, **Veh 22352**
Spur tracks, stopping, **Veh 22452, 22453**
Stop signs in addition to railroad signals, **Veh 21355**
Stopping, **Veh 22450 et seq.**
Automated enforcement systems, **Veh 21362.5**

TRAFFIC RULES AND REGULATIONS
—Cont'd

Railroad crossings—Cont'd

Stopping—Cont'd

Automated enforcement systems
—Cont'd

Notice, violations, **Veh 40518,
40520**

Railroads,

Automated rail crossing enforcement
system, **Veh 21362.5**

Building movers, notice of transportation across tracks, **Veh 35789**

Drivers handbook, safety, **Veh 1656.3**

Parking vehicles, **Veh 22521**

Removal of parked or standing vehicles
from right of way, **Veh 22656**

Rapid transit districts, **Veh 21113**

Rates and charges,

Impounding, ante

Parking, ante

Toll on crossings, **Veh 23301 et seq.**

Towing or removal,

Offstreet parking facilities, **Veh 22952**

Vehicular crossings, **Veh 23271, 23272**

Ratio of weight to length, axle limits, **Veh
35551**

Rear projection of load, length limitations,
Veh 35410

Reasonable and prudent speed, **Veh 22350**

Rebuttal evidence, police report, **Veh
40806**

Reckless driving, **Veh 23103, 40000.24**

Alcohol and drug education program,
parole and probation, **Veh 23103.5**

Alcoholic beverages, second or subsequent offenses, **Veh 23103.5**

Arrest, procedure, **Veh 40303**

Bodily injury, causing, **Veh 23104**

Drivers licenses, revocation or suspension, **Veh 13200, 13201**

Driving during suspension, **Veh 14601**

Drug and alcohol education program,
parole and probation, **Veh 23103.5**

Fines and penalties, **Veh 23105**

Great bodily injury, **Veh 23104**

Guilty plea, **Veh 23103.5**

Impounding vehicles, **Veh 14602.7**

Investigation by department, **Veh 13800
et seq.**

Juveniles committed to youth authority,
Veh 41500

Nolo contendere plea, **Veh 23103.5**

Off highway vehicles, **Veh 38316**

Bodily injuries, **Veh 38317**

Misdemeanors, **Veh 40000.24**

Parking, private off street facility, **Veh
21107.8**

Parole and probation, alcohol and drug
education program, **Veh 23103.5**

Photography and pictures, sound recordings, **Veh 40008**

Point count, **Veh 12810**

Road rage, generally, post

Second or subsequent offenses, alcohol
involved, **Veh 23103.5**

TRAFFIC RULES AND REGULATIONS
—Cont'd

Reckless driving—Cont'd

Sentence and punishment, **Veh 23104,
23105, 40000.15**

Snowmobiles, **Veh 23128**

Traffic violator schools, continuance, attendance, exemptions, **Veh 41501**

Records and recordation,

Abstract of record,

Dismissal of charges, employee size
or weight law violations, **Veh
40003**

Offenses, forwarding to state, **Veh
1803.5**

Crimes and offenses, ante

Driving privilege, revocation or suspension, evidence, **Veh 40832**

Driving under the influence, ante

Electronic recording, **Veh 1806**

Evidence, revocation or suspension of
driving privilege, **Veh 40832**

Fees, violation records, defendants, assessment, **Veh 40508.6**

Handicapped persons, permanent disability, **Veh 22511.55, 22511.58**

Ignition interlock devices, driving under
the influence, **Veh 23575**

Inspection and inspectors, **Veh 1808**

Motor carriers, safety regulations, **Veh
34500 et seq.**

Prior convictions, **Veh 13209**

Revocation or suspension of driving
privilege, evidence, **Veh 40832**

Sale of information, **Veh 1810 et seq.**

Tour bus, driving record, reports, **Veh
1808.1**

Violations, **Veh 1802**

Recreational vehicles, appurtenances,
width of vehicle or load, **Veh 35103**

Recycling, covering loads, **Veh 23115**

Red flags. Flags, ante

Red lights, **Veh 21453, 21457, 25269**

Bicycles, equipment, **Veh 21201**

Definitions, **Veh 375**

Emergency vehicles, exemptions, **Veh
21055**

Fines and penalties, running red light,
Veh 42001.15

Public policy, **Veh 30**

School buses, **Veh 22112**

Reduction of weight limits, cities, **Veh
35701**

Reflectors, **Veh 24607**

Bicycles, **Veh 21201**

Front and side, **Veh 24608**

Motorized scooters, **Veh 21223**

Rear mounting, **Veh 24607**

Refunds,

Bail, **Veh 42201.6**

Trial by written declaration, **Veh
40902**

Fees and penalties, **Veh 42230 et seq.**

Refusal, permit, exceeding maximum size,
weight, **Veh 35782**

TRAFFIC RULES AND REGULATIONS
—Cont'd

Refuse. Garbage and refuse, generally,
ante

Registration,

Commercial vehicles,

Additional weight fees, partial year
registration, **Veh 9702, 9704,
9706**

Adjustments, **Veh 1678**

Weight fees, partial year registration,
Veh 9407, 9700

Infractions, notice to correct, **Veh
40303.5**

Trolley coaches, application of law, **Veh
21051**

Violations, proof of correction, dismissal, **Veh 40522**

Rejection of applications, return of fees,
Veh 42230

Release. Impounding, ante

Release on promise to appear. Arrest,
ante

Removal of vehicles,

Abandoned vehicles on private property
after accident, **Veh 22653**

Disabled vehicles, transportation department employees, **Veh 22654**

Disposition of vehicles, **Veh 22660**

Driving under the influence, second and
subsequent offenses, **Veh 14602.8**

Law enforcement, volunteers, **Veh
22651.05**

Obstructing traffic, **Veh 22654**

Parking, ante

Stolen vehicles on private property, **Veh
22653**

Trash, governmental agencies, **Veh
23113**

Repair of roadway, exemption from driving on right side, **Veh 21650**

Repetitive driving past traffic control
points, **Veh 21100**

Reports, **Veh 1803 et seq.**

Accidents, ante

Convictions, **Veh 1803 et seq.**

Crimes and offenses, prior convictions,
Veh 42004

Driving under the influence, ante

Electronic recording, **Veh 1806**

Evidence, ante

Failure to report violations, misfeasance, **Veh 1805**

Fines and penalties, prior convictions,
Veh 42004

Infractions, prior convictions, **Veh 42004**

Juvenile traffic offenders, **Veh 1816**

Motorsports, semitrailers, length, special
permits, **Veh 35401.5**

Negligence actions, admissibility of reports, findings of department, **Veh
40833**

Night court assessment, **Veh 42006**

Notations, **Veh 1818**

TRAFFIC

TRAFFIC RULES AND REGULATIONS
—Cont'd

Reports—Cont'd

Parking, Long Beach, left hand parking, two way roadways, pilot programs, **Veh 22502**

Police reports, evidence on guilty plea, **Veh 40806**

Second and subsequent offenses, department informational reports, **Veh 42004**

Stolen or embezzled vehicles, removal, **Veh 22651, 22653**

Violations, **Veh 1803 et seq.**

Res judicata, civil actions, effect of conviction, **Veh 40834**

Rescue, bicycles, peace officers, exemptions, **Veh 21200**

Residence districts. Business or residence districts, generally, ante

Resolutions, enactment of regulations, **Veh 32**

Reversal of conviction, abstract of record, **Veh 1803.3**

Riders, towing bicycles, sleds, carrying riders, **Veh 21712**

Ridesharing, parking, exclusive use spaces, **Veh 22507.1**

Riding on vehicle, restrictions, **Veh 21712**

Riding trails, unauthorized vehicles, crimes and offenses, **Veh 23127**

Right lane,
Bicycles, **Veh 21202**
Motorized scooters, rules of the road, **Veh 21228**
Pedestrians walking outside of business or residence district, **Veh 21956**
Three lane roadways, use, **Veh 21659**

Right of way, **Veh 21800 et seq.**
Abandoned vehicles, removal, **Veh 22650 et seq.**
Alleys, entering or crossing highway from, **Veh 21804**
Animals, horseback riders, **Veh 21805**
Approaching yield right of way sign, **Veh 21803**
Authorized emergency vehicles, **Veh 21806, 21807**
Bicycles, drivers handbook, **Veh 1656.3**
Blind persons, **Veh 21963 et seq.**
Bridle paths, horseback riders, **Veh 21805**
Crossings, horseback riders, **Veh 21805**
Crosswalks,
Jaywalkers, **Veh 21954**
Pedestrians, **Veh 21950**
Definitions, **Veh 525**
Drivers handbook, **Veh 1656.3**
Dumping on highway, **Veh 23112, 23113**
Electric personal assistive mobility devices, **Veh 21281.5**
Emergency vehicles, **Veh 21806, 21807**
Entrance, **Veh 21802, 21804**
Equestrian crossings, horseback riders, **Veh 21805**

TRAFFIC RULES AND REGULATIONS
—Cont'd

Right of way—Cont'd

Horseback riders, equestrian crossings, **Veh 21805**

Impounding vehicles, freeways, **Veh 22651**

Intersections, generally, ante

Left turn,
Alley or private road, **Veh 21804**
Intersections, **Veh 21800, 21801**
Marked crosswalks, pedestrians, **Veh 21950**

Narrow roadways, **Veh 21661**

Pedestrians, ante

Personal assistive mobility devices, **Veh 21281.5**

Prima facie speed limits, **Veh 22352**

Private roads or driveways, entering or crossing highway, **Veh 21804**

Removal of parked or standing vehicles, **Veh 22650 et seq.**

Sidewalks, pedestrians, **Veh 21952**

Speed limits, **Veh 22352**

Streetcars, yielding to emergency vehicles, **Veh 21806, 21807**

Terminating highways, intersection with continuing cross highways, **Veh 21800**

Through highways, entrance, yielding, **Veh 21451, 21802**
Uncontrolled intersections, left turn, **Veh 21800**

Turning on red, yielding, **Veh 21453**

Uncontrolled intersections, **Veh 21800**

Unmarked crosswalks, pedestrians, **Veh 21950**

Vehicle approaching uncontrolled intersections, **Veh 21800**

Visually handicapped persons, **Veh 21963 et seq.**

Yielding right of way, generally, post

Right side of roadway,
Approaching vehicles, passing, **Veh 21660**
Bicycle riders, **Veh 21202**
Divided highways, driving, **Veh 21651**
Driving and operation, **Veh 21650**
Mountain driving, warning, **Veh 21662**
Passing overtaken vehicle, **Veh 21754, 21755**
Slow moving vehicles, operation, **Veh 21654, 21655**
Three lane roadway, overtaking and passing, **Veh 21659**

Right turns, **Veh 22100 et seq.**
Bicycle riders, **Veh 21202**
Lanes marked for, **Veh 22100**
Movement of vehicle, safety, **Veh 22107**
One way roadways, **Veh 22100**
Red lights, **Veh 21453**
Slow moving vehicles, **Veh 21654**
Designated lanes, **Veh 21655**
Traffic Signs and Signals, this index

TRAFFIC RULES AND REGULATIONS
—Cont'd

Road or driving test, interference with driver or mechanism, exemption, **Veh 21701**

Road rage,
Drivers licenses, revocation or suspension, **Veh 13210, 13351.8**
Driving schools, courses of study, **Veh 11113**
Traffic violator schools, courses of study, **Veh 11219**
Sentence and punishment, **Veh 13210**

Roadside rest areas,
Motor vehicles, removal, **Veh 22651**
Violations, **Veh 22520.6**

Roadway design features, prohibiting entry, exit, local authorities, **Veh 21101**

Rocks, highway dumping, **Veh 23112, 23113**

Roller skating, **Veh 21113, 21969**
Towing skaters, **Veh 21712**

Routes, explosives, **Veh 31614**
Transportation, state fire marshall, **Veh 31614, 31616, 31617**

Rubbish. Garbage and refuse, generally, ante

Running red light, **Veh 21453**
Fines and penalties, **Veh 42001.15**

Safety, **Veh 2900 et seq., 34500 et seq.**
Funds, **Veh 42200**
Nets, width of vehicles or load, **Veh 35100**
Participation, **Veh 2909, 2910**
Representative, appointment, **Veh 2901**
Zones, **Veh 21709**
Driving or operation, **Veh 21709**
Speed, passing trolley coach, **Veh 21756**
Stopping, standing or parking vehicles, **Veh 22500**
Trolley coach, passing speed, **Veh 21756**

Safety enhancement double fine zones, **Veh 42010**

Sales,
Driving under the influence, ante
Hazardous substances and waste, illegal dumping, nuisance, **Veh 23112.7**
Roadside rest areas, vista points, **Veh 22520.5**

Samples, driving under the influence, chemical tests, **Veh 23614**

San Diego County, garbage trucks, weight limits, **Veh 35701**

San Francisco City and County, parking, buses, videotape, transit only traffic lanes, **Veh 40240 et seq.**

San Luis Obispo, length, combinations of vehicles, exemptions, **Veh 35401**

Santa Barbara County, length, combinations of vehicles, exemptions, **Veh 35401**

Schedules, speed, unlawful, **Veh 34501.3**

School buildings and grounds,
Crosswalks, guards, **Veh 40000.7, 42200**

TRAFFIC RULES AND REGULATIONS
—Cont'd
School buildings and grounds—Cont'd
Local authority closing streets, **Veh 21102, 21103**
Prima facie speed limits, **Veh 22352**
Speed, post
Stopping vehicles or animals, local regulation, **Veh 21113**
School buses, **Veh 22500.5**
Approaching vehicles, stopping, **Veh 22454, 22454.5**
Bus stops, approval of highway patrol, **Veh 22504**
Cellular radio telephones, **Veh 23125**
Crimes and offenses, cellular radio telephones, **Veh 23125**
Distances between vehicles, **Veh 21704**
Drivers licenses, suspension, third or subsequent offense, **Veh 22454.5**
Intersections, passing, **Veh 22454, 22454.5**
Lanes designated, **Veh 21655**
Length, crossing control arms, **Veh 35400**
Loading or unloading, transit bus stops, **Veh 22500.5**
Overtaking and passing, ante
Public or private driveways, stopping, **Veh 22500**
Railroad crossings, stopping, **Veh 22452, 22452.5**
Crossing guards, **Veh 21100**
Passengers, imputed negligence, **Veh 22453**
Second and subsequent offenses, approaching vehicles, stopping, **Veh 22454.5**
Slow moving vehicles, designated lanes, **Veh 21655**
Speed limits, **Veh 22406, 22407**
Stopping,
Railroad crossings, **Veh 22452**
Passengers, imputed negligence, **Veh 22453**
Special stops, **Veh 22454, 22454.5**
State highways, ordinances, approval, **Veh 22501**
Third and subsequent offenses, stopping, approaching vehicles, **Veh 22454.5**
Unincorporated areas, bus stops, **Veh 22504**
Youth buses, **Veh 27906.5**
School for traffic violators. Traffic Violator Schools, generally, this index
Schools and school districts, **Veh 21113**
Bus stops, approval of highway patrol, **Veh 22504**
Crossing guards,
County contracts, **Veh 42201**
Disobedience, **Veh 40000.7**
Fines and penalties, **Veh 42001.1**
Distribution, **Veh 1656**

TRAFFIC RULES AND REGULATIONS
—Cont'd
Schools and school districts—Cont'd
Driver education,
Interference with driver or mechanism, exemption, **Veh 21701**
Local authorities closing streets, **Veh 21101**
Motor vehicle violators, administration fees, **Veh 42007, 42007.1**
Traffic safety fund, compensation of school crossing, **Veh 42200**
Scooters, driving under the influence, **Veh 40303**
Searches and seizures,
Driving under the influence, second and subsequent offenses, **Veh 14602.8**
Impounding, generally, ante
Removal of parked or standing vehicles, **Veh 22650 et seq.**
Safety belts, mandatory use, **Veh 27315**
Seasonal limitations, permits to exceed maximum size, weight, **Veh 35782**
Seatbelts. Motor Vehicles, this index
Second and subsequent offenses,
Animals, transporting, infractions, **Veh 42001.4**
Driving under the influence, ante
Exhaust systems, noise pollution, decals, **Veh 27202.1**
Explosives, transportation, **Veh 31618**
Hazardous substances and waste, transportation, **Veh 32002**
Infractions, fines and penalties, **Veh 42001**
Inspection and inspectors, failure to stop and submit, **Veh 42002.1**
Leakage or spilling of loads on highways, **Veh 40000.16**
Noise pollution, exhaust systems, decals, **Veh 27202.1**
Passengers, trunk, **Veh 21712**
Removal of vehicles, **Veh 22651.2**
Reports, **Veh 24004**
Speed contest on highways, **Veh 23109.5**
Trunk, passengers, **Veh 21712**
Weight limitations, violations, **Veh 42030**
Security deposit following accident, evidence in civil actions, **Veh 40833**
Selective devices, gates, restricting access, **Veh 21101.6**
Semitrailers,
Combination, length, exemptions, **Veh 35401.5**
Length, **Veh 35414**
Senior care centers, prima facie speed limits, **Veh 22352**
Sentence and punishment,
Drag racing, **Veh 23109.1**
Driving under the influence, ante
Inspection and inspectors, failure to stop, **Veh 42002.1**
Reckless driving, **Veh 23105**
Serious traffic violations, motor carriers, speed, **Veh 22406.1**

TRAFFIC RULES AND REGULATIONS
—Cont'd
Service roads, entering or leaving highway, **Veh 21652**
Sheriffs,
Direction in emergency situation, **Veh 21707**
Following emergency vehicles, **Veh 21706**
Shifting gears, carriers stopping at railroad crossings, **Veh 22452**
Shipping instructions, explosives, **Veh 31612**
Shoulders, motorcycles, prohibition of operation, **Veh 21714**
Shovels, motor carried equipment, length of booms or masts, **Veh 35407**
Sidewalks,
Access ramp, handicapped persons, parking restrictions, **Veh 22522**
Bicycles, local regulations, **Veh 21100**
Driving on sidewalk, **Veh 21663**
Electric carts, local regulation, **Veh 21114.5**
Motorized scooters, **Veh 21235**
Parking, **Veh 22500**
Access ramp, handicapped persons, **Veh 22522**
Pedestrians, right of way, driving over sidewalk, **Veh 21952**
Roller skating, local regulation, **Veh 21969**
Toll roads and bridges, vehicular crossings, **Veh 23331**
Signs and signals. Traffic Signs and Signals, generally, this index
Single lanes,
Driving or operation, **Veh 21658**
Roadway divided into two or more lanes, **Veh 21658**
Single permit for excessive size or weight, **Veh 35791**
Sirens, **Veh 27000 et seq.**
Emergency vehicles, exemption from traffic laws, **Veh 21055**
Escorts, police and traffic officers, **Veh 21057**
Peace officers, willful flight, **Veh 2800.1**
Public policy, **Veh 30**
Right of way of emergency vehicles, **Veh 21806, 21807**
Standards and specifications, adoption and enforcement, **Veh 26103**
Size, **Veh 35000 et seq.**
Arrest, refusal to stop for inspection, **Veh 40303**
Counties over 4,000,000, islands, **Veh 21100.5, 35404**
Crimes and offenses, **Veh 35784, 40001**
Damage to highways or bridges, torts, **Veh 17302**
Emergency vehicles, exemption, **Veh 35002**
Employees, violations,
Arrest, employers failure to answer charges, **Veh 40005**

TRAFFIC

TRAFFIC RULES AND REGULATIONS
—Cont'd
Size—Cont'd
Employees, violations—Cont'd
Codefendants, owners, **Veh 40003**
Escort vehicles, pilot cars, **Veh 472, 27904**
Excessive size, single permit, **Veh 35791**
Explosives, transportation, **Veh 31615**
Fees, licenses and permits, variances, **Veh 35795**
Fines and penalties, special permits, **Veh 35784, 35784.5**
Height, **Veh 35250 et seq.**
Inspection and inspectors, **Veh 2813**
Arrest, procedure, **Veh 40303**
Length, **Veh 35400 et seq.**
Licenses and permits, **Veh 35780 et seq.**
Metric equivalent, **Veh 35100.1**
Operation without compliance, **Veh 40001**
Pilot cars, **Veh 472, 27904**
Rules and regulations, **Veh 32**
Single permit, excessive size, **Veh 35791**
Special permits, variances, **Veh 35780 et seq.**
Weights, **Veh 35550 et seq.**
Width of vehicle or load, **Veh 35100 et seq.**
Skateboards, **Veh 21113, 21967, 21968**
Skiing, **Veh 21959**
Towing skiers, **Veh 21712**
Sleds, towing sleds carrying riders, **Veh 21712**
Slow moving vehicles,
Agricultural machinery and equipment, emblem, display, **Veh 36508**
Blocking traffic, minimum speed limit, **Veh 22400**
Congested roads, diversion of vehicles, **Veh 21101.2**
Definitions, turning out of highway, **Veh 21656**
Designated lanes, **Veh 21655**
Distances between vehicles, **Veh 21704**
Driving and operation, **Veh 21654 et seq.**
Emblem, **Veh 24615**
Agricultural machinery and equipment, **Veh 36508**
Exemption, use of right side of roadway, **Veh 21650**
Golf carts, **Veh 21115**
Grades, overtaking and passing, **Veh 21758**
Implements of husbandry, lighting, **Veh 25251.1**
Lanes designated, **Veh 21655, 21658**
Log hauling over bridge or causeway, **Veh 35785**
Maximum speed limits, **Veh 22406 et seq.**
Metal tires, maximum speed limits, **Veh 22410**
Minimum speed limit, **Veh 22400**

TRAFFIC RULES AND REGULATIONS
—Cont'd
Slow moving vehicles—Cont'd
Obstructing traffic, minimum speed limit, **Veh 22400**
Operation, **Veh 21654 et seq.**
Overtaking and passing, ante
Right side of roadway,
Exemption, **Veh 21650**
Operation, **Veh 21654**
Solid tires, gross weights, speed limits, **Veh 22409**
Tires, speed limits, metal cars in contact with highway, **Veh 22410**
Turning, post
Snow. Ice and snow, generally, ante
Snowmobiles, unlawful operation, **Veh 23128**
Sobriety checkpoints, **Veh 2814.2**
Soliciting rides, hitchhiking, **Veh 21957**
Solid tire vehicles, gross weight,
Limits, **Veh 35600**
Speed, **Veh 22409**
Solid waste. Garbage and refuse, generally, ante
Sound recordings, reckless driving, following too closely, interference, **Veh 40008**
South coast air quality management district, speed limits, **Veh 22365**
Spanish language, **Veh 1656**
Special downward speed zoning, **Veh 22358.5**
Special events, temporary closing of streets, local regulations, **Veh 21101**
Special mobile equipment, width restrictions, exemption, **Veh 35104**
Special penalty assessments, night court assessments, **Veh 42006**
Special permits, weight limits, variances, **Veh 35780 et seq.**
Terminal Island freeway, **Veh 35700.5**
Special regulations, vehicular crossings, toll roads and bridges, **Veh 23330 et seq.**
Special stops required, **Veh 22450 et seq.**
Specifications, local authorities, uniform standards, **Veh 21100.1**
Speed, **Veh 22348 et seq., 22406 et seq.**
Agricultural machinery and equipment, **Veh 22406 et seq., 36400**
Air pollution, south coast air quality management district, **Veh 22365**
Alleys, **Veh 22352**
Arrest,
Contest or exhibition on highway, **Veh 22651.6, 40303**
Notice to appear, **Veh 40503**
Official uniform and vehicle, **Veh 40804**
Basic Speed Law, **Veh 22350, 22362**
Blocking traffic, minimum speed limit, **Veh 22400**
Boundary line streets and highways, **Veh 22359**
Bridges, **Veh 22402 et seq.**

TRAFFIC RULES AND REGULATIONS
—Cont'd
Speed—Cont'd
Burden of proof, speed traps, **Veh 40803**
Buses, drawing another vehicle, **Veh 22406, 22407**
Business or residence districts,
Local highways linking districts, **Veh 22360**
Narrow streets, **Veh 22358.3**
Prima facie speed limits, **Veh 22352**
Caldecott tunnel, reduced speed limit, **Veh 31301**
Change, prima facie limits, **Veh 22352**
Clocks, local authority, **Veh 22358.3**
Combinations of vehicles, length, exemptions, **Veh 35401**
Commercial vehicles, serious traffic violations, **Veh 22406.1**
Complaint, speeding charge, **Veh 40503**
Construction work, **Veh 22362**
Contests. Drag racing, generally, ante
Contractor or employees working on roadway, **Veh 22362**
Conviction of violation,
Evidence, **Veh 40831**
Speed traps, jurisdiction, **Veh 40805**
Crimes and offenses, **Veh 22351, 22405, 40000.15**
Bridges, tubes, **Veh 22405**
Drag racing, generally, ante
Speed traps, burden of proof, **Veh 40803**
Tank vehicles, flammable liquids, **Veh 22406.5**
Decrease,
Grades and grading, streets, **Veh 22413**
State highways, **Veh 22354, 22354.5**
Downward speed zoning, **Veh 22358.5**
Drivers licenses, revocation or suspension, **Veh 13200, 13200.5**
Driving under the influence, enhanced sentence, **Veh 23582**
Electric personal assistive mobility devices, **Veh 21281.5**
Elevated structures, **Veh 22402 et seq.**
Engineering and traffic surveys, **Veh 22354 et seq.**
Escort officers, **Veh 21057**
Evidence, ante
Excess speed, **Veh 22351**
Exhibitions on highway, arrest, procedure, **Veh 40303**
Existing conditions, regard for existing conditions, **Veh 22350**
Explosives, transports, **Veh 21655, 22406, 22407**
Farm labor buses or trucks, **Veh 22406, 22407**
Fines and penalties, **Veh 42000, 42000.5**
Second and subsequent offenses, **Veh 22348**
Tank vehicles, flammable liquids, **Veh 22406.5**
Following too closely, **Veh 21703**

TRAFFIC RULES AND REGULATIONS
—Cont'd
Speed—Cont'd
Following too closely—Cont'd
Photography and pictures, sound recordings, **Veh 40008**
Freeways, **Veh 22355, 22356**
Golf carts, **Veh 21115**
Grades and grading,
Decrease, streets, **Veh 22413**
Descending, **Veh 22407**
Gross weight, solid tire vehicles, **Veh 22409**
Hearings,
Maximum speed on bridges, **Veh 22404**
State highways, increase or decrease, **Veh 22354.5**
Horseback riding, Norco, **Veh 22353**
Ice or snow, **Veh 22363**
Impounding vehicles, **Veh 22651.6**
Indictment or information, contents, **Veh 40503**
Infractions, **Veh 22406.1**
Intersections, prima facie limits, **Veh 22352**
Jamming devices, **Veh 28150, 40000.15**
Jurisdiction of offense, speed traps, **Veh 40805**
Juvenile delinquents and dependents, **Veh 13355**
Lanes,
Multiple lane highways, **Veh 22361**
State highways, **Veh 22364**
Laser jamming devices, **Veh 28150, 40000.15**
Lawful speed, **Veh 22351, 22352**
Local authorities,
Prima facie limits, **Veh 22352**
Speed limit, **Veh 22358.3**
Local limits, adjustment, **Veh 22357 et seq.**
Log book, motor carriers, presumption, **Veh 34501.3**
Logging vehicles, **Veh 26457**
Bridges or causeways, **Veh 35785**
Low speed vehicles. Motor Vehicles, this index
Manufactured housing, private roads, **Veh 21107.9**
Maximum limit, **Veh 22349**
Metal tire in contact with highway, **Veh 22410**
Minimum speed limit, **Veh 22400**
Mobilehomes and mobilehome parks, private roads, **Veh 21107.9**
Moderate density residential districts, **Veh 22352**
Motorized scooters, **Veh 21228, 21235, 22411**
Multiple lane highways, **Veh 22361**
Narrow streets, **Veh 22358.3**
Norco, horseback riding, **Veh 22353**
Notice,
Appear, arrest, **Veh 40503**

TRAFFIC RULES AND REGULATIONS
—Cont'd
Speed—Cont'd
Notice—Cont'd
Increase, maximum speed limit, **Veh 22366**
Obstructing traffic, minimum limits, **Veh 22400**
Off highway vehicles, **Veh 38305, 38310**
Exemption of emergency vehicles, **Veh 21055**
Official uniform and vehicle, arresting officer, **Veh 40804**
Ordinances,
Business or residence districts, narrow streets, **Veh 22358.3**
Prima facie speed limits, **Veh 22357 et seq.**
Overtaking and passing, generally, ante
Parking, private off street facility, enforcement, **Veh 21107.8**
Personal assistive mobility devices, **Veh 21281.5**
Point system, drivers license, **Veh 12810**
Prima facie speed limits, **Veh 22352**
Air pollution, south coast air quality management district, **Veh 22365**
Bridges, **Veh 22405**
Business or residence districts, narrow streets, **Veh 22358.3**
Linking districts, **Veh 22360**
Complaint, **Veh 40503**
Evidence, negligence actions, **Veh 40831**
Excess speed, **Veh 22351**
Ice or snow, **Veh 22363**
Indictment or information, **Veh 40503**
Local authorities, adjustment of limits, **Veh 22357 et seq.**
Local limits, adjustment, **Veh 22357 et seq.**
Multiple lane highways, **Veh 22361**
Narrow streets, business or residence districts, **Veh 22358.3**
Negligence, evidence of violation, **Veh 40831**
Notice to appear, **Veh 40503**
Presumption, **Veh 41100**
Public parks, narrow streets, **Veh 22358.3**
Reduction, designated lanes, **Veh 21655**
Snow conditions, **Veh 22363**
State highways, decrease, **Veh 22354**
Streets,
Adjustment by local authorities, **Veh 22357 et seq.**
Grade exceeding ten per cent, **Veh 22413**
Surveys, public works department, **Veh 22354 et seq.**
Prudent regard for weather, visibility, **Veh 22350**
Racing. Drag racing, generally, ante

TRAFFIC RULES AND REGULATIONS
—Cont'd
Speed—Cont'd
Radar,
Jamming devices, **Veh 28150, 40000.15**
Speed traps, burden of proof, **Veh 40803**
Railway crossings, **Veh 22352**
Reasonable and prudent, **Veh 22350**
Reduced limit, Caldecott tunnel, **Veh 31301**
Safety, regard for existing conditions, **Veh 22350**
Schedules, hours of services, logbooks, **Veh 34501.3**
School buildings and grounds, **Veh 22352**
Decrease of local limits, **Veh 22358.4**
Increase of local limits, **Veh 22357**
School buses, **Veh 22406, 22407**
Second and subsequent violations, **Veh 13355, 22348**
Senior citizen centers or facilities, prima facie limits, **Veh 22352**
Serious traffic violations, **Veh 22406.1**
Slow moving vehicles, generally, ante
Snow or ice, **Veh 22363**
Solid tire vehicles, **Veh 22409**
South coast air quality management district, **Veh 22365**
Special downward speed zoning, **Veh 22358.5**
Speed traps, evidence, **Veh 40801 et seq.**
State highways,
Bridges and structures, maximum limits, **Veh 22402 et seq.**
Decrease in speed limits, **Veh 22354**
Hearings, increase or decrease, **Veh 22354.5**
Lane limits, **Veh 22364**
Variable limits, **Veh 22355**
Street railways, crossings, **Veh 22352**
Streets,
Adjustment by local authorities, **Veh 22357 et seq.**
Decreasing limits on grades, **Veh 22413**
Surface of highway, existing conditions, **Veh 22350**
Surveys, engineering and traffic studies, **Veh 22354 et seq.**
Tank vehicles, flammable liquids, **Veh 22406.5**
Tires,
Metal tire in contact with highway, **Veh 22410**
Solid tire vehicles, gross weight, **Veh 22409**
Towing vehicles, **Veh 22406, 22407**
Traffic officers, **Veh 21057**
Traps, speed traps, **Veh 40801 et seq.**
Trolley coach overtaken at safety zone, passing, **Veh 21756**
Truck tractors, **Veh 22406, 22407**

TRAFFIC

TRAFFIC RULES AND REGULATIONS
—Cont'd
Speed—Cont'd
Tubes, maximum limits, **Veh 22402 et seq.**
Tunnels, maximum limits, **Veh 22402 et seq.**
Turning out of highway, **Veh 21656**
Two lane, undivided highway, **Veh 22349**
Variable speed limits, state highways, **Veh 22355**
Visibility, regard for existing conditions, **Veh 22350**
Weather, regard for conditions, **Veh 22350**
Weight of vehicle, solid tires, gross weight, **Veh 22409**
Width of highway, regard for existing conditions, **Veh 22350**
Working on roadway, **Veh 22362**
Zoning, special downward speed zoning, **Veh 22358.5**
Speed traps, **Veh 40801 et seq.**
Spilling load or contents on highway, **Veh 23114**
Spur tracks, railroad crossings, stopping, **Veh 22452, 22453**
Standards, local authorities, uniform standards, **Veh 21100.1**
Standing vehicles, **Veh 22500 et seq.**
Abandonment, removal, **Veh 22650 et seq.**
Adjacent curbs on roadway, **Veh 22502**
Unincorporated areas, **Veh 22504**
Airports, municipal airports, **Veh 21113**
Blocking wheels on hills, **Veh 22509**
Brakes of unattended vehicles, setting, **Veh 22515**
Bridges, **Veh 22500**
State highways, local ordinances, **Veh 22501**
Commercial vehicles,
Loading or unloading, **Veh 22502**
Local authorities, powers, **Veh 22507.5**
Crossings, toll roads and bridges, **Veh 23333**
Crosswalks, **Veh 22500**
Designated areas, prohibited, **Veh 22505**
Disabled persons, exemption, **Veh 22511.5**
Disabled vehicles, **Veh 22504**
Doors, opening on moving traffic, **Veh 22517**
Double parking, **Veh 22500**
Emergency vehicles, overtaking and passing, **Veh 21809**
Excavations, **Veh 22500**
Exemptions, public utilities, **Veh 22512**
Explosives, **Veh 31614**
Transports, **Veh 31616**
Fire hydrants, **Veh 22514**
Fire lanes, **Veh 22500.1**
Fire station entrance, **Veh 22500**
Freeways, **Veh 21718**

TRAFFIC RULES AND REGULATIONS
—Cont'd
Standing vehicles—Cont'd
Grades, unattended vehicles, blocking wheels, **Veh 22509**
Impounding, **Veh 22651**
Intersections, **Veh 22500**
Lighted parking lamps, **Veh 24800 et seq.**
Lights, dimming headlamps, **Veh 24401**
Local authorities, **Veh 22506 et seq.**
Local regulation, **Veh 21113**
Locked vehicles, duties, **Veh 22516**
Motors of unattended vehicles, stopping, **Veh 22515**
Obstructing traffic, **Veh 22500**
Off highway vehicles subject to identification, **Veh 38020**
Offstreet parking, ordinances or resolutions, **Veh 22519**
Opening doors on moving traffic, **Veh 22517**
Ordinances or resolutions, offstreet parking, **Veh 22519**
Parking, generally, ante
Private driveways, **Veh 22500**
Public utilities, exemption, **Veh 22512**
Removal, **Veh 22650 et seq., 22654**
Safety zones, **Veh 22500**
Sidewalks, **Veh 22500**
Snow areas, **Veh 22510**
State highways, local ordinances, **Veh 22501**
Stopping motor and setting brakes, **Veh 22515**
Sweeping streets, designated hours, prohibition or restriction of standing vehicles, **Veh 22507.6**
Tow trucks, overtaking and passing, **Veh 21809**
Transportation department, overtaking and passing, **Veh 21809**
Unincorporated areas, **Veh 22504**
Utility vehicles, exemption, **Veh 22512**
Vehicular crossings, toll roads and bridges, **Veh 23333**
Stands, taxicabs and public carriers, regulation, **Veh 21112**
Starting,
Off highway vehicles, **Veh 38312**
Safety, **Veh 22106**
State, applicability of traffic laws to state vehicles, **Veh 21052**
State buildings, stopping, paths, driveways or grounds, **Veh 21113**
State highways,
Bridges, stopping, standing or parking vehicles, **Veh 22500, 22501**
Decrease, speed limits, **Veh 22354**
Disabled vehicles, parking or stopping, **Veh 22505**
Lane speed limits, **Veh 22364**
Parking, ante
Prima facie speed limits, decrease, **Veh 22354**
Skiing or tobogganing across, **Veh 21959**

TRAFFIC RULES AND REGULATIONS
—Cont'd
State highways—Cont'd
Speed, generally, ante
Stopping,
Bridges, **Veh 22500**
Disabled vehicles, **Veh 22505**
Local ordinances, **Veh 22501**
Weight limits, changes, **Veh 35650 et seq.**
State institutions, animal or vehicle, stopping, standing, driveways, paths or grounds, **Veh 21113**
State police, removal of abandoned vehicles from private property after accident, **Veh 22653**
Statements,
Driving under the influence, advisory statements, **Veh 23593**
Evidence, **Veh 40903**
Statute of limitations. Limitation of actions, generally, ante
Stolen vehicles, removal of parked or standing vehicles, **Veh 22650 et seq.**
Stop intersections, local regulations, **Veh 21101**
Stopped traffic, diverting vehicles, **Veh 21101.2**
Stopping, **Veh 21110, 22500 et seq.**
Abandoned vehicles, removal, **Veh 22650 et seq.**
Adjacent curbs on roadway, **Veh 22502**
Unincorporated areas, **Veh 22504**
Agricultural machinery and equipment, **Veh 36510**
Airports, municipal airports, **Veh 21113**
Animals, passing, **Veh 21759**
Antigridlock Act, **Veh 22526**
Approaching vehicles,
Crosswalks, **Veh 21951**
Fines and penalties, **Veh 42001.17**
Entrance of highway or intersection, **Veh 21802, 22450 et seq.**
Backing vehicle, highway, safety, **Veh 22106**
Blocking wheels, grades, **Veh 22509**
Brakes, stopping requirement, **Veh 26454 et seq.**
Bridges, **Veh 22500 et seq.**
State highways, local regulation, **Veh 22501**
Buses, ante
Business districts, commercial vehicles, **Veh 22502**
Checkpoints,
Air pollution, emissions, **Veh 2814.1**
Sobriety checkpoints, **Veh 2814.2**
Combined vehicle inspection and sobriety checkpoint, **Veh 2814.2**
Commercial vehicles, loading or unloading, **Veh 22502**
Crossings, vehicular crossings, toll roads and bridges, **Veh 23333**
Crosswalks, **Veh 22450, 22500**
Vehicles stopped for pedestrians, **Veh 21951**

TRAFFIC RULES AND REGULATIONS
  —Cont'd
Stopping—Cont'd
  Crosswalks—Cont'd
    Vehicles stopped for pedestrians
      —Cont'd
      Fines and penalties, **Veh 42001.17**
  Definitions, motor vehicles, **Veh 587**
  Disabled persons, exemption, **Veh
    22511.5**
  Disabled vehicles,
    State highways, **Veh 22505**
    Unincorporated areas, **Veh 22504**
  Distance requirements,
    Airbrakes, emergency stopping sys-
      tem, **Veh 26508**
    Brakes, **Veh 26454 et seq.**
    Exemptions, **Veh 26457**
  Doors, opening on moving traffic, **Veh
    22517**
  Double parking, **Veh 22500**
  Emergencies, yielding right of way, **Veh
    21806, 21807**
  Entrance of through highway, **Veh
    21802**
  Excavations, **Veh 22500**
  Exemptions, public utilities, **Veh 22512**
  Explosives,
    Transportation, **Veh 31611**
    Transports, **Veh 31616**
  Fire hydrants, **Veh 22514**
  Fire lanes, **Veh 22500.1**
  Fire stations, **Veh 22500**
  Freeways, **Veh 21718**
    Tow trucks, **Veh 22513**
  Gate crossings, railroad, **Veh 22451 et
    seq.**
  Grades, blocking wheels, **Veh 22509**
  Horse drawn vehicles, overtaking and
    passing, **Veh 21759**
  Impounding vehicles, **Veh 22651**
    Speed contests, **Veh 22651.6**
  Imputed negligence, passenger for hire,
    failure of driver to stop at railroad
    crossing, **Veh 22453**
  Inspection and inspectors, emissions,
    Veh 2814.2
  Intersections, **Veh 22450 et seq., 22500**
    Right of way,
      All directions controlled by stop
        sign, **Veh 21800**
      Stop signs controlling all directions,
        Veh 21800
      Terminating highway intersecting
        continuing cross highway, yield-
        ing right of way, **Veh 21800**
      Vehicle stopped for pedestrians in
        crosswalk, **Veh 21951**
        Fines and penalties, **Veh 42001.17**
  Lighted parking lamps, **Veh 24800 et
    seq.**
  Local regulation, **Veh 21113**
  Logging vehicles, distance requirements,
    Veh 26457
  Look and listen, grade crossings, **Veh
    22452**

TRAFFIC RULES AND REGULATIONS
  —Cont'd
Stopping—Cont'd
  Motor carriers, railroad crossings, **Veh
    22452, 22453**
  Negligence, passenger for hire, failure
    of driver to stop at railroad cross-
    ing, **Veh 22453**
  Obstructing traffic, **Veh 22500**
  Off highway vehicles subject to identifi-
    cation, **Veh 38020**
  Offstreet parking, ordinances, **Veh
    22519**
  Opening doors on moving traffic, **Veh
    22517**
  Ordinances,
    Offstreet parking, **Veh 22519**
    State highways, bridges, **Veh 22501**
  Passengers for hire, failure of driver to
    stop at railroad crossing, imputed
    negligence, **Veh 22453**
  Pedestrians, ante
  Points, violation points, Antigridlock
    Act violations, **Veh 12810.4**
  Private driveways, **Veh 22500**
  Public utility vehicles,
    Exemption, **Veh 22512**
    Warning devices, **Veh 25301**
  Railroad crossings, ante
  Red lights, generally, ante
  Removal of vehicles, **Veh 22650 et seq.**
  Safety zones, **Veh 22500**
  School buses, ante
  Seat belts, mandatory use, **Veh 27315**
  Sidewalks, **Veh 22500**
  Snow areas, **Veh 22510**
  Sobriety checkpoints, **Veh 2814.2**
  Special stops, **Veh 22450 et seq.**
  Starting vehicle on highway, safety, **Veh
    22106**
  State highways, ante
  Taxicabs, crosswalks, **Veh 22500**
  Through highway entrance, **Veh 21802**
  Tow trucks, **Veh 22513**
  Traffic movement impeded or blocked,
    Veh 22400
  Train signals, **Veh 22451 et seq.**
  Transit grade crossings, **Veh 22451**
  Tubes or tunnels, **Veh 22500**
  Unattended vehicles, stopping motor
    and setting brakes, **Veh 22515**
  Unincorporated areas, **Veh 22504**
  Utility vehicles, exemption, **Veh 22512**
  Vehicles stopped for pedestrians in
    crosswalk, **Veh 21951**
    Fines and penalties, **Veh 42001.17**
  Vehicular crossings, toll roads and
    bridges, **Veh 23333**
  Yield right of way signs, **Veh 21803**
Stopping traffic, pedestrians, **Veh 21950**
Storage,
  Driving under the influence, second and
    subsequent offenses, **Veh 14602.8**
  Fees,
    Improper removal of parked vehicle,
      Veh 22658

TRAFFIC RULES AND REGULATIONS
  —Cont'd
Storage—Cont'd
  Fees—Cont'd
    Notice, **Veh 22651**
    Hearings, **Veh 22852**
      Driving under the influence, second
        and subsequent offenses, **Veh
        14602.8**
      Intoxicating liquors, opened container,
        Veh 23225
    Notice, fees, **Veh 22651**
    Opened container, intoxicating liquors,
      Veh 23225
    Parked or standing vehicles, obstructing
      traffic, **Veh 22654**
    Release, proof of current registration,
      Veh 22850.3
    Taxicabs, **Veh 21100.4**
Street railways,
  Application of laws, **Veh 21051**
  Emergency vehicles, yielding right of
    way, **Veh 21806, 21807**
  Failure to obey signals, **Veh 21462**
  Overtaking and passing,
    Left side, **Veh 21756**
    Passengers alighting or boarding, **Veh
      21756**
  Prima facie speed limit at crossings, **Veh
    22352**
  Right of way, yielding to emergency ve-
    hicles, **Veh 21806, 21807**
  Safety zones, driving or operation, **Veh
    21709**
  Speed, prima facie limit at crossings,
    Veh 22352
Street use restrictions, local agencies, **Veh
  9400.7, 9400.8**
Streetsweepers,
  Exemptions, **Veh 21060**
  Parking, photography and pictures, en-
    forcement, **Veh 40245 et seq.**
Structural materials, load length limita-
  tion, **Veh 35414**
Structures, weight limits, **Veh 35750 et seq.**
Studies, driving under the influence, igni-
  tion interlock devices, **Veh 23575.1**
Subpoenas, infractions, **Veh 40901**
Substandard width lane, motorized scoot-
  ers, rules of the road, **Veh 21228**
Subways, local authorities, powers, **Veh
  21109**
Suits. Actions and proceedings, generally,
  ante
Summary of laws, publication, **Veh 1656**
Supersedeas or stay, driving under the in-
  fluence,
  Alcohol education and treatment pro-
    grams, **Veh 23640**
  Sentence and punishment, **Veh 23600**
Supplemental traffic patrol services, high-
  way patrol, **Veh 2410.5**
Surface of highway, speed, regard for ex-
  isting conditions, **Veh 22350**
Surveys, speed, engineering and traffic
  studies, **Veh 22354 et seq.**

TRAFFIC

TRAFFIC RULES AND REGULATIONS
—Cont'd

Sweeping streets, vehicle parking or standing prohibitions or restrictions during designated hours, **Veh 22507.6**

Swerving, towed train of vehicles, **Veh 21711**

Swill. Garbage and refuse, generally, ante

Synopsis, publication, **Veh 1656**

Tailgating, **Veh 21703**
    Photography and pictures, sound recordings, crimes and offenses, **Veh 40008**

Tank containers, loads and loading, **Veh 31540**

Tank vehicles, grade crossing stopping, **Veh 22452**
    Passengers, imputed negligence, **Veh 22453**

Tap, traffic assistance programs, traffic violator schools, monitoring, **Veh 11205.2, 11205.4**

Taxicabs, **Veh 21100 et seq.**
    Crosswalks, stopping to load or unload passengers, **Veh 22500**
    Impounding, **Veh 21100.4**
    Intoxicating liquors, occupant drinking or possessing, **Veh 23229**
    Public or private driveways, stopping, **Veh 22500**
    Seat belts, **Veh 27315**
    Stands, local regulation, **Veh 21112**
    Stopping to load or unload passengers, **Veh 22500**

Telecommunications,
    Eight hundred (800) numbers, trucks transporting workmen, **Veh 2429**
    Wireless telecommunications, **Veh 23123**
        Children and minors, **Veh 23124**
        Point system, **Veh 12810.3**
        School buses, mass transit, **Veh 23125**

Television, vehicles taking pictures, length, **Veh 35409**

Temporarily appointed personnel, Enforcement, **Veh 21100**
    Failure to obey, **Veh 21100.3**

Temporary closing, streets, local regulation, **Veh 21101**

Terminal Island freeway, special permits, overweight vehicles, **Veh 35700.5**

Terminals, motor carriers, safety regulations, **Veh 34500 et seq.**

Terminating highway, intersection with continuing cross highway, right of way, **Veh 21800**

Testimony. Evidence, generally, ante

Tests,
    Driving under the influence, ante
    Dynamic stability, **Veh 35101**
    Motorsports, semitrailers, length, special permits, **Veh 35401.5**
    Traffic safety program, **Veh 2900 et seq.**

Text messages, infractions, **Veh 23123.5**

TRAFFIC RULES AND REGULATIONS
—Cont'd

Theft,
    Investigating officers, distinctive uniform and vehicle, exemption, **Veh 40800, 40804**
    Removal of parked or standing vehicles, **Veh 22650 et seq.**

Third class counties, commercial vehicles, weight limit, **Veh 35712**

Three lane roadway, **Veh 21659**
    Turns, **Veh 22100**

Three wheeled vehicles,
    Helmets, application of laws, **Veh 27803**
    Seat belts, application of laws, **Veh 27315.1**
        Children and minors, **Veh 27368**

Throwing lighted substances on highway, motorists, **Veh 23111**

Throwing or projecting substances at vehicles, **Veh 23110**
    Off highway vehicles, **Veh 38318**

Thumbprints, arrest, **Veh 40303**
    Nonresidents, **Veh 40305, 40305.5, 40500, 40504**

Timber and lumber,
    Field loaded unprocessed bulk forest products, weight restrictions, penalties, **Veh 42030**
    Loads and loading,
        Railroad crossings, **Veh 22452, 22453**
        Trucks transporting, flashing amber warning lights, **Veh 25275**
        Tandem axles, weight, **Veh 35552**

Time,
    Arrested person, appearance, **Veh 40501**
    Explosives, transportation, review, **Veh 31616.5**
    Hours of driving, **Veh 34506**
        Carriers, **Veh 21702**
    Limitations, permits to exceed maximum size, weight, **Veh 35782**
    Parking or standing vehicles, ordinances, **Veh 22507**
    Sweeping streets, parking or standing vehicle prohibitions or restrictions, **Veh 22507**

Tires,
    Limits, weight, **Veh 35600**
    Pneumatic tires, maximum width of vehicle or load, **Veh 35101**
    Speed,
        Metal car in contact with highway, **Veh 22410**
        Solid tires, gross weight, **Veh 22409**
    Waste tire haulers, registration, **Veh 31560**

Title to property,
    Passenger, **Veh 17158**
    Proof of ownership, parking violations, **Veh 40900**
    Removal of vehicles, **Veh 22650 et seq.**
    Responsibility, unlawful operation, **Veh 40001**

Tobogganing across roadways, **Veh 21959**

TRAFFIC RULES AND REGULATIONS
—Cont'd

Toll roads and bridges,
    Crossings, generally, ante
    Interchanges, **Veh 23250 et seq.**

Towing. Motor Vehicles, this index

Toy vehicles, towing toy vehicles carrying riders, **Veh 21712**

Tractors, farm tractors. Agricultural Machinery and Equipment, generally, this index

Traffic assistance programs, traffic violator schools, monitoring, **Veh 11205.2, 11205.4**

Traffic citations, forms, uniform misdemeanor and traffic citation, **Veh 40508**

Traffic control points, cruising, **Veh 21100**

Traffic officer enforcing code provisions, distinctive uniform and vehicle, **Veh 40800**

Traffic Signs and Signals, generally, this index

Traffic Violator Schools, generally, this index

Trailer buses, speed, **Veh 22406**

Trailers,
    Almond trailers, weight limitations, towing, **Veh 36627**
    Distances between vehicles, exemption, **Veh 21704**
    Length limitations, **Veh 35401**
        Exemptions, **Veh 35401.5**
    Mobilehomes and mobilehome parks, generally, ante

Trails, riding and hiking trails, unauthorized vehicle operation, **Veh 23127**

Train of vehicles,
    Accident, presumption of violation, **Veh 41104**
    Passenger vehicle combinations, **Veh 21715**
    Swerving, **Veh 21711**

Training, traffic safety program, **Veh 2900 et seq.**

Transit development boards, **Veh 21113**

Transit districts, **Veh 21113**

Transit grade crossings, stopping, **Veh 22451**

Transit systems, cellular radio telephones, **Veh 23125**

Transportation department, standing vehicles, overtaking and passing, **Veh 21809**

Traps, speed traps, illegal evidence, **Veh 40801 et seq.**

Trash. Garbage and refuse, generally, ante

Treatment programs. Driving under the influence, ante

Trespass, vehicular crossings, toll roads and bridges, **Veh 23332**

Trial,
    Failure to appear, bail forfeiture, **Veh 40512.5**
    Scheduling, **Veh 40519**

TRAFFIC RULES AND REGULATIONS
—Cont'd

Triple axle semitrailers, length, **Veh 35401.3**

Trolley coaches. Street railways, generally, ante

Truck tractors, speed limits, **Veh 22406, 22407**

Trunk, passengers, **Veh 21712**

Trusses, width of vehicle or load, stacks, **Veh 35780.5**

Tubes. Tunnels, generally, post

Tunnels,
Approaching vehicles, left side of roadway, **Veh 21752**
Caldecott tunnel, explosives and flammable substances, **Veh 31301**
Cargo tank vehicle regulation, **Veh 34020.5**
Local regulation, **Veh 21109**
Overtaking and passing, **Veh 21752**
Parking, **Veh 22500**
Pedestrians, failure to use, **Veh 21953**
Removal of parked or standing vehicles, **Veh 22650 et seq.**
Speed limits, **Veh 22402 et seq.**
Stopping, standing or parking vehicles, **Veh 22500**

Tuolumne County, weights, Old Priest Grade, **Veh 35715.1**

Turn signals,
Garbage trucks, **Veh 21059**
Motorcycles, **Veh 24951**

Turning, **Veh 22100 et seq.**
Business or residence district, **Veh 22102, 22103**
Divided highways, **Veh 21651**
Double lines, **Veh 21460**
Fire stations, **Veh 22104**
Intersections, **Veh 22100**
Lanes, turning from middle lane, **Veh 22100**
Left turns, generally, ante
Local authorities, powers, **Veh 22113**
Middle lane, **Veh 22100**
Motorized scooters, rules of the road, **Veh 21229**
Movement of vehicle, safety, **Veh 22107**
Off highway vehicles, **Veh 38314**
Emergency vehicles, exemptions, **Veh 21055**
Ordinance prohibiting certain movements, **Veh 22113**
Parallel lines, **Veh 21460**
Red lights, **Veh 21453**
Residence districts, **Veh 22103**
Right side of roadway, exemption from operation, **Veh 21650**
Right turns, generally, ante
Safety, **Veh 22107**
Slow moving vehicles, **Veh 21654**
Designated lanes, **Veh 21655**
Turning out of highway, **Veh 21656**
Terminating highway, middle lane, **Veh 22100**

TRAFFIC RULES AND REGULATIONS
—Cont'd

Turning—Cont'd
Three lane highway, middle lane, **Veh 22100**
Two way turning lanes, **Veh 21460.5**
U turns, generally, post
Yielding right of way, **Veh 21451**

Two lane highways,
Overtaking and passing, left side, **Veh 21751**
Slow moving vehicles, turning out of highway, **Veh 21656**
Speed limit, undivided highways, **Veh 22349**
Turning out, slow moving vehicles, **Veh 21656**

Two way turning lanes, offenses, **Veh 21460.5**

U turns,
Business district, **Veh 22102**
Definitions, **Veh 665.5**
Divided highways, **Veh 21651**
Business districts, **Veh 22102**
Double lines, **Veh 21460**
Fire stations, **Veh 22104**
Intersections,
Business districts, **Veh 22102**
Residence districts, **Veh 22103**
Traffic signals, **Veh 22100.5**
Parallel lines, pavement markings, **Veh 21460**
Residence districts, intersections, **Veh 22103**
Right of way, **Veh 21801**
Signals controlling intersection, **Veh 22100.5**
Traffic signs permitting, **Veh 21451**
Two way left turn lanes, **Veh 21460.5**
Visibility, **Veh 22105**

Unattended vehicles. Standing vehicles, generally, ante

Unclaimed property. Abandoned or unclaimed property, generally, ante

Undertakings,
Bail, generally, ante
Permit to exceed maximum size, weight, protecting highways and bridges, **Veh 35782**

Uniform misdemeanor and traffic citation, form, **Veh 40508**

Uniform traffic penalty schedule, **Veh 40310**

Uniforms,
Arresting speed violators, official uniform and vehicle, **Veh 40804**
Traffic officers enforcing code provisions, **Veh 40800**

Unimproved county highways, reduction of weight limits, **Veh 35706**

Unincorporated areas, parking, **Veh 22504**

United States,
Conviction for violation of code required by federal law, inadmissibility, **Veh 40830**

TRAFFIC RULES AND REGULATIONS
—Cont'd

United States—Cont'd
Violation of code required by federal law, defenses, **Veh 41401**

Unmarked crosswalks,
Jaywalkers, yielding right of way, **Veh 21954**
Overtaking and passing, vehicles stopped for pedestrians, **Veh 21951**
Fines and penalties, **Veh 42001.17**
Pedestrian right of way, **Veh 21950**

Use of particular highways by certain vehicles, local regulations, **Veh 21101**

Use restrictions,
Local agencies, **Veh 9400.7, 9400.8**
Streets or highways, local agencies, **Veh 9400.7, 9400.8**

Utility vehicles, stopping, **Veh 22502, 22512**

Van or tank containers, loads and loading, **Veh 31540**

Variances, weight limits, agreements and permits, **Veh 35780 et seq.**

Vehicular crossings. Crossings, generally, ante

Vending, ice cream trucks, **Veh 22456**

Veterans,
Disabled veterans, generally, ante
Parking, fines and penalties, **Veh 42001.13**

Viaducts,
Approaching vehicles, left side of roadway, **Veh 21752**
Local regulation, **Veh 21109**
Overtaking and passing, **Veh 21752**
Removal of parked or standing vehicles, **Veh 22650 et seq.**

View obstructed, overtaking and passing, restrictions, **Veh 21752**

Viewpoints, removal of vehicles, **Veh 22651**

Violator schools. Traffic Violator Schools, generally, this index

Visibility,
Limitations, restricted highway use, **Veh 2812.5**
Speed, regard for existing conditions, **Veh 22350**
U turns, **Veh 22105**

Vista points, violations, **Veh 22520.6**

Visually handicapped persons, right of way, **Veh 21963 et seq.**

Volunteers, law enforcement, removal of vehicles, **Veh 22651.05**

Waiver,
Complaint,
Filing of verified complaint, **Veh 40513**
Persons owning or controlling vehicles, **Veh 40002**
Filing of verified complaint, **Veh 40513**
Impounding vehicles, administrative cost, **Veh 22850.5**
Infractions, constitutional rights, **Veh 40901**

TRAFFIC

TRAFFIC RULES AND REGULATIONS
—Cont'd

Waiver—Cont'd

Limitation of actions, written pleas in lieu of personal appearance, **Veh 40519**

Pleading, written plea, waiver of right to trial within statutory period, **Veh 40519**

Wall panels, width of vehicle or load, stacks, **Veh 35780.5**

War and civil defense, police escort vehicles, sirens and speed, **Veh 21057**

Warning lights, private security agency vehicles, **Veh 25279**

Removal, **Veh 22651**

Warnings,

Horn warning, mountain highways, **Veh 21662**

Loads, removal or covering, **Veh 35783.5**

Warrants,

Arrest, ante

Automated warrant system, **Veh 40508.5**

Failure to correct violations, **Veh 40618**

Impounding vehicles, flight from peace officers and reckless driving, **Veh 14602.7**

Service, **Veh 2411**

Waste. Garbage and refuse, generally, ante

Water well drilling and servicing equipment, length, **Veh 35407**

Watering vehicles, exemptions, **Veh 21060**

Weather, speed, regard for existing conditions, **Veh 22350**

Weekend courts, special assessments, **Veh 42006**

Weekend service of sentence program, driving under the influence, **Veh 23536, 23580**

Weighmasters, records, criminal or civil proceedings, **Veh 35557**

Weights, **Veh 35000 et seq., 35550 et seq.**

Agreements,

Overweight loads, **Veh 35788**

Variances, **Veh 35780 et seq.**

Application for permit to increase, **Veh 35781**

Arrest,

Failure to submit vehicle, **Veh 40303**

Refusal to stop for inspection, **Veh 40303**

Axle weight, **Veh 35550 et seq., 35551.5**

Excess and gross weight and axle weight as one offense, **Veh 42031**

Front axle weight, **Veh 35550**

Loading facilities, request for weighing before vehicle leaves, **Veh 35558**

Brakes,

Equipment of vehicles over seven tons, **Veh 26301**

Stopping distance requirements, **Veh 26455**

Bridges, limits, **Veh 35750 et seq.**

TRAFFIC RULES AND REGULATIONS
—Cont'd

Weights—Cont'd

Carson City, overweight vehicles, special permits, **Veh 35700.5**

Certificates, load removal, **Veh 2803**

Christensen Belotti Act, **Veh 35552**

Commercial vehicles, ante

Containers, intermodal terminals, scales, **Veh 35580, 35581**

Contractors, exemption of licensed contractor, **Veh 35704**

Contracts,

Transporting, **Veh 35788**

Variances, **Veh 35780 et seq.**

Contributions, overloaded vehicles, use, **Veh 35788**

Cotton module movers, **Veh 35555**

County bridges, maximum weights, **Veh 35754**

County highways, limitations, **Veh 35700 et seq., 35706 et seq.**

Crimes and offenses, **Veh 40000.7, 40000.23, 40001 et seq., 42030 et seq.**

Bridges or structures, **Veh 35753**

Evidence, **Veh 35557**

State highways, violation of decreased restriction, **Veh 35655**

Violation of permit, **Veh 35784**

Damage to highways or bridges, tort liability, **Veh 17301, 17302**

Decreases, limits,

Bridges and other structures, **Veh 35750 et seq.**

State highway limit changes, **Veh 35651**

Emergency vehicles, exemption, **Veh 35002**

Employees, violations,

Arrest, employers failure to answer charges, **Veh 40005**

Codefendants, owners, **Veh 40003**

Dismissal of charges, abstract of record, **Veh 40003**

Employer failing to answer charges, **Veh 40005**

Enactment of regulations, **Veh 32**

Evidence, criminal or civil proceedings, **Veh 35557**

Exceeding maximum limits, special permits, **Veh 35780 et seq.**

Excess, **Veh 42031**

Fees, **Veh 9406.1**

Registration, **Veh 9554.2**

Exemptions, **Veh 35001, 35002, 35551.5**

Axle limits, **Veh 35553**

Commercial vehicles, **Veh 35714**

Explosives, transportation, **Veh 31615**

Speed limit, **Veh 22407**

Fees, **Veh 9400 et seq.**

Excess, **Veh 9406.1**

Exemptions, **Veh 9107, 9410**

Vehicles manufactured before designated time, **Veh 9401**

Insignia, display, **Veh 5206**

TRAFFIC RULES AND REGULATIONS
—Cont'd

Weights—Cont'd

Fees—Cont'd

Licenses and permits, variances, **Veh 35795**

Field loaded unprocessed bulk, agricultural and forest products or livestock, **Veh 42030**

Fines and penalties, **Veh 42030, 42031**

Bridges, causeways, viaducts, **Veh 35753**

Load greater than highway will bear, **Veh 35655**

Special permits,

Failure to obtain, **Veh 35784.5**

Violating terms and conditions, **Veh 35784**

Fleet vehicles, decals, **Veh 9400.1**

Front axle weight, **Veh 35550**

Hearings,

Bridges and other structures, decreasing limits, **Veh 35751**

Reduction of limits, **Veh 35705**

State highway limit changes, **Veh 35652, 35653**

Highway operation of vehicles, application of law, **Veh 35000**

Improved county highways, reduction of limits, **Veh 35707**

Increases, state highway limit changes, **Veh 35650**

Infractions, **Veh 4000.6**

Inspection and inspectors, **Veh 2809**

Arrest, procedure, **Veh 40303**

Weighmaster records, **Veh 35557**

Intermodal containers, terminals, scales, **Veh 35580, 35581**

Investigations and investigators, decreases for bridges or other structures, **Veh 35751**

License contractor, exemption, **Veh 35704, 35716**

Licenses and permits, **Veh 35780 et seq.**

Overweight vehicles, Terminal Island freeway, **Veh 35700.5**

Local authorities, powers, **Veh 35700 et seq.**

Log hauling, **Veh 35552**

Axle limitations, exemption, **Veh 35785**

Long Beach, special permits, overweight vehicles, **Veh 35700.5**

Los Angeles, overweight vehicles, special permits, **Veh 35700.5**

Maximum, Oakland, **Veh 35655.5**

Metal tires, gross weight limit, **Veh 35601**

Municipalities, increases or decreases, **Veh 35700 et seq.**

New vehicles, sales, **Veh 24009**

Notice,

Hearing, state highway limit changes, **Veh 35652**

Reduction of limits, **Veh 35705**

TRAFFIC RULES AND REGULATIONS
—Cont'd
Weights—Cont'd
Old Priest Grade, Tuolumne County, **Veh 35715.1**
Operation without compliance with provisions, **Veh 40001 et seq.**
Ordinances, **Veh 35700 et seq.**
Public utilities, exemption, **Veh 35704, 35714**
Ratio of weight to length, **Veh 35551**
Reloading, carriers, **Veh 2803**
Santa Clara County, state highway route 85, **Veh 35722**
Single permit, excessive weight, **Veh 35791**
Snow removal equipment, exemption, **Veh 35001**
Solid tires, gross weight, **Veh 35600**
Speed limits, **Veh 22409**
Special permits, **Veh 35780 et seq.**
Terminal Island freeway, overweight vehicles, **Veh 35700.5**
Speed limits, solid tire vehicles, gross weight, **Veh 22409**
State highways,
Bridges, dangerous or weak condition, limits, **Veh 35755**
Changes, **Veh 35650 et seq.**
Stopping distance requirement, brakes, **Veh 26455**
Street railways, application of law, **Veh 21051**
Structural limits, **Veh 35750 et seq.**
Suspension of sentence, **Veh 42030**
Tables,
Axle limits, **Veh 35551.5**
Two or more consecutive axles, **Veh 35551**
Tandem axles, **Veh 35551**
Terminal Island freeway, overweight vehicles, special permits, **Veh 35700.5**
Timber and lumber,
Axle weight limits of vehicles transporting logs, **Veh 35552**
Log hauling permits, **Veh 35785**
Tire limits, **Veh 35600, 35601**
Solid tires, speed limits, **Veh 22409**
Tow trucks, fees, **Veh 9400.1**
Tuolumne County, Old Priest Grade, **Veh 35715.1**
Two or more consecutive axles, tables, **Veh 35551**
Unimproved county highways, reduction of limits, **Veh 35706**
Variances, permits and agreements, **Veh 35780 et seq.**
Wheel loads, **Veh 35550**
Wheel loads, **Veh 35550**
Wheels, blocking when parking on hills, **Veh 22509**
White reflectors, motorized scooters, **Veh 21223**
Width of roadway,
Exemption from driving on right side, **Veh 21650**

TRAFFIC RULES AND REGULATIONS
—Cont'd
Width of roadway—Cont'd
Speed, regard for existing conditions, **Veh 22350**
Zoning, special downward speed zoning, **Veh 22358.5**
Width of vehicle or load, **Veh 35000 et seq., 35100 et seq.**
Aerodynamic devices, **Veh 35110**
Agricultural products, loose loads, **Veh 35102**
Amber light, **Veh 25803**
Arrest, refusal to stop for inspection, **Veh 40303**
Building materials, trusses, wall panels, **Veh 35780.5**
Clearance, **Veh 25100 et seq.**
Commercial coaches, **Veh 35789.5**
Common carriers of passengers for hire, coaches or buses operated by, **Veh 35106, 35107**
Cotton module movers, **Veh 35100.5**
Crimes and offenses, **Veh 40000.7, 40001 et seq.**
Dynamic stability, tests, **Veh 35101**
Emergency vehicles, exemption, **Veh 35002**
Employees, violation,
Codefendants, owners, **Veh 40003**
Employer failing to answer charges, **Veh 40005**
Enactment of regulations, **Veh 32**
Equipment, extension beyond permissible limits, **Veh 35109, 35110**
Exceeding maximum limits, special permit, **Veh 35780 et seq.**
Exemptions, **Veh 35104**
Factory built housing, **Veh 35789.5, 35790.1**
Fees, licenses and permits, variances, **Veh 35795**
Flags, red flags, left front and left rear, **Veh 25104**
Highway construction or maintenance equipment, exemption, **Veh 35104**
Highway operation, application of law, **Veh 35000**
Inspection and inspectors, arrest, procedure, **Veh 40303**
Licenses and permits, **Veh 35780 et seq.**
Additional width, **Veh 35109**
Lights,
Clearance lamps, **Veh 25100**
Projection beyond permissible limits, **Veh 35109**
Manufactured housing, **Veh 35789.5 et seq.**
Mirrors, **Veh 35109**
Mobilehomes, **Veh 35790.1**
Appendages, **Veh 35789.5**
Operation without compliance with regulation, **Veh 40001 et seq.**
Ordinance permitting excess of limits, **Veh 35105**

TRAFFIC RULES AND REGULATIONS
—Cont'd
Width of vehicle or load—Cont'd
Passenger coaches or buses operated in urban or suburban service, **Veh 35106, 35107**
Passenger vehicles, projecting loads, **Veh 35111**
Pneumatic tires, **Veh 35101**
Projecting equipment, **Veh 35109, 35110**
Recreational vehicles, appurtenances, **Veh 35103**
Red flag or cloth, display at sides, **Veh 25104**
Side marker lamps, **Veh 25100**
Snow removal equipment, exemption, **Veh 35001**
Special mobile equipment, exemption, **Veh 35104**
Special permits, variances, **Veh 35780 et seq.**
Trusses, wall panels, stacks, **Veh 35780.5**
Variances, permits, **Veh 35780 et seq.**
Willful misconduct, **Veh 40000.14**
Owner as passenger, **Veh 17158**
Wireless telecommunications. Telecommunications, ante
Witnesses,
Police reports, rebuttal, **Veh 40806**
Speed traps, incompetency of officer or person assisting in arrest, **Veh 40804**
Work permits, driving under the influence, **Veh 23538, 23562**
Work release programs, driving under the influence, **Veh 23536, 23580**
Working on roadway, speed limits, **Veh 22362**
Wrecked vehicles, removal, **Veh 22650 et seq.**
Written declaration, infractions, trial, **Veh 40902**
Yellow parallel lines, driving to left, **Veh 21460**
Yellow reflectors, motorized scooters, **Veh 21223**
Yielding right of way,
Animals, horseback riders, **Veh 21805**
Approaching yield right of way sign, **Veh 21803**
Authorized emergency vehicles, **Veh 21806, 21807**
Buses, signs and signals, education, **Veh 24617**
Crosswalks, pedestrians, **Veh 21950**
Entrance of through highway, **Veh 21802, 21804**
Equestrian crossings, **Veh 21805**
Jaywalkers, **Veh 21954**
Left turn at intersection, **Veh 21801**
Overtaken vehicle, **Veh 21753**
Pedestrians, **Veh 21950 et seq.**
Private road or driveway, **Veh 21804**
Sidewalks, pedestrians, **Veh 21952**
Signs, stopping, **Veh 21803**
Through highway entrance, **Veh 21802**

TRAFFIC

TRAFFIC RULES AND REGULATIONS
—Cont'd
Yielding right of way—Cont'd
Turning vehicles, **Veh 21451**
Uncontrolled intersections, **Veh 21800**
Youth buses, loading or discharging children, **Veh 2816**
Youthful drunk driver visitation program, **Veh 23509 et seq.**
Zero emission electric vehicles, parking, designated spaces, **Veh 22511, 22511.1, 42001.6**
Zones,
Safety, ante
Speed,
Special downward speed zoning, **Veh 22358.5**
Working on roadways, **Veh 22362**

TRAFFIC SAFETY PROGRAM
Generally, **Veh 2900 et seq.**

TRAFFIC SCHOOLS
Traffic Violator Schools, generally, this index

TRAFFIC SIGNS AND SIGNALS
Generally, **Veh 21350 et seq.**
Abatement, nuisance, **Veh 21467**
Adjacent intersections, pedestrians, duties, **Veh 21955**
Affidavits of nonliability, automated enforcement systems, **Veh 40520**
Agricultural machinery and equipment,
Hand and arm signals, **Veh 22110**
Lamp signals, **Veh 22110**
Airports and landing fields, private roads, **Veh 21108**
Animals,
Abandoned or unclaimed property, crimes and offenses, **Veh 21376**
Bridle paths, designation, **Veh 21805**
Equestrian crossings, designation, **Veh 21805**
Livestock crossings, **Veh 21464**
Obedience to signals, **Veh 21462**
Open livestock range, designation, **Veh 21365**
Overtaking and passing, caution, **Veh 21759**
Approach sign, railroad crossing, **Veh 21362**
Area reflectorizing material, motor vehicle, use, **Veh 25500**
Arm signals, turning, **Veh 22110, 22111**
Arrows,
Green arrow signal, **Veh 21451**
Red arrow signal, **Veh 21453**
Yellow arrow signal, **Veh 21452**
Attaching materials, interference, **Veh 21464**
Automated enforcement systems, **Veh 21455.5 et seq.**
Definitions, **Veh 210**
Notice, violations, **Veh 40518, 40520**
Photography and pictures, post
Railroad crossings, **Veh 22451**

TRAFFIC SIGNS AND SIGNALS—Cont'd
Avoiding collision, obedience to signals, **Veh 21462**
Axle limits, weight restriction, **Veh 35551**
Bicycles, this index
Blinding lights, display, **Veh 21466**
Blocking traffic, minimum speed limit, **Veh 22400**
Boundaries, business or residence district, speed restrictions, **Veh 21358**
Bridges,
Automatic enforcement systems, **Veh 21455.5 et seq.**
Notice, violations, **Veh 40518, 40520**
County bridges, weight limits, **Veh 35754**
Local regulation, **Veh 21109**
Maximum speed limit, **Veh 22404, 22405**
Speed, protection of structure, **Veh 22403**
State highway bridges, weight limits, **Veh 35755**
Weight limits, **Veh 35752**
State highway bridges, **Veh 35755**
Bridle paths, right of way, **Veh 21805**
Broken lines, driving to left, **Veh 21460**
Buses,
Identification lamps and signs, **Veh 25350**
Lighted display signs, **Veh 25400**
Stops, school buses, **Veh 22504**
Business or residential districts,
Boundaries, speed signs, placement, **Veh 21358**
Speed,
Boundaries of districts, **Veh 21357, 21358**
Local highways linking districts, **Veh 22360**
Narrow streets, **Veh 22358.3**
Caution signal, **Veh 21452**
Crimes and offenses, application of law, **Veh 21450**
Checkpoints,
Air pollution, emissions, **Veh 2814.1**
Sobriety checkpoints, **Veh 2814.2**
Circular green signal, **Veh 21451**
Circular red signal, **Veh 21453**
Circular yellow signal, **Veh 21452**
Citations, automatic enforcement systems, **Veh 21455.5 et seq.**
Closing of highways or roads, **Veh 2812**
Commercial vehicles, **Veh 35713**
Local regulations, **Veh 21101 et seq.**
Private roads, public use, **Veh 21107.5 et seq.**
Colleges and universities,
Freeway directional signs, **Veh 21375**
Use of driveways and paths, **Veh 21113**
Collision, obedience to signals, exemption, **Veh 21462**
Colored lights, pedestrian movements, **Veh 21456.1**
Colors, curb markings, **Veh 21458**
Combined use highways, off highway vehicles, **Veh 38026**

TRAFFIC SIGNS AND SIGNALS—Cont'd
Commercial establishments, private roads, **Veh 21107.6**
Commercial vehicles,
Closing highways, **Veh 35713**
Identification lamps, **Veh 25350**
Parking, standing or stopping, **Veh 22502**
Common carrier vehicles, identification lamp and signs, **Veh 25350**
Compliance with code, presumption, **Veh 41101**
Concurrent signals, pedestrians, obedience to signals, **Veh 21456.1**
Confidential or privileged information, automated enforcement systems, photographic records, **Veh 21455.5**
Confirmation, speed signs, **Veh 21369**
Construction, **Veh 21367**
State highways, intersections, **Veh 21370**
Contractors or employees working on roadway, speed limits, **Veh 22362**
Contracts, automatic enforcement systems, manufacturers and manufacturing, **Veh 21455.5, 21455.6**
Counties, this index
Crimes and offenses, **Veh 21450 et seq.**
Abatement, nuisance, **Veh 21467**
Caution signs, **Veh 21452**
Application of law, **Veh 21450**
Curbs, marking, **Veh 21458**
Distinctive roadway markings, **Veh 21459**
Dont walk, definitions, **Veh 21456**
Double lines, **Veh 21460**
Failure to obey official devices, **Veh 21461, 21462**
Pedestrians, **Veh 21461.5**
Flashing signals, obedience, **Veh 21457**
Go signs, application of law, **Veh 21450**
Green or go signal, **Veh 21451**
Interference with devices, **Veh 21464**
Lights,
Blinding or dazzling lights, **Veh 21466**
Colored lights, application of law, **Veh 21450**
Manual signals, illegal operation, **Veh 21463**
Nuisance, abatement, **Veh 21467**
Obedience to official devices, **Veh 21461, 21462**
Pedestrians, failure to obey signs or signals, **Veh 21461.5**
Red lights, **Veh 21453**
Roadway markings, **Veh 21459**
School crossing guard, **Veh 2815**
Infraction convictions, **Veh 42001.1**
Stop signals, **Veh 21453**
Application of law, **Veh 21450**
Stop signs, post
Traffic actuated signals, illegal operation, **Veh 21463**
Turning at intersections, **Veh 22101**
Two way turning lanes, **Veh 21460.5**
Unauthorized devices, **Veh 21465**
Walk, definitions, **Veh 21456**

TRAFFIC SIGNS AND SIGNALS—Cont'd

Crimes and offenses—Cont'd
Yellow or caution signal, **Veh 21452**
Crossings,
Animal crossings, **Veh 21364**
Equestrian crossings, designation, **Veh 21805**
Livestock crossings, **Veh 21364**
Railroad crossings, generally, post
Toll roads and bridges, **Veh 23300, 23334**
Crosswalks,
Dont walk, definitions, **Veh 21456**
Intersections, designation of single legal intersection, **Veh 21361**
Local regulation, **Veh 21106**
Movements authorized by signals and light, **Veh 21450 et seq.**
School buildings and grounds, **Veh 21368**
Single legal intersection, designation, **Veh 21361**
Stopping vehicle, special stop requirements, **Veh 22450 et seq.**
Wait, definitions, **Veh 21456**
Walk, definitions, **Veh 21456**
Yielding right of way, **Veh 21451**
Cruising, control area, **Veh 21100**
Curbs and gutters,
Disabled vehicles, warning signals, **Veh 25300**
Handicapped persons, exclusive use parking spaces, designation, **Veh 21458, 22511.7, 22511.8, 22511.9**
Marking for parking and stopping, **Veh 21458**
Dazzling lights, display, **Veh 21466**
Deaf children, **Veh 21351.7**
Death or injury ensuing while defacing, **Veh 21464**
Defacing, offenses, **Veh 21464**
Description, devices, **Veh 21400**
Destruction. Removal or destruction, generally, post
Detour signs, **Veh 21363**
Diffused vehicle lights resembling signs, **Veh 25401**
Disabled vehicles, warning signals and devices, **Veh 25300 et seq.**
Disabled veterans, parking spaces, **Veh 22511.5 et seq.**
Discharging children, youth buses, **Veh 2816**
Display,
Blinding or dazzling light, **Veh 21466**
Unofficial signal, **Veh 21465**
Distinctive roadway markings, **Veh 21459**
Divided highways,
Disabled vehicles, warning signals, **Veh 25300**
Markings, **Veh 21651**
Dont walk, definitions, **Veh 21456**
Double parallel solid lines, offenses, **Veh 21460**
Driving to left of distinctive roadway markings, **Veh 21459, 21460**

TRAFFIC SIGNS AND SIGNALS—Cont'd

Driving under the influence, monuments and memorials, damages, **Veh 17300 et seq.**
Duration of signal, turning, **Veh 22108**
Educational institutions, use of grounds, **Veh 21113**
Electric interurban railway, warning approach signs, **Veh 21362**
Elevated structures, maximum speed limit, **Veh 22404, 22405**
Emergencies, obedience to signals, avoiding collisions, **Veh 21462**
Emergency Vehicles, this index
Enforcement systems. Automated enforcement systems, generally, ante
Entrance,
Automatic enforcement systems, **Veh 21455.5 et seq.**
Notice, violations, **Veh 40518, 40520**
Flashing red signals, **Veh 21802**
Highway or intersection, stop sign, **Veh 21355**
Toll roads and bridges, vehicular crossing, **Veh 23300**
Equipment, motor carriers, **Veh 25300 et seq.**
Erecting and maintaining, **Veh 21350 et seq.**
Evidence, restrictions on speed, presumption, authority to erect, **Veh 41100**
Exits, alleys, driver warnings, pedestrians and bicyclists, **Veh 21356.5**
Felonies. Crimes and offenses, generally, ante
Fines and penalties,
Interference with, **Veh 21464**
Red lights, failure to stop, **Veh 42001.15**
Special misdemeanors, **Veh 42001**
Weight restriction, violation, **Veh 42030**
Fire hydrants, parking distance, **Veh 22514**
Fire lanes, **Veh 22500.1**
Flagmen,
Railway grade crossings, speed limits, applicability, **Veh 22352**
Train signals, **Veh 22451 et seq.**
Flashing signals. Lights and lighting, post
For sale signs, removal of vehicle, **Veh 22651.9**
Form of devices, **Veh 21400**
Freeways,
Automatic enforcement systems, **Veh 21455.5 et seq.**
Notice, violations, **Veh 40518, 40520**
Colleges and universities, directional signs, **Veh 21375**
Restriction on use, **Veh 21960**
Speed limits, **Veh 22355, 22356**
Funeral procession, peace officers signals or directions, disregarding, **Veh 2817**
Fusees, disabled vehicles, **Veh 25300 et seq., 25305**
Go signs, **Veh 21451**
Crimes and offenses, application of law, **Veh 21450**

TRAFFIC SIGNS AND SIGNALS—Cont'd

Golf carts, use of local highways, **Veh 21115**
Governmental agencies, application of law, representatives, **Veh 21054**
Grade crossings,
Necessity of stopping, **Veh 22452**
Railroad crossings, generally, post
Grades, speed limits, decreasing on streets, **Veh 22413**
Green, definitions, **Veh 21451**
Guidelines, devices near schools, **Veh 21372**
Guideposts,
Injury, removal, **Veh 21464**
Interference with, **Veh 21464**
Hand and arm signals,
Bicycles, **Veh 22111**
Turning, **Veh 22110, 22111**
Handicapped persons,
Location, parking, **Veh 22511.10, 22511.11**
Parking spaces, **Veh 21458, 22511.7 et seq.**
Hearings, automated enforcement systems, **Veh 21455.6**
Hiking trails, unauthorized vehicles, **Veh 23127**
Hills, disabled vehicles, warning signals, **Veh 25300**
Historical landmarks, markers and monuments, interference with, **Veh 21464**
Horse drawn vehicles, overtaking and passing, **Veh 21759**
Horseback riders,
Equestrian crossings, right of way, **Veh 21805**
Trails, unauthorized vehicles, **Veh 23127**
Hospital districts, use of driveways and path, **Veh 21113**
Housing project, local authorities, **Veh 21111**
Ice and snow conditions, speed, restrictions, **Veh 22363**
Ice cream trucks, **Veh 22456**
Illuminated traffic signals, **Veh 21457**
Industrial or spur tracks, **Veh 22452**
Infrared transmitters, crimes and offenses, **Veh 21464**
Inoperative traffic control signal, right of way, **Veh 21800**
Inspection and inspectors, emissions, **Veh 2814.2**
Interference with, **Veh 21464**
Intersections,
Automatic enforcement systems, **Veh 21455.5 et seq.**
Notice, violations, **Veh 40518, 40520**
Bridle paths, designation, **Veh 21805**
Construction zones, state highways, **Veh 21370**
Crosswalks, local regulation, **Veh 21106**
Equestrian crossings, designation, **Veh 21805**
Flashing signals. Lights and lighting, post

TRAFFIC

TRAFFIC SIGNS AND SIGNALS—Cont'd
Intersections—Cont'd
Inoperative traffic control signal, right of way, **Veh 21800**
Local authorities, permission for state highway placement and maintenance, **Veh 21353**
Markings for turning, **Veh 22101**
Name signs, streets, **Veh 21366**
Prima facie speed limits, changing, **Veh 22352**
Private roads, local authorities, **Veh 21360**
Right of way, yield signs, **Veh 21803**
School buses, flashing red lamps, **Veh 22112**
Single legal intersection, designation, **Veh 21361**
Speed, prima facie limits, changing, **Veh 22352**
State highways, placement and maintenance, **Veh 21352**
Stop signs, placement and maintenance, **Veh 21355**
Stopping,
Special stops, **Veh 22450 et seq.**
Yield right of way signs, **Veh 21803**
Street name signs, **Veh 21366**
Through highways, local authorities, **Veh 21354**
Turning, **Veh 22101**
Yield right of way signs, **Veh 21356**
Knocking down or removal, **Veh 21464**
Lanes,
Designation, slow moving vehicles, **Veh 21655**
Slow moving traffic, **Veh 21658**
Speed limits, state highways, **Veh 22364**
State highways, placement and maintenance, **Veh 21352**
Turning at intersections, **Veh 22101**
Two way turning lanes, **Veh 21460.5**
Leases, motor vehicles, automated enforcement systems, affidavits of nonliability, **Veh 40520**
Left side of road,
Distinctive roadway markings, restrictions, **Veh 21459**
Double lines, **Veh 21460**
Left side of vehicle, hand and arm signals, **Veh 22111**
Left turns,
Arm and hand signals, **Veh 22111**
Continuous signal, duration, **Veh 22108**
Double lines, **Veh 21460**
Duration of signal, **Veh 22108**
Flashing signal, **Veh 22454**
Intersection, motor vehicles, **Veh 21801, 22101**
Markings or signs, **Veh 22101**
Motor vehicles turning into private road or alley, **Veh 21804**
Movement of vehicle, **Veh 22107**
Parallel lines, **Veh 21460**
Prohibition, **Veh 22101**
Time, duration of signal, **Veh 22108**

TRAFFIC SIGNS AND SIGNALS—Cont'd
Left turns—Cont'd
Two way turning lanes, **Veh 21460.5**
Lights and lighting,
Colored lights, offenses, application of law, **Veh 21450**
Description of devices, **Veh 21400**
Display of blinding or dazzling lights, **Veh 21466**
Flashing signals, **Veh 21456**
Fines and penalties, **Veh 42001.15**
Green arrow replaced by flashing red or yellow signals, **Veh 22454**
Obedience, **Veh 21457**
Red lamps,
School bus, **Veh 22112, 22454**
Through highway entrances, stopping, **Veh 21802**
School buses, **Veh 22112**
Schools and school districts, **Veh 21372**
Turning, **Veh 22110**
Vehicular obedience, **Veh 21457**
Yield right of way, **Veh 21802**
Nuisance, prohibited light, removal, **Veh 21467**
Pedestrians, **Veh 21450 et seq., 21456.1**
Red lights. Traffic Rules and Regulations, this index
Specifications, **Veh 21400**
Standards, devices, **Veh 21400**
Vehicular movements authorized, **Veh 21450 et seq.**
Livestock, open range, **Veh 21365**
Livestock crossings, **Veh 21364**
Loading children, youth buses, **Veh 2816**
Loads and loading,
Operation without, removal or covering of sign, **Veh 35783.5**
School buses, flashing red lamps, **Veh 22112**
Local authorities,
Intersections, designation of single legal intersection, **Veh 21361**
Metric and standard signs, placement and maintenance, **Veh 21351.3**
Powers, **Veh 21351**
Speed limits, streets, **Veh 22357 et seq.**
State highways permission, **Veh 21353**
Stop signs, **Veh 21355**
Railroad crossings, **Veh 21351.5**
Through highways, designation, **Veh 21354**
Timing signals, **Veh 22401**
Tourist directions, **Veh 21374**
Turning at intersections, **Veh 22101**
Uniform standards, **Veh 21100.1**
Yield right of way signs, **Veh 21356**
Local regulations, **Veh 21100 et seq., 21354**
Location, handicapped persons, parking, **Veh 22511.10, 22511.11**
Maintenance and replacement, **Veh 21350 et seq.**
Manual or traffic actuated, illegal operation, **Veh 21463**

TRAFFIC SIGNS AND SIGNALS—Cont'd
Markers and marking,
Crosswalks, single intersection, **Veh 21361**
Curbs, parking and stopping, **Veh 21458**
Distinctive roadway markings, **Veh 21459**
Divided highways, **Veh 21651**
Double lines, **Veh 21460**
Fire hydrants, stopping or parking, **Veh 22514**
Interference with, **Veh 21464**
Left side of roadway, restriction from, **Veh 21459**
Left turn, two way turning lanes, **Veh 21460.5**
Parking meter zones, **Veh 22508**
Roadways, **Veh 21459**
School crosswalks, **Veh 21368**
Single intersection, crosswalks, **Veh 21361**
Specifications, **Veh 21400**
Turning at intersections, **Veh 22101**
Two way turning lanes, **Veh 21460.5**
Unofficial signs, **Veh 21465**
Maximum weights,
Bridges or other structures, **Veh 35752**
State highways, **Veh 35654**
Memorials, damages, **Veh 17300 et seq.**
Metric and standard signs, placement and maintenance, local authorities, **Veh 21351.3**
Mileage signs, metric and standard, placement and maintenance, local authorities, **Veh 21351.3**
Minimum speed limit, **Veh 22400**
Misdemeanors. Crimes and offenses, generally, ante
Mobile infrared transmitters, crimes and offenses, **Veh 21464**
Monuments and memorials, damages, **Veh 17300 et seq.**
Motor carriers,
Identification signs, display, **Veh 27900 et seq.**
Warning signals and devices, **Veh 25300 et seq.**
Motor vehicle license fee fund, street name signs, **Veh 21366**
Motorcycles, traffic actuated signals, **Veh 21450.5**
Movements authorized by signals and light, **Veh 21450 et seq.**
Municipalities, this index
Names, signal controlled intersections, **Veh 21366**
Negligence, damages, tort liability, **Veh 17300 et seq.**
Nonglaring vehicle lights, resembling signs, **Veh 25401**
Nonliability, affidavits, automated enforcement systems, **Veh 40520**
Notice,
Automated enforcement systems, **Veh 21455.5**
Violations, **Veh 40518, 40520**

TRAFFIC SIGNS AND SIGNALS—Cont'd

Notice—Cont'd

Local traffic laws, **Veh 21103**

Nuisance, prohibited sign, removal, **Veh 21467**

Private ownership, exemption from local regulation, **Veh 21107.5 et seq.**

Turning at intersections, **Veh 22101**

Nuisance, abatement, **Veh 21467**

Obedience to official devices, **Veh 21461, 21462**

Off highway vehicles, **Veh 38280 et seq.**

Malicious removal or alteration, **Veh 38318.5**

Public lands, **Veh 38302**

Offenses. Crimes and offenses, generally, ante

Official signals, **Veh 21450**

Official traffic control devices, **Veh 21400, 21401**

Definitions, **Veh 440**

One way roadway, **Veh 21657**

Official traffic control signal,

Definitions, **Veh 445**

Inoperative, right of way, **Veh 21800**

Location at other than intersection, **Veh 21455**

Stop signs, removal, **Veh 21355**

Oil and gas pipelines, construction and maintenance, vehicles, warning lights, **Veh 25260.1**

One way roadways,

Designation of lanes or part of roadway, **Veh 21657**

Stop signs, placement and maintenance, **Veh 21355**

Open livestock range, **Veh 21365**

Ordinances closing highways, **Veh 35713**

Overtaking and passing,

Double lines, **Veh 21460**

Slow moving vehicles, **Veh 21654**

Yielding by overtaken vehicle, **Veh 21753**

Parallel lines, driving to left, **Veh 21460**

Parked vehicles, removal, **Veh 22651, 22658**

Parking,

Bordering state parks, **Veh 22505**

Commercial vehicles, conditions for applicability of local ordinances or resolutions, **Veh 22502**

Disabled vehicles, warning signals, **Veh 25300 et seq.**

Handicapped persons, **Veh 21458, 22511.7 et seq.**

Access ramps, **Veh 22522**

Inoperable parking meters, **Veh 22508.5**

Meter zones, **Veh 22508**

Ordinances, **Veh 22507**

Privately owned parking facilities, public parking prohibited, **Veh 22511.8**

Public utility vehicles, **Veh 22512**

Removal of vehicles, **Veh 22651, 22658**

Snow areas, **Veh 22510**

State highways, **Veh 22505, 22506**

TRAFFIC SIGNS AND SIGNALS—Cont'd

Passenger common carriers, identification lamps and signs, **Veh 25350**

Pedestrians,

Alley exits, driver warnings, **Veh 21356.5**

Application of law, offenses, **Veh 21450**

Caution signal, **Veh 21452**

Concurrent signals, obedience to walk, wait or don't walk signals, **Veh 21456.1**

Control signals, **Veh 21456**

Crosswalks, generally, ante

Dont walk, definitions, **Veh 21456**

Failure to obey signs or signals, **Veh 21461.5**

Manual or traffic actuated signal to cross roadway, operation, **Veh 21463**

Movement authorized by signals and lights, **Veh 21450 et seq.**

Obedience to signals, **Veh 21456.1, 21462**

Use of sidewalks, vehicular crossings, **Veh 23331**

Wait, definitions, **Veh 21456**

Walk, definitions, **Veh 21456**

Yellow or caution signal, **Veh 21452**

Yielding right of way, facing green or go signal, **Veh 21451**

Penalties. Fines and penalties, generally, ante

Photography and pictures,

Automated enforcement systems, **Veh 210, 21455.5 et seq.**

Notice, violations, **Veh 40518, 40520**

Notice, automated enforcement systems, violations, **Veh 40518, 40520**

Placement and maintenance, **Veh 21350 et seq.**

Presumption,

Correctness of speed restriction signs, **Veh 41100**

Validity, **Veh 41101**

Prima facie evidence, maximum speed, bridges, tubes, **Veh 22405**

Prima facie speed limits, change, **Veh 22352**

Private roads,

Airports and landing fields, **Veh 21108**

Application of law, local regulations, public institutions, **Veh 21113**

Closing to public use, **Veh 21107.5 et seq.**

Commercial establishments, **Veh 21107.6**

Definitions, local regulation, **Veh 21107.7**

Housing project, local regulation, **Veh 21111**

Intersection with highway, **Veh 21360**

Left turn, **Veh 21804**

Local regulation, **Veh 21107 et seq.**

Placement, **Veh 21360**

Notice of private ownership, exemption from local regulation, **Veh 21107.5 et seq.**

TRAFFIC SIGNS AND SIGNALS—Cont'd

Private roads—Cont'd

Public institutions, application of law, local regulation, **Veh 21113**

Public use, **Veh 21107.5**

Stop signs, **Veh 21360**

Public buildings and grounds, local regulation, **Veh 21113**

Public employees and equipment, application of traffic rules and regulations, **Veh 21053**

Public institutions, use of driveways, paths, **Veh 21113**

Public nuisance, prohibited signal, **Veh 21467**

Public use of private roads, local regulation, **Veh 21107.5**

Public utilities commission, powers, **Veh 21468**

Public utility vehicles,

Parking or stopping, **Veh 22512**

Warning devices, **Veh 25301**

Punishment. Crimes and offenses, generally, ante

Radar, automated enforcement systems, **Veh 21455.6**

Railroad crossings,

Approaching signs, **Veh 21362**

Automated enforcement systems, **Veh 22451**

Notice, violations, **Veh 40518, 40520**

Devices, train signals, **Veh 22451 et seq.**

Stop signs at crossings controlled by automatic signals, **Veh 21355**

Flagmen, **Veh 22451 et seq.**

Gate crossings, stopping, **Veh 22451 et seq.**

Industrial tracks, stopping, **Veh 22452, 22453**

Local authorities, state highway placement and maintenance, **Veh 21353**

Local regulation, **Veh 21110**

Photography and pictures, automated enforcement systems, **Veh 22451**

Notice, violations, **Veh 40518, 40520**

Prima facie speed limits, **Veh 22352**

Speed, changing prima facie limits, **Veh 22352**

Stop requirements, **Veh 22450 et seq.**

Stop signs, post

Train signals, **Veh 22451 et seq.**

Warning approach signal, official traffic control devices, **Veh 21400, 21401**

Warning approach signs, **Veh 21362**

Raised pavement markers, double lines, **Veh 21460**

Ratification, speed signs, **Veh 21369**

Rebuttable presumption, code compliance, **Veh 41100, 41101**

Red lights. Traffic Rules and Regulations, this index

Reduction of weight limits, county improved highways, **Veh 35710**

Reflectorizing material, use, **Veh 25500**

Removal or destruction,

Interference with devices, **Veh 21464**

TRAFFIC

TRAFFIC SIGNS AND SIGNALS—Cont'd
Removal or destruction—Cont'd
  Nuisances, abatement, **Veh 21467**
  Stop signs, **Veh 21355**
  Traffic device, guide post or historical marker, **Veh 21464**
Rental cars, automated enforcement systems, affidavits of nonliability, **Veh 40520**
Requests, installation of devices, school boards, **Veh 21373**
Residential districts. Business or residential districts, generally, ante
Riding trails, unauthorized vehicles, **Veh 23127**
Right of way, **Veh 21356, 21802**
  Inoperative control signal, **Veh 21800**
  Prima facie speed limits, intersections governed by yield signs, **Veh 22352**
  Uncontrolled intersections, application of law, **Veh 21800**
Right side of roadway, slow moving vehicles, **Veh 21654**
Right turns,
  Arm and hand signals, **Veh 22111**
  Duration of signal, **Veh 22108**
  Markings or signs, **Veh 22101**
  Movement of vehicle, **Veh 22107**
Running red light, **Veh 21453**
  Fines and penalties, **Veh 42001.15**
Safety zones,
  Caution signals, **Veh 21452**
  Stopping, standing or parking vehicles, **Veh 22500**
School buildings and grounds,
  Closing streets, local authorities, **Veh 21102, 21103**
  Crosswalks, marking, **Veh 21368**
  Device guidelines, **Veh 21372**
  Requests for devices, **Veh 21373**
  Speed, prima facie limits, applicability, **Veh 22352**
  Surveys, **Veh 21373**
  Use of driveways and paths, **Veh 21113**
School buses, **Veh 22454**
  Display, **Veh 27906**
  Flashing red lamps, **Veh 22112**
Schools and school districts,
  Approach signs, flashing signals, **Veh 21372**
  Crossing guard, **Veh 2815**
    Disregarding, fines and penalties, **Veh 42001.1**
  Crosswalks, marking, **Veh 21368**
  Guidelines for devices, **Veh 21372**
  Requests, installation of devices, **Veh 21373**
  Speed limits, prima facie limits, **Veh 22352**
Semaphores,
  Changing devices, **Veh 21464, 25352**
  Local authorities, state highways, **Veh 21353**
  State highways, placement and maintenance, **Veh 21352**

TRAFFIC SIGNS AND SIGNALS—Cont'd
Senior care centers, speed, prima facie limits, **Veh 22352**
Sentence and punishment. Crimes and offenses, generally, ante
Shape of devices, **Veh 21400**
Shooting devices, **Veh 21464**
Sidewalks, vehicular crossings, toll roads and bridges, **Veh 23331**
Single intersections, marking, **Veh 21361**
Slow moving vehicles,
  Decreasing maximum speed limit, **Veh 22407**
  Lanes designated, **Veh 21655, 21658**
  Right side of roadway, **Veh 21654**
  Turning out of highway, **Veh 21656**
Snow areas, parking, **Veh 22510**
Snow conditions, speed restrictions, **Veh 22363**
Sobriety checkpoints, **Veh 2814.2**
Special stops, **Veh 22450 et seq.**
Specifications,
  Devices, **Veh 21400**
  Local authorities, uniform standards, **Veh 21100.1**
Speed,
  Arm and hand signals, sudden decrease, **Veh 22111**
  Automated enforcement systems, **Veh 21455.6**
  Blocking traffic, minimum speed limit, **Veh 22400**
  Bridges, maximum limit, **Veh 22404, 22405**
  Business or residential districts, ante
  Changing prima facie speed limits, **Veh 22352**
  Confirmation, signs in place on January, 1, 1960, **Veh 21369**
  Contractors or employees working on roadway, **Veh 22362**
  Decreasing speed limits,
    Grades, streets, **Veh 22413**
    Slow moving vehicles, **Veh 22407**
    State highways, **Veh 22354**
  Elevated structures, maximum limits, **Veh 22404, 22405**
  Freeways, **Veh 22355, 22356**
  Hand signals, sudden decrease, **Veh 22111**
  Ice and snow conditions, **Veh 22363**
  Intersections, prima facie limits, changing, **Veh 22352**
  Lane speed limits, state highways, **Veh 22364**
  Local authorities, streets, **Veh 22357 et seq.**
  Maximum limit, bridges, tubes, **Veh 22404, 22405**
  Metric and standard signs, placement and maintenance, local authorities, **Veh 21351.3**
  Minimum speed limit, **Veh 22400**
  Narrow streets, business or residence districts, **Veh 22358.3**

TRAFFIC SIGNS AND SIGNALS—Cont'd
Speed—Cont'd
  Official traffic control devices, **Veh 21400, 21401**
  Presumptions,
    Authority to erect, **Veh 41100**
    Correctness of speed restriction signs, **Veh 41100**
  Prima facie evidence,
    Bridges, tubes, **Veh 22405**
    Change, **Veh 22352**
    Intersections, **Veh 22352**
    Railway crossings, prima facie limits, **Veh 22352**
  Ratification, signs in place on January 1, 1960, **Veh 21369**
  Residential districts, **Veh 21357, 21358**
  Snow conditions, **Veh 22363**
  Special speed limits, **Veh 21359**
  State highways,
    Bridges, tubes, **Veh 22404, 22405**
    Decrease, **Veh 22354**
    Lane limits, **Veh 22364**
  Sudden decrease,
    Hand and arm signals, **Veh 22111**
    Rearward vehicle, **Veh 22109**
  Timing of traffic signals, **Veh 22401**
  Tubes, maximum limits, **Veh 22404, 22405**
  Tunnels, maximum limits, **Veh 22404, 22405**
  Working on roadways, **Veh 22362**
Speed bumps, status, **Veh 440**
Standards,
  Description of devices, **Veh 21400**
  Local authorities, uniform standards, **Veh 21100.1**
Standing vehicles,
  Commercial vehicles, conditions for applicability of local regulations, **Veh 22502**
  Ordinances, **Veh 22507**
State authority, placement and maintenance, **Veh 21350**
State highways, **Veh 21350 et seq.**
  Automatic enforcement systems, **Veh 21455.5 et seq.**
    Notice, violations, **Veh 40518, 40520**
  Bridges, weight limits, **Veh 35755**
  Construction zones, intersections, **Veh 21370**
  Devices, **Veh 21352**
  Driving under the influence, monuments and memorials, damages, **Veh 17300 et seq.**
  Intersection, designation of single legal intersection, **Veh 21361**
  Lane speed limits, **Veh 22364**
  Local authorities, permission, **Veh 21353**
  Open livestock range, **Veh 21365**
  Parking, **Veh 22505, 22506**
  Speed limits, **Veh 22354**
    Bridges, tubes, **Veh 22404, 22405**
    Lane limits, **Veh 22364**
  Stop signs, **Veh 21352, 21355**
    Railroad crossings, **Veh 21351.5**

I–228

TRAFFIC SIGNS AND SIGNALS—Cont'd
State highways—Cont'd
  Weight limits, bridges, **Veh 35755**
State institutions, use of driveways and
  paths, **Veh 21113**
Stock crossings, **Veh 21364**
  Official traffic control devices, **Veh
  21400, 21401**
Stop signs,
  Bridle paths, **Veh 21805**
  Commercial vehicles,
    Conditions for applicability of local
      ordinances or resolutions, **Veh
      22502**
    Inspection, **Veh 2813**
  Crimes and offenses,
    Application of law, **Veh 21450**
    Fines and penalties, **Veh 42001.15**
  Description of devices, **Veh 21400,
    21401**
  Entrance to intersection, placement,
    Veh 21355
  Equestrian crossings, **Veh 21805**
  Erected prior to January 1, 1957, **Veh
    21401**
  Form, **Veh 21400**
  Intersection, placement, **Veh 21355**
  Local authorities, permission for place-
    ment and maintenance on state
    highway, **Veh 21353**
  Local highway, **Veh 21355**
  Local regulations, **Veh 21101**
  Notice of local traffic laws, **Veh 21103**
  Official traffic control devices, defini-
    tions, **Veh 440**
  Placement, local authorities, **Veh 22450**
  Prima facie speed limits, **Veh 22352**
  Private roads, **Veh 21360**
  Railroad crossings, **Veh 21351.5, 22450
    et seq.**
    Additional stop signs, **Veh 21355**
    Local regulation, **Veh 21110**
    Train actuated control devices, **Veh
      21355**
  Removal, intersection control by official
    signals, **Veh 21355**
  School buses, **Veh 22454, 22504**
    Display, **Veh 27906**
  Shape, **Veh 21400, 21401**
  Special stops, **Veh 22450 et seq.**
  Specifications, **Veh 21400, 21401**
  Speed, prima facie limits, **Veh 22352**
  State highways, **Veh 21352**
  Through highways,
    Local regulation, **Veh 21101, 21354**
    Right of way, **Veh 21802**
  Train signals, **Veh 22451**
  Yielding right of way, through highways,
    Veh 21802
Stopping,
  Arm and hand signals, **Veh 22111**
  Local authorities, **Veh 22506**
  Movement of vehicle, **Veh 22109**
  Ordinances, **Veh 22507**
  Railroad crossings, **Veh 22450 et seq.**

TRAFFIC SIGNS AND SIGNALS—Cont'd
Stopping—Cont'd
  Rearward vehicle, opportunity for sig-
    nal, **Veh 22109**
  School buses, flashing red lamps, **Veh
    22112**
  Sudden decrease of speed signal, **Veh
    22109**
Street name signs,
  Official traffic control devices, **Veh
    21400, 21401**
  Signal controlled intersections, **Veh
    21366**
Street railways, approach signs, **Veh 21362**
Streetcars, obedience to signals, **Veh 21462**
Subways, local regulation, **Veh 21109**
Sudden decrease of speed,
  Hand and arm signals, **Veh 22111**
  Rearward vehicle, **Veh 22109**
Surveys, school buildings and grounds, in-
  stallation of devices, **Veh 21373**
Tax fund, street name signs, payment out
  of, **Veh 21366**
Three lane highways, driving in center or
  left lane, **Veh 21659**
Time,
  Turning, duration of signal, **Veh 22108**
  Yellow lights, automatic enforcement
    systems, **Veh 21455.7**
Timing of traffic signals, speed, **Veh 22401**
Toll roads and bridges, vehicular crossings,
  Veh 23334
  Entrance, **Veh 23300**
  Officers, **Veh 23253**
Tort liability, damages, **Veh 17300 et seq.**
Tourist oriented directional signs, **Veh
  21374**
Traffic actuated signals,
  Bicycles, **Veh 21450.5**
  Illegal operation, **Veh 21463**
Traffic safety fund, devices, **Veh 42200**
Train signals, railroad crossings, **Veh
  22451 et seq.**
Training, **Veh 21401**
Transmitters, mobile infrared transmitters,
  crimes and offenses, **Veh 21464**
Trolley coaches, lighted display signs, **Veh
  25400**
Tubes and tunnels,
  Local regulation, **Veh 21109**
  Maximum speed limit, **Veh 22403,
    22404, 22405**
Turn signals, **Veh 22100 et seq.**
Turning, **Veh 22107 et seq.**
  Arm signals, **Veh 22110, 22111**
  Continuous signal, duration, **Veh 22108**
  Double lines, **Veh 21460**
  Green or go signal, **Veh 21451**
  Hand and arm signals, **Veh 22110, 22111**
  Intersections, **Veh 22101**
  Lamp signal, **Veh 22110**
  Left turns, generally, ante
  Markings or signs, intersections, **Veh
    22101**
  Method of signaling, **Veh 22110**
  Movement of vehicle, **Veh 22107**

TRAFFIC SIGNS AND SIGNALS—Cont'd
Turning—Cont'd
  Parallel lines, **Veh 21460**
  Red lights, **Veh 21453**
  Right turns, generally, ante
  Slow moving vehicles, turning off high-
    ways, **Veh 21656**
  Time, duration of signal, **Veh 22108**
  Two way turning lanes, **Veh 21460.5**
  U turns, **Veh 21451**
U turns,
  Double lines, **Veh 21460**
  Green or go signal, **Veh 21451**
  Parallel lines, pavement markings, **Veh
    21460**
Upraised hand symbol, **Veh 21456, 21456.1**
Utility vehicles, warning signals, parked,
  stopped or standing vehicles, **Veh
  25301**
Vandalism, **Veh 21464**
Vehicular and pedestrian movements au-
  thorized, **Veh 21450 et seq.**
Vehicular crossings, toll roads and bridges,
  Veh 23253, 23300, 23334
Vehicular parking, bordering state parks,
  Veh 22505
Veterans, disabled veterans, parking
  spaces, **Veh 22511.5 et seq.**
Viaducts, local regulation, **Veh 21109**
Wait or dont walk, definitions, **Veh 21456**
Walk, definitions, **Veh 21456**
Walking person symbol, **Veh 21456.1**
Warning lights, construction zones, **Veh
  21367**
Warnings, automatic enforcement systems,
  Veh 21455.5
Warrants, school devices, guidelines, **Veh
  21372, 21373**
Watercourse banks, motor vehicle opera-
  tion restrictions, **Veh 21116**
Weapons, shooting devices, **Veh 21464**
Weights,
  Axle limits, **Veh 35551**
  Bridges, **Veh 35752**
    State highway bridges, **Veh 35755**
  Commercial vehicles, closing highways,
    Veh 35713
  County bridges, **Veh 35754**
  County improved highways, reduction of
    limits, **Veh 35710**
  Fines and penalties, **Veh 42030**
  Intercounty streets, **Veh 35719**
  Notice, **Veh 35718**
  Reduction by cities, **Veh 35701**
  State highway bridges, **Veh 35755**
White parallel lines, driving to left, **Veh
  21460**
Wilfully or negligently damaging, liability,
  Veh 17300 et seq.
Windshields, **Veh 26708**
Work warning signs, specifications, **Veh
  21400**
Working on roadway, speed limits, **Veh
  22362**
Yellow, definitions, **Veh 21452**

TRAFFIC

TRAFFIC SIGNS AND SIGNALS—Cont'd

Yellow flashing lights,
Replacement of green arrow, **Veh 21454**
Vehicular obedience, **Veh 21457**
Yellow lights, time, automatic enforcement systems, **Veh 21455.7**
Yellow parallel lines, driving to left, **Veh 21460**
Yield signs,
Intersections, entrances, **Veh 21356**
Official traffic control devices, **Veh 21400, 21401**
Speed, changing prima facie limits, controlled highways, **Veh 22352**
Stopping, **Veh 21803**
Yielding for passing, overtaking vehicle, audible signal, **Veh 21753**
Youth buses, loading or discharging children, **Veh 2816**
Zones, speed, working on roadway, **Veh 22362**

TRAFFIC VIOLATOR SCHOOL INSTRUCTOR
Definitions, **Veh 626.4, 626.6**

TRAFFIC VIOLATOR SCHOOL OWNER
Definitions, **Veh 626.8**

TRAFFIC VIOLATOR SCHOOLS
Generally, **Veh 11200 et seq.**
Actions and proceedings, fraudulent practices, damages, **Veh 11203.5**
Administrative services, contracts, **Veh 11222**
Agent for service of process, **Veh 11202**
Aggressive driving, courses of study, **Veh 11219**
Attendance, **Veh 42005, 42005.1**
Average daily attendance of public educational institution, inclusion, **Veh 42005.5**
Bail,
Continuance, attendance, **Veh 41501, 42005**
Forfeitures,
Installment payments, fees, **Veh 42007**
Proof of completion, **Veh 40512.6**
Bicycles, right of way, courses of study, **Veh 11219.3**
Bonds (officers and fiduciaries), **Veh 11202**
Deposit in lieu of bond, **Veh 11203**
License cancellation, **Veh 11216**
Cancellation, classes, fees, **Veh 11219.5**
Certificate of completion, crimes and offenses, **Veh 11202**
Certificates and certification, license certificates, **Veh 11204**
Instructors, **Veh 11207**
Change of ownership, corporate structure or address, notice, **Veh 11213**
Character and reputation, licenses and permits, **Veh 11206.5**
Commercial motor vehicles, **Veh 42005**
Complaints, reports, **Veh 11208.5**
Compromise and settlement, accusation against licensee, **Veh 11218**

TRAFFIC VIOLATOR SCHOOLS—Cont'd

Confidential or privileged information,
Attendance as punishment, **Veh 1808.7**
Conviction, **Veh 1803.5, 1808.7**
Records and recordation, **Veh 1808.10, 11212, 42005**
Consumer protection, disclosure, **Veh 11200**
Continuance,
Abstract of record, **Veh 1803.5**
Attendance, **Veh 41501**
Continuing education, **Veh 11204**
Contracts, administrative services, **Veh 11222**
Conviction,
Confidential or privileged information, **Veh 1803.5, 1808.7**
Continuance, attendance, **Veh 41501, 42005**
Corporations, refusal to issue license, **Veh 11211**
Course completion, notice, **Veh 11200**
Courses of study, **Veh 11219**
Court approved programs, licenses and permits, **Veh 11202**
Court ordered attendance, **Veh 42005**
Studies, **Veh 42005.1**
Courthouse construction fund, fees, deposit, **Veh 42007.1**
Damages, fraudulent practices, actions against school, **Veh 11203.5**
Death of licensee, temporary license, **Veh 11204**
Definitions, **Veh 626**
Final determination, discrimination, **Veh 11216.2**
Deposit in lieu of bond, **Veh 11203**
Disclosure, consumer protection, **Veh 11200**
Discrimination, handicapped persons, **Veh 11216.2**
Division, types of businesses, **Veh 1670**
Driving under the influence, continuance, attendance, exemptions, **Veh 41501**
Examiners and examinations,
Instructors licenses, **Veh 11206**
Renewal, **Veh 11207**
Operators licenses, **Veh 11202.5**
Reexamination, **Veh 11220**
Failure to attend, **Veh 40000.25**
Offenses, **Veh 42005**
Fees,
Administrative fees, **Veh 42007.1**
Allocation, **Veh 42007.3**
Attendance, **Veh 42007, 42007.1**
Conversion to bail, forfeiture, **Veh 40512.6**
Licenses, **Veh 11208**
Receipts, **Veh 11219.5**
Reports, **Veh 11208.5**
Traffic assistance programs, monitoring, **Veh 11205.2**
Fraud, actions or damages, **Veh 11203.5**
Guilty plea, continuance, attendance, **Veh 41501, 42005**

TRAFFIC VIOLATOR SCHOOLS—Cont'd

Handicapped persons, accommodation, **Veh 11202**
Hearings,
License suspension or revocation, **Veh 11215, 11217**
Refusal to issue license, **Veh 11211**
Hit and run drivers, continuance, attendance, exemptions, **Veh 41501**
Installment payments, fees, **Veh 42007**
Instructors licenses, **Veh 11206 et seq.**
Internet, course completion, notice, **Veh 11200**
Lesson plans, **Veh 11202**
Licenses and permits, **Veh 11200 et seq.**
Cancellation, **Veh 11216**
Certificate, **Veh 11204**
Instructors, **Veh 11207**
Character and reputation, **Veh 11206.5**
Continuing education, **Veh 11204**
Crimes and offenses, **Veh 11216.5**
Qualifications, **Veh 11211**
Criteria, **Veh 11202**
Fees, **Veh 11208**
Reinstatement, **Veh 11217**
Instructors, **Veh 11206, 11207**
Moral turpitude, crimes involving, suspension or revocation, **Veh 11216.5**
Operators, **Veh 11202.5**
Probationary license, **Veh 11204**
Instructors, **Veh 11207**
Refusal to issue, **Veh 11211**
Reinstatement, fee, **Veh 11217**
Renewal, **Veh 11204**
Failure to renew, **Veh 11209**
Instructors licenses, **Veh 11207**
Revocation or suspension, **Veh 11211, 11215, 11215.5, 11215.7, 11216.2, 11216.5, 11217**
Renewal, **Veh 11209**
Temporary license, death of licensee, **Veh 11204**
Temporary permits, **Veh 11210**
Time, renewal, **Veh 11204**
Instructors, **Veh 11207**
List of schools, **Veh 11205**
Monitoring, traffic assistance programs, **Veh 11205.4**
Motorcycles, right of way, courses of study, **Veh 11219.3**
No contest, continuance, attendance, **Veh 41501, 42005**
Notice,
Change of ownership, corporate structure or address, **Veh 11213**
Course completion, **Veh 11200**
License revocation or suspension, **Veh 11215, 11217**
Office, place of business, **Veh 1670, 1671**
Operators, character and reputation, licenses and permits, **Veh 11206.5**
Partnerships, refusal to issue license, **Veh 11211**
Pedestrians, courses of study, **Veh 11219.3**
Place of business, license cancellation, **Veh 11216**

TRAFFIC VIOLATOR SCHOOLS—Cont'd
Probationary licenses, **Veh 11204**
    Instructors, **Veh 11207**
Process, new address or termination of
    business, **Veh 11217.5**
Public educational institutions, average
    daily attendance, inclusion, **Veh
    42005.5**
Railroad crossings, **Veh 42001.16**
Reckless driving, continuance, attendance,
    exemptions, **Veh 41501**
Records and recordation,
    Confidential or privileged information,
        Veh 1808.10, 42005
    Students, **Veh 11212**
Referrals, court ordered attendance, **Veh
    42005**
Reports, **Veh 11208.5**
Revocation, licenses, **Veh 11215.5**
Right of way, courses of study, **Veh
    11219.3**
Road rage, courses of study, **Veh 11219**
    Sentence and punishment, **Veh 13210**
Rules and regulations, **Veh 11219**
Service of process, **Veh 11202**
    New address or termination of business,
        Veh 11217.5
Stipulated penalties, accusation against li-
    censee, **Veh 11218**
Student records, **Veh 11212**
Studies, court ordered, **Veh 42005.1**
Suspension or revocation, licenses, **Veh
    11215.5**
Temporary permits, **Veh 11210**
Time, licenses and permits, renewal, **Veh
    11204**
    Instructors, **Veh 11207**
Traffic assistance programs, **Veh 11205.2,
    11205.4**
Two or more types of businesses, division
    between, **Veh 1670**

TRAILER BUS
Definition and regulation, **Veh 636**

TRAILER COACHES
Generally, **Veh 34500 et seq.**
Definitions, **Veh 635**
Registration, **Veh 5350 et seq., 6703**
    Fees, **Veh 9250, 9250.1**

TRAILER PARKS
Mobilehomes and Mobilehome Parks,
    generally, this index

TRAILERS
Agricultural Machinery and Equipment,
    this index
Applications, permanent trailer identifica-
    tion plates, **Veh 5015**
Boats and Boating, this index
Brakes, **Veh 26304**
    Use in lieu of service brake control, **Veh
    26458.5**
Camp Trailers, generally, this index
Certificates and certification, permanent
    trailer identification plates, **Veh
    5014.1, 5016**

TRAILERS—Cont'd
Commercial vehicles, towing, weight fees,
    Veh 9400
    Exemption, vehicles manufactured be-
        fore designated time, **Veh 9401**
Cotton Trailers, generally, this index
Definitions,
    Camp trailer, **Veh 242**
    Vehicle Code, **Veh 630**
Dismantlers, business signs, **Veh 11514**
Display, permanent trailer identification
    plates, **Veh 5017**
Dollies,
    Permanent trailer identification plates,
        Veh 468
    Registration, **Veh 4000**
Drivers licenses, restricted, towing live-
    stock trailers, **Veh 12804.14**
Environmental license plates, **Veh 5101 et
    seq.**
Farm trailers, registration, exemption, **Veh
    36109**
Fees,
    Permanent trailer identification plates,
        Veh 5014.1
    Transfers, **Veh 5016**
    Special interest license plates, **Veh 5060**
Financial statements and reports, special
    interest license plates, **Veh 5060**
Fleet vehicles, permanent trailer identifi-
    cation plates, **Veh 5301**
Funds, special interest license plates, **Veh
    5060**
Identification plates. Permanent trailer
    identification plates, generally, post
Inspection and inspectors, registration,
    commercial vehicles, gross weight,
    Veh 4000.6
License plates,
    Permanent trailer identification plates,
        generally, post
    Special interest plates, **Veh 5060**
Livestock trailers, towing, restricted driv-
    ers licenses, **Veh 12804.14**
Lost or destroyed property, permanent
    trailer identification plates, **Veh 4458,
    5017**
Markets and marketing, special interest
    license plates, **Veh 5060**
Mobilehomes and Mobilehome Parks,
    generally, this index
Motor Carriers, generally, this index
Notice,
    Lost or stolen plates, **Veh 4458**
    Special interest license plates, **Veh 5060**
Permanent trailer identification plates,
    Veh 468, 5011, 5014.1 et seq.
    Distinguishing marks, **Veh 5000**
    Environmental license plates, **Veh 5101
        et seq.**
    Fleet vehicles, **Veh 5301**
    Lost or stolen plates, **Veh 4458**
Promotions, special interest license plates,
    Veh 5060
Reflectors, **Veh 24607, 24611**

TRAILERS—Cont'd
Registration, **Veh 4000 et seq.**
    Commercial vehicles, gross weight, **Veh
        4000.6**
    Exemption, newly discharged military
        personnel entering state, **Veh 6703**
    Farm trailers, exemption, **Veh 36109**
    Weight fees, **Veh 9400**
Restricted drivers licenses, livestock trail-
    ers, towing, **Veh 12804.14**
Safety regulations, **Veh 34500 et seq.**
Shade trailers, registration, exemptions,
    Veh 36105
Snow tires, **Veh 27459**
Stop lamps, **Veh 24603**
Tail lamps, **Veh 24600**
Theft, permanent trailer identification
    plates, **Veh 4458**
Tire traction devices, **Veh 27454, 27459 et
    seq.**
Towing equipment, safety connections,
    Veh 29004.5
Towing livestock trailers, restricted drivers
    licenses, **Veh 12804.14**
Traffic Rules and Regulations, this index
Transfer of property, permanent trailer
    identification plates, **Veh 5014.1, 5017**
Weight fees, **Veh 9400**

TRAILS
Recreational Trails, generally, this index

TRAINED NURSES
Nurses, generally, this index

TRAINING
Buses, youth bus drivers, **Veh 2423**
Driving Schools, generally, this index
Emergency medical dispatchers, highway
    patrol, **Veh 2422**
Highway Patrol, this index
Medical Care and Treatment, this index
Motor Vehicles, this index
Motorcycles, safety, **Veh 2932**
Nurses, this index
Off highway vehicles, **Veh 38007**
    Children and minors, **Veh 38504.1,
        38504.2**
Paratransit vehicles, drivers, **Veh 12517.5**
Peace Officers, this index
Police, this index
Traffic signs and signals, **Veh 21401**
Youth bus drivers, **Veh 2423, 12523**

TRAINS
Railroads, generally, this index

TRAMWAYS
Street Railways, generally, this index

TRANSCRIPT OF RECORD
Administrative Law and Procedure, gener-
    ally, this index

TRANSFER OF POWERS AND DUTIES
Highway patrol, state police division, **Veh
    2250.1**

TRANSFER

TRANSFER OF PROPERTY

Motor vehicles, semitrailers, permanent trailer identification plates, **Veh 5017**

Trailers, permanent trailer identification plates, **Veh 5014.1, 5017**

TRANSFEREES

Definitions, motor vehicles, **Veh 640**

TRANSIT DEVELOPMENT BOARDS

Traffic rules and regulations, **Veh 21113**

TRANSIT DISTRICTS

Abandoned or unclaimed property, motor vehicles, appraisal and appraisers, **Veh 22855**

Air pollution, heavy duty vehicles, emission standards, **Veh 28114**

Alameda Contra Costa transit district, buses, bicycles, transportation, length, **Veh 35400.7**

Animals, standing, **Veh 21113**

Bicycles, riding or parking on grounds, **Veh 21113**

Heavy duty vehicles, emission standards, **Veh 28114**

Motor vehicles,
   Emission standards, **Veh 28114**
   Low emission vehicles, **Veh 28113**
   Traffic districts, **Veh 21113**

Motorized bicycles, riding or parking on public grounds, **Veh 21113**

Roller skating, riding or parking on public grounds, **Veh 21113**

Santa Cruz metropolitan transit district, buses, right of way, signs and signals, **Veh 24617**

Skateboarding, riding or parking on public grounds, **Veh 21113**

Stopped vehicles, **Veh 21113**

Traffic rules and regulations, **Veh 21113**

Vehicles. Motor vehicles, generally, ante

TRANSIT SYSTEMS

Accidents, reports, **Veh 16002**

Paratransit Vehicles, generally, this index

Reports, accidents, **Veh 16002**

Traffic rules and regulations, cellular radio telephones, **Veh 23125**

TRANSPLANTS

Anatomical Gifts, generally, this index

TRANSPORTATION

Animals, this index

Atomic Energy, this index

Automated rail crossing enforcement system, rail transit, **Veh 21362.5**

Buses, generally, this index

Car pools. Motor Vehicles, this index

Commercial passenger vehicles, financial responsibility, **Veh 16500 et seq.**

Corridors. Highways and Roads, this index

Dangerous materials, drivers licenses and operation certificates, agricultural hazardous materials, transportation, **Veh 12804.2**

TRANSPORTATION—Cont'd

Drivers licenses, inadequate facilities, junior permits, **Veh 12513**

Dwelling house or building across railroad tracks, notice, **Veh 35789**

Electric personal assistive mobility devices, **Veh 21280 et seq.**

Explosives, this index

Fireworks, this index

Flammable liquids, **Veh 34001 et seq.**

Hazardous Substances and Waste, this index

Highway patrol, injured persons, **Veh 2406**

Highways and Roads, generally, this index

Hospitals, this index

Kitchen Grease, this index

Local vehicle license fee surcharge, San Francisco City and County, **Veh 9250.12**

Manufactured housing, permits for movement, **Veh 35790**

Mass Transit, generally, this index

Mentally Retarded and Developmentally Disabled Persons, this index

Paratransit Vehicles, generally, this index

Passengers, limitation on driving hours, **Veh 21702**

Peace Officers, this index

Personal assistive mobility devices, **Veh 21280 et seq.**

Persons injured in accident, **Veh 20016**

Railroads, generally, this index

Rapid transit districts. Transit Districts, generally, this index

Rapid transit systems. Transit Systems, generally, this index

San Francisco City and County, local vehicle license fee surcharge, **Veh 9250.12**

School Buses, generally, this index

School pupils. School Buses, generally, this index

Schools and School Districts, this index

State highways. Highways and Roads, this index

Timber and Lumber, this index

Traffic safety program, **Veh 2900 et seq.**

Transit Districts, generally, this index

Transit Systems, generally, this index

Vanpooling, generally, this index

Workmen in trucks,
   Eight hundred (800) numbers, **Veh 2429**
   Equipment, **Veh 31400**

TRANSPORTATION DEPARTMENT

Impounding, parked or standing vehicles, **Veh 22654**

Motor vehicles, authority to impound, employees, **Veh 22654**

Officers and employees, impounding, parked or standing vehicles, **Veh 22654**

Traffic rules and regulations, standing vehicles, overtaking and passing, **Veh 21809**

TRANSPORTATION DISTRICTS

Transit Districts, generally, this index

TRANSPORTATION FUND

State Treasury, this index

TRANSPORTERS

Motor Vehicles, this index

TRAP WAGON

Definitions, agricultural machinery and equipment, **Veh 36016**

TRASH

Solid Waste, generally, this index

TRAVEL TRAILERS

Camp Trailers, generally, this index

Mobilehomes and Mobilehome Parks, generally, this index

TRAVELING EXPENSES

Highway Patrol, this index

TREASURERS

County Treasurers, generally, this index

TREASURY

State Treasury, generally, this index

TREES

Advertisements. Outdoor Advertising, generally, this index

Outdoor Advertising, generally, this index

Products. Timber and Lumber, generally, this index

TRESPASS

Motor Vehicles, this index

Traffic rules and regulations, vehicular crossings, toll roads and bridges, **Veh 23332**

TRIAL

Continuance, traffic rules and regulations, Arrest for infraction, **Veh 40306**
   Police or traffic officer reports, rebuttal, **Veh 40806**

Costs, generally, this index

Process, generally, this index

Traffic Rules and Regulations, this index

TRIAL COURTS

Courts, generally, this index

TROLLEY COACHES

Street Railways, generally, this index

TRONA JOINT UNIFIED SCHOOL DISTRICT

Coach bus, inspection, **Veh 545.5**

TRUANTS

Schools and School Districts, this index

TRUCK TRACTORS

Definitions, **Veh 655**

Motor Carriers, generally, this index

TRUCKS

Motor Carriers, generally, this index

TRUSSES

Definitions, motor vehicles, **Veh 657**

Traffic rules and regulations, width of vehicle or load, stacks, **Veh 35780.5**

TRUST FUNDS
Court facilities trust fund, night court, assessments, traffic rules and regulations, **Veh 42006**

TRUSTS AND TRUSTEES
Motor vehicles, sales, application of law, **Veh 12121**

TUITION
Driving schools, mature driver improvement courses, **Veh 1676**

TUNNELS
Caldecott tunnel, explosive or flammable liquids, transportation, **Veh 31301**
Cargo tank vehicles, flammable liquids, **Veh 21109**
Explosives,
   Caldecott tunnel, transportation, **Veh 31301**
   Vehicle transporting, avoidance, **Veh 31614**
Local authorities, powers, **Veh 21109**
Traffic Rules and Regulations, this index

TUOLUMNE COUNTY
Highways and roads, Old Priest Grade, weights, **Veh 35715.1**
Traffic rules and regulations, weights, Old Priest Grade, **Veh 35715.1**

TURN SIGNALS
Motor Carriers, this index
Motor Vehicles, this index
Motorcycles, **Veh 24951**

TURNING
Traffic Rules and Regulations, this index
Traffic Signs and Signals, this index

TWO LANE, UNDIVIDED HIGHWAY
Definitions, speed limit, **Veh 22349**

TWO WAY COMMUNICATION DEVICES
Buses, **Veh 24018**

U TURNS
Traffic Rules and Regulations, this index
Traffic Signs and Signals, this index

ULEV
Definitions, motor vehicles, air pollution, decals, **Veh 5205.5**

ULTRALOW EMISSION VEHICLES
Decals, **Veh 5205.5, 21655.9, 40000.13**
   Forgery, counterfeiting, **Veh 4463**

UNCLAIMED PROPERTY
Abandoned or Unclaimed Property, generally, this index

UNCONSCIOUS PERSONS
Motor vehicles, blood tests, driving under influence of alcohol or drugs, **Veh 13353**

UNDERTAKINGS
Bail, generally, this index

UNDERTAKINGS—Cont'd
Bonds (Officers and Fiduciaries), generally, this index

UNDOCUMENTED VESSELS
Ships and Shipping, this index

UNIFORMS
Bulletproof vests, highway patrol, **Veh 2259.5**
Handicapped parking, special enforcement units, **Veh 22507.9**
Highway Patrol, this index
Motor vehicle offenses, investigating officers, exemption, **Veh 40804**
Toll takers, vehicular crossings, **Veh 23252**
Traffic officers, distinctive uniform, **Veh 40800**

UNINCORPORATED ASSOCIATIONS
Associations and Societies, generally, this index

UNINSURED MOTOR VEHICLE
Definitions, insurance, **Veh 16000.7**

UNINSURED MOTORISTS
Motor Vehicle Insurance, this index

UNITED STATES
Emergency vehicles, definitions, **Veh 165**
Military Forces, generally, this index
Motor Vehicle Insurance, this index
Motor vehicles,
   Air pollution, **Veh 2814, 27153 et seq.**
   Conviction for violation of code required by federal law, inadmissibility, **Veh 40830**
   Emergency vehicles, **Veh 165**
   Fees, exemptions, **Veh 9101, 9103**
   Financial responsibility, exemption, **Veh 16051**
   Offenses, required by federal law, inadmissibility of conviction in negligence action, **Veh 40830**
   Officers or employees operating, license, exemption, **Veh 12501**
   Out of service orders, failure to comply, **Veh 2800**
   Registration, **Veh 4155**
   Safety glazing material standards, **Veh 26704**
   Special license plates, **Veh 5001**
   Violation of code required by federal law, defenses, **Veh 41401**
Officers and employees, addresses, confidentiality, **Veh 1808.4**
Public lands, motor vehicles, irrigation and irrigation districts, machinery and equipment, inspection and inspectors, **Veh 2810.2**
Ships and shipping, exemptions, **Veh 9873**
Traffic rules and regulations, violation of code required by federal law,
   Defense, **Veh 41401**
   Inadmissibility of conviction in negligence action, **Veh 40830**

UNITED STATES AGENCIES AND INSTITUTIONS
Traffic rules and regulations, **Veh 41401**

UNITED STATES POSTAL SERVICE
Electric carts, sidewalk use, local regulation, **Veh 21114.5**
Officers and employees, electric carts, sidewalk use, local regulation, **Veh 21114.5**
Sidewalks, electric carts, local regulation, **Veh 21114.5**

UNITED STATES TERRITORIES AND POSSESSIONS
Motor vehicle violations, drivers license revocation or suspension, **Veh 13352**

UNIVERSITIES
Colleges and Universities, generally, this index

UNIVERSITY OF CALIFORNIA
Colleges and Universities, this index

UNLADEN WEIGHT
Definitions, motor vehicles, **Veh 660, 661**

URBAN OR SUBURBAN SERVICE
Definitions, width of vehicles, **Veh 35107**

URBAN RENEWAL
Housing Authorities, generally, this index

URINE
Driving under influence of alcohol or drugs, tests, **Veh 13353, 23158**

USE
Definitions, registration and transfer of vessel, **Veh 9840**

USE FUEL TAX
Transportation fund. State Treasury, this index

USE TAXES
Sales and Use Taxes, generally, this index

USED CAR LOTS
Motor Vehicles, this index

USED VEHICLES
Motor Vehicles, this index

UTILITIES
Public Utilities, generally, this index

UTILITY TRAILERS
Trailers, generally, this index

VACATING OR SETTING ASIDE
Judgments and Decrees, this index

VACUUM BRAKES
Motor vehicles, **Veh 26520 et seq.**

VACUUM HOSES
Motor vehicles, nonconforming equipment, sales, **Veh 24005**

VALUATION
Motor Vehicles, this index

VAN OR TANK CONTAINERS
Traffic rules and regulations, loads and
loading, **Veh 31540**

VANDALISM
Children and Minors, this index
Delay or suspension of driving privileges,
Veh 13202.6
Driving privileges, delay or suspension,
Veh 13202.6
Malicious Mischief, generally, this index
Suspension of driving privileges, **Veh
13202.6**
Traffic signs and signals, **Veh 21464**

VANPOOL VEHICLES
Definitions, **Veh 668**

VANPOOLING
Financial responsibility, motor vehicle in-
surance, **Veh 16020.3**
Fire extinguishers, **Veh 34509**
First aid kit, **Veh 34509**
Inspection and inspectors, safety, **Veh
34509**
Insurance, motor vehicle insurance, finan-
cial responsibility, **Veh 16020.3**
Maintenance, **Veh 34509**
Motor vehicle insurance, financial respon-
sibility, **Veh 16020.3**
Records and recordation, maintenance,
Veh 34509
Signs, **Veh 34509**
State highways, bus stops, utilization, **Veh
22525**
Weight, fees, exemption, **Veh 9107**

VANS
Paratransit Vehicles, generally, this index

VECTOR CONTROL DISTRICTS
Mosquito Abatement or Vector Control
Districts, generally, this index

VEGETATION
Weeds, generally, this index

VEHICLE
Generally, **Veh 1 et seq.**
Motor Vehicles, generally, this index

VEHICLE CODE
Generally, **Veh 1 et seq.**
Actions and proceedings, pending actions,
Veh 4
Application, uniformity, **Veh 21**
Construction, **Veh 2, 6**
Continuation of existing law, **Veh 2**
Definitions, **Veh 11 et seq., 100 et seq.**
Delegation of powers and duties, **Veh 8**
English language, written instruments, **Veh
9**
Headings, construction, **Veh 7**
Mail and mailing, notice, **Veh 22**
Notice, mail and mailing, **Veh 22**
Pending actions, **Veh 4**
Reference to statutes, **Veh 10**
Severability, **Veh 5**
Tenure of office, **Veh 3**

VEHICLE CODE—Cont'd
Title, **Veh 1**
Uniformity of application, **Veh 21**
Vested rights, **Veh 4**
Written instruments, English language,
Veh 9

VEHICLE EMISSIONS
Motor vehicles. Air Pollution, this index

VEHICLE INSPECTION AND REPAIR FUND
Deposits, emission control fines and penalties, **Veh 9250.18**

VEHICLE VERIFIERS
Generally, **Veh 11300 et seq.**

VEHICLE WEIGHT LIMITS ACT
Generally, **Veh 35551**

VEHICLES
Generally, **Veh 1 et seq.**
Motor Vehicles, generally, this index

VENDOR AND PURCHASER
Definitions, private party vehicle markets,
Veh 12102
Motor vehicles department, message dis-
play systems, contracts, **Veh 1656.5**

VENISON
Deer. Fish and Game, this index

VENTURA COUNTY
South coast air quality management district. Air Pollution, this index

VENTURA COUNTY STATE COLLEGE
Colleges and Universities, generally, this
index

VENUE
Motor Vehicles, this index

VESSELS
Boats and Boating, generally, this index
Definitions, registration and transfer, **Veh
9840**
Ships and Shipping, generally, this index

VETERANS
Benefits, drivers licenses, applications, **Veh
12811**
Blind Persons, this index
Definitions. Disabled veterans, post
Disabled veterans,
Curbs, marking for parking, **Veh 21458**
Definitions, parking exemptions, **Veh
295.7**
Motor Vehicles, this index
Parking,
Curbs, marking, **Veh 21458**
Handicapped zones, **Veh 22511.5 et
seq.**
Traffic Rules and Regulations, this in-
dex
Drivers licenses,
Benefits, applications, **Veh 12811**
Discharge, continuation, **Veh 12817**

VETERANS—Cont'd
Fees, prisoners of war, special motor vehi-
cle license plates, **Veh 5101.5**
Fines and penalties, parking, **Veh 42001.13**
Foreign states, parking exemptions, **Veh
22511.5**
Handicapped persons. Disabled veterans,
generally, ante
Licenses and permits, prisoners of war,
motor vehicle license plates, **Veh
5101.5**
Motor Vehicles, this index
Motorcycles, this index
Paraplegics, motor vehicle fees, exemp-
tions, **Veh 9105**
Parking,
Disabled veterans, exemptions, placards,
Veh 9105
Fines and penalties, **Veh 42001.13**
Meters, license plates, special plates,
rates and charges, exemptions, **Veh
22511.3**
Placards, disabled veterans, parking, **Veh
22511.5 et seq.**
Prisoners of war. Military Forces, this
index
Traffic Rules and Regulations, this index

VETERANS AFFAIRS DEPARTMENT
Motor vehicles, license plates, special
plates, **Veh 5156**

VETERANS ORGANIZATIONS
Motor Vehicles, this index
Traffic rules and regulations, disabled veterans, parking exemptions, **Veh
22511.5 et seq.**

VETERINARIANS
Drugs and Medicine, generally, this index
Medical waste. Hazardous Substances
and Waste, this index
Medicine. Drugs and Medicine, general-
ly, this index

VIADUCTS
Explosives, vehicle transporting, avoid-
ance, **Veh 31614**
Local authorities, powers, **Veh 21109**
Traffic Rules and Regulations, this index
Weight of motor vehicle, restriction, **Veh
35753**

VIDEO DISPLAY DEVICES
Solid waste, motor carriers, **Veh 27000**
Fines and penalties, **Veh 42001.20**

VIDEOTAPE
Motor vehicles, equipment, **Veh 27602**

VINES
Grapes and Grapevines, generally, this index

VISIBILITY
Traffic Rules and Regulations, this index

VISION
Blind Persons, generally, this index

VISION—Cont'd
Eyes and Eyesight, generally, this index

VISITATION
Driving under the influence, youthful drunk driver visitation program, **Veh 23509 et seq.**
Traffic rules and regulations, youthful drunk driver visitation program, **Veh 23509 et seq.**
Youthful drunk driver visitation program, **Veh 23509 et seq.**

VISUALLY IMPAIRED PERSONS
Blind Persons, generally, this index

VITAL STATISTICS
Birth certificates,
 Fraud, motor vehicle identification card, **Veh 13007.5**
 Identification cards, verification, **Veh 13007.5**

VOCATIONAL EDUCATION
Correctional Institutions, this index
Driving Schools, generally, this index

VOCATIONAL NURSING
Blood tests, intoxicated driver, **Veh 23158**
Driving while intoxicated, blood tests, **Veh 23158**
Motor vehicles, driving while intoxicated, blood tests, **Veh 23158**

VODKA
Alcoholic Beverages, generally, this index

VOLTAGE
Motor vehicle lighting equipment, **Veh 24252**

VOLUNTEER FIREFIGHTERS AND FIRE DEPARTMENTS
Firefighters and Fire Departments, this index

VOLUNTEERS
Ambulances, drivers, emergency medical training, exemptions, **Veh 12527**
Definitions, law enforcement, **Veh 22651.05**
Law enforcement, motor vehicles, removal, **Veh 22651.05**
Motor vehicles, law enforcement, removal, **Veh 22651.05**
Traffic rules and regulations, law enforcement, removal of vehicles, **Veh 22651.05**

VOTERS AND VOTING
Elections, generally, this index

VOTERS REGISTRATION LAW
Registration of voters. Elections, this index

WAGES
Compensation and Salaries, generally, this index

WALL PANELS
Traffic rules and regulations, width of vehicle or load, stacks, **Veh 35780.5**

WALLET GUN
Weapons, generally, this index

WALLS
Advertisements. Outdoor Advertising, generally, this index
Outdoor Advertising, generally, this index

WAR AND CIVIL DEFENSE
Motor vehicle offenses, conviction of offenses required by governors order, inadmissibility in negligence actions, **Veh 40830**
Police escorts, national emergency personnel and supplies, siren and speed, **Veh 21057**
Prisoners of war. Military Forces, this index
Traffic rules and regulations, violation required by orders, of Act, defense, **Veh 41402**
Veterans, generally, this index

WARDS
Guardian and Ward, generally, this index

WARNING SIGNALS AND DEVICES
Motor Vehicles, this index

WARNINGS
Alley exits, watching for pedestrians and bicyclists, **Veh 21356.5**
Pocket bikes, stickers, **Veh 9955**
Traffic signs and signals, automatic enforcement systems, **Veh 21455.5**

WARRANTIES
Motor Vehicles, this index
Recreational vehicles, franchises, **Veh 3075**

WARRANTS
Highway patrol, authority to serve, **Veh 2411**
Motor Vehicles, this index
Searches and Seizures, this index
Traffic Rules and Regulations, this index

WASTE
Hazardous Substances and Waste, generally, this index
Radioactive waste. Atomic Energy, generally, this index
Solid Waste, generally, this index

WATER CARRIERS
Ships and Shipping, generally, this index

WATER CONSERVATION DISTRICTS
Levees and Flood Control, generally, this index

WATER QUALITY
San Mateo County, storm water, managers and management, **Veh 9250.5**
Storm water, San Mateo County, managers and management, **Veh 9250.5**

WATER STORAGE
Agricultural vehicles equipped with water tanks, registration, exemption, **Veh 36101**

WATER TANKS
Agricultural vehicles equipped with water tanks, registration, exemption, **Veh 36101**

WATER TENDER VEHICLES
Definitions, motor vehicles, **Veh 676.5**
Flashing amber warning lights, display, **Veh 25281**

WATER WAGONS
Special highway construction equipment, definitions, **Veh 565**

WATER WELLS
Drilling machinery,
 Length exemptions, drought areas, **Veh 35400**
 Motor carried equipment, length, **Veh 35407**

WATERCRAFT
Boats and Boating, generally, this index
Ships and Shipping, generally, this index

WATERFOWL
Fish and Game, generally, this index

WATERS AND WATER COURSES
Boats and Boating, generally, this index
Definitions, registration and transfer of vessels, **Veh 9840**
Fish and Game, generally, this index
Levees and Flood Control, generally, this index
Motor vehicle operation restrictions on banks, **Veh 21116**
Public Policy, generally, this index

WAYS
Highways and Roads, generally, this index

WEAPONS
Assault and Battery, this index
Concealed weapons, motor vehicles, children and minors, drivers licenses, suspension, **Veh 13202.4**
Crimes and offenses, second and subsequent offenses, children and minors, concealed weapons, **Veh 13202.4**
Destructive devices. Explosives, generally, this index
Explosives, generally, this index
Highway Patrol, this index
Motor carriers, explosives, transportation, **Veh 31600 et seq.**
Motor vehicles,
 Concealed weapons, children and minors, drivers licenses, suspension, **Veh 13202.4**
 Discharging, off highway vehicles, **Veh 38318**

WEAPONS—Cont'd

Motor vehicles—Cont'd

Drivers licenses,

Children and minors, concealed weapons, revocation or suspension, **Veh 13202.4**

Use of vehicle as, revocation or suspension, **Veh 13351.5**

Report of bullet marks, **Veh 10653**

Transportation of smokeless powder, **Veh 31619**

Off highway vehicles, discharging at vehicle or occupant, **Veh 38318**

Traffic signs and signals, interference with, shooting, **Veh 21464**

WEARING APPAREL

Uniforms, generally, this index

WEATHER

Motor vehicles, headlamps, inclement weather, **Veh 24400**

Traffic rules and regulations, speed, regard for existing conditions, **Veh 22350**

WEEDS

Amber lights, control vehicles, **Veh 25261**

Lights and lighting, weed control vehicles, **Veh 25261**

Motor vehicles, amber warning lights, weed control vehicles, **Veh 25261**

Mowers, special highway construction equipment, definitions, **Veh 565**

WEEKEND SERVICE OF SENTENCE PROGRAM

Driving under the influence, **Veh 23536, 23580**

WEIGHTS AND MEASURES

Buses, this index

Certificates and certification,

Fees, payment, **Veh 5206**

Motor vehicles, load removal, **Veh 2803**

Crimes and offenses, motor vehicles, gross weight, **Veh 42030.1**

Damages to highway or bridge due to excess weight, liability, **Veh 17301**

Inspection and inspectors, commercial vehicles, registration, **Veh 4000.6**

Instruments used, certification as accurate, **Veh 2809**

Metric system, traffic signs, **Veh 21351.3**

Traffic Rules and Regulations, this index

Traffic Signs and Signals, this index

Unladen weight, definitions, motor vehicles, **Veh 660, 661**

WELDERS

Special highway construction equipment, definitions, **Veh 565**

WHEELCHAIRS

Buses, this index

Handicapped parking, special enforcement units, motorized, **Veh 22507.9**

Motor vehicles, license plates, lifts, carriers, obstructions, **Veh 5201**

WHEELCHAIRS—Cont'd

Public transit vehicles, safety certification, **Veh 34501.1**

WHISKEY

Alcoholic Beverages, generally, this index

WHITE CANES

Blind Persons, this index

WHITE LIGHTS

Emergency vehicles, flashing lights, **Veh 25258**

WHITETOP

Weeds, generally, this index

WHOLESALERS

Motor Vehicles, this index

WIDTH

Door handles, hinges, cable cinchers and chain binders, **Veh 35110**

Motor carriers, inspection, **Veh 2802**

Traffic Rules and Regulations, this index

Weights and Measures, generally, this index

WILD ANIMALS AND BIRDS

Fish and Game, generally, this index

WILDERNESS AREAS

Off highway vehicles, **Veh 38301.3**

WILDLIFE

Fish and Game, generally, this index

WILDLIFE AREAS

Fish and Game, this index

WILLFULLY

Definitions, gross polluters, motor vehicle emissions, crimes and offenses, **Veh 27156**

WILLS

Administrators, executors and administrators. Probate Proceedings, this index

Anatomical Gifts, generally, this index

Gifts, Devises and Bequests, generally, this index

Probate Proceedings, generally, this index

WINDOWS

Motor Vehicles, this index

WINDSHIELD WIPERS

Motor vehicles,

Maintenance in good operating condition, **Veh 26707**

Self operating wipers, **Veh 26706**

WINDSHIELDS

Agricultural machinery and equipment, exemptions, **Veh 36515, 36520**

Motorcycles, **Veh 26701, 26705**

WIRELESS TELECOMMUNICATIONS

Telecommunications, this index

WIRELESS TELEPHONE AUTOMOBILE SAFETY ACT

Generally, **Veh 12810.3, 23123**

WITNESSES

Motor Vehicles, this index

Privileges and Immunities, generally, this index

Reports, accidents, common carriers, **Veh 20009**

Subpoenas, generally, this index

Traffic Rules and Regulations, this index

WOMEN

Midwives, generally, this index

WOOD

Timber and Lumber, generally, this index

WOODLANDS

Forests and Forestry, generally, this index

WORDS AND PHRASES

Abandoned vehicle abatement, funds, **Veh 22710**

Ability to pay, traffic judgments, **Veh 42003**

Ability to respond in damages, motor vehicle insurance, **Veh 102**

Actual fraud, motor vehicles, license revocations, **Veh 11705**

Advertisement, motor vehicles, dealers, **Veh 11614, 11713.1**

Aerodynamic devices, motor carriers, width of vehicle or load, **Veh 35110**

Affiliate, motor vehicles, engine manufacturer different from vehicle manufacturer, **Veh 9980**

Agency, arrest, quotas, peace officers, **Veh 41601.5**

Agricultural irrigation supplies, motor vehicles, public lands, inspection and inspectors, **Veh 2810.2**

Agricultural water well boring rig, **Veh 105**

Air brakes, motor vehicles, **Veh 108**

Alcoholic beverages, motor vehicles, **Veh 109**

All terrain vehicle safety instructor, instructional programs, safety training, **Veh 111.3**

All terrain vehicle safety training organization, instructional programs, safety training, **Veh 111.5**

All terrain vehicles, instructional programs, safety training, **Veh 111**

Alley, motor vehicles, **Veh 110**

Amber, motor vehicle equipment, **Veh 112**

Amphibious vehicles, registration, **Veh 9872.5**

Antisiphoning device, motor vehicles, **Veh 28110**

Antiterrorism activities, antiterrorism fund, **Veh 5066**

Application, motor vehicles, consumer protection, recovery corporation, **Veh 12200**

Approaches, vehicular crossings, **Veh 23255**

WORDS AND PHRASES—Cont'd

Appropriate victims, youthful drunk driver visitation program, **Veh 23517**

Appurtenances, recreational vehicles, width, **Veh 35103**

Area of responsibility, motor vehicles, franchises, **Veh 11713.3**

Armored car, **Veh 115**

Arrest quota, peace officers, **Veh 41600**

Authorized emergency vehicle, **Veh 165**

Auto buying service, **Veh 166**

Autobroker, **Veh 166**

Autoette, **Veh 175**

Automated enforcement system, traffic rules and regulations, **Veh 210**

Automated rail crossing enforcement system, traffic rules and regulations, **Veh 210**

Automatic bale wagon, motor vehicles, **Veh 36011**

Automobile dismantler, **Veh 220, 221**

Automobile dismantlers tow vehicle, **Veh 615**

Automobile driver training, **Veh 223**

Autonomous technology, motor vehicles, **Veh 38750**

Autonomous vehicles, **Veh 38750**

Auxiliary dolly, motor vehicles, **Veh 225**

Axle, motor vehicles, **Veh 230**

B train assembly, motor vehicles, **Veh 230.5**

Bail, traffic rules and regulations, amnesty, **Veh 42008.7**

Bicycle dealer, **Veh 39006**

Bicycle path, **Veh 231.5**

Bicycle path crossings, **Veh 231.6**

Bicycles, **Veh 231**
  Licenses, **Veh 39000**
  Traffic rules and regulations, **Veh 21200**

Bike path, **Veh 231.5**

Blind, traffic rules and regulations, **Veh 21965**

Board, motor vehicles, **Veh 232**

Bulk packaging,
  Hazardous substances and waste, route notification, **Veh 32050**
  Transportation of inhalation hazards, **Veh 32101**

Bumpers, motor vehicles, **Veh 28071**

Buses, **Veh 233**
  Limousines, **Veh 14602.9**

Business, motor vehicles, **Veh 234**

Business and residence districts, motor vehicles, **Veh 240**

Business day, motor vehicles, private property, removal, **Veh 22658**

Business district, motor vehicles, **Veh 235**

Business representative, motor vehicles, **Veh 236**

Buy here pay here, motor vehicles, dealers, used vehicles, **Veh 241, 241.1**

Cable television company, **Veh 25274**

California highway patrol, **Veh 2102**

Camp trailer, **Veh 242**

Camper, motor vehicles, **Veh 243**

Cancellation, drivers licenses, **Veh 13100**

WORDS AND PHRASES—Cont'd

Car share vehicles, parking, exclusive use spaces, **Veh 22507.1**

Cargo body, motor carriers, hazardous substances and waste, **Veh 32001**

Cargo tank, motor vehicle load, **Veh 34003**

Carryall, motor vehicles, **Veh 245**

Cash price,
  Motor vehicle sales, **Veh 11713.1**
  Used vehicles, cancellation option agreements, conditional sales, **Veh 11713.21**

Casual drivers, driving records, **Veh 1808.1**

Cause of action, financial responsibility, motor vehicle insurance, **Veh 16251**

Certificate of compliance, motor vehicles, **Veh 246**

Certified paramedic, blood test, **Veh 23158**

Certified record of permanent exportation,
  Inspection and cancellation of titles, vehicles, **Veh 6161**
  Motor vehicles, **Veh 6161**

Charter party carriers, limousines, **Veh 14602.9**

Chop shop, motor vehicles, **Veh 250**

Citation, peace officers arrest quota, **Veh 41601**

City,
  Motor vehicles, **Veh 255**
  Traffic safety fund, **Veh 42200**

Clean air stickers, motor vehicles, forgery, counterfeiting, **Veh 4463**

Clean fuel vehicle, **Veh 257**

Closed course, off highway vehicle registration, **Veh 38014**

Collector, historic vehicles, **Veh 5051**

Collector motor vehicle, **Veh 259**

Combustible liquids, motor vehicle load, **Veh 34003**

Commercial drivers license, regulation, **Veh 15210**

Commercial motor vehicle,
  Permits, **Veh 34601**
  Regulation, **Veh 15210**

Commercial purchaser, motor vehicle sales, **Veh 11713.1**

Commercial vehicle, **Veh 260**

Commissioner,
  Highway patrol, **Veh 265**
  Motorcycle safety, **Veh 2930**

Community service, vandalism, defacing property, **Veh 13202.6**

Component parts for passenger motor vehicles, **Veh 5505**

Computer vendors, motor vehicles, dealers, records and recordation, privacy, **Veh 11713.25**

Confidential dealer computer records, motor vehicles, privacy, **Veh 11713.25**

Consignments, motor vehicle dealers, **Veh 266**

Construction vehicles, backup devices or alarms, **Veh 27000**

Constructive fraud, motor vehicles, license revocations, **Veh 11705**

WORDS AND PHRASES—Cont'd

Consumers,
  Autobroker registration, **Veh 11735**
  Motor vehicles, consumer protection, recovery corporation, **Veh 12200**

Controlled substance, commercial motor vehicle and driver regulation, **Veh 15210**

Conviction,
  Commercial motor vehicles, **Veh 15210**
  Concealed weapons, minors, **Veh 13202.4**
  Drivers licenses, **Veh 13202.5**
    Compact, **Veh 15021**
  Nolo contendere pleas, driving school licenses, **Veh 11110.7**
  Vandalism, defacing property, **Veh 13202.6**

Cooking equipment, recreational vehicles, **Veh 28060**

Cotton module mover, agricultural machinery and equipment, **Veh 36012**

Counter report of a property damage accident, motor vehicles, **Veh 20015**

County, motor vehicles, **Veh 270, 9250.12**

Course provider, driving schools, mature driver improvement courses, **Veh 1675**

Court facilities trust fund, night court, assessments, traffic rules and regulations, **Veh 42006**

Court supervised program, traffic schools, administrative fees, **Veh 42007**

Credit card,
  Motor vehicles,
    Impounding, **Veh 14602.6, 14602.7**
      Driving under the influence, second and subsequent offenses, **Veh 14602.8**
      Repossessors and repossession, **Veh 23118**
    Towing, storage, **Veh 22651.1, 22658**
  Taxicabs, impounding, **Veh 21100.4**

Crib sheet, motor vehicle drivers license examinations, **Veh 273**

Cribbing device, motor vehicle drivers license examinations, **Veh 273**

Critical need to drive,
  Children and minors, revoked or suspended licenses, driving while intoxicated, **Veh 13353.8**
  Drivers licenses, **Veh 13202.5**

Crossing control arm, school buses, length, **Veh 35400**

Crosswalk, **Veh 275**

Cruising, traffic control points, **Veh 21100**

Darkness, motor vehicles, **Veh 280**

Day, motor vehicles, forfeitures, unlicensed drivers, **Veh 14607.6**

Dealer, motor vehicles, **Veh 285, 286**

Dealer computer systems, motor vehicles, records and recordation, privacy, **Veh 11713.25**

Dealership, recreational vehicles, franchises, **Veh 3072**

WORDS

WORDS AND PHRASES—Cont'd

Deceit, motor vehicles, license revocation, **Veh 11705**

Declaration that the vehicle will not be permanently located outside the United States, **Veh 6161**

Inspection and cancellation of titles, **Veh 6161**

Declared combined gross weight, motor vehicles, **Veh 288**

Declared gross vehicle weight, motor vehicles, **Veh 289**

Department,
Highway patrol, **Veh 2101**
Equipment of vehicles, **Veh 24000**
Motor vehicles, **Veh 290, 38750**
Traffic rules and regulations, **Veh 21000**

Deployed, motor vehicles, registration, renewal, military forces, waiver, **Veh 9560**

Designated commercial zone, foreign commercial motor carriers, **Veh 34517**

Designated local transportation officers, taxicabs, impounding, **Veh 21100.4**

Direction and control, commercial vehicles, employers, powers and duties, **Veh 15242**

Director, motor vehicles, **Veh 295**

Disabled person, parking permits, **Veh 295.5**

Disabled person placard, motor vehicles, **Veh 4461, 4463**

Disabled veterans, parking, **Veh 295.7**

Disqualification, commercial motor vehicle and driver regulation, **Veh 15210**

Distributor, motor vehicles, **Veh 296**

District, buses, bicycles, length, Sacramento City and County, **Veh 35400.8**

District attorney, motor vehicles, forfeitures, unlicensed drivers, **Veh 14607.6**

Dollies, motor vehicles, **Veh 225**

Double parallel solid lines, traffic signs and signals, **Veh 21460**

Drawbar, motor vehicles, **Veh 300**

Driveaway towaway operation, motor vehicles, **Veh 303**

Driver, motor vehicles, **Veh 305**

Driver records, motor carriers, maintenance facilities, inspection, **Veh 34501.12**

Drivers licenses,
Fraudulent license, **Veh 14610**
Motor vehicles, **Veh 310**

Driving a commercial vehicle under the influence, **Veh 15210**

Driving instructor, driving schools, **Veh 310.4**

Driving record history, motor vehicles, license suspension or revocation, **Veh 14601.3**

Driving school operator, **Veh 310.8**

Driving school owner, **Veh 311**

Driving schools, **Veh 310.6**

Drugs,
Motor vehicles, **Veh 312**
Vehicle Code, **Veh 312**

WORDS AND PHRASES—Cont'd

Ecological reserve, highway access, **Veh 21117**

Economic automobile theft, **Veh 10901**
Prevention, **Veh 10901**

Effective oversight, parking enforcement, processing agencies, **Veh 40200.6**

Electric personal assistive mobility device, **Veh 313**

Electronic wireless communications devices, traffic rules and regulations, **Veh 23124**

Eligible claims, motor vehicles, consumer protection, recovery corporation, **Veh 12200**

Eligible family members, Gold Star Families, motor vehicles, special license plates, **Veh 5156**

Emergency, motor vehicles, size and weight limitation exemptions, **Veh 35002**

Emergency ambulance, resuscitation equipment, **Veh 2418.5**

Emergency move, motor carriers, **Veh 34631.5**

Emergency response situation, transporting persons in back of trucks, **Veh 23116**

Emergency road service,
Motor vehicles, **Veh 2436**
Tow truck driver certification, **Veh 2430.1**

Emergency roadside assistance, motor vehicles, **Veh 2436**

Emergency vehicles, **Veh 165**

Employer,
Commercial motor vehicle and driver regulation, **Veh 15210**
Emergency roadside assistance, **Veh 2436**
Tow truck driver certification, **Veh 2430.1**

Employing, motor carriers, reports, replacement, **Veh 34501.18**

Encumbered funds, motor vehicles, registration, fingerprints and fingerprinting, fees, **Veh 9250.19**

Engaged in a business, station wagons, weight fees, **Veh 9404**

Engineering and traffic survey, motor vehicles, **Veh 627**

Environmental license plates, motor vehicles, **Veh 5103**

EPAMD, electric personal assistive mobility devices, **Veh 313**

Essential parts, motor vehicles, **Veh 315**

Established place of business, motor vehicles, **Veh 320**

Evidence of financial responsibility,
Drivers license examination, **Veh 12804.9**
Motor vehicle financial responsibility, **Veh 16020**

Explosives, transportation on highway, **Veh 31600**

WORDS AND PHRASES—Cont'd

Export,
Inspection and cancellation of titles, exported vehicles, **Veh 6161**
Motor vehicles, **Veh 6161**

Express consent, motor vehicles, dealers, computers, records and recordation, privacy, **Veh 11713.25**

Expressways, counties, **Veh 314**

Extralegal load, **Veh 320.5**

Facsimile of a light bar, motor vehicles, **Veh 27606**

Factory built building, school buildings, motor vehicles, **Veh 321**

Family, motor vehicles, license plates, special plates,
Congressional Medal of Honor, **Veh 5101.6**
Firefighters and fire departments, **Veh 5101.2**
Military forces, decorations for valor, **Veh 5101.4**
Prisoners of war, **Veh 5101.5**
Purple Heart recipients, **Veh 5101.8**

Family members, motor vehicles, franchises, sales, **Veh 11713.3**

Farm labor vehicle, **Veh 322**

Farm products, motor carriers, hours of service, **Veh 34501.2**

Farm trailer, agricultural machinery and equipment, **Veh 36010**

Fatality, commercial motor vehicles, **Veh 15210**

Felonies, commercial motor vehicle and driver regulation, **Veh 15210**

Final determination, traffic violators schools, discrimination, **Veh 11216.2**

Fines, traffic rules and regulations, amnesty, **Veh 42008.7**

Fire apparatus, emergency vehicles, **Veh 35002**

Fire chief, hazardous substances and waste, route notification, **Veh 32050**

Firefighting equipment, drivers licenses, **Veh 12804.11**

First point of processing or packing, motor carriers, hours of service, **Veh 34501.2**

First stage manufacturers, house cars, **Veh 11930**

Flammable liquids, motor vehicle load, **Veh 34003**

Fleet owner, inspection and maintenance stations, **Veh 2525**

For hire, paratransit vehicles, **Veh 462**

For hire motor carrier of property, permits, **Veh 34601**

Foreclosure documents, limousines, **Veh 14602.9**

Foreign,
Jurisdiction, motor vehicles, **Veh 325**
Vehicle, **Veh 330**

Former prisoner of war, license plates, **Veh 324.5**

Frame, motor vehicle ground clearance, **Veh 24008.5**

WORDS AND PHRASES—Cont'd

Frame heights, motor vehicle ground clearance, **Veh 24008.5**

Franchise, motor vehicles, **Veh 331**

Franchisee, motor vehicles, **Veh 331.1**

Franchisor, motor vehicles, **Veh 331.2**

Fraud,
    Lessor retailers, **Veh 11613**
    Motor vehicles, license revocations, **Veh 11705**

Freeway, **Veh 332**

Freeway service patrol,
    Emergency roadside assistance, **Veh 2436**
    Tow truck driver certification, **Veh 2430.1**

Front end assembly, motor vehicles, **Veh 5505**

Full time, motor carriers, officers and employees, reports, replacement, **Veh 34501.18**

Fund,
    Motor carriers, motor vehicle account, **Veh 34602**
    Motorcycle safety, **Veh 2930**

Funeral escort, Los Angeles County, **Veh 21100.7**

Funeral procession, Los Angeles County, **Veh 21100.7**

Gantry truck, **Veh 335**

Garage, **Veh 340**

General public paratransit vehicle, **Veh 336**

General supervision, phlebotomy technicians, driving under the influence, blood tests, **Veh 23158**

Golf cart, **Veh 345**

Goods or services, motor vehicles, dealers, rates and charges, **Veh 11713.19**

Green, traffic signals, **Veh 21451**

Gross combination weight rating,
    Commercial motor vehicle and driver regulation, **Veh 15210**
    Motor vehicles, **Veh 350**

Gross vehicle weight rating,
    Commercial motor vehicle and driver regulation, **Veh 15210**
    Motor vehicles, **Veh 350**

Guaranteed traffic arrest bail bond, **Veh 40305.5**

Guaranteed traffic arrest bail bond certificate, **Veh 40305.5**

GVWR, motor vehicles ground clearance, **Veh 24008.5**

Harmful waste matter, illegal dumping, traffic rules and regulations, impounding, **Veh 23112.7**

Hazardous materials, transportation, **Veh 353**

Hazardous substances, highway spill containment and abatement, **Veh 2452**

Health care professional, motor vehicles, **Veh 12804.9**

Heavy duty, transit district vehicles, emission standards, **Veh 28114**

WORDS AND PHRASES—Cont'd

Highway, **Veh 360, 591**
    Motor vehicles, **Veh 592**

Highway service organization, emergency roadside assistance, **Veh 2436**

Historic vehicles, special identification plates, **Veh 5004**

Home state, Drivers License Compact, **Veh 15021**

House car, **Veh 362**

Housing authorities, traffic rules and regulations, **Veh 21113**

Ice cream truck, commercial vending vehicles, **Veh 22456**

Identifiable vehicle component, motor vehicle theft, **Veh 2805**

Identification, off highway vehicles, **Veh 38013**

Illegal dumping, traffic rules and regulations, impounding, **Veh 23112.7**

Immediate safety hazard, agricultural machinery and equipment, **Veh 24002.5, 31402**

Immediately, driving under the influence, Notice, suspension order, **Veh 13382**
    Parole and probation, drivers licenses, revocation or suspension, **Veh 13389**
    Reports, **Veh 13380**
        Children and minors, **Veh 13388**

Imminent hazard, commercial motor vehicles, **Veh 15210**

Implement of husbandry, **Veh 36005**
    Traffic rules and regulations, **Veh 36000**

Imprisonment, driving under influence of alcohol or drugs, second and subsequent offenses, **Veh 23580**

Incentive, motor vehicle sales, **Veh 11713.1**

Incident command at the scene of an on highway hazardous substance incident, **Veh 2454**

Inclement weather, motor vehicles, headlamps, **Veh 24400**

Incompetent operator, traffic rules and regulations, **Veh 12809**

Information, motor vehicles, keys, **Veh 9954**

Infractions, **Veh 40000.1, 40000.3**

Inhalation hazards, transportation, **Veh 32101**

Inoperable parking meters, **Veh 22508.5**

Inoperable parking payment centers, **Veh 22508.5**

Inspection and maintenance station, fleet owners, **Veh 2525**

Inspection stop, transportation of inhalation hazards, **Veh 32101**

Intermodal chassis, **Veh 34505.9**
    Ocean marine terminals, intermodal roadability inspection program, **Veh 34505.9**
    Safety regulations, **Veh 34505.9**

Intersection, **Veh 365**

Intoxicating liquors, motor vehicles, **Veh 109**

Issuing agency, toll evasion, **Veh 40250**

WORDS AND PHRASES—Cont'd

Itemized invoices, motor vehicles, towing, **Veh 22651**

Judgment, financial responsibility, motor vehicle insurance, **Veh 16250**

Land, drinking, motor vehicles, **Veh 23220**

Legal owners,
    Motor vehicles, **Veh 370**
    Registration and transfer of vessels, **Veh 9840**

Lessee, lease contracts, **Veh 371**

Lessor, motor vehicle lease contracts, **Veh 372**

Lessor retailer, motor vehicle leasing, **Veh 373**

Licensed renderer, inedible kitchen grease, **Veh 2460**

Light bar, motor vehicles, **Veh 27606**

Light duty, low emission vehicles, **Veh 28113**

Lighting equipment, motor vehicles, **Veh 375**

Limit line, motor vehicles, **Veh 377**

Liquefied petroleum gas, motor vehicles, **Veh 380**

Load, motor vehicles, **Veh 655**

Local agencies, parking, buses, videotape, transit only traffic lanes, **Veh 40240**

Local authorities, motor vehicles, **Veh 385**

Local entities, tow truck driver certification, **Veh 2430.1**

Local public agency, streetsweeping, parking, enforcement, **Veh 40246**

Local street or road, speed traps, **Veh 40802**

Location, night court, assessments, traffic rules and regulations, **Veh 42006**

Locked container, open containers, motor vehicles, **Veh 23225**

Logging dolly, motor vehicles, **Veh 385.2**

Logging vehicles, **Veh 385.3**

Low speed vehicle, **Veh 385.5, 21250**

Maintenance facility or terminal, motor vehicle safety inspections, **Veh 34515**

Maintenance records, motor carriers, inspection, **Veh 34501.12**

Major component parts for motorcycles, **Veh 5505**

Major component parts for trucks, truck type or bus type vehicles, motor vehicles, **Veh 5505**

Managerial employee, motor vehicle licenses, dealers, manufacturers, **Veh 386**

Manufactured homes, motor vehicles, **Veh 387**

Manufacturer, motor vehicles,
    Autonomous vehicles, **Veh 38750**
    Bumpers, **Veh 24011.3**

Manufacturer branch, motor vehicles, **Veh 389**

Mass transit vehicle, high occupancy vehicle lanes, **Veh 21655.5**

Maximum penalties, handicapped persons, parking,
    Placards, **Veh 22511.55**

WORDS

WORDS AND PHRASES—Cont'd

Maximum penalties, handicapped persons, parking—Cont'd
Temporary placards, **Veh 22511.59**
May, **Veh 15**
Medium duty, low emission vehicles, **Veh 28113**
Metal tire, **Veh 395**
Minor component parts for motorcycles, **Veh 5505**
Minors, motor vehicles, **Veh 17700**
Mobile billboard advertising displays, **Veh 395.5**
Mobile electronic devices, motor vehicle insurance, financial responsibility, evidence, **Veh 16028**
Moped, **Veh 406**
Motor carrier, **Veh 34501.12**
Safety regulations, **Veh 408**
Motor carrier of property, permits, **Veh 34601**
Motor driven cycle, **Veh 405**
Motor truck, **Veh 410**
Motor vehicle dealership,
Franchises, satellite warranty facilities, **Veh 3062**
Recreational vehicles, franchises, **Veh 3072**
Motor vehicle operated for compensation to transport persons, low emission vehicles, **Veh 28113**
Motor vehicle speed contests, crimes and offenses, **Veh 23109**
Motor vehicles, **Veh 415**
Keys, information, **Veh 9954**
Seatbelts, **Veh 27315**
Motorcycles, **Veh 400**
Motorized bicycles, **Veh 406**
Motorized quadricycle, vehicle registration, **Veh 407**
Motorized scooters, **Veh 407.5**
Motorized tricycle, vehicle registration, **Veh 407**
Motorsports, semitrailers, length, special permits, **Veh 35401.5**
Mufflers, motor vehicles, **Veh 425**
Multiple lane highway, school buses, stopping, overtaking, **Veh 22454**
Negligent operator, traffic rules and regulations, **Veh 12810.5**
New motor vehicle dealer, **Veh 426**
New vehicle, **Veh 430**
Newspaper display advertisements, motor vehicles, sales, **Veh 11713.1**
NMVTIS (national motor vehicle title information system), dealers, used vehicles, history, reports, disclosure, **Veh 11713.26**
NMVTIS (national motor vehicle title information system) data providers, dealers, used vehicles, history, reports, disclosure, **Veh 11713.26**
NMVTIS (national motor vehicle title information system) operators, dealers, used vehicles, history, reports, disclosure, **Veh 11713.26**

WORDS AND PHRASES—Cont'd

NMVTIS (national motor vehicle title information system) vehicle history reports, dealers, used vehicles, disclosure, **Veh 11713.26**
No damage, motor vehicle bumper strength notices, **Veh 24011.3**
Noncommercial motor vehicle, **Veh 15210**
Nonrepairable vehicle, motor vehicles, **Veh 431**
Nonrepairable vehicle certificate, motor vehicles, **Veh 432**
Nonresident, motor vehicles, **Veh 435**
Nonresident commercial drivers license, **Veh 15210**
Nonresident daily commuter, registration exemption, **Veh 435.5**
Normal business hours, motor vehicles, towing, **Veh 22658**
Oaths, motor vehicles, **Veh 16**
Occupant handholds, off highway vehicles, **Veh 38604**
Ocean marine terminal, **Veh 34505.9**
Intermodal roadability inspection program, **Veh 34505.9**
Safety regulations, **Veh 34505.9**
Off highway motor vehicles, **Veh 38006**
Off highway vehicle registration, **Veh 38012**
Off highway motorcycle, **Veh 436**
Official traffic control device, **Veh 440**
Official traffic control signal, **Veh 445**
Offstreet parking facility, **Veh 4000**
Drivers licenses, **Veh 12500, 14605**
Removal of vehicles, **Veh 22651**
Operate,
Ignition interlock devices, **Veh 23575**
Traffic signs and signals, automatic enforcement systems, **Veh 21455.5**
Operator, motor vehicles, autonomous vehicles, **Veh 38750**
Original drivers license, **Veh 455**
Out of service orders, motor vehicles, **Veh 2800**
Owned, ignition interlock devices, **Veh 23575**
Owner,
Inspection and cancellation of titles, exported vehicles, **Veh 6161**
Motor vehicles, **Veh 460, 6161**
Registration and transfer of vessels, **Veh 9840**
Paging, buses, illuminated signs, **Veh 25353**
Santa Monica, advertisements, **Veh 25353.1**
University of California, Irvine, **Veh 25354**
Paratransit vehicle, **Veh 462**
Parking, motor vehicles, **Veh 463**
Parking lamps, vehicle lighting equipment, **Veh 24801**
Parking penalty, **Veh 40200.4**
Participant, motor vehicles, consumer protection, recovery corporation, **Veh 12200**

WORDS AND PHRASES—Cont'd

Participation in the pull notice system, driving records, **Veh 1808.1**
Parts car, historic vehicles, **Veh 5051**
Passenger motor vehicle, **Veh 27315.3**
Passenger restraint system, school buses, **Veh 27316, 27316.5**
Passenger transportation vehicles, trailer buses, **Veh 464**
Passenger vehicles, **Veh 465**
Bumper strength, **Veh 24011.3**
Damage control, **Veh 34710**
Pay by plate toll payment, traffic rules and regulations, **Veh 23302**
Peace officer,
Inedible kitchen grease, **Veh 2460**
Motor vehicle violations, written notice, **Veh 40600**
Pedestrians, **Veh 467**
Pedicabs, **Veh 467.5**
Permanent, serious injury, hit and run drivers, **Veh 20001**
Permanently affixed, motor vehicles, advertisements, **Veh 21100**
Personally identifiable consumer data, motor vehicles, dealers, computers, records and recordation, privacy, **Veh 11713.25**
Persons, motor vehicles, lessor retailers, **Veh 11613**
Persons authorized by law to receive the information, motor vehicle drivers license records, **Veh 1807.5**
Pickup truck, **Veh 471**
Pilot car, escort vehicles, **Veh 472**
Pneumatic tire, **Veh 485**
Pocket bikes, **Veh 473**
Pole or pipe dolly, motor vehicles, **Veh 475**
Power brake, **Veh 480**
Power unit, motor carriers, owner operators, **Veh 34624**
Private carrier, permits, **Veh 34601**
Private party vehicle markets, **Veh 12102**
Operators, **Veh 12102**
Private road or driveway, **Veh 490**
Private school, motor vehicles, **Veh 492**
Privately owned and maintained roads, traffic rules and regulations, **Veh 21107.7**
Processing agency,
Parking enforcement, **Veh 40200.6**
Toll evasion, **Veh 40253**
Professional education, traffic violator schools, **Veh 11204**
Program,
Motorcycle safety, **Veh 2930**
Youthful drunk driver visitation program, **Veh 23512**
Properly restrained by a safety belt, motor vehicles, **Veh 27315**
Public transportation agencies, standing vehicles, **Veh 21113**
Purchased, motor vehicles, size and weight limitations, **Veh 35002**
Racing vehicle, **Veh 286**
Driving schools, **Veh 11101**

WORDS AND PHRASES—Cont'd

Real estate development offering golf facilities, regulation of golf cart traffic, **Veh 21115**

Rear clip, motor vehicles, **Veh 5505**

Rear facing auxiliary lamp, motor vehicles, **Veh 24616**

Reasonable access, length of vehicles, **Veh 35400**

Reckless driving, punishment, **Veh 23103**

Recording device, motor vehicles, **Veh 9951**

Recovery corporations, motor vehicles, consumer protection, **Veh 12200**

Recovery fund, motor vehicles, consumer protection, **Veh 12200**

Recreational off highway vehicles, **Veh 500**

Recreational vehicle,
Fire extinguishers, **Veh 28060**
Reports of stored vehicles, **Veh 10658**

Recreational vehicle franchises, **Veh 331.3**

Recreational vehicle line make, franchises, **Veh 3072**

Recut or regrooved tires, motor vehicle equipment, **Veh 27460.5, 27461**

Refrigerator van, motor vehicle equipment, **Veh 28000**

Regional or local entity,
Child passenger restraint systems, **Veh 2430.2**
Emergency roadside assistance, **Veh 2436**
Tow truck driver certification, **Veh 2430.1**

Register, motor vehicles, noise limits, **Veh 27200**

Registered locksmiths, motor vehicles, **Veh 9954**

Registered owner,
Motor vehicles, **Veh 505**
Keys, information, **Veh 9954**
Registration and transfer of vessels, **Veh 9840**
Toll roads and bridges, evasion, **Veh 40250**

Registered owner or lessee, motor vehicles, smog impact fees, foreign states, **Veh 1673**

Registered transporter, inedible kitchen grease, **Veh 2460**

Registrant, motor vehicles, **Veh 8200**

Registration, off highway vehicles, **Veh 38013**

Registration service, motor vehicles, **Veh 505.2**

Registration year, motor vehicles, **Veh 506**

Regular and periodic training, peace officers, pursuit, **Veh 17004.7**

Relevant market area, motor vehicles, **Veh 507**

Remanufactured vehicle, **Veh 507.5**

Remanufacturer, motor vehicles, **Veh 507.8**

Remove and store a vehicle, abandoned vehicles, **Veh 22655.3**

Renter, **Veh 508**

WORDS AND PHRASES—Cont'd

Repair shop, motor vehicles, **Veh 510**

Repeat violator, toll roads and bridges, evasion, notice, time, **Veh 40254**

Repossessors tow vehicle, **Veh 615**

Representative sample, motor carriers, maintenance facilities, inspection, **Veh 34501.12**

Representatives, motor vehicles, **Veh 512**

Rescue team, emergency vehicles, liability, resuscitation attempts, **Veh 165.5**

Residence district, motor vehicles, **Veh 515**

Resident, motor vehicles, **Veh 516**

Residue,
Hazardous substances and waste, route notification, **Veh 32050**
Transportation of inhalation hazards, **Veh 32101**

Resuscitator, ambulance equipment, **Veh 2418.5**

Retail establishment, motor vehicles, notice, removal, **Veh 22658**

Retail sales, motor vehicles, **Veh 520**

Retarder, motor vehicles, **Veh 521**

Reverse, traffic convictions, **Veh 1803.3**

Revived salvage vehicle, **Veh 521.5**

Revocation, drivers licenses, **Veh 13101**

Ridesharing, **Veh 522**
Motor vehicles, **Veh 522**

Right of way, motor vehicles, **Veh 525**

Road, Vehicle Code, **Veh 527**

Roadside rest area or viewpoint, motor vehicles, removal, **Veh 22651**

Roadways, **Veh 530**

Safe parking place, transportation of inhalation hazards, **Veh 32101**

Safe stopping place, transportation of inhalation hazards, **Veh 32101**

Safety bumper, length of buses, **Veh 35400**

Safety glazing material, motor vehicles, **Veh 535**

Safety zone, motor vehicles, **Veh 540**

Sales, motor vehicles, **Veh 5901**

Salvage pool, motor vehicles, **Veh 543**

Salvage vehicle rebuilder, **Veh 543.5**

Satellite warranty facility, motor vehicles, franchises, **Veh 3062**

Satisfactory evidence, parking violations, impoundment or immobilization, **Veh 22651.8**

School pupil activity bus, **Veh 546**

School transportation vehicle, drivers, drugs and medicine, alcoholic beverages, tests, **Veh 34520.3**

School zone, speed traps, **Veh 40802**

Schoolbus, **Veh 545**

Schoolbus accident, motor vehicles, **Veh 12517.1**

Second or subsequent conviction, motor vehicles, driving with suspended license, **Veh 14602.5**

Second stage manufacturers, house cars, **Veh 11930**

Secondhand dealer, private party vehicle markets, **Veh 12101**

WORDS AND PHRASES—Cont'd

Semitrailer, **Veh 550, 630**

Serious bodily injury, motor vehicles, flight from peace officers, **Veh 2800.3**

Serious traffic violation,
Commercial motor vehicle and driver regulation, **Veh 15210**
Speed limits, **Veh 22406**

Shade trailers, **Veh 531**

Shall, **Veh 15**

Short term, drivers license, motorized bicycles, **Veh 12804.9**

Sidewalk, **Veh 555**

Signature, motor vehicles, **Veh 17**

Silage, agricultural machinery and equipment, registration, exemption, **Veh 36101**

Slow moving vehicles, turning out of highway, **Veh 21656**

Snowmobile, **Veh 557**

Solid tire, **Veh 560**

Spark ignition marine engines, certificates and certification, brands, marks and labels, **Veh 9853.7**

Special consideration, parking ticket processing contracts, **Veh 40200.5**

Special construction equipment, **Veh 565**
Motor vehicles, **Veh 570**

Special interest vehicle, historical vehicles, **Veh 5051**

Special mobile equipment, **Veh 575**

Special situation farm products, motor carriers, hours of service, **Veh 34501.2**

Specially constructed vehicle, **Veh 580**

Speed trap, **Veh 40802**

State,
Commercial motor vehicle and driver regulation, **Veh 15210**
Drivers License Compact, **Veh 15021**
Driving under the influence, nonresidents, **Veh 13353.5**

State agency, motor vehicles, license plates, special plates, **Veh 5151**

State of domicile, motor vehicles, **Veh 12505**

State of principal use, registration and transfer of vessels, **Veh 9840**

Station wagon, **Veh 585**

Stop or stopping, motor vehicles, **Veh 587**

Stop signal arm, school buses, **Veh 25257**

Streaming, buses, illuminated signs, **Veh 25353**
Santa Monica, advertisements, **Veh 25353.1**
University of California, Irvine, **Veh 25354**

Street, **Veh 590, 591**

Street rod vehicle, **Veh 5051**

Street sweeping parking lanes, photography and pictures, enforcement, **Veh 40246**

Streetsweepers, parking, photography and pictures, enforcement, **Veh 40246**

Subdivision, **Veh 11**

SULEV, motor vehicles, air pollution, decals, **Veh 5205.5**

WORDS

WORDS AND PHRASES—Cont'd

Supplemental restraint system, motor vehicles, **Veh 593**

Suspension, drivers licenses, **Veh 13102**

Tank vehicle,
Commercial motor vehicle and driver regulation, **Veh 15210**
Motor vehicle load, **Veh 34003**

Taxicab, signs, **Veh 27908**

Terminal,
Motor carriers, **Veh 595**
Traffic rules and regulations, length of vehicles or combinations, **Veh 35401.5**

Terminating highway, uncontrolled intersections, right of way, **Veh 21800**

Through highway, **Veh 600**

Tiller operators, firefighters and fire departments, drivers licenses, **Veh 12804.11**

Tire traction devices, **Veh 605**

Tire tread, **Veh 610**

Title,
Inspection and cancellation of titles, exported vehicles, **Veh 6161**
Motor vehicles, **Veh 6161**

Toll evasion penalty, **Veh 40252**

Toll facility, emergency vehicles, rates and charges, vehicular crossings, exemptions, **Veh 23301.5**

Toll highway, motor vehicles, **Veh 611**

Toll road, motor vehicles, **Veh 611**

Total bail, traffic schools, administrative fees, **Veh 42007**

Total loss salvage vehicle, **Veh 544**

Tour bus, **Veh 612**

Tow dolly, motor vehicles, **Veh 617**

Tow truck, **Veh 615**
Coupling towed vehicles, **Veh 29004**

Tow truck driver,
Certification, **Veh 2430.1**
Emergency roadside assistance, **Veh 2436**

Towed vehicle, motor carriers, owner operators, **Veh 34624**

Traditionally used route, garbage trucks, San Diego County, **Veh 35701**

Traffic, **Veh 620**

Traffic assistance programs, traffic violator schools, **Veh 11205.2**

Traffic officer, **Veh 625**

Traffic violator school, **Veh 626**

Traffic violator school branch or classroom location, **Veh 626.2**

Traffic violator school instructor, **Veh 626.4**

Traffic violator school operator, **Veh 626.6**

Traffic violator school owner, **Veh 626.8**

Trailer, **Veh 630**

Trailer bus, traffic regulation, **Veh 636**

Trailer coach, **Veh 635**

Trained volunteers, law enforcement, **Veh 22651.05**

Transfer of responsibility, night court, assessments, traffic rules and regulations, **Veh 42006**

WORDS AND PHRASES—Cont'd

Transferee, motor vehicles, **Veh 640**

Transit only traffic lanes, parking, San Francisco City and County, buses, videotape, **Veh 40240**

Transporter, **Veh 645**

Trap wagon, agricultural machinery and equipment, **Veh 36016**

Trolley coach, **Veh 650**

Truck tractor, **Veh 655**

Trusses,
Motor vehicles, **Veh 657**
Traffic rules and regulations, width of vehicle or load, **Veh 35780.5**

Two lane, undivided highway, speed limit, **Veh 22349**

Two way communication devices,
Buses, **Veh 24018**
Motor carriers, hazardous substances and waste, **Veh 32001**

U turn, definitions, **Veh 665.5**

ULEV, motor vehicles, air pollution, decals, **Veh 5205.5**

Unauthorized motor vehicle, riding and hiking trails, **Veh 23127**

Underpaid fees, motor carriers, registration, apportionment, foreign states, **Veh 8058**

Undocumented vessel, registration and transfer, **Veh 9840**

Unfair discrimination, motor vehicles, franchises, **Veh 11713.3**

Uninsured motor vehicle, insurance, **Veh 16000.7**

Unladen weight, motor vehicles, **Veh 660, 661**

Urban and suburban service, common carriers of passengers for hire, **Veh 35107**

Urgent, emergency vehicles, toll roads and bridges, rates and charges, vehicular crossings, exemptions, **Veh 23301.5**

Use, registration and transfer of vessels, **Veh 9840**

Used vehicle, **Veh 665**

Utility terrain vehicles, **Veh 531**

Utility trailers, **Veh 667**

Vanpool vehicles, **Veh 668**

Vehicle, **Veh 670, 6161**
Fees, exemptions, **Veh 9105**
Ignition interlock devices, **Veh 23575**
Inspection and cancellation of titles, exports, **Veh 6161**
Registration, nonoperation of vehicle, **Veh 4604**

Vehicle frame, **Veh 670.5**

Vehicle identification number, motor vehicles, **Veh 671**

Vehicle manufacturer, **Veh 672**

Vehicle salesperson, **Veh 675**

Vehicle verifiers, motor vehicles, **Veh 675.5**

Vehicular crossing, traffic rules and regulations, **Veh 23254**

Vendor, private party vehicle markets, **Veh 12102**

WORDS AND PHRASES—Cont'd

Verification acceptable to the department, motor vehicle records, suppression, **Veh 1808.21**

Vessels, registration and transfer, **Veh 9840**

Video event recorders, motor vehicles, **Veh 26708**

Viewpoint, removal of vehicles, **Veh 22651**

Wait, traffic signals, **Veh 21456**

Walk, traffic signals, **Veh 21456**

Wall panels, traffic rules and regulations, width of vehicle or load, **Veh 35780.5**

Waste matter, illegal dumping, traffic rules and regulations, impounding, **Veh 23112.7**

Water tender vehicle, motor vehicles, **Veh 676.5**

Waters of this state, registration and transfer of vessels, **Veh 9840**

Wear a safety helmet, motorcycles, motor driven cycles and motorized vehicles, **Veh 27803**

Whistle tip, motor vehicles, exhaust systems, **Veh 27150.3**

Willful failure, motor carriers, alcoholic beverages, tests, labor and employment, **Veh 34623**

Willful or wanton disregard for the safety of persons or property, peace officers, escape, **Veh 2800.2**

Willfully,
Motor carriers, controlled substances and alcohol use, **Veh 34520**
Motor vehicle emissions standards, gross polluters, crimes and offenses, **Veh 27156**

Write, send or read a text based communication, traffic rules and regulations, infractions, **Veh 23123.5**

Written evidence of the brokers valid surety bond, motor carriers, construction, nonprofit organizations, **Veh 34510.5**

Year, disabled person parking placards, **Veh 22511.55**

Year round registration, motor vehicles, **Veh 676**

Youth bus, **Veh 680**

WORK FURLOUGHS

Jails, this index

WORK PERMITS

Schools and School Districts, this index

WORKERS COMPENSATION

Driving schools, **Veh 11103.2**

Handicapped parking, special enforcement units, **Veh 22507.9**

Highway Patrol, this index

Motor Carriers, this index

Motor vehicles, financial responsibility, **Veh 16454**

Perjury, driving schools, compliance, **Veh 11103.2**

WORKSHOPS
Manufacturers and Manufacturing, generally, this index

WORLD WAR II
Veterans, generally, this index

WORLD WAR VETERANS
Veterans, generally, this index

WRECKS AND WRECKERS
Boats, undocumented vessels, termination of certificates of number and ownership, **Veh 9864**
Dismantlers. Motor Vehicles, this index
Ships and Shipping, this index

WRIT OF ERROR
Appeal and Review, generally, this index

WRITING
Evidence, this index
Motor vehicles, tow trucks, private property, removal, **Veh 22658**

WRONGFUL DEATH
Motor vehicles,
Damages, **Veh 17151**
Tort liability, **Veh 17000 et seq.**

YACHT AND SHIP BROKERS AND SALESPERSONS
Sales and use taxes, vessels, collection, **Veh 9858.5**

YELLOW
Definitions, traffic signals, **Veh 21452**

YELLOW STAR THISTLE
Weeds, generally, this index

YIELD RIGHT OF WAY ACT
Generally, **Veh 21800 et seq.**

YIELD SIGNS
Traffic Signs and Signals, this index

YOUTH AUTHORITY
Juvenile Facilities Division, generally, this index

YOUTH BUSES
Generally, **Veh 12523**
Certificates and certification, **Veh 2807.3, 12523**
Drivers, post Endorsement, **Veh 13369 et seq.**
Courses of instruction, drivers, first aid, **Veh 12522**
Crimes and offenses, **Veh 40000.21**
Equipment, maintenance and operation, **Veh 34506**
Loading or discharging children, **Veh 2816**
Criminal history information, drivers, certificates and certification, **Veh 12517.3**
Definitions, **Veh 680**
Discharging children, crimes, **Veh 2816**
Drivers, certificates and certification,
Criminal history information, **Veh 12517.3**
Drugs and medicine, revocation, **Veh 13376**
Fingerprints and fingerprinting, **Veh 12517.3**
First aid, courses of instruction, **Veh 12522**
Revocation or suspension, **Veh 12806.5**
Drivers licenses, **Veh 12523**
Revocation, **Veh 13371**
Drugs and medicine, drivers, certificates and certification, revocation, **Veh 13376**

YOUTH BUSES—Cont'd
Equipment, crimes and offenses, **Veh 34506**
Fees,
Drivers certificates, **Veh 12523**
Inspection and inspectors, **Veh 2807.3**
Fingerprints and fingerprinting, drivers, certificates and certification, **Veh 12517.3**
First aid, courses of instruction, drivers, **Veh 12522**
Inspection and inspectors, **Veh 2807.3**
Loading children, crimes, **Veh 2816**
Maintenance, crimes, **Veh 34506**
Operating certificate, **Veh 12523**
Operation, crimes, **Veh 34506**
Safety regulations, **Veh 34500 et seq.**
Seatbelts, operators, **Veh 12523**
Sex offenses, drivers, license revocation, **Veh 13369 et seq.**
Signs and signals, **Veh 27906.5**

YOUTHFUL DRUNK DRIVER VISITATION PROGRAM
Generally, **Veh 23509 et seq.**

YOUTHFUL OFFENDERS
Juvenile Delinquents and Dependents, generally, this index

ZONING AND PLANNING
Outdoor Advertising, generally, this index
Traffic rules and regulations, downward speed zoning, legislative intent, **Veh 22358.5**
Trucks, driving in residential areas, **Veh 35712**

†